CW00383099

The Form Book®
JUMPS ANNUAL 2010–2011

The BHA's Official Record

The complete record of all Jump racing from 25 April 2010 to 23 April 2011

Published by Raceform Ltd
Compton, Newbury, Berkshire, RG20 6NL

A catalogue record for this book is available from the British Library.

ISBN 978-1-906820-69-5

Printed and bound in the UK by Polestar Wheatons, Exeter

CONTENTS

Editor: Graham Dench

Head of Analysis Team: Ashley Rumney

Race Analysts & Notebook Writers:
Tom Abbott, Gavin Beech, Dave Bellingham, Mark Brown,
Tom Byrne, Steffan Edwards, Walter Glynn, Jeremy Grayson,
Niall Hannity, Joseph Isherwood, David Lawrence, Richard Lowther,
Iain Mackenzie, Lee McKenzie, Tim Mitchell, Dave Moon,
Sandra Noble, David Orton, Steve Payne, Rodney Pettinga,
David Revers, Ashley Rumney, Colin Russell, Andrew Sheret,
Steve Taylor, David Toft, Ron Wood, Richard Young.

Production: Ashley Rumney & Richard Lowther

The Form Book

Jumps Annual **2010–2011**

Welcome to the 2010-2011 edition of *The Form Book Jumps Annual*. Race details contain Racing Post Ratings assessing the merit of each individual performance, speed figures for every horse that clocks a worthwhile time, weight-for-age allowances, stall positions for every race and the starting price percentage, in addition to the traditional features.

A race Focus is included after the result and endeavours to combiner the opinions o fthe notebook writer, the handicapper, speed figure expert and, where appropriate, the paddock observer in order to provide a snapshot of the merit of each individual race. The extended Notebook comments are printed below each race and cover all horses which are considered worthy of inclusion by our expert race-readers and analysts. The comments provide an analysis of the winning performance and, where applicable, explain possible reasons for improvement or attempt to explain why any horse failed to run to its best. More importantly, our team will also indicate the conditions under which horses are likely to be seen to best advantage.

The official record

THE FORM BOOK records comprehensive race details of every domestic race, every major Irish Graded race and every foreign event in which a British-trained runner participated. In the **NOTEBOOK** section, extended interpretation is provided for all runners worthy of a mention, including all placed horses and all favourites. Generally speaking, the higher the class of race, the greater the number of runners noted.

MEETING BACK REFERENCE NUMBER is the Raceform number of the last meeting run at the track and is shown to the left of the course name.

THE OFFICIAL GOING, shown at the head of each meeting, is recorded as follows: Hard; Firm; Good to firm; Good; Good to soft; Soft; Heavy. All-Weather: FST (Fast); STD (Standard); SLW (Slow). There may be variations for non-British meetings.

Where appropriate, is a section indicating track bias and any differences to the official going indicated by race times.

THE WEATHER is shown below to the date for selected meetings.

VISIBILITY is good unless otherwise stated.

RACE NUMBERS for foreign races carry the suffix 'a' in the race header and in the index.

RACE TITLE is the name of the race as shown in the Racing Calendar.

COMPETITIVE RACING CLASSIFICATIONS are shown on a scale from Class 1 to Class 6. All Graded races are Class 1.

THE RACE DISTANCE is given for all races, and is accompanied by the number of fences or hurdles and number of flights bypassed or omitted (if any).

OFFICIAL RACE TIME as published in the Racing Calendar is followed in parentheses by the time when the race actually started. This is followed by the race class, age restrictions, handicap restrictions and the official rating of the declared top weight.

PRIZE MONEY shows penalty values for each placing; winner's prizemoney in bold type, remainder in parentheses.

IN THE RACE RESULT, the figures to the far left of each horse (under Form) shows the most recent form figures. The figure in bold is the finishing position in this race as detailed below.

1...40 - finishing positions first to fortieth; **b** - brought down; **c** - carried out; **f** - fell; **p** - pulled up; **r** - refused; **ro** - ran out; **s** - slipped up; **u** - unseated rider; **v** - void race.

THE OFFICIAL DISTANCES between the horses are shown on the left-hand side immediately after their position at the finish.

NUMBER OF DAYS SINCE PREVIOUS RUN is the superscript figure immediately following the horse name and suffix.

PREVIOUS RACEFORM RACE NUMBER is the boxed figure to the right of the horse's name.

THE HORSE'S AGE is shown immediately before the weight carried.

WEIGHTS shown are actual weights carried.

OFFICIAL RATING is the superior figure directly after the horse's weight in the race result.

In handicaps, this figure is displayed in bold, and indicates the official BHA rating, at entry, from which the horse raced, after the following adjustments had been made:
(i) Overweight carried by the rider.
(ii) The number of pounds out of the handicap (if applicable).
(iii) Penalties incurred after the publication of the weights.
In non-handicaps, the rating is provided for information only, and is the bare BHA rating, at entry, with no adjustments.

HEADGEAR is shown immediately before the jockey's name and in parentheses and expressed as: **b** (blinkers); **v** (visor); **h** (hood); **e** (eyeshield); **c** (eyecover); **p** (sheepskin cheekpieces); **t** (tongue tie). A superscript 1 indicates the aid is being worn for the first time.

THE JOCKEY is shown for every runner followed, in superscript, by apprentice allowances in parentheses.

CONDITIONAL JOCKEYS' ALLOWANCES The holders of conditional jockeys' licences, under the provisions of Rule 109(ii) (a) are permitted to claim the following allowances in Jumps races:

7lb until they have won 15 races;

thereafter 5lb until they have won 35 such races;

thereafter 3lb until they have won 65 such Flat races.

These allowances can be claimed in the steeplechases, hurdle races and National Hunt flat races set out below, with the exception of races confined to conditional jockeys:
(a) All handicaps except the Grand National Steeplechase
(b) All selling races.
(c) All weight-for-age races classified 3, 4, 5, and 6.
(d) All National Hunt Flat races

RACING POST RATINGS, which record the level of performance attained in this race for each horse, appear in the column headed RPR. These are the work of handicapper Steve Mason, who heads a dedicated team dealing with Jumps races for Raceform and sister publication, the *Racing Post*.

THE TRAINER is shown for every runner.

COMMENT-IN-RUNNING is shown for each horse in an abbreviated form. Details of abbreviations appear later in this section.

STARTING PRICES appear below the jockey in the race result. The favourite indicator appears to the right of the Starting Price;1 for the favourite, 2 for the second-favourite and 3 for third-favourite. Joint favourites share the same number.

RACE TIMES in Great Britain are shown to a tenth of a second. Figures in parentheses following the time show the number of seconds faster or slower than the Raceform Median Time for the course and distance.

RACEFORM MEDIAN TIMES are compiled from all races run over the course and distance in the preceding five years. Times equal to the median are shown as (0.00). Times under the median are preceded by minus, for instance, 1.8 seconds under the median would be shown (-1.8). Record times are displayed as follows (1.2 under best).

GOING CORRECTION appears against each race to allow for changing conditions of the ground. It is shown to a tenth of a second and indicates the adjustment per furlong against the median time. The going based on the going correction is shown in parentheses and is recorded in the following stages:

HD (Hard); F (Firm); GF (Good to firm); G (Good); GS (Good to soft); S (Soft); HVY (Heavy).

WEIGHT-FOR-AGE allowances are given where applicable for mixed-age races.

STARTING PRICE PERCENTAGE follows the going correction and weight-for-age details, and gives the total SP percentage of all runners that competed. It precedes the number of runners taking part in the race.

Bookmakers have historically tended to bet to a margin of around 2% per horse (i.e. 110% for a five-runner race and 120% if there are ten runners). If the over-round is any bigger than this the market can be considered unduly skewed in their favour. However, percentages are usually significantly smaller at the big meetings, especially in handicaps, and in recent years the influence of betting exchanges and the arrival of 'new blood' among on course bookmakers has contributed to a general narrowing of the 'over round'.

SELLING DETAILS (where applicable) and details of any claim are given. Friendly claims are not detailed.

SPEED RATINGS appear below the race time and going correction. They are the work of time expert Dave Bellingham and differ from conventional ratings systems in that they are an expression of a horse's ability in terms of lengths-per-mile, as opposed to pounds in weight. They are not directly comparable with BHA and Racing Post ratings.

The ratings take no account of the effect of weight, either historically or on the day, and this component is left completely to the user's discretion. What is shown is a speed rating represented in its purest form, rather than one that has been altered for weight using a mathematical formula that treats all types of horses as if they were the same.

A comparison of the rating achieved with the 'par' figure for the grade of race - the rating that should be achievable by an everage winner in that class of race- will both provide an at-a-glance indication of whether or not a race was truly run and also highlight the value of the form from a time perspective.

In theory, if a horse has a best speed figure five points superior to another and both run to their best form in a race over a mile, the first horse should beat the second by five lengths. In a race run over two miles, the margin should be ten lengths and so on.

Before the speed figures can be calculated, it is necessary to establish a set of standard or median times for every distance at every track, and this is done by averaging the times of all winners over a particular trip going back several years. No speed ratings are produced when insufficient races have been run over a distance for a reliable median time to be calculated.

Once a meeting has taken place, a raw unadjusted speed rating is calculated for each winner by calculating how many lengths per mile the winning time was faster or slower than the median for the trip. A difference of 0.2 of a second equals one length. The raw speed ratings of all winners on the card are then compared to the 'par' figure for the class of race. The difference between the 'raw' speed rating and the 'par' figure for each race is then noted, and both the fastest and slowest races are discarded before the rest are averaged to produce the going allowance or track variant. This figure gives an idea as to how much the elements, of which the going is one, have affected the final times of each race.

The figure representing the going allowance is then used to adjust how fast the winners would have run on a perfectly good surface with no external influences, including the weather. The ratings for beaten horses are worked out by taking the number of lengths they were behind the winner, adjusting that to take into account the distance of the race, and deducting that figure from the winner's rating. The reader is left with a rating which provides an instant impression of the value of a time performance.

The speed 'pars' below act as benchmark with which to compare the speed figures earned by each horse in each race. A horse that has already exceeded the 'par' for the class he is about to run in is of special interest, especially if he has done it more than once, as are horses that have consistently earned higher figures than their rivals.

Class 1 Grade One	117
Class 1 Grade Two	115
Class 1 Grade Three	113
Class 1 Listed	111
Class 2	109
Class 3	107
Class 4	105
Class 5	103
Class 6	101

Allowances need to be made for younger horses and for fillies. These allowances are as follows.

3-y-o	Jul / Aug	-3
	Sep / Oct	-2
	Nov / Dec	-1

Races contested by mares only -3

TOTE returns include a £1 stake. Exacta dividends are shown in parentheses. The Computer Straight Forecast dividend is preceded by the letters CSF, Computer Tricast is preceded by CT and Tote Trio dividend is preceded by the word Trio. Jackpot, Placepot and Quadpot details appear at the end of the meeting to which they refer.

OWNER is followed by the breeder's name and the trainer's location.

STEWARDS' INQUIRIES are included with the result, and any suspensions and/or fines incurred. Objections by jockeys and officials are included, where relevant.

HISTORICAL FOCUS details occasional points of historical significance.

FOCUS The Focus section has been enhanced to help readers distinguish good races from bad races and reliable form from unreliable form, by drawing together the opinions of handicapper, time expert and paddock watcher and interpreting their views in a punter-friendly manner.

NOTEBOOK horses marked with the symbol are those deemed by our racereaders especially worthy of note in future races.

OFFICIAL EXPLANATIONS, where the horse is deemed to have run well above or below expectation, are included in the Notebook section.

Key to racereaders' initials

WG....................Walter Glynn
KH......................Keith Hewitt
RL................Richard Lowther
IM..................Iain MacKenzie
LM....................Lee McKenzie
TM......................Tim Mitchell
JN.............Jonathan Neesom
DO....................Darren Owen
SP........................Steve Payne
CR....................Colin Roberts
JR.....................Joe Rowntree
JS........................John Santer
ST........................Steve Taylor
RY.................Richard Young

Abbreviations and their meanings

Paddock comments

gd sort - well made, above average on looks
h.d.w - has done well, improved in looks
wl grwn - well grown, has filled to its frame
lengthy - longer than average for its height
tall - tall
rangy - lengthy and tall but in proportion, covers a deal of ground
scope - scope for physical development
str - strong, powerful looking
w'like - workmanlike, ordinary in looks
lt-f - light-framed, not much substance
cmpt - compact
neat - smallish, well put together
leggy - long legs compared with body
angular - unfurnished behind the saddle, not filled to frame
unf - unfurnished in the midriff, not filled to frame
narrow - not as wide as side appearance would suggest
small - lacks any physical scope
nt grwn - not grown
lw - looked fit and well
bkwd - backward in condition
t - tubed
swtg - sweating
b (off fore or nr fore) - bandaged in front
b.hind (off or nr) - bandaged behind

At the start

stdd s - jockey purposely reins back the horse
dwlt - missed the break and left for a short time
s.s - slow to start, left longer than a horse that dwelt
s.v.s - started very slowly
s.i.s - started on terms but took time to get going
ref to r - either does not jump off, or travels a few yards and then stops
rel to r - tries to pull itself up in mid-race
w.r.s - whipped round start

Position in the race

led - in lead on its own
disp ld - upsides the leader

w ldr - almost upsides the leader
w ldrs - in a line of three or more disputing the lead
prom - on the heels of the leaders, in the front third of the field
trckd ldr(s) - just in behind the leaders giving impression that it could lead if asked
chsd ldr - horse in second place
chsd clr ldrs - horse heads main body of field behind two clear leaders
chsd ldrs - horse is in the first four or five but making more of an effort to stay close to the pace than if it were tracking the leaders.
clsd - closed
in tch - close enough to have a chance
hdwy - making ground on the leader
gd hdwy - making ground quickly on the leader, could be a deliberate move
sme hdwy - making some ground but no real impact on the race
stdy hdwy - gradually making ground
ev ch - upsides the leaders when the race starts in earnest
rr - at the back of main group but not detached
bhd - detached from the main body of runners
hld up - restrained as a deliberate tactical move
nt rcvr - lost all chance after interference, mistake etc.
wknd - stride shortened as it began to tire
lost tch - had been in the main body but a gap appeared as it tired
lost pl - remains in main body of runners but lost several positions quickly

Riding

effrt - short-lived effort
pushed along - received urgings with hands only, jockey not using legs
rdn - received urgings from the saddle, including use of the whip
hrd rdn - received maximum assistance from the saddle including use of whip
drvn - received forceful urgings, jockey putting in a lot of effort and using whip
hrd drvn - jockey very animated, plenty of kicking, pushing and reminders

Finishing comments

jst failed - closing rapidly on the winner and probably would have led a stride after the line
r.o - jockey's efforts usually involved to produce an increase in pace without finding an appreciable turn of speed
r.o wl - jockey's efforts usually involved to produce an obvious increase in pace without finding an appreciable turn of speed
unable qckn - not visibly tiring but does not possess a sufficient change of pace
one pce - not tiring but does not find a turn of speed, from a position further out than unable qckn
nt r.o. - did not consent to respond to pressure
styd on - going on well towards the end, utilising stamina
nvr able to chal - unable to produce sufficient to reach a challenging position
nvr nr to chal - in the opinion of the racereader, the horse was never in a suitable position to challenge.
nrst fin - nearer to the winner in distance beaten than at any time since the race had begun in earnest
nvr nrr - nearer to the winner position-wise than at any time since the race had begun in earnest
rallied - responded to pressure to come back with a chance having lost its place
no ex - unable to sustain its run
bttr for r - likely to improve for the run and experience
rn green - inclined to wander and falter through inexperience
too much to do - left with too much leeway to make up

Winning comments

v.easily - a great deal in hand
easily - plenty in hand
comf - something in hand, always holding the others
pushed out - kept up to its work with hands and heels without jockey resorting to whip or kicking along and wins fairly comfortably
rdn out - pushed and kicked out to the line, with the whip employed
drvn out - pushed and kicked out to the line, with considerable effort and the whip employed
all out - nothing to spare, could not have found any more
jst hld on - holding on to a rapidly diminishing lead, could not have found any more if passed
unchal - must either make all or a majority of the running and not be challenged from an early stage

Complete list of abbreviations

a - always
abt - about
a.p - always prominent
appr - approaching
awrdd - awarded
b.b.v - broke blood-vessel
b.d - brought down
bdly - badly
bef - before
bhd - behind
bk - back
blkd - baulked
blnd - blundered
bmpd - bumped
bnd - bend
btn- beaten
bttr - better
c - came
ch - chance
chal - challenged
chse - chase
chsd - chased
chsng - chasing
circ - circuit
cl - close
clr - clear
clsd - closed
comf - comfortably
cpld - coupled
crse - course
ct - caught
def - definite
dismntd - dismounted
disp - disputed
dist - distance
div - division
drvn - driven
dwlt - dwelt
edgd - edged
effrt - effort

ent - entering
ev ch - every chance
ex - extra
f - furlong
fin - finished
fnd - found
fnl - final
fr - from
gd - good
gng - going
gp - group
grad - gradually
grnd - ground
hd - head
hdd - headed
hdwy - headway
hld - held
hmpd - hampered
imp - impression
ins - inside
j.b - jumped badly
j.w - jumped well
jnd - joined
jst - just
kpt - kept
l - length
ld - lead
ldr - leader

lft - left
mod - moderate
m - mile
m.n.s - made no show
mde - made
mid div - mid division
mstke - mistake
n.d - never dangerous
n.g.t - not go through
n.m.r - not much room
nk - neck
no ex - no extra
nr - near
nrr - nearer
nrst fin - nearest finish
nt - not
nvr - never
one pce - one pace
out - from finish
outpcd - outpaced
p.u - pulled up
pce - pace
pckd - pecked
pl - place
plcd - placed
plld - pulled
press - pressure
prog - progress

prom - prominent
qckly - quickly
qckn - quicken
r - race
racd - raced
rch - reach
rcvr - recover
rdn - ridden
rdr - rider
reard - reared
ref - refused
rn - ran
rnd - round
r.o - ran on
rr - rear
rspnse - response
rt - right
s - start
sddle - saddle
shkn - shaken
slt - slight
sme - some
sn - soo
spd- speed
st - straight
stmbld - stumbled
stdd - steadied
stdy - steady

strly - strongly
styd - stayed
styng - staying
s. u - slipped up
swtchd - switched
swvd - swerved
tk - took
t.k.h - took keen hold
t.o - tailed off
tch - touch
thrght - throughout
trbld - troubled
trckd - tracked
u.p - under pressure
u.str.p- under strong pressure
w - with
w.r.s - whipped round start
wd - wide
whn - when
wknd - weakened
wl - well
wnr - winner
wnt - went
1/2-wy - halfway

Racing Post Ratings

Raceform Ratings for each horse are listed after the Starting Price and indicate the actual level of performance attained in that race. The figure in the back index represents the BEST public form that Raceform's Handicappers still believe the horse capable of reproducing.

To use the ratings constructively in determining those horses best-in in future events, the following procedures should be followed:

(i) In races where all runners are set to carry the same weight, no calculations are necessary. The horse with the highest rating is best in.

(ii) In races where all runners are set to carry different weights, add one point to the Raceform Rating for every pound less than 12 st to be carried; deduct one point for every pound more than 12 st.

For example,

Horse	Age & Weight	Adj. from 12st	RRbase rating	Adj. rating
Voy Por Ustedes	8-12-00	0	170	170
Petit Robin	6-11-12	+2	168	170
Well Chief	10-11-10	+4	167	171
Twist Magic	7-11-06	+8	162	170

Therefore Well Chief is top-rated (best-in)

NB No adjustments are made for weight for age in Racing Post ratings. The official weight for age scale is displayed for information purposes while any live weight for age conditions are displayed underneath each individual result.

The following symbols are used in conjunction with the ratings:

++ almost certain to prove better

+ likely to prove better

d disappointing (has run well below best recently)

? form hard to evaluate, may prove unreliable

t tentative rating based on race-time

Weight adjusted ratings for every race are published daily in Raceform Private Handicap. For subscription terms please contact the Subscription Department on (01635) 578080.

The Official Scale of Weight, Age & Distance (Jumps)

The following scale should only be used in conjuction with the Official ratings published in this book. Use of any other scale will introduce errors into calculations. The allowances are expressed as the number of pounds that is deemed the average horse in each group falls short of maturity at different dates and distances.
N.B. Southern Hemisphere horses receive different allowances.

Scale of Weight for Age for Steeple Chases and Hurdle Races

HURDLE RACES

The allowances, assessed in lbs, which three-year-olds and four-year-olds will receive from five-year-olds and upwards

Distance		JAN		FEB		MAR		APR		MAY		JUNE		JULY		AUG		SEPT		OCT		NOV		DEC	
Miles	Age	1/15	16/31	1/14	15/29	1/15	16/31	1/15	16/30	1/15	16/31	1/15	16/30	1/15	16/31	1/15	16/31	1/15	16/30	1/15	16/31	1/15	16/30	1/15	16/31
2	3	–	–	–	–	–	–	–	–	22	22	21	21	20	20	19	19	18	18	17	17	16	15	14	13
	4	12	11	10	9	8	7	6	5	4	4	3	3	2	2	1	1	–	–	–	–	–	–	–	–
2½	3	–	–	–	–	–	–	–	–	23	23	22	22	21	21	20	20	19	19	18	18	17	16	15	14
	4	13	12	11	10	9	8	7	6	5	5	4	4	3	3	2	2	1	1	–	–	–	–	–	–
3	3	–	–	–	–	–	–	–	–	24	24	23	23	22	22	21	21	20	20	19	19	18	17	16	15
	4	14	13	12	11	10	9	8	7	6	6	5	5	4	4	3	3	2	2	1	1	–	–	–	–

STEEPLECHASES

The allowances, assessed in lbs, which four-year-olds and five-year-olds will receive from five-year-olds and upwards

Distance		JAN		FEB		MAR		APR		MAY		JUNE		JULY		AUG		SEPT		OCT		NOV		DEC	
Miles	Age	1/15	16/31	1/14	15/29	1/15	16/31	1/15	16/30	1/15	16/31	1/15	16/30	1/15	16/31	1/15	16/31	1/15	16/30	1/15	16/31	1/15	16/30	1/15	16/31
2	4	–	–	–	–	–	–	–	–	18	18	17	17	16	15	14	13	12	11	10	9	8	7	6	5
	5	4	3	2	1	–	–	–	–	–	–	–	–	–	–	–	–	–	–	–	–	–	–	–	–
2½	4	–	–	–	–	–	–	–	–	19	19	18	18	17	16	15	14	13	12	11	10	9	8	7	6
	5	5	4	3	2	1	–	–	–	–	–	–	–	–	–	–	–	–	–	–	–	–	–	–	–
3	4	–	–	–	–	–	–	–	–	20	20	19	19	18	17	16	15	14	13	12	11	10	9	8	7
	5	6	5	4	3	2	1	–	–	–	–	–	–	–	–	–	–	–	–	–	–	–	–	–	–

Course Descriptions

COURSE	COMMENT
AINTREE	Two left-handed courses. Grand National circuit, 2m2f, is flat and has big fences with drop on landing side and a long run-in. Mildmay Course, 1m3f, flat with conventional fences, is sharper than the hurdles course.
ASCOT	Right-handed, galloping, last mile mainly uphill, with stiff fences. Circuit 1m5f.
AYR	Left-handed, mainly flat. Circuit 1m4f.
BANGOR	Left-handed, sharp and flat with a long run-in. Circuit 1m4f.
CARLISLE	Right-handed, undulating, stiff and galloping. Circuit 1m5f
CARTMEL	Left-handed, sharp and undulating, with stiff fences and a 4f run-in for chases. Circuit 1m
CATTERICK	Left-handed, sharp and undulating, suiting handy types. Circuit 1m3f.
CHELTENHAM *(old course)*	Left-handed, galloping, undulating and testing track with stiff fences. Circuit 1m4f.
CHELTENHAM *(new course)*	Left-handed, galloping, undulating and testing track with stiff fences. Circuit 1m4½f.
CHEPSTOW	Left-handed and undulating. Going can be very testing. Circuit 1m7f.
DONCASTER	Left-handed, galloping, generally flat. Heavy ground rare. Circuit 2m.
EXETER	Right-handed and undulating. Stiff test of stamina. Circuit 2m.
FAKENHAM	Left-handed, sharp, undulating, suiting nippy types. Circuit 1m.
FFOS LAS	Left-handed, galloping flat track. Circuit 1m6f.
FOLKESTONE	Right-handed, undulating oval of 1m2f
FONTWELL	Left-handed hurdle course. Figure-of-eight chase course does not suit long-striding gallopers. Ground can be testing. Circuit 1m.
HAYDOCK	Left-handed, flat and galloping. Chase course now on hurdles track and with portable fences. Suits gallopers but new course sharper than the old track. Ciruit 1m4f.
HEREFORD	Right-handed, sharpish and generally flat. Suits nippy types. Circuit 1m4f.
HEXHAM	Left-handed, severe and undulating, placing emphasis on stamina. Circuit 1m4f.

HUNTINGDON	Right-handed and galloping. Circuit 1m4f.
KELSO	Left-handed and undulating. Hurdles course of 1m1f is sharp, more so than 1m 3f chase track, which has 2f run-in.
KEMPTON	Right-handed triangular course, practically flat. Circuit 1m5f.
LEICESTER	Right-handed and undulating, placing emphasis on stamina. Circuit 1m6f.
LINGFIELD	Left-handed, undulating and sharp. Chase circuit 1m5f, hurdles run on flat course.
LUDLOW	Right-handed. Chase course flat with sharp bends, circuit 1m4f. Hurdles track, 150y longer, slightly undulating, with easier bends.
MARKET RASEN	Right-handed oval, sharp and somewhat undulating. Circuit 1m2f.
MUSSELBURGH	Right-handed virtually flat track with sharp turns. Circuit 1m3f.
NEWBURY	Left-handed, flat and galloping, with stiff fences. Circuit 1m7f.
NEWCASTLE	Left-handed, with uphill finish. Going can be very testing. Circuit 1m6f.
NEWTON ABBOT	Left-handed oval, sharp with short run-in. Circuit 1m2f.
PERTH	Right-handed and flat, with tight bends. Chase course has long run-in. Circuit 1m 2f.
PLUMPTON	Left-handed, undulating, sharp. Circuit 1m1f.
SANDOWN	Right-handed with stiff uphill finish. Chase course tricky, especially for novices. Hurdles run on flat course. Circuit 1m5f.
SEDGEFIELD	Left-handed, undulating oval, sharp bends. Chase course has easy fences. Circuit 1m2f.
SOUTHWELL	Left-handed oval, approx 1m round, with six portable fences. Outside half of jumps course used in summer.
STRATFORD	Left-handed, flat and sharp, with short finishing straight. Circuit 1m2f.
TAUNTON	Right-handed oval, on the sharp side with short run-in. Circuit 1m2f.
TOWCESTER	Right-handed, with last mile uphill. Very testing. Circuit 1m6f.
UTTOXETER	Left-handed with some undulations. Hurdle course is inside chase course. Circuit 1m3f.
WARWICK	Left-handed, with tight turns and short run-in. Circuit 1m5f.
WETHERBY	Left-handed oval, with easy bends. Track modifications and changes to fences mean course is less testing than in the past. Circuit 1m4f.
WINCANTON	Right-handed rectangular track, mainly flat. Circuit 1m3f.

LUDLOW (R-H)

Sunday, April 25

OFFICIAL GOING: Good to firm (good in places; chs 8.3 hdl 8.2)

Bends moved to provide fresh ground but impact on distances not known.

Wind: Light across Weather: Cloudy

1 LUDLOW GOLF CLUB CLAIMING HURDLE (9 hdls) 2m

2:00 (2:00) (Class 4) 4-Y-0+ **£2,927** (£859; £429; £214)

Form RPR

110- **1** **Marodima (FR)**[37] 4711 7-12-0 145 APMcCoy 123+
(Rebecca Curtis) *swvd lft s: mde all: rdn appr 3 out: hit last: drvn out* **1/7**[1]

1P2- **2** *3 1/4* **Blacktoft (USA)**[31] 4847 7-11-10 116 (e) PaulMoloney 114
(Evan Williams) *chsd wnr: hit 2nd: nt fluent 5th: ev ch 3 out: rdn appr last: no ex towards fin* **11/1**[2]

5UP- **3** *2* **Rapide Plaisir (IRE)**[129] 2934 12-11-0 98 (t) CharliePoste 103
(Richard Lee) *prom: ev ch 3 out: rdn appr last: styd on same pce flat* **28/1**

140- **4** *37* **Roisin's Prince (IRE)**[21] 5015 8-11-0 100 (t) AidanColeman 77
(Matt Sheppard) *chsd ldrs: mstke 4th: outpcd bef next: t.o* **22/1**[3]

3m 42.8s (-6.70) **Going Correction** -0.60s/f (Firm) **4** Ran SP% **103.6**
Speed ratings (Par 105): **92,90,89,70**
CSF £2.02 TOTE £1.10; EX 1.40.Marodima claimed by Mr J. E. Snowden for £12,000.
Owner Mark & Lavinia Sherwood **Bred** Earl La Vastine Et Al **Trained** Newport, Dyfed

FOCUS
The bends were moved to provide fresh ground. False wings in all fences (except the water) six yards from the inside. Jockeys involved in the first reported that the ground was riding as described. It was steadily run and the winner was 20lb+ below his level.

NOTEBOOK
Marodima(FR), taking a big drop in grade after running in the County Hurdle last time, had at least 25lb in hand on his rivals but was well below his best in victory. After going badly out to his left when the tapes rose, he never got more than a few lengths clear and he made fairly heavy weather of landing the odds, probably finding this ground plenty quick enough.
Blacktoft(USA) likes to lead but that was never a realistic option with Marodima in the field. He ran respectably and was breathing down the winner's neck on the home turn before failing to quicken. Some of his hurdling lacked fluency. (op 10-1)
Rapide Plaisir(IRE) had the least chance on adjusted official figures and performed with credit on this first start since December, but he was held after an awkward leap two from home. He was wearing a tongue tie for the first time. (op 33-1 tchd 40-1)
Roisin's Prince(IRE) was struggling before they turned into the back straight.

2 TOTESPORTGAMES.COM NOVICES' CHASE (13 fncs) 2m

2:30 (2:30) (Class 3) 5-Y-0+ **£6,319** (£1,907; £982; £520)

Form RPR

242- **1** **West With The Wind**[41] 4651 5-10-12 0 PaulMoloney 128+
(Evan Williams) *mde all and sn clr: mstke 5 out: hit last: unchal* **1/1**[1]

3- **2** *21* **Remember Bampi**[12] 5176 6-10-5 0 (tp) JimmyDerham(7) 100
(Simon Burrough) *prom: chsd wnr 3rd to 6th: wnt 2nd again 5 out but nvr any ch w wnr: j.rt last* **11/1**[3]

34P- **3** *44* **Sunsetten (IRE)**[72] 4018 6-10-9 123 MrOGreenall(3) 70
(Henry Daly) *chsd wnr to 3rd: wknd after 5 out: t.o whn blnd next* **11/8**[2]

/53- **4** *90* **Huntingford (IRE)**[29] 4882 7-10-13 0 ow6 MrGBarfoot-Saunt(5) —
(Tracey Barfoot-Saunt) *bhd fr 4th: t.o: wnt bdly rt 4 out* **50/1**

0- **P** **Not Another Barney (IRE)**[52] 4411 7-10-12 0 JamieMoore —
(Helen Nelmes) *hld up: hdwy to chse wnr 6th tl mstke 5 out: sn wknd: t.o whn p.u bef 2 out* **20/1**

3m 51.8s (-6.70) **Going Correction** -0.375s/f (Good) **5** Ran SP% **107.2**
Speed ratings: **101,90,68,23,—**
CSF £10.43 TOTE £1.90: £1.10, £1.60; EX 7.10.
Owner Mrs Janet Davies **Bred** Newsells Park Stud **Trained** Llancarfan, Vale Of Glamorgan

FOCUS
A poor novice chase for the money, with only two realistic contenders. The easy winner was value for further and is rated to his mark.

NOTEBOOK
West With The Wind had been runner-up to decent sorts on both his previous tries over fences, sandwiching a well-beaten effort behind Marodima over hurdles here. Quickly in a clear lead, he was given a breather down the back, allowing the others to close, before drawing away for an effortless win. With Sunsetten running so poorly he had nothing to beat, and his jumping could let him down on a track with stiffer fences. He brushed through the top of several and walked right through the last without losing momentum. (op 4-5)
Remember Bampi failed to complete in five successive point-to-points before dropping back in trip to finish third in a novice chase at Exeter. He was no match for the winner but picked up a bit more prize-money and looks to be improving at a lowly level. (op 10-1)
Sunsetten(IRE) looked the only danger to the winner and this drop in trip seemed likely to suit after he failed to see out 2m4f on his chasing debut. He had not jumped well that day and it was the same story here, as he failed to get involved in the race and was well adrift when blundering badly at the fourth from home. It would be no surprise to see him revert to hurdles. Official explanation: trainer said gelding finished distressed (op 2-1)

3 TOTESPORTBINGO.COM H'CAP HURDLE (11 hdls) 2m 5f

3:05 (3:05) (Class 3) (0-120,118) 4-Y-0+
£6,262 (£1,850; £925; £463; £231; £116)

Form RPR

56F- **1** **Valento**[31] 4849 5-11-2 108 JasonMaguire 123+
(Kim Bailey) *hld up: racd keenly: hdwy after 8th: led 3 out: hung rt thereafter: nt fluent last: drvn out* **14/1**

212- **2** *7* **Tabaran (FR)**[2] 5365 7-11-4 117 7ex (tp) OliverDayman(7) 124
(Alison Thorpe) *sn prom: led 7th: hdd 3 out: rdn after next: styd on same pce last* **4/1**[1]

F3P- **3** *6* **Wild Tonto (IRE)**[173] 2051 7-11-4 110 PaddyBrennan 112
(Nigel Twiston-Davies) *hld up: hdwy appr 3 out: j.rt next: sn rdn: wknd last* **10/1**

001- **4** *6* **Parlesotho (FR)**[7] 5253 7-11-11 117 7ex CharliePoste 113
(Ben Case) *mid-div: hdwy appr 3 out: wknd after next* **7/1**[2]

466- **5** *1* **Cool Bob (IRE)**[2] 5359 7-9-11 96 (t) MrLRPayter(7) 90
(Matt Sheppard) *prom: lost pl after 2nd: hdwy appr 3 out: sn wknd* **7/1**[2]

000- **6** *7* **Lyster (IRE)**[15] 5136 11-10-0 92 oh4 TomMessenger 80
(David Evans) *hld up: rdn appr 3 out: nvr on terms* **40/1**

262- **7** *1* **Key Cutter (FR)**[31] 4849 6-11-12 118 (t) WillKennedy 105
(Paul Webber) *led to 2nd: led 5th to 7th: wknd 3 out* **8/1**[3]

400/ **8** *13* **Enchanted Approach (IRE)**[36] 7-9-7 92 oh2 RobertKirk(7) 67
(Lady Susan Brooke) *chsd ldr tl led 2nd: wandered into next: hdd 5th: wknd after 4 out: bhd whn blnd 2 out: t.o* **66/1**

/62- **9** *3 1/4* **Benedict Spirit (IRE)**[25] 4721 5-11-3 109 (v) ChristianWilliams 81
(David Evans) *prom: hit 6th: mstke 8th: sn rdn and wknd: t.o* **7/1**[2]

003- **10** *84* **Singapore Reef (FR)**[7] 5245 4-10-12 110 DarylJacob —
(Nick Williams) *chsd ldrs tl rdn and wknd wl bef 3 out: t.o* **4/1**[1]

3P4- **P** **Brimley**[24] 4967 7-10-10 105 LeeStephens(3) —
(Ann Price) *chsd ldrs: lost pl 4th: bhd fr 6th: t.o whn p.u bef next* **66/1**

462- **P** **Highland River**[20] 5051 4-9-8 99 JimmyDerham(7) —
(Aytach Sadik) *hld up: bhd fr 7th: t.o whn p.u bef 2 out* **28/1**

31P- **P** **Screenscraper (IRE)**[65] 4143 5-11-3 109 PaulMoloney —
(Evan Williams) *mid-div: rdn appr 3 out: sn wknd: t.o whn p.u bef last: dismntd* **25/1**

4m 58.4s (-16.40) **Going Correction** -0.60s/f (Firm)
WFA 4 from 5yo+ 7lb **13** Ran SP% **117.1**
Speed ratings (Par 107): **107,104,102,99,99 96,96,91,90,58 —,—,—**
Tote Swingers: 1&2 £20.60, 1&3 £40.00, 2&3 £11.10 CSF £66.89 CT £596.65 TOTE £12.10: £3.80, £1.80, £2.40; EX 97.20.
Owner Mr & Mrs Nigel Blackwell **Bred** D J And Mrs Deer **Trained** Andoversford, Gloucs

FOCUS
A fair handicap hurdle run at a solid pace. The winner improved to the level of his best Flat form, with the second to his mark.

NOTEBOOK
Valento had not been in much form of late and was an early faller here last time, but this longer trip did the trick. Travelling well into contention before showing ahead three from home, he then began to hang to his right, veering close to the chase track after a mistake at the final flight. He liked this ground and his in-form trainer is likely to run him under a penalty. (op 16-1 tchd 12-1)
Tabaran(FR) came here in excellent form and was on a hat-trick after being awarded a race at Newton Abbot a couple of days earlier. He ran another solid race under his penalty and is a good guide to this form. (op 5-1)
Wild Tonto(IRE) was without the cheekpieces and tongue tie on this first start since November and debut for the Twiston-Davies yard. Running his best race for a long while, he improved going well but could not quicken up in the straight. (op 17-2)
Parlesotho(FR) was ahead of the handicapper under the penalty she picked up when beating fellow mares at Stratford. She performed creditably but this quick reappearance was not ideal for her. (op 9-2)
Cool Bob(IRE) was in action just two nights earlier and could never get involved. This was not a bad effort but he has now managed no wins and just one placed run in 28 career starts. (op 12-1)
Key Cutter(FR) had finished second on three of his last four outings, but is racing off a career-high mark now and faded after losing his lead four from home. (op 9-1)
Singapore Reef(FR) did not see out this longer trip. Official explanation: trainer said, regarding running, that the race may have come too soon for the gelding
Brimley Official explanation: jockey said gelding was unsuited by the good to firm (good in places) ground and lost a shoe
Screenscraper(IRE) Official explanation: jockey said gelding lost its action

4 WELSH GUARDS ASSOCIATION NOVICES' HURDLE (9 hdls) 2m

3:40 (3:40) (Class 4) 4-Y-0+ **£4,228** (£1,241; £620; £310)

Form RPR

1 **Honorary Title (IRE)**[205] 1594 5-10-12 0 RichardJohnson 117+
(Tim Vaughan) *chsd ldrs: led appr 3 out: clr last: shkn up and styd on wl* **2/1**[1]

03- **2** *11* **Lucaindubai (IRE)**[66] 4118 4-10-7 0 PaulMoloney 102
(Evan Williams) *plld hrd and prom: chsd wnr after 3 out: styd on same pce appr last* **9/1**[3]

6P- **3** *3 1/2* **Icy Colt (ARG)**[70] 4059 4-10-0 0 (p) WillKennedy 91
(Paul Webber) *chsd ldr to appr 3 out: styd on same pce fr next* **66/1**

156- **4** *8* **Cresswell Bubbles**[186] 1853 7-10-5 0 PaddyBrennan 89
(Nigel Twiston-Davies) *hld up in tch: rdn appr 3 out: wknd next* **9/1**[3]

52- **5** *14* **Golden Button (IRE)**[48] 4490 5-10-5 0 (t) JasonMaguire 78
(Kim Bailey) *led: clr 4th: hdd appr 3 out: wkng whn hit next* **7/2**[2]

005- **6** *6* **Abulharith**[99] 3458 4-10-7 0 TomScudamore 73
(Michael Scudamore) *hld up: rdn and wknd bef 3 out* **33/1**

5F- **7** *22* **Sarika (FR)**[11] 5180 4-10-7 0 DarylJacob 53
(Nick Williams) *hld up: a in rr: racd keenly: blnd 4th: rdn after 6th: sn wknd: t.o* **2/1**[1]

8 *8* **Red Dagger (IRE)**[15] 4-10-4 0 GerardTumelty(3) 46
(Richard Price) *hld up: a in rr: rdn and wknd after 6th: t.o* **80/1**

P **Breadstick**[233] 4-9-11 0 TommyPhelan(3) —
(Christopher Nenadich) *a last and nt jump wl: t.o fr 4th: p.u bef 3 out* **80/1**

3m 38.6s (-10.90) **Going Correction** -0.60s/f (Firm)
WFA 4 from 5yo+ 6lb **9** Ran SP% **115.8**
Speed ratings (Par 105): **103,97,95,91,84 81,70,66,—**
Tote Swingers: 1&2 £17.60, 1&3 £53.70, 2&3 £2.00 CSF £21.25 TOTE £3.40: £2.30, £2.90, £25.50; EX 17.50.
Owner Pearn's Pharmacies Ltd **Bred** J Mernagh **Trained** Aberthin, Vale of Glamorgan

FOCUS
No more than a modest novice hurdle, but it was solidly run. The winner ran to his mark.

NOTEBOOK
Honorary Title(IRE), a bumper winner who made the frame in a couple of hurdles in the autumn for Paul Nolan in Ireland, was too good for some limited opposition on this debut for the Vaughan yard and was value for further. Likely to be given another run before connections decide whether to put him away until the autumn, he handles easier underfoot conditions. (tchd 9-4)
Lucaindubai(IRE) ran a promising race on his hurdling debut at Ffos Las in February and he again performed with credit, keeping on over this shorter trip without troubling the winner. A stiffer 2m could be what he wants. (tchd 8-1)
Icy Colt(ARG) showed little in his two previous starts and this was an improvement, with the cheekpieces not harming his cause. (op 50-1)
Cresswell Bubbles, making her hurdles debut on this first run in six months, has had just four starts but is already on her third trainer. She will need to improve to win over hurdles but has the option of races against her own sex. (op 8-1)
Golden Button(IRE), who was tried in a tongue-tie, made the running but was already on the retreat when blundering two from home. (tchd 4-1)
Abulharith has stamina limitations, even on this quicker ground, but he may not be without hope when switched to handicaps.
Sarika(FR) was always towards the back and this may have come too soon for him after his Cheltenham fall. (op 5-2)

5 TOTESPORTCASINO.COM H'CAP CHASE (17 fncs) 2m 4f

4:15 (4:14) (Class 3) (0-120,125) 5-Y-0+
£7,514 (£2,220; £1,110; £555; £277; £139)

Form RPR

054- **1** **Warpath (IRE)**[204] 1605 9-11-7 113 PaulMoloney 129+
(Evan Williams) *chsd ldr tl mstke 13th: led 2 out: mstke last: styd on wl* **5/1**[3]

5U4- **2** *5* **Magnetic Pole**[31] 4850 9-10-8 100 (p) CharliePoste 108
(Richard Lee) *prom: mstke 1st: chsd ldr 13th: rdn after 2 out: styd on same pce last* **8/1**

035- **3** 2 3/4 **Tyup Pompey (IRE)**[24] 4969 9-10-6 **101** LeeStephens(3) 105
(Ann Price) *chsd ldrs: nt fluent 9th(water): outpcd 12th: rdn appr 4 out: rallied flat: r.o to go 3rd nr fin* **7/1**

15P/ **4** *hd* **Neutrino**[534] 2047 8-10-7 **99** (p) RodiGreene 104
(David Bridgwater) *hld up: hdwy appr 4 out: rdn after 2 out: hung lft and styd on same pce flat* **33/1**

063- **5** 2 1/2 **Markila (FR)**[24] 4969 7-11-8 **114** RichardJohnson 116
(Henry Daly) *hld up: mstke 8th: plenty to do 5 out: r.o flat: nvr nrr* **7/2**[2]

621- **6** *1* **Sou'Wester**[7] 5259 10-11-12 **125** 7ex SamTwiston-Davies(7) 126
(Colin Tizzard) *prom: rdn after 5 out: wknd last* **2/1**[1]

144- **7** *4* **Gleann An Sagart**[287] 930 8-11-10 **116** TomScudamore 117+
(Michael Scudamore) *led: j.lft: hdd 2 out: wknd last* **9/1**

P6P- **P** **Scalini's (IRE)**[32] 4824 10-9-11 **92** oh14 (p) TommyPhelan(3) —
(Christopher Nenadich) *sn wl bhd: t.o fr 4th: p.u bef 12th* **66/1**

4m 53.3s (-11.10) **Going Correction** -0.375s/f (Good) course record **8** Ran SP% **110.3**
Speed ratings: **107,105,103,103,102 102,100,—**
Tote Swingers: 1&2 £7.40, 1&3 £7.90, 2&3 £9.70 CSF £40.23 CT £261.55 TOTE £6.90: £1.90, £2.90, £2.10; EX 51.00.
Owner R J Gambarini **Bred** Mrs Sue Hill **Trained** Llancarfan, Vale Of Glamorgan

FOCUS
A fair handicap chase run at a brisk pace, and solid form. All bar the pulled-up Scalini's were still in contention as they turned for home.

NOTEBOOK
Warpath(IRE) had come down to a mark the best part of a stone lower than when last winning nearly two years ago, and he had gone well when fresh in the past, so an absence since October was unlikely to pose a problem. Despite a less than immaculate round of jumping, he came away from the second-last to win a shade comfortably. (op 9-2)
Magnetic Pole was never far from the pace and posted a solid effort. Other than a mistake at the first he jumped well enough, and he turned around last month's form with a couple of these. (op 9-1)
Tyup Pompey(IRE), a place ahead of today's runner-up last time, has not won since taking this contest off a 2lb higher mark 12 months ago. He appreciated this return to better ground and stayed on well on the run-in after jumping the last in sixth place. (op 6-1)
Neutrino had not run since November 2008 and this was a pleasing return to action. He had been dropped 8lb during his absence and is now operating off his last winning mark. (op 25-1)
Markila(FR) stayed on without quite getting into contention on this faster ground. (op 4-1)
Sou'Wester was anchored under the penalty for his Wincanton victory over 2m. Official explanation: trainer said race possibly came too soon for gelding (op 15-8 tchd 7-4)
Gleann An Sagart ⊠ was responsible for setting the pace and was only headed going to the second-last. He was still in third place over the final fence but got in close and was relegated four places on the run-in. He should improve for his first run since July and he can pay his way through the summer. (op 10-1 tchd 11-1)

6 MCGRATH FOR SKIPS HUNTERS' CHASE (FOR THE LUDLOW GOLD CUP) (17 fncs) 2m 4f
4:45 (4:45) (Class 5) 6-Y-0+ **£2,186** (£677; £338; £169)

Form RPR

/PF- **1** **Whataboutya (IRE)**[8] 5233 9-11-3 115 (p) MissJennyCarr(7) 125+
(Jonjo O'Neill) *prom: hmpd by loose horse and lost pl 2nd: hdwy 6th: chsd ldr after 3 out: led flat: shkn up and styd on wl* **6/1**[3]

334- **2** 3 1/2 **Distant Thunder (IRE)**[17] 5106 12-11-3 102 (t) MrJHamer(7) 116
(Miss Jane Western) *hld up: hdwy 10th: led appr 4 out: rdn and hdd flat: styd on same pce* **3/1**[2]

4/4- **3** *11* **Emotional Article (IRE)**[14] 10-11-3 123 MrAWadlow(7) 106
(Mrs Belinda Clarke) *chsd ldr 2nd tl hmpd by loose horse 5th: remained handy tl rdn and wknd bef last* **6/1**[3]

060/ **4** *13* **Fairwood Present (IRE)**[22] 12-11-3 0 MrJRJarrett(7) 92
(John Buxton) *prom: chsd ldr 6th tl led 13th: rdn and hdd bef next: wknd bef 2 out* **17/2**

630- **5** 4 1/2 **Give Me Love (FR)**[8] 5233 10-11-3 82 (b) MrJackTurner(7) 88
(F L Matthews) *led to 13th: wknd next* **33/1**

5P6- **6** *72* **Made In France (FR)**[44] 4562 10-11-3 70 MrJHooper(7) 16
(Miss Helen Herrick) *hld up: plld hrd: hdwy 6th: wknd 11th: t.o* **66/1**

223- **P** **Cheeky Lad**[299] 829 10-12-0 115 MrNickWilliams —
(T M Stephenson) *rel to r: a in rr: t.o whn p.u bef 11th* **5/2**[1]

P44- **P** **Enitsag (FR)**[7] 11-11-7 99 MrJFlook(7) —
(S Flook) *hld up: rdn after 9th: a in rr: t.o whn p.u bef 11th* **10/1**

2/P- **P** **Donovan (NZ)**[14] 11-11-3 0 (p) MrBFurnival(7) —
(Mrs C J Robinson) *mid-div: dropped to rr 4th: t.o fr 9th: p.u bef 12th* **25/1**

/UP- **U** **Saucy Bingo (IRE)**[31] 4845 8-11-3 100 MrAMaskill(7) —
(Miss Helen Herrick) *w ldr whn uns rdr 1st* **25/1**

6F4/ **U** **Orvita (FR)**[29] 8-11-3 0 MrDNelmes(7) 82
(K A Nelmes) *hld up: a in rr: bhd fr 10th: t.o whn blnd and uns rdr last* **25/1**

4m 57.4s (-7.00) **Going Correction** -0.375s/f (Good) **11** Ran SP% **117.7**
Speed ratings: **99,97,93,88,86 57,—,—,—,— —**
Tote Swingers: 1&2 £4.60, 1&3 £5.50, 2&3 £3.70 CSF £23.91 TOTE £7.40: £2.50, £1.30, £2.50; EX 32.20.
Owner John P McManus **Bred** Mrs Maggie Wilson **Trained** Cheltenham, Gloucs

FOCUS
A very moderate hunter chase rated through the second.

NOTEBOOK
Whataboutya(IRE), a fair chaser for Noel Meade in Ireland, had failed to complete in two starts in this sphere. He became his connections' first string following the defection of Good Company and ultimately won comfortably under a tidy ride after a loose horse had hampered him a couple of times. (op 7-1 tchd 15-2)
Distant Thunder(IRE) is understandably not the horse he once was but he is still capable of operating respectably at this level. Equipped with a tongue tie for the first time, he struck the front turning into the straight but could not hold off the winner from the last. (op 10-3 tchd 5-2)
Emotional Article(IRE)'s limitations have been exposed in point-to-points since his second over course and distance on his British debut in February. Keen to post, he was never far from the action before eventually fading between the last two. (op 9-2)
Fairwood Present(IRE), who has been very lightly raced in recent years, was never far from the pace and led briefly early in the straight before fading. (op 14-1)
Cheeky Lad was reluctant to race on this first start since last summer and trailed the field until pulling up. (tchd 3-1)

7 JENKINSONS CATERERS INTERMEDIATE OPEN NATIONAL HUNT FLAT RACE 2m
5:15 (5:15) (Class 5) 4-6-Y-0 **£2,276** (£668; £334; £166)

Form RPR

3- **1** **Barthelemy**[31] 4853 5-11-3 0 APMcCoy 99+
(Nicky Henderson) *hld up in tch: led on bit over 1f out: readily* **13/8**[1]

2 *4* **Royale's Charter** 4-10-12 0 DarylJacob 87+
(Nick Williams) *hld up: hdwy 4f out: rdn and hung rt over 1f out: styd on to go 2nd ins fnl f: no ch w wnr* **5/1**[3]

0- **3** *5* **Steel Bullet (IRE)**[29] 4893 4-10-12 0 AlanO'Keeffe 82
(Jennie Candlish) *led 1f: chsd ldrs: led again over 4f out: rdn and hdd over 1f out: wknd ins fnl f* **16/1**

\- **4** *8* **Verde Goodwood** 4-10-5 0 LeightonAspell 67
(Oliver Sherwood) *hld up: hdwy over 3f out: sn rdn: wknd over 2f out* **7/1**

5 3/4 **Definite Dawn (IRE)**[147] 6-11-3 0 RichardJohnson 78
(Tim Vaughan) *hld up: hdwy 1/2-way: rdn over 3f out: wknd over 2f out* **3/1**[2]

00- **6** *hd* **Taylors Secret**[60] 4235 4-10-12 0 TomMessenger 73
(Shaun Lycett) *prom: racd keenly: rdn over 3f out: wknd over 2f out* **40/1**

00- **7** *28* **Al Sirat**[134] 2842 4-10-12 0 ChristianWilliams 45
(Brendan Powell) *sn chsng ldr: rdn over 3f out: sn wknd: t.o* **25/1**

6- **8** *dist* **Beck's Bolero (IRE)**[31] 4853 4-10-12 0 PaulMoloney —
(Evan Williams) *led after 1f: hung lft and hdd over 4f out: sn wknd and eased: t.o* **12/1**

9 *dist* **Irish Love** 4-10-12 0 LiamTreadwell —
(Roy Brotherton) *hld up: rdn and wknd 5f out: t.o* **25/1**

3m 42.2s (-1.70) **Going Correction** -0.60s/f (Firm)
WFA 4 from 5yo+ 6lb **9** Ran SP% **116.0**
Speed ratings: **80,78,75,71,71 71,57,—,—**
Tote Swingers: 1&2 £3.20, 1&3 £8.00, 2&3 £11.10 CSF £9.92 TOTE £2.40: £1.10, £1.70, £5.30; EX 13.00 Place 6: £67.42 Place 5: £58.10 .
Owner Howard Spooner **Bred** Lord Fairhaven **Trained** Upper Lambourn, Berks

FOCUS
There was no great pace on in this ordinary bumper. The winner produced a step forward.

NOTEBOOK
Barthelemy had shown ability when third on his debut over course and distance, and the winner of that race Big Time Billy had boosted the form by winning the mares' Listed bumper at Aintree. This faster ground was up his street and he ran out a very fluent winner. He should make the grade over hurdles. (op 7-4)
Royale's Charter is a half-brother to winning hurdler Fleur De Vassy out of a useful chaser at around 3m. He was a little reluctant to go to post but ran a promising race, staying on well to go second inside the final furlong. This was too sharp for him and he looks to have a future. (op 9-2)
Steel Bullet(IRE) attracted support first time out at Newbury and he showed ability here, leading in the straight but unable to hold off the winner and second.
Verde Goodwood is a half-sister to useful jumpers Winsley, Argento Luna and Lyes Green, and she showed enough on this debut to suggest she will be paying her way. (op 15-2)
Definite Dawn(IRE)'s win in an Irish point in November came in very different ground. (op 7-2)
Beck's Bolero(IRE), just under 7l behind Barthelemy here last month, made the running, but he had steering problems and was virtually pulled-up going into the home turn. Official explanation: jockey said gelding hung badly left-handed (op 11-1)
T/Plt: £143.70 to a £1 stake. Pool: £49,280.99. 250.29 winning tickets. T/Qpdt: £68.40 to a £1 stake. Pool: £3,608.22. 39.02 winning tickets. CR

WETHERBY (L-H)
Sunday, April 25

OFFICIAL GOING: Good (good to firm in places; 7.5)
Wind: light 1/2 behind Weather: overcast, heavy rainstorm race 3 & 4

8 NATIONAL FESTIVAL CIRCUS IS HERE TODAY MAIDEN HURDLE (12 hdls) 2m 6f
2:20 (2:20) (Class 5) 4-Y-0+ **£2,055** (£599; £299)

Form RPR

1 **Thyne For Deploy (IRE)**[31] 4857 6-10-7 109 APHeskin(7) 111
(Michael Hourigan, Ire) *chsd ldrs: wnt clr 2nd appr 3 out: rdn to ld narrowly last: edgd rt: hld on towards fin* **15/8**[1]

002- **2** 1/2 **Teenage Kicks (IRE)**[20] 5039 5-11-0 102 WarrenMarston 111
(Pam Sly) *trckd ldrs: led after 9th: hdd last: crowded: no ex nr fin* **9/4**[2]

663- **3** *22* **Carmela Maria**[39] 4680 5-10-7 90 KeithMercer 86
(Mike Sowersby) *chsd ldrs: wnt clr 3rd appr 3 out: one pce* **7/1**

356- **4** *7* **Pair Of Kings (IRE)**[26] 4942 5-11-0 0 BrianHughes 87
(Alan Swinbank) *trckd ldrs: fdd fr 3 out* **25/1**

000- **5** *18* **Baileys Surprise (IRE)**[35] 4752 8-10-11 86 AdrianLane(3) 73
(Tracy Waggott) *nt fluent: in rr: hdwy 8th: nvr nr ldrs* **40/1**

663- **6** *20* **Almond Court (IRE)**[14] 5140 7-10-2 79 JamesHalliday(5) 50
(Robert Johnson) *in rr: hdwy 6th: sn chsng ldrs: wknd appr 3 out* **14/1**

0- **7** *11* **Davids City (IRE)**[46] 4509 6-11-0 0 RichieMcGrath 48
(Geoffrey Harker) *in rr: mstke 1st: hdwy 7th: wknd 9th* **50/1**

/00- **8** *3* **Ruby Queen (IRE)**[61] 4210 8-10-7 0 PaddyAspell 39
(Geoffrey Harker) *in rr: sme hdwy 6th: drvn and lost pl after next: sn bhd* **100/1**

04- **9** *3* **Orkney (IRE)**[14] 5146 5-11-0 0 DougieCostello 43
(Julie Camacho) *in rr: hdwy 7th: lost pl after 9th* **13/2**[3]

540- **10** *28* **Mzuri Bay**[66] 4123 5-11-0 0 MarkGrant 21
(Brendan Duke) *nt jump wl: mid-div: bhd fr 8th: blnd 3 out: t.o* **40/1**

0/0- **P** **Simhal**[54] 4368 6-10-11 0 MichaelO'Connell(3) —
(Clive Mulhall) *chsd ldrs: drvn 6th: wknd qckly: t.o whn p.u bef next* **200/1**

P- **P** **Molesden Glen (IRE)**[151] 2513 4-10-5 0 CampbellGillies(3) —
(Simon Waugh) *led: blnd 10th: sn hdd: wknd next: bhd whn p.u bef last* **100/1**

006- **P** **Warmaster (IRE)**[14] 5140 6-10-11 93 JamesO'Farrell(3) —
(Howard Johnson) *nt jump wl in rr: bhd and reminders 6th: t.o whn p.u bef 3 out* **22/1**

P- **P** **Valonty**[49] 4468 8-10-11 0 (tp) RyanMania(3) —
(Brian Storey) *trckd ldrs: wknd qckly 6th: t.o whn p.u bef next* **100/1**

0- **P** **Bzhamij Ai (SLO)**[10] 5199 6-10-7 0 (b[1]) JanFaltejsek —
(George Charlton) *chsd ldrs: stmbld 3rd: wknd qckly after 7th: t.o 9th: p.u bef next* **40/1**

5m 28.4s (1.60) **Going Correction** +0.225s/f (Yiel)
WFA 4 from 5yo+ 7lb **15** Ran SP% **119.0**
Speed ratings (Par 103): **106,105,97,95,88 81,77,76,75,65 —,—,—,—,—**
Tote Swingers: 1&2 £2.10, 1&3 £7.10, 2&3 £3.60 CSF £5.72 TOTE £3.30: £1.50, £1.30, £3.00; EX 7.20.
Owner Miss M M Hourigan **Bred** Cecil Ashe **Trained** Patrickswell, Co Limerick
⊠ Stewards' Enquiry : Jan Faltejsek caution: used whip when mare showed no response.

FOCUS
The front pair drew clear in what was a moderate maiden hurdle.

NOTEBOOK
Thyne For Deploy(IRE), representing the previous day's Bet365 Gold Cup winning trainer/jockey combination, had been struggling through the softer ground back home, and he appreciated the faster surface on offer here, eventually mastering the runner-up and shaping as though there could be improvement to come at 3m. (tchd 2-1)
Teenage Kicks(IRE) ran his best race over hurdles when second at Fakenham latest, and he tried to stretch the winner on this drop in trip, but was joined at the last and just lost out on the run-in. He stays well, and can win a minor race. (op 3-1)

Carmela Maria fared best of the remainder and can do better back in handicaps.
Pair Of Kings(IRE) should have a future in handicaps. (op 22-1)
Orkney(IRE) should have done better, but on the plus side he should get a workable handicap mark. (tchd 6-1 and 7-1 in a place)
Molesden Glen(IRE) Official explanation: jockey said gelding had a breathing problem

9 BOOK TICKETS ON-LINE @ WETHERBYRACING.CO.UK H'CAP CHASE (16 fncs) 2m 4f 110y

2:55 (2:55) (Class 4) (0-100,103) 5-Y-0+ **£3,252** (£955; £477; £238)

Form RPR
U65- **1** **Nothingbutthetruth (IRE)**[44] 4554 6-11-10 **98**.................... PhilKinsella 113+
(Tim Pitt) *hld up: hdwy to trck ldrs 12th: upsides whn lft in ld 4 out: drvn clr fr 2 out* **7/1**[3]
165- **2** *7* **Pistol Basc (FR)**[19] 5077 6-11-1 **89**.................... KeithMercer 95
(Ferdy Murphy) *prom: drvn and lft 3rd 4 out: 2 l 3rd last: kpt on to take n.d 2nd nr fin* **9/4**[1]
530- **3** *½* **Ginger's Lad**[19] 5073 6-10-1 **75**.................... BrianHughes 81
(Michael Easterby) *chsd ldrs: chalng whn lft 2nd 4 out: hit last: lost 2nd nr line* **11/2**[2]
P50- **4** *17* **Lindseyfield Lodge (IRE)**[14] 5139 9-10-8 **85**......(p) MichaelMcAlister(3) 79
(Robert Johnson) *led: hdd after 12th: wknd next: modest 4th whn mstke 2 out* **11/1**
/3P- **5** *5* **Reasonably Sure (IRE)**[27] 4931 10-10-2 **76**....................(v) BarryKeniry 64
(Patrick Morris) *chsd ldrs: outpcd 10th: lost pl 12th* **11/2**[2]
P44- **6** *30* **Crofton Arch**[31] 4836 10-10-0 **74** oh8....................(p) PaddyAspell 38
(John Dixon) *chsd ldrs: lost pl 9th: sn bhd: t.o 12th* **22/1**
/P0- **P** **Nifty Roy**[333] 495 10-11-7 **98**.................... JamesO'Farrell(3) —
(Barry Murtagh) *stdd s: detached in rr: bhd fr 10th: t.o 12th: p.u bef next* **40/1**
3F5- **U** **Ice Image (IRE)**[14] 5139 8-11-1 **89**....................(t) JanFaltejsek —
(George Charlton) *w ldrs: led after 12th: jnd whn blnd and uns rdr next* **11/2**[2]
450- **P** **Arctic Rock**[49] 4472 7-9-10 **80** ow2.................... BarryBrowne(10) —
(Geoffrey Harker) *mstkes: prom: lost pl 7th: sn bhd: sddle slipped: p.u bef 9th* **14/1**

5m 9.90s (2.10) **Going Correction** +0.225s/f (Yiel) **9** Ran SP% **111.2**
Speed ratings: **105,102,102,95,93 82,—,—,—**
Tote Swingers: 1&2 £2.00, 1&3 £8.80, 2&3 £3.30 CSF £22.85 CT £89.69 TOTE £8.60: £3.30, £1.10, £2.30; EX 26.40.
Owner Ferrybank Properties Limited **Bred** P A Byrne **Trained** Norton, N Yorks

FOCUS
This was a moderate handicap chase.

NOTEBOOK
Nothingbutthetruth(IRE), held when unseating on his one previous outing over fences, had run well off similar marks over hurdles in the past and he jumped well down the straight to run out a ready winner. He remains capable of better over fences. (op 13-2)
Pistol Basc(FR) failed to stay 3m1f at the course last time, but he was found wanting for pace on this drop in trip, keeping on late to take second. (op 2-1)
Ginger's Lad, who was backed beforehand, almost certainly cost himself second with a mistake at the last, but there will be other days for this lightly raced sort. (tchd 5-1)
Reasonably Sure(IRE) was backed beforehand but couldn't deliver a challenge. (op 8-1 tchd 5-1)
Ice Image(IRE) was again undone by his shoddy jumping, unseating when still just in front four out. (op 7-1 tchd 5-1)
Arctic Rock Official explanation: jockey said saddle slipped (op 7-1 tchd 5-1)

10 WETHERBY RACECOURSE FOR CONFERENCES & EVENTS LADY RIDERS' H'CAP HURDLE (9 hdls) 2m 110y

3:30 (3:30) (Class 5) (0-95,99) 4-Y-0+ **£2,055** (£599; £299)

Form RPR
P52- **1** **More Like It (IRE)**[14] 5145 10-11-2 **92**....................(p) MissCCundall(7) 95
(Peter Niven) *prom: outpcd after 3rd: hdwy appr 3 out: led appr last: kpt on* **11/2**[3]
00P- **2** *2 ¼* **Nobel (FR)**[30] 4863 9-9-7 **69** oh1....................(p) MissSamanthaDrake(7) 70
(Brian Storey) *chsd ldrs: upsides between last 2: styd on same pce run-in* **25/1**
660- **3** *1 ¾* **Humourous (IRE)**[190] 1790 8-9-11 **73**....................(t) MissJRRichards(7) 72
(Brian Storey) *led: hdd appr 3 out: upsides between last 2: kpt on same pce* **12/1**
40P- **4** *4 ½* **Evelith Regent (IRE)**[86] 3721 7-10-1 **77**.............. MissCarolineHurley(7) 72
(John Davies) *stdd s: t.k.h: hdwy appr 3 out: led after 2 out: hdd appr last: sn wknd* **14/1**
00U- **5** *3 ¾* **Archie's Wish**[19] 5076 6-9-10 **72**.................... MissEStead(7) 65
(Micky Hammond) *chsd ldrs: lft in ld 2 out: sn hdd: hung lft and wknd last* **7/1**
020- **6** *3* **Mister Fizzbomb (IRE)**[11] 5072 7-10-11 **85**....................(v) MissADeniel(5) 75
(John Wainwright) *w ldr: hdd appr 3 out: wknd 2 out* **11/2**[3]
066- **7** *9* **King's Majesty (IRE)**[4] 5318 8-11-2 **90**......... GemmaGracey-Davison(5) 71
(Tim Pitt) *stdd s: in rr: hdwy 6th: sn drvn: wknd appr 2 out* **7/2**[1]
561- **8** *5* **Dobravany (IRE)**[14] 5145 6-11-9 **99**....................(v) MissKLMorgan(7) 76
(Kevin Morgan) *stdd s: in rr: nvr on terms* **4/1**[2]
000- **9** *49* **Sea Cove**[135] 2820 10-11-3 **93**.................... MissECSayer(7) 26
(Dianne Sayer) *mid-div: lost pl after 4th: sn bhd: t.o 6th* **10/1**
/PP- **U** **Perez (IRE)**[75] 3952 8-9-7 **69** oh7....................(v) MissLAlexander(7) 82+
(Wilf Storey) *trckd ldrs: led appr 3 out and sn 10 l clr: 15 l infront whn tried to refuse: swvd rt and uns rdr 2 out* **50/1**

4m 7.80s (12.00) **Going Correction** +0.675s/f (Soft) **10** Ran SP% **114.7**
Speed ratings (Par 103): **98,96,96,94,92 90,86,84,61,—**
Tote Swingers: 1&2 £29.60, 1&3 £26.80, 2&3 £18.50 CSF £119.27 CT £1572.67 TOTE £4.60: £1.10, £5.30, £5.40; EX 178.20.
Owner Sandy Lodge Racing Club & P D Niven **Bred** Tom O'Connor **Trained** Barton-le-Street, N Yorks

FOCUS
A low-grade handicap hurdle.

NOTEBOOK
More Like It(IRE), back to form when second in a selling handicap hurdle at Market Rasen latest (behind Dobravany), is currently rated 5lb lower than over fences and he simply stayed on too well for his rivals, coming through to take it up before the last, having been outpaced. (op 9-2 tchd 6-1)
Nobel(FR), who was 1lb 'wrong' at the weights, has shown no worthwhile form for three years, so this rather came from out of nowhere. The better ground was clearly a help, but it remains to be seen whether he can repeat the form.
Humourous(IRE) ran a fair enough race on this first start for 190 days, keeping on once headed.
Evelith Regent(IRE), who stopped quickly having himself been overtaken at the last. (op 16-1)
King's Majesty(IRE), well beaten at Southwell just four days earlier, was well supported, but never really threatened, fading having tried to close. (op 4-1 tchd 9-2)
Dobravany(IRE) was another who failed to get involved, and failed by some way to confirm recent form with the winner. Official explanation: trainer had no explanation for the poor form shown other than the gelding tends to be unreliable. (tchd 9-2)

Perez(IRE), who had failed to complete on his last three outings, was in the process of running his best race as a hurdler and was set to lose his maiden tag prior to trying to refuse and unseating. (op 40-1)

11 YORKSHIRE POST LADIES DAY - 20TH MAY H'CAP CHASE (18 fncs) 3m 1f

4:00 (4:01) (Class 3) (0-130,118) 5-Y-0+ **£6,505** (£1,910; £955; £477)

Form RPR
0F3- **1** **Dawn Ride (IRE)**[19] 5075 9-11-1 **107**....................(p) BarryKeniry 117+
(Micky Hammond) *trckd ldrs: smooth hdwy appr 4 out: led on bit 3 out: shkn up and drew clr last 75yds* **10/3**[3]
241- **2** *3* **Killard Point (IRE)**[19] 5077 11-11-12 **118**.................... AndrewThornton 125
(Caroline Bailey) *led: nt fluent: reminders after 9th: hdd 13th: led after next: hdd 3 out: kpt on same pce run-in* **11/10**[1]
5/5- **3** *44* **Hold The Bid (IRE)**[19] 5075 10-11-7 **113**.................... HenryOliver 97
(Sue Smith) *jnd ldr1st: nt fluent 2nd: jnd ldr 12th: led next: hdd after 14th: wknd 3 out: t.o last* **3/1**[2]
664- **4** *32* **Water Taxi**[43] 4577 9-11-6 **112**.................... GrahamLee 56
(Ferdy Murphy) *hld up in last: jnd ldrs 9th: hit 13th: outpcd whn blnd and lost pl next: sn wl bhd: t.o and completed in own time* **13/2**

6m 28.2s (18.80) **Going Correction** +0.675s/f (Soft) **4** Ran SP% **109.0**
Speed ratings: **107,106,91,81**
CSF £7.76 TOTE £4.60; EX 11.30.
Owner Belarus 2 Partnership **Bred** David Lyons **Trained** Middleham Moor, N Yorks

FOCUS
A competitive handicap chase, despite there being just the four runners.

NOTEBOOK
Dawn Ride(IRE) returned to something like his best, making it course win number four. He had found the trip too sharp when only third last time, and could be called the winner from some way out, cantering to the front three out and coming away after the last. (tchd 3-1 and 7-2)
Killard Point(IRE), 4lb higher than when winning over course and distance earlier in the month, didn't jump as well as he can, but again gave his all, and simply wasn't good enough. (op 11-8 tchd 6-4 in places)
Hold The Bid(IRE) ended up well beaten, but it's possible he still needed this, as it was only his second run back from a lengthy break. (tchd 11-4)
Water Taxi gradually became detached having made mistakes. (op 4-1)

12 WETHERBY RACES "FAMILY DAY" (S) H'CAP HURDLE (11 hdls) 2m 4f

4:35 (4:35) (Class 5) (0-90,88) 4-7-Y-0 **£2,055** (£599; £299)

Form RPR
550- **1** **Zelos Diktator**[9] 5216 4-11-2 **84**.................... WayneHutchinson 85
(Rose Dobbin) *in rr: hdwy 8th: sn chsng ldrs: led 2 out: nt fluent last: styd on to forge clr run-in* **10/1**
606- **2** *4* **Cosmetic**[49] 4471 5-10-10 **75**.................... JamesO'Farrell(3) 78
(Howard Johnson) *chsd ldrs: ev ch 2 out: j.lft last: kpt on same pce* **20/1**
005- **3** *4* **Lifes A Mystery (IRE)**[152] 2493 7-10-1 **63**....................(p) RichieMcGrath 63
(Pauline Robson) *chsd ldrs: led 7th: hdd 2 out: one pce appr last* **3/1**[1]
540- **4** *1 ¼* **Naughty Diesel**[19] 5072 7-10-8 **75**....................(t) JamesHalliday(5) 74
(Robert Johnson) *hld up in rr: hdwy 7th: chsng ldrs 3 out: nt fluent last: fdd* **14/1**
060- **5** *¾* **Lukey Luke**[20] 5038 7-11-4 **80**.................... PeterBuchanan 78
(James Turner) *in rr: hdwy 7th: one pce fr 2 out* **25/1**
40P- **6** *11* **Pugnacity**[49] 4471 6-10-10 **75**.................... RyanMania(3) 68
(Dianne Sayer) *chsd ldrs: upsides 2 out: wknd appr last* **6/1**[2]
000- **7** *¾* **Toujours Souriante**[11] 3688 4-10-4 **72**.................... PaddyAspell 55
(Tracy Waggott) *in rr: hdwy 8th: wknd 2 out* **10/1**
4F0- **8** *nk* **Still Calm**[46] 4510 6-11-8 **87**....................(t) MichaelMcAlister(3) 76
(Maurice Barnes) *mid-div: hdwy to chse ldrs 6th: wknd 2 out* **28/1**
P03- **9** *53* **Daarth**[55] 4353 5-11-11 **87**....................(tp) MarkGrant 33
(Brendan Duke) *mid-div: bhd fr 8th: t.o* **9/1**[3]
6P0- **P** **Masra**[34] 4779 7-11-11 **87**.................... GrahamLee —
(Alan Kirtley) *in rr: nt fluent: drvn 5th: sn bhd: t.o whn p.u bef 3 out* **25/1**
0/0- **P** **Noble Edge**[52] 3895 7-10-7 **76**....................(t) KyleJames(7) —
(Lee James) *t.k.h: w ldrs: led after 2nd: hdd 7th: sn wknd: t.o whn p.u bef 3 out* **20/1**
4U0- **P** **Blue Jet (USA)**[68] 4094 6-11-12 **88**....................(b[1]) KeithMercer —
(Mike Sowersby) *chsd ldrs: wkng whn mstke 8th: bhd whn p.u bef 3 out* **33/1**
0/0- **P** **Miss Cruisecontrol**[350] 234 5-11-5 **86**.................... MarcGoldstein(5) —
(Jim Best) *toward rr: drvn and wknd 6th: sn bhd: t.o whn p.u bef 3 out* **14/1**
PPU- **P** **Luce Bay**[89] 3669 7-11-1 **77**....................(b) WarrenMarston —
(Richard Phillips) *led: racd keenly: hdd after 2nd: reminders 5th: lost pl after 8th: bhd whn p.u bef 2 out* **20/1**
35P- **P** **Hazy Oaks**[14] 5145 7-11-9 **85**....................(p) JamesReveley —
(Philip Kirby) *mid-div: lost pl 8th: sn bhd: t.o whn p.u bef next* **12/1**
06U- **P** **If You Knew Suzy**[13] 5166 5-10-8 **70**.................... PhilKinsella —
(Ron Barr) *mid-div: wknd 7th: t.o whn p.u bef 3 out* **33/1**
050- **P** **Spruzzo**[46] 4509 4-10-7 **80**....................(b[1]) PaulCallaghan(5) —
(C W Thornton) *sn bhd: reminders 3rd: t.o 5th: p.u bef next* **50/1**
000- **P** **Great Vintage (IRE)**[86] 3726 5-10-0 **62** oh3....................(b[1]) BrianHughes —
(Peter Niven) *sn trcking ldrs: wknd after 8th: bhd whn p.u bef 2 out* **16/1**

5m 22.6s (23.10) **Going Correction** +1.025s/f (Soft)
WFA 4 from 5yo+ 7lb **18** Ran SP% **127.6**
Speed ratings: **94,92,90,90,90 85,85,85,63,— —,—,—,—,— —,—,—**
Tote Swingers: 1&2 £78.20, 1&3 £16.20, 2&3 £23.40 CSF £200.94 CT £762.47 TOTE £11.70: £2.90, £2.60, £1.60, £4.00; EX 370.10.There was no bid for the winner.
Owner Tremousser Partnership **Bred** The Duke Of Roxburghe's Stud **Trained** South Hazelrigg, Northumbria
⊠ Stewards' Enquiry : James O'Farrell one-day ban: careless riding (May 9)

FOCUS
An open-looking selling handicap hurdle.

NOTEBOOK
Zelos Diktator ⊠ had failed to reach the places in five previous starts over hurdles, but he was really helped by the further drop in grade, and actually ran out a rather comfy winner. It would be unwise to get carried away, but he certainly looks capable of winning again. Official explanation: trainer said, regarding apparent improvement in form, that the gelding had benefited from the step up in trip, the drop in grade and by being settled further back in the field. (op 14-1 tchd 9-1)
Cosmetic appreciated the better ground and left behind her disappointing Sedgefield running, keeping on without being able to match the winner. (op 18-1)
Lifes A Mystery(IRE) hadn't run since November, so it entitled to improve, and he certainly looks capable of winning something similar. (op 7-2)
Naughty Diesel failed to get home having made a good forward move. (op 16-1)
Lukey Luke made a little late headway, but was never close enough to challenge. (op 28-1)

Pugnacity was another to weaken having moved well. (op 8-1)

13 JCT600 - CHRYSLER - JEEP - DODGE BEGINNERS' CHASE (18 fncs) 2m 6f 110y

5:05 (5:06) (Class 4) 5-Y-0+ **£3,332** (£1,034; £557)

Form RPR

0P4- **1** **Le Platino (GER)**31 4834 8-11-0 95 (p) BrianHughes 108+
(Brian Storey) *j.rt: mde all: wnt 10 l clr 14th: reminders and 30 l ahd bef next: unchal* **85/40**2

52P- **2** 37 **Greenbelt**14 5153 9-11-0 118 KeithMercer 81
(George Moore) *chsd wnr: shkn up 8th: sn rdn: dropped modest last 13th: wnt poor 2nd 4 out: blnd last* **4/6**1

0P6- **3** 61 **Stolen Light (IRE)**36 4732 9-10-11 75 (b) MichaelO'Connell(3) 30
(Andrew Crook) *racd keenly: chsd wnr 9th: rdn 12th: wknd 4 out: bhd whn mstkes next 2: wl t.o* **12/1**

\- **P** **Aurifex (IRE)**722 6-11-0 0 PaddyAspell —
(Paul Murphy) *t.k.h in last: hung rt and j. violently rt: lost tch 9th: t.o whn p.u bef next* **9/1**3

5m 58.2s (21.20) **Going Correction** +1.025s/f (Soft) 4 Ran SP% **109.7**
Speed ratings: **104,91,69,—**
CSF £4.22 TOTE £4.10; EX 5.00.
Owner John Wade **Bred** Carlton Consultants Ltd **Trained** Boltonfellend, Cumbria

FOCUS
A weak beginners' chase, especially in the absence of likely favourite Baren De Doc.

NOTEBOOK
Le Platino(GER), rated just 95, made all for an easy success, jumping well and really pressing on a long way from the finish. The form is worth very little, and he will now find it a lot tougher back in handicaps, but this was only his third start over fences, so he may yet improve. (op 9-4 tchd 2-1)
Greenbelt lacks scope for fences and was blown away by a less-exposed type. It's likely that he will continue to struggle to get his head in front. (op 10-11)
Stolen Light(IRE) managed to get round, but achieved little. (op 10-1 tchd 14-1)
Aurifex(IRE) took a real grip and didn't appear to like going this way round. Official explanation: jockey said gelding hung right (op 6-1)

14 ROYAL PIGEON RACING ASSOCIATION NOVICES' HURDLE (9 hdls) 2m 110y

5:35 (5:37) (Class 4) 4-Y-0+ **£2,740** (£798; £399)

Form RPR

445- **1** **Chief Bucaneer (IRE)**144 2646 7-10-12 0 JanFaltejsek 115+
(George Charlton) *t.k.h: trckd ldrs: nt fluent: j.rt 5th: chalng whn blnd 3 out: styd on to ld nr fin* **7/4**1

060- **2** ½ **The Magic Bishop**39 4683 5-10-12 0 PhilKinsella 110
(Malcolm Jefferson) *w ldrs: led 4th: kpt on wl fr 3 out: hdd and no ex cl home* **22/1**

436- **3** 33 **Bucephalus (IRE)**3 5333 6-10-9 104 (t) MichaelMcAlister(3) 91+
(Maurice Barnes) *chsd ldrs: wknd appr 2 out: tired and eased run-in* **3/1**2

004- **4** 13 **Cornish Castle (USA)**46 4510 4-10-7 90 BarryKeniry 68
(Joss Saville) *mid-div: blnd 3rd: sn given reminders: outpcd 6th: poor 4th whn mstke and rdr briefly lost iron 2 out* **9/2**3

2- **5** 1 **Solo Choice**20 4876 4-10-4 0 CampbellGillies(3) 67
(Ian McInnes) *led to 4th: wknd rapidly 6th: sn bhd* **7/1**

340- **6** 79 **Hooked On Line (IRE)**20 5050 5-10-12 0 WarrenMarston 9
(Pam Sly) *stdd s: t.k.h in rr: blnd 6th: sn t.o* **14/1**

P **Shaftesbury Avenue (USA)**22 7-10-12 0 PaddyAspell —
(Ian McInnes) *in rr: wknd and t.o 4th: p.u bef next* **33/1**

P **Minnis Bay (CAN)**43 6-10-12 0 GrahamLee —
(Ferdy Murphy) *in rr: bhd fr 4th: t.o whn p.u bef 3 out* **14/1**

06- **F** **Secret Desert**19 5076 4-10-4 0 AdrianLane(3) —
(Paul Murphy) *in tch: trcking ldrs whn fell 4th* **25/1**

00- **P** **Little Miss Foozle**60 4235 6-10-2 0 BrianHughes(3) —
(Peter Niven) *in rr: bhd fr 4th: t.o whn p.u after 6th* **50/1**

UP- **P** **Camomile**54 4368 4-10-0 0 ow3 JamesO'Farrell(3) —
(Tracy Waggott) *in rr: bhd fr 4th: t.o whn p.u bef 3 out* **150/1**

0- **P** **Indienne Etoile**14 5138 6-10-0 0 JamesHalliday(5) —
(Robert Johnson) *in rr: bhd fr 4th: t.o whn p.u bef 3 out* **100/1**

4m 11.8s (16.00) **Going Correction** +1.025s/f (Soft)
WFA 4 from 5yo+ 6lb 12 Ran SP% **120.1**
Speed ratings (Par 105): **103,102,87,81,80 43,—,—,—,— —,—**
Tote Swingers: 1&2 £20.70, 1&3 £3.90, 2&3 £12.60 CSF £47.02 TOTE £2.90: £1.60, £5.10, £1.70; EX 68.80 Place 6: £345.31 Place 5: £277.04.
Owner George A Charlton **Bred** Gabriel White **Trained** Stocksfield, Northumberland

FOCUS
A modest novices' hurdle.

NOTEBOOK
Chief Bucaneer(IRE) did remarkably well to win considering his poor jumping, and can safely be rated a good bit better than the bare form. Despite making numerous errors, including one two out which looked to have handed the race to the winner, he made good ground on the flat and just got there in time. His jumping will need to be addressed if he is to defy a penalty, but he clearly has an engine. (op 11-4)
The Magic Bishop, well held on all three starts in bumpers, travelled well on this hurdles debut, but couldn't shake the winner off, and was eventually run down. He is clearly nothing special, but can win races. (op 18-1)
Bucephalus(IRE) couldn't handle two less exposed types. (op 11-4 tchd 5-2)
Cornish Castle(USA) will stand more of a chance back in handicaps. (tchd 4-1)
T/Jkpt: Not won. T/Plt: £598.20 to a £1 stake. Pool: £65,192.82. 79.55 winning tickets. T/Qpdt: £350.60 to a £1 stake. Pool: £4,264.09. 9.00 winning tickets. WG

FFOS LAS (L-H)

Monday, April 26

OFFICIAL GOING: Good to firm (good in places; 8.5)
Wind: Moderate against for Race 1, gradually to nil Weather: Sunny

15 FELINFOEL BREWERY DAY NOVICES' HURDLE (11 hdls) 2m 6f

5:20 (5:20) (Class 4) 4-Y-0+ **£2,602** (£764; £382)

Form RPR

65/ **1** **Native Taipan (IRE)**537 2009 8-10-13 0 APMcCoy 105+
(Rebecca Curtis) *hld up in rr: impr to ld 3 out: rdn between last 2: gd jump last: r.o: a doing enough cl home* **15/8**2

U32- **2** 1 **Acrai Rua (IRE)**25 4968 7-10-13 122 PaulMoloney 105+
(Evan Williams) *led: j. slowly 1st and 5th: hdd after 4 out: stl chalng 3 out: hung lft u.p and nt qckn appr last: continued to hang and styd on run-in: hld cl home* **8/13**1

00- **3** 22 **Classic Bavard**21 5048 8-10-13 0 TomScudamore 89
(Hughie Morrison) *racd in 2nd pl: led after 4 out: hdd 3 out: wknd 2 out: eased whn btn bef last* **14/1**3

5m 27.7s (9.70) 3 Ran SP% **103.4**
CSF £3.36 TOTE £2.60; EX 2.70.
Owner Miss Rebecca Curtis **Bred** James Ryan **Trained** Newport, Dyfed

FOCUS
This was never going to take much winning, with three of the original six declared not taking part. Not an easy race to put a figure on and the favourite is rated a stone below his best.

NOTEBOOK
Native Taipan(IRE) got the better of the favourite to make a winning hurdles debut. He had shaped reasonably well in a couple of bumpers in late 2008, and relished this longer distance, holding on well having taken the last in his stride. He will find life tougher under a penalty, but will be kept on the go and should find another suitable opportunity at some stage. (op 2-1)
Acrai Rua(IRE) had shown fair form in two previous hurdles, latterly being beaten by the smart but enigmatic Kennel Hill, so it was disappointing he could not capitalise on this easier opportunity, making life hard for his rider by hanging. He won't be seen at his best until chasing, but he can make his mark in handicap hurdles first. (op 4-7)
Classic Bavard showed more than he had done previously. For all that, he may have been flattered, and he should do better in handicaps. (op 10-1)

16 DOUBLE DRAGON NATIONAL ALE OF WALES H'CAP HURDLE (12 hdls) 3m

5:50 (5:51) (Class 5) (0-95,95) 4-Y-0+ **£1,951** (£573; £286; £143)

Form RPR

424- **1** **Midnight Gold**171 2096 10-11-11 **94** (p) WayneHutchinson 107+
(Peter Bowen) *led fr 1st: mde rest: j. slowly 7th: pressed fr 2 out: rdn appr last: r.o wl and plld clr run-in* **5/1**2

05F- **2** 6 **Back In Business (IRE)**37 4728 10-11-7 **90** (p) PaulMoloney 99
(Evan Williams) *trckd ldrs: chsd wnr appr 3 out: rdn and hung lft whn chalng fr 2 out: no ex run-in* **9/2**1

/P2- **3** dist **Strand Line (IRE)**16 5135 10-11-2 **92** PeterHatton(7) 69
(Lisa Day) *prom: rdn after 4 out: sn wl outpcd: n.d to front pair fr 3 out* **8/1**

414- **4** 1 **Paradise Expected**8 5257 7-11-12 **95** RichardJohnson 71
(Tim Vaughan) *hld up: pushed along fr bef 8th: woefully outpcd appr 3 out: kpt on modly fr 2 out: no imp* **13/2**

400- **5** 3¾ **Rocky Lane (IRE)**131 2909 6-11-11 **94** (t) JackDoyle 66
(Victor Dartnall) *led to 1st: trckd ldrs after: rdn and wknd after 4 out* **12/1**

P06- **6** 19 **Mangonel**8 5258 6-9-9 **69** oh5 (v) IanPopham(5) 24
(Stuart Howe) *prom: rdn and wknd appr 3 out: n.d whn mstke 2 out* **11/2**3

7 2½ **Tinalliat (FR)**324 7-11-2 **92** MrJFMathias(7) 45
(David Rees) *hld up: rdn and outpcd after 4 out: sn dropped away* **25/1**

0P5- **8** 4½ **Welsh Jaunt**32 4851 5-10-6 **82** MissIsabelTompsett(7) 31
(Brian Eckley) *hld up: rdn after 4 out: sn wl bhd* **14/1**

005- **P** **Septos**25 4968 6-10-11 **87** MrMPrice(7) —
(Richard Price) *in tch: rdn appr 3rd: lost pl 5th and bhd: t.o 7th: p.u bef 4 out* **16/1**

001- **P** **Walls Way**49 4483 6-11-2 **90** LeeEdwards(5) —
(Tony Carroll) *mstkes: a in rr: rdn after 6th: t.o 7th: p.u* **11/2**3

5m 55.4s (8.40) **Going Correction** -0.425s/f (Good) 10 Ran SP% **114.1**
Speed ratings (Par 103): **105,103,91,91,90 83,82,81,—,—**
toteswingers: 1&2 £5.50, 1&3 £8.10, 2&3 £13.10 CSF £27.64 CT £176.10 TOTE £5.90: £1.70, £2.50, £1.40; EX 29.00.
Owner Blue Skyes **Bred** Barton Stallion Partnership **Trained** Little Newcastle, Pembrokes

FOCUS
Few got into this handicap hurdle. The first two are both better over fences but produced hurdles personal bests.

NOTEBOOK
Midnight Gold made pretty much all the running. Rated 20lb lower over hurdles compared with fences, he was ridden positively and found extra from the last to win with a bit in hand. He can win again over hurdles when conditions are similar. (op 13-2)
Back In Business(IRE), a faller over fences at the course latest, had earlier run well off this mark over hurdles, and he looked a big danger to the winner. However, not for the first time, he didn't find as much as expected. (op 11-2)
Strand Line(IRE) has found some form and again ran well enough to suggest he has it in him to win a small race. (op 15-2 tchd 7-1)
Paradise Expected never got close enough to challenge, keeping on having been outpaced. (op 9-2)
Rocky Lane(IRE) dropped right away on this handicap debut, looking as though he didn't stay the 3m. (op 11-1)
Walls Way, 5lb higher than when winning at the course last time (runner-up behind), failed to reproduce the form. He was never jumping well and was eventually pulled up. (op 5-1 tchd 9-2)

17 CELTIC GOLD LAGER - WALES' PREMIUM LAGER NOVICES' H'CAP CHASE (18 fncs) 3m

6:25 (6:25) (Class 4) (0-115,102) 5-Y-0+ **£3,903** (£1,146; £573; £286)

Form RPR

416- **1** **Backfromthecongo (IRE)**22 5016 9-11-7 **97** (bt) JohnnyFarrelly 112+
(Richard Lee) *led 1st: mde rest: pckd 8th but gd rnd of jumping in the main: wnt sltly rt-handed fnl 4 fences: asserted bef last: r.o wl* **5/2**2

6P4- **2** 4½ **Brenin Cwmtudu**45 4571 7-11-9 **102** DPFahy(3) 113
(Evan Williams) *hld up bhd ldrs: mstke 3rd: j. slowly 4th: chsd wnr 11th: rdn after 2 out: sn no imp: kpt on same pce run-in* **10/3**3

033- **3** 10 **Gentleman Jimmy**15 5157 10-11-9 **99** TomScudamore 100
(Hughie Morrison) *hld up bhd ldrs: attempted to chal 4 out: outpcd fr 2 out* **7/4**1

4/3- **4** 17 **Sir Monty (USA)**9 5229 8-11-12 **102** (p) TomO'Brien 87
(Peter Bowen) *led to 1st: chsd wnr: dropped to last pl 12th: mstke and wknd 13th: j.rt whn toiling 4 out* **4/1**

6m 21.7s (-1.30) **Going Correction** -0.425s/f (Good) 4 Ran SP% **108.0**
Speed ratings: **85,83,80,74**
CSF £10.37 TOTE £4.60; EX 7.10.
Owner D Cound, J Jackson & A Compton **Bred** Stan Doyle **Trained** Byton, H'fords

FOCUS
Front-runners are often favoured over fences here, and Backfromthecongo made just about all. The first two are rated to form.

NOTEBOOK
Backfromthecongo(IRE) made just about all, jumping better than the runner-up down the straight and finding plenty for pressure. He had won nicely at the course last month, off 6lb lower, but won't always have things go his way. (op 11-4)
Brenin Cwmtudu improved on his Wincanton effort, keeping on right the way to the line, and would have given the winner more of a race had he been ridden more positively. We have still to see the best of him. (tchd 3-1 and 7-2)
Gentleman Jimmy has been in fair form, but it's been a while since he won a race, and he ultimately proved disappointing back in third. (op 2-1)

Sir Monty(USA) was the first one in trouble and got left well behind from the turn in. (op 11-4)

18 FELINFOEL BREWERY CAMBRIAN BEST BITTER H'CAP CHASE

(17 fncs) **2m 5f**

7:00 (7:00) (Class 2) (0-150,145) 5-Y£10,139 (£2,995; £1,497; £748; £374)

Form				RPR
3P2-	**1**		**Postmaster**[8] 5244 8-10-9 **128**............................ PaulMoloney (Evan Williams) *hld up: blnd 6th: hdwy 4 out: effrt to ld narrowly last: r.o and a doing enough* **6/1**	136
064-	**2**	*nk*	**Stan (NZ)**[10] 5208 11-11-0 **133**............................ AidanColeman (Venetia Williams) *trckd ldrs: wnt 2nd 5th: led 12th: j. sltly rt 2 out: hdd narrowly last: rallied gamely and pushed wnr all the way* **6/1**	141
121-	**3**	*2 ¾*	**Herons Well**[10] 5215 7-11-0 **133**............................(p) APMcCoy (Rebecca Curtis) *hld up: hdwy 12th: chal fr 4 out: stl chalng for press whn pckd last: no ex fnl 75yds* **6/4**[1]	140
P21-	**4**	*10*	**Silver Adonis (IRE)**[18] 5096 9-10-5 **124**............................(p) DarylJacob (Dr Richard Newland) *chsd ldrs: stl in contention appr 2 out: wknd last* **4/1**[2]	121
/34-	**5**	*1 ¼*	**Lord Henry (IRE)**[156] 2417 11-11-12 **145**............................ RichardJohnson (Philip Hobbs) *nt jump wl: hld up: hdwy to chse ldrs whn mstke 4 out: wknd 2 out* **15/2**	141
PPP-	**6**	*67*	**Psychomodo**[16] 5132 8-11-7 **140**............................(t) JimmyMcCarthy (Brendan Powell) *led: mstke 10th: hdd 12th: wknd appr 4 out: t.o* **33/1**	74
3F2-	**P**		**Coq Hardi (FR)**[10] 5206 9-10-10 **129**............................(t) TomO'Brien (Tim Vaughan) *chsd ldr to 5th: remained in tch tl wknd after 13th: bhd whn p.u bef 3 out: dismntd: lame* **11/2**[3]	—

5m 20.1s (-9.90) **Going Correction** -0.425s/f (Good) 7 Ran SP% **118.7**
Speed ratings: **109,108,107,104,103 78,—**
toteswingers: 1&2 £4.20, 1&3 £2.30, 2&3 £2.50 CSF £42.46 TOTE £5.80: £1.50, £2.60; EX 37.30.

Owner The Bill & Ben Partnership **Bred** Juddmonte Farms **Trained** Llancarfan, Vale Of Glamorgan

FOCUS

Decent handicap chase form with a small personal best from the winner. The second was a stone off his best old form.

NOTEBOOK

Postmaster just got the better of Stan in the finish. The winner, who had finished runner-up in a novices' chase at Ascot just eight days earlier, won the race with a superior kick after the last and remains capable of better under similar conditions. (op 13-2)

Stan(NZ), who ran his best race in ages when fifth at Cheltenham latest, was always likely to be suited by the step back up in trip, and he jumped really well under a positive ride. However, despite a spirited effort, he couldn't fend off the winner. He remains well weighted, and can end his losing run if kept on the go. (tchd 11-2 and 7-1)

Herons Well has been progressing really well, winning three of his last four, but he had been beaten off 9lb lower on his last outing in a handicap, and couldn't race on with the front pair from the last. (op 2-1)

Silver Adonis(IRE), 9lb higher than when last winning a handicap, could find no extra from before the last, and may still have been feeling the effects of his Aintree Fox Hunters' heroics. (op 3-1 tchd 9-2 and 5-1 in a place)

Lord Henry(IRE) had the ground in his favour, and looked interesting on this rise in distance, but he has never been the most fluent of jumpers, and again had trouble with several of his fences. (op 8-1)

Psychomodo needs to go right-handed. (op 25-1)

Coq Hardi(FR) was dismounted having been pulled up, something evidently going amiss. Official explanation: jockey said gelding pulled up lame (op 9-1)

19 CELTIC PRIDE - WALES' FAVOURITE PREMIUM ALE MARES' H'CAP HURDLE

(3 hdls 5 omitted) **2m**

7:30 (7:39) (Class 4) (0-115,115) 4-Y-O+ **£2,602** (£764; £382; £190)

Form				RPR
432-	**1**		**Madame Mado (FR)**[54] 4378 6-11-4 **105**............................ APMcCoy (Nicky Henderson) *trckd ldrs: wnt 2nd appr 1st: led last (over 6f out): a in command after: drew clr over 1f out: easily* **8/13**[1]	117+
020-	**2**	*3 ¼*	**Boogie Dancer**[8] 5261 6-10-8 **98**............................ HarrySkelton(3) (Stuart Howe) *hld up: hdwy last (over 6f out): chsd wnr in vain fr over 3f out: kpt on ins fnl f but nvr any ch* **9/1**[3]	95
534-	**3**	*4 ½*	**Stir On The Sea (IRE)**[8] 5253 4-10-10 **109**............................ AodhaganConlon(7) (Rebecca Curtis) *racd keenly: led for 1f on long run to 1st: remained prom: j. slowly last: pushed along after: one pce fr over 2f out* **16/1**	97
P04-	**4**	*3 ½*	**Garafena**[183] 1918 7-10-3 **90**............................ TomScudamore (Richard Lee) *hld up bhd ldrs: j. slowly 2nd: rdn over 3f out on long run-in: sn outpcd* **14/1**	80
402-	**5**	*6*	**Dabaratsa (FR)**[30] 4880 7-11-7 **108**............................(vt) RichardJohnson (Tim Vaughan) *racd keenly: led after 1f on long run to 1st: hdd last (over 6f out): rdn over 4f out: wknd over 2f out* **4/1**[2]	92
14-	**6**	*27*	**Halling Gal**[12] 5180 4-11-9 **115**............................ PaulMoloney (Evan Williams) *hld up: struggling over 3f out on long run-in: sn bhd* **9/1**[3]	70

3m 44.1s (-4.90) **Going Correction** -0.425s/f (Good)
WFA 4 from 5yo+ 6lb 6 Ran SP% **114.5**
Speed ratings (Par 105): **102,100,98,96,93 79**
toteswingers: 1&2 £1.20, 1&3 £4.50, 2&3 £18.70 CSF £7.34 TOTE £1.40: £1.10, £5.60; EX 5.60.

Owner Paul Murphy **Bred** Isabelle Plessis And Bertrand Plessis **Trained** Upper Lambourn, Berks

FOCUS

With all hurdles in the straight being taken out due to the sun, only three flights were jumped in total, and there was obviously an extremely long run from the last down the back straight to the line. A big step up from the facile winner who was value for a lot further.

NOTEBOOK

Madame Mado(FR), who was always in control having gone on, and just had to be ridden out to score. An opening mark of 105 was clearly lenient, and this wasn't a strong heat, but she looks more than capable of winning again, with her having the option of novice events. (op 10-11 tchd 5-4 in a place)

Boogie Dancer bounced back from a disappointing effort at Wincanton, keeping on for second without ever looking a threat to the winner. (tchd 17-2 and 10-1)

Stir On The Sea(IRE) stayed on the best she could without shaping a like a future winner. Official explanation: jockey said filly hung right (op 12-1)

Garafena could be worth another chance in a more truly-run race. (tchd 16-1)

Dabaratsa(FR) failed to get home having been free in front. (tchd 9-2)

Halling Gal hasn't gone on at all from her debut win, and the way she got left behind was rather disconcerting. (op 7-1 tchd 10-1)

20 FELINFOEL BREWERY DRAGON STOUT STANDARD OPEN NATIONAL HUNT FLAT RACE

2m

8:05 (8:06) (Class 6) 4-6-Y-O **£1,626** (£477; £238; £119)

Form				RPR
	1		**Manikon Eros (IRE)** 5-11-3 0............................ APMcCoy (Rebecca Curtis) *mde most: rdn over 2f out whn running green: clr over 1f out: r.o wl* **5/6**[1]	113+
02-	**2**	*10*	**Kilmore West (IRE)**[21] 5035 5-11-3 0............................ RichardJohnson (Tim Vaughan) *hld up bhd ldrs: hdwy 5f out: effrt to chse ldrs over 3f out: wnt 2nd u.p over 2f out: no imp on wnr: one pce fnl f* **2/1**[2]	104
40-	**3**	*4 ½*	**Seren Cwmtudu (IRE)**[11] 5199 6-10-7 0............................ DPFahy(3) (Evan Williams) *w wnr: rdn over 4f out: outpcd and lost 2nd over 2f out: wknd fnl f* **7/1**[3]	93
	4	*2 ½*	**Grandads Horse** 4-10-12 0............................ JackDoyle (Alan Jones) *trckd ldrs tl rdn and wknd over 4f out* **18/1**	93
30-	**5**	*8*	**Santamina (IRE)**[21] 5050 4-10-12 0............................ TomO'Brien (Peter Bowen) *hld up bhd ldrs: struggling over 4f out: sn dropped away and hung lft: nvr a danger* **12/1**	86

3m 40.2s (-3.20) **Going Correction** -0.425s/f (Good)
WFA 4 from 5yo+ 6lb 5 Ran SP% **113.3**
Speed ratings: **103,98,95,94,90**
CSF £2.86 TOTE £2.20: £1.80, £1.60; EX 2.40.

Owner G Costelloe **Bred** Justin Casey **Trained** Newport, Dyfed

FOCUS

A weak bumper but the winner looks a decent recruit.

NOTEBOOK

Manikon Eros(IRE), having been sent clear turning in, kept finding for a ready debut success. A son of Old Vic, he will probably be suited by softer ground in future, and will need to improve to defy a penalty in stronger company, but obviously remains open to improvement. (op Evens)

Kilmore West(IRE), a former point winner in heavy ground, was second in a bumper on testing ground at Chepstow, and he didn't do too badly considering conditions would have been plenty quick enough. (op 13-8)

Seren Cwmtudu(IRE) won't be capable of winning until she jumps a hurdle. (op 11-1 tchd 12-1)

Grandads Horse, a son of St Leger winner Bollin Eric, was well held and will struggle to win a bumper. (op 25-1 tchd 28-1)

Santamina(IRE) will need further over hurdles.

T/Plt: £100.60 to a £1 stake. Pool: £54,124.59. 392.75 winning tickets. T/Qpdt: £29.10 to a £1 stake. Pool: £6,784.18. 172.10 winning tickets. DO

TOWCESTER (R-H)

Monday, April 26

OFFICIAL GOING: Good to firm (good in places; 9.4)

Hurdle course dolled out wide but impact on distances not quantified.

Wind: almost nill Weather: suuny but cloudy

21 MACINTYRE HUDSON CLAIMING HURDLE

(11 hdls) **2m 5f**

2:20 (2:21) (Class 5) 4-Y-O+ **£2,276** (£668; £334; £166)

Form				RPR
PF5-	**1**		**Shore Thing (IRE)**[34] 4810 7-11-5 130............................(tp) JimmyMcCarthy (Charles Egerton) *cl up: hit 5th: rdn bef 3 out: chal bef 2 out: led between last two: a holding rival after* **4/1**[1]	113
PP2-	**2**	*1 ¼*	**Irish Legend (IRE)**[30] 4895 10-11-0 115............................ SamTwiston-Davies(7) (Bernard Llewellyn) *hld up and t.k.h: trckd ldrs: stdy prog 7th: led gng wl bef 2 out: sn pushed along: hdd between last two: kpt on same pce* **5/1**[2]	114
3P4-	**3**	*15*	**Dusty Dane (IRE)**[30] 4895 8-10-10 106............................(t) TomO'Connor(5) (Bill Turner) *midfield: rdn and effrt after 8th: wnt poor 3rd 2 out: nvr looked like chalng* **8/1**	93
330-	**4**	*32*	**Sparkling Montjeu (IRE)**[9] 5229 5-10-12 95............................ AndrewTinkler (George Baker) *chsd ldrs: rdn and wknd after 8th: wl bhd after next* **12/1**	58
P/0-	**5**	*¾*	**Wee Forbees (IRE)**[9] 5231 8-11-5 115............................ BrianHughes (Michael Easterby) *led or disp ld tl led 8th: rdn and hdd bef 2 out: dropped out qckly* **6/1**[3]	66
00P-	**6**	*7*	**Utern**[100] 3451 6-10-6 80............................ AidanColeman (Venetia Williams) *cl up: rdn and fdd 8th: wl bhd whn mstke 2 out: t.o* **14/1**	44
	7	*1*	**Poacher's Dream (IRE)**[37] 8-11-3 0............................ FelixDeGiles (Jonathen de Giles) *midfield: rdn 7th: struggling next: t.o after 3 out* **50/1**	54
005-	**8**	*15*	**Little Blackbeetle**[30] 4895 5-10-10 0............................ WillKennedy (Paul Webber) *led or disp ld: rdn 7th: cl 2nd next: nt run on and sn wl btn: t.o* **40/1**	32
000-	**9**	*9*	**Aldiruos (IRE)**[156] 2415 10-11-9 106............................ SamThomas (Tony Carroll) *rdn in rr: nvr keen: struggling u.p 5th: t.o fr 7th* **25/1**	36
P/P-	**P**		**The Iron Giant (IRE)**[36] 8-10-6 66............................ MissCareyWilliamson(7) (Diana Weeden) *sn bhd: t.o 7th: p.u 2 out* **250/1**	—
/2P-	**P**		**Highest Esteem**[34] 4810 6-11-5 110............................(be[1]) JamieMoore (Gary Moore) *bhd: effrt 6th: struggling whn put hd in air after 8th and lost tch: blnd 3 out: p.u 2 out* **9/1**	—
5-	**P**		**Spiritonthemount (USA)**[15] 5155 5-11-1 0............................(b) LiamTreadwell (Peter Hiatt) *bhd: rdn 5th: t.o 7th: p.u 2 out* **40/1**	—
	P		**Killowenabbey (IRE)**[130] 2942 6-11-3 0............................(t) SeamusDurack (Debra Hamer) *chsd ldrs tl 8th: sn btn: losing 5th whn nt fluent and eased after 3 out: p.u next* **5/1**[2]	—
0-	**P**		**Double Tangle**[13] 5173 7-10-12 0............................ AlexMerriam(3) (Peter Hiatt) *midfield: drvn 7th: fnd nil: btn whn mstke 8th: t.o and p.u 2 out* **100/1**	—

5m 18.2s (-9.00) **Going Correction** -0.875s/f (Firm) 14 Ran SP% **115.2**
Speed ratings (Par 103): **104,103,97,85,85 82,82,76,73,— —,—,—,—**
toteswingers: 1&2 £2.80, 1&3 £7.00, 2&3 £6.50 CSF £21.87 TOTE £5.20: £2.00, £1.30, £3.20; EX 23.60.Shore Thing was claimed by B J Llewellyn for £8,000.

Owner Vineste **Bred** Airlie Stud And Sir Thomas Pilkington **Trained** Chaddleworth, Berks

FOCUS

A decent sized field for this claimer and not a bad race of its type, but the first two drew right away. There is a case for rating the race up to 12lb higher.

NOTEBOOK

Shore Thing(IRE) had plenty in hand judged on official ratings but had lost his form of late and had to prove his stamina for the longer trip. With cheekpieces back on instead of blinkers, he came through to take the advantage between the last two and held off the persistent runner-up. (op 7-2 tchd 10-3)

Irish Legend(IRE) had 17lb to find with the winner judged on official ratings but travelled well and kept fighting once headed. This was an encouraging first run for his new trainer and he will find easier tasks at this level, especially as he is versatile regarding trip and ground. (op 6-1)

Dusty Dane(IRE) ran on from the rear but was beaten a fair way and will appreciate a return to further. He was in turn clear of the rest. (op 15-2 tchd 13-2)
Sparkling Montjeu(IRE) got a reminder with a full circuit to go, but ran on and will be better off in low-grade handicaps. (op 14-1)
Wee Forbees(IRE) made much of the running but was quite keen early and, after being headed turning in, dropped away quickly up the hill. He will be of more interest on a sharper track like Sedgefield, where he has gone well in the past. (tchd 7-1)
Killowenabbey(IRE) was well backed on his first start in Britain and run for the yard but was struggling a fair way from home on the fastest ground he has tackled under rules. (op 7-1 tchd 9-2)

22 SAFENAMES.NET BEGINNERS' CHASE (14 fncs) 2m 3f 110y
2:50 (2:50) (Class 4) 5-Y-0+ **£3,252** (£955; £477; £238)

Form RPR
332- **1** **The Ferbane Man (IRE)**[21] 5032 6-10-9 0 .... DeanColeman(5) 84+
(Tim Vaughan) *led fr 2nd: travelled wl and j. soundly: jnd between last two: looked idle but a doing jst enough and asserted cl home* **1/1**[1]
PP4- **2** *½* **Lonesome Boatman (IRE)**[16] 5133 10-10-11 68 .... CharlieHuxley(3) 83
(Arthur Whitehead) *mstke 4th: last tl 5th: tk 3rd bef 11th: sn rdn: wnt 2nd 2 out: drew upsides idling wnr between last two: ev ch u.p tl no ex cl home* **7/1**
1PP- **3** *16* **Benmore Boy (IRE)**[15] 5147 7-11-0 0 ....(p) AndrewThornton 71
(Henrietta Knight) *handy on outside: chsd wnr fr 9th tl lost 2nd and hit 2 out: fining v weakly whn mstke last* **7/2**[3]
00P- **4** *34* **Kilvergan Boy (IRE)**[57] 4330 6-11-0 97 .... PaddyBrennan 33
(Nigel Twiston-Davies) *led tl mstke 2nd: nt fluent and nt gng freely after: str reminders after 6th: lost 2nd at 9th: 4th at next: t.o 3 out* **3/1**[2]
P3P- **5** *dist* **Mr Parson (IRE)**[16] 5133 10-10-11 45 .... CharlieStudd(3) —
(Simon Lewis) *rdn 4th: lost tch after next: t.o bef 8th: continued v slowly* **100/1**

5m 1.40s (-16.80) **Going Correction** -0.875s/f (Firm) course record **5** Ran SP% **110.7**
Speed ratings: **98,97,91,77,61**
CSF £8.33 TOTE £1.80: £1.60, £3.00; EX 5.90.
Owner Aidan & Gerard Flynn **Bred** Oliver Loughlin **Trained** Aberthin, Vale of Glamorgan
■ Stewards' Enquiry : Charlie Studd two-day ban: used whip when out of contention (May 10-11)

FOCUS
A very moderate beginners' chase and a small field but it produced a good finish. The form is rated through the second with the winner 3st below his best.

NOTEBOOK
The Ferbane Man(IRE) jumped into the lead at the first ditch and made the rest of the running. A heavy-ground point winner, this was much the fastest going he had faced under rules but he handled it well and his proven stamina, aided by a good jump at the final fence, proved decisive. (op 8-13 tchd 11-10)
Lonesome Boatman(IRE) was held up early but looked to be struggling in pursuit of the leaders turning out of the back straight. However, he came through to challenge at the second-last only to find the winner too determined. He also went close here last spring, and a return to handicapping may offer him the best chance of going one better. (op 12-1)
Benmore Boy(IRE), having only his second run over fences, travelled well for most of the way and looked the most likely winner at the third-last. However, when he was asked for his effort the response was limited and he was soon beaten. It appeared he did not stay. (op 5-1 tchd 3-1)
Kilvergan Boy(IRE) was chased along to lead early but lost the advantage with an error at the second, and was getting reminders before halfway prior to dropping out. (op 4-1 tchd 9-2 and 11-4)

23 WEATHERBYS BLOODSTOCK INSURANCE H'CAP HURDLE (8 hdls) 2m
3:20 (3:20) (Class 4) (0-110,110) 4-Y-0+ **£3,903** (£1,146; £573; £286)

Form RPR
P46- **1** **Alph**[56] 4362 13-11-5 110 .... MrTJCannon(7) 117+
(Roger Teal) *hld up: prog 5th: led gng wl sn after 3 out: 4l clr bef last: rdn out* **13/2**[3]
/02- **2** *5* **Helen Wood**[36] 4760 7-11-4 105 ....(bt) HaddenFrost(3) 107
(David Pipe) *t.k.h in midfield: effrt on heels of ldrs 3 out: wnt 2nd bef next: drvn between last two: sn no imp and wl hld* **12/1**
365- **3** *¾* **Wingull (IRE)**[40] 4680 6-10-10 94 .... AndrewTinkler 95
(George Baker) *settled in rr: stdy prog 3 out: wnt 3rd at last: rdn and catching 2nd nr fin but wnr clr* **6/1**[2]
FF6- **4** *5* **Foreign King (USA)**[81] 2406 6-11-3 101 .... AndrewThornton 98
(Seamus Mullins) *towards rr tl 5th: effrt on outer to go 3rd bef 2 out: flattered briefly: rdn and sn btn: lost 3rd at last: fin weakly* **9/2**[1]
006- **5** *10* **Books Review**[29] 4918 6-10-11 95 .... SeamusDurack 81
(Debra Hamer) *pushed along and nt gng wl in last pair: lost tch bef 4th: plodded past faders fr bef two out: no ch* **14/1**
423- **6** *6* **Spider Boy**[27] 4937 13-10-1 90 ....(b) GemmaGracey-Davison(5) 70
(Zoe Davison) *prom: led bef 4th tl sn after 3 out: rdn and sn lost pl* **13/2**[3]
0P0- **7** *6* **Nothing Is Forever (IRE)**[18] 5105 6-11-7 108 .... SeanQuinlan(3) 82
(Liam Corcoran) *cl up: chal ldrs 5th: rdn and lost pl qckly next* **9/2**[1]
03P- **8** *6* **Mr Melodious**[61] 4242 4-11-5 108 ....(b) PaddyBrennan 71
(Nigel Twiston-Davies) *in rr and u.p bef 4th: nvr keen after: struggling bef 3 out* **16/1**
240- **9** *16* **Classic Fly (FR)**[18] 5105 7-11-1 99 ....(p) NickScholfield 51
(Arthur Whiting) *led tl bef 4th: reminders and lost pl after next: t.o* **8/1**
P06- **10** *1½* **Genies Lamp (IRE)**[42] 4654 6-10-3 92 ....(p) PeterToole(5) 43
(Warren Greatrex) *chsd ldrs: rdn to chal for ld 3 out: fdd bdly up hill: t.o* **12/1**

3m 54.2s (-13.70) **Going Correction** -0.875s/f (Firm)
WFA 4 from 6yo+ 6lb **10** Ran SP% **116.4**
Speed ratings (Par 105): **99,96,96,93,88 85,82,79,71,70**
toteswingers: 1&2 £16.10, 1&3 £105.80, 2&3 £25.70 CSF £79.58 CT £494.11 TOTE £8.70: £2.70, £2.60, £1.60; EX 101.20.
Owner Andy Chard **Bred** G A And Mrs Antill **Trained** Ashtead, Surrey

FOCUS
A modest but fairly competitive handicap hurdle. The winner's best run for a year, with the second another very well in on his old form.

NOTEBOOK
Alph, formerly a useful sort who had been placed in graded company, gained his first success since scoring at Kempton two and a half years ago. He was rated 138 then but managed to take this off a mark two stones lower, and has more races in him at a similar level. (op 8-1 tchd 6-1)
Helen Wood is another who has not scored for more than two years, although she was absent for much of that time. Another who has slipped down the weights, this was her best effort since returning to action, although she never really troubled the winner on ground that may have been faster than ideal. (op 8-1 tchd 14-1)
Wingull(IRE) has handled this going in the past and was backed. He crept into contention from three out but never looked like reeling in the first two. (op 15-2)
Foreign King(USA) is well suited by fast ground and was backed into favouritism. He appeared to have his chance before failing to pick up from the penultimate flight and might have needed the run after a break. (op 4-1)
Nothing Is Forever(IRE) gained his sole success on fast ground but was too keen early and paid for it up the hill. (op 11-2 tchd 4-1)
Classic Fly(FR) Official explanation: trainer said gelding bled from the nose

24 WEATHERBYS PRINTING SERVICES H'CAP CHASE (18 fncs) 3m 110y
3:50 (3:50) (Class 4) (0-105,100) 5-Y-0 **£4,435** (£1,310; £655; £327; £163)

Form RPR
P05- **1** **Basoda**[17] 5120 7-11-9 100 ....(t) SeanQuinlan(3) 112+
(Kim Bailey) *bhd and on outer: hmpd 4th: blnd 5th: plenty to do tl 5th and drvn to make prog bef 3 out: 6l 3rd next: styd on dourly to ld after last: gd ride* **16/1**
245- **2** *1¼* **Early Wings (GER)**[43] 4611 8-10-10 84 .... AndrewThornton 95
(Caroline Bailey) *trckd ldrs: effrt on outside to go cl 2nd at 15th: led 3 out: sn hdd: led again bef next: ct and no ex after last* **9/2**[1]
40U- **3** *9* **Impact Zone**[3] 5361 6-10-5 79 .... BrianHughes 81
(Michael Easterby) *prom: bmpd at 8th: chal 3 out: led on long run to next but rdn and hdd bef fence: lost 2nd at last and fdd* **8/1**
02P- **4** *22* **Jacarado (IRE)**[17] 5120 12-10-11 85 ....(v) HenryOliver 65
(Robin Dickin) *midfield: rdn 7th: u.p 10th: struggling bef 3 out* **14/1**
452- **5** *1¼* **Well Mick (IRE)**[22] 5016 9-10-3 77 ....(p) FelixDeGiles 56
(Jonathen de Giles) *last pair: rdn bef 10th: r.o u.p after last but nvr put himself into r* **9/2**[1]
P5U- **6** *20* **Gershwinner (IRE)**[39] 4707 7-11-11 99 .... JasonMaguire 58
(Donald McCain) *reminders 3rd: bhd: mstke 10th: effrt to go fair 5th at 15th: fdd tamely after next: t.o and eased* **11/2**[2]
65S- **7** *10* **Nearly A Breeze**[16] 5133 10-10-4 81 ....(b) ChrisHonour(3) 30
(Chris Down) *cl up: 2nd at 6th: led 11th: 4l clr next: hmpd by loose horse 15th: hdd next: 3rd whn blnd 3 out and lost any ch: t.o* **18/1**
FP0- **8** *34* **Irish Guard**[68] 4097 9-11-0 95 .... AnthonyFreeman(7) 10
(John O'Neill) *led 2nd tl hdd u.p 11th: 6th and fading qckly whn blnd 14th: bdly t.o* **14/1**
300- **P** **Alcatras (IRE)**[61] 4240 13-10-11 85 ....(p) AndrewGlassonbury —
(John Ryall) *nt a fluent: cl up tl 6th: dropped in rr 11th: blnd 13th: sn lost tch: t.o and p.u 2 out* **40/1**
P **Schindlers Tune (IRE)**[9] 5240 10-11-11 99 .... SamThomas —
(Daniel Mark Loughnane, Ire) *tended to lack fluency: led tl 2nd: lost pl and j. slowly 6th: rallied to go 2nd 13th tl 15th: sn wknd: t.o and p.u 2 out* **28/1**
5P6- **F** **Bobby Bullock (IRE)**[43] 4611 8-10-8 82 .... PaddyBrennan —
(Michael Scudamore) *last tl fell heavily 4th* **10/1**
45P- **P** **Prof De L'Isle (FR)**[30] 4898 7-11-12 100 ....(p) AndrewTinkler —
(Henry Daly) *reminders 4th: a gng bdly: in rr 6th: t.o and p.u after 9th* **16/1**
U52- **U** **The Brig At Ayr**[47] 4513 6-10-0 74 oh1 .... KeithMercer —
(John Weymes) *midfield tl stmbld and uns rdr 4th* **7/1**[3]

6m 11.9s (-25.00) **Going Correction** -0.875s/f (Firm) **13** Ran SP% **120.7**
Speed ratings: **105,104,101,94,94 87,84,73,—,— —,—,—**
toteswingers: 1&2 £24.80, 1&3 £38.80, 2&3 £11.90 CSF £89.85 CT £639.14 TOTE £22.30: £5.60, £2.10, £3.30; EX 154.50.
Owner Angie & Michael Storey **Bred** S V Parry **Trained** Andoversford, Gloucs

FOCUS
A good-sized field for this moderate staying chase and another good finish. The winner improved to the level of his hurdles form.

NOTEBOOK
Basoda, a heavy-ground winner over hurdles, has had jumping problems over fences but has improved in that respect since switched to a sounder surface. He recovered from a bad peck on the first circuit, and ran on really well from three out, landing just behind the leader at the last and outstaying him on the run-in. This should help his confidence and he can build on this in the short-term.
Early Wings(GER) has run well a number of times but has yet to win. He looked as though he would break the duck when going on at the last ditch and was still in front at the last, only to be run down on the flat. He is capable of winning races and will probably be kept on the go. (op 7-1)
Impact Zone is relatively inexperienced over fences but travelled well for a long way, only to tire from the penultimate fence. He can win a small race this summer, possibly over a shorter trip. (op 7-1 tchd 6-1)
Jacarado(IRE) knows his way around here but was never really involved until staying on late. (op 11-1)
Well Mick(IRE) never got competitive on this faster ground. (op 7-1 tchd 4-1)
Gershwinner(IRE) soon lost a good early pitch and looked well held early on the second circuit before keeping on up the hill. (op 9-2)
Nearly A Breeze went on down the far side on the second circuit but was hampered by a loose horse at the fourth-last, and headed soon after, dropped away from the next. (tchd 16-1 and 20-1)
Prof De L'Isle(FR) Official explanation: jockey said gelding never travelled

25 TCA ENGINEERING LTD NOVICES' HURDLE (8 hdls) 2m
4:20 (4:20) (Class 4) 4-Y-0+ **£3,252** (£955; £477; £238)

Form RPR
/24- **1** **Lidar (FR)**[136] 2813 5-10-12 0 .... RobertThornton 107+
(Alan King) *led 3rd: shkn up bef 2 out where hrd pressed but lft in command: racd lazily but drew clr last: pushed out* **4/6**[1]
150- **2** *3¼* **De Forgotten Man (IRE)**[40] 4676 5-10-12 0 .... WarrenMarston 99
(Martin Keighley) *wnt 2nd at 5th tl bef 2 out where rdn and lft 2nd again: kpt on but no match for wnr bef last* **11/4**[2]
064- **3** *6* **Like Ice**[21] 5057 5-10-12 0 .... JamieMoore 93
(Philip Middleton) *led bef 2nd tl 3rd: prom tl rdn and outpcd bef 2 out where impeded and lft 3rd: one pce and n.d after* **28/1**
336- **4** *nk* **Tricky Tree (IRE)**[21] 5048 4-10-4 0 .... SeanQuinlan(3) 89
(Pam Sly) *midfield: rdn and outpcd bef 2 out where impeded: kpt on in battle for modest 3rd* **11/1**[3]
0P- **5** *12* **Stevie Bull (IRE)**[59] 4279 5-10-12 0 .... ColinBolger 81
(Chris Gordon) *racd keenly early: wnt 3rd and j. slowly 4th: rdn after next: sn btn: struggling whn j. slowly 2 out* **66/1**
500/ **6** *5* **Sparkling Brook (IRE)**[51] 7-10-5 0 .... PaddyBrennan 69
(Nigel Twiston-Davies) *hld up: 8 l last at 5th: no ch after next* **40/1**
006- **7** *18* **Nehemiah**[17] 5115 6-10-12 0 .... AndrewThornton 58
(Henrietta Knight) *midfield: rdn on outer bef 3 out: fdd tamely up hill* **20/1**
/F5- **8** *30* **Call Me Dave**[22] 5012 9-10-9 0 .... EamonDehdashti(3) 28
(John E Long) *set crawl tl hdd bef 2nd: hrd rdn and dropped bk last after 5th: hopelessly t.o* **100/1**
550- **F** **Mid Valley**[116] 2038 7-10-12 92 .... LeightonAspell 100
(J R Jenkins) *plld hrd: last tl after 4th: 2nd and chalng strly whn fell 2 out: dead* **40/1**

4m 5.20s (-2.70) **Going Correction** -0.875s/f (Firm)
WFA 4 from 5yo+ 6lb **9** Ran SP% **110.6**
Speed ratings (Par 105): **71,69,66,66,60 57,48,33,—**
toteswingers: 1&2 £1.80, 1&3 £5.50, 2&3 £8.00 CSF £2.32 TOTE £1.70: £1.02, £1.20, £5.70; EX 2.90.
Owner High 5 **Bred** Mme Danielle De La Heronniere **Trained** Barbury Castle, Wilts

FOCUS
A couple of fair performers have won this in recent seasons but the result might have been different had Mid Valley not fallen two out. The winner was value for further but is rated below his best in a steadily run event.

NOTEBOOK
Lidar(FR), a fine, big gelding, was keen early on but seemed happier when allowed to go on at the third. He wandered around going into his hurdles, as though he was adjusting himself to jump them and, after his main challenger fell two out, kept galloping up the hill to hold off his market rival. He may have one more run if his trainer can find suitable ground for him and looks sure to improve with experience. (op 8-15 tchd 8-11 in places)
De Forgotten Man(IRE) finished well beaten in the Festival bumper but had previously scored here and settled better than the favourite on this hurdling debut. He chased his market rival into the straight but could make no impression. He can win races, but might need more ease in the ground. (op 10-3 tchd 5-2 and 7-2 in places)
Like Ice, another who was quite keen early, did not fare badly on this hurdling debut and could well have a small race in him. (op 33-1)
Tricky Tree(IRE) was held up out the back before staying on without ever posing a threat. He now qualifies for handicaps and could make his mark in that sphere at a modest level. (op 16-1)
Mid Valley was held up out the back early but made good ground up the hill, and was on the winner's quarters when taking a heavy fall at the second-last. Sadly it proved fatal. (op 33-1)

26 DALEPAK LTD SUPPORTS COBBLERS YOUTH H'CAP CHASE (12 fncs) 2m 110y
4:55 (4:55) (Class 4) (0-105,105) 5-Y-0+ **£3,903** (£1,146; £573; £286)

Form				RPR
235-	**1**		**Devils River (IRE)**[21] [5044] 8-10-12 91..........................(p) AndrewTinkler (Anna Brooks) *ldng pair: led 5th tl 7th: led 9th tl rdn and hdd 2 out: led again last: drew clr but all out* **4/1**[3]	97
660-	**2**	*5*	**Coach Lane**[29] [4917] 9-11-11 104.. SamThomas (Venetia Williams) *wnt 2nd at 6th: led 7th tl 9th: led again 2 out and rdn: finding nthing after: hdd last and plodded on unenthusiastically* **10/3**[1]	106
654-	**3**	*11*	**Nesnaas (USA)**[168] [2192] 9-11-4 104................................... DavidBass[(7)] (Mark Rimell) *pushed along and lost tch bef 4th where j.lft: wl adrift in last after: 18 l last at 9th: plugged on after 2 out: nt pushed flat* **12/1**	95
P6U-	**4**	*3*	**Launde (IRE)**[18] [5096] 11-11-12 105....................................... ColinBolger (Chris Gordon) *led 2nd tl 5th: rdn next: lost tch after 9th: kpt gng slowly* **4/1**[3]	92
34U-	**5**	*12*	**Croon**[7] [5289] 8-11-1 94.. NickScholfield (Andy Turnell) *mstke 4th: hld up: wnt 3rd after 3 out and flattered briefly: stopped to nil up hill: lft poor 3rd briefly 2 out* **9/2**	69
310-	**U**		**Nawow**[83] [2156] 10-11-3 101...(p) PeterToole[(5)] (Matt Hazell) *led tl 2nd: cl up tl rdn 3 out: 7 l 3rd and racing awkwardly whn mstke and uns rdr 2 out* **7/2**[2]	92

4m 5.50s (-10.60) **Going Correction** -0.875s/f (Firm) 6 Ran SP% **111.2**
Speed ratings: **89,86,81,80,74** —
toteswingers: 1&2 £2.30, 1&3 £9.40, 2&3 £9.50 CSF £17.53 TOTE £3.40: £1.20, £3.70; EX 20.70.
Owner T L Brooks & Sue Price **Bred** Ian Fair **Trained** Alderton, Northants

FOCUS
A moderate handicap chase but quite competitive, as reflected by the market. A small chase personal best from the winner.

NOTEBOOK
Devils River(IRE) has a good record at this track but he likes to make the running and got no peace at the head of affairs. He kept fighting off his rivals but looked beaten when the runner-up went on at the second-last. However, he responded to pressure when switched towards the rail before the final fence and proved strongest on the flat. (tchd 7-2 and 9-2)
Coach Lane, whose last win was at this track over hurdles, travelled well for much of the way and looked the winner two out. However, he could not respond when the winner rallied, although this was his best effort for a while. (op 7-2)
Nesnaas(USA) was in the rear until running on past beaten rivals but was never involved. (op 9-1)
Launde(IRE) tried to take the winner on for the lead early but was struggling from around halfway. (op 7-2 tchd 9-2)
Croon moved up to threaten the leaders going to three out but his effort petered out soon after. (tchd 5-1 and 6-1 in places)
Nawow had beaten today's winner here last May and was better off at the weights this time. He was never that far away, but was third and beaten when blundering away his rider at the second-last. (op 9-2)

27 TOTEPOOL A BETTER WAY TO BET MARES' STANDARD OPEN NATIONAL HUNT FLAT RACE 2m
5:30 (5:30) (Class 5) 4-6-Y-O **£1,951** (£573; £286; £143)

Form				RPR
021-	**1**		**The Strawberry One**[15] [5150] 5-10-12 0.................. AnthonyFreeman[(7)] (David Arbuthnot) *pressed ldrs: rdn to ld 2f out: sn urged clr: v easily* **6/4**[1]	106+
65-	**2**	*10*	**Desolait**[11] [5200] 5-10-5 0................................(t) SamTwiston-Davies[(7)] (Nigel Twiston-Davies) *chsd ldrs: rdn and outpcd 4f out: 5th st: rallied and styd on u.p: wnt poor 2nd 50yds out* **7/2**[2]	89+
65-	**3**	*2 3/4*	**Hill Forts Gloria (IRE)**[43] [4620] 5-10-5 0...................... JimmyDerham[(7)] (Seamus Mullins) *slt ld 10f: remained prom tl 3rd and rdn st: 2nd but outpcd by wnr 2f out: lost 2nd fnl 50yds* **9/1**	88
3-	**4**	*6*	**Himayna**[27] [4945] 6-10-9 0... RichardKilloran[(3)] (Tim Vaughan) *bhd: 8l last and rdn 1/2-way: outpcd after: plugged on in st despite hanging bdly lft: no ch* **9/2**[3]	81
5-	**5**	*1/2*	**Kykate**[33] [4819] 4-10-7 0..(t) TomMessenger (Thomas Kinsey) *cl 2nd tl led 6f out: rdn and hdd 2f out: sn wknd and edging lft* **33/1**	75
0-	**6**	*3/4*	**Viking Gold**[21] [5042] 6-10-7 0... DeanColeman[(5)] (Tim Vaughan) *midfield: rdn 5f out: struggled on* **25/1**	79
	7	*3 1/4*	**Muzey's Princess** 4-10-0 0... BrianToomey[(7)] (Michael Mullineaux) *in last pair: rdn 1/2-way: struggling fnl 5f: t.o* **28/1**	71
	8	*13*	**Time Legend** 4-10-7 0.. WarrenMarston (Martin Keighley) *chsd ldrs tl 4th and drvn and outpcd st: eased fnl f: t.o* **15/2**	58

3m 55.5s (-6.80) **Going Correction** -0.875s/f (Firm)
WFA 4 from 5yo+ 6lb 8 Ran SP% **112.4**
Speed ratings: **82,77,75,72,72 72,70,63**
toteswingers: 1&2 £2.00, 1&3 £4.30, 2&3 £5.60 CSF £6.45 TOTE £2.40: £1.10, £1.30, £3.00; EX 5.40 Place 6: £39.68 Place 5: £21.48.
Owner Miss Kykie Allsopp **Bred** Miss Carolyn A B Allsopp **Trained** Compton, Berks

FOCUS
A few runners with experience in this mares' bumper and the only previous winner turned this into a procession. Ordinary form.

NOTEBOOK
The Strawberry One settled behind the leaders and, once asked to assert, quickly went on and just drew further and further away. If she can transfer her ability to hurdles she should be able to win her share. (op 9-4 after early 11-4 in places)
Desolait improved on her debut on good ground last time and ran creditably without threatening the winner in the straight. (op 11-4)
Hill Forts Gloria(IRE) shared much of the pacemaking and, although unable to respond immediately when headed, kept on well for pressure. She should be suited by the switch to hurdles. (op 7-1 tchd 13-2)
Himayna was well beaten on soft ground on her debut but was being pushed along at an early stage this time before keeping on up the hill, and the fast ground may not have suited. (op 5-1 tchd 6-1)
Kykate improved on her bumper debut on soft and helped make the running but, after going to the front off the bend, was soon headed and tired in the last quarter-mile. (op 22-1)
T/Plt: £34.70 to a £1 stake. Pool: £62,966.59. 1,324.22 winning tickets. T/Qpdt: £20.60 to a £1 stake. Pool: £3,915.66. 140.26 winning tickets. IM

28 - 29a (Foreign Racing) - See Raceform Interactive

SEDGEFIELD (L-H)
Tuesday, April 27

OFFICIAL GOING: Good to firm (good in places on chase course; chs 8.4, hdl 8.6)
Wind: light 1/2 behind Weather: fine

30 TOTEPLACEPOT MAIDEN HURDLE (10 hdls) 2m 4f
5:50 (5:50) (Class 4) 4-Y-0+ **£2,862** (£840; £420; £209)

Form				RPR
224-	**1**		**Cailin Na Ri (IRE)**[242] [1321] 7-10-7 112.............................. DenisO'Regan (Martin Todhunter) *mde all: rdn appr last: kpt on wl* **9/4**[2]	100+
222-	**2**	*7*	**Mr Syntax (IRE)**[57] [4357] 6-11-0 124.................................... BrianHughes (Tim Fitzgerald) *chsd wnr: mstke 1st: hit 3 out: rdn appr next: one pce* **4/11**[1]	102+
0-	**3**	*23*	**Just Dan**[15] [5169] 4-10-2 0 ow1... MrGRSmith[(7)] (David Thompson) *chsd ldrs: drvn 7th: tk poor 3rd after 3 out* **100/1**	72
606-	**4**	*39*	**Alfie Bet**[181] [1957] 6-10-11 0.......................................(t) MichaelMcAlister[(3)] (Maurice Barnes) *t.k.h: chsd ldrs and shkn up 5th: wknd after 3 out: sn bhd: lame* **28/1**[3]	38
PPP-	**5**	*34*	**One More Cent**[8] [5273] 5-10-4 0.................................... JamesO'Farrell[(3)] (Dianne Sayer) *t.k.h: dropped in rr 3rd: sn bhd: t.o 7th* **250/1**	—
P-	**P**		**Moscow Player (IRE)**[8] [5273] 5-10-7 0...................... MrJohnDawson[(7)] (John Wade) *in rr: bhd fr 7th: sn t.o: p.u bef 2 out* **80/1**	—

5m 0.10s (7.40) **Going Correction** +0.375s/f (Yiel)
WFA 4 from 5yo+ 7lb 6 Ran SP% **110.2**
Speed ratings (Par 105): **112,109,100,84,70** —
toteswingers: 1&2 £1.02, 1&3 £5.80, 2&3 £2.80 CSF £3.50 TOTE £4.60: £1.40, £1.10; EX 4.00.
Owner Barry Brown **Bred** Jim McDonald **Trained** Orton, Cumbria

FOCUS
As the betting suggested, this was a most uncompetitive maiden hurdle and one in which the two market leaders had the race to themselves from some way out. The gallop was just an ordinary one. The winning rider described the ground as "a bit dead and a bit rough in places". The winner is rated to his mark.

NOTEBOOK
Cailin Na Ri(IRE), proven under the conditions, looked the only feasible danger to the market leader and she ran right up to her best on this first outing since August. Her jumping was accurate and, while this was not much of a race, she has a decent attitude and may be able to win again this summer. (op 5-2 tchd 11-4 and 3-1 in places)
Mr Syntax(IRE), who carried his head high, looked the pick of the weights in this uncompetitive event but, although he travelled strongly for a long way, his jumping was less fluent than the winner's and he was below the pick of his form on the quickest ground he has tackled to date. He has been placed on all his starts and, while he is capable of picking up a similar race on an easier surface, this confirms he is not one to be taking too short a price about. (op 2-5 tchd 1-3 and 4-9 in places)
Just Dan, a very moderate and inconsistent Flat maiden on the Flat, may be flattered by his proximity in a race run at just an ordinary gallop. He'll be suited by the step into low-grade handicaps and a stiffer test of stamina may also be in his favour.
Alfie Bet should be seen in a more favourable light when switched to moderate handicaps but he will have to show a good deal more before he is a solid betting proposition. The vet reported he returned injured. (op 20-1)

31 TOTEEXACTA (S) HURDLE (QUALIFIER FOR JOHN WADE SELLING SERIES FINAL) (10 hdls) 2m 4f
6:20 (6:20) (Class 5) 4-Y-0+ **£1,691** (£496; £248; £124)

Form				RPR
323-	**1**		**Bewery Man (IRE)**[32] [4879] 9-10-13 104................................ GrahamLee (Ferdy Murphy) *trckd ldrs: led appr 2 out: kpt on strly: v comf* **1/2**[1]	97+
00F-	**2**	*6*	**Oh Yah Dancer (IRE)**[47] [4532] 8-11-4 89..........................(p) BarryKeniry (George Bewley) *chsd ldrs: wnt 2nd 2 out: no ch w wnr* **9/1**[3]	89
500-	**3**	*4*	**Parisian Knight (IRE)**[40] [4708] 7-10-8 74 ow2........................ MrGCrow[(7)] (A M Crow) *wnt prom 4th: drvn 6th: one pce appr 2 out: tk 3rd sn after last* **22/1**	82
F00-	**4**	*6*	**Still Calm**[2] [12] 6-10-10 87....................................(t) MichaelMcAlister[(3)] (Maurice Barnes) *t.k.h: jnd ldrs 5th: led after 7th: hdd appr 2 out: 3rd last: wknd run-in* **5/1**[2]	75
50P-	**5**	*12*	**Spruzzo**[2] [12] 4-10-2 80... PaulCallaghan[(5)] (C W Thornton) *chsd ldrs: reminders and lost pl 2nd: bhd fr 5th: sn t.o* **25/1**	56
0PP-	**6**	*11*	**Tickateal**[40] [4708] 10-10-10 90....................................(b) JamesO'Farrell[(3)] (Alan Lockwood) *overj. and nrly lost rdr 1st: chsd ldrs: lost pl after 7th: sn bhd: blnd last* **12/1**	51
P0P/	**7**	*43*	**Gala Queen**[3] 10-10-6 0.. AndrewThornton (William Young) *j.lft: led tl after 7th: wknd qckly after next: sn t.o* **100/1**	1

5m 6.10s (13.40) **Going Correction** +0.375s/f (Yiel)
WFA 4 from 6yo+ 7lb 7 Ran SP% **110.2**
Speed ratings (Par 103): **100,97,96,93,88 84,67**
toteswingers: 1&2 £2.60, 1&3 £4.20, 2&3 £6.90 CSF £5.27 TOTE £1.90: £1.60, £3.10; EX 3.50.There was no bid for the winner.
Owner Ferdy Murphy **Bred** Mrs Kay Curtis **Trained** West Witton, N Yorks

FOCUS
A low-grade race that lost much of its interest with a couple of early morning defections. An ordinary gallop quickened around halfway but this time was around six seconds slower than the opener. The winner was value for further and is rated close to form.

NOTEBOOK
Bewery Man(IRE) faced a straightforward task at the weights and did not have to improve to win with any amount in hand. He is a reliable sort who should continue to give a good account in this type of event. (tchd 4-9 early 4-7 in places)
Oh Yah Dancer(IRE) doesn't look the most straightforward of individuals but he ran well in the face of a stiff task under his optimum conditions in first-time cheekpieces. The switch back to ordinary handicaps will see him in a more favourable light but he is not one for maximum faith. (op 13-2)

Parisian Knight(IRE) was not disgraced in the face of a very stiff task. He too will be suited by the return to low-grade handicaps and, on this evidence, he will be worth another try over a bit further. (op 20-1)

Still Calm, turned out after his exertions on Sunday, also had a tough task at the weights in relation to the winner but is probably a bit better than the bare facts suggest after taking a strong hold. The return to shorter may suit better but his overall record means he remains one to have reservations about. (op 13-2 tchd 9-2)

Tickateal Official explanation: jockey said gelding hung left throughout

32 SENDRIG CONSTRUCTION NOVICES' CHASE (16 fncs) 2m 4f

6:50 (6:50) (Class 4) 5-Y-0+ **£3,802** (£1,123; £561; £280; £140)

Form RPR

223- **1** **Knockavilla (IRE)**[45] 4579 7-10-12 125 .... BrianHughes 114+
(Howard Johnson) *free to post: led after 1st: mde rest: 5 l ahd last: eased nr fin* **10/11**[1]

340- **2** 3 ¾ **Dontpaytheferryman (USA)**[45] 4591 5-10-12 0 .... KeithMercer 108
(Brian Ellison) *led tl after 1st: chsd wnr: one pce fr 2 out* **4/1**[2]

060- **3** 18 **Another Dark Rum**[8] 5271 6-10-12 97 .... RichieMcGrath 93
(John Weymes) *wnt prom 5th: oiutpced 12th: modest 3rd after next: one pce* **28/1**

040- **4** 3 **Magellan Straits**[146] 2645 6-10-12 0 .... TjadeCollier 88
(Sue Smith) *wnt prom 5th: outpcd 12th: one pce fr next* **15/2**

430- **5** 14 **Follow On**[38] 4735 8-10-9 0 ....(t) MichaelMcAlister(3) 76
(Maurice Barnes) *sn pushed along: dropped in rr 8th: sn bhd* **18/1**

623- **6** 1 ¾ **Ellandshe (IRE)**[33] 4834 10-10-12 50 ....(b) AndrewThornton 74
(William Young) *w ldrs: reminders 8th: wknd 11th: sn bhd* **40/1**

006- **7** 4 ½ **Braden Brook (IRE)**[42] 4666 7-10-5 0 ....(t) MrJohnDawson(7) 70
(John Wade) *prom: reminders and outpcd 9th: sn lost pl and bhd* **100/1**

/FU- **8** 8 **Big Burrows (IRE)**[130] 2954 8-10-12 0 .... GrahamLee 63
(Ferdy Murphy) *nt fluent: in rr: mstke 7th: sme hdwy 11th: sn lost pl* **11/2**[3]

/PP- **F** **Deer Fin (IRE)**[33] 4833 8-10-12 0 .... PaddyAspell —
(Andrew Wilson) *in rr: bhd fr 8th: last whn fell 2 out* **150/1**

4m 59.9s (-3.10) **Going Correction** +0.025s/f (Yiel) **9** Ran SP% **112.3**
Speed ratings: **107,105,98,97,91 90,89,85,—**
toteswingers: 1&2 £1.90, 1&3 £10.30, 2&3 £11.50 CSF £4.78 TOTE £2.30: £1.20, £1.10, £10.30; EX 5.50.
Owner Andrea & Graham Wylie **Bred** Michael Heskin **Trained** Billy Row, Co Durham

FOCUS

A fair event for the track in which the gallop was a reasonable one. The winner was value for further but didn't need to improve.

NOTEBOOK

Knockavilla(IRE), keen to post but who settled better in the race, appreciated the return to this trip on a sound surface but did not have to better previous efforts to win with something in hand at the fifth attempt over fences. He's a capable sort for this time of year and he should be able to defy a penalty in this grade. (op 6-5 tchd 5-4)

Dontpaytheferryman(USA) ⊠ , a 118-rated hurdler, had his limitations exposed in the Imperial Cup at Sandown in March but shaped with a good deal of promise on this chase debut in this less-competitive event. He goes well in testing ground and, on this evidence, he is sure to win a race over fences. (tchd 3-1)

Another Dark Rum ⊠ bettered the form of his chasing debut over this shorter trip and against better opposition. He travelled strongly for a long way, was not knocked about when clearly held and he will be of more interest returned to ordinary handicaps. (op 25-1)

Magellan Straits is rated 118 over hurdles but has yet to match that in three starts over fences and he was quickly left behind when the tempo increased leaving the back straight. His best efforts over hurdles were around 2m on good and softer ground and he is not one to write off yet. (op 7-1)

Big Burrows(IRE), a strapping individual who has the physique to progress over fences, was the disappointment of the race. His round was littered with jumping errors and, although a more galloping track would probably have suited better, he will be one to watch until he brushes up in the jumping department. Official explanation: jockey said gelding jumped poorly throughout (op 5-1)

33 TOTEPOOL DURHAM NATIONAL H'CAP CHASE (22 fncs) 3m 4f

7:20 (7:20) (Class 3) (0-130,130) 5-Y-0+

£15,555 (£4,602; £2,300; £1,150; £575; £290)

Form RPR

002- **1** **General Hardi**[15] 5167 9-10-0 104 oh6 .... BrianHughes 111
(John Wade) *chsd ldrs: led after 18th: styd on gamely run-in* **11/1**

4F3- **2** 2 **Neptune Equester**[21] 5073 7-10-2 106 .... PhilKinsella 111
(Brian Ellison) *hld up in rr: hdwy 15th: sn chsng ldrs: wnt 2nd 3 out: upsides last: hung lft: kpt on same pce* **4/1**[1]

5U1- **3** 8 **Leac An Scail (IRE)**[8] 5274 9-11-0 125 7ex .... AlexanderVoy(7) 124
(Sue Smith) *chsd ldrs: drvn 15th: outpcd 4 out: wnt modest 3rd 2 out* **7/1**

434- **4** 22 **Justwhateverulike (IRE)**[16] 5141 9-10-8 112 ....(p) PaddyAspell 92
(Sandy Forster) *prom: outpcd 4 out: wknd after 2 out* **6/1**[3]

633- **5** 1 ½ **Description (IRE)**[12] 5195 8-11-5 123 .... HenryOliver 100
(Sue Smith) *chsd ldrs: wknd after 2 out* **6/1**[3]

040- **6** 2 **Daldini**[17] 5126 8-11-4 122 .... TjadeCollier 97
(Sue Smith) *t.k.h in rr: hdwy 17th: wknd 3 out* **16/1**

03P- **7** 3 ½ **Quattrocento (FR)**[31] 4890 6-11-1 119 ....(p) TomO'Brien 94
(Peter Bowen) *prom: mstke 2nd: outpcd 4 out: wknd between last 2* **9/2**[2]

031- **8** 7 **Lucky Nellerie (FR)**[32] 4878 11-10-10 114 .... KeithMercer 80
(Ferdy Murphy) *led 2nd: j.rt: hdd 14th: drvn 17th: lost pl 4 out* **6/1**[3]

/0U- **9** 13 **Mr Pointment (IRE)**[8] 5274 11-11-9 130 .... AdrianLane(3) 84
(Paul Murphy) *ld to 2nd: w ldrs: led 14th tl after 18th: wknd after 4 out: sn bhd* **40/1**

/00- **P** **Cerium (FR)**[17] 5127 9-11-12 130 .... GrahamLee —
(Paul Murphy) *in rr: reminders 12th and 14th: bhd 16th: p.u bef 18th* **16/1**

7m 5.10s (1.10) **Going Correction** +0.025s/f (Yiel) **10** Ran SP% **116.1**
Speed ratings: **99,98,96,89,89 88,87,85,82,—**
toteswingers: 1&2 £16.70, 1&3 £18.20, 2&3 £11.10 CSF £56.00 CT £336.36 TOTE £15.70: £4.50, £2.30, £2.90; EX 85.30.
Owner John Wade **Bred** Mrs A Yearley **Trained** Mordon, Co Durham

FOCUS

A valuable prize and a better quality event than last year's renewal. An ordinary gallop saw the field bunched up starting the final circuit but the two bottom weights pulled clear from the penultimate fence. The winner was 3lb off his best with the next two close to their marks.

NOTEBOOK

General Hardi had only won once in his previous 30 starts under rules but turned in an improved performance to beat an unexposed type from 6lb out of the handicap. His jumping was sound, he appreciated the step to this trip and it will be interesting to see if this can be built on next time. (op 14-1 tchd 16-1)

Neptune Equester ⊠ posted his best effort on this handicap debut upped markedly in distance and is the one to take from the race. Although he drifted to his left in the closing stages, he saw this trip out well enough, finished clear of the remainder and appeals strongly as the sort to win a race over fences. (op 5-1)

Leac An Scail(IRE), a recent Hexham scorer, was far from disgraced turned out under his penalty over this trip for the first time. He will be 3lb lower in future and shapes as though he will stay even further. (tchd 13-2)

Justwhateverulike(IRE) wasn't totally disgraced after being less than fluent at a couple of obstacles. He should not be inconvenienced by the return to around 3m but he will have to improve to win a competitive handicap from his current mark. (op 15-2 tchd 8-1)

Description(IRE) had been shaping as though a stiffer test would suit on his last couple of starts but he did not see out this trip (first try at the distance) as well as the principals. The drop back to around 3m should be more to his liking. (op 5-1 tchd 13-2)

Daldini shaped a bit better than the bare form after racing keenly for much of the way and was not surprisingly found out in the last half-mile. The return to shorter will suit but he is not the most predictable of individuals. (tchd 14-1 and 20-1)

Quattrocento(FR) again disappointed after making mistakes and his form has been patchy since winning in December. (op 11-2)

Lucky Nellerie(FR), last year's winner, could never get clear of the field on this ground and will be better served by easier underfoot conditions. (tchd 13-2)

34 TOTESWINGER H'CAP HURDLE (8 hdls) 2m 1f

7:50 (7:50) (Class 3) (0-135,116) 4-Y-0+

£6,262 (£1,850; £925; £463; £231; £116)

Form RPR

404/ **1** **Breaking Storm (IRE)**[532] 2144 7-11-8 112 .... RichieMcGrath 112+
(Kate Walton) *chsd ldrs: outpcd 3 out: rallied next: led run-in: edgd rt: styd on wl* **16/1**

112- **2** 2 **Samizdat (FR)**[15] 5169 7-11-2 109 .... RyanMania(3) 107
(Dianne Sayer) *trckd ldrs: led after 3 out: hdd run-in: no ex* **11/1**

416- **3** ¾ **Crosby Jemma**[8] 5275 6-11-1 105 .... BrianHughes 101
(Mike Sowersby) *t.k.h: trckd ldrs: upsides last: no ex* **10/1**

200- **4** ½ **Overrule (USA)**[11] 5213 6-11-11 115 .... GrahamLee 111
(Brian Ellison) *in rr: hdwy 5th: chsng ldrs 2 out: styd on same pce run-in* **3/1**[2]

003- **5** ¾ **Cool Operator**[30] 4909 7-11-11 115 .... WilsonRenwick 111
(Howard Johnson) *led tl after 3 out: hmpd on outer between last 2: one pce* **11/2**[3]

244- **6** 1 **Longdale**[187] 1858 12-10-8 98 .... JamesReveley 92
(Martin Todhunter) *in rr: detached 3 out: hdwy between last 2: one pce run-in* **22/1**

2P5- **7** ½ **Bijou Dan**[20] 2221 9-11-11 115 .... BarryKeniry 109
(George Moore) *in rr: drvn along 4th: reminders next: sn outpcd: kpt on fr 2 out: gng on at fin but nvr a threat* **14/1**

161- **8** 3 ¼ **Stagecoach Pearl**[137] 2818 6-11-7 116 .... ShaneByrne(5) 108+
(Sue Smith) *t.k.h: jnd ldrs 1st: one pce appr 2 out* **11/4**[1]

022- **9** 36 **Calculaite**[33] 4838 9-11-10 114 .... DenisO'Regan 73
(Martin Todhunter) *chsd ldrs: lost pl 5th: t.o 2 out* **6/1**

4m 9.90s (3.00) **Going Correction** +0.375s/f (Yiel) **9** Ran SP% **115.7**
Speed ratings (Par 107): **107,106,105,105,105 104,104,102,85**
toteswingers: 1&2 £26.20, 1&3 £8.20, 2&3 £28.50 CSF £173.06 CT £1852.11 TOTE £17.60: £4.00, £2.40, £5.20; EX 160.20.
Owner Yarm Racing Partnership **Bred** Miss Marie Harding **Trained** Middleham Moor, N Yorks

FOCUS

A fair handicap in which the pace was reasonable. They finished in a heap but the form looks solid enough.

NOTEBOOK

Breaking Storm(IRE), absent for over a year with tendon problems, was easy to back but showed that he retains all his ability and demonstrated a gritty attitude dropped in trip for his seasonal debut. The return to 2m4f will not inconvenience and it will be interesting to see if this can be built on. (op 12-1)

Samizdat(FR) is in the form of his life and ran another game race from this career-high mark. He handles soft ground and should continue to give a good account in this type of event. (tchd 10-1 and 12-1)

Crosby Jemma is high enough in the weights but followed a below-par run at Hexham with a creditable one after travelling strongly for a long way. However, she is going to have to raise her game to win a similar event from her current mark. (op 33-1)

Overrule(USA) ⊠ had disappointed on his two previous starts but fared much better returned to this track. He left the impression he would be worth a try over a bit further, is in good hands and is lightly raced enough over hurdles to be open to a bit of improvement. (op 5-2)

Cool Operator, down in distance and back on a sound surface, was far from disgraced after re-adopting front-running tactics. He won't be inconvenienced by the return to further and may be capable of a bit better in this sphere. (op 13-2)

Longdale, from a yard among the winners, also left the impression that the return to further would suit and he should be better for this first start since October. (op 20-1)

Stagecoach Pearl, who was 8lb higher than when posting a career-best effort at Doncaster in December, attracted support but proved disappointing. However, given he raced with the choke out for much of the way and that he's only lightly raced, he will be worth another chance in similar company. (op 7-2)

35 OAKLEY-WEST AUCKLAND FOR MITSUBISHI DEALS STANDARD OPEN NATIONAL HUNT FLAT RACE 2m 1f

8:20 (8:20) (Class 6) 4-6-Y-0 **£1,431** (£420; £210; £104)

Form RPR

3/0- **1** **Sir Frank (IRE)**[347] 324 5-11-3 0 .... BrianHughes 109
(Alan Swinbank) *trckd ldrs: led over 2f out: kpt on wl: hrd rdn and hld on towards fin* **3/1**[2]

6- **2** hd **Call Me Bill (IRE)**[31] 4886 4-10-12 0 .... TomO'Brien 104
(Peter Bowen) *chsd ldrs: pushed along 7f out: drvn over 3f out: rallied to chse wnr appr fnl f: ev ch ins fnl f: no ex nr fin* **16/1**

53- **3** 15 **Steel Edge (IRE)**[69] 4109 5-11-3 0 .... GrahamLee 96
(Ferdy Murphy) *w ldrs: ev ch tl wknd appr fnl f* **9/1**

4 5 **Jingoism (USA)** 4-10-12 0 .... KeithMercer 84
(Brian Ellison) *in rr: bhd and drvn 7f out: styd on fnl f* **13/2**[3]

143- **5** ¾ **Bridlingtonbygones (IRE)**[36] 4785 5-11-10 0 .... SamThomas 95
(Karen McLintock) *trckd ldrs: drvn over 3f out: lost pl 2f out* **13/8**[1]

43- **6** 1 ½ **Jersey Boys**[71] 4076 4-10-12 0 .... WilsonRenwick 82
(Howard Johnson) *trckd ldrs: t.k.h: led over 3f out: edgd rt and hdd over 2f out: sn wknd* **7/1**

7 2 **Island Sprite (IRE)** 6-10-10 0 .... DenisO'Regan 78
(Martin Todhunter) *towards rr: pushed along 7f out: outpcd and lost pl over 4f out* **10/1**

8 10 **Auld Farmer** 6-11-3 0 .... PaddyAspell 75
(Christopher Wilson) *led: hdd over 2f out: sn wknd: bhd whn eased nr fin* **66/1**

P **Fertiflirt** 4-9-12 0.. AndrewCooper(7) —
(Ray Craggs) *in rr: reminders after 6f: bhd 7f out: t.o whn p.u over 3f out* **100/1**

4m 10.9s (9.60) **Going Correction** +0.375s/f (Yiel)
WFA 4 from 5yo+ 6lb **9** Ran SP% **116.4**
Speed ratings: **92,91,84,82,82 81,80,75,—**
toteswingers:1&2 £4.90, 2&3 £19.80, 1&3 £6.20 CSF £50.05 TOTE £5.60: £2.90, £6.80, £1.20; EX 46.60 Place 6: £133.18 Place 5: £132.62 .
Owner Frank Hanson **Bred** Mrs G Galvin **Trained** Melsonby, N Yorks
⊠ Stewards' Enquiry : Brian Hughes one-day ban: used whip with excessive frequency (May 11)

FOCUS
Probably a fair bumper for the track but one that took less winning than seemed likely beforehand with the market leader disappointing. The gallop was an ordinary one but the first two pulled clear in the closing stages. Big steps up from the first two, who finished clear.

NOTEBOOK
Sir Frank(IRE) attracted support and turned in an improved effort and found plenty for pressure on this first run for nearly a year (had been given plenty of time to develop). He is in good hands and, although this was not the strongest of bumpers, he may well be capable of a little better. (op 9-2)
Call Me Bill(IRE) ⊠ didn't show much when starting at a shortish price on his debut but, although fairly easy in the market this time, turned in a much-improved display. He pulled clear of the remainder and is capable of winning a similar race when the emphasis is on stamina but his future lies over jumps. (op 12-1)
Steel Edge(IRE), ridden more prominently than on his two previous outings, travelled strongly for a long way and probably ran to a similar level in a race run at just an ordinary gallop. He should fare better over further when sent hurdling. (op 15-2)
Jingoism(USA), an expensive yearling picked up by current connections last year, has several useful Flat winners in his pedigree and he made up plenty of late ground after getting badly outpaced before halfway. He is in good hands and should improve for this experience. (op 7-1 tchd 8-1)
Bridlingtonbygones(IRE) looked to have solid claims in this company under his penalty but carried his head high and dropped away fairly tamely in the straight. This was disappointing but he will be worth another chance when sent hurdling. (op 11-8 tchd 5-4 and 7-4 and 15-8 in places)
Jersey Boys, from a yard back among the winners, failed to match his previous form and he will have to settle better than he has done so far if he is to progress when sent over hurdles. (op 13-2)
T/Plt: £88.60 to a £1 stake. Pool: £72,614.45. 598.24 winning tickets. T/Qpdt: £78.30 to a £1 stake. Pool: £6,305.91. 59.58 winning tickets. WG

WINCANTON (R-H)

Tuesday, April 27

OFFICIAL GOING: Good to firm
Wind: mild breeze across Weather: fine but cloudy

36 WINCANTON H'CAP HURDLE (10 hdls) 2m 4f
2:20 (2:20) (Class 4) (0-100,100) 4-Y-0+ **£2,927** (£859; £429; £214)

Form RPR

4F3- **1** **Bollywood (IRE)**[7] [5295] 7-9-7 **74** oh7.......................... EdGlassonbury(7) 80
(Alison Batchelor) *in tch: struggling to hold pl 7th: hdwy u.p 2 out: sn hung rt: led after last: styd on strly to draw clr* **5/2**[1]

2/ **2** *4* **Ace High Blue (IRE)**[636] [1072] 8-11-12 **100**.....................(t) PaulMoloney 102
(Evan Williams) *trckd ldrs: led 6th: rdn after 2 out: hdd sn after last: kpt on same pce* **9/1**

405- **3** *4 ½* **Marigolds Way**[4] [5365] 8-11-9 **100**................................... HarrySkelton(3) 98
(Ron Hodges) *trckd ldrs: rdn in cl 3rd gng to 2 out: styd on same pce* **11/2**[2]

36- **4** *1 ¾* **Uncle Bunge (IRE)**[19] [5102] 4-11-3 **97**.............................. JasonMaguire 87
(Liam Corcoran) *hld up: hdwy 3 out: sn rdn to chse ldr: styd on same pce fr next* **7/1**[3]

230- **5** *29* **Young Tot (IRE)**[9] [5261] 12-10-9 **86**............................ RichardKilloran(3) 53
(Carroll Gray) *led tl 5th: rdn after 7th: wknd after 2 out: eased* **12/1**

56- **6** *1 ¾* **Quatre Huit (FR)**[22] [5040] 6-11-12 **100**.......................... RichardJohnson 65
(Tim Vaughan) *hld up in last trio: rdn bef 3 out: no imp: wknd next: eased* **12/1**

205- **7** *3 ¼* **Le Toto**[46] [4573] 7-11-7 **95**.. LeightonAspell 57
(Oliver Sherwood) *hld up in last pair: nt fluent 4th: hdwy after 3 out: sn rdn: wknd next: eased* **7/1**[3]

PP2- **P** **Mansolias (FR)**[17] [5136] 6-10-7 **81**.................................(b) CharliePoste —
(Sophie Leech) *prom: led 5th tl nt fluent next: sn rdn: wknd after 3 out: p.u bef last: dismntd* **11/2**[2]

4m 37.7s (-19.10) **Going Correction** -0.975s/f (Hard)
WFA 4 from 6yo+ 7lb **8** Ran SP% **109.7**
Speed ratings (Par 105): **105,103,101,100,89 88,87,—**
toteswingers: 1&2 £7.00, 1&3 £4.10, 2&3 £9.50 CSF £22.77 CT £102.57 TOTE £3.70: £1.60, £2.60, £1.20; EX 27.80.
Owner Mrs Alison Batchelor **Bred** Glashare House Stud **Trained** Petworth, W Sussex

FOCUS
The ground remained quick, officially being described as good to firm. Ordinary handicap, the winner rated to his mark despite being 7lb wrong.

NOTEBOOK
Bollywood(IRE), racing from 7lb out of the handicap, had run much more promisingly when third at Towcester latest, and he was in need of this longer trip, staying on strongly having been outpaced to win comfortably. (op 10-3)
Ace High Blue(IRE), an ex-Irish performer who hadn't been seen since July 2008, went on early and briefly looked the winner, but he was conceding tons of weight to Bollywood, and proved no match on the run-in. (op 5-1)
Marigolds Way, making a quick reappearance, held her chance in the straight, but lacked the acceleration of the front pair. (op 15-2)
Uncle Bunge(IRE), making his handicap debut, briefly looked a threat, having made headway, but couldn't quicken on with the ground looking too fast for him. (op 8-1)
Le Toto looked a possible improver, so it was disappointing to see such a tame finishing effort. (op 6-1 tchd 11-2)
Mansolias(FR) Official explanation: jockey said gelding lost its action; vet said gelding pulled up lame

37 CHAMPAGNE LANSON NOVICES' HURDLE (10 hdls) 2m 4f
2:50 (2:50) (Class 4) 4-Y-0+ **£2,602** (£764; £382; £190)

Form RPR

335- **1** **Quedillac (FR)**[43] [4642] 6-10-13 105.............................. RichardJohnson 111+
(Tim Vaughan) *trckd ldr: jnd ldr 6th: led after 3 out: in command sn after: comf* **11/4**[2]

541- **2** *13* **Five Out Of Five (IRE)**[34] [4823] 6-11-6 0.........................(t) PaulMoloney 99
(Evan Williams) *led: qcknd pce whn jnd 6th: hit next: rdn and hdd after 3 out: no ch w wnr fr next: hit last* **8/15**[1]

5PP- **3** *1 ¼* **Dust In Time**[30] [4916] 5-10-8 0.....................................(p) TomO'Connor(5) 91
(Bill Turner) *chsd ldrs: pushed along fr 4th: outpcd 6th: plugged on fr 2 out: hit last* **40/1**

540- **4** *31* **Irish Airman (IRE)**[48] [4522] 5-10-10 0.............................. HarrySkelton(3) 72
(Paul Nicholls) *chsd ldrs: 3rd whn outpcd 6th: pckd whn lost 3rd 2 out: wknd: eased run-in* **16/1**

50- **5** *62* **Smiles Better**[31] [4899] 5-10-10 0.. ChrisHonour(3) —
(Chris Down) *a in last pair: lost tch after 6th: t.o* **100/1**

00- **P** **Kericho**[78] [3931] 5-10-13 0... RobertThornton —
(Alan King) *nvr fluent: sn niggled along in last pair: losing tch whn hit 6th: p.u bef next* **14/1**[3]

4m 35.2s (-21.60) **Going Correction** -0.975s/f (Hard) **6** Ran SP% **107.9**
Speed ratings (Par 105): **110,104,104,91,67 —**
toteswingers: 1&2 £1.10, 1&3 £2.80, 2&3 £3.20 CSF £4.36 TOTE £3.20: £1.60, £1.10; EX 5.00.
Owner Mrs M Findlay **Bred** Dominique Gouin And Carole Piton **Trained** Aberthin, Vale of Glamorgan

FOCUS
An uncompetitive novices' hurdle. The winner is rated in line with his previous best.

NOTEBOOK
Quedillac(FR) had disappointed on his handicap debut at Plumpton, when finding the ground too soft, but he proved a different proposition back on this faster surface, and scooted clear of the favourite for an easy success. Now off the mark over hurdles, it would be no surprise if he were to follow up. (op 10-3 tchd 5-2)
Five Out Of Five(IRE), who made all when winning at Hereford latest, had faster conditions to contend with and let himself down by making a few sloppy mistakes. He was ultimately left well behind, and may struggle to defy the penalty under these conditions. (op 8-13 tchd 4-6 in places)
Dust In Time, pulled up on two of his three starts over hurdles, ran a much-improved race, though there is a good chance he was flattered. He will find easier opportunities in handicaps. (op 33-1 tchd 50-1)
Irish Airman(IRE) is clearly not very good, and probably won't be with Paul Nicholls for much longer. (op 11-1)
Kericho jumped poorly and showed little, eventually being pulled up. (op 10-1)

38 EDUCATION PLANNING AND DATA SOLUTIONS H'CAP CHASE (21 fncs) 3m 1f 110y
3:20 (3:20) (Class 3) (0-125,123) 5-Y-0+ **£6,982** (£2,387)

Form RPR

4P4- **1** **Triggernometry**[9] [5258] 9-10-5 **102**......................................(bt) JoeTizzard 117+
(Colin Tizzard) *trckd ldr: led appr 3 out: clr 2 out: eased nr fin* **2/1**[2]

5P5- **2** *12* **Terrible Tenant**[30] [4917] 11-10-2 **106**............................. JimmyDerham(7) 106
(Seamus Mullins) *led: rdn and hdd appr 3 out: sn hld* **9/2**[3]

FP2- **F** **Minella Four Star (IRE)**[11] [5212] 7-11-12 **123**................ RobertThornton —
(Alan King) *trckd ldr: hit 2nd: fell heavily next* **5/6**[1]

6m 20.2s (-19.30) **Going Correction** -0.975s/f (Hard) **3** Ran SP% **106.1**
Speed ratings: **90,86,—**
CSF £8.14 TOTE £2.90; EX 5.60.
Owner The Butterwick Syndicate **Bred** H T Cole **Trained** Milborne Port, Dorset

FOCUS
Only three runners remained, and one of those, the favourite Minella Four Star, departed as early as the third fence. The first two are rated on similar lines to this race last year.

NOTEBOOK
Triggernometry, who beat the runner-up in the race last year, was always travelling strongly and he had the race in the bag taking three out. He had slipped to a mark just 3lb higher than last year, and may well win again while in this sort of form. (op 9-4)
Terrible Tenant, 4lb higher than when winning over C&D last May, had everything in his favour, but always looked an easy target for the winner and he was readily left trailing having been headed before the first in the straight. (op 3-1)
Minella Four Star(IRE), already twice a faller over fences, was just 1lb higher than when a good second at Chepstow latest, and looked the one to beat, but he was untidy at the second, and took a heavy fall at the next. It remains to be seen how this affects his confidence. (op 10-11 tchd 4-5 and evens in a place)

39 WINCANTON NOVICES' CHASE (21 fncs) 3m 1f 110y
3:50 (3:50) (Class 4) 5-Y-0+ **£3,577** (£1,050; £525)

Form RPR

262- **1** **Nom De Guerre (IRE)**[10] [5231] 8-10-12 116.......................... DarylJacob 116+
(Ben De Haan) *j.w: mde most: hdd after 9th tl 14th: styd on wl fr 3 out: pushed out: dismntd* **5/6**[1]

523- **2** *2* **Now Listen To Me**[171] [2130] 7-10-12 112.........................(t) NickScholfield 113
(Paul Nicholls) *racd keenly: trckd ldrs: led sn after 9th: hit 12th: narrowly hdd 14th: mstke 3 out: sn rdn: styd on but a being hld fr next* **11/10**[2]

356- **3** *29* **Orion Star (IRE)**[288] [938] 8-10-5 68..........................(p) JimmyDerham(7) 89
(Seamus Mullins) *trckd wnr tl after 9th: trckd ldng pair: nt fluent 13th (water): nudged along fr 14th: one pce fr after 4 out* **20/1**[3]

6m 32.1s (-7.40) **Going Correction** -0.975s/f (Hard) **3** Ran SP% **106.9**
Speed ratings: **72,71,62**
CSF £2.15 TOTE £1.90; EX 1.90.
Owner Mr & Mrs Nicholas Tatman **Bred** Keith Douglas **Trained** Lambourn, Berks

FOCUS
A virtual match, and things would have been closer between the front two had the runner-up jumped better in the straight. It was slowly run and the first two are rated below their best.

NOTEBOOK
Nom De Guerre(IRE) certainly deserved a win, having run many creditable races in defeat over fences, and his superior jumping was the difference. He was dismounted after the race, and has broken blood-vessels in the past, however, so clearly isn't one to be getting carried away with. (op Evens)
Now Listen To Me didn't really settle, and his rider allowed him to go on before the tenth. He still looked a big danger in the straight, despite having been headed, but notable mistakes at both the third- and second-last sealed his fate. He can pick up a small race, but doesn't look one to take a short price about. (op Evens tchd 6-5 in a place)
Orion Star(IRE) was never going to make an impact, and did well to last as long as he did. (op 16-1 tchd 22-1)

40 WINNING POST H'CAP HURDLE (8 hdls) 2m
4:20 (4:20) (Class 4) (0-100,99) 4-Y-0+ **£2,602** (£764; £382; £190)

Form RPR

002- **1** **Regional Counsel**[4] [5357] 6-11-7 **94**.................................(t) WillKennedy 102+
(Alex Hales) *plld hrd early: trckd ldrs: led 2 out: mstke last: jst hld on: all out: dismntd and did nt return to wnrs enclosure* **4/1**[3]

000- **2** *nk* **Forest Rhythm (IRE)**[92] [3651] 6-11-3 **97**.....................(t) JimmyDerham(7) 103
(Seamus Mullins) *in tch: rdn after 3 out: styd on fr after next: str run fnl 120yds: swtchd rt nr fin: jst failed* **16/1**

56F- **3** *1 ½* **Jenny Potts**[9] [5261] 6-11-5 **97**.. GilesHawkins(5) 102
(Chris Down) *prom: slipped on bnd bef 3rd: lft in ld appr 4th tl nt fluent 2 out: sn rdn: kpt on same pce fr last* **3/1**[2]

600- 4 8 **Bazart**[47] 4539 8-11-5 **99** MissIsabelTompsett(7) 96
(Bernard Llewellyn) *trckd ldrs: rdn whn mstke 2 out: one pce after* **11/2**
100- 5 5 **Weststern (GER)**[35] 4812 7-11-12 **99** (t) JamieMoore 90
(Gary Moore) *hld up: cl enough whn rdn after 3 out: one pce fr next* **8/1**
402- 6 ½ **Crazy Bold (GER)**[9] 5255 7-11-3 **95** LeeEdwards(5) 86
(Tony Carroll) *hld up: wnt lft 5th: sn rdn: little imp fr next* **11/4**[1]
600- 7 22 **Shipboard Romance (IRE)**[10] 5234 5-10-11 **89** PeterToole(5) 58
(Mark Rimell) *sn trcking ldrs: rdn after 3 out: wknd next: t.o* **25/1**
506- P **Magistrate (IRE)**[11] 5216 5-10-11 **84** (b[1]) NickScholfield —
(Andy Turnell) *led tl lost action and p.u bef 4th: dead* **28/1**

3m 37.7s (-11.20) **Going Correction** -0.975s/f (Hard) **8** Ran SP% **111.3**
Speed ratings (Par 105): **89,88,88,84,81 81,70,—**
toteswingers: 1&2 £8.30, 1&3 £4.10, 2&3 £8.90 CSF £56.70 CT £210.18 TOTE £4.00: £1.10, £4.50, £1.70; EX 61.40.
Owner A S Helaissi **Bred** Cheveley Park Stud Ltd **Trained** Wardington, Oxon

FOCUS

A moderate handicap hurdle but the form should work out.

NOTEBOOK

Regional Counsel, runner-up at Bangor just four days earlier, failed to settle, but was always well placed, and bounced off the quick ground, just doing enough to hold on having been untidy at the last. He was dismounted after the line, however, and looked to have broken down.
Forest Rhythm(IRE) looked a likely improver for this better ground, and he would have got up in another stride or two, coming with a strong run after the last. He is completely unexposed and it will be disappointing if he fails to win this summer, with a stiffer test likely to suit at some stage. (op 14-1)
Jenny Potts, still in front when falling at the last over C&D just nine days earlier, briefly lost her footing on the bend racing away from the stands, but recovered to lead and she stayed on the best she could without being able to fend off the front pair. (op 7-2 tchd 4-1)
Bazart's run gave a bit more encouragement, although not enough to suggest he is about to win. (op 7-1 tchd 9-2)
Crazy Bold(GER), off the same mark as when second at Stratford latest, proved bitterly disappointing, never threatening to get into it having been held up, and only beating one home. (op 3-1 tchd 10-3)

41 WINCANTON GOLF COURSE NOVICES' HURDLE (8 hdls) 2m
4:50 (4:50) (Class 4) 4-Y-0+ **£2,665** (£827; £445)

Form RPR
400- 1 **Marc Aurele (IRE)**[32] 4871 5-10-5 110 (t) MrRMahon(7) 116+
(Paul Nicholls) *mde all: kpt on wl to draw clr fr last: drvn out* **3/1**[2]
33/- 2 11 **Gremlin**[11] 4896 6-10-12 0 (p) WillKennedy 109+
(Dai Burchell) *trckd ldrs: wnt 2nd after 4th: nt fluent 2 out: sn rdn: kpt on but nt gng pce of wnr fr last* **1/1**[1]
50- 3 13 **Diamond Eclipse (IRE)**[12] 5194 4-10-7 0 DarylJacob 92+
(Nick Williams) *w wnr tl after 4th: chsd ldng pair: rdn after 3 out: one pce fr next: hit last: eased run-in* **11/2**
044- P **Raspbary**[35] 4799 4-10-0 102 JimmyDerham(7) —
(Seamus Mullins) *chsd ldrs: nt fluent 3rd: rdn after 3 out: sn wknd: p.u bef next* **9/2**[3]

3m 33.7s (-15.20) **Going Correction** -0.975s/f (Hard)
WFA 4 from 5yo+ 6lb **4** Ran SP% **108.6**
Speed ratings (Par 105): **99,93,87,—**
CSF £6.67 TOTE £2.90; EX 6.00 Place 6: £76.83 Place 5: £44.36.
Owner Ged Mason & Sir Alex Ferguson **Bred** Haras Du Mezeray And Ecurie Demgalop **Trained** Ditcheat, Somerset

FOCUS

An open novices' handicap. A step up from the winner with the second setting the level.

NOTEBOOK

Marc Aurele(IRE) left behind his dismal handicap efforts on this faster ground, appreciating the change to more forceful tactics and making just about all. He looked vulnerable when the favourite came in pursuit of him early in the straight, but kept finding under a fine ride, and was going away again at the line. He will be kept on the go, and is set to go chasing at some stage. (tchd 11-4 and 5-2 in places)
Gremlin, in good form on the AW this year, had some okay form to his name over hurdles when with Alan King, and he looked the one to beat, but didn't find as much as expected, and was ultimately well held. (op 5-4 tchd 11-8)
Diamond Eclipse(IRE) is more of a handicap prospect, and looks to need more time. (op 4-1)
Raspbary was eventually pulled up having dropped away and looks more of a long-term prospect. (op 4-1)
T/Plt: £485.30 to a £1 stake. Pool: £45,203.71. 67.99 winning tickets. T/Qpdt: £77.40 to a £1 stake. Pool: £3,286.86. 31.40 winning tickets. TM

KELSO (L-H)

Wednesday, April 28

OFFICIAL GOING: Good to firm (good in places; watered; 7.5)
Wind: Fairly strong, half against Weather: Cloudy

42 JEDFOREST DEER PARK MAIDEN HURDLE (8 hdls) 2m 110y
5:50 (5:50) (Class 4) 4-Y-0+ **£3,252** (£955; £477; £238)

Form RPR
222- 1 **Saveiro (FR)**[22] 5076 6-11-0 117 BrianHughes 122
(Alan Swinbank) *pressed ldr: led 4 out: hrd pressed fr 2 out: drvn and kpt on gamely run-in* **5/2**[2]
245- 2 ¾ **Al Qeddaaf (IRE)**[20] 5094 4-10-9 125 JasonMaguire 117
(Donald McCain) *trckd ldng pair: wnt 2nd 3 out: effrt next: ev ch run-in: kpt on: hld towards fin* **4/7**[1]
355- 3 28 **Devil Water**[7] 5310 7-10-11 111 HarryHaynes(3) 96
(James Ewart) *set decent gallop to 4 out: cl up tl rdn and no ex bef 2 out* **20/1**
4 ½ **Imperial Breeze (IRE)**[45] 4628 5-11-0 0 DougieCostello 96
(J J Lambe, Ire) *in tch: stdy hdwy and cl up 3 out: drvn and outpcd fr next* **16/1**[3]
30P- 5 10 **King Penda (IRE)**[54] 4412 7-10-11 0 FearghalDavis(3) 87
(Nicky Richards) *hld up: stdy hdwy after 3rd: outpcd 1/2-way: rallied bef 2 out: sn no imp* **33/1**
00- 6 6 **Stormion (IRE)**[41] 4706 5-11-0 0 PeterBuchanan 81
(Lucinda Russell) *nt fluent on occasions: sn towards rr: outpcd 1/2-way: plugged on fr 2 out: nvr on terms* **80/1**
UP- 7 7 **Quine Des Ormeaux (FR)**[43] 4663 6-10-1 0 ow1 AlexanderVoy(7) 69
(Stuart Coltherd) *blnd 1st: towards rr: hdwy 4th: rdn and in tch 3 out: wknd bef next* **200/1**
/P0- 8 7 **Samaret**[17] 5138 5-10-0 0 GarryWhillans(7) 62
(Harriet Graham) *hmpd 1st: bhd: struggling 1/2-way: nvr on terms* **200/1**
350- 9 nk **Just Maddie**[70] 4104 6-10-4 100 (p) RyanMania(3) 61
(Rayson Nixon) *blnd 1st: prom tl rdn and wknd bef 3 out* **66/1**
606- 10 1¼ **See The Legend**[17] 5138 5-10-7 0 PaddyAspell 60
(Sandy Forster) *hmpd 1st: bhd: struggling bef 4th: nvr on terms* **33/1**
000- 11 22 **Hollows Gift (IRE)**[17] 5138 5-11-0 0 RichieMcGrath 47
(Barry Murtagh) *hmpd 1st: bhd: no ch fr 1/2-way: t.o* **200/1**
00- 12 25 **Emirate Isle**[2] 2749 6-11-0 0 JamesReveley 25
(Brian Storey) *in tch: outpcd whn hit 4 out: sn wknd: t.o* **40/1**
5- 13 15 **Foxes Delight (IRE)**[32] 6-10-7 0 (t) AlistairFindlay(7) 11
(Jane Walton) *nt fluent: in tch tl hit and wknd 4 out: t.o* **100/1**
/0F- P **Harrys Double (IRE)**[159] 2407 6-10-11 0 (p) GaryBerridge(3) —
(Joseph Bewley) *nt fluent in rr: struggling 4th: sn t.o: p.u bef 2 out* **125/1**
260- F **Power Flow (IRE)**[38] 4752 5-11-0 0 PhilKinsella —
(Peter Atkinson) *midfield whn fell heavily 2nd* **66/1**
/00- P **Blaqjack (IRE)**[80] 3922 6-10-11 0 JamesO'Farrell(3) —
(Michael Smith) *midfield: struggling bef 4th: tailing off whn p.u after next* **200/1**

3m 56.0s (-5.80) **Going Correction** -0.15s/f (Good)
WFA 4 from 5yo+ 6lb **16** Ran SP% **119.2**
Speed ratings (Par 105): **107,106,93,93,88 85,82,79,78,78 68,56,49,—,— —**
toteswingers:1&2:£1.10, 1&3:£9.50, 2&3:£5.20 CSF £4.05 TOTE £2.90: £1.10, £1.70, £2.50; EX 4.60.
Owner Ian John Clark **Bred** Satwa Farm **Trained** Melsonby, N Yorks

FOCUS

This was a match between the first two in the betting and they came a long way clear of their rivals, but the market got it wrong. The winner improved to the level of his best bumper form with the next three below form.

NOTEBOOK

Saveiro(FR) opened his account at the seventh attempt as a hurdler and, despite having finished second on his previous three outings, there was no faulting his attitude here. The quicker ground over this shorter trip looked to make all the difference. (op 11-4)
Al Qeddaaf(IRE) finished a well-beaten fifth in a Grade 1 at Aintree against his own age 20 days earlier and was, unsurprisingly, all the rage on this return to a lower level. He moved like the best horse in the race and looked set to go about his business nearing the home straight. However, he came under pressure after getting the second-last wrong and couldn't get past the winner. It may be the ground was quicker than he cares for, but he is obviously flattered by his new mark at this stage. (op 4-6 tchd 8-11 inplaces)
Devil Water cut out the running with the winner until failing to go the pace when that one asserted three out. He kept on gamely and ideally needs a stiffer test, but is another currently flattered by his official mark. (op 18-1)
Imperial Breeze(IRE) moved nicely into contention, but was left behind when the race got really serious and probably needs a stiffer test. He now has the option of handicaps.
King Penda(IRE), who cost £115,000, ran with a fair bit more encouragement and should benefit from a step up in trip when going handicapping. (op 25-1)
Samaret Official explanation: jockey said mare hung right throughout

43 CHARLESWORTH GROUP NOVICES' H'CAP CHASE (17 fncs) 2m 6f 110y
6:20 (6:20) (Class 3) (0-120,112) 5-Y-0+ **£6,505** (£1,910; £955; £477)

Form RPR
256- 1 **Quick Will (FR)**[46] 4578 6-11-9 **112** HarryHaynes(3) 121
(James Ewart) *hld up in tch: hdwy to ld 13th: hrd pressed fr 2 out: styd on gamely u.p to assert towards fin* **10/1**
601- 2 1½ **Phone In**[12] 5202 7-11-12 **112** PeterBuchanan 120
(Lucinda Russell) *chsd ldrs: rdn after 13th: rallied next: disp ld 2 out to run-in: drvn and kpt on: hld nr fin* **11/10**[1]
20P- 3 33 **Border Reiver**[33] 4862 6-11-2 **102** (bt[1]) RichieMcGrath 85
(Tim Easterby) *led to 13th: rallied and ev ch 3 out: mstke and wknd fr next* **11/4**[2]
4 dist **On Gossamer Wings (IRE)**[24] 5028 6-11-5 **105** DougieCostello 47
(J J Lambe, Ire) *nt fluent: cl up: drvn and outpcd bef 3 out: lost tch after next: virtually p.u run-in* **9/1**
42P- P **Sierra Victor (IRE)**[159] 2412 7-10-2 **88** WilsonRenwick —
(P Monteith) *hld up in tch: outpcd bef 5th: p.u bef next* **9/2**[3]

5m 42.4s (-2.10) **Going Correction** -0.525s/f (Firm) **5** Ran SP% **111.6**
Speed ratings: **82,81,70,56,—**
CSF £23.01 TOTE £11.30: £3.50, £2.50; EX 25.30.
Owner W H Whitley, C Davidson **Bred** Michel Rivaillon **Trained** Langholm, Dumfries & G'way

FOCUS

A moderate handicap, decimated by non-runners. A step up from the winner on the best of his hurdles form with slight improvement from the second on his recent win.

NOTEBOOK

Quick Will(FR) completed the task in game fashion on this switch to chasing. He put in some indifferent jumps early on but, when he did meet a fence right, he looked very good in that department. His attitude was spot-on in the home straight and he is obviously a better stayer in this sphere. He has now gained both his wins at this venue. (tchd 16-1)
Phone In was hiked up 10lb for his Ayr success 12 days earlier. He came under pressure around the 12th fence, but wasn't getting a good sight at his fences as the leader went out to his right and was soon back on the bridle when getting past that rival. His rider took a look over his shoulder turning for home, but it proved to be overconfidence as his mount lacked the resolution of the winner. It wouldn't be surprising to see some headgear back on after this. (op 11-8)
Border Reiver was equipped with first-time blinkers and proved popular. He set out from the front, but didn't get an easy lead and didn't help his cause by tending to jump to his right. He was easily beaten off when the first pair kicked on and looks one to avoid. Official explanation: jockey said gelding had a breathing problem (op 10-3 tchd 9-4)
On Gossamer Wings(IRE) was making his handicap debut on quicker ground and his fate was apparent before the home turn. (op 15-2 tchd 10-1)
Sierra Victor(IRE) Official explanation: jockey said gelding lost its action but returned sound

44 JUSTIN & SUSAN GREIG WEDDING CELEBRATION H'CAP HURDLE (10 hdls) 2m 2f
6:50 (6:50) (Class 3) (0-135,125) 4-Y-0+ **£5,204** (£1,528; £764; £381)

Form RPR
300- 1 **Hazeldene**[37] 4783 8-10-1 **103** RyanMania(3) 111+
(George Charlton) *mde all: sn clr: rdn bef 2 out: styd on strly run-in* **9/2**[3]
/P0- 2 6 **Nevertika (FR)**[12] 5207 9-10-13 **115** HarryHaynes(3) 117
(James Ewart) *hld up in tch: hdwy and cl up 3 out: rdn and chsd wnr last: styd on same pce run-in* **7/2**[1]
26/- 3 1¾ **Nine Stories (IRE)**[397] 4742 5-11-10 **123** BrianHughes 126+
(Howard Johnson) *hld up in midfield: stdy hdwy and in tch whn blnd 2 out: sn outpcd: kpt on run-in: no imp* **14/1**
053- 4 1 **Premier Dane (IRE)**[12] 5207 8-11-9 **125** (b[1]) FearghalDavis(3) 124
(Nicky Richards) *hld up: stdy hdwy 4 out: chsd wnr bef 2 out to last: sn no ex* **4/1**[2]
214- 5 6 **Cassius (IRE)**[11] 5224 8-11-7 **120** GrahamLee 114
(Bruce Mactaggart) *chsd (clr) wnr tl rdn and outpcd bef 2 out* **4/1**[2]
236- 6 29 **The Panama Kid (IRE)**[12] 5202 6-11-7 **120** PhilKinsella 88
(Malcolm Jefferson) *prom chsng gp: hit 6th: wknd bef next: t.o* **8/1**

/00- **7** *3* **Modicum (USA)**46 4578 8-11-2 115 WilsonRenwick 80
(Rose Dobbin) *hld up: reminders after 5th: struggling fr next: t.o* **16/1**
206- **8** *4* **Sea Storm (IRE)**35 4814 12-10-11 110 PaddyAspell 71
(James Moffatt) *hld up: struggling after 6th: sn btn: t.o* **22/1**
26P- **P** **Sunarri (IRE)**53 4436 6-10-11 110 TimmyMurphy —
(George Charlton) *j.rt: hld up: wknd and p.u bef 6th* **12/1**
4m 22.6s (-4.40) **Going Correction** -0.15s/f (Good) 9 Ran SP% **116.1**
Speed ratings (Par 107): **103,100,99,99,96 83,82,80,—**
toteswingers:1&2:£7.50, 1&3:£16.70, 2&3:£15.70 CSF £21.24 CT £204.01 TOTE £6.60: £2.40, £2.70, £5.70; EX 27.60.
Owner George A Charlton **Bred** J I A Charlton **Trained** Stocksfield, Northumberland

FOCUS
A weak handicap for the class. The fourth helps to set the level which looks very solid. The winner is rated back to his best.

NOTEBOOK
Hazeldene did plenty through the early parts, but kept finding once the challengers loomed up around three out and ultimately made all with something left up his sleeve. He had something to prove coming into this, but his yard is among the winners at present and the aggressive tactics over this shorter trip worked out. He has also now posted both wins on a sound surface.
Nevertika(FR) proved reluctant to jump off and clearly has his quirks. This was better from him in defeat, though, and while he is one to tread carefully with there is little doubt he can find a race off this sort of mark. (op 4-1 tchd 10-3)
Nine Stories(IRE) was returning from a 13-month absence and the market suggested the run would be needed. He ran a big race, however, and would have most likely finished second had he not made a mistake at the penultimate flight. He has time on his side and should come on nicely for the run.
Premier Dane(IRE) failed to raise his game for the application of first-time blinkers on this drop in trip, but wasn't disgraced under top weight and helps to set the level. (tchd 9-2)
Cassius(IRE) wasn't able to find an extra gear when it mattered and needs softer ground, but he is high enough in the weights at present. (op 11-2)
Sunarri(IRE) Official explanation: jockey said gelding was unsuited by the good to firm (good in places) ground

45 JOHN N. DUNN GROUP LTD/SOL20 H'CAP HURDLE (11 hdls) 2m 6f 110y
7:20 (7:20) (Class 3) (0-130,128) 4-Y-0+
£7,514 (£2,220; £1,110; £555; £277; £139)

Form RPR
231- **1** **Coastley (IRE)**16 5166 8-10-4 113 MrJARichardson(7) 126+
(David Carr) *chsd ldrs: wnt 2nd 7th: effrt and chal 2 out: led bef last: drifted lft run-in: styd on wl* **9/2**3
222- **2** *5* **Pontop (IRE)**6 5338 7-10-11 120 AlistairFindlay(7) 128
(George Charlton) *led: rdn and jnd 2 out: hdd bef last: kpt on same pce run-in* **2/1**1
P/4- **3** *12* **Wot Way Chief**17 5147 9-10-7 114 JamesHalliday(5) 111
(Malcolm Jefferson) *trckd ldrs: outpcd bef 2 out: plugged on fr last: no imp* **16/1**
361- **4** *9* **The Gloves Are Off (IRE)**17 5147 7-10-12 119 GilesHawkins(5) 109
(Sue Smith) *in tch: hdwy and cl up appr 3 out: rdn and outpcd bef next* **12/1**
U4P- **5** *3 ¼* **Corkage (IRE)**11 5226 7-11-12 128 (b1) PeterBuchanan 113
(Lucinda Russell) *chsd ldr to 7th: rdn and outpcd bef 2 out: n.d after* **22/1**
453- **6** *5* **Tension Point**185 1912 6-10-13 120 (t) MissLHorner(5) 100
(Chris Grant) *midfield: outpcd whn nt fluent 3 out: sn n.d* **18/1**
052- **7** *7* **Its Tough (IRE)**12 5203 7-10-0 102 oh2 WilsonRenwick 76
(P Monteith) *hld up: rdn after 4 out: nvr rchd ldrs* **15/2**
3- **8** *½* **City Of Doral**14 5186 8-11-0 116 DougieCostello 89
(J J Lambe, Ire) *t.k.h in midfield: outpcd 3 out: sn btn* **18/1**
5P3- **9** *nk* **Harmony Brig (IRE)**12 5206 11-11-4 120 (b) RichieMcGrath 93
(Nicky Richards) *t.k.h: hld up: hung lft and outpcd 4 out: sn btn* **40/1**
001- **10** *3* **Ameeq (USA)**10 5248 8-11-2 125 BrianToomey(7) 95
(Dr Richard Newland) *hld up: drvn after 4 out: nvr on terms* **4/1**2
1/P- **11** *13* **Browneyes Blue (IRE)**37 4783 12-10-8 110 PaddyAspell 69
(James Moffatt) *midfield: outpcd bef 7th: no ch after* **50/1**
160- **P** **Little Lu (IRE)**54 4416 8-10-13 115 BrianHughes —
(Alan Swinbank) *hld up: rdn after 4 out: nvr on terms: p.u and dismntd on run-in* **18/1**
5m 33.4s (-7.60) **Going Correction** -0.15s/f (Good) 12 Ran SP% **121.4**
Speed ratings (Par 107): **107,105,101,97,96 95,92,92,92,91 86,—**
toteswingers:1&2:£2.40, 1&3:£12.50, 2&3:£9.10 CSF £14.39 CT £137.22 TOTE £6.80: £2.30, £1.10, £7.90; EX 18.60.
Owner David Carr **Bred** Walter Zieg **Trained** Hexham, Northumberland

FOCUS
A modest handicap, run at an uneven gallop and it paid to race handily. On the face of it the winner produced a big step up.

NOTEBOOK
Coastley(IRE) followed up his Sedgefield success on this switch to handicap company. He was perfectly placed when it mattered and was well on top at the finish, so looks well worth turning out under a penalty while in such form. (op 6-1)
Pontop(IRE), 2lb higher, has now found one too good on five of his last six outings. He had the run of the race and is one to swerve for win-only betting. (op 11-4 tchd 10-3 in plcaes)
Wot Way Chief would have enjoyed a more truly run race despite this being a stiffer test and he reversed last-time-out form with The Gloves Are Off. (op 14-1)
The Gloves Are Off(IRE) failed to really see out the longer trip off a 6lb higher mark. (op 9-1)
Its Tough(IRE) got badly outpaced before staying on and is better than he could show. (op 9-1 tchd 11-1)
Ameeq(USA) went unpenalised for his recent Ascot success and, although his response when asked to improve was disappointing, he was another never in with a chance from out the back. Official explanation: trainer had no explanation for the poor form shown (tchd 9-2 in places)
Little Lu(IRE) Official explanation: jockey said mare was struck into

46 ATTHERACES.COM H'CAP CHASE (19 fncs) 3m 1f
7:55 (7:55) (Class 3) (0-120,120) 5-Y-0+ **£6,505** (£1,910; £955; £477)

Form RPR
420- **1** **Top Dressing (IRE)**48 4533 9-11-1 109 BrianHughes 122+
(Howard Johnson) *hld up towards rr: hdwy bef 3 out: led last: styd on strly to go clr run-in* **18/1**
61P- **2** *9* **Seize**9 5274 8-10-13 107 GrahamLee 112
(Ferdy Murphy) *hld up: hdwy and in tch 1/2-way: effrt and ev ch last: kpt on run-in: nt pce of wnr* **12/1**
06P- **3** *4 ½* **Nile Moon (IRE)**134 2893 9-10-6 100 (b) PaddyAspell 101
(Ann Hamilton) *chsd ldrs: slt ld 15th to last: sn no ex* **8/1**3
6P3- **4** *7* **Minouchka (FR)**17 5141 10-10-11 108 GaryBerridge(3) 103
(Simon Shirley-Beavan) *chsd ldrs: ev ch 15th: drvn and outpcd 3 out: plugged on run-in: no imp* **10/1**
063- **5** *5* **Harry Flashman**9 5274 9-10-8 102 PeterBuchanan 93
(Donald Whillans) *chsd ldrs: effrt after 2 out: wknd fr last* **4/1**2
33F- **6** *29* **Ocarina (FR)**39 4734 8-10-2 99 HarryHaynes(3) 78
(James Ewart) *t.k.h: mde most to 15th: rallied to dispute ld next: hit 2 out: sn wknd: eased whn no ch run-in* **4/1**2
/50- **7** *62* **Bill's Echo**12 5204 11-11-10 118 (b) SamThomas 26
(Alistair Whillans) *hld up: hdwy and in tch 1/2-way: rdn and wknd bef 3 out: virtually p.u run-in* **25/1**
U5P- **P** **Snowy (IRE)**34 4836 12-10-1 95 WilsonRenwick —
(P Monteith) *prom tl lost pl 8th: struggling fr 10th: t.o whn p.u bef 14th* **11/1**
3/4- **P** **Ring Street Roller (IRE)**12 5205 10-11-4 112 (b) DougieCostello —
(J J Lambe, Ire) *nt fluent: hld up: struggling fr 13th: t.o whn p.u bef last* **8/1**3
231- **P** **Something Silver**34 4836 9-10-0 94 oh1 (v) RichieMcGrath —
(Jim Goldie) *chsd ldrs: lost pl bef 12th: t.o whn p.u bef 3 out* **7/2**1
6m 14.0s (-17.50) **Going Correction** -0.525s/f (Firm) 10 Ran SP% **118.7**
Speed ratings: **107,104,102,100,98 89,69,—,—,—**
toteswingers:1&2:£15.30, 1&3:£21.30, 2&3:£17.60 CSF £211.10 CT £1875.69 TOTE £27.60: £6.80, £4.80, £3.30; EX 211.10.
Owner Group Captain J A Prideaux **Bred** Andrew Pierce **Trained** Billy Row, Co Durham

FOCUS
This was wide open and they went a sound gallop. Fair form with the first two rated to their best.

NOTEBOOK
Top Dressing(IRE) came with a well-timed challenge under his in-form rider and eventually pulled right away. The decent gallop was right up his street, as was the good ground, and he obviously stays well. The handicapper will now hike him back up, but he didn't have the hardest of races and would have to be of strong interest if able to turn out under a penalty. (op 16-1)
Seize showed his latest effort to be all wrong and ran a solid race in defeat, but the handicapper now looks to have his measure. (op 9-1)
Nile Moon(IRE) was last seen pulling up 134 days previously, so this was a lot better. This is his time of year and dropping back in trip should only help. (op 9-1)
Minouchka(FR), as was the case over C&D last time, hit a flat spot before staying on again late in the day. The ground was probably quick enough for her liking. (op 7-1)
Harry Flashman had good claims on his recent form nd showed a real liking for this venue over hurdles. He failed to get a good trip through the race, though, and got in too low at his fences after failing to get into a good rhythm. He looks worth dropping back in trip.
Something Silver, effectively 5lb higher, attracted support over this longer trip. He dropped out a long way from home, perhaps because of the quicker ground. Official explanation: jockey said gelding was unsuited by the good to firm (good in places) ground (op 4-1tchd 9-2 in places)

47 RADIO BORDERS CASH FOR KIDS STANDARD OPEN NATIONAL HUNT FLAT RACE 2m 110y
8:25 (8:25) (Class 5) 4-6-Y-O **£1,951** (£573; £286; £143)

Form RPR
1 **Storm Kirk** 4-10-6 0 EwanWhillans(5) 88
(Alistair Whillans) *hld up on outside: stdy hdwy over 6f out: effrt and ev ch over 2f out: led ins fnl f: styd on wl* **7/2**2
2 *2* **Kvarner Riviera (IRE)** 4-10-11 0 PhilKinsella 86
(Malcolm Jefferson) *hld up in tch: stdy hdwy over 4f out: effrt and ev ch over 1f out: hung lft ins fnl f: r.o* **6/1**3
3 *shd* **Golden View (IRE)**368 5-11-2 0 DougieCostello 91
(J J Lambe, Ire) *set modest gallop: rdn over 2f out: hdd ins fnl f: kpt on same pce* **10/1**
03/- **4** *6* **La Bacouetteuse (FR)**428 4118 5-10-9 0 NathanMoscrop(7) 85
(Simon Shirley-Beavan) *hld up: stdy hdwy over 6f out: chsng ldrs and rdn over 2f out: sn one pce* **16/1**
- **5** *1 ¼* **Whiteadder** 5-11-2 0 WilsonRenwick 84
(Rose Dobbin) *hld up: rdn along 3f out: no imp fnl 2f* **25/1**
6 *1* **Connie Beauchamp**39 6-10-4 0 JamesHalliday(5) 76
(Elliott Cooper) *pressed ldr tl rdn and outpcd over 2f out: n.d after* **50/1**
7 *3* **Cool Water** 5-10-2 0 AlexanderVoy(7) 73
(John Wade) *t.k.h: hld up in tch: rdn 3f out: no imp fr 2f out* **50/1**
8 *17* **Flash Flight (IRE)** 5-10-13 0 JamesO'Farrell(3) 63
(Michael Smith) *t.k.h: midfield: struggling over 3f out: sn btn* **28/1**
U- **P** **Nipper Nial**5 5376 5-11-2 0 JasonMaguire —
(R MacDonald) *prom: hmpd and lost action bnd over 3f out: sn p.u* **20/1**
- **R** **Diamond MM (IRE)** 4-10-4 0 BrianHughes —
(Alan Swinbank) *t.k.h: trckd ldrs: stl gng wl whn ducked lft and rn out bnd over 3f out* **4/5**1
3m 59.6s (3.40) **Going Correction** -0.15s/f (Good)
WFA 4 from 5yo+ 6lb 10 Ran SP% **123.0**
Speed ratings: **86,85,85,82,81 81,79,71,—,—**
toteswingers:1&2:£4.30, 1&3:£7.00, 2&3:£5.10 CSF £24.70 TOTE £9.80: £3.40, £2.00, £1.20; EX 19.70 Place 6 £126.97; Place 5 £119.17.
Owner W J E Scott & Mrs M A Scott **Bred** Mrs D H Mathias **Trained** Newmill-On-Slitrig, Borders

FOCUS
A modest bumper which has been rated through the fourth.

NOTEBOOK
Storm Kirk showed a very good attitude on his debut to come out on top. He is not from a stable usually associated with first-time-out bumper winners, but the market suggested a big run was expected and this Flat-bred 4-y-o clearly has a future. (op 5-1 tchd 11-2)
Kvarner Riviera(IRE), whose yard won this last season, crept into things going nicely off the home turn and, despite hanging left under pressure, held every chance. He just found the winner that bit too speedy, but has plenty of scope and should be up to going one better before long. (op 13-2)
Golden View(IRE) came into this having won at the third attempt in the Irish pointing field a year ago and got a positive ride. He gave his all and it rates a pleasing debut effort on ground that suits. (op 8-1 tchd 11-1)
La Bacouetteuse(FR) was last seen finishing third on his second outing at Catterick in February last year. He shaped as though the run would do him good and looks ready to go hurdling. (op 14-1 tchd 20-1)
Diamond MM(IRE) has a Flat pedigree for around 1m2f and is held in high regard. She was going well within herself prior to unseating and it came as a shock as she hadn't shown any distinct signs of greenness prior to that. (op 10-11)

T/Plt: £326.70 to a £1 stake. Pool: £77429.68. 173.01 winning tickets. T/Qpdt: £166.90 to a £1 stake. Pool: £6791.01. 30.10 winning tickets. RY

SOUTHWELL (L-H)

Wednesday, April 28

OFFICIAL GOING: Good (8.1)

Penultimate fence in home str. omitted on all circuits of chase course. Fences 7yds ins. line used on April 21, golf club bend 5yds o/s, home bend 5yds ins.
Wind: light 1/2 against Weather: fine and sunny

48 SOUTHWELL-RACECOURSE.CO.UK H'CAP CHASE (11 fncs 2 omitted) 2m

2:30 (2:30) (Class 5) (0-95,92) 5-Y-0+ **£2,602** (£764; £382; £190)

Form RPR

244- **1** **Mad Professor (IRE)**[7] 5318 7-9-9 **68**.........................(p) JoeCornwall(7) 80+
(John Cornwall) *chsd ldrs: styd on fr 3 out: wnt 2nd next: led appr last: drvn clr* **5/2**[1]

F06- **2** *7* **Braddock Island**[96] 3589 7-11-12 **92**................................... KeithMercer 98
(Mrs S Sunter) *chsd ldrs: wnt 2nd 6th: led appr 2 out: hdd appr last: no ex* **12/1**

00F- **3** *4 1/2* **Ajzal (IRE)**[28] 4964 6-11-3 **83**...(b) FelixDeGiles 86
(Tom George) *t.k.h: led: hdd appr 2 out: hung rt and sn btn* **11/4**[2]

564- **4** *3* **Peak Seasons (IRE)**[4] 5390 7-10-3 **76**......................... StevenGagan(7) 76
(Michael Chapman) *w ldrs: drvn 6th: wl outpcd 3 out: kpt on between last 2* **12/1**

4P0- **5** *40* **Bright Sparky (GER)**[65] 3530 7-11-6 **89**......................(b) MrOGreenall(3) 57
(Michael Easterby) *prom: hit 5th and sn given reminders: lost pl bef next: sn bhd: t.o last whn hmpd 3 out* **9/1**

430- **6** *1 1/4* **Stuff Of Dreams**[17] 5139 5-11-5 **92**................................ PaulGallagher(7) 59
(Ferdy Murphy) *hit 1st: in tch: outpcd and reminders 7th: sn bhd: t.o 3 out* **9/1**

205- **U** **Thievery**[47] 4574 9-11-9 **89**... RichardJohnson —
(Henry Daly) *j.rt: blnd 2nd: bhd fr 6th: t.o 6th whn blnd and uns rdr 3 out* **9/2**[3]

4m 10.0s **Going Correction** +0.075s/f (Yiel) **7** Ran SP% **108.8**
Speed ratings: **103,99,97,95,75 75,—**
toteswingers:1&2:£6.40, 1&3:£2.00, 2&3:£10.60 CSF £26.59 CT £76.89 TOTE £3.10: £1.60, £8.10; EX 50.90.

Owner J R Cornwall **Bred** Jerry Murphy **Trained** Long Clawson, Leics

FOCUS
A weak contest and the winner is rated in line with his recent hurdle runs. The middle fence in the home straight was missed out all meeting, and jockeys who rode in the opener considered the ground to be on the easy side of good.

NOTEBOOK
Mad Professor(IRE), without a victory since the middle of 2008 and down in trip, attracted plenty of market interest on his return to fences and won by a clear margin. Rated just 68, it was not that easy to work out why he was so strongly fancied, even allowing for a low weight and weak opposition, but the money was well placed and easily landed. (op 3-1 tchd 9-4)
Braddock Island, trained again by his owner after leaving Chris Grant, is a nice, big sort who shapes as though further will suit. He took over from the long-time leader in the home straight but lacked a gear change once in front. (op 11-1)
Ajzal(IRE) ran his best race for a long time before falling at the final fence at Hereford on his last outing, and looked the one to beat if none the worse for that effort. His jockey made an enterprising move with a circuit to go, gaining a healthy advantage, but he capitulated quickly once joined and looked a weak finisher. (tchd 3-1)
Peak Seasons(IRE), making a quick return, was prominent early but got outpaced when the tempo increased. He was never a serious threat.
Bright Sparky(GER), wearing blinkers again, won at Wolverhampton when last seen but failed to show the same sparkle back over fences. Official explanation: jockey said gelding lost a shoe (op 7-1)
Thievery had been well beaten in two starts this year after a winter break and was jumping moderately before unseating Richard Johnson. (op 5-1)

49 PLAY GOLF AT SOUTHWELL GOLF CLUB NOVICES' H'CAP CHASE (18 fncs 3 omitted) 3m 2f

3:05 (3:06) (Class 4) (0-105,105) 5-Y-0+ **£6,330** (£1,965; £1,058)

Form RPR

P44- **1** **Grenoli (FR)**[10] 5251 9-9-7 **79** oh1.................................(bt) JoeCornwall(7) 101+
(John Cornwall) *led 2nd: wnt clr 13th: 40 l ahd last: heavily eased* **9/2**[1]

231- **2** *36* **Tanners Court**[17] 5152 13-11-7 **105**.................................... IanPopham(5) 91
(Claire Dyson) *led to 2nd: chsd ldrs: pushed along 12th: wnt modest 3rd 15th: kpt on to take 2nd towards fin* **11/2**[3]

633- **3** *3/4* **Katalak (IRE)**[19] 5120 7-11-7 **100**.. FelixDeGiles 86
(Jonathen de Giles) *trckd ldrs: chsd wnr fr 10th: outpcd 13th: lost 2nd nr line* **6/1**

6PP- **P** **Blackanblue**[32] 4898 11-9-11 **81**...................................... LeeEdwards(5) —
(Alan Hollingsworth) *unruly and reluctant s: s.s: j. poorly detached in last: sme hdwy 5th: reminders and dropped bk next: sn t.o: p.u bef 10th* **20/1**

/4F- **P** **The Artful Fox**[22] 9-9-7 **79** oh10...................................... HenryBrooke(7) —
(Mike Sowersby) *in tch: hdwy 13th: modest 5th whn mstke 3 out: distant 4th whn blnd next: p.u bef last* **14/1**

542- **P** **Omme Antique (FR)**[20] 5104 8-10-9 **88**................................ AidanColeman —
(Venetia Williams) *in tch: outpcd and lost pl 13th: distant 5th whn p.u bef 2 out* **5/1**[2]

403- **P** **Midnight Diamond (IRE)**[32] 4898 7-10-0 **79** oh7...........(p) KeithMercer —
(Lisa Williamson) *in rr: bhd fr 8th: t.o 7th whn p.u bef 2 out* **14/1**

U51- **P** **Minella For Food (IRE)**[36] 4793 7-11-8 **101**..................(p) PaulMoloney —
(Evan Williams) *chsd ldrs: modest 3rd whn blnd 14th: sn wknd: distant 6th whn p.u bef 2 out* **11/1**

543- **P** **Feeling Peckish (USA)**[23] 5040 6-9-7 **79** oh4..............(t) PeterHatton(7) —
(Michael Chapman) *chsd ldrs: reminders 6th: lost pl 12th: sn t.o: p.u bef 14th* **9/1**

U22- **U** **Greenandredparson (IRE)**[9] 5272 7-10-11 **97**........... PaulGallagher(7) —
(Paul Murphy) *hld up in rr: hit 11th: reminders and lost pl after 12th: poor 7th whn blnd and uns rdr 14th* **15/2**

6m 54.5s (15.70) **Going Correction** +0.075s/f (Yiel) **10** Ran SP% **112.7**
Speed ratings: **78,66,66,—,— —,—,—,—,—**
toteswingers:1&2:£8.40, 1&3:£7.00, 2&3:£4.70 CSF £29.04 CT £147.31 TOTE £4.40: £2.00, £2.00, £1.10; EX 30.10.

Owner J R Cornwall **Bred** Jerome Miceli **Trained** Long Clawson, Leics

FOCUS
The pace was ordinary in this staying contest. A big step up from the winner who was well in on recent runs, with the second rated 2st+ off his recent C/D win.

NOTEBOOK
Grenoli(FR) won by a wide margin from 1lb out of the handicap. The jockey deserves plenty of credit for his tactics, but the form will not be reliable, and the handicapper is sure to make his life hard, especially as he is already due to go up 10lb from the weekend. (op 5-1 tchd 11-2)
Tanners Court, up 5lb for winning over C&D last time, when beating a 14-y-o, plugged on but was never a threat. (tchd 6-1)
Katalak(IRE), who had looked an unlucky loser last time, travelled well throughout but lacked any acceleration once his rider asked for an effort. (op 7-2)

50 SOUTHWELL RACECOURSE HORSE TRIALS MARES' MAIDEN HURDLE (9 hdls) 2m

3:40 (3:40) (Class 4) 4-Y-0+ **£3,425** (£998; £499)

Form RPR

3- **1** **Martha Elizabeth (IRE)**[42] 4684 5-10-12 103........................ APMcCoy 96
(Liam Lennon, Ire) *trckd ldrs: led narrowly appr 2 out: nt fluent and sn hdd: crowded and upsides last: styd on to ld last stride* **13/8**[1]

5F3- **2** *shd* **Chip N Pin**[9] 5275 6-10-12 96... DenisO'Regan 95
(Tim Easterby) *chsd ldrs: led narrowly appr 2 out: sn hdd: led after 2 out: edgd rt and jnd appr last: hdd post* **7/2**[2]

0- **3** *5* **Timoca (IRE)**[91] 3688 5-10-12 0... PaulMoloney 92
(Evan Williams) *chsd ldrs 3 l 3rd and one pce whn mstke last* **11/1**

0/0- **4** *12* **Camino Real**[19] 5115 7-10-12 0...(t) RhysFlint 81
(Jim Old) *chsd ldrs: one pce fr 3 out: 4th whn mstke last* **14/1**

203- **5** *2 1/2* **Be My Light (IRE)**[51] 4495 4-10-7 0.................................... FelixDeGiles 74
(Charlie Longsdon) *in rr: nt fluent 4th: hdwy 7th: kpt on: nvr a factor* **14/1**

005- **6** *1 1/4* **Hopeand**[45] 4606 5-10-9 95... AdamPogson(3) 80
(Charles Pogson) *led: hdd appr 2 out: 5th and wkng whn hit last* **25/1**

460- **7** *1* **River Beauty**[15] 5172 6-10-12 100..................................... AndrewTinkler 78
(Nicky Henderson) *chsd ldrs: rdn 3 out: wknd appr next* **11/2**[3]

1/4- **8** *7* **Eterna**[17] 5155 10-10-12 0.. ColinBolger 72
(Alan McCabe) *in rr: hdwy u.p 3 out: wknd appr next* **20/1**

9 *10* **Tuppenny Piece**[177] 4-10-7 0.. RobertThornton 59
(Alan King) *prom: nt fluent 5th and 6th: lost pl after 3 out: eased next* **12/1**

000- **10** *21* **Golden Smog (IRE)**[32] 4899 4-10-4 0........................... BernieWharfe(3) 42
(Ian Williams) *in rr: bhd fr 3 out: t.o* **66/1**

00P- **11** *shd* **Tara Isle**[62] 4257 6-10-12 0... RichardJohnson 47
(Henry Daly) *in rr-div: rdn 3 out: sn wknd: eased appr next: sn bhd: t.o* **33/1**

0- **12** *54* **Betty Browneyes**[20] 5102 5-10-12 0................................ SeamusDurack 4
(Tom George) *t.k.h in midfield: lost pl 3 out: sn wl t.o: eventually completed* **33/1**

00P- **13** *32* **My Clementine (IRE)**[7] 5317 5-10-9 0.............................. MrOGreenall(3) —
(Michael Easterby) *sn detached in rr: reminders 3rd: t.o 6th: eventually completed* **100/1**

4m 5.70s (8.60) **Going Correction** +0.575s/f (Soft)
WFA 4 from 5yo+ 6lb **13** Ran SP% **122.0**
Speed ratings (Par 105): **101,100,98,92,91 90,90,86,81,71 71,44,28**
toteswingers:1&2:£2.90, 1&3:£9.30, 2&3:£11.10 CSF £6.76 TOTE £2.50: £1.10, £1.70, £5.10; EX 9.70.

Owner Martin Duffy **Bred** Maurice Graig **Trained** Newry, Co. Down

FOCUS
As is generally the case in these events, only a few could be given a serious chance. The first two are rated to their marks.

NOTEBOOK
Martha Elizabeth(IRE), the highest-rated of those with an official mark, ran well on her previous start and set the standard. She was always close to the front of the chasing bunch and rallied bravely to deny the runner-up. The intention is to keep her on the go during the summer, as her jockey feels she will like the quick ground. (op 15-8 tchd 2-1)
Chip N Pin attracted market support and looked set to collect the prize when hitting the front after two out. However, she started to falter once in the lead, edging right under pressure, and was passed only a few yards from the winning line. (op 11-2)
Timoca(IRE), who has a BHA mark of 86 on the Flat, was disappointing on her only previous run over hurdles at Musselburgh in January, but shaped better in this after being covered up. A mistake at the last almost certainly did not make any difference to the final outcome. (op 8-1)
Camino Real, wearing a tongue tie for the first time, ran a fair race and may be better over further. (op 12-1)
Be My Light(IRE), having her first outing over hurdles, caught the eye after being towards the rear in the early stages. (op 16-1)
Hopeand enjoyed an easy lead and led turning in. This seemed a fair performance, but she might be flattered by it. (op 18-1)
River Beauty has become disappointing this season and never looked like being involved in the finish. (op 13-2)

51 MEMBERSHIP AT SOUTHWELL GOLF CLUB H'CAP HURDLE (9 hdls) 2m

4:15 (4:15) (Class 4) (0-115,109) 4-Y-0+ **£4,553** (£1,337; £668; £333)

Form RPR

061- **1** **Exulto (IRE)**[10] 5261 5-11-4 **101**....................................... RichardJohnson 108+
(Philip Hobbs) *hld up wl in tch: hdwy on ins whn forced to check bnd after 3 out: led after 2 out: kpt on wl u.p run-in: a holding on* **6/4**[1]

5P2- **2** *1 1/2* **Dalaram (IRE)**[50] 4497 10-11-5 **109**.........................(t) AnthonyFreeman(7) 114
(Sean Curran) *trckd ldrs: hit 5th: sn lost pl: rallied after 3 out: wnt 2nd between last 2: 2 l down last: styd on same pce* **9/1**

0F0- **3** *11* **Peaceful Means (IRE)**[10] 5253 7-11-1 **103**.................. DeanColeman(5) 98
(J Jay) *hld up wl in tch: jnd ldrs 3 out: led appr next: hdd sn after 2 out: wknd appr last* **20/1**

254- **4** *11* **Pure Faith (IRE)**[171] 2146 6-11-10 **107**.................................. TomO'Brien 95
(Peter Bowen) *trckd ldrs: led 3 out: hdd appr next: wknd after 2 out* **9/4**[2]

30- **5** *21* **Wee Sonny (IRE)**[12] 4684 4-10-6 **101**.............................. MarkQuinlan(7) 66
(Liam Lennon, Ire) *chsd ldrs: wknd appr 2 out: sn bhd* **10/1**

525- **6** *10* **Wheelavit (IRE)**[202] 1665 7-11-10 **107**...........................(t) LiamTreadwell 69
(Claire Dyson) *mde most to 3rd: lost pl after 3 out* **20/1**

222- **P** **Irish Symphony (IRE)**[29] 4941 6-11-9 **109**.................... CharlieHuxley(3) —
(John Mackie) *w ldr: narrow ld 3rd: hdd 3 out: lost pl and p.u bef next* **6/1**[3]

4m 4.00s (6.90) **Going Correction** +0.575s/f (Soft)
WFA 4 from 5yo+ 6lb **7** Ran SP% **113.7**
Speed ratings (Par 105): **105,104,98,93,82 77,—**
toteswingers:1&2:£3.80, 1&3:£7.70, 2&3:£20.20 CSF £15.13 TOTE £2.50: £1.60, £6.90; EX 18.00.

Owner Sir Peter O'Sullevan **Bred** Ennistown Stud **Trained** Withycombe, Somerset

FOCUS
Plenty of these runners pulled hard early, which counted against them in the final stages. The winner is rated a bit better than the bare result.

NOTEBOOK

Exulto(IRE), who is already due to go up 11lb for his victory at Wincanton, settled better than some. Anchored in rear, he made good headway once the race took shape and found plenty under pressure to get the better of the runner-up. (op 7-4 tchd 15-8)

Dalaram(IRE) has never looked the easiest horse to predict, but he did run well when last seen in March. Raised 8lb for that effort, he lost his place a couple of times for a few strides, but had every chance in the home straight. He is still capable of running well when at his best. (op 8-1 tchd 10-1)

Peaceful Means(IRE) got to the lead turning in and put up her best performance for this trainer. (tchd 22-1)

Pure Faith(IRE), having his first run since being beaten 9l in November by Totesport Trophy winner and Cheltenham festival runner-up Get Me Out Of Here, was making his handicap debut but was one of those who took a keen grip. A big sort, he should have lots more to come. (op 2-1)

Wee Sonny(IRE) won a maiden on his last start over hurdles but started to fade on the home bend. (op 11-1 tchd 12-1 and 9-1)

Wheelavit(IRE), having his first run since October, dropped out after being prominent over the first few hurdles. (op 16-1)

Irish Symphony(IRE), runner-up on her last three outings, pulled hard towards the head of affairs and weakened quickly coming to two out. This was clearly not her true form and she is entitled to another chance. Official explanation: trainer said mare lost its action (op 8-1 tchd 9-1)

52 GOLF AND RACING AT SOUTHWELL RACECOURSE MARES' (S) HURDLE (9 hdls) 2m

4:50 (4:50) (Class 5) 4-Y-0+ **£2,740** (£798; £399)

Form				RPR
234-	**1**		**Tharaya**[41] 4704 5-11-0 83 KeithMercer (James Turner) *hld up wl in tch: smooth hdwy to go handy 3rd sn after 3 out: shkn up appr next: led on bit between last 2: rdn clr run-in: eased towards fin* **15/8**[2]	110+
030-	**2**	*12*	**Cloudier**[16] 5167 9-11-0 97 RichardJohnson (Tim Vaughan) *chsd ldrs: pushed along 5th: led 3 out: hdd between last 2: no ch w wnr* **7/4**[1]	96
060-	**3**	*shd*	**Knar Mardy**[23] 5047 5-10-11 81 AdamPogson[(3)] (Charles Pogson) *chsd ldrs: nt fluent 5th: wnt cl 2nd 3 out: hung lft between last 2: kpt on same pce* **3/1**[3]	96
P-	**4**	*61*	**Glan Lady (IRE)**[258] 1195 4-10-9 0 JodieMogford (Graham Smith) *t.k.h: trckd ldrs: rdn after 3 out: wknd qckly appr 2 out: sn bhd: wl t.o* **80/1**	36
U40-	**5**	*2 ½*	**Can't Remember**[164] 2307 5-11-0 78 PaulGallagher[(7)] (Robert Johnson) *tk fierce hold: trckd ldrs: wknd 3 out: sn bhd: wl t.o* **11/1**	46
03P-	**6**	*10*	**Bob's Sister (IRE)**[94] 3634 7-10-7 75 AnthonyFreeman[(7)] (Martin Bosley) *led: clr 2nd to 4th: hdd 3 out: sn lost pl and bhd: wl t.o* **12/1**	30

4m 7.70s (10.60) **Going Correction** +0.575s/f (Soft)
WFA 4 from 5yo+ 6lb **6** Ran SP% **113.4**
Speed ratings (Par 103): **96,90,89,59,58 53**
toteswingers:1&2:£1.40, 1&3:£1.40, 2&3:£1.80 CSF £5.90 TOTE £3.70: £1.50, £1.10; EX 5.90.There was no bid for the winner.
Owner Miss S J Turner **Bred** Barry Walters Catering **Trained** Norton-le-Clay, N Yorks

FOCUS

Moderate form. The winner can probably rate higher and the second was again well below his best.

NOTEBOOK

Tharaya has been fairly consistent since going over hurdles and this was a deserved first success. Much bigger than the majority of her rivals, she won nicely and has the scope to be slightly better than this grade. Surprisingly, there were no bids for her at the subsequent auction. (op 11-4)

Cloudier was successful the last time she was tried in this grade (mainly well beaten in handicaps and in one run over fences since), and was the other runner who appeared to be handed a golden opportunity when the Evan Williams-trained favourite was withdrawn. However, although she kept on going, she came under pressure leaving the back straight and always looked like being picked up by the winner. (op 11-10)

Knar Mardy, without cheekpieces this time, has not shown a great deal since leaving Nicky Henderson in January (she often disappointed for that trainer), but made the runner-up work hard for that placing. (op 7-1)

Glan Lady(IRE) pulled hard early but showed a modicum of promise. (op 40-1)

Can't Remember had no chance on official figures after a lengthy absence and was awash with sweat before the field jumped off. She also pulled far too hard. (op 10-1 tchd 12-1)

Bob's Sister(IRE), third in a seller last November, went clear at one point but faded tamely when challenged. (op 8-1)

53 4TH SEPTEMBER GB ENDURANCE RIDE AT SOUTHWELL MAIDEN OPEN NATIONAL HUNT FLAT RACE 2m

5:25 (5:25) (Class 6) 4-6-Y-0 **£1,644** (£479; £239)

Form				RPR
22-	**1**		**Mawsem (IRE)**[17] 5158 4-10-13 0 AndrewTinkler (George Baker) *in tch: hdwy to chse clr ldr over 5f out: led over 2f out: decisive advantage 1f out: jst lasted home* **13/8**[1]	103+
	2	*1 ¼*	**Spring Snow (USA)** 4-10-13 0 RhysFlint (Alan Swinbank) *in tch: sn pushed along: styd on to go 6 l 2nd 1f out: hung rt and styd on strly: nt quite rch wnr* **4/1**[2]	99
0-	**3**	*5*	**Ruling Party**[83] 3852 5-11-4 0 RobertThornton (Alan King) *mid-div: hdwy 6f out: kpt on same pce to take 3rd 1f out* **14/1**	100
	4	*3 ¼*	**Tammys Hill (IRE)**[131] 2963 5-11-4 0 PaulMoloney (Liam Lennon, Ire) *prom: wnt 2nd 2f out: wknd fnl f* **8/1**[3]	98
5-	**5**	*17*	**Emperor Charlie**[29] 4945 6-11-4 0 KeithMercer (Ferdy Murphy) *in rr: drvn 6f out: styd on fnl 2f: nvr on terms* **28/1**	84
	6	*1 ½*	**Newton Tonic** 5-11-4 0 WillKennedy (Alex Hales) *in rr-div: hdwy 6f out: nvr a factor* **20/1**	83
0-	**7**	*3 ½*	**Cherry Star (FR)**[189] 1853 6-11-4 0 RichardJohnson (Noel Chance) *in rr: hdwy 6f out: eased fnl 2f* **16/1**	85+
0-	**8**	*9*	**Counttoten (IRE)**[15] 5178 5-11-4 0 LeightonAspell (Oliver Sherwood) *chsd ldrs: drvn 6f out: lost pl over 4f out* **33/1**	73
/6-	**9**	*1 ½*	**Purrfect Hero (IRE)**[136] 2862 5-11-4 0 APMcCoy (Jonjo O'Neill) *chsd ldrs: lost pl over 3f out: eased over 2f out* **9/1**	82+
06P-	**10**	*½*	**Flockton Tobouggie**[4] 5391 4-10-10 0 MrOGreenall[(3)] (Michael Easterby) *led: sn clr: hdd over 2f out: wknd over 1f out* **40/1**	66
	11	*½*	**Rivermouth** 5-11-4 0 WayneHutchinson (Alan King) *mid-div: reminders 9f out: lost pl over 7f out: sn bhd* **10/1**	71
0/	**12**	*50*	**Middleton Red (IRE)**[529] 2215 6-11-4 0 JodieMogford (Graham Smith) *chsd ldrs: drvn 6f out: lost pl over 4f out: eased and t.o over 2f out: eventually completed* **150/1**	31
	13	*14*	**Mlini (IRE)** 4-10-6 0 DaleSwift[(7)] (Tim Etherington) *mid-div: lost pl over 8f out: t.o over 5f out: eventually completed* **20/1**	15
0-	**14**	*25*	**Missing The Craic**[23] 5050 4-10-6 0 (t) AnthonyFreeman[(7)] (Sean Curran) *in rr: drvn after 6f: sn bhd: t.o 7f out: eventually completed* **100/1**	—

4m 1.10s (9.60) **Going Correction** +0.575s/f (Soft)
WFA 4 from 5yo+ 6lb **14** Ran SP% **120.9**
Speed ratings: **99,98,95,94,85 85,83,78,78,77 77,52,45,33**
toteswingers:1&2:£2.50, 1&3:£7.90, 2&3:£12.50 CSF £6.84 TOTE £2.10: £1.10, £1.40, £3.90; EX 11.00 Place 6 £8.33; Place 5 £3.55.
Owner George Baker & Partners **Bred** 6c Racing **Trained** Whitsbury, Hants

FOCUS

Probably an ordinary bumper. The winner is rated to his mark.

NOTEBOOK

Mawsem(IRE) had shown more than enough in two previous starts to win a race of this nature and he duly collected victory after being well positioned throughout. It would not be the biggest shock to see him tried on the Flat at some stage. (op 5-2)

Spring Snow(USA), who cost $130,000 as a yearling but was sold last July for 6,000gns, got nicely backed but was too green in the chasing pack to hold his position. He looked to be going nowhere leaving the back straight, but suddenly started to get the idea and finished strongly. (op 5-1 tchd 11-2)

Ruling Party improved from his debut and stayed on well. The better ground may have been in his favour. (op 17-2)

Tammys Hill(IRE) shaped nicely in a Downpatrick bumper after winning the final of this three starts in points by 10l, but was arguably a little disappointing in this when considering he had four starts behind him. He may want further to be seen at his best. (op 7-1)

Emperor Charlie ran on from a long way off the pace and will surely need more time, as well as a stiffer course. (op 25-1)

Cherry Star(FR), absent since last October, was not given a hard time down the home straight when it was obvious he would not be involved in the finish. Official explanation: jockey said gelding had no more to give (op 12-1)

Purrfect Hero(IRE), the first foal of a smart racemare, disappointed in a Hereford bumper on debut and did so again. (op 15-2)

T/Plt: £11.00 to a £1 stake. Pool: £54778.83. 3615.65 winning tickets. T/Qpdt: £2.70 to a £1 stake. Pool: £4851.90. 1295.26 winning tickets. WG

HEREFORD (R-H)

Thursday, April 29

OFFICIAL GOING: Good changing to good to soft after race 5 (4.20)

Wind: Brisk across Weather: Overcast, light rain

54 WYE VALLEY BREWERY H'CAP HURDLE (8 hdls) 2m 1f

2:20 (2:20) (Class 5) (0-90,90) 4-Y-0+ **£2,602** (£764; £382; £190)

Form				RPR
362-	**1**		**Skye But N Ben**[21] 5100 6-11-6 87 (b) MarcGoldstein[(5)] (Jim Best) *trckd ldr: led 4th: c wl clr fr 3 out: pushed out* **5/1**[1]	105+
6/6-	**2**	*19*	**Boomtown**[48] 4573 5-11-8 84 (t) LiamTreadwell (Claire Dyson) *chsd ldrs: wnt wl hld 2nd after 2 out* **11/1**	85
056-	**3**	*3 ¾*	**Ghaill Force**[10] 5285 8-10-5 77 AshleyBird[(10)] (Paddy Butler) *chsd ldrs: styd on for wl hld 3rd after 2 out* **10/1**	75
P5U-	**4**	*6*	**New Rackheath (IRE)**[61] 4296 7-10-13 78 DPFahy[(3)] (Evan Williams) *chsd ldrs: wnt 2nd after 4th: no ch w wnr fr next: rdn 3 out: wknd and lost 2nd after 2 out* **13/2**[3]	71
542-	**5**	*2*	**Wee Ziggy**[12] 5229 7-10-11 80 BrianToomey[(7)] (Michael Mullineaux) *in rr tl styd on fr 3 out: sme prog fr next but nvr a threat* **6/1**[2]	74
43U-	**6**	*7*	**Secret Cavern (USA)**[163] 2346 8-10-3 72 MarkQuinlan[(7)] (James Evans) *towards rr: sme prog fr 2 out* **14/1**	58
634-	**7**	*6*	**Just Mossie**[284] 1002 5-11-5 86 TomO'Connor[(5)] (Bill Turner) *chsd ldrs: rdn 3 out: wknd next* **14/1**	67
060-	**8**	*2 ¾*	**Brad's Luck (IRE)**[8] 5318 4-11-9 90 (b) SeamusDurack (Michael Blanshard) *bhd fr 1/2-way* **28/1**	64
056/	**9**	*3*	**Mr Tambourine Man (IRE)**[368] 2 9-10-12 77 LeeStephens[(3)] (Katie Stephens) *a bhd* **20/1**	54
156-	**10**	*5*	**Golden Square**[46] 4614 8-11-7 88 LeeEdwards[(5)] (Tony Carroll) *chsd ldrs tl rdn and wknd 5th* **8/1**	61
PP5-	**11**	*23*	**Send For Tim (IRE)**[38] 4789 7-9-9 62 oh1 JohnKington[(5)] (F Jordan) *sn bhd* **50/1**	16
04P/	**12**	*19*	**Risk Challenge (USA)**[504] 2725 8-10-3 68 (p) DerekLaverty[(3)] (William Davies) *led tl hdd 4th: wknd qckly* **25/1**	7
U00-	**F**		**Rustler**[161] 2380 8-11-4 80 SamJones (Mary Evans) *sn bhd: mod prog whn fell last* **66/1**	69
340-	**P**		**Mr Deal**[48] 4573 4-11-8 89 (p) JimmyMcCarthy (Eve Johnson Houghton) *sn bhd: t.o whn p.u bef last* **11/1**	—
000-	**U**		**Rossbrin (IRE)**[37] 4809 5-11-5 81 AndrewTinkler (Anna Brooks) *stmbld and uns rdr s* **9/1**	—

3m 59.56s (0.16) **Going Correction** 0.0s/f (Good) **15** Ran SP% **120.0**
Speed ratings (Par 103): **99,90,88,85,84 81,78,77,75,73 62,53,—,—,—**
toteswingers: 1&2 £20.60, 1&3 £11.10, 2&3 £23.90 CSF £55.35 CT £538.66 TOTE £5.60: £2.00, £5.30, £3.80; EX 101.60.
Owner N J Sillett **Bred** Charles And David Hodge **Trained** Lewes, E Sussex

FOCUS

This was a very weak handicap and most were in trouble a long way out. A big step up from the winner with the second to his mark.

NOTEBOOK

Skye But N Ben, with blinkers replacing cheekpieces, deservedly got off the mark as a hurdler and proved far too strong for his opposition. He was never far away and sensibly kicked for home before the home turn, which often proves to be a winning move at this venue. He was 6lb higher for finishing second in a seller last time and will go up again plenty for this should the handicapper take the form literally, so it wouldn't be at all surprising to see him successfully defy a penalty. (op 6-1 tchd 13-2)

Boomtown stayed on to win the race for second and is slowly going the right way. A stiffer test is probably what he needs. (op 16-1)

Ghaill Force, with the cheekpieces abandoned, rallied under pressure nearing the last and this plating-class maiden helps to put the form into perspective. (op 11-1)

New Rackheath(IRE) was returning to hurdling after a two-month break and was another that shaped as though this was too sharp. (op 6-1 tchd 7-1)

Wee Ziggy found himself well out of his ground when the race got serious and caught the eye staying on steadily late on. He is a confirmed hold-up horse, though, and this track over the shorter trip was not for him. (op 11-2 tchd 13-2)

55 BUTTY BACH H'CAP HURDLE (10 hdls) 2m 4f
2:50 (2:50) (Class 4) (0-110,110) 4-Y-0+ **£2,992** (£878; £439; £219)

Form RPR
550- **1** **Astracad (FR)**[64] 4231 4-10-13 **103** PaddyBrennan 109+
(Nigel Twiston-Davies) *in rr but in tch: hdwy after 5th: wnt 2nd 3 out: led appr 2 out: c wl clr home turn and in n.d whn wnt bdly lft and mstke last: eased run-in* **3/1**[2]
P10- **2** *18* **Victory Surge (IRE)**[92] 3686 6-11-3 **101** APMcCoy 101+
(Jonjo O'Neill) *in rr but in tch: hdwy 5th: rdn along 7th: chsd wnr appr 2 out: effrt to cl u.p sn after but nvr any ch and wknd wl bef last* **5/1**[3]
646- **3** *5* **Thehonourablelady**[21] 5105 9-11-0 **98** (bt) RhysFlint 85
(John Flint) *chsd ldrs: hit 6th: rdn 3 out: styd on to take mod 3rd fnl flight* **8/1**
1F0- **4** *5* **Manjam (IRE)**[23] 3864 6-10-12 **96** TomScudamore 79
(Rebecca Curtis) *chsd ldr: disp ld fr 5th tl slt ld 4 out: hdd appr 2 out: sn no ch: lost mod 3rd fnl flight* **11/4**[1]
306- **5** *3* **Root Cause**[24] 5043 7-11-7 **105** (b[1]) JasonMaguire 85
(Donald McCain) *chsd ldr: lft w slt advantage 5th tl narrowly hdd 4 out: hit 3 out: wknd fr 2 out* **17/2**
P00- **6** *20* **Ryans Good Time (IRE)**[12] 5234 8-10-6 **90** (t) JodieMogford 54
(Nikki Evans) *in tch: rdn 3rd and 4th: in rr whn bdly hmpd 5th: nvr in contention after* **40/1**
3/0- **7** *16* **Timpo (FR)**[359] 154 7-11-7 **105** RichardJohnson 56
(Henry Daly) *towards rr: lost tch fr 5th* **20/1**
662- **F** **Mayor Of Kilcock**[21] 5105 7-11-1 **106** MrJMahot(7) —
(James Danahar) *led tl lost footing on landing and fell 5th* **5/1**[3]
4m 52.7s (-2.80) **Going Correction** 0.0s/f (Good)
WFA 4 from 6yo+ 7lb **8** Ran SP% **113.8**
Speed ratings (Par 105): **105,97,95,93,92 84,78,—**
CSF £18.49 CT £106.83 TOTE £4.20: £2.00, £2.10, £1.90; EX 20.10.
Owner H R Mould **Bred** Charlotte Thoreau **Trained** Naunton, Gloucs

FOCUS
A moderate handicap, run at a fair gallop. A step up from the easy winner and the second to form.

NOTEBOOK
Astracad(FR) appreciated the easing surface and shed his maiden tag with a bloodless display on his debut in a handicap. He travelled by far the best throughout the race and had things wrapped up before making a mess of the final flight, which looked down to inexperience. The longer trip clearly helped and this juvenile remains open to improvement, but turning out under a penalty may be the most sensible option as the handicapper will now have his say. Official explanation: trainer said, regarding apparent improvement in form, that the gelding was better suited by the faster ground. (op 4-1)
Victory Surge(IRE), returning from a three-month layoff, was the only one to make a real race of it with the winner. He needed plenty of driving to get into contention, though, and ultimately got outstayed by that rival. Perhaps the run will do him good. (op 9-2 tchd 11-2)
Thehonourablelady showed up a little more encouragingly on this debut for her new yard, but looks to be struggling with the handicapper. Now could be the time to try chasing again. (tchd 15-2)
Manjam(IRE) was popular on this debut for Rebecca Curtis and was a winner on his previous visit to the track. He was in trouble before the penultimate flight though, and may enjoy stepping up in trip. (tchd 5-2 and 3-1)

56 MORGAN PUBLIC HOUSE IN MALVERN NOVICES' H'CAP CHASE (16 fncs) 2m 5f 110y
3:20 (3:20) (Class 4) (0-110,110) 5-Y-0+ **£3,519** (£1,287)

Form RPR
205- **1** **Badger Foot (IRE)**[39] 4766 5-11-12 **110** APMcCoy 114+
(Jonjo O'Neill) *trckd ldr whn lft in ld 10th: mde rest and a gng easily: won on bit* **2/1**[2]
4/0- **2** *3 ¾* **Haoyunma (IRE)**[19] 5135 8-9-12 **85** oh12 ow1 SeanQuinlan(3) 75
(Harry Chisman) *lft in 2nd 10th: styd in tch w v easy wnr but nvr any ch* **20/1**
250- **U** **Over The Flow**[48] 4566 8-10-4 **95** NathanSweeney(7) —
(Bob Buckler) *tried to refuse and uns rdr 1st* **6/4**[1]
62P- **P** **Denny Mac (IRE)**[174] 2096 9-11-9 **107** (t) JasonMaguire —
(Liam Corcoran) *led tl p.u lame 10th* **9/4**[3]
5m 29.1s (9.10) **4** Ran SP% **108.9**
CSF £20.44 TOTE £2.20; EX 20.10.
Owner John P McManus **Bred** J Moran **Trained** Cheltenham, Gloucs

FOCUS
This race fell into the winner's lap and the form is suspect. The winner is value for further.

NOTEBOOK
Badger Foot(IRE) always looked to have things under control once left in front, but the runner-up proved game and ensured he had to be kept up to his work. This initial success should boost Badger Foot's confidence nicely and he is open to improvement at this sort of level, but it's hard to know just what he achieved here. (op 15-8)
Haoyunma(IRE) showed the clear benefit of her return from injury 19 days earlier and this was just her second outing for the stable. Like the winner, it's hard to know just what she achieved here and the handicapper will no doubt put her up a deal, but she's worth a chance to prove the run to be no fluke. (op 16-1 tchd 12-1)
Over The Flow was well backed for her chasing debut, but got no further than the first after proving a real madam. (op 2-1 tchd 11-4)
Denny Mac(IRE) was unfortunately found to have broken down. (op 2-1 tchd 11-4)

57 BARRELS HEREFORD H'CAP CHASE (12 fncs) 2m
3:50 (3:50) (Class 3) (0-130,130) 5-Y-0+ **£6,337** (£1,872; £936; £468)

Form RPR
353- **1** **Tyup Pompey (IRE)**[4] 5 9-9-11 **104** oh3 LeeStephens(3) 112+
(Ann Price) *hld up in rr but wl in tch: hdwy to trck ldr after 6th: led 4 out: c readily clr fr 2 out: comf* **11/2**
050- **2** *6* **Huguenot (IRE)**[11] 5261 7-11-2 **120** TomO'Brien 123
(Philip Hobbs) *trckd ldrs: wnt 2nd and rdn fr 2 out: kpt on but nvr any ch w wnr* **4/1**[3]
333- **3** *10* **Almaydan**[40] 4726 12-11-12 **130** (b) RobertThornton 128
(Richard Lee) *w ldr to 3rd: j. slowly and lost position 6th: sn reminders and no ch fr next: styd on to take wl hld 3rd appr last* **9/4**[2]
P12- **4** *6* **Line Artic (FR)**[13] 5210 6-11-9 **127** LiamHeard 120
(Chris Down) *mde most tl blnd 8th and hdd 4 out: lost 2nd 2 out: wknd rapidly and lost 3rd appr last* **11/8**[1]
3m 55.25s (-8.35) **Going Correction** -0.325s/f (Good) **4** Ran SP% **108.3**
Speed ratings: **107,104,99,96**
CSF £23.64 TOTE £7.80; EX 16.40.
Owner Mrs A Price **Bred** Rosetown Syndicate **Trained** Norton, Powys

FOCUS
A tight handicap and the form should be treated with a little caution. The winner is rated to the best of last season's form.

NOTEBOOK
Tyup Pompey(IRE), third at Ludlow over 2m4f four days earlier, was out of the handicap and the outsider of the quartet. That did not reflect his true chance, however, as he had finished third in this race last season when behind Hugeunot off a 9lb higher mark. Considering he was 13lb better off with that one this year and the easing ground was in his favour, it's not surprising he came out on top, and he got a ride in the race. His profile strongly suggests he is one to oppose again next time, though. (tchd 5-1 and 6-1)
Huguenot(IRE) likes this venue, but could have done without the rain and could have settled better. He still finished a clear second-best, is evidently much happier over fences, and there will be other days for him. (tchd 10-3)
Almaydan attracted support with the easing ground expected to be in his favour. It was a little surprising to see him ridden so positively early on, but he was still going nicely prior to losing all chance with a bad leap at the sixth fence. Looking at the way he rallied from two out, he would have surely gone very close with a clear round. (op 5-2 tchd 11-4)
Line Artic(FR) was back on a right-handed track, but wasn't allowed an easy lead and is another that could have done without the surface easing. She didn't help her cause with a mistake at the eighth, but judging by the way she eventually folded this run likely came too soon after her good effort at Cheltenham 13 days earlier. (tchd 13-8)

58 PERTEMPS PEOPLE DEVELOPMENT GROUP MAIDEN HURDLE (7 hdls 1 omitted) 2m 1f
4:20 (4:20) (Class 5) 4-Y-0+ **£2,602** (£764; £382; £190)

Form RPR
2/ **1** **Roodolph**[518] 2455 6-11-0 0 JimmyMcCarthy 116+
(Eve Johnson Houghton) *in tch: hdwy fr 3rd: chsd ldr 3 out: chal 2 out: sn led: drvn and idled appr last and run-in but a doing enough* **11/4**[2]
422- **2** *3 ½* **Niceonefrankie**[230] 1421 4-10-9 108 AidanColeman 105
(Venetia Williams) *chsd ldrs: rdn to go 2nd after 2 out: kpt on bhd idling wnr but nvr any ch* **6/1**[3]
P0U- **3** *9* **Just One Thing (IRE)**[7] 5340 5-11-0 0 PaulMoloney 104
(Evan Williams) *led: rdn 3 out: jnd 2 out and hdd sn after and wknd into 3rd* **10/1**
032- **4** *9* **Blue Spartan (IRE)**[11] 5260 5-11-0 0 (t) RobertThornton 96
(Charlie Mann) *in rr tl rdn and sme prog 3 out but nvr gng pce to rch ldng trio* **15/8**[1]
136- **5** *13* **Sir Bere (FR)**[15] 5180 4-10-2 0 AodhaganConlon(7) 82
(Rebecca Curtis) *chsd ldrs: hit 4th: wknd after 3 out* **9/1**
6 *20* **Burnthill (IRE)**[74] 5-11-0 0 LiamTreadwell 69
(Claire Dyson) *prom: j. slowly 1st: j. slowly 3rd and bhd* **25/1**
5- **7** *9* **Kaliski (IRE)**[24] 5030 6-10-7 0 RhysFlint 55
(David Brace) *chsd ldrs: hit 2nd: wknd bef 3 out: no ch whn mstke 2 out* **66/1**
8 *3* **I Can Run Can You (IRE)** 4-10-9 0 APMcCoy 55
(Jonjo O'Neill) *j. modly: rdn 3rd: a bhd* **7/1**
9 *104* **Billy Beetroot (USA)**[145] 4-10-6 0 LeeStephens(3) —
(Katie Stephens) *j. poorly: t.o fr 3rd* **66/1**
4m 1.30s (1.90) **Going Correction** +0.20s/f (Yiel)
WFA 4 from 5yo+ 6lb **9** Ran SP% **114.2**
Speed ratings (Par 103): **103,101,97,92,86 77,73,71,—**
toteswingers: 1&2 £2.80, 1&3 £6.50, 2&3 £5.80 CSF £19.34 TOTE £4.20: £2.20, £1.10, £3.80; EX 18.30.
Owner Mrs R F Johnson Houghton **Bred** Mrs H Johnson Houghton & Mrs R F Johnson Hought **Trained** Blewbury, Oxon

FOCUS
A moderate maiden hurdle in which the second and third set the level. The flight after the winning post was omitted.

NOTEBOOK
Roodolph was last seen finishing second on his hurdling debut back in November 2008 and that form was head and shoulders above anything any of his rivals here had yet to show. It was just a case of whether he was ready to do himself justice after the absence, but he had actually won a 7f charity race at Ascot recently and his stable has been among the winners on the Flat. Given a copybook ride, he had the race sewn up off the home turn and it was probably a case of him idling on the run-in. He should go on from this. (op 5-2)
Niceonefrankie ⊠ was having his first outing for 230 days and posted a pleasing return. He should come on nicely for the run and is in the right hands to find a race or two during the summer. (tchd 11-2 and 7-1)
Just One Thing(IRE) showed his previous outing to be no fluke, but did get very much the run of things from the front. He should appreciate stepping up in trip when switching to a handicap. (op 12-1)
Blue Spartan(IRE) was entitled to go close on his previous level and would have likely benefited from a more positive ride, but may not be the most straightforward. (op 9-4)
Billy Beetroot(USA) Official explanation: jockey said gelding was unsuited by the good ground

59 ROSE & LION IN BROMYARD NOVICES' H'CAP HURDLE (9 hdls 2 omitted) 2m 6f 110y
4:50 (4:50) (Class 5) (0-95,95) 4-Y-0+ **£1,951** (£573; £286; £143)

Form RPR
040- **1** **Musical Wedge**[32] 4916 6-11-4 **90** TommyPhelan(3) 95
(Claire Dyson) *in rr tl hdwy 6th: chsd ldrs to 3 out: slt ld wl bef 2 out: drvn out run-in* **33/1**
6PP- **2** *½* **Poppy Gregg**[35] 2299 5-10-0 **72** (v) EamonDehdashti(3) 77
(Dr Jeremy Naylor) *in rr: pushed along 5th: hdwy 4 out: chsd wnr fr 2 out and kpt on u.p appr last but a jst hld run-in* **4/1**[1]
/PP- **3** *4* **Inchloch**[15] 5184 8-11-7 **90** (t) LiamTreadwell 91
(Claire Dyson) *chsd ldrs: rdn and cl 3rd 2 out: styd on same pce appr last* **8/1**
0/0- **4** *10* **Enchanted Approach (IRE)**[4] 3 7-11-0 **90** RobertKirk(7) 82
(Lady Susan Brooke) *t.k.h: pressed ldrs tl lft in narrow ld bnd after 6th: hdd 3 out: wknd 2 out* **40/1**
030- **5** *13* **No More Whispers (IRE)**[45] 4654 5-11-12 **95** PaulMoloney 76
(Evan Williams) *in rr: hdwy u.p whn hit 3 out: nvr any ch after* **12/1**
P40- **6** *12* **Answer Me (IRE)**[12] 5234 7-11-7 **90** WayneHutchinson 60
(John Spearing) *chsd ldrs: led 3 out: hdd wl bef 2 out and wknd qckly* **20/1**
/0P- **7** *17* **Oshkosh (IRE)**[46] 4618 9-11-9 **95** SeanQuinlan(3) 50
(Kim Bailey) *chsd ldrs to 6th* **14/1**
6P3- **8** *5* **The Fox's Decree**[13] 5216 6-11-7 **90** WarrenMarston 40
(Martin Keighley) *chsd ldrs fr 5th: chal 6th and n.m.r bnd sn after: wknd 3 out* **6/1**[3]
643- **9** *21* **Rawaaj**[50] 4510 4-11-0 **90** (t) JasonMaguire 14
(Donald McCain) *chsd ldrs to 4 out* **4/1**[1]
060- **10** *10* **Mamba (GER)**[52] 4493 8-10-9 **78** LiamHeard —
(Chris Down) *chal to 6th: wknd 4 out* **40/1**

505- **P** **Chit Chat**[29] 4963 5-11-6 **89** APMcCoy —
(Jonjo O'Neill) *rdn and bhd 4th: sme hdwy u.p 3 out: sn wknd: p.u bef last* **5/1**[2]

06P- **R** **Albert Park (IRE)**[50] 4519 9-9-8 **70** (p) AnthonyFreeman(7) —
(John Upson) *led tl rn out bnd after 6th* **12/1**

5m 34.3s (-3.70)
WFA 4 from 5yo+ 7lb **12** Ran SP% **116.7**
toteswingers: 1&2 £45.40, 1&3 £29.60, 2&3 £7.80 CSF £157.82 CT £1185.66 TOTE £50.50: £9.60, £1.70, £3.00; EX 430.50.
Owner D J Dyson **Bred** Wood Farm Stud **Trained** Cleeve Prior, Worcs

FOCUS
The flight after the winning post was omitted. A poor novice handicap, run at an ordinary gallop. The first three dominated and the winner is on the upgrade.

NOTEBOOK
Musical Wedge proved the most resolute in the home straight and shed his maiden tag. He had something to prove coming here, but it was his first run in a handicap and he has evidently now found his level. Official explanation: trainer said, regarding apparent improvement in form, that the gelding was much more settled before and during the race. (op 28-1 tchd 25-1)
Poppy Gregg was a market mover on this return to hurdling as she had shown improvement on the AW since her last outing in this sphere since being equipped with a visor. She crept into the race going well turning for home, but didn't prove too willing when asked for everything and it is not hard to see why she goes in headgear. This was still her best run yet. (op 11-2 tchd 7-2)
Inchloch hit a flat spot before staying on again and this was a lot more like it again from him. The addition of a first-time tongue tie clearly helped and he could build on this back on a more galloping circuit. (op 10-1)
Enchanted Approach(IRE) ran better than was the case at Ludlow four days earlier and could be on a fair mark judged on her bumper form, if consenting to build on this. However, her proximity really sums up the strength of this contest. (tchd 33-1)

60 WONDERFUL HPA INTERMEDIATE OPEN NATIONAL HUNT FLAT RACE 2m 1f
5:20 (5:20) (Class 6) 4-6-Y-O **£1,507** (£439; £219)

Form RPR

4- **1** **Scoter Fontaine (FR)**[9] 5301 4-10-12 0 APMcCoy 101+
(Rebecca Curtis) *trckd ldr: led 1/2-way: green and hung bdly lft over 2f out but nvr in any danger: readily* **2/5**[1]

25- **2** *16* **Edlomond (IRE)**[33] 4899 4-10-9 0 (t) MrOGreenall(3) 82
(Bill Turner) *towards rr: hdwy 5f out: wnt 2nd over 3f out: edgd lft and green over 2f out: nvr any ch w wnr but wl clr of 3rd* **11/1**[3]

00- **3** *20* **Toxic Asset**[182] 1970 5-11-3 0 RhysFlint 69
(John Flint) *led tl hdd 1/2-way: lost pl and poor 5th 5f out: styd on again to take mod 3rd cl home* **14/1**

4 *3/4* **Toomyvara (IRE)** 6-11-3 0 LiamTreadwell 68
(Nick Gifford) *chsd ldrs: rdn to go 2nd briefly 4f out: wknd 3f out: lost poor 3rd cl home* **12/1**

0- **5** *13* **Bahr Nothing (IRE)**[54] 4429 4-10-12 0 RichardJohnson 52
(Henry Daly) *in rr tl hdwy to press ldrs fr 1/2-way: wknd over 3f out* **6/1**[2]

6 *4* **My Idea** 4-10-12 0 TomO'Brien 48
(Anabel L M King) *chsd ldrs tl wknd u.p over 4f out* **14/1**

7 *19* **Bridge Street Boy** 5-11-0 0 LeeStephens(3) 36
(Susan Johnson) *t.k.h: lost tch fr 1/2-way* **50/1**

0- **8** *51* **Floating Cloud**[12] 5235 6-10-10 0 CharliePoste —
(Trevor Wall) *wl bhd fr 1/2-way* **100/1**

0- **9** *89* **Castle Legend**[137] 2862 5-11-0 0 CharlieStudd(3) —
(Simon Lewis) *t.k.h chsd ldrs to 1/2-way: sn t.o* **66/1**

4m 3.24s (9.44) **Going Correction** +0.20s/f (Yiel)
WFA 4 from 5yo+ 6lb **9** Ran SP% **119.5**
Speed ratings: **85,77,68,67,61 59,50,—,—**
toteswingers: 1&2 £2.80, 1&3 £4.30, 2&3 £11.80 CSF £6.72 TOTE £1.80: £1.10, £2.80, £5.90; EX 6.90 Place 6: £807.59, Place 5: £58.04..
Owner G Costelloe **Bred** Gilbert Mesnil & Mme Louise Mesnil **Trained** Newport, Dyfed

FOCUS
A weak bumper dominated by the progressive winner, who was value for further but didn't need to be at his best.

NOTEBOOK
Scoter Fontaine(FR) ⊠ made his debut in the prestigious Goffs Land Rover Bumper at the Punchestown Festival last week, finishing fourth, and was unsurprisingly all the rage in this much lesser company. He completed the task in clear-cut fashion, despite still running distinctly green when in front, and his success made it 5-5 for his stable in such races at the track. Defying a penalty shouldn't be too much of an issue for this well-bred 4-y-o. (op 1-2)
Edlomond(IRE) travelled nicely into contention, but it was clear turning for home he would have to play second fiddle to the winner. He has a future once sent hurdling and helps to set the standard here. (op 10-1)
Toxic Asset raced from the front and would have probably been better off going off quicker, looking at the way he rallied for third late on. This was an improved effort on debut for his new connections. (op 12-1)
Toomyvara(IRE)'s dam was placed in one of these and he hails from a yard well capable of success in the bumper sphere. He ran with some encouragement and really the experience looked needed. (op 9-1)
Bahr Nothing(IRE) was faced with an easier assignment than on debut 54 days previously and looked a big player when making his move from off the pace. It proved to be short-lived, however, and he could have probably done without the ground easing. (tchd 5-1 and 13-2)
Castle Legend Official explanation: jockey said gelding had a breathing problem
T/Plt: £1,540.30 to a £1 stake. Pool: £69,208.17. 32.8 winning tickets. T/Qpdt: £456.50 to a £1 stake. Pool: £4626.80. 7.50 winning tickets. ST

HUNTINGDON (R-H)
Thursday, April 29

OFFICIAL GOING: Good (good to firm in places)
The open ditch in front of the stands was omitted - ground under repair.
Wind: Light half-against Weather: Overcast

61 PAUL RACKHAM CHAMPION NOVICES' HUNTERS' CHASE (17 fncs 2 omitted) 3m
5:40 (5:41) (Class 6) 5-Y-0+ **£961** (£314; £169)

Form RPR

1 **Belavard (IRE)**[12] 10-11-5 0 MrJMQuinlan(7) 76
(Mrs J Quinlan) *nt fluent and j.lft thrght: led tl after 10th: led again 13th: hdd whn blnd 3 out: sn wknd: lft 2nd last: rallied to ld and hung lft flat: drvn out* **2/1**[2]

2 *5* **Red In Bed (IRE)**[11] 6-11-2 0 (t) MrMatthewSmith(3) 62
(Matthew Smith) *hld up: hdwy 8th: wknd after 3 out: 22 l down whn lft in ld last: hdd and no ex flat* **12/1**[3]

P/0- **3** *43* **Maree Hall (IRE)**[12] 9-11-9 77 MrRHFowler(3) 35
(Martin Ward) *chsd wnr to 5th: remained handy tl wknd appr 10th: t.o fr next: lft remote 3rd last* **12/1**[3]

5P5/ **F** **Native Bob (IRE)**[19] 6-11-9 0 MrJOwen(3) 94+
(J M Turner) *prom: racd keenly: chsd wnr 5th tl led after 10th: hdd 13th: led again bef 3 out: clr sn after: 22 l ahd and gng easily whn fell last* **5/6**[1]

U **O Ellie (IRE)**[11] 6-11-5 0 (p) MrRichardCollinson(7) —
(Miss Katie Thory) *hld up in tch: mstke 12th: 4th whn blnd and uns rdr 3 out* **16/1**

6m 26.8s (16.50) **Going Correction** -0.05s/f (Good) **5** Ran SP% **109.2**
Speed ratings: **70,68,54,—,—**
CSF £19.93 TOTE £2.00: £1.10, £4.10; EX 17.30.
Owner Mrs J Quinlan **Bred** Michael C Gunn **Trained** Newmarket, Suffolk
⊠ The first winner under rules for both jockey Jack Quinlan and his mother Joanne Quinlan, the trainer.

FOCUS
Despite the title a poor novices' hunters' chase, run on ground eased by 2mm of afternoon rain. The faller is rated in line with his hurdles form. The open ditch in front of the stands was omitted in order to carry out repair work.

NOTEBOOK
Belavard(IRE), with some fair bumper form and two pointing successes, was a very fortunate winner. He looked well beaten by Native Bob until that one subsided after the final fence and, in the end, it was merely superior stamina to the runner-up that got him home in front. His jumping was not convincing, exhibiting a mix of caution and clumsiness, but he did battle on gamely. Connections feel he is better going left-handed. (op 13-8)
Red In Bed(IRE), placed in seven points but still to win, often makes the running but was held up in third place for much of this contest. She momentarily threatened the winner at the last but found little on the run-in and did not seem to see out the trip. (op 16-1)
Maree Hall(IRE), a winning pointer in Ireland and second in a chase off a mark of 102 in 2007, had not shown much on his more recent efforts and again ran poorly. He was getting reminders by halfway and tailed off long before the home turn. (tchd 16-1)
Native Bob(IRE), fifth from an official mark of 92 in a handicap hurdle a year ago, had since won two point-to-points and was well-supported to add to those victories. All appeared to be going the way of favourite backers until he screwed on landing after the final fence and crumpled to the ground. (op 10-11 tchd 4-5)

62 VINDIS ST IVES NOVICES' HURDLE (10 hdls) 2m 4f 110y
6:10 (6:15) (Class 4) 4-Y-0+ **£2,927** (£859; £429; £214)

Form RPR

003- **1** **Vincitore (FR)**[39] 4758 4-10-7 0 FelixDeGiles 109+
(Charlie Longsdon) *a.p: racd keenly: jnd ldr 2 out: rdn and hmpd flat: styd on u.p to ld towards fin* **6/1**[3]

263- **2** *hd* **American Cricket (IRE)**[18] 5147 9-10-13 115 (p) WillKennedy 115+
(Alex Hales) *led: nt fluent 5th: jnd 2 out: hrd rdn and hung lft flat: hdd towards fin* **4/7**[1]

00P- **3** *15* **Alexander Beetle**[39] 4758 5-10-13 0 (p) SamThomas 100
(Henrietta Knight) *chsd ldr to 2nd: remained handy tl lost pl 4th: drvn along after 6th: wknd bef last* **16/1**

302/ **4** *3 3/4* **Last One Standing**[381] 5005 6-10-13 0 JamieGoldstein 98
(Sheena West) *chsd ldr 2nd: j.rt 4th: nt fluent 6th: lost 2nd 3 out: wknd bef last* **9/2**[2]

220- **5** *2 1/4* **Keep Talking (IRE)**[53] 4466 6-10-10 0 AlexMerriam(3) 98
(Neil King) *got loose prior to the s: hld up: racd keenly: hdwy 4th: chsd ldr 3 out: ev ch whn blnd next: wknd last* **33/1**

P60- **6** *5* **Not A Bob (IRE)**[18] 5154 5-10-10 0 RichieMcLernon(3) 91
(Jonjo O'Neill) *hld up: rdn after 6th: wknd appr 2 out* **25/1**

4m 53.6s (-5.40) **Going Correction** -0.125s/f (Good)
WFA 4 from 5yo+ 7lb **6** Ran SP% **108.8**
Speed ratings (Par 105): **105,104,99,97,96 95**
toteswingers: 1&2 £1.30, 1&3 £9.30, 2&3 £5.00 CSF £9.71 TOTE £5.80: £2.30, £1.10; EX 12.10.

Owner Cavenham Stud **Bred** Mme Isabelle Garcon **Trained** Over Norton, Oxon

FOCUS
A moderate novice hurdle run at a muddling pace. Ordinary form.

NOTEBOOK
Vincitore(FR), who had shown promise on his only previous start over hurdles, was stepping up trip and it seemed to suit him. He travelled easily in midfield for the first part of the race and was clearly going best four out. He moved up to join the front-running second between the last two flights and, although he was headed and intimidated on the run-in, he refused to give best. (tchd 11-2 and 7-1)
American Cricket(IRE), a sound third from a mark of 115 on his latest start, set the standard on that form and appeared to run somewhere near peak form. He was always either leading or disputing the lead and jumped soundly, but he could not match the winner's pace from the final flight. (op 8-11 tchd 4-5 in places)
Alexander Beetle, pulled up behind Vincitore on his latest start, was fitted with first-time cheekpieces and the result was markedly better. He did not look an easy ride, racing in snatches and coming under pressure three out, but this was his most encouraging effort for some time. (tchd 25-1)
Last One Standing, a bumper winner at Southwell in 2008 and runner-up last time out, was reappearing after a 381-day layoff and ran as if the race was needed. He disputed the lead for a long way, but tired in the closing stages. (tchd 4-1 and 5-1)
Keep Talking(IRE), twice runner-up in bumpers in October and making his hurdling debut, bolted before the start and, although he did not seem to take too much out of himself in doing so, was losing ground at the finish. (op 16-1)

63 TOTEPOOL £25,000 FREE BET GIVEAWAY H'CAP CHASE (11 fncs 1 omitted) 2m 110y
6:40 (6:43) (Class 5) (0-90,90) 5-Y-0+ **£3,082** (£898; £449)

Form RPR

405- **1** **Lord Gunnerslake (IRE)**[24] 5052 10-9-11 **64** (v) RichardKilloran(3) 81+
(Tim Vaughan) *hld up: pushed along 7th: hdwy 3 out: led after next: clr whn j.rt last: drvn out* **9/2**[2]

226- **2** *13* **Wiesenfurst (GER)**[39] 4763 6-11-5 **83** JamieMoore 88
(Gary Moore) *hld up in tch: pushed along 8th: rdn appr 2 out: styd on same pce: wnt 2nd nr fin* **15/2**[3]

4P0- **3** *2 1/4* **Fort Severn (IRE)**[24] 5043 6-11-9 **90** (v) RichieMcLernon(3) 93
(Brendan Powell) *chsd ldrs: led after 3 out: hdd after next: sn rdn: wknd flat: lost 2nd nr fin* **10/1**

221- **4** *16* **Bid Art (IRE)**[7] 5331 5-11-7 **85** 7ex (t) DarylJacob 76
(Jamie Snowden) *led: mstke 5th: hdd after next: rdn appr 2 out: wknd bef last: t.o* **1/1**[1]

634- **5** *1 1/4* **Safe Investment (USA)**[11] 5244 6-11-9 **87** (p) AndrewThornton 74
(Ben Pollock) *hld up: rdn appr 3 out: nvr on terms: t.o* **20/1**

400- **6** *2 1/4* **Laharna**[24] 5040 10-11-12 **90** (t) LeightonAspell 75
(Lucy Wadham) *hld up: nt fluent 4th: hdwy 3 out: rdn and wknd bef last: t.o* **10/1**

5P0- **7** 1 1/4 **Gainsborough's Art (IRE)**[65] 4214 5-11-6 **87**.............(b) ChrisHonour(3) 73
(Chris Down) *chsd ldr: nt fluent 4th: led after 6th: hdd after 3 out: sn rdn: wkng whn mstke next: t.o* **16/1**

/1P- **8** 18 **Ilewin Tom**[235] 1394 7-10-8 **72**... JamesDavies 40
(Gary Brown) *hld up in tch: racd keenly: pushed along 8th: wknd after next: t.o* **18/1**

005- **F** **Simplified**[58] 4372 7-9-7 **64** oh5....................................... StevenGagan(7) —
(Michael Chapman) *a bhd: t.o whn fell 2 out* **66/1**

4m 7.80s (-2.40) **Going Correction** -0.05s/f (Good) **9** Ran SP% **115.5**
Speed ratings: **103,96,95,88,87 86,86,77,—**
toteswingers: 1&2 £6.80, 1&3 £6.50, 2&3 £13.00 CSF £38.00 CT £320.60 TOTE £6.00: £3.00, £1.20, £2.90; EX 40.00.
Owner Select Racing Syndicates I **Bred** T Keane **Trained** Aberthin, Vale of Glamorgan

FOCUS
A weak handicap chase, with the top-weight rated just 90, but the pace was sound enough. The form is rated through the second to his mark.

NOTEBOOK
Lord Gunnerslake(IRE) is inconsistent and a 1-38 chasing record going into this indicated that he has not been easy to win with. He was having only his fourth run for current connections, however, and this was a marked improvement. Victory looked unlikely early in the race, when he was pushed along and given reminders, but he made powerful progress from three out and led before the last. A strong gallop seems to suit him. (op 5-1)
Wiesenfurst(GER), a fair second from a mark of 80 at Folkestone in March, had run poorly last time out, but this was better. Held up in midfield for much of the race, he started to launch a challenge turning for home and stayed on well up the run-in to grab second. (op 13-2)
Fort Severn(IRE), bumper placed here for previous connections, was tried in a visor for only the second time and it seemed to bring about some improvement. He was always prominent and took the lead briefly two out, but could offer only token resistance when the winner swept past. (op 16-1)
Bid Art(IRE), whose form last term had been progressive at a modest level, was carrying a 7lb penalty for his all-the-way win at Fontwell seven days previously and it proved too much for him. He again set out to make all, perhaps running too freely for his own good, but was overtaken in mid-race and lost ground in the closing stages. (op 11-10)
Safe Investment(USA), still a maiden over both hurdles and fences, was never in a threatening position and looks exposed off his current mark.
Laharna collected from a rating 4lb higher than this at Plumpton in February 2009, but has largely disappointed since and again failed to convince that he is a winner waiting to happen. (op 9-1)

64 TOTEPOOL, BETTER CHOICE, BETTER VALUE H'CAP HURDLE (10 hdls) 2m 5f 110y
7:10 (7:11) (Class 4) (0-110,108) 4-Y-0+ **£3,252** (£955; £477; £238)

Form RPR

4P0/ **1** **Purely By Chance**[16] 5096 5-11-8 **107**......................... GerardTumelty(3) 117+
(Jeff Pearce) *hld up: hdwy 3rd: reminders next: led after 3 out: clr next: hit last: styd on wl* **10/1**

624- **2** 14 **Yonder**[48] 4569 6-11-3 **99**...(t) TomScudamore 98
(Hughie Morrison) *chsd ldr to 5th: nt fluent next: hit 7th: sn rdn: wknd 2 out: wnt 2nd bef last* **3/1**[2]

500- **3** 2 **Miller's Dawn**[16] 5172 6-11-5 **101**.....................................(p) SamThomas 96
(Henrietta Knight) *hld up: hdwy appr 6th: rdn and wknd appr 2 out: wnt 3rd towards fin* **7/2**[3]

430- **4** 2 3/4 **Kristallo (GER)**[26] 2664 5-11-9 **105**..................................(b) WillKennedy 99
(Paul Webber) *trckd ldrs: racd keenly: wnt 2nd 5th: led 7th tl after 3 out: sn rdn: wknd next: lost 3rd towards fin* **9/2**

0FP- **5** 22 **Cave Of The Giant (IRE)**[34] 4869 8-11-7 **103**............(p) SeamusDurack 78
(Tim McCarthy) *prom: rdn after 5th: wknd next: t.o* **22/1**

0P5- **6** 26 **Tuscany Star (IRE)**[10] 5291 7-10-13 **98**....................(tp) AlanCreighton(3) 53
(Edward Creighton) *chsd ldrs: lost pl 3rd: sn pushed along: drvn along after 5th: wknd next: t.o* **16/1**

F21- **7** 40 **Alfloramoor**[37] 4812 8-11-7 **106**...................................(p) AdamPogson(3) 29
(Charles Pogson) *led: racd keenly: hdd 7th: sn rdn and wknd: t.o* **11/4**[1]

5m 7.30s (-3.30) **Going Correction** -0.125s/f (Good) **7** Ran SP% **111.4**
Speed ratings (Par 105): **101,95,95,94,86 76,62**
toteswingers: 1&2 £5.80, 1&3 £5.40, 2&3 £2.80 CSF £38.64 CT £124.10 TOTE £6.20: £1.90, £2.20; EX 34.70.
Owner Lady Green **Bred** Lady Jennifer Green **Trained** Newmarket, Suffolk

FOCUS
A run-of-the-mill handicap hurdle, but run at a decent pace. The winner improved towards the level of her Flat form.

NOTEBOOK
Purely By Chance, successful in novice company in 2008, had not run over jumps for 375 days. She has been kept busy on the all-weather, though, and ran out a decisive winner. Held up early on, she responded to a reminder at halfway and had moved into second before three out. Asked to go about her business from the next flight, she soon quickened away and, despite a clumsy jump at the last, collected with a fair bit in hand. (op 8-1)
Yonder, whose bumper and Flat form suggested she might not be badly treated on this handicap hurdle debut, had run only a fair race last time out, but fared better here. She was always prominent and might have finished closer to the winner had she not made quite bad mistakes at both the fifth-last and fourth-last hurdles. (tchd 11-4)
Miller's Dawn had made mistakes on each of his previous outings over hurdles, but had fared slightly better in cheekpieces last time out. His jumping was not too bad here, but, having travelled in midfield for much of the race, he never posed a serious threat to the first two. (tchd 4-1)
Kristallo(GER), twice in the frame in fair novice company and fit from a sound run on the all-weather, was making his handicap debut over jumps. He was up with the pace from the outset, taking the lead on the far side on the final circuit, but lost significant momentum with a poor jump three from home. (op 5-1)
Cave Of The Giant(IRE), without a victory since January 2008, was never in contention. He was at the back of the field for the majority of the journey and took fifth largely as a result of others mistakes. Official explanation: , without a victory since January 2008, was never in contention. He was at the back of the field for the majority of the journey and took fifth largely as a result of others mistakes.
Tuscany Star(IRE) Official explanation: jockey said gelding was unsuited by the good (good to firm places) ground
Alfloramoor Official explanation: trainer said gelding ran too free

65 TOTEPOOL A BETTER WAY TO BET H'CAP CHASE (15 fncs 1 omitted) 2m 4f 110y
7:40 (7:40) (Class 4) (0-115,115) 5-Y-0+ **£3,252** (£955; £477; £238)

Form RPR

23P- **1** **American World (FR)**[19] 5131 6-11-6 **109**...........................(t) APMcCoy 117+
(Brendan Powell) *hld up: wnt 3rd 4th: chsd ldr 12th: led appr 2 out: sn clr: comf* **1/1**[1]

PF4- **2** 3 1/4 **Pairc Na Gcapall (IRE)**[41] 4719 8-11-9 **115**...............(p) AlexMerriam(3) 118
(Neil King) *chsd ldr tl led briefly 7th: lost 2nd 12th: sn drvn along: wnt 2nd again after 2 out: kpt on u.p but nvr any ch w wnr* **7/2**[3]

000- **3** 16 **Sunday City (JPN)**[12] 5231 9-11-7 **110**...........................(b) PaddyAspell 104
(Donald McCain) *led: mstke 6th: hdd briefly next: rdn and hdd appr 2 out: wknd bef last* **8/1**

464- **4** 43 **Ice Bucket (IRE)**[10] 5281 10-11-10 **113**...........................(p) SamThomas 69
(Henrietta Knight) *chsd ldrs: lost pl 4th: sn drvn along: wl bhd fr 6th: t.o* **3/1**[2]

5m 3.50s (-1.80) **Going Correction** -0.05s/f (Good) **4** Ran SP% **108.3**
Speed ratings: **101,99,93,77**
CSF £4.84 TOTE £2.20; EX 4.70.
Owner John P McManus **Bred** Mme Chantel Hamon **Trained** Upper Lambourn, Berks

FOCUS
A small field but a good gallop to this weak handicap. The winner is rated to his mark.

NOTEBOOK
American World(FR), successful in this race last season, had been placed twice - including from this rating - in March. Refitted with a tongue-tie, which had been left off last time out, he won readily. Content to sit in third until approaching the third-last, he eased into second from that point and then led before two out. He idled on the run-in, allowing the second to make ground, but was never in any danger. He can be rated better than the winning margin. (op 11-10 tchd 10-11 and 6-5 in places)
Pairc Na Gcapall(IRE), twice successful on this course in the spring of 2009, had shown only occasional glimpses of form since. Considering that, he posted a decent effort here, always figuring prominently and staying on well in the home straight. (op 10-3 tchd 3-1)
Sunday City(JPN), capable of winning a handicap hurdle off 124 at his peak in 2007, has been only lightly raced in the past two seasons and, on the basis of this form, has to be considered a shadow of his former self. He led for a long way, jumping boldly, but made a mistake two out and tired quickly. (op 13-2)
Ice Bucket(IRE), without a win since scoring here off 104 in 2008, has found life harder from a rating in the 110s and ran a shocker here. Always in last place, he was nudged along from an early stage but failed to respond with any enthusiasm. (op 7-2 tchd 4-1)

66 TOTEPOOL RACING'S BIGGEST SUPPORTER H'CAP HURDLE (12 hdls) 3m 2f
8:10 (8:10) (Class 4) (0-105,105) 4-Y-0+ **£2,927** (£859; £429; £214)

Form RPR

001- **1** **Wor Rom (IRE)**[8] 5315 6-10-1 **80**..................................(p) JohnnyFarrelly 92+
(Elliott Cooper) *hld up: hdwy 7th: mstke 3 out: sn rdn: led last: drvn out* **10/3**[2]

043- **2** 1 1/4 **Knock Em Dead (IRE)**[37] 4798 6-11-5 **98**...........................(b) APMcCoy 109+
(Jonjo O'Neill) *chsd ldrs: led and mstke 9th: hit 3 out: rdn bef next: hdd last: styd on same pce flat* **3/1**[1]

602- **3** 10 **Phare Isle (IRE)**[24] 5043 5-11-7 **105**............................. JamesHalliday(5) 109+
(Ben Case) *hld up: racd keenly: hdwy after 9th: ev ch 2 out: sn rdn: wknd flat* **11/2**

110- **4** 8 **Earcomesthedream (IRE)**[21] 5107 7-11-5 **101**..........(b) HarrySkelton(3) 97
(Peter Pritchard) *hld up: hdwy 9th: wknd appr last* **5/1**[3]

P43- **5** 9 **Attorney General (IRE)**[33] 4895 11-11-1 **97**............(bt¹) AlexMerriam(3) 85
(Neil King) *hld up: drvn along after 8th: sme hdwy 3 out: wknd bef next* **8/1**

PPP- **6** 15 **Shergill (IRE)**[8] 5315 9-10-6 **85**...................................... TomScudamore 61
(Shaun Lycett) *chsd ldr: led appr 8th: hdd next: sn rdn: wknd bef 3 out: t.o* **25/1**

022- **7** 13 **Konigsbote (GER)**[24] 5053 8-11-3 **96**............................(b) PaulMoloney 62
(Sophie Leech) *prom: rdn 8th: wknd appr 3 out: t.o* **17/2**

436- **8** 47 **Gunnadoit (USA)**[7] 5330 5-10-10 **92**.............................. ChrisHonour(3) 20
(Neil King) *led: pushed along after 5th: hdd bef 8th: sn wknd: t.o* **20/1**

0P6- **P** **Eskimo Pie (IRE)**[33] 4895 11-10-4 **86** ow6.................(b) AdamPogson(3) —
(Charles Pogson) *p.u bef 3 out* **20/1**

6m 15.8s (-7.10) **Going Correction** -0.125s/f (Good) **9** Ran SP% **115.1**
Speed ratings (Par 105): **105,104,101,99,96 91,87,73,—**
toteswingers: 1&2 £1.60, 1&3 £3.40, 2&3 £3.80 CSF £13.64 CT £52.46 TOTE £7.20: £3.50, £1.10, £1.10; EX 11.00 Place 6: £65.91, Place 5: £26.21.
Owner Campbell Cooper & Halley **Bred** Jerry Halley **Trained** Brigham, Cumbria
⊠ Stewards' Enquiry : Johnny Farrelly three-day ban: used whip with excessive frequency (May 13-15)

FOCUS
No more than an ordinary handicap hurdle, but competitive nevertheless. The first two stood out at the weights and the winner is rated in line with his recent win.

NOTEBOOK
Wor Rom(IRE), a winner from this mark when fitted with first-time cheekpieces over 3m at Southwell on his latest start, once again wore that headgear. He is due to go up 11lb at the end of this week, so his form chance was obvious, and he battled hard to notch a gallant victory. Never far off the pace, he took the lead two flights out and could be named the winner from that point on. How he will fare once raised in the ratings, however, remains to be seen. (op 11-4 tchd 5-2)
Knock Em Dead(IRE), successful off this mark at Newton Abbot in August last year, had posted a fair third from 100 at Exeter last time out and again ran well. Always in the front rank, travelling nicely, he led three from home, only to be overhauled by the better-handicapped winner. (op 4-1 tchd 11-4)
Phare Isle(IRE), runner-up behind the multiple winner Flower Haven here last time out, had been raised 10lb since that effort and it found him out. He ran creditably, making ground from a midfield position approaching three out, but was ultimately well held. (op 5-1)
Earcomesthedream(IRE), twice a winner last month with the second success coming off a mark of 92, had been well beaten from this rating on his latest start and it appears he now needs some mercy from the handicapper. He tried to go with the first two from three out but was left behind in the home straight. (op 7-1)
Attorney General(IRE), whose rating has dropped dramatically since a good run at Cheltenham in November, failed to take advantage, despite being fitted with first-time blinkers. (op 14-1)
T/Plt: £160.20 to a £1 stake. Pool: £48,815.88. 222.40 winning tickets. T/Qpdt: £43.30 to a £1 stake. Pool: £4,770.43. 81.44 winning tickets. CR

67a - 74a (Foreign Racing) - See Raceform Interactive

BANGOR-ON-DEE (L-H)
Friday, April 30

OFFICIAL GOING: Good to soft (soft in places) changing to soft after race 2 (6.20)
Shared bends reduced advertised chase distances by about circa 100yds.
Wind: Blustery. Weather: squally showers

75 LADY MOSTYN MEMORIAL RED CROSS WEEK (S) HURDLE (9 hdls) 2m 1f
5:50 (5:50) (Class 5) 4-Y-0+ **£2,055** (£599; £299)

Form RPR

P- **1** **Killowenabbey (IRE)**[4] 21 6-10-5 0.................(tp) AodhaganConlon(7) 80
(Debra Hamer) *trckd ldrs: led 6th: rdn and creeping along fr 3 out: lft w 2 l advantage 2 out: hung on gamely although floundering nr fin* **7/4**[1]

50/ **2** *nk* **He's A Sheila**[348] 7-10-2 0 JoshWall(10) 80
(Trevor Wall) *last and rdn after 3rd: hdwy 5th: wnt 3rd 3 out: rdn whn lft 2nd next: 2 l down last: plugged on wl and jst failed* **40/1**
422- **3** *15* **Sonic Anthem (USA)**[169] 1897 8-10-9 99 DannyCook(3) 75
(Barry Leavy) *cl 2nd tl led 5th tl 6th: rdn after next: stl w wnr whn blnd bdly 2 out and lost all ch* **7/4**[1]
50U- **4** *30* **The Randy Bishop**[153] 2578 10-10-7 93 LeeEdwards(5) 50
(Tony Carroll) *bhd: effrt 5th: wnt modest 3rd but rdn next: lost pl 3 out: t.o and v tired 2 out* **11/2**[2]
0/0- **P** **Gumlayloy**[338] 496 11-10-5 0 (t) RobertKirk(7) —
(George Jones) *prom tl stopped to nil after 4th: sn wl t.o: p.u 3 out* **80/1**
0- **P** **Willie Ever**[7] 5352 6-10-5 0 MrSWDrinkwater(7) —
(David Bridgwater) *flattened 2nd: slt ld tl 5th: stopped to nil: p.u 3 out* **25/1**
00P- **P** **Rockman**[7] 5352 9-10-5 64 PeterHatton(7) —
(Patricia Rigby) *rdn and struggling 4th: wl t.o whn p.u next* **100/1**
P **Bansha (IRE)**[6] 4-10-7 0 JamesDavies —
(Alan Bailey) *chsd ldrs: rdn after 4th: wl t.o whn p.u 3 out* **6/1**[3]

4m 30.9s (20.00) **Going Correction** +0.875s/f (Soft)
WFA 4 from 5yo+ 6lb 8 Ran SP% **110.9**
Speed ratings (Par 103): **87,86,79,65,— —,—,—**
Tote Swingers: 1&2 £16.60, 1&3 £1.10, 2&3 £10.90 CSF £62.50 TOTE £3.00: £1.10, £13.40, £1.02; EX 55.50.There was no bid for the winner.
Owner Mrs D A Hamer **Bred** Malachy Hanley **Trained** Nantycaws, Carmarthens

FOCUS
This was a poor and uncompetitive seller. The winner is rated 2st off his best with the second in line with his bumper form.

NOTEBOOK
Killowenabbey(IRE) only made his debut for this yard on Monday, when pulled up after coming in for support at Towcester, and he was suited by the change in the ground, having acted in soft conditions in Ireland. Tried in cheekpieces for the first time, he challenged four from home and was left a couple of lengths to the good two out, before scrambling home with nothing to spare. He returned with a lacerated leg which needed stitching. Official explanation: trainer said, regarding apparent improvement in form, that the gelding was better suited by the flatter track and drop in distance. (op 9-4)
He's A Sheila showed just a hint of ability in a couple of bumpers but had been pulled up on each of his five starts in point-to-points. Off the track for nearly a year and debuting over hurdles on his first run for the yard, he seemed to be struggling in rear for the first half of the race but stayed on steadily to move on to the leaders' heels at the second-last. Running on after the last, but just held, he probably needs slightly further. (op 33-1)
Sonic Anthem(USA) was runner-up in a couple of better sellers than this when last seen back in the autumn and has winning form after an absence on the Flat. Upsides the winner, but beginning to tire, when he blundered badly at the second-last, he has shown his form on fast ground and the rain was against him. (op 13-8 tchd 2-1)
The Randy Bishop, reverting to hurdles after a five-month break and lowered into selling company for the first time, was struggling shortly after the fourth-last. (tchd 9-2 and 13-2)

76 HAVEAGO@STANJAMES.COM NOVICES' HURDLE (9 hdls) 2m 1f
6:20 (6:20) (Class 4) 4-Y-0+ **£3,252** (£955; £477; £238)

Form RPR
623- **1** **Osric (IRE)**[34] 4891 7-10-12 122 APMcCoy 116+
(Nicky Henderson) *racd keenly: wnt 3rd at 5th and 2nd after 3 out: shkn up whn hit next: swtchd ins and led last: sn clr* **8/11**[1]
341- **2** *5* **Master Fong (IRE)**[8] 5340 4-11-0 114 (b) JasonMaguire 113
(Donald McCain) *led at stdy pce: rdn whn j.rt 2 out and again whn hdd last: no ch w wnr after* **6/1**[3]
051- **3** *14* **Accordingtoemandem (IRE)**[53] 4490 6-11-5 124 PaddyBrennan 105
(Ian Williams) *t.k.h in 3rd: jnd ldr 5th tl 3 out: drvn and lost 2nd wl bef next: sn no ch: fin weakly* **11/4**[2]
164- **4** *8* **Red Not Blue (IRE)**[37] 4823 7-10-12 0 AndrewThornton 90
(Simon Earle) *rn wout shoes: chsd ldr tl 4th: reminder next: lost tch bef 3 out* **25/1**
/P4- **5** *14* **National Obsession (IRE)**[25] 5030 7-10-12 0 AidanColeman 82
(Venetia Williams) *ballooning jumps and v careful in last pair: rdn 6th: struggling after* **25/1**
5/0- **P** **Oxford Circus**[19] 5146 8-10-12 0 AndrewTinkler —
(Anna Brooks) *last pair: hit 4th: j. slowly 5th: lost tch bef 3 out: poor 5th whn p.u bef 2 out: dismntd* **66/1**

4m 30.2s (19.30) **Going Correction** +0.875s/f (Soft)
WFA 4 from 5yo+ 6lb 6 Ran SP% **108.0**
Speed ratings (Par 105): **89,86,80,76,69 —**
Tote Swingers: 1&2 £1.60, 1&3 £1.10, 2&3 £1.50 CSF £5.15 TOTE £2.20: £1.40, £1.10; EX 4.50.

Owner Mr & Mrs R Kelvin Hughes **Bred** P Turley And Sons **Trained** Upper Lambourn, Berks

FOCUS
A modest novice hurdle run at a steady pace and in a time just 0.7sec quicker than the seller. The form is rated around the second and fourth and could be piched higher around the winner.

NOTEBOOK
Osric(IRE) had the best chance on adjusted BHA ratings but he needed to work to land the odds. He was well on top at the end though, after switching to the inside of the runner-up, and will be seen to better effect in a stronger-run race. That could mean a move back into handicaps rather than carrying a penalty in novice company. (tchd 4-6 and 4-5)
Master Fong(IRE), who is not very big, had plenty on at the weights under the penalty for his arguably fortunate win at Uttoxeter. Making the running, he jumped out to his right at both the last two flights when the pressure was on and could not hold off the favourite. (op 9-2)
Accordingtoemandem(IRE) stopped quickly on the home turn, lookering to be floundering in the conditions. He had gained his win on good ground at Stratford, form not boosted by runner-up Golden Button next time. (op 7-2 tchd 4-1)
Red Not Blue(IRE) is from a yard which has had few runners in recent months due to a virus. Dropped in trip, he ended up well held, but he is the type to do better in handicaps. (tchd 22-1 and 28-1)
National Obsession(IRE) showed a poor hurdling technique and trailed throughout. (op 33-1)

77 STANJAMES.COM NOVICES' H'CAP CHASE (12 fncs) 2m 1f 110y
6:50 (6:50) (Class 4) (0-100,95) 5-Y-0+ **£3,577** (£1,050; £525; £262)

Form RPR
04U- **1** **Star Tenor (IRE)**[7] 5371 8-11-4 87 PaddyAspell 97
(Sandy Forster) *trckd ldrs: j. ahd 7th: rdn clr bef 2 out: hld on dourly flat: all out* **11/2**
621- **2** *1 1/4* **Chicago Alley**[25] 5049 9-11-0 88 LeeEdwards(5) 99+
(Tony Carroll) *t.k.h: several positions: nt fluent 6th: mstke 9th: chsd wnr 3 out: outpcd bef next: rallied and nt fluent last: styd on cl home* **11/8**[1]
000- **3** *5* **Winged Farasi**[44] 4677 6-11-12 95 TjadeCollier 99
(Joanne Foster) *j. slowly 1st: pressed ldrs tl rdn and outpcd after 3 out: plugged on* **11/1**
504- **4** *11* **Ruby Valentine (FR)**[66] 4214 7-10-11 80 AndrewThornton 74
(Jim Wilson) *handy tl rdn on outside 7th: nt gng wl after: fdd tamely wl bef 2 out* **3/1**[2]
463- **P** **Cordier**[9] 5313 8-11-2 88 (tp) RichieMcLernon(3) —
(John Mackie) *led at muddling pce tl hit 7th: last and struggling bef 3 out: t.o and p.u next* **9/2**[3]

4m 31.5s (9.40) **Going Correction** +0.30s/f (Yiel) 5 Ran SP% **109.0**
Speed ratings: **91,90,88,83,—**
CSF £13.85 TOTE £14.60: £10.80, £1.02; EX 29.10.
Owner Anne & Tony Howarth **Bred** William Durkan **Trained** Kirk Yetholm, Borders

FOCUS
The going was officially amended to soft all round prior to this race. This was a very moderate novice handicap chase, although the pace appeared reasonable and the form has a solid look to it.

NOTEBOOK
Star Tenor(IRE) was essentially a plater over hurdles and he had not shone in two previous starts over fences, albeit facing an unrealistic task latest. Jumping soundly, he led five from home and saw it out well enough. He stays further and does not mind better ground. (op 17-2 tchd 10-1)
Chicago Alley went up 12lb for her recent win at Huntingdon but still looked fairly treated on her old form. After taking a keen hold through the first part of the race and putting in several poor leaps, she was staying on again after the last. She might not be one to give up on back on better ground and returned to further. (op 5-4 tchd 6-5)
Winged Farasi is a pretty ordinary hurdler and he may not be easy to place over fences, although to be fair he did jump pretty safely on this chasing debut before fading out of contention. (op 10-1)
Ruby Valentine(FR) gained her sole win over hurdles at this track, but did not show a great deal of promise on this chase debut. (op 7-2 tchd 11-4)
Cordier dropped away tamely once headed and was eventually pulled up. (op 4-1)

78 BELUCKY@STANJAMES.COM WYNNSTAY HUNT H'CAP CHASE (15 fncs) 2m 4f 110y
7:20 (7:20) (Class 3) (0-135,135) 5-Y-0+ **£8,238** (£2,433; £1,216; £608; £304)

Form RPR
252- **1** **Storymaker**[9] 5309 9-10-10 119 PaddyAspell 129+
(Sandy Forster) *mstke 1st and rdr lost iron: stdy hdwy 5th: last of three gng clr at 10th: rdn after 3 out: styd on to ld after next: kpt gng stoutly flat* **11/2**
031- **2** *1 1/4* **Picaroon**[7] 5360 6-11-4 132 7ex DeanColeman(5) 142+
(Tim Vaughan) *cl up: blnd 9th: led bef next: duelled for ld after tl drvn and hdd after 2 out: blnd last: kpt on flat* **4/1**[1]
U- **3** *2 1/2* **Yabora (FR)**[35] 4868 5-11-5 128 JasonMaguire 134
(Charlie Longsdon) *a ldng trio: w ldr fr 3 out tl next: drvn and one pce bef last* **16/1**
P1P- **4** *16* **Just Smudge**[141] 2790 8-10-12 121 AidanColeman 111
(Venetia Williams) *chsd ldrs: rdn and outpcd by ldng trio fr 10th: mod 4th whn dived over 3 out: no ch after* **16/1**
2U5- **5** *6* **Magic Sky (FR)**[12] 5247 10-11-6 132 MrOGreenall(3) 116
(Milton Harris) *bhd: rdn 5th: 8 l last at 1/2-way: effrt to midfield but u.p 10th: no ch after* **14/1**
54P- **6** *4 1/2* **Mister Quasimodo**[20] 5126 10-11-5 128 (b) JoeTizzard 107
(Colin Tizzard) *towards rr: rdn and lost tch 10th: wl bhd 3 out* **22/1**
250- **7** *16* **Private Be**[43] 4702 11-11-12 135 TomO'Brien 98
(Philip Hobbs) *struggling in last and rdn after 9th: t.o 11th* **9/2**[2]
3B0- **P** **Gaelic Flight (IRE)**[14] 5204 12-11-3 126 (t) WillKennedy —
(Jeremy Scott) *hit 1st: pushed along and nt gng wl 5th: struggling 9th: t.o and p.u 3 out* **16/1**
00U- **P** **Boomshakalaka (IRE)**[21] 5111 10-10-13 122 AndrewTinkler —
(Nicky Henderson) *cl up tl dropped to rr 9th: t.o and p.u 2 out* **14/1**
542- **F** **Master Somerville**[34] 4883 8-10-7 116 (b) RichardJohnson —
(Henry Daly) *rdn 6th: dropping to rr u.p 7th: fell 8th* **5/1**[3]
10P- **P** **Saphir Des Bois (FR)**[27] 4988 6-11-8 134 (p) RichieMcLernon(3) —
(Jonjo O'Neill) *set gd pce tl hdd after 9th: lost pl rapidly u.p: t.o and p.u 2 out* **17/2**

5m 11.7s (2.60) **Going Correction** +0.30s/f (Yiel) 11 Ran SP% **116.1**
Speed ratings: **107,106,105,99,97 95,89,—,—,— —**
Tote Swingers: 1&2 £6.30, 1&3 £21.30, 2&3 £24.70 CSF £28.27 CT £332.78 TOTE £13.50: £4.10, £1.10, £1.70; EX 37.60.
Owner J M & Miss H M Crichton, Miss S Forster **Bred** Ms Susan Perriam **Trained** Kirk Yetholm, Borders

FOCUS
A worthwhile prize and a competitive handicap, run at a good pace. The first three came clear and the form looks solid. The first two are rated in line with their most recent efforts.

NOTEBOOK
Storymaker came here in good heart with three seconds in his last four starts, and the horse that beat him last time at Perth, Nedzer's Return, won again there two days later. The leading pair were going better than him when he went in pursuit on the home turn, but he got to the front at the last and stayed on well to give his trainer and jockey a double on the night. He was officially a pound ahead of the handicapper here and may struggle a bit when he is reassessed. (op 13-2)
Picaroon was 6lb well-in. Unbeaten in two completed starts over fences, he led travelling strongly six from home but had to work to shrug off the third and had just been headed by the winner when he walked through the last. He was coming back for more on the short run-in and will remain one to be interested in even when his new mark takes effect, although there is certainly room for improvement in his jumping. The soft ground did not inconvenience him. (op 9-2 tchd 5-1)
Yabora(FR), having his second run since arriving from France, had underfoot conditions to suit and ran well for a long way until fading between the last two fences. He is only five and looks a good recruit for his yard. (op 20-1)
Just Smudge ⊠ shaped with promise on this first outing since December and there are more races to be won with this relatively unexposed gelding, although he did not prove the most consistent in a light campaign last season. (tchd 18-1)
Magic Sky(FR) was not disgraced but could never really get into the race after a slightly slow start. He is pretty consistent and is due to be dropped a pound now. (op 16-1)
Private Be was down in grade and should have liked the ground, but never got into it. (op 5-1 tchd 11-2)
Gaelic Flight(IRE) Official explanation: trainer's rep said gelding was unsuited by the soft ground (op 9-1 tchd 8-1)
Master Somerville usually runs well here, but he could not dominate with Saphir Des Bois in the field and he was already going backwards when he fell early on the final circuit. (op 9-1 tchd 8-1)
Saphir Des Bois(FR) made the running in the first-time headgear but did not offer much when headed. (op 9-1 tchd 8-1)

79 JAMES GRIFFITH MEMORIAL NOVICES' HUNTERS' CHASE (18 fncs) 3m 110y
7:50 (7:51) (Class 6) 5-Y-0+ **£1,249** (£387; £193; £96)

Form RPR
20/ **1** **Horsham Lad (IRE)**[48] 6-12-0 0 MrRBurton 122+
(F M O'Brien) *taken steadily first circ: prog gng wl on outer 10th: led 14th: pushed clr after 3 out: nvr looked like being ct: quite impressive* **13/8**[1]

PPP/ **2** *10* **Springfield Dante**[19] 9-11-7 0.. HenryBrooke(7) 111
(Nick Kent) *midfield: nt fluent 11th: effrt and mstke 14th: wnt 10 l 2nd 2 out: kpt on gamely but no ch w wnr* **16/1**

3 *7* **Ballyeightra Cross (IRE)**[19] 6-12-0 0................................ MrTGreenall 103
(G D Hanmer) *bhd and nt fluent: 9th whn blnd bdly 12th: effrt and mstke 15th: wnt 2nd after 3 out tl next: drvn and sn wknd* **5/1**[3]

P04- **4** *9* **Cash In Hand (IRE)**[9] 5314 10-11-7 88......................(b) AdamWedge(7) 94
(R Harvey) *led tl 14th: gave up qckly u.p after 3 out* **12/1**

5 *12* **Keenans Reserve (IRE)**[19] 9-11-11 0............................ MrGBrewer(3) 82
(G D Hanmer) *chsd ldrs: rdn 14th: lost tch qckly wl bef 2 out* **22/1**

/P5- **6** *32* **Brookview Lad (IRE)**[29] 4972 7-11-7 0............................ MrRJarrett(7) 50
(R Smart) *midfield: effrt to press ldrs 13th: rdn whn mstke 15th: 6th and fading whn blnd 3 out: sn t.o* **33/1**

324- **7** *4 1/2* **Shraden Edition**[24] 13-11-7 87.. MrBFurnival(7) 46
(P A Jones) *chsd ldrs tl drvn and wknd qckly 13th: wl t.o after 3 out* **10/1**

/12- **P** **Accumulus**[61] 4329 10-11-11 115...................................... MrRBandey(7) —
(Geoffrey Deacon) *j.lft and detached in last pair: nvr gng wl: t.o 12th: p.u 15th* **9/2**[2]

235/ **P** **Willie Wong (IRE)**[25] 8-11-7 0..(t) MrWKinsey(7) —
(W R Kinsey) *prom tl rdn and wknd and mstke 13th: t.o and p.u 2 out* **12/1**

P **Mrsilverlining (IRE)**[27] 8-11-7 0.. MrJFlook(7) —
(Miss I H Pickard) *mstke 5th: prom tl wknd qckly and blnd 12th: sn t.o: crawled over 13th and p.u next* **66/1**

P **Lilly De Rome**[342] 7-11-0 0..................................(t) MrJamieJenkinson(7) —
(Mrs Edward Crow) *reluctant to set off and lost many l: nt jump wl: jst in tch 8th tl 10th: t.o and p.u 14th* **40/1**

6m 26.9s (7.10) **Going Correction** +0.30s/f (Yiel) **11 Ran SP% 114.5**
Speed ratings: **100,96,94,91,87 77,76,—,—,— —**
Tote Swingers: 1&2 £10.50, 1&3 £3.70, 2&3 £29.00 CSF £27.35 TOTE £3.60: £1.10, £9.70, £1.50; EX 32.20.
Owner Mr & Mrs William Rucker **Bred** Mrs Jean O'Brien **Trained** Naunton, Gloucs

FOCUS
An interesting race of its type. The winner looks a smart hunter and can rate higher.

NOTEBOOK
Horsham Lad(IRE) has progressed very well in point-to-points this spring, winning a maiden, a restricted and an intermediate, and he took another step up the ladder with a comfortable win on his debut over regulation fences. He will run in the John Corbet Cup at Stratford at the end of the month, the champion novice hunter chase, and should have no problem with the 3m4f trip there. A nice young prospect, he races in the same colours as 2009 Foxhunter winner Cappa Bleu. (tchd 6-4)
Springfield Dante won a maiden point at Tabley last time and this was a thoroughly creditable hunter chase debut, but he was no match for the promising winner. (op 12-1)
Ballyeightra Cross(IRE), recent winner of a restricted point on the same Tabley card, ran well under a patient ride but his jumping lacked fluency. (op 6-1 tchd 7-1)
Cash In Hand(IRE) had been second in each of the last three renewals of this and he ran respectably again, but is without a win in 22 hunter chase starts now. (op 16-1)
Accumulus, runner-up to subsequent Aintree Fox Hunter's second Moncadou at Fontwell last time, was again ridden well off the pace, but this time he jumped sketchily and out to his left and he could never get into it. Official explanation: trainer said gelding lost a shoe (op 7-2 tchd 3-1)

80 STANJAMES.COM H'CAP HURDLE (9 hdls) 2m 1f
8:20 (8:21) (Class 3) (0-135,127) 4-Y-0+ **£6,970** (£2,059; £1,029; £514; £257)

Form RPR

236- **1** **Son Of Flicka**[37] 4817 6-11-10 **125**.................................... JasonMaguire 130+
(Donald McCain) *lft 2nd at 3rd: led 6th: rdn bef 2 out where blnd: hld on wl fr last* **3/1**[1]

144- **2** *2 3/4* **Dancewiththedevil (IRE)**[188] 1898 9-11-2 **117**............ RichardJohnson 120
(C Roberts) *settled towards rr: mstke 5th: effrt next: 4th and rdn and trying to chal whn nt fluent 2 out: wnt 2nd at last: no imp on wnr* **13/2**

215- **3** *1 1/4* **Mohayer (IRE)**[35] 4873 8-11-9 **124**... APMcCoy 124
(Jonjo O'Neill) *hld up in rr: crept clsr fr 5th: cajoled into 2nd bef 2 out: ch between last two: fnd little and lost 2nd at last* **10/3**[2]

030- **4** *2 1/4* **Pepporoni Pete (IRE)**[181] 2002 9-11-3 **118**....................(p) CharliePoste 118+
(Milton Harris) *racd keenly and cl up: wnt 2nd 3 out tl rdn bef next: 4th and outpcd whn blnd last* **14/1**

410- **5** *3/4* **Mickmacmagoole (IRE)**[90] 3739 8-10-9 **120**............... JSMcGarvey(10) 117
(Evan Williams) *hld up: pushed along after 4th: rdn and effrt next: on heels of ldrs on long run to two out: one pce and btn whn hit last* **16/1**

112- **6** *19* **Ocean Transit (IRE)**[105] 3006 5-10-9 **113**.................. GerardTumelty(3) 91
(Richard Price) *bhd: rdn 5th: lost tch next* **12/1**

644- **7** *10* **Karky Schultz (GER)**[18] 4737 5-11-1 **123**......................... MrRMahon(7) 91
(James Eustace) *led and clr w one rival: lft 10 l ahd 3rd: pressed after next: hdd 6th: drvn and dropped out rapidly after 3 out* **11/2**[3]

P3P/ **8** *34* **Charlie Yardbird (IRE)**[426] 4220 9-11-7 **127**................ DeanColeman(5) 61
(Tim Vaughan) *cl up tl 6th: fdd next: t.o bef 2 out: sn eased* **20/1**

30- **F** **Black Coffee**[20] 5128 5-11-1 **123**.. DavidBass(7) —
(Nicky Henderson) *w ldr and clr of rest tl fell 3rd* **13/2**

4m 22.6s (11.70) **Going Correction** +0.875s/f (Soft) **9 Ran SP% 115.1**
Speed ratings (Par 107): **107,105,105,104,103 94,90,74,—**
Tote Swingers: 1&2 £2.10, 1&3 £2.60, 2&3 £5.30 CSF £23.04 CT £67.87 TOTE £4.30: £3.10, £4.80, £1.10; EX 22.50 Place 6 £8.57, Place 5 £6.45..
Owner Twenty Four Seven Recruitment **Bred** Chieveley Manor Stud **Trained** Cholmondeley, Cheshire

FOCUS
A fair handicap hurdle and solid enough form with the winner rated back to his best.

NOTEBOOK
Son Of Flicka hit the front four from home and held on willingly to win his second race at Bangor from two visits. The drop back in trip suited him. (op 9-2 tchd 11-4)
Dancewiththedevil(IRE) is a consistent sort and he ran well on this first start since October. Although he remains on a career-high mark, there looks no reason why he should not pay his way in the coming months. (op 5-1 tchd 15-2)
Mohayer(IRE) travelled well into contention but could not quicken up from the second-last. He did not mind the rain-softened ground and had been dropped 3lb by the handicapper. (op 9-2)
Pepporoni Pete(IRE), another returning from a lengthy winter break, travelled well for a long way but was just held when flattening the last. This was a pleasing reappearance but he does not hold any secrets from the handicapper. (op 16-1)
Mickmacmagoole(IRE), whose last two wins have been in sellers, ran quite well on this return from a three-month break but could never quite get into the action. (op 10-1)
Ocean Transit(IRE) was one of the first beaten and has questions to answer after her lacklustre run on the Flat on her previous start. (op 9-1)
Charlie Yardbird(IRE) faded on this first start since February 2009, but should last longer next time. (op 16-1)
T/Plt: £5.90 to a £1 stake. Pool: £59,833.57. 7,327.03 winning tickets. T/Qpdt: £4.60 to a £1 stake. Pool: £4,281.78. 677.82 winning tickets. IM

FONTWELL (L-H)
Friday, April 30

OFFICIAL GOING: Good changing to good (good to firm in places) after race 1 (5.40)
Rail movement increased chases by circ 65yds per circuit and hurdles by 20yds per circuit.
Wind: Moderate, half-behind. Weather: dry

81 WILLIAMS ROOFING CONTRACTORS LTD H'CAP CHASE (13 fncs) 2m 2f
5:40 (5:40) (Class 4) (0-105,105) 5-Y-0+ **£4,228** (£1,241; £620; £310)

Form RPR

06P- **1** **Good Old Days (IRE)**[164] 2343 11-10-13 **95**.................. SeanQuinlan(3) 108+
(Kim Bailey) *sn trcking ldrs: led 9th: clr after 3 out: r.o wl: pushed out* **8/1**

5/3- **2** *3 3/4* **Maxwil**[11] 5286 5-11-12 **105**.. ColinBolger 114+
(Pat Phelan) *in tch: tk clsr order 7th: wnt 2nd bef 4 out: 1 l down whn hit 3 out: hld whn mstke next: kpt on* **15/2**[3]

4PP- **3** *8* **Post It**[8] 5331 9-10-0 **86** ow4... MattGriffiths(7) 85
(Ron Hodges) *hld up last: rdn and hdwy after 4 out: styd on same pce fr next: wnt 3rd towards fin* **16/1**

322- **4** *1/2* **Space Cowboy (IRE)**[8] 5331 10-10-0 **79** oh5..................(b) JamieMoore 78
(Gary Moore) *in tch: tk clsr order 6th: chal for 2nd fr 4 out: rdn bef next: styd on same pce: no ex fr last: lost 3rd towards fin* **7/2**[1]

325- **5** *4* **Morestead (IRE)**[11] 5280 5-11-0 **100**.....................(p) AnthonyFreeman(7) 95
(Brendan Powell) *tendency to jump rt: disp tl 9th: sn rdn: one pce fr after next* **17/2**

54P- **6** *16* **One Cornetto (IRE)**[31] 4936 11-10-13 **92**........................ LiamTreadwell 73
(Nick Gifford) *disp tl 9th: sn rdn: wknd after 4 out* **14/1**

P0P- **P** **Maggie Mathias (IRE)**[20] 5135 9-10-6 **85**.................... JimmyMcCarthy —
(Brendan Powell) *hld up: wnt lft 5th: qckly lost tch: p.u bef 8th* **10/1**

12P- **P** **Majy D'Auteuil (FR)**[29] 4969 8-11-11 **104**....................... RobertThornton —
(Alan Jessop) *trckd ldrs: struggling 7th: sn bhd: p.u after 9th* **7/2**[1]

6P4- **U** **Bushwacker (IRE)**[101] 3524 6-11-1 **101**........................ JimmyDerham(7) —
(Seamus Mullins) *hld up: mstke 5th: awkward whn uns rdr next* **11/2**[2]

4m 29.6s (-5.10) **Going Correction** -0.275s/f (Good) **9 Ran SP% 114.9**
Speed ratings: **100,98,94,94,92 85,—,—,—**
Tote Swingers: 1&2 £12.50, 1&3 £26.10, 2&3 £24.10 CSF £65.51 CT £936.98 TOTE £9.90: £2.90, £2.20, £6.60; EX 57.20.
Owner Mr & Mrs K R Ellis **Bred** John Muldoon **Trained** Andoversford, Gloucs

FOCUS
The ground had been watered but the rain stayed away and the going was changed to Good, Good to Firm in places after this race. A moderate handicap chase in which several had something to prove. Solid enough form at its level.

NOTEBOOK
Good Old Days(IRE), well suited by fast ground, he scored twice late last summer including over C&D (off 7lb lower), before his form tailed off. Fresh from a break since November, he came through to lead five out and gradually shook off his rivals. He could well follow up and looks set for a good summer. (op 9-1)
Maxwil had run reasonably on his chasing debut and first start for the yard last time and again performed with credit. However, he compromised his chance with a couple of errors in the straight and did well to finish so close. He should be able to win over fences before long. (op 13-2)
Post It was a capable sort three years ago but endured a long absence afterwards. This was her best effort since her return to action, and she looks reasonably handicapped if she can build on it. (tchd 18-1)
Space Cowboy(IRE) was racing from 5lb out of the handicap but had been running reasonably well and was sent off favourite. He had his chance but lacked an extra gear in the straight. (op 9-2)
Morestead(IRE) made the running but gradually faded once the winner went on. He might need to return to longer trips. (op 7-1)
Maggie Mathias(IRE) was struck into according to her jockey. Official explanation: jockey said mare was struck into (op 9-1 tchd 12-1)
Majy D'Auteuil(FR), a dual course winner, was a disappointment, losing his place quickly at around the halfway mark, so may have had excuses and his rider reported the gelding stopped quickly. Official explanation: jockey said gelding stopped quickly (op 9-1 tchd 12-1)

82 CHANCELLOROFTHEFORMCHECKER.CO.UK PEPE RUFINO MEMORIAL MAIDEN HURDLE (10 hdls) 2m 4f
6:10 (6:10) (Class 5) 4-Y-0+ **£2,276** (£668; £334; £166)

Form RPR

532- **1** **Calon Crwbin**[38] 4809 5-11-0 118....................................(t) JohnnyFarrelly 123+
(Alison Thorpe) *trckd ldrs: led 4th: clr next: wnt rt 3 out: hung rt on bnd sn after: awkward next: r.o wl: pushed out: comf* **13/8**[1]

200- **2** *5* **Smooth Classic (IRE)**[80] 3946 6-11-0 0.................... WayneHutchinson 118+
(Warren Greatrex) *mid-div: stdy prog fr 6th: wnt 2nd after next: rdn after 2 out: kpt on for wl clr 2nd but no ch w wnr* **9/4**[2]

06- **3** *41* **Bon Spiel**[12] 5243 6-11-0 0.. ColinBolger 82
(Chris Gordon) *trckd ldrs: rdn after 7th: wknd after 3 out: t.o* **5/1**[3]

0- **4** *19* **Western Palm (IRE)**[11] 5278 7-11-0 0.................................... DarylJacob 69
(Charlie Mann) *hld up towards rr: prog 5th: wnt 4th after 7th: sn rdn: wknd 3 out: blnd next: t.o* **25/1**

5 *9* **Savannah**[594] 3698 7-10-7 0.. KeithBowens(7) 57
(Luke Comer, Ire) *mid-div: hit 4th: sn struggling towards rr: wknd bef 3 out: t.o* **16/1**

U- **6** *6* **Atabaas Allure (FR)**[8] 5328 4-10-1 0.. RodiGreene 38
(Chris Gordon) *nt fluent: a wl in rr: t.o* **18/1**

/56- **7** *1 3/4* **Bruff Academy (IRE)**[125] 3060 7-11-0 94.......................... LiamTreadwell 50
(Nick Gifford) *led tl hit 3rd: chsd ldrs: wknd after 6th: t.o* **10/1**

00- **8** *2 1/4* **Jack Fawaz (IRE)**[21] 5115 4-10-1 0............................... GarethThomas(7) 42
(Pat Phelan) *mid-div: struggling towards rr 5th: wknd after 7th: t.o* **80/1**

0PP- **P** **Towmater**[38] 4809 6-11-0 0... TomScudamore —
(Charlie Longsdon) *chsd ldr: reminders after 2nd: led 3rd tl next: chsd wnr tl after 7th: wknd 3 out: p.u bef next* **22/1**

4m 41.4s (-18.00) **Going Correction** -0.675s/f (Firm)
WFA 4 from 5yo+ 7lb **9 Ran SP% 115.2**
Speed ratings (Par 103): **109,107,91,83,79 77,76,75,—**
Tote Swingers: 1&2 £1.80, 1&3 £3.10, 2&3 £2.90 CSF £5.43 TOTE £2.70: £1.50, £1.50, £1.10; EX 5.40.
Owner Hanford's Chemist Ltd **Bred** R W And Mrs B D Neale **Trained** Bronwydd Arms, Carmarthens

FOCUS
An ordinary maiden hurdle that was weakened by late withdrawals and had no strength in depth. A small step up from the winner.

NOTEBOOK

Calon Crwbin ⊠ set a reasonable standard off a mark of 118. Given a positive ride, he went on at the third, soon opened up an advantage and never looked like being reeled in. He did tend to lug right on the home turn and after the last, but kept running and can be found further suitable opportunities this spring. He is likely to stay over hurdles in the short term. (op 7-4 tchd 2-1)

Smooth Classic(IRE), tackling fast ground for the first time, was held up early before moving up at halfway. He chased the winner for most of the last circuit but could make little impression. He does qualify for a handicap mark now, though. (op 2-1 tchd 5-2)

Bon Spiel tracked the leaders for most of the way but was left behind on the second circuit. He is another for whom handicaps beckon. (tchd 9-2)

Western Palm(IRE) never really got into contention but showed his first sign of ability, and is yet another who will probably be contesting a handicap before long. (op 20-1)

83 ELITE HELICOPTERS FLYING H'CAP CHASE (19 fncs) 3m 2f 110y

6:40 (6:40) (Class 5) (0-90,88) 5-Y-0+ **£2,602** (£764; £382; £190)

Form RPR

6PP- **1** **Boardroom Dancer (IRE)**[46] 4641 13-9-7 **62**............. JimmyDerham(7) 72
(Suzy Smith) *sn led: hdd 15th: sn rdn: kpt chsng ldr: 4 l down last: rallied gamely: styd on to regain ld nr finsh* **11/2**[3]

452- **2** *hd* **Mighty Moose (IRE)**[20] 5133 10-11-5 **86**.......................... IanPopham(5) 96
(Jeremy Scott) *prom: led 15th: 4 l clr u.p last: no ex whn ct nr fin* **7/2**[1]

004- **3** *10* **Great Ocean Road (IRE)**[22] 5103 7-11-6 **82**.................... PaulMoloney 85+
(Charlie Mann) *hld up last: stdy hdwy fr 14th: wnt 3rd after 4 out: rdn after next: styd on same pce* **9/1**

005- **4** *5* **Monsieur Georges (FR)**[26] 5007 10-9-9 **62** oh4........... JohnKington(5) 59
(F Jordan) *hld up: nudged along after 9th: rdn after 13th: no ch fr bef 4 out: styd on fr 3 out: wnt 4th sn after last* **16/1**

002- **5** *nk* **El Batal (IRE)**[11] 5288 9-11-5 **88**.............................(p) AnthonyFreeman(7) 86
(Sean Curran) *in tch: reminders after 12th: rdn after 15th: one pce fr after 4 out* **9/1**

012- **6** *12* **You Can Of Course (IRE)**[164] 2353 7-11-6 **82**...........(v) DougieCostello 67
(Neil Mulholland) *trckd ldrs: rdn after 4 out: sn hld: wknd last: lost 4th sn after* **4/1**[2]

/P0- **P** **Ballyboe Boy (IRE)**[24] 5072 11-10-4 **66**..........................(tp) JamieMoore —
(Shaun Harris) *mid-div: blnd 5th: rdn after 13th: wknd after 15th: bhd whn p.u bef 3 out* **20/1**

5F5- **P** **Strolling Vagabond (IRE)**[25] 5056 11-10-0 **62**............. JamieGoldstein —
(John Upson) *chsd ldrs early: struggling in last 7th: t.o whn p.u bef 11th* **12/1**

314- **P** **Fourpointone**[7] 5361 9-11-10 **86**.................................(p) TomScudamore —
(Michael Scudamore) *prom whn lost action and p.u bef 4th* **4/1**[2]

6m 51.5s (-9.60) **Going Correction** -0.275s/f (Good) **9** Ran SP% **115.9**
Speed ratings: **103,102,99,98,98 94,—,—,—**
Tote Swingers: 1&2 £5.80, 1&3 £8.40, 2&3 £5.10 CSF £26.02 CT £171.30 TOTE £7.80: £3.30, £1.50, £4.80; EX 29.00.
Owner Dr D J Meecham Jones & T A Fowler **Bred** Patrick Higgins **Trained** Lewes, E Sussex
⊠ Stewards' Enquiry : Ian Popham fifteen-day ban: usede whip with excessive frequency and in wrong place causing gelding to be wealed (May 21,23, 25-Jun 3 & Jun 5-7)

FOCUS

This very moderate staying handicap chase was run at a reasonable pace and produced a dramatic finish. The winner was well in on his bedst form and returned to something like his best.

NOTEBOOK

Boardroom Dancer(IRE) is lightly raced and does not have the best completion record, having pulled up in three of his previous five starts, but he clearly retains ability and put up a game effort to get back up close home. After making the running he looked in trouble when headed by the runner-up five out but kept fighting and found more as that rival tired from the last to snatch the race. There is no guarantee he will be able to reproduce this next time but he is well handicapped on his best form. Official explanation: trainer said, regarding apparent improvement in form, that the gelding was able to dominate on better ground. (op 15-2 tchd 8-1 and 5-1)

Mighty Moose(IRE) suffered his second narrow defeat in successive starts. He looked to have this won halfway up the straight but his rider went for everything between the last two fences and his mount had nothing left with which to repel the winner's renewed effort. He deserves a change of luck. (op 4-1)

Great Ocean Road(IRE), a former pointer making his chasing debut in this country, was given a patient ride and looked a big threat turning in but his effort petered out early in the straight. Despite his age he has still to fill his ample frame. (op 11-2)

Monsieur Georges(FR) merely stayed on past beaten rivals in the straight. (op 20-1)

El Batal(IRE) was never far away but could not respond to pressure from halfway around the final lap. (tchd 10-1)

You Can Of Course(IRE), returning from a break, moved up onto the heels of the leaders with a circuit to go but faded tamely when pressure was applied. (op 7-2)

Fourpointone was pulled up early having gone wrong. Official explanation: jockey said gelding went wrong (op 9-2)

84 TRAVIS PERKINS H'CAP HURDLE (11 hdls) 2m 6f 110y

7:10 (7:10) (Class 5) (0-95,95) 4-Y-0+ **£2,276** (£668; £334; £166)

Form RPR

463- **1** **Alldunnandusted (IRE)**[37] 4821 6-11-4 **94**................. JimmyDerham(7) 103+
(Seamus Mullins) *hld up in rr of midfield: hdwy 7th: rdn to chse ldrs after 3 out: led last: styd on wl: rdn out* **6/1**[2]

503- **2** *3 ½* **Play A Cord (IRE)**[204] 1663 7-10-1 **77**..........................(p) MarkQuinlan(7) 83
(Neil Mulholland) *mid-div: hdwy 7th: led appr 2 out: sn rdn: mstke and hdd last: kpt on but no ex* **16/1**

662- **3** *6* **Pete The Feat (IRE)**[25] 5055 6-11-2 **85**.......................... MattieBatchelor 86
(Anna Newton-Smith) *led tl 5th: chsd ldrs: ev ch 3 out: sn sltly outpcd: styd on again fr last: wnt 3rd nr fin* **10/1**

45P- **4** *nk* **Ease And Grace**[36] 4851 6-11-9 **92**.. JackDoyle 91
(Emma Lavelle) *chsd ldrs: hit 7th: ev ch 3 out: sn rdn: styd on same pce* **8/1**[3]

0F5- **5** *shd* **Ocean Du Moulin (FR)**[25] 5039 8-11-7 **90**........................(vt) DarylJacob 89
(Jamie Snowden) *in tch: nt fluent 7th: rdn after 3 out: styd on same pce fr next* **11/1**

F61- **6** *nk* **Pearly Star**[11] 5290 9-11-7 **95** 7ex..............................(b) MarcGoldstein(5) 94
(Jim Best) *chsd ldr: led 5th: rdn and hdd appr 2 out: styd on same pce: no ex whn lost 3rd towards fin* **5/1**[1]

4P0- **7** *1* **Free To Air**[12] 5258 7-10-10 **79**.....................................(v[1]) LeightonAspell 77
(Oliver Sherwood) *hld up towards rr: hdwy after 3 out: sn rdn: nvr threatened to get on terms: styd on same pce* **11/1**

1P5- **8** *9* **Osokenda**[38] 4798 10-11-5 **88**.. NickScholfield 80
(Jeremy Scott) *hld up towards rr: tk clsr order 5th: rdn after 7th: wknd 2 out* **9/1**

625- **9** *15* **Command Marshal (FR)**[13] 5229 7-11-9 **92**................ TomScudamore 75
(Michael Scudamore) *hld up bhd: hdwy 8th: sn rdn: nvr on terms w ldrs: wknd bef 2 out: t.o* **10/1**

0PU- **10** *21* **Fly Direct (IRE)**[99] 3572 7-11-12 **95**............................. ChristianWilliams 53
(Lawney Hill) *mid-div: rdn 6th: wknd bef 8th: t.o* **5/1**[1]

0P0- **11** *45* **Little Roxy (IRE)**[21] 5117 5-11-4 **87**..................................... FelixDeGiles —
(Anna Newton-Smith) *mid-div tl wknd after 8th: t.o* **33/1**

3/P- **P** **Migigi**[341] 439 10-10-8 **77**... SamThomas —
(Michael Roberts) *struggling 5th: a bhd: t.o whn p.u bef 7th* **50/1**

6P/- **P** **Major Upset (IRE)**[387] 4904 7-9-13 **75**...................... AnthonyFreeman(7) —
(John Upson) *mid-div: trcking ldrs whn lost action and p.u after 5th* **25/1**

5m 25.1s (-17.40) **Going Correction** -0.675s/f (Firm) **13** Ran SP% **118.2**
Speed ratings (Par 103): **103,101,99,99,99 99,99,95,90,83 —,—,—**
Tote Swingers: 1&2 £19.30, 1&3 £8.40, 2&3 £23.90 CSF £93.48 CT £950.43 TOTE £6.00: £1.80, £9.70, £3.70; EX 83.30.
Owner C R Dunning **Bred** Miss D Keegan & D Feeley **Trained** Wilsford-Cum-Lake, Wilts

FOCUS

A big field for this low-grade handicap hurdle in which a number were returning from absences.

NOTEBOOK

Alldunnandusted(IRE) had questions to answer regarding his ability to handle the ground. However, he seemed well suited by it, creeping into contention at the end of the back straight and then proving far too good for the runner-up after taking the lead at the final flight. There looks to be more to come with his rider expecting him to improve again. (op 8-1)

Play A Cord(IRE) was having her first start since October and ran well, although no match for the winner. However, she carried her head awkwardly under pressure and might not be the most straightforward. (op 33-1)

Pete The Feat(IRE) helped cut out the early pacemaking but looked in trouble leaving the back straight, only to rally in the closing stages and come out best in a blanket finish for third.

Ease And Grace, who was making her handicap debut on the fastest ground she has so far encountered, was never far away but could not pick up under pressure. (op 7-1 tchd 9-1)

Ocean Du Moulin(FR), who has fallen in the weights without producing much in the way of a revival, was also never far away but could not pick up under pressure. (op 16-1)

Pearly Star, penalised for a recent win at Plumpton, helped set the pace but, after being headed at the penultimate flight, was treading water and lost three places on the run-in. (op 11-2 tchd 6-1)

Fly Direct(IRE), making his first start for the yard, was backed earlier in the day but was in trouble a long way from home on ground that should have suited. (op 9-2)

85 NEILMULHOLLANDRACING.COM H'CAP CHASE (16 fncs) 2m 6f

7:40 (7:40) (Class 4) (0-115,113) 5-Y-0+ **£4,228** (£1,241; £620; £310)

Form RPR

662- **1** **Double The Trouble**[14] 5219 9-11-1 **102**.......................... NickScholfield 113+
(Andy Turnell) *trckd ldr: led 5th: hit 12th: rdn and hdd 3 out: hit next: edgd rt but led sn after last: styd on wl fnl 100yds: rdn out* **4/1**[2]

320- **2** *2 ¼* **Marc Of Brilliance (USA)**[15] 5195 7-11-2 **110**............. JoshuaMoore(7) 117
(Gary Moore) *hld up bhd ldng gp: nudged along and hdwy after 11th: rdn in cl 3rd 3 out: ev ch sn after last: kpt on but no ex* **7/1**

012- **3** *2 ¼* **Royal Kicks (FR)**[21] 5118 9-10-10 **104**.......................... JimmyDerham(7) 112+
(Suzy Smith) *travelled wl bhd ldrs: awkward 12th: rdn after 4 out: nvr quite ev ch fr next: styd on same pce: wnt 3rd nr fin* **9/4**[1]

320- **4** *nk* **Herewearagain (IRE)**[15] 5195 7-11-12 **113**.......................(b[1]) RhysFlint 118
(Philip Hobbs) *trckd ldr: led 3 out: sn rdn: rchd for last: hdd sn after: no ex fnl 100yds* **9/2**[3]

243- **5** *30* **Topless (IRE)**[39] 4791 9-11-1 **102**.................................(tp) DougieCostello 80
(Neil Mulholland) *chsd ldrs: hmpd 2nd: rdn after 11th: wknd appr 3 out: t.o* **6/1**

262- **6** *dist* **Cockatoo (USA)**[25] 5044 7-11-11 **112**..............................(b) JamieMoore —
(Gary Moore) *j.lft often: hld up bhd ldrs: in last pair fr 4th: effrt to cl 9th: wknd 12th: p.u bef 4 out* **10/1**

62P- **P** **The Jolly Spoofer (IRE)**[46] 4646 8-11-5 **109**..............(p) AlexMerriam(3) —
(Diana Grissell) *led tl 5th: chsd ldrs tl struggling 8th: t.o whn p.u bef 11th* **18/1**

5m 37.5s (-5.50) **Going Correction** -0.275s/f (Good) **7** Ran SP% **110.1**
Speed ratings: **99,98,97,97,86 —,—**
Tote Swingers: 1&2 £9.60, 1&3 £1.70, 2&3 £4.70. CSF £28.56 CT £71.20 TOTE £6.60: £2.60, £2.20; EX 34.40.
Owner Mrs M R Taylor **Bred** L G Kimber **Trained** Broad Hinton, Wilts

FOCUS

This modest handicap chase produced another close finish. The second is rated in line with his good recent run here.

NOTEBOOK

Double The Trouble had gained all his previous wins on stiff, right-handed tracks over shorter but put his stamina to good use over this longer trip. He made much of the running but hit five out and looked in trouble when headed at the first in the straight. He rallied well under pressure and the momentum gained by a quick jump at the last carried him to the front again. This is his ground. (op 7-2)

Marc Of Brilliance(USA) gained his last hurdles success here and ran well against more experienced chasers. He just could not hold the renewed effort of the winner. (op 8-1)

Royal Kicks(FR) was never far away but was rather keen under restraint and could not pick up in the closing stages. He did though confirm previous form with the fourth on 7lb worse terms. (op 11-4)

Herewearagain(IRE) was 7lb better off with today's third compared with their previous meeting and was wearing blinkers for the first time. He looked the most likely winner when going to the front at the last ditch but he had nothing in reserve when challenged on either side at the final fence, and was run out of the placings after the last. (tchd 4-1)

Topless(IRE), representing the stable that sponsored the race, found this an insufficient test. (tchd 11-2)

86 HARDINGS CATERING H'CAP HURDLE (9 hdls) 2m 2f 110y

8:10 (8:10) (Class 4) (0-115,115) 4-Y-0+ **£3,903** (£1,146; £573; £286)

Form RPR

5P0- **1** **Forget It**[14] 5213 5-11-2 **105**.. JamieMoore 113+
(Gary Moore) *cl up: wnt 3rd after 6th: rdn after 3 out: led next: hrd rdn run-in: jst hld on: all out* **5/2**[1]

350- **2** *nse* **Bolton Hall (IRE)**[202] 1694 8-10-13 **102**................................(tp) RhysFlint 109
(Keith Goldsworthy) *led: hit 6th: rdn and hdd 2 out: drifted rt but rallied wl run-in: jst failed* **6/1**

014- **3** *17* **Sonning Star (IRE)**[26] 5009 6-11-12 **115**......................(b) LiamTreadwell 107
(Nick Gifford) *w ldr: rdn and ev ch after 3 out: hld fr next: wknd bef last* **11/4**[2]

65U- **4** *33* **Rock Me (IRE)**[121] 2600 5-11-0 **103**............................(p) ChristianWilliams 65
(Lawney Hill) *trckd ldrs: rdn after 6th: sn wknd: t.o* **5/1**[3]

100- **5** *8* **Stratford Stroller (IRE)**[77] 4017 6-11-7 **110**.................(t) DougieCostello 65
(Jonjo O'Neill) *trckd ldrs: rdn after 3 out: sn wknd* **5/1**[3]

0/U- **6** *14* **White On Black (GER)**[50] 4539 9-11-2 **112**................ JimmyDerham(7) 54
(Steven Dixon) *a last: lost tch 6th: t.o* **12/1**

4m 20.2s (-14.10) **Going Correction** -0.675s/f (Firm) **6** Ran SP% **110.5**
Speed ratings (Par 105): **102,101,94,80,77 71**
Tote Swingers: 1&2 £6.30, 1&3 £3.00, 2&3 £5.30. CSF £16.74 CT £40.11 TOTE £3.10: £2.30, £2.40; EX 20.60 Place 6 £347.57, Place 5 £65.65..
Owner The Cockpit Crew **Bred** Mrs J Chandris **Trained** Lower Beeding, W Sussex
⊠ Stewards' Enquiry : Rhys Flint caution: used whip with excessive frequency.
Jamie Moore caution: used whip with excessive frequency.

FOCUS
The field for this modest contest was almost cut in half by withdrawals but it produced a desperate finish. The winner is rated back to something like his best.
NOTEBOOK
Forget It had been struggling in mainly better company following a promising start over hurdles early last year. He came through to lead at the second last but then did not find as much as looked likely, and in the end hung on by the skin of his teeth. He apparently came back with a superficial cut on his near fore which could be the reason; he has the size to make a chaser in time. (tchd 9-4)
Bolton Hall(IRE) stays further than this and had run well on both previous visits here. Having his first start since October, he made the running and then dug really deep under pressure and was unlucky to be beaten on the nod. He should be able to gain compensation if given time to get over this hard race. (op 11-2)
Sonning Star(IRE) back on a track where he has previously been successful, was tackling the quickest ground he has encountered over hurdles. He was never far away but had nothing more to offer when coming under pressure early in the straight. (tchd 3-1)
Rock Me(IRE) returning from a break following a spell over fences and with track and ground to suit, dropped away with a circuit to go.
Stratford Stroller(IRE) was quickly left behind from the last on the far side. (op 6-1)
T/Plt: £219.20 to a £1 stake. Pool: £80,856.58. 269.17 winning tickets. T/Qpdt: £21.80 to a £1 stake. Pool: £8,399.80. 285.07 winning tickets. TM

HEXHAM (L-H)
Saturday, May 1

OFFICIAL GOING: Good (good to firm in places; 7.7)
Wind: Breezy, half behind Weather: Overcast

87 NORTHUMBERLAND CLUBS FOR YOUNG PEOPLE (S) HURDLE (8 hdls) 2m 110y
5:50 (5:50) (Class 5) 4-Y-O+ **£2,055** (£599; £299)

Form RPR
011- **1** **Along The Nile**[22] 4810 8-11-8 120 (b) JamesReveley 122+
(Keith Reveley) *hld up in tch: stdy hdwy bef 2 out: led bef last: drvn clr run-in* **11/8**[1]
P16- **2** *8* **The Duke's Speech (IRE)**[188] 1913 9-11-0 0 GrahamLee 104
(Ferdy Murphy) *nt fluent on occasions: in tch: hdwy whn lft 2nd after 4th: ev ch 2 out to bef last: kpt on run-in: nt pce of wnr* **11/4**[2]
551- **3** *1 ½* **Prioryjo**[19] 5169 7-11-1 100 (p) WilsonRenwick 103
(Martin Todhunter) *in tch: lft 3rd after 4th: effrt bef last: one pce run-in* **7/1**
/05- **4** *1 ¾* **Wee Forbees (IRE)**[5] 21 8-10-11 115 MrOGreenall(3) 100
(Michael Easterby) *led tl rdn and hdd bef last: one pce run-in* **9/2**[3]
P04- **5** *6* **Woody Valentine (USA)**[7] 5388 9-11-5 112 AlexanderVoy(7) 107
(Evelyn Slack) *chsd ldrs: lost pl 4th: outpcd bef 2 out: rallied briefly between last 2: 5th and wkng whn hit last* **12/1**
300- **P** **Qaasi (USA)**[52] 4509 8-10-7 74 KyleJames(7) —
(Ian Brown) *pressed ldr tl p.u after 4th* **40/1**
4m 19.3s (1.90) **Going Correction** -0.025s/f (Good) **6** Ran SP% **109.6**
Speed ratings (Par 103): **94,90,89,88,85 —**
.The winner was bought in for 4,500gns. The Duke's Speech was claimed by Mrs S Leech for £6,000\n\x\x
Owner William Hoey **Bred** Lucayan Stud Ltd And Whatton Manor Stud **Trained** Lingdale, Redcar & Cleveland
FOCUS
Despite the numbers this was an interesting little seller.
NOTEBOOK
Along The Nile, held up early, travelled and jumped smoothly throughout and would take a lot of beating in similar company over the coming weeks. (op 6-5 tchd 11-10 and 6-4)
The Duke's Speech(IRE), who has a good record fresh, travelled well on his drop in grade for the first time, but was unable to quicken after the last. He has bled from the nose in the past, and possibly, not one to take a short price about. (op 4-1)
Prioryjo, rated 100, found this tougher than the race she won at Sedgefield. It looks like she ran to form here. (tchd 8-1)
Wee Forbees(IRE) was well held, just like he was at Towcester earlier in the week. His losing run on the racecourse stretches back over two years now. (op 6-1)
Woody Valentine(USA), back over hurdles, ran okay without really threatening to win. Rated 112, he might not be the easiest to place. (op 17-2 tchd 8-1)
Qaasi(USA) Official explanation: jockey said gelding lost its action but returned sound

88 IAN STRAKER MEMORIAL TROPHY (HANDICAP CHASE) (15 fncs) 2m 4f 110y
6:25 (6:25) (Class 4) (0-105,105) 5-Y-O+ **£5,204** (£1,528; £764; £381)

Form RPR
4F6- **1** **Baltic Pathfinder (IRE)**[25] 5073 6-11-6 99 HenryOliver 113+
(Sue Smith) *prom: hit 11th: rdn to ld bef 2 out: edgd lft and styd on wl u.p run-in* **10/1**
50F- **2** *1* **Emotive**[37] 4838 7-10-4 86 CampbellGillies(3) 97
(Barry Murtagh) *hld up: stdy hdwy bef 10th: effrt after 2 out: chsd wnr run-in: edgd rt: kpt on: hld nr fin* **25/1**
P54- **3** *2 ½* **Crow Spinney**[59] 4379 7-10-13 95 MrOGreenall(3) 104
(Michael Easterby) *hld up: mstke 3rd: hdwy and prom 11th: effrt and ch between last 2: one pce and lost 2nd run-in* **33/1**
F5U- **4** *6* **Ice Image (IRE)**[6] 9 8-10-10 89 JanFaltejsek 92
(George Charlton) *hld up: hdwy and in tch 6th: effrt bef 2 out: one pce last* **14/1**
644- **5** *7* **I'm Your Man**[12] 5271 11-10-11 97 (p) AlexanderVoy(7) 97
(Evelyn Slack) *led to 3rd: cl up: ev ch 10th to 3 out: wknd appr last* **7/1**[2]
053- **6** *8* **Smugglers Bay (IRE)**[15] 5202 6-11-6 99 (b) BrianHughes 89
(Tim Easterby) *hld up: rdn bef 3 out: no imp bef next* **7/1**[2]
/5F- **7** *¾* **Bardolet (IRE)**[12] 5272 7-10-11 90 JamesReveley 79
(Keith Reveley) *midfield: hit and lost pl 7th: rallied and in tch bef 3 out: wknd fr next* **13/2**[1]
120- **8** *½* **Manoubi**[19] 5167 11-10-9 88 GrahamLee 77
(Martin Todhunter) *hld up outside: hdwy and in tch 9th: drvn and outpcd after next: no imp bef 3 out* **15/2**[3]
446- **9** *10* **Crofton Arch**[6] 9 10-10-0 79 oh13 (p) PaddyAspell 59
(John Dixon) *midfield: hdwy and in tch 4 out: wknd fr next* **66/1**
131- **10** *1 ¼* **Duke Of Malfi**[37] 4838 7-11-7 100 (p) PeterBuchanan 79
(Lucinda Russell) *cl up: led bef 9th: hdd bef 2 out: wknd bef last* **15/2**[3]
02P- **11** *8* **It's A Roofer (IRE)**[182] 2007 10-11-8 101 RichieMcGrath 73
(Kate Walton) *in tch: lost pl bef 8th: n.d after* **14/1**
F0P- **12** *12* **Norminster**[12] 5271 9-10-5 89 (p) JamesHalliday(5) 50
(Rayson Nixon) *hld up: hdwy into midfield 7th: outpcd bef 10th: struggling fr 4 out* **40/1**
2P3- **P** **Tully Hill**[12] 5272 9-9-12 82 oh7 ow3 EwanWhillans(5) —
(Kevin Hunter) *cl up: led 3rd to bef 9th: struggling fr next: t.o whn p.u bef last* **16/1**
U60- **U** **Janal (IRE)**[19] 5167 7-10-0 79 oh11 KeithMercer —
(Stuart Coltherd) *trckd ldrs: hit and uns rdr 2nd* **33/1**
13- **F** **St Killian's Run (IRE)**[20] 5139 6-11-12 105 WilsonRenwick —
(P Monteith) *hld up: fell heavily 2nd* **7/1**[2]
5m 11.0s (-2.50) **Going Correction** +0.025s/f (Yiel) **15** Ran SP% **116.3**
Speed ratings: **105,104,103,101,98 95,95,95,91,90 87,83,—,—,—**
toteswingers:1&2:£80.40, 1&3:£105.40, 2&3:£131.80 CSF £231.78 CT £7660.64 TOTE £10.40: £4.20, £9.30, £8.60; EX 357.90.
Owner John Regan & John Conroy **Bred** Christopher Maye **Trained** High Eldwick, W Yorks
FOCUS
A wide-open 0-105 handicap chase, run at a sound pace.
NOTEBOOK
Baltic Pathfinder(IRE) lost his maiden tag at his fifth attempt over fences. He held every chance when he crashed out at Sedgefield on his penultimate start, but jumped better here and it didn't look like he was doing a lot when hitting the front. The six-year-old can win again for a yard among the winners. (tchd 11-1)
Emotive, up in trip ran well. This was only his third try over fences and can go one better on the evidence of this, that said, he doesn't have a great strike-rate. (op 20-1)
Crow Spinney, 8lb lower over fences, also ran with credit and this point-to-point winner can make her mark as well at some point.
Ice Image(IRE), a 21-race maiden, jumped better here and can also have his day in the sunshine, if able to build on this. (tchd 16-1)
Duke Of Malfi, in front three from home, clearly didn't stay and can be forgiven this below-par run. Official explanation: trainer had no explanation for the poor form shown (op 11-2 tchd 9-2)
St Killian's Run(IRE) got no further than the second fence.

89 ARUP H'CAP HURDLE (10 hdls) 2m 4f 110y
6:55 (6:55) (Class 3) (0-125,122) 4-Y-O+ **£6,179** (£1,814; £907; £453)

Form RPR
224- **1** **Cash Man (IRE)**[7] 5387 9-10-5 108 AlexanderVoy(7) 113
(Evelyn Slack) *cl up: led 3rd: mde rest: edgd lft and hld on gamely u.p fr last* **12/1**
/05- **2** *½* **Magical Legend**[16] 5196 9-11-12 122 (t) PaulMoloney 127
(Sophie Leech) *chsd ldrs: effrt after 2 out: rallied and ev ch run-in: edgd lft and hld nr fin* **8/1**
222- **3** *1 ¼* **Pontop (IRE)**[3] 45 7-11-10 120 JanFaltejsek 123
(George Charlton) *hld up: nt fluent and pushed along 4 out: hdwy between last 2: chsd ldrs run-in: no ex towards fin* **11/8**[1]
641- **4** *1 ¾* **Heavenly Chorus**[12] 5275 8-10-10 106 JamesReveley 108
(Keith Reveley) *hld up: nt fluent and outpcd 3 out: rallied bef last: one pce run-in* **10/1**
2F2- **5** *½* **Mini Minster**[12] 5275 8-10-8 104 GrahamLee 105
(Peter Atkinson) *cl up: effrt and ev ch 2 out: no ex run-in* **9/2**[2]
44U- **6** *10* **Night Force**[8] 5372 7-11-1 111 BrianHughes 105
(Howard Johnson) *hld up in tch: drvn after 3 out: wknd fr next* **7/1**[3]
116- **7** *1 ¼* **Mister Pete (IRE)**[26] 4731 7-10-4 100 (p) RichieMcGrath 91
(Chris Grant) *led to 3rd: cl up tl wknd fr 2 out* **14/1**
8 *62* **Cantrell (IRE)**[27] 5023 7-10-5 101 BarryKeniry 36
(H Smyth, Ire) *in tch tl wknd bef 2 out: t.o* **22/1**
5m 7.80s (-4.70) **Going Correction** -0.025s/f (Good) **8** Ran SP% **111.7**
Speed ratings (Par 107): **107,106,106,105,105 101,101,77**
toteswingers:1&2:£14.00, 1&3:£4.30, 2&3:£4.40 CSF £96.37 CT £213.32 TOTE £15.20: £3.10, £1.50, £1.10; EX 73.30.
Owner A Slack **Bred** John P Coughlan **Trained** Hilton, Cumbria
FOCUS
A 0-125 handicap hurdle with the top weight 3lb below the ceiling rating.
NOTEBOOK
Cash Man(IRE), back over hurdles off a 3lb lower mark than his recent chasing exploits, showed a willing attitude to last home. He has been successful on all sorts of ground and, as long as the handicapper doesn't overreact, he should continue to pay his way. (op 9-1 tchd 14-1)
Magical Legend has only had a few runs for current connections. She has dropped down to a winning mark and can go one better shortly. (op 5-1)
Pontop(IRE) was placed yet again. Runner-up only three days earlier, he didn't travel as well here but came home well. He deserves to get his head in front again. (op 7-4 tchd 5-4)
Heavenly Chorus appeared to run bang up to form. (op 8-1)
Mini Minster again ran her race. (op 11-2 tchd 6-1)
Mister Pete(IRE) was racing here off 10lb higher than his last Newcastle success, which came on much softer ground, and he struggled. (op 12-1)

90 THOMPSON PRUDHOE HEART OF ALL ENGLAND MAIDEN HUNTERS' CHASE (19 fncs) 3m 1f
7:30 (7:30) (Class 4) 5-Y-O+ **£3,123** (£968; £484; £242)

Form RPR
5- **1** **Special Portrait (IRE)**[6] 6-11-7 0 (t) MrWKinsey(7) 106
(Mark Hughes) *hld up in tch: stdy hdwy 1/2-way: effrt and led last: drvn out run-in* **20/1**
2 *hd* **Poppy Day**[20] 7-11-0 0 MissJoannaMason(7) 99
(I M Mason) *prom: effrt after 2 out: ev ch last: kpt on run-in: hld nr fin* **13/8**[1]
43F- **3** *11* **Father Murtagh (IRE)**[20] 10-11-7 90 (v[1]) MrsFreyaBrewer(7) 97
(Mrs Freya Brewer) *t.k.h: cl up: led after 2 out to last: wknd run-in* **20/1**
3P4- **4** *4 ½* **Ardnaclancy (IRE)**[40] 4784 7-11-7 0 MrJARichardson(7) 94
(Andrew Richardson) *mstkes: hld up on outside: outpcd 1/2-way: plugged on fr 2 out: nvr rchd ldrs* **8/1**[3]
3/2- **5** *2 ¼* **Athoss**[13] 8-11-7 0 MrRMSmith(7) 90
(Robert Smith) *hld up in tch: hdwy 12th: effrt on outside after 2 out: wknd appr last* **28/1**
/40- **6** *hd* **Buckstruther (IRE)**[13] 8-11-7 84 MrMEnnis(7) 90
(Alistair Bell) *mstkes: prom: hit and lost pl 7th: struggling 14th: styd on fr 2 out: no imp* **5/2**[2]
/FF- **7** *3* **Gun Smith**[11] 5297 8-11-7 0 HenryBrooke(7) 87
(Nick Kent) *nt jump wl: bhd: hdwy u.p bef 3 out: no imp fr next* **18/1**
643- **8** *10* **Cherryland**[34] 4908 7-11-7 97 NathanMoscrop(7) 78
(Philip Kirby) *led to 3rd: led 6th to 10th: led 4 out to 2 out: wknd bef last* **10/1**
U4P- **9** *29* **Silk Parasol (IRE)**[28] 4985 8-11-0 71 MrJBewley(7) 45
(Alan J Brown) *hld up: outpcd after 4 out: btn next* **40/1**
3F3- **10** *56* **Know The Ropes (IRE)**[28] 4985 10-11-7 67 (v) CallumWhillans(7) —
(Mrs L A Coltherd) *t.k.h: cl up: led 12th to 4 out: rallied: wknd after 2 out* **50/1**
0PP/ **P** **Harwood Dale**[13] 10-11-11 0 (v[1]) MrGBrewer(3) —
(Mrs Freya Brewer) *cl up: led 3rd to 6th: led 10th to 12th: wknd after next: t.o whn p.u bef 15th* **33/1**

P/ **P** **Thatsthereasonwhy (IRE)**[13] 9-11-7 0 MrJohnDawson(7) —
(Ms Lucinda Broad) *in tch: outpcd after 4 out: btn whn blnd next: sn p.u* **100/1**

P **Dystonia's Revenge (IRE)**[13] 5-11-7 0 MissCWalton(7) —
(Mrs Sheena Walton) *bhd: lost tch 7th: p.u bef last* **25/1**

6m 33.5s (1.30) **Going Correction** +0.025s/f (Yiel) **13** Ran SP% **117.3**
Speed ratings: **98,97,94,92,92 92,91,88,78,60 —,—,—**
toteswingers:1&2:£4.40, 1&3:£19.20, 2&3:£14.10 CSF £51.39 TOTE £24.50: £4.70, £1.30, £6.20; EX 30.50.
Owner Mark Hughes **Bred Trained** Wigton, Cumbria
■ The first winner under rules for Mark Hughes.

FOCUS
A prestigious and long-established prize, but at the end of the day a low-grade maiden hunter chase run a decent pace and what the form is worth is questionable. The first two pulled clear.

NOTEBOOK
Special Portrait(IRE) had being doing well in the point-to-point field and he jumped well throughout. He's only a six-year-old so there could still be more to come.
Poppy Day came here with five successive pointing wins behind her, including the prestigious Grimthorpe Gold Cup over 4m1f latest. On her hunter chase debut, she had every chance at the last and went down fighting. She should remain competitive in similar contests. (op 6-4 tchd 11-8)
Father Murtagh(IRE) ran well in his first-time visor. (op 25-1)
Ardnaclancy(IRE) stayed on well after racing very wide throughout. (op 11-1)
Gun Smith, a faller on his last two starts, would have been closer but yet again the fences got in the way at certain stages. (op 16-1)

91 PETER BEAUMONT HAPPY RETIREMENT NOVICES' CHASE (15 fncs) 2m 4f 110y
8:00 (8:02) (Class 4) 5-Y-0+ **£3,903** (£1,146; £573; £286)

Form RPR
/22- **1** **Logans Run (IRE)**[41] 4753 7-10-12 119 BrianHughes 121
(Howard Johnson) *chsd ldr: rdn to ld after 2 out: hld on wl u.p run-in* **5/4**[1]
100- **2** *1* **Diavoleria**[16] 5196 7-10-2 0 MrOGreenall(3) 113
(Michael Easterby) *hld up in tch: stdy hdwy and cl up bef 3 out: effrt next: chsd wnr run-in: r.o* **6/4**[2]
2F4- **3** *1 ¼* **Blue Shark (FR)**[60] 4369 8-10-12 120 GrahamLee 119
(Malcolm Jefferson) *led to after 2 out: sn drvn: rallied: one pce run-in* **7/1**[3]
P2P- **4** *86* **Charming Knight (IRE)**[40] 4784 9-10-5 90 AlistairFindlay(7) 42
(Jane Walton) *trckd ldrs tl wknd fr 4 out: virtually p.u run-in* **28/1**
046- **P** **Grand Award**[36] 4867 5-10-12 0 LeightonAspell —
(Don Cantillon) *in tch: blnd 10th: sn outpcd: t.o whn p.u bef 3 out* **11/1**

5m 13.8s (0.30) **Going Correction** +0.025s/f (Yiel) **5** Ran SP% **108.7**
Speed ratings: **100,99,99,66,—**
CSF £3.56 TOTE £2.10: £1.10, £1.10; EX 3.90.
Owner Andrea & Graham Wylie **Bred** Dunmanway Breeding Club **Trained** Billy Row, Co Durham
■ Stewards' Enquiry : Brian Hughes two-day ban: used whip with excessive frequency (May 15-16)

FOCUS
The first three in the betting dominated the finish.

NOTEBOOK
Logans Run(IRE) got off the mark over fences at the sixth attempt. Appearing not to do a lot when hitting the front, he hasn't many miles on the clock this season and should be able to win again under a penalty. (op 10-11)
Diavoleria, rated 118 over hurdles, ran well on her chasing debut. Jumping well throughout, she can go one better at this time of year. (op 15-8 tchd 5-4)
Blue Shark(FR), having his fifth start over fences, had every chance at the last. Coming from a yard among the winners, his mark off 120 would appear to flatter him. (op 11-1)
Charming Knight(IRE) may find life easier in low-grade handicaps. (op 33-1)
Grand Award struggled and was eventually pulled up. (tchd 10-1 and 12-1)

92 DAVE (DC) COLLINS MEMORIAL NOVICES' HURDLE (12 hdls) 3m
8:30 (8:30) (Class 4) 4-Y-0+ **£3,425** (£998; £499)

Form RPR
1- **1** **Thyne For Deploy (IRE)**[6] 8 6-10-13 109 APHeskin(7) 122+
(Michael Hourigan, Ire) *led to 2nd: trckd ldrs: led 2 out: styd on strly to go clr run-in* **11/10**[1]
/24- **2** *7* **Inner Steel (IRE)**[33] 4932 5-10-13 0 LeightonAspell 109
(Don Cantillon) *plld hrd: prom: hdwy and ev ch 2 out to bef last: kpt on same pce run-in* **11/2**[3]
231- **3** *18* **Grand Zouki (FR)**[20] 5156 5-11-6 119 BarryKeniry 99
(George Moore) *cl up: hdwy and led briefly bef 2 out: wknd bef last* **15/8**[2]
63F- **4** *6* **Little Wizard (IRE)**[162] 2407 8-10-6 0 AlistairFindlay(7) 89
(George Charlton) *mstkes: cl up: led 5th to 7th: drvn and outpcd bef 2 out: n.d after* **12/1**
300- **5** *12* **Sambelucky (IRE)**[12] 5273 5-10-13 0 JamesReveley 78
(Keith Reveley) *in tch: outpcd after 3 out: shortlived effrt after next: sn btn* **22/1**
/PP- **6** *16* **Birnies Boy**[25] 5076 6-10-13 0 RichieMcGrath 62
(Brian Storey) *t.k.h: led 2nd: hit next: hdd 5th: led 7th to bef 2 out: sn struggling* **100/1**
0/0- **7** *5* **Flapjack Crumbly**[20] 5146 7-10-13 0 HenryOliver 57
(Sue Smith) *in tch: blnd 8th: wknd fr 3 out* **40/1**
0- **8** *134* **Betty's Run**[144] 2762 8-10-6 0 PaddyAspell —
(Lynn Siddall) *nt fluent: hld up: struggling 1/2-way: t.o fr 3 out* **125/1**
0F0- **P** **Snap Decision**[12] 5273 8-10-1 0 (p) JamesHalliday(5) —
(Rayson Nixon) *hld up: struggling 8th: t.o whn p.u bef 2 out* **100/1**
P- **P** **Mujada**[19] 5166 5-10-3 0 MrOGreenall(3) —
(Michael Easterby) *bhd: drvn and outpcd 1/2-way: struggling 8th: t.o whn p.u bef 2 out* **200/1**

6m 9.30s (-3.90) **Going Correction** -0.025s/f (Good) **10** Ran SP% **115.5**
Speed ratings (Par 105): **105,102,96,94,90 85,83,50,—,—**
toteswingers:1&2:£4.50, 1&3:£1.50, 2&3:£3.80 CSF £7.80 TOTE £2.20: £1.10, £1.20, £1.20; EX 9.60 Place 6 £46.64; Place 5 £38.44.
Owner Miss M M Hourigan **Bred** Cecil Ashe **Trained** Patrickswell, Co Limerick

FOCUS
A 3m novice hurdle lacking strength in depth, the early pace was steady.

NOTEBOOK
Thyne For Deploy(IRE) ran out an impressive winner. Also a winner last Sunday at Wetherby, this was only his fifth start and has got the size and scope to jump fences in due course. (op 5-4)
Inner Steel(IRE) ran a solid race on his first try over hurdles. Time might prove he ran into an above-average winner and his shrewd trainer should have little problem placing him to go one better at this time of year. (op 9-2)
Grand Zouki(FR) proved a little disappointing. A good second at Musselburgh earlier in the year, it might prove he's better on a flat track. His mark off 119 looks harsh on the evidence of this. (op 2-1)
Little Wizard(IRE) showed up well enough for a while and will find life easier in modest handicaps. (op 14-1 tchd 16-1)

T/Plt: £60.40 to a £1 stake. Pool: £55,995.64. 675.84 winning tickets. T/Qpdt: £2.80 to a £1 stake. Pool: £6,017.14. 1,572.67 winning tickets. RY

UTTOXETER (L-H)
Saturday, May 1

OFFICIAL GOING: Chase course - soft; hurdle course - good to soft (good places in straight) (chs 5.8, hdl 7.3)
Penultimate fence omitted in all chases; Final hurdle in the back straight omitted in all hurdle races.
Wind: virtually nil Weather: overcast

93 TOTEPLACEPOT MAIDEN HURDLE (DIV I) (9 hdls 1 omitted) 2m
1:35 (1:35) (Class 5) 4-Y-0+ **£1,626** (£477; £238; £119)

Form RPR
01- **1** **Total Submission**[20] 5158 5-11-0 0 WarrenMarston 109+
(Martin Keighley) *chsd ldrs: wnt 2nd after 4th: wnt clr w ldr after 6th: rdn to ld wl bef 3 out: j.big 3 out: kpt on u.p flat* **3/1**[1]
0- **2** *1 ¼* **Blue Monster (IRE)**[56] 4452 6-11-0 0 APMcCoy 108
(Nicky Henderson) *midfield: bdly bmpd by rival 3rd: niggled along after 4th: 7th and outpcd after 6th: stl modest 6th 2 out: styd on to chse wnr sn after last: kpt on: nvr quite getting to wnr* **3/1**[1]
64- **3** *6* **Flicka's Witness (IRE)**[81] 3957 5-11-0 0 JasonMaguire 103+
(Donald McCain) *t.k.h: in tch: j. bdly lft and bmpd rival 3rd: chsd ldng pair and rdn after 6th: wnt 2nd after 3 out: no imp between last 2: btn whn hit last* **13/2**[3]
0/4- **4** *1 ¼* **The Grifter**[35] 4891 8-11-0 0 AndrewGlassonbury 102
(John Ryall) *j. bdly rt thrght: chsd ldr tl after 4th: outpcd after 6th: rallied u.p bef 2 out: kpt on flat* **5/1**[2]
5- **5** *1 ½* **Sphere (IRE)**[149] 2664 5-10-7 0 AndrewTinkler 93
(John Mackie) *hld up towards rr: hdwy to chse ldng trio after 6th: wnt 3rd and hit 3 out: no prog after* **15/2**
4- **6** *6* **Jobekani (IRE)**[9] 5340 4-10-7 0 DerekLaverty(3) 91
(Lisa Williamson) *midfield whn blnd 1st: towards rr after: mstke 4th: rdn and lost tch after 6th: kpt on again between last 2: no threat to ldrs* **33/1**
600- **7** *shd* **Overyou**[16] 5200 5-10-7 0 JohnnyFarrelly 86
(Elliott Cooper) *wl bhd: sme hdwy 6th: sn lost tch w ldrs: plugged on steadily u.p fr 3 out: nvr trbld ldrs* **100/1**
2F- **8** *hd* **Strictly Business**[35] 4894 5-11-0 0 PaddyBrennan 93
(Tom George) *nt a fluent: led: wnt clr w wnr after 6th: rdn and hdd wl bef next: lost 2nd after 3 out: 4th and wkng whn mstke next* **10/1**
4- **9** *4* **Mr Chippy (IRE)**[31] 4959 6-11-0 0 DougieCostello 89
(Ian Williams) *a towards rr: rdn and struggling after 6th: n.d* **14/1**
60- **10** *29* **Knottage Hill (IRE)**[9] 5340 5-11-0 0 AidanColeman 63
(Reg Hollinshead) *t.k.h: chsd ldrs tl 5th: lost pl u.p next: t.o 2 out* **100/1**
11 *6* **Ruby Delta**[448] 5-11-0 0 CharliePoste 58
(Alan Juckes) *j. novicey: midfield whn j.rt and pckd 1st: j. slowly next: dropped to rr 5th: lost tch after next: t.o* **66/1**

3m 56.5s (1.30) **Going Correction** -0.175s/f (Good)
WFA 4 from 5yo+ 18lb **11** Ran SP% **113.9**
Speed ratings (Par 103): **89,88,85,84,84 81,80,80,78,64 61**
toteswingers:1&2:£2.60, 1&3:£5.00, 2&3:£5.60 CSF £11.26 TOTE £4.20: £1.50, £1.70, £2.00; EX 12.30.
Owner Mrs Louise Jones **Bred** S Hadley **Trained** Condicote, Gloucs

FOCUS
The weaker-looking of the two divisions and run in a slightly slower time.

NOTEBOOK
Total Submission, making his hurdling debut, beat a subsequent bumper winner on his previous outing and shaped like a stayer in this under a positive ride. The trainer reported afterwards that his horse will have a summer break and come back for races over further in the autumn.
Blue Monster(IRE) was easily beaten on his British debut in a bumper at Newbury, after returning from a long absence, and looked like being thrashed again at halfway, but McCoy kept pushing away and in the end the pair were catching Total Submission as the winning line approached. (op 10-3 tchd 7-2 and 4-1 in places)
Flicka's Witness(IRE) made a satisfactory debut over hurdles and seems sure to find a race if kept on the go during the summer. (op 10-1)
The Grifter ■ showed ability on his return to action last time (his first outing over hurdles) but gave himself no chance of taking this by jumping wildly out to his right. If he had kept straight at the hurdles, he possibly would have won. (op 9-2)
Sphere(IRE) ■ again hinted at having enough ability to win a race over Jumps, but might be one for handicaps. (op 7-1)
Strictly Business cut out a lot of the running but weakened in the home straight. (op 8-1)

94 TOTESWINGER BETTING H'CAP HURDLE (11 hdls 1 omitted) 2m 4f 110y
2:05 (2:05) (Class 2) 4-Y-0+ **£15,208** (£4,492; £2,246; £1,123; £561)

Form RPR
114- **1** **Bella Haze**[16] 5196 8-10-13 139 MrDGPrichard(7) 146+
(Phillip Dando) *chsd ldng pair tl led 7th: pushed clr 3 out: in command fr next: rdn out* **12/1**
403- **2** *8* **Tobago Bay**[39] 4802 5-10-10 129 (p) JamieGoldstein 129
(Sheena West) *chsd ldr tl 7th: rdn and chsd wnr bef 3 out: kpt on same pce and no imp after 3 out* **16/1**
630- **3** *3* **Afsoun (FR)**[23] 5099 8-11-12 145 AndrewTinkler 142
(Nicky Henderson) *led tl 7th: 3rd and drvn bef 3 out: plugged on u.p but no threat to wnr fr 2 out* **25/1**
10F- **4** *¾* **Busker Royal**[13] 5248 7-9-13 125 DavidBass(7) 123
(Nicky Henderson) *in tch: mstke 2nd: chsd ldrs and drvn bef 3 out: no imp: btn whn hit 2 out* **5/1**[2]
111- **5** *¾* **Federstar (GER)**[15] 5203 8-10-13 132 CharliePoste 130
(Milton Harris) *chsd ldrs: mstke 5th: rdn wl bef 3 out: one pce and no ch w wnr fr 3 out* **14/1**
0F5- **6** *4 ½* **Frontier Dancer (IRE)**[14] 5222 6-10-13 132 PaddyBrennan 125
(Nigel Twiston-Davies) *in tch in midfield: drvn after 6th: no prog u.p bef 3 out: wl btn 2 out* **8/1**
10U- **7** *6* **Shadow Dancer (IRE)**[15] 5201 5-10-7 126 APMcCoy 113
(Jonjo O'Neill) *hld up in rr early: pogess 5th: chsd ldrs and reminders after 7th: wknd bef 2 out* **11/4**[1]
101- **8** *17* **Sir Harry Ormesher**[23] 5099 7-11-12 145 RobertThornton 116
(Alan King) *in tch towards rr: hdwy 6th: drvn and struggling after 7th: wl btn next: eased after last: t.o* **11/2**[3]
14P- **9** *2 ½* **Raslan**[16] 5197 7-11-4 137 (tp) TimmyMurphy 106
(David Pipe) *hld up in last: reminders after 4th: hmpd 5th and detached last bef next: lost tch after 6th: t.o bef 3 out* **25/1**

223- **10** *5* **Arkose (IRE)**[56] 4450 6-10-9 **128** LeightonAspell 92
(Oliver Sherwood) *in tch towards rr: rdn and btn after 7th: t.o 3 out: eased after last* **20/1**

400- **11** *3 ½* **Chief Yeoman**[22] 5113 10-10-13 **132** AidanColeman 93
(Venetia Williams) *in tch towards rr: rdn and struggling after 6th: t.o bef 3 out: eased after last* **25/1**

532- **12** *15* **Persian Run (IRE)**[13] 5256 6-10-8 **127** JoeTizzard 75
(Colin Tizzard) *chsd ldrs: lost pl u.p after 6th: t.o bef 3 out: eased after last* **14/1**

600- **U** **Nampour (FR)**[21] 5128 5-10-10 **134** GilesHawkins(5) —
(Philip Hobbs) *hld up in tch towards rr tl stmbld and uns rdr 5th* **16/1**

4m 55.3s (-8.70) **Going Correction** -0.175s/f (Good) **13** Ran SP% **118.9**
Speed ratings (Par 109): **109,105,104,104,104 102,100,93,92,90 89,83,—**
toteswingers:1&2:£70.70, 1&3:£10.40, 2&3:£58.90 CSF £173.78 CT £4600.45 TOTE £16.10: £4.10, £4.50, £7.10; EX 175.70.

Owner P Dando **Bred** Phillip C And Mrs Kathryn M Dando **Trained** Peterston-Super-Ely, S Glamorg

FOCUS
The pace seemed good as the field charged off, and the front three grabbed something of an advantage. It looked likely that they had set the race up for the remainder, but they all responded to pressure and took all three places.

NOTEBOOK
Bella Haze, the only mare in the field, is a credit to her connections and pulled out another outstanding performance. Recording her fifth win of the year off a 29lb higher mark than the first of those victories in February, she was value for a bit more than the winning margin. If the rain comes and the going is on the easy side, she may head to the Swinton Hurdle, but if it remains on the quick side she will either be put away for later in the year or be covered by a stallion. (op 10-1)

Tobago Bay, wearing cheekpieces for the first time, likes to be handy, so was always close to the pace. He was ridden along rounding the home bend but never stopped trying all the way to the line. The handicapper still has him about right but that is not to say he cannot win a handicap at a slightly lower level soon. (op 14-1)

Afsoun(FR) was not the most fancied of the Henderson pair but was another to keep going all the way to the finish. If the handicapper leaves him alone after dropping him 5lb, he may be able to win a handicap this summer if kept on the go.

Busker Royal had every chance off his light weight but his jumping was not always the most fluent when it needed to be. (op 6-1)

Federstar(GER), chasing a fourth successive victory, was 12lb than last time and that appeared to tell in the latter stages. (op 12-1)

Frontier Dancer(IRE) got pushed along early but stayed on down the home straight, without suggesting he is about to win. (op 15-2 tchd 7-1 and 9-1)

Shadow Dancer(IRE) took some stoking along to get into a challenging position and then found little once asked to quicken again. His record suggests that a right-handed course might be best for him. He seemed to edge left under pressure here. (op 7-2)

Sir Harry Ormesher was mounted on the course and ran disappointingly for no obvious reason. His victory at Aintree possibly took a lot out of him. (op 6-1 tchd 13-2)

Arkose(IRE) making his handicap debut, can be given another chance in less-demanding company. (op 16-1)

95 TOTEEXACTA BETTING H'CAP CHASE (14 fncs 2 omitted) 2m 5f
2:40 (2:40) (Class 5) (0-90,90) 5-Y-O+ **£2,602** (£764; £382; £190)

Form RPR

P21- **1** **Gunship (IRE)**[21] 5133 9-10-13 **84** (b) JimmyDerham(7) 102+
(Cathy Hamilton) *led 2nd: mde rest: drew wl clr fr 3 out: easily* **7/1**

542- **2** *21* **Bertenbar**[26] 5049 6-11-1 **79** SamThomas 75
(Henrietta Knight) *chsd ldrs: chsd wnr 10th: rdn wl bef 3 out: no ch w wnr fr 3 out* **7/2**[2]

652- **3** *1* **Pistol Basc (FR)**[6] 9 6-11-4 **89** PaulGallagher(7) 84
(Ferdy Murphy) *hld up in rr: hdwy into midfield 6th: rdn 8th: chsd ldng pair after 10th: hrd drvn and wl btn bef 3 out* **10/3**[1]

3PP- **4** *32* **Extra Smooth**[70] 4172 9-11-12 **90** TomMessenger 53
(Chris Bealby) *chsd ldrs: rdn and struggling after 10th: 4th and t.o bef 3 out* **16/1**

U24- **5** *2 ½* **Rash Moment (FR)**[20] 5151 11-11-8 **86** (p) TomScudamore 47
(Michael Scudamore) *towards rr: sme hdwy into midfield: 7th: no prog and u.p whn j. slowly 8th: t.o wl bef 3 out* **8/1**

00U- **6** *3* **Final Bid (IRE)**[22] 5116 7-10-12 **81** MrGBarfoot-Saunt(5) 39
(Tracey Barfoot-Saunt) *a bhd: reminders and no rspnse 4th: lost tch u.p 7th: wl t.o 10th: plugged on* **40/1**

54P- **P** **Major Euro (IRE)**[31] 4964 13-10-12 **76** LiamTreadwell —
(S J Gilmore) *alway bhd: rdn and lost tch after 7th: t.o whn p.u 10th* **25/1**

1/2- **P** **Ossmann (IRE)**[328] 632 10-11-10 **88** PaddyBrennan —
(Tom George) *led tl 2nd: chsd wnr after: rdn 8th: lost 2nd 10th: fdd rapidly and p.u next* **11/2**[3]

0/5- **P** **Doubly Sharp (USA)**[350] 333 7-11-7 **85** AndrewThornton —
(Caroline Bailey) *a bhd: mstke 1st: lost tch u.p after 7th: t.o and p.u 10th* **16/1**

P **De Danu (IRE)**[45] 4696 7-11-0 **78** JohnnyFarrelly —
(Aidan Anthony Howard, Ire) *t.k.h: hld up in tch: rdn and struggling after 8th: losing tch whn p.u 11th* **12/1**

006- **P** **Saddlers Mount (IRE)**[20] 5152 6-10-8 **77** (v[1]) DeanColeman(5) —
(J Jay) *in tch but nvr gng wl: j. slowly 1st: reminders 4th: lost pl and rdn 6th: lost tch 8th: wl bhd whn p.u 10th* **20/1**

5m 25.0s (1.50) **Going Correction** +0.10s/f (Yiel) **11** Ran SP% **114.8**
Speed ratings: **101,93,92,80,79 78,—,—,—,— —**
toteswingers:1&2:£4.60, 1&3:£5.10, 2&3:£2.70 CSF £31.25 CT £96.94 TOTE £7.50: £1.90, £2.00, £1.80; EX 33.80.

Owner M W Hoskins **Bred** Thomas Abbey **Trained** Kington Magna, Dorset

FOCUS
A one-horse affair from an early stage. This is weak form.

NOTEBOOK
Gunship(IRE) easily gained the lead he so enjoys. His rivals appeared to ignore him out in front and were then unable to close him down. Stamina was never going to be a problem to this three-time 3m winner, and he will need to be turned out quickly before the handicapper can get his hands on him. (op 13-2)

Bertenbar travelled strongly on the bridle but found little off it. (op 5-1)

Pistol Basc(FR) eventually got into contention after being held up but was never going to play a part in the finish. (op 7-2)

Extra Smooth deserves a mention for travelling nicely, albeit well off the pace, for much of the race. (op 12-1)

Major Euro(IRE) Official explanation: jockey said gelding lost a shoe

Ossmann(IRE) Official explanation: jockey said gelding never travelled

96 TOTETRIFECTA BETTING H'CAP HURDLE (9 hdls 1 omitted) 2m
3:15 (3:16) (Class 3) (0-125,119) 4-Y-0 **£6,337** (£1,872; £936; £468; £234)

Form RPR

605- **1** **Dishdasha (IRE)**[15] 5213 8-11-8 **115** (t) SeamusDurack 123+
(Alison Thorpe) *t.k.h: hld up in tch towards rr: hdwy 5th: chsd ldr 3 out: led next: rdn clr last: r.o wl: comf* **13/2**

350- **2** *2 ½* **Spare Me**[27] 5015 7-9-13 **99** JimmyDerham(7) 104
(Milton Harris) *chsd ldr tl 3rd: lost pl but stl in tch in midfield whn j.lft 5th: rdn bef 3 out: kpt on u.p fr next: styd on flat to go 2nd towards fin: nvr gng pce to chal wnr* **25/1**

603- **3** *1* **Numide (FR)**[28] 4986 7-11-12 **119** (be) JamieMoore 123
(Gary Moore) *hld up in tch in rr: hdwy wl bef 3 out: chsd ldng pair 3 out: chsd wnr bef last: no imp and one pce flat: lost 2nd towards fin* **5/1**[2]

F53- **4** *1 ½* **Celticello (IRE)**[39] 4810 8-11-3 **110** TomO'Brien 113
(Michael Quinlan) *in tch in midfield: rdn and unable qck wl bef 3 out: rallied u.p bef 2 out: kpt on u.p flat: unable to rch ldrs* **14/1**

505- **5** *3* **Ffos Las Diamond (IRE)**[54] 4486 6-11-11 **118** APMcCoy 119
(Nicky Henderson) *chsd ldrs: wnt 2nd 3rd: led next: rdn and blnd 3 out: hdd next: wknd after 2 out and btn whn nt fluent last* **9/4**[1]

F50- **6** *nse* **Marino Prince (FR)**[13] 5255 5-10-0 **93** DougieCostello 93
(Barry Leavy) *t.k.h: chsd ldrs: rdn and unable qck bef 3 out: wknd between last 2* **14/1**

420- **7** *14* **Elaala (USA)**[13] 5253 8-11-6 **116** DannyCook(3) 104
(Barry Leavy) *hld up in tch in rr: rdn and wknd bef 3 out: wl btn 2 out* **20/1**

030- **8** *4* **Wizard Of Us**[47] 4656 10-10-2 **95** (p) RodiGreene 79
(Michael Mullineaux) *led tl 4th: chsd ldr after: rdn after 6th: wknd u.p 3 out: wl btn whn nt fluent last* **22/1**

641- **9** *3 ½* **I'm In The Pink (FR)**[13] 5255 6-11-11 **118** ChristianWilliams 99
(David Evans) *t.k.h: hld up in tch in midfield: effrt and n.m.r bnd bef 3 out: sn rdn: wknd bef 2 out* **11/2**[3]

350- **10** *9* **Danny Zuko (IRE)**[160] 2444 7-11-2 **109** JasonMaguire 82
(Donald McCain) *in tch in rr: pushed along after 5th: rdn and lost tch bef 3 out* **7/1**

3m 52.1s (-3.10) **Going Correction** -0.175s/f (Good)
WFA 4 from 5yo+ 18lb **10** Ran SP% **114.9**
Speed ratings (Par 107): **100,98,98,97,96 95,88,86,85,80**
toteswingers:1&2:£19.40, 1&3:£8.90, 2&3:£21.50 CSF £148.29 CT £876.57 TOTE £8.70: £2.40, £5.80, £2.20; EX 194.90 TRIFECTA Not won..

Owner Tristar **Bred** Locsot Srl **Trained** Bronwydd Arms, Carmarthens

FOCUS
An even pace was set but plenty of these could be seen taking a grip in behind.

NOTEBOOK
Dishdasha(IRE), who shaped respectably on his return from a break at Cheltenham last time, forged clear once asked to quicken from about two out. It was a fine performance but he is not be the most reliable of horses to be backing next time. (op 9-2)

Spare Me was another to move well under restraint before staying on after the last. This was a big improvement on what he did on his previous outing. (op 16-1)

Numide(FR) is not looking the easiest ride nowadays. Held up towards the rear, he made up ground during the race and had a clear shot down the home straight. However, he did not pick up that strongly and made no impact after the final hurdle. (op 11-2 tchd 6-1)

Celticello(IRE), beaten in a claimer on his previous start, went strongly for a long way and was not disgraced, but his proximity limits the form. (op 11-1 tchd 10-1)

Ffos Las Diamond(IRE), who was back with Nicky Henderson after leaving his care for a few runs, helped to set a fair pace, but a few in behind him travelled nicely. He was readily left behind when under pressure. (op 9-2 tchd 2-1)

I'm In The Pink(FR), raised 9lb for his Stratford success, pulled hard and was making an effort when getting short of room on the bend. The jockey was not hard on his mount once their chance was gone. (op 5-1)

97 TOTEPLACEPOT MAIDEN HURDLE (DIV II) (9 hdls 1 omitted) 2m
3:50 (3:50) (Class 5) 4-Y-0+ **£1,626** (£477; £238; £119)

Form RPR

232- **1** **Lion On The Prowl (IRE)**[26] 5050 6-11-0 0 (t) JasonMaguire 110+
(Kim Bailey) *t.k.h: chsd ldrs: led 3 out: sn drvn clr: nt fluent 2 out: j.lft last: styd on wl* **4/1**[3]

3- **2** *3 ¾* **Hilfiger (GER)**[26] 5048 5-11-0 0 RobertThornton 106+
(Ian Williams) *plld hrd: hld up wl in tch: rdn and effrt 3 out: disp 2nd and mstke 2 out: chsd wnr bef last: kpt on same pce u.p flat* **10/3**[2]

3- **3** *1 ¾* **Zakatal**[58] 4399 4-10-10 0 (t) RichardJohnson 100
(Philip Hobbs) *trckd ldrs: pushed along briefly after 5th: n.m.r bnd bef 3 out: rdn to chal and blnd 3 out: nt qckn w wnr bef next: one pce fr 2 out* **11/8**[1]

4 *2 ¾* **Hypnotic Gaze (IRE)**[36] 4-10-10 0 AndrewTinkler 97
(John Mackie) *t.k.h: hld up in tch in rr: hdwy to trck ldrs after 6th: hmpd and mstke 3 out: kpt on same pce fr next* **40/1**

05P- **5** *8* **Milandale (IRE)**[92] 3716 5-11-0 0 PaddyBrennan 93
(Tom George) *t.k.h: hld up in tch towards rr: hdwy to chse ldrs after 4th: rdn bef 3 out: outpcd next: no threat to ldrs after* **28/1**

60- **6** *5* **Wizaller**[48] 4620 5-10-7 0 AndrewThornton 81
(Henrietta Knight) *in tch towards rr: hdwy after 5th: mstke 6th: rdn and struggling bef 3 out: wl btn 2 out* **66/1**

7 *6* **Isario (GER)**[174] 5-11-0 0 (t) WillKennedy 82
(Noel Chance) *t.k.h: hld up wl in tch: rdn bef 3 out: wknd bef 2 out* **25/1**

0- **8** *¾* **Kashubian Quest**[44] 4706 4-10-10 0 TjadeCollier 79
(Sue Smith) *pressed ldr: mstke 1st: ev ch bef 3 out: wknd qckly 3 out: wl btn whn blnd 2 out* **66/1**

435- **9** *10* **Nodanawink**[15] 5214 7-10-11 0 AdrianLane(3) 74
(Donald McCain) *led: j.lft 1st: hdd and blnd 3 out: sn wknd* **33/1**

- **10** *22* **Calypso Bay (IRE)**[12] 4-10-10 0 APMcCoy 45
(Jonjo O'Neill) *t.k.h: hld up towards rr: dropped to last and mstke 6th: sn lost tch: t.o fr 3 out* **8/1**

- **P** **Soccerjackpot (USA)**[106] 6-11-0 0 TomO'Brien —
(Alan Jones) *t.k.h: hld up in tch in midfield: dropped to rr after 5th lost tch wl bef 3 out: t.o whn p.u 2 out* **20/1**

3m 55.5s (0.30) **Going Correction** -0.175s/f (Good)
WFA 4 from 5yo+ 18lb **11** Ran SP% **116.7**
Speed ratings (Par 103): **92,90,89,87,83 81,78,78,73,62 —**
toteswingers:1&2:£2.30, 2&3:£2.20, 1&3:£1.40 CSF £16.76 TOTE £4.50: £1.10, £1.70, £1.40; EX 17.70.

Owner Kim Bailey Racing Partnership II **Bred** Abergwaun Farms **Trained** Andoversford, Gloucs

FOCUS
This is not a result to take seriously, as they went slowly early and sprinted up the home straight.

NOTEBOOK

Lion On The Prowl(IRE) collected his first win of any description on his debut over hurdles. He showed a good attitude under pressure and jumped well in the main, so should go close under a penalty if running again in the next few weeks. (op 7-2)

Hilfiger(GER) ⊠ either needs to learn to settle or have a much stronger gallop to chase, as he took a fierce grip again under restraint. He clearly has plenty of ability. (op 7-2 tchd 4-1)

Zakatal, wearing a first-time tongue-tie, lost his place for a few strides down the back straight but was back in the firing line turning in. He gave the impression he is less about speed and more about stamina, despite running well. (op 15-8)

Hypnotic Gaze(IRE) ⊠ was not given a hard time on his hurdling debut and caught the eye. The slight concern with him is that he was winless from quite a few tries on the Flat, but he should be given a chance to make his mark over Jumps.

Milandale(IRE) ⊠ was not completely disgraced and caught the eye with his finishing effort. (op 33-1)

Calypso Bay(IRE), having his first outing over hurdles, hit the first in the back straight and never got into the race. The jockey was quick to accept that he was not going to get involved on the home bend. (op 15-2 tchd 6-1)

Soccerjackpot(USA), a four-time winner at up to just over 1m on the Flat, pulled very hard on his hurdling debut and gave himself no chance of getting home. No doubt he will find his level in time. Official explanation: jockey said gelding pulled up distressed (op 14-1)

98 TOTEPOOL H'CAP CHASE (FOR THE TOM WRAGG TROPHY) (LISTED RACE) (15 fncs 3 omitted) 3m

4:25 (4:25) (Class 1) 5-Y-0+

£28,505 (£10,695; £5,355; £2,670; £1,340; £670)

Form RPR

52F- **1** **Auroras Encore (IRE)**[14] 5223 8-11-1 **139** .... TjadeCollier 150+
(Sue Smith) *chsd ldrs: wnt 2nd bef 11th: hmpd by loose horse bnd after next: rallied u.p 2 out: led bef last: styd on strly to draw clr flat* **12/1**

031- **2** *6* **Forzy Origny (FR)**[26] 5046 8-11-1 **139** .... RobertThornton 144+
(Alan King) *led: rdn after 3 out: gd jump next: rdn and hdd bef last: wknd flat* **5/1**[2]

4PF- **3** *1 3/4* **That's Rhythm (FR)**[14] 5223 10-10-11 **135** .... DenisO'Regan 137
(Martin Todhunter) *in tch in midfield: rdn and outpcd 10th: rallied after 12th: chsd ldng pair on long run between last 2: plugged on same pce after* **16/1**

311- **4** *4 1/2* **Midnight Chase**[16] 5195 8-10-13 **137** .... DougieCostello 135
(Neil Mulholland) *w ldr tl 8th: lost 2nd after 11th: lost pl bef next: rdn wl bef 3 out: no threat to ldrs after* **7/1**[3]

044- **5** *1 1/2* **Lead On (IRE)**[9] 5338 9-11-1 **139** .... TomO'Brien 135
(Philip Hobbs) *bhd: rdn and struggling 10th: wl bhd 12th: plugged on fr 3 out: nvr trbld ldrs* **20/1**

U/0- **6** *6* **Bronte Bay (IRE)**[20] 5067 7-10-9 **133** ....(b[1]) APMcCoy 123
(Paul W Flynn, Ire) *t.k.h early: hld up in tch: chsd ldng trio and drvn after 12th: wknd after 3 out* **9/2**[1]

4FF- **7** *2* **Pablo Du Charmil (FR)**[21] 5127 9-11-12 **150** ....(t) TomScudamore 138
(David Pipe) *in tch: chsd ldng pair 12th: rdn bef next: wknd 2 out* **16/1**

11F- **S** **Eric's Charm (FR)**[21] 5127 12-11-11 **149** .... LeightonAspell —
(Oliver Sherwood) *chsd ldrs: j. slowly and lost pl 2nd: in rr whn slipped up after 5th* **8/1**

51P- **P** **Victorias Groom (GER)**[44] 4702 8-10-8 **132** .... PaddyBrennan —
(Lucy Wadham) *in tch in midfield: chsd ldrs 8th: mstke 9th: sn rdn and struggling: wl btn whn p.u 12th* **12/1**

P12- **U** **Burren Legend (IRE)**[17] 5181 9-10-3 **132** .... JayPemberton(5) —
(Richard Rowe) *in tch towards rr whn uns rdr 6th* **5/1**[2]

1P3- **P** **Pocket Aces (IRE)**[84] 3891 8-10-11 **135** .... AidanColeman —
(Richard Rowe) *in tch towards rr: rdn and struggling after 10th: t.o whn p.u 3 out* **25/1**

PP0- **P** **Kornati Kid**[16] 5197 8-10-13 **137** .... RichardJohnson —
(Philip Hobbs) *a in rr: hmpd 6th: rdn and lost tch after 9th: t.o 12th tl p.u 3 out* **10/1**

6m 10.8s (-4.30) **Going Correction** +0.10s/f (Yiel) **12** Ran SP% **120.0**
Speed ratings: **111,109,108,106,106 104,103,—,—,— —,—**
toteswingers:1&2:£17.40, 1&3:£56.60, 2&3:£10.20 CSF £73.59 CT £984.65 TOTE £15.80: £4.40, £2.80, £4.80; EX 135.60.
Owner Mrs Alicia Skene & W S Skene **Bred** Mountarmstrong Stud **Trained** High Eldwick, W Yorks

FOCUS

A strong field for a valuable prize even though two fancied horses, Ogee and Ouzbeck, were taken out beforehand. The pace appeared to be at least good, but it did pay to be prominent.

NOTEBOOK

Auroras Encore(IRE) is a talented individual but has not always been the easiest to predict. A first-fence faller in the Scottish National when last seen, he stayed on the tail of the leader throughout before keeping on the stronger from two out. He is possibly the sort that can be aimed at the Aintree National next year.

Forzy Origny(FR) ⊠ , 17lb higher than when winning on his return to fences last time, set out to make every yard but could not last home, hard though he tried. He remains a horse to have on your side even though defeated here. (op 11-2 tchd 6-1)

That's Rhythm(FR), without cheekpieces this time, was another who went early in the Scottish National. He got behind at one stage and needed urging along, but kept on finding and stayed on well.

Midnight Chase, up 12lb since the last of his two successive victories, had no problems with the distance. He will get further judged on the way he kept on again after the last. (op 6-1)

Lead On(IRE), back over fences, got behind before making ground. He was never in with a serious chance of making an impact. (op 16-1)

Bronte Bay(IRE), in first-time blinkers, had every chance and no excuses. It has been a long time since he won. (op 11-2 tchd 6-1)

Pablo Du Charmil(FR), an early faller in the Grand National, ran well but was anchored by his big weight from three out. (op 14-1)

99 SIR STANLEY CLARKE MEMORIAL H'CAP CHASE (11 fncs 1 omitted) 2m

5:00 (5:00) (Class 4) (0-105,104) 5-Y-0+ **£3,837** (£1,158; £596; £315)

Form RPR

602- **1** **Coach Lane**[5] 26 9-11-12 **104** .... AidanColeman 113+
(Venetia Williams) *trckd ldrs: cruised upsides ldrs between last 2: led last: rdn to assert flat: comf* **10/3**[2]

P01- **2** *2 1/2* **Folie A Deux (IRE)**[47] 4653 8-11-2 **94** .... JoeTizzard 99
(Colin Tizzard) *chsd ldr: dived and blnd 2nd: led after 4th: hdd and rdn 3 out: drvn and stl ev last: nt pce of wnr flat* **5/2**[1]

316- **3** *6* **Troodos Jet**[25] 5072 9-9-11 **78** ....(p) RyanMania(3) 77
(Dianne Sayer) *trckd ldrs: pushed into ld 3 out: rdn between last 2: hdd and stmbld last: sn btn* **10/3**[2]

654- **4** *20* **Arumun (IRE)**[21] 5131 9-11-6 **98** .... TomScudamore 75
(Michael Scudamore) *racd keenly: led: dived 1st: hdd after 4th: styd w ldr tl bef 3 out: wknd u.p bef 2 out* **7/1**

321- **P** **Glimmer Of Light (IRE)**[26] 5052 10-10-12 **93** ....(bt) CharlieHuxley(3) —
(Dr Richard Newland) *in tch: dropped to last and reminders after 4th: sn lost interest: lost tch after next: t.o whn j. slowly 6th and immediately p.u* **4/1**[3]

4m 2.00s (6.40) **Going Correction** +0.10s/f (Yiel) **5** Ran SP% **107.2**
Speed ratings: **88,86,83,73,—**
CSF £11.57 TOTE £4.00: £1.50, £1.80; EX 13.30.
Owner B Moore & E C Stephens **Bred** Juddmonte Farms **Trained** Kings Caple, H'fords

FOCUS

All the runners, except for Glimmer Of Light, who lost interest early, had a chance on the final bend, but three took control heading to two out. This, however, is not form to trust.

NOTEBOOK

Coach Lane, making a fairly quick reappearance and without a win for almost two years, travelled strongly and pulled out enough when sent to the front to gain victory. This, however, is not form to trust. (tchd 7-2)

Folie A Deux(IRE) ⊠ , up 9lb for winning on his only run for Nigel Hawke last time, was harried for the lead and made a mistake at the second. His jockey soon had him back in the action but the horse was forced to rally again coming to the final fence after looking held. He was not beaten far and can be given another chance. (op 11-4 tchd 3-1)

Troodos Jet, who ran over hurdles last time, got to the lead going fairly well but weakened on the approach to the final fence. A stumble after jumping it ended whatever chance he had. (op 7-2)

Arumun(IRE) sat next to the runner-up in the early stages but was a spent force soon after turning into the home straight. (op 11-2)

Glimmer Of Light(IRE), last year's winner, lost interest passing the winning line for the first time and soon got well behind. He was pulled up at an early stage. Official explanation: jockey said gelding lost its action but returned sound (tchd 7-2)

100 BET TOTEPOOL TO SUPPORT YOUR SPORT NOVICES' H'CAP HURDLE (10 hdls 2 omitted) 2m 6f 110y

5:30 (5:30) (Class 5) (0-95,95) 4-Y-0+ **£1,951** (£573; £286; £143)

Form RPR

U11- **1** **Liz's Dream**[10] 5311 10-11-2 **92** ....(tp) MrTomDavid(7) 102+
(Lisa Harrison) *hld up in rr: hdwy 7th: trckd ldrs wl bef 3 out: rdn to chse ldr bef 2 out: drvn to ld last: hld on cl home* **5/2**[1]

463- **2** *nk* **Entertain Me**[48] 4609 6-11-8 **91** .... CharliePoste 101+
(Robin Dickin) *chsd ldrs: nt fluent 1st: wnt 2nd 6th: led wl bef 3 out: drvn and kpt on wl 2 out: mstke and hdd last: rallied gamely flat: no ex and hld cl home* **9/1**

2P1- **3** *11* **Richard The Third**[42] 4741 6-11-11 **94** .... AndrewThornton 94
(John Harris) *hld up towards rr: hdwy into midfield bef 3rd: wnt 2nd after 7th tl after 3 out: sn outpcd by ldrs: 4th and wl btn last: wnt 3rd nr fin* **5/1**[2]

000- **4** *nk* **Cockney Prince (IRE)**[54] 4489 5-11-7 **90** .... APMcCoy 89
(Jonjo O'Neill) *hld up in tch: mstke 6th: j. slowly next: hdwy to chse ldrs bef 3 out: rdn and btn 2 out: j. slowly last: lost 3rd nr fin* **5/2**[1]

065- **5** *31* **Books Review**[5] 23 6-11-5 **95** ....(p) AodhaganConlon(7) 71
(Debra Hamer) *chsd ldrs: rdn after 7th: wknd next: t.o* **25/1**

625- **6** *14* **Just For Jean (IRE)**[42] 4741 5-11-11 **94** .... JasonMaguire 52
(Donald McCain) *t.k.h: hld up towards rr: rdn and stuggling 6th: lost tch 7th: t.o whn j.rt 3 out* **17/2**[3]

034- **7** *3 3/4* **Pavanne (IRE)**[27] 5015 5-11-5 **88** .... WarrenMarston 43
(Martin Keighley) *in tch towards rr: reminders after 2nd: rdn 5th: stl in tch: drvn and wkng whn nt fluent 3 out: t.o* **10/1**

000- **8** *2 1/4* **Departed (IRE)**[22] 5120 6-11-9 **95** ....(b[1]) SeanQuinlan(3) 48
(Richard Phillips) *led: blnd 1st: hdd and drvn after 7th: sn wknd: t.o 2 out* **33/1**

0/5- **P** **Conkering (USA)**[103] 3516 7-11-6 **92** .... RichieMcLernon(3) —
(Jonjo O'Neill) *chsd ldr tl 6th: sn rdn and lost pl: wl bhd next: t.o whn p.u 3 out* **25/1**

06P- **P** **Good To Be Grey**[20] 5152 8-11-11 **94** ....(p) RodiGreene —
(Reg Hollinshead) *in tch in midfield: rdn and struggling 6th: lost tch next: t.o whn p.u 3 out* **33/1**

5m 26.8s (-4.10) **Going Correction** -0.175s/f (Good) **10** Ran SP% **117.0**
Speed ratings (Par 103): **100,99,96,95,85 80,79,78,—,—**
toteswingers:1&2:£2.70, 1&3:£3.00, 2&3:£17.00 CSF £24.01 CT £104.14 TOTE £3.30: £1.80, £2.60, £1.20; EX 38.10 Place 6: £284.31, Place 5: £189.52..
Owner David Alan Harrison **Bred** D A Harrison **Trained** Aldoth, Cumbria

FOCUS

A modest contest.

NOTEBOOK

Liz's Dream, chasing a hat-trick, was given a wonderfully patient ride to get into contention but had to work hard to gain the victory. The handicapper can not raise him very much, which should help his cause. (op 7-2)

Entertain Me ⊠ hit the front leaving the back straight and had plenty of her rivals in trouble once there. Still going well turning in, she kept finding a bit more every time her jockey asked for a response and she went down fighting. (op 7-1)

Richard The Third, raised 7lb for winning over the course last time, was slightly up in trip and did not help his cause by being keen. (op 13-2)

Cockney Prince(IRE), up in trip for his handicap debut, rarely looked like winning. He has plenty to prove now. (op 9-4 tchd 2-1)

T/Plt: £276.00 to a £1 stake. Pool: £77,892.36. 206.00 winning tickets. T/Qpdt: £13.80 to a £1 stake. Pool: £6,493.99. 347.80 winning tickets. SP

101a - 128a (Foreign Racing) - See Raceform Interactive

EXETER (R-H)

Tuesday, May 4

OFFICIAL GOING: Good to firm

Wind: Virtually nil Weather: dry

129 FARMERS FRIEND OF EXETER MAIDEN HURDLE (8 hdls) 2m 1f

5:50 (5:50) (Class 4) 4-Y-0+ **£2,602** (£764; £382; £190)

Form RPR

250- **1** **Shalamiyr (FR)**[39] 4871 5-11-0 112 .... RichardJohnson 109+
(Philip Hobbs) *mde virtually all: hdd briefly 3 out: kpt on: rdn out* **2/1**[1]

022- **2** *5* **Spent**[30] 5012 5-11-0 112 .... SeamusDurack 106+
(Alison Thorpe) *hld up: bhd 2nd: hdwy after next: rdn to chse ldng pair 3 out: styd on to chse wnr last but a being hld* **3/1**[3]

000- **3** *3 1/2* **Shinnecock Bay**[144] 2818 6-11-0 95 ....(b[1]) LeightonAspell 100
(Oliver Sherwood) *hld up: rdn appr 3 out: styd on steadily fr 3 out: wnt 3rd run-in: nvr trbld ldrs* **16/1**

242- **4** *3/4* **Googoobarabajagal (IRE)**[1] 4643 4-10-10 111 .... TomScudamore 95
(Stuart Kittow) *mid-div: hdwy 5th: rdn bef next: sn one pce* **11/4**[2]

0- **5** *3/4* **Recurring Dream**[244] 1374 4-10-3 0 .... JohnnyFarrelly 87
(John Flint) *trckd ldrs: rdn to take narrow advantage 3 out: sn hdd: chsd wnr tl no ex fr bef last* **16/1**

/05- **6** *5* **Adeus Ayrton (IRE)**^{54} 4541 6-11-0 0 RhysFlint 93
(Philip Hobbs) *hld up: rdn and prog after 5th: wnt 4th next: hit 2 out: wknd* **10/1**

606- **7** *nse* **Keep Guessing**^{34} 4959 7-11-0 99 WayneHutchinson 93
(Warren Greatrex) *hld up: rdn appr 3 out: no imp* **25/1**

0- **8** *1 1/2* **Mccauley (IRE)**^{129} 3064 7-10-7 0 JimmyDerham$^{(7)}$ 92
(Nick Mitchell) *in tch: nt fluent 5th: hit 3 out: sn rdn: fnd little* **33/1**

9 *20* **Trew Style**^{557} 8-10-11 0 SeanQuinlan$^{(3)}$ 71
(David Rees) *t.k.h: trckd ldr: hit 3rd: rdn after 5th: sn wknd: t.o* **80/1**

P **As Cold As Ice**^{1129} 10-10-7 0 NickScholfield —
(Linda Blackford) *trckd ldr tl wknd appr 5th: t.o whn p.u bef 3 out: b.b.v* **150/1**

3m 57.1s (-18.40) **Going Correction** -1.175s/f (Hard)
WFA 4 from 5yo+ 18lb **10** Ran SP% **114.5**
Speed ratings (Par 105): **96,93,92,91,91 88,88,88,78,—**
Tote Swingers: 1&2 £1.80, 1&3 £5.80, 2&3 £13.70 CSF £8.03 TOTE £1.90: £1.02, £1.40, £8.70; EX 7.80.
Owner Mrs R J Skan **Bred** H H The Aga Khan's Studs Sc **Trained** Withycombe, Somerset

FOCUS

A moderate maiden hurdle that was never going to take much winning. They finished in a heap and the form is rated around the front three.

NOTEBOOK

Shalamiyr(FR), who has been crying out for some decent ground, made all the running to win his first race. Placed behind a couple of smart sorts towards the end of last year, the winner ran no sort of race in bad ground on his recent handicap debut but settled better than he has in the past and stayed on well to score with a bit in hand. He carried his head a tad high, but that can be put down to greenness, as this scopey sort looks to be learning all the time. He remains a horse to keep on side, and it will be a surprise if he doesn't win again. (op 9-4)
Spentwas another suited by drier ground, but he made a notable early blunder and couldn't match the winner in the straight. This wasn't a bad effort considering his jumping, and a minor race should come his way eventually. (op 9-4)
Shinnecock Bay showed much improved form in the first-time blinkers, staying on take third, but it remains to be seen whether the headgear works as well a second time. (tchd 20-1)
Googoobarabajagal(IRE), who ran on the Flat at Chepstow 24 hours earlier, should have given Shalamiyr more of a race judging on his earlier hurdles efforts. He won't be seen at his best until he goes handicapping. (op 4-1)
Recurring Dream, beaten miles on her sole previous outing over hurdles last September, joined the winner two out, but ultimately didn't get home. (op 14-1 tchd 20-1)
Adeus Ayrton(IRE) will do better once handicapping.
As Cold As Ice Official explanation: trainer said mare bled from the nose

130 CHAMPAGNE LANSON 250TH ANNIVERSARY H'CAP CHASE (12 fncs) 2m 1f 110y

6:20 (6:20) (Class 4) (0-110,111) 5-Y-0+ **£3,903** (£1,146; £573; £286)

Form RPR

P50- **1** **Passato (GER)**^{86} 3912 6-11-5 103 (t) RobertThornton 120+
(Joanna Davis) *trckd ldrs: nudged along after 5th: rdn to ld 4 out: kpt on wl: rdn out* **3/1**^{1}

P4-U **2** *2 3/4* **Bushwacker (IRE)**^{4} 81 6-10-10 101 JimmyDerham$^{(7)}$ 115+
(Seamus Mullins) *in tch: nt fluent 3rd: hdwy after 8th: styd on same pce fr 4 out: wnt 2nd 2 out: kpt on but a being hld by wnr* **11/2**^{3}

/60- **3** *7* **Mutual Respect (IRE)**^{22} 5167 8-10-9 96 DPFahy$^{(3)}$ 102
(Evan Williams) *hld up bhd ldrs: hit 8th: rdn bef 4 out: styd on same pce: wnt 3rd last* **11/2**^{3}

P32- **4** *8* **Quick Fix (IRE)**^{37} 4914 8-11-8 106 (t) PaddyBrennan 106+
(Tom George) *trckd ldr: led 7th: rdn and hdd 4 out: hld whn hit 2 out: wknd* **7/2**^{2}

PPP- **5** *7* **Knapp Bridge Boy**^{195} 1848 10-10-0 84 oh2 LiamTreadwell 74
(James Payne) *hld up last tl wnt 6th bef 5th: sn rdn: nvr on terms* **20/1**

32F/ **6** *27* **De Luain Gorm (IRE)**^{397} 4827 12-11-5 110 MrGGallagher$^{(7)}$ 73
(Chris Down) *led: sn clr: hdd 7th: wknd bef 4 out: t.o* **7/1**

/P1- **P** **Sea Saffron**^{90} 3817 9-11-1 102 HaddenFrost$^{(3)}$ —
(James Frost) *struggling in rr after 4th: t.o and p.u bef 4 out* **11/2**^{3}

3m 58.7s (-20.30) **Going Correction** -1.00s/f (Hard) course record **7** Ran SP% **110.6**
Speed ratings: **105,103,100,97,94 82,—**
Tote Swingers: 1&2 £4.70, 1&3 £2.80, 2&3 £6.60 CSF £18.47 CT £80.05 TOTE £2.00: £1.10, £4.20; EX 19.30.
Owner P Ponting **Bred** Gestut Hof Ittlingen **Trained** East Garston, Berks
⊠ Stewards' Enquiry : Mr G Gallagher one-day ban: used whip when out of contention (tbn)

FOCUS

A low-grade handicap chase. Solid form in a fast time for the grade.

NOTEBOOK

Passato(GER), likely to have benefited from a spin over hurdles last time, likes a fast surface and there was no doubting the result once this strong stayer took over at the first in the straight. He had slipped to a mark 3lb lower than when last successful and may well win again this summer, having performed well off much higher marks than this in the past. (op 11-4 tchd 5-2 and 7-2 in a place)
Bushwacker(IRE), who unseated his rider latest, travelled well and stayed on nicely having been outpaced, but he was never going to reach the winner. Any improvement on this should see him good enough to land a minor race. (op 15-2)
Mutual Respect(IRE) ran an improved race, but he hasn't won since his bumper days. (op 15-2)
Quick Fix(IRE) stopped rather tamely from two out having made a lot of the running and jumping well, but it's possible the ground was a tad quick. (tchd 10-3 and 4-1)
De Luain Gorm(IRE) didn't last home on this return from a lengthy absence, finishing a well-beaten last. (op 11-1)
Sea Saffron, 9lb higher than when winning in soft ground at the course earlier in the year, was never going on this much quicker surface. Official explanation: jockey said gelding never travelled (op 10-3)

131 PETER HAHN CASHMERE CLASSIC H'CAP HURDLE (12 hdls) 2m 7f 110y

6:50 (6:50) (Class 3) (0-130,130) 4-Y-0+ **£5,204** (£1,528; £764; £381)

Form RPR

042- **1** **Very Cool**^{21} 5175 8-10-11 115 (bt) TomScudamore 121+
(David Pipe) *prom: led whn nt fluent 7th: rdn after 3 out: styd on gamely: drvn out* **5/2**^{1}

UP4- **2** *1 3/4* **Silverburn (IRE)**^{21} 5175 9-11-4 125 DPFahy$^{(3)}$ 130+
(Evan Williams) *trckd ldrs: chal 3 out: sn rdn: ev ch whn wnt lft last: no ex* **17/2**

43P- **3** *5* **Cold Mountain (IRE)**^{11} 5365 8-10-4 115 JimmyDerham$^{(7)}$ 113
(Seamus Mullins) *mid-div: hdwy after 9th: sn rdn: chsd ldng pair fr 3 out: kpt on same pce* **25/1**

043- **4** *12* **Midas Way**^{16} 5248 10-11-2 120 (p) PaddyBrennan 109
(Patrick Chamings) *hld up: hdwy whn stmbld bdly 8th: nt fluent next: sn rdn: one pce fr 3 out* **7/1**^{2}

34B- **5** *2 1/2* **Thedeboftheyear**^{21} 5175 6-11-0 118 LiamHeard 102
(Chris Down) *mid-div: hdwy 9th to trck ldrs: rdn bef next: wknd 2 out* **17/2**

P/2- **6** *10* **Karanja**^{24} 5132 11-11-12 130 JackDoyle 104
(Simon Burrough) *mid-div tl struggling in last quartet 9th: nvr bk on terms* **15/2**^{3}

005- **7** *1 3/4* **Knight Legend (IRE)**^{18} 5207 11-11-0 118 (t) RichardJohnson 90
(Philip Hobbs) *led: wnt lft 1st 2: hdd 7th: rdn after 9th: wknd 3 out* **7/1**^{2}

U30- **8** *shd* **Lordsbridge (USA)**^{19} 5195 8-10-13 117 NickScholfield 91
(Andy Turnell) *hld up: rdn after 9th: no imp* **12/1**

15P/ **9** *53* **I'm Supreme (IRE)**^{524} 2437 8-9-9 104 oh2 GilesHawkins$^{(5)}$ 23
(Philip Hobbs) *trckd ldrs tl wknd bef 3 out: virtually p.u* **14/1**

635- **10** *1* **Orchard King (IRE)**^{21} 5175 9-11-2 120 (p) JohnnyFarrelly 38
(Alison Thorpe) *mid-div: rdn after 9th: sn wknd: eased fr next: virtually p.u* **12/1**

34P- **11** *1* **Barnhill Brownie (IRE)**^{146} 2778 7-11-2 120 (t) RhysFlint 37
(Philip Hobbs) *trcking ldrs whn sltly hmpd 1st: nt fluent next: lost pl: on tail end of gp but drvn fr after 6th: t.o* **11/1**

5m 26.2s (-32.80) **Going Correction** -1.175s/f (Hard) **11** Ran SP% **120.6**
Speed ratings (Par 107): **107,106,104,100,99 96,96,95,77,77 77**
Tote Swingers: 1&2 £3.80, 1&3 £15.70, 2&3 £45.70 CSF £25.33 CT £445.11 TOTE £4.30: £2.80, £4.30, £9.50; EX 37.40.
Owner N G Mills **Bred** Mrs N G Mills **Trained** Nicholashayne, Devon

FOCUS

The first three came clear in what had the look of a fair handicap hurdle. The form could be rated up to 7lb higher with the first pair a stone better than this over hurdles at their best.

NOTEBOOK

Very Cool, runner-up over course and distance last time, was 2lb higher, but he has clearly found his best form again and kept battling under strong pressure to assert on the run-in. He clearly likes it here, but may prove vulnerable when competing off his new higher mark. (op 3-1 tchd 10-3)
Silverburn(IRE) continues to plummet in the weights and he ran easily his best race of the year so far, just not being able to stay on as strongly as the winner. (op 7-1)
Cold Mountain(IRE) was much improved back in third, but is hardly on the best mark at present. (tchd 22-1)
Midas Way has been running well of late, but was a little below his best here. (tchd 15-2 and 8-1 in a place)
Thedeboftheyear, brought down at the first on her recent course outing, continues to look too high at the weights. (op 11-1)
Karanja never got into it under top weight. (op 8-1)
Knight Legend(IRE) failed to get home having made a lot of the running. (tchd 13-2)

132 LEONARD COOMBE MASTER SADDLERS AND COUNTRY LIFE NOVICES' H'CAP CHASE (18 fncs) 3m

7:20 (7:20) (Class 5) (0-95,94) 5-Y-0+ **£2,602** (£764; £382; £190)

Form RPR

563- **1** **Orion Star (IRE)**^{7} 39 8-9-7 68 (p) JimmyDerham$^{(7)}$ 89+
(Seamus Mullins) *mde all: rchd for 2nd and 9th: wnt lft 4 out and 3 out: styd on: all out* **5/1**^{2}

236- **2** *1/2* **Local Present (IRE)**^{15} 5280 7-11-3 88 HarrySkelton$^{(3)}$ 107
(Ron Hodges) *trckd ldrs: rdn appr 4 out: wnt 2nd sn after 2 out: styd on fr last: hld nr fin* **8/1**^{3}

322- **3** *9* **Montana Gold (IRE)**^{11} 5361 9-11-4 86 (p) RichardJohnson 97
(Tim Vaughan) *trckd ldrs: rdn 4 out: styng on same pce whn pckd 2 out* **4/1**^{1}

4P5- **4** *3 3/4* **Whatcanisay**^{24} 5133 11-10-1 72 (t) HaddenFrost$^{(3)}$ 78
(James Frost) *mid-div: rdn and hdwy to chse ldng quartet after 14th: styd on same pce fr 3 out* **8/1**^{3}

02P- **5** *6* **Brandy And Pep (IRE)**^{57} 4487 6-10-2 70 JohnnyFarrelly 70
(Miss J Lightholder, Ire) *mid-div: trckd ldrs 6th: rdn after 4 out: cl 2nd whn hmpd 3 out: wknd bef last* **16/1**

P65- **6** *21* **The Composer**^{21} 5176 8-10-7 75 JimmyMcCarthy 54
(Michael Blanshard) *in tch: rdn after 14th: wknd 4 out* **25/1**

6PP- **7** *55* **New Mill Moll**^{52} 4588 7-10-6 81 (t) MattGriffiths$^{(7)}$ —
(Kevin Bishop) *hmpd 2nd: a towards rr: t.o fr after 14th* **16/1**

030- **8** *22* **Daarth**^{9} 12 5-11-5 87 (tp) MarkGrant —
(Brendan Duke) *nt fluent 1st: trckd ldrs tl 8th: sn in rr: t.o* **40/1**

46F/ **P** **Misttori Belle**^{23} 7-9-9 68 oh4 (t) GilesHawkins$^{(5)}$ —
(Philip Hobbs) *trckd ldrs: jnd wnr 7th tl 14th: wknd bef next: p.u bef 2 out* **10/1**

64B- **P** **Oxford De Lagarde (FR)**^{13} 5313 8-11-12 94 (t) AidanColeman —
(Mairi Wilson) *hld up towards rr: hit 7th: reminders: wknd bef 4 out: bhd whn p.u bef 2 out* **16/1**

442- **P** **Turnworth (IRE)**^{13} 5312 7-11-8 90 RobertThornton —
(R H & Mrs S Alner) *mid-div tl blnd bdly 8th (water): towards rr whn fatally injured and p.u after 10th* **4/1**^{1}

34P- **P** **Normandy Landings**^{44} 4761 7-11-3 85 (t) DougieCostello —
(Neil Mulholland) *hld up: wnt midfield 9th: rdn after 14th: wknd bef next: p.u bef 2 out* **14/1**

5m 48.1s (-21.20) **Going Correction** -1.00s/f (Hard) **12** Ran SP% **118.6**
Speed ratings: **95,94,91,90,88 81,63,55,—,— —,—**
Tote Swingers: 1&2 £10.70, 1&3 £6.40, 2&3 £9.70 CSF £45.33 CT £177.58 TOTE £3.50: £1.10, £2.40, £1.30; EX 46.70.
Owner C A Green **Bred** Dr J O'Keeffe **Trained** Wilsford-Cum-Lake, Wilts

FOCUS

A competitive handicap chase. The winner should still be competitive when reassessed.

NOTEBOOK

Orion Star(IRE), running off his lowest mark yet in a handicap, comes from a yard in good form at present, and he kept finding off the front for a deserved success. The cheekpieces have clearly been a big help and he remains capable of better under similar conditions. (op 9-2 tchd 4-1)
Local Present(IRE) really chased the winner hard after the last, drawing clear of the remainder in the process, and this stiffer test was clearly to his liking. He's yet to win over fences but should put that right at some point. (op 10-1)
Montana Gold(IRE) has now finished either second or third on all five starts over fences, but he is still a maiden at the age of nine, and the return of cheekpieces failed to improve him. (op 7-2)
Whatcanisay has shown a bit more the last twice and isn't badly weighted. (op 15-2 tchd 7-1)
Brandy And Pep(IRE) was unfortunate as he was about to jump level with the winner when hampered badly by him three out, and he quickly emptied. He deserves another chance. (op 14-1)
Misttori Belle, racing from 4lb out of the handicap on this return to rules (been in good form in points), showed up well to a point, but she was beaten very quickly. (op 11-2)
Turnworth(IRE) landed awkwardly at the tenth and appeared to fatally injure himself. (op 11-2)

133 BATHWICK TYRES INTERMEDIATE HUNTERS' CHASE (SERIES FINAL) (18 fncs) 3m

7:50 (7:50) (Class 4) 5-Y-0+ **£3,038** (£949; £474; £237; £118)

Form RPR

050- **1** **Glacial Call (IRE)**^{17} 7-10-10 0 (b^{1}) MrRHawkins$^{(7)}$ 95+
(Mrs N Frost) *trckd ldr: led after 14th: styd on wl: comf* **7/2**^{3}

3- **2** *9* **Brook Castle (IRE)**[21] 5177 8-11-10 0..................(p) MrJoshuaGuerriero 92+
(T W Dennis) *hld up: hdwy after 14th: wnt 4th next: sn rdn: styd on fr next: wnt 2nd run-in: no ch w wnr* **3/1**[2]

3 *3 ¾* **Deloughtane (IRE)**[17] 10-11-3 0..................................(p) MissAPearn(7) 90
(R M Woollacott) *trckd ldrs tl lost pl 9th: hdwy 14th: rdn to dispute 2nd whn hit last 4: no ex flat* **11/1**

5U- **4** *11* **Walter De Wodeland**[11] 5369 9-11-3 0............................. MissJBuck(7) 79
(Miss J Du Plessis) *in tch: jnd ldrs 7th: mstke 10th: led 13th tl after next: kpt chsng wnr: wknd bef last* **9/4**[1]

5 *4 ½* **Karley**[10] 9-11-10 0.. MissPGundry 73
(Polly Gundry) *hld up: sme mod late prog: n.d* **11/1**

4/ **6** *8* **Party Pictures (IRE)**[10] 7-11-7 0................................ MrDEdwards(3) 67
(A J Farrant) *hld up last: hdwy after 14th: sn rdn: 5th and hld whn blunder 3 out: wkng whn nt fluent next* **16/1**

P/5- **7** *5* **Moment Of Magic (IRE)**[23] 7-11-7 0..........................(b¹) MrRMahon(3) 60
(Kathleen Sanderson) *trckd ldrs: rdn after 12th: wknd after 14th* **12/1**

8 *18* **Quantocks Lastbrat**[24] 11-11-5 0....................................... MrMWall(5) 42
(Miss G Langley) *led tl 13th: wknd after next: t.o* **66/1**

P/6- **U** **Flinski (IRE)**[3] 15-11-3 79...(t) MrLRowe(7) —
(Mrs Diane Wilson) *in tch: hit 2nd: blnd and uns rdr 10th* **22/1**

0PP/ **P** **Grande Bretagne (FR)**[24] 11-11-7 0.............................. MattGriffiths(3) —
(Mrs S Prouse) *mid-div: wnt 4th 12th: rdn after 14th: sn wknd: bhd whn p.u bef last* **50/1**

5m 49.0s (-20.30) **Going Correction** -1.00s/f (Hard) **10** Ran SP% **116.0**
Speed ratings: **93,90,88,85,83 80,79,73,—,—**
Tote Swingers: 1&2 £2.70, 1&3 £12.90, 2&3 £9.80 CSF £14.76 TOTE £3.20: £1.10, £1.70, £4.90; EX 13.40.
Owner Mrs J E Brake **Bred** Dennis Deas Andrew **Trained** Buckfastleigh, Devon

FOCUS
Not the strongest hunter chase, it has been rated around the second and fourth.

NOTEBOOK
Glacial Call(IRE), who had been doing well in points until beaten at odds of 1-8 last time, ran out a cosy winner in the first-time blinkers, pressing on once in front and staying on strongly. She may well win again in this sphere. (op 4-1 tchd 9-2 in a place)
Brook Castle(IRE), a well-beaten third over course and distance latest, was ridden under restraint and stayed on for a clear second, but he never got close to the winner. (op 11-4 tchd 9-4)
Deloughtane(IRE), an easy point winner last time, didn't run too badly and gave the impression a slightly easier test may suit. (op 10-1 tchd 12-1)
Walter De Wodeland, still going well when unseating last time, had his chance and simply failed to get home. (op 11-4)

134 BATHWICK TYRES HAPPY BIRTHDAY CHARLOTTE CONDITIONAL JOCKEYS' NOVICES' H'CAP HURDLE (10 hdls) 2m 3f
8:20 (8:20) (Class 5) (0-95,93) 4-Y-0+ **£1,951** (£573; £286; £143)

Form RPR
/00- **1** **Nomad (FR)**[293] 960 9-10-7 **74**... HarrySkelton 79
(Carroll Gray) *hld up bhd: hdwy u.p after 7th: wnt 4th after 3 out: styd on to go 2nd whn hit last: lft in ld fnl 75yds: rdn out* **33/1**

424- **2** *2 ¼* **Waarid**[15] 5291 5-11-4 **93**..(b) JosephAkehurst(8) 97+
(Gary Moore) *in tch: rdn and ev ch 3 out tl last: kpt on but no ex whn lft 2nd run-in* **7/1**[2]

PPU- **3** *4* **Sanpor (IRE)**[57] 4487 7-11-7 **88**... DPFahy 87
(Miss J Lightholder, Ire) *hld up towards rr: hdwy 7th: narrow ld u.p 3 out: hdd next: no ex: lft 3rd flat* **22/1**

020- **4** *4 ½* **Lansdowne Princess**[24] 5135 8-11-1 **82**........................... GilesHawkins 77
(Gerald Ham) *towards rr: nudged along and hung lft 4th: hdwy after 7th to hold ev ch 3 out: kpt on same pce* **11/1**

615- **5** *4 ½* **Hammer**[11] 5364 5-11-4 **90**..(bt) OliverDayman(5) 80
(Alison Thorpe) *mid-div: hdwy and travelling okay after 7th: rdn after 3 out: sn one pce* **8/1**[3]

004- **6** *2* **Knockvicar (IRE)**[16] 5256 8-10-10 **80**................. SamTwiston-Davies(3) 69
(Richard Mitchell) *hld up towards rr: hdwy 5th: rdn after 7th: hmpd on bnd bef 3 out: one pce fr next* **25/1**

000- **7** *7* **Mrs Overall**[125] 3177 5-10-12 **87**................................ NathanSweeney(8) 68
(Bob Buckler) *struggling in rr after 4th: nvr on terms* **40/1**

645- **8** *1 ½* **Seaquel**[14] 5295 4-11-4 **90**.. CharlieHuxley 65
(Andrew Haynes) *mid-div early: bhd and struggling 6th: pckd next: nvr bk on terms* **17/2**

460- **9** *5* **Lupita (IRE)**[16] 5243 6-10-4 **74**....................................(t) JimmyDerham(3) 49
(Derrick Scott) *led tl after 7th: sn wknd* **12/1**

P00- **10** *8* **Ninogaro (FR)**[34] 4963 5-10-2 **69**.....................................(v¹) JohnKington 36
(Linda Blackford) *prom tl wknd after 5th* **80/1**

204- **11** *½* **Mistress Eva**[11] 5367 5-10-10 **77**............................ AndrewGlassonbury 43
(Sophie Leech) *prom: rdn after 7th: wknd bef 3 out* **28/1**

463- **12** *11* **Regain Du Charbonneau (FR)**[12] 5339 5-11-9 **93**(v¹) JohnnyFarrelly(3) 48
(David Pipe) *trckd ldrs: led after 7th: rdn and wknd rapidly appr 3 out* **7/2**[1]

2P0- **P** **Charlotte Street (IRE)**[56] 4501 8-10-4 **71**..................(vt) GerardTumelty —
(Warren Greatrex) *mid-div rdn appr 5th: wknd after 6th: t.o whn p.u bef 3 out* **12/1**

06P- **U** **Cappagh (IRE)**[21] 5172 5-11-6 **90**......................................(p) RhysFlint(3) 98+
(Philip Hobbs) *rn in snatches in tch: hdwy u.p to chal 3 out: led 2 out: 2 l clr and in command whn veered bdly lft and uns rdr 75yds fr line* **7/2**[1]

4m 22.2s (-20.50) **Going Correction** -1.175s/f (Hard)
WFA 4 from 5yo+ 18lb **14** Ran SP% **120.6**
Speed ratings (Par 103): **96,95,93,91,89 88,85,85,83,79 79,74,—,—**
Tote Swingers: 1&2 £119.30, 1&3 £119.30, 2&3 £42.60. CSF £240.85 CT £5182.68 TOTE £58.60: £16.60, £1.10, £9.40; EX 584.60 Place 6 £133.87, Place 5 £84.43..
Owner A P Helliar **Bred** Marc Trinquet **Trained** Moorland, Somerset

FOCUS
A dramatic finish to this weak handicap hurdle, Cappagh, who had the race in the bag, veering sharply left on the run-in and getting rid of Rhys Flint. The third is rated to form, with the unseater rated a 3l winner.

NOTEBOOK
Nomad(FR), who hadn't run since finishing well beaten in a seller last summer, was left to collect when Cappagh veered left and unseated his rider on the run-in. Understandably dismissed in the betting, he was well weighted on a couple of pieces of form from a couple of years back and would have finished a decent second but for the incident. It remains to be seen whether he can build on this, however. (op 40-1)
Waarid travelled well and had his chance, but not for the first time failed to find as much as had seemed likely. (op 6-1 tchd 11-2)
Sanpor(IRE) is best known as a chaser, but was right there until two out. He could win again with a few pounds less on his back. (op 16-1)
Lansdowne Princess made headway to challenge in the straight, but couldn't race on in the end. Official explanation: jockey said mare hung left-handed throughout (op 10-1)
Mistress Eva (op 25-1)
Regain Du Charbonneau(FR) stopped quickly in the first-time visor and clearly failed to run his race. He had looked a likely winner at some stage prior to this and perhaps deserves another chance. (tchd 10-3)
Cappagh(IRE), who was strong in the market, had the first-time cheekpieces to assist with his concentration, but they only worked up to a point. He was being niggled and pushed throughout the race but did respond, and had asserted, only to veer badly left as soon as Flint struck him with the whip after the last. He clearly has the ability to win a race, and will be helped by a stiffer test, but backing him evidently comes with risks attached. (tchd 4-1)
T/Plt: £29.40 to a £1 stake. Pool: £65,760.76. 1,631.54 winning tickets. T/Qpdt: £9.70 to a £1 stake. Pool: £5,814.78. 441.12 winning tickets. TM

FAKENHAM (L-H)
Tuesday, May 4

OFFICIAL GOING: Good to firm (good in places; 9.4)
Wind: fresh, behind Weather: overcast, dry

135 YOUR DUTY TO VOTE 6TH MAY (S) HURDLE (9 hdls) 2m
2:20 (2:20) (Class 5) 4-Y-0+ **£2,740** (£798; £399)

Form RPR
31F- **1** **What's Up Doc (IRE)**[24] 1879 9-10-12 108................. ChristianWilliams 107+
(Lawney Hill) *led: nt fluent 4th: hdd 6th: styd chsng ldrs: n.m.r on inner after 3 out: led 2 out: rdn bef last: kpt on wl flat* **9/4**[2]

P1- **2** *1 ¾* **Kanad**[29] 5036 8-10-13 121.......................................(bt) PeterToole(5) 111
(Charlie Mann) *chsd ldrs: bmpd 1st: rdn and ev ch 2 out: stl ev ch bef last: nt qckn and btn flat* **10/11**[1]

3 *12* **Wicklewood**[19] 4-10-1 0..(v) MattCrawley(7) 89
(Christine Dunnett) *t.k.h: hld up towards rr: carried wd bnd after 1st: rdn and gd hdwy 6th: chsd ldrs u.p 3 out: outpcd by ldng pair sn after 2 out: plugged on flat to go 3rd last stride* **66/1**

06P- **4** *shd* **Bold Policy (IRE)**[49] 4665 7-10-12 97.............................(v) CharliePoste 93
(Milton Harris) *chsd ldr: mstke 4th: led 6th: hdd and hit 2 out: outpcd by ldng pair wl bef last: lost 3rd last stride* **12/1**

4F4- **5** *4* **Jordan's Light (USA)**[33] 4966 7-11-4 105............................... APMcCoy 95
(David Evans) *chsd ldrs: carried wd bnd after 1st: sn rcvrd: rdn and nt qckn after 3 out: wl btn between last 2* **6/1**[3]

FUP- **6** *1 ½* **Vogarth**[28] 2788 6-10-5 82.. StevenGagan(7) 87
(Michael Chapman) *in tch in midfield: mstke 6th: rdn and no prog bef 3 out: wl btn between last 2* **50/1**

0/3- **7** *34* **Renege The Joker**[193] 1877 7-10-7 0............ GemmaGracey-Davison(5) 53
(Sean Regan) *t.k.h: hld up in tch towards rr: carried wd bnd after 1st: rdn and struggling after 5th: t.o fr 3 out* **66/1**

000/ **8** *4* **Favouring (IRE)**[77] 979 8-10-5 0................................. GaryRutherford(7) 49
(Michael Chapman) *in tch whn hung rt bnd after 1st: dropped in rr 4th: lost tch after next: wl t.o fr 3 out* **100/1**

F **Persian Tomcat (IRE)**[14] 4-10-1 0.. MrJBanks(7) —
(Julia Feilden) *mstkes: j. awkwardly 1st: chsd ldrs: stl in tch but u.p whn fell 3 out* **22/1**

0- **P** **Midnight Jack**[15] 5284 5-10-12 0..................................(t) AndrewThornton —
(Ben Pollock) *j. slowly 1st and 2nd: a last: reminders after 3rd: t.o 5th tl p.u 3 out* **66/1**

3m 49.9s (-15.50) **Going Correction** -0.875s/f (Firm)
WFA 4 from 5yo+ 18lb **10** Ran SP% **116.9**
Speed ratings (Par 103): **103,102,96,96,94 93,76,74,—,—**
.The winner was bought in for 7,000gns. Kanad was claimed by M. F. Harris for £6000.\n\x\x
Owner M B Clarke **Bred** James J Monaghan **Trained** Aston Rowant, Oxon

FOCUS
The market leaders dominated this seller and are a bit better than this grade. The winner is rated to the best of his hurdles form.

NOTEBOOK
What's Up Doc(IRE), third in this last year, ran out a game winner on this return to hurdling and is clearly an improved performer. He would have found this test sharp enough, but kept battling away under pressure and his hurdling was more fluent than the runner-up. There should be more of these to be won with him, especially on a stiffer track. Connections will now aim to run him back on the level at Brighton next week. (op 13-8 tchd 5-2 in places)
Kanad, best in at the weights, resumed winning ways on his debut in this company at this venue last time and was popular despite this being a drop back in trip. He got a bump at the first flight, which didn't help, but it was really his attitude that cost him when it mattered most. He isn't the most natural of jumpers over hurdles these days and is one to tread carefully with. (op 5-4)
Wicklewood was a 40-rated maiden on the Flat. He took time to settle, but got the hang of things down the back straight and the switch of discipline looked to rekindle some enthusiasm.
Jordan's Light(USA) had a fairly tough task with the first two at the weights, but he was never in contention and needs a stiffer test. (op 11-2)

136 TOTEPOOL H'CAP CHASE (16 fncs) 2m 5f 110y
2:50 (2:50) (Class 5) (0-90,90) 5-Y-0+ **£3,252** (£955; £477; £238)

Form RPR
2F1/ **1** **Mattaking (IRE)**[488] 3148 7-11-12 **90**...................................(p) SamJones 98+
(Renee Robeson) *a travelling wl: chsd ldr tl 3rd: styd handy: led 11th: clr 2 out: rdn bef last: idling u.p but a doing enough flat* **7/1**

644- **2** *1* **Peak Seasons (IRE)**[6] 48 7-10-0 **71**........................ GaryRutherford(7) 77+
(Michael Chapman) *mstkes: in tch in midfield: rdr lost iron 3rd: mstke and lost pl 8th: rdn after 11th: lft 5th 13th: chsd wnr after 3 out: kpt on u.p flt but nvr gng pce to chal wnr* **12/1**

/PP- **3** *4* **The Iron Giant (IRE)**[8] 21 8-9-12 **69**............. MissCareyWilliamson(7) 71
(Diana Weeden) *in tch in rr: mstke 6th: hdwy and hit 12th: lft 6th 13th: rdn to chse ldng trio after 3 out: keeping on same pce whn lft 3rd and sltly hmpd last* **66/1**

43P- **4** *11* **Feeling Peckish (USA)**[6] 49 6-10-4 **75**...................(t) StevenGagan(7) 65
(Michael Chapman) *a towards rr: pushed along after 5th: struggling u.p 11th: plugged on same pce u.p fr 3 out: lft modest 4th last: nvr trbld ldrs* **12/1**

043- **5** *3* **Donald Will Do (IRE)**[13] 5312 10-11-6 **84**................... AndrewThornton 71
(Caroline Bailey) *led tl 11th: sn rdn: lft 3rd and drvn 13th: wknd next: wl btn 2 out* **4/1**[2]

P0-P **6** *4 ½* **Ballyboe Boy (IRE)**[4] 83 11-10-2 **66**...........................(bt) JamieMoore 52
(Shaun Harris) *chsd ldr 3rd tl 11th: hrd drvn and lft 2nd 13th tl next: sn wknd* **28/1**

1U4- **P** **Wishes Or Watches (IRE)**[12] 5331 10-9-12 **69**....... AnthonyFreeman(7) —
(John Upson) *mistskes: a towards rr: j.rt 6th: losing tch whn p.u 12th* **20/1**

441- **U** **Mad Professor (IRE)**[6] 48 7-10-4 **75** 7ex................(p) JoeCornwall(7) —
(John Cornwall) *uns rdr 1st* **11/4**[1]

440- **U** **Great Tsar (IRE)**64 4354 7-10-8 79 (v1) MrTomDavid(7) —
(Tim Vaughan) *chsd ldrs: mstke 6th and 10th: pushed along to chse wnr after 12th: uns rdr next* **11/2**

00P- **F** **Dunbrody House**42 4798 6-11-12 90 (p) BrianHughes 92
(Peter Bowen) *in tch: mstke 2nd: lft 4th 13th: wnt 3rd sn after next: nt fluent 2 out: one pce and hld whn fell last* **5/1**3

5m 29.5s (-12.30) **Going Correction** -0.70s/f (Firm) **10** Ran SP% **116.3**
Speed ratings: **94,93,92,88,87 85,—,—,—,—**
toteswingers: 1&2 £2.40, 1&3 £34.60, 2&3 £57.40 CSF £81.28 CT £5017.38 TOTE £5.20: £1.30, £3.00, £12.80; EX 55.30.
Owner The Ravenstone Partnership **Bred** John McConvey **Trained** Tyringham, Bucks

FOCUS
A weak handicap full of characters and the comeback winner was the only one to put in a clean round. The first two are better than the bare result.

NOTEBOOK
Mattaking(IRE) was having his first outing since getting off the mark over C&D back in January 2009. He came in for support earlier in the day and his yard is well capable of readying one after a layoff, but drifted right out in the on-course betting ring. Handily ridden on the inside, he jumped best of all in the race and Sam Jones's decision to assert going out onto the final circuit was a winning one. He was idling from the penultimate fence, so rates value for further and is clearly still on an upwards curve. One will have to be very mindful of the bounce factor next time, however. (op 9-2)
Peak Seasons(IRE) again looked a tricky ride. He emerged as the most serious threat to the winner in the home straight and this was much more like it from him, but he remains one to avoid for win-only purposes. (op 11-1)
The Iron Giant(IRE), another pulled up on his most recent outing, was never seriously competitive on this return to chasing and is flattered by his finishing position. (op 50-1)
Donald Will Do(IRE) returned to something like his best at Southwell last week, but threw in the towel here when headed at the 11th fence. (op 11-2 tchd 7-2)
Mad Professor(IRE) won well at Southwell last time, but got no further than the first here and it looked something of a soft exit by his rider. (op 5-1)
Great Tsar(IRE) went in a first-time visor on this return from a 64-day break. His jumping went to pot nearing the final circuit, but he was coming back prior to eventually unseating and remains one of the hardest jumpers to win with currently in training. (op 5-1)
Dunbrody House attracted support on this switch to fences. He was staying on gamely after hitting a flat spot around four out and would have been placed but for falling at the last. (op 5-1)

137 SIS LIVE NOVICES' HURDLE (13 hdls) 2m 7f 110y
3:20 (3:21) (Class 3) 4-Y-0+ **£5,854** (£1,719; £859; £429)

Form RPR

23- **1** **Oursininlaw (IRE)**45 4723 6-10-13 0 PaulMoloney 109
(Evan Williams) *chsd ldrs: wnt 2nd 3 out: rdn and ev ch 2 out: rdn to ld but wanting to hang lft between last 2: rdn out* **11/1**

/4P- **2** ¾ **Oedipe (FR)**66 4306 8-10-13 0 APMcCoy 108
(Nicky Henderson) *j.w: led: hrd pressed and rdn 2 out: hdd between last 2: unable qck flat* **5/6**1

0- **3** ¾ **Little Carmela**12 5328 6-10-3 0 AlexMerriam(3) 101+
(Neil King) *hld up in tch: hdwy after 9th: cl 3rd and rdn bef 2 out: stl ev ch and nt fluent last: unable qck flat* **25/1**

022- **4** 8 **Kilmore West (IRE)**8 20 5-10-6 0 MrTomDavid(7) 100
(Tim Vaughan) *in tch in midfield: blnd 1st: chsd ldrs and hanging lft whn rdn after 3 out: outpcd bef next* **5/1**3

P10- **5** ¾ **Talenti (IRE)**43 4787 7-11-5 125 (t) ChristianWilliams 104
(Lawney Hill) *in tch in midfield: j.lft 2nd: j. 5th: rdn and unable qck after 3 out: btn whn j. slowly 2 out* **9/2**2

000- **6** 3 ¼ **Ashmolian (IRE)**51 4612 7-10-8 85 (p) GemmaGracey-Davison(5) 96
(Zoe Davison) *t.k.h: hld up in tch in rr hdwy after 9th: rdn and no prog after 3 out: wl btn next* **50/1**

000- **7** 22 **Grand Article (IRE)**38 4897 6-10-13 82 (p) CharliePoste 73
(Paul Cowley) *t.k.h: chsd ldr: mstke 5th: lost 2nd 3 out: sn wknd u.p: wl btn next* **80/1**

424- **8** 79 **Saintly Lady (IRE)**29 5035 5-10-6 0 BrianHughes —
(Peter Bowen) *in tch in last trio: nt fluent 3rd: blnd and dropped to last 7th: rallied but j. slowly 8th and 9th: tailing off whn stmbld 10th: continued wl t.o* **9/1**

5m 41.0s (-25.40) **Going Correction** -0.875s/f (Firm) **8** Ran SP% **114.8**
Speed ratings (Par 107): **107,106,106,103,103 102,95,68**
toteswingers: 1&2 £4.00, 1&3 £19.80, 2&3 £9.30 CSF £21.59 TOTE £10.90: £1.10, £1.20, £7.30.
Owner R E R Williams **Bred** P And B Turley **Trained** Llancarfan, Vale Of Glamorgan

FOCUS
A modest novice event. The first three came clear and the winner stepped up but the second was well below his chase form.

NOTEBOOK
Oursininlaw(IRE) came out on top under a strong ride and the step up in trip clearly made the difference. This was just his second outing over hurdles and his first win to date, so there ought to be more to come on this sort of ground. (op 9-1 tchd 12-1)
Oedipe(FR) has lost his way over fences but still boasts an official rating of 134 in that sphere. He was belatedly having his first outing as a hurdler and set out to make all. He did things well enough through the race, but McCoy continually looked in behind to see where the challengers were and it was always going to be a case of what there was in the locker when they emerged. That happened from two out and, although he did respond once headed, the suspicion is that it was down to his rider that he finished so close in the end. (op Evens tchd 11-10 in places)
Little Carmela ⊠ proved game under pressure and wasn't beaten at all far. This was a marked improvement on her hurdling debut, a recent switch of yard looks to have done her good and she too enjoyed the longer trip. It would not surprise to see her go in next time. (op 33-1)
Kilmore West(IRE) attracted support yet spoilt his chance with some sloppy jumping. (op 4-1 tchd 7-2)
Talenti(IRE) was running here as connections believe he has been overrated on a mark of 125 and they look to be right. The step up in trip was not expected to be much of a problem, but he could have jumped better and didn't look to enjoy this ultra-tight circuit. (op 5-1 tchd 4-1)

138 AT THE RACES NOVICES' CHASE (18 fncs) 3m 110y
3:50 (3:50) (Class 3) 5-Y-0+ **£7,330** (£2,275; £1,225)

Form RPR

012- **1** **Pheidias (IRE)**23 5153 6-11-4 119 (p) DavidEngland 124+
(Pam Sly) *chsd ldrs: lft 3rd 7th: pushed along next: rdn to ld 13th: clr bef 2 out: racing v lazily u.p between last 2: a doing enough flat* **5/2**2

321- **2** 3 **The Ferbane Man (IRE)**8 22 6-10-13 0 DeanColeman(5) 122+
(Tim Vaughan) *mstkes: chsd ldr tl lft disputing ld 7th: mstke 12th: hdd 13th: lft clr 2nd 3 out: blnd and rdr lost iron next: rallied as wnr idled between last 2: blnd and rdr dropped reins last: one pce flat* **9/2**

PP- **3** 125 **Delgany Run**15 5279 7-10-12 0 (p) AndrewThornton —
(Ben Pollock) *bhd: mstke and rdn 10th: lost tch next: hopelessly t.o fr 13th: lft poor 3rd 3 out* **50/1**

/50- **F** **Earth Magic (IRE)**46 4715 10-10-12 124 PaulMoloney —
(Evan Williams) *led tl fell 7th* **4/1**3

161- **F** **King Ar Aghaidh (IRE)**21 5176 9-11-4 0 DarylJacob —
(David Arbuthnot) *hld up in last pair: lft 4th and hmpd 7th: hdwy and trckd ldrs 13th: disputing 1 l 2nd and stl gng ok whn fell 3 out* **9/4**1

/45- **U** **Sparrow Hills (IRE)**143 2838 6-10-12 0 (tp) SamThomas —
(Charlie Mann) *chsd ldr: lft disputing ld 7th: mstke and pckd 12th: hdd 14th: wknd qckly 15th: poor 4th whn blnd and uns rdr 3 out* **8/1**

6m 13.4s (-22.30) **Going Correction** -0.70s/f (Firm) **6** Ran SP% **110.6**
Speed ratings: **107,106,—,—,— —**
toteswingers: 1&2 £2.20, 1&3 £5.80, 2&3 £5.10 CSF £13.67 TOTE £2.60: £1.10, £3.90.
Owner G A Libson D L Bayliss G Taylor P M Sly **Bred** Ballymacoll Stud Farm Ltd **Trained** Thorney, Cambs

FOCUS
A novice chase notable for sloppy jumping and the winner badly idled from two out. The first two just about ran to form.

NOTEBOOK
Pheidias(IRE) was not at all fluent through the race, but put his best foot forward on the final circuit and being in front won him the day. His jumping improved when he was in the lead, but he continually idled and his rider needed to be at his strongest to get him home. His laziness was highlighted by the runner-up coming back despite nearly unseating at the second last, so he is obviously quirky but this is his trip and he is now 2-2 over C&D. (op 3-1 tchd 9-4)
The Ferbane Man(IRE) had to work hard to open his account at over 2m3f Towcester eight days earlier and proved easy to back on this contrasting track. He would have very possibly followed up had he not made a right hash of the second-last, at which his rider did very well to get him back going afterwards, and also got the last wrong - again his rider emerging with top marks for maintaining the partnership. Providing he can iron out the errors he could just rate higher in time and returning to easier ground may also suit. (op 11-4)
Delgany Run was predictably outclassed from the tenth fence, but jumped round and was rewarded with just over £1,000 for doing so. (tchd 66-1)
Earth Magic(IRE) was the one to beat according to official figures and was going nicely out in front prior to falling, obviously too early to tell how he would have fared. (op 9-2 tchd 7-2)
King Ar Aghaidh(IRE) wasn't convincing when winning on his chasing debut and had not been foot perfect prior to eventually crashing out. (op 9-2 tchd 7-2)

139 YOUR VOTE WILL COUNT FOX HUNTERS' CHASE (FOR THE TURNER FAMILY TROPHY) (18 fncs) 3m 110y
4:20 (4:20) (Class 6) 5-Y-0+ **£1,318** (£405; £202)

Form RPR

323- **1** **Kadount (FR)**13 5314 12-11-7 115 MrJOwen(3) 120+
(J M Turner) *t.k.h: chsd ldr tl 13th: led 2 out: sn clr: eased towards fin* **13/8**2

UU4- **2** 18 **Thistlecraft (IRE)**16 11-11-3 102 (v1) AdamWedge(7) 100
(Miss Laura Morgan) *chsd ldrs tl wnt 2nd 13th: led and mstke 15th: drvn and hdd after 3 out: no ch w wnr between last 2* **10/1**

3 9 **Jumbul Sale**16 11-10-13 0 MissRachelKing(7) 90
(Mrs Alana Cowley) *led tl 13th: led and after 3 out: hdd next: sn btn: blnd last* **8/1**3

PU3- **4** 20 **Cool Running (IRE)**17 5233 10-11-10 124 MrAJBerry 81
(Jonjo O'Neill) *a last: nt a fluent: mstke and rdn 13th: struggling 15th: no imp whn blnd 2 out: wl btn after: j.v.slowly last: eased flat* **1/1**1

6m 15.1s (-20.60) **Going Correction** -0.70s/f (Firm) **4** Ran SP% **108.3**
Speed ratings: **104,98,95,88**
CSF £12.97 TOTE £3.60; EX 8.50.
Owner J M Turner **Bred** Roger Le Texier **Trained** Bury St Edmunds, Suffolk

FOCUS
The easy winner handed his stable an amazing 19th success in this race.

NOTEBOOK
Kadount(FR) bounced back to winning ways in ready fashion, handing his trainer an amzing 19th success in the race. He had won this event in 2008 and finished third in it last year behind a Jonjo O'Neill hotpot. With Jonjo's representative this season failing to run his race he didn't have to really raise his game to score, but still did the job in good style and will be high on confidence now. Connections aim to bring him back next term for another crack. (op 6-4 tchd 7-4)
Thistlecraft(IRE) posted his best effort of the current campaign, but was easily shaken off by the winner and remains a shadow of his former self. (tchd 12-1)
Jumbul Sale, a six-time winner between the flags, ran a sound enough race from the front on this debut over regulation fences. (tchd 17-2)
Cool Running(IRE) proved very lacklustre and, while something may have been amiss here, he has now looked on his last two outings as though some headgear may be required. Official explanation: trainer said gelding was unsuited by the track (op 6-5 tchd 10-11and 5-4 in places)

140 REMEMBER TO VOTE 6TH MAY MARES' H'CAP HURDLE (11 hdls) 2m 4f
4:50 (4:50) (Class 4) (0-105,103) 4-Y-0+ **£3,903** (£1,146; £573; £286)

Form RPR

223- **1** **Another Storm**15 5291 8-11-10 101 DarylJacob 103+
(Ben Case) *t.k.h: in tch: chsd ldr 5th: rdn to ld between last: drvn and racd idly bef last: a doing enough flat: drvn out* **2/1**1

F03- **2** ¾ **Peaceful Means (IRE)**6 51 7-11-7 103 DeanColeman(5) 104+
(J Jay) *hld up in tch in rr: mstke 7th: hdwy bef next: rdn to dispute 2nd between last 2: kpt on u.p flat* **4/1**2

211- **3** ¾ **Shropshirelass**15 5291 7-11-1 97 GemmaGracey-Davison(5) 96
(Zoe Davison) *chsd ldr tl 5th: lost pl next: hdwy to chse ldrs after 3 out: disputing 2nd and drvn between last 2: one pce flat* **9/2**3

540- **4** 2 **Aega**13 5317 5-10-13 93 (p) AlexMerriam(3) 91
(Neil King) *led: rdn after 3 out: hdd between last: nt fluent and dropped to 4th last: no ex flat* **16/1**

4/4- **5** 28 **What's For Tea**15 5285 5-10-10 97 (p) AshleyBird(10) 66
(Paddy Butler) *in tch: hdwy to chse ldrs 6th: rdn bef 3 out: wknd bef 2 out: dismntd after fin: lame* **16/1**

353- **P** **Lucky Score (IRE)**12 5328 4-11-1 100 RichardKilloran(3) —
(Mouse Hamilton-Fairley) *in tch in last pair: blnd 4th: sn rdn and nt look keen: lost tch 6th: wl t.o whn mstke 8th and immediately p.u* **11/2**

620- **P** **Sophisticated Lady**35 4939 7-10-1 78 JamieMoore —
(Neil King) *chsd ldrs: rdn and unable qck 8th: drvn and btn next: eased and p.u bef 2 out* **7/1**

4m 55.4s (-17.20) **Going Correction** -0.875s/f (Firm)
WFA 4 from 5yo+ 19lb **7** Ran SP% **111.2**
Speed ratings (Par 105): **99,98,98,97,86 —,—**
toteswingers: 1&2 £3.30, 1&3 £3.30, 2&3 £5.00 CSF £10.07 TOTE £2.70: £1.40, £3.40; EX 12.20 Place 6: £143.10 Place 5: £113.81 .
Owner Case Racing Partnership **Bred** D A Wales **Trained** Edgcote, Northants

FOCUS
A tricky mares' handicap. The winner is rated to his best of this season's form.

NOTEBOOK
Another Storm belatedly got her head back in front under a good ride. She was taken into the race nearing the final circuit, hurdling fluently, and asked to win the race off the home turn. Her ears were pricked from the moment she hit the front and, while her attitude could not be faulted, it's a good bet she was holding something back for herself. This track suited her and she now heads off for her summer break. (op 9-4 tchd 5-2)
Peaceful Means(IRE), third at Southwell six days earlier, ran her race yet looks a touch flattered by her proximity to the winner. This was a good effort under top weight and she deserves a change of fortune. (op 5-1)
Shropshirelass was bidding for a hat-trick and had beaten the winner at Plumpton 15 days previously. She was unable to confirm that form on this contrasting track off a 3lb higher mark, but still ran well and could well get back to winning ways when reverting to a stiffer track. (op 3-1)
Aega was making her handicap debut in first-time cheekpieces. She got an easy time out in front early on, but was hard pressed throughout the final circuit and did well in the circumstances. (op 20-1)
Lucky Score(IRE) Official explanation: jockey said filly made a bad mistake never travelled thereafter
Sophisticated Lady Official explanation: jockey said mare lost its action and pulled up
T/Plt: £69.80 to a £1 stake. Pool: £48238.68, 503.80 winning tickets. T/Qpdt: £14.00 to a £1 stake. Pool: £3754.18, 198.43 winning tickets. SP

141 - 147a (Foreign Racing) - See Raceform Interactive

CHELTENHAM (L-H)
Wednesday, May 5

OFFICIAL GOING: Good (7.8)
Wind: Light behind Weather: Overcast

148 LADY HOOPER HUNTERS' CHASE (14 fncs) 2m 110y
5:35 (5:37) (Class 5) 5-Y-0+ **£2,186** (£677; £338; £169)

Form RPR
0/4- **1** **Shooters Wood (IRE)**[12] 5369 6-11-0 0 MrRLee(7) 109+
(Miss C Baylis) *chsd ldrs: led 3rd: jnd 2 out: rdn appr last: hung rt flat: styd on* **9/1**
6P2- **2** ¾ **Ryeman**[12] 5369 8-11-7 90 (vt1) MrJoshuaGuerriero 107
(Andrew Jackson) *led to 3rd: remained handy: chsd wnr 8th: chal 2 out: sn rdn: hung rt flat: styd on u.p* **10/3²**
/3P- **3** 5 **Innocent Rebel (USA)**[25] 9-11-0 98 (t) MissCRoddick(7) 103
(Mrs K Heard) *hld up: hdwy 5th: rdn after 3 out: styd on same pce fr next* **10/1**
/F1- **4** 1 ¾ **Farmer Frank**[31] 5018 7-11-12 0 MrSFMagee(3) 110
(Nick Kent) *a.p: rdn appr 2 out: styd on same pce* **3/1¹**
064- **5** 33 **Ralahine (IRE)**[11] 7-11-0 90 (t) MrPJTolman(7) 71
(Sirrell Griffiths) *prom: mstke 3rd: wknd appr 3 out: t.o* **22/1**
6/0- **6** nk **Even Homer Nods (IRE)**[46] 9-11-4 0 (t) MrRMahon(3) 71
(A F Gorman) *hld up: rdn after 9th: nvr on terms: t.o* **20/1**
3U4- **7** ½ **Alroyal (GER)**[17] 5254 11-11-6 105 MrDGPrichard(5) 75
(Ian Prichard) *hld up: rdn and bhd fr 9th: t.o* **8/1³**
00P- **8** ½ **Calgary Jock**[17] 5249 9-11-0 0 MrHKinchin(7) 70
(Mrs J Marles) *hld up: hdwy 8th: rdn and wknd appr 2 out: t.o* **50/1**
402- **9** 12 **Mr Goofy (IRE)**[15] 5297 9-11-4 98 MrTWeston(3) 59
(Michael Scudamore) *hld up in tch: lost pl after 3rd: mstke 6th (water): nvr gng afterwards: t.o* **8/1³**
2/5- **10** 1 ½ **Smart Boy Prince (IRE)**[24] 9-11-0 0 MrLRPayter(7) 58
(Miss C C Jones) *prom to 8th: sn lost pl: t.o* **33/1**
6- **P** **Redskyatnight**[10] 9-11-0 0 MissHannahWatson(7) —
(H J Franklin) *hld up: a in rr: t.o whn p.u bef 10th* **100/1**
POP/ **P** **Sullivan's Cascade (IRE)**[3] 12-11-0 0 MrJFlook(7) —
(Miss I H Pickard) *prom to 10th: sn wknd: t.o whn p.u bef 2 out* **100/1**
P/3- **P** **Lan Na Lamh (IRE)**[34] 4972 10-10-7 0 MrDJGriffiths(7) —
(P S Davies) *hld up: hdwy appr 5th: wknd 8th: t.o whn p.u bef 2 out* **25/1**
256/ **P** **Grand Silence (IRE)**[17] 7-11-0 0 (b1) MrJEngland(7) —
(S Joynes) *in rr whn mstke 1st: bhd fr 5th: t.o whn p.u bef 10th* **18/1**
66P- **P** **Marado (IRE)**[17] 9-11-0 55 MrDHilton(7) —
(Simon Lewis) *mid-div: wknd 7th: t.o whn p.u bef 2 out* **200/1**
60P- **P** **Lethal Gun (IRE)**[18] 8-11-0 64 MrJBanks(7) —
(Richard Mitchell) *chsd ldrs: hmpd after 4th: sn lost pl: blnd and rdr lost iron next: t.o whn p.u bef 2 out:* **200/1**
P **Clash (IRE)**[18] 7-11-0 0 (t) MrTGarner(7) —
(Miss L Thomas) *chsd ldrs: mstke 7th: wknd after next: t.o whn p.u bef 2 out* **66/1**
4m 6.10s (-0.60) **Going Correction** -0.075s/f (Good) **17** Ran SP% **117.0**
Speed ratings: **98,97,95,94,78 78,78,78,72,71 —,—,—,—,— —,—**
toteswingers: 1&2 £7.00, 1&3 £34.40, 2&3 £10.60 CSF £36.07 TOTE £11.60: £3.50, £1.30, £2.80; EX 50.50.
Owner W A Harrison-Allan **Bred** Oliver Walsh **Trained** Warminster, Wilts
⊠ The first winner under rules for Camilla Baylis and Rob Lee.

FOCUS
A rare hunter chase over the trip and the first four came right away from the remainder. The second and third are the best guides.

NOTEBOOK
Shooters Wood(IRE) got a positive ride and proved more resolute than the runner-up when it mattered up the run-in. He had finished behind that rival at Newton Abbot 12 days earlier, but that was his debut in this sphere and the switch in tactics over this shorter trip did the trick. There should be more to come from him in this sphere. (op 10-1)
Ryeman finished third in this last term. He had a first-time visor replacing his usual cheekpieces and got a peach of a ride, but simply didn't want it as much as the winner when asked to win the race. He remains one to swerve for win-only purposes, but is consistent and sets the level. (op 9-2 tchd 5-1)
Innocent Rebel(USA) was staying on well after the last and clearly lacked the speed for this sharper test. (op 15-2)
Farmer Frank, well backed, had done the job gamely at Towcester last time out. The drop in distance on this stiff track wasn't as much of a concern as his penalty, though, and it was probably that which did for him. Reverting to easier ground can see him back to winning ways. (op 11-4 tchd 9-4)
Ralahine(IRE) Official explanation: vet said gelding finished lame
Alroyal(GER) Official explanation: vet said gelding bled from the nose

149 INNSWORTH TECHNOLOGY PARK CHAMPION HUNTERS' CHASE (22 fncs) 3m 2f 110y
6:10 (6:10) (Class 4) 5-Y-0+ **£4,684** (£1,452; £726; £363)

Form RPR
UF5- **1** **Take The Stand (IRE)**[20] 5198 14-11-8 108 (p) MrMByrne(5) 135+
(Peter Bowen) *mde all: mstke 18th: rdn and mstke last: styd on wl* **20/1**
612- **2** 2 ¼ **Templer (IRE)**[20] 5198 9-11-10 130 MattGriffiths(3) 133+
(Philip Hobbs) *a.p: chsd wnr 15th: chal 3 out: rdn last: styd on same pce flat* **9/4¹**
1P6- **3** 15 **Southwestern (IRE)**[14] 5325 11-11-13 131 MrNHarris 119
(Jeremy Scott) *hld up: hdwy 17th: rdn and wknd last* **5/1³**
211- **4** 11 **Theatre Diva (IRE)**[20] 5198 9-10-13 120 MissJBuck(7) 102
(Miss J Du Plessis) *hld up in tch: tk clsr order 15th: wknd appr 2 out* **7/2²**
316- **5** 5 **Tikram**[17] 5249 13-11-7 121 (p) JoshuaMoore(3) 104
(Gary Moore) *chsd wnr to 14th: sn outpcd: rallied 17th: wknd appr 2 out* **28/1**
5/2- **6** 4 ½ **Billyvoddan (IRE)**[14] 5314 11-11-0 116 (b) MrLRPayter(7) 94
(Phillip Rowley) *prom: chsd wnr 14th to next: wknd after 16th* **7/1**
101- **7** 63 **Drybrook Bedouin**[27] 5106 8-11-8 119 MrSAllwood(5) 68
(Peter Shaw) *prom: j.rt: mstke 12th: rdn bef next: wknd after 16th: t.o* **11/2**
110- **P** **Breaking Silence (IRE)**[20] 5198 9-11-13 119 (t) MrAJBerry —
(Jonjo O'Neill) *hld up: nt fluent: pushed along 7th: hdwy 11th: mstke 13th: wknd after 15th: t.o whn p.u bef 4 out* **20/1**
6m 49.4s (-4.40) **Going Correction** -0.075s/f (Good) **8** Ran SP% **110.5**
Speed ratings: **104,103,98,95,94 92,74,—**
toteswingers: 1&2 £16.20, 1&3 £21.40, 2&3 £4.40 CSF £63.41 TOTE £20.90: £3.60, £1.30, £1.70; EX 69.80.
Owner F W Ridge **Bred** James Phelan **Trained** Little Newcastle, Pembrokes

FOCUS
A strong hunter chase, run at an uneven gallop. The winner produced a small step up on his previous best in this grade.

NOTEBOOK
Take The Stand(IRE) bounced right back to form and was most game in fending off Templer up the home straight, repeating his success in the race in 2008. He finished fifth and some way adrift of the runner-up over C&D last month, but was able to get a soft lead here and his rider got it spot on from the front. He looked vulnerable turning for home, but his attitude won him the day and it has to rate as a fine training feat. (op 18-1)
Templer(IRE) threw it away when badly idling here last month and was unsurprisingly held on to for longer this time. He counted against the winner pulling out more from the home turn, though, and his jumping under pressure was not as fluent as that rival. This ground was just about quick enough for him and there are still more prizes to be won with him in this sphere. (op 3-1 tchd 7-2 in a place)
Southwestern(IRE) made his move nearing the fifth-last and looked a big threat on the final turn. He was readily left behind when the first pair locked horns, however, and this rather confirms he is on the downgrade. No doubt he will be back later this month for another crack at Stratford's Champion Hunters' Chase. (op 9-2)
Theatre Diva(IRE) got up late on to repel Templer over C&D last time out and was 4lb worse off. This wasn't run at such a strong gallop, though, and she was unable to go with him from three out. (op 3-1)
Tikram came under pressure a long way out and bravely kept battling away. This could just persuade connections to hold off his retirement. (op 25-1)
Billyvoddan(IRE) went down by a whisker at Southwell last time, but this return to a more demanding circuit saw him down tools shortly after going out onto the final circuit. (op 8-1)
Drybrook Bedouin, who won a sub-standard renewal of the Intermediate Final at this meeting last year, was disappointing. He tended to jump to his right almost throughout and perhaps something was amiss. (op 9-2)
Breaking Silence(IRE) failed to respond positively for the return of a tongue tie and was the first in trouble. He now has it to prove. (op 16-1)

150 CONNOLLY'S RED MILLS INTERMEDIATE POINT-TO-POINT CHAMPIONSHIP FINAL HUNTERS' CHASE (20 fncs 1 omitted) 3m 1f 110y
6:45 (6:48) (Class 4) 5-Y-0+ **£4,372** (£1,355; £677; £338)

Form RPR
4- **1** **Bradley**[11] 6-11-0 0 MrSWDrinkwater(7) 113
(F M O'Brien) *hld up: hdwy 16th: 23 l down 2 out: clsd gap to 14 l down last: styd on stoutly to ld nr fin* **16/1**
21- **2** 1 **William Somers**[29] 9-11-6 0 (t) MrMWall(5) 119+
(T F Sage) *j. slowly 1st: led bef next: clr 6th: mstke 8th: blnd 3 out: rdn appr last: wknd on the long run-in: hung rt and hdd nr fin* **2/1¹**
0/5- **3** 27 **Oca De Thaix (FR)**[12] 5362 8-11-2 79 MrDGPrichard(5) 89
(R E Luke) *prom: racd keenly: wknd fr 16th* **25/1**
4 9 **Raleagh House (IRE)**[24] 8-11-4 0 MrTWeston(3) 80
(Miss E Alvis) *chsd ldrs tl wknd fr 16th* **13/2³**
5S3/ **5** hd **One Cool Knight (IRE)**[38] 7-11-0 0 MrJBanks(7) 84
(Mrs K Hobbs) *hld up: hdwy 7th: chsd ldr 13th: rdn and wknd appr last: lost 2nd on the long run-in: collapsed and died after the r* **12/1**
FP0/ **6** 1 ¾ **Adieu Mari (FR)**[24] 7-11-2 0 MissJCoward(5) 78
(Mrs C A Coward) *hld up: hdwy 13th: wknd 16th* **18/1**
5/P- **7** 56 **Cluthe Boy (IRE)**[10] 7-11-2 0 (t) MissSSharratt(5) 28
(Miss S Sharratt) *a in rr: hit 12th: t.o* **33/1**
3PP/ **8** 26 **Prince Car (FR)**[18] 7-11-0 95 (t) MrMatthewBarber(7) 4
(Marc Barber) *mid-div: bhd fr 11th: t.o* **40/1**
/PP- **F** **Buckingham Bill (IRE)**[29] 10-11-0 80 MrMWilesmith(7) —
(Mrs C Wilesmith) *mid-div: hdwy 9th: 6th whn fell 11th* **20/1**
P- **P** **Plunge (IRE)**[12] 5362 8-11-4 90 (p) HarryChalloner(3) —
(Miss Katy Jane Price) *sn in rr: t.o whn p.u bef last* **40/1**
5/4- **P** **One To Note (IRE)**[11] 7-11-0 0 (p) MrTJCannon(7) —
(David Phelan) *prom: pushed along 8th: wknd 15th: t.o whn p.u bef last* **50/1**
U **Nomadic Dreamer**[30] 7-11-0 0 MrLRPayter(7) —
(Phillip Rowley) *hld up: hit 4th: hmpd and uns rdr 11th* **11/2²**
4P- **P** **Jolly Boys Outing (IRE)**[20] 5198 7-11-0 0 MissHannahWatson(7) —
(Rosemary Gasson) *in rr: bhd whn hmpd 11th: sn p.u* **28/1**
F **Lotta Presents (IRE)**[25] 7-11-4 0 MrJOwen(3) —
(John Ferguson) *led tl after 1st: chsd ldr to 13th: 3rd and wkng whn fell 3 out: fatally injured* **13/2³**
0/ **U** **Rosies Peacock**[30] 7-11-0 0 MrJFMathias(7) —
(D H Llewellyn) *sn bhd: t.o whn mstke and uns rdr 11th* **20/1**
6m 32.8s (-5.40) **Going Correction** -0.075s/f (Good) **15** Ran SP% **120.8**
Speed ratings: **105,104,96,93,93 93,75,67,—,— —,—,—,—,—**
toteswingers: 1&2 £12.90, 1&3 £38.20, 2&3 £7.50 CSF £45.72 TOTE £14.30: £4.10, £1.10, £9.50; EX 78.40.
Owner J C Collett **Bred** P A Broad **Trained** Naunton, Gloucs
⊠ Stewards' Enquiry : Mr M Wall one-day ban: used whip with excessive frequency (tbn)

FOCUS
A cracking race of its type. It was run at a decent gallop and few got involved, but there were changing fortunes in the home straight. The first two are good hunters and finished well clear. The final fence was bypassed.

NOTEBOOK

Bradley got taken off his feet and looked a lost cause nearing the third-last but as the leaders began to wilt up the home straight, he started to motor. He still had about ten lengths to find nearing the next and the fact they bypassed the last allowed his momentum to sustain. He could be a touch flattered by this, but arrived here having won his last three points and is clearly still improving.

William Somers was penalised for his success in this sphere at Chepstow and made a very brave bid to make all. His jumping wasn't as fluent on this sounder surface, indeed he whacked the third-last, but he has to be considered an unlucky loser and still emerges as the best horse at the weights. This must have been especially galling for his jockey, who normally rides the winner. (op 9-4 tchd 15-8 and 5-2 in a place)

Oca De Thaix(FR) was never seriously competitive and didn't look the most willing, but clearly stays very well.

Raleagh House(IRE), a winner of four of his last five points, hit a flat spot on the final circuit and was never really going thereafter. (op 6-1 tchd 7-1)

One Cool Knight(IRE), a winner of his last three between the flags, was the only one to make a real race of it with William Somers on the final circuit but sadly he collapsed and died after the race. (op 11-1)

Adieu Mari(FR) took a real walk in the betting ring and posted a laboured effort. (op 12-1 tchd 20-1)

Nomadic Dreamer came in for big support, but was far from fluent out the back prior to departing. (op 15-2 tchd 5-1 and 8-1 in a place)

151 HUNT STAFF BENEFIT SOCIETY COLIN NASH MEMORIAL HUNTERS' CHASE (FOR THE UNITED HUNTS CHALLENGE CUP)

(21 fncs) **3m 1f 110y**

7:20 (7:23) (Class 4) 6-Y-O+ **£3,435** (£1,065; £532; £266)

Form				RPR
433/	1		**The Cool Guy (IRE)**[452] 3785 10-11-0 0 MrGPhillips(7) — (N J Phillips) *trckd ldr: racd keenly: led 4th to 17th: led again next: clr 2 out: nt fluent last: styd on wl* **20/1**	133+
5/1-	2	10	**Marblehead (IRE)**[18] 8-11-2 126 (b) MrMWall(5) — (F M O'Brien) *hld up in tch: wnt 3rd 7th tl chsd wnr 13th: led 17th to next: rdn appr 2 out: styd on same pce* **9/4**[1]	122
3F4-	3	8	**Nobody Tells Me (FR)**[24] 9-11-7 105 MissPGundry — (E Walker) *prom: racd keenly: outpcd 4 out: styd on to go 3rd nr fin* **10/1**	115
200-	4	nk	**James Pine (IRE)**[11] 11-11-7 111 MrJETudor — (Sue Wilson) *chsd ldrs: rdn whn lft 3rd 4 out: wknd appr last: lost 3rd nr fin* **11/2**[3]	116
315-	5	9	**Oranger (FR)**[17] 5254 8-11-4 105 (b) MrAndrewMartin(3) — (Andrew J Martin) *hld up: pushed along 8th: bhd fr 14th* **20/1**	108
144-	6	17	**Gentle George**[22] 5177 7-11-7 124 MrOGreenall — (S Flook) *led tl mstke and hdd 4th: chsd ldrs tl lost pl 8th: mstke 14th: sn wknd: t.o* **10/3**[2]	91
	7	10	**Artic Fire (IRE)**[30] 11-11-0 0 MrRMason(7) — (Craig Pilgrim) *hld up: a in rr: bhd fr 14th: t.o* **40/1**	82
30/	8	8	**Freedomofthecity (IRE)**[32] 8-11-0 0 MrJBanks(7) — (Miss L Thomas) *hld up: drvn along 10th: bhd fr 14th: t.o* **80/1**	75
1-	U		**Mad Victor (IRE)**[32] 9-11-2 0 MissCAllen(5) — (Miss S M Taylor) *hld up: hdwy 10th: cl 3rd and gng okay whn blnd and uns rdr 4 out* **10/3**[2]	—
P	P		**Mrsilverlining (IRE)**[5] 79 8-11-0 0 MrJFlook(7) — (Miss I H Pickard) *prom: mstke 1st: chsd ldr 6th to 13th: sn rdn: wknd after 16th: t.o whn p.u bef 2 out* **200/1**	—
PP-	P		**Stormy Chance (IRE)**[18] 9-11-0 0 MissRachelKing(7) — (Miss Emma Crew) *a in rr: nt jump wl: t.o whn p.u bef 15th* **150/1**	—

6m 42.5s (4.30) **Going Correction** -0.075s/f (Good) **11 Ran SP% 115.8**

Speed ratings: **90,86,84,84,81 76,73,70,—,— —**

toteswingers: 1&2 £10.70, 1&3 £20.40, 2&3 £12.30 CSF £65.18 TOTE £27.20: £6.40, £1.10, £3.00; EX 109.50.

Owner Frosty's Four **Bred** Kieran Strain **Trained** Bibury, Gloucs

⊠ Stewards' Enquiry : Mr Andrew Martin one-day ban: used whip without giving gelding time to respond (tbn)

FOCUS

A good hunter chase, but they went no gallop and the form has to rate as suspect. The third and fourth set the level.

NOTEBOOK

The Cool Guy(IRE) was making his debut in this sphere after a 452-day layoff. Despite the absence it was surprising to see him go off at such a big price as he was clearly fit enough and would have won half the track in his pomp. He also scored as he pleased despite pulling hard early on and taking a few liberties at his fences, so the engine is still obviously in tact. It wouldn't be surprising to see him now aimed at the big one back here next year, but connections could well aim him at the Champion Hunters' Chase at Stratford later this month. However, the bounce factor would have to be of some concern were that to materialise. (op 14-1)

Marblehead(IRE), representing the connections of the previous winner Bradley, was surprisingly not asked to lead early on and that was probably the cause for the crawling early gallop. He wouldn't have beaten the winner, but had he adopted his customary tactics he would have likely given him more of a race. (op 3-1)

Nobody Tells Me(FR) was staying on dourly having let the leaders get away from him (op 12-1 tchd 9-1)

James Pine(IRE), winner of this in 2007 and still in front when unseating at the final fence last year, failed to raise his game for having James Tudor aboard. (op 13-2)

Gentle George ran no sort of race. The decision to turn him out again after his lifeless effort at Exeter completely backfired on his connections and he once more looked to be crying out for a break. (op 7-2)

Mad Victor(IRE) was still going strongly prior to giving his rider no chance of staying aboard and he would have no doubt made the winner work harder, if not succeeded with a clear round. These fences ultimately proved too stiff for him. (op 3-1 tchd 7-2)

152 WARNERS MOTOR GROUP HUNTERS' CHASE (27 fncs) 4m 1f

7:55 (7:56) (Class 4) 5-Y-O+ **£3,435** (£1,065; £532; £266)

Form				RPR
034-	1		**Martha's Kinsman (IRE)**[18] 5233 11-11-0 119 MrAWadlow(7) — (Henry Daly) *t.k.h: trckd ldrs: led 9th: jnd fr 15th to 17th: pushed along fr 4 out: styd on strly fr 2 out: c clr run-in* **5/1**[2]	124+
1/0-	2	13	**It's Like That (IRE)**[19] 5212 10-12-1 114 MrAJBerry — (Jonjo O'Neill) *mid-div fr 8th: j. slowly 13th: stdy hdwy fr 18th to chse wnr fr 21st: stl gng ok after 3 out: rdn 2f out and styd on same pce* **12/1**	121+
204-	3	3 1/4	**Dennis The Legend**[20] 5198 9-11-12 112 MrRMahon(3) — (Grant Cann) *in tch fr 9th: hit 17th: blnd 19th and lost position: hdwy 22nd: hit 4 out: whe styng on: rallied fr 3 out and styd on wl fr 2 out to cl on 2nd run-in but no ch w wnr* **6/1**[3]	119+
10-	4	15	**King's Wood (IRE)**[24] 9-11-8 0 (b) MrDEdwards(3) — (A J Farrant) *chsd ldrs: mstke 8th: styd on to take 3rd 4 out: wl there whn blnd 3 out: wknd sn after* **12/1**	101
/33-	5	6	**Florida Dream (IRE)**[20] 5198 11-11-0 105 MrSWDrinkwater(7) — (Mrs C Twiston-Davies) *chsd ldrs: wnt 2nd 20th to next: styd front rnk to 4 out: wknd fr 3 out* **17/2**	90
/	6	1 1/2	**Up There (IRE)**[18] 9-11-8 0 (tp) MrLRPayter(7) — (Mrs N Sheppard) *j. slowly 2nd: in rr: hit 12th: sme prog fr 22nd but nvr rchd ldrs* **33/1**	96
/P5-	7	6	**The Venetian (IRE)**[18] 9-11-7 92 (p) MrJoshuaGuerriero — (Miss G G Haywood) *in rr: hit 7th and 8th: hdwy 16th and in tch 20th: wknd after 4 out* **33/1**	82
3P2-	P		**Mr Ed (IRE)**[40] 4872 12-11-10 115 (p) MrMByrne(5) — (Peter Bowen) *in rr: rdn: hdwy and hit 17th: wknd 22nd: t.o whn p.u bef 2 out: dismntd* **15/2**	—
F/1-	P		**Fair Question (IRE)**[32] 4985 12-11-8 125 MrJHamer(7) — (Donald McCain) *led 3rd to 4th: chsd ldrs tl wknd 12th: wl bhd 17th: t.o whn p.u bef 22nd* **10/3**[1]	—
P05-	P		**Waynesworld (IRE)**[29] 12-11-4 90 MrTWeston(3) — (Mrs Marilyn Scudamore) *in rr and hmpd 10th: styd in rr tl t.o and p.u bef 3 out* **25/1**	—
0/2-	P		**Ossmoses (IRE)**[70] 4234 13-11-0 0 HenryBrooke(7) — (Mrs Alison Christmas) *hit 4th and sn towards rr: hit 7th: t.o whn p.u after 17th* **8/1**	—
500-	P		**Walton Way**[11] 10-11-0 72 MrHKinchin(7) — (Miss G Stephens) *pressed ldrs: blnd 7th: styd upsides: hit 14th: stl chalng whn blnd 18th: wknd 21st: t.o whn p.u bef 23rd* **66/1**	—
54U-	P		**Ben Ryan (IRE)**[18] 11-11-0 74 (p) MrRHodges(7) — (S Rea) *t.k.h: chsd ldrs tl wknd fr 18th: t.o whn p.u bef 22nd* **100/1**	—
6-	P		**Tricky Tangler (IRE)**[17] 8-11-0 0 (p) MrJBanks(7) — (Mrs E Mitchell) *towards rr modest of way tl t.o and p.u bef 3 out* **66/1**	—
0/	P		**Ataraxia**[17] 8-10-11 0 (b[1]) MattGriffiths(3) — (Mrs Sue Popham) *chsd ldrs to 15th: wknd fr 17th: t.o whn p.u bef 3 out* **40/1**	—
U/5-	P		**Saddlers Blaze (IRE)**[30] 8-11-4 57 (t) HarryChalloner(3) — (Edward Creighton) *led to 3rd: led 4th to 9th: wknd 15th: t.o whn p.u bef 21st* **50/1**	—
0PP-	P		**Prelude D'Estruval (FR)**[3] 7-11-0 76 (b) MissKWood(7) — (Miss N L Elliott) *j. poorly and in rr tl t.o whn p.u bef 21st* **100/1**	—
	U		**Sweden (IRE)**[29] 6-11-7 0 MrJETudor — (Mrs Edward Crow) *in tch whn blnd bdly and uns rdr 10th* **14/1**	—

8m 44.0s (-5.90) **Going Correction** -0.075s/f (Good) **18 Ran SP% 128.6**

Speed ratings: **104,100,100,96,94 94,93,—,—,— —,—,—,—,— —,—,—**

toteswingers: 1&2 £24.80, 1&3 £8.20, 2&3 £13.70 CSF £62.55 TOTE £6.90: £2.40, £3.90, £2.40; EX 99.30.

Owner Barlow, Hartley and Brereton **Bred** Michael Ward-Thomas, Susan Lady Barlow & Richard H **Trained** Stanton Lacy, Shropshire

FOCUS

A wide-open marathon hunter chase. The winner won easily in the end and the first four are all rated close to their marks.

NOTEBOOK

Martha's Kinsman(IRE) broke his duck in this sphere at the third time of asking pretty much as he pleased. He wasn't at his best at Bangor last time and things didn't too look to good for him here as he pulled his way into the lead. However, he kept finding for pressure after the third-last and actually passed the post with something to spare. This longer trip was evidently just what he wanted and his trainer later said he may now send him for the Horse & Hound Cup. (op 7-1 tchd 15-2)

It's Like That(IRE) ran better than the bare form when backed on his return at this venue in handicap company last month. He travelled sweetly into contention from five out and looked the most likely winner. He couldn't get past the winner try as he might, though, and it was probably a case of his stamina deserting him. (op 9-1)

Dennis The Legend stays all day long and his last outing at this track 20 days ago suggested he would be a player in this. He continually made mistakes, however, and really his rider deserves credit for getting to finish so close. (op 13-2)

King's Wood(IRE), another who stays very well, ran a solid race under a positive ride on this return to regulation fences and would have been much closer had he not hit three out. (op 14-1)

Florida Dream(IRE) met support, but was held from the fourth-last and may well benefit for the return some headgear. (op 11-1 tchd 8-1)

The Venetian(IRE), back to winning ways between the flags last time, looked a possible threat when staying on from out the back. His attitude under pressure was that willing, though, and it's not hard to see why he wears headgear. (op 28-1)

Fair Question(IRE) was a bloodless winner when the mud was flying on his return from injury in this division last time out and had previously scored quicker ground. He was unable to dictate, but manner in which he downed tools from halfway would suggest he bounced. Official explanation: jockey said gelding was unsuited by the good ground (tchd 11-4)

Ataraxia Official explanation: jockey said mare had a breathing problem (tchd 11-4)

153 NIGEL DIMMER HUNTERS' CHASE (17 fncs) 2m 5f

8:25 (8:26) (Class 5) 5-Y-O+ **£2,186** (£677; £338; £169)

Form				RPR
1P1-	1		**Bob Hall (IRE)**[17] 5249 9-12-1 129 (t) MrAJBerry — (Jonjo O'Neill) *hld up: pushed along 11th: hdwy next: rdn to ld flat: styd on wl* **13/8**[1]	128
342-	2	4 1/2	**Distant Thunder (IRE)**[10] 6 12-11-0 102 (t) MrJHamer(7) — (Miss Jane Western) *a.p: rdn to ld appr last: hdd and unable qck flat* **11/2**[2]	116
/03-	3	5	**Mustangsallyrally (IRE)**[25] 9-12-1 111 (p) MrNickWilliams — (R Barber) *chsd ldrs: led 12th: rdn and hdd bef last: no ex flat* **12/1**	121
10U/	4	20	**Mighty Matters (IRE)**[761] 4865 11-11-0 127 MrJFMathias(7) — (Charlie Longsdon) *hld up: hdwy 8th: ev ch 2 out: wknd bef last* **6/1**[3]	97+
0/5-	5	13	**Power King (IRE)**[11] 8-11-4 101 L-BdrSallyRandell(7) — (Mrs J E Hawkins) *chsd ldrs: lost pl after 5th: rallied 10th: wknd after 4 out* **25/1**	86
12P/	6	2 3/4	**John Diamond (IRE)**[18] 9-11-0 0 AdamWedge(7) — (Helen Needham) *hld up: hdwy 5th: wknd appr 3 out* **12/1**	79
P/3-	7	9	**Holy Joe (FR)**[31] 5018 13-11-2 0 MissJCoward(5) — (Mrs C A Coward) *chsd ldrs: led 3rd to 12th: wknd appr 3 out* **25/1**	71
04P/	8	3 1/2	**Dr Cerullo**[10] 9-11-7 0 MissPGundry — (E Walker) *bhd fr 5th* **14/1**	68
0/2-	9	12	**New Street Express (IRE)**[17] 9-11-2 0 ow2 MrPBlagg(7) — (Paul Blagg) *hld up: mstke 9th: hdwy next: wknd after 11th* **66/1**	59
344-	10	5	**Some Timbering (IRE)**[31] 5018 11-11-0 0 MrDJGriffiths(7) — (P S Davies) *prom to 9th* **66/1**	53
P/1-	11	32	**Fergal's Find (IRE)**[17] 11-11-4 0 (t) MissAEStirling(7) — (F M O'Brien) *chsd ldrs tl wknd 13th* **33/1**	28
6U4-	12	36	**Launde (IRE)**[9] 26 11-11-10 105 ow2 MrAWard-Thomas(7) — (Chris Gordon) *led to 3rd: lost pl after 6th: bhd fr 8th* **50/1**	—
/U2-	13	5	**Molostiep (FR)**[46] 10-11-4 103 MrRMahon(3) — (Susan Nock) *mid-div: hdwy 9th: wknd after 11th* **10/1**	—

F **Gentleman Anshan (IRE)**[24] 6-11-0 0.............. MissHannahWatson(7) —
(Rosemary Gasson) *hld up: hdwy 7th: wknd 3 out: bhd whn fell next* **33/1**

5m 14.9s (-4.50) **Going Correction** -0.075s/f (Good) **14** Ran SP% **117.4**
Speed ratings: **105,103,101,93,88 87,84,83,78,76 64,50,48,—**
toteswingers:1&2 £2.40, 2&3 £9.90, 1&3 £5.00 CSF £9.38 TOTE £2.50: £1.30, £2.00, £2.80; EX 9.80 Place 6: £72.97 Place 5: £20.74.
Owner John P McManus **Bred** Katom **Trained** Cheltenham, Gloucs

FOCUS
A good hunter chase, and solid form rated through the runner-up.

NOTEBOOK
Bob Hall(IRE) made it five wins from his last six outings in this sphere and those that backed him have his rider Alan Berry to thank. The winner went in snatches throughout the final lap and looked a lost cause three from home. His rider kept niggling at him, however, and as those in front began to feel the pinch he really found his stride. He was well on top at the finish and is no doubt a very classy hunter on his day. His only defeat in his last six came when he failed to run his race in the big one here in March and, despite never having previously won at the track, he did finish second in a Jewson Handicap back in 2007. (op 11-8)
Distant Thunder(IRE) came into this in good heart and was produced to lead at the last. Not for the first time he failed to find an extra gear when in front and isn't one for win-only betting, but still rates the benchmark here. (op 8-1)
Mustangsallyrally(IRE) proved very easy to back despite his yard having a good record in the race and this track promising to suit. He ran a much-improved race and, for all that he finds winning hard, is a consistent performer. (op 9-1)
Mighty Matters(IRE) looked like he was going to make a winning comeback as he travelled easily to a share of the lead three out. He blew up, however, nearing the final fence and was very tired at the finish. (tchd 11-2)
T/Plt: £115.00 to a £1 stake. Pool: £65,626.38, 416.40 winning tickets. T/Qpdt: £24.50 to a £1 stake. Pool: £7,200.30, 217.00 winning tickets. CR

61 HUNTINGDON (R-H)

Wednesday, May 5

OFFICIAL GOING: Good to soft (good in places)
Open ditch in front of the stands omitted in all chases.
Wind: nil Weather: overcast

154 RACING UK NOVICES' HURDLE (8 hdls) 2m 110y
5:20 (5:21) (Class 4) 4-Y-0+ **£2,602** (£764; £382; £190)

Form RPR

31- **1** **Clerk's Choice (IRE)**[16] 5278 4-10-12 133...................... TomMolloy(3) 115+
(Michael Banks) *chsd ldr: led 3 out: clr bef next: wnt lft and nt fluent last: v easily* **1/3[1]**

6P5- **2** *6* **Himrayn**[26] 5115 7-10-12 0.. GerardTumelty 101
(Anabel L M King) *t.k.h: chsd ldrs: rdn to chse clr wnr bef 2 out: no imp but kpt on* **40/1**

0- **3** *4* **Valkyrie (IRE)**[13] 5328 4-10-3 0 ow2................................ PaulMoloney 89+
(Nick Littmoden) *racd keenly: led: wanderd bdly 1st: clr after 3rd: mstke 4th and 5th: hdd 3 out: rdn and outpcd by wnr bef next: wl hld whn hit last* **28/1**

4 *4* **Iron Man Of Mersey (FR)**[28] 4-10-3 0......................... LeeEdwards(5) 90
(Tony Carroll) *t.k.h: hld up towards rr: j.lft 1st: hdwy and mstke 5th: chsd ldrs and rdn after 3 out: no ch w wnr bef 2 out: mstke last* **66/1**

5 *3/4* **Swiss Guard**[61] 4-10-8 0.. RichardJohnson 89
(Tim Vaughan) *in tch in midfield: hit 5th: rdn and outpcd after 3 out: plugged on same pce after* **14/1[3]**

F- **6** *3 3/4* **Day Time Run (IRE)**[60] 4440 6-10-9 0............................ AlexMerriam(3) 90
(Diana Grissell) *in tch in midfield: rdn and btn bef 2 out: wl btn whn mstke last* **25/1**

7 *4* **Silver Roque (FR)**[184] 4-10-8 0... APMcCoy 81
(Henrietta Knight) *t.k.h: chsd ldrs: rdn and btn after 3 out: wknd qckly* **11/2[2]**

050- **8** *11* **Kaybeew**[43] 4809 5-10-12 0... PaddyBrennan 74
(Nigel Twiston-Davies) *hld up in rr: nt fluent 3rd: reminders and no rspnse 4th: lost tch bef 3 out* **20/1**

000- **9** *1 1/4* **Still Royal**[38] 4907 4-10-8 0.. DougieCostello 68
(John Davies) *hld up in rr: rdn and lost tch bef 3 out* **200/1**

10 *2 3/4* **Sufficient Warning**[76] 6-10-12 0..................................... DarylJacob 70
(Ralph Smith) *t.k.h: hld up in midfield: rdn and wknd 3 out: sn wl bhd* **150/1**

P- **11** *9* **Aughcarra (IRE)**[30] 5045 5-10-9 0................................ SeanQuinlan(3) 61
(Harry Chisman) *t.k.h: hld up in rr: hdwy after 4th: rdn and hit 3 out: sn wknd: t.o* **250/1**

050/ **12** *7* **Patrick Dee**[417] 4467 5-10-5 0.. MattCrawley(7) 54
(Christine Dunnett) *hld up in midfield: mstke 5th: rdn and wknd bef 3 out: wl bhd whn j.lft last 2: t.o* **250/1**

3m 50.0s (-4.90) **Going Correction** -0.20s/f (Good)
WFA 4 from 5yo+ 18lb **12** Ran SP% **115.0**
Speed ratings (Par 105): **103,100,98,96,96 94,92,87,86,85 81,77**
toteswingers: 1&2 £6.00, 1&3 £5.90, 2&3 £33.10 CSF £27.11 TOTE £1.30: £1.02, £6.90, £4.90; EX 24.20.
Owner M C Banks **Bred** N Coman **Trained** Waresley, Cambs

FOCUS
An uncompetitive novice hurdle in which the winner is value for further but below the level of his recent win.

NOTEBOOK
Clerk's Choice(IRE) made easy work of this. Tracking the leader, he quickened clear round the final turn and came home unchallenged. Despite some clumsy jumping, this was an effortless performance against moderate opposition. Rated 133, following a comprehensive defeat of the 128-rated Aather at Kempton last month, he might be able to pick up another soft contest as a novice before putting his rating to the test. Connections are considering turning him out at Uttoxeter on Saturday if the ground is no softer than it was here, and they might not rule out a return to the Flat at some stage. (op 2-5 after early 1-2 in places)
Himrayn moved up to track the winner in the back straight and was given every chance but, not surprisingly, did not have the pace near the finish. He has only been lightly raced over the past couple of years but now seems to be on the way back, and this was as good as could be expected against an experienced ex-Flat rival. (op 33-1)
Valkyrie(IRE), who set the pace, was all over the place going to the first and still looked green at the last, but to her credit she did not capitulate too badly once headed and should continue to improve with more experience. (op 25-1)
Iron Man Of Mersey(FR) pulled too hard and though he managed to latch on to the back of the leading pack turning in, he was running on empty near the finish. He was only a poor performer on the Flat, but could do a bit better if learning to settle over hurdles. (op 100-1)
Swiss Guard made some progress to be in contention wide of the pack in the back straight, but that was as good as it got, and this former Aiden O'Brien inmate remains disappointing. (tchd 12-1)
Silver Roque(FR) was an interesting hurdling debutant, having won on his sole Flat outing at Nantes in France and with his dam related to Fred Winter winner Sanctuaire. However, despite travelling well enough, he was soon outpaced from the home turn and was eased when beaten. He may have needed the run and may prove better on softer ground. (op 8-1)

155 TURFTV NOVICES' CHASE (15 fncs 1 omitted) 2m 4f 110y
5:55 (5:55) (Class 4) 5-Y-0+ **£4,553** (£1,337; £668; £333)

Form RPR

123- **1** **Circus Of Dreams**[39] 4892 7-11-5 117..........................(v) LeightonAspell 128+
(Oliver Sherwood) *chsd ldr tl led 4th: hrd pressed whn j.lft and collided w rival 2 out: hdd bef last: lft in clr ld and hmpd last: hmpd by loose horse flat: swtchd lft fnl 100yds: kpt on* **9/1**

211- **2** *4* **Samurai Way**[43] 4807 8-11-12 125.................................... AidanColeman 128
(Venetia Williams) *in tch in midfield: hdwy 8th: mstke and reminders 11th: drvn after 3 out: outpcd next: lft 3rd last: kpt on same pce flat: wnt 2nd last stride* **6/1[3]**

503/ **3** *shd* **Important Business (IRE)**[495] 2932 7-10-12 0.................... SamJones 114
(Renee Robeson) *hld up in rr: hdwy 9th: chsd ldng pair and rdn bef 2 out: unable qck and btn whn lft 2nd last: kpt on one pce flat: lost 2nd last stride* **10/1**

/00- **4** *nk* **Squadron**[60] 4426 6-10-12 0... JimmyMcCarthy 115+
(Alan King) *nt a fluent: towards rr: mstke and struggling 9th: poor 6th 3 out: styd on bef next: lft 5th last: styd on strly flat: nt rch ldrs* **4/1[2]**

301- **5** *19* **Diablo (IRE)**[14] 5307 8-11-5 130.. PaddyBrennan 111+
(Nigel Twiston-Davies) *led tl 4th: nt fluent 7th: chsd ldr after: pushed along 11th: drvn bef 3 out: wknd bef 2 out: wl btn whn lft 4th last: eased flat* **3/1[1]**

0U5- **6** *31* **Master Darcy**[86] 3934 8-10-12 0.. ColinBolger 72
(Laura Mongan) *racd keenly: chsd ldrs: struggling whn blnd bdly 11th: t.o fr 3 out* **66/1**

3- **7** *3/4* **Delgany Gunner**[15] 5293 6-10-12 0.............................. AndrewThornton 71
(Ben Pollock) *bhd: blnd bdly 2nd: lost tch 7th: t.o fr 9th* **150/1**

436- **8** *33* **Sea Cliff (IRE)**[260] 1245 6-10-12 0...(t) APMcCoy 38
(Jonjo O'Neill) *mstkes: chsd ldrs early: steadily lost pl due to modest jumping: bhd 7th: t.o fr 12th* **16/1**

000- **U** **Songe (FR)**[27] 5099 6-10-12 0.. TomScudamore 122+
(Charlie Longsdon) *chsd ldng pair: wnt 2nd 3 out: ev ch whn j.rt and collided w rival 2 out: rdn to ld bef last: j.rt, blnd and uns rdr last* **3/1[1]**

5m 0.20s (-5.10) **Going Correction** -0.20s/f (Good) **9** Ran SP% **111.4**
Speed ratings: **101,99,99,99,92 80,79,67,—**
toteswingers: 1&2 £4.10, 1&3 £7.40, 2&3 £10.40 CSF £59.34 TOTE £15.40: £4.00, £1.10, £4.50; EX 41.30.
Owner David Knox **Bred** David Knox **Trained** Upper Lambourn, Berks

FOCUS
With a couple of formerly classy hurdlers and several chasing winners in the field, this was quite a competitive contest and it produced a dramatic finish. The form makes sense.

NOTEBOOK
Circus Of Dreams, after setting a good pace, had all bar Songe beaten by the second-last, but as both of them began to tire at that stage they collided over that fence. He kept going against the inside rail, but when his challenger departed at the last and wandered to his right it was touch and go for a moment whether Leighton Aspell could switch his mount in time to veer towards the winning line. In the end, he was a deserving winner who is at his best when allowed to dominate. Connections might look for another race this month, and would not rule out a drop back to 2m. (op 12-1)
Samurai Way stayed on well considering he put in several low jumps and never looked to be travelling that well. He had beaten today's winner at Towcester in March but is now creeping up the weights and remains vulnerable under a double penalty in novice company. (op 4-1)
Important Business(IRE) ran well on his first start since December 2008 and will benefit from this experience with his stable in good form at the moment. (op 16-1 tchd 18-1)
Squadron jumped ponderously early on and did not seem to relish the prospect of fences, and was practically tailed off with half a circuit to go. However, between the last in the back straight and the first in the home straight, he went into overdrive to cut down the gap, gaining all the way to the line. If he can improve his jumping, then a step back up in trip would look ideal. (op 5-1)
Diablo(IRE) tried to take on the winner from the front but was beaten off by the final circuit and weakened out of it. His Perth win last month came over 3m and he looked to struggle off this faster pace. (op 11-4)
Songe(FR) raced keenly and with his ears back, but still travelled as well as he has for some time. He was just beginning to tire when bumping the winner at the second- last but was keeping on when diving at the last and parting company with his jockey. (op 10-3 tchd 7-2)

156 SAFEGUARD ELECTRICAL INSTALLATIONS H'CAP CHASE (15 fncs 1 omitted) 2m 4f 110y
6:30 (6:30) (Class 4) (0-100,100) 5-Y-0+ **£4,553** (£1,337; £668; £333)

Form RPR

213- **1** **Brimham Boy**[35] 4962 8-11-10 98..................................(t) WarrenMarston 110+
(Martin Keighley) *chsd ldr tl led 4th: mde rest: mstke 7th: rdn bef 2 out: kpt on gamely: drvn out* **11/2[2]**

534- **2** *5* **Noble Future**[26] 5120 8-10-12 86...................................... AidanColeman 93
(Venetia Williams) *chsd ldrs: drvn after 3 out: chsd wnr last: kpt on same pce u.p and no imp flat* **9/2[1]**

441- **3** *4* **High Jack (IRE)**[16] 5280 8-11-12 100.............................. NickScholfield 104
(Andy Turnell) *in tch in midfield: hdwy 8th: chsd wnr 3 out: rdn and unable qck bef 2 out: mstke and lost 2nd last: wknd flat* **11/2[2]**

/P6- **4** *5* **Ede's**[26] 5119 10-10-4 78... ColinBolger 78
(Pat Phelan) *in tch towards rr: rdn and hdwy after 5th: chsd ldrs and drvn 3 out: 4th and no imp whn mstke 2 out* **10/1**

43U- **5** *7* **Grand Bay (USA)**[77] 4097 9-11-8 96................................(t) APMcCoy 90
(Jonjo O'Neill) *hld up towards rr: mstke 4th: hdwy 9th: chsd wnr 12th tl mstke 3 out: rdn and btn bef next: j.rt 2 out* **7/1**

0FP- **6** *4 1/2* **Ouragan Lagrange (FR)**[51] 4637 8-11-2 90...................... JamieMoore 78
(Gary Moore) *in tch: mstke 5th: hdwy after 8th: chsd wnr 10th tl 12th: wkng whn j. slowly 3 out: wl btn bef next* **12/1**

4U2- **7** *2* **Kercabellec (FR)**[11] 5390 12-9-7 74 oh5........................ JoeCornwall(7) 60
(John Cornwall) *in tch in midfield: mstke 1st: rdn and struggling 11th: wl hld fr 3 out* **11/1**

35P- **8** *1 3/4* **Play The Rock (FR)**[41] 4836 7-10-12 86................ AndrewGlassonbury 71
(Philip Kirby) *j.rt: a bhd: struggling u.p 11th: nvr trbld ldrs* **14/1**

3P0- **9** *1/2* **Sarobar (IRE)**[155] 2626 10-10-12 86................................ LiamTreadwell 70
(John Spearing) *t.k.h early: hld up in midfield: dropped to rr 5th: last whn mstke next: rdn and struggling 8th: no ch fr next* **20/1**

0R- **P** **Iphar (FR)**[161] 2505 9-11-7 95... DavidEngland —
(Giles Smyly) *racd keenly: chsd ldr 4th tl 8th: sn pushed along: wknd 11th: t.o whn p.u 2 out* **40/1**

/P1- **P** **Bold Punt (IRE)**[52] 4604 8-11-12 **100**............................(p) PaddyBrennan —
(Tom George) *led: mstke 1st: mstke 3rd: hdd next: styd prom: chsd wnr and hit 8th: lost 2nd 10th: wkng whn blnd next: sn p.u* **13/2**[3]

5m 2.30s (-3.00) **Going Correction** -0.20s/f (Good) **11** Ran SP% **113.8**
Speed ratings: **97,95,93,91,89 87,86,85,85,— —**
toteswingers: 1&2 £4.90, 1&3 £4.30, 2&3 £5.10 CSF £30.26 CT £141.60 TOTE £3.40: £1.10, £1.50, £2.00; EX 26.00.
Owner Davids Thorpe & Cowie **Bred** Miss T M Hammond **Trained** Condicote, Gloucs

FOCUS
There was little strength in depth but it was run at a reasonable pace, though the finishing time was around three seconds slower than the earlier, and classier, novice chase.

NOTEBOOK
Brimham Boy had a battle for the early lead, but by virtue of keeping up a relentless pace and jumping soundly he was able to dominate. The pack was poised leaving the back straight, but the winner showed a gutsy attitude to keep on best. He did not stay over 3m last time, but had previously won with plenty to spare over a similar trip, and is still improving. (op 6-1 tchd 5-1)
Noble Future is generally consistent and once again ran his race, but he lacks any sort of finishing pace which means he keeps getting beaten at all sorts of trips. (op 5-1)
High Jack(IRE) plugged on but was tiring near the finish and could pose no threat. He won well last time to end a lengthy spell in a handicap-enforced wilderness, but after that win he was raised to a similar mark that had proved beyond him in the past. (op 9-2)
Ede's is attractively weighted over fences compared to his hurdling mark and ran well enough considering he is not at his best on right-handed tracks. (op 12-1)
Grand Bay(USA) did not jump that fluently but still made steady progress in the back straight. He was travelling ominously well to the home turn but once again found little from that point and he remains an enigma. (op 6-1)
Bold Punt(IRE) was too keen early on but tended to slow into the fences, and despite moving up to the lead again midway, he had already expended too much energy to maintain his position. (op 6-1 tchd 8-1)

157 DAVID MARKS 50TH BIRTHDAY H'CAP HURDLE (9 hdls 1 omitted) 2m 5f 110y
7:05 (7:06) (Class 4) (0-105,105) 4-Y-0+ **£2,927** (£859; £429; £214)

Form RPR
4/4- **1** **Legion D'Honneur (UAE)**[22] 5172 5-11-9 **102**............ RichardJohnson 108+
(Chris Down) *hld up in tch in midfield: hdwy to chse ldrs after 5th: led bef 2 out: rdn and j.lft last 2: edging lft flat but hld on wl* **5/1**[3]
124/ **2** ½ **Ring Bo Ree (IRE)**[452] 3787 7-11-4 **97**............................ PaddyBrennan 103+
(Tom George) *t.k.h: hld up towards rr: clipped heels and stmbld after 1st: hdwy bypassing 7th: rdn to chal and j.lft 2 out: drvn and mstke last: unable qck flat* **9/2**[2]
225/ **3** 8 **Mvuto**[371] 56 5-11-5 **105**.. MattCrawley(7) 104
(Lucy Wadham) *chsd ldrs: led 6th: rdn and hdd bef 2 out: outpcd by ldng pair 2 out: kpt on one pce* **16/1**
000- **4** 14 **Thompson**[81] 4043 6-11-4 **97**....................................... WayneHutchinson 83
(Richard Phillips) *in tch: nt fluent 5th: rdn bef 3 out: wknd bef 2 out* **28/1**
040- **5** 8 **Dundry**[22] 5172 9-11-8 **101**..(p) JamieMoore 81
(Gary Moore) *in tch in midfield: mstke 6th: hdwy bypassing next: rdn bef 3 out: wknd wl bef 2 out* **14/1**
0P5- **6** 4 ½ **Barlin Bay**[14] 5317 6-10-0 **82** oh15 ow3......................... TommyPhelan(3) 56
(Harry Chisman) *hld up in last trio: rdn and effrt wl bef 3 out: no prog and wl btn 3 out: plugged on past btn horse fr 2 out: nvr trbld ldrs* **125/1**
/04- **7** shd **Patrixtoo (FR)**[30] 5038 9-10-0 **79** oh4.............................. AndrewTinkler 53
(Tim Fitzgerald) *hld up in rr: hdwy bypassing 7th: rdn and no hdwy 3 out: wl btn bef next* **20/1**
0PP- **8** 1 ¼ **Zahra's Place**[17] 5253 7-11-5 **105**......................... SamTwiston-Davies(7) 78
(Neil King) *hld up in tch in rr: hdwy wl bef 3 out: rdn and no prog whn mstke 3 out: wl btn bef next* **12/1**
633- **9** 8 **Carmela Maria**[10] 8 5-10-11 **90**....................................... KeithMercer 56
(Mike Sowersby) *chsd ldr tl led 2nd: hdd 6th: sn rdn and lost pl: wl bhd 3 out: t.o* **11/1**
54P/ **10** 15 **Little Bit Of Hush (IRE)**[80] 10-10-6 **88**........................... AlexMerriam(3) 40
(Neil King) *led tl 2nd: chsd ldr after tl 6th: wknd wl bef 3 out: t.o 2 out* **25/1**
/00- **11** 23 **Go All Out (IRE)**[52] 4618 7-11-9 **105**................................ SeanQuinlan(3) 36
(Richard Phillips) *in tch in midfield: rdn and struggling wl bef 3 out: t.o bef 2 out* **66/1**
003- **R** **Crystal Prince**[31] 5015 6-10-6 **85**......................................(tp) FelixDeGiles —
(Charlie Longsdon) *hld up in tch in rr: gd hdwy on inner and wl in tch whn short of room: rn out and uns rdr bnd bef 3 out* **14/1**
440- **F** **Mistress To No One**[35] 4960 7-11-8 **101**.....................(t) WarrenMarston —
(Martin Keighley) *towards rr whn fell heavily 2nd: fatally injured* **9/1**
/50- **P** **Ede's The Best**[59] 4463 6-11-4 **97**.. ColinBolger —
(Pat Phelan) *in tch in midfield: pushed along after 5th: rdn and struggling after 6th: t.o whn p.u 2 out* **33/1**
/20- **P** **Old Brigade (IRE)**[69] 4262 6-10-11 **90**.................................(t) APMcCoy —
(Jonjo O'Neill) *chsd ldrs: wnt 2nd bef 3 out: rdn and btn bef next: 7th and wl btn whn eased and p.u 2 out* **10/3**[1]
400- **P** **Argentis (FR)**[98] 3681 5-11-0 **93**..................................(t) JimmyMcCarthy —
(Charlie Morlock) *hld up in tch in rr: rdn and toiling after 6th: t.o whn p.u 2 out* **40/1**

5m 2.10s (-8.50) **Going Correction** -0.20s/f (Good) **16** Ran SP% **122.9**
Speed ratings (Par 105): **107,106,103,98,95 94,94,93,90,85 77,—,—,—,— —**
toteswingers: 1&2 £2.10, 1&3 £17.70, 2&3 £30.60 CSF £26.68 CT £346.91 TOTE £6.50: £1.60, £2.50, £6.60, £8.20; EX 36.70.
Owner F Down,V Holland,J T Measures,P Holland **Bred** Darley **Trained** Mutterton, Devon

FOCUS
A fair contest that saw some reasonable performances from the placed horses. A step up from the winner with the second to his mark. The seventh flight was bypassed.

NOTEBOOK
Legion D'Honneur(UAE) ran well at Exeter last month on his return from a year-long absence. That fitness edge proved crucial at the finish as he found enough to repel a sustained challenge from the last. He is lightly raced and improving, and this could have proved a lenient mark. His previous absence was more to do with changing stables and settling in rather than recovering from an injury, and connections were keen to keep hold of this promising chasing type. (tchd 13-2)
Ring Bo Ree(IRE) attracted sustained market support on his first start since February last year. He was poised to fight out the finish with the winner although he never looked quite likely to get on top, but pulled well clear of the third, who had been with the leading duo turning for home. If he improves for this run he should gain compensation. (op 4-1)
Mvuto raced prominently throughout despite some ponderous jumping at times, and she was still with the leaders until getting outpaced from the final turn. She was a bit fresh on her first run for a year and did not get home, but should come on for this. (op 12-1)
Thompson made a mistake at the first in the back straight and was struggling from then on, and could do no more than plug on. He has been dropping down the weights but might need to continue the slide to be competitive. (op 25-1 tchd 33-1)
Dundry was around seven lengths behind the winner when they met at Exeter last month, but could not get competitive on similar terms and looks moderate. (op 11-1)

Old Brigade(IRE) was travelling well poised on the shoulders of the leaders before reportedly hanging badly on the home bend and was soon pulled up. Official explanation: jockey said, regarding running, that the gelding made an error at the third last flight and then hung badly. (op 11-2)

158 HUNTINGDON RACECOURSE H'CAP CHASE (17 fncs 2 omitted) 3m
7:40 (7:40) (Class 4) (0-110,108) 5-Y-0+ **£4,683** (£1,375; £687; £343)

Form RPR
P43- **1** **Roseneath (IRE)**[32] 4983 6-11-1 **97**................................(p) PaulMoloney 117+
(Alex Hales) *hld up in rr: stdy prog 11th: trckd ldr gng wl bef 2 out: led between last 2: sn clr: shkn up and wl in command flat: easily* **9/2**[2]
B1P- **2** 15 **Darn Hot**[27] 5105 6-11-9 **108**.. ChrisHonour(3) 112+
(Chris Down) *t.k.h: hld up in tch in rr: hdwy after 10th: chsd ldr 13th: led 3 out: rdn and blnd 2 out: hdd between last 2: sn btn* **20/1**
441- **3** 11 **Grenoli (FR)**[7] 49 9-10-7 **96** 7ex.................................(bt) JoeCornwall(7) 91+
(John Cornwall) *j.lft: led tl 3 out: sn rdn: 3rd and wl btn next: mstke last* **6/1**[3]
P45- **4** 1 ½ **Sycho Fred (IRE)**[16] 5271 9-10-0 **82**.................................(t) KeithMercer 72
(Mike Sowersby) *chsd ldrs: pushed along and dropped in rr 10th: struggling u.p 13th: lost tch next: wnt poor 4th 2 out: plugged on u.p flat* **11/1**
3P3- **5** 32 **Pantalaimon**[52] 4617 9-11-10 **106**................................... RichardJohnson 67
(Henry Daly) *chsd ldr: reminders 6th: mstke next: more reminders after 9th: lost 2nd 13th: struggling u.p next: wl btn after 3 out: t.o 2 out* **4/1**[1]
252- **P** **Thai Vango (IRE)**[98] 3682 9-11-9 **105**.............................. PaddyBrennan —
(Nigel Twiston-Davies) *chsd ldrs: rdn and struggling 13th: wl btn 3 out: t.o whn p.u next: b.b.v* **4/1**[1]
203- **P** **Arctic Shadow**[36] 4943 8-11-7 **108**................................ DeanColeman(5) —
(Tim Vaughan) *chsd ldrs: hit 10th: pushed along whn blnd bdly 12th: nt rcvr and sn lost tch: p.u next* **20/1**
5U2- **F** **Lord Brunello (IRE)**[51] 4644 8-11-3 **99**...................(p) ChristianWilliams —
(Lawney Hill) *racd in last trio: blnd 1st: last whn fell 9th* **15/2**
1P4- **P** **Porta Vogie (IRE)**[19] 5219 8-11-8 **104**................................ JodieMogford —
(Graeme McPherson) *a towards rr: mstke 1st: hmpd and mstke 12th: sn toiling u.p: t.o whn p.u 2 out* **10/1**

6m 3.10s (-7.20) **Going Correction** -0.20s/f (Good) **9** Ran SP% **111.2**
Speed ratings: **104,99,95,94,84 —,—,—,—**
toteswingers: 1&2 £36.00, 1&3 £10.50, 2&3 £27.50 CSF £75.55 CT £524.00 TOTE £5.20: £2.50, £5.10, £2.60; EX 109.10.
Owner The Strathclyders **Bred** N J Connors **Trained** Wardington, Oxon

FOCUS
This was run at a searching pace and those that tried to go with the leader were labouring on the final circuit, leaving two hold-up horses to benefit. A big step forward from the easy winner.

NOTEBOOK
Roseneath(IRE) was ridden patiently until making stealthy progress throughout the final circuit, only being produced to challenge at the last, from where he won authoritatively. He is best when able to pick off rivals in a strongly run race, so the way the race fell apart suited him best. He is inexperienced over fences but both his wins have been over course and distance, so this looks the type of track where he can find his ideal conditions. (op 13-2)
Darn Hot was also ridden patiently, but made her forward move first, taking up the running leaving the back straight. She blundered at the second last, handing the initiative to the winner, but she was beginning to tire slightly at that stage. She reportedly suffered an irregular heartbeat when pulling up at Taunton last month, but with connections reassured that she is back to full health she will be kept on the go. (op 18-1 tchd 22-1 and 25-1 in places)
Grenoli(FR) set the pace but could not get an easy lead. He kept up the gallop longer than the early challengers, who were all struggling by the final circuit, but he finally ran out of steam before the last. If he can manage to dominate he can regain the winning thread. (op 9-2 tchd 13-2)
Sycho Fred(IRE) did not jump that fluently and was never able to get competitive as a result, but made some good late headway. (op 14-1)
Pantalaimon raced prominently but was never going that well, carrying his tail high early on and needing reminders before halfway, and though he responded he was already struggling by the final circuit. (tchd 9-2)
Thai Vango(IRE) was another to race prominently until he found the pace too much and dropped away on the final circuit. This was his first run since January and it is conceivable he may have needed this Official explanation: vet said gelding had bled (op 9-2 tchd 3-1)

159 HUNTINGDON H'CAP HURDLE (8 hdls) 2m 110y
8:10 (8:12) (Class 4) (0-115,115) 4-Y-0+ **£2,927** (£859; £429; £214)

Form RPR
344- **1** **Stage Acclaim (IRE)**[27] 5107 5-11-5 **115**............ SamTwiston-Davies(7) 118
(Dr Richard Newland) *led tl 3rd: styd prom: ev ch and rdn 3 out: mstke next: led between last 2: styd on gamely flat* **11/2**
U26- **2** ¾ **Saltagioo (ITY)**[22] 5172 6-11-1 **104**.............................. WayneHutchinson 106
(Alan King) *t.k.h: hld up in tch: rdn to chse ldng pair bef 2 out: pressing ldrs whn hit last: unable qck u.p flat: wnt 2nd nr fin* **4/1**[2]
FU2- **3** ½ **Mega Watt (IRE)**[42] 4828 5-10-13 **102**............................. AidanColeman 104+
(Venetia Williams) *trckd ldrs: jnd ldrs gng wl 5th: led bef 3 out: hit 2 out: narrowly hdd between last 2: rdn and nt qckn flat: lost 2nd nr fin* **3/1**[1]
643- **4** 6 **Rebel Dancer (FR)**[17] 5255 5-11-3 **106**.........................(t) RichardJohnson 101
(Philip Hobbs) *t.k.h: hld up in rr: hdwy 5th: chsd ldng pair and rdn bef 2 out: wknd between last 2* **9/2**[3]
544- **5** 8 **Mon Michel (IRE)**[34] 4970 7-11-7 **110**...............................(p) JamieMoore 100
(Gary Moore) *racd in last pair: pushed along after 5th: rdn and edging rt bef 2 out: no prog and wl btn between last 2* **6/1**
163- **6** 7 **Crosby Jemma**[8] 34 6-11-1 **104**.. KeithMercer 86
(Mike Sowersby) *wl in tch in midfield: rdn after 3 out: sn btn* **8/1**
126- **7** 7 **Three Ships**[139] 2934 9-10-8 **100**.................................... CharlieHuxley(3) 76
(S Wynne) *chsd ldng pair: rdn after 3 out: btn bef next* **16/1**
360- **8** 23 **Nicky Nutjob (GER)**[17] 5255 4-11-0 **107**.......................... GerardTumelty 58
(Jeff Pearce) *racd keenly: w ldr tl led 3rd: mstke 5th: sn rdn and hdd bef next: wl btn after 3 out* **25/1**

3m 49.0s (-5.90) **Going Correction** -0.20s/f (Good)
WFA 4 from 5yo+ 18lb **8** Ran SP% **113.7**
Speed ratings (Par 105): **105,104,104,101,97 94,91,80**
toteswingers: 1&2 £6.60, 1&3 £3.20, 2&3 £3.40 CSF £27.83 CT £77.41 TOTE £8.20: £2.70, £2.10, £1.70; EX 31.70 Place 6: £99.90 Place 5: £74.69.
Owner G Carstairs **Bred** Oaks Stud **Trained** Claines, Worcs

FOCUS
A three-way battle from the last in a competitive handicap. Solid handicap form with the first two rated to their marks.

NOTEBOOK
Stage Acclaim(IRE) raced prominently and stuck to the task in courageous style. Although he could never shake off the pursuers, he was able to keep up the gallop and that was enough to prevail, as he lacks a change of gear and is therefore best when able to sustain an even pace. He has only been with current connections for about four weeks and will be kept on the go, possibly stepping up in trip. (op 7-1)

Saltagioo(ITY) was driven to close up as the leaders threatened to get away, and he stuck to the task, staying on right to the line. He has looked a bit short of pace, so the minimum trip on a fast track would not have been to his advantage. (op 5-1)
Mega Watt(IRE) made smooth progress to look the likely winner turning in, but he found less than expected on his handicap debut. He had not shown much previously, but evidently has some ability. (op 9-2)
Rebel Dancer(FR) was very keen held up in rear, and he still carried his head high when allowed to go after the leaders, but he was unable to make up the ground. He is beginning to look rather awkward. (op 4-1 tchd 5-1)
Mon Michel(IRE) was never travelling that well and could only make modest headway from a rear position. He is on a reasonable mark based on the height of his form two years ago, but a resurgence is looking unlikely at present. (op 9-2)
T/Plt: £51.00 to a £1 stake. Pool £47,821.16, 683.52 winning tickets. T/Qpdt: £15.40 to £1 stake. Pool £6,012.32, 287.23 winning tickets. SP

42 KELSO (L-H)

Wednesday, May 5

OFFICIAL GOING: Good (good to firm in places; 7.4)
Wind: Slight, half against Weather: Overcast, dry

160 NICHOLSON BROS. (S) H'CAP CHASE (17 fncs) 2m 6f 110y
2:05 (2:05) (Class 5) (0-95,95) 5-Y-0+ **£2,276** (£668; £334; £166)

Form RPR
504- **1** **Lindseyfield Lodge (IRE)**10 [9] 9-10-13 **85**....(p) MichaelMcAlister(3) 97+
(Robert Johnson) *led 1st: mde rest: clr after 2 out: nt fluent last: styd on strly* **14/1**
255- **2** *7* **Instant Shot (IRE)**54 [4555] 7-10-5 **74**.............................. RichieMcGrath 80
(Jim Goldie) *led to 1st: cl up: effrt after 2 out: one pce run-in* **7/1**2
005- **3** *8* **Smart Man**11 [5389] 8-10-2 **74**..(p) HarryHaynes(3) 72
(Evelyn Slack) *a.p: rdn bef 3 out: kpt on same pce after next* **16/1**
443- **4** *8* **Red Dynamite**19 [5219] 9-11-3 **89**.............................. MichaelO'Connell(3) 80
(Geoffrey Harker) *nt fluent: hld up: hdwy and in tch bef 3 out: outpcd between last 2* **9/2**1
055- **5** *2* **Skipping Chapel**41 [4836] 9-10-2 **74**................................(t) AdrianLane(3) 63
(N W Alexander) *in tch: drvn along 3 out: no imp after next* **9/1**3
/1P- **6** *1 ½* **Cash On Friday**16 [5272] 9-11-12 **95**.............................. WilsonRenwick 82
(P Monteith) *hld up in tch: outpcd after 13th: n.d after* **16/1**
3P5- **7** *4 ½* **Reasonably Sure (IRE)**10 [9] 10-10-6 **75**...................(v) BrianHughes 58
(Patrick Morris) *cl up: outpcd after 3 out: wknd fr next* **11/1**
4P0- **8** *14* **Bullies Acre (IRE)**55 [4535] 10-9-11 **69** oh5..............(p) CampbellGillies(3) 40
(Barry Murtagh) *hld up towards rr: struggling fr 12th: nvr on terms* **40/1**
00P- **9** *6* **Kalmo Bay (FR)**16 [5272] 7-11-1 **91**................................ MissCWalton(7) 56
(Ferdy Murphy) *midfield: outpcd 12th: struggling after next* **33/1**
000- **10** *15* **Sea Cove**10 [10] 10-11-4 **90**.. RyanMania(3) 42
(Dianne Sayer) *towards rr: struggling 12th: sn btn* **33/1**
PPP- **11** *16* **Sierra Peak (IRE)**13 [5334] 6-11-2 **85**.............................. DenisO'Regan 23
(Martin Todhunter) *in tch: mstke 6th: rdn and wknd fr 4 out* **14/1**
06P- **P** **Witness Run (IRE)**16 [5272] 10-11-2 **85**.............................. PaddyAspell —
(Sandy Thomson) *sn bhd: struggling 1/2-way: t.o whn p.u bef 3 out* **16/1**
544- **F** **Political Pendant**32 [4983] 9-10-6 **80**........................(p) JamesHalliday(5) —
(Rayson Nixon) *hld up last: fell heavily 2nd* **7/1**2
343- **P** **Viel Gluck (IRE)**23 [5167] 7-11-11 **94**.................................... GrahamLee —
(Ferdy Murphy) *nt fluent: bhd: reminders 11th: struggling after next: t.o whn p.u bef 3 out* **9/2**1

5m 47.1s (2.60) **Going Correction** -0.425s/f (Good) **14** Ran SP% **119.0**
Speed ratings: **78,75,72,70,69 68,67,62,60,55 49,—,—,—**
toteswingers: 1&2 £41.60, 1&3 not won, 2&3 not won. CSF £107.83 CT £1603.38 TOTE £16.30: £5.60, £3.80, £4.20; EX 203.40.There was no bid for the winner.
Owner Toon Racing **Bred** Mrs M Brophy **Trained** Newburn, Tyne & Wear

FOCUS
A rare selling handicap chase, so not form to be getting excited about, and most of these are unreliable types in any case. The first two are rated to their marks. Surprisingly, given a few of these are iffy jumpers, there weren't many incidents at the fences.

NOTEBOOK
Lindseyfield Lodge(IRE), who travelled and jumped well out in front, had this in the bag a long way out, finally breaking his duck at the 14th time of asking over fences. A mistake at the last didn't really hinder his momentum, as he was travelling so much better than his rivals, and his rider didn't have to get overly serious on the run-in to assert again. He had not been in great form recently, but the step up to this trip seemed to help and, more importantly, he got into a good rhythm at the head of affairs. (op 18-1)
Instant Shot(IRE) was always chasing the leader and he kept on well enough to post something like a career-best, but wasn't good enough. (op 17-2)
Smart Man shaped with more promise than in recent outings.
Red Dynamite, dropped in grade, once again ran as though he can find a small race at some point. (op 4-1 tchd 7-2)
Witness Run(IRE) Official explanation: jockey said gelding lost its action
Viel Gluck(IRE) Official explanation: trainer said gelding was lame left-hind

161 SIS CONDITIONAL JOCKEYS' NOVICES' H'CAP HURDLE (8 hdls) 2m 110y
2:35 (2:36) (Class 4) (0-105,102) 4-Y-0+ **£2,797** (£821; £410; £205)

Form RPR
353- **1** **Beidh Tine Anseo (IRE)**41 [4837] 4-11-2 **99**.............. CampbellGillies(3) 121+
(Lucinda Russell) *rrd and fell over bkwards at s: in tch: smooth hdwy 3 out: led gng wl run-in: shkn up briefly and sn wl clr: readily* **3/1**1
622- **2** *14* **Mountskip**19 [5216] 6-10-4 **83**.. AlexanderVoy(3) 86
(Rose Dobbin) *prom: ev ch after 3 out: led appr last to run-in: kpt on but no ch w ready wnr* **13/2**2
135- **3** *1 ¼* **Barron Watlass (IRE)**29 [5074] 6-11-11 **101**................ MichaelO'Connell 103
(George Moore) *trckd ldrs: led bef 2 out to appr last: kpt on same pce run-in* **9/1**3
003- **4** *1* **Piccolo Pride**149 [2749] 5-11-0 **95**..................................(t) MrDarylMillar(5) 97
(Maurice Barnes) *hld up towards rr: smooth hdwy and prom after 3 out: effrt next: one pce fr last* **18/1**
P00- **5** *5* **King's Chorister**46 [4730] 4-10-0 **80** oh5..........................(t) HarryHaynes 72
(Barry Murtagh) *hld up: hdwy bef 3 out: rdn and no imp bef next* **40/1**
50P- **6** *½* **Arctic Rock**10 [9] 7-9-8 **80** ow2..................................(p) BarryBrowne(10) 77
(Geoffrey Harker) *led: rn wd bnd bef 4th: hdd bef 2 out: sn outpcd: n.d after* **33/1**
6P5- **7** *3* **Claude Carter**12 [5374] 6-11-9 **102**................................ EwanWhillans(3) 95
(Alistair Whillans) *prom: carried wd bnd bef 4th: drvn and outpcd after 3 out: n.d after* **12/1**
633- **8** *1 ¼* **Solis (GER)**12 [5374] 7-11-0 **93**... RyanMania(3) 85
(P Monteith) *t.k.h: in tch: outpcd 3 out: sn btn* **13/2**2
404- **9** *1 ½* **Naughty Diesel**10 [12] 7-9-11 **78** oh1 ow2.......................(t) AshleyBird(5) 69
(Robert Johnson) *hld up: pushed along bef 2 out: nvr rchd ldrs* **16/1**
065- **10** *1 ¾* **Cuigny (FR)**53 [4580] 7-11-3 **96**...................................(bt) GarryWhillans(3) 85
(Simon Shirley-Beavan) *hld up on outside: mstke 1st: struggling after 3rd: n.d after* **22/1**
05P- **11** *1 ¼* **Saujana**150 [2732] 6-11-2 **95**.. KyleJames(3) 83
(Joseph Bewley) *midfield: rdn and outpcd bef 4th: btn fnl 3* **33/1**
065- **12** *2 ¼* **Giant Star (USA)**41 [4837] 7-9-6 **76** oh3.............................. PaulNorton(8) 62
(Jim Goldie) *hld up: rdn along after 4 out: nvr on terms* **10/1**
/40- **13** *1 ½* **Hernando Cortes**141 [2890] 6-10-11 **87**............................ JamesHalliday 72
(Martin Todhunter) *hld up: struggling 4 out: nvr on terms* **25/1**
260- **14** *3 ½* **Arabian Silk (IRE)**51 [4650] 4-10-11 **94**........................(t) JohnKington(3) 72
(Donald McCain) *in tch: reminders after 3rd: drvn fr 1/2-way: wknd fnl 3* **20/1**
PPU- **15** *2 ½* **Perez (IRE)**10 [10] 8-9-9 **76** oh14..............................(v) PaulGallagher(5) 55
(Wilf Storey) *prom tl nt fluent and wknd fr 3 out* **14/1**
0/0- **P** **Danehill Silver**41 [4835] 6-10-9 **85**.................................. FearghalDavis —
(Brian Storey) *midfield: outpcd whn sddle slipped and p.u bef 3 out* **80/1**

3m 57.3s (-4.50) **Going Correction** -0.125s/f (Good)
WFA 4 from 5yo+ 18lb **16** Ran SP% **118.8**
Speed ratings (Par 105): **105,98,97,97,95 94,93,92,92,91 90,89,88,87,86 —**
toteswingers: 1&2 £2.30, 1&3 £10.30, 2&3 £14.40 CSF £19.71 CT £160.32 TOTE £3.60: £1.20, £1.70, £2.50, £4.40; EX 14.30.
Owner Ian D Miller **Bred** J S Bolger **Trained** Arlary, Perth & Kinross
■ Stewards' Enquiry : Paul Gallagher one-day ban: used whip when out of contention (May 19)
Ryan Mania caution: used whip when out of contention
Barry Browne four-day ban: careless riding (May 19,21-23)
Kyle James caution: used whip when out of contention
John Kington caution: used whip when out of contention

FOCUS
More modest fare. A massive step up from the winner but there should be more to come. The form appears pretty solid.

NOTEBOOK
Beidh Tine Anseo(IRE) is going the right way now, having initially taken time to acclimatise to life with Lucinda Russell, and this former 90-rated Flat performer in Ireland relished tackling a sound surface for the first time over hurdles. Despite causing problems at the start, where he unshipped his rider, the son of Rock Of Gibraltar travelled eyecatchingly well off the pace, before moving smoothly through to take over after the last and clearing right way with plenty still left in the locker. Unexposed and open to plenty more improvement in handicaps, he looks the type who ought to be capable of defying a rise in the weights. (op 11-4 tchd 5-2)
Mountskip is also progressing at a lowly level since being switched to handicaps and a sound surface, and he posted another encouraging effort. (op 7-1 tchd 6-1)
Barron Watlass(IRE) was made to look a little one-paced in the straight and appears better suited by a stiffer test of stamina. (op 10-1)
Piccolo Pride travelled strongly before not finding much for pressure, although a mistake at the second-last didn't help.
Danehill Silver Official explanation: jockey said saddle slipped

162 DRYBURGH ABBEY HOTEL NOVICES' H'CAP CHASE (FOR THE HADDINGTON JUBILEE CUP) (19 fncs) 3m 1f
3:05 (3:07) (Class 3) (0-135,128) 5-Y-0+ **£6,505** (£1,910; £955)

Form RPR
1P1- **1** **Gilsland (IRE)**13 [5341] 7-10-9 **111**..................................(b) JasonMaguire 115+
(Donald McCain) *nt fluent on occasions: mde all: hesitated 4th: blnd 15th: hrd pressed fr 3 out: hung rt run-in: hld on wl* **5/6**1
513- **2** *nk* **Heez A Steel (IRE)**21 [5185] 9-11-5 **128**........................ AlistairFindlay(7) 131
(George Charlton) *pressed wnr: rdr dropped whip after 6th: ev ch 3 out: outpcd appr last: rallied run-in: kpt on: jst hld* **7/4**2
22U- **3** *2 ¼* **Greenandredparson (IRE)**7 [49] 7-9-11 **102** oh6......... AdrianLane(3) 103
(Paul Murphy) *nt fluent: chsd ldrs: outpcd 4 out: rallied 2 out: chsd wnr bef last to run-in: one pce last 200yds* **11/2**3

6m 33.2s (1.70) **Going Correction** -0.425s/f (Good) **3** Ran SP% **106.3**
Speed ratings: **80,79,79**
CSF £2.61 TOTE £1.50; EX 2.70.
Owner Brendan Richardson and Jon Glews **Bred** The Well Dunne Racing Syndicate **Trained** Cholmondeley, Cheshire
■ Stewards' Enquiry : Adrian Lane caution: used whip with excessive frequency

FOCUS
Only three runners, but a race chock full of jumping errors. It was steadily run and the winner is rated below his best.

NOTEBOOK
Gilsland(IRE) was less than fluent and was almost brought to a standstill when ploughing through the fifith-last, but he recovered remarkably well before boxing on gamely and just holding off a rallying Heez A Steel in a driving finish. He doesn't look straightforward as he needed urging along with a circuit to go, and then wandered around a bit in front, but to his credit he stayed on gamely after the last under strong driving. (tchd evens in places)
Heez A Steel(IRE) was far from fluent at some of his fences but having looked like he was about to drop away after the second-last, he rallied despite his rider having lost his whip, and finished his race strongly. (op 15-8 tchd 13-8)
Greenandredparson(IRE) had a bit on from 6lb out of the handicap, so he fared quite well, especially given his shaky jumping technique, but he looks a risky proposition whatever the company over fences. (op 9-2 tchd 6-1)

163 CHEVIOT MARQUEES NOVICES' H'CAP HURDLE (11 hdls) 2m 6f 110y
3:40 (3:40) (Class 4) (0-110,110) 4-Y-0+ **£2,797** (£821; £410; £205)

Form RPR
U3P- **1** **Jurisdiction**103 [3588] 6-11-3 **101**.. GrahamLee 120+
(Rose Dobbin) *cl up: led 3rd to next: w ldr: led bef 4 out: clr next: eased run-in* **6/1**
205- **2** *12* **Mini Beck**24 [5142] 11-11-5 **110**..................................... AlexanderVoy(7) 116
(Sandy Thomson) *prom: effrt after 3 out: chsd wnr between last 2: no imp run-in* **5/1**3
00U- **3** *9* **Paddington Bob (IRE)**13 [5339] 6-10-1 **85**...................... RichieMcGrath 83
(Pauline Robson) *trckd ldrs: drvn 4 out: effrt and chsd wnr bef 2 out to between last 2: no ex* **7/4**1
464- **4** *29* **Fly Tipper**46 [4736] 10-9-7 **84** oh20.................................. PaulGallagher(7) 56
(Wilf Storey) *in tch: outpcd whn blnd 7th: n.d after* **40/1**
122- **5** *2 ½* **Samizdat (FR)**8 [34] 7-11-8 **109**.. RyanMania(3) 79
(Dianne Sayer) *led to 3rd: led next to bef 4 out: lost 2nd bef 2 out: eased whn btn* **4/1**2
3P6- **6** *13* **Doodlebop (IRE)**16 [5273] 7-10-0 **84** oh2..........................(p) PaddyAspell 42
(Ann Hamilton) *hld up: hdwy and prom after 3rd: struggling 7th: btn fr next* **12/1**
F3F- **7** *16* **Watch The Wind**29 [5074] 9-9-9 **86** oh6 ow2.................... MissCWalton(7) 29
(James Walton) *bhd: struggling 1/2-way: nvr on terms* **22/1**

F/P- **8** 3 3/4 **Saddlers' Supreme (IRE)**[327] 686 8-10-4 **88** JamesReveley 28
(Martin Todhunter) *cl up: disputing ld whn wnt rt and lost pl 2nd: struggling 7th: sn btn* **20/1**

500- **9** 26 **Just Maddie**[7] 42 6-10-11 **99** (p) JamesHalliday(5) 17
(Rayson Nixon) *bhd: struggling 1/2-way: sn btn* **40/1**

5P5- **P** **I Witness (IRE)**[24] 5140 8-10-2 **93** AlistairFindlay(7) —
(Jane Walton) *in tch: lost pl 4th: struggling fr 1/2-way: t.o whn p.u bef 3 out* **14/1**

5P0- **P** **Qolloure (FR)**[55] 4534 6-10-8 **95** GaryBerridge(3) —
(Simon Shirley-Beavan) *trckd ldrs tl wknd fr 7th: t.o whn p.u bef 3 out* **11/1**

5m 39.6s (-1.40) **Going Correction** -0.125s/f (Good) **11** Ran SP% **124.0**
Speed ratings (Par 105): **97,92,89,79,78 74,68,67,58,— —**
toteswingers: 1&2 £4.00, 1&3 £4.00, 2&3 £4.20 CSF £37.10 CT £75.96 TOTE £7.90: £1.80, £1.40, £1.10; EX 31.00.
Owner River Tweed Syndicate **Bred** Mrs J Cadzow **Trained** South Hazelrigg, Northumbria

FOCUS
A big step up from the winner in this ordinary handicap with the second rated to his mark.

NOTEBOOK
Jurisdiction, a good-ground bumper winner, had flopped in three outings over hurdles, all on soft ground, but into handicaps for the first time, and back on his favoured surface, he proved a completely different proposition. Always travelling strongly, he cruised clear after the third last and was in no danger after the last flight of hurdles. He looks a decent tool granted these conditions and is open to plenty more improvement. (op 8-1)
Mini Beck ⊠ travelled really strongly off the pace, but could not close the gap when push came to shove in the straight. He remains a maiden but this, along with one or two of his previous efforts, mark him down as one who is capable of winning off this sort of mark. (tchd 9-2)
Paddington Bob(IRE) was a relatively warm order after unseating when holding a winning chance at Uttoxeter last time, but he came under pressure down the back and was never making any impression on the leader. (op 15-8 tchd 2-1)
Fly Tipper, a long-standing maiden, plugged on for a well beaten fourth.
Samizdat(FR)'s stamina ran out, but he ran a good race up to a point and is one to be interested in back in trip. (op 6-1 tchd 7-1)
Saddlers' Supreme(IRE) Official explanation: jockey said mare had a breathing problem

164 FLEET BAR, EYEMOUTH H'CAP CHASE (21 fncs) 3m 4f
4:20 (4:21) (Class 4) (0-110,108) 5-Y-0+ **£3,382** (£993; £496; £248)

Form RPR

P34- **1** **Minouchka (FR)**[7] 46 10-11-5 **108** MissKBryson(7) 117+
(Simon Shirley-Beavan) *hld up in tch: outpcd whn hit 15th: rallied and in tch bef 3 out: hdwy to ld run-in: styd on strly* **13/2**

1P2- **2** 4 **Seize**[7] 46 8-11-11 **107** GrahamLee 112
(Ferdy Murphy) *hld up: hdwy and cl up 16th: ev ch 3 out: led last: hdd run-in: kpt on same pce* **5/2**[1]

P22- **3** 1 1/2 **Reckless Venture (IRE)**[48] 4707 9-10-8 **90** (t) PeterBuchanan 93
(Lucinda Russell) *prom: effrt bef 2 out: ev ch and rdn bef last: one pce run-in* **4/1**[2]

211- **4** 4 **Rosie All Over**[13] 5342 8-11-8 **104** (p) JasonMaguire 104
(Donald McCain) *cl up: led 9th: rdn 4 out: hdd last: outpcd run-in* **9/2**[3]

21P- **5** 3 **Old Noddy (IRE)**[16] 5272 10-10-9 **91** (b[1]) BrianHughes 87
(A M Crow) *mde most to 9th: cl up: drvn 4 out: rallied: wknd bef last* **15/2**

5P5- **6** 68 **Windy Hills**[16] 5272 10-10-0 **89** (p) MissJRRichards(7) 24
(Nicky Richards) *in tch: outpcd 16th: sn btn: t.o* **9/1**

/60- **P** **Prince Of Slane**[16] 5271 11-9-11 **82** oh17 (v[1]) CampbellGillies(3) —
(Chris Grant) *disp ld to 8th: lost pl 12th: struggling 15th: t.o whn p.u bef 3 out* **11/1**

7m 10.0s (-15.40) **Going Correction** -0.425s/f (Good) **7** Ran SP% **110.2**
Speed ratings: **105,103,103,102,101 82,—**
toteswingers: 1&2 £3.30, 1&3 £3.80, 2&3 £2.20 CSF £22.20 TOTE £7.50: £2.60, £1.30; EX 14.00.
Owner Mrs P M Shirley-Beavan **Bred** Michel Du Jonchay & Jean-Claude Cherasse **Trained** Abbotrule, Borders
⊠ Stewards' Enquiry : Jason Maguire six-day ban: used whip causing minor weal (May 19-24)

FOCUS
A decent gallop to this handicap. The winner is rated back to her 2009 form with the next two to their marks.

NOTEBOOK
Minouchka(FR), who was patiently ridden, swept up the inside after the last fence to win on her final racecourse start. The winner is now off to stand as a broodmare. (op 6-1 tchd 7-1)
Seize was well backed and looked the most likely winner when jumping to the front at the last, but he was readily brushed aside by Minouchka in the final 150 yards. This was his second consecutive decent effort in defeat and he is clearly in good heart. (op 3-1 tchd 9-4)
Reckless Venture(IRE) doesn't have a great strike-rate but he ran his race, in a little stronger company than is often the case. (op 9-2)
Rosie All Over, who was behind Seize at Ayr in March off the same terms, came into this in cracking shape having won her last two but she didn't see this out as well as some of her rivals. (op 11-4)

165 FORSYTHS OF WOOLER NOVICES' HUNTERS' CHASE (19 fncs) 3m 1f
4:55 (4:55) (Class 6) 5-Y-0+ **£1,561** (£484; £242; £121)

Form RPR

FPP- **1** **Benbeoch**[11] 11-11-9 81 (p) MrCDawson(3) 96+
(Sandy Thomson) *dictated modest gallop: shkn up to go clr after 2 out: kpt on wl run-in: eased towards fin: unchal* **7/2**[3]

5/ **2** 14 **Lady Brig**[11] 11-10-12 0 MissKBryson(7) 71
(Mrs Wendy Hamilton) *prom: outpcd 14th: rallied 3 out: rdn after next: styd on run-in: wnt 2nd cl home: no ch w wnr* **11/10**[1]

5/P- **3** nse **Silver Palomino**[32] 4985 9-11-5 70 MissLAlexander(7) 77
(Mrs L A Coltherd) *chsd wnr: rdn after 2 out: one pce run-in* **40/1**

43-0 **4** 11 **Cherryland**[4] 90 7-11-5 97 (p) NathanMoscrop(7) 68
(Philip Kirby) *mstkes: hld up: outpcd 13th: hdwy to chse ldrs bef 2 out: wknd last* **3/1**[2]

F **Temple Green**[17] 8-11-0 0 AlistairFindlay(5) —
(Mrs J Martin-Mayland) *in tch: outpcd bef 14th: rallied and in tch whn blnd 3 out: 7 l 5th whn fell next* **10/1**

00P/ **P** **What A Cliche**[24] 7-11-5 0 MrECameron(7) —
(R A Wilson) *j.rt on occasions: in tch: hdwy 1/2-way: rdn 3 out: sltly hmpd and wknd next: t.o whn p.u bef last* **20/1**

6m 41.2s (9.70) **Going Correction** -0.425s/f (Good) **6** Ran SP% **111.1**
Speed ratings: **67,62,62,58,— —**
toteswingers: 1&2 £1.60, 1&3 £9.60, 2&3 £7.80 CSF £8.05 TOTE £5.50: £2.50, £2.40; EX 9.10.
Owner Mr & Mrs A M Thomson **Bred** Mrs E J Deans **Trained** Lambden, Berwickshire

FOCUS
A weak hunter chase. The easy winner was heading for this sort of figure when falling here earlier in the season.

NOTEBOOK
Benbeoch, who fell two out when clear in a race here in February, made amends in style having jumped and travelled strongly at the head of affairs. His form is littered with falls and pulled-ups, but there was nothing wrong with his jumping here, and he proved that he's a capable chaser by cruising home with his head in his chest. (tchd 10-3)
Lady Brig has a good strike-rate in points but she was well beaten on her only previous run under rules and, despite this weaker company, she could never get a blow in on Benbeoch. (op 11-8 tchd Evens and 6-4 in a place)
Silver Palomino raced a bit too keenly early and, having chased the leader throughout, could only plug on at the one pace. (op 28-1)
Cherryland, who hasn't been seeing out his races very well, didn't get home once again but that may have been as much to do with some sloppy jumping that stamina. (op 4-1)

166 TIMEFORM BETFAIR RACING CLUB H'CAP HURDLE (10 hdls) 2m 2f
5:25 (5:25) (Class 4) (0-115,110) 4-Y-0+ **£2,797** (£821; £410; £205)

Form RPR

024- **1** **Maska Pony (IRE)**[14] 5315 6-10-11 **90** GrahamLee 98+
(George Moore) *w ldr: led whn hit 3 out: hrd pressed last: styd on gamely to assert last 150yds* **9/2**[1]

30P- **2** 3 1/4 **Annibale Caro**[200] 1793 8-11-9 **102** JamesReveley 106
(Jim Goldie) *hld up and bhd: smooth hdwy bef 3 out: chal gng wl last: rdn run-in: no ex last 150yds* **11/2**[2]

500- **3** 14 **Painted Sky**[12] 5357 7-11-0 **93** BrianHughes 86
(Richard Fahey) *trckd ldrs: effrt and rdn whn blnd last: sn outpcd by first two* **10/1**

23F- **4** 1 1/4 **Nevsky Bridge**[16] 5275 8-10-12 **96** JamesHalliday(5) 86
(Martin Todhunter) *hld up: hdwy and in tch bef 2 out: rdn whn hit last: sn outpcd* **8/1**[3]

640- **5** 2 **Safin (GER)**[54] 4554 10-10-0 **79** oh2 TomMessenger 67
(Sue Bradburne) *trckd ldrs: hit and rdn 3 out: outpcd between last 2* **25/1**

/55- **6** 1 1/4 **Player (FR)**[213] 1624 7-11-6 **99** PaddyAspell 86
(Ann Hamilton) *hld up towards rr: hdwy and in tch appr 3 out: outpcd fr next* **18/1**

U20- **7** 1/2 **Goldan Jess (IRE)**[173] 2257 6-11-5 **105** KyleJames(7) 92
(Philip Kirby) *trckd ldrs: rdn bef 2 out: wknd last* **8/1**[3]

200- **8** 9 **Wensleydale Web**[16] 5275 8-11-1 **94** DenisO'Regan 73
(Martin Todhunter) *hld up: hdwy bef 3 out: rdn and wknd bef next* **22/1**

506- **9** 5 **Benmadigan (IRE)**[19] 5207 8-11-7 **103** FearghalDavis(3) 77
(Nicky Richards) *bhd: hdwy into midfield after 4 out: wknd fr next* **9/1**

P00- **10** 1/2 **Midnite Blews (IRE)**[17] 5255 5-10-11 **93** (t) MichaelMcAlister(3) 67
(Maurice Barnes) *led to bef 3 out: rdn and wknd fr next* **22/1**

066- **11** 3 1/4 **Marsool**[45] 4755 4-11-3 **100** JasonMaguire 67
(Donald McCain) *hld up: struggling bef 3 out: sn btn* **10/1**

045- **12** 43 **Front Rank (IRE)**[14] 5308 10-11-9 **105** RyanMania(3) 37
(Dianne Sayer) *prom: reminders after 1st: lost pl bef 6th: lost tch fr next* **10/1**

300- **13** 60 **Long Distance (FR)**[24] 5142 5-11-11 **104** (b[1]) PeterBuchanan —
(Lucinda Russell) *hld up: struggling after 4 out: sn btn: virtually p.u run-in* **33/1**

100- **P** **Ethan's Star (IRE)**[297] 916 8-11-0 **96** HarryHaynes(3) —
(William Young) *prom: lost pl qckly after 5th: sn p.u* **25/1**

4m 29.8s (2.80) **Going Correction** -0.125s/f (Good)
WFA 4 from 5yo+ 18lb **14** Ran SP% **117.7**
Speed ratings (Par 105): **88,86,80,79,78 78,78,74,71,71 70,51,24,—**
toteswingers: 1&2 £1.60, 1&3 £9.60, 2&3 £7.80 CSF £26.47 CT £237.41 TOTE £3.70: £1.10, £2.80, £5.70; EX 24.00 Place 6: £44.91 Place 5: £6.98.
Owner Mrs J M Gray **Bred** Twelve Oaks Stud Establishment **Trained** Middleham Moor, N Yorks

FOCUS
An ordinary handicap. The first two finished clear and are rated to their marks.

NOTEBOOK
Maska Pony(IRE) proved a tough horse to pass and battled on really gamely to assert again and win going away. This was his first success and, having failed to get home over longer trips this year, the drop back to 2m2f on a sound surface seemed to suit him well. He is relatively unexposed in handicaps and he is certainly at the right end of the weights so there is scope for progress. (op 11-2)
Annibale Caro was given a fine ride and, having made stealthy headway around the outside, bagged that favoured far rail. He cruised up to challenge at the final flight but was beaten off by a stronger stayer in the end. Still, he finished miles clear of the rest and is clearly capable of going one better soon. (op 7-2)
Painted Sky attracted significant market support despite having run a stinker at Bath last time, and fared infinitely better. He was held when blundering at the last but this was a much more encouraging run and he is back down below his last winning mark. (op 20-1 tchd 9-1)
Nevsky Bridge proved that his latest fall hasn't dented her confidence by running well enough. (op 10-1)
Safin(GER) kept on for pressure and shaped with more promise than in recent starts. (op 28-1)
Benmadigan(IRE) Official explanation: jockey said gelding never travelled
Ethan's Star(IRE) Official explanation: jockey said gelding pulled up lame
T/Plt: £149.20 to a £1 stake. Pool: £48304.24, 236.19 winning tickets. T/Qpdt: £8.40 to a £1 stake. Pool: £4353.56, 380.90 winning tickets. RY

NEWTON ABBOT (L-H)
Thursday, May 6

OFFICIAL GOING: Good (good to soft in places)
All bends moved but effect on distances not notified.
Wind: virtually nil Weather: light rain

167 THE WINNING POST RESTAURANT "NATIONAL HUNT" MAIDEN HURDLE (DIV I) (8 hdls) 2m 3f
2:05 (2:05) (Class 4) 4-Y-0+ **£3,382** (£993; £496; £248)

Form RPR

342- **1** **Express Leader**[23] 5173 7-11-0 119 NickScholfield 120+
(Paul Nicholls) *trckd clr ldr: clsd on ldr 5th: led 3 out: sn clr: v easily* **11/10**[1]

5- **2** 14 **Gambo (IRE)**[77] 4117 4-10-9 0 PaulMoloney 97
(Evan Williams) *hld up in rr of mid-div: hdwy 6th: outpcd 3 out: staqyed on again fr next: wnt 2nd bef last: no ch w wnr* **9/1**

226- **3** 2 **Magical Treasure**[42] 4846 6-11-0 0 PaddyBrennan 101
(Sophie Leech) *in tch: outpcd appr 6th: styd on fr 2 out* **16/1**

243- **4** 3 1/2 **Lord Landen (IRE)**[55] 4572 5-11-0 110 AidanColeman 98
(Rachel Hobbs) *racd freely: led: clr tl 5th: hdd 3 out: sn rdn and no ch w wnr: wknd after 2 out* **3/1**[2]

000- **5** 3 **Evening Haze**[68] 4301 6-10-0 0 MrDGPrichard(7) 89
(Phillip Dando) *mid-div: trckd ldrs 4th: rdn after 3 out: one pce fr next* **80/1**

520- **6** *11* **Powerfullbeat**[246] 1379 6-10-7 0 .... MrRMahon(7) 85
(Kathleen Sanderson) *mid-div tl wknd 3 out* **66/1**

4P5/ **7** *7* **Royal Arms**[760] 4899 8-11-0 0 .... ChristianWilliams 79
(C Roberts) *struggling 4th: a in rr* **100/1**

122- **8** *10* **Swing State**[31] 5057 5-11-0 0 .... MattieBatchelor 70
(Tony Carroll) *mid-div: hdwy after 5th to trck ldrs: rdn after 3 out: sn wknd* **11/2**[3]

9 *2* **Bobbits Way**[197] 5-11-0 0 .... TomO'Brien 68
(Alan Jones) *chasd ldrs: rdn after 6th: wknd after 3 out* **12/1**

5PU- **10** *50* **Dolly Grey**[28] 5104 7-10-7 88 .... (t) SeamusDurack 16
(Grant Cann) *chsd ldrs early: in rr fr 4th: t.o* **100/1**

/50- **11** *1* **Bold Exit (IRE)**[136] 3007 5-10-4 0 .... CiaranMckee(10) 22
(Tom George) *struggling 4th: t.o fr after next* **50/1**

P **Hows The Boy** 7-11-0 0 .... JackDoyle —
(Victor Dartnall) *a in rr: t.o 5th: p.u bef 2 out* **40/1**

4m 30.8s (-3.10) **Going Correction** 0.0s/f (Good)
WFA 4 from 5yo+ 18lb 12 Ran SP% **120.7**
Speed ratings (Par 105): **106,100,99,97,96 91,88,84,83,62 62,—**
toteswingers: 1&2 £5.20, 1&3 £5.90, 2&3 £8.40 CSF £12.92 TOTE £2.70: £2.40, £5.10, £6.20; EX 12.30.
Owner R Metherell & J George & Mrs L Squire **Bred** Mrs J F Maitland-Jones **Trained** Ditcheat, Somerset

FOCUS
The opening novice hurdle was run at a strong pace which had the field strung out from a long way. The easy winner was value for further and is rated to his mark.

NOTEBOOK
Express Leader ran out an easy winner having raced prominently throughout. His jumping still has room for improvement and now he has broken his maiden status over hurdles he could take a similar race under a penalty; although he would not want the ground too fast. In time he will make a chaser as well. (tchd 6-5)
Gambo(IRE) had shown promise on his hurdling debut at Ffos Las and he ran creditably and fared best of those who were held up. Natural progression should see him winning soon. (op 12-1)
Magical Treasure was under pressure with a circuit to go and if he is to win over hurdles it will be over a longer trip, possibly in handicaps.
Lord Landen(IRE) is officially rated 110 and set a strong pace and was getting tired when not jumping fluently at the final two flights of hurdles. He could easily drop in trip but should be winning over hurdles before long. (op 4-1)

168 THE WINNING POST RESTAURANT "NATIONAL HUNT" MAIDEN HURDLE (DIV II) (8 hdls) 2m 3f
2:35 (2:35) (Class 4) 4-Y-O+ **£3,382** (£993; £496; £248)

Form RPR

032- **1** **Lucaindubai (IRE)**[11] 4 4-10-9 0 .... PaulMoloney 125+
(Evan Williams) *mde all: gng clrwhn hit 3 out: eased run-in* **2/1**[2]

210- **2** *15* **Caught By Witness (IRE)**[15] 5323 5-11-0 0 .... WarrenMarston 115+
(Milton Harris) *t.k.h: trckd ldrs: wnt 2nd 6th: hit next: rdn appr 2 out: sn btn: mstke last* **8/11**[1]

400- **3** *30* **Mzuri Bay**[11] 8 5-11-0 0 .... MarkGrant 90
(Brendan Duke) *chsd wnr to 6th: wknd next* **40/1**

2F-0 **4** *23* **Strictly Business**[5] 93 5-11-0 0 .... PaddyBrennan 66
(Tom George) *hld up in rr: hdwy 6th: wnt distant 4th 2 out* **9/1**[3]

/P0- **5** *19* **Rich Kayf**[20] 5214 6-10-7 0 .... L-BdrSallyRandell(7) 49
(John O'Shea) *trckd ldrs: wknd after 6th: lost distant 4th 2 out* **100/1**

/50- **6** *7* **Magusta (GER)**[36] 4959 6-11-0 0 .... (t) DarylJacob 42
(Jamie Snowden) *in rr: sme hdwy 5th: wknd 3 out: sn bhd* **28/1**

7 *½* **Seaview Lad (IRE)**[39] 7-10-7 0 .... NathanSweeney(7) 42
(Bob Buckler) *mid-div: wknd 6th: sn bhd: t.o next* **50/1**

505- **8** *9* **Smiles Better**[9] 37 5-10-11 0 .... ChrisHonour(3) 34
(Chris Down) *in rr: bhd fr 6th: sn t.o* **66/1**

4P0- **P** **Nobel Play**[18] 5260 6-10-0 0 .... AodhaganConlon(7) —
(Debra Hamer) *mid-div: reminders 5th: sn bhd: t.o whn p.u bef 2 out* **100/1**

40- **P** **Commanche Luke**[283] 1064 7-11-0 0 .... ChristianWilliams —
(C Roberts) *nt fluent in rr: bhd and reminders 5th: t.o whn p.u bef 2 out* **25/1**

5- **P** **Raise Your Hopes (IRE)**[52] 4652 7-11-0 0 .... NickScholfield —
(Linda Blackford) *in rr: bhd whn reminders 4th: t.o 6th: p.u bef 2 out* **66/1**

4m 32.0s (-1.90) **Going Correction** 0.0s/f (Good)
WFA 4 from 5yo+ 18lb 11 Ran SP% **117.9**
Speed ratings (Par 105): **104,97,85,75,67 64,64,60,—,— —**
toteswingers: 1&2 £1.02, 2&3 £13.60, 1&3 not won CSF £3.79 TOTE £3.40: £1.10, £1.10, £7.90; EX 5.10.
Owner R J Gambarini **Bred** Martin Cullinane **Trained** Llancarfan, Vale Of Glamorgan

FOCUS
The second race of the afternoon saw another winner make all, and it was marginally the slower division. The winner is rated up nearly a stone and there was no strength in depth.

NOTEBOOK
Lucaindubai(IRE) made every yard and is clearly learning fast having run green last time. He jumped more fluently and is open to progression but he may now be put away for a short spell as his trainer feels he could benefit from a break. He ought to be able to win over hurdles again when reappearing. (tchd 15-8)
Caught By Witness(IRE) showed plenty of ability in bumpers and never looked like reaching the winner but he showed more than enough to suggest he will be winning over hurdles before long. (op 5-6 tchd 10-11)
Mzuri Bay was under pressure from a long way out and looked as if he has an attitude problem. He may struggle to win races. (op 33-1)
Strictly Business was not given a hard time and he is now eligible for a mark. He could be up to winning a low-grade handicap. (op 17-2)

169 HAPPY 65TH BIRTHDAY ALLAN TWYFORD H'CAP CHASE (16 fncs) 2m 5f 110y
3:05 (3:05) (Class 4) (0-110,109) 5-Y-O+ **£3,968** (£1,165; £582; £290)

Form RPR

/FP- **1** **Magical Harry**[54] 4586 10-10-12 95 .... AidanColeman 110+
(Anthony Honeyball) *in tch: travelling wl whn joining ldrs 4 out: led sn after 3 out: pushed clr appr last: comf* **20/1**

521- **2** *9* **Maurisca (FR)**[12] 5390 5-11-9 106 .... FelixDeGiles 115+
(Charlie Longsdon) *mid-div: trcking ldrs whn mstke 9th: rdn whn led briefly 3 out: hld fr after next: landed v awkwardly last* **4/1**[2]

2F2- **3** *1 ¼* **Cloud Nine (IRE)**[17] 5280 7-11-12 109 .... TomScudamore 114
(David Pipe) *nt a fluent in narrow ld: rdn and hdd 3 out: sn one pce* **7/2**[1]

351- **4** *¾* **Quedillac (FR)**[9] 37 6-11-8 105 .... RichardJohnson 111+
(Tim Vaughan) *trckd ldrs: rdn appr 4 out: styd on same pce fr after next* **7/2**[1]

643- **5** *¾* **Shanahan (IRE)**[13] 5366 9-11-1 101 .... (p) SeanQuinlan(3) 106
(Liam Corcoran) *hld up towards rr: hdwy fr 11th: rdn in 6th after 3 out: one pce fr next: blnd last* **16/1**

420- **6** *1 ¼* **Sula's Legend**[173] 2277 9-11-4 108 .... MarkQuinlan(7) 110
(Neil Mulholland) *hld up towards rr: sme late prog fr 3 out: nvr trbld ldrs* **16/1**

50-U **7** *10* **Over The Flow**[7] 56 8-10-5 95 .... NathanSweeney(7) 88
(Bob Buckler) *a towards rr* **25/1**

/00- **8** *1 ½* **Sninfia (IRE)**[147] 2799 10-11-1 105 .... MattGriffiths(7) 99
(Kevin Bishop) *prom: mstke 7th (water): rdn and ev ch 3 out: sn wknd* **16/1**

402- **9** *20* **River Ripples (IRE)**[40] 4898 11-10-12 95 .... (p) PaddyBrennan 68
(Tom George) *trckd ldrs: rdn after 12th: wknd qckly after next* **11/1**

2UP- **10** *71* **Dune Raider (USA)**[64] 4389 9-11-5 105 .... LeeStephens(3) 14
(David Evans) *bhd fr 3rd: t.o fr after 9th* **20/1**

00P- **P** **Sordid Secret (IRE)**[68] 4295 7-11-2 99 .... PaulMoloney —
(Evan Williams) *a towards rr: t.o whn p.u bef 4 out* **33/1**

F10- **P** **Power Shared (IRE)**[36] 4960 6-11-6 103 .... WayneHutchinson —
(Pat Murphy) *mid-div: early bhd 7th: t.o whn p.u bef 10th* **8/1**[3]

5m 26.0s (4.60) **Going Correction** +0.35s/f (Yiel) 12 Ran SP% **117.8**
Speed ratings: **105,101,101,101,100 100,96,96,88,63 —,—**
toteswingers:1&2 £27.00, 2&3 £7.00, 1&3 £22.10 CSF £96.84 CT £357.68 TOTE £28.90: £6.00, £1.10, £2.00; EX 130.20.
Owner A Honeyball **Bred** R And J Micklethwait **Trained** Seaborough, Dorset

FOCUS
A competitive looking handicap which turned into a procession and saw another winner who was towards the fore throughout. Solid form which should work out.

NOTEBOOK
Magical Harry travelled supremely well throughout and drew clear to win easily. In the past he has had tendon problems and has been known to bleed, but if his trainer can keep him sound he ought to be competitive in similar races as he comes to himself at this time of year. Official explanation: trainer had no explanation for the apparent improvement of form, or why the gelding stopped quickly turning into the home straight at Chepstow, but said that it does come into its own at this time of the year (tchd 25-1)
Maurisca(FR), who is already better over fences than he was over hurdles, was raised 9lb for his victory last time and gave another bold showing today. He should remain competitive in similar races.
Cloud Nine(IRE) is still a maiden and would be better if stepped up in trip, but he is becoming disappointing. (op 4-1)
Quedillac(FR) was an easy winner over hurdles last time but looked one-paced on his British chase debut. He could prove difficult to place now as his handicap mark does not look the most generous.
Shanahan(IRE) reverted to type and found nothing off the bridle. He is very hard to win with. (op 14-1)
Sninfia(IRE) travelled well for a long way on her first start for Kevin Bishop and if she can find any improvement she can acquit herself well throughout the summer. (op 20-1)
Dune Raider(USA) Official explanation: jockey said the gelding was not keen to race without its customary blinkers.
Power Shared(IRE) Official explanation: jockey said that the gelding was never travelling' vet said the gelding had an irregular heartbeat

170 EMMA H'CAP HURDLE (8 hdls) 2m 3f
3:45 (3:45) (Class 3) (0-130,128) 4-Y-O+ **£6,463** (£1,909; £954; £477; £238)

Form RPR

305- **1** **Nortonthorpe Lad (IRE)**[12] 5393 8-11-4 120 .... (p) APMcCoy 128+
(Alison Thorpe) *in rr: pushed along 4th: led bef 2 out: clr appr last: drvn out* **7/2**[1]

010- **2** *9* **Robo (FR)**[136] 3004 5-10-11 113 .... RichardJohnson 114+
(Philip Hobbs) *chsd ldrs: led bef 3 out: hdd appr next: wl btn whn hit last* **10/1**

100- **3** *5* **I Hear A Symphony (IRE)**[28] 5099 8-11-9 125 .... PaddyBrennan 119
(Charlie Longsdon) *in rr: hdwy 3 out: one pce and sn mod 3rd* **11/2**[3]

141- **4** *5* **Agente Romano (USA)**[52] 4652 5-11-2 118 .... PaulMoloney 107
(Evan Williams) *led 2nd: hdd bef 6th: sn lost pl: kpt on to take modest 4th 2 out* **8/1**

010- **5** *½* **Freddy's Star (IRE)**[20] 5217 8-10-11 118 .... KeiranBurke(5) 107
(Gerald Ham) *wnt prom 5th: outpcd after next: kpt on run-in* **33/1**

050- **6** *8* **Mister Benedictine**[15] 5319 7-11-3 119 .... (t) MarkGrant 100
(Brendan Duke) *chsd ldrs: rdn after 6th: hdd bef 3 out: sn wknd* **16/1**

400- **7** *1* **Jocheski (IRE)**[17] 5282 6-10-11 113 .... AndrewThornton 93
(Tony Newcombe) *mid-div: lost pl 6th: sme hdwy 3 out: sn wknd* **12/1**

FF0- **8** *15* **Armenian Boy (FR)**[202] 1777 7-11-2 118 .... (t) TomScudamore 85
(David Pipe) *in rr: hdwy to chse ldrs 5th: wknd after next: sn bhd: t.o and eased 2 out* **5/1**[2]

310- **P** **Tritonville Lodge (IRE)**[12] 5393 8-11-10 126 .... JackDoyle —
(Emma Lavelle) *led to 2nd: lost pl and blnd 6th: t.o whn p.u bef next* **9/1**

614- **P** **Sebastiano (FR)**[44] 4803 7-10-6 115 .... JoshuaMoore(7) —
(Gary Moore) *in rr: bhd whn p.u bef 4th* **14/1**

011- **P** **Santera (IRE)**[40] 4880 6-10-10 112 .... TimmyMurphy —
(Andrew Haynes) *lost pl 5th: sn bhd: t.o whn p.u bef 3 out* **13/2**

4m 30.3s (-3.60) **Going Correction** 0.0s/f (Good) 11 Ran SP% **121.0**
Speed ratings (Par 107): **107,103,101,99,98 95,95,88,—,— —**
toteswingers: 1&2 £11.90, 1&3 £6.60, 2&3 £16.90 CSF £39.93 CT £194.54 TOTE £4.20: £2.40, £4.00, £3.30; EX 26.30.
Owner Don Jenkins **Bred** Mrs Kathleen McElroy **Trained** Bronwydd Arms, Carmarthens

FOCUS
A strongly run race which saw the eventual winner under pressure from an early stage. The overall form looks fair for the grade.

NOTEBOOK
Nortonthorpe Lad(IRE) ran promisingly last time at Sandown and was flat out in the early stages, but he benefited from the strong pace. He had good form last season before losing his way, and another win is not out of the question on this showing. (tchd 4-1)
Robo(FR) is a chasing sort who ran well on his second start in handicaps. He is suited by better ground and can still progress over hurdles, if he improves his jumping. In time he will be a chaser. (op 15-2)
I Hear A Symphony(IRE) is not the most consistent and struggled here. He is not well handicapped and could be difficult to win with. (op 9-1)
Agente Romano(USA) should be more competitive on his favoured firm summer ground. (op 6-1)
Armenian Boy(FR) hails from a yard in good form but he found the overnight rain against him. (op 8-1)
Tritonville Lodge(IRE) Official explanation: jockey said the gelding lost its action
Sebastiano(FR) Official explanation: jockey said the gelding was never travelling; vet said the gelding had an irregular heartbeat

Santera(IRE) Official explanation: jockey said the mare moved poorly

171 SOUTH WEST RACING CLUB NOVICES' H'CAP HURDLE (8 hdls) 2m 1f
4:20 (4:20) (Class 5) (0-95,95) 4-Y-0+ £2,123 (£619; £309)

Form RPR
62-1 1 **Skye But N Ben**[7] [54] 6-11-9 92 7ex................................(b) APMcCoy 101+
(Jim Best) *led 2nd: mde rest: drew ahd after 3 out: idled and kpt up to work: kpt on* **8/15**[1]
646- 2 7 **Windpfeil (IRE)**[18] [5260] 4-11-8 95.. ColinBolger 89
(Simon Burrough) *in tch: rdn to chse wnr after 3 out: kpt on but nvr any imp on wnr* **16/1**
PP0- 3 ½ **Art Man**[4] [5172] 7-11-4 90... HaddenFrost(3) 90
(James Frost) *mid-div: hit 5th: rdn after 3 out: styd on fr next: wnt 3rd nr fin* **33/1**
4P3/ 4 nse **Justabout**[407] [4705] 7-11-2 85.. JoeTizzard 83
(Colin Tizzard) *led tl 2nd: trckd ldrs: rdn after 3 out: styd on same pce* **14/1**
040- 5 ½ **Broadway Allstar (IRE)**[17] [5290] 5-11-2 88.................... SeanQuinlan(3) 87
(Liam Corcoran) *trckd ldrs: rdn after 3 out: kpt on same pce* **22/1**
5F0- 6 2¾ **Commit To Memory**[18] [5255] 5-11-10 93........................ LeightonAspell 88+
(Jimmy Fox) *hld up towards rr: styd on past btn horses fr after 3 out: nvr a danger* **40/1**
4/6- 7 3¼ **Monkhair (IRE)**[43] [4831] 5-10-8 77.................................. MattieBatchelor 70
(Tony Carroll) *in tch: rdn after 3 out: sn one pce* **20/1**
0/P- 8 25 **Zelos (IRE)**[361] [233] 6-11-2 85...(bt) RodiGreene 55
(David Bridgwater) *trckd wnr fr 2nd: ev ch whn mstke 5th: sn rdn: wknd sn after next: t.o* **66/1**
06B- 9 23 **Majestic Bull (USA)**[46] [4765] 4-11-3 90................................... JackDoyle 35
(Susan Gardner) *a towards rr: hmpd 4th: t.o fr next* **20/1**
433- P **Tar (IRE)**[24] [5169] 6-11-12 95..(v) RichardJohnson —
(Tim Vaughan) *a in rr: t.o whn p.u after 4th* **10/1**[3]
633- P **Laneguy (FR)**[25] [5155] 5-11-12 95.................................... PaddyBrennan —
(Tom George) *a towards rr: t.o whn p.u bef 2 out* **9/1**[2]
5F0- F **Haling Park (UAE)**[141] [2661] 4-11-4 91................................ JamieMoore —
(Gary Moore) *trcking ldrs whn fell heavily 4th* **25/1**

4m 10.7s (5.00) **Going Correction** 0.0s/f (Good)
WFA 4 from 5yo+ 18lb **12** Ran SP% **121.5**
Speed ratings (Par 103): **88,84,84,84,84 82,81,69,58,— —,—**
toteswingers: 1&2 £5.80, 1&3 £12.40, 2&3 £47.10 CSF £9.43 CT £170.05 TOTE £1.60: £1.30, £3.70, £8.30; EX 11.30.
Owner N J Sillett **Bred** Charles And David Hodge **Trained** Lewes, E Sussex

FOCUS
A moderate handicap, and it would be unwise to go overboard about the form. The winner was 5lb below his recent winning level with the second and third rated to their marks.

NOTEBOOK
Skye But N Ben was an easy winner at Hereford last time and under his penalty he scored well despite idling in front. The handicapper will now have his say and it is likely he will be dropped into selling company after having a small break. (op 8-13 tchd 4-6 in places)
Windpfeil(IRE) has shown promise in his qualifying runs for a mark and he ran creditably on his handicap debut. He ought to be competitive in similar races in the summer but he does not look the most straightforward of rides.
Art Man showed his first meaningful piece of form over hurdles, however his hurdling was not always fluent and he will need to improve if he is to win races. (op 28-1)
Justabout is a tall horse who goes best fresh but he ran only moderately and winning races could prove challenging with him.
Commit To Memory made some good late progress and is capable of better but he is still a maiden.
Tar(IRE) Official explanation: jockey said that the gelding was never travelling

172 PADDOCK RESTAURANT CLAIMING HURDLE (8 hdls) 2m 3f
4:55 (4:55) (Class 5) 4-Y-0+ £2,055 (£599; £299)

Form RPR
3P3- 1 **Wild Tonto (IRE)**[11] [3] 7-11-10 110.............................. PaddyBrennan 116+
(Nigel Twiston-Davies) *mid-div: smooth hdwy after 3 out to ld bef next: rdn whn idled after next: kpt on* **3/1**[2]
122/ 2 6 **Nanga Parbat (FR)**[661] [920] 9-11-3 118........................... MrRMahon(7) 111
(Paul Nicholls) *trckd ldrs: hit 4th: led after 3 out: rdn and hdd bef next: kpt on same pce* **4/1**[3]
2P6- 3 2¼ **Fourty Acers (IRE)**[40] [4884] 10-11-4 123.......................(vt) JohnnyFarrelly 103
(David Pipe) *led: rdn appr 6th: hit 3 out: sn rdn: one pce sn after* **15/8**[1]
3P0- 4 1½ **Mr Melodious**[10] [23] 4-10-9 108.. DavidEngland 92
(Nigel Twiston-Davies) *mid-div tl dropped in rr 5th: plugged fr after 3 out: wnt 4th whn hit last* **28/1**
150- 5 8 **Michigan Assassin (IRE)**[18] [5258] 8-10-13 105...... AodhaganConlon(7) 98
(Debra Hamer) *trckd ldrs: t.k.h: hit 3rd: mstke 3 out: sn rdn: wknd* **20/1**
6 6 **The Clubhousebee (IRE)**[189] [1978] 6-10-6 107............. MattGriffiths(7) 84
(Kevin Bishop) *hld up towards rr: hdwy appr 6th: led whn mstke 3 out: sn rdn and hdd: wknd next* **9/1**
100- 7 3 **Bubbs**[13] [5365] 8-10-11 87.. RodiGreene 78
(Nick Ayliffe) *chsd ldrs tl 5th: sn in rr* **40/1**
502- 8 13 **Alrafid (IRE)**[106] [2095] 11-11-0 108......................................(b) JamieMoore 69
(Gary Moore) *a towards rr* **16/1**
614- 9 14 **Pips Assertive Way**[259] [1258] 9-10-9 94........................ MattieBatchelor 52
(Tony Carroll) *chsd ldr tl 5th: sn in rr* **33/1**
210- 10 1 **Stance**[13] [5365] 11-11-0 104...(p) LeightonAspell 56
(Peter Hedger) *a bhd* **12/1**
404- R **Mix N Match**[13] [5364] 6-10-11 92....................................... HaddenFrost(3) —
(James Frost) *mid-div: hdwy 5th: abt to join ldr and travelling wl whn rn out 3 out* **22/1**

4m 37.7s (3.80) **Going Correction** 0.0s/f (Good)
WFA 4 from 6yo+ 18lb **11** Ran SP% **121.3**
Speed ratings (Par 103): **92,89,88,87,84 82,80,75,69,68 —**
toteswingers: 1&2 £3.00, 1&3 £2.70, 2&3 £3.30 CSF £15.23 TOTE £5.30: £2.00, £1.10, £1.80; EX 14.50.Mix N Match was claimed by Sarah J. Minton for £5000.
Owner Walters Plant Hire Ltd **Bred** Thomas Matthews **Trained** Naunton, Gloucs

FOCUS
An ordinary claimer which contained some very moderate and slow horses. The winner is rated to his mark and the fourth is the best guide.

NOTEBOOK
Wild Tonto(IRE) ran well on his first start for Nigel Twiston-Davies and this drop in grade saw him return to the winner's enclosure. If kept to this grade he should remain competitive. (tchd 11-4 and 7-2)
Nanga Parbat(FR) had a spell on the sidelines with leg problems and he ran well for long enough to suggest he still retains some ability. In a similar race he can win before long but he is very one-paced. (op 9-2 tchd 5-1)
Fourty Acers(IRE) has not won for a long time and is unlikely to do so unless he improves his attitude. (op 5-2)
Mr Melodious is badly handicapped and his only realistic chances come in sellers and claimers. However, he looks like he will struggle to win a race as he is so slow. (op 25-1)
Mix N Match was travelling well when running out at the third from home. In low-grade handicaps he should be winning soon. (op 16-1)

173 TEIGN SUITE RESTAURANT HUNTERS' CHASE (20 fncs) 3m 2f 110y
5:25 (5:25) (Class 6) 6-Y-0+ £1,054 (£324; £162)

Form RPR
550- 1 **Apollo Blaze (IRE)**[23] [5177] 9-11-7 92................................ MissJBuck(7) 98
(Mrs P J Shaw) *mde virtually all: j.rt more often than nt: lft in clr advantage 15th: unchal after: styd on* **20/1**
51P/ 2 3 **Alambique (IRE)**[12] 11-11-7 0.. MrRHawkins(7) 95
(T W Dennis) *in tch: slow jump 10th: sn nudged along: lft 2nd 15th: rdn after 4 out: styd on same pce fr next* **6/1**[3]
642- 3 49 **Thirtytwo Red (IRE)**[23] [5177] 9-12-0 98................... MrJoshuaGuerriero 51
(R J Alford) *chsd ldrs tl lost pl 13th: sn no ch: t.o: wnt remote 3rd fnl stride* **7/4**[1]
/60- 4 nse **Beau Supreme (IRE)**[11] 13-11-11 85................................ MrRMahon(3) 51
(B Sanderson) *trckd ldrs: rdn appr 14th: wknd 4 out: lft remote 3rd last tl fnl stride* **12/1**
334- 5 5 **Charles Street**[256] [1293] 8-11-7 95... MrJPark(7) 47
(Mrs T Porter) *hld up: wknd 14th: t.o* **11/1**
2/F- R **Paddy The Piper (IRE)**[11] 13-11-7 0.............................. MrMHeard(7) 51
(J Heard) *in tch: rdn after 15th: wnt 3rd next: wknd 3 out: ref last* **9/1**
P/U- R **Mioche D'Estruval (FR)**[12] 10-11-7 0.......................... MrBenRobarts(7) —
(A J Farrant) *slow 1st: a bhd tailing off whn ref 15th* **10/1**
/65- P **Thunder Child**[13] [5369] 10-11-11 76................................ MattGriffiths(3) —
(Mrs Sue Popham) *in tch: rdn after 13th: sn wl bhd: p.u after 4 out* **22/1**
1/0- F **Pertinent (FR)**[26] 7-11-11 116...(t) MrDCollins(7) —
(C R Whittaker) *trckd ldrs: disp fr 12th tl fell 15th* **4/1**[2]

6m 55.0s (10.40) **Going Correction** +0.35s/f (Yiel) **9** Ran SP% **114.9**
Speed ratings: **98,97,82,82,81 —,—,—,—**
toteswingers: 1&2 £7.00, 1&3 £3.60, 2&3 £3.10 CSF £134.60 TOTE £32.60: £7.00, £3.50, £1.10; EX 321.50 Place 6: £5.52 Place 5: £3.30.
Owner Paul Harvey **Bred** John Costello **Trained** Looe, Cornwall

FOCUS
A very ordinary hunter chase, but there is a case for rating the race a few pounds higher.

NOTEBOOK
Apollo Blaze(IRE) won his point-to-point over 3m4f last season and he kept on gamely to score. He is a slow horse who stays well and his connections are aiming him at the John Corbet Cup at Stratford at the end of the month as long as the ground has some cut in it. (op 16-1)
Alambique(IRE) is another who is slow and stays well. He ran well for the capable Richard Hawkins, suggesting if he were to run in a similar race on a more demanding track he could win. (op 3-1)
Thirtytwo Red(IRE) is woefully one-paced and will need to run on a stiffer track if he is to win a similar race. (op 5-2)
Beau Supreme(IRE) is a previous hunter chase winner but age has caught up with him and he will struggle to be competitive outside of point-to-points. (op 16-1)
Paddy The Piper(IRE) is not good enough for hunter chases and was a long way behind when refusing at the last. (op 12-1)
T/Plt: £7.60 to a £1 level stake. Pool: £45,552.57, 4,348.03 winning tickets T/Qpdt: £5.60 to a £ level stake. Pool:£3,727.40, 485.70 winning tickets TM

[8]WETHERBY (L-H)
Thursday, May 6

OFFICIAL GOING: Good
Wind: fresh 1/2 against Weather: overcast, breezy and cool

174 WETHERBY RACECOURSE SHOWGROUND FOR OUTDOOR EVENTS CONDITIONAL JOCKEYS' NOVICES' HURDLE (9 hdls) 2m 110y
5:45 (5:45) (Class 4) 4-Y-0+ £2,740 (£798; £399)

Form RPR
02F- 1 **Kosta Brava (FR)**[42] [4838] 6-10-12 94.................................. RyanMania 110+
(Howard Johnson) *j.rt: chsd ldrs: wnt 2nd 3rd: led after 6th: 15 l ahd whn mstke last: eased run-in* **5/1**[3]
00-0 2 9 **Overyou**[5] [93] 5-10-2 0... KyleJames(3) 89+
(Elliott Cooper) *hld up: hdwy 6th: wnt 15 l 2nd appr 2 out: kpt on: no ch w wnr* **25/1**
06F- 3 27 **Secret Desert**[11] [14] 4-10-3 0...................................... PaulGallagher(5) 68
(Paul Murphy) *prom: one pce fr 6th: tk modest 3rd and hit last* **50/1**
020- 4 1¼ **Kris Kin Line (IRE)**[25] [5146] 4-10-5 0............................. JohnKington(3) 69
(Donald McCain) *prom: reminders 4th: one pce fr 6th* **6/1**
350- 5 8 **Knockaveen (IRE)**[56] [4531] 5-10-5 0.................................. EwanWhillans 58
(Andrew Crook) *chsd ldrs: rdn 6th: wknd next* **9/1**
25- 6 9 **Solo Choice**[11] [14] 4-10-8 0.. FearghalDavis 52
(Ian McInnes) *rr-divsion: drvn 5th: wknd next* **25/1**
602- 7 4 **The Magic Bishop**[11] [14] 5-10-9 0........................... JamesHalliday(3) 52
(Malcolm Jefferson) *led: hdd after 6th: wknd appr 2 out: tired 5th last: heavily eased* **6/4**[1]
8 nk **Too Tall**[169] 4-10-2 0...(t) MrTomDavid(6) 48
(Tim Vaughan) *t.k.h: sn trcking ldrs: wknd appr 2 out* **7/2**[2]
P0- 9 35 **Sandman (GER)**[47] [4730] 5-10-12 0..................................... HarryHaynes 20
(William Amos) *stdd s: in rr: bhd whn mstke 5th: t.o* **80/1**
P- P **Shaftesbury Avenue (USA)**[11] [14] 7-10-12 0.........(b) CampbellGillies —
(Ian McInnes) *chsd ldr: drvn 3rd: sn wknd: wl bhd whn j.v.slowly next: sn p.u* **150/1**
00P- P **Little Miss Foozle**[11] [14] 6-10-5 0.................................. CharlieHuxley —
(Peter Niven) *in rr: blnd 3rd: sn t.o and p.u* **150/1**
00P- P **City In The Sky**[17] [5273] 4-10-0 0 ow2............................ AlexanderVoy(3) —
(Mike Sowersby) *in rr: blnd and rdr briefly lost iron 2nd: t.o 5th: p.u bef 3 out* **200/1**
PP- P **Valonty**[11] [8] 8-10-12 0...(tp) MichaelO'Connell —
(Brian Storey) *chsd ldrs: lost pl after 3rd: t.o whn p.u bef next* **200/1**

4m 5.60s (9.80) **Going Correction** +0.50s/f (Soft)
WFA 4 from 5yo+ 18lb **13** Ran SP% **116.4**
Speed ratings (Par 105): **96,91,79,78,74 70,68,68,51,— —,—,—**
toteswingers:1&2:£15.20, 1&3:£15.20, 2&3:Not won CSF £107.20 TOTE £6.40: £1.60, £7.80, £5.90; EX 273.50.
Owner Andrea & Graham Wylie **Bred** Guy Blasco **Trained** Billy Row, Co Durham

FOCUS
A dry spell saw nearly 60mm of water applied to the home straight with a further 30mm on the back straight since last Wednesday. The riders reported the ground to be over-watered and on the slow side. A modest novice hurdle that did not take as much winning as seemed likely with the two market leaders disappointing. The gallop was a reasonable one. The winner produced a big step forward but the form is believable.

NOTEBOOK

Kosta Brava(FR) is only rated 94 but he took advantage of the disappointing runs of the market leaders to win in clear-cut fashion returned to hurdles. This represented his best effort yet, he won't get a penalty and, although this was not much of a race, he may be capable of a little better. (op 6-1)

Overyou, from a yard among the winners, had hinted at ability on her hurdle debut and ran to a similar level this time. Her future lies in low-grade handicaps over further. (op 18-1)

Secret Desert again had his limitations exposed over hurdles and is likely to remain vulnerable in this type of event. (op 66-1 tchd 80-1)

Kris Kin Line(IRE) again failed to reproduce his Catterick form over this trip on this sound surface and a stiffer test of stamina and the switch to low-grade handicaps will suit. (op 8-1)

The Magic Bishop, who raced with the choke out and failed by a long chalk to reproduce his recent encouraging course and distance run, was the disappointment. It is possible this watered ground did not suit and it is too soon to write him off. Official explanation: trainer was unable to offer any explanation for the poor performance shown (tchd 11-8 and 13-8)

Too Tall, a consistent sort up to 1m4f for Luca Cumani, attracted support but dropped out very tamely on this hurdle debut and first run since November in the first-time tongue-tie after racing freely. (op 10-3 tchd 3-1)

Little Miss Foozle Official explanation: jockey said the mare had lost its action

Valonty Official explanation: jockey said the gelding had lost its action

175 "PARTY IN THE PADDOCK" - 3RD JUNE NOVICES' H'CAP CHASE (16 fncs) 2m 4f 110y

6:15 (6:23) (Class 4) (0-110,109) 5-Y-0+ **£3,252** (£955; £477; £238)

Form RPR

651- **1** **Nothingbutthetruth (IRE)**[11] 9 6-11-8 **105** 7ex........ DougieCostello 123+
(Tim Pitt) *hld up: hdwy to trck ldrs 9th: upsides 12th: hit next: led 2 out: clr last. eased run-in* **5/2**[2]

446- **2** *22* **Scale Bank (IRE)**[60] 4467 7-11-12 **109**........ BrianHughes 108
(Alan Swinbank) *led to 2nd: narrow ld appr 4 out: mstke 3 out: hdd and hit next: sn wknd* **6/1**[3]

202- **3** *6* **Persian Prince (IRE)**[160] 2545 10-9-12 **88**........ MrJohnDawson(7) 79
(John Wade) *t.k.h: led 2nd: hdd approaqching 4 out: sn wl outpcd* **7/1**

5/4- **4** *9* **Ragador**[25] 5149 9-11-10 **107**........ HenryOliver 92
(Sue Smith) *chsd ldrs: blnd 9th: sn drvn: lost pl 12th* **10/1**

03P- **5** *58* **Black Apache (IRE)**[33] 4990 6-11-11 **108**........ JasonMaguire 39
(Donald McCain) *nt jump wl: lost pl and blnd 11th: sn t.o: eventually completed* **12/1**

232- **U** **Lord Collingwood (IRE)**[13] 5353 9-10-5 **88**........ AndrewTinkler —
(Nigel Tinkler) *chsd ldrs: blnd bdly and uns rdr 4th* **7/4**[1]

5m 11.1s (3.30) **Going Correction** +0.30s/f (Yiel) **6** Ran SP% **108.5**

Speed ratings: **105,96,94,90,68** —

toteswingers:1&2:£5.10, 1&3:£5.10, 2&3:£6.90 CSF £16.04 TOTE £2.60: £1.10, £1.70; EX 12.60.

Owner Ferrybank Properties Limited **Bred** P A Byrne **Trained** Norton, N Yorks

FOCUS

A modest handicap but one that lost much of its interest when the well-backed market leader unshipped his rider early on. The gallop was a modest one.

NOTEBOOK

Nothingbutthetruth(IRE) had shown improved form to win over course and distance on his penultimate start and probably did not have to improve too much to follow up in a race where his main market rival departed early on and where several of his rivals made jumping errors. However, he's clearly in good fettle and may have a bit more to offer over fences. (op 7-4)

Scale Bank(IRE) has been a frustrating sort since gifted a race over hurdles just over a year ago and he found less than anticipated after ploughing through the third-last fence. The drop back to 2m on genuinely good ground may suit but he doesn't look one to be taking too short a price about. (op 5-1 tchd 7-1)

Persian Prince(IRE), a moderate maiden, was allowed to set his own pace but he capitulated turning for home on this first run since November. He has yet to win in 20 starts under rules and, although this was not his true form, he may not be one to make too many excuses for. (tchd 17-2)

Ragador was very easy to back but, after making a bad mistake in the back straight, failed to confirm the form he showed after a lengthy break last month. However, he is in good hands and it's too soon to write him off. (op 13-2)

Lord Collingwood(IRE), very well backed, was on the same mark as when running well at Bangor last month but gave his rider little chance of staying aboard in the early stages. He has yet to win a race is probably worth another chance. (op 7-2)

176 YORKSHIRE POST LADIES' DAY - 20TH MAY H'CAP HURDLE (12 hdls) 2m 6f

6:50 (6:51) (Class 4) (0-100,99) 4-Y-0+ **£3,082** (£898; £449)

Form RPR

0PP- **1** **Flying Doctor**[58] 4503 7-9-13 **75**........ HarryHaynes(3) 91+
(Elliott Cooper) *trckd ldrs: led 3 out: drvn and styd on strly fr next* **6/1**[1]

024- **2** *3 ¼* **Boyoboy (IRE)**[19] 5234 6-11-3 **90**........ DougieCostello 100
(George Moore) *mid-div: hdwy to chse ldrs 9th: wnt 2nd 2 out: kpt on: no imp* **7/1**[2]

263- **3** *25* **Miss Tarantella**[30] 5074 7-10-9 **85**........(t) MichaelMcAlister(3) 73
(Maurice Barnes) *hld up: hdwy 7th: sn chsng ldrs: upsides 3 out: wknd next* **10/1**

605- **4** *9* **Lukey Luke**[11] 12 7-10-7 **80**........ KeithMercer 59
(James Turner) *in rr: hdwy 9th: one pce fr 2 out* **14/1**

040- **5** *3* **Rokinhorsescience (FR)**[19] 5229 6-11-12 **99**........(b) RichieMcGrath 76
(Jonjo O'Neill) *t.k.h: wnt prom 4th: led briefly appr 3 out: wknd 2 out* **11/1**

006- **6** *24* **Apache Blue (IRE)**[14] 5334 6-11-7 **94**........ BrianHughes 49
(Howard Johnson) *chsd ldrs: reminders 4th: lost pl 6th: hdwy u.p 9th: sn wknd* **16/1**

54P- **7** *¾* **What's Occurrin**[47] 4736 6-11-8 **95**........(p) LiamHeard 49
(Tim Walford) *led: hit 6th: hdd & wknd appr 3 out* **12/1**

000- **8** *¾* **Toujours Souriante**[11] 12 4-10-0 **78** oh6........ PaddyAspell 27
(Tracy Waggott) *in rr: drvn along and in tch 5th: bhd fr 9th* **9/1**[3]

111- **9** *14* **Mardood**[41] 4879 5-11-6 **93**........(p) DenisO'Regan 34
(Chris Grant) *rr-divsion: drvn and sme hdwy 9th: wknd appr next* **7/1**[2]

/40- **10** *5* **Airedale Lad (IRE)**[329] 669 9-10-0 **80**........ MrJohnDawson(7) 17
(Karen Tutty) *chsd ldrs: lost pl 9th* **25/1**

/00- **11** *10* **Short Straw (IRE)**[56] 4531 7-9-12 **74** oh9 ow1........ RyanMania(3) 2
(Barry Murtagh) *in rr: wl bhd fr 8th* **33/1**

060- **P** **Vicentio**[168] 2387 11-9-9 **73** oh9........(p) JamesHalliday(5) —
(Tim Fitzgerald) *in rr: wl bhd whn p.u bef 9th* **28/1**

603- **P** **Humourous (IRE)**[11] 10 8-10-0 **73**........(t) GrahamLee —
(Brian Storey) *chsd ldrs: drvn 7th: wknd qckly and p.u bef 3 out* **10/1**

20P- **P** **Cute N You Know It**[44] 4811 7-10-0 **78**........ EwanWhillans(5) —
(Andrew Crook) *chsd ldrs: lost pl and blnd 8th: sn bhd: t.o whn p.u bef 3 out* **12/1**

00P- **P** **Vallani (IRE)**[13] 5374 5-10-9 **82**........ PeterBuchanan —
(J Barclay) *in rr: bhd fr 7th: t.o whn p.u bef 3 out* **50/1**

0U5- **P** **Archie's Wish**[11] 10 6-9-11 **73** oh1........ CampbellGillies(3) —
(Micky Hammond) *trckd ldrs: wknd 9th: bhd whn p.u bef 2 out* **16/1**

5m 34.6s (7.80) **Going Correction** +0.50s/f (Soft)

WFA 4 from 5yo+ 19lb **16** Ran SP% **121.8**

Speed ratings (Par 105): **105,103,94,91,90 81,81,81,76,74 70,—,—,—,— —**

toteswingers:1&2:£34.00, 1&3:£14.10, 2&3:£9.20 CSF £45.78 CT £423.42 TOTE £10.60: £2.60, £1.10, £3.30, £6.30; EX 74.40.

Owner Tom McNicholas **Bred** London Thoroughbred Services Ltd & J Gaines **Trained** Brigham, Cumbria

FOCUS

A moderate handicap run at a reasonable gallop but one in which the first two pulled clear over the last two flights.

NOTEBOOK

Flying Doctor ⊠ had shown precious little previously for a yard that has been among the winners but he's plummeted in the weights and justified the strong market confidence to win in decisive fashion. Testing ground doesn't seem to suit him but, on this evidence, he should be able to win again in the near future. Official explanation: trainer said, regarding the apparent improvment of form, that at Newcastle the gelding had been unsuited by the soft going (op 15-2)

Boyoboy(IRE) ⊠ is an unexposed sort who turned in an improved effort upped in trip but had the misfortune to bump into one so favourably treated. He pulled a long way clear of the remainder and it should only be a matter of time before he goes one better. (tchd 6-1)

Miss Tarantella is a fairly reliable yardstick but she had her limitations firmly exposed behind a well-handicapped and behind a progressive sort. There will be easier opportunities in this grade.

Lukey Luke isn't fully exposed over hurdles and may be capable of a bit better granted a stiffer test of stamina. (op 18-1)

Rokinhorsescience(FR) again didn't get home and his best trip has yet to be established.

Mardood came here on the back of three consecutive victories but turned in a laboured effort after a short break and was beaten too far out to blame the longer trip. He is probably worth another chance. Official explanation: jockey said the gelding failed to stay the 2m 6 furlongs today

177 WETHERBY RACECOURSE FOR WEDDING RECEPTIONS H'CAP CHASE (13 fncs) 2m

7:20 (7:23) (Class 4) (0-115,115) 5-Y-0+ **£3,252** (£955; £477; £238)

Form RPR

233- **1** **Storm Surge (IRE)**[41] 4864 7-10-9 **98**........ DenisO'Regan 107+
(Martin Todhunter) *racd keenly: trckd ldr: narrow advantage 8th: 3 l ahd whn blnd 4 out: narrowly hdd run-in: hrd rdn and rallied to ld post* **10/3**[2]

1F1- **2** *shd* **The Kealshore Kid (IRE)**[15] 5313 6-10-9 **101**........ MichaelO'Connell(3) 108
(George Moore) *wnt prom 5th: wnt 2nd appr 4 out: upsides 2 out: tk narrow ld run-in: hdd post* **2/1**[1]

660- **3** *28* **King's Majesty (IRE)**[11] 10 8-10-0 **89** oh1........ DougieCostello 71
(Tim Pitt) *wnt prom 5th: outpcd 9th: tk distant 3rd last* **16/1**

123- **4** *9* **Silver Steel (FR)**[178] 2192 7-11-9 **112**........(t) GrahamLee 86
(Richard Ford) *hld up: hdwy and prom 5th: outpcd 4 out: 10 l 3rd whn mstke 2 out: wknd last* **8/1**

21-P **5** *17* **Glimmer Of Light (IRE)**[5] 99 10-10-1 **93**........(bt) CharlieHuxley(3) 51
(Dr Richard Newland) *chsd ldrs: lost pl 8th: sn bhd* **8/1**

015- **6** *23* **Jim Tango (FR)**[19] 5230 6-11-12 **115**........(b) JasonMaguire 53
(Donald McCain) *wl away: led: j.lft: hdd 8th: lost pl appr next: sn bhd* **7/2**[3]

400- **P** **Trafalgar Man (IRE)**[239] 1415 9-10-10 **99**........ TomMessenger —
(Micky Hammond) *j.rt 2nd: hdwy and prom 5th: wnt bdly wrong and p.u gng to 9th* **12/1**

3m 55.5s (-0.30) **Going Correction** +0.30s/f (Yiel) **7** Ran SP% **114.4**

Speed ratings: **112,111,97,93,84 73,—**

toteswingers:1&2:£1.80, 2&3:£8.60, 1&3:£25.80 CSF £10.96 CT £89.43 TOTE £3.80: £1.20, £4.70; EX 13.70.

Owner Alex Pimbley **Bred** T Fleming **Trained** Orton, Cumbria

FOCUS

A fair handicap run at a reasonable gallop. The form is rated around the front two.

NOTEBOOK

Storm Surge(IRE) has sometimes looked as though he's saving a bit for himself but he showed a good attitude after a blunder turning for home to notch his second win over fences. A truly run race over this trip on good and softer ground are his requirements and it will be interesting to see if this can be built on. (op 4-1)

The Kealshore Kid(IRE)'s record over fences is one of steady improvement and, although worried out of it in the closing stages, this represented his best effort yet. He finished a long way clear of the remainder and is capable of scoring again in this sphere. (op 9-4)

King's Majesty(IRE) has mainly been disappointing since his last win in 2008 and, although plugging on to take a distant third, didn't do anywhere enough to suggest he'll soon be taking advantage of his declining mark. (op 14-1 tchd 12-1)

Silver Steel(FR) proved easy to back and was a long way below his best on this first run since November. This run may well have been needed and this usually consistent sort is worth another chance. (op 13-2)

Jim Tango(FR) dropped away very tamely back over this trip after setting a decent gallop and, although he's won two of his last six starts over fences, he's not the most predictable of animals. (op 11-2)

178 YORKSHIRE POINT-TO-POINT ASSOCIATION HUNTERS' CHASE (18 fncs) 3m 1f

7:55 (7:56) (Class 6) 5-Y-0+ **£1,318** (£405; £202)

Form RPR

1U1- **1** **Eliza Doalott (IRE)**[17] 5276 8-11-12 106........ MrGBrewer(3) 113+
(Mrs M Stirk) *j.w: travelled strly: jnd ldrs 7th: led on bit 4 out: hit 2 out: shkn up run-in: pushed out* **5/6**[1]

P22- **2** *3 ¾* **Pen Gwen (FR)**[17] 5276 7-11-7 105........ HenryBrooke(7) 104
(Kate Walton) *trckd ldrs: led 14th: hdd next: kpt on fr 2 out: no imp* **9/4**[2]

PPP/ **3** *41* **One Five Eight**[11] 11-11-9 0........(p) MissJCoward(5) 67
(Mrs C A Coward) *led to 1st: lost pl 9th: rallied next: wnt modest 3rd appr 4 out: sn wl outpcd* **33/1**

006/ **4** *4* **Blandings Castle**[11] 9-11-7 0........ MissGTutty(7) 64
(Karen Tutty) *led 1st: hdd 14th: wl outpcd appr next* **25/1**

5 *22* **Johnny Venture (IRE)**[11] 11-12-0 0........ MrSWalker 44
(C C Pimlott) *wnt prom 10th: stmbld 12th: blnd and lost pl 14th: bhd fr 3 out* **12/1**[3]

6m 26.1s (16.70) **Going Correction** +0.30s/f (Yiel) **5** Ran SP% **99.8**

Speed ratings: **95,93,80,79,72**

CSF £2.49 TOTE £1.50: £1.30, £1.30; EX 2.20.Brize Norton was withdrawn. Price at time of withdrawal 8/1. Rule 4 applies to all bets - deduction 10p in the pound

Owner Mrs M Stirk **Bred** J Day **Trained** Laverton, N Yorks

⊠ Brize Norton (8/1) was withdrawn after proving unruly and injuring the rider leaving the paddock. Deduct 10p in the £ under R4.

FOCUS

An uncompetitive hunter chase in which the gallop was ordinary. The two market leaders pulled clear off the home turn and the cosy winner is value for further.

NOTEBOOK

Eliza Doalott(IRE) ⊠ is a very capable sort with a fine strike-rate and ran up to her best to extend her winning run to six when confirming recent placings with the runner-up, even on worse terms. She isn't very big and has little margin for error with her jumping but she's got an engine and, although options are open with her (would be interesting if switched back to hurdles) is the type to win more races. (op 10-11 tchd Evens and 11-10 in a place)

Pen Gwen(FR) has been running well and posted another solid effort, although he was beaten further by the winner (who was worse off at the weights) than he was at Hexham last month. He is capable of winning a run-of-the-mill event. (op 5-2)

One Five Eight will have to fare a good deal better if he is to win a race in this sphere. (op 25-1 tchd 18-1)

Blandings Castle had the run of the race but was quickly left behind once overtaken and his best chance of success these days remains in the point-to-point field. (op 20-1)

179 GREAT ANTIQUES FAIR HERE - 29TH MAY H'CAP HURDLE (9 hdls) 2m 110y

8:25 (8:25) (Class 4) (0-110,108) 4-Y-0+ **£3,082** (£898; £449)

Form				RPR
513-	**1**		**Hi Dancer**[31] 5043 7-11-6 **107** ... GilesHawkins(5) (Ben Haslam) *trckd ldrs: led on bit after 6th: rdn 5 l clr last: kpt rt up to work* **5/1**[2]	111+
031-	**2**	*3*	**Ballysimon (IRE)**[30] 5072 6-10-13 **98** ... HarryHaynes(3) (James Ewart) *led to 4th: kpt on to chse wnr between last 2: styd on run-in* **5/1**[2]	98
4F3-	**3**	*7*	**Flash Harriet**[44] 4812 6-10-6 **91** ... RichieMcLernon(3) (John Mackie) *hld up: hdwy 6th: 4th and one pce whn mstke 2 out* **10/1**	87
F32-	**4**	*1¼*	**Chip N Pin**[8] 50 6-11-0 **96** ... (b) DenisO'Regan (Tim Easterby) *trckd ldrs: chsd wnr 3 out: wknd between last 2* **3/1**[1]	90
242-	**5**	*1*	**Patriot (IRE)**[15] 5310 6-10-8 **93** ... (t) MichaelMcAlister(3) (Maurice Barnes) *chsd ldrs: blnd 4th: one pce fr 3 out* **7/1**[3]	85
025-	**6**	*14*	**Dabaratsa (FR)**[10] 19 7-11-5 **108** ... (vt) MrTomDavid(7) (Tim Vaughan) *chsd ldrs: mstke 5th: lost pl next: sn bhd* **9/1**	90
040-	**7**	*17*	**Motive (FR)**[71] 4233 9-11-11 **107** ... BrianHughes (Howard Johnson) *in tch: drvn 6th: lost pl appr next: sn bhd* **7/1**[3]	71
600-	**U**		**White Lightening (IRE)**[45] 4781 7-10-1 **90** ... (b) MrJohnDawson(7) (John Wade) *chsd ldrs: lost pl appr 2 out: last and wl bhd whn blnd and uns rdr last* **33/1**	—
422-	**R**		**Tipsy Indian**[41] 4879 7-10-3 **92** ... GaryRutherford(7) (Sue Smith) *chsd ldr: led 4th: hdd after 6th: sn wknd: poor 6th whn rn out and uns rdr 2 out* **11/1**	—

4m 9.10s (13.30) **Going Correction** +0.50s/f (Soft)
WFA 4 from 6yo+ 18lb **9** Ran SP% **113.7**
Speed ratings (Par 105): **88,86,83,82,82 75,67,—,—**
toteswingers:1&2:£9.10, 1&3:£12.60, 2&3:£3.80 CSF £30.08 CT £238.67 TOTE £3.00: £1.10, £4.70, £4.00; EX 27.20 Place 6 £87.18; Place 5 £16.80.
Owner R Tocher **Bred** Mrs E Roberts **Trained** Middleham Moor, N Yorks

FOCUS

A modest handicap in which the gallop was ordinary. The first two are rated to their marks.

NOTEBOOK

Hi Dancer raced keenly but was always well placed in a race run at an ordinary gallop and skipped clear rounding the home turn to register an improved effort. He would have been even better suited by a truer gallop and this versatile sort may be able to win more races. (tchd 11-2)

Ballysimon(IRE) ⊠ was raised 23lb for an improved course-and-distance victory last month, but confirmed that was no fluke and left the impression that an even stiffer test of stamina would have suited better. The return to further may help and he may have further progress to make. (op 7-1)

Flash Harriet has yet to win a race but posted another creditable effort and, although she tended to carry her head a shade high, was another to shape as though the return to further would be more to her liking. (op 17-2 tchd 12-1)

Chip N Pin, who came very close to losing her maiden status last time, looked to have decent claims with the blinkers refitted but, not for the first time, looked to be saving a bit for herself once pressure was applied. She will be 4lb higher in future and is not really one for skinny odds. (op 10-3 tchd 5-2)

Patriot(IRE) was again below the form that saw him just touched off at Ayr in soft ground in March. He has yet to win a race and will have to show a bit more before he is a solid betting proposition. (op 8-1 tchd 13-2)

Motive(FR), winner of this race in 2008, looked to have plenty in his favour, but registered a tame effort after a short break. His form since that last win has been very patchy and he remains one to tread carefully with. (op 11-2 tchd 5-1)

T/Plt: £15.60 to a £1 stake. Pool £39,310.94 - 1,831.42 winning tickets. T/Qpdt: £3.40 to a £1 stake. Pool £3,272.27 - 711.62 winning tickets. WG

[36]WINCANTON (R-H)

Thursday, May 6

OFFICIAL GOING: Good to firm (good in places)

Wind: Moderate across Weather: Overcast

180 BATHWICK TYRES YEOVIL NOVICES' HURDLE (10 hdls 1 omitted) 2m 6f

5:35 (5:35) (Class 4) 4-Y-0+ **£2,602** (£764; £382; £190)

Form				RPR
122-	**1**		**Prescelli (IRE)**[17] 5282 6-10-12 105 ... (b) TomO'Brien (Keith Goldsworthy) *mde all: pushed clr wl bef 2 out: unchal* **11/8**[1]	110+
01-	**2**	*39*	**Elevenses**[57] 4516 6-11-2 0 ... HarrySkelton(3) (Paul Nicholls) *in rr tl stdy hdwy 4 out: trckd wnr 3 out and clsd to win 3 l after 3 out: sn rdn and lft bhd bnd appr 2 out but wl clr of 3rd* **9/4**[2]	78
311-	**3**	*12*	**Brandy Butter**[12] 5385 4-11-7 113 ... (bt) TomScudamore (David Pipe) *chsd ldr: rdn 6th: blnd 4 out: dropped bk to distant 4th after 3 out: styd on to take poor 3rd sn after last* **6/1**[3]	68
0F0-	**4**	*8*	**Sweet Request**[3] 3811 6-9-12 35 ... KeithBowens(7) (Dr Jeremy Naylor) *in rr tl sme hdwy and hit 3 out: tk mod 3rd wl bef 2 out: wknd into poor 4th sn after last* **200/1**	47
05F-	**5**	*22*	**Chapolimoss (FR)**[156] 2621 6-10-12 0 ... (t) SamThomas (Jonjo O'Neill) *in rr: mod prog into 5th 3 out: sn wknd* **13/2**	29
6-	**6**	*27*	**Whenwehadmoney (IRE)**[40] 4881 6-10-12 0 ... PaulMoloney (Evan Williams) *t.k.h: hmpd 1st: chsd ldrs: hit 5th: wknd* **12/1**	2
602-	**7**	*1¼*	**Watoscar (IRE)**[18] 5250 5-10-12 0 ... ChristianWilliams (Rachel Hobbs) *in tch and t.k.h: early: wl bhd after 6th* **50/1**	1
6P6-	**8**	*11*	**Saffron Spring**[18] 5256 7-9-12 0 ... MarkQuinlan(7) (Mrs S P Stretton) *chsd ldrs to 5th* **200/1**	—
	U		**Mik**[36] 4-10-4 0 ... EamonDehdashti(3) (Dr Jeremy Naylor) *distracted and j.v.slowly 1st: awkward: mstke and uns rdr 2nd* **150/1**	—
00P-	**U**		**Letcombe Brook**[27] 5117 4-10-7 0 ... JimmyMcCarthy (Charlie Morlock) *veered bdly lft: tried to refuse and uns rdr 1st* **100/1**	—

5m 11.2s (-15.30) **Going Correction** -0.625s/f (Firm) **10** Ran SP% **112.8**
Speed ratings (Par 105): **102,87,83,80,72 62,62,58,—,—**
toteswingers: 1&2 £2.00, 1&3 £2.70, 2&3 £3.10 CSF £4.60 TOTE £2.30: £1.10, £1.30, £1.90; EX 6.30.
Owner S F Barlow **Bred** Thomas Coleman **Trained** Yerbeston, Pembrokes

FOCUS

A poor novice event. The winner is only rated in line with the previous best.

NOTEBOOK

Prescelli(IRE) made all to deservedly resume winning ways on her return from handicap company. She was given a copybook ride from the front by Tom O'Brien and had the race in the bag off the home turn. The handicapper will probably raise her again for this, but she is the type to defy a double penalty against her own sex as summer ground obviously suits. (op 13-8 tchd 7-4)

Elevenses won a dire novice event at Fontwell last time out and was firmly put in his place under his penalty. He still finished a clear second-best and should appreciate a fence before too long. (op 2-1 tchd 15-8)

Brandy Butter was chasing a hat-trick, but both of his previous wins came in selling company and he was easily beaten off in this hotter company. A mark of 114 greatly flatters him. (op 5-1)

Sweet Request is officially rated just 35, so while this was better from her, the fact she was fighting it out for third place sums up the strength of the race.

Chapolimoss(FR) failed to take a hand on this return to action in a first-time tongue tie and, while a more positive ride may have helped his cause, is one to tread carefully with until showing more signs of enthusiasm. (op 15-2 tchd 6-1)

181 HOLBROOK HOUSE RESTAURANT & SPA H'CAP CHASE (21 fncs) 3m 1f 110y

6:05 (6:05) (Class 3) (0-120,120) 5-Y-0+ **£5,854** (£1,719; £859; £429)

Form				RPR
P53-	**1**		**Sir Bathwick (IRE)**[18] 5258 11-11-6 **114** ... (tp) TomScudamore (David Pipe) *mde all: drvn and styd on gamely fr 3 out: unchal* **4/1**[2]	128+
U63-	**2**	*3¾*	**Newbay Bob**[31] 5034 10-10-6 **107** ... (p) MrRGHenderson(7) (Nick Mitchell) *chsd wnr thrght: rdn and no imp 4 out but responded fr 2 out and styd on run-in but nvr a serious threat* **10/1**	115
053-	**3**	*9*	**Hoof It Harry (IRE)**[18] 5257 9-9-9 **94** ... JimmyDerham(5) (Paul Henderson) *in tch 10th: hdwy 12th: rdn fr 17th: nvr nr wnr and styd on same pce fr 3 out* **7/1**	92
526-	**4**	*17*	**Classic Clover**[168] 2393 10-10-0 **94** oh3 ... (t) AidanColeman (Colin Tizzard) *in tch: hdwy 10th: rdn to stay in tch 14th: wknd 4 out* **9/1**	82
232-	**5**	*37*	**Now Listen To Me**[9] 39 7-11-4 **112** ... (t) APMcCoy (Paul Nicholls) *towards rr tl stdy hdwy and in tch 15th: hit 17th: wknd qckly appr 4 out* **5/2**[1]	85
415-	**6**	*77*	**Over The Creek**[13] 5373 11-11-12 **120** ... (bt) GerrySupple (David Pipe) *hit 1st and 2nd: blnd 10th: t.o 12th* **5/1**[3]	—
11U-	**P**		**Tank Buster**[91] 3851 10-10-9 **106** ... RichardKilloran(3) (Carroll Gray) *blnd 9th and bhd: t.o 12th: p.u bef next* **14/1**	—
630-	**P**		**Romping Home (IRE)**[14] 5342 7-11-7 **115** ... PaulMoloney (Evan Williams) *in rr tl sme hdwy 15th: wknd 17th: t.o whn p.u bef 3 out* **12/1**	—

ms (-399.50) **8** Ran SP% **111.2**
toteswingers: 1&2 £10.50, 1&3 £7.30, 2&3 £11.70 CSF £39.13 CT £260.45 TOTE £6.30: £1.70, £3.10, £2.70; EX 41.40.
Owner Mrs S Clifford **Bred** Patrick Keane **Trained** Nicholashayne, Devon

FOCUS

A moderate handicap where it paid to race handily. The winner is a much better chaser than hurdler and the second ran to his mark.

NOTEBOOK

Sir Bathwick(IRE) was returning to chasing off an 8lb higher mark, but was still well treated on his previous best efforts and he won most decisively from the front. He was able to get an easy lead, but still had them strung out in behind and it was clear turning for home that he was the one to be on. It was his first success since late 2007 and it wouldn't be surprising to see him out under a penalty. (op 5-1 tchd 7-2)

Newbay Bob was the only one to try to keep tabs on the winner and got rewarded with second as a result. He stays all day and really wants an easier surface, so this was a respectable effort. (tchd 9-1 and 11-1)

Hoof It Harry(IRE), who attracted some support, turned in just about his best effort to date over fences and has now been third over C&D the last twice. (op 15-2 tchd 8-1)

Classic Clover always tends to go in snatches and did so again here. It was his first run for 168 days, though, and he did enough to suggest it would be to his benefit. (op 8-1)

Now Listen To Me was bidding to enhance his stable's excellent record in the race. He is a tricky ride, but not even Tony McCoy could get him to show more enthusiasm. Even allowing for the fact this may have come soon enough, he has now become one to swerve at all costs. (op 3-1 tchd 2-1)

Tank Buster Official explanation: jockey said the gelding finished distressed

182 BATHWICK TYRES TAUNTON NOVICES' HURDLE (8 hdls) 2m

6:35 (6:36) (Class 4) 4-Y-0+ **£2,602** (£764; £382; £190)

Form				RPR
1-	**1**		**Barrel Of Fun (IRE)**[31] 5051 4-11-1 0 ... (t) APMcCoy (Jim Best) *w ldr tl def advantage after 3 out: drvn to assert fr 2 out: styd on strly run-in* **13/8**[1]	113+
553-	**2**	*5*	**Fidelis (IRE)**[18] 5260 6-10-12 105 ... DarylJacob (Ben De Haan) *hld up in mid-div: stdy hdwy 3 out: chsd wnr appr 2 out: sn rdn: no imp appr last* **3/1**[2]	104
0-	**3**	*14*	**Red Army Commander (IRE)**[18] 5260 5-10-12 0 ... AndrewThornton (Neil Mulholland) *t.k.h: mstke 2nd and sn rr: stl plenty to do fr 2 out: styd on wl as others hmpd sn after last and tk wl hld 3rd cl home* **100/1**	89
0U-	**4**	*¾*	**Tartan Tie**[43] 4822 6-10-5 0 ... (t) OliverDayman(7) (Alison Thorpe) *chsd ldrs: rdn and no imp 2 out: no ch w ldng duo whn hmpd sn after last* **20/1**	91+
03-	**5**	*shd*	**Timoca (IRE)**[8] 50 5-10-5 0 ... PaulMoloney (Evan Williams) *chsd ldrs: rdn and one pce whn mstke 2 out: no ch after* **9/2**[3]	84
6/4-	**6**	*6*	**Cadeaux Cerise (IRE)**[16] 5294 6-10-5 0 ... JackDoyle (Andrew Haynes) *mde most tl hdd after 3 out: wknd 2 out and readily hld whn hmpd sn after last* **22/1**	81+
	7	*8*	**Lean Burn (USA)**[51] 4-10-5 0 ... DannyCook(3) (John Panvert) *in rr: sme hdwy 3 out: rdn and btn bef next* **66/1**	70
55-	**8**	*2¼*	**Kapborg (FR)**[16] 5296 4-10-1 0 ... TomScudamore (David Pipe) *in rr: rdn appr 2 out and mstke: no ch whn blnd last* **33/1**	61
	9	*12*	**The Grey One (IRE)**[13] 7-10-5 0 ... ChrisDavies(7) (Milton Bradley) *plld v hrd: hit 2nd: blnd 3rd: wknd 3 out* **33/1**	60
0/0-	**10**	*16*	**Bolanderi (USA)**[21] 5194 5-10-12 0 ... NickScholfield (Andy Turnell) *chsd ldrs: rdn 3 out: wknd sn after* **9/1**	44

F **Tignello (IRE)**[235] 5-10-9 0 .... HarrySkelton(3) 104+
(Paul Nicholls) *hld up in rr tl stdy hdwy 3 out: styd on fr 2 out: dipsuting 4 l 2nd and hld whn fell last* **16/1**

3m 43.7s (-5.20) **Going Correction** -0.625s/f (Firm) **11** Ran SP% **114.6**
Speed ratings (Par 105): **88,85,78,78,78 75,71,69,63,55** —
toteswingers: 1&2 £1.80, 1&3 £17.20, 2&3 £33.30 CSF £5.88 TOTE £3.20: £1.90, £1.10, £9.20; EX 7.90.
Owner Fruits Incorporated **Bred** Barronstown Stud **Trained** Lewes, E Sussex

FOCUS
There was just an ordinary gallop on here, which caused most to run freely, and again it paid to be up front. Due to the steady pace the form is suspect but the winner is entitled to rate a lot higher than this on Flat form.

NOTEBOOK
Barrel Of Fun(IRE) made just about all to follow up his Plumpton win a month earlier. He was facing much quicker ground here, but had shown useful maiden form as a Flat performer when in Ireland and it caused him no trouble. Tony McCoy kicked him for home at the right time and, despite wandering a little nearing the penultimate flight, was always in command in the home straight. Things will not be so simple under a double penalty and he was really gifted this by his rivals, but further improvement is not ruled out. (tchd 6-4 and 7-4)
Fidelis(IRE) found this easier than some of the assignments he has faced and he was very well backed to open his account. He was close enough if good enough when the winner asserted and again his attitude could have been more convincing under pressure. There should be a small race for him this summer, but he isn't one to place much faith in. (op 9-2 tchd 11-4)
Red Army Commander(IRE) was motoring home on the run-in and was the chief sufferer of the lack of an early pace. This was a vast improvement on his hurdling debut and he could be an improver, but at first glance he does little for the form. Official explanation: jockey said, regaridng the running and riding, that his instructions were to try and get the gelding settled, as he had been very free on his only previous run over hurdles. He added that the gelding made a bad mistake at the second hurdle when in mid-division, and having lost his position he asked for an effort turning out of the back straight and the gelding stayed on through beaten horses from the second last
Tartan Tie now qualifies for handicaps and should improve in that sphere. (op 16-1 tchd 14-1)
Timoca(IRE) produced a lacklustre effort. She probably found it coming soon enough, though, and is now eligible for a mark. (op 7-2)
Tignello(IRE) was a 54-rated maiden on the level and had abundant chances in that sphere. He was very easy to back for this hurdling debut, but has joined the top yard for his new career and was booked for second prior to falling at the last. A stronger gallop may even have seen him a debut winner with a clear round and hurdling looks like it may well see him in a much better light, but this was anything but an ideal introduction. (op 14-1)

183 ROYAL BATH & WEST SHOW NOVICES' H'CAP CHASE (13 fncs) 2m
7:10 (7:10) (Class 4) (0-100,100) 5-Y-0+ **£3,252** (£955; £477; £238)

Form RPR

P06- **1** **Randjo (FR)**[13] 5364 5-11-1 **89** .... JamieMoore 99+
(R H & Mrs S Alner) *mde virtually: strly pressed fr 6th: styd on to assert fr 3 out: hld on all out run-in* **13/2**

51U- **2** *nk* **Chilbury Hill (IRE)**[18] 5259 7-11-7 **95** .... WayneHutchinson 103
(Kevin Bishop) *chsd ldrs: hit 6th: styd on to chse wnr 3 out: kpt on wl u.p appr last: fin wl but a jst hld* **4/1**[3]

2/2- **3** *2 1/4* **Ace High Blue (IRE)**[9] 36 8-11-12 **100** ....(t) PaulMoloney 106
(Evan Williams) *hld up in rr but in tch: hdwy 9th: disp 2nd fr 3 out: hit 2 out: one pce appr last* **11/4**[1]

/65- **4** *15* **Beauchamp Viking**[14] 5331 6-9-13 **78** ....(t) JimmyDerham(5) 70
(Simon Burrough) *chsd ldrs: chal 6th: stmbld 7th: mstke 9th: upsides 4 out: wknd bef next* **14/1**

654/ **5** *11* **Knightsbridge Hill (IRE)**[19] 8-9-11 **76** oh3 ow2 .... KeiranBurke(5) 55
(Patrick Rodford) *in rr and rdn along fr 6th: sn chsng ldrs: wknd 8th* **10/1**

0F3- **6** *27* **Ajzal (IRE)**[8] 48 6-10-9 **83** ....(b) FelixDeGiles 35
(Tom George) *blnd 3rd: chsd ldrs: rdn 5th: chal fr 6th: rdn 9th: wknd qckly 4 out* **3/1**[2]

F56- **7** *3 1/2* **Finnish Melody**[17] 5286 6-9-7 **74** oh2 .... EdCookson(7) 22
(Andy Turnell) *sn bhd: no ch whn mstke 4 out* **33/1**

460- **8** *1/2* **Compton Star**[18] 5261 10-9-9 **74** oh5 .... IanPopham(5) 22
(Ron Hodges) *nvr travelling: blnd 7th: a bhd* **12/1**

3m 53.73s (-6.17) **Going Correction** -0.25s/f (Good) **8** Ran SP% **111.4**
Speed ratings: **105,104,103,96,90 77,75,75**
toteswingers: 1&2 £4.10, 1&3 £2.40, 2&3 £2.50 CSF £31.62 CT £85.32 TOTE £5.40: £1.10, £1.10, £1.30; EX 30.70.
Owner P M De Wilde **Bred** Denis Fontaine **Trained** Droop, Dorset

FOCUS
An ordinary novice handicap. Straightforward form, rated through the second.

NOTEBOOK
Randjo(FR) ⊠ showed improvement for the switch to fences and he landed his first win since coming over from France in very gutsy fashion. He had obviously schooled well at home as he was aggressively ridden into the first fence and it was his jumping that won him the day when under maximum pressure from four out. He looks a lazy sort so probably had a deal left in the tank at the finish and there should be more to come from him as a chaser, despite a likely rise. (op 8-1 tchd 6-1)
Chilbury Hill(IRE) had won over C&D two runs back and was booked for a place prior to unseating here 16 days earlier. He travelled nicely into contention and looked a big player when asked for his effort coming to three out. He found the winner too resolute, however, and is probably a little flattered by his proximity at the finish. He has developed into a likeable sort of late and rates the benchmark. (op 11-4)
Ace High Blue(IRE) travelled sweetly before flattening out over hurdles on his debut for this stable nine days earlier and was dropped in trip for this chasing debut. He jumped well enough and had every chance, but just looked to find this sharp enough. It was a good effort considering the run came plenty quick enough and he should be winning before long. (op 5-2 tchd 9-4)
Beauchamp Viking posted his best effort of any description and really paid for running with too much enthusiasm in the early parts. If he could settle better, he may just be able to build on this. (op 16-1 tchd 12-1)
Knightsbridge Hill(IRE) has been struggling in points this year, but this was his debut for the stable and he did enough to think he could find improvement over a longer trip. (op 14-1)
Ajzal(IRE) again made a positive move in the race only to weaken right out of things when it mattered. (op 10-3 tchd 4-1)

184 WINCANTON RACECOURSE WESSEX AREA CHAMPION HUNTERS' CHASE (21 fncs) 3m 1f 110y
7:40 (7:41) (Class 4) 5-Y-0+ **£3,123** (£968; £484; £242)

Form RPR

6/1- **1** **Ask Again**[23] 5177 11-11-9 107 .... MissSarahWest(7) 123+
(Miss Sarah West) *slt advantage to 6th: styd pressing ldr: nt fluent 13th: one pce whn ldr qcknd appr 3 out: rallied fr next and led after last as ldr blnd: styd on wl* **5/2**[2]

102- **2** *1 1/2* **Turthen (FR)**[19] 5233 9-12-6 136 .... MissCTizzard 129+
(C St V Fox) *trckd ldrs: led 15th: qcknd appr 3 out: sn pushed along: drvn into last and blnd: hdd sn after and styd on same pce* **4/6**[1]

2P0/ **3** *32* **Coolers Quest**[18] 11-11-0 0 .... MrJBarnes(5) 79
(Mrs R Ford) *chsd ldrs tl rdn and lost tch w ldng duo fr 17th: t.o* **28/1**

104/ **4** *8* **Trade Off (IRE)**[19] 12-11-7 0 .... MrSAllwood(5) 78
(Miss L Alner) *w wnr: slt ld fr 6th: hdd 15th: wknd fr 17th: t.o* **12/1**[3]

P/P- **5** *5* **Own Line**[19] 11-11-5 107 ....(p) MrRobertHawker(7) 73
(Miss S L Gould) *chsd ldrs: hit 9th: chal 13th: wknd and mstke 17th: t.o* **18/1**

P **Lutteur Bleu (FR)**[19] 11-11-9 0 .... MissAGoschen(3) —
(Mrs Angela Davis) *sn t.o: p.u bef 7th* **33/1**

6m 31.38s (-8.12) **Going Correction** -0.25s/f (Good) **6** Ran SP% **107.9**
Speed ratings: **102,101,91,89,87** —
toteswingers: 1&2 £1.10, 1&3 £7.10, 2&3 £5.20 CSF £4.40 TOTE £2.80: £1.10, £1.50; EX 4.50.
Owner C D J West **Bred** R Jenks **Trained** Wedmore, Somerset

⊠ Stewards' Enquiry : Miss C Tizzard one-day ban: used whip without giving time to repsond

FOCUS
The two market leaders predictably dominated this hunter chase and the form is rated around them.

NOTEBOOK
Ask Again had rather found the race falling into his lap at Exeter last time out and had been well beaten by Turthen when the pair met between the flags in February, but this quick ground enabled him to keep tabs on his main rival throughout the final circuit. He is a very likeable performer. (op 11-4 tchd 9-4)
Turthen(FR) had got the upper hand and was booked for repeat success prior to throwing it away with a final-fence blunder. He is a class above this lot on his day, but he hasn't been at his very best all year and the one worry here was the quick ground. He would have won with a better leap at the last, but it was surely the ground which made his jumping stickier than usual. (tchd 8-11 and 4-5 in a place)
Coolers Quest won the race for third and ran respectably enough (op 20-1)
Trade Off(IRE) seems best when allowed an easy lead and continues on the downgrade. (tchd 10-1)
Lutteur Bleu(FR) Official explanation: jockey said gelding was never travelling

185 FRYS ELECTRICAL H'CAP HURDLE (8 hdls) 2m
8:15 (8:15) (Class 4) (0-100,100) 4-Y-0+ **£2,602** (£764; £382; £190)

Form RPR

002- **1** **Forest Rhythm (IRE)**[9] 40 6-11-4 **97** .... JimmyDerham(5) 113+
(Seamus Mullins) *trckd ldrs: chal 2 out: led sn after: clr last: easily* **7/2**[2]

525- **2** *10* **Petito (IRE)**[32] 5009 7-11-9 **100** ....(b) TommyPhelan(3) 103
(Mark Gillard) *chsd ldrs: chal 3 out: led sn after: rdn appr 2 out: hdd sn after: no ch w wnr but kpt on for 2nd* **12/1**

PP0/ **3** *3 3/4* **Looks The Business (IRE)**[12] 1109 9-11-0 **88** .... NickScholfield 87
(Andrew Haynes) *chsd ldrs: hrd drvn appr 2 out: styd on same pce* **16/1**

5F6- **4** *2 1/4* **Casual Style**[14] 5340 4-11-6 **98** ....(t) TomScudamore 91
(David Pipe) *hld up in rr tl stdy hdwy appr 3 out: chsd ldrs and rdn appr 2 out: styd on same pce* **12/1**

420- **5** *3/4* **Rowan River**[110] 3456 6-11-0 **88** ....(tp) RichardJohnson 86
(Alison Thorpe) *chsd ldrs: mstke 2nd: rdn appr 2 out: sn one pce: mstke last* **4/1**[3]

/00- **6** *10* **Honeycombe**[18] 5261 9-9-7 **74** oh6 .... MarkQuinlan(7) 60
(Mrs S P Stretton) *chsd ldrs: chal 5th: slt ld 4 out: hdd sn after 3 out: wknd bef next* **40/1**

030- **7** *5* **Mista Rossa**[16] 5295 5-11-1 **89** ....(p) DarylJacob 70
(Jamie Snowden) *in rr: rdn appr 3 out: nvr in contention* **22/1**

000- **8** *12* **Slam**[18] 5260 5-11-4 **92** .... PaddyBrennan 61
(Tom George) *in rr: rdn appr 3 out: sme prog appr 2 out: nvr anywhere nr ldrs and sn btn* **9/4**[1]

0U3- **9** *8* **Toi Express (IRE)**[195] 1880 14-10-1 **82** .... MissJBuck(7) 43
(Susan Gardner) *chsd ldr to 4th: wknd qckly bef 4 out* **40/1**

015- **10** *48* **Loom (GER)**[162] 2504 8-11-12 **100** ....(b) GerrySupple 13
(David Pipe) *a bhd: t.o* **33/1**

/2F- **P** **Hot Choc (IRE)**[56] 4537 8-10-5 **84** .... IanPopham(5) —
(John Ryall) *led: wnt rt and blnd 2nd: nvr fluent after: hdd 4 out: sn wknd: t.o whn p.u bef 2 out* **9/1**

600- **P** **Doric Echo**[39] 4913 4-10-10 **88** .... JamieMoore —
(Charlie Morlock) *in rr: hmpd 3rd: no ch fr 3 out: t.o whn p.u bef last* **40/1**

3m 36.52s (-12.38) **Going Correction** -0.625s/f (Firm)
WFA 4 from 5yo+ 18lb **12** Ran SP% **118.9**
Speed ratings (Par 105): **105,100,98,97,96 91,89,83,79,55** —,—
toteswingers: 1&2 £5.30, 1&3 £15.00, 2&3 £91.40 CSF £41.71 CT £589.14 TOTE £3.40: £2.40, £4.90, £3.70; EX 31.30 Place 6 £22.84; Place 5 £19.17.
Owner New Forest Racing Partnership **Bred** Vincent Walsh **Trained** Wilsford-Cum-Lake, Wilts

FOCUS
An ordinary handicap, run at a strong gallop and there was an easy winner who produced a step up on his recent run.

NOTEBOOK
Forest Rhythm(IRE) bounced back to form when second over course and distance off this mark nine days earlier and went one better with an easy success. The strong gallop played right into his hands and it was clear coming to the second-last he had only to stay on his feet to win. He was eased down near the finish and his best option is surely to try and find something under a penalty before the handicapper can reassess him. (op 11-4 tchd 4-1)
Petito(IRE) ran one of his better races for the return to quick ground and, despite being no match for the winner, was not at all disgraced under top weight. He remains a longstanding maiden, however. (op 14-1)
Looks The Business(IRE) showed the benefit of a recent spin on the AW and posted a fair effort under a positive ride. He can be placed to find another race off this mark during the summer. (op 11-1)
Casual Style was making her handicap debut and was restrained out the back. She did her best to close from three out, but couldn't sustain her effort and still has to prove she stays the trip. (op 11-1 tchd 9-1)
Rowan River had her chance, but again ran out when under pressure and cannot be considered a betting proposition. (op 6-1)
Slam was very useful when trained on the Flat and whose last run in novice company caught the attention of the stewards. He was very well backed but his rider overdid the waiting tactics and he never figured. Slam looked disinterested, however, when asked for an effort and staying the trip is clearly a big problem. His yard is also out of form at present. (op 10-3 tchd 2-1)
T/Plt: £219.30 to a £1 stake. Pool £42,192.10 - 150.40 winning tickets. T/Qpdt: £10.40 to a £1 stake. Pool £6,117.45 - 434.90 winning tickets. ST

186 - 189a (Foreign Racing) - See Raceform Interactive

COMPIEGNE (L-H)
Thursday, May 6

OFFICIAL GOING: Turf: very soft

190a PRIX GENERAL DE SAINT-DIDIER (CHASE) (CONDITIONS) (5YO+) (TURF) 2m 5f
4:25 (12:00) 5-Y-0+ **£8,495** (£4,247; £2,477; £1,681; £796)

RPR

1 **Baulon (FR)**[10] 6-10-8 0....(p) BastienBenard —
(C Lerner, France) **17/1**

2 3 **Nascar (FR)**[46] 7-10-8 0....(p) AdelineGadras —
(Mlle M-L Mortier, France) **15/1**

3 hd **Parkhalkevi (FR)**[15] 5-10-8 0.... JeremyDaSilva(4) —
(Y Fouin, France) **9/1**

4 ¾ **Micadou (FR)**[1054] 10-11-5 0.... StevenLeVot(4) —
(G Macaire, France) **11/2**[2]

5 4 **Yanky Sundown (FR)**[200] 5-10-8 0.... BorisChameraud —
(P Bigot, France) **42/1**

6 8 **Lutteur Dancer (FR)**[225] 5-10-10 0.... MorganRegairaz —
(Y Fouin, France) **33/10**[1]

7 2½ **Olivia Des Bordes (FR)**[319] [781] 8-10-3 0....(p) PACarberry —
(F-M Cottin, France) **8/1**

8 1 **Olazuro Du Mou (FR)**[609] 8-10-8 0....(p) BenoitDelo —
(M De Montfort, France) **17/1**

9 ¾ **Fandor Chalet (FR)**[15] 8-10-12 0....(p) KevinNabet(5) —
(J-L Henry, France) **77/1**

10 3 **Rural Mag (FR)**[39] 5-10-10 0.... GregoryAdam —
(M Rolland, France) **9/1**

0 **Petelo D'Ha (FR)**[316] 7-10-10 0.... JonathanNattiez —
(L Postic, France) **15/2**[3]

0 **Ty Perrine (FR)**[22] 7-11-0 0.... SylvainDehez —
(F Cheyer, France) **17/1**

0 **Masterly (FR)**[596] 7-10-8 0.... XavierHondier —
(Mlle M-L Mortier, France) **53/1**

F **Soleil Fix (FR)**[27] [5118] 9-10-8 0....(b) MrDHDunsdon —
(Nick Gifford) *midfield tl fell 8th* **78/1**

P **Robe Longue (FR)**[15] 5-10-12 0....(p) DavidCottin —
(F-M Cottin, France) **21/1**

P **Duo Cubar (FR)**[10] 5-10-3 0.... LudovicSolignac —
(B Lefevre, France) **112/1**

5m 32.0s (332.00) **16** Ran SP% **116.6**
PARI-MUTUEL (all including 1 euro stakes): WIN 18.10; PLACE 6.30, 4.10, 3.50; DF 152.80; SF 331.50.
Owner Jean-Pierre Lefebvre **Bred** Robert Aubaud **Trained** France

AINTREE (L-H)
Friday, May 7

OFFICIAL GOING: Good (chs 8.3, hdl 8.4)

All bends on Mildmay course moved but imapct on distances not known.
Wind: Fresh across Weather: Cloudy

191 HILTON LIVERPOOL NOVICES' HURDLE (11 hdls) 2m 4f
6:05 (6:05) (Class 4) 4-Y-0+ **£3,252** (£955; £477; £238)

Form RPR

21- 1 **Mostly Bob (IRE)**[21] [5214] 7-11-5 0.... RichardJohnson 124+
(Philip Hobbs) *hld up: nt fluent 2nd: hdwy 7th: rdn after next: sn outpcd: rallied and hit 2 out: led and mstke last: styd on wl* **3/1**[1]

215- 2 5 **Worth A King'S**[20] [5220] 4-11-0 118.... JasonMaguire 115
(Donald McCain) *chsd ldrs: rdn after 8th: ev ch appr last: styd on same pce flat* **20/1**

332- 3 1¾ **Lamboro Lad (IRE)**[180] [2147] 5-10-12 112.... APMcCoy 110
(Peter Bowen) *led and nt fluent 2nd: set stdy pce: mstke 3rd: hdd 6th: led again 3 out: hdd last: no ex flat* **6/1**

2P1- 4 2¾ **Promising Anshan (IRE)**[45] [4809] 5-11-0 123....(t) PeterToole(5) 114
(Charlie Mann) *chsd ldrs: rdn appr 3 out: styd on same pce appr last* **5/1**[3]

114/ 5 1½ **Araldur (FR)**[461] [3666] 6-10-12 0.... RobertThornton 106+
(Alan King) *hld up in tch: nt fluent 5th: led after next: hdd 3 out: wknd last* **7/2**[2]

/06- 6 3¾ **Stand Clear**[14] [5354] 5-10-5 0.... GrahamLee 94
(Ferdy Murphy) *hld up: hld up: sme hdwy appr 3 out: nvr on terms* **66/1**

U- 7 10 **Murcar**[26] [5155] 5-10-12 0.... JohnnyFarrelly 95+
(Alison Thorpe) *prom: racd keenly: mstke 8th: ev ch 3 out: rdn and wknd appr last* **12/1**

250- 8 10 **Oh No Not Harry (FR)**[22] [5194] 5-10-12 114.... DougieCostello 81
(Ian Williams) *hld up: j.rt and wknd 3 out: t.o* **13/2**

006- 9 6 **Red Tanber (IRE)**[16] [5310] 7-10-12 57.... KeithMercer 75
(Bruce Mactaggart) *hld up: wknd 6th: t.o* **150/1**

0P2- 10 6 **Meet The Critics (IRE)**[19] [5243] 7-10-12 0.... AidanColeman 69
(Brendan Powell) *led to 2nd: chsd ldr tl led again 6th: sn hdd: wknd 3 out: t.o* **10/1**

600- 11 1¾ **Winter Alchemy (IRE)**[15] [5333] 5-10-9 0.... FearghalDavis(3) 68
(Nicky Richards) *hld up: wknd 6th: t.o* **100/1**

00- 12 78 **Plaisir De Montot (FR)**[43] [4833] 7-10-9 0.... GaryBerridge(3) —
(Simon Shirley-Beavan) *hld up: mstke 5th: hdwy next: wknd 7th: t.o* **150/1**

5m 1.30s (0.60) **Going Correction** -0.20s/f (Good)
WFA 4 from 5yo+ 19lb **12** Ran SP% **116.9**
Speed ratings (Par 105): **90,88,87,86,85 84,80,76,73,71 70,39**
toteswingers: 1&2 £3.50, 1&3 £2.10, 2&3 £25.00 CSF £59.46 TOTE £3.90: £2.20, £4.20, £2.40; EX 43.70.
Owner Favourites Racing XXVI **Bred** Mrs Mary Gallagher **Trained** Withycombe, Somerset

FOCUS
The winning jockey in the first described the ground as 'just on the fast side of good'. This was a reasonable novices' hurdle, but it was only steadily run in a slow time compared with the later handicap, and the form may not prove too solid. It has been rated around the first two.

NOTEBOOK
Mostly Bob(IRE) did not travel particularly well and was under the shove back in eighth place turning into the home straight, but he soon began a forward move and stayed on to win going away in the end. This was a decent performance under the penalty for his Uttoxeter win and there is more to come from him when the emphasis is placed more on stamina over this trip. He may switch to fences soon, although he is not the biggest. (op 11-4 tchd 5-2)
Worth A King'Swas another to stay on from an unpromising position. He had every chance, but could do little to prevent the winner from pulling away from him up the run-in. This is his trip. (op 14-1)
Lamboro Lad(IRE) was back in front three out but could pull out no extra from the last. He spent time in the air over the hurdles and still looks to have strengthening to do, but this was a pleasing return from six months off. He will not mind going back over 3m. (op 7-1 tchd 5-1)
Promising Anshan(IRE) was an easy winner at Southwell over subsequent scorer Calon Cwrbin and was the pick on official figures, but this was disappointing. He made a mistake at the first down the far side and lacked the pace to get involved up the home straight. A stronger gallop would have suited him. (op 11-2 tchd 6-1)
Araldur(FR) had been sidelined since January 2009. He raced keenly and took up the running down the back, only to fade out of things between the last two flights. Still unproven over this far, he looks to retain plenty of ability and should be sharper for this. (op 9-2)
Stand Clear ⊠ made late progress from the rear, showing enough for her to be of interest when she switches to minor handicap company.
Murcar raced prominently for a long way but had been rather keen early on and he did not get home. He won at an extended 2m on the Flat so this trip ought to have been within reach. (op 11-1)

192 RADIO CITY 96.7 ROSSIE AND CO. BREAKFAST NOVICES' CHASE (12 fncs) 2m
6:35 (6:36) (Class 4) 5-Y-0+ **£4,553** (£1,337; £668; £333)

Form RPR

232- 1 **Miss Sarenne (FR)**[63] [4423] 5-10-5 121.... AndrewTinkler 125
(Nicky Henderson) *chsd ldrs: hit 8th: led appr 3 out: rdn bef last: styd on gamely* **5/2**[3]

421- 2 ½ **West With The Wind**[12] [2] 5-11-5 0.... PaulMoloney 139
(Evan Williams) *led 1st: hdd 5th: led again appr 9th: hdd bef 3 out: rdn after next: ev ch last: rdr dropped whip sn after: edgd lft flat: styd on* **15/8**[1]

6/- 3 dist **Askmeroe (IRE)**[30] [5090] 7-11-5 126.... PCarberry 114+
(A J Martin, Ire) *led tl nt fluent 1st: chsd ldr: led 5th: hdd appr 9th: rdn and wknd 2 out: eased: t.o* **9/4**[2]

004- 4 65 **Overrule (USA)**[10] [34] 6-10-12 0.... KeithMercer 42
(Brian Ellison) *hld up: mstke 4th: lost tch next: bhd whn hit 6th: t.o* **7/1**

3m 57.0s (-3.00) **Going Correction** +0.10s/f (Yiel) **4** Ran SP% **106.6**
Speed ratings: **111,110,93,60**
CSF £7.45 TOTE £2.70; EX 6.00.
Owner John P McManus **Bred** J B De Balanda, F Hoffet Et Al **Trained** Upper Lambourn, Berks

FOCUS
The bends on the chase course had been moved to provide fresh ground. A fair novice chase run at a sound pace, it provided a rousing finish. The winner is rated to her previous chase best, with a personal best from the second.

NOTEBOOK
Miss Sarenne(FR) just prevailed on this return to chasing. In receipt of a stone from her two principal opponents, she tracked them before slipping through on the inside to lead off the home turn. The runner-up renewed his challenge, but she held him off gamely. Her jumping had been sloppy on her earlier efforts over fences but that criticism could not be levelled at her on the better ground here. (op 15-8 tchd 11-4)
West With The Wind had not jumped too well when winning easily at Ludlow, but he did not do much wrong in that department here. He did not have things his own way up front this time, but rallied willingly after the winner headed him before the third-last and went down fighting. (op 2-1 tchd 7-4)
Askmeroe(IRE) made all at Fairyhouse on his latest start but was taken on for the lead here. Dropping away from the second-last, he looks in need of considerably slower ground and possibly a right-handed track. (op 11-4 tchd 3-1)
Overrule(USA) did not jump with much confidence on this chase debut and was last throughout. This trip is sharp enough for him. (op 9-1)

193 BETDAQ BETTING EXCHANGE H'CAP HURDLE (13 hdls) 3m 110y
7:05 (7:05) (Class 3) (0-125,125) 4-Y-0+ **£5,204** (£1,528; £764; £381)

Form RPR

304- 1 **Alderley Rover (IRE)**[23] [5184] 6-11-1 114.... JasonMaguire 121+
(Donald McCain) *hld up: hdwy appr 3 out: rdn to ld bef last: styd on wl* **6/1**[2]

530- 2 3¼ **Solway Minstrel**[21] [5203] 13-9-13 103.... EwanWhillans(5) 106
(Lisa Harrison) *led: rdn and hdd whn nt fluent last: styd on same pce* **16/1**

3 1¼ **Meadows Thyne (IRE)**[23] [5191] 9-10-9 108.... PCarberry 110+
(A J Martin, Ire) *hld up: hdwy 3 out: rdn appr last: styd on: nt rch ldrs* **5/1**[1]

416- 4 2 **Elusive Muse**[21] [5217] 4-10-3 115.... OliverDayman(7) 109
(Alison Thorpe) *hld up: hdwy 5th: rdn appr last: styd on same pce* **16/1**

125- 5 9 **Ballyvesey (IRE)**[23] [5184] 5-10-5 104....(p) TomO'Brien 96
(Peter Bowen) *hld up: hdwy appr 8th: wknd bef last* **6/1**[2]

653- 6 2 **Or Jaune (FR)**[32] [5046] 8-11-6 119....(b) JamieMoore 110
(Gary Moore) *prom: chsd ldr 8th: rdn and wknd appr last* **16/1**

030- 7 9 **Giovanna**[62] [4442] 9-11-7 123.... SeanQuinlan(3) 108
(Richard Phillips) *prom: rdn after 9th: wknd 2 out* **16/1**

004- 8 11 **Civil Servant**[14] [5374] 5-10-4 110....(t) SamTwiston-Davies(7) 82
(Nigel Twiston-Davies) *hld up: rdn appr 3 out: n.d: t.o* **20/1**

641- 9 13 **Tribe**[20] [5231] 8-11-12 125.... WillKennedy 85
(Paul Webber) *hld up: sme hdwy u.p appr 3 out: sn wknd: t.o* **12/1**

425- 10 10 **River Logic (IRE)**[15] [5349] 7-11-6 119....(t) KeithMercer 70
(J Hetherton) *mid-div: hdwy 5th: drvn along 8th: wknd after 10th: t.o* **11/1**[3]

10- 11 6 **Daurica**[189] [1986] 6-11-12 125.... SamJones 71
(Renee Robeson) *chsd ldr to 8th: wknd after 10th: t.o* **25/1**

P/5- 12 1¼ **Gee Dee (IRE)**[26] [5147] 9-10-13 112.... HenryOliver 57
(Sue Smith) *chsd ldrs: rdn and lost pl after 7th: wknd 9th: t.o* **20/1**

415- 13 1½ **Bescot Springs (IRE)**[28] [5119] 5-11-1 114....(p) RichardJohnson 58
(Philip Hobbs) *prom: rdn after 10th: wknd 3 out: t.o* **12/1**

2/5- P **The Whisperer (IRE)**[197] [1857] 9-11-12 125.... SamThomas —
(Nicky Richards) *hld up: a in rr: t.o whn p.u bef 3 out* **33/1**

201- P **Bollin Fiona**[42] [4863] 6-9-13 105.... CallumWhillans(7) —
(Donald Whillans) *mid-div: nt fluent and lost pl 2nd: sn dropped to last pl and nt fluent afterwards: bhd whn hit 8th: t.o whn p.u bef 3 out* **20/1**

6P/- P **Oberon Moon (IRE)**[496] [2999] 9-11-1 114.... RobertThornton —
(Alan King) *prom tl rdn and wknd after 10th: t.o whn p.u bef next* **28/1**

046- P **Stow**[48] [4739] 5-11-7 120.... AidanColeman —
(Venetia Williams) *mid-div: mstkes 3rd and 6th: rdn appr 8th: wknd next: t.o whn p.u bef 3 out* **12/1**

6m 5.50s (-10.80) **Going Correction** -0.20s/f (Good)
WFA 4 from 5yo+ 20lb **17** Ran SP% **124.7**
Speed ratings (Par 107): **109,107,107,106,104 103,100,97,92,89 87,87,86,—,— —,—**
toteswingers: 1&2 £33.70, 1&3 £20.20, 2&3 £59.40 CSF £88.24 CT £528.72 TOTE £6.40: £2.10, £5.70, £2.20, £4.10; EX 153.40.
Owner Alec Craig & Andrew Dick **Bred** Miss Kitty O'Connor **Trained** Cholmondeley, Cheshire

FOCUS
A competitive handicap hurdle run at a sound gallop, and the form looks solid. The winner is on the upgrade.

NOTEBOOK
Alderley Rover(IRE) travelled notably well before improving on the long turn out of the back straight. He had to work to get on top approaching the last, but was well in command at the line. The extended 3m on this flat track was not a problem and he is settling better these days. He has the scope to make a nice chaser. (op 8-1)
Solway Minstrel was third in this race last year and has now been placed on all three visits to Aintree. He ran a game race from the front and lost nothing in defeat. Other than the last flight, which he did not meet quite right, his hurdling was a pleasure to watch. (op 25-1)
Meadows Thyne(IRE) was up considerably in the weights after his recent Gowran win. Another to come from off the pace, he was staying on after the last but too late to get to the first two. (op 11-2)
Elusive Muse is a progressive young stayer and this was another solid effort. His run under a penalty last time may have come too quickly for him and he was 3lb lower here, with the stronger gallop a plus. (op 20-1)
Ballyvesey(IRE), well supported, ran creditably without quite reaching a challenging position. He could not replicate Cheltenham form with tonight's winner but that was probably due to an improved effort on Alderley Rover's part. (op 5-1 tchd 9-2)
Or Jaune(FR) ran respectably switched back to hurdles but faded after rapping the third-last when right behind the leaders.
Giovanna is back down to her last winning mark but was 9lb lower when winning this race 12 months ago. She faded out of the picture from the second-last.
Tribe was bumped up 9lb for his comfortable Bangor win. He made eyecatching progress down the back but came under pressure before the home turn and dropped away. Official explanation: jockey said gelding made a mistake fourth last and never travelled (op 10-1)
Bescot Springs(IRE) remains 7lb higher than when winning two starts back and may not have stayed this longer trip. He seems more at home in softer ground. (op 16-1)

194 BETDAQ.CO.UK H'CAP CHASE (12 fncs) — 2m
7:40 (7:40) (Class 3) (0-135,133) 5-Y-O+ **£7,604** (£2,246; £1,123; £561; £280)

Form — RPR

313- **1** **Quito Du Tresor (FR)**[20] 5225 6-10-10 **120**............... CampbellGillies(3) 127
(Lucinda Russell) *led: rdn and hdd after 2 out: 3 1/2 l down and hld whn lft in ld last: styd on* **7/2**[1]

216- **2** *2* **Drever Route (IRE)**[26] 5141 7-10-12 **119**.............................. DarylJacob 125
(Howard Johnson) *a.p: rdn to chse ldr and mstke 3 out: styng on same pce whn lft 2nd and hmpd last* **9/1**

642- **3** *5* **Stan (NZ)**[11] 18 11-11-12 **133**... AidanColeman 135+
(Venetia Williams) *trckd ldrs: rdn after 2 out: no ex whn lft 3rd and hmpd last* **4/1**[2]

556- **4** *3 3/4* **Enfant De Lune (FR)**[127] 3190 6-10-10 **117**.................. RobertThornton 110
(Alan King) *prom: mstke 4 out: wknd after 2 out: lft 4th and hmpd last* **16/1**

154- **5** *10* **My Moment (IRE)**[63] 4415 7-11-12 **133**......................... RichardJohnson 120
(Henry Daly) *chsd ldr: hit 3rd: rdn appr 3 out: sn wknd* **11/1**

46F- **6** *1 1/2* **Charingworth (IRE)**[21] 5204 7-11-3 **124**............................. GrahamLee 112
(Ferdy Murphy) *hld up: nvr on terms* **8/1**

F33- **7** *hd* **Vinmix De Bessy (FR)**[21] 5208 9-11-2 **123**......................(p) JamieMoore 111
(Gary Moore) *hld up: mstke 10th: rdn next: n.d* **12/1**

6P4- **8** *11* **Tramantano**[15] 5337 11-11-11 **132**.................................(b) PaddyBrennan 108
(Nigel Twiston-Davies) *hld up: hdwy u.p 9th: wknd next* **7/1**[3]

631- **9** *29* **Nelson Du Ronceray (FR)**[15] 5337 9-11-2 **123**............ WilsonRenwick 73
(P Monteith) *hld up: mstke 2nd: bhd whn hit 5th: t.o* **12/1**

61F- **F** **Master Nimbus**[15] 5343 10-11-3 **124**.......................... DougieCostello 136+
(John Quinn) *hld up in tch: led after 2 out: 3 1/2 l clr and gng wl whn fell last* **15/2**

3m 58.7s (-1.30) **Going Correction** +0.10s/f (Yiel) **10** Ran SP% **117.2**
Speed ratings: **107,106,103,101,96 95,95,90,75,—**
toteswingers: 1&2 £9.00, 1&3 £9.30, 2&3 £13.20 CSF £35.25 CT £132.15 TOTE £3.30: £1.10, £3.80, £2.60; EX 36.00.
Owner Mrs Jo Tracey **Bred** Mme Claude Menard & Jacques Cherel **Trained** Arlary, Perth & Kinross

FOCUS
A competitive and truly run handicap chase. The winner was fortunate and the faller was heading for a personal best, but this is fairly solid form.

NOTEBOOK
Quito Du Tresor(FR) ran out a fortunate winner. That said, the six-year-old had run a bold race from the front, only relinquishing his lead after the second-last. He gets further than this and jumps pretty well, although he did show a tendency to go slightly out to his right. Racing off his proper mark having run well from out of the weights at Ayr, he was not adversely affected by the removal of his cheekpieces. The Summer Plate at Market Rasen is reportedly his target. (tchd 4-1)
Drever Route(IRE) was never far from the action and stuck on for a creditable second after a mistake three out and being slightly hampered by the faller at the last. The 3m1f was too far for him at Kelso but he may get a bit further than tonight's trip. (op 12-1)
Stan(NZ) ran creditably but then again he should have done as he was officially 5lb ahead of the handicapper. He may prefer further these days. (op 5-1)
Enfant De Lune(FR) ran well on this handicap debut and first start since New Year's Eve, keeping on again after losing his pitch when short of room going into the cross fence. He will be suited by a step up in trip. (op 14-1)
My Moment(IRE) tracked the winner for much of the way before weakening quickly in the straight. He does not look straightforward. (op 14-1 tchd 10-1)
Charingworth(IRE) ☒ found this too sharp and is definitely not one to give up on when returned to 2m4f. (tchd 13-2)
Tramantano has a decent record at this venue but he was never going that well this time. (op 13-2 tchd 6-1)
Nelson Du Ronceray(FR), who had Tramantano behind when winning off 4lb lower at Perth, jumped markedly out to his right and was soon toiling. He was without the cheekpices here. Official explanation: jockey said gelding made a mistake in back straight and lost its confidence (op 9-1)
Master Nimbus moved well through the race and it looked all over when he quickened ahead after two out, only for him to take a crunching fall. The same happened at Uttoxeter on his previous start and it is to be hoped he gets over this second successive tumble, as he would have been an impressive winner. (op 7-1 tchd 8-1)

195 INKERMAN NOVICES' HUNTERS' CHASE (16 fncs) — 2m 4f
8:10 (8:11) (Class 6) 5-Y-O+ **£1,743** (£665)

Form — RPR

PF6/ **1** **Hivikos (FR)**[13] 7-11-9 0..(t) MrMWall(5) 105
(Mrs P J Buckler) *chsd ldr to 3rd: remained handy: wnt 2nd again after 8th: led 10th: rdn clr 3 out: chal and stl slt ld whn lft wl clr last* **15/2**

25P- **2** *120* **Oscar Royal (IRE)**[14] 5369 9-11-7 117........................... MrTEllis(7) —
(F A Hutsby) *led and clr to 4th: hdd 10th: wknd 4 out: sn t.o: lft remote 2nd last* **12/1**

21U- **U** **Carrick Oscar (IRE)**[29] 5096 10-12-1 119...................... MrJFMathias(7) —
(Tim Vaughan) *mstke and uns rdr 1st* **5/2**[2]

5/1- **F** **Port Talbot (IRE)**[14] 5369 9-12-1 0.............................. MrLukeMorgan(3) 106
(P W Mason) *hld up and bhd: mstke 2nd: hdwy to go 3rd 9th: chsd wnr 4 out: rdn and ev ch whn hung lft and fell last* **13/2**[3]

1- **F** **Quotica De Poyans (FR)**[46] 4784 6-11-11 0................ MissKBryson(7) —
(Simon Shirley-Beavan) *prom: chsd ldr 3rd tl after 8th: dropped to last pl next: wnt 7 l 3rd and stl appearing to be gng okay whn fell 3 out* **10/11**[1]

5m 8.10s (-0.10) **Going Correction** +0.10s/f (Yiel) **5** Ran SP% **113.7**
Speed ratings: **104,—,—,—,—**
CSF £67.01 TOTE £10.40: £6.60, £5.00; EX 107.10.
Owner Mrs P J Buckler **Bred** Jean-Christian Raymond **Trained** Cirencester, Gloucs
☒ A winner with her first runner under rules for trainer Nell Buckler.

FOCUS
An eventful novice hunter chase, and not form to take seriously. The winner is rated value for 3l.

NOTEBOOK
Hivikos(FR) was a modest chaser for Paul Nicholls in 2008/9, but he had made all in a couple of restricted point-to-points this spring. After showing ahead in the back straight, he kicked off the home turn and looked just about in command when he was left well clear at the last. His own jumping had not been especially fluent. (op 12-1)
Oscar Royal(IRE), whose keenness to get on with things had caused a false start, reverted to his usual trailblazing tactics. He offered nothing when headed but inherited a very remote second place. (op 16-1 tchd 11-1)
Port Talbot(IRE)'s Newton Abbot win had been boosted at Cheltenham on Wednesday evening by a couple that he beat. After a shaky round of jumping, he came through to pose a threat between the last two fences but appeared held when he came down at the last. (op 8-11 tchd 11-10)
Quotica De Poyans(FR) was unbeaten coming into this, but his record looked in jeopardy when he made errors at successive fences on the final circuit and dropped to the rear. He was attempting to close, but had work to do, when he came down at the first in the straight. (op 8-11 tchd 11-10)

196 BJORN AGAIN AT AINTREE FRIDAY 11TH JUNE H'CAP HURDLE (11 hdls) — 2m 4f
8:40 (8:40) (Class 3) (0-125,124) 4-Y-O+ **£5,204** (£1,528; £764; £381)

Form — RPR

50-1 **1** **Astracad (FR)**[8] 55 4-10-7 **110** 7ex.............................. PaddyBrennan 118+
(Nigel Twiston-Davies) *hld up: hdwy 8th: led appr 3 out: edgd lft flat: drvn out* **3/1**[1]

202- **2** *2* **Baaher (USA)**[46] 4781 6-9-10 **104**.................................. PaulNorton(10) 115+
(Jim Goldie) *hld up: hdwy appr 3 out: rdn and ev ch last: styd on u.p* **33/1**

544- **3** *1 1/2* **Pure Faith (IRE)**[9] 51 6-10-9 **107**...................................... TomO'Brien 115
(Peter Bowen) *hld up: hdwy appr 3 out: rdn and ev ch last: styd on same pce flat* **9/1**

051- **4** *1* **Extreme Conviction (IRE)**[20] 5229 6-10-6 **104**................ WillKennedy 111
(John Berry) *hld up: hdwy 6th: rdn appr last: no ex flat* **9/1**

122- **5** *1/2* **Tabaran (FR)**[12] 3 7-10-12 **117**.................................(tp) OliverDayman(7) 124
(Alison Thorpe) *prom: chsd ldr 6th to 8th: rdn 2 out: styd on same pce last* **7/1**[2]

532- **6** *5* **E Major**[32] 5038 5-10-12 **110**.. SamJones 113
(Renee Robeson) *hld up: hdwy 3 out: sn rdn: nt pce to chal* **14/1**

432- **7** *1 3/4* **To Arms**[21] 5217 8-11-12 **124**..................................(tp) ChristianWilliams 125
(Lawney Hill) *hld up: hdwy appr 3 out: rdn after next: wknd flat* **16/1**

12F- **8** *7* **Share Option**[28] 5119 8-11-2 **119**...................................... LeeEdwards(5) 114
(Tony Carroll) *hld up: hdwy appr 3 out: rdn and wknd bef last* **25/1**

145- **9** *15* **Cassius (IRE)**[9] 44 8-11-8 **120**... GrahamLee 101
(Bruce Mactaggart) *hld up: nvr on terms: t.o* **16/1**

116- **10** *nk* **Still At Lunch (IRE)**[147] 2808 7-11-9 **121**...................... RichieMcGrath 102
(Kate Walton) *chsd ldr 2nd to 6th: wknd appr 3 out: t.o* **16/1**

114- **11** *nk* **Word Of Warning**[16] 5308 6-11-3 **115**............................ DenisO'Regan 96
(Martin Todhunter) *prom tl rdn and wknd 2 out: t.o* **17/2**[3]

64U- **12** *1 1/2* **Simple Jim (FR)**[16] 5319 6-10-12 **110**.............................. KeithMercer 89
(J Hetherton) *hld up: a in rr: hmpd 5th: t.o* **20/1**

155- **13** *30* **Mumbles Pier (IRE)**[19] 5255 5-11-1 **113**................................ APMcCoy 65
(Peter Bowen) *prom: chsd ldr 8th: ev ch appr 3 out: sn wknd: t.o* **14/1**

10P- **14** *1/2* **Peters Star (IRE)**[34] 4991 8-11-1 **116**...........................(b) AdrianLane(3) 68
(Donald McCain) *chsd ldrs: mstke 4th: rdn 7th: sn wknd: t.o* **28/1**

P2F- **15** *29* **Ouste (FR)**[19] 5246 8-10-7 **105**..................................(bt) RichardJohnson 31
(Alison Thorpe) *led and sn clr: nt fluent 4th: hit 8th: hdd & wknd appr 3 out: t.o* **20/1**

350- **16** *21* **Moment Present (FR)**[19] 5248 5-11-6 **118**.....................(tp) PaulMoloney 25
(Charlie Mann) *mid-div: dropped in rr 5th: t.o* **28/1**

241/ **17** *9* **Option Money (IRE)**[389] 4997 8-11-4 **116**.................... AndrewThornton 15
(Peter Salmon) *hld up: mstke 6th: bhd fr 8th: t.o* **66/1**

P0-1 **F** **Forget It**[7] 86 5-11-0 **112** 7ex.. JamieMoore —
(Gary Moore) *hld up: fell 5th* **16/1**

4m 53.1s (-7.60) **Going Correction** -0.20s/f (Good)
WFA 4 from 5yo+ 19lb **18** Ran SP% **129.6**
Speed ratings (Par 107): **107,106,105,105,105 103,102,99,93,93 93,92,80,80,68 60,56,—**
toteswingers:1&2:£57.00, 1&3:£14.80, 2&3:£82.70 CSF £121.14 CT £857.58 TOTE £3.40: £1.10, £6.50, £3.30, £2.00 Place 6 £1,363.43, Place 5 £564.53..
Owner H R Mould **Bred** Charlotte Thoreau **Trained** Naunton, Gloucs

FOCUS
A competitive handicap hurdle and the form looks solid and should work out. The finish was dominated by those near the foot of the handicap.

NOTEBOOK
Astracad(FR) looked an improving young hurdler when winning at Hereford last week and he was officially 8lb well in under the penalty. He made smooth progress to lead turning in and showed a good attitude to fend off the runner-up after the last. Easier conditions shouldn't trouble him as the rain was getting into the ground at Hereford. (op 4-1 tchd 11-4)
Baaher(USA) was at the back for much of the trip and was slightly hampered by a faller at the last with a lap to go. He improved to look a threat at the final flight, but the winner proved too strong. The return to this longer trip suited and this was a pleasing effort, but he lacks consistency and remains a maiden.
Pure Faith(IRE) was alongside the winner at the final flight but was just found out over this longer trip. He is due to be dropped 2lb in future handicaps. (op 10-1)
Extreme Conviction(IRE) ran well off this 7lb higher mark but lacked a change of gear late on. (op 17-2)
Tabaran(FR) was 1lb well in. He was renewing his effort late on and continues to run consistently well. (op 8-1)
E Major ☒ was 8lb higher than when beaten by handicap good thing Woodlark Island last time. He was staying on nicely at the end and his first hurdles win should not be far away.
To Arms ran with credit in the combination of tongue tie and cheekpieces for the first time.
Still At Lunch(IRE) could not get to the front on this first start since December and eventually faded after racing prominently. (tchd 18-1)
Word Of Warning ran better than his finishing position suggests back over this longer trip. (op 7-1)
Ouste(FR), back over hurdles after a heavy chase fall last time, held a clear lead for a long way but came back to his field before the home turn. (op 22-1)
T/Plt: £825.60 to a £1 stake. Pool: £74,538.54 - 65.90 winning tickets. T/Qpdt: £454.10 to a £1 stake. Pool: £5,707.35 - 9.30 winning tickets. CR

197a - 205a (Foreign Racing) - See Raceform Interactive

HAYDOCK (L-H)

Saturday, May 8

OFFICIAL GOING: Good changing to good (good to firm in places) after race 3 (3.00). Other races run under rules of Flat racing.

Rail realignment increased distances on round course by 10yds. All races run on inside chase course and hurdle races run over shorter than advertised.

Wind: Moderate, half-behind Weather: Fine

206 TOTEQUADPOT LONG DISTANCE H'CAP HURDLE 3m 1f

3:00 (3:00) (Class 2) 4-Y-0+

£15,655 (£4,625; £2,312; £1,157; £577; £290)

Form	Pos	Dist	Horse / details	RPR
461-	1		**Picture This (IRE)**[23] 5197 7-10-7 **129** .... HarrySkelton(3) (Paul Nicholls) *hld up: hdwy 8th and a travelling wl: led jst bef last: drvn clr and styd on wl run-in* **6/1**[2]	145+
310-	2	6	**Barafundle (IRE)**[23] 5197 6-10-8 **127** .... AlanO'Keeffe (Jennie Candlish) *chsd ldrs: wnt 2nd 5th: led 6th: hdd after 4 out: rdn to regain ld 3 out: hdd jst bef last: kpt on same pce and no ch w wnr run-in* **40/1**	136+
04F-	3	7	**Amber Brook (IRE)**[23] 5196 9-11-7 **140** .... JasonMaguire (Nigel Twiston-Davies) *hld up: hdwy appr 4 out: chsd ldrs 2 out: hung lft u.p fr bef last: styd on but no imp on front 2 run-in* **33/1**	142
541-	4	2 1/4	**Al Co (FR)**[22] 5217 5-10-13 **132** .... APMcCoy (Jonjo O'Neill) *midfield: hdwy 8th: effrt to chse ldrs 3 out: styd on same pce fr bef last* **5/1**[1]	132
233-	5	1 3/4	**Sangfroid**[5] 5393 6-10-9 **128** .... DarylJacob (Nick Williams) *in tch: pushed along after 4 out: effrt to chse ldrs appr 2 out: styd on same pce after* **12/1**	126
313-	6	1/2	**Soft Spoken Guy (IRE)**[17] 5306 7-10-10 **132** ....(t) MichaelMcAlister(3) (Maurice Barnes) *in tch: led after 4 out: hdd 3 out: rdn and stl chalng 2 out: 3rd and u.p whn slipped on landing last: sn wknd* **28/1**	133+
034-	7	3 1/4	**Fin Vin De Leu (GER)**[20] 5245 4-10-2 **127** .... PaulMoloney (Charlie Mann) *hld up: hdwy appr 4 out: kpt on same pce u.p fr 2 out: nvr able to chal ldrs* **33/1**	116
20P-	8	3/4	**Erzen (IRE)**[51] 4699 5-11-0 **133** .... AndrewTinkler (Nicky Henderson) *midfield: rdn along after 6th: lost pl 7th: struggling to keep up w ldrs and no imp after* **22/1**	127
12F-	9	1/2	**Superior Wisdom (IRE)**[21] 5223 10-10-11 **130** .... WillKennedy (Alex Hales) *in tch: rdn after 4 out: no real imp on ldrs: wknd 2 out* **25/1**	124
101-	10	1	**Captive Audience (IRE)**[21] 5228 7-11-7 **140** .... TomScudamore (Rebecca Curtis) *j.rt: led 1st to 3rd: remained w ldr tl 4 out: wknd 3 out* **12/1**	133
212-	11	32	**Pokanoket (IRE)**[22] 5205 7-10-1 **125** .... JamesHalliday(5) (Malcolm Jefferson) *racd keenly: prom: led 3rd to 6th: remained handy: rdn and wknd appr 2 out* **22/1**	89
441-	12	33	**Mous Of Men (FR)**[14] 5393 7-10-8 **127** ....(t) TimmyMurphy (David Pipe) *bhd: struggling 4 out: nvr able to get on terms: eased whn wl btn bef last: t.o* **9/1**[3]	61
201-	13	6	**Love Of Tara**[32] 5076 8-10-11 **130** .... WarrenMarston (Martin Keighley) *in tch: nt fluent 7th: u.p and wknd 4 out: t.o* **14/1**	59
P00-	14	16	**Elzahann (IRE)**[42] 4884 8-10-6 **125** .... GrahamLee (Ferdy Murphy) *bhd: blnd bdly 5th: nvr gng after: t.o* **10/1**	39
/PF-	P		**Jaunty Flight**[28] 5126 8-11-12 **145** .... MrTGreenall (Oliver Sherwood) *in rr: struggling whn j. slowly 6th: sn lost tch: t.o whn p.u bef 7th* **80/1**	—
P41-	P		**Oscar Bay (IRE)**[28] 5132 8-11-2 **138** ....(b) HaddenFrost(3) (James Frost) *a bhd: struggling 7th: t.o whn p.u bef 4 out* **33/1**	—
514-	F		**Wychwoods Legend**[22] 5212 7-10-3 **122** ....(t) WayneHutchinson (Martin Keighley) *chsd ldrs: lost pl 4th: pushed along and struggling whn fell 8th* **11/1**	—
010-	P		**Alderluck (IRE)**[29] 5113 7-11-2 **135** ....(v) LiamTreadwell (Nick Gifford) *led to 1st: remained prom tl wknd 7th: t.o whn p.u bef 3 out* **40/1**	—
0F0-	P		**Heathcliff (IRE)**[29] 5113 8-10-8 **127** ....(b) RobertThornton (Richard Lee) *midfield but nvr travelling: lost pl appr 7th: t.o whn p.u bef 4 out* **25/1**	—
212-	P		**Viking Blond (FR)**[15] 5372 5-10-3 **129** ....(b) SamTwiston-Davies(7) (Nigel Twiston-Davies) *chsd ldrs: rdn appr 6th: u.p after: wknd bef 8th: t.o whn p.u bef 3 out* **14/1**	—
F31-	P		**Penylan Star (IRE)**[25] 5173 5-10-5 **124** .... RichardJohnson (Philip Hobbs) *a bhd: t.o whn p.u bef 3 out* **14/1**	—

5m 31.7s (-36.30)

WFA 4 from 5yo+ 20lb **21** Ran SP% **128.5**

Tote Swingers: 1&2 £1.10, 1&3 £3.70, 2&3 £4.50 CSF £239.29 CT £7247.23 TOTE £5.60: £1.90, £7.20, £11.00, £1.90; EX 1065.40.

Owner Sir Alex Ferguson, Ged Mason & Ron Wood **Bred** Dominick Vallely **Trained** Ditcheat, Somerset

⊠ Stewards' Enquiry : Will Kennedy one-day ban: used whip when out of contention (May 23)

FOCUS

They went a sound pace for what was a good staying handicap hurdle. Step ups from the first two with the sixth setting the level.

NOTEBOOK

Picture This(IRE) bounced back to his best when decisively winning a decent staying handicap at Cheltenham latest (appreciated the better ground), and an 11lb rise was nowhere near enough to stop him. Always travelling supremely well, it looked a question when, not if, he asserted all the way up the straight, and Harry Skelton decided to put the race to bed approaching the last. He can expect another stern rise, but it may not matter as connections plan to go chasing with him in the autumn. (op 9-2 tchd 13-2)

Barafundle(IRE) had been progressing well until finishing miles behind the winner at Cheltenham, but that was clearly not his true form and he didn't go down without a fight off 14lb better terms, but was well and truly put in his place from the last. He should make a fine 3m chaser. (op 33-1)

Amber Brook(IRE), a faller at Cheltenham latest, had earlier finished fourth in the David Nicholson Mares' race at the festival and she showed herself to be none the worse for her recent spill, staying on well once the race was all over.

Al Co(FR), who appreciated the better ground when winning off 6lb lower at Uttoxeter, didn't run at all badly and remains open to further progress, being just a 5-y-o. (op 8-1)

Sangfroid, narrowly denied on the Flat the other day, boxed on best he could without being good enough. (op 14-1)

Soft Spoken Guy(IRE) ran a fine race under a positive ride, and would have been battling it out for the places had he not lost his footing on touching down after the last. (tchd 25-1)

Fin Vin De Leu(GER), trying this trip for the first time, made a little late headway and clearly has a future as a decent handicapper.

Erzen(IRE) was another to make small late gains. (op 20-1)

Mous Of Men(FR), 7lb higher than when winning over 2m4f at Sandown latest, was never going (op 8-1)

Elzahann(IRE), 3lb higher than when winning last year, was never going after a blunder at the fifth. (op 11-1 tchd 12-1)

Jaunty Flight Official explanation: jockey said mare was unsuited by the good (good to firm places) ground (op 10-1)

Oscar Bay(IRE) Official explanation: jockey said gelding never travelled (op 10-1)

Alderluck(IRE) Official explanation: jockey said gelding finished distressed (op 10-1)

Penylan Star(IRE) looked to be progressing, but he was never travelling on this handicap debut. (op 10-1)

207 TOTESPORT.COM SWINTON H'CAP HURDLE GRADE 3 2m 110y

3:35 (3:35) (Class 1) 4-Y-0+

£42,757 (£16,042; £8,032; £4,005; £2,010; £1,005)

Form	Pos	Dist	Horse / details	RPR
104-	1		**Eradicate (IRE)**[21] 5222 6-10-1 **132** .... DavidBass(7) (Nicky Henderson) *midfield: hdwy appr 3 out: nt fluent 2 out: led appr last: drvn out and r.o wl* **16/1**	141+
111-	2	2 3/4	**Overturn (IRE)**[21] 5222 6-11-0 **138** .... JasonMaguire (Donald McCain) *chsd ldrs: led appr 3 out: rdn and hdd bef last: styd on u.p run-in: one pce fnl 100yds* **9/2**[1]	143
512-	3	2	**Issaquah (IRE)**[28] 5128 8-10-11 **140** .... JamesHalliday(5) (Malcolm Jefferson) *midfield: hdwy 3 out: pushed along to chse ldrs appr 2 out: r.o run-in: nrst fin* **33/1**	142
52-	4	2 1/4	**Toubab (FR)**[70] 4307 4-10-3 **131** .... PTownend (Paul Nicholls) *midfield: hdwy 4 out: rdn to chal 2 out: no ex run-in* **16/1**	128
211-	5	nk	**Conquisto**[27] 5146 5-10-7 **131** .... KeithMercer (Steve Gollings) *led: hdd 4 out: stl chalng 2 out: nt qckn appr last: kpt on run-in but no further imp* **8/1**[2]	131
023-	6	2 1/2	**Arcalis**[21] 5222 10-11-0 **138** .... APMcCoy (Howard Johnson) *midfield: hdwy u.p 3 out: styd on run-in: nt rch ldrs* **8/1**[2]	136
211-	7	3	**William's Wishes (IRE)**[17] 5316 5-10-10 **134** .... PaulMoloney (Evan Williams) *midfield: hdwy appr 4 out: effrt whn nt fluent 3 out: styd on same pce fr 2 out* **16/1**	129
000-	8	7	**Mutual Friend (USA)**[50] 4711 6-10-11 **138** ....(b) HaddenFrost(3) (David Pipe) *midfield: hdwy 4 out: rdn and outpcd 2 out: no imp after* **33/1**	127
020-	9	hd	**Ellerslie Tom**[224] 1536 8-10-11 **135** ....(t) DarylJacob (Alison Thorpe) *prom: hit 4th: rdn and nt qckn appr 2 out: wknd bef last* **33/1**	123
6P0-	10	4	**Helium (FR)**[14] 5393 5-10-3 **127** ....(t) LeightonAspell (Nick Gifford) *bhd: styd on fr 2 out: nvr able to rch chalng position* **40/1**	112
310-	11	2 1/2	**Zarinava (IRE)**[53] 4662 6-10-13 **137** .... DenisO'Regan (Mrs John Harrington, Ire) *hld up: rdn after 4 out: sme hdwy 3 out: one pce and no imp fr 2 out* **25/1**	120
2P2-	12	nk	**Aather (IRE)**[19] 5278 5-10-4 **128** ....(t) TimmyMurphy (Alan Fleming) *hld up: pushed along after 4 out: j.rt fnl 3: sme hdwy 2 out: nvr on terms w ldrs* **16/1**	110
101-	13	1 1/2	**Hunterview**[21] 5220 4-10-8 **136** ....(b) TomScudamore (David Pipe) *chsd ldrs tl rdn and wknd after 4 out* **14/1**	113
0-	14	18	**Cooper's Crest (IRE)**[15] 5382 7-10-6 **130** .... MDarcy (Sabrina J Harty, Ire) *chsd ldrs: u.p and wknd after 3 out* **25/1**	95
341-	15	2 1/4	**Noble Request (FR)**[21] 5225 9-10-12 **136** .... RichardJohnson (Philip Hobbs) *hld up: rdn and outpcd after 4 out: nvr on terms* **14/1**	99
300-	16	nse	**Hibiki (IRE)**[132] 3084 6-10-6 **130** ....(p) TomO'Brien (Philip Hobbs) *bhd: niggled along appr 4th: nvr on terms* **33/1**	93
111-	17	14	**Ciceron (IRE)**[16] 5333 4-10-10 **138** .... AidanColeman (Venetia Williams) *midfield: hdwy 4 out: effrt 3 out: wknd 2 out* **11/1**[3]	84
262-	18	nk	**Gloucester**[21] 5222 7-10-7 **131** .... SamThomas (Michael Scudamore) *a bhd* **14/1**	81
031-	19	6	**Dee Ee Williams (IRE)**[28] 5128 7-11-12 **150** ....(b) LiamTreadwell (Nick Gifford) *in tch: lost pl 4th: dropped aways and bhd 4 out* **18/1**	94
105-	20	26	**Dan Breen (IRE)**[29] 5108 5-11-1 **139** .... JohnnyFarrelly (David Pipe) *chsd ldrs: mstke 5th: rdn and wknd after 4 out: t.o* **16/1**	60
12V-	21	2 1/2	**Is It Me (USA)**[147] 2840 7-10-11 **135** ....(t) CharliePoste (Sophie Leech) *a bhd: t.o fr 5th* **100/1**	54
/11-	22	7	**Acambo (GER)**[321] 776 9-11-2 **140** .... GrahamLee (David Pipe) *bhd: pushed along appr 4 out: nvr on terms* **33/1**	53
12F-	P		**Black Jack Blues (IRE)**[20] 5250 7-10-13 **137** ....(t) RobertThornton (Rebecca Curtis) *prom: led 4 out: hdd bef 3 out: wkng whn blnd 2 out: bhd whn p.u bef last* **16/1**	—

3m 42.8s (-21.40) **Going Correction** -0.725s/f (Firm)

WFA 4 from 5yo+ 18lb **23** Ran SP% **135.1**

Speed ratings (Par 113): **113,111,110,109,109 108,106,103,103,101 100,100,99,91,90 90,83,83,80,68 67,63,—**

Tote Swingers:1&2:£48.90, 2&3:£145.20, 1&3:£145.20 CSF £85.44 CT £2465.79 TOTE £24.30: £4.00, £1.80, £8.50, £4.70; EX 164.40 TRIFECTA Not won..

Owner A D Spence **Bred** Sir Eric Parker **Trained** Upper Lambourn, Berks

FOCUS

A cracking renewal of what is always a highly competitive handicap, this year the race being stacked with unexposed, up-and-coming hurdlers. They went a good gallop, and the right horses filled the frame. Solid form.

NOTEBOOK

Eradicate(IRE), a well-held fourth in the Scottish Champion Hurdle, was back to a mark 3lb higher than when winning comfortably at Musselburgh at the start of last season, and he appreciated the quick ground and well-run race to produce a career-best effort, quickly asserting before the last and doing the bare minimum once in front. David Bass admitted to getting there a little too soon, and it will be interesting to see whether connections opt to go chasing with the son of Montjeu. (op 20-1)

Overturn(IRE), put up 8lb for his all-the-way win in the Scottish Champion Hurdle, wasn't ridden as aggressively in this larger field, being content to chase the early pace, but he emerged as a big threat in the straight and went on two out. In the end he was done for speed, but he kept on well, and his trainer's immediate thoughts were to raise him in trip next time. That will be it for now over hurdles, but don't be surprised if he pops up in one of two good Flat races, currently being rated 93 in that sphere. The Ascot Stakes may be the race for him. (op 6-1)

Issaquah(IRE) has found her form again and, despite being 4lb higher than when runner-up at Aintree, she battled on doggedly to take third.

Toubab(FR), who has yet to win but finished second to subsequent Triumph Hurdle winner Soldantino in the Adonis, had been given a mark of 131, which seemed fair, and he went well for a long way, but in the end was done for pace on this quicker ground. He is still a maiden over hurdles, but that won't be the case for long, and he should make a nice chaser one day. (op 12-1)

Conquisto, on a hat-trick after two easy wins in minor novice hurdles, mark of 131, took them along until the straight, but he didn't give in and only backed out of it approaching the last. (op 10-1)

Arcalis has found some form again, finishing second in the County and third off this mark in the Scottish Champion Hurdle, but he lacked the pace to get involved on this quick ground. (op 11-1 tchd 12-1)
William's Wishes(IRE), on a hat-trick after a couple of easy wins in novice hurdles, was found wanting for speed, but this wasn't a bad effort from a mark of 134 on his handicap debut.
Mutual Friend(USA), edging back down the weights and now 3lb higher than when winning at Cheltenham in October, did his usual trick of travelling well only to find little, but he will find easier opportunities.
Hunterview, a flop off 11lb lower in the Fred Winter, had things all his own way when winning a novice hurdle at Ayr and didn't take to this more competitive field. (op 11-1)
Cooper's Crest(IRE) Official explanation: jockey said mare ran flat
Ciceron(IRE), a progressive 4-y-o chasing a four-timer, was 25lb higher than when winning at Wincanton two starts back and never got into this stronger contest. (op 10-1)
Dee Ee Williams(IRE) had shot up 11lb for winning comfortably at Aintree and failed to reproduce the form. Official explanation: jockey said gelding finished distressed (op 20-1 tchd 22-1)

208 TOTESPORT 0800 221 221 BEGINNERS' CHASE (15 fncs) 2m 4f
4:10 (4:10) (Class 3) 5-Y-0+ **£9,107** (£2,674; £1,337; £667)

Form RPR
410- **1** **Tara Royal**[30] 5099 5-11-0 0 JasonMaguire 137+
(Donald McCain) *racd keenly: hld up: hit 7th: clsd 4 out: led appr 2 out: rdn clr bef last: all out towards fin* **9/4**[1]
22- **2** ½ **Cool Friend (IRE)**[68] 4355 7-10-7 124 NickScholfield 127
(Jeremy Scott) *trckd ldrs: wnt 2nd 4th: led 3 out: hdd appr 2 out: rdn and nt qckn bef last and lost grnd on wnr: styd on run-in: gaining towards fin* **9/4**[1]
33B- **3** ½ **Bluegun (IRE)**[43] 4868 8-11-0 123 RichardJohnson 135
(Philip Hobbs) *w ldr: led 4th: nt fluent 4 out: sn hrd pressed: hdd 3 out: wl outpcd 2 out: rallied run-in: styd on and clsd on ldrs towards fin* **6/1**[3]
50-F **4** 82 **Earth Magic (IRE)**[4] 138 10-11-0 124 PaulMoloney 60
(Evan Williams) *led: hdd 4th: j. slowly and bhd 6th: rousted along sn after to get on terms briefly: bhd 7th: lost tch 9th: t.o* **14/1**
F20- **P** **Mahonia (IRE)**[50] 4715 7-11-0 135 PTownend —
(Paul Nicholls) *cl up: blnd 8th: mstke 9th: wknd 4 out: bhd whn p.u bef 2 out: b.b.v* **5/2**[2]
4m 50.9s (-19.10) **Going Correction** -0.725s/f (Firm) course record 5 Ran SP% **111.1**
Speed ratings: **109,108,108,75,—**
CSF £8.02 TOTE £2.50: £1.10, £1.60; EX 8.70.
Owner T G Leslie **Bred** Cobhall Court Stud **Trained** Cholmondeley, Cheshire

FOCUS
A fair novice chase. The winner should go on to rate higher.

NOTEBOOK
Tara Royal won this nicely. His jumping was impressive at the first time of asking, especially over these fences. A keen sort, he again took a good hold and had to be reigned back after several quick jumps, but quickly asserted once allowed to stride on going to two out and, although in the end he only just held on, he didn't appear to be doing a lot in front and was probably getting a little tired. He will need to learn to settle if he is to mix it at a higher level, but he's a likeable sort who warrants keeping on side for the time being. (tchd 3-1 in a place)
Cool Friend(IRE), runner-up on all four previous starts over fences, including twice behind smart mare Carole's Legacy, was again made to settle for second. She kept on right the way to the line and will find a race at some stage. (op 11-4)
Bluegun(IRE) failed to win in four starts over fences last season and doesn't look the most natural chaser, but he stuck to his task having been headed and can probably win a chase at one of the minor tracks through the summer. (tchd 11-2 and 13-2)
Earth Magic(IRE), a faller at Fakenham just four days earlier, got round in his own time. (op 10-1)
Mahonia(IRE), runner-up to Mad Max on his second and final start over fences last season, dropped away quickly and was reported to have bled from the nose. Official explanation: jockey said gelding bled from the nose (tchd 9-4)

[87]HEXHAM (L-H)
Saturday, May 8

OFFICIAL GOING: Good to soft (good in places) changing to good (good to soft in places) after race 1 (2:15)
Final flight in the back straight omitted in all hurdle races; worn ground.
Wind: Fresh, half behind Weather: Cloudy, dry

209 CHAMPIONS 60:60 "NATIONAL HUNT" NOVICES' HURDLE (6 hdls 2 omitted) 2m 110y
2:15 (2:15) (Class 4) 4-Y-0+ **£5,138** (£1,497; £749)

Form RPR
020- **1** **Montoya's Son (IRE)**[15] 5370 5-10-9 112 JamesO'Farrell(3) 98
(Howard Johnson) *hld up in tch: rdn and outpcd bef last: styd on wl run-in: led nr fin* **5/1**
242- **2** hd **Twentynineblack (FR)**[43] 4865 6-10-9 108 AdrianLane(3) 98
(Donald McCain) *prom: smooth hdwy to ld bef last: rdn run-in: kpt on: hdd nr fin* **3/1**[2]
441- **3** nk **Pyracantha**[27] 5138 5-11-5 114 BarryKeniry 105
(Alan Swinbank) *pressed ldr: led briefly bef last: sn rdn: kpt on wl run-in: hld cl home* **7/2**[3]
053- **4** 7 **Attaglance**[27] 5144 4-10-1 0 KyleJames(7) 88
(Malcolm Jefferson) *prom: drvn and outpcd bef last: kpt on run-in: no imp* **11/1**
012- **5** 5 **Quatro Pierji (FR)**[27] 5138 6-11-5 114 (p) PaddyAspell 93
(James Moffatt) *j.rt: led to bef last: wknd run-in* **9/4**[1]
300- **6** 11 **Fentara**[27] 5146 5-10-6 0 ow1 LiamHeard 69
(Tim Walford) *towards rr: drvn and outpcd after 2 out (usual 3 out): no imp bef last* **125/1**
/05- **7** ½ **Daniel's Dream**[79] 4126 10-10-7 63 (p) EwanWhillans(5) 74
(John Dixon) *trckd ldrs tl rdn and wknd passing usual 2 out* **250/1**
000- **8** ¾ **Lisdonagh House (IRE)**[72] 4258 8-10-12 82 AndrewThornton 73
(Lynn Siddall) *bhd: drvn and outpcd 3rd: shortlived effrt between last 2: nvr on terms* **40/1**
100- **9** 4 **Sheriff Hall (IRE)**[47] 4785 5-10-12 0 RichieMcGrath 69
(George Charlton) *t.k.h: hld up outside: hdwy 1/2-way: wknd bef last* **14/1**
00- **10** 28 **Ontrack (IRE)**[15] 5370 6-10-12 0 WilsonRenwick 41
(Rose Dobbin) *bhd: lost tch 3rd: nvr on terms: t.o* **100/1**
P06- **11** shd **Transact (IRE)**[27] 5155 5-10-9 0 HarryHaynes(3) 41
(Andrew Wilson) *in tch tl wknd after 3 out: t.o* **300/1**
0PP- **12** 27 **Murphys Future**[17] 5310 5-10-9 0 RyanMania(3) 14
(George Foster) *midfield: lost pl 3rd: struggling fr next: t.o* **200/1**
4m 8.60s (-8.80) **Going Correction** -0.45s/f (Good)
WFA 4 from 5yo+ 18lb 12 Ran SP% **115.1**
Speed ratings (Par 105): **102,101,101,98,96 90,90,90,88,75 75,62**
toteswingers:1&2:£2.80, 1&3:£2.70, 2&3:£1.20 CSF £20.52 TOTE £6.00: £1.70, £1.40, £1.90; EX 21.30.
Owner Andrea & Graham Wylie **Bred** Dr Marie Madden **Trained** Billy Row, Co Durham
Stewards' Enquiry : Adrian Lane one-day ban: used whip with excessive frequency (May 23)
James O'Farrell two-day ban: used whip with excessive frequency down shoulder in the forehand (May 23,25)

FOCUS
The last hurdle down the back was omitted, leaving a long run between the final two flights. A moderate race with just a handful of serious contenders, but the highest-rated horses came to the fore and, though the first three finished in a heap, the form looks reliable.

NOTEBOOK
Montoya's Son(IRE) was patiently ridden, letting the leaders get slightly away up the final hill where he looked a little awkward, but he got going from the last to cut down his rivals in time. He still looks to be learning the game which could account for the improvement he found here. His best run previously had been when second to subsequent winner Lord Villez at Newcastle, and it may be that stiff tracks will suit best. Official explanation: trainer said, regarding apparent improvement in form, that the gelding appreciated the better ground. (op 13-2)
Twentynineblack(FR) was always prominent but seemed to need to find extra effort to stay on terms up the hill before striking for home from the last. He nearly stayed in front but was just coming to the end of his reserves near the line. (tchd 10-3)
Pyracantha tracked the leader until taking it up climbing the final hill and rallied once headed to be going on again near the line. Penalised after conquering Quatro Pierji last time, he put in a sound effort and could win again while there is some give in the ground. (op 11-4 tchd 5-2)
Attaglance made some good progress on the final circuit but was beaten from the last. This was a reasonable hurdling debut against more established contenders and he should improve on this. (op 16-1)
Quatro Pierji(FR) was well backed to gain revenge over Pyracantha last time. He set just a reasonable pace but was soon outpaced from the top of the hill. A previous C&D winner in a lesser race, he was outclassed and the penalty for the earlier win did not help either, though he is best on stiff tracks. (op 11-4 tchd 3-1)

210 SHIRE (S) HURDLE (6 hdls 2 omitted) 2m 110y
2:45 (2:45) (Class 5) 4-Y-0+ **£2,740** (£798; £399)

Form RPR
404- **1** **Dunaskin (IRE)**[46] 4810 10-11-1 123 (b) KyleJames(7) 112
(Brian Ellison) *prom: drvn and nt keen after 3rd: outpcd 2 out (usual 3 out): rallied bef last: styd on strly run-in to ld nr fin* **3/1**[1]
51-3 **2** 1¼ **Prioryjo**[7] 87 7-10-8 100 (p) PaulGallagher(7) 104
(Martin Todhunter) *cl up: led after 2 out (usual 3 out): sn clr: rdn bef last: no ex and hdd nr fin* **5/1**
212- **3** 3¼ **Dr Valentine (FR)**[15] 5352 4-11-1 104 PaddyAspell 101
(Ann Duffield) *hld up: hdwy to chse clr ldr passing omitted 2 out: sn rdn: kpt on same pce fr last* **7/2**[2]
00- **4** 22 **Sunset Resort (IRE)**[16] 5333 5-10-12 0 (t) AndrewThornton 78
(Maurice Barnes) *nt jump wl: bhd and detached: hdwy bef last: nvr on terms* **40/1**
253- **5** 1½ **Josephine Malines**[14] 5385 6-10-9 102 CampbellGillies(3) 77
(Ann Duffield) *prom: drvn after 2 out (usual 3 out): wknd between last 2* **7/1**
05-4 **6** 10 **Wee Forbees (IRE)**[7] 87 8-10-9 99 (b1) MrOGreenall(3) 68
(Michael Easterby) *in tch: hdwy to ld 3 out (usual 4 out) to next: wknd between last 2* **4/1**[3]
051/ **7** 8 **Alloro**[19] 4112 6-11-5 92 PeterBuchanan 68
(Alan Kirtley) *led to 3 out (usual 4 out): rdn and wknd after next* **33/1**
/00- **P** **Abstinence (IRE)**[53] 4665 7-10-12 105 WilsonRenwick —
(Howard Johnson) *hld up: rdn 3 out (usual 4 out): wknd fr next: t.o whn p.u bef last* **10/1**
F06- **P** **Tombov (FR)**[21] 5220 4-10-5 68 (p) HarryHaynes(3) —
(James Ewart) *t.k.h: outpcd whn blnd 2 out (usual 3 out): wknd qckly: t.o whn p.u bef last* **33/1**
405- **P** **Can't Remember**[10] 52 5-10-9 78 RyanMania(3) —
(Robert Johnson) *a bhd: struggling 3 out (usual 4 out): sn btn: t.o whn p.u bef last* **50/1**
4m 13.8s (-3.60) **Going Correction** -0.45s/f (Good)
WFA 4 from 5yo+ 18lb 10 Ran SP% **115.8**
Speed ratings (Par 103): **90,89,87,77,76 72,68,—,—,—**
toteswingers:1&2:£5.00, 1&3:£3.50, 2&3:£3.50 CSF £17.92 TOTE £3.60: £1.50, £1.90, £1.50; EX 9.60.There was no bid for the winner.
Owner Koo's Racing Club **Bred** J P And Miss M Mangan **Trained** Norton, N Yorks

FOCUS
A good early pace and a run for home with half a circuit to go decimated the field so there were just three in contention near the finish.

NOTEBOOK
Dunaskin(IRE) was awkward at the first, after which his jumping never found any fluency, and he did not look to be enjoying things. However, the blinkers were back on and galvanized him enough to stick to the task, and once the final flight had been clumsily negotiated he found a change of gear to gallop past two tiring rivals. Although rated 18lb higher than his nearest rival he did not look likely to convert that notional superiority to success for much of the way, notwithstanding he was not ideally suited by the track. (op 11-4)
Prioryjo got first run on the field and began to stretch clear in the back straight. That effort meant she was getting very tired near the finish and could not quite hang on. She is a reliable and capable performer in this grade but is usually better on less testing tracks. (op 6-1)
Dr Valentine(FR) made good progress in the back straight but by this time Prioryjo had made a bid for home. That gave him little option but to chase down the leader and, though he made up ten lengths or more, he was legless from the last. He is only a 4yo and is capable of being a factor in this grade. (tchd 9-2)
Sunset Resort(IRE) was outpaced early but made some late progress past tiring rivals but was never a threat.
Josephine Malines, the weaker of the two Ann Duffield runners, was up there until the pace increased but was soon beaten off. (op 8-1)
Wee Forbees(IRE) was near the head of affairs but soon retreated once the pace lifted. He was rated 134 over fences at his peak but has not won for two years and looks on the downgrade. (op 5-1)

211 GORDON HOPPER H'CAP CHASE (19 fncs) 3m 1f
3:15 (3:15) (Class 5) (0-95,91) 5-Y-0+ **£3,425** (£998; £499)

Form RPR
0P6- **1** **Finbin (IRE)**[19] 5271 8-11-4 **86** (t) FearghalDavis(3) 106+
(Henry Hogarth) *chsd ldrs: drvn and ev ch whn blnd 3 out: led after next: drvn out fr last* **12/1**

644- **2** *6* **Shulmin**[35] 4981 10-10-0 **65** oh3 .... PeterBuchanan 79
(Carol Ferguson) *hld up: hdwy and in tch 1/2-way: effrt bef 3 out: chsd wnr between last 2: no imp run-in* **7/1**[2]

4PU- **3** *10* **Hasper**[19] 5272 12-11-5 **91** .... MrGCrow(7) 95
(Sandy Forster) *rn in snatches: prom: effrt bef 3 out: plugged on after next: no imp* **12/1**

60-U **4** *8* **Janal (IRE)**[7] 88 7-10-3 **68** .... WilsonRenwick 64
(Stuart Coltherd) *hld up: effrt and rdn after 4 out: no imp fr next* **18/1**

545- **5** *nk* **Cinaman (IRE)**[27] 5151 6-10-1 **73** .... AlexanderVoy(7) 71
(Roger Fisher) *hld up: hdwy and prom 6th: led 12th: jst in front whn blnd bdly 2 out: sn hdd: wknd bef last* **8/1**[3]

4FP- **6** *2 1/4* **The Artful Fox**[10] 49 9-9-11 **69** .... HenryBrooke(7) 63
(Mike Sowersby) *chsd ldrs tl rdn and outpcd after 4 out: n.d after* **16/1**

0U3- **7** *2* **Impact Zone**[12] 24 6-10-11 **79** ....(p) MrOGreenall(3) 71
(Michael Easterby) *s.v.s: hld up: jnd pack 4th: effrt after 4 out: wknd fr 2 out* **4/1**[1]

5U1- **8** *47* **Rexmehead (IRE)**[27] 5151 9-11-1 **80** ....(b) PaddyAspell 30
(Andrew Wilson) *nt fluent on occasions: hld up: outpcd 14th: sn struggling* **10/1**

P30- **P** **Glacial Rambler (IRE)**[42] 11-9-11 **65** oh5 .... AdrianLane(3) —
(Stuart Coltherd) *chsd ldrs tl blnd and lost pl 13th: t.o whn p.u bef next* **25/1**

PU5- **P** **The Green Hat (IRE)**[35] 4983 10-10-4 **76** .... MissLAlexander(7) —
(Theresa Gibson) *blnd and dropped in rr 3rd: nvr on terms after: t.o whn p.u bef 15th* **11/1**

P32- **P** **Benny The Piler (IRE)**[19] 5271 10-11-8 **90** ....(p) HarryHaynes(3) —
(Carol Ferguson) *led to 12th: wknd and p.u 4 out* **8/1**[3]

0U2- **P** **Editors Rose (IRE)**[35] 4981 7-10-10 **82** ....(p) KyleJames(7) —
(Tim Walford) *t.k.h: cl up to 4 out: sn wknd: p.u bef next* **7/1**[2]

6m 30.0s (-2.20) **Going Correction** -0.025s/f (Good) **12** Ran SP% **115.0**
Speed ratings: **102,100,96,94,94 93,92,77,—,— —,—**
toteswingers:1&2:£48.90, 1&3:£145.20, 2&3:£145.20 CSF £92.02 CT £1035.42 TOTE £16.50: £3.90, £1.90, £5.30; EX 54.30.
Owner Hogarth Racing **Bred** J Mangan **Trained** Stillington, N Yorks

FOCUS
A weak affair.

NOTEBOOK
Finbin(IRE) jumped quite slowly and kept losing ground because of this but once the race got serious on the final circuit he moved up to challenge the leader Cinaman and, with his rival fluffing the last in the back straight, he took up the running and stayed out in front in gutsy fashion. He put up a poor show when tailed off over C&D last time, but that was his first run for five months and he may have needed that. Improvement was expected this time off a mark back down to his last winning level. Official explanation: trainer had no explanation regarding the apparent improvement in form (tchd 14-1)
Shulmin was given plenty of time to eat into the winner's lead but could not get there. This track does not play to her strengths, but she looks on an attractive mark and it would be a shame if she could not capitalise on it. (op 6-1 tchd 11-2)
Hasper lost ground with a mistake at the ninth and though he finished well he could never mount a serious challenge. This veteran, with only a couple of slowly run hunter chase victories in his record, looks up against it off his current mark. (op 16-1)
Janal(IRE) was already feeling the pace down the back and the step up in trip did not elicit the necessary improvement. (op 14-1)
Cinaman(IRE) was a bit too keen in front, but rallied when challenged by the winner until clouting the second-last and losing all chance. He would not have won but would have finished closer. (tchd 7-1)
Impact Zone made some progress on the final circuit after a sluggish start, but his effort was all too brief. He should have enough ability to win but does not look suited by stiff tracks. (op 9-2 tchd 5-1)
Benny The Piler(IRE) Official explanation: jockey said gelding never travelled
Editors Rose(IRE) Official explanation: jockey said mare hung left throughout

212 BEST DRESSED LADY 2009 H'CAP HURDLE (10 hdls 2 omitted) 3m
3:50 (3:50) (Class 4) (0-100,99) 4-Y-0+ **£4,878** (£1,432; £716; £357)

Form RPR

PP-1 **1** **Flying Doctor**[2] 176 7-10-6 **82** 7ex .... RichieMcLernon(3) 99+
(Elliott Cooper) *in tch gng wl: smooth hdwy to ld last: drew clr run-in: v easily* **9/4**[1]

214- **2** *11* **Solway Ally**[16] 5334 7-11-7 **97** ....(p) HarryHaynes(3) 102+
(Lisa Harrison) *led to 4th: led bef 6th: rdn and hdd last: plugged on run-in: no ch w wnr* **7/1**[3]

323- **3** *7* **Auberge (IRE)**[57] 4556 6-10-7 **80** .... FelixDeGiles 77+
(A M Crow) *in tch: blnd 7th: outpcd bef 2 out (usual 3 out): rallied bef last: nrst fin* **9/1**

636- **4** *2 1/4* **Almond Court (IRE)**[13] 8 7-10-3 **79** .... RyanMania(3) 72
(Robert Johnson) *chsd ldrs tl rdn and no ex bef last* **22/1**

0P0- **5** *1 3/4* **Papa Drew (IRE)**[16] 5334 6-10-10 **83** .... JamesReveley 74
(Andrew Parker) *hld up: drvn along and effrt between last 2: sn no imp* **16/1**

0F2- **6** *10* **Oh Yah Dancer (IRE)**[11] 31 8-11-2 **89** ....(p) BarryKeniry 71
(George Bewley) *bhd: struggling 3 out (usual 4 out): shortlived effrt after next: btn bef last* **20/1**

004- **7** *nk* **Jane Doe**[51] 4708 7-10-7 **87** .... GarryWhillans(7) 69
(Harriet Graham) *chsd ldrs tl wknd bef last* **16/1**

UU6- **8** *7* **It's A Discovery (IRE)**[21] 5234 9-11-5 **95** .... AdrianLane(3) 71
(Donald McCain) *chsd ldrs tl rdn and wknd passing omitted 2 out* **28/1**

022/ **9** *1/2* **Hooky's Hope**[414] 4601 7-9-8 **74** .... GaryRutherford(7) 49
(Harriet Graham) *cl up: chal 2 out untl wknd bef last* **28/1**

6P0- **10** *27* **Capybara (IRE)**[67] 4366 12-10-9 **85** .... FearghalDavis(3) 36
(Henry Hogarth) *midfield: struggling 1/2-way: btn after 2 out (usual 3 out)* **40/1**

00P- **P** **Easter Queen**[16] 5334 8-10-10 **83** .... PaddyAspell —
(Robert Goldie) *cl up: led 4th to bef 6th: wknd fr next: t.o whn p.u bef last* **66/1**

0/P- **P** **Clueless**[62] 4471 8-10-9 **85** ....(p) CampbellGillies(3) —
(Carol Ferguson) *midfield: struggling after 2 out (usual 3 out): t.o whn p.u bef last* **50/1**

52F- **P** **Delightfully (FR)**[22] 5203 6-11-12 **99** ....(v) PeterBuchanan —
(Lucinda Russell) *midfield: lost pl and p.u bef 6th* **16/1**

0/0- **P** **Letterpress (IRE)**[60] 4505 6-11-5 **95** .... JamesO'Farrell(3) —
(Howard Johnson) *hld up: struggling bef 3 out (usual 4 out): t.o whn p.u bef last* **20/1**

501- **P** **Zelos Diktator**[13] 12 4-10-13 **92** .... RichieMcGrath —
(Rose Dobbin) *hld up: rdn 3 out (usual 4 out): btn after next: t.o whn p.u bef last* **14/1**

022- **P** **Monsieur Cadou (FR)**[46] 4798 5-11-10 **97** .... PaddyBrennan —
(Tom George) *hld up: struggling after 7th: t.o whn p.u bef last* **4/1**[2]

5m 59.4s (-13.80) **Going Correction** -0.45s/f (Good)
WFA 4 from 5yo+ 20lb **16** Ran SP% **124.2**
Speed ratings (Par 105): **105,101,99,98,97 94,94,91,91,82 —,—,—,—,— —**
toteswingers:1&2:£14.50, 1&3:£12.70, 2&3:£9.80 CSF £16.72 CT £127.43 TOTE £2.80: £1.70, £2.40, £2.00, £3.40; EX 13.80.
Owner Tom McNicholas **Bred** London Thoroughbred Services Ltd & J Gaines **Trained** Brigham, Cumbria

FOCUS
A comfortable romp by an in-form and well-handicapped winner.

NOTEBOOK
Flying Doctor travelled well and looked the likeliest winner from half a mile out, swooping past the long-time leader for a comfortable success. He had looked a forlorn hope since leaving the Nicky Richards yard last summer, starting at not less than 40-1 in his next four races and performing poorly. However, with his rating at an all-time low, sprung back to form at Wetherby two days earlier and, showing no ill effects from that recent run, quickly cemented that form before the handicapper's reassessment. (op 2-1 tchd 7-4 and 5-2 in places)
Solway Ally, in first-time cheekpieces, was always in the front rank, as usual, and tried to fight off a strong challenge in the back straight, but she had no answer giving 15lb to the winner. This was another game effort at this trip, but she is beginning to pay for her consistency with the handicapper. (op 9-1)
Auberge(IRE) made a mistake and lost position six out so did quite well to rally under pressure, although by that stage there was no pegging back the first two. On this evidence she is on a handy enough mark to gain a first win if avoiding costly errors. (op 10-1 tchd 11-1)
Almond Court(IRE) was well placed but could only plug on. She goes best at this track but was third in this race last year and has not improved.
Monsieur Cadou(FR) Official explanation: trainer's rep said gelding was unsuited by the faster ground

213 TANT PIS CONDITIONAL JOCKEYS' H'CAP CHASE (15 fncs) 2m 4f 110y
4:25 (4:25) (Class 4) (0-115,112) 5-Y-0+ **£5,480** (£1,597; £799)

Form RPR

3F6- **1** **Ocarina (FR)**[10] 46 8-10-7 **96** ....(p) HarryHaynes(3) 105+
(James Ewart) *cl up: effrt after 2 out: led run-in: styd on wl u.p* **4/1**[1]

24-1 **2** *2 1/2* **Cash Man (IRE)**[7] 89 9-11-8 **111** .... AlexanderVoy(3) 117
(Evelyn Slack) *chsd ldrs: led 4 out: hrd pressed and rdn 2 out: hdd run-in: kpt on same pce* **11/2**[2]

6P3- **3** *14* **Nile Moon (IRE)**[10] 46 9-10-13 **99** ....(b) FearghalDavis 92
(Ann Hamilton) *prom: rdn along fr 1/2-way: rallied: wnt mod 3rd after 2 out: plugged on: no ch w first two* **4/1**[1]

P05- **4** *4 1/2* **Livingonaknifedge (IRE)**[43] 4866 11-10-6 **92** .... SamJones 81
(Richard Guest) *hld up: rdn to improve after 4 out: no imp fr 2 out* **16/1**

244- **5** *6* **Just For Men (IRE)**[41] 4911 10-11-4 **109** .... PaulGallagher(5) 97+
(Martin Todhunter) *mstke 1st: hld up: hdwy and prom 4 out: rdn and outpcd whn hit 2 out: sn btn* **13/2**[3]

34P- **6** *3 1/2* **Babe Heffron (IRE)**[41] 4915 9-11-9 **109** .... RichieMcLernon 90
(Tom George) *led to 4 out: rdn and wknd fr 2 out* **10/1**

FPP- **7** *7* **Nelliedonethat (IRE)**[27] 5141 10-10-11 **100** .... CampbellGillies(3) 74
(Lucinda Russell) *in tch: lost pl 6th: struggling fr 10th* **20/1**

060- **P** **Bleu Pois (IRE)**[22] 5203 8-11-7 **110** .... JamesO'Farrell(3) —
(Howard Johnson) *hld up: struggling after 9th: sn lost tch: t.o whn p.u bef 3 out* **25/1**

463- **P** **Quicuyo (GER)**[17] 5309 7-11-9 **112** .... RyanMania(3) —
(P Monteith) *chsd ldrs: blnd 4 out: wknd next: t.o whn p.u bef last* **4/1**[1]

5m 10.3s (-3.20) **Going Correction** -0.025s/f (Good) **9** Ran SP% **112.3**
Speed ratings: **105,104,98,97,94 93,90,—,—**
toteswingers:1&2:£3.70, 1&3:£4.60, 2&3:£7.50 CSF £25.79 CT £91.45 TOTE £5.50: £1.70, £1.70, £2.00; EX 32.00.
Owner Mrs Ray Calder **Bred** Bernard Cypres **Trained** Langholm, Dumfries & G'way

FOCUS
Several were keen to get to the front in a competitive handicap, but it still paid to race prominently.

NOTEBOOK
Ocarina(FR) has not won for more than two years but he has put up some decent performances in the interim, certainly good enough to be competitive here. Always placed near the front, he was outpaced up the final hill, but once on the downhill homeward run he stayed on resolutely. His jumping was adequate enough to suggest he has regained the confidence lost after falling at Newcastle in March, but he would need to find some more consistency than he has shown to date to make a quick follow-up a tasty proposition. Official explanation: trainer said, regarding apparent improvement in form, that the gelding appreciated the return to 2 1/2m and the re-application of cheekpieces. (op 11-2)
Cash Man(IRE), reverting to fences after winning over this trip here a week ago, was quite keen early and went for home up the final hill but was just outstayed near the finish. Giving 15lb to the winner must have had an impact. (op 5-1 tchd 6-1)
Nile Moon(IRE) began to labour on the final circuit so did relatively well to keep on for third, but he might need to be dropped in grade to make an impact. (op 7-2 tchd 10-3)
Livingonaknifedge(IRE) was never able to get competitive and, judging on this effort, looks a way off capitalising on a plummeting handicap mark. (op 14-1)
Just For Men(IRE) did not jump fluently enough to keep on terms but he made some headway on the final circuit before his progress was halted by a mistake at the last in the back straight. (op 6-1)
Babe Heffron(IRE) could not shake off the challengers for the lead and weakened tamely up the final climb. (op 8-1)
Quicuyo(GER) Official explanation: jockey said gelding finished distressed

214 SAFE JOURNEY 60:60 NOVICES' HURDLE (8 hdls 2 omitted) 2m 4f 110y
5:00 (5:00) (Class 4) 4-Y-0+ **£5,138** (£1,497; £749)

Form RPR

601- **1** **Solway Sam**[15] 5370 7-11-5 123 .... RichieMcGrath 125+
(Lisa Harrison) *t.k.h early: a cl up: hdwy to ld bef last: drew clr run-in* **7/4**[2]

42-5 **2** *12* **Patriot (IRE)**[2] 179 6-10-12 93 ....(t) AndrewThornton 104
(Maurice Barnes) *prom: led between last 2: hdd bef last: hung lft run-in: no ch w wnr* **14/1**

044- **3** *13* **Wave Power (IRE)**[48] 4755 6-10-12 107 .... WilsonRenwick 92
(Howard Johnson) *hld up: rdn and hdwy after 2 out (usual 3 out): chsd ldrs between last 2: wknd bef last* **14/1**

44P- **4** *11* **Aint She The Lady (IRE)**[27] 5157 6-10-2 103 .... HarryHaynes(3) 75
(Roger Fisher) *in tch: outpcd after 3 out (usual 4 out): no imp between last 2* **14/1**

PPP- **5** *5* **Stolen Moments (FR)**[56] 4590 9-10-12 0 .... PaddyAspell 78
(James Moffatt) *midfield: outpcd bef 3 out (usual 4 out): sn struggling* **20/1**

221- **6** *15* **Soulard (USA)**[20] 5246 7-10-12 0 .... PaddyBrennan 64
(Tom George) *led tl hdd between last 2: sn wknd* **11/8**[1]

000- **7** *18* **Alexander Oats**[17] 5305 7-10-9 0 .... JamesO'Farrell(3) 48
(Robert Goldie) *bhd: struggling bef 3 out (usual 4 out): nvr on terms* **200/1**

055- 8 10 **Bach Street Girl (IRE)**[34] 5017 6-10-2 0 AdrianLane(3) 32
(Lynn Siddall) *bhd: struggling after 5th: nvr on terms* **100/1**
451- P **Chief Bucaneer (IRE)**[13] 14 7-11-2 0 RyanMania(3) —
(George Charlton) *nt fluent: chsd ldrs: blnd bdly 3 out: wknd after next: t.o whn p.u and dismntd bef last* **10/1**3
0P- P **Indienne Etoile**[13] 14 6-10-2 0 CampbellGillies(3) —
(Robert Johnson) *bhd: lost tch 5th: p.u bef 2 out (usual 3 out)* **200/1**

5m 4.00s (-8.50) **Going Correction** -0.45s/f (Good) **10 Ran SP% 114.3**
Speed ratings (Par 105): **98,93,88,84,82 76,69,66,—,—**
toteswingers:1&2:£5.00, 1&3:£11.90, 2&3:£10.20 CSF £24.71 TOTE £2.80: £1.30, £3.40, £2.70; EX 29.20 Place 6: £67.60 Place 5: £42.59.
Owner David Alan Harrison **Bred** D A Harrison **Trained** Aldoth, Cumbria

FOCUS
A reasonable contest but the form is mitigated as two of the main contenders failed to run up to their best. The winner, though, was very impressive.

NOTEBOOK
Solway Sam was always going comfortably just behind the leader. He was given plenty of time to mount a challenge and won decisively. Successful over 2m at Perth last month, he brushed aside the penalty with ease and coped with the step up in trip in similar fashion. He had to win purely on ratings but even though he was only doing what was expected this big chasing type out of Double Trigger looks to have a promising future. (op 11-4 tchd 3-1 in places)
Patriot(IRE) stuck to the task but was just outclassed. Despite being reasonably consistent he is still looking for that first win, but his rating of 93 suggests handicaps might prove more fruitful. (op 11-1)
Wave Power(IRE) made some late progress under pressure but could never make an impression. He had plenty to find on official ratings and is probably better on softer ground. (op 16-1)
Soulard(USA) had been racing over fences this year, winning a 0-130 contest at Ascot last time, and the market expected him to convert that form to hurdles. He was going well enough in the lead until the final hill where, like his stablemate in the previous race, he faded tamely. He came into this race in good form so perhaps the long journey from his yard was a factor. Official explanation: jockey said gelding never travelled (op 11-10 tchd Evens and 6-4 in places)
Chief Bucaneer(IRE), based on his recent Wetherby success, had more to find under a penalty than the winner. However, he was going well enough until blundering the third last and he lost all confidence. Official explanation: jockey said gelding stumbled badly after second last hurdle and lost its action (op 7-1)
T/Plt: £71.40 to a £1 stake. Pool: £52,532.39 - 537.03 winning tickets. T/Qpdt: £54.00 to a £1 stake. Pool: £3,171.76 - 43.40 winning tickets. RY

PLUMPTON (L-H)
Sunday, May 9

OFFICIAL GOING: Good to firm (hdl 9.3, chs 9.4)
Split bends with hurdle and chase rails in early season position but impact on distances not known.
Wind: modest, behind Weather: overcast, chilly

215 TOM, ELLA AND SOPHIE MAIDEN HURDLE (DIV I) (9 hdls) 2m
2:10 (2:10) (Class 5) 4-Y-0+ **£1,712** (£499; £249)

Form RPR
406- 1 **Ardmaddy (IRE)**[21] 5261 6-10-7 98 (b) JoshuaMoore(7) 103+
(Gary Moore) *hld up in tch: trckd ldr sn after 3 out: shkn up to ld bef 2 out: rdn and drew wl clr between last 2: kpt up to work and r.o strly flat* **9/2**3
403- 2 10 **J'Adhere (FR)**[16] 5358 5-11-0 0 TomScudamore 94
(Tim Vaughan) *plld hrd: hld up in midfield: hdwy bef 3 out: trckd ldng pair wl bef 2 out: chsd wnr 2 out: sn rdn and fnd little: wl btn bef last* **3/1**2
/4- 3 9 **Randomer**[20] 5287 7-10-4 0 (p) AshleyBird(10) 84
(Paddy Butler) *racd freely: led: mstke 1st: hdd bef 3 out: rdn and btn bef 2 out: wl btn 4th whn hmpd last: wnt modest 3rd flat* **33/1**
635- 4 5 **Alwaysonthemove**[58] 4568 6-11-0 0 ColinBolger 84+
(Laura Mongan) *plld hrd: chsd ldrs: mstke 2nd: led bef 3 out: rdn and hdd bef 2 out: wknd qckly 2 out: 3rd and wl btn whn j. bdly rt last: sn lost 3rd pl* **6/1**
00- 5 20 **Goring Two (IRE)**[90] 3933 5-10-9 0 MarcGoldstein(5) 59
(Diana Grissell) *chsd ldr: rdn and lost pl bef 6th: wknd bef 3 out: t.o* **100/1**
00-0 6 2 1/4 **Jack Fawaz (IRE)**[9] 82 4-10-3 0 GarethThomas(7) 53
(Pat Phelan) *chsd ldrs: nt fluent 2nd: lost pl and rdn after 4th: lost tch bef 3 out: t.o* **100/1**
0- 7 1 3/4 **Nomoretaxes (BRZ)**[104] 3659 8-10-11 0 (t) BernieWharfe(3) 55
(Debbie Mountain) *t.k.h: hld up towards rr: hdwy to chse ldrs 5th: pressing ldrs next: rdn and wknd qckly after 3 out: t.o* **66/1**
P **Simone Martini (IRE)**[19] 5-11-0 0 (t) WarrenMarston —
(Milton Harris) *hld up in tch in rr tl p.u qckly 6th* **40/1**
52- U **Onemix**[55] 4650 4-10-0 0 RichardKilloran(3) —
(Nicky Henderson) *stmbld and uns rdr s* **6/5**1
000- U **Keckerrockernixes (IRE)**[17] 5332 4-10-5 0 JayPemberton(5) —
(Richard Rowe) *hld up towards rr tl uns rdr 3rd* **66/1**

3m 43.8s (-17.00) **Going Correction** -1.275s/f (Hard)
WFA 4 from 5yo+ 18lb **10 Ran SP% 113.3**
Speed ratings (Par 103): **91,86,81,79,69 67,67,—,—,—**
Tote Swingers: 1&2 £3.30, 1&3 £8.90, 2&3 £21.20 CSF £17.79 TOTE £4.00: £1.10, £1.20, £7.30; EX 15.40.
Owner Blue Crocodile **Bred** Frank Dunne **Trained** Lower Beeding, W Sussex

FOCUS
The first division of the maiden hurdle was blown wide-open when short-price favourite Onemix stumbled and unseated her rider a few strides after setting off.

NOTEBOOK
Ardmaddy(IRE) was always travelling nicely and quickly went clear having taken over at the first in the straight. He has had chances in the past but may do better back in handicaps now that he has got his head in front. (op 5-1 tchd 4-1)
J'Adhere(FR), who refused to settle, became the one to beat when the favourite departed, and he had his chance but lacked the necessary pace on this drop to 2m. (op 11-2 tchd 11-4)
Randomer was soon up on the pace and showed enough to suggest he will have a future in low-grade handicaps. (op 40-1)
Alwaysonthemove stopped quickly having pulled hard. (op 4-1)
Simone Martini(IRE) Official explanation: vet said gelding pulled up lame (op 11-10 tchd 6-4, Evens in places)
Onemix, who was mulish in the paddock, stumbled and unseated her rider after a couple of strides, leaving the race wide open. (op 11-10 tchd 6-4, Evens in places)

216 TOM, ELLA AND SOPHIE MAIDEN HURDLE (DIV II) (9 hdls) 2m
2:40 (2:40) (Class 5) 4-Y-0+ **£1,712** (£499; £249)

Form RPR
004/ 1 **Blue Eyed Eloise**[59] 1926 8-10-7 0 AndrewGlassonbury 98
(Brian McMath) *t.k.h: hld up towards rr: hdwy bef 6th: chsd ldr 3 out: ev ch and j.rt 2 out: drvn to ld flat: kpt on wl* **7/2**3
2- 2 hd **Gulf President**[260] 1281 4-10-10 0 TomScudamore 101
(Tim Vaughan) *in tch in midfield: hdwy to ld 6th: rdn after 3 out: drvn between last 2: hdd flat: kpt on but a jst hld after* **3/1**1
/40- 3 3 3/4 **Al Amaan**[21] 5260 5-10-9 112 (t) IanPopham(5) 101
(Paul Nicholls) *hld up wl in tch towards rr: hdwy 6th: chsd ldrs next: rdn and styd on same pce fr 2 out* **7/2**3
552- 4 7 **Navajo Nation (IRE)**[16] 5367 4-10-5 100 (p) TomO'Connor(5) 90
(Bill Turner) *hld up in tch towards rr: hdwy after 5th: chsd ldrs 3 out: rdn and unable qck 2 out: one pce and hld whn blnd bdly last* **12/1**
0- 5 9 **Pursuit Of Purpose**[17] 5328 4-9-12 0 GemmaGracey-Davison(5) 74
(Philip Sharp) *t.k.h: chsd ldrs: wnt 2nd after 2nd tl 5th: sn lost pl: bhd bef 3 out: hdwy u.p wl bef 2 out: no imp ent st* **200/1**
P- 6 3/4 **Cubism**[21] 5243 4-10-10 0 WarrenMarston 80
(Milton Harris) *t.k.h: chsd ldrs: wnt 2nd 5th tl next: sn lost pl: no ch after 3 out* **25/1**
40F- 7 13 **Goring One (IRE)**[20] 5282 5-11-0 104 JamieGoldstein 71
(Diana Grissell) *t.k.h: chsd ldr tl after 2nd: styd handy tl lost pl after 5th: wl bhd after 3 out* **14/1**
00- 8 1 **Out To Impress (IRE)**[34] 5057 5-10-11 0 EamonDehdashti(3) 70
(Murty McGrath) *led tl 6th: sn rdn: wknd qckly after 3 out* **200/1**
402- 9 shd **Mid Wicket (USA)**[20] 5285 4-10-7 110 RichardKilloran(3) 66
(Mouse Hamilton-Fairley) *in tch: mstke 2nd: chsd ldrs 6th: wknd qckly u.p wl bef 2 out* **10/3**2
P **Oscar Brando (IRE)**[350] 7-10-4 0 AshleyBird(10) —
(Paddy Butler) *hld up in last pl: rdn and effrt 3 out: midfield and no threat to ldrs whn lost action: p.u and dismntd bef 2 out* **100/1**

3m 42.8s (-18.00) **Going Correction** -1.275s/f (Hard)
WFA 4 from 5yo+ 18lb **10 Ran SP% 112.7**
Speed ratings (Par 103): **94,93,92,88,84 83,77,76,76,—**
Tote Swingers: 1&2 £2.60, 1&3 £2.80, 2&3 £2.40 CSF £14.20 TOTE £3.70: £1.20, £1.80, £1.80; EX 14.90.
Owner Chocolate Factory **Bred** Miss M E Steele **Trained** Newmarket, Suffolk

FOCUS
This looked the stronger of the two divisions.

NOTEBOOK
Blue Eyed Eloise eventually got the best of her duel with the runner-up. Not seen over hurdles since October 2007 prior to this, she has subsequently won a couple of times on the Flat, despite not standing much racing due to injury, but she jumped well here and saw it out better than expected. She is open to limited improvement. (op 9-2)
Gulf President, off since finishing a well-beaten second to top juvenile Barizan on his debut last August, was never far away and had his chance, but couldn't get away from the winner and was worn down. (op 2-1)
Al Amaan has been disappointing, but there were positives to take from this. He will benefit from a stronger pace and not for the first time shaped as though he will stay further, so probably has a future in low-grade handicaps. (op 4-1 tchd 5-1)
Navajo Nation(IRE) has been struggling to get his head in front in sellers and claimers, so fourth was about the best he could have hoped for.
Pursuit Of Purpose stepped up markedly on her debut effort and clearly isn't useless. (op 150-1)
Mid Wicket(USA) had shown improved form at the course latest, but couldn't build on that, and the way he dropped away was rather disconcerting. (op 4-1 tchd 3-1)

217 ALAN WATSON 50TH BIRTHDAY H'CAP HURDLE (14 hdls) 3m 1f 110y
3:10 (3:10) (Class 5) (0-95,94) 4-Y-0+ **£2,055** (£599; £299)

Form RPR
P1B- 1 **My Matilda**[17] 5339 7-10-7 **75** TomScudamore 87
(Lawney Hill) *chsd ldng pair: wnt 2nd after 7th: clr w ldr 11th: mstke 3 out: rdn and swtchd rt bef 2 out: led last: styd on wl* **4/1**3
P62- 2 1 1/2 **King Raven (IRE)**[40] 4939 8-10-12 **83** (v) DannyCook(3) 93
(Mark Rimell) *j.big at times: led: clr w wnr 11th: rdn 2 out: j.big and rdn 2 out: hdd last: one pce u.p flat* **7/2**2
P35- 3 22 **Hail The King (USA)**[271] 1192 10-10-8 **76** JamieGoldstein 64
(R M Carson) *hld up in rr: hdwy after 10th: wnt modest 3rd 3 out: no imp on ldrs bef next and wl btn 2 out* **11/1**
650- 4 6 **The Saucy Snipe**[81] 3935 4-10-1 **82** MrDGPrichard(7) 58
(Daniel O'Brien) *nt a fluent: hld up in tch towards rr: pushed along and struggling after 10th: wl btn bef 3 out: wnt poor 4th bef 2 out* **25/1**
/00- 5 hd **Eddystone (IRE)**[19] 5295 6-9-10 **69** (vt) GemmaGracey-Davison(5) 51
(Linda Jewell) *t.k.h early: hld up in tch towards rr: hdwy into midfield 7th: rdn after 9th: no prog u.p 11th: wl btn 3 out* **25/1**
25U- 6 1 1/2 **Not For Diamonds (IRE)**[55] 4642 10-11-5 **94** MrKevinJones(7) 74
(Seamus Mullins) *in tch on outer: blnd 5th: rdn and struggling whn mstke 10th: wl btn bef 3 out* **8/1**
004- 7 14 **Smart N Sharp (IRE)**[160] 2612 7-9-7 **68** oh4 (t) PeterHatton(7) 34
(Linda Jewell) *hld up in tch towards rr: hdwy 7th: chsd clr ldng pair 11th: no hdwy and wknd u.p sn after next* **33/1**
PPP- 8 49 **Sterling Moll**[49] 4767 7-10-6 **77** DerekLaverty(3) —
(W De Best-Turner) *in tch: mstke 6th: rdn 8th: bhd and losing tch whn mstke 10th: t.o bef 3 out* **40/1**
031- F **Geography (IRE)**[35] 5007 10-11-3 **85** (p) AndrewGlassonbury —
(Jim Best) *t.k.h: hld up in tch towards rr tl fell 2nd* **10/3**1
PP4- P **Lahinch Lad (IRE)**[28] 5152 10-9-8 **69** (p) MissCLWills(7) —
(Brendan Powell) *led tl 6th: chsd ldr after tl rdn and wknd qckly bef 11th: t.o whn p.u 2 out* **12/1**
PP3- P **Dust In Time**[12] 37 5-11-6 **93** (p) TomO'Connor(5) —
(Bill Turner) *in tch: niggled along 4th: dropped to last pl and reminders 7th: lost tch u.p 9th: p.u bef 11th* **8/1**

6m 1.80s (-27.00) **Going Correction** -1.275s/f (Hard)
WFA 4 from 5yo+ 20lb **11 Ran SP% 116.6**
Speed ratings (Par 103): **90,89,82,80,80 80,76,61,—,— —**
Tote Swingers: 1&2 £4.00, 2&3 £40.20 CSF £17.91 CT £142.64 TOTE £6.60: £1.90, £1.50, £4.60; EX 18.80.
Owner L G Kimber **Bred** L G Kimber **Trained** Aston Rowant, Oxon

FOCUS
A low-grade staying handicap hurdle. The favourite Geography came down at the second hurdle.

NOTEBOOK

My Matilda, brought down early last time, had earlier beaten King Raven in heavy ground at Fontwell, and was weighted to confirm the form, which she ultimately did following a long struggle. This much quicker ground clearly wasn't as suitable, but she stays well, and remains capable of better for her in-form yard. (op 9-2 tchd 5-1 in a place)

King Raven(IRE) travelled well up on the speed and looked to have everything in trouble running down hill, but he couldn't shake off his old rival and was eventually run down. (op 5-1)

Hail The King(USA) is well handicapped on old form and has clearly benefited from a nice break. He travelled well until getting outpaced and could pick up a small race at some stage this summer. (op 12-1 tchd 10-1)

The Saucy Snipe struggled with his jumping and never got into it. (op 33-1)

Eddystone(IRE) was never close enough to challenge. (op 28-1 tchd 33-1)

Geography(IRE) came down at the second hurdle, leaving the race open. (op 9-4)

218 VI NICHOL 90TH BIRTHDAY NOVICES' H'CAP CHASE (18 fncs) 3m 2f

3:40 (3:40) (Class 4) (0-105,105) 5-Y-0 **£4,399** (£1,311; £663; £340; £177)

Form RPR

610- **1** **Ethiopia**[18] 5315 7-10-8 **94** .... NathanSweeney(7) 106+
(Bob Buckler) *pressed ldr: led 14th: rdn bef 2 out: kpt on wl between last* **13/2**[3]

650- **2** 1 1/4 **Oamaru Stone (IRE)**[96] 3807 7-11-0 **100** .... MrRMahon(7) 109
(Paul Nicholls) *in tch: niggled along 7th: 4th whn mstke 14th: sn rdn along: wnt 2nd whn j.rt and collided w rival 2 out: n.m.r between last 2: styd on same pce flat* **4/1**[2]

U62- **3** 1 1/4 **Plane Painter (IRE)**[17] 5329 6-11-9 **102** ....(p) WarrenMarston 112+
(Brendan Powell) *led: mstke 12th: hdd 14th: hit next: 4th and outpcd u.p after 3 out: rallied bef last: kpt on flat* **3/1**[1]

P31- **4** 8 **Allterrain (IRE)**[20] 5288 7-10-11 **97** .... MrSJO'Donovan(7) 98
(Norma Twomey) *chsd ldrs: clsd 14th: chsd wnr and mstke 3 out: sn drvn: lost 2nd and bmpd next: wknd bef last: eased whn wl btn flat* **4/1**[2]

64P- **5** dist **Hemington**[24] 5198 7-11-4 **97** .... TomScudamore 51
(Michael Scudamore) *in tch: blnd 3rd: mstke 10th: rdn and struggling after 13th: no ch 15th: t.o* **4/1**[2]

3P0/ **P** **Alfabet Souk**[71] 9-9-7 **79** oh22 ....(bt) MrDGPrichard(7) —
(Bernard Llewellyn) *rn wout declared tongue strap: nvr gng wl: sn detached in last and jumping slowly: rdn and lost tch after 7th: t.o whn p.u 13th* **18/1**

P **My Fella (IRE)**[392] 4968 7-11-7 **105** .... JimmyDerham(5) —
(Seamus Mullins) *t.k.h: hld up in tch: mstke 12th: immediately struggling and losing tch whn p.u next* **11/1**

6m 23.7s (-27.00) **Going Correction** -0.90s/f (Hard) **7** Ran SP% **111.9**
Speed ratings: **105,104,104,101,87 —,—**
Tote Swingers: 1&2 £5.70, 1&3 £3.90, 2&3 £2.50 CSF £31.48 CT £92.58 TOTE £12.80: £5.00, £6.10; EX 34.70.
Owner Nick Elliott **Bred** Mrs C Van Straubenzee & Mrs J N Humphreys **Trained** Henley, Somerset

FOCUS

An interesting novices' handicap chase in which the first two were both having their first start over fences.

NOTEBOOK

Ethiopia, a winner over hurdles at the track, was soon disputing it at a fair clip and jumped well on the whole. He kept finding for strong pressure, and with the runner-up being unable to switch out to challenge coming into the last, he had the momentum to hold on. Only seven, he clearly stays really well, and should be a regular in these low-grade staying/marathon handicap chases at the small tracks. (op 7-1 tchd 6-1)

Oamaru Stone(IRE), a former point winner who looked devoid of pace over hurdles, jumped well and is clearly going to make a better chaser. He found himself outpaced running down the hill, but came strong in the straight, and this one-paced galloper may well have won had his rider been able to switch him out to challenge approaching the last, as he was a bit short for room and then couldn't pick up well enough on the run-in. (tchd 7-2 and 9-2)

Plane Painter(IRE) is consistent and kept on dourly. (tchd 11-4, 10-3 in a place)

Allterrain(IRE), up 8lb for his C&D win, was already in trouble when bumping with the runner-up two out, and he soon emptied. (op 7-2)

Hemington has been struggling to win in hunter chases and it was surprising to see support for him on this return to handicaps. (op 6-1)

219 BLUEBELL RAILWAY 50TH ANNIVERSARY CLAIMING HURDLE (9 hdls) 2m

4:10 (4:10) (Class 5) 4-Y-0+ **£2,055** (£599; £299)

Form RPR

101- **1** **Marodima (FR)**[14] 1 7-11-12 **141** .... TomO'Brien 117+
(Jamie Snowden) *mde all: sn clr: mstke 3 out and last: unchal* **4/9**[1]

004- **2** 15 **Bazart**[12] 40 8-11-1 **97** .... JimmyDerham(5) 96
(Bernard Llewellyn) *racd in last pair: lft 2nd 4th: rdn and no imp after 3 out: wl btn after* **11/4**[2]

34-0 **3** 57 **Just Mossie**[10] 54 5-10-11 **84** ....(p) TomO'Connor(5) 35
(Bill Turner) *racd in last pair: lft and hmpd 4th: sn lost tch: t.o fr 6th* **16/1**[3]

030- **U** **Rosoff (IRE)**[73] 4262 8-11-3 **89** ....(b) GemmaGracey-Davison(5) —
(Laura Mongan) *chsd clr wnr tl blnd and uns rdr 4th* **20/1**

3m 39.0s (-21.80) **Going Correction** -1.275s/f (Hard) **4** Ran SP% **106.6**
Speed ratings (Par 103): **103,95,67,—**
CSF £1.97 TOTE £1.40; EX 1.80.Marodima was subject to a friendly claim for £12,000.
Owner Coles & Garbett Families Partnership **Bred** Earl La Vastine Et Al **Trained** Ebbesbourne Wake, Wilts

FOCUS

This was little more than a canter round for Marodima.

NOTEBOOK

Marodima(FR) was miles clear at the weights and made every yard of the running to make a winning debut for the yard, having been claimed 14 days earlier. He's not yet weighted out of handicaps, although isn't in quite as good a form as he was earlier in the year, so may be best kept to this sort of level for the time being. He's got "terrible legs" and also bleeds according to his trainer, which is worth bearing in mind. (op 1-3)

Bazart, officially rated 44lb inferior to the winner, was a clear second from an early stage and never held any chance of beating the winner. (op 7-2 tchd 5-2)

Just Mossie quickly began to struggle having been slightly hampered. (tchd 14-1)

Rosoff(IRE) departed at the fourth. (op 16-1 tchd 22-1)

220 STEWART NASH 60TH BIRTHDAY AMATEUR RIDERS' H'CAP HURDLE (12 hdls) 2m 5f

4:40 (4:40) (Class 4) (0-110,107) 4-Y-0+ **£2,810** (£871; £435; £217)

Form RPR

606- **1** **There's No Panic (IRE)**[25] 5184 5-11-4 **102** .... MrRMahon(3) 108+
(Paul Nicholls) *chsd ldrs: wnt 2nd after 8th: rdn to ld 3 out: drvn between last 2: styd on wl flat* **11/4**[1]

161- **2** 4 1/2 **Canni Thinkaar (IRE)**[67] 4388 9-11-9 **107** ....(b) JoshuaMoore(3) 106
(Jim Best) *led: clr w wnr after 9th: hdd and hit next: sn rdn: kpt on same pce u.p after* **3/1**[2]

221- **3** 1/2 **Tarabela**[22] 5234 7-10-9 **97** .... MrDSymes-Meineck(7) 97
(Gerald Ham) *hld up wl bhd: gd hdwy 8th: outpcd by ldng pair next: mstke 3 out: sn chsng clr ldng pair: clsd 2 out: blnd last: no imp flat* **7/1**

46-3 **4** 5 **Thehonourablelady**[10] 55 9-10-7 **95** ....(tp) ThomasFlint(7) 88
(John Flint) *hld up wl off the pce in midfield: hdwy 7th: chsd clr ldng pair after 9th: rdn and no prog after 3 out* **7/2**[3]

5P5- **5** nk **Wricksons Bridge (IRE)**[50] 4724 6-10-11 **99** ....(p) MrMLurcock(7) 93
(Keith Goldsworthy) *racd off the pce in midfield: mstke 2nd: nt fluent next: clsd on ldrs after 7th: disputing 3rd but outpcd 9th: 5th and wl btn after 3 out* **16/1**

53P- **6** 11 **Signs Of Love (FR)**[104] 3656 7-11-3 **105** .... MrJBanks(7) 87
(Noel Chance) *hld up wl off the pce in last trio: clsd and in tch after 7th: rdn after next: 6th and wl btn bef 3 out* **14/1**

2/0- **7** 25 **Monash Lad (IRE)**[20] 5291 8-10-4 **90** ....(p) MissZoeLilly(5) 47
(Michelle Bryant) *hld up wl off the pce in last pair: sme hdwy 7th: rdn and toiling after next: t.o fr 3 out* **33/1**

1/0- **U** **Top Ram (IRE)**[34] 10-11-3 **105** .... MrNHenderson(7) —
(Chris Gordon) *racd off the pce in midfield: bmpd along and lost pl after 7th: lost tch bef 3 out: wl bhd whn slt mstke and rdr lost iron 2 out: eventually rolled off bef last* **12/1**

2P-P **P** **The Jolly Spoofer (IRE)**[9] 85 8-11-4 **104** .... MrPGHall(5) —
(Diana Grissell) *w ldr: hit 2nd: lost 2nd after 6th: dropped out rapidly 9th: wl t.o whn p.u 2 out* **25/1**

4m 52.7s (-29.60) **Going Correction** -1.275s/f (Hard) **9** Ran SP% **113.4**
Speed ratings (Par 105): **105,103,103,101,101 96,87,—,—**
Tote Swingers: 1&2 £2.10, 1&3 £4.00, 2&3 £5.20 CSF £11.54 CT £49.97 TOTE £4.30: £2.20, £1.02, £3.70; EX 8.60.
Owner The Stewart Family **Bred** J R Weston **Trained** Ditcheat, Somerset

FOCUS

Few got into this amateur riders' handicap hurdle.

NOTEBOOK

There's No Panic(IRE) came out nicely on top. Always travelling best, he went on three out and was quickly clear but had chased the good pace early and did idle a bit. He found plenty for pressure, though, and won with plenty in hand. This is his time of year, as he needs good ground, and he will be sent chasing at some stage, so looks certain to win again. (op 5-2 tchd 2-1)

Canni Thinkaar(IRE) has been in cracking form, winning four of his last five since joining connections, but he left himself vulnerable in disputing the early lead at a good clip and, though he kept on valiantly, he had been put in his place by the winner some way out. (op 10-3 tchd 7-2)

Tarabela, 5lb higher than when winning at Bangor, made good headway with a circuit to run and then stayed on well to bustle up the front pair, but never actually looked like winning. She may have been second but for a mistake at the last. Her jockey, who was having his first ride, looked very competent. (op 11-2)

Thehonourablelady never got close enough to challenge, but did keep on. (op 13-2)

Wricksons Bridge(IRE) was well outpaced in the end.

221 BRIAN SPENCER MEMORIAL H'CAP CHASE (14 fncs) 2m 4f

5:10 (5:11) (Class 4) (0-110,107) 5-Y-0 **£4,383** (£1,295; £647; £324; £161)

Form RPR

/4F- **1** **Take A Mile (IRE)**[20] 5289 8-10-12 **98** .... JimmyDerham(5) 112+
(Seamus Mullins) *chsd ldng pair: led 3 out: rdn clr between last 2: j.rt last: idling and drvn flat: a gng to hold on* **7/2**[2]

4P4- **2** nk **Pilgrims Lane (IRE)**[167] 2465 6-11-12 **107** .... WarrenMarston 119
(Milton Harris) *wl bhd: clsd on ldng trio 8th: wnt 2nd and hit 2 out: outpcd by wnr between last 2: rallied as wnr idled flat: kpt on u.p* **7/1**

611- **3** 4 **Putney Bridge**[16] 5358 8-11-10 **105** ....(bt) TomO'Brien 115+
(Keith Goldsworthy) *w ldr and set fast gallop: led 10th: rdn and hdd 3 out: drvn and lost 2nd 2 out: one pce and hld whn blnd last* **11/10**[1]

1U0- **4** 24 **Maximix**[20] 5280 7-11-6 **101** ....(b) AndrewGlassonbury 84
(Gary Moore) *sn bhd and nvr looking happy: mstke 1st: sme hdwy and pushed along but hanging rt 9th: no hdwy and wl btn fr next* **8/1**

532- **5** 31 **Sumdancer (NZ)**[20] 5289 8-10-13 **99** ....(p) MarcGoldstein(5) 62
(Michael Madgwick) *led at fast gallop: hdd and rdn 10th: wknd rapidly after 3 out: t.o and eased flat* **11/2**[3]

4m 49.9s (-17.40) **Going Correction** -0.90s/f (Hard) course record **5** Ran SP% **108.8**
Speed ratings: **98,97,96,86,74**
CSF £23.63 TOTE £3.80: £1.60, £2.70; EX 12.70.
Owner Mrs G Elliott **Bred** Gerry Flannery **Trained** Wilsford-Cum-Lake, Wilts

FOCUS

A competitive handicap chase, despite the small field, and the early pace was a good one.

NOTEBOOK

Take A Mile(IRE) was still in front when hampered, causing his rider to lose his irons and the saddle to slip, before falling at the last here last time, and he had 4lb more on his back this time. However, he adopted the stalking position in behind the early pace and assumed control three out. He was idling on the run-in and had to survive one final challenge, but just managed to hold on for a deserved victory. (tchd 3-1 and 4-1)

Pilgrims Lane(IRE) was likely to do better at some stage and he has clearly benefited from a break. Held up well off the early pace, he gradually closed to challenge and may well have won but a mistake two out, but there will be other days for the 6-y-o. (op 8-1)

Putney Bridge has been on a roll over hurdles and looked very well weighted on this return to fences, but Tom O'Brien got him involved in a battle for the lead and his jumping cracked under pressure down the back straight. He kept on best he could and there will be other days for him. (op 13-8)

Maximix was soon in trouble and didn't look at all happy on the ground. (op 11-2)

Sumdancer(NZ) goes well here and often runs his race, but for some reason his rider seemed intent on leading, despite the horse having stamina doubts, and he ultimately dropped right out. (op 9-2)

222 SUSANNA HALL STANDARD OPEN NATIONAL HUNT FLAT RACE 2m 2f

5:40 (5:42) (Class 6) 4-6-Y-0 **£1,712** (£499; £249)

Form RPR

402- **1** **Dirty Deal**[71] 4301 6-10-9 0 .... TomO'Brien 100+
(John Flint) *taken down early: plld hrd: w ldr tl led after 5f: mde rest: rdn clr wl over 2f out: in command whn hung rt 1f out: styd on wl* **10/3**[2]

2 6 **Willy Be Lucky (IRE)** 4-10-7 0 .... JimmyDerham(5) 97+
(Seamus Mullins) *hld up in last pl: hdwy 9f out: chsd ldrs and rdn over 3f out: chsd wnr over 1f out: kpt on same pce and no imp after* **13/2**

3U- **3** 3/4 **Karoshdee**[19] 5296 5-10-6 0 .... EamonDehdashti(3) 92
(John E Long) *in tch in midfield: hdwy to chse ldng pair 4f out: rdn and unable qck 3f out: kpt on same pce fnl 2f* **11/1**

4- **4** 3 1/2 **Cloudy Wager**[67] 4391 5-10-4 0 .... MarcGoldstein(5) 89
(Diana Grissell) *in tch: rdn along fr 1/2-way: 7th and wl outpcd: kpt on steadily u.p fnl 2f: nt pce to rch ldrs* **14/1**

3- **5** 5 **Playtime Ben (IRE)**[17] 5332 5-11-2 0 .... TomScudamore 91
(Peter Hedger) *hld up in last pair: hdwy 6f out: rdn to chse clr wnr over 2f out tl over 1f out: wknd fnl f* **7/2**[3]

63- **6** *15* **Quidam Blue (FR)**[19] 5296 6-10-13 0 RichardKilloran(3) 81
(Tim Vaughan) *t.k.h: hld up in tch towards rr: hdwy to chse ldrs 8f out: rdn to chse wnr 4f out tl over 2f out: wknd: eased whn no ch ins fnl f* **3/1**[1]

7 *6* **Rapid Exit (IRE)** 5-11-2 0 WarrenMarston 70
(Brendan Powell) *t.k.h: chsd ldrs: wnt 2nd 9f out tl 4f out: sn wknd u.p* **12/1**

0- **8** *2* **Late Red**[60] 4522 5-10-9 0 CharlieWallis(7) 68
(Jamie Poulton) *t.k.h: hld up in tch in last trio: hdwy 7f out: rdn and wknd wl over 3f out: t.o* **25/1**

0- **9** *4 1/2* **Combat King (IRE)**[22] 5235 6-10-13 0 DerekLaverty(3) 63
(Norma Twomey) *in tch in midfield: nt clr and run and lost pl over 8f out: lost tch 5f out: t.o* **33/1**

500- **10** *2 1/2* **She's Sassy (IRE)**[34] 5042 5-10-9 0 ColinBolger 54
(Suzy Smith) *led but rn green and wandering arnd: hdd 5f out: lost pl qckly and rdn over 8f out: lost tch 6f out: t.o* **33/1**

11 *21* **The Ridge**[15] 6-11-2 0 AndrewGlassonbury 40
(Michael Scudamore) *t.k.h: in tch on outer tl wknd rapidly 4f out: wl t.o and eased ins fnl f* **66/1**

4m 8.10s (-18.90) **Going Correction** -1.275s/f (Hard)
WFA 4 from 5yo+ 4lb **11** Ran SP% **117.5**
Speed ratings: **91,88,88,86,84 77,74,74,72,70 61**
Tote Swingers: 1&2 £7.80, 1&3 £7.20, 2&3 £22.10 CSF £24.52 TOTE £3.40: £1.30, £2.80, £2.70; EX 21.10 Place 6: £47.94 Place 5: £19.17.
Owner K C Trotman **Bred** Winton Bloodstock Ltd **Trained** Kenfig Hill, Bridgend

FOCUS
They dawdled in what was a weak bumper.

NOTEBOOK
Dirty Deal, runner-up in heavy ground at Chepstow, was always to the fore and galloped on well, despite wandering a little in the straight, to get off the mark at the fourth attempt. She will have a future at a lowly level over hurdles. (op 3-1 tchd 7-2)
Willy Be Lucky(IRE), representing last year's winning trainer/jockey combination, is related to Westender and he did well considering the lack of pace. He would have been closer but for getting a bump before the straight, and is probably the one to take from the race. (op 7-1 tchd 15-2)
Karoshdee, who hung badly left and unseated her rider at Towcester last time, appreciated the return to a left-handed track and confirmed the promise she showed on debut. (op 12-1)
Cloudy Wager again showed ability and has a future over hurdles. (op 9-1)
Playtime Ben(IRE) failed to build on his debut effort, but will do better once racing over further in hurdle races. (op 5-1)
Quidam Blue(FR) was below par, but had earlier shown promise and is another likely to do better in hurdles. (tchd 10-3)
She's Sassy(IRE) proved troublesome, first appearing to cock her jaw at the stable bend, and then causing interference as she dropped back through the field down the back. (op 40-1)
T/Plt: £40.10. Pool: £66,116.19 - 1,201.94 winning units. T/Qpdt: £15.70. Pool: £4,736.46 - 22.34 winning units. SP

[93]UTTOXETER (L-H)
Sunday, May 9

OFFICIAL GOING: Good to firm (good in places; hdl 7.6, chs 7.5)
Final hurdle in back straight and second-last fence omitted due to ground being under repair.
Wind: light 1/2 behind Weather: fine and sunny, becoming overcast and very cool

223 MICKLEY STUD WINNERS FOR ALL SEASONS "NATIONAL HUNT" NOVICES' HURDLE (DIV I) (12 hdls 2 omitted) 3m
1:30 (1:30) (Class 4) 4-Y-0+ **£2,536** (£744; £372; £186)

Form RPR

642- **1** **Identity Parade (IRE)**[18] 5317 6-10-6 103 JasonMaguire 105+
(Donald McCain) *mde all: styd on wl fr 3 out: drvn out* **3/1**[2]

4F4- **2** *8* **Woodmore (IRE)**[15] 5386 6-10-13 110 KeithMercer 102
(Steve Gollings) *chsd ldrs: wnt 2nd 9th: kpt on: no imp* **6/1**

5P4- **3** *2 1/2* **Anadama (IRE)**[30] 5117 6-10-6 0 RobertThornton 92
(Alan King) *chsd ldrs: one pce appr 3 out: wnt 3rd next* **11/2**

454- **4** *25* **Supreme Plan (IRE)**[44] 4867 7-10-10 114 SeanQuinlan(3) 86+
(Kim Bailey) *in rr: hdwy 9th: wnt modest 3rd 3 out: wknd 2 out* **5/2**[1]

431- **5** *4 1/2* **Bringewood Belle**[16] 5354 7-10-9 105 TommyPhelan(3) 71
(John Needham) *chsd ldrs: lost pl appr 3 out: sn bhd* **10/3**[3]

0/0- **P** **Limestone Boy (IRE)**[46] 4826 8-10-6 70 TrevorWhelan(7) —
(Rob Summers) *chsd ldrs: reminders 9th: sn lost pl and bhd: t.o whn p.u bef 3 out* **100/1**

/00- **P** **Our Little Dreamer (IRE)**[280] 1120 6-10-10 0 RichieMcLernon(3) —
(Jonjo O'Neill) *stdd s: t.k.h in rr: reminders and lost pl 8th: hung rt and sn bhd: t.o whn p.u bef 2 out* **40/1**

003- **U** **Roman Landing**[21] 5250 6-10-13 0 JackDoyle —
(Peter Pritchard) *chsd ldrs: lost pl 9th: t.o last whn leather broke and uns rdr run-in* **66/1**

5m 50.5s (-14.70) **Going Correction** -0.675s/f (Firm) **8** Ran SP% **111.2**
Speed ratings (Par 105): **97,94,93,85,83 —,—,—**
Tote Swingers: 1&2 £6.10, 1&3 £1.90, 2&3 £6.90 CSF £19.89 TOTE £3.30: £1.20, £2.30, £1.80; EX 22.20.
Owner Racegoers Club Owners Group **Bred** Mrs M Doran **Trained** Cholmondeley, Cheshire

FOCUS
A modest-looking novice contest in which the two unpenalised mares dominated the outcome. The final flight on the back straight was omitted for all races over hurdles, and the winner's time was almost 6 seconds slower than Aberdale's time in the second divison.

NOTEBOOK
Identity Parade(IRE), up about half a mile in trip, set off in front and comfortably held her rivals as they tried to challenge. Connections will need to find a similarly weak affair for her to carry a penalty in, although she will have the option of competing against only her sex as well. (op 5-2 tchd 10-3)
Woodmore(IRE), who was a bit disappointing over 2m3f on his previous outing, seemed to appreciate the trip and ran encouragingly. (op 15-2 tchd 8-1)
Anadama(IRE), trying 3m for the first time, needed to be woken up with a few reminders at around halfway, and may have only finished third due to Supreme Plan hitting two out quite hard. (op 7-1 tchd 9-2)
Supreme Plan(IRE) hit two out and his rider was not hard on his mount after that error. (op 11-4)
Bringewood Belle won over 2m4f at Bangor last time and was running under a 6lb penalty in this. She did not look to be enjoying it at various stages of the race and one has to conclude she doesn't stay 3m. Official explanation: trainer had no explanation for the poor form shown (op 3-1)
Our Little Dreamer(IRE) Official explanation: jockey said gelding hung badly right-handed throughout

224 BETFRED NOVICES' HURDLE (9 hdls 1 omitted) 2m
2:00 (2:00) (Class 4) 4-Y-0+ **£2,862** (£840; £420; £209)

Form RPR

3/2- **1** **Gremlin**[12] 41 6-10-12 102 (p) RobertThornton 92+
(Dai Burchell) *trckd ldrs: wnt 2nd appr 3 out: led bef 2 out: in command whn lft clr last: eased towards fin* **4/5**[1]

10- **2** *12* **Life Long (IRE)**[94] 3846 6-10-12 0 GerardTumelty 81+
(Anabel L M King) *chsd ldrs: reminders 6th: lft modest 3rd and hmpd 2 out: lft 15 l 2nd and hmpd last* **8/1**[3]

0 **3** *17* **I Can Run Can You (IRE)**[10] 58 4-10-5 0 RichieMcLernon(3) 59
(Jonjo O'Neill) *in tch: outpcd 6th: lft poor 3rdh whn hmpd last* **14/1**

06- **4** *nk* **Allformary**[34] 5045 4-9-12 0 SeanQuinlan(3) 51
(Kim Bailey) *in rr: outpcd and bhd 6th: kpt on fr 2 out* **10/1**

/ **5** *2 3/4* **John Potts**[16] 5-10-12 0 JodieMogford 59
(Brian Baugh) *in rr: hdwy appr 3 out: poor 4th whn j.rt last* **25/1**

0- **6** *2 1/2* **Red Dagger (IRE)**[14] 4 4-10-5 0 CharlieHuxley(3) 53
(Richard Price) *in tch: lost pl 5th: sn bhd* **100/1**

P/0- **7** *dist* **Bernshaw**[16] 5352 5-10-12 70 PaddyAspell 17
(James Turner) *in rr: bhd fr 4th: t.o 6th: hmpd 2 out: eventually completed* **100/1**

0- **F** **A Nod And A Wink (IRE)**[17] 5340 6-10-5 0 TomMessenger —
(Shaun Lycett) *hld up in rr: bhd fr 4th: t.o whn fell 2 out* **66/1**

0- **F** **Hannicean**[23] 2040 6-10-12 0 DougieCostello 85
(Ian Williams) *led 2nd: hdd bef 2 out: 6 l 2nd and wl hld whn fell last* **9/2**[2]

000- **F** **Decent Lord (IRE)**[57] 4584 6-10-12 66 AlanO'Keeffe 81
(Jennie Candlish) *led to 2nd: 6 l 3rd and wl btn whn fell 2 out* **16/1**

0P- **P** **Oxus (IRE)**[17] 5340 5-10-12 0 LeightonAspell —
(William Clay) *in rr: t.o 5th: p.u bef 2 out* **100/1**

0PU- **P** **Passive Interest**[17] 5340 5-10-2 0 AdrianLane(3) —
(Ray Peacock) *bhd fr 4th: t.o 6th: p.u bef 2 out* **50/1**

3m 50.6s (-4.60) **Going Correction** -0.675s/f (Firm)
WFA 4 from 5yo+ 18lb **12** Ran SP% **116.8**
Speed ratings (Par 105): **84,78,69,69,67 66,46,—,—,— —,—**
Tote Swingers: 1&2 £33.10, 2&3 £1.80 CSF £7.67 TOTE £1.80: £1.30, £1.70, £1.90; EX 4.50.
Owner Jason Tucker **Bred** Catridge Farm Stud Ltd **Trained** Briery Hill, Blaenau Gwent

FOCUS
This looked to be nothing more than a moderate contest. Only three had any hope of winning throughout.

NOTEBOOK
Gremlin, a dual winner on the all-weather in April, was a disappointing favourite last time when he had cheekpieces on for the first time, but had the race set up for him here and won in authoritative style. His confidence will have been boosted if nothing else. Connections indicated afterwards that he may go to Cartmel next at the end of this month. (tchd 8-11and 5-6 in places)
Life Long(IRE), having his first run over hurdles, stayed on strongly after being outpaced (he was also hampered by two fallers in front of him) and may have finished second even if Hannicean had stayed upright. (op 15-2 tchd 13-2)
I Can Run Can You(IRE) showed little recently on his first attempt on a racecourse but probably ran a bit better here. (op 16-1 tchd 12-1)
Allformary, beaten over 49l on both of her previous starts over hurdles, might do better in handicaps. (op 14-1 tchd 16-1)
Hannicean has been running respectably on the all-weather for Ian Williams since his only previous run over hurdles for another stable, and quickly established a healthy lead while being keen. At one point it looked as though he may have enough of a lead to hang on, but he tired down the home straight and fell at the final hurdle when in second. (op 7-2 tchd 5-1)

225 BETEX PLC "NATIONAL HUNT" NOVICES' HURDLE (DIV II) (12 hdls 2 omitted) 3m
2:30 (2:30) (Class 4) 4-Y-0+ **£2,536** (£744; £372; £186)

Form RPR

401- **1** **Aberdale (IRE)**[28] 5155 6-11-2 120 (t) RichieMcLernon(3) 123+
(Jonjo O'Neill) *trckd ldrs: wnt 2nd 8th: led next: hung rt: hit 3 out: pushed 7 l ahd last: eased fnl 100yds* **10/11**[1]

F4-2 **2** *6* **Pairc Na Gcapall (IRE)**[10] 65 8-10-10 110 (p) AlexMerriam(3) 106
(Neil King) *led to 4th: outpcd 9th: kpt on to take 4 l 2nd 3 out: no ch w wnr* **9/2**[2]

0/P- **3** *9* **Ballyoliver**[175] 2297 6-10-13 0 JasonMaguire 99
(Kim Bailey) *trckd ldr: led 4th: hdd 9th: wknd run-in* **9/2**[2]

563- **4** *31* **A Fistful Of Euros**[26] 5173 6-10-1 0 GilesHawkins(5) 62
(Chris Down) *sn modest 4th: t.o 9th* **10/1**[3]

00- **P** **Coppingers Court (IRE)**[22] 5228 9-10-13 0 BarryKeniry —
(Rachel Hobbs) *in rr: t.o whn mstke 6th: p.u bef 3 out* **100/1**

P5/0 **P** **Royal Arms**[3] 167 8-10-13 0 ChristianWilliams —
(C Roberts) *berhind fr 5th: p.u after 7th: fatally injured* **33/1**

646- **P** **Silk And Roses**[18] 5317 7-10-3 0 MichaelMcAlister(3) —
(David Thompson) *sn modest 5th: wknd 8th: sn t.o: p.u bef 3 out* **66/1**

6- **P** **Luther (IRE)**[30] 5117 7-10-13 0 RobertThornton —
(Alan King) *bhd fr 7th: t.o 9th: p.u bef next* **10/1**[3]

0- **P** **Solway Dornal**[191] 1991 5-10-8 0 EwanWhillans(5) —
(Lisa Harrison) *sn wl bhd: t.o 4th: p.u bef 3 out* **33/1**

0P0- **P** **My Clementine (IRE)**[11] 50 5-10-6 0 WilsonRenwick —
(Michael Easterby) *sn wl bhd and drvn along: p.u bef 3 out* **66/1**

5m 44.8s (-20.40) **Going Correction** -0.675s/f (Firm) **10** Ran SP% **116.8**
Speed ratings (Par 105): **107,105,102,91,— —,—,—,—,—**
Tote Swingers: 1&2 £5.60, 2&3 £1.60 CSF £5.29 TOTE £1.90: £1.10, £1.80, £1.60; EX 4.20.
Owner Trevor Hemmings **Bred** Simon Lambert **Trained** Cheltenham, Gloucs

FOCUS
It was difficult to see past the favourite taking the second division of the staying maiden even though he was a little weak in the market.

NOTEBOOK
Aberdale(IRE), wearing a tongue-tie for the first time, looked head and shoulders above his rivals on form, especially after winning by 15l at Southwell on his previous start. Trying 3m for the first time, he sat just off the good gallop set and got to the lead on the final bend. He tended to wander once in front but, once straightened out, won in comfortable style. His build does suggest he will win races over fences when sent over them. (op 8-11 tchd Evens)
Pairc Na Gcapall(IRE), having his first run over hurdles since November 2008, is only modest over fences and was ridden along quite early. It did look for a while that he would lose touch, but he responded to pressure and kept on nicely. (op 4-1)

Ballyoliver, absent since pulling up behind Tell Massini at Cheltenham last November, had plenty to find with Aberdale on their meeting in a course bumper and was well held by that rival again after setting a strong pace once in front. One would imagine that around a tighter track, he will be hard to catch. (op 8-1)

226 DELAMERE WARRINGTON NOVICES' CHASE (14 fncs 2 omitted) 2m 6f 110y

3:00 (3:01) (Class 4) 5-Y-O+ **£3,295** (£973; £486; £243; £121)

Form RPR

613- **1** **Tisfreetdream (IRE)**[21] 5251 9-11-5 120............................(p) JackDoyle 115+
(Peter Pritchard) *led 2nd: blnd 5th: 4l clr 2 out: rdn out* **13/8**[1]

UU2- **2** *6* **Lord Larsson**[36] 4979 7-10-12 0...................................... DougieCostello 102
(Malcolm Jefferson) *hld up: wnt prom 5th: chsd wnr after 11th: hit next: kpt on one pce* **2/1**[2]

P/ **3** *½* **Gothic Charm (IRE)**[33] 8-10-12 0................................ ChristianWilliams 102
(Rachel Hobbs) *chsd ldrs: one pce fr 3 out* **16/1**

053- **4** *41* **Little Girl**[17] 5341 12-10-5 66... PaddyAspell 58
(Ray Peacock) *in rr: bhd and drvn 7th: tk distant 4th after 3 out* **66/1**

335- **5** *28* **Young Yozza**[36] 4987 8-10-5 61.. JoeCornwall(7) 40
(David Pearson) *in rr: bhd and drvn 7th: kpt on fr 3 out: tk distant 5th appr 2 out* **14/1**

563- **6** *1 ½* **Busy Times**[47] 4809 8-10-12 0.. DenisO'Regan 38
(John Spearing) *t.k.h: nt jump wl: led to 2nd: blnd 8th: wknd appr 3 out: sn eased and bhd* **3/1**[3]

6- **7** *12* **Harvey May (IRE)**[160] 2610 8-10-5 0....................(b[1]) AnthonyFreeman(7) 28
(John Upson) *chsd ldrs: outpcd whn mstke 8th: sn bhd* **25/1**

PP0- **U** **Smiling Applause**[28] 5154 11-10-9 0.........................(b[1]) SeanQuinlan(3) —
(Harry Chisman) *last whn blnd bdly 1st and uns rdr* **100/1**

5m 42.9s (-5.60) **Going Correction** -0.875s/f (Firm) **8** Ran SP% **115.3**

Speed ratings: **74,71,71,57,47 47,43,—**

Tote Swingers: 1&2 £1.60, 1&3 £8.60, 2&3 £11.30 CSF £5.51 TOTE £2.60: £1.30, £1.10, £4.00; EX 3.90.

Owner Woodland Generators & D R Pritchard **Bred** Cornelius O'Riordan **Trained** Whatcote, Warwicks

FOCUS

A novice chase that lacked much depth, although it was made a bit more open by the withdrawal of likely favourite Masked Man. The fence that is usually the second-last was omitted for all chases on the card, leaving only three to be jumped in the home straight.

NOTEBOOK

Tisfreetdream(IRE) is at his best when stamina comes into play, so it was a smart move by his jockey to get him up near the head of affairs early. He was not always foot perfect, but he made no serious errors and stayed on strongly all the way to the winning line. His trainer reported that he suffers from back problems, which could have accounted for his slightly disappointing effort at Stratford last time. He will be kept on the go in the summer. (op 6-5)

Lord Larsson has looked talented but had failed to complete over fences until his previous start. Taking a 6f step up in distance, he, as is usual, was keen under restraint and got a little way off the leading bunch at one point. Steadily brought through to have every chance, he kept on and seems sure to win a race over fences if his jumping holds out under pressure. (op 11-4)

Gothic Charm(IRE) shaped really well on his first outing for Rebecca Curtis after showing moderate form between the flags last season. (op 18-1)

Busy Times did not show much over hurdles but did win Irish points back in 2008. Sent to the front from the start, his jumping was erratic and he was not able to hold a position. He did briefly come back into contention after losing his place, but was then left behind again before the home straight. He was reported to have finished distressed. Official explanation: trainer said gelding finished distressed (op 7-2)

227 "CADET 150" (S) HURDLE (10 hdls 2 omitted) 2m 6f 110y

3:30 (3:30) (Class 5) 4-8-Y-0 **£1,691** (£496; £248; £124)

Form RPR

241- **1** **House Of Bourbon (IRE)**[182] 2147 7-10-8 115........(vt) DeanColeman(5) 111+
(Tim Vaughan) *chsd ldrs: wnt 2nd after 7th: narrow ld next: kpt on: hrd rdn: hld on wl towards fin* **5/2**[1]

5PP- **2** *2* **King Of Castile**[56] 4603 6-10-13 109............................(vt[1]) RichieMcGrath 109
(Evan Williams) *chsd ldr: led 7th: hdd appr next: kpt on: rallied and almost upsides last: hld last 75yds* **9/2**[3]

400- **3** *11* **Money Finder**[20] 5290 7-10-3 80...................................... HaddenFrost(3) 92
(Roger Curtis) *chsd ldrs: modest 32rd after 7th* **100/1**

P0-4 **4** *13* **Mr Melodious**[3] 172 4-10-7 103....................................(b) DavidEngland 83
(Nigel Twiston-Davies) *chsd ldrs: sn drvn along: one pce 4th fr 7th* **14/1**

222- **5** *15* **Lady Pilot**[34] 5036 8-10-6 118.. DougieCostello 67
(Jim Best) *in rr: pushed along 5th: sme hdwy 3 out: nvr on terms* **11/4**[2]

00- **6** *3 ¼* **Be Ashored**[67] 4384 5-10-13 0.. DenisO'Regan 71
(Nicky Vaughan) *hld up in rr: hdwy 7th: wknd appr 2 out* **100/1**

03- **7** *8* **Just Dan**[12] 30 4-10-0 0... MrJohnDawson(7) 58
(David Thompson) *prom: drvn 5th: wknd after next* **33/1**

0P0- **8** *1* **Rosie Larkin (IRE)**[60] 4512 6-10-6 60..........................(t) TomMessenger 56
(Joss Saville) *in rr: bhd fr 6th* **100/1**

54P/ **9** *1* **Amazing Request**[385] 5101 6-10-6 0.................. MissIsabelTompsett(7) 62
(Bernard Llewellyn) *in rr: sme hdwy 7th: wknd 2 out* **28/1**

030- **10** *3* **Insignia (IRE)**[18] 5318 8-10-13 81....................................... BrianHughes 59
(Karen Tutty) *led to 7th: sn lost pl and bhd* **25/1**

030- **11** *46* **What Luck (IRE)**[188] 2039 8-10-6 78.......................... AnthonyFreeman(7) 18
(Sean Curran) *chsd ldrs: lost pl 6th: sn bhd: t.o next: eventually completed* **16/1**

P60- **P** **Original Fly (FR)**[64] 4438 8-10-13 95...........................(p) JasonMaguire —
(Donald McCain) *chsd ldrs: drvn 2nd: lost pl next: detached in last whn p.u bef 6th* **9/1**

5U-4 **P** **Rock Me (IRE)**[9] 86 5-10-13 101...........................(p) ChristianWilliams —
(Lawney Hill) *in rr: bhd fr 7th: t.o whn p.u bef last* **12/1**

PPU- **P** **Moonlight Rose**[15] 5385 6-10-6 0....................................... RodiGreene —
(Christopher Kellett) *in rr: sn bhd: t.o 6th: p.u after next* **150/1**

5m 19.1s (-11.80) **Going Correction** -0.675s/f (Firm)

WFA 4 from 5yo+ 19lb **14** Ran SP% **117.5**

Speed ratings: **93,92,88,83,78 77,74,74,74,73 57,—,—,—**

Tote Swingers: 1&2 £3.40, 1&3 £29.10, 2&3 £34.10 CSF £13.36 TOTE £4.80: £3.30, £1.80, £30.20; EX 15.20.There was no bid for winner.

Owner Mrs Gill Owens **Bred** Darley **Trained** Aberthin, Vale of Glamorgan

⊠ Stewards' Enquiry : Dean Coleman three-day ban: used whip with excessive frequency down shoulder in the forehand (May 23-25)

FOCUS

Not many of these made much appeal on their recent form, so this had the look of a weak event, even for the grade.\n

NOTEBOOK

House Of Bourbon(IRE) won a novice hurdle when last seen on the racecourse in November, so it was a little bit of a surprise to see him in this grade on his first outing since. Settled behind the two that gained an advantage with a circuit to go, he claimed the runner-up on the bend but did not extend away as seemed likely. That said, he did not give up in the battle and held on. (tchd 9-4)

King Of Castile, with a visor on for the first time to go with the tongue-tie he had already worn, was pulled up on his two previous starts, so hardly looked the most obvious winner of this despite a couple of fair efforts before that. However, that did not stop his being backed and running really well under a positive ride. A similar contest is within his range. (op 6-1)

Money Finder had shown a modicum of ability in limited tries before this and ran well down in selling company for the first time.

Mr Melodious did not run too badly in a claiming hurdle the previous Thursday and again here, but did not look the easiest of rides. (op 12-1)

Lady Pilot was well treated with some of these on official figures and finished a close second in a similar contest at Fakenham last time. Held up towards the rear in this, she seemed unable to make any headway when the race took shape and could only run on at the one pace down the home straight. (op 9-4 tchd 3-1)

228 REG HOLLINSHEAD CONDITIONAL JOCKEYS' H'CAP HURDLE (9 hdls 1 omitted) 2m

4:00 (4:01) (Class 5) (0-95,95) 4-Y-0+ **£1,951** (£573; £286; £143)

Form RPR

110- **1** **Nono Le Sage (FR)**[21] 5261 6-11-4 **90**.......................(t) JohnnyFarrelly(3) 99+
(David Pipe) *trckd ldrs: qcknd to ld appr 2 out: 4l clr last: hld on towards fin* **11/2**[2]

00-U **2** *½* **Rossbrin (IRE)**[10] 54 5-10-12 **81**.................................... CharlieHuxley 87
(Anna Brooks) *chsd ldrs: wnt 2nd last: kpt on wl: no ex towards fin* **12/1**

000- **3** *8* **Spate River**[69] 4359 5-11-1 **87**..................................(t) RichieMcLernon(3) 88+
(Jonjo O'Neill) *in tch: hdwy 6th: chsd ldrs: outpcd appr 2 out: 4th and styng on whn blnd last: tk modest 3rd towards fin* **3/1**[1]

345- **4** *1 ¼* **General Smith**[21] 5261 11-11-2 **90**................................... MarkQuinlan(5) 88
(James Evans) *chsd ldrs 3rd: wnt 2nd 5th: wknd last* **11/2**[2]

056- **5** *3 ¼* **Abulharith**[14] 4 4-10-8 **84**.. AlexanderVoy(3) 75
(Michael Scudamore) *chsd ldrs: outpcd 3 out: kpt on run-in* **20/1**

40-6 **6** *shd* **Answer Me (IRE)**[10] 59 7-11-2 **85**................................. GilesHawkins 80
(John Spearing) *led tl hdd appr 2 out: sn fdd* **10/1**

500- **7** *1* **M'Lady Eliza**[19] 5295 5-11-2 **85**....................................... DeanColeman 79
(Joanne Priest) *in rr: kpt on fr 3 out: nvr a factor* **22/1**

FF0- **8** *4* **Zizou (IRE)**[19] 5295 7-11-3 **92**.................................... AnthonyFreeman(6) 82
(Sean Curran) *chsd ldrs: upsides 3 out: wknd appr next* **20/1**

405- **9** *2 ¼* **Amwell Brave**[63] 4460 9-11-10 **93**...................................... HaddenFrost 81
(J R Jenkins) *in rr: sme hdwy 3 out: sn wknd: blnd last* **33/1**

/P0- **10** *3* **Besi**[217] 1632 8-11-0 **83**... EwanWhillans 69
(Lisa Harrison) *hld up towards rr: hdwy appr 3 out: sn chsng ldrs: lost pl bef 2 out* **8/1**

044- **11** *1 ½* **Cornish Castle (USA)**[14] 14 4-11-3 **90**........................... RyanMania 70
(Joss Saville) *chsd ldr to 5th: lost pl after 3 out* **28/1**

/6P- **12** *36* **Marlborough Sound**[44] 4877 11-11-12 **95**...................... FearghalDavis 47
(James Turner) *in rr: drvn 6th: sn bhd: t.o 3 out* **33/1**

50-6 **F** **Marino Prince (FR)**[8] 96 5-11-8 **91**..................................... PeterToole 88
(Barry Leavy) *chsd ldrs: 5th and keeping on same pce whn fell 2 out* **7/1**[3]

3m 48.3s (-6.90) **Going Correction** -0.675s/f (Firm)

WFA 4 from 5yo+ 18lb **13** Ran SP% **119.4**

Speed ratings (Par 103): **90,89,85,85,83 83,82,80,79,78 77,59,—**

Tote Swingers: 1&2 £50.70, 1&3 £1.90, 2&3 £13.80 CSF £60.57 CT £235.00 TOTE £4.80: £1.80, £3.00, £2.10; EX 130.70.

Owner 3 To 1 Syndicate **Bred** Yves Bourdin Et Al **Trained** Nicholashayne, Devon

FOCUS

The pace seemed only ordinary for this low-grade handicap, so the form may not be reliable. Plenty of them were in a bunch heading to the second-last.

NOTEBOOK

Nono Le Sage(FR) had his attempt at a hat-trick halted by Exulto, who had gone on to win again, but looked the one to give the favourite the most to do on form. Never far away, he was produced to take up the running down the home straight and won by a narrow margin. He looks big enough to jump fences in time. (op 9-2 tchd 6-1)

Rossbrin(IRE), whose jockey was unshipped at the start last time, could be seen travelling well for a lot of the race, but got outpaced before running on again. (tchd 11-1 and 14-1)

Spate River, fitted with a tongue-tie for the first time, had shown little over hurdles for Jonjo O'Neil since being purchased out of the Chris Wall stable. The ground did look more suitable here for this useful sort on the Flat, and a mark of 87 on his handicap debut seemed very good if rediscovering his Flat form. Settled just in behind, this was far more encouraging and he can win something over hurdles if faced with a realistic task. (op 9-2 tchd 11-4)

General Smith attracted some market support and travelled strongly towards the front. He momentarily hit the front in the home straight but the winner soon swept passed him. (op 8-1)

Abulharith got left behind when the tempo increased but ran on strongly after the final hurdle. (tchd 25-1)

Answer Me(IRE), taking a big drop in trip, hardly looked the most obvious winner on what he had done recently and weakened steadily after leading for much of the contest. (op 14-1)

M'Lady Eliza seemed to put in a respectable effort but may have been flattered. (op 20-1)

Besiwas supported down from 20-1 in places in the morning but made no impression. (op 9-2)

Marino Prince(FR) was not disgraced over C&D last time and was keeping on when falling two out. He would not have won but could have been somewhere near the third. (op 8-1)

229 TIM LEADBEATER H'CAP CHASE (17 fncs 3 omitted) 3m 2f

4:30 (4:30) (Class 4) (0-110,110) 5-Y-0+ **£3,295** (£973; £486; £243; £121)

Form RPR

130- **1** **Shammy Buskins**[23] 5219 8-11-6 **104**........................(p) ChristianWilliams 116+
(Lawney Hill) *in rr: mstke 9th: hdwy and in tch whn hit 11th: outpcd 13th: hdwy after 4 out: 12 l down 2 out: 6 l 4th last: styd on strly to ld last 75yds* **9/1**

3P4- **2** *1 ¾* **Alexanderthegreat (IRE)**[16] 5356 12-11-9 **107**.............. AidanColeman 116
(Venetia Williams) *w ldr: led after 4 out: hdd and no ex last 50yds* **8/1**

U35- **3** *2* **Prophete De Guye (FR)**[62] 4494 7-10-6 **90**......................... FelixDeGiles 97
(James Evans) *t.k.h: hdwy to trck ldrs 7th: rallied and chal last: kpt on same pce* **7/1**[2]

4 *5* **Proform Native (IRE)**[49] 8-11-8 **106**................................. DenisO'Regan 110
(David Rees) *in tch: hdwy to chse ldrs 12th: ev ch fr 3 out: fdd last* **9/1**

513- **5** *25* **Sesame Rambler (IRE)**[17] 5329 11-11-0 **103**.................... PeterToole(5) 83
(R H & Mrs S Alner) *chsd ldrs: lost pl 9th: hdwy 11th: lost pl next* **14/1**

5/2- **6** *1 ¾* **Sandyzar (IRE)**[36] 11-10-2 **93**...............................(p) MrRGHenderson(7) 72
(Nick Mitchell) *chsd ldrs: hit 11th: sn lost pl and bhd* **7/1**[2]

261- **7** *1 ¾* **Power Pack Jack (IRE)**[43] 4898 7-11-4 **102**..................(b) DavidEngland 79
(Nigel Twiston-Davies) *led: blnd 4 out: sn hdd: wknd qckly appr 2 out: sn bhd* **5/1**[1]

03- **8** *33* **Chorizo (IRE)**[198] 1876 9-11-10 **108**.................................... PaddyAspell 55
(Richard Guest) *in rr: drvn 9th: bhd fr 12th: t.o 3 out* **15/2**[3]

55P- **P** **Ballygalley Bob (IRE)**[26] 5174 9-11-8 **106**.................(b[1]) LeightonAspell —
(Oliver Sherwood) *chsd ldrs: mstke 11th: wknd 13th: bhd whn p.u bef 3 out* **10/1**

The Form Book, Raceform Ltd, Compton, RG20 6NL

051- **P** **Basoda**[13] 24 7-11-10 **108**......(t) JasonMaguire —
(Kim Bailey) *in rr: drvn in last 3rd: detached 7th: blnd next: sn p.u* **5/1**[1]

6m 37.6s (-12.40) **Going Correction** -0.875s/f (Firm) **10** Ran SP% **117.0**
Speed ratings: **105,104,103,102,94 94,93,83,—,—**
Tote Swingers: 1&2 £8.20, 2&3 £13.00 CSF £78.80 CT £538.39 TOTE £4.90: £1.10, £2.70, £3.40.
Owner P J Morgan **Bred** D I Bare **Trained** Aston Rowant, Oxon

FOCUS
There were a couple of confirmed front-runners in this staying chance, which meant the gallop was at least sensible for the trip.

NOTEBOOK
Shammy Buskins enjoyed the return to staying distances after a modest effort over 2m5f last time, his first run after a break, but it still took all of Christian Williams's strength to get him home, as victory looked remote after jumping two out. Still in fourth jumping the last, he seems to love quick ground but will have work to do next time, as this success came off a career-high mark. (tchd 10-1)
Alexanderthegreat(IRE) has come sharply down the weights and ran a cracker in this. He could seen going well throughout and was only mugged close to the winning line. He jumped superbly in the main and was unfortunate to be worn down. (op 15-2 tchd 13-2)
Prophete De Guye(FR) was another to travel strongly during the race, but he could not quicken under pressure down the home straight when he needed to get to the front and push on. However to his credit, he kept going and still had a chance coming to the last. (op 11-1)
Proform Native(IRE), successful in a 3m point in Ireland on his previous start, was having his first run for this trainer and shaped with more than enough promise to suggest he will be winning soon.
Power Pack Jack(IRE) had been raised 11lb for a wide-margin success last time when blinkers were fitted for the first time. He had the run of the race out in the lead but found only the one pace from three out, and looked tired thereafter. (op 13-2)
Chorizo(IRE), having his first start since last October, never got competitive. (op 6-1)
Ballygalley Bob(IRE) is coming down the weights but ran too freely in the first-time blinkers here to get home. (op 7-1)
Basoda, raised 8lb for winning a staying chase at Towcester, had seemed to make some progress since having a tongue-tie fitted, but he got behind almost from the outset here and was pulled up early. Official explanation: trainer had no explanation for the poor form shown (op 7-1)

230 DRAYTON MANOR PARK MARES' STANDARD OPEN NATIONAL HUNT FLAT RACE 2m

5:00 (5:01) (Class 6) 4-6-Y-O **£1,431** (£420; £210; £104)

Form RPR

42- **1** **Pure Anticipation (IRE)**[165] 2508 5-10-12 0......JohnnyFarrelly 99
(Tim Vaughan) *chsd ldrs: wnt 2nd 6f out: led over 2f out: styd on wl fnl 2f* **20/1**

2 2 ½ **Bellaboosh (IRE)** 4-10-8 0......AndrewTinkler 92
(Nicky Henderson) *mid-div: drvn after 4f: hdwy over 3f out: chsd wnr over 2f out: no imp* **7/4**[1]

4- **3** 3 ½ **Lady Jannina**[28] 5150 4-10-8 0......ChristianWilliams 89
(Henry Daly) *in rr: drvn and hdwy 5f out: styd on to take 3rd 1f out* **15/2**[3]

20- **4** 1 ¾ **Some Secret**[108] 3576 5-10-9 0......ChrisHonour(3) 92
(Chris Down) *hld up in rr: drvn 7f out: styd on fnl f* **25/1**

52- **5** ¾ **Tsarinova**[17] 5332 5-10-12 0......RobertThornton 91
(Alan King) *chsd ldrs: one pce fnl 3f* **8/1**

20- **6** 7 **Definitley Lovely**[57] 4592 5-10-9 0......(t) TomMolloy(3) 85
(Nigel Twiston-Davies) *led after 1f: hdd over 3f out: wknd 2f out* **16/1**

34- **7** 1 **Himayna**[13] 27 6-10-7 0......DeanColeman(5) 84
(Tim Vaughan) *chsd ldrs: drvn over 4f out: one pce fnl 3f* **28/1**

8 2 ¾ **Alexander Road (IRE)** 5-10-9 0......AdrianLane(3) 81
(Donald McCain) *hld up in mid-div: lost pl 7f out: no ch after* **9/1**

3- **9** 7 **Sara's Smile**[28] 5150 4-10-8 0......JasonMaguire 71
(Donald McCain) *t.k.h: led 1f: chsd ldrs: lost pl over 3f out* **7/2**[2]

3/ **10** ¾ **Inner Pride**[391] 4991 5-10-12 0......LeightonAspell 74
(Don Cantillon) *in tch: lost pl over 3f out: lame* **20/1**

11 2 ¼ **Mystic Echo** 4-10-8 0......RichieMcGrath 68
(John Davies) *stdd s: in rr: bhd fnl 5f* **50/1**

12 18 **Stephie** 4-10-8 0......WilsonRenwick 52
(Michael Easterby) *in rr: bhd fnl 4f* **20/1**

3m 42.5s (-7.10) **Going Correction** -0.675s/f (Firm)
WFA 4 from 5yo+ 4lb **12** Ran SP% **120.0**
Speed ratings: **90,88,87,86,85 82,81,80,76,76 75,66**
Tote Swingers: 1&2 £2.80, 1&3 £5.60, 2&3 £4.50 CSF £65.42 TOTE £19.00: £3.20, £1.50, £1.80; EX 53.10 Place 6: £9.49 Place 5: £3.25 .
Owner Cloud Nine **Bred** Mrs Christine Kelly **Trained** Aberthin, Vale of Glamorgan

FOCUS
Although the pace was only ordinary, as these contests tend to be, this appeared to be a fair race of its type.

NOTEBOOK
Pure Anticipation(IRE), absent since a fair effort in a heavy-ground bumper at Chepstow in November and surprisingly weak in the betting market, was given a positive ride and always looked likely to collect after turning in. A daughter of a modest staying chaser, she is one to follow when sent over hurdles. (op 9-1)
Bellaboosh(IRE), a half-sister to Topsham Belle, the winner of her only start in bumper company, seemed to lack the scope of some of her rivals, but her heart could not be faulted. Well backed before the off, she was going nowhere at halfway but fought on well under pressure down the home straight to claim second. (op 11-4)
Lady Jannina, another to get market support, appeared to at least run as well as she did on her first start, but further and time is probably needed with her. (op 14-1)
Some Secret had shown ability on her first outing but disappointed on her next start. This was better but she may not be completely straightforward. (op 16-1)
Tsarinova continues to make a bit of progress but, like the third, seems sure to be effective over much further or on a stiffer course. (op 7-1)
Definitley Lovely, wearing a tongue-tie for the first time, ran well on her first start but was beaten a long way in a Listed event next time. Back down to a more suitable level, she helped to set the pace but was left behind when it increased. (op 8-1)
Himayna never looked likely to win but ran a bit better than her final position suggested. (op 20-1)
Alexander Road(IRE), wearing a noseband on her first start, stayed on really well after getting behind at one point. This was a promising effort. (op 12-1)
Sara's Smile raced too keenly early to have much left for the finish. She had finished in front of Lady Jannina last time. Official explanation: jockey said filly ran too free (op 4-1 tchd 10-3)
Inner Pride reportedly finished lame. Official explanation: vet said mare finished lame right-fore (op 16-1)
T/Plt: £7.70. Pool: £52,191.32 - 4,898.06 winning units. T/Qpdt: £3.60. Pool: £3,221.22 - 658.18 winning units. WG

WORCESTER (L-H)

Sunday, May 9

OFFICIAL GOING: Good (good to firm in places; chs 7.5, hdl 7.6)
Shared Cathedral bend on inside line. Home straight chase bend on inner line and home straight hurdle bend 10metres outside chase bend.
Wind: Light against Weather: Cloudy with sunny spells

231 2ND SKIN LINGERIE CHARITY BRA CHAIN H'CAP HURDLE (DIV I) (12 hdls) 3m

1:50 (1:52) (Class 4) (0-110,110) 4-Y-0+ **£2,602** (£764; £382; £190)

Form RPR

3U3- **1** **Rifleman (IRE)**[189] 2020 10-10-5 **89**......(t) CharliePoste 96+
(Richard Lee) *a.p: led after 4 out: styd on u.p* **12/1**

02-3 **2** 1 ¾ **Phare Isle (IRE)**[10] 66 5-11-2 **105**......JamesHalliday(5) 110+
(Ben Case) *hld up: hdwy 4 out: ev ch 2 out: rdn flat: styd on same pce* **7/2**[2]

0F4- **3** 6 **Hohlethelonely**[39] 4960 6-11-5 **103**......AidanColeman 102
(Venetia Williams) *mid-div: hdwy 4 out: rdn bef next: styd on same pce appr last: wnt 3rd flat* **8/1**

665- **4** 2 ¼ **Cool Bob (IRE)**[14] 3 7-10-10 **94**......(t) PaddyBrennan 92
(Matt Sheppard) *chsd ldrs: ev ch fr 3 out tl no ex last: lost 3rd flat* **8/1**

266- **5** 1 ¾ **Mauricetheathlete (IRE)**[20] 5282 7-11-3 **106**......SamTwiston-Davies(5) 101
(Martin Keighley) *chsd ldr tl led 7th: hdd after 4 out: sn rdn: styd on same pce appr last* **3/1**[1]

P00- **6** 5 **Gilwen Glory (IRE)**[43] 4889 7-11-9 **110**......DPFahy(3) 100
(Evan Williams) *mid-div: hdwy 8th: drvn along appr 3 out: hrd rdn after next: sn wknd* **13/2**[3]

/0-4 **7** 11 **Enchanted Approach (IRE)**[10] 59 7-9-11 **88**......RobertKirk(7) 67
(Lady Susan Brooke) *led to 7th: wknd appr 3 out: bhd whn hit next* **25/1**

020- **8** 3 ¾ **Arctic Watch**[21] 5258 5-11-2 **100**......(t) MarkGrant 75
(Brendan Duke) *hld up: wknd after 4 out* **50/1**

033- **9** 6 **Solitary Palm (IRE)**[17] 5330 7-11-0 **98**......LiamTreadwell 67
(Brian Forsey) *chsd ldrs: rdn after 4 out: wknd bef next* **9/1**

0PP- **10** 17 **Owlsley**[31] 5101 8-10-0 **84** oh13......(t) WayneHutchinson 36
(Jim Old) *hld up: rdn after 4 out: wknd bef next: t.o* **50/1**

/1P- **11** 29 **Rien A Perdre (FR)**[343] 543 9-11-0 **105**......MrTomDavid(7) 28
(Graeme McPherson) *hld up: racd keenly: effrt appr 3 out: sn wknd: t.o* **12/1**

0U-6 **P** **Final Bid (IRE)**[8] 95 7-10-7 **91**......WillKennedy —
(Tracey Barfoot-Saunt) *hld up: mstke 7th: sn rdn and wknd: t.o whn p.u bef 4 out* **50/1**

5m 36.9s (-7.70) **Going Correction** -0.275s/f (Good) **12** Ran SP% **117.9**
Speed ratings (Par 105): **101,100,98,97,97 95,91,90,88,82 73,—**
Tote Swingers: 1&2 £5.40, 1&3 £15.50, 2&3 £9.80 CSF £53.55 CT £361.62 TOTE £13.70: £4.30, £1.30, £6.70; EX 35.80.
Owner John Jackson & Mike Bevan **Bred** James Hanly, Trevor Stewart & Anthony Stroud **Trained** Byton, H'fords

FOCUS
The ground had been watered to maintain the good, good to firm in places going. This was the weaker of the two divisions of a modest staying 0-110 handicap hurdle run at a modest pace.

NOTEBOOK
Rifleman(IRE) has only scored once and that was over fences back in 2006 although he has plenty of placed efforts to his name. He travelled well for most of the way and, after taking it up three out, stayed on well enough. He goes well fresh, but is quite exposed. (op 11-1 tchd 10-1)
Phare Isle(IRE) looked a big danger on the home bend after making steady progress down the back straight but could only stay on at the same pace from two out. He is relatively lightly raced and has put in improved performances on his last two runs since being stepped up in trip. (tchd 4-1)
Hohlethelonely looked well in on his first try at the trip which he saw out well enough without threatening the front two. (op 9-1)
Cool Bob(IRE) is still a maiden after 29 starts and after taking it up at the last in the back straight fought on well enough before tiring going to the last. (op 17-2)
Mauricetheathlete(IRE) had run well in a better heat last time and was fancied to get off the mark here. He sat prominently for most of the way but could only stay on at the same pace. Official explanation: trainer said gelding ran flat (op 4-1)
Gilwen Glory(IRE) was trying the trip for the first time and appeared not to quite get home. (op 9-1 tchd 6-1)
Rien A Perdre(FR) is versatile as regards trip and will be better for the outing for he probably payed the price for racing too keenly on his return to action after being sidelined for 343 days. (op 9-1)

232 2ND SKIN LINGERIE CHARITY BRA CHAIN H'CAP HURDLE (DIV II) (12 hdls) 3m

2:20 (2:20) (Class 4) (0-110,110) 4-Y-0+ **£2,602** (£764; £382; £190)

Form RPR

/25- **1** **Haldibari (IRE)**[6] 1851 6-10-6 **95**......SamTwiston-Davies(5) 106+
(Shaun Lycett) *mde virtually all: clr fr 3 out: styd on wl* **12/1**[3]

U35- **2** 13 **Fresh Air And Fun (IRE)**[21] 5246 7-11-10 **108**......APMcCoy 109+
(Jonjo O'Neill) *hld up: hdwy 8th: rdn to chse wnr appr 3 out: styd on same pce fr next: eased whn btn fnl 100yds* **11/2**[2]

/PP- **3** 4 **In Media Res (FR)**[90] 3937 9-11-9 **110**......CharlieStudd(3) 104
(Charlie Longsdon) *chsd ldrs: rdn appr 3 out: sn wknd* **33/1**

063- **4** 4 ½ **Louis Pasteur (IRE)**[21] 5256 5-11-0 **101**......HarrySkelton(3) 91
(Nick Mitchell) *hld up in tch: rdn after 9th: wknd bef next* **14/1**

424- **5** 2 ¼ **Azulada Bay (IRE)**[20] 5282 6-11-0 **105**......DavidBass(7) 92
(Mark Rimell) *prom tl rdn and wknd 3 out* **5/2**[1]

P10- **6** 1 ¼ **Synonymy**[169] 2434 7-10-4 **88**......(b) NickScholfield 74
(Michael Blanshard) *hld up in tch: rdn after 4 out: wknd bef next* **14/1**

1P3- **7** 23 **Comprimario (IRE)**[49] 4762 4-11-2 **106**......(b) PaddyBrennan 63
(Nigel Twiston-Davies) *prom tl rdn 9th: sn wknd: t.o* **14/1**

050- **8** 7 **The Boss Rock (IRE)**[42] 4913 7-10-7 **91**......(t) WayneHutchinson 47
(Jim Old) *hld up: rdn and wknd 4 out: t.o* **25/1**

PP0- **9** 21 **Nishnash**[20] 5282 7-10-6 **90**......(p) AndrewThornton 25
(Jim Wilson) *mid-div: wknd 9th: t.o* **50/1**

/20- **10** 8 **Feel The Force (IRE)**[20] 5282 6-11-7 **105**......TimmyMurphy 32
(Alan Fleming) *hld up: a in rr: t.o whn j.lft 2 out* **18/1**

432- **11** 30 **Flexi Time (IRE)**[16] 5359 6-11-7 **105**......(b) RichardJohnson —
(Alison Thorpe) *chsd wnr: led briefly appr 7th: rdn and wknd bef 3 out: t.o* **5/2**[1]

U46- **P** **Investment Wings (IRE)**[19] 5295 8-10-0 **84** oh8........(tp) LiamTreadwell —
(P Kelsall) *hld up: a in rr: t.o whn p.u bef 3 out* **33/1**

5m 37.6s (-7.00) **Going Correction** -0.275s/f (Good)
WFA 4 from 5yo+ 20lb **12** Ran SP% **117.2**
Speed ratings (Par 105): **100,95,94,92,92 91,84,81,74,72 62,—**
Tote Swingers: 1&2 £5.40, 1&3 £15.50, 2&3 £9.80 CSF £74.35 CT £2134.73 TOTE £20.30: £4.50, £2.30, £12.10; EX 129.20.
Owner Nicholls Family **Bred** His Highness The Aga Khan's Studs S C **Trained** Clapton-on-the-Hill, Gloucs

FOCUS
The second division was run at a similar ordinary pace.

NOTEBOOK
Haldibari(IRE) made all and, after kicking clear at the last in the back straight, he never looked like being caught. He has been generally a little disappointing but this was a better effort to get off the mark. He will probably have one more outing over hurdles before switching his attention to fences. (op 14-1)
Fresh Air And Fun(IRE), better known as a chaser, ran a sound enough race returning to hurdles but he could never lay down a serious challenge to the winner although running out a clear second. (op 4-1)
In Media Res(FR) was having his first try at the trip after failing to complete the last twice. He seemed to see it out but was another who could only muster the same pace where it mattered. (op 28-1)
Louis Pasteur(IRE), on what looked a reasonable mark of 101 on his handicap debut, also looks very one-paced and would be of better interest when tackling fences.
Azulada Bay(IRE) has been performing consistently in similar contests, but was another who could only muster the same pace. (op 7-2 tchd 4-1)
Flexi Time(IRE) Official explanation: vet said gelding finished distressed

233 LADBROKES AT WORCESTER RACECOURSE H'CAP CHASE (12 fncs) 2m
2:50 (2:51) (Class 4) (0-110,110) 5-Y-0+ **£3,252** (£955; £477; £238)

Form RPR
233- **1** **My Condor (IRE)**[173] 2346 9-9-10 **85**.............................. JohnKington(5) 96
(Donald McCain) *led to 4th: led again 7th: styd on wl u.p* **8/1**[3]
P00- **2** 4 ½ **Mibleu (FR)**[226] 1533 10-11-7 **110**.................................. KeiranBurke(5) 117
(R H & Mrs S Alner) *hld up: hdwy 5th: chsd wnr after 8th: rdn 2 out: styd on same pce flat* **25/1**
02-1 **3** 1 ¼ **Coach Lane**[8] 99 9-11-11 **109**.. AidanColeman 115+
(Venetia Williams) *hld up: blnd 1st: hdwy appr 4 out: styd on u.p to go 3rd nr fin* **5/1**[2]
UP3- **4** nk **Rapide Plaisir (IRE)**[14] 1 12-11-2 **103**....................(t) MrOGreenall(3) 108
(Richard Lee) *hld up: hdwy 6th: hit last: styd on: lost 3rd nr fin* **16/1**
P01- **5** 25 **Quel Bruere (FR)**[84] 4058 6-11-1 **106**.........................(vt) MrTomDavid(7) 84
(Graeme McPherson) *chsd ldrs: led 4th: blnd 6th: hdd next: rdn and wknd 4 out: t.o* **5/1**[2]
543- **6** 7 **Nesnaas (USA)**[13] 26 9-10-12 **103**...............................(v[1]) DavidBass(7) 74
(Mark Rimell) *chsd ldrs to 7th: t.o* **20/1**
OPO- **U** **Caliban (IRE)**[144] 2914 12-10-1 **90**.................................. LeeEdwards(5) —
(Sally-Anne Wheelwright) *prom tl mstke and lost pl 4th: towards rr whn blnd and uns rdr next* **66/1**
033- **P** **No Greater Love (FR)**[17] 5331 8-10-4 **88**...................... PaddyBrennan —
(Charlie Longsdon) *hld up: mstke 3rd: blnd 5th: sn p.u* **8/1**[3]
/54- **U** **Erdeli (IRE)**[21] 5261 6-11-4 **102**.......................................(t) WillKennedy —
(Paul Webber) *chsd ldrs: mstke 4th: lost pl after next: in rr whn blnd and uns rdr 7th* **5/1**[2]
114- **P** **Benefit Game (IRE)**[249] 1378 6-11-3 **101**............................... APMcCoy —
(Jonjo O'Neill) *hld up: bhd fr 3rd: t.o whn p.u bef 3 out* **3/1**[1]
4FP- **P** **Lucky Dancer**[201] 1839 5-11-12 **110**.................................. PaulMoloney —
(Evan Williams) *hld up: bhd fr 6th: t.o whn p.u bef 4 out* **20/1**

3m 50.4s (-1.20) **Going Correction** -0.275s/f (Good) **11** Ran SP% **118.0**
Speed ratings: **92,89,89,88,76 72,—,—,—,— —**
Tote Swingers: 1&2 £28.60, 1&3 £7.60, 2&3 £20.60 CSF £180.29 CT £1105.21 TOTE £12.90: £3.40, £12.20, £2.70; EX 126.00.
Owner D McCain **Bred** Mrs Claire Lonergan **Trained** Cholmondeley, Cheshire

FOCUS
A modest 0-110 handicap chase.

NOTEBOOK
My Condor(IRE) set a decent pace for this modest 0-110 handicap chase to have all but two of his rivals in trouble from a fair way out. He kept enough in reserve to fight off the persistent challenge of the runner-up in the straight to run out a deserving winner. His usual headgear was removed but he does not normally find too much in the latter stages of his races and has been rather frustrating overall. He was well handicapped for this but will probably struggle in the future after being reassessed. (op 9-1)
Mibleu(FR) was returning to action after 200 days and ran creditably in defeat. He laid down a persistent challenge to the winner in the straight but his jumping to his right proved ultimately quite costly and lack of a run probably told from the last. (op 22-1)
Coach Lane had been tried at staying trips throughout the winter but returned to form when dropped back recently. He could never get involved as he was always struggling to hold his position before staying on from two out to snatch third near the line. (op 9-2 tchd 6-1)
Rapide Plaisir(IRE) had his chance turning in but could never lay down a serious threat and stayed on at the same pace only to lose third close home.
Quel Bruere(FR) scored with first-time blinkers last time out and was well fancied to repeat the effort, but after sitting with the winner most of the way weakened tamely before hitting four out. (op 6-1 tchd 13-2)
No Greater Love(FR) Official explanation: jockey said gelding jumped poorly
Benefit Game(IRE) was disappointing after being held up off the pace he could never make any inroads on the leaders when asked and was pulled up after a mistake four out. Official explanation: jockey said gelding jumped poorly

234 LADBROKES BEGINNERS' CHASE (18 fncs) 2m 7f
3:20 (3:20) (Class 4) 5-Y-0+ **£3,252** (£955; £477; £238)

Form RPR
223- **1** **Mont Present (FR)**[22] 5226 6-11-0 120.......................... RichardJohnson 113+
(Philip Hobbs) *hld up: hdwy 9th: rdn after 2 out: r.o to ld nr fin* **15/8**[1]
P42- **2** ¾ **Picture In The Sky (IRE)**[41] 4927 9-10-9 119..... SamTwiston-Davies(5) 110
(Susan Nock) *chsd ldrs: led 12th to 14th: rdn and ev ch flat: r.o* **14/1**
222- **3** nk **Horseshoe Reef (AUS)**[28] 5154 7-11-0 0.......................... DarylJacob 110
(Jamie Snowden) *chsd ldrs: led after 5th: hdd 12th: led again 14th: rdn and hdd nr fin* **18/1**
/1P- **4** 1 ¾ **I'm The Decider (IRE)**[319] 809 8-11-0 0...........................(p) APMcCoy 108
(Jonjo O'Neill) *hld up: hdwy appr 4 out: sn rdn: unable qck nr fin* **9/2**[2]
422- **5** 11 **Silver Bay**[23] 5215 9-11-0 113.. SamJones 97
(Oliver Sherwood) *chsd ldrs: rdn and wknd appr last* **14/1**
4/P- **6** 6 **Hell's Bay (FR)**[167] 2478 8-10-11 0............................ HarrySkelton(3) 92
(Paul Nicholls) *hld up: hdwy 9th: hit 11th: wknd appr last* **5/1**[3]
223- **7** 6 **Cadoudalas (FR)**[56] 4618 7-10-11 110............................ MrOGreenall(3) 90
(Richard Lee) *hld up in tch: cl enough 4 out: mstke and wknd 2 out: nt fluent last* **9/1**
P **Moynalveylad (IRE)**[16] 5377 10-10-11 0..................(bt) TommyPhelan(3) —
(David Anthony O'Brien, Ire) *hld up: in rr whn hmpd 11th: t.o whn p.u bef 4 out* **100/1**
6PP- **U** **Tarkesar (IRE)**[56] 4612 8-10-9 71.................................(b) LeeEdwards(5) —
(Carole Ikin) *a in rr: bhd whn mstke and uns rdr 11th* **100/1**
P22- **B** **Haar**[21] 5251 6-11-0 124.. NickScholfield —
(Andy Turnell) *nt jump wl in rr: bhd whn b.d 11th* **15/2**
0/F- **P** **Willowpattern**[31] 5101 7-10-7 0............................... WayneHutchinson —
(Martin Keighley) *led tl after 5th: chsd ldrs: mstke 9th: wknd 12th: t.o whn p.u bef 4 out* **33/1**
F **Foxtown Girl (IRE)**[14] 8-10-2 0.................................(t) DonalDevereux(5) —
(David Anthony O'Brien, Ire) *prom: mstke 5th: j.lft 9th: sn given reminders: in rr whn fell 11th* **66/1**

5m 42.1s (-0.50) **Going Correction** -0.275s/f (Good) **12** Ran SP% **116.4**
Speed ratings: **89,88,88,88,84 82,80,—,—,— —,—**
Tote Swingers: 1&2 £9.50, 1&3 £5.40, 2&3 £21.80 CSF £29.53 TOTE £2.60: £1.10, £5.10, £4.60; EX 33.10.
Owner Thurloe 50 **Bred** Snc Ste Entrainment Artu Jean-Yves Et Al **Trained** Withycombe, Somerset

FOCUS
A competitive staying novice chase which produced a thrilling finish after a good pace.

NOTEBOOK
Mont Present(FR)'s rider deserves plenty of credit for getting him up in the closing stages after looking set for another placed effort. Always in touch, he was under some strong pressure turning in, although not losing his pitch, but was not finding enough to get on terms until a strong run from the last saw him prevail. He disapointed slightly during the winter but that was due to the ground as he does need a decent surface. He will probably carry on through the summer where he can pay his way. (op 9-4)
Picture In The Sky(IRE) could not justify favouritism in a weak contest at Towcester but this was a much better performance. Racing prominently throughout he held every chance in the straight and stuck to his guns well all the way to the line. He can get off the mark if repeating this effort. (tchd 16-1)
Horseshoe Reef(AUS) made a bold effort from the front and looked the winner jumping the last only to get collared nearing the finish. He was a consistent performer over hurdles without winning but his turn over fences does not look too far away. (op 12-1)
I'm The Decider(IRE) produced a decent effort after his break and this progressive hurdler looks more than capable of making his presence felt in this sphere. He moved through from the rear to challenge in the straight and kept on well from the last. (op 5-1 tchd 11-2)
Hell's Bay(FR), a Grade 2 winner over hurdles in 2008, looked to have a very bright future but this was a second disappointing effort over fences so he is best watched at present. (op 10-3)
Willowpattern Official explanation: vet said mare pulled up lame

235 LADBROKES H'CAP HURDLE (8 hdls) 2m
3:50 (3:50) (Class 3) (0-125,125) 4-Y-0+ **£4,878** (£1,432; £716; £357)

Form RPR
60P- **1** **Pascha Bere (FR)**[31] 5099 7-11-12 **125**.......................(p) LiamTreadwell 134+
(Nick Gifford) *mde all: shkn up and styd on wl flat* **6/1**[2]
4F3- **2** 6 **Cool Touch (IRE)**[44] 4873 7-11-2 **115**.............................. PaddyBrennan 118
(Nigel Twiston-Davies) *hld up: racd keenly: hdwy 5th: chsd wnr 2 out: sn rdn: styd on same pce flat* **4/1**[1]
010- **3** 1 ½ **Alazan (IRE)**[55] 4648 4-11-0 **117**.................................... RichardJohnson 115
(Philip Hobbs) *hld up: hdwy appr 3 out: rdn after next: styd on same pce flat* **7/1**
256- **4** 1 ½ **Wheelavit (IRE)**[11] 51 7-10-2 **104**...........................(t) TommyPhelan(3) 106
(Claire Dyson) *nt fluent 1st: chsd wnr to next: remained handy: wnt 2nd again 5th tl rdn 2 out: no ex last* **28/1**
014- **5** 2 ½ **Sun Quest**[31] 5105 6-9-13 **105**.. RobertKirk(7) 103
(Steven Dixon) *chsd ldr after 2nd to 5th: sn rdn: styd on same pce fr 3 out* **10/1**
312- **6** 1 ¾ **Ring For Time**[23] 5209 7-11-0 **113**.. WillKennedy 109
(Dai Burchell) *hld up: rdn and outpcd 5th: styd on flat* **9/1**
11-1 **7** 1 ½ **Along The Nile**[8] 87 8-11-7 **120**................................(b) JamesReveley 114
(Keith Reveley) *hld up: bhd 3rd: hdwy 3 out: wknd next* **8/1**
6P2- **8** 7 **Playing With Fire (IRE)**[16] 5355 6-11-2 **115**...................... CharliePoste 104
(Robin Dickin) *hld up in tch: rdn and wknd appr 3 out* **16/1**
355- **9** 7 **Lepido (ITY)**[55] 4656 6-10-6 **105**...............................(b) TimmyMurphy 89
(Gary Moore) *hld up: hdwy appr 3 out: wknd bef next* **6/1**[2]
331- **10** 63 **Dean's Grange**[30] 5115 5-11-5 **118**... JoeTizzard 35
(Colin Tizzard) *mid-div: hdwy 4th: rdn and wknd appr 3 out* **13/2**[3]

3m 39.1s (-8.20) **Going Correction** -0.275s/f (Good)
WFA 4 from 5yo+ 18lb **10** Ran SP% **113.9**
Speed ratings (Par 107): **109,106,105,104,103 102,101,98,94,63**
Tote Swingers: 1&2 £6.50, 1&3 £9.20, 2&3 £7.70 CSF £30.08 CT £171.10 TOTE £8.90: £2.40, £1.30, £2.90; EX 24.90.
Owner Mr and Mrs Mark Tracey **Bred** S N C Regnier Et Al **Trained** Findon, W Sussex

FOCUS
A competitive handicap hurdle run at a fair pace.

NOTEBOOK
Pascha Bere(FR) produced a decent performance. This was a much deserved all-the-way success after contesting some decent handicaps throughout the winter including being placed in a couple of Listed events. The drop in class obviously was beneficial and fitting of cheek-pieces also seemed to help his cause. Connections felt he got ran off his feet a bit last time at Aintree so this was a good effort. (tchd 13-2)
Cool Touch(IRE) had been highly tried on debut for this yard and was a respectable third in a decent contest at Newbury. He was well supported for this. He moved through from the rear to chase the winner going to two out but was readily brushed aside soon after. (op 7-2)
Alazan(IRE) had been a beaten favourite on both tries in handicap company but he could only keep on at the same pace after mounting a challenge three out. His yard do well with this type during the summer and he should be capable of picking up a race off this mark. (op 17-2)
Wheelavit(IRE) had come on for his previous outing and ran respectably contesting a higher grade than usual. He held every chance when making a costly mistake three out. (op 33-1)
Sun Quest is running respectably at present and this was another solid effort. (op 14-1 tchd 9-1)
Ring For Time also put up another solid effort. (op 12-1)
Along The Nile, coming here on the back of a hat-trick, could never find the pace to get on terms after being held up. (op 6-1)

236 LADBROKES H'CAP CHASE (15 fncs) 2m 4f 110y
4:20 (4:20) (Class 3) (0-135,132) 5-Y-0+ **£5,854** (£1,719; £859; £429)

Form RPR
541- **1** **Warpath (IRE)**[14] 5 9-11-2 **122**...................................... PaulMoloney 131+
(Evan Williams) *chsd ldrs: led 15th: drvn out* **10/1**
211- **2** 1 **Prince Des Marais (FR)**[19] 5292 7-10-12 **118**........... AndrewThornton 127+
(Caroline Bailey) *a.p: racd keenly: ev ch last: styd on u.p* **7/1**[3]

355- **3** *4 ½* **Safari Adventures (IRE)**[18] 5309 8-10-10 **119**.......... CampbellGillies(3) 122
(Lucinda Russell) *led: mstke 4th: nt fluent 8th: rdn and hdd last: no ex flat* **11/1**

462- **4** *½* **Cossack Dancer (IRE)**[16] 5360 12-11-0 **120**..............(p) MattieBatchelor 121
(Mark Bradstock) *chsd ldr: mstke 1st: outpcd 4 out: swtchd lft appr last: r.o wl flat* **11/1**

U32- **5** *½* **Nikos Extra (FR)**[22] 5226 6-11-6 **126**......................... WayneHutchinson 127
(Alan King) *hld up: hdwy 11th: styd on towards fin: nt trble ldrs* **3/1**[1]

022- **6** *1 ¼* **Good Company (IRE)**[35] 5018 10-11-4 **124**........................ APMcCoy 124
(Jonjo O'Neill) *hld up: blnd 5th: hdwy 11th: rdn whn nt clr run and swtchd rt appr last: no ex flat* **6/1**[2]

004- **7** *10* **Nikola (FR)**[18] 5309 9-11-2 **127**........................... SamTwiston-Davies(5) 118
(Nigel Twiston-Davies) *chsd ldrs: ev ch 4 out: wknd last* **11/1**

4PF- **8** *15* **Silmi**[96] 3812 6-11-0 **120**.. CharliePoste 97
(Sophie Leech) *prom to 8th: t.o* **20/1**

604- **9** *27* **Flake**[22] 5232 10-10-11 **117**... TjadeCollier 64
(Sue Smith) *bhd fr 6th: t.o* **20/1**

322- **10** *6* **Kew Jumper (IRE)**[21] 5252 11-10-13 **119**........................ NickScholfield 60
(Andy Turnell) *got loose prior to the s: hld up: rdn and wknd after 11th: t.o* **10/1**

2PU- **P** **Battlecry**[30] 5111 9-11-12 **132**.. PaddyBrennan —
(Nigel Twiston-Davies) *racd in last pl tl p.u after 2nd* **9/1**

620- **P** **Free Gift**[200] 1852 12-11-1 **121**...(p) DarylJacob —
(R H & Mrs S Alner) *hld up: blnd 2nd: p.u bef next* **25/1**

36P- **P** **Amble Forge (IRE)**[78] 4171 8-10-10 **116**.............................(t) JoeTizzard —
(Colin Tizzard) *hld up: mstke 1st: in rr whn hit 10th: t.o whn p.u bef 4 out* **25/1**

4m 57.0s (-9.70) **Going Correction** -0.275s/f (Good) **13** Ran SP% **122.2**
Speed ratings: **107,106,104,104,104 104,100,94,84,81 —,—,—**
Tote Swingers: 1&2 £20.50, 1&3 £18.70, 2&3 £7.40 CSF £76.68 CT £794.21 TOTE £8.40: £3.90, £3.00, £4.50; EX 61.80 TRIFECTA Not won..
Owner R J Gambarini **Bred** Mrs Sue Hill **Trained** Llancarfan, Vale Of Glamorgan
⊠ Stewards' Enquiry : Nick Scholfield one-day ban: used whip when out of contention (May 23)

FOCUS
A decent 0-135 handicap chase run at a sound pace.

NOTEBOOK
Warpath(IRE) made light of a slipping mark when scoring at Ludlow when returning from seven-month break and was coming here off a 9lb higher mark. He travelled well behind the pacesetters and his rider allowed himself a look between his legs turning in only to see the majority of the field right on his tail. He made a mistake when challenging three out and neither was he particularly fluent two out, but led at the last and held on gamely. He does not hold many secrets but it is good heart at present. (op 9-1)
Prince Des Marais(FR) had been getting his act together of late after a wind operation and came here seeking his hat-trick. He travelled as well as the winner turning in with his rider not asking any questions until the last neared. He had to be switched on the run-in and kept on well to the line. It might have been interesting had his rider decided to commit him a little earlier. He is clearly in good health at present and should be capable adding to his tally. (op 13-2 tchd 6-1)
Safari Adventures(IRE) ran with plenty of credit but after trying to make all, he was coninually let down by going to his right at the fences. He has done all his winning at 2m but he saw this further half mile out well. (op 10-1)
Cossack Dancer(IRE) is a consistent performer at this level and put in another sound effort. Always up with the pace he stayed on at the same pace from four out. (tchd 12-1)
Nikos Extra(FR) is another to have been running consistently and was sent off favourite for this. He had to be given some reminders after the ninth and could never get on terms in the straight. (op 10-3 tchd 11-4)
Good Company(IRE) was returning to handicapping after a bout of hunter chasing recently. He came through to chase the leaders entering the straight but could never quite lay down a challenge before being hampered by the runner up going to the last. (op 15-2)
Battlecry Official explanation: jockey said gelding hit the first fence and lost its action
Free Gift Official explanation: jockey said gelding made a bad mistake at second fence and felt wrong

237 STORAGE KING FOR SPACE 01905 23449 INTERMEDIATE NH FLAT RACE (CONDITIONAL/AMATEURS) (DIV I) 2m

4:50 (4:52) (Class 6) 4-6-Y-0 **£1,370** (£399; £199)

Form RPR

1 **Kells Belle (IRE)** 4-10-0 0.. DavidBass(7) 102+
(Nicky Henderson) *hld up: hdwy over 4f out: shkn up to ld ins fnl f: edgd lft: r.o* **13/8**[1]

2 *1 ¼* **Arthur's Pass** 6-10-8 0... CiaranMckee(10) 112+
(Tom George) *chsd ldrs: led over 2f out: rdn over 1f out: hdd and unable qck ins fnl f* **11/2**

/22- **3** *12* **Thomas Wild**[26] 5179 5-10-11 0....................................... MattGriffiths(7) 100
(Philip Hobbs) *disp stdy pce 2f: chsd ldr tl led again over 6f out: rdn and hdd over 2f out: hung rt and wknd over 1f out* **3/1**[2]

6- **4** *1 ½* **Thoresby (IRE)**[55] 4649 4-10-9 0.................................. JamesHalliday(5) 95
(Ben Case) *hld up in tch: rdn and nt clr run 3f out: wknd 2f out* **5/1**[3]

0- **5** *9* **Midnight Place**[80] 4123 5-10-11 0..........................(t) MrRobertHawker(7) 90
(Richard Hawker) *hld up: rdn 6f out: hdwy u.p 3f out: hung lft and wknd over 2f out* **100/1**

0- **6** *¾* **Hidden Pleasure**[16] 5368 5-10-4 0................................... MrBenClarke(7) 82
(Nerys Dutfield) *hld up: hdwy 1/2-way: rdn and wknd over 3f out* **33/1**

7 *2 ½* **Ellie Wiggins** 4-10-4 0.. HarrySkelton(3) 75
(Bob Buckler) *disp stdy pce 2f: chsd ldrs tl rdn and wknd 3f out* **14/1**

8 *½* **Go Ruby Go** 6-10-4 0.. AdamWedge(7) 79
(Kevin Morgan) *hld up: racd keenly: hdwy 7f out: rdn and wknd over 2f out* **16/1**

0- **9** *9* **Yarlington Mill**[45] 4853 5-10-11 0..................................... MrJFlook(7) 77
(Edward Bevan) *plld hrd and prom: led after 2f: hdd over 6f out: rdn and wknd over 3f out: t.o* **100/1**

0- **10** *75* **Tenitemsplustoast**[58] 4575 4-10-9 0................................ KeiranBurke(5) —
(Patrick Rodford) *chsd ldrs: lost pl over 5f out: sn bhd: t.o* **66/1**

3m 47.4s (5.70) **Going Correction** -0.275s/f (Good)
WFA 4 from 5yo+ 4lb **10** Ran SP% **114.1**
Speed ratings: **74,73,67,66,62 61,60,60,55,18**
Tote Swingers: 1&2 £4.50, 1&3 £2.80, 2&3 £5.60 CSF £2.90 TOTE £2.90: £1.30, £2.30, £1.10; EX 14.80.
Owner Brian,Gwen,Terri & Kelly Griffiths **Bred** Brian And Gwen Griffiths **Trained** Upper Lambourn, Berks

FOCUS
An ordinary bumper run at a steady pace until they quickened turning out of the back straight with the front two coming clear and shaping as promising types.

NOTEBOOK
Kells Belle(IRE) looked fit and she had been pleasing in her prep work at home. She ran out a comfortable winner after travelling well for most of the way and only had to be pushed out to assert inside the final furlong. She was rather green when she hit the front but did all she was asked. (op 15-8 tchd 9-4)
Arthur's Pass took it up entering the straight and drew clear with the winner soon after but had no more to give when headed inside the final furlong. He looks capable of going one better in a similar comtest. (op 7-1 tchd 5-1)
Thomas Wild has now been placed on all four starts in bumpers. He raced prominently but could not quicken when the two principals drew clear in the straight and he sets just an ordinary standard. (op 5-2 tchd 2-1 and 10-3)
Thoresby(IRE) had shown promise on debut and again here. He lost his place down the back straight but moved back into contention turning in but could only keep on at the same pace. (op 8-1)

238 STORAGE KING FOR SPACE 01905 23449 INTERMEDIATE NH FLAT RACE CONDITIONAL AND AMATEURS') (DIV II) 2m

5:20 (5:23) (Class 6) 4-6-Y-0 **£1,370** (£399; £199)

Form RPR

2/3- **1** **Thecircleoftrust (FR)**[350] 442 5-10-8 0....................(t) CiaranMckee(10) 111+
(Tom George) *chsd ldrs: led 2f out: r.o wl* **6/1**[3]

23- **2** *5* **Islamouth**[92] 3901 6-10-11 0... JasonFavell(7) 106
(Kim Bailey) *trckd ldrs: racd kenly: led over 9f out: rdn and hdd 2f out: styd on same pce ins fnl f* **4/1**[2]

3 *2 ½* **Journeyman (IRE)** 4-10-7 0.. DavidBass(7) 99
(Nicky Henderson) *hld up: pushed along 6f out: hdwy over 2f out: r.o wl ins fnl f: nrst fin* **1/1**[1]

4 *1* **Grey Gold (IRE)** 5-11-1 0.. MrOGreenall(3) 102
(Richard Lee) *chsd ldrs: rdn over 3f out: hung lft and no ex fnl f* **20/1**

0- **5** *8* **Tocatchaprince (IRE)**[50] 4742 4-11-0 0......................... GerardTumelty 92+
(Alan King) *hld up: hdwy over 5f out: wknd over 2f out* **12/1**

6 *4 ½* **Rolline (IRE)** 5-10-4 0... MrDPick(7) 82
(Stuart Kittow) *plld hrd and prom: lost pl over 6f out: n.d after* **33/1**

0- **7** *3* **Russian Conquest**[34] 5035 4-10-11 0............................... HarrySkelton(3) 82
(Seamus Mullins) *hld up: hdwy over 4f out: wknd 3f out* **33/1**

8 *9* **Buckden (IRE)** 6-10-11 0.. MrJRoche(7) 77
(Sue Smith) *hld up: hdwy 1/2-way: wknd over 3f out: t.o* **25/1**

0- **9** *20* **The Dark Witch**[34] 5042 6-10-4 0................................. MissECrossman(7) 50
(Alan Blackmore) *plld hrd and prom: led after 2f: hdd over 9f out: wknd 6f out: t.o* **100/1**

10 *2* **Gemini June (IRE)** 6-10-4 0.. MrDHiskett(7) 48
(Martin Keighley) *hld up in tch: racd keenly: wknd over 3f out: t.o* **20/1**

04- **11** *28* **Original Prankster (IRE)**[66] 4405 5-10-13 0...... SamTwiston-Davies(5) 27
(Nigel Twiston-Davies) *plld hrd: led 2f: remained handy tl rdn 7f out: wknd 5f out: t.o* **18/1**

3m 37.0s (-4.70) **Going Correction** -0.275s/f (Good) **11** Ran SP% **117.5**
Speed ratings: **100,97,96,95,91 89,88,83,73,72 58**
Tote Swingers: 1&2 £3.50, 1&3 £2.70, 2&3 £2.00 CSF £7.70 TOTE £7.70: £1.80, £1.50, £1.10; EX 38.60 Place 6: £545.09 Place 5: £206.34.
Owner Mike Stratford and Steve Hurn **Bred** Martine Head **Trained** Slad, Gloucs

FOCUS
The second division of the bumper was run at a better pace than the first division and again delivered some promising performances.

NOTEBOOK
Thecircleoftrust(FR) was well backed and his supporters were rewarded with quite a comfortable success. He tracked the leaders before taking it up over two furlongs out only to be having to be pushed out to assert. He had shown some promise previously and was returning from 350-day absence. Should build upon this when switched to hurdling as he looks a promising sort. (op 12-1)
Islamouth set the standard on a RPR of 116 and probably ran to that level. He took the lead halfway down the back straight and stayed on well enough when headed over two furlongs out. As with the winner he looks capable of holding his own when switched to hurdling. (op 9-2 tchd 7-2)
Journeyman(IRE) was struggling from a long way out but to his credit stayed on well in the straight. He will have benefited from the outing. (op 10-11)
Grey Gold(IRE) made an encouraging debut, he turned in holding every chance but could not sustain the effort and ultimately was run out of third spot nearing the finish but was clear of the remainder. (op 16-1)
Original Prankster(IRE) Official explanation: jockey said gelding lost its action
T/Jkpt: Not won. T/Plt: £165.80. Pool: £72,514.46 - 319.18 winning units. T/Qpdt: £18.10. Pool: £5,599.09 - 227.96 winning units. CR

239 - 248a (Foreign Racing) - See Raceform Interactive

[21]TOWCESTER (R-H)

Monday, May 10

OFFICIAL GOING: Good to firm
Wind: light half across Weather: overcast and cold

249 NIFTYLIFT MAIDEN HURDLE (11 hdls) 2m 5f

6:00 (6:03) (Class 4) 4-Y-0+ **£3,577** (£1,050; £525; £262)

Form RPR

63-2 **1** **Entertain Me**[9] 100 6-10-7 98.. CharliePoste 109+
(Robin Dickin) *cl up: led bef 7th: 7 l clr 2 out: mstke last: rdn and kpt on wl flat* **11/4**[1]

24-2 **2** *5* **Yonder**[11] 64 6-10-7 99...(t) TomScudamore 102
(Hughie Morrison) *mounted on crse and taken down early: racd keenly and prom: mstke 3rd: disp ld briefly 8th: rdn and outpcd bef 2 out where regained mod 2nd: no ch w wnr* **5/1**[2]

052- **3** *10* **Silver Phoenix**[48] 4811 6-10-2 68....................................(p) IanPopham(5) 93
(Caroline Keevil) *settled midfield: effrt gng wl bef 3 out: wnt 2nd and rdn but outpcd by wnr bef next: sn reluctant in 3rd and racing awkwardly* **12/1**

00-3 **4** *2 ½* **Miller's Dawn**[11] 64 6-11-0 100.....................................(p) SamThomas 97
(Henrietta Knight) *chsd ldrs: rdn in 4th 3 out: woefully one pce and n.d after* **8/1**

0P0- **5** *35* **Dancing Legend**[20] 5294 4-9-13 0.................................. SeanQuinlan(3) 50
(Nigel Twiston-Davies) *bhd: lost tch 5th: struggling bdly fr 7th: sn t.o* **66/1**

0- **6** *5* **Poacher's Dream (IRE)**[14] 21 8-11-0 0.............................. ColinBolger 57
(Jonathen de Giles) *bhd: lost tch 4th: t.o and rdn 7th: mstke 3 out* **150/1**

5/0- **R** **Chouromanesco (FR)**[177] 2272 7-11-0 0........................ MattieBatchelor —
(Mark Bradstock) *plld v hrd and hanging violently lft: led 3rd tl 4th: unrideable whn rn off crse after next* **33/1**

/00- **F** **Jays Cottage**[31] 5117 7-10-9 0..................................... MichaelMurphy(5) —
(Jim Old) *poor 13th whn fell 4th* **125/1**

/40- **P** **Ironical (IRE)**[86] 4042 6-11-0 0... PaddyBrennan —
(Nigel Twiston-Davies) *chsd ldrs: rdn and no rspnse 7th: 6th whn hung bdly lft after next: virtually unrideable after: p.u after 3 out* **6/1**[3]

P52- **P** **Bobbisox (IRE)**[57] 4609 5-10-7 98.. FelixDeGiles —
(Alex Hales) *terrible mstke 2nd and rdr lost iron: nvr nr ldrs after: struggling after 6th: t.o and p.u 3 out* **11/4**[1]

0P/ **P** **Joli Al**^{382} [5165] 6-10-9 0 .... MarcGoldstein(5) —
(Michael Roberts) *t.k.h v briefly: tried to run out 2nd: wknd 4th: sn hopelessly t.o: p.u 6th: dismntd* **200/1**

0/ **P** **Pretti Woman (FR)**^{439} [4138] 7-10-7 0 .... SeamusDurack —
(Michael Roberts) *drvn and struggling 5th: sn hopelessly t.o: p.u 6th* **150/1**

00P- **P** **Eros Moon (IRE)**^{17} [5354] 6-11-0 0 .... (b^{1}) RobertThornton —
(Alan King) *plld hrd and v awkward: sn led: hdd 3rd: led again 5th: hdd bef 7th: sn downed tools: t.o and p.u 2 out* **25/1**

0- **P** **Delgany Diva**^{35} [5050] 5-10-7 0 .... AndrewThornton —
(Ben Pollock) *hanging violently lft and unrideable: already t.o whn bdly hmpd 4th: sn p.u* **250/1**

5m 11.3s (-15.90) **Going Correction** -1.375s/f (Hard)
WFA 4 from 5yo+ 19lb **14** Ran SP% **114.4**
Speed ratings (Par 105): **97,95,91,90,77 75,—,—,—,— —,—,—,—**
toteswingers:1&2:£3.30, 1&3:£16.60, 2&3:£16.00 CSF £15.79 TOTE £4.80: £1.70, £1.10, £5.00; EX 12.70.
Owner Mrs A L Merry **Bred** Mrs A L Merry **Trained** Atherstone on Stour, Warwicks

FOCUS
A poor race and the future is bleak for quite a few of these, some of whom were getting detached before halfway. A group of three drew clear leaving the back. The first two are rated to their marks.

NOTEBOOK
Entertain Me began to pour it on approaching the second-last flight and, although she made a bit of a mess of the final obstacle, this improving mare had the race in safekeeping on the short run-in. Her last couple of runs have been much more encouraging after a slow start to her career and she confirmed that promise by posting an authoritative performance. (op 7-2)
Yonder, who went to post very early, was always front rank but she was readily brushed aside by the winner and her best efforts so far have come on much easier tracks than this. (op 7-2)
Silver Phoenix, just as at Southwell last time, travelled smoothly into contention but could only plug on at the one pace when coming under pressure. However, given she is rated over two stone inferior to the pair in front of her, she has performed with credit and would have be of interest if dropped in grade. (op 16-1)
Miller's Dawn plugged on without ever really looking like getting on terms and doesn't seem to be progressing, while the rest were in a different county.
Chouromanesco(FR) Official explanation: jockey said gelding hung badly left
Ironical(IRE) Official explanation: jockey said gelding hung badly left
Bobbisox(IRE) Official explanation: trainer had no explanation for the poor form shown
Joli Al Official explanation: vet said gelding pulled up lame
Delgany Diva Official explanation: jockey said mare jumped poorly and hung badly left

250 NIFTYLIFT (S) HURDLE (8 hdls) 2m
6:30 (6:30) (Class 5) 4-8-Y-O **£1,951** (£573; £286; £143)

Form RPR

5/P- **1** **Den Maschine**^{17} [5352] 5-10-12 0 .... TomO'Brien 115+
(John Flint) *trckd ldrs: effrt gng wl to ld 3 out: kpt wandering but drawing clr bef next: wl in command appr last* **8/1**^{3}

343- **2** *10* **Stir On The Sea (IRE)**^{14} [19] 4-10-1 105 .... TomScudamore 89
(Rebecca Curtis) *prom: t.k.h: led bef 3 out where hdd: sn drvn: one pce and wl hld fr 2 out* **13/8**^{1}

026- **3** *7* **Kirkhammerton (IRE)**^{17} [5357] 8-11-2 100 .... DannyCook(3) 100
(Barry Leavy) *prom: hmpd 4th: drvn and ev ch bef 3 out: lost tch w ldrs bef next* **12/1**

433- **4** *7* **Bari Bay**^{32} [5100] 4-9-10 69 .... JimmyDerham(5) 76
(Seamus Mullins) *lost tch 2nd: hmpd 4th: plugged on into 4th 3 out: rdn and struggling wl bef next* **18/1**

/5-P **5** *31* **Doubly Sharp (USA)**^{9} [95] 7-11-5 0 .... (b) AndrewThornton 62
(Caroline Bailey) *plld hrd: led tl hdd bef 3 out: gave up instantly: t.o next* **50/1**

440- **6** *1 ¾* **Vacario (GER)**^{31} [5119] 6-11-5 113 .... (bt^{1}) RichardJohnson 60
(Charlie Mann) *j. and hung lft and sulking thrght: lost tch 2nd: t.o whn hmpd 5th* **11/4**^{2}

603- **7** *1 ¾* **Knar Mardy**^{12} [52] 5-10-7 81 ow5 .... (p) AdamPogson(3) 50
(Charles Pogson) *hld up last: lost tch 2nd: t.o next: impeded 4th* **16/1**

36P- **P** **Decree Nisi**^{214} [1673] 7-11-5 0 .... (v) LiamTreadwell —
(P Kelsall) *lost tch 2nd: nvr keen: t.o 5th: wnt wrong and p.u 2 out* **100/1**

0P0/ **F** **Musical Affair**^{563} [1822] 6-10-5 0 .... WillKennedy —
(F Jordan) *6th whn stmbld and fell after 2nd* **250/1**

6P-4 **B** **Bold Policy (IRE)**^{6} [135] 7-11-5 97 .... (b^{1}) WarrenMarston —
(Milton Harris) *prom: drvn into 4th and b.d* **12/1**

505- **F** **Kelly Manor (IRE)**^{20} [5294] 6-10-0 87 .... (v^{1}) LeeEdwards(5) —
(Tony Carroll) *pressed ldr tl fell 4th* **12/1**

3m 44.5s (-23.40) **Going Correction** -1.375s/f (Hard)
WFA 4 from 5yo+ 18lb **11** Ran SP% **113.4**
Speed ratings: **103,98,94,91,75 74,73,—,—,— —**
toteswingers:1&2:£7.80, 1&3:£24.40, 2&3:£6.70 CSF £21.21 TOTE £12.20: £3.90, £1.10, £5.00; EX 55.70.There was no bid for the winner
Owner Paul Morgan **Bred** York Stut & Stald Rainbow **Trained** Kenfig Hill, Bridgend

FOCUS
The easy winner was value for further but this is probably not strong selling form with the runner-up a stone off her Ffos Las level.

NOTEBOOK
Den Maschine left behind previous hurdling efforts to score in some style. Always travelling smoothly, he cruised upsides form choice Stir On The Sea after the third last before skipping clear, despite still looking quite green and immature, and pinging the last in the manner of a horse capable of holding his own in better company in time. It transpired that this five-year-old went wrong when pulling up at Bangor last month but he proved here that he is not without considerable ability and, in hammering the 105-rated runner-up while conceding 11lb, he posted a pretty smart performance for the grade. (op 10-1)
Stir On The Sea(IRE) ran with credit in a handicap last time and looked to have leading claims on her first start in selling company but she's been a touch unfortunate to bump into a dark one. She has finished clear of the rest and is more than capable of winning in this grade. (op 6-4 tchd 11-8 and 7-4)
Kirkhammerton(IRE) also appreciated the drop back to selling company having been below par in a handicap at Bangor last time but he was made to look quite one-paced and his wins, on the Flat and one success over hurdles, have all come on flatter tracks. (op 10-1 tchd 14-1)
Bari Bay, a 69-rated maiden, fared best of the rest but her form is a long way shy of what is normally required to win, even in this grade. (op 20-1 tchd 22-1)
Vacario(GER) was never going in the first-time blinkers and looked totally out of love with the game. A dark cloud hangs over him now. Official explanation: jockey said gelding never travelled (op 5-2 tchd 9-4)

Decree Nisi Official explanation: vet said gelding pulled up lame

251 NIFTYLIFT H'CAP CHASE (18 fncs) 3m 110y
7:00 (7:00) (Class 4) (0-100,96) 5-Y-0+**£4,435** (£1,310; £655; £327; £163)

Form RPR

32P- **1** **Gerrard (IRE)**^{57} [4611] 12-10-4 **79** .... (b) SamTwiston-Davies(5) 94+
(Althea Barclay) *trckd ldrs gng wl: lft 3rd after 11th: led bef 15th: 14 l clr 2 out: rdn and wl in command after* **6/1**

452- **2** *7* **Early Wings (GER)**^{14} [24] 8-11-5 **89** .... AndrewThornton 95
(Caroline Bailey) *j. slowly 3rd: midfield: clsd to 2nd after 11th: 3rd and rdn and outpcd after 15th: wnt 2nd bef 2 out: kpt plodding on but nvr looked like catching wnr* **4/1**^{1}

U46- **3** *19* **Caspar Of Tarsus (IRE)**^{30} [5133] 7-11-2 **89** .... EamonDehdashti(3) 81+
(Gerald Ham) *rdr lost iron 1st: belted several fences: chsd ldrs: rdn 12th: wnt 8 l 3rd 3 out: sn outpcd: wl btn whn j.rt and rdr wnt sideways two out* **12/1**

PP1- **4** *16* **Arceye**^{17} [5361] 13-10-8 **81** .... (p) DerekLaverty(3) 51
(William Davies) *chsd ldrs tl hit 10th and 11th: sn wl bhd: t.o 3 out* **9/1**

2P4- **5** *8* **Jacarado (IRE)**^{14} [24] 12-11-0 **84** .... (v) HenryOliver 46
(Robin Dickin) *j. slowly 5th: rdn and no zest after: struggling 12th: laboured on: t.o 3 out* **12/1**

400- **6** *3 ¾* **Ash High (IRE)**^{75} [4240] 7-11-8 **92** .... PaddyBrennan 53
(Nigel Twiston-Davies) *pressed ldr: drew upsides 9th tl lft in ld 11th: hdd after 15th: fdd bdly up hill: out on his feet after last* **14/1**

040- **P** **Khazar (FR)**^{19} [5312] 7-11-5 **89** .... (t) APMcCoy —
(Jonjo O'Neill) *midfield: mstke 6th: u.p 9th: nt co-operating after: j.v.slowly 11th: t.o and p.u 3 out* **10/1**

525- **P** **Well Mick (IRE)**^{14} [24] 9-10-6 **76** .... FelixDeGiles —
(Jonathen de Giles) *nvr gng wl: last and rdn 6th: t.o 10th: p.u 12th* **5/1**^{2}

5U6- **U** **Gershwinner (IRE)**^{14} [24] 7-11-12 **96** .... (b^{1}) JasonMaguire —
(Donald McCain) *racd keenly: led: jnd 9th: w ldr whn stmbld and uns rdr 11th* **11/2**^{3}

1P4- **U** **Commanche Dream**^{26} [5185] 7-11-2 **86** .... MattieBatchelor —
(Simon Lewis) *bhd: rdn 6th: mstke 8th and struggling after: 45 l last whn pckd and rdr toppled off 3 out* **25/1**

6m 17.7s (-19.20) **Going Correction** -0.625s/f (Firm) **10** Ran SP% **111.3**
Speed ratings: **105,102,96,91,89 87,—,—,—,—**
toteswingers:1&2:£3.70, 1&3:£14.30, 2&3:£11.40 CSF £29.61 CT £269.28 TOTE £4.60: £1.40, £1.80, £3.30; EX 35.40.
Owner Mrs Althea Barclay **Bred** Niall Delany **Trained** Oddington, Gloucs

FOCUS
A moderate handicap and a slow-motion finish. The winner posted his best figure for a while with the second rated to his mark.

NOTEBOOK
Gerrard(IRE) threw in a stinker when last seen but, given a break since, he bounced back to something like his best to register track win number two. Although 3lb higher than when scoring here last term, the 12-year-old is competitive off this sort of mark when on a going day and, having gone clear turning in the straight, two good jumps sealed the race for him. (op 13-2)
Early Wings(GER) posted yet another solid effort in defeat, keeping on stoutly up the run in to close on the winner, but he remains winless after 26 starts over jumps which has to be cause for concern.
Caspar Of Tarsus(IRE), another with a poor strike-rate, has struggled since winning at Hereford in February and he could never land a blow here, although conditions may have been a bit quicker than ideal. (tchd 11-1)
Arceye's poor jumping contributed his downfall and he's far too inconsistent nowadays. (op 11-1)
Jacarado(IRE) was also slow at some of his fences and was a spent force by the home turn. (op 17-2 tchd 8-1)
Well Mick(IRE) attracted some support beforehand but was never travelling and his best efforts have all come on an easier surface. (op 7-1)

252 NIFTYLIFT H'CAP HURDLE (8 hdls) 2m
7:30 (7:31) (Class 4) (0-105,102) 4-Y-0**£4,119** (£1,216; £608; £304; £152)

Form RPR

P00/ **1** **Jeu De Roseau (IRE)**^{742} [22] 6-10-6 **82** .... DenisO'Regan 91+
(Chris Grant) *j. deliberately 1st: towards rr: rdn and hdwy bef 3 out: stl 4th and struggling to pick up bef 2 out: drvn and sustained run to ld last: sn asserted flat: fine ride* **6/4**^{1}

335- **2** *1* **Ruby Crown**^{36} [5015] 8-11-5 **95** .... JasonMaguire 102
(Kim Bailey) *last and reminders after 2nd: gd prog on inner after 3 out: 5 l 4th 2 out: hrd drvn to jump last w wnr: fnd less than him after but fine ride* **8/1**^{3}

321- **3** *1 ½* **Midnight Spirit**^{17} [5363] 10-11-3 **100** .... (tp) AnthonyFreeman(7) 106
(Frederick Sutherland) *racd freely in 2nd or 3rd: rdn to ld bef 2 out: hdd nring last: kpt on cl home* **12/1**

F0-4 **4** *9* **Manjam (IRE)**^{11} [55] 6-11-5 **95** .... (tp) APMcCoy 93
(Rebecca Curtis) *led at str pce: rdn and hdd bef 2 out: no ex appr last* **5/1**^{2}

32P- **5** *11* **Perlon (FR)**^{43} [4918] 5-11-0 **97** .... JoshuaMoore(7) 83
(Gary Moore) *hld up: effrt 3 out: sn drvn: 5th and wkng bef next* **25/1**

061- **6** *1 ½* **Miss Mamma Wagga (IRE)**^{20} [5295] 7-11-0 **90** .... ChristianWilliams 74
(Lawney Hill) *a bhd: virtually t.o whn mstke 5th: plugged on* **11/1**

F00- **7** *2 ¾* **Eddie Dowling**^{43} [4918] 5-10-9 **85** .... (tp) CharliePoste 68
(Milton Harris) *chsd ldrs: effrt 3 out: briefly 3rd and rdn bef next: btn whn mstke 2 out* **66/1**

653- **8** *1 ½* **Wingull (IRE)**^{14} [23] 6-11-4 **94** .... AndrewTinkler 74
(George Baker) *bhd early: struggling bef 3 out* **12/1**

521- **9** *6* **More Like It (IRE)**^{15} [10] 10-11-5 **95** .... (p) BrianHughes 69
(Peter Niven) *chsd ldrs: rdn after 4th: btn next* **20/1**

304- **10** *nk* **Witch Of The Wave (IRE)**^{21} [5290] 4-11-1 **95** .... (t) RobertThornton 67
(Joanna Davis) *pressed ldrs: blnd and reminder 4th: 3rd whn blnd 3 out: nt rcvr: nt pushed fr next* **20/1**

053- **11** *nk* **Tora Petcha (IRE)**^{179} [2240] 7-11-6 **99** .... DannyCook(3) 72
(Barry Leavy) *pressed ldrs: drvn bef 5th: nt run on and sn btn* **16/1**

135- **12** *2 ¼* **Tom O'Tara**^{17} [5357] 6-11-8 **98** .... AidanColeman 69
(Robin Dickin) *midfield: rdn bef 3 out: sn struggling* **16/1**

/00- **P** **Gilded Youth**^{355} [401] 6-11-2 **92** .... MattieBatchelor —
(Simon Lewis) *plld frenetically: sn w ldr tl stopped to nil bef 4th: t.o and p.u next* **66/1**

3m 46.4s (-21.50) **Going Correction** -1.375s/f (Hard)
WFA 4 from 5yo+ 18lb **13** Ran SP% **119.6**
Speed ratings (Par 105): **98,97,96,92,86 86,84,83,80,80 80,79,—**
toteswingers:1&2:£4.20, 1&3:£5.80, 2&3:£8.40 CSF £13.30 CT £109.71 TOTE £2.20: £1.10, £2.10, £8.60; EX 17.50.
Owner W Raw **Bred** P Connolly **Trained** Newton Bewley, Co Durham

⊠ Jeu De Roseau was part of an enormous four-horse gamble orchestrated by his former trainer Barney Curley.

FOCUS
A modest handicap hurdle and a race dominated by the monumental gamble on the winner. The winner can rate higher and the next two ran to their marks.

NOTEBOOK
Jeu De Roseau(IRE) was as big as 25-1 in the morning, yet was sent off a 6-4 favourite. Not seen for just over two years, the six-year-old showed very little when last seen but bits and pieces of earlier form, not least when just 3l behind Won In The Dark, entitled him to huge respect off this lowly mark of 82. Although his hurdling was not entirely fluent early, it improved as the race progressed as he made headway up the inside and, produced upsides at the last, he pinged it before staying on strongly to land the plunge under a fine ride. (op 9-4 tchd 5-4)
Ruby Crown appreciate the return to a sound surface and put up an improved performance. She went down all guns blazing and seems to like this venue. (op 15-2 tchd 13-2)
Midnight Spirit, who was always front rank, wasn't great at the second last but he maintained his good run of form with another solid effort despite having been hiked up 8lb. (tchd 10-1)
Manjam(IRE) got outpaced by the principals after the last but he's better suited by a stiffer test of stamina so this wasn't a bad run at all. (op 6-1)

253 NIFTYLIFT HUNTERS' CHASE (18 fncs) 3m 110y
8:00 (8:00) (Class 6) 5-Y-0+ **£1,561** (£484; £242; £121)

Form RPR
1/1- **1** **Coolefind (IRE)**[19] 5314 12-11-13 119 .... MrJonathanBailey(7) 119+
(W J Warner) *enthusiastic chsng ldr: clsd on bit 2 out: led between last two: sn in command* **4/5**[1]
0U3- **2** *4 1/2* **Fruitfull Citizen (IRE)**[7] 10-11-2 92 .... MsLucyJones(7) 100
(Simon Jones) *generally j. beautifull: led: rdn and hdd between last two: kpt on gamely but outclassed by wnr* **15/2**[3]
025- **3** *28* **Oopsmylord (IRE)**[23] 5233 8-12-2 115 .... MrDMansell 82
(S Flook) *blnd bdly 4th: nt fluent 10th: last of three gng clr after next: 10 l 3rd and outpcd 15th: no ch fr next: bmpd along and jst hld poor 3rd* **4/1**[2]
P2U- **4** *nse* **Back Nine (IRE)**[22] 13-11-13 95 .... (t) MrJHamer(7) 83
(Miss Jane Western) *rdn fr 6th: outpcd 11th: 4th but 10 l fr ldrs next: plugged on for driving fr 2 out and nrly snatched poor 3rd* **15/2**[3]
41P- **5** *33* **Picabo Kid (USA)**[9] 7-11-9 111 .... MissBAndrews(7) 46
(Mrs C H Covell) *rdn in spurs: drvn fr 7th: lost tch 11th: t.o 13th* **11/1**
0/ **P** **Bouncing Bob**[22] 9-11-5 0 .... MrJGoss(7) —
(Miss Jo Pearson) *rdn 10th: struggling next: blnd 15th: t.o last whn crashed over 2 out and p.u* **40/1**

6m 15.1s (-21.80) **Going Correction** -0.625s/f (Firm) **6** Ran SP% **109.9**
Speed ratings: **109,107,98,98,88 —**
toteswingers:1&2:£2.20, 1&3:£1.10, 2&3:£3.20 CSF £7.16 TOTE £1.50: £1.10, £2.60; EX 6.20.
Owner Mrs Judy Wilson **Bred** Michael Gowen **Trained** Northampton, Northants

FOCUS
An uncompetitive hunter chase. The winner was value for further and the first two are rated pretty much to their marks.

NOTEBOOK
Coolefind(IRE) proved different class under a cool ride. Always stalking the leader, he sauntered upsides approaching the last before going clear on the run-in to enhance an already hugely impressive strike-rate. (op 5-6 tchd 10-11 in places)
Fruitfull Citizen(IRE) gave it a good go from the front, jumping big and bold at times, but she was a sitting duck in the straight. (op 7-1)
Oopsmylord(IRE) made a bad mistake early. He soon recovered but was struggling leaving the back and was left behind. (tchd 9-2)

254 NIFTYLIFT MAIDEN OPEN NATIONAL HUNT FLAT RACE 2m
8:30 (8:30) (Class 5) 4-6-Y-0 **£1,951** (£573; £286; £143)

Form RPR
25- **1** **Ben Cee Pee M (IRE)**[30] 5137 5-11-2 0 .... LeightonAspell 105+
(Oliver Sherwood) *t.k.h trcking ldrs on inner: produced to ld over 1f out: sn clr: rdn out* **5/1**[3]
000- **2** *2 3/4* **Meridiem**[35] 5050 6-11-2 0 .... TomScudamore 99
(Sean Regan) *bhd: effrt on inner 3f out: rdn to go 2nd 1f out: no ch w wnr* **66/1**
3 *1 1/2* **Midnight King** 4-10-12 0 .... AndrewTinkler 94
(George Baker) *trckd ldrs: rdn to go 2nd over 1f out: rn green and hung rt and faltered: 3rd and no ex 1f out* **4/1**[1]
524- **4** *3 3/4* **Brooklyn Bay**[23] 5235 5-10-11 0 .... JamesHalliday(5) 94
(Malcolm Jefferson) *led at v modest pce for 5f: rdn to ld again over 2f out: hdd and wavered and wknd over 1f out* **9/2**[2]
4- **5** *3 1/4* **Tears From Heaven (USA)**[16] 5391 4-10-12 0 .... BrianHughes 87
(Peter Niven) *prom: drvn and ev ch over 2f out: fdd over 1f out* **9/2**[2]
06- **6** *2 1/2* **Golden Celebration**[18] 5332 4-10-12 0 .... ColinBolger 84
(Chris Gordon) *stdd in last: stl 8 l last 5f out: plugged on but no ch* **20/1**
7 *1 1/4* **Restless Harriet** 4-10-5 0 .... CharliePoste 76
(Robin Dickin) *trckd ldrs: slt ld on outer 3f out tl rdn and hdd over 2f out: fdd over 1f out* **25/1**
8 *2* **Old Emily Rose** 5-10-4 0 .... SamTwiston-Davies(5) 78
(Althea Barclay) *v green and awkward in rr: rdn 6f out: btn 3f out* **22/1**
9 *1 3/4* **Barnack** 4-10-9 0 .... SeanQuinlan(3) 79
(Pam Sly) *towards rr and green: btn 3f out* **11/2**
0- **10** *3/4* **Sunnyhill Gal**[54] 4683 4-10-0 0 .... JimmyDerham(5) 71
(Milton Harris) *towards rr: effrt 4f out: btn over 2f out* **14/1**
11 *1 1/2* **Hunting Red**[65] 5-10-9 0 .... FelixDeGiles 74
(Jonathen de Giles) *slt ld after 5f tl rdn and hdd 3f out: lost pl qckly* **25/1**
12 *4 1/2* **Harry Masters**[29] 6-10-9 0 .... MrJFlook(7) 76
(Edward Bevan) *in tch 12f* **50/1**

3m 57.6s (-4.70) **Going Correction** -1.375s/f (Hard)
WFA 4 from 5yo+ 4lb **12** Ran SP% **115.3**
Speed ratings: **56,54,53,52,50 49,48,47,46,46 45,43**
toteswingers:1&2:£24.80, 1&3:£13.20, 2&3:not won CSF £314.25 TOTE £4.70: £1.90, £25.00, £5.80; EX 264.10 Place 6 £19.19; Place 5 £10.19.
Owner CPM Group Limited **Bred** Daniel Fogarty **Trained** Upper Lambourn, Berks

FOCUS
Probably just an average bumper. The winner was value for further.

NOTEBOOK
Ben Cee Pee M(IRE) confirmed the promise of his Southwell debut by posting an authoritative success, despite racing very freely in the early stages. He took over on the inside turning for home before really finding his stride up the hill to maintain a healthy advantage and give the impression he'll stay much further, especially if learning to settle better. (tchd 11-2)
Meridiem had been thrashed on all three previous starts but this was an infinitely better performance and he travelled like quite a decent horse off the pace before finding plenty for pressure. It's hard to know what inspired this huge improvement, but he's clearly not the poor performer he looked previously. (tchd 80-1)
Midnight King was a bit too keen for his own good early but he shaped with promise, despite wandering around in the final couple of furlongs, and ought to improve for this experience. (op 7-1)
Brooklyn Bay has shaped with promise on all starts and he was clear of the remainder. Connections think he'll be a much better horse next year over hurdles. (tchd 4-1)
Tears From Heaven(USA) dropped away in the closing stages (as he did on debut) and hasn't really built on his Market Rasen run, but he might fare better back on a less demanding track.
T/Plt: £21.70. Pool: £580,074.35 - 2,684.48 winning units. T/Qpdt: £8.60. Pool: £5,794.39 - 497.39 winning units. IM

255a - 262a (Foreign Racing) - See Raceform Interactive

[167]NEWTON ABBOT (L-H)
Tuesday, May 11

OFFICIAL GOING: Good (good to firm in places;7.4)
Wind: virtuall nil Weather: light rain at times

263 PADDOCK RESTAURANT MARES' NOVICES' HURDLE (8 hdls) 2m 3f
6:00 (6:00) (Class 4) 4-Y-0+ **£3,740** (£1,098; £549; £274)

Form RPR
32F- **1** **Synthe Davis (FR)**[20] 5317 5-10-12 115 .... APMcCoy 89+
(Nicky Henderson) *in tch: wnt cl 3rd 3 out: rdn to ld 2 out: kpt on: rdn out* **8/11**[1]
332- **2** *1 1/2* **Way Back When**[36] 5042 5-10-12 0 .... RobertThornton 85
(Alan King) *in tch: nt fluent 2nd: rdn to dispute cl 3rd after 3 out: kpt on: wnt 2nd sn after last* **4/1**[2]
035- **3** *nk* **Be My Light (IRE)**[13] 50 4-10-7 0 .... PaddyBrennan 80
(Charlie Longsdon) *hld up: hdwy appr 6th: rdn after 3 out: styd on: wnt 3rd run-in* **11/2**[3]
004- **4** *1 1/4* **Detroit Red**[18] 5363 4-10-4 0 .... HaddenFrost(3) 79
(Martin Hill) *prom: rdn to ld after 3 out: hdd next: no ex whn lost 2nd/3rd run-in* **20/1**
066- **5** *2 3/4* **Mangonel**[15] 16 6-10-12 72 .... (v) RodiGreene 81
(Stuart Howe) *led: rdn and hdd after 3 out: kpt on tl no ex appr last* **40/1**
55-0 **6** *5* **Kapborg (FR)**[5] 182 4-10-7 0 .... (t) TomScudamore 71
(David Pipe) *hld up: rdn after 3 out: no imp* **25/1**
0- **7** *5* **Just Lola**[32] 5122 6-10-5 0 .... (t) MarkQuinlan(7) 71
(Neil Mulholland) *a towards rr* **100/1**
8 *31* **Illegale (IRE)**[211] 4-10-7 0 .... AidanColeman 35
(Venetia Williams) *mid-div tl wknd after 3 out: t.o* **10/1**
9 *dist* **Dunnicks County**[16] 7-10-7 0 .... KeiranBurke(5) —
(Patrick Rodford) *chsd ldrs tl after 5th: sn wl t.o* **200/1**
0P/ **P** **River Conquest**[45] 6-10-12 0 .... DougieCostello —
(Neil Mulholland) *chsd ldrs tl dropped in rr 5th: wknd next: t.o whn p.u bef 2 out* **100/1**

4m 36.1s (2.20) **Going Correction** -0.125s/f (Good)
WFA 4 from 5yo+ 18lb **10** Ran SP% **115.9**
Speed ratings (Par 105): **90,89,89,88,87 86,83,69,—,—**
toteswingers: 1&2 £1.90, 1&3 £2.20, 2&3 £3.20 CSF £3.74 TOTE £1.80: £1.10, £1.10, £1.30; EX 3.80.
Owner Sir Robert Ogden **Bred** Claude Quellier **Trained** Upper Lambourn, Berks

FOCUS
A weak mares' novice event, run at an ordinary gallop. The winner is rated more than two stone below her best.

NOTEBOOK
Synthe Davis(FR) got off the mark as a hurdler at the eighth time of asking, but had to work hard to land the odds. She did take a heavy fall at Southwell 20 days earlier, so this should get her back on track. It will be interesting to see whether she turns out at Aintree Friday, but remains a likely candidate to head to the Sales next week. (op 4-6 tchd 8-13 and 4-5 in places)
Way Back When, placed in all three of her outings in bumpers, is going to need further as a hurdler on the evidence of this outing. She may have also found the ground quick enough for her liking and can be found an opening in the coming weeks. (tchd 9-2)
Be My Light(IRE), up in trip, attracted support and would have gone plenty closer had she not wandered about under pressure coming to the second-last. She now has to prove that was not down to temperamental issues. (op 9-1)
Detroit Red posted a solid effort under a positive ride on this step up in trip and probably ran close enough to her previous level, so helps to set the standard. (op 16-1)
Mangonel only gave way coming to the last, but she had the run of the race and is rated 72, so rather sums up the strength of this race.

264 WINNING POST (S) HURDLE (8 hdls) 2m 3f
6:30 (6:30) (Class 5) 4-Y-0+ **£2,055** (£599; £299)

Form RPR
022- **1** **Helen Wood**[15] 23 7-10-5 105 .... (bt) TomScudamore 109+
(David Pipe) *trckd ldrs: lft in ld appr 3 out: rdn after 2 out: mstke last: kpt on: drvn out* **5/2**[1]
053- **2** *1 1/2* **Cantabilly (IRE)**[8] 4966 7-10-5 112 .... MattGriffiths(7) 113
(Ron Hodges) *mid-div: hdwy to trck ldng pair appr 6th: lft 2nd bef 3 out: sn rdn: kpt on to draw wl clr of remainder: a being hld by wnr* **3/1**[2]
/P0- **3** *27* **Intac (IRE)**[18] 5365 8-11-4 102 .... JoeTizzard 95
(Colin Tizzard) *mid-div: rdn into 5th at the 6th: plugged on after 3 out: nvr any ch: wnt modest 3rd last* **16/1**
P00- **4** *6* **Go Free**[64] 4483 9-10-5 85 .... CharlieWallis(7) 84
(John O'Shea) *trckd ldrs: rdn appr 6th: lft 3rd 3 out: sn no ch: lost modest 3rd last* **33/1**
145- **5** *2 1/4* **Brigadore (USA)**[22] 5290 7-10-13 90 .... (p) KeiranBurke(5) 87
(Patrick Rodford) *trckd ldrs tl 3rd: sn drvn in midfield: nvr any threat after* **20/1**
0PU- **6** *8* **Triple Bluff**[45] 4895 7-10-9 96 .... HaddenFrost(3) 74
(James Frost) *slowly away: rcvrd into midfield 3rd: rdn after 6th: nvr any danger* **14/1**
00P/ **7** *nse* **Supreme Royal (IRE)**[8] 8-10-12 0 .... TomO'Brien 74
(Philip Hobbs) *nvr bttr than mid-div: wknd 3 out* **18/1**
5/6- **8** *2 1/4* **Water King (USA)**[22] 5290 11-10-12 85 .... BarryKeniry 72
(Robert Stronge) *rdn after 5th: a in rr* **20/1**
04-0 **9** *shd* **Mistress Eva**[7] 134 5-10-5 77 .... JohnnyFarrelly 65
(Sophie Leech) *chsd ldrs: reminders after 4th: wknd 6th* **40/1**
2P3- **10** *8* **Galant Eye (IRE)**[22] 5290 11-10-7 79 .... GilesHawkins(5) 65
(Chris Down) *a towards rr* **16/1**
000- **11** *13* **Captain Walcot**[33] 5100 4-10-4 69 .... (p) HarrySkelton(3) 48
(Carroll Gray) *a bhd: t.o* **100/1**
/00- **12** *dist* **Pacte Noir (FR)**[49] 4793 7-10-12 0 .... (t) AndrewThornton 22
(Tony Newcombe) *mid-div: hit 5th: sn bhd: t.o* **100/1**
415- **P** **Beautiful Vision (IRE)**[46] 4861 10-11-4 119 .... (tp) PaulMoloney —
(Evan Williams) *led 2nd tl p.u appr 3 out: dismntd* **7/2**[3]
000- **P** **How Realee (IRE)**[22] 5285 7-10-12 72 .... (t) DavidDennis —
(Nigel Hawke) *led tl 2nd: prom: rdn after 5th: sn wknd: t.o whn p.u bef 2 out* **100/1**

4m 26.8s (-7.10) **Going Correction** -0.125s/f (Good)
WFA 4 from 5yo+ 18lb **14** Ran SP% **117.4**
Speed ratings (Par 103): **109,108,97,94,93 90,90,89,89,85 80,66,—,—**

The winner bought in for 4,800gns. Cantabilly was subject to a friendly claim.
Owner Mrs Elizabeth King **Bred** Mrs J A Gawthorpe **Trained** Nicholashayne, Devon

FOCUS
The first pair dominated this strongly run seller and the form is straightforward.

NOTEBOOK
Helen Wood was left in front three out and, despite idling from the penultimate flight, resumed winning ways on this drop in class over a longer trip. She was entitled to win at the weights, but rates value for further and can pick up more of these during the summer. Connections subsequently bought her back in for £4,800. (op 7-4)
Cantabilly(IRE) was dropped in grade for this return to hurdling and was well backed. He closed on the idling winner after that rival hit the last, but was always being held and may well benefit for the application of some headgear. (op 9-2)
Intac(IRE) lacked the pace to get involved, but this was better and returning to softer ground in this class should help.
Beautiful Vision(IRE) had won one of these on his last outing over hurdles and got a positive ride, but looked a sitting duck prior to quickly pulling up nearing the third-last. Official explanation: jockey said gelding lost its action (op 4-1 tchd 3-1)

265 CHAMPION'S 60:60 CHARITY CHALLENGE NOVICES' CHASE (13 fncs) 2m 110y
7:00 (7:01) (Class 4) 5-Y-0+ **£4,798** (£1,489; £802)

Form RPR
22F- **1** **Cockney Trucker (IRE)**[23] 5244 8-10-12 130 RichardJohnson 143+
(Philip Hobbs) *j.rt: lft in ld 2nd: nt fluent whn hdd 7th: narrow ld next: clr after 3 out: pushed out: comf* **5/4**[1]
000- **2** 3 1/4 **Simarian (IRE)**[53] 4715 5-10-12 0 PaulMoloney 134+
(Evan Williams) *trckd wnr fr 2nd tl rdn after 8th: styd on again after 3 out: wnt 2nd bef last: kpt on but no ch w wnr* **3/1**[3]
51- **3** 21 **Lady An Co (FR)**[57] 4651 5-10-9 133 HarrySkelton(3) 125+
(Paul Nicholls) *travelled wl for most of way: trckd wnr fr 2nd: led 7th tl next: rdn after 3 out: sn hld by wnr: wnt rt next: wknd last* **2/1**[2]
3PP- **U** **King Caine (IRE)**[98] 3809 8-10-12 118 ChristianWilliams —
(Alan Jones) *led: j.lft, hit wing and rdr lost irons 1st: rdr nvr rcvrd whn wnt lft next: jinked rt and uns rdr next* **16/1**

4m 8.00s (1.50) **Going Correction** +0.075s/f (Yiel) **4** Ran SP% **108.7**
Speed ratings: **99,97,87,—**
CSF £5.36 TOTE £1.60; EX 6.40.
Owner Mrs Karola Vann **Bred** Gerald Monahan **Trained** Withycombe, Somerset

FOCUS
An interesting novice chase despite the size of the field. The winner is value for further and rated to his mark.

NOTEBOOK
Cockney Trucker(IRE) belatedly opened his account over fences. He was left in a clear lead when King Caine shot his rider out of the saddle at the second fence and was messed about by that horse for the next couple of fences. He got into a good rhythm on the back straight, though, and won the race when stretching clear nearing the final turn. He was probably idling in the home straight and tended to jump out to his right through the race, but this was certainly a deserved success. Connections intend to keep him on the go to increase his confidence and, providing they can sort out his jumping, he ought to be capable of further success. (op 11-8 tchd 13-8 in a place)
Simarian(IRE) has not won for a long time, but has struggled with the handicapper over hurdles and was officially rated 142 at best in that sphere, so had to be of interest on this switch to chasing. He jumped adequately early on, but tended to go in snatches passing the stands for the first time and lost ground by being deliberate on the back straight. He consented to run on from the home turn and was motoring late on, looking a brief threat to the winner. Hopefully, the experience will see him prove sharper next time and, should that play out, he would rate a decent prospect for this time of year. (op 11-4 tchd 7-2)
Lady An Co(FR) was penalised for her Taunton win 57 days earlier, but still looked a big player here. He jumped up going strongly on the back straight, but was in trouble shortly after a fine leap to lead at the seventh fence. The manner in which she faded would suggest something may have been amiss. (op 9-4)

266 "SPONSOR'S NAME HERE" NOVICES' HURDLE (10 hdls) 2m 6f
7:30 (7:30) (Class 4) 4-Y-0+ **£3,707** (£1,088; £544; £271)

Form RPR
P- **1** **Red Twist**[28] 5173 5-10-9 0 BernieWharfe(3) 112+
(Martin Hill) *hld up in last pair: hdwy into cl 4th 3 out: gd run on inner to ld on home bnd: hit next: kpt on wl* **33/1**
322- **2** 3 **Acrai Rua (IRE)**[15] 15 7-10-12 120 APMcCoy 108
(Evan Williams) *trckd ldr: led 7th: rdn whn hdd 3 out: remained w ev ch whn hung lft off fnl bnd: hld fr next: kpt on same pce* **11/8**[1]
330/ **3** nk **Prince Tom**[495] 3145 6-10-7 0 IanPopham(5) 108
(Paul Nicholls) *trckd ldrs: hit 1st: rdn w ch home bnd: kpt on same pce fr next* **11/4**[2]
PP0- **4** 3/4 **Russian Song (IRE)**[44] 4913 6-10-12 0 TomScudamore 107
(Colin Tizzard) *trckd ldrs: sltly outpcd 3 out: styd on again fr next* **6/1**[3]
030- **5** 13 **Avec Moi Ce Soir (IRE)**[63] 4497 7-10-12 109 JoeTizzard 95
(Colin Tizzard) *trckd ldrs: narrow advantage travelling wl after 3 out: rdn and hdd bef next: wknd qckly* **9/1**
6 2 1/4 **Sobre Tresor (FR)**[30] 4-10-7 0 DavidDennis 87
(Nigel Hawke) *in tch: rdn appr 7th: wknd after 3 out* **50/1**
P62- **7** 11 **Quelclasse (FR)**[22] 5287 6-10-12 88 BarryKeniry 81
(Robert Stronge) *led: hdd whn blnd 7th: sn rdn: wknd after 3 out* **25/1**
/35- **8** 16 **Tim Henry (IRE)**[184] 2147 7-10-7 0 KeiranBurke(5) 65
(Patrick Rodford) *in tch tl wknd after 3 out: t.o* **13/2**
P **Sunrise Court** 11-10-5 0 ChrisDavies(7) —
(Peter Purdy) *nt a fluent: a in rr: t.o whn p.u bef 2 out: lame* **200/1**

5m 28.7s (8.50) **Going Correction** -0.125s/f (Good)
WFA 4 from 5yo+ 19lb **9** Ran SP% **115.6**
Speed ratings (Par 105): **79,77,77,77,72 71,67,62,—**
toteswingers: 1&2 £8.50, 1&3 £23.90, 2&3 £1.60 CSF £81.24 TOTE £57.60: £7.40, £2.10, £2.80; EX 126.10.
Owner Martin Hill **Bred** Meon Valley Stud **Trained** Littlehempston, Devon

FOCUS
This was an ordinary novice hurdle and they went a steady gallop until nearing the fourth-last. The form is suspect but the winner is rated in line with his Flat best.

NOTEBOOK
Red Twist had shaped a bit better than the bare form of his hurdling debut when pulling up at Exeter last month and showed himself to be a fair performer with a ready success. He was only poor when trained on the Flat, but came good when faced with good ground at the second attempt in the pointing field and this switch to quicker ground made all the difference. He travelled sweetly into contention before getting a dream run up the inside turning for home and was in no real danger thereafter. The should be more to come.
Acrai Rua(IRE) had his chance, but was laboured from the top of the home straight and has now run below his mark over this trip the last twice. Returning to a little further back on softer ground could see him back in a better light, though. Official explanation: jockey said gelding hung right-handed off final bend (op Evens tchd 10-11)
Prince Tom was having his first run for Paul Nicholls and making his hurdling debut after a 495-day absence. He never seriously looked like justifying support, but got the trip and left the impression he would benefit a deal for the run. Easier ground may also suit ideally. (op 9-2 tchd 5-1)
Russian Song(IRE), up in trip, would have enjoyed a more truly run race and this was certainly his most encouraging effort as a hurdler. His previous bumper form suggests he can rate higher and he is one to note when going handicapping. (op 8-1 tchd 9-1)
Avec Moi Ce Soir(IRE) was very disappointing on his handicap debut last time out, but had previously looked a horse of some promise. He looked a likely winner nearing the home straight, but wasn't helped when the runner-up came into him off the bend. He faded tamely soon after. It may be that he failed to get home and dropping back in trip on easier ground could well do the trick. (op 8-1 tchd 10-1)
Sunrise Court Official explanation: trainer said gelding hung left at each hurdle and finished lame

267 RACECOURSE FOR YOUR HOSPITALITY REQUIREMENTS H'CAP HURDLE (10 hdls) 2m 6f
8:00 (8:00) (Class 4) (0-115,115) 4-Y-0+ **£3,382** (£993; £496; £248)

Form RPR
065- **1** **Norisan**[61] 4539 6-10-1 90 (t) AidanColeman 97
(Alan Jones) *hld up bhd: stdy prog fr after 6th: pushed along fr 3 out: tended to lean lft: wnt 2nd next: led narrowly last: r.o* **20/1**
25-1 **2** 1/2 **Haldibari (IRE)**[2] 232 6-10-8 102 7ex SamTwiston-Davies(5) 108
(Shaun Lycett) *prom: led 4th: rdn after 3 out: narrowly hdd last: kpt on but no ex* **9/4**[1]
300- **3** 16 **Consulate (IRE)**[23] 5255 6-11-5 115 MrDEdwards(7) 107
(Gordon Edwards) *hld up towards rr: stdy hdwy fr after 6th: rdn to chse ldr after 3 out tl next: fdd* **28/1**
456- **4** 1 3/4 **Young Albert (IRE)**[22] 5291 9-11-5 111 TomMolloy(3) 101
(Charlie Longsdon) *hld up towards rr: rdn after 7th: plugged on fr after 3 out: wnt modest 4th flat* **16/1**
00U- **5** 1 **Mr Straffan (IRE)**[18] 5365 7-9-11 89 oh4 HaddenFrost(3) 81
(Martin Hill) *mid-div: hdwy 7th: rdn after 3 out: wknd after next: nt fluent last: lost 4th flat* **20/1**
031- **6** 14 **Nulato (IRE)**[30] 5154 7-11-12 115 RobertThornton 92
(Alan King) *in tch: tk clsr order after 6th: rdn to chse ldr sn after 3 out: wknd next* **4/1**[2]
U6F- **7** 7 **Legal Glory (IRE)**[32] 5120 10-9-9 89 oh5 GilesHawkins(5) 60
(Ron Hodges) *trckd ldrs: rdn after 7th: wknd after 3 out: t.o* **17/2**
14P/ **8** 17 **Thumbprint (IRE)**[554] 1994 8-11-1 104 (t) JoeTizzard 59
(Colin Tizzard) *prom: hit 2nd: grad lost pl: bhd fr 5th: t.o* **16/1**
024- **9** 1 1/2 **Converti**[19] 5326 6-10-12 108 LucyBarry(7) 62
(Audrey Manners) *led tl 4th: drvn after 6th: sn bhd: t.o* **25/1**
32P- **10** 11 **Occasionally Yours (IRE)**[252] 1369 6-10-11 100 DavidDennis 44
(Nigel Hawke) *mid-div: hdwy 6th: jnd ldrs sn after: wknd sn after 3 out: t.o* **40/1**
01P- **11** 6 **Sir Harry Cool**[36] 5039 7-10-11 103 DannyCook(3) 42
(John Panvert) *prom tl 7th: sn wknd: t.o* **8/1**[3]
6F0/ **12** 2 1/2 **Crathorne (IRE)**[304] 208 10-11-5 115 (t) OliverDayman(7) 51
(Alison Thorpe) *hit 6th: a in rr: t.o* **25/1**
PP0- **P** **A Haon A Do (IRE)**[18] 5364 8-10-4 93 (b) AndrewGlassonbury —
(Gerald Ham) *mid-div: rdn whn mstke 3 out: sn wknd: t.o whn p.u bef last* **28/1**
F- **P** **Kauto The Kid (FR)**[25] 5202 5-11-7 113 HarrySkelton(3) —
(Paul Nicholls) *hld up towards rr: sme hdwy after 6th: rdn bef 3 out: wknd sn after: t.o whn p.u bef last* **12/1**

5m 14.7s (-5.50) **Going Correction** -0.125s/f (Good) **14** Ran SP% **118.4**
Speed ratings (Par 105): **105,104,99,98,98 92,90,84,83,79 77,76,—,—**
toteswingers: 1&2 £20.20, 1&3 £73.30, 2&3 £59.10 CSF £61.21 CT £1322.67 TOTE £34.10: £10.20, £1.02, £18.80; EX 118.80.
Owner BPD Ltd **Bred** The National Stud Owner Breeders Club Ltd **Trained** Coedkernew, Newport

FOCUS
A moderate handicap, run at a sound gallop and the first pair came clear. The winner is entitled to rate higher on his Flat form.

NOTEBOOK
Norisan, a big eye-catcher last time out in better company, got up on the run-in and won with something to spare. He got a lovely ride through the race, coming from last to first, and looked to have something left in the tank when cajoled to the front near the finish. He had something to prove on this ground and over the trip, but he evidently stays fine nowadays. This 6-y-o was formerly Listed class in his heyday on the Flat and it wouldn't be surprising to see him win again if consenting to maintain his current mood, as the first-time tongue tie clearly worked the oracle. (op 16-1)
Haldibari(IRE) had bolted up at Worcester two days earlier and was way ahead of the handicapper under his penalty. He made a brave bid to follow up and was only mugged late on, finish well clear of the rest. It will probably be chasing next for him. (op 7-4)
Consulate(IRE) was taking another drop back down in grade and ran a big race. He enjoyed the way the race was run, but looked to make his effort plenty soon enough over this longer trip and ultimately failed to see it out anything like the first pair. His turn looks to be nearing again, though he may have to go back up in class. (op 25-1)
Young Albert(IRE) was reported to have hated the quick ground on his previous outing and here it looked fast enough for his liking here. It was an effort he could build on when reverting to slightly easier ground as he is now fairly handicapped, but he is not the easiest of rides. (op 12-1)
Mr Straffan(IRE) turned in his most encouraging display yet from 4lb out of the weights. (op 25-1)
Nulato(IRE) found disappointingly little when push came to shove and was eventually well beaten on this handicap debut. Perhaps a return to a sharper test is required, but now he has to prove he is up to this level. (op 11-2 tchd 7-2)

268 NEWTONABBOTRACING.COM H'CAP HUNTERS' CHASE (16 fncs) 2m 5f 110y
8:30 (8:32) (Class 4) 5-Y-0+ **£3,646** (£1,138; £569; £284; £142)

Form RPR
42-2 **1** **Distant Thunder (IRE)**[6] 153 12-11-0 102 (t) MrJHamer(7) 118
(Miss Jane Western) *trckd ldrs: led sn after 2 out: pushed out* **5/2**[3]
/13- **2** 3/4 **Blu Teen (FR)**[33] 5096 10-12-4 116 (t) MrRMahon(3) 130
(D J Staddon) *trckd ldrs: rdn after 3 out: wnt 2nd last: styd on* **9/4**[2]
P2-2 **3** 2 3/4 **Ryeman**[6] 148 8-10-2 90 (vt) MrRHawkins(7) 101
(Andrew Jackson) *j.w: prom: led 9th: rdn after 3 out: hdd sn after next: no ex* **2/1**[1]
05P- **4** 23 **Dutch Bill**[10] 9-10-12 100 MrJCole(7) 90
(J Cole) *led tl 9th: chsd ldrs: hit 4 out: sn wknd*
620- **5** hd **Doof (IRE)**[8] 10-10-10 98 MissJBuck(7) 88
(L Jefford) *reluctant to line up: dwlt: rcvrd to trck ldrs 6th: hit 8th: wknd after 4 out* **7/1**

44-0 **U** **Some Timbering (IRE)**[6] 153 11-10-6 **90**......(b) MissIsabelTompsett(3) —
(P S Davies) *trckd ldrs: hit 3rd: dropped to last 6th: mstke 9th: struggling whn mstke and uns rdr 11th* **25/1**

5m 20.2s (-1.20) **Going Correction** +0.075s/f (Yiel) **6** Ran SP% **113.8**
Speed ratings: **105,104,103,95,95 —**
toteswingers:1&2 £1.30, 2&3 £2.40, 1&3 £1.70 CSF £9.13 TOTE £2.90: £1.10, £1.20; EX 8.80 Place 6: £14.64 Place 5: £13.42.
Owner Mrs Susan Humphreys **Bred** Daniel C And Patrick Keating **Trained** Chard, Somerset

FOCUS
A rare handicap for the hunter chase division and a tricky puzzle to solve. It was run at a solid gallop and the first three dominated. Sound form.

NOTEBOOK
Distant Thunder(IRE) finally got his head back in front and registered a first win under rules since landing a Grade 2 novice chase back in 2005. He has become a very difficult horse to get right, but the race was run to suit and, taking it up two from home, getting a stone from the top weight saw him last home in front. This should do his confidence a power of good. (tchd 9-4)
Blu Teen(FR), who ran an excellent race over the National fences at Aintree last month, was conceding upwards of a stone all around. It was his jumping which caught him out here, but it was still a commendable effort and he is really at his best on easier ground. (op 5-2)
Ryeman held every chance and ran a solid race, but had a leading chance at these weights and remains one to swerve for win-only betting. (op 9-4 tchd 11-4)
Dutch Bill couldn't go with them on the back straight. (op 16-1)
Doof(IRE) never seriously looked like bettering his third in the race last year. (op 8-1 tchd 17-2)
T/Plt: £10.20. Pool:£75,866.56 - 5,387.63 winning tickets. T/Qpdt: £7.60. Pool:£4,311.46 - 418.48 winning tickets TM

269 - 271a (Foreign Racing) - See Raceform Interactive

129 EXETER (R-H)

Wednesday, May 12

OFFICIAL GOING: Good to firm (chs 9.6, hdl 9.5)
Wind: Virtually nil Weather: Light rain at times with sunny periods, persistent light rain from 4.15pm.

272 BATHWICK TYRES TAUNTON NOVICES' H'CAP HURDLE (10 hdls) 2m 3f
2:20 (2:20) (Class 4) (0-100,99) 4-Y-0+ **£2,602** (£764; £382; £190)

Form RPR
00-1 **1** **Nomad (FR)**[8] 134 9-9-10 **74**.. IanPopham(5) 78+
(Carroll Gray) *hld up towards rr: pushed along and hdwy appr 3 out: led after 2 out: kpt on wl* **10/3**[1]
P3-0 **2** 1 3/4 **The Fox's Decree**[13] 59 6-11-3 **90**............................(t) WarrenMarston 92
(Martin Keighley) *trckd ldrs: rdn appr 3 out: ev ch 2 out: nt fluent last: kpt on to snatch 2nd nr fin* **9/1**
56-3 **3** hd **Ghaill Force**[13] 54 8-9-8 **77**..(p) AshleyBird(10) 79
(Paddy Butler) *racd keenly: prom: led 3rd: rdn whn hrd pressed fr 3 out: hdd after 2 out: kpt on but no ex* **9/1**
/6-2 **4** 1 3/4 **Boomtown**[13] 54 5-10-12 **85**..(t) LiamTreadwell 85
(Claire Dyson) *trckd ldrs: rdn after 7th: hit 3 out: kpt on same pce* **9/2**[3]
3P0/ **5** 2 3/4 **Award Winning (IRE)**[444] 9-10-1 **79**............................ TomO'Connor(5) 77
(John Berwick) *in tch: rdn to chse ldrs 3 out: kpt on same pce* **33/1**
63-0 **6** 3 1/4 **Regain Du Charbonneau (FR)**[8] 134 5-11-6 **93**...(tp) TomScudamore 87
(David Pipe) *rn in snatches: hld up bhd: rdn appr 3 out: no imp tl styd on past btn horses run-in* **4/1**[2]
000- **7** 1 **Spring Haze**[19] 5363 5-9-8 **74**.. MrDGPrichard(7) 67
(Phillip Dando) *led tl 3rd: prom: rdn appr 3 out: one pce fr 2 out* **20/1**
00-3 **8** nk **Shinnecock Bay**[8] 129 6-11-8 **95**......................................(b) APMcCoy 89
(Oliver Sherwood) *hld up towards rr: hdwy 7th: ev ch whn nt fluent 3 out: sn rdn: one pce fr next* **9/2**[3]
04-6 **9** 1 **Knockvicar (IRE)**[8] 134 8-10-7 **80**.................................... JohnnyFarrelly 72
(Richard Mitchell) *mid-div: cl up on inner appr 3 out: sn rdn: one pce after* **25/1**
60-0 **10** 27 **Mamba (GER)**[13] 59 8-9-12 **74** oh2 ow1...................... ChrisHonour(3) 39
(Chris Down) *mid-div tl wknd 7th: t.o* **33/1**
/0P- **11** 46 **Paradise Regained (FR)**[19] 5365 7-11-8 **95**..................... PaulMoloney 14
(Sophie Leech) *struggling 5th: a bhd: t.o* **28/1**

4m 32.8s (-9.90) **Going Correction** -0.775s/f (Firm) **11** Ran SP% **117.4**
Speed ratings (Par 105): **89,88,88,87,86 84,84,84,83,72 53**
toteswingers: 1&2 £3.30, 1&3 £3.70, 2&3 £20.20 CSF £30.37 CT £245.74 TOTE £4.30: £1.70, £3.50, £2.40; EX 39.60.
Owner A P Helliar **Bred** Marc Trinquet **Trained** Moorland, Somerset

FOCUS
A moderate handicap hurdle. It was steadily run but the first four were all close to their marks.

NOTEBOOK
Nomad(FR), a lucky winner at the course last week, escaped a penalty for that success (due to go up 6lb in future), and he ground it out best having got to the front after the second-last. He is clearly in good form, but will find life tougher in future handicaps.
The Fox's Decree has still to win a race, but this represented easily his best effort to date over hurdles, and he gave the impression he will stay a bit further. (op 7-1)
Ghaill Force came into this without a win in 52 starts and, for all that he ran another good race in defeat, he is going to remain vulnerable. (op 10-1 tchd 11-1)
Boomtown ran better at Hereford last time and he backed that up with another sound effort, suggesting he will be winning at some stage. (op 13-2 tchd 7-1)
Award Winning(IRE), not seen under rules for 629 days, had previous course form with the winner and he shaped most encouragingly on this first start in 15 months. (tchd 40-1)
Regain Du Charbonneau(FR), who disappointed behind the winner in a first-time visor last week, had cheekpieces this time but raced lazily and made only moderate late headway. (op 8-1)
Shinnecock Bay, due to go up 9lb for his third at the course last week, came to hold his chance in the straight but found little. (op 10-3 tchd 5-2)

273 SAM LOUGHRIDGE DIAMOND EDGE H'CAP HURDLE (12 hdls) 2m 7f 110y
2:50 (2:50) (Class 4) (0-100,97) 4-Y-0+ **£2,602** (£764; £382; £190)

Form RPR
6P-U **1** **Cappagh (IRE)**[8] 134 5-11-5 **90**... APMcCoy 112+
(Philip Hobbs) *mid-div on outer: hdwy 7th: rdn appr 3 out: swtchd rt to chal 2 out: led bef last: styd on wl to assert flat* **15/8**[1]
P04- **2** 3 1/4 **Captain Becket**[19] 5365 7-10-11 **85**............................ HaddenFrost(3) 101
(James Frost) *hld up early: trckd ldrs 6th: led appr 3 out: sn rdn: hdd appr last: wl clr of remainder but sn hld by wnr* **10/3**[2]
24P- **3** 21 **Bring It On Home**[19] 5365 6-11-7 **92**.................................. PaulMoloney 87
(Sophie Leech) *towards rr: reminders fr 5th: plugged on past btn horses fr 3 out: wnt modest 3rd nr fin: nvr any danger to ldrs* **9/1**
F5-5 **4** 1 1/4 **Ocean Du Moulin (FR)**[12] 84 8-11-4 **89**.......................(vt) DarylJacob 85
(Jamie Snowden) *prom: led whn hit 5th: rdn and hdd appr 3 out: sn btn: lost modest 3rd towards fin* **17/2**
PP-6 **5** 4 **Shergill (IRE)**[13] 66 9-10-9 **80**...................................... TomScudamore 70
(Shaun Lycett) *in tch: rdn after 7th: no ch fr next* **18/1**
0P4- **6** 1/2 **Kilvergan Boy (IRE)**[16] 22 6-11-4 **94**............... SamTwiston-Davies(5) 83
(Nigel Twiston-Davies) *hld up: mid-div after 6th: rdn after 7th: wnt 4th 9th but nvr threatened ldrs: no ch fr next: lost 2 pls flat* **16/1**
4/0- **7** 6 **Always Cruising (USA)**[24] 5261 5-11-7 **97**...................... JohnKington(5) 80
(Linda Blackford) *hld up towards rr: hit 6th: rdn bef next: no imp* **33/1**
00-0 **8** 3/4 **Ninogaro (FR)**[8] 134 5-10-0 **71** oh2...................(v) AndrewGlassonbury 53
(Linda Blackford) *mid-div tl wknd appr 3 out* **100/1**
522- **9** 2 1/4 **Flag Flier**[170] 2482 7-10-7 **85**.. NathanSweeney(7) 65
(Bob Buckler) *mid-div tl after 8th* **9/1**
P/P- **10** 11 **Here To Eternity (IRE)**[32] 5135 9-10-0 **71** oh1...................... RodiGreene 40
(Sarah Robinson) *led tl 5th: w ldr tl rdn appr 7th: wknd wl bef 3 out* **100/1**
5S0- **11** 12 **Nearly A Breeze**[16] 24 10-10-13 **87**............................(b) ChrisHonour(3) 44
(Chris Down) *trckd ldrs tl rdn 7th: sn bhd: t.o* **22/1**
5P-4 **P** **Ease And Grace**[12] 84 6-11-6 **91**................................(t) AidanColeman —
(Emma Lavelle) *trckd ldrs tl 9th: sn rdn: wknd qckly: p.u bef 3 out:* **8/1**[3]

5m 34.8s (-24.20) **Going Correction** -0.775s/f (Firm) **12** Ran SP% **119.9**
Speed ratings (Par 105): **109,107,100,100,99 97,97,96,96,92 88,—**
toteswingers: 1&2 £2.20, 1&3 £5.90, 2&3 £8.00 CSF £8.63 CT £45.25 TOTE £3.00: £1.40, £1.70, £3.00; EX 10.20.
Owner John P McManus **Bred** Legends Stud **Trained** Withycombe, Somerset

FOCUS
The front pair drew clear in this modest handicap hurdle. A step up from the winner and the first two should be competitive when reassessed.

NOTEBOOK
Cappagh(IRE), who threw the race away when jinking sharply left and unseating his rider on the run-in last week (gifting it to the winner of the first race), was able to atone. Due to race off 9lb higher in future, he has been crying out for this longer distance, and never looked like repeating the antics of last week under McCoy, being brought against the rail in the straight and staying on well having led at the last. It will be harder next time, and it would come as no surprise were connections to switch him to fences at some stage. (op 7-4 tchd 9-4)
Captain Becket went on at the first in the straight, but soon had the winner to worry about, and he simply couldn't stay on as well. He pulled a long way clear of the remainder, so can expect to go up a few pounds, but is clearly in good form. (op 7-2 tchd 3-1)
Bring It On Home never got going until the race was all over, coming under pressure a long way out and keeping on late to take third. (op 17-2 tchd 8-1)
Ocean Du Moulin(FR) got tired having been up there a long way and was run out of the third nearing the line. (op 8-1 tchd 9-1)
Ease And Grace stopped rather quickly and there was presumably something amiss. (op 10-1)

274 BETFAIR H'CAP CHASE (18 fncs) 3m
3:20 (3:20) (Class 4) (0-115,115) 5-Y-0+ **£4,553** (£1,337; £668; £333)

Form RPR
P53- **1** **Ballycarney (IRE)**[23] 5200 9-11-2 **112**........................ MrJJO'Donovan(7) 127+
(Emma Lavelle) *hld up bhd ldrs: wnt 2nd 10th: led 12th: rdn after 3 out: styd on wl* **13/8**[1]
320- **2** 7 **River Indus**[26] 5212 10-11-2 **105**... DarylJacob 111
(Bob Buckler) *trckd ldr: led 4th tl 7th: outapeced 14th: styd on again fr 4 out: wnt 2nd bef last: no ch w wnr* **5/1**[3]
P52- **3** 3 1/4 **Terrible Tenant**[15] 38 11-10-9 **103**............................ JimmyDerham(5) 106
(Seamus Mullins) *led tl 4th: led 7th tl 12th: rdn after 14th: styd on same pce fr 4 out* **8/1**
P43- **4** 1 3/4 **Dusty Dane (IRE)**[16] 21 8-10-13 **109**...........................(t) MarkQuinlan(7) 110
(Bill Turner) *hld up bhd ldrs: rdn after 12th: wnt cl 4th 14th: styd on same pce fr 4 out* **8/1**
22P- **5** 30 **Skipper's Lad (IRE)**[137] 3062 8-11-7 **110**...........................(bt) JoeTizzard 86
(Colin Tizzard) *hld up bhd ldrs: nudged along after 10th: hdwy 12th: rdn to chse wnr 4 out: wknd after next* **4/1**[2]
003- **P** **Pauillac (FR)**[22] 5292 7-11-4 **107**..(vt) APMcCoy —
(David Pipe) *chsd ldrs early: reminders after 3rd: nvr travelling after: bhd whn stmbld 8th: grad lost tch: p.u bef 14th* **7/1**
/PP- **F** **Strong Coffee**[186] 2127 8-11-12 **115**....................................(p) SamJones —
(Oliver Sherwood) *trckd ldrs: cl 6th but pushed along whn fell 12th* **25/1**

5m 47.7s (-21.60) **Going Correction** -0.775s/f (Firm) **7** Ran SP% **113.3**
Speed ratings: **105,102,101,101,91 —,—**
toteswingers: 1&2 £1.90, 1&3 £1.70, 2&3 £8.90 CSF £10.35 CT £48.63 TOTE £2.50: £1.80, £2.50; EX 13.30.
Owner Elite Racing Club **Bred** Aaron Metcalfe **Trained** Wildhern, Hants

FOCUS
An ordinary handicap chase. The winner is rated up 10lb, with the second back to something like his best.

NOTEBOOK
Ballycarney(IRE) took over early down the back and stayed on strongly in the straight to win with a fair bit in hand. He had promised to be suited by this trip when second over 2m4f at Kempton the time before, on what was only his second start for the yard, and he looks capable of better still. (op 15-8)
River Indus was never far away and kept on dourly for second, but was never in with a chance against the comfy winner. (op 9-2 tchd 11-2)
Terrible Tenant likes a fast surface and this represented a step forward on his Wincanton effort (second of two to finish). He's fairly weighted again. (op 15-2)
Dusty Dane(IRE), well held at a lowly level over hurdles the last twice, isn't at all badly weighted over fences and he ran well on this return to handicap company. (op 11-1)
Skipper's Lad(IRE), still 9lb above his last winning mark, moved well for a long way on this first start in 137 days, and simply got tired from the third-last. He will be of interest next time. (op 9-2 tchd 5-1)
Pauillac(FR) was in trouble from an early stage and didn't look at ease on the ground. (op 11-2)
Strong Coffee appeared to be struggling when coming down seven out. (op 11-2)

275 CITY OF EXETER CHALLENGE CUP MARES' NOVICES' HURDLE (8 hdls) 2m 1f
3:55 (3:55) (Class 4) 4-Y-0+ **£2,602** (£764; £382; £190)

Form RPR
1 **Tout Regulier**[39] 5001 6-10-7 0.................................... DonalDevereux(5) 107+
(Peter Bowen) *disp ld tl clr advantage 3rd: drew clr fr 3 out: unextended: eased run-in* **10/3**[2]
2 4 1/2 **Frosted Grape (IRE)**[25] 5236 4-10-8 110....................... TomScudamore 88
(David Pipe) *disp tl 3rd: sn rdn to chse wnr: lost 2nd after 5th: regained 2nd bef last: no ch w v easy wnr* **4/6**[1]
00-5 **3** 4 1/2 **Evening Haze**[6] 167 6-10-5 0...................................... MrDGPrichard(7) 89
(Phillip Dando) *trckd ldrs: wnt 2nd appr 3 out: sn rdn: no ch w wnr: lost 2nd bef last* **7/1**[3]
0U0- **4** 32 **Gabrielle Da Vinci**[27] 5200 4-10-3 0.................... SamTwiston-Davies(5) 51
(Nigel Twiston-Davies) *trckd ldrs: rdn after 5th: wknd 3 out: t.o* **18/1**
5 16 **Farncombe (IRE)**[49] 4-10-3 0.. JohnKington(5) 35
(Michael Scudamore) *hld up 5th: wnt 2nd after 5th tl rdn bef 3 out: sn wknd: t.o* **22/1**

P **Special Bond**[459] 4-10-8 0 ...... RodiGreene —
(Kevin Bishop) *a last: lost tch fr 5th: t.o whn p.u bef 2 out* **22/1**

4m 0.20s (-15.30) **Going Correction** -0.775s/f (Firm)
WFA 4 from 6yo+ 18lb **6** Ran SP% **109.5**
Speed ratings (Par 105): **105,102,100,85,78** —
toteswingers: 1&2 £1.50, 1&3 £2.20, 2&3 £1.80 CSF £5.88 TOTE £3.40: £1.30, £1.30; EX 8.60.
Owner G A Moore **Bred** Miss M E Steele **Trained** Little Newcastle, Pembrokes

FOCUS

A weak mares' novices' hurdle. The winner was up 6lb on her best Irish form.

NOTEBOOK

Tout Regulier, an ex-Irish mare, ran out a most easy winner. Having established herself in front from the third, it was clear from some way out that she was going much the best, and with the favourite running a rather laboured race in second, she had the luxury of being eased after the last. She was bought with summer jumping in mind, and will probably have one more run over hurdles before she goes chasing. (op 3-1 tchd 7-2)
Frosted Grape(IRE), placed six times without winning in Ireland, was well supported to make a winning debut for the yard, but she was going without the blinkers she usually wears, and failed to travel with any zest. She did run on again when the result was beyond doubt, but doesn't look straightforward, and clearly needs the headgear reapplied. (op 8-11 tchd 4-5 and 5-6 in places and 10-11 in a place)
Evening Haze seems to be going the right way, albeit slowly, and this half-sister to the yard's admirable hurdler Bella Haze can do better with further experience. (op 13-2 tchd 6-1)
Gabrielle Da Vinci looked in need of the experience on this hurdles debut. (op 11-1)
Farncombe(IRE) stopped quickly having been second on the turn in. (op 16-1)

276 HEAVITREE BREWERY H'CAP CHASE (12 fncs) 2m 1f 110y

4:30 (4:30) (Class 4) (0-100,99) 5-Y-0+ **£3,903** (£1,146; £573; £286)

Form				RPR
F64-	1		**Foreign King (USA)**[16] 23 6-11-7 **99** ...... JimmyDerham(5) (Seamus Mullins) *hld up: stdy prog to go 3rd 8th: clsd on ldng pair sn after: j.rt fr 4 out: led appr 2 out: kpt on wl* **11/2**[3]	114+
32-	2	9	**Remember Bampi**[17] 2 6-10-10 **90** ......(tp) NathanSweeney(7) (Simon Burrough) *in tch: rdn after 8th: styd on same pce fr 4 out: wnt 2nd appr last: no ch w wnr* **4/1**[2]	96
PP-3	3	½	**Post It**[12] 81 9-10-2 **82** ...... MattGriffiths(7) (Ron Hodges) *in tch: blnd 7th: rdn after 8th: no real imp tl styd on fr 2 out: wnt 3rd run-in* **7/1**	87
F06-	4	2¼	**Kirbys Glen (IRE)**[62] 4541 8-10-7 **85** ...... KeiranBurke(5) (Patrick Rodford) *trckd ldrs: narrow advantage 5th: rdn after 4 out: hdd bef 2 out: fdd last* **20/1**	86
01-2	5	1¾	**Folie A Deux (IRE)**[11] 99 8-11-7 **94** ...... JoeTizzard (Colin Tizzard) *led tl hit 5th: reminders: pressed ldr: rdn and ev ch appr 4 out: fdd appr last* **3/1**[1]	93
U0P-	6	7	**Tilly Shilling (IRE)**[160] 2662 6-10-0 **73** oh1 ...... RodiGreene (Kevin Bishop) *hld up: nt fluent early: hit 4th: rdn after 8th: hit 2 out: wknd* **40/1**	65
60-0	P		**Compton Star**[6] 183 10-9-9 **73** oh4 ......(b[1]) IanPopham(5) (Ron Hodges) *chsd ldrs tl after 6th: sn in rr: p.u bef 4 out* **14/1**	—
P0P-	P		**Bollitree Bob**[24] 5259 9-11-7 **94** ...... DarylJacob (Jamie Snowden) *p.u after 1st: dismntd: lame* **20/1**	—
1U3-	P		**One Of The Boys (IRE)**[150] 2861 9-11-7 **94** ...... APMcCoy (Tim Vaughan) *chsd ldrs tl wknd after 7th: bhd whn p.u bef 4 out: b.b.v* **3/1**[1]	—

4m 5.60s (-13.40) **Going Correction** -0.775s/f (Firm) course record **9** Ran SP% **116.5**
Speed ratings: **98,94,93,92,92 88,—,—,—**
toteswingers: 1&2 £5.30, 1&3 £4.90, 2&3 £6.90 CSF £27.97 CT £157.05 TOTE £6.40: £1.80, £2.90; EX 30.70.
Owner John Collins **Bred** Jayeff 'B' Stables **Trained** Wilsford-Cum-Lake, Wilts

FOCUS

Not a race that took much winning, but the form has a solid look to it.

NOTEBOOK

Foreign King(USA), on his chasing debut, proved good enough under top weight. He may still have needed his latest run at Towcester, when tiring badly, and once put into the race here, his jumping improved. Although tending to go out to his right in the straight, he always looked in control having taken over before two out, and is clearly going to make a better chaser than hurdler. (op 6-1 tchd 5-1)
Remember Bampi came through to take second on the run-in, and very much ran like a horse in need of a stiffer test. (op 11-2)
Post It was another who got going all too late, having taken a while to recover from a blunder at the open ditch down the back. She may well be up to winning another minor race. (op 9-1)
Kirbys Glen(IRE) was ridden with a bit more restraint than usual early on this return to fences and ran more promisingly. He still didn't get home, though, and remains a maiden under rules. (op 25-1)
Folie A Deux(IRE), off the same mark as when second at Uttoxeter, was ridden positively, but had been headed before the straight and faded late on. (op 5-2 tchd 10-3)
Bollitree Bob was pulled up and dismounted after the first, something evidently having gone amiss. Official explanation: jockey said gelding was lame (op 5-2)
One Of The Boys(IRE) stopped quickly on this first start in five months and something was clearly not right. Official explanation: vet said gelding bled from the nose (op 5-2)

277 BATHWICK TYRES PLYMOUTH STANDARD OPEN NATIONAL HUNT FLAT RACE 2m 1f

5:05 (5:05) (Class 6) 4-6-Y-0 **£1,626** (£477; £238; £119)

Form				RPR
	1		**Kings Riches (IRE)** 5-10-13 0 ...... DonalDevereux(5) (Peter Bowen) *hld up in last: hdwy to chse ldr 3f out: led over 1f out: pushed out* **6/4**[1]	98+
000-	2	2¼	**Dashing Patriarch**[19] 5368 5-10-11 0 ...... MrMLurcock(7) (Malcolm Beck) *t.k.h: trckd ldrs: plld way through to join ldrs after 6f: led 3f out: hung bdly lft sn after: c bk rt but hdd over 1f out: no ex fnl f* **7/1**	94
60-	3	3½	**Beck's Bolero (IRE)**[17] 7 4-11-0 0 ...... PaulMoloney (Evan Williams) *hld up 4th: rdn over 3f out: sn chsng ldng pair: styd on same pce* **7/1**	86
0/	4	19	**Court Gamble (IRE)**[747] 5206 6-10-11 0 ...... JoeTizzard (Nerys Dutfield) *t.k.h: trckd ldr: led over 4f out: sn rdn: hdd over 3f out: wknd* **6/1**[3]	64
	5	2	**Lord Hugo** 5-10-13 0 ...... JimmyDerham(5) (Seamus Mullins) *racd green: led: hdd over 4f out: sn rdn: wknd 3f out* **9/4**[2]	69

4m 12.9s (4.10) **Going Correction** -0.775s/f (Firm) **5** Ran SP% **110.1**
Speed ratings: **59,57,56,47,46**
CSF £12.12 TOTE £2.30: £3.30, £8.70; EX 13.10 Place 6 £19.35, Place 5 £7.46.
Owner Mrs Karen Bowen **Bred** Miss Helena Gaskin **Trained** Little Newcastle, Pembrokes

FOCUS

A farcical contest that basically turned into a 3f sprint. It has been given a token rating through the second.

NOTEBOOK

Kings Riches(IRE), whose dam was a 3m chase winner, knew his job well enough to score at the first time of asking. He achieved very little, though, and we will see a truer test of his ability next time. (op 2-1)
Dashing Patriarch, who pulled very hard early, had three previous runs to his name, but he still looked very green in the straight, hanging badly out to his left and handing the winner the advantage. He should stay further over hurdles, but is clearly moderate. (op 15-2 tchd 13-2)
Beck's Bolero(IRE) had steering difficulties latest, and he again failed to settle, being unable to make any impression on the front pair in the final furlong. (op 4-1)
T/Plt: £48.10 to a £1 stake. Pool: £55,056.48. 834.09 winning tickets. T/Qpdt: £14.00 to a £1 stake. Pool: £3,347.39. 176.60 winning tickets. TM

81 FONTWELL (L-H)

Wednesday, May 12

OFFICIAL GOING: Good (good to firm in places; 7.5)
Wind: Almost nil Weather: Cloudy

278 PREMIER EQUINE ART - KEITH BURDON 01273 491220 H'CAP CHASE (15 fncs) 2m 4f

1:55 (1:55) (Class 5) (0-90,83) 5-Y-0+ **£2,602** (£764; £382; £190)

Form				RPR
05-1	1		**Lord Gunnerslake (IRE)**[13] 63 10-11-5 **76** ......(v) RichardJohnson (Tim Vaughan) *occasionally j.rt: trckd ldrs: cl up fr 9th: chsd ldr after 4 out: led 2 out: rdn clr: comf* **9/4**[1]	89+
22-4	2	9	**Space Cowboy (IRE)**[12] 81 10-11-3 **74** ......(b) JamieMoore (Gary Moore) *hld up in tch: cl enough 4 out: sn pushed along and fnd nil: wnt 3rd and mstke 3 out: plugged on to take 2nd flat* **7/2**[2]	78
/P2-	3	4	**Sean Og (IRE)**[52] 4763 8-10-6 **63** ......(t) FelixDeGiles (Jonathen de Giles) *led to 3rd: chsd ldr tl lost pl briefly 9th: effrt to ld 4 out: hdd 2 out: wknd flat* **9/2**[3]	64
025-	4	12	**Monty's Moon (IRE)**[21] 5312 8-10-9 **73** ......(b) MrBJPoste(7) (Rachel Hobbs) *in tch: mstkes 5th and 10th: chal 4 out: wkng whn blnd 3 out* **10/1**	66
105-	5	51	**Mr Floppy (IRE)**[43] 4939 9-11-7 **78** ...... LeightonAspell (Alison Batchelor) *hld up and sn detached in last: pushed along and no prog 9th: t.o after next* **7/1**	21
54P-	P		**Lutin Collonges (FR)**[63] 4518 11-10-9 **66** ...... SeamusDurack (Michael Roberts) *a towards rr: lost tch 9th: sn t.o: p.u bef 4 out: b.b.v* **16/1**	—
306-	F		**Open Range (IRE)**[20] 5331 10-10-6 **63** ow2 ...... AndrewThornton (George Wareham) *led 3rd: nt fluent 6th and 11th: hdd and mstke next: wknd rapidly: 30 l 5th whn fell heavily last* **10/1**	56

5m 0.50s (-6.80) **Going Correction** -0.425s/f (Good) **7** Ran SP% **107.7**
Speed ratings: **96,92,90,86,65** —,—
toteswingers: 1&2 £1.10, 1&3 £3.40, 2&3 £3.50 CSF £9.60 CT £25.99 TOTE £2.60: £1.80, £2.20; EX 7.80.
Owner Select Racing Syndicates I **Bred** T Keane **Trained** Aberthin, Vale of Glamorgan

FOCUS

A decidedly poor contest. The winner was better than this in the past and the next three are all rated in line with their recent from.

NOTEBOOK

Lord Gunnerslake(IRE) was slightly outpaced around the final turn, but Johnson was just biding his time and he had plenty in reserve to assert from the second-last to pull well clear. He had improved for the fitting of a visor at Huntingdon two weeks ago and the headgear worked again here. He had gone up 12lb for that win, but this was such a weak contest that an in-form horse could nullify any weights rise. Connections plan to make good use of their in-form winner before the handicapper gets his say, and he is entered for a hurdle at Uttoxeter on Saturday and at Towcester next week. (tchd 2-1)
Space Cowboy(IRE) did not jump that fluently, but made steady progress on the final circuit and stayed on past the weakening leader, though he could make no inroads into the winner's advantage. He has not won for two and a half years, but goes a bit better at his local track. (op 10-3 tchd 9-2)
Sean Og(IRE) vied for the early lead, took up the running when that rival weakened, and opened up a bit of a gap around the final turn. However, that was as good as it got and he was running on empty from the second-last. He had put up his best performance for some time on his return from a break at this track in March and this was a reasonable run once again, without looking potentially winning form. (tchd 4-1)
Lutin Collonges(FR) Official explanation: jockey said gelding bled from both nostrils (op 18-1 tchd 8-1)
Open Range(IRE) attracted some market support to improve on his belated chase debut three weeks ago. However, he was too free in the lead and began to weaken from four out, and was very tired when falling at the last. (op 18-1 tchd 8-1)

279 NUTTY'S 50 YEARS OF PASO DOBLE MAIDEN HURDLE (9 hdls) 2m 2f 110y

2:30 (2:30) (Class 4) 4-Y-0+ **£3,577** (£1,050; £525; £262)

Form				RPR
00-	1		**Harvest Song (IRE)**[23] 5278 4-10-9 0 ...... WillKennedy (Henrietta Knight) *disp ld after 1st tl def advantage sn after 3 out: forged ahd after 2 out: wl in command whn veered rt after last* **40/1**	109+
3-	2	5	**Hadron Collider (FR)**[24] 5243 5-10-9 0 ...... PeterToole(5) (Charlie Mann) *trckd ldrs: mstke 6th: rdn to go 2nd after 3 out: chal and mstke next: wl hld after* **7/2**[3]	109
	3	2¼	**Oscar Close (IRE)**[22] 3066 5-11-0 115 ...... AndrewTinkler (George Baker) *disp ld after 1st tl sn after 3 out: rdn and one pce bef next* **2/1**[1]	105
532-	4	2½	**Wizard Of Odds**[51] 4786 8-10-11 110 ......(t) MrDHDunsdon(3) (Nick Gifford) *reluctant to join others at s: led to after 1st: restrained bhd ldrs and nt fluent after: shkn up in 4th after 3 out: no rspnse* **11/4**[2]	105
	5	9	**Rainiers Girl**[98] 4-9-9 0 ...... MrTJCannon(7) (Roger Teal) *in tch towards rr: rdn after 5th: clinging on to bk of gp after: abt 12 l down whn blnd bdly 2 out: no imp after* **80/1**	83
0P5-	6	24	**Stevie Bull (IRE)**[16] 25 5-10-11 0 ...... CharlieStudd(3) (Chris Gordon) *a in rr: nt gng wl fr 2nd: lost tch 6th: wl bhd fr 3 out* **40/1**	73
30U-	7	1½	**First Bay (IRE)**[68] 4413 4-10-9 106 ......(p) RichardJohnson (Keith Goldsworthy) *trckd ldrs: mstke 6th: wknd rapidly bef next: t.o* **9/2**	69
	P		**Canongate**[272] 6-11-0 0 ...... JackDoyle (Emma Lavelle) *hld up: jst in tch 6th: sn fdd and eased: t.o whn p.u bef 2 out* **14/1**	—

P **Bower Island (IRE)**[18] 6-11-0 0 .... ColinBolger —
(Chris Gordon) *racd freely: w ldrs to 3rd: wknd next: t.o whn p.u bef 6th*
66/1

4m 21.9s (-12.40) **Going Correction** -0.725s/f (Firm)
WFA 4 from 5yo+ 18lb **9** Ran SP% **114.7**
Speed ratings (Par 105): **97,94,93,92,89 79,78,—,—**
toteswingers: 1&2 £20.00, 1&3 £52.70, 2&3 £1.60 CSF £176.26 TOTE £35.20: £3.70, £1.90, £1.40; EX 308.10.
Owner The Queen **Bred** Swettenham Stud **Trained** West Lockinge, Oxon

FOCUS
An ordinary maiden hurdle. The winner produced a massive step up on his previous form.

NOTEBOOK
Harvest Song(IRE) raced up with the lead throughout and could be called the winner some way from home, and despite veering away from the whip towards the paddock exit on the run-in, he soon straightened up to win with some authority. This was only his third run over hurdles, so it might have been more about greenness as the 4-y-o readily kept up the effort when asked. Costing 290,000gns as a yearling, he had looked an expensive flop on the Flat and he has had some problems, but has improved for each run over hurdles and looks to have some potential. A big immature type, he will be put away now until the autumn and connections are confident of him jumping fences in time. Official explanation: trainer had no explanation for the apparent improvement in form
Hadron Collider(FR) was beginning to feel the pressure three out, but rallied well to challenge the winner before the last. He looked to hold a strong chance based on his debut run at Ascot last month, but the stable are out of form at present and he ran as if just below his best. (op 11-4 tchd 5-2)
Oscar Close(IRE) was up with the leaders from the start until getting outpaced from the final turn. His form on predominantly soft ground in Ireland over the winter gave him a good chance here, but there were worries about him coping with faster ground based on his recent exploits on the Flat. He did not lack fluency on the ground here, just pace, so maybe softer ground will continue to suit best. (op 11-4)
Wizard Of Odds was fractious before the start, but jumped off well enough. His jumping was clumsy and he was beginning to feel the pace half a mile out. He has been knocking at the door of a first hurdling success this year, but the first-time tongue tie did not help him see out the trip and his attitude looks questionable. (op 9-4 tchd 2-1)
Stevie Bull(IRE) Official explanation: jockey said gelding never travelled
First Bay(IRE) Official explanation: jockey said gelding had a breathing problem
Canongate Official explanation: jockey said gelding had a breathing problem

280 CRABBIES ALCOHOLIC GINGER BEER H'CAP CHASE (19 fncs) 3m 2f 110y
3:00 (3:00) (Class 5) (0-95,92) 5-Y-0+ **£2,602** (£764; £382; £190)

Form RPR
22-3 **1** **Montana Gold (IRE)**[8] 132 9-11-6 **86** .... RichardJohnson 95
(Tim Vaughan) *hld up in midfield: smooth prog to go 2nd 15th: chal next: upsides and rdn on inner fr 3 out: drvn ahd nr fin* **9/4**[1]
05-4 **2** ½ **Monsieur Georges (FR)**[12] 83 10-10-0 **66** oh9 .... WillKennedy 74
(F Jordan) *sn prom: jnd ldr 6th: led 13th: mstke 4 out and rdn: jnd next: battled on wl: hdd nr fin* **12/1**
621- **3** ½ **Siouxme (IRE)**[20] 5329 8-11-2 **82** .... LeightonAspell 89
(Alison Batchelor) *hld up last early: smooth prog to go 3rd 15th: chal on outer 3 out: upsides last: nt qckn nr fin* **11/2**[2]
6P0- **4** 26 **Brookfieldshector (IRE)**[32] 5134 6-10-0 **71** ....(t) MichaelMurphy(5) 55
(Mike Hammond) *nt a fluent: in tch: reminders 12th: rdn to go 4th sn after 4 out: lft bhd by ldrs bef next* **18/1**
P4-P **5** 16 **Lahinch Lad (IRE)**[3] 217 10-10-3 **69** ....(p) OwynNelmes 38
(Brendan Powell) *led 2nd: jnd 6th: hdd 13th: lost pl u.p 15th: wl btn after 4 out* **15/2**[3]
422- **6** 32 **Honour's Dream (FR)**[58] 4641 7-11-12 **92** ....(p) ColinBolger 32
(Chris Gordon) *cl up tl rdn and lost pl 15th: wkng whn mstke next: t.o* **11/2**[2]
11- **P** **Kappelhoff (IRE)**[38] 5011 13-10-9 **75** ....(b) MattieBatchelor —
(Lydia Richards) *a in rr: last whn mstke 9th: wknd 12th: t.o whn p.u bef 14th* **8/1**
F5-P **P** **Strolling Vagabond (IRE)**[12] 83 11-9-9 **66** oh8...(b) MarcGoldstein(5) —
(John Upson) *led to 2nd: reminders 7th: wknd u.p bef 14th: t.o whn p.u bef 3 out* **18/1**
FP-6 **P** **Ouragan Lagrange (FR)**[7] 156 8-11-10 **90** .... JamieMoore —
(Gary Moore) *w.w: wl in tch 15th: drvn and no rspnse next: wl btn after: poor 6th whn p.u bef last* **9/1**

6m 47.3s (-13.80) **Going Correction** -0.425s/f (Good) **9** Ran SP% **112.6**
Speed ratings: **103,102,102,95,90 80,—,—,—**
toteswingers: 1&2 £9.70, 1&3 £3.20, 2&3 £4.80 CSF £27.90 CT £131.39 TOTE £2.70: £1.10, £3.60, £1.70; EX 32.80.
Owner Brian Jones **Bred** Cecil Ashe **Trained** Aberthin, Vale of Glamorgan

FOCUS
A very ordinary handicap chase. The winner and third are rated in line with their decent recent runs.

NOTEBOOK
Montana Gold(IRE) jumped fluently, particularly at the tricky fences in the back straight each time, and that stood him in good stead at the finish, giving him enough in reserve to get up near the line. He has not looked the most resolute in a battle in the past, and there were echoes of that here, but he has been generally consistent since switched to fences this year and that form gave him a strong chance of breaking his maiden. (op 3-1after 4-1 in a place)
Monsieur Georges(FR) raced prominently, taking up the lead on the final circuit, and showed plenty of grit to remain in contention to the line. On this running he should be able to pick up a weak race, but he is none too consistent with a losing run over fences now stretching to 26. (op 16-1)
Siouxme(IRE) was travelling best of all as she moved into a menacing position on the home turn, but she could not convert her apparent advantage and she was out-battled in the end. Having scored over C&D three weeks ago and raised just 2lb for that success, more might have been expected although she was carrying a stone more this time round which may have been a factor. (op 9-2)
Lahinch Lad(IRE) was going reasonably well in the lead, but soon capitulated once headed on the final circuit and remains out of form. (op 17-2 tchd 13-2)

281 WEATHERBYS BANK BEGINNERS' CHASE (16 fncs) 2m 6f
3:35 (3:35) (Class 4) 5-Y-0+ **£4,228** (£1,241; £620; £310)

Form RPR
20-2 **1** **Marc Of Brilliance (USA)**[12] 85 7-10-7 112 .... JoshuaMoore(7) 122+
(Gary Moore) *mstke 1st: hld up in 4th: wnt 3rd 11th: effrt 3 out: rdn to ld next: styd on wl* **6/1**[3]
43P- **2** 2¾ **Cast Cada (IRE)**[56] 4670 7-11-0 128 ....(t) RichardJohnson 121
(Charlie Mann) *trckd ldr: led 10th: gng strly 4 out: hdd and n.m.r 2 out: one pce after* **7/4**[2]
540- **3** 17 **Elusive Dream**[88] 4032 9-11-0 0 ....(t) HarrySkelton 113+
(Paul Nicholls) *nt a fluent: trckd ldng pair: wnt 2nd 11th: drvn to chal on inner whn bmpd 2 out and stmbld bdly: nt rcvr and eased* **6/4**[1]
603- **4** 37 **Swainson (USA)**[52] 4759 9-11-0 0 .... OwynNelmes 70
(Helen Nelmes) *a in last pair and struggling: tk poor 4th bef 3 out* **80/1**
/02- **P** **Alaghiraar (IRE)**[29] 5176 6-11-0 110 .... JackDoyle —
(Emma Lavelle) *led: j. wildly first 4 fences (rdr lost iron briefly after 1st): hdd and drvn 10th: wkng whn mstke next: t.o whn p.u bef 3 out* **12/1**
2P4- **F** **Near The Water (IRE)**[52] 4762 6-11-0 0 .... LeightonAspell 65
(Richard Rowe) *hld up in detached last: nvr remotely involved: wnt poor 4th briefly 4 out: over 50 l down in 5th whn fell heavily last* **9/1**

5m 29.9s (-13.10) **Going Correction** -0.425s/f (Good) **6** Ran SP% **109.6**
Speed ratings: **106,105,98,85,— —**
toteswingers: 1&2 £2.90, 1&3 £2.40, 2&3 £1.10 CSF £16.84 TOTE £6.90: £2.40, £1.10; EX 19.90.
Owner Nick Peacock **Bred** Darley **Trained** Lower Beeding, W Sussex

FOCUS
An interesting beginners' chase. Ordinary form rated around the first two, with the third over a stone off his recent hurdles form.

NOTEBOOK
Marc Of Brilliance(USA) crept into the race and though he was a bit slow at the last in the back straight as the pace was quickening, he stuck to the task, with ears flat back against his head, to forge out a gutsy success. Although he was winning over fences at the seventh attempt, he has been generally consistent and as he goes well on fast ground, he might continue to run well. He does look a bit exposed though, which is a modifier for the overall level of form for this race. (op 15-2 tchd 11-2)
Cast Cada(IRE) jumped neatly and looked to be going well enough, but was readily outpaced from the last. With a rating of 128 already over fences, more might have been expected. However, this was the second of the stable's horses to show they are coming into form, if not having arrived at peak fitness yet, so there might be more to come. (op 11-4)
Elusive Dream looked to be destined for big things after a promising season as a novice hurdler, but after falling in a Grade 1 hurdle at Ascot in December 2008 he has never looked the same. He handled the switch to fences well enough, and looked a threat when getting bumped at the second last, pecking on landing and losing all chance, but this was a softer contest than he has been used to so he still has it all to prove. (op 11-10 tchd 7-4)

282 WEATHERBYS BLOODSTOCK INSURANCE H'CAP HURDLE (10 hdls) 2m 4f
4:10 (4:10) (Class 4) (0-115,115) 4-Y-0+ **£4,228** (£1,241; £620; £310)

Form RPR
046- **1** **Pro Pell (IRE)**[61] 4568 5-11-3 **106** .... JamieMoore 114+
(Gary Moore) *trckd ldrs in 6th: cl up 3 out: pushed along and prog to ld sn after 2 out: rdn clr* **11/2**[2]
50-2 **2** 5 **Bolton Hall (IRE)**[12] 86 8-11-4 **107** ....(tp) RichardJohnson 111
(Keith Goldsworthy) *led 3rd to 6th: rdn bef next: dropped to 6th after 3 out: rallied on inner and mstke 2 out: sn wnt 2nd: no imp on wnr* **11/2**[2]
405- **3** 6 **Prince Du Seuil (FR)**[34] 5105 7-11-3 **106** .... RobertThornton 105
(Alan King) *trckd ldng trio: wnt 2nd 3 out: effrt ld and hit 2 out hrd: sn hdd and fnd nil: nt fluent last: drvn to hold on to 3rd* **11/1**
202- **4** 1½ **Kijivu**[24] 5253 5-10-7 **96** ....(bt) FelixDeGiles 92
(Alastair Lidderdale) *w ldrs: led after 6th: kicked on bef next: hdd and no ex 2 out* **8/1**
F1P/ **5** 9 **Zero (IRE)**[403] 4854 7-11-12 **115** .... JackDoyle 104
(Emma Lavelle) *hld up last: stdy prog 7th to trck ldrs 3 out: sn rdn: wknd bef 2 out* **11/1**
342- **6** 7 **Restezen D'Armor (FR)**[65] 4492 5-10-10 **99** .... PaddyBrennan 80
(Charlie Longsdon) *hld up in rr: nt fluent 2nd: stdy prog after 6th: disp 2nd after 3 out: rdn and wknd tamely bef next* **11/4**[1]
442- **7** 5 **Ray Diamond**[23] 5291 5-11-4 **112** ....(v) MarcGoldstein(5) 89
(Michael Madgwick) *trckd ldrs in 5th: blnd 4th: rdn after 6th: sn struggling: wl bhd after 3 out* **9/1**
020- **8** 6 **Henry Hook (IRE)**[47] 4869 6-11-3 **106** .... TomO'Brien 77
(Victor Dartnall) *hld up in rr: struggling fr 5th: last and losing tch bef 7th: sn no ch* **7/1**[3]
0P2- **9** 53 **Art Exhibition (IRE)**[51] 4790 5-11-1 **109** ....(bt) PeterToole(5) 32
(Charlie Mann) *led to 3rd: w ldrs to 5th: wknd rapidly after next: t.o 3 out* **16/1**

4m 42.1s (-17.30) **Going Correction** -0.725s/f (Firm) **9** Ran SP% **113.6**
Speed ratings (Par 105): **105,103,100,100,96 93,91,89,68**
toteswingers: 1&2 £5.80, 1&3 £14.40, 2&3 £11.90 CSF £35.47 CT £319.23 TOTE £6.20: £1.50, £1.90, £3.20; EX 20.00.
Owner Mrs Julie Middleton **Bred** Mrs P De Stacpoole **Trained** Lower Beeding, W Sussex

FOCUS
A moderate handicap where they finished fairly strung out behind the progressive winner. The form is rated around the second.

NOTEBOOK
Pro Pell(IRE) was niggled going onto the final circuit, and though he was coping well enough he looked to be travelling worst of the leaders turning for home, but he kept finding enough and had settled the race before the last. He had not shown much in soft-ground novice hurdles over the winter, but raced with more promise on better ground at Sandown in March. On the face of it he did not look that well treated for his handicap debut, but he won a bumper on fast ground last autumn and clearly improved for faster conditions again. A big chasing type, connections plan to send him over fences before too long. (tchd 9-2)
Bolton Hall(IRE) raced prominently until starting to feel the pace on the final circuit, but he kept going to stay on again. He is genuine and consistent, running another good race at this track, but is now on a career-high mark and that might have an impact. (tchd 4-1)
Prince Du Seuil(FR) was still travelling well in the back straight, taking up the running from the home turn, but did not find that much and was one-paced near the finish. His mark has been on the slide, but he needs this to continue plus more give in the ground to capitalise. (op 8-1 tchd 12-1)
Kijivu seemed to enjoy herself in the lead and was travelling well until the second last, where she could find no more. She is generally consistent and often runs above her mark, but is all too vulnerable to better finishers. (op 17-2 tchd 7-1)
Restezen D'Armor(FR) was well backed after his promising effort at Stratford last time and looked to be on favourable mark, but after moving up well and looking set to be a threat he hit the third last and weakened tamely thereafter. (op 9-2 tchd 5-1 in a place)

283 "FONTWELL PHIL" NOVICES' H'CAP CHASE (13 fncs) 2m 2f
4:45 (4:45) (Class 5) (0-90,90) 5-Y-0+ **£2,602** (£764; £382; £190)

Form RPR
26-2 **1** **Wiesenfurst (GER)**[13] 63 6-11-5 **83** ....(p) JamieMoore 92
(Gary Moore) *chsd ldrs: rdn in 5th after 7th: no prog and looked btn tl styd on bef 3 out: wnt 2nd and chal 2 out: sn led: drvn out* **3/1**[1]
005- **2** 2¼ **Battlefield Bob (IRE)**[21] 5316 6-11-7 **85** .... AndrewThornton 93+
(Caroline Bailey) *hld up in rr: smooth prog 6th to go 2nd after next: hit 9th: led next: rdn and hdd after 2 out: one pce* **6/1**
21-4 **3** 11 **Bid Art (IRE)**[13] 63 5-11-5 **90** ....(t) MrRMahon(7) 87
(Jamie Snowden) *led at str pce: hit 9th: hdd next: and sn dropped to 3rd: grad fdd* **4/1**[2]

/30- **4** 3 1/4 **Rudinero (IRE)**[21] 5318 8-10-9 **78**........ PeterToole(5) 72
(Barry Brennan) *hld up in rr: gng bttr than most 1/2-way and prog 8th: rdn next: wnt 2nd after 4 out: mstke next and immediately wknd* **9/2**[3]

/30- **5** 4 **Maybe A Malt (IRE)**[20] 5328 8-11-1 **79**........ LeightonAspell 71
(Richard Rowe) *nt fluent: hld up in detached last: nvr remotely involved: wnt poor 6th after 4 out: styd on steadily wout any great press* **25/1**

545- **P** **King Diamond (FR)**[52] 4763 9-10-3 **67**........(p) WillKennedy —
(F Jordan) *prom to 7th: sn wknd u.p: t.o whn p.u bef 3 out* **11/1**

F0P- **F** **Drombeg Pride (IRE)**[205] 1837 6-10-4 **73**........ MarcGoldstein(5) —
(Gerry Enright) *mostly chsd ldr tl after 7th: wknd 9th: abt 20 l down and gng slowly whn stmbld and fell 2 out* **22/1**

0- **P** **Tinalliat (FR)**[16] 16 7-11-4 **89**........(p) MrJFMathias(7) —
(David Rees) *chsd ldrs to 4th: dropped to rr next: in last pair and toiling after 7th: t.o whn p.u bef 3 out* **33/1**

P0-3 **P** **Fort Severn (IRE)**[13] 63 6-11-8 **89**........(v) RichieMcLernon(3) —
(Brendan Powell) *chsd ldrs: lost pl and str reminders 7th: rallied and cl up after 9th: 4th and wkng whn blnd 3 out: p.u bef last* **11/2**

4m 38.1s (3.40) **Going Correction** -0.425s/f (Good) **9** Ran SP% **112.3**
Speed ratings: **75,74,69,67,65 —,—,—,—**
toteswingers: 1&2 £4.40, 1&3 £2.40, 2&3 £5.50 CSF £20.36 CT £70.76 TOTE £2.60: £1.10, £3.80, £1.20; EX 23.20.

Owner G L Moore **Bred** Gestut Elsetal **Trained** Lower Beeding, W Sussex

FOCUS
A poor novice handicap in which the winner is rated to form.

NOTEBOOK
Wiesenfurst(GER) was feeling the pace heading out onto the final circuit and his chance looked to have evaporated, but he kept finding more and was suddenly in the mix two out, from where he kept up the gallop to win well, giving his stable their third winner at the meeting. He had been struggling for consistency but his last run was respectable enough, finishing second behind Lord Gunnerslake, who won earlier on the card, and gives a handle on the form. (op 7-2 tchd 4-1 and 5-2)

Battlefield Bob(IRE), after travelling sweetly, could find no more when challenged and flashed his tail under pressure near the finish. This was a vast improvement on his hurdling efforts and he should be up to going one better, although that finishing effort is a slight cause for concern. (op 10-1)

Bid Art(IRE) jumped well in the lead, but he set off at a strong pace and could not keep up the gallop. This was another sound effort back at the scene of his first success, but the handicapper is not letting him off lightly. (op 7-2 tchd 9-2)

Rudinero(IRE) took a while to warm to the switch to chasing, jumping slowly early on, which anchored him in rear. That played to his advantage as he did not get involved in the pace up front and he plugged on past beaten horses, but he was never in with a shout. (op 11-2)

King Diamond(FR) Official explanation: jockey said gelding never travelled

284 FREE RACING WITH ODDSCHECKER.COM WEDNESDAYS INTERMEDIATE OPEN NATIONAL HUNT FLAT RACE — 1m 6f
5:15 (5:17) (Class 6) 4-6-Y-0 — **£1,431** (£420; £210; £104)

Form — RPR

\- **1** **Batonnier (FR)** 4-10-12 0........ RobertThornton 98+
(Alan King) *hld up in tch: prog to go 2nd 4f out: led over 2f out: sn pressed: shkn up and r.o wl* **10/11**[1]

0- **2** 2 **Marching Song (USA)**[33] 5122 4-10-12 0........ NickScholfield 95+
(Andy Turnell) *hld up in last pair: smooth prog fr 4f out: poised to chal over 2f out: chsd wnr after: r.o but a hld* **4/1**[2]

3 10 **Landenstown Pearl (IRE)** 4-10-5 0........ JamieMoore 76
(Seamus Mullins) *hld up in rr: effrt 6f out: outpcd over 3f out: rdn over 2f out: styd on to take 3rd fnl f* **9/2**[3]

4 8 **Jimmy The Brave** 4-10-7 0........ MarcGoldstein(5) 74
(Gerry Enright) *hld up in last pair: prog 5f out gng wl: chsd ldng pair 2f out but outpcd: lost 3rd fnl f* **20/1**

0- **5** 3 1/4 **Erehwon**[11] 6-10-11 0........ GilesHawkins(5) 74
(Philip Hobbs) *led by up to 5 l: hdd over 2f out: immediately outpcd* **20/1**

6 6 **Transinski (IRE)** 4-10-12 0........ FelixDeGiles 63
(Alastair Lidderdale) *chsd ldr: pushed along 7f out: lost pl qckly over 4f out: no ch after* **16/1**

0- **7** 2 3/4 **Manolete (IRE)**[66] 4466 4-10-12 0........ RichardJohnson 59
(Ralph Smith) *cl up: wnt 2nd briefly over 4f out: wknd qckly over 2f out* **10/1**

0- **8** 8 **Poesmulligan (IRE)**[23] 5284 4-10-12 0........ AndrewThornton 50
(Linda Jewell) *uns rdr and bolted bef s: chsd ldrs to over 4f out: sn dropped to rr and btn* **66/1**

0- **9** 8 **Acceptance**[221] 1607 5-10-9 0........ HarrySkelton 37
(Laura Mongan) *t.k.h: hld up: wknd over 5f out: sn bhd* **33/1**

3m 16.8s (-14.30) **9** Ran SP% **119.5**
toteswingers: 1&2 £3.30, 1&3 £2.90, 2&3 £3.90 CSF £4.71 TOTE £2.20: £1.10, £1.10, £1.30; EX 5.10 Place 6 £30.60, Place 5 £20.71.

Owner H R Mould **Bred** Olivier Delegue **Trained** Barbury Castle, Wilts

FOCUS
No strength in depth in this slowly run bumper but decent performances from the two market leaders.

NOTEBOOK
Batonnier(FR) steadily moved into contention, struck for home in the straight and stayed on powerfully. He looked very green for this debut, but was ridden to learn a lot from this experience, racing amongst horses and coming through despite a bit of buffeting, and showed plenty of ability to keep up the gallop. He was steady rather than flashy, suggesting this French-bred gelding will blossom once given a test of stamina. (op 6-5 tchd 5-4)

Marching Song(USA) was patiently ridden in rear and still had around five lengths to find on the winner as they went around the final turn. He made up the ground stylishly but could not get past the winner, which was slightly disappointing in the circumstances. He did not look to get the trip over 2m at Kempton and may need more time if he is to get the trip over jumps. (tchd 7-2)

Landenstown Pearl(IRE) made some progress from a rear position but could not get near the front two. She is related to several jumps winners, but the stable does not have many bumper successes, so this was as good as could be expected. (tchd 5-1)

Jimmy The Brave made some headway to be a challenger turning for home, but she was soon outclassed and faded out of it.

T/Plt: £14.30 to a £1 stake. Pool: £54,692.10. 2,772.93 winning tickets. T/Qpdt: £8.80 to a £1 stake. Pool: £3,296.69. 276.64 winning tickets. JN

PERTH (R-H)
Wednesday, May 12
OFFICIAL GOING: Good to firm (good in places; 7.0)
Wind: Breezy, half against Weather: Fine

285 LONDON HILL DRY GIN MARES' INTERMEDIATE HURDLE (10 hdls) — 2m 4f 110y
5:50 (5:51) (Class 4) 4-Y-0+ — **£2,602** (£764; £382; £190)

Form — RPR

0/1- **1** **Smuglin**[180] 2261 7-11-5 120........ JasonMaguire 109+
(Donald McCain) *nt fluent: chsd ldr: sn drvn: led appr next: drvn clr run-in* **2/1**[2]

033- **2** 10 **Proficiency**[20] 5334 5-10-12 95........(v) PaddyAspell 94
(Sue Bradburne) *led to appr 2 out: rdn and kpt on same pce* **8/1**[3]

3 9 **Dark Halo (IRE)**[59] 4628 5-10-12 0........(p) GrahamLee 85
(C A McBratney, Ire) *prom: drvn and outpcd after 4 out: plugged on fnl 2: no imp* **33/1**

2/5- **4** 14 **Posh Bird (IRE)**[26] 5205 7-11-5 115........(p) AELynch 79
(I R Ferguson, Ire) *chsd ldrs: drvn and outpcd 3 out: btn next* **6/5**[1]

206- **5** 21 **Catleen (IRE)**[57] 4663 6-10-12 0........ PeterBuchanan 53
(S R B Crawford, Ire) *nt fluent: hld up: n.m.r bnd after 6th: drvn and wknd fr next* **10/1**

0P6- **6** 12 **Be Smart (IRE)**[18] 5238 5-10-7 85........(t) MJBolger(5) 43
(Valentine Donoghue) *prom: hit 3rd: rdn and outpcd 4 out: wknd fr next* **50/1**

600- **7** 38 **Kalatime (IRE)**[215] 1681 7-11-0 72........(p) JamesHalliday(5) 15
(William Young) *sn bhd: lost tch 1/2-way: t.o* **100/1**

334/ **F** **Harveys Spirit (IRE)**[28] 5188 5-10-12 91........ DenisO'Regan —
(A J Martin, Ire) *t.k.h: hld up: hdwy and in tch 4 out: wknd bef next: 7th and wl btn whn fell heavily 2 out and down for sme time* **12/1**

5m 3.40s (-3.50) **Going Correction** -0.20s/f (Good) **8** Ran SP% **112.6**
Speed ratings (Par 105): **98,94,90,85,77 72,58,—**
toteswingers: 1&2 £2.00, 1&3 £7.80, 2&3 £14.80 CSF £17.42 TOTE £3.60: £2.10, £1.60, £12.20; EX 13.40.

Owner Broadband Partnership **Bred** R F Broad **Trained** Cholmondeley, Cheshire

FOCUS
A mares' intermediate hurdle lacking strength in depth, it was run at a steady pace and the first two home, who pulled clear, were ridden handily throughout. The winner is rated 7lb off her best.

NOTEBOOK
Smuglin, having her first start since being successful at Newcastle last November, stayed on the best from the last to run out a ready winner in the end. Rated 120, it proved an ideal opportunity for the lightly raced seven-year-old, and although she will be harder to place from now on, she is in the right hands and should stay further in due course. (op 6-4)

Proficiency, dropping back in trip, ran a solid race and looked the most likely winner turning for home. Rated 25lb below the winner, connections will be hoping the handicapper doesn't over react. She can lose her maiden tag over hurdles in a small handicap. (op 15-2)

Dark Halo(IRE) stayed on without really threatening to land a blow. She is lightly raced over hurdles and will also find life easier in modest handicaps. (op 40-1)

Posh Bird(IRE) had a chance at the weights, but in the end proved disappointing. She might prefer easier ground, but can only be watched next time after this effort. (op 6-4)

286 SIS NOVICES' H'CAP HURDLE (8 hdls) — 2m 110y
6:20 (6:20) (Class 5) (0-95,95) 4-Y-0+ — **£2,397** (£698; £349)

Form — RPR

33-0 **1** **Solis (GER)**[7] 161 7-11-7 **93**........(p) RyanMania(3) 95
(P Monteith) *chsd clr ldr: chal 2 out: led bef next: drvn out fr last* **10/3**[2]

P- **2** 1 3/4 **November Papa Golf (IRE)**[348] 524 10-11-7 **90**........ DenisO'Regan 90
(A J Martin, Ire) *hld up: hdwy 2 out: chsd wnr run-in: hrd rdn and kpt on towards fin* **9/1**

00-5 **3** 3 1/4 **King's Chorister**[7] 161 4-9-13 **75**........(t) CampbellGillies(3) 70
(Barry Murtagh) *t.k.h: chsd ldrs: hit 4th: effrt 2 out: one pce last* **5/2**[1]

500- **4** 16 **Middlemarch (IRE)**[38] 4576 10-11-12 **95**........(v) RichieMcGrath 80
(Jim Goldie) *nt fluent: led and clr to bef 3 out: hdd bef next: wknd between last 2* **16/1**

6/P- **5** 61 **Shopfrontspecialist (IRE)**[28] 5188 7-11-2 **90**........ MJBolger(5) 18
(Valentine Donoghue) *chsd ldrs to 3 out: sn wknd: eased whn no ch run-in* **8/1**[3]

634- **6** 3/4 **Night Knight (IRE)**[48] 4837 4-10-10 **88**........(v) MissLHorner(5) 12
(Chris Grant) *nt fluent: hld up: hit and struggling 3 out: t.o* **10/3**[2]

000- **U** **The Dunion**[21] 5310 7-10-2 **71**........ BrianHughes 54
(R MacDonald) *chsd ldrs: drvn and outpcd 3 out: lft 13 l 5th whn jinked rt and uns rdr last* **20/1**

/P-0 **F** **Saddlers' Supreme (IRE)**[7] 163 8-11-5 **88**........(t) JamesReveley 88
(Martin Todhunter) *hld up in tch: hdwy bef 2 out: 1 l 2nd and styng on whn fell heavily last* **16/1**

3m 57.5s (-2.20) **Going Correction** -0.20s/f (Good)
WFA 4 from 7yo+ 18lb **8** Ran SP% **112.4**
Speed ratings (Par 103): **97,96,94,87,58 58,—,—**
toteswingers: 1&2 £7.30, 2&3 £2.60 CSF £31.35 CT £85.02 TOTE £4.30: £1.40, £5.20, £1.10; EX 25.20.

Owner Dennis J Coppola **Bred** Stiftung Gestut Fahrhof **Trained** Rosewell, Midlothian

FOCUS
A weak 0-95 novices' handicap run at a sound pace and unlikely to throw up many future winners. The form reads sound enough.

NOTEBOOK
Solis(GER), wearing cheekpieces, got his head in front at the 20th attempt over hurdles. He jumped better here and this will have done his confidence no harm. However, his overall profile would suggest he is not one to take a short price about next time out. (op 4-1 tchd 9-2 and 3-1)

November Papa Golf(IRE), a point-to-point winner four years ago, threw down a strong challenge at the final flight. His shrewd trainer might be able to get this lightly raced 10-year-old to go one better. (op 6-1)

King's Chorister, having his fifth start over hurdles, travelled well throughout and didn't help himself with a untidy jump at the last. A small race should come his way if he can continue to progress. (op 7-2)

Night Knight(IRE), who was wearing a visor for the first time over jumps, though had one on when successful on the Flat. He stopped quickly after jumping three from home. Official explanation: jockey said gelding would not face the visor (op 5-2 tchd 7-2)

Saddlers' Supreme(IRE) was in the process of running a good race when taking a heavy fall at the last. (op 20-1)

287 PETER K. DALE LTD NOVICES' H'CAP CHASE (18 fncs) 3m

6:50 (6:50) (Class 4) (0-110,105) 5-Y-0+ **£4,553** (£1,337; £668; £333)

Form RPR

05P- **1** **Solway Bay**[19] 5373 8-11-1 **97**....(t) HarryHaynes(3) 118+
(Lisa Harrison) *hld up in tch: stdy hdwy 12th: effrt 3 out: led last: styd on wl u.p* **12/1**

FF5- **2** 3 3/4 **Hurricane Jack**[55] 4709 7-10-4 **83**....(bt[1]) PeterBuchanan 102
(Lucinda Russell) *led: rdn bef 2 out: hdd last: kpt on same pce* **13/2**

3 4 **King Roonah**[223] 1586 6-10-11 **90**.... JasonMaguire 105
(Gordon Elliott, Ire) *hld up in tch: smooth hdwy to chse ldr 13th: effrt and ev ch whn mstke 3 out: sn outpcd: nt fluent next: 3rd and hld whn j.rt last* **3/1**[1]

0F-2 **4** shd **Emotive**[11] 88 7-10-9 **91**.... CampbellGillies(3) 104
(Barry Murtagh) *bhd: pushed along 13th: hdwy bef 4 out: kpt on fr next: nvr able to chal* **8/1**

003- **5** 30 **Too Cool To Fool (IRE)**[85] 4096 7-10-9 **88**.... RichieMcGrath 79
(Jim Goldie) *nt fluent: hld up: rdn 12th: shortlived effrt 14th: wknd fr next* **7/2**[2]

P41- **6** 22 **Le Platino (GER)**[17] 13 8-11-12 **105**....(p) BrianHughes 71
(Brian Storey) *chsd ldrs: blnd and lost pl 12th: struggling fr next* **6/1**[3]

106/ **P** **Ziggy Zen**[13] 70 11-10-9 **95**....(t) KMDonoghue(7) —
(David Anthony O'Brien, Ire) *bhd: reminders and struggling 8th: t.o whn p.u bef 12th* **20/1**

P50- **P** **Art Bank**[62] 4532 7-10-0 **79** oh15.... PaddyAspell —
(Sue Bradburne) *chsd ldrs tl lost pl 12th: t.o whn p.u bef 4 out* **40/1**

051- **P** **Dallas Bell**[45] 4908 8-11-1 **99**.... EwanWhillans(5) —
(Alistair Whillans) *chsd ldrs tl wknd 13th: t.o whn p.u bef 4 out* **15/2**

6m 12.4s (-8.00) **Going Correction** -0.20s/f (Good) 9 Ran SP% **112.6**
Speed ratings: **105,103,102,102,92 85,—,—,—**
toteswingers: 1&2 £30.10, 1&3 £30.10, 2&3 £5.20 CSF £85.14 CT £295.23 TOTE £16.50: £6.60, £3.30, £3.20; EX 80.50.
Owner David Alan Harrison **Bred** D A Harrison **Trained** Aldoth, Cumbria

FOCUS
A 3m novices' handicap chase for horses rated 0-110, though the top weight was 5lb below the ceiling rating. It was run at an even pace. Easy form to rate.

NOTEBOOK
Solway Bay is 7lb lower over fences, and dropping back in trip after pulling up in the Highland National last time appeared to do the trick. Coming from a yard going well, there is little reason to suggest he won't remain competitive over the coming months. Official explanation: trainer said, regarding apparent improvement in form, that the gelding had jumped well and all the yard's horses have been running well of late. (op 16-1)
Hurricane Jack, wearing blinkers for the first time, is a half-brother to the yard's very useful chaser Silver By Nature. His jumping held up well and he should have little trouble going one better next time as long as the blinkers have the desired effect again. (op 9-1 tchd 10-1)
King Roonah kept on in third place. This was his first run for his trainer, who does vey well here, and he would be of interest if coming back over possibly down in trip. (op 2-1)
Too Cool To Fool(IRE) tended to run in snatches on his first try over fences. (op 4-1)
Le Platino(GER), a winner of a very weak chase at Wetherby last time, made a mistake going out on the final circuit and was soon beaten. (op 15-2 tchd 8-1 in a place)
Dallas Bell Official explanation: jockey said gelding bled from the nose

288 GLENGOYNE HIGHLAND SINGLE MALT SCOTCH WHISKY CONDITIONAL JOCKEYS' H'CAP HURDLE (8 hdls) 2m 110y

7:20 (7:20) (Class 4) (0-115,115) 4-Y-0+ **£3,252** (£955; £477; £238)

Form RPR

53-1 **1** **Beidh Tine Anseo (IRE)**[7] 161 4-10-10 **106** 7ex.... CampbellGillies(3) 120+
(Lucinda Russell) *prom: led gng wl after 2 out: shkn up and qcknd clr run-in: readily* **8/13**[1]

02-2 **2** 6 **Baaher (USA)**[5] 196 6-10-7 **104**.... PaulNorton(8) 110
(Jim Goldie) *hld up and bhd: hdwy bef 2 out: chsd wnr run-in: kpt on: no imp* **4/1**[2]

600- **3** 1/2 **Regent's Secret (USA)**[156] 2751 10-10-11 **100**....(v) EwanWhillans 107
(Jim Goldie) *hld up: hdwy bef 2 out: chsd wnr bef last to run-in: one pce* **33/1**

053- **4** 5 **Border Tale**[19] 5357 10-10-9 **106**....(b) JamesSmith(8) 108
(James Moffatt) *led 2nd: hdd after 2 out: outpcd fr last* **14/1**

5/ **5** 4 **Tetouan**[590] 1531 6-11-3 **114**.... KMDonoghue(8) 111
(Gordon Elliott, Ire) *hld up: hdwy and prom bef 2 out: sn outpcd* **16/1**

446- **6** 2 3/4 **Longdale**[15] 34 12-10-3 **97**.... PaulGallagher(5) 93
(Martin Todhunter) *hld up in tch: hdwy to chse ldrs 3 out: hit next: sn wknd* **33/1**

1- **7** 3 3/4 **Caulkin (IRE)**[9] 117 7-11-12 **115**.... JamesHalliday 108
(I R Ferguson, Ire) *chsd ldrs: ev ch gng wl bef 2 out: sn rdn and wknd* **20/1**

050- **8** 12 **Soubriquet (IRE)**[156] 2751 7-10-11 **105**....(t) MrDarylMillar(5) 86
(Maurice Barnes) *in tch: outpcd bef 3 out: sn wknd* **33/1**

00-0 **9** 7 **Sea Cove**[7] 160 10-10-1 **90**.... RyanMania 65
(Dianne Sayer) *prom tl rdn and lost pl 3 out: sn struggling* **66/1**

6P4- **10** 7 **Rossini's Dancer**[21] 5310 5-10-8 **97**.... AlexMerriam 65
(Sue Bradburne) *led to 2nd: cl up: hit next: rdn and wknd bef 2 out* **50/1**

11 dist **Golan Guy (IRE)**[35] 5086 5-11-8 **111**.... RTDunne —
(A J Martin, Ire) *hld up: nt fluent and rdn 3 out: wknd bef next: virtually p.u run-in* **10/1**[3]

3m 53.2s (-6.50) **Going Correction** -0.20s/f (Good)
WFA 4 from 5yo+ 18lb 11 Ran SP% **120.6**
Speed ratings (Par 105): **107,104,103,101,99 98,96,91,87,84 37**
toteswingers: 1&2 £1.50, 1&3 £5.20, 2&3 £8.80 CSF £3.51 CT £42.86 TOTE £1.60: £1.20, £1.10, £7.60; EX 3.20.
Owner Ian D Miller **Bred** J S Bolger **Trained** Arlary, Perth & Kinross

FOCUS
A competitive little handicap run at a sound pace. Solid form. The easy winner was again value for further and can go on to rate higher.

NOTEBOOK
Beidh Tine Anseo(IRE) is clearly going the right way. Carrying a 7lb penalty for his recent Kelso success, he was still 11lb well in and it proved a very easy task. His earlier juvenile form looks rock solid as well and, despite his hike in the weights, he will still be one to follow on this better ground at this time of year. (op 8-11 tchd 4-5 in places)
Baaher(USA), who is still a maiden over hurdles, ran well considering how keen he was early in the contest. Due to go up 4lb at the weekend, he can go one better shortly and time might well prove this is strong form for this time of year. (op 5-1)
Regent's Secret(USA) again ran a solid race at his favourite track (all three jumping wins have been here). He can continue to be competitive, especially at this track. (op 25-1)
Border Tale again ran his race and could do with a little help from the handicapper. (op 12-1 tchd 16-1)

289 STEADFAST SCOTLAND MAIDEN HURDLE (10 hdls) 2m 4f 110y

7:50 (7:50) (Class 5) 4-Y-0+ **£2,276** (£668; £334; £166)

Form RPR

1 **What A Riddle (IRE)**[185] 2173 7-11-0 0.... DenisO'Regan 112+
(A J Martin, Ire) *hld up: stdy hdwy 4 out: effrt and disp ld last: led run-in: jst hld on* **16/1**

035- **2** nse **Malin Bay (IRE)**[19] 5370 5-10-11 0.... FearghalDavis(3) 113+
(Nicky Richards) *hld up in midfield: stdy hdwy to chse ldrs 3 out: led bef next: sn rdn: hdd run-in: rallied: jst failed* **8/1**

252- **3** 14 **Pegasus Prince (USA)**[21] 5305 6-11-0 110.... BrianHughes 101
(John Wade) *chsd ldrs: drvn bef 3 out: rallied: one pce after next* **7/2**[3]

503- **4** 5 **Fool's Wildcat (USA)**[35] 5086 5-10-9 95....(t) MJBolger(5) 97
(Valentine Donoghue) *hld up: effrt u.p bef 3 out: no imp fr next: hld whn hit last* **66/1**

0U6- **5** 18 **Soldiers Tree (IRE)**[21] 5305 5-11-0 0....(t) PaddyAspell 79
(Sue Bradburne) *chsd ldrs: drvn after 3 out: wknd bef next* **50/1**

022- **6** 9 **Eighteen Carat (IRE)**[19] 5354 6-11-0 108.... JasonMaguire 76
(Donald McCain) *cl up: led 4 out: hdd whn nt fluent 2 out: wknd* **3/1**[2]

00- **7** 49 **Wellesley**[20] 5333 4-10-2 0.... GarryWhillans(7) 21
(Donald Whillans) *a bhd: struggling fnl circ: t.o* **80/1**

044- **8** 2 1/4 **Mr Tallyman**[19] 5370 4-10-9 112.... BarryKeniry 19
(Micky Hammond) *t.k.h: trckd ldrs: rdn and outpcd whn blnd 2 out: sn btn* **10/1**

PP- **9** 5 **Molesden Glen (IRE)**[17] 8 4-10-6 0....(t) CampbellGillies(3) 15
(Simon Waugh) *led to 4 out: rallied and ev ch 3 out: wknd bef next* **100/1**

3- **10** 14 **Apache Country**[21] 5305 6-10-7 0....(t) KMDonoghue(7) 7
(Gordon Elliott, Ire) *in tch: drvn 4 out: wknd fr next* **5/2**[1]

P **Daasij (IRE)**[215] 5-11-0 0.... PeterBuchanan —
(J Barclay) *a bhd: struggling fr 1/2-way: t.o whn p.u after 2 out* **25/1**

P **Osbaldeston (IRE)** 7-11-0 0.... WilsonRenwick —
(Rose Dobbin) *nt fluent: a bhd: t.o whn p.u bef 2 out* **50/1**

P **Kiltartan (IRE)**[45] 5-11-0 0.... SamThomas —
(Miss Clare Judith Macmahon, Ire) *trckd ldrs: rdn and wknd after 4 out: t.o whn p.u bef 2 out* **14/1**

P **Bernie'Stheboss (IRE)**[59] 5-10-7 0....(t) GrahamLee —
(David Anthony O'Brien, Ire) *a bhd: struggling 1/2-way: t.o whn p.u bef 4 out* **50/1**

5m 1.00s (-5.90) **Going Correction** -0.20s/f (Good)
WFA 4 from 5yo+ 19lb 14 Ran SP% **122.0**
Speed ratings (Par 103): **103,102,97,95,88 85,67,66,64,59 —,—,—,—**
toteswingers: 1&2 £26.30, 1&3 £26.30, 2&3 £7.20 CSF £136.53 TOTE £16.70: £3.70, £3.50, £2.20; EX 411.50.
Owner P A Byrne **Bred** S Slater **Trained** Summerhill, Co. Meath
■ Stewards' Enquiry : Denis O'Regan one-day ban: careless riding (May 26)
Fearghal Davis caution: used whip with excessive frequency.

FOCUS
Probably just an ordinary maiden hurdle run at a sound pace and the first three pulled well clear. Big steps up from the first two.

NOTEBOOK
What A Riddle(IRE), lightly raced, had been second on much easier ground in a maiden hurdle at Tramore over two years ago. Easy to back here, he stayed on well and can score again if able to stay sound and get back on the track at this time of year. (op 12-1)
Malin Bay(IRE), who had finished behind the disappointing Mr Tallyman here last time out, is clearly going the right way and a similar contest can go his way in the coming weeks. (op 9-1)
Pegasus Prince(USA), rated 110, appeared to run his race and is the one to put the form in some context. (op 9-2)
Eighteen Carat(IRE), from an in-form yard, was also well below par. There is room for improvement in the jumping department with him. (op 11-4)
Apache Country, wearing a tonguestrap, was very disappointing, beaten before three from home. He can only be watched after this. (op 10-3)

290 ISLE OF SKYE BLENDED SCOTCH WHISKY H'CAP CHASE (12 fncs) 2m

8:20 (8:21) (Class 4) (0-115,115) 5-Y-0+ **£5,854** (£1,719; £859; £429)

Form RPR

P55- **1** **Seeyaaj**[270] 1220 10-11-1 **107**....(t) CampbellGillies(3) 119+
(Lucinda Russell) *prom: smooth hdwy to ld 2 out: styd on strly fr last* **8/1**

554- **2** 3 **Storm Prospect**[31] 5139 7-10-6 **95**....(b) PeterBuchanan 103
(Lucinda Russell) *bhd: pushed along 1/2-way: hdwy bef 4 out: effrt next: chsd wnr run-in: kpt on: no imp* **2/1**[1]

204- **3** 2 **All For The Cause (IRE)**[60] 4579 8-11-12 **115**.... BarryKeniry 120
(Nicky Richards) *hld up: stdy hdwy 1/2-way: effrt and chsd wnr bef last to run-in: edgd rt and no ex* **6/1**

210- **4** 10 **Yankee Holiday (IRE)**[48] 4836 10-9-8 **90**.... PaulGallagher(7) 88
(Sue Bradburne) *cl up: led 6th to 2 out: wknd and lost 2nd last* **11/2**[3]

200- **5** 16 **Flaming Heck**[39] 4984 13-9-10 **92**.... AlexanderVoy(7) 74
(Lucy Normile) *prom: outpcd 5 out: rallied next: wknd fr 3 out* **14/1**

220- **6** 20 **Calculaite**[15] 34 9-11-11 **114**.... JamesReveley 78
(Martin Todhunter) *led to 6th: cl up tl rdn and wknd bef 3 out* **9/1**

0P-0 **7** 15 **Norminster**[11] 88 9-9-11 **89** oh5....(p) RyanMania(3) 39
(Rayson Nixon) *bhd: outpcd 1/2-way: lost tch bef 4 out* **25/1**

U4F- **P** **Tranos (USA)**[18] 5390 7-10-2 **91**.... GrahamLee —
(Micky Hammond) *in tch: nt fluent and outpcd 4th: p.u bef next* **4/1**[2]

3m 58.0s (-4.70) **Going Correction** -0.20s/f (Good) 8 Ran SP% **114.6**
Speed ratings: **103,101,100,95,87 77,70,—**
toteswingers: 1&2 £4.10, 1&3 £5.70, 2&3 £3.20 CSF £25.62 CT £104.47 TOTE £13.60: £3.90, £1.10, £2.90; EX 23.60.
Owner Brahms & Liszt **Bred** Milton Park Stud Partnership **Trained** Arlary, Perth & Kinross

FOCUS
An even gallop for this 0-115 2m handicap chase, which was full of horses with questions to answer. The winner is rated back to form with the next two setting the level.

NOTEBOOK
Seeyaaj, having his first run since last August, is clearly in good heart and should continue to pay his way. (tchd 7-1)
Storm Prospect, a previous course winner, appeared to run his race. That said, his last win was nearly two years ago and he doesn't look one to take a short price about in his bid to go one better next time. (tchd 9-4)
All For The Cause(IRE) is now a maiden over fences after 13 starts. He could do with some help from the handicapper and deserves to get his head in front at some point. (op 13-2 tchd 7-1)
Yankee Holiday(IRE) weakened quickly; he also doesn't have the best strike-rate. (op 5-1 tchd 9-2)

Tranos(USA) Official explanation: jockey said gelding pulled up lame

291 WATSON'S TRAWLER DARK RUM H'CAP HURDLE (12 hdls) 3m 110y
8:50 (8:50) (Class 4) (0-115,110) 4-Y-0+ **£3,903** (£1,146; £573; £286)

Form RPR
042- **1** **Ballymacduff (IRE)**[20] 5334 6-11-2 **100**..........(t) JanFaltejsek 110+
(George Charlton) *t.k.h: cl up: shkn up and ev ch last: sn led: kpt on strly* **6/1**[3]
553- **2** 2 3/4 **Maolisa (IRE)**[85] 4092 8-9-12 **85**.......... CampbellGillies(3) 93+
(S R B Crawford, Ire) *led: rdn bef 2 out: nt fluent last: sn hdd: kpt on same pce run-in* **11/1**
PP4- **3** 2 1/2 **Dundock**[51] 4783 9-10-8 **97**.......... EwanWhillans(5) 100
(Alistair Whillans) *mstkes: chsd ldrs: drvn bef 2 out: kpt on same pce bef last* **13/2**
404- **4** 4 1/2 **Summer Soul (IRE)**[26] 5207 8-11-12 **110**..........(p) PeterBuchanan 109
(Lucinda Russell) *hld up towards rr: effrt and rdn whn hit 2 out: sn no imp* **11/1**
305- **5** 6 **Follow On**[15] 32 8-10-9 **96**..........(t) MichaelMcAlister(3) 90
(Maurice Barnes) *hld up: hdwy u.p and in tch 3 out: outpcd fr next* **22/1**
05-2 **6** 4 **Mini Beck**[7] 163 11-11-5 **110**.......... AlexanderVoy(7) 102
(Sandy Thomson) *trckd ldrs: hit 7th: rdn and wknd bef 2 out* **9/2**[2]
P12- **7** 23 **Solway Bee**[20] 5339 10-10-4 **91**..........(p) HarryHaynes(3) 61
(Lisa Harrison) *prom: drvn after 3 out: wknd bef next* **3/1**[1]
/P0- **8** 2 3/4 **Browneyes Blue (IRE)**[14] 45 12-11-7 **105**.......... PaddyAspell 72
(James Moffatt) *midfield: outpcd after 4 out: btn bef 2 out* **28/1**
502/ **9** 2 3/4 **Valley Of Giants**[53] 4747 8-11-11 **109**..........(p) JasonMaguire 74
(Gordon Elliott, Ire) *in tch: lost pl whn blnd 7th: effrt u.p after 4 out: wknd next* **13/2**
P42/ **10** 72 **Baileys Encore**[28] 5188 7-10-11 **100**..........(t) MJBolger(5) —
(Valentine Donoghue) *mstkes in rr: outpcd whn blnd 4 out and next: t.o* **33/1**
0/6- **P** **Foodbroker Founder**[18] 10-11-2 **107**.......... MissLAlexander(7) —
(N W Alexander) *nt fluent in rr: struggling fnl circ: t.o whn p.u bef 3 out* **66/1**
P **All The Cousins (IRE)**[46] 4904 10-11-11 **109**.......... DenisO'Regan —
(A J Martin, Ire) *midfield: n.m.r bnd after 7th: lost pl: p.u and dismntd after next* **10/1**

6m 8.90s (-1.00) **Going Correction** -0.20s/f (Good) **12** Ran SP% **122.1**
Speed ratings (Par 105): **93,92,91,89,87 86,79,78,77,54 —,—**
toteswingers: 1&2 £26.60, 1&3 £19.90, 2&3 £7.10 CSF £68.82 CT £452.38 TOTE £6.00: £1.90, £6.50, £3.60; EX 85.90 Place 6 £48.41, Place 5 £14.73.
Owner George A Charlton **Bred** Hugh J Holohan **Trained** Stocksfield, Northumberland

FOCUS
A wide-open 3m handicap hurdle open to horses rated 0-115, though the top weight was 5lb below the ceiling rating. There was an even pace and the first two home were prominent throughout. A big step forward from the winner.

NOTEBOOK
Ballymacduff(IRE), although keen early, lost his maiden tag in good style and should remain competitive at this time of the year. He is clearly going the right way. (op 13-2 tchd 7-1)
Maolisa(IRE), a point-to-point winner, appeared to stay this trip well enough and can go one better in similar company. (op 14-1)
Dundock, 7lb lower than for his last win, stayed on strongly from the last. His best form has come on easier ground and he isn't one to give up on. (op 6-1 tchd 15-2 and 8-1 in places)
Summer Soul(IRE), from an in-form yard, ran okay but it's a long time since his last win. (op 12-1)
Solway Bee weakened quickly after holding every chance three from home. (op 7-2)
All The Cousins(IRE) was pulled up and dismounted, appearing to go wrong. (op 5-1)
T/Plt: £42.90 to a £1 stake. Pool: £68,985.97. 1,171.66 winning tickets. T/Qpdt: £15.10 to a £1 stake. Pool: £6,152.60. 299.57 winning tickets. RY

FOLKESTONE (R-H)
Thursday, May 13
OFFICIAL GOING: Good (good to firm in places; 7.5)
Wind: virtually nil Weather: bright, chilly

292 NIGEL COLLISON FUELS LTD NOVICES' HUNTERS' CHASE (FOR THE GUY PEATE MEMORIAL CHALLENGE TROPHY) (19 fncs) 3m 2f
5:35 (5:35) (Class 6) 5-Y-0+ **£1,318** (£405; £202)

Form RPR
203/ **1** **Delightful Cliche**[10] 9-11-11 0.......... MissGAndrews(3) 109+
(S R Andrews) *led to 2nd: chsd ldrs after: lost pl 6th: hdwy to chse ldng pair 8th: lft in ld 13th: mde rest: mstke 3 out: rdn clr between last 2: in command whn idled and hung lft flat: fnd ex whn pressed nr fin* **3/1**[3]
P/2- **2** nk **He's On His Way (IRE)**[10] 11-11-11 0..........(p) JoshuaMoore(3) 107
(David Phelan) *sn niggled along in rr: hdwy into midfield 9th: lft 3rd and sltly hmpd 13th: sn rdn: mstke next: drvn to chse wnr 3 out: outpcd next: rallied as wnr idled flat: hld nr fin* **2/1**[1]
F/5- **3** 4 1/2 **Ambrosinni**[26] 8-12-0 0.......... MrPYork 102
(P York) *towards rr: mstke 4th: pushed along and hdwy 12th: lft 2nd next: rdn and pressing wnr whn hit next: drvn after 3 out: one pce whn hit next* **5/2**[2]
025/ **4** 11 **Supa Tramp**[38] 7-11-11 0.......... MrPBull(3) 94+
(Mrs Suzy Bull) *hld up in last trio: hdwy to chse ldrs whn j. slowly 12th: lft 4th and sltly hmpd next: rdn and wknd bef 2 out* **13/2**
P32/ **5** 33 **Master Brew**[10] 12-11-7 0..........(p) MrWHickman(7) 58
(Mrs Alison Hickman) *j. slowly 1st: in tch tl struggling and dropped to last after 10th: lost tch 14th: t.o 3 out* **25/1**
00F/ **6** 3 3/4 **Balableu (FR)**[10] 8-11-7 0.......... MissCDouglas(7) 54
(Mrs Diane Broad) *t.k.h: chsd ldrs: dived 2nd: chsd ldr 4th tl 12th: rdn and struggling 16th: rallied briefly after next: wknd qckly bef 2 out: t.o* **28/1**
040/ **F** **Achieved**[5] 7-11-9 0..........(b[1]) MrGGallagher(5) —
(Daniel O'Brien) *j. bdly rt: racd freely: led 2nd tl fell 13th* **14/1**
334/ **P** **Roaringwater (IRE)**[18] 11-11-7 0..........(b) MissCHaydon(7) —
(Miss C M E Haydon) *chsd ldrs tl lost pl 8th: bhd 11th: lost tch 14th: t.o 3 out tl p.u last* **20/1**
P **Cotton Bay (IRE)**[61] 7-11-7 0..........(p) MrMGorman(7) —
(Mrs C M Gorman) *chsd ldrs tl lost pl 11th: lost tch 13th: t.o whn p.u 15th* **40/1**

6m 24.4s (-18.70) **Going Correction** -0.775s/f (Firm) **9** Ran SP% **121.4**
Speed ratings: **97,96,95,92,81 80,—,—,—**
toteswingers:1&2:£2.20, 1&3:£2.40, 2&3:£1.10 CSF £10.05 TOTE £4.90: £2.10, £1.90, £1.90; EX 10.40.
Owner Mrs P Rogers **Bred** Mrs P Sly **Trained** Luton, Beds
⊠ Stewards' Enquiry : Mr W Hickman one-day ban: used whip when out of contention (tbn)
Mr P York caution: used whip with excessive frequency

FOCUS
A moderate hunter chas in which the winner is rated to his rules mark.

NOTEBOOK
Delightful Cliche has been performing with credit in points this season and was given a good ride by the capable Gina Andrews to score, despite idling and hanging left close home. He is a strong stayer, who has a good attitude and who should acquit himself well in hunter chases. (op 4-1tchd 9-2 in a place)
He's On His Way(IRE) won his last three starts in points but was under pressure from a long way out. He kept trying for Joshua Moore and he nearly caught the winner. He ought to be up to winning a hunter chase but will need a sterner test to do so. Better ground would also suit him better. (op 7-4 tchd 13-8)
Ambrosinni, who is not the biggest, scored in his Members' race at Penshurst in March. He ran creditably here, but never threatened to score. He looks one paced and may struggle to be competitive outside of point-to-points. (op 11-4)
Supa Tramp came in for support before the off but ultimately was not good enough. He would also appreciate the ground on the easy side. (op 7-1 tchd 11-2)

293 GRANT'S CHERRY BRANDY SOUTH EAST NOVICES' HUNTERS' CHASE (15 fncs) 2m 5f
6:05 (6:05) (Class 5) 5-Y-0+ **£2,637** (£811; £405)

Form RPR
1 **Fort View (IRE)**[26] 6-11-7 0..........(p) MrRGHenderson(7) 102
(Polly Gundry) *chsd ldrs: rdn after 3 out: drvn to chse wnr between last 2: styd on wl flat to ld fnl 110yds* **3/1**[2]
2 1/2 **Behind The Scenes (IRE)**[32] 8-11-9 0.......... MrPGHall(5) 102
(Mrs D H McCarthy) *w ldr tl led 9th: j.lft and rdn 2 out: hung lft u.p flat: hdd and no ex fnl 100yds* **20/1**
/U4- **3** 2 3/4 **Divine Intavention (IRE)**[10] 6-11-7 0.......... MrNdeBoinville(7) 99
(Sue Wilson) *t.k.h: hld up in midfield: hdwy to chse ldrs 9th: rdn after 11th: chsd wnr u.p bef 2 out: one pce and btn between last 2* **8/1**
0/P- **4** 29 **Spartan Place**[46] 10-12-0 90.......... MrPYork 77+
(R Gurney) *nt a fluent: led tl 9th: styd w ldr: mstke 10th: rdn bef 3 out: drvn after 3 out: wknd qckly ent st: fin slowly* **4/1**[3]
5 4 **Good Return (FR)**[26] 7-11-7 0..........(t) MrDMaxwell(7) 66
(Mrs Kim Smyly) *hld up in last trio: clsd and in tch 8th: nudged along and struggling next: wl btn 12th: t.o* **13/2**
24P/ **6** 10 **Greek Star**[10] 9-11-7 0.......... MrRichardCollinson(7) 56
(H Hill) *chsd ldrs: lost pl 6th: rdn and struggling 9th: t.o fr 3 out* **28/1**
7 4 1/2 **Jonlahy (IRE)**[10] 11-11-7 0.......... MrJMQuinlan(7) 51
(Mrs J Quinlan) *hld up in last trio: j.lft 1st: mstke next: hdwy and in tch 8th: 5th and outpcd after 10th: wl btn 3 out: t.o* **22/1**
P5/F **P** **Native Bob (IRE)**[14] 61 6-11-11 0.......... MrJOwen(3) —
(J M Turner) *t.k.h: chsd ldrs tl lost pl rapidly and dropped to last 7th: eased and p.u bef next* **5/2**[1]
P **General Willie**[19] 8-11-7 0.......... L-BdrJSole(7) —
(C J Lawson) *hld up in last trio: clsd and in tch 8th: j.lft next and immediately struggling: t.o whn p.u 11th* **25/1**

5m 4.20s (-18.00) **Going Correction** -0.775s/f (Firm) **9** Ran SP% **114.4**
Speed ratings: **103,102,101,90,89 85,83,—,—**
toteswingers:1&2:£14.50, 1&3:£4.40, 2&3:£10.50 CSF £57.47 TOTE £5.70: £2.40, £2.30, £1.10; EX 43.80.
Owner Guy Henderson **Bred** Noel Delahunty **Trained** Axminster, East Devon

FOCUS
An uncompetitive hunter chase but it comes out quite well on time compared with other races over the trip.

NOTEBOOK
Fort View(IRE) is a tall individual who looked a bit weak last year. He scored in his last two point-to-point starts this time and made a winning start to his hunter chase career. He was under pressure from a long way out but kept responding to the rider's urgings. He can continue to progress as he is only six and a longer trip is sure to suit him. (op 7-2)
Behind The Scenes(IRE) was left clear on his sole start in an English point last time. He stepped up on that effort and could still be open to improvement, but may find point-to-points easier to win than hunter chases. His jumping in Ireland, when trained by Arthur Moore, was always suspect.
Divine Intavention(IRE) ran well in his point-to-point last time but he lacks the class to win hunter chases under his inexperienced rider. This is his right trip, and he is worth trying under a professional. (tchd 15-2)
Spartan Place won his last three points in good style but found the quicker ground against him and that saw his jumping problems re-surface. He is going to struggle in hunter chases. (op 7-2)
Good Return(FR) was well backed but never looked like scoring under his owner-rider, who was never able to get competitive. (op 14-1)
Native Bob(IRE) failed to settle and ultimately shaped as though something went wrong. He was reported to have hated the ground. Official explanation: jockey said he thought gelding had gone wrong; vet said gelding was found to be sound (op 2-1)

294 HAMLET OAK FRAMED BUILDINGS MAIDEN HUNTERS' CHASE (FOR THE CUCKOO MAIDEN CHALLENGE CUP) (15 fncs) 2m 5f
6:40 (6:40) (Class 6) 5-Y-0+ **£1,318** (£405; £202)

Form RPR
UP2/ **1** **More Trouble (IRE)**[18] 9-12-0 0..........(b) MrJETudor 97+
(Alan Hill) *nt a fluent: alway pressing for ld: clr w ldr after 9th: led 3 out: clr and wl in command bef next: pushed out* **15/8**[1]
P/P- **2** 7 **Captain's Legacy**[19] 9-11-11 0..........(b[1]) MrPBull(3) 91+
(Miss E Leppard) *w ldrs tl led 8th: clr w wnr fr 10th: mstke and hdd 3 out: no ch w wnr bef next but kpt on for clr 2nd* **16/1**
/5-P **3** 21 **Saddlers Blaze (IRE)**[8] 152 8-11-7 57..........(t) AdamWedge(7) 67
(Edward Creighton) *chsd ldrs: rdn and outpcd 10th:5th and no ch w ldrs 3 out: styd on flat to snatch 3rd last stride* **18/1**
4/0- **4** shd **The Tailor Carey (IRE)**[10] 11-11-7 90..........(p) MrMGorman(7) 68
(Mrs C M Gorman) *t.k.h: hld up in tch towards rr: hdwy 7th: chsd ldrs 10th: sn outpcd by ldng pair: wnt 3rd 11th: wl btn after 3 out: lost 3rd last stride* **12/1**
PF5- **5** 6 **High Toby**[23] 5297 11-11-7 79.......... MrTCheesman(7) 61
(Eric George) *hld up in tch towards rr: effrt and in tch after 8th: struggling and rdn after next: wl bhd fr 12th* **25/1**
/2-0 **6** 2 1/2 **New Street Express (IRE)**[8] 153 9-11-7 0.......... MrPBlagg(7) 58
(Paul Blagg) *prom: led 2nd tl 8th: outpcd by ldng pair 10th: 4th and wl btn after 3 out: t.o* **7/1**[3]
7 2 **Man From Moscow**[19] 7-11-7 0.......... MrWHickman(7) 56
(Mrs Alison Hickman) *in tch in midfield: struggling whn wnt wd and rdn after 9th: wl bhd fr 11th: t.o bef 2 out* **22/1**
P **Lord Snow (IRE)**[46] 9-11-9 0.......... MrNPearce(5) —
(N Pearce) *a in rr: mstke 6th: lost tch after 9th: t.o 3 out tl p.u next* **8/1**
4P0/ **P** **Tobougg Welcome (IRE)**[25] 6-11-9 0.......... MrPGHall(5) —
(Miss Rose Grissell) *j. v poorly in last: sn lost tch: t.o 6th tl p.u 9th* **12/1**

U4P- **P** **Nessa**10 7-11-7 0 MrPYork —
(P York) *a towards rr: pushed along 8th: rdn and struggling whn mstke 10th: t.o whn p.u 2 out* **3/1**2

5m 8.10s (-14.10) **Going Correction** -0.775s/f (Firm) **10** Ran SP% **118.1**
Speed ratings: **95,92,84,84,82 81,80,—,—,—**
toteswingers:1&2:£21.30, 1&3:£11.80, 2&3:£21.30 CSF £33.49 TOTE £3.40: £2.80, £6.60, £8.70; EX 27.40.
Owner I R Mann **Bred** Mrs B Collins **Trained** Aston Rowant, Oxfordshire

FOCUS
The winner proved a class apart here and is rated in line with his best hurdles form.

NOTEBOOK
More Trouble(IRE) had won six of his last eight starts in points and now added an easy hunter chase success to his tally. He is a quirky sort whose jumping is not always fluent but his blinkers helped him concentrate and he had the assistance of a top jockey. He has plenty of ability and he ought to be capable of winning again in this sphere. He could go summer jumping from the Lawney Hill yard, and he is sure to do well. (op 7-4)
Captain's Legacy was sporting blinkers for the first time and they brought about some improvement. However, he was not always in rhythm with his rider and could struggle in this sphere in the future. (op 14-1)
Saddlers Blaze(IRE) had been performing poorly in hunter chases recently but a change of jockey bought about some improvement. He is only moderate and will find it hard to win races under rules (op 20-1)
The Tailor Carey(IRE) is an inconsistent sort who shows his best form going right handed. He kept trying for his rider but ultimately was not good enough. (op 8-1)

295 SHEPHERD NEAME UNITED HUNTS OPEN CHAMPION HUNTERS' CHASE (22 fncs) 3m 7f
7:15 (7:15) (Class 4) 6-Y-0+ **£3,123** (£968; £484; £242)

Form RPR
6/2- **1** **Teeton Bollinger**12 9-11-5 0 (p) MrNPearce(5) 96+
(Mrs Joan Tice) *nt a fluent: sn pushed along: chsd ldrs: reminders after 15th: rdn 17th: chsd ldr 19th: looked btn 2 out: swtchd rt and styd on dourly to chal last: led fnl 75yds: edgd lft under towards fin: all out* **11/10**1

2 1/2 **The Camerengo (IRE)**12 10-11-3 0 (b1) AdamWedge(7) 95
(A R Corbett) *t.k.h: chsd ldrs: jnd ldrs 15th: led after 17th: looked wnr 2 out: sn rdn and nt look keen: jnd last: hdd and edgd lft fnl 75yds:* **7/1**

3 20 **Wee Fly (FR)**12 8-11-3 0 MissPGundry 68
(Ross Oliver) *racd on outer: led tl 4th: chsd ldr tl led again 8th tl 12th: outpcd by ldng pair and j. bdly rt 3 out: wl btn bef next* **10/3**2

0- **4** 49 **Lord Fitzroy**12 11-11-3 0 MissABush(7) 26
(Mrs O Bush) *a in last pair and sn niggled along: clsd and in tch 8th: struggling and pushed along again after 13th: lost tch and t.o fr 16th* **33/1**

P2P/ **P** **Inishturk (IRE)**10 11-11-3 0 MissBAndrews(7) —
(S R Andrews) *in tch tl dropped to last pair and pushed along 6th: nvr gng wl after and rdn along at times: lost tch after 13th: t.o and p.u wl bef 2 out* **16/1**

U **Flowersoftherarest (IRE)**10 7-11-7 0 (p) JoshuaMoore(3) —
(David Phelan) *chsd ldr tl led 4th: mstke and hdd 8th: led again 12th: mstke 14th: hdd after 17th: 4th and btn whn: j. across: mstke and uns rdr 3 out* **9/2**3

7m 43.9s (-9.00) **Going Correction** -0.775s/f (Firm) **6** Ran SP% **110.2**
Speed ratings: **80,79,74,62,— —**
toteswingers:1&2:£1.30, 1&3:£1.10, 2&3:£3.40 CSF £9.02 TOTE £1.60: £1.10, £4.60; EX 7.80.
Owner Mrs Joan Tice **Bred** Mrs Joan Tice **Trained** Pytchley, Northants
☒ Stewards' Enquiry : Mr N Pearce one-day ban: used whip with excessive frequency (tbn)

FOCUS
The first pair dominated this marathon hunter chase. Ordinary hunter frorm, the winner rated to his mark.

NOTEBOOK
Teeton Bollinger went one place better than he did in this race last year. He is a strong stayer who never travelled or jumped with any fluency but he was the beneficiary of a tremendous ride from Nick Pearce. He clearly did not like the quicker ground but, returned to a softer surface, he is sure to do well in staying races. (op 11-8)
The Camerengo(IRE) built up a good record in points and was not at fault when carried out last time. He raced awkwardly from three out and carried his head high in the closing stages but his capable rider got the best out of him. He might just win a hunter chase if age does not catch up with him and a try in a novices chase might not be over-optimistic. (op 6-1 tchd 11-2)
Wee Fly(FR) had scored in a couple of modest Cornish points and raced on the outside under his veteran rider. He lacked the class of the leading pair and is more likely to resume his career in the pointing field. (op 11-4)
Lord Fitzroy lacks the class to be competitive in hunter chases and did not seem to want to stride out on the ground. (op 40-1)

296 GUILLAINE OVENDEN 95TH BIRTHDAY OPEN HUNTERS' CHASE (FOR THE STUART ADAMSON MEMORIAL TROPHY) (10 fncs 8 omitted) 3m 1f
7:50 (7:55) (Class 6) 5-Y-0+ **£1,318** (£405; £202)

Form RPR
23-1 **1** **Kadount (FR)**9 [139] 12-12-1 115 MrJOwen(3) 120+
(J M Turner) *a trvelling wl: trckd ldrs tl wnt 2nd 7th: led bef 2 out: sn clr: v easily* **6/5**1

13P- **2** 8 **Blaze Ahead (IRE)**35 [5096] 10-11-11 104 (p) MissCLWills(7) 100
(Brendan Powell) *w ldr tl led after 6th: clr w wnr on v long run bef 2 out: hdd ent st: sn btn: hit 2 out: plugged on for clr 2nd* **6/1**3

/15- **3** 20 **Badger**5 10-12-1 93 MrsCLTaylor(7) 86
(Mrs C L Dennis) *in tch: niggled along after 6th: 3rd and outpcd by ldng pair 3 out (stl 7f out): wl btn bef 2 out* **8/1**

POU/ **4** 16 **Sorry Al (IRE)**10 10-11-7 0 (p) MrRStearn(7) 60
(S J Stearn) *led tl after 6th: sn rdn and struggling: wl btn whn mstke actual 3 out: t.o* **10/1**

056/ **5** 15 **Beluga (IRE)**32 11-11-7 0 MajGFWheeler(7) 45
(Miss Rose Grissell) *sn wl bhd in last: shkn up and qcknd to cl after 6th: struggling again after next: wl btn on long run bef 2 out* **40/1**

P- **6** 3/4 **Gunner Be Quick**10 8-11-7 0 MrRTory(7) 44
(Mrs Monica Tory) *towards rr: mstke and pushed along 6th: rallied to chse ldrs next: wknd jumping actual 3 out: t.o wl bef 2 out* **20/1**

7 dist **Ah Come On Tom (IRE)**10 11-11-7 0 MrLiamWard(7) —
(Mrs J Quinlan) *dropped to rr after mstke 3rd: t.o fr 6th* **33/1**

5/P- **P** **Honourable Spider**38 11-11-11 0 MrPBull(3) —
(Mrs Suzy Bull) *chsd ldrs: clsd up and wl in tch after 6th: rdn and btn bef actual 3 out: wl bhd whn p.u 2 out* **7/2**2

6m 0.80s (-35.00) **Going Correction** -0.775s/f (Firm) **8** Ran SP% **112.3**
Speed ratings: **101,98,92,86,82 81,65,—**
toteswingers:1&2:£1.70, 1&3:£2.40, 2&3:£7.80 CSF £8.67 TOTE £2.50: £1.40, £1.10, £1.80; EX 6.70.
Owner J M Turner **Bred** Roger Le Texier **Trained** Bury St Edmunds, Suffolk

FOCUS
Another hunter chase with an easy winner. He was value for further and is rated to his mark. The fences in the back straight were omitted on both circuits.

NOTEBOOK
Kadount(FR), a previous course winner over 2m, scored in a hunter chase at Fakenham last time and registered a quick double. He is a talented horse in this grade and connections will try to find a similar opportunity for him before the season ends. He looked particularly well and thrives when the ground is fast. (op 11-10 tchd Evens and 5-4)
Blaze Ahead(IRE) has been running creditably and kept trying here. He shows his best form right-handed and deserves to win a race. (op 11-2 tchd 5-1)
Badger chased home the capable Lady Myfanwy last time, but was not able to concede weight all round here. He kept trying and is capable in points but has only won once under rules, in a spectacularly bad contest. (tchd 15-2)
Sorry Al(IRE) has only shown moderate form in points and he is highly unlikely to be winning under rules. (op 16-1)
Honourable Spider hated this ground. (op 4-1)

297 EDENBRIDGE@NFUMMTUAL.CO.UK CENTENARY OPEN HUNTERS' CHASE (FOR THE UNITED HUNTS CUP) (14 fncs 1 omitted) 2m 5f
8:20 (8:21) (Class 6) 5-Y-0+ **£1,318** (£405; £202)

Form RPR
100/ **1** **Oscatello (USA)**19 10-12-4 0 MissPGundry 129+
(Ross Oliver) *chsd ldrs: led after 9th: mde rest: drew wl clr after 3 out: mstke next: r.o wl: easily* **2/1**2

/40- **2** 17 **Master T (USA)**19 11-11-11 0 MrPBull(3) 105
(Mrs Suzy Bull) *t.k.h: hld up in midfield: dropped to last pair after 6th: hdwy after 8th: 4th and wl outpcd after 3 out: wnt modest 2nd after last: no ch w wnr* **16/1**

4PP/ **3** 4 **Portland Bill (IRE)**11 10-11-11 0 MissAGoschen(3) 102
(Miss A Goschen) *chsd ldrs tl rdn and outpcd after 10th: 3rd wl btn after 3 out: plugged on but no ch after* **12/1**

31F- **4** 14 **Predateur (FR)**49 [4852] 7-12-1 125 MrNSutton(7) 105+
(Giles Smyly) *in tch in midfield: hdwy to press wnr 10th: mstke 12th: btn after next: stl 2nd whn j. awkwardly and sprawled on landing last: sn lost 2 pls* **7/1**3

0/0- **5** 20 **Reflex Blue**5 13-11-7 0 (b) MissCDouglas(7) 67
(Rex Smith) *led tl after 9th: wkng whn mstke next: t.o fr 3 out* **80/1**

600/ **P** **Celtic Star (IRE)**26 12-11-7 0 (t) L-BdrJSole(7) —
(Miss J Wickens) *in tch towards rr: struggling and rdn after 9th: lost tch after next: t.o whn p.u bef 2 out* **80/1**

664- **P** **Mr Tee Pee (IRE)**19 10-11-7 89 MrMBraxton(7) —
(Miss Rose Grissell) *chsd ldr 2nd tl 4th: sn lost pl: lost tch and swishing tail after 8th: wl t.o whn p.u 2 out* **7/1**3

424/ **P** **Gold Heart (FR)**40 8-11-9 0 (t) MrNPearce(5) —
(Miss C P Holliday) *nvr jumping w any fluency: in rr: hdwy on inner to chse ldrs after 8th: rdn and btn 11th: 5th and wl btn after 3 out: p.u next* **6/4**1

60P/ **P** **Latalanta (FR)**32 7-11-7 0 MrBBentley(7) —
(Mrs P A Tetley) *a towards rr: struggling and lost tch 10th: t.o whn p.u 2 out: dismntd* **33/1**

5m 4.70s (-17.50) **Going Correction** -0.775s/f (Firm) **9** Ran SP% **117.3**
Speed ratings: **102,95,94,88,81 —,—,—,—**
toteswingers:1&2:£11.20, 1&3:£9.90, 2&3:£11.70 CSF £31.61 TOTE £2.00: £1.02, £5.20, £4.00; EX 37.00 Place 6 £40.40; Place 5 £34.79.
Owner Ross Oliver **Bred** Highland Farms Inc **Trained** Newquay, Cornwall

FOCUS
Yet another very easy winner on the night. The form is rated around the second and third.

NOTEBOOK
Oscatello(USA) scored in his previous two point-to-point starts in Cornwall. He quickened clear of his rivals nicely to make a winning start to his hunter chase career. He had some decent form for Philip Hobbs in his younger days (before sustaining a leg injury) and was a cut above these. He is sure to be a force in races of this nature in the future. (op 11-4)
Master T(USA) is a perennial runner-up in points and filled that spot again here. He is unlikely to be a force in hunter chases next season, as he is an elderly performer. (op 14-1)
Portland Bill(IRE) has had his limitations exposed in points and looked in need of a stiffer test having got outpaced at a crucial stage in the race. (tchd 14-1)
Predateur(FR) would have been placed but for a bad blunder at the last. He has a suspect attitude and appears not to stay this trip. (op 9-2)
Gold Heart(FR) ran well below par and was in trouble from a long way out. His jumping lacked fluency throughout and the firm ground was doubtless against him. He could be worth another chance granted softer conditions in early 2011. (op 13-8)
T/Plt: £45.00 to a £1 stake. Pool: £47,893.71. 775.24 winning tickets. T/Qpdt: £14.10 to a £1 stake. Pool: £4,505.85. 235.00 winning tickets. SP

1LUDLOW (R-H)
Thursday, May 13

OFFICIAL GOING: Good (good to firm in places; 7.7)
Wind: Almost nil Weather: Fine but cool

298 ST JOHN AMBULANCE AND BRITISH RED CROSS CONDITIONAL JOCKEYS' (S) HURDLE (9 hdls) 2m
5:25 (5:25) (Class 5) **£2,276** (£668; £334; £166)

Form RPR
25- **1** **Ajman (IRE)**31 [5169] 5-10-9 0 (t) DPFahy(3) 93+
(Evan Williams) *racd keenly: handy: wnt 2nd and chal appr 3 out: led 2 out: edgd lft and drvn clr run-in* **12/1**

15-5 **2** 5 **Hammer**9 [134] 5-10-13 90 (bt) OliverDayman(5) 94
(Alison Thorpe) *hld up: hdwy appr 3 out: wnt 2nd and chal 2 out: outpcd by wnr after last: no ex cl home* **5/1**2

43- **3** 1/2 **Stravita**20 [5352] 6-10-5 80 PeterToole 81
(Reg Hollinshead) *midfield: hdwy 4 out: effrt to chse ldrs 3 out: styd on same pce run-in* **13/2**3

P50- **4** 8 **Welsh Jaunt**17 [16] 5-10-4 79 ow2 (p) KyleJames(3) 75
(Brian Eckley) *hld up: struggling whn mstke 4 out: sme hdwy bef 3 out: no real imp on ldrs: hung lft run-in whn n.d* **33/1**

4-03 **5** 3 1/2 **Just Mossie**4 [219] 5-10-13 84 (v1) MarkQuinlan(5) 83
(Bill Turner) *trckd ldrs: rdn and outpcd appr 3 out: sn btn* **28/1**

4P/0 **6** 3 1/2 **Risk Challenge (USA)**14 [54] 8-10-12 65 RichardKilloran 74
(William Davies) *hld up: nt fluent 3rd: hdwy 4 out: sn chsd ldrs: wknd 3 out* **66/1**

2-11 **7** 1 1/4 **Skye But N Ben**7 [171] 6-11-8 108 (b) AndrewGlassonbury 85
(Jim Best) *led 2nd to 3rd: remained prom: led after 5th: rdn and hrd pressed whn j.rt 3 out: j.rt and mstke whn hdd 2 out: sn wknd* **8/11**1

50/2 **8** 4 1/2 **He's A Sheila**[13] 75 7-10-2 0 (p) JoshWall(10) 69
(Trevor Wall) *towards rr: rdn after 3rd: nvr on terms w ldrs* **12/1**

0 **F** **Trew Style**[9] 129 8-10-9 0 MrTomDavid(3) 74
(David Rees) *racd keenly: prom: chal after 4 out: wknd bef 3 out: 7th and no ch whn fell last* **50/1**

0P0- **P** **Wait For The Light**[20] 5364 6-10-12 83 (b) RichieMcLernon —
(Sophie Leech) *a cajoled along: led to 2nd: led 3rd: hdd after 5th: wknd 4 out: t.o whn p.u bef 3 out* **33/1**

3m 44.4s (-5.10) **Going Correction** -0.225s/f (Good) **10** Ran SP% **116.1**
Speed ratings: **103,100,100,96,94 92,92,89,—,—**
Tote Swingers: 1&2 £7.90, 1&3 £5.60, 2&3 £4.30 CSF £67.58 TOTE £12.00: £2.50, £1.30, £2.00; EX 77.40.There was no bid for the winner. Stravita was claimed by Mr J. J. Best for £6,000.
Owner R P R O'Neil **Bred** Pat McDonnell **Trained** Llancarfan, Vale Of Glamorgan

FOCUS
A very ordinary seller, lacking depth. The winner produced a step up.

NOTEBOOK
Ajman(IRE), an encouraging second on his hurdling debut, had disappointed in a visor last time out. The headgear was dispensed with here and, after figuring prominently for most of the race, he showed no signs of shirking the issue. He quickened to hit the front two out and stayed on well for a decisive victory. (tchd 11-1)
Hammer, who beat Skye But N Ben by half a length on easy ground at Taunton last month, was 8lb better off here and upheld that form. Held up early on, he made progress from halfway and chased the winner gamely from the last. (op 11-2 tchd 13-2)
Stravita, rated 80 after two first-four placings in low-grade hurdles last season, looks a fair guide to the form. She was another to come from behind, having raced in midfield for much of the contest. (tchd 7-1)
Welsh Jaunt has been dropping down the ratings recently but, based on this display, even a mark of 79 flatters her. She stayed on in the home straight but never looked likely to bother the winner.
Skye But N Ben, successful in handicaps at Hereford and Newton Abbot in the past couple of weeks, was well backed to complete a hat-trick. He ran poorly this time, though, jumping markedly right from the third-last and fading tamely in the closing stages. (op 4-5 tchd 4-6)

299 LYCETTS INSURANCE BROKERS NOVICES' H'CAP HURDLE (9 hdls) 2m
5:55 (5:55) (Class 4) (0-110,105) 4-Y-0+ **£3,903** (£1,146; £573; £286)

Form RPR

442- **1** **Vertueux (FR)**[62] 4563 5-11-2 **100** LeeEdwards(5) 108+
(Tony Carroll) *in tch: hmpd 1st and rdr lost irons for a spell: led appr 3 out: r.o wl to draw clr run-in: eased cl home* **15/2**

53-2 **2** 8 **Fidelis (IRE)**[7] 182 6-11-12 **105** DarylJacob 107+
(Ben De Haan) *hld up: hdwy 4 out: chsd wnr 3 out: rdn abt 3 l down whn blnd last: no ex run-in* **9/2**[3]

055- **3** 7 **Decision**[24] 5278 4-11-4 **101** (t) ChristianWilliams 90
(Lawney Hill) *led: pushed along and hdd appr 3 out: wknd bef last* **15/8**[1]

500- **4** 9 **Weet In Nerja**[26] 5229 4-10-8 **91** RodiGreene 71
(James Unett) *chsd ldr tl rdn and wknd appr 3 out* **20/1**

305- **5** nk **Gratification**[138] 3023 7-11-7 **100** LeightonAspell 84
(Oliver Sherwood) *chsd ldrs: nt fluent 1st: wknd after 4 out* **16/1**

240- **6** 4 **Ten Pole Tudor**[21] 5333 5-11-12 **105** TomScudamore 89
(Michael Scudamore) *hld up: hit 4 out: sme hdwy u.p appr 3 out but nvr a threat* **20/1**

533- **7** 28 **Everyman**[32] 5154 6-10-13 **99** HarryChalloner(7) 54
(John Bryan Groucott) *j.rt 1st: chsd ldrs: wknd 4 out: toiling whn blnd 3 out* **25/1**

U00- **U** **Danzig Fox**[66] 4489 5-10-6 **85** AndrewGlassonbury —
(Michael Mullineaux) *hld up in midfield whn jinked and uns rdr 4th* **66/1**

43-4 **U** **Rebel Dancer (FR)**[8] 159 5-11-11 **104** (t) RichardJohnson —
(Philip Hobbs) *hld up: hmpd and uns rdr 4th* **3/1**[2]

0- **U** **Lord Francois (FR)**[150] 2889 5-11-1 **99** DeanColeman(5) —
(Tim Vaughan) *hld up: hmpd and uns rdr 4th* **28/1**

3m 43.6s (-5.90) **Going Correction** -0.225s/f (Good)
WFA 4 from 5yo+ 18lb **10** Ran SP% **113.9**
Speed ratings (Par 105): **105,101,97,93,92 90,76,—,—,—**
Tote Swingers: 1&2 £1.30, 1&3 £4.80, 2&3 £2.90 CSF £37.56 CT £88.82 TOTE £14.80: £4.20, £2.70, £1.02; EX 27.10.
Owner John Rutter **Bred** Roger Baudouin **Trained** Cropthorne, Worcs

FOCUS
A run-of-the-mill novices' handicap hurdle. A step up from the winner with the second to his best.

NOTEBOOK
Vertueux(FR), up 5lb since finishing second at Sandown in March, made light of that rise in the ratings. His jumping was not all that convincing, as he made a mistake at the first and another at the last, but he was never in danger after leading at the third-last. (op 13-2)
Fidelis(IRE), who lined up still a maiden but with a string of fair runs to his name, is pretty consistent and seems a decent guide to the form. Held up early on, he started to make progress turning for home and, although he was no match for the winner, stayed on well in the home straight. (tchd 4-1)
Decision, from a yard in good form, had posted his best previous effort when fifth at Kempton last time out, so this was a little disappointing. Well backed, he set out to make all but faded after being headed at the third-last. (op 2-1 tchd 7-4)
Weet In Nerja was dropping back in distance after running over 2m4f last time out but seemed to find even this trip beyond him, backpedalling in the closing stages after chasing the pace until the home straight. (op 25-1)
Rebel Dancer(FR) was one of three to exit the race at the fourth. (op 7-2)

300 TANNERS WINES H'CAP CHASE (22 fncs) 3m 1f 110y
6:30 (6:30) (Class 3) (0-130,130) 5-Y-0+
£7,514 (£2,220; £1,110; £555; £277; £139)

Form RPR

53-1 **1** **Tyup Pompey (IRE)**[14] 57 9-10-2 **109** LeeStephens(3) 112+
(Ann Price) *in tch: mstke and led 3 out: styd on wl run-in to draw clr* **12/1**

443- **2** 4 **Ginolad (AUS)**[26] 5230 10-11-2 **120** AidanColeman 117
(Venetia Williams) *midfield: hdwy after 5 out: sn chsd ldrs: styd on u.p run-in: tk 2nd post: no imp on wnr* **10/1**

PP2- **3** nse **De Soto**[27] 5211 9-11-7 **125** (t) WillKennedy 123
(Paul Webber) *chsd ldrs: wnt 2nd 15th: chalng 4 out: sn rdn: kpt on u.p tl no ex fnl 100yds: lost 2nd post* **7/1**

00P- **4** 5 **Chiaro (FR)**[26] 5223 8-11-7 **125** (b) TomO'Brien 117
(Philip Hobbs) *midfield: hdwy 9th: effrt to chse ldrs 4 out: one pce fr last* **9/2**[2]

2P4- **5** 3 1/4 **Cousin Nicky**[54] 4727 9-11-0 **118** DavidEngland 108
(Giles Smyly) *prom: led 6th: rdn and hdd 3 out: wknd last* **16/1**

304- **6** 27 **Boychuk (IRE)**[29] 5181 9-11-7 **130** (b) GilesHawkins(5) 95
(Philip Hobbs) *bhd: hdwy appr 6th: rn in snatches tl dropped bhd 14th (water): n.d after* **5/1**[3]

10P- **7** 3 1/4 **Seymar Lad (IRE)**[215] 1696 10-11-9 **127** JackDoyle 89
(Emma Lavelle) *led: hdd 6th: remained prom: lost pl 14th (water): bhd after 5 out* **14/1**

21P- **P** **Sea Wall**[319] 824 8-11-2 **120** APMcCoy —
(Jonjo O'Neill) *hld up: struggling 17th: bhd whn p.u bef 3 out* **4/1**[1]

0P5- **P** **Shouldhavehadthat (IRE)**[29] 5181 8-11-3 **121** AndrewTinkler —
(Nicky Henderson) *hld up: hdwy appr 15th: rdn and wknd 17th: bhd whn p.u bef 3 out* **8/1**

115- **P** **Winsley Hill**[26] 5232 8-11-10 **128** DougieCostello —
(Neil Mulholland) *midfield: wknd 5 out: t.o whn p.u bef 4 out* **20/1**

6m 27.4s (-7.90) **Going Correction** -0.125s/f (Good) **10** Ran SP% **112.6**
Speed ratings: **107,105,105,104,103 94,93,—,—,—**
Tote Swingers: 1&2 £24.10, 1&3 £30.30, 2&3 £16.30 CSF £119.26 CT £903.48 TOTE £19.00: £5.80, £5.30, £1.50; EX 102.00.
Owner Mrs A Price **Bred** Rosetown Syndicate **Trained** Norton, Powys

FOCUS
A fair handicap chase, featuring plenty with form, but several had something to prove. A surprise personal best from the winner.

NOTEBOOK
Tyup Pompey(IRE), already twice a winner on this course, had been raised 5lb since collecting at Hereford in April, but the extra proved no hindrance. Never far off the pace, he took close order before the home turn and led three out. He hit the second-last, but he lost little momentum and stayed on bravely. This was his first run over this far. (op 10-1)
Ginolad(AUS), with only patchy form in novice company since arriving from Australia, was making his handicap debut and did enough to suggest his mark is not unreasonable. Held up in midfield for much of the contest, he stayed on well in the home straight while others were weakening. (op 12-1 tchd 14-1)
De Soto, successful from a mark of 120 last August, had shown little on more recent outings, but ran much better here. Always in the leading group, he edged into second two out and battled on gamely but was just pushed into third on the line. (op 11-2 tchd 5-1)
Chiaro(FR), pulled up in the Scottish National on his previous run, had been dropped 4lb and was well backed. He never looked likely to collect, appearing to lack a change of gear in the closing stages. (op 7-1)
Sea Wall, a Ffos Las winner last June, broke a blood vessel on his only subsequent outing and was returning from a 319-day layoff. He was supported in the betting, suggesting someone thought his wellbeing was assured, but he never figured with a serious chance. (tchd 7-2)

301 BOB CHAMPION 60:60 CHALLENGE HUNTERS' CHASE (17 fncs) 2m 4f
7:05 (7:05) (Class 5) 5-Y-0+ **£2,186** (£677; £338; £169)

Form RPR

/43- **1** **Emotional Article (IRE)**[18] 6 10-11-3 117 MrAWadlow(7) 111
(Mrs Belinda Clarke) *led: hdd 9th (water): remained pressing ldr: rdn to regain ld last: styd on u.p: a doing enough whn pressed cl home* **10/3**[2]

0/4- **2** 3/4 **Fairwood Present (IRE)**[18] 6 12-11-3 0 MrRJarrett(7) 111+
(John Buxton) *chsd ldr: led 9th (water): rdn appr 3 out: j.rt and hdd last: rallied to press wnr towards fin but a looked hld* **7/1**[3]

PF1- **3** 7 **Whataboutya (IRE)**[18] 6 9-11-7 115 (p) MissJennyCarr(7) 110
(Jonjo O'Neill) *hld up: chsd ldng pair 13th: effrt and hdwy to cl 4 out: one pce and no firther imp fr last* **10/11**[1]

4/U- **4** 25 **Orvita (FR)**[18] 6 8-11-3 0 MrDNelmes(7) 82
(K A Nelmes) *bhd: nt fluent 6th and reminders: plodded on modly fr 4 out: nt trble ldrs* **28/1**

3FP- **5** 3 1/4 **Little Rocker (IRE)**[25] 5249 9-11-7 107 MrBFurnival(7) 83
(R Smart) *midfield early: bhd fr 5th: struggling after* **11/1**

0FP/ **6** 22 **So Many Questions (IRE)**[11] 10-11-3 0 MrJHamer(7) 59
(G C Evans) *midfield early: struggling 10th: nvr on terms* **20/1**

7 4 1/2 **Hocinail (FR)**[19] 6-11-3 0 MrNDeakin(7) 55
(P Goldsworthy) *reluctant to line-up: chsd clr ldrs: wknd 13th* **14/1**

6-P **P** **Redskyatnight**[8] 148 9-11-3 0 MissHannahWatson(7) —
(H J Franklin) *hld up in rr div: toiling fnl circ: wl bhd whn p.u bef 3 out* **50/1**

5m 1.00s (-3.40) **Going Correction** -0.125s/f (Good) **8** Ran SP% **113.1**
Speed ratings: **101,100,97,87,86 77,76,—**
Tote Swingers: 1&2 £3.30, 1&3 £1.60, 2&3 £1.80 CSF £25.28 TOTE £6.20: £2.70, £1.10, £1.10; EX 21.50.
Owner Mrs Belinda Clarke **Bred** Gerry O'Sullivan **Trained** Bridgnorth, Shropshire

FOCUS
A modest hunter chase. The winner was rated 130+ in Ireland but was nowhere near that level here.

NOTEBOOK
Emotional Article(IRE), third behind Whataboutya last time out, turned that form around in style. In the lead early on - and well clear at one stage - he was overtaken by the runner-up on the far side and looked booked for second three out. He kept battling, though, and, when Fairwood Present jumped right at the last, he took advantage for a game success. (tchd 3-1 and 7-2)
Fairwood Present(IRE), fourth behind Whataboutya 18 days previously, on only his second outing in a year, might have been expected to improve for that run and arguably did so. Looking set for victory three out, where he was in the lead and going better than the eventual winner, he jumped significantly right at the last and then wandered under pressure on the run-in. But for that, he might well have prevailed. (op 9-1)
Whataboutya(IRE), successful over course and distance on his latest start, is officially rated 115 but ran well short of that here. Held up in the early stages, with his rider apparently confident he could bridge the gap to the first two, he made only limited progress when asked to quicken. This was disappointing (op 5-6)
Orvita(FR) did best of the rest and, given his modest profile, that does not augur well for those further behind. (op 25-1)

302 HATFIELDS JAGUAR H'CAP HURDLE (12 hdls) 3m
7:40 (7:40) (Class 3) (0-125,125) 4-Y-O+ **£6,020** (£1,778; £889; £444; £222)

Form RPR

654- **1** **Moghaayer**[49] 4849 5-10-11 **110** AndrewTinkler 120+
(Nicky Henderson) *hld up: hdwy after 4 out: led 3 out: drvn out and styd on wl run-in* **10/1**

063- **2** 5 **Markington**[20] 5365 7-11-0 **113** (b) TomO'Brien 118
(Peter Bowen) *trckd ldrs: mstke and outpcd 8th: rallied fr 3 out: styd on to take 2nd run-in: no imp on wnr* **15/2**

0/6- **3** 3/4 **Toby Belch (IRE)**[28] 5197 7-11-7 **120** RobertThornton 124
(Henry Daly) *hld up: hdwy 8th: pushed along after 8th: chsd wnr u.p jst after last: styd on same pce but lost 2nd run-in* **11/2**[2]

22-1 **4** 14 **Prescelli (IRE)**[7] 180 6-10-13 **112** 7ex (b) TomScudamore 103
(Keith Goldsworthy) *prom: led on long run appr 3 out: hit and hdd 3 out: wknd last* **7/1**[3]

16-4 **5** 3 1/2 **Elusive Muse**[6] 193 4-10-3 **115** OliverDayman(7) 98
(Alison Thorpe) *midfield: hdwy 4 out: pushed along appr 3 out whn chsd ldrs: styd on same pce fr 2 out* **7/2**[1]

4P-0 **6** *8* **Barnhill Brownie (IRE)**[9] 131 7-11-2 **120**..................(t) GilesHawkins(5) 101
(Philip Hobbs) *in tch: lost pl 3rd: bhd 4th: kpt on modly fr 3 out: no imp on ldrs* **33/1**

P3-1 **7** *2 3/4* **Wild Tonto (IRE)**[7] 172 7-11-4 **117** 7ex.......................... PaddyBrennan 98+
(Nigel Twiston-Davies) *wandered appr 1st: in tch: pushed along after 4 out: sn outpcd* **10/1**

404- **8** *1/2* **Roisin's Prince (IRE)**[18] 1 8-10-0 **99** oh1................(t) AidanColeman 77
(Matt Sheppard) *prom tl wknd 8th* **66/1**

116- **9** *88* **Englishtown (FR)**[263] 1292 10-11-7 **123**.......................... MrAJBerry(3) 22
(Jonjo O'Neill) *prom fr 2nd: wknd 4 out* **33/1**

340- **S** **Kristoffersen**[35] 5107 10-10-7 **106**...................................... OwynNelmes —
(Helen Nelmes) *hld up: pushed along whn hmpd and uns rdr on bnd appr 3 out* **28/1**

05-2 **P** **Magical Legend**[12] 89 9-11-12 **125**...............................(t) CharliePoste —
(Sophie Leech) *trckd ldrs: rdn and ev ch appr 3 out: sn btn: bhd whn p.u bef last* **18/1**

P4-2 **F** **Silverburn (IRE)**[9] 131 9-11-12 **125**................................ PaulMoloney 130
(Evan Williams) *led: hdd appr 3 out: u.p in 3rd and hld whn fell last: winded* **7/1**[3]

P0/1 **S** **Purely By Chance**[14] 64 5-11-5 **118**....................(b) WayneHutchinson —
(Jeff Pearce) *midfield: hdwy 8th: chal 4 out: pushed along and losing pl whn slipped up on bnd appr 3 out* **25/1**

211- **S** **Tarvini (IRE)**[173] 2434 5-11-3 **116**...(p) APMcCoy —
(Jonjo O'Neill) *hld up: struggling whn hmpd and uns rdr on bnd appr 3 out* **12/1**

5m 42.7s (-9.60) **Going Correction** -0.225s/f (Good)
WFA 4 from 5yo+ 20lb **14** Ran SP% **120.2**
Speed ratings (Par 107): **107,105,105,100,99 96,95,95,66,— —,—,—,—**
Tote Swingers: 1&2 £19.80, 1&3 £12.40, 2&3 £7.70 CSF £79.50 CT £463.38 TOTE £12.50: £3.70, £4.00, £2.60; EX 125.50.
Owner The Ten From Seven **Bred** Goldford Stud **Trained** Upper Lambourn, Berks

FOCUS
A fair handicap, and solid form which should work out.

NOTEBOOK
Moghaayer, a winner on his hurdling debut and with only four jump races under his belt, was the least exposed of these and made his handicap mark of 110 look a serious under-assessment with a decisive success over this longer trip. Held up in the early stages, he made eyecatching progress as the field approached the home turn and was second three out. Quickening well from there on, he had a clear lead at the last and stayed on strongly. His immediate future probably depends on how much his rating rises, but he may run again this summer. (op 12-1 tchd 14-1)
Markington was 10lb higher than for his latest victory, but had run well from this mark at Newton Abbot last time out, so the form looks sound. Never far away, despite a mistake five out, he stayed on in the home straight without troubling the comfortable winner. (op 6 1)
Toby Belch(IRE), twice successful as a novice in 2008, has been raced sparingly since. His sixth at Cheltenham in April was encouraging, though, and he again ran well enough to suggest he can notch a victory in the near future. He passed a few in the home straight and a stiffer course might suit him. (op 6-1 tchd 13-2)
Prescelli(IRE), with a decent record on this course, was carrying a 7lb penalty for her win here seven days previously and it found her out. She was always in the leading group, but could stay on at only one pace in the closing stages. (op 6-1 tchd 15-2)
Elusive Muse, a winner at Taunton in April and fourth at Aintree on his latest start, was well supported, but, after turning for home in the first six, could never mount a meaningful challenge. (op 9-2 tchd 10-3)
Silverburn(IRE), second from this mark at Exeter last week and due to go up 5lb, led for much of the race and was still battling away gamely when falling at the last while disputing third. Down for some time before getting to his feet, provided all is well with him he should remain competitive (tchd 15-2)

303 TONY MORGAN RETIREMENT NOVICES' HURDLE (11 hdls) 2m 5f
8:10 (8:11) (Class 4) 4-Y-O+ **£3,903** (£1,146; £573; £286)

Form RPR
230- **1** **Firm Order (IRE)**[34] 5119 5-10-12 114.............................. WillKennedy 113+
(Paul Webber) *trckd ldrs: wnt 2nd 4 out: led appr 3 out but pressed by runner-up: r.o wl to draw clr run-in* **3/1**[2]

125- **2** *9* **Anquetta (IRE)**[48] 4867 6-10-12 0.. APMcCoy 106+
(Nicky Henderson) *hld up: hdwy 7th: chal wnr fr 3 out: no ex run-in* **4/6**[1]

0-40 **3** *4* **Enchanted Approach (IRE)**[4] 231 7-9-12 88.............. MissLBrooke(7) 93
(Lady Susan Brooke) *led: hdd appr 3 out: sn outpcd: kpt on u.p fr 2 out but n.d to front pair* **33/1**

00- **4** *1* **Downward Spiral (IRE)**[33] 5137 5-10-12 0........................ AlanO'Keeffe 99
(Jennie Candlish) *trckd ldrs: lost pl 6th: nt fluent and outpcd 4 out: rallied u.p fr 3 out: no imp on ldrs and one pce fr 2 out* **33/1**

5 *33* **Paddy Rielly (IRE)**[296] 5-10-12 0.......................................(t) TomO'Brien 69
(John Flint) *racd keenly: hld up in rr: pushed along appr 3 out: nvr a danger* **16/1**

564- **P** **Cresswell Bubbles**[18] 4 7-10-5 0.............................. PaddyBrennan —
(Nigel Twiston-Davies) *chsd ldr to 4 out: sn wknd: t.o whn p.u bef 3 out* **11/2**[3]

5m 3.90s (-10.90) **Going Correction** -0.225s/f (Good) **6** Ran SP% **112.1**
Speed ratings (Par 105): **111,107,106,105,93 —**
Tote Swingers: 1&2 £1.10, 2&3 £6.90 CSF £5.60 TOTE £3.20: £1.20, £1.10; EX 5.60.
Owner The Syndicators **Bred** Edmund Arthur **Trained** Mollington, Oxon

FOCUS
A weak novice hurdle. The winner is rated back to the level of his good Warwick run but the second was a stone off.

NOTEBOOK
Firm Order(IRE), second at Fakenham in January and third at Warwick in February, is officially rated 114, which puts the form into perspective. Always in the front rank, he took the lead three out and stayed on well in the closing stages. He is likely to find it difficult to shrug off a penalty and may now be best campaigned in handicaps. (op 7-2)
Anquetta(IRE), an encouraging second at Ffos Las in February, had run poorly in soft ground on his only subsequent outing at Newbury and was again very disappointing. Underfoot conditions can hardly have been an excuse this time and he now has a fair bit to prove. (op 4-7 tchd 8-11)
Enchanted Approach(IRE)'s proximity is a further indictment of the form. She took the field along until the turn for home and the first two did not finish that far in front of her, even though she tired in the closing stages. (op 25-1)
Downward Spiral(IRE), who had won a maiden point in Ireland but shown little in two bumpers since, was always in midfield and made no progress in the home straight. (op 40-1 tchd 25-1)
Cresswell Bubbles ran with the choke out. (op 6-1 tchd 5-1)

304 NSPCC INTERMEDIATE OPEN NATIONAL HUNT FLAT RACE 2m
8:40 (8:40) (Class 5) 4-6-Y-O **£2,276** (£668; £334; £166)

Form RPR
4- **1** **Thanks For Coming**[54] 4729 4-10-10 0...................................... APMcCoy 82+
(Nicky Henderson) *racd keenly: hld up in tch: hdwy over 2f out: chsd ldr wl over 1f out: r.o to ld ins fnl f: pushed out cl home* **11/8**[1]

016- **2** *3/4* **Cityar (FR)**[182] 2245 6-11-0 0.. CharlieWallis(7) 91
(John O'Shea) *hld up: hdwy on outside over 2f out: rdn over 1f out: styd on to take 2nd ins fnl f: gng on at fin* **14/1**

03- **3** *3/4* **Steel Bullet (IRE)**[18] 7 4-10-10 0...................................... AlanO'Keeffe 79
(Jennie Candlish) *racd keenly: prom: led over 4f out: tried to dash away 2f out: rdn over 1f out: hdd ins fnl f: kpt on u.p but hld after* **11/4**[2]

4 *5* **Lucky Sun** 4-10-10 0.. SeamusDurack 74
(Brian Eckley) *hld up: hdwy bef 1/2-way: pushed along 5f out: chsd ldrs 3f out: one pce over 1f out* **25/1**

0- **5** *6* **William Percival (IRE)**[26] 5235 4-10-10 0........................ AndrewTinkler 68
(Henry Daly) *in tch: rdn to chal 2f out: wknd over 1f out* **8/1**

0- **6** *1 1/4* **Singapore Harbour (IRE)**[49] 4853 4-10-3 0.................. LeightonAspell 60
(Oliver Sherwood) *trckd ldrs: pushed along 2f out: rdn and wknd over 1f out* **20/1**

50- **7** *1* **Les Andelys**[159] 2716 4-10-3 0... MattCrawley(7) 66
(Terry Clement) *led: hdd over 4f out: rdn 2f out: wknd wl over 1f out* **20/1**

8 *1/2* **La Chemme** 4-10-3 0... HarrySkelton 58
(Reg Hollinshead) *hld up: pushed along bhd ldrs over 2f out: nvr able to chal* **7/1**[3]

P- **9** *27* **Hennerwood Beech**[73] 4358 5-10-7 0.................................. TomO'Brien 35
(Richard Price) *prom tl wknd 3f out* **33/1**

3m 46.4s (2.50) **Going Correction** -0.225s/f (Good)
WFA 4 from 5yo+ 4lb **9** Ran SP% **115.4**
Speed ratings: **84,83,83,80,77 77,76,76,62**
Tote Swingers: 1&2 £4.10, 1&3 £1.20, 2&3 £3.90 CSF £21.23 TOTE £3.00: £2.70, £2.80, £1.10; EX 17.00 Place 6 £79.14; Place 5 £29.07.
Owner Unchartered Waters **Bred** The National Stud **Trained** Upper Lambourn, Berks

FOCUS
A moderate bumper where they finished in a heap. The winner is rated below the level of his debut run.

NOTEBOOK
Thanks For Coming had managed only fourth when sent off at odds-on in his sole previous race, but that form set the standard and he justified market support. He was hardly impressive, however, getting outpaced on the home turn and needing strong driving to get to the front. He looks a stayer, judged on this run, and will surely benefit from a stiffer test when sent hurdling. (op Evens tchd 6-4)
Cityar(FR), successful in this discipline here in October, had managed only sixth under his penalty last time out, so the fact that he could finish a close second underlines the weakness of this event. He made ground from the rear turning for home and stayed on in the closing stages.
Steel Bullet(IRE), third over course and distance 18 days previously, again ran adequately, but it is becoming clear that he has only limited ability. He disputed the lead from the outset, but looked one-paced in the home straight. (op 3-1)
Lucky Sun, a newcomer related to both fair point and hurdle performers, showed a glimpse of ability, staying on in the closing stages, but will need to improve to win an ordinary race of this type. (op 33-1)
William Percival(IRE) had revealed only limited talent when ninth of 15 at Bangor last month and again suggested he is no superstar. (tchd 15-2)
T/Plt: £89.70 to a £1 stake. Pool: £43,628.88. 354.85 winning tickets. T/Qpdt: £21.10 to a £1 stake. Pool: £4,736.30. 165.90 winning tickets. DO

[285]PERTH (R-H)
Thursday, May 13

OFFICIAL GOING: Good to firm (good in places; 7.5)
Wind: Fresh, half behind Weather: Overcast

305 SHEEP DIP WHISKY INTERMEDIATE HURDLE (12 hdls) 3m 110y
2:20 (2:20) (Class 4) 4-Y-O+ **£2,602** (£764; £382; £190)

Form RPR
112- **1** **Cool Mission (IRE)**[26] 5228 6-11-11 133........................... JasonMaguire 127+
(Donald McCain) *mde all: stdy pce: niggled fr 1/2-way: drvn bef 2 out: styd on wl* **10/11**[1]

312- **2** *5* **Caerlaverock (IRE)**[32] 5140 5-11-5 126................................ GrahamLee 117
(Rose Dobbin) *chsd wnr tl nt fluent and outpcd 4 out: rallied to take 2nd pl bef 2 out: kpt on fr last: nt pce of wnr* **9/2**[3]

B- **3** *2 1/2* **Leggy Lad (IRE)**[22] 5321 7-10-12 125........................ MrMMcConville(7) 113
(Stephen McConville, Ire) *prom: hdwy after 7th: chsd wnr 4 out to bef 2 out: hung rt: kpt on same pce* **4/1**[2]

564- **4** *17* **Pair Of Kings (IRE)**[18] 8 5-10-13 0................................ BrianHughes 93
(Alan Swinbank) *t.k.h: chsd ldrs tl outpcd bef 4 out: no imp fr next* **18/1**

600- **5** *38* **The Sheepdipper**[21] 5333 6-10-6 85.............................. AlexanderVoy(7) 52
(Lucy Normile) *nt fluent: hld up: outpcd bef 4 out: sn btn: t.o* **100/1**

6 *3 1/2* **Tamayo (IRE)**[270] 1233 10-10-13 107.. AELynch 49
(I R Ferguson, Ire) *hld up: blnd 7th: struggling fr next: t.o* **7/1**

6m 8.10s (-1.80) **Going Correction** -0.325s/f (Good) **6** Ran SP% **109.3**
Speed ratings (Par 105): **89,87,86,81,69 67**
toteswingers:1&2:£1.10, 1&3:£1.10, 2&3:£3.40 CSF £5.19 TOTE £1.50: £1.10, £3.30; EX 4.20.
Owner T G Leslie **Bred** Mrs Eleanor Kent **Trained** Cholmondeley, Cheshire

FOCUS
The rail and hurdle sites were moved to the outermost positions to provide the runners with fresh ground. Sound form.

NOTEBOOK
Cool Mission(IRE), who was well beaten over this distance last time under a double penalty in a novice event, made really hard work of grinding out success. His rider deserves lots of credit for getting the best out of his horse, who took a lot of driving from an early stage. If the handicapper makes his life too difficult, one would imagine that he'll go over fences sooner rather than later. (tchd 4-5 and Evens in a place)
Caerlaverock(IRE) did not seem to get home over 2m6f on his latest outing but plugged on well over this longer trip. (tchd 11-2)
Leggy Lad(IRE) was struggling when brought down in a Grade 3 contest over this distance at Punchestown in April, but moved up going well in this as the tempo increased. However, once looking dangerous, his effort soon levelled out and he kept on at the one pace. (tchd 9-2)
Pair Of Kings(IRE) didn't really threaten after being keen but has time on his side. (op 22-1)
Tamayo(IRE), a chase winner having his first run over hurdles, was representing a trainer going for his fourth successive victory in this contest. A large sort, he was still moving well when hitting the seventh really hard. That was probably enough to end his chance. (op 8-1)

306 SCOTTISH SPCA MAIDEN CHASE (12 fncs) 2m
2:50 (2:50) (Class 5) 5-Y-O+ **£2,927** (£859; £429; £214)

Form RPR
0/ **1** **Del Rio (IRE)**[99] 3837 7-11-0 135.. AELynch 112+
(J T R Draper, Ire) *hld up in tch: hdwy and prom 7th: led 4 out: 2 l in front whn blnd bdly and hdd next: 6 l down last: styd on u.p to ld towards fin* **10/11**[1]

2 2 1/4 **Mayo Abbey (IRE)**[12] 7-11-0 0 JasonMaguire 104
(Gordon Elliott, Ire) *chsd ldrs: lft 2nd 4 out: lft in ld next: 6 l clr last: rdn and hung rt run-in: hdd and no ex towards fin* 4/1[2]

/2-5 3 nse **Athoss**[12] [90] 8-10-7 0 MrJBewley(7) 103
(Robert Smith) *hld up: outpcd 1/2-way: effrt u.p 4 out: styd on wl fr last: nrst fin* 22/1

603- 4 6 **Another Dark Rum**[16] [32] 6-11-0 97 RichieMcGrath 98
(John Weymes) *prom: effrt bef 3 out: outpcd fr last* 12/1

456- 5 9 **Isla Pearl Fisher**[32] [5139] 7-11-0 82 PaddyAspell 89
(N W Alexander) *bhd: struggling bef 7th: plugged on fr last: nvr on terms* 33/1

553- 6 1 3/4 **Devil Water**[15] [42] 7-10-11 110 HarryHaynes(3) 87
(James Ewart) *cl up: drvn and outpcd whn checked 4 out: sn btn* 8/1

FC0- P **More Shennanigans**[63] [4535] 9-10-11 70 RyanMania(3) —
(Jean McGregor) *in tch: outpcd after 6th: t.o whn p.u bef 3 out* 100/1

664- F **Poseidon (GER)**[20] [5375] 8-11-0 102 BrianHughes —
(John Wade) *led: jst hdd whn fell 4 out* 13/2[3]

3m 57.5s (-5.20) **Going Correction** -0.325s/f (Good) 8 Ran SP% **112.8**
Speed ratings: **100,98,98,95,91 90,—,—**
toteswingers:1&2:£1.10, 1&3:£10.00, 2&3:£30.40 CSF £4.88 TOTE £1.70: £1.10, £2.00, £4.20; EX 4.40.
Owner Mrs P J Conway **Bred** Mrs P J Conway **Trained** Kilsallaghan, Co Dublin
⊠ Stewards' Enquiry : A E Lynch two-day ban: used whip with excessive frequency (May 27-28)

FOCUS
A modest event. The winner was better than the bare result but is rated over a stone below his best.

NOTEBOOK
Del Rio(IRE), who had good form over fences in Ireland, looked a very unlikely winner after making a big blunder three out while in the lead. However, his jockey did well to sit that error and then conjure another effort out of him, making Del Rio's stamina come into play as others weakened in front of him. One would imagine he will be kept on the go, as his trainer reported that they came over for the better ground. (op 6-4)
Mayo Abbey(IRE), representing last season's winning trainer, easily won his most recent start, an Irish point, on similar ground and was left in front when the winner made a mistake. In front over the final fence, he found his stride shorten after the last as he hung, and was caught. It was a great start to his career under rules and he seems sure to win soon if raced through the summer. (op 11-4 tchd 9-2)
Athoss, a winning pointer, was taking a big drop in trip after running in a 3m1f hunter chase, and did not hit full stride until turning into the home straight. He stayed on strongly and would have been challenging Del Rio within another 50 yards. (op 18-1)
Another Dark Rum ⊠ once again caught the eye and must be given consideration wherever he runs next. (op 11-1)
Devil Water, a pointing winner in the past, had a couple of runs in hunter chases at about this time last year but has been running over hurdles since. Back over fences, he travelled smoothly in the early stages but was beaten at around halfway.
Poseidon(GER) led at a sensible pace and was still there when falling, although he seemed about to be claimed when departing. (tchd 6-1)

307 HAVEAGO@STANJAMES.COM CLAIMING HURDLE (8 hdls) 2m 110y
3:25 (3:26) (Class 5) 4-6-Y-0 **£2,276** (£668; £334)

Form RPR
604- 1 **Right Or Wrong (IRE)**[20] [5371] 6-11-8 121 (tp) JasonMaguire 118+
(Gordon Elliott, Ire) *mde all: drew clr bef 2 out: v easily* 1/5[1]

004- 2 26 **Still Calm**[16] [31] 6-10-9 80 (t) MichaelMcAlister(3) 82
(Maurice Barnes) *chsd ldrs: lft 2nd 4 out: rdn and wknd bef 2 out* 6/1[2]

3 61 **Castelli (IRE)**[213] 4-11-0 0 BrianHughes 23
(Howard Johnson) *nt fluent: chsd wnr tl overj. and sprawled bdly 4 out: sn lost tch: t.o* 13/2[3]

3m 58.5s (-1.20) **Going Correction** -0.325s/f (Good)
WFA 4 from 5yo+ 18lb 3 Ran SP% **111.0**
Speed ratings: **89,76,48**
CSF £2.12 TOTE £1.10; EX 1.70.
Owner A M Egan/Ms Annie Flora Joan Bowles **Bred** Castlemartin Stud And Skymarc Farm **Trained** Trim, Co Meath

FOCUS
Four non-runners left a very uncompetitive event. The winner stood out and is rated 6lb off his best.

NOTEBOOK
Right Or Wrong(IRE), given an uncomplicated ride with the cheekpieces/tongue-tie back on, had little to beat but did it very easily and his confidence will have been boosted. (early 4-9 in a place and 2-5 in places)
Still Calm, beaten 16l in a seller on his previous outing, never landed any sort of blow. (op 13-2 tchd 7-1)
Castelli(IRE), a well-bred sort who had shown little on the Flat for Jim Bolger, was beaten at halfway after he over-jumped the fourth-last and sprawled on landing. (op 9-2 tchd 7-1)

308 TIMOTHY HARDIE JEWELLERS H'CAP CHASE (18 fncs) 3m
4:00 (4:00) (Class 3) (0-125,123) 5-Y-0+ **£5,854** (£1,719; £859; £429)

Form RPR
055- 1 **Sheriff Hutton (IRE)**[27] [5203] 7-11-12 123 LiamHeard 135+
(Tim Walford) *cl up: led 9th: mde rest: rdn 3 out: hrd pressed last: edgd lft and styd on gamely run-in* 8/1

PP- 2 2 1/4 **Bear Witness (IRE)**[20] [5373] 8-11-3 114 SamThomas 121
(S R B Crawford, Ire) *cl up: led 3rd to 5th: cl up: effrt and chsd wnr bef 2 out: ev ch last: edgd rt and one pce run-in* 5/1[2]

0PP- 3 17 **Or De Grugy (FR)**[22] [5309] 8-11-9 120 PaddyAspell 112
(Sue Bradburne) *led to 3rd: led 5th to 9th: styd upsides: drvn bef 2 out: sn outpcd by first two* 33/1

201- 4 hd **Top Dressing (IRE)**[15] [46] 9-11-8 119 BrianHughes 112
(Howard Johnson) *blnd bdly 1st: sn rcvrd and in tch: rdn bef 4 out: outpcd fr next* 7/1

1- 5 9 **Bally Wall (IRE)**[26] [5226] 7-11-5 116 AELynch 99
(I R Ferguson, Ire) *hld up: hdwy after 14th: rdn and wknd fr 3 out* 9/4[1]

0P0- 6 21 **Native Coral (IRE)**[27] [5203] 12-11-7 121 FearghalDavis(3) 85
(Nicky Richards) *hld up: hdwy and in tch bef 4 out: wknd next* 16/1

511- P **Catch The Perk (IRE)**[27] [5206] 13-11-10 121 PeterBuchanan —
(Lucinda Russell) *in tch: hdwy to chal 12th: wknd fr 14th: t.o whn p.u bef 3 out* 11/2[3]

10P- P **Kells Castle**[20] [5373] 8-11-4 115 (vt) JasonMaguire —
(Gordon Elliott, Ire) *in tch: pushed along fr 7th: struggling 12th: j. slowly next and sn p.u* 8/1

/01- P **Oscar Honey (IRE)**[49] [4833] 9-11-9 120 GrahamLee —
(Rose Dobbin) *nt fluent: hld up: struggling 14th: t.o whn p.u bef 3 out* 16/1

6m 7.90s (-12.50) **Going Correction** -0.325s/f (Good) 9 Ran SP% **112.2**
Speed ratings: **107,106,100,100,97 90,—,—,—**
toteswingers:1&2:£8.10, 1&3:£23.40, 2&3:£19.10 CSF £46.80 CT £1238.60 TOTE £10.10: £2.40, £1.90, £8.30; EX 57.60.
Owner Richard Adcock Joe Grindal Nigel Skinner **Bred** Joe Slattery **Trained** Sheriff Hutton, N Yorks
⊠ Stewards' Enquiry : Brian Hughes one-day ban: careless riding (May 27)

FOCUS
A fair handicap chase. The winner stepped forward on his previous chase form and the race could be rated up to 3lb higher.

NOTEBOOK
Sheriff Hutton(IRE), back over fences, could be spotted going well for much of the race and then showed a pleasing attitude when challenged over the final two fences. This was his first win in handicap company over fences (he won off 115 over hurdles), so he is likely to struggle off higher marks despite having age of his side. (op 6-1)
Bear Witness(IRE) ⊠, who was hampered at the second fence last time out and reportedly lost his action, travelled well throughout and was at least upsides Sheriff Hutton jumping the final fence, but could not get past him. (op 8-1)
Or De Grugy(FR) had been pulled up on his previous two starts, so this was obviously a lot better. He jumped nicely under a prominent ride in the early stages.
Top Dressing(IRE), raised 10lb for a comfortable success at Kelso, made a bad mistake at the first but was comfortably back on terms starting their final circuit. His jumping was not as fluent as it could have been, but he did keep going under pressure. (op 5-1)
Bally Wall(IRE) has looked a thorough stayer and won a fair-looking contest at Ayr on his previous outing, but failed to reproduce that sort of form here. He would have wanted a stiffer test of stamina and is not one to give up on yet. (op 5-2 tchd 2-1)
Kells Castle looked too high in the weights on his winning form and did not seem in the best of moods. (op 18-1 tchd 14-1)
Oscar Honey(IRE), the fortunate winner of a novice hurdle last time, never looked happy and made no impression. (op 18-1 tchd 14-1)

309 MCEWENS OF PERTH H'CAP HURDLE (10 hdls) 2m 4f 110y
4:35 (4:35) (Class 3) (0-135,130) 4-Y-0+ **£4,683** (£1,375; £687; £343)

Form RPR
/03- 1 **Hearthstead Dream**[21] [5338] 9-11-2 120 JasonMaguire 125+
(Gordon Elliott, Ire) *bhd and sn niggled along: hdwy 4 out: rdn to ld appr last: kpt on wl: eased nr fin* 4/1[2]

U06- 2 6 **Santa's Son (IRE)**[22] [5308] 10-11-5 123 (t) BrianHughes 123
(Howard Johnson) *prom gng wl: chsd ldr 4 out: rdn to ld bef 2 out: hdd appr last: one pce run-in* 7/1[3]

U35- 3 2 1/4 **Los Nadis (GER)**[13] [5338] 6-11-5 126 RyanMania(3) 125
(P Monteith) *chsd ldrs: effrt bef 2 out: nt fluent last: one pce* 7/1[3]

001- 4 1 **Hazeldene**[15] [44] 8-10-10 114 JanFaltejsek 111
(George Charlton) *led: clr 1st to 4th: hdd bef 2 out: rallied: no ex bef last* 7/2[1]

143- 5 14 **Tarkani (IRE)**[5] [3068] 7-10-1 110 (tp) MJBolger(5) 94
(Valentine Donoghue) *hld up: hdwy bef 3 out: rdn and wknd bef next* 9/1

35U- 6 3 1/4 **Currahee**[27] [5203] 6-10-8 115 (t) MichaelMcAlister(3) 96
(Maurice Barnes) *chsd ldrs: outpcd bef 4 out: n.d after* 11/1

4P5- 7 6 **Corkage (IRE)**[15] [45] 7-11-7 125 (p) PeterBuchanan 101
(Lucinda Russell) *sn last and nt keen: struggling fnl circ: kpt on fr 2 out: nvr on terms* 17/2

22-5 8 2 **Samizdat (FR)**[8] [163] 7-10-2 109 HarryHaynes(3) 83
(Dianne Sayer) *hld up in midfield: hdwy 4 out: rdn and wknd after next* 7/1[3]

046- 9 1/2 **Astarador (FR)**[21] [5338] 8-11-12 130 WilsonRenwick 104
(Howard Johnson) *sn towards rr: struggling bef 4 out: btn next* 22/1

35P- 10 51 **Kempski**[46] [4909] 10-10-0 104 oh4 (b) KeithMercer 32
(Rayson Nixon) *chsd ldrs: rdn and lost pl bef 4 out: sn struggling: t.o* 33/1

4m 56.15s (-10.75) **Going Correction** -0.325s/f (Good) 10 Ran SP% **115.9**
Speed ratings (Par 107): **107,104,103,103,98 96,94,93,93,74**
toteswingers:1&2:£7.30, 1&3:£7.00, 2&3:£7.10 CSF £32.22 CT £190.37 TOTE £4.50: £1.90, £2.70, £2.40; EX 32.70.
Owner M J Wasylocha **Bred** G And Mrs Middlebrook **Trained** Trim, Co Meath

FOCUS
A fair handicap run at a good pace. Solid form.

NOTEBOOK
Hearthstead Dream had gone a long time without winning a race, and you had to go back to January 2007 for his last victory over hurdles. He was travelling ominously well on the final bend before landing flat-footed after three out, seemingly stopping his progress again. However, galvanised under pressure, he slowly but steadily made up the ground and got the better of the tiring runner-up after the final hurdle. (op 7-2)
Santa's Son(IRE), up 4f in trip, eased his way to the front after pulling hard throughout and returned to something resembling his best form. (op 9-1)
Los Nadis(GER) looked fairly treated on his win over C&D at about this time in 2009 and kept on well after being outpaced after three out. (op 11-2 tchd 5-1)
Hazeldene, raised a whopping 11lb for his all-the-way victory at Kelso last time, is a confirmed front-runner. His rider appeared to give him a good ride, slowing the gallop at one stage before kicking on again, but he still found three too good for him. (op 9-2)
Tarkani(IRE) appears too high in the weights and ran like a horse that needs to be lowered a few pounds. (op 11-1)
Currahee was another who seemed high in the handicap judged on his two previous handicap successes, and made no impression. (op 14-1)
Corkage(IRE), with cheekpieces back on, is starting to look an awkward ride. (op 10-1)
Samizdat(FR) is probably at his best when there is ease in the ground. (op 6-1)
Astarador(FR) Official explanation: jockey said gelding hung right throughout

310 YOUNG HORSE CHAMPION NOVICES' HUNTERS' CHASE (FOR THE LINLITHGOW & STIRLINGSHIRE HUNT CHALLENGE CUP) (15 fncs) 2m 4f 110y
5:05 (5:05) (Class 5) 5-7-Y-0 **£1,873** (£581; £290; £145)

Form RPR
50- 1 **Scotch Warrior**[11] 6-11-6 0 ow1 MrRMSmith(7) 105+
(Robert Smith) *chsd ldrs: led 4 out: drew clr fr next* 14/1

2 47 **Chapmans Peak (IRE)**[10] 7-11-9 0 MrCDawson(3) 62
(C T Dawson) *cl up: led 7th to 4 out: outpcd by wnr fr next* 8/1[3]

P/P- 3 3/4 **Barry The Cracker**[5] 7-11-5 0 MrMEnnis(7) 61
(G F White) *t.k.h: prom: chal 4 out: outpcd fr next* 16/1

4 34 **Beau Traveller**[5] 7-11-5 0 MrJBewley(7) 30
(Miss Bianca Dunk) *led to 7th: cl up: hit 9th: blnd next: struggling fr 4 out* 11/1

/00- U **Quinder Spring (FR)**[19] 6-11-5 0 MrGJCockburn(7) —
(Lucinda Russell) *nt fluent: hld up in tch: uns rdr 5th* 8/13[1]

P Oojar[18] 6-11-9 0 MrGBrewer(3) —
(Jane Makin) *in tch: outpcd after 10th: wknd after next: t.o whn p.u bef 4 out* **7/2**[2]

5m 19.1s (5.10) **Going Correction** -0.325s/f (Good) **6** Ran SP% **116.1**
Speed ratings: **77,59,58,45,— —**
toteswingers:1&2:£5.50, 2&3:£4.50 CSF £108.63 TOTE £14.90: £6.20, £3.00; EX 121.30.

Owner R Michael Smith **Bred** Miss Jayne Butler **Trained** Galston, E Ayrshire

⊠ The first winner under rules both as trainer and jockey for Michael Smith.

FOCUS
This looked a competitive little event, with all the runners finishing either first or second on their previous outing. The winner looks decent but the form doesn't amount to much.

NOTEBOOK
Scotch Warrior didn't run too badly last time in a point and took this in effortless style once fending off his rivals. He probably won't be any star but, like all of the others in this, he has age on his side. Both of his victories now, including the one in points, have come over 2m4f on quick ground. (op 12-1)

Chapmans Peak(IRE), a recent maiden point winner, had nothing left to offer once Scotch Warrior shot clear. (op 11-2)

Barry The Cracker, a recent restricted point winner, was left behind over the last four fences. (op 14-1)

Quinder Spring(FR), a multiple winner since going into points, hit the fifth and his jockey had no chance of staying abaord. (op 4-6)

Oojar Official explanation: jockey said gelding was unsuited by the good to firm (good in places) ground (op 4-6)

311 LADIES' DAY STANDARD OPEN NATIONAL HUNT FLAT RACE 2m 110y
5:40 (5:43) (Class 6) 4-6-Y-O **£1,712** (£499; £249)

Form				RPR
	1		**Aikman (IRE)**[40] 6-10-9 0 MrTDavidson(7) (James Ewart) *mde all: shkn up and styd on strly to go clr fnl 2f* **20/1**	111+
15-	**2**	*8*	**Priceless Art (IRE)**[33] 5129 5-11-9 0 BrianHughes (Alan Swinbank) *prom: hdwy to chse wnr over 5f out: effrt and rdn 3f out: one pce fnl 2f* **10/11**[1]	111
	3	*½*	**Wither Hills (IRE)** 4-10-5 0 KMDonoghue(7) (I R Ferguson, Ire) *hld up: smooth hdwy on outside 1/2-way: chsd ldrs over 4f out: effrt over 2f out: one pce fnl 2f* **14/1**	100
1-	**4**	*2*	**Corky Dancer**[221] 1629 5-11-6 0 RyanMania(3) (P Monteith) *hld up in midfield: outpcd over 5f out: rallied over 2f out: kpt on: no imp* **8/1**[2]	109
	5	*7*	**Shan Valley (IRE)** 4-9-12 0 AlexanderVoy(7) (Lucy Normile) *prom: rdn and hung lft over 2f out: sn outpcd* **28/1**	85
	6	*8*	**Bertie Milan (IRE)**[88] 5-11-2 0 PaddyAspell (Sue Bradburne) *trckd ldrs: drvn and outpcd over 5f out: n.d after* **20/1**	88
4-	**7**	*1*	**Shooting Times**[24] 5277 5-10-11 0 JamesHalliday(5) (Andrew Parker) *in tch: lost pl after 6f: drvn 1/2-way: sme late hdwy: nvr on terms* **66/1**	87
	8	*2*	**Dizzy River (IRE)** 5-11-2 0 RichieMcGrath (George Charlton) *hld up: hdwy and prom 1/2-way: rdn and wknd fr 2f out* **8/1**[2]	86
	9	*3¾*	**Knockando** 5-11-2 0 PeterBuchanan (Lucinda Russell) *hld up in midfield: hmpd and lost pl after 2f: drvn and outpcd 1/2-way: n.d after* **14/1**	82
	10	*29*	**Hey There Tiger (IRE)** 5-10-9 0 KeithMercer (George Foster) *towards rr: drvn and outpcd 1/2-way: nvr on terms* **100/1**	49
	11	*1*	**Isla Patriot** 4-10-9 0 CampbellGillies(3) (N W Alexander) *bhd: struggling after 6f: nvr on terms* **100/1**	51
4-	**12**	*1*	**Tammys Hill (IRE)**[15] 53 5-11-2 0 SamThomas (Liam Lennon, Ire) *trckd ldrs tl rdn and wknd over 4f out: eased whn no ch* **12/1**	54
	13	*7*	**Money Tree** 4-10-12 0 JasonMaguire (Donald McCain) *t.k.h: prom: outpcd over 6f out: sn wknd* **11/1**[3]	44
	14	*29*	**Whiskey Mist (IRE)**[75] 6-10-9 0 MrMMcConville(7) (Stephen McConville, Ire) *t.k.h: trckd ldrs tl wknd 6f out* **40/1**	22
	15	*16*	**Hurryonharry** 4-10-12 0 (t) JamesReveley (Brian Storey) *hld up in midfield: drvn and outpcd 1/2-way: sn btn* **100/1**	3

3m 49.8s (-4.30) **Going Correction** -0.325s/f (Good)
WFA 4 from 5yo+ 4lb **15** Ran SP% **123.8**
Speed ratings: **107,103,103,102,98 95,94,93,91,78 77,77,73,60,52**
toteswingers:1&2:£11.20, 1&3:£86.70, 2&3:£10.00 CSF £37.92 TOTE £31.40: £6.90, £1.10, £6.40; EX 89.30 Place 6 £214.10; Place 5 £151.57.Snow Easy was withdrawn. Price at time of withdrawal 80/1. Rule 4 does not apply

Owner G E Davidson & S J Houliston **Bred** Gerry Carroll **Trained** Langholm, Dumfries & G'way

FOCUS
The runner-up set a fair standard and the winner looks decent.

NOTEBOOK
Aikman(IRE) ⊠ , unbeaten in three British points, and having his ninth start in total, won in convincing style after leading from the off. This looked an impressive victory, even allowing for his experience advantage, so hopefully he will go on to prove himself a decent prospect. (op 14-1)

Priceless Art(IRE), beaten just over 15l in a Grade 2 bumper at Aintree last time, set a good standard for the others to aim at and moved into contention powerfully. He was unable to go with the winner as that horse quickened again, and one would imagine we may see him on the Flat at some stage. (op 11-10)

Wither Hills(IRE) ⊠ caught the eye with the way he made up ground and looks sure to win something similar in due course. He has a bit of size about him. (op 12-1)

Corky Dancer won a bumper when last on the racecourse back in October of last year (form of which is ordinary) and finished strongly after getting outpaced. He doesn't look the biggest. (op 9-1 tchd 10-1)

Shan Valley(IRE) raced prominently and stuck to her task well despite looking green. (op 33-1)

Bertie Milan(IRE) cost connections £40,000 at the Cheltenham sales last month after showing promise in Irish points. He threatened to get involved as the tempo increased but could only find the one pace under pressure.

Dizzy River(IRE) ⊠ , who looked the owner's first string on caps, hinted at having ability before not getting home. (op 10-1 tchd 15-2)

Tammys Hill(IRE) had been running quite well in his previous starts in bumpers but was beaten before the field turned back into the home straight for the final time. (op 11-1 tchd 9-1)

T/Plt: £109.10 to a £1 stake. Pool: £49,141.17. 328.51 winning tickets. T/Qpdt: £43.00 to a £1 stake. Pool: £3,478.06. 59.80 winning tickets. RY

LE LION-D'ANGERS (R-H)
Thursday, May 13

OFFICIAL GOING: Turf: very soft

312a PRIX ANJOU-LOIRE CHALLENGE (CHASE) (CROSS-COUNTRY) (LISTED RACE) (6YO+) (TURF) 4m 4f 110y
3:50 (12:00) 6-Y-0+
£44,601 (£21,805; £12,884; £8,920; £4,955; £3,469)

			RPR
1		**Another Jewel (IRE)**[21] 5347 8-10-10 0 JLCullen (Denis Paul Murphy, Ire) *hld up: hdwy to chse ldrs fr 1/2-way: chal ldr appr last: sn led and styd on wl* **102/10**	—
2	*2½*	**Ninon De Grissay (FR)**[1166] 9-10-6 0 AnthonyThierry (F-H Hayeres, France) **12/1**	—
3	*2½*	**Ni Plus Ni Moins (FR)**[1628] 9-10-6 0 (p) OlivierJouin (P Journiac, France) **68/10**[3]	—
4	*3*	**Phakos (FR)** 7-10-10 0 DavidCottin (P Cottin, France) **9/2**[2]	—
5	*dist*	**L'Aubergiste (FR)**[802] 6-10-10 0 JonathanPay (J-L Guillochon, France) **12/1**	—
6	*dist*	**Lusty (FR)**[767] 9-10-10 0 (p) SebastienZuliani (C Le Galliard, France) **40/1**	—
F		**Pass Me By**[61] 11-10-10 0 TomMessenger (Suzy Smith) *hld up: towards rr whn fell 14th* **39/1**	—
F		**Chriseti (FR)**[530] 10-10-10 0 (b) JulienJouin (E Leenders, France) **3/1**[1]	—
P		**Semiramiss (FR)**[529] 6-10-6 0 JeromeZuliani (P Quinton, France) **20/1**	—
F		**Quart Monde (FR)**[37] 6-10-10 0 JonathanPlouganou (F Nicolle, France) **12/1**	—
F		**Oke Prince (FR)** 8-10-10 0 StephaneJuteau (J Follain, France) **68/10**[3]	—
F		**Natacha Rochelaise (FR)** 9-10-6 0 (p) DavidVerry (P Quinton, France) **16/1**	—

10m 23.45s (623.45) **12** Ran SP% **116.4**
PARI-MUTUEL (all including 1 euro stakes): WIN 11.20; PLACE 4.10, 2.90, 2.40; DF 71.70.
Owner Frank Magee **Bred** Tony And Michael O'Brien **Trained** Enniscorthy, Co Wexford

NOTEBOOK
Another Jewel(IRE) was an easy winner of what is probably Europe's longest race.

191 AINTREE (L-H)
Friday, May 14

OFFICIAL GOING: Good (8.4)
Wind: Light, across Weather: Fine

313 ALMOND RESORTS MARES' H'CAP HURDLE (11 hdls) 2m 4f
5:30 (5:31) (Class 4) (0-115,115) 4-Y-0+ **£3,577** (£1,050; £525; £262)

Form				RPR
111-	**1**		**Flower Haven**[28] 5216 8-10-12 **108** EdGlassonbury(7) (Victor Dartnall) *midfield: hdwy appr 7th: led 3 out: rdn in duel w runner-up run-in and hdd briefly: styd on gamely and jst prevailed* **9/4**[1]	113
202-	**2**	*hd*	**Boogie Dancer**[18] 19 6-10-9 **98** HarrySkelton (Stuart Howe) *hld up: hdwy 4 out: chsd ldrs 3 out: wnt 2nd 2 out: str chal fr last: led briefly in duel w wnr run-in: jst wnt down* **15/2**[3]	103
PF3-	**3**	*4½*	**Laureate Des Loges (FR)**[26] 5253 6-11-5 **108** AndrewTinkler (Henry Daly) *hld up: hdwy to chse ldrs appr 3 out: hit 2 out: chsd ldng pair whn j.lft last: styd on same pce and no imp run-in* **8/1**	109
F2-5	**4**	*shd*	**Mini Minster**[13] 89 8-11-1 **104** GrahamLee (Peter Atkinson) *in tch: clsd 6th: rdn and outpcd appr 3 out: styd on wl fr last: gng on at fin* **17/2**	105
001-	**5**	*5*	**Princess Rainbow (FR)**[34] 5130 5-11-3 **106** AlanO'Keeffe (Jennie Candlish) *racd keenly: prom: led after 4 out: hdd 3 out: hung rt-handed: wknd appr last* **8/1**	102
142-	**6**	*10*	**Last Of The Bunch**[25] 5273 5-11-6 **109** BrianHughes (Alan Swinbank) *in tch: nt fluent 6th and lost pl briefly: chalng 3 out: pushed along and wknd bef last* **5/1**[2]	96
42P-	**7**	*¾*	**Itstooearly**[71] 4401 7-10-5 **94** PaddyAspell (James Moffatt) *hld up: pushed along 3 out: kpt on fr 2 out wout troubling ldrs* **20/1**	81
06/-	**8**	*2¾*	**Bollin Ruth**[432] 4362 8-10-7 **103** CallumWhillans(7) (Donald Whillans) *midfield: nt fluent 7th: pushed along 4 out: wknd bef 3 out* **33/1**	87
02P-	**9**	*3¾*	**Hot Tottie (IRE)**[50] 4851 6-11-1 **104** SeamusDurack (Jeremy Scott) *prom: pushed along after 4 out: wknd appr 3 out* **20/1**	85
324-	**10**	*24*	**Obara D'Avril (FR)**[10] 1552 8-10-1 **95** PaulCallaghan(5) (Simon West) *nt fluent at times: bhd: sme hdwy appr 2 out: nvr able to trble ldrs: wknd bef last* **16/1**	54
450-	**11**	*9*	**Zepnove (IRE)**[26] 5253 4-10-9 **106** (p) AlexMerriam(3) (Neil King) *led: hdd after 4 out: sn rdn and wknd* **33/1**	52

4m 59.4s (-1.30) **Going Correction** +0.075s/f (Yiel)
WFA 4 from 5yo+ 19lb **11** Ran SP% **113.2**
Speed ratings (Par 105): **105,104,103,103,101 97,97,95,94,84 81**
toteswingers: 1&2 £2.90, 2&3 £6.00, 1&3 £13.80. CSF £17.71 CT £111.80 TOTE £2.50: £1.10, £3.10, £3.20; EX 19.90.
Owner Gentlemen Don't Work On Mondays **Bred** J B Haggas **Trained** Brayford, Devon

FOCUS
A competitive 0-115 mares' handicap hurdle run at a fair pace with a cracking finish fought out between the two principals. Solid handicap form.

NOTEBOOK
Flower Haven was trying to defy a 16lb hike in the ratings since scoring over 2m5f at Uttoxeter and duly did so in a determined fashion to complete a four-timer. She took up the running going to two out but was soon under strong driving when challenged. She came out on top on the run to the line with her stamina probably proving the difference. There is the possibility she will return here for a conditional jockeys mares' race next time but, connections are very keen on giving her a spin on the flat where she has an attractive mark of 40. (op 5-2 tchd 11-4 in places)
Boogie Dancer has mainly been campaigned at 2m but she is a gutsy little performer who normally runs her race. She lost little in defeat here as she was probably only denied by the stamina of the winner in a protracted duel from two out only to go down by a narrow margin. She can find compensation over the summer in similar contests. (op 13-2 tchd 17-2)

Laureate Des Loges(FR) returned to some sort of form on the evidence of finishing third last time, albeit being beaten a fair way. This was a better performance again after moving through from the rear she looked as though she could figure in the finish but, she only stayed on at the same pace after a mistake two out not helping her cause. (tchd 7-1)
Mini Minster has been steadily recapturing her form this year but got outpaced going to three out. She finished strongly and this was a solid effort. (op 9-1)
Princess Rainbow(FR) ran too free before leading at the last in the back straight. She hung right when headed and was tiring when getting the second last wrong. (op 15-2)
Last Of The Bunch was disappointing on her handicap debut and now has something to prove off this mark. (op 6-1 tchd 9-2)

314 BETDAQ THE BETTING EXCHANGE H'CAP CHASE (19 fncs) 3m 1f
6:00 (6:01) (Class 3) (0-135,132) 5-Y-0+ **£6,505** (£1,910; £955; £477)

Form RPR
3PP- **1** **Victor Daly (IRE)**[305] 936 9-10-7 **118** JimmyDerham(5) 123+
(Martin Keighley) *chsd ldrs: wnt 2nd 10th: led 14th: abt 10 l clr appr 3 out: rdn and hdd bef last: rallied u.p to regain ld towards fin* **5/1**[1]
461- **2** ½ **Briery Fox (IRE)**[26] 5247 12-11-8 **128** LeightonAspell 134+
(Henry Daly) *hld up: hdwy 15th: wnt chsng clr ldr whn nt fluent 2 out: clsd rapidly to ld appr last: hdd towards fin* **11/1**
P15- **3** 17 **Go West (IRE)**[28] 5212 9-10-8 **114** PaddyBrennan 107
(Nigel Twiston-Davies) *chsd ldr to 10th: pushed along after 11th: outpcd 15th: kpt on to take 3rd 2 out: sn no imp* **9/1**
21P- **4** 5 **Western Gale (IRE)**[27] 5223 7-10-12 **118** DenisO'Regan 103
(Martin Todhunter) *towards rr: mstke 9th: pushed along after 11th: u.p 13th: sme hdwy 15th: nvr able to land a blow* **10/1**
4P1- **5** 8 **Radetsky March (IRE)**[28] 5219 7-11-0 **120** JasonMaguire 98
(Mark Bradstock) *led: nt fluent 13th: hdd 14th: rdn and wknd appr 2 out* **5/1**[1]
/00- **6** 78 **College Ace (IRE)**[201] 1925 9-11-6 **126** (tp) SamJones 34
(Renee Robeson) *in tch: pushed along and outpcd 12th: bhd sn after* **33/1**
PU-P **P** **Battlecry**[5] 236 9-11-7 **132** SamTwiston-Davies(5) —
(Nigel Twiston-Davies) *chsd ldrs: nt fluent 4th and 5th: sn lost pl: bhd and struggling after 8th: t.o whn p.u after 11th* **12/1**
04P- **P** **Aleron (IRE)**[51] 4816 12-10-11 **117** (p) DougieCostello —
(John Quinn) *midfield: mstke 10th: wknd bef 15th: t.o whn p.u bef 2 out* **14/1**
066- **U** **Calatagan (IRE)**[28] 5204 11-11-2 **127** JamesHalliday(5) —
(Malcolm Jefferson) *hld up in rr: hit 5th: blnd and uns rdr 7th* **16/1**
P/1- **P** **Direct Flight (IRE)**[359] 402 12-11-1 **121** (t) NickScholfield —
(Jeremy Scott) *midfield: bhd after 11th: struggling after: t.o whn p.u bef 14th* **16/1**
531- **P** **Sagalyrique (FR)**[27] 5232 6-11-6 **126** (p) RobertThornton —
(Alan King) *midfield: hdwy 4th: mstke 6th: handy tl pushed along and outpcd appr 4 out: wknd bef 3 out: bhd whn p.u bef last* **11/2**[2]
001- **P** **Back Exit (IRE)**[25] 5281 7-10-11 **117** (t) TomO'Brien —
(Philip Hobbs) *in tch: lost pl 4th: reminders bef 11th: toiling whn blnd 14th: t.o whn p.u bef 3 out* **8/1**[3]

6m 28.5s (-1.50) **Going Correction** +0.075s/f (Yiel) **12** Ran SP% **116.3**
Speed ratings: **105,104,99,97,95 70,—,—,—,— —,—**
toteswingers: 1&2 £12.20, 2&3 £17.00, 1&3 £27.30. CSF £57.67 CT £483.31 TOTE £5.30: £1.60, £4.20, £1.10; EX 70.70.
Owner C B Compton **Bred** Joseph O'Dwyer **Trained** Condicote, Gloucs

FOCUS
A strong pace helped make this competitive handicap chase produce another cracking finish. The second ran to his mark and the winner is capable of better.

NOTEBOOK
Victor Daly(IRE) regained the initiative after looking beaten going to the last and rallied gamely, after getting his second wind, to get back up towards the finish. He won this race two years ago when with Heather Dalton and, although, there was money to support him throughout the day connections felt he would need this. He will come on for this and will be kept on the go through the summer. (op 11-2 tchd 9-2)
Briery Fox(IRE) is a grand old servant running yet again with plenty of credit. He came though from the back off the strong pace and seemed to have the measure of the winner when taking it up going to the last but got run out of it nearing the finish. (op 10-1 tchd 12-1)
Go West(IRE) raced up with the pace for much of the way but was struggling to make any impact when it quickened and was beaten turning into the straight. (op 8-1)
Western Gale(IRE) outclassed in the Scottish National after winning a weak novice chase, was feeling the pinch when the pace quickened and could never get involved. (tchd 11-1)
Radetsky March(IRE) was another to have been well-supported after winning over 2m5f last time but after ensuring the strong pace failed to see out the step up to three miles. (op 8-1)

315 SIKA CENTENARY NOVICES' HURDLE (9 hdls) 2m 110y
6:30 (6:30) (Class 4) 4-Y-0+ **£3,903** (£1,146; £573; £286)

Form RPR
43- **1** **Praxiteles (IRE)**[106] 3695 6-10-12 115 APMcCoy 124+
(Rebecca Curtis) *prom: led appr 3 out: drew clr after last: r.o wl* **7/2**[3]
2 10 **Heron Bay**[202] 6-10-12 0 TomO'Brien 115+
(Peter Bowen) *hld up in tch: hdwy to chse ldrs 3 out: rdn appr last: wnt 2nd run-in: no ch w wnr* **9/1**
241- **3** ½ **Lidar (FR)**[18] 25 5-11-5 117 RobertThornton 122+
(Alan King) *hld up: hdwy 4th: wnt 2nd and chalng 3 out: sn rdn: outpcd by wnr bef last: styd on same pce after* **7/4**[1]
62- **4** 7 **Devotion To Duty (IRE)**[27] 5220 4-10-8 0 PeterBuchanan 106
(Lucinda Russell) *in tch: effrt to chse ldrs 3 out: u.p whn hit last: wknd* **10/1**
44U- **5** 13 **Double Handful (GER)**[36] 5094 4-10-8 0 (b[1]) AidanColeman 95
(Venetia Williams) *hld up: outpcd fr 2 out: nvr a danger* **20/1**
221- **6** 9 **Saveiro (FR)**[16] 42 6-11-5 125 BrianHughes 95
(Alan Swinbank) *led: hdd appr 3 out: wknd bef 2 out:* **10/3**[2]
6- **7** 3¼ **Wilbury Star (IRE)**[184] 2228 4-10-8 0 AndrewTinkler 81
(Nicky Henderson) *prom: lost pl 2nd: hdwy to chse ldrs whn nt fluent 4th: wknd 4 out* **20/1**
01- **P** **Reverend Green (IRE)**[57] 3419 4-10-8 0 LiamHeard —
(Chris Down) *racd keenly: in tch: wknd appr 3 out: t.o whn p.u bef 2 out* **40/1**

4m 2.70s (-3.50) **Going Correction** +0.075s/f (Yiel)
WFA 4 from 5yo+ 18lb **8** Ran SP% **112.7**
Speed ratings (Par 105): **111,106,106,102,96 92,90,—**
toteswingers: 1&2 £9.60, 2&3 £1.40, 1&3 £3.70. CSF £31.77 TOTE £4.70: £1.30, £3.00, £1.90; EX 37.90.
Owner Walters Plant Hire Ltd **Bred** Ballymacoll Stud Farm Ltd **Trained** Newport, Dyfed

FOCUS
A decent novice hurdle for the time of year run at just a fair pace. A big step up from the winner with the fourth and fifth helping set the level.

NOTEBOOK
Praxiteles(IRE) had only produced a couple of satisfactory efforts over hurdles to date after winning a 1m4f maiden on the Flat and needed to step up on those appearances to land this, which he duly did in a decent manner. Always racing prominently he clattered three out before taking the lead, only having to be pushed clear. Clearly going the right way, he was well-supported in the morning and connections have not ruled out a return to the Flat. (op 4-1 tchd 9-2 in places)
Heron Bay had been bought by new connections for 12,500gns out of Chris Wall's yard after being ultimately disappointing on the Flat. He travelled and hurdled well enough but could only stay on at the same pace in the straight. Headgear might be an option as he no doubt retains plenty of ability and if connections can rekindle his enthusiasm he can go one better as this was a pleasing effort. (op 11-1 tchd 12-1)
Lidar(FR) laid down a strong challenge in the straight but looked one paced when the winner kicked two out. He looks as though he would appreciate a step up in trip. (op 13-8)
Devotion To Duty(IRE) chased the leaders for much of the way but he clattered a couple of hurdles before weakening going to the last. (op 9-1)
Double Handful(GER) now qualifies for a mark after being highly tried in first time blinkers last time although never threatening to get involved after struggling from a fair way out. (op 18-1)
Saveiro(FR) was slightly disappointing after winning last time. He folded tamely when headed in the straight and looks to be on a high enough mark of 125. (op 3-1 tchd 7-2)

316 MAMMA MIA! AT THE ECHO ARENA H'CAP HURDLE (9 hdls) 2m 1f
7:05 (7:06) (Class 3) (0-135,131) 4-Y-0+ **£5,854** (£1,719; £859; £429)

Form RPR
115- **1** **The Jigsaw Man (IRE)**[144] 3004 6-11-6 **125** APMcCoy 137+
(Rebecca Curtis) *mde all: j. awkwardly 1st: looked in command fr 3 out: rdn to go clr appr last: r.o wl* **7/2**[1]
P62- **2** 10 **Dantari (IRE)**[20] 5393 5-11-5 **127** DPFahy(3) 128
(Evan Williams) *chsd wnr tl rdn and outpcd after 4 out: kpt on u.p to retake 2nd 3 out: had battle for pls after: no imp on wnr and no ch fr last* **13/2**
143- **3** ¾ **Forty Thirty (IRE)**[210] 1779 4-10-11 **125** MarcGoldstein(5) 121
(Sheena West) *bhd: hdwy after 4 out: chsd ldrs appr 3 out: sn chal for 2nd: nt fluent 2 out: kpt on u.p* **16/1**
30-F **4** 14 **Black Coffee**[14] 80 5-10-11 **123** DavidBass(7) 111
(Nicky Henderson) *chsd ldrs: rdn along after 5th: chsd wnr after 4 out to 3 out: wknd after 2 out* **16/1**
0/6- **5** 3½ **Salute Him (IRE)**[70] 321 7-10-13 **118** DenisO'Regan 103
(A J Martin, Ire) *hld up: hdwy 4th: chsd wnr appr 3 out tl lost pl at flight: wknd 2 out* **11/2**[2]
5U0- **6** 4 **High Bird Humphrey**[138] 3084 11-10-0 **108** (p) MichaelNaughton(3) 89
(Simon West) *bhd: nt fluent 3rd: sme hdwy 3 out: nvr able to trble ldrs* **28/1**
410- **7** 7 **Well Disguised (IRE)**[23] 5308 8-9-11 **109** GarryWhillans(7) 84
(Donald Whillans) *midfield: rdn and outpcd appr 3 out: nvr on terms w ldrs* **33/1**
U10- **8** 4½ **Olympian (FR)**[28] 5213 8-11-3 **122** JamieMoore 93
(Philip Middleton) *midfield: rdn and outpcd appr 3 out: nvr a danger* **16/1**
36-1 **9** 2¾ **Son Of Flicka**[14] 80 6-11-12 **131** JasonMaguire 99
(Donald McCain) *chsd ldrs tl pushed along and wknd 4 out* **8/1**
242- **10** 7 **Nearby**[23] 5308 6-11-6 **125** TomO'Brien 87
(Philip Hobbs) *midfield: lost pl 5th: rdn and bhd after 4 out: nvr a threat* **6/1**[3]
V02- **11** 41 **Divers (FR)**[28] 5213 6-11-6 **125** GrahamLee 50
(Ferdy Murphy) *midfield: mstke and lost pl 4th: bhd after* **7/1**
050- **P** **Cheshire Prince**[56] 4721 6-10-13 **121** AlexMerriam(3) —
(Neil King) *in tch: mstke 4th: wknd 5th: pushed along after 4 out: t.o whn p.u bef last* **10/1**

4m 9.30s (-4.40) **Going Correction** +0.075s/f (Yiel)
WFA 4 from 5yo+ 18lb **12** Ran SP% **122.0**
Speed ratings (Par 107): **113,108,107,101,99 97,94,92,91,87 69,—**
toteswingers: 1&2 £6.60, 2&3 £7.50, 1&3 £57.50. CSF £27.77 CT £331.98 TOTE £4.10: £1.80, £2.40, £5.60; EX 34.40.
Owner LL R P Racing **Bred** P J O'Connor **Trained** Newport, Dyfed

FOCUS
A fair handicap hurdle. The impressive winner improved to the level promised by his smart bumper form.

NOTEBOOK
The Jigsaw Man(IRE) trounced his rivals in what looked a competitive heat beforehand. The drop back in trip ensured he would make this a good gallop and he ran his rivals ragged in the home straight. The softer conditions at Ffos Las were blamed for his disappointing run last time and there were concerns that the ground had eased too much here. His future over hurdles now lies in the handicapper's assessment but connections feel he could develop into a better chaser as he is obviously still progressing. (op 6-1)
Dantari(IRE) ran with plenty of credit. Dropped back in trip after some solid efforts in decent handicaps, he chased the winner for much of the way and was under pressure to do so from a long way out. He stuck to his task well and will appreciate a step back up in distance again. (op 9-1 tchd 6-1)
Forty Thirty(IRE) ran a solid race tackling older opposition on handicap debut. He battled it out for second throughout the home straight, although never posing a threat to the winner. (op 12-1)
Black Coffee ran a similar race to the runner-up before tiring going to the last and this should serve as a good confidence booster after having a nasty fall last time. (tchd 14-1)
Salute Him(IRE) moved through to track the winner entering the straight, looking to be travelling particularly well. But, when asked to close could not to do so and was soundly beaten. (op 9-2 tchd 7-1)

317 BETDAQ.CO.UK H'CAP HUNTERS' CHASE (19 fncs) 3m 1f
7:40 (7:42) (Class 3) (0-125,115) 5-Y-0**£6,025** (£1,898; £960; £492; £257)

Form RPR
F5-1 **1** **Take The Stand (IRE)**[9] 149 14-12-2 **115** 7ex (p) MrMByrne(5) 129+
(Peter Bowen) *led: hdd appr 4th: led again 5th: drew clr fr 2 out: mstke last: pushed out* **7/4**[1]
P11- **2** 4½ **Lisadell King (IRE)**[26] 5254 10-12-4 **114** MrGMaundrell(3) 121+
(G C Maundrell) *racd keenly: hld up: impr to trck ldrs 5th: outpcd after 4 out: mstke 3 out: chsd clr wnr appr last: no imp* **7/2**[3]
00-4 **3** 14 **James Pine (IRE)**[9] 151 11-11-13 **111** MrMWall(5) 104
(Sue Wilson) *chsd ldrs: wnt 2nd 5th: sn pressing wnr tl rdn appr 3 out: wknd bef last* **11/4**[2]
0P4- **4** 8 **Thunder Hawk (IRE)**[33] 5143 10-10-6 **92** (p) MissLAlexander(7) 78
(Mrs L A Coltherd) *in tch: nt fluent 4th: j. slowly and bhd 6th: struggling fr 12th: n.d after* **9/2**
1U4- **5** 23 **Belem Ranger (IRE)**[6] 10-12-0 **110** MrCDawson(3) 80
(Mrs J Warwick) *hld up: nt fluent 12th: outpcd fr 13th: n.d after* **11/1**

PP-P **F** **Prelude D'Estruval (FR)**[9] 152 7-10-0 **86** oh10.........(b) MissKWood(7) —
(Miss N L Elliott) *handy: pckd bdly 1st: led appr 4th: hdd 5th: lost pl 7th: fell 8th* **33/1**

6m 35.0s (5.00) **Going Correction** +0.075s/f (Yiel) **6** Ran SP% **114.7**
Speed ratings: **95,93,89,86,79** —
toteswingers: 1&2 £1.10, 2&3 £1.50, 1&3 £3.70. CSF £8.89 TOTE £1.90: £1.10, £2.40; EX 4.00.

Owner F W Ridge **Bred** James Phelan **Trained** Little Newcastle, Pembrokes

FOCUS
A rare heat in which this hunter chase is run as a handicap. Just an ordinary pace with this small field. There is a case for rating the race up to 6lb higher.

NOTEBOOK
Take The Stand(IRE) was always going to take all the beating off a mark of 114, and duly did so after making virtually all. There was a slight scare when he launched himself at the last, but he had already put the race to bed. He will now go to Stratford for the W+S Recycling Championship Hunter Chase at the end of the month, a race which he has been placed in twice before. (op 5-4)
Lisadell King(IRE), as with the winner racing off 114, has been making giant strides this season winning three hunter chases. He looked to be the only one with the profile that could trouble the winner but, after sitting behind the leaders much of the way, could only stay on at the same pace in the straight. A mistake three out did not aid his cause and he should be capable of regaining the winning thread. (op 11-4 tchd 4-1)
James Pine(IRE) was quietly fancied to land this but, after mixing it with the winner from the start, was in trouble entering the straight before weakening approaching the last. (op 5-1)

318 JOCKEY CLUB CATERING CONDITIONAL JOCKEYS' H'CAP HURDLE (13 hdls) 3m 110y
8:15 (8:16) (Class 4) (0-105,105) 4-Y-0+ **£3,903** (£1,146; £573; £286)

Form RPR
24-2 **1** **Boyoboy (IRE)**[8] 176 6-10-11 **90**................................ MichaelO'Connell 104+
(George Moore) *hld up: hdwy appr 8th: led bef 3 out: rdn bef last: r.o wl to draw clr fnl 100yds* **3/1**[1]

P-11 **2** *4* **Flying Doctor**[6] 212 7-10-10 **89** 14ex........................... RichieMcLernon 100+
(Elliott Cooper) *trckd ldrs and travelled wl: wnt 2nd to chal whn hit 3 out: rdn bef last: no ex fnl 100yds* **10/3**[2]

0P2- **3** *¾* **Manadam (FR)**[23] 5311 7-11-9 **105**........................ CampbellGillies(3) 114
(Lucinda Russell) *hld up: hdwy appr 3 out: chsd ldrs u.p bef 2 out: styd on wl towards fin: nt quite pce to chal* **11/1**

50P- **4** *2 ½* **Sparkling Zola**[55] 4736 8-10-0 **82**................................ EwanWhillans(3) 88
(Alistair Whillans) *dropped to midfield 2nd: rdn and hdwy whn mstke 3 out: styd on whn edgd lft u.p run-in* **66/1**

244- **5** *16* **Bled (FR)**[22] 5339 5-10-6 **88**..(b) JohnKington(3) 80
(Donald McCain) *led: reminder after 1st: hdd appr 3 out: sn rdn: wknd bef last* **16/1**

003- **6** *5* **Charlie Bucket**[23] 5310 7-10-5 **90**................................ GarryWhillans(6) 77
(Donald Whillans) *bhd: hdwy appr 9th: chsd ldrs bef 3 out: wknd bef last* **28/1**

10-4 **7** *4* **Earcomesthedream (IRE)**[15] 66 7-11-7 **100**.............(b) HarrySkelton 84
(Peter Pritchard) *bhd: pushed along after 4 out: hdwy to chse ldrs appr 3 out: unable to chal: no further imp on ldrs bef last* **10/1**

0P3- **8** *2* **Magical Island**[23] 5315 7-9-11 **79**....................................(b) DavidBass(3) 61
(Sophie Leech) *trckd ldrs: mstke 7th: wkng u.p whn mstke 3 out* **16/1**

321- **9** *27* **Glen Rouge (IRE)**[22] 5339 9-10-4 **83**.................................... RyanMania 40
(James Moffatt) *midfield: nt fluent 5th: wkng whn mstke 3 out* **11/1**

25-5 **10** *9* **Ballyvesey (IRE)**[7] 193 5-11-8 **104**........................ DonalDevereux(3) 53
(Peter Bowen) *in tch: lost pl bef 8th: struggling 4 out: n.d after* **13/2**[3]

30-P **11** *19* **Glacial Rambler (IRE)**[6] 211 11-10-0 **79** oh19............. JamesHalliday 11
(Stuart Coltherd) *prom tl rdn and wknd after 4 out* **100/1**

PP0- **12** *3* **Papradon**[62] 4584 6-9-12 **80**.......................(b) SamTwiston-Davies(3) 10
(Nigel Twiston-Davies) *trckd ldrs tl rdn and wknd appr 3 out* **25/1**

36P- **P** **Scaramouche**[39] 5055 10-10-3 **92**..................................(tp) JoshEvans(10) —
(Ben De Haan) *hld up: rdr lost iron briefly 4th: u.p after 4 out: t.o whn p.u bef last* **33/1**

04-0 **P** **Jane Doe**[6] 212 7-10-8 **87**.. HarryHaynes —
(Harriet Graham) *nt fluent: prom: rdn and wknd after 8th: t.o whn p.u bef 3 out* **16/1**

630- **P** **Knight Woodsman**[78] 4262 6-11-3 **99**........................... AlexMerriam(3) —
(Neil King) *bhd: pushed along and gng nowhere after 7th: t.o whn p.u bef 9th: b.b.v* **25/1**

6m 15.8s (-0.50) **Going Correction** +0.075s/f (Yiel) **15** Ran SP% **121.4**
Speed ratings (Par 105): **103,101,101,100,95 93,92,92,83,80 74,73,—,—,—**
toteswingers: 1&2 £1.30, 2&3 £8.40, 1&3 £7.30. CSF £12.63 CT £99.71 TOTE £3.90: £1.60, £2.20, £4.60; EX 7.30.

Owner Geoff & Sandra Turnbull **Bred** E Farrell **Trained** Middleham Moor, N Yorks

FOCUS
A decent sized field contested this modest staying conditional jockeys' handicap hurdle run at a good pace with the front four finishing well clear of the remainder. Solid handicap form.

NOTEBOOK
Boyoboy(IRE) travelled well throughout before taking up the running three out. He always held enough in reserve to repel any challenges thereafter and stayed on strongly to score. He met the runner-up on better terms than last time and was well supported to turn the tables. He saw out this step up in trip well and can be found a similar opportunity to follow up. (tchd 5-2 and 7-2 in places)
Flying Doctor, who had to defy a 14lb penalty and is due to be racing of a mark a further 6lb higher in the future, came here to complete a quick hat-trick. After holding every chance before blundering three out he looked as though he was capable of doing so, but the turn around at the weights with the winner duly told by the next. He stuck to his task well, but it will be difficult for him now in future. (op 9-4)
Manadam(FR) is rather frustrating but did run one of his better races. He was patiently ridden but a smooth run up the inner on the home bend saw him come with a chance. Once ridden his effort flattened briefly before closing again after the last. (op 16-1)
Sparkling Zola looked a beaten horse when entering the back straight but, came there with a chance turning in. He wandered in the straight without managing to lay down a serious threat but drew well clear of the fifth after the last. (op 50-1)
Bled(FR) took them along at a decent pace and kept pressing the leaders until tiring going to the last. (op 12-1)
Charlie Bucket came there travelling well in the straight only to fail to see out the trip. (op 25-1)

319 LIVERPOOL VOLKSWAGEN STANDARD OPEN NATIONAL HUNT FLAT RACE 2m 1f
8:45 (8:49) (Class 5) 4-6-Y-0 **£1,951** (£573; £286; £143)

Form RPR
1- **1** **Problema Tic (FR)**[46] 4932 4-11-5 0.. APMcCoy 114
(Nicky Henderson) *mde all: rdn over 1f out: pressed ins fnl f: r.o gamely and on top towards fin* **4/1**[1]

2 *¾* **Morgan's Bay** 5-11-2 0... AndrewTinkler 110
(Henry Daly) *in tch: rdn to take 2nd over 1f out: str chal and upsides ins fnl f: nt qckn cl home* **8/1**[2]

3 *6* **Lexicon Lad (IRE)**[33] 5-11-2 0.. PaddyBrennan 105
(Tom George) *trckd ldrs: wnt 2nd and chalng 2f out tl over 1f out: outpcd by front pair fnl f* **25/1**

4 *3 ¾* **Native Breeze (IRE)** 5-10-9 0.. TomO'Brien 95
(Philip Hobbs) *hld up: hdwy whn plenty to do 3f out: styd on fnl 2f: nrst fin* **25/1**

- **5** *¾* **Rival D'Estruval (FR)** 5-11-2 0..................................... TimmyMurphy 101
(Pauline Robson) *midfield: hdwy to chse ldrs after 5f: stl handy over 2f out: rdn over 1f out: kpt on same pce fnl f* **33/1**

6 *6* **Benheir (IRE)** 4-10-12 0.. RobertThornton 91
(Henry Daly) *in tch: rdn over 3f out: one pce fnl 2f* **33/1**

7 *1* **Lively Baron (IRE)** 5-10-13 0.. AdrianLane(3) 95
(Donald McCain) *midfield: hdwy after 5f: rn green u.p whn chsng ldrs 3f out: wknd over 1f out* **28/1**

8 *1* **Blenheim Brook (IRE)**[117] 5-11-2 0.................................. PeterBuchanan 94
(Lucinda Russell) *hld up: hdwy over 3f out: one pce fnl 2f* **16/1**

9 *1 ½* **Blazing Bay (IRE)** 5-10-9 0.. PaddyAspell 85
(James Moffatt) *hld up: nt clr run 4f out: kpt on fnl 2f: nvr trbld ldrs* **66/1**

10- **10** *½* **Tale Of Tanganyika (FR)**[34] 5129 4-11-5 0......................... KeithMercer 95
(Tom Tate) *racd keenly: chsd wnr: chalng over 2f out: sn lost 2nd: wknd over 1f out* **4/1**[1]

4- **11** *4* **His Lordship**[21] 5368 6-11-2 0... NickScholfield 88
(Grant Cann) *hld up: pushed along over 3f out: nvr a danger* **33/1**

12 *11* **Tullyraine (IRE)**[90] 6-10-11 0............................... SamTwiston-Davies(5) 78
(Nigel Twiston-Davies) *trckd ldrs: niggled along 5f out: wknd over 2f out* **28/1**

13 *½* **Honour The King (IRE)** 4-10-7 0............................. DonalDevereux(5) 74
(Peter Bowen) *in rr: pushed along 6f out: nvr on terms* **20/1**

14 *shd* **Foot The Bill**[166] 5-11-2 0... DougieCostello 78
(Patrick Holmes) *midfield: pushed along and wknd over 2f out* **25/1**

15 *13* **Mwaleshi** 5-11-2 0.. JasonMaguire 66
(Donald McCain) *racd keenly in midfield: wknd over 2f out* **4/1**[1]

16 *½* **North Brook (IRE)** 5-10-11 0.. EwanWhillans(5) 66
(Alistair Whillans) *midfield tl wknd over 3f out* **66/1**

17 *3 ½* **Velvet Vic (IRE)** 4-10-7 0... JamesHalliday(5) 59
(Malcolm Jefferson) *a bhd* **25/1**

18 *4 ½* **Glenfly (IRE)** 5-11-2 0.. SeamusDurack 58
(Philip Hobbs) *in tch: rdn and wknd 4f out* **9/1**[3]

19 *41* **Smart Command (IRE)** 6-11-2 0.. GrahamLee 22
(Ferdy Murphy) *a bhd: struggling 1/2-way: t.o* **66/1**

4m 10.7c (3.30) **Going Correction** +0.075s/f (Yiel) **19** Ran SP% **127.3**
Speed ratings: **95,94,91,90,89 86,86,85,85,85 83,77,77,77,71 71,69,67,48**
toteswingers: 1&2 £36.80, 2&3 £44.70, 1&3 £56.70. CSF £31.62 TOTE £3.20: £2.30, £3.50, £12.00; EX 44.10 Place 6: £20.03 Place 5: £12.40.

Owner Sir Robert Ogden **Bred** Julien Merienne & Mrs Maryvonne Merienne **Trained** Upper Lambourn, Berks

FOCUS
A well-contested bumper with plenty of promising types and produced, at least, a couple of exciting sorts for next season. Usually a decent bumper, this was run at a good pace. The race could have been rated up to 7lb higher.

NOTEBOOK
Problema Tic(FR) had been a market drifter when landing an ordinary heat at Towcester but it was thought he would benefit from the run and stayed very well. With that in mind he made this a decent gallop from the front and showed a likeable attitude when put to the sword early in the straight to hold on well. Hailing from a top yard and related to some useful jumpers, he should be worth following especially as he was only a four-year-old defying a penalty. (op 5-2)
Morgan's Bay had come in for some morning support and was a shade unlucky that he has bumped into a type as promising as this. He laid down a serious challenge from over two furlongs only giving best nearing the finish but drawing clear of the third. This was a very encouraging effort and he also looks worth keeping on the right side of. (op 9-1)
Lexicon Lad(IRE) was unruly beforehand as he had been in the preliminaries of his point-to-point. Another very promising performance as he held every chance in the straight before fading slightly in the final furlong. (op 33-1)
Native Breeze(IRE) did best of those racing well off the pace and was doing all her best work up the home straight. (op 20-1)
Rival D'Estruval(FR) was sat just off the pace and stayed on well enough without being to harshly treated. A nice introduction that he should benefit from.
Benheir(IRE) got outpaced entering the straight but stayed on again in the final furlong.
T/Plt: £43.90. Pool of £96,345.27 - 1,601.79 winning tickets T/Qpdt: £6.10. Pool of £5,728.70 - 689.20 winning tickets DO

320 - 326a (Foreign Racing) - See Raceform Interactive

75 BANGOR-ON-DEE (L-H)
Saturday, May 15

OFFICIAL GOING: Good (good to firm in places; 8.1)
Wind: moderate 1/2 behind Weather: mainly fine

327 WREXHAM "NATIONAL HUNT" MAIDEN HURDLE (9 hdls) 2m 1f
1:50 (1:50) (Class 4) 4-Y-0+ **£3,122** (£916; £458; £228)

Form RPR
42-2 **1** **Twentynineblack (FR)**[7] 209 6-11-0 108........................ JasonMaguire 111+
(Donald McCain) *t.k.h in tch: wnt 2nd 3 out: led next: 4 l clr whn hit last: eased towards fin* **5/4**[1]

46-P **2** *7* **Grand Award**[14] 91 5-10-11 0.. AdrianLane(3) 99
(Donald McCain) *hld up in rr: hdwy 6th: sn chsng ldrs: hung lft and wnt 2nd between last 2: no ch w wnr* **40/1**

020- **3** *3* **Alpine Breeze (IRE)**[36] 5114 4-10-3 0............................ LeightonAspell 88+
(Don Cantillon) *hld up: hdwy to chse ldrs 5th: drvn whn j.rt 3 out: one pce fr next: mstke last* **9/4**[2]

600- **4** *3* **The Chazer (IRE)**[45] 4963 5-11-0 107................................. CharliePoste 93
(Richard Lee) *chsd ldrs: hmpd 2nd: one pce appr 2 out* **14/1**

5 *6* **Study Troubles (IRE)**[27] 6-10-11 0.................................. BTO'Connell(3) 88
(Philip Fenton, Ire) *chsd ldrs: wknd after 3 out: j. bdly lft last* **25/1**

300- **6** *2 ¾* **Acquisitive (FR)**[22] 5370 4-10-5 0........................ SamTwiston-Davies(5) 82
(Nigel Twiston-Davies) *in rr: hdwy 5th: chsng ldrs 3 out: wknd after next* **25/1**

7 *3* **Rendezvous Bay (IRE)**[13] 108 6-10-7 0........................ MrNiallTerry(7) 81
(A J Martin, Ire) *in rr: kpt on fr 2 out: nvr on terms* **33/1**

0/0- **8** *7* **Steptoe**[94] 3972 5-11-0 0.. APMcCoy 76+
(Nicky Henderson) *t.k.h: led: clr 3rd to 3 out: hdd and mstke 2 out: wknd qckly and sn eased* **8/1**[3]

6/0- **9** *5* **She'Solovely**[156] 2786 6-10-7 0 .... LiamTreadwell 62
(Martin Wilesmith) *stdd s: t.k.h in rr: bhd fr 5th* **125/1**

06P- **10** *68* **Beat In Time**[21] 5386 4-10-0 0 .... RichieMcLernon(3) —
(John Mackie) *prom: hmpd 2nd: lost pl after 4th: t.o 6th* **100/1**

0/0- **P** **Lago Verde (SWI)**[113] 3590 5-11-0 0 .... WillKennedy —
(Paul Webber) *j. bdly: t.k.h: trckd ldrs: blnd and lost pl 2nd: bhd fr 4th: t.o whn p.u bef 2 out* **100/1**

5P-5 **P** **Milandale (IRE)**[14] 97 5-11-0 0 .... PaddyBrennan —
(Tom George) *chsd ldrs: lost pl 3 out: 8th and bhd whn p.u bef next* **16/1**

4m 9.20s (-1.70) **Going Correction** -0.175s/f (Good)
WFA 4 from 5yo+ 18lb **12 Ran SP% 114.7**
Speed ratings (Par 105): **97,93,92,90,88 86,85,82,79,47 —,—**
Tote Swingers: 1&2 £5.30, 1&3 £1.30, 2&3 £16.00 CSF £63.85 TOTE £1.80: £1.02, £11.40, £2.00; EX 59.50.
Owner Tracey Gaunt & David Gibbons **Bred** Bernard Soulhol **Trained** Cholmondeley, Cheshire

FOCUS
A weak novice hurdle run at a fair pace with the free-running Steptoe soon clear before weakening rapidly when headed by the winner two out.

NOTEBOOK
Twentynineblack(FR) was a warm order to get off the mark at the ninth time and duly did so. Travelling well for most of the way he came through with ease to track the winner three out. He led on the bit two out before clattering the last with the race in safe-keeping. His mark of 108 looks workable but there is a possibility he will now be put away for the summer. (op Evens)
Grand Award, stablemate to the winner, had not progressed since landing a Worcester bumper and had disappointed over fences last time. He was a little flat-footed when the tempo increased three out but stayed on to challenge for second from the next, although never threatening the winner. He will have to repeat this effort before he can be of interest but at least this was a return to some sort of form. (op 33-1)
Alpine Breeze(IRE) had been performing creditably in bumpers, most recently a Listed affair when eighth, and ran with promise on this hurdling debut. She was another to be challenging for second from two out but could only stay on at the same pace. Her breeding suggests that she would appreciate a step up in trip. (op 7-2)
The Chazer(IRE) was not particularly fluent at some of his hurdles but appeared to appreciate the step back in trip and this was a satisfactory performance. (op 12-1)
Study Troubles(IRE), an Irish raider and winning pointer, got outpaced after chasing the leader until three out before staying on again going to the last. (op 22-1)

328 GORDON ROWLANDS LIFETIME IN RACING NOVICES' H'CAP HURDLE (11 hdls) 2m 4f
2:20 (2:20) (Class 4) (0-110,106) 4-Y-0+ **£3,415** (£1,002; £501; £250)

Form RPR

050- **1** **Hurricane Electric (IRE)**[62] 4602 5-10-0 80 oh1 .... JodieMogford 86+
(Graeme McPherson) *t.k.h: w ldrs: led 3rd: blnd 8th: mstke 2 out: kpt on wl: nvr really threatened* **50/1**

0- **2** *2 ¼* **Silver Accord (IRE)**[101] 3819 7-11-8 102 .... LeightonAspell 103
(Oliver Sherwood) *chsd ldrs 5th: wnt 2nd 8th: kpt on fr 2 out: nvr able land blow* **12/1**

0P5- **3** *3 ¼* **Mohi Rahrere (IRE)**[29] 5217 7-11-5 104 .... PeterToole(5) 102
(Barry Leavy) *mid-div: hdwy 7th: styd on fr 2 out: wnt 3rd appr last* **12/1**

31-2 **4** *3 ¼* **Ballysimon (IRE)**[9] 179 6-11-5 102 .... HarryHaynes(3) 97
(James Ewart) *led: j.rt and hdd 3rd: one pce appr 2 out* **9/2**[1]

42-5 **5** *6* **Wee Ziggy**[5] 54 7-9-7 80 .... BrianToomey(7) 70
(Michael Mullineaux) *stdd s: tk fierce hold in rr: hdwy after 8th: effrt appr 2 out: sn rdn: wknd between last 2* **6/1**[2]

51P- **6** *4 ½* **The Brimmer (IRE)**[22] 5359 6-11-7 106 .... JimmyDerham(5) 92
(Seamus Mullins) *nt fluent in rr: sme hdwy 8th: sn rdn: nvr nr ldrs* **12/1**

2P0- **7** *3 ¾* **Bankstair (FR)**[300] 1005 6-10-10 90 ....(t) PaddyBrennan 76+
(Nigel Twiston-Davies) *in rr: wnt prom 6th: 4th and rdn whn nt fluent 3 out: 5th and wkng whn nt fluent last* **8/1**[3]

250- **8** *16* **Tiger Dream**[27] 5255 5-11-9 106 .... ChrisHonour(3) 74
(Chris Down) *chsd ldrs: drvn 6th: lost pl 8th: sn t.o* **25/1**

1P5- **9** *9* **Star Galaxy (IRE)**[22] 5360 10-11-2 96 ....(b) TomO'Brien 56
(John Flint) *mid-div: outpcd 5th: lost pl 3 out: sn bhd* **11/1**

30-4 **10** *11* **Kristallo (GER)**[16] 64 5-11-11 105 ....(b) WillKennedy 55
(Paul Webber) *chsd ldrs: wknd 3 out: sn bhd: t.o next* **10/1**

F3-3 **11** *4* **Flash Harriet**[9] 179 6-10-7 90 .... RichieMcLernon(3) 36
(John Mackie) *wnt prom 5th: lost pl 7th: t.o 2 out* **9/2**[1]

20-4 **P** **Kris Kin Line (IRE)**[9] 174 4-11-6 105 ....(b1) JasonMaguire —
(Donald McCain) *chsd ldrs: lost pl after 6th: sn bhd: t.o whn p.u bef 3 out* **11/1**

4m 51.2s (-6.20) **Going Correction** -0.175s/f (Good)
WFA 4 from 5yo+ 19lb **12 Ran SP% 116.4**
Speed ratings (Par 105): **105,104,102,101,99 97,95,89,85,81 79,—**
Tote Swingers: 1&2 £27.20, 1&3 £28.90, 2&3 £17.50 CSF £553.62 CT £7483.07 TOTE £75.20: £12.30, £6.30, £3.20; EX 1868.70.
Owner J Barrass & R W Orr **Bred** Azienda Agricola Il Poderuccio **Trained** Upper Oddington, Gloucs

FOCUS
A moderate 0-110 handicap hurdle run at a steady pace until the tempo increased after the seventh.

NOTEBOOK
Hurricane Electric(IRE) proved just that to belie odds of 50-1 in coming out on top. He was rather keen off the steady pace before taking it up at the fourth. He increased the pace after four out but, barring a couple of mistakes at the next two he had the field in trouble. He tended to hang to his left staying on strongly to score. Hard to assess the performance granted that connections were also quite surprised, so it remains to be seen whether the form is up to much. Official explanation: trainer said, regarding apparent improvement in form, that the gelding was better suited by the left-handed track and the slightly quicker ground.
Silver Accord(IRE) had been regressing since a promising start to hurdling and was tackling handicap company for the first time. He chased the winner form four out but could never quite get on terms. (op 10-1)
Mohi Rahrere(IRE) looks modest on past performances, so casts a shadow over the form. He stayed on past beaten horses after two out but never troubled the principals. (op 16-1)
Ballysimon(IRE) ran a sound enough race after travelling prominently but looks to be struggling since being raised in the ratings after his Wetherby success. (tchd 4-1)
Wee Ziggy is exposed and could never get involved off the steady early pace. (op 8-1)

329 BANGORONDEERACES.CO.UK NOVICES' CHASE (15 fncs) 2m 4f 110y
2:55 (2:55) (Class 4) 5-Y-0+ **£4,065** (£1,193; £596; £298)

Form RPR

PP1- **1** **Otage De Brion (FR)**[28] 5230 8-11-5 132 ....(t) FelixDeGiles 140+
(Charlie Longsdon) *racd freely: led to 7th: led 11th: styd on wl fr 2 out: shkn up run-in: a in command* **4/1**[3]

403- **2** *2 ¼* **Always Bold (IRE)**[29] 5217 5-10-12 0 .... JasonMaguire 124
(Donald McCain) *mstke 1st: chsd ldrs: wnt modest 3rd 3 out: 7 l 2nd next: 2 l down last: kpt on: no real imp* **9/4**[2]

V31- **3** *21* **Wessex King (IRE)**[25] 5293 6-11-5 0 .... AndrewTinkler 113
(Henry Daly) *hld up: wnt prom 5th: led 7th: hdd 11th: wknd 2 out* **8/1**

3B-3 **4** *30* **Bluegun (IRE)**[7] 208 8-10-12 128 .... TomO'Brien 78
(Philip Hobbs) *chsd ldrs: nt fluent 2nd: reminders 4th: drvn 6th: wknd 11th: t.o 2 out* **85/40**[1]

411- **5** *50* **Masked Man (IRE)**[26] 5279 7-11-12 130 .... RobertThornton 47
(Alan King) *chsd ldrs: 3rd and outpcd whn drvn 10th: wknd 3 out: sn wl bhd: t.o next* **7/1**

P43- **P** **Bob's Temptation**[45] 4964 11-10-9 54 ....(tp) TommyPhelan(3) —
(Jim Wilson) *j.rt: in rr: bhd whn mstke 8th: sn t.o: p.u bef 12th* **100/1**

PP-U **U** **King Caine (IRE)**[4] 265 8-10-12 118 .... ChristianWilliams —
(Alan Jones) *t.k.h detached in last: poor 6th whn blnd and uns rdr 10th* **33/1**

4m 57.9s (-11.20) **Going Correction** -0.55s/f (Firm) **7 Ran SP% 110.3**
Speed ratings: **99,98,90,78,60 —,—**
Tote Swingers: 1&2 £1.40, 1&3 £7.70, 2&3 £4.90 CSF £12.99 TOTE £6.80: £4.20, £1.10; EX 17.30.
Owner Sir Robert Ogden **Bred** Philippe Lamotte D'Argy **Trained** Over Norton, Oxon

FOCUS
Just an ordinary pace for this tricky novice chase where a case could be made for five of the seven.

NOTEBOOK
Otage De Brion(FR) repeated his effort over C&D last month to win with a bit more in hand than the official margin would suggest. His jumping is his forte as he is rather quick over his obstacles and travels with plenty of zest throughout his races. The switch to fences and a return to a sound surface has brought about a resurgence in form. He will probably be taking up his engagement at Doncaster sales next week. (op 9-2)
Always Bold(IRE), on his chasing debut after looking in the grasp of the handicapper over hurdles, made a pleasing start. He jumped well and, although, flattered going to the last, the winner always had enough in hand to hold him at bay. Only a five-year-old, he should be capable of going one better before long. (op 11-4)
Wessex King(IRE) faced a stiffer task under a penalty since scoring at Towcester but ran with some credit. He disputed from the seventh and looked to be the main rival to the winner before tiring two out. He had been campaigned at 2m and it would be questionable that he stayed this extra half mile. (op 7-1 tchd 13-2)
Bluegun(IRE), with the ground in his favour, was disappointing and he has still to get his act together over fences. (op 5-2)
Masked Man(IRE) was trying to defy a double penalty in a race his stable has won the last three renewals. He was beaten too far out to suggest the penalty had anything to do with this running. (tchd 4-1 in places)

330 TURFTV.CO.UK H'CAP CHASE (15 fncs) 2m 4f 110y
3:30 (3:30) (Class 4) (0-115,115) 5-Y-0+ **£4,878** (£1,432; £716; £357)

Form RPR

P23- **1** **Grand Slam Hero (IRE)**[157] 2777 9-11-10 113 ....(t) PaddyBrennan 131+
(Nigel Twiston-Davies) *hld up: hdwy to trck ldrs 7th: led appr 2 out: 6 l ahd last: eased: v comf* **5/1**[2]

12-3 **2** *2 ¾* **Royal Kicks (FR)**[15] 85 9-10-10 104 .... JimmyDerham(5) 112
(Suzy Smith) *chsd ldrs: kpt on fr 2 out: hung lft and tk 2nd run-in: no ch w wnr* **9/2**[1]

P31- **3** *3 ¼* **Josear**[37] 5104 8-11-4 112 .... GilesHawkins(5) 117
(Chris Down) *w ldrs: led 10th: hdd 2 out: lost 2nd run-in* **11/1**

021- **4** *1 ¾* **Tighe Caster**[34] 5149 11-11-2 112 .... MrTomDavid(7) 114
(Graeme McPherson) *mid-div: hdwy to chse ldrs 9th: 5th whn rdr dropped whip sn after 2 out: kpt on same pce* **14/1**

332- **5** *nk* **Tot Of The Knar**[28] 5230 8-11-6 114 .... DonalDevereux(5) 117
(Peter Bowen) *in rr: hit 4th: hdwy 6th: hmpd next: chsng ldrs 9th: one pce appr 2 out* **7/1**[3]

P2P- **6** *nk* **Pamak D'Airy (FR)**[22] 5375 7-11-8 111 .... KeithMercer 114
(Henry Hogarth) *trckd ldrs: drvn whn mstke 11th: one pce fr 3 out* **16/1**

52U- **7** *20* **Kack Handed**[28] 5230 7-11-12 115 .... AndrewTinkler 99
(Henry Daly) *t.k.h: led 3rd: hdd 10th: wknd appr 2 out* **10/1**

056- **8** *10* **Marked Man (IRE)**[177] 2379 14-10-7 96 .... DenisO'Regan 71
(Richard Lee) *prom: wknd after 12th: bhd whn mstke 2 out* **16/1**

2F3- **9** *21* **Or D'Oudairies (FR)**[34] 5149 8-11-4 107 ....(t) GrahamLee 63
(Peter Salmon) *hld up in rr: j.rt 7th: shkn up and prom 9th: sn lost pl: bhd fr 12th* **8/1**

00-3 **P** **Sunday City (JPN)**[16] 65 9-11-4 107 ....(b) JasonMaguire —
(Donald McCain) *led to 3rd: lost pl 7th and sn p.u* **14/1**

004- **P** **Miss Phoebe (IRE)**[28] 5230 5-11-8 111 .... DavidEngland —
(Giles Smyly) *prom: lost pl 12th: bhd whn p.u sn after last: lame* **22/1**

650- **P** **Dais Return (IRE)**[230] 1553 6-11-7 110 .... APMcCoy —
(Jonjo O'Neill) *in rr: last and struggling whn blnd 8th: sn bhd: p.u bef 11th* **8/1**

4m 58.7s (-10.40) **Going Correction** -0.55s/f (Firm) **12 Ran SP% 116.4**
Speed ratings: **97,95,94,94,93 93,86,82,74,— —,—**
Tote Swingers: 1&2 £2.20, 1&3 £11.50, 2&3 £18.40 CSF £28.06 CT £237.56 TOTE £5.10: £2.00, £2.40, £3.50; EX 38.20.
Owner Walters Plant Hire Ltd **Bred** Lady Rathdonnell **Trained** Naunton, Gloucs

FOCUS
A competitive 0-115 handicap chase run at a sound pace.

NOTEBOOK
Grand Slam Hero(IRE) looked in good nick for his return to action after an absence of 157 days and was well supported to make it a winning one, which he duly did in a convincing manner. Jumping well in the midfield, he closed readily onto the tails of the leaders before taking it up two out and soon putting the race to bed, easing down nearing the finish. Also marking his return to his former trainer this was a decent effort but, no doubt, he will have to step up on this when reassessed. (op 4-1 tchd 11-2)
Royal Kicks(FR) is versatile as regards ground and after some pleasing efforts of late recorded another solid performance off his highest mark for the best part of two years. He had his chance going to two out but could only stay on without threatening the winner. (op 13-2)
Josear normally likes to front-run but failed to get there until the tenth. That being said, she is honest and it did not affect the result. She was readily brushed aside by the winner after two out but ran with credit in a stronger contest. (op 7-1)
Tighe Caster had risen 8lb for his recent success. He was close enough if good enough three out, but could not find the pace to get on terms. (op 16-1)
Tot Of The Knar was making progress when getting hampered at the seventh but still managed to get into contention three out. She stayed on at the same pace but this formerly useful hurdler is steadily slipping down to a reasonable mark. (op 8-1 tchd 9-1 in places)
Pamak D'Airy(FR) is inconsistent, but did respond to pressure although never troubling the principals. (op 18-1)
Or D'Oudairies(FR) Official explanation: jockey said gelding had a breathing problem
Sunday City(JPN) Official explanation: jockey said gelding was struck into behind

Miss Phoebe(IRE) Official explanation: vet said mare finished lame

331 STUTE PINNINGTON MEMORIAL H'CAP HURDLE (9 hdls) 2m 1f
4:05 (4:05) (Class 3) (0-120,120) 4-Y-0+ **£6,505** (£1,910; £955; £477)

Form RPR

10-3 **1** **Alazan (IRE)**[6] 235 4-11-5 **117** TomO'Brien 120+
(Philip Hobbs) *hld up: hdwy 6th: chsng ldrs whn hmpd next: led 2 out: 1 1/2 l ahd last: hrd rdn and hld on wl* **10/3**[2]

313- **2** *1/2* **Aohna (FR)**[173] 2470 5-11-0 **108** RobertThornton 113+
(Alan King) *chsd ldrs: hmpd 3 out: styd on to take 2nd last: kpt on wl: no ex clsng stages* **10/1**

44-2 **3** *3/4* **Dancewiththedevil (IRE)**[15] 80 9-11-5 **118** DonalDevereux(5) 122+
(C Roberts) *chsd ldrs: hmpd 3 out: led appr next: sn hdd: kpt on wl run-in* **6/1**[3]

011- **4** *9* **Knight In Purple**[22] 5357 6-11-4 **112** (v) AndrewTinkler 109
(John Mackie) *in rr: hdwy to chse ldrs 5th: upsides whn hit 2 out: wknd appr last* **3/1**[1]

210- **5** *9* **Haarth Sovereign (IRE)**[40] 5045 6-11-5 **113** (t) ChristianWilliams 99
(Lawney Hill) *in rr: effrt and nt fluent 6th: lost pl appr 2 out* **14/1**

011- **6** *3* **The Good Guy (IRE)**[198] 1973 7-11-12 **120** JodieMogford 103
(Graeme McPherson) *led: hit 3rd: hdd 6th: wknd next* **12/1**

10-5 **7** *3/4* **Freddy's Star (IRE)**[9] 170 8-11-2 **117** DavidBass(7) 99
(Gerald Ham) *chsd ldrs: lft in ld 3 out: hdd appr next: sn wknd* **16/1**

100- **8** *8* **Ravati (IRE)**[169] 2544 4-10-12 **115** MissLHorner(5) 86
(Chris Grant) *hld up towards rr: sme hdwy 4th: lost pl 6th: sn bhd* **33/1**

500- **9** *65* **Very Stylish (IRE)**[116] 3531 6-10-13 **107** APMcCoy 24
(Jonjo O'Neill) *prom: lost pl 3rd: bhd and drvn 5th: t.o 3 out* **10/1**

41/0 **U** **Option Money (IRE)**[8] 196 8-10-10 **111** KyleJames(7) —
(Peter Salmon) *prom: drvn 5th: lost pl next: bhd whn hmpd by loose horse and rdr knocked out of the sddle after 3 out* **40/1**

520- **F** **Kind Heart**[26] 5275 4-11-0 **112** JasonMaguire —
(Donald McCain) *t.k.h: trckd ldr: led 6th: fell next* **14/1**

4m 5.30s (-5.60) **Going Correction** -0.175s/f (Good)
WFA 4 from 5yo+ 18lb **11** Ran SP% **112.8**
Speed ratings (Par 107): **106,105,105,101,96 95,95,91,60,—,—**
Tote Swingers: 1&2 £4.10, 1&3 £7.00, 2&3 £12.50 CSF £35.16 CT £189.63 TOTE £3.70: £1.20, £2.00, £2.10; EX 41.20.
Owner Mrs Caren Walsh & R J Budge **Bred** D G Iceton **Trained** Withycombe, Somerset

FOCUS
A competitive 0-120 handicap hurdle run at a reasonable pace.

NOTEBOOK
Alazan(IRE) made a pleasing return to action earlier in the week when third at Worcester and with conditions to suit was fancied to get off the mark for the season. He was badly hampered when left in a close third three out but soon came back on an even keel. Taking it up two out he quickened well to have enough in hand when getting things all wrong at the last, but held on well. He has learnt to settle a lot better now and will be kept going through the summer with a chance he might tackle fences as a four-year-old. (op 5-1)
Aohna(FR), on her handicap debut after six months off, was travelling as well as the winner on the heels of the leaders when also being badly hampered three out. She, again, was soon back on the bridle and ran on well from the last but, could not reel in the winner. She can make her presence felt over the summer in similar contests. (op 8-1)
Dancewiththedevil(IRE) was another who was travelling just as well when hampered at the same flight and looked the main danger, but he could not quicken with the winner when asked. Another solid effort nonetheless. (op 5-1 tchd 9-2)
Knight In Purple, a further 9lb higher, held every chance when also being slightly hampered but could not match the pace of the front three when they quickened after the second last. (tchd 5-2)
Very Stylish(IRE) Official explanation: jockey said gelding had a breathing problem
Kind Heart was racing quite keenly behind the long-time leader before being allowed to go on after four out. She crashed out at the next causing interference to all three principals. She was still travelling well and this was quite nasty. Hopefully her confidence won't be affected. (tchd 16-1)

332 PATRICK BURLING DEVELOPMENTS MARES' STANDARD OPEN NATIONAL HUNT FLAT RACE (DIV I) 2m 1f
4:40 (4:40) (Class 5) 4-6-Y-0 **£2,055** (£599; £299)

Form RPR

1 **Heather Royal** 4-10-8 0 APMcCoy 106+
(Nicky Henderson) *hld up: smooth hdwy to trck ldrs 7f out: led 2f out: pushed out* **5/4**[1]

1- **2** *2 3/4* **Dorabelle (IRE)**[29] 5218 5-11-5 0 JasonMaguire 111
(Donald McCain) *trckd ldrs: rdn over 3f out: chsd wnr fnl 2f: styd on same pce fnl f* **7/2**[2]

26- **3** *2 3/4* **Natural Spring**[36] 5114 5-10-12 0 ColinBolger 102
(Suzy Smith) *chsd ldr: led over 3f out: hdd 2f out: one pce* **4/1**[3]

6- **4** *12* **Sapphire Rouge (IRE)**[30] 5199 4-10-3 0 JimmyDerham(5) 87
(Seamus Mullins) *chsd ldrs: outpcd over 3f out: lost pl over 2f out* **33/1**

5- **5** *nk* **Bianco Fuji**[70] 4452 5-10-12 0 LeightonAspell 91
(Oliver Sherwood) *in rr whn hung rt bnd after 4f: hdwy 7f out: outpcd over 4f out: hdwy to chse ldrs 3f out: sn wknd* **8/1**

6 *17* **Calusa Catrina (IRE)** 5-10-12 0 TomO'Brien 76
(Philip Hobbs) *in rr: hdwy 7f out: drvn and outpcd over 4f out: lost pl over 2f out* **16/1**

002- **7** *18* **Dark Sensation**[22] 5368 5-10-5 0 MrDPick(7) 59
(Stuart Kittow) *led: hdd over 3f out: wknd over 2f out: eased fnl f* **16/1**

5- **8** *17* **Call Me Friday**[30] 5199 4-10-1 0 MrJBanks(7) 40
(Matthew Salaman) *mid-div: lost pl over 4f out: sn t.o* **50/1**

5- **9** *28* **Wood Burner**[32] 5179 5-10-12 0 LiamHeard 19
(Chris Down) *sn chsng ldrs: drvn 7f out: lost pl over 5f out: sn bhd* **50/1**

10 *121* **Silk Rose** 6-10-12 0 AlanO'Keeffe —
(Martin Wilesmith) *in rr: drvn 7f out: sn t.o* **66/1**

3m 58.4s (-6.90) **Going Correction** -0.175s/f (Good)
WFA 4 from 5yo+ 4lb **10** Ran SP% **117.9**
Speed ratings: **109,107,106,100,100 92,84,76,62,29**
Tote Swingers: 1&2 £2.80, 1&3 £1.10, 2&3 £1.80 CSF £5.61 TOTE £2.30: £1.10, £2.10, £1.60; EX 7.30.
Owner Mrs Rita Brown **Bred** Mrs Rita Brown **Trained** Upper Lambourn, Berks

FOCUS
An average mares' bumper run at an ordinary pace.

NOTEBOOK
Heather Royal, well related and well supported, hails from a top stable and did little wrong to land this, having only to be pushed out after taking the lead over a furlong out. A half-sister to the high-class chaser Barbers Shop, she obviously has plenty going for her. She can only improve for this as she was rather green when hitting the front. (op 15-8)
Dorabelle(IRE) was trying to defy a penalty for her Uttoxeter success last month and confirmed her promise. She did her best to keep pressing the winner after coming under pressure over two furlongs out but was always being held inside the distance. (op 4-1 tchd 9-2)
Natural Spring was runner-up in a decent contest at Ascot first time out and this was another pleasing effort. She took over the lead at the three marker but could only stay on at the same pace in the latter stages, although pulling well clear of the remainder. (op 7-2)
Sapphire Rouge(IRE) ran with a degree of promise but could not live with the principals when the pace quickened (op 28-1 tchd 25-1)
Bianco Fuji was under pressure from a long way out, but to her credit kept finding if never enough. (op 7-1)

333 PATRICK BURLING DEVELOPMENTS MARES' STANDARD OPEN NATIONAL HUNT FLAT RACE (DIV II) 2m 1f
5:15 (5:15) (Class 5) 4-6-Y-0 **£2,055** (£599; £299)

Form RPR

4- **1** **With Grace**[73] 4384 5-10-7 0 DonalDevereux(5) 98+
(Peter Bowen) *hld up: hdwy to trck ldr 5f out: shkn up to ld over 1f out: drvn out* **10/1**[3]

0- **2** *2* **Diamond MM (IRE)**[17] 47 4-10-8 0 GrahamLee 92
(Alan Swinbank) *hld up: hdwy on ins over 4f out: swtchd rt over 2f out: sn chsng ldrs: styd on same pce to take 2nd ins fnl f: no real imp* **2/1**[2]

3 *1 3/4* **Copper Kate (IRE)**[181] 6-10-12 0 TomO'Brien 95
(John Flint) *led: drvn along 6f out: hdd over 1f out: hung lft and kpt on same pce ins fnl f* **25/1**

4 *3 1/2* **Playful Rose (IRE)** 4-10-8 0 AndrewTinkler 87
(Henry Daly) *in rr: hdwy to chse ldrs over 3f out: one pce fnl 2f* **25/1**

0- **5** *1* **Kaituna (IRE)**[59] 4683 4-10-8 0 LeightonAspell 86
(Oliver Sherwood) *hld up in rr: hdwy 4f out: one pce fnl 2f* **33/1**

6 *4* **Jessie Gwendoline (IRE)** 4-10-8 0 JasonMaguire 82
(Donald McCain) *chsd ldrs: drvn 6f out: wknd fnl 2f* **10/1**[3]

7 *3 3/4* **Rinca Deas (IRE)** 5-10-7 0 JimmyDerham(5) 82
(Seamus Mullins) *in rr: styd on fnl 2f: nvr a factor* **18/1**

8 *7* **China Sky (IRE)** 5-10-12 0 APMcCoy 83+
(Nicky Henderson) *chsd ldrs: drvn 7f out: plld wd bnd over 4f out: w ldrs over 2f out: lost pl over 1f out: eased ins fnl f* **10/11**[1]

9 *3 1/4* **Tooney Malooney** 5-10-12 0 DougieCostello 72
(Neil Mulholland) *chsd ldrs: lost pl over 2f out* **33/1**

10 *13* **Rabbit Lewis** 5-10-7 0 LeeEdwards(5) 59
(Tom Gretton) *chsd ldrs: drvn 6f out: lost pl over 3f out: sn bhd* **66/1**

11 *9* **Charmouth Girl** 4-10-8 0 FelixDeGiles 46
(John Mackie) *in rr: hdwy 7f out: lost pl over 4f out: sn bhd* **50/1**

4m 4.30s (-1.00) **Going Correction** -0.175s/f (Good)
WFA 4 from 5yo+ 4lb **11** Ran SP% **126.2**
Speed ratings: **95,94,93,91,91 89,87,84,82,76 72**
Tote Swingers: 1&2 £9.80, 2&3 £46.80 CSF £31.30 TOTE £8.20: £1.50, £1.10, £6.40; EX 48.30.

Owner Shade Oak Stud **Bred** Shade Oak Stud **Trained** Little Newcastle, Pembrokes

FOCUS
The weaker of the two divisions of the mares' bumpers and the slower. Again the Henderson stable looked to hold a strong hand with the well-bred China Sky, but it proved to be those with the benefit of racecourse experience who came out on top.

NOTEBOOK
With Grace had clearly progressed since her fourth over C&D on her debut and ran out a deserving winner. She stayed on well after taking up the running but it is hard to assess this performance based on her previous bumper as nothing has boosted or knocked the form. (op 8-1 tchd 11-1)
Diamond MM(IRE) was backed to make amends for running off the course when travelling well on her debut. She confirmed her promise but could stay on only at the same pace after closing under pressure from two furlongs out. (op 10-3)
Copper Kate(IRE), a maiden pointer in Ireland, made full use of her experience by trying to make all. She had no more to offer when headed in the straight. (op 16-1 tchd 28-1)
Playful Rose(IRE) had her chance over two furlongs out but could only muster the same pace. (op 20-1 tchd 28-1)
Kaituna(IRE) was caught slightly flat-footed after losing her position over three furlongs out and could never get back on terms. (op 25-1)
China Sky(IRE) had nowhere to go over three furlongs out and had to be switched wide for her effort but was a spent force entering the final two furlongs. (op 11-10 tchd 11-8 in a place and 5-4 in places)

334 NORTH WESTERN AREA POINT TO POINT CHAMPIONSHIP HUNTERS' CHASE (18 fncs) 3m 110y
5:45 (5:46) (Class 4) 5-Y-0+ **£3,123** (£968; £484; £242)

Form RPR

P/1- **1** **Ice Tea (IRE)**[28] 5233 10-12-4 130 (b) MrRBurton 138+
(Mrs S K McCain) *led 2nd: styd on fr 15th: pushed along to draw clr run-in* **4/5**[1]

15P- **2** *10* **Border Fusion**[12] 11-12-4 120 MrTGreenall 130+
(G D Hanmer) *hld up in rr: hdwy 10th: wnt 2nd 13th: 3 l down and no imp whn mstke last* **7/2**[2]

P12- **3** *44* **Vicario**[12] 9-12-1 102 MrJHamer(7) 98
(Mrs S K McCain) *led to 2nd: shkn up 7th: sn outpcd: reminders 9th: tk modest 3rd 14th: t.o 2 out* **7/1**[3]

5PP/ **4** *26* **Ballyvoge (IRE)**[42] 9-11-11 0 HarryChalloner(3) 61
(R J Bevis) *chsd ldrs: wknd 14th: sn bhd: t.o 3 out* **11/1**

P5-6 **5** *36* **Brookview Lad (IRE)**[15] 79 7-11-7 0 MrBFurnival(7) 29
(R Smart) *chsd ldrs: wnt 2nd 5th: wknd 13th: sn bhd: t.o15th* **66/1**

/PP- **F** **Inching Closer**[6] 13-11-7 0 MrAWadlow(7) —
(R J Hewitt) *in rr: drvn 6th: bhd and reminders 8th: t.o whn fell 10th* **40/1**

262- **P** **Von Origny (FR)**[27] 5254 9-11-7 102 (p) MrWKinsey(7) —
(Mrs Corrine Wynne) *prom: lost pl 11th: sn bhd: t.o whn p.u bef 14th* **14/1**

5m 58.6s (-21.20) **Going Correction** -0.55s/f (Firm) **7** Ran SP% **109.2**
Speed ratings: **111,107,94,85,74 —,—**
Tote Swingers: 1&2 £1.30, 1&3 £2.00, 2&3 £2.20 CSF £3.69 TOTE £1.90: £1.30, £1.10; EX 3.10 Place 6: £133.62 Place 5: £106.45.
Owner D A Malam **Bred** Eugene McDermott **Trained** Cholmondeley, Cheshire

FOCUS
A hunter chase restricted to those who had qualified to run in the North West area.

NOTEBOOK
Ice Tea(IRE) was sent off a warm favourite to land this after taking the notable scalp of Turthen over C&D last month. He made all at a fair pace and apart from a couple of mistakes at the third and second last did so with the minimum of fuss. Rated 138 at his peak and the switch to pointing/hunter chasing appears to have rekindled his enthusiasm and he can continue to be a force in this sphere. (op 5-6 tchd 10-11)
Border Fusion was trying to land this for the fourth consecutive year. He is coming back to hand but was held when blundering at the last. (op 3-1)
Vicario, a stablemate of the winner, has been in good form since switching codes, but he travelled in snatches and never posed a serious threat. (op 13-2)
Ballyvoge(IRE) chased the winner for much of the way, but was beaten a long way after tiring from the fourth last. (op 12-1)
T/Plt: £179.90. Pool £65473.96 - 265.54 winning tickets. T/Qpdt: £9.20. Pool £4623.30 - 369.62 winning tickets. WG

[223]UTTOXETER (L-H)

Saturday, May 15

OFFICIAL GOING: Good (good to firm in places; 7.8)

Second last fence omitted in all chases and first hurdle in back straight omitted due to ground under repair.

Wind: Light against Weather: Cloudy with sunny spells

335 MOUNT ARGUS OPEN HUNTERS' CHASE (16 fncs 2 omitted) 3m

5:20 (5:20) (Class 6) 5-Y-O+ **£874** (£271; £135; £67)

Form RPR

20F- **1** **Keepitsecret (IRE)**[260] 1320 9-12-6 134 MrAJBerry 110+
(Jonjo O'Neill) *j.big 1st: nt a fluent afterwards: hld up: hdwy 11th: mstke next: rdn appr 2 out: led flat: styd on u.p* **15/8**[2]

U4-2 **2** *nk* **Thistlecraft (IRE)**[11] 139 11-11-5 102 (v) AdamWedge(7) 100
(Miss Laura Morgan) *hld up: hdwy 8th: rdn after 3 out: styd on wl u.p* **13/2**[3]

55P- **3** *¾* **Pastek (FR)**[14] 7-11-5 66 MissCLBrown(7) 99
(Martin Peaty) *chsd ldrs: led 9th: hdd 4 out: rdn appr 2 out: styd on* **33/1**

0/1- **4** *1 ¼* **Leading Man (IRE)**[23] 5335 10-11-9 0 NathanMoscrop(7) 104+
(Mrs V Dobbin) *hld up: hdwy 8th: led 4 out: rdn and lost action appr last: hdd flat: eased nr fin: dismntd after line* **6/4**[1]

000/ **5** *53* **Tomillielou**[14] 9-11-7 0 (p) MissSPhizacklea(5) 51
(Miss H L Phizacklea) *led tl after 1st: chsd ldr to 7th: rdn bef 9th: wknd 11th: t.o* **40/1**

04-4 **P** **Cash In Hand (IRE)**[15] 79 10-11-5 80 (b) MrDPeters(7) —
(R Harvey) *chsd ldrs: reminder after 6th: lost pl next: wknd 9th: t.o whn p.u bef 4 out* **16/1**

/33- **P** **Star Double (ITY)**[14] 10-11-5 0 MrJonathanBailey(7) —
(Mrs Fleur Hawes) *led after 1st: hdd and mstke 9th: wknd appr 3 out: t.o whn p.u bef next* **9/1**

6m 11.1s (-4.00) **Going Correction** -0.025s/f (Good) **7** Ran SP% **109.4**

Speed ratings: **105,104,104,104,86 —,—**

Tote Swingers: 1&2 £10.30, 1&3 £3.50, 2&3 £12.80 CSF £13.19 TOTE £2.20: £1.50, £3.70; EX 14.10.

Owner Mrs Gay Smith **Bred** Paul Ryan **Trained** Cheltenham, Gloucs

⊠ Stewards' Enquiry : Mr A J Berry four-day ban: used whip with excessive frequency without giving gelding time to respond (tbn)

FOCUS

An exciting finish to this low-value hunter chase with four fighting out the finish from the last.

NOTEBOOK

Keepitsecret(IRE) had not run since taking a heavy fall at Ffos Las last August, but was the one to beat on previous rules form and ratings. For most of the way victory did not look likely as he jumped very slowly, getting in close to a few and occasionally jumping out to the right. That he was still in with a chance turning for home was testament to his jockey's perseverance and, getting his best jump of the race at the last, he was able to get on top in the battle to the line. He was the one to beat on rules form and evidently still retains ability, but he will need to jump more fluently if he is to feature in any of the bigger prizes this summer. (op 6-4)

Thistlecraft(IRE) continued a return to form that began with a well-beaten second at Fakenham last week. Taking up the running on the final circuit, he was headed around the final turn but rallied well to be gaining rapidly at the finish. (op 8-1)

Pastek(FR) has been plying his trade in points this year, in the main running respectably until failing to fire in a 4m contest two weeks ago. This was a better effort and he stayed on well to the line. However, he was very moderate when last running under rules a year ago, so this puts the form into context.

Leading Man(IRE) was looking to continue the success gained at Perth last month. Making stealthy progress to lead on the home turn, he was swamped at the last and faded tamely into fourth. The ground looked to be firmer than he liked so he might be worth another chance. (op 7-4)

Star Double(ITY) Official explanation: jockey said gelding pulled up lame

336 FREEEASYBETS.COM H'CAP HURDLE (DIV I) (10 hdls 2 omitted) 2m 4f 110y

5:50 (5:51) (Class 5) (0-95,94) 4-Y-O+ **£1,951** (£573; £286; £143)

Form RPR

64-4 **1** **Red Not Blue (IRE)**[15] 76 7-11-10 92 AndrewThornton 98+
(Simon Earle) *hld up: hdwy and hit 4th: led 2 out: lft clr last: rdn out* **6/1**[2]

0-U2 **2** *5* **Rossbrin (IRE)**[6] 228 5-10-13 81 CharliePoste 84+
(Anna Brooks) *chsd ldrs: rdn after 7th: styng on same pce whn lft 2nd last* **2/1**[1]

144- **3** *¾* **Paradise Expected**[19] 16 7-11-7 94 DeanColeman(5) 94
(Tim Vaughan) *hld up: hdwy 6th: rdn bef 3 out: styd on same pce fr next: lft 3rd last* **10/1**

25-0 **4** *6* **Command Marshal (FR)**[15] 84 7-11-8 90 TomScudamore 85
(Michael Scudamore) *hld up: hdwy appr 3 out: sn rdn: wknd bef last* **7/1**[3]

U03- **5** *38* **Present Your Case (IRE)**[24] 5317 5-11-8 90 (t) DarylJacob 50
(Ben Case) *hld up: hdwy after 7th: mstke and wknd next: t.o* **9/1**

33P- **6** *13* **Solway Blue**[22] 5374 8-11-2 87 (tp) HarryHaynes(3) 36
(Lisa Harrison) *hld up: mstke 4th: hdwy appr 3 out: sn wknd: t.o* **6/1**[2]

30-0 **7** *3* **Wizard Of Us**[14] 96 10-11-7 89 (p) RodiGreene 35
(Michael Mullineaux) *prom: lost pl 2nd: pushed along 4th: wknd 7th: t.o* **20/1**

006- **8** *12* **Pezula**[28] 5229 4-10-1 77 SeanQuinlan(3) 7
(Richard Phillips) *chsd ldrs: mstke 6th: sn rdn and wknd: t.o* **20/1**

00-6 **P** **Ryans Good Time (IRE)**[16] 55 8-10-12 80 (t) JodieMogford 80
(Nikki Evans) *led: hit 7th: hdd 2 out: 2nd whn wnt lame bef last: p.u and dismntd flat* **33/1**

6P-0 **F** **Albert Park (IRE)**[16] 59 9-9-9 70 (p) AnthonyFreeman(7) —
(John Upson) *chsd ldrs: rdn after 6th: wknd bef 3 out: t.o whn fell last* **14/1**

0PP- **P** **Stafford Charlie**[52] 4821 4-9-9 75 oh5 ow2 CharlieWallis(7) —
(John O'Shea) *chsd ldr tl hit 7th: sn rdn: wknd bef next: t.o whn p.u bef last* **66/1**

4m 50.7s (-13.30) **Going Correction** -0.925s/f (Hard)

WFA 4 from 5yo+ 19lb **11** Ran SP% **114.1**

Speed ratings (Par 103): **88,86,85,83,69 64,62,58,—,— —**

Tote Swingers: 1&2 £4.70, 1&3 £7.40, 2&3 £5.90 CSF £17.53 CT £117.72 TOTE £5.50: £2.20, £1.50, £1.80; EX 17.60.

Owner Mrs Sara Meehan **Bred** William Hubbert **Trained** Tytherington, Wilts

FOCUS

A competitive low-grade handicap and the field were still bunched on the home turn. With the top weights prominent at the finish the form held up.

NOTEBOOK

Red Not Blue(IRE) hugged the rail before delivering his challenge, and outstayed the rest. He won a bumper at this track and ran quite well when stepped up in class at Cheltenham last November, but had shown nothing in two previous hurdle starts. On that evidence he was fairly treated for his handicap debut and it brought about the necessary improvement. He has had injury problems, including twice breaking his pelvis, but connections maintain he can be decent when sound. (op 9-2)

Rossbrin(IRE) chased down the winner but could not land a blow. On his running over 2m here last week he held every chance, where he stayed on late into second with a finishing time that put him ahead of the handicapper, especially as he went un-penalisedfor that run. However, he maybe lacks pace near the business end as he finished in similar style again.

Paradise Expected made good late progress but could get no nearer. Back down to a more suitable trip after looking not to stay 3m recently, she ran respectably from a high enough mark, but often cannot string more than two decent efforts together. (tchd 9-1)

Command Marshal(FR) was ridden patiently before making headway to challenge wide of the bunch from the home turn. He has looked out of form this spring but showed a bit more back at this more suitable trip, although he has received no leniency from the handicapper. (op 11-1)

Present Your Case(IRE) was still in with a chance on her handicap debut until she got in close to the first in the home straight and weakened thereafter, but was found to have finished lame. Official explanation: jockey said mare never travelled (op 17-2)

Solway Blue lost several lengths when hampered midway, and though he made up some ground he was never on terms. His best runs have come on right-handed tracks but the recently employed tongue-tie has not brought about the desired improvement. (op 15-2)

Ryans Good Time(IRE) was challenging the winner when seeming to go wrong before the last. (op 28-1)

337 DERBYSHIRE COUNTY CRICKET CLUB NOVICES' HURDLE (10 hdls 2 omitted) 2m 4f 110y

6:20 (6:20) (Class 4) 4-Y-O+ **£2,602** (£764; £382; £190)

Form RPR

15-2 **1** **Worth A King'S**[8] 191 4-10-11 119 AdrianLane(3) 107+
(Donald McCain) *led and mstke 1st: hdd whn j.big next: remained w ldr tl led again 6th: clr whn hit last: comf* **4/5**[1]

06- **2** *10* **Douglas**[28] 5235 5-10-12 0 MarkGrant 91
(Roger Curtis) *hld up in tch: rdn after 7th: chsd wnr 3 out: sn outpcd* **25/1**

6 **3** *6* **Burnthill (IRE)**[16] 58 5-10-12 0 LiamTreadwell 85
(Claire Dyson) *racd keenly: led to 1st: led next: hdd 6th: chsd wnr to 3 out: wknd bef next* **28/1**

40- **4** *13* **Telling Stories (IRE)**[12] 4231 4-9-9 0 (t) MichaelMurphy(5) 60
(Barry Leavy) *hld up: reminder 5th: hdwy next: rdn and wknd bef 3 out* **14/1**

0- **5** *12* **Tucumcari (IRE)**[206] 1849 5-10-12 0 JimmyMcCarthy 60
(Brendan Powell) *hld up: hdwy after 3rd: wknd appr 7th: t.o* **12/1**[3]

4/0- **6** *2* **Celts Espere**[22] 5354 7-10-12 0 TomMessenger 58
(Chris Bealby) *prom: racd keenly: pushed along and lost pl 4th: bhd fr 6th: t.o* **20/1**

0P-P **P** **Little Miss Foozle**[9] 174 6-10-7 0 ow2 AndrewThornton —
(Peter Niven) *hld up: mstke 3rd: bhd whn hit 6th: t.o whn p.u bef 2 out* **100/1**

4- **P** **Imperial Breeze (IRE)**[17] 42 5-10-12 97 RobertThornton —
(J J Lambe, Ire) *trckd ldrs: racd keenly: wknd 3 out: bhd whn p.u bef last* **15/8**[2]

060- **P** **Solo Roma (IRE)**[25] 5296 6-10-12 0 WillKennedy —
(F Jordan) *j.rt 1st: bhd and j. slowly next: t.o whn p.u bef 6th* **100/1**

4m 55.1s (-8.90) **Going Correction** -0.925s/f (Hard)

WFA 4 from 5yo+ 19lb **9** Ran SP% **118.7**

Speed ratings (Par 105): **79,75,72,67,63 62,—,—,—**

Tote Swingers: 1&2 £9.80, 1&3 £8.20, 2&3 £52.00 CSF £28.19 TOTE £1.50: £1.02, £5.40, £5.50; EX 19.00.

Owner David A Price **Bred** Wretham Stud **Trained** Cholmondeley, Cheshire

FOCUS

Little strength in depth, and the favourite won as expected.

NOTEBOOK

Worth A King'S was a bit clumsy over his hurdles, but always looked to be in control and stretched clear down the home straight. He was the one to beat, having finished second in a better race at Aintree last week, and did not have to be at his best to gain his second hurdling success. (op 8-13 tchd 5-6 and 10-11 in places)

Douglas began to feel the pressure towards the end of the back straight but kept on to run a reasonable debut over hurdles. He had shown a glimmer of ability when belying his long odds in a bumper last month, and on this evidence he could win a weak race over hurdles.

Burnthill(IRE), a former point winner, helped set the pace and rallied once headed, but could find no more. This was better than his first run over hurdles last month, but he might improve for a longer trip. (tchd 25-1)

Telling Stories(IRE) was under pressure as they headed out on to the final circuit, and though he tried to keep tabs on the leaders he could get no nearer and looks as moderate over jumps as he has been on the Flat. (op 16-1)

Imperial Breeze(IRE) raced too freely early on but was still on terms with the winner until fading rapidly from the third last, eventually pulling up as if something was amiss. (op 3-1)

338 BANNER MARQUEES H'CAP HURDLE (9 hdls 1 omitted) 2m

6:50 (6:50) (Class 5) (0-95,95) 4-Y-O+ **£1,951** (£573; £286; £143)

Form RPR

000- **1** **Shipboard Romance (IRE)**[18] 40 5-10-11 85 (t) PeterToole(5) 96
(Mark Rimell) *hld up: hdwy appr 7th: chsd ldr 2 out: rdn to ld flat: styd on* **16/1**

45-4 **2** *1 ¾* **General Smith**[6] 228 11-11-0 90 MarkQuinlan(7) 99
(James Evans) *hld up: hdwy to ld 3 out: rdn and hdd flat: no ex towards fin* **9/2**[2]

46-2 **3** *18* **Windpfeil (IRE)**[9] 171 4-11-1 95 (b) NathanSweeney(7) 86
(Simon Burrough) *trckd ldrs: racd keenly: ev ch 3 out: blnd next: sn rdn: nt run on* **9/1**[3]

10-1 **4** *3 ¼* **Nono Le Sage (FR)**[6] 228 6-11-7 90 (t) TomScudamore 82
(David Pipe) *hld up in tch: chsd ldr appr 3 out: sn ev ch: mstke and wknd next* **5/6**[1]

/00- **5** *½* **Ton-Chee**[25] 5295 11-11-0 86 CharlieHuxley(3) 76
(Arthur Whitehead) *trckd ldrs: plld hrd: led 6th: rdn and hdd next: sn wknd* **28/1**

00-P **6** *3* **Gilded Youth**[5] 252 6-11-6 92 CharlieStudd(3) 79
(Simon Lewis) *hld up: sme hdwy appr 3 out: sn rdn and wknd* **50/1**

034- **7** *17* **Louis Ludwig (IRE)**[22] 5352 5-11-4 87 (bt) TomMessenger 59
(Chris Bealby) *chsd ldr: rdn after 6th: wknd bef next: t.o* **16/1**

0P5- **8** *2* **Pembo**[22] 5352 5-10-0 74 (b) MichaelMurphy(5) 44
(Mike Hammond) *led to 6th: wkng whn mstke next: t.o* **33/1**

P0-5 **9** *24* **Rich Kayf**[9] 168 6-9-9 71 ow1 CharlieWallis(7) 19
(John O'Shea) *hld up and a bhd: t.o* **14/1**

P/0- **P** **Bobering**[22] 5352 10-9-13 **71** ow2 TommyPhelan(3) —
(Brian Baugh) *hld up and a bhd: t.o whn p.u bef 3 out* **66/1**

/64- **P** **Breeze With Ease (IRE)**[148] 2960 6-11-12 **95** (b[1]) RobertThornton —
(J J Lambe, Ire) *hld up: hdwy 5th: wknd after next: t.o whn p.u bef 3 out* **20/1**

3m 49.4s (-5.80) **Going Correction** -0.925s/f (Hard)
WFA 4 from 5yo+ 18lb **11** Ran SP% **115.8**
Speed ratings (Par 103): **77,76,67,65,65 63,55,54,42,— —**
Tote Swingers: 1&2 £15.70, 1&3 £64.40, 2&3 £2.30 CSF £82.33 CT £700.99 TOTE £19.60: £3.90, £1.90, £1.50; EX 177.00.
Owner Mrs S E Lindley **Bred** John Flynn **Trained** Leafield, Oxon

FOCUS
This was run at a reasonable pace with the field beginning to string out by the final circuit.

NOTEBOOK
Shipboard Romance(IRE) had barely been sighted in three runs this spring, but the combination of dropping down the handicap and the reapplication of the tongue-tie for the first time in a year helped find the necessary improvement. Moving into contention, her jockey bided his time letting the second go for home, and swooped after the last to register her first win at the twelfth attempt. Official explanation: trainer said, regarding apparent improvement in form, that the mare benefited from a change in tactics and the reapplication of a tongue strap. (tchd 14-1)
General Smith was full of running as he came wide of the pack to deliver his challenge in the home straight, but he had been out in front for a long time as the line approached and he had no answer as the winner pounced. This was another good run from this consistent sort, and if he could save a bit more at the finish he might end his long losing spell. (op 6-1)
Windpfeil(IRE) was well placed to challenge but could only run on at one pace when it mattered. He did not run to his rating on his handicap debut last time but more might have been expected with blinkers reapplied for the first time since his only success on the Flat. (op 6-1)
Nono Le Sage(FR) was well supported in his bid for a quick-fire C&D double off the same mark, but although he looked a serious threat turning in he was labouring before the second last. He did complete a double at Warwick in March off a 15lb lower mark, but those were his first two runs after a break and he may need a rest now. (op 10-11 tchd Evens and 4-5)
Ton-Chee was poised to strike and indeed took up the running in the back straight, but he had used up too much energy early on and was a spent force by the home straight. (op 20-1)

339 DERBYSHIRE COUNTY CRICKET CLUB H'CAP CHASE (10 fncs 2 omitted) 2m
7:25 (7:25) (Class 4) (0-105,102) 5-Y-0 **£3,421** (£1,010; £505; £252; £126)

Form RPR

1-P5 **1** **Glimmer Of Light (IRE)**[9] 177 10-11-0 **90** (b) DenisO'Regan 98+
(Dr Richard Newland) *mde all: clr fr 5th: eased nr fin* **7/2**[1]

26-3 **2** *8* **Kirkhammerton (IRE)**[5] 250 8-11-3 **100** HarryChalloner(7) 100
(Barry Leavy) *hld up: r.o to go 2nd last: no ch w wnr* **9/1**

10U- **3** *7* **Nawow**[19] 26 10-11-6 **101** (p) PeterToole(6) 96
(Matt Hazell) *prom: chsd wnr 3 out: sn rdn: no imp tl wknd last* **7/1**

12P- **4** *nk* **Red Jester**[150] 2920 9-11-12 **102** LiamHeard 95
(Gerald Ham) *chsd wnr tl nt fluent 3 out: styd on same pce* **6/1**[3]

/5-P **5** *11* **Conkering (USA)**[14] 100 7-10-11 **90** RichieMcLernon(3) 73
(Jonjo O'Neill) *hld up: hdwy 5th: rdn and wknd appr 3 out* **7/1**

3U-6 **6** *5* **Secret Cavern (USA)**[16] 54 8-9-7 **76** oh4 MarkQuinlan(7) 55
(James Evans) *hld up: rdn after 4 out: wknd bef next* **11/2**[2]

4U5- **7** *52* **Croon**[19] 26 8-10-13 **89** NickScholfield 21
(Andy Turnell) *chsd ldrs tl rdn and wknd after 4 out: t.o* **7/1**

/56- **P** **Popcorn Rosie**[304] 961 7-10-6 **87** GilesHawkins(5) —
(Chris Down) *bhd fr 4th: t.o whn p.u and dismntd after 2 out* **11/2**[2]

3m 53.2s (-2.40) **Going Correction** -0.025s/f (Good) **8** Ran SP% **114.8**
Speed ratings: **105,101,97,97,91 89,63,—**
Tote Swingers: 1&2 £5.50, 1&3 £4.80, 2&3 £7.40 CSF £33.92 CT £208.65 TOTE £4.70: £2.30, £3.70, £1.10; EX 40.50.
Owner D & D Coatings Ltd **Bred** The Earl Of Harrington **Trained** Claines, Worcs

FOCUS
Last year's winner was taking no prisoners in his bid for a repeat win, seizing the initiative from the start and not allowing anything else a look-in.

NOTEBOOK
Glimmer Of Light(IRE) was ridden with much more restraint when taking this contest last year, but this time he raced enthusiastically in the lead and kept up the gallop, never seeing a rival. He seemed to improve for having the tongue-tie left off this time, and the booking of Denis O'Regan on his only ride of the meeting must have been a factor. He did not build on that success last year, but this time he has 3lb more to play with when he heads off to the sales on Tuesday. (op 9-2)
Kirkhammerton(IRE) languished for a long time near the rear of the field, looking to discover any fluency on his chasing debut, but he stayed on well past tiring rivals to gain a couple of lengths on the winner near the line. If he learns from this experience he could prove better over fences than his modest hurdling form. (op 17-2 tchd 8-1)
Nawow tracked the winner but had to give up the ghost and could only plug on. He has tended to need his first run after a break in the past, and with him unseating on his reappearance at Towcester last time, perhaps he needed this as well. (op 5-1)
Red Jester tried to chase down the winner but found the task beyond him. This was still a reasonable reappearance after a five month absence, and although he is 6lb higher than his last winning mark, he goes well on fast ground and should come on for this. (op 7-2)
Conkering(USA), making his chasing debut, lost confidence at the fences as the race progressed, so this was no more encouraging than his moderate performances over hurdles. (op 15-2 tchd 8-1)
Croon struggles to stay 2m and has offered little encouragement now in three runs following a winter break. (op 8-1)

340 AMBER CLAIMS MANAGEMENT MARES' H'CAP HURDLE (12 hdls 2 omitted) 3m
7:55 (7:55) (Class 4) (0-115,112) 4-Y-0+ **£2,602** (£764; £382; £190)

Form RPR

25P- **1** **Ambrose Princess (IRE)**[29] 5205 5-11-12 **112** (p) TomScudamore 120
(Michael Scudamore) *led: mstke 9th: sn hdd: rallied to ld flat: styd on u.p* **7/1**[3]

00-3 **2** *½* **Money Finder**[6] 227 7-9-11 **86** oh6 HaddenFrost(3) 94
(Roger Curtis) *chsd wnr after 2nd: led after 9th: rdn and hdd flat: styd on* **9/2**[2]

025- **3** *8* **Devon Native (IRE)**[107] 3698 7-11-6 **109** ChrisHonour(3) 110
(Chris Down) *prom: rdn appr 2 out: no ex last* **8/1**

643- **4** *3 ¼* **Dot's Delight**[25] 5294 6-11-2 **107** PeterToole(5) 105
(Mark Rimell) *hld up: hdwy after 8th: rdn appr last: wknd flat* **11/1**

00-0 **5** *4* **Sninfia (IRE)**[9] 169 10-10-4 **90** RodiGreene 84
(Kevin Bishop) *hld up: hdwy appr 3 out: wknd next* **14/1**

14-2 **6** *9* **Solway Ally**[7] 212 7-10-11 **100** (p) HarryHaynes(3) 86
(Lisa Harrison) *prom: lost pl 6th: rallied 8th: rdn and wknd appr 2 out* **15/8**[1]

001- **7** *5* **Romance Dance**[24] 5317 7-11-5 **105** PaulMoloney 87
(Sophie Leech) *hld up: hdwy 8th: wknd 3 out* **12/1**

206- **8** *32* **Xtravaganza (IRE)**[35] 5134 5-10-12 **98** DarylJacob 51
(Jamie Snowden) *hld up: rdn after 8th: wknd next* **33/1**

0/6- **P** **Tastes Like More (IRE)**[28] 5231 8-11-0 **100** (p) JasonMaguire —
(Donald McCain) *chsd wnr tl after 2nd: remained handy tl rdn and lost pl after 7th: sn bhd: t.o whn p.u bef 3 out* **8/1**

P0- **P** **Chocolat (IRE)**[37] 5105 5-11-3 **110** MrSJO'Donovan(7) —
(Emma Lavelle) *hld up: mstke 4th: hdwy 7th: wknd after next: t.o whn p.u bef 3 out* **28/1**

5m 39.8s (-25.40) **Going Correction** -0.925s/f (Hard) **10** Ran SP% **116.8**
Speed ratings (Par 105): **105,104,102,101,99 96,95,84,—,—**
Tote Swingers: 1&2 £5.50, 1&3 £4.80, 2&3 £7.40 CSF £39.24 CT £260.44 TOTE £7.90: £3.00, £2.20, £1.80; EX 56.00.
Owner The Yes No Wait Sorries **Bred** Tally-Ho Stud **Trained** Bromsash, Herefordshire

FOCUS
Just a steady pace that enabled two horses that raced prominently throughout to battle it out and pull clear from the last.

NOTEBOOK
Ambrose Princess(IRE) adopted her customary front-running role and looked to have run her race when headed round the final turn, but she kept finding more and rallied to get up on the line for a gusty success. She had flopped on her two previous attempts at this trip, but they were in much better company and, back in a more realistic grade, she proved a thoroughly competent and genuine staying hurdler. (op 6-1)
Money Finder had run her best race over hurdles at this track six days earlier and she would have gained her first win had it not been for the rallying of the winner. Racing from out of the weights here, she will not be unexposed next time and that might prove problematic, although there could still be a an opportunity in a lower-grade contest first. (op 7-1)
Devon Native(IRE), on her first outing since January, was right there in the home straight but was eventually outpaced. She still has to prove she stays this far, but should not be written off over this trip, on fast ground at least, as she may have needed this.
Dot's Delight, stepping up to three miles, was held up to get the trip. She made good progress to join the leaders on the home turn travelling well, but just emptied near the finish. She might not have stayed but still looks in good enough form to win off her current mark. (op 15-2)
Sninfia(IRE) has been struggling for form over fences, and though she was off a much more tempting mark for her first run over hurdles for more than two years, she has not proved effective at this trip. (op 12-1)
Solway Ally was well backed to improve upon her second at Hexham a week ago off just a 3lb higher mark, but she ran in snatches, did not look that happy on the ground and could do no more than plug on. (op 5-2)

341 MICHAEL SHILTON 25 YEARS AT UTTOXETER H'CAP HURDLE (DIV II OF 5.50) (10 hdls 2 omitted) 2m 4f 110y
8:30 (8:30) (Class 5) (0-95,93) 4-Y-0+ **£1,951** (£573; £286; £143)

Form RPR

/34- **1** **Sir Monty (USA)**[19] 17 8-11-12 **93** (p) TomO'Brien 99+
(Peter Bowen) *led to 3 out: rallied to ld next: hrd rdn flat: all out* **6/1**[3]

P05- **2** *1 ¼* **Smart John**[184] 2244 10-11-7 **91** CharlieStudd(3) 95
(Simon Lewis) *chsd ldrs: hit 1st: ev ch 2 out: styd on u.p* **33/1**

0U6/ **3** *½* **Maizy Missile (IRE)**[676] 870 8-10-4 **71** PaulMoloney 76
(Mary Evans) *chsd ldrs: rdn and ev ch 2 out: styd on u.p* **20/1**

050- **4** *8* **Snark (IRE)**[48] 4918 7-11-4 **90** JimmyDerham(5) 87
(Simon Earle) *chsd wnr 2nd: led 3 out: hdd next: wknd last* **14/1**

005- **5** *4* **Mylo**[45] 4960 12-11-9 **90** APMcCoy 83
(Jonjo O'Neill) *hld up: hdwy u.p 6th: sn outpcd: n.d after* **11/4**[1]

35-0 **6** *4* **Nodanawink**[14] 97 7-11-7 **88** JasonMaguire 77
(Donald McCain) *chsd ldrs: rdn after 5th: wknd after 3 out* **8/1**

/25- **7** *2 ¾* **Jerry Lee (IRE)**[28] 5234 7-10-8 **75** (p) WillKennedy 62
(F Jordan) *hld up in tch: racd keenly: rdn and wkng whn blnd 2 out* **4/1**[2]

053- **8** *¾* **Lifes A Mystery (IRE)**[20] 12 7-10-0 **67** oh4 (p) RichieMcGrath 53
(Pauline Robson) *hld up: effrt after 7th: nvr on terms* **4/1**[2]

00F- **9** *13* **Blazing Tommy**[23] 5339 7-9-7 **67** oh1 (b) JasonFavell(7) 41
(Kim Bailey) *hld up: a in rr: t.o whn hmpd 2 out* **14/1**

00P- **10** *12* **Dickie Valentine**[52] 4821 5-11-6 **87** WarrenMarston 51
(Richard Phillips) *hld up: mstke 2nd: rdn after 4th: nvr on terms: t.o whn bmpd 2 out* **20/1**

300/ **P** **Mustakhlas (USA)**[144] 3921 9-10-13 **80** JodieMogford —
(Brian Baugh) *hld up: a bhd: t.o whn p.u bef 2 out* **50/1**

4m 58.2s (-5.80) **Going Correction** -0.925s/f (Hard) **11** Ran SP% **119.8**
Speed ratings (Par 103): **74,73,73,70,68 67,66,65,60,56 —**
Tote Swingers: 1&2 £29.20, 1&3 £72.70, 2&3 £47.50 CSF £185.95 CT £3700.99 TOTE £8.20: £3.30, £6.00, £10.80; EX 92.40 Place 6: £96.64 Place 5: £48.07 .
Owner Saith O Ni & Karen Bowen **Bred** D Holt And Dana Holt **Trained** Little Newcastle, Pembrokes

FOCUS
Just a steady pace saw four in a line coming to the second last, before the early leader found he had left enough for a late surge. The final time was significantly slower than the first division of this handicap.

NOTEBOOK
Sir Monty(USA) led from the start, and though he was hassled for the lead, his fluent jumping and willing attitude enabled him to fight off the challengers for a game success. After a reasonably encouraging return from a year off the track at Bangor he could not build on that next time over fences at Ffos Las, but he seemed much happier over hurdles and had to make use of a career-low mark here. (tchd 11-2)
Smart John was always in touch with the winner and stuck to the task but was eventually outbattled. Like the winner he had been rated much higher in the past, and it may have just been his six month absence that was the deciding factor.
Maizy Missile(IRE) was still poised to challenge when fluffing the last and losing some momentum. This was her first outing since July 2008 and, if she progresses from this, she is on a tempting enough mark to gain her first success. (op 16-1)
Snark(IRE) headed the winner and was still with the leading quartet coming to the second last, but he could find no more and his challenge petered out. He is beginning to look harshly treated. (op 16-1)
Mylo plugged on but had been niggled from a long way out and did not look entirely happy on the ground. (op 5-2)
Mustakhlas(USA) Official explanation: jockey said gelding was unsuited by the good to firm ground

T/Plt: £110.50. Pool: £54,361.95 - 358.81 winning units. T/Qpdt: £56.20. Pool: £5,487.81 - 72.22 winning units. CR

342 - 348a (Foreign Racing) - See Raceform Interactive

MARKET RASEN (R-H)

Sunday, May 16

OFFICIAL GOING: Good (good to firm in places on chase course; chs 7.9, hdl 7.6)

Wind: fresh 1/2 against Weather: mainly fine

349 JOURNAL MAIDEN HURDLE (8 hdls) 2m 1f
2:00 (2:03) (Class 4) 4-Y-0+ **£2,740** (£798; £399)

Form RPR

602- **1** **Rubipresent (IRE)**23 5370 6-10-9 0............................ JamesHalliday(5) 100+
(Malcolm Jefferson) *chsd ldrs: outpcd 2 out: swtchd lft between last 2: 5th last: styd on strly to ld last 50yds* **3/1**2

535- **2** ¾ **Favours Brave**22 5386 4-10-10 100.................................... DenisO'Regan 95
(Tim Easterby) *led: hdd and no ex clsng stages* **12/1**

452- **3** 6 **Al Qeddaaf (IRE)**18 42 4-10-10 125............................ JasonMaguire 90
(Donald McCain) *chsd ldr: drvn to chal 2 out: one pce run-in* **4/6**1

00P- **4** 4 ½ **Earl Grez (FR)**40 5076 5-11-0 0.. JamesReveley 89
(Philip Kirby) *chsd ldrs: 3rd and one pce whn hit last* **125/1**

000- **5** ½ **Fulofanoyance**22 5391 5-11-0 0.................................... DougieCostello 88
(Malcolm Jefferson) *towards rr: hdwy 3 out: kpt on fr next: nvr rchd ldrs* **66/1**

5-5 **6** ¾ **Sphere (IRE)**15 93 5-10-7 0.. AndrewTinkler 81
(John Mackie) *trckd ldrs: hit 2 out: one pce* **16/1**

0/ **7** shd **Im Ova Ere Dad (IRE)**115 2628 7-11-0 0........................ LeightonAspell 87
(Don Cantillon) *hld up in rr: hdwy 3 out: kpt on fr next* **12/1**

200- **8** nk **Magnushomesdotcom (IRE)**161 2731 6-10-11 0(t) MichaelMcAlister(3) 88
(Maurice Barnes) *towards rr: drvn and hdwy next: hit 2 out: kpt on* **66/1**

9 1 ½ **King's Icon (IRE)**36 5-11-0 0.. GrahamLee 87
(Michael Wigham) *chsd ldrs: wknd run-in* **10/1**3

P- **10** 29 **Minnis Bay (CAN)**21 14 6-11-0 0.................................... KeithMercer 57
(Ferdy Murphy) *in rr: bhd fr 2 out* **80/1**

P00- **11** 9 **Driving Seat**174 2483 6-11-0 0.. RodiGreene 48
(Michael Mullineaux) *stdd s: t.k.h in rr: bhd fr 4th: t.o 3 out* **125/1**

F- **12** 25 **James Junior**22 5385 4-10-10 0...................................... WilsonRenwick 19
(Peter Niven) *gave problems gng to s: stdd s: j. bdly lft 1st: bhd fr 4th: t.o 6th* **125/1**

4m 17.5s (10.80) **Going Correction** +0.20s/f (Yiel)
WFA 4 from 5yo+ 18lb 12 Ran SP% **121.9**
Speed ratings (Par 105): **82,81,78,76,76 76,76,75,75,61 57,45**
toteswingers: 1&2 £10.10, 1&3 £1.20, 2&3 £3.40 CSF £38.29 TOTE £3.70: £1.20, £2.70, £1.10; EX 34.90.
Owner J H Wilson **Bred** Miss Mary O'Sullivan **Trained** Norton, N Yorks

FOCUS
The rails were moved out 2-3yards round the whole course. The ground rode generally good but faster in places, according to a jockey involved in the first. An ordinary maiden hurdle in which the runner-up set only a moderate pace and the form may not prove entirely solid.

NOTEBOOK
Rubipresent(IRE) was caught in a flat spot on the home turn and his chance did not look obvious when he jumped the last in a share of third place, but he flew up the run-in to snatch the race. Runner-up to subsequent winner Solway Sam last time, he is on the upgrade and there is further improvement in him when he steps back up in trip. He will make a chaser in time. (tchd 11-4)
Favours Brave, who hurdled well, tried to make all and looked in control touching down over the last, but he was mown down by the winner's strong finish. He is by Galileo out of an Ebor winner so should be worth another try at further. (op 18-1)
Al Qeddaaf(IRE) was never far away and he came to challenge for the lead two out, but he could not pick up under pressure. He has now spurned two chances at odds-on since his good effort at Aintree and isn't one for maximum faith. (tchd 8-11)
Earl Grez(FR) had shown nothing for his previous yard but he ran a much more promising race on his debut for this stable back down in trip.
Fulofanoyance ⊠ , the winner's stablemate, shaped pleasingly on this hurdling debut and looks one to keep an eye on.
Sphere(IRE) was trying to stay on in sixth place when she lost her hind legs on landing over the second-last. She is now eligible for handicaps and should be kept in mind. (tchd 18-1)
Im Ova Ere Dad(IRE) has won six times on the Flat since his one previous try over hurdles in December 2006. After racing keenly in rear, he was never nearer than at the end.
King's Icon(IRE), without the headgear for this hurdles debut, showed up for a long way but still has his stamina to prove after weakening in the latter stages. (op 12-1)
Driving Seat Official explanation: jockey said regarding running and riding, that his orders were to settle the gelding which was very keen and ridden in a ring bit and Kineton, before making the best of his way home, it was the first run over hurdles and pulled for a mile but, when asked for an effort it was completely empty.

350 FUSSEY ENGINEERING H'CAP HURDLE (8 hdls) 2m 1f
2:30 (2:30) (Class 4) (0-110,109) 4-Y-0+ **£3,252** (£955; £477; £238)

Form RPR

026- **1** **Crazy Bold (GER)**19 40 7-10-9 97.................................. LeeEdwards(5) 105+
(Tony Carroll) *trckd ldrs: led appr 2 out: mstke: styd on strly* **6/1**2

03-2 **2** 4 **Peaceful Means (IRE)**12 140 7-11-3 105.................. DeanColeman(5) 108
(J Jay) *hld up in rr: hdwy after 3 out: 5th last: styd on to take 2nd run-in: kpt on: nt rch wnr* **9/2**1

F00- **3** 2 ¾ **Aggravation**90 4072 8-10-10 98.. MissLHorner(5) 99
(Chris Grant) *hld up in rr: hdwy on wd outside 5th: chsd wnr last: kpt on same pce* **40/1**

02P- **4** 1 ¾ **Elk Trail (IRE)**23 5357 5-11-9 106.......................................(p) RodiGreene 105
(Michael Mullineaux) *led: hdd appr 2 out: hrd rdn and one pce* **12/1**

P00- **5** ½ **Golden Future**79 3721 7-10-12 95.. GrahamLee 95
(Peter Niven) *chsd ldrs: wnt 2nd 3 out: one pce appr 2 out* **22/1**

500- **6** 3 ¾ **Dark Energy**25 5308 6-11-12 109..(t) SamThomas 104+
(Michael Scudamore) *hld up towards rr: hdwy 3 out: nvr nr ldrs* **14/1**

200- **7** 8 **Prize Fighter (IRE)**58 4721 8-10-12 95.............................. PaddyAspell 83
(Lynn Siddall) *hld up in rr: hdwy 3 out: 7th and no imp whn blnd next* **12/1**

002- **8** 3 ¼ **Keep Gunin (IRE)**24 5340 5-11-3 105............................ ShaneByrne(5) 90
(Sue Smith) *in tch: lost pl 3 out* **10/1**

03-4 **9** 6 **Piccolo Pride**11 161 5-10-9 95........................(t) MichaelMcAlister(3) 78
(Maurice Barnes) *prom: rdn 3 out: no imp whn mstke next: blnd next* **6/1**2

416- **10** 33 **Shilpa (IRE)**35 5146 5-11-10 107.................................... RobertThornton 57
(Alan King) *chsd ldrs: lost pl appr 2 out: bhd and eased run-in: t.o* **8/1**3

045- **11** 3 **Cocoa Key (IRE)**27 5273 6-11-2 104........................(p) JamesHalliday(5) 51
(Malcolm Jefferson) *chsd ldrs: rdn 5th: sn lost pl: t.o 2 out: eased run-in* **6/1**2

400- **P** **Classic Fly (FR)**20 23 7-10-13 99.................................. HaddenFrost(3) —
(Arthur Whiting) *chsd ldrs: lost pl appr 2 out: sn p.u* **12/1**

4m 10.1s (3.40) **Going Correction** +0.20s/f (Yiel) 12 Ran SP% **117.8**
Speed ratings (Par 105): **100,98,96,96,95 94,90,88,85,70 68,—**
toteswingers: 1&2 £6.10, 1&3 £6.90, 2&3 £58.40 CSF £33.50 CT £1000.48 TOTE £7.60: £1.50, £2.30, £6.90; EX 34.80.
Owner Mrs Susan Keable **Bred** Frau B Radner **Trained** Cropthorne, Worcs

FOCUS
A competitive handicap hurdle. The pace was sound and the time was more than seven seconds quicker than the earlier novice race. The form has a solid look to it, with prominent racers and hold-up horses both involved in the finish.

NOTEBOOK
Crazy Bold(GER) was always travelling well and he shrugged off a mistake two out, just as he had eased into the lead, to win comfortably. He recorded back-to-back wins last May, his most recent victories, and this is his time of year. (tchd 11-2)
Peaceful Means(IRE) was held up at the back of the field and was under pressure before the straight. She was no better than fourth over the last but stayed on well up the run-in, suggesting a return to further will suit her. Although she is in good heart at present, she is currently 9lb higher than her last winning mark and may remain vulnerable. (op 11-2)
Aggravation improved on the outside of the field to get involved and touched down in second place over the last. This was his best run over hurdles, with the sounder surface a help. (op 33-1)
Elk Trail(IRE) downed tools quickly at Bangor last time but had things more his own way in front here and only relinquished his lead going to the second-last. (tchd 14-1)
Golden Future chased the pace for much of the trip and this was a creditable effort on this first start since February. (tchd 20-1)
Dark Energy has been dropped 3lb since his recent return from a break and should be spot on with this outing under his belt. (op 12-1)
Keep Gunin(IRE), making his handicap debut, shaped as if finding this too sharp. (op 9-1)
Piccolo Pride was found wanting and again made mistakes. Official explanation: jockey said gelding never travelled
Cocoa Key(IRE) disappointed in the first-time cheekpieces. (op 8-1)

351 LEGSBY ROAD H'CAP HURDLE (10 hdls) 2m 5f
3:00 (3:01) (Class 4) (0-115,115) 4-Y-0+ **£3,903** (£1,146; £573; £286)

Form RPR

50-2 **1** **Spare Me**15 96 7-10-13 102.. WarrenMarston 107+
(Milton Harris) *trckd ldrs: led appr 2 out: hit 2 out: hrd rdn run-in: hld on gamely* **7/1**

025- **2** nk **Bobble Hat Bob (FR)**52 4849 5-11-6 109....................(p) DougieCostello 113
(Jonjo O'Neill) *in rr: hdwy 3 out: wnt 4th 2 out: styd on to chal run-in: no ex nr fin* **4/1**1

3PP- **3** 1 ¼ **Springfield Raki**179 2365 6-11-12 115................................ KeithMercer 118
(Steve Gollings) *chsd ldrs: chal 2 out: upsides last: styd on same pce fnl 150yds* **14/1**

420- **4** 11 **Mcqueen (IRE)**238 1481 10-10-11 105.............................. PeterToole(5) 98
(Barry Leavy) *chsd ldr: wknd appr 2 out* **14/1**

004- **5** 2 **Ovthenight (IRE)**28 5255 5-11-4 114.......................... MissGAndrews(7) 105
(Pam Sly) *in rr: reminders 7th: nvr a threat* **5/1**2

P50- **6** shd **Bijou Dan**19 34 9-11-11 114.. BarryKeniry 105
(George Moore) *in rr: wnt prom 4th: outpcd and lost pl 6th: no threat after* **6/1**3

4P0/ **7** 15 **Reel Missile**1079 547 11-10-6 98.................................. AdamPogson(3) 86+
(Charles Pogson) *led: hdd 2 out: sn wknd: heavily eased run-in* **12/1**

012- **P** **Muntami (IRE)**22 5389 9-10-11 105.............................. DeanColeman(5) —
(John Harris) *prom: rdn and wknd 3 out: last whn p.u bef next* **13/2**

60-0 **P** **Nicky Nutjob (GER)**11 159 4-10-8 102.............................. GerardTumelty —
(Jeff Pearce) *hld up: mstke 1st: p.u bef 2nd* **20/1**

302- **S** **Nomadic Warrior**47 4937 5-10-10 99..........................(p) TomMessenger —
(John Holt) *clipped heels and slipped up sn after s* **6/1**3

5m 17.9s (9.10) **Going Correction** +0.20s/f (Yiel)
WFA 4 from 5yo+ 19lb 10 Ran SP% **116.9**
Speed ratings (Par 105): **105,104,104,100,99 99,93,—,—,—**
toteswingers: 1&2 £2.50, 1&3 £53.30, 2&3 £7.20 CSF £35.90 CT £386.22 TOTE £6.10: £1.60, £1.80, £6.00; EX 38.30.
Owner John Rawlings **Bred** Gleadhill House Stud Ltd **Trained** Herridge, Wiltshire

FOCUS
A fair handicap hurdle run at a reasonable pace.

NOTEBOOK
Spare Me, put up 3lb after finishing second at Uttoxeter, showed good battling qualities to repel the third before holding off the runner-up. All three of his hurdles wins have come at this course, the previous two on soft ground. (tchd 13-2)
Bobble Hat Bob(FR), with cheekpieces on in place of blinkers, put a modest effort at Ludlow behind him and stayed on well to issue a strong challenge to the winner after the last. He was just held, but there did not seem much wrong with his attitude. (op 11-2)
Springfield Raki, having his seventh consecutive run here, had every chance between the final two flights but couldn't quicken. This was a pleasing return after six months off and he looks worth trying at this sort of trip again. (op 12-1)
Mcqueen(IRE) had not run under rules since September, but he won a charity Flat race at Uttoxeter the previous weekend. Unable to lead as he would have liked, he faded from the second-last. (op 12-1)
Ovthenight(IRE) could never get involved over this longer trip. (op 7-1)
Bijou Dan, upped in trip for this second run back, was outpaced after a slight mistake down the far side. (tchd 13-2)
Reel Missile, who had not been seen for nearly three years, made the running until blowing up going to the second-last. (op 16-1)
Muntami(IRE), a three-time course winner, was beaten before he was pulled up on the home turn. His rider reported that the gelding's boot had slipped down over his joint. Official explanation: jockey said gelding lost its action and on dismounting found that the boot had slipped over its joint (op 6-1 tchd 7-1)
Nicky Nutjob(GER) Official explanation: jockey said colt lost its action after mistake first hurdle and was later pulled up but subsequently reported to have returned sound (op 6-1 tchd 7-1)
Nomadic Warrior had barely gone a few strides when he stumbled badly and gave his jockey no chance of staying aboard. (op 6-1 tchd 7-1)

352 FUSSEY PILING H'CAP CHASE (14 fncs) 2m 6f 110y
3:30 (3:30) (Class 4) (0-115,112) 5-Y-0+ **£3,903** (£1,146; £573; £286)

Form RPR

416/ **1** **North Island (IRE)**503 3070 8-11-2 107.......................... DonalDevereux(5) 119+
(Peter Bowen) *led: hdd and hit 9th: led 3 out: styd on gamely run-in* **8/1**

/54- **2** 1 ½ **Lawaaheb (IRE)**34 5167 9-10-11 97.. LiamHeard 103
(Tim Walford) *trckd ldrs: chal 2 out: kpt on same pce fnl 150yds* **13/2**2

05-1 **3** 3 **Badger Foot (IRE)**17 56 5-11-9 112.......................... RichieMcLernon(3) 115
(Jonjo O'Neill) *trckd ldrs: drvn after 4 out: kpt on same pce to take 3rd last* **10/1**

125- **4** 2 ¾ **Our Jim**56 4756 8-11-10 110.. JasonMaguire 111
(Donald McCain) *w ldrs: led 9th: rdn and hdd 3 out: one pce fr next* **4/1**1

3-0 **5** *1¾* **Chorizo (IRE)**^{7} 229 9-11-8 **108**.......... PaddyAspell 107
(Richard Guest) *chsd ldrs: rdn after 4 out: outpcd 2 out: kpt on run-in* **12/1**

/53- **6** *nse* **Hold The Bid (IRE)**^{21} 11 10-11-4 **109**.......... ShaneByrne$^{(5)}$ 108
(Sue Smith) *mstkes: chsd ldrs: hit 4 out: one pce fr next* **10/1**

661- **7** *29* **Toulouse Express (IRE)**^{34} 5167 11-10-12 **103**.......(v) JamesHalliday$^{(5)}$ 76
(Robert Johnson) *chsd ldrs: lost pl appr 3 out: sn bhd* **12/1**

214- **8** *11* **Oniz Tiptoes (IRE)**^{27} 5288 9-10-9 **98**..........(v) HarryHaynes$^{(3)}$ 61
(John Wainwright) *j.lft: in rr: drvn 7th: bhd fr 10th* **7/1**^{3}

644- **9** *48* **Water Taxi**^{21} 11 9-11-10 **110**.......... GrahamLee 30
(Ferdy Murphy) *last whn mstke and reminders 1st: in rr: blnd 9th: sn bhd: t.o 3 out* **20/1**

0PP- **P** **Kings Brook**^{69} 4494 10-9-11 **90**.......... JoeCornwall$^{(7)}$ —
(John Cornwall) *t.k.h in rr: blnd 9th: bhd whn p.u bef next* **28/1**

622- **P** **Sea Venture (IRE)**^{35} 5149 8-11-10 **110**.......... RobertWalford —
(Tim Walford) *hld up in rr: sme hdwy 8th: lost pl and struggling whn p.u bef 4 out* **7/1**^{3}

50P- **P** **Pingaro De La Vire (FR)**^{35} 5149 7-11-0 **107**.......... MrDMaxwell$^{(7)}$ —
(Giles Smyly) *in rr: blnd bdly and rdr lost irons 9th: bhd whn p.u bef next* **20/1**

5m 36.6s (-9.40) **Going Correction** -0.425s/f (Good) **12** Ran SP% **116.0**
Speed ratings: **99,98,97,96,95 95,85,81,65,— —,—**
toteswingers: 1&2 £30.30, 1&3 £19.10, 2&3 £17.00 CSF £57.10 CT £528.72 TOTE £9.10: £3.30, £2.90, £2.60; EX 69.80.
Owner Steve & Jackie Fleetham **Bred** John Smyth **Trained** Little Newcastle, Pembrokes

FOCUS
Ordinary handicap chase form although the pace was solid.

NOTEBOOK
North Island(IRE) made just about all the running and won with a bit to spare, idling with his ears pricked late on. He had not run since December 2008 due to a leg problem, but had been dropped 5lb since his absence and his in-form trainer had him fully tuned up for this return. (op 17-2)
Lawaaheb(IRE) shaped well after a break at Sedgefield and stepped up on that. He travelled well and had every chance at the last but got in slightly too close and could not get back at the winner. (op 8-1)
Badger Foot(IRE) found this much more competitive than the two-finisher novice handicap he won at Hereford, but he ran well, staying on after being slightly outpaced by the leaders entering the home turn. (op 8-1)
Our Jim ran commendably on this return from a short break but remains 8lb above his previous winning mark. (op 9-2 tchd 7-2)
Chorizo(IRE) is inconsistent and has not won since scoring off 8lb lower over course and distance last July, but this was a reasonable effort. (tchd 14-1)
Hold The Bid(IRE), a dual course winner, made a few errors and could never quite get to the leaders. (op 11-1 tchd 12-1)
Kings Brook Official explanation: trainer said gelding had a breathing problem (op 6-1)
Sea Venture(IRE), a stablemate of the runner-up, began to struggle down the back and was eventually pulled up. He still has to prove he can stay this far. (op 6-1)
Pingaro De La Vire(FR) Official explanation: jockey said that his stirrup iron broke (op 6-1)

353 G.D. BOLTS NOVICES' H'CAP CHASE (14 fncs) 2m 4f
4:00 (4:00) (Class 4) (0-105,105) 5-Y-O+ **£3,252** (£955; £477; £238)

Form RPR

21-2 **1** **Chicago Alley**^{16} 77 9-10-5 **89**.......... LeeEdwards$^{(5)}$ 104+
(Tony Carroll) *hld up in rr: hmpd in 2nd: hdwy 7th: sn trcking ldrs: led appr 3 out: hit 3 out: hdd 2 out: upsides last: styd on to ld last 150yds* **6/1**^{2}

/02- **2** *2¼* **Indian Pipe Dream (IRE)**^{22} 5388 8-11-12 **105**..........(tp) KeithMercer 117+
(Steve Gollings) *w ldrs: hit 4 out: led and blnd 2 out: hdd and no ex run-in* **8/1**^{3}

32-U **3** *6* **Lord Collingwood (IRE)**^{10} 175 9-10-9 **88**.......... AndrewTinkler 95
(Nigel Tinkler) *in rr: hit 6th: hdwy appr 3 out: kpt on to take n.d 3rd sn after last* **7/2**^{1}

0U1- **4** *1¼* **Champtho (FR)**^{23} 5353 5-11-8 **101**.......... LeightonAspell 106
(Oliver Sherwood) *trckd ldrs: chal 3 out: one pce fr next* **6/1**^{2}

34-5 **5** *2½* **Safe Investment (USA)**^{17} 63 6-10-6 **85**..........(p) DenisO'Regan 87
(Ben Pollock) *in rr: mstke 10th: hdwy to chse ldrs next: one pce fr 3 out* **33/1**

41-U **6** *1½* **Mad Professor (IRE)**^{12} 136 7-9-7 **79** oh3..........(p) JoeCornwall$^{(7)}$ 80
(John Cornwall) *chsd ldrs: outpcd appr 3 out: kpt on fr 2 out* **9/1**

04-1 **7** *3¼* **Lindseyfield Lodge (IRE)**^{11} 160 9-10-11 **93**....(p) MichaelMcAlister$^{(3)}$ 92
(Robert Johnson) *led: hdd appr 3 out: fdd 2 out* **12/1**

515- **8** *9* **Overbranch**^{27} 5275 7-11-4 **102**..........(b) JamesHalliday$^{(5)}$ 94
(Malcolm Jefferson) *prom: hdwy to chse ldrs 4 out: hi t3 out: wknd appr last* **14/1**

404- **9** *4½* **King Of Leon (FR)**^{37} 5115 6-11-9 **102**.......... SamThomas 88
(Henrietta Knight) *in rr: hmpd 2nd: drvn 9th: sme hdwy 4 out: sn wknd* **12/1**

2P-0 **10** *14* **It's A Roofer (IRE)**^{15} 88 10-11-7 **100**.......... RichieMcGrath 73
(Kate Walton) *chsd ldrs: lost pl after 4 out: sn bhd* **20/1**

40-5 **11** *1¼* **Rokinhorsescience (FR)**^{10} 176 6-11-6 **99**.......... DougieCostello 71
(Jonjo O'Neill) *in rr: hmpd 2nd: bhd fr 10th* **14/1**

404- **F** **Magellan Straits**^{19} 32 6-11-7 **105**.......... ShaneByrne$^{(5)}$ —
(Sue Smith) *mid-div: fell 2nd* **9/1**

0P2- **P** **Itea Du Fau (FR)**^{24} 5342 5-11-12 **105**.......... RobertThornton —
(Alan King) *chsd ldrs: wknd 3 out: bhd whn p.u bef 3 out* **16/1**

4m 54.3s (-11.40) **Going Correction** -0.425s/f (Good) **13** Ran SP% **124.2**
Speed ratings: **105,104,101,101,100 99,98,94,92,87 86,—,—**
toteswingers: 1&2 £12.80, 2&3 £8.90, 1&3 £5.10 CSF £56.36 CT £199.44 TOTE £6.50: £2.30, £2.20, £2.00; EX 52.60.
Owner Lavender Hill Stud L L C **Bred** Mrs J L Egan **Trained** Cropthorne, Worcs

FOCUS
This was a competitive novice handicap run at a decent pace, and the form should hold up.

NOTEBOOK
Chicago Alley was hampered by a faller at the second before making steady progress on the second circuit. In front briefly three from home, she rallied well to get up back up on the run-in. She had shaped when second at Bangor last time as if this longer trip and better ground would suit, and so it proved. (op 7-1)
Indian Pipe Dream(IRE), also runner-up over course and distance on his one previous chase start, had just taken it up when he went through the top of the second-last, and he could not hold off the mare on the run-in. The switch to fences seems to have rekindled his enthusiasm. (op 10-1)
Lord Collingwood(IRE) closed up from the rear to look a threat, but could not race on with the leaders from the second-last. He might be worth returning to 3m. (op 11-2)
Champtho(FR), who beat Lord Collingwood a head at Bangor and was 3lb worse off, ran a creditable race and still gives the impression he has more to offer. (op 11-2)
Safe Investment(USA) stayed on from the rear without posing a threat. (op 28-1)
Mad Professor(IRE), who was effectively 11lb higher than when scoring over 2m two starts back, was another who never really looked like winning. (op 10-1 tchd 11-1)
Lindseyfield Lodge(IRE), 8lb higher than when winning a Kelso selling chase recently, was responsible for setting the pace, but was swallowed up early in the home straight.
Overbranch was not disgraced on this first run over fences since December 2008 but will need to improve to score. (op 16-1)
King Of Leon(FR), another hampered by the early faller, was always towards the rear on this chasing debut. (op 17-2)

354 GEOSTAR HUNTERS' CHASE (14 fncs) 2m 6f 110y
4:30 (4:30) (Class 6) 5-Y-O+ **£988** (£304; £152)

Form RPR

F1-4 **1** **Farmer Frank**^{11} 148 7-11-13 0.......... HenryBrooke$^{(7)}$ 122+
(Nick Kent) *trckd ldrs: led appr 2 out: drew clr run-in* **6/4**^{1}

15-5 **2** *13* **Oranger (FR)**^{11} 151 8-11-13 102..........(b) MrAndrewMartin$^{(3)}$ 106
(Andrew J Martin) *w ldr: outpcd appr 3 out: kpt on to take modest 2nd run-in* **8/1**

160- **3** *10* **Think Lucky**^{233} 1529 7-11-9 99.......... MrlSmith$^{(7)}$ 98
(Mrs N Naughton) *chsd ldrs: led 3 out: hdd appr next: in 2nd and wl hld whn mstke last: hung lft: wknd and lost 2nd on run-in* **20/1**

/3P- **4** *6* **Scotland Yard (UAE)**^{25} 5314 7-11-5 100.......... AdamWedge$^{(7)}$ 88
(Mrs Fleur Hawes) *chsd ldrs: outpcd 10th: kpt on to take modest 4th run-in* **20/1**

/60- **5** *4½* **Itzacliche (IRE)**^{22} 10-11-9 0..........(b^{1}) MissJRRichards$^{(7)}$ 90
(Nicky Richards) *mde most: hdd 3 out: wknd rapidly run-in* **9/2**^{2}

/40- **6** *15* **Caramia (FR)**^{64} 9-11-9 107..........(p) MissGAndrews$^{(3)}$ 70
(Miss S Klug) *prom: drvn 7th: lost pl 10th: sn bhd* **7/1**

06P/ **7** *7* **Pouilly (FR)**^{71} 7-11-9 0.......... MrMatthewSmith$^{(3)}$ 64
(Mrs Fleur Hawes) *hld up: hdwy 8th: chsng ldrs after 4 out: sn hrd drvn: wknd appr next* **18/1**

445/ **P** **Stroom Bank (IRE)**^{13} 10-11-5 0.......... MrOHopkins-Fagan$^{(7)}$ —
(Simon Andrews) *prom: reminders and lost pl 7th: sn bhd: t.o whn p.u after next* **50/1**

/0F- **P** **High Skies**^{58} 4720 7-12-3 113.......... MrTWeston$^{(3)}$ —
(Dr Richard Newland) *in rr: hdwy 8th: rdn and lost pl 4 out: bhd whn p.u bef 2 out* **6/1**^{3}

5m 40.8s (-5.20) **Going Correction** -0.425s/f (Good) **9** Ran SP% **112.8**
Speed ratings: **92,87,84,81,80 75,72,—,—**
toteswingers: 1&2 £3.60, 1&3 £8.30, 2&3 £13.50 CSF £13.49 TOTE £2.60: £2.20, £1.10, £5.20; EX 15.00.
Owner R J Jackson **Bred** F S Jackson **Trained** Brigg, Lincs
■ Henry Brooke's first winner under rules.

FOCUS
A modest hunter chase.

NOTEBOOK
Farmer Frank came away in nice style once sent to the front before the second-last. Held under a penalty over 2m at Cheltenham last time, he was suited by the return to this more suitable trip and should win plenty more of these. (op 15-8 tchd 11-8)
Oranger(FR) was always up with the pace and rallied on the flat to claim second. (op 17-2)
Think Lucky, formerly with David Pipe and running in only his third chase, had not been seen since September and was missing the usual headgear. He showed up prominently, but was held when he clouted the last and lost second. (op 18-1 tchd 16-1)
Itzacliche(IRE), winner of his last two starts in ladies' opens, was previously unbeaten in three vists to Market Rasen, including this race two years ago. After making a lot of the running in his first-time blinkers, shadowed by Oranger, he weakened quickly when headed in the straight. (tchd 4-1 and 5-1)
Stroom Bank(IRE) Official explanation: trainer said gelding finished distressed and was lame left-fore (op 5-1 tchd 13-2)
High Skies was upsides the winner when falling at the last on his British debut two months ago but was always in the rear division here before pulling up. Official explanation: trainer said gelding finished distressed (op 5-1 tchd 13-2)

355 HOST YOUR HEN PARTY HERE STANDARD OPEN NATIONAL HUNT FLAT RACE 2m 1f
5:00 (5:00) (Class 6) 4-6-Y-O **£1,507** (£439; £219)

Form RPR

4- **1** **Kasbadali (FR)**^{55} 4792 5-11-2 0.......... LeightonAspell 107
(Oliver Sherwood) *in rr: drvn 7f out: gd hdwy over 2f out: chal ins fnl f: styd on to ld fnl strides* **18/1**

03- **2** *shd* **Sweet Irony (FR)**^{85} 4158 4-10-12 0.......... RobertThornton 103
(Alan King) *tk fierce hold in rr: hdwy to trck ldrs after 5f: smooth hdwy to ld over 2f out: rdn and kpt on fnl f: hdd post* **10/3**^{1}

3 *3¼* **Moufatango (FR)** 4-10-9 0.......... FearghalDavis$^{(3)}$ 100
(Nicky Richards) *in rr: hdwy 6f out: chal 2f out: one pce fnl f* **28/1**

4 *7* **Jukebox Melody (IRE)** 4-10-7 0.......... JamesHalliday$^{(5)}$ 93
(Malcolm Jefferson) *chsd ldrs: pushed along 7f out: hung lft bnd over 3f out: wknd over 1f out* **8/1**

5 *½* **Mrs Eff** 4-9-12 0.......... HenryBrooke$^{(7)}$ 85
(Kate Walton) *in rr: last and drvn after 6f: sn bhd: styd on fnl 3f* **33/1**

2- **6** *1* **Spring Snow (USA)**^{18} 53 4-10-12 0.......... BarryKeniry 91
(Alan Swinbank) *chsd ldrs: drvn 6f out: outpcd over 2f out: one pce* **7/2**^{2}

7 *1½* **Tippering (IRE)** 5-11-2 0.......... TjadeCollier 94
(Sue Smith) *w ldr: led over 3f out: hdd over 2f out: wknd over 1f out* **16/1**

30- **8** *½* **The Wee Midget**^{236} 1498 5-10-13 0.......... HaddenFrost$^{(3)}$ 93
(Arthur Whiting) *t.k.h in rr: hdwy 6f out: outpcd over 2f out: one pce* **50/1**

9 *3¾* **Jomade (IRE)** 4-10-12 0.......... JasonMaguire 86
(Kim Bailey) *chsd ldrs: lost pl 2f out* **4/1**^{3}

10 *1½* **Whiskey Ridge (IRE)** 4-10-12 0.......... KeithMercer 84
(Sue Smith) *chsd ldrs: outpcd over 4f out: one pce fnl 3f* **28/1**

0- **11** *2¼* **Searree**^{364} 357 5-10-9 0.......... PaddyAspell 79
(James Turner) *mid-div: outpcd and lost pl over 4f out* **80/1**

2- **12** *2¼* **Cloudy Joe (IRE)**^{24} 5344 4-10-9 0.......... AdamPogson$^{(3)}$ 80
(Charles Pogson) *led: qcknd 7f out: hdd over 3f out: wknd 2f out* **12/1**

13 *29* **Cardigan Island (IRE)** 5-10-11 0.......... DonalDevereux$^{(5)}$ 55
(Peter Bowen) *in rr: drvn 6f out: t.o over 3f out* **7/1**

0- **14** *26* **Funky Beat**^{41} 5050 4-10-5 0.......... TomMessenger 18
(John Holt) *stdd s: hld up in rr: sme hdwy 6f out: sn lost pl and bhd: t.o over 3f out* **150/1**

4m 12.3s (11.20) **Going Correction** +0.20s/f (Yiel)
WFA 4 from 5yo 4lb **14** Ran SP% **121.4**
Speed ratings: **81,80,79,76,75 75,74,74,72,72 70,69,56,44**
toteswingers: 1&2 £29.20, 1&3 £7.60, 2&3 £33.60 CSF £75.58 TOTE £14.40: £3.50, £2.00, £12.40; EX 89.80 Place 6: £61.23 Place 5: £51.95.
Owner T D J Syder **Bred** Olivier Delegue **Trained** Upper Lambourn, Berks

FOCUS
A reasonable bumper for the track and time of year. The pace was steady for the first half of the contest but it picked up appreciably down the back straight, and those that were to the fore at this stage paid the price for trying to keep up the gallop for so long. The form may not stand up.

NOTEBOOK
Kasbadali(FR) let the leaders get on with things and was only tenth turning into the home straight but he stayed on and produced a strong run to get up on the line for an unlikely victory. He stepped up on what he showed on his debut at Plumpton in March but may be flattered by the way this race was run. (op 12-1)
Sweet Irony(FR), third at Ascot when last seen in February, failed to settle until the pace lifted. He led going nicely into the straight and looked set to win only to be cut down in the final strides. He should have a decent future. (op 7-2 tchd 4-1)
Moufatango(FR), who is not the biggest, is a half-brother to several winners, including decent jumper Persian Isle. He was outpaced by the leaders early in the straight but soon found his stride and briefly found himself in second place at the quarter-mile pole. (op 25-1)
Jukebox Melody(IRE) represented the stable that had won the last two runnings of this event with useful pair McMurrough and Mac Aeda. A decent type, he ran creditably and improvement should be forthcoming as he was noticeably green, hanging more than once. (op 12-1)
Mrs Eff was one of the first under pressure at the back of the pack but stayed on through beaten horses. (op 28-1)
Spring Snow(USA) paid for chasing the pace and did well to finish as close as he did. (op 9-2)
Tippering(IRE), from the family of Supreme Novices' Hurdle winner Destriero and smart chaser Carruthers, was close up in second when the winner kicked, forcing him into racing much earlier than was desirable. Not surprisingly, he could not sustain his effort but he should be capable of better.
Jomade(IRE), one of the better lookers in the field and well supported ahead of this debut, is another who failed to last home after chasing the pace when it quickened. (op 7-2 tchd 9-2)
Cloudy Joe(IRE) made the running, and it was no surprise to see him drop right away after quickening the pace the best part of a mile from home. (op 9-1)
T/Jkpt: £16,081.60. Pool of £22,650.27 - 1.00 winning tickets T/Plt: £58.00. Pool of £74,557.15 - 936.88 winning tickets T/Qpdt: £27.20. Pool of £3,827.78 - 104.00 winning tickets WG

STRATFORD (L-H)
Sunday, May 16
OFFICIAL GOING: Good (good to firm in places; 9.1)
Wind: Light against Weather: Cloudy with sunny spells

356 SALFORD PRIORS NOVICES' HURDLE (DIV I) (9 hdls) 2m 110y
2:20 (2:20) (Class 4) 4-Y-0+ **£4,228** (£1,241; £620; £310)

Form RPR
31-1 **1** **Clerk's Choice (IRE)**[11] 154 4-11-5 131 TomMolloy(3) 125+
(Michael Banks) *led tl after 4th: led again next: hdd 6th: led 3 out: mstke last: shkn up and styd on wl flat* **4/6**[1]
2/1 **2** *1 1/4* **Roodolph**[17] 58 6-11-5 128 JimmyMcCarthy 118
(Eve Johnson Houghton) *trckd ldrs: mstke 4th: chsd wnr appr 2 out: ev ch last: unable qck towards fin* **85/40**[2]
3 *5* **Clear Sailing**[58] 7-10-12 0 PaddyBrennan 107+
(Ian Williams) *hld up: hdwy 3 out: rdn appr last: no ex flat* **8/1**[3]
0 **4** *14* **The Grey One (IRE)**[10] 182 7-10-5 0 ChrisDavies(7) 92
(Milton Bradley) *hld up: hdwy after 3 out: wknd bef next* **50/1**
6B-0 **5** *8* **Majestic Bull (USA)**[10] 171 4-10-8 85 (p) JackDoyle 80
(Susan Gardner) *chsd ldrs: led 6th: hdd next: wknd bef 2 out* **100/1**
-0 **6** *1 1/4* **Calypso Bay (IRE)**[15] 97 4-10-8 0 APMcCoy 80
(Jonjo O'Neill) *j. slowly 1st: w ldrs tl rdn appr 6th: wknd next* **12/1**
0F0- **7** *1* **Racingisdreaming (USA)**[91] 4055 4-10-8 96 (t) TomScudamore 78
(David Pipe) *hld up: pushed along 5th: wknd after 3 out* **20/1**
0 **8** *21* **Billy Beetroot (USA)**[17] 58 4-10-5 0 LeeStephens(3) 57
(Katie Stephens) *chsd ldrs: led after 4th: hdd and j. slowly next: wknd after 3 out: t.o* **150/1**
4m 4.70s (8.70) **Going Correction** +0.575s/f (Soft) **8** Ran SP% **119.2**
Speed ratings (Par 105): **102,101,99,92,88 88,87,77**
toteswingers: 1&2 £1.02, 1&3 £2.00, 2&3 £2.70 CSF £2.54 TOTE £1.60: £1.10, £1.10, £1.90; EX 2.70.
Owner M C Banks **Bred** N Coman **Trained** Waresley, Cambs
FOCUS
Straightforward novice form.
NOTEBOOK
Clerk's Choice(IRE) has not looked back since making his debut in this sphere in March and landed the hat-trick with a fairly straightforward display. He took it up nearing three out and was always doing enough to hold off his challengers in the home straight, despite being made to work by the runner-up after hitting the last. Looking at official figures he ran up to his mark, and he has probably yet to peak as a hurdler, but whether he will be able to defy it in a handicap remains to be seen. (op 8-11)
Roodolph was the only one to go with the winner nearing the business end and posted a solid race in defeat, this being his second run back from an injury. He will not always bump into a rival like the winner during the summer and can defy his penalty. (op 5-2)
Clear Sailing won three claimers on the AW earlier this year and was having his first run for new connections. He gets 1m4f on the level, so stamina was not expected to be an issue, and he turned in an encouraging effort. He just looked to be racing somewhat awkwardly as the first pair got away from him in the home straight, but should learn for the experience and find a race or two this summer.
The Grey One(IRE) again proved keen under restraint, but that was largely down the ordinary gallop and this was a definite step in the right direction. He should find more opportunities now he is eligible for a mark. (tchd 66-1)
Billy Beetroot(USA) Official explanation: jockey said gelding hung right; vet said gelding lost its left-fore shoe

357 PAXFORD NOVICES' CHASE (14 fncs) 2m 4f
2:50 (2:52) (Class 3) 5-Y-0+ **£6,805** (£2,340)

Form RPR
21F- **1** **Baily Storm (IRE)**[182] 2296 8-10-12 0 DarylJacob 131+
(Tim Vaughan) *chsd ldrs: mstke 3rd: rdn whn lft 2nd and hmpd 2 out: led last: all out* **11/4**[2]
220- **2** *hd* **Classic Swain (USA)**[197] 2002 5-10-12 0 (bt) APMcCoy 130+
(Paul Nicholls) *nt fluent especially at the ditches: led: j. slowly and hdd 2nd where rdr dropped whip: chsd ldr: pushed along 8th: lft in ld after 2 out: hdd last: styd on* **8/15**[1]
55-0 **F** **Mumbles Pier (IRE)**[9] 196 5-10-12 0 TomO'Brien 125
(Peter Bowen) *w ldr tl led 2nd: slt ld and stl gng okay whn stmbld and fell 2 out* **11/2**[3]
4m 54.9s (0.70) **Going Correction** +0.125s/f (Yiel) **3** Ran SP% **107.3**
Speed ratings: **103,102,—**
CSF £4.81 TOTE £3.20; EX 5.50.
Owner Chasing Gold Ltd **Bred** J Harold-Barry **Trained** Aberthin, Vale of Glamorgan
FOCUS
A fair little novice chase.

NOTEBOOK
Baily Storm(IRE) was returning from a sizeable break and making his chasing debut. He is officially rated a stone inferior to Classic Swain over hurdles, but was rated on 129 before losing his form in that sphere and has always looked more of a chasing type. He wasn't always foot perfect, but his jumping got better when it mattered and he came with a well-timed challenge in the home straight. He only just edged the verdict, but is entitled to improve a deal for the experience and should enjoy reverting to further as a chaser. (op 7-2)
Classic Swain(USA) was a very short price for a chasing debutant that wears headgear and was returning from a 197-day break. He lacked fluency and tended to go in snatches, but looked to be in control after being left in front two from home. It was clear after the next he was in trouble, though, and it was only down to his rider's unparalleled strength on the run-in that he finished so close in the end, despite McCoy having lost his whip at the second fence. Perhaps dropping back in trip would help. (op 1-2 tchd 4-9 and 4-7 in a place)
Mumbles Pier(IRE), rated 110 over hurdles, has been waiting to get over fences and was in the process of running a big race prior to crumpling on landing after the penultimate fence. His jumping had been the most convincing in the race prior to that and he was far from done with at the time. (tchd 7-1)

358 MEON HILL MARES' NOVICES' (S) HURDLE (9 hdls) 2m 110y
3:20 (3:21) (Class 5) 4-Y-0+ **£1,951** (£573; £286; £143)

Form RPR
5- **1** **Bonzeno Queen (IRE)**[30] 5218 5-10-7 0 DPFahy(3) 96+
(Evan Williams) *hld up: hdwy 6th: lft 2nd 2 out: r.o to ld towards fin* **8/1**
F6-4 **2** *2* **Casual Style**[10] 185 4-10-6 95 (t) TomScudamore 91
(David Pipe) *trckd ldrs: racd keenly: mstke 6th: led appr 2 out: sn clr: rdn and hdd towards fin* **5/2**[1]
3 *13* **A Dream Come True**[97] 5-10-10 0 JodieMogford 82
(Graeme McPherson) *j. slowly 1st: bhd: mstke 6th: hdwy appr 2 out: wknd bef last* **28/1**
40-5 **4** *12* **Broadway Allstar (IRE)**[10] 171 5-10-10 88 TimmyMurphy 72
(Liam Corcoran) *chsd ldrs tl rdn and wknd bef 2 out* **11/4**[2]
0/ **5** *11* **Berry Hill Lass (IRE)**[519] 2332 6-10-3 0 (vt[1]) CharlieWallis(7) 64
(John O'Shea) *hld up: hdwy 5th: ev ch after 3 out: rdn and wkng whn hmpd next: t.o* **33/1**
6 *1 3/4* **Par Excellence**[64] 7-10-10 0 NickScholfield 61
(Jeremy Scott) *hld up: hdwy after 5th: rdn and wknd appr 2 out: t.o* **50/1**
/4P- **7** *1* **Covey (IRE)**[185] 2244 9-10-3 88 L-BdrSallyRandell(7) 59
(John O'Shea) *prom tl lost pl 5th: sn bhd: t.o* **25/1**
P4- **8** *4 1/2* **Glan Lady (IRE)**[18] 52 4-10-3 0 AlexMerriam(3) 51
(Graham Smith) *hld up: wknd 6th: t.o* **100/1**
9 *24* **Montiboli (IRE)**[41] 5-10-10 0 DarylJacob 33
(Gordon Edwards) *plld hrd and prom: led 3rd: mstke and hdd 6th: wknd after 3 out: t.o* **14/1**
10 *33* **Magics Gold (IRE)**[392] 8-10-3 0 MissJBuck(7) 4
(James Danahar) *a in rr: bhd whn hmpd 4th: t.o* **100/1**
P30- **F** **Lady Sorcerer**[41] 5038 5-10-10 90 JamieMoore —
(Alan Jarvis) *mid-div: fell 4th* **4/1**[3]
U **Carhue Princess (IRE)**[683] 4-10-6 0 PaulMoloney 88
(Evan Williams) *hld up: hdwy 6th: wkng whn hmpd and uns rdr 2 out* **33/1**
430- **B** **Ravine Rose**[206] 1861 4-10-6 84 (t) CharliePoste —
(Ben Case) *hld up: b.d 4th* **25/1**
25-6 **F** **Just For Jean (IRE)**[15] 100 5-10-7 90 (b[1]) AdrianLane(3) 95
(Donald McCain) *led to 3rd: led again 6th: hdd and wkng whn fell 2 out* **7/1**
4m 2.40s (6.40) **Going Correction** +0.575s/f (Soft)
WFA 4 from 5yo+ 18lb **14** Ran SP% **126.5**
Speed ratings (Par 103): **107,106,99,94,89 88,87,85,74,58 —,—,—,—**
toteswingers: 1&2 £5.60, 2&3 £25.90, 1&3 not won. CSF £28.87 TOTE £9.50: £2.70, £1.70, £7.40; EX 28.10.The winner was bought in for 7,000gns.
Owner John Crawley **Bred** John Crawley **Trained** Llancarfan, Vale Of Glamorgan
FOCUS
The first pair dominated this mares' novice seller.
NOTEBOOK
Bonzeno Queen(IRE) was making her hurdling debut in lowly company and she got up late in the day to land a gamble. She was given time to find her feet and came under pressure after getting into a prominent position nearing the home turn. The runner-up went clear at that stage, but the winner's stamina kicked into play after the second-last and she was always going to reel in that rival on the run-in. She should only improve for the outing and, despite this being a poor contest, she is probably a fair bit better than this grade. Connections bought her back in for 7,000gns afterwards. (op 22-1)
Casual Style, down in grade, again proved headstrong, but her rider must have felt confident as he sent on for home off the final turn. She wandered about coming to the last and paid for refusing to settle as the winner began to find her full stride. No doubt she can win races in this class, though, as she was well clear of the remainder. (op 2-1)
A Dream Come True came into this hurdling debut for new connections with something to prove having lost her way on the level. Her new yard is an up-and-coming one, however, and while she failed to threaten this was a performance she is entitled to build on. (op 25-1 tchd 33-1)
Carhue Princess(IRE) was still fighting for a place prior to unseating. (op 13-2 tchd 15-2)
Just For Jean(IRE), in first-time blinkers, was booked for a place prior to falling. (op 13-2 tchd 15-2)

359 CHARLES LEA MEMORIAL H'CAP HURDLE (FOR THE CHARLES LEA MEMORIAL TROPHY) (14 hdls) 3m 3f
3:50 (3:50) (Class 4) (0-115,114) 4-Y-0+ **£4,553** (£1,337; £668; £333)

Form RPR
006- **1** **Lyster (IRE)**[21] 3 11-9-11 **88** oh3 LeeStephens(3) 99+
(David Evans) *hld up: hdwy 11th: rdn to ld appr 2 out: styd on wl* **4/1**[2]
002- **2** *10* **Mac Halen (IRE)**[25] 5315 7-10-9 **100** DPFahy(3) 102
(Evan Williams) *hld up: hdwy 9th: rdn after 3 out: styng on same pce whn wnt 2nd last* **5/1**
501/ **3** *2 3/4* **Nabouko (FR)**[35] 9-10-13 **101** (b[1]) TomScudamore 101
(Susan Nock) *chsd ldr tl led 4th: hdd after 3 out: sn rdn: wknd last* **33/1**
002- **4** *3/4* **Aqualung (FR)**[38] 5107 6-11-12 **114** (t) LiamTreadwell 114
(Claire Dyson) *prom: chsd ldr 10th: led after 3 out: rdn and hdd bef next: wknd last* **16/1**
P55- **5** *11* **Alfadora**[41] 5046 10-10-2 **90** (t) CharliePoste 79
(Milton Harris) *hld up: hdwy after 10th: rdn and wknd appr 2 out* **11/1**
F42- **6** *1 1/4* **Hampton Court**[24] 5330 5-10-5 **98** JimmyDerham(5) 86
(Seamus Mullins) *hld up: hdwy 9th: rdn and wknd appr 2 out* **9/2**[3]
10-1 **7** *7* **Ethiopia**[7] 218 7-9-13 **94** NathanSweeney(7) 76
(Bob Buckler) *led to 4th: chsd ldr to 10th: rdn and wknd appr 2 out* **15/2**
364- **8** *2 3/4* **Dont Tell The Wife (IRE)**[151] 2918 7-10-11 **106** DavidBass(7) 85
(Nicky Henderson) *chsd ldrs: drvn along after 10th: sn wknd* **7/2**[1]
5P/0 **9** *9* **I'm Supreme (IRE)**[12] 131 8-10-12 **100** TomO'Brien 71
(Philip Hobbs) *chsd ldrs: drvn along after 10th: wknd appr 2 out: t.o* **14/1**

0/0- **10** *70* **Dr Dream (IRE)**[50] 4897 6-9-8 **89** oh7 ow1....................(b) CharlieWallis(7) —
(John O'Shea) *prom: lost pl 9th: bhd fr 11th: t.o* **50/1**

000- **P** **Petrus De Sormain (FR)**[185] 2246 7-10-8 **103**.............(t) MarkQuinlan(7) —
(James Evans) *hld up: hdwy 7th: wknd 10th: t.o whn p.u bef 2 out* **33/1**

636- **P** **Intersky Music (USA)**[13] 2162 7-11-6 **108**............................ APMcCoy —
(Jonjo O'Neill) *hld up in tch: lost pl after 6th: rallied appr 11th: rdn and wkng whn p.u bef 2 out* **14/1**

PPP- **P** **Paddleyourowncanoe (IRE)**[23] 5365 9-11-5 **110**.......(b[1]) TomMolloy(3) —
(Emma Baker) *hld up in tch: wknd after 10th: t.o whn p.u bef 2 out* **66/1**

6m 40.7s (12.10) **Going Correction** +0.575s/f (Soft) **13** Ran SP% **125.7**
Speed ratings (Par 105): **105,102,101,101,97 97,95,94,91,71 —,—,—**
toteswingers: 1&2 £10.20, 2&3 £49.70 1&3 not won. CSF £25.76 CT £605.99 TOTE £7.30: £2.30, £3.10, £12.40; EX 42.00.

Owner M D Jones **Bred** B D Darrer **Trained** Pandy, Monmouths

FOCUS
A wide-open staying handicap and an easy winner.

NOTEBOOK
Lyster(IRE) attracted support and came home a most decisive winner. He had previously looked out of sorts since resuming from a long layoff this year, but was running over a trip short of his best and it was his first outing beyond 3m since his last win, which came over 3m2f in 2008. That came off a mark of 88, so while he was 3lb out of the handicap here he was still on a good mark if bouncing back. (op 9-2 tchd 5-1)

Mac Halen(IRE) plugged on to win the race for second, but never held any chance with the winner. He is up to breaking his duck this summer, but could have done without the handicapper upping him 5lb for his second at Southwell last time. (op 7-1)

Nabouko(FR) had cut little ice between the flags this year, but Tom Scudamore was a positive jockey booking and he was equipped with first-time blinkers for this return to hurdling. Positively ridden, looking at the way he kept on under pressure he could have probably done with making this even more of a test. It wouldn't be surprising to see him sent chasing soon.

Aqualung(FR) was 3lb higher on this debut for new connections and posted a sound enough effort under top weight. (op 12-1)

Dont Tell The Wife(IRE) was well backed on his return to action, but the distress signals were soon being sent out by his rider after he walked through the eighth flight. He plugged on for pressure, but fitness shouldn't have been an issue with him and this leaves him with something to prove. (op 6-1)

Intersky Music(USA) Official explanation: vet said gelding returned lame

360 SALFORD PRIORS NOVICES' HURDLE (DIV II) (9 hdls) 2m 110y
4:20 (4:20) (Class 4) 4-Y-0+ **£4,228** (£1,241; £620; £310)

Form RPR

UF6- **1** **Battle Group**[56] 4760 5-10-12 0.. TomScudamore 105+
(David Pipe) *s.s: hld up and bhd: pushed along and hdwy after 3 out: led next: r.o strly* **16/1**

336- **2** *3* **Apache Dawn**[221] 1660 6-10-9 97.............................. EamonDehdashti(3) 97+
(Aytach Sadik) *a.p: racd keenly: ev ch and hmpd 2 out: no ex flat* **14/1**

5- **3** *5* **Ask Archer**[23] 5363 5-10-12 0... PaulMoloney 90
(Evan Williams) *prom: racd keenly: lost pl 4th: hdwy appr 2 out: nt trble ldrs* **12/1**[3]

1/0- **4** *3 ¾* **Duke Of Burgundy (FR)**[30] 3881 7-10-12 0....................(t) AlanO'Keeffe 87
(Jennie Candlish) *set stdy pce tl hdd appr 3rd: chsd ldr: led again after 5th: mstke next: rdn and hdd 2 out: wkng whn j.rt last* **20/1**

10- **5** *1 ½* **Super Kenny (IRE)**[38] 5094 4-11-1 0.................................... APMcCoy 90+
(Nicky Henderson) *trckd ldrs: ev ch whn mstke 2 out: sn wknd* **1/3**[1]

000- **6** *1 ¾* **Golden Smog (IRE)**[18] 50 4-10-1 0............................... PaddyBrennan 72
(Ian Williams) *hld up: hdwy after 3 out: rdn and wknd bef next* **100/1**

P-6 **7** *nk* **Cubism**[7] 216 4-10-8 0.. CharliePoste 79
(Milton Harris) *hld up: nt fluent 1st: nvr nr to chal* **33/1**

43- **8** *4* **Esprit De Fer (FR)**[36] 5130 6-10-7 102.....................(t) MichaelMurphy(5) 79
(Rob Summers) *trckd ldr: racd keenly: rdn and ev ch appr 2 out: sn wknd* **9/1**[2]

0-3 **9** *4 ½* **Red Army Commander (IRE)**[10] 182 5-10-12 0...... AndrewThornton 74
(Neil Mulholland) *hld up: hdwy 6th: wknd after 3 out* **22/1**

10 *10* **The Snatcher (IRE)**[202] 7-10-9 0.................................... SeanQuinlan(3) 64
(Richard Phillips) *mid-div: plld hrd: rdn and wknd 3 out: t.o* **33/1**

5- **11** *31* **Highway Magic (IRE)**[41] 5036 4-10-8 0.................................. SamJones 29
(Alan Jarvis) *hld up: plld hrd: hdwy to ld appr 3rd: sn clr: hdd after 5th: wknd bef 3 out: t.o* **80/1**

4m 10.2s (14.20) **Going Correction** +0.575s/f (Soft) **11** Ran SP% **122.5**
Speed ratings (Par 105): **89,87,85,83,82 81,81,79,77,73 58**
toteswingers: 1&2 £39.00, 1&3 £12.20, 2&3 £4.20 CSF £188.36 TOTE £20.90: £3.90, £4.00, £2.70; EX 441.20.

Owner Jolly Boys Outing **Bred** Juddmonte Farms Ltd **Trained** Nicholashayne, Devon

FOCUS
This second divison of the novice hurdle was notable for the favourite flopping, but the winner still impressed.

NOTEBOOK
Battle Group ⊠ , a former bumper winner, failed to complete on his first two outings in this sphere and then looked out of sorts when making his debut for David Pipe 56 days earlier. He was ridden right out the back here and with just a steady pace on, looked like being one of the back numbers through the first half. However, he began picking off the stragglers on the back straight and emerged to the leaders full of running nearing the penultimate flight. He wasn't clever at it, but that didn't stop him from coming right away and he looked to have any amount in hand passing the line. This better ground was a big help to him and switching to Pond House has clearly also been a big benefit. He ought to have little trouble getting further and it will be fascinating to see how he fares under a penalty now that his confidence will be high. It may also be that his trainer sends him into handicaps next, though. (op 18-1 tchd 20-1)

Apache Dawn is a 96-rated maiden over hurdles and the fact he shaped a little better than the bare form does put the overall form into perspective. He has shaped better than his mark at times in defeat, though, and perhaps his turn is nearing. (tchd 12-1)

Ask Archer ran close enough to the level of his hurdling debut 23 days previously and now has the option of handicaps. (op 14-1)

Duke Of Burgundy(FR) would have found this sharp enough on his second run over hurdles and probably missed a trick not going off quicker than he did, but this was still a more encouraging effort from him.

Super Kenny(IRE) created a good impression when winning over C&D on debut two runs back and found it all happening too quickly when pitched into a Grade 1 next time. He was expected to win, and win well, but the writing was on the wall for him before he got the second-last all wrong. This obviously wasn't his true running and it wouldn't be surprising to see him rate higher as he strengthens up, as he is in the right hands. Official explanation: trainer had no explanation for the poor form shown (tchd 3-10 and 4-11 and 2-5 in a place)

Cubism Official explanation: jockey said gelding ran too freely

Red Army Commander(IRE) Official explanation: vet said gelding had been struck into

361 MORETON-IN-MARSH H'CAP CHASE (12 fncs) 2m 1f 110y
4:50 (4:50) (Class 3) (0-135,125) 5-Y-0+
£6,262 (£1,850; £925; £463; £231; £116)

Form RPR

P4-2 **1** **Pilgrims Lane (IRE)**[7] 221 6-10-3 **107**........................ JimmyDerham(5) 118+
(Milton Harris) *hld up: hdwy after 2 out: chsd ldr last: rdn and n.m.r flat: r.o to ld nr fin* **9/1**

002- **2** *1 ¼* **Norborne Bandit (IRE)**[24] 5343 9-10-8 **107**...................(p) HarrySkelton 114
(Evan Williams) *a.p: led appr 2 out: rdn flat: hdd nr fin* **9/1**

50-2 **3** *8* **Huguenot (IRE)**[17] 57 7-11-5 **118**...................................... TomO'Brien 120+
(Philip Hobbs) *hld up: hdwy 9th: hit 2 out: sn rdn: wknd bef last* **7/1**[3]

150- **4** *4 ½* **Kirby's Vic (IRE)**[156] 2811 10-10-10 **109**.........................(b) DavidEngland 105
(Nigel Twiston-Davies) *chsd ldrs: lft 2nd 4th: led next: hdd appr 2 out: wknd bef last* **20/1**

11-2 **5** *38* **Prince Des Marais (FR)**[7] 236 7-11-5 **118**................ AndrewThornton 79
(Caroline Bailey) *hld up: hdwy 8th: wknd appr 2 out: t.o* **3/1**[2]

11P- **6** *39* **Some Touch (IRE)**[90] 4075 10-11-12 **125**.............................. DarylJacob 50
(Howard Johnson) *chsd ldr tl lft in ld 4th: hdd next: j.lft 6th: wknd 9th: bhd whn hit next: t.o* **16/1**

1/5- **U** **Merchant Red (USA)**[37] 5118 7-11-12 **125**.....................(b[1]) WillKennedy —
(Paul Webber) *hld up: hdwy whn hmpd and uns rdr 6th* **16/1**

131- **U** **Kikos (FR)**[24] 5343 8-11-8 **121**.. SamJones —
(Renee Robeson) *led tl mstke and uns rdr 4th* **7/1**[3]

32-1 **U** **Miss Sarenne (FR)**[9] 192 5-11-8 **121**.................................... APMcCoy —
(Nicky Henderson) *hld up: mstke and uns rdr 4th* **11/4**[1]

4m 6.10s (-1.00) **Going Correction** +0.125s/f (Yiel) **9** Ran SP% **113.2**
Speed ratings: **107,106,102,100,84 66,—,—,—**
toteswingers: 1&2 £12.60, 1&3 £16.10, 2&3 £12.50 CSF £83.12 CT £599.01 TOTE £12.20: £3.30, £3.40, £2.50; EX 100.60.

Owner Mrs D J Brown **Bred** J Mangan **Trained** Herridge, Wiltshire

⊠ Stewards' Enquiry : Harry Skelton four-day ban: careless riding (May 30-Jun 2)

FOCUS
What was already not a strong race for the grade lost a fair bit of its interest when the two last-time-out winners both unseated at the fourth fence. The overall form should be treated with a degree of caution.

NOTEBOOK
Pilgrims Lane(IRE) had finished a narrow second at Plumpton a week earlier and, given a well-judged ride, went one better to gain compensation on this drop back in trip. He allowed the second first run, but his rider didn't panic and he rates value for a little further as he was impeded by the loose horse when trying to get in front after the last. (op 11-1)

Norborne Bandit(IRE), who again took time to settle, looked to have stolen a winning advantage when kicking on after the penultimate fence. His stride began to shorten after the last, however, and he proved a sitting duck for the winner. If he would consent to settle better he would have little trouble going in off this mark. (op 17-2)

Huguenot(IRE) had to be of interest from a handicapping point of view considering he was 2lb lower than when chasing home a subsequent winner on his previous outing. He looked held before a less than fluent jump two out, though, and perhaps this track wasn't for him. (op 13-2)

Kirby's Vic(IRE) gave his all and should improve for the run, but looks in need of a drop back down in grade. Official explanation: vet said gelding was lame (op 16-1)

Prince Des Marais(FR) was turning out quickly after his good second at Worcester and turned in a lifeless effort, even allowing for this test being too sharp for him. Official explanation: jockey said gelding ran flat (op 10-3 tchd 11-4)

Kikos(FR)'s rider stood no chance of staying aboard at the fourth. (op 13-2 tchd 8-1)

Miss Sarenne(FR), off the mark as a chaser at Aintree last time, unseated independently of Kikos at the fourth but was perhaps distracted by that rival. (op 13-2 tchd 8-1)

362 HOOK NORTON STANDARD OPEN NATIONAL HUNT FLAT RACE 2m 110y
5:20 (5:20) (Class 6) 4-6-Y-O **£1,626** (£477; £238; £119)

Form RPR

1 **Poungach (FR)** 4-10-12 0.. HarrySkelton 102+
(Paul Nicholls) *mde all: rdn over 2f out: clr fr over 1f out: comf* **9/4**[2]

2 *8* **Traditional Bob (IRE)** 5-11-2 0.. JodieMogford 99
(Graeme McPherson) *hld up in tch: outpcd over 2f out: rallied to chse wnr fnl f: no imp* **16/1**

3 *4* **Sohappyharry** 4-10-9 0.. DPFahy(3) 93+
(Jane Mathias) *hld up: hdwy over 6f out: rdn and hmpd 2f out: styd on same pce* **18/1**

4 *4 ½* **Point Blank (IRE)** 4-10-12 0..(t) APMcCoy 87
(Jonjo O'Neill) *trckd ldrs: rdn and hung lft fr over 2f out: wknd over 1f out* **13/8**[1]

0- **5** *2 ¾* **Christy Ring (IRE)**[27] 5284 5-11-2 0.................................... JamieMoore 89
(John Berry) *hld up: hdwy over 6f out: rdn over 3f out: wknd over 2f out* **7/2**[3]

0- **6** *14* **Jim Job Jones**[33] 5179 6-10-9 0.................................... MarkQuinlan(7) 76
(Neil Mulholland) *trckd ldrs: rdn over 6f out: wknd over 3f out: t.o* **40/1**

7 *14* **Thomas Bell (IRE)** 6-10-9 0.. CharlieWallis(7) 63
(John O'Shea) *hld up: rdn over 5f out: sn wknd: t.o* **17/2**

8 *nk* **Fen Farm** 5-10-13 0.. TomMolloy(3) 63
(Emma Baker) *hld up in tch: rdn over 5f out: wknd over 3f out: t.o* **50/1**

0-0 **9** *11* **Yarlington Mill**[7] 237 5-11-2 0... LiamTreadwell 53
(Edward Bevan) *plld hrd and prom: jnd wnr after 2f: rdn over 7f out: wknd over 6f out: t.o* **80/1**

3m 59.9s (9.50) **Going Correction** +0.575s/f (Soft)
WFA 4 from 5yo+ 4lb **9** Ran SP% **118.4**
Speed ratings: **100,96,94,92,90 84,77,77,72**
toteswingers: 1&2 £6.60, 1&3 £8.90, 2&3 £21.50 CSF £38.20 TOTE £2.90: £1.20, £3.80, £2.90; EX 38.40 Place 6: £664.35 Place 5: £620.48.

Owner Bromley, Nicholls & Webb **Bred** Gheorghe Codre **Trained** Ditcheat, Somerset

⊠ Stewards' Enquiry : A P McCoy one-day ban: careless riding (May 30)

FOCUS
Probably a fair bumper.

NOTEBOOK
Poungach(FR), a half-brother to a winning hurdler/chaser in France, was bought for £20,000 in December and, on this showing, it to be looks money well spent. He evidently stays very well and would appeal as the sort to defy a penalty if connections keep him on the go during the summer months. His yard has a cracking record in bumpers at this course. (op 2-1 tchd 11-4)

Traditional Bob(IRE) ⊠ , bred to make his mark over fences in due course, met support and turned in a pleasing debut effort. He travelled up sweetly to get into contention, but lacked the tactical speed to go with the winner as that one kicked off the home turn. He kept on to finish a clear second-best and has a future. (tchd 20-1)

Sohappyharry emerged late in the day with a strong challenge, but wasn't done any favours when hampered soon after turning for home. It didn't make any real difference to the overall result, but he rates better than the bare form and should come on a bundle for this initial outing. (op 16-1)

Point Blank(IRE), whose unraced dam is related to Champion Hurdlers Granville Again and Morely Street, cost £60,000 and the market suggested he was well fancied. He looked to be going better than the winner nearing the home turn, but his effort under pressure was disappointing. He did wear a tongue tie for this racecourse debut and, looking at the way he backed out of it, perhaps there is a more serious issue with his breathing. His next outing should reveal more. Official explanation: jockey said gelding hung left (op 2-1 tchd 11-8)
Christy Ring(IRE) was a big market mover when failing to figure on his debut at Kempton and he left the impression here that he would have finished closer under a more positive ride. (tchd 4-1)
T/Plt: £940.90. Pool of £76,448.19 - 59.31 winning tickets. T/Qpdt: £365.80. Pool of £4,796.08 - 9.70 winning tickets CR

363 - 369a (Foreign Racing) - See Raceform Interactive

263 NEWTON ABBOT (L-H)

Monday, May 17

OFFICIAL GOING: Good (good to soft in places) changing to good after race 2 (2.50)
Wind: virtually nil Weather: Sunny

370 DICEY REILLYS, TEIGNMOUTH NOVICES' HURDLE (10 hdls) 2m 6f
2:20 (2:20) (Class 4) 4-Y-O+ **£3,707** (£1,088; £544; £271)

Form RPR
4P-2 **1** **Oedipe (FR)**[13] 137 8-10-12 0 APMcCoy 121+
(Nicky Henderson) *mde all: hit 3 out: sn rdn and hrd pressed: hit last: hld on wl: drvn out* **13/8**[1]
3-3 **2** ½ **Zakatal**[16] 97 4-10-7 111 (t) TomO'Brien 115+
(Philip Hobbs) *in tch: trckd ldrs after 6th: chalng whn nt fluent 2 out: rdn and ev ch last: nt qckn* **3/1**[2]
3 10 **Jetnova (IRE)**[386] 5-10-12 0 RobertThornton 109
(Alan King) *in tch: trckd ldrs and nudged along after 6th: rdn and ev ch whn hit 2 out: fdd last* **14/1**
54-4 **4** 1 **Supreme Plan (IRE)**[8] 223 7-10-12 114 (tp) JasonMaguire 107
(Kim Bailey) *hld up bhd: stdy hdwy fr after 6th: rdn to chse ldrs after 3 out: styd on same pce* **7/1**
351- **5** 6 **Five Star Wilsham (IRE)**[37] 5134 6-11-5 0 WillKennedy 109
(Jeremy Scott) *prom: rdn after 3 out: wknd next* **5/1**[3]
/15- **6** 4½ **Great Mates (IRE)**[337] 717 6-10-12 0 HarrySkelton 97
(Paul Nicholls) *hld up towards rr: hdwy to trck ldrs 7th: rdn after 3 out: wknd next* **16/1**
245/ **7** 11 **Hello Hector**[540] 2382 7-10-12 0 JoeTizzard 86
(Colin Tizzard) *a towards rr* **28/1**
PP-0 **8** 13 **New Mill Moll**[13] 132 7-10-0 0 ow2 (t) MattGriffiths(7) 68
(Kevin Bishop) *mid-div: rdn appr 7th: wknd bef 3 out* **100/1**
20-6 **9** 39 **Powerfullbeat**[11] 167 6-10-5 0 MrRMahon(7) 34
(Kathleen Sanderson) *mid-div tl wknd 7th: t.o* **33/1**
0-0 **10** 12 **Mccauley (IRE)**[13] 129 7-10-7 0 JimmyDerham(5) 22
(Nick Mitchell) *prom tl 7th: sn wknd: t.o* **50/1**
06- **11** 42 **Viking Gold**[21] 27 6-10-5 0 DarylJacob —
(Tim Vaughan) *rdn after 6th: a towards rr: t.o* **50/1**
0 **12** 1¼ **Seaview Lad (IRE)**[11] 168 7-10-5 0 NathanSweeney(7) —
(Bob Buckler) *mid-div tl 6th: sn bhd: t.o* **200/1**
5m 16.3s (-3.90) **Going Correction** -0.15s/f (Good)
WFA 4 from 5yo+ 19lb 12 Ran SP% **116.6**
Speed ratings (Par 105): **101,100,97,96,94 93,89,84,70,66 36,36**
toteswingers: 1&2 £1.50, 2&3 £3.90, 1&3 not won. CSF £6.20 TOTE £3.20: £1.10, £1.80, £3.20; EX 7.30.
Owner W J Brown **Bred** Bruno Vagne **Trained** Upper Lambourn, Berks

FOCUS
A competitive novices' hurdle for the time of year which saw the leading pair draw clear. Ordinary form.

NOTEBOOK
Oedipe(FR) was turned over at odds-on last time at Fakenham, but he justified favouritism and benefited from a typically strong ride from A P McCoy. He takes plenty of driving and clearly does not retain all of his ability (once rated 140 over fences) but in similar races over the summer he can remain competitive. He is now bound for the Doncaster sales. (op 2-1 tchd 9-4)
Zakatal has now been placed in all three of his starts over hurdles. He gave the winner a good race but did not look straightforward in the closing stages. His trainer reports he has a breathing problem which will require an operation at some stage. He can win races. (op 10-3 tchd 5-2)
Jetnova(IRE) was making his first start for the Alan King yard after a year off and he ought to come on for this run. Similar races should fall his way. (op 9-1)
Supreme Plan(IRE) was tried in cheekpieces and a tongue tie, but he found this shorter trip on a sharp track against him and looks slow. (op 12-1)
Five Star Wilsham(IRE) won on his hurdling debut last time but was found out in this better race under a penalty. He has enough ability to win again, but would need a less competitive race to do so. (op 4-1)
Great Mates(IRE) is a half-brother to Racing Demon, but again failed to see his race out. He looks a horse with problems and his hanging right in the home straight was far from encouraging. (op 9-1)

371 RED LION HOTEL, TIVERTON NOVICES' H'CAP CHASE (16 fncs) 2m 5f 110y
2:50 (2:50) (Class 4) (0-100,98) 5-Y-O+ **£4,358** (£1,279; £639; £319)

Form RPR
0-U0 **1** **Over The Flow**[11] 169 8-11-6 92 DarylJacob 101
(Bob Buckler) *in tch: wnt 3rd whn hit 10th: chal after 3 out: rdn to ld bef last: styd on wl: rdn out* **7/1**[3]
253- **2** 1¾ **Spirit Of Lake (IRE)**[26] 5318 8-10-11 83 AndrewThornton 90
(Karen George) *trckd ldr: led 5th: rdn whn hrd pressed 2 out: hdd bef last: no ex* **9/2**[1]
P3/4 **3** 14 **Justabout**[11] 171 7-10-10 82 JoeTizzard 75
(Colin Tizzard) *led tl 5th: chsd ldr: rdn after 11th: one pce fr 4 out* **9/2**[1]
540- **4** 3½ **Outclass**[54] 4821 8-10-0 72 oh8 DavidEngland 62
(Harry Chisman) *in tch: rdn after 4 out: sn one pce* **28/1**
/30- **5** 13 **Glad Big (GER)**[28] 5280 8-11-12 98 WarrenMarston 75
(Richard Phillips) *mid-div: wnt 4th and sn rdn after 4 out: wknd after 3 out* **11/1**
03U- **6** 4½ **Killing Me Softly**[24] 5366 9-10-5 77 LiamTreadwell 49
(Brian Forsey) *towards rr: drvn along fr 9th: nvr a danger* **9/1**
PU-0 **7** 19 **Dolly Grey**[11] 167 7-11-0 86 (t) TomO'Brien 39
(Grant Cann) *mid-div: struggling after 10th: sn in rr: t.o* **33/1**
00-4 **P** **Go Free**[6] 264 9-11-4 97 CharlieWallis(7) —
(John O'Shea) *mid-div: tendency to jump rt at times: rdn after 11th: sn wknd: bhd whn p.u bef 4 out* **22/1**
/0-2 **P** **Haoyunma (IRE)**[18] 56 8-10-4 79 SeanQuinlan(3) —
(Harry Chisman) *allways towards rr: rdn after 9th: sn lost tch: p.u bef 11th* **12/1**
F42- **P** **Oncle Kid (FR)**[50] 4917 8-11-7 98 JimmyDerham(5) —
(Paul Henderson) *mid-div whn p.u bef 3rd: dismntd* **11/2**[2]
000- **P** **Barton Alf**[34] 5172 6-11-8 94 DougieCostello —
(Neil Mulholland) *prom tl wknd after 9th: p.u bef 11th* **12/1**
004- **P** **Bernie The Banker**[57] 4765 6-11-8 94 DavidDennis —
(W W Dennis) *a towards rr: bhd whn p.u bef 4 out* **12/1**
5m 22.2s (0.80) **Going Correction** 0.0s/f (Good) 12 Ran SP% **116.4**
Speed ratings: **98,97,92,91,86 84,77,—,—,— —,—**
toteswingers: 1&2 £8.80, 1&3 £9.20, 2&3 £5.00 CSF £38.01 CT £158.99 TOTE £11.50: £2.80, £1.40, £2.00; EX 33.80.
Owner Mrs Heather Dunn, Mrs Anne Collier **Bred** Mrs H R Dunn **Trained** Henley, Somerset

FOCUS
A shocking race in which the 12 contestants had run 193 times between them, gaining a mere eight wins and four of those were contributed by Killing Me Softy, who has not won since 2005. The winner is rated in line with the best of his hurdles form.

NOTEBOOK
Over The Flow wasn't given a hard time when last seen over C&D (tried to refuse at the first on chasing debut.). Her jumping was more assured on this occasion and she ran on well to shed her maiden status at the 18th attempt.. However, it would be unwise to back her next time given the low quality of this race. (op 17-2)
Spirit Of Lake(IRE) was well backed for his chasing debut and he jumped soundly. He was not progressive over hurdles so it would be optimistic to expect a win next time. (op 15-2 tchd 4-1)
Justabout ran well on his return to action at this venue last time, but downed tools a long way from home here and he is not one to trust. (op 5-1 tchd 4-1)
Outclass is a low-grade maiden from a stable who have yet to send out a winner from 36 tries. She was racing from 8lb out of the handicap and her proximity to the places underlines again how poor a race it was.
Glad Big(GER) has yet to show any form since returning from a long absence and is one to treat with caution. (op 9-1)
Killing Me Softly looked far from keen throughout. (op 17-2 tchd 8-1)
Oncle Kid(FR) Official explanation: jockey said gelding lost its action (op 20-1)
Bernie The Banker came in for some support but his jumping was not up to scratch and he looks poorly handicapped in any case. (op 20-1)

372 PAR INN H'CAP HURDLE (8 hdls) 2m 3f
3:20 (3:20) (Class 3) (0-135,135) 4-Y-0+ **£6,495** (£1,918; £959; £479; £239)

Form RPR
22-5 **1** **Tabaran (FR)**[10] 196 7-10-2 118 (tp) OliverDayman(7) 124+
(Alison Thorpe) *mid-div: hdwy 6th: rdn to ld appr 2 out: styd on strly: comf* **9/2**[1]
1P3- **2** 6 **Humbel Ben (IRE)**[164] 2690 7-10-3 112 HarrySkelton 113+
(Alan Jones) *in tch: travelling wl and led briefly appr 2 out: sn rdn and hld: kpt on same pce* **6/1**[2]
140- **3** ½ **Akarshan (IRE)**[23] 5393 5-10-11 123 DPFahy(3) 123
(Evan Williams) *hld up towards rr of midfield: hdwy 6th: rdn to chse ldrs after 3 out: styd on same pce fr next* **16/1**
134- **4** 3½ **Mohanad (IRE)**[23] 5393 4-10-4 123 MarcGoldstein(5) 115
(Sheena West) *trckd ldr: led 3rd: rdn and hdd appr 2 out: kpt on same pce* **6/1**[2]
0/2- **5** nk **Mae Cigan (FR)**[14] 4486 7-10-2 111 JimmyMcCarthy 108
(Michael Blanshard) *in tch: nt fluent 6th: sn rdn: styd on same pce fr 3 out: lame* **10/1**
F20- **6** 10 **Working Title (IRE)**[60] 4698 8-11-10 133 APMcCoy 122
(Nicky Henderson) *trckd ldrs: rdn and ev ch appr 2 out: wknd qckly* **15/2**[3]
10F- **7** 14 **Like A Duke (FR)**[29] 5252 7-10-3 112 TomScudamore 87
(Colin Tizzard) *a towards rr* **25/1**
50-1 **8** 1¾ **Shalamiyr (FR)**[13] 129 5-10-6 115 TomO'Brien 88
(Philip Hobbs) *trckd ldrs: rdn after 5th: wknd after 3 out* **12/1**
42U- **9** 1 **The Real Deal (IRE)**[33] 5182 9-10-12 121 DarylJacob 94
(Nick Williams) *led tl 3rd: chsd ldrs: rdn after 5th: wknd 3 out* **15/2**[3]
0-50 **10** ¾ **Freddy's Star (IRE)**[2] 331 8-10-8 117 WillKennedy 89
(Gerald Ham) *a towards rr* **33/1**
00-U **11** nk **Nampour (FR)**[9] 94 5-11-6 134 GilesHawkins(5) 106
(Philip Hobbs) *towards rr of midfield: rdn after 5th: sn btn* **12/1**
503- **12** 17 **Baccalaureate (FR)**[33] 5180 4-11-1 129 (t) PaddyBrennan 80
(Nigel Twiston-Davies) *mid-div: rdn after 5th: wknd after next: t.o* **22/1**
/00- **13** 11 **Oslot (FR)**[177] 2417 8-11-11 134 NickScholfield 80
(Paul Nicholls) *nvr travelling: a in rr* **28/1**
4P-0 **14** 74 **Raslan**[16] 94 7-11-12 135 (tp) TimmyMurphy 15
(David Pipe) *nvr travelling: sn in rr: t.o fr after 5th* **20/1**
4m 27.5s (-6.40) **Going Correction** -0.15s/f (Good)
WFA 4 from 5yo+ 18lb 14 Ran SP% **120.0**
Speed ratings (Par 107): **107,104,104,102,102 98,92,91,91,91 90,83,79,48**
toteswingers: 1&2 £4.70, 1&3 £19.20, 1&3 not won. CSF £29.13 CT £404.39 TOTE £5.50: £1.90, £2.70, £5.80; EX 35.40.
Owner Mrs A M Thorpe **Bred** S A Aga Khan **Trained** Bronwydd Arms, Carmarthens

FOCUS
The going was officially changed to good before this competitive handicap hurdle. The form has a solid look to it.

NOTEBOOK
Tabaran(FR) has been performing with credit throughout the early part of the summer season and deserved to win this for his capable claiming rider who gets on well with him. He is not very big so the fact that he was carrying such a light weight was an advantage. Alison Thorpe does well with this kind of horse and it would not be a surprise if he was to progress further, perhaps in the fashion of the likes of former or present stablemates Treaty Flyer and Rushneeyriver. (op 13-2)
Humbel Ben(IRE) was well supported on his handicap debut and travelled smoothly before hanging and finding little off the bridle. He is clearly capable of winning races, but has a question mark over his attitude now. (tchd 11-2)
Akarshan(IRE) proved he can act on a left-handed track with a staying-on third here. However he will need to find some improvement if he is to win again as the handicapper may have his measure. (tchd 18-1)
Mohanad(IRE) ran creditably over hurdles at Sandown last time, but never looked like playing a part in the finish. He will need to improve if he is to win over hurdles and his trainer is now 38 runners and 142 days without a winner. (tchd 11-2)
Mae Cigan(FR) ran well at Ffos Las on his last hurdling start, but he lacked the ability to land a telling blow. He will be better in a lower-grade race. Official explanation: vet said gelding was lame left-fore (op 15-2)
Working Title(IRE) was disappointing over fences at the Cheltenham Festival last time and he is now winless from seven tries in handicap company over hurdles. (op 9-1)
Like A Duke(FR) has been having troubles jumping fences, but could never get into this. (op 20-1)
Nampour(FR) needs some respite from the handicapper if he is to return to winning ways. (tchd 14-1)
Oslot(FR) won the Galway Plate in 2008, but has lost his way since and now has plenty to prove.

Raslan began to sulk as soon as he realised he had to race. (op 16-1)

373 WOLBOROUGH INN, NEWTON ABBOT H'CAP CHASE (13 fncs) 2m 110y

3:50 (3:50) (Class 4) (0-115,114) 5-Y-0+ **£4,358** (£1,279; £639; £319)

Form RPR

/53- **1** **Earth Dream (IRE)**[308] 934 7-11-5 **114** .... MrRMahon(7) 124+
(Paul Nicholls) *chsd ldrs: rdn to ld 3 out: pckd last: kpt on: drvn out* **9/4**[2]

64-1 **2** *3* **Foreign King (USA)**[5] 276 6-10-13 **106** 7ex .... JimmyDerham(5) 113
(Seamus Mullins) *hld up in last pair: wnt 2nd 3 out: sn rdn: kpt on but being hld by wnr* **5/4**[1]

2F/6 **3** *26* **De Luain Gorm (IRE)**[13] 130 12-10-12 **107** .... MrGGallagher(7) 93
(Chris Down) *led after 1st: rdn and hdd 3 out: sn wknd* **8/1**

305- **4** *dist* **Young Tot (IRE)**[20] 36 12-10-8 **101** .... IanPopham(5) 48
(Carroll Gray) *struggling in last pair 6th: sn lost tch: t.o* **25/1**

440- **F** **Gleann An Sagart**[22] 5 8-11-12 **114** .... TomScudamore —
(Michael Scudamore) *led tl after 1st: w ldr whn fell 7th: fatally injured* **4/1**[3]

4m 4.30s (-2.20) **Going Correction** 0.0s/f (Good) **5** Ran SP% **110.2**
Speed ratings: **105,103,91,73,—**
CSF £5.77 TOTE £2.80: £1.10, £2.40; EX 6.20.

Owner Mrs Catherine Penny **Bred** Gerald McStay **Trained** Ditcheat, Somerset

FOCUS
A modest handicap chase and the form is rated around the first two.

NOTEBOOK
Earth Dream(IRE) made a winning return after a ten-month absence on only his second chasing start. His trainer reported he would be better over a longer trip so the strong pace helped him in that respect. He can remain competitive over the summer. (op 11-4 tchd 3-1and 10-3 in a place)
Foreign King(USA) was an easy winner on his chasing debut at Exeter last time, but he did not look at home on this tight course. He is likely to be hit hard by the handicapper for his previous success and could find life more difficult. (op Evens)
De Luain Gorm(IRE) set off in front, but was quickly left behind by two classier rivals once he was headed. He will need to find significant improvement if he is to be competitive at the age of 12. (op 10-1 tchd 15-2)
Young Tot(IRE) was never travelling and looks a light of former days. (op 20-1)

374 BISHOP JOHN DE GRANDISSON, BISHOPSTEIGNTON (S) HURDLE (8 hdls) 2m 3f

4:20 (4:20) (Class 5) 4-Y-0+ **£2,055** (£599; £299)

Form RPR

31P- **1** **Mhilu (IRE)**[212] 1784 8-11-0 0 .... (bt) APMcCoy 115+
(Gary Brown) *in tch: led gng wl after 3 out: clr whn wnt rt next: rdn out flat* **10/11**[1]

P0 3 **2** *0* **Intac (IRE)**[6] 264 8-11-5 102 .... JoeTizzard 107
(Colin Tizzard) *chsd ldrs: drvn thrght fnl circ in tch: plugged on after 3 out: wnt 2nd nr fin: no ch w wnr* **9/2**[3]

63U- **3** *¾* **Super Fly**[63] 4656 8-10-9 100 .... (p) DonalDevereux(5) 101
(Debra Hamer) *mid-div: hdwy whn hit 6th: rdn to chse ldrs after 3 out: styd on same pce* **11/4**[2]

3PP- **4** *2* **Casual Garcia**[69] 4497 5-11-2 102 .... (b) TommyPhelan(3) 105
(Mark Gillard) *hld up in mid-div: hdwy appr 6th: rdn and ev ch after 3 out: sn hld: one pce fr next* **25/1**

010/ **5** *9* **Lesmoir**[444] 4182 8-11-0 0 .... AndrewThornton 91
(Tony Newcombe) *hld up: rdn after 3 out: sme late prog: nvr a factor* **14/1**

/P0- **6** *7* **Galantos (GER)**[204] 1926 9-11-0 90 .... (p) SeamusDurack 85
(Jane Southcombe) *led 2nd tl after next: styd prom: led appr 6th: rdn and hdd after 3 out: fdd bef next* **33/1**

-035 **7** *½* **Just Mossie**[4] 298 5-10-9 84 .... (b) TomO'Connor(5) 85
(Bill Turner) *trckd ldrs: rdn after 3 out: sn wknd* **33/1**

PU-6 **8** *40* **Triple Bluff**[6] 264 7-10-11 96 .... (b[1]) HaddenFrost(3) 49
(James Frost) *trckd ldrs: led after 3rd: rdn and hdd bef 6th: sn wknd: t.o* **12/1**

05P/ **P** **Man Overboard**[37] 8-10-4 0 .... QuintonJones(10) —
(Gary Brown) *sn detached: t.o whn p.u after 3 out* **33/1**

0P0- **P** **Silver Emblem**[74] 4411 5-10-7 68 .... (p) LiamHeard —
(Colin Heard) *struggling in rr 4th: t.o whn p.u bef 6th* **100/1**

4m 33.3s (-0.60) **Going Correction** -0.15s/f (Good) **10** Ran SP% **125.3**
Speed ratings (Par 103): **95,91,90,90,86 83,83,66,—,—**
toteswingers: 1&2 £2.50, 1&3 £2.30, 2&3 £3.20 CSF £6.00 TOTE £2.10: £1.30, £1.10, £1.50; EX 8.90.There was no bid for the winner.

Owner Anthony Tory **Bred** D J Fitzpatrick **Trained** East Garston, Berks

FOCUS
An uncompetitive selling hurdle which saw the champion jockey benefit at Rodi Greene's expense after the withdrawal of paper favourite Financialregulator (reported travel problems), who is trained by Mhilu's former handler Gordon Elliott. The easy winner was over a stone off his old mark with the next four all close to their marks.

NOTEBOOK
Mhilu(IRE) was making his debut for the Gary Brown yard (he rents stables from the winning rider) and, despite jumping right at all the flights of hurdles, won with consummate ease under replacement jockey A.P.McCoy to land a gamble. He is not the most straightforward but at this low grade he can remain a force. (tchd 11-10)
Intac(IRE) was trounced in a seller over C&D last week. He was under pressure from a long way out here and looked slow, but he is at least running in the right grade. (op 9-1)
Super Fly isn't the most reliable but turned in one of his better efforts in cheekpieces (replacing the usual visor). He is another who is no better than plating class. (op 10-3)
Casual Garcia was picked up cheaply by current connections a couple of weeks ago and a drop to selling company didn't bring about much improvement. He looked unwilling off the bridle. (op 20-1)
Lesmoir won his bumper here in August 2007 but was never in contention on his first start for 15 months. He should strip fitter for this and a low-grade race could fall his way.
Triple Bluff was representing the Jimmy Frost yard who had won the previous three runnings of this race but this representative gave up tamely once headed. (op 11-1 tchd 10-1)

375 SOUTH PACIFIC BAR, TEIGNMOUTH STANDARD OPEN NATIONAL HUNT FLAT RACE 2m 1f

4:50 (4:51) (Class 6) 4-6-Y-0 **£1,747** (£509; £254)

Form RPR

1 **Mr Hudson (IRE)**[51] 5-10-9 0 .... MrRMahon(7) 102+
(Paul Nicholls) *mde all: hung rt ent fnl bnd: rdn over 2f out: styd on wl to assert fnl f: rdn out* **9/2**[3]

10- **2** *5* **Milgen Bay**[37] 5129 4-11-5 0 .... LeightonAspell 100
(Oliver Sherwood) *trckd ldrs: rdn to chse wnr over 2f out: kpt on but readily hld ins fnl f* **14/1**

4- **3** *1¼* **Grandads Horse**[21] 20 4-10-12 0 .... TomO'Brien 92
(Alan Jones) *w wnr tl rdn over 3f out: sltly outpcd: styd on again fnl f: wnt 3rd towards fin* **40/1**

4 *½* **Long Row** 4-10-5 0 .... TimmyMurphy 84
(Stuart Howe) *hld up towards rr: nudged along and stdy prog fr over 2f out: styd on fnl f: nrst fin* **66/1**

2- **5** *shd* **Maggie Aron**[156] 2842 4-9-12 0 .... MrTomDavid(7) 84
(Tim Vaughan) *trckd ldrs: rdn 3f out: styd on same pce fnl 2f* **11/1**

6 *¾* **Weldone Honey** 5-10-2 0 .... MrMByrne(7) 88
(Peter Bowen) *mid-div: styd on same pce fnl 2f* **22/1**

7 *nk* **Lieutenant Miller** 4-10-12 0 .... APMcCoy 90
(Nicky Henderson) *in tch: nudged along 1/2-way: rdn to chse ldrs over 3f out: one pce fnl 2f: edgd lft fnl f* **13/8**[1]

8 *8* **Littledean Jimmy (IRE)** 5-10-9 0 .... CharlieWallis(7) 87
(John O'Shea) *hld up towards rr: rdn over 3f out: sme late prog: nvr a danger* **40/1**

9 *3¾* **Le Roi Max (FR)** 6-11-2 0 .... PaddyBrennan 86
(Nigel Twiston-Davies) *hld up towards rr: rdn into midfield over 4f out: wknd fnl f* **10/1**

10 *19* **Mr Bachster (IRE)** 5-11-2 0 .... JackDoyle 67
(Victor Dartnall) *mid-div: rdn over 4f out: wknd over 3f out* **4/1**[2]

11 *1½* **Right Move (IRE)** 5-10-11 0 .... IanPopham(5) 65
(Caroline Keevil) *mid-div: rdn over 4f out: wknd over 2f out* **100/1**

12 *14* **Bardolf (IRE)** 4-10-12 0 .... RobertThornton 49
(Alan King) *nvr bttr than mid-div* **10/1**

13 *4* **Bonny Prince Luso (IRE)** 5-11-2 0 .... NickScholfield 49
(Stuart Kittow) *mid-div tl wknd over 4f out* **66/1**

0- **14** *14* **Rabbitkettle Lake (IRE)**[53] 4853 6-11-2 0 .... JimmyMcCarthy 37
(Michael Blanshard) *mid-div tl wknd 5f out: t.o* **100/1**

15 *14* **Hartland Point** 5-10-9 0 .... MrMLurcock(7) 24
(Malcolm Beck) *a towards rr* **150/1**

16 *46* **Dunnicks Spindle** 4-10-0 0 .... KeiranBurke(5) —
(Patrick Rodford) *mid-div tl 7f out: t.o* **150/1**

4m 4.60s (4.50) **Going Correction** -0.15s/f (Good) **16** Ran SP% **125.0**
Speed ratings: **83,80,80,79,79 79,79,75,73,64 64,57,55,49,42 20**
toteswingers: 1&2 £11.80, 1&3 £32.80, 2&3 £24.00 CSF £65.21 TOTE £5.60: £1.60, £5.40, £11.20; EX 61.20 Place 6: £21.53 Place 5: £15.33.

Owner Mark Tincknell **Bred** Margo & Julie Harty **Trained** Ditcheat, Somerset

FOCUS
A potentially informative bumper which could herald several winners. An easy race to rate.

NOTEBOOK
Mr Hudson(IRE) made a winning debut in a Larkhill maiden point from which the fifth Fort View has subsequently won a hunter chase. He then chased home the potentially useful Master Flight at that venue last time. This good-topped gelding from the Barber/Nicholls yard still has plenty to learn but he could develop into a good performer. (op 7-1 tchd 4-1)
Milgen Bay ran well under his penalty for his in-form yard. His proximity shows that the form has some credence and he can acquit himself well once sent hurdling. (op 12-1)
Grandads Horse has run well in both his starts in bumpers, suggesting he will be better when presented with a longer trip over hurdles.
Long Row is a Flat-bred filly who ran creditably on her debut, but she is likely to fare better on the level than over hurdles in the future. Her yard is winless since last May.
Maggie Aron was receiving plenty of weight but was unable to make it tell. She is related to stayers so could do better in time. (op 17-2)
Weldone Honey hails from a yard which is in great form but shaped as if a longer trip would suit. (op 20-1)
Lieutenant Miller is a small, lengthy sort who is related to the useful General Millar. He was sent off favourite but showed no immediate sparkle, and may need to strengthen. (op 5-4)
Mr Bachster(IRE), a half-brother to bumper winner Mic's Delight, was well backed. He could never land a telling blow and will need to learn plenty from this. (op 7-1)
Bardolf(IRE) looked in need of the run and that proved the case in the race. In time he can do better. (op 14-1)
T/Plt: £35.00. Pool £75,880.51 - 1,578.50 winning tickets T/Qpdt: £11.40. Pool £4,948.11 - 318.86 winning tickets TM

376 - 378a (Foreign Racing) - See Raceform Interactive

249 TOWCESTER (R-H)

Tuesday, May 18

OFFICIAL GOING: Good to firm (10.3)
Wind: nil Weather: sunny and muggy

379 TONY MERRY AND FRIENDS AT GG.COM MAIDEN HURDLE (10 hdls) 2m 3f 110y

6:10 (6:11) (Class 4) 4-Y-0+ **£3,252** (£955; £477; £238)

Form RPR

U-0 **1** **Murcar**[11] 191 5-10-9 0 .... GilesHawkins(5) 114+
(Alison Thorpe) *t.k.h: wandering into sme hurdles: led tl wandered bdly 5th: led again 7th: drew clr w one rival sn after 3 out: gng best fr next: drvn out* **7/4**[1]

550- **2** *3½* **Naughty Naughty**[73] 4425 5-10-7 92 .... JimmyMcCarthy 100
(Brendan Powell) *cl up: taking t.k.h 5th: rdn to go 2nd 3 out: sn 5 l bhd wnr: kpt on but a hld after* **7/1**

26-3 **3** *27* **Magical Treasure**[12] 167 6-11-0 0 .... PaulMoloney 83
(Sophie Leech) *midfield: disp 4th and rdn 3 out: lost tch qckly: wnt poor 3rd after last* **4/1**[3]

0/P- **4** *shd* **Knightsbridgelives (IRE)**[45] 7-11-0 100 .... (t) ChristianWilliams 80
(Lawney Hill) *plld hrd: hit 4th: dashed up fr last to ld jst after 5th: hdd 7th: sn fdd after next: 17 l 3rd 2 out: lost 3rd after last* **14/1**

U-6 **5** *2* **Atabaas Allure (FR)**[18] 82 4-10-2 0 .... ColinBolger 66
(Chris Gordon) *in rr div: effrt 7th: disp 4th and in tch 3 out: sn wknd* **40/1**

P6-0 **6** *13* **Saffron Spring**[12] 180 7-10-0 64 .... MarkQuinlan(7) 59
(Mrs S P Stretton) *taken down early and mounted on crse: nt fluent in rr div: pushed along 3rd: rdn and lost tch bef 3 out: t.o next* **150/1**

00P/ **P** **Sykalino (FR)**[552] 2155 7-11-0 0 .... TimmyMurphy —
(Alan Fleming) *hld up in rr: lost tch 6th: t.o bef 3 out: p.u next* **25/1**

643- **P** **Like Ice**[22] 25 5-11-0 0 .... JamieMoore —
(Philip Middleton) *racd in 3rd tl 7th: drvn and wknd bef next: bdly t.o whn p.u bef last* **11/4**[2]

4m 51.7s (-17.90) **Going Correction** -0.975s/f (Hard)
WFA 4 from 5yo+ 18lb **8** Ran SP% **109.1**
Speed ratings (Par 105): **96,94,83,83,82 77,—,—**
toteswingers:1&2:£2.80, 1&3:£2.60, 2&3:£4.40 CSF £13.26 TOTE £1.80: £1.02, £3.30, £1.60; EX 12.50.

Owner Centaur Global Partnership I **Bred** John W Ford And Peter J Skinner **Trained** Bronwydd Arms, Carmarthens

FOCUS
A weak event run at a muddling pace. Improvement from the winner with the second rated to his mark.

NOTEBOOK
Murcar, officially rated 72 when least seen on the Flat, had shown a modicum of ability in this sphere at Aintree 11 days previously and improved on that effort to score with a bit in hand. Well backed, he set out to make all the running and, apart from a brief spell in mid-race, he was always at the head of affairs. He made a meal of the fifth from home, jinking left before getting over it, but, after getting back on an even keel, was never seriously threatened. (tchd 15-8)
Naughty Naughty finished second here on her hurdling debut and, as three subsequent outings had been disappointing, it seems fair to assume she enjoys racing at Towcester. Held up in the early stages, she chased the winner from three out and stayed on gamely to the end. (op 8-1 tchd 6-1)
Magical Treasure, third over 2m3f at Newton Abbot on his hurdling debut 12 days previously, is bred to appreciate this stiffer test and, after becoming outpaced turning for home, finished well to grab second on the line. An even longer trip may now beckon. (op 3-1)
Knightsbridgelives(IRE), whose form for Alan King was only modest, has cut little ice in recent point-to-points, but posted a better effort here. He quickened to grab the lead in mid-race, chased the pace when re-headed by the winner and lost third only in the dying strides. (op 18-1 tchd 12-1)
Atabaas Allure(FR), whose two previous starts over hurdles had produced nothing to get excited about, once again ran only moderately.
Saffron Spring also revealed strictly limited ability, figuring towards the rear for much of the race and looking one-paced in the home straight. (op 125-1)

380 HAYGAIN HAY STEAMERS NOVICES' (S) HURDLE (8 hdls) 2m
6:40 (6:41) (Class 5) 4-Y-0+ **£1,951** (£573; £286; £143)

Form RPR
45-0 **1** **Seaquel**14 [134] 4-9-12 90....(v1) CharlieHuxley(3) 97+
(Andrew Haynes) *mde all: 7 l clr 2 out: kpt up the gallop to score readily* **9/4**1
33-4 **2** *8* **Bari Bay**8 [250] 4-9-10 69.... JimmyDerham(5) 89
(Seamus Mullins) *bhd: effrt and rdn in 5th whn mstke 3 out: wnt 3rd bef 2 out and 2nd between last two: nvr looked like rching wnr* **9/2**3
0U-4 **3** *12* **The Randy Bishop**18 [75] 10-10-7 90.... LeeEdwards(5) 89
(Tony Carroll) *nrly a 2nd: rdn and outpcd by wnr after 3 out: lost 2nd between last two: fin weakly* **14/1**
40-5 **4** *18* **Dundry**13 [157] 9-10-12 98....(p) JamieMoore 69
(Gary Moore) *pressed ldrs: wnt 3rd and rdn 3 out: wknd qckly bef next: reluctant between last two: lft remote 4th at last* **11/4**2
/50- **5** *8* **Cripsey Brook**167 [2640] 12-10-12 95....(b) JamesReveley 61
(Keith Reveley) *bhd: blnd 3rd: modest prog in 6th whn hit 3 out: sn struggling* **7/1**
0 **6** *75* **Sufficient Warning**13 [154] 6-10-12 0.... DarylJacob —
(Ralph Smith) *bhd: lost tch 5th: hopelessly t.o whn blnd last* **50/1**
520/ **P** **Monets Masterpiece (USA)**405 [4906] 7-10-12 0....(t) LiamTreadwell —
(P Kelsall) *last whn pckd bdly 1st: lost tch and mstke 2nd: trailed rnd: bdly t.o whn p.u 2 out* **40/1**
4P/0 **U** **Amazing Request**9 [227] 6-10-5 0.... MissIsabelTompsett(7) —
(Bernard Llewellyn) *towards rr: mstke 4th: lost tch after next: wnt 30 l 4th but blnd and uns rdr last* **16/1**
0 **P** **Ruby Delta**17 [93] 5-10-12 0....(b) CharliePoste —
(Alan Juckes) *plld hrd and looked awkward: 3rd tl wnt 2nd briefly bef 5th: wknd qckly u.p next: t.o and p.u 2 out* **66/1**
P **Extracurricular (USA)**25 4-10-1 0.... KeithMercer —
(Steve Gollings) *chsd ldrs tl 5th: bdly t.o whn p.u 2 out* **28/1**
/0P- **P** **London Times (IRE)**258 [1375] 5-10-9 85.... CharlieStudd(3) —
(Simon Lewis) *uns rdr leaving paddock: chsd ldrs tl lost grnd rapidly u.p bef 3 out: t.o and p.u next* **40/1**
3m 48.2s (-19.70) **Going Correction** -0.975s/f (Hard)
WFA 4 from 5yo+ 18lb 11 Ran SP% **112.4**
Speed ratings (Par 103): **110,106,100,91,87 49,—,—,—,— —**
toteswingers:1&2:£3.40, 1&3:£8.60, 2&3:£10.80 CSF £11.72 TOTE £3.50: £1.10, £1.30, £4.80; EX 12.20.There was no bid for the winner
Owner Allan Drewett **Bred** Michael E Broughton **Trained** Limpley Stoke, Bath
FOCUS
A weak race, short on depth, but the first two are on the upgrade.
NOTEBOOK
Seaquel was fitted with a first-time visor after flopping on her latest start and the headgear made all the difference. Strongly supported beforehand, she grabbed the lead immediately the tapes went up and made all. The opposition was nothing special, but she scored with plenty in hand and may collect again in this grade, if the visor continues to have the desired effect. (op 3-1)
Bari Bay, third from a rating of 68 in a selling handicap hurdle at Taunton in April, provides a fair guide to the form. Held up early on, she started to make progress four out but, after making a mistake at the third-last, had little chance of catching the winner. (op 8-1)
The Randy Bishop, a winning novice chaser, had run poorly in this grade on his return to hurdling 18 days earlier and, while this was an improvement, it would be wise not to get carried away with what he achieved. To his credit, he was always chasing the pace and jumped adequately. (op 12-1)
Dundry lined up still a maiden over hurdles, but his fourth at Plumpton in March was the best jumps form of offer, so this performance was disappointing. He was never closer than fourth and finished in that spot with the help of Amazing Request's blunder at the final flight. (op 2-1)
Monets Masterpiece(USA) Official explanation: jockey said he thought gelding was lame but pulled up sound
Amazing Request might well have taken fourth had he not unseated his rider at the last. He was disputing that position when jumping too clumsily for the partenership to stay intact.

381 ZEDZED.UK.COM E-COMMERCE H'CAP CHASE (12 fncs) 2m 110y
7:10 (7:10) (Class 5) (0-95,95) 5-Y-0+ **£3,252** (£955; £477; £238)

Form RPR
65-4 **1** **Beauchamp Viking**12 [183] 6-10-2 76....(t) JimmyDerham(5) 92+
(Simon Burrough) *nt fluent 3rd: dropped out last tl after 5th: 8 l 6th 3 out: sn impr on inner: wnt 2nd 2 out and led last: readily drew clr* **13/2**3
5-11 **2** *4* **Lord Gunnerslake (IRE)**6 [278] 10-11-0 83 7ex....(v) APMcCoy 93
(Tim Vaughan) *pushed along early: wnt 3rd at 6th and 2nd at 9th: led 3 out: rdn bef next: hdd last: plugged on wout recrse to whip* **1/1**1
62F- **3** *9* **Jardin De Vienne (FR)**27 [5313] 8-11-5 95....(v1) BrianToomey(7) 96
(Renee Robeson) *towards rr: effrt on outer but rdn bef 3 out: disp 2nd briefly next: reluctant up the hill and sn gave up* **7/1**
F06- **4** *27* **Transvestite (IRE)**28 [2387] 8-11-7 90....(t) SamJones 64
(Tor Sturgis) *towards rr: qckly tailed himself off after 5th: plugged on bef 2 out to go remote 4th cl home* **20/1**
P/3- **5** *1 1/4* **Jose Bove**58 [4763] 8-11-0 83....(t) WillKennedy 56
(Henrietta Knight) *led: hdd 3 out: drvn bef next where lost 2nd: fdd tamely* **4/1**2
F55- **6** *14* **Dasher Reilly (USA)**170 [2602] 9-10-1 73.... EamonDehdashti(3) 32
(Aytach Sadik) *sn off the bridle: in rr and struggling 6th: t.o after 3 out* **28/1**
/30- **7** *7* **Un Autre Espere**364 [372] 11-9-5 70 oh11 ow1....(b) JoshWall(10) 22
(Trevor Wall) *t.k.h: pressed ldr: mstke 8th: lost 2nd at next and dropped out rapidly: t.o: fin reluctantly* **66/1**
000- **8** *33* **The Darling Boy**84 [4216] 5-11-6 89.... PaddyBrennan 8
(Tom George) *chsd ldrs: hit 8th: drvn after next: sn struggling: t.o* **9/1**
4m 0.50s (-15.60) **Going Correction** -0.975s/f (Hard) 8 Ran SP% **115.5**
Speed ratings: **97,95,90,78,77 71,67,52**
toteswingers:1&2:£2.60, 1&3:£9.10, 2&3:£1.70 CSF £14.21 CT £47.96 TOTE £12.60: £3.70, £1.10, £1.70; EX 26.50.
Owner Mrs Maureen Emery **Bred** E Penser **Trained** West Buckland, Somerset
FOCUS
A modest event with the top-weight rated 95. A big step forward from the winner with the second rated to his mark.
NOTEBOOK
Beauchamp Viking, never in the first three in 14 previous outings, had earned his best finishing position when fourth last time out and improved again here. In rear early and still well adrift three out, he started to make eyecatching progress at the next and jumped into the lead at the last. Just what the form amounts to is hard to judge, but this was much his best display and the handicapper will surely take note. (op 7-1 tchd 8-1 and 6-1)
Lord Gunnerslake(IRE), bidding for a hat-trick after victories at Huntingdon and Fontwell, was carrying a 7lb penalty and it proved too much for him. Held up in touch early on, he was booted into the lead approaching two out in an attempt to out-slog his rivals. He could not shrug off the winner, though, and was made to look one-paced on the run-in. Perhaps this race, his second in six days, came too soon. (tchd 10-11 and 11-10)
Jardin De Vienne(FR), a sound second from a mark of 94 at Leicester in March, was just 1lb higher here, but ran moderately. He made a mistake at the fourth, which caused him to lose valuable ground, and third was the best place he ever held. (op 9-2)
Transvestite(IRE), a decent Flat performer but largely disappointing over hurdles, ran an extraordinary race on this first try over fences. Fitted with a first-time tongue-strap, he was tailed off at one stage, but picked up in the home straight and was staying on strongly at the finish. (tchd 18-1)
Jose Bove, a course-and-distance winner in 2008, had run encouragingly following a long absence fitted with a tongue-tie last time out. Despite wearing it again here, he ran as if breathing might have been a problem, as he faded dramatically after taking the field along until the third-last. (op 7-1)
The Darling Boy Official explanation: vet said gelding bled from the nose

382 GEORGE SINGH H'CAP HURDLE (10 hdls) 2m 3f 110y
7:40 (7:40) (Class 4) (0-115,112) 4-Y-0+ **£3,903** (£1,146; £573; £286)

Form RPR
00-6 **1** **Ashmolian (IRE)**14 [137] 7-9-9 86 oh1....(p) GemmaGracey-Davison(5) 98+
(Zoe Davison) *hld up in last pair tl 6th: stdy prog after 3 out to go 2nd on inner bef 2 out: rdn to ld last: asserted cl home* **4/1**3
63-1 **2** *3/4* **Alldunnandusted (IRE)**18 [84] 6-10-10 101.... JimmyDerham(5) 112+
(Seamus Mullins) *chsd ldrs: wnt 3rd gng wl 3 out: led bef next: drvn and hdd last: no ex fnl 100yds* **5/2**1
62-F **3** *20* **Mayor Of Kilcock**19 [55] 7-10-13 106.... AnthonyFreeman(7) 97
(James Danahar) *racd freely in ld: clr 3rd tl 5th: rdn and hdd bef 2 out: racd w high hd carriage after and nt run on: poor 3rd whn hit last* **3/1**2
166- **4** *5* **Thenameescapesme**194 [2081] 10-10-13 99.... JasonMaguire 85
(Kim Bailey) *trckd ldrs: wnt 2nd 3 out: sn rdn: lost pl bef next and plodded home* **9/2**
PP3- **5** *2* **Benmore Boy (IRE)**22 [22] 7-11-12 112....(p) PaulMoloney 96
(Henrietta Knight) *rdn after 5th: lost tch 7th: wl adrift 3 out: v mod late prog* **8/1**
/05- **6** *1/2* **Tifoso (FR)**13 [4464] 5-11-9 109....(e) SamJones 94
(Richard Guest) *settled in rr: prog after 5th: 4th next: fdd tamely wl bef 2 out* **20/1**
14-0 **7** *3 1/4* **Pips Assertive Way**12 [172] 9-10-6 92.... MattieBatchelor 73
(Tony Carroll) *pressed ldr tl 7th: rdn and wknd bef 2 out* **22/1**
62P- **8** *50* **Highland River**8 [3] 4-10-5 99.... EamonDehdashti(3) 25
(Aytach Sadik) *lost pl after 4th: bmpd along next: lost tch 7th: hopelessly t.o* **25/1**
4m 47.2s (-22.40) **Going Correction** -0.975s/f (Hard)
WFA 4 from 5yo+ 18lb 8 Ran SP% **115.8**
Speed ratings (Par 105): **105,104,96,94,93 93,92,72**
toteswingers:1&2:£3.00, 1&3:£3.50, 2&3:£2.60 CSF £14.63 CT £33.62 TOTE £4.30: £1.50, £2.00, £1.60; EX 17.50.
Owner The Secret Circle **Bred** Hascombe And Valiant Studs **Trained** Hammerwood, E Sussex
FOCUS
A run-of-the-mill contest. The winner was well in on his best and is rated to his mark.
NOTEBOOK
Ashmolian(IRE) lined up still a maiden after 13 starts, but he has fair form from way back and was well supported beforehand. Held up in rear for much of the race, he began to edge into contention at the third-last and was second two out. He challenged the runner-up at the last, just rising ahead, and showed much the better speed on the run-in. Racing from 1lb out of the handicap here, he is sure to take a hit from the handicapper. (op 7-1)
Alldunnandusted(IRE), a consistent performer who scored at Fontwell 18 days previously, had been raised 7lb for that success and did his utmost to notch a follow-up. Always travelling nicely, he was third three out and led at the next, but could not match the winner's pace from the final flight. (tchd 2-1 and 11-4)
Mayor Of Kilcock, runner-up on his first start for this stable at Taunton in April, had fallen early on his latest start but displayed no signs of confidence-loss when leading until the third-last. He was quickly left behind when the first two quickened up, but kept plugging away bravely in the closing stages. (op 4-1)
Thenameescapesme, returning to hurdling for the first time in almost two years, was making his first appearance in any discipline for 194 days. He was entitled to need the outing and, after mounting a brief challenge approaching three out, faded in the home straight. (op 5-1 tchd 6-1)
Benmore Boy(IRE), twice successful on this course and switching back to hurdles after a poor run over fences, was easy in the betting and rather disappointing. He never figured with a serious chance. (op 5-1)
Highland River Official explanation: vet said gelding finished lame

383 CITY LINK - BREAST CANCER H'CAP CHASE (18 fncs) 3m 110y
8:10 (8:12) (Class 5) (0-95,91) 5-Y-0+ **£3,252** (£955; £477; £238)

Form RPR
436- **1** **Overton Lad**156 [2858] 9-10-9 74....(b) JackDoyle 87+
(Peter Pritchard) *j. slowly 2nd: j.v.slowly 3rd and reminder: 2nd much of way: led after 3 out: sn 4 l clr: styd on stoutly* **8/1**
4/5- **2** *10* **Von Galen (IRE)**52 9-11-11 90.... SamThomas 92+
(Michael Scudamore) *chsd ldrs: wnt 3rd at 13th: chsd wnr bef 2 out: rdn and no imp after* **10/1**
02-5 **3** *16* **El Batal (IRE)**18 [83] 9-11-0 86....(p) AnthonyFreeman(7) 70
(Sean Curran) *mstkes: chsd ldrs: and u.p 14th: struggling and looking awkward fr 3 out: tk poor 3rd after last* **7/1**3

P0-0 **4** ½ **Sarobar (IRE)**13 156 10-11-4 **83**.................................... LiamTreadwell 65
(John Spearing) *chsd ldrs: lost pl 12th: 25 l 6th 2 out: plugged on* **33/1**

55P- **5** 3¾ **Sam Cruise**24 5390 9-11-7 **86**.....................................(t) ChristianWilliams 64
(Steve Gollings) *on his toes and rdn down wout irons: uns rdr in false s: led: clr early: hdd after 3 out: 3rd and fading after next: lost two pls fr last* **10/1**

05-4 **6** ¾ **Livingonaknifedge (IRE)**10 213 11-11-12 **91**.................... SamJones 69
(Richard Guest) *last at 5th: hdwy to midfield 11th: hrd drvn 14th: 5th and btn after 3 out* **20/1**

P1-4 **7** 20 **Arceye**8 251 13-10-13 **81**...(p) DerekLaverty(3) 39
(William Davies) *settled 3rd: wnt 2nd at 7th: 3rd and rdn whn mstke 11th: dropped out qckly: t.o after 3 out* **10/1**

43-5 **8** 30 **Donald Will Do (IRE)**14 136 10-11-4 **83**.................(p) AndrewThornton 11
(Caroline Bailey) *dropped to rr and rdn bef 10th: nt keen after: t.o 3 out* **8/1**

P42- **P** **Lonesome Boatman (IRE)**22 22 10-10-6 **74**.......... CharlieHuxley(3) —
(Arthur Whitehead) *nt jump wl in rr: reminders 4th: nvr gng wl: lost tch 14th: t.o 3 out: p.u 2 out* **11/4**1

140- **P** **Man Of The Moment**44 5016 8-11-12 **91**........................(b) JamieMoore —
(Jim Best) *rdn in last and sulking bef 7th: t.o after 11th: j. slowly 13th: p.u next* **4/1**2

6m 10.8s (-26.10) **Going Correction** -0.975s/f (Hard) **10** Ran SP% **116.4**
Speed ratings: **102,98,93,93,92 92,85,76,—,—**
toteswingers:1&2:£6.20, 1&3:£21.10, 2&3:£69.30 CSF £83.29 CT £590.54 TOTE £10.10: £2.70, £5.10, £3.20; EX 111.80.
Owner D R Pritchard **Bred** D R Pritchard **Trained** Whatcote, Warwicks

FOCUS
A modest event, but it looked very open on paper. The winner was well in on his best form but this still rates a step forward.

NOTEBOOK
Overton Lad, who broke his duck over fences at Warwick in October, was having his first run for 156 days. He has run well here before, though, and took this contest by a wide margin. Always prominent, despite a couple of early mistakes, he shot to the front two out and scored easing down. This trip clearly suits him and he may be improving, but the handicapper will surely take note of his comfortable success.
Von Galen(IRE) was having his first run for new connections, after landing a weak point-to-point on his most recent start, and they are likely to have gained satisfaction from this performance. Held up early on, he made progress approaching the fourth-last and stayed on encouragingly in the home straight. (tchd 9-1)
El Batal(IRE), runner-up from a mark 2lb higher in April, was taking a drop in distance and lacked the pace to make a major impact. Never too far away, he fought on gamely without ever threatening to collect. (op 12-1)
Sarobar(IRE) had finished third over this trip at Southwell in November, but was another who looked short of pace at the business end. He kept plugging away, having been held up in touch for much of the contest, but made little progress late on. (op 25-1)
Sam Cruise was fractious beforehand and unseated his rider before the start. He took the field along in the early stages before establishing a clear lead in mid-race, but he had been overhauled by the second-last and back-pedalled from that point. (op 17-2)
Lonesome Boatman(IRE) Official explanation: vet said gelding finished distressed

384 GG.COM CONDITIONAL JOCKEYS' MARES' H'CAP HURDLE (8 hdls) 2m
8:40 (8:40) (Class 5) (0-95,95) 4-Y-0+ **£2,602** (£764; £382; £190)

Form RPR
35-2 **1** **Ruby Crown**8 252 8-11-12 **95**.. RichardKilloran 107+
(Kim Bailey) *bhd: rdn 5th: hdwy 3 out: 6th and reminders st: styd on wl to ld between last two: sn clr: eased cl home* **11/8**1

/6-0 **2** 6 **Monkhair (IRE)**12 171 5-10-3 **75**.. LeeEdwards(3) 80
(Tony Carroll) *plld hrd: chsd ldrs: effrt gng wl to ld bef 2 out: rdn and hdd between last two: sn outpcd by wnr* **8/1**

20-5 **3** 7 **Rowan River**12 185 6-11-0 **88**......................................(t) OliverDayman(5) 85
(Alison Thorpe) *wl bhd: stl last but one at 5th: prog in 8 l 4th 2 out: nvr trbld ldrs after but plugged on* **7/1**3

/4-5 **4** 5 **What's For Tea**14 140 5-10-13 **90**..................................(p) AshleyBird(8) 83
(Paddy Butler) *chsd ldrs: 5th and rdn st: wnt 3rd 2 out: wkng whn blnd last* **28/1**

/4-6 **5** 3½ **Cadeaux Cerise (IRE)**12 182 6-11-9 **95**......................... DavidBass(3) 85
(Andrew Haynes) *led: mstke 3 out: rdn and hdd bef next: mod 5th and fading whn blnd last* **14/1**

P03- **6** 1¼ **Petit Fleur**188 2230 8-11-4 **90**.................................... AnthonyFreeman(3) 77
(Julian Smith) *hld up and keen: effrt 3 out: fdd bef next* **14/1**

00-6 **7** 7 **Honeycombe**12 185 9-10-0 **69** oh1...................................... HarrySkelton 49
(Mrs S P Stretton) *chsd ldr after 2nd tl 3 out: drvn and fdd bef next* **25/1**

600- **8** 2 **Lady Of Ashcott**117 3571 4-9-9 **76**................................. MarkQuinlan(8) 50
(Neil Mulholland) *midfield: rdn and btn 3 out* **20/1**

P0/F **9** 5 **Musical Affair**8 250 6-10-0 **69** oh10................................... HaddenFrost 42
(F Jordan) *last pair: lost tch after 5th* **66/1**

000- **10** 4 **Frosty's Gift**179 2406 6-10-7 **76**...(p) JohnKington 45
(Jimmy Fox) *towards rr: effrt on outer in 7th st: sn fdd* **40/1**

044- **P** **Garafena**22 19 7-11-4 **87**... GilesHawkins —
(Richard Lee) *prom: hrd rdn 3 out: 3rd and fading st: sn eased: p.u last* **6/1**2

430- **P** **Phoenix Enforcer**15 2641 4-10-9 **82**.........................(v1) RichieMcLernon —
(George Baker) *prom: lost pl 3 out: t.o and p.u next* **22/1**

F0-F **P** **Haling Park (UAE)**12 171 4-10-10 **91**......................... JosephAkehurst(8) —
(Gary Moore) *t.k.h: chsd ldrs tl wknd 3 out: p.u next* **14/1**

3m 53.8s (-14.10) **Going Correction** -0.975s/f (Hard)
WFA 4 from 5yo+ 18lb **13** Ran SP% **120.3**
Speed ratings (Par 103): **96,93,89,87,85 84,81,80,77,75 —,—,—**
toteswingers:1&2:£4.90, 1&3:£3.00, 2&3:£13.30 CSF £11.88 CT £62.00 TOTE £2.00: £1.10, £3.70, £1.20; EX 13.90 Place 6 £13.56; Place 5 £9.28.
Owner I F W Buchan **Bred** I F W Buchan **Trained** Andoversford, Gloucs

FOCUS
A poor contest, lacking depth, and there was a decisive win from the well-backed favourite. The winner is rated to her recent level.

NOTEBOOK
Ruby Crown, whose three career victories made her the obvious choice even under top weight, collected in style, despite getting slightly outpaced before the third-last. She had finished second on her latest start and, against these rivals, she had far too many guns. She needed to be vigorously nudged along to get to the front after the second-last, but once she took the lead the result was never in doubt. (op 13-8 tchd 5-4)
Monkhair(IRE) lined up still a maiden, but has made the frame from higher marks in the past and was far from disgraced in taking second against a rival due to go up 7lb after this. She was never far away and led briefly two out but could not match the winner's finishing kick. (op 12-1)
Rowan River, second from a mark of 85 in December, had found life tougher in two subsequent outings and for a long way here seemed likely to be out with the washing. She finished with a flourish, though, passing several rivals in the home straight, and this was a better effort. (op 13-2 tchd 6-1)
What's For Tea, reported lame after seeming to find 2m4f at Fakenham too far last time, appeared to handle this trip well enough, without suggesting she is a winner waiting to happen. In touch throughout, she kept going gamely in the home straight. (op 22-1)
Cadeaux Cerise(IRE), still lightly-raced and a moderately encouraging fourth here in April, set out to make all. She was still in front three out, but could not respond when asked to rally as the first two went past. (tchd 16-1)
T/Plt: £41.00. Pool £88,751.52 - 1,579.80 winning tickets T/Qpdt: £14.40. Pool £5,546.64 - 284.72 winning tickets IM

385a - 392a (Foreign Racing) - See Raceform Interactive

160 KELSO (L-H)
Wednesday, May 19

OFFICIAL GOING: Good to firm (good in places; 7.9)
Wind: Breezy, half against Weather: Overcast, dry

393 ROBIN BEATON IS RETIRING CONDITIONAL JOCKEYS' H'CAP HURDLE (10 hdls) 2m 2f
2:10 (2:10) (Class 4) (0-115,115) 4-Y-0+ **£3,577** (£1,050; £525; £262)

Form RPR
06-0 **1** **Benmadigan (IRE)**14 166 8-10-9 **101**.......................... FearghalDavis(3) 108+
(Nicky Richards) *hld up in tch: rdn and hdwy bef 2 out: led run-in: edgd rt: kpt on wl* **5/1**2

0/0- **2** 2¾ **Smarties Party**19 2820 7-10-9 **98**................................. MichaelO'Connell 102
(C W Thornton) *prom: hdwy to ld after 3 out: rdn next: hdd run-in: edgd lft and kpt on u.p towards fin* **11/2**3

11-0 **3** 3 **Mardood**13 176 5-10-2 **91**..(p) CampbellGillies 93
(Chris Grant) *w ldrs: led 3rd to next: ev ch and rdn 2 out: one pce last* **11/2**3

31-0 **4** 2 **Nelson Du Ronceray (FR)**12 194 9-11-9 **115**............(p) RyanMania(3) 115
(P Monteith) *hld up in tch: hdwy to chse ldrs bef 3 out: rdn and outpcd appr next: rallied bef last: no imp run-in* **13/2**

150- **5** 3¼ **Leith Walk (IRE)**28 5311 7-10-2 **97**............................... GarryWhillans(6) 94
(Donald Whillans) *hld up on outside: drvn and outpcd after 4 out: rallied bef 2 out: no imp fr last* **3/1**1

6P-P **6** 3¼ **Witness Run (IRE)**14 160 10-10-0 **89** oh9....................(p) HarryHaynes 83
(Sandy Thomson) *cl up: led 4th to after 3 out: wknd after next* **25/1**

66-0 **7** 8 **Marsool**14 166 4-10-1 **97**...(p) JohnKington(3) 79
(Donald McCain) *led to 3rd: cl up tl rdn and wknd fr 2 out* **5/1**2

5P-0 **8** 6 **Saujana**14 161 6-10-0 **92**.. KyleJames(3) 73
(Joseph Bewley) *t.k.h: nt fluent: prom: reminders 6th: sn lost pl: struggling fr next* **7/1**

4m 19.9s (-7.10) **Going Correction** -0.75s/f (Firm)
WFA 4 from 5yo+ 18lb **8** Ran SP% **118.8**
Speed ratings (Par 105): **85,83,82,81,80 78,75,72**
toteswingers: 1&2 £6.40, 1&3 £11.90, 2&3 £7.80 CSF £33.96 CT £159.04 TOTE £4.30: £1.20, £3.30, £1.10; EX 41.00.
Owner Jimmy Dudgeon **Bred** Neilie O'Mahony **Trained** Greystoke, Cumbria
⊠ Stewards' Enquiry : Kyle James caution: used whip when out of contention

FOCUS
A moderate contest run at a slow tempo in the early stages. Straightforward form and the winner is rated back to his best.

NOTEBOOK
Benmadigan(IRE), beaten over 30l on two of his last three starts, always gave the impression that he had a bit in reserve despite being ridden along a couple of times after two out. He found enough after the final hurdle to send him to the front, and stayed there once stretching away. (tchd 6-1)
Smarties Party, having her first run over hurdles since December, has run respectably on the Flat (last two starts were a little disappointing, however) and for a few strides seemed to have stolen this off the final bend once sprinting into an advantage. She kept fighting away under pressure but found the winner too strong after the last hurdle. (op 13-2)
Mardood, dropped in trip again, held every chance after being given a prominent ride and seemed to run up to his best. The jockey reported that his mount stumbled on the bend. (op 6-1)
Nelson Du Ronceray(FR), back over hurdles, appears to be at his best when there is cut in the ground, so this was not a bad performance. Official explanation: jockey said gelding stumbled on bend turning into home straight (tchd 6-1)
Leith Walk(IRE), taking a big drop in trip, was pushed into contention leaving the back straight but found only the one pace. (op 7-2 tchd 4-1)
Marsool, the only 4-y-o in the line-up, had cheekpieces on for the first time and was behind Benmadigan last time over C&D. He rarely threatened. (tchd 11-2)

394 NFU MUTUAL RISK MANAGEMENT SERVICES NOVICES' CHASE (19 fncs) 3m 1f
2:45 (2:45) (Class 4) 5-Y-0+ **£5,415** (£1,969)

Form RPR
00-2 **1** **Diavoleria**18 91 7-10-5 0.. DenisO'Regan 119+
(Michael Easterby) *trckd ldrs: nt fluent 6th: and 15th: lft 2nd next: led gng wl appr last: drvn and hld on wl run-in* **11/10**1

0/6- **2** ½ **River Alder**364 389 12-10-2 0.. RyanMania(3) 115
(J M Dun) *chsd ldr to 10th: cl up: lft in ld 4 out: hdd appr last: rallied run-in: kpt on: hld nr fin* **7/1**

12P- **U** **Mr Woods**26 5375 8-11-5 124... JamesReveley —
(Harriet Graham) *j.rt: led: jst hdd whn mstke and uns rdr 11th* **9/2**3

561- **F** **Quick Will (FR)**21 43 6-11-2 115...................................... HarryHaynes(3) —
(James Ewart) *in tch: hdwy to chse ldr 10th: lft in ld next: 1 l in front and gng wl whn fell 4 out* **9/4**2

/00- **P** **Warnell View**194 2105 7-10-12 0.. PeterBuchanan —
(Rayson Nixon) *nt jump wl: blnd and bhd fr 2nd: t.o whn p.u bef 13th* **100/1**

6m 16.2s (-15.30) **Going Correction** -0.475s/f (Good) **5** Ran SP% **110.1**
Speed ratings: **105,104,—,—,—**
CSF £8.91 TOTE £1.70: £1.10, £4.70; EX 7.30.
Owner Mrs A Blanchard **Bred** R And Mrs Blanchard **Trained** Sheriff Hutton, N Yorks

FOCUS
A tight novice chase, but it proved an eventful heat. The winner is rated close to her hurdles best.

NOTEBOOK
Diavoleria, who was hampered by the fall of Quick Will, just held on after idling once in the lead. She is now a winner of a bumper, a hurdle race and a chase, so one would imagine connections are delighted to have completed the full set. (op 6-5 tchd 5-4 and Evens)
River Alder, who last tried chasing back in 2006 and was returning from a year off, made a few small errors at the fences but rallied strongly once the winner started to do nothing in front. (op 10-1)

Mr Woods, pulled up in handicap company last time, set a good standard considering he is rated 124. Tried over 3m again for the first time since January, he set off in front (he usually races prominently) but jumped out to his right throughout - something he has done in the past. He held a good advantage at once stage but had been passed when departing. (op 5-2 tchd 11-4)
Quick Will(FR), a winner on his chasing debut last time at this course over 2m6f, took it up going nicely on their final circuit but got a bit low four out and paid the price. (op 5-2 tchd 11-4)

395 HUNTER PROPERTY FUND MANAGEMENT H'CAP CHASE (12 fncs) 2m 1f

3:20 (3:20) (Class 4) (0-115,115) 5-Y-0+ **£3,903** (£1,146; £573; £286)

Form RPR

P2P- **1** **Carrietau**[26] 5375 7-11-9 **115**..........(bt) RyanMania(3) 122+
(Barry Murtagh) *j.w: mde all: sn clr: given breather 1/2-way: qcknd bef last: unchal* **7/4**[1]

31-0 **2** *7* **Duke Of Malfi**[18] 88 7-10-11 **100**..........(p) PeterBuchanan 101
(Lucinda Russell) *prom: drvn and outpcd 1/2-way: effrt and chsd ldrs 3 out: rdn and kpt on fr last: tk 2nd nr fin: nt rch wnr* **7/4**[1]

15-6 **3** *1 1/4* **Jim Tango (FR)**[13] 177 6-11-7 **113**..........(b) AdrianLane(3) 112
(Donald McCain) *chsd wnr: effrt after 2 out: rdn and one pce last: edgd rt and lost 2nd nr fin* **6/1**[3]

/0P- **4** *30* **Well Oiled (IRE)**[199] 2024 9-10-5 **94**.......... PaddyAspell 66
(Sandy Forster) *bhd: outpcd after 5th: hdwy and in tch bef 3 out: wknd after next* **4/1**[2]

4m 9.20s (-8.80) **Going Correction** -0.475s/f (Good) **4** Ran SP% **107.0**
Speed ratings: **101,97,97,83**
CSF £5.23 TOTE £2.40; EX 5.90.
Owner Anthony White **Bred** John Ellis **Trained** Low Braithwaite, Cumbria

FOCUS
A weakish handicap where the winner dominated. He is rated to his mark.

NOTEBOOK
Carrietau's rider set a sensible gallop and made sure he had enough in hand to quicken again at the end to secure victory. This success came off a career-high handicap mark, so the gelding will find probably things difficult next time. (tchd 13-8)
Duke Of Malfi didn't jump fluently early and got behind as a result. He never held any chance of victory but fought on well to get into second. His profile suggests that much easier ground suits him best. (op 2-1)
Jim Tango(FR) put up a better performance than last time but was easily held. (op 7-2)
Well Oiled(IRE), having his first run since November, made no impression and did not convince with his jumping. (op 7-1)

396 KLEINWORT BENSON H'CAP HURDLE (11 hdls) 2m 6f 110y

3:55 (3:55) (Class 3) (0-130,128) 4-Y-0+ **£5,204** (£1,528; £764; £381)

Form RPR

5P-1 **1** **Solway Bay**[7] 287 8-9-13 **104**..........(t) HarryHaynes(3) 109
(Lisa Harrison) *hld up: hdwy and swtchd rt after 2 out: led run-in: styd on strly* **13/2**

311- **2** *2* **Coastley (IRE)**[21] 45 8-11-11 **127**.......... JamesReveley 130
(David Carr) *chsd ldr: led last: rdn: hung lft and hdd run-in: kpt on same pce towards fin* **11/2**

514- **3** *2 1/4* **Lawgiver (IRE)**[33] 5217 9-10-10 **112**.......... GrahamLee 113
(Marjorie Fife) *prom: effrt and rdn bef 2 out: kpt on u.p run-in* **16/1**

536- **4** *3 1/2* **Tension Point**[21] 45 6-10-13 **120**..........(t) MissLHorner(5) 118
(Chris Grant) *hld up: effrt bef 2 out: no imp fr last* **12/1**

U12- **5** *2 3/4* **Mcmurrough (IRE)**[33] 5201 6-11-7 **128**.......... JamesHalliday(5) 124
(Malcolm Jefferson) *nt fluent on occasions: in tch: effrt 3 out: outpcd after next* **4/1**[2]

231- **6** *11* **Humbie (IRE)**[58] 4783 6-10-13 **115**.......... TimmyMurphy 102
(Pauline Robson) *set modest gallop: rdn bef 2 out: hdd last: sn btn* **2/1**[1]

000- **7** *31* **Modicum (USA)**[21] 44 8-10-7 **109**..........(t) WilsonRenwick 67
(Rose Dobbin) *trckd ldrs: rdn after 3 out: wknd fr next* **40/1**

22-3 **P** **Pontop (IRE)**[18] 89 7-11-11 **127**.......... JanFaltejsek —
(George Charlton) *hld up: struggling 1/2-way: t.o whn p.u bef 3 out* **9/2**[3]

5m 18.4s (-22.60) **Going Correction** -0.75s/f (Firm) **8** Ran SP% **116.2**
Speed ratings (Par 107): **109,108,107,106,105 101,90,—**
toteswingers: 1&2 £5.20, 1&3 £6.50, 2&3 £12.10 CSF £42.71 CT £551.20 TOTE £8.60: £2.20, £1.10, £4.30; EX 41.90.
Owner David Alan Harrison **Bred** D A Harrison **Trained** Aldoth, Cumbria

FOCUS
A fair handicap for the class and sound enough form with the winner rated to his best.

NOTEBOOK
Solway Bay, back over hurdles after winning a chase on his previous start, continued the good run of form by his trainer with a gutsy success. Held up, he made stealthy headway approaching the final hurdle (he was in about fourth when jumping it) and stayed on strongly up the hill to gain victory. The quick ground was in his favour and he may complete the hat-trick. (op 10-1)
Coastley(IRE), chasing a third successive success off a 14lb higher mark than his last victory, is far from exposed and ran another solid race. He was giving plenty of weight to Solway Bay, so it was another step in the right direction and he remains one to follow. (op 5-1 tchd 4-1)
Lawgiver(IRE), slightly disappointing last time at Uttoxeter, was a bit keen early but stayed on well in the final half a furlong. (op 14-1 tchd 12-1)
Tension Point, over 30l behind Coastley on his previous outing, took a good grip under his jockey and was caught flat-footed as the pace increased. (op 11-1 tchd 10-1)
Mcmurrough(IRE)p, a previous C&D winner, was dropping in trip slightly but never seemed happy. To his credit, he did keep going and was staying on and will probably be going chasing in the near future. (op 11-2 tchd 6-1)
Humbie(IRE), having his fourth consecutive start over C&D, was 9lb higher than last time (when claiming his first victory) but enjoyed an easy lead. He was still in front turning in but folded quickly after the final hurdle. This was probably a bit too much too soon. (op 13-8 tchd 5-2)
Modicum(USA) has dropped a lot in the weights over hurdles after some very moderate efforts and was fitted with a tongue-tie for the first time. He was close up for a while but found little once the sprint started. (op 33-1)
Pontop(IRE) had a very consistent profile coming into this but was in trouble early in the contest. It is difficult to know why he ran so moderately. (op 13-2)

397 SCOTT COPPOLA NOVICES' HURDLE (10 hdls) 2m 2f

4:30 (4:30) (Class 4) 4-Y-0+ **£3,252** (£955; £477; £238)

Form RPR

3- **1** **Balnagore**[27] 5333 6-10-12 0.......... PeterBuchanan 93+
(Lucinda Russell) *led to 7th: cl up: drvn to ld bef last: hld on wl u.p run-in* **11/4**[2]

3-01 **2** *hd* **Solis (GER)**[7] 286 7-11-2 90..........(p) RyanMania(3) 99
(P Monteith) *trckd ldrs: drvn 3 out: rallied bef last: styd on wl run-in: jst hld* **9/2**[3]

0/0- **3** *1 1/2* **Choctaw Nation**[235] 1541 6-10-7 0.......... JamesHalliday(5) 91
(Malcolm Jefferson) *hld up: effrt bef 2 out: hung lft and flashed tail after last: styng on wl whn hung rt and flashed tail again last 150yds* **20/1**

4 *3* **Waldvogel (IRE)**[131] 6-10-12 0.......... SamThomas 92+
(Nicky Richards) *nt fluent on occasions: in tch: hdwy to chse ldrs 4 out: effrt and ev ch between last 2: no ex run-in* **1/1**[1]

00- **5** *6* **Hippolytus**[28] 5310 5-10-9 0.......... CampbellGillies(3) 83
(Lucinda Russell) *in tch: effrt bef 2 out: wknd after last* **28/1**

00-4 **6** *3/4* **Sunset Resort (IRE)**[11] 210 5-10-9 92..........(t) MichaelMcAlister(3) 82
(Maurice Barnes) *hld up: drvn and effrt bef 2 out: wknd fr last* **50/1**

00-0 **7** *nk* **Sheriff Hall (IRE)**[11] 209 5-10-12 0.......... TimmyMurphy 82
(George Charlton) *t.k.h: cl up: led 7th to bef last: wknd run-in* **9/1**

0U- **P** **Acclaim To Fame (IRE)**[28] 5305 4-10-1 0.......... CallumWhillans(7) —
(Donald Whillans) *t.k.h: prom to 4 out: struggling next: t.o whn p.u bef 2 out* **80/1**

4m 18.3s (-8.70) **Going Correction** -0.75s/f (Firm)
WFA 4 from 5yo+ 18lb **8** Ran SP% **116.3**
Speed ratings (Par 105): **89,88,88,86,84 83,83,—**
CSF £15.28 TOTE £3.80: £1.10, £1.10, £4.30; EX 11.80.
Owner K Alexander **Bred** Mrs S A Lloyd **Trained** Arlary, Perth & Kinross

FOCUS
Ordinary novice form rated through the runner-up.

NOTEBOOK
Balnagore, a fair middle-distance sort on the Flat for John Dunlop, was a little free in front early but found plenty when asked to quicken approaching the final hurdle. He gained an advantage from that point but only just held on from a moderate rival, so the form does not look strong. However, the trainer reported that he has more to come and had improved from his first start for them. He will be kept on the go. (op 3-1)
Solis(GER) won a handicap off 93 last time (cheekpieces on for the first time) and will be going up 3lb from the weekend. He emerges as the best horse at the weights, and seems on the upgrade. (op 13-2 tchd 7-1)
Choctaw Nation, having his first start for Malcolm Jefferson, stayed on to catch the eye but looks far from a straightforward ride. It would not be a surprise to see headgear on him next time. (op 25-1)
Waldvogel(IRE) never managed to win for Luca Cumani and you had to go back to 2007 in Germany for his last success. Making his hurdling debut, het he was in with every chance coming to the last when pecking after it. The trainer said there would be more to come from his horse next time, and maybe he will be better on a flat track, but one had the impression the winner would have had his measure no matter what happened here. (op 5-6)
Sheriff Hall(IRE) pulled very hard early and predictably weakened up the hill. He needs to settle better to give himself any chance. (op 11-1 tchd 12-1)

398 CHARLIE BROWN UNITED BORDER OPEN HUNTERS' CHASE (19 fncs) 3m 1f

5:05 (5:05) (Class 6) 5-Y-0+ **£1,561** (£484; £242; £121)

Form RPR

553/ **1** **Moment Of Madness (IRE)**[10] 12-11-7 0.......... MrMWalford(5) 106
(Mrs M Stirk) *mde all: pushed along bef last: hld on wl run-in* **7/1**[2]

F20- **2** *3/4* **Anshan Spirit (IRE)**[30] 5276 12-10-12 97.......... MrRWGreen(7) 98
(R W Green) *hld up: hdwy and in tch 12th: effrt after 2 out: chsd wnr 2 out: kpt on run-in and looked dangerous last 200yds: hld towards fin* **12/1**[3]

URU- **3** *3 1/4* **Floreana (GER)**[27] 5335 9-10-12 95..........(p) MissLAlexander(7) 95
(Mrs A J Boswell) *hld up: hdwy into midfield 7th: lost pl whn hit 15th: rallied after 2 out: kpt on run-in: nt rch first two* **40/1**

125- **4** *nk* **Areyacoddinmee (IRE)**[30] 5276 10-11-9 89..........(b) MrGRSmith(7) 105
(Mrs Elaine Smith) *midfield: hdwy and cl up 1/2-way: hit 15th: outpcd 3 out: rallied after last: kpt on* **100/1**

P4-4 **5** *3/4* **Ardnaclancy (IRE)**[18] 90 7-11-5 0.......... MrJARichardson(7) 101
(Andrew Richardson) *chsd ldrs: pushed along 3 out: one pce fr last* **25/1**

413- **6** *1 1/4* **Silver Sedge (IRE)**[30] 5276 11-11-13 113..........(t) MrJBewley(7) 107
(Ann Hamilton) *hld up: hdwy to chse ldrs bef last to run-in: wknd* **7/1**[2]

7 *2* **Davy Boy Legend (IRE)**[11] 7-11-5 0.......... MrDOckenden(7) 98
(Josie Ross) *midfield: lost pl 5th: no imp tl hdwy bef last: kpt on run-in: n.d* **16/1**

PP-1 **8** *2 1/4* **Benbeoch**[14] 165 11-11-13 92..........(p) MrCDawson(3) 99
(Sandy Thomson) *cl up: chsd wnr fr 11th to bef last: wknd run-in* **16/1**

F22- **9** *10* **Dix Villez (FR)**[17] 11-11-5 106..........(p) MrAWaugh(7) 85
(Simon Waugh) *mstkes: prom tl wknd fr 3 out* **14/1**

/P-3 **10** *32* **Silver Palomino**[14] 165 9-11-9 70.......... MrTDavidson(3) 53
(Mrs L A Coltherd) *prom to 3 out: sn wknd: t.o* **100/1**

15P- **11** *1 1/4* **Almost Blue (IRE)**[17] 8-11-9 99.......... MrJamieAlexander(7) 56
(N W Alexander) *bhd: struggling 1/2-way: t.o* **50/1**

P54- **U** **Doris's Gift**[16] 9-11-5 66..........(b) MrAdamNicol(7) —
(T Glass) *prom: rdn 8th: losing pl whn blnd and uns rdr next* **50/1**

U1-1 **F** **Eliza Doalott (IRE)**[13] 178 8-11-10 114.......... MrGBrewer(3) —
(Mrs M Stirk) *hld up: fell 6th* **4/6**[1]

6m 16.0s (-15.50) **Going Correction** -0.475s/f (Good) **13** Ran SP% **123.3**
Speed ratings: **105,104,103,103,103 102,102,101,98,88 88,—,—**
toteswingers: 1&2 £10.40, 1&3 £25.60, 2&3 £26.40 CSF £83.26 TOTE £5.80: £1.20, £3.50, £5.90; EX 99.70.
Owner Mrs R A G Haggie **Bred** William Hubbert **Trained** Laverton, N Yorks

FOCUS
The winner dictated in this moderate hunter chase and they finished in something of a heap. The winner was close to his mark.

NOTEBOOK
Moment Of Madness(IRE) put up a splendid round of jumping under a prominent ride, and held on well under pressure. This was his first win under rules since 2005. (op 5-1)
Anshan Spirit(IRE), who won this race from 2006-2008, came with a spirited late challenge to finish a clear second-best. (op 14-1 tchd 16-1)
Floreana(GER), who had failed to finish on her last two starts but was runner-up in this last year, came home strongly yet did not have time to get on terms. (op 33-1)
Areyacoddinmee(IRE), with the blinkers back on, was hard ridden down the back straight and was another coming home strongly in the last half a furlong.
Benbeoch, an easy C&D winner earlier this month, sat just behind the winner throughout the final circuit but lacked that horse's stamina after the final fence.
Eliza Doalott(IRE), chasing her sixth victory in a row, came down early with an uncharacteristic error. (op 5-6 tchd evens in places)

399 KELSOGOLFCLUB.COM STANDARD OPEN NATIONAL HUNT FLAT RACE 2m 110y

5:40 (5:40) (Class 6) 4-6-Y-0 **£1,626** (£477; £238; £119)

Form RPR

34- **1** **Freddie Brown**[38] 5144 6-11-2 0.......... JanFaltejsek 103
(George Charlton) *t.k.h: prom: smooth hdwy to ld over 1f out: drvn and edgd rt: hld on wl* **11/2**[3]

\- **2** *2 1/4* **Pasture Bay (IRE)** 4-10-12 0.......... TimmyMurphy 97+
(George Charlton) *hld up: gd hdwy 2f out: styd on wl fnl f to take 2nd cl home: nt rch wnr* **7/2**[1]

23- **3** *3/4* **Mr Jay Dee (IRE)**[64] 4669 5-11-2 0 ..... BrianHughes 100
(Alan Swinbank) *trckd ldrs: effrt and ev ch over 1f out: edgd rt: one pce fnl f: lost 2nd cl home* **9/2**[2]

4 *2 3/4* **Thurnham** 4-10-12 0 ..... JamesReveley 93
(Keith Reveley) *hld up: shkn up and hdwy 2f out: kpt on fnl f: nvr nr ldrs* **11/2**[3]

5 *1* **Orraloon** 4-10-5 0 ..... GarryWhillans(7) 92
(Donald Whillans) *racd keenly: cl up: pushed along fr over 3f out: plugged on fnl f: no imp* **12/1**

203- **6** *nk* **Finellas Fortune**[227] 1629 5-9-13 0 ..... SamuelWelton(10) 89
(George Moore) *cl up: led over 2f out to 1f out: sn one pce* **16/1**

6- **7** *7* **Connie Beauchamp**[21] 47 6-10-4 0 ..... EwanWhillans(5) 82
(Elliott Cooper) *prom: drvn and outpcd over 3f out: n.d after* **18/1**

8 *3/4* **Crushed Ice** 4-10-7 0 ..... JamesHalliday(5) 84
(Malcolm Jefferson) *led to over 2f out: sn rdn and wknd* **9/2**[2]

9 *nk* **Ladies Pride (IRE)** 5-10-6 0 ..... AdrianLane(3) 81
(Bruce Mactaggart) *bhd: pushed along over 4f out: nvr able to chal* **40/1**

5- **10** *4 1/2* **Whiteadder**[21] 47 5-11-2 0 ..... WilsonRenwick 83
(Rose Dobbin) *trckd ldrs: ev ch 3f out: wknd fr 2f out* **16/1**

0- **11** *22* **Darden Burn (IRE)**[69] 4536 4-10-5 0 ..... MrJARichardson(7) 57
(David Carr) *midfield: hdwy and prom over 5f out: wknd over 3f out* **80/1**

0- **12** *1* **Master Woodsman**[32] 5227 4-10-9 0 ..... MichaelMcAlister(3) 56
(Edwin Tuer) *trckd ldrs tl wknd over 3f out* **50/1**

13 *nk* **Roi's Last Runner** 5-10-9 0 ..... GarethThomas(7) 60
(Barry Murtagh) *hld up: hdwy into midfield 1/2-way: wknd over 3f out* **100/1**

14 *128* **Twin Edge** 5-10-6 0 ..... RyanMania(3) —
(George Foster) *w.r.s and lost many l s: rcvrd and jnd pack after 4f: wknd over 5f out: t.o* **80/1**

3m 47.6s (-8.60) **Going Correction** -0.75s/f (Firm)
WFA 4 from 5yo+ 4lb **14** Ran SP% **121.9**
Speed ratings: **90,88,88,87,86 86,83,83,82,80 70,69,69,—**
toteswingers: 1&2 £6.00, 1&3 £5.80, 2&3 £6.40 CSF £25.13 TOTE £8.60: £2.70, £1.10, £3.10; EX 29.00 TRIFECTA Place 6: £510.66 Place 5: £213.33 .
Owner J R Jeffreys **Bred** J R Jeffreys **Trained** Stocksfield, Northumberland

FOCUS
A modest bumper in which the winner is rated close to his previous best.

NOTEBOOK
Freddie Brown, having his third consecutive start in a C&D bumper, seemed one to take on but he got going at the right time to gain an advantage, one he kept all the way to the line. He will be put away now and go hurdling in the autumn. (op 5-1 tchd 9-2)
Pasture Bay(IRE), a 20,000euro purchase, whose dam is an unraced half-sister to Silver Birch, finished strongly and may have given the winner more to think about had he started his challenge a bit earlier. (op 4-1 tchd 9-2)
Mr Jay Dee(IRE) shaped nicely on his debut but was somewhat disappointing last time. This was better and he may win something similar if connections keep him in these contests, but a switch to jumping would not surprise. (op 10-3 tchd 3-1)
Thurnham, the first foal of a dam that won two bumpers for this stable, was last rounding the final bend but came home so strongly that he passed nine rivals up the home straight. He would have been a bigger threat given a positive ride. (op 7-2)
Orraloon shaped with a bit of promise on his debut and showed signs of ability. (op 16-1 tchd 18-1)
Finellas Fortune travelled strongly on her return to action and ran satisfactorily.
Crushed Ice, a half-brother to winners, including stablemate Mac Aeda, was supported but did not get home after racing prominently. (op 10-1)
T/Plt: £499.100. Pool:£55575.620 - 81.28 winning tickets. T/Qpdt: £159.60. Pool:£3580.23 - 16.60 winning tickets. RY

[30]SEDGEFIELD (L-H)

Wednesday, May 19

OFFICIAL GOING: Good to firm (good in places; 6.1)
Wind: light 1/2 behind Weather: overcast

400 FREE RACING WITH ODDSCHECKER.COM WEDNESDAY'S NOVICES' HURDLE (8 hdls) 2m 1f

6:30 (6:30) (Class 4) 4-Y-0+ **£2,862** (£840; £420; £209)

Form RPR

35-3 **1** **Barron Watlass (IRE)**[14] 161 6-11-5 101 ..... BarryKeniry 105+
(George Moore) *trckd ldrs: wnt 2nd after 3 out: led between last 2: sn hdd: styd on to ld last 75yds* **4/1**[2]

2 *1/2* **Heart Of Dubai (USA)**[11] 5-10-12 0 ..... TomMessenger 97+
(Micky Hammond) *hld up in mid-div: hdwy to go handy 3rd after 3 out: narrow ld appr last: hdd and no ex run-in* **50/1**

1-1 **3** *4* **Barrel Of Fun (IRE)**[13] 182 4-11-8 121 ..... (t) JohnnyFarrelly 105+
(Jim Best) *w ldr: led 4th: rdn appr 2 out: hdd between last 2: fdd run-in* **4/9**[1]

UPP- **4** *16* **Camomile**[24] 14 4-9-12 0 ..... MichaelO'Connell(3) 70
(Tracy Waggott) *hld up in rr: hdwy 3 out: tk modest 4th run-in* **200/1**

5 *2 1/4* **Island Chief**[8] 4-10-1 0 ..... BrianToomey(7) 81+
(Kevin Ryan) *j. poorly: blnd 1st 2: in rr: hdwy 5th: 4th whn stmbld landing 2 out: j.lft last: sn wknd* **33/1**

P4- **6** *3 3/4* **Barbarian**[103] 3868 4-10-8 0 ..... KeithMercer 73
(Alan Brown) *chsd ldrs: wknd after 3 out* **16/1**

05-0 **7** *7* **Daniel's Dream**[11] 209 10-10-12 70 ..... (p) PaddyAspell 71
(John Dixon) *led to 4th: reminders next: lost pl after 3 out* **100/1**

65- **8** *1 1/4* **Musca (IRE)**[307] 973 6-10-5 0 ..... MrJohnDawson(7) 70
(John Wade) *t.k.h: sn trcking ldrs: blnd 3 out: outpcd appr next: sn wknd* **100/1**

00- **9** *2* **Everaard (USA)**[52] 3945 4-10-8 0 ..... RichieMcGrath 64
(Kate Walton) *prom: lost pl 3 out* **40/1**

0/0- **10** *1 1/2* **Steel Giant (USA)**[222] 1679 5-10-5 0 ..... KyleJames(7) 67
(Malcolm Jefferson) *in rr: bhd fr 5th* **40/1**

6- **11** *15* **Takaatuf (IRE)**[62] 4706 4-10-8 0 ..... GrahamLee 51
(John Hellens) *racd keenly: trckd ldrs: hit 4th: lost pl 3f out: eased appr next: sn bhd* **12/1**[3]

4m 5.80s (-1.10) **Going Correction** 0.0s/f (Good) **11** Ran SP% **115.1**
Speed ratings (Par 105): **102,101,99,92,91 89,86,85,84,84 76**
toteswingers: 1&2 £20.30, 1&3 £1.10, 2&3 £23.30 CSF £151.90 TOTE £3.60: £1.02, £10.90, £1.50; EX 313.80.
Owner JBSRP John Barry ROn **Bred** M Cleary **Trained** Middleham Moor, N Yorks

FOCUS
After a dry day the ground was described as good to firm, good in places. A very weak novices' hurdle run at a steady pace and what looked a good opportunity for the favourite proved anything but. The winner is rated to his mark.

NOTEBOOK
Barron Watlass(IRE), rated 101 and penalised for a win at this track in a modest handicap in March, puts the form in some context. Not doing a lot when hitting the front, he has the size to jump fences in due course and should remain competitive back in small handicaps, as long as the handicapper doesn't over react, which he shouldn't. (tchd 7-2 and 9-2)
Heart Of Dubai(USA) ran well on his hurdling debut. Only rated 46 on the Flat, he can go one better in similar company at this time off the year. (op 33-1)
Barrel Of Fun(IRE) proved very disappointing. Carrying his head high, he could have done with a stronger pace and some company up front. There is no way he ran anywhere near his mark off 121 and not one to take a short price about in similar company. (op 4-7)
Camomile, from an in-form yard, stayed on late and will find life easier in modest handicaps in due course.
Island Chief, struggling in claimers and sellers and the Flat of late, showed promise on his first start over hurdles, but there is plenty of room for improvement in the jumping department with him.

401 T MANNERS & SONS 150TH ANNIVERSARY BEGINNERS' CHASE (15 fncs 1 omitted) 2m 4f

7:00 (7:00) (Class 4) 5-Y-0+ **£4,055** (£1,198; £599; £299; £149)

Form RPR

FU0- **1** **Big Burrows (IRE)**[22] 32 8-11-0 0 ..... GrahamLee 123+
(Ferdy Murphy) *wnt prom 8th: led 13th: 4 l clr omitted last: drvn rt out* **9/1**

402- **2** *4 1/2* **Dontpaytheferryman (USA)**[22] 32 5-11-0 0 ..... KeithMercer 118
(Brian Ellison) *j.rt: led to 5th: lft in ld 8th: hdd 11th: regained 2nd normal 2 out: styd on same pce* **2/1**[1]

256- **3** *7* **Bugsy's Boy**[68] 4211 6-11-0 0 ..... AndrewTinkler 113
(George Baker) *chsd ldrs: hmpd 8th: led 11th: hdd 13th: one pce fr normal 2 out* **4/1**[3]

614- **4** *33* **The Gloves Are Off (IRE)**[21] 45 7-11-0 0 ..... TjadeCollier 86
(Sue Smith) *j.rt: chsd ldrs: drvn 7th: lost pl 9th: sn bhd: t.o 12th: tk distant 4th nr fin* **7/2**[2]

64-F **5** *nk* **Poseidon (GER)**[6] 306 8-10-7 102 ..... MrJohnDawson(7) 86
(John Wade) *chsd ldrs: hmpd 8th: outpcd and drvn 10th: t.o omitted 2 out* **16/1**

16-0 **F** **Still At Lunch (IRE)**[12] 196 7-11-0 0 ..... RichieMcGrath —
(Kate Walton) *w ldr: led 5th: fell 8th: fatally injured* **4/1**[3]

4m 59.4s (-3.60) **Going Correction** 0.0s/f (Good) **6** Ran SP% **111.4**
Speed ratings: **107,105,102,89,89 —**
toteswingers: 1&2 £19.30, 1&3 £3.90, 2&3 £5.70 CSF £27.95 TOTE £13.00: £5.70, £1.70; EX 39.30.
Owner Mrs J Morgan **Bred** Pat Hickey **Trained** West Witton, N Yorks

FOCUS
A weak beginners' chase run at an even pace. A big step up from Big Burrows but he threatened this sotrt of figure over hurdles, with the second to his mark. The final fence was bypassed.

NOTEBOOK
Big Burrows(IRE) got off the mark at the fourth attempt over fences, turning around course form with Dontpaytheferryman. Falling and unseating on his first two tries over fences, he jumped better here, and certainly has the size to carry a penalty at this time off year. (op 10-1 tchd 11-1)
Dontpaytheferryman(USA), who was runner-up over course and distance on his chasing debut last month, tended to jump to the right throughout here, and ran in snatches. He would definitely prefer easier ground, and if getting it, can go one better at this time of the year. (op 7-4)
Bugsy's Boy, Having his first start over fences, jumped well enough, but didn't strike as a winner waiting to happen. (op 5-1)
The Gloves Are Off(IRE), having his eighth start over fences, was struggling with a circuit to go and can only be watched after this. (op 4-1)

402 JOHN WADE EQUINE FIBRE & RUBBER (S) H'CAP HURDLE (QUALIFIER) (8 hdls) 2m 1f

7:30 (7:33) (Class 5) (0-95,95) 4-7-Y-0 **£1,951** (£573; £286; £143)

Form RPR

604- **1** **Authentic Act (IRE)**[15] 4552 6-9-11 69 oh3 ..... MichaelO'Connell(3) 84+
(Martin Todhunter) *trckd ldrs: hmpd on ins bnd bef 2 out: led appr 2 out: wnt 6 l clr last: heavily eased clsng stages* **7/2**[1]

05-P **2** *8* **Can't Remember**[11] 210 5-10-6 78 ..... HarryHaynes(3) 81
(Robert Johnson) *chsd ldsers: wnt cl 2nd 2 out: kpt on same pce* **20/1**

0P-6 **3** *4* **Arctic Rock**[14] 161 7-10-9 78 ..... (v[1]) PaddyAspell 77
(Geoffrey Harker) *in rr: hdwy to chse ldrs 4th: 3rd and wl btn whn mstke last* **7/1**[3]

33-P **4** *2 1/2* **Tar (IRE)**[13] 171 6-11-5 95 ..... (v) MrTomDavid(7) 93
(Tim Vaughan) *chsd ldrs: led after 3 out: hdd appr next: 3rd whn stmbld on landing: wknd between last 2* **11/1**

206- **5** *8* **Mister Fizzbomb (IRE)**[24] 10 7-10-7 83 ..... (v) AlexanderVoy(7) 74
(John Wainwright) *w ldrs: lost pl appr 2 out* **9/1**

500- **6** *hd* **Bold Indian (IRE)**[26] 2835 6-10-6 75 ..... KeithMercer 65
(Mike Sowersby) *hld up in rr: hdwy to chse ldrs 3 out: rdn and wknd appr next* **16/1**

216- **7** *7* **Freedom Flying**[113] 3672 7-11-0 90 ..... (p) KyleJames(7) 75
(Philip Kirby) *sn drvn along in rr: reminders 3rd: bhd fr next: nvr on terms* **15/2**

00-U **8** *3 3/4* **White Lightening (IRE)**[13] 179 7-10-11 87 ..... (b) MrJohnDawson(7) 69
(John Wade) *in rr: sme hdwy appr 2 out: wknd between last 2* **16/1**

P46- **9** *5* **Bold Pioneer (USA)**[38] 5151 7-10-8 77 ..... (t) GrahamLee 55
(Richard Ford) *racd wd: w ldrs: led 4th: hdd after 3 out: wknd appr next* **8/1**

605- **P** **Norman Beckett**[59] 4769 7-11-6 89 ..... (bt) JohnnyFarrelly —
(Jim Best) *led: hdd: mstke and reminders 3rd: reluctant and lost pl next: sn bhd: t.o 3 out: p.u bef next* **11/2**[2]

4m 5.90s (-1.00) **Going Correction** 0.0s/f (Good)
WFA 4 from 5yo+ 18lb **10** Ran SP% **107.8**
Speed ratings: **102,98,96,95,91 91,88,86,83,—**
toteswingers: 1&2 £24.10, 1&3 £3.20, 2&3 £33.20 CSF £59.62 CT £394.26 TOTE £3.00: £1.10, £8.40, £3.00; EX 55.40.The winner bought in for 5,800gns.
Owner Mr & Mrs Ian Hall **Bred** Gestut Ammerland **Trained** Orton, Cumbria
⊠ Night Knight was withdrawn (10/1, vet's advice at s). Deduct 5p in the £ under R4.

FOCUS
Despite four course-and-distance winners in the line up, this was only a run of the mill seller. It was run at an even pace. The easy winner was value for further.

NOTEBOOK
Authentic Act(IRE) won in decisive style. Denied a clear run before the penultimate flight, he idled when hitting the front. He hasn't had many chances over hurdles and is at the right end of the handicap to remain competitive. (op 4-1)
Can't Remember ran better here, she doesn't have the best of strike-rates and not one to take a short price about in a quest to go one better next time. (op 33-1)
Arctic Rock, wearing a first-time visor, stayed on and might be worth a try over further in this grade. (op 8-1)
Tar(IRE), from an in-form yard, was well held and looks badly handicapped on what he has achieved. (tchd 10-1)

Bold Pioneer(USA) got very warm beforehand and remains 2lb higher than his victory over course and distance, which was a long time ago. (op 9-1)

403 CRABBIE'S ALCOHOLIC GINGER BEER H'CAP CHASE (16 fncs) 2m 4f

8:00 (8:00) (Class 4) (0-100,100) 5-Y-O+ **£4,055** (£1,198; £599; £299; £149)

Form RPR

02-3 **1** **Persian Prince (IRE)**[13] 175 10-10-5 **86**.................. MrJohnDawson(7) 102+
(John Wade) *mde all: lft clr 2 out: rdn out* **8/1**

44-5 **2** *28* **I'm Your Man**[18] 88 11-11-1 **96**..................................(p) AlexanderVoy(7) 93
(Evelyn Slack) *chsd ldrs: wnt 2nd 4th: 3 l down and hld whn blnd bdly 2 out: lft 16 l 2nd last* **11/2**[3]

20P- **3** *11* **High Stand Lad**[26] 5374 8-11-12 **100**................................ DenisO'Regan 85
(Martin Todhunter) *chsd ldrs: one pce fr 4 out: lft modest 3rd last* **14/1**

4U-1 **4** *5* **Star Tenor (IRE)**[19] 77 8-11-3 **91**...................................... PaddyAspell 72
(Sandy Forster) *in rr: hdwy 7th: chsng ldrs 10th: drvn 4 out: wknd after next: lft poor 4th last* **5/1**[2]

264- **5** *10* **Naval Attache**[28] 5312 8-10-5 **82**..................................(p) DerekLaverty(3) 55
(Fred Kirby) *j.rt: in tch: reminders 7th: lost pl 10th: hung rt sn bhd* **11/1**

0U2- **6** *10* **Letham Island (IRE)**[45] 5015 6-11-9 **100**................(tp) RichardKilloran(3) 65
(Tim Vaughan) *in rr: bhd whn mstke 6th: t.o 11th* **8/1**

00-3 **F** **Winged Farasi**[19] 77 6-11-7 **95**.. TjadeCollier 99
(Joanne Foster) *hdwy to chse ldrs 7th: hrd drvn appr 3 out: kpt on and 10 l 2nd whn fell last* **18/1**

3P-6 **U** **Solway Blue**[4] 336 8-10-10 **87**.. HarryHaynes(3) —
(Lisa Harrison) *hld up in rr: j.rt 1st: hit 9th: 7th and outpcd whn stmbld and uns rdr 11th* **10/1**

303- **F** **Ginger's Lad**[24] 9 6-10-1 **75**...(p) BrianHughes —
(Michael Easterby) *chsd ldrs: blnd 8th: disputing 2nd whn fell 12th* **11/4**[1]

5m 0.30s (-2.70) **Going Correction** 0.0s/f (Good) **9** Ran SP% **110.3**

Speed ratings: **105,93,89,87,83 79,—,—,—**

toteswingers:1&2 £6.80, 2&3 £43.20, 1&3 £60.90 TOTE £7.80: £2.60, £1.50, £4.40; EX 25.10.

Owner John Wade **Bred** Miller's Bloodstock Ltd **Trained** Mordon, Co Durham

■ The first winner under rules for John Dawson, who is having a good season in point-to-points.

■ Stewards' Enquiry : Mr John Dawson two-day ban: used whip when clearly winning (tbn)

FOCUS

A very ordinary 0-100 handicap chase, the early pace was even.

NOTEBOOK

Persian Prince(IRE), who made all, deserved to get his head in front after running consistently all season. At the age of ten, he is fully exposed and the handicapper shouldn't be too harsh. He should remain competitive in similar company. (op 9-1 tchd 15-2)

I'm Your Man again ran a solid race and didn't help his chances with a mistake at the penultimate fence. (op 7-1)

High Stand Lad, coming from a yard among the winners, looks high enough in the weights. (op 16-1)

Star Tenor(IRE), 4lb higher for his Bangor success, never landed a blow and will need to bounce back after this. Official explanation: jockey said gelding was unsuited by the track (op 9-2)

Naval Attache Official explanation: jockey said gelding hung and jumped right

Letham Island(IRE) Official explanation: jockey said mare lost its confidence after making an early mistake

Winged Farasi would have finished second, but took a heavy fall at the last. This was only his second start over fences, and if none the worse for this, he can continue to pay his way. (op 7-2 tchd 4-1 in places)

Ginger's Lad, tried in cheekpieces, departed five from home. (op 7-2 tchd 4-1 in places)

404 PHOENIX SECURITY H'CAP CHASE (13 fncs) 2m 110y

8:30 (8:30) (Class 5) (0-90,92) 5-Y-O+ **£2,602** (£764; £382; £190)

Form RPR

P35- **1** **Schinken Otto (IRE)**[9] 5216 9-11-6 **86**................... JamesHalliday(5) 97+
(Malcolm Jefferson) *trckd ldrs: led sn after 2 out: 2 l ahd last: styd on wl* **9/2**[2]

16-3 **2** *7* **Troodos Jet**[18] 99 9-11-2 **77**..(p) BrianHughes 82
(Dianne Sayer) *trckd ldrs: mstke 5th: wnt 2nd between last 2: kpt on same pce* **4/1**[1]

0-U4 **3** *¾* **Janal (IRE)**[11] 211 7-10-4 **65**... WilsonRenwick 69
(Stuart Coltherd) *in rr: styd on fr 2 out: lft 5th last: styd on to take 3rd last 50yds: kpt on towards fin* **7/1**[3]

46-0 **4** *1 ¾* **Crofton Arch**[18] 88 10-10-5 **66**...................................(p) PaddyAspell 69
(John Dixon) *reminders after s: w ldr: one pce fr 2 out* **14/1**

32P- **5** *3 ½* **Mischief Man**[113] 3677 8-11-6 **86**...................................... ShaneByrne(5) 87
(Sue Smith) *chsd ldrs: outpcd 4 out: 5th whn hit next: one pce* **9/2**[2]

P63- **6** *1 ¼* **Stolen Light (IRE)**[24] 13 9-10-6 **70**....................(b) MichaelO'Connell(3) 70
(Andrew Crook) *in rr: mstke 4th: in tch 7th: hit next: sn outpcd: one pce fr 3 out* **28/1**

/P-P **7** *8* **Clueless**[11] 212 8-11-2 **80**...(p) HarryHaynes(3) 73
(Carol Ferguson) *in rr: kpt on fr 3 out: hmpd and lft modest 7th last* **16/1**

004- **8** *42* **Mezuzah**[38] 5145 10-11-12 **87**..(p) TjadeCollier 46
(Joanne Foster) *in rr: bhd fr 9th: t.o 3 out* **33/1**

0-P6 **P** **Ballyboe Boy (IRE)**[15] 136 11-10-0 **61** oh5...................(bt) KeithMercer —
(Shaun Harris) *in rr: drvn 5th: sn lost pl: bhd fr 9th: t.o last whn p.u bef last* **33/1**

33-1 **F** **My Condor (IRE)**[10] 233 9-11-12 **92** 7ex........................ JohnKington(5) 93
(Donald McCain) *led: hdd sn after 2 out: 4th and wkng whn fell last* **4/1**[1]

4m 10.9s (2.30) **Going Correction** 0.0s/f (Good) **10** Ran SP% **110.7**

Speed ratings: **94,90,90,89,87 87,83,63,—,—**

toteswingers:1&2 £4.80, 2&3 £3.70, 1&3 £5.40 CSF £21.84 CT £116.43 TOTE £8.30: £3.00, £1.90, £3.50; EX 32.30.

Owner John Donald **Bred** T Burns And Mrs P F N Fanning **Trained** Norton, N Yorks

FOCUS

A good gallop for this 0-90 chase, which was basically a seller all but in name. The winner took advantage of a good mark.

NOTEBOOK

Schinken Otto(IRE), 16lb lower than for his last win, stayed on past some weak finishers to land his first victory in well over two years. (op 11-2)

Troodos Jet again travelled well but didn't find that much. That said, he might prefer easier ground. (tchd 7-2)

Janal(IRE), rated only 65, stayed on strongly from the last and will need to go back up in trip in a bid to find that first win over fences. (op 8-1)

My Condor(IRE), a winner last time out at Worcester, made the early running but was well held when crashing out at the final fence. Despite coming from a respected yard, he is never one to take a short price about. (op 11-4)

405 THORN ACADEMY OF LIGHT H'CAP HURDLE (10 hdls) 2m 5f 110y

9:00 (9:00) (Class 5) (0-95,95) 4-Y-O+ **£2,211** (£649; £324; £162)

Form RPR

0P6- **1** **Pugnacity**[24] 12 6-10-1 **73**.. RyanMania(3) 83+
(Dianne Sayer) *trckd ldrs: smooth hdwy to go handy 2nd after 3 out: shkn up to ld 2 out: 3 l ahd last: pushed out* **7/2**[1]

0F0- **2** *3 ½* **Wotchalike (IRE)**[28] 5311 8-10-13 **82**..................................(p) GrahamLee 89
(Shelley Johnstone) *chsd ldrs: led 3 out: hdd 2 out: kpt on same pce* **12/1**

550- **3** *6* **Knight Valliant**[28] 5311 7-10-13 **85**.............................. JamesO'Farrell(3) 87
(Barbara Butterworth) *hmpd 1st: in rr: hdwy and prom 6th: kpt on to take modest 3rd 2 out* **8/1**

P22- **4** *26* **Sharadiyn**[43] 5072 7-11-9 **95**.. MichaelO'Connell(3) 76
(Clive Mulhall) *chsd ldrs: wknd between last 2* **13/2**[3]

40-5 **5** *2 ½* **Safin (GER)**[14] 166 10-10-8 **77**.. TomMessenger 53
(Sue Bradburne) *in tch: effrt 3 out: wknd appr next* **11/1**

003- **6** *11* **Parisian Knight (IRE)**[22] 31 7-10-8 **77**............................ BrianHughes 43
(A M Crow) *led: hdd 3 out: wknd appr next* **6/1**[2]

P00- **7** *¾* **Appeal Denied (IRE)**[33] 5203 8-11-7 **90**............................ PaddyAspell 55
(Sandy Forster) *mid-div: outpcd 3 out: lost pl bef next* **12/1**

P00/ **8** *8* **Ramblees Holly**[960] 1565 12-10-0 **74**............................ JamesHalliday(5) 32
(Robert Wood) *chsd ldrs: outpcd after 5th: lost pl after 3 out: bhd whn eased run-in* **25/1**

636- **9** *hd* **Pay On (IRE)**[54] 4863 7-10-2 **76**...................................(p) EwanWhillans(5) 34
(Alistair Whillans) *in rr whn blnd 1st: bhd and drvn 4th: t.o 7th* **10/1**

000/ **10** *17* **Tirol Livit (IRE)**[11] 7-9-11 **73** ow1..................................(p) MrJohnDawson(7) 16
(John Wainwright) *w ldrs: lost p;lace after 3 out: sn bhd* **33/1**

060- **11** *7* **Kochanski (IRE)**[70] 4512 4-10-11 **85**..................................(t) KeithMercer 16
(John Weymes) *in rr: hit 1st: bhd whn mstken 3 out* **16/1**

32-P **P** **Benny The Piler (IRE)**[11] 211 10-10-13 **85**...............(p) HarryHaynes(3) —
(Carol Ferguson) *chsd ldrs: lost pl after 5th: t.o whn p.u bef 7th* **10/1**

5m 14.1s (-0.50) **Going Correction** 0.0s/f (Good)

WFA 4 from 6yo+ 19lb **12** Ran SP% **115.5**

Speed ratings (Par 103): **100,98,96,87,86 82,81,79,78,72 70,—**

toteswingers:1&2 £7.20, 2&3 £22.00, 1&3 £6.20 CSF £44.22 CT £314.74 TOTE £3.80: £1.80, £4.90, £1.90; EX 56.80 Place 6: £52.05 Place 5: £45.97.

Owner Anthony White **Bred** Old Mill Stud And S C Williams **Trained** Hackthorpe, Cumbria

FOCUS

Another low-grade handicap hurdle in which the early pace was steady and the first two pulled clear. The first three ran pretty much to their marks.

NOTEBOOK

Pugnacity, back down to her last winning mark, was well backed throughout the morning. She travelled well throughout and won well in the end. All of her three wins have come at this track, but it will require a career best to follow up once the handicapper has had his say. (op 10-3 tchd 3-1)

Wotchalike(IRE), 2lb higher than his last win last July, also travelled well. Clearly in good heart, he should remain competitive.

Knight Valliant was very confidently ridden from off the pace, and with more forcing tactics he can pick up a small race. (op 9-1)

Sharadiyn has been hit hard by the handicapper for a couple of place efforts of late, and on the evidence of this will continue to struggle of his current mark. (op 6-1 tchd 11-2)

Pay On(IRE)was always struggling after making a bad mistake at the first.

Benny The Piler(IRE) Official explanation: jockey said gelding never travelled

T/Plt: £71.50. Pool: £85,062.73 - 868.40 winning tickets. T/Qpdt: £32.20. Pool:£5,759.32 - 132.00 winning tickets. WG

[231]WORCESTER (L-H)

Wednesday, May 19

OFFICIAL GOING: Good to firm

Wind: Almost nil Weather: Overcast but warm

406 HARGREAVE HALE STOCKBROKERS HUNTERS' CHASE (18 fncs) 2m 7f

5:50 (5:51) (Class 6) 5-Y-O+ **£1,186** (£365; £182)

Form RPR

/0-2 **1** **It's Like That (IRE)**[14] 152 10-12-0 114........................... MrAJBerry 119
(Jonjo O'Neill) *hld up and bhd: nt fluent 1st: hdwy 14th: sn rdn: chsd ldr 2 out: styd on u.p to ld towards fin* **10/11**[1]

F4-3 **2** *nk* **Nobody Tells Me (FR)**[14] 151 9-11-5 105........................ MissCAllen(5) 115
(E Walker) *hld up: hdwy 10th: led after 12th: rdr looked over wrong shoulder flat: rdn and hdd towards fin* **7/2**[2]

3 *22* **Stormy Bob (IRE)**[16] 11-10-13 0.. MrLRPayter(7) 90
(Mrs C Wilesmith) *chsd ldr: blnd 3rd: led 11th: hdd after next: wknd bef last* **20/1**

U/ **4** *1 ¾* **May Be Possible (IRE)**[44] 11-11-1 0............................ MrDavidTurner(5) 87
(Mrs G Bryan) *prom tl wknd 13th* **33/1**

050/ **5** *3 ¼* **Avesomeofthat (IRE)**[11] 9-10-13 0..................................(t) MissHLewis(7) 86
(Miss Hannah Lewis) *hld up: blnd 7th: hdwy 10th: chsd ldr 5 out: wkng whn mstke 2 out* **11/1**

0/1- **P** **Winning Counsel (IRE)**[16] 8-11-0 0.............................. MrsAlexDunn(7) —
(Miss A Smith-Maxwell) *led at gd pce: j. slowly 2nd: hdd 11th: wknd 14th: t.o whn p.u bef next* **13/2**[3]

P **Mister Kay Bee**[16] 9-11-6 0..(b) MrDMansell —
(Miss J Houldey) *hld up: bhd fr 9th: t.o whn p.u bef next* **28/1**

0/ **P** **Su Bleu (IRE)**[10] 8-10-13 0.. MrSWDrinkwater(7) —
(Paul King) *prom: hit 9th: wkng whn j.rt 11th: sn p.u* **20/1**

5m 38.6s (-4.00) **Going Correction** -0.175s/f (Good) **8** Ran SP% **112.2**

Speed ratings: **99,98,91,90,89 —,—,—**

toteswingers: 1&2 £2.90, 1&3 £8.90, 2&3 £38.00 CSF £4.07 TOTE £2.00: £1.80, £1.10, £5.10; EX 5.30.

Owner John P McManus **Bred** Mrs S Brennan **Trained** Cheltenham, Gloucs

FOCUS

An uncompetitive hunter chase. The firfst two are rated pretty much to their marks.

NOTEBOOK

It's Like That(IRE) was never jumping or travelling with any fluency and seemed to be toiling down the back, but his rider kept rowing away on him and his extra stamina came into play, eventually getting on top close home. He had finished second over 4m1f at Cheltenham last time, but won't be able to afford such a laboured performance in a better race. (op 11-10 tchd 5-4 and 4-5)

Nobody Tells Me(FR) took over after the 12th and looked far the likeliest winner turning in, but the favourite slowly ate into his advantage and he was worn down close home. (op 9-2 tchd 3-1)

Stormy Bob(IRE) stopped quickly from two out. (op 33-1)

Avesomeofthat(IRE) found little and was disappointing. (op 6-1 tchd 12-1)

Winning Counsel(IRE) jumped slowly and was quickly brushed aside. (op 5-1)

407 CHELTENHAM AND THREE COUNTIES CLUB "NATIONAL HUNT" NOVICES' HURDLE (8 hdls) 2m

6:20 (6:20) (Class 4) 4-Y-0+ **£2,927** (£859; £429; £214)

Form | | | | RPR
200/ **1** **Washango (IRE)**[810] 4185 8-10-0 0 SamTwiston-Davies(5) 95+
(Shaun Lycett) *hld up in tch: tk clsr order 3 out: rdn to ld fnl 100yds: r.o wl* **11/2**[3]
43-4 **2** *1 3/4* **Lord Landen (IRE)**[13] 167 5-10-12 110 AidanColeman 100
(Rachel Hobbs) *racd keenly: w ldr tl led after 2nd: slipped bnd sn after: rdn and hdd last: rallied flat: outpcd towards fin* **1/1**[1]
21-3 **3** *hd* **Midnight Spirit**[9] 252 10-10-12 100 (tp) AnthonyFreeman(7) 106
(Frederick Sutherland) *prom: trckd ldr appr 3rd: chal 2 out: led last: rdn and hdd fnl 100yds: nt qckn* **10/3**[2]
600- **4** *10* **Nobby Kivambo (IRE)**[84] 4236 5-10-12 90 WarrenMarston 89
(Brendan Powell) *hld up and bhd: hdwy after 5th: styd on same pce fr 3 out* **20/1**
0-53 **5** *11* **Evening Haze**[7] 275 6-9-12 0 MrDGPrichard(7) 71
(Phillip Dando) *prom: rdn after 3 out: wknd appr last* **6/1**
0PP- **6** *41* **Achiltibuie (IRE)**[26] 5354 5-10-12 0 (p) ChristianWilliams 37
(Dai Burchell) *racd keenly: led: hdd after 2nd: slipped bnd sn after: wknd after 5th: t.o* **66/1**
UPP- **7** *15* **Simbamead**[154] 2912 5-10-9 0 (p) AlexMerriam(3) 22
(Michael Mullineaux) *hld up in tch: rdn 4th: wknd next: t.o* **33/1**
8 *10* **Secret Shared (IRE)**[39] 6-10-5 0 MrJBanks(7) 12
(Richard Mitchell) *hld up: pushed along after 3rd: wknd next: t.o* **100/1**

3m 41.6s (-5.70) **Going Correction** -0.40s/f (Good) 8 Ran SP% **112.9**
Speed ratings (Par 105): **98,97,97,92,86 66,58,53**
toteswingers: 1&2 £1.90, 1&3 £2.50, 2&3 £1.50 CSF £11.58 TOTE £5.40: £1.20, £1.10, £1.10.
Owner The Berryman Lycett Experience **Bred** Dr D B A Silk **Trained** Clapton-on-the-Hill, Gloucs

FOCUS
A very ordinary novice hurdle but the form makes sense.

NOTEBOOK
Washango(IRE) overcame an 810-day absence to make it second time lucky over hurdles. She had shown some fair place form in bumpers back in 2007, and the way she stayed on to assert in the final half furlong suggests she will have no trouble getting further. (op 7-2 tchd 10-3)
Lord Landen(IRE), who slipped and lost his footing racing out on to the final circuit, failed to settle early and, though this drop in trip should have suited, he couldn't quicken in the straight, rallying late to reclaim second. He may find life easier in handicaps, but needs to relax before he can win. (op 5-4)
Midnight Spirit, winner of a maiden hurdle at Chepstow before placing off 100 in a handicap, looked vulnerable under a penalty, but came there travelling strongly in the straight and looked the likely winner. He couldn't quicken from the last, though, and lost out on second. (tchd 3-1 and 7-2)
Nobby Kivambo(IRE) is only rated 90 and showed enough to suggest he will be competitive in handicaps.
Evening Haze ended up well held and doesn't look to be progressing. (op 9-1 tchd 11-2)

408 DINNER IN THE SEVERN RESTAURANT BEGINNERS' CHASE (18 fncs) 2m 7f

6:50 (6:50) (Class 4) 5-Y-0+ **£3,252** (£955; £477; £238)

Form | | | | RPR
120- **1** **Baddam**[15] 5113 8-11-0 0 DougieCostello 125+
(Ian Williams) *led and nt fluent early: hdd 2nd: chsd ldr: led again after 5th: clr fr 10th: eased flat* **6/4**[1]
4/P- **2** *23* **Cullahill (IRE)**[36] 5175 8-11-0 0 (t) HarrySkelton 99+
(Bob Buckler) *hld up: hdwy 13th: wknd bef 4 out: wnt remote 2nd 3 out* **7/1**[3]
35-0 **3** *15* **Orchard King (IRE)**[15] 131 9-10-7 0 (b) OliverDayman(7) 81
(Alison Thorpe) *chsd ldrs tl wknd 5 out: t.o* **17/2**
262- **4** *14* **Another Trump (NZ)**[177] 2467 6-11-0 0 APMcCoy 74
(Jonjo O'Neill) *nt fluent: hld up and bhd: hdwy to chse wnr 5 out: wknd bef next: blnd and lost 2nd 3 out: t.o* **9/4**[2]
5 *dist* **Smart Dwellie**[444] 7-11-0 0 ColinBolger 27
(Kevin Bishop) *led 2nd: hdd after 5th: chsd ldr: wkng whn blnd 5 out: t.o* **40/1**
233- **U** **Silver Story**[18] 7-10-9 0 DeanColeman(5) —
(Tim Vaughan) *chsd ldrs: disputing 2nd whn mstke and uns rdr 11th* **7/1**[3]
/04- **U** **Sprowler**[26] 5358 6-10-7 0 AnthonyFreeman(7) —
(Joanna Davis) *hld up: mstke 1st: bhd whn blnd and uns rdr 7th* **80/1**

5m 43.6s (1.00) **Going Correction** -0.175s/f (Good) 7 Ran SP% **110.0**
Speed ratings: **91,83,77,72,59 —,—**
toteswingers: 1&2 £3.70, 1&3 £2.40, 2&3 £6.20 CSF £11.66 TOTE £2.10: £1.20, £5.20; EX 10.90.
Owner N Martin **Bred** Mrs V Rapkins **Trained** Portway, Worcs

FOCUS
This was won in dominant fashion by Baddam, who was a 133-rated hurdler at his best and can rate higher over fences.

NOTEBOOK
Baddam made most of the running and, after being slow at a couple early on, jumped well on this first start over fences. He was in total control from a long way out and never saw a challenge. The form is worth nothing, but he may win again if finding the right opportunity. (op 9-4 tchd 11-8)
Cullahill(IRE), making his chasing debut, popped round in his own time and comfortably took second, his jockey very much having an eye on the future. (op 8-1 tchd 13-2)
Orchard King(IRE), pulled up on his one previous try over fences (15 months ago), never posed a threat and was beaten a long way. (op 8-1 tchd 10-1)
Another Trump(NZ), rated 123 over hurdles, made his share of mistakes on this first start over fences and was beaten well before the straight. (op 5-2 tchd 11-4)
Silver Story was still very much in contention and may well have finished second but for unseating. (op 7-2)

409 LADIES DAY 5 JUNE NOVICES' HURDLE (12 hdls) 3m

7:20 (7:21) (Class 4) 4-Y-0+ **£2,927** (£859; £429; £214)

Form | | | | RPR
3P-1 **1** **American World (FR)**[20] 65 6-10-13 109 (t) APMcCoy 114+
(Brendan Powell) *hld up: hdwy 8th: rdn appr 3 out: mstkes last 2 flight: swtchd rt flat: styd on wl u.p to ld towards fin* **2/1**[1]
00-3 **2** *1* **Mzuri Bay**[13] 168 5-10-13 0 (t) MarkGrant 110
(Brendan Duke) *chsd ldrs: rdn to ld flat: sn hung lft: hdd towards fin* **16/1**
5/1- **3** *1 1/2* **Native Taipan (IRE)**[23] 15 8-11-5 0 RobertThornton 114
(Rebecca Curtis) *led to 8th: led again 4 out: rdn and hdd flat: styd on same pce* **2/1**[1]
13-1 **4** *10* **Brimham Boy**[14] 156 8-10-13 0 (t) WarrenMarston 98
(Martin Keighley) *chsd ldr tl led 8th: hdd next: sn rdn: wknd appr last* **11/4**[2]
/25- **5** *3 1/4* **Off Gallivanting**[26] 5368 5-10-10 0 RichieMcLernon(3) 96+
(Jonjo O'Neill) *hld up: hdwy 5th: wknd 2 out* **10/1**[3]
6 *30* **Lightning Moley (IRE)**[395] 7-10-13 0 (t) AndrewThornton 65
(Tracey Watkins) *hld up: dropped in rr 7th: wknd after 4 out: t.o: fin lame* **25/1**
P4-U **7** *6* **Commanche Dream**[9] 251 7-10-10 0 CharlieStudd(3) 59
(Simon Lewis) *prom tl rdn and wknd appr 3 out: t.o* **50/1**
500- **P** **Nether Stream (IRE)**[27] 5344 6-10-8 0 SamTwiston-Davies(5) —
(Shaun Lycett) *hld up: wknd appr 3 out: 6th whn p.u bef next* **50/1**

5m 38.6s (-6.00) **Going Correction** -0.40s/f (Good) 8 Ran SP% **116.1**
Speed ratings (Par 105): **94,93,93,89,88 78,76,—**
toteswingers: 1&2 £5.80, 1&3 £1.20, 2&3 £6.30 CSF £33.02 TOTE £3.20: £2.30, £3.30, £1.02; EX 36.50.
Owner John P McManus **Bred** Mme Chantel Hamon **Trained** Upper Lambourn, Berks

FOCUS
Tony McCoy really pulled this one out of the fire aboard American World. Ordinary novice hurdle form.

NOTEBOOK
American World(FR) looked booked for third 100 yards from the line, having blundered at the last, but he rallied strongly and was lifted across the line. A winner over fences last month, he proved fully effective on this return to hurdles, which he had never previously won over, and saw the trip out better than some may have expected. He is only six and may still be improving. (tchd 15-8 and 9-4)
Mzuri Bay, well beaten on both previous starts over hurdles, proved a different proposition in the first-time tongue tie and looked the winner after the last, but having hung across to the rail, he was run down close home. He could pick up a small race if improving again. (op 20-1)
Native Taipan(IRE), all out to win at Ffos Las, had more on here under a penalty and his rider tried to make use of his stamina, but he couldn't quicken on the flat. (op 5-2 tchd 13-8)
Brimham Boy, a winner off 98 over fences latest, had never previously won over hurdles and he failed to get home having been bang there turning in. (op 10-3 tchd 7-2)
Off Gallivanting, who showed a bit of ability in bumpers, moved up well down the back, but didn't pick up in the straight and his stamina appeared to give way. (op 17-2 tchd 12-1)
Lightning Moley(IRE) Official explanation: vet said gelding finished stiff
Nether Stream(IRE) Official explanation: jockey said gelding hung left-handed

410 RED DEVILS FAMILY FUN DAY 6 JUNE H'CAP HURDLE (10 hdls) 2m 4f

7:50 (7:50) (Class 5) (0-95,95) 4-Y-0+ **£2,055** (£599; £299)

Form | | | | RPR
26F/ **1** **Cash Back**[1312] 1694 10-10-5 81 RachaelGreen(7) 91+
(Anthony Honeyball) *hld up: hdwy after 7th: chsd ldr 2 out: shkn up and r.o to ld nr fin* **16/1**
2P2- **2** *hd* **Basford Lass**[28] 5318 5-11-6 89 (b) AlanO'Keeffe 98
(Jennie Candlish) *led: clr last: rdn flat: hdd nr fin* **9/1**[3]
P0P- **3** *7* **Mujamead**[56] 4821 6-11-1 84 ChristianWilliams 86
(Sally-Anne Wheelwright) *chsd ldrs: outpcd 6th: rallied 3 out: styd on same pce fr last* **33/1**
UF0- **4** *10* **Kentmere (IRE)**[94] 2663 9-11-12 95 SamJones 89
(Paul Webber) *prom: chsd ldr appr 3 out to next: sn rdn: wknd last* **11/1**
04-0 **5** *3* **Witch Of The Wave (IRE)**[9] 252 4-11-7 95 (tp) RobertThornton 79
(Joanna Davis) *hld up: hdwy 5th: lost pl after next: n.d after* **11/1**
432/ **6** *nse* **Penric**[897] 2606 10-10-7 83 LucyBarry(7) 72
(Martin Bosley) *hld up: hdwy 7th: wknd bef next* **40/1**
04-2 **7** *4 1/2* **Captain Becket**[7] 273 7-10-13 85 HaddenFrost(3) 69
(James Frost) *chsd ldr tl rdn and wknd appr 3 out* **13/8**[1]
61-6 **8** *4* **Pearly Star**[19] 84 9-11-7 95 (b) MarcGoldstein(5) 75
(Jim Best) *chsd ldrs: rdn after 7th: wknd bef next* **9/1**[3]
04-0 **9** *2 1/4* **Mix N Match**[13] 172 6-11-6 92 EamonDehdashti(3) 70
(Gerald Ham) *hld up: pushed along 6th: hdwy next: wknd bef 3 out* **16/1**
00P- **10** *29* **Tribunel**[33] 5216 6-10-12 84 SeanQuinlan(3) 33
(Kim Bailey) *hld up: bhd fr 5th: t.o* **40/1**
46F- **P** **Satindra (IRE)**[73] 4470 6-10-11 85 (p) LeeEdwards(5) —
(Carole Ikin) *hld up in tch: rdn 5th: sn wknd: t.o whn p.u bef 3 out* **18/1**
P05- **P** **Cricket Boy**[65] 4654 6-11-7 90 (b) APMcCoy —
(David Pipe) *hld up in tch: mstke 2nd: pushed along after 4th: wknd 6th: t.o whn p.u bef 3 out* **13/2**[2]
5-0 **P** **Kaliski (IRE)**[20] 58 6-11-6 89 TomO'Brien —
(David Brace) *hld up: pushed along after 4th: bhd fr next: t.o whn p.u bef 7th* **40/1**

4m 37.9s (-9.50) **Going Correction** -0.40s/f (Good)
WFA 4 from 5yo+ 19lb 13 Ran SP% **115.4**
Speed ratings (Par 103): **103,102,100,96,94 94,93,91,90,79 —,—,—**
toteswingers: 1&2 £15.90, 2&3 £56.20, 1&3 £74.70 CSF £143.99 CT £4599.13 TOTE £27.90: £9.00, £2.00, £14.20; EX 323.80.
Owner Neil & Susie Dalgren **Bred** Trefusis Farm **Trained** Seaborough, Dorset

FOCUS
A moderate handicap hurdle. The winner is rated to his 2006 mark.

NOTEBOOK
Cash Back, returning from a 1,312-day absence and backed, had only run four times over hurdles previously, his best effort coming when second in a selling hurdle, but he was clearly straight enough and stayed on strongly close home to deny long-time leader Basford Lass. Winning off a mark of just 81, it remains to be seen which way he goes from this. (op 25-1)
Basford Lass, beaten 24l when second at Southwell last time, was soon in front and made them all go, but having looked the winner taking the last, she could not quite hang on. (op 8-1 tchd 7-1)
Mujamead was under pressure a long way out, but did keep plugging away and ended up a clear third.
Kentmere(IRE), who has been running well on the Flat, was never far away and had his chance, but his stamina gave out from the second-last. (tchd 9-1 and 12-1)
Witch Of The Wave(IRE) kept on again but never posed a threat. (op 14-1)
Captain Becket, a good second over 3m at Exeter latest, looked the one to beat and was ridden positively on this drop in trip, but he did not find for pressure and dropped out rather tamely. (op 15-8)
Satindra(IRE) Official explanation: trainer said gelding had a breathing problem (op 4-1)
Cricket Boy received an early reminder and stopped quickly having briefly rallied down the back. (op 4-1)

411 WORCESTER-RACECOURSE.CO.UK H'CAP CHASE (16 fncs 2 omitted) 2m 7f

8:20 (8:20) (Class 3) (0-135,135) 5-Y-0 **£5,703** (£1,684; £842; £421; £210)

Form | | | | RPR
41-P **1** **Oscar Bay (IRE)**[11] 206 8-11-8 134 (b) HaddenFrost(3) 142+
(James Frost) *a.p: pushed along 10th: hmpd bnd appr 4 out: styd on u.p to ld nr fin* **15/2**
216- **2** *1 1/4* **Sou'Wester**[24] 5 10-11-4 127 (p) JoeTizzard 133
(Colin Tizzard) *hld up: hdwy 10th: chsd ldr appr 4 out: led bef last: rdn and hdd nr fin* **10/1**

5U2- **3** *6* **Mizen Raven (IRE)**[277] 1215 7-10-13 **122**.............................. APMcCoy 122
(Paul Nicholls) *chsd ldr tl led 9th: rdn and hdd appr last: wknd towards fin* **2/1**[1]

04-3 **4** *½* **Dennis The Legend**[14] 152 9-10-3 **112**.............................. NickScholfield 113
(Grant Cann) *hld up: hdwy 5th: rdn 4 out: styd on same pce fr 2 out* **3/1**[2]

41-1 **5** *5* **Warpath (IRE)**[10] 236 9-11-6 **129** 7ex.............................. PaulMoloney 125
(Evan Williams) *chsd ldr 10th tl rdn appr 4 out: wknd 2 out* **4/1**[3]

16-2 **6** *7* **The Duke's Speech (IRE)**[18] 87 9-10-12 **121**................ CharliePoste 112+
(Sophie Leech) *hld up: hdwy appr 4 out: wkng whn mstke 2 out* **25/1**

20-P **7** *57* **Free Gift**[10] 236 12-10-12 **121**..(p) DarylJacob 52
(R H & Mrs S Alner) *led to 9th: wknd after 11th: t.o* **16/1**

PP6- **P** **Psychomodo**[23] 18 8-11-12 **135**..............................(t) JimmyMcCarthy —
(Brendan Powell) *w.r.s and wl bhd: j.rt 3rd: managed to get win a couple of l of the rr gp gng to the 9th: sn wknd: t.o whn p.u and dismntd bef the 12th: lame* **25/1**

5m 34.2s (-8.40) **Going Correction** -0.175s/f (Good) course record **8** Ran SP% **112.8**
Speed ratings: **107,106,104,104,102 100,80,—**
toteswingers:1&2 £15.70, 2&3 £5.30, 1&3 £4.30 CSF £72.91 CT £204.17 TOTE £8.20: £2.30, £3.30, £1.10; EX 101.70.

Owner G Thompson **Bred** Gabriel White **Trained** Scorriton, Devon

FOCUS
A decent little handicap chase. The winner is rated to his best 2009 form.

NOTEBOOK
Oscar Bay(IRE), a winner off 2lb lower over hurdles last month, was pulled up last time, but he did not look badly weighted on this return to fences and, despite being squeezed and dropping back to sixth turning in, he stayed on best over the last couple of fences, really picking up well after the last to get on top. This was his first win at a trip that clearly suits now. (op 10-1)

Sou'Wester, disappointing off 2lb lower at Ludlow last time, had earlier won well at Wincanton and this represented a return to that sort of form, just failing to stay on as strongly as the winner. (tchd 9-1 and 12-1)

Mizen Raven(IRE) failed to improve on this first start for Paul Nicholls, fading from the last and ending up comfortably held. (tchd 15-8)

Dennis The Legend lacked the speed to make an impact in the straight and ideally needs a stiffer test. (op 9-2)

Warpath(IRE), chasing a hat-trick, again looked a major player under a penalty, but he was under pressure before the straight and faded disappointingly. (op 11-4 tchd 9-2 in a place)

412 CONFERENCING AND EVENTS AT WORCESTER RACECOURSE STANDARD OPEN NATIONAL HUNT FLAT RACE 2m
8:50 (8:51) (Class 6) 4-6-Y-O **£1,712** (£499; £249)

Form RPR

1 **The Merry Giant (IRE)** 4-11-0 0.............................. APMcCoy 98
(Rebecca Curtis) *chsd ldrs: rdn over 3f out: chal over 2f out: hung lft over 1f out: led ins fnl f: styd on u.p* **4/5**[1]

0- **2** *½* **Railway Diva (IRE)**[39] 5137 6-10-11 0.............................. RobertThornton 94
(Tim Vaughan) *chsd ldr tl led over 3f out: rdn and hung lft over 1f out: hdd ins fnl f: styd on* **20/1**

3 *1¼* **Alaska River (IRE)** 4-10-7 0.............................. MarkGrant 89
(Brendan Duke) *hld up: hdwy over 5f out: rdn and hung lft fr over 1f out: r.o* **40/1**

4- **4** *2* **Sothisisit (FR)**[30] 5284 4-11-0 0..............................(t) DougieCostello 94
(Jonjo O'Neill) *hld up in tch: rdn over 3f out: hung lft over 1f out: styd on same pce ins fnl f* **8/1**

00- **5** *1¼* **Basford Tara**[34] 5200 5-10-11 0.............................. AlanO'Keeffe 90
(Jennie Candlish) *chsd ldrs: outpcd over 2f out: rallied and swtchd rt over 1f out: styd on* **16/1**

065- **6** *6* **Smart Freddy**[30] 5283 4-11-0 0.............................. ChristianWilliams 87
(Lawney Hill) *sn led: rdn and hdd over 2f out: wknd over 1f out* **6/1**[3]

7 *1¾* **Sheezatreasure (IRE)** 5-10-11 0.............................. DavidDennis 82
(James Evans) *hld up: hdwy over 4f out: wknd 2f out* **66/1**

8 *4* **Pathlow (IRE)** 4-11-0 0.............................. TomO'Brien 81
(Anabel L M King) *hld up: hdwy over 5f out: wknd over 2f out:* **11/2**[2]

0- **9** *4* **Time Legend**[23] 27 4-10-2 0.............................. JimmyDerham(5) 70
(Martin Keighley) *hld up: nvr on terms* **40/1**

10 *14* **Miss Harriet** 5-10-4 0.............................. MrJMahot(7) 60
(Rachel Hobbs) *hld up: hdwy 1/2-way: wknd over 3f out: t.o* **40/1**

11 *8* **Glad Schipi (FR)** 5-10-11 0.............................. FelixDeGiles 52
(Tor Sturgis) *hld up: bhd fnl 6f: t.o* **33/1**

12 *5* **Kingston Orla** 5-10-11 0.............................. NickScholfield 47
(Andrew Haynes) *hld up: bhd fnl 6f: t.o* **50/1**

0 **13** *21* **Bridge Street Boy**[20] 60 5-11-1 0.............................. LeeStephens(3) 33
(Susan Johnson) *mid-div: dropped in rr over 6f out: t.o* **100/1**

3m 42.1s (0.40) **Going Correction** -0.40s/f (Good)
WFA 4 from 5yo+ 4lb **13** Ran SP% **121.7**
Speed ratings: **83,82,82,81,80 77,76,74,72,65 61,59,48**
toteswingers:1&2 £10.20, 2&3 £91.00, 1&3 £22.00 CSF £25.75 TOTE £2.40: £1.40, £3.80, £15.80; EX 21.10 Place 6: £30.76 Place 5: £24.14 .

Owner John P McManus **Bred** Cathal Ennis **Trained** Newport, Dyfed

FOCUS
As is often the case in bumpers, the pace was a steady one. Ordinary form.

NOTEBOOK
The Merry Giant(IRE), representing a jockey-trainer combination that has an excellent record together, especially in bumpers, was strong at the head of the market and just did enough to make a winning debut. He was unimpressive, but has scope to do better over jumps and will stay further. (op 6-5 tchd 5-4)

Railway Diva(IRE) bounced back from a poor effort at Chepstow and made the favourite give everything he had. She is only moderate, but should have a future over hurdles. (op 16-1)

Alaska River(IRE) made a satisfactory debut, keeping on for third despite hanging. (op 50-1 tchd 33-1)

Sothisisit(FR) failed to improve much on his debut effort, the application of a tongue-tie making no real difference. (op 4-1)

Basford Tara showed ability again and will want further over hurdles. (op 11-1 tchd 10-1)

Smart Freddy would have gone close to winning this if he had reproduced his latest Kempton fifth. (op 7-1)

T/Plt: £119.90. Pool: £59,053.51- 359.46 winning tickets T/Qpdt: £62.10. Pool: £5,111.61 - 60.85 winning tickets . CR

413 - 419a (Foreign Racing) - See Raceform Interactive

[174] WETHERBY (L-H)
Thursday, May 20

OFFICIAL GOING: Good (good to firm in places; 8.8)
Wind: moderate 1/2 behind Weather: fine and sunny

420 COUNTRY WEEK (S) HURDLE (11 hdls) 2m 4f
2:00 (2:00) (Class 5) 4-7-Y-O **£2,055** (£599; £299)

Form RPR

PP-2 **1** **King Of Castile**[11] 227 6-10-12 109..............................(vt) APMcCoy 111
(Evan Williams) *w ldr: sn drvn along: led 6th: hdd 3 out: led last: drvn rt out* **4/5**[1]

413- **2** *2¼* **Jimbatai (IRE)**[27] 5360 7-10-5 0.............................. MrPJTolman(7) 109
(Tim Vaughan) *trckd ldrs: wnt 3rd 5th: wnt 2nd 8th: led next: rdn and hung rt after 2 out: hdd last: edgd lft and no ex* **9/4**[2]

033- **3** *44* **Starbougg**[16] 3454 6-10-5 100..............................(b[1]) JamesReveley 62
(Keith Reveley) *in rr: drvn 8th: sn outpcd: wnt poor 3rd 3 out* **9/1**[3]

/PP- **4** *3¼* **Rahy's Crown (USA)**[59] 4787 7-10-9 0..............................(p) CharlieStudd(3) 66
(Philip Sharp) *in rr: reminders 6th: wnt modest 3rd after 8th: outpcd appr next: sn lft wl bhd* **150/1**

03-0 **5** *44* **Just Dan**[11] 227 4-10-0 90.............................. MrJohnDawson(7) 22
(David Thompson) *chsd ldng pair: mstke and dropped bk 4th: reminders after next: t.o 7th* **66/1**

/00- **P** **Luna Landing**[16] 4104 7-10-12 114..............................(b) GrahamLee —
(Jedd O'Keeffe) *led: hdd 6th: hit next: and 8th: sn lost pl: poor 5th whn p.u bef 3 out* **9/1**[3]

4m 51.1s (-8.40) **Going Correction** -0.325s/f (Good)
WFA 4 from 6yo+ 19lb **6** Ran SP% **108.5**
Speed ratings: **103,102,84,83,65 —**
toteswingers:1&2:£1.10, 1&3:£5.40, 2&3:£6.10 CSF £2.69 TOTE £1.50: £1.10, £1.60; EX 2.50.There was no bid for winner. Jimbatai was claimed by Barry Leavey for £6,000

Owner D P Barrie & M J Rees **Bred** Matthews Breeding And Racing Ltd **Trained** Llancarfan, Vale Of Glamorgan

FOCUS
The front pair drew well clear in this selling hurdle. They are decent for the grade and are rated to their marks.

NOTEBOOK
King Of Castile came out on top despite looking in trouble turning in. He responded really well to strong riding from McCoy and had rallied to take a narrow lead again at the last. This was his first ever victory and he should remain competitive at this level. (op 11-10)

Jimbatai(IRE), a winner off 110 over fences two starts back, looked to be travelling much the best turning in on this drop in grade/return to hurdles, but he couldn't get away from the winner, having gone on, and was reclaimed at the last. (tchd 2-1)

Starbougg fared best of the remainder, but achieved little. (op 8-1 tchd 10-1)

Luna Landing, the highest-rated of these, stopped quickly and has completely lost his form. (op 11-2)

421 PARTY IN THE PADDOCK ON 3RD JUNE MARES' MAIDEN HURDLE (9 hdls) 2m 110y
2:30 (2:30) (Class 5) 4-Y-0+ **£2,055** (£599; £299)

Form RPR

22- **1** **Astrolibra**[28] 5328 6-11-0 103.............................. APMcCoy 110+
(Mark H Tompkins) *w ldr: led 2nd: hit 2 out: pushed rt out* **4/11**[1]

03-0 **2** *3½* **Knar Mardy**[10] 250 5-10-11 81.............................. AdamPogson(3) 104
(Charles Pogson) *chsd ldrs: wnt 2nd appr 3 out: kpt on: no real imp* **25/1**

24-0 **3** *17* **Saintly Lady (IRE)**[16] 137 5-10-9 0.............................. DonalDevereux(5) 89
(Peter Bowen) *led to 2nd: chsd wnr: rdn 6th: one pce fr next: snatched poor 3rd nr line* **12/1**[3]

0-3 **4** *nse* **Valkyrie (IRE)**[15] 154 4-10-10 0.............................. PaulMoloney 89
(Nick Littmoden) *chsd ldrs: one pce fr 3 out: 11 l 3rd whn blnd bdly last* **9/2**[2]

0-5 **5** *27* **Pursuit Of Purpose**[11] 216 4-10-5 0........... GemmaGracey-Davison(5) 60
(Philip Sharp) *chsd ldrs to 3rd: hdwy 6th: wknd appr next* **50/1**

50-5 **6** *14* **Knockaveen (IRE)**[14] 174 5-11-0 0.............................. BrianHughes 52
(Andrew Crook) *in rr: bhd fr 4th: t.o 6th* **25/1**

00/- **7** *15* **I Feel Fine**[6] 608 7-11-0 0.............................. PeterBuchanan 38
(Alan Kirtley) *stdd s: in rr: hdwy 4th: wknd after 6th: sn wl bhd: t.o* **200/1**

3m 53.7s (-2.10) **Going Correction** -0.325s/f (Good)
WFA 4 from 5yo+ 18lb **7** Ran SP% **109.3**
Speed ratings (Par 103): **91,89,81,81,68 62,54**
toteswingers:1&2:£4.90, 1&3:£1.90, 2&3:£22.40 CSF £12.08 TOTE £1.50: £1.10, £5.50; EX 11.20.

Owner Mystic Meg Limited **Bred** Mystic Meg Limited **Trained** Newmarket, Suffolk

FOCUS
A weak mares' hurdle. The winner stood out and is rated 10lb below her best.

NOTEBOOK
Astrolibra made near enough all the running and never looked in any danger. She had to be kept up to her work, and will find life tougher under a penalty, but could win again at some stage. (op 4-9 tchd 1-2 in a place)

Knar Mardy went second leaving the back straight and kept on in valiant pursuit of the winner without ever looking likely to trouble her. (op 22-1 tchd 20-1)

Saintly Lady(IRE) clearly needs further and was fortunate to take third. She has the ability to win over hurdles when upped in trip. (op 9-1)

Valkyrie(IRE) blundered badly at the last and lost third. She is capable of winning a little race. (op 5-1 tchd 11-2)

422 LIFE & STYLE NOVICES' CHASE (13 fncs) 2m
3:05 (3:05) (Class 4) 5-Y-0+ **£3,252** (£955; £477; £238)

Form RPR

00-0 **1** **Mutual Friend (USA)**[12] 207 6-10-12 0....................(b) TomScudamore 134+
(David Pipe) *sn trcking ldr: led 4 out: qcknd 5 l clr last: easily* **4/9**[1]

610- **2** *8* **Stagecoach Pearl**[23] 34 6-10-12 0.............................. TjadeCollier 123+
(Sue Smith) *tk fierce hold: j.lft: trckd ldrs: upsides 4 out: styd on same pce fr 2 out* **3/1**[2]

P22- **3** *15* **Blacktoft (USA)**[25] 1 7-10-12 0..............................(e) PaulMoloney 111+
(Evan Williams) *set str pce: hdd 4 out: one pce fr next: eased run-in* **12/1**[3]

0P- **4** *29* **Executive's Hall (IRE)**[60] 4753 6-10-12 0.............................. KeithMercer 78
(Andrew Crook) *nt fluent: chsd ldrs: outpcd and lost pl 4th: drvn 7th: hdwy to chse ldrs 4 out: sn wknd: bhd whn mstke next* **14/1**

3m 44.9s (-10.90) **Going Correction** -0.55s/f (Firm) course record **4** Ran SP% **108.6**
Speed ratings: **105,101,93,79**
CSF £2.29 TOTE £1.30; EX 2.00.

Owner Pond House Racing **Bred** Gainsborough Farm Llc **Trained** Nicholashayne, Devon

FOCUS
The easy winner was value for further and to the level of his previous chase form. The runner-up looks a certain future chase winner.
NOTEBOOK
Mutual Friend(USA), a 135-rated hurdler, was found what looked a great opportunity to get off the mark over fences, and he duly won with ease. A horse who has often failed to find for pressure in the past, he didn't have to come off the bridle having gone on soon after the fourth-last, and could be the type to run up a sequence this summer, with him relishing a fast surface. (tchd 1-2 after early 8-13 in a place)
Stagecoach Pearl ⊠ , a 114-rated hurdler, was very keen and couldn't match the classier winner, but he jumped well in the main and showed more than enough to suggest he will be winning races over fences. (op 11-4)
Blacktoft(USA), twice beaten in claiming hurdles this year, didn't run badly and will find easier opportunities. (op 10-1)
Executive's Hall(IRE) came in for a bit of support beforehand, but he was under strong pressure and beaten before they reached the straight. (op 66-1 tchd 12-1)

423 "DRESSING ROOM - HARROGATE" BEST DRESSED LADY H'CAP HURDLE (9 hdls) 2m 110y
3:40 (3:41) (Class 4) (0-115,112) 4-Y-0+ **£2,602** (£764; £382; £190)

Form RPR
341- **1** **Tharaya**[22] 52 5-10-9 **95** ... KeithMercer 110+
(James Turner) *trckd ldr: led 2 out: wnt 6 l clr last: easily* **15/8**[1]
6- **2** *9* **Two Left Boots (FR)**[240] 1492 6-11-7 **112** ... DeanColeman(5) 115
(Tim Vaughan) *stdd s: t.k.h: trckd ldrs 3rd: upsides whn hit 3 out: rdn and hung lft between last 2: kpt on same pce* **5/2**[2]
560- **3** *1* **Kayf Commander**[39] 5147 7-10-10 **96** ... AndrewTinkler 97
(Mel Brittain) *led: hdd 2 out: kpt on same pce* **5/1**
40-0 **4** *3* **Motive (FR)**[14] 179 9-11-2 **102** ... BrianHughes 100
(Howard Johnson) *chsd ldrs: upsides 3 out: one pce fr next: lame* **7/2**[3]
000- **5** *1 ¾* **Waldo Winchester (IRE)**[65] 4666 7-9-4 **86** oh1 ... AndrewCooper(10) 86
(Tracy Waggott) *trckd ldrs: upsides 3 out: hit next: hung lft and one pce* **8/1**

3m 56.5s (0.70) **Going Correction** -0.325s/f (Good) **5** Ran SP% **113.4**
Speed ratings (Par 105): **85,80,80,78,78**
CSF £7.39 TOTE £3.00: £1.10, £1.30; EX 6.10.
Owner Miss S J Turner **Bred** Barry Walters Catering **Trained** Norton-le-Clay, N Yorks
FOCUS
A moderate and slowly run handicap hurdle. Another step up from the winner with the next pair a few pounds off their best.
NOTEBOOK
Tharaya, easy winner of a selling hurdle latest, was 12lb higher than when last contesting a handicap but, judging by the way she won this, she is a much-improved mare. Always travelling strongly, she readily drew clear having led two out, and connections will no doubt try and get her out under a penalty. (op 2-1 tchd 9-4 and 5-2 in a place)
Two Left Boots(FR), making his debut for the yard, raced keenly under restraint, but readily made his ground and held every chance in the straight, but was left for dead by the winner. He did stay on for second, though, and can probably win something similar. (tchd 3-1)
Kayf Commander had the run of things out in front, but was readily brushed aside and didn't have the pace over this trip. (op 6-1)
Motive(FR) unfortunately finished lame. (op 4-1 tchd 10-3)

424 WETHERBYRACING.CO.UK LADY RIDERS' H'CAP HURDLE (13 hdls) 3m 1f
4:15 (4:15) (Class 5) (0-95,95) 4-Y-0+ **£2,055** (£599; £299)

Form RPR
-112 **1** **Flying Doctor**[6] 318 7-11-5 **95** ... MissJennyCarr(7) 107+
(Elliott Cooper) *hld up: hdwy to trck ldrs 5th: led on bit 2 out: smoothly* **9/4**[1]
P6-1 **2** *3 ¼* **Finbin (IRE)**[12] 211 8-11-4 **94** ... (t) MissGAndrews(7) 96+
(Henry Hogarth) *rn in snatches: drvn 6th: hdwy appr 3 out: styd on one pce fr next: kpt on to take n.d 2nd towards fin* **4/1**[2]
0P-P **3** *¾* **Cute N You Know It**[14] 176 7-9-9 **71** ... (b) MissIsabelTompsett(7) 71
(Andrew Crook) *w ldr: led 8th: hdd 2 out: kpt on same pce* **8/1**
64-4 **4** *5* **Fly Tipper**[15] 163 10-9-7 **69** oh5 ... MissLAlexander(7) 66
(Wilf Storey) *hld up in rr: jnd ldrs 7th: wknd appr last* **12/1**
P0-0 **5** *17* **Rosie Larkin (IRE)**[11] 227 6-9-7 **69** oh9 ... (t) MissSamanthaDrake(7) 50
(Joss Saville) *chsd ldrs: outpcd appr 3 out: grad wknd* **66/1**
30-0 **6** *2 ¼* **Insignia (IRE)**[11] 227 8-10-5 **81** ... (p) MissGTutty(7) 62
(Karen Tutty) *in rr: bhd fr 3 out: 6th whn blnd last* **50/1**
33-0 **7** *½* **Carmela Maria**[15] 157 5-10-11 **87** ... (p) MissCCundall(7) 65
(Mike Sowersby) *wnt prom 4th: rdn along 9th: lost pl next* **12/1**
300- **8** *1 ¼* **General Simara**[28] 5339 6-10-4 **80** ... MissBAndrews(7) 57
(Tony Carroll) *mid-div: drvn after 7th: lost pl appr 3 out* **33/1**
P00- **P** **Fortune's Fool**[183] 2367 11-9-7 **69** oh8 ... MrsJoanneBrown(7) —
(Ian Brown) *trckd ldrs 4th: hmpd and lost pl 10th: sn bhd: t.o whn p.u after 2 out* **100/1**
FPU- **P** **Maclean**[145] 3025 9-10-7 **81** ... GemmaGracey-Davison(5) —
(Philip Sharp) *in rr: bhd and drvn 8th: t.o whn p.u bef 3 out* **40/1**
03-P **U** **Humourous (IRE)**[14] 176 8-9-9 **71** ... (t) MissJRRichards(7) —
(Brian Storey) *led: hdd 8th: w ldr whn mstke and uns rdr 10th* **18/1**
321- **P** **Rusty Red (IRE)**[26] 5387 7-11-7 **95** ... MissLHorner(5) —
(Chris Grant) *wnt prom 5th: drvn and hit 9th: lost pl appr 3 out: 6th whn p.u after 3 out: lame* **8/1**
63-3 **P** **Miss Tarantella**[14] 176 7-10-9 **85** ... (t) MissAngelaBarnes(7) —
(Maurice Barnes) *t.k.h: w ldr: sddle sn slipped: p.u bef 2nd* **13/2**[3]
340- **P** **I See A Star**[71] 4513 7-11-1 **91** ... MissEStead(7) —
(Micky Hammond) *w ldrs: lost pl appr 3 out: wl bhd whn p.u bef last* **25/1**

6m 16.6s (0.10) **Going Correction** -0.325s/f (Good) **14** Ran SP% **120.6**
Speed ratings (Par 103): **86,84,84,83,77 76,76,76,—,— —,—,—,—**
toteswingers:1&2:£2.30, 1&3:£5.80, 2&3:£9.50 CSF £11.18 CT £63.09 TOTE £3.30: £1.50, £2.00, £2.80; EX 9.00.
Owner Tom McNicholas **Bred** London Thoroughbred Services Ltd & J Gaines **Trained** Brigham, Cumbria
⊠ Stewards' Enquiry : Miss Samantha Drake one-day ban: used whip when out of contention
FOCUS
A low-grade lady riders' handicap hurdle. The easy winner was value for further and is rated to his best. The form could be rated a fair bit higher.
NOTEBOOK
Flying Doctor, whose hat-trick bid had come unstuck six days earlier, was back in a weaker contest and won in a canter. Considering he had an extra 6lb on his back this time it was probably a fair effort, and it would be no surprise to see him take his chance again at Hexham next week. (op 11-4 tchd 3-1)
Finbin(IRE), 8lb higher than when winning over fences earlier in the month, ran his race on this return to hurdles without being good enough. (op 3-1)
Cute N You Know It has become well handicapped, and she left behind several poor efforts in finishing third with the blinkers back on. (op 10-1 tchd 12-1)
Fly Tipper didn't get home in the end, but this still wasn't bad from 5lb 'wrong'. (op 18-1)
Maclean Official explanation: jockey said gelding lost its action
Humourous(IRE) was still in contention when unseating.
Rusty Red(IRE) Official explanation: jockey said gelding finished lame
Miss Tarantella Official explanation: jockey said saddle slipped

425 "HATMAKERS OF THE NORTH" H'CAP CHASE (18 fncs) 3m 1f
4:45 (4:45) (Class 4) (0-115,115) 5-Y-0+ **£3,252** (£955; £477; £238)

Form RPR
F32- **1** **Neptune Equester**[23] 33 7-11-8 **111** ... KeithMercer 123+
(Brian Ellison) *hld up wl in tch: jnd ldrs 12th: led 2 out: wnt clr run-in: v readily* **5/2**[1]
4P2- **2** *8* **Our Hero (IRE)**[27] 5356 7-11-12 **115** ... (t) RichieMcGrath 121+
(Charlie Longsdon) *trckd ldrs: effrt 4 out: 3 l 2nd and wl hld whn stmbld landing last* **10/3**[2]
P3P- **3** *nk* **Shrewd Investor (IRE)**[27] 5373 10-11-2 **108** ... (p) FearghalDavis(3) 113
(Henry Hogarth) *chsd ldr: led appr 4 out: hdd and hit 2 out: kpt on same pce* **11/1**
12P- **4** *19* **Milesian King (IRE)**[238] 1518 9-10-11 **100** ... (t) ChristianWilliams 87
(Lawney Hill) *trckd ldrs: drvn appr 4 out: wknd 3 out* **11/2**
F31- **5** *½* **Dawn Ride (IRE)**[25] 11 9-11-9 **112** ... (p) BarryKeniry 98
(Micky Hammond) *in tch in last: drvn 14th: lost pl next: modest 5th whn blnd 2 out* **7/1**
U22- **6** *23* **Darina's Boy**[39] 5152 14-10-0 **89** oh3 ... TjadeCollier 54
(Sue Smith) *led: rdn 14th: hdd appr next: sn lost pl and bhd* **4/1**[3]

5m 58.9s (-10.50) **Going Correction** -0.55s/f (Firm) course record **6** Ran SP% **107.9**
Speed ratings: **105,102,102,96,96 88**
toteswingers:1&2:£1.40, 1&3:£4.20, 2&3:£5.60 CSF £10.55 TOTE £2.30: £1.10, £1.40; EX 6.80.
Owner Kristian Strangeway **Bred** Mrs Joanna Daniell **Trained** Norton, N Yorks
FOCUS
This was probably a fair handicap chase. The winner is on the upgrade and the form could be rated higher.
NOTEBOOK
Neptune Equester fully deserved this first win over fences. He had been raised 5lb for finishing a good second at Sedgefield last time and his abundant stamina was again there for all to see, clearing right away in the end. This was only his sixth start and he remains open to further progress. (tchd 11-4)
Our Hero(IRE), runner-up off this mark at Market Rasen latest, looked vulnerable under top weight, but again ran well. He did blunder at the last, but it didn't affect the result. (op 7-2 tchd 3-1)
Shrewd Investor(IRE) went on before the straight and had his chance, but wasn't helped by a mistake two out. (op 8-1)
Milesian King(IRE), returning from a 238-day absence, comes from a yard that does well at this time of year and he should improve. (op 15-2 tchd 8-1)
Dawn Ride(IRE), who won here last time, was beaten too far for the 5lb rise to be blamed. Official explanation: jockey said gelding ran flat (op 9-2)
Darina's Boy has been running well in defeat of late, but couldn't reproduce his best this time. (op 9-2 tchd 5-1)

426 RACING AGAIN NEXT THURSDAY - 27TH MAY NOVICES' HURDLE (11 hdls) 2m 4f
5:15 (5:15) (Class 4) 4-Y-0+ **£2,740** (£798; £399)

Form RPR
2- **1** **Mr Moonshine (IRE)**[39] 5155 6-10-12 0 ... TjadeCollier 125+
(Sue Smith) *mde all: hit 7th: qcknd next: drew clr appr 2 out: pushed out* **9/2**[3]
P11- **2** *10* **Quo Video (FR)**[27] 5359 6-11-12 120 ... APMcCoy 130
(Tim Vaughan) *chsd ldrs: wnt 2nd 8th: sn drvn: rdn next: no imp* **4/7**[1]
53- **3** *23* **Dice (IRE)**[31] 5273 4-10-7 0 ... DenisO'Regan 92
(Chris Grant) *hmpd sltly and lft 2nd at 2nd: 3rd and outpcd whn hit 3 out: sn wknd* **11/4**[2]
4 *92* **Danderdandan**[569] 4-10-4 0 ... CharlieStudd(3) —
(Philip Sharp) *nt fluent in last: bhd fr 4th: t.o 6th* **200/1**
000- **F** **Morecambe Bay**[31] 5277 5-10-12 0 ... HenryOliver —
(David Thompson) *chsd wnr: fell 2nd* **100/1**

4m 51.7s (-7.80) **Going Correction** -0.325s/f (Good)
WFA 4 from 5yo+ 19lb **5** Ran SP% **110.0**
Speed ratings (Par 105): **102,98,88,52,—**
CSF £7.90 TOTE £6.60: £3.80, £1.10; EX 7.80 Place 6 £2.88; Place 5 £2.62.
Owner Mrs S Smith **Bred** T McIlhagga **Trained** High Eldwick, W Yorks
FOCUS
A big step forward from the easy winner, with the form rated through the runner-up.
NOTEBOOK
Mr Moonshine(IRE) put up quite a nice performance, making all the running and staying on strongly to win with plenty in hand. He had finished second to a very useful sort on his hurdles debut at Southwell and the 14lb he was receiving from the favourite was a big factor. He may well defy the penalty. (tchd 6-1)
Quo Video(FR), shouldered with a double penalty, had won a couple of handicaps, the last of them off 109, and he found the weight concession too much against a potentially useful rival. (op 5-6)
Dice(IRE) was unable to step up on his Hexham third, but is at least eligible for handicaps now. (op 2-1)
T/Plt: £6.20. Pool:£44,047.73 - 5,146.27 winning tickets T/Qpdt: £5.80. Pool:£3,341.84 - 422.98 winning tickets WG

379 TOWCESTER (R-H)
Friday, May 21

OFFICIAL GOING: Good to firm (9.3)
Wind: Nil. Weather: very hot and sunny

427 GLAZERITE WINDOWS LTD H'CAP CHASE (14 fncs) 2m 3f 110y
6:20 (6:21) (Class 4) (0-115,115) 5-Y-0+ **£3,577** (£1,050; £525; £262)

Form RPR
41-3 **1** **High Jack (IRE)**[16] 156 8-10-11 **100** ... NickScholfield 111+
(Andy Turnell) *mde virtually all: readily drew clr bef 2 out where 6 l ahd: rdn and styd on wl after: nt fluent last* **15/8**[1]
23P- **2** *21* **Presentandcorrect (IRE)**[195] 2127 9-11-7 **115**... SamTwiston-Davies(5) 105
(Nigel Twiston-Davies) *trckd ldrs: wnt 2nd 3 out: rdn and outpcd bef next: fighting a losing battle after* **11/2**
334- **3** *6* **Rockiteer (IRE)**[42] 5118 7-11-12 **115** ... RichardJohnson 102
(Henry Daly) *cl 2nd and w ldr at times: rdn 3 out: wknd after next: blnd and pckd last* **4/1**[2]
030- **4** *30* **Borora**[35] 5219 11-11-2 **105** ... CharliePoste 59
(Richard Lee) *chsd ldrs: rdn and mstke 6th: hit 9th and outpcd: labouring bdly after* **6/1**

136- **5** *9* **Rio Laine**[169] 2663 5-11-3 **106**..(p) PaddyBrennan 51
(Tom George) *cl up: rdn and wknd bdly after 3 out* **12/1**

660- **6** *4 ½* **Games (IRE)**[150] 2663 9-10-11 **100**..(p) RodiGreene 41
(Christopher Kellett) *nt jump wl in last and nvr gng wl: rdn 9th: t.o 11th* **100/1**

23F- **P** **Pistolet Dove (IRE)**[28] 5353 8-11-0 **103**..............................(b) APMcCoy —
(Philip Hobbs) *pressed ldrs: rdn 10th: reluctant after: lost tch 3 out: t.o and p.u next* **5/1**[3]

5m 2.20s (-16.00) **Going Correction** -0.825s/f (Firm) course record **7** Ran SP% **109.8**
Speed ratings: **99,90,88,76,72 70,—**
Tote Swingers: 1&2 £2.40, 1&3 £2.40, 2&3 £2.50 CSF £11.75 TOTE £2.00: £1.10, £4.10; EX 12.40.
Owner M Tedham **Bred** Mrs Maura McSweeney **Trained** Broad Hinton, Wilts

FOCUS
A moderate race run at a comfortable pace.

NOTEBOOK
High Jack(IRE) set the pace, doing everything within his comfort zone, and when headed down the back his jockey just let him carry on in his own rhythm until asserting before the final climb and stretching effortlessly clear, despite diving at the last. He came into this race with the best recent form, and was able to capitalise on his relatively low weight back at his favourite track to notch up his fourth course success. These factors evidently held more importance than his rating, as he was 0-8 when rated 100 or more before this victory. That might not leave much leeway for the future, though. Connections suggested that, having been on the go throughout the winter, he will have a well-deserved break now. (op 2-1 tchd 9-4 and 85-40 in a place)
Presentandcorrect(IRE) challenged before the home turn but was soon beaten off, although he did plug on again up the hill. Having been absent since November, he might come on for this and could be better on a tighter track. He is now 0-13 over fences but is better in the warmer months and looks capable of winning a small race. (op 7-2 tchd 13-2)
Rockiteer(IRE) was given every chance but he lacked a finishing effort up the hill and was a tired horse when diving at the last. He was able to be competitive off this sort of mark over hurdles, but his chasing form looks beneath that level. (op 9-2 tchd 7-2)
Borora, who was sweating profusely beforehand, was just struggling to keep tabs on the leaders and was never really travelling that well, jumping out to the right as he tired up the hill. Despite being given a chance by the handicapper, he has largely been out of form since last autumn. (op 7-1 tchd 11-2)
Rio Laine is best on flat tracks and did not get up the hill, but might come on for his first start since December. (tchd 11-1)
Games(IRE) is a moderate maiden who has not taken to fences and was never jumping with any fluency.
Pistolet Dove(IRE) did not jump with much fluency, getting low at several fences and landing steeply on occasion. He has been unable to build on his chasing debut success at Leicester in December and still has something to prove. (op 7-1 tchd 9-2)

428 VEKA PLC NOVICES' HURDLE (10 hdls) 2m 3f 110y
6:50 (6:51) (Class 4) 4-Y-0+ **£2,927** (£859; £429; £214)

Form RPR

F3-2 **1** **Cool Touch (IRE)**[12] 235 7-10-12 115.............................. PaddyBrennan 105+
(Nigel Twiston-Davies) *lobbing along in 3rd tl wnt 2nd at 7th: led 3 out: clr and cantering bef next* **2/11**[1]

336- **2** *15* **Saint Espiegle (FR)**[30] 5315 6-10-7 82...................... MichaelMurphy[(5)] 85
(Rob Summers) *2nd tl led 6th: rdn and hdd 3 out: hopelessly outclassed by wnr after* **10/1**[3]

/U4- **3** *19* **Lygon Legend**[40] 5154 7-10-12 0.. NickScholfield 68
(Peter Hiatt) *set v slow pce tl 6th: lost 2nd at next: nt hrd rdn in hopeless pursuit after* **7/1**[2]

P/06 **4** *27* **Risk Challenge (USA)**[8] 298 8-10-9 65...................... DerekLaverty[(3)] 39
(William Davies) *plld hrd: in tch tl 6th: sn struggling: eased and t.o bef 2 out* **50/1**

U **P** **Mik**[15] 180 4-10-4 0.. EamonDehdashti[(3)] —
(Dr Jeremy Naylor) *mstkes and nvr able to keep up: woefully t.o whn eventually p.u 3 out* **80/1**

P **Miss Mardy Pants (IRE)**[54] 5-10-5 0............................ GerardTumelty —
(Charlie Morlock) *overj. 1st: j. indifferently and barely raised a gallop: woefully t.o whn eventually p.u 3 out* **100/1**

4m 56.3s (-13.30) **Going Correction** -0.60s/f (Firm)
WFA 4 from 5yo+ 18lb **6** Ran SP% **110.4**
Speed ratings (Par 105): **102,96,88,77,— —**
Tote Swingers: 1&2 £1.10, 1&3 £1.02, 2&3 £4.00 CSF £2.90 TOTE £1.10: £1.10, £1.80; EX 2.30.

Owner Seamus Murphy **Bred** Peter Casey **Trained** Naunton, Gloucs

FOCUS
A desperately poor race.

NOTEBOOK
Cool Touch(IRE) boasted a rating at least 36lb higher than his exposed rivals and simply had to win this. He duly had the race in the bag from the home turn. Although he was not always travelling that comfortably, he hardly had to break sweat to confirm his superiority in this field. He had looked a bit one-paced on flatter tracks over 2m, so this trip and track were ideal, and he cemented his last run when a good second in a reasonable handicap this month, although he will not find many easier opportunities. He will be kept on the go in small races at similar trips this summer to keep his confidence high. (tchd 1-6 and 1-5 in a place)
Saint Espiegle(FR) took up the running in the back straight and briefly matched strides with the winner, but he was soon labouring. He has a slightly awkward-looking high knee action and looks slow, even for Towcester. (tchd 11-1)
Lygon Legend set a reasonable pace for a circuit, but he weakened out of contention in his bumper and hurdle starts and continued that tendency here. (op 8-1)
Risk Challenge(USA), who was too free and not fluent enough, was beaten after a circuit. He is an unpromising selling-class hurdler who has not suggested a revival this spring since returning from a lengthy absence. (op 66-1)
Miss Mardy Pants(IRE) Official explanation: jockey said mare hung left

429 GLAZERITE WINDOWS LTD MAIDEN CHASE (14 fncs) 2m 3f 110y
7:20 (7:20) (Class 4) 5-Y-0+ **£3,252** (£955; £477; £238)

Form RPR

4-U2 **1** **Bushwacker (IRE)**[17] 130 6-10-9 104........................ JimmyDerham[(5)] 96+
(Seamus Mullins) *sme minor errors: wnt 2nd at 4th: hit 8th: u.p bef 2 out: led appr last: clr but wobbling bdly after last: fin at a crawl* **6/4**[2]

P5-6 **2** *7* **Tuscany Star (IRE)**[22] 64 7-10-7 93..............................(t) AdamWedge[(7)] 89
(Edward Creighton) *hit 2nd: chsd ldrs: j. slowly 7th and drvn: disp 2nd briefly at 11th: wknd u.p bef 2 out: forced into 2nd fnl strides* **33/1**

20-4 **3** *hd* **Hereweareagain (IRE)**[21] 85 7-11-0 113........................(b) TomO'Brien 88
(Philip Hobbs) *led fr 4th: hrd drvn and hdd bef 2 out: downed tools completely: barely walking up the hill after last: lost 2nd nr fin* **1/1**[1]

/43- **4** *18* **Thyne Spirit (IRE)**[53] 4927 11-11-0 58.............................. ColinBolger 70
(Simon Lewis) *rdn 3rd: struggling after: t.o after 7th: wnt remote 4th bef last* **100/1**

3-0 **5** *1 ¾* **Delgany Gunner**[16] 155 6-11-0 0.................................. AndrewThornton 68
(Ben Pollock) *led tl 4th: rdn bef 10th: lost tch next: t.o 3 out* **33/1**

6 *10* **Himalayan Express**[13] 6-11-0 0.. FelixDeGiles 58
(Charlie Longsdon) *j. slowly 1st: chsd ldrs tl lost tch qckly bef 3 out and hung lft: t.o* **12/1**[3]

/PP- **P** **Byzantina Fair**[141] 3192 8-10-7 0.. SamJones —
(Henrietta Knight) *j.rt 2nd: lost tch 4th: t.o 7th: continued pointlessly tl eventually p.u 3 out* **25/1**

5m 10.3s (-7.90) **Going Correction** -0.825s/f (Firm) **7** Ran SP% **108.4**
Speed ratings: **82,79,79,71,71 67,—**
Tote Swingers: 1&2:£18.10, 2&3:£18.10, 1&3:£1.02 CSF £35.44 TOTE £2.60: £1.40, £14.40; EX 58.70.
Owner Darren Anderson **Bred** Mrs Margaret Whelan **Trained** Wilsford-Cum-Lake, Wilts

FOCUS
Just three still in contention as they came up the straight, but fortunes changed up the hill as the favourite weakened out of it.

NOTEBOOK
Bushwacker(IRE) got in close to several fences and was generally hesitant, but he stuck to the task and, when the favourite faltered, he was poised to take his chance. He wandered around near the finish but stayed on well enough. He has been plagued by jumping errors but still showed some improvement at Exeter last time and was able to build on that here. The bare form of this race does not suggest obvious progression, but connections intend to keep him on the go and are confident he can win again. (op 13-8 tchd 7-4)
Tuscany Star(IRE) raced quite keenly and had to be driven to stay on terms with the two market leaders, but he plugged on to get up past the favourite on the line. He had bits and pieces of form over hurdles but is taking time to get his act together over fences.
Hereweareagain(IRE), the highest-rated of the field, looked to be running up to his rating as he took the lead turning in, but he was in trouble as soon as he met the rising ground and had legs of jelly from the last. This is not the first time he has weakened at the finish, so stiff tracks do not seem an obvious fit. (tchd 10-11 and 11-10 in a place)
Thyne Spirit(IRE) is lightly raced but his best previous run was when second in this corresponding race five years ago, and he does not look like breaking his maiden any time soon.
Delgany Gunner raced more prominently this time but was beaten before the home turn. Although he now qualifies for handicaps, he would have to improve considerably to win a race. (op 40-1)
Himalayan Express did not jump that fluently but was still in touch, wide of the pack, until the home turn. After his poor form in points, this was a minuscule step in the right direction. (op 10-1)
Byzantina Fair, making her chasing debut, jumped too slowly to play a part. (op 18-1)

430 NETWORK VEKA H'CAP HURDLE (8 hdls) 2m
7:50 (7:50) (Class 4) (0-105,105) 4-Y-0+ **£2,927** (£859; £429; £214)

Form RPR

133- **1** **Woodlark Island (IRE)**[28] 5359 4-11-5 **102**..............(tp) TomScudamore 105+
(David Pipe) *led: wavered 3rd: rdn and blnd 3 out: hdd next: drvn to ld again last: all out: v game* **9/2**[2]

64B- **2** *shd* **Topflight Wildbird**[30] 5312 7-11-7 **100**............................ RobertThornton 107+
(Alan King) *racd keenly on heels of ldrs tl drvn after 5th: outpcd bef next: rallied to ld 2 out: jst hdd last: ev ch after tl btn on nod* **8/1**

560- **3** *3 ¼* **Points Of View**[142] 3180 5-11-5 **101**.................................. SeanQuinlan[(3)] 105+
(Kim Bailey) *hld up in rr: rdn 5th: hdwy next: pressing ldng pair whn mstke 2 out: hanging lft after: btn bef last* **8/1**

034- **4** *12* **Sweet Seville (FR)**[82] 1477 6-11-5 **105**............................ MattCrawley[(7)] 96
(Michael Squance) *towards rr: rdn and lost tch after 5th: plugged on to go poor 4th after last* **66/1**

1-33 **5** *2* **Midnight Spirit**[2] 407 10-11-0 **100**......................(tp) AnthonyFreeman[(7)] 89+
(Frederick Sutherland) *cl up: ev ch 3 out: rdn and wknd qckly sn after next: lost 4th after last* **10/3**[1]

P00- **6** *8* **Nothing Is Forever (IRE)**[25] 23 6-11-10 **103**.................. DarylJacob 84
(Liam Corcoran) *t.k.h in midfield: rdn and lost tch wl bef 2 out: clambered over last* **20/1**

04-2 **7** *1 ½* **Bazart**[12] 219 8-11-4 **97**.. ChristianWilliams 76
(Bernard Llewellyn) *mstke 3rd: in midfield: rdn and struggling wl bef 2 out* **8/1**

06-1 **8** *11* **Ardmaddy (IRE)**[12] 215 6-11-5 **105** 7ex.....................(b) JoshuaMoore[(7)] 73
(Gary Moore) *chsd ldrs: brief effrt bef 3 out: sn hrd rdn and struggling* **9/1**

2P-5 **9** *5* **Perlon (FR)**[11] 252 5-11-4 **97**.. JamieMoore 60
(Gary Moore) *pressed ldr tl 3 out: rdn and dropped out qckly* **14/1**

236- **P** **Spider Boy**[25] 23 13-10-4 **88**.....................(p) GemmaGracey-Davison[(5)] —
(Zoe Davison) *last and nvr gng wl: rdn and lost tch after 4th: t.o and p.u 2 out* **18/1**

2F-0 **P** **Ouste (FR)**[14] 196 8-11-2 **100**....................................(bt) GilesHawkins[(5)] —
(Alison Thorpe) *t.k.h towards rr: mstkes 2nd and 4th: lost tch 3 out: p.u next* **7/1**[3]

3m 56.0s (-11.90) **Going Correction** -0.60s/f (Firm)
WFA 4 from 5yo+ 18lb **11** Ran SP% **115.3**
Speed ratings (Par 105): **105,104,103,97,96 92,91,86,83,— —**
Tote Swingers: 1&2:£4.60, 2&3:£15.30, 1&3:£9.50 CSF £39.81 CT £279.59 TOTE £4.10: £1.30, £5.30, £3.20; EX 47.50.
Owner Eminence Grise Partnership **Bred** Stone Ridge Farm **Trained** Nicholashayne, Devon

FOCUS
A competitive handicap featuring a gritty battle from the second-last, and the first two went past the post together.

NOTEBOOK
Woodlark Island(IRE) managed to battle back to wrest the victory in gutsy fashion. Leading throughout, the challengers were poised turning in but he kept finding more and, by virtue of a fluent leap at the last, he found just enough near the line. He had been in good form this spring with two wins in eight days, but the edge had been lost in his next two runs. However, with four weeks to recover, he was able to bounce back to form. Connections suggested the stiff finish helped as he really needs further, and he will be kept on the go for the time being. (tchd 5-1)
Topflight Wildbird challenged from the second-last and looked set to go on to victory, but she just lifted her head near the post and let the winner back in. Despite this, she could still be considered an unlucky loser as she lost some momentum at the third-last as the pace was picking up, then found herself trapped behind horses and had to be switched wide to deliver her challenge, so these efforts might just have taken the edge off her finish. She has shown little, especially over fences, since finishing second at this track a year ago in a better race, but she seems better at this track over hurdles, so could gain compensation. (tchd 9-1)
Points Of View lost ground at the third-last but continued making good progress from the rear until weakening up the hill. He was a bit keen after his 142-day absence and might still be a bit weak, but looks to have a race in him. (op 15-2)
Sweet Seville(FR) dropped to the back of the field midway before staying on again late on, and might have needed this return from a layoff, although she still looks stiffly handicapped on previous efforts. (op 100-1)
Midnight Spirit has been in good form and rated a strong contender if able to run to form in his sixth start in as many weeks. Although he was going best of all three out, he faded up the hill and looks in need of a break. (op 7-2)
Nothing Is Forever(IRE) got warm beforehand and was never really in it, but although the ground was possibly against him, he is at least dropping towards a more realistic mark. (op 25-1)
Spider Boy Official explanation: jockey said gelding was never travelling

Ouste(FR) Official explanation: jockey said gelding had a breathing problem

431 GLAZERITE SOUTH WEST DIVISION H'CAP CHASE (18 fncs) 3m 110y
8:20 (8:20) (Class 4) (0-115,111) 5-Y-O+ **£3,577** (£1,050; £525; £262)

Form RPR
1U6- **1** **Lucky Luk (FR)**[163] 2777 11-11-2 **104**...........................(p) SeanQuinlan(3) 121+
(Kim Bailey) *hdwy 7th: effrt 3 out: led bef next where 5 l clr: in command after: eased after last* **5/1**[2]
20-2 **2** 9 **River Indus**[9] 274 10-11-6 **105**.. DarylJacob 112
(Bob Buckler) *pressed ldr tl led 14th: gng wl after 3 out but hdd bef next: plugged on but sn no ch w wnr* **11/2**[3]
P4-2 **3** 2 **Alexanderthegreat (IRE)**[12] 229 12-11-8 **107**............... AidanColeman 114+
(Venetia Williams) *cl up: chal and blnd 3 out: sn one pce in 3rd but kpt battling gamely* **11/2**[3]
U2-F **4** 4 ½ **Lord Brunello (IRE)**[16] 158 8-11-0 **99**....................(p) ChristianWilliams 102+
(Lawney Hill) *nt jump wl in last: 8 l last at 13th: blnd 14th: kpt on fr 2 out wout getting nr ldrs* **9/1**
52-3 **5** 19 **Terrible Tenant**[9] 274 11-10-13 **103**............................ JimmyDerham(5) 85
(Seamus Mullins) *led tl 14th: wknd tamely wl bef 2 out* **7/1**
342- **6** nk **Pinerock (IRE)**[40] 5157 6-11-11 **110**.......................................(p) APMcCoy 91
(Jonjo O'Neill) *landed awkwardly 1st: bhd: hdwy 9th: cajoled along in 6th at 15th: no rspnse and struggling after next* **7/2**[1]
P60- **7** 47 **Keltic Lord**[217] 1780 14-10-13 **98**....................................... NickScholfield 32
(Peter Hiatt) *prom to 8th: struggling 15th: t.o after next* **28/1**
13-5 **U** **Sesame Rambler (IRE)**[12] 229 11-11-4 **103**................. RobertWalford —
(R H & Mrs S Alner) *rdn 7th: nvr looked to be gng wl after: in rr and 10 l fr ldr whn mstke and uns rdr 3 out* **22/1**
03P- **P** **Bubble Boy (IRE)**[32] 5281 11-11-5 **111**..................(t) AnthonyFreeman(7) —
(Brendan Powell) *drvn fr 3rd: lost tch bef 10th: t.o and p.u next* **16/1**
P0P- **P** **The Hollow Bottom**[27] 5387 9-11-6 **105**.......................(b) PaddyBrennan —
(Nigel Twiston-Davies) *chsd ldrs: rdn and wknd 3 out: eased and j.rt next: p.u last* **14/1**

6m 12.8s (-24.10) **Going Correction** -0.825s/f (Firm) **10** Ran SP% **112.5**
Speed ratings: **105,102,101,100,93 93,78,—,—,—**
Tote Swingers: 1&2 £15.80, 1&3 £2.90, 2&3 £3.30 CSF £32.08 CT £154.35 TOTE £5.80: £3.00, £1.30, £2.40; EX 37.10.
Owner Mrs E A Kellar **Bred** Pierre Sayet & Maurice Marlin **Trained** Andoversford, Gloucs

FOCUS
A reasonably competitive event.

NOTEBOOK
Lucky Luk(FR), who won this race last year, excels round here and stayed on much the best. He was a bit keen on his return from a five-month absence, and looked a bit ring-rusty at a few of the fences, but he tends to go well on his first two runs following a break. With freshness, ground, track and stable form in his favour, he readily brushed aside the 5lb higher mark since last year's victory just three runs back. Connections stressed that the light campaign is because fast ground is essential for him. If conditions are suitable, he might take up an entry at Sedgefield next week, but the overall plan is another crack at the Velka Pardubicka. (op 9-2 tchd 11-2)
River Indus was always prominent and ran a sound race, but was outstayed by the winner. This was another genuine effort from this consistent performer, but he has not been able to convert this to victory since December 2008, and stiff tracks such as this do not seem the obvious venue to achieve that. (op 9-2)
Alexanderthegreat(IRE) moved up to mount a challenge but nearly unseated his rider at the open ditch three out and his bid was effectively over. Although he has not won for three years, he is in better form of late and, despite his advancing years, is on a tempting-enough mark to capitalise in a weak race. (op 5-1 tchd 9-2)
Lord Brunello(IRE) made up some ground late on but never jumped fluently enough to enable him to hold a competitive position. (op 11-1 tchd 12-1)
Terrible Tenant led until the third-last but does not really stay this far on stiff tracks. (op 8-1 tchd 6-1)
Pinerock(IRE) faced a stiff-enough task on his chasing debut and he showed his inexperience with some hesitant jumping. He got tired on the final climb, wandering around and jumping right, but should improve for this taster. (op 9-2 tchd 3-1)

432 MACO UK "NATIONAL HUNT" NOVICES' HURDLE (8 hdls) 2m
8:50 (8:52) (Class 4) 4-Y-O+ **£2,927** (£859; £429; £214)

Form RPR
03-2 **1** **J'Adhere (FR)**[12] 215 5-10-12 0.................................... RichardJohnson 100+
(Tim Vaughan) *plld v hrd: mstkes: last tl after 3rd: effrt and mstke 5th: led on bit next: clr after 2 out: v easily* **2/1**[2]
0PP- **2** 4 ½ **Ana Buachaill Dana**[57] 4841 8-10-12 79.......................... LeightonAspell 91
(Tom Gretton) *led at slow pce tl rdn and hdd bef 3 out: no ch w wnr fr next: wnt 2nd at last* **100/1**
3-21 **3** 4 **Entertain Me**[11] 249 6-10-12 98... CharliePoste 87
(Robin Dickin) *wnt 2nd bef 4th: led appr 3 out where nt fluent and hdd: sn outpcd by wnr: fading whn lost 2nd at last* **8/11**[1]
/04- **4** 28 **Camino Real**[23] 50 7-10-5 0... TimmyMurphy 58
(Jim Old) *t.k.h: hld up in rr: lost tch 4th: nt being given a hrd time whn hit 2 out* **7/1**[3]
P0-P **5** 8 **A Haon A Do (IRE)**[10] 267 8-10-5 93................................(p) LiamHeard 44
(Gerald Ham) *chsd ldr tl rdn bef 4th: rdn and fdd bef 3 out: sn wl bhd* **50/1**
/04- **6** 7 **Mikeys Sister**[31] 5296 5-10-0 0... LeeEdwards(5) 37
(Tony Carroll) *blnd 1st: bhd: lost tch bef 4th where mstke: t.o 3 out* **40/1**

4m 0.40s (-7.50) **Going Correction** -0.60s/f (Firm) **6** Ran SP% **109.1**
Speed ratings (Par 105): **94,91,89,75,71 68**
Tote Swingers: 1&2:£11.60, 2&3:£14.70, 1&3:£1.02 CSF £93.81 TOTE £2.30: £1.10, £12.10; EX 102.30 Place 6 £55.22, Place 5 £32.98..
Owner David Lovell **Bred** Henri Soler & Mathieu Daguzan-Garr **Trained** Aberthin, Vale of Glamorgan

FOCUS
Another moderate race.

NOTEBOOK
J'Adhere(FR) pulled hard and that helped contribute to some clumsy jumping early on, but once he was allowed to make his move he stayed on well. He has taken a while to get the hang of things over hurdles, and has not finished that strongly in the past, but once his keen-going tendencies settle down he has enough pace to win again. (tchd 15-8)
Ana Buachaill Dana was fractious before the start and was too free in the early stages, but he stayed on again from the last into second. His form has been decidedly moderate, especially on softer ground, but he showed a bit of improvement on this faster surface. (op 66-1)
Entertain Me moved into the lead three out as she had done when victorious at this track 11 days ago, but she could not shake off the winner and eventually faded. That previous victory was over a longer trip, so it was disappointing that she did not stay on better, but this was her third run in three weeks and it may have contributed to a jaded effort. (op 10-11)
Camino Real still looked as if she has plenty to learn over hurdles and, without the aid of a tongue-tie this time, she tired from the last. She might fare better now she is qualified for handicaps, but still needs to improve if she is to match the promise of her bumper runs of 2007. (op 11-2 tchd 8-1)

T/Plt: £43.30. Pool: £63,850.88. 1,074.93 winning units. T/Qpdt: £14.20. Pool: £4,695.66. 244.60 winning units. IM

433 - 435a (Foreign Racing) - See Raceform Interactive

[135]FAKENHAM (L-H)
Sunday, May 23

OFFICIAL GOING: Good to firm (9.2)
Wind: Gentle breeze, half against Weather: Sunny, very hot

436 CHAMPION'S 60:60 CHARITY CHALLENGE NOVICES' H'CAP HURDLE (13 hdls) 2m 7f 110y
2:25 (2:25) (Class 4) (0-100,93) 4-Y-O+ **£4,553** (£1,337; £668; £333)

Form RPR
0-61 **1** **Ashmolian (IRE)**[5] 382 7-11-6 **92** 7ex.......(p) GemmaGracey-Davison(5) 98
(Zoe Davison) *t.k.h: hld up in rr: hdwy 9th: chsd ldrs after next: rdn to chse ldr bef last: 2 l down and looked hld last: kpt on flat to ld last stride* **7/4**[1]
03-2 **2** shd **Play A Cord (IRE)**[23] 84 7-10-13 **80**..........................(p) DougieCostello 87
(Neil Mulholland) *hld up in tch: hdwy to chse ldr 10th: pushed ahd bef last: 2 l clr last: rdn and put hd in air flat: nt run on and hdd last stride* **10/3**[2]
00-0 **3** 11 **Grand Article (IRE)**[19] 137 6-11-1 **82**...............................(p) CharliePoste 81
(Paul Cowley) *chsd ldr: nt fluent 9th: led next: rdn bef 2 out: hdd between last 2: wknd flat* **10/1**
005/ **4** 32 **Fort Royal (IRE)**[940] 1852 11-10-0 **67** oh8........................... JamieMoore 34
(Jeff Pearce) *hld up in tch in last pair: hdwy and mstke 9th: sn pushed along: struggling after next: lft modest 4th and j.rt 3 out: t.o: dismntd after fin* **20/1**
04-0 **5** 31 **Smart N Sharp (IRE)**[14] 217 7-9-7 **67** oh3...................(t) PeterHatton(7) 6
(Linda Jewell) *in tch towards rr: nt fluent 1st and 2nd: rdn and struggling after 9th: t.o whn hmpd 3 out* **33/1**
P0-0 **6** 41 **Nishnash**[14] 232 7-10-13 **80**..(p) AndrewThornton —
(Jim Wilson) *in tch in midfield: nt fluent and dropped to rr 8th: lost tch: next: wl t.o bef 3 out* **20/1**
00P- **F** **Builteoir (IRE)**[85] 4296 8-10-10 **77**..................................... PaulMoloney —
(Evan Williams) *chsd ldrs: rdn 10th: disputing 3rd and struggling whn fell heavily 3 out* **7/2**[3]
40-4 **P** **Aega**[19] 140 5-11-9 **93**..(p) AlexMerriam(3) —
(Neil King) *led tl 10th: sn rdn and btn: lft modest 5th and bdly hmpd 3 out: p.u bef next* **10/1**

5m 48.7s (-17.70) **Going Correction** -0.975s/f (Hard) **8** Ran SP% **112.3**
Speed ratings (Par 105): **90,89,86,75,65 51,—,—**
toteswingers: 1&2 £1.90, 1&3 £5.40, 2&3 £4.50 CSF £7.83 CT £41.72 TOTE £2.40: £1.10, £1.60, £2.70; EX 8.10.
Owner The Secret Circle **Bred** Hascombe And Valiant Studs **Trained** Hammerwood, E Sussex

FOCUS
A low-grade novices' handicap. The winner looks the best guide to the form.

NOTEBOOK
Ashmolian(IRE), penalised for his Towcester win just a few days earlier, needed every yard of this extra distance as, having looked beaten coming to the last, he stayed on strongly to get up in the final stride. He is clearly in top form, but things are going to get a lot tougher. (op 9-4)
Play A Cord(IRE) looked to be travelling much the best having taken the lead two out and seemed to have the race in the bag jumping the last, but she carried her head high after the last and was nabbed on the line. She isn't the strongest of finishers, which may explain why she is still a maiden. (op 11-4 tchd 7-2)
Grand Article(IRE) stopped quickly once beaten in the straight. (op 16-1)
Builteoir(IRE) was looking in big trouble when he fell heavily at the third from home, badly hampering the struggling Aega in the process. (op 10-3 tchd 3-1)
Aega Official explanation: trainer said mare pulled up lame (op 10-3 tchd 3-1)

437 LIGHT DRAGOONS H'CAP CHASE (FOR THE PRINCE OF WALES CUP) (18 fncs) 3m 110y
2:55 (2:55) (Class 4) (0-100,100) 5-Y-O+ **£5,204** (£1,528; £764; £381)

Form RPR
60-3 **1** **Mutual Respect (IRE)**[19] 130 8-11-8 **96**............................ PaulMoloney 116+
(Evan Williams) *chsd ldr after 2nd: clr w ldr fr 7th: led 12th tl hdd and mstke 14th: rdn after 3 out: led sn after next: sn in command: eased towards fin* **3/1**[2]
3P-4 **2** 12 **Feeling Peckish (USA)**[19] 136 6-9-7 **74** oh2...............(t) PeterHatton(7) 78
(Michael Chapman) *j.rt at times: racd in last trio: lost tch 8th: t.o fr 12th: wnt poor 3rd bef 3 out: plugged on to 2nd sn after last: no ch w wnr* **5/1**
PP-3 **3** 13 **The Iron Giant (IRE)**[19] 136 8-9-10 **77** oh5 ow3 MissCareyWilliamson(7) 70
(Diana Weeden) *chsd ldrs tl 3rd: sn dropped into last trio: struggling and lost tch 8th: t.o fr 12th: wnt poor 4th bef 3 out: plugged on to go 3rd nr fin* **16/1**
U-43 **4** ¾ **The Randy Bishop**[5] 380 10-11-7 **100**.......................(v[1]) LeeEdwards(5) 95
(Tony Carroll) *racd keenly: led: clr w rival and hit 7th: mstke: pckd and hdd 12th: led again 14th: mstke 2 out: sn hdd and immediately btn: stl 2nd but v tired whn blnd bdly last: lost 2 pls flat* **11/1**
F1/1 **5** 49 **Mattaking (IRE)**[19] 136 7-11-9 **97**......................................(p) SamJones 45
(Renee Robeson) *rousted along s: racd in midfield: reminder and hdwy to chse clr ldng pair after 7th: several slow jumps and no prog after: rdn: reluctant and lost tch w ldrs after 13th: t.o in last fr 3 out* **5/2**[1]
4P/0 **P** **Little Bit Of Hush (IRE)**[18] 157 10-10-8 **85**.................. AlexMerriam(3) —
(Neil King) *chsd ldr tl after 2nd: 4th and lost tch on ldng trio after 8th: t.o and rdn after 13th: p.u next* **12/1**
43-5 **P** **Shanahan (IRE)**[17] 169 9-11-12 **100**........................(p) RichardJohnson —
(Liam Corcoran) *hld up in last: hmpd and mstke 4th: losing tch and mstke 8th: t.o 12th tl p.u bef last* **7/2**[3]

6m 18.4s (-17.30) **Going Correction** -0.575s/f (Firm) **7** Ran SP% **114.4**
Speed ratings: **104,100,96,95,80 —,—**
toteswingers: 1&2 £3.60, 1&3 £5.30, 2&3 £9.30 CSF £18.49 TOTE £6.90: £7.00, £10.00; EX 21.10.
Owner R E R Williams **Bred** Highfort Stud **Trained** Llancarfan, Vale Of Glamorgan

FOCUS
A modest handicap chase with the winner's two main market rivals running poorly. The form is rated around the second and third.

NOTEBOOK
Mutual Respect(IRE), who didn't run too badly off this mark at Exeter latest, was clear with The Randy Bishop a long way from the finish and was never in any danger having seen him off by the second-last. He did make one notable blunder five out, and could do with being a bit quicker at his fences, but this was only his seventh start over them. (op 11-4 tchd 5-2)
Feeling Peckish(USA), racing from 2lb 'wrong', often goes well here and he kept plodding away for a well-beaten second. (op 13-2 tchd 9-2)

The Iron Giant(IRE), 5lb out of the handicap, also has his rider putting up 3lb overweight and he was always going to struggle. (op 14-1)
The Randy Bishop raced with the choke out in the first-time visor and that took its toll in the final couple of furlongs. (op 10-1)
Mattaking(IRE), 7lb higher than when winning here on his recent return from a lengthy absence, simply wasn't on a going day. He raced and jumped lazily and didn't look over enthused when asked to up his effort. This wasn't his form, but a disconcerting display none the less. (op 5-2 after early 3-1 in places, tchd 11-4)
Little Bit Of Hush(IRE) Official explanation: trainer said gelding bled from the nose (tchd 9-2)
Shanahan(IRE) was never going having been slightly interfered with early and his rider eventually accepted the situation. Official explanation: vet said gelding pulled up lame (tchd 9-2)

438 REX CARTER MEMORIAL H'CAP CHASE (16 fncs) 2m 5f 110y
3:25 (3:25) (Class 3) (0-130,125) 5-Y-0+ **£6,505** (£1,910; £955; £477)

Form RPR
654- **1** **Dead Or Alive (IRE)**[30] 5360 7-11-5 **118**....................(t) RichardJohnson 125
(Tim Vaughan) *chsd ldrs: wnt 2nd 8th: j. upsides ldr 3 out: outj. next: rdn between last 2: bttr jump last and sn chalng again: drvn ahd fnl 100yds: styd on wl* **7/2**[2]
5U2- **2** *2 1/4* **Quarrymount**[44] 5120 9-10-4 **103**.. ColinBolger 110+
(Chris Gordon) *led: mstke and jnd 3 out: outj. rival and forged ahd again next: rdn between last 2: pckd last: sn hrd pressed: hdd fnl 100yds: sn btn: eased towards fin* **5/2**[1]
236- **3** *2* **Cool Roxy**[35] 5247 13-11-2 **115**.. LiamTreadwell 119
(Alan Blackmore) *chsd ldr tl 8th: 3rd and rdn 12th: kpt on gamely but one pce fr pce fr 3 out: hld whn mstke last* **5/2**[1]
500- **4** *38* **Commemoration Day (IRE)**[17] 5111 9-11-11 **124**.........(b) JamieMoore 93
(Gary Moore) *in tch in last pair: j. slowly 5th and nt look happy after: rdn after 8th: lost tch qckly bef 13th: t.o* **5/1**[3]
6PP- **5** *36* **Heathcote**[50] 4988 8-11-9 **125**.................................... EamonDehdashti(3) 61
(Gary Moore) *a last: nvr jumping fluently or gng wl: mstke 6th: lost tch after mstke 12th: t.o fr 3 out* **7/1**

5m 25.2s (-16.60) **Going Correction** -0.975s/f (Hard) **5** Ran SP% **108.5**
Speed ratings: **107,106,105,91,78**
CSF £12.42 TOTE £3.60: £1.50, £1.60; EX 13.40.
Owner T Vaughan **Bred** J R Weston **Trained** Pencoed, Bridgend

FOCUS
A fair handicap chase. The winner is rated close to his best, with the second up 7lb on his chase form.

NOTEBOOK
Dead Or Alive(IRE) raced past Quarrymount on the run-in, the latter having pecked on landing. The winner hadn't been in the best of form but his mark has dropped back to his last winning one, and he was able to return right back to his best. He was in cracking form this time a year ago, and it would be no surprise were he to win again. Official explanation: trainer had no explanation for the apparent improvement in form shown (op 9-2 tchd 3-1)
Quarrymount, back to form when second off 1lb lower at Kempton, was putting in a dour display and had started to get on top again when getting in close at the last and losing momentum, eventually getting run down. He deserves to win again. (op 11-4 tchd 3-1)
Cool Roxy, 11 times a winner here, was on a career-low mark over fences and it was no surprise to see him run well, though neither was a surprise that there were a couple too good for him. He entered into well deserved retirement after the race. (op 2-1 tchd 15-8 and 11-4)
Commemoration Day(IRE) looked moody and stopped quickly. (op 11-2 tchd 9-2)
Heathcote gave himself no chance with sloppy jumping. (tchd 6-1)

439 BETFAIR NOVICES' HURDLE (9 hdls) 2m
4:00 (4:00) (Class 4) 4-Y-0+ **£3,252** (£955; £477; £238)

Form RPR
010- **1** **Moonstreaker**[44] 5108 7-11-2 119.................................. AdamPogson(3) 101+
(Charles Pogson) *j.rt: mde all: pressed after 3 out: readily drew clr fr 2 out: easily* **1/3**[1]
3 **2** *18* **Wicklewood**[19] 135 4-10-1 0..(v) MattCrawley(7) 72
(Christine Dunnett) *hld up in tch: lft 3rd 2nd: chsd wnr and blnd 6th: rdn to press wnr after 3 out: struggling whn mstke next: wl btn whn hit last* **10/1**
/3-0 **3** *3* **Renege The Joker**[19] 135 7-10-5 0................................ MissCBoxall(7) 73
(Sean Regan) *t.k.h: hld up in rr: hdwy and mstke 6th: chsd ldng pair bef next: rdn and mstke 2 out: btn whn hmpd by loose horse bnd bef last* **80/1**
PP0- **4** *20* **Souchang (IRE)**[30] 5367 5-9-12 0................................(b) MarkQuinlan(7) 46
(Susan Gardner) *chsd ldrs: j. awkwardly and lft 2nd tl 6th: sn lost pl and drvn: t.o after 3 out* **100/1**
5- **5** *18* **Tribal Rule**[31] 5340 4-10-8 0...(t) PaulMoloney 31
(Evan Williams) *t.k.h: hld up in last pair: rdn and btn after 6th: mstke next: t.o bef 2 out* **13/2**[2]
020- **U** **Chalice Welcome**[13] 4722 7-10-9 85.............................. AlexMerriam(3) —
(Neil King) *chsd wnr tl j. awkwardly and uns rdr 2nd* **7/1**[3]

3m 55.3s (-10.10) **Going Correction** -0.975s/f (Hard)
WFA 4 from 5yo+ 18lb **6** Ran SP% **112.2**
Speed ratings (Par 105): **86,77,75,65,56 —**
toteswingers: 1&2 £1.80, 1&3 £5.30, 2&3 £7.60 CSF £4.92 TOTE £1.40: £1.10, £2.10; EX 5.20.
Owner Wordingham Plant Hire **Bred** Hellwood Stud Farm **Trained** Farnsfield, Notts

FOCUS
A straightforward win for the favourite who only needed to match his previous best.

NOTEBOOK
Moonstreaker found this significantly easier than the Grade 2 he contested at Aintree last month. A ready winner at Market Rasen the time before, he made all the running and, despite jumping as though he would be suited by going the other way round, everything went smoothly. He can be placed to win again through the summer. (op 1-2 tchd 8-15 and 4-7 in places)
Wicklewood, a well-beaten third in a selling hurdle at the course on debut, did best of the remainder, though it's hard to say whether this was much of an improvement. (op 9-1 tchd 11-1)
Renege The Joker was making a race of it for second when squeezed up against he rail by a loose horse after the second-last, but it probably didn't affect his finishing position. (op 66-1)
Tribal Rule was disappointing, considering he had showed promise on his hurdles debut. (op 7-2)
Chalice Welcome got no further than the second, unseating in dramatic fashion. (op 8-1)

440 HAPPY BIRTHDAY TODAY LINDA TAYLOR BEGINNERS' CHASE (12 fncs) 2m 110y
4:35 (4:35) (Class 4) 5-Y-0+ **£4,553** (£1,337; £668; £333)

Form RPR
F0F- **1** **Treaty Flyer (IRE)**[29] 5392 9-10-7 0.................................. JohnnyFarrelly 116+
(Alison Thorpe) *j.w: chsd ldrs tl wnt 2nd 3rd: gd jump to join ldr next: led 7th: drew clr fr 3 out: eased after last: v easily* **4/5**[1]
0/0- **2** *15* **El Presidente (IRE)**[79] 4417 5-10-11 115.....................(b) AlexMerriam(3) 98
(Neil King) *sn led and racd keenly: jnd 4th: mstke and hdd 7th: rdn and btn after 3 out: no ch w wnr but plugged on for clr 2nd* **6/1**[3]
04-4 **3** *17* **Ruby Valentine (FR)**[23] 77 7-10-7 78........................ AndrewThornton 74
(Jim Wilson) *chsd ldng trio: in tch tl pushed along and struggling bdly 7th: lost tch next: wnt poor 3rd between last 2* **10/1**
446- **4** *12* **Galley Slave (IRE)**[48] 5038 5-10-7 62................................ PeterHatton(7) 69
(Michael Chapman) *a bhd: j. slowly 4th and 5th: lost tch 7th: sn t.o* **20/1**
324- **P** **Edgefour (IRE)**[15] 2351 6-10-7 0.. CharliePoste —
(Ben Case) *t.k.h: chsd ldr tl 3rd: chsd ldng pair after: mstke 7th: rdn and wknd qckly after next: dropped to last and t.o after 2 out: p.u last* **3/1**[2]

4m 5.00s (-11.60) **Going Correction** -0.575s/f (Firm) **5** Ran SP% **108.7**
Speed ratings: **104,96,88,83,—**
CSF £5.93 TOTE £1.90: £1.10, £3.30; EX 4.80.
Owner Atlantic Racing And R W Huggins **Bred** Mrs M Brophy **Trained** Bronwydd Arms, Carmarthens

FOCUS
A weak beginners' chase and easy for the winner with his main market rival running poorly. The form is rated around the third.

NOTEBOOK
Treaty Flyer(IRE) skipped round to win for the first time over fences at the third attempt. She has raced solely over hurdles for the past year and a half, progressing into a 132-rated performer, and would probably have finished second to Ashkazar at Sandown last time but for taking a heavy fall. She showed no signs of a dent in confidence, though, being quick and fluent at her fences, and she may well defy a penalty in the right company. (op 5-6 tchd 10-11)
El Presidente(IRE) didn't run too badly in a handicap at Doncaster on his chasing debut, but he had plenty to find with the favourite at the weights and was left trailing. He needs to improve his jumping. (op 13-2 tchd 9-2)
Ruby Valentine(FR), rated just 78, kept on for a remote third. (op 14-1)
Edgefour(IRE) looked a live contender but she was quickly beaten off and the way she stopped suggests something may have been amiss. Official explanation: jockey said mare stopped quickly (op 11-4 tchd 5-2)

441 RAY ATHERTON MEMORIAL LADY AMATEUR RIDERS' H'CAP HURDLE (11 hdls) 2m 4f
5:10 (5:10) (Class 5) (0-90,90) 4-Y-0+ **£2,637** (£811; £405)

Form RPR
4P4- **1** **Moon Melody (GER)**[49] 5007 7-10-9 **76**............. MissIsabelTompsett(3) 83
(Evan Williams) *chsd ldrs: led 8th tl bef next: rdn and ev ch last: led again fnl 100yds: kpt on* **9/2**[2]
56-5 **2** *1/2* **Abulharith**[14] 228 4-10-7 **83**... MissJBuck(7) 85
(Michael Scudamore) *hld up in tch: hdwy to chse ldng pair after 8th: rdn and hdwy on inner to ld bef last: sn edging rt: hdd fnl 100yds: no ex and hung rt towards fin* **11/2**[3]
5/5- **3** *1 1/4* **Ruby Isabel (IRE)**[32] 5318 6-10-11 **82**......................... MissJennyCarr(7) 89
(Tim Vaughan) *hld up in tch in last trio: hdwy to trck ldrs after 5th: led gng wl after 8th: mstke next and 2 out: hdd and rdn between last 2: fnd little but stl ev ch last: btn flat: clr run and eased towards fin* **4/1**[1]
30-0 **4** *8* **Mista Rossa**[6] 185 5-11-5 **83**... MissLHorner 84
(Jamie Snowden) *hld up wl in rr: stdy hdwy bef 3 out: wnt 6th 2 out: no imp on ldrs after but kpt on to go 4th sn after last: nvr gng pce to rch ldrs* **11/1**
20-P **5** *5* **Sophisticated Lady**[19] 140 7-10-7 **78**...................... MissJCWilliams(7) 72
(Neil King) *hld up in last trio: pushed along after 7th: rdn and hdwy 3 out: no prog and wl hld fr next* **16/1**
0FP/ **6** *8* **Misty Gem (IRE)**[384] 9-10-0 **71**................................ MissSMStaveley(7) 58
(Philip Kirby) *racd keenly: sn led: hdd 6th: wknd qckly next: wl btn 2 out* **25/1**
S54- **7** *2 3/4* **Call Me Sir (IRE)**[61] 4798 8-10-13 **80**.............................. MissLGardner(3) 65
(Susan Gardner) *chsd ldr after 1st tl 8th: rdn and wknd qckly bef next: wl btn bef 2 out* **9/2**[2]
6-33 **8** *1 1/2* **Ghaill Force**[11] 272 8-10-9 **78**..(p) MissZoeLilly(5) 61
(Paddy Butler) *in tch in midfield: hdwy to chse ldrs and mstke 7th: hit next: sn rdn: wknd bef 3 out* **9/2**[2]
36-0 **9** *54* **Gunnadoit (USA)**[24] 66 5-11-5 **90**..............................(v[1]) MissCBoxall(7) 25
(Neil King) *chsd ldrs tl rdn and lost pl after 4th: bhd fr 6th: lost tch after next: t.o fr 3 out* **12/1**

4m 51.3s (-21.30) **Going Correction** -0.975s/f (Hard)
WFA 4 from 5yo+ 19lb **9** Ran SP% **115.7**
Speed ratings (Par 103): **103,102,102,99,97 93,92,92,70**
toteswingers: 1&2 £4.40, 1&3 £5.60, 2&3 £5.10 CSF £29.82 CT £106.91 TOTE £5.40: £2.30, £1.70, £1.70; EX 32.40 Place 6 £14.08, Place 5 £9.59.
Owner R E R Williams **Bred** R Hartmann **Trained** Llancarfan, Vale Of Glamorgan

FOCUS
A moderate handicap hurdle for lady riders. Straightforward form around the front pair.

NOTEBOOK
Moon Melody(GER) had the assistance of one of the better riders and the pair got on top close home, being helped by the runner-up edging out to his right. This was the lowest mark he has been on in over a year, and it will take a step forward for him to go in off a higher mark, especially as it was just his second win at the 58th attempt under both codes. (op 5-1)
Abulharith remains a maiden, but this was the closest he has ever come, and he would have been even closer but for hanging late on. This new trip may have been a tad too far. (op 13-2 tchd 7-1)
Ruby Isabel(IRE) may have moved to prominence too early as her finishing effort was rather tame. A more restrained ride over the trip may enable her to pick up a small race. (op 10-3)
Mista Rossa, well held on the Flat just six days earlier, has still to win a race over hurdles and he never got close enough to challenge. (op 10-1)
Call Me Sir(IRE) failed to run his race, possibly find the drop in trip on quick ground against him. (op 5-1 tchd 11-2)
T/Plt: £31.70 to a £1 stake. Pool: £5,2390.69. 1,203.28 winning tickets. T/Qpdt: £7.40 to a £1 stake. Pool: £4,274.77. 423.50 winning tickets. SP

305 PERTH (R-H)
Sunday, May 23

OFFICIAL GOING: Good to soft (soft in places; 6.3)
Wind: Almost nil Weather: Sunny, hot

442 PROVOST'S PLATE CHALLENGE TROPHY NOVICES' HURDLE (10 hdls) 2m 4f 110y
2:15 (2:15) (Class 4) 4-Y-0+ **£2,602** (£764; £382; £190)

Form RPR
U11- **1** **Nedzer's Return (IRE)**[30] 5375 8-10-12 145.........................(t) APMcCoy 119+
(Gordon Elliott, Ire) *trckd ldrs: clsd 4 out: led after next: drew clr fr 2 out: easily* **1/3**[1]
F- **2** *17* **Huncheon Wells (IRE)**[20] 120 8-10-7 94......... SamTwiston-Davies(5) 104+
(R T J Wilson, Ire) *pressed ldr: led 4 out to after next: plugged on same pce fr 2 out* **10/1**[3]

33-2 **3** 7 **Proficiency**[11] 285 5-10-5 96 (v) PaddyAspell 86
(Sue Bradburne) *led to 4 out: drvn and outpcd after next: no imp fr 2 out* **6/1²**

4 3 ½ **Elcanos (GER)**[70] 4629 7-10-12 0 PCarberry 94+
(A J Martin, Ire) *hld up: hit 4th: stdy hdwy to trck ldrs whn nt fluent 3 out: effrt bef next: sn one pce: 3rd and hld whn blnd last* **16/1**

5 20 **Hesaposer (IRE)**[126] 3498 4-10-7 0 BrianHughes 67
(Gordon Elliott, Ire) *midfield: drvn and outpcd after 4 out: n.d after* **50/1**

06-5 **6** 22 **Catleen (IRE)**[11] 285 6-10-5 0 PeterBuchanan 45
(S R B Crawford, Ire) *hld up: rdn bef 4 out: nvr on terms* **28/1**

03-4 **7** 3 **Fool's Wildcat (USA)**[5] 388 5-10-12 95 (tp) RobertThornton 49
(Valentine Donoghue) *in tch: effrt after 4 out: wknd next* **20/1**

8 9 **Cape Secret (IRE)**[14] 240 7-10-12 0 DenisO'Regan 41
(Gordon Elliott, Ire) *hld up: struggling 4 out: nvr on terms* **25/1**

P **9** 20 **Daasij (IRE)**[11] 289 5-10-12 0 GrahamLee 23
(J Barclay) *t.k.h early: hld up: struggling bef 4 out: nvr on terms* **50/1**

0/ **P** **Some Lad (IRE)**[389] 53 5-10-9 0 RyanMania(3) —
(Mrs A C Hamilton) *prom: blnd and lost pl 6th: t.o whn p.u next* **66/1**

0-P **P** **Solway Dornal**[14] 225 5-10-7 0 EwanWhillans(5) —
(Lisa Harrison) *bhd: struggling 4th: t.o whn p.u bef 6th* **100/1**

5m 15.5s (8.60) **Going Correction** +0.60s/f (Soft)
WFA 4 from 5yo+ 19lb **11** Ran SP% **122.7**
Speed ratings (Par 105): **107,100,97,96,88 80,79,75,68,— —**
toteswingers: 1&2 £1.80, 1&3 £1.40, 2&3 £4.70 CSF £4.82 TOTE £1.40: £1.02, £2.30, £1.30; EX 4.20.
Owner Ms Annie Flora Joan Bowles **Bred** P M Dwyer **Trained** Trim, Co Meath

FOCUS
The ground was officially eased to good, good to soft in places before the opener and it was visibly kicking up in places in the race. The winner did not need to get close to his chase form.

NOTEBOOK
Nedzer's Return(IRE) was raised 17lb after winning back-to-back races over fences at this venue last month, which forced connections to go novice hurdling, and he had been found a simple task on his debut in this sphere. He did things easily, running out a most decisive winner, and should have little trouble defying a penalty in something similar. (op 4-11 tchd 1-2 in places)
Huncheon Wells(IRE), who like the winner is better known for his exploits over fences, was given a positive ride and kept on gamely to win the race for second. With an official mark rated 51lb the winner's inferior, he obviously faced a very tough task on this return to hurdling and emerged with credit.
Proficiency, second over C&D last time, was awash with sweat and folded off the home turn after cutting out most of the running. She is a tricky sort to get right and her ideal trip remains open to debate. (op 5-1)
Elcanos(GER) looked a big player when making up ground nearing the home turn under a typical waiting ride by his jockey, but he had nothing left in the tank when push came to shove. The run may have been needed, but he looks a shadow of the horse that ran on the Flat when trained in Germany. (op 14-1)

443 UNIVERSAL INSPECTION (UK) NOVICES' H'CAP CHASE (15 fncs) 2m 4f 110y
2:45 (2:45) (Class 3) (0-120,112) 5-Y-0+ **£5,854** (£1,719; £859; £429)

Form RPR
053- **1** **Sotovik (IRE)**[30] 5375 9-10-13 104 EwanWhillans(5) 112+
(Alistair Whillans) *led to 4 out: sn drvn along: one pce after next: 15 l down whn lft clr last: drvn out* **9/1**

2-53 **2** 9 **Athoss**[10] 306 8-10-10 103 MrJBewley(7) 97
(Robert Smith) *prom: drvn and outpcd fr 5 out: lft 19 l 2nd last: plugged on: eased cl home and jst hld on for 2nd* **8/1**

3 **3** shd **Meadows Thyne (IRE)**[16] 193 9-11-11 111 PCarberry 102+
(A J Martin, Ire) *nt fluent: hld up last: effrt u.p after 5 out: no imp fr next: lft 40 l 4th last: styd on wl run-in: jst failed to snatch 2nd* **11/4²**

54-3 **4** 4 **Crow Spinney**[22] 88 7-10-9 98 MrOGreenall(3) 85
(Michael Easterby) *in tch: drvn and outpcd fr 5 out: lft 32 l 3rd last: kpt on run-in: no imp* **9/1**

012- **P** **Phone In**[25] 43 7-11-12 112 PeterBuchanan —
(Lucinda Russell) *sn cl up: drvn fr 8th: struggling after next: t.o whn p.u bef 4 out* **7/2³**

3 **F** **King Roonah**[11] 287 6-10-4 90 (t) BrianHughes 122+
(Gordon Elliott, Ire) *trckd ldrs: led 4 out: drew clr after next: 15 l in front whn fell last* **2/1¹**

5m 26.2s (12.20) **Going Correction** +0.30s/f (Yiel) **6** Ran SP% **113.3**
Speed ratings: **88,84,84,83,— —**
toteswingers: 1&2 £11.40, 1&3 £4.40, 2&3 £5.80 CSF £70.00 TOTE £12.80: £5.10, £4.30; EX 107.30.
Owner Jethart Justice **Bred** Timothy Fennessy **Trained** Newmill-On-Slitrig, Borders

FOCUS
A moderate novice handicap, run at an ordinary gallop. King Roonah would have trotted up but for falling at the last and has been rated a 17-length winner.

NOTEBOOK
Sotovik(IRE) rates a very lucky winner, with King Roonah falling when in front at the last. He was a tired horse passing the winning line. (op 8-1)
Athoss failed to raise his game as might have been expected for the step up in trip, but that was likely down to the ground turning soft. He was eased down late on and very nearly got caught out for second place as Meadows Thyne rattled home on the run-in. (op 13-2)
Meadows Thyne(IRE) failed to have a cut at his fences early on and that cost him, but he may jump better in this sphere back on a sounder surface. (op 4-1)
Phone In never looked that happy and was eventually pulled up as though something went amiss. Official explanation: jockey said gelding never travelled (tchd 10-3)
King Roonah looks much improved for the change of stable and had the race at his mercy when coming down at the last fence. He was well suited by this drop back in trip and, providing he emerges from the race without a hitch, there should be races still to be won with him. (tchd 10-3)

444 FUGRO-ROVTECH LTD H'CAP CHASE (12 fncs) 2m
3:15 (3:15) (Class 4) (0-115,115) 5-Y-0+ **£5,204** (£1,528; £764; £381)

Form RPR
220- **1** **The Rocking Dock (IRE)**[19] 146 9-11-11 114 (tp) APMcCoy 128
(Gordon Elliott, Ire) *cl up: led 5 out to bef next: drvn bef 3 out: rallied u.p to ld last: rdn out* **10/3²**

22-1 **2** 7 **Helen Wood**[12] 264 7-11-9 112 (bt) TomScudamore 120+
(David Pipe) *cl up: led bef 4 out: rdn 2 out: hdd last: no ex* **3/1¹**

2-13 **3** 36 **Coach Lane**[14] 233 9-11-6 109 AidanColeman 84
(Venetia Williams) *prom: rdn and outpcd whn mstke 4 out: sn btn* **5/1**

344- **4** 29 **Prince Tam**[64] 4732 6-10-0 89 oh3 (p) PeterBuchanan 48+
(Lucinda Russell) *led to 5 out: wknd after next: eased whn no ch run-in* **7/1**

0P-2 **P** **Annibale Caro**[18] 166 8-11-3 106 JamesReveley —
(Jim Goldie) *hld up in tch: wknd qckly after 6th: p.u next* **11/2**

04-3 **P** **All For The Cause (IRE)**[11] 290 8-11-12 115 BarryKeniry —
(Nicky Richards) *nt fluent on occasions: hld up: struggling bef 7th: t.o whn p.u bef 3 out* **4/1³**

4m 5.50s (2.80) **Going Correction** +0.30s/f (Yiel) **6** Ran SP% **112.6**
Speed ratings: **105,101,83,69,— —**
toteswingers: 1&2 £3.30, 1&3 £1.30, 2&3 £1.70 CSF £14.14 TOTE £4.10: £3.20, £2.00; EX 11.70.
Owner M Carle **Bred** Richard Galvin **Trained** Trim, Co Meath

FOCUS
This was a wide-open handicap. The first two dominated from four out and there was a slow-motion finish. The winner is rated up 5lb.

NOTEBOOK
The Rocking Dock(IRE) bounced back to winning ways with a game effort under a typically never-say-die ride from Tony McCoy. He jumped particularly well but looked in trouble as Helen Wood skipped clear into the home straight. He refused to give in, however, and as that rival began to tire his stamina kicked into play. This was a lot more like it from him and his form figures at the course now read 322P1. (op 7-2)
Helen Wood was bought back in by connections after winning a seller over hurdles last time out and was well treated back over fences on her previous best efforts. She looked all over the winner three out but her stamina gave way coming to the last. (op 4-1)
Coach Lane should have enjoyed the easing surface but his fate was apparent a long way out and his recent revival looks to have come to an end. (op 4-1)
Prince Tam, 3lb out of the handicap, set out to make all but was a sitting duck at the fourth-last. (tchd 13-2 and 15-2)
Annibale Caro Official explanation: trainer said gelding had a fibrillating heart

445 LIGHTHOUSE CLUB CONSTRUCTION INDUSTRY CHARITY NOVICES' H'CAP HURDLE (FOR THE SILVER CUP) (8 hdls) 2m 110y
3:45 (3:45) (Class 4) (0-105,104) 4-Y-0+ **£3,252** (£955; £477; £238)

Form RPR
052- **1** **Wind Shuffle (GER)**[16] 5333 7-11-12 104 GrahamLee 116
(Jim Goldie) *led: rdn 2 out: hdd last: rallied u.p to regain ld last 25yds: gamely* **4/1²**

2 1 ¼ **Cabernet Sauvignon**[7] 366 4-11-8 104 APMcCoy 111
(Gordon Elliott, Ire) *chsd ldrs: hdwy to go 2nd bef 2 out: effrt and led last: hdd and no ex last 25yds* **4/7¹**

/P-5 **3** 14 **Shopfrontspecialist (IRE)**[11] 286 7-10-7 85 RobertThornton 83
(Valentine Donoghue) *in tch: hdwy to chse ldrs bef 2 out: drvn and wknd between last 2* **12/1**

P-6U **4** 17 **Solway Blue**[4] 403 8-10-4 85 HarryHaynes(3) 68
(Lisa Harrison) *hld up in last: rdn bef 2 out: sn btn* **5/1³**

P4-0 **5** 1 ¼ **Rossini's Dancer**[11] 288 5-11-1 93 PaddyAspell 75
(Sue Bradburne) *chsd wnr tl rdn and wknd bef 2 out* **14/1**

4m 7.60s (7.90) **Going Correction** +0.60s/f (Soft)
WFA 4 from 5yo+ 18lb **5** Ran SP% **114.7**
Speed ratings (Par 105): **105,104,97,89,89**
CSF £7.40 TOTE £4.10: £1.20, £1.30; EX 7.90.
Owner Mrs S Bruce & Mrs L Mackay **Bred** Gestut Elsetal **Trained** Uplawmoor, E Renfrews

FOCUS
This was a very ordinary novice handicap, run at a fair enough gallop. The form is rated around the first three.

NOTEBOOK
Wind Shuffle(GER) proved most game under maximum pressure from the penultimate flight and deservedly opened his account as over hurdles at the fifth attempt. The decision to ride him from the front was a wise move and there could be a little more to come from him in this sphere. (op 7-2)
Cabernet Sauvignon predictably travelled up going strongly at the top of the home straight, but again he found little when asked to win the race. His attitude will rightly come under scrutiny after this. (tchd 4-6 tchd 8-11 in a place)
Shopfrontspecialst(IRE) shaped an awful lot better than had been the case over C&D last time out, but it is no coincidence she is yet to win a race. (op 14-1 tchd 11-1)
Solway Blue was never in the hunt on this return hurdling. (op 13-2)
Rossini's Dancer lacked fluency and was done with from the third-last. (op 16-1 tchd 9-1)

446 NEWWAVE RECRUITMENT SCOTLAND PERTH GOLD CUP H'CAP CHASE (18 fncs) 3m
4:20 (4:20) (Class 2) (0-145,138) 5-Y-0+ **£13,010** (£3,820; £1,910; £954)

Form RPR
0P2- **1** **Ollie Magern**[31] 5336 12-11-8 134 PaddyBrennan 147
(Nigel Twiston-Davies) *j.w: led: rdn and styd on strly to draw clr fr last* **14/1**

53-1 **2** 12 **Sir Bathwick (IRE)**[17] 181 11-10-9 121 (tp) TomScudamore 124
(David Pipe) *chsd wnr thrght: effrt bef 2 out: outpcd fr last* **3/1¹**

342- **3** ¾ **Go Silver Bullet (FR)**[31] 5337 9-10-8 120 PeterBuchanan 122
(Lucinda Russell) *trckd ldrs: effrt 3 out: one pce between last 2* **14/1**

/05- **4** 1 ¾ **Piano Star**[22] 104 10-11-10 136 (p) RobertThornton 138
(Michael Cunningham, Ire) *hld up: hdwy and in tch appr 4 out: rdn and outpcd 2 out: n.d after* **25/1**

43-2 **5** 2 ½ **Ginolad (AUS)**[10] 300 10-10-8 120 AidanColeman 118
(Venetia Williams) *hld up: drvn and outpcd 13th: styd on fr 2 out: nvr rchd ldrs* **8/1**

11-P **6** 11 **Catch The Perk (IRE)**[10] 308 13-10-5 120 CampbellGillies(3) 108
(Lucinda Russell) *hld up towards rr: outpcd and detached after 12th: sme late hdwy: nvr on terms* **20/1**

112- **7** ¾ **Flemross (IRE)**[20] 117 7-10-12 129 SamTwiston-Davies(5) 117
(R T J Wilson, Ire) *nt fluent on occasions: trckd ldrs: rdn whn hit 4 out: wknd bef next* **10/1**

0UP- **8** 2 ¾ **Lothian Falcon**[29] 5395 11-11-1 127 RobertWalford 112
(Peter Maddison) *midfield: hit 12th: rdn and outpcd whn hit 4 out: sn btn* **16/1**

/50- **9** 33 **Hoopy (IRE)**[147] 3103 8-11-3 129 (bt¹) APMcCoy 84
(Gordon Elliott, Ire) *nt fluent 1st and 2nd: in tch: drvn and reminders bef 12th: nt fluent 5 out: sn wknd* **7/2²**

222- **P** **Doc Row (IRE)**[56] 4911 10-10-3 115 WilsonRenwick —
(P Monteith) *hld up on outside: rdn and outpcd bef 12th: sn btn: p.u bef next* **9/1**

2/2- **P** **Jack The Blaster**[118] 3666 10-11-1 127 BrianHughes —
(Howard Johnson) *hld up: struggling 12th: p.u bef next* **15/2³**

P/ **P** **Militant (FR)**[9] 10-10-12 124 PCarberry —
(Gordon Elliott, Ire) *nt fluent: hld up: blnd and nrly uns rdr 6th: struggling fr 11th: p.u bef 13th* **33/1**

6m 25.1s (4.70) **Going Correction** +0.30s/f (Yiel) **12** Ran SP% **120.0**
Speed ratings: **104,100,99,99,98 94,94,93,82,— —,—**
toteswingers: 1&2 £14.20, 1&3 £30.40, 2&3 £15.70 CSF £57.32 CT £624.00 TOTE £14.40: £3.20, £1.90, £3.70; EX 36.50.
Owner Roger Nicholls **Bred** R Nicholls And T Smith **Trained** Naunton, Gloucs

FOCUS
The feature race was run at a sound enough gallop but nothing landed a significant blow from behind. Ollie Magern's best run since the Charlie Hall, with the next pair a few pounds off their recent best.
NOTEBOOK
Ollie Magern made every yard a winning one and finally ended his losing run, which stretched back to 2007. He has been given a chance by the handicapper of late and a repeat of his latest second off this mark over C&D proved good enough. This should boost his confidence no end. (op 9-1)
Sir Bathwick(IRE) was 7lb higher than when resuming winning ways on quicker ground at Wincanton earlier in the month. With the winner in the race, he was unable to dictate but was always in second place and posted a game effort. (op 4-1)
Go Silver Bullet(FR) does find this trip stretching his stamina, so the fact he was handy throughout and held third place strongly suggests it was a big advantage to race near the lead. He deserves to get his head back in front.
Piano Star emerged looking a threat on the back straight, but didn't help his cause by hitting the third-last. He was well held after that, but did fare best of those coming from behind and would have found the ground easy enough. (op 22-1)
Ginolad(AUS) was never seriously involved and looks to need more prominent handling. (op 10-1 tchd 11-1)
Hoopy(IRE)'s chance was apparent soon after the halfway stage and the first-time blinkers looked to have a negative effect. Official explanation: jockey said gelding never travelled (op 10-3)

447 BELUCKY@STANJAMES.COM H'CAP HURDLE (10 hdls) 2m 4f 110y
4:55 (4:55) (Class 3) (0-125,120) 4-Y-0+ **£4,878** (£1,432; £716; £357)

Form RPR
04-4 **1** **Summer Soul (IRE)**[11] [291] 8-10-12 **109**...............(p) CampbellGillies(3) 124+
(Lucinda Russell) *chsd ldrs: drvn and outpcd after 6th: rallied bef 3 out: led appr next: clr whn edgd lft between last 2: eased towards fin* **6/1**[3]
P5-0 **2** *18* **Corkage (IRE)**[10] [309] 7-11-12 **120**...............(p) PeterBuchanan 118
(Lucinda Russell) *bhd: pushed along 1/2-way: hdwy bef 3 out: chsd (clr) wnr last: no imp* **10/1**
12U- **3** *17* **Bathwick Man**[253] [1292] 5-11-12 **120**...............(tp) TomScudamore 103
(David Pipe) *w ldr: led 3 out to appr next: sn btn* **3/1**[1]
3FU- **4** *4 1/2* **Strobe**[10] [4108] 6-9-10 **97** ow2...............(p) AlexanderVoy(7) 78
(Lucy Normile) *slt ld to 3 out: ev ch tl wknd bef next: hld whn j.rt last* **22/1**
55-6 **5** *1* **Player (FR)**[18] [166] 7-10-2 **96**............... PaddyAspell 74
(Ann Hamilton) *hld up towards rr: outpcd 1/2-way: n.d after* **14/1**
43-5 **6** *4 1/2* **Tarkani (IRE)**[10] [309] 7-11-0 **108**...............(tp) RobertThornton 82
(Valentine Donoghue) *in tch tl rdn and wknd bef 3 out* **12/1**
233- **7** *3* **Black Jacari (IRE)**[21] [1251] 5-11-10 **118**............... JamesReveley 89
(Philip Kirby) *hld up: shortlived effrt after 4 out: btn bef 2 out* **14/1**
2-22 **8** *43* **Baaher (USA)**[11] [288] 6-11-0 **108**............... GrahamLee 40
(Jim Goldie) *t.k.h: hld up: effrt and hdwy bef 3 out: wknd bef next* **10/3**[2]
/20- **P** **Key Time (IRE)**[42] [5147] 8-11-3 **111**............... BrianHughes —
(Howard Johnson) *chsd ldrs tl wknd bef 4 out: t.o whn p.u bef 2 out* **12/1**
P **Mickey Monk (IRE)**[20] [116] 5-10-11 **105**............... APMcCoy —
(Gordon Elliott, Ire) *prom: lost pl 6th: sn struggling: t.o whn p.u bef 7th* **6/1**[3]

5m 15.5s (8.60) **Going Correction** +0.60s/f (Soft) **10** Ran SP% **118.8**
Speed ratings (Par 107): **107,100,93,91,91 89,88,72,—,—**
toteswingers: 1&2 £9.20, 1&3 £6.20, 2&3 £9.20 CSF £64.99 CT £217.48 TOTE £8.10: £2.50, £2.90, £1.60; EX 82.70.
Owner Bissett Racing **Bred** Moyglare Stud Farm Ltd **Trained** Arlary, Perth & Kinross
FOCUS
This modest handicap was another race on the card where it proved hard to get involved from off the pace, despite it being run at a sound gallop. The winner was back to his 2008 C/D form.
NOTEBOOK
Summer Soul(IRE) took up the running with a fine leap two out and was in no danger thereafter. This was just his second win as a hurdler, but he has always looked a horse that could make the grade in this sphere and his proven stamina on this drop back in trip was a real advantage. (op 7-1 tchd 15-2)
Corkage(IRE) stayed on dourly from out the back to hand his stable a one-two. He wasn't travelling with any purpose early on but kept on gamely for a clear second. (op 12-1)
Bathwick Man attracted support on this return to hurdling. He got a positive ride but his lack of a recent run seemed to tell from the penultimate flight and it wouldn't be surprising to see him last longer next time. (op 11-4 tchd 7-2)
Strobe performed a lot more encouragingly on his return from chasing. He is on a good mark if able to build on this. (op 16-1)
Tarkani(IRE) Official explanation: jockey said gelding had a breathing problem
Baaher(USA) Official explanation: jockey said gelding had a breathing problem
Mickey Monk(IRE), making his British debut, proved easy to back and this clearly wasn't his true form. Perhaps the easing ground was against him, but he does have something to prove. Official explanation: jockey said gelding was unsuited by the good to soft (soft in places) ground (op 11-2)

448 SIS STANDARD OPEN NATIONAL HUNT FLAT RACE 2m 110y
5:30 (5:30) (Class 6) 4-6-Y-O **£1,712** (£499; £249)

Form RPR
10- **1** **Lovey Dovey (IRE)**[44] [5114] 6-10-11 0............... MrStevenCrawford(5) 114+
(S R B Crawford, Ire) *cl up: led over 6f out: hung lft 2f out: edgd rt and styd on strly fnl f* **3/1**[3]
62- **2** *7* **Call Me Bill (IRE)**[26] [35] 4-10-12 0............... TomO'Brien 104
(Peter Bowen) *cl up: effrt over 2f out: kpt on same pce ins fnl f* **5/2**[2]
6- **3** *14* **Float My Boat**[59] [4839] 4-10-12 0............... PCarberry 91
(S R B Crawford, Ire) *hld up: stdy hdwy over 4f out: effrt over 2f out: sn outpcd: edgd rt and no imp fnl f* **14/1**
0- **4** *2 3/4* **Jacks Grey**[31] [5351] 5-11-2 0............... APMcCoy 93
(I R Ferguson, Ire) *hld up: stdy hdwy to chse ldrs 5f out: rdn and outpcd fr 2f out* **9/4**[1]
5- **5** *30* **Minden March**[57] [4886] 5-10-9 0............... RobertWalford 59
(Peter Maddison) *hld up: drvn and outpcd over 5f out: sn wknd* **40/1**
6 *24* **Monashee (IRE)** 5-11-2 0............... DenisO'Regan 44
(George Charlton) *t.k.h: prom tl wknd fr 3f out* **9/2**
0/ **7** *4* **Lookin Daggers (IRE)**[555] [2202] 6-10-9 0............... MrJBewley(7) 41
(George Bewley) *cl up tl wknd over 4f out* **50/1**
8 *4* **Over The Clyde**[15] 5-10-13 0............... RyanMania(3) 37
(William Young) *led to over 6f out: sn struggling* **66/1**

4m 4.70s (10.60) **Going Correction** +0.60s/f (Soft)
WFA 4 from 5yo+ 4lb **8** Ran SP% **115.1**
Speed ratings: **99,95,89,87,73 62,60,58**
toteswingers: 1&2 £1.30, 1&3 £5.30, 2&3 £8.10 CSF £10.98 TOTE £4.40: £1.50, £1.40, £2.20; EX 10.70 Place 6 £76.14, Place 5 £71.40.
Owner S R B Crawford **Bred** Hugh Suffern Bloodstock Ltd **Trained** Larne, Co Antrim
FOCUS
The first pair came nicely clear in this reasonable bumper and the form is rated around them.
NOTEBOOK
Lovey Dovey(IRE) was outclassed in Listed company at Aintree last month but was better than the bare form there and showed her true colours again on this return to a smaller track. She was idling when in front but never looked like throwing it away and rates a nice prospect for novice hurdling against her own sex. (op 7-2 tchd 4-1)
Call Me Bill(IRE), touched off at Sedgefield 26 days previously, could have probably done without the ground softening. He kept on gamely under pressure and was clear of the rest but was always being held by the winner. (op 9-4 tchd 2-1)
Float My Boat stepped up on the level of his debut at Ayr and left the impression he may have got closer under a more positive ride. This former point winner will need further once sent hurdling. (op 7-1)
Jacks Grey made his debut at the Punchestown Festival last month and had McCoy aboard this time. He travelled nicely into contention but found just the same pace when it mattered and is another that may need firmer ground. (op 3-1)
T/Plt: £109.50 to a £1 stake. Pool: £67,290.33. 448.44 winning tickets. T/Qpdt: £9.90 to a £1 stake. Pool: £5,933.49. 440.70 winning tickets. RY

449 - 455a (Foreign Racing) - See Raceform Interactive

[209]HEXHAM (L-H)
Tuesday, May 25

OFFICIAL GOING: Good to firm (7.9)
Last flight in back straight omitted on all circuits on hurdle course.
Wind: Breezy, half behind Weather: Overcast, dull

456 ST. JOHN LEE AMATEUR RIDERS' NOVICES' H'CAP HURDLE (6 hdls 2 omitted) 2m 110y
6:35 (6:35) (Class 5) (0-95,93) 4-Y-0+ **£2,307** (£709; £354)

Form RPR
22-2 **1** **Mountskip**[20] [161] 6-10-10 **84**............... MrAdamNicol(7) 93+
(Rose Dobbin) *trckd ldrs: smooth hdwy to ld last: qckng clr: readily* **7/4**[1]
3F-4 **2** *11* **Little Wizard (IRE)**[24] [92] 8-11-7 **93**............... AlistairFindlay(5) 90
(George Charlton) *mde most tl nt fluent and hdd last: sn drvn: kpt on same pce* **13/2**[3]
200/ **3** *2 3/4* **Devils And Dust (IRE)**[9] 9-10-1 **75**...............(p) MissGTutty(7) 69
(Karen Tutty) *cl up: chal 2 out (usual 3 out) to last: sn outpcd* **33/1**
03-6 **4** *4 1/2* **Parisian Knight (IRE)**[6] [405] 7-10-7 **79** ow2............... MrGCrow(5) 69
(A M Crow) *hld up: hdwy and prom 3rd: rdn and wknd bef last* **8/1**
563- **5** *30* **Teenando (IRE)**[66] [4734] 10-10-9 **83**............... MrJRoche(7) 43
(Sue Smith) *chsd ldrs: lost pl 2nd: outpcd and struggling after next: nvr on terms after* **6/1**[2]
40-0 **6** *15* **Hernando Cortes**[20] [161] 6-11-3 **84**............... MrOGreenall 29
(Martin Todhunter) *mstkes: hld up: rdn bef 3 out (usual 4 out): wknd fr next* **7/1**
P3P- **7** *1* **Glengap (IRE)**[216] [1848] 7-10-3 **77**............... MrPJTolman(7) 21
(Elliott Cooper) *hld up in tch: stdy hdwy and cl up 2 out (usual 3 out): rdn and wknd bef last* **9/1**
P/0- **P** **Gala Queen**[28] [31] 10-10-0 **74** oh10 ow7...............(tp) MrJohnDawson(7) —
(William Young) *w ldrs: hit 2nd: sn pushed along and lost pl: t.o 2 out: p.u bef last* **66/1**
/0-P **P** **Danehill Silver**[20] [161] 6-11-1 **85**............... MrMSeston(3) —
(Brian Storey) *t.k.h: prom: mstke 3 out (usual 4 out): p.u bef next* **40/1**
40-P **S** **I See A Star**[5] [424] 7-11-3 **91**............... MissEStead(7) —
(Micky Hammond) *hld up last: slipped and fell sme way bef 1st* **12/1**

4m 10.4s (-7.00) **Going Correction** -0.55s/f (Firm) **10** Ran SP% **112.2**
Speed ratings (Par 103): **94,88,87,85,71 64,63,—,—,—**
toteswingers: 1&2 £4.60, 1&3 £5.30, 2&3 £21.60 CSF £13.12 CT £263.71 TOTE £2.70: £2.10, £1.10, £12.40; EX 8.50.
Owner The Kwick Syndicate **Bred** Mrs K Walton **Trained** South Hazelrigg, Northumbria
⊠ Adam Nicol's first winner under rules.
FOCUS
A poor contest, lacking depth. The winner is arguably worth further.
NOTEBOOK
Mountskip, runner-up on each of his last three starts, has been creeping up the ratings but it made no difference here. Held up in touch in the early stages, he eased closer to the pace three out and went second approaching the last. Jumping well there, he quickly left the rest behind and won eased down. Those he beat were not up to much but he can collect again if sensibly placed. (tchd 13-8)
Little Wizard(IRE), fourth in novice company here last time out, was taking a sharp drop in distance for this and set out to make the running. He was headed briefly early on, but held a clear advantage three out, which he forfeited only when the winner took control over the last. Not surprisingly, he stayed on well enough, but was never a threat on the run-in. (op 11-2)
Devils And Dust(IRE), second in two handicaps in 2007 but still a maiden after 27 races, was making his first appearance under rules for 896 days. He did not fare too badly, chasing the pace throughout, but his presence in third serves to underline the weakness of this contest. (op 20-1)
Parisian Knight(IRE), third in a Sedgefield seller a month previously, was trying 2m over hurdles for the first time and lacked the pace to make a major impact. Disputing second at the second-last, he was beaten when the principals quickened. (op 9-1 tchd 10-1)
Glengap(IRE) was the only other runner to figure with a chance once the turn for home began, but he soon tired and dropped away tamely approaching the last. Official explanation: jockey said gelding had a breathing problem (op 8-1 tchd 10-1and 6-1 in a place)
Danehill Silver Official explanation: jockey said saddle slipped

457 S & N GOOD LUCK MAIDEN HURDLE (8 hdls 2 omitted) 2m 4f 110y
7:05 (7:05) (Class 4) 4-Y-0+ **£2,740** (£798; £399)

Form RPR
2-52 **1** **Patriot (IRE)**[17] [214] 6-10-11 105...............(t) MichaelMcAlister(3) 103+
(Maurice Barnes) *chsd ldrs: led bef last: drifted lft and kpt on strly run-in* **9/4**[2]
- **2** *4* **Symphonica (IRE)**[19] [188] 7-10-7 106............... APMcCoy 92
(Gordon Elliott, Ire) *t.k.h: led to bef last: outpcd whn nt fluent last: kpt on u.p run-in* **7/4**[1]
000- **3** *4 1/2* **Nearly Sunday**[44] [5140] 5-10-0 0............... GarryWhillans(7) 87
(Donald Whillans) *chsd ldrs: drvn and outpcd 2 out (usual 3 out): rallied to chse (clr) ldrs bef last: kpt on run-in* **66/1**
00-5 **4** *23* **Sambelucky (IRE)**[24] [92] 5-11-0 0............... JamesReveley 71
(Keith Reveley) *hld up: outpcd bef 2 out (usual 3 out): n.d after* **12/1**
51- **5** *2* **Lackamon**[58] [4912] 5-11-0 0............... TjadeCollier 69
(Sue Smith) *chsd ldrs tl rdn and wknd passing omitted 2 out* **7/2**[3]
44- **6** *1/2* **Accordingtotheboss (IRE)**[33] [5333] 5-10-11 0............... FearghalDavis(3) 68
(Nicky Richards) *t.k.h: hld up in tch: rdn and wknd passing omitted 2 out* **7/1**

0- **P** **Modestine**[36] 5273 8-10-3 0 ow3 AlistairFindlay(7) —
(Jane Walton) *nt jump wl: bhd: hdwy and prom 3rd: struggling fr 5th: t.o whn p.u next* **100/1**

5m 5.00s (-7.50) **Going Correction** -0.55s/f (Firm)
WFA 4 from 5yo+ 19lb 7 Ran SP% **112.0**
Speed ratings (Par 105): **92,90,88,80,79 79,—**
toteswingers: 1&2 £1.30, 1&3 £26.10, 2&3 £16.60 CSF £6.54 TOTE £2.60: £1.10, £1.10; EX 6.70.
Owner K Barker **Bred** David Magnier And Cobra Bloodstock **Trained** Farlam, Cumbria

FOCUS
A modest event in which few boasted worthwhile form. The third and the slow time are worries but the winner has been rated to his best.

NOTEBOOK
Patriot(IRE), second on three of his last five outings and officially rated 105, took this without being hard-pressed. Second for the majority of the race, he joined the pace-setting runner-up as they turned into the home straight and quickly asserted his superiority. He hung to his left on the run-in, ending up under the far rail, but had plenty in hand at the finish. (op 7-2)
Symphonica(IRE) had not been beaten far when fifth in a Clonmel handicap last time out on her first start for seven months and seemed sure to improve. It is doubtful that she did, however, as after racing keenly and setting the pace until approaching the final flight, she was soon outpaced. (tchd 2-1)
Nearly Sunday, down the field in two bumpers and her only previous hurdle race, she showed her first glimmer of form by taking third. She was in front early on and close up for much of rest of the contest but lacked the pace to stay with the first two from the home turn. (tchd 50-1)
Sambelucky(IRE) had hinted at ability in bumpers but, as on his two previous outings over hurdles, was comprehensively outpointed. He was never closer than fourth and beaten a long way. (op 16-1)
Lackamon Official explanation: jockey said, regarding the running and riding, that his instructions were to sit handy, get him jumping and give him every chance to win. He added that the gelding needed softer ground and had been feeling the fast ground coming down the hill. The trainer confirmed these instructions.

458 THANK YOU ANTHONY WOOD NOVICES' CHASE (17 fncs 2 omitted) 3m 1f
7:35 (7:36) (Class 4) 5-Y-0+ **£4,664** (£1,448; £779)

Form RPR
11-4 **1** **Midnight Chase**[24] 98 8-11-12 137 DougieCostello 130+
(Neil Mulholland) *led to 4 out: regained ld appr next: rdn clr after 2 out: eased run-in* **8/11**[1]
44-F **2** *12* **Political Pendant**[20] 160 9-10-2 80 (p) RyanMania(3) 89
(Rayson Nixon) *prom: drvn and outpcd after 13th: rallied between last 2: styd on to chse (clr) wnr run-in: no imp* **80/1**
5U-6 **3** *2 ¾* **Currahee**[12] 309 6-10-9 0 (t) MichaelMcAlister(3) 94
(Maurice Barnes) *nt fluent: chsd ldrs: outpcd 4 out: rallied to chse (clr) wnr whn j.lft last: sn no ex and lost 2nd run-in* **14/1**[3]
4/5- **F** **Ballylanigan (IRE)**[10] 347 8-11-5 128 (b) APMcCoy 100
(Gordon Elliott, Ire) *chsd wnr: hit 13th: led 4 out to appr next: outpcd after 2 out: lost 2nd bef last: 15 l 3rd whn hmpd and fell heavily last* **6/4**[2]

6m 20.4s (-11.80) **Going Correction** -0.375s/f (Good) 4 Ran SP% **105.8**
Speed ratings: **103,99,98,—**
CSF £14.91 TOTE £1.70; EX 15.60.
Owner Lady Clarke **Bred** Conkwell Grange Stud Ltd **Trained** Burlescombe, Devon

FOCUS
A numerically disappointing turnout and it looked a match on form. The winner was value for further but is still rated 10lb off. The second fence after the winning post was omitted on both circuits due to low sun.

NOTEBOOK
Midnight Chase, fourth in a handicap last time out and officially rated 137, set the standard and won well. He took the lead immediately after the start and, although headed briefly four out, soon took up the running again and was well clear by the final fence. He shrugged off a double-penalty here and should find further suitable openings at this level. (op 10-11)
Political Pendant is rated just 80 over fences, so the fact that she could finish second indicates how little the winner needed to achieve to win. She was last for much of the race, but stayed on dourly while others were faring less well. (op 50-1)
Currahee, successful off a mark of 104 over hurdles a year ago, was making his chasing debut and, apart from an error at the sixth, jumped adequately. Having raced in third early on, he looked booked for second approaching the final fence but faded tamely on the run-in. (op 11-1 tchd 16-1)
Ballylanigan(IRE), rated 128 and stepping up in trip after scoring over 2m6f at Kilbeggan ten days previously, chased the winner for most of the race. He was tiring rapidly, however, when falling heavily at the last. Fortunately, he got up and appeared no worse for the experience. (op 11-8)

459 WEDDING DAY H'CAP HURDLE (8 hdls 2 omitted) 2m 4f 110y
8:05 (8:05) (Class 5) (0-90,90) 4-Y-0+ **£2,740** (£798; £399)

Form RPR
0/0- **1** **Fair Spin**[36] 2100 10-10-4 68 (v) BarryKeniry 73
(Micky Hammond) *prom: rdn passing omitted 2 out: led run-in: styd on wl* **6/1**[2]
0P5- **2** *¾* **King Penda (IRE)**[27] 42 7-11-9 90 FearghalDavis(3) 94
(Nicky Richards) *hld up: hdwy and prom 5th: drvn bef 2 out: rallied passing omitted 2 out: ev ch run-in: edgd lft: hld towards fin* **16/1**
3F **3** *3 ¼* **King Roonah**[2] 443 6-11-12 90 (t) APMcCoy 91
(Gordon Elliott, Ire) *t.k.h: cl up: led 2 out: drvn bef last: hdd run-in: kpt on same pce* **1/1**[1]
36-0 **4** *6* **Pay On (IRE)**[6] 405 7-10-7 76 (b[1]) EwanWhillans(5) 72
(Alistair Whillans) *cl up: effrt bef last: rdn and outpcd run-in* **22/1**
024- **5** *15* **Harcas (IRE)**[21] 914 8-11-5 83 DenisO'Regan 65
(Martin Todhunter) *hld up: outpcd bef 2 out (usual 3 out): hdwy bef last: sn no imp* **10/1**
00-0 **6** *6* **Toujours Souriante**[19] 176 4-10-2 71 (p) PaddyAspell 43
(Tracy Waggott) *led to 2nd: cl up tl outpcd 3 out (usual 4 out): n.d after* **9/1**[3]
2/P- **7** *2 ¼* **Belanak (IRE)**[51] 5023 7-11-10 88 TomO'Brien 63
(Michael Cunningham, Ire) *hld up: stdy hdwy and in tch after 2 out (usual 3 out): rdn and wknd bef last* **22/1**
0F6- **8** *4* **Mr Midaz**[76] 4510 11-10-13 77 PeterBuchanan 48
(Donald Whillans) *hld up towards rr: mstke and reminder 4th: rdn and outpcd 2 out (usual 3 out): n.d after* **16/1**
040- **9** *2* **Sadler's Cove (FR)**[83] 4396 12-10-7 78 (tp) MrSFMagee(7) 47
(J K Magee, Ire) *hld up in tch: outpcd 3 out (usual 4 out): sn n.d* **50/1**
44-0 **10** *16* **Cornish Castle (USA)**[16] 228 4-11-1 84 (p) TomMessenger 34
(Joss Saville) *nt fluent in rr: struggling 3 out (usual 4 out): nvr on terms* **25/1**
46P- **P** **Panthers Run**[36] 5271 10-10-10 74 (t) DougieCostello —
(Jonathan Haynes) *in tch tl rdn and outpcd after 2 out (usual 3 out): sn btn: p.u bef last* **40/1**
550- **P** **Douglas Julian**[282] 1226 8-11-1 79 HenryOliver —
(Sue Smith) *led 2nd to 2 out: wknd passing omitted 2 out: p.u bef last* **25/1**

5m 5.50s (-7.00) **Going Correction** -0.55s/f (Firm)
WFA 4 from 6yo+ 19lb 12 Ran SP% **115.9**
Speed ratings (Par 103): **91,90,89,87,81 79,78,76,76,69 —,—**
toteswingers: 1&2 £15.80, 1&3 £3.70, 2&3 £5.80 CSF £79.34 CT £172.30 TOTE £5.20: £1.40, £6.20, £1.02; EX 97.80.
Owner Bendery Properties Holdings Ltd **Bred** A S Reid **Trained** Middleham Moor, N Yorks

FOCUS
A modest event, with the top-weight rated 90, but it looked quite competitive. The winner is rated in line with the best of his recent form.

NOTEBOOK
Fair Spin had not scored over hurdles since 2006, but he won on the Flat at Pontefract last month and that victory seems to have rekindled his fire. Never far away here, he eased into fourth three flights from home and came to challenge for the lead shortly after the last. Quickening well, he squeezed between the second and third on the run-in and scored going away. (op 5-1)
King Penda(IRE), whose fifth at Kelso a month earlier had suggested he was improving, did even better here. Keen in the early stages, when held up towards the rear, he made progress from three out and went second jumping the last. He did nothing wrong thereafter but was outpaced by the winner. (op 14-1)
King Roonah fell at the final fence when set to win a handicap chase very easily off the same mark at Perth two days previously. Re-fitted with a tongue-tie in his bid for compensation and well supported beforehand, he was in the front rank until taking the lead three out, but could never establish a telling advantage and was outpaced from the final flight. (op 6-4)
Pay On(IRE), who notched his only win two years ago and finished tailed off last time out, ran much better here. Never far away, and in the lead briefly mid-race, he stayed on at one pace in the home straight.
Harcas(IRE), second over 2m1f at Sedgefield last summer, was up 2lb for this step back up in trip and it proved too much. He did stay on late, though, having been held up in rear in the early stages. (op 8-1 tchd 12-1)

460 BETFAIR H'CAP CHASE (12 fncs) 2m 110y
8:35 (8:35) (Class 4) (0-105,105) 5-Y-0+ **£5,854** (£1,719; £859; £429)

Form RPR
54-4 **1** **Arumun (IRE)**[24] 99 9-11-1 94 SamThomas 101
(Michael Scudamore) *hld up: hdwy and in tch 4 out: effrt after next: led run-in: drvn and jst hld on* **12/1**
5U-4 **2** *nse* **Ice Image (IRE)**[24] 88 8-10-3 89 AlistairFindlay(7) 96+
(George Charlton) *chsd ldr: led bef last to run-in: rallied: jst failed* **9/1**
F1-2 **3** *1 ¼* **The Kealshore Kid (IRE)**[19] 177 6-11-9 102 BarryKeniry 108
(George Moore) *hld up: stdy hdwy and in tch 3 out: effrt next: edgd lft and styd on u.p run-in* **5/2**[1]
41-4 **4** *5* **Heavenly Chorus**[24] 89 8-11-5 98 JamesReveley 99
(Keith Reveley) *hld up: hdwy bef 3 out: rdn and kpt on run-in: nt rch ldrs* **11/2**[3]
C0-P **5** *1* **More Shennanigans**[12] 306 9-10-0 79 oh9 KeithMercer 79
(Jean McGregor) *midfield: rdn 4 out: effrt u.p next: no imp after 2 out* **40/1**
54-2 **6** *nse* **Storm Prospect**[13] 290 7-11-4 97 (b) PeterBuchanan 97
(Lucinda Russell) *hld up: hdwy and in tch 3 out: rdn next: no imp bef last* **7/2**[2]
-P51 **7** *5* **Glimmer Of Light (IRE)**[10] 339 10-11-6 99 (b) DenisO'Regan 95
(Dr Richard Newland) *led 1st: set decent gallop: rdn and hdd bef last: wknd run-in* **12/1**
21-0 **8** *10* **More Like It (IRE)**[15] 252 10-11-4 97 (p) BrianHughes 84
(Peter Niven) *led to 1st: cl up tl rdn and wknd bef 2 out* **20/1**
0-00 **9** *1 ½* **Sea Cove**[13] 288 10-10-0 82 RyanMania(3) 68
(Dianne Sayer) *midfield: lost pl 3rd: struggling 4 out: btn next* **33/1**
04-F **10** *¾* **Magellan Straits**[9] 353 6-11-12 105 TjadeCollier 90
(Sue Smith) *prom tl rdn and wknd fr 3 out* **10/1**
200/ **11** *50* **Skiddaw Jones**[692] 820 10-10-7 89 (t) MichaelMcAlister(3) 29
(Maurice Barnes) *t.k.h: chsd ldrs: hit 7th: rdn and wknd fr 3 out* **40/1**

4m 1.00s (-8.80) **Going Correction** -0.375s/f (Good) 11 Ran SP% **113.2**
Speed ratings: **105,104,104,102,101 101,99,94,93,93 69**
toteswingers: 1&2 £16.80, 1&3 £19.00, 2&3 £10.10 CSF £104.75 CT £356.39 TOTE £17.10: £4.70, £2.80, £1.50; EX 87.50.
Owner Mark Blandford **Bred** J W George **Trained** Bromsash, Herefordshire

FOCUS
A run-of-the-mill handicap chase. The winner is rated in line with his best form of the past year and with small chase personal bests from the next two.

NOTEBOOK
Arumun(IRE), with one win in his last 25 starts, has been slipping down the ratings and took advantage with a gutsy victory. Held up early on, he began to make progress four out and was third jumping the third-last. He took second at the last and, after a battle with the runner-up, edged into the lead close home. He should not go up too much for this so has sound prospects of staying competitive. Official explanation: trainer had no explanation for the apparent improvement in form shown
Ice Image(IRE), who had fallen on three of six previous chase starts but had not been beaten far when getting round, again showed he is on a fair mark. Always close to the pace, he quickened to hit the front at the last and, responding gamely to driving, was unfortunate to lose out on the nod. (tchd 10-1)
The Kealshore Kid(IRE), already successful twice this year, was only 1lb higher than when second at Wetherby last time out but even that seemed to take its toll, as he could not quite match the first two on the run-in. This was game effort, however, as he was under pressure three fences from home. (op 3-1 tchd 9-4)
Heavenly Chorus, successful here from this mark over hurdles in April, posted a solid performance reverting to fences. Held up in rear early on, she made steady progress in the home straight and was staying on at the finish. (op 4-1)
Storm Prospect, second from a mark 2lb lower at Perth 13 days previously, often gets behind in his races and could never really mount a meaningful challenge. (tchd 4-1)

461 HEXHAM RACECOURSE CARAVAN SITE H'CAP HURDLE (10 hdls 2 omitted) 3m
9:05 (9:05) (Class 5) (0-95,102) 4-Y-0+ **£2,602** (£764; £382; £190)

Form RPR
0P-4 **1** **Sparkling Zola**[11] 318 8-10-8 82 EwanWhillans(5) 99+
(Alistair Whillans) *hld up in tch: hdwy after 2 out (usual 3 out): led last: drvn clr* **7/2**[2]
PP-6 **2** *4 ½* **Birnies Boy**[24] 92 6-10-6 75 (t) RichieMcGrath 87
(Brian Storey) *led: rdn and hdd last: edgd lft and styd on same pce run-in* **40/1**
1121 **3** *4 ½* **Flying Doctor**[5] 424 7-11-12 102 7ex MrPJTolman(7) 111
(Elliott Cooper) *hld up: hdwy passing omitted 2 out: effrt last: no imp run-in* **6/4**[1]
36-4 **4** *10* **Almond Court (IRE)**[17] 212 7-10-4 76 RyanMania(3) 75
(Robert Johnson) *cl up: rdn after 2 out (usual 3 out): wknd bef last* **7/2**[2]

0-P0 **5** *9* **Glacial Rambler (IRE)**[11] 318 11-9-9 **69** oh9............ JamesHalliday(5) 60
(Stuart Coltherd) *cl up tl rdn and wknd bef last* **66/1**
22/0 **6** *2 3/4* **Hooky's Hope**[17] 212 7-9-8 **70**.................... GarryWhillans(7) 58
(Harriet Graham) *prom: chsd ldr 2 out (usual 3 out): wknd bef last* **9/1**[3]
0-05 **7** *52* **Rosie Larkin (IRE)**[5] 424 6-10-0 **69** oh9..................(t) TomMessenger 11
(Joss Saville) *midfield: hit and outpcd 3 out (usual 4 out): lost tch after next* **33/1**
60-P **8** *29* **Vicentio**[19] 176 11-10-0 **69** oh5.................................(p) GrahamLee —
(Tim Fitzgerald) *hld up: rdn and wknd qckly passing omitted 2 out* **28/1**
1P-5 **P** **Old Noddy (IRE)**[20] 164 10-11-8 **91**...........................(b) BrianHughes —
(A M Crow) *cl up tl p.u after 4th: collapsed and died* **12/1**

5m 58.1s (-15.10) **Going Correction** -0.55s/f (Firm) **9** Ran SP% **112.5**
Speed ratings (Par 103): **103,101,100,96,93 92,75,65,—**
toteswingers: 1&2 £8.80, 1&3 £1.50, 2&3 £13.70 CSF £116.52 CT £288.74 TOTE £3.70: £1.40, £15.60, £1.10; EX 138.60 Place 6 £7.27, Place 5 £4.43.
Owner Mrs L M Whillans **Bred** Victor G And Mrs Izabel Palmer **Trained** Newmill-On-Slitrig, Borders

FOCUS
Another modest contest but solid form rated around the winner and third.

NOTEBOOK
Sparkling Zola, having only her sixth run over hurdles, was 13lb better off with Flying Doctor than when they met at Aintree 11 days previously and turned the form around. Patiently ridden in the early stages, she took closer order approaching two out and was second at the final flight. Quickening well, she led on the run-in and won going away. The handicapper will take note. (op 11-4)
Birnies Boy, who showed his first glimpse of form when sixth over C&D last time out, was given an excellent front-running ride and almost pulled off a massive shock. He was still in front at the last and, even though the winner had too much pace for him, he battled bravely up the run-in. (op 50-1)
Flying Doctor, already successful three times this month, was carrying a 7lb penalty for his most recent victory and the extra weight proved beyond him. Held up in the early stages, he made a move three out and was third at the second-last. He could not muster a change of gear, though, and made no further progress. (tchd 13-8)
Almond Court(IRE) lined up still a maiden, but several of her better efforts have come here and revised weights gave her a chance of reversing the form of her fourth behind Flying Doctor on her previous start. She was unable to do so, however, and, after figuring prominently for much of the race, she tired late on. (op 6-1)
Glacial Rambler(IRE), rated just 69 and racing from 9lb out of the weights, helps put the form into perspective. Second three flights from home, he faded in the home straight. (op 100-1)
Hooky's Hope, twice second from this mark in 2008-09, had not been disgraced when ninth after a 414-day layoff but did not appear to progress from that run. She was in the first four for most of the way but back-pedalled from two flights out. (op 13-2 tchd 6-1)
T/Plt: £9.40 to a £1 stake. Pool: £94,517.11. 7,300.23 winning tickets. T/Qpdt: £4.60 to a £1 stake. Pool: £6,325.85. 996.79 winning tickets. RY

154 HUNTINGDON (R-H)
Tuesday, May 25

OFFICIAL GOING: Good to firm (8.9)
Open ditch in front of the stands and last fence in the back straight omitted on all circuits on chase course.
Wind: Light, against Weather: Overcast

462 CHAMPAGNE LANSON VINTAGE CONDITIONAL JOCKEYS' (S) H'CAP HURDLE (8 hdls) 2m 110y
6:20 (6:20) (Class 5) (0-95,95) 4-Y-0+ **£2,055** (£599; £299)

Form RPR
/064 **1** **Risk Challenge (USA)**[4] 428 8-10-0 **67** oh2................ RichardKilloran 79+
(William Davies) *hld up: hdwy appr 3 out: led after next: clr last: comf* **20/1**
506- **2** *9* **Masterpoint**[34] 5312 10-10-7 **77**...................................... MrTomDavid(3) 76
(Richard Harper) *prom: j. slowly 4th: chsd wnr appr 2 out: styd on same pce last* **66/1**
00-0 **3** *4* **Eddie Dowling**[15] 252 5-11-0 **81**...............................(tp) JimmyDerham 76
(Milton Harris) *hld up: hdwy appr 3 out: styd on to go 3rd towards fin: nvr nrr* **8/1**[3]
56-0 **4** *1 1/4* **Golden Square**[26] 54 8-11-4 **88**.................................. LeeEdwards(3) 82
(Tony Carroll) *prom: rdn after 5th: led 3 out: rdn and hdd after next: wknd flat* **8/1**[3]
0P-0 **5** *1/2* **Dickie Valentine**[10] 341 5-10-13 **80**..........................(b) GerardTumelty 74
(Richard Phillips) *hld up: hdwy appr 2 out: swtchd rt and wknd bef last* **40/1**
UP5- **6** *7* **We'Re Delighted**[50] 5047 5-11-7 **91**.............................(t) AlexMerriam(3) 78
(Neil King) *hld up in tch: rdn after 3 out: wknd next* **11/1**
6-42 **7** *18* **Casual Style**[9] 358 4-11-7 **95**..............................(t) JohnnyFarrelly(3) 62
(David Pipe) *trckd ldrs: racd keenly: ev ch 3 out: wknd bef next: t.o* **5/1**[2]
00-4 **8** *shd* **Weet In Nerja**[12] 299 4-11-2 **87**............................ SamTwiston-Davies 54
(James Unett) *trckd ldr: racd keenly: rdn and wknd after 3 out: t.o* **18/1**
30-P **9** *6* **Phoenix Enforcer**[7] 384 4-10-11 **82**.......................(b[1]) RichieMcLernon 44
(George Baker) *led and mstke 1st: hdd 3 out: sn wknd: t.o* **28/1**
5-P5 **10** *23* **Doubly Sharp (USA)**[15] 250 7-11-1 **82**............................(b) SamJones 27
(Caroline Bailey) *chsd ldrs: rdn after 5th: wknd bef next: t.o* **25/1**
50U- **11** *7* **Quiditch D'Ouxy (FR)**[205] 2027 6-10-10 **80**...................... DavidBass(3) 19
(Mark Hoad) *hld up: bhd and rdn 4th: t.o* **20/1**
330- **P** **Royal Prodigy (USA)**[22] 5261 11-11-3 **84**........................ HarrySkelton —
(Ron Hodges) *hld up: bhd and riddeafter 3rd: t.o whn p.u bef 3 out* **10/1**
F0-0 **P** **Zizou (IRE)**[16] 228 7-11-3 **90**.................................. AnthonyFreeman(6) —
(Sean Curran) *hld up: bhd whn p.u and dismntd after 3rd* **11/1**
00-3 **F** **Painted Sky**[20] 166 7-11-7 **93**...................................... NathanSweeney(5) —
(Richard Fahey) *hld up in tch: racd keenly: wkng whn fell 3 out* **11/4**[1]

3m 44.2s (-10.70) **Going Correction** -0.675s/f (Firm) **14** Ran SP% **117.3**
Speed ratings (Par 103): **98,93,91,91,91 87,79,79,76,65 62,—,—,—**
toteswingers: 1&2 £89.70, 1&3 £40.50, 2&3 £118.50 CSF £886.54 CT £10876.19 TOTE £34.30: £9.70, £21.80, £3.80; EX 1187.80.The winner was sold to M F Harris for 4,750gns.
Owner Bill Davies **Bred** Juddmonte Farms Inc **Trained** Wigmore, H'fords

FOCUS
A poor selling handicap, confined to conditional riders. There was a sound gallop on. The easy winner was value for further.

NOTEBOOK
Risk Challenge(USA) settled a lot better than had been the case when beaten a long way at Towcester four days earlier and ultimately couldn't have broken his duck over hurdles with much more ease. He had fallen a long way from grace since winning nicely on his debut in a Ludlow bumper in 2006 and was 2lb out of the handicap even in this lowly grade. It was only this problematic horse's fourth run back from injury for the stable, however, and it will not be surprising to see him take up one of his entries later in the week as he will escape a penalty. He was subsequently bought by Milton Harris. Official explanation: trainer's rep said, regarding the apparent improvement in form shown, gelding appeared to have benefited from being raced over a shorter trip on a firmer surface and from being dropped in class (op 25-1)
Masterpoint wasn't fluent at times on this return to hurdling and drop in class, but this was a much more encouraging display. He really wants further, so his proximity does little for those in behind, but this should help restore his confidence when going back over fences.
Eddie Dowling was taking a drop in grade and has plummeted in the weights this year. He shaped as though the trip was on the sharp side but has now found his level. (op 12-1 tchd 7-1)
Golden Square proved very easy to back. He came under pressure a fair way out, but kept battling and rates the most sensible guide for the form. (op 13-2)
Dickie Valentine would have been closer with a better round of jumping. (op 33-1)
We'Re Delighted found very little for pressure in the home straight. (op 16-1)
Casual Style proved keen and looked to be making heavy weather of it prior to departing. (op 7-2)
Royal Prodigy(USA) Official explanation: jockey said gelding never travelled (tchd 3-1 and 10-3 in places)
Painted Sky proved keen and looked to be making heavy weather of it prior to departing. (tchd 3-1 and 10-3 in places)

463 BETFAIR H'CAP CHASE (13 fncs 3 omitted) 2m 4f 110y
6:50 (6:50) (Class 4) (0-110,110) 5-Y-0+ **£3,577** (£1,050; £525; £262)

Form RPR
F4-5 **1** **Jordan's Light (USA)**[2] 135 7-10-10 **97**....................(v) LeeStephens(3) 103+
(David Evans) *hld up: hdwy 10th: styd on wl to ld towards fin* **12/1**
50-P **2** *1 3/4* **Dais Return (IRE)**[10] 330 6-11-6 **107**....................... RichieMcLernon(3) 112+
(Jonjo O'Neill) *chsd ldrs: mstke 4th: hit next: led 6th: rdn appr 2 out: hung rt bef last: hdd towards fin* **14/1**
6P-1 **3** *nk* **Good Old Days (IRE)**[25] 81 11-11-2 **103**.................... SeanQuinlan(3) 108
(Kim Bailey) *mid-div: hdwy 7th: mstke 9th: rdn and ev ch flat: unable qck towards fin* **9/2**[2]
361- **4** *3 1/2* **Sarahs Gift (IRE)**[50] 5040 7-11-4 **102**.......................(t) ChristianWilliams 103
(Lawney Hill) *hld up: hdwy 10th: rdn after 2 out: no ex fr last* **4/1**[1]
43-6 **5** *2* **Nesnaas (USA)**[16] 233 9-10-6 **97**..................................(v) DavidBass(7) 96
(Mark Rimell) *hld up: hdwy 8th: rdn after 3 out: styd on same pce fr next* **10/1**
02-P **6** *12* **Alaghiraar (IRE)**[13] 281 6-11-5 **110**........................(p) MrSJO'Donovan(7) 98
(Emma Lavelle) *chsd ldr: rdn after 3 out: wknd next* **9/1**
0U-3 **7** *10* **Nawow**[10] 339 10-10-13 **100**...(p) PeterToole(3) 79
(Matt Hazell) *hld up: effrt and mstke 3 out: sn wknd* **8/1**[3]
U4-0 **P** **Launde (IRE)**[20] 153 11-11-3 **101**.. ColinBolger —
(Chris Gordon) *mid-div: mstke 6th: sn bhd: t.o whn p.u bef 3 out* **10/1**
21-1 **P** **Gunship (IRE)**[24] 95 9-10-8 **97**..............................(b) JimmyDerham(5) —
(Cathy Hamilton) *led: mstke 2nd: hdd & wknd 6th: p.u bef next* **4/1**[1]

4m 53.8s (-11.50) **Going Correction** -0.40s/f (Good) **9** Ran SP% **111.8**
Speed ratings: **105,104,104,102,102 97,93,—,—**
toteswingers: 1&2 £21.20, 1&3 £15.00, 2&3 £12.80 CSF £148.76 CT £863.65 TOTE £16.20: £4.30, £5.90, £1.70; EX 197.20.
Owner J R B Williams **Bred** Lantern Hill Farm Llc **Trained** Pandy, Monmouths

FOCUS
This competitive handicap was a truly run race and the form looks fair. The first two can probably do a bit better.

NOTEBOOK
Jordan's Light(USA) didn't do a great deal to help his rider during the race and lacked fluency but still came out on top where it mattered. He found things happening all too quickly over hurdles in a seller at Fakenham on his penultimate outing, but shaped better on the Flat two days previously and the stiffer test was much more in his favour. His overall profile suggests he is one to be against next time, however. (op 10-1)
Dais Return(IRE) ran an awful lot better than was the case on his debut for the yard ten days earlier and gave his all under a positive ride. It was just his second outing over fences and so he is entitled to improve for the experience, and stepping up in distance should help. (op 12-1)
Good Old Days(IRE) was 8lb higher than when winning on his comeback 25 days earlier and posted a sound enough effort over this stiffer test, but does seem happier over a shorter trip. (op 5-1)
Sarahs Gift(IRE) had been upped 6lb for his Fakenham success 50 days earlier. He was rather taken off his feet early on but improved as the race went on and held every chance. The handicapper does now look to have his measure. (op 7-2)
Launde(IRE) Official explanation: jockey said gelding never travelled (op 10-3)
Gunship(IRE) ensured there was no hanging about early on, but he was pulled up shortly after being headed passing the stands for the first time and quickly dismounted. Official explanation: jockey said gelding finished distressed (op 10-3)

464 VINDIS ST IVES NOVICES' CHASE (10 fncs 2 omitted) 2m 110y
7:20 (7:20) (Class 4) 5-Y-0+ **£3,577** (£1,050; £525)

Form RPR
41-0 **1** **Noble Request (FR)**[17] 207 9-11-5 136...................... RichardJohnson 141+
(Philip Hobbs) *hld up: pushed along 5th: chsd ldr next: led appr 2 out: sn clr: comf* **4/5**[1]
00-U **2** *9* **Songe (FR)**[20] 155 6-10-12 0.................................. TomScudamore 119
(Charlie Longsdon) *trckd ldr: plld hrd: led 2nd: sn clr: rdn and hdd bef 2 out: sn outpcd* **2/1**[2]
33F- **3** *nk* **Wade Farm Billy (IRE)**[31] 5393 6-10-12 0......................... JamieMoore 119
(Gary Moore) *set stdy pce to 2nd: chsd ldr to 6th: rdn appr and mstke 2 out: styd on same pce* **9/2**[3]

4m 5.30s (-4.90) **Going Correction** -0.40s/f (Good) **3** Ran SP% **107.1**
Speed ratings: **95,90,90**
CSF £2.72 TOTE £1.80; EX 2.90.
Owner Mrs Karola Vann **Bred** Patrick Chedeville & Antoinette Tamagni **Trained** Withycombe, Somerset

FOCUS
A fair little novice chase and the penalised winner won as he was entitled to. He can rate a lot higher.

NOTEBOOK
Noble Request(FR) showed his true colours on this return to fences and scored easily under a penalty. He bided his time before taking it up full of running nearing the home turn and was in no real danger thereafter. He has now won his last two races in this sphere and, although not the force of old, will be high on confidence after this. It wouldn't be surprising to see him defy a double penalty. (op 10-11 tchd 8-11 and evens in places)
Songe(FR) pulled his way to the front early on and jumped well enough but there was very little in the tank when the winner asserted. He probably paid for running with the choke out and the ground was quick enough for him, but one fears his big chance to get off the mark was probably when unseating here at the last on his previous outing. (op 15-8)

Wade Farm Billy(IRE) looked in trouble when the tempo increased up on the far side, but rallied and would have been second had he jumped the last two fences with more fluency. He is not in the same league as the winner and probably rates a better guide to the form than the runner-up. (tchd 11-2)

465 SDC NOVICES' HURDLE (8 hdls) 2m 110y

7:50 (7:51) (Class 4) 4-Y-0+ **£2,602** (£764; £382; £190)

Form RPR

5P- **1** **Freedom Fire (IRE)**[15] 3079 4-10-8 0 JamieMoore 109+
(Gary Moore) *trckd ldrs: plld hrd: wnt 2nd after 3 out: led last: drvn out* **8/1**[3]

2/12 **2** *1 3/4* **Roodolph**[9] 356 6-11-5 128 JimmyMcCarthy 118+
(Eve Johnson Houghton) *set stdy pce tl hdd after 3rd: chsd ldr: led again 3 out: rdn and hdd whn nt fluent last: styd on same pce flat* **4/6**[1]

200/ **3** *30* **Mulaazem**[455] 3180 7-10-5 0 DavidBass(7) 84
(Derek Frankland) *prom: mstke 4th: rdn and wknd after 3 out: lft remote 3rd last: t.o* **66/1**

4 *1/2* **Cool The Heels (IRE)**[22] 5-10-12 0 JackDoyle 84
(Emma Lavelle) *hld up and bhd: nvr nr to chal: t.o* **40/1**

4 **5** *16* **Iron Man Of Mersey (FR)**[20] 154 4-10-3 0 LeeEdwards(5) 65
(Tony Carroll) *hld up: hdwy 4th: mstke and rdr lost iron next: sn rdn: j.lft and wknd 3 out: bhd whn blnd next: t.o* **14/1**

0/6- **6** *18* **Shake On It**[45] 1251 6-10-12 0 LeightonAspell 53
(Mark Hoad) *hld up: plld hrd: hdwy to ld after 3rd: hdd & wknd 3 out: t.o* **50/1**

32-4 **F** **Blue Spartan (IRE)**[26] 58 5-10-12 104 (t) DarylJacob 108
(Charlie Mann) *chsd ldrs: cl 3rd but rdn whn fell last* **11/4**[2]

3m 41.8s (-13.10) **Going Correction** -0.675s/f (Firm)
WFA 4 from 5yo+ 18lb **7** Ran SP% **110.3**
Speed ratings (Par 105): **103,102,88,87,80 71,—**
toteswingers: 1&2 £1.80, 1&3 £16.40, 2&3 £8.70 CSF £13.52 TOTE £6.70: £1.90, £1.20; EX 18.00.
Owner The Horse Players Two **Bred** Ennistown Stud **Trained** Lower Beeding, W Sussex

FOCUS
An ordinary novice hurdle, run at an uneven gallop. The winner can rate higher on his Flat form.

NOTEBOOK
Freedom Fire(IRE) had not convinced on his two previous outings as a hurdler, but has been in fair form on the level since and this quicker ground proved much more to his liking. His jumping was accurate when it mattered and he looks the sort that will progress through the summer months, especially when faced with a stiffer test. (tchd 6-1)
Roodolph was free out in front early and could have settled better when headed by the keen-going Shake On It. He took it up again turning for home, but was rather worried out of things by the winner and may have found the ground a little quicker than he cares for. (op 8-11 tchd 5-6)
Mulaazem was returning to hurdling after a 455-day layoff and making his debut for another new trainer. He was outpaced when things got serious and rates flattered by his finishing position, but should benefit a deal for the run. A return to plating company in due course could see him finally back to winning ways. (op 80-1 tchd 100-1)
Cool The Heels(IRE), a 57-rated maiden on the Flat, has joined a decent operation for his new career but showed his inexperience throughout.
Blue Spartan(IRE) had been well beaten by the runner-up on his previous outing, but was back on quicker ground and raced more handily this time. He shaped more encouragingly as a result, but was held by the first pair prior to falling at the last and his confidence could take quite a knock. (op 3-1 tchd 5-2)

466 MIKE VANBERGEN 80TH BIRTHDAY HUNTERS' CHASE (15 fncs 4 omitted) 3m

8:20 (8:23) (Class 6) 5-Y-0+ **£936** (£290; £145; £72)

Form RPR

3P-2 **1** **Blaze Ahead (IRE)**[12] 296 10-11-7 104 (p) MissCLWills(7) 99+
(Brendan Powell) *pushed along to chse ldr: led 2nd: hdd 4th: led again after 6th: rdn and hdd 2 out: rallied to ld fnl 100yds: styd on wl* **11/2**[3]

6/P- **2** *3 1/2* **Spanchil Hill**[17] 10-11-3 78 MrPPrince(7) 92
(Mrs A S Hodges) *a.p: led last: rdn and hung rt flat: hdd and no ex fnl 100yds* **25/1**

16-5 **3** *2 1/4* **Tikram**[20] 149 13-11-11 121 (p) JoshuaMoore(3) 93
(Gary Moore) *hld up in tch: outpcd 9th: rallied appr 2 out: r.o wl to go 3rd towards fin* **6/4**[1]

03/1 **4** *1 1/2* **Delightful Cliche**[12] 292 9-11-11 0 MissGAndrews(3) 92
(S R Andrews) *led to 2nd: led again 4th: hdd after 6th: chsd ldr tl led again 2 out: rdn and hdd last: no ex flat: lost 3rd towards fin* **11/4**[2]

P0/3 **5** *39* **Coolers Quest**[19] 184 11-10-12 0 MrJBarnes(5) 46
(Mrs R Ford) *prom: rdn after 3 out: wknd bef next: t.o* **16/1**

4P-P **6** *16* **Jolly Boys Outing (IRE)**[20] 150 7-11-3 0 MissHannahWatson(7) 38
(Rosemary Gasson) *hld up: rdn 3 out: nvr on terms: t.o* **20/1**

2/P- **7** *1* **Celestial Dragon (IRE)**[24] 9-11-3 92 MissRachelKing(7) 37
(James Richardson) *hld up in tch: rdn after 3 out: sn wknd: tailing off whn j.lft and hit 2 out: blnd last: t.o* **10/1**

P6/ **8** *3/4* **It Plays Itself (IRE)**[22] 11-11-5 0 MrRJBarrett(5) 37
(Miss K Young) *prom: lost pl 6th: hdwy 11th: rdn and wknd after 3 out: t.o* **66/1**

4P/6 **9** *10* **Greek Star**[12] 293 9-11-3 0 MrRichardCollinson(7) 28
(H Hill) *hld up: rdn after 8th: a in rr: wkng wheh hit 3 out* **80/1**

10 *12* **Pirate Depp (IRE)**[24] 6-11-3 0 MrTEllis(7) 17
(G J Tarry) *chsd ldrs tl rdn and wknd after 3 out* **40/1**

2 **11** *6* **Red In Bed (IRE)**[26] 61 6-11-0 0 (t) MrMatthewSmith(3) 4
(Matthew Smith) *hld up: blnd 8th: bhd fr 11th: t.o* **33/1**

56/5 **P** **Beluga (IRE)**[12] 296 11-11-3 0 MajGFWheeler(7) —
(Miss Rose Grissell) *hld up: a in rr: mstke 11th: t.o whn p.u bef 3 out* **66/1**

5m 57.0s (-13.30) **Going Correction** -0.40s/f (Good) **12** Ran SP% **115.2**
Speed ratings: **106,104,104,103,90 85,84,84,81,77 75,—**
toteswingers: 1&2 £13.80, 1&3 £3.70, 2&3 £11.60 CSF £117.95 TOTE £5.20: £1.80, £3.20, £1.50; EX 109.40.
Owner Mrs S Clifford **Bred** John R Cox **Trained** Upper Lambourn, Berks

FOCUS
A modest hunter chase, run at a good gallop. The form is rated through the second.

NOTEBOOK
Blaze Ahead(IRE), a clear second-best at Folkestone last time, was always front rank and signed off on his career with a very game success. (op 6-1 tchd 7-1)
Spanchil Hill looked to have plenty on his plate on this return to regulation fences, but he travelled best of all through the race and posted a greatly improved effort considering the ground would have been quick enough for him. (op 22-1)
Tikram had registered his last success in this event 12 months ago. He lost out by hitting a flat spot at halfway, but was motoring again in the home straight. He now heads off for an honourable retirement. (op 15-8 tchd 11-8)
Delightful Cliche cut out most of the running along with the winner and made a bold bid to follow up his Folkestone success of 12 days earlier. (op 3-1 tchd 10-3)
Beluga(IRE) Official explanation: jockey said gelding was struck into

467 HUNTINGDON H'CAP HURDLE (12 hdls) 3m 2f

8:50 (8:50) (Class 4) (0-105,104) 4-Y-0+ **£2,602** (£764; £382; £190)

Form RPR

06-1 **1** **Lyster (IRE)**[9] 359 11-10-11 92 7ex LeeStephens(3) 102+
(David Evans) *hld up: hdwy 8th: led and nt fluent 2 out: edgd rt flat: comf* **15/8**[1]

PP-4 **2** *4* **Casual Garcia**[8] 374 5-11-7 102 (bt) TommyPhelan(3) 106
(Mark Gillard) *a.p: led 3 out: rdn and hdd next: ev ch last: no ex flat* **16/1**

241- **3** *7* **Midnight Gold**[29] 16 10-11-7 104 (p) DonalDevereux(5) 102
(Peter Bowen) *led to 9th: sn rdn: styd on same pce fr 3 out* **9/2**[2]

62-2 **4** *3 3/4* **King Raven (IRE)**[16] 217 8-10-12 90 (v) TomScudamore 84
(Mark Rimell) *chsd ldrs: led 9th: hdd 3 out: sn rdn: wknd bef last* **5/1**[3]

6F-0 **5** *3 1/2* **Legal Glory (IRE)**[14] 267 10-10-1 84 GilesHawkins(5) 75
(Ron Hodges) *hld up: hdwy 6th: wknd 3 out: bhd whn hit next* **22/1**

0P-0 **6** *49* **Oshkosh (IRE)**[26] 59 9-10-4 85 SeanQuinlan(3) 32
(Kim Bailey) *chsd ldrs: rdn and wknd appr 3 out* **14/1**

P0-0 **P** **Free To Air**[25] 84 7-10-0 78 oh2 (v) SamJones —
(Oliver Sherwood) *hld up: mstke 4th: wknd 8th: t.o whn p.u bef 3 out* **8/1**

P-65 **P** **Shergill (IRE)**[13] 273 9-9-9 78 oh3 SamTwiston-Davies(5) —
(Shaun Lycett) *chsd ldr to 7th: sn rdn: wknd bef next: t.o whn p.u bef 2 out* **7/1**

6-00 **P** **Gunnadoit (USA)**[2] 441 5-10-9 90 (v) AlexMerriam(3) —
(Neil King) *sn pushed along and prom: bhd fr 6th: t.o whn p.u bef 2 out* **25/1**

6m 1.70s (-21.20) **Going Correction** -0.675s/f (Firm) **9** Ran SP% **114.0**
Speed ratings (Par 105): **105,103,101,100,99 84,—,—,—**
toteswingers: 1&2 £12.50, 1&3 £2.40, 2&3 £12.30 CSF £30.62 CT £120.11 TOTE £2.50: £1.10, £5.60, £1.60; EX 51.10 Place 6 £137.24, Place 5 £15.62.
Owner M D Jones **Bred** B D Darrer **Trained** Pandy, Monmouths

FOCUS
A moderate staying handicap. The winner is rated back to his best.

NOTEBOOK
Lyster(IRE) had been 3lb out of the weights when winning at Stratford nine days earlier, so was effectively just 4lb higher with a 7lb penalty. He was very well backed to follow up and duly obliged in good style. He had to dig deep after an error two out, but had travelled supremely well to that point. If he can be found another similar task in the next week then he would no doubt again take all the beating. (op 2-1 tchd 7-4)
Casual Garcia, third on his previous outing over C&D, had been picked up at the sales by new connections with a view to going eventing. He was the only one to make a real race of it with the winner from the home turn and probably found himself in front sooner than ideal, but it made no difference to the result. The first-time tongue tie had a positive effect. (tchd 14-1)
Midnight Gold was up in trip and 10lb higher than when winning on his return to hurdling at Ffos Las 29 days earlier. He was in trouble immediately after being headed but rallied to get third and evidently stays the trip. (op 10-3)
King Raven(IRE) took it up after the fourth-last but his stamina appeared to give way from the final turn and being raised 7lb for finishing second at Plumpton looks somewhat harsh.
Free To Air Official explanation: vet said gelding bled from the nose
T/Plt: £391.70 to A £1 stake. Pool: £59,803.45. 111.45 winning tickets. T/Qpdt: £4.10 to a £1 stake. Pool: £5,458.48. 970.13 winning tickets. CR

400 SEDGEFIELD (L-H)

Wednesday, May 26

OFFICIAL GOING: Chase course - good (8.0); hurdle course - good to firm (good in places; 8.1)
Wind: Moderate, half against Weather: Overcast, persistent light rain

468 FREE RACING WITH ODDSCHECKER.COM NOVICES' HURDLE (8 hdls) 2m 1f

2:20 (2:20) (Class 4) 4-Y-0+ **£2,992** (£878; £439; £219)

Form RPR

363- **1** **Bucephalus (IRE)**[11] 14 6-10-9 96 (t) MichaelMcAlister(3) 112+
(Maurice Barnes) *trckd ldrs: led after 3 out: wnt 10 l clr last: easily* **9/1**[3]

41-3 **2** *16* **Pyracantha**[18] 209 5-11-5 114 BrianHughes 102
(Alan Swinbank) *trckd ldrs: rdn to go 5 l 2nd 2 out: no ch w wnr* **10/11**[1]

PP-0 **3** *5* **Molesden Glen (IRE)**[14] 289 4-10-5 0 (t) CampbellGillies(3) 86
(Simon Waugh) *chsd ldrs: one pce appr 2 out* **100/1**

35-2 **4** *4* **Favours Brave**[10] 349 4-10-8 100 RichieMcGrath 83
(Tim Easterby) *hld up: hdwy 5th: one pce fr next: wnt modest 4th appr 2 out* **6/4**[2]

0P-4 **5** *9* **Earl Grez (FR)**[10] 349 5-10-12 0 JamesReveley 78
(Philip Kirby) *hdwy to trck ldrs 3rd: outpcd whn mstke 3 out: sn wknd* **22/1**

65-0 **6** *25* **Musca (IRE)**[7] 400 6-10-5 86 MrJohnDawson(7) 56
(John Wade) *t.k.h: led: hdd after 3 out: wknd qckly: t.o next* **66/1**

0- **7** *36* **First Lord (FR)**[39] 5235 6-10-12 0 APMcCoy 24
(Ronald O'Leary, Ire) *nt fluent in rr: reminders after 3rd: bhd fr 5th: t.o next* **14/1**

0-0 **8** *3/4* **Kashubian Quest**[25] 97 4-10-8 0 TjadeCollier 19
(Sue Smith) *in rr: pushed along 4th: sn bhd: t.o whn mstke 3 out* **33/1**

4m 2.90s (-4.00) **Going Correction** -0.10s/f (Good)
WFA 4 from 5yo+ 18lb **8** Ran SP% **118.8**
Speed ratings (Par 105): **105,97,95,93,89 77,60,59**
toteswingers: 1&2 £4.20, 1&3 £23.90, 2&3 £21.90 CSF £19.04 TOTE £10.60: £1.90, £1.02, £15.00; EX 19.80.
Owner T A Barnes **Bred** Michael J Kinane **Trained** Farlam, Cumbria

FOCUS
This weak novice hurdle was run at a sound enough gallop and most knew their fate at the top of the home straight.

NOTEBOOK
Bucephalus(IRE) took up the running at the third-last and was not in any serious danger thereafter. He had been officially eased 8lb since his previous outing as a hurdler, but this was a lot more like it from him and the undulating track evidently suited. His confidence will now be high, but he would look vulnerable under a penalty. Official explanation: trainer said, regarding the apparent improvement in form shown, he had no explanation for the poor run last time, but the stable appeared to be hitting form at present (op 10-1 tchd 11-1)
Pyracantha came under pressure just as the winner went to the front and, although he rallied gamely, was always being held under his penalty. He was still a clear second-best and will appreciate returning to an easier surface. (tchd 5-6 and Evens)
Molesden Glen(IRE) turned in by far his best effort to date and the drop back to this trip proved a lot more suitable for him. He is now eligible for a mark.

Favours Brave, who had tried to make all when second at Market Rasen last time out, produced a lacklustre display. Ridden with a lot more restraint this time, the switch in tactics failed to work out as he got badly outpaced from three out. Getting so edgy beforehand cannot have helped his cause. (op 2-1 tchd 9-4)

469 DYLAN ROBERT MEALE MEMORIAL NOVICES' CHASE (13 fncs) 2m 110y
2:50 (2:50) (Class 4) 5-Y-O+ **£4,182** (£1,235; £617)

Form RPR

20-0 **1** **Ellerslie Tom**[18] 207 8-10-12 0 ....(t) DarylJacob 123+
(Alison Thorpe) *mde all: 5 l clr 2 out: sn rdn: unchal* **4/6**[1]

2 *1 ½* **Financialregulator (IRE)**[25] 104 6-10-12 105 .... APMcCoy 120
(Gordon Elliott, Ire) *chsd wnr 5th: pushed along 4 out: kpt on and 3 l down last: styd on but unable chal* **9/2**[3]

46-2 **3** *35* **Scale Bank (IRE)**[20] 175 7-10-12 108 .... BrianHughes 89
(Alan Swinbank) *nt fluent: chsd wnr to 5th: nt fluent next: outpcd and lost pl 7th: sn lost tch* **11/4**[2]

4m 8.90s (0.30) **Going Correction** -0.10s/f (Good) **3** Ran SP% **104.8**
Speed ratings: **95,94,77**
CSF £3.45 TOTE £1.40; EX 2.50.
Owner Don Jones **Bred** Catridge Farm Stud Ltd **Trained** Bronwydd Arms, Carmarthens

FOCUS
An uncompetitive event.

NOTEBOOK
Ellerslie Tom faced a straightforward task to belatedly open his account over fences. Making all, he still wasn't that convincing, lacking fluency early on, and had to work in order to fend off the runner-up after the last. That was likely down to him idling, though, and he has the class to defy a penalty at this time of year. (op 8-15 tchd 1-2)
Financialregulator(IRE) has been very disappointing over hurdles in Ireland, but was making his chasing debut on only his second outing for Gordon Elliot. He had plenty to find with the winner at the weights so this was obviously much more encouraging, and he looks sure to be placed to win a race over jumps this summer. (tchd 4-1 and 6-1)
Scale Bank(IRE)also had a lot to find with the winner, but did have the benefit of more recent experience as a chaser, and had won his only race over hurdles at this venue. The drop back in trip didn't help, but he really lost out with some sloppy jumping on the back straight and is one to tread carefully with. (op 10-3 tchd 5-2)

470 JOHN WADE EARTHWORKS & DEMOLITION (S) HURDLE (QUALIFIER) (8 hdls) 2m 1f
3:25 (3:25) (Class 5) 4-Y-O+ **£1,691** (£496; £248; £124)

Form RPR

5/2- **1** **Arisea (IRE)**[104] 651 7-10-5 104 .... GrahamLee 104+
(Ferdy Murphy) *hld up: smooth hdwy 5th: wnt 2nd after 3 out: led appr next: nudged clr between last 2: 12 l ahd last: easily* **3/1**[2]

04-1 **2** *11* **Right Or Wrong (IRE)**[13] 307 6-11-4 119 ....(tp) APMcCoy 104
(Gordon Elliott, Ire) *chsd ldr: led 3 out: rdn and hdd appr next: no ch w wnr* **4/7**[1]

0-U0 **3** *9* **White Lightening (IRE)**[7] 402 7-10-5 87 ....(bt) MrJohnDawson(7) 91+
(John Wade) *sn chsng ldrs: wnt modest 3rd appr 2 out: 5 l 3rd whn nt fluent last* **28/1**

20- **4** *6* **San Silvestro (IRE)**[9] 1502 5-10-5 0 .... PaulGallagher(7) 85
(Ann Duffield) *led after 1st: hdd 3 out: wknd appr next* **14/1**[3]

5-P2 **5** *16* **Can't Remember**[7] 402 5-10-8 78 .... HarryHaynes(3) 72+
(Robert Johnson) *chsd ldrs: outpcd and lost pl 3 out* **16/1**

0- **6** *2 ¼* **Castle Myth (USA)**[15] 725 4-10-8 0 ....(t) KeithMercer 64
(Brian Ellison) *in rr: bhd fr 3rd: t.o 5th* **20/1**

/00- **7** *8* **Monfils Monfils (USA)**[59] 2641 8-10-12 89 .... JamesReveley 61
(Ron Barr) *led tl after 1st: drvn 5th: wknd next* **28/1**

PP0- **8** *nk* **Franklee**[65] 4779 7-10-5 0 .... GaryRutherford(7) 61
(Harriet Graham) *in rr: distant 8th whn blnd and rdr briefly lost irons 3 out: sme hdwy appr next: nvr on terms* **150/1**

0/0- **9** *20* **Whatevertheweather**[24] 6-10-12 0 .... PaddyAspell 43
(Sandy Forster) *in rr: reminders after 2nd: t.o 5th* **80/1**

PP-4 **10** *24* **Camomile**[7] 400 4-10-1 0 .... PeterBuchanan 10
(Tracy Waggott) *mid-div: short lived effrt 3 out: sn lost pl and bhd* **25/1**

4m 3.80s (-3.10) **Going Correction** -0.10s/f (Good)
WFA 4 from 5yo+ 18lb **10** Ran SP% **118.6**
Speed ratings (Par 103): **103,97,93,90,83 82,78,78,68,57**
toteswingers: 1&2 £1.30, 1&3 £12.10, 2&3 £7.80 CSF £5.07 TOTE £3.10: £1.10, £1.10, £7.20; EX 7.60.The winner was bought in for 5,000gns. Can't Remember was claimed by Mrs A. M. Thorpe for £4,500.
Owner Ferdy Murphy **Bred** Agricola S A S Di Frederica Rinaldini **Trained** West Witton, N Yorks

FOCUS
A fair seller.

NOTEBOOK
Arisea(IRE) ran out a most decisive winner on this return from a 104-day break, and her first outing over hurdles since last June. Making her debut for Ferdy Murphy, she got a lovely sit through the race under a jockey who rides this course so well. It was clear coming to the penultimate flight she was going to do the business and there should be plenty more prizes in this grade to be won with her. (op 9-2)
Right Or Wrong(IRE) resumed winning ways in a dire claimer at Perth last time, when not having to come out of second gear, and while this was tougher it still represented another good opportunity. He wasn't able to dictate so easily here and again showed why he wears headgear when pressed by the winner. (op 8-15 tchd 1-2)
White Lightening(IRE) posted his best effort since winning a handicap in this class over C&D just over a year ago, staying on well down the home straight. (tchd 25-1)
San Silvestro(IRE) was given a positive ride on this return from the Flat, but was done with shortly after three out. (tchd 16-1)

471 DYLAN MEALE MEMORIAL H'CAP CHASE (21 fncs) 3m 3f
4:00 (4:00) (Class 4) (0-105,95) 5-Y-O+ **£4,722** (£1,776)

Form RPR

6-12 **1** **Finbin (IRE)**[6] 424 8-11-9 95 ....(t) FearghalDavis(3) 106+
(Henry Hogarth) *trckd ldrs: lft cl 2nd 5th: led 13th: drew 7 l clr last: heavily eased run-in* **13/8**[1]

PU-3 **2** *2 ½* **Hasper**[18] 211 12-10-13 89 .... MrGCrow(7) 90
(Sandy Forster) *chsd ldrs: lft in front 5th: hdd 13th: remained upsides tl 2 l down 2 out: kpt on run-in: greatly flattered* **9/2**[3]

12-0 **F** **Solway Bee**[14] 291 10-11-2 90 .... EwanWhillans(5) —
(Lisa Harrison) *narrow ldr: fell 5th* **7/1**

36-1 **U** **Overton Lad**[8] 383 9-10-12 81 7ex ....(b) JackDoyle —
(Peter Pritchard) *chsd ldrs: reminders 2nd: bdly hmpd and uns rdr 5th* **3/1**[2]

2U-3 **B** **Greenandredparson (IRE)**[21] 162 7-11-6 92 .... AdrianLane(3) —
(Paul Murphy) *racd in last but wl in tch: bdly hmpd and b.d 5th* **5/1**

7m 1.40s (12.40) **Going Correction** -0.10s/f (Good) **5** Ran SP% **110.4**
Speed ratings: **77,76,—,—,—**
CSF £9.22 TOTE £2.80; EX 6.80.
Owner Hogarth Racing **Bred** J Mangan **Trained** Stillington, N Yorks

FOCUS
Not a strong race for the grade and there was high drama at the fifth fence. The first two met at Hexham and Hasper ran to form while Finbin, who was value for 8l, is rated up 3lb.

NOTEBOOK
Finbin(IRE) confirmed his Hexham form with his sole remaining rival despite being 9lb worse off. He was lucky not to have come down himself in the drama at the fifth, as he got hampered. He is evidently right at the top of his game at present and further improvement over this sort of test cannot be ruled out. There is a chance he could turn out quickly at Cartmel on Monday. (op 15-8)
Hasper was the one that missed the trouble at the fifth and found himself in front thereafter. The writing was on the wall for him turning into the home straight, however, but he was still game in defeat. (op 5-1 tchd 4-1)
Solway Bee clipped the top of the fifth and fell, bringing down both Greenandredparson and Overton Lad in the process. (op 9-1 tchd 10-1)
Overton Lad galloped round loose for most of the way after getting back to his feet. (op 9-1 tchd 10-1)

472 PHOENIX SECURITY H'CAP HURDLE (8 hdls) 2m 1f
4:35 (4:35) (Class 4) (0-110,109) 4-Y-O+ **£2,992** (£878; £439; £219)

Form RPR

5-21 **1** **Ruby Crown**[8] 384 8-11-2 102 .... SeanQuinlan(3) 107
(Kim Bailey) *hld up: hdwy to chse ldrs 4th: narrow ld appr 2 out: rdn and edgd lft between last 2: all out* **3/1**[1]

1-32 **2** *shd* **Prioryjo**[18] 210 7-11-5 102 ....(p) GrahamLee 107
(Martin Todhunter) *trckd ldrs: upsides 2 out and last: jst failed* **7/1**

00-0 **3** *10* **Midnite Blews (IRE)**[21] 166 5-10-3 89 ....(t) MichaelMcAlister(3) 85
(Maurice Barnes) *led after 2nd: hit 5th: hdd appr 2 out: sn wknd* **8/1**

5-46 **4** *10* **Wee Forbees (IRE)**[18] 210 8-11-0 97 .... WilsonRenwick 84
(Michael Easterby) *bhd and drvn 4th: tk poor 4th after 3 out* **9/1**

53-4 **5** *28* **Border Tale**[14] 288 10-11-8 105 ....(b) PaddyAspell 67
(James Moffatt) *chsd ldrs: drvn 3rd: sn lost pl and bhd* **9/2**[2]

605- **6** *33* **Switched Off**[18] 4666 5-11-3 100 ....(b[1]) BrianHughes 32
(Michael Easterby) *sn chsng ldrs: hit 5th: wknd next: t.o 2 out: virtually p.u* **9/1**

2-50 **P** **Samizdat (FR)**[13] 309 7-11-9 109 .... RyanMania(3) —
(Dianne Sayer) *chsd ldrs: reminders after 1st: wknd 3 out: t.o whn p.u bef next* **5/1**[3]

020- **P** **Haka Dancer (USA)**[16] 2547 7-11-7 104 .... JamesReveley —
(Philip Kirby) *led tl after 2nd: w ldrs: wknd rapidly 3 out: sn t.o: p.u bef next* **10/1**

4m 4.80s (-2.10) **Going Correction** +0.025s/f (Yiel) **8** Ran SP% **112.6**
Speed ratings (Par 105): **105,104,100,95,82 66,—,—**
toteswingers: 1&2 £11.10, 1&3 £3.80, 2&3 £6.00 CSF £23.41 CT £149.31 TOTE £4.00: £2.30, £1.10, £2.90; EX 13.60.
Owner I F W Buchan **Bred** I F W Buchan **Trained** Andoversford, Gloucs

FOCUS
The course endured showers before this moderate handicap and it had visibly got into the ground. It was run at a sound gallop and there was a cracking finish between the two mares. Both are rated up a few pounds on their recent marks.

NOTEBOOK
Ruby Crown just did enough to fend off Prioryjo where it mattered and followed up her Towcester success eight days earlier off a 7lb higher mark. The doubt beforehand was how she would handle this contrasting track, but it suited and this was her first success going left handed. The sort that holds her form well, she should at least remain competitive after another likely rise. (op 9-4 tchd 2-1)
Prioryjo has lots of form around here and so nearly landed her first win in handicap company. She came into this having been placed on her two previous outings and was well clear of the remainder here, so richly deserves another winning turn. (op 6-1)
Midnite Blews(IRE) was a sitting duck for the first pair, but this was a lot better from him and he fared by far the best of those that raced on the pace. He could have done without the ground easing, and his turn may not be that far off again. (op 14-1)
Wee Forbees(IRE) plugged on from out the back without ever looking that happy. (op 8-1 tchd 10-1)
Samizdat(FR) was done with around three from home. Something was evidently amiss with him. (op 13-2)

473 JOHN WADE DEMOLITION NOVICES' H'CAP CHASE (16 fncs) 2m 4f
5:05 (5:05) (Class 5) (0-95,95) 5-Y-O+ **£2,732** (£802; £401; £200)

Form RPR

03-F **1** **Ginger's Lad**[7] 403 6-10-6 75 ....(p) BrianHughes 82+
(Michael Easterby) *chsd ldrs: wnt cl 2nd 4 out: led and hit last: edgd lft: hld on towards fin* **9/2**[2]

P6-1 **2** *½* **Pugnacity**[7] 405 6-9-13 71 .... RyanMania(3) 78
(Dianne Sayer) *j.rt 1st: sn chsng ldrs: kpt on run-in: tk 2nd nr fin* **7/2**[1]

2-31 **3** *1* **Persian Prince (IRE)**[7] 403 10-11-3 93 7ex .... MrJohnDawson(7) 100+
(John Wade) *led: hdd last: crowded: cl 2nd but hld whn eased nr fin* **7/2**[1]

P-P0 **4** *¾* **Clueless**[7] 404 8-10-11 80 ....(p) PeterBuchanan 85
(Carol Ferguson) *hdwy to chse ldrs 8th: styd on same pce run-in* **33/1**

-U43 **5** *hd* **Janal (IRE)**[7] 404 7-10-0 69 oh4 ....(p) WilsonRenwick 74
(Stuart Coltherd) *chsd ldrs: pushed along 8th: outpcd appr 2 out: kpt on between last 2: nvr able to chal* **13/2**[3]

-6U4 **6** *15* **Solway Blue**[3] 445 8-10-13 85 .... HarryHaynes(3) 77
(Lisa Harrison) *in rr: hdwy 10th: sn chsng ldrs: wknd between last 2* **25/1**

00P/ **7** *76* **Exit Forty Four (IRE)**[483] 3609 8-10-6 75 .... JamesReveley —
(Martin Todhunter) *in rr: bhd fr 7th: t.o 11th* **28/1**

536- **P** **Downing Street (IRE)**[260] 1413 9-11-12 95 ....(vt) AlanO'Keeffe —
(Jennie Candlish) *in rr: sme hdwy 11th: chsng ldrs next: 7th and wl hld whn p.u sn after 3 out* **8/1**

FU0- **P** **Patchoulie Conti (FR)**[35] 5318 7-11-0 88 .... ShaneByrne(5) —
(Sue Smith) *hmpd 1st: in rr: bhd whn p.u bef 11th* **25/1**

3-04 **P** **Cherryland**[21] 165 7-11-5 88 ....(b[1]) RichieMcGrath —
(Philip Kirby) *w ldr: reminders 9th: wknd next: bhd whn p.u after 4 out* **16/1**

000/ **P** **Flag Hill**[38] 7-10-0 69 oh5 .... PaddyAspell —
(Peter Atkinson) *in rr: hdwy to chse ldrs 10th: wknd 4 out: bhd whn p.u bef 2 out* **10/1**

5m 1.80s (-1.20) **Going Correction** +0.025s/f (Yiel) **11** Ran SP% **116.1**
Speed ratings: **103,102,102,102,102 96,65,—,—,—,—**
toteswingers: 1&2 £4.60, 1&3 £4.40, 2&3 £2.90 CSF £20.13 CT £61.24 TOTE £5.90: £1.70, £1.40, £1.30; EX 23.80.
Owner W H & Mrs J A Tinning **Bred** W H Tinning **Trained** Sheriff Hutton, N Yorks
■ Stewards' Enquiry : Mr John Dawson seven-day ban: failed to ride out for 2nd place (Jul 21, Aug 19, Oct 15, 19, 21, 24, 31)

FOCUS
An open handicap that saw the field strung out from an early point. The first five all held a chance of sorts after the penultimate fence and the bunch finish suggests the form is limited.

NOTEBOOK

Ginger's Lad eventually came out on top and landed his first win of any description at the 16th time of asking. He wasn't done with prior to falling in the race won by Persian Prince at Wetherby a week earlier, and the recent application of cheekpieces looks to have made the difference. (op 5-1)

Pugnacity, who landed a third win over hurdles at the course a week earlier, travelled nicely through the race and gave her all under pressure. This was a solid return to fences, where she is currently rated 10lb lower, and she is capable of breaking her duck in this sphere in the coming weeks. (op 4-1 tchd 9-2)

Persian Prince(IRE) made a bold bid to follow up under his penalty and deserves extra credit as he did most of the donkey work. He rates a solid benchmark. (op 11-4 tchd 4-1 in a place)

Clueless tended to run somewhat in snatches through the first half, but got interested as the race went on and turned in a much-improved effort for the longer trip.

Janal(IRE) was supported throughout the day, but despite the cheekpieces being back on, she proved hard work for her rider. Her best trip in this sphere also remains open to debate. (op 8-1)

Patchoulie Conti(FR) Official explanation: jockey said mare lost its action

474 BUY TV BRACKETS AT EBAY MCGOW123 MAIDEN OPEN NATIONAL HUNT FLAT RACE — 2m 1f

5:35 (5:35) (Class 6) 4-6-Y-O — **£1,431** (£420; £210; £104)

Form — RPR

03- **1** **Noble Scholar (IRE)**[37] 5277 5-11-4 0.............................(t) BrianHughes 98+
(Alan Swinbank) *mid-div: hdwy to chse ldrs 7f out: chal over 2f out: led over 1f out: jst hld on* **11/4**[2]

0- **2** *hd* **Island Sprite (IRE)**[29] 35 6-10-11 0.............................. JamesReveley 91
(Martin Todhunter) *hld up in rr: hdwy 6f out: drvn over 4f out: styd on wl to take 3rd over 1f out: jst hld* **33/1**

3 *1 ¾* **Not So Sure Dick (IRE)**[38] 5-11-4 0.................................. SamThomas 96
(George Baker) *trckd ldrs: led 6f out: hdd over 1f out: kpt on same pce* **15/8**[1]

4 *1 ¾* **Harsh But Fair** 4-11-0 0.. WilsonRenwick 91
(Michael Easterby) *mid-div: hdwy 6f out: chsng ldrs 4f out: one pce fnl 2f* **9/2**[3]

0- **5** *12* **Cool Water**[28] 47 5-10-4 0.. AlexanderVoy(7) 76
(John Wade) *w ldrs: wknd 3f out* **33/1**

0 **6** *3 ½* **Mystic Echo**[17] 230 4-10-7 0.. RichieMcGrath 68
(John Davies) *chsd ldrs: outpcd over 3f out: grad wknd* **50/1**

0- **7** *12* **Why So Serious**[66] 4757 4-10-7 0............................... CallumWhillans(7) 63
(Donald Whillans) *in rr-div: sn drvn along: outpcd 5f out: sn wknd* **9/1**

5- **8** *32* **Big Sam**[37] 5277 5-11-4 0... GrahamLee 35
(Martin Todhunter) *mid-div: reminders 9f out: lost pl 5f out: bhd and eased over 2f out: sn t.o* **10/1**

9 *5* **Miss Vivian (IRE)**[31] 4-10-0 0.. MrJBewley(7) 19
(David Thompson) *chsd ldrs: drvn 6f out: wknd over 4f out: sn bhd: t.o* **33/1**

0- **10** *55* **Auld Farmer**[29] 35 6-11-4 0.. PaddyAspell —
(Christopher Wilson) *led tl 6f out: wknd qckly 4f out: sn bhd: t.o over 2f out* **100/1**

11 *30* **Buymequick (IRE)** 5-10-4 0.. MrJohnDawson(7) —
(Ron Barr) *in rr: lost tch 7f out and sn wl t.o: sn virtually p.u* **50/1**

4m 5.50s (4.20) **Going Correction** +0.025s/f (Yiel)
WFA 4 from 5yo+ 4lb — **11** Ran SP% **112.5**
Speed ratings: **91,90,90,89,83 81,76,61,59,33 19**
toteswingers: 1&2 £7.00, 1&3 £2.20, 2&3 £12.10 CSF £95.72 TOTE £3.50: £1.40, £10.60, £1.10; EX 57.30 Place 6 £6.53, Place 5 £3.89.
Owner Mrs B Watson **Bred** Moyglare Stud Farm Ltd **Trained** Melsonby, N Yorks

FOCUS

There was an average gallop on in this ordinary bumper and the first four came well clear. The form is rated around the winner.

NOTEBOOK

Noble Scholar(IRE) just did enough to last home in front and enhanced his trainer's decent record in the race. He made his move turning for home and gamely got on top nearing the business end. It was his first success at the third attempt and the first-time tongue tie had the desired effect. (op 13-8)

Island Sprite(IRE) only just missed out but was always getting there that bit too late. She hit a flat spot after trying to get involved down the back straight, but stayed on stoutly inside the final 2f. This was a vast improvement on her C&D debut 29 days earlier. (op 16-1)

Not So Sure Dick(IRE) was making his debut for new connections and proved popular. He was given a positive ride and held every chance. His Irish point win came on quick ground and the easing surface was probably not ideal. (op 11-4)

Harsh But Fair did best of the newcomers and this Flat-bred colt should come on a bundle for the outing. (op 6-1 tchd 4-1)

T/Plt: £6.70 to a £1 stake. Pool: £59,501.75. 6,427.44 winning tickets. T/Qpdt: £3.30 to a £1 stake. Pool: £4,577.02. 1,005.32 winning tickets. WG

48 SOUTHWELL (L-H)

Wednesday, May 26

OFFICIAL GOING: Good (good to firm in places) changing to good after race 1 (6.20)

Golf Club bend moved to outside, home straight bend on inside.

Wind: Light against Weather: Overcast turning to light rain from the 4th race

475 BEST ODDS GUARANTEED AT TOTESPORT.COM H'CAP CHASE (16 fncs) — 2m 4f 110y

6:20 (6:20) (Class 4) (0-105,103) 5-Y-O+ — **£5,204** (£1,528; £764; £381)

Form — RPR

-112 **1** **Lord Gunnerslake (IRE)**[8] 381 10-10-9 86............(v) RichardJohnson 94+
(Tim Vaughan) *chsd ldrs: rdn appr 3 out: mstke next: led last: styd on wl* **5/2**[1]

106- **2** *5* **Morenito (FR)**[284] 1214 7-11-2 93..................................(p) PaddyBrennan 96
(Tom George) *chsd ldr tl led 3rd: hdd 6th: led 8th: nt fluent next: sn hdd: led 10th: rdn appr 3 out: hdd last: wknd towards fin* **4/1**[3]

0-31 **3** *2 ¼* **Mutual Respect (IRE)**[3] 437 8-11-12 103 7ex................. PaulMoloney 106+
(Evan Williams) *led to 3rd: led 6th to 8th: led after next: hdd 10th: hit 11th: drvn along after 13th: mstke 3 out: styd on same pce appr last* **11/4**[2]

U42- **4** *nk* **Magnetic Pole**[31] 5 9-11-12 103...................................(p) CharliePoste 104
(Richard Lee) *chsd ldrs: rdn after 13th: ev ch appr last: wknd flat* **13/2**

1U1- **5** *4* **Ponchatrain (IRE)**[120] 3669 10-10-13 90....................... WarrenMarston 89+
(Martin Keighley) *prom: mstke 10th: sn outpcd: n.d after* **11/2**

432/ **P** **Personal Column**[414] 4895 6-11-11 102................................ SamJones —
(Tor Sturgis) *hld up: pushed along 7th: wknd 9th: t.o whn p.u bef 11th* **16/1**

5m 30.3s (15.30) **Going Correction** +0.075s/f (Yiel) — **6** Ran SP% **109.8**
Speed ratings: **73,71,70,70,68 —**
toteswingers: 1&2: £1.80, 1&3: £1.70, 2&3: £2.50 CSF £12.43 TOTE £2.90: £1.30, £3.50; EX 12.90.
Owner Select Racing Syndicates I **Bred** T Keane **Trained** Aberthin, Vale of Glamorgan

FOCUS

Good ground (good to firm in places), and a GoingStick reading of 8.2 for this modest jumps card. Quite a competitive handicap chase but it was littered with jumping errors from all of the runners.

NOTEBOOK

Lord Gunnerslake(IRE), a bargain-basement buy, continued his fine run of form by rallying strongly after the second-last (where he was very untidy) to assert on the run-in. The step back up to 2m4f suited this gelding and, despite being 22lb higher than when scoring at Huntingdon in April, he made it three wins from four starts, all of which have come on a sound surface. It would be no surprise if his winning run continued. (op 3-1)

Morenito(FR) was always mixing it with Mutual Respect at the head of affairs but, although he held the advantage turning for home, he was outstayed in the closing stages. Still, this was a very decent effort on the back of a 284-day absence and he'll find more races on his favoured fast ground if holding this level of form through the summer. (op 100-30 tchd 3-1)

Mutual Respect(IRE), an easy recent Fakenham winner, could never recover from a bad mistake at the sixth-last fence, but to his credit he rallied in the closing stages having looked as though he might drop right away leaving the back. (op 3-1 tchd 7-2)

Magnetic Pole was bang in the race early in the straight but he dropped out of contention and this mark looks high enough for now. (op 11-2 tchd 7-1)

Ponchatrain(IRE) was struggling from some way out but he ideally needs easier conditions to show his best. (tchd 5-1 and 6-1)

476 FREE RACING POST FORM AT TOTESPORT.COM BEGINNERS' CHASE (19 fncs) — 3m 110y

6:50 (6:50) (Class 4) 5-Y-O+ — **£4,110** (£1,198; £599)

Form — RPR

3P-2 **1** **Cast Cada (IRE)**[14] 281 7-11-0 128................................(t) PaulMoloney 127+
(Charlie Mann) *led: reminders after 9th: rdn after 16th: hdd whn lft clr next: styd on u.p* **7/4**[1]

244- **2** *2 ¼* **Zemsky (IRE)**[105] 3973 7-11-0 131................................... AndrewTinkler 125
(Nicky Henderson) *chsd ldrs: mstke 14th: rdn after 16th: sn outpcd: lft 2nd and hmpd 3 out: rallying whn mstke last: styd on u.p* **9/4**[2]

1P-4 **3** *26* **I'm The Decider (IRE)**[17] 234 8-11-0 0.............................(p) APMcCoy 106
(Jonjo O'Neill) *hld up: j.big over the first 2: hdwy 6th: hit 13th: wknd next: lft remote 3rd 3 out* **4/1**

F00 **F** **Billie Magern**[123] 3603 6-11-0 0... PaddyBrennan 135+
(Nigel Twiston-Davies) *trckd ldr: mstke 6th: rdn to ld whn fell 3 out* **7/2**[3]

6m 25.5s (-0.50) **Going Correction** +0.075s/f (Yiel) — **4** Ran SP% **109.4**
Speed ratings: **103,102,93,—**
CSF £6.14 TOTE £3.60; EX 5.00.
Owner R E Good **Bred** Enda Hunston **Trained** Upper Lambourn, Berks

FOCUS

A tight little beginners' chase.

NOTEBOOK

Cast Cada(IRE) broke his duck at the sixth time of asking over fences, but whether that would have been the case if Billie Magern had not crashed out at the second-last when upsides and seemingly going better, is another question. He jumped pretty soundly at the head of affairs but he was given reminders after the ninth fence and was he was coming under pressure when left clear. He deserved this success having been pretty consistent since switched to fences, but whether he can defy a penalty or hold his own off this sort of mark in a handicap remains to be seen. (op 9-4 tchd 5-2 and 13-8)

Zemsky(IRE)'s jumping again lacked fluency and, although he briefly looked like he might catch Cast Cada after the last, the effort petered out. He settled much better this time but is still not the finished article over fences. (op 2-1 tchd 11-4)

I'm The Decider(IRE) began to lose touch with the front three when slow over the 13th and could never get back into it. He may fare better back on slightly slower ground. (op 7-2 tchd 3-1)

Billie Magern ⊠ , a full-brother to the stable's high-class staying chaser Ollie Magern, was making his debut over the larger obstacles having won four times over hurdles, all on a sound surface. He jumped well up until his departure and it will not be long before he makes amends. Indeed, he could easily prove very useful in the long term.

477 BET TOTEPOOL AT TOTESPORT.COM NOVICES' H'CAP CHASE (13 fncs) — 2m

7:20 (7:20) (Class 4) (0-105,103) 5-Y-O+ — **£4,795** (£1,397; £699)

Form — RPR

441- **1** **Master Charm (FR)**[33] 5362 6-11-12 103...................... RichardJohnson 118+
(Tim Vaughan) *chsd ldrs: j.lft 3rd: blnd and lost pl next: hdwy appr 3 out: led bef next: stdd into last: styd on wl* **4/7**[1]

005- **2** *7* **Weststern (GER)**[29] 40 7-11-6 97.................................(t) JamieMoore 102
(Gary Moore) *hld up: hmpd 3rd: hdwy 5th: rdn and ev ch appr 2 out: j.lft and no ex last* **16/1**

1-U6 **3** *3 ¾* **Mad Professor (IRE)**[10] 353 7-9-7 77 oh1.................(p) JoeCornwall(7) 77
(John Cornwall) *hld up: drvn along after 4 out: styd on flat: nvr trbld ldrs* **10/1**

03-4 **4** *1 ¼* **Another Dark Rum**[13] 306 6-11-6 97.................................. KeithMercer 98+
(John Weymes) *w ldr tl led after 3rd: clr 6th: mstke 3 out: rdn and hdd whn blnd next: wknd bef last* **8/1**[3]

05-2 **5** *3* **Battlefield Bob (IRE)**[14] 283 6-10-12 89..................... AndrewThornton 87
(Caroline Bailey) *chsd ldrs: lft 2nd 9th: mstke 3 out: wknd bef next* **6/1**[2]

6-32 **B** **Kirkhammerton (IRE)**[11] 339 8-11-2 100.................. HarryChalloner(7) —
(Barry Leavy) *hld up: hdwy 6th: disputing cl 4th whn b.d 9th* **16/1**

300- **F** **Overspin**[360] 540 7-10-12 89.. WillKennedy —
(Paul Webber) *led tl after 3rd: chsd ldr: cl 2nd whn fell 9th* **33/1**

4m 9.20s (-0.80) **Going Correction** +0.075s/f (Yiel) — **7** Ran SP% **112.8**
Speed ratings: **105,101,99,99,97 —,—**
toteswingers: 1&2 £4.60, 1&3 £2.50, 2&3 £6.10 CSF £10.42 TOTE £1.60: £1.10, £6.60; EX 11.60.
Owner David Lovell **Bred** Scea Du Haras Des Sablonets **Trained** Aberthin, Vale of Glamorgan

FOCUS

A modest affair.

NOTEBOOK

Master Charm(FR) got the job done pretty easily in the end but his supporters had one or two very nervous moments, especially in the early stages of this contest. A bad blunder at the fourth fence was the worst of his mistakes but his jumping wasn't great all the way round and his class carried him to success. He has now won two from two since joining Tim Vaughan having bolted up in a 3m hunter chase at Chepstow last time and the change of scenery has clearly worked wonders, as it does with so many of the horses Vaughan gets. He'll probably be stepped back up in trip and looks the type who could easily rattle up a sequence. (op 8-11)

Weststern(GER), making his chasing debut, didn't fare too badly but was no match for the winner. He is handicapped up to his best on hurdles form, but on this evidence might be capable of a bit better in this sphere. (op 12-1)
Mad Professor(IRE)'s sole chase win (from 17 previous starts) came off an 8lb lower mark and, although he rallied in the closing stages, he is vulnerable in this grade. (op 9-1)
Another Dark Rum blundered the third- and second-last fences, which ended his challenge. (op 15-2 tchd 9-1)
Battlefield Bob(IRE) once again failed to see his race out. (op 13-2 tchd 11-2)

478 JOHN COOK'S 80TH BIRTHDAY (S) HURDLE (11 hdls) 2m 4f 110y
7:50 (7:50) (Class 5) 4-Y-O+ **£2,055** (£599; £299)

Form RPR
P5F/ **1** **Dont Call Me Derek**[854] 3264 9-10-12 0 APMcCoy 111+
(Dr Richard Newland) *trckd ldrs: racd keenly: led after 4th: mstke next: clr fr 8th: canter* **3/1**[2]
10-5 **2** *24* **Talenti (IRE)**[22] 137 7-11-5 120 (t) ChristianWilliams 95
(Lawney Hill) *led and j.big 1st: mstke 2nd: hdd after 4th: chsd wnr to 8th: sn outpcd: wnt remote 2nd again after 3 out* **10/11**[1]
6F-P **3** *19* **Satindra (IRE)**[7] 410 6-10-9 85 (tp) SeanQuinlan(3) 71
(Carole Ikin) *hld up: hdwy 7th: wknd next: wnt remote 3rd appr 2 out: t.o* **22/1**
P0-U **4** *3 ¾* **Smiling Applause**[17] 226 11-10-12 64 (b) DavidEngland 68
(Harry Chisman) *chsd ldrs: pushed along 5th: wknd 8th: t.o* **100/1**
40-6 **5** *28* **Vacario (GER)**[16] 250 6-11-2 110 (tp) PeterToole(3) 50
(Charlie Mann) *chsd ldr to 4th: rdn and wknd 3 out: t.o* **6/1**[3]
PF- **P** **Transfered (IRE)**[35] 5317 4-9-11 0 TommyPhelan(3) —
(Lucinda Featherstone) *plld hrd: hld up and a bhd: t.o whn p.u bef 7th* **33/1**
40-4 **P** **Telling Stories (IRE)**[11] 337 4-9-7 80 HarryChalloner(7) —
(Barry Leavy) *hld up: bhd and pushed along 5th: wknd 7th: t.o whn p.u bef 2 out* **12/1**
5- **P** **Ingenue**[8] 2661 4-10-0 0 (v) JamieMoore —
(Paul Howling) *hld up: hdwy 4th: chsd wnr 8th tl wknd after next: t.o whn p.u bef 2 out* **8/1**

5m 17.3s (6.60) **Going Correction** +0.20s/f (Yiel)
WFA 4 from 6yo+ 19lb **8 Ran SP% 118.8**
Speed ratings (Par 103): **95,85,78,77,66 —,—,—**
toteswingers: 1&2 £1.80, 1&3 £13.80, 2&3 £11.30 CSF £6.56 TOTE £4.30: £2.10, £1.02, £7.50; EX 8.40.There was no bid for the winner.
Owner D & D Coatings Ltd **Bred** Whitsbury Manor Stud **Trained** Claines, Worcs

FOCUS
A uncompetitive seller.

NOTEBOOK
Dont Call Me Derek ⊠ turned this into a procession, jumping fluently and coming home alone despite being heavily eased. He hadn't been seen since January 2008, but his new connections were clearly confident he was well enough to land this given the strength of morning support. On this evidence he'd be a shoo-in back in a handicap off a 43lb lower mark than at his peak, so it will be interesting to see if he is out again quickly before the Handicapper has a chance to react. (op 13-8)
Talenti(IRE)'s mark of 120 is very flattering on this evidence. He was unfortunate to bump into such a classy rival dropped to this grade for the first time and can probably find a small race at this level, but he doesn't strike as the most reliable. (op 6-4)
Satindra(IRE) plugged on for third to offer a little more encouragement than when last seen. (op 28-1 tchd 33-1)
Vacario(GER) appears to have lost the plot and is one to avoid now. (op 15-2 tchd 9-1, 11-2)
Ingenue dropped away as if something was amiss. Official explanation: trainer's rep said filly had a breathing problem and lost a shoe (op 17-2 tchd 9-1)

479 BET TOTEPOOL ON 0800 221 221 H'CAP HURDLE (9 hdls) 2m
8:20 (8:21) (Class 3) (0-120,120) 4-Y-O+ **£5,854** (£1,719; £859; £429)

Form RPR
313- **1** **Tiger O'Toole (IRE)**[40] 5213 5-11-7 115 PaulMoloney 122+
(Evan Williams) *hld up: hdwy 5th: nt clr run appr 2 out: led last: styd on wl* **11/4**[1]
3-22 **2** *1 ¾* **Peaceful Means (IRE)**[4] 350 7-10-6 105 MichaelMurphy(5) 108
(J Jay) *hld up: hdwy after 3 out: led next: hdd last: styd on same pce flat* **4/1**[2]
36-2 **3** *14* **Apache Dawn**[10] 360 6-10-0 97 EamonDehdashti(3) 87
(Aytach Sadik) *hld up in tch: plld hrd: lost pl appr 5th: rallied 6th: ev ch appr 2 out: wknd last* **12/1**
01F- **4** *6* **Viable**[51] 5044 8-11-1 116 MissGAndrews(7) 101
(Pam Sly) *trckd ldrs: plld hrd: ev ch 2 out: sn rdn and wknd* **12/1**
14-3 **5** *1 ¾* **Sonning Star (IRE)**[26] 86 6-11-7 115 LiamTreadwell 98
(Nick Gifford) *hld up: pushed along 4th: hdwy sn after: rdn 3 out: wknd bef last* **8/1**
103- **6** *7* **Slip**[9] 4482 5-11-5 113 RobertThornton 90
(Conor Dore) *hld up: hdwy 4th: outpcd after 6th: rallied appr 2 out: sn wknd: t.o* **14/1**
00-0 **7** *6* **Very Stylish (IRE)**[11] 331 6-10-13 107 APMcCoy 79
(Jonjo O'Neill) *led: rdn and hdd 2 out: sn wknd: t.o* **20/1**
500- **8** *16* **Stumped**[62] 4849 7-10-6 100 (p) WarrenMarston 57
(Milton Harris) *chsd ldrs: mstke 4th: rdn and wknd bef 2 out: t.o* **13/2**[3]
44-5 **9** *6* **Mon Michel (IRE)**[21] 159 7-10-12 106 (b[1]) JamieMoore 58
(Gary Moore) *hld up in tch: rdn and ev ch appr 2 out: sn wknd: t.o* **7/1**
46P- **10** *19* **Royal Max (IRE)**[38] 5245 4-10-10 115 (vt) StevenGagan(7) 46
(Michael Chapman) *w ldr tl wknd 3 out: t.o* **33/1**
3P/0 **P** **Charlie Yardbird (IRE)**[26] 80 9-11-12 120 RichardJohnson —
(Tim Vaughan) *hld up: p.u after 4th: lame* **22/1**

3m 57.5s (0.40) **Going Correction** +0.20s/f (Yiel)
WFA 4 from 5yo+ 18lb **11 Ran SP% 117.7**
Speed ratings (Par 107): **107,106,99,96,95 91,88,80,77,68 —**
toteswingers: 1&2 £3.40, 1&3 £8.00, 2&3 £12.90 CSF £14.07 CT £113.75 TOTE £4.70: £2.70, £1.10, £8.50; EX 18.90.
Owner Ms S Howell **Bred** Mrs Jayne M Gollings **Trained** Llancarfan, Vale Of Glamorgan

FOCUS
Steady rain changed the ground to good all over before this contest, and it looked like it was getting into the ground. This had quite an open feel to it on paper but it was a two horse race by the final flight.

NOTEBOOK
Tiger O'Toole(IRE) ⊠ jumped to the front at the last and saw it out much stronger than Peaceful Means, who looked the most likely winner when poaching a couple of lengths on her nearest rival after the second-last. He travelled well through the first half of the contest but seemed to hit a flat spot leaving the back before picking up once again after the second last flight. There wasn't much of a gallop on here and a stronger-run race would suit this progressive grey. He is one to keep on the right side of. (op 5-2)
Peaceful Means(IRE) ⊠ , who moved into contention with eye-catching ease up the inside, traded at 1-5 on the exchanges when skipping clear in the straight, but she couldn't fend off the strong finish of the winner. She doesn't win that often but on this evidence she's capable of defying her current mark. (op 5-1)
Apache Dawn ⊠ has only won one of his 46 previous starts but his performance deserves marking up given he ran so freely through the first half of the race. A stronger pace will definitely help but his win-to-run record is clearly a big concern. (op 10-1)
Viable, another who was very keen early, also deserves extra credit as his best performances have all come on right-handed tracks, while his trainer reported beforehand that the easing of the going wouldn't have been a help to him.
Sonning Star(IRE) was not helped by the drop back to 2m and weakened having held every chance. (tchd 9-1)
Stumped, the morning gamble, was beaten a long way out. (op 7-1)

480 HOSPITALITY AT SOUTHWELL RACECOURSE NOVICES' H'CAP HURDLE (11 hdls) 2m 4f 110y
8:50 (8:50) (Class 4) (0-105,101) 4-Y-O+ **£3,425** (£998; £499)

Form RPR
0P1- **1** **Restart (IRE)**[35] 5318 9-11-3 95 TommyPhelan(3) 98+
(Lucinda Featherstone) *hld up in tch: led 2 out: mstke last: rdn out* **10/3**[1]
50-1 **2** *2 ¼* **Hurricane Electric (IRE)**[11] 328 5-10-12 87 JodieMogford 86
(Graeme McPherson) *led: rdn and hdd 2 out: styd on same pce flat* **11/2**[3]
2-55 **3** *2* **Wee Ziggy**[11] 328 7-9-10 78 BrianToomey(7) 75+
(Michael Mullineaux) *hld up: racd keenly: hdwy appr 2 out: rdn to go 3rd flat: nvr trbld ldrs* **11/2**[3]
0/6- **4** *1 ¾* **Sparkling Brook (IRE)**[30] 25 7-10-7 82 PaddyBrennan 78
(Nigel Twiston-Davies) *hld up: hdwy 7th: rdn appr last: no ex flat* **12/1**
430- **5** *shd* **Sagunt (GER)**[38] 5261 7-11-5 101 (t) AnthonyFreeman(7) 97
(Sean Curran) *hld up in tch: rdn appr last: styd on same pce flat* **9/2**[2]
0- **6** *1 ¾* **Baltimore Patriot (IRE)**[23] 1693 7-11-6 95 MarkGrant 89
(Roger Curtis) *trckd ldrs: rdn appr 2 out: no ex last* **14/1**
25-6 **7** *12* **Solo Choice**[20] 174 4-10-10 90 KeithMercer 68
(Ian McInnes) *hld up: hit 7th: rdn and wknd bef 2 out* **28/1**
22-2 **8** *3* **Pen Gwen (FR)**[20] 178 7-11-4 100 HenryBrooke(7) 80
(Kate Walton) *chsd ldr: nt fluent 4th: mstke 8th: rdn and wknd bef 2 out* **6/1**
433- **9** *27* **Pure Crystal**[180] 2334 4-10-13 100 MrJMQuinlan(7) 51
(Michael Quinlan) *hld up: a in rr: bhd fr 7th: t.o* **12/1**
6PF- **10** *nk* **Gatien Du Tertre (FR)**[35] 5312 6-10-9 84 (b[1]) DavidDennis 40
(Frank Sheridan) *mid-div: hdwy 5th: rdn 8th: wknd bef 2 out: t.o* **10/1**

5m 27.3s (16.60) **Going Correction** +0.20s/f (Yiel)
WFA 4 from 5yo+ 19lb **10 Ran SP% 120.9**
Speed ratings (Par 105): **76,75,74,73,73 73,68,67,57,56**
toteswingers: 1&2:£3.80, 1&3:£5.80, 2&3:£8.10 CSF £23.42 CT £100.98 TOTE £3.90: £2.00, £3.10, £2.60; EX 19.90 Place 6 £10.56, Place 5 £5.78.
Owner J Roundtree **Bred** Acacia Holdings **Trained** Atlow, Derbyshire

FOCUS
A moderate bunch for this novices' handicap hurdle and the early pace was very steady.

NOTEBOOK
Restart(IRE), a recent course winner, deserves real credit for defying a 20lb hike in the handicap and he would have won even more decisively had he not been very awkward at the final two flights. He looks a different horse since returning from a break and on this evidence there is no reason why he can't complete the hat-trick. (op 9-2)
Hurricane Electric(IRE) ran at least as well as when winning at Bangor last time off 7lb lower and is another revitalised performer. (op 6-1)
Wee Ziggy ⊠ was the big eye-catcher, makinge stealthy headway from the back of the field without his rider resorting to maximum pressure and it wasn't until after the last that he was given the office, where he finished well. The big drawback is his record which now reads no wins from 34 starts (17 over hurdles), which indicates it's probably unwise to get too carried away. Official explanation: jockey said gelding was unsuited by the good going (op 8-1)
Sparkling Brook(IRE) hadn't shown a great deal in five previous outings but, fitter for a spin at Towcester last month after well over a year off the track, she shaped with much more encouragement, throwing down a big challenge leaving the back and keeping on well. There is more to come from her. (op 15-2)
Sagunt(GER), for whom the step up to this trip brought about an improved effort, is unexposed over this distance and could be one to keep an eye on. (op 4-1)
T/Plt: £16.40 to a £1 stake. Pool: £79,239.88. 3,517.79 winning tickets. T/Qpdt: £4.70 to a £1 stake. Pool: £6,453.08. 1,013.80 winning tickets. CR

481 - 487a (Foreign Racing) - See Raceform Interactive

420 WETHERBY (L-H)
Thursday, May 27

OFFICIAL GOING: Good (good to firm in places; 8.8)
Wind: moderate 1/2 behind Weather: fine

488 TURFTV.CO.UK MARES' NOVICES' HURDLE (11 hdls) 2m 4f
5:45 (5:45) (Class 4) 4-Y-O+ **£2,602** (£764; £382; £190)

Form RPR
3-02 **1** **Knar Mardy**[7] 421 5-10-7 81 AdamPogson(3) 104
(Charles Pogson) *chsd ldrs: wnt handy 2nd appr 3 out: swtchd lft appr 2 out: chalng whn lft in ld last: sn wnt clr* **17/2**
22-1 **2** *10* **Astrolibra**[7] 421 6-11-3 103 APMcCoy 110+
(Mark H Tompkins) *trckd ldrs: led appr 3 out: j.lft 2 out: jnd whn blnd bdly last: nt rcvr* **15/8**[2]
241- **3** *14* **Cailin Na Ri (IRE)**[30] 30 7-11-3 114 DenisO'Regan 89
(Martin Todhunter) *trckd ldr: led after 8th: hdd appr next: fr 2 out: one pce* **13/8**[1]
1 **4** *3 ¼* **Tout Regulier**[15] 275 6-10-12 108 DonalDevereux(5) 86
(Peter Bowen) *led: hit 4th: hdd after 8th: wknd 2 out* **9/2**[3]
P-PP **5** *97* **Little Miss Foozle**[12] 337 6-10-10 0 AndrewThornton —
(Peter Niven) *in rr: pushed along 5th: lost pl and hit next: t.o 8th* **300/1**
P/ **6** *¾* **Coniston**[842] 3739 7-10-10 0 TjadeCollier —
(Sue Smith) *in rr whn hmpd 2nd: bhd fr 5th: t.o 8th* **50/1**
304- **P** **Just Jennings (IRE)**[64] 4819 5-10-3 0 AlexanderVoy(7) —
(John Norton) *nt fluent: j.rt: bhd and drvn 5th: sn t.o: p.u bef 7th* **40/1**

4m 57.1s (-2.40) **Going Correction** +0.05s/f (Yiel) **7 Ran SP% 106.3**
Speed ratings (Par 105): **106,102,96,95,56 56,—**
toteswingers: 1&2 £3.90, 1&3 £7.70, 2&3 £1.10 CSF £22.08 TOTE £6.80: £1.60, £3.10; EX 38.80.
Owner Wordingham Plant Hire **Bred** Brian And Gwen Griffiths **Trained** Farnsfield, Notts

FOCUS
There was 2mm of rain overnight, but the ground remained on the firm side. This was a modest mares' hurdle to start proceedings. The winner reversed C&D form with the runner-up, helped by the latter's error.

NOTEBOOK

Knar Mardy started at a decent price (much longer was available in the morning) considering she was entitled to respect after finishing second to Astrolibra here a week ago, and now had the advantage of a 7lb pull. Bought out of the Henderson yard for just 5,500gns, she was finally getting off the mark at the 15th attempt, but her attitude seems fine and she appeared to have a fair bit left at the finish. She may be up to scoring again in a mares' handicap. (op 16-1 tchd 8-1)

Astrolibra raced with tongue lolling in the home straight, but she still held a slight advantage when a terrible blunder at the last ruined her chance. It would undoubtedly have been very close, but she was certainly not guaranteed to have held on. (op 9-4)

Cailin Na Ri(IRE) made the frame in six of seven races for another trainer last summer and, although she made all at Sedgefield for this yard a month ago, she reverted to looking one-paced. (tchd 6-4 and 15-8)

Tout Regulier won a mares' maiden point in Ireland and a mares' hurdle in which the second horse looked anything but genuine at Exeter, but she was firmly put in her place here. Fences beckon and she might be a bit better over them. (op 5-2)

Just Jennings(IRE) was making her hurdling debut after four tries in soft-ground bumpers (ran well once), and she consistently jumped right and seemed to hate the firmish surface. Official explanation: trainer said mare was unsuited by the good (good to firm in places) ground (op 100-1)

489 VOLKSWAGEN APPROVED USED CARS H'CAP CHASE (18 fncs) 2m 6f 110y

6:15 (6:18) (Class 4) (0-105,105) 5-Y-0+ **£3,252** (£955; £477; £238)

Form RPR

43-4 **1** **Red Dynamite**[22] 160 9-10-7 **89**.........................(p) MichaelO'Connell(3) 101+
(Geoffrey Harker) *jnd ldrs 8th: led 10th: drvn 3 out: rdn and wandered between last 2: all out* **9/2**[3]

P3-3 **2** *3 1/4* **Nile Moon (IRE)**[19] 213 9-11-6 **99**.........................(b) PaddyAspell 105
(Ann Hamilton) *led: hdd 10th: rallied and jnd wnr after 14th: kpt on same pce fr 2 out* **3/1**[2]

5P1- **3** *12* **Wizards Dust**[34] 5356 8-11-9 **102**.........................(b) APMcCoy 97
(Donald McCain) *w ldr: drvn 10th: wknd 2 out: j.rt last* **5/4**[1]

/4-4 **4** *34* **Ragador**[21] 175 9-11-7 **105**......................... ShaneByrne(5) 70
(Sue Smith) *chsd ldrs: reminders 5th and 9th: hmpd bnd bef 10th: hrd rdn 14th: appr next: sn bhd: t.o* **17/2**

P/4- **P** **Neutrino**[32] 5 8-11-6 **99**.........................(p) RodiGreene —
(David Bridgwater) *chsd ldrs: reminders 7th: drvn 9th: lost pl and hit 12th: sn bhd: t.o whn p.u bef 4 out* **17/2**

5m 34.8s (-2.20) **Going Correction** +0.05s/f (Yiel) **5** Ran SP% **108.7**
Speed ratings: **105,103,99,87,—**
CSF £17.65 TOTE £6.80: £2.50, £1.70; EX 17.10.

Owner A S Ward **Bred** N B Mason **Trained** Thirkleby, N Yorks

FOCUS

A poor event.

NOTEBOOK

Red Dynamite, wearing first-time cheekpieces, got off the mark at the 15th attempt in this woeful handicap chase. He has looked to have some ability on occasions, but lacks a battling attitude and his most recent defeat was in a seller. He was doing very little out in front but the others were doing even less. At least he always gets round, and he did not go unbacked, but he will never be one to have any faith in. (op 13-2 tchd 7-1)

Nile Moon(IRE) completed a double at Kelso 13 months ago, but he is extremely one-paced and could never muster enough speed to get to the idling winner in this slow-motion finish. (op 11-4 tchd 5-2)

Wizards Dust was being partnered by McCoy for the first time in 29 races (won five), but the maestro could get no sort of tune out of this extremely moody individual, who had his ears flat back and was declining to co-operate from soon after halfway. (op 11-8 tchd 13-8)

Ragador was the only one not to be sporting some kind of headgear, but this giant-sized maiden 9-y-o was never travelling and ran a shocker. (op 9-1 tchd 8-1)

Neutrino comes from a yard which has not had a winner for 201 days and he had already turned it in starting the final circuit. (op 11-2)

490 RACING UK ON SKY CHANNEL 432 H'CAP HURDLE (9 hdls) 2m 110y

6:50 (6:50) (Class 5) (0-90,88) 4-Y-0+ **£2,055** (£599; £299)

Form RPR

00-5 **1** **Ton-Chee**[12] 338 11-11-6 **85**.........................(t) CharlieHuxley(3) 98+
(Arthur Whitehead) *hld up in rr: gd hdwy after 5th: led 3 out: hung bdly lft between last 2: mstke last: kpt on wl* **33/1**

0P2- **2** *5* **Nobel (FR)**[32] 10 9-10-0 **69**.........................(p) MissJCoward(7) 77+
(Brian Storey) *trckd ldrs: led 5th: hdd 3 out: swtchd rt after 2 out: kpt on to take 2nd nr fin* **20/1**

04-1 **3** *hd* **Authentic Act (IRE)**[8] 402 6-10-8 **73** 7ex......................... MichaelO'Connell(3) 80
(Martin Todhunter) *mid-div: hdwy 5th: wnt 2nd after next: swtchd rt between last 2: kpt on same pce: lost pl in last strides* **7/4**[1]

00P- **4** *17* **Flashy Max**[118] 3721 5-11-5 **81**.........................(b[1]) GrahamLee 73
(Jedd O'Keeffe) *led: hit 3rd: hdd 5th: outpcd appr 3 out: kpt on to take modest 4th last* **25/1**

5-00 **5** *1* **Daniel's Dream**[8] 400 10-10-5 **70**.........................(b[1]) HarryHaynes(3) 61
(John Dixon) *j.lft: mid-div: outpcd 5th: 9th 3 out: 6th last: styd on* **25/1**

/P0- **6** *2* **Song In My Heart (IRE)**[263] 1402 5-11-9 **85**......................... APMcCoy 74
(Jonjo O'Neill) *hld up in rr: hdwy 5th: chsng ldrs next: outpcd appr 3 out: wknd last* **7/1**[2]

0P4- **7** *13* **Evelith Regent (IRE)**[32] 10 7-10-7 **76**......................... BrianToomey(7) 53
(John Davies) *stdd s: hld up in last: mstke 4th: sme hdwy 3 out: nvr on terms* **33/1**

U5-P **8** *shd* **Archie's Wish**[21] 176 6-10-4 **66**......................... BarryKeniry 43
(Micky Hammond) *mid-div: hdwy 5th: chsng ldrs next: lost pl appr 3 out* **22/1**

000- **9** *2* **Laybach (IRE)**[57] 4958 6-10-10 **75**......................... GaryBerridge(3) 50
(Michael Quinlan) *mid-div: lost pl after 5th* **12/1**

P0/3 **10** *2 3/4* **Looks The Business (IRE)**[21] 185 9-11-10 **86**......................... NickScholfield 59
(Andrew Haynes) *prom: outpcd appr 3 out: 6th and wkng whn hit 2 out* **9/1**[3]

P-63 **11** *12* **Arctic Rock**[8] 402 7-11-2 **78**.........................(v) PaddyAspell 40
(Geoffrey Harker) *in rr: bhd fr 6th* **16/1**

00-P **12** *2 3/4* **Fortune's Fool**[7] 424 11-9-7 **62** oh1......................... HenryBrooke(7) 21
(Ian Brown) *a towards rr: bhd fr 6th* **66/1**

P0-U **13** *4* **Caliban (IRE)**[18] 233 12-11-4 **85**......................... LeeEdwards(5) 41
(Sally-Anne Wheelwright) *chsd ldrs: lost pl 5th: sn bhd: t.o 3 out* **100/1**

00-P **14** *9* **Qaasi (USA)**[26] 87 8-10-5 **74**......................... KyleJames(7) 22
(Ian Brown) *in rr: hit 3rd: bhd fr 6th* **50/1**

/P-0 **P** **Zelos (IRE)**[21] 171 6-11-6 **82**.........................(bt) RodiGreene —
(David Bridgwater) *chsd ldrs: rdn 5th: lost pl and p.u bef 3 out* **50/1**

000- **U** **Cedar Falls (USA)**[122] 3659 5-10-1 **63** oh34 ow1......(vt[1]) RichieMcGrath —
(Gary Brown) *towards rr whn stmbld bdly landing 1st and uns rdr* **16/1**

00-F **P** **Decent Lord (IRE)**[18] 224 6-10-8 **70**......................... AlanO'Keeffe —
(Jennie Candlish) *nt jump wl: w ldrs: lost pl after 6th: bhd whn p.u bef next* **9/1**[3]

3m 54.0s (-1.80) **Going Correction** +0.05s/f (Yiel) **17** Ran SP% **117.4**
Speed ratings (Par 103): **106,103,103,95,95 94,88,87,87,85 80,78,76,72,— —,—**
toteswingers: 1&2 £50.30, 1&3 £65.40, 2&3 £5.40 CSF £538.23 CT £1777.06 TOTE £41.90: £6.40, £5.20, £1.02, £5.50; EX 673.30.

Owner A J Whitehead **Bred** Auldyn Stud Ltd **Trained** Aston on Clun, Shropshire

FOCUS

Everything pointed to this being no more than a glorified seller and so it proved. Some of the interest was removed when the Jim Best pair who were due to make their debuts for the yard, Hoar Frost and Mycenean Prince, failed to turn up. They willl be worth noting when they do appear in this sort of grade.

NOTEBOOK

Ton-Chee has been on the go for nine years and sprang a 33-1 surprise, as he did when winning a seller 14 months ago. He wore a tongue-strap for only the second time (the first was five years ago) and it may have been helpful. He is inconsistent and fully exposed and only seven months away from his 12th birthday, so connections, who have a very small string at their Shropshire base, did well to extract this success.

Nobel(FR) used to be decent for Rose Dobbin, but it is three years since he won and he is only modest now. (op 22-1 tchd 25-1)

Authentic Act(IRE) won twice on the Flat in Germany and picked up a fast-ground seller at Sedgefield last week, but was firmly put in his place. He is now due a weight hike and may need to return to the lowest level if he is to score again. (op 9-4 tchd 5-2 in a place)

Flashy Max showed no real promise, trailing home a long way behind the first three. (op 28-1 tchd 22-1)

Daniel's Dream, a long-standing maiden, did get up a head of steam close home. (op 40-1)

Song In My Heart(IRE) was a market springer, although this Irish Flat winner had been beaten 30l or far more in six previous attempts for this stable. Off the bridle and struggling a long way out, there is apparently not much to work on. (op 12-1 tchd 6-1)

Laybach(IRE) was reported well backed by some quarters, but after drifting from 6-1 to double those odds he ran no race at all. (op 6-1)

491 HOLD YOUR CHRISTMAS PARTY HERE NOVICES' CHASE (16 fncs) 2m 4f 110y

7:25 (7:25) (Class 4) 5-Y-0+ **£3,252** (£955; £477; £238)

Form RPR

31-2 **1** **Picaroon**[27] 78 6-11-12 138......................... RichardJohnson 111+
(Tim Vaughan) *mde all: blnd 3rd: qcknd appr 4 out: j.rt after: clr 3 out: eased towards fin* **1/6**[1]

60-3 **2** *9* **King's Majesty (IRE)**[21] 177 8-10-12 85......................... DougieCostello 86
(Tim Pitt) *wnt prom 4th: chsd wnr after 12th: sn upsides: one pce fr 3 out* **16/1**[3]

P0-0 **3** *1* **Browneyes Blue (IRE)**[15] 291 12-10-12 0......................... PaddyAspell 85
(James Moffatt) *in last: drvn and wl outpcd 8th: wnt 3rd 3 out: one pce* **10/1**[2]

0P-4 **4** *14* **Executive's Hall (IRE)**[7] 422 6-10-12 0......................... KeithMercer 73+
(Andrew Crook) *chsd wnr: hit 10th and 12th: wknd 2 out* **25/1**

5m 5.40s (-2.40) **Going Correction** +0.05s/f (Yiel) **4** Ran SP% **104.5**
Speed ratings: **106,102,102,96**
CSF £3.21 TOTE £1.10; EX 2.70.

Owner David Lovell **Bred** Darley **Trained** Aberthin, Vale of Glamorgan

FOCUS

A one-horse race.

NOTEBOOK

Picaroon was withdrawn the previous day (vet's certificate) from a slightly more valuable race at Sedgefield in which he would have faced only three rivals, and he made mincemeat of that number here. Bred by Darley and an Irish bumper winner for the enthusiastic veteran amateur Barry Connell, he was picked up by current connections for 22,000gns and is gradually paying his way, with three wins already this year. He was very secure after one early mistake, and never broke sweat trouncing vastly inferior rivals. His run of success should continue. (tchd 2-11)

King's Majesty(IRE), whose far more adept stable companion Nothingbutthetruth was withdrawn in the morning, was left to pick up second prize. It is just possible that he will now suffer from an unfavourable reaction from the Handicapper, which is hardly going to help his cause. (op 11-1 tchd 10-1)

Browneyes Blue(IRE) is very much in the old boys' league and he has shown no sparkle since an apparent setback in 2007, when he was twice successful at Cartmel (where he is trained) and once at Perth. (op 11-1)

Executive's Hall(IRE) was too slow to win any of his maiden points in Ireland, and was totally out of his depth here. (op 28-1 tchd 22-1)

492 WETHERBYRACING.CO.UK NOVICES' HURDLE (13 hdls) 3m 1f

8:00 (8:00) (Class 4) 4-Y-0+ **£2,602** (£764; £382; £190)

Form RPR

21-2 **1** **The Ferbane Man (IRE)**[23] 138 6-10-13 0.........................(p) RichardJohnson 90+
(Tim Vaughan) *trckd ldr: drvn to chal 3 out: led next: sn rdn and hung lft: gained upper hand nr fin: all out* **30/100**[1]

PP-5 **2** *nk* **Stolen Moments (FR)**[19] 214 9-10-13 110......................... PaddyAspell 88
(James Moffatt) *set modest pce: qcknd 7th: drvn and jnd 3 out: narrowly hdd next: no ex towards fin* **4/1**[2]

0-46 **3** *7* **Sunset Resort (IRE)**[8] 397 5-10-10 92.........................(t) MichaelMcAlister(3) 82
(Maurice Barnes) *t.k.h: wnt prom 3rd: drvn appr 3 out: one pce fr 2 out* **14/1**[3]

4 *108* **Blackthirteen (IRE)** 6-10-13 0......................... TjadeCollier —
(Joanne Foster) *t.k.h: trckd ldrs: nt fluent 2nd: lost pl 8th: sn bhd: t.o 10th* **40/1**

6m 26.3s (9.80) **Going Correction** +0.05s/f (Yiel) **4** Ran SP% **106.0**
Speed ratings (Par 105): **86,85,83,—**
CSF £1.83 TOTE £1.20; EX 1.60.

Owner Aidan & Gerard Flynn **Bred** Oliver Loughlin **Trained** Aberthin, Vale of Glamorgan

FOCUS

The very short-priced favourite finally asserted, but only after some heart-stopping moments for any intrepid punters.

NOTEBOOK

The Ferbane Man(IRE) was a modest Irish pointer, and only won a three-finisher maiden from 14 attempts. He beat four others in a Towcester chase despite idling (hence the first time cheekpieces, which did not really seem especially helpful) but a conditional put up a circus act on him when narrowly beaten at Fakenham next time, where he lost an iron two out and was almost decanted and then dropped his reins at the last. This was only his second hurdle and it was a good piece of placing by connections, but Richard Johnson needed all his strength to get him home, and he would need something very similar to follow up. (op 1-4)

Stolen Moments(FR), decent a long time ago, pulled up in his final three handicap chases (in good company) for Alan King, so this was a bit better and he tried hard enough, but the value of the form is almost non-existent. (op 6-1)

Sunset Resort(IRE) pulls hard and makes mistakes, and has already been trounced in a seller. (op 12-1)

493 GO RACING AT CATTERICK ON SATURDAY OPEN HUNTERS' CHASE (16 fncs) 2m 4f 110y

8:30 (8:31) (Class 6) 5-Y-O+ **£1,318** (£405; £202)

Form RPR

1/2- **1** **Bow School (IRE)**[39] 9-11-11 0 MrWKinsey(7) 120+
(Mrs A C Hamilton) *chsd ldrs: led 3 out: hit next: hld on gamely* **11/1**

1-41 **2** *nk* **Farmer Frank**[11] 354 7-12-1 0 HenryBrooke(7) 123
(Nick Kent) *chsd ldrs: led 4 out: hdd next: kpt on wl: no ex towards fin* **7/4**[1]

/6F- **3** *14* **Line Ball (IRE)**[36] 5314 9-12-0 0 (p) MrAJBerry 102
(Jonjo O'Neill) *rn in snatches: reminders 5th: chsng ldrs 7th: plld wd after 12th: upsides next: one pce fr 3 out* **10/3**[2]

00P/ **4** *2 ½* **Cottam Phantom**[12] 9-11-9 0 MissJCoward(5) 100
(Mrs C A Coward) *chsd ldr: led 11th: hdd after next: one pce fr 3 out* **18/1**

/U5- **5** *3 ¾* **Strong Weld**[24] 13-11-7 114 (tp) MrRJenkins(7) 97
(Mrs N Sheppard) *led to 11th: regained lde after next: hdd 4 out: 5th whn hit 2 out: wknd towards fin* **7/2**[3]

4/2- **6** *18* **Madison De Vonnas (FR)**[19] 10-11-11 0 MrGBrewer(3) 80
(Mrs Freya Brewer) *towards rr: hdwy to chse ldrs 12th: wknd appr 3 out* **20/1**

PPP/ **7** *dist* **Nirvana Du Bourg (FR)**[54] 9-11-7 0 (p) MrGRSmith(7) 50
(R A Wilson) *chsd ldrs: lost pl appr 4 out: sn bhd: t.o 4 out* **40/1**

3/0- **P** **Vital Spark**[19] 11-11-7 103 (b) MissHDukes(7) —
(O R Dukes) *sn bhd: t.o 5th: p.u bef next* **40/1**

2P1- **P** **Over To Joe**[19] 10-12-1 0 (p) MrMSeston(3) —
(C C Pimlott) *chsd ldrs: lost pl 8th: bhd fr 10th: t.o whn p.u bef 4 out* **16/1**

P **Zaffman (IRE)**[19] 9-11-7 0 MrSCharlton(7) —
(David Pritchard) *hit 5th: bhd fr 7th: sn t.o: p.u bef 12th* **100/1**

5m 30.0s (22.20) **Going Correction** +0.05s/f (Yiel) **10** Ran SP% **111.8**
Speed ratings: **59,58,53,52,51 44,30,—,—,—**
toteswingers: 1&2 £4.00, 1&3 £11.90, 2&3 £1.20 CSF £30.12 TOTE £19.20: £1.70, £1.02, £2.90; EX 44.90.
Owner J P G Hamilton **Bred** Andrew Kiernan **Trained** Cavers, Borders

NOTEBOOK

Bow School(IRE) has had a chequered career, with hanging or jumping errors sometimes counting against him, but he has never lacked ability at best, and after landing three points in 2008 he went on to pick up two chases for Howard Johnson. 2m4f is his ideal trip, and dropping down in distance after only making the frame in two spring points clearly suited him. (op 17-2 tchd 12-1)
Farmer Frank has been in good heart this year and gave the lightweight Henry Brooke (looks promising) a first win under rules at Market Rasen 11 days ago. He did nothing wrong, but the concession of 4lb to an animal of similar ability was just beyond him. He is still a youngster, and should do well over similar trips in this company next year. (op 9-4)
Line Ball(IRE) is typical of the once useful rules performers that Jonjo O'Neill tries to rejuvenate in hunter chases. From the way this one failed to travel (off the bridle after one jump and gave up very quickly in the straight) he has a real challenge on his hands. (op 9-4)
Cottam Phantom had won his last three points but apparently had more to do here, and he lost touch from three out with the rider motionless. Official explanation: jockey said gelding had a breathing problem (op 12-1)
Strong Weld is a gutsy old horse but only seems effective in points these days. (op 9-2)

494 "PARTY IN THE PADDOCK" NEXT THURSDAY H'CAP HURDLE (11 hdls) 2m 4f

9:05 (9:05) (Class 4) (0-115,113) 4-Y-O+ **£2,602** (£764; £382; £190)

Form RPR

2-54 **1** **Mini Minster**[13] 313 8-11-3 104 GrahamLee 105
(Peter Atkinson) *led: qcknd 6th: 3 l ahd last: hld on gamely* **8/1**

12-6 **2** *¾* **Ring For Time**[18] 235 7-11-12 113 WillKennedy 113
(Dai Burchell) *chsd ldrs: drvn 8th: chsd wnr 2 out: kpt on wl run-in: jst hld* **15/2**

3-3P **3** *3 ½* **Miss Tarantella**[7] 424 7-9-11 87 oh2 (t) MichaelMcAlister(3) 84
(Maurice Barnes) *prom: chsd wnr 3 out: styd on same pce fr next* **8/1**

6-01 **4** *4* **Benmadigan (IRE)**[8] 393 8-10-11 101 FearghalDavis(3) 95
(Nicky Richards) *t.k.h in midfield: hdwy to chse ldrs 3 out: one pce fr next* **9/2**[1]

340- **5** *13* **Lady Wright (IRE)**[40] 5229 7-10-7 97 MrOGreenall(3) 79
(Michael Easterby) *hld up towards rr: hdwy to chse ldrs 8th: rdn and wknd appr 2 out* **7/1**[3]

24-5 **6** *2* **Azulada Bay (IRE)**[18] 232 6-11-2 103 (p) TomScudamore 83
(Mark Rimell) *towards rr: kpt on fr 3 out: nvr on terms* **6/1**[2]

60-3 **7** *nk* **Kayf Commander**[7] 423 7-10-9 96 AndrewTinkler 76
(Mel Brittain) *in rr: hdwy to chse ldrs 8th: wknd 2 out: mstke and j. slowly last* **16/1**

460- **8** *21* **Terenzium (IRE)**[20] 5338 8-11-2 110 (v) AlexanderVoy(7) 71
(Micky Hammond) *t.k.h: trckd ldrs: wknd 3 out* **8/1**

/00- **9** *23* **Tyrrhenian**[36] 5311 7-10-3 90 WilsonRenwick 30
(Rose Dobbin) *chsd ldrs: wknd 8th: t.o next* **33/1**

1/0U **10** *19* **Option Money (IRE)**[12] 331 8-11-6 107 AndrewThornton 30
(Peter Salmon) *chsd ldrs: lost pl 8th: sn bhd: t.o next* **50/1**

0-1F **F** **Forget It**[20] 196 5-11-10 111 JamieMoore —
(Gary Moore) *hld up in rr: hit 2nd: hdwy and prom whn stmbld bdly landing 7th and fell* **8/1**

00-0 **P** **Still Royal**[22] 154 4-9-9 94 oh8 ow2 BrianToomey(7) —
(John Davies) *chsd ldrs: blnd 8th: sn lost pl: t.o whn p.u bef next* **80/1**

4m 59.9s (0.40) **Going Correction** +0.05s/f (Yiel)
WFA 4 from 5yo+ 19lb **12** Ran SP% **113.2**
Speed ratings (Par 105): **101,100,99,97,92 91,91,83,73,66 —,—**
toteswingers: 1&2 £9.40, 1&3 £18.00, 2&3 £23.60 CSF £63.52 CT £494.47 TOTE £11.80: £3.80, £4.00, £3.20; EX 84.30 Place 6: £23.36 Place 5: £7.03 .
Owner P G Atkinson **Bred** D G Atkinson **Trained** Yafforth, N Yorks

FOCUS

Unlike much of what had gone before, this looked fairly competitive.

NOTEBOOK

Mini Minster, a diminutive home-bred, has always had her heart in the right place, but she does not find it easy to score and both previous successes were at Hexham, most recently two years ago. There will not be many meetings for her in the north over the summer, so perhaps she will have a break until the autumn. (op 10-1)
Ring For Time does not appear to be particularly well handicapped, but there are a plethora of Worcesters for her in the next few months, and being a trier she deserves to score again. 2m4f is possibly ideal. (op 8-1)
Miss Tarantella is at the foot of the handicap but has always found it hard to get her head in front. She prefers easier surfaces. (op 10-1)
Benmadigan(IRE), unpenalised for the most recent of his five wins, did not come in for any significant market support, and after pulling hard he failed to run his race. Three outings in May have perhaps taken their toll, and he is essentially better than this. (op 10-3)
Forget It was Jamie Moore's only ride of the night, but after making the very long haul from Brighton he was an early faller. It was the same scenario at Aintree on his previous attempt, which must have peeved connections no end. (op 15-2 tchd 9-1)
T/Plt: £52.00 to a £1 stake. Pool: £45,566.37 - 638.95 winning ticket. T/Qpdt: £2.30 to a £1 stake. Pool: £4,249.61- 1,331.72 winning tickets. WG

495 - 497a (Foreign Racing) - See Raceform Interactive

356 STRATFORD (L-H)

Friday, May 28

OFFICIAL GOING: Good to firm (good in places on chase course; 9.0)
Chase course rails moved in 7m reducing distances by about 30yds per circuit and hurdle rails moved in 10m reducing distances about 60yds per circuit.
Wind: Almost Nil Weather: Sunny but overcast

498 W+S RECYCLING NOVICES' H'CAP CHASE (15 fncs) 2m 5f 110y

6:20 (6:20) (Class 4) (0-115,117) 5-Y-O+ **£4,553** (£1,337; £668; £333)

Form RPR

4-21 **1** **Pilgrims Lane (IRE)**[12] 361 6-12-2 117 7ex PeterToole(3) 132+
(Milton Harris) *hld up in last: stdy prog 11th: led gng best 2 out: clr last: pushed out: readily* **6/1**[3]

4-34 **2** *4 ½* **Crow Spinney**[5] 443 7-10-11 98 MrOGreenall(3) 104
(Michael Easterby) *t.k.h: sn 2nd: led 11th: rdn and hdd 2 out: outpcd bef last where mstke* **6/1**[3]

464- **3** *6* **Distiller (IRE)**[75] 4608 6-11-9 107 PaddyBrennan 106
(Nigel Twiston-Davies) *pressed ldrs: rdn 11th: lost tch w ldng pair 2 out: plugged on* **5/1**[2]

4F-1 **4** *1 ½* **Take A Mile (IRE)**[19] 221 8-11-1 104 JimmyDerham(5) 104+
(Seamus Mullins) *hld up: dropped bk last and rdn 10th: plugged on fr 2 out: contested 3rd at last: one pce* **5/1**[2]

1P-0 **5** *1 ¾* **Sir Harry Cool**[17] 267 7-10-11 95 DavidEngland 92
(John Panvert) *midfield: mstke 3 out: struggling next: ev ch of 3rd whn mstke last* **25/1**

U04- **6** *22* **Uncle Eli (IRE)**[27] 4637 8-11-4 102 JackDoyle 76
(Richard Rowe) *mstke 3rd: j. slowly 4th: cl up tl 10th: dropped bk last and mstke 12th: sn wl bhd* **4/1**[1]

00-5 **7** *1* **Stratford Stroller (IRE)**[28] 86 6-11-10 108 (t) APMcCoy 81
(Jonjo O'Neill) *bhd: hit 9th: last whn mstke 11th: rdn and btn next* **14/1**

F33- **P** **Rudivale (IRE)**[90] 4296 8-10-7 91 JoeTizzard —
(Colin Tizzard) *led and t.k.h: hdd 11th: t.o 3 out: p.u last* **4/1**[1]

5m 0.40s (-14.60) **Going Correction** -0.525s/f (Firm) course record **8** Ran SP% **112.4**
Speed ratings: **105,103,101,100,100 92,91,—**
toteswingers:1&2:£9.90, 1&3:£4.00, 2&3:£4.20 CSF £40.15 CT £191.29 TOTE £6.90: £1.70, £3.90, £3.50; EX 51.60.
Owner Mrs D J Brown **Bred** J Mangan **Trained** Herridge, Wiltshire
⊠ Stewards' Enquiry : David England two-day ban: careless riding (Jun 11-12)

FOCUS

A run-of-the-mill 0-115 novice handicap chase run at an ordinary pace with most of the field holding some sort of chance four out.

NOTEBOOK

Pilgrims Lane(IRE), due to rise 10lb, won this as he liked carrying a 7lb penalty. He was held up well off the pace before making smooth progress in the back straight to take it up turning in, only having to be nudged clear. This was a fair effort under top weight but life will become more challenging off his new mark. (op 9-2)
Crow Spinney needs a quick surface and ran another satisfactory race with conditions to suit. He tracked the leader before taking the lead in the back straight but was fighting a losing battle with the winner and was soon brushed aside before pecking at the last. He should be capable of picking up a similar contest off this mark.
Distiller(IRE) looked to be potentially well handicapped after some modest efforts over fences after winning off a mark of 122 over hurdles. He struggled to hold his place in the back straight when the tempo increased and just stayed on from two out. (op 9-2 tchd 11-2)
Take A Mile(IRE) had the winner back in a close second when scoring at Plumpton on similar terms but, after losing his pitch when hampered going out on the final circuit, he could only stay on at the same pace. (op 4-1)
Sir Harry Cool jumped well enough on his second try over fences and had his chance but he is not the most consistent. (op 22-1)
Uncle Eli(IRE) looked well beforehand and was the subject of a gamble but his supporters knew their fate a fair way out as he dropped away tamely. (op 15-2 tchd 7-2)

499 HAPPY 60TH BIRTHDAY JONATHAN BOURNE HUNTERS' CHASE (12 fncs) 2m 1f 110y

6:50 (6:50) (Class 5) 6-Y-O+ **£2,498** (£774; £387; £193)

Form RPR

2-23 **1** **Ryeman**[17] 268 8-11-10 98 (vt) MrJoshuaGuerriero 107+
(Andrew Jackson) *prom: 2nd at 9th: led and edgd lft 2 out: 3 l clr and looked in command last: idled and rdn flat: fnd ex cl home* **4/1**[2]

/4-2 **2** *1 ¼* **Fairwood Present (IRE)**[15] 301 12-11-3 0 MrRJarrett(7) 102
(John Buxton) *chsd ldrs: effrt 11th: rdn and cl up whn impeded 2 out: wnt 2nd at last: r.o gamely flat but no ex fnl 100yds* **5/1**[3]

5U-4 **3** *5* **Walter De Wodeland**[24] 133 9-11-3 0 MissJBuck(7) 99+
(Miss J Du Plessis) *blnd 7th: mde most tl hdd 2 out: lost 2nd at last: fdd flat* **11/2**

43-1 **4** *10* **Emotional Article (IRE)**[15] 301 10-11-7 120 MrWKinsey(7) 91
(Mrs Belinda Clarke) *chsd ldrs: nt fluent 9th and outpcd: poor 6th 2 out: plugged on* **15/2**

0P-0 **5** *1 ¾* **Calgary Jock**[23] 148 9-11-3 0 MrHKinchin(7) 85
(Mrs J Marles) *blnd 4th: pressed ldrs: nt jump wl: losing tch whn mstke 3 out* **33/1**

/5-0 **6** *4* **Smart Boy Prince (IRE)**[23] 148 9-11-7 0 (p) MrTWeston(3) 81
(Miss C C Jones) *w ldr or cl 2nd tl rdn and fdd 2 out* **33/1**

22-6 **7** *39* **Good Company (IRE)**[19] 236 10-11-10 123 (b[1]) MrAJBerry 42
(Jonjo O'Neill) *mstkes and sn lost tch: nvr gng wl enough: struggling after 8th* **9/4**[1]

/PP- **8** *5* **Media Man (IRE)**[37] 5314 10-11-3 88 MrRWinks(7) 37
(P Winks) *hmpd 1st: nt jump wl in rr: t.o fr 7th* **33/1**

0/5- **9** *19* **Waziri (IRE)**[41] 9-11-7 0 MrDEdwards(3) 18
(A S T Holdsworth) *t.o fr 7th* **33/1**

00/P **10** *1 ¼* **Celtic Star (IRE)**[15] 297 12-11-3 0 (bt) L-BdrJSole(7) 17
(Miss J Wickens) *wl bhd whn mstke 4th: t.o fr 9th* **150/1**

53U- **11** *31* **Irish Stream (USA)**[20] 12-11-3 62 ReverendSBeveridge(7) —
(Mrs E Mitchell) *cl up tl 5th: struggling 8th: bdly t.o* **66/1**

P66- **F** **Made In France (FR)**[26] 10-11-3 70 .... MrJHooper(7) —
(Miss Helen Herrick) *sn lost tch: mstkes and rdr ungainly: hopelessly t.o whn crashing fall last* **100/1**

P/P- **U** **Borouj (IRE)**[5] 8-11-3 0 ....(p) MrJosephProctor(7) —
(Miss C D Richardson) *10th and tailing off whn blnd and uns rdr 11th* **66/1**

1F-4 **F** **Predateur (FR)**[15] 297 7-12-1 120 .... MrNSutton(7) —
(Giles Smyly) *fell heavily 1st* **10/1**

4m 3.00s (-4.10) **Going Correction** -0.525s/f (Firm) **14** Ran SP% **120.1**
Speed ratings: **88,87,85,80,80 78,60,58,50,49 35,—,—,—**
toteswingers:1&2:£5.30, 1&3:£5.10, 2&3:£6.80 CSF £23.79 TOTE £4.50: £1.40, £1.70, £2.90; EX 24.10.
Owner Denis Williams **Bred** D Williams **Trained** Witheridge, Devon

FOCUS
A modest hunter chase run at a decent pace.

NOTEBOOK
Ryeman had become difficult to win with, although he had run some fair races over varying trips, especially at Cheltenham in first-time blinkers over this trip. He travelled well before taking the lead turning in and had to be driven out when idling on the run-in before veering left nearing the finish. He holds few secrets but it might be worth chancing him in a handicap during the summer. (op 9-2 tchd 5-1)
Fairwood Present(IRE) had been in good form since returning from nearly a year off and once again performed with credit. He came through with an effort after two out and laid down a strong challenge when the winner idled after the last. He looked held when short of room near the finish. (op 17-2 tchd 9-1 and 9-2)
Walter De Wodeland had failed to get round or home over longer trips on three previous tries in hunter chases although he was travelling particularly well when unseating. Dropping back to this trip seemed to be ideal and he took them along at a decent clip before headed by the winner turning for home. He rallied well after the last when the winner idled until fading in the final 75 yards. (op 9-1)
Emotional Article(IRE) had beaten the runner-up at Ludlow but could never got competitive here. (op 11-2)
Smart Boy Prince(IRE) Official explanation: vet said gelding was struck into left-hind
Good Company(IRE), in first-time blinkers, was badly hampered at the first. (op 2-1 tchd 5-2)

500 BORDEAUX-UNDISCOVERED.CO.UK NOVICES' HURDLE (9 hdls) 2m 110y
7:20 (7:20) (Class 3) 4-Y-0+
£6,262 (£1,850; £925; £463; £231; £116)

Form RPR

3 **1** **Clear Sailing**[12] 356 7-10-12 0 .... DougieCostello 113+
(Ian Williams) *plld hrd: hld up: gng wl 3 out: clsd to ld and wnt lft next: sn drvn and racing idly: kpt on to maintain advantage after last* **9/1**

12- **2** 1 ¾ **Monetary Fund (USA)**[44] 5180 4-11-0 125 .... APMcCoy 113+
(Nicky Henderson) *prom: wnt 2nd at 5th: rdn and w ldr whn impeded 2 out: sltly outpcd and swtchd rt bef last: rallied to go 2nd cl home* **15/8**[1]

3-21 **3** ½ **Cool Touch (IRE)**[7] 428 7-11-4 118 .... PaddyBrennan 116
(Nigel Twiston-Davies) *pressed ldr tl led 4th: rdn and hdd 2 out: 2nd and one pce whn pckd last* **9/4**[2]

/P-1 **4** ½ **Den Maschine**[18] 250 5-11-4 0 .... TomO'Brien 115
(John Flint) *cl up: ev ch bef 2 out: hld after but kpt on wl fr last* **17/2**

152- **5** 1 ¼ **Action Impact (ARG)**[53] 5045 6-11-4 120 ....(b) JamieMoore 113
(Gary Moore) *pressed ldrs: rdn and ev ch bef 2 out: one pce bef last* **6/1**[3]

41-0 **6** 3 ¼ **I'm In The Pink (FR)**[6] 96 6-11-8 116 .... ChristianWilliams 114
(David Evans) *pressed ldrs: mstke 3 out: rdn and nt qckn fr next* **12/1**

06- **7** ¾ **Minneapolis**[39] 5278 5-10-12 0 .... LeightonAspell 103
(Alison Batchelor) *plld hrd in rr: nvr trbld ldrs but styng on nicely after last: promising* **33/1**

060- **8** 10 **Welcome Wonder**[43] 5199 6-10-0 0 .... MichaelMurphy(5) 86
(John Allen) *bhd: struggling 3 out* **100/1**

003- **9** 19 **Classic Bavard**[32] 15 8-10-12 0 ....(t) TomScudamore 74
(Hughie Morrison) *led and j.rt: hdd 4th: wknd and j. slowly 6th* **66/1**

10 dist **Frame And Cover**[25] 4-9-8 0 .... AnthonyFreeman(7) 18
(Joanna Davis) *j. bdly in rr: lost tch u.p 5th: bdly t.o* **300/1**

P **Savanna's Gold**[29] 6-10-0 0 .... JayPemberton(5) —
(Richard Rowe) *nt jump wl in rr: j. slowly 5th: t.o whn p.u 2 out* **250/1**

3m 48.5s (-7.50) **Going Correction** -0.25s/f (Good)
WFA 4 from 5yo+ 18lb **11** Ran SP% **114.2**
Speed ratings (Par 107): **107,106,105,105,105 103,103,98,89,68 —**
toteswingers:1&2:£5.60, 1&3:£6.00, 2&3:£1.80 CSF £26.42 TOTE £7.50: £1.80, £1.10, £1.70; EX 31.10.
Owner C Owen **Bred** Juddmonte Farms Ltd **Trained** Portway, Worcs

FOCUS
A fair novice hurdle run at a muddling pace resulting in six holding a good chance turning in.

NOTEBOOK
Clear Sailing won four claimers on the all-weather before making a promising start to his hurdling career. He was a little keen early on in the rear off this muddling pace but travelled sweetly tracking the leaders going to three out. He wandered about a little when laying down his challenge two out but had enough pace to hold the runner-up at bay after the last. His rider thought he got there plenty soon enough as he is not the most straightforward but felt he should be capable of following up under a penalty. (op 8-1)
Monetary Fund(USA) had taken well to hurdling, winning on his debut then runner-up to a respected rival last time. He had his chance going to two out before being caught a little flat-footed but ran on again from the last to regain second. The pace of the race would not have suited, so he could return to winning ways before long. (op 7-4)
Cool Touch(IRE) set the standard with a rating of 118 and ran a solid effort in defeat. Always racing prominently, he was sticking to his task well when hard-pressed, but a mistake when headed at the last was costly and he could not match the winners pace soon after. (op 11-4 tchd 2-1)
Den Maschine looked a good deal better than the grade when trouncing his rivals in a seller last time. This was a sound effort back in novice company and he should be capable of winning again. (op 9-1 tchd 10-1)
Action Impact(ARG) had blinkers re-fitted after failing to follow up his Plumpton success. He was keen in the midfield before making an effort after three out but could only stay on at the same pace from the next. (op 13-2 tchd 7-1)
I'm In The Pink(FR) has been performing creditably back on the Flat of late and again ran a sound race reverting to hurdles, but at the weights he was always going to find this a stiff task. (op 11-1 tchd 9-1)

501 IRISH THOROUGHBRED MARKETING H'CAP CHASE (20 fncs) 3m 4f
7:50 (7:50) (Class 3) (0-125,125) 5-Y-0 **£6,337** (£1,872; £936; £468; £234)

Form RPR

43-4 **1** **Dusty Dane (IRE)**[16] 274 8-10-0 106 ....(t) MarkQuinlan(7) 114
(Bill Turner) *chsd ldrs: clsd on ldng pair 10th: led 2 out: rdn and hld on gamely flat* **14/1**

30-1 **2** 1 ¼ **Shammy Buskins**[19] 229 8-10-12 111 ....(p) ChristianWilliams 118
(Lawney Hill) *bhd: rdn and outpcd 15th: 6th after 3 out: r.o strly after 2 out: wnt 2nd flat: too much to do* **9/2**[1]

4-23 **3** 3 ½ **Alexanderthegreat (IRE)**[7] 431 12-10-11 110 .... AidanColeman 114+
(Venetia Williams) *cl up in chsng gp: chal for ld 17th tl 2 out: kpt on gamely but no ex bef last: fin lame* **13/2**[3]

4-22 **4** 8 **Pairc Na Gcapall (IRE)**[19] 225 8-10-13 115 ....(p) AlexMerriam(3) 111
(Neil King) *sn led at fast pce: hdd 17th: sn drvn: dropped out qckly bef 2 out* **10/1**

102- **5** 5 **Petite Margot**[35] 5373 11-11-3 116 .... PaddyBrennan 106
(Nigel Twiston-Davies) *j. slowly in rr: rdn and struggling 15th* **15/2**

P41- **6** 4 ½ **Triggernometry**[31] 38 9-10-12 111 ....(bt) JoeTizzard 97
(Colin Tizzard) *towards rr: mstke 16th: rallied briefly: rdn and sn wknd* **16/1**

211- **7** 11 **Painter Man (FR)**[40] 5257 8-11-7 120 ....(bt) TomScudamore 98
(David Pipe) *led tl 1st: sn chsng clr ldng pair: clsd 10th: rdn 17th: ev ch 2 out: drvn and fdd between last two* **5/1**[2]

UP0- **P** **King Harald (IRE)**[75] 4619 12-11-6 119 .... MattieBatchelor —
(Mark Bradstock) *prom v briefly: sn making mstkes and nt keen in rr: lost tch 6th: t.o and p.u 12th* **22/1**

0P-0 **F** **Seymar Lad (IRE)**[15] 300 10-11-12 125 ....(p) JackDoyle —
(Emma Lavelle) *blnd bdly 1st: fell 2nd* **28/1**

PP5/ **P** **What A Scientist (IRE)**[406] 5068 10-10-2 106 ..... SamTwiston-Davies(5) —
(Nigel Twiston-Davies) *mstkes 1st and 3rd: nvr gng wl: rdn 6th: t.o and p.u 11th* **9/1**

41-3 **P** **Grenoli (FR)**[23] 158 9-9-10 102 ....(bt) JoeCornwall(7) —
(John Cornwall) *pressed ldr at fast pce and clr of rest tl 9th: lost 2nd bef 17th: fdd rapidly: t.o and p.u after 2 out* **18/1**

25-4 **F** **Our Jim**[12] 352 8-10-8 110 .... AdrianLane(3) —
(Donald McCain) *fell 1st* **13/2**[3]

6m 44.2s (-18.80) **Going Correction** -0.525s/f (Firm) course record **12** Ran SP% **118.0**
Speed ratings: **105,104,103,101,99 98,95,—,—,— —,—**
toteswingers:1&2:£41.50, 1&3:£36.70, 2&3:£6.90 CSF £77.65 CT £459.98 TOTE £28.10: £4.60, £1.50, £2.70; EX 134.20.
Owner E A Brook **Bred** Martin Moloney **Trained** Sigwells, Somerset

FOCUS
An ordinary 0-125 staying chase with the front three receiving a bit of a fright on the home bend when a loose horse crashed through the rails.

NOTEBOOK
Dusty Dane(IRE) has been beaten in sellers and claimers over hurdles recently. He was the last of the principals to come under pressure and stayed on stoutly when taking the lead going to the last. It's difficult to gauge the performance and, although this was his best success to date, he does not possess the strongest of profiles. (op 12-1)
Shammy Buskins confirmed his placing with the third on 7lb worse terms but ran a strange sort of race. He was under pressure and making no in-roads from the midfield from the beginning of the back straight. He then stayed on strongly going to the last to go second on the run to the line, but it was all too late as he was never going to reel in the winner. (op 13-2 tchd 4-1)
Alexanderthegreat(IRE) ran another solid race in defeat and, after taking the lead after three out, never gave best under strong driving until going to the last. He is in good form and slipping to a reasonable mark after failing to win for three years, but unfortunately finished lame. Official explanation: vet said gelding pulled up lame (op 17-2)
Pairc Na Gcapall(IRE) had shaped better since cheekpieces were applied and this was another good effort. He vied for the lead for much of the way but was beginning to tire when hampered by the loose horse on the home bend. (op 11-1)
Petite Margot ran in snatches towards the rear although she did stay on past beaten horses going to the last but was never going to catch the leaders. (tchd 8-1)
Triggernometry was under pressure a long way out which caused some untidy jumping, but he was a spent force on the home bend.
Painter Man(FR) folded tamely after holding every chance two out. (op 4-1)
What A Scientist(IRE) Official explanation: jockey said gelding was unsuited by the good to firm (good in places) ground

502 POINTTOPOINT.CO.UK CHAMPION NOVICES' HUNTERS' CHASE (FOR THE JOHN CORBET CUP) (20 fncs) 3m 4f
8:20 (8:21) (Class 2) 5-Y-0+
£12,004 (£3,750; £1,874; £938; £468; £236)

Form RPR

4P-5 **1** **Hemington**[19] 218 7-11-10 95 .... MrTWeston 108+
(Michael Scudamore) *cl up: 2 l 3rd 2 out: rdn to chal last: lft in ld and r.o wl: cosily* **28/1**

4-1 **2** 2 ¼ **Bradley**[23] 150 6-11-10 0 .... MrMWall 106
(F M O'Brien) *hld up: prog 11th: hrd drvn bef 17th: nt fluent next: one l 2nd 2 out: drvn to chal and ev ch last: wnt lft flat: r.o u.p but a hld* **7/2**[2]

P2/1 **3** 12 **More Trouble (IRE)**[15] 294 9-11-10 0 ....(b) MrJETudor 97+
(Alan Hill) *nt a fluent: bhd early: prog 12th: mstkes 14th and 17th: 10 l 4th and btn 2 out: lft 3rd at last* **16/1**

/32- **4** 1 ½ **Minsgill Mans**[13] 12-11-10 98 .... MrJFMathias 93
(J W Tudor) *prom: lost pl 9th: n.d fr 13th: lft poor 4th at last* **33/1**

5P-3 **5** 34 **Pastek (FR)**[13] 335 7-11-10 78 .... MissCLBrown 59
(Martin Peaty) *a bhd: no ch fr 13th: t.o* **50/1**

163- **6** 14 **Penny Doc (IRE)**[35] 5369 9-11-10 115 .... MrPYork 45
(P York) *bhd: v bdly hmpd 12th: no ch after: t.o* **15/2**

50-1 **7** 2 ¾ **Apollo Blaze (IRE)**[22] 173 9-11-10 95 .... MissJBuck 42
(Mrs P J Shaw) *a bhd: no ch fr 13th: mstke 17th: t.o* **22/1**

11-2 **F** **Lisadell King (IRE)**[14] 317 10-11-10 114 .... MrGMaundrell 108+
(G C Maundrell) *hld up: hdwy 9th: led 16th: rdr adjsting goggles between last two: jnd and fell last* **4/1**[3]

2 **P** **The Camerengo (IRE)**[15] 295 10-11-10 0 ....(b) AdamWedge —
(A R Corbett) *mstke 3rd: reminder 4th: chsd ldrs to 12th: nt run on: p.u 15th* **28/1**

PP/2 **P** **Springfield Dante**[28] 79 9-11-10 0 .... MrJoshuaGuerriero —
(Nick Kent) *last whn p.u 12th: lame* **25/1**

/2-1 **F** **Teeton Bollinger**[15] 295 9-11-10 0 ....(p) MrNPearce —
(Mrs Joan Tice) *prom: 4th and gng strly at 11th: fell next* **14/1**

0PF- **P** **Royal Tender (IRE)**[12] 6-11-3 56 ....(p) MrDMansell —
(Dai Williams) *led tl 5th: lft in ld 10th tl 15th: lost pl rapidly: p.u 2 out* **100/1**

3- **P** **Good Egg (IRE)**[37] 5325 7-11-10 0 .... MrCMMurphy —
(Lady J Fowler, Ire) *sn bhd: t.o and p.u 17th* **11/4**[1]

50-1 **P** **Glacial Call (IRE)**[24] 133 7-11-3 0 ....(b) MrRHawkins —
(Mrs N Frost) *led 5th tl blnd 10th: led again 15th tl 16th: 4th and wkng whn j. bdly rt 2 out: t.o and p.u last* **20/1**

6m 55.8s (-7.20) **Going Correction** -0.525s/f (Firm) **14** Ran SP% **118.9**
Speed ratings: **89,88,84,84,74 70,70,—,—,— —,—,—,—**
toteswingers:1&2 £31.00, 1&3 £21.30, 2&3 £7.10 CSF £118.79 TOTE £35.10: £6.20, £2.10, £5.30; EX 89.20.

Owner Horse Passport Agency Racing **Bred** Andrew And Mrs S R B Davis **Trained** Bromsash, Herefordshire

FOCUS

A well-contested competitive championship novice hunter chase run at a true pace with some promising types, but it lost a bit of its lustre with the withdraw of probable favourite Horsham Lad.

NOTEBOOK

Hemington had been third in this race last season with his rider believing he would be a stronger horse with another year on his back and that proved to be the case. He was laying down a strong challenge when left in the lead at the last but had to be driven out to hold on. Reported not to have come down the hill in handicap company last time at Plumpton and not unfancied by connections returning here, he's only a seven-year-old so still has scope for improvement. (op 20-1)

Bradley stays very well which stood him in good stead when scoring at Cheltenham last time. He was a little untidy at the tenth and was soon being niggled along to hold his place before the rider becoming more aggressive turning out on the final circuit. To his credit, he stuck to his task well and was left with every chance at the last but drifted to his left just failing to collar the winner. Official explanation: vet said gelding finished lame (op 5-1 tchd 3-1)

More Trouble(IRE) opened his account in hunter chases at Folkestone last time after a successful time in points. An early mistake did not help his cause but he could never get on terms with the leaders. (op 12-1)

Minsgill Mans is a fair performer in points but has struggled to open his account in hunter chases and this was stiff task for him to do so. He put up a fair effort but never threatened the principals. (op 22-1 tchd 20-1)

Lisadell King(IRE) has had a very good season and is a very likeable sort so it was unfortunate to see him crash out at the last when still holding a narrow advantage. (op 11-2)

Springfield Dante Official explanation: jockey said gelding pulled up lame; vet said gelding bled from the nose (op 11-2)

503 JENKINSONS CATERERS H'CAP HURDLE (14 hdls) 3m 3f

8:50 (8:50) (Class 3) (0-135,132) 4-Y-0+ **£5,204** (£1,528; £764; £381)

Form RPR

43-4 **1** **Midas Way**^{24} [131] 10-11-0 **120** (p) PaddyBrennan 124+
(Patrick Chamings) *trckd ldrs: led bef 11th: clr appr 2 out: idled flat and rdn out: a doing enough* **12/1**

2U-0 **2** *2 ½* **The Real Deal (IRE)**^{11} [372] 9-11-1 **121** DarylJacob 120
(Nick Williams) *trckd ldrs: rdn to chse wnr bef 2 out: kpt on but a hld* **14/1**

P-06 **3** *2 ¾* **Barnhill Brownie (IRE)**^{15} [302] 7-10-9 **115** TomO'Brien 111
(Philip Hobbs) *pressed ldrs: rdn 3 out: one pce fr next* **25/1**

6-11 **4** *nk* **Lyster (IRE)**^{3} [467] 11-9-11 **99** 14ex LeeStephens(3) 104+
(David Evans) *hld up in rr but wl in tch: effrt to midfield whn blnd 3 out: sn drvn and n.d after* **9/2**^{2}

P0-4 **5** *4 ½* **Russian Song (IRE)**^{17} [266] 6-10-1 **107** TomScudamore 99
(Colin Tizzard) *trckd ldrs: effrt 3 out: chsd wnr briefly bef next: nt run on* **6/1**^{3}

40-S **6** *nk* **Kristoffersen**^{15} [302] 10-10-0 **106** WillKennedy 97
(Helen Nelmes) *bhd: 8 l last and rdn after 9th: n.d after 3 out* **20/1**

001- **7** *¾* **Ouzbeck (FR)**^{44} [5181] 8-11-12 **132** JackDoyle 122
(Emma Lavelle) *settled towards rr: bandage flapping off fr 10th: in tch tl rdn and wknd after 3 out* **13/2**

3P-3 **8** *1 ¾* **Cold Mountain (IRE)**^{24} [131] 8-10-4 **115** JimmyDerham(5) 104
(Seamus Mullins) *in tch tl rdn 10th: sn struggling* **14/1**

6-45 **9** *91* **Elusive Muse**^{15} [302] 4-10-3 **115** RichardJohnson —
(Alison Thorpe) *plld hrd: led 4th tl hdd bef 11th: wknd bef 2 out and sn virtually p.u* **3/1**^{1}

P22- **F** **Irish Legend (IRE)**^{11} [21] 10-10-4 **115** SamTwiston-Davies(5) —
(Bernard Llewellyn) *hld up: trcking ldrs whn fell 8th: fatally injured* **16/1**

30-0 **F** **Giovanna**^{21} [193] 9-11-0 **120** RobertThornton —
(Richard Phillips) *prom tl fell 7th* **8/1**

400- **P** **Horseford Hill**^{223} [1519] 6-10-9 **115** SamThomas —
(Miss J R Tooth) *in tch tl dropped bk last and rdn 10th: t.o and p.u after 3 out* **50/1**

6m 23.1s (-5.50) **Going Correction** -0.25s/f (Good)
WFA 4 from 6yo+ 20lb **12** Ran SP% **119.4**
Speed ratings (Par 107): **98,97,96,96,95 94,94,94,67,—,—,—**
toteswingers:1&2 £27.40, 1&3 £25.80, 2&3 £33.10 CSF £162.38 CT £4086.58 TOTE £15.20: £3.50, £4.70, £10.20; EX 145.30 Place 6 £509.77; Place 5 £189.04.

Owner Mrs Alexandra J Chandris **Bred** Mrs J Chandris **Trained** Baughurst, Hants

FOCUS

A competitive, if modest, handicap hurdle with plenty coming here off the back of decent runs run at an ordinary pace.

NOTEBOOK

Midas Way raced prominently throughout before taking a definite advantage after three out and had the race in the bag when hitting two out. He finished third in this heat last year and had shown he was in good order with some fair placed efforts of late, so he was entitled to figure here. It will get harder once he is reassessed as he has never won off a mark higher than his current one. (op 11-1)

The Real Deal(IRE) is better known as a staying chaser but has been trying his luck over hurdles of late. This was a sound enough performance and he stayed on well enough but is fairly exposed.

Barnhill Brownie(IRE) has been disappointing since a promising start to his career and was another that could only stay on at the same pace. (tchd 28-1)

Lyster(IRE) had bounced right back to form winning his last two starts but struggled to get involved under his double penalty. (op 7-2)

Russian Song(IRE) had shown a bit more than previous hurdling experience when fourth last time. He had his chance going to three out before his effort flattened. (op 9-1)

T/Plt: £1,634.50 to a £1 stake. Pool:£94,672.07 - 42.28 winning tickets T/Qpdt: £163.90 to a £1 stake. Pool:£6,224.70 - 28.10 winning tickets IM

504 - 513a (Foreign Racing) - See Raceform Interactive

CARTMEL (L-H)

Saturday, May 29

OFFICIAL GOING: Good

Wind: light 1/2 against Weather: raining

514 COUNTRY REFRESHMENTS NOVICES' HURDLE (11 hdls) 2m 6f

6:00 (6:00) (Class 4) 4-Y-0+ **£2,927** (£859; £429; £214)

Form RPR

42-1 **1** **Identity Parade (IRE)**^{20} [223] 6-10-9 113 AdrianLane(3) 105
(Donald McCain) *mde all: hrd rdn run-in: all out* **9/4**^{1}

06-6 **2** *nk* **Stand Clear**^{22} [191] 5-10-5 0 GrahamLee 98
(Ferdy Murphy) *hld up in rr: gd hdwy after 3 out: chal last: no ex towards fin* **8/1**

F4-2 **3** *6* **Woodmore (IRE)**^{20} [223] 6-10-12 110 KeithMercer 99
(Steve Gollings) *chsd wnr: styd on same pce run-in* **5/1**^{3}

4 *4 ½* **Nobetter Buachaill (IRE)**^{367} [508] 8-10-5 0 EJO'Connell(7) 95
(J J Lambe, Ire) *hld up: hdwy after 3 out: kpt on run-in* **40/1**

3/P- **5** *shd* **Atlantic Coast (IRE)**^{389} [161] 6-10-12 110 (b) TomO'Brien 96
(Peter Bowen) *chsd ldrs: 4th and one pce whn mstke last* **14/1**

23-1 **6** *5* **Oursininlaw (IRE)**^{25} [137] 6-11-2 109 DPFahy(3) 100
(Evan Williams) *chsd ldrs: 6th and wkng whn mstke last* **5/2**^{2}

P-52 **7** *4* **Stolen Moments (FR)**^{2} [492] 9-10-12 110 PaddyAspell 87
(James Moffatt) *in rr: hdwy 8th: lost pl 2 out* **11/2**

P **8** *8* **Osbaldeston (IRE)**^{17} [289] 7-10-12 0 WilsonRenwick 80
(Rose Dobbin) *in rr: hdwy 7th: wknd 2 out: bhd whn mstke last* **66/1**

06- **9** *61* **Fifth Sea Lord (IRE)**^{46} [5179] 5-10-7 0 LeeEdwards(5) 25
(Tom Gretton) *t.k.h: trckd ldrs: wkng whn mstke 3 out: hit 2 out: sn t.o* **100/1**

P- **P** **Rahood (IRE)**^{26} 8-10-5 0 (p) MrMGarnett(7) —
(F Jestin) *nt fluent: chsd ldrs: lost pl 6th: t.o whn p.u after 8th* **150/1**

5m 25.8s (-3.50) **Going Correction** -0.075s/f (Good) **10** Ran SP% **114.8**
Speed ratings (Par 105): **103,102,100,99,99 97,95,92,70,—**
toteswingers:1&2:£5.70, 1&3:£4.30, 2&3:£5.60 CSF £20.55 TOTE £3.10: £1.10, £3.00, £1.10; EX 18.70.

Owner Racegoers Club Owners Group **Bred** Mrs M Doran **Trained** Cholmondeley, Cheshire

FOCUS

This was not a bad novice hurdle for the time of year, although it lacked depth. The winner and fourth are rated to their marks.

NOTEBOOK

Identity Parade(IRE) had been progressing with each run, winning at Uttoxeter last time out, and was well supported. She broke quickly and made all, jumping nicely throughout. She came under pressure turning into the home straight, but battled on gamely and was always holding the runner-up. (op 11-4 tchd 2-1)

Stand Clear, not disgraced when sixth at Aintree three weeks previously, was stepping up in trip and saw it out well. Held up in rear early on, she began to makle progress approaching the third-last and jumped the next in fourth. She did her utmost to overhaul the winner and can't be faulted for effort, but was just unable to get alongside in the closing stages. (op 7-1)

Woodmore(IRE), successful in an Irish bumper, had finished an encouraging 8l second behind the winner at Uttoxeter on his most recent outing and, better off at the weights, got a little closer here. He was always prominent, but could not muster the pace of the first two from the final flight. (op 6-1)

Nobetter Buachaill(IRE), having his first run for a new stable, showed his first real glimpse of form. Nobody should get too excited about what he achieved but, having been held up for much of the race, he was closest at the finish. (op 28-1)

Atlantic Coast(IRE), who showed promise in two starts in 2008-09, was returning from a 389-day layoff and ran as if the race might bring him on. He was third two out, having been towards the front for much of the journey, but faded in the closing stages. (op 15-2)

Oursininlaw(IRE), who scored at Fakenham 25 days previously, had a 7lb penalty for that win and never looked like shrugging it off. He was never closer than third and lost three places from the third-last. (op 11-4)

515 ROOFING CONSULTANTS LTD (S) HURDLE (8 hdls) 2m 1f 110y

6:30 (6:30) (Class 5) 4-Y-0+ **£1,951** (£573; £286; £143)

Form RPR

04-1 **1** **Dunaskin (IRE)**^{21} [210] 10-11-4 120 (b) PaddyAspell 112+
(Richard Guest) *chsd ldr: dropped bk 3 out: hit next: 5th last: styd on wl to ld last 75yds* **7/2**^{1}

100- **2** *2 ¾* **Lets Go Girls**^{102} [4096] 6-10-5 95 GrahamLee 95
(James Moffatt) *chsd ldrs: led 1f out: hdd and no ex fnl 75yds* **9/1**

50-0 **3** *3* **Danny Zuko (IRE)**^{28} [96] 7-10-9 105 (p) AdrianLane(3) 99
(Donald McCain) *chsd ldrs: led 3 out: hdd between last 2: led last: hdd 1f out: kpt on same pce* **5/1**^{3}

04-5 **4** *1 ¼* **Woody Valentine (USA)**^{28} [87] 9-10-12 111 TjadeCollier 99
(Evelyn Slack) *chsd ldrs: rdn 5th: outpcd 2 out: handy 6th whn hit last: kpt on to take 4th nr fin* **10/1**

53-5 **5** *1* **Josephine Malines**^{21} [210] 6-10-5 98 KeithMercer 90
(Ann Duffield) *led to 3 out: led between last 2: hdd last: sn hmpd: fdd fnl 150yds* **8/1**

364- **6** *6* **Turbo Shandy**^{51} [4614] 7-10-12 90 ChristianWilliams 92
(Dai Burchell) *in rr: hdwy 5th: sn chsng ldrs: wknd run-in* **9/1**

20-6 **7** *7* **Calculaite**^{17} [290] 9-10-12 110 DenisO'Regan 86
(Martin Todhunter) *towards rr: hdwy to chse ldrs 3 out: wknd between last 2* **8/1**

26-0 **8** *14* **Three Ships**^{24} [159] 9-10-9 97 CharlieHuxley(3) 73
(S Wynne) *in rr: hdwy 4th: rdn and outpcd whn hit next: sn bhd* **16/1**

30R- **R** **Sacrilege**^{5} [3601] 5-10-7 125 (b) PaulCallaghan(5) —
(Michael Chapman) *slowly away: reluctant and nt fluent in last: t.o 2nd: ref to r after 4th* **4/1**^{2}

4m 7.70s (-5.50) **Going Correction** -0.075s/f (Good) **9** Ran SP% **116.1**
Speed ratings (Par 103): **109,107,106,105,105 102,99,93,—**
toteswingers:1&2:£6.70, 1&3:£3.10, 2&3:£5.10 CSF £35.31 TOTE £4.10: £2.00, £2.10, £2.40; EX 36.90.There was no bid for the winner.

Owner Miss Alison Ibbotson **Bred** J P And Miss M Mangan **Trained** Stainforth, S Yorks

FOCUS

Better than many sellers and competitive on paper. The winner is rated a stone off his best.

NOTEBOOK

Dunaskin(IRE), a course winner last year and successful at this level at Hexham on his last start, overcame a serious mistake to score. Keen early on, he raced in second for much of the journey and was arguably going best three out. However, he clouted that hurdle hard and dropped back quickly, apparently having lost his chance. Somehow he recovered the lost ground and made powerful progress to get back into contention at the final flight, from where he quickened up smartly to grab the lead 100 yards from the post. (op 3-1 tchd 4-1)

Lets Go Girls, a winner at Wetherby in December but disappointing since, posted much her best performance of this year. Always in the leading group, she stayed on well in the closing stages. (op 8-1)

Danny Zuko(IRE), without a victory since the 2008-09 season, was fitted with cheekpieces for his first run in selling company and they seemed to help. He was never far off the pace and went into third at the third-last. He could not find much under pressure from the next, but this was not a bad effort. (op 6-1)

Woody Valentine(USA), successful three times at this level, was slightly disappointing. Backed at double-figure odds beforehand, he was never in contention after racing in midfield for much of the contest. (op 14-1)

Josephine Malines, a course and distance winner in 2009, set out to make all, but was overtaken at the third-last. She briefly regained the lead when the winner made his error, but was comprehensively outpaced in the closing stages.

Turbo Shandy lined up with a 0-16 record over hurdles and,although he made progress to get to the heels of the leaders two from home, he did not look likely to break his losing sequence.

516 BURLINGTON STONE H'CAP CHASE (14 fncs) 2m 5f 110y
7:00 (7:00) (Class 4) (0-100,100) 5-Y-0+ **£3,903** (£1,146; £573; £286)

Form				RPR
44-2	**1**		**Shulmin**[21] 211 10-10-0 **74** oh8 ... PeterBuchanan (Carol Ferguson) *in rr: hdwy to chse ldrs 8th: led appr last: styd on wl* **6/1**[3]	91+
F-24	**2**	*7*	**Emotive**[17] 287 7-11-0 **91** ... CampbellGillies(3) (Barry Murtagh) *in rr: hdwy 9th: wnt 2nd over 1f out: no imp* **11/2**[2]	103
6-04	**3**	*9*	**Crofton Arch**[10] 404 10-10-0 **74** oh10 ... (p) PaddyAspell (John Dixon) *led after 2nd: hdd 4 out: one pce between last 2* **25/1**	77
45-4	**4**	*6*	**Sycho Fred (IRE)**[24] 158 9-10-7 **81** ... (t) KeithMercer (Mike Sowersby) *chsd ldrs: one pce fr 3 out* **11/2**[2]	79
33-1	**5**	*2¾*	**Storm Surge (IRE)**[23] 177 7-11-12 **100** ... DenisO'Regan (Martin Todhunter) *trckd ldrs: wnt 2nd sn after last: wknd over 1f out* **5/2**[1]	95
44-2	**6**	*1¼*	**Peak Seasons (IRE)**[25] 136 7-9-8 **75** ... StevenGagan(7) (Michael Chapman) *led tl after 2nd: w ldr: led 11th: hdd appr last: hung rt and wknd fnl 2f* **11/2**[2]	70
23P-	**7**	*26*	**Corporation (IRE)**[6] 453 6-11-5 **100** ... (p) EJO'Connell(7) (J J Lambe, Ire) *in rr: hdwy and prom 8th: lost pl 10th: sn bhd* **15/2**	71
0-3F	**F**		**Winged Farasi**[10] 403 6-11-7 **95** ... TjadeCollier (Joanne Foster) *nt jump wl in rr: hdwy 8th: wknd 10th: t.o 3 out: fell last* **12/1**	—

5m 16.0s (-9.40) **Going Correction** -0.30s/f (Good) **8** Ran SP% **112.3**
Speed ratings: **105,102,99,97,96 95,86,—**
toteswingers:1&2:£5.40, 1&3:£21.10, 2&3:£34.00 CSF £37.57 CT £757.50 TOTE £5.00: £1.30, £3.40, £8.10; EX 23.40.
Owner F S Storey **Bred** J Wade **Trained** Dalston, Cumbria

FOCUS
A modest event, with the top weight rated 100. Pretty solid form.

NOTEBOOK
Shulmin, second at Hexham three weeks previously, was racing from 8lb out of the handicap, but comfortably overcame that apparent disadvantage. In rear early on, she made progress mid-race and was fourth approaching the third-last. She jumped into second at that fence, took the lead at the last and stayed on well up the long run-in. She is sure to take a hefty hit from the handicapper, but appears to be improving. (tchd 5-1)
Emotive, whose two previous efforts this month had been solid enough and who is rated 91, seems a plausible yardstick for the form. Ridden patiently, he made good progress from the final fence and was the only one to mount a serious challenge to the winner in the closing stages. (tchd 5-1)
Crofton Arch, whose only career victory came over course and distance, again showed his liking for the track. Racing from 10lb out of the handicap, he disputed the lead from the outset and, despite being overtaken at the third-last, kept battling away.\n\x\x , whose only career victory came over course and distance, again showed his liking for the track. Racing from 10lb out of the handicap, he disputed the lead from the outset and, despite being overtaken at the third-last, kept battling away. (op 20-1)
Sycho Fred(IRE), back on the same mark as when scoring at Catterick in December, ran his best race since. Always chasing the pace, he stuck to his guns even after the winner surged away. (op 7-1 tchd 15-2)
Storm Surge(IRE), successful over 2m at Wetherby 23 days previously, was 2lb higher for this step up in trip and the combination seemed to find him out. He disputed third for much of the race, but weakened quickly from the final fence.
Peak Seasons(IRE), a course winner over hurdles, had been raised 4lb for finishing second in this discipline on his most recent start and the extra weight proved too much on this occasion. He disputed the lead until the final fence, but dropped away tamely from that point. (op 6-1)

517 STICKY TOFFEE PUDDING INTERMEDIATE H'CAP CHASE (18 fncs) 3m 2f
7:35 (7:35) (Class 5) (0-95,95) 5-Y-0+ **£3,252** (£955; £477; £238)

Form				RPR
56-	**1**		**Volcanic Rock (IRE)**[37] 5347 10-11-10 **93** ... MrDerekO'Connor (John Anthony Staunton, Ire) *hld up in rr: stdy hdwy 12th: jnd ldrs gng wl 2 out: led 2f out: shkn up and wnt clr 1f out: easily* **7/2**[1]	105+
31P-	**2**	*8*	**Onthegoagain (IRE)**[26] 117 9-11-8 **91** ... DenisO'Regan (J J Lambe, Ire) *hld up: hdwy to trck ldrs 9th: led 2 out: hdd and readily outpcd by wnr run-in* **6/1**[3]	94+
FP-6	**3**	*16*	**The Artful Fox**[21] 211 9-9-7 **69** oh5 ... HenryBrooke(7) (Mike Sowersby) *prom: outpcd 11th: rallied 13th: one pce fr 2 out* **11/1**	56
U6-U	**4**	*6*	**Gershwinner (IRE)**[19] 251 7-11-9 **95** ... (b) AdrianLane(3) (Donald McCain) *w ldrs: 6th and wkng whn blnd last* **6/1**[3]	75
F60-	**5**	*7*	**Bathwick Breeze**[280] 1286 6-11-12 **95** ... (b) TomScudamore (David Pipe) *chsd ldrs: hit 10th: wknd appr last* **9/1**	72
611-	**6**	*39*	**Copper's Gold (IRE)**[40] 5272 6-11-12 **95** ... (b) PeterBuchanan (Lucinda Russell) *led: hdd 2 out: wknd qckly sn after last: t.o* **4/1**[2]	34
PP-0	**7**	*11*	**Sierra Peak (IRE)**[24] 160 6-10-11 **80** ... JamesReveley (Martin Todhunter) *in rr: hdwy and prom 9th: lost pl 14th: sn bhd* **33/1**	9
5P-5	**8**	*68*	**Sam Cruise**[11] 383 9-11-0 **83** ... (t) ChristianWilliams (Steve Gollings) *w ldr: blnd 5th: hit 12th: lost pl 14th: sn t.o: virtually p.u run-in* **12/1**	—
2-PP	**P**		**Benny The Piler (IRE)**[10] 405 10-11-7 **90** ... (p) BrianHughes (Carol Ferguson) *prom: blnd 6th: bhd 9th: t.o whn p.u bef 13th* **20/1**	—
0P-F	**P**		**Dunbrody House**[25] 136 6-11-7 **90** ... (p) TomO'Brien (Peter Bowen) *nt fluent in rr: bhd fr 12th: t.o whn p.u after 14th* **9/1**	—

6m 34.4s (-0.50) **Going Correction** -0.30s/f (Good) **10** Ran SP% **114.5**
Speed ratings: **88,85,80,78,76 64,61,40,—,—**
toteswingers:1&2:£5.70, 1&3:£9.50, 2&3:£15.00 CSF £24.89 CT £207.38 TOTE £4.60: £1.70, £1.40, £3.00; EX 25.60.
Owner P T McNamara **Bred** Mrs Karen A Sinnott **Trained** Tubber, Co. Galway

FOCUS
A poor contest, the top weight being rated just 95, and several looked seriously out of form. The winner is rated in line with his best Irish form.

NOTEBOOK
Volcanic Rock(IRE), still a maiden under rules, had shown promise when sixth in Punchestown's La Touche Cup on his latest start and was well backed beforehand. Ridden patiently, he was out the back in the early stages and did not start to make ground until approaching the third-last. He went into third at the next, moved up a place at the last and then quickened decisively. Pushed out with hands and heels, he won easily and seems sure to take a big hike from the handicapper, so connections may want to get him out again quickly under a penalty. (op 6-1)
Onthegoagain(IRE), a winner on his latest start over fences, had twice disappointed over hurdles subsequently. Back in his favoured discipline, he showed a lot more, easing into contention approaching three out and hitting the front at the final fence. He could not match the winner, but still ran a cracker. (op 7-1 tchd 5-1)
The Artful Fox, racing from 5lb out of the handicap, also performed with credit, although he never threatened the first two. In midfield for most of the race, he stayed on in the closing stages. (op 14-1 tchd 10-1)
Gershwinner(IRE), beaten only three-quarters of a length in this race a year earlier, was 9lb lower this time around but failed to take advantage. He raced in second for a long way, still holding that position approaching two out, but could not sustain his effort. (op 9-2)
Bathwick Breeze had fallen on his only previous start over fences and made more than one mistake here. His two worst errors came at the tenth and 11th and they obviously took their toll, as he faded in the closing stages. (op 6-1)
Copper's Gold(IRE), successful at Musselburgh and Hexham on his last two starts, had seemed to be progressing. He has taken a couple of hits from the handicapper lately, though, and they appear to have left him vulnerable. Official explanation: trainer had no explanation for the poor form shown (tchd 7-2)

518 ROYAL OAK INN NOVICES' CHASE (12 fncs) 2m 1f 110y
8:10 (8:10) (Class 4) 5-Y-0+ **£3,252** (£955; £477; £238)

Form				RPR
020-	**1**		**Thumbs Up**[49] 5128 5-10-12 0 ... GrahamLee (Donald McCain) *set slow pce: hdd after 2nd: hdd 4th: trckd ldr: hit last: led 2f out: rdn rt out* **6/4**[2]	119+
0-01	**2**	*¾*	**Mutual Friend (USA)**[9] 422 6-11-5 135 ... (b) TomScudamore (David Pipe) *led 4th: qcknd 7th: hdd 2f out: rallied fnl 150yds: a being hld* **6/5**[1]	125+
162-	**3**	*6*	**Watch Out**[41] 5258 6-10-12 0 ... (tp) ChristianWilliams (Dai Burchell) *hld up: chsd ldrs 9th: wnt 3rd sn after last: one pce fnl 2f* **16/1**	112
PP-3	**4**	*24*	**Springfield Raki**[13] 351 6-10-12 0 ... KeithMercer (Steve Gollings) *nt fluent: j. slowly 2nd: sn led: j. slowly and hdd next: lost pl 7th: sn bhd* **6/1**[3]	88
05/	**5**	*53*	**James Caird (IRE)**[1001] 1320 10-10-5 0 ... SClements(7) (J Clements, Ire) *hit 1st: trckd ldrs: outpcd 3 out: wknd qckly sn after last: t.o: virtually p.u* **40/1**	58

4m 53.4s (34.50) **Going Correction** -0.30s/f (Good) **5** Ran SP% **108.1**
Speed ratings: **11,10,8,—,—**
CSF £3.71 TOTE £2.30: £1.10, £1.70; EX 4.40.
Owner T G Leslie **Bred** London Thoroughbred Services Ltd **Trained** Cholmondeley, Cheshire

FOCUS
A disappointing turnout numerically and run at an absurdly slow early pace. The rating is limited by the proximity of the third.

NOTEBOOK
Thumbs Up, successful three times over hurdles last season and rated 127 in that sphere, was making his chasing debut and jumped well enough. He did make a mistake at the last, but it barely checked his momentum and, once he quickened off the home turn, victory was assured. He has been waiting for some time to try fences, with connections keen to find a sharp 2m for him. Given the right track, he should score again. (op 2-1 tchd 11-4)
Mutual Friend(USA) is not altogether straightforward, but his smooth victory at Wetherby nine days previously had earned him an official mark of 135, which set a fair standard for the others to aim at. He probably did not run to his best, however, as he was obliged to make more of the running than is ideal and, after jumping the last in front, was soon headed by the winner. He tried to fight back on the long run-in, but never looked likely to regain the advantage. (op 8-11 tchd 4-6)
Watch Out, winner of a handicap hurdle from a mark of 80 in March, was handed a tough test on this switch to fences and his presence in third underlines the dubious nature of the form. He was last for much of the race, but made progress from three out and stayed on far better than those behind him. (op 12-1)
Springfield Raki, third under top weight in a Market Rasen handicap hurdle 13 days earlier, was trying fences for the first time and did not entirely convince with his jumping. Having led early, he made a costly error at the eighth and was left behind when the first three quickened. (op 10-1)
James Caird(IRE), a triple winner on the Flat in his younger days with Mark Tompkins, had shown little over jumps for his current connections and was returning from a 1001-day layoff. He made a mistake at the first, pulled hard in mid-race and was left trailing after another error at the second-last. (op 22-1)

519 GEOFF'S LAST HURDLE MAIDEN HURDLE (8 hdls) 2m 1f 110y
8:40 (8:41) (Class 5) 4-Y-0+ **£2,276** (£668; £334; £166)

Form				RPR
/01-	**1**		**Sir Frank (IRE)**[32] 35 5-11-0 0 ... BrianHughes (Alan Swinbank) *trckd ldrs: led after 2 out: styd on run-in: hld on towards fin* **5/1**[3]	111+
225-	**2**	*½*	**Duty Free (IRE)**[8] 1358 6-11-0 109 ... PaddyAspell (James Moffatt) *trckd ldrs: wnt cl 2nd after 2 out: no ex towards fin* **7/2**[2]	110+
03P-	**3**	*10*	**Beat The Shower**[48] 5146 4-10-10 107 ... GrahamLee (Peter Niven) *hld up: j. slowly 2nd: hdwy after 4th: 4th last: kpt on* **11/1**	96
-	**4**	*5*	**Kingsmoss (IRE)**[20] 240 5-11-0 124 ... DenisO'Regan (J J Lambe, Ire) *in tch: drvn 5th: 3rd and one pce whn hit last* **7/4**[1]	97
6-P2	**5**	*9*	**Grand Award**[14] 327 5-10-11 106 ... AdrianLane(3) (Donald McCain) *t.k.h: led tl after 3rd: w ldr: led 5th: hdd after 2 out: sn wknd* **8/1**	86
2P-0	**6**	*11*	**Itstooearly**[15] 313 7-9-11 92 ... JamesSmith(10) (James Moffatt) *in rr: sme hdwy 3 out: nvr on terms* **16/1**	68
0-02	**7**	*5*	**Overyou**[23] 174 5-10-4 0 ... HarryHaynes(3) (Elliott Cooper) *s.s: sme hdwy 3 out: wknd after next* **20/1**	63
40-	**8**	*5*	**Great Esteem (IRE)**[68] 4785 5-11-0 0 ... JimmyMcCarthy (Charles Egerton) *nt jump wl in rr: bhd whn blnd 2 out* **25/1**	67
0/4-	**9**	*½*	**Marieschi (USA)**[64] 4874 6-11-0 0 ... KeithMercer (Roger Fisher) *j. slowly: chsd ldrs: wknd 3 out* **66/1**	65
4-6	**10**	*1¾*	**Jobekani (IRE)**[28] 93 4-10-7 0 ... DerekLaverty(3) (Lisa Williamson) *wnt prom 4th: sn lost pl and bhd* **50/1**	59
-005	**11**	*1¼*	**Daniel's Dream**[2] 490 10-10-11 70 ... (b) RyanMania(3) (John Dixon) *w ldrs: led after 3rd: hdd 5th: lost pl appr 3 out* **66/1**	62

4m 11.6s (-1.60) **Going Correction** -0.075s/f (Good)
WFA 4 from 5yo+ 18lb **11** Ran SP% **114.1**
Speed ratings (Par 103): **100,99,95,93,89 84,82,79,79,78 78**
toteswingers:1&2:£7.40, 2&3:£9.30, 1&3:£20.50 CSF £21.59 TOTE £8.10: £3.60, £1.10, £4.60; EX 24.80.
Owner Frank Hanson **Bred** Mrs G Galvin **Trained** Melsonby, N Yorks

FOCUS
Not much depth to this and the first two came home clear. The winner looks the type to rate higher.

NOTEBOOK
Sir Frank(IRE), successful in a Sedgefield bumper in April, was making his hurdling debut and coped like an old hand. Never far off the pace, jumping nicely, he went second two out and hit the front at the last. He stayed on gamely when challenged by the second on the run-in and looks as if he will handle a longer trip. He may well be able to shrug off a penalty in minor novice company. (op 3-1)
Duty Free(IRE), fairly consistent but limited for his previous stable, was making his first jumping appearance for these connections and did them proud. He was in rear early on, but made good progress in mid-race and jumped into second at the last. He gave it a good shot on the run-in but could not quite match the winner's drive to the line. (op 4-1 tchd 9-2)

Beat The Shower, third two starts back at Market Rasen, had been pulled up on his only subsequent start, but fared a good deal better here. He proved easily best of the four-year-olds and should find a small race somewhere down the line. (op 17-2)
Kingsmoss(IRE), twice in the frame from three previous outings over hurdles and officially rated 124, did not run to that mark. Held up in touch early on, he improved to take third approaching three out, but soon began to back-pedal when pressure was applied. (op 11-4)
Grand Award, an encouraging second on his first start for this yard two weeks previously, raced too keenly for his own good. He also made one or two mistakes and, after leading until the third-last, dropped back in the closing stages. (tchd 6-1)
Itstooearly is still a maiden and did little to indicate she will rectify that in the near future. She did make some late progress, but what she achieved is nothing to get excited about. (tchd 18-1)

520 ANDREA ROBINSON CELEBRATION H'CAP HURDLE (8 hdls) 2m 1f 110y
9:10 (9:11) (Class 5) (0-90,91) 4-Y-0+ **£2,602** (£764; £382; £190)

Form				RPR
P42-	**1**		**Ardesia (IRE)**[81] 4503 6-11-5 **81** BrianHughes (Tina Jackson) *trckd ldr: led appr 3 out: wnt clr between last 2: pushed out* **7/1**[3]	93+
345-	**2**	*10*	**Devils Delight (IRE)**[72] 4704 8-10-13 **75** PaddyAspell (James Moffatt) *chsd ldrs: wnt 2nd 2 out: kpt on same pce* **15/2**	76
663-	**3**	*10*	**Royal Flynn**[11] 4865 8-11-3 **86** (p) HenryBrooke[(7)] (Kate Walton) *chsd ldrs: wnt 3rd 2 out: kpt on one pce* **11/1**	81+
50-3	**4**	*2*	**Knight Valliant**[10] 405 7-11-6 **85** JamesO'Farrell[(3)] (Barbara Butterworth) *wnt prom 4th: one pce fr 2 out* **17/2**	76
0-06	**5**	*¾*	**Hernando Cortes**[4] 456 6-11-8 **84** (p) DenisO'Regan (Martin Todhunter) *led: hdd appr 3 out: wknd between last 2* **16/1**	74
05-	**6**	*19*	**Temple Place (IRE)**[63] 4897 9-11-10 **86** (t) TomO'Brien (Alan Jones) *hld up in rr: sme hdwy 5th: wknd appr 2 out* **14/1**	65
0-PP	**7**	*½*	**Danehill Silver**[4] 456 6-11-6 **85** RyanMania[(3)] (Brian Storey) *mid-div: wknd 5th: hit last* **33/1**	57
00-5	**8**	*25*	**The Sheepdipper**[16] 305 6-11-2 **85** AlexanderVoy[(7)] (Lucy Normile) *prom: lost pl 4th: sn bhd: t.o 3 out* **33/1**	34
033-	**9**	*2*	**Pinewood Legend (IRE)**[273] 1335 8-11-12 **88** (t) GrahamLee (Peter Niven) *in rr: hit running rail after 1st: sme hdwy 5th: wknd 2 out* **6/1**[2]	36
2-21	**10**	*5*	**Mountskip**[4] 456 6-12-1 **91** 7ex WilsonRenwick (Rose Dobbin) *in rr: drvn 5th: sn wknd: bhd fr 2 out* **6/4**[1]	34

4m 12.2s (-1.00) **Going Correction** -0.075s/f (Good)
WFA 4 from 6yo+ 18lb **10** Ran SP% **115.8**
Speed ratings (Par 103): **99,94,90,89,88 80,80,69,68,66**
toteswingers:1&2:£11.00, 1&3:£9.80, 2&3:£9.00 CSF £58.24 CT £568.40 TOTE £8.60: £2.40, £3.20, £3.10; EX 51.70 Place 6 £56.30; Place 5 £32.15.
Owner A Jackson **Bred** Patrick J Farrington **Trained** Liverton, Cleveland

FOCUS
A modest event in which few had serious claims. The winner is rated back to his best 2009 form.

NOTEBOOK
Ardesia(IRE) lined up without a win since 2007, but his most recent second at Newcastle suggested he was not out of this and he absolutely bolted up. He disputed the lead from the start, always travelling nicely, and jumped into the lead at the second-last. He quickly established a clear advantage and was not hard-ridden to come home well ahead. The handicapper will note this performance and respond with a significant hike to his rating. (op 8-1)
Devils Delight(IRE) has compiled a consistent record, albeit at a low level, and had run well here before, so seems a plausible yardstick for the form. She was held up in touch for most of race, making progress to go second approaching two out, but was no match for the comfortable winner. (op 11-2 tchd 8-1)
Royal Flynn is still a maiden in this discipline, but he was 4lb lower than when third at Carlisle in March and seems to have dropped to a level from which he can be competitive. He was unable to go with the winner after three out, but stayed on well enough to suggest a small race can eventually come his way. (op 12-1)
Knight Valliant had finished third from this mark at Sedgefield ten days earlier, but fared markedly less well in this event. A mistake mid-race cannot have helped his cause. (tchd 7-1)
Hernando Cortes has not shown a lot lately and the refitting of cheekpieces did not seem to spark him up. He cut out his fair share of the running, but dropped away tamely once headed. (op 12-1)
Mountskip, who had gained reward for his previous consistency when winning at Hexham four days earlier, ran poorly, even allowing for the fact that he was carrying a 7lb penalty for that 11-length success. Perhaps this came to quickly for him. (op 7-4 tchd 15-8)
T/Plt: £140.20 to a £1 stake. Pool:£58,061.48 - 302.30 winning tickets T/Qpdt: £24.40 to a £1 stake. Pool:£5,095.01 - 154.35 winning tickets WG

[498]STRATFORD (L-H)
Saturday, May 29

OFFICIAL GOING: Hurdle course - good to firm (good in places); chase course - good (good to firm in places) changing to good all over after race 1 (5:50)
Chase course rails moved in 7m reducing distances by about 30yds per circuit and hurdle rails moved in 10m reducing distances about 60yds per circuit.
Wind: Moderate, half against Weather: Showers

521 MARK FOSSEY CUP H'CAP HURDLE (FOR THE CLAIREFONTAINE CHALLENGE TROPHY) (9 hdls) 2m 110y
5:50 (5:50) (Class 3) (0-135,135) 4-Y-0+
£8,766 (£2,590; £1,295; £648; £323; £162)

Form				RPR
13-1	**1**		**Tiger O'Toole (IRE)**[3] 479 5-10-13 **122** 7ex PaulMoloney (Evan Williams) *t.k.h: trckd ldrs: led 2 out: drvn out* **9/4**[1]	127+
43-3	**2**	*3*	**Forty Thirty (IRE)**[15] 316 4-10-12 **125** JamieGoldstein (Sheena West) *hld up in rr: smooth hdwy and in tch 3 out: chsd wnr run-in: nt qckn* **4/1**[2]	122
30-4	**3**	*2 ¼*	**Pepporoni Pete (IRE)**[29] 80 9-10-9 **118** (p) CharliePoste (Milton Harris) *t.k.h: pressed ldr: hit 4th: led after 3 out: hdd next: one pce* **12/1**	118
05-1	**4**	*3 ½*	**Dishdasha (IRE)**[4] 96 8-11-1 **124** (t) SeamusDurack (Alison Thorpe) *t.k.h towards rr: hdwy 5th: wnt 3rd at next: hrd rdn 3 out: sn outpcd* **4/1**[2]	120
461-	**5**	*9*	**Alph**[33] 23 13-10-0 **116** MrTJCannon[(7)] (Roger Teal) *towards rr: drvn along and mod effrt 3 out: 5th and no imp whn hit 2 out* **11/1**	105
4-23	**6**	*3 ½*	**Dancewiththedevil (IRE)**[14] 331 9-10-6 **120** DonalDevereux[(5)] (C Roberts) *in tch: outpcd 6th: sn struggling* **13/2**[3]	105
2V-0	**7**	*8*	**Is It Me (USA)**[21] 207 7-11-7 **130** (t) JohnnyFarrelly (Sophie Leech) *in tch to 5th: sn bhd* **25/1**	107
P20-	**8**	*hd*	**Border Castle**[42] 5222 9-11-12 **135** NickScholfield (Michael Blake) *chsd ldrs: rdn and wknd after 5th: bhd whn j.lft last* **20/1**	112
124-	**9**	*nk*	**Palmito (IRE)**[184] 2516 6-10-4 **113** PaddyBrennan (Nigel Twiston-Davies) *led: hit 5th: hdd & wknd qckly after 3 out* **14/1**	90

3m 50.6s (-5.40) **Going Correction** -0.325s/f (Good)
WFA 4 from 5yo+ 18lb **9** Ran SP% **115.4**
Speed ratings (Par 107): **99,97,96,94,90 89,85,85,85**
toteswingers:1&2:£2.50, 1&3:£5.10, 2&3:£10.00 CSF £12.08 CT £86.75 TOTE £3.50: £2.00, £2.10, £3.20; EX 16.00.
Owner Ms S Howell **Bred** Mrs Jayne M Gollings **Trained** Llancarfan, Vale Of Glamorgan

FOCUS
A damp evening with heavy rain beforehand forced the ground to be changed from the official good to firm (good in places on the chase track) to good all round on both courses. The withdraws of Exulto, Osric and Australia Day made this a little less interesting but nonetheless it remained a competitive 0-135 hurdle with some hardened handicappers at the top of their game tackling two progressive types. It was run at just an ordinary pace until it quickened going to three out. The winner is on the upgrade.

NOTEBOOK
Tiger O'Toole(IRE) was ridden closer to the pace than usual after hitting a flat spot when winning at Southwell last week for which he was carrying a 7lb penalty. Once hitting the front two out he kept on well to win with a little in hand. He remains on an upward curve and is one to keep on the right side of. Connections will be eyeing either one of the valuable handicaps over the summer at Newton Abbot, Market Rasen or Galway for the winner as they feel he could develop into something quite smart. (op 10-3)
Forty Thirty(IRE) had been given a break after a successful time as a juvenile and made a pleasing return to action off this mark on his handicap debut at Aintree earlier this month. This was another solid effort after moving through from the rear to chase the winner going to the last though not finding the pace to get on terms. He looks capable of going one better before long. (op 5-1)
Pepporoni Pete(IRE) ran another fair race on his second run since a break and looks to be on good terms with himself, but he holds few secrets. He took up the running after three out and, once headed at the next, kept on well enough. (op 10-1)
Dishdasha(IRE) was in good order after winning over hurdles at Uttoxeter and a pleasing effort back on the Flat earlier in the week. He settled better than he can but could not muster the pace to lay down a serious challenge. (tchd 9-2)
Alph is a grand old servant to connections and again acquitted himself creditably after being risen 6lb for his Towcester success. He could never get on terms with the leaders after being held up off the pace. (op 12-1)

522 KEOGH AND HOWS AMATEUR RIDERS' H'CAP HURDLE (10 hdls) 2m 3f
6:20 (6:28) (Class 4) (0-110,109) 4-Y-0+ **£2,498** (£774; £387; £193)

Form				RPR
3-12	**1**		**Alldunnandusted (IRE)**[11] 382 6-11-5 **109** MrKevinJones[(7)] (Seamus Mullins) *hld up and bhd: gd hdwy 7th: led 3 out: wnt lft after 2 out: blnd last: hrd drvn and hld on run-in: all out* **5/2**[1]	116+
545-	**2**	*nse*	**Just Victor**[179] 2630 5-11-1 **105** (t) MrJonathanBailey[(7)] (Paul Webber) *sn trcking ldrs: disp 2nd on bit at 6th: sltly hmpd by wnr and shkn up after 2 out: str chal run-in: jst pipped* **8/1**	112+
4-00	**3**	*1*	**Pips Assertive Way**[11] 382 9-10-1 **89** RobertKirk[(5)] (Tony Carroll) *mid-div: outpcd 5th: rdn and hdwy fr 3 out: styd on wl run-in: clsng at fin* **16/1**	94+
P4-6	**4**	*10*	**Kilvergan Boy (IRE)**[17] 273 6-10-7 **90** MrSWaley-Cohen (Nigel Twiston-Davies) *disp 2nd pl: drvn along 7th: wknd appr 2 out* **10/1**	86
406-	**5**	*7*	**Sheikhman (IRE)**[45] 9-10-6 **92** MattGriffiths[(3)] (Stephen Hughes) *prom in chsng gp: drvn along after 6th: steadily fdd* **8/1**	82
66-5	**6**	*¾*	**Mauricetheathlete (IRE)**[20] 231 7-11-1 **105** MrNSlatter[(7)] (Martin Keighley) *sn wl bhd: j. slowly 2nd: hrd rdn 5th: styd on u.p fr 3 out* **4/1**[2]	94
PP-P	**7**	*2 ¾*	**Paddleyourowncanoe (IRE)**[13] 359 9-10-10 **100** (bt) MrJBanks[(7)] (Emma Baker) *mid-div: rdn and sme hdwy 7th: outpcd fr 3 out* **40/1**	87
F/63	**8**	*21*	**De Luain Gorm (IRE)**[12] 373 12-11-2 **104** MrGGallagher[(5)] (Chris Down) *led: sn clr: hdd and hrd rdn after 3 out: sn wknd* **33/1**	72
2-F3	**9**	*½*	**Mayor Of Kilcock**[11] 382 7-11-6 **106** MrTWeston[(3)] (James Danahar) *a towards rr: drvn along and struggling fr 6th* **13/2**[3]	73
1P4/	**10**	*30*	**Swift Sailor**[26] 9-11-3 **105** (p) MrMWall[(5)] (Derek Frankland) *mid-div: j. slowly 5th: rdn and j.rt 6th: sn struggling* **40/1**	45
200-	**11**	*6*	**Monzon (FR)**[202] 2153 10-9-12 **88** oh1 ow5 MrCChapman[(7)] (Chris Gordon) *sn wl bhd* **40/1**	23
0/0-	**P**		**Dancing Hill**[333] 830 11-10-1 **89** MrDGPrichard[(5)] (Kevin Bishop) *s.s: a t.o: p.u bef 2 out* **40/1**	—
	P		**Aisemma (IRE)**[42] 5238 6-10-0 **88** MrMByrne[(5)] (Peter Bowen) *mid-div: mstke 2nd: sddle slipped and p.u bef next* **20/1**	—
3P-5	**P**		**Black Apache (IRE)**[23] 175 6-11-6 **108** (b) MrJHamer[(5)] (Donald McCain) *prom tl wknd 5th: btn whn bmpd next: wl bhd whn p.u bef 7th* **16/1**	—

4m 26.6s (-4.90) **Going Correction** -0.325s/f (Good) **14** Ran SP% **122.4**
Speed ratings (Par 105): **105,104,104,100,97 97,95,87,86,74 71,—,—,—**
toteswingers:1&2:£5.20, 1&3:£18.30, 2&3:£36.30 CSF £21.98 CT £263.59 TOTE £4.10: £1.70, £2.70, £4.50; EX 31.70.
Owner C R Dunning **Bred** Miss D Keegan & D Feeley **Trained** Wilsford-Cum-Lake, Wilts
⊠ The first winner under rules for Kevin Jones.

FOCUS
In direct contrast to the opening heat this featured modest performers overall, thus resulting in a weakish affair for this amateur riders' handicap hurdle. With White On Black reluctant to race before being withdrawn there were three false starts, but the race produced a cracking finish nonetheless. The tiome is decent for the grade and the form is rated positively.

NOTEBOOK
Alldunnandusted(IRE) was set a difficult task off top weight and being held up way off the leaders, but he proved up to the task in the end, although he was all out in doing so. His rider, scoring for the first time, reported that he did not intend on sitting so far out of his ground, but after three false starts it was just the way things panned out. He will be kept on the go during the summer. (tchd 3-1)
Just Victor on paper looked to have strong claims on his 21-length fourth to Menorah at Warwick in November and was desperately unlucky not to score. Always in touch he moved through to track the winner after three out before laying down a serious challenge and receiving a hefty bump after two out. He held a very narrow advantage at the last but could not hold on to that, only losing on the nod. This was a weak affair and he was in here off a reasonable mark. (op 17-2 tchd 7-1)
Pips Assertive Way, returning to a track she acts well round, lost her pitch after three out but stayed on strongly from after the next and was closing well at the finish. Failing to hold her ground three out appeared to prove rather costly as she probably would have won this. (op 20-1 tchd 22-1)
Kilvergan Boy(IRE) had lost his form badly after a successful debut on soft in January 2009. He chased the leaders for most of the way without laying down any significant threat before tiring going to the last. (tchd 9-1 and 11-1)

Mauricetheathlete(IRE) was well supported last time out in a stronger heat but was not so here. He never got competitive. (op 6-1)

523 JON PINFOLD INDUSTRIAL CLEANERS H'CAP CHASE (12 fncs) 2m 1f 110y

6:50 (6:50) (Class 3) (0-135,132) 5-Y-O+ **£9,427** (£2,809; £1,422; £729; £381)

Form RPR

50-1 **1** **Passato (GER)**[25] 130 6-10-7 **113**................................(t) RobertThornton 132+
(Joanna Davis) *prom: led 6th: qcknd clr fr 2 out: easily* **5/1**[3]

50-6 **2** *17* **Mister Benedictine**[23] 170 7-10-11 **117**...............................(t) MarkGrant 118
(Brendan Duke) *t.k.h towards rr: smooth hdwy 8th: mstke 3 out: one pce: wnt 2nd nr fin* **16/1**

2-1U **3** *nk* **Miss Sarenne (FR)**[13] 361 5-11-1 **121**................................ APMcCoy 121
(Nicky Henderson) *hld up in rr: hdwy 8th: chsd wnr fr 3 out: one pce next: lost 2nd nr fin* **11/4**[1]

141- **4** *9* **Tempting Paradise (IRE)**[40] 5289 7-10-4 **110**................... PaulMoloney 102
(Evan Williams) *chsd ldrs tl hrd rdn and wknd 4 out* **8/1**

02-2 **5** *6* **Norborne Bandit (IRE)**[13] 361 9-10-3 **109**....................(p) HarrySkelton 99
(Evan Williams) *hld up in rr: sme hdwy and fair 6th whn blnd 3 out: nt rcvr: sn bhd* **11/2**

05-0 **F** **Knight Legend (IRE)**[25] 131 11-11-7 **132**...............(t) GilesHawkins(5) 128
(Philip Hobbs) *in tch: effrt and cl up 4 out: mstke and outpcd next: disputing 10 l 2nd whn fell last* **9/1**

33-0 **P** **Vinmix De Bessy (FR)**[22] 194 9-11-2 **122**.......................(p) JamieMoore —
(Gary Moore) *towards rr: mstke 5th and dropped to last: sn drvn along: p.u after 7th* **16/1**

32P- **P** **Leamington Lad (IRE)**[45] 5183 7-11-6 **126**...................(b) PaddyBrennan —
(Nigel Twiston-Davies) *sn led: hdd 6th: wknd after 8th: wl bhd whn p.u bef last* **9/2**[2]

/5-U **P** **Merchant Red (USA)**[13] 361 7-11-5 **125**........................(b) SamThomas —
(Paul Webber) *prom tl j. slowly 5th (water): bhd fr 7th: p.u bef 2 out* **14/1**

4m 6.50s (-0.60) **Going Correction** -0.15s/f (Good) **9** Ran SP% **116.4**

Speed ratings: **95,87,87,83,80** —,—,—,—

toteswingers:1&2:£10.70, 1&3:£2.40, 2&3:£39.50 CSF £75.08 CT £264.05 TOTE £3.50: £1.10, £6.60, £2.90; EX 118.30.

Owner P Ponting **Bred** Gestut Hof Ittlingen **Trained** East Garston, Berks

FOCUS

A tricky 0-135 handicap chase with most of the field either trying to recapture their form or having questions to answer regarding their fencing. The form could be rated up to 5lb higher.

NOTEBOOK

Passato(GER) had slipped in the weights prior to winning at Exeter and was back up 10lb here, but that was readily brushed aside with an emphatic success. The winner, a very clean jumper, took the lead in the back straight and never looked like being caught, scoring with ease. He probably won a bit too far for the handicapper to have his say, but he seems in good nick after his winter break and will be kept on the go throughout the summer (op 11-2 tchd 9-2)

Mister Benedictine had not recaptured his form since running a close second over hurdles in September. This was a step back in the right direction on his return to fences and he eventually wore down Miss Sarrene to snatch second, though never held any chance with Passato.

Miss Sarenne(FR) has not been the most fluent since tackling fences which has hindered her progress, but she is only a five-year-old and clearly has ability. She could never get on terms with the winner's superior pace but jumped well enough this time. (op 7-2)

Tempting Paradise(IRE) was tackling better company than of late, but after disputing for much of the way he was beaten leaving the back straight. (op 7-1)

Knight Legend(IRE) was in the process over running his best race since crossing the Irish Sea, and he was staying on to challenge for second when crashing out at the last. (op 16-1)

Vinmix De Bessy(FR) Official explanation: jockey said gelding never travelled (op 16-1)

524 LLEWELLYN HUMPHREYS H'CAP CHASE (IN MEMORY OF GEORGE JONES, FOR THE GAMBLING PRINCE TROPHY) (13 fncs 2 omitted) 2m 5f 110y

7:20 (7:20) (Class 2) (0-140,140) 5-Y-O+ **£10,019** (£2,960; £1,480; £740; £369; £1815)

11F- **1** **King Troy (IRE)**[224] 1785 8-11-12 **140**................................... JackDoyle 149+
(Alan King) *mid-div: mstke 6th: hdwy next: led after 2 out: drvn out* **13/2**[3]

213- **2** *1 ¾* **Herons Well**[33] 18 7-11-0 **135**................................ AodhaganConlon(7) 140
(Rebecca Curtis) *chsd ldrs: led 7th: nt fluent 2 out: sn hdd: kpt on u.p* **11/2**[2]

2PP- **3** *1 ¾* **Tanks For That (IRE)**[42] 5226 7-11-6 **134**....................... AndrewTinkler 136
(Nicky Henderson) *hld up in rr: hdwy 8th: chal 2 out: styd on same pce* **16/1**

16/1 **4** *7* **North Island (IRE)**[13] 352 8-9-10 **115**........................ DonalDevereux(5) 111
(Peter Bowen) *prom tl outpcd 3 out* **9/2**[1]

500- **5** *3 ¼* **Bill's Echo**[31] 46 11-10-1 **115**.......................................(b) DougieCostello 108
(Alistair Whillans) *towards rr: rdn and sme hdwy fr 3 out: n.d* **7/1**

2PP- **6** *4 ½* **Buck The Legend (IRE)**[45] 5181 8-11-2 **130**.................. PaddyBrennan 122
(Nigel Twiston-Davies) *chsd ldrs: disp ld 7th: blnd bdly next: sn lost pl* **14/1**

52-1 **7** *nk* **Storymaker**[29] 78 9-10-11 **128**.................................... FearghalDavis(3) 117
(Sandy Forster) *mid-div: rdn and no hdwy fr 3 out* **8/1**

551- **8** *7* **Overclear**[36] 5366 8-11-10 **138**................................... RichardJohnson 121
(Victor Dartnall) *a towards rr: rdn and struggling fr 8th* **13/2**[3]

01P- **9** *39* **Nelson's Spice (IRE)**[118] 3779 9-11-2 **130**............................. APMcCoy 78
(Jonjo O'Neill) *a towards rr: no ch fr 9th* **12/1**

10P- **10** *39* **Lord Jay Jay (IRE)**[35] 5394 10-11-6 **137**.......................(p) LeeStephens(3) 50
(David Evans) *led tl mstke and lost pl 7th (water): wl bhd fr 9th* **22/1**

P21- **P** **Postmaster**[33] 18 8-11-9 **137**... PaulMoloney —
(Evan Williams) *a bhd: no ch fr 8th: p.u bef last* **14/1**

5- **P** **Benbradagh (IRE)**[26] 118 7-10-0 **114** oh1...................... JohnnyFarrelly —
(I R Ferguson, Ire) *prom to 6th: wl bhd whn p.u bef 8th* **28/1**

5m 6.50s (-8.50) **Going Correction** -0.15s/f (Good) **12** Ran SP% **118.5**

Speed ratings: **109,108,107,105,104 102,102,99,85,71** —,—

toteswingers:1&2:£9.50, 1&3:£31.00, 2&3:£28.10 CSF £43.13 CT £556.06 TOTE £8.60: £3.30, £3.80, £9.20; EX 37.60.

Owner Alan King **Bred** Mrs Matthew Banville **Trained** Barbury Castle, Wilts

FOCUS

A decent pace for this open-looking 0-140 handicap chase with most of the field in good form. The winner looked to score with something in hand.

NOTEBOOK

King Troy(IRE) had been in fine fettle over fences last year before falling at Cheltenham in October and had not been seen since. He travelled well for much of the way before joining the leaders three out and jumped well until getting a little close to the last and losing momentum. He had to be shaken up to re-assert but won with a little more in hand than the official margin suggests. (op 15-2 tchd 8-1 and 11-2)

Herons Well has been running well for his in-form stable and this was another solid performance. He led for much of the way and kept on well when headed after two out to still hold a chance after the last but could not find any extra. A likeable sort, he looks sure to add to his tally. (tchd 5-1)

Tanks For That(IRE) had failed to complete on his last two starts, albeit at the festival and when stepped up to 3m last time, but this was a better effort. He travelled smoothly and held every chance after two out but had no more to give nearing the last.

North Island(IRE), who missed 2009, made a winning return to action at Market Rasen 13 days ago and the 8lb rise seemed fair enough. He chased the leaders and had his chance in the back straight but faded from the second-last. (op 5-1)

Bill's Echo was well supported throughout the day but could never get involved. (op 11-1)

525 W+S RECYCLING STRATFORD FOXHUNTERS CHAMPION HUNTERS' CHASE (52ND RUNNING) (20 fncs) 3m 4f

7:55 (7:56) (Class 2) 5-Y-O+

£18,006 (£5,625; £2,811; £1,407; £702; £354)

Form RPR

/2B- **1** **Roulez Cool**[26] 7-12-0 148.. MrSWaley-Cohen 137+
(Robert Waley-Cohen) *hld up in tch: tk clsr order 7th: nt fluent 13th (water): led 15th: drvn to hold on run-in* **2/1**[1]

12-2 **2** *3 ¼* **Templer (IRE)**[24] 149 9-12-0 126.................................... MattGriffiths 135
(Philip Hobbs) *in tch: chsd ldrs 11th: rdn 16th: chalng whn blnd bdly last: nt rcvr* **10/1**

5-11 **3** *nk* **Take The Stand (IRE)**[15] 317 14-12-0 126........................(p) MrMByrne 135
(Peter Bowen) *prom: mstke 4 out, drvn along and sltly outpcd after 2 out: styd on to regain 3rd nr fin: dismntd after line* **11/1**

02-2 **4** *nk* **Turthen (FR)**[23] 184 9-12-0 136.. MissCTizzard 133
(C St V Fox) *hld up towards rr: hdwy 15th: rdn to press wnr and ch run-in: no ex fnl 50yds* **6/1**[3]

P6-3 **5** *17* **Southwestern (IRE)**[24] 149 11-12-0 131............................ MrDEdwards 117
(Jeremy Scott) *held up and bhd: hdwy and in tch 4 out: mstke next: no further prog* **16/1**

/1-1 **6** *13* **Ice Tea (IRE)**[14] 334 10-12-0 130......................................(b) MrRBurton 106
(Mrs S K McCain) *led: hit 14th: hdd next: wknd 4 out* **7/2**[2]

/FF- **7** *5* **Simonsberg (IRE)**[26] 120 7-12-0 127.................................... MrNPearce 101
(I R Ferguson, Ire) *j. slowly 2nd: mstkes 10th and 12th: a bhd* **16/1**

/1-1 **8** *6* **Coolefind (IRE)**[19] 253 12-12-0 119............................ MrJonathanBailey 96
(W J Warner) *plld hrd: prom to 14th: losing pl whn mstke and rdr lost iron 16th* **16/1**

34-1 **P** **Martha's Kinsman (IRE)**[24] 152 11-12-0 120.................. JakeGreenall —
(Henry Daly) *chsd ldrs tl wknd 14th: wl bhd whn p.u bef 2 out* **22/1**

5P-2 **P** **Border Fusion**[14] 334 11-12-0 120...................................... MrTGreenall —
(G D Hanmer) *a bhd: mstke 14th: no ch after: p.u bef 2 out* **25/1**

214- **P** **Silver Adonis (IRE)**[33] 18 9-12-0 124.............................(p) MrTWeston —
(Dr Richard Newland) *in tch: rdn 4 out: sn struggling: bhd whn p.u after 2 out* **25/1**

4-34 **P** **Dennis The Legend**[10] 411 9-12-0 112.............................. MrOGreenall —
(Grant Cann) *a towards rr: mstke 11th: wl bhd whn p.u bef 15th* **20/1**

/1-2 **P** **Marblehead (IRE)**[24] 151 8-12-0 126....................................(b) MrMWall —
(F M O'Brien) *chsd ldrs tl wknd 15th: bhd whn blnd 4 out: sn p.u* **16/1**

01-0 **F** **Drybrook Bedouin**[24] 149 8-12-0 119.................................. MrSAllwood —
(Peter Shaw) *mid-div: nt fluent 4th: rdn and outpcd 15th: bhd whn fell last* **50/1**

5-52 **P** **Oranger (FR)**[13] 354 8-12-0 102...............................(p) MrAndrewMartin —
(Andrew J Martin) *prom: blnd 1st: wknd 8th: wl bhd whn mstke 12th: p.u bef 3 out* **66/1**

7m 2.00s (-1.00) **Going Correction** +0.20s/f (Yiel) **15** Ran SP% **131.1**

Speed ratings: **109,108,107,107,103 99,97,96**,—,— —,—,—,—,—

toteswingers:1&2:£6.70, 1&3:£3.60, 2&3:£7.90 CSF £23.66 TOTE £3.70: £1.70, £4.50, £4.50; EX 37.10.

Owner Robert Waley-Cohen **Bred** Upton Viva Stud **Trained** Ratley, Warwicks

FOCUS

A good pace and a decent renewal for this prestigious hunter chase in its 52nd year. The winner was a stone off his best in victory with the next two close to their recent marks.

NOTEBOOK

Roulez Cool, a former Listed winner over fences in France and comfortably the top-rated in the field off a mark of 148, ran out the winner in workmanlike fashion. He had his confidence restored in a point-to-point since being brought down, when struggling, in the foxhunter at the festival. He was soon settled in the midfield before moving through to take the lead at the 15th. He looked to be idling and had to be ridden out after the last but this was his first try at a trip of this distance and he had been in front for a long time. The 7-y-o had put on a bit of weight since winning his point and connections feel he is still maturing. He will be kept to this division next season where his primary target will again be the Cheltenham Foxhunter. (op 9-4 tchd 5-2 and 11-4 in places)

Templer(IRE) was a useful handicapper in his prime and has been enjoying his spell in the hunter chasing ranks, and this was another fine performance. Soon up with the pace, he was under pressure chasing the winner in the back straight but stuck to his guns well and looked as though he might hold a chance before a costly mistake at the last. He regained second on the run to the line but any chance he had had vanished. (op 12-1)

Take The Stand(IRE), placed in the last two runnings of this and winner at Cheltenham last time when out-battling the runner-up here, deserves all the credit that is reaped upon him for the grand old servant he is and this was yet another gutsy display. As is his customary role being up with the pace his never-say-die attitude kept him in with a chance even after clouting one down the back straight. He stayed on strongly from the last, only just being denied for second. Unfortunately he was dismounted after the line.

Turthen(FR) could possibly have won the foxhunter last year had he stayed up the hill, and again it was evident here as he posed the biggest threat coming to the last only to fade in the final 75 yards. Given a fine ride here to be produced at the perfect time, he will remain a force in this sphere. (op 8-1)

Southwestern(IRE), last year's winner, had not been in the form of old this season, and after moving comfortably through to be close enough, faded when coming under pressure after the second-last.

Ice Tea(IRE), rejuvenated since switching to this sphere having won his last two races, took them along at a decent pace before being headed at the 15th. He had no more to give in the back straight and was soundly beaten. (op 5-1)

526 INTERBRANDS EUROPE LADIES' HUNTERS' CHASE (FOR THE STRATFORD MILLENNIUM ROSE BOWL) (17 fncs) 2m 7f

8:30 (8:30) (Class 5) 6-Y-O+ **£2,498** (£774; £387; £193)

Form RPR

/23- **1** **Cannon Bridge (IRE)**[48] 12-10-3 109................................. MissHLewis(7) 108+
(P S Davies) *mde all at gd gallop: clr after 2 out: rdn out: readily* **12/1**

26P- **2** *4 ½* **Lady Myfanwy**[14] 9-10-0 99.. L-BdrSallyRandell(7) 100
(Mrs Myfanwy Miles) *chsd ldrs: lost pl 11th: sn bhd: styd on wl to take 2nd at last: nt pce of wnr run-in* **3/1**[2]

F1-3 **3** *6* **Whataboutya (IRE)**[16] 301 9-10-11 115..................(p) MissJennyCarr(7) 105
(Jonjo O'Neill) *prom: lost pl 13th: rallied 3 out: one pce fr next* **4/1**[3]

05P/ **4** *1* **The General Lee (IRE)**[17] 8-10-3 .... MissLBrooke(7) 96
(Phillip Rowley) *mid-div: hdwy 11th: disp 2nd 4 out: outpcd fr 2 out* **40/1**

1-U **5** *8* **Mad Victor (IRE)**[24] 151 9-11-0 .... MissPGundry 92
(Miss S M Taylor) *bhd: pushed along early: effrt and in tch 13th: wknd 2 out* **7/4**[1]

F **6** *nse* **Gentleman Anshan (IRE)**[24] 153 6-10-3 LucyBarry(7) 87
(Rosemary Gasson) *hld up in rr: hdwy 3 out: chsd wnr next tl wknd appr last* **66/1**

5/ **7** *½* **That Look**[618] 1307 7-10-11 MissGAndrews(3) 91
(Don Cantillon) *chsd ldrs: pckd 1st: lost pl 8th: rallied 10th: drvn along 3 out: sn outpcd* **6/1**

355/ **8** *6* **Scotmail Too (IRE)**[26] 9-10-7 ow2 MissSSharratt(5) 83
(Miss S Sharratt) *in tch: nt fluent 2nd (water): sn towards rr: last at 8th: struggling fr 11th* **22/1**

3P-3 **9** *hd* **Innocent Rebel (USA)**[24] 148 9-10-6 98 ow3 (t) MissCRoddick(7) 84
(Mrs K Heard) *chsd wnr: mstke 4th: wknd 4 out* **14/1**

5m 47.0s (5.40) **Going Correction** +0.20s/f (Yiel) **9** Ran SP% **118.3**
Speed ratings: **98,96,94,94,91 91,91,88,88**
toteswingers:1&2:£10.40, 1&3:£13.00, 2&3:£4.40 CSF £50.18 TOTE £14.70: £3.00, £2.00, £2.00; EX 68.90.
Owner K Pritchard **Bred** Tony McKiernan **Trained** Bromyard, H'fords

FOCUS
A lady riders' staying hunter chase run at a sound pace which resulted in the reversal of placings from the corresponding race last season. Ordinary form.

NOTEBOOK
Cannon Bridge(IRE) made the most of an enterprising ride from the front to run out a deserved winner after taking lengths off his rivals with his fencing before kicking clear going to the last. A faller last time out but in good form this spring and deserved to go one better than his narrow defeat in this last year. (tchd 14-1)
Lady Myfanwy lost her pitch going out on the final circuit and appeared to be fighting a losing battle to get back on terms, but to her credit she began to pick them off one-by-one after the second last but the winner was always had more than enough in hand. (op 7-2)
Whataboutya(IRE) had been enjoying his spell in the hunter chasing ranks, but after chasing the leaders could only stay on at the same pace from two out. (op 5-1 tchd 6-1)
The General Lee(IRE) is another to have been in reasonable form, but never posed a serious threat.
Mad Victor(IRE) had been well-supported throughout the day and was sent off favourite. Held up early on he made some progress going out on the final circuit but was soon under pressure and never could get on terms. (op 2-1)

527 SIS NOVICES' H'CAP HURDLE (9 hdls) 2m 110y
9:00 (9:00) (Class 4) (0-105,103) 4-Y-0+ **£3,252** (£955; £477; £238)

Form RPR

P-60 **1** **Cubism**[13] 360 4-11-0 **95** (t) WarrenMarston 96+
(Milton Harris) *mde all: set modest pce: j.rt 5th: qcknd next: clr after 3 out: easily* **15/2**

3B3- **2** *4* **Space Telescope (IRE)**[177] 2667 4-11-7 **102** APMcCoy 96
(Jonjo O'Neill) *pressed wnr: hrd rdn 3 out: one pce fr next* **2/1**[1]

6-02 **3** *hd* **Monkhair (IRE)**[11] 384 5-10-0 **77** oh1 MattieBatchelor 75
(Tony Carroll) *plld hrd: cl up: pressed ldrs 6th: rdn and styd on same pce fr 3 out* **11/4**[2]

400/ **4** *3 ¼* **Troys Steps**[431] 4689 6-10-0 **77** oh5 TomMessenger 72
(Sandy Forster) *chsd ldrs: drvn along and outpcd fr 3 out* **66/1**

00-1 **5** *1 ¼* **Shipboard Romance (IRE)**[14] 338 5-10-12 **92** (t) PeterToole(3) 86
(Mark Rimell) *t.k.h in rr: effrt 3 out: nt pce to chal* **3/1**[3]

00-U **6** *½* **Danzig Fox**[16] 299 5-10-5 **85** CharlieStudd(3) 78
(Michael Mullineaux) *hld up in 6th: outpcd 6th: no imp* **66/1**

/60- **7** *6* **Boo**[89] 2239 8-11-1 **92** (v) RodiGreene 79
(James Unett) *plld hrd: chsd ldrs: rdn 6th: sn wknd* **16/1**

20-0 **8** *54* **Henry Hook (IRE)**[17] 282 6-11-12 **103** JamieMoore 36
(Victor Dartnall) *a in rr: last and struggling 5th: sn wl bhd* **11/1**

4m 13.0s (17.00) **Going Correction** +0.55s/f (Soft)
WFA 4 from 5yo+ 18lb **8** Ran SP% **114.0**
Speed ratings (Par 105): **82,80,80,78,77 77,74,49**
toteswingers:1&2:£3.70, 1&3:£7.20, 2&3:£4.20 CSF £23.46 CT £51.29 TOTE £12.30: £3.50, £1.10, £1.10; EX 31.50 Place 6 £65.00; Place 5 £44.48.
Owner Barbara Woodcock & Christopher Shankland **Bred** Darley **Trained** Herridge, Wiltshire

FOCUS
A weak novice handicap hurdle. They finished in a bit of a heap off a slow pace and the form is suspect.

NOTEBOOK
Cubism ran out a very easy winner. He had not shown a great deal on the Flat in Ireland and possessed a similar profile in three attempts over hurdles so far. A tongue-tie applied for the first time and handicap debut off a mark of 95 did just the trick. He raced a little keenly in the lead and immediately had the race in the bag when quickening clear after three out. (op 11-2 tchd 10-1)
Space Telescope(IRE), a winner over 7f in Ireland and had shown promise since switching to hurdles got in here off a mark of 102 and attracted support. He raced prominently throughout and held every chance three out before being readily outpaced by the winner. He ought to be capable of going one better with his connections. (tchd 9-4)
Monkhair(IRE) has returned from an absence in fair form and this was another sound effort but he was another who could not match the pace of the winner. (op 4-1)
Troys Steps was up against it from out of the weights, but made a satisfactory handicap debut after a long absence. (op 50-1)
Shipboard Romance(IRE), a winner of an ordinary heat last time, was another who could only muster the same pace. (op 9-2 tchd 11-4)
T/Plt: £36.10 to a £1 stake. Pool:£96,093.36 - 1,943.00 winning tickets T/Qpdt: £15.70 to a £1 stake. Pool:£6,558.47 - 309.02 winning tickets LM

[278]FONTWELL (L-H)
Sunday, May 30

OFFICIAL GOING: Good (good to firm in places; watered; 7.5)
Rail realignment increased chases by 30yds per circuit, Hurdles as advertised.
Wind: fresh across Weather: sunny

528 BELLWAY HOMES "NATIONAL HUNT" MAIDEN HURDLE (9 hdls) 2m 2f 110y
2:00 (2:01) (Class 4) 4-Y-0+ **£3,252** (£955; £477; £238)

Form RPR

054- **1** **I Need A Hero (IRE)**[39] 5305 5-11-0 0 (t) JackDoyle 96
(Sarah Humphrey) *mid-div: hdwy after 5th: cl up whn c wd on home bnd: rdn after next: led sn after last: kpt on wl* **16/1**

2 *3* **Crimson Canyon (IRE)** 4-10-9 0 DougieCostello 88
(Jonjo O'Neill) *hld up in last trio: hdwy after 5th: rdn to ld after 2 out: hdd after last: kpt on but no ex* **14/1**[3]

3 *2 ¼* **Rimini (FR)**[27] 5-11-0 0 PaulMoloney 92
(David Rees) *trckd ldrs: rdn and ev ch whn nt fluent 2 out: kpt on same pce* **7/1**[2]

060- **4** *5* **Nehemiah**[34] 25 6-11-0 97 WillKennedy 86
(Henrietta Knight) *trckd ldrs: wnt 2nd after 3rd: cl 5th and rdn whn nt fluent 2 out: one pce after* **33/1**

0-4 **5** *1 ½* **Western Palm (IRE)**[30] 82 7-10-11 0 PeterToole(3) 85
(Charlie Mann) *in tch: rdn and cl enough whn c wd fnl bnd: one pce fr next* **25/1**

6P4- **6** *22* **Saddlewood (IRE)**[38] 5328 7-10-7 0 (t) DarylJacob 58
(Jamie Snowden) *a towards rr: t.o fr after 3 out* **7/1**[2]

0/2- **7** *3 ¼* **Conflictofinterest**[383] 271 8-11-0 0 (t) NickScholfield 69
(Paul Nicholls) *led tl after 1st: led 3rd: rdn whn hdd after 2 out: wknd qckly: t.o* **4/11**[1]

00-U **8** *4* **Keckerrockernixes (IRE)**[21] 215 4-10-9 0 LeightonAspell 54
(Richard Rowe) *a towards rr: t.o fr after 3 out* **100/1**

P **Georgie's Grey**[71] 8-11-0 0 JamieMoore —
(Diana Grissell) *j. bdly rt: led after 1st tl 3rd: sn dropped in rr: t.o whn p.u bef 6th* **33/1**

00-0 **P** **Out To Impress (IRE)**[21] 216 5-10-11 0 EamonDehdashti(3) —
(Murty McGrath) *trckd ldrs: struggling 5th: sn bhd: t.o whn p.u bef last* **100/1**

4m 21.2s (-13.10) **Going Correction** -1.20s/f (Hard)
WFA 4 from 5yo+ 18lb **10** Ran SP% **122.6**
Speed ratings (Par 105): **79,77,76,74,74 64,63,61,—,—**
toteswingers:1&2:£9.50, 1&3:£8.00, 2&3:£4.00 CSF £193.54 TOTE £16.30: £2.60, £3.10, £1.70; EX 173.90.
Owner Mrs S J Humphrey **Bred** Martin Brickley **Trained** West Wratting, Cambs

FOCUS
The ground was described as quick but safe by riders in the first. This maiden hurdle seriously lacked depth, and with the odds-on favourite bombing out and the race steadily run this is not form to get excited about. The fourth and fifth help set the level.

NOTEBOOK
I Need A Hero(IRE) had run a respectable race at Perth last month for a different yard and was dropping back in trip here on only his third run over hurdles. Carried wide by some scrimmaging on the home turn, he soon recovered his stride and stayed on to assert on the run-in. He is entitled to improve further on this but might well struggle under a penalty in novice company. Apparently the plan is to switch this winning pointer to fences before long.
Crimson Canyon(IRE), out of a half-sister to the high-class hurdler/chaser Foreman, was keen through the early parts on his debut. He was another involved in the trouble leaving the back straight but came through to hold every chance before the winner asserted. (op 12-1)
Rimini(FR) came here in good form in modest Welsh point-to-points and he ran respectably on this hurdles debut. There is room for improvement in his jumping and he will not mind a stiffer test of stamina.
Nehemiah only plugged on at the one pace over the last two flights.
Western Palm(IRE) came off the bridle after being forced wide on the turn having travelled quite well to that point. (op 33-1)
Saddlewood(IRE) had run an improved race against fellow mares here last time but she failed to step up on that and trailed all the way. (op 15-2)
Conflictofinterest, placed in graded company two seasons ago, was easily the highest-rated horse on show at the meeting with an official mark of 133, and this looked a simple opportunity for him to break his duck on his first start since finishing second on his chasing debut a year ago. After making much of the running, he found nothing when tackled between the last two flights and dropped away rapidly. He was reported by the vet to have an irregular heartbeat. Official explanation: vet said gelding had an irregular heartbeat (op 2-5 touched 4-9 in a place)
Georgie's Grey Official explanation: jockey said gelding jumped right throughout

529 FOLLOW SUMMER JUMPING WITH CHANCELLOROFTHEFORMCHECKER.CO.UK NOVICES' H'CAP CHASE (16 fncs) 2m 6f
2:30 (2:30) (Class 5) (0-95,95) 5-Y-0+ **£2,992** (£878; £439; £219)

Form RPR

53-3 **1** **Hoof It Harry (IRE)**[24] 181 9-11-9 **92** RichardJohnson 109+
(Paul Henderson) *cl up: jnd ldr after 10th: led 12th: drew wl clr fr 3 out: wnt rt and mstke last: comf* **9/4**[1]

30-4 **2** *18* **Rudinero (IRE)**[18] 283 8-10-5 **77** PeterToole(3) 72
(Barry Brennan) *trckd ldrs: chsd wnr appr 4 out: rdn sn after: no ch w wnr fr 3 out* **13/2**

30-5 **3** *2* **Maybe A Malt (IRE)**[18] 283 8-10-7 **76** LeightonAspell 71
(Richard Rowe) *cl up whn blnd bdly and nrly uns rdr 2nd: dropped to last 7th: wnt 4th bef 4 out: sn rdn: styd on same pce fr next* **16/1**

04-3 **4** *5* **Great Ocean Road (IRE)**[30] 83 7-10-13 **82** PaulMoloney 72
(Charlie Mann) *hld up: wnt 4th appr 4 out: sn rdn into 3rd: wandered after 3 out and 2 out: no ch w ldrs* **9/2**[3]

22-0 **5** *12* **Konigsbote (GER)**[31] 66 8-11-12 **95** JohnnyFarrelly 75
(Sophie Leech) *cl up: nudged along after 4th: rdn after 11th: sn wknd* **12/1**

/00- **6** *nk* **Strath Gallant**[123] 3682 7-11-7 **95** (b[1]) JimmyDerham(5) 75
(Suzy Smith) *trckd ldr: rdn after 9th: sn lost pl: wknd 12th* **16/1**

6P0- **P** **Nebeltau (GER)**[102] 4102 8-10-4 **76** RichieMcLernon(3) —
(Jonjo O'Neill) *led: 5 l clr 5th tl 8th: hdd 12th: wkng whn hit 4 out: p.u bef next* **11/1**

6-21 **P** **Wiesenfurst (GER)**[18] 283 6-11-8 **91** (p) JamieMoore —
(Gary Moore) *hld up in tch: reminders after 9th: rdn after next: wknd 12th: p.u bef 4 out* **10/3**[2]

5m 32.4s (-10.60) **Going Correction** -0.40s/f (Good) **8** Ran SP% **113.2**
Speed ratings: **103,96,95,93,89 89,—,—**
toteswingers:1&2:£4.70, 1&3:£6.70, 2&3:£22.20 CSF £17.14 CT £184.00 TOTE £3.00: £1.30, £1.40, £3.80; EX 16.20.
Owner Paul Henderson **Bred** David O'Connell **Trained** Rockbourne, Hants

FOCUS
Rail alignments meant that all chases were run over 30 yards further per circuit. The pace was sound in this low-grade novice handicap so the form should stand up. The easy winner is value for further.

NOTEBOOK
Hoof It Harry(IRE) had run respectably on his last two tries over fences and was nudged down the weights here. After jumping to the front five from home he steadily drew clear before giving his supporters an anxious moment when going badly out to his right at the last. Otherwise, he jumped soundly and can probably pick up another similarly modest event, particularly if turned out under a penalty in the next fortnight. (op 11-4)
Rudinero(IRE), back up in trip on only his second try over fences, ran a fair race but could not prevent the winner pulling away from him from the third-last. (op 9-1)
Maybe A Malt(IRE) had been dropped 3lb since her chasing debut (behind Wiesenfurst) here recently. After nearly unseating Leighton Aspell at the second, she could never get into the action but stayed on over this longer trip for a well-beaten third. (op 14-1)
Great Ocean Road(IRE) was still going fairly well in third place when he got in too close to the fourth-last, and he was quickly on the retreat from there. (op 3-1 tchd 5-1)
Nebeltau(GER) seemed to enjoy bowling along in front but was immediately beaten once headed five from home and soon pulled up. His form over fences is very poor. (op 14-1)

Wiesenfurst(GER) had today's second and third behind when scoring over 2m2f here earlier this month. Raised 8lb for that, he was in trouble before his stamina for this longer trip could be seriously put to the test and was well adrift when pulling up. Connections could offer no explanation for this disappointing run. Official explanation: trainer had no explanation for the poor form shown (op 14-1)

530 DON CLARK 50TH BIRTHDAY H'CAP HURDLE (11 hdls) 2m 6f 110y
3:00 (3:00) (Class 4) (0-115,115) 4-Y-0+ **£3,252** (£955; £477; £238)

Form RPR

/00- **1** **Soliya (FR)**[116] [3815] 6-11-4 **110**....(t) HaddenFrost[(3)] 118
(David Pipe) *mde all at decent pce: galloped on relentlessly: unchal* **7/1**[3]

06-1 **2** *16* **There's No Panic (IRE)**[21] [220] 5-11-1 **111**.... MrDGPrichard[(7)] 106
(Paul Nicholls) *mid-div early: disp 2nd fr 5th: rdn after 3 out: no ch w wnr fr after next: styd on same pce* **7/2**[1]

U65- **3** *4 ½* **Swordsman (GER)**[24] [5248] 8-11-5 **115**....(tp) MrTJCannon[(7)] 105
(Chris Gordon) *mid-div: drvn along fr after 3rd: styd on same pce fr 2 out: wnt 3rd towards fin: nvr any ch* **12/1**

6-34 **4** *½* **Thehonourablelady**[21] [220] 9-10-5 **94**....(tp) TomO'Brien 83
(John Flint) *mid-div: hdwy after 7th: disp 2nd and rdn after 3 out: one pce fr next: lost 3rd towards fin* **8/1**

0-22 **5** *8* **Bolton Hall (IRE)**[18] [282] 8-11-5 **108**....(tp) RichardJohnson 91
(Keith Goldsworthy) *chsd ldrs: rdn after 7th: outpcd 3 out: nvr any ch after* **9/2**[2]

FP-P **6** *4* **Lucky Dancer**[21] [233] 5-11-4 **110**.... DPFahy[(3)] 88
(Evan Williams) *mid-div: rdn after 3 out: wknd bef next* **40/1**

02-0 **7** *53* **Alrafid (IRE)**[24] [172] 11-10-11 **100**....(b) JamieMoore 31
(Gary Moore) *hld up towards rr: prog into midfield 5th: rdn after 3 out: wknd qckly: t.o* **25/1**

44P- **8** *10* **Fongoli**[114] [3534] 4-10-10 **105**....(v) LeightonAspell 21
(Brendan Powell) *racd wd: mid-div tl 5th: sn in rr: t.o* **33/1**

03P- **9** *29* **Notmorebrandy (IRE)**[69] [4787] 6-10-5 **99**.... MarcGoldstein[(5)] —
(Diana Grissell) *chsd ldrs tl 7th: t.o fr next* **50/1**

PP-3 **P** **In Media Res (FR)**[21] [232] 9-11-3 **109**.... CharlieStudd[(3)] —
(Charlie Longsdon) *chsd ldrs: rdn after 8th: one pce fr next: btn 7th whn p.u bef last: dismntd* **12/1**

1P/5 **F** **Zero (IRE)**[18] [282] 7-11-12 **115**.... JackDoyle —
(Emma Lavelle) *hld up towards rr: fell 7th* **10/1**

P3-5 **P** **Benmore Boy (IRE)**[12] [382] 7-11-7 **110**.... WillKennedy —
(Henrietta Knight) *mid-div tl 5th: losing tch whn hmpd after 7th: sn p.u* **28/1**

320- **P** **Viva Colonia (IRE)**[41] [5282] 5-11-7 **110**....(t) PaulMoloney —
(Charlie Mann) *a towards rr: t.o whn p.u after 7th* **16/1**

32-0 **P** **Flexi Time (IRE)**[21] [232] 6-11-2 **106**....(b) JohnnyFarrelly —
(Alison Thorpe) *mid-div: drvn along fr 4th: towards rr whn p.u after 7th* **8/1**

5m 11.5s (-31.00) **Going Correction** -1.20s/f (Hard)
WFA 4 from 5yo+ 19lb **14** Ran SP% **120.1**
Speed ratings (Par 105): **105,99,97,97,94 93,75,71,61,— —,—,—,—**
toteswingers:1&2:£8.80, 1&3:£30.00, 2&3:£35.20 CSF £30.75 CT £297.75 TOTE £8.30: £3.10, £1.80, £6.00; EX 49.40.
Owner Eminence Grise Partnership **Bred** Guy Cherel **Trained** Nicholashayne, Devon

FOCUS
An ordinary handicap hurdle. The winner is rated back to her 2009 best. She set a stiff pace and a number of these never got into the race.

NOTEBOOK
Soliya(FR) did not show much in a light campaign last season but she was clearly refreshed by a lengthy break and the first time tongue-tie had a beneficial effect. This game and enthusiastic mare made every yard, keeping up the gallop in relentless fashion and pulling away again from the home turn. She had dropped to an attractive mark on her best form and was evidently well suited by the lively surface. (op 6-1)
There's No Panic(IRE) was found out by a 9lb rise for his Plumpton win. He stalked the winner through the final circuit but she had his measure before the home turn and he could only keep going at the same pace for second. There seems no reason to suggest that he did not run his race and he confirmed his Plumpton superiority over the fourth home. (op 9-2)
Swordsman(GER), a winner on the Flat since his last hurdles run, was on and off the bridle from an early stage and looked hard work for his jockey. He was well held in fourth jumping the final flight but stayed on well to grab third.
Thehonourablelady, 10lb better off with the favourite on their meeting at Plumpton, moved briefly into second place on the home turn but could make no further inroads and weakened on the run-in.
Bolton Hall(IRE) had been runner-up on his last two starts, both at this track, but he was being shoved along to remain in touch with a full circuit left this time. (tchd 4-1)
Lucky Dancer, pulled up over fences last time, was not discredited on this handicap hurdle bow.
In Media Res(FR) ran fairly well for a long way but was beaten when pulled up and dismounted before the last. His rider reported that he was never travelling. Official explanation: jockey said gelding never travelled
Benmore Boy(IRE) Official explanation: jockey said gelding never travelled
Viva Colonia(IRE) Official explanation: jockey said gelding never travelled
Flexi Time(IRE) Official explanation: jockey said gelding jumped poorly

531 CHICHESTER PREMIER INN H'CAP CHASE (19 fncs) 3m 2f 110y
3:35 (3:35) (Class 5) (0-95,85) 5-Y-0+ **£2,927** (£859; £429; £214)

Form RPR

/P5- **1** **Gaining Ground (IRE)**[178] [2665] 10-10-0 **59** oh3....(v[1]) JodieMogford 78+
(Graeme McPherson) *led after 1st: tendency to jump rt: hit 3rd: drew wl clr after 13th: unchal after: awkward and stmbld bdly 15th: nt fluent 3 out: tired run-in but remained wl clr* **5/1**

P4-1 **2** *26* **Moon Melody (GER)**[7] [441] 7-11-3 **76**.... PaulMoloney 69
(Evan Williams) *hld up last: hit 13th: wnt 3rd u.p gng to 4 out: wnt remote 2nd sn after but nvr any ch w wnr* **10/3**[2]

5-42 **3** *7* **Monsieur Georges (FR)**[18] [280] 10-10-10 **69**.... WillKennedy 53
(F Jordan) *trckd ldrs: reminders after 10th: rdn after 13th: sn no ch: t.o* **7/2**[3]

00P/ **4** *10* **Mandalay Bay (IRE)**[22] 10-10-5 **64**.... ColinBolger 44
(Chris Gordon) *trckd wnr fr 5th: could nt go w wnr after 13th: no ch after: wknd after 4 out: t.o* **8/1**

PP-1 **P** **Boardroom Dancer (IRE)**[30] [83] 13-10-5 **69**.... JimmyDerham[(5)] —
(Suzy Smith) *led tl after 1st: trckd ldr tl lost pl 6th: nt travelling after: t.o whn p.u bef 11th* **9/4**[1]

306- **P** **Mr Presley (IRE)**[134] [3454] 6-11-2 **75**....(b) DougieCostello —
(Jonjo O'Neill) *hld up: wnt cl 4th at the 6th: mstke 9th: wknd 14th: t.o whn p.u bef 3 out* **10/1**

6m 50.4s (-10.70) **Going Correction** -0.40s/f (Good) **6** Ran SP% **112.9**
Speed ratings: **99,91,89,86,— —**
toteswingers:1&2:£4.90, 1&3:£3.20, 2&3:£1.90 CSF £22.38 CT £64.63 TOTE £5.70: £2.60, £2.50; EX 27.80.
Owner The Gaining Ground Partnership **Bred** Friday Chub **Trained** Upper Oddington, Gloucs

FOCUS
An appalling long-distance handicap. Following two withdrawals the top weight was racing off a mark of only 76. The winner produced a big step up on his previous rules form and ther's a case for rating the form up to a stone higher.

NOTEBOOK
Gaining Ground(IRE) came in for support and he rewarded his followers with a wide-margin win. Making virtually all, he had opened up an unassailable lead with a full circuit to run but had to survive a stumble five from home and was getting tired late on after being out in front so long. Officially rated just 56, but 3lb out of the weights here, he was tailed off in a couple of novice events on his only previous chase ventures and had not been seen since December, but he is a winning pointer in cheekpieces and had a first-time visor here. Suited by this sort of ground, he is certainly at the right end of the handicap and he might win again, although he will be going up a fair way in the weights for this. (op 11-1)
Moon Melody(GER), successful off the same mark over hurdles on his latest start, struggled into a remote second before the home turn but never threatened to reduce the gap to the winner. He is not the best of jumpers. (op 2-1)
Monsieur Georges(FR) ran creditably over course and distance last time, but was raised 3lb for that. This thoroughly exposed performer has just a single win to his name from 57 career starts. (tchd 10-3 and 4-1)
Mandalay Bay(IRE), runner-up in a couple of weak point-to-points recently, was ultimately well beaten on this chasing debut under rules. (op 13-2 tchd 6-1)
Boardroom Dancer(IRE) went up 7lb for his win here last week. He seemed to lose interest when unable to hold his early lead and dropped through the field before being pulled up. (op 10-3)

532 3663 FIRST FOR FOOD SERVICE H'CAP HURDLE (10 hdls) 2m 4f
4:10 (4:10) (Class 5) (0-95,94) 4-Y-0+ **£2,276** (£668; £334; £166)

Form RPR

5-04 **1** **Command Marshal (FR)**[15] [336] 7-11-6 **88**.... RichardJohnson 99+
(Michael Scudamore) *hld up towards rr off str pce: smooth hdwy fr after 5th: jnd ldrs after 7th: led bef 2 out: qcknd clr last: readily* **9/4**[1]

52-3 **2** *8* **Silver Phoenix**[20] [249] 6-11-7 **89**....(p) TomO'Brien 88
(Caroline Keevil) *hld up towards rr: smooth hdwy after 6th: wnt 2nd and travelling ok gng to 2 out: sn rdn: kpt on but nt pce of wnr* **8/1**

510- **3** *7* **Kilshannig (IRE)**[134] [3451] 5-11-9 **94**....(t) MrAJBerry[(3)] 91+
(Jonjo O'Neill) *mid-div: stmbld and wnt rt 2nd: hmpd on bnd after 4th and lost pl: nudged along and hdwy 6th: reminders after 3 out: led briefly sn after: rdn and styd on same pce fr next* **7/1**[3]

0-P5 **4** *26* **A Haon A Do (IRE)**[9] [432] 8-10-11 **79**....(p) LiamHeard 48
(Gerald Ham) *chsd ldrs: led 7th tl rdn after 3 out: sn wknd: t.o* **25/1**

523- **5** *2 ¾* **Magic Merlin**[55] [5047] 9-11-1 **83**.... JamieMoore 50
(Charlie Morlock) *mid-div: rdn after 7th: wknd next: t.o* **6/1**[2]

/0-0 **6** *1 ¾* **Always Cruising (USA)**[18] [273] 5-11-8 **90**.... NickScholfield 55
(Linda Blackford) *mid-div tl wknd after 7th: t.o* **10/1**

/40- **7** *2 ¼* **Fantastic Morning**[ccc] [441] 6-10-7 **75**.... WillKennedy 38
(F Jordan) *disp ld tl 7th: sn rdn: wknd after 3 out: t.o* **40/1**

5P/P **8** *22* **Man Overboard**[13] [374] 8-10-6 **84**.... QuintonJones[(10)] 27
(Gary Brown) *mid-div tl wknd after 6th: sn t.o* **33/1**

415/ **P** **Native American**[1016] [1182] 8-10-12 **80**.... JackDoyle —
(Tim McCarthy) *chsd ldrs tl after 4th: grad dropped in rr: t.o whn p.u after 6th* **16/1**

555- **P** **Himba**[38] [5330] 7-10-4 **72**.... LiamTreadwell —
(Nick Gifford) *chsd ldrs: drvn along fr 4th: wknd after 6th: t.o whn p.u after 6th* **8/1**

/4-3 **P** **Randomer**[21] [215] 7-10-8 **86**....(p) AshleyBird[(10)] —
(Paddy Butler) *disp tl 7th: wknd 3 out: t.o whn p.u bef 2 out* **11/1**

000/ **P** **Capeleira (IRE)**[435] [4633] 5-10-10 **78**.... LeightonAspell —
(Richard Rowe) *hit 1st: sn t.o: p.u after 6th* **20/1**

4m 41.1s (-18.30) **Going Correction** -1.20s/f (Hard) **12** Ran SP% **117.1**
Speed ratings (Par 103): **88,84,82,71,70 69,68,60,—,— —,—**
toteswingers:1&2:£4.70, 1&3:£3.50, 2&3:£6.20 CSF £19.59 CT £110.75 TOTE £3.40: £1.90, £3.50, £1.50; EX 17.70.
Owner Eddie Moss **Bred** Werner Wolf **Trained** Bromsash, Herefordshire

FOCUS
A moderate handicap hurdle run at a brisk gallop. A step up from the winner with the next two close to their marks.

NOTEBOOK
Command Marshal(FR), who was well backed, sat off the pace for the first circuit, sensibly enough, before closing going nicely. Showing ahead on the home turn, he came away to score in very comfortable style. He seems to like this track and has notched two wins here, the first of them coming back in the autumn off a 9lb lower mark. (op 3-1 touched 10-3 in places)
Silver Phoenix ruined her handicap mark when third in a Towcester maiden hurdle and was no less than 25lb higher than when runner-up in a handicap the time before. Ridden from off the pace, she was still going well when moving into second two from home but was soon left trailing by the winner. (op 6-1 tchd 9-1)
Kilshannig(IRE), a winner at Southwell two runs back, had his ground on this first run since January. Niggled along from an early stage, he stayed on for third and might prefer a more galloping track or a step up in trip. (op 6-1)
A Haon A Do(IRE) ran her best race since arriving in this country and even led for a few strides, but after hanging on the home turn she was soon beaten.
Himba Official explanation: jockey said gelding never travelled (op 12-1)
Randomer, on his handicap debutant, duelled for the lead at a fast pace. Unsurprisingly, his exertions told in the end and he was eventually tailed off. (op 12-1)

533 WORTHING AUDI TT CHALLENGE H'CAP CHASE (13 fncs) 2m 2f
4:50 (4:51) (Class 5) (0-90,90) 5-Y-0+ **£2,602** (£764; £382; £190)

Form RPR

40-P **1** **Khazar (FR)**[20] [251] 7-11-4 **85**.... RichieMcLernon[(3)] 93
(Jonjo O'Neill) *chsd ldrs: rdn after 9th: wnt 2nd after 4 out: led jst bef last: kpt on: drvn out* **11/1**

P-33 **2** *3* **Post It**[18] [276] 9-10-11 **82**.... MattGriffiths[(7)] 87
(Ron Hodges) *trckd ldr tl 4th: remained cl up: led after 7th: rdn 6 l clr after 4 out: hdd whn wnt rt last: no ex* **5/1**

2-42 **3** *26* **Space Cowboy (IRE)**[18] [278] 10-10-10 **74**....(b) JamieMoore 57
(Gary Moore) *chsd ldrs: outpcd after 8th: prog u.p into 3rd 3 out: wknd bef last* **9/4**[1]

5U-4 **4** *6* **New Rackheath (IRE)**[31] [54] 7-10-11 **78**.... DPFahy[(3)] 54
(Evan Williams) *chsd ldrs: rdn after 4 out: wknd 2 out* **7/2**[3]

06-F **P** **Open Range (IRE)**[18] [278] 10-10-2 **66** oh5 ow2.... LeightonAspell —
(George Wareham) *a last: losing tch whn wnt rt 8th: sn t.o: p.u bef 2 out* **20/1**

1-43 **P** **Bid Art (IRE)**[18] [283] 5-11-7 **90**....(t) JimmyDerham[(5)] —
(Jamie Snowden) *set decent pce: hdd after 7th: sn rdn to remain chsng ldrs tl wknd 3 out: p.u bef last* **5/2**[2]

4m 30.2s (-4.50) **Going Correction** -0.40s/f (Good) **6** Ran SP% **111.3**
Speed ratings: **94,92,81,78,— —**
toteswingers:1&2:£3.30, 1&3:£3.90, 2&3:£1.70 CSF £60.71 CT £164.77 TOTE £8.10: £2.40, £2.40; EX 52.00.

Owner John P McManus **Bred** H H The Aga Khan's Studs Sc **Trained** Cheltenham, Gloucs

FOCUS

A weak handicap chase and not form to treat too seriously. The pace was sound and the firwst two ran to their marks.

NOTEBOOK

Khazar(FR) looked in trouble when ridden along in fourth place on the second circuit, but he responded to chase the winner on the entrance to the straight and got to the front before the last, which he brushed through. He had shown little aptitude or enthusiasm for fences previously but was well in on his old hurdles form having been dropped no less than 19lb since March. (tchd 10-1 and 12-1)

Post It was bustled along to lead with a circuit to run and seemed in command turning for home, but she soon began to look vulnerable and was eventually worn down. She acts well on a sound surface and is running creditably, but is only moderate. (op 7-2)

Space Cowboy(IRE) could not build on his 2m4f course second to subsequent winner Lord Gunnerslake and merely struggled on for a soundly beaten third. (tchd 5-2)

New Rackheath(IRE) was well held on this return to fences and probably needs softer ground. (op 9-2)

Bid Art(IRE), who made the running again, did not hold on to his lead until much past halfway and was well beaten when eventually pulling up. He has now been found wanting three times since winning off 12lb lower over course and distance last month. (op 3-1)

534 RACINGPOST.COM MEMBERS CLUB H'CAP HURDLE (9 hdls) 2m 2f 110y

5:25 (5:25) (Class 4) (0-115,114) 4-Y-0+ **£3,252** (£955; £477; £238)

Form				RPR
00-0	1		**Stumped**[4] 479 7-10-12 **100** ....(t) DarylJacob (Milton Harris) *hld up towards rr: hdwy 6th: wnt 2nd after 3 out: led last: rdn out* **6/1**[3]	104+
02-1	2	¾	**Forest Rhythm (IRE)**[24] 185 6-11-3 **110** .... JimmyDerham[(5)] (Seamus Mullins) *hld up towards rr: hdwy fr 3 out: pushed along in 3rd after next: rdn after last: kpt on but nt pce to chal wnr* **11/4**[1]	113+
00-3	3	3 ¼	**Consulate (IRE)**[19] 267 6-11-5 **114** .... MrDEdwards[(7)] (Gordon Edwards) *trckd ldrs: led after 3 out: sn rdn: hdd whn hit last: kpt on same pce* **7/1**	114
03P-	4	4 ½	**Just Beware**[42] 5253 8-10-0 **93** ....(p) GemmaGracey-Davison[(5)] (Zoe Davison) *hld up towards rr: hdwy 3 out: sn rdn: styd on same pce fr next* **25/1**	88
031-	5	5	**Mayberry**[38] 5328 5-11-6 **108** .... JackDoyle (Emma Lavelle) *hld up bhd: shocking mstke 2nd and fortunate to stay up: hdwy after 6th: rdn to chse ldrs 2 out: 4th and btn whn awkward last: fdd* **4/1**[2]	102+
1P-0	6	7	**Rien A Perdre (FR)**[21] 231 9-10-10 **105** .... MrTomDavid[(7)] (Graeme McPherson) *led tl after 3 out: sn rdn and hung lft: wknd next* **16/1**	89
6-10	7	8	**Ardmaddy (IRE)**[9] 430 6-11-3 **105** ....(b) JamieMoore (Gary Moore) *in tch: effrt after 3 out: wknd next* **14/1**	82
2/2-	8	2 ¼	**Harlequinn Danseur (IRE)**[31] 159 5-10-12 **100** ....(p) TomO'Brien (John Flint) *trckd ldrs: ev ch 3 out: sn rdn: wknd bef 2 out* **11/1**	75
/01-	9	7	**King Of The Titans (IRE)**[266] 1395 7-11-3 **112** .... CharlieWallis[(7)] (Patrick Gilligan) *in tch: rdn whn rn wd on bnd after 3 out: wknd next* **8/1**	81
/0P-	10	3 ½	**Dream Catcher (SWE)**[127] 3610 7-11-8 **110** .... DougieCostello (Jonjo O'Neill) *wnt lft 1st: mid-div: rdn whn rn wd on bnd after 3 out: wknd next* **20/1**	75
01P/	11	40	**King Gabriel (IRE)**[405] 5119 8-11-9 **114** .... PeterToole[(3)] (Barry Brennan) *mid-div tl wknd appr 6th: t.o* **20/1**	43

4m 18.6s (-15.70) **Going Correction** -1.20s/f (Hard) **11 Ran SP% 118.8**

Speed ratings (Par 105): **85,84,83,81,79 76,73,72,69,67 50**

toteswingers:1&2:£5.80, 1&3:£7.60, 2&3:£6.70 CSF £22.99 CT £121.02 TOTE £5.90: £1.90, £1.80, £2.40; EX 31.30 Place 6 £688.26; Place 5 £128.95.

Owner Crew Bourgeois **Bred** Wyck Hall Stud Ltd **Trained** Herridge, Wiltshire

FOCUS

An ordinary handicap hurdle run at a fair pace, and the form looks solid for the grade. The winner can probably step up on this.

NOTEBOOK

Stumped was well supported at Southwell on Wednesday on his debut for the yard and the money was down again. Fitted with a tongue tie, but with the cheekpieces omitted, he found plenty after leading at the last. He had not shown much for some time but was very attractively handicapped on the form he had been showing a year or so ago. (op 7-1)

Forest Rhythm(IRE) came from off the pace and chased the winner after the last without getting to him. The 13lb rise for his Wincanton win told but he remains in good heart. (op 10-3 tchd 7-2)

Consulate(IRE), dropped in trip after finishing third last time, showed in front leaving the back straight and was only collared at the last. There is no reason why he shouldn't continue to run with credit. (tchd 6-1 and 15-2)

Just Beware was getting plenty of weight from all her rivals and she stayed on determinedly for fourth. She last won in September 2008 but has made the frame a dozen times since. (op 33-1)

Mayberry landed a mares' novice hurdle here last time and looked fairly treated for this handicap debut. Held up in last place, she made a bad blunder at the second but recovered well enough and improved into third place two from home before the effort flattened out. She might be worth another chance. (op 3-1)

Rien A Perdre(FR) ran respectably from the front on this drop in trip.

King Of The Titans(IRE), one of several on the day to run wide on the bend leaving the back, is entitled to improve for this first run since winning here back in September. (touched 10-1 in a place)

T/Plt: £1,070.40 to a £1 stake. Pool:£73,686.61 - 50.25 winning tickets T/Qpdt: £49.40 to a £1 stake. Pool:£6,206.64 - 92.80 winning tickets TM

335 UTTOXETER (L-H)

Sunday, May 30

OFFICIAL GOING: Good changing to good (good to firm in places) after race 4 (3:50)

Penultimate fence omitted on all circuits of the chase course. Final flight in the back straight omitted on all circuits of the hurdle course.

Wind: Fresh against Weather: Cloudy with sunny spells

535 DOUGLAS FAMILY MARES' NOVICES' HURDLE (9 hdls 1 omitted) 2m

2:10 (2:12) (Class 4) 4-Y-0+ **£2,732** (£802; £401; £200)

Form				RPR
52-U	1		**Onemix**[21] 215 4-9-13 104 .... DavidBass[(7)] (Nicky Henderson) *chsd ldr tl led 5th: clr 2 out: rdn and wandered bef last: styd on wl* **5/2**[2]	105+
2-	2	10	**Rose Street (IRE)**[174] 2749 6-10-10 0 .... TimmyMurphy (Pauline Robson) *prom: chsd wnr 6th: shkn up after 3 out: styd on same pce fr next* **4/9**[1]	100
0-	3	7	**Tuppenny Piece**[32] 50 4-10-6 0 .... RobertThornton (Alan King) *chsd ldrs: rdn appr 3 out: wknd next* **12/1**	90
0-5	4	9	**Recurring Dream**[26] 129 4-10-6 0 .... TomScudamore (John Flint) *prom: rdn appr 3 out: wknd bef next* **8/1**[3]	82
6	5	49	**Par Excellence**[14] 358 7-10-10 0 .... SamThomas (Jeremy Scott) *hld up: hdwy after 6th: wknd bef 3 out: t.o* **66/1**	42
5	6	3	**Farncombe (IRE)**[18] 275 4-10-1 0 .... JohnKington[(5)] (Michael Scudamore) *hld up: bhd fr 6th: t.o* **33/1**	35
	7	14	**Miss Markham (IRE)**[310] 5-10-3 0 .... PeterHatton[(7)] (Patricia Rigby) *s.s: a bhd: t.o* **150/1**	26
0/	8	31	**Poca A Poca (IRE)**[283] 4659 6-10-10 0 .... AidanColeman (Rachel Hobbs) *hld up: hdwy 6th: wknd bef next: t.o* **100/1**	—
5P0/	U		**Silver Sonnet**[441] 4506 7-10-10 0 .... CharliePoste (Ben Case) *hld up: mstke and uns rdr 3rd* **80/1**	—
P0-P	P		**Nobel Play**[24] 168 6-10-10 0 ....(tp) ChristianWilliams (Debra Hamer) *led: mstke 3rd: hdd and nt fluent 5th: wknd bef next: t.o whn p.u bef last* **100/1**	—

3m 48.9s (-6.30) **Going Correction** -0.525s/f (Firm)

WFA 4 from 5yo+ 18lb **10 Ran SP% 124.9**

Speed ratings (Par 105): **94,89,85,81,56 55,48,32,—,—**

toteswingers:1&2:£1.10, 1&3:£3.00, 2&3:£1.20 CSF £4.51 TOTE £3.90: £1.10, £1.10, £2.40; EX 4.40.

Owner S W Group Logistics Limited **Bred** Ken Knox **Trained** Upper Lambourn, Berks

FOCUS

After 12mm of rain on Saturday the going had eased to Good. One fence and a hurdle were omitted on all circuits. Little strength in depth in an uncompetitive event, and so it proved with four pulling well clear of the rest. The form is rated around the first two.

NOTEBOOK

Onemix first had to prove her willingness to take part after unseating at the start at Plumpton last time, but she jumped off sweetly to take up a prominent position throughout. Moving into the lead in the back straight, she kept going to gradually pull clear of her rivals. She met several of the early flights awkwardly, and in general seems less than straightforward but she seemed willing enough, with no undue pressure applied, to take a small step in the right direction. (tchd 9-4 and 11-4)

Rose Street(IRE) was the best of these on the Flat and was all the rage to convert that ability on just her second hurdling start. Taken wide, she was within striking distance of the winner but never looked like getting there. She was not helped by a hesitant jump turning into the straight and a tendency to jump right. She may have needed her first run since December, but the market support she attracted suggested many thought this would not be a problem, so this was a disappointing effort. (op 8-11)

Tuppenny Piece was niggled to stay on terms leaving the back straight and though she kept on she got tired in the closing stages. This was still an improvement on her hurdling debut at Southwell a month ago and a similar step up could see her pick up a small handicap. (op 11-1)

Recurring Dream stayed on better than she had at Exeter last time, but she could do no more than plod on and failed to make an impact. She might do better now she qualifies for handicaps. (op 7-1)

Par Excellence tried to go with the leading quartet but she was struggling from the turn in and was eased after a tired leap at the third last.

536 ALWAYS WAINING BEGINNERS' CHASE (12 fncs 3 omitted) 2m 4f

2:45 (2:46) (Class 4) 5-Y-0+ **£3,581** (£1,081; £556; £294)

Form				RPR
41-0	1		**Mous Of Men (FR)**[22] 206 7-11-0 126 ....(t) TomScudamore (David Pipe) *chsd ldr tl led 7th: nt fluent 10th: hdd 2 out: sn rdn: rallied to ld fnl 50yds* **11/10**[1]	121+
03/3	2	¾	**Important Business (IRE)**[25] 155 7-11-0 0 .... SamJones (Renee Robeson) *a.p: chsd wnr 10th: led 2 out: sn rdn: hdd and unable qck fnl 50yds* **4/1**[3]	117
1-2	3	37	**Kanad**[26] 135 8-11-0 0 ....(t) WarrenMarston (Milton Harris) *hld up: hmpd by loose horse 7th: rdn and wknd appr 3 out: t.o* **7/1**	91
	4	22	**Double Bank (IRE)**[14] 7-11-0 105 .... AidanColeman (A J Kennedy, Ire) *led: hdd whn hmpd by loose horse 7th: chsd wnr to 10th: rdn and wknd bef 3 out: t.o* **25/1**	64
542-	U		**Franchoek (IRE)**[115] 3849 6-11-0 122 .... RobertThornton (Alan King) *blnd and uns rdr 1st* **11/4**[2]	—

5m 8.70s (3.20) **Going Correction** -0.225s/f (Good) **5 Ran SP% 110.6**

Speed ratings: **84,83,68,60,—**

CSF £6.08 TOTE £2.10: £1.40, £2.40; EX 5.00.

Owner D A Johnson **Bred** Scea La Reigniere **Trained** Nicholashayne, Devon

FOCUS

Much of the interest dissipated early with the departure of Franchoek at the first, but it still produced a stirring finish. The winner is rated a bit better than the bare result.

NOTEBOOK

Mous Of Men(FR), with trip and ground to suit, was well backed for his chasing debut. Scudamore had reportedly been responsible for most of the schooling, which is why he replaced the owner's retained jockey this time. Indeed, prior knowledge of the gelding seemed essential, as he looks to be a bit of a slow learner. Hesitant at several fences and getting in close to others, he continued in the lead by virtue of his flat speed, but looked beaten when outjumped at the last in the back straight. However, he saved his best jump for last and, with the leader there for the taking, he was roused for a final thrust to get up near the line. On this evidence his chasing form may fall short of his hurdling ability, but he does have some pace and could win more chases if his jumping improves. (op 6-4 tchd 13-8)

Important Business(IRE) had something to find on hurdles ratings, but had put up an encouraging display following a break on his chasing debut last time. That experience looked likely to pay dividends as he soared into the lead with a fluent jump in the back straight. However, it was still a way from home and he began to idle on the long run to the last, allowing the winner to get back to him. Had the second last had not been omitted today it might have been in his favour. He has not won a race yet, but looks capable of doing so if he can sustain the run to the line. (tchd 7-2)

Kanad, formerly a useful hurdler, had to be dropped to selling company to gain a win last month and has changed hands since. He was keen on this switch back to fences and could never get on terms. It did not help matters when Franchoek careered into him at the sixth, but it made little difference. (op 11-2 tchd 5-1)

Double Bank(IRE) had failed to make an impact in points of late so, although he led early on, it was no surprise to see him drop away mid-race.

Franchoek(IRE) dived at the first and gave Robert Thornton no chance, sending him crashing to the ground. He continued to gallop loose and, when trying another jump, dived left and collided with Kanad. He does not look a natural over fences. (op 5-2 tchd 3-1)

537 DOUGLAS FAMILY CONDITIONAL JOCKEYS' (S) HURDLE (9 hdls 1 omitted) 2m

3:15 (3:15) (Class 5) 4-8-Y-0 **£1,691** (£496; £248; £124)

Form				RPR
U2-6	1		**Letham Island (IRE)**[11] 403 6-10-2 109 ....(vt[1]) DeanColeman[(3)] (Tim Vaughan) *chsd ldr: nt fluent 6th: rdn appr 3 out: led after next: sn clr: easily* **5/1**[3]	110+

53-0 **2** *19* **Tora Petcha (IRE)**[20] 252 7-10-12 96 MichaelMurphy 99
(Barry Leavy) *prom: outpcd after 6th: rallied to go 2nd flat: no ch w wnr* **14/1**

441- **3** *½* **Tri Nations (UAE)**[37] 5352 5-11-1 115 (tp) JohnKington(3) 104
(Donald McCain) *led: hdd & wknd after 2 out: lost 2nd flat* **6/4**[1]

52-4 **4** *8* **Navajo Nation (IRE)**[21] 216 4-10-3 100 (p) MarkQuinlan(5) 86
(Bill Turner) *hld up: nt fluent 3rd: hdwy 6th: rdn and wknd appr 2 out* **15/2**

050/ **5** *10* **Turkish Sultan (IRE)**[37] 1 7-10-7 82 (p) ChrisDavies(5) 81
(Milton Bradley) *hld up: rdn and wknd bef 3 out: t.o* **50/1**

1-10 **6** *14* **Along The Nile**[21] 235 8-11-4 118 (b) AlexMerriam 74
(Graham Smith) *chsd ldrs: mstke and pushed along 6th: wknd bef 3 out: t.o* **5/2**[2]

3m 44.5s (-10.70) **Going Correction** -0.525s/f (Firm)
WFA 4 from 5yo+ 18lb 6 Ran SP% **105.6**
Speed ratings: **105,95,95,91,86 79**
toteswingers:1&2:£10.20, 1&3:£1.90, 2&3:£3.20 CSF £52.11 TOTE £5.10: £2.00, £5.10; EX 67.60.The winner was bought in for 7,400gns.
Owner Diamond Racing Ltd **Bred** Rathasker Stud **Trained** Aberthin, Vale of Glamorgan

FOCUS
This was run at a steady early pace so, despite two early leaders taking each other on, they still had enough to increase the pace midway to see off the chasers. The winner is rated to her mark.

NOTEBOOK
Letham Island(IRE) looked to be coming off worst in the battle for the lead and had to be driven to stay on terms around the home turn, but she stuck to the task and, finding a second wind, pulled well clear of toiling rivals up the straight. The fitting of a visor to replace the normally worn cheekpieces helped offset her lack of pace, as 2m on this easy track looks on the short side, but she does possess enough strength and stamina to keep her in contention in moderate grade. (op 10-3)
Tora Petcha(IRE) was caught out when the pace increased mid-race but he plugged on to snatch second from the tiring favourite on the line. This was a small improvement on his reappearance run at Towcester last time, but overall he seems on the downgrade. (op 11-1)
Tri Nations(UAE) was hassled for the lead and looked to have got the better of that battle when stretching into a clear lead in the back straight, but he had no resistance when challenged again and was very tired by the last. (op 7-4 tchd 15-8)
Navajo Nation(IRE) moved up to track the leaders down the back, but he had no answer as they pulled clear again in the home straight. Although he has yet to win, he could change that given fast ground in similar grade. (op 17-2)
Turkish Sultan(IRE) looks to have little ability over hurdles. (tchd 40-1)
Along The Nile was never going well on his first start for new connections. (tchd 9-4)

538 BOWEL CANCER UK MAIDEN HURDLE (10 hdls 2 omitted) 2m 4f 110y
3:50 (3:50) (Class 5) 4-Y-0+ £1,951 (£573; £286; £143)

Form RPR

32-3 **1** **Lamboro Lad (IRE)**[23] 191 5-10-9 112 DonalDevereux(5) 118+
(Peter Bowen) *chsd ldr tl led 4th: c clr fr 2 out: blnd last: easily* **11/8**[1]

P24- **2** *9* **Chesapeake (IRE)**[186] 2506 6-11-0 118 SamThomas 106+
(Jonjo O'Neill) *mid-div: hdwy 6th: rdn appr 3 out: wnt 2nd and wknd after next* **4/1**[2]

1/0- **3** *2 ¼* **Necromancer (IRE)**[84] 4461 7-11-0 0 AidanColeman 103
(Venetia Williams) *prom: mstke 1st: chsd wnr 7th: sn rdn: styd on same pce fr 3 out* **14/1**

06-2 **4** *18* **Douglas**[15] 337 5-11-0 0 MarkGrant 91+
(Roger Curtis) *prom: chsd wnr after 7th tl blnd and wknd 2 out* **13/2**[3]

6 **5** *8* **Sobre Tresor (FR)**[19] 266 4-10-9 0 DavidDennis 73
(Nigel Hawke) *mid-div: hdwy after 5th: rdn and wknd bef 3 out: t.o* **80/1**

/0-0 **6** *1 ½* **Chouromanesco (FR)**[20] 249 7-11-0 0 MattieBatchelor 77
(Mark Bradstock) *hld up: hdwy 7th: sn rdn: wknd 3 out: t.o* **50/1**

00-6 **7** *23* **Be Ashored**[21] 227 5-11-0 0 DenisO'Regan 56
(Nicky Vaughan) *hld up: rdn after 7th: n.d: t.o* **100/1**

P/ **8** *3* **Rootheday (IRE)**[27] 10-10-11 0 DerekLaverty(3) 54
(Michael Mullineaux) *led to 4th: chsd wnr tl wknd bef 7th: t.o* **200/1**

/0-6 **9** *½* **Celts Espere**[15] 337 7-11-0 0 TomMessenger 53
(Chris Bealby) *chsd ldrs: rdn after 6th: wknd next: t.o* **100/1**

/66- **10** *6* **Peter Sent**[63] 4916 8-11-0 0 PaddyBrennan 48
(Tom George) *hld up: a in rr: t.o* **16/1**

11 *5* **Sarah's Boy**[25] 5-11-0 0 (t) TomScudamore 43
(David Pipe) *hld up in tch: wknd after 7th: t.o* **8/1**

12 *17* **Naturally Royal** 7-11-0 0 ChristianWilliams 28
(Lawney Hill) *hld up: in rr and rdn after 5th: t.o after next* **25/1**

P **Watch The Master**[278] 4-10-9 0 CharliePoste —
(Ben Case) *hld up: blnd 4th: wknd and p.u bef 6th* **150/1**

P **Hinton Luciana** 7-10-7 0 AndrewTinkler —
(Nicky Henderson) *hld up: hdwy 5th: rdn and wknd after 7th: t.o: p.u bef 2 out* **11/1**

4m 48.7s (-15.30) **Going Correction** -0.525s/f (Firm)
WFA 4 from 5yo+ 19lb 14 Ran SP% **117.6**
Speed ratings (Par 103): **108,104,103,96,93 93,84,83,83,80 78,72,—,—**
toteswingers:1&2:£1.80, 1&3:£6.60, 2&3:£7.50 CSF £6.33 TOTE £2.30: £1.20, £1.80, £3.70; EX 6.80.
Owner Margaret and Raymond John **Bred** Dan And Mrs Margaret O'Neill **Trained** Little Newcastle, Pembrokes

FOCUS
Just a moderate maiden but some reasonable performances. The winner is on the upgrade.

NOTEBOOK
Lamboro Lad(IRE) ⊠ set what looked no more than a comfortable pace and the field was still grouped down the back, but he kept up the gallop and it was enough to put the rest under pressure. He made a couple of errors, most notably at the last, but it did not stop his momentum and he did it effortlessly. The competition might not have been that strong, but this was an impressive performance. (op 2-1)
Chesapeake(IRE) was well in touch but could not make an impression on the winner. However, considering this was his first run since November and he might be better on easier ground, this was an encouraging run. (op 7-2 tchd 9-2)
Necromancer(IRE) jumped big at the first and was hesitant early on, betraying his lack of experience. That put him on the back foot throughout, but he managed to remain prominent for much of the way so should do better in time, perhaps when tackling handicaps. (tchd 12-1 and 16-1)
Douglas tried to chase down the winner but dived at the second last and lost all chance. He weakened from there but overall ran better than the margin of defeat suggests. (op 8-1 tchd 5-1)
Sobre Tresor(FR) was an indifferent pointer and will need to find a good deal of improvement to feature under rules. (op 66-1)
Sarah's Boy was up with the pack when making a mistake in the back straight that cost him momentum, and his chance was effectively over before it could be seen if the tongue-tie would help him last home on his hurdling debut.
Watch The Master Official explanation: jockey said gelding lost its action

539 RICHARD AND LISA OLDHAM WEDDING ANNIVERSARY H'CAP HURDLE (10 hdls 2 omitted) 2m 4f 110y
4:25 (4:31) (Class 4) (0-105,103) 4-Y-0+ £2,732 (£802; £401; £200)

Form RPR

4-41 **1** **Red Not Blue (IRE)**[15] 336 7-11-7 98 AndrewThornton 110+
(Simon Earle) *prom: chsd ldr 4th: led after 7th: clr last: comf* **2/1**[1]

00/1 **2** *6* **Jeu De Roseau (IRE)**[20] 252 6-11-2 93 DenisO'Regan 100+
(Chris Grant) *hld up: hdwy 7th: rdn appr 3 out: wnt 2nd bef last: no imp* **9/2**[3]

1/0- **3** *2 ¼* **Accumulate**[77] 4601 7-11-1 95 DerekLaverty(3) 98
(Bill Moore) *prom: rdn to chse wnr appr 3 out: wknd bef last* **33/1**

P1-3 **4** *15* **Richard The Third**[29] 100 6-11-3 94 SamJones 83
(John Harris) *hld up: rdn 6th: nvr trbld ldrs* **3/1**[2]

/5P- **5** *16* **Come On Eddie**[50] 5135 7-10-0 77 oh2 (p) GerardTumelty 52
(Anabel L M King) *prom: rdn after 7th: wknd next: t.o* **20/1**

2P-0 **6** *2 ¾* **Occasionally Yours (IRE)**[19] 267 6-11-6 97 DavidDennis 69
(Nigel Hawke) *led: hdd after 7th: sn rdn: wknd next: t.o* **25/1**

06P- **7** *6* **Captain Marlon (IRE)**[70] 4766 9-11-3 94 (t) JoeTizzard 61
(Colin Tizzard) *mid-div: hdwy appr 7th: rdn and wknd bef next: t.o* **16/1**

00P- **8** *3* **Filippo Lippi (IRE)**[46] 5184 5-11-6 97 (b) SamThomas 61
(Jonjo O'Neill) *hld up: rdn and wknd after 7th: t.o* **12/1**

P/0- **P** **Carlton Scroop (FR)**[12] 401 7-10-12 94 MichaelMurphy(5) —
(J Jay) *hld up: plld hrd: a bhd: t.o whn p.u bef 2 out* **12/1**

6P- **P** **Rapid Return (IRE)**[280] 1293 7-11-1 95 SeanQuinlan(3) —
(Richard Phillips) *mid-div: rdn and wknd bef 6th: t.o whn p.u bef next* **33/1**

00P- **P** **Firedog (IRE)**[69] 4790 6-11-2 93 AidanColeman —
(Venetia Williams) *chsd ldr to 4th: remained handy tl rdn and wknd after 7th: t.o whn p.u bef next* **9/1**

4m 50.1s (-13.90) **Going Correction** -0.525s/f (Firm) 11 Ran SP% **122.3**
Speed ratings (Par 105): **105,102,101,96,90 89,86,85,—,— —**
toteswingers:1&2:£3.20, 1&3:£17.40, 2&3:£17.10 CSF £11.78 CT £229.59 TOTE £2.70: £1.10, £1.50, £8.00; EX 12.80.
Owner Mrs Sara Meehan **Bred** William Hubbert **Trained** Tytherington, Wilts
⊠ Ring Boo Ree (4/1) withdrawn after getting loose bef s; deduct 20p in £ from all bets at board prices prior to withdrawal.

FOCUS
Solid form, with another step forward from the winner.

NOTEBOOK
Red Not Blue(IRE), after the withdrawal of the original favourite, was left with a theoretically easier task and he took full advantage. Always prominent, he went for home over the rise in the back straight, got first run on the field and was never in danger from then on. He has been a late recruit to jumping due to injury problems, including a broken pelvis, but now he is sound and in form he made light work of the 6lb rise following his handicap debut success last time. (old market op 7-2)
Jeu De Roseau(IRE) was the subject of a market plunge when returning from a two-year absence to be successful at Towcester last time. Though he ran well again, steadily making progress in the final mile, he was never able to get to the winner. The 11lb rise could not have helped, but he was beaten by a better horse on the day. (old market tchd 6-1)
Accumulate was a bit keen on his first run since March but he was still on terms round the final turn before running out of steam from the last. He had some ability three years ago but did not show much on his return from a lengthy absence in March. This suggests he is finally going the right way. (old market tchd 28-1)
Richard The Third met trouble in running when making headway, but the winner had got first run and was already clear. A C&D winner off a 7lb lower mark in March, he was outclassed here. (old market op 5-1 tchd 11-2, new market op 10-3)
Come On Eddie ran a bit better in first-time cheekpieces, without looking like he will trouble the judge any time soon. (old market op 33-1)

540 DOUGLAS FAMILY H'CAP CHASE (15 fncs 3 omitted) 3m
5:05 (5:05) (Class 4) (0-110,110) 5-Y-0+ £3,548 (£1,048; £524; £262; £131)

Form RPR

35-3 **1** **Prophete De Guye (FR)**[21] 229 7-10-7 91 FelixDeGiles 103+
(James Evans) *trckd ldrs: confidently rdn: led appr last: shkn up and styd on* **3/1**[1]

0-43 **2** *7* **James Pine (IRE)**[16] 317 11-11-5 110 MrMWall(7) 115
(Sue Wilson) *chsd ldr tl led 4 out: rdn and hdd appr last: styd on same pce* **8/1**

601- **3** *19* **Petroupetrov (FR)**[51] 5120 7-11-0 101 SeanQuinlan(3) 90
(Richard Phillips) *hld up: hdwy 7th: rdn appr 3 out: mstke and wknd next* **9/2**[2]

55-5 **4** *1* **Alfadora**[14] 359 10-10-7 91 (t) CharliePoste 79
(Milton Harris) *hld up: drvn along 11th: sn lost tch: wnt mod 4th and hit last* **5/1**[3]

450- **5** *5* **Good Harvest (IRE)**[153] 3128 7-11-3 101 SamThomas 87
(Jonjo O'Neill) *hld up: mstke 8th: hit 10th: hdwy next: drvn to chse wnr after 4 out: blnd and wknd 2 out* **8/1**

26-4 **6** *4* **Classic Clover**[24] 181 10-10-7 91 (tp) AidanColeman 69
(Colin Tizzard) *led: reminders 8th: tried to pull up bnd by stables sn after: hdd 4 out: rdn and wknd appr 2 out* **9/2**[2]

5PP- **7** *52* **Bernard**[47] 5174 10-10-2 91 DonalDevereux(5) 22
(Kevin Bishop) *prom: mstkes 1st and 10th: wknd next: t.o* **8/1**

6m 6.30s (-8.80) **Going Correction** -0.225s/f (Good) 7 Ran SP% **111.4**
Speed ratings: **105,102,96,96,94 93,75**
toteswingers:1&2:£4.60, 1&3:£2.50, 2&3:£5.60 CSF £24.61 CT £101.97 TOTE £3.40: £1.90, £2.90; EX 23.30.
Owner Elegant Clutter Ltd **Bred** G A E C Delorme Gerard & Vincent **Trained** Broadwas, Worcs

FOCUS
A modest race, and the cosy winner is rated in line with his best run.

NOTEBOOK
Prophete De Guye(FR) was taken down to the start early and was keen in the race but travelled well and was looking the likeliest winner throughout the final circuit. His jockey was anxious not to get to the lead too soon, but once asked he had plenty in reserve for a comfortable success. He had run well over a longer trip at this track last time and was able to progress off just a 1lb higher mark. The manner of his victory suggests he could win again, but overall his win ratio, two from 28, is not convincing. (op 7-2 tchd 4-1 and 11-4)
James Pine(IRE) was always near the head of affairs and kept on well enough, but lacked the finishing pace of the winner. However, he handled the switch from hunter chasing to handicaps well, especially off a stiff enough mark. (op 7-1 tchd 9-1)
Petroupetrov(FR) had gained a rare success on his chasing debut at Kempton last month, but was unable to build on that. He jumped low at several fences and was already under pressure before the turn in. He was tired when diving at the second last. (op 7-2)
Alfadora hit several fences, and he began to lose touch in the back straight before staying on a bit near the finish without ever being in contention. He won over fences at this track a year ago but since falling in his next race at Fakenham has not been the same force. (op 9-2 tchd 11-2)

Good Harvest(IRE) jumped a bit carefully and was under pressure from the home turn, giving the impression he needed the run following a five-month break. (tchd 6-1)
Classic Clover needed some encouragement, but generally responded to maintain the lead until fading in the home straight. He might still be a way off hitting form, but it would not surprise if he picked up a weak race or two this summer. (tchd 4-1 and 5-1)

541 DOUGLAS FAMILY H'CAP HURDLE (9 hdls 1 omitted) 2m
5:40 (5:40) (Class 4) (0-115,110) 4-Y-0+ **£2,732** (£802; £401; £200)

Form RPR
060- **1** **Quipe Me Posted (FR)**[41] 5282 6-11-7 **105**........................ SamThomas 109+
(Jonjo O'Neill) *hld up: hdwy 6th: led appr and hit last: drvn out* **14/1**
55-3 **2** 2¾ **Decision**[17] 299 4-10-4 **99**..........................(t) DavidBass(7) 95
(Lawney Hill) *trckd ldrs: led appr 2 out: rdn and hdd bef last: styd on same pce flat* **3/1**[3]
01-5 **3** 1¼ **Princess Rainbow (FR)**[16] 313 5-11-7 **105**...................... AlanO'Keeffe 104
(Jennie Candlish) *led: rdn and hdd 3 out: styd on same pce flat* **6/1**
00-0 **4** ¾ **Ravati (IRE)**[15] 331 4-11-3 **110**.................................. MissLHorner(5) 104
(Chris Grant) *prom: rdn after 3 out: styd on same pce fr last* **33/1**
5-42 **5** 9 **General Smith**[15] 338 11-10-3 **94**................................ MarkQuinlan(7) 86
(James Evans) *hld up: hdwy and n.m.r after 6th: rdn and wknd appr last* **11/4**[2]
2 **6** 23 **Frosted Grape (IRE)**[18] 275 4-11-5 **107**........................(b) GerrySupple 72
(David Pipe) *hld up: reminders after 5th: wknd next: t.o* **11/1**
0/0- **7** ½ **Top Achiever (IRE)**[43] 5229 9-10-8 **95**.......................... DerekLaverty(3) 64
(Bill Moore) *prom: drvn along 5th: wknd after next: hit 2 out: t.o* **33/1**
U2-3 **P** **Mega Watt (IRE)**[25] 159 5-11-6 **104**.............................. AidanColeman —
(Venetia Williams) *chsd ldr tl led 3 out: hdd bef next: p.u bef last: dismntd* **9/4**[1]

3m 48.1s (-7.10) **Going Correction** -0.525s/f (Firm)
WFA 4 from 5yo+ 18lb **8** Ran SP% **117.6**
Speed ratings (Par 105): **96,94,94,93,89 77,77,—**
toteswingers:1&2:£11.70, 1&3:£6.50, 2&3:£6.30 CSF £58.67 CT £286.05 TOTE £16.70: £3.10, £1.50, £2.20; EX 72.80 Place 6 £59.64; Place 5 £47.41.
Owner Scoobyless Partnership **Bred** Gheorghe Codre **Trained** Cheltenham, Gloucs

FOCUS
A steady pace saw six still in a bunch coming to the second last, and the final time was under a second quicker than the opening mares' hurdle. Fair handicap form.

NOTEBOOK
Quipe Me Posted(FR) was restrained in rear until making good progress in the back straight and staying on strongly near the finish. Given the steady pace, the style of his victory was all the more creditable. He did not stay when tried over further this spring and while this drop in trip suited he seemed to have more in the way of stamina than speed to call on at the finish. (op 12-1 tchd 16-1)
Decision raced prominently and though he was readily outpaced he still kept on. He has not achieved much over hurdles but is slowly going the right way and might benefit from stepping up in trip. (op 9-2 tchd 5-1)
Princess Rainbow(FR) was right there to the second last but could only stay on at the one pace and may need a stiffer track or softer ground to be seen to best advantage. (op 9-2)
Ravati(IRE) looked harshly treated after his juvenile success last October and, though he is gradually coming down the weights, he might need this trend to continue for the time being. (op 28-1)
General Smith again raced freely but was still right there turning in. The 11-y-o has not won for three years and is vulnerable to more sprightly finishers. (op 4-1)
Mega Watt(IRE) helped dictate the pace until two out but had been swamped when pulling up quickly and it is to be hoped that nothing is amiss. Official explanation: jockey said gelding lost its action but returned sound (op 5-2 tchd 7-4 and 11-4 in places)
T/Plt: £35.70 to a £1 stake. Pool:£67,935.73 - 1,386.16 winning tickets T/Qpdt: £17.70 to a £1 stake. Pool:£4,421.91 - 184.70 winning tickets CR

542 - 546a (Foreign Racing) - See Raceform Interactive

[514]CARTMEL (L-H)
Monday, May 31

OFFICIAL GOING: Good
Bends moved out 2-3 metres.
Wind: Light, half-behind. Weather: fine and sunny

547 A F CONNELL MARES' NOVICES' (S) HURDLE (8 hdls) 2m 1f 110y
2:10 (2:11) (Class 5) 4-Y-0+ **£1,951** (£573; £286; £143)

Form RPR
654- **1** **Dream Risk (FR)**[17] 2661 4-10-6 98...................................... GrahamLee 100+
(Kate Walton) *trckd ldrs: t.k.h: wnt cl 2nd 3 out: led between last 2: wnt clr run-in: eased towards fin* **2/1**[1]
43-2 **2** 9 **Stir On The Sea (IRE)**[21] 250 4-10-3 105...................... HaddenFrost(3) 87
(James Frost) *t.k.h: trckd ldr: led appr 3 out: hdd between last 2: no ch w wnr* **9/4**[2]
5-1 **3** 11 **Bonzeno Queen (IRE)**[15] 358 5-11-0 0.............................. DPFahy(3) 88
(Evan Williams) *hld up: hdwy to chse ldrs 3 out: one pce fr next* **7/2**[3]
4 9 **Grethel (IRE)**[226] 6-10-3 0.. JamesSmith(7) 76+
(Alan Berry) *chsd ldrs: mstke 1st: outpcd 5th: one pce fr 2 out* **25/1**
0-0 **5** 4 **Searree**[15] 355 5-10-10 0... PeterBuchanan 69
(James Turner) *in rr: hdwy 5th: one pce fr 2 out* **40/1**
05-F **6** 29 **Simplified**[32] 63 7-10-3 0... StevenGagan(7) 43
(Michael Chapman) *led tl appr 3 out: sn wknd* **66/1**
P00- **7** 9 **Samaret**[33] 42 5-10-3 0.. GarryWhillans(7) 35
(Harriet Graham) *in rr: bhd fr 3rd* **100/1**
05-F **8** ¾ **Kelly Manor (IRE)**[21] 250 6-10-5 87............................(v) LeeEdwards(5) 35
(Tony Carroll) *chsd ldrs: wknd 3 out* **12/1**
/00- **9** 13 **Little Lily Morgan**[55] 5072 7-10-10 66................................. PaddyAspell 23
(Robin Bastiman) *in rr: reminders 5th: sn bhd: t.o 3 out* **16/1**
5F0- **P** **Pacific Bay (IRE)**[21] 4370 4-10-6 78.................................... BrianHughes —
(Richard Ford) *mid-div: lost pl 3 out: blnd next: t.o whn p.u bef last* **20/1**
P **Truckers Storm (IRE)**[29] 7-10-3 0.................... MissRachelBlackmore(7) —
(A J Kennedy, Ire) *unruly s: s.s and gave rdr real problems: t.o and j. poorly: p.u after 5th* **33/1**
00- **P** **One Under (IRE)**[199] 2265 5-10-7 0................................ FearghalDavis(3) —
(Nicky Richards) *mid-div: lost pl 5th: t.o 3 out: p.u bef last* **40/1**

4m 8.60s (-4.60) **Going Correction** -0.10s/f (Good)
WFA 4 from 5yo+ 18lb **12** Ran SP% **118.8**
Speed ratings (Par 103): **106,102,97,93,91 78,74,74,68,— —,—**
Tote Swingers:1&2:£1.10, 2&3:£1.10, 1&3:£1.90 CSF £6.44 TOTE £3.10: £1.30, £1.30, £1.50; EX 7.30.The winner was bought in for 8,800gns.
Owner Keep The Faith Partnership **Bred** Trainers House Enterprises Ltd **Trained** Middleham Moor, N Yorks

FOCUS
A moderate mares' seller which saw an impressive winner. The placed horses set the level.

NOTEBOOK
Dream Risk(FR) had run well in juvenile novice hurdles last winter, despite having a tendency to hang left and hinder her chances. Connections bought her to this left-handed track on faster ground and she won impressively. She ought to be up to winning a similarly low-grade race over the summer. Connections clearly think there is something to work with as they bought her in for £8,800. (op 10-3 tchd 15-8)
Stir On The Sea(IRE) was making her debut for this yard, having been runner-up for the Rebecca Curtis yard at Towcester last time. Once again she raced keenly in the early stages, but ran her race and this is clearly her level. She will need to find a moderate seller if she is to win a race over the summer. (op 2-1 tchd 5-2)
Bonzeno Queen(IRE) ran out an impressive winner at Stratford last time, but she looked moderate on this occasion. She will need to improve on this effort. (op 5-2)
Grethel(IRE) was supported at big prices, but was too keen early and her jumping was not good enough. It could prove challenging to win with her over hurdles. (op 50-1)
Little Lily Morgan was backed at big prices, but ran woefully. She is clearly going to struggle. (op 25-1)
Pacific Bay(IRE) Official explanation: jockey said filly made a mistake second and lost its action

548 ROOFING CONSULTANTS LTD FOUR YEARS OLD NOVICES' HURDLE (8 hdls) 2m 1f 110y
2:45 (2:45) (Class 4) 4-Y-0 **£2,927** (£859; £429; £214)

Form RPR
3-11 **1** **Beidh Tine Anseo (IRE)**[19] 288 4-10-9 120............ CampbellGillies(3) 110+
(Lucinda Russell) *trckd ldrs: led on bit after 2 out: v cheekily* **2/5**[1]
2 1½ **Andhaar**[28] 4-10-12 0.. KeithMercer 102+
(Steve Gollings) *mstkes: chsd ldrs: 5th last: styd on to take flattered 2nd last 150yds* **10/1**
22- **3** 3¼ **Classic Contours (USA)**[10] 1746 4-10-12 114.............. DougieCostello 96
(John Quinn) *lft in ld 1st: hdd 4th: led 3 out: hdd after 2 out: kpt on same pce* **8/1**[3]
4 3 **Johnmanderville**[16] 4-10-12 0.. WilsonRenwick 95+
(Noel Wilson) *led: j. slowly and hdd 1st: chsd ldrs: one pce fr 2 out* **33/1**
41-2 **5** 2 **Master Fong (IRE)**[31] 76 4-11-2 119.............................(b) AdrianLane(3) 100
(Donald McCain) *w ldrs: led and blnd 4th: hdd next: one pce fr 2 out* **9/2**[2]
6-0 **6** ½ **Takaatuf (IRE)**[12] 400 4-10-12 0... GrahamLee 91
(John Hellens) *in rr: outpcd 5th: kpt on fr 2 out: nvr a factor* **50/1**
5 **7** 5 **Swiss Guard**[26] 154 4-10-7 0.. DeanColeman(5) 89+
(Tim Vaughan) *chsd ldrs: hit 3 out: hung lft and wknd appr last* **16/1**
PP- **8** 73 **Markadam**[72] 4730 4-10-12 0.. JohnnyFarrelly 21
(Elliott Cooper) *prom: lost pl 4th: sn bhd: t.o 3 out* **50/1**

4m 8.60s (-4.60) **Going Correction** -0.10s/f (Good) **8** Ran SP% **122.6**
Speed ratings: **106,105,103,102,101 101,99,66**
Tote Swingers: 1&2 £1.60, 1&3 £1.60, 2&3 £9.70 CSF £6.72 TOTE £1.50: £1.10, £2.50, £2.30; EX 6.60.
Owner Ian D Miller **Bred** J S Bolger **Trained** Arlary, Perth & Kinross

FOCUS
A good quality race for the time of year, which could contain several winners over the summer. The overall form looks decent rated through the third, and the runner-up can rate a lot higher.

NOTEBOOK
Beidh Tine Anseo(IRE) was unpenalised for his last two successes in conditional jockeys' handicap hurdles. He travelled with ease throughout and never looked in any danger under Gillies, who is now 3-3 on him. The switch back to novice company was a clever piece of placing by his trainer and a valuable handicap hurdle at Perth in June could be the target. (op 4-9 after early 4-6 in a place and 4-7 in places)
Andhaar is officially rated 80 on the flat and he stayed 1m4f in that sphere, so staying the trip over hurdles was no problem. However, his jumping will need to improve if he is to progress, but a win over hurdles should be within his compass. Connections reported he was unsuited by the track and will return to a more conventional course for his next start. (op 8-1)
Classic Contours(USA) has now finished placed in all three hurdles starts. He shaped as if a race over hurdles should fall his way before long. (op 7-1)
Johnmanderville's jumping was not good enough, despite the fact he looks a nice jumping sort.
Master Fong(IRE) turned in a laboured effort. (op 5-1 tchd 6-1)
Swiss Guard shaped with promise and it would be no surprise if he was up to winning races over the summer. Official explanation: jockey said colt hung left-handed closing stages (op 14-1)

549 TOTEPOOL FLEXI BETTING H'CAP CHASE (20 fncs) 3m 6f
3:20 (3:20) (Class 4) (0-105,104) 5-Y-0+ **£3,903** (£1,146; £573; £286)

Form RPR
4-21 **1** **Shulmin**[2] 516 10-10-0 **78** 7ex oh5.................................. PeterBuchanan 92+
(Carol Ferguson) *hld up in rr: hdwy to trck ldrs 14th: led 4 out: wnt clr run-in: easily* **4/1**[1]
03-P **2** 10 **Pauillac (FR)**[19] 274 7-11-6 **101**....................................... HaddenFrost(3) 102
(David Pipe) *mstkes: hld up in midfield: hdwy to trck ldrs 9th: outpcd 12th: rallied 15th: hit 3 out: styd on to take modest 2nd 2f out* **25/1**
5F2- **3** 2½ **Back In Business (IRE)**[35] 16 10-11-0 **92**.................(p) PaulMoloney 89
(Evan Williams) *chsd ldrs: drvn and outpcd 16th: styd on to take modest 3rd last 150yds* **4/1**[1]
106- **4** 9 **Lavenoak Lad**[38] 5373 10-11-9 **104**.................................(t) RyanMania(3) 95
(Simon Burrough) *chsd ldrs: hit 10th and 13th: 3rd whn mstke last: grad wknd* **14/1**
241- **5** nse **Hever Road (IRE)**[40] 5312 11-10-4 **89**............................. JoeCornwall(7) 81
(David Pearson) *mstkes: prom: lost pl 10th: rallied 15th: outpcd next: mstke 3 out: kpt on run-in* **14/1**
-121 **6** 1 **Finbin (IRE)**[5] 471 8-11-7 **102** 7ex...............................(t) FearghalDavis(3) 91
(Henry Hogarth) *chsd ldrs: reminders after 2nd and 7th: hit 10th: outpcd 14th: lost pl 4 out* **13/2**[2]
34P- **7** 1 **Stop The Show (IRE)**[50] 5152 9-10-8 **86**.......................(p) TimmyMurphy 74
(Richard Phillips) *trckd ldrs: jnd ldrs 14th: wnt 2nd and mstke 2 out: wknd bdly fnl 2f* **10/1**
0P3- **8** 16 **Esme Rides A Gaine**[42] 5271 8-10-9 **87**............................. PaddyAspell 59
(Christopher Wilson) *mde most: hdd 4 out: wknd sn after last* **15/2**
P-42 **9** 22 **Feeling Peckish (USA)**[8] 437 6-9-7 **78** oh6.................. StevenGagan(7) 31
(Michael Chapman) *nt fluent in last: j.rt: bhd fr 9th: t.o 15th* **12/1**
6-U4 **10** 50 **Gershwinner (IRE)**[2] 517 7-11-0 **95**..............................(b) AdrianLane(3) 3
(Donald McCain) *w ldr: wknd qckly 3 out: wl bhd last: t.o* **7/1**[3]
U43- **P** **Saddler's Way (IRE)**[184] 2575 7-10-8 **93** ow3.................. MrGCrow(7) —
(A M Crow) *in rr: bhd and drvn 9th: t.o 16th: blnd 3 out: p.u bef next* **14/1**

7m 29.8s (-6.40) **Going Correction** -0.10s/f (Good) **11** Ran SP% **118.2**
Speed ratings: **104,101,100,98,98 97,97,93,87,74 —**
toteswingers: 1&2 £14.30, 1&3 £5.30, 2&3 £11.70 CSF £90.44 CT £430.43 TOTE £4.90: £1.70, £5.70, £1.90; EX 155.20.
Owner F S Storey **Bred** J Wade **Trained** Dalston, Cumbria

FOCUS
On paper a competitive handicap which turned into a one-horse race from some way out. The first two are rated to their best.

NOTEBOOK

Shulmin ran out an easy winner here on Saturday over 2m5f and this strong-staying mare coped with the longer trip easily. She is likely to take a hefty rise in the weights after her two wins, and connections report she will have a break now as fast ground is not really to her liking. (op 9-2 tchd 7-2)

Pauillac(FR) is a moody sort who turned in one of his better displays upped in trip. His jumping was not always fluent and as usual his attitude was poor. It would be unwise to expect a similar showing next time. (op 20-1)

Back In Business(IRE) is not the most fluent of jumpers, but he once again made the frame on his return to fences. Under pressure from a long way out, he plugged on late to claim a place. He has now dropped 10lb below his last winning mark, but hardly shaped as a certain next time out winner. (op 9-2 tchd 7-2)

Lavenoak Ladis an out-and-out stayer who ran creditably. Making his fair share of mistakes was not a help to his chances, but the Handicapper looks in charge now. (op 11-1)

Hever Road(IRE) ended a losing spell that went back five years when winning at Leicester in March. Since then he went on to score at Southwell, but found this 4lb higher mark beyond him. (op 12-1 tchd 11-1)

Finbin(IRE) struggled to cope with a 6lb penalty for a recent win and will need to produce career-best efforts if he is to win off this mark, but this track still probably was not for him. (op 9-2)

Stop The Show(IRE) bled from the nose last time but travelled well here before finishing weakly, which is usual for him. He is one to be wary of. (op 12-1)

550 BET TOTEPOOL ON ALL UK RACING BEGINNERS' CHASE (14 fncs) 2m 5f 110y

3:55 (3:55) (Class 4) 5-Y-O+ **£3,252** (£955; £477; £238)

Form RPR

00-2 **1** **Simarian (IRE)**[20] 265 5-11-0 0 .... PaulMoloney 124+
(Evan Williams) *led: hit 8th and reminders: narrowly hdd next: w ldr: hit 3 out: led 2f out: all out* **9/4**[1]

135- **2** *hd* **Last Flight (IRE)**[281] 1292 6-10-2 0 ....(p) DonalDevereux(5) 115
(Peter Bowen) *trckd ldrs: led 9th: narrowly hdd 2f out: no ex nr fin* **11/4**[2]

02-2 **3** *5* **Indian Pipe Dream (IRE)**[15] 353 8-11-0 108 ....(tp) KeithMercer 117
(Steve Gollings) *w wnr: outpcd 2 out: kpt on same pce run-in* **7/2**

03-1 **4** *43* **Hearthstead Dream**[18] 309 9-11-0 127 .... BrianHughes 84+
(Gordon Elliott, Ire) *nt fluent: chsd ldrs: outpcd 9th: modest 5th whn mstke 2 out: tk poor 4th 2f out* **3/1**[3]

0/ **5** *16* **Ballycolin**[24] 202 7-11-0 110 .... PeterBuchanan 70
(I A Duncan, Ire) *chsd ldrs: hit 8th: wknd 2 out: eased whn lost distant 4th 2f out* **14/1**

35-5 **6** *100* **Young Yozza**[22] 226 8-10-7 61 .... JoeCornwall(7) —
(David Pearson) *mstke 1st: sn detached in last and drvn along: t.o fr 5th: eventually completed* **50/1**

5m 17.7s (-7.70) **Going Correction** -0.10s/f (Good) **6** Ran SP% **113.3**
Speed ratings: **110,109,108,92,87 —**
Tote Swingers: 1&2 £2.00, 1&3 £2.60, 2&3 £1.50 CSF £9.32 TOTE £3.50: £2.00, £1.20; EX 8.20.

Owner Peter Conway **Bred** His Highness The Aga Khan's Studs S C **Trained** Llancarfan, Vale Of Glamorgan

FOCUS

Another above average race for the time of year, which produced an exciting battle between the leading pair on the long run for home. The placed horses offer the best guides to the form.

NOTEBOOK

Simarian(IRE) ran well on his chasing debut at Newton Abbot last time and, despite not always travelling well, he battled to shed his maiden tag over fences. His jumping may need to be more fluent if he is to be upped in class. A similar race under a penalty should be within his reaches and a valuable handicap in August could be a target.

Last Flight(IRE) was a good quality hurdler who ran well on her chasing debut. She jumped well and although carrying her head awkwardly she battled right to the line. Trying hard and good jumping, together with her class, should see he win races over fences. (op 4-1)

Indian Pipe Dream(IRE) has now finished placed in his last three chase starts, but looked awkward under pressure. He is clearly in good heart, but is hard to win with and his last success was in August 2008. (op 4-1 tchd 10-3)

Hearthstead Dream was making his chasing debut, but his jumping was not up to scratch and is not an obvious chasing type. (op 9-4 tchd 7-2)

551 WICKS WASTE MANAGEMENT MAIDEN HUNTERS' CHASE (FOR THE FRASER CUP) (14 fncs) 2m 5f 110y

4:30 (4:30) (Class 6) 5-Y-O+ **£1,249** (£387; £193; £96)

Form RPR

4-45 **1** **Ardnaclancy (IRE)**[12] 398 7-11-5 0 .... MrJARichardson(7) 111+
(Andrew Richardson) *chsd ldr: rn wd bnd after last: led over 2f out: drvn rt out* **4/1**[3]

26- **2** *6* **What Of It (IRE)**[50] 5143 7-11-5 0 .... CaptTWCEdwards(7) 105
(Tom George) *led: hdd over 2f out: kpt on same pce* **3/1**[1]

4BP- **3** *1* **Lagosta (SAF)**[15] 10-11-7 86 .... MrJHamer(5) 104
(S J Graham) *chsd ldrs: wnt 3rd 4 out: styd on fnl f* **8/1**

3F-3 **4** *13* **Father Murtagh (IRE)**[22] 10-11-9 90 ....(v) MrGBrewer(3) 92
(Mrs Freya Brewer) *swvd rt s: wnt prom 3rd: wknd between last 2* **9/2**

/P-0 **5** *½* **Cluthe Boy (IRE)**[26] 150 7-11-7 0 ....(t) MissSSharratt(5) 92
(Miss S Sharratt) *in rr: bhd 8th: styd on run-in: nrst fin* **16/1**

55P/ **6** *1¾* **The Stickler**[16] 11-11-5 0 ....(p) MrGRSmith(7) 91
(Mrs Elaine Smith) *chsd ldrs: outpcd 2 out: sn btn* **9/1**

-532 **7** *1¼* **Athoss**[8] 443 8-11-7 105 ow2 .... MrRMSmith(7) 93
(Robert Smith) *chsd ldrs: outpcd 3 out: wl btn whn hit last* **7/2**[2]

030/ **8** *½* **Wilfie Wild**[28] 14-11-9 0 .... MissTJackson(3) 90
(Mrs Lynne Ward) *in rr: outpcd 9th: hit 3 out: modest 4th last: wknd fnl 2f* **25/1**

/P-3 **9** *89* **Barry The Cracker**[18] 310 7-11-5 0 .... MrMEnnis(7) 9
(G F White) *stdd s: hld up detached in last: hdwy whn hit 9th: wknd 4 out: eased whn bhd run-in: virtually p.u* **22/1**

5m 19.8s (-5.60) **Going Correction** -0.10s/f (Good) **9** Ran SP% **120.6**
Speed ratings: **106,103,103,98,98 97,97,97,64**
Tote Swingers: 1&2 £2.20, 1&3 £10.90, 2&3 £3.00 CSF £17.94 TOTE £5.00: £1.90, £1.70, £3.10; EX 21.70.

Owner David Carr **Bred** Patrick Hayes **Trained** Hexham, Northumberland

FOCUS

An ordinary hunter chase in which the winner is on the upgrade. The third is rated to his mark.

NOTEBOOK

Ardnaclancy(IRE) had good form in points last season, but something had amiss in the early part of the season, hence his poor showings. He bounced back to form here and scored well, despite his rider looking over the wrong shoulder close home. Still young, he could progress from this and can give another bold show next time. (op 5-1 tchd 7-2)

What Of It(IRE) usually makes the running and found this track more to his liking unlike Kelso last time. He responded well to his rider's wild urgings and should run well in similar hunter chases next season. Fast ground suits him best. (op 4-1 tchd 9-2)

Lagosta(SAF) had the assistance of top amateur rider Josh Hamer and he had been in good form in points this season. This was a respectable run to round off his season. It remains to be seen if he can progress from this given his age. (op 5-1)

Father Murtagh(IRE) had been blighted by errors in his recent points and looks to be regressing aged ten, having run poorly here. (op 11-2 tchd 6-1)

Cluthe Boy(IRE) is a dual point winner this year, but found this trip too short. He would only be of interest in hunter chases over a longer trip. (tchd 20-1)

Athoss, whose rider put up 2lb overweight, was a disappointment on his favoured fast ground and was later reported never to be travelling Official explanation: jockey said gelding never travelled (op 4-1)

552 A F CONNELL FRIENDS AND FAMILY NOVICES' H'CAP HURDLE (10 hdls 1 omitted) 2m 6f

5:05 (5:05) (Class 5) (0-95,95) 4-Y-O+ **£2,602** (£764; £382; £190)

Form RPR

0U-3 **1** **Paddington Bob (IRE)**[26] 163 6-10-12 81 .... TimmyMurphy 86
(Pauline Robson) *trckd ldrs: wnt cl 2nd normal 3 out: led bef omitted last: kpt on: all out* **11/4**[1]

46-4 **2** *½* **Galley Slave (IRE)**[8] 440 5-9-7 69 oh1 .... StevenGagan(7) 74
(Michael Chapman) *in rr: gd hdwy 7th: chsng ldrs next: led sn after normal 2 out: hdd bef omitted last: hrd rdn and kpt on wl fnl 2f: jst hld* **12/1**

05-4 **3** *2½* **Lukey Luke**[25] 176 7-10-7 76 .... KeithMercer 78
(James Turner) *mid-div: hdwy 8th: styd on wl fr normal 2 out: tk modest 3rd bef omitted last: styd on wl fnl f* **7/1**

43-0 **4** *19* **Rawaaj**[32] 59 4-10-13 90 .... AdrianLane(3) 70
(Donald McCain) *chsd ldrs: wknd normal 2 out* **8/1**

000- **5** *20* **Apache Brave (IRE)**[74] 4708 7-10-1 70 ....(p) BrianHughes 37
(Henry Hogarth) *chsd ldrs: wknd normal 2 out* **16/1**

04-0 **6** *13* **Naughty Diesel**[26] 161 7-10-1 75 ....(t) JamesHalliday(5) 31
(Robert Johnson) *stdd s: hld up in rr: kpt on fr normal 2 out: nvr on terms* **12/1**

PP/ **7** *18* **Make It Blossom (IRE)**[564] 2171 8-10-11 80 .... DenisO'Regan 19
(John G Carr, Ire) *led: hdd sn after normal 2 out: sn lost pl* **22/1**

006- **8** *27* **Strumble Head (IRE)**[72] 4723 5-11-2 85 .... TomO'Brien —
(Peter Bowen) *chsd ldrs: wknd 8th* **11/2**[3]

05P- **9** *17* **Hows Trix (IRE)**[289] 1221 10-10-13 89 .... PaulGallagher(7) —
(Ferdy Murphy) *nt fluent in rr: bhd fr 7th* **20/1**

01-P **10** *11* **Zelos Diktator**[23] 212 4-11-2 90 .... GrahamLee —
(Rose Dobbin) *chsd ldrs: wknd 7th: eased extended run-in: t.o* **9/2**[2]

P0-0 **P** **Besi**[22] 228 8-10-9 81 .... HarryHaynes(3) —
(Lisa Harrison) *s.i.s: drvn 5th: sn bhd: t.o whn mstke 8th: sn p.u* **16/1**

0/0 **P** **Quick Man (FR)**[214] 1968 6-10-8 80 .... FearghalDavis(3) —
(Nicky Richards) *in rr: bhd fr 8th: t.o whn p.u after normal 2 out: lame* **14/1**

5m 24.4s (-4.90) **Going Correction** -0.10s/f (Good)
WFA 4 from 5yo+ 19lb **12** Ran SP% **126.8**
Speed ratings (Par 103): **104,103,102,96,88 84,77,67,61,57 —,—**
Tote Swingers: 1&2 £12.70, 1&3 £4.60, 2&3 £27.20 CSF £39.39 CT £224.29 TOTE £3.50: £1.70, £4.10, £2.50; EX 51.50.

Owner Mr & Mrs Raymond Anderson Green **Bred** Eamonn And Liam O'Donovan **Trained** Kirkharle, Northumberland

FOCUS

A weak novice handicap with the first three pretty much to their marks.

NOTEBOOK

Paddington Bob(IRE) was third over this trip at Kelso last time and travelled well for Timmy Murphy here. The sharper track appeared to suit him well and his rider's strength got him home. He would need to improve further if he is to win again. (op 3-1 tchd 10-3 and 4-1 in a place)

Galley Slave(IRE) showed improved form at this trip, but his chance was not helped when his rider became unbalanced by-passing the final flight of hurdles. The fact he is winless in 57 career starts and his trainer is on a losing run stretching back 158 runners puts this race into context. (op 16-1 tchd 18-1)

Lukey Luke was staying on late having found himself in an unpromising position jumping the last. He has shown only moderate form in the past and will need to improve if he is to shed his maiden tag. (op 15-2 tchd 8-1)

Rawaaj was racing without the tongue tie he has had on his last two starts, but that made little difference. Another poor showing leaves him with plenty of questions to answer. (op 7-1)

Zelos Diktator shaped as a non-stayer at Hexham last time, but was a big disappointment here. His sole win came in a seller and that is probably his level. (op 5-1)

Quick Man(FR) Official explanation: vet said gelding finished lame

553 PSR MARQUEE HIRE CONDITIONAL JOCKEYS' H'CAP HURDLE (11 hdls 1 omitted) 3m 2f

5:40 (5:40) (Class 4) (0-110,108) 4-Y-O+ **£3,903** (£1,146; £573; £286)

Form RPR

1213 **1** **Flying Doctor**[6] 461 7-11-12 108 .... JohnnyFarrelly 116+
(Elliott Cooper) *hld up: trckd ldrs 3rd: led on bit bef last: heavily eased: cheekily* **5/1**[2]

21-0 **2** *1¼* **Glen Rouge (IRE)**[17] 318 9-10-0 82 oh2 .... RyanMania 84
(James Moffatt) *in rr: hdwy to chse ldrs 5th: kpt on to take 2nd last: no ch w eased down wnr* **17/2**

0-32 **3** *11* **Money Finder**[16] 340 7-10-11 93 .... HaddenFrost 86
(Roger Curtis) *w ldr: led normal 3 out: hdd appr last: wknd run-in* **7/1**

05-5 **4** *20* **Follow On**[19] 291 8-10-7 94 ....(t) MrDarylMillar(5) 68
(Maurice Barnes) *chsd ldrs 3rd: hmpd and lost pl 7th: sn bhd: tk remote 4th last* **16/1**

061- **5** *11* **Ripalong Lad (IRE)**[234] 1684 9-11-9 108 ....(p) DonalDevereux(3) 72
(Peter Bowen) *sn chsng ldrs: led after 7th: hdd normal 3 out: wknd rapidly bef last* **11/1**

4-26 **6** *6* **Solway Ally**[16] 340 7-11-4 100 ....(p) HarryHaynes 63
(Lisa Harrison) *led: hdd 8th: wknd after normal 2 out: bhd and eased last* **11/2**[3]

4-21 **F** **Boyoboy (IRE)**[17] 318 6-11-12 108 .... MichaelO'Connell —
(George Moore) *hld up: hdwy to trck ldrs 6th: fell next: fatally injured* **9/4**[1]

14-0 **P** **Oniz Tiptoes (IRE)**[15] 352 9-11-4 100 ....(v) CampbellGillies —
(John Wainwright) *in tch: hmpd and lost pl 7th: sn bhd: t.o normal 2 out: p.u run-in* **14/1**

/0P- **P** **Quality Control (IRE)**[64] 4908 9-11-2 106 .... PaulGallagher(8) —
(Ferdy Murphy) *in rr: lost pl 8th: sn bhd: p.u after next* **14/1**

3PP- **P** **Mewstone**[69] 4796 7-11-1 105 .... CiaranMckee(8) —
(Tom George) *chsd ldrs: hit 5th: sn lost pl: bhd whn p.u after 7th: lame* **33/1**

6m 20.0s (-6.10) **Going Correction** -0.10s/f (Good) **10** Ran SP% **116.3**
Speed ratings (Par 105): **105,104,101,95,91 89,—,—,—,—**
Tote Swingers: 1&2 £10.60, 1&3 £7.30, 2&3 £13.50 CSF £46.86 CT £299.01 TOTE £5.10: £2.30, £3.30, £3.00; EX 62.00 Place 6 £7.17, Place 5 £6.48..

Owner Tom McNicholas **Bred** London Thoroughbred Services Ltd & J Gaines **Trained** Brigham, Cumbria

FOCUS

A moderate handicap and the progressive winner rates value for a good bit further with the runner-up rated to his Uttoxeter mark..

NOTEBOOK

Flying Doctor recorded his fourth win this spring and once again did so with ease. He was set too much to do last time, but under a professional rider he readily drew clear. This horse has been a credit to his trainer, holds an entry here on Wednesday, and if all is well he will take that up. Judged on this he could take come stopping. (op 11-2 tchd 9-2)

Glen Rouge(IRE) was racing from 2lb out of the handicap here and ran creditably. He is not always the heartiest of battlers and has only one win from 23 starts. (op 9-1 tchd 8-1)

Money Finder had showed improved form when upped in trip at Uttoxeter the last twice. Another longer trip was not against her, she is holding her form well, but the Handicapper could be in charge now. (tchd 6-1 and 15-2)

Follow On was never travelling with great purpose and is becoming hard to predict. (tchd 14-1)

Ripalong Lad(IRE) had won 2-3 of his last chasing starts, but he has been absent since October 2009. He shaped as if he needed the run and it would not be a surprise if he were to improve on this. (op 10-1 tchd 12-1)

Boyoboy(IRE) sadly took a fatal fall at the seventh. (op 3-1 tchd 7-2 in a place)

T/Plt: £10.90 to a £1 stake. Pool:£51,647.43 - 3,435.62 winning tickets T/Qpdt: £5.80 to a £1 stake. Pool:£2,666.10 - 336.30 winning tickets WG

[427]TOWCESTER (R-H)

Monday, May 31

OFFICIAL GOING: Good (good to firm in places; 10.1)

Hurdle course dolled out to middle position.

554 HAYGAIN HAY STEAMERS MAIDEN HURDLE (8 hdls) 2m

2:15 (2:15) (Class 5) 4-Y-O+ **£2,602** (£764; £382; £190)

Form RPR

22-2 **1** **Niceonefrankie**[32] 58 4-10-10 114 .... AidanColeman 113+
(Venetia Williams) *chsd ldr tl led after 2nd: mde rest: mstke 3 out: drew clr wl bef next: eased after last: easily* **3/1**[2]

2 *9* **Scene Two**[232] 4-10-10 0 .... RichardJohnson 101
(Philip Hobbs) *hld up wl in tch: chsd clr wnr bef 2 out: no imp u.p between last 2: kpt on* **13/2**

200- **3** *1 ½* **Apache Chant (USA)**[50] 5142 6-10-7 103 .... AnthonyFreeman[(7)] 104
(Tony Carroll) *in tch in midfield: mstke 3rd: rdn and outpcd after 5th: rallied u.p bef 2 out: wnt 3rd last: kpt on but no ch w wnr* **9/1**

2-2 **4** *½* **Gulf President**[22] 216 4-10-10 110 .... TomScudamore 101+
(Tim Vaughan) *led tl after 2nd: chsd wnr after: mstke 5th: rdn and hit next: sn outpcd by wnr and 4th 2 out: plugged on same pce after* **4/1**[3]

6-23 **5** *7* **Apache Dawn**[5] 479 6-10-11 100 .... EamonDehdashti[(3)] 97
(Aytach Sadik) *in tch in midfield: pushed along 3 out: no prog and wl btn bef next* **8/1**

65- **6** *2* **Monreale (GER)**[27] 5103 6-11-0 0 .... (t) APMcCoy 98+
(David Pipe) *hld up in tch towards rr: hdwy into midfield 4th: rdn and pressing for 2nd whn wandered bdly 2 out: wknd and wl btn whn mstke last* **5/2**[1]

5 **7** *26* **Rainiers Girl**[19] 279 4-9-10 0 .... MrTJCannon[(7)] 57
(Roger Teal) *t.k.h: chsd ldrs: mstke 2nd: wknd qckly bef 3 out: t.o fr 2 out* **25/1**

60/ **8** *5* **Surdoue**[83] 1501 10-10-9 0 .... JohnKington[(5)] 63
(Michael Scudamore) *t.k.h: hld up in rr: mstke 2nd: lost tch bef 3 out: t.o fr 2 out* **200/1**

0-P6 **9** *¾* **Gilded Youth**[16] 338 6-11-0 90 .... ColinBolger 62
(Simon Lewis) *t.k.h: chsd ldrs tl wknd u.p bef 3 out: t.o fr 2 out* **100/1**

R **Captain Flack**[67] 4-10-10 0 .... TomMessenger —
(Giles Bravery) *t.k.h early: dropped to last 3rd: losing tch whn j. slowly next: tailing off whn rn out 5th* **100/1**

00-6 **F** **Golden Smog (IRE)**[15] 360 4-10-3 0 .... PaddyBrennan —
(Ian Williams) *a in rr: mstke 1st and 3rd: rdn and wl btn bef 3 out: t.o whn wandered and fell 2 out* **66/1**

3m 51.1s (-16.80) **Going Correction** -0.775s/f (Firm)

WFA 4 from 6yo+ 18lb **11** Ran SP% **115.8**

Speed ratings (Par 103): **111,106,105,105,102 101,88,85,85,— —**

Tote Swingers: 1&2 £1.50, 1&3 £7.00, 2&3 £7.10 CSF £22.27 TOTE £4.30: £1.80, £1.80, £2.30; EX 19.50.

Owner The Gambling Cousins **Bred** Mrs M E Jones **Trained** Kings Caple, H'fords

FOCUS

A modest maiden hurdle though the winning time was good. There is more to come from the winner and the third, fourth and fifth set the level.

NOTEBOOK

Niceonefrankie looked worth trying around a more demanding course after three staying-on second place efforts either side of his winter break, and he rewarded late market support in this opener. Aidan Coleman's decision to kick on after three out proved the race-winning move, and the partnership always looked to have matters well under control from that point on. This will do plenty for his confidence and he could prove up to defying a penalty in a small summer novice. Connections plan to keep him on the go if the ground allows it. (op 9-2)

Scene Two hadn't been seen since winning a Goodwood 1m4f handicap off 71 for Luca Cumani last October, but looked fit and well for this hurdling debut. The quirks displayed even in victory there (veering everywhere under pressure) did not resurface when asked for his effort, and he was simply beaten by a horse evidently better suited to this test. He should find a small opening. (op 11-2)

Apache Chant(USA) is winless after 15 hurdles tries and had been well beaten in a Kelso handicap off 105 last time, but stayed on reasonably well late on. His overall profile tempers confidence he'll produce a comparable effort next time. (op 12-1)

Gulf President came under pressure a fair way out and didn't build on his near-miss at Plumpton last time, though in mitigation two mistakes mid-race may have cost him a deal of impetus. (op 9-2 tchd 11-2)

Monreale(GER), who met with late market hostility, was starting to respond to his rider's industry when jinking to his right two out cost him all chance. He does at least qualify for a mark now. (op 15-8 tchd 11-4)

555 JENKINSONS CATERERS CLAIMING HURDLE (8 hdls) 2m

2:50 (2:50) (Class 5) 4-Y-O+ **£1,951** (£573; £286; £143)

Form RPR

3 **1** **A Dream Come True**[15] 358 5-10-4 0 .... JodieMogford 90+
(Graeme McPherson) *t.k.h: chsd ldr and wandering into hurdles: lft in ld 5th: mde rest: drew clr after 2 out: easily* **12/1**[3]

00 **2** *8* **Billy Beetroot (USA)**[15] 356 4-10-4 0 .... LeeStephens[(3)] 83
(Katie Stephens) *hld up in last: lft 4th 5th: hdwy to chse wnr bef 2 out: rdn and btn wl bef last* **50/1**

0-0P **3** *3* **Nicky Nutjob (GER)**[15] 351 4-10-10 102 .... GerardTumelty 84
(Jeff Pearce) *a in last pair: lft cl 3rd 5th: rdn and wanting to hang after 3 out: swtchd rt jst bef 2 out: no prog and wl hld whn mstke last* **14/1**

106- **4** *6* **Miss Nightshade**[43] 5253 6-10-10 110 .... (t) DarylJacob 80
(Jamie Snowden) *chsd ldng pair tl lft 2nd 5th: mstke next: wknd u.p bef 2 out: last and btn whn mstke 2 out* **7/2**[2]

1P-1 **R** **Mhilu (IRE)**[14] 374 8-10-11 121 .... (vt[1]) APMcCoy —
(Gary Brown) *led tl rn out 5th* **1/3**[1]

3m 59.9s (-8.00) **Going Correction** -0.775s/f (Firm)

WFA 4 from 5yo+ 18lb **5** Ran SP% **113.6**

Speed ratings (Par 103): **89,85,83,80,—**

CSF £183.05 TOTE £12.90: £4.40, £6.10; EX 827.60.Mhilu claimed by Mr T. Vaughan for £5,000.

Owner The Futures Bright Partnership **Bred** D K Ivory **Trained** Upper Oddington, Gloucs

FOCUS

The complexion of this ordinary contest changed entirely at the fifth flight. The race took little winner but could be rated a lot higher.

NOTEBOOK

A Dream Come True, winless away from the Polytrack on the level and well held on her hurdling debut in a Stratford novice seller last time, picked up the pieces when the favourite ran out. She had raced a touch awkwardly and taken a grip early in the contest, so the fact she was still able to come home in splendid isolation (even idling a touch up the run-in) doesn't speak volumes for those she beat. (op 11-1)

Billy Beetroot(USA) had finished last on both previous hurdles starts, beaten an aggregate of over 210 lengths. This was clearly better, but it didn't require much effort on the part of the winner to brush him off up the straight. (op 40-1)

Nicky Nutjob(GER) hasn't followed up his Wetherby Listed juvenile win of last last October in seven subsequent hurdles starts, and maybe two heavy defeats at Cheltenham right after that victory have left a mark. The drop to claiming grade and return to a stiff 2m did not inspire the revival connections hoped for, and he's looking increasingly hard to win with. (op 12-1)

Miss Nightshade offered very little response for increased pressure turning in despite not having raced as keenly as she sometimes does. (op 4-1)

Mhilu(IRE), who had gone about his business more pleasingly than his four rivals up to the fifth flight, ran out to the right of the hurdle, taking a dividing rail with him. He is likely to get a number of chances to make amends during the summer, though few necessarily as easy as this. (op 2-5)

556 TONY CLARK BEGINNERS' CHASE (16 fncs) 2m 6f

3:25 (3:25) (Class 4) 5-Y-O+ **£3,252** (£955; £477; £238)

Form RPR

34F- **1** **Baren De Doc (IRE)**[39] 5327 7-11-0 112 .... (p) RichardJohnson 109+
(Tim Vaughan) *in tch: lft 3rd 2nd: led 6th tl after 9th: led again 11th: mde rest: rdn clr after 2 out: wl in command last: eased towards fin* **2/1**[2]

P/3 **2** *11* **Gothic Charm (IRE)**[22] 226 8-11-0 0 .... ChristianWilliams 95
(Rachel Hobbs) *j.lft: bmpd rival and stmbld 1st: in tch: rdn to chse ldng pair sn after 3 out: no ch w wnr between last 2: plugged on to go 2nd fnl 50yds* **6/1**[3]

1/1- **3** *1* **Dreamy Sweeney (IRE)**[394] 114 8-11-0 0 .... APMcCoy 95+
(Nicky Henderson) *t.k.h: hld up in tch in last: mstke 7th: hdwy next: pressed wnr gng wl 11th: mstke 13th: ev ch and rdn 2 out: wknd wl bef last: tired flat and lost 2nd fnl 50yds* **4/5**[1]

43-4 **4** *20* **Thyne Spirit (IRE)**[10] 429 11-11-0 58 .... ColinBolger 73
(Simon Lewis) *led tl hdd 6th: reminders bef next: lost pl briefly after 7th: hdwy u.p to ld after 9th tl 11th: wknd rapidly after 3 out: wl btn whn j.rt last* **66/1**

6-0 **5** *46* **Harvey May (IRE)**[22] 226 8-10-7 0 .... AnthonyFreeman[(7)] 27
(John Upson) *chsd ldr tl 5th: reminders bef next: rdn and struggling bef 12th: 5th and wl btn whn blnd bdly 3 out: t.o* **50/1**

5-62 **P** **Tuscany Star (IRE)**[10] 429 7-10-7 98 .... (t) AdamWedge[(7)] —
(Edward Creighton) *rn in snatches: j.lft and bmpd rival 1st: in tch: j. slowly 3rd: drvn and wknd 12th: t.o whn p.u 2 out* **14/1**

004- **F** **Wham Bang**[45] 5209 6-10-11 88 .... SeanQuinlan[(3)] —
(Robin Mathew) *chsd ldng pair tl fell 2nd* **20/1**

5m 33.3s (-19.70) **Going Correction** -0.775s/f (Firm) **7** Ran SP% **118.1**

Speed ratings: **104,100,99,92,75 —,—**

Tote Swingers: 1&2 £2.20, 2&3 £1.10 CSF £14.64 TOTE £2.70: £1.60, £2.10; EX 15.10.

Owner Oceans Six **Bred** Colin Wright **Trained** Aberthin, Vale of Glamorgan

FOCUS

A thinly contested beginners' chase. The winner is rated to his mark and is value for further with the form backed up by the runner-up.

NOTEBOOK

Baren De Doc(IRE), a faller at Fontwell last time, was essentially foot-perfect on this occasion and had more to worry about from a loose horse than his rivals over the last third of the contest. (op 4-1)

Gothic Charm(IRE) was given time to get back into the race after a mid-air collision with Tuscany Star at the first, but never really held a winning chance and merely boxed on past the disappointing favourite close home. Low-grade handicaps are likely to prove his level eventually. (tchd 11-2)

Dreamy Sweeney(IRE) looked to have been found a gilt-edged opportunity to open his account over fences as long as a 394-day absence could be overcome. He did much to compromise his chances, however, taking a strong hold and not jumping with any great alacrity from an early stage (a sideways leap at the second ditch was particularly alarming). His challenge up the straight was pretty limited despite the aid of the outer rail after the last, and while he's entitled to have learned something from the experience, on this evidence it would be brave to take short odds about him, even in a similarly ordinary race next time unless something comes to light. (op 8-13 tchd 5-6 and 10-11 in places)

Thyne Spirit(IRE) ran okay to a point before all the driving to keep him at the head of affairs finally took its toll. (op 50-1)

557 GG.COM BANK HOLIDAY RACING EXCELLENCE "HANDS AND HEELS" H'CAP HURDLE (FOR CONDITIONAL JOCKEYS) (9 hdls 1 omitted) 2m 3f 110y

4:00 (4:00) (Class 5) (0-95,90) 4-Y-O+ **£2,602** (£764; £382; £190)

Form RPR

6P-0 **1** **Marlborough Sound**[22] 228 11-11-4 85 .... HenryBrooke[(3)] 93+
(James Turner) *hld up in tch in midfield: hdwy to trck ldrs gng wl bef 3 out: led wl bef 2 out: in command between last 2: easily* **16/1**

/42- **2** *7* **Present**[48] 2346 6-10-5 69 .... MattCrawley 70
(Diana Weeden) *t.k.h early: hld up in tch towards rr: rdn and effrt to chse clr wnr after 3 out: no imp whn mstke next: plugged on for clr 2nd* **9/1**

P3-0 **3** *8* **Galant Eye (IRE)**[20] 264 11-10-13 77 .... TrevorWhelan 69
(Chris Down) *in tch towards rr: rdn and no prog bef 3 out: hmpd 3 out: nt clr run ent st: styd on to go modest 3rd between last: no ch w wnr* **10/1**

06-2 **4** *5* **Masterpoint**[6] 462 10-10-10 77 .... AdamWedge[(3)] 64
(Richard Harper) *in tch: rdn and effrt bef 3 out: plugged on same pce and no ch w ldrs fr bef 2 out* **7/1**

3-42 **5** 2 3/4 **Bari Bay**[13] 380 4-10-12 86.. MrKevinJones(5) 69+
(Seamus Mullins) *t.k.h early: hld up in rr: hmpd 5th: effrt and mstke 3 out: no prog and wl btn next* **5/1**[3]

45P- **6** 3/4 **Dolans Bay (IRE)**[56] 5049 9-10-3 70.............................. AshleyBird(3) 54
(Jim Best) *chsd ldrs: wnt 2nd after 2nd: rdn and outpcd by ldng pair bef 2 out: edgd rt and wknd 2 out* **7/2**[1]

3P0- **7** 3 **The Boat Shed (IRE)**[172] 2792 4-11-2 90......................(t) MrTGarner(5) 66
(Brendan Duke) *led: wandered 2nd: hdd 6th: styd prom tl wknd qckly after 3 out* **20/1**

56/0 **8** 4 1/2 **Mr Tambourine Man (IRE)**[32] 54 9-10-7 74.............. MrTJCannon(3) 51
(Katie Stephens) *t.k.h: hld up in last pair: gd hdwy on inner to ld 6th: rdn and hdd after 3 out: sn wknd* **25/1**

4P6- **9** 15 **Ticket To Ride (FR)**[56] 5049 12-9-9 64..................(tp) MissBAndrews(5) 25
(Jim Wilson) *chsd ldr tl after 2nd: chsd ldrs after but wanting to hang rt and sn niggled along: rdn and dropped to last bef 3 out: lost tch wl bef 2 out: t.o* **18/1**

0-11 **U** **Nomad (FR)**[19] 272 9-11-2 80.. EdGlassonbury —
(Carroll Gray) *hld up in tch tl rr tl mstke and uns rdr 5th* **4/1**[2]

P0-6 **P** **Galantos (GER)**[14] 374 9-11-7 85..................................(p) MarkQuinlan —
(Jane Southcombe) *in tch tl rdn and wknd qckly sn after 3 out: wl bhd whn p.u last* **18/1**

6P-P **R** **Good To Be Grey**[30] 100 8-11-12 90.........(v1) MissPernillaHermansson —
(Reg Hollinshead) *towards rr whn rn out and uns rdr 1st* **25/1**

4m 52.4s (-17.20) **Going Correction** -0.775s/f (Firm)
WFA 4 from 6yo+ 18lb **12** Ran SP% **119.3**
Speed ratings (Par 103): **103,100,97,95,93 93,92,90,84,— —,—**
Tote Swingers: 1&2 £6.30, 1&3 £28.70, 2&3 £19.00 CSF £149.43 CT £1520.17 TOTE £20.70: £6.10, £4.70, £4.60; EX 216.10.
Owner J R Turner **Bred** Mrs I H Lowe **Trained** Norton-le-Clay, N Yorks

FOCUS
Eventful fare. the winner is rated to old course form with the runner-up to her mark.

NOTEBOOK
Marlborough Sound travelled notably kindly towards the rear of a bunched field before being sent on at the foot of the hill, and a less than fluent jump at the last cost him no momentum. Evidently hard to train, having stood just ten previous starts in six years, he is nevertheless 2-2 at Towcester with this victory (and his North Yorkshire-based trainer has now won with his last three runners here). Future prospects may depend on both his wellbeing and how much of the 10lb drop he received following his last outing is reapplied. (op 12-1)
Present threaded nicely through the pack turning in to emerge as the main danger with two to jump, but an error at that flight ended her challenge abruptly. It's not certain how much she would have found having proven keen in midfield early on in any case, and she can't be classed as unlucky. (tchd 8-1 and 10-1)
Galant Eye(IRE) caught some of the backwash of back-pedalling front-runners that Present managed to miss, but he wasn't going as well as either that one or the winner at the time and he was clear third best on the day. This was his first place finish outside of selling grade since December 2003. (op 14-1)
Masterpoint's best jumps form has all been recorded around far sharper tracks than this. (op 8-1)
Bari Bay, second in a 2m novice seller here last time, wasn't done too many favours by Nomad's departure, but her over-keenness and error three out were all of her own making. She's a bit better than this. (op 4-1)
Dolans Bay(IRE) ultimately disappointed as favourite for the fourth race running. (op 4-1)
Nomad(FR), seeking a hat-trick, gave Ed Glassonbury a crashing fall before his forward move had begun in earnest. (op 20-1)
Good To Be Grey ran out on the opposite side of the same hurdle which caused the problems in the claimer. (op 20-1)

558 NORMAN ATKINSON H'CAP CHASE (12 fncs) 2m 110y
4:35 (4:35) (Class 5) (0-95,84) 5-Y-O+ £2,998 (£971; £501)

Form RPR
/5-3 **1** **Ruby Isabel (IRE)**[8] 441 6-11-10 82.............................. RichardJohnson 94+
(Tim Vaughan) *chsd ldng pair: lft 2nd 3rd: j.rt next: clsng whn lft in ld 3 out: pushed along between last 2: hmpd by loose horse and nt fluent last: rdn and readily asserted flat* **2/1**[2]

5-41 **2** 2 3/4 **Beauchamp Viking**[13] 381 6-11-7 84......................(t) JimmyDerham(5) 92+
(Simon Burrough) *hld up wl bhd: wnt 3rd whn mstke and stmbld 6th: mstke next: lft 2nd 3 out: pushed along between last 2: lft w ch last: drvn and btn fnl 150yds* **1/1**[1]

06-P **3** 19 **Saddlers Mount (IRE)**[30] 95 6-10-6 69...............(t) MichaelMurphy(5) 56
(J Jay) *a in last pair: j. slowly and reminders 2nd: nvr looked happy after: lft 3rd 3 out: drvn and wl btn bef 2 out* **4/1**[3]

30-0 **F** **Un Autre Espere**[13] 381 11-9-7 61 ow3..........................(b) JoshWall(10) —
(Trevor Wall) *led: lft clr 3rd: mstke 8th: 3 l clr but coming bk to field whn fell 3 out* **20/1**

PP4- **U** **Simiola**[41] 5293 11-10-0 58 oh5.. ColinBolger —
(Simon Lewis) *t.k.h: chsd ldr tl uns rdr 3rd* **25/1**

4m 6.70s (-9.40) **Going Correction** -0.775s/f (Firm) **5** Ran SP% **111.9**
Speed ratings: **91,89,80,—,—**
CSF £4.74 TOTE £2.80: £1.30, £1.20; EX 2.80.
Owner M Khan X2 **Bred** Patrick Doyle **Trained** Aberthin, Vale of Glamorgan

FOCUS
A pretty poor contest with jumping errors occasionally to the fore, but at least the pace was decent. The winner can rate higher and the runner-up sets the standard.

NOTEBOOK
Ruby Isabel(IRE) gave the best jumping display on her chase debut and had enough in reserve having been left in front three out to repel the runner-up comfortably enough in the end. She got to race here off a hurdles mark that had dipped 12lb in a light campaign over the last 12 months, and it will be interesting to see if this half-sister to the Listed chase winner Valley Ride proves any more capable of defying higher marks in her new vocation. (op 6-4 tchd 11-8)
Beauchamp Viking's mistake from which he recovered to win a similar C&D event last time had come earlier in the contest than the two he made here, and either that, or an 8lb higher mark, conspired to thwart the follow-up bid. Closing to within a length just after the last was as good as it got before the winner reasserted. He may be able to remain competitive in small handicaps, though there aren't too many summer jumping courses suitable for the pronounced hold-up tactics which have served him better of late. (op 11-10 tchd 6-5)
Saddlers Mount(IRE), a dual Irish point winner, hated every minute of this and is impossible to recommend as a future winner at present despite a tumbling mark. (op 6-1 tchd 7-1)
Un Autre Espere, 62l behind the runner-up last time, had already nudged one fence and was being reeled in by the winner when coming down. (op 16-1)

559 GG.COM NOVICES' HURDLE (12 hdls) 3m
5:10 (5:10) (Class 4) 5-Y-O+ £2,927 (£859; £429; £214)

Form RPR
00-4 **1** **Downward Spiral (IRE)**[18] 303 5-10-12 0...................... AlanO'Keeffe 110+
(Jennie Candlish) *mde all: drew wl clr after 3 out: mstke 2 out: rdn between last 2: eased after last* **8/1**[3]

0-5 **2** 17 **Tucumcari (IRE)**[16] 337 5-10-12 0.............................. JimmyMcCarthy 90
(Brendan Powell) *t.k.h: hld up in tch: hdwy to chse wnr bef 3 out: n.m.r on inner and hit doll after 3 out: sn rdn and btn* **10/1**

12-1 **3** 5 **Pheidias (IRE)**[27] 138 6-10-12 0....................................(p) DavidEngland 85
(Pam Sly) *rn in snatches and rdn along at times: chsd ldrs: wnt 2nd 7th tl bef 3 out: hrd drvn and btn 3 out* **5/6**[1]

0-32 **4** 31 **Mzuri Bay**[12] 409 5-10-12 107...(t) MarkGrant 54
(Brendan Duke) *j.lft 1st: chsd ldr tl 6th: rdn bef 8th: wknd u.p bef 3 out: t.o 2 out* **9/4**[2]

050- **P** **Billy Smith**[204] 2153 7-10-5 76.................................... AnthonyFreeman(7) —
(John Upson) *chsd ldrs: nt fluent 2nd: dropped to last and rdn after 5th: lost tch bef 7th: wl t.o whn p.u 3 out* **16/1**

6m 4.90s (-10.10) **Going Correction** -0.775s/f (Firm) **5** Ran SP% **111.4**
Speed ratings: **85,79,77,67,—**
CSF £65.77 TOTE £5.40: £1.60, £4.10; EX 26.90 Place 6 £9,057.34, Place 5 £3,617.43..
Owner P and Mrs G A Clarke **Bred** John Bates **Trained** Basford Green, Staffs

FOCUS
A staying hurdle weakened appreciably by the defection of the two market leaders, and with the eventual favourite disappointing badly it took little winning. The form is difficult to assess.

NOTEBOOK
Downward Spiral(IRE) gave an authoritative display of front-running on his first try back over this trip since winning his sole Irish point start (3m, good) last October, turning the screw before the homeward turn and kept going by his rider until close home. Connections opined that this test was just what the doctor ordered for their gelding. While the form might not amount to much, it wouldn't surprise to see him dominate some limited summer opposition in another 3m novice hurdle around the likes of Worcester before long. (op 9-2)
Tucumcari(IRE) was left momentarily short of room on the inner when Downward Spiral kicked on, but such was the superiority of the winner it seems unlikely that it cost him a winning opportunity. Another to emerge from the Irish pointing field, albeit without a win, he hadn't been getting home over shorter trips than this previously and may need more time to strengthen. Handicaps are at least open to him now. (op 7-1)
Pheidias(IRE)'s recent good work over fences, including two wins, had been recorded around sharp, left-hand tracks. The driving that this lazy individual came under from a long way out hasn't been unusual to see during that purple patch, but the very limited response this time certainly was, and the safest conclusion to draw could be that he didn't enjoy this very different course. (op 11-10 after early 6-4 and 5-4 in places)
Mzuri Bay, who had hung left late on at Worcester last time, was inclined to jump that way in the very early stages here, and was already under pressure with over a mile to run. A return to flat, left-hand courses seems advisable. Official explanation: trainer said gelding ran flat (op 5-2)
T/Plt: £8,764.30 to a £1 stake. Pool:£48,023.63 - 4.00 winning tickets T/Qpdt: £146.50 to a £1 stake. Pool:£4,238.70 - 21.40 winning tickets SP

560 - 562a (Foreign Racing) - See Raceform Interactive

[15]FFOS LAS (L-H)
Tuesday, June 1

OFFICIAL GOING: Good to firm (good in places; 8.1)
Wind: Fresh, across, becoming light after race 2 Weather: Sunny

563 PHONELINE BRECON AND ADEPT TELECOM NOVICES' HURDLE (8 hdls) 2m
6:25 (6:25) (Class 4) 4-Y-O+ £2,602 (£764; £382; £190)

Form RPR
040- **1** **U B Carefull**[44] 5243 7-10-5 109.................................. MrPJTolman(7) 118+
(Sirrell Griffiths) *taken down early: trckd ldng trio fr 3rd: sltly outpcd after 5th: clsd 3 out: led next: rdn and styd on wl* **28/1**

43-1 **2** 3 1/4 **Praxiteles (IRE)**[18] 315 6-11-5 128... APMcCoy 122
(Rebecca Curtis) *trckd ldng pair: wnt cl 2nd after 5th: led 3 out: hdd and rdn 2 out: nt qckn* **8/13**[1]

/14- **3** 1 1/4 **Old McDonald**[29] 114 5-10-12 0.................................. PaddyBrennan 114+
(N F Glynn, Ire) *trckd ldr: led 5th: hdd and hit 3 out: sn u.p and dropped to 3rd: kpt on fr last* **7/4**[2]

6-0 **4** 13 **Wilbury Star (IRE)**[18] 315 4-10-9 0.................................. AndrewTinkler 98
(Nicky Henderson) *trckd ldng trio to 3rd: j. slowly next and reminders: outpcd 5th: rdn bef 3 out: no imp* **33/1**

5-3 **5** 37 **Ask Archer**[16] 360 5-10-12 0.. PaulMoloney 73
(Evan Williams) *t.k.h: hld up in last pair: nvr nrr than whn nudged into modest 5th after 5th: mstke 3 out: sn eased: t.o* **25/1**[3]

0F **6** 3/4 **Trew Style**[19] 298 8-10-9 0.. SeanQuinlan(3) 72
(David Rees) *led to 5th: wknd rapidly bef next: eased after 2 out: t.o* **150/1**

P **Majd Aljazeera**[141] 4-10-2 0.......................................(t) OliverDayman(7) —
(Alison Thorpe) *a in rr: wknd rapidly 5th: wl t.o bef next: p.u bef 2 out* **80/1**

3m 38.2s (-10.80) **Going Correction** -1.10s/f (Hard)
WFA 4 from 5yo+ 17lb **7** Ran SP% **110.4**
Speed ratings (Par 105): **95,93,92,86,67 67,—**
toteswingers:1&2:£1.70, 1&3:£2.90, 2&3:£1.10 CSF £46.24 TOTE £29.30: £10.20, £1.10; EX 34.80.
Owner S G Griffiths **Bred** A J Wall **Trained** Nantgaredig, Carmarthenshire

FOCUS
A modest novices' hurdle but not bad for the time of year. the runner-up is rated to his mark and the form should work out.

NOTEBOOK
U B Carefull landed the spoils at 28-1 with the front three pulling clear in the straight. The winner had failed to show much since switching his attention to hurdling being tailed off when last seen at Ascot in April. Settled nicely behind the leaders before taking up the running 2f out. A very nervy horse so taken to post early, but connections have always thought he has ability. If his temperament holds up there is no reason why he cannot follow up. (tchd 20-1 and 33-1)
Praxiteles(IRE) won nicely at Aintree last time out and was a warm order at odds-on to follow up here. He travelled well tracking the leaders before taking it up after three out, but could only muster the same pace when headed from the next. His rider reported that it was riding a little loose on top. (tchd 8-11 and 10-11 in a place)
Old McDonald was a useful performer in bumpers and was fancied to make a winning hurdling debut. He jumped well enough on the whole, but a mistake when leading three out saw him come under pressure and headed. He stayed on well, albeit without getting back on terms, and should be winning before long. (op 15-8 tchd 13-8)
Wilbury Star(IRE) finished a long way behind Praxiteles at Aintree and never landed a blow here although, he did stay on in the straight. He was a 75-rated performer on the Flat, so has possibilities when sent handicapping now he qualifies for a mark. (op 25-1)

Ask Archer never settled off the steady pace and, after moving through into a close enough fourth, weakened tamely. Official explanation: jocley said the gelding ran too freely early on (tchd 28-1)

564 M & A SOLICITORS NOVICES' H'CAP CHASE (15 fncs) 2m 3f 110y

6:55 (6:55) (Class 4) (0-110,110) 5-Y-0+ **£3,903** (£1,146; £573; £286)

Form RPR

50-5 **1** **Michigan Assassin (IRE)**[26] 172 8-11-3 **105**........ AodhaganConlon(7) 121
(Debra Hamer) *led 2nd: jnd 4 out: sn rdn: battled on wl u.p to gain upper hand after last* **11/1**

11-3 **2** *3/4* **Putney Bridge**[23] 221 8-11-10 **105**..........(tp) TomO'Brien 120
(Keith Goldsworthy) *led to 2nd: trckd ldr: nt fluent 6th: chal and upsides fr 4 out gng wl: rdn and stl upsides last: outbattled flat* **11/8**[1]

36-0 **3** *39* **Sea Cliff (IRE)**[27] 155 6-11-12 **107**..........(t) APMcCoy 91
(Jonjo O'Neill) *nt a fluent: hld up in 4th: clsd on ldrs bef 4 out: wknd rapidly after 3 out: fin tired* **7/1**[3]

4 *41* **Thewritinonthewall**[21] 269 5-11-10 **105**..........(b) PaddyBrennan 48
(N F Glynn, Ire) *trckd ldng pair: mstke 11th: sn rdn to chal: wknd rapidly fr 4 out and j.v.slowly after: t.o* **8/1**

/2-3 **P** **Ace High Blue (IRE)**[26] 183 8-11-7 **102**..........(t) PaulMoloney —
(Evan Williams) *hld up in last: nt fluent 6th: 10l bhd ldr whn blnd 10th: sn t.o: j. slowly and markedly rt 4 out and next: p.u bef 2 out* **15/8**[2]

4m 47.5s (-18.50) **5** Ran SP% **108.8**
CSF £27.14 TOTE £16.80: £5.10, £1.80; EX 34.70.
Owner C A Hanbury **Bred** George Ward **Trained** Nantycaws, Carmarthens

FOCUS
A weak novices' handicap chase that lost a lot of its interest when Master Charm pulled out, but it produced a good battle in the straight. The runner-up is rated to the best of his chasing form.

NOTEBOOK
Michigan Assassin(IRE) took over at the head of affairs after the second and showed a good attitude to get back up after being narrowly headed two out. Sprang a surprise when winning at Taunton over hurdles returning from a break, but had performed below that standard since, including in a claimer. He jumped well on this his chasing debut, but hardly inspires confidence to repeat the effort. (tchd 12-1)
Putney Bridge, reasonably treated compared to his hurdle mark, ran a solid race but, after taking a narrow advantage, could not shake off the persistent challenge of the winner. He was run out of it towards the finish. (op 13-8 tchd 7-4)
Sea Cliff(IRE) took a while to warm to his fencing, but came here holding every chance turning in. He weakened when put under pressure. (op 5-1)
Thewritinonthewall was another who weakened tamely when put under pressure going to four out and was well beaten. (op 6-1)
Ace High Blue(IRE) was disappointing. He lost touch very quickly after a mistake at the tenth and was pulled up. (op 9-4 tchd 7-4)

565 FRANCES GRIFFITHS MEMORIAL NOVICES' CHASE (13 fncs) 2m

7:30 (7:30) (Class 4) 5-Y-0+ **£4,228** (£1,241; £620; £310)

Form RPR

21-2 **1** **West With The Wind**[25] 192 5-11-5 0.......... PaulMoloney 148+
(Evan Williams) *led 2nd: gained grnd on runner-up most fences: blnd 8th: wl in command fr 4 out: eased flat* **7/2**[2]

15-1 **2** *14* **The Jigsaw Man (IRE)**[18] 316 6-10-12 0.......... APMcCoy 130+
(Rebecca Curtis) *j. sketchily and lost grnd most fences: led to 2nd: mstke 6th: rdn and no imp on wnr 4 out: n.d after* **4/9**[1]

3 *34* **Mister Bishop (IRE)**[163] 2995 5-10-12 0.......... PaddyBrennan 94
(Paul John Gilligan, Ire) *immediately outpcd: won battle for remote 3rd fr 1/2-way: no ch ldng pair whn mstke 4 out* **16/1**

5-0F **4** *33* **Mumbles Pier (IRE)**[16] 357 5-10-12 0.......... TomO'Brien 69
(Peter Bowen) *already outpcd whn blnd 1st: lost battle for remote 3rd fr 1/2-way: t.o: j. last as runner-up fin* **6/1**[3]

3m 48.0s (-17.00) **Going Correction** -1.10s/f (Hard) **4** Ran SP% **111.6**
Speed ratings: **98,91,74,57**
CSF £6.06 TOTE £3.00; EX 11.90.
Owner Mrs Janet Davies **Bred** Newsells Park Stud **Trained** Llancarfan, Vale Of Glamorgan

FOCUS
A small field for this novice chase but a decent pace and a fair contest for the time of year. The winner is still on the upgrade, while the runner-up is rated 10lb off his best hurdling mark.

NOTEBOOK
West With The Wind ran out an impressive winner. Apart from a mistake in the back straight, his jumping was good and he hardly came off the bridle to win as he liked. A Flat and dual hurdle winner who is bettering that form since switching to fences and looks as though there is further improvement to come. He was not a natural when schooling initially over fences but he learnt a lot at Aintree last time and this was a fluent performance. He likes top-of-the-ground and will be kept on the go throughout the summer. (tchd 9-2)
The Jigsaw Man(IRE) had been forced to go chasing sooner than they wished after the Handicapper had raised the 6-y-o a stone for his latest success at Aintree. He is not very big and his jumping was not that convincing on this chasing debut. He was struggling to match the winner's fluency at the fences going down the back straight and was always being held at bay in the home straight. However, he is a likeable individual who can only build on this. (op 4-7 tchd 8-13 in a place)
Mister Bishop(IRE) had kept some decent company over hurdles so was a bit of an unknown quantity now tackling fences. He was always adrift of the principals but jumped soundly enough. (tchd 14-1 and 18-1)
Mumbles Pier(IRE) had jumped well before falling on chasing debut when looking the likely winner. As with the third he was soon trailing in the wake of the front pair. Apart from a mistake at the first he fenced satisfactory and in lesser company could figure with his confidence restored. (op 11-2 tchd 5-1)

566 M & A SOLICITORS H'CAP HURDLE (3 hdls 5 omitted) 2m

8:00 (8:04) (Class 3) (0-120,113) 4-Y-0+ **£4,878** (£1,432; £716; £357)

Form RPR

25-1 **1** **Ajman (IRE)**[19] 298 5-10-3 **93**..........(t) DPFahy(3) 98+
(Evan Williams) *trckd ldr: gng easily 4f out: led by-passing 2 out: rdn and kpt on wl* **15/2**

124- **2** *3 1/4* **Screaming Brave**[57] 5048 4-11-9 **113**.......... JamieGoldstein 112
(Sheena West) *hld up in 6th: smooth prog to go 3rd 4f out: rdn to chal over 1f out: hung lft but kpt on to take 2nd fnl f* **15/2**

33-1 **3** *2* **Woodlark Island (IRE)**[11] 430 4-11-4 **108**..........(tp) TomScudamore 105
(David Pipe) *led: urged along after last (6f out): hdd u.p by-passing 2 out: one pce* **9/4**[1]

4 *22* **Adare Manor (IRE)**[241] 1609 6-11-12 **113**.......... APMcCoy 93
(Jonjo O'Neill) *t.k.h: hld up in last pair: latched on to ldng gp 5f out: outpcd 4f out: no ch after* **8/1**

0-44 **5** *1/2* **Manjam (IRE)**[22] 252 6-10-8 **95**..........(tp) PaddyBrennan 75
(Rebecca Curtis) *prom: rdn after last (6f out): sn lost tch: plugged on* **11/2**[3]

4-20 **6** *1/2* **Bazart**[11] 430 8-10-3 **95**..........(p) JimmyDerham(5) 74
(Bernard Llewellyn) *trckd ldrs: pushed along over 5f out: sn lost tch and no ch* **8/1**

622/ **7** *10* **Mad Moose (IRE)**[403] 5205 6-10-13 **105**.......... SamTwiston-Davies(5) 75
(Nigel Twiston-Davies) *trckd ldrs: rdn in 4th 6f out: wknd 4f out* **4/1**[2]

000- **8** *52* **Blue Express (IRE)**[135] 3487 11-10-13 **100**..........(t) PaulMoloney 24
(Evan Williams) *hld up in last pair: mstke 1st: struggling after: t.o after last (6f out)* **20/1**

3m 34.0s (-15.00) **Going Correction** -1.10s/f (Hard)
WFA 4 from 5yo+ 17lb **8** Ran SP% **116.7**
Speed ratings (Par 107): **106,104,103,92,92 91,86,60**
toteswingers:1&2:£13.10, 1&3:£3.60, 2&3:£1.90 CSF £62.22 CT £168.46 TOTE £7.30: £2.20, £3.40, £1.10; EX 84.90.
Owner R P R O'Neil **Bred** Pat McDonnell **Trained** Llancarfan, Vale Of Glamorgan

FOCUS
The front three pulled well clear of the remainder in the home straight. The winner can rate higher and the placed horses are rated pretty much to their marks.

NOTEBOOK
Ajman(IRE), winner of a seller on debut for Evan Williams last time, was believed to be up against it now stepping up in class. However, he stuck to his task well after taking up the running going around the bypassed second last. He is going the right way and likes fast ground, but the form of this cannot be taken literally. (op 7-1 tchd 9-1)
Screaming Brave is not particularly well-treated but ran a sound enough race. He held every chance in the straight but threw away any chance he had of winning by hanging onto the chase course in the final 150 yards. (op 5-1)
Woodlark Island(IRE) had made decent progress since being fitted with cheekpieces, winning back-to-back handicaps over longer trips, and had been raised a further 6lb for his recent success over this distance. He tried to make all, but once headed could only stay on at the same pace. A step back up in trip should see him add to his tally. (op 7-2 tchd 2-1 and 4-1 in a place)
Adare Manor(IRE), the best of these on the Flat and with only a second to his name in a maiden hurdle after seven attempts, looked to be on a high enough mark. His effort petered out quite soon in the straight after closing on the leaders. (op 9-1 tchd 10-1)
Manjam(IRE) has failed to recapture his form this season and can only be watched at present. (op 6-1 tchd 5-1)

567 M & A SOLICITORS H'CAP CHASE (9 fncs 9 omitted) 3m

8:35 (8:36) (Class 3) (0-130,125) 5-Y-O+ **£5,703** (£1,684; £842; £421; £210)

Form RPR

23-1 **1** **Grand Slam Hero (IRE)**[17] 330 9-11-12 **125**..........(t) PaddyBrennan 136+
(Nigel Twiston-Davies) *hld up in 4th: smooth prog to go 2nd over 3f out: led over 1f out: hung lft fnl f: drvn out* **15/8**[1]

P2-3 **2** *1* **De Soto**[19] 300 9-11-12 **125**..........(t) WillKennedy 133
(Paul Webber) *led at modest pce: slow jumps early: kicked on 4f out: hdd over 1f out: styd on: a hld* **11/2**[3]

1P-P **3** *16* **Sea Wall**[19] 300 8-11-6 **119**.......... APMcCoy 113
(Jonjo O'Neill) *hld up in 5th: rdn and effrt 4f out: sn outpcd: n.d after* **5/1**[2]

005- **4** *4* **William Butler (IRE)**[44] 5252 10-11-0 **116**.......... DPFahy(3) 106
(Evan Williams) *t.k.h: mostly trckd ldr fr 2nd tl wknd over 3f out* **16/1**

110- **5** *30* **Incentivise (IRE)**[46] 5212 7-10-7 **111**.......... MichaelMurphy(5) 74
(C Roberts) *chsd ldr to 2nd: mstke 7th: sn rdn and wknd: t.o 4f out* **8/1**

120- **P** **Sydney Sling (IRE)**[181] 2642 5-11-2 **115**.......... PaulMoloney —
(Evan Williams) *hld up: blnd 3rd and p.u: fatally injured* **16/1**

5m 52.4s (-30.60) **Going Correction** -1.10s/f (Hard) **6** Ran SP% **89.7**
Speed ratings: **107,106,101,100,90** —
toteswingers:1&2:£1.20, 1&3:£1.10, 2&3:£2.10 CSF £7.74 TOTE £2.60: £1.50, £2.90; EX 7.40.
Owner Walters Plant Hire Ltd **Bred** Lady Rathdonnell **Trained** Naunton, Gloucs

FOCUS
With the low sun again taking out all the fences in the home straight, only ten of the 18 fences were jumped in this modest staying handicap chase. The race could be rated higher but is limited by not much strength in depth.

NOTEBOOK
Grand Slam Hero(IRE) was 5lb above his highest ever winning mark, but this looked a good opportunity to defy that which he duly did. Settled behind the leaders he laid down his challenge from the omitted four out until leading bypassing two out. His future is really in the hands of the Handicapper, but he should not be too unfairly treated for this success as all of these hold few secrets. (tchd 13-8 and 2-1)
De Soto had run respectably since being raised 5lb for his Bangor success – this being another fair effort. He tried to make all but looked to be up against it when headed, although he did draw clear of the remainder. (op 5-1)
Sea Wall was disappointing after breaking a blood vessel previously, so had something to prove. He flattered in the straight, but was ultimately soundly beaten. (op 6-1 tchd 9-2)
William Butler(IRE) was back on a reasonable mark but has not recaptured his form of late. He kept pressing for third in the straight without threatening the principals. (op 11-1)
Incentivise(IRE) had shown decent progress to score twice at Chepstow before failing to figure in a competitive heat at Cheltenham. He tracked the leader early, but a mistake at the tenth soon had him in trouble finishing a long way behind. (op 9-1)
Sydney Sling(IRE) unfortunately received a fatal injury after blundering at the third and had to be pulled up. (op 12-1)

568 IRISH THOROUGHBRED MARKETING MARES' STANDARD OPEN NATIONAL HUNT FLAT RACE 2m

9:05 (9:05) (Class 6) 4-6-Y-0 **£1,712** (£499; £249)

Form RPR

2-5 **1** **Maggie Aron**[15] 375 4-10-9 0.......... RichardJohnson 101+
(Tim Vaughan) *t.k.h: hld up in last trio: gd prog and squeezed through 3f out: led over 2f out: r.o wl and sn clr* **11/4**[1]

4- **2** *5* **Verde Goodwood**[37] 7 4-10-9 0.......... LeightonAspell 93
(Oliver Sherwood) *hld up in last trio: prog on inner over 4f out: chal and upsides 3f out: chsd wnr over 2f out: r.o but readily outpcd* **8/1**

3 *8* **Bachley Gale**[56] 5-10-12 0.......... APMcCoy 88
(Keith Goldsworthy) *hld up in last trio: prog and cl up 4f out: rdn 3f out: sn outpcd: kpt on to take 3rd 1f out* **9/2**[3]

06- **4** *1/2* **My Viking Bay (IRE)**[47] 5200 6-10-5 0.......... CharlieWallis(7) 88
(John O'Shea) *hld up in midfield: prog to join ldrs over 4f out: upsides 3f out: sn wl outpcd* **14/1**

66- **5** *2* **Thorpey's Girl (IRE)**[39] 5368 5-10-5 0.......... OliverDayman(7) 86
(Alison Thorpe) *hld up towards rr: prog on outer to join ldrs over 4f out: upsides 3f out: sn outpcd* **16/1**

6 **6** *8* **Weldone Honey**[15] 375 5-10-7 0.......... DonalDevereux(5) 79
(Peter Bowen) *prom: pushed along over 6f out: effrt to ld over 4f out to over 2f out: wknd* **4/1**[2]

7 *nk* **Me Too (IRE)**[29] 5-10-12 0.......... BarryKeniry 79
(Liam Corcoran) *hld up in midfield: prog and cl up 5f out: rdn to chal over 3f out: wknd over 2f out* **12/1**

6 **8** *2 1/4* **Rolline (IRE)**[23] 238 5-10-12 0 TomScudamore 77
(Stuart Kittow) *t.k.h: trckd ldrs: lost pl 6f out: sn wl in rr: plugged on again 3f out* **8/1**
9 *12* **Miss Tilly Oscar (IRE)**[30] 4-10-2 0 MrJFlook(7) 63
(Edward Bevan) *fractious preliminaries: prom: rdn to chal over 4f out: wknd 3f out* **18/1**
10 *3/4* **Lynford Nakita** 4-10-9 0 TomO'Brien 62
(Caroline Keevil) *settled in rr: lost tch fr 5f out: no ch after* **33/1**
P- **11** *20* **Gift Of Freedom (IRE)**[47] 5199 5-10-12 0 PaddyBrennan 47
(Nigel Twiston-Davies) *led 5f: rdn over 6f out: wknd over 4f out: t.o* **16/1**
0- **12** *4 1/2* **Ginger Jalapeno**[90] 4384 4-10-4 0 GilesHawkins(5) 40
(Edward Bevan) *t.k.h: led after 5f to over 4f out: wknd rapidly: t.o* **50/1**
P-0 **13** *111* **Hennerwood Beech**[19] 304 5-10-12 0 GerardTumelty —
(Richard Price) *t.k.h: prom: wknd rapidly 7f out: sn wl t.o* **80/1**

3m 36.1s (-7.30) **Going Correction** -1.10s/f (Hard)
WFA 4 from 5yo+ 3lb 13 Ran SP% **124.6**
Speed ratings: **86,83,79,79,78 74,74,72,66,66 56,54,—**
toteswingers:1&2:£5.80, 1&3:£2.80, 2&3:£14.90 CSF £26.46 TOTE £4.10: £1.70, £5.00, £1.10; EX 18.40 Place 6 £50.82; Place 5 £31.08.
Owner J S Hughes **Bred** R J & S A Carter **Trained** Aberthin, Vale of Glamorgan

FOCUS
Not much to go on but overall form suggests just a modest mares' bumper run at an ordinary pace with plenty in with a chance turning in. There were big steps up from the first two but the form looks believable rated around some of those out of the placings.

NOTEBOOK
Maggie Aron had previous experience which held her in good stead as she romped away with this. Held up at the back she made good headway on the final bend to be travelling strongly on the heels of the leaders before quickening right away after taking the lead. She shapes as though she will be seen to good effect when upped in trip over hurdles. (op 3-1)
Verde Goodwood made eye-catching headway on the final bend to take the lead. Once headed she couldn't cope with the injection of pace from the winner. However, this was another encouraging effort as she drew clear of the remainder. (op 15-2 tchd 13-2)
Bachley Gale had been well supported throughout the day after failing to show a great deal in points. She stayed on well enough in the straight without ever laying down a serious threat. (op 13-2 tchd 7-1)
My Viking Bay(IRE) laid down a strong challenge entering the straight, but just kept on at the same pace in the final 2f. (op 10-1)
Thorpey's Girl(IRE) was another to hold every chance, but her effort flattened out entering the final furlong.
Weldone Honey had met with interference on her debut and had every chance here but could only muster the same pace until weakening entering the final furlong. (tchd 6-1)
T/Plt: £19.20 to a £1 stake. Pool:£70,157.29 - 2,657.09 winning tickets T/Qpdt: £11.40 to a £1 stake. Pool:£5,372.44 - 345.74 winning tickets JN

569 - 575a (Foreign Racing) - See Raceform Interactive

[547] CARTMEL (L-H)
Wednesday, June 2

OFFICIAL GOING: Good (good to soft in places, soft on woodside)
Both bends moved out a further 3metres and course at outermost configuration.
Wind: light 1/2 behind Weather: fine and sunny

576 GIBSONS OF KENDAL NOVICES' HURDLE (8 hdls) 2m 1f 110y
2:20 (2:22) (Class 4) 4-Y-0+ **£2,927** (£859; £429; £214)

Form RPR
2-21 **1** **Twentynineblack (FR)**[18] 327 6-11-5 112 JasonMaguire 109+
(Donald McCain) *hld up towards rr: stdy hdwy 5th: led on inner sn after last: shkn up and styd on strly: v readily* **13/8**[1]
3- **2** *3 1/4* **Silverlord (FR)**[362] 351 6-10-12 0 GrahamLee 98
(Gordon Elliott, Ire) *nt jump wl: chsd ldrs: kpt on to take 2nd over 1f out: no ch w wnr* **8/1**
12-5 **3** *nk* **Quatro Pierji (FR)**[25] 209 6-11-5 113 (p) PaddyAspell 104
(James Moffatt) *chsd ldr: led 3 out: j.rt last: sn hdd: kpt on same pce* **5/1**[2]
451- **4** *4 1/2* **Sadler's Star (GER)**[79] 4645 7-11-5 107 (p) DenisO'Regan 100
(Michael Blake) *towards rr: hdwy 2 out: kpt on run-in* **7/1**[3]
5-31 **5** *2 1/2* **Barron Watlass (IRE)**[14] 400 6-11-12 105 BarryKeniry 105
(George Moore) *chsd ldrs: one pce run-in* **15/2**
2 **6** *1 1/4* **Heart Of Dubai (USA)**[14] 400 5-10-12 0 TomMessenger 89
(Micky Hammond) *hld up in rr: hdwy 5th: sn chsng ldrs: one pce fr 2 out* **12/1**
244- **7** *3/4* **Nelson's Chief**[64] 4945 4-10-9 0 BrianHughes 86
(Alan Swinbank) *t.k.h: chsd ldrs: rdn appr 2 out: fdd run-in* **9/1**
8 *3/4* **Red Skipper (IRE)**[37] 5-10-12 0 KeithMercer 88
(Noel Wilson) *nt fluent: chsd ldrs: sn drvn along: outpcd sn after 2 out* **50/1**
0- **9** *17* **Oh Landino (GER)**[52] 5138 5-10-12 0 WilsonRenwick 73
(P Monteith) *in rr: bhd fr 5th* **100/1**
P0 **10** *13* **Daasij (IRE)**[10] 442 5-10-12 0 PeterBuchanan 61
(J Barclay) *in rr: mstke 1st: bhd fr 5th* **125/1**
/0-4 **11** *1* **Duke Of Burgundy (FR)**[17] 360 7-10-12 0 (t) AlanO'Keeffe 60
(Jennie Candlish) *j.rt: led: hit 5th: hdd next: wknd between last 2: eased* **20/1**

4m 17.8s (4.60) **Going Correction** +0.475s/f (Soft)
WFA 4 from 5yo+ 17lb 11 Ran SP% **116.3**
Speed ratings (Par 105): **108,106,106,104,103 102,102,102,94,88 88**
toteswingers: 1&2 £1.70, 1&3 £2.00, 2&3 £3.00. CSF £15.00 TOTE £2.50: £1.10, £1.70, £2.20; EX 13.60.
Owner Tracey Gaunt & David Gibbons **Bred** Bernard Soulhol **Trained** Cholmondeley, Cheshire

FOCUS
Both bends were moved out 3m to their outermost position. Riders in the first confirmed that underfoot conditions were rather patchy. This was an ordinary novice hurdle run at a fairly modest pace. The easy winner is on the upgrade.

NOTEBOOK
Twentynineblack(FR) is a consistent type and he followed up last month's Bangor win in good style. Settling well before improving his position before halfway, he nipped through on the inside to lead off the home turn and quickly scooted clear. He may need to revert to handicap company now as he will be saddled with a double penalty in novice races. (op 7-4 tchd 6-4)
Silverlord(FR), trained by James Lambe when third on his hurdles debut, was having his first start for his new yard. Never far away, he could not match the winner's pace off the home turn. He is capable of winning over hurdles, but needs to jump better and may not be straightforward. (op 13-2 tchd 6-1)
Quatro Pierji(FR) tracked the pace and took it up three from home, but he jumped out to his right at the final flight, something he has done before, and could not fend off the winner. (op 13-2 tchd 7-1)
Sadler's Star(GER), sold out of Alan King's yard after winning a seller and his trainer's first runner with a full licence, stayed on from the rear without reaching a challenging position. (op 11-2)
Barron Watlass(IRE) was close enough between the final two flights but could not prevent the leaders from leaving him behind after the last. (op 9-1)
Heart Of Dubai(USA), runner-up to Barron Watlass at Sedgefield and 7lb better off with him, travelled well for some way but faded from the second-last. (op 10-1)
Nelson's Chief is not the biggest and failed to get home on this hurdles bow. (op 18-1)
Red Skipper(IRE), another lacking hurdling experience, was keeping on for pressure and might get a bit further.
Duke Of Burgundy(FR) cut out a lot of the running but showed a tendency to jump right. He dropped away quickly once headed. Official explanation: jockey said gelding jumped right throughout (op 18-1)

577 CORRIE & CO MARES' MAIDEN HURDLE (11 hdls) 2m 6f
2:50 (2:52) (Class 5) 4-Y-0+ **£2,276** (£668; £334; £166)

Form RPR
P2-2 **1** **Basford Lass**[14] 410 5-11-0 95 (b) AlanO'Keeffe 101+
(Jennie Candlish) *mde all: hit last: styd on u.p* **11/4**[1]
4-03 **2** *1 3/4* **Saintly Lady (IRE)**[13] 421 5-10-9 0 DonalDevereux(5) 98+
(Peter Bowen) *chsd ldrs: wnt 2nd 8th: stmbld landing 2 out: rallied and upsides last: hung rt over 1f out: hung lft ins fnl f: kpt on same pce* **8/1**[3]
53-2 **3** *7* **Maolisa (IRE)**[21] 291 8-10-11 90 CampbellGillies(3) 91
(S R B Crawford, Ire) *chsd wnr: one pce appr last* **9/2**[2]
0-3 **4** *nk* **Little Carmela**[29] 137 6-10-11 0 AlexMerriam(3) 91
(Neil King) *in tch: drvn 7th: one pce fr 3 out* **11/4**[1]
6-56 **5** *3* **Catleen (IRE)**[10] 442 6-11-0 0 PeterBuchanan 89
(S R B Crawford, Ire) *in tch: hdwy to chse ldrs 7th: wknd last* **11/1**
4 **U** **Grethel (IRE)**[2] 547 6-10-7 0 JamesSmith(7) —
(Alan Berry) *prom: blnd and uns rdr 4th* **33/1**
46-P **P** **Silk And Roses**[24] 225 7-10-7 0 (b[1]) KyleJames(7) —
(David Thompson) *chsd ldrs: lost pl 8th: t.o 3 out: p.u between last 2* **80/1**
60-0 **P** **Arabian Silk (IRE)**[28] 161 4-10-10 90 JasonMaguire —
(Donald McCain) *chsd ldrs: drvn 8th: wknd next: eased 2 out: sn wl bhd and p.u* **9/1**
300- **P** **Flying Feathers (IRE)**[223] 1860 6-11-0 0 PaddyAspell —
(James Moffatt) *in rr: bhd fr 5th: t.o whn p.u after 7th: lame* **22/1**
6-0 **P** **Connie Beauchamp**[14] 399 6-10-11 0 HarryHaynes(3) —
(Elliott Cooper) *nt fluent in rr: sn drvn along: t.o 5th: p.u after 7th* **16/1**
P **Back To Normality (IRE)**[40] 7-11-0 0 GrahamLee —
(B R Hamilton, Ire) *in rr: drvn 5th: sn bhd: t.o whn p.u bef 8th* **33/1**
0-P **P** **Modestine**[8] 457 8-10-7 0 AlistairFindlay(7) —
(Jane Walton) *in tch: lost pl 5th: sn bhd: t.o whn p.u bef 8th* **100/1**

5m 38.0s (8.70) **Going Correction** +0.475s/f (Soft)
WFA 4 from 5yo+ 18lb 12 Ran SP% **119.3**
Speed ratings (Par 103): **103,102,99,99,98 —,—,—,—,— —,—**
toteswingers: 1&2 £7.10, 1&3 £3.40, 2&3 £11.10. CSF £25.24 TOTE £3.20: £1.10, £3.60, £1.60; EX 29.80.
Owner Alan Baxter **Bred** L A C Ashby Newhall Estate Farm **Trained** Basford Green, Staffs

FOCUS
A very modest mares' maiden. The winner is rated to her mark.

NOTEBOOK
Basford Lass, the pick of those with official ratings, had gone close on more than one occasion and was caught in the final strides in a Worcester handicap latest. Again sent out in front, she survived an error at the last and battled on willingly enough to see off the runner-up.
Saintly Lady(IRE), who travelled keenly, recovered from a peck two out to hold every chance on the lengthy run-in before edging to her right under pressure and conceding defeat. She improved for the step back up in trip. (op 11-1)
Maolisa(IRE), like the winner, was runner-up in a handicap last time. Always up with the pace, she led for a few strides before the third-last and weakened after the next. (op 4-1)
Little Carmela found things happening too quickly and was off the bridle with a full circuit to run, but stayed on and almost snatched third. She needs a return to further. (op 3-1 tchd 10-3)
Catleen(IRE), a stablemate of the third, improved to look a possible threat before her effort flattened out. (op 16-1 tchd 10-1)
Arabian Silk(IRE) Official explanation: jockey said filly had a breathing problem

578 MARL SPEED OF LIGHT H'CAP CHASE (12 fncs) 2m 1f 110y
3:25 (3:31) (Class 5) (0-95,94) 5-Y-0+ **£3,252** (£955; £477; £238)

Form RPR
-043 **1** **Crofton Arch**[4] 516 10-10-0 68 oh4 (p) PaddyAspell 77
(John Dixon) *wnt 2f after false s: mde all: drvn 4 out: kpt on gamely* **7/1**
46-0 **2** *2 1/2* **Bold Pioneer (USA)**[14] 402 7-10-2 70 (t) GrahamLee 78
(Richard Ford) *nt jump wl: t.k.h in rr: stdy hdwy 4 out: 5th last: 3rd and swtchd rt 2f out: kpt on to take 2nd clsng stages* **9/1**
64-6 **3** *3/4* **Turbo Shandy**[4] 515 7-11-8 90 (p) TomO'Brien 97
(Dai Burchell) *hld up: hdwy 7th: wnt 2nd last: styd on same pce fnl 2f* **4/1**[2]
U-14 **4** *11* **Star Tenor (IRE)**[14] 403 8-11-6 91 FearghalDavis(3) 89
(Sandy Forster) *chsd ldrs: wknd over 2f out* **14/1**
6-32 **5** *5* **Troodos Jet**[14] 404 9-10-9 77 (p) BrianHughes 71
(Dianne Sayer) *chsd ldrs: wknd over 2f out* **5/1**[3]
35-1 **6** *7* **Schinken Otto (IRE)**[14] 404 9-11-7 94 JamesHalliday(5) 83
(Malcolm Jefferson) *uns rdr: rn loose and j. 1 fence after false s: chsd ldrs: lost pl after 4 out* **8/1**
00-5 **7** *34* **Flaming Heck**[21] 290 13-11-1 90 AlexanderVoy(7) 45
(Lucy Normile) *charged tapes: uns rdr and j. 1 fence after false s: chsd ldrs: hit 2nd: drvn and lost pl 6th: t.o 4 out* **16/1**
U-42 **8** *5* **Ice Image (IRE)**[8] 460 8-11-0 89 AlistairFindlay(7) 40
(George Charlton) *chsd ldrs: wknd rapidly last: eased and sn wl bhd* **3/1**[1]
3P-0 **9** *52* **Glengap (IRE)**[8] 456 7-10-6 77 HarryHaynes(3) —
(Elliott Cooper) *chsd ldrs: lost pl 8th: sn bhd: t.o next* **16/1**

4m 26.5s (7.60) **Going Correction** +0.475s/f (Soft) 9 Ran SP% **113.7**
Speed ratings: **102,100,100,95,93 90,75,73,49**
toteswingers: 1&2 £9.70, 1&3 £7.60, 2&3 £7.10. CSF £65.58 CT £285.29 TOTE £11.10: £3.60, £4.90, £2.80; EX 79.70.
Owner Mrs E M Dixon **Bred** Mrs E M Dixon **Trained** Thursby, Cumbria

FOCUS
A very ordinary handicap chase which was delayed following a false start. The winer stepped up on his recent run and the second ran to his mark.

NOTEBOOK
Crofton Arch, racing from 4lb out of the handicap, but a respectable third here four nights earlier, made all the running and kept going bravely to record only the second win of his career. The first came at this track more than three years ago. (op 9-1)
Bold Pioneer(USA), representing a stable with an excellent record at this course, was keen in rear and jumped the first few fences stickily. He made steady improvement on the final circuit, but was briefly stuck behind horses before the home turn and when in the clear he was unable to quicken up. He is clearly capable of winning over fences. (op 8-1)
Turbo Shandy, another ridden from off the pace, was run out of second on the lengthy run-in and this was certainly better than he offered in a selling hurdle here on Saturday. (tchd 9-2)
Star Tenor(IRE) ran a better race back down in trip but was held from the home turn. (tchd 16-1)

Troodos Jet was another unable to quicken up on the long run home, at least overturned Sedgefield running with Schinken Otto.
Schinken Otto(IRE) was one of two to break loose from their riders in the false start. (op 13-2)
Flaming Heck, the other who got loose beforehand, was unable to lead and soon lost interest. (op 14-1)
Ice Image(IRE) was officially 2lb ahead of the handicapper after being beaten a nose at Hexham last time. He chased the pace before weakening disappointingly following a mistake three from home. Official explanation: trainer's rep said gelding was unsuited by the good (good to soft in places) ground (tchd 7-2)

579 BURLINGTON STONE CARTMEL GRAND VETERANS' H'CAP CHASE (20 fncs) 3m 6f

3:55 (3:57) (Class 3) (0-125,115) 10-Y-0+ **£6,505** (£1,910; £955; £477)

Form RPR
2/4- **1** **Lydon House**[40] 5373 11-11-10 **113**....(bt) JasonMaguire 119+
(Gordon Elliott, Ire) *chsd ldr 4th: led 8th: styd on strly to forge clr run-in: eased towards fin* **2/1**[1]
P2-P **2** *15* **Mr Ed (IRE)**[28] 152 12-11-7 **115**.... DonalDevereux(5) 107
(Peter Bowen) *rn in snatches: trckd ldrs: wnt 2nd 4 out: kpt on same pce run-in* **8/1**
30P- **3** *2 3/4* **Master Sebastian**[66] 4911 11-11-4 **107**.... PeterBuchanan 96
(Lucinda Russell) *chsd ldrs: outpcd 4 out: tk modest 3rd sn after last: kpt on* **15/2**[3]
53-4 **4** *22* **Little Girl**[24] 226 12-10-0 **89** oh23.... PaddyAspell 58
(Ray Peacock) *led to 8th: drvn 11th: lost pl 15th* **33/1**
21P/ **5** *80* **Sporting Rebel (IRE)**[18] 10-11-9 **115**.... HaddenFrost(3) 12
(James Frost) *chsd ldrs: 3rd 4 out tl wknd rapidly sn after last: eased and sn t.o: virtually p.u nr fin* **9/1**
P64- **P** **Victory Gunner (IRE)**[85] 4498 12-11-3 **106**.... TomMessenger —
(C Roberts) *reminders after 1st: chsd ldrs: drvn 11th: lost pl and hit next: sn bhd: t.o whn p.u bef 15th* **15/2**[3]
232- **P** **Michigan D'Isop (FR)**[46] 5232 10-11-4 **107**.... TomO'Brien —
(John Ryall) *in rr: mstke 10th: lost pl 12th: last whn p.u bef 3 out* **5/2**[2]

7m 47.5s (11.30) **Going Correction** +0.475s/f (Soft) **7** Ran SP% **109.5**
Speed ratings: **103,99,98,92,71 —,—**
toteswingers: 1&2 £6.60, 1&3 £6.40, 2&3 £6.30. CSF £16.37 CT £88.57 TOTE £2.10: £1.10, £2.90; EX 18.80.
Owner Michael Lydon **Bred** I P Crane **Trained** Trim, Co Meath

FOCUS
No Chabrimal Minster, successful in the last three runnings, and not a strong field for this old-timers' marathon. The easy winner is rated back to his 2008 course mark.

NOTEBOOK
Lydon House was in front with two circuits to run and was clear with his race won when idling on the final bend. The proven stayer had only a Down Royal hunter chase to his name under rules, but has also won six point-to-points in Ireland. (op 9-4 tchd 15-8)
Mr Ed(IRE), without his usual cheekpieces, could not trouble the winner in the latter stages but ran a thoroughly respectable race, which was good to see after he had been pulled up and dismounted last time. (op 12-1)
Master Sebastian never got close enough to deliver a challenge but did plug on for third over this longer trip. (tchd 7-1 and 8-1)
Little Girl was a well-beaten fourth from 23lb out of the handicap. (op 40-1)
Sporting Rebel(IRE) raced prominently for a long way on this return to the racecourse proper but he failed to see out the trip. He had been well beaten when third in a 4m point two starts back. Official explanation: jockey said, regarding riding, that the gelding started to whinny on the final turn and he felt it prudent to ease down (op 7-1)
Victory Gunner(IRE), who had shown signs of a revival last time, was beaten by halfway. (op 8-1 tchd 7-1)
Michigan D'Isop(FR), whose yard won back-to-back runnings of this with Sir Frosty in 2005-6, did not jump well and was adrift when pulling up. Official explanation: jockey said gelding jumped poorly throughout (op 8-1 tchd 7-1)

580 TOWN AND COUNTRY EVENTS HUNTERS' CHASE (FOR THE HORACE D. PAIN MEMORIAL TROPHY) (16 fncs 2 omitted) 3m 2f

4:30 (4:30) (Class 6) 5-Y-0+ **£1,249** (£387; £193; £96)

Form RPR
P4-4 **1** **Thunder Hawk (IRE)**[19] 317 10-11-9 86....(p) MrTDavidson(3) 101
(Mrs L A Coltherd) *led to 4th: chsd ldrs: 3rd 4 out: wnt 5 l 2nd over 1f out: styd on wl to ld nr fin* **22/1**
3/14 **2** *1* **Delightful Cliche**[8] 466 9-11-13 0.... MissGAndrews(3) 106+
(S R Andrews) *chsd ldrs: led 11th: 12 l ahd sn after last: hrd rdn and idled: ct nr fin* **13/2**
22-P **3** *6* **Doc Row (IRE)**[10] 446 10-11-7 115.... MrGCrow(5) 95
(P Monteith) *chsd ldrs: led 7th: to 11th: chsd wnr: wknd over 1f out* **5/2**[2]
4-22 **4** *11* **Thistlecraft (IRE)**[18] 335 11-11-5 102....(v) AdamWedge(7) 88+
(Miss Laura Morgan) *chsd ldrs: hit 6th: wknd 2 out* **12/1**
25-4 **5** *55* **Areyacoddinmee (IRE)**[14] 398 10-11-9 105....(b) MrGRSmith(7) 39
(Mrs Elaine Smith) *sn detached in rr: hrd rdn and hdwy 11th: wknd rapidly 3 out: sn wl bhd: t.o* **12/1**
/1-P **U** **Fair Question (IRE)**[28] 152 12-12-1 125....(p) MrJHamer(5) —
(Donald McCain) *led 4th: hdd 7th: hit 9th: reminders next: 5th and chsng ldrs whn blnd and uns rdr 5 out* **2/1**[1]
00/- **P** **Oaklands Luis**[25] 11-11-9 0.... MrCDawson(3) —
(R G Russ) *in rr: wnt prom 7th: lost pl after 11th: t.o whn p.u bef 4 out* **33/1**
P1P- **U** **Optimistic Harry**[4] 11-11-9 80.... MissSamanthaDrake(7) —
(Miss S A Drake) *mid-div whn blnd and uns rdr 1st* **16/1**
F10/ **P** **Proud Andees (IRE)**[32] 11-11-13 0.... MrGBrewer(3) —
(G D Hanmer) *prom: lost pl and hit 7th: bhd fr 11th: t.o whn p.u bef 3 out* **6/1**[3]

6m 45.8s (10.90) **Going Correction** +0.475s/f (Soft) **9** Ran SP% **118.1**
Speed ratings: **102,101,99,96,79 —,—,—,—**
toteswingers: 1&2 £13.30, 1&3 £9.40, 2&3 £4.70. CSF £160.41 TOTE £28.80: £6.30, £1.10, £1.80; EX 110.10.
Owner Robert Millerbakewell **Bred** J P N Parker **Trained** Selkirk, Borders
Stewards' Enquiry : Miss G Andrews caution: used whip with excessive frequency
Mr T Davidson three-day ban: used whip with excessive frequency wothout giving gelding time to respond (tbn)

FOCUS
A modest hunter chase run at a sound gallop, and a race where the complexion changed on the punishing run-in. The winner is rated back to the level of his 2009 best.

NOTEBOOK
Thunder Hawk(IRE) was well beaten in this race a year ago and appeared up against it on official ratings. He looked booked for third place jumping the final fence, but his rider never stopped urging him along and he collared the flagging leader in the last few strides. (op 25-1 tchd 20-1)
Delightful Cliche seemed sure to win when clear and still going well on the home turn, but he began to idle after being out in front so long and was cut down late on. He is pretty consistent but perhaps not straightforward. (op 8-1)
Doc Row(IRE), reverting to hunter chasing, ran his race with no excuses and is essentially hard to win with. (op 7-2 tchd 4-1 in places)
Thistlecraft(IRE), runner-up on both his starts last month but without a win since November 2007, was well held back in fourth. (op 14-1)
Fair Question(IRE) lost his lead and looked less than enthusiastic when dropping back through the field. He was attempting to rally, but under pressure, when he blundered away his rider five from home. (op 5-1 tchd 13-2)
Proud Andees(IRE) never looked like adding to his 2008 victory in this race. (op 5-1 tchd 13-2)

581 ANDY YOOL BUILDING & HEATING H'CAP HURDLE (10 hdls 1 omitted) 2m 6f

5:05 (5:06) (Class 4) (0-115,116) 4-Y-0+ **£4,553** (£1,337; £668; £333)

Form RPR
4-41 **1** **Summer Soul (IRE)**[10] 447 8-11-10 **116** 7ex....(p) CampbellGillies(3) 123+
(Lucinda Russell) *prom: pushed along 6th: chsd ldrs 3 out: led last: drvn out* **11/4**[1]
36-P **2** *4 1/2* **Downing Street (IRE)**[7] 473 9-11-8 **111**....(vt) AlanO'Keeffe 116+
(Jennie Candlish) *in rr: gd hdwy 3 out: cl 2nd whn taken wd appr last: blnd: regained 2nd over 1f out: no imp* **16/1**
4-12 **3** *11* **Cash Man (IRE)**[25] 213 9-11-2 **112**.... AlexanderVoy(7) 107+
(Evelyn Slack) *w ldr: led bef 3 out: taken wd and hdd last: wknd over 1f out: eased towards fin* **11/2**[3]
0-21 **4** *1 1/4* **Spare Me**[17] 351 7-11-1 **107**.... PeterToole(3) 100
(Milton Harris) *in rr: mstke 1st: hdwy 4 out: chsng ldrs 2 out: one pce* **5/1**[2]
PF-0 **5** *3/4* **Silmi**[24] 236 6-11-12 **115**.... MarkGrant 106
(Sophie Leech) *chsd ldrs: hit 4 out: one pce fr 2 out* **12/1**
34-1 **6** *1 1/4* **Sir Monty (USA)**[18] 341 8-10-11 **100**....(b) TomO'Brien 89
(Peter Bowen) *chsd ldrs: one pce fr 2 out* **9/1**
535- **7** *6* **Rare Coincidence**[43] 4534 9-11-0 **103**....(p) KeithMercer 87
(Roger Fisher) *led: hdd appr 3 out: wknd next* **10/1**
1F0/ **8** *40* **Puy D'Arnac (FR)**[25] 2764 7-11-3 **106**.... BrianHughes 79+
(Alan Swinbank) *hld up in rr: hdwy 6th: chsng ldrs 3 out: wknd next: sn heavily eased and bhd: t.o* **5/1**[2]
132- **9** *10* **Heir To Be**[269] 1390 11-11-12 **115**....(b) DenisO'Regan 54
(Michael Blake) *in rr: drvn 4 out: sn bhd: t.o 2 out* **16/1**
005/ **P** **Karelian**[536] 2763 9-11-11 **114**.... GrahamLee —
(Ferdy Murphy) *in rr: nt fluent: t.o 6th: p.u bef 4 out* **33/1**
6/P- **P** **Solent (IRE)**[50] 4017 8-11-9 **112**.... DougieCostello —
(John Quinn) *trckd ldrs: lost pl and blnd 4 out: t.o whn p.u bef next* **14/1**

5m 39.1s (9.80) **Going Correction** +0.475s/f (Soft) **11** Ran SP% **123.5**
Speed ratings (Par 105): **101,99,95,94,94 94,92,78,74,— —**
toteswingers: 1&2 £16.90, 1&3 £5.10, 2&3 £25.50. CSF £48.83 CT £239.11 TOTE £4.30: £2.00, £5.30, £2.50; EX 76.90.
Owner Bissett Racing **Bred** Moyglare Stud Farm Ltd **Trained** Arlary, Perth & Kinross

FOCUS
A fair handicap hurdle and the form seems sound even though things became a bit messy at the final flight. The first two are rated to their marks.

NOTEBOOK
Summer Soul(IRE) arrived here in good nick and even with the penalty for his Perth win he was officially 7lb ahead of the handicapper. Missing the trouble at the last, he led on the home turn and saw it out well enough. Things will be tougher from his new mark. (op 10-3 tchd 7-2)
Downing Street(IRE) was in last place and going nowhere with a circuit to run. He eventually responded to pressure and made up a huge amount of ground to have every chance at the last, only to bungle the flight. He cannot be guaranteed to reproduce this effort.
Cash Man(IRE), runner-up over fences last time, led before the third-last but could never shake off his pursuers. He was headed at the final flight after his rider started to steer him past the obstacle, which had been bypassed on the previous circuit, only to realise that he needed to jump it this time. The gelding would have finished closer otherwise and remains in good heart. (op 13-2)
Spare Me was 5lb higher than when a game winner at Market Rasen and that appeared to tell in the latter stages. (op 8-1)
Silmi, another switching back from fences, made a couple of jumping errors.
Sir Monty(USA), racing off a 7lb higher mark, could not go with the principals from the second-last. (tchd 10-1)
Puy D'Arnac(FR), running over hurdles for the first time since late 2008, travelled well for a long way and is one to keep an eye on back over shorter. (tchd 4-1)

582 PAUL ELLIS CONGRATULATES BLACKPOOL'S PREMIERSHIP PROMOTION CONDITIONAL JOCKEYS' H'CAP HURDLE (8 hdls) 2m 1f 110y

5:35 (5:37) (Class 4) (0-105,105) 4-Y-0+ **£3,252** (£955; £477; £238)

Form RPR
42-1 **1** **Ardesia (IRE)**[4] 520 6-10-6 **88** 7ex.... AlexanderVoy(3) 95+
(Tina Jackson) *w ldrs: led 4th: briefly hdd 3 out: styd on strly fr 2 out: decisively* **7/4**[1]
00-5 **2** *3 3/4* **Golden Future**[17] 350 7-11-1 **94**.... RyanMania 96
(Peter Niven) *chsd ldrs: wnt 2nd 2 out: kpt on: no real imp* **15/2**[2]
00-0 **3** *8* **Wensleydale Web**[28] 166 8-11-0 **93**.... JamesHalliday 88
(Martin Todhunter) *t.k.h: trckd ldrs 3rd: one pce fr 2 out* **8/1**[3]
45-0 **4** *6* **Front Rank (IRE)**[28] 166 10-11-5 **98**....(p) JamesO'Farrell 87
(Dianne Sayer) *led to 4th: led briefly 3 out: outpcd 2 out: sn wknd* **9/1**
006- **5** *11* **Lady Rusty (IRE)**[104] 4124 4-10-10 **95**....(p) CampbellGillies(3) 72
(Lucinda Russell) *hld up: hdwy 5th: chsng ldrs 2 out: sn wknd* **10/1**
6/-0 **6** *1 3/4* **Bollin Ruth**[19] 313 8-11-4 **103**.... GarryWhillans(6) 81
(Donald Whillans) *in rr: nvr on terms* **22/1**
5/0- **7** *14* **Hollies Favourite (IRE)**[77] 4693 7-11-4 **100**.... AlexMerriam(3) 65
(Neil King) *t.k.h: jnd ldrs 3rd: wknd qckly 2 out* **40/1**
P-06 **8** *12* **Itstooearly**[4] 519 7-10-13 **92**.... HarryHaynes 47
(James Moffatt) *in tch: drvn and lost pl after 4th: sn bhd* **10/1**
P5-0 **P** **Claude Carter**[28] 161 6-11-7 **100**.... MichaelO'Connell —
(Alistair Whillans) *nt jump wl: chsd ldrs: reminders 4th: lost pl after 5th: bhd whn p.u bef 2 out* **12/1**

4m 19.5s (6.30) **Going Correction** +0.475s/f (Soft)
WFA 4 from 5yo+ 17lb **9** Ran SP% **101.9**
Speed ratings (Par 105): **105,103,99,97,92 91,85,79,—**
toteswingers: 1&2 £3.10, 1&3 £3.40, 2&3 £6.10. CSF £11.62 CT £44.18 TOTE £1.80: £1.02, £3.10, £2.40; EX 13.70 Place 6: £63.79, Place 5: £44.57..
Owner A Jackson **Bred** Patrick J Farrington **Trained** Liverton, Cleveland

FOCUS
A moderate handicap hurdle which was weakened by the withdrawal at the start of the mulish Financialregulator (5/2, deduct 20p in the £ under R4). The winner is rated to his best.

NOTEBOOK
Ardesia(IRE) was 7lb well in under the penalty for his comfortable win over this trip here on Saturday evening and he had little problem following up. Making most of the running from halfway, he came clear off the final turn to score in ready fashion. (op 2-1 tchd 5-2)

Golden Future confirmed the promise of his reappearance at Market Rasen and was unfortunate to run up against an in-form rival. (op 8-1 tchd 7-1)
Wensleydale Web has a good record at this unique track and she ran creditably again, putting some lacklustre efforts at other venues behind her. (op 7-1)
Front Rank(IRE) performed respectably with the cheekpieces refitted.
Lady Rusty(IRE), back in cheekpieces for this handicap debut and first start since February, went well for a long way but weakened between the last two flights. She might need a bit further. (tchd 9-1)
T/Jkpt: Not won. T/Plt: £118.50 to a £1 stake. Pool: £58,241.87. 358.69 winning tickets. T/Qpdt: £73.30 to a £1 stake. Pool: £3,449.73. 34.80 winning tickets. WG

528 FONTWELL (L-H)
Wednesday, June 2

OFFICIAL GOING: Good (good to firm in places)
Rail realignment increased chases by 40yds a circuit and hurdles by 15yds a circuit.
Wind: Almost nil Weather: Sunny and warm

583 ELIZABETH CLARK'S 50TH BIRTHDAY NOVICES' HURDLE (11 hdls) 2m 6f 110y
2:30 (2:30) (Class 4) 4-Y-O+ **£2,602** (£764; £382; £190)

Form RPR
42-1 **1** **Pure Anticipation (IRE)**[24] 230 5-10-5 0 RichardJohnson 103+
(Tim Vaughan) *hld up in rr: hdwy 6th: mstke 8th: rdn appr 2 out: mstke last: styd on to ld run-in* **7/4**[1]
/13- **2** *1 3/4* **Like A Hurricane (IRE)**[40] 5355 7-11-2 115 CharlieHuxley(3) 115+
(Alan King) *trckd ldrs: drvn to chse ldr whn mstke 2 out: styd on same pce* **5/2**[3]
U-01 **3** *hd* **Murcar**[15] 379 5-11-5 112 JohnnyFarrelly 116+
(Alison Thorpe) *prom: led 7th and wnt 4 l ahd: blnd 3 out: drvn along and mstke last: hdd and one pce run-in* **2/1**[2]
4 *23* **Leitra House (IRE)**[368] 7-10-12 0 NickScholfield 88
(Jeremy Scott) *plld hrd: in tch: blnd 1st: effrt 8th: wknd 3 out* **28/1**
PP-P **5** *40* **Byzantina Fair**[12] 429 8-10-5 0 AndrewThornton 43
(Henrietta Knight) *chsd ldr: j.rt 1st: led appr 2nd: blnd 5th: hdd and mstke 7th: sn bhd* **66/1**
P **Pallaton**[30] 4-10-7 0 JimmyMcCarthy —
(Brendan Powell) *sn bhd: rdn 3rd: no ch fr 8th: p.u bef 2 out* **80/1**
P **Cash Crisis (IRE)**[25] 5-10-0 0 MichaelMurphy(5) —
(Mike Hammond) *led: j.rt 1st: hdd and j. path appr 2nd: lost pl 5th: bhd whn p.u after 7th* **14/1**

5m 28.3s (-14.20) **Going Correction** -0.55s/f (Firm)
WFA 4 from 5yo+ 18lb 7 Ran SP% **111.1**
Speed ratings (Par 105): **102,101,101,93,82** —,—
toteswingers: 1&2 £1.10, 1&3 £2.00, 2&3 £1.10. CSF £6.28 TOTE £3.30: £2.10, £1.20; EX 7.20.
Owner Cloud Nine **Bred** Mrs Christine Kelly **Trained** Aberthin, Vale of Glamorgan

FOCUS
The complexion of this modest novices' hurdle changed quickly, with Murcar, who was a couple of lengths up and looking the winner, blundering at the last and being run down by both Pure Anticipation and Like A Hurricane. Ordinary but sound form.

NOTEBOOK
Pure Anticipation(IRE), who won her third and final start in a bumper at Uttoxeter, wasn't always as quick as some of these at her hurdles, but that was understandable, and she impressed with her attitude on the run-in, really knuckling down and staying on well. This sort of trip clearly suits, and she may well defy the penalty, with 3m unlikely to be a problem. (op 2-1 tchd 5-2)
Like A Hurricane(IRE) has looked in need of this trip, but he faced no easy task in trying to give 14lb to the winner. He ran really well, however, keeping on again having been a bit slow two out. (op 2-1 tchd 11-4)
Murcar, off the mark at Towcester last time, was ridden positively and really did kick on. A mistake three out didn't halt his momentum, and he still looked the winner coming into the last, but he was again untidy and could find no extra on the final climb to the line. Though beaten this time, he will be winning again at some stage, with a shorter trip unlikely to be a problem. (op 9-4 tchd 7-4)
Cash Crisis(IRE) Official explanation: jockey said mare lost its action

584 FREE RACING WITH ODDSCHECKER.COM WEDNESDAYS NOVICES' H'CAP CHASE (13 fncs) 2m 2f
3:00 (3:01) (Class 4) (0-110,107) 5-Y-O+ **£3,903** (£1,146; £573)

Form RPR
P0-0 **1** **Bankstair (FR)**[18] 328 6-10-7 88 (t) PaddyBrennan 99+
(Nigel Twiston-Davies) *led after 1st: 2-3 l ahd whn nt fluent fnl 3 fences: drvn out* **2/1**[2]
/3-2 **2** *3 1/4* **Maxwil**[33] 81 5-11-12 107 ColinBolger 114
(Pat Phelan) *chsd wnr fr 4th: mstke 3 out: hrd rdn and one pce fr next* **7/4**[1]
/21- **3** *59* **Karasakal (IRE)**[184] 2612 7-11-10 105 (b[1]) JamieMoore 84+
(Gary Moore) *led tl after 1st: cl up tl wknd appr 3 out: eased* **7/4**[1]

4m 36.8s (2.10) **Going Correction** -0.075s/f (Good) 3 Ran SP% **106.1**
Speed ratings: **92,90,64**
CSF £5.43 TOTE £3.30; EX 4.50.
Owner Hugh Doubtfire **Bred** Jean Biraben Et Al **Trained** Naunton, Gloucs

FOCUS
A trappy affair, despite there being just the three runners, and Paddy Brennan excelled on the winner, who improved by 6lb on his best hurdles form.

NOTEBOOK
Bankstair(FR) was ridden positively and upped the gallop racing out on to the final circuit. He got in a bit close to all three fences down the straight, but jumped well in the main and showed a likeable attitude, suggesting he can win again if not put up too much by the handicapper. (op 3-1)
Maxwil, the only one with previous chasing experience, had finished second at the course latest and again appeared to run his race, but he couldn't stay on as well as the winner. His turn will come eventually. (op 6-4 tchd 15-8)
Karasakal(IRE) hadn't run since romping home in heavy ground at Folkestone last November, and was only 7lb higher here, but he raced freely in the first-time blinkers and was dropped by the front pair from four out. He has the size to make a go of it chasing, but may do better without headgear. (op 11-8 tchd 5-4)

585 CHILDREN'S TRUST TADWORTH SPONSORED BY STURTS H'CAP HURDLE (9 hdls) 2m 2f 110y
3:35 (3:35) (Class 5) (0-90,90) 4-Y-O+ **£1,951** (£573; £286; £143)

Form RPR
P0-0 **1** **Papradon**[19] 318 6-10-6 75 SamTwiston-Davies(5) 88
(Nigel Twiston-Davies) *mde all: set gd pce: rdn appr 2 out: hit last: drvn to hold on run-in* **10/1**
POP/ **2** *2 1/4* **Rosenblatt (GER)**[720] 673 8-10-10 74 JodieMogford 85
(M S Tuck) *hld up in midfield: smooth hdwy 6th: trckd wnr on bit after 3 out: rdn appr last: nt qckn* **16/1**
4-54 **3** *13* **What's For Tea**[15] 384 5-11-1 89 (p) AshleyBird(10) 89
(Paddy Butler) *in tch: effrt 6th: one pce fr 3 out: disputing 3rd and hld whn blnd 2 out* **28/1**
0641 **4** *7* **Risk Challenge (USA)**[8] 462 8-10-1 65 CharliePoste 58
(Milton Harris) *t.k.h in midfield: mstke 3rd: sn lost pl: sme hdwy 3 out: nt trble ldrs* **15/8**[1]
5U4- **5** *3* **Lady Florence**[6] 5047 5-11-1 79 JimmyMcCarthy 69
(Alan Coogan) *chsd ldng pair most of way: hit 5th: outpcd fr 3 out* **10/1**
3-06 **6** *1* **Regain Du Charbonneau (FR)**[21] 272 5-11-12 90(tp) TomScudamore 79
(David Pipe) *outpcd and sn wl bhd: mstke 2nd: rdn and passed btn horses fr 6th* **6/1**[3]
00-4 **7** *2 1/4* **Nobby Kivambo (IRE)**[14] 407 5-11-12 90 APMcCoy 77
(Brendan Powell) *bhd: rdn after 5th: modest effrt 3 out: nvr nr ldrs* **3/1**[2]
U-65 **8** *10* **Atabaas Allure (FR)**[15] 379 4-10-9 77 RodiGreene 51
(Chris Gordon) *mid-div: effrt appr 6th: wknd 3 out* **25/1**
B-05 **9** *3 1/4* **Majestic Bull (USA)**[17] 356 4-11-3 85 (p) JackDoyle 56
(Susan Gardner) *chsd wnr tl wknd qckly after 3 out: fin lame* **22/1**
30-P **P** **Royal Prodigy (USA)**[8] 462 11-11-6 84 (b) AndrewTinkler —
(Ron Hodges) *sn chsng ldrs: hrd rdn 5th: wknd appr next: wl bhd whn p.u bef 2 out* **25/1**
0P0- **P** **Iveragh Lad (IRE)**[44] 5285 10-9-7 64 (b) RobertKirk(7) —
(Steven Dixon) *sn bhd: t.o 4th: p.u bef 6th: lame* **100/1**
0/F0 **P** **Musical Affair**[15] 384 6-10-0 64 oh5 WillKennedy —
(F Jordan) *sn bhd: no ch fr 5th: wl bhd whn p.u bef 2 out* **66/1**
0U-0 **P** **Quiditch D'Ouxy (FR)**[8] 462 6-11-2 80 (b[1]) DarylJacob —
(Mark Hoad) *chsd ldrs: hrd rdn and wknd 6th: btn whn blnd 3 out: bhd whn p.u bef next* **50/1**

4m 22.3s (-12.00) **Going Correction** -0.55s/f (Firm)
WFA 4 from 5yo+ 17lb 13 Ran SP% **118.1**
Speed ratings (Par 103): **103,102,96,93,92 91,91,86,85**,— —,—,—
toteswingers: 1&2 £36.30, 1&3 £22.40, 2&3 £65.90. CSF £138.23 CT £4277.49 TOTE £13.90: £3.10, £6.00, £5.10; EX 155.40.
Owner N A Twiston-Davies **Bred** B Whitehouse **Trained** Naunton, Gloucs

FOCUS
A weak race and little got into it. A step up from the winner but the form looks believable.

NOTEBOOK
Papradon took them along at a decent gallop and kept on dourly when strongly pressed in the straight, getting off the mark at the tenth attempt over hurdles despite a mistake at the last. He was 13lb lower than when placed at Wetherby in December, and the more aggressive ride over this shorter trip plainly suited him well. Official explanation: trainer said, regarding apparent improvement in form, that the gelding was able to dominate in a less competitive race. (op 12-1)
Rosenblatt(GER) ran a massive race on this first start in nearly two years, travelling well but unable to get past the determined winner. It remains to be seen which way he goes from this, but he can probably win something small if progressing. (op 20-1 tchd 14-1)
What's For Tea kept on late and may be capable of a hurdle success once down a few pounds. (op 33-1)
Risk Challenge(USA), a winner at Huntingdon, escaped a penalty and could race off 2lb lower here (was out of handicap last time), but never got close enough to challenge. (tchd 9-4)
Lady Florence, just beaten on the Flat at Brighton the other day, was struggling down the back straight and gradually faded on this return to hurdles. (op 17-2)
Regain Du Charbonneau(FR) is a tough ride and he only got going once the race was all over. (op 9-1 tchd 11-2)
Nobby Kivambo(IRE) was disappointing, getting behind early and failing to get involved. (op 11-4 tchd 9-4)
Majestic Bull(USA) Official explanation: vet said gelding pulled up lame
Iveragh Lad(IRE) Official explanation: vet said gelding pulled up lame

586 PLATINUM AND LACE BAR GENTLEMENS CLUB H'CAP CHASE (16 fncs) 2m 6f
4:05 (4:06) (Class 4) (0-115,111) 5-Y-O+ **£4,228** (£1,241; £620; £310)

Form RPR
03-3 **1** **Mustangsallyrally (IRE)**[28] 153 9-11-5 111 (p) MrRMahon(7) 118
(Paul Nicholls) *hld up in tch: trckd ldrs 10th: rdn appr 3 out: styd on to ld fnl 50yds* **7/2**[1]
P63- **2** *1 1/4* **Misty Dancer**[45] 5246 11-11-11 110 AidanColeman 116
(Venetia Williams) *cl up: jnd ldrs 6th: led 11th to 4 out: led appr 3 out: hrd rdn and kpt on run-in: hdd fnl 50yds* **9/1**
1U6- **3** *2 3/4* **Moulin De La Croix**[67] 4888 6-10-13 103 (t) SamTwiston-Davies(5) 108+
(Nigel Twiston-Davies) *trckd ldrs: led briefly 4 out: drvn along and one pce fr 2 out* **10/1**
530- **4** *2* **Lidjo De Rouge (FR)**[44] 5280 11-11-6 105 RichardJohnson 107
(Paul Henderson) *hld up towards rr: hdwy and in tch 10th: rdn after 4 out: styd on run-in* **7/1**
25-5 **5** *1 1/2* **Morestead (IRE)**[33] 81 5-10-11 96 (p) JimmyMcCarthy 97
(Brendan Powell) *prom: led 3rd tl 11th: outpcd and btn 4 out* **17/2**
U0-4 **6** *36* **Maximix**[24] 221 7-11-1 100 (b) JamieMoore 76
(Gary Moore) *bhd: sme hdwy into midfield and rdn 11th: n.d: 6th and no ch whn blnd last* **25/1**
34P- **P** **Green Gamble**[43] 5292 10-11-4 108 MarcGoldstein(5) —
(Diana Grissell) *in rr whn j. slowly 1st: hdwy into midfield 4th: jnd ldrs 4 out: 5th and btn whn mstke next: bhd whn p.u after 2 out* **50/1**
0-22 **P** **River Indus**[12] 431 10-11-6 105 DarylJacob —
(Bob Buckler) *led tl 3rd: wknd 10th: bhd whn p.u after 4 out* **9/2**[2]
2P-4 **P** **Milesian King (IRE)**[13] 425 9-10-13 98 (t) ChristianWilliams —
(Lawney Hill) *mid-div: lost pl 5th: sn bhd and rdn: t.o whn p.u bef 3 out* **5/1**[3]
/3P- **P** **Vial De Kerdec (FR)**[237] 1664 7-11-0 102 RichardKilloran(3) —
(Mark Bradstock) *nvr gng or jumping wl: sn towards rr: wl bhd fr 1/2-way: t.o whn p.u bef 3 out* **8/1**
2PP- **P** **Orfeo Conti (FR)**[45] 5252 8-11-9 108 (b) PaulMoloney —
(Henrietta Knight) *prom tl wknd qckly 10th: t.o whn p.u bef 3 out* **16/1**

5m 38.5s (-4.50) **Going Correction** -0.075s/f (Good) 11 Ran SP% **122.0**
Speed ratings: **105,104,103,102,102 89**,—,—,—,— —
toteswingers: 1&2 £6.40, 1&3 £10.70, 2&3 £12.40. CSF £36.84 CT £297.54 TOTE £5.20: £1.60, £3.30, £3.80; EX 41.20.
Owner H B Geddes **Bred** John Cotter **Trained** Ditcheat, Somerset

FOCUS
A solid gallop made this a good test. The first two are rated to the best of their recent form.

NOTEBOOK

Mustangsallyrally(IRE), formerly a useful chaser in Ireland, had been beaten in two hunter chases since arriving in Britain, but the switch to Paul Nicholls should bring out the best in him. On a fair mark which can be exploited during the summer now he has shown he acts on fast ground, he travelled well for much of the race but only got on top late in the day, and a return to 3m would be no problem. (op 9-2 tchd 5-1)

Misty Dancer has been hit-and-miss (mainly miss) since having a purple patch in 2006 and 2007, but he had been putting it together better in recent outings and this was another solid effort. He is well handicapped compared with his best and, while nobody would claim he can ever reproduce that form again, he does look capable of winning off his current mark. (op 15-2 tchd 7-1)

Moulin De La Croix had been unconvincing on soft ground since being stepped back up in trip, but this was a much better effort. Having briefly looked the winner four out, she did not fail through lack of stamina. (op 11-1 tchd 9-1)

Lidjo De Rouge(FR) bounced back from a poor run last time. He has done well at this trip in the past, but the way he was finally picking up when the race was over suggests a return to 3m would suit him on fast conditions like these. (op 8-1 tchd 9-1)

Morestead(IRE) has the build of a chaser but he lacks a turn of foot, so races at 3m plus are worth considering. (op 10-1 tchd 8-1)

River Indus was disappointing, failing to reproduce two good recent seconds, but he was reported to be never travelling. He has done well round here in the past, but his best recent runs have been on more testing tracks, and he probably need a stiffer test these days. Official explanation: jockey said gelding never travelled and pulled up (op 6-1 tchd 7-1)

Milesian King(IRE) was another who soon looked unhappy. He seems to have lost his form. (op 6-1 tchd 7-1)

587 MARY BROSNAN CONDITIONAL JOCKEYS' H'CAP HURDLE (11 hdls) 2m 6f 110y

4:40 (4:40) (Class 5) (0-90,89) 4-Y-O+ **£1,951** (£573; £286; £143)

Form — RPR

3-22 **1** **Play A Cord (IRE)**[10] 436 7-10-9 **80**..........(b[1]) MarkQuinlan(8) 88
(Neil Mulholland) *hld up in rr: smooth hdwy 8th: drvn to ld appr last: clr run-in: styd on wl* **4/1**[2]

1B-1 **2** *6* **My Matilda**[24] 217 7-11-4 **84**.......... DavidBass(3) 87
(Lawney Hill) *chsd ldrs: hrd rdn 3 out: kpt on to take 2nd run-in* **4/1**[2]

UP/- **3** *1 ½* **Arctic Ghost**[32] 10-11-1 **86**..........(v[1]) ChrisDavies(8) 90+
(Philip Hobbs) *led after 1st: hit 5th and 7th: rdn 3 out: hdd and btn whn mstke last* **20/1**

P-OF **4** *2 ¾* **Albert Park (IRE)**[18] 336 9-10-1 **64**..........(p) SamTwiston-Davies 63
(John Upson) *hld up in tch: wnt prom and rdn 3 out: one pce fr next* **14/1**

36-P **5** *2* **Spider Boy**[12] 430 13-11-2 **82**..........(b) GemmaGracey-Davison(3) 79
(Zoe Davison) *prom: rdn to chse wnr after 3 out: wknd appr last* **20/1**

234- **6** *1 ¼* **Eastwell Smiles**[30] 4811 6-11-7 **84**..........(t) RichieMcLernon 83
(Richard Phillips) *led tl after 1st: prom tl wknd 2 out* **17/2**[3]

1121 **7** *7* **Lord Gunnerslake (IRE)**[7] 475 10-11-9 **86**..........(v) RichardKilloran 80+
(Tim Vaughan) *rdn nrly all the way: a struggling in rr: passed btn horses fr 3 out* **7/2**[1]

50-4 **8** *17* **Snark (IRE)**[18] 341 7-11-12 **89**.......... JimmyDerham 64
(Simon Earle) *a towards rr: rdn and n.d fr 7th* **16/1**

00-5 **9** *27* **Eddystone (IRE)**[24] 217 6-9-10 **64**..........(vt) PeterHatton(5) 14
(Linda Jewell) *mid-div: sltly hmpd 1st: wknd 7th: sn bhd* **28/1**

31-F **P** **Geography (IRE)**[24] 217 10-11-8 **85**..........(p) MarcGoldstein —
(Jim Best) *bhd tl p.u and dismntd bef 6th: lame* **11/1**

F-05 **F** **Legal Glory (IRE)**[8] 467 10-11-7 **84**.......... GilesHawkins —
(Ron Hodges) *prom whn fell 1st* **12/1**

24P- **P** **The Pious Prince (IRE)**[44] 5290 9-10-12 **78**..........(b) JohnnyFarrelly(3) —
(David Pipe) *sn towards rr: rdn 6th: no ch whn blnd 8th: wl bhd whn p.u bef 2 out* **14/1**

P5-0 **P** **Send For Tim (IRE)**[34] 54 7-10-0 **63** oh9.......... JohnKington —
(F Jordan) *mid-div: stmbld 6th: rdn and wknd after next: wl bhd whn p.u bef 2 out* **100/1**

5m 28.1s (-14.40) **Going Correction** -0.55s/f (Firm) **13** Ran SP% **122.0**

Speed ratings (Par 103): **103,100,100,99,98 98,95,89,80,— —,—,—**

toteswingers: 1&2 £4.10, 1&3 £17.20, 2&3 £25.40. CSF £20.39 CT £294.61 TOTE £4.80: £1.80, £1.80, £9.50; EX 17.30.

Owner Neil Mulholland Racing Club **Bred** C J And Mrs D Hodgins **Trained** Burlescombe, Devon

FOCUS

A low-grade handicap hurdle in which the first two are rated to their marks.

NOTEBOOK

Play A Cord(IRE) took over coming to the last and stayed on strongly. A runner-up on her last two starts, latterly over 3m, she was clearly helped by the application of blinkers instead of cheekpieces here and this in-form mare can continue to pay her way. (op 5-1)

My Matilda, 9lb higher than when winning at Plumpton, is a really strong stayer and she was doing her best work in he final 2f, but never actually looked like winning. She may be up to defying this mark back over a longer trip. (op 5-1)

Arctic Ghost had a first-time visor on for this first start for Philip Hobbs. He has been running without success in points, but went well for a long way under a positive ride. (op 14-1)

Albert Park(IRE), who had failed to complete on each of his last three starts, falling when tailed off last time, at least got round and gave the impression there is a race in him if building some confidence. (op 28-1)

Spider Boy didn't run badly, but it was no surprise to see a few of the younger ones do him for speed. (op 22-1)

Lord Gunnerslake(IRE) never went a yard, being ridden pretty much throughout, and he could only plod on late past beaten horses. Official explanation: jockey said gelding never travelled (tchd 9-2)

Geography(IRE) Official explanation: jockey said gelding pulled up lame

588 SPORTING APPOINTMENTS NOVICES' H'CAP CHASE (19 fncs) 3m 2f 110y

5:15 (5:15) (Class 4) (0-105,103) 5-Y-O+ **£3,903** (£1,146; £573; £286)

Form — RPR

36-2 **1** **Local Present (IRE)**[29] 132 7-11-2 **93**.......... APMcCoy 107+
(Ron Hodges) *cl up: led 14th: clr 3 out: rdn appr last: comf* **6/4**[1]

50-2 **2** *8* **Oamaru Stone (IRE)**[24] 218 7-11-5 **103**.......... MrRMahon(7) 109
(Paul Nicholls) *led: rdn 10th: hdd and outpcd 14th: rallied 4 out: one pce: wnt 10 l 2nd at last* **5/2**[2]

/3P- **3** *4 ½* **Turbulance (IRE)**[30] 8-11-12 **103**..........(p) RichardJohnson 107+
(Bernard Llewellyn) *chsd ldr most of way: hrd rdn and nt pce of wnr fr 3 out: lost 2nd at last* **7/1**

0-10 **4** *3* **Ethiopia**[17] 359 7-11-9 **100**.......... AidanColeman 100
(Bob Buckler) *cl up: mstke 4th: outpcd 13th: disputing 3rd whn mstke 15th: sn btn* **11/2**[3]

2-F4 **5** *1* **Lord Brunello (IRE)**[12] 431 8-11-7 **98**..........(p) ChristianWilliams 98
(Lawney Hill) *a last: mstkes 9th: 11th and 12th: rdn and struggling after* **7/1**

6m 55.5s (-5.60) **Going Correction** -0.075s/f (Good) **5** Ran SP% **109.0**

Speed ratings: **105,102,101,100,100**

CSF £5.72 TOTE £2.30: £1.10, £2.30; EX 5.70.

Owner Miss R Dobson, P Hart, R Hodges **Bred** John Quane **Trained** Charlton Mackrell, Somerset

FOCUS

Just a modest handicap chase. Easy to rate form.

NOTEBOOK

Local Present(IRE) gained a much deserved victory. Not beaten far off a 5lb lower mark at Exeter latest, McCoy sent him on plenty early enough here, and he could be called the winner from six out. He seems to be progressing and, although this wasn't a great race, he may well win again. (op 5-2 tchd 11-4 in places)

Oamaru Stone(IRE), a bit unlucky not to beat Ethiopia at Plumtpon on his chasing debut, was entitled to confirm the form with the weight difference, but he was no match for the winner, plodding on again to take second having been readily outpaced. He's a slow horse, but jumps well, and will no doubt find a suitable opportunity at some point. (op 9-4 tchd 11-4)

Turbulance(IRE), winner of a point-to-point latest, has yet to win under rules, but he went well for a long way, in the end just getting outstayed for second. (op 5-1 tchd 9-2)

Ethiopia had been held over hurdles since winning at Plumpton, and for all that he ran better on this return to fences, he couldn't confirm form with the runner-up and wasn't so effective under this less-aggressive ride. (op 9-2)

Lord Brunello(IRE) wasn't beaten far, despite finishing last of the five, but he has yet to win and is another who looks rather slow. (op 11-2)

589 BRENDAN POWELL RACING STANDARD OPEN NATIONAL HUNT FLAT RACE 2m 2f 110y

5:45 (5:46) (Class 6) 4-6-Y-O **£1,431** (£420; £210; £104)

Form — RPR

6- **1** **Midnight Macarena**[58] 5042 5-10-9 0.......... LeightonAspell 105+
(Lucy Wadham) *hld up in rr: gd hdwy on outer 3f out: led 2f out: pushed clr* **16/1**

2 *1 ¾* **Billy Merriott (IRE)** 4-10-5 0.......... MrRMahon(7) 105
(Paul Nicholls) *chsd ldrs: led 5f out tl 2f out: styd on same pce* **13/2**

3 *2 ¾* **Junior Jack**[30] 5-11-2 0.......... WarrenMarston 107
(Martin Keighley) *t.k.h in midfield: rdn 4f out: styd on to take 3rd 2f out* **9/2**[2]

4 *14* **E Street Boy** 4-10-12 0.......... APMcCoy 90
(Brendan Powell) *hld up in midfield: hdwy 6f out: chsd ldr 4f out tl wknd over 2f out* **3/1**[1]

5 *½* **St Enoder**[30] 5-10-9 0.......... NickScholfield 87
(Brendan Powell) *hld up in rr: promising hdwy 5f out: sn trcking ldrs: rdn and btn 2f out* **25/1**

6 *1 ¾* **Glory Nights**[60] 5005 6-10-11 0.......... SamTwiston-Davies(5) 92
(Dr Richard Newland) *prom: rdn 5f out: btn 3f out* **9/2**[2]

5- **7** *11* **Catch The Rascal (IRE)**[41] 5332 4-10-0 0.......... JimmyDerham(5) 71
(Seamus Mullins) *towards rr: rdn 7f out: wl bhd 5f out: modest late hdwy* **16/1**

8 *1* **Miltara (IRE)** 5-10-9 0.......... AndrewThornton 82
(Diana Grissell) *hld up in midfield on outer: tk clsr order 5f out: wknd and eased over 2f out* **25/1**

9 *½* **Track Star (IRE)** 5-11-2 0.......... RichardJohnson 85
(Luke Dace) *in tch: wnt prom 4f out: rdn and wknd 2f out* **6/1**[3]

10 *9* **Downe Payment (IRE)** 5-10-4 0.......... MarcGoldstein(5) 66
(Diana Grissell) *chsd ldr: led 6f out tl 5f out: wknd 4f out* **20/1**

06-6 **11** *50* **Golden Celebration**[23] 254 4-10-9 0.......... CharlieStudd(3) 24
(Chris Gordon) *chsd ldrs: led after 8f tl 6f out: wknd over 4f out: bhd and eased fnl 3f: t.o* **50/1**

12 *3* **Ice Boru (IRE)** 4-10-0 0.......... MichaelMurphy(5) 14
(Mike Hammond) *plld hrd: prom: rdn 7f out: sn wknd: t.o fnl 5f* **40/1**

13 *shd* **West Bay Hoolie** 4-10-12 0.......... JamieMoore 21
(Helen Nelmes) *a in rr: t.o fnl 5f* **66/1**

0 **14** *1 ¼* **Hunting Red**[23] 254 5-10-9 0.......... FelixDeGiles 17
(Jonathen de Giles) *led 8f: wknd 5f out: wl bhd fnl 3f: t.o* **66/1**

4m 18.0s (-10.70) **Going Correction** -0.55s/f (Firm)

WFA 4 from 5yo+ 3lb **14** Ran SP% **120.6**

Speed ratings: **100,99,98,92,92 91,86,86,86,82 61,59,59,59**

toteswingers: 1&2 £16.90, 1&3 £19.40, 2&3 £11.70. CSF £110.35 TOTE £18.70: £7.10, £2.00, £1.60; EX 131.80 Place 6: £411.22, Place 5: £240.53.

Owner J J W Wadham **Bred** Mrs Elizabeth Gordon Lennox **Trained** Newmarket, Suffolk

FOCUS

An ordinary bumper, run at a steady early gallop and the first three came clear up the home straight. They look reasonable prospects.

NOTEBOOK

Midnight Macarena had run below market expectations on her debut at Fakenham, but settled a lot better this time and ran out a determined winner. She was produced with her chance off the home turn and this stiffer track was much more to her liking. She is bred to enjoy a trip when sent over jumps and there should be more to come. (op 14-1 tchd 12-1)

Billy Merriott(IRE) ran a big race in defeat. He was only picked off by the winner late on and should come on a good deal for the outing. (op 9-2)

Junior Jack is a half-brother to Love Of Tara, a 130-rated hurdler for the same connections, and had fallen on his sole outing between the flags last month. He got outpaced a fair way out, but was keeping on well at the finish and this rates an encouraging introduction. (op 8-1)

E Street Boy's dam is a half-sister to his stable's former classy chaser Colonel Frank, who failed to win one of these. He was another that lacked the tactical pace when it mattered and left the impression the outing would do him good. (tchd 11-4 and 7-2)

St Enoder showed her best form in the pointing field when third on her final outing in that sphere and ran as though she needs a stiffer test. Her breeding fully backs up that opinion. (op 16-1)

T/Plt: £1,093.60 to a £1 stake. Pool: £53,287.43. 35.57 winning tickets. T/Qpdt: £122.10 to a £1 stake. Pool: £4,587.83. 27.80 winning tickets. LM

370 NEWTON ABBOT (L-H)

Thursday, June 3

OFFICIAL GOING: Good to firm (good in places; 8.3)

Course at innermost configuration.

Wind: fresh across Weather: sunny

590 NATIONAL COASTWATCH INSTITUTION MAIDEN HURDLE (8 hdls) 2m 1f

2:30 (2:32) (Class 4) 4-Y-O+ **£3,382** (£993; £496; £248)

Form — RPR

26-2 **1** **Saltagioo (ITY)**[10] 159 6-11-0 107.......... WarrenMarston 111+
(Milton Harris) *trckd ldr: slt ld whn hit 5th: asserted bef 2 out: r.o strly: readily* **4/1**[2]

252- **2** *9* **Souter Point (USA)**[46] 5245 4-10-11 120..........(b[1]) APMcCoy 98
(Nicky Henderson) *trckd ldrs: jnd wnr 5th: rdn after 3 out: fnd little: sn btn* **10/11**[1]

236- **3** *5* **Sahrati**[95] 3130 6-11-0 115.......... PaulMoloney 96+
(Michael Blake) *mid-div: rdn bef 3 out: styd on same pce* **11/2**[3]

F **4** 1 ½ **Tignello (IRE)**[28] 182 5-11-0 0 HarrySkelton 96+
(Paul Nicholls) *mid-div: blnd 2nd: hdwy 3 out: sn chsd clr ldng pair: no imp whn nt fluent 2 out: fdd last* **7/1**

0P-6 **5** nk **Tilly Shilling (IRE)**[22] 276 6-10-2 0 (b) GilesHawkins(5) 87
(Kevin Bishop) *mid-div: rdn and styd on fr after 3 out: mstke next: wnt 3rd last: no ch w ldng pair* **100/1**

00-0 **6** 13 **Spring Haze**[22] 272 5-10-0 70 (p) MrDGPrichard(7) 74
(Phillip Dando) *led tl 5th: wknd after 3 out* **100/1**

0- **7** 1 **Grit (IRE)**[46] 5260 5-11-0 0 RodiGreene 80
(Nick Ayliffe) *trckd ldrs: rdn bef 3 out: wknd bef 2 out* **40/1**

0/5- **8** 4 ½ **Shame The Devil (IRE)**[26] 245 5-11-0 0 DavidDennis 78
(James Evans) *hld up towards rr: nt fluent 5th and 3 out: little imp* **100/1**

P **9** 7 **Special Bond**[22] 275 4-10-1 0 ow4 MattGriffiths(7) 63
(Kevin Bishop) *a towards rr* **100/1**

04 **10** nk **The Grey One (IRE)**[18] 356 7-10-7 0 ChrisDavies(7) 68
(Milton Bradley) *dwlt bdly: 20 l last: jnd tail end of main gp 3rd but nvr a factor* **25/1**

-P **P** **Soccerjackpot (USA)**[33] 97 6-10-11 0 RichardKilloran(3) —
(Alan Jones) *a towards rr: t.o 3 out: p.u bef next* **14/1**

3m 56.6s (-9.10) **Going Correction** -0.50s/f (Good)
WFA 4 from 5yo+ 17lb 11 Ran SP% **117.2**
Speed ratings (Par 105): **101,96,94,93,93 87,86,84,81,81 —**
Tote Swingers: 1&2 £1.90, 1&3 £2.70, 2&3 £2.50 CSF £8.20 TOTE £5.40: £2.20, £1.02, £1.80; EX 9.50.
Owner Mrs D Dewbery **Bred** Az Ag Francesca **Trained** Herridge, Wiltshire

FOCUS
This had looked a competitive contest but it was weakened slightly by a couple of withdrawals prior to the off. It was steadily run and the winner produced a step up.

NOTEBOOK
Saltagioo(ITY), having his first run for Milton Harris since being claimed from Alan King's stable last time on the Flat, showed the most commitment under pressure to prevail. He can win a couple of races during the summer round some tight tracks. (op 5-1)
Souter Point(USA), blinkered for the first time, appeared to have the best hurdling form on offer and was rated 5lb higher than any of his rivals with official marks. He was upsides the winner when they started to go clear but did not look the most willing under pressure. (tchd 5-4 tchd 11-8 in places)
Sahrati, beaten when evens favourite for a 1m3f Kempton claimer last time, put in a couple of decent performances in three attempts last season over hurdles but gave himself a handicap in this by taking a strong hold under restraint early. Outpaced at around halfway, he was still in fifth coming to the final hurdle but kept on strongly to grab third. (op 9-2 tchd 4-1 and 13-2)
Tignello(IRE) was running a decent race on his first outing for this stable before falling at the last on his previous start, and came through with a promising effort halfway down the back straight, but it never seemed likely that he would get to the first two and a error two out saw him start to weaken. At least he managed to complete this time, despite a couple of errors, which should boost his confidence. (op 9-1 tchd 13-2)
Tilly Shilling(IRE), with blinkers refitted on her return to hurdling, did not look completely straightforward under pressure at some stages but gave the impression she could win something weak during the summer.

591 SEE WILL YOUNG HERE 24 JULY "NATIONAL HUNT" NOVICES' HURDLE (8 hdls) 2m 3f

3:00 (3:00) (Class 4) 4-Y-0+ **£3,707** (£1,088; £544; £271)

Form RPR
23-1 **1** **Osric (IRE)**[34] 76 7-11-5 120 APMcCoy 130+
(Nicky Henderson) *cl up: jnd ldr 6th: led appr 2 out: sn clr: comf* **10/11**[1]

32-1 **2** 14 **Calon Crwbin**[34] 82 5-11-5 125 (t) JohnnyFarrelly 115
(Alison Thorpe) *led: rdn and hdd appr 2 out: sn hld by wnr* **5/4**[2]

04-4 **3** 9 **Detroit Red**[23] 263 4-9-12 90 HaddenFrost(3) 87
(Martin Hill) *trckd ldr tl 6th: sn rdn to chse ldng pair: one pce fr after 3 out* **25/1**

003- **4** 25 **Klampenborg**[47] 5235 5-10-12 0 TomScudamore 73
(Michael Scudamore) *trckd ldrs: little slow 1st: rdn and wknd 3 out* **12/1**[3]

00P- **5** 29 **Oxlea Lass**[96] 4295 5-9-12 0 MarkQuinlan(7) 37
(James Frost) *hld up bhd ldrs tl lost tch 5th: t.o* **100/1**

16-2 **F** **Cityar (FR)**[21] 304 6-10-5 0 CharlieWallis(7) —
(John O'Shea) *nvr particularly fluent in last: awkward 4th: wknd after 3 out: wl bhd whn fell last* **28/1**

4m 19.0s (-14.90) **Going Correction** -0.50s/f (Good)
WFA 4 from 5yo+ 17lb 6 Ran SP% **112.8**
Speed ratings (Par 105): **111,105,101,90,78 —**
Tote Swingers: 1&2 £1.02, 1&3 £2.20, 2&3 £2.60 CSF £2.43 TOTE £1.90: £1.10, £1.10; EX 2.20.
Owner Mr & Mrs R Kelvin Hughes **Bred** P Turley And Sons **Trained** Upper Lambourn, Berks

FOCUS
An uncompetitive contest. The easy winner is rated in line with his previous best.

NOTEBOOK
Osric(IRE), who reportedly hasn't been the easiest to train, took a while to get the hang of things but looked decent last time when winning by 5l at Bangor. He took this by a much wider margin after travelling up to the long-time leader going well, but there was a couple of times when he needed pushing along to get up and past the leader before gaining an advantage. One would imagine further or a stiffer course would be no problem. That is probably it now until the autumn. (op 5-6 tchd Evens)
Calon Crwbin also took his first race last time by 5l, after a few attempts, and set off to make every yard. He did respond quite well to pressure but was firmly put in his place. (op 13-8)
Detroit Red had run respectably on his previous two starts but was no match for the pair that kicked on in the latter stages, albeit she was not beaten that far by the runner-up. (op 18-1)
Klampenborg was readily left behind before three out on his hurdling debut. (op 16-1)
Cityar(FR), the winner of one of his four starts in bumpers, jumped moderately on his hurdling debut and fell when well behind. (op 20-1)

592 OUR FRIENDS AT SIS H'CAP CHASE (13 fncs) 2m 110y

3:30 (3:36) (Class 3) (0-125,121) 5-Y-0+ £7,129 (£2,106; £1,053; £526; £263)

Form RPR
/630 **1** **De Luain Gorm (IRE)**[5] 522 12-10-9 104 AidanColeman 124+
(Chris Down) *j.w: mde all: qcknd clr after 3 out: readily* **12/1**

2-12 **2** 11 **Helen Wood**[11] 444 7-11-3 112 (bt) TomScudamore 120
(David Pipe) *trckd wnr: rdn after 4 out: nt pce of wnr after 3 out: styd on same pce* **7/2**[2]

53-1 **3** 2 ¾ **Earth Dream (IRE)**[17] 373 7-11-5 121 MrRMahon(7) 128
(Paul Nicholls) *trckd wnr: rdn after 4 out: kpt on same pce: no ch w wnr but disputing 2nd whn hit last: no ex* **9/2**[3]

0-23 **4** 13 **Huguenot (IRE)**[18] 361 7-11-4 118 GilesHawkins(5) 113
(Philip Hobbs) *chsd ldrs: pushed along after 7th: mstke 4 out: sn rdn: one pce fr next* **5/1**

-211 **5** 4 **Pilgrims Lane (IRE)**[6] 498 6-11-5 119 7ex JimmyDerham(5) 112
(Milton Harris) *hld up bhd ldrs: outpcd after 4 out: wknd after next: fin lame* **2/1**[1]

331- **6** 74 **Cortinas (GER)**[206] 2192 8-11-10 119 (tp) PaulMoloney 43
(Charlie Mann) *hld up bhd ldrs: nt fluent 4th (water): blnd 8th: sn lost tch: t.o* **16/1**

00-2 **P** **Mibleu (FR)**[25] 233 10-10-10 110 KeiranBurke(5) —
(R H & Mrs S Alner) *j. sltly rt at times: quite keen: hld up: wnt 4th 7th: wnt 3rd 4 out: rdn whn nt fluent 3 out (water): sn wknd: wnt bdly rt next: p.u bef last* **14/1**

3m 58.2s (-8.30) **Going Correction** -0.30s/f (Good) 7 Ran SP% **110.6**
Speed ratings: **107,101,100,94,92 57,—**
Tote Swingers: 1&2 £11.90, 1&3 £10.70, 2&3 £3.00 CSF £50.98 CT £210.47 TOTE £13.40: £7.10, £1.70; EX 67.90.
Owner Mrs M Trueman **Bred** Mrs Martina Dollard **Trained** Mutterton, Devon

FOCUS
Six of the seven that ran in this finished in the first three last time, so this seemed a reasonable contest, but it appeared that the winner, the only horse not to place last time, stole it from the front. The winner is rated back to his 2009 form.

NOTEBOOK
De Luain Gorm(IRE), who was well behind Earth Dream last time he ran over fences, has been running poorly since returning from a broken pelvis but he was allowed an easy time of it in front and did not set a really strong gallop. Aidan Coleman replaced a 7lb claiming rider and got his fractions right in front, increasing the tempo at the right time to gain a crucial advantage. If connections can get him out quickly, he can follow up. (op 20-1)
Helen Wood, the winner of a selling hurdle two starts previously, was a fair second back over fences last time and seemed to run up to her best without ever looking likely to peg back the leader. (op 10-3 tchd 11-4 and 4-1)
Earth Dream(IRE), 7lb higher than when winning over C&D on his return from a lengthy layoff last month, raced prominently but was one paced from some way out. (op 4-1)
Huguenot(IRE), beaten over 9l by Pilgrims Lane last time, was pushed along halfway down the back straight and never figured. (op 9-2 tchd 4-1)
Pilgrims Lane(IRE), chasing a hat-trick, was 12lb higher here than when winning the first of his two wins and played no part at any stage. He probably wants further. (op 5-2 tchd 3-1)
Cortinas(GER), absent since winning a 2m Southwell handicap last November, was 9lb higher here and ruined his chance by pulling very hard early. He then made a bad mistake at the eighth and could never get involved. (op 22-1 tchd 14-1)
Mibleu(FR), who won this race last season, did make a brief attempt to get competitive starting round the final bend but he was already under pressure when hitting three out and might have hurt himself as he was pulled up after the next. (op 8-1)

593 NEWTON ABBOT RACECOURSE LADY RIDERS' (S) H'CAP HURDLE (10 hdls) 2m 3f

4:00 (4:01) (Class 5) (0-95,95) 4-Y-0+ **£2,055** (£599; £299)

Form RPR
56/- **1** **Public Esteem (IRE)**[61] 9-11-5 95 (p) MrsAlexDunn(7) 104
(Dr Richard Newland) *chsd ldr: led 6th: sn rdn: hdd after 3 out: led bef next: hld on: all out* **10/1**

P/0U **2** hd **Amazing Request**[16] 380 6-9-11 73 (p) MissIsabelTompsett(7) 84+
(Bernard Llewellyn) *mid-div: nt fluent 3 out: rdn and hdwy bef next: styd on fr last: jst hld* **8/1**

U-4P **3** 4 **Rock Me (IRE)**[25] 227 5-11-5 95 (tp) LucyBarry(7) 102
(Lawney Hill) *mid-div: hdwy 6th: rdn to ld after 3 out: hdd bef next: styd on same pce* **25/1**

3U-6 **4** ¾ **Killing Me Softly**[17] 371 9-10-3 79 (v) MissJBuck(7) 83
(Brian Forsey) *hld up towards rr: hit 1st: struggling 6th: styd on appr 2 out: nvr trbld ldrs* **16/1**

1-60 **5** 1 ¼ **Pearly Star**[15] 410 9-11-5 93 (b) GemmaGracey-Davison(5) 96
(Jim Best) *chsd ldrs: rdn after 6th: one pce fr after 3 out* **5/1**[1]

50/5 **6** 5 **Turkish Sultan (IRE)**[4] 537 7-10-6 82 (p) MissBAndrews(7) 80
(Milton Bradley) *mid-div: effrt 3 out: one pce fr next* **33/1**

000- **7** nse **Low Delta (IRE)**[75] 4731 10-11-2 92 MissGAndrews(7) 90
(Michael Blake) *hld up towards rr: rdn appr 3 out: styd on fr 2 out: nvr a danger* **14/1**

3-03 **8** 3 ¼ **Galant Eye (IRE)**[3] 557 11-10-1 77 MissCBoxall(7) 72
(Chris Down) *sme mod late hdwy: mainly towards rr* **15/2**[3]

0-4P **9** nk **Go Free**[17] 371 9-10-9 85 (p) L-BdrSallyRandell(7) 79
(John O'Shea) *in tch: rdn bef 6th: wnt 3rd 3 out: 5th and hld whn stmbld bdly 2 out* **12/1**

05-4 **10** 10 **Young Tot (IRE)**[17] 373 12-10-8 84 MissZoeLilly(7) 68
(Carroll Gray) *led tl 6th: sn rdn: wknd after 3 out* **33/1**

0P-0 **11** 7 **Paradise Regained (FR)**[22] 272 7-10-11 87 (p) MissHannahWatson(7) 64
(Sophie Leech) *mid-div: effrt 3 out: sn wknd* **40/1**

0-0P **12** 2 ¾ **Compton Star**[22] 276 10-9-10 72 (b) MissAliceMills(7) 47
(Ron Hodges) *a towards rr: t.o* **22/1**

4-60 **P** **Knockvicar (IRE)**[22] 272 8-9-12 74 MissJennyCarr(7) —
(Richard Mitchell) *reminders in rr fr 3rd: t.o whn p.u bef 6th* **12/1**

0-03 **P** **Eddie Dowling**[9] 462 5-10-5 81 (tp) MissCRoddick(7) —
(Milton Harris) *in tch tl wknd 3 out: bhd whn p.u bef last* **7/1**[2]

0U-5 **P** **Mr Straffan (IRE)**[23] 267 7-10-9 85 MissCLWills(7) —
(Martin Hill) *in tch tl wknd appr 3 out: bhd whn p.u bef last* **5/1**[1]

4m 23.5s (-10.40) **Going Correction** -0.50s/f (Good) 15 Ran SP% **122.2**
Speed ratings (Par 103): **101,100,99,98,98 96,96,94,94,90 87,86,—,—,—**
Tote Swingers: 1&2 £24.10, 1&3 £22.80, 2&3 £43.90 CSF £84.10 CT £1969.62 TOTE £13.60: £2.80, £3.90, £6.90; EX 134.40.There was no bid for the winner.
Owner Mrs K R Smith-Maxwell **Bred** Neil R Tector **Trained** Claines, Worcs

FOCUS
The pace looked strong, which meant plenty of these came under pressure at the halfway point. The first six home were all wearing headgear of some description. The third to sixth help set the level.

NOTEBOOK
Public Esteem(IRE), who has been running fairly consistently in points, used his stamina to good effect once towards the head of affairs, but only just held on in a close finish. It is not easy to know whether he will repeat this effort next time, or have the race run to suit. (op 9-1)
Amazing Request, with the cheekpieces back on, attracted market support and went close to collecting for those who backed him in the win market, but he didn't jump that fluently on occasions, and also gave the impression he is not one to completely trust. (op 16-1)
Rock Me(IRE), with a tongue-tie fitted for the first time, came through to have every chance but did not get home as strongly as the first two. (op 22-1)
Killing Me Softly really caught the eye with the way he finished, and would have been a bigger threat to the first two had his effort come a bit earlier. (op 12-1)
Pearly Star was never far away but did not finish as strongly as those in front of him. (op 11-2 tchd 6-1)
Go Free looked held when hitting two out hard. (op 20-1)

Mr Straffan(IRE) was very disappointing after losing his position. (tchd 9-2 and 11-2 in a place)

594 EMMA BEGINNERS' CHASE (16 fncs) 2m 5f 110y
4:30 (4:30) (Class 5) 5-Y-0+ £2,797 (£821; £410; £205)

Form				RPR
034-	1		**Gee Dee Nen**[108] 4080 7-11-0 0 .... JamieMoore (Gary Moore) *j.w: led tl after 2nd: prom: led 9th: rdn after 4 out: holding runner-up fr next: styd on wl* **5/2**[2]	131+
20-2	2	4 ½	**Classic Swain (USA)**[18] 357 5-11-0 0 .... (t) NickScholfield (Paul Nicholls) *hld up bhd ldrs: tk clsr order 6th: rdn and ev ch after 4 out: kpt on same pce fr next* **13/8**[1]	128
50-0	3	17	**Moment Present (FR)**[27] 196 5-11-0 0 .... TomScudamore (Charlie Mann) *trckd ldrs: slow 11th: sn rdn: outpcd fr 4 out* **6/1**	110
5	4	¾	**Smart Dwellie**[15] 408 7-11-0 0 .... RodiGreene (Kevin Bishop) *prom early: trckd ldrs fr 3rd: slow next: rdn after 11th: outpcd fr 4 out* **66/1**	109
22-3	5	13	**Horseshoe Reef (AUS)**[25] 234 7-11-0 0 .... DarylJacob (Jamie Snowden) *led after 2nd tl 9th: trckd wnr: rdn after 11th: outpcd 4 out: wknd after next* **3/1**[3]	102+
32-2	6	24	**Remember Bampi**[22] 276 6-10-9 90 .... (tp) JimmyDerham[(5)] (Simon Burrough) *hld up bhd ldrs: struggling 10th: wknd 4 out* **14/1**	72
0P/P	F		**Sullivan's Cascade (IRE)**[29] 148 12-10-7 0 .... MrJFlook[(7)] (Edward Bevan) *in tch tl nt fluent 7th (water): sn bhd: fell 10th: fatally injured* **100/1**	—

5m 14.4s (-7.00) **Going Correction** -0.30s/f (Good) 7 Ran SP% **115.1**
Speed ratings: **100,98,92,91,87 78,—**
Tote Swingers: 1&2 £3.30, 1&3 £2.70, 2&3 £3.00 CSF £7.47 TOTE £2.70: £1.70, £1.10; EX 9.50.

Owner Chris Duggan & Brendan Gilligan **Bred** Kingwood Bloodstock **Trained** Lower Beeding, W Sussex

FOCUS
A modest beginners' chase. The winner is rated in line with her hurdles best.

NOTEBOOK
Gee Dee Nen, without any headgear for his chasing debut, looked like he needed a bit of urging in a prominent position early, but he kept finding a little bit more for strong pressure throughout the final stages and maintained the lead he gained. (tchd 9-4)

Classic Swain(USA), without blinkers this time but wearing a sheepskin noseband, is a classy sort to be chasing at this time of the year, although he has looked best on quick ground. He didn't look a natural over fences on his first start over them at Stratford and once again here, so the jury is still out as to whether he likes chasing. (op 2-1)

Moment Present(FR) won a couple of novice events last May, but was slightly disappointing thereafter. Having his first chasing experience, he made a satisfactory start over fences but was never going to trouble the first two. (op 10-1 tchd 12-1)

Smart Dwellie, who went down before the others, kept plugging away and was not completely disgraced.

Horseshoe Reef(AUS) shaped nicely on his first start over fences in a competitive event (2m7f), but a couple of mistakes at different points of the race appeared to knock his confidence. He doesn't look the quickest and may want a return to around 3m. (op 5-2 tchd 10-3)

595 CAR BOOT SALE HERE 27TH JUNE H'CAP HURDLE (8 hdls) 2m 1f
5:00 (5:00) (Class 4) (0-105,105) 4-Y-0+ £3,317 (£974; £487; £243)

Form				RPR
56-4	1		**Wheelavit (IRE)**[25] 235 7-11-11 104 .... (t) LiamTreadwell (Claire Dyson) *mde all: hit last: kpt on wl: pushed out* **15/2**	110+
0-51	2	1 ½	**Ton-Chee**[7] 490 11-10-6 92 7ex .... (t) CDTimmons[(7)] (Arthur Whitehead) *trckd ldrs: wnt 2nd travelling ok 3 out: rdn whn wnt lft 2 out: kpt on* **6/1**	95
243-	3	¾	**Olivino (GER)**[22] 2301 9-11-2 102 .... MissIsabelTompsett[(7)] (Bernard Llewellyn) *mid-div: hdwy whn short of room after 3 out: rdn in cl 3rd whn sltly hmpd 2 out: kpt on but no ex fr last* **5/1**[3]	105
-601	4	8	**Cubism**[5] 527 4-11-6 102 7ex .... (t) WarrenMarston (Milton Harris) *trckd ldrs: rdn after 3 out: one pce fr next* **9/2**[2]	93
065/	5	3 ½	**Querido (USA)**[22] 8-10-5 89 .... (t) JimmyDerham[(5)] (Simon Burrough) *in tch: rdn after 3 out: sn one pce* **33/1**	80
433-	6	4	**Watergate (IRE)**[41] 5364 4-11-2 105 .... (t) MrRMahon[(7)] (Paul Nicholls) *cl up: rdn in 3rd after 3 out: wknd after next* **5/2**[1]	89
P-50	7	2 ½	**Perlon (FR)**[13] 430 5-10-13 92 .... JamieMoore (Gary Moore) *a towards rr* **16/1**	76
0-U	8	1	**Lord Francois (FR)**[21] 299 5-10-13 99 .... MrTomDavid[(7)] (Tim Vaughan) *hit 3rd and last: a towards rr* **25/1**	82
F0-0	9	15	**Racingisdreaming (USA)**[18] 356 4-10-7 89 .... (t) TomScudamore (David Pipe) *a towards rr: t.o* **14/1**	54
00-6	P		**Nothing Is Forever (IRE)**[13] 430 6-11-6 99 .... DarylJacob (Liam Corcoran) *in tch: rdn after 3 out: lost action and sn p.u: dismntd* **8/1**	—

3m 54.7s (-11.00) **Going Correction** -0.50s/f (Good)
WFA 4 from 5yo+ 17lb 10 Ran SP% **119.9**
Speed ratings (Par 105): **105,104,103,100,98 96,95,95,87,—**
Tote Swingers: 1&2 £9.00, 1&3 £5.40, 2&3 £9.20 CSF £53.97 CT £251.79 TOTE £10.10: £3.80, £3.80, £2.10; EX 49.70 Place 6: £79.30 Place 5: £69.75..

Owner Miss C Dyson **Bred** John Bourke **Trained** Cleeve Prior, Worcs

FOCUS
A moderate handicap hurdle but solid form with the first three to their marks.

NOTEBOOK
Wheelavit(IRE) set a pace that suited him. A couple of times he looked like being closed down, but the horse was brave and responded to pressure, finding just enough to win for the first time since taking this contest last year. (op 13-2 tchd 8-1)

Ton-Chee, a 33/1 winner at Wetherby last time, travelled strongly on the tail of the leader and seemed sure to get past at some stage. However, Wheelavit didn't want to give up and Ton-Chee could not get to the front. He dwarfed most of his rivals, so it wouldn't be a surprise to see him go back over fences again soon, especially as he is due to go up another 7lb from the weekend. (op 15-2)

Olivino(GER) can sometimes hit a flat spot but, as is usual, he runs on well in the final stages. The handicapper seems to have him about right, so is the best guide to the level here. (op 9-2 tchd 11-2)

Cubism, 7lb higher than his win last time, did not lead this time and lost his place after three out before staying on again. It might be that he needs to lead. (op 10-3 tchd 5-1)

Watergate(IRE) attracted market support but once again disappointed. (op 4-1)

T/Plt: £175.30 to a £1 stake. Pool: £63.723.69 - 265.34. T/Qpdt: £122.90 to a £1 stake. Pool: £3,090.13 - 18.60. TM

535 UTTOXETER (L-H)
Thursday, June 3

OFFICIAL GOING: Good to firm (good in places; chs 7.4; hdl 7.8)
The third hurdle in the back straight was omitted in all hurdle races. The second last fence was omitted in all chases. - ground under repair.
Wind: Light behind Weather: Warm sunny

596 LADIES AT RACES "NATIONAL HUNT" NOVICES' HURDLE (9 hdls 1 omitted) 2m
5:50 (5:50) (Class 4) 4-Y-0+ £2,732 (£802; £401; £200)

Form				RPR
44-3	1		**Pure Faith (IRE)**[27] 196 6-10-12 109 .... TomO'Brien (Peter Bowen) *led after 1st: a gng easily: wl in command 2 out* **1/2**[1]	119+
	2	10	**Yeomanry**[57] 5086 5-10-12 0 .... DougieCostello (Ian Williams) *led tl stdd after 1st: chsd wnr bef 5th: rdn and wl hld whn hit 2 out* **3/1**[2]	109
	3	31	**O'Callaghan Strand (AUS)** 4-10-0 0 .... WillKennedy (Jonjo O'Neill) *t.k.h in rr: outpcd whn mstke 6th: lft poor 3rd at last* **11/1**[3]	65
0P-	4	3 ¼	**Carraigh Na Loine**[197] 2361 5-10-12 0 .... SamThomas (Jonjo O'Neill) *hld up: wnt 3rd at 6th: lost tch bef 3 out: 22 l 3rd next: blnd last and sn 4th: bttr for r* **40/1**	77
PP-0	5	8	**Simbamead**[15] 407 5-10-9 0 .... (p) CharlieStudd[(3)] (Michael Mullineaux) *chsd wnr after 1st: tl rdn bef 5th: sn struggling bdly: t.o 3 out* **100/1**	66
4-0	6	28	**Mr Chippy (IRE)**[33] 93 6-10-12 0 .... TomMessenger (Ian Williams) *bhd: reminders bef 5th: sn lost tch: t.o 3 out* **14/1**	38
	U		**Humbel Lad (IRE)**[31] 6-10-2 0 .... CraigGallagher[(10)] (Richard Guest) *t.k.h: chsd ldrs tl rdn and lost tch bef 6th: 37 l 6th whn uns rdr 2 out* **66/1**	—

3m 50.4s (-4.80) **Going Correction** -0.425s/f (Good)
WFA 4 from 5yo+ 17lb 7 Ran SP% **111.6**
Speed ratings (Par 105): **95,90,74,72,68 54,—**
toteswingers: 1&2 £1.02, 1&3 £3.00, 2&3 £5.90 CSF £2.22 TOTE £1.30: £1.10, £2.20; EX 2.20.

Owner P Bowling,S Scott,R Harvey & K Bowen **Bred** P J Carmody **Trained** Little Newcastle, Pembrokes

FOCUS
An uncompetitive novice hurdle and a slow time compared with other races over the trip. The form is rated around the first two.

NOTEBOOK
Pure Faith(IRE), placed off 107 at Aintree latest, was down in trip and faced a much simpler task in this event. Soon in front, he could always be called the winner, readily drawing clear to score with plenty in hand. He looks capable of defying a penalty in the right company. (op 4-6)

Yeomanry was the only one to get anywhere near the winner, but he was readily left trailing and probably needs further. (op 9-4 tchd 10-3 in a place)

O'Callaghan Strand(AUS) plugged on to take a modest third and will do better over further in time. (op 12-1)

Carraigh Na Loine is a likely type for handicaps further down the line. (op 33-1)

597 PIMM'S NOVICES' H'CAP CHASE (15 fncs 3 omitted) 3m
6:20 (6:20) (Class 4) (0-105,105) 5-Y-0 £3,421 (£1,010; £505; £252; £126)

Form				RPR
0P-P	1		**Sordid Secret (IRE)**[28] 169 7-11-0 96 .... DPFahy[(3)] (Evan Williams) *trckd ldrs: prom and gng wl fr 10th: led after 12th: hdd after 2 out: nt fluent last: strly rdn to ld again fnl 50yds* **7/1**[3]	107+
4-55	2	¾	**Safe Investment (USA)**[18] 353 6-10-4 83 .... (p) AndrewThornton (Ben Pollock) *t.k.h in rr: prog 10th: wnt 2nd after 12th: led after 2 out: urged along and ct 50yds out* **10/1**	93
20-P	3	1 ½	**Old Brigade (IRE)**[29] 157 6-10-11 90 .... (t) WillKennedy (Jonjo O'Neill) *bhd and nt fluent: mstkes 9th and 11th: last of 6 w ch after next: effrt 2 out: sn 3rd: rdn and tried to chal last: v one pce flat* **11/2**[2]	98
/02-	4	7	**Mealagh Valley (IRE)**[42] 5341 9-11-3 103 .... DavidBass[(7)] (Ben De Haan) *last after slow jump 4th: mstkes 5th and 6th: rallied 11th: 5th after next: wnt 3rd briefly but no imp 2 out: plodded on u.p* **7/2**[1]	106
0-2P	5	6	**Haoyunma (IRE)**[17] 371 8-9-11 79 oh7 .... SeanQuinlan[(3)] (Harry Chisman) *wnt 2nd at 6th: led 10th: hdd after 12th: rdn and wknd after 3 out* **25/1**	75
/5-2	6	9	**Von Galen (IRE)**[16] 383 9-10-11 90 .... SamThomas (Michael Scudamore) *trckd ldrs fr 4th tl fdd u.p bef 3 out* **7/2**[1]	82
03P-	7	5	**Midnight Diamond (IRE)**[36] 49 7-9-7 79 oh7 .... (p) HarryChalloner[(7)] (Lisa Williamson) *nt fluent: nvr looked to be gng wl: prom tl rdn 6th: in rr 8th: t.o fr 12th* **16/1**	62
12-	8	38	**Tanners Court**[36] 49 13-11-9 105 .... TommyPhelan[(3)] (Claire Dyson) *led tl 10th: lost tch bef 3 out: t.o and eased next* **7/1**[3]	54
5-06	P		**Nodanawink**[19] 341 7-10-1 85 .... JohnKington[(5)] (Donald McCain) *prom: j. slowly 9th and rdn: stopped to nil: p.u after next* **9/1**	—

6m 6.80s (-8.30) **Going Correction** -0.425s/f (Good) 9 Ran SP% **113.6**
Speed ratings: **96,95,95,92,90 87,86,73,—**
toteswingers: 1&2 £59.50, 1&3 £11.90, 2&3 £43.10 CSF £71.02 CT £411.72 TOTE £6.20: £2.60, £4.40, £1.30; EX 47.30.

Owner R E R Williams **Bred** Joseph And William Morgan **Trained** Llancarfan, Vale Of Glamorgan

FOCUS
A low-grade novices' handicap chase. The winner was a bit better than the bare result and can probably rate higher.

NOTEBOOK
Sordid Secret(IRE), pulled up on her recent debut over fences, is a former point winner and it was no surprise to see her leave that initial chase effort behind, travelling well throughout and battling back gamely to assert close home. She clearly stays well, and shouldn't be put up too much, so can probably win again. Official explanation: trainer said, regarding apparent improvement in form, that the mare has had a history of injury but, having recovered her fitness, appeared to benefit from being run over 3m for the first time. (op 10-1)

Safe Investment(USA) showed improved form for the longer trip, but he didn't settle that well early, and having taken over coming to two out, he found himself done by a stronger stayer close home. He should come on again and can soon win a small race. (op 11-1)

Old Brigade(IRE) did well to finish as close as he did considering his jumping, but for all that he stayed on to not be beaten far, he never actually looked like winning. (op 4-1)

Mealagh Valley(IRE), runner-up in a novices' chase over C&D latest, looked the one to beat if able to reproduce that form on this switch to handicaps, but he made a couple of mistakes and in the end couldn't race on with the front trio. (tchd 4-1)

Von Galen(IRE) was rather disappointing considering he had finished second off this mark at Towcester last time. This clearly wasn't his true form. (op 10-3 tchd 3-1)

598 PIMM'S (S) HURDLE (9 hdls 1 omitted) 2m
6:55 (6:56) (Class 5) 4-8-Y-0 £1,691 (£496; £248; £124)

Form RPR

2-61 **1** **Letham Island (IRE)**[4] 537 6-10-0 109....................(vt) DeanColeman(5) 109+
(Tim Vaughan) *settled in 3rd pl: wnt 2nd at 5th: led 6th: 5 l clr 3 out: rdn and last and racd idly: nvr looked like being ct* **11/4**[2]

5-01 **2** *9* **Seaquel**[16] 380 4-10-5 96..(v) CharlieHuxley(3) 105
(Andrew Haynes) *hld up: effrt after 6th: sn drvn: wnt 2nd 3 out: no imp whn mstkes 2 out and last* **10/1**

14- **3** *12* **Calzaghe (IRE)**[7] 4362 6-10-12 113.. APMcCoy 98
(Jim Best) *hld up: wnt 3rd at 6th: sn 2nd but u.p: relegated 3rd whn mstke 3 out: no ch after* **4/1**[3]

22-3 **4** *11* **Sonic Anthem (USA)**[34] 75 8-10-9 99........................... PeterToole(3) 86
(Barry Leavy) *led tl after 1st: chsd clr ldr tl lost pl 5th: 20 l 4th 2 out* **12/1**

605/ **5** *11* **Celtic Warrior (IRE)**[23] 1550 7-10-12 95...................... AndrewThornton 76
(John Harris) *a bhd: labouring after 6th: t.o next* **40/1**

0U0- **P** **Border Fox**[12] 3895 7-10-5 89.....................................(t) MrJackSalmon(7) —
(Peter Salmon) *tk fierce hold: led after 1st: 12 l clr 4th: hdd 6th and dropped out rapidly: t.o and p.u last* **40/1**

610- **P** **Dobravany (IRE)**[39] 10 6-11-4 99.............................(v) LeightonAspell —
(Kevin Morgan) *reluctant and toiling in last: t.o 5th: p.u after next* **40/1**

00P- **P** **Rathrockscourt (IRE)**[72] 4794 7-10-12 109........................ TomO'Brien —
(Victor Dartnall) *t.k.h in midfield: p.u 3rd: lame* **6/4**[1]

3m 44.0s (-11.20) **Going Correction** -0.425s/f (Good)
WFA 4 from 6yo+ 17lb **8** Ran SP% **110.8**
Speed ratings: **111,106,100,95,89 —,—,—**
toteswingers: 1&2 £2.40, 1&3 £1.90, 2&3 £10.80 CSF £26.68 TOTE £3.70: £1.70, £3.70, £1.02; EX 26.50.The winner was bought by J. Singh for 6,800gns.
Owner Diamond Racing Ltd **Bred** Rathasker Stud **Trained** Aberthin, Vale of Glamorgan

FOCUS
This took little winning once the favourite Rathrockscourt, who had won on both previous starts at this level, pulled up lame before the third hurdle. The winner was the form pick and is rated to his mark.

NOTEBOOK
Letham Island(IRE), easy winner of a similar race at the course just four days earlier, was left with little to beat once the favourite pulled up, and despite giving the impression she was running about a bit in front, she always looked in control. Favoured by the weights this time, she is clearly a fair sort at this level and it would be no surprise were she to go in again. (op 3-1)

Seaquel's mistakes at the last two hurdles made no difference to where she finished. She had won a similar race for novices last time, and stood no realistic chance against the winner at the weights, so it was a fair effort. (op 8-1)

Calzaghe(IRE) was a bit disappointing, having been the highest-rated runner in the field. He didn't really respond to strong pressure and had no obvious excuse. (op 3-1)

Rathrockscourt(IRE), who had won on both previous starts at this level, pulled up lame before the third hurdle. Official explanation: vet said gelding pulled up lame right-fore (op 9-4 tchd 11-8)

599 MEDIA RESOURCES H'CAP CHASE (17 fncs 3 omitted) 3m 2f
7:25 (7:27) (Class 4) (0-115,114) 5-Y-0 £3,421 (£1,010; £505; £252; £126)

Form RPR

/FP- **1** **Andrew Nick (IRE)**[56] 5106 8-11-2 111........................... AdamWedge(7) 119
(Matt Hazell) *chsd ldrs: rdn 10th: outpcd u.p after 14th: 10 l 3rd 3 out: styd on dourly to ld after last: sn clr* **11/1**

3F0- **2** *3 1/4* **Winchester Red**[256] 1481 8-11-11 113................................ PaulMoloney 119+
(Evan Williams) *t.k.h in rr: 5th at 13th: smooth prog to 2nd next: sn led: 7 l clr 2 out: flagged bdly after being 2 l ahd last: sn hdd and fin weakly* **8/1**

P1-3 **3** *2* **Wizards Dust**[7] 489 8-10-11 102..................................(b) AdrianLane(3) 106
(Donald McCain) *led tl 3rd: 2nd tl led again 9th: hdd after 14th: unenthusiastic fr next: mstke next and lost 2nd: plugged on* **5/1**[3]

U6-1 **4** *8* **Lucky Luk (FR)**[13] 431 11-11-9 114.............................(p) SeanQuinlan(3) 110
(Kim Bailey) *rdn early: trckd ldrs: 4th and drvn at 13th: 10 l 4th and btn bef 3 out: plodding on whn mstke last* **9/2**[2]

00P- **5** *32* **Foxesbow (IRE)**[133] 3572 6-10-13 101....................................... APMcCoy 78
(Jonjo O'Neill) *bhd: in tch after 13th: wknd next: eased 2 out* **5/1**[3]

P/00 **6** *24* **I'm Supreme (IRE)**[18] 359 8-11-10 112.............................. TomO'Brien 58
(Philip Hobbs) *chsd ldrs: mstkes 5th and 12th: struggling 14th: mstke next: t.o after* **16/1**

423- **7** *19* **Ballinruane (IRE)**[189] 2534 11-10-0 88......................(vt1) TomMessenger 17
(S Wynne) *led 3rd tl 9th: pressed ldr tl after 13th: blnd next and lost tch: t.o and eased* **11/2**

15-3 **P** **Go West (IRE)**[20] 314 9-11-11 113................................. PaddyBrennan —
(Nigel Twiston-Davies) *blnd 2nd: nvr fluent or gng w any zest in last after: sn drvn: lost tch 11th: p.u after next* **4/1**[1]

6m 35.5s (-14.50) **Going Correction** -0.425s/f (Good) **8** Ran SP% **112.2**
Speed ratings: **105,104,103,100,91 83,77,—**
toteswingers: 1&2 £47.00, 1&3 £11.40, 2&3 £17.30 CSF £88.70 CT £495.01 TOTE £22.80: £7.30, £1.80, £2.90; EX 130.80.
Owner W F Caudwell **Bred** Mrs Ann McGrath **Trained** Wantage, Oxon

FOCUS
Just a modest handicap chase but the fiorm makes sense rated through the second and third.

NOTEBOOK
Andrew Nick(IRE) had failed to complete in two hunter chase starts this year but was running a decent race until falling in the first of them, and found himself on a mark 2lb lower than when last successful. His stamina really kicked in down the straight and, having looked an unlikely winner taking 3 out, he ran on strongly to end up winning going away. Official explanation: trainer said, regarding apparent improvement in form, that the gelding sustained an injury when falling in February and had taken time to come right, adding that it may have benefited from being dropped in the handicap and racing on a firmer surface. (op 16-1 tchd 18-1)

Winchester Red, who was going to win when falling at the last on his latest outing over fences in August 2009, was very fresh on this first start of the year and, having raced into a clear lead, started to tire badly on the run to the last and was run down comprehensively by the winner. (op 5-1)

Wizards Dust is a bit moody and didn't like it when the runner-up went on, in the end just plugging on for third. (op 11-2)

Lucky Luk(FR) was a bit idle early and, despite bucking up his ideas, never looked like winning, the 10lb he was raised for winning at Towcester proving too much. (op 4-1)

Foxesbow(IRE) failed to improve for the step back up in trip. (op 8-1)

I'm Supreme(IRE) failed to improve for the return to fences.

Ballinruane(IRE) did a bit too much in the first-time visor and suffered late on. (op 6-1 tchd 4-1)

Go West(IRE) seemed to be unnerved by a mistake at the second as he was never going a yard afterwards. Official explanation: jockey said gelding never travelled (tchd 10-3)

600 HOLIDAY LOUNGE MARES' H'CAP HURDLE (9 hdls 1 omitted) 2m
8:00 (8:01) (Class 5) (0-95,95) 4-Y-0+ £2,081 (£611; £305; £152)

Form RPR

-023 **1** **Monkhair (IRE)**[5] 527 5-10-2 76.. LeeEdwards(5) 90+
(Tony Carroll) *midfield: effrt and nt clr run bef 3 out: rcvrd and sn chsng ldr: mstke 2 out: led last: being urged clr whn rdr dropped whip 1/2-way up run-in: dossing and ears pricked after* **7/2**[2]

2P4- **2** *4* **Hoar Frost**[99] 4237 5-11-5 88.. APMcCoy 98
(Jim Best) *trckd ldrs: led bef 3 out: rdn and hdd last: kpt on gamely and wl clr of rest but no match for wnr fnl 100yds* **5/2**[1]

060- **3** *23* **Artic Bliss**[44] 5295 8-10-4 73... FelixDeGiles 63
(Charlie Longsdon) *racd keenly: jnd ldrs 2nd: rdn after 6th: outpcd by ldng pair after 3 out: wnt poor 3rd after last* **16/1**

00-0 **4** *1/2* **M'Lady Eliza**[25] 228 5-11-0 83.. AlanO'Keeffe 72
(Joanne Priest) *bhd: clsd on outer bef 3 out: sn rdn and outpcd by ldng pair: fading next: 18 l 3rd at last* **14/1**

254/ **5** *7* **Miss Molly Be Rude (IRE)**[919] 2462 8-10-3 72............. RobertWalford 55
(Tim Walford) *nvr bttr than midfield: blnd 4th: drvn and wknd bef 3 out* **11/1**

25B- **6** *2 1/2* **Location**[17] 1374 4-10-6 85.. TrevorWhelan(7) 63
(Ian Williams) *bhd: last after 4th: short-lived effrt after 6th: struggling in mod 6th at next* **9/2**[3]

P4-0 **7** *8* **Glan Lady (IRE)**[18] 358 4-10-5 80................................ CharlieHuxley(3) 51
(John Mackie) *bhd: rdn 4th: blnd 5th: nt fluent 6th: struggling after: t.o* **33/1**

160- **8** *57* **Berriedale**[13] 1625 4-11-2 95... PaulGallagher(7) 14
(Ann Duffield) *hit 2nd: 2nd tl led 5th: rdn and hdd and swishing tail bef 3 out: sn gave up: bdly t.o* **16/1**

03-5 **P** **Timoca (IRE)**[28] 182 5-11-12 95.. PaulMoloney —
(Evan Williams) *led tl hdd and reminders 5th: lost pl rapidly next: t.o and p.u wl bef 3 out* **11/2**

3m 47.8s (-7.40) **Going Correction** -0.425s/f (Good)
WFA 4 from 5yo+ 17lb **9** Ran SP% **114.1**
Speed ratings (Par 103): **101,99,87,87,83 82,78,50,—**
toteswingers: 1&2 £1.50, 1&3 £21.80, 2&3 £17.40 CSF £12.87 CT £119.55 TOTE £4.30: £1.10, £1.70, £6.30; EX 14.30.
Owner Group 1 Racing (1994) Ltd **Bred** James J Monaghan **Trained** Cropthorne, Worcs

FOCUS
This was a moderate mares' handicap hurdle. The first two finished clear and produced steps forward.

NOTEBOOK
Monkhair(IRE) won with a bit in hand, leading soon after the last and getting well on top, despite her rider losing his whip. She was making a quick reappearance, having been third at Stratford just five days earlier, and is clearly thriving on racing. (op 4-1 tchd 9-2)

Hoar Frost tried to kick away in the straight, and she successfully managed to drop them all bar the winner, who eventually mastered her after the last. She's very modest and will go up a bit for this, but can find a small race at some point. (op 3-1 tchd 10-3 in a place)

Artic Bliss did best of the remainder but was beaten a long way. (tchd 14-1)

M'Lady Eliza looks likely to do better over further. (op 12-1 tchd 10-1)

Timoca(IRE) gave up the ghost quickly once headed and was pulled up, having become tailed off. (op 6-1)

601 CHEMTECH H'CAP HURDLE (10 hdls 2 omitted) 2m 6f 110y
8:35 (8:35) (Class 4) (0-110,110) 4-Y-0+ £2,732 (£802; £401; £200)

Form RPR

24/2 **1** **Ring Bo Ree (IRE)**[29] 157 7-11-5 103............................ PaddyBrennan 115+
(Tom George) *stdd in rr: effrt and lost action briefly after 6th: chal 3 out: led and wnt lft jst after last: sn clr: pushed out* **11/4**[1]

32-6 **2** *2 1/2* **E Major**[27] 196 5-11-12 110... JimmyMcCarthy 119
(Renee Robeson) *sn in midfield: effrt after 7th: rdn to ld bef 3 out: hdd after last and crossed and snatched up: kpt on wl after but a hld* **4/1**[2]

20-4 **3** *21* **Mcqueen (IRE)**[18] 351 10-11-2 103................................... PeterToole(3) 92
(Barry Leavy) *prom: 2nd and rdn after 7th: fdd next: 20 l 3rd at last* **7/1**

30-P **4** *7* **Romping Home (IRE)**[28] 181 7-11-12 110........................ PaulMoloney 93
(Evan Williams) *bhd: sme prog 7th: rdn and lost tch bef 3 out* **14/1**

06-5 **5** *6* **Root Cause**[35] 55 7-11-2 100...(b) APMcCoy 77
(Donald McCain) *t.k.h: prom: wnt 2nd at 6th: led gng wl after next: hdd bef 3 out: dropped out qckly* **6/1**[3]

61-2 **6** *3 3/4* **Canni Thinkaar (IRE)**[25] 220 9-11-7 110...............(b) MarcGoldstein(5) 84
(Jim Best) *cl 2nd: hit 2nd and 3rd: led 4th: hdd u.p after 7th: 7 l 3rd and fading 2 out* **9/1**

PP0- **7** *24* **Woodlands Gem (IRE)**[42] 5339 8-10-1 85.....................(tp) CharliePoste 37
(Peter Pritchard) *rdn 3rd: nvr gng wl in rr: struggling 7th: t.o* **33/1**

15P- **P** **Tayman (IRE)**[203] 2246 8-11-4 107....................(p) SamTwiston-Davies(5) —
(Nigel Twiston-Davies) *led but nvr travelling freely: rdn and hdd 4th: sn lost interest: wl bhd whn p.u 7th* **9/1**

0-40 **P** **Earcomesthedream (IRE)**[20] 318 7-11-0 98..................(bt) JackDoyle —
(Peter Pritchard) *nt fluent 5th and drvn in last: t.o and p.u after 6th* **6/1**[3]

5m 20.4s (-10.50) **Going Correction** -0.425s/f (Good) **9** Ran SP% **117.3**
Speed ratings (Par 105): **101,100,92,90,88 87,78,—,—**
toteswingers: 1&2 £2.20, 1&3 £2.20, 2&3 £5.70 CSF £14.88 CT £69.80 TOTE £3.90: £1.50, £1.50, £2.00; EX 15.00.
Owner Miss Judith Wilson **Bred** Albert Sherwood **Trained** Slad, Gloucs

FOCUS
An ordinary handicap hurdle. The first two are on the upgrade and finished clear.

NOTEBOOK
Ring Bo Ree(IRE), a non-runner here last weekend having got loose before the race, was having his second start back from injury, and despite being 6lb higher than when runner-up at Huntingdon last month, always looked to be going strongly and got well on top from the last. He did hamper the runner-up after the last but it made no difference to the result. He has the scope to do better still, especially over fences. (op 5-2 tchd 3-1 in places)

E Major took over three out and tried to kick on but couldn't shake the winner and was already beaten when slightly cut up soon after the last. (op 9-2 tchd 5-1)

Mcqueen(IRE) is back on a decent mark but is rather exposed and fared about as well as could have been expected back in third. (op 15-2)

Romping Home(IRE) never got close enough to challenge. Official explanation: jockey said mare never travelled (op 12-1 tchd 11-1)

Root Cause travelled really well but had been a bit keen early and failed to get home. (op 13-2)

Tayman(IRE) Official explanation: jockey said gelding never travelled

Earcomesthedream(IRE) Official explanation: jockey said gelding never travelled

602 MEDIA RESOURCES STANDARD OPEN NATIONAL HUNT FLAT RACE 2m

9:05 (9:07) (Class 6) 4-6-Y-O **£1,431** (£420; £210; £104)

Form RPR

6/4- **1** **Seam Of Diamonds**364 596 5-10-6 0 CharlieHuxley(3) 100+
(John Mackie) *midfield: rdn and effrt 3f out: led over 1f out: grad plugged clr* **33/1**

2 2 1/4 **Rody (FR)** 5-11-2 0 PaddyBrennan 105
(Tom George) *prom: led gng wl over 3f out: rdn and hdd over 1f out: plodded on* **7/2**2

2- **3** 13 **Coral Cove**99 4235 5-11-2 0 SeamusDurack 92+
(John Mackie) *t.k.h: prom tl rdn and wknd over 2f out: wnt poor 3rd wl ins fnl f* **5/1**3

4 1/2 **Sunsalve (IRE)**438 6-11-2 0 APMcCoy 91+
(Rebecca Curtis) *led at stdy pce tl rdn and hdd over 3f out: grad fdd: lost 3rd fnl 50yds* **5/4**1

50- **5** 13 **Instant Decision (IRE)**84 4536 4-10-13 0 TomO'Brien 75
(Peter Bowen) *prom tl rdn and wknd wl over 2f out* **18/1**

6 4 **Lukeys Luck** 4-10-13 0 AlanO'Keeffe 71
(Richard Ford) *hld up towards rr: effrt 4f out: chsd ldrs over 3f out: rn green and wl btn over 2f out* **12/1**

7 1 1/4 **Orlittlebylittle** 4-10-10 0 AdrianLane(3) 70
(Donald McCain) *rdn over 5f out: labouring after* **12/1**

0 **8** 10 **Pathlow (IRE)**15 412 4-10-13 0 GerardTumelty 60
(Anabel L M King) *prom tl fdd bdly 5f out: t.o* **33/1**

9 27 **Satch**81 4-10-13 0 TomMessenger 33
(Thomas Kinsey) *bhd: struggling fnl 5f: bdly t.o* **80/1**

0-5 **10** 41 **Midnight Place**25 237 5-10-11 0 (t) DeanColeman(5) —
(Richard Hawker) *bhd: struggling 1/2-way: t.o fnl 3f* **40/1**

11 dist **Alhudhud (USA)** 4-10-13 0 (t) LeightonAspell —
(Kevin Morgan) *bhd: pushed along and struggling 1/2-way: hopelessly t.o fnl 4f: eventually walked across line* **12/1**

3m 44.6s (-5.00) **Going Correction** -0.425s/f (Good)
WFA 4 from 5yo+ 3lb **11** Ran SP% **121.2**
Speed ratings: **95,93,87,87,80 78,78,73,59,39 —**
toteswingers: 1&2 £45.20, 1&3 £4.80, 2&3 £2.00 CSF £148.39 TOTE £51.30: £12.20, £2.00, £1.20; EX 488.40 Place 6: £58.08 Place 5: £54.13 .
Owner N J Sessions **Bred** J And E Shally **Trained** Church Broughton , Derbys

FOCUS
The front pair drew clear in what was a modest bumper.

NOTEBOOK
Seam Of Diamonds, well held in two previous starts, readily closed on the strong travelling runner-up and stayed on much the stronger, her previous experience being the difference-maker. She will stay further over hurdles and remains capable of better, being just a 5-y-o.
Rody(FR), half-brother to a French chase winner, travelled much the best and looked the likeliest winner when taking over, but he ran about a bit under pressure, looking green, and had to settle for second. This was a promising start and he should learn a bit. (op 4-1 tchd 9-2)
Coral Cove, second in a soft-ground Doncaster bumper in February, was readily outpaced in the straight on this much faster surface. (op 4-1 tchd 11-2)
Sunsalve(IRE), representing a jockey/trainer combination with an excellent record in bumper, was last seen winning a point-to-point in March 2009, and he looked to get tired in the straight. Quite a big horse, it's possible the ground would have been plenty fast enough too, and he will do better over hurdles. (op 6-4 tchd 13-8 and 7-4 in a place)
T/Plt: £83.00 to a £1 stake. Pool:£53,896.02 - 473.87 winning ticket. T/Qpdt: £20.40 to a £1 stake. Pool:£5,856.07 211.70 winning tickets. IM

488 WETHERBY (L-H)

Thursday, June 3

OFFICIAL GOING: Good (good to firm in places)
Wind: light 1/2 against Weather: fine and sunny

603 COCKTAILS IN THE CARIBBEAN MARQUEE (S) HURDLE (12 hdls) 2m 6f

6:00 (6:00) (Class 5) 4-7-Y-O **£1,884** (£549; £274)

Form RPR

-021 **1** **Knar Mardy**7 488 5-10-8 93 AdamPogson(3) 106+
(Charles Pogson) *hld up: jnd ldrs 7th: led on bit 3 out: drvn out run-in* **11/4**2

P-21 **2** 1 3/4 **King Of Castile**14 420 6-11-4 111 (vt) RichardJohnson 111
(Evan Williams) *mde most tl drvn and hdd after 6th: led next: hdd 3 out: styd on and 1 l down whn mstke last: kpt on same pce* **1/1**1

64-4 **3** 53 **Pair Of Kings (IRE)**21 305 5-10-12 100 BrianHughes 57
(Alan Swinbank) *w ldr: reminders 2nd: led briefly after 6th: wl outpcd appr 3 out: sn lft wl bhd* **8/1**

00-0 **4** 22 **Kalatime (IRE)**22 285 7-10-6 72 (p) JamesHalliday(5) 37
(William Young) *prom: drvn and lost pl 7th: t.o 8th: wnt remote 4th 3 out* **80/1**

00/0 **5** dist **Tirol Livit (IRE)**15 405 7-10-5 72 (p) MrJohnDawson(7) —
(John Wainwright) *trckd ldrs: drvn and lost pl 7th: t.o 9th: tk distant 5th last* **100/1**

6 12 **Sammy Pat (IRE)**11 450 6-10-12 0 AELynch —
(Michael O'Hare, Ire) *trckd ldrs: blnd 6th: rdn 9th: sn wknd: t.o next: distant 5th whn virtually p.u sn after last* **4/1**3

5m 23.4s (-3.40) **Going Correction** 0.0s/f (Good) **6** Ran SP% **110.0**
Speed ratings: **106,105,86,78,60 42**
toteswingers: 1&2 £1.60, 1&3 £2.00, 2&3 £1.80 CSF £5.87 TOTE £5.80: £2.00, £1.10; EX 8.50.There was no bid for winner
Owner Wordingham Plant Hire **Bred** Brian And Gwen Griffiths **Trained** Farnsfield, Notts

FOCUS
A steady gallop for this run-of-the-mill seller and it revolved around the two recent course winners. Both are rated close to their recent winning form.

NOTEBOOK
Knar Mardy, a winner of a mares' novice hurdle here last week, travelled well throughout and was well in at the weights. She looks straightforward and should continue to pay her in this grade, at this time of the year. (tchd 7-2)
King Of Castile, up 2lb and 2f from his recent win in similar grade, never travelled with any zest and his jumping lacked fluency on occasions. A mark of 111 would appear to flatter him, but he is in the right hands to stay competitive in this grade for the time being. (op 11-10 tchd 6-5)
Pair Of Kings(IRE), coming from an in-form yard, also never travelled with much purpose and can only be watched on the evidence of this. (tchd 13-2)
Sammy Pat(IRE), well backed beforehand, looked like taking a hand in proceedings four from home but quickly stopped to nothing, and he is another one that can only be watched at present. Official explanation: trainer said gelding scoped dirty (tchd 11-4)

604 WETHERBYRACING.CO.UK NOVICES' H'CAP HURDLE (9 hdls) 2m 110y

6:30 (6:30) (Class 5) (0-95,95) 4-Y-0+ **£1,884** (£549; £274)

Form RPR

6P/- **1** **Dereks (IRE)**461 4185 8-11-11 94 JasonMaguire 110+
(Jim Best) *j. boldly: mde all at str pce: styd on wl: drvn out: unchal* **7/4**1

00-0 **2** 3 3/4 **Everaard (USA)**15 400 4-11-2 88 (p) GrahamLee 98
(Kate Walton) *chsd ldrs: clr 2nd and rdn 6th: kpt on: 4 l down last: no imp* **11/1**

00-5 **3** 19 **Hippolytus**15 397 5-11-4 87 PeterBuchanan 83
(Lucinda Russell) *mid-div: hdwy 3 out: wnt remote 3rd last: lame* **17/2**3

0-53 **4** 4 1/2 **King's Chorister**22 286 4-9-13 74 (t) CampbellGillies(3) 64
(Barry Murtagh) *in rr: hdwy to chse ldrs 6th: modest 3rd 2 out: wknd last* **4/1**2

00P/ **5** 3/4 **Mulligan's Pride (IRE)**602 1623 9-9-4 69 oh3 (v) JamesSmith(10) 60
(James Moffatt) *in rr: hdwy to chse ldrs 5th: one pce fr 3 out* **25/1**

P4-6 **6** 2 **Barbarian**15 400 4-11-4 90 KeithMercer 76
(Alan Brown) *prom: lost pl and mstke 3 out: kpt on fr next* **18/1**

22-4 **7** 1/2 **Sharadiyn**15 405 7-11-7 95 JamesHalliday(5) 84
(Clive Mulhall) *chsd ldrs: 4th and one pce whn mstke 2 out* **10/1**

34-6 **8** nk **Night Knight (IRE)**22 286 4-10-11 88 (p) MissLHorner(5) 74
(Chris Grant) *in rr: hdwy 6th: modest 3rd 3 out: one pce* **16/1**

PU-0 **9** 2 1/4 **Perez (IRE)**7 161 8-10-0 76 (vt) MissLAlexander(7) 63
(Wilf Storey) *towards rr: hdwy 6th: wknd next* **16/1**

-065 **10** 14 **Hernando Cortes**5 520 6-11-1 84 (p) DenisO'Regan 58
(Martin Todhunter) *prom: lost pl 6th: sn bhd* **12/1**

5-P0 **11** nse **Archie's Wish**7 490 6-10-0 69 oh3 BarryKeniry 43
(Micky Hammond) *in rr: reminders and hdwy after 6th: wknd next* **40/1**

-PP0 **12** 21 **Danehill Silver**5 520 6-10-13 85 RyanMania(3) 40
(Brian Storey) *nt fluent: prom: reminders 4th: sn lost pl: bhd 3 out: sn t.o* **33/1**

0-P0 **P** **Qaasi (USA)**7 490 8-9-13 75 ow1 (t) KyleJames(7) —
(Ian Brown) *in rr: bhd fr 6th: t.o whn p.u bef 2 out* **50/1**

3m 53.9s (-1.90) **Going Correction** 0.0s/f (Good)
WFA 4 from 5yo+ 17lb **13** Ran SP% **120.2**
Speed ratings (Par 103): **104,102,93,91,90 89,89,89,88,81 81,71,—**
toteswingers: 1&2 £8.10, 1&3 £2.80, 2&3 £7.90 CSF £21.52 CT £137.31 TOTE £3.50: £1.10, £7.90, £1.80; EX 36.80.
Owner Miss J S Dollan **Bred** D Wall **Trained** Lewes, E Sussex

FOCUS
Very few landed any sort of blow in this modest novice handicap hurdle. It was run at a sound pace thanks to the well-backed winner Dereks. The first two home pulled clear of the remainder and the winner is capable of better.

NOTEBOOK
Dereks(IRE), coming back after a long layoff on his first start for Jim Best, was well handicapped on old form and won with ease. Jumping well throughout, the handicapper will obviously have his say, but he should be able to win again, especially at this time of the year. (op 15-8 tchd 2-1)
Everaard(USA), wearing cheekpieces on his handicap debut, ran well. Coming from a yard among the winners this week, he can go one better as long as the handicapper doesn't overreact as he was a long way clear of the remainder. (op 14-1)
Hippolytus was quite useful on the Flat and ran well here, but unfortunately finished lame. Official explanation: jockey said gelding finished lame (op 7-1)
King's Chorister should have his day in the sunshine at some point (op 5-1)
Sharadiyn had some good place form to his name before this. He got very warm beforehand and is better than this. (op 12-1)
Perez(IRE) Official explanation: trainer said gelding scoped dirty

605 NIDDVALE.CO.UK NOVICES' CHASE (18 fncs) 3m 1f

7:05 (7:05) (Class 4) 5-Y-0+ **£3,252** (£955; £477; £238)

Form RPR

32-1 **1** **Neptune Equester**14 425 7-11-5 120 KeithMercer 121
(Brian Ellison) *led: hdd 10th: hit 13th: led after 4 out: hrd rdn hld on wl run-in* **6/4**2

1-21 **2** 1 **The Ferbane Man (IRE)**7 492 6-11-5 115 (p) RichardJohnson 122+
(Tim Vaughan) *chsd ldrs: hit 7th: blnd 14th: chal 3 out: no ex fnl 75yds* **8/1**3

03-2 **3** 5 **Always Bold (IRE)**19 329 5-10-12 0 JasonMaguire 112
(Donald McCain) *trckd ldrs: led and qcknd 10th: hdd after 4 out: outpcd next: rallied and 2 l 3rd whn hit last: one pce: eased towards fin* **11/10**1

00/P **4** dist **Flag Hill**8 473 7-10-12 64 (t) PaddyAspell 64
(Peter Atkinson) *prom: outpcd 10th: t.o 4 out: 5th whn blnd last: tk 4th nr line* **100/1**

5- **5** 1 **Willie Martin (IRE)**81 4634 5-10-12 0 AELynch 63
(Michael O'Hare, Ire) *chsd ldrs: drvn 14th: wknd next: remote 4th whn blnd 3 out: eased and lost distant 4th nr fin* **11/1**

6m 7.10s (-2.30) **Going Correction** -0.10s/f (Good) **5** Ran SP% **108.1**
Speed ratings: **109,108,107,91,91**
CSF £11.96 TOTE £3.70: £4.90, £7.10; EX 11.70.
Owner Koo's Racing Club **Bred** Mrs Joanna Daniell **Trained** Norton, N Yorks

FOCUS
Despite only five runners in this novice chase, it was an interesting little contest. The early pace was steady before the tempo quickened at halfway. The first two are rated pretty much to their marks.

NOTEBOOK
Neptune Equester, rated 120, put in another polished display. He looks like he will stay even further and another novice chase at this time of year is his for the taking. (op 15-8)
The Ferbane Man(IRE), a winner over hurdles here last week, ran well. Rated 115, time might prove he ran into an above-average recruit for this time off the year. (op 6-1)
Always Bold(IRE), rated 130 over hurdles, also ran well on his second start over fences. A beginners' chase should prove a straightforward task for him with his respected yard keeping up their fine form. (op 6-5 tchd Evens)
Willie Martin(IRE) was easily brushed aside on his first try over fences. (op 15-2)

606 BETFAIR H'CAP HURDLE (12 hdls) 2m 6f

7:35 (7:35) (Class 3) (0-135,120) 4-Y-0+ **£4,878** (£1,432; £716; £357)

Form RPR

11-S **1** **Tarvini (IRE)**21 302 5-11-5 116 (p) RichieMcLernon(3) 120+
(Jonjo O'Neill) *in rr: drvn to chse ldrs 4th: rdn appr 3 out: 4th 2 out: styd on and 1 l down and sltly hmpd last: kpt on to ld fnl stride* **8/1**

60-0 **2** shd **Terenzium (IRE)**7 494 8-11-2 110 (p) BarryKeniry 115
(Micky Hammond) *trckd ldrs: led 2 out: j.lft last: hdd post* **14/1**

53/ **3** 12 **Vincent Pipe (IRE)**265 1431 8-10-9 103 AELynch 98
(Michael O'Hare, Ire) *trckd ldrs: narrow ld 3 out: hdd next: wknd last* **5/1**3

/10- **4** *16* **Olifan D'Oudairies (FR)**50 5188 8-10-11 **105**...............(tp) BrianHughes 84
(J Larkin, Ire) *led to 7th: led after 9th: hdd appr next: lost pl appr 2 out: tk poor 4th sn after last* **5/1**3

66-U **5** *shd* **Calatagan (IRE)**20 314 11-11-4 **117**........................... JamesHalliday(5) 96
(Malcolm Jefferson) *hdwy and in tch 8th: sn drvn: outpcd and lost pl appr next* **11/1**

P30- **6** *13* **Come Out Firing (IRE)**72 4802 8-11-11 **119**.................. TimmyMurphy 86
(Michael Blake) *trckd ldrs: led 7th tl after 9th: led bridely appr next: wknd qckly after 2 out: poor 4th whn j. bdly lft last: virtually p.u* **12/1**

000- **7** *23* **Aldiruos (IRE)**38 21 10-10-11 **105**.................................... TjadeCollier 51
(Tony Carroll) *prom: drvn 7th: sn lost pl: t.o 2 out* **28/1**

-541 **P** **Mini Minster**7 494 8-11-3 **111** 7ex.. GrahamLee —
(Peter Atkinson) *chsd ldrs: drvn 7th: lost pl 9th: sn bhd: p.u bef next* **3/1**1

4-0 **F** **Word Of Warning**27 196 6-11-5 **113**............................... DenisO'Regan —
(Martin Todhunter) *hld up: fell 4th* **4/1**2

5m 22.6s (-4.20) **Going Correction** 0.0s/f (Good) **9** Ran SP% **115.6**
Speed ratings (Par 107): **107,106,102,96,96 92,83,—,—**
toteswingers: 1&2 £12.10, 1&3 £10.80, 2&3 £17.20 CSF £107.39 CT £617.97 TOTE £8.70: £2.70, £3.50, £2.00; EX 67.20.
Owner John P McManus **Bred** His Highness The Aga Khan's Studs S C **Trained** Cheltenham, Gloucs

FOCUS
A handicap hurdle open to horses rated 0-135, but the top-weight Come Out Firing, who stopped very quickly, was rated 16lb below the ceiling rating. However, there were five previous course winners and the pace appeared even. A step up from the winner.

NOTEBOOK
Tarvini(IRE) got up under a strong ride close home. He has appeared to have improved for the step up in trip and should have no problem staying 3m in due course. However it will require a career best when the handicapper has had his say. (op 7-1)
Terenzium(IRE), travelled well and looked the most likely winner approaching the final flight. He is back on a winning mark and can go one better shortly. (op 9-1)
Vincent Pipe(IRE), who is still a maiden, ran with credit and he will find easier opportunities than this. (op 9-2 tchd 11-2)
Mini Minster was struggling four from home and soon pulled up. Back-to-back wins have been something she has struggled with in the past, she can bounce back in due course, but the handicapper could be charge for the time being. Official explanation: jockey said race came too soon (op 5-1)
Word Of Warning got no further than the fourth hurdle. (op 5-1)

607 "PARADISE STEEL BAND" MAIDEN CLAIMING HURDLE (9 hdls) 2m 110y
8:10 (8:12) (Class 5) 4-Y-O+ **£1,884** (£549; £274)

Form RPR

420- **1** **Players Please (USA)**87 4492 6-11-4 107....................... TimmyMurphy 108+
(Michael Blake) *mde virtually all: jnd 3 out: 3 l ahd whn j. bdly rt last: hrd rdn and styd on wl* **11/4**2

0-44 **2** *4* **Mr Melodious**25 227 4-10-8 100...................................(b) DavidEngland 92
(Nigel Twiston-Davies) *chsd ldrs: drvn along 4th: outpcd 3 out: rallied and 4th whn hit last: styd on to take 2nd clsng stages* **15/2**

3 *1* **Totoman**249 1558 5-11-8 0.. RichardJohnson 107
(Tim Vaughan) *trckd ldrs: upsides 3 out: kpt on same pce run-in* **7/4**1

/40- **4** *½* **Turner Brown (IRE)**41 5384 6-11-9 0...................................... AELynch 108+
(Michael O'Hare, Ire) *jnd ldrs 6th: upsides next: 3 l 2nd whn j.rt last: one pce* **11/2**3

63-P **5** *31* **Cordier**34 77 8-11-2 0.. BrianHughes 71
(John Mackie) *chsd ldrs: lost pl and modest 5th whn mstke 3 out* **50/1**

00-6 **6** *nk* **Bold Indian (IRE)**15 402 6-10-11 71................................. KeithMercer 66
(Mike Sowersby) *in rr: sme hdwy appr 3 out: sn wknd* **100/1**

7 *3¾* **Lava Steps (USA)**16 4-10-11 0.. PaddyAspell 63
(Paul Midgley) *hld up in rr: hdwy 4th: outpcd 6th: lost pl appr next* **50/1**

33-3 **8** *1¾* **Starbougg**14 420 6-10-7 94...(b) JamesReveley 57
(Keith Reveley) *prom: dropped out 3rd: bhd fr 6th* **9/1**

0-6 **9** *6* **Castle Myth (USA)**8 470 4-10-7 0....................................(t) LiamHeard 52
(Brian Ellison) *in rr: bhd fr 6th* **33/1**

04- **10** *31* **Gordon Road (IRE)**20 3915 4-11-1 0........................ RichieMcLernon(3) 35
(Michael Quinlan) *in rr: bhd fr 6th: sn t.o* **12/1**

3m 55.7s (-0.10) **Going Correction** 0.0s/f (Good)
WFA 4 from 5yo+ 17lb **10** Ran SP% **115.7**
Speed ratings (Par 103): **100,98,97,97,82 82,80,80,77,63**
toteswingers: 1&2 £6.00, 1&3 £1.30, 2&3 £3.40 CSF £23.06 TOTE £3.10: £1.10, £2.10, £1.70; EX 20.80.
Owner Staverton Owners Group **Bred** 6 C Racing Limited **Trained** Trowbridge, Wilts
⊠ Michael Blake's first winner as a licensed trainer.

FOCUS
An ordinary maiden claiming hurdle. The early pace was even and the race is highly unlikely to throw up many winners. The first two are rated to their marks.

NOTEBOOK
Players Please(USA) was always prominent and won with a bit in hand on his first run for current connections (trainer's first winner). He is currently rated 107, but would be dangerous back in similar company. (op 7-2 tchd 4-1)
Mr Melodious, best in at the weights, was ridden at halfway and stayed on to take second close home. Wearing blinkers, he is not one to take a short price about in a bid to go one better next time. (tchd 7-1)
Totoman, having his first run for Tim Vaughan, ran all right to a point, but this would appear to be his level. (op 11-10)
Turner Brown(IRE) had a chance turning for home but wasn't able to give the weight away at the business end. (op 15-2)
Castle Myth(USA) Official explanation: jockey said gelding had a breathing problem

608 WETHERBY RACECOURSE & CONFERENCE CENTRE H'CAP CHASE (18 fncs) 2m 6f 110y
8:45 (8:45) (Class 3) (0-125,125) 5-Y-O+ **£5,854** (£1,719; £859; £429)

Form RPR

454- **1** **Bale O'Shea (IRE)**106 4104 6-10-6 **105**.................................... AELynch 117+
(Michael O'Hare, Ire) *hld up: hdwy 14th: sn trcking ldrs: cl 3rd 3 out: styd on strly to ld last 50yds* **9/2**2

51-1 **2** *3* **Nothingbutthetruth (IRE)**28 175 6-11-2 **115**.............. DougieCostello 123+
(Tim Pitt) *hld up in rr: stdy hdwy to trck ldrs 14th: led 2 out: hdd and no ex fnl 50yds* **5/2**1

2P3- **3** *1½* **Chernik (IRE)**40 5387 9-10-10 **109**................................ WilsonRenwick 115
(Micky Hammond) *trckd ldrs: led appr 4 out: hdd 2 out: styd on same pce run-in* **12/1**

53-6 **4** *12* **Hold The Bid (IRE)**18 352 10-10-8 **107**............................. KeithMercer 102
(Sue Smith) *in rr: hdwy to chse ldrs 14th: one pce whn j.lft 3 out* **17/2**

412- **5** *15* **Killard Point (IRE)**39 11 11-11-2 **118**........................ AdamPogson(3) 100
(Caroline Bailey) *chsd ldr: wknd 3 out* **11/1**

62-4 **6** *17* **Cossack Dancer (IRE)**25 236 12-11-7 **120**................(p) JasonMaguire 86
(Mark Bradstock) *led tl appr 4 out: lost pl appr 2 out: 6th and eased last* **11/2**3

P2-2 **7** *¾* **Seize**29 164 8-10-8 **107**.. GrahamLee 73
(Ferdy Murphy) *rn in snatches: reminders 4th: lost pl and bhd 14th* **8/1**

112- **8** *4½* **Native City (IRE)**237 1684 8-10-11 **113**..................... RichieMcLernon(3) 75
(Jonjo O'Neill) *chsd ldrs: hit 8th and reminders: drvn 12th: lost pl appr 4 out* **20/1**

F6-1 **9** *2¼* **Baltic Pathfinder (IRE)**33 88 6-10-7 **106**......................... TjadeCollier 66
(Sue Smith) *chsd ldrs: drvn 10th: lost pl 14th: sn bhd: blnd 3 out* **10/1**

01P- **10** *16* **Brave Rebellion**43 5309 11-11-12 **125**............................ JamesReveley 70
(Keith Reveley) *trckd ldrs: effrt 4 out: outpcd whn bmpd next: 7th and bhd whn j. bdly rt last: heavily eased* **25/1**

5m 30.2s (-6.80) **Going Correction** -0.10s/f (Good) **10** Ran SP% **117.5**
Speed ratings: **107,105,105,101,96 90,89,88,87,81**
toteswingers: 1&2 £4.70, 1&3 £10.70, 2&3 £6.70 CSF £17.00 CT £127.31 TOTE £4.90: £1.40, £1.80, £3.80; EX 25.10.
Owner Mrs Tracey O'Hare **Bred** P Hore **Trained** Castlebellingham, Co. Louth

FOCUS
Quite a competitive handicap chase run at a sound pace, and the first two home were held up in the early stages. The cosy winner is rated up 7lb on his best hurdles form.

NOTEBOOK
Bale O'Shea(IRE) got off the mark at the first attempt over fences, jumping well throughout. He is at the right end of the handicap and should have plenty of options in a bid to follow up. (tchd 11-2)
Nothingbutthetruth(IRE), looking for his third course success, also travelled and jumped well throughout of a 10lb higher mark than his last win. Time might prove he ran into a well-handicapped horse. (op 11-4 tchd 3-1)
Chernik(IRE) appeared to have every chance turning for home but remains 14lb higher than his only chase win, which came well over a year ago. (op 16-1)
Hold The Bid(IRE) also ran his race but could do with some help from the handicapper as well. (op 8-1 tchd 15-2)
Killard Point(IRE) weakened quickly turning for home on ground that would have been quick enough for the previous course winner. (op 10-1 tchd 9-1)
Native City(IRE) will be better for this run. (op 14-1)
Baltic Pathfinder(IRE) could never land a blow. (op 11-1 tchd 12-1)

609 RACING AGAIN ON WEDNESDAY 13TH OCTOBER STANDARD OPEN NATIONAL HUNT FLAT RACE 2m 110y
9:15 (9:17) (Class 6) 4-6-Y-O **£1,507** (£439; £219)

Form RPR

62-2 **1** **Call Me Bill (IRE)**11 448 4-10-8 0............................. DonalDevereux(5) 101+
(Peter Bowen) *mde all: increased pce 6f out: styd on strly fnl 4f to go clr over 1f out* **13/8**1

2 *10* **Thornton Alice** 5-10-9 0.. PeterBuchanan 87
(Ian McInnes) *trckd ldrs: chal over 4f out: styd on same pce fnl 2f* **33/1**

3 **3** *nk* **Moufatango (FR)**18 355 4-10-10 0............................. FearghalDavis(3) 91
(Nicky Richards) *hld up: hdwy to trck ldrs after 6f: rdn over 3f out: kpt on same pce fnl 2f* **11/4**2

03- **4** *1¾* **Wicked Streak (IRE)**40 5391 5-11-2 0................................. BarryKeniry 92
(Micky Hammond) *t.k.h: hdwy to trck ldrs after 6f: drvn over 3f out: one pce fnl 2f* **14/1**

0- **5** *3¾* **Darkan Road**74 4757 5-11-2 0... JanFaltejsek 88
(George Charlton) *in rr: outpcd over 4f out: kpt on one pce fnl 2f* **16/1**

6 *5* **First Watch** 5-11-2 0... JasonMaguire 83
(Martin Keighley) *trckd ldrs: rdn over 3f out: wknd 2f out* **7/2**3

0- **7** *2* **Bonnie Baloo**53 5150 4-10-6 0.. SamJones 71
(Shaun Harris) *hld up: hdwy 6f out: drvn over 4f out: sn wl outpcd* **100/1**

5-5 **8** *1¼* **Minden March**11 448 5-10-9 0.. DougieCostello 73
(Peter Maddison) *t.k.h: trckd ldrs: pushed along 6f out: outpcd 3f out: sn lost pl* **50/1**

9 *59* **Silverwort** 4-10-10 0.. CampbellGillies(3) 18
(Mike Sowersby) *t.k.h: trckd wnr: drvn 6f out: sn lost pl: t.o fnl 3f: virtually p.u* **33/1**

44- **R** **Johann Sabestian (IRE)**108 4083 5-10-13 0.........(t) RichieMcLernon(3) —
(Jonjo O'Neill) *w.r.s: ref to r: tk no part* **12/1**

4m 5.30s (15.10) **Going Correction** 0.0s/f (Good)
WFA 4 from 5yo 3lb **10** Ran SP% **116.1**
Speed ratings: **64,59,59,58,56 54,53,52,17,—**
toteswingers: 1&2 £19.70, 1&3 £1.10, 2&3 £9.30 CSF £67.94 TOTE £2.20: £1.10, £8.10, £1.50; EX 76.00 Place 6: £30.91 Place 5: £26.07.
Owner W Bryan **Bred** Robert McCarthy **Trained** Little Newcastle, Pembrokes

FOCUS
An ordinary bumper run at a steady pace that was weakened further when Johann Sabestian refused to take any part at the start. Probably not form to dwell on.

NOTEBOOK
Call Me Bill(IRE) got off the mark at the fourth attempt. The 4-y-o had shown a decent level on his last couple of starts and should be able to make his mark over hurdles at this time of year.
Thornton Alice made a nice start on her racecourse debut and would be of interest in a mares'-only next time.
Moufatango(FR), third on his debut, also filled that place again. He might find life easier over hurdles in due course.
Wicked Streak(IRE) is another who should do better over hurdles.
First Watch weakened quickly after having a chance turning for home.
T/Plt: £66.30 to a £1 stake. Pool:£38,584.32 - 424.77 winning tickets. T/Qpdt: £44.90 toa £1 stake. Pool:£3,624.23- 59.60 winning tickets. WG

610 - 623a (Foreign Racing) - See Raceform Interactive

456 HEXHAM (L-H)
Saturday, June 5

OFFICIAL GOING: Good to firm (watered; 8.7)
Wind: Slight, half against Weather: Sunny, warm

624 GREATRUN.ORG "NATIONAL HUNT" NOVICES' HURDLE (10 hdls) 2m 4f 110y
2:15 (2:15) (Class 4) 4-Y-O+ **£2,945** (£858; £429)

Form RPR

1 **Majestic Mayhem (IRE)**29 203 7-10-12 0........................ BarryKeniry 115+
(George Moore) *cl up: chsd ldr 6th: led bef last: drew clr: readily* **9/4**2

01-1 **2** *12* **Sir Frank (IRE)**7 519 5-11-5 0.. BrianHughes 111+
(Alan Swinbank) *trckd ldrs: effrt and wnt 2nd bef last: sn rdn and kpt on same pce* **4/5**1

P-62 **3** *10* **Birnies Boy**11 461 6-10-12 77...(t) GrahamLee 94
(Brian Storey) *led tl hdd bef last: sn rdn and wknd* **14/1**

00-3 **4** *nk* **Nearly Sunday**11 457 5-9-12 0.................................... GarryWhillans(7) 86
(Donald Whillans) *in tch: drvn and outpcd 4 out: rallied after 2 out: no imp bef last* **14/1**

00-0 **5** *6* **Magnushomesdotcom (IRE)**[20] 349 6-10-9 0..(t) MichaelMcAlister(3) 88
(Maurice Barnes) *nt fluent: hld up: rdn and outpcd 4 out: rallied after next: no imp fnl 2* **28/1**

5-65 **6** *½* **Player (FR)**[13] 447 7-10-12 93................................ PaddyAspell 88
(Ann Hamilton) *chsd ldr to 6th: outpcd next: rallied 2 out: hung lft and no imp bef last* **11/1**[3]

305- **7** *96* **Santamina (IRE)**[40] 20 4-10-3 0......................... DonalDevereux(5) —
(Peter Bowen) *in tch: drvn and outpcd 6th: struggling fr next* **25/1**

P-P **8** *dist* **Rahood (IRE)**[7] 514 8-10-6 0 ow1.............................. MrMGarnett(7) —
(F Jestin) *bhd: lost tch fr 5th: t.o* **200/1**

/0P- **P** **Simhal**[41] 8 6-10-12 0.. TomMessenger —
(Clive Mulhall) *hld up: struggling 5th: sn lost tch: t.o whn p.u bef 4 out* **200/1**

5m 2.90s (-9.60) **Going Correction** -0.775s/f (Firm)
WFA 4 from 5yo+ 18lb **9** Ran SP% **116.3**
Speed ratings (Par 105): **87,82,78,78,76 76,39,—,—**
toteswinger: 1&2 £1.02, 1&3 £10.80, 2&3 £6.70 CSF £4.53 TOTE £3.70: £1.40, £1.10, £2.90; EX 5.50.
Owner J B Wallwin **Bred** D Hickey **Trained** Middleham Moor, N Yorks

FOCUS
Dry weather overnight and a very warm day meant conditions were quick. After a good early pace three pulled well clear from the back straight in an uncompetitive contest. The winner is the type to rate higher.

NOTEBOOK
Majestic Mayhem(IRE) was prominent throughout and about to challenge when jumping slowly at the last in the back straight, but he still had stamina reserves to call on as he regained the lead and stayed on to go clear in the straight. The triple Irish point-to-point winner had been found a relatively straightforward opportunity for his hurdling debut and utilised his superior stamina on a track that played to his strengths. (op 5-2)
Sir Frank(IRE) had to contend with a penalty, following his win a week earlier and a step up in trip, and they proved his undoing. He was a little bit keen early on but travelled well enough to look the most potent danger in the back straight. That all changed, however, up the final hill, where he was soon labouring, and he did not get home on this stiff track. (op 8-11 tchd 4-6 and 5-6 in places)
Birnies Boy set a good pace and was still right there with the leading trio as they drew clear in the back straight. Having been second last time in a low-grade handicap over a longer distance at this track, the intention might have been to run the finish out of his rivals. However, those tactics exposed his own stamina limitations instead, and he only just clung on for third. (op 11-1)
Nearly Sunday nearly caught the long-time leader on the line, but other than that she was never competitive. She will need handicaps and longer distances to elicit any improvement. (tchd 16-1)

625 JUNIOR GREAT NORTH RUN NOVICES' CHASE (15 fncs) 2m 4f 110y
2:45 (2:45) (Class 4) 5-Y-0+ **£3,252** (£955; £477; £238)

Form RPR

1F-1 **1** **Baily Storm (IRE)**[20] 357 8-11-5 0.............................. DarylJacob 107
(Tim Vaughan) *cl up: led 7th to 9th: styd upsides: led and drvn after 2 out: hrd pressed run-in: all out* **2/9**[1]

2PP- **2** *nse* **Sierra Victor (IRE)**[38] 43 7-10-9 88........................ RyanMania(3) 100
(P Monteith) *in tch: stdy hdwy 4 out: rdn bef 2 out: rallied and str chal after last: kpt on wl: jst hld* **7/1**[2]

66/ **3** *7* **Miss Sunflower**[6] 8-9-12 0...................................(p) MissTJackson(7) 87
(Tina Jackson) *t.k.h: cl up: led 9th to after 2 out: rallied: wknd run-in* **14/1**

U5-P **4** *32* **The Green Hat (IRE)**[28] 211 10-10-5 67.................... HenryBrooke(7) 61
(Theresa Gibson) *led to 7th: prom tl outpcd 4 out: n.d after* **12/1**[3]

236- **5** *19* **Ellandshe (IRE)**[39] 32 10-10-7 50........................(b) JamesHalliday(5) 42
(William Young) *prom tl rdn and wknd after 3 out* **12/1**[3]

5m 15.4s (1.90) **Going Correction** -0.35s/f (Good) **5** Ran SP% **116.4**
Speed ratings: **82,81,79,67,59**
CSF £3.14 TOTE £1.20: £1.02, £2.80; EX 2.50.
Owner Chasing Gold Ltd **Bred** J Harold-Barry **Trained** Aberthin, Vale of Glamorgan
■ Stewards' Enquiry : Daryl Jacob caution: used whip down shoulder in the forehand.

FOCUS
This may have lacked strength in depth, but it produced a cracking finish, with the first two locked in battle up the home straight. The race was steadily run and the winner is rated 20lb+ below his best, with the second setting the level.

NOTEBOOK
Baily Storm(IRE) was a bit novicey at the early fences, but improved as the pace lifted in the back straight. Covering the leader's move up the final hill left him vulnerable to any closers, but he showed tenacity to rally again near the line for the second narrow success of his fledgling chasing career. As the only previous winner under rules in the field, he might have been expected to win with much more ease. This might indicate that he could ultimately lack progression over fences, but his fighting spirit should help his chances. (op 1-4 tchd 2-7)
Sierra Victor(IRE) jumped slowly at the water with a circuit to go and was consequently under pressure as the pace began to increase, but he made steady progress to emerge as a strong challenger in the back straight. He battled on and just about headed the winner but lacked his rival's edge. If this effort does not ruin his handicap mark, he could conceivably gain his first win in a moderate contest. (tchd 13-2)
Miss Sunflower took up the running and increased the pace in the back straight, but she was the first of the leaders to crack from the home turn. She has been successful in a couple of point-to-points but has limitations at this level. (op 16-1 tchd 12-1)
The Green Hat(IRE), who attracted some market support, set a steady early pace but as soon as it began to increase he was struggling with a circuit to go. (op 20-1)
Ellandshe(IRE) was keen early on and did not jump fluently enough to stay with the pack. (op 14-1 tchd 11-1)

626 GREAT NORTH CITY GAMES H'CAP CHASE (19 fncs) 3m 1f
3:20 (3:20) (Class 4) (0-115,115) 5-Y-0+ **£3,562** (£1,038; £519)

Form RPR

635- **1** **Harry Flashman**[38] 46 9-10-12 101.......................... PeterBuchanan 111
(Donald Whillans) *cl up: led 2nd: mde rest: rdn and kpt on wl bef last* **2/1**[1]

32-5 **2** *3¼* **Tot Of The Knar**[21] 330 8-11-5 113.......................... DonalDevereux(5) 120
(Peter Bowen) *t.k.h: cl up: wnt 2nd 12th: effrt after 2 out: kpt on u.p fr last* **3/1**[2]

1P-4 **3** *12* **Western Gale (IRE)**[22] 314 7-11-12 115....................... DenisO'Regan 111
(Martin Todhunter) *hld up in tch: drvn and outpcd after 4 out: tk mod 3rd after last: no ch w first two* **3/1**[2]

1P-6 **4** *7* **Cash On Friday**[31] 160 9-10-6 95............................(p) WilsonRenwick 85
(P Monteith) *prom: effrt bef 2 out: wknd bef last* **17/2**

313- **P** **Panama At Once**[43] 5373 10-10-11 100......................(p) TomMessenger —
(Joss Saville) *led to 2nd: cl up: lost pl 12th: wknd 14th: t.o whn p.u bef 4 out* **6/1**[3]

430- **P** **Guerilla (AUS)**[45] 5311 10-10-2 98 oh8 ow9...............(p) AlexanderVoy(7) —
(Lucy Normile) *nt jump wl: sn wl bhd: t.o whn p.u bef 10th* **20/1**

6m 19.8s (-12.40) **Going Correction** -0.35s/f (Good) **6** Ran SP% **112.9**
Speed ratings: **105,103,100,97,— —**
toteswinger: 1&2 £2.70, 1&3 £1.30, 2&3 £5.20 CSF £8.85 TOTE £3.40: £1.80, £2.00; EX 9.40.
Owner A Gilchrist M Kent P Wylie **Bred** Allan Gilchrist **Trained** Hawick, Borders

FOCUS
A reasonably competitive handicap dictated throughout by the market leader. Ordinary form, with the winner rated to his best.

NOTEBOOK
Harry Flashman soon took up the running, setting a comfortable pace and jumping more fluently than the others. He was briefly niggled up the final hill but soon asserted again to hold off the challenge of the second. He won at this track a year ago but has largely been overmatched since. He still came into the race with a solid chance based on his two-length third in a better race at this track in April, and that experience enabled him to complete this task with ease. (op 9-4 tchd 5-2 in places)
Tot Of The Knar made a few of her customary jumping errors, but still travelled well to pose a threat in the back straight before facing the final hill, where her stamina reserves began to empty. She can get this trip on easier tracks and looks in good form, but her jumping remains an issue. (op 5-2 tchd 2-1 in places)
Western Gale(IRE) raced at the rear of the main pack and was struggling to stay in touch, but he plugged on to get third near the line. This was a better effort than his previous two outings this spring on his return to action, but the C&D winner needs some give in the ground, as he lacks a bit of speed. (op 7-2)
Cash On Friday travelled well through the final circuit until the top of the hill, where he weakened and lost third place. He won on his comeback from a long absence at Carlisle in March but has not been able to reproduce that form. (op 8-1 tchd 9-1)
Panama At Once got in close to the ninth and his jumping became increasingly erratic until he was pulled up when out of contention. He did not have an easy task off a 13lb higher mark than his last win over C&D in April, but this was not his true form. Official explanation: jockey said gelding was unsuited by the good to firm ground (op 5-1)
Guerilla(AUS) Official explanation: jockey said gelding has lost its confidence over fences (op 5-1)

627 NOVA INTERNATIONAL CLASSIC H'CAP HURDLE (8 hdls) 2m 110y
3:50 (3:51) (Class 2) 4-Y-0+
£12,524 (£3,700; £1,850; £926; £462; £232)

Form RPR

031- **1** **Inventor (IRE)**[43] 5355 5-11-5 134.............................. JasonMaguire 142+
(Donald McCain) *prom: stdy hdwy after 3 out: led bef last: rdn clr run-in* **3/1**[1]

06-2 **2** *6* **Santa's Son (IRE)**[23] 309 10-10-7 125....................(t) AdamPogson(3) 127
(Charles Pogson) *t.k.h: prom: hdwy 1/2-way: led bef 2 out to bef last: kpt on: nt pce of wnr* **10/1**

40-3 **3** *14* **Akarshan (IRE)**[19] 372 5-10-6 124.............................. DPFahy(3) 113
(Evan Williams) *midfield: drvn to improve bef 2 out: plugged on fr last: no imp* **9/2**[2]

2/1- **4** *3¼* **Danish Rebel (IRE)**[15] 5374 6-10-2 124 ow7..............(t) AlistairFindlay(7) 110
(George Charlton) *cl up: led 2nd: hdd bef 2 out: wknd bef last* **16/1**

35-3 **5** *nk* **Los Nadis (GER)**[10] 309 6-10-8 126.............................. RyanMania(3) 113
(P Monteith) *in tch: drvn and outpcd after 3 out: rallied bef last: no imp* **10/1**

25-2 **6** *6* **Duty Free (IRE)**[7] 519 6-10-0 115 oh1.......................... PaddyAspell 95
(James Moffatt) *midfield: rdn bef 4 out: hdwy and prom after next: rdn and wknd between last 2* **14/1**

4/1- **7** *1¼* **Breaking Storm (IRE)**[39] 34 7-10-0 115........................ GrahamLee 94
(Kate Walton) *bhd: drvn along 1/2-way: sme late hdwy: nvr on terms* **8/1**

0-43 **8** *¾* **Pepporoni Pete (IRE)**[7] 521 9-10-5 120.......................(p) BrianHughes 99
(Milton Harris) *chsd ldrs tl rdn and wknd fr 2 out* **9/1**

11-2 **9** *10* **Coastley (IRE)**[17] 396 8-10-7 129.............................. MrJARichardson(7) 99
(David Carr) *hld up: rdn after 3 out: btn next* **13/2**[3]

1-04 **10** *3¾* **Nelson Du Ronceray (FR)**[17] 393 9-10-0 115............ WilsonRenwick 81
(P Monteith) *hld up: hdwy after 3 out: wknd fr next* **28/1**

01-1 **11** *27* **Marodima (FR)**[27] 219 7-11-5 141.............................. MrRMahon(7) 83
(Jamie Snowden) *led to 2nd: cl up tl lost pl 3 out: sn struggling* **11/1**

11-0 **12** *50* **Acambo (GER)**[28] 207 9-11-8 137.............................. JohnnyFarrelly 34
(David Pipe) *hld up: drvn bef 4 out: sn btn: t.o* **12/1**

4m 0.20s (-17.20) **Going Correction** -0.775s/f (Firm) **12** Ran SP% **127.8**
Speed ratings (Par 109): **109,106,99,98,97 95,94,94,89,87 74,51**
toteswinger: 1&2 £5.80, 1&3 £2.90, 2&3 £5.00 CSF £36.74 CT £142.68 TOTE £3.80: £1.50, £3.70, £1.40.
Owner The MerseyClyde Partnership **Bred** Brendan Holland And P Connell **Trained** Cholmondeley, Cheshire

FOCUS
A competitive event and, with several front-runners in the field, the pace was generous and two pulled clear from the top of the hill. Arguably a step up from the winner, with a hurdles best from the second.

NOTEBOOK
Inventor(IRE) has gone well when ridden prominently, but he did not get involved in the early pace this time and that was a sensible move. He travelled well to cut down the leader coming to the home turn and stayed on well for a comfortable success. Having won three times as a novice last season, he was not disgraced at the Cheltenham and Aintree festivals and, with that experience proving invaluable, this was a much easier target and he should win more races. (tchd 11-4)
Santa's Son(IRE) took up the running in the back straight and began to draw clear, and he shook off all bar the winner to finish a long way in front of the third. He has generally been better over fences, and though he may just lack a bit of pace for hurdling, he is on a comparatively reasonable mark and a continuation of his good form should bring compensation for his new, in-form stable. One slight note of caution is that he has seemed better when relatively fresh. (op 9-1)
Akarshan(IRE) made some late progress past tiring rivals but could make no inroads into the leaders' advantage. He has been struggling off an 8lb higher mark since winning at Towcester in March, but stiff tracks do suit him, albeit in easier grades. (op 13-2)
Danish Rebel(IRE) helped set the pace until tiring up the final hill and fading, and in general he might be better on easier ground and in a lower grade. (op 14-1)
Los Nadis(GER) made progress in the back straight but was unable to mount a challenge on a track that is probably too stiff for him. (tchd 12-1)
Duty Free(IRE) made progress in the back straight and, although outclassed, this run suggests he could pick up his first hurdling victory if his sights are lowered. (op 16-1)
Coastley(IRE) Official explanation: jockey said gelding was unsuited by the track
Marodima(FR) Official explanation: trainer said gelding finished distressed

628 FILMNOVA HUNTERS' CHASE (15 fncs) 2m 4f 110y
4:25 (4:25) (Class 6) 5-Y-0+ **£1,318** (£405; £202)

Form RPR

-451 **1** **Ardnaclancy (IRE)**[5] 551 7-11-9 0.......................... MrJARichardson(7) 121
(Andrew Richardson) *cl up: led 3rd to 5th: rdn and outpcd 2 out: rallied and chal last: led run-in: pushed out* **17/2**

-113 **2** *1* **Take The Stand (IRE)**[7] 525 14-12-1 126..................(p) MrMByrne(5) 125
(Peter Bowen) *led: hit and hdd 3rd: led 5th: hdd whn nt fluent 3 out: regained ld next: hdd run-in: kpt on* **6/4**[1]

2-20 **3** *8* **Pen Gwen (FR)**[10] 480 7-11-5 105.............................. HenryBrooke(7) 109
(Kate Walton) *prom: drvn and outpcd after 3 out: rallied bef last: kpt on run-in: nt rch first two* **8/1**[3]

60-3 **4** *19* **Think Lucky**[20] 354 7-11-9 99 MrISmith(7) 96
(Mrs N Naughton) *hld up: mstke 4th: outpcd after 4 out: plugged on between last 2: nvr on terms* **18/1**

5 *3/4* **Rakerin Lad (IRE)**[6] 7-11-5 0 MrMEnnis(7) 91
(Mrs S Taylor) *hld up: hdwy and in tch whn mstke 4 out: sn outpcd: no imp fr next* **33/1**

50-1 **6** *8* **Scotch Warrior**[23] 310 6-11-9 0 MrRMSmith(7) 88
(Robert Smith) *bhd: blnd 2nd: hdwy and prom 10th: led bef 3 out to next: wknd bef last* **10/1**

7 *13* **Victor (IRE)**[6] 7-11-5 0 MrSCharlton(7) 72
(Miss Victoria Easterby) *midfield: hdwy and in tch bef 3 out: wknd after next* **33/1**

P **Sendeed (USA)**[21] 8-11-7 0 (tp) MrGCrow(5) —
(Ms Lucinda Broad) *prom tl wknd 3 out: t.o whn p.u bef last* **50/1**

/2-1 **U** **Bow School (IRE)**[9] 493 9-12-1 0 MrWKinsey(5) —
(Mrs A C Hamilton) *t.k.h: prom: blnd 2nd: hit and uns rdr 8th* **9/4**[2]

6/0- **P** **Benwell**[6] 9-11-5 0 MrGRSmith(7) —
(G T Sunter) *bhd: struggling fnl circ: t.o whn p.u bef last* **66/1**

U **Pirate D'Estruval (FR)**[6] 7-11-7 0 ow2 MrSimonRobinson(7) —
(S J Robinson) *t.k.h in midfield: lost pl 5th: t.o whn uns rdr 4 out* **100/1**

5m 8.00s (-5.50) **Going Correction** -0.35s/f (Good) **11** Ran SP% **117.1**
Speed ratings: **96,95,92,85,85 82,77,—,—,— —**
toteswinger: 1&2 £6.00, 1&3 £8.50, 2&3 £2.20 CSF £22.30 TOTE £10.40: £2.30, £1.20, £2.50; EX 16.30.

Owner David Carr **Bred** Patrick Hayes **Trained** Hexham, Northumberland

⊠ Stewards' Enquiry : Mr M Byrne seven-day ban: used whip with excessive frequency (tbn)
Mr I Smith three-day ban: used whip with excessive freaquency (tbn)

FOCUS
A reasonable contest with last year's winner just denied on the run from the last. Solid form, and the winner is on the upgrade.

NOTEBOOK
Ardnaclancy(IRE) won a string of point-to-points last year but he has taken a while to get the hang of things in hunter chases. He finally came good when dropped in trip at Cartmel earlier in the week, and now, having hit peak form, racing over a similar trip and with youth on his side, he was able to get the better of a gallant veteran. However, he got a bit outpaced in the back straight before finishing well and may ultimately need further. (op 15-2 tchd 7-1 and 9-1)

Take The Stand(IRE) may be a light of former days and better over longer distances, but his inherent class enables him to remain competitive in this grade, and the 14-year-old was bidding to win the race for a second year. It was a gallant attempt to draw the sting out his rivals, and he nearly did it, but eventually the market leader had to give way to younger legs. (op 13-8 tchd 11-8)

Pen Gwen(FR) was soundly beaten over hurdles ten days earlier but fared better back in this sphere. He has been consistent in hunter chases this spring, finishing second three times, but he lacks pace where it matters and the hurdles experience did not impart the necessary impetus. (tchd 9-1)

Think Lucky had shown little on his return to action at Market Rasen last month, and that trend continued. He looks a long way off the form of his Stratford win last summer, but seems to need several runs to find his form, and might improve for the refitting of a tongue-tie. (op 16-1 tchd 22-1)

Bow School(IRE) had good enough form to feature, but has a tendency to make mistakes, and that trend continued until he parted company with his jockey mid-race. (op 11-4)

629 GREAT NORTH RUN JUVENILE HURDLE (8 hdls) 2m 110y
4:55 (4:55) (Class 4) 3-Y-O **£2,945** (£858; £429)

Form RPR

1 **Lucky Quay (IRE)**[192] 3-10-12 0 (b[1]) JohnnyFarrelly 91+
(David Pipe) *mde all: hit 2 out: rdn clr bef last* **11/4**[2]

2 *22* **Sansili**[40] 3-10-7 0 DonalDevereux(5) 72+
(Peter Bowen) *cl up: rdn and outpcd after 2 out: rallied to chse wnr bef last: no imp* **15/8**[1]

3 *1 1/4* **Anchorage Boy (USA)**[47] 3-10-9 0 AlexMerriam(3) 69
(Amy Weaver) *nt fluent: cl up tl rdn and outpcd 2 out: no imp after* **12/1**

4 *6* **Mr Mohican (IRE)**[18] 3-10-12 0 GrahamLee 64
(Ann Duffield) *t.k.h: prom: chsd wnr after 2 out: wknd bef last* **7/1**

5 *36* **Henry Havelock**[5] 3-10-12 0 DenisO'Regan 31
(Chris Grant) *nt jump wl: sn bhd: struggling fr 1/2-way: t.o* **3/1**[3]

P **Another Grand (IRE)**[354] 3-10-5 0 OliverWilliams(7) —
(Ruth Carr) *nt fluent: bhd: struggling 1/2-way: t.o whn p.u bef last* **20/1**

P **Dark Gem** 3-10-0 0 PaulCallaghan(5) —
(Simon West) *t.k.h: hld up: outpcd 3rd: shortlived effrt after 3 out: sn btn: t.o whn p.u bef last* **25/1**

4m 15.2s (-2.20) **Going Correction** -0.775s/f (Firm) **7** Ran SP% **115.2**
Speed ratings: **74,63,63,60,43 —,—**
toteswinger 1&2 £1.10, 1&3 £3.50, 2&3 £7.50 CSF £8.79 TOTE £3.10: £2.10, £1.50; EX 9.60
Place 6 £3.81, Place 5 £3.37.

Owner M H Dixon & Cinque Ports Syndicate **Bred** M H Dixon **Trained** Nicholashayne, Devon

FOCUS
Little to go on, with none of the runners having run over hurdles in this early-season juvenile contest. A very slow time compared with the earlier handicap.

NOTEBOOK
Lucky Quay(IRE) exhibited fitness and some professionalism in his jumping, typical of the stable's newcomers, and the combination of a good pace and fluent jumping had his rivals in trouble on the final circuit. He already has blinkers fitted, but responded well to them and looks capable of picking up similar events over the summer. (tchd 5-2)

Sansili was just a moderate performer on the Flat, but, with the yard in good form, he was well backed here. His jumping was not as fluent as the winner and his challenge was only a brief one as he soon began to tire up the final hill. He may need time to strengthen up but does not look that good at this stage. (tchd 7-4 and 2-1)

Anchorage Boy(USA) slowed into the first, ballooned some early jumps and generally betrayed his greenness. He managed to stay in touch for a long way considering his jumping, but will need to improve to feature in this sphere. (op 9-1)

Mr Mohican(IRE) raced prominently but paid the price for trying to challenge in the back straight and finished well beaten off. He should improve but whether that will be good enough is open to question. (op 9-1)

Henry Havelock managed to complete was something of a surprise, as he was spooked at the sight of the first hurdle and he did not jump with any confidence thereafter. (op 10-3 tchd 7-2)

T/Plt: £5.80 to a £1 stake. Pool: £41,834.13. 5260.14 winning units. T/Qpdt: £5.80 to a £1 stake. Pool: £2,463.00. 311/80 winning units. RY

406 WORCESTER (L-H)
Saturday, June 5

OFFICIAL GOING: Good (good to firm in places; chs 7.6; hdl 7.4)
All bends on inside racing line.
Wind: Nil Weather: Overcast and humid

630 MALVERNSPA HOTEL HEALTH CLUB & RESTAURANT NOVICES' H'CAP HURDLE (12 hdls) 3m
1:55 (1:56) (Class 5) (0-95,95) 4-Y-0+ **£2,055** (£599; £299)

Form RPR

2-32 **1** **Silver Phoenix**[6] 532 6-11-6 **89** (p) TomO'Brien 101+
(Caroline Keevil) *hld up: hdwy 8th: led 1/2-way up the run-in: styd on wl* **11/1**

3-02 **2** *3* **The Fox's Decree**[24] 272 6-11-8 **91** (t) WarrenMarston 100
(Martin Keighley) *hld up: hdwy after 9th: led 3 out: rdn and hdd 1/2-way up the run-in: styd on same pce* **16/1**

U3-1 **3** *9* **Rifleman (IRE)**[27] 231 10-11-5 **95** (t) JakeGreenall(7) 96
(Richard Lee) *hld up: hdwy 8th: rdn appr 3 out: ev ch next: no ex flat* **7/1**[3]

65-4 **4** *10* **Cool Bob (IRE)**[27] 231 7-11-10 **93** (t) PaddyBrennan 83
(Matt Sheppard) *led: hdd 3 out: rdn and wknd last* **8/1**

423- **5** *13* **Immense (IRE)**[66] 4960 6-11-2 **92** (t) TrevorWhelan(7) 69
(Ian Williams) *hld up: hdwy after 8th: hung rt and wknd after next: t.o* **7/2**[1]

F00/ **6** *13* **Stowford Press (IRE)**[77] 7-11-3 **86** (t) JodieMogford 50
(Nikki Evans) *hld up: bhd 4th: t.o* **50/1**

6/ **7** *6* **Isle Of Inishmore (IRE)**[42] 7-11-12 **95** RichardJohnson 53
(Tim Vaughan) *hld up in tch: chsd ldr 9th: wknd after next: eased bef last: t.o* **4/1**[2]

4-05 **8** *10* **Witch Of The Wave (IRE)**[17] 410 4-11-5 **93** (t) RobertThornton 36
(Joanna Davis) *chsd ldr tl rdn after 8th: wknd bef 3 out: t.o* **11/1**

P5-6 **9** *39* **Stevie Bull (IRE)**[24] 279 5-11-11 **94** ColinBolger 3
(Chris Gordon) *chsd ldrs tl rdn and wknd appr 9th: t.o* **40/1**

P **10** *74* **Aisemma (IRE)**[7] 522 6-11-2 **85** SeamusDurack —
(Peter Bowen) *hld up: hdwy 8th: rdn and wknd next: t.o* **33/1**

2-U3 **P** **Lord Collingwood (IRE)**[20] 353 9-11-5 **88** (p) AndrewTinkler —
(Nigel Tinkler) *prom tl rdn and wknd bef 9th: t.o whn p.u bef next* **15/2**

00-4 **P** **Thompson**[31] 157 6-11-9 **92** AidanColeman —
(Richard Phillips) *prom: rdn 7th: wknd bef next: t.o whn p.u bef 9th* **18/1**

00-0 **P** **Go All Out (IRE)**[31] 157 7-11-9 **95** SeanQuinlan(3) —
(Richard Phillips) *hld up: bhd fr 6th: t.o whn p.u bef next* **33/1**

36-2 **P** **Saint Espiegle (FR)**[15] 428 6-11-7 **95** MichaelMurphy(5) —
(Rob Summers) *prom: outpcd 8th: rallied after next: blnd 3 out: sn p.u* **25/1**

5m 32.7s (-11.90) **Going Correction** -0.60s/f (Firm)
WFA 4 from 5yo+ 19lb **14** Ran SP% **119.5**
Speed ratings (Par 103): **95,94,91,87,83 79,77,73,60,36 —,—,—,—**
toteswingers: 1&2 £23.80, 1&3 £7.20, 2&3 £39.60 CSF £160.86 CT £1329.43 TOTE £12.80: £2.60, £6.00, £2.40; EX 134.00.

Owner Mrs L R Lovell **Bred** Mrs Lynda R Lovell **Trained** Blagdon, Somerset

FOCUS
A tricky but moderate staying novices' handicap hurdle, which proved to be quite a lively betting heat on going described as good, good to firm in places after watering. The winner improved to the level of her bumper form.

NOTEBOOK
Silver Phoenix received a hefty 21lb rise in the weights when third over 2m5f at Towcester, but proved she could handle that when second next time out dropped back slightly in trip. She saw out this trip well after coming under pressure in the straight to draw clear in the final 100 yards and score in workmanlike fashion. A further rise in the weights will now make life difficult. (op 15-2)

The Fox's Decree had the ground he prefers and was being stepped up to 3m after some fair placed efforts recently. He was caught slightly flat-footed at the middle hurdle in the back but moved through travelling well when taking the lead three out. He saw out this trip well enough but had nothing left when collared in the final 100 yards.

Rifleman(IRE) had to defy a 6lb rise for his success in a C&D handicap, which saw him compete off his highest mark for three years. He made steady progress down the back straight to hold every chance turning in, but a mistake two out saw his effort flatten out. (op 11-2)

Cool Bob(IRE) is slipping down the weights but remains a maiden after 30 starts now. He took them along at a reasonable pace until headed three out. Once again, it looks like 3m is stretching his stamina. (op 9-1)

Immense(IRE)'s best efforts have been on an easier surface and he was struggling to hold his midfield position in the back straight before staying on from two out. (op 9-2 tchd 11-2)

Stowford Press(IRE) Official explanation: jockey said mare never travelled

Isle Of Inishmore(IRE) was sent off as joint-favourite after winning a maiden point and having his first run for Tim Vaughan. He travelled well turning in when holding every chance but folded tamely when asked a question. Official explanation: jockey said gelding had a breathing problem (tchd 7-2)

Lord Collingwood(IRE) Official explanation: vet said gelding pulled up lame

631 ANNE SIMS SPECIAL BIRTHDAY CELEBRATION BEGINNERS' CHASE (17 fncs 1 omitted) 2m 7f
2:30 (2:30) (Class 4) 5-Y-0+ **£3,610** (£1,313)

Form RPR

/P-2 **1** **Cullahill (IRE)**[17] 408 8-11-0 0 (t) HarrySkelton 111+
(Bob Buckler) *led to 2nd: led again 4th: j.rt 8th: clr fr 13th: easily* **5/1**[3]

5-03 **2** *40* **Orchard King (IRE)**[17] 408 9-10-7 0 (p) OliverDayman(7) 81
(Alison Thorpe) *hld up: hdwy and lft chsng wnr 7th: j. slowly 11th: mstke and wknd next: t.o* **9/1**

42-6 **U** **Hampton Court**[20] 359 5-10-9 0 JimmyDerham(5) —
(Seamus Mullins) *blnd and uns rdr 1st* **10/1**

21P- **U** **Factotum**[190] 2552 6-11-0 0 APMcCoy —
(Jonjo O'Neill) *trckd ldrs: blnd and uns rdr 3rd* **4/5**[1]

340- **F** **Bally Sands (IRE)**[52] 5184 6-11-0 113 (p) WarrenMarston —
(Robin Mathew) *chsd ldrs tl fell 7th* **9/2**[2]

0- **P** **Time'Ll Tell**[70] 5-11-0 0 (t) SamJones —
(Fiona Kehoe) *led 2nd to 4th: wknd 9th: t.o whn p.u bef 13th* **66/1**

5m 43.4s (0.80) **Going Correction** -0.35s/f (Good) **6** Ran SP% **111.0**
Speed ratings: **84,70,—,—,— —**
toteswingers: 1&2 £7.10 CSF £41.88 TOTE £5.40: £2.30, £3.60; EX 23.30.

Owner Nick Elliott **Bred** P P O'Dwyer **Trained** Henley, Somerset

FOCUS
This proved to be a modest and incident-packed contest. The second fence in the home straight was bypassed on the second circuit. There may be more to come from the winner.

NOTEBOOK
Cullahill(IRE), who cut out most of the running, came home in his own time after drawing clear down the back straight. He produced some respectable efforts as a hurdler back in 2008, but he missed all of 2009 and failed to take the eye on two runs since. However, he gave a slightly more encouraging display on his chasing debut when well behind Baddam here last time. He confirmed his superiority over the runner-up here, which is about all that can be taken out of the race. (op 3-1 tchd 11-4)
Orchard King(IRE) has struggled to regain the form which saw him win three staying handicap hurdles last year, and that remains the case after holding no chance from the back straight. (op 11-1)
Factotum unseated his rider on this chase debut after blundering at the third (op 6-5 tchd 5-4)

632 MATALAN MAIDEN HURDLE (DIV I) (10 hdls) 2m 4f
3:00 (3:03) (Class 4) 4-Y-0+ **£2,276** (£668; £334; £166)

Form RPR
15-6 **1** **Great Mates (IRE)**[19] 370 6-11-0 0 HarrySkelton 110+
(Paul Nicholls) *hld up: hdwy 5th: chsd ldr 2 out: hung rt after last: rdn to ld 1/2-way up the run-in: styd on wl* **5/1**[3]
306- **2** *2 1/2* **Rappel D'Estruval (FR)**[115] 3978 5-11-0 108 PaddyBrennan 107
(Tom George) *hld up: hdwy 5th: led after 7th: rdn and hdd 1/2-way up the run-in: styd on same pce* **11/2**
320- **3** *6* **Our Guardian Angel (IRE)**[130] 3670 6-10-7 0 (t) RichardJohnson 94
(Tim Vaughan) *hld up: hdwy 6th: rdn appr last: wknd flat* **4/1**[2]
4 *3 1/4* **Unleashed (IRE)**[56] 5-11-0 0 PaulMoloney 98
(Charlie Mann) *hld up: hdwy appr 3 out: rdn and hung lft bef last: sn wknd* **3/1**[1]
51-5 **5** *2 1/2* **Lackamon**[11] 457 5-11-0 0 TjadeCollier 95
(Sue Smith) *chsd ldrs: rdn and wknd appr last* **12/1**
P0P/ **6** *18* **The Boat (IRE)**[28] 8-11-0 69 ChristianWilliams 77
(Lawney Hill) *hld up: hdwy appr 3 out: sn wknd and eased: t.o* **9/1**
7 *30* **Exiles Return (IRE)**[28] 8-10-7 0 MrNdeBoinville[(7)] 47
(Sue Wilson) *plld hrd: trckd clr ldr: ev ch after 4 out: rdn and wkng whn blnd 2 out: t.o* **50/1**
5/P- **8** *102* **Piper Royal**[75] 4787 6-11-0 0 FelixDeGiles —
(Nicky Henderson) *chsd ldrs tl wknd after 7th: eased: t.o* **8/1**
0/5 **U** **Berry Hill Lass (IRE)**[20] 358 6-10-0 0 (vt) CharlieWallis[(7)] —
(John O'Shea) *in rr whn swvd and uns rdr after 1st* **33/1**
/5P- **P** **Tram Express (FR)**[48] 5250 6-10-9 0 SamTwiston-Davies[(5)] —
(Shaun Lycett) *led and sn wl clr: wknd and hdd after 7th: t.o whn p.u bef next* **28/1**
00-U **P** **Cedar Falls (USA)**[9] 490 5-11-0 28 RodiGreene —
(Gary Brown) *hld up: bhd fr 5th: t.o whn p.u bef 3 out* **40/1**
P **P** **Watch The Master**[6] 538 4-10-10 0 AidanColeman —
(Ben Case) *hld up: a in rr: t.o whn p.u bef 3 out* **100/1**
5 **P** **Lord Hugo**[24] 277 5-10-9 0 JimmyDerham[(5)] —
(Seamus Mullins) *hld up: bhd fr 5th: t.o whn p.u after 7th* **50/1**

4m 36.4s (-11.00) **Going Correction** -0.60s/f (Firm)
WFA 4 from 5yo+ 18lb **13** Ran SP% **119.6**
Speed ratings (Par 105): **98,97,94,93,92 85,73,—,—,— —,—,—**
toteswingers: 1&2 £3.90, 1&3 £13.30, 2&3 £4.20 CSF £31.66 TOTE £4.60: £1.70, £2.00, £1.60; EX 20.10.
Owner Jim Lewis **Bred** Con O'Keeffe **Trained** Ditcheat, Somerset

FOCUS
A weak maiden hurdle, run at a fair pace. The first two are rated to their marks but this is not form to get carried away with it.

NOTEBOOK
Great Mates(IRE) had won a Stratford bumper quite decisively but had often looked a weak finisher, including when only sixth on his hurdling debut. Patiently ridden from the rear, he made steady progress to be chasing the leader going to two out. He had to be shaken up and wandered on the run-in before getting the stand side rail and running on well to score. He finished well here, although he was running green when asked to go about his task. He looks as though he is progressing and will be kept on the go throughout the summer. (op 6-1 tchd 9-2)
Rappel D'Estruval(FR) has not shown a terrific amount of promise to date but had earned a mark of 108 and set the standard. He travelled like the winner when taking over after the seventh. He held on to the advantage in the straight before being outstayed by the winner in the final 100 yards. (op 5-1)
Our Guardian Angel(IRE) had some placed form to his name in bumpers but had been absent since a fairly moderate hurdling debut in January. This was a better effort but, after being close enough three out, he could only stay on at the same pace. (op 5-1)
Unleashed(IRE) ran creditably in Listed company when with Henry Cecil, and was backed down to favouritism here on his hurdling debut. He lost his place at the middle hurdle down the back and was soon pushed along. He could never get back on terms, although he stayed on again from two out. (op 11-4 tchd 4-1)
Lackamon, an Irish point winner who landed a Hexham bumper in March, made a satisfactory start to his hurdling career last time. He made a similar effort here and held a chance turning in, but he was soon under pressure and found only the one pace. (tchd 11-1)
Piper Royal is a half-brother to high-class chaser Barbers Shop but after a promising debut in his bumper, was reported to have bled internally on hurdling debut. He remains one to be cautious of after this showing. (tchd 10-1)

633 JOHN WILLIAM DEELEY CLASSIC H'CAP HURDLE (10 hdls) 2m 4f
3:35 (3:35) (Class 3) (0-135,135) 4-Y-0+ **£4,878** (£1,432; £716; £357)

Form RPR
6-10 **1** **Son Of Flicka**[22] 316 6-11-6 129 APMcCoy 134
(Donald McCain) *hld up: hdwy after 7th: sn rdn: styd on u.p to ld nr fin* **10/1**
100- **2** *shd* **Rajeh (IRE)**[8] 2035 7-11-3 126 PaddyBrennan 131
(John Spearing) *hld up: hdwy 6th: led last: rdn and hung lft flat: hdd nr fin* **6/1**[3]
6F1- **3** *9* **Valento**[41] 3 5-10-8 120 SeanQuinlan[(3)] 117
(Kim Bailey) *hld up: hdwy 7th: rdn appr last: wknd flat* **12/1**
0F-4 **4** *3 1/2* **Busker Royal**[35] 94 7-10-9 125 DavidBass[(7)] 118
(Nicky Henderson) *chsd ldrs: led 6th: hdd 3 out: rdn and wknd flat* **7/2**[1]
0P-1 **5** *2 1/2* **Pascha Bere (FR)**[27] 235 7-11-12 135 (p) LiamTreadwell 125+
(Nick Gifford) *chsd ldrs: led 3 out: hdd last: wknd flat* **7/1**
2-51 **6** *3 1/4* **Tabaran (FR)**[19] 372 7-10-11 127 (tp) OliverDayman[(7)] 114
(Alison Thorpe) *hld up: hdwy 4th: rdn and wknd appr last* **11/2**[2]
014- **7** *3/4* **Parlesotho (FR)**[41] 3 7-10-11 120 CharliePoste 106
(Ben Case) *mid-div: drvn along and dropped to rr 6th: n.d after* **16/1**
10-P **8** *1/2* **Tritonville Lodge (IRE)**[30] 170 8-11-3 126 JackDoyle 112
(Emma Lavelle) *led to 6th: rdn and wknd after 2 out* **33/1**
220- **9** *2 3/4* **Special Envoy (FR)**[57] 5113 8-11-8 134 RichardKilloran[(3)] 117
(Nicky Henderson) *prom: rdn appr 3 out: wknd after next* **25/1**
V-00 **10** *6* **Is It Me (USA)**[7] 521 7-11-2 125 (t) PaulMoloney 102
(Sophie Leech) *chsd ldrs tl wknd 5th* **33/1**
10-0 **11** *1* **Daurica**[29] 193 6-10-4 120 BrianToomey[(7)] 96
(Renee Robeson) *mid-div: hdwy 4th: wknd after 7th* **25/1**
03-2 **12** *3 1/4* **Tobago Bay**[35] 94 5-11-7 130 (p) JamieGoldstein 103
(Sheena West) *chsd ldr to 6th: rdn and wknd after next: t.o* **7/1**
P-00 **13** *14* **Raslan**[19] 372 7-11-10 133 (tp) GerrySupple 92
(David Pipe) *hld up: bhd fr 5th: t.o: t.o* **28/1**
6/1- **14** *15* **Estate**[72] 4849 8-10-11 120 TomScudamore 64
(David Pipe) *prom tl rdn and wknd 6th: t.o* **15/2**

4m 31.5s (-15.90) **Going Correction** -0.60s/f (Firm) course record **14** Ran SP% **128.3**
Speed ratings (Par 107): **107,106,103,101,100 99,99,99,98,95 95,93,88,82**
toteswingers: 1&2 £31.10, 1&3 £29.70, 2&3 £17.40 CSF £70.39 CT £752.68 TOTE £11.20: £3.40, £3.40, £3.90; EX 155.10.
Owner Twenty Four Seven Recruitment **Bred** Chieveley Manor Stud **Trained** Cholmondeley, Cheshire

FOCUS
A competitive handicap hurdle. There were plenty with a chance turning in after a decent pace was set, and it ended with a cracking finish being fought out between the two principals. There is a case for rating the race a few pounds higher.

NOTEBOOK
Son Of Flicka was right up to his best when scoring at Bangor in April but was well beaten at Aintree two weeks ago on similar ground. This was as game an effort as they come and he showed a very willing attitude under a great ride. Held up off the pace he was niggled along in the back straight before closing on the home bend. Under pressure when taking over at the last, he looked to be fighting a losing battle when narrowly headed, but he found enough as the finish neared to regain the upper hand. (tchd 11-1)
Rajeh(IRE) had conditions to suit and was coming here in good form off the back of a winning run on the flat eight days ago. He lost nothing in defeat after taking up the lead soon after the last, but he could not find enough to repel the renewed thrust of the winner. He looks a decent sort for this time of year and should be respected in similar affairs. (tchd 11-2)
Valento had gone up 12lb for a recent success and was taking on stiffer company. He never quite got competitive after moving through to chase the leaders but he stayed on well enough.
Busker Royal was off a reasonable mark and had his chances, but he could only stay on at the same pace in the straight. (op 11-2)
Pascha Bere(FR) was back up 10lb for landing a less competitive event over 2m and this was another fair effort back up 4f. He raced prominently before leading three out, but he could not match the pace of the front pair from the last before fading towards the finish. (op 8-1)
Tabaran(FR) was unable to lay down a serious challenge.
Estate ran no sort of race after sweating up beforehand. (op 8-1)

634 BAXIECOGEN.COM GENERATE YOUR OWN ELECTRICITY NOVICES' H'CAP CHASE (12 fncs) 2m
4:10 (4:11) (Class 4) (0-115,111) 5-Y-0+ **£3,252** (£955; £477; £238)

Form RPR
114- **1** **Elite Land**[15] 5357 7-11-12 111 KeithMercer 122+
(Brian Ellison) *hld up and bhd: hdwy appr 4 out: chsd ldr 2 out: led and hit last: styd on wl* **5/1**[2]
123- **2** *7* **Blossom King (FR)**[159] 3126 6-11-10 109 PaddyBrennan 113
(Tom George) *chsd ldr tl led 5th: hit 3 out: hdd last: no ex flat* **5/1**[2]
1U-2 **3** *4 1/2* **Chilbury Hill (IRE)**[30] 183 7-11-0 99 LiamHeard 98
(Kevin Bishop) *prom: chsd ldr appr 4 out: mstke next: lost 2nd 2 out: wknd bef last* **5/1**[2]
0-32 **4** *1 1/2* **King's Majesty (IRE)**[9] 491 8-10-0 85 DougieCostello 82
(Tim Pitt) *hld up: stmbld 8th: hdwy appr 4 out: rdn and wknd bef last* **10/1**
2U-0 **5** *4 1/2* **Kack Handed**[21] 330 7-11-12 111 RichardJohnson 106
(Henry Daly) *led: mstke 2nd: hdd 5th: remained handy tl blnd and wknd 2 out* **2/1**[1]
4-44 **6** *10* **Ragador**[9] 489 9-11-1 100 TjadeCollier 83
(Sue Smith) *chsd ldrs: mstke 4th: drvn along after 5th: hit 7th: wknd appr 4 out* **8/1**
2F-3 **7** *35* **Jardin De Vienne (FR)**[18] 381 8-10-2 94 (v) BrianToomey[(7)] 42
(Renee Robeson) *prom tl wknd after 5th: t.o* **7/1**[3]
66P- **8** *2* **Moneywise (IRE)**[105] 4164 6-11-6 105 APMcCoy 51
(Jonjo O'Neill) *hld up: hdwy 6th: wknd 3 out: j.rt next: t.o* **15/2**

3m 47.5s (-4.10) **Going Correction** -0.35s/f (Good) **8** Ran SP% **127.8**
Speed ratings: **96,92,90,89,87 82,64,63**
toteswingers: 1&2 £9.30, 1&3 Not won, 2&3 £3.40 CSF £34.13 CT £138.77 TOTE £4.50: £1.30, £2.30, £2.30; EX 29.70.
Owner Dan Gilbert **Bred** T Umpleby **Trained** Norton, N Yorks

FOCUS
A fair event. The winner stepped up on his previous jumps efforts but the form looks believable.

NOTEBOOK
Elite Land, a decent dual-purpose performer, won this convincingly under a patient ride. Coming through from the rear to take it up at the last, he only had to be shaken up to draw clear. Twice successful in March over hurdles, and a runner-up on the flat a fortnight ago, he was clearly in good heart. He is a versatile performer who lacks chasing experience but, on this evidence, he fences well and should be capable of handling a higher mark. (op 9-2)
Blossom King(FR) had not been seen since a costly slip when third at Leicester. He took it up in the back straight but after a bad stumble three out, was soon pushed along before being headed at the last and readily brushed aside. This was a pleasing return to action with the yard beginning to hit form.
Chilbury Hill(IRE) has been running creditably since switching to fences on varying ground, and this was a similar effort. He chased the leaders throughout but was struggling when diving to his left and hitting two out.
King's Majesty(IRE) was up against it here and could never get involved. (tchd 9-1)
Kack Handed, who was well backed, took them along at a fair pace until headed in the back straight. He remained chasing the leaders until hitting two out and weakening. (op 4-1)
Moneywise(IRE) had not shown a great deal in four runs over fences and this was another disappointing effort. (op 7-1)

635 MATALAN MAIDEN HURDLE (DIV II) (10 hdls) 2m 4f
4:40 (4:40) (Class 4) 4-Y-0+ **£2,276** (£668; £334; £166)

Form RPR
25-5 **1** **Off Gallivanting**[17] 409 5-11-0 0 APMcCoy 107+
(Jonjo O'Neill) *a.p: chsd ldr 5th: led appr 3 out: rdn and hung rt flat: styd on u.p* **9/4**[2]
3-2 **2** *1* **Hadron Collider (FR)**[24] 279 5-10-11 114 PeterToole[(3)] 107+
(Charlie Mann) *trckd ldrs: chal 3 out: nt fluent next: hrd rdn and edgd rt flat: styd on* **4/5**[1]
04-U **3** *5* **Sprowler**[17] 408 6-10-9 0 JimmyDerham[(5)] 101
(Joanna Davis) *chsd ldrs: ev ch 3 out: rdn and swtchd lft flat: no ex fnl 100yds* **33/1**
64- **4** *49* **Karzelle**[89] 4495 6-11-0 0 PaddyBrennan 52
(John Spearing) *hld up: blnd 1st: mstke 5th: a bhd: t.o* **14/1**
5 *1/2* **Dawn Storm (IRE)**[31] 5-10-11 0 SeanQuinlan[(3)] 52
(Rachel Hobbs) *hld up: drvn along 5th: lost tch next: t.o* **33/1**

The Form Book, Raceform Ltd, Compton, RG20 6NL

6 3/4 **Market Bob (IRE)**[21] 8-10-11 0 .... LeeStephens(3) 51
(Ann Price) *w ldr tl after 1st: sn lost pl: bhd and rdn 4th: t.o* **8/1**[3]
PU-P **7** *17* **Passive Interest**[27] 224 5-10-7 0 .... ColinBolger 27
(Ray Peacock) *led: hdd & wknd appr 3 out: t.o* **66/1**
4 **8** *16* **Cool The Heels (IRE)**[11] 465 5-11-0 0 .... JackDoyle 18
(Emma Lavelle) *prom: blnd 7th: sn wknd: t.o* **12/1**
9 *2* **Roc De Guye (FR)**[448] 5-11-0 0 .... DavidDennis 16
(James Evans) *hld up: hdwy 6th: wknd after 7th: t.o* **25/1**
P- **P** **Wild Lyph**[226] 1861 4-10-10 0 .... DougieCostello —
(Neil Mulholland) *chsd ldr after 1st: wknd qckly 5th: t.o whn p.u bef 7th* **80/1**
0- **P** **Autumn's Quest**[363] 637 7-10-7 0 .... LiamTreadwell —
(Teresa Spearing) *hld up: bhd fr 4th: t.o whn p.u bef 3 out* **50/1**

4m 41.5s (-5.90) **Going Correction** -0.60s/f (Firm)
WFA 4 from 5yo+ 18lb **11** Ran SP% **126.2**
Speed ratings (Par 105): **87,86,84,65,64 64,57,51,50,— —**
toteswingers: 1&2 £1.10, 1&3 £16.70, 2&3 £17.50 CSF £4.78 TOTE £4.10: £1.60, £1.02, £10.00; EX 5.10.
Owner John P McManus **Bred** Mrs S J Brasher **Trained** Cheltenham, Gloucs

FOCUS
The less competitive of the two divisions of the 2m4f maiden hurdle was run at an ordinary pace with the front three drawing well clear of the remainder. The winner improved to the level of his bumper form.

NOTEBOOK
Off Gallivanting tracked the leaders before taking the lead three out. Idling from the last, he had the advantage of the near rail to hold on well. He had been raced in cheekpieces on his third bumper run, but they were left off when he appeared not to see out the 3m trip here last time. Although he could probably in time get further, at this stage he clearly appreciated the drop back in distance. (op 7-2)
Hadron Collider(FR) was a warm order to get off the mark at the third time of asking after boasting the strongest level of form, but was always being held after holding every chance three out. He ought to be capable of going one better shortly. (op 10-11 tchd Evens)
Sprowler hinted at ability in his sole bumper start but had been soundly beaten on two previous tries over hurdles. This was a more encouraging effort. He could not match the front two from the last, but was well clear of the remainder.
Karzelle could never get involved on his hurdling debut and was beaten a long way. (op 12-1 tchd 11-1)
Roc De Guye(FR) Official explanation: vet said gelding finished distressed

636 MATALAN VALERIE LEWIS MEMORIAL H'CAP CHASE (15 fncs) 2m 4f 110y
5:10 (5:10) (Class 3) (0-135,123) 5-Y-O+ **£5,703** (£1,684; £842; £421; £210)

Form RPR
442- **1** **Polyfast (FR)**[47] 5279 7-11-8 **119** .... AndrewTinkler 127+
(Nicky Henderson) *hld up in tch: nt fluent 4 out: led last: rdn clr flat* **5/1**[3]
42-U **2** *10* **Franchoek (IRE)**[6] 536 6-11-11 **122** .... APMcCoy 118
(Alan King) *chsd ldrs: led 5th: rdn and hdd last: wknd flat* **3/1**[2]
1-25 **3** *nse* **Prince Des Marais (FR)**[20] 361 7-11-12 **123** .... AndrewThornton 121+
(Caroline Bailey) *hld up: hdwy 8th: chsd ldr 10th: rdn and ev ch 2 out: wknd flat* **8/1**
35F- **4** *15* **Stagecoach Amber (USA)**[307] 1122 8-11-3 **119** .... ShaneByrne(5) 100
(Sue Smith) *led to 2nd: chsd ldr fr there to 5th: rdn appr 4 out: mstke and wknd next* **9/1**
3-11 **5** *10* **Tyup Pompey (IRE)**[23] 300 9-11-2 **116** .... LeeStephens(3) 87
(Ann Price) *prom: pushed along 7th: wknd bef 4 out: t.o* **10/1**
0-P0 **6** *8* **Free Gift**[17] 411 12-10-13 **117** .... (p) DavidBass(7) 80
(R H & Mrs S Alner) *led 2nd to 5th: sn rdn: wknd after 11th: t.o* **16/1**
5PF- **7** *6* **Osolomio (IRE)**[120] 3869 7-11-8 **119** .... AlanO'Keeffe 76
(Jennie Candlish) *hld up: a in rr: mstke 5th: j.rt 8th: wknd 11th: t.o* **12/1**
/25- **P** **Loita Hills (IRE)**[48] 5249 10-11-9 **120** .... RichardJohnson —
(Philip Hobbs) *hld up: bhd whn j.rt 3rd and 4th: sn p.u* **11/4**[1]

4m 55.4s (-11.30) **Going Correction** -0.35s/f (Good) **8** Ran SP% **112.1**
Speed ratings: **107,103,103,97,93 90,88,—**
toteswingers: 1&2 £1.90, 1&3 £3.00, 2&3 £6.50 CSF £20.27 CT £115.51 TOTE £4.70: £1.30, £1.70, £2.70; EX 25.00.
Owner W J Brown **Bred** Patrick Boiteau **Trained** Upper Lambourn, Berks

FOCUS
A competitive 0-135 2m4f handicap chase run at just an ordinary pace. The winner is rated to the level of his Kempton win.

NOTEBOOK
Polyfast(FR) had not won since his rather fortunate success at Kempton on Boxing Day, but he had performed to that level when runner-up last time. He had to be driven along turning in before taking the lead at the last and drawing clear soon after. Underfoot conditions are a big factor to him and he also goes well fresh. Therefore, coming here off the back of a 47-day break stood him in good stead. (tchd 9-2 and 11-2)
Franchoek(IRE) has not really taken to fences in five starts. He does not look as though he will reach the lofty heights he did as a juvenile over hurdles and has dropped to a mark of 122. Under a positive ride and taking it up at the first in the back straight, he remained there until headed at the last where he found no extra. (op 9-2 tchd 11-4)
Prince Des Marais(FR) has been a revelation since having a wind operation. He narrowly failed to complete his hat-trick last month but has remained on a workable mark. He travels well in his races and looked strong before landing awkwardly four out. He was soon under pressure after that but was rallying before getting the last wrong. (op 13-2)
Stagecoach Amber(USA) had not run for 307 days and will benefit from the outing. He sat prominently for most of the way before tiring turning in. (op 10-1)
Tyup Pompey(IRE) put up a career best last time when winning at his beloved Ludlow last time, earning a 7lb rise. He was under pressure six out and was a spent force in the straight. (op 8-1)
Loita Hills(IRE) had been campaigned unsuccessfully, albeit respectably, in hunter chases but returned to handicap company on a handy looking mark. He jumped badly right and was never travelling before pulling up at the fifth. Official explanation: jockey said gelding jumped right-handed; vet said gelding was lame (op 3-1)

637 TOMORROW IS WORCESTER'S FAMILY FUN RACE DAY INTERMEDIATE OPEN NATIONAL HUNT FLAT RACE 2m
5:40 (5:40) (Class 6) 4-6-Y-O **£1,712** (£499; £249)

Form RPR
1 **Mossley (IRE)**[111] 4-10-13 0 .... APMcCoy 121+
(Nicky Henderson) *hld up in tch: led on bit over 1f out: canter* **4/6**[1]
2 **2** *6* **Arthur's Pass**[27] 237 6-11-2 0 .... PaddyBrennan 112
(Tom George) *a.p: chsd ldr 4f out: led over 2f out: rdn and hdd over 1f out: styd on same pce fnl f* **3/1**[2]
3 *7* **Tara Rose**[61] 5-10-6 0 .... LeeStephens(3) 96
(David Evans) *led: rdn and hdd over 2f out: wknd over 1f out* **12/1**[3]
5- **4** *11* **Glacial Harry**[49] 5235 4-10-6 0 .... PeterHatton(7) 89
(Reg Hollinshead) *hld up: hdwy u.p fr over 3f out: sn hung lft: n.d* **16/1**
44-R **5** *16* **Johann Sabestian (IRE)**[2] 609 5-10-13 0 .... (p) RichieMcLernon(3) 76
(Jonjo O'Neill) *prom: chsd ldr over 6f out: rdn over 4f out: wknd over 3f out: sn hung lft: t.o* **25/1**
0 **6** *12* **The Ridge**[27] 222 6-11-2 0 .... TomScudamore 64
(Michael Scudamore) *hld up: bhd 1/2-way: nvr on terms: t.o* **66/1**
0 **7** *1 3/4* **La Chemme**[23] 304 4-10-6 0 .... HarrySkelton 52
(Reg Hollinshead) *chsd ldrs tl rdn and wknd over 4f out: t.o* **33/1**
6 **8** *7* **My Idea**[37] 60 4-10-13 0 .... GerardTumelty 52
(Anabel L M King) *hld up in tch: racd keenly: wknd 6f out: t.o* **33/1**
9 *1 1/4* **Red Whisper** 6-10-11 0 .... MichaelMurphy(5) 54
(Rob Summers) *hld up: hdwy u.p over 4f out: sn wknd: t.o* **33/1**
0 **10** *5* **Right Move (IRE)**[19] 375 5-11-2 0 .... TomO'Brien 49
(Caroline Keevil) *prom tl wknd 6f out: t.o* **50/1**
4- **11** *121* **Mini Shower**[50] 5218 6-10-5 0 ow3 .... MrSJO'Donovan(7) —
(Norma Twomey) *chsd ldr tl wknd qckly over 6f out: eased fnl 4f: t.o* **28/1**
6 **12** *38* **Transinski (IRE)**[24] 284 4-10-13 0 .... FelixDeGiles —
(Alastair Lidderdale) *chsd ldrs: rdn 1/2-way: sn wknd: t.o* **66/1**
0- **U** **Kirkton**[161] 3027 5-10-9 0 .... AndrewThornton —
(Jim Wilson) *in rr and hung lft most of way tl hung rt and uns rdr 9f out* **100/1**

3m 33.0s (-8.70) **Going Correction** -0.60s/f (Firm)
WFA 4 from 5yo+ 3lb **13** Ran SP% **120.6**
Speed ratings: **97,94,90,85,77 71,70,66,66,63 —,—,—**
toteswingers: 1&2 £1.02, 1&3 £5.10, 2&3 £5.90 CSF £2.35 TOTE £2.00: £1.20, £1.10, £2.60; EX 2.30 Place 6: £405.95, Place 5: £100.63..
Owner Michael Buckley **Bred** Pipe View Stud **Trained** Upper Lambourn, Berks

FOCUS
A fair pace for this bumper. The easy winner looks a smart redcruit, and the second set a decent standard.

NOTEBOOK
Mossley(IRE) ran out a very comfortable winner. Settled off the pace, he moved through the field travelling well entering the straight to take over the lead 2f out and sauntered home. Out of a Listed winner on the flat, who is a half-sister to the useful chaser Commanche Court, he was still holding a narrow advantage when falling on his sole start in an Irish point. This was a likeable performance and, with his connections, he can only build on this. He will now be turned away for the summer. (op Evens)
Arthur's Pass ran with plenty of credit when chasing home a promising sort here last time, the pair clear of the remainder. Again this was another encouraging effort after attracting plenty of support in the market beforehand, but he was readily held by the winner. (op 5-2 tchd 9-4)
Tara Rose had been placed in a couple of points but had since joined a respected yard. She used her pointing experience to her advantage and set off at a fair pace, which probably played to the strengths of the winner. She stayed on at the same pace when headed over 3f out. (op 10-1)
Glacial Harry was beaten 20 lengths in a similar contest at Bangor on his debut and ran to that level again here, never posing a threat. (op 14-1 tchd 18-1)
Johann Sabestian(IRE), after a couple of initial promising efforts, blotted his copybook by refusing to start last time in a tongue-tie. The tongue-tie was left off this time in favour of cheekpieces. He had his chance entering the straight but soon faded. (op 10-1)
T/Plt: £105.50 to a £1 stake. Pool: £44,180.32. 305.47 winning tickets. T/Qpdt: £14.00 to a £1 stake. Pool: £3,241.22. 171.30 winning tickets. CR

638 - 644a (Foreign Racing) - See Raceform Interactive

[630]WORCESTER (L-H)
Sunday, June 6

OFFICIAL GOING: Good (good to firm in places; watered) changing to good to soft after race 3 (3.10)
All bends moved out 3-5metres from the inner line used on Saturday increasing distances by about 20yds.
Wind: Light behind Weather: Rain clearing after race 3

645 LADBROKES CONDITIONAL JOCKEYS' H'CAP HURDLE (DIV I) (10 hdls) 2m 4f
2:10 (2:12) (Class 4) (0-100,100) 4-Y-0+ **£2,602** (£764; £382; £190)

Form RPR
P00- **1** **Cannon Fire (FR)**[73] 4849 9-10-10 **87** .... DPFahy(3) 105+
(Evan Williams) *a.p: chsd ldr 3 out: led next: r.o wl* **8/1**
-041 **2** *12* **Command Marshal (FR)**[7] 532 7-11-4 **95** 7ex .... DavidBass(3) 102
(Michael Scudamore) *hld up: hdwy appr 3 out: chsd wnr after 2 out: hung lft and wknd flat* **2/1**[1]
02-4 **3** *2 1/4* **Kijivu**[25] 282 5-11-7 **95** .... (bt) GilesHawkins 101
(Alastair Lidderdale) *chsd ldr 2nd tl led appr 6th: clr bef 3 out: hdd next: wknd last* **9/2**[2]
20-4 **4** *4 1/2* **Lansdowne Princess**[33] 134 8-10-8 **82** .... RhysFlint 83
(Gerald Ham) *hld up: pushed along appr 3 out: nvr nrr* **6/1**[3]
03-6 **5** *shd* **Petit Fleur**[19] 384 8-10-10 **87** .... AnthonyFreeman(3) 88
(Julian Smith) *hld up: hdwy appr 5th: chsd ldr 7th: sn rdn: wknd last* **25/1**
030- **6** *3/4* **Edgevine**[84] 4612 6-11-3 **91** .... SamJones 91
(Paul Webber) *chsd ldrs: lost pl 4th: rallied next: rdn appr 3 out: wknd last* **28/1**
0- **7** *3 3/4* **Makena (FR)**[29] 8-11-7 **95** .... (p) DonalDevereux 92
(David Rees) *hld up: racd keenly: hdwy after 7th: sn rdn: wknd next: no ch whn rdr dropped whip flat* **12/1**
04P- **8** *2* **Ballingaddy (IRE)**[88] 4518 7-11-0 **88** .... (t) DeanColeman 83
(Lawney Hill) *hld up: rdn and wknd after 7th* **20/1**
00-0 **9** *14* **Lady Of Ashcott**[19] 384 4-9-6 **78** oh7 .... MarkQuinlan(8) 56
(Neil Mulholland) *prom to 5th: t.o* **66/1**
3P-6 **10** *50* **Signs Of Love (FR)**[28] 220 7-11-10 **98** .... JohnnyFarrelly 35
(Noel Chance) *chsd ldrs: pushed along after 4th: sn lost pl: t.o fr 6th* **33/1**
P0- **11** *37* **Skip The Present (IRE)**[228] 1851 7-11-2 **90** .... MichaelMurphy —
(John Spearing) *plld hrd: trckd ldr to 2nd: remained handy tl wknd 7th: t.o* **7/1**
PFP- **P** **Badly Bruised (IRE)**[133] 3629 9-11-12 **100** .... (b) GerardTumelty —
(Martin Keighley) *led: hdd appr 6th: wknd next: t.o whn p.u bef 3 out* **16/1**

4m 49.6s (2.20) **Going Correction** +0.25s/f (Yiel)
WFA 4 from 5yo+ 18lb **12** Ran SP% **119.5**
Speed ratings (Par 105): **105,100,99,97,97 97,95,94,89,69 54,—**
Tote Swingers: 1&2 £4.40, 1&3 £5.30, 2&3 £2.80 CSF £23.92 CT £84.57 TOTE £11.80: £3.30, £1.10, £1.50; EX 26.80.
Owner R E R Williams **Bred** Gilles And Mrs Forien **Trained** Llancarfan, Vale Of Glamorgan

FOCUS
All bends moved out 3-5 metres on to fresh ground. The track was watered during the morning and there was a spell of heavy rain shortly before racing. The riders in the first reported that the ground was definitely affected and was riding on the soft side of good, but the official going description was not amended until after the third. Division one of this very modest handicap hurdle. The pace was sound and the form should prove solid. The well-in winner was 8lb off his best 2009 form. The time reflected the easy underfoot conditions but was 4.8secs quicker than the second division.

NOTEBOOK
Cannon Fire(FR) had shown little in his last few starts but that was reflected by a steady fall in his rating and he was able to race off no less than 25lb lower than as recently as November. He was reported to have had a breathing problem last time and the tongue tie was left off here. Leading two from home and drawing clear on the run-in for a ready success, he avoids a penalty for this win in a conditionals' race and will be of obvious interest if turned out before he can be reassessed. The ease in the ground suited him. (op 14-1)
Command Marshal(FR) won comfortably at Fontwell the previous Sunday but could not follow up under a penalty. After making rather laboured progress to put himself into contention, he was left trailing by the winner from the last, but probably gave his running. (op 6-4)
Kijivu has been performing well and this was another solid effort, but after skipping clear before the straight she was untidy three from home and soon overhauled. She has made the frame in six of her last seven starts without managing to win. (op 5-1)
Lansdowne Princess clocked up defeat number 34 but made late progress for fourth and a win should come her way in the end. (op 7-1 tchd 11-2)
Petit Fleur, dropped 3lb and back up in trip, moved into contention on the home turn before her effort began to flatten out. (op 33-1)
Edgevine, returning from a break, was administered reminders with a full circuit to run and did well to remain in contention for as long as she did. (op 25-1)
Makena(FR) has done very well between the flags in Wales this spring but was well held on this first run over hurdles in Britain. (op 11-1 tchd 10-1)

646 LADBROKES CONDITIONAL JOCKEYS' H'CAP HURDLE (DIV II) (10 hdls) 2m 4f
2:40 (2:40) (Class 4) (0-100,100) 4-Y-0+ **£2,602** (£764; £382; £190)

Form				RPR
3U-5	**1**		**Grand Bay (USA)**[32] 156 9-11-9 **98**........(t) RichieMcLernon(3) (Jonjo O'Neill) *hld up: hdwy appr 3 out: shkn up to ld fnl 100yds: r.o wl* **17/2**	101+
P5-0	**2**	*3 1/2*	**Star Galaxy (IRE)**[22] 328 10-11-4 **90**........(b) RhysFlint (John Flint) *chsd ldrs: led last: rdn and hdd fnl 100yds: no ex* **11/1**	90
22P-	**3**	*nse*	**Festival Dreams**[57] 5135 5-11-9 **95**........(p) HaddenFrost (Joanna Davis) *chsd ldr tl led after 4th: rdn and hdd last: styd on same pce* **11/2**[3]	95
000-	**4**	*1 1/4*	**Vintage Fabric (USA)**[224] 1926 8-11-9 **95**........(t) GerardTumelty (Nigel Hawke) *chsd ldrs: lost pl after 4th: wnt prom again next: rdn appr 3 out: styd on* **16/1**	94
-003	**5**	*1*	**Pips Assertive Way**[8] 522 9-11-4 **93**........LeeEdwards(3) (Tony Carroll) *led tl after 4th: eveny ch whn mstke 3 out: styd on same pce flat* **11/4**[1]	92
450/	**6**	*2 3/4*	**Diego Velasquez (IRE)**[91] 6-11-4 **90**........(t) HarrySkelton (Patrick Griffin, Ire) *hld up: hdwy appr 3 out: rdn after next: styd on same pce* **10/1**	86
553-	**7**	*13*	**Am I Blue**[71] 4880 4-11-10 **100**........DeanColeman (Mrs D Thomas) *hld up: a in rr: bhd fr 7th* **18/1**	80
064-	**8**	*1 1/2*	**Lukie Victor (IRE)**[72] 4879 9-10-12 **87**........DPFahy(3) (Evan Williams) *hld up in tch: rdn and wknd after 2 out* **3/1**[2]	69
/0-P	**9**	*8*	**Dancing Hill**[8] 522 11-11-0 **86**........JohnnyFarrelly (Kevin Bishop) *prom: j. slowly 5th: wknd bef 3 out* **40/1**	61
550-	**F**		**Scotsbrook Cloud**[224] 1926 5-11-2 **88**........DonalDevereux (C Roberts) *hld up: rdn appr 3 out: wkng whn fell next* **12/1**	—

4m 54.4s (7.00) **Going Correction** +0.25s/f (Yiel) **10** Ran SP% **116.3**
Speed ratings (Par 105): **96,94,94,94,93 92,87,86,83,—**
Tote Swingers: 1&2 £28.40, 1&3 £5.60, 2&3 £8.80 CSF £95.84 CT £563.31 TOTE £10.10: £2.80, £3.90, £2.20; EX 68.90.
Owner John P McManus **Bred** Rosemont Farm Llc **Trained** Cheltenham, Gloucs

FOCUS
Division two of this event was run at only a steady pace, and the time was the best part of five seconds slower than for division one. A step up from the winner on his previous British best.

NOTEBOOK
Grand Bay(USA) was a maiden going into this after 19 previous starts, including chases on his last three runs, but the 9yo finally broke his duck. He has flattered to deceive on many occasions, but this time scored comfortably under a patient ride, still only in a share of fourth place over the last before cutting down the leaders under hands and heels. This will have done his confidence no harm at all but it may be prudent not to count on him following up. (op 8-1 tchd 9-1)
Star Galaxy(IRE) won five times over fences in the latest season but had gone off the boil before this better effort. He seemed to like these brush hurdles and showed in front going to the last, only for the winner to claim him on the run-in. (op 14-1)
Festival Dreams, returning from a two-month break, wore cheekpieces in place of blinkers. In a narrow lead from halfway until the final flight, he rallied on the run-in and nearly grabbed second. (op 5-1 tchd 6-1)
Vintage Fabric(USA), having his first run since the autumn, has been shown some leniency by the handicapper and he stayed on again for fourth. (tchd 20-1)
Pips Assertive Way made a lot of the running and was still right there two from home, but could not race on from there. (tchd 5-2)
Diego Velasquez(IRE), who has been making the frame in west country point-to-points, was keeping on late on this return to hurdles for his new Irish yard. (op 6-1)
Lukie Victor(IRE), from the yard successful in the first division, has become very well handicapped on his best form of a year ago but will need to show more. (op 11-2 tchd 11-4)

647 LADBROKES BEGINNERS' CHASE (15 fncs) 2m 4f 110y
3:10 (3:10) (Class 4) 5-Y-0+ **£3,332** (£1,034; £557)

Form				RPR
33-U	**1**		**Silver Story**[18] 408 7-11-0 0........RichardJohnson (Tim Vaughan) *chsd ldrs: lft 2nd 4th: led next: hdd 7th: lft in ld next: blnd 4 out: sn hdd: led again 2 out: rdn out* **9/4**[2]	115+
2FP-	**2**	*7*	**Vic's World (IRE)**[45] 5342 8-10-4 92........HaddenFrost(3) (James Frost) *a.p: hmpd 8th: rdn to chse wnr last: styd on same pce* **9/1**	96
U45-	**3**	*18*	**Chevy To The Levy (IRE)**[328] 934 8-11-0 110........APMcCoy (John O'Shea) *hld up: hdwy 5th: mstke: hmpd and lft 2nd 8th: lft in ld after 4 out: hdd 2 out: wknd flat* **5/1**[3]	93
P	**F**		**My Fella (IRE)**[28] 218 7-10-9 102........JimmyDerham(5) (Seamus Mullins) *hld up: lost tch 11th: sn t.o: fell last* **20/1**	—
54	**U**		**Smart Dwellie**[3] 594 7-11-0 0........ColinBolger (Kevin Bishop) *led tl blnd and uns rdr 4th* **40/1**	—
1/4-	**F**		**Apartman (CZE)**[43] 5392 5-11-0 0........NickScholfield (Paul Nicholls) *chsd ldr tl lft in ld 4th: hdd next: led again 7th: fell next* **5/4**[1]	—

5m 16.4s (9.70) **Going Correction** +0.45s/f (Soft) **6** Ran SP% **109.1**
Speed ratings: **99,96,89,—,—,—**
Tote Swingers: 1&2 £3.10, 1&3 £4.10, 2&3 £12.20 CSF £19.51 TOTE £2.80: £1.90, £3.60; EX 11.60.
Owner N B Jones **Bred** The Earl Of Burlington **Trained** Aberthin, Vale of Glamorgan

FOCUS
A modest beginners' chase which took less winning following the fall of the favourite. The winner was value for further with the next two to their marks.

NOTEBOOK
Silver Story had unshipped his rider here last time and his jumping almost let him down again as he made a shuddering blunder at the last ditch, four from home. To his credit he was back in front two fences later and came away for a comfortable win. A return to 3m should play to his strengths. (op 5-2 tchd 2-1 and 3-1 in a place)
Vic's World(IRE) generally runs with credit when completing and this was another example as she stayed on for second. She is modest, but should pick up a small race one day. (tchd 10-1)
Chevy To The Levy(IRE) looked set to be the beneficiary when left in the lead by the winner's blunder four out, but could not hold on and was well held in the end. He looks very ordinary, but this was a satisfactory return after nearly a year off. (op 11-2 tchd 6-1 and 9-2)
Apartman(CZE) was making his chasing debut having been outclassed in a conditions hurdle at Sandown at the end of last season on his one previous run for the champion trainer. He was back in front, having been jumping soundly, when he took off too soon at the open ditch in the back straight. He appeared to be unhurt, but this nasty fall won't have done his confidence any good. (op 11-10)

648 LADBROKES INTERMEDIATE HURDLE (8 hdls) 2m
3:40 (3:40) (Class 4) 4-Y-0+ **£2,927** (£859; £429; £214)

Form				RPR
5-	**1**		**Ghimaar**[99] 4304 5-10-12 0........APMcCoy (Nicky Henderson) *chsd ldr tl led appr and hit 3 out: clr whn mstke last: easily* **7/2**[3]	134+
312-	**2**	*12*	**Now This Is It (IRE)**[245] 1624 6-11-2 127........CampbellGillies(3) (S R B Crawford, Ire) *chsd ldrs: mstke 4th: outpcd fr 2 out: wnt 2nd post* **13/8**[1]	124
34-4	**3**	*nse*	**Mohanad (IRE)**[20] 372 4-11-2 123........JamieGoldstein (Sheena West) *trckd ldrs: racd keenly: chsd wnr appr 3 out: rdn and wknd last: lost 2nd post* **9/4**[2]	121
20-F	**4**	*12*	**Kind Heart**[22] 331 4-10-9 112........JasonMaguire (Donald McCain) *led: rdn and hdd appr 3 out: wknd bef next* **8/1**	105
6-	**5**	*40*	**Calon**[44] 5363 4-9-9 0........MrJEngland(7) (Evan Williams) *hld up: rdn and wknd appr 3 out: t.o* **50/1**	60
-335	**P**		**Midnight Spirit**[16] 430 10-10-12 105........(tp) AnthonyFreeman(7) (Frederick Sutherland) *hld up: wknd 5th: t.o whn p.u bef 3 out* **14/1**	—
0-6	**U**		**Red Dagger (IRE)**[28] 224 4-10-9 0........GerardTumelty (Richard Price) *hld up: mstke 4th: wknd next: t.o whn blnd and uns rdr 2 out* **150/1**	—

3m 48.8s (1.50) **Going Correction** +0.25s/f (Yiel)
WFA 4 from 5yo+ 17lb **7** Ran SP% **111.5**
Speed ratings (Par 105): **106,100,99,93,73 —,—**
Tote Swingers: 1&2 £1.10, 1&3 £2.70, 2&3 £1.70 CSF £9.43 TOTE £6.40: £3.90, £1.10; EX 8.90.
Owner Martin George **Bred** Hunscote House Farm Stud **Trained** Upper Lambourn, Berks

FOCUS
The official going was belatedly amended to good to soft before this race. This was weakened by withdrawals but was still a reasonable intermediate hurdle. The pace was fairly steady. Solid form, with the easy winner value for further.

NOTEBOOK
Ghimaar had finished last of the five to get round on his jumping debut at Kempton in February, but that was in the Grade 2 Dovecote Hurdle and this was a considerable drop in class. Always up with the pace before leading on the home turn, he came right away for a very easy win, and this smart Flat performer for Dermot Weld is capable of rating higher in this sphere. On the downside, his jumping technique has room for improvement. (op 5-2)
Now This Is It(IRE) ◆ is trained in Ireland but has never run there. He travelled quite well but could not go with the leaders when the pace quickened up early in the home straight. Staying on after the last to grab second, strongly suggesting that this was too sharp for him, he can win again back over a more suitable trip. (op 5-2)
Mohanad(IRE) is a decent performer with an official rating of 123 and he appeared to run his race. He went after the winner off the home turn and although he quickly had no chance with that rival, he looked comfortably second best until caught for that position on the post. The ease in the ground may have been against him. (op 5-2 tchd 2-1)
Kind Heart, who took a crunching fall last time, made a lot of the running before weakening on the home turn. (op 13-2)

649 LADBROKES H'CAP CHASE (DIV I) (18 fncs) 2m 7f
4:10 (4:10) (Class 5) (0-90,90) 5-Y-0+ **£2,055** (£599; £299)

Form				RPR
050-	**1**		**Clifden Boy (IRE)**[355] 740 8-10-11 **75**........(b[1]) APMcCoy (Jim Best) *mde all: clr fr 12th: unchal: eased flat* **9/4**[1]	100+
226-	**2**	*21*	**Classic Rock**[81] 4679 11-11-7 **85**........(p) JimmyMcCarthy (James Unett) *chsd wnr thrght: rdn after 14th: styd on same pce* **11/1**	84
0-04	**3**	*19*	**Sarobar (IRE)**[19] 383 10-11-3 **81**........LiamTreadwell (John Spearing) *hld up: mstke 8th: wnt remote 3rd 4 out: nvr on terms: t.o* **10/1**	63
U1-5	**4**	*58*	**Ponchatrain (IRE)**[11] 475 10-11-12 **90**........GerardTumelty (Martin Keighley) *chsd ldrs tl rdn and wknd after 14th: fin tired: t.o* **5/1**[3]	20
060-	**5**	*19*	**Day Du Roy (FR)**[80] 4709 12-10-0 **64** oh3........PaddyAspell (Lynn Siddall) *wnt prom 4th: wknd 10th: t.o* **33/1**	—
24-5	**P**		**Rash Moment (FR)**[36] 95 11-11-6 **84**........(p) TomScudamore (Michael Scudamore) *hld up: hdwy appr 10th: wknd 12th: t.o whn p.u bef 14th* **9/1**	—
P5-0	**P**		**Reasonably Sure (IRE)**[32] 160 10-10-1 **72**........BrianToomey(7) (Patrick Morris) *prom to 8th: t.o fr 11th: p.u bef last* **12/1**	—
P-33	**P**		**The Iron Giant (IRE)**[14] 437 8-9-10 **67**........MissCareyWilliamson(7) (Diana Weeden) *hld up: bhd whn blnd 8th: t.o fr 12th: p.u bef last* **14/1**	—
55-6	**P**		**Dasher Reilly (USA)**[19] 381 9-10-1 **70**........JimmyDerham(5) (Aytach Sadik) *chsd ldrs: lost pl 4th: bhd fr 7th: t.o whn p.u bef 10th* **28/1**	—
005/	**P**		**Blejan Eyhre**[43] 8-10-5 **69**........PaddyBrennan (Tom George) *hld up: mstke 9th: pushed along and hdwy bef next: wknd 11th: t.o whn p.u bef 12th* **7/2**[2]	—

5m 57.8s (15.20) **Going Correction** +0.75s/f (Soft) **10** Ran SP% **117.8**
Speed ratings: **103,95,89,68,62 —,—,—,—,—**
Tote Swingers: 1&2 £6.60, 1&3 £6.20, 2&3 £17.10 CSF £27.73 CT £211.63 TOTE £3.20: £1.10, £4.00, £3.90; EX 35.80.
Owner The Jam Boys **Bred** Maurice Harrington **Trained** Lewes, E Sussex

FOCUS
A very weak handicap chase and not form to treat seriously, but the easy winner is rated to the level of his best hurdles form.

NOTEBOOK
Clifden Boy(IRE), off the track for nearly a year and previously trained by Sarah Robinson, made all the running on his debut for the Best yard. McCoy got him into a rhythm, jumping nicely in front, and the gelding drew away to score unchallenged. The first-time blinkers had a positive effect and he is likely to be seen out soon under a penalty. He would not want the ground any easier than this. (op 11-4 tchd 2-1)
Classic Rock chased the winner all the way and plugged on for a well beaten second. He is hard to win with but this was another solid run following a short break. (op 17-2)

Sarobar(IRE), who made a bad blunder at the second-last with a circuit to run, stayed on from the back to claim a remote third. (op 9-1)
Ponchatrain(IRE) was out on his feet in third as far out as the home turn. (op 11-2 tchd 6-1)
Day Du Roy(FR) Official explanation: trainer said gelding was found to be very stiff and jarred up on return home
Blejan Eyhre won a maiden point when last seen in April but made one or two mistakes and was eventually pulled up on this debut over regulation fences. (tchd 4-1)

650 LADBROKES H'CAP CHASE (DIV II) (18 fncs) 2m 7f
4:40 (4:41) (Class 5) (0-90,88) 5-Y-0+ **£2,055** (£599; £299)

Form RPR
3/43 **1** **Justabout**[20] [371] 7-11-3 **79**....(t) JoeTizzard 96
(Colin Tizzard) *chsd ldr: led 13th: rdn appr last: styd on u.p* **6/1**[3]
P5-4 **2** *5* **Whatcanisay**[33] [132] 11-10-5 **70**....(t) HaddenFrost(3) 82
(James Frost) *hld up: hdwy 14th: chsd wnr 3 out: hit next: rdn appr last: no imp flat* **7/2**[2]
542- **3** *dist* **Misamon (FR)**[15] 7-11-8 **84**.... PaulMoloney 65
(David Rees) *hld up: hdwy 12th: rdn and wknd after 14th: t.o* **9/4**[1]
25-4 **4** *1* **Monty's Moon (IRE)**[25] [278] 8-9-13 **68**....(b) MrBJPoste(7) 48
(Rachel Hobbs) *hld up: hdwy 6th: chsd wnr 13th: rdn whn blnd 4 out: sn wknd: t.o* **15/2**
/6P- **P** **Caislean Na Deirge (IRE)**[378] [448] 12-10-3 **72**....(p) MarkQuinlan(7) —
(Neil Mulholland) *led 3rd to 12th: wknd 14th: t.o whn p.u bef 4 out* **14/1**
06-4 **U** **Transvestite (IRE)**[19] [381] 8-11-12 **88**....(t) SamJones —
(Tor Sturgis) *bhd and nt fluent: detached whn blnd and uns rdr 11th* **33/1**
6P-P **P** **Rapid Return (IRE)**[7] [539] 7-11-6 **82**....(b[1]) RobertThornton —
(Richard Phillips) *chsd ldrs: lost pl and reminders 6th: bhd fr 8th: t.o whn p.u after next* **14/1**
6F/P **P** **Misttori Belle**[33] [132] 7-10-2 **64**....(t) TomO'Brien —
(Philip Hobbs) *hld up: hdwy 10th: hmpd and wknd 12th: t.o whn p.u bef 4 out* **8/1**
1P-0 **P** **Ilewin Tom**[38] [63] 7-10-4 **71**.... DonalDevereux(5) —
(Gary Brown) *led to 2nd: chsd ldrs tl j. slowly 11th: wknd next: t.o whn p.u bef 13th* **12/1**

6m 3.00s (20.40) **Going Correction** +0.75s/f (Soft) **9** Ran SP% **114.1**
Speed ratings: **94,92,80,79,**— —,—,—,—
Tote Swingers: 1&2 £3.60, 1&3 £2.30, 2&3 £3.40 CSF £27.84 CT £60.90 TOTE £4.60: £2.00, £1.10, £1.50; EX 19.90.
Owner Brocade Racing **Bred** H T Cole **Trained** Milborne Port, Dorset
■ Stewards' Enquiry : Joe Tizzard five-day ban: used whip in manner to cause gelding to be wealed (Jun 20, 22,23,25,27)

FOCUS
The second division of the staying chase and another desperate affair, slow compared with division one. The form is rated through the runner-up.

NOTEBOOK
Justabout, equipped with a tongue tie for the first time, made a lot of the running and, after looking to be idling in front, stayed on well from the last. The son of smart chaser Dubacilla has taken a long time to record his first ever win and it will be interesting to see if he can build on this. (op 5-1)
Whatcanisay has not been running badly and he plodded on dourly for second, but a mistake two from home ended lingering hopes that he might catch the winner. (op 9-2)
Misamon(FR) has been running quite well in open point-to-points this spring. Back under rules, he was never really travelling and was receiving reminders after the fifth, but kept going to secure a distant third. (op 3-1)
Monty's Moon(IRE), despite some sketchy jumping, looked a threat to the winner turning out of the back straight, only to weaken quickly from there. (op 8-1 tchd 7-1)
Ilewin Tom Official explanation: jockey said gelding failed to act on the good to soft ground

651 JOHN BARLOW 50TH BIRTHDAY CELEBRATION H'CAP HURDLE (12 hdls) 3m
5:10 (5:10) (Class 4) (0-115,115) 4-Y-0+ **£2,927** (£859; £429; £214)

Form RPR
000- **1** **Two Miles West (IRE)**[160] [3120] 9-11-8 **111**.... APMcCoy 123+
(Jonjo O'Neill) *hld up: hdwy 8th: chsd ldr after 4 out: led next: clr last: eased towards fin* **8/1**
4-44 **2** *4 ½* **Supreme Plan (IRE)**[20] [370] 7-11-7 **110**....(tp) JasonMaguire 111
(Kim Bailey) *hld up: hdwy after 4 out: chsd wnr 2 out: sn outpcd* **10/1**
/0-0 **3** *4 ½* **Timpo (FR)**[38] [55] 7-10-11 **100**.... RichardJohnson 97
(Henry Daly) *mid-div: hdwy 7th: led 4 out: sn rdn and hdd: outpcd bef next: kpt on flat* **20/1**
04-0 **4** *½* **Roisin's Prince (IRE)**[24] [302] 8-10-6 **95**....(t) AidanColeman 92
(Matt Sheppard) *hld up: hdwy 8th: outpcd after 4 out: styd on flat* **16/1**
640- **5** *15* **Deep Reflection**[73] [4849] 10-10-7 **101**....(v) JimmyDerham(5) 84
(Martin Keighley) *mid-div: hdwy 7th: led after 4 out: rdn and hdd next: wknd appr last* **10/1**
5-12 **6** *49* **Haldibari (IRE)**[26] [267] 6-11-3 **111**.... SamTwiston-Davies(5) 50
(Shaun Lycett) *chsd ldrs: led 4th to 6th: pushed along next: rdn and wknd after 4 out: t.o* **9/2**[2]
0-32 **7** *51* **Intac (IRE)**[20] [374] 8-11-4 **107**.... JoeTizzard —
(Colin Tizzard) *led to 4th: led 6th to appr 8th: wknd bef next: t.o* **8/1**
3/1- **P** **Island Arrow (IRE)**[402] [77] 9-11-4 **107**.... AndrewTinkler —
(George Baker) *hld up: a in rr: t.o whn p.u bef 8th* **12/1**
64-0 **P** **Dont Tell The Wife (IRE)**[21] [359] 7-10-9 **105**....(b) DavidBass(7) —
(Nicky Henderson) *chsd ldrs: nt fluent 4th and 5th: sn given reminders: led appr 8th: hdd & wknd bef next: t.o whn p.u bef last* **6/1**[3]
063- **P** **Ellen Tilley**[68] [4940] 6-11-7 **110**.... RobertThornton —
(Alan King) *chsd ldrs: pushed along 7th: wknd and p.u bef 9th* **4/1**[1]
4P0- **P** **Starlight Air**[162] [3021] 7-10-11 **100**.... LiamTreadwell —
(John Spearing) *prom tl p.u and dismntd bef 6th* **12/1**

5m 54.6s (10.00) **Going Correction** +0.55s/f (Soft) **11** Ran SP% **118.9**
Speed ratings (Par 105): **105,103,102,101,96 80,63,**—,—,—,—
Tote Swingers: 1&2 £12.30, 1&3 £37.30, 2&3 £38.90 CSF £85.75 CT £1553.08 TOTE £7.50: £3.00, £3.10, £7.60; EX 105.20.
Owner John P McManus **Bred** Tower Bloodstock **Trained** Cheltenham, Gloucs

FOCUS
A fair handicap hurdle run at a sound pace. The easy winner was value for further.

NOTEBOOK
Two Miles West(IRE) had not shown much on his last few starts and had been absent from the track since late December, but he had dropped to a mark just a pound higher than when scoring over course and distance last summer. Held up off the good gallop, he led early in the home straight and came away for a comfortable win, value for further. He will still be well handicapped on his best form after a rise for this but has never been too consistent and cannot be guaranteed to reproduce this level of performance. (op 10-1 tchd 7-1)
Supreme Plan(IRE) ◆ ran a fair race on this switch to handicap company and stamina is clearly his strong suit. He is still lightly raced over hurdles and is steadily getting his act together, so should get off the mark before long. (op 11-1 tchd 9-1)
Timpo(FR), dropped 5lb for this second run back after a break, stayed on under pressure for a soundly beaten third.
Roisin's Prince(IRE) was well held but did hint that he might have more stamina than had previously looked the case. (op 14-1)
Deep Reflection, who led briefly leaving the back straight, did not appear to see out the trip. (op 8-1)
Haldibari(IRE), in good form of late but a further 9lb higher this time, was one of three to help set a strong pace and he did not get home. Official explanation: jockey said gelding never travelled (op 4-1)
Island Arrow(IRE) Official explanation: jockey said gelding stopped quickly (op 9-2 tchd 5-1)
Ellen Tilley was beaten before her stamina for this trip could be put to the test. (op 9-2 tchd 5-1)
Starlight Air Official explanation: jockey said mare was struck into and lost its action (op 9-2 tchd 5-1)

652 NEU-SERVO H'CAP CHASE (12 fncs) 2m
5:40 (5:40) (Class 5) (0-95,97) 5-Y-0+ **£2,397** (£698; £349)

Form RPR
U-44 **1** **New Rackheath (IRE)**[7] [533] 7-10-6 **78**....(b[1]) DPFahy(3) 90+
(Evan Williams) *chsd ldr to 4th: remained handy: led 3 out: sn clr: rdn and idled flat: jst hld on* **5/1**[3]
0-P5 **2** *¾* **More Shennanigans**[12] [460] 9-10-1 **73**.... RyanMania(3) 80
(Jean McGregor) *prom: chsd ldr 4th tl led 8th: hdd 4 out: sn outpcd: styd on flat* **6/1**
3-1F **3** *nk* **My Condor (IRE)**[18] [404] 9-11-8 **91**....(p) JasonMaguire 98
(Donald McCain) *led to 8th: swtchd rt and outpcd bef 3 out: styd on flat* **7/2**[2]
40-U **4** *4* **Great Tsar (IRE)**[33] [136] 7-10-10 **79**....(v) RichardJohnson 84
(Tim Vaughan) *prom: mstke 6th: led appr 4 out: hdd next: sn outpcd* **3/1**[1]
P-65 **5** *4 ½* **Tilly Shilling (IRE)**[3] [590] 6-10-1 **70**....(b) RodiGreene 69
(Kevin Bishop) *hld up: drvn along 8th: nvr trbld ldrs* **6/1**
6P-0 **6** *2 ½* **Captain Marlon (IRE)**[7] [539] 9-11-11 **94**....(t) JoeTizzard 90
(Colin Tizzard) *hld up and bhd: r.o flat: nvr nr to chal* **8/1**
PP0/ **7** *61* **Mustamad**[440] [4683] 7-10-0 **69** oh2.... ColinBolger 4
(Chris Gordon) *chsd ldrs: drvn along 5th: wknd 7th: t.o whn j. bdly rt last 4 fences* **33/1**
60-6 **P** **Games (IRE)**[16] [427] 9-11-10 **93**.... JimmyMcCarthy —
(Christopher Kellett) *blnd 1st: sn bhd: t.o whn blnd 8th: sn p.u* **33/1**
3-P4 **P** **Tar (IRE)**[18] [402] 6-11-5 **95**.... MrTomDavid(7) —
(Tim Vaughan) *hld up: mstke 5th: t.o whn blnd 8th: sn p.u* **14/1**

4m 7.30s (15.70) **Going Correction** +0.75s/f (Soft) **9** Ran SP% **116.1**
Speed ratings: **90,89,89,87,85 83,53,**—,—
Tote Swingers: 1&2 £5.80, 1&3 £4.20, 2&3 £6.80 CSF £35.57 CT £117.05 TOTE £5.70: £2.30, £2.10, £1.60; EX 37.90 Place 6: £54.10 Place 5: £36.59.
Owner David M Williams **Bred** Andrew English **Trained** Llancarfan, Vale Of Glamorgan

FOCUS
A low-grade handicap which produced a slow-motion finish. The idling winner was value for further.

NOTEBOOK
New Rackheath(IRE) won off 6lb higher over course and distance for Chris Down at this fixture a year ago but had been well beaten in his recent outings. The first-time blinkers had a galvanising effect and the easier ground helped, but after taking it up three out he idled in front and did not win by as clear a margin as he had promised to. (op 9-2)
More Shennanigans, a Scottish raider, had been dropped 5lb since his latest start. He was outpaced by the leaders early in the home straight but rallied to go second at the last and was closing on the flagging winner at the line. (op 11-2 tchd 5-1 and 13-2)
My Condor(IRE), who had made the running to past halfway, plugged on to be beaten only a length or so in the end having seemed held. (op 4-1 tchd 9-2 and 5-1 in a place)
Great Tsar(IRE), a frustrating Great Tsar again made errors but he looked a threat at one stage and was still in second place heading down to the final fence. Official explanation: vet said gelding lost a right-fore plate (op 4-1)
T/Plt: £40.30 to a £1 stake. Pool: £72,675.05. 1,316.08 winning tickets. T/Qpdt: £9.10 to a £1 stake. Pool: £4,737.56. 382.52 winning tickets. CR

653 - 659a (Foreign Racing) - See Raceform Interactive

590 NEWTON ABBOT (L-H)
Monday, June 7

OFFICIAL GOING: Good (good to firm in places) changing to good (good to soft in places) after race 1 2:30
Hurdle course dolled out 3yds but impact on distances not quantified.
Wind: Strong across Weather: wet and windy

660 ATTHERACES SKY 415 H'CAP HURDLE (12 hdls) 3m 3f
2:30 (2:31) (Class 4) (0-105,104) 4-Y-0+ **£3,382** (£993; £496; £248)

Form RPR
02-2 **1** **Mac Halen (IRE)**[22] [359] 7-11-7 **102**.... DPFahy(3) 111+
(Evan Williams) *cl up: led after 3 out: clr next: wnt lft last: comf* **11/8**[1]
00-0 **2** *17* **Bubbs**[32] [172] 8-10-9 **87**.... RodiGreene 82
(Nick Ayliffe) *led tl 6th: w ldr: rdn whn nt fluent 9th: styd on to chse wnr 2 out but nvr any ch* **7/1**
22-0 **3** *3 ½* **Flag Flier**[26] [273] 7-10-7 **85**.... RichardJohnson 77
(Bob Buckler) *cl up: effrt after 3 out: one pce fr next* **7/2**[2]
P4-3 **4** *2 ¾* **Anadama (IRE)**[29] [223] 6-11-8 **100**.... RobertThornton 90
(Alan King) *trckd ldr: reminders after 8th: rdn after next: one pce fr after 3 out* **5/1**[3]
-P54 **5** *2 ¾* **A Haon A Do (IRE)**[8] [532] 8-9-10 **79**....(p) DonalDevereux(5) 66
(Gerald Ham) *trckd ldrs: led 6th: rdn and hdd after 3 out: fdd fr next* **16/1**
00-0 **6** *27* **Mrs Overall**[34] [134] 5-10-6 **84**.... HarrySkelton 65+
(Bob Buckler) *cl up: rdn appr 9th: wknd bef 2 out: t.o* **10/1**

6m 40.6s (-0.40) **Going Correction** +0.05s/f (Yiel) **6** Ran SP% **108.5**
Speed ratings (Par 105): **102,96,95,95,94 86**
toteswingers:1&2:£2.20, 1&3:£1.70, 2&3:£5.30 CSF £10.45 CT £23.59 TOTE £1.60: £1.10, £4.60; EX 10.50.
Owner Keith And Sue Lowry **Bred** Matthew Brady **Trained** Llancarfan, Vale Of Glamorgan

FOCUS
A modest race which didn't take much winning. The easy winner is rated back to his best.

NOTEBOOK
Mac Halen(IRE) cleared right away after three out to win with ease. Although 2lb higher than when second at Stratford latest, he had the most solid credentials of this lot, and he may progress a bit now he has finally won a race. (op 9-4)
Bubbs is back on a decent mark and ran much more encouragingly, although she was no match for the winner. (op 9-2)
Flag Flier bounced back from a poor effort at Exeter, although she was still beaten quite a long way. (op 4-1 tchd 3-1)
Anadama(IRE) failed to improve for the switch to handicaps. (op 11-4)
A Haon A Do(IRE) ran well for a long way, but did stop quickly once headed. (op 18-1 tchd 20-1)

Mrs Overall didn't improve as expected for the longer trip. (op 12-1 tchd 9-1)

661 ATTHERACES.COM WITH FREE TIMEFORM (S) HURDLE (8 hdls) 2m 1f
3:00 (3:01) (Class 5) 4-Y-0+ **£2,055** (£599; £299)

Form RPR
4-20 **1** **Captain Becket**[19] 410 7-10-11 95 HaddenFrost(3) 96
(James Frost) *hld up: rdn after 5th: hdwy after 3 out: chsd ldr bef next: 5 l 2nd and hld whn lft in ld after last: lucky* **6/1**[2]
2-44 **2** 4 ½ **Navajo Nation (IRE)**[8] 537 4-10-6 100 (p) TomO'Connor(5) 99+
(Bill Turner) *trckd ldrs: led after 3 out: 5 l clr and in command whn mstke: stmbld and slipped bdly last: sn hdd: nt rcvr* **12/1**
4P-0 **3** 8 **Fongoli**[8] 530 4-10-5 105 (b) AnthonyFreeman(7) 83
(Brendan Powell) *chsd ldrs: pushed along frequently: rdn after 5th: styd on same pce fr after 3 out* **16/1**
65/5 **4** 4 ½ **Querido (USA)**[4] 595 8-10-9 89 (t) JimmyDerham(5) 81
(Simon Burrough) *hld up: hdwy to trck ldr 5th: rdn and ev ch after 3 out: fdd next* **25/1**
22-5 **5** 4 ½ **Lady Pilot**[29] 227 8-10-7 113 APMcCoy 70
(Jim Best) *nvr travelling in rr: nvr any danger* **5/6**[1]
-420 **6** dist **Casual Style**[13] 462 4-10-4 95 (vt[1]) TomScudamore —
(David Pipe) *led: nt a fluent: rdn after 5th: hdd after 3 out: wknd qckly* **6/1**[2]
F-P **P** **Kauto The Kid (FR)**[27] 267 5-11-0 110 HarrySkelton —
(Paul Nicholls) *trckd ldr: rdn after 5th: wknd qckly after 3 out: p.u bef next* **17/2**[3]

4m 5.00s (-0.70) **Going Correction** +0.05s/f (Yiel)
WFA 4 from 5yo+ 17lb 7 Ran SP% **111.1**
Speed ratings (Par 103): **103,100,97,95,92** —,—
toteswingers:1&2:£7.20, 1&3:£11.40, 2&3:£14.10 CSF £63.58 TOTE £7.30: £3.20, £6.00; EX 55.30.There was no bid for the winner.
Owner Share My Dream **Bred** J D Frost **Trained** Scorriton, Devon

FOCUS
Not much of a selling hurdle and the outcome changed dramatically when Navajo Nation, who was clear and had the race in the bag, stumbled and slipped badly at the last, handing it to Captain Becket. The runner-up is rated a 6l winner.

NOTEBOOK
Captain Becket was booked for second when the leader blundered badly at the last. He had a bit on at the weights, but had finished runner-up off 85 over 3m at Exeter two starts back, and this trip looked a bit on the short side.
Navajo Nation(IRE), well beaten in this grade latest, had earlier finished fourth in a maiden hurdle at Plumpton, and he was set to score for the first time until getting the last all wrong. He should gain compensation at some point, but this was a golden opportunity squandered. (tchd 14-1)
Fongoli kept plugging away but looked hard work.
Querido(USA) is rated just 89, but did at least shape with a bit of promise. (op 16-1)
Lady Pilot, who was best in at the weights, proved most disappointing. She was never going a yard, and as her latest run also suggested, it looks like she's completely lost her form. Official explanation: trainer's rep had no explanation for the poor form shown (op 10-11 tchd Evens and 11-10 in places)
Casual Style did too much in the first-time visor and stopped very quickly having been headed. (tchd 9-2)
Kauto The Kid(FR) has done nothing since joining current connections and even this drop into selling company didn't help. (op 10-1 tchd 8-1)

662 ATTHERACES VIRGIN 534 NOVICES' HURDLE (8 hdls) 2m 3f
3:30 (3:30) (Class 3) 4-Y-0+ **£6,523** (£1,969; £1,014; £537)

Form RPR
412- **1** **Five Out Of Five (IRE)**[41] 37 6-11-4 115 (t) PaulMoloney 122+
(Evan Williams) *mde virtually all: rchd for 2nd: hit 3 out: hdd briefly: pushed clr gng to 2 out: comf* **8/11**[1]
P-1 **2** 12 **Red Twist**[27] 266 5-11-1 0 BernieWharfe(3) 112+
(Martin Hill) *hld up: hdwy to join wnr after 5th: rdn to ld briefly after 3 out: kpt on for clr 2nd but hld by wnr fr next* **9/2**[3]
65 **3** 12 **Sobre Tresor (FR)**[8] 538 4-10-8 0 DavidDennis 89
(Nigel Hawke) *trckd wnr tl after 5th: sn rdn: outpcd fr next: regained 3rd last* **25/1**
401- **4** 5 **Alhaque (USA)**[50] 5245 4-11-4 120 JamieMoore 95
(Gary Moore) *chsd ldrs: hit 3rd: rdn appr 6th: sn outpcd: wknd after 2 out: lost 3rd last* **11/4**[2]
P **Upstairs**[344] 6-10-5 0 MrRMahon(7) —
(Paul Henderson) *t.o 5th: sn p.u* **66/1**
P **Ogmore Junction (IRE)**[54] 5-10-12 0 RhysFlint —
(John Flint) *trckd ldrs: rdn after 5th: wknd next: p.u bef 3 out* **40/1**

4m 32.2s (-1.70) **Going Correction** +0.05s/f (Yiel)
WFA 4 from 5yo+ 17lb 6 Ran SP% **110.5**
Speed ratings (Par 107): **105,99,94,92**,—,—
toteswingers:1&2:£1.90, 1&3:£2.40, 2&3:£6.10 CSF £4.41 TOTE £1.50: £1.20, £2.40; EX 4.00.
Owner Mr & Mrs William Rucker **Bred** The Three Rivers Racing Syndicate **Trained** Llancarfan, Vale Of Glamorgan

FOCUS
This proved a rather comfortable success in the end for Five Out Of Five. Ordinary form with the first three running to their marks.

NOTEBOOK
Five Out Of Five(IRE)'s stamina really kicked in once straightening for home. Beaten when an odds-on favourite at Wincanton latest, the slower ground helped on this occasion, and regardless of whether he wins again or not over hurdles, he is going to make a fine chaser. (op 10-11tchd Evens in a place)
Red Twist could have done without the rain, but he still travelled well to a point. He was ultimately dropped by the winner, but will appreciate a return to further. (op 4-1 tchd 7-2)
Sobre Tresor(FR) plugged on late and will be of much more interest once handicapping. Official explanation: jockey said gelding lost its action (tchd 33-1)
Alhaque(USA), withdrawn from Worcester the previous day, could have done without the rain and he never looked like winning, coming under strong pressure before fading and losing out on third. (op 5-2 tchd 3-1)

663 ATTHERACES.COM ROYAL ASCOT MEGASITE H'CAP CHASE (16 fncs) 2m 5f 110y
4:00 (4:00) (Class 4) (0-115,115) 5-Y-0+ **£4,033** (£1,184; £592; £295)

Form RPR
3P-2 **1** **Presentandcorrect (IRE)**[17] 427 9-11-7 115 SamTwiston-Davies(5) 123
(Nigel Twiston-Davies) *wnt rt 1st: trckd ldrs: rdn into narrow ld 2 out: styd on u.str.p: all out* **6/1**[3]
U4-0 **2** ½ **Alroyal (GER)**[33] 148 11-10-9 105 MrDGPrichard(7) 112
(Phillip Dando) *hld up: tk clsr order to trck ldrs 9th: rdn after 4 out: styd on wl fr last: wnt 2nd and clsng on wnr nring fin* **10/1**
FP-1 **3** nk **Magical Harry**[32] 169 10-11-3 106 AidanColeman 113
(Anthony Honeyball) *led after 2nd: rdn after 3 out: narrowly hdd next: ch last: no ex: lost 2nd nring fin* **9/4**[1]
0-43 **4** dist **Hereweareagain (IRE)**[17] 429 7-11-10 113 (bt) TomO'Brien —
(Philip Hobbs) *led tl after 2nd: trckd ldr tl nt fluent 4 out: sn rdn: wkng whn awkward next (water)* **9/2**[2]
324- **P** **On You Go (IRE)**[271] 1418 9-11-10 113 APMcCoy —
(Jonjo O'Neill) *hld up: reminders after 9th: cl enough whn rdn after 11th: wknd 4 out: bhd whn p.u bef 2 out* **9/2**[2]
20-6 **P** **Sula's Legend**[32] 169 9-10-11 107 MarkQuinlan(7) —
(Neil Mulholland) *sn pushed along in last pair: wknd 4 out: bhd whn p.u bef 2 out* **9/2**[2]
564- **P** **Coup De Tabac (FR)**[179] 2796 6-10-13 102 (t) DavidDennis —
(Nigel Hawke) *trckd ldrs: struggling whn slow jump 10th: sn bhd: t.o whn p.u bef 4 out* **12/1**

5m 26.5s (5.10) **Going Correction** +0.375s/f (Yiel) 7 Ran SP% **116.4**
Speed ratings: **105,104,104**,—,—,—,—
Swingers:1&2:£14.50, 1&3:£3.30, 2&3:£7.30 CSF £59.56 TOTE £8.90: £4.00, £6.50; EX 77.30.
Owner Robroy Racing 2 **Bred** Daniel N O'Donovan **Trained** Naunton, Gloucs

FOCUS
No more than a modest handicap chase, made up of exposed chaser, but it produced a really good finish. The winner is rated back to his best.

NOTEBOOK
Presentandcorrect(IRE), still a maiden over fences coming into this, had run well at Towcester on his return from a break and showed the benefit of that outing here, edging ahead two out and grimly holding on. (op 11-2)
Alroyal(GER), who has been running in hunter chases, is a previous C&D winner, and he really came home well, but never quite looked like getting up. (op 14-1 tchd 16-1)
Magical Harry, raised 11lb for last month's ready course success, could easily have backed out of it once joined by the winner, but he kept grinding away and did enough to suggest he is capable of scoring off this mark. (op 11-4 tchd 3-1and 10-3 in a place)
Hereweareagain(IRE) finished very tired at Towcester on his latest start and was again found wanting in the latter part of the race. (op 6-1)
On You Go(IRE) was under pressure early and proved disappointing. (op 7-2)
Sula's Legend never loked like winning and was eventually pulled up. (op 7-2)

664 ATTHERACES.COM FREE RACE REPLAYS H'CAP HURDLE (8 hdls) 2m 1f
4:30 (4:31) (Class 4) (0-115,115) 4-Y-0+ **£3,382** (£993; £496; £248)

Form RPR
F6-1 **1** **Battle Group**[22] 360 5-11-4 107 TomScudamore 118+
(David Pipe) *patiently rdn in rr: smooth hdwy after 5th: jnd ldr travelling wl after 3 out: led next: sn hung lft: mstke last: r.o strly: readily* **10/3**[2]
0-01 **2** 3 **Stumped**[8] 534 7-10-13 107 7ex JimmyDerham(5) 111+
(Milton Harris) *hld up: hdwy after 3 out: wnt 2nd next: sn rdn: kpt on but nt pce of wnr* **3/1**[1]
F3P- **3** 6 **O'Toole (IRE)**[247] 1605 11-11-7 115 GilesHawkins(5) 111
(Caroline Keevil) *led: mstke 3rd: hdd on long run to 5th: rdn bef 3 out: kpt on same pce* **28/1**
0U3- **4** ½ **Pool Of Knowledge (FR)**[77] 4786 4-10-10 102 AidanColeman 94
(Venetia Williams) *trckd ldrs: led after 3 out: rdn and hdd bef next: kpt on same pce* **3/1**[1]
030/ **5** hd **Moon Star (GER)**[11] 2919 9-11-7 115 MichaelMurphy(5) 110
(Barry Brennan) *w ldr: rdn after 5th: styd chsng ldrs: kpt on same pce fr 2 out* **6/1**[3]
0F-0 **6** 14 **Like A Duke (FR)**[21] 372 7-11-6 109 JoeTizzard 93
(Colin Tizzard) *racd keenly: trckd ldrs: led on long run to 5th: rdn and hdd after 3 out: wknd qckly* **8/1**
0-00 **7** 15 **Henry Hook (IRE)**[9] 527 6-10-11 100 JamieMoore 69
(Victor Dartnall) *t.k.h early: hld up: struggling after 4th: wknd after 3 out: t.o* **16/1**
465- **8** ½ **Darfour**[28] 2686 6-10-6 98 BernieWharfe(3) 66
(Martin Hill) *hld up: hdwy 5th: sn rdn: wknd after 3 out: t.o* **10/1**

4m 5.20s (-0.50) **Going Correction** +0.05s/f (Yiel)
WFA 4 from 5yo+ 17lb 8 Ran SP% **116.9**
Speed ratings (Par 105): **103,101,98,98,98 91,84,84**
toteswingers:1&2:£2.90, 1&3:£9.00, 2&3:£15.60 CSF £14.53 CT £237.32 TOTE £3.70: £1.60, £1.60, £7.20; EX 11.80.
Owner Jolly Boys Outing **Bred** Juddmonte Farms Ltd **Trained** Nicholashayne, Devon

FOCUS
A modest handicap hurdle that was won in ready fashion by Battle Group, despite blundering his way through the last. He is on the upgrade.

NOTEBOOK
Battle Group won this with plenty in hand, despite blundering his way through the last. Cosy winner of a novices' hurdle at Stratford latest, an opening mark of 107 looked fair, and he could be called the winner before they reached the straight. The switch to hold-up tactics has been the making of this former highly strung sort, and though a sizeable rise will follow, it would be no surprise were he to go in again. (op 3-1 tchd 5-2 and 7-2 in places and 4-1 in a place)
Stumped, shouldering a 7lb penalty for last week's Fontwell success, moved into a challenging position before the straight, but he proved no match for the winner. (op 7-2 tchd 4-1)
O'Toole(IRE), who was returning from a 247-day absence, shaped encouragingly. Ideally suited by quick ground, and better over fences, he could be one to watch out for in the coming weeks. (op 16-1 tchd 33-1)
Pool Of Knowledge(FR) came there travelling best three out, but he was strongly pressed before the straight and finished rather weakly. He will do better on a genuinely fast surface. (op 7-2)
Moon Star(GER) kept on without ever looking the winner on this return to hurdles. (op 11-1)
Like A Duke(FR) isn't a natural hurdler, but is merely getting his confidence back before returning to fences (had major problems with his jumping). (op 17-2)

665 ATTHERACES.COM BE A VIRTUAL OWNER CONDITIONAL JOCKEYS' H'CAP CHASE (20 fncs) 3m 2f 110y
5:00 (5:01) (Class 5) (0-95,92) 5-Y-0+ **£2,764** (£811; £405; £202)

Form RPR
6-46 **1** **Classic Clover**[8] 540 10-11-11 91 (t) SamTwiston-Davies 107+
(Colin Tizzard) *trckd ldrs: rdn appr 14th: led 16th: drew clr after 3 out: kpt up to work* **8/1**
2-53 **2** 14 **El Batal (IRE)**[20] 383 9-10-13 85 (p) AnthonyFreeman(6) 80
(Sean Curran) *mid-div: slow jump 7th: reminder: sn in rr: rdn after 14th: styd on fr 2 out: wnt 2nd run-in: nvr any ch w wnr* **5/1**[3]
12-6 **3** 1 **You Can Of Course (IRE)**[38] 83 7-10-6 80 (v) MarkQuinlan(8) 74
(Neil Mulholland) *mid-div: hdwy 14th: rdn to chse wnr after 4 out: no ch fr after next: lost 2nd run-in* **7/2**[1]
6-1U **4** nk **Overton Lad**[12] 471 9-11-3 83 (b) HarrySkelton 81+
(Peter Pritchard) *prom: nt fluent 4th (water): mstke 12th: sn drvn: led after next: mstke 14th: hdd 16th: one pce fr after 4 out* **4/1**[2]

0/0- **5** *1* **Zi Missile (IRE)**[396] 191 6-10-1 70 DPFahy(3) 65
(Evan Williams) *hld up: hdwy 13th: trcking ldrs whn clipped heels and stmbld on bnd after 14th: rdn after 4 out: plugged on: hit 2 out and last* **10/1**

P00- **6** *20* **Wasntme (IRE)**[45] 5361 7-11-5 85 (bt) HaddenFrost 66
(Colin Tizzard) *mid-div tl dropped in rr 10th: nvr a danger after: wknd after 3 out* **20/1**

54/5 **7** *12* **Knightsbridge Hill (IRE)**[32] 183 8-10-2 71 (p) KeiranBurke(3) 41
(Patrick Rodford) *trckd ldrs: rdn after 10th: wknd 15th: t.o* **16/1**

005/ **P** **Lord Lescribaa (FR)**[23] 7-11-0 83 (b1) RhysFlint(3) —
(Philip Hobbs) *led: mstke 11th (water): hdd after 13th: prom whn hmpd on bnd after 14th: wknd after 16th: p.u bef 3 out* **6/1**

606- **P** **Know Your Place**[196] 2470 6-11-9 92 RichieMcLernon(3) —
(Jonjo O'Neill) *hld up: blnd 8th: hdwy whn mstke 14th: sn rdn: wknd next: p.u bef 16th* **17/2**

P0-4 **P** **Brookfieldshector (IRE)**[26] 280 6-10-2 68 (t) MichaelMurphy —
(Mike Hammond) *a towards rr: bhd whn p.u bef 16th* **12/1**

6m 56.2s (11.60) **Going Correction** +0.375s/f (Yiel) **10** Ran SP% **122.2**
Speed ratings: **97,92,92,92,92 86,82,—,—,—**
toteswingers:1&2:£7.60, 1&3:£7.20, 2&3:£3.50 CSF £51.10 CT £170.61 TOTE £9.10: £2.40, £1.60, £2.10; EX 67.10 Place 6 £530.57; Place 5 £314.88.
Owner John and Heather Snook **Bred** M H Ings **Trained** Milborne Port, Dorset

FOCUS
Few got into this low-grade handicap chase. The easy winner is rated value for further and to the level of his best old form.

NOTEBOOK
Classic Clover, a well-beaten sixth at Uttoxeter last week, had the cheekpieces left off and he seemed to appreciate taking a lead early on. Having gone on before three out, though, he started to come clear, and was ridden out to win with plenty in hand. He's going to receive a hit from the handicapper now, however, and it would be a surprise were he to follow up. (tchd 9-1)
El Batal(IRE), 11lb below his last winning mark, improved on his recent Towcester third, but was still well beaten. (op 6-1 tchd 9-2)
You Can Of Course(IRE) travelled well, but didn't really find for pressure and ended up well held, losing out on second late in the day. (op 6-1)
Overton Lad threw in a few sloppy jumps, but did keep on dourly to his credit, in the end just missing out on the places.
Zi Missile(IRE), making her chase debut, ran better than the bare form suggests, stumbling and making a couple of mistakes when trying to close. Her trainer may get a win out of her yet. (op 11-1 tchd 12-1 and 9-1)
Lord Lescribaa(FR), who has generally been doing well in points, had first-time blinkers on for this return to rules, and he was in trouble soon after getting slightly hampered. (op 9-2)
Know Your Place never got into it and was disappointing under top weight. (op 9-2)
T/Plt: £207.20. to a £1 stake. Pool:£72,240.03 - 254.40 winning tickets T/Qpdt: £14.50. to a £1 stake. Pool:£5,334.26 - 270.70 winning tickets TM

666a - 673a (Foreign Racing) - See Raceform Interactive

[327]BANGOR-ON-DEE (L-H)
Tuesday, June 8

OFFICIAL GOING: Good (good to soft in places; 7.8)
Hurdle track at widest configuration, chase course at winter alignment and shared bends.
Wind: Almost nil Weather: Partly cloudy developing to showers

674 TRACY WILLIAMS BIRTHDAY JUVENILE HURDLE (9 hdls) 2m 1f
6:50 (6:50) (Class 4) 3-Y-O **£3,425** (£998; £499)

Form RPR

1 **Beyond (IRE)**[92] 3-10-12 0 APMcCoy 90+
(Evan Williams) *sn led: hdd 2nd: wandered arnd most of way: distracted by running out ldr and lft in ld 4th: clr appr last: easily* **8/13**[1]

2 *11* **Glen Lass**[57] 3-10-5 0 (p) DarylJacob 70+
(Jamie Snowden) *hld up: hmpd and mstke 1st: mstke 3rd: effrt and hdwy to chse ldrs appr 3 out: wnt 2nd bef 2 out: no ch w wnr bef last* **5/1**[2]

3 *5* **Gulf Punch**[2] 3-10-2 0 PeterToole(3) 63
(Milton Harris) *in rr: struggling after 5th: blnd 3 out: plugged on u.p but no imp* **28/1**

4 *17* **Clayton Flick (IRE)**[14] 3-10-12 0 HarrySkelton 58
(Andrew Haynes) *hld up racing keenly: hdwy after 4th: chsd wnr and nt fluent 5th: lost 2nd appr 2 out: wknd long bef last* **33/1**

R **High Holborn (IRE)**[45] 3-10-12 0 TomScudamore —
(David Pipe) *chsd ldr: nt fluent 1st: led 2nd: rn out and uns rdr 4th* **5/1**[2]

P **Gypsy Jazz (IRE)**[45] 3-10-5 0 (t) AlanO'Keeffe —
(Jennie Candlish) *plld hrd: prom: wandered appr 1st: remained in tch: bdly hmpd and by loose horse after 4th: bhd after: t.o whn p.u bef 2 out* **14/1**[3]

U **Dinkie Short**[98] 3-10-5 0 DavidBass(7) —
(Ben De Haan) *hld up: hdwy whn nt fluent 4th: sn chsd wnr tl 5th: wandered and uns rdr 4 out* **40/1**

F **Snore No More (IRE)**[44] 3-10-9 0 RyanMania(3) —
(Stuart Coltherd) *prom: hmpd 1st: j. sideways and fell 2nd* **66/1**

U **Sefton Park**[19] 3-10-12 0 (b) PaddyBrennan —
(Charles Egerton) *in tch: mstke and hmpd 1st: j. awkwardly and uns rdr 4th* **16/1**

4m 17.2s (6.30) **Going Correction** 0.0s/f (Good) **9** Ran SP% **118.1**
Speed ratings: **85,79,77,69,— —,—,—,—**
toteswingers: 1&2 £1.40, 1&3 £6.30, 2&3 £13.20 CSF £4.24 TOTE £1.20: £1.02, £1.90, £7.00; EX 3.70.
Owner R J H Geffen **Bred** Pat Fullam **Trained** Llancarfan, Vale Of Glamorgan

FOCUS
There were incidents aplenty in this juvenile contest, and one could be forgiven for thinking that none of these had ever seen a hurdle before. It was slowly run and is not form to dwell on, for all that the winner has potential.

NOTEBOOK
Beyond(IRE) was kept up the front and out of trouble, and cruised home for an easy success. A promising sort on the Flat, winning two of his three starts, he should learn a good deal from this and, though he ultimately beat little, it would be a surprise were he not to defy a penalty. (tchd 4-6)
Glen Lass, a five-time winner in claiming company on the Flat, had little go her way, being hampered on a couple of occasions, but the winner was in a different league anyway. She too will be much wiser with this run under her belt. (op 7-1)
Gulf Punch, an 18-race maiden on the Flat who had run at Brighton only two days earlier, plugged on for third, but didn't shape with any obvious promise for the future.
Clayton Flick(IRE), another without a win on the Flat, looked a doubtful stayer on this hurdles debut and was the last of those to finish, not getting home having raced keenly.
High Holborn(IRE), a Flat maiden sold for £5,000, was plenty keen enough, even after he had been allowed to stride on, and he ran out at the fourth. (op 9-2 tchd 7-2)
Gypsy Jazz(IRE), badly hampered by a loose horse running away after the fifth, was set to finish last until being pulled up before two out. (op 9-2 tchd 7-2)
Dinkie Short, rated 53 on the Flat, still appeared to have plenty of running left in him when being put off by the loose horse ducking and unseating his rider coming into the fourth-last. He may well have been second. (op 9-2 tchd 7-2)
Snore No More(IRE) took a really awkward-looking fall at the second. (op 9-2 tchd 7-2)
Sefton Park, an expensive failure on the Flat, jumped sketchily and got rid of his rider at the fourth. (op 9-2 tchd 7-2)

675 JUNE H'CAP HURDLE (9 hdls) 2m 1f
7:20 (7:20) (Class 3) (0-120,112) 4-Y-O+ **£5,204** (£1,528; £764; £381)

Form RPR

0-03 **1** **Danny Zuko (IRE)**[10] 515 7-11-5 105 (b1) JasonMaguire 112+
(Donald McCain) *in tch: hit 4 out: rdn after 3 out and lft abt 9 l 2nd: prog u.p appr 2 out: rdn to ld jst bef last where nt fluent: styd on towards fin* **7/2**[3]

001- **2** *1 3/4* **Marc Aurele (IRE)**[42] 41 5-11-3 110 (t) MrRMahon(7) 114
(Paul Nicholls) *led: clr 5th: lft abt 9 l clr after 3 out: rdn and hdd jst bef last where mstke: kpt on same pce and hld towards fin* **3/1**[2]

214/ **3** *10* **Garrulous (UAE)**[538] 3030 7-11-7 107 RichardJohnson 101
(Tim Vaughan) *chsd ldrs: rdn whn sltly hmpd 3 out: sn wknd* **17/2**

3P0- **4** *8* **Phoenix Eye**[218] 2038 9-10-10 103 BrianToomey(7) 90
(Michael Mullineaux) *nt fluent: hld up: struggling 3 out: sn wl btn* **25/1**

24-0 **5** *shd* **Obara D'Avril (FR)**[8] 313 8-10-2 93 PaulCallaghan(5) 80
(Simon West) *hld up: struggling 3 out: nvr landed a blow* **8/1**

5-11 **U** **Ajman (IRE)**[7] 566 5-10-11 100 7ex (t) DPFahy(3) 104+
(Evan Williams) *chsd ldr: abt 6 l down whn overj.: stmbld and uns rdr 3 out* **7/4**[1]

4m 7.80s (-3.10) **Going Correction** 0.0s/f (Good) **6** Ran SP% **109.1**
Speed ratings (Par 107): **107,106,101,97,97** —
toteswingers: 1&2 £2.30, 1&3 £7.00, 2&3 £7.10 CSF £13.74 TOTE £4.20: £2.10, £2.50.
Owner Gilbert, Pattison and Rooney **Bred** Mrs Siobhan O'Connor **Trained** Cholmondeley, Cheshire

FOCUS
They went a decent gallop in what was an ordinary handicap hurdle. The winner was back to form and the second close to his mark, while the unseater was probably headed for another best.

NOTEBOOK
Danny Zuko(IRE), a previous C&D winner, had finished third in a selling hurdle at Cartmel latest, but was only 2lb higher than when last winning. However, the application of first-time blinkers enabled him to get his head back in front, chasing down the long-time leader and just staying on the better despite a few untidy jumps. (op 6-1)
Marc Aurele(IRE) ◆ appreciated being allowed to stride on when winning at Wincanton last time and he looked very capable of winning this off 110. However, the rain wouldn't have been in his favour, and he was eventually worn down. He remains capable of better back on a faster surface, and his aggressive style should be rewarded back on a more speed-favouring track. (op 9-4)
Garrulous(UAE) didn't fare too badly on this return from a lengthy absence and his new trainer is likely to get a win out of him at some stage. (op 9-2)
Ajman(IRE) may well have completed the hat-trick had he not skidded on landing and unseated his rider a few strides after three out. Penalised for his Ffos Las victory, he had just gone in pursuit of the runner-up when departing, and was a few lengths ahead of the eventual winner, so would surely have gone close. (op 15-8)

676 1ST BATALLION THE ROYAL WELSH H'CAP CHASE (12 fncs) 2m 1f 110y
7:50 (7:50) (Class 4) (0-115,113) 5-Y-O+ **£4,553** (£1,337; £668; £333)

Form RPR

1-21 **1** **Chicago Alley**[23] 353 9-10-4 96 LeeEdwards(5) 112+
(Tony Carroll) *racd w plenty of zest: led appr 2nd: mde rest: a looked in full control fr 4 out: clr after last: easily* **85/40**[2]

55-1 **2** *7* **Seeyaaj**[27] 290 10-11-12 113 (t) PeterBuchanan 114
(Lucinda Russell) *trckd ldrs: chsd wnr appr 7th tl bef 3 out and again bef 2 out: no ch bef last* **13/2**

532- **3** *1 3/4* **Kilkenny All Star (IRE)**[48] 5313 9-11-6 112 ShaneByrne(5) 110
(Sue Smith) *led: hdd appr 2nd: chsd wnr tl bef 7th and again bef 3 out tl bef 2 out: u.p and wl btn appr last* **7/4**[1]

5-63 **4** *6* **Jim Tango (FR)**[20] 395 6-11-11 112 (b) JasonMaguire 105
(Donald McCain) *racd keenly: hld up: pushed along bhd ldrs appr 2 out: no imp and wl hld sn after* **9/1**

-133 **5** *30* **Coach Lane**[16] 444 9-11-7 108 AidanColeman 74
(Venetia Williams) *hld up: niggled along appr 4 out: outpcd after 3 out: dropped away* **9/2**[3]

4m 23.0s (0.90) **Going Correction** 0.0s/f (Good) **5** Ran SP% **109.9**
Speed ratings: **98,94,94,91,78**
CSF £14.69 TOTE £2.20: £1.10, £2.30.
Owner Lavender Hill Stud L L C **Bred** Mrs J L Egan **Trained** Cropthorne, Worcs

FOCUS
What had looked a tight little handicap chase was actually won with ease by in-form mare Chicago Alley, who was value for further. The pace was only steady.

NOTEBOOK
Chicago Alley, who despite pulling hard even when allowed to stride on, powered away from her rivals. It hadn't been the plan to lead, but nothing else wanted to, and at least connections now know she can make the running if necessary. Both previous wins had been over further than this, but she is clearly versatile with regards to distance too, and though she can expect another rise, she may be up to defying it in this current mood. (op 11-4)
Seeyaaj, up 6lb for his Perth victory, was attempting to concede 17lb to the winner, and although he stayed on best for second, he was well and truly put in his place by the mare. (op 7-2)
Kilkenny All Star(IRE), just denied at Southwell last time, was up 3lb and seemed happy to take a lead off the winner, but he was then made to look very one-paced at the business end. (op 11-4)
Jim Tango(FR) was ridden with more restraint than usual, a tactic which didn't seem to suit the 6-y-o, who found little when asked to close. (op 13-2 tchd 6-1)
Coach Lane appears to be losing his form following a good spell earlier in the year. (tchd 5-1)

677 EDWARD SYMMONS H'CAP CHASE (15 fncs) 2m 4f 110y
8:20 (8:20) (Class 4) (0-100,100) 5-Y-O+ **£4,228** (£1,241; £620; £310)

Form RPR

/4-P **1** **Neutrino**[12] 489 8-11-10 98 (v) TomScudamore 118+
(David Bridgwater) *in tch: led 4 out: clr appr 2 out: easily* **11/1**

-464 **2** *14* **Wee Forbees (IRE)**[13] 472 8-11-12 100 DenisO'Regan 103+
(Michael Easterby) *led: hdd 11th: chsd wnr 3 out: u.p and no imp fr bef 2 out* **6/1**

P-4B **3** *2* **Bold Policy (IRE)**[29] 250 7-11-4 95 (p) PeterToole(3) 95
(Milton Harris) *in rr: niggled along appr 9th: outpcd fr 3 out: plugged on to take 3rd bef last: one pce* **9/1**

324- **4** *2 1/2* **Pipers Legend**[190] 2608 11-11-2 90 (b) AidanColeman 88
(Sarah Humphrey) *chsd ldr: led 11th: hdd 4 out: rdn and wknd after 3 out* **11/2**

06-2 **5** *19* **Morenito (FR)**[13] 475 7-11-7 **95**....................(p) PaddyBrennan 85
(Tom George) *chsd ldrs: hmpd 9th: effrt to chal 11th: wknd appr 2 out* **7/4**[1]

66-4 **P** **Thenameescapesme**[21] 382 10-11-6 **94**.................... JasonMaguire —
(Kim Bailey) *hld up: j. slowly 9th: sn dropped away: t.o whn p.u bef 4 out* **5/1**[3]

U435 **U** **Janal (IRE)**[13] 473 7-9-11 **74** oh5.................... RyanMania(3) —
(Stuart Coltherd) *chsd ldrs tl blnd bdly and uns rdr 3rd* **4/1**[2]

5m 6.10s (-3.00) **Going Correction** 0.0s/f (Good) **7** Ran SP% **121.0**
Speed ratings: **105,99,98,97,90** —,—
toteswingers:1&2 £20.30, 2&3 £10.90, 1&3 £20.60 CSF £77.09 CT £634.21 TOTE £21.40: £10.70, £6.50; EX 130.30.
Owner Building Bridgies **Bred** D R Wellicome **Trained** Icomb, Gloucs

FOCUS
This was just a modest handicap chase lacking strength in depth. The winner is rated back to his best.

NOTEBOOK
Neutrino hasn't always looked the most genuine, but he received a nice ride from Tom Scudamore, who sent him on soon after four out, and the pair galloped clear to win easily. Given his inconsistent profile, it's hard to say what he'll do next time, but as he'll be carrying extra weight, the percentage call would be to oppose. Official explanation: trainer's representative said, regarding the apparent improvement of form, that the gelding appeared to have benefitted from the refitting of a visor (op 10-1 tchd 9-1)
Wee Forbees(IRE) ran well on this return to fences, leading for quite a bit of the race before hitting a brief flat spot and then staying on again. (op 8-1)
Bold Policy(IRE), who has been running over hurdles, had yielded one fair effort from four previous tries over fences, but all he could manage here was a laboured third. (op 10-1 tchd 11-1)
Pipers Legend was beaten soon after he was headed four out. (op 6-1 tchd 5-1)
Morenito(FR) made a few mistakes and couldn't repeat his recent Southwell second, looking unsuited by the rain that fell. Official explanation: jockey was unable to offer any explanation for the poor performance shown (op 2-1 tchd 9-4 in places)
Thenameescapesme was particularly disappointing, dropping right out before being pulled up. (op 6-1)
Janal(IRE) got no further than the third. (op 6-1)

678 RACING EXCELLENCE "HANDS AND HEELS" NOVICES' H'CAP HURDLE (CONDITIONALS AND AMATEURS') (9 hdls) 2m 1f
8:50 (8:50) (Class 4) (0-105,103) 4-Y-0+ **£3,903** (£1,146; £573; £286)

Form RPR

-012 **1** **Seaquel**[5] 598 4-11-2 **96**....................(v) EdGlassonbury 102+
(Andrew Haynes) *mde all: shkn up appr last: styd on wl* **9/4**[1]

35P- **2** *3 1/2* **Wisteria Lane (IRE)**[208] 2244 7-9-11 **77** oh2.................... AdamWedge(3) 80
(Anabel L M King) *chsd ldrs: wnt 2nd 5th: pushed along and no imp on wnr fr 2 out* **8/1**

P5-2 **3** *5* **Himrayn**[34] 154 7-11-7 **101**.................... MrOJMurphy(3) 101
(Anabel L M King) *hld up: nt fluent 4 out: pushed along and hdwy whn nt fluent 3 out: kpt on same pce fr 2 out* **7/1**

00-3 **4** *nse* **Apache Chant (USA)**[8] 554 6-11-12 **103**.................... AodhaganConlon 101
(Tony Carroll) *in tch: effrt to chse ldrs 4 out: kpt on same pce fr 2 out* **5/1**[3]

0-6F **5** *5* **Marino Prince (FR)**[30] 228 5-10-13 **90**....................(b[1]) TrevorWhelan 84
(Barry Leavy) *hld up: niggled along appr 4 out and outpcd: plugged on u.p but no imp fr 2 out* **17/2**

0-U6 **6** *8* **Danzig Fox**[10] 527 5-10-1 **81**.................... GaryRutherford(3) 69
(Michael Mullineaux) *plld hrd: prom: pushed along 5th: wknd after 3 out* **33/1**

60-3 **7** *6* **Points Of View**[18] 430 5-11-9 **103**.................... JasonFavell(3) 87
(Kim Bailey) *t.k.h: hld up: carried hd awkwardly: hdwy appr 5th: blnd 4 out: nt fluent 3 out: sn wknd* **6/1**

500- **8** *1/2* **Santo Thomas (FR)**[72] 4913 4-11-4 **98**.................... MarkQuinlan 78
(Venetia Williams) *hld up: pushed along 4 out: outpcd after 3 out* **9/2**[2]

5/0- **9** *76* **Arch**[359] 435 7-11-7 **98**....................(t) MrGCrow 11
(A M Crow) *chsd ldr to 5th: sn wknd: t.o* **66/1**

4m 11.2s (0.30) **Going Correction** 0.0s/f (Good)
WFA 4 from 5yo+ 17lb **9** Ran SP% **118.5**
Speed ratings (Par 105): **99,97,95,94,92 88,86,85,50**
toteswingers: 1&2 £7.60, 1&3 £2.20, 2&3 £17.50 CSF £21.58 CT £111.95 TOTE £2.50: £1.10, £4.20, £2.20; EX 52.20.
Owner Allan Drewett **Bred** Michael E Broughton **Trained** Limpley Stoke, Bath

FOCUS
Not much of a race and in-form mare Seaquel led throughout. She was thrown in on her Uttoxeter effort and was a bit off that here.

NOTEBOOK
Seaquel is in good form and led throughout. She has been competing at a lower level, winning and then finishing second just five days ago in selling company, but she was in full control of this from some way out and stayed on well to score despite a mistake at the last. She won't pick up a penalty, so can compete off the same mark for now and will no doubt be out again shortly. (op 10-3)
Wisteria Lane(IRE), racing from 2lb out of the handicap, stuck on well on this return from a 208-day absence but was always coming off second-best. (op 12-1)
Himrayn, runner-up in a novice hurdle at Huntingdon last month, made a satisfactory handicap debut and looks sure to find a small race at some point. (op 8-1)
Apache Chant(USA) looked vulnerable under top weight and was comfortably held. (op 6-1 tchd 7-1)
Santo Thomas(FR) made mistakes and would probably have been better off had it not rained. He's sure to come good at some point, and deserves another chance. (tchd 4-1)

679 BANGORONDEERACES.CO.UK NOVICES' HURDLE (11 hdls) 2m 4f
9:20 (9:20) (Class 4) 4-Y-0+ **£2,927** (£859; £429; £214)

Form RPR

233- **1** **Spirit Of Adjisa (IRE)**[108] 4152 6-10-12 119.................... RichardJohnson 125+
(Tim Vaughan) *sn led: clr and in full control whn mstke 2 out: v easily* **8/15**[1]

5-21 **2** *24* **Worth A King'S**[24] 337 4-11-8 119.................... JasonMaguire 115+
(Donald McCain) *sn chsd wnr: reminder appr 4 out: no ch fr bef 2 out* **9/4**[2]

64-3 **3** *8* **Flicka's Witness (IRE)**[38] 93 5-10-9 0.................... AdrianLane(3) 96
(Donald McCain) *plld hrd: prom: blnd bdly 3rd and gd rcvry fr rdr: hit 5th: wknd appr 3 out* **9/1**[3]

4 *dist* **Twentypoundluck (IRE)**[44] 5-10-12 0.................... HarrySkelton 63
(Patrick Griffin, Ire) *hld up: rdn appr 3 out: sn dropped away* **16/1**

0-0 **5** *91* **Betty's Run**[38] 92 8-10-5 0.................... WillKennedy —
(Lynn Siddall) *hld up: pushed along appr 6th: t.o bef 7th* **125/1**

4m 55.8s (-1.60) **Going Correction** 0.0s/f (Good) **5** Ran SP% **112.7**
Speed ratings (Par 105): **103,93,90**,—,—
CSF £2.22 TOTE £1.30: £1.10, £1.70; EX 2.00 Place 6: £211.40 Place 5: £161.86.
Owner Darr, Johnson, Weston & Whitaker **Bred** C J Haughey J Flynn And E Mulhern **Trained** Aberthin, Vale of Glamorgan

FOCUS
An uncompetitive novice hurdle. The progressive winner can rate higher on Flat form.

NOTEBOOK
Spirit Of Adjisa(IRE) looked a very strong favourite, especially in receipt of 10lb from the runner-up, and he made just about all for an easy success. His jumping wasn't as fluent as it might have been, but he is a fair sort for time of year and looks sure to defy a penalty. (op 4-7 tchd 1-2 and 8-13 in places)
Worth A King'S, winning for the second time at Uttoxeter last month, faced a very tough task against the favourite at the weights and was well and truly put in his place. (op 2-1 tchd 5-2)
Flicka's Witness(IRE), who blundered badly at the third, has plenty of scope about him and it was no disgrace that two ex-Flat racers proved too good for him. He was well held, but isn't going to reach his potential until he goes chasing. (op 10-1 tchd 12-1)
Twentypoundluck(IRE) was readily outpaced and looks in need of time. (op 18-1 tchd 20-1)
T/Plt: £82.90 to a £ stake. Pool:£72,927.30 - 642.05 winning tickets T/Qpdt: £34.80 to a £ stake. Pool:£6,187.56 - 131.40 winning tickets DO

475 SOUTHWELL (L-H)
Tuesday, June 8

OFFICIAL GOING: Good (good to soft in places; 8.0)
Golf Club bend 5m inside, home straight bend 5m outside line utilised on May 26th.
Wind: almost nil Weather: cool and cloudy

680 BET WORLD CUP FOOTBALL - BETDAQ H'CAP CHASE (21 fncs) 3m 2f
6:05 (6:05) (Class 4) (0-115,114) 5-Y-0+ **£3,577** (£1,050; £525; £262)

Form RPR

P-63 **1** **The Artful Fox**[10] 517 9-9-9 **88** oh24.................... SamTwiston-Davies(5) 98
(Mike Sowersby) *settled towards rr: effrt after 18th: rdn and disp 2nd 3 out: jnd ldr last: led on nod* **14/1**

41-3 **2** *nse* **Midnight Gold**[14] 467 10-11-7 **114**....................(p) DonalDevereux(5) 125+
(Peter Bowen) *trckd ldrs: j. slowly 11th: led gng wl bef 3 out: drvn and jnd last: pipped on post* **10/3**[1]

00-5 **3** *8* **Bill's Echo**[10] 524 11-11-12 **114**....................(b) DougieCostello 120+
(Alistair Whillans) *dropped out last: mstke 5th: effrt after 18th: disp 2nd gng wl 3 out: ev ch next: fnd nil whn rdn and sn btn* **11/2**

-313 **4** *4* **Mutual Respect (IRE)**[13] 475 8-11-3 **105**.................... PaulMoloney 106
(Evan Williams) *nt fluent 3rd: hit 13th: trckd ldrs: shkn up bef 2 out: sn btn* **7/2**[2]

63-5 **5** *6* **Teenando (IRE)**[14] 456 10-10-1 **89**.................... TjadeCollier 83
(Sue Smith) *nt a fluent: prom: rdn 15th: tdd bef 3 out* **8/1**

01P- **6** *1* **Simply Smashing (IRE)**[46] 5373 10-10-9 **104**....................(t) KyleJames(7) 99
(Philip Kirby) *prom: pushed along 7th: 2nd and drvn whn mstke 15th: sn struggling: last at 18th* **4/1**[3]

4-10 **P** **Lindseyfield Lodge (IRE)**[23] 353 9-10-4 **92**....................(p) JamieMoore 87
(Robert Johnson) *taken down early: led and 20 l clr early: tended to jump rt: pressed fr 14th: drvn and hdd bef 3 out: sn lost pl: p.u last* **8/1**

7m 3.10s (24.30) **Going Correction** +0.475s/f (Soft) **7** Ran SP% **109.6**
Speed ratings: **81,80,78,77,75 75**,—
toteswingers: 1&2 £10.30, 1&3 £12.00, 2&3 £3.90 CSF £56.30 TOTE £26.30: £14.70, £1.10; EX 110.20.
Owner Mrs E A Verity **Bred** F T Gibbon And Son **Trained** Goodmanham, E Yorks

FOCUS
A very ordinary handicap and a big step up from the surprise winner.

NOTEBOOK
The Artful Fox had to be kept interested by his jockey and was driven up to hold a challenging position, but he still had plenty left. Meeting the last on a good stride, he had enough impetus to hold off the second in a battle to the line. He was 24lb out of the handicap here due to having shown very little in his chasing career under rules, but the light weight made just enough difference. Despite his connections' surprise, some late market support suggested that someone thought he could do better. (op 25-1)
Midnight Gold has been in good form over hurdles this spring, and made a bold attempt to convert that form off a slightly higher mark over fences. He was travelling best of all up the straight, but the winner had a bit more momentum as well as a weight advantage, and that proved the difference. (op 3-1)
Bill's Echo did not jump at all fluently, but he still managed to make good progress from the rear of the field to emerge as a challenger in the home straight. However, when he needed a good jump at the last, he did not find it and could not recover. He has taken time to come into form since a year-long layoff, but finally looks to be getting there. That said, his jumping is a worry, even though he might need faster ground. (op 5-1 tchd 6-1)
Mutual Respect(IRE) began to come under pressure in the back straight and ran a bit flat, not helped by the 9lb higher mark imposed since gaining his first win over fences last month. (op 3-1)
Simply Smashing(IRE) looked like a big danger until clouting one in the back straight, after which his jumping went to pieces. He might need stiffer tracks to show his best. (op 5-1 tchd 7-2)

681 BET MULTIPLES - BETDAQ H'CAP CHASE (16 fncs) 2m 4f 110y
6:35 (6:35) (Class 4) (0-115,119) 5-Y-0+ **£3,768** (£1,098; £549)

Form RPR

1-32 **1** **Putney Bridge**[7] 564 8-11-2 **105**....................(tp) TomO'Brien 125+
(Keith Goldsworthy) *mde all: hit 8th: 6 l clr whn mstke 3 out: pushed out: unchal* **10/11**[1]

4F-1 **2** *23* **Baren De Doc (IRE)**[8] 556 7-11-9 **119** 7ex....................(p) MrTomDavid(7) 119
(Tim Vaughan) *nvr really gng wl and nt a fluent: rdn to chse wnr fr 11th: wl hld bef 3 out* **9/2**[2]

4-F0 **3** *18* **Magellan Straits**[14] 460 6-10-11 **100**.................... TjadeCollier 83
(Sue Smith) *cl up: u.p 11th: lost tch 13th: wnt poor 3rd bef 3 out: t.o* **13/2**

0P-P **4** *43* **The Hollow Bottom**[18] 431 9-10-8 **102**.................... SamTwiston-Davies(5) 46
(Nigel Twiston-Davies) *chsd wnr tl after 9th: j. slowly 10th and rdn: sn struggling: t.o bef 3 out* **10/1**

-U21 **P** **Bushwacker (IRE)**[18] 429 6-10-13 **107**.................... JimmyDerham(5) —
(Seamus Mullins) *in tch: hit 8th and 9th: mstke 12th: lost poor 3rd bef 3 out: 4th whn p.u next* **5/1**[3]

5m 22.2s (7.20) **Going Correction** +0.475s/f (Soft) **5** Ran SP% **109.7**
Speed ratings: **105,96,89,73**,—
CSF £5.52 TOTE £1.60: £1.02, £4.20; EX 5.60.
Owner Mrs L A Goldsworthy **Bred** I Norman **Trained** Yerbeston, Pembrokes

FOCUS
A modest handicap. The winner stepped up on his previous chase form.

NOTEBOOK
Putney Bridge jumped well bowling along in the lead and though the pace did not look that strong, his rivals began to drop away on the final circuit. Despite a small blunder in the home straight, he was far enough clear not to be troubled. This was his first win over fences, but he showed he had the ability after getting caught on the run-in at Ffos Las last week and on this track he had no trouble seeing out the trip. He holds several entries, including at Stratford on Sunday, and reportedly is better on firmer ground. (op 11-8)

Baren De Doc(IRE) finally gained his first chase win last week and looked well treated for a follow-up victory if he could translate Towcester form to this tight track so soon after his last race. However, his jumping let him down and, though he tried to catch the winner, he had given away too much of an advantage to be a serious threat. (tchd 5-1)

Magellan Straits tracked the winner for a way until finding the pressure too much and he weakened in the back straight. His best form over hurdles was on soft ground and he might need similar over fences. (op 9-1 tchd 6-1)

The Hollow Bottom tracked the winner until the final circuit, but soon dropped tamely away. He had something to prove after being pulled up in his last two outings and that remains the case. (op 8-1 tchd 11-1)

Bushwacker(IRE) was travelling quite well and was making some headway when a blunder in the back straight stopped him in his tracks and he was eventually pulled up. (op 11-4)

682 MEMBERSHIP AT SOUTHWELL GOLF CLUB H'CAP HURDLE (11 hdls) 2m 4f 110y

7:05 (7:05) (Class 4) (0-115,115) 4-Y-0+ **£2,740** (£798; £399)

Form RPR

00-1 **1** **Cannon Fire (FR)**[2] 645 9-10-0 **89** oh2 .... PaulMoloney 109+
(Evan Williams) *settled 3rd: jnd ldr 6th: led gng easily next: drew rt away bef 2 out: heavily eased fnl 100yds* **4/9**[1]

2P-4 **2** *27* **Elk Trail (IRE)**[23] 350 5-11-3 **106** .... (p) RodiGreene 92
(Michael Mullineaux) *drvn at various stages: nvr really travelling: led briefly 6th: chsd wnr and clr of rest after next: no ch bef 2 out* **15/2**[3]

P-06 **3** *1* **Rien A Perdre (FR)**[9] 534 9-11-2 **105** .... JodieMogford 89
(Graeme McPherson) *nt fluent 2nd: led tl hdd 6th: drvn to ld again sn after: hdd 7th: wknd and mstke next: 20 l 3rd bef 2 out* **10/1**

/0U0 **4** *nk* **Option Money (IRE)**[12] 494 8-10-11 **100** .... AndrewThornton 83
(Peter Salmon) *last pair: rdn and lost tch bef 7th: plugged on after 2 out and catching remote plcd horses after last* **25/1**

2/0- **P** **Welcome Stranger**[204] 2332 10-10-13 **109** .... PeterHatton(7) —
(Louise Davis) *chsd ldrs: wknd qckly 7th: t.o and p.u 2 out* **40/1**

24-P **P** **Edgefour (IRE)**[16] 440 6-11-2 **105** .... TomO'Brien —
(Ben Case) *last pair: rdn 6th: t.o 7th: mstke next: p.u 2 out* **7/1**[2]

5m 20.4s (9.70) **Going Correction** +0.475s/f (Soft) **6 Ran SP% 108.9**
Speed ratings (Par 105): **100,89,89,89,—** —
toteswingers: 1&2 £1.30, 1&3 £1.80, 2&3 £3.20 CSF £4.29 TOTE £1.40: £1.10, £5.40; EX 3.80.
Owner R E R Williams **Bred** Gilles And Mrs Forien **Trained** Llancarfan, Vale Of Glamorgan

FOCUS
An uncompetitive event dominated by a well-handicapped favourite, who was value for further and is rated in line with his best 2009 hurdles form.

NOTEBOOK
Cannon Fire(FR) travelled supremely well throughout, eased into the lead in the back straight and sauntered clear without encountering a challenge. He spent the winter in the doldrums but after a spring break bounced back to form to take advantage of a career-low mark two days earlier and was all the rage to follow up. His trainer was anxious to capitalise quickly especially as the 9-y-o escaped a penalty for that earlier win before the handicapper could act. (tchd 1-2 in places)

Elk Trail(IRE) was keen, held back from the early lead and began to feel the pressure with a circuit to go, but he kept responding as best he could until tiring in the straight. This was a valiant effort but he did not stay and was up against a lightly weighted and well-handicapped winner in any case. (op 8-1 tchd 7-1)

Rien A Perdre(FR) led until the final circuit and plugged on once headed, but the dual hunter chase winner lacks pace over hurdles. (op 8-1 tchd 15-2)

Option Money(IRE) made up some ground to gain on the early leader, but was never competitive. He has been struggling to find any form over hurdles this spring and, while this was a little bit better, he still has some way to go to make use of his falling handicap mark. (tchd 28-1)

Edgefour(IRE) put in a laboured effort and was eventually pulled up. Official explanation: vet said that the mare had an elevated heart and respiratory rate for a significant period after the race (op 8-1)

683 BETDAQ THE BETTING EXCHANGE "NATIONAL HUNT" NOVICES' HURDLE (9 hdls) 2m

7:35 (7:35) (Class 4) 4-Y-0+ **£2,740** (£798; £399)

Form RPR

623- **1** **Lady Soughton (IRE)**[64] 5030 5-10-5 0 .... RobertThornton 93+
(Tim Vaughan) *lft in ld 4th: gng best bef 2 out: 6 l clr last: readily* **11/4**[2]

3-16 **2** *2 3/4* **Oursininlaw (IRE)**[10] 514 6-11-5 110 .... PaulMoloney 101
(Evan Williams) *hld up: nt fluent 5th and rdn: drvn to chse wnr bef 2 out: no imp after: racing unwillingly w high hd carriage* **4/6**[1]

U **3** *10* **Humbel Lad (IRE)**[5] 596 6-10-2 0 .... CraigGallagher(10) 84
(Richard Guest) *cl up tl rdn and lost tch after 3 out: plodded on* **66/1**

006- **4** *15* **Princess Laila (IRE)**[233] 1814 5-10-5 0 .... DougieCostello 62
(Ian Williams) *t.k.h in rr: wknd bef 2 out* **16/1**

0 **5** *4* **Buckden (IRE)**[30] 238 6-10-12 0 .... TjadeCollier 67
(Sue Smith) *t.k.h early: lft 2nd at 4th: nt fluent 3 out and rdn: lost 2nd bef 2 out and mstke there whn wkng* **25/1**

F-6 **U** **Day Time Run (IRE)**[34] 154 6-10-9 100 .... AlexMerriam(3) —
(Diana Grissell) *led at modest pl tl veered bef 4th: looked to run out and dumped rdr on landing side* **7/1**[3]

4m 4.50s (7.40) **Going Correction** +0.475s/f (Soft) **6 Ran SP% 110.4**
Speed ratings (Par 105): **100,98,93,86,84** —
toteswingers: 1&2 £1.10, 1&3 £10.80, 2&3 £8.90 CSF £4.97 TOTE £4.20: £1.80, £1.02; EX 3.90.
Owner Owen Promotions Limited **Bred** Forenaghts Stud And Dermot Cantillon **Trained** Aberthin, Vale of Glamorgan

FOCUS
A weak novice event in which the winner improved to his bumper mark.

NOTEBOOK
Lady Soughton(IRE) was the one to benefit from a canny ride, taking up the running on the final circuit before injecting some pace before the home turn that caught her rivals flat-footed. She quickly opened up a gap and kept up the gallop so that two minor blunders at the final two flights did little to dent her advantage. She was well beaten on her hurdling debut in April, but that was on heavy ground and she looked much more at ease on better going, though she will do well to defy a penalty next time. (op 15-8 tchd 7-4)

Oursininlaw(IRE) had won over nearly a mile further last month, so was vulnerable trying to defy a penalty if there was a lack of pace. As the winner stretched for home he was caught out, but rallied to be gaining close home, though the winner was too far clear by that stage. Returning to a longer trip might help. (op 6-5 tchd 5-4)

Humbel Lad(IRE) was keen racing wide of the pack, but had no answer once the winner had quickened away and could only stay on at one pace. He has been out of form in points this spring and unseated his jockey on his hurdling debut, so this represents an improvement. (tchd 50-1)

Princess Laila(IRE) was very keen on her first start since October, but made a bit of headway before tiring and should come on for this hurdling debut. (op 10-1)

Buckden(IRE), making his hurdling debut, was under pressure from some way out and tired before the last and failed to improve on his sole bumper run a month ago. (tchd 20-1)

684 SOUTHWELL-RACECOURSE.CO.UK MARES' MAIDEN HURDLE (11 hdls) 2m 4f 110y

8:05 (8:05) (Class 5) 4-Y-0+ **£2,260** (£659; £329)

Form RPR

20-3 **1** **Alpine Breeze (IRE)**[24] 327 4-10-10 0 .... LeightonAspell 109+
(Don Cantillon) *settled in 3rd pl: wnt 2nd after 3 out: jnd ldr next: led narrowly and wavered nring last: drvn and hung lft flat: asserted cl home* **2/1**[1]

522/ **2** *1 1/4* **Rith Bob (IRE)**[58] 7-11-0 102 .... PaulMoloney 113+
(David Rees) *led at brisk pce: pckd bdly 8th: drvn and jnd 2 out: hdd last: battled on v gamely but hld whn hmpd 75yds out* **5/1**[2]

10- **3** *21* **Pickworth (IRE)**[60] 5114 5-10-7 0 .... KyleJames(7) 91
(Philip Kirby) *sn off the bridle: reminders after 1st: bhd tl rdn and hdwy 6th: last of four w ch 3 out: lost tch qckly bef next* **12/1**

0-2 **4** *25* **Railway Diva (IRE)**[20] 412 6-11-0 0 .... RobertThornton 69
(Tim Vaughan) *cl up: pressed ldr fr 7th tl fdd bdly after 3 out: t.o* **5/1**[2]

5 *10* **The Great Outdoors (IRE)**[73] 4900 6-11-0 0 .... JackDoyle 60
(Sarah Humphrey) *midfield: rdn after 6th: t.o next* **80/1**

3P4- **6** *6* **Tenawa**[48] 5317 8-11-0 89 .... AndrewThornton 54
(Karen George) *mounted on crse: chsd ldrs: rdn and lost tch 6th: t.o next* **20/1**

/06- **7** *50* **Arctic Flow**[61] 5103 6-10-9 0 .... IanPopham(5) 9
(Caroline Keevil) *chsd ldrs tl rdn after 6th: t.o after next: fin eventually* **125/1**

P **Le Petit Vigier**[31] 4-10-10 0 .... (t) PaddyAspell —
(Patrick Holmes) *chsd ldrs tl hrd rdn after 6th: t.o and j. slowly next: p.u 2 out* **200/1**

P0/U **P** **Silver Sonnet**[9] 535 7-11-0 0 .... CharliePoste —
(Ben Case) *stopped to nil after 6th: t.o and p.u next* **66/1**

/0P- **U** **Moscow Jewel (IRE)**[96] 4399 6-10-9 0 .... JohnKington(5) —
(Richard Price) *blnd bdly and uns rdr 1st* **80/1**

50-2 **P** **Naughty Naughty**[21] 379 5-11-0 100 .... JimmyMcCarthy —
(Brendan Powell) *chsd ldrs: rdn after 6th: t.o next: p.u 2 out* **11/2**[3]

240- **P** **Himitas (FR)**[284] 1322 5-11-0 0 .... JodieMogford —
(Graeme McPherson) *j. slowly 2nd: last at 3rd: sme hdwy after 6th: nvr nr ldrs: poor 6th 3 out: t.o and p.u 2 out* **22/1**

5-P **P** **Ingenue**[13] 478 4-10-10 0 .... (bt) JamieMoore —
(Paul Howling) *blnd 1st: last tl 3rd: t.o 7th: p.u 2 out* **33/1**

652- **P** **Desolait**[43] 27 5-10-9 0 .... (t) SamTwiston-Davies(5) —
(Nigel Twiston-Davies) *pressed ldr tl 6th: rdn and lost pl next: poor 5th 3 out: t.o and p.u 2 out* **9/1**

5m 15.9s (5.20) **Going Correction** +0.475s/f (Soft)
WFA 4 from 5yo+ 18lb **14 Ran SP% 117.0**
Speed ratings (Par 103): **109,108,100,91,87 84,65,—,—,— —,—,—,—**
toteswingers: 1&2 £4.00, 1&3 £8.10, 2&3 £9.60 CSF £10.85 TOTE £2.50: £1.30, £2.20, £4.50; EX 13.00.
Owner Don Cantillon **Bred** D E Cantillon **Trained** Newmarket, Suffolk

FOCUS
A weak mares' maiden where the first pair dominated. They both produced improved form.

NOTEBOOK
Alpine Breeze(IRE) was always within striking distance of the leader and moved out to challenge on the home turn, but could not cruise past and had to get the better of a determined battle to score. She showed some greenness by veering towards the inside rail after the last and squeezed up the second, but already held the advantage. Having shown promise in bumpers she has now transferred that ability to hurdles. Her trainer confirmed that, like her dam, she is a tough character, but will be off for a summer break now. (op 7-2 tchd 15-8)

Rith Bob(IRE) set a good pace. Despite diving at the middle one down the back, she soon regained her momentum to try valiantly to repel the sustained challenge of the winner when getting squeezed against the rail after the last. But it would not have made a difference to the outcome. The winner of four minor points this year, she looks up to winning under rules as well. (op 9-2 tchd 6-1)

Pickworth(IRE) was driven along for a long way but stuck to it to chase the leaders round the final turn until having no more to give in the straight. A winner of a Catterick bumper, she has since switched stables and should improve for this hurdling debut. (op 14-1 tchd 16-1)

Railway Diva(IRE) raced prominently and challenged in the back straight, but her effort soon petered out and, after showing some promise in bumpers and Irish points, more might have been expected. (op 4-1)

Naughty Naughty Official explanation: jockey said that the mare was never travelling

Himitas(FR) Official explanation: jockey that the mare jumped awkwardly and was never travelling thereafter

Desolait Official explanation: very said that the mare had a breathing problem

685 BOOK TICKETS ONLINE AT SOUTHWELL-RACECOURSE.CO.UK H'CAP HURDLE (13 hdls) 3m 110y

8:35 (8:35) (Class 3) (0-135,130) 4-Y-0+ **£6,505** (£1,910; £955; £477)

Form RPR

0FP- **1** **Valley Ride (IRE)**[163] 3083 10-11-4 **127** .... (p) DonalDevereux(5) 132+
(Peter Bowen) *trckd ldrs: gng wl 3 out: drvn bef next where disp 2nd: led last: styd on wl* **6/1**

36-4 **2** *1 1/2* **Tension Point**[20] 396 6-10-9 **118** .... (t) MissLHorner(5) 121
(Chris Grant) *settled cl last: pushed along after 8th: led on outer after 3 out and sn 3 l clr but rdn: hdd last: hung rt whn hld flat* **5/1**

-063 **3** *4* **Barnhill Brownie (IRE)**[11] 503 7-10-4 **115** .... (t) MrSParish(7) 114
(Philip Hobbs) *plld hrd: cl up: led bef 9th: nt fluent 10th and rdn: hdd after 3 out: disp 2nd and ev ch 2 out: wknd qckly bef last* **7/2**[3]

4-2F **4** *8* **Silverburn (IRE)**[26] 302 9-11-12 **130** .... PaulMoloney 123
(Evan Williams) *set mod pce tl hdd and nt fluent 9th: drvn and btn after 3 out* **11/4**[2]

P2-3 **5** *68* **Manadam (FR)**[25] 318 7-10-8 **112** .... CharliePoste 63
(Anthony Middleton) *prom: rdn and dropped out tamely bef 3 out: eased next: t.o after* **9/4**[1]

6m 33.9s (26.40) **Going Correction** +0.475s/f (Soft) **5 Ran SP% 110.6**
Speed ratings (Par 107): **76,75,74,71,49**
CSF £32.90 TOTE £16.80: £10.70, £1.40; EX 40.60.
Owner Saith O Ni & Ednyfed & Elizabeth Morgan **Bred** Patrick Doyle **Trained** Little Newcastle, Pembrokes

FOCUS
A fair little handicap, and easy form to rate.

NOTEBOOK

Valley Ride(IRE) travelled well and his rider waited patiently to deliver his challenge. It took a while for him to get on top once asked for an effort, but he always looked likely to prevail and eventually wore down his rival to win quite cosily. This was his first outing since pulling up at Kempton in December, so although he can go well fresh he may just have needed this. He was a decent chaser last year who lost his way after scoring at Market Rasen in September, but he has been given plenty of time to recover and connections were able to capitalise on his lower rating over hurdles. The plan now is an entry in the Summer National at Uttoxeter. (op 4-1 tchd 15-2)

Tension Point was niggled along from an early stage and was never going that well, but he found a second wind coming to the home turn to move into the lead. He did everything in his power to repel the winner but ultimately may have hit the front too soon. He was well handicapped on his best form and has hit form again, cementing his good run at Kelso last time in a good time. If he continues in this vein he might again be interesting in the handicap hurdle on Summer Plate day at Market Rasen next month. (op 4-1 tchd 6-1)

Barnhill Brownie(IRE) was too keen in the race and his young jockey had quite a time holding on to him, but he was still there until the home straight. The reapplication of the tongue-tie seems in his favour and he looks as if he is coming into form. (tchd 11-4)

Silverburn(IRE) has been in the wilderness for a long while, but hinted at a return to some sort of form when second at Exeter last month before taking a heavy fall at Ludlow next time. Setting a comfortable pace, he seemed to be going well enough until weakening tamely in the back straight, and that glimmer seems to have dulled again. (op 3-1 tchd 5-2)

Manadam(FR), on his first start for new connections, was well supported but was under pressure in the back straight and could not go with them. The market move might suggest that more is to come, but he has been running below his handicap level for a year now. (op 10-3 tchd 2-1)

686 PLAY GOLF AT SOUTHWELL GOLF CLUB MARES' STANDARD OPEN NATIONAL HUNT FLAT RACE — 2m

9:05 (9:05) (Class 6) 4-6-Y-0 — **£1,507** (£439; £219)

Form				RPR
4-1	**1**		**With Grace**[24] 333 5-11-0 0 DonalDevereux(5) (Peter Bowen) *trckd ldrs gng wl: led 3f out: clr over 1f out: galloped on stoutly* **7/2**[2]	110+
3	**2**	*6*	**Alaska River (IRE)**[20] 412 4-10-9 0 MarkGrant (Brendan Duke) *chsd ldrs: rdn over 3f out: wnt 2nd 1f out: no ch w wnr* **11/1**	92
	3	*2 ½*	**Music In The Air** 6-10-12 0 CharliePoste (Robin Dickin) *prom: rdn 5f out: led 4f out tl hdd and chsd wnr vainly 3f out: lost 2nd 1f out: plugged on* **66/1**	92
0-2	**4**	*4*	**Diamond MM (IRE)**[24] 333 4-10-9 0 BrianHughes (Alan Swinbank) *t.k.h chsng ldrs: effrt 4f out: 3rd and shkn up 3f out: little rspnse: btn wl over 1f out* **11/10**[1]	85
3	**5**	*2 ½*	**Landenstown Pearl (IRE)**[27] 284 4-10-4 0 JimmyDerham(5) (Seamus Mullins) *bhd: looked outpcd 1/2-way: effrt to chse clr ldng quartet 3f out: unable to chal* **18/1**	83
	6	*10*	**Helena Of Troy** 4-10-9 0 TjadeCollier (Sue Smith) *led at slow pce for 6f: prom tl rn green and wknd 4f out: t.o* **33/1**	73
3	**7**	*hd*	**Bachley Gale**[7] 568 5-10-12 0 RhysFlint (Keith Goldsworthy) *chsd ldrs: rdn 5f out: sn btn: t.o* **12/1**	75
	8	*½*	**Nonobu (UAE)** 4-10-9 0 AndrewTinkler (George Baker) *hld up: effrt 1/2-way: wknd 4f out: poor 6th st: t.o* **5/1**[3]	72
	9	*11*	**Pocket Rocket Too** 6-10-9 0 AlexMerriam(3) (Neil King) *struggling 1/2-way: t.o* **40/1**	64
	10	*7*	**Kissing Lessons** 5-10-5 0 MrRichardCollinson(7) (Patrick Leech) *chsd ldrs: fdd bdly wl over 3f out: t.o* **50/1**	57
	11	*6*	**Ringadingadoo** 5-10-12 0 LiamTreadwell (Joanne Priest) *plld hrd: led after 6f: hdd 4f out and rapidly lost pl: t.o* **33/1**	51
0	**12**	*11*	**Rabbit Lewis**[24] 333 5-10-5 0 MrJHamer(7) (Tom Gretton) *t.o after 6f* **125/1**	40
	13	*5*	**Willos Silvergirl** 4-10-9 0 TomO'Brien (Keith Goldsworthy) *rdn and struggling 1/2-way: sn t.o* **20/1**	32

4m 6.10s (14.60) **Going Correction** +0.475s/f (Soft)
WFA 4 from 5yo+ 3lb — **13** Ran SP% **125.1**
Speed ratings: **82,79,77,75,74 69,69,69,63,60 57,51,49**
toteswingers:1&2 £7.50, 2&3 £99.70, 1&3 £73.80 CSF £41.71 TOTE £2.80: £1.10, £4.50, £30.60; EX 42.10 Place 6: £42.57 Place 5: £14.34.
Owner Shade Oak Stud **Bred** Shade Oak Stud **Trained** Little Newcastle, Pembrokes

FOCUS

An ordinary mares' bumper that was steadily run. It was won by a progressive performer.

NOTEBOOK

With Grace had to defy a penalty following her win at Bangor last month, but her jockey's claim partially offset that nominal disadvantage. Travelling wide of the pack, she challenged on the home turn and eventually came clear up the straight for an authoritative success. She gave the impression that stamina is her forte, so she should continue to do well once sent over jumps. (op 4-1 tchd 3-1)

Alaska River(IRE) made some progress out wide to stay on late, but she could not eat into the winner's advantage. This was a reasonable run representing a stable that does not tend to target bumpers, and she should improve for longer distances. (op 6-1)

Music In The Air, also from a yard that rarely has bumper winners, was driven up to challenge in the back straight, and remained there under sufferance until eventually crying enough on her racecourse debut. (op 50-1)

Diamond MM(IRE) was attempting to gain revenge on her Bangor conqueror With Grace and was better off at the weights this time. However, once again she raced too keenly and had nothing in reserve at the finish. She will need to learn to settle is she is to stay 2m. (op 6-4 tchd 13-8 in places)

T/Plt: £45.30 to a £1 stake. Pool: £71,482.43 - 1,149.66 winning tickets T/Qpdt: £11.60 to a £1 stake. Pool: £6,717.04 - 428.10 winning tickets IM

583 FONTWELL (L-H)

Thursday, June 10

OFFICIAL GOING: Good (good to firm in places) changing to good after race 1 (6.30)

Rail realignment increased chase by about 50yds per circuit and hurdles by 25yds per circuit.

Wind: Moderate, against. Weather: Showers before racing, then dull

687 BET365.COM BEGINNERS' CHASE (13 fncs) — 2m 2f

6:30 (6:30) (Class 4) 5-Y-0+ — **£3,903** (£1,146; £573; £286)

Form				RPR
4/	**1**		**Nintytwo Team (IRE)**[37] 145 8-11-0 130 AELynch (Paul John Gilligan, Ire) *cl up: led 4 out: clr fr next: j.rt last: easily* **3/1**[3]	124+
1-23	**2**	*15*	**Kanad**[11] 536 8-10-9 120 JimmyDerham(5) (Milton Harris) *t.k.h towards rr: j. slowly 1st: nt fluent and rdn 6th: sme hdwy 9th: kpt on at one pce to take mod 2nd nr fin* **14/1**	105
54-1	**3**	*½*	**I Need A Hero (IRE)**[11] 528 5-11-0 (t) JackDoyle (Sarah Humphrey) *prom: chsd wnr and easily outpcd 3 out: lost 2nd nr fin* **13/2**	104
03-4	**4**	*1 ¾*	**Swainson (USA)**[29] 281 9-11-0 OwynNelmes (Helen Nelmes) *hld up in rr: mod effrt 8th: no imp fr 4 out* **50/1**	102
00-0	**5**	*½*	**Hibiki (IRE)**[33] 207 6-11-0 (p) RichardJohnson (Philip Hobbs) *chsd ldrs: hit 4th: lost pl and rdn 7th: in rr whn nt fluent next: blnd 9th: n.d after* **5/2**[2]	104
	6	*3 ¾*	**Diaco (IRE)**[572] 2228 6-10-11 RichieMcLernon(3) (Jonjo O'Neill) *t.k.h towards rr: rdn 9th: sn struggling* **20/1**	98
3F-3	**7**	*33*	**Wade Farm Billy (IRE)**[16] 464 6-11-0 JamieMoore (Gary Moore) *led tl 4 out: hrd rdn and wknd 2 out: no ch whn j.rt last: virtually p.u run-in* **9/4**[1]	90+

4m 41.5s (6.80) **Going Correction** -0.025s/f (Good) — **7** Ran SP% **111.1**
Speed ratings: **83,76,76,75,75 73,58**
Tote Swingers:1&2:£23.80, 2&3:£6.30, 1&3:£4.90. CSF £36.36 TOTE £4.80: £3.10, £5.70; EX 56.20.
Owner Hurl 'N' Ball Syndicate **Bred** Donal Brazil **Trained** Athenry, Co Galway

FOCUS

Some rain had eased the ground a little. The beginners' chase was a reasonable contest in which two leaders took the field along at a good pace.The winner can rate higher over fences but the fourth limits this form for now.

NOTEBOOK

Nintytwo Team(IRE) ◆ had been doing well in handicap hurdles in his native Ireland this spring, but fell on his chasing debut last month. This small field was a much easier test however, and, ridden patiently early, he swooped into the lead before the final bend and stayed on for a clear-cut success. On this evidence he should be at least as good a chaser as he was over hurdles and he reportedly heads to Galway next. (op 7-2 tchd 9-2)

Kanad was slow over the open ditch on the first circuit and took a while to recover his composure before staying on well but all too late. The tongue-tie was left off today, which did not seem to make a great deal of difference, but he still needs to improve his jumping. (op 16-1)

I Need A Hero(IRE) joined the leader at the seventh and stayed on once headed by the winner. Considering he would have been outclassed had this been over hurdles, this was a solid debut run over fences. (op 17-2 tchd 5-1)

Swainson(USA) lacked fluency over the early fences and took a long time to finally get going. He gained his sole hurdling success at this track last year but still has some way to go to match that level over fences. (tchd 66-1)

Hibiki(IRE), the market leader, was a decent hurdler who may have just crept too high in the weights for that sphere and was making his chasing debut. He travelled well early on but made a small mistake at the fourth, which was followed by a more significant mistake at the seventh and he lost all confidence mid-race, before staging a late rally. He needs to prove his courage over fences before being trusted with too much money again. (op 9-4 tchd 7-4)

Diaco(IRE) was having his first run since his only previous start in an Irish maiden hurdle late in 2008, and after getting outpaced on the final circuit he should come on for the run. (op 12-1)

Wade Farm Billy(IRE) was a bit keen setting the early pace and he weakened badly, wandering around after the last, and has to prove he can last home. (op 5-2)

688 CASINO AT BET365 NOVICES' H'CAP HURDLE (9 hdls) — 2m 2f 110y

7:00 (7:00) (Class 5) (0-95,91) 4-Y-0+ — **£2,211** (£649; £324; £162)

Form				RPR
-221	**1**		**Play A Cord (IRE)**[8] 587 7-10-12 **84** (b) MarkQuinlan(7) (Neil Mulholland) *hld up towards rr: hdwy 6th: led after 2 out: drvn clr* **5/4**[1]	91+
440-	**2**	*4 ½*	**Appointment**[49] 5328 5-11-12 **91** (p) JamieGoldstein (Sheena West) *prom: led 6th tl hdd and hrd rdn 3 out: regained 5l 2nd whn mstke last: one pce* **5/1**[3]	95
0-40	**3**	*7*	**Nobby Kivambo (IRE)**[8] 585 5-11-11 **90** RichardJohnson (Brendan Powell) *prom: led after 5th tl mstke next: led 3 out: blnd next: sn hdd & wknd* **5/2**[2]	91+
/30-	**4**	*24*	**Hawk Gold (IRE)**[220] 2039 6-10-5 **77** (b) AshleyBird(7) (Michelle Bryant) *t.k.h in 5th: rdn 6th: sn outpcd* **20/1**	52
4-05	**P**		**Smart N Sharp (IRE)**[18] 436 7-9-9 **65** oh1 (tp) GemmaGracey-Davison(5) (Linda Jewell) *led tl after 5th: sn wknd: bhd whn p.u bef 3 out* **16/1**	—
00/P	**P**		**Capeleira (IRE)**[11] 532 5-10-13 **78** (b[1]) LeightonAspell (Richard Rowe) *mstke and dropped to last at 1st: blnd 2nd: struggling after: wl bhd whn p.u bef 6th* **28/1**	—
505-	**P**		**Princess Soraya**[195] 2550 4-10-11 **80** JimmyMcCarthy (Brendan Powell) *chsd ldrs: mstke 4th: wknd 5th: sn lost tch: wl bhd whn p.u after 3 out* **16/1**	—

4m 35.6s (1.30) **Going Correction** -0.025s/f (Good)
WFA 4 from 5yo+ 17lb — **7** Ran SP% **109.7**
Speed ratings (Par 103): **96,94,91,81,—,—,—**
Tote Swingers:1&2:£1.10, 2&3:£2.90, 1&3:£1.50 CSF £7.48 TOTE £2.70: £2.50, £1.70; EX 5.00.
Owner Neil Mulholland Racing Club **Bred** C J And Mrs D Hodgins **Trained** Burlescombe, Devon

FOCUS

Just a weak contest, there for the taking by the only previous winner in the field. The first three are rated pretty much to their marks.

NOTEBOOK

Play A Cord(IRE), the only previous winner in the line-up, duly obliged. Moving up to stalk the leader down the back, she met some resistance from that rival but she stayed on well, so was able to impose her superiority. Connections had found a straightforward opportunity for the mare, and she looked well handicapped in this race, but she ran as if she would be more effective returned to longer trips. Blinkers have reportedly helped her focus and have brought about her recent improvement. (op 10-11 tchd 11-8)

Appointment had moved up to the lead when jumping slowly at the last in the back straight at a crucial stage. She was beginning to get outpaced but stayed on well again towards the finish. The fitting of cheekpieces and the way she ran suggests she might do better over further. (op 11-2 tchd 6-1 and 4-1)

Nobby Kivambo(IRE) was just getting outpaced as the winner challenged leaving the back straight, but he did not go down without a fight, though his jumping lost fluency in the closing stages and that did not help. (op 4-1 tchd 2-1)

Hawk Gold(IRE) was outpaced on the final circuit and could only plod on. This was his first run since last November and he ran as if he would benefit from the outing. (op 14-1)

Smart N Sharp(IRE) Official explanation: jockey said mare lost its action and pulled up

689 BET365 H'CAP CHASE (13 fncs) — 2m 2f

7:30 (7:30) (Class 5) (0-95,95) 5-Y-0+ — **£2,602** (£764; £382; £190)

Form				RPR
0-01	**1**		**Bankstair (FR)**[8] 584 6-11-12 **95** 7ex (t) PaddyBrennan (Nigel Twiston-Davies) *hld up in midfield: hdwy to chse ldr 8th: mstke next: jnd ldr and blnd 2 out: led appr last: rdn clr* **3/1**[1]	112+

1-25 **2** *7* **Folie A Deux (IRE)**29 276 8-11-10 93..........................(t) SeamusDurack 103
(Colin Tizzard) *led: wnt clr 5th: c bk fr 8th: mstke 4 out: hdd appr last: one pce* **5/1**2

42-3 **3** *20* **Misamon (FR)**4 650 7-11-1 84..(b) PaulMoloney 75
(David Rees) *early reminders: in tch: chsd ldr 3rd tl 8th: sn outpcd* **3/1**1

0P/4 **4** *1 3/4* **Mandalay Bay (IRE)**11 531 10-9-11 69 oh5................. CharlieStudd(3) 58
(Chris Gordon) *outpcd in rr: sme hdwy fr 4 out: nvr trbld ldrs* **25/1**

0-P1 **5** *9* **Khazar (FR)**11 533 7-11-6 92 7ex.............................. RichieMcLernon(3) 76
(Jonjo O'Neill) *mid-div: rdn after 7th: disp mod 3rd appr 3 out: sn wknd* **8/1**3

3-65 **6** *27* **Nesnaas (USA)**16 463 9-11-5 95....................................(v) DavidBass(7) 52
(Mark Rimell) *outpcd in rr: j. slowly 3rd and 4th: no ch fr 8th* **12/1**

-423 **P** **Space Cowboy (IRE)**11 533 10-10-2 74...........(b) EamonDehdashti(3) —
(Gary Moore) *hld up towards rr: rdn after 7th: sn lost tch: wl bhd whn p.u bef last* **17/2**

33-P **P** **No Greater Love (FR)**32 233 8-11-5 88..................... TomScudamore —
(Charlie Longsdon) *chsd ldrs early: losing pl whn j. slowly 4th: sn struggling in rr: wl bhd whn p.u bef 3 out* **12/1**

-21P **P** **Wiesenfurst (GER)**11 529 6-11-8 91..............................(b) JamieMoore —
(Gary Moore) *chsd ldrs: drvn along fr 7th: mstke 8th: btn whn hit next: wl bhd whn p.u bef 2 out* **10/1**

4m 37.4s (2.70) **Going Correction** -0.025s/f (Good) **9** Ran SP% **116.6**
Speed ratings: **93,89,81,80,76 64,—,—,—**
Tote Swingers:1&2:£3.20, 2&3:£3.90, 1&3:£3.20 CSF £19.17 CT £48.47 TOTE £5.10: £2.40, £2.50, £1.10; EX 20.50.
Owner Hugh Doubtfire **Bred** Jean Biraben Et Al **Trained** Naunton, Gloucs

FOCUS
This was run at a relentless pace and few were able to get into it. This was a step up from the winner while the runner-up is rated to his mark.

NOTEBOOK
Bankstair(FR) settled in the chasing pack before moving up to stalk the long-time leader in the back straight, travelling best of all. The pair engaged in a dour battle up the straight, and though he dived at the second-last, he had done a bit less early on and hence had more to call on at the finish. Having scored over C&D last week, this was a marginally better race but the penalty allowed him to be fairly well treated for the follow-up. There is the possibility that he might not be able to sustain the good form, notwithstanding the handicapper's reaction. (op 5-2)
Folie A Deux(IRE) is best with an uncontested lead and, reunited with Seamus Durack, who was aboard for his last success, the pair fought to get in front. He had most of the field in trouble after a circuit until the winner loomed up ominously, but he still went down battling. Ultimately the first-time tongue-tie could not help him quite last home, although the pace was a bit too strong and the ground may just have been easier than ideal. (op 9-2 tchd 4-1)
Misamon(FR), a remote third on his return from a ten-month absence just four days previously, was well backed to leave that effort behind. He was prominent for a long way but found chasing the strong pace too much and he was struggling from half a mile out. (op 7-1 tchd 11-4)
Mandalay Bay(IRE) made some late progress but was never able to be competitive. He may not have stayed 3m2f at this track last time, but generally has struggled outside of pointing company. (tchd 33-1)
Khazar(FR), another bidding for a repeat success over C&D under a penalty, was keen early on but jumped hesitantly at the strong pace, and though he made some headway late on his effort was over all too quickly. (op 7-1)

690 POKER AT BET365 NOVICES' HURDLE (10 hdls) 2m 4f
8:00 (8:00) (Class 4) 4-Y-0+ **£3,252** (£955; £477; £238)

Form RPR

11-2 **1** **Quo Video (FR)**21 426 6-11-12 120........................... RichardJohnson 130
(Tim Vaughan) *mde all: set modest pce: hit 3rd and 4th: qcknd 7th: hrd rdn and hit last: hld on gamely* **1/1**1

2F-1 **2** *nk* **Synthe Davis (FR)**30 263 5-10-12 115.......................... LeightonAspell 116
(Laura Mongan) *prom: blnd 2nd: chsd wnr fr 7th: str chal run-in: kpt on wl* **5/1**3

2-12 **3** *19* **Forest Rhythm (IRE)**11 534 6-11-0 110.................(t) JimmyDerham(5) 106
(Seamus Mullins) *hld up in rr: hdwy 7th: drvn to go 4 l 3rd appr 2 out: wknd appr last* **13/8**2

0-U0 **4** *14* **Keckerrockernixes (IRE)**11 528 4-10-3 .... JayPemberton(5) 79
(Richard Rowe) *bhd: sme hdwy 5th: outpcd appr 7th* **100/1**

5 *39* **Oaklea**60 6-10-12 .... DarylJacob 44
(Liam Corcoran) *t.k.h: in tch: wnt 2nd at 3rd: j. slowly next: lost 2nd pl and wknd 7th* **66/1**

P0- **6** *21* **Desert Fever**260 1500 4-10-8 .... PaddyBrennan 19
(Nigel Twiston-Davies) *hld up towards rr: brief effrt 6th: bhd fr next* **25/1**

P **Platinum Bounty**50 4-10-1 .... DougieCostello —
(Neil Mulholland) *plld hrd: chsd ldrs tl blnd 6th: sn bhd: wl bhd whn p.u bef 2 out* **66/1**

4m 58.7s (-0.70) **Going Correction** -0.025s/f (Good)
WFA 4 from 5yo+ 18lb **7** Ran SP% **112.6**
Speed ratings (Par 105): **100,99,92,86,71 62,—**
Tote Swingers:1&2:£1.10, 2&3:£1.10, 1&3:£1.10 CSF £6.43 TOTE £1.70: £1.10, £1.80; EX 5.90.
Owner Folly Road Racing Partners (1996) **Bred** Dominique Clayeux & Haras De Saint-Voir
Trained Aberthin, Vale of Glamorgan

FOCUS
A small field but still a tight affair with the three previous winners dominating off a steady pace. The form is ordinary with the runner-up the best guide.

NOTEBOOK
Quo Video(FR) dictated the pace throughout, quickened it up down the back straight, and knuckled down in determined fashion for the battle from the last. He had disappointed at Wetherby last month but this was a much better showing, especially since he was giving weight away all round thanks to a double penalty. He did have things his own way here, but is versatile regarding running style, and his fighting spirit should see him continue to go well. (op 7-4 tchd 15-8)
Synthe Davis(FR) moved up to mount a challenge from the back straight, but she was never really getting the better of the winner, though she gave her all from the last. Her win in a mares' novice event at Newton Abbot last month was a notch below this level, so this run suggests she is improving. (op 4-1 tchd 7-2)
Forest Rhythm(IRE) allowed the leaders to get away somewhat before making up ground to latch on to them in the back straight. However, he is more about speed than stamina and that mid-race move dented his finishing effort. (op 5-4)

691 BET365.COM H'CAP CHASE (19 fncs) 3m 2f 110y
8:30 (8:31) (Class 4) (0-110,109) 5-Y-0+ **£3,903** (£1,146; £573; £286)

Form RPR

P-30 **1** **Cold Mountain (IRE)**13 503 8-11-4 106...................... JimmyDerham(5) 123+
(Seamus Mullins) *a gng wl: hld up in 4th: trckd ldng pair 4 out: led 2 out: sn clr: easily* **14/1**

3-31 **2** *22* **Hoof It Harry (IRE)**11 529 9-11-2 99 7ex.................... RichardJohnson 98
(Paul Henderson) *prom: led 4 out tl hdd and easily outpcd by wnr 2 out: 2nd and btn whn mstke last* **9/4**1

65-3 **3** *17* **Swordsman (GER)**11 530 8-11-10 107.............................(t) ColinBolger 89
(Chris Gordon) *prom: reminders 1st: 7th and 10th: led 14th tl 4 out: wknd appr next* **14/1**

5-55 **4** *17* **Morestead (IRE)**8 586 5-10-13 96..............................(p) AidanColeman 63
(Brendan Powell) *led: j. slowly 4th: hdd 14th: sn rdn and wknd* **12/1**

64-3 **5** *48* **Distiller (IRE)**13 498 6-11-10 107.................................. PaddyBrennan 30
(Nigel Twiston-Davies) *racd mainly in 6th: rdn 9th: wknd 14th* **6/1**3

2-6U **P** **Hampton Court**5 631 5-11-0 97.................................. AndrewThornton —
(Seamus Mullins) *nt jump wl: towards rr: mod effrt 14th: sn outpcd: 5th and no ch whn p.u bef last* **8/1**

41-6 **P** **Triggernometry**13 501 9-11-12 109.........................(bt) TomScudamore —
(Colin Tizzard) *in tch: hrd rdn and lost pl 12th: sn wl bhd: p.u bef 14th* **16/1**

21-3 **P** **Siouxme (IRE)**29 280 8-10-1 84... LeightonAspell —
(Alison Batchelor) *bhd: j. slowly 3rd: sme hdwy 10th: wknd 14th: wl bhd whn p.u bef 3 out* **11/4**2

6m 56.8s (-4.30) **Going Correction** -0.025s/f (Good) **8** Ran SP% **109.7**
Speed ratings: **105,98,93,88,74 —,—,—**
Tote Swingers:1&2:£6.50, 2&3:£15.50, 1&3:£28.60 CSF £43.94 CT £425.09 TOTE £17.30: £3.80, £1.02, £6.40; EX 56.00.
Owner Woodford Valley Racing **Bred** Skymarc Farm **Trained** Wilsford-Cum-Lake, Wilts

FOCUS
A competitive handicap run at a steady pace with most of the field still bunched as they headed out on to the final circuit. The winner improved on previous efforts with the runner-up rated in line with previous form at the trip.

NOTEBOOK
Cold Mountain(IRE) settled much better than he had over hurdles last time, travelling comfortably and biding his time before serving up to the favourite, and proving he had greater depths of stamina. He has not been as good as a chaser as he is over hurdles, but that is reflected in his rating, and on this form he is catching up over fences and might have a chance once he is reassessed. However, the plan is to give him a summer break now. (tchd 16-1)
Hoof It Harry(IRE) has improved for each run over fences, culminating in a wide-margin victory at this track 11 days ago, yet still had the benefit of running with a penalty. He travelled well at the head of affairs and looked the likeliest winner for much of the way until his stamina emptied and he scrambled over the last. (tchd 2-1)
Swordsman(GER) does not look a natural over fences and needed plenty of driving throughout, but it is a testament to his latent ability that he was able to remain up there for so long. Although his chase rating is no longer related to his hurdling ability, it still looks too high. (op 10-1)
Morestead(IRE) led for a long way but was stepping up in trip and did not get home. (op 10-1)
Distiller(IRE) had been outpaced over 5f shorter at Stratford two weeks ago, but this step back up in trip looked a good opportunity to make use of a favourable mark. However, his jumping was sluggish throughout and it seems that he has problems jumping off ground with any give in it. (op 9-2)
Siouxme(IRE) was well supported off her light weight to add to her success in a four-runner handicap over C&D in April. Held up early, she made some progress a circuit out but was soon outpaced, and was outclassed. (op 7-2 tchd 5-2)

692 BET365 H'CAP HURDLE (11 hdls) 2m 6f 110y
9:00 (9:00) (Class 5) (0-95,95) 4-Y-0+ **£2,211** (£649; £324; £162)

Form RPR

2-24 **1** **King Raven (IRE)**16 467 8-11-7 90..........................(v) TomScudamore 107+
(Mark Rimell) *hld up in tch: wnt 3rd after 7th: lft 5l 2nd at next: led appr 2 out: sn rdn wl clr* **5/2**2

42P- **2** *36* **Colonial Jim (IRE)**72 4939 7-10-9 78...........................(b1) DougieCostello 61
(Neil Mulholland) *pressed ldr: led 6th: jnd whn lft 5l ahd at 8th: hdd appr 2 out: wknd qckly* **6/1**3

6-P5 **3** *7* **Spider Boy**8 587 13-10-8 82.......................(b) GemmaGracey-Davison(5) 56
(Zoe Davison) *chsd ldrs: hrd rdn 7th: sn outpcd* **12/1**

6-FP **4** *3* **Open Range (IRE)**11 533 10-10-1 70 oh5 ow1............ LeightonAspell 42
(George Wareham) *towards rr: mstkes 2nd and 7th: mod 4th fr 3 out: n.d* **33/1**

FP-5 **5** *16* **Cave Of The Giant (IRE)**42 64 8-11-12 95............(p) SeamusDurack 52
(Tim McCarthy) *in tch: drvn along and outpcd 4th: struggling after: n.d fr 7th* **18/1**

/P-4 **6** *11* **Knightsbridgelives (IRE)**23 379 7-11-9 92...........(t) ChristianWilliams 39
(Lawney Hill) *led: hit 3rd: hdd 6th: wknd next: 4th and btn whn hmpd 8th* **18/1**

0-11 **F** **Cannon Fire (FR)**2 682 9-11-6 94 7ex............................. MrJETudor(5) —
(Evan Williams) *trckd ldrs: moved up to dispute ld and gng wl whn fell 8th* **5/6**1

0-50 **P** **Eddystone (IRE)**8 587 6-10-0 69 oh5.............................(tp) JamieMoore —
(Linda Jewell) *nvr gng wl and frequent reminders in rr: p.u bef 4th* **33/1**

5m 40.4s (-2.10) **Going Correction** -0.025s/f (Good) **8** Ran SP% **121.5**
Speed ratings (Par 103): **102,89,87,86,80 76,—,—**
Tote Swingers:1&2:£1.50, 2&3:£6.10, 1&3:£2.90 CSF £19.49 CT £154.28 TOTE £3.10: £1.20, £2.40, £2.70; EX 16.00 Place 6 £63.92, Place 5 £11.58..
Owner J J King **Bred** R Ryan **Trained** Leafield, Oxon

FOCUS
This looked a straightforward opportunity for Cannon Fire to gain his third win in five days, but he exited four from home. The form is not easy to rate with the winner up a stone on his previous best hurdles mark.

NOTEBOOK
King Raven(IRE) was able to cruise home after the departure of the market leader. Tracking the favourite in the early stages, he was still going well enough a few lengths off the leaders in the back straight, but once the favourite had departed he was able to sweep into the lead off the home bend against little resistance. He has been tried at a variety of trips but seemed destined to continually find one too good and, although he may have been fortunate this time he has gradually been coming into form. (op 4-1)
Colonial Jim(IRE) ran well for a long way in first-time blinkers but had no answer as the winner went by and he was tired jumping the last, but he should come on for this first start in ten weeks. (op 5-1)
Spider Boy has been kept busy this year and ran another consistent race, but the veteran is finding life tougher now. (tchd 14-1)
Open Range(IRE) was never competitive and looks a decidedly moderate maiden.
Cave Of The Giant(IRE) has been tumbling down the weights, but unfortunately has the form to match and ran another lacklustre race. (op 16-1 tchd 20-1)
Knightsbridgelives(IRE) pulled too hard at Towcester last time and it was the case again here. (op 14-1)
Cannon Fire(FR) was going well in his bid for a quick hat-trick and was just about to take up the lead when catching the top bar of the fourth-last flight and crumpling on landing. (op 4-6 tchd 10-11)
T/Plt: £163.60 to a £1 stake. Pool: £55,559.84 - 247.81 winning tickets. T/Qpdt: £19.90 to a £1 stake. Pool: £5,215.33 - 193.30 winning tickets. LM

[596]UTTOXETER (L-H)

Thursday, June 10

OFFICIAL GOING: Good (7.0)

Wind: Light, behind. Weather: Overcast with the odd spot of rain

693 JENKINSONS CATERERS FIRST CHOICE FOR WEDDINGS MAIDEN HURDLE (10 hdls 2 omitted) 2m 4f 110y

6:40 (6:40) (Class 4) 4-Y-0+ £2,732 (£802; £401; £200)

Form RPR
36-3 **1** **Sahrati**[7] 590 6-11-0 115 TimmyMurphy 118+
(Michael Blake) *chsd ldrs: led appr 3 out: hdd bef next: led again gng to the last: rdn out* **15/8**[1]
620- **2** *6* **Benedict Spirit (IRE)**[37] 3 5-11-0 109 (p) RhysFlint 112
(John Flint) *chsd ldrs: led appr 2 out: rdn and hdd bef last: styd on same pce flat* **7/2**[2]
00- **3** *4* **Hermoso (IRE)**[106] 4242 5-10-9 0 SamTwiston-Davies(5) 108
(Nigel Twiston-Davies) *hld up: hdwy appr 3 out: rdr lost iron briefly sn after: rdn after 2 out: styd on same pce* **9/1**
-P25 **4** *5* **Grand Award**[12] 519 5-11-0 102 JasonMaguire 106+
(Donald McCain) *hld up: hdwy whn blnd 3 out: n.d after* **7/1**
5 *8* **Swiss Art (IRE)**[30] 4-10-3 0 OliverDayman(7) 93
(Alison Thorpe) *hld up: hdwy and blnd 3 out: wknd next* **25/1**
/34- **6** *21* **You Never Said (IRE)**[75] 4881 6-11-0 108 (t) APMcCoy 77
(Charles Egerton) *hld up: hdwy 7th: ev ch whn mstke 3 out: sn wknd: t.o* **9/2**[3]
7 *4* **Soggy Dollar**[38] 5-10-11 0 AlexMerriam(3) 73
(Neil King) *mid-div: mstke 7th: hdwy appr 3 out: wknd bef next: t.o* **80/1**
6 **8** *7* **Himalayan Express**[20] 429 6-11-0 0 (p) FelixDeGiles 67
(Charlie Longsdon) *chsd ldr tl rdn and wknd appr 3 out* **80/1**
00-5 **9** *34* **Basford Tara**[22] 412 5-10-7 0 AlanO'Keeffe 29
(Jennie Candlish) *mde most tl hdd & wknd appr 3 out: t.o* **14/1**
/0P- **10** *88* **Newgatehopeful**[79] 4809 6-10-7 0 (t) MrJohnWilley(7) —
(Mark Campion) *a in rr: t.o fr 4th* **100/1**
P **Appeal To Paddy (IRE)**[26] 6-11-0 0 (p) DavidEngland —
(Matt Sheppard) *a in rr: bhd and rdn 5th: t.o whn p.u bef 7th* **40/1**
PP-6 **P** **Achiltibuie (IRE)**[22] 407 5-11-0 51 (p) TomO'Brien —
(Dai Burchell) *chsd ldrs tl wknd after 7th: t.o whn p.u bef 2 out* **66/1**
0- **P** **Pay The Russian**[62] 5121 4-10-10 0 TomMessenger —
(Neil King) *prom: racd keenly: blnd 1st: mstke 6th: wknd next: t.o whn p.u bef 2 out* **100/1**

5m 2.00s (-2.00) **Going Correction** -0.125s/f (Good)
WFA 4 from 5yo+ 18lb 13 Ran SP% **116.6**
Speed ratings (Par 105): **98,95,94,92,89 81,79,77,64,30 —,—,—**
Tote Swingers: 1&2 £2.90, 1&3 £4.40, 2&3 £6.10 CSF £7.94 TOTE £3.10: £1.10, £1.90, £3.40; EX 10.00.
Owner Mrs Val Butcher **Bred** Darley **Trained** Trowbridge, Wilts

FOCUS

Despite 9.5mm of rain in the previous 24 hours, the ground remained good, and the clerk of the course reported there were some slower patches in the back straight and some quicker ones in the home straight. This was a maiden hurdle that lacked strength in depth, the first two are rated below their best with the fourth setting the level. The pace was fairly steady and the last hurdle in the back straight was omitted.

NOTEBOOK

Sahrati, a decent handicapper on the Flat, had strong claims on the pick of his four-race hurdle form, including when one place behind a 120-rated rival in third in a 2m1f Newton Abbot maiden hurdle on his comeback/debut for a new yard the previous week. He gradually worked his way to the front against the far rail early in the straight and showed a good attitude to forge clear. He looks a professional type who jumps fluently and has a bit of scope for further progress. (op 7-4)

Benedict Spirit(IRE), a five-time winner on the Flat who was a fair sixth off a mark of 82 in a 2m1f Bath handicap last time, gave it a decent shot with cheekpieces re-applied back over hurdles for a new stable. Lightly raced in this sphere, he went close off 107 at Fakenham in March and adds some solidity to the form. (tchd 10-3 and 4-1)

Hermoso(IRE) attracted a bit of support and showed some promise on his first run for a high-profile yard after 106 days off. The most pleasing part of this display was how smoothly he moved into contention before his effort flattened out. He kept on well to land a maiden point in Ireland in October, and this was the first sign of him translating that ability over hurdles. (op 11-1)

Grand Award had a bit to find on figures and compromised his chance by taking a strong hold. The former point and bumper winner is hard to predict and needs to learn to settle better to fulfil his potential. (op 13-2)

Swiss Art(IRE), a multiple 7f-1m winner on Fibresand, showed a bit of promise without really proving his stamina on his hurdle debut. (op 20-1)

You Never Said(IRE) was in the thick of things three out but he weakened quite quickly and may have had stamina issues at the trip. (tchd 4-1 and 11-2)

694 CRABBIE'S ALCOHOLIC GINGER BEER NOVICES' H'CAP CHASE (13 fncs 2 omitted) 2m 4f

7:10 (7:10) (Class 4) (0-110,112) 5-Y-0+ £3,453 (£1,042; £537; £284)

Form RPR
-4B3 **1** **Bold Policy (IRE)**[2] 677 7-10-9 95 (p) PeterToole(3) 104
(Milton Harris) *racd keenly: hdwy 3rd: hmpd 8th: chsd ldr 3 out: led after next: sn rdn: styd on* **11/2**[3]
0-51 **2** *7* **Michigan Assassin (IRE)**[9] 564 8-11-8 112 7ex AodhaganConlon(7) 119+
(Debra Hamer) *led 2nd: mstke 5th: slt ld whn blnd 2 out: sn hdd and rdn: no ex flat: edgd lft towards fin* **13/8**[1]
0-50 **3** *13* **Stratford Stroller (IRE)**[13] 498 6-11-8 105 (t) APMcCoy 96
(Jonjo O'Neill) *hld up: hdwy 9th: disp cl 2nd 3 out: sn rdn: wknd appr last* **8/1**
00-6 **4** *7* **Ash High (IRE)**[31] 251 7-10-0 88 SamTwiston-Davies(5) 73
(Nigel Twiston-Davies) *chsd ldrs: rdn after 10th: wknd next* **7/2**[2]
5P-2 **P** **Oscar Royal (IRE)**[34] 195 9-11-12 109 LiamTreadwell —
(Peter Hiatt) *led to 2nd: chsd ldr: blnd 8th: rdn and wknd appr 3 out: t.o whn p.u bef last* **13/2**
P5P- **P** **Little Al**[71] 4960 7-11-0 97 (p) SamJones —
(Oliver Sherwood) *hld up: bhd fr 5th: drvn along next: sn t.o: p.u bef 10th* **11/1**

5m 3.80s (-1.70) **Going Correction** -0.125s/f (Good) 6 Ran SP% **108.5**
Speed ratings: **98,95,90,87,—,—**
Tote Swingers: 1&2 £2.20, 1&3 £2.90, 2&3 £1.50. CSF £14.53 TOTE £5.80: £3.10, £1.10; EX 17.20.
Owner Mrs D Dewbery **Bred** Mrs E Tector **Trained** Herridge, Wiltshire

FOCUS

An uncompetitive handicap chase with the winner rated back to his best. The second last fence in the back straight was omitted.

NOTEBOOK

Bold Policy(IRE) has looked short of tactical pace at times and could only plug on into a 16l third in a Bangor handicap chase on Tuesday. He needed to step up here and put in a much more fluent performance to end a 17-month losing run and register his second career win on the 21st attempt. He is well treated on his old form but has a very patchy profile in recent times, and would not be certain to repeat this form next time. (tchd 6-1)

Michigan Assassin(IRE) put in a feisty trailblazing display when making a successful start to his chase career at Ffos Las nine days earlier. Things looked to be going well for a long way in his bid to defy a penalty but the weak favourite seemed to lose concentration before scrambling over the second last. He deserves a bit of credit for rallying after that mistake but could not land a blow on the winner who got away. (op 11-8 tchd 7-4)

Stratford Stroller(IRE) was well beaten on his chase debut last time after a few quiet runs. He was involved in the main action here before fading early in the straight and may be able to build on this slight hint of a revival. (op 7-1)

Ash High(IRE) was well backed but driven along and going nowhere some way out on this drop back in trip. It is still early days for the dual Irish point winner who is in good hands, but he is one to be a bit wary of until he finds some form and consistency. (op 9-2 tchd 10-3)

Oscar Royal(IRE) made some mistakes and dropped away to add a fourth consecutive tailed off/pulled up effort to his record. (tchd 7-1)

695 SPIFFINGLY REFRESHING CRABBIE'S ALCOHOLIC GINGER BEER H'CAP CHASE (15 fncs 3 omitted) 3m

7:40 (7:41) (Class 4) (0-110,109) 5-Y-0 £3,421 (£1,010; £505; £252; £126)

Form RPR
01-3 **1** **Petroupetrov (FR)**[11] 540 7-11-4 101 RobertThornton 105+
(Richard Phillips) *chsd ldr: led 2nd to next: led 7th: rdn appr last: styd on* **11/1**
5-4F **2** *2 1/2* **Our Jim**[13] 501 8-11-12 109 JasonMaguire 109
(Donald McCain) *led and nt fluent 1st: hdd next: led 3rd to 7th: chsd wnr: drvn along appr 3 out: ev ch last: no ex flat* **7/1**
31-4 **3** *1 1/4* **Allterrain (IRE)**[32] 218 7-10-8 98 ow1 MrSJO'Donovan(7) 97
(Norma Twomey) *a.p: ev ch 3 out: sn rdn: styd on same pce last* **25/1**
5-31 **4** *2 1/4* **Prophete De Guye (FR)**[11] 540 7-11-1 98 7ex FelixDeGiles 95
(James Evans) *hld up in tch: rdn after 3 out: styd on same pce appr last* **9/4**[1]
2P-5 **5** *hd* **Skipper's Lad (IRE)**[29] 274 8-11-12 109 (bt) JoeTizzard 106
(Colin Tizzard) *chsd ldrs: rdn after 3 out: styd on same pce appr last* **11/1**
4P-0 **6** *11* **Stop The Show (IRE)**[10] 549 9-10-3 86 (p) TimmyMurphy 73
(Richard Phillips) *hld up: hdwy 12th: wknd after 3 out* **13/2**[3]
60P- **7** *6* **Mokum (FR)**[60] 5141 9-11-0 102 LeeEdwards(5) 83
(Tony Carroll) *hld up: hdwy 9th: rdn and wknd 3 out* **16/1**
P5/P **8** *2 1/2* **What A Scientist (IRE)**[13] 501 10-11-3 105 (b) SamTwiston-Davies(5) 84
(Nigel Twiston-Davies) *prom: lost pl after 3rd: hdwy 8th: mstke 10th: drvn along after 12th: wknd after next* **16/1**
60-0 **P** **Keltic Lord**[20] 431 14-11-0 97 LiamTreadwell —
(Peter Hiatt) *in rr fr 2nd: bhd fr 9th: t.o whn p.u bef last* **50/1**
03-P **P** **Arctic Shadow**[36] 158 8-11-6 108 DeanColeman(5) —
(Tim Vaughan) *prom: lost pl 4th: bhd whn p.u after 7th* **16/1**
0F0- **P** **Ocheekobee (IRE)**[81] 4764 7-9-11 83 oh3 SeanQuinlan(3) —
(Richard Phillips) *a in rr: hit 2nd: bhd fr 9th: blnd 11th: t.o whn p.u bef 2 out* **25/1**
43-2 **P** **Knock Em Dead (IRE)**[42] 66 6-11-9 106 (b) APMcCoy —
(Jonjo O'Neill) *hld up: hdwy 5th: mstke 10th: wkng whn blnd 3 out: sn p.u* **9/2**[2]

6m 8.60s (-6.50) **Going Correction** -0.125s/f (Good) 12 Ran SP% **118.8**
Speed ratings: **105,104,103,103,102 99,97,96,—,— —,—**
Tote Swingers: 1&2 £16.00, 1&3 £35.40, 2&3 £49.60 CSF £85.39 CT £1896.61 TOTE £15.20: £4.20, £1.60, £8.90; EX 104.40.
Owner Robert Brown & Partners **Bred** Gheorghe Codre **Trained** Adlestrop, Gloucs

FOCUS

A minor handicap chase with the placed horses rated pretty much to their marks. The first three home were in those positions throughout.

NOTEBOOK

Petroupetrov(FR) got off the mark stepped up to this trip on chase debut at Kempton in April. He was a well held third over C&D last time but bounced back with a gritty effort under a positive ride to make it 2-3 over fences. He looks a tough customer who may be able to dominate some more staying handicaps. (op 12-1)

Our Jim put in a solid effort and has bounced back from an early fall at Stratford last time. He does not have a lot of leeway off this mark but is generally consistent and should continue to run well. (tchd 13-2)

Allterrain(IRE), an ex-Irish pointer, ran another solid race but his progress seems to have levelled out since showing improved form to win off 8lb lower at Plumpton in April.

Prophete De Guye(FR) did the job well under a confident ride over C&D last time. He was strongly supported to follow up but he was a bit keen and not entirely fluent, and could never quite land a serious blow in a race where the leaders didn't stop. (op 10-3)

Skipper's Lad(IRE) kept on well on his second run back from a layoff. He came good with a tongue-strap applied last year and remains well treated on his near-miss off 1lb lower at Ascot in November. (op 8-1)

Knock Em Dead(IRE), second to a well handicapped rival over hurdles last time, put in some sketchy jumps before dropping away and being pulled up off 8lb higher on his chase debut after six weeks off. (op 5-1 tchd 15-2)

696 JENKINSONS CATERERS FOR RACECOURSE HOSPITALITY (S) HURDLE (8 hdls 2 omitted) 2m

8:10 (8:11) (Class 5) 4-8-Y-0 £1,691 (£496; £248; £124)

Form RPR
P-10 **1** **Mhilu (IRE)**[10] 555 8-11-5 121 (bt) APMcCoy 118+
(Tim Vaughan) *trckd ldr: led 6th: hdd 3 out: rdn after 2 out: j.rt last: led flat: hung lft: drvn out* **9/4**[2]
41-3 **2** *5* **Tri Nations (UAE)**[11] 537 5-10-12 115 (tp) JasonMaguire 106
(Donald McCain) *chsd ldrs: led 3 out: rdn and j.rt last: hdd flat: styd on same pce* **3/1**[3]
3-02 **3** *3 1/4* **Tora Petcha (IRE)**[11] 537 7-10-9 96 DannyCook(3) 102
(Barry Leavy) *hld up in tch: racd keenly: outpcd after 3 out: r.o flat: wnt 3rd nr fin* **12/1**
14R- **4** *3/4* **Zafar (IRE)**[51] 5293 7-10-12 127 (t) RhysFlint 101
(John Flint) *hld up: pushed along and hdwy appr 3 out: rdn after next: wknd flat: lost 3rd nr fin* **15/8**[1]
3-10 **5** *13* **Wild Tonto (IRE)**[28] 302 7-11-0 117 SamTwiston-Davies(5) 97
(Nigel Twiston-Davies) *led: hdd and mstke 6th: rdn and wknd 2 out: nt fluent last* **5/1**
002 **6** *3 3/4* **Billy Beetroot (USA)**[10] 555 4-10-6 0 LeeStephens(3) 82
(Katie Stephens) *hld up: rdn and wknd 3 out* **33/1**

3m 59.4s (4.20) **Going Correction** -0.125s/f (Good)
WFA 4 from 5yo+ 17lb 6 Ran SP% **117.9**
Speed ratings: **84,81,79,79,73 71**
Tote Swingers: 1&2 £2.30, 1&3 £8.50, 2&3 £5.70 CSF £10.31 TOTE £3.70: £3.40, £1.10; EX 8.60.The winner was sold for £6,000 to Paul Rich.

The Form Book, Raceform Ltd, Compton, RG20 6NL

Owner Diamond Racing Ltd **Bred** D J Fitzpatrick **Trained** Aberthin, Vale of Glamorgan

FOCUS

Four of the runners had an official rating between 115 and 127 in this selling hurdle. The time was slow and the first two are rated below their best with the third and sixth the best guides.

NOTEBOOK

Mhilu(IRE) progressed into a quite useful novice chaser for Gordon Elliot last year and then easily took a Newton Abbot seller for another yard on return to action last month. He inexplicably ran out when hot favourite in a claiming hurdle last time but put that blip behind him with a resolute performance on debut for Tim Vaughan. Best on fast ground, he stays quite a bit further than this and his tendency to jump to the right here, suggests he may appreciate the switch back to a right-handed track. (op 2-1 tchd 5-2)

Tri Nations(UAE) put in a creditable effort in his bid to improve his career record to 5-15. His hurdle profile is not particularly progressive, but he looks an uncomplicated and willing type who should be able to find some more decent opportunities in 2m events on fast ground. (op 4-1)

Tora Petcha(IRE) did well to grab some minor money in a race where he had quite a bit to find with most of his rivals. (op 16-1)

Zafar(IRE), rated 127 after a hat-trick of novice hurdle wins in cheekpieces last summer, looked a strong contender dropped into this grade after an abortive chase debut in April, but he found a limited response and was eventually quite well held. (op 11-4)

Wild Tonto(IRE) couldn't stay with the leaders when the pace quickened on his first try at 2m since January 2007. A return to 2m4f-2m6f will suit but a current handicap mark of 117 looks on the high side. (op 4-1)

697 JENKINSONS CATERERS NOVICES' H'CAP HURDLE (8 hdls 2 omitted) 2m

8:40 (8:40) (Class 5) (0-95,101) 4-Y-0+ **£2,081** (£611; £305; £152)

Form				RPR
0231	**1**		**Monkhair (IRE)**[7] 600 5-10-10 **83** 7ex .... LeeEdwards(5) (Tony Carroll) *hld up: hdwy 5th: led appr 2 out: hrd rdn towards fin: all out* **5/2**[2]	93+
0-01	**2**	*nse*	**Papradon**[8] 585 6-10-9 **82** 7ex .... SamTwiston-Davies(5) (Nigel Twiston-Davies) *a.p: chsd ldr 6th: outpcd 3 out: rallied last: r.o u.p: jst failed* **5/1**[3]	89
P/-1	**3**	*2*	**Dereks (IRE)**[7] 604 8-12-0 **101** 7ex .... MarcGoldstein(5) (Jim Best) *led: nt fluent 4th: rdn and hdd appr 2 out: styd on* **2/1**[1]	107
060-	**4**	*1*	**Avanos (FR)**[96] 4425 5-11-5 **94** .... KyleJames(7) (Philip Kirby) *hld up: r.o u.p appr last: nrst fin* **20/1**	98
5-F0	**5**	*6*	**Kelly Manor (IRE)**[10] 547 6-10-12 **87** .... AnthonyFreeman(7) (Tony Carroll) *hld up: hdwy appr 3 out: styd on same pce fr next* **33/1**	86
0-53	**6**	*4 ½*	**Rowan River**[23] 384 6-11-6 **88** ....(tp) JohnnyFarrelly (Alison Thorpe) *prom: rdn appr 3 out: wkng whn mstke last* **16/1**	83
0F	**7**	*6*	**Saddlers' Supreme (IRE)**[29] 286 8-11-3 **85** ....(t) DenisO'Regan (Martin Todhunter) *hld up: pushed along bef 3 out: n.d* **12/1**	74
3-P5	**8**	*8*	**Cordier**[7] 607 8-11-8 **90** .... BrianHughes (John Mackie) *prom: rdn after 6th: wknd 3 out* **25/1**	72
32	**9**	*2 ½*	**Wicklewood**[18] 439 4-11-7 **95** ....(v) AlexMerriam(3) (Christine Dunnett) *hld up: sme hdwy appr 3 out: sn wknd* **25/1**	72
05-0	**10**	*33*	**Amwell Brave**[32] 228 9-11-9 **91** .... RobertThornton (J R Jenkins) *hld up: sme hdwy appr 3 out: sn wknd and eased: t.o* **22/1**	41
4-66	**11**	*8*	**Barbarian**[7] 604 4-11-5 **90** ....(v) KeithMercer (Alan Brown) *chsd ldr to 6th: wknd bef next: t.o* **20/1**	30
P/P-	**P**		**Muraqeb**[382] 444 10-9-11 **68** oh4 .... SeanQuinlan(3) (Harry Chisman) *a in rr: bhd and rdn after 4th: t.o whn p.u bef 3 out* **66/1**	—
0-34	**P**		**Valkyrie (IRE)**[21] 421 4-11-7 **92** .... SamThomas (Nick Littmoden) *chsd ldrs: rdn and wknd after 6th: t.o whn p.u bef 2 out* **12/1**	—

3m 54.6s (-0.60) **Going Correction** -0.125s/f (Good)

WFA 4 from 5yo+ 17lb **13** Ran SP% **125.8**

Speed ratings (Par 103): **96,95,94,94,91 89,86,82,80,64 60,—,—**

Tote Swingers:1&2:£1.60, 2&3:£3.40, 1&3:£1.90 CSF £15.17 CT £31.19 TOTE £3.40: £1.10, £3.00, £1.30; EX 17.40.

Owner Group 1 Racing (1994) Ltd **Bred** James J Monaghan **Trained** Cropthorne, Worcs

FOCUS

A fairly hot race for the grade and the three market leaders who were all last-time-out winners filled the first three places. the winner looks progressive but the placed horses are rated below their recent winning marks.

NOTEBOOK

Monkhair(IRE) got off the mark on the 12th attempt over hurdles when landing a C&D mares' event last week. This looked tougher but she was 1lb well in under a penalty and just held on after kicking into a decisive lead early in the straight. She looks the type who needs a bit of coaxing but has improved for her new trainer and may be able to win again. (op 3-1 tchd 10-3)

Papradon has taken a bit of time to get to grips with this discipline but a switch to positive tactics and drop in trip sparked improvement when winning over 2m2f at Fontwell last week and he almost managed to run down the winner in his bid to defy a penalty in this stronger race. A return to a bit further will suit and he should be able to gain compensation for this near-miss.

Dereks(IRE) was well backed and in command at an early stage when scoring on stable debut after a long break at Wetherby last week. He looked potentially well treated under a penalty but couldn't fight off a couple of improvers in his bid to follow up. (op 9-4 tchd 11-4)

Avanos(FR), tailed off at 100-1 on handicap debut in March, showed plenty of promise to finish just behind three in-form rivals on his return for a new trainer after 96 days off. (op 16-1)

Kelly Manor(IRE) put in a better effort with headgear removed but she has yet to reach the frame in 13 starts over hurdles.

698 HOOPS AND SILKS WITH JENKINSONS CATERERS H'CAP HURDLE (10 hdls 2 omitted) 2m 4f 110y

9:10 (9:10) (Class 5) (0-95,95) 4-Y-0+ **£2,081** (£611; £305; £152)

Form				RPR
00-3	**1**		**Spate River**[32] 228 5-11-4 **87** .... APMcCoy (Jonjo O'Neill) *hld up in tch: racd keenly: led 3 out: styd on wl* **2/1**[1]	102+
4-64	**2**	*3 ¾*	**Kilvergan Boy (IRE)**[12] 522 6-11-2 **90** .... SamTwiston-Davies(5) (Nigel Twiston-Davies) *a.p: rdn to chse wnr 2 out: edgd lft and no ex flat* **9/2**[2]	98
6-00	**3**	*6*	**Three Ships**[12] 515 9-11-5 **95** .... AdamWedge(7) (S Wynne) *hld up in tch: plld hrd: hit 7th: rdn appr 3 out: stmbld next: styd on same pce* **25/1**	98
0P-3	**4**	*13*	**Mujamead**[22] 410 6-11-1 **84** .... RobertThornton (Sally-Anne Wheelwright) *chsd ldrs: hit 6th: led after next: hdd 3 out: sn rdn and wknd* **7/1**	75
0-U4	**5**	*9*	**Smiling Applause**[15] 478 11-10-0 **69** oh5 .... DavidEngland (Harry Chisman) *hld up: pushed along and bhd 3rd: nvr on terms: t.o* **33/1**	51
P2-2	**6**	*9*	**Nobel (FR)**[14] 490 9-10-0 **76** ....(p) MissJCoward(7) (Brian Storey) *chsd ldr: led after 2nd: hdd after 7th: wknd next: t.o* **8/1**	50
F-P3	**7**	*8*	**Satindra (IRE)**[15] 478 6-10-9 **81** ....(tp) SeanQuinlan(3) (Carole Ikin) *hld up: drvn along 6th: n.d: t.o* **25/1**	48
013-	**8**	*13*	**Danse Macabre (IRE)**[61] 5136 11-10-13 **87** ....(b) LeeEdwards(5) (Tony Carroll) *hld up: drvn along after 5th: bhd fr 7th: t.o* **10/1**	42
005-	**9**	*3 ¾*	**Robbmaa (FR)**[23] 4894 5-10-5 **74** .... MattieBatchelor (Tony Carroll) *hld up: a in rr: t.o* **28/1**	26
U-6P	**10**	*49*	**Final Bid (IRE)**[32] 231 7-10-8 **77** .... TomMessenger (Tracey Barfoot-Saunt) *mid-div: bhd fr 5th: t.o* **33/1**	—
POU/	**F**		**Delightful Touch (FR)**[423] 5000 9-9-9 **69** oh5 .... MarcGoldstein(5) (Gerald Ham) *hld up: racd keenly: hdwy whn stmbld and fell after 7th* **50/1**	—
04P-	**P**		**Dashing Bach (IRE)**[231] 1863 6-10-11 **80** .... JohnnyFarrelly (Alison Thorpe) *led to 2nd: mstke next: chsd ldrs tl rdn and wknd after 7th: t.o whn p.u bef next* **22/1**	—
6-52	**U**		**Abulharith**[18] 441 4-11-0 **87** .... SamThomas (Michael Scudamore) *chsd ldrs: rdn 3 out: 4th and wkng whn mstke and uns rdr last* **6/1**[3]	82

5m 7.90s (3.90) **Going Correction** -0.125s/f (Good)

WFA 4 from 5yo+ 18lb **13** Ran SP% **121.8**

Speed ratings (Par 103): **87,85,83,78,74 71,68,63,62,43 —,—,—**

Tote Swingers: 1&2 £6.90, 1&3 £19.80, 2&3 £4.10 CSF £10.73 CT £179.75 TOTE £2.20: £1.02, £3.40, £8.30; EX 16.80 Place 6 £48.26, Place 5 £32.87..

Owner John P McManus **Bred** Firman And Webster Bloodstock **Trained** Cheltenham, Gloucs

FOCUS

A modest handicap hurdle which was won in good style by the well backed favourite. He is entitled to rate higher and there should be more to come.

NOTEBOOK

Spate River, a useful handicapper at around 1m on the Flat, stepped up on his previous moderate form as hurdler when third over 2m on handicap debut here last time. This longer trip posed no problem and he did the job in smooth style with a tongue tie removed and McCoy booked. He idled in the closing stages, so was value for more than the winning margin and looks the type who could climb the ranks in handicaps on good or quicker ground now that something has clicked. (op 11-4 tchd 3-1)

Kilvergan Boy(IRE) plugged on well and was the only runner to pose any sort of threat to the winner in the home straight. His mark has tumbled and a competitive edge seems to have returned recently. (op 11-2 tchd 6-1)

Three Ships shaped with some promise on his third run back from a break. He is hard to predict and has recorded just one win since December 2007 but he did defy this mark at Ludlow last October. (tchd 22-1)

Mujamead was placed from out of the blue at Worcester last time and backed that up with a fair effort under a positive ride. A drop in trip could suit and he is hard to ignore at this level off a mark that has tumbled 31lb since last March, but his form is prone to wild swings and his last success was in November 2008. (op 6-1 tchd 11-2)

Nobel(FR), a runner-up over 2m at Wetherby the last twice, weakened tamely off 7lb higher under a forcing ride back up in trip. This was a bit disappointing from a horse who was a dual 2m4f winner in his youth. (op 7-1)

T/Plt: £48.20 to a £1 stake. Pool: £63,024.52 - 953.40 winning tickets. T/Qpdt: £26.70 to a £1 stake. Pool: £4,256.96 - 117.60 winning tickets. CR

699 - 705a (Foreign Racing) - See Raceform Interactive

313 AINTREE (L-H)

Friday, June 11

OFFICIAL GOING: Good (8.5)

Hurdle course on inside line.

Wind: moderate 1/2 against Weather: fine

706 WHITE EVENTS CONDITIONAL JOCKEYS' MARES' H'CAP HURDLE (11 hdls) 2m 4f

6:00 (6:00) (Class 4) (0-115,114) 4-Y-0+ **£3,903** (£1,146; £573; £286)

Form				RPR
-213	**1**		**Entertain Me**[21] 432 6-10-7 **105** .... ChristopherWard(10) (Robin Dickin) *trckd ldrs: led 2 out: drew clr last: pushed out* **22/1**	113+
01-0	**2**	*7*	**Romance Dance**[27] 340 7-11-3 **105** .... DonalDevereux (Sophie Leech) *led to 3rd: w ldrs: outpcd appr 2 out: kpt on to take modest 2nd last 50yds* **33/1**	107
11-1	**3**	*2 ¼*	**Flower Haven**[28] 313 8-11-4 **114** .... EdGlassonbury(8) (Victor Dartnall) *t.k.h: jnd ldrs 6th: led appr 3 out: hdd next: wknd run-in* **11/4**[1]	114
	4	*15*	**Dizzy Rascal**[6] 641 6-10-4 **98** ....(p) APHeskin(6) (Michael Hourigan, Ire) *prom: sn drvn along: reminders 5th: lost pl appr 3 out: hmpd next* **15/2**[3]	85
11-3	**5**	*9*	**Shropshirelass**[38] 140 7-10-8 **99** .... GemmaGracey-Davison(3) (Zoe Davison) *in rr: nt fluent 1st: sme hdwy 8th: sn lost pl: bhd whn hmpd 2 out* **18/1**	77
02-2	**6**	*1 ¾*	**Boogie Dancer**[28] 313 6-11-1 **103** .... HarrySkelton (Stuart Howe) *hld up: nt fluent 4th: hdwy 7th: wknd appr 3 out: bhd whn hmpd 2 out* **8/1**	80
54-1	**7**	*2 ¼*	**Dream Risk (FR)**[11] 547 4-10-13 **105** 7ex .... CampbellGillies (Kate Walton) *w ldr: led 3rd: hdd appr 3 out: sn wknd* **6/1**[2]	77
4B-2	**U**		**Topflight Wildbird**[21] 430 7-10-11 **105** .... CDTimmons(6) (Alan King) *chsd ldrs: 5th and hrd rdn whn mstke and uns rdr 3 out* **11/1**	—
/0-2	**F**		**Smarties Party**[23] 393 7-10-12 **100** .... RhysFlint (C W Thornton) *in tch: outpcd and drvn 7th: hdwy next: 5th and one pce whn fell 2 out* **9/1**	79
2-U1	**P**		**Onemix**[12] 535 4-10-13 **111** 7ex .... DavidBass(6) (Nicky Henderson) *nt fluent and lost pl 3rd: reminders and prom 6th: lost pl appr 3 out: sn bhd: t.o whn p.u bef last* **6/1**[2]	—
-020	**P**		**Overyou**[13] 519 5-10-3 **91** .... JohnnyFarrelly (Elliott Cooper) *in rr: bhd 5th: mstke 6th: hung bdly rt: t.o whn p.u bef next* **40/1**	—

4m 55.2s (-5.50) **Going Correction** -0.30s/f (Good)

WFA 4 from 5yo+ 18lb **11** Ran SP% **111.4**

Speed ratings (Par 105): **99,96,95,89,85 85,84,—,—,— —**

toteswingers: 1&3 not won, 2&3 £27.80, 1&3 £13.30 CSF £504.20 CT £2568.40 TOTE £26.40: £5.00, £12.50, £1.10; EX 639.90.

Owner Mrs A L Merry **Bred** Mrs A L Merry **Trained** Atherstone on Stour, Warwicks

■ Stewards' Enquiry : A P Heskin caution: used whip without giving mare time to respond.

FOCUS

On a bright and breezy evening the ground was described as good all around. What looked a quite competitive mares' handicap hurdle probably didn't take as much winning as a couple of the fancied runners ran below par. The early pace was only moderate but the the first two made small steps up with the third to form.

NOTEBOOK

Entertain Me, whose inexperienced rider took off a valuable 10lb, found a good opportunity to get back to winning ways. The step back up in trip appeared to suit and she can continue to pay her way at this time of the year. (op 25-1)

Romance Dance did not appear to stay 3m last time out but ran well enough here. She doesn't hold any secrets from the Handicapper, though. (op 20-1)

Flower Haven, unbeaten in four starts for current connections, again ran her race under top weight. Travelling and jumping well throughout, life will now be tougher for her off her new mark. (tchd 3-1)
Dizzy Rascal, wearing cheekpieces, never really threatened to land a blow. (op 12-1 tchd 7-1)
Dream Risk(FR), a winner of a poor seller last time out at Cartmel over 2m, appeared to get run of the race and this is as good as she is under her 7lb penalty. Rated only 55 on the Flat, she will struggle off an 8lb higher mark in future handicaps, unless the Handicapper steps in and helps out, in which he surely should. (op 5-1 tchd 9-2)
Topflight Wildbird wasn't done with when unseating three from home. (op 10-1 tchd 12-1)
Onemix doesn't convince with his jumping and is not one to take a short price about. Official explanation: jockey said filly made a mistake and never travelled (op 10-1 tchd 12-1)
Overyou Official explanation: jockey said mare hung badly right (op 10-1 tchd 12-1)

707 BETDAQ THE BETTING EXCHANGE H'CAP CHASE (16 fncs) 2m 4f
6:35 (6:35) (Class 3) (0-125,125) 5-Y-0+ **£6,505** (£1,910; £955; £477)

Form | | | | RPR
55-3 **1** **Safari Adventures (IRE)**[33] 236 8-11-4 **120**............ CampbellGillies(3) 136+
(Lucinda Russell) *j.rt: t.k.h whn mstke 1st: nt fluent 9th: wnt 3l ahd 2 out: sn wnt clr: easily* **5/4**[1]
63-2 **2** *19* **Misty Dancer**[9] 586 11-10-11 **110**.............................. AidanColeman 108
(Venetia Williams) *chsd ldrs: wnt handy 2nd after 4 out: one pce fr 2 out: 10 l down whn stmbld bdly landing last* **7/4**[2]
2-60 **3** *2* **Good Company (IRE)**[14] 499 10-11-10 **123**........................ APMcCoy 119
(Jonjo O'Neill) *hld up: hdwy and prom 7th: mstke 9th: hit 4 out: sn 3rd and rdn: one pce* **5/1**[3]
0U/4 **4** *63* **Mighty Matters (IRE)**[37] 153 11-11-5 **125**.................... MrJFMathias(7) 62
(Charlie Longsdon) *chsd wnr: upsides 7th: wknd after 4 out: wl bhd whn j.rt 2 out: t.o* **9/1**

5m 9.90s (1.70) **Going Correction** +0.175s/f (Yiel) **4** Ran SP% **107.5**
Speed ratings: **103,95,94,69**
CSF £3.90 TOTE £1.80; EX 3.90.
Owner Mrs P K Clark, P G Stephen & H McCaig **Bred** Mrs James Wigan & London TB Services Ltd **Trained** Arlary, Perth & Kinross

FOCUS
A disappointing turnout for this 0-125 handicap chase. The winner is rated up 6lb but the race could be rated higher.

NOTEBOOK
Safari Adventures(IRE) took a while to warm to his jumping and it will be interesting to see what the Handicapper does to him, as it would appear all of his opposition ran below par. Versatile regarding ground, he is rated 120 and it will require a career-best to follow up, where ever he goes next. (op 6-4 tchd 13-8 and 7-4 in places)
Misty Dancer, very well handicapped on old form, kept on in second. His losing run stretches back over three years now and he doesn't look one to take a short price a bout in a bid to go one better next time out. (op 13-8 tchd 6-4)
Good Company(IRE), running here without the blinkers, ran in snatches. He might prefer easier ground but is badly handicapped on the evidence of this and can only be watched for the time being. (op 9-2 tchd 4-1)
Mighty Matters(IRE), having only his second start back after a long layoff, showed up well before getting very tired three from home, he also needs a hand from the Handicapper as, at the age of 11, isn't getting any younger. Official explanation: jockey said gelding hung right (op 8-1 tchd 11-1)

708 KENYON FRASER H'CAP HURDLE (13 hdls) 3m 110y
7:05 (7:05) (Class 3) (0-125,125) 4-Y-0+ **£6,505** (£1,910; £955; £477)

Form | | | | RPR
63-2 **1** **Markington**[29] 302 7-11-3 **116**..(b) TomO'Brien 130+
(Peter Bowen) *chsd ldrs: styd on to ld between last 2: rdn clr run-in* **11/2**[2]
55-1 **2** *10* **Sheriff Hutton (IRE)**[29] 308 7-11-12 **125**........................ RobertWalford 129
(Tim Walford) *trckd ldrs: led 3 out: hdd between last 2: styd on same pce* **16/1**
5-02 **3** *1 3/4* **Corkage (IRE)**[19] 447 7-11-7 **120**..............................(p) PeterBuchanan 121
(Lucinda Russell) *mid-div: chsd ldrs 5th: hung lft and kpt on same pce to take modest 3rd last* **14/1**
3-56 **4** *4 1/2* **Tarkani (IRE)**[5] 656 7-10-6 **105**.......................................(tp) PaulMoloney 103
(Valentine Donoghue) *mid-div: hit 9th: hdwy next: hung lft and one pce fr next* **33/1**
2131 **5** *1* **Flying Doctor**[11] 553 7-10-2 **108**................................ MissJennyCarr(7) 106+
(Elliott Cooper) *trckd ldrs: ev ch 3 out: wknd last* **5/2**[1]
42-1 **6** *6* **Very Cool**[38] 131 8-11-9 **122**...............................(bt) JohnnyFarrelly 114
(David Pipe) *w ldr: led 9th: hung lft and hdd 3 out: wknd between last 2* **10/1**
30-2 **7** *19* **Solway Minstrel**[35] 193 13-10-5 **107**............................ HarryHaynes(3) 81
(Lisa Harrison) *led: drvn 8th: hdd next: wknd appr 2 out* **10/1**
6-P2 **8** *6* **Downing Street (IRE)**[9] 581 9-10-11 **110**....................(vt) AlanO'Keeffe 81
(Jennie Candlish) *in rr: bhd and drvn 8th: mstke last: kpt on* **11/1**
-611 **9** *5* **Ashmolian (IRE)**[19] 436 7-9-11 **101**..........(p) GemmaGracey-Davison(5) 65
(Zoe Davison) *in rr: bhd fr 8th: nvr a factor* **20/1**
16-0 **10** *30* **Englishtown (FR)**[29] 302 10-11-9 **122**...............................(p) APMcCoy 59
(Jonjo O'Neill) *hld up: hdwy 7th: lost pl after 10th: t.o* **14/1**
P5-6 **11** *10* **Barlin Bay**[37] 157 6-9-11 **99** oh35.................................. SeanQuinlan(3) 27
(Harry Chisman) *in rr: wnt prom 9th: lost pl after next: t.o 3 out* **100/1**
15-P **12** *4* **Winsley Hill**[29] 300 8-11-2 **122**.. MarkQuinlan(7) 46
(Neil Mulholland) *chsd ldrs: lost pl appr 3 out: sn bhd: t.o* **50/1**
P16/ **P** **Oakapple Express**[580] 2064 10-10-7 **109**.................. CampbellGillies(3) —
(Geoffrey Harker) *nt fluent: prom: lost pl after 7th: sn bhd: t.o whn p.u after next* **40/1**
33 **P** **Meadows Thyne (IRE)**[19] 443 9-10-12 **111**.................. JasonMaguire —
(A J Martin, Ire) *mid-div: lost pl 10th: t.o whn p.u bef last* **8/1**[3]
0P-0 **P** **Peters Star (IRE)**[35] 196 8-11-2 **115**.......................(b) TimmyMurphy —
(Donald McCain) *chsd ldrs: drvn 4th: lost pl next: sn bhd: t.o 8th: p.u bef next* **16/1**
01U- **P** **Darstardly Dick (IRE)**[55] 5230 7-11-2 **122**...............(b) EdGlassonbury(7) —
(Victor Dartnall) *in rr: mstke 2nd: in rr fr 7th: t.o 3 out: p.u bef last* **16/1**

6m 4.10s (-12.20) **Going Correction** -0.30s/f (Good) **16** Ran SP% **125.7**
Speed ratings (Par 107): **107,103,103,101,101 99,93,91,89,80 77,75,—,—,— —**
toteswingers: 1&2 £0.00, 1&3 £13.80, 2&3 £62.30 CSF £88.43 CT £1201.29 TOTE £6.30: £2.00, £2.40, £2.80, £8.20; EX 109.80.
Owner Ron Stepney **Bred** Minster Enterprises Ltd **Trained** Little Newcastle, Pembrokes

FOCUS
A competitive 0-125 handicap hurdle ran at an even pace. The winner is rated in line with his Flat form and the race looks solid through the placed horses.

NOTEBOOK
Markington is already on a career-high mark, but his trainer does well at this time of year and the gelding can remain competitive off an even higher mark. He has been schooled over fences and might have a go at that sphere shortly and also a spin on the Flat could be on the cards as well, so he has plenty of options. (op 15-2 tchd 5-1)
Sheriff Hutton(IRE), a winner over fences last time out, ran with credit here under top weight and is holding his form well. (tchd 18-1)
Corkage(IRE), coming from a stable going well, also appeared to run bang to form but remains on a high enough mark. (op 12-1)
Tarkani(IRE), who has been busy of late, ran well up to his best. (op 25-1)
Flying Doctor was taking a step up in grade. He ran up to form for his 7lb claimer who had ridden him to victory in the past, but he is also handicapped to his very best form. (op 3-1)
Very Cool found himself in front soon enough.
Oakapple Express Official explanation: jockey said gelding lost its action but returned sound (op 7-1)
Meadows Thyne(IRE) never threatened to land a blow. Official explanation: trainer had no explanation for the poor form shown (op 7-1)

709 BETDAQ.CO.UK H'CAP CHASE (12 fncs) 2m
7:40 (7:40) (Class 3) (0-135,135) 5-Y-0+ **£6,505** (£1,910; £955; £477)

Form | | | | RPR
3/ **1** **Smack That (IRE)**[86] 4686 8-10-10 **122**............................ PeterToole(3) 129+
(Milton Harris) *hld up: wnt prom 5th: led on bit 3 out: sprinted clr after next: v easily* **14/1**
31-U **2** *18* **Kikos (FR)**[26] 361 8-10-12 **121**... SamJones 109
(Renee Robeson) *j.rt: led: hdd 4th: led 8th: hdd 3 out: 12 l down whn mstke last* **5/1**[3]
13-1 **3** *4 1/2* **Quito Du Tresor (FR)**[35] 194 6-10-10 **122**............(p) CampbellGillies(3) 112+
(Lucinda Russell) *w ldr: led 4th: hdd 8th: 4th and outpcd whn stmbld bdly landing and almost lost rdr 4 out: kpt on to take modest 3rd run-in* **13/8**[2]
PP-3 **4** *14* **Tanks For That (IRE)**[13] 524 7-11-12 **135**........................ APMcCoy 114
(Nicky Henderson) *nt fluent: jnd ldrs 5th: drvn after 9th: 3rd and outpcd whn hit next: sn btn: lost modest 3rd and heavily eased run-in* **5/4**[1]

3m 59.9s (-0.10) **Going Correction** +0.175s/f (Yiel) **4** Ran SP% **105.9**
Speed ratings: **107,98,95,88**
CSF £62.57 TOTE £6.70; EX 31.40.
Owner Christopher Shankland & Mrs Ruth Nelmes **Bred** Andrew Pierce **Trained** Herridge, Wiltshire

FOCUS
Despite there only being four runners, this 0-135 handicap chase was run at a sound pace. The winner was impressive and can score again.

NOTEBOOK
Smack That(IRE) ran out a ready winner on his debut for Milton Harris. His two previous wins come on heavy ground but he clearly relished the good ground here, travelling and jumping well throughout. He would be dangerous in a novice chase with a penalty at this time of the year and should be followed. He is entered to run over hurdles on Sunday at Stratford, and would be very interesting if turning up. (op 10-1 tchd 9-1)
Kikos(FR) jumped well here and time might prove he ran into a well-handicapped horse. He remains 1lb higher than his last winning mark. (op 9-2 tchd 11-2)
Quito Du Tresor(FR), a fortunate winner over C&D last time out, was travelling well when making a bad mistake three from home, which paid to his chance, he can bounce back in due course. (op 5-4 tchd 7-4)
Tanks For That(IRE), dropping down in trip, never appeared happy, carrying his tail awkwardly throughout, he has clearly got issues and can only be watched after this below-par effort. Official explanation: trainer's rep said gelding was unsuited by the track (op 15-8)

710 KLM JOURNEYS OF INSPIRATION NOVICES' HURDLE (11 hdls) 2m 4f
8:15 (8:15) (Class 4) 4-Y-0+ **£3,903** (£1,146; £573; £286)

Form | | | | RPR
01-1 **1** **Solway Sam**[34] 214 7-11-12 125.. APMcCoy 134+
(Lisa Harrison) *chsd ldrs: nt fluent 6th: sn outpcd: hit 8th: rallied appr 3 out: wnt 2nd after 3 out: 2 l down last: styd on to ld last 150yds* **3/1**[2]
2-31 **2** *1/2* **Lamboro Lad (IRE)**[12] 538 5-11-0 112...................... DonalDevereux(5) 125
(Peter Bowen) *led: qckna 6th: hit next: hdd run-in: kpt on same pce clsng stages* **15/8**[1]
213- **3** *34* **Nodforms Violet (IRE)**[181] 2836 6-10-12 0........................ GrahamLee 90
(Karen McLintock) *nt fluent: w ldr: hit 3rd: drvn along 7th: wknd 3 out: 15 l 3rd whn mstke last* **15/8**[1]
2-21 **4** *7* **Niceonefrankie**[11] 554 4-11-1 114.............................. AidanColeman 90
(Venetia Williams) *trckd ldrs: hrd drvn 2nd whn hit 3 out: sn btn and nt fluent last 2: eased run-in* **8/1**[3]
0-60 **5** *6* **Be Ashored**[12] 538 5-10-12 0.. JackDoyle 76
(Nicky Vaughan) *hld up in last: outpcd and lost pl 7th: no ch after* **80/1**

4m 55.0s (-5.70) **Going Correction** -0.30s/f (Good)
WFA 4 from 5yo+ 18lb **5** Ran SP% **106.9**
Speed ratings (Par 105): **99,98,85,82,80**
CSF £8.71 TOTE £3.60: £3.00, £1.40, £4.60, £8.71.
Owner David Alan Harrison **Bred** D A Harrison **Trained** Aldoth, Cumbria
■ Stewards' Enquiry : Donal Devereux one-day ban: used whip with excessive frequency (Jun 25)

FOCUS
Despite there only being five runners in this novice hurdle, it was made up of three previous hurdle winners and a bumper winner. The early pace was steady and the first two are progressive, with the third and fourth well below form.

NOTEBOOK
Solway Sam landed a hat-trick under a fine ride from McCoy. Rated 125, he clearly has an engine and, although he won't be easy to place now, he has the size to jump fences. (op 9-4 tchd 10-3 in places)
Lamboro Lad(IRE), rated 126 and an impressive winner at Uttoxeter recently, looked the most likely winner going to the last hurdle. A similar contest is his for the taking in the coming weeks. (op 2-1)
Nodforms Violet(IRE), who was coming back from a break, has shown ability on all of his starts so far. He raced prominently before getting tired and will find easier assignments than this in the coming weeks. (op 11-4 tchd 7-4)
Niceonefrankie, rated 116, had a bit of work to do at the weights, and so it proved. He is in the right hands to get back on the winning track at some point. (op 5-1)
Be Ashored will find life easier in modest handicaps in due course. (op 66-1)

711 MEDICASH HEALTHCARE MAIDEN HURDLE (9 hdls) 2m 110y
8:50 (8:50) (Class 4) 4-Y-0+ **£3,903** (£1,146; £573; £286)

Form | | | | RPR
2 **1** **Heron Bay**[28] 315 6-11-0 0.. TomO'Brien 117+
(Peter Bowen) *chsd clr ldr: led 6th: hrd rdn and styd on run-in: hld on wl towards fin* **4/5**[1]
F- **2** *3/4* **Phoenix Flight (IRE)**[20] 4894 5-11-0 0............................ TimmyMurphy 116+
(James Evans) *hld up in rr: gd hdwy pulling hrd to join ldrs 6th: upsides whn hit 2 out: no ex towards fin* **5/1**[3]
3 *2 1/2* **Russian George (IRE)**[35] 4-10-11 0................................ KeithMercer 111+
(Steve Gollings) *hld up in rr: hdwy appr 3 out: 3rd whn awkward jump 2 out: 6l down last: styd on* **4/1**[2]
4 *22* **Hi Wycombe (IRE)**[11] 562 6-10-9 0................................(p) APHeskin(5) 91
(Michael Hourigan, Ire) *chsd ldrs: wknd appr 2 out* **14/1**
4 **5** *6* **Elcanos (GER)**[19] 442 7-11-0 103..(t) APMcCoy 85
(A J Martin, Ire) *hdwy 6th: sn chsng ldrs: wknd after 3 out: eased run-in* **7/1**

P-0 **6** *7* **Aughcarra (IRE)**[37] 154 5-10-11 0 SeanQuinlan(3) 78
(Harry Chisman) *in rr: sme hdwy 6th: sn lost pl and bhd* **100/1**
0 **7** *14* **Miss Markham (IRE)**[12] 535 5-10-0 0 PeterHatton(7) 57
(Patricia Rigby) *trckd ldrs: wknd 3 out: sn bhd* **150/1**
0-PP **8** *72* **Solway Dornal**[19] 442 5-10-11 0 HarryHaynes(3) —
(Lisa Harrison) *j.lft 1st: lost pl 6th: sn bhd: t.o whn j. violently rt 2 out* **80/1**
P **Laurollie**[1221] 8-10-1 0 ow4 DerekSmith(10) —
(Bill Moore) *reluctant ldr: t.k.h and wl clr 2nd: hdd 6th: wknd rapidly: t.o whn p.u bef next* **100/1**
U **Echo Dancer**[49] 4-10-1 0 JoshWall(10) —
(Trevor Wall) *t.k.h: bmpd and uns rdr 1st* **25/1**

4m 12.2s (6.00) **Going Correction** -0.30s/f (Good)
WFA 4 from 5yo+ 17lb **10** Ran SP% **119.1**
Speed ratings (Par 105): **73,72,71,61,58 55,48,14,—,—**
toteswingers:1&2 £1.80, 2&3 £6.40, 1&3 £1.70 CSF £5.60 TOTE £2.00: £1.20, £1.70, £1.30; EX 5.60 Place 6: £672.89 Place 5: £239.88.
Owner Gwilym J Morris **Bred** Car Colston Hall Stud **Trained** Little Newcastle, Pembrokes

FOCUS
Plenty of deadwood in this novice hurdle but it also had a few above average recruits for this time of the year. A very steady pace and the race didn't develop to after halfway. It will throw up plenty of future winners with the fourth the best guide to the level.

NOTEBOOK
Heron Bay, very useful on the Flat (rated 105 in his prime and also tasted Royal Ascot success) made a very good start to his hurdling career over C&D last month and went one better in determined style. Coming from a yard going well, he will have little trouble in defying a penalty and it will be interesting to see how far he can go in this sphere. A return to the Flat could also be on the agenda. (op Evens)
Phoenix Flight(IRE) wasn't suited by the steady early pace and was very keen. A winner of 74 on the Flat recently, he can go one better shortly, especially in a true run race. This was a step in the right direction after falling on his hurdling debut. (op 4-1)
Russian George(IRE), rated 82 on the Flat, made a good start to his hurdles career. He looked like he will come on plenty for this experience and will have little trouble taking a novices' hurdle at this time of the year. (op 9-2)
Hi Wycombe(IRE), rated 84, had no chance at the weights, but probably ran up to form.
T/Plt: £1,514.40 to a £1 stake. Pool of £52,550.76 - 25.33 winning tickets. T/Qpdt: £58.90 to a £1 stake. Pool of £4,411.93 - 55.38 winning tickets. WG

349 MARKET RASEN (R-H)
Friday, June 11

OFFICIAL GOING: Good (good to firm in places; hdl 7.1, chs 7.6)
Rails moved out 2-3yards around whole course and hurdles and chases running on shared line on the Wood Bend.
Wind: almost nil Weather: warm and sunny

712 LUCIE JONES PERFORMING HERE 21ST AUGUST NOVICES' HURDLE (8 hdls) 2m 1f
2:00 (2:00) (Class 4) 4-Y-0+ **£2,740** (£798; £399)

Form RPR
02-1 **1** **Rubipresent (IRE)**[26] 349 6-11-0 119 JamesHalliday(5) 116+
(Malcolm Jefferson) *led tl appr 2nd: pckd 5th: rdn and outpcd bef 2 out: rallied last: styd on gamely to ld fnl 100yds* **3/1**[2]
63-1 **2** *½* **Bucephalus (IRE)**[16] 468 6-11-2 110 (t) MichaelMcAlister(3) 115+
(Maurice Barnes) *prom: rdn after 3 out: led next: mstke last: hdd 100yds out: kpt on u.p* **11/2**[3]
4 **3** *1 ½* **Hypnotic Gaze (IRE)**[41] 97 4-10-9 0 AndrewTinkler 103
(John Mackie) *hld up: effrt gng wl after 3 out: rdn and nt qckn last: kpt on to snatch 3rd* **6/1**
2 **4** *hd* **Andhaar**[11] 548 4-10-9 0 KeithMercer 104
(Steve Gollings) *numerous mstkes or slow jumps and t.k.h: led bef 2nd: mstke 3 out: hdd next: ev ch whn mstke last: wknd flat: lost 3rd cl home* **15/8**[1]
51-4 **5** *23* **Sadler's Star (GER)**[9] 576 7-11-5 107 (p) TimmyMurphy 92
(Michael Blake) *hld up trcking ldrs: wknd 2 out: wnt lft last: eased flat* **11/2**[3]
4-5 **6** *10* **Tears From Heaven (USA)**[32] 254 4-10-9 0 BrianHughes 69
(Mrs S Sunter) *sn last: rdn and struggling 3 out: sn wl bhd* **50/1**
U **Royal Entourage**[244] 5-10-5 0 KyleJames(7) 82
(Philip Kirby) *chsd ldrs: rdn and lost tch after 3 out: poor 6th whn blnd and uns rdr last* **20/1**

4m 13.5s (6.80) **Going Correction** +0.10s/f (Yiel)
WFA 4 from 5yo+ 17lb **7** Ran SP% **111.6**
Speed ratings (Par 105): **88,87,87,86,76 71,—**
toteswingers:1&2:£1.30, 1&3:£6.40, 2&3:£5.80 CSF £18.77 TOTE £4.00: £1.80, £2.10; EX 13.70.
Owner J H Wilson **Bred** Miss Mary O'Sullivan **Trained** Norton, N Yorks

FOCUS
An interesting little novices' hurdle and the first four are rated close to pre-race marks.

NOTEBOOK
Rubipresent(IRE) faced a tougher ask under the penalty, but he again saw his race out strongly, eventually getting on top in the final half furlong. He is clearly on the up and may have even more to come back at 2m4f. (op 5-2 tchd 9-4)
Bucephalus(IRE), rated 9lb inferior to the winner, got to the front two out and had his chance, but couldn't hold on. He should find another opening, possibly in handicaps. (op 9-2)
Hypnotic Gaze(IRE) improved on his debut effort, travelling well until being unable to quicken late on, and he should have no trouble winning a maiden hurdle, at least. (op 17-2)
Andhaar, second at Cartmel on debut, made a lot of the running and didn't do too badly considering his jumping lacked fluency. A further mistake at the last cost him dear, and in the end he lost out on the places, but he will have no trouble winning if he can be slicker at his hurdles. (op 5-2 tchd 3-1)
Sadler's Star(GER), finally off the mark at Stratford in March, ran creditably last time, but this was well below what he is capable of. (op 9-2 tchd 4-1)

713 BOB CHAMPION'S 60:60 CHARITY CHALLENGE NOVICES' H'CAP HURDLE (10 hdls) 2m 3f
2:30 (2:30) (Class 4) (0-100,100) 4-Y-0+ **£2,602** (£764; £382; £190)

Form RPR
/0-3 **1** **Choctaw Nation**[23] 397 6-10-13 92 JamesHalliday(5) 96
(Malcolm Jefferson) *settled towards rr: prog in 5th: gng wl on outside 3 out: 4th at last: drvn along and responded gamely to ld cl home* **16/1**
0-02 **2** *hd* **Everaard (USA)**[8] 604 4-10-10 88 (p) GrahamLee 89+
(Kate Walton) *racd enthusiastically: lft in ld 1st tl hdd bef 6th: led again 3 out: drvn and ct fnl strides* **15/8**[1]
-553 **3** *1 ¼* **Wee Ziggy**[16] 480 7-10-5 79 RodiGreene 82
(Michael Mullineaux) *heavily restrained s and wl off the pce in the rr tl 3 out: rapid prog next: stl 5th at last but dashed past two rivals nr fin: too much to do* **18/1**
6-42 **4** *½* **Galley Slave (IRE)**[2] 552 5-9-7 74 oh6 StevenGagan(7) 78
(Michael Chapman) *bhd and pulling hrd: rapid prog 4th: led bef 6th: hdd 3 out: bmpd along and stl ev ch last: nt qckn and lost 3rd nr fin* **12/1**
3-21 **5** *hd* **J'Adhere (FR)**[21] 432 5-11-10 98 RichardJohnson 101+
(Tim Vaughan) *heavily restrained s: wl in rr tl prog 7th: 4th whn mstke 2 out: rdn and nt qckn flat: lost 4th nr fin* **5/2**[2]
00/- **6** *4 ½* **Northern Lad (IRE)**[477] 4019 8-11-6 94 TomScudamore 92
(Jim Best) *hld up towards rr: effrt on ins on long run to 2 out: kpt on steadily wout landing a blow after* **10/1**
4P-4 **7** *2 ¼* **Aint She The Lady (IRE)**[34] 214 6-11-5 100 MrTomDavid(7) 96
(Tim Vaughan) *midfield: rdn and outpcd wl bef 2 out: kpt on flat* **16/1**
3-1 **8** *9* **Balnagore**[23] 397 6-11-8 96 PeterBuchanan 83
(Lucinda Russell) *cl up and t.k.h: mstke 5th: rdn and lost pl 3 out* **8/1**[3]
232- **9** *1 ¼* **Montiyra (IRE)**[84] 4717 6-10-9 83 PaddyAspell 68
(Lynn Siddall) *trckd ldrs tl rdn and wknd 2 out* **25/1**
550- **10** *11* **Raisthorpe**[116] 4071 6-10-11 85 BrianHughes 59
(Tim Fitzgerald) *pressed ldrs: rdn after 3 out: wknd bef next* **100/1**
U0P- **P** **Blue Jet (USA)**[47] 12 6-10-4 85 AlexanderVoy(7) —
(Mike Sowersby) *taken down early: a last: lost tch and j. slowly 6th: j. bdly rt next: sn t.o: p.u after jumping rt 3 out* **100/1**
005/ **P** **Victorias**[408] 52 5-10-3 77 KeithMercer —
(Andrew Crook) *midfield: lost tch wl bef 2 out: t.o and p.u last* **40/1**
0-00 **F** **Kashubian Quest**[16] 468 4-10-8 86 TjadeCollier —
(Sue Smith) *led tl virtually ref 1st: racd promly but erratically: rdn and ev ch 3 out: wkng rapidly whn fell next* **66/1**

4m 51.3s (11.90) **Going Correction** +0.10s/f (Yiel)
WFA 4 from 5yo+ 17lb **13** Ran SP% **118.0**
Speed ratings (Par 105): **78,77,77,77,77 75,74,70,69,65 —,—,—**
toteswingers:1&2:£3.60, 1&3:£28.50, 2&3:£11.50 CSF £46.30 CT £574.36 TOTE £18.00: £3.70, £1.50, £4.80; EX 62.10.
Owner Ian L Davies/Mrs Rita Lee **Bred** Juddmonte Farms Ltd **Trained** Norton, N Yorks

FOCUS
This was a modest novices' handicap hurdle but a step up from the winner and the third and fifth give the form a fairly solid look.

NOTEBOOK
Choctaw Nation didn't look straightforward when third at Kelso latest, flashing his tail on several occasions, but he was always set to do better once handicapping, and he received a fine ride from Halliday, who kidded him along and produced a fine rally to get up on the line. He has the potential to do better, but is clearly a bit tricky. (tchd 20-1)
Everaard(USA), runner-up off this mark on his recent handicap debut, looked the one to beat and went on again three out, but he couldn't repel the winner's late surge. He can pick up a small race at some stage. (op 9-4 tchd 5-2)
Wee Ziggy may well have taken this had he been ridden a tad closer the pace. He can race keenly, but was simply left with too much to do here, flying home in the straight and just getting up for third. (op 14-1)
Galley Slave(IRE), who was 6lb 'wrong' at the weights, ran a good race. He didn't quite get home having refused to settle. (op 14-1)
J'Adhere(FR) looked potentially interesting off a mark of 98 on this handicap debut, but having made his ground from the rear to challenge, could find no extra late on. (op 7-2 tchd 9-4)
Northern Lad(IRE) never got into it having been held up. (op 13-2)
Kashubian Quest raced erratically up with the pace before eventually fading.

714 DEBORAH SERVICES BEGINNERS' CHASE (14 fncs) 2m 4f
3:00 (3:00) (Class 4) 5-Y-0+ **£3,903** (£1,146; £573; £286)

Form RPR
/25- **1** **Edgeover**[200] 2473 8-11-0 116 DenisO'Regan 128+
(Paul Webber) *taken down early: hld up in rr: hdwy 9th: wnt 2nd gng strly bef 3 out: led on bit last and lft wl clr: impressive* **11/2**[2]
/04- **2** *31* **Viper**[78] 4848 8-11-0 0 SamThomas 95+
(Dr Richard Newland) *hld up trcking ldrs: rdn and outpcd 3 out: 12 l 3rd next: lft poor 2nd at last* **6/1**[3]
P0/0 **3** *6* **Reel Missile**[26] 351 11-10-11 0 AdamPogson(3) 90+
(Charles Pogson) *taken down early: led: 6 l clr early: pressed and j. slowly 8th: jst hdd 10th tl next: led again tl rdn and hdd and qckly outpcd bef 3 out: lft 3rd at last* **17/2**
P-34 **4** *½* **Springfield Raki**[13] 518 6-11-0 0 KeithMercer 88
(Steve Gollings) *j. slowly: rdn all the way: chsd ldrs tl outpcd 10th: plugged on but n.d after* **18/1**
04-2 **5** *nse* **Still Calm**[29] 307 6-10-11 0 (t) MichaelMcAlister(3) 87
(Maurice Barnes) *mstkes: in tch tl looking outpcd and blnd 9th: sn drvn: btn after next* **80/1**
62-4 **6** *15* **Another Trump (NZ)**[23] 408 6-10-11 0 RichieMcLernon(3) 74
(Jonjo O'Neill) *consistently lacked fluency in rr: last at 9th: sn rdn and struggling: j. bdly rt last* **12/1**
/52- **U** **Ikorodu Road**[196] 2551 7-11-0 124 JasonMaguire 125
(Martin Keighley) *pressed ldr: slt ld 9th tl 10th: led again bef 3 out: rdn next: jnd and gng worst of pair whn blnd last and uns rdr* **8/11**[1]

4m 51.5s (-14.20) **Going Correction** -0.475s/f (Good) **7** Ran SP% **112.3**
Speed ratings: **109,96,94,94,93 87,—**
toteswingers:1&2:£4.50, 1&3:£8.50, 2&3:£5.50 CSF £35.95 TOTE £7.00: £3.80, £5.40; EX 33.30.
Owner D Allen **Bred** Mrs J K M Oliver **Trained** Mollington, Oxon

FOCUS
A fair beginners' chase in which the winner is rated a three-length winner from the faller.

NOTEBOOK
Edgeover held strong claims on the form shown when second to French Opera at Ascot last October and he had already mastered Ikorodu Road when that one departed at the last. A strong-travelling sort, he looks capable of defying a penalty before going handicapping. (op 5-1 tchd 6-1)
Viper, making his debut for a new yard, showed enough to make him of interest once handicapping. (op 13-2 tchd 7-1)
Reel Missile was ultimately left trailing on this return to fences (op 9-1 tchd 11-1)
Springfield Raki will find easier opportunities in low-grade handicaps. (op 14-1 tchd 20-1)

Ikorodu Road, off since finishing second off 119 at Newbury last November, looked the one to beat on that form, but he had been headed and looked booked for second when blundering and unseating his rider at the last. This wasn't his day, but he will have no trouble winning races over fences. (op 10-11)

715 BETFAIR H'CAP HURDLE (10 hdls) 2m 3f

3:35 (3:35) (Class 3) (0-125,120) 4-Y-0+ **£6,505** (£1,910; £955; £477)

Form RPR

33-0 **1** **Black Jacari (IRE)**[19] 447 5-11-2 **117**.................. KyleJames[(7)] 116
(Philip Kirby) *t.k.h and prom: lost pl 7th: sn rdn: 7th next: 7 l 5th st: rallied bef last: surged past ldng trio on long run-in to get up cl home* **16/1**

0-62 **2** ¾ **Mister Benedictine**[13] 523 7-11-9 **117**..................(t) MarkGrant 116+
(Brendan Duke) *hld up: trckd ldrs gng wl fr 5th: tk ld w ears pricked and hit 2 out: rdn flat: ct cl home* **8/1**

/43- **3** 2 **Wot Way Chief**[44] 45 9-11-1 **114**.................. JamesHalliday[(5)] 111
(Malcolm Jefferson) *hld up: mstke 5th: prog 3 out: 4th bef next: rdn and sustained effrt fr 2 out: disp 2nd and ev ch last: nt qckn fnl 100yds* **5/1**[2]

2U-3 **4** 2¾ **Bathwick Man**[19] 447 5-11-11 **119**..................(tp) TomScudamore 113
(David Pipe) *pressed ldr tl led 7th: drvn and hdd nring 2 out: disp 2nd at last: wknd flat* **4/1**[1]

44-1 **5** 6 **Stage Acclaim (IRE)**[21] 159 5-11-7 **120**.......... SamTwiston-Davies[(5)] 108
(Dr Richard Newland) *sn pressing ldrs: effrt 3 out: 3rd and rdn bef next: wknd between last two* **11/2**[3]

0-04 **6** 7 **Ravati (IRE)**[12] 541 4-10-7 **110**.................. MissLHorner[(5)] 86
(Chris Grant) *hld up in rr: outpcd by ldrs fr wl bef 2 out* **14/1**

11-6 **7** 1¾ **The Good Guy (IRE)**[27] 331 7-11-11 **119**.................. JodieMogford 98
(Graeme McPherson) *taken down early: led tl 7th: qckly lost pl* **16/1**

14-4 **8** 4½ **The Gloves Are Off (IRE)**[23] 401 7-11-6 **119**.......... GilesHawkins[(5)] 93
(Sue Smith) *cl up: rdn and lost pl 3 out: no ch whn mstke next* **20/1**

1P6- **9** 2¼ **Holoko Heights**[136] 3668 5-11-10 **118**..................(v[1]) RichardJohnson 90
(Tim Vaughan) *hld up in rr: 7 l last whn j. slowly 6th and lost tch: prog after 3 out to take mod 6th next: no ex* **8/1**

0-33 **10** 7 **Consulate (IRE)**[12] 534 6-11-6 **114**.................. DarylJacob 81
(Gordon Edwards) *nt a fluent: prom tl wknd 3 out* **4/1**[1]

236- **11** 2 **King Ozzy (IRE)**[161] 3216 6-11-3 **111**.................. GerardTumelty 74
(Martin Keighley) *bhd: rdn 3 out: no rspnse and sn btn* **12/1**

4m 37.9s (-1.50) **Going Correction** +0.10s/f (Yiel)
WFA 4 from 5yo+ 17lb **11 Ran SP% 125.2**
Speed ratings (Par 107): **107,106,105,104,102 99,98,96,95,92 91**
toteswingers:1&2:not won, 1&3:£5.50, 2&3:£11.80 CSF £146.57 CT £753.47 TOTE £18.20: £5.40, £2.10, £2.40; EX 132.70.
Owner Keith Sivills **Bred** Allevamento Gialloblu S R L **Trained** Castleton, N Yorks

FOCUS
A competitive handicap hurdle with the winner and third rated to their marks.

NOTEBOOK
Black Jacari(IRE), well beaten at Perth on his recent return to hurdles, didn't look at all badly weighted and he came with a strong late run to deny Mister Benedictine, who looked to have done enough. This was a likeable effort, considering he had been shuffled back through the pack, and he appeals as the type with more to offer. (op 14-1)
Mister Benedictine travelled best for much of the way, and found plenty to fend off the third, but he had no answer when the winner swept past close home. He remains on a lengthy losing run, but that should end at some point if he can reproduce this sort of form.
Wot Way Chief was produced to hold every chance under a fine ride, but couldn't race on with the front pair from the last. He's ideally suited by a bit further. (op 15-2 tchd 9-2)
Bathwick Man, well ahead of the winner at Perth, didn't get home again stronger stayers having been ridden positively and was disappointing. (op 5-1 tchd 6-1)
Stage Acclaim(IRE), raised 5lb for his Huntingdon victory, didn't get home over this longer trip. (op 7-1 tchd 8-1)
The Good Guy(IRE) Official explanation: jockey said gelding hung left throughout
Consulate(IRE) made mistakes and proved disappointing. (op 6-1 tchd 7-2)

716 JAMIE ARCHER IN CONCERT 21ST AUGUST H'CAP CHASE (14 fncs) 2m 6f 110y

4:10 (4:10) (Class 4) (0-110,109) 5-Y-0+ **£3,252** (£955; £477; £238)

Form RPR

3-05 **1** **Chorizo (IRE)**[26] 352 9-11-4 **106**.................. JamesHalliday[(5)] 121+
(Richard Guest) *pressed ldr gng wl: chal and hit last: rdn to ld fnl 50yds: hld on gamely* **9/2**[3]

6/-1 **2** hd **Public Esteem (IRE)**[8] 593 9-10-2 **92**..................(p) MrsAlexDunn[(7)] 105
(Dr Richard Newland) *led: slt advantage whn outj. rival last: urged along and hdd 50yds out: kpt on wl* **7/2**[2]

5-44 **3** 9 **Sycho Fred (IRE)**[13] 516 9-10-0 **83** oh5..................(t) GrahamLee 87
(Mike Sowersby) *pressed ldrs: rdn 3 out: 4 l 3rd and btn next* **9/2**[3]

1-00 **4** 4½ **More Like It (IRE)**[17] 460 10-10-10 **93**..................(p) BrianHughes 92
(Peter Niven) *nt a fluent: chsd ldrs: rdn 10th: cajoled along on heels of ldrs bef 3 out: btn next: mstke last* **28/1**

2-23 **5** 7 **Indian Pipe Dream (IRE)**[11] 550 8-11-11 **108**..........(tp) KeithMercer 101
(Steve Gollings) *already pushed along whn j. slowly 2nd: rdn rest of way and nt keen on outside: mstke 8th: struggling after* **15/8**[1]

3P-3 **6** 7 **Shrewd Investor (IRE)**[22] 425 10-11-8 **108**..........(p) FearghalDavis[(3)] 93
(Henry Hogarth) *pressed ldng pair: rdn and lost pl 11th: btn bef next* **11/1**

05-5 **7** 46 **Gratification**[29] 299 7-11-0 **97**.................. LeightonAspell 36
(Oliver Sherwood) *hld up in tch: nt fluent 10th: wknd bef 3 out: j. bdly rt next: eased and t.o* **12/1**

5m 31.8s (-14.20) **Going Correction** -0.475s/f (Good) **7 Ran SP% 112.8**
Speed ratings: **105,104,101,100,97 95,79**
toteswingers:1&2:£3.80, 1&3:£3.60, 2&3:£4.40 CSF £20.48 CT £73.29 TOTE £5.10: £1.40, £2.50; EX 18.30.
Owner EERC **Bred** N J Henderson And Mrs S A Aston **Trained** Stainforth, S Yorks

FOCUS
A moderate handicap chase with the first two rated to their best.

NOTEBOOK
Chorizo(IRE), still 6lb higher than when winning over C&D last July, had looked in need of both previous outings this year and he overcame a mistake at the last to score, holding on well from the gritty runner-up. (op 5-1 tchd 13-2)
Public Esteem(IRE), winner of a selling handicap hurdle at Newton Abbot last week, has some previous experience of fences, and is a point winner, so it was no surprise to see him run well on this return to chasing. He could pick up a small race off this sort of mark. (op 4-1 tchd 3-1)
Sycho Fred(IRE), racing from 5lb 'wrong', ran a more encouraging race and will be suited by a return to further. (op 5-1 tchd 11-2)
More Like It(IRE), 6lb below his last winning chase mark, ran a bit better than his finishing position suggests. (op 22-1 tchd 33-1)
Indian Pipe Dream(IRE) was laboured from an early stage and failed to reproduce his earlier course form. (op 9-4 tchd 13-8)

717 LLOYD DANIELS SINGING HERE 21ST AUGUST H'CAP HURDLE (10 hdls) 2m 5f

4:45 (4:45) (Class 4) (0-105,105) 4-Y-0+ **£2,602** (£764; £382; £190)

Form RPR

FU-4 **1** **Strobe**[19] 447 6-10-9 **95**..................(p) AlexanderVoy[(7)] 106+
(Lucy Normile) *prom: swishing tail 1/2-way: led bef 2 out where mstke: rdn clr fr next* **12/1**

P-01 **2** 8 **Marlborough Sound**[11] 557 11-10-6 **85**.................. PaddyAspell 91+
(James Turner) *hld up: effrt to chse ldrs 7th: hmpd next: sn rdn in 4th: tried to rally 2 out: wnt 2nd last: outpcd by wnr flat* **11/4**[1]

10-3 **3** 2 **Kilshannig (IRE)**[12] 532 5-10-12 **94**..................(t) RichieMcLernon[(3)] 94
(Jonjo O'Neill) *nt fluent 1st: chsd ldrs: mstke and rdn 7th: chsd wnr 2 out: no imp whn mstke last* **5/1**[2]

0-02 **4** 19 **Terenzium (IRE)**[8] 606 8-11-12 **105**..................(p) BarryKeniry 87
(Micky Hammond) *prom: led after 5th: rdn and hdd bef 2 out: dropped out rapidly: poor 4th whn blnd last* **11/2**[3]

456- **5** 2½ **Montevetro**[50] 5339 5-10-4 **83**.................. AndrewTinkler 66
(William Clay) *j. poorly and nvr gng wl or looking keen in rr: lost tch: bdly hmpd 3 out: t.o after* **13/2**

005- **6** 11 **Golden Alchemist**[54] 5258 7-11-9 **102**..................(p) RobertThornton 74
(Mark Usher) *dropped to rr after 5th and sn rdn: struggling fr next: hmpd 3 out: t.o after* **11/2**[3]

00/0 **7** 2¼ **Ramblees Holly**[23] 405 12-9-9 **79** oh5.................. JamesHalliday[(5)] 43
(Robert Wood) *towards rr: rdn and lost tch 6th: t.o after 3 out* **33/1**

603- **F** **Adjami (IRE)**[11] 5389 9-10-1 **80**..................(p) LiamTreadwell —
(John Harris) *sn led: hdd after 5th: prom and gng wl whn fell 3 out* **14/1**

40-5 **B** **Lady Wright (IRE)**[15] 494 7-11-2 **95**.................. DenisO'Regan —
(Michael Easterby) *settled in rr: effrt 6th: pressing ldrs whn b.d 3 out* **13/2**

5m 15.9s (7.10) **Going Correction** +0.10s/f (Yiel) **9 Ran SP% 118.1**
Speed ratings (Par 105): **105,101,101,93,93 88,87,—,—**
toteswingers:1&2:£9.40, 1&3:£15.30, 2&3:£4.40 CSF £47.29 CT £193.74 TOTE £19.20: £5.80, £2.80, £2.40; EX 82.80.
Owner Miss P A & P J Carnaby **Bred** Old Mill Stud **Trained** Duncrievie, Perth & Kinross

FOCUS
A modest handicap hurdle in which the winner was back to his 2009 best with the third to his mark.

NOTEBOOK
Strobe travelled well throughout and stayed on strongly to draw right away after the last. Now rated 5lb lower than when winning his one previous race at Musselburgh, there was a bit of promise in his latest Perth effort, and the better ground here clearly suited him well. (op 10-1)
Marlborough Sound closed right up coming to two out and had his chance, but proved no match for the winner. (op 9-2)
Kilshannig(IRE) was another who closed up coming to the second-last, and held every chance, but like the runner-up, could do nothing as the winner galloped clear. (op 9-2)
Terenzium(IRE)'s finishing effort was surprisingly weak considering he had finished second over 2m6f at Wetherby last time. (op 5-2)
Montevetro was also badly affected in the incident three out. (op 10-1)
Golden Alchemist Official explanation: jockey said gelding returned lame
Adjami(IRE) was still going well when coming down. (op 8-1)
Lady Wright(IRE) was still bang there when brought down by the fall of the strong-travelling Adjami. (op 8-1)

718 STUART "QUICKLY" MURFIN MEMORIAL STANDARD OPEN NATIONAL HUNT FLAT RACE 2m 1f

5:15 (5:16) (Class 6) 4-6-Y-0 **£1,507** (£439; £219)

Form RPR

15-2 **1** **Priceless Art (IRE)**[29] 311 5-11-9 0.................. BrianHughes 120+
(Alan Swinbank) *w ldr: led after 4f: cantered clr 3f out: hrd hld* **1/3**[1]

2 7 **Fill The Power (IRE)** 4-10-13 0.................. TjadeCollier 93
(Sue Smith) *chsd ldrs: rdn 4f out: wnt 2nd 2f out: no ch w effrtless wnr* **16/1**

3 4½ **Tealissio** 4-10-13 0.................. LeightonAspell 89
(Lucy Wadham) *settled in rr: clsd over 3f out: disp 2nd but rdn 2f out: wknd over 1f out* **6/1**[2]

4 7 **Up And Away (IRE)**[33] 5-11-2 0.................. AndrewThornton 85
(Caroline Bailey) *prom: t.k.h early: wnt 2nd 6f out tl rdn 2f out: sn wknd* **12/1**

5 13 **Robello** 6-11-2 0.................. RobertThornton 72
(Richard Phillips) *midfield: drvn 1/2-way: struggling 4f out: plodded on* **10/1**[3]

0 **6** 2 **Old Emily Rose**[32] 254 5-10-4 0.................. SamTwiston-Davies[(5)] 63
(Althea Barclay) *chsd ldrs: rdn 5f out: lost tch 3f out: t.o* **33/1**

0- **7** 5 **Muzey's Princess**[46] 27 4-10-6 0.................. RodiGreene 55
(Michael Mullineaux) *w wnr 4f: rdn and wknd 1/2-way: t.o fnl 3f* **100/1**

0- **8** 1¾ **Carrifran (IRE)**[244] 1692 5-10-9 0.................. DougieCostello 56
(Malcolm Jefferson) *t.k.h towards rr: rdn 1/2-way: t.o fnl 3f* **20/1**

0 **9** nse **Whiskey Ridge (IRE)**[26] 355 4-10-13 0.................. TomMessenger 60
(Sue Smith) *midfield: struggling 4f out: t.o fnl 3f* **25/1**

10 dist **Captain Tee Gee** 4-10-6 0.................. StevenGagan[(7)] —
(Michael Chapman) *plld hrd briefly: detached in last: hopelessly t.o fr 1/2-way: btn quarter of a m* **66/1**

P **Monty's Fortune**[34] 5-10-9 0.................. AlexanderVoy[(7)] —
(Mike Sowersby) *plld v hrd: midfield whn rn wd and p.u 10f out: dismntd* **125/1**

4m 8.10s (7.00) **Going Correction** +0.10s/f (Yiel)
WFA 4 from 5yo+ 3lb **11 Ran SP% 126.8**
Speed ratings: **87,83,81,78,72 71,68,68,68,21 —**
toteswingers:1&2:£6.70, 1&3:£2.10, 2&3:£9.40 CSF £8.85 TOTE £1.40: £1.02, £4.80, £1.40; EX 13.60 Place 6 £288.90; Place 5 £132.62.
Owner Matthew Green & David Manasseh **Bred** Lady Bamford **Trained** Melsonby, N Yorks

FOCUS
A weak bumper but an impressive winner.

NOTEBOOK
Priceless Art(IRE) had easily the strongest profile of these and readily defied the penalty. Disappointing at Perth last time having earlier finished fifth in the Aintree Championship Bumper, he looks a bright hurdling prospect and is likely to win again if kept on the go. (op 8-15)
Fill The Power(IRE), from a yard whose newcomers often need a run, kept galloping away for second and showed a good deal of ability. He will be suited by a stiffer test once sent hurdling. (op 12-1)
Tealissio, the second foal of a bumper winner, shaped nicely enough back in third and should improve. (op 11-2 tchd 5-1)
Up And Away(IRE), runner-up in a couple of points, was readily outpaced in the straight and will do better once tackling a longer distance over hurdles. (op 11-1)
Monty's Fortune Official explanation: jockey said saddle slipped

T/Plt: £617.10 to a £1 stake. Pool:£39,735.22 - 47.00 winning tickets T/Qpdt: £81.20 to a £1 stake. Pool:£4,091.43 - 37.25 winning tickets IM

719 - 725a (Foreign Racing) - See Raceform Interactive

624 HEXHAM (L-H)

Saturday, June 12

OFFICIAL GOING: Good to soft (good in places; 7.3)

Wind: Slight, half against Weather: Overcast

726 TERESA DUCHETT MARES' NOVICES' HURDLE (8 hdls) 2m 110y
1:55 (1:55) (Class 4) 4-Y-0+ **£3,425** (£998; £499)

Form				RPR
1-2	1		**Dorabelle (IRE)**28 [332] 5-10-10 0 JasonMaguire (Donald McCain) *trckd ldrs: rdn to ld bef last: styd on wl run-in* **8/11**1	91+
41-1	2	3/4	**Tharaya**23 [423] 5-11-10 105 KeithMercer (James Turner) *hld up in tch: pushed along after 2 out: hdwy to chse wnr bef last: kpt on run-in* **85/40**2	104+
P06-	3	7	**Zoenicibel**127 [3871] 6-10-5 87 JamesHalliday(5) (Malcolm Jefferson) *cl up: led bef 4 out to bef 2 out: ev ch bef last: one pce run-in* **11/1**3	83
0-	4	8	**Orpen Bid (IRE)**291 [1303] 5-10-7 0 RyanMania(3) (A M Crow) *led to bef 4 out: led bef 2 out to bef last: sn wknd* **100/1**	75
0-	5	1	**Flying Bella**15 [512] 4-10-0 0 EJO'Connell(7) (J J Lambe, Ire) *hld up in tch: rdn and outpcd 2 out: n.d after* **20/1**	71
6-	6	33	**Marillos Proterras**17 [814] 4-10-7 0 GrahamLee (Ann Duffield) *nt fluent in rr: pushed along fr 4th: wknd fr 3 out: t.o* **16/1**	38

4m 19.7s (2.30) **Going Correction** -0.075s/f (Good)
WFA 4 from 5yo+ 17lb **6** Ran SP% **109.9**
Speed ratings (Par 105): **91,90,87,83,83 67**
toteswingers: 1&2 £1.02, 1&3 £3.10, 2&3 £4.50 CSF £2.45 TOTE £1.60: £1.10, £1.50; EX 2.30.
Owner Brendan Richardson **Bred** Tommy James **Trained** Cholmondeley, Cheshire

FOCUS

A fair mares' novice hurdle to start proceedings.

NOTEBOOK

Dorabelle(IRE) was making her debut over hurdles and was odds-on to win, having already shown plenty of ability in bumpers. She gave her supporters a few scares and was rather green and novicey, but eventually got the job done well, and this stocky mare looks the type to progress with experience. (tchd 4-5)

Tharaya faced a tough task under her double penalty but went down fighting and was certainly not disgraced. She can produce some finishing speed at this level and will probably be able to win a handicap if not over-burdened. She is big enough to be worth considering over fences. (op 2-1 tchd 15-8)

Zoenicibel comes from a stable in form but was only gaining her second placing from seven attempts.This race may have been too slowly run to be ideal for her. (op 22-1)

Orpen Bid(IRE) was mounted on the course and gave some trouble at the start. Even at this slow speed, she seemed to be struggling for stamina. (tchd 80-1)

Flying Bella is small and was firmly put in her place in the closing stages. (op 14-1 tchd 11-1)

Marillos Proterras is not a natural over jumps yet. (op 40-1)

727 PROSPECT ESTATES H'CAP HURDLE (8 hdls) 2m 110y
2:30 (2:30) (Class 4) (0-110,107) 4-Y-0+ **£4,228** (£1,241; £620; £310)

Form				RPR
3P-3	1		**Beat The Shower**14 [519] 4-11-12 107 GrahamLee (Peter Niven) *hld up in tch: stdy hdwy bef 2 out: rdn to ld bef last: hld on wl run-in* **5/1**2	104+
/-06	2	1 1/4	**Bollin Ruth**10 [582] 8-10-12 97 CallumWhillans(7) (Donald Whillans) *hld up in tch: drvn and outpcd bef 2 out: rallied bef last: chsd wnr run-in: r.o* **12/1**	95
040-	3	2	**Weetfromthechaff**12 [2595] 5-11-2 97 (t) MichaelMcAlister(3) (Maurice Barnes) *t.k.h: cl up: rdn and led briefly bef last: hit last: one pce run-in* **40/1**	94
0-03	4	3 3/4	**Wensleydale Web**10 [582] 8-11-0 92 DenisO'Regan (Martin Todhunter) *t.k.h: hld up in tch: outpcd 2 out: rallied bef last: no imp run-in* **6/1**3	83
2-11	5	1 1/2	**Ardesia (IRE)**10 [582] 6-11-4 96 BrianHughes (Tina Jackson) *chsd ldrs: drvn and outpcd 2 out: rallied bef last: sn no imp* **5/6**1	86
0/F-	6	4 1/2	**Hair Of The Dog**214 [2222] 6-10-1 82 CampbellGillies(3) (William Amos) *mde most to bef last: sn rdn and wknd* **16/1**	68
	7	16	**King Benny (IRE)**139 [3640] 6-11-3 95 JohnnyFarrelly (Elliott Cooper) *t.k.h: cl up: chal 3rd: rdn and wknd after 2 out* **12/1**	66
00-0	8	11	**Prize Fighter (IRE)**27 [350] 8-11-0 92 PaddyAspell (Lynn Siddall) *hld up: hdwy and prom 3 out: rdn and wknd next* **18/1**	50

4m 17.1s (-0.30) **Going Correction** -0.075s/f (Good) **8** Ran SP% **114.5**
Speed ratings (Par 105): **97,96,95,93,93 90,83,78**
toteswingers: 1&2 £9.00, 2&3 £12.30, 1&3 not won. CSF £59.40 CT £2130.82 TOTE £7.50: £1.90, £3.80, £6.80; EX 55.80.
Owner Mrs Kate Young **Bred** C P E Brooks **Trained** Barton-le-Street, N Yorks

FOCUS

About five seconds faster than the mares' race, and a fine ride by Graham Lee on the winner.

NOTEBOOK

Beat The Shower was being urged along after only one flight of hurdles, but was always persuaded to keep in touch. This Catterick Flat winner has already been placed in a 2m3f hurdle, and he probably found this trip a bare minimum for requirements. He showed a feisty attitude in the paddock and often lashed out with his hind legs, but buckled down well to his work to defy top weight. However, with Ardesia under-performing badly, this was not a great race. (op 7-1)

Bollin Ruth tries hard but is only small. She has won at Hexham before and made a valiant attempt after the last. She deserves another success, but may need to slip a bit more in the handicap. (op 9-1 tchd 8-1)

Weetfromthechaff casts doubts on the strength of the form as he has never won. He would have finished a bit closer had he not crashed over the last. (op 33-1)

Wensleydale Web is a dual Cartmel scorer but is a ten-time Hexham loser and never looked like breaking that hoodoo. (op 11-2 tchd 7-1)

Ardesia(IRE) had scored twice in four days at Cartmel and only had a ten-day break since. He had enough on his plate at these weights but was already weary well before the last, and may need a break. (op 11-8 tchd 6-4 in a place)

Hair Of The Dog has not learned to settle. (op 12-1 tchd 10-1)

King Benny(IRE) raced keenly for a long way and must not be written off yet. Official explanation: jockey said gelding ran too free and hung left-handed (op 15-2)

Prize Fighter(IRE) has not won over hurdles since 2005 and remains badly out of form. (op 12-1)

728 LORDS TAVERNERS H'CAP CHASE (12 fncs) 2m 110y
3:05 (3:05) (Class 4) (0-115,114) 5-Y-0+ **£5,204** (£1,528; £764; £381)

Form				RPR
F5P-	1		**Ormus**49 [5390] 7-10-1 89 (p) KeithMercer (Christopher Wilson) *prom: effrt after 2 out: led run-in: styd on wl* **15/2**3	104
10-2	2	1 3/4	**Stagecoach Pearl**23 [422] 6-11-7 114 ShaneByrne(5) (Sue Smith) *t.k.h: chsd ldrs: ev ch 3 out: led after next: hdd run-in: kpt on same pce* **3/1**2	127
-242	3	10	**Emotive**14 [516] 7-10-0 91 CampbellGillies(3) (Barry Murtagh) *nt fluent: hld up in tch: outpcd 5th: rallied and in tch 7th: rdn bef 3 out: hdwy bef last: no ch w first two* **3/1**2	98+
0P-4	4	5	**Well Oiled (IRE)**24 [395] 9-10-2 90 (tp) PaddyAspell (Sandy Forster) *led to 3rd: led 5th to after 2 out: wknd bef last* **10/1**	90
1-44	5	8	**Heavenly Chorus**18 [460] 8-10-9 97 GrahamLee (Keith Reveley) *bhd: outpcd 5th: rallied and in tch 7th: mstke next: rdn and outpcd 3 out: n.d after* **9/4**1	92
2P-4	6	19	**Red Jester**28 [339] 9-10-13 101 LiamHeard (Gerald Ham) *led to 3rd: cl up: rdn 5th: rallied: wknd fr 3 out* **14/1**	77

4m 1.80s (-8.00) **Going Correction** -0.325s/f (Good) **6** Ran SP% **108.3**
Speed ratings: **105,104,99,97,93 84**
toteswingers: 1&2 £8.50, 1&3 £8.50, 2&3 £3.50 CSF £28.43 TOTE £12.10: £5.30, £2.30.
Owner David Bartlett **Bred** Mrs Andrea Bartlett **Trained** Manfield, N Yorks

FOCUS

Generally hard to win with types and the result was something of a surprise.

NOTEBOOK

Ormus had only scored once in 24 previous attempts, over hurdles at Musselburgh 15 months ago. He was tailed off and pulled-up last time out, but first-time cheekpieces may have helped his concentration, and he jumped better than he often does. It would be unwise to be carried away with this form. Official explanation: trainer said, regarding apparent improvement in form, that the gelding benefited from the application of cheek pieces and a lay-off of 49 days. (op 9-1 tchd 10-1)

Stagecoach Pearl was trying to concede 13lb or more to his rivals and looked like succeeding between the last two, but his three previous wins were on flat tracks and he rather ran out of steam at the end. It was a decent performance nonetheless. (tchd 11-4)

Emotive had run well at Cartmel but he has only scored once in 29 races and the drop back to the minimum trip and a few jumping errors conspired against him. He was staying on at the end, and needs to run over further. (tchd 5-2)

Well Oiled(IRE) was beaten for the 11th time over fences and dropped out of contention tamely. (op 9-1)

Heavenly Chorus scored over hurdles here in April but looked moody and could only be persuaded to get into contention briefly. She awaits a first success over fences after ten tries. Official explanation: trainer said mare jumped poorly throughout (op 11-4 tchd 2-1)

Red Jester had come a very long way for this, and he has previously done well on hilly tracks such as Towcester, but he took a walk in the market and trailed home. Official explanation: jockey said gelding never travelled (op 15-2)

729 POLA MINERALS H'CAP HURDLE (10 hdls) 2m 4f 110y
3:40 (3:40) (Class 4) (0-110,110) 4-Y-0+ **£4,553** (£1,337; £668; £333)

Form				RPR
/0-1	1		**Fair Spin**18 [459] 10-9-9 84 oh9 (v) JamesHalliday(5) (Micky Hammond) *cl up: led bef last: drew clr run-in* **9/2**2	91+
U-31	2	8	**Paddington Bob (IRE)**12 [552] 6-10-4 88 GrahamLee (Pauline Robson) *led: nt fluent 3 out: hdd bef last: kpt on same pce* **11/8**1	86
-521	3	2 3/4	**Patriot (IRE)**18 [457] 6-11-8 109 (t) MichaelMcAlister(3) (Maurice Barnes) *t.k.h: cl up: rdn 2 out: kpt on same pce last* **13/2**	105
P-41	4	nk	**Sparkling Zola**18 [461] 8-10-7 98 GarryWhillans(7) (Alistair Whillans) *hld up in tch: outpcd 3 out: rallied bef last: no imp run-in* **11/2**3	93
4	5	43	**Nobetter Buachaill (IRE)**14 [514] 8-11-0 105 EJO'Connell(7) (J J Lambe, Ire) *hld up in tch: effrt 2 out: wknd qckly between last 2* **18/1**	62
360-	6	46	**Yachvili (IRE)**11 [571] 7-11-12 110 JohnnyFarrelly (J J Lambe, Ire) *cl up tl wknd qckly fr 2 out* **16/1**	25
50-5	F		**Leith Walk (IRE)**24 [393] 7-10-5 96 CallumWhillans(7) (Donald Whillans) *in tch: rdn after 3 out: 5l 5th and outpcd whn fell next* **8/1**	—

5m 8.10s (-4.40) **Going Correction** -0.075s/f (Good) **7** Ran SP% **111.3**
Speed ratings (Par 105): **105,101,100,100,84 66,—**
toteswingers: 1&2 £1.60, 2&3 £6.40, 1&3 not won. CSF £10.88 TOTE £4.10: £2.70, £3.20; EX 14.90.
Owner Bendery Properties Holdings Ltd **Bred** A S Reid **Trained** Middleham Moor, N Yorks

FOCUS

Four previous course winners on show here, and a third success at the track for Fair Spin.

NOTEBOOK

Fair Spin has been tumbling down the weights, and this sometimes irresolute sort came here on the back of a success at Pontefract in April. He travelled strongly throughout and saw the race out with plenty of determination on a course which brings out the best in him. He was 9lb out of the weights but that did not stop him from making it three wins in a row. (tchd 4-1 and 5-1)

Paddington Bob(IRE) was a well-backed favourite to follow up his Cartmel success, but he had had to pull out all the stops to beat the perennial maiden Galley Slave there, and found himself outspeeded before the last. He looks rather one-paced but has the size to win chasing. (op 9-4)

Patriot(IRE) was a long time in winning but finally got off the mark at the 17th attempt here last month. He is consistent enough but this return to a handicap made things tough for him. (tchd 9-2)

Sparkling Zola stayed on after getting outpaced and was seen to far better advantage when she won over 3m here. (op 9-2 tchd 7-1)

Nobetter Buachaill(IRE) is more of a chaser on looks. (op 12-1)

Yachvili(IRE) won over C&D two years ago but this effort was very tame. (op 10-1)

730 LADY TAVERNERS H'CAP CHASE (15 fncs) 2m 4f 110y
4:10 (4:10) (Class 4) (0-100,99) 5-Y-0+ **£5,204** (£1,528; £764; £381)

Form				RPR
P3-P	1		**Tully Hill**42 [88] 9-10-0 73 oh1 GrahamLee (Kevin Hunter) *led to 8th: chsd ldr: effrt after 2 out: led run-in: edgd lft: hld on wl* **7/1**	78
U-32	2	1 1/2	**Hasper**17 [471] 12-10-9 89 MrGCrow(7) (Sandy Forster) *hld up: nt fluent 9th: hdwy 11th: effrt after 2 out: kpt on wl run-in* **4/1**2	93
3-F1	3	hd	**Ginger's Lad**17 [473] 6-10-6 79 (p) BrianHughes (Michael Easterby) *prom: hmpd 8th: drvn and outpcd after 2 out: rallied to chse wnr run-in: lost 2nd cl home* **3/1**1	82
5-P4	4	nk	**The Green Hat (IRE)**7 [625] 10-10-1 81 oh6 ow8 MrJohnDawson(7) (Theresa Gibson) *cl up: led 8th: rdn and hdd run-in: kpt on same pce* **20/1**	84+
51-P	5	7	**Dallas Bell**31 [287] 8-11-9 99 CampbellGillies(3) (Alistair Whillans) *in tch: drvn and outpcd after 3 out: no imp fr next* **5/1**3	96

6P-P **6** ½ **Panthers Run**[18] 459 10-10-6 79 ....(t) DougieCostello 75
(Jonathan Haynes) *bhd: drvn and outpcd 1/2-way: kpt on fr 2 out: nvr rchd ldrs* **28/1**
-P04 **7** 83 **Clueless**[17] 473 8-10-7 80 ....(p) PeterBuchanan 2
(Carol Ferguson) *in tch: lost pl bef 9th: struggling fr 11th: t.o* **13/2**
0-50 **P** **Flaming Heck**[10] 578 13-10-7 87 .... AlexanderVoy(7) —
(Lucy Normile) *sn bhd and detached: t.o whn p.u bef 9th* **18/1**
2P-5 **P** **Mischief Man**[24] 404 8-10-11 84 .... TjadeCollier —
(Sue Smith) *chsd ldrs: blnd bdly 8th: wknd 5 out: p.u bef next* **8/1**
5m 12.9s (-0.60) **Going Correction** -0.325s/f (Good) **9** Ran SP% **112.1**
Speed ratings: **88,87,87,87,84 84,52,—,—**
toteswingers: 1&2 £10.40, 1&3 £24.40, 2&3 £7.70 CSF £34.71 CT £100.91 TOTE £7.50: £1.90, £1.50, £1.70; EX 37.60.
Owner K Hunter **Bred** R D And Mrs J S Chugg **Trained** Natland, Cumbria

FOCUS
A moderate contest.

NOTEBOOK
Tully Hill often runs well for a long way but is normally easy to catch, and he finally won under rules (picked up an Irish point in 2005) at the 28th time of asking, giving his trainer Kevin Hunter a first success. He had given a bold display here in April but was eventually third beaten 31l, and this was another masterclass in the saddle from Lee, who did not panic when he was overtaken at halfway, and wrested back the advantage soon after the last. A follow up will not be easy. Official explanation: trainer had no explanation, regarding apparent improvement in form. (tchd 6-1)
Hasper won a hunter chase here last year but can be let down by his jumping and has a tendency to run in snatches. He looked as if he might mow down the leaders coming to the last but had given the winner just too much rope. (op 5-1 tchd 7-2)
Ginger's Lad needed 14 chances before he finally won and was made to look flat-footed a long way out. (op 5-2)
The Green Hat(IRE), trained within sight of the course and missing an eye, made a bold bid to lead from halfway and looked like holding on at the foot of the hill, but three rivals passed him from the last. Softer ground and possibly cheekpieces might work the oracle. (op 25-1)
Clueless Official explanation: jockey said gelding made a mistake and never travelled thereafter
Flaming Heck was very flighty last time and sulked badly here. (tchd 16-1)
Mischief Man had no hope of recovering after a bad blunder at halfway. Official explanation: jockey said gelding felt wrong behind after making bad mistake (tchd 16-1)

731 HADRIAN HEALTH CARE STANDARD OPEN NATIONAL HUNT FLAT RACE (DIV I) 2m 110y
4:45 (4:46) (Class 6) 4-6-Y-O **£1,370** (£399; £199)

Form RPR
03-1 **1** **Noble Scholar (IRE)**[17] 474 5-11-10 0 .... BrianHughes 106
(Alan Swinbank) *cl up: led over 4f out: hrd pressed over 1f out: hld on gamely fnl f* **4/1**[2]
2 *hd* **Aupcharlie (IRE)** 4-10-11 0 .... MrJPMcKeown(3) 96
(P E Collins, Ire) *hld up in midfield: hdwy over 4f out: effrt and chal over 1f out: kpt on fnl f: jst hld* **5/2**[1]
3- **3** 5 **Ciannte (IRE)**[50] 5-10-5 0 .... MrStevenCrawford(5) 87
(S R B Crawford, Ire) *trckd ldrs: effrt over 3f out: one pce appr fnl f* **4/1**[2]
1-4 **4** 5 **Corky Dancer**[30] 311 5-11-3 0 .... AlexanderVoy(7) 96
(P Monteith) *prom: outpcd 4f out: rallied over 2f out: no imp fnl f* **4/1**[2]
3/4- **5** 11 **La Bacouetteuse (FR)**[45] 47 5-11-3 0 .... PaddyAspell 78
(Simon Shirley-Beavan) *hld up: pushed along over 4f out: effrt 3f out: no imp fnl 2f* **22/1**
6 15 **Alta Rock (IRE)** 5-11-3 0 .... TjadeCollier 63
(Sue Smith) *uns rdr and loose bef s: hld up: hdwy and prom after 4f:* **33/1**
7 1 **Pollard (IRE)**[21] 4-11-0 0 .... JohnnyFarrelly 59
(I R Ferguson, Ire) *hld up on ins: drvn over 4f out: btn fnl 3f* **10/1**[3]
0 **8** 11 **Go Ruby Go**[34] 237 6-10-3 0 .... AdamWedge(7) 44
(Kevin Morgan) *bhd: struggling 1/2-way: nvr on terms* **50/1**
0 **9** *nk* **Hurryonharry**[30] 311 4-10-7 0 ....(t) MrJohnDawson(7) 48
(Brian Storey) *set slow pce: hdd over 4f out: sn wknd* **250/1**
10 15 **Balwyllo (IRE)** 5-11-3 0 .... BarryKeniry 36
(Ben Haslam) *prom tl wknd over 4f out* **28/1**
P **Ontario Lass (IRE)** 4-10-7 0 .... GrahamLee —
(Ferdy Murphy) *bhd: broke down and p.u 1/2-way* **14/1**
4m 15.2s (2.50) **Going Correction** -0.075s/f (Good)
WFA 4 from 5yo+ 3lb **11** Ran SP% **117.4**
Speed ratings: **91,90,88,86,81 73,73,68,68,61 —**
toteswingers: 1&2 £2.20, 1&3 £4.00, 2&3 £4.40 CSF £13.81 TOTE £5.60: £1.90, £1.90, £1.60; EX 22.90.
Owner Mrs B Watson **Bred** Moyglare Stud Farm Ltd **Trained** Melsonby, N Yorks
■ Stewards' Enquiry : Brian Hughes caution: used whip with excessive frequency.
Mr J P McKeown one-day ban: used whip with excessive frequency (tbn)

FOCUS
Shenanigans before the race, with Alta Rock unseating on the way to the start, and Peasant Law having to be withdrawn after an anti-social act in the paddock. The race was run at a crawl. Noble Scholar had won narrowly at Sedgefield and followed up in battling fashion. He is a good-sized individual and should win over hurdles. His trainer is an expert at producing horses to defy penalties in bumpers.

NOTEBOOK
Noble Scholar(IRE) had won narrowly at Sedgefield and followed up in battling fashion. He is a good-sized individual and should win over hurdles. His trainer is an expert at producing horses to defy penalties in bumpers (op 9-2)
Aupcharlie(IRE) is a leggy, unfurnished sort and was sent off favourite, perhaps because he is a half-brother to winners including the smart French hurdler La Grande Dame. He gave his all, and could be worth sending over from Ireland again to contest a similar event. (op 11-4 tchd 10-3 and 9-4)
Ciannte(IRE) is not very big, but has won an Irish point and been a good third in a bumper at Perth. Perhaps the first two were slightly better than average, so there is hope for her. (op 5-1)
Corky Dancer won at Kelso in the autumn, but he looked too small to be able to carry the penalty. (op 9-2)
Ontario Lass(IRE) Official explanation: vet said filly pulled up lame

732 HADRIAN HEALTH CARE STANDARD OPEN NATIONAL HUNT FLAT RACE (DIV II) 2m 110y
5:15 (5:22) (Class 6) 4-6-Y-O **£1,370** (£399; £199)

Form RPR
10-1 **1** **Lovey Dovey (IRE)**[20] 448 6-11-1 0 .... MrStevenCrawford(5) 122+
(S R B Crawford, Ire) *cl up: led 1/2-way: drew clr fr over 2f out: easily* **5/4**[1]
00/ **2** 11 **Be My Deputy (IRE)**[451] 4570 5-11-3 0 .... PaddyAspell 107
(Richard Guest) *hld up: stdy hdwy over 4f out: effrt over 3f out: chsd wnr ent fnl f: no imp* **22/1**
3 10 **Milano Supremo (IRE)**[36] 203 5-11-3 0 .... DenisO'Regan 98
(Chris Grant) *cl up: effrt over 3f out: no ex fr 2f out: lost 2nd ent fnl f* **7/4**[2]
2-6 **4** 2½ **Spring Snow (USA)**[27] 355 4-11-0 0 .... BrianHughes 92
(Alan Swinbank) *hld up in tch: drvn and outpcd 1/2-way: rallied over 2f out: nvr rchd ldrs* **5/1**[3]
5 8 **Oh Right (IRE)**[55] 6-11-0 0 .... RyanMania(3) 87
(Dianne Sayer) *led to 1/2-way: cl up tl rdn and wknd fr 3f out* **66/1**
644- **6** 1¾ **Janie's Encore**[280] 1388 5-10-10 0 .... GrahamLee 78
(Malcolm Jefferson) *t.k.h: chsd ldrs: drvn and outpcd 4f out: wknd 3f out* **22/1**
4- **7** ¾ **Jingoism (USA)**[46] 35 4-11-0 0 .... KeithMercer 81
(Brian Ellison) *hld up on outside: outpcd 1/2-way: n.d after* **25/1**
06 **8** 6 **Mystic Echo**[17] 474 4-10-7 0 .... DougieCostello 68
(John Davies) *in tch: outpcd over 5f out: sn btn* **100/1**
9 21 **Beano Boy** 5-11-3 0 .... PeterBuchanan 57
(Brian Storey) *midfield: outpcd 1/2-way: n.d after* **66/1**
0-0 **10** 6 **Why So Serious**[17] 474 4-11-0 0 ....(b[1]) WilsonRenwick 48
(Donald Whillans) *t.k.h: in tch: rdn over 5f out: wknd 4f out* **66/1**
P **Llobo** 4-11-0 0 .... TomMessenger —
(F Jestin) *bhd: lost tch 1/2-way: p.u over 5f out* **66/1**
4m 9.90s (-2.80) **Going Correction** -0.075s/f (Good)
WFA 4 from 5yo+ 3lb **11** Ran SP% **117.0**
Speed ratings: **103,97,93,91,88 87,87,84,74,71 —**
toteswingers: 1&2 £0.00, 1&3 £1.02, 2&3 £8.50 CSF £34.92 TOTE £2.40: £1.10, £4.10, £1.10; EX 40.90 Place 6 £37.42; Place 5 £34.74.
Owner S R B Crawford **Bred** Hugh Suffern Bloodstock Ltd **Trained** Larne, Co Antrim

FOCUS
A much better pace than division one, so the winning time was five seconds quicker. All bar the first four started at huge prices and did not belie their odds.

NOTEBOOK
Lovey Dovey(IRE) is a grand little mare who has now won three bumpers plus an Irish point. She ran right away from the opposition coming up the hill and never looked like being caught. Hopefully she can translate her ability to hurdling. (op 13-8)
Be My Deputy(IRE) is very tall and was returning from a long absence, having shaped like a stayer previously. He was not knocked about but kept going in good style and should win races. (op 14-1 tchd 25-1)
Milano Supremo(IRE) was making his first appearance for this yard, having shown promise in Ireland, although he did hang badly left when second in a tongue-tie last time. He was well backed suggesting the ability is there, and he is large enough to make a hurdler, which could be his job eventually, although a bit of improvement will be needed. (op 11-4 tchd 6-4)
Spring Snow(USA) has been disappointing, but seems to need more time and a much longer trip. (tchd 11-2)
Beano Boy Official explanation: jockey said gelding had a breathing problem
T/Plt: £134.90 to a £1 stake. Pool: £52,974.62 - 286.60 winning ticket. T/Qpdt: £21.30 to a £1 stake. Pool: £4,333.07 - 149.90 winning tickets. RY

521 STRATFORD (L-H)
Sunday, June 13

OFFICIAL GOING: Hurdle course - good to firm (good in places); chase course - good (good to firm in places)
All bends moved out increasing distances by about 6m per circuit.
Wind: Virtually nil Weather: Partly cloudy, bright spells

733 ALLENS CARAVANS NOVICES' HURDLE (9 hdls) 2m 110y
2:10 (2:10) (Class 3) 4-Y-O+ **£4,878** (£1,432; £716; £357)

Form RPR
3-2 **1** **Hilfiger (GER)**[43] 97 5-10-12 111 .... RobertThornton 116+
(Ian Williams) *w ldr tl led 2nd: mde rest at fast gallop: clr 6th: in command whn hit last: eased towards fin* **4/1**[3]
P-14 **2** 5 **Den Maschine**[16] 500 5-11-4 116 .... RhysFlint 115
(John Flint) *chsd ldng pair: wnt 2nd 6th: 2 l down and rdn bef 2 out: btn between last 2: plugged on for clr 2nd* **6/1**
526- **3** 9 **Danimix (IRE)**[280] 1398 5-10-7 0 .... DonalDevereux(5) 100+
(Peter Bowen) *racd off the pce in midfield: mstke 2nd: rdn and sme prog bef 6th: wnt 3rd bef 2 out: no imp on ldng pair after: n.d* **25/1**
S- **4** 16 **Society Venue**[148] 2856 5-10-12 0 .... TomScudamore 86
(Michael Scudamore) *sn wl bhd in last trio: virtually t.o 3rd: sme hdwy and modest 7th bef 6th: rdn to go 4th bef 2 out: nvr on terms* **50/1**
-213 **5** 1¼ **Cool Touch (IRE)**[16] 500 7-11-4 118 .... PaddyBrennan 92
(Nigel Twiston-Davies) *chsd ldng trio: mstke 5th: rdn and struggling whn hit next: wl btn 3 out* **7/4**[1]
6-21 **6** 4 **Saltagioo (ITY)**[10] 590 6-11-4 120 .... APMcCoy 89
(Milton Harris) *led tl mstke and hdd 2nd: w wnr after: hit 4th: 3rd and struggling whn mstke 6th: stl 3rd but wl btn next: wknd* **9/4**[2]
60-0 **7** 22 **Welcome Wonder**[16] 500 6-10-0 0 .... MichaelMurphy(5) 54
(John Allen) *nt fluent: sn wl bhd in last trio: t.o after 4th* **200/1**
50 **8** 37 **Swiss Guard**[13] 548 4-10-9 0 .... RichardJohnson 25
(Tim Vaughan) *nt jump fluently: sn toiling in last trio: t.o after 4th: burst blood vessel* **14/1**
P **Astania**[63] 5-9-12 0 .... MattGriffiths(7) —
(Philip Hobbs) *racd off the pce in midfield: mstke 1st: 5th and rdn after 4th: sn struggling and wknd after next: t.o whn p.u last* **33/1**
05-P **P** **Princess Soraya**[3] 688 4-10-2 80 ....(p) AidanColeman —
(Brendan Powell) *v reluctant to leave paddock: chsd ldrs but nvr on terms: rdn and reluctant after 5th: sn dropped to rr: t.o whn p.u 3 out* **100/1**
3m 48.7s (-7.30) **Going Correction** -0.30s/f (Good)
WFA 4 from 5yo+ 17lb **10** Ran SP% **118.3**
Speed ratings (Par 107): **105,102,98,90,90 88,78,60,—,—**
toteswingers: 1&2 £2.80, 1&3 £26.80, 2&3 £10.80 CSF £27.62 TOTE £5.50: £2.80, £2.40, £6.60; EX 31.90.
Owner Patrick Kelly **Bred** Gestut Hof Ittlingen **Trained** Portway, Worcs

FOCUS
This was a fair novices' hurdle.

NOTEBOOK
Hilfiger(GER), placed on both previous starts, seemed to appreciate the faster going and prospered under a positive ride, galloping on strongly and winning comfortably, despite getting the last wrong. A fair sort on the Flat in Germany, he appeals as the type with more to offer, and should be good enough to defy a penalty. (op 9-2 tchd 7-2)
Den Maschine, whose win came in a selling hurdle, has twice run well under a penalty now, and gives the impression he can win again in the right company. (op 13-2)
Danimix(IRE) improved markedly on his initial effort over hurdles and should do so again once faced with a stiffer test of stamina.
Society Venue, who had slipped up on one previous try over hurdles, made some late gains having got himself a long way back and should improve again for the experience. (op 100-1)

Cool Touch(IRE), ahead of the runner-up when third at the course latest, ran a laboured race, making mistakes under strong pressure and finishing weakly. This clearly wasn't his true form. (op 11-4 tchd 13-8)
Saltagioo(ITY) was another to disappoint, making several errors and ultimately dropping right out. (op 15-8 tchd 5-2)
Swiss Guard Official explanation: trainer said colt bled from the nose
Astania Official explanation: trainer said mare finished distressed

734 AVON CARAVAN PARK STRATFORD H'CAP CHASE (14 fncs) 2m 4f
2:40 (2:41) (Class 4) (0-115,116) 5-Y-O+ **£4,553** (£1,337; £668; £333)

Form RPR
6301 **1** **De Luain Gorm (IRE)**[10] 592 12-11-13 **116**.................... AidanColeman 132+
(Chris Down) *j. boldly: chsd ldr untl led 3rd: rdn bef last: in command whn hit last: eased flat* **9/2**[3]
2F1/ **2** 3 ¾ **Tampa Boy (IRE)**[426] 4988 8-11-1 **104**................................ CharliePoste 114
(Milton Harris) *chsd ldrs: wnt 2nd 6th: rdn after 2 out: kpt on trying but no imp on wnr after* **17/2**
62P- **3** 17 **Prince Noora (IRE)**[221] 2055 9-10-12 **101**..................(t) RichardJohnson 95
(Tim Vaughan) *hld up in last trio: hdwy 8th: struggling and rdn 11th: 4th and wl btn 2 out: wnt modest 3rd bef last* **5/1**
215- **4** 7 **Silver Dollars (FR)**[82] 4800 9-10-13 **102**................................ DarylJacob 90
(David Arbuthnot) *chsd ldrs: wnt 3rd 9th: rdn and no prog 11th: wl btn 2 out: lost 3rd bef last* **5/1**
4-12 **5** 6 **Foreign King (USA)**[27] 373 6-11-1 **109**..................... JimmyDerham(5) 94
(Seamus Mullins) *mstkes: a in rr: blnd 4th: rdn and struggling 11th: wl btn 2 out* **11/4**[1]
164- **P** **Glengarra (IRE)**[246] 1690 13-11-7 **110**..........................(tp) TimmyMurphy —
(Liam Corcoran) *led tl 3rd: chsd ldrs after tl dropped out rapidly after slow jump 9th: t.o whn p.u 3 out* **25/1**
14-P **U** **Benefit Game (IRE)**[35] 233 6-10-12 **101**................................ APMcCoy —
(Jonjo O'Neill) *bhd: rdn and effrt 10th: j. slowly next: 6th and wl btn whn blnd bdly and uns rdr 3 out* **4/1**[2]

4m 44.2s (-10.00) **Going Correction** -0.30s/f (Good) **7** Ran SP% **112.6**
Speed ratings: **108,106,99,96,94** —,—
toteswingers: 1&2 £16.10, 1&3 £3.90, 2&3 £13.30 CSF £38.30 TOTE £8.40: £5.70, £6.70; EX 56.70.
Owner Mrs M Trueman **Bred** Mrs Martina Dollard **Trained** Mutterton, Devon

FOCUS
They went a really good gallop in this handicap chase.

NOTEBOOK
De Luain Gorm(IRE) really pressed on once in front and keeping up the gallop remarkably well to supplement his Newton Abbot victory, despite being 12lb higher. His jumping was again an asset, and despite being a 12-y-o, he seems in the form of his life. (op 6-1 tchd 7-1)
Tampa Boy(IRE), who hadn't run since winning over hurdles at Fakenham 426 days ago, was able to perform off the same mark on this return to fences (well beaten one previous try), and he was the only one capable of staying with the winner, but couldn't match him. Official explanation: vet said gelding lost a right-fore shoe (op 8-1 tchd 9-1)
Prince Noora(IRE) remains 8lb higher than when last winning. (tchd 9-2)
Silver Dollars(FR) has a similar problem, in that he's 12lb above his last winning mark and clearly not up to winning off it. (op 11-2 tchd 6-1)
Foreign King(USA), some way ahead of the winner at Newton Abbot last time out, was in trouble quite a way out and never jumped well enough to mount a challenge. (op 7-2 tchd 5-2)
Benefit Game(IRE)'s jumping was again his downfall. (op 7-2 tchd 3-1)

735 NIGEL MUNN MEMORIAL H'CAP CHASE (17 fncs) 2m 7f
3:15 (3:15) (Class 3) (0-135,133) 5-Y-O **£6,337** (£1,872; £936; £468; £234)

Form RPR
-321 **1** **Putney Bridge**[5] 681 8-10-7 **114** 7ex................................(tp) TomO'Brien 133+
(Keith Goldsworthy) *mde all: clr fr 12th: rdn and kpt on wl between last 2: eased after last: comf* **3/1**[1]
53-1 **2** 12 **Ballycarney (IRE)**[32] 274 6-11-1 **122**.................................... JackDoyle 125
(Emma Lavelle) *chsd wnr tl after 8th: 3rd and wl outpcd 12th: wl btn 2 out: kpt on u.p flat to regain 2nd towards fin* **5/1**[3]
11-0 **3** 1 **Painter Man (FR)**[16] 501 8-10-13 **120**......................(bt) TomScudamore 122
(David Pipe) *chsd ldr tl wnt 2nd after 8th: rdn after 2 out: no imp on wnr and wl btn last: lost 2nd towards fin* **12/1**
2-52 **4** 2 ¾ **Tot Of The Knar**[8] 626 8-10-1 **113**..........................(p) DonalDevereux(5) 115
(Peter Bowen) *in tch in midfield: mstke 9th: rdn after next: sme hdwy u.p and blnd 13th: wnt modest 4th 3 out: nvr trbld wnr* **9/2**[2]
2-13 **5** 10 **Pheidias (IRE)**[13] 559 6-10-13 **120**...............................(p) DavidEngland 112
(Pam Sly) *chsd ldrs: nt a fluent and rdn along at times: drvn and struggling 11th: 4th and no ch w wnr fr 14th* **28/1**
PP-6 **6** 2 ¾ **Buck The Legend (IRE)**[15] 524 8-11-7 **128**................... PaddyBrennan 116
(Nigel Twiston-Davies) *mstkes: in midfield tl dropped to rr and mstke 8th: rdn and sme hdwy into midfield 14th: plugged on but nvr on terms w wnr* **16/1**
3-25 **7** 3 ¼ **Ginolad (AUS)**[21] 446 10-10-12 **119**.................................. AidanColeman 104
(Venetia Williams) *hld up towards rr: hdwy and wl in tch 9th: rdn and btn after 13th: wl btn 3 out* **16/1**
16-2 **8** 22 **Sou'Wester**[25] 411 10-11-8 **129**..(p) JoeTizzard 94
(Colin Tizzard) *a in rr: lost tch 12th: t.o 3 out* **16/1**
6-26 **9** 12 **The Duke's Speech (IRE)**[25] 411 9-10-12 **119**............... PaulMoloney 74
(Sophie Leech) *a bhd: j.rt 3rd: lost tch 12th: t.o fr 14th* **50/1**
P2-2 **10** 4 **Our Hero (IRE)**[24] 425 7-10-8 **115**..............................(tp) LiamTreadwell 66
(Charlie Longsdon) *in tch in midfield tl rdn and struggling 11th: sn bhd: t.o fr 14th* **9/1**
1F3- **11** 1 ½ **Present Gale (IRE)**[227] 1974 8-10-7 **117**.................... RichieMcLernon(3) 67
(Jonjo O'Neill) *in tch in midfield: mstke 9th: rdn and struggling 12th: wl btn 3 out* **25/1**
B0-P **12** ½ **Gaelic Flight (IRE)**[44] 78 12-11-4 **125**..........................(t) WillKennedy 110+
(Jeremy Scott) *chsd ldrs: mstke 6th and 13th: sn wknd: t.o after 2 out: virtually p.u after last* **33/1**
2PP- **13** 43 **Nostringsattached (IRE)**[50] 5395 9-11-12 **133**..................(p) APMcCoy 43
(Jonjo O'Neill) *hld up in midfield: rdn and no prog after 12th: wl btn next: t.o fr 3 out: burst blood vessel* **10/1**
455- **U** **Cruchain (IRE)**[101] 4402 7-10-10 **117**............................ DougieCostello —
(Jonjo O'Neill) *hld up in last pair: mstke 9th: rdn and no real prog after 11th: 9th and no ch whn blnd bdly and uns rdr 2 out* **16/1**

5m 37.5s (-4.10) **Going Correction** -0.30s/f (Good) **14** Ran SP% **122.4**
Speed ratings: **95,90,90,89,86 85,83,76,72,70 70,70,55**,—
toteswingers: 1&2 £2.30, 1&3 £4.40, 2&3 £12.40 CSF £18.73 CT £163.62 TOTE £3.20: £1.40, £2.60, £3.60; EX 18.50.
Owner Mrs L A Goldsworthy **Bred** I Norman **Trained** Yerbeston, Pembrokes

FOCUS
What had looked a competitive handicap chase was turned into a rout by Putney Bridge.

NOTEBOOK
Putney Bridge made every yard and stayed on strongly to defy the penalty he picked up for winning at Southwell earlier in the week. Still well handicapped on his hurdles form (rated 125), he is a dangerous horse when allowed an uncontested lead and may bid for a quick-fire hat-trick at Ffos Las later in the week. (op 9-2)
Ballycarney(IRE) looked a decent prospect when winning at Exeter, but he had a 10lb rise to overcome and proved no match for the winner. He did stay on again for second, though, and may be the sort to appreciate a marathon test. (tchd 11-2)
Painter Man(FR)'s good run of form came to an end when well beaten off this mark at the course last time, and for all that he ran better here, the impression was left that this mark is beyond him. (op 9-1 tchd 17-2)
Tot Of The Knar was unable to build on her Hexham second, failing to improve for the cheekpieces. (op 11-2)
Pheidias(IRE) had been beaten a long way off 3lb lower on his one previous try in a handicap and was again well held, for all that he wasn't disgraced. (op 25-1)
Buck The Legend(IRE) made errors and got well behind before plugging on late. (op 14-1)
Gaelic Flight(IRE) Official explanation: vet said gelding was struck into
Nostringsattached(IRE) Official explanation: trainer said gelding bled from the nose

736 ALLENS PARK HOMES H'CAP HURDLE (9 hdls) 2m 110y
3:50 (3:50) (Class 3) (0-130,124) 4-Y-O **£6,337** (£1,872; £936; £468; £234)

Form RPR
5-14 **1** **Dishdasha (IRE)**[15] 521 8-11-5 **124**...........................(t) OliverDayman(7) 127
(Alison Thorpe) *in tch in midfield: hdwy to press ldrs on outer after 3 out: unable qck whn sltly hmpd and swtchd lft sn after 2 out: lft w ev ch after last: kpt on wl to ld nr fin* **8/1**
611- **2** hd **Exulto (IRE)**[46] 51 5-11-0 **112**.................................... RichardJohnson 115
(Philip Hobbs) *hld up in last pair: hdwy to trck ldrs 3 out: rdn and effrt bef 2 out: looked hld in 2nd whn lft in ld sn after last: drvn and hdd nr fin* **9/4**[1]
13-2 **3** ¾ **Aohna (FR)**[29] 331 5-10-12 **110**...................................... RobertThornton 116+
(Alan King) *chsd ldng pair: wnt 2nd after 6th: rdn to ld bef 2 out: j.rt 2 out: looking wnr whn stmbld on landing and nrly uns rdr last: sn hdd: nt rcvr and styd on same pce after* **10/3**[3]
-012 **4** 1 ¼ **Stumped**[6] 664 7-10-7 **105**...(t) DarylJacob 106
(Milton Harris) *in tch in rr: pushed along after 5th: hdwy and rdn to chse ldrs after 3 out: kpt on same pce between last 2* **11/4**[2]
41-4 **5** 7 **Agente Romano (USA)**[38] 170 5-11-6 **118**....................... PaulMoloney 116+
(Evan Williams) *chsd ldr tl led 6th: blnd bdly 3 out: drvn and hdd bef 2 out: wknd between last 2* **7/1**
304- **6** 9 **Nordwind (IRE)**[262] 1515 9-11-9 **124**....................................... DPFahy(3) 111
(Evan Williams) *hld up in last pair: clsd and wl in tch 6th: drvn and wknd qckly after 3 out* **22/1**
43P- **7** 24 **Olympian Boy (IRE)**[199] 2262 0-10-0 **100**..................... TomScudamore 71
(Anabel L M King) *led tl 6th: dropping out and towards rr whn mstke next: lost tch bef 2 out: t.o* **16/1**

3m 48.7s (-7.30) **Going Correction** -0.30s/f (Good) **7** Ran SP% **114.4**
Speed ratings (Par 107): **105,104,104,103,100 96,85**
toteswingers: 1&2 £4.30, 1&3 £4.40, 2&3 £2.30 CSF £27.08 CT £72.51 TOTE £8.60: £4.30, £2.10; EX 30.60.
Owner Tristar **Bred** Locsot Srl **Trained** Bronwydd Arms, Carmarthens

FOCUS
The outcome of this handicap hurdle would surely have been different had Aohna not nearly unseated Robert Thornton at the last, losing momentum and leaving it to Dishdasha and Exulto to fight it out.

NOTEBOOK
Dishdasha(IRE) had finished fourth off this mark at the course last time, and his useful rider's 7lb claim was the difference maker, getting up in the final stride. It would be a surprise were he to follow up off a higher mark, however. (tchd 7-1 and 9-1)
Exulto(IRE), 11lb higher than when winning at Southwell in April, was closing on the eventual third when gifted with the lead after the last, but he couldn't quite hang on. The 5-y-o is clearly still progressing. (op 3-1)
Aohna(FR) ◆, not beaten far when second off 2lb lower on her reappearance, travelled well and looked all over the winner having taken over before the straight, but she stumbled on landing at the last, and despite a good recovery from her rider, her chance had gone. She will probably go up a bit for this, but can gain compensation at some stage. (op 3-1 tchd 4-1)
Stumped, making a quick reappearance, has been in good form under similar conditions, and he came to hold every chance in the straight, but couldn't quite get level and was then slightly impeded when already held on the run-in. (tchd 5-2)
Agente Romano(USA) was always going to struggle having made a right mess of the third-last. (op 13-2)

737 RAYFORD CARAVAN PARK STRATFORD NOVICES' H'CAP HURDLE (12 hdls) 2m 6f 110y
4:25 (4:25) (Class 4) (0-100,100) 4-Y-O+ **£3,252** (£955; £477; £238)

Form RPR
210- **1** **Miss Saffron**[64] 5136 7-10-11 **85**... JackDoyle 93+
(Susan Gardner) *t.k.h: hld up in rr: stdy prog fr 7th: chsd ldr bef 3 out: led wl bef 2 out: in command whn nt fluent last: eased towards fin* **8/1**[3]
-022 **2** 2 **The Fox's Decree**[8] 630 6-11-3 **96**............................(t) JimmyDerham(5) 100
(Martin Keighley) *in tch in midfield hdwy bef 3 out: rdn to chse wnr bef 2 out: styd on one pce u.p between last 2* **9/2**[2]
5-44 **3** 5 **Cool Bob (IRE)**[8] 630 7-11-3 **91**..................................(t) PaddyBrennan 92
(Matt Sheppard) *t.k.h: hld up towards rr: stdy hdwy bef 8th: pushed along and chsd ldrs after 3 out: rdn to go 3rd 2 out: no imp after* **8/1**[3]
-241 **4** 4 **King Raven (IRE)**[3] 692 8-11-9 **97** 7ex.....................(v) TomScudamore 98+
(Mark Rimell) *in tch in midfield tl blnd bdly and dropped to last pair 3rd: pushed along and sme prog after 8th: modest and drvn after 3 out: plugged on u.p to go 4th flat: nvr trbld ldrs* **3/1**[1]
0-44 **5** 1 **Lansdowne Princess**[7] 645 8-10-1 **82**.............................. DavidBass(7) 79
(Gerald Ham) *chsd ldrs: lft 3rd at 3rd: mstke 5th: led 8th: rdn and hit 3 out: sn hdd: short of room at bnd wl bef 2 out: wknd u.p* **11/1**
0P6- **6** hd **Utern**[48] 21 6-10-6 **80**.. AidanColeman 75
(Venetia Williams) *hld up in tch: hdwy to chse ldrs after 7th: wnt 3rd bef 3 out: wknd u.p wl bef 2 out* **40/1**
-403 **7** 11 **Enchanted Approach (IRE)**[31] 303 7-10-9 **90**........... MissLBrooke(7) 75
(Lady Susan Brooke) *t.k.h: chsd ldrs: rdn and wknd bef 3 out* **40/1**
2P-0 **8** 11 **Hot Tottie (IRE)**[30] 313 6-11-12 **100**.............................. SeamusDurack 75
(Jeremy Scott) *hld up in rr: mstke 4th: rdn and struggling whn j. slowly 8th: sn wl bhd* **50/1**
06-0 **9** 1 **Strumble Head (IRE)**[13] 552 5-10-9 **83**.......................(p) TomO'Brien 57
(Peter Bowen) *chsd ldrs: lft 2nd 3rd tl bef 3 out: wknd qckly u.p wl bef 2 out* **25/1**
-442 **10** nk **Mr Melodious**[10] 607 4-11-2 **100**.......................(b) SamTwiston-Davies(5) 69
(Nigel Twiston-Davies) *in tch in midfield: rdn w no rspnse 8th: wl btn 3 out* **11/1**

P/-3 **11** *20* **Arctic Ghost**[11] 587 10-10-5 **86**....................(v) ChrisDavies(7) 42
(Philip Hobbs) *mstkes: chsd ldr tl lft in ld 3rd: mstke and hdd 6th: rdn and wknd bef 8th: wl bhd whn hit 3 out: t.o* **17/2**

U0P- **P** **Cool Cliche**[51] 5362 8-10-9 **83**.................... PaulMoloney —
(Evan Williams) *midfield and sn rdn along: reminders and hdwy to chse ldrs 3rd: dropped to rr and rdn w no rspnse 5th: lost tch qckly after: wl t.o 9th tl p.u 2 out* **14/1**

600- **P** **River Beauty**[46] 50 6-11-4 **95**.................... PeterToole(3) —
(Barry Brennan) *a in rr: mstke 2nd: rdn and lost tch bef 8th: wl t.o whn p.u 2 out* **33/1**

2-21 **U** **Basford Lass**[11] 577 5-11-10 **98**....................(b) AlanO'Keeffe —
(Jennie Candlish) *led tl blnd bdly and uns rdr 3rd* **17/2**

5m 17.9s (-10.20) **Going Correction** -0.30s/f (Good)
WFA 4 from 5yo+ 18lb **14** Ran SP% **123.4**
Speed ratings (Par 105): **105,104,102,101,100 100,96,93,92,92 85,—,—,—**
toteswingers: 1&2 £8.30, 1&3 £10.00, 2&3 £7.20 CSF £44.03 CT £308.78 TOTE £9.60: £3.50, £1.90, £3.60; EX 57.20.
Owner P A Tylor & G N Noye **Bred** P A Tylor **Trained** Longdown, Devon

FOCUS
An ordinary novice handicap that was won in good fashion by Miss Saffron.

NOTEBOOK
Miss Saffron asserted leaving the back straight and stayed on well to win with a bit in hand. A heavy-ground winner in March, she is clearly versatile with regards to going, and remains capable of better, this being just her eighth start. (op 15-2)
The Fox's Decree, up 5lb from last time, has now finished second on his last three outings. He was clear of the remainder and certainly deserves to win a race. (op 6-1)
Cool Bob(IRE) plugged on without being able to challenge. (op 9-1)
King Raven(IRE), penalised for his easy Fontwell success three days earlier, gave himself plenty to do when making a telling blunder at the third and he could never recover, making laboured late progress. (tchd 10-3 and 7-2 in places)
Lansdowne Princess was in trouble having hit three out, and she could find no extra once tightened against the rail on the run to two out. (op 12-1)
Utern showed a bit more, for all that she didn't see it out. (op 33-1 tchd 50-1)
River Beauty Official explanation: trainer said mare was unsuited by the good to firm (good in places) ground

738 ALLENS CARAVAN HOLIDAY HOMES NOVICES' CHASE (17 fncs) 2m 7f
4:55 (4:55) (Class 4) 5-Y-0+ **£4,553** (£1,337; £668; £333)

Form RPR

00-F **1** **Billie Magern**[18] 476 6-10-12 0.................... PaddyBrennan 128+
(Nigel Twiston-Davies) *chsd ldng pair tl wnt 2nd 8th: led bef 14th: rdn and kpt on wl between last 2: a holding runner-up flat* **3/1**[2]

35-2 **2** *1 ½* **Last Flight (IRE)**[13] 550 6-10-0 0....................(p) DonalDevereux(5) 119+
(Peter Bowen) *hld up in tch in midfield: hdwy to chse ldrs gng wl 10th: chsd wnr 15th and sn wl clr of rivals: kpt on wl u.p flat but quite nvr able to chal wnr* **15/8**[1]

/1-F **3** *34* **Port Talbot (IRE)**[37] 195 9-11-5 0.................... LeightonAspell 103
(Oliver Sherwood) *t.k.h: hld up wl bhd: mstke 1st and 8th: blnd 12th: plugged on past btn horses to go poor 3rd bef last: nvr on terms: t.o* **25/1**

4 *6* **Teri D Trixter (IRE)**[42] 5-10-12 0.................... JasonMaguire 89
(Denis Paul Murphy, Ire) *led and set gd gallop: hdd bef 14th: 3rd and wl btn after 3 out: lost poor 3rd bef last: t.o* **50/1**

320- **5** *5* **Walamo (GER)**[199] 2526 6-10-12 0....................(t) RichardJohnson 86
(Tim Vaughan) *in tch in midfield: hdwy to chse ldrs and mstke 9th: rdn and mstke 11th: sn struggling: wl btn 14th: t.o* **12/1**

/UP- **6** *4 ½* **The Hairy Mutt (IRE)**[15] 8-10-5 **99**.................... MissLBrooke(7) 80
(Lady Susan Brooke) *a bhd in last trio: j. rigth 3rd: blnd 7th: lost tch 12th: t.o fr 2 out* **50/1**

611- **7** *36* **City Heights (IRE)**[52] 5327 8-11-5 **116**.................... TimmyMurphy 55
(David Arbuthnot) *in tch: j. slowly and lost pl 6th and 7th: rallied and hdwy to chse ldrs 12th: rdn and btn bef 14th: t.o and eased wl bef last* **8/1**

1P-U **8** *8* **Factotum**[8] 631 6-10-12 0.................... APMcCoy 41
(Jonjo O'Neill) *nt a fluent: a struggling in last pair: niggled along fr 5th: lost tch 12th: wl t.o fr 14th* **7/2**[3]

13-1 **P** **Tisfreetdream (IRE)**[35] 226 9-11-12 **120**....................(p) JackDoyle —
(Peter Pritchard) *chsd ldr tl 8th: losing pl whn mstke 11th: tailing off whn mstke 13th: p.u next* **14/1**

5m 32.7s (-8.90) **Going Correction** -0.30s/f (Good) **9** Ran SP% **115.2**
Speed ratings: **103,102,90,88,86 85,72,69,—**
toteswingers: 1&2 £2.80, 1&3 £10.60, 2&3 £14.50 CSF £9.36 TOTE £4.60: £1.50, £1.40, £5.70; EX 10.30.
Owner Roger Nicholls **Bred** Roger Nicholls **Trained** Naunton, Gloucs

FOCUS
The front pair came well clear in what looked a fair novice chase.

NOTEBOOK
Billie Magern, just about to assert when falling at Southwell on his recent chase debut, showed no signs of a dent in confidence and a good jump at the last sealed it for him. A brother to former high-class chaser Ollie Magern, he looks capable of better over fences, and it would be a surprise were he not to go in again at some stage. (op 11-4 tchd 5-2)
Last Flight(IRE), narrowly denied by a decent sort on her chasing debut at Cartmel, ensured the winner didn't have things all his own way, keeping on right the way to the line, but she was always coming off second-best. She should have no trouble getting off the mark before long. (op 9-4 tchd 5-2)
Port Talbot(IRE), still in with a chance when falling at the last in a novices' hunter chase at Aintree latest, appeared to be struggling for much of the way, but his jumping improved as the race went on, and he plugged on late past beaten horses. (op 16-1)
Teri D Trixter(IRE), who fell on his final start in points, showed up well for a long way and will find easier opportunities. (op 33-1)
Walamo(GER), making his chase debut, may have needed this first run in 199 days. (op 16-1 tchd 10-1)
The Hairy Mutt(IRE) (op 66-1)
City Heights(IRE) didn't jump as well as he had done previously and was quickly beaten having jumped badly left at the open ditch down the back. (op 13-2, tchd 9-1 in places)
Factotum agained jumped moderately and needs more time/experience. (op 4-1 tchd 9-2 and 3-1)
Tisfreetdream(IRE) was saddled with a double penalty and failed to run his race. (tchd 12-1 and 16-1)

739 RIVERSIDE CARAVAN PARK STRATFORD STANDARD OPEN NATIONAL HUNT FLAT RACE 2m 110y
5:30 (5:30) (Class 6) 4-6-Y-0 **£1,712** (£499; £249)

Form RPR

1 **Vicpol (ITY)** 4-10-9 0.................... TomO'Connor(5) 108+
(Bill Turner) *chsd ldrs: wnt 2nd 4f out: pushed into ld wl over 1f out: sn clr and r.o strly: easily* **80/1**

2 *12* **Whereveryougoigo (IRE)** 4-11-0 0.................... TomO'Brien 97
(Peter Bowen) *in tch in midfield: sltly outpcd and pushed along over 6f out: hdwy on outer 5f out: chsd ldrs and unable qck over 2f out: kpt on fnl f to go 2nd nr fin: no ch w wnr* **9/4**[1]

2- **3** *1 ½* **Jump Up**[54] 5296 4-11-0 0.................... APMcCoy 96
(Keith Goldsworthy) *chsd ldrs: wnt 2nd over 9f out: led 6f out: drvn and hdd wl over 1f out: sn outpcd by wnr and wl btn fnl f: lost 2nd nr fin* **4/1**[2]

3 **4** *4 ½* **Sohappyharry**[28] 362 4-10-11 0.................... DPFahy(3) 92
(Jane Mathias) *hld up in tch in midfield: hdwy 1/2-way: rdn to chse ldng pair wl over 2f out: wknd 2f out* **14/1**

5 *4 ½* **Superior Knight** 6-11-3 0.................... DavidDennis 91
(James Evans) *in tch towards rr: pushed along and outpcd wl over 5f out: styd on past btn horses steadily fnl 2f: no ch w ldrs* **50/1**

63-6 **6** *1 ¼* **Quidam Blue (FR)**[35] 222 6-11-3 0.................... RichardJohnson 90
(Tim Vaughan) *hld up wl bhd: gd prog 5f out: chsd ldng quartet and rdn wl over 2f out: sn struggling and wknd fnl 2f* **17/2**

5-4 **7** *9* **Glacial Harry**[8] 637 4-10-7 0.................... PeterHatton(7) 79
(Reg Hollinshead) *sn chsng ldr tl over 9f out: styd in tch but hanging and racing awkwardly after: wknd u.p over 3f out* **20/1**

3 **8** *1 ½* **Not So Sure Dick (IRE)**[18] 474 5-11-3 0.................... AndrewTinkler 80
(George Baker) *hld up wl in tch in midfield: rdn and effrt 6f out: wknd qckly wl over 3f out: wl btn fnl 2f* **12/1**

3- **9** *9* **Sheila's Rose (IRE)**[69] 5042 5-10-3 0.................... CDTimmons(7) 65
(Barry Brennan) *hld up wl in tch in midfield: hdwy on inner to chse ldrs 5f out: nt clr run and shuffled bk over 4f out: no ch after* **6/1**[3]

03-3 **10** *3 ¼* **Steel Bullet (IRE)**[31] 304 4-11-0 0.................... AlanO'Keeffe 66
(Jennie Candlish) *t.k.h: hld up in tch towards rr: hdwy on outer to press ldrs 4f out: fdd rapidly and wd bnd 2f out: sn wl bhd* **20/1**

11 *¾* **Smoking (FR)**[91] 4-11-0 0.................... RobertThornton 66
(Alan King) *t.k.h: chsd ldrs tl rdn and wknd qckly 4f out: wl bhd fnl 2f* **9/1**

12 *32* **Snope**[141] 5-11-3 0.................... DarylJacob 40
(Jamie Snowden) *racd freely: led tl 6f out: dropped out rapidly over 4f out: t.o wl over 2f out* **50/1**

13 *1 ¼* **Total Effects (IRE)** 6-11-3 0.................... TomScudamore 39
(Anabel L M King) *a bhd: rdn and struggling 7f out: t.o fnl 3f* **16/1**

14 *28* **Macindi Starr** 4-10-2 0.................... GemmaGracey-Davison(5) 4
(Zoe Davison) *a bhd: rdn and struggling bdly 1/2-way: wl t.o fnl 5f* **66/1**

3m 45.8s (-4.60) **Going Correction** -0.30s/f (Good)
WFA 4 from 5yo+ 3lb **14** Ran SP% **122.0**
Speed ratings: **98,92,91,89,87 86,82,81,77,76 75,60,60,46**
toteswingers: 1&2 £61.20, 1&3 £20.40, 2&3 £5.70 CSF £251.89 TOTE £86.30: £15.80, £1.30, £1.60; EX 212.50 Place 6 £217.66, Place 5 £64.72.
Owner Paul Thorman **Bred** Giacinto Guglielmi Et Al **Trained** Sigwells, Somerset

FOCUS
An open-looking bumper, highlighted by the victory of 80-1 shot Vicpol.

NOTEBOOK
Vicpol(ITY), though an 80-1 outsider, ran right away with it, powering clear having taken over inside the final 2f and winning easily. A half-brother to four Flat winners in Italy, it was hard not to be taken with the manner in which he settled things, but defying a penalty in this is never easy.
Whereveryougoigo(IRE), half-brother to an Irish point winner, took time to pick up and the winner was away and gone by the time he hit top stride. He should improve on this and is going to appreciate a stiffer test over hurdles. (op 9-2 tchd 2-1)
Jump Up, runner-up at Towcester on debut, was ridden positively and had his chance, but couldn't quicken on. (op 10-3 tchd 3-1)
Sohappyharry again showed ability and will do better over hurdles. (tchd 16-1)
Superior Knight, a son of Superior Premium, made a little late headway and should improve. (op 40-1)
Sheila's Rose(IRE), a promising third at Fakenham on debut, could make no impression having been a bit tight for room and lost her place. (tchd 13-2)
T/Plt: £381.80 to a £1 stake. Pool: £68,385.98. 130.74 winning tickets. T/Qpdt: £24.60 to a £1 stake. Pool: £6,734.84. 202.22 winning tickets. SP

740 - 742a (Foreign Racing) - See Raceform Interactive

468 SEDGEFIELD (L-H)
Monday, June 14

OFFICIAL GOING: Good (good to firm in places on hurdle course; chs 7.9, hdl 8.1)
The last fence was omitted in both chases.
Wind: fresh 1/2 against Weather: bright and breezy

743 PAXTONS POWERING AHEAD WITH CASE IH JUVENILE HURDLE (7 hdls 1 omitted) 2m 1f
2:30 (2:30) (Class 4) 3-Y-0 **£2,992** (£878; £439; £219)

Form RPR

1 **Meetings Man (IRE)**[11] 3-10-12 0.................... BarryKeniry 89+
(Micky Hammond) *trckd ldrs: led appr 2 out and hit flight: wandered and j.lft last: drvn rt out* **4/1**[2]

1 **2** *2* **Lucky Quay (IRE)**[9] 629 3-11-5 0....................(b) TomScudamore 91+
(David Pipe) *led: reluctant and drvn bnd after 3rd: hrd drvn at the omitted 3 out: hdd appr 2 out: rallied run-in: a hld* **2/5**[1]

4 **3** *17* **Mr Mohican (IRE)**[9] 629 3-10-12 0.................... KeithMercer 66
(Ann Duffield) *chsd ldrs: drvn 5th: wknd appr 2 out* **18/1**

4 *¾* **Alphacino**[24] 3-10-12 0.................... AndrewThornton 65
(Ben Haslam) *chsd ldr: wknd appr 2 out: hung lft: lost 3rd nr line* **66/1**

P **5** *½* **Another Grand (IRE)**[9] 629 3-10-5 0.................... OliverWilliams(7) 65
(Ruth Carr) *in rr: bdly hmpd 2nd: poor 5th omitted 3 out: sme hdwy appr 2 out: nvr on terms* **100/1**

P **Petrocelli**[13] 3-10-12 0.................... GrahamLee —
(Alan McCabe) *nt jump wl in rr: bhd fr 3rd: t.o whn p.u after next* **25/1**

3 **B** **Anchorage Boy (USA)**[9] 629 3-10-9 0.................... AlexMerriam(3) —
(Amy Weaver) *prom: hmpd 1st: bdly hmpd and b.d 2nd* **33/1**

U **Pobs Trophy**[209] 3-10-12 0.................... PaddyAspell —
(Richard Guest) *w ldr whn wandered bdly and uns rdr 1st* **100/1**

P **Vito Volterra (IRE)**[6] 3-10-9 0.................... JamesO'Farrell(3) —
(Michael Smith) *j. bdly: j. bdly lft 2nd: reminders after next: sn bhd: t.o whn p.u bef 2 out* **11/1**[3]

P **Tantsor (FR)**[54] 3-10-12 0.................... WilsonRenwick —
(Paul Midgley) *in rr: sme hdwy 4th: reminders next: sn wknd: t.o whn p.u bef 2 out* **100/1**

P **P** **Dark Gem**[9] 629 3-10-2 0.................... MichaelNaughton(3) —
(Simon West) *in rr: hmpd 1st: reminders after 3rd: bhd fr 5th: t.o whn p.u bef 2 out* **100/1**

4m 9.30s (2.40) **Going Correction** -0.35s/f (Good) **11** Ran SP% **117.3**
Speed ratings: **80,79,71,70,70 —,—,—,—,— —**
CSF £6.07 TOTE £4.20: £1.20, £1.02, £3.90; EX 7.10.

Owner Paul R Snook **Bred** Hakan Keles **Trained** Middleham Moor, N Yorks

FOCUS

The third-last flight was bypassed. A weak juvenile event and the form is straightforward. The winner should rate higher.

NOTEBOOK

Meetings Man(IRE), having travelled strongly, quickly came under pressure and ran down the last, allowing Lucky Quay another crack at him, but he pulled out enough to hold off that rival, with the pair well clear, to make a winning start over hurdles. He has been in good form on the level this summer, where he is rated 64, and he is entitled to derive considerable benefit from this first hurdles outing. (op 7-2)

Lucky Quay(IRE), penalised for an easy win at Hexham, had things his own way out in front but was being niggled along three out and could never shake off the better travelling winner. He plugged on but this has to go as slightly disappointing even though he has finished clear of the rest. (op 4-9 tchd 1-2 in a place)

Mr Mohican(IRE) was 29l behind Lucky Quay at Hexham and has closed the gap slightly this time, but in truth was never troubling the front pair. (op 22-1 tchd 28-1)

Alphacino, whose best form came at 7f on the Flat, ran well for a long way on hurdles debut before getting tired in the closing stages and will probably fare better on a sharper track. (op 50-1 tchd 80-1)

Another Grand(IRE), who was pulled up behind Lucky Quay at Hexham, fared much better this time, keeping on from a long way back, which suggests stamina isn't a major concern despite his four Flat runs coming over 5-6f. (op 80-1)

744 PAXTONS AND INDEPENDENT TWINE - WRAP AND TWINE NOVICES' HURDLE (10 hdls) 2m 4f

3:00 (3:00) (Class 4) 4-Y-0+ **£2,992** (£878; £439; £219)

Form				RPR
6-62	1		**Stand Clear**[16] 514 5-10-5 108 ... GrahamLee (Ferdy Murphy) *hld up in rr: blnd and sddle briefly slipped 5th: hdwy 7th: sn trcking ldrs: wnt 2nd appr 2 out: swtchd rt between last 2: styd on to ld nr fin* **2/1**[1]	104+
41-3	2	hd	**Cailin Na Ri (IRE)**[18] 488 7-10-12 110 ... DenisO'Regan (Martin Todhunter) *led: kpt on u.p run-in: hdd last strides* **7/2**[3]	109
4-	3	14	**Kembla Grange (IRE)**[107] 4317 4-10-8 117 ... BrianHughes (C A McBratney, Ire) *towards rr: hdwy to chse ldrs 7th: drvn and outpcd 3 out: kpt on to take modest 3rd sn after last* **22/1**	91
P0	4	4 ½	**Osbaldeston (IRE)**[16] 514 7-10-12 0 ... WilsonRenwick (Rose Dobbin) *prom: modest 3rd 2 out: wknd last* **100/1**	91
-013	5	3	**Murcar**[12] 583 5-11-5 115 ... JohnnyFarrelly (Alison Thorpe) *chsd ldr: rdn 3 out: wknd next* **3/1**[2]	97
0U-4	6	49	**Tartan Tie**[39] 182 6-10-12 0 ... (t) DarylJacob (Alison Thorpe) *chsd ldrs: outpcd and mstke 6th: sn bhd: t.o after 3 out* **11/1**	39
	7	12	**Serious Intent (IRE)**[806] 4827 8-10-12 0 ... RichardJohnson (C A McBratney, Ire) *chsd ldrs: wknd qckly after 7th: t.o after next* **5/1**	27
U/	8	21	**Ford Of Wells (IRE)**[226] 2017 9-10-12 100 ... HarrySkelton (Patrick Griffin, Ire) *trckd ldrs: wknd qckly 7th: sn bhd: t.o after next* **100/1**	6
U3	9	3 ½	**Humbel Lad (IRE)**[6] 683 6-10-2 0 ... CraigGallagher(10) (Richard Guest) *in tch: outpcd after 5th: sn bhd: t.o 7th* **66/1**	—

4m 52.5s (-0.20) **Going Correction** -0.35s/f (Good)

WFA 4 from 5yo+ 18lb **9** Ran SP% **113.4**

Speed ratings (Par 105): **98,97,92,90,89 69,64,56,55**

toteswingers: 1&2 £1.80, 1&3 £32.50, 2&3 £10.70 CSF £9.15 TOTE £3.40: £1.30, £1.10, £5.50; EX 9.20.

Owner Beautifully Bred Partnership **Bred** Mrs R Crank **Trained** West Witton, N Yorks

FOCUS

The first pair came clear in a dramatic finish in this modest novice hurdle. A step up from the winner.

NOTEBOOK

Stand Clear made a bad mistake at the fifth flight where her rider did remarkably well to stay in the saddle. Because of the error, Lee had one foot out of the irons and his saddle had slipped, but he appeared fairly happy within a couple of furlongs and began to make stealthy headway up the inside to chase the long-time leader through into the straight. Still to get on terms at the last, it appeared the mare was held, but Lee galvanised his mount to produce a stirring late charge and take advantage of the 7lb she was receiving from the penalised Cailin Na Ri. (op 6-4)

Cailin Na Ri(IRE) posted an excellent effort in defeat, not least because she was pressed for the lead by Murcar three out. After shaking off the attentions of that rival, she appeared to be staying on well enough to hold off Stand Clear but was grabbed on the line. She is a hard mare to pass when allowed to dominate and will win more races. (op 3-1 tchd 9-2)

Kembla Grange(IRE) was racing over this trip and on a sound surface for the first time but kept plugging away and looks the type to fare better on slower ground, where normally speedier rivals will be slowed down. (op 20-1)

Osbaldeston(IRE) stepped up on what he'd shown in two previous starts, sticking on well enough to finish three lengths in front of Murcar, which is an encouraging level of performance given what that rival has been doing in recent starts.

Murcar threw the gauntlet down to Cailin Na Ri three out but soon came under pressure and ultimately dropped away disappointingly. (op 7-2 tchd 11-4)

Serious Intent(IRE) was struggling some way out but, given this was his first outing since March 2008, he's entitled to come on a good deal and the fact that connections are persevering with this 8-y-o suggests he's got ability. (op 9-1 tchd 4-1)

745 JOHN WADE GROUP PREMIER (S) H'CAP HURDLE (FINAL) (9 hdls 1 omitted) 2m 4f

3:30 (3:30) (Class 5) 4-Y-0+

£6,262 (£1,850; £925; £463; £231; £116)

Form				RPR
F00-	1		**Planetarium**[11] 3917 5-10-7 90 ... (p) WilsonRenwick (P Monteith) *trckd ldrs: hit 4th: led after 8th: styd on u.p* **4/1**[1]	96+
16-0	2	3 ¾	**Freedom Flying**[26] 402 7-9-13 89 ... (p) KyleJames(7) (Philip Kirby) *chsd ldrs: drvn fr 3rd: kpt on extended run-in: tk 2nd nr line* **9/1**	92
06-5	3	¾	**Mister Fizzbomb (IRE)**[10] 402 7-9-11 83 oh4 ... (v) CampbellGillies(3) (John Wainwright) *led: hdd after 8th: kpt on same pce extended run-in: lost 2nd cl home* **10/1**	85
-322	4	6	**Prioryjo**[19] 472 7-11-5 109 ... AlexanderVoy(7) (Martin Todhunter) *hld up: stdy hdwy to trck ldrs 6th: effrt appr normal 2 out: sn rdn: lost 3rd passing omitted last* **8/1**[3]	107
50P-	5	32	**Amjad**[80] 4863 13-9-7 83 oh10 ... (p) GaryRutherford(7) (Simon West) *sn lost tch in last: t.o 7th: plodded on extended run-in* **100/1**	51
6-02	6	4	**Bold Pioneer (USA)**[12] 578 7-10-0 83 oh12 ... (t) KeithMercer (Richard Ford) *hld up in rr: sme hdwy whn hit 7th: poor 5th after next: wknd extended run-in* **14/1**	48
00-0	7	nse	**Monfils Monfils (USA)**[19] 470 8-10-0 83 oh2 ... PeterBuchanan (Ron Barr) *chsd ldrs: drvn 7th: sn lost pl* **33/1**	47
-50P	8	21	**Samizdat (FR)**[19] 472 7-11-5 105 ... RyanMania(3) (Dianne Sayer) *w ldrs: wknd 8th* **12/1**	51
-630	9	1 ½	**Arctic Rock**[18] 490 7-10-1 84 oh9 ow1 ... (b[1]) DougieCostello (Geoffrey Harker) *in rr: lost pl after 5th: sn bhd* **17/2**	28
-U03	10	2	**White Lightening (IRE)**[19] 470 7-10-7 90 ... (bt) BrianHughes (John Wade) *chsd ldrs: lost pl 8th* **16/1**	32
/2-1	F		**Arisea (IRE)**[19] 470 7-11-4 108 ... GarryWhillans(7) (James Moffatt) *hld up in midfield: fell 6th* **13/2**[2]	—
231-	P		**Bewery Man (IRE)**[48] 31 9-11-7 104 ... GrahamLee (Ferdy Murphy) *hld up in rr: hmpd 5th: sn p.u* **4/1**[1]	—

4m 50.2s (-2.50) **Going Correction** -0.35s/f (Good) **12** Ran SP% **118.2**

Speed ratings (Par 103): **103,101,101,98,86 84,84,75,75,74** —,—

toteswingers: 1&2 £10.50, 1&3 £15.00, 2&3 £31.60 CSF £40.22 CT £340.56 TOTE £7.20: £3.00, £4.20, £4.60; EX 53.60.There was no bid for the winner.

Owner G M Cowan **Bred** Goldford Stud And P E Clinton **Trained** Rosewell, Midlothian

FOCUS

The final flight was bypassed. A competitive seller, unsurprisingly given the prize money on offer. The form is sound.

NOTEBOOK

Planetarium landed a bit if a touch having been backed throughout the day. His trainer reported afterwards that this horse needs fast ground to show his best, but consistency isn't one of the grey's strong points so he's no good thing to repeat this form even if conditions were as suitable next time. (op 7-2)

Freedom Flying ran a moody sort of race, racing prominently but soon getting reminders before getting outpaced. However she rallied to the cause and finished her race better than anything. She isn't one to have much confidence in but this is her grade and she clearly has the ability to win a similar event if in the mood. (op 10-1 tchd 12-1)

Mister Fizzbomb(IRE) ran well from the front but is winless from 18 starts over hurdles now. (op 18-1 tchd 20-1)

Prioryjo travelled well but didn't get home and is much more effective over trips around 2m. (op 6-1 tchd 5-1)

White Lightening(IRE) Official explanation: jockey said gelding hung left-handed

Bewery Man(IRE) Official explanation: jockey said gelding lost its action

746 PAXTONS SUPPORTING CUSTOMERS WITH PEREGRINE FINANCE H'CAP CHASE (14 fncs 2 omitted) 2m 4f

4:00 (4:00) (Class 4) (0-115,112) 5-Y-O+ **£3,802** (£1,123; £561; £280; £140)

Form				RPR
50-0	1		**Soubriquet (IRE)**[33] 288 7-11-2 105 ... (t) MichaelMcAlister(3) (Maurice Barnes) *prom: led appr last: kpt on: all out* **18/1**	117
021-	2	½	**General Hardi**[48] 33 9-11-12 112 ... BrianHughes (John Wade) *chsd ldrs: wnt 2nd last: styd on towards fin: jst hld* **9/2**[2]	124
3-32	3	12	**Nile Moon (IRE)**[18] 489 9-10-10 99 ... (b) FearghalDavis(3) (Ann Hamilton) *chsd ldrs: reminders 7th and 9th: outpcd 2 out: kpt on to take modest 3rd last 75yds* **9/4**[1]	100
000-	4	2 ¾	**Broadway Star (FR)**[138] 3691 7-11-0 100 ... WilsonRenwick (Rose Dobbin) *j.rt in rr: mstke 4th: hdwy 11th: 4th whn rdr lost whip sn after last: tk 3rd 2f out: wknd fnl 100yds* **8/1**	99
43-	5	9	**Indiana Gold (FR)**[81] 4843 6-10-12 98 ... DarylJacob (Alison Thorpe) *trckd ldrs: led 3 out: hdd appr last: wknd over 2f out* **5/1**[3]	88
61-0	6	9	**Toulouse Express (IRE)**[29] 352 11-10-10 103 ... (v) MrAdamNicol(7) (Robert Johnson) *led after 1st: reminders 9th: hdd 3 out: wknd appr last: eased towards fin* **9/1**	85
05/P	P		**Karelian**[12] 581 9-11-8 108 ... GrahamLee (Ferdy Murphy) *nt fluent detached in last: reminders 5th: hit next: t.o 8th: p.u after next* **12/1**	—
15P/	P		**Back To The Wind (IRE)**[734] 659 8-11-3 103 ... (t) TomScudamore (David Pipe) *led tl after 1st: w ldr: reminders 11th: sn wknd: t.o whn p.u bef last* **13/2**	—

4m 51.0s (-12.00) **Going Correction** -0.475s/f (Good) **8** Ran SP% **113.0**

Speed ratings: **105,104,100,98,95 91**,—,—

toteswingers: 1&2 £13.10, 1&3 £9.00, 2&3 £2.30 CSF £95.62 CT £256.44 TOTE £20.70: £5.20, £1.70, £1.80.

Owner Minstrel's Double Racing **Bred** Stonethorn Stud Farms Ltd **Trained** Farlam, Cumbria

FOCUS

An open handicap chase in which the pace was generous. It is worth being fairly positive about the form.

NOTEBOOK

Soubriquet(IRE) had been out of sorts over hurdles over the winter and on his sole start this year, but he proved a different proposition switching back to fences, and bounced right back to his best. Despite getting reminders quite early on, Soubriquet worked his way into contention before joining Indiana Gold at the second last and kicking on for home. He had enough in the tank to hold off the late thrust of General Hardi and land his first win in 14 months. (op 16-1)

General Hardi does most of his racing over much further than this. He got slightly outpaced two out but came home strongly to close right in on the winner at the line and is one to be with back up in trip. (op 5-1 tchd 6-1)

Nile Moon(IRE) rallied to get third having got outpaced leaving the back, but he lacks a change of gear over this trip and both wins have come over further. (op 10-3)

Broadway Star(FR) shaped with some promise on this first try over fences, especially as his rider dropped his whip shortly after the last fence, and is entitled to improve on this. He might want to go the other way around, though, as he jumped to his right on more than one occasion. (op 11-1)

Indiana Gold(FR) looked a huge threat when moving smoothly to the front leaving the back but, not for the first time, his stamina soon gave way and he's an interesting proposition back in trip. (op 4-1 tchd 6-1)

747 PAXTONS NO 1 FOR JCB LANDPOWER H'CAP CHASE (11 fncs 2 omitted) 2m 110y

4:30 (4:30) (Class 4) (0-100,96) 5-Y-O+**£3,802** (£1,123; £561; £280; £140)

Form				RPR
5-31	1		**Ruby Isabel (IRE)**[14] 558 6-11-4 88 ... RichardJohnson (Tim Vaughan) *hld up: wnt prom 6th: led 8th: rdn 7 l clr 1f out: eased towards fin* **5/6**[1]	107+
-325	2	10	**Troodos Jet**[12] 578 9-10-7 77 ... (p) BrianHughes (Dianne Sayer) *trckd ldrs: wnt handy in 2nd 3 out: rdn last: one pce* **13/2**[3]	85
-324	3	9	**King's Majesty (IRE)**[9] 634 8-11-0 84 ... (v[1]) DougieCostello (Tim Pitt) *in rr: outpcd 6th: sme hdwy 2 out: kpt on to take modest 3rd 1f out* **10/1**	84
5-16	4	hd	**Schinken Otto (IRE)**[12] 578 9-11-10 94 ... GrahamLee (Malcolm Jefferson) *led: hdd 7th: outpcd appr 2 out* **9/1**	94
00/0	5	¾	**Skiddaw Jones**[20] 460 10-10-12 85 ... (t) MichaelMcAlister(3) (Maurice Barnes) *chsd ldr: led and blnd 7th: hdd next: one pce fr 2 out* **80/1**	84
0431	6	19	**Crofton Arch**[12] 578 10-10-3 73 ... (p) PeterBuchanan (John Dixon) *chsd ldrs: reminders 5th: lost pl 7th: t.o last* **6/1**[2]	55
3-44	7	3	**Another Dark Rum**[19] 477 6-11-12 96 ... KeithMercer (John Weymes) *in rr: outpcd 6th: bhd fr 3 out: wknd run-in* **16/1**	75

-144 **8** *18* **Star Tenor (IRE)**[12] [578] 8-11-3 **90**.............................. FearghalDavis(3) 53
(Sandy Forster) *chsd ldrs: drvn 7th: lost pl and hit 3 out: t.o last* **20/1**

4m 2.10s (-6.50) **Going Correction** -0.475s/f (Good) **8** Ran SP% **113.1**
Speed ratings: **96,91,87,86,86 77,76,67**
toteswingers: 1&2 £3.00, 1&3 £2.70, 2&3 £6.50 CSF £7.12 CT £31.33 TOTE £1.90: £1.50, £1.10, £2.40; EX 6.70.
Owner M Khan X2 **Bred** Patrick Doyle **Trained** Aberthin, Vale of Glamorgan

FOCUS
A weak handicap, run at a brisk gallop. The easy winner is on the upgrade.

NOTEBOOK
Ruby Isabel(IRE) travelled strongly, took over heading to the fourth-last and gradually asserted from her only realistic danger Troodos Jet on the long run-in after the last. She made light of the 6lb rise she incurred for her chasing debut success and looks the type who could run up a sequence in this sphere. She is down to run in a similar event at Newton Abbot tomorrow evening. (op 10-11 tchd 4-5 and 11-10 in places)
Troodos Jet was the only one to make a race of it with the winner but he was readily left behind after the last. All of his wins have come on ground with the word 'soft' in the description, but he handles a sound surface well enough. (op 8-1 tchd 17-2)
King's Majesty(IRE) kept on from off the pace without ever threatening and his losing run now stands at 22. (op 8-1)
Schinken Otto(IRE) was not helped by being taken on for the lead and paid the price. (op 15-2 tchd 10-1)
Crofton Arch couldn't reproduce his Cartmel form and he has yet to produce anything like his best in four runs at this venue. (op 13-2)

748 TRADERSBETTINGEXCHANGE.CO.UK H'CAP HURDLE (8 hdls) 2m 1f
5:00 (5:00) (Class 4) (0-105,105) 4-Y-0+ **£3,252** (£955; £477; £238)

Form RPR

0-52 **1** **Golden Future**[12] [582] 7-11-2 **95**.............................. BrianHughes 104+
(Peter Niven) *trckd ldrs: wnt 2nd after 3 out: led appr 2 out: 6 l clr whn hit last: rdn out* **9/2**[2]

100/ **2** *6* **Film Festival (USA)**[10] [1739] 7-11-12 **105**.............................. KeithMercer 107
(Brian Ellison) *chsd ldr: led 2nd: hdd appr 2 out: styd on same pce* **8/1**[3]

0-03 **3** *15* **Midnite Blews (IRE)**[19] [472] 5-10-7 **89**..............(t) MichaelMcAlister(3) 79
(Maurice Barnes) *chsd ldrs: hit 3 out: wl outpcd appr next* **10/1**

00-2 **4** *2* **Lets Go Girls**[16] [515] 6-10-12 **101**.............................. JamesSmith(10) 88
(James Moffatt) *in rr: hdwy 5th: one pce appr 2 out* **10/1**

-000 **5** *10* **Sea Cove**[20] [460] 10-10-6 **88**..............................(p) RyanMania(3) 66
(Dianne Sayer) *chsd ldrs: drvn 5th: lost pl after 3 out* **40/1**

0-14 **6** *55* **Nono Le Sage (FR)**[30] [338] 6-11-4 **97**..............(t) TomScudamore 25
(David Pipe) *in tch: wnt prom 5th: sn rdn: wknd next: t.o* **3/1**[1]

00-0 **7** *15* **Wellesley**[33] [289] 4-10-3 **85**.............................. PeterBuchanan —
(Donald Whillans) *in rr: bhd fr 4th: t.o next* **28/1**

00-3 **P** **Aggravation**[29] [350] 8-11-0 **98**.............................. MissLHorner(5) —
(Chris Grant) *hld up towards rr: blnd bdly 2nd: sddle slipped sn p.u* **16/1**

0P-4 **P** **Flashy Max**[18] [490] 5-10-2 **81**..............................(b) WilsonRenwick —
(Jedd O'Keeffe) *in rr: bhd fr 4th: t.o next: p.u bef 2 out* **10/1**

0/2- **P** **Rolecarr (IRE)**[390] [395] 7-10-8 **90**.............................. JamesO'Farrell(3) —
(Ann Hamilton) *in rr: t.o 5th: p.u bef 2 out* **12/1**

206- **F** **Strevelyn**[66] [1746] 4-10-6 **88**.............................. GrahamLee —
(Ann Duffield) *t.k.h: led: hdd 2nd: wd bnd after 3rd: 3rd whn fell next* **18/1**

0-30 **P** **Kayf Commander**[18] [494] 7-11-0 **93**.............................. AndrewTinkler —
(Mel Brittain) *nt fluent in rr: mstke 3rd: t.o 5th: p.u bef next* **16/1**

P-03 **P** **Molesden Glen (IRE)**[19] [468] 4-10-2 **87**..............(t) CampbellGillies(3) —
(Simon Waugh) *chsd ldrs: p.u bef 3rd* **16/1**

-210 **U** **Mountskip**[16] [520] 6-10-9 **98**.............................. MrAdamNicol(10) —
(Rose Dobbin) *hld up: hdwy and handy 5th whn rdr knocked out of sddle and uns rdr 4th* **14/1**

4m 3.40s (-3.50) **Going Correction** -0.35s/f (Good)
WFA 4 from 5yo+ 17lb **14** Ran SP% **121.8**
Speed ratings (Par 105): **94,91,84,83,78 52,45,—,—,— —,—,—,—**
toteswingers: 1&2 £5.70, 1&3 £7.60, 2&3 £16.00 CSF £40.51 CT £351.29 TOTE £4.10: £1.50, £3.70, £3.10; EX 37.20.
Owner The Little Ice Club **Bred** Larksborough Stud Limited **Trained** Barton-le-Street, N Yorks

FOCUS
A moderate handicap and a comfortable winner, who is improving towards the level of his Flat form.

NOTEBOOK
Golden Future travelled all over his rivals. He went away from Film Festival two out, but gave his backers a scare when getting the last flight all wrong and very nearly coming down. The partnership remained intact, though, and he was driven out to land his first success over hurdles at the tenth time of asking. He is improving and might be capable of overcoming a rise in the weights. (op 8-1 tchd 4-1)
Film Festival(USA), who was on the sharp end throughout, ran well in second having not been seen in this sphere since 2008, and both of his hurdles wins have come over this course and distance, so he clearly likes this place. Although higher in the weights nowadays, on this evidence he can find further success over hurdles. (op 13-2)
Midnite Blews(IRE) was left behind leaving the back straight but kept plugging away and is attractively handicapped nowadays, so is no forlorn hope. (op 12-1 tchd 9-1)
Lets Go Girls also stayed on, but struggled to make an impact having been bumped up 6lb for her latest Cartmel second and this mark may well be beyond her. (op 8-1)
Nono Le Sage(FR) has clearly gone off the boil. Official explanation: trainer's rep had no explanation for the poor form shown (tchd 7-2 and 4-1 in a place)
Aggravation Official explanation: jockey said saddle slipped
Rolecarr(IRE) Official explanation: jockey said gelding never travelled
Kayf Commander Official explanation: jockey said gelding never travelled
Molesden Glen(IRE) Official explanation: jockey said gelding lost its action

749 JOHN WADE H'CAP HURDLE (13 hdls) 3m 3f 110y
5:30 (5:30) (Class 5) (0-95,95) 4-Y-0+ **£2,471** (£725; £362; £181)

Form RPR

345- **1** **Patrixbourne**[328] [1019] 7-10-6 **75**..............................(v[1]) RichardJohnson 77+
(Tim Vaughan) *chsd ldrs: led after 3 out: drvn rt out* **15/8**[1]

1-02 **2** *1 ½* **Glen Rouge (IRE)**[14] [553] 9-10-11 **83**.............................. RyanMania(3) 84
(James Moffatt) *in rr: hmpd bnd after 8th: hdwy to chse ldrs 4 out: wnt 2nd appr last: kpt on* **9/1**

3 **3** *1* **Dark Halo (IRE)**[33] [285] 5-11-5 **88**..............................(p) GrahamLee 87
(C A McBratney, Ire) *hld up in rr: hdwy to trck ldrs whn blnd 7th: chsd wnr appr 2 out: kpt on same pce run-in* **20/1**

225- **4** *4 ½* **Steveys Lad (IRE)**[53] [5339] 7-10-9 **85**.............................. KyleJames(7) 81
(Philip Kirby) *chsd ldrs: led briefly 3 out: 4th and btn whn mstke last* **9/2**[2]

23-3 **5** *11* **Auberge (IRE)**[37] [212] 6-10-11 **80**.............................. FelixDeGiles 65
(A M Crow) *chsd ldrs: drvn 5th: wknd sn after 2 out* **5/1**[3]

42-2 **6** *4* **Present**[14] [557] 6-9-12 **74** ow2.............................. MattCrawley(7) 56
(Diana Weeden) *t.k.h in rr: hdwy 10th: wknd appr 2 out* **12/1**

000/ **7** *48* **First Fought (IRE)**[22] 8-10-7 **76**..............................(t) TjadeCollier 14
(Joanne Foster) *in rr: hdwy 8th: lost pl sn after 3 out: sn bhd t.o* **50/1**

60-5 **8** *1 ¼* **Itzacliche (IRE)**[29] [354] 10-10-7 **83**.............................. MissJRRichards(7) 20
(Nicky Richards) *in rr: outpcd 9th: sn bhd: t.o 3 out* **22/1**

-3P3 **9** *4* **Miss Tarantella**[18] [494] 7-11-2 **88**..............(t) MichaelMcAlister(3) 22
(Maurice Barnes) *wnt prom 7th: wknd after 3 out: sn bhd: t.o* **16/1**

P00/ **10** *4* **Weather Permitting (IRE)**[16] 7-11-8 **91**..............(tp) TomScudamore 21
(David Pipe) *w ldrs: led after 8th: hdd 3 out: lost pl appr next and sn bhd: heavily eased and virtually p.u run-in: t.o* **9/1**

06-4 **P** **Lavenoak Lad**[14] [549] 10-11-12 **95**..............................(t) AidanColeman —
(Simon Burrough) *chsd ldrs: hit 7th: sn reminders and lost pl: t.o 10th: p.u bef 2 out* **16/1**

-10P **P** **Lindseyfield Lodge (IRE)**[6] [680] 9-10-12 **88**..........(p) OliverWilliams(7) —
(Robert Johnson) *t.k.h: led: clr 2nd to 4th: hdd after 8th: sn lost pl and bhd: t.o whn p.u bef 3 out* **33/1**

6m 48.6s (-3.40) **Going Correction** -0.35s/f (Good) **12** Ran SP% **123.1**
Speed ratings (Par 103): **90,89,89,88,84 83,70,69,68,67 —,—**
toteswingers: 1&2 £5.40, 1&3 £13.00, 2&3 £18.70 CSF £19.68 CT £275.30 TOTE £3.00: £1.80, £1.90, £6.80; EX 25.90 Place 6: £17.01 Place 5: £15.56 .
Owner Diamond Racing Ltd **Bred** Mrs Hugh Maitland-Jones **Trained** Aberthin, Vale of Glamorgan

FOCUS
A poor staying handicap, but fairly sound form.

NOTEBOOK
Patrixbourne ◆ was sent on leaving the back and got the job done despite idling approaching the last flight. She had enough in the locker to get the job done though and finished with her ears pricked, so it would be no surprise were she to have more to offer, especially now in the care of Tim Vaughan, who has proved himself masterful at improving horses from other yards. (op 9-4 tchd 7-4)
Glen Rouge(IRE) has been generally consistent this year and he finished his race strongly, suggesting he can win off this sort of mark. (op 7-1)
Dark Halo(IRE) ◆ recovered well from a mistake at the fifth-last when on the improve. This lightly-raced mare soon worked her way on to the heels of the leaders and stayed on nicely up the straight. She'll likely soon be winning. (tchd 18-1)
Steveys Lad(IRE) kept battling away for pressure despite the absence of the headgear that had been on board for his four previous outings, but is becoming quite exposed now and struggling to find that winning opportunity. (op 8-1)
Auberge(IRE) had been shaping as though she might improve for this stiffer test of stamina and she was weighted to reverse Ayr form with Glen Rouge but, whilst running creditably, she couldn't build on previous efforts. (op 6-1)
T/Plt: £36.40 to a £1 stake. Pool: £58,997.35 - 1,181.01 winning tickets. T/Qpdt: £20.00 to a £1 stake. Pool: £3,874.11 - 143.10 winning tickets. WG

750 - 753a (Foreign Racing) - See Raceform Interactive

660 NEWTON ABBOT (L-H)
Tuesday, June 15

OFFICIAL GOING: Good (good to firm in places) changing to good to firm (good in places) after race 1 (6.15)
All bends moved but impact on distances not quantified.
Wind: quite strong breeze across Weather: cloudy with sunny periods

754 SIS MAIDEN HURDLE (8 hdls) 2m 1f
6:15 (6:16) (Class 4) 4-Y-0+ **£3,707** (£1,088; £544; £271)

Form RPR

05- **1** **Tin Pot Man (IRE)**[87] [4723] 4-10-11 0..............................(t) PaulMoloney 99+
(Evan Williams) *trckd ldr: led briefly 2nd: rdn to chse ldr bef 2 out: led sn after last: r.o wl: rdn out* **18/1**

2 *1 ¼* **Coeur De Lionne (IRE)**[116] 6-11-0 0..............................(t) HarrySkelton 103+
(Paul Nicholls) *in tch: smooth hdwy to ld appr 2 out: looked in command whn m green and wandered last: sn hdd: nt rcvr* **2/1**[2]

26 **3** *10* **Frosted Grape (IRE)**[16] [541] 4-10-4 103..................(b) TomScudamore 80
(David Pipe) *led tl 2nd: trckd ldrs: rdn after 3 out: sn outpcd by ldng pair* **4/1**[3]

F- **4** *12* **Pegasus Lad (USA)**[58] [5260] 4-10-11 0.............................. JackDoyle 75
(Linda Blackford) *led 2nd tl after 4th: trckd ldrs: rdn and ev ch after 3 out: wknd next* **33/1**

3 **5** *3 ¾* **O'Callaghan Strand (AUS)**[12] [596] 4-9-11 0.............. RichieMcLernon(3) 60
(Jonjo O'Neill) *mid-div: mstke 3 out: sn rdn: wknd next* **28/1**

5-06 **6** *14* **Kapborg (FR)**[35] [263] 4-10-1 0..............................(t) HaddenFrost(3) 50
(David Pipe) *hld up towards rr: rdn and sme prog after 3 out: wknd next* **25/1**

2 **7** *1 ½* **Crimson Canyon (IRE)**[16] [528] 4-10-11 0.............................. APMcCoy 56
(Jonjo O'Neill) *in tch: awkward and rdr lost iron briefly 1st: nt fluent 2nd and 5th: rdn after 3 out: sn wknd* **15/8**[1]

P0 **8** *2 ¾* **Special Bond**[12] [590] 4-10-4 0.............................. RodiGreene 46
(Kevin Bishop) *mid-div: rdn and sme hdwy after 3 out: nvr trbld ldrs* **100/1**

0 **9** *4* **Lean Burn (USA)**[23] [182] 4-10-8 0..............................(bt) DannyCook(3) 49
(John Panvert) *trckd ldrs: led after 4th: rdn and hdd bef 2 out: sn wknd* **40/1**

66-5 **10** *¾* **Thorpey's Girl (IRE)**[14] [568] 5-10-0 0.............................. OliverDayman(7) 44
(Alison Thorpe) *mid-div: mstke 2nd: rdn after 4th: sn in rr* **25/1**

11 *5* **Heavenly Saint**[228] 5-10-0 0.............................. PeterHatton(7) 39
(Lisa Day) *nt fluent 2nd: a towards rr* **100/1**

6- **12** *13* **Colour Trooper (IRE)**[288] [1359] 5-11-0 0..............................(t) JohnnyFarrelly 33
(David Pipe) *a towards rr* **16/1**

P **Whos Counting**[842] 6-10-0 0.............................. MattGriffiths(7) —
(Kevin Bishop) *hld up towards rr: stmbld bdly and sddle slipped 3rd: nt rcvr and p.u bef next* **150/1**

S- **F** **Tobizzy**[58] [5260] 4-9-11 0.............................. EdGlassonbury(7) —
(Linda Blackford) *mid-div whn fell 5th* **100/1**

4m 1.20s (-4.50) **Going Correction** -0.45s/f (Good)
WFA 4 from 5yo+ 17lb **14** Ran SP% **119.4**
Speed ratings (Par 105): **92,91,86,81,79 72,72,70,68,68 66,60,—,—**
Tote Swingers: 1&2 £8.40, 1&3 £7.00, 2&3 £1.80 CSF £53.00 TOTE £38.10: £9.70, £1.50, £1.10; EX 87.90.
Owner R E R Williams **Bred** Michael Rogers **Trained** Llancarfan, Vale Of Glamorgan

FOCUS
Drama in this average maiden hurdle when the leader jinked before the last, lost momentum and in so doing surrendered the victory. The first two look above average for the time of year.

NOTEBOOK
Tin Pot Man(IRE) had been outpaced as the leader eased to the front around the final turn, kept up the chase and was therefore in the ideal position to benefit. The pair finished clear of the remainder, so although he may have been a fortunate winner it was still a fair performance. He needed to improve on his two previous hurdles efforts, and the first-time tongue-tie and better ground helped elicit that improvement. (op 16-1)

Coeur De Lionne(IRE) was a bit wayward at the early flights but was travelling best of all as he eased into the lead coming into the straight. It looked a question of how far, but he idled in front and veered right and left before the last, which just cost him enough momentum to lose the race. A four-time winner over middle distances on the Flat, this was his debut over hurdles and he should gain compensation with this experience behind him. (op 9-4)
Frosted Grape(IRE) held a good position but was well beaten off in the straight. She has had plenty of chances but is now 0-13 over jumps and looks exposed.
Pegasus Lad(USA) led to halfway before fading and needs to prove his stamina over hurdles. (op 25-1)

755 HAVE YOUR EXHIBITION HERE H'CAP CHASE (13 fncs) 2m 110y
6:45 (6:45) (Class 5) (0-95,95) 5-Y-O+ **£2,797** (£821; £410; £205)

Form				RPR
2-33	1		**Misamon (FR)**[5] 689 7-11-4 **84**........(v) PaulMoloney (David Rees) *led tl nt fluent 7th: chsd ldr: rdn after 3 out: rallied to ld last: styd on strly: rdn out* 10/1[3]	98
/20-	2	3	**Inmate (IRE)**[334] 971 9-11-7 **87**........ CharliePoste (Robin Dickin) *w wnr: led 7th: rdn after 3 out: hdd last: no ex* 25/1	98
-311	3	hd	**Ruby Isabel (IRE)**[1] 747 6-12-1 **95** 7ex........ RichardJohnson (Tim Vaughan) *hld up: hdwy fr 8th: rdn after 3 out: wnt 3rd whn hit next: kpt on fr last* 1/1[1]	107
4-63	4	3 ¾	**Turbo Shandy**[13] 578 7-11-10 **90**........ TomO'Brien (Dai Burchell) *hld up: stdy prog fr 9th: rdn after 3 out: styd on same pce* 10/1[3]	97
F35-	5	2 ¾	**My Pal Val (IRE)**[37] 10-11-8 **91**........(t) DannyCook(3) (John Panvert) *hld up: plenty to do 4 out: rdn and prog after 3 out: styd on same pce fr next: nvr nrr* 22/1	96
554-	6	4 ½	**Shindig**[57] 5289 8-11-9 **89**........(tp) RhysFlint (John Flint) *mid-div: hdwy 8th: rdn after 4 out: nvr able to mount chal: fdd last* 22/1	90
P-06	7	15	**Captain Marlon (IRE)**[9] 652 9-11-12 **92**........(t) JoeTizzard (Colin Tizzard) *trckd ldrs: wnt 3rd 7th: mstke 8th: rdn after 3 out: wkng whn blnd 2 out* 22/1	86+
56P-	8	1 ¼	**Only Dreams (IRE)**[58] 5259 9-11-4 **91**........ MrJBanks(7) (Nick Lampard) *mid-div tl wknd after 4 out* 25/1	77
-412	9	1	**Beauchamp Viking**[15] 558 6-11-5 **85**........(t) AndrewThornton (Simon Burrough) *hld up: hdwy into midfield 9th: sn rdn: wknd after 3 out* 7/2[2]	71
0-0F	10	20	**Un Autre Espere**[15] 558 11-9-4 **66** oh8........(b) JoshWall(10) (Trevor Wall) *chsd ldrs: rdn after 6th: wknd 8th: t.o* 66/1	33
-655	11	7	**Tilly Shilling (IRE)**[9] 652 6-10-4 **70**........(t) RodiGreene (Kevin Bishop) *mid-div: reminders after 5th: rdn after next: sn in rr: t.o* 20/1	31
PP-5	P		**Knapp Bridge Boy**[42] 130 10-11-2 **82**........ LiamTreadwell (James Payne) *mid-div: wnt lft 1st: mstke 2nd: in rr fr 7th: t.o whn p.u after 3 out* 33/1	—

4m 2.20s (-4.30) **Going Correction** -0.175s/f (Good) 12 Ran SP% **120.3**
Speed ratings: **103,101,101,99,98 96,89,88,88,78 75,—**
Tote Swingers: 1&2 £0.00, 1&3 £3.70, 2&3 £21.60 CSF £210.89 CT £471.30 TOTE £7.30: £1.40, £8.50, £1.20; EX 233.00.
Owner The Supreme Racing Club **Bred** Alain Ranson **Trained** Clarbeston, Pembrokes

FOCUS
Two duelling leaders maintained a strong pace to the line, meaning few could get a look in. Ordinary but sound form.

NOTEBOOK
Misamon(FR) had been well backed for his two races earlier this month, but had come up short. Although this trip looked shorter than ideal, by helping to set the pace he was able to run the sting out of his rivals. He got a bit outpaced down the back, but had a fitness edge over his rival for the lead and was able to reassert in the home straight for a hard-fought first success over jumps. (tchd 11-1)
Inmate(IRE) helped cut out the pace and was only beaten as the lack of a recent run told in the closing stages. He has gone well fresh in the past, but that usually results in him finishing second, and it was the same again. However, on a similar track he could be interesting next time, especially if able to run off a lighter weight to help sustain that pace to the line.
Ruby Isabel(IRE) was well backed after winning at Sedgefield the previous day. She made progress in the back straight to close down the leaders, but that recent run looked to have taken the edge off her and a low jump at the last meant she could make no further impression. (tchd 10-11, 11-10 in places and 5-4 in a place)
Turbo Shandy was stretched into a couple of jumping errors and could never get competitive. (tchd 11-1)
My Pal Val(IRE), who has been running in points this year, was held up early and made some progress but could never get into it, though he should improve for this outing for his new connections. (op 18-1 tchd 16-1)
Captain Marlon(IRE) was in the process of running his best race for a while but he hit the second-last when about to challenge and his effort was effectively over. (op 18-1 tchd 25-1)

756 NEWTON ABBOT RACES H'CAP HURDLE (8 hdls) 2m 3f
7:15 (7:15) (Class 3) (0-135,135) 4-Y-O **£6,337** (£1,872; £936; £468; £234)

Form				RPR
P3-2	1		**Humbel Ben (IRE)**[29] 372 7-10-5 **114**........ PaddyBrennan (Alan Jones) *trckd ldrs: rdn after 3 out: nt fluent next: wandered sltly whn chalng bef last: led run-in: r.o wl: rdn out* 11/4[1]	116+
62-2	2	1 ¼	**Dantari (IRE)**[32] 316 5-11-2 **128**........ DPFahy(3) (Evan Williams) *led: rdn and hdd after 3 out: kpt chsng ldrs: n.m.r but rallied last: kpt on: regained 2nd line* 5/1[2]	128
624-	3	nse	**Whenever**[63] 5173 6-10-7 **116**........ RobertThornton (Richard Phillips) *a.p: rdn to ld whn nt fluent 2 out: sn hung lft: nt fluent last: sn hdd no ex: lost 2nd line* 10/1	117
3-32	4	1 ½	**Forty Thirty (IRE)**[17] 521 4-11-2 **129**........ APMcCoy (Sheena West) *hld up towards rr: hdwy 6th: rdn to dispute cl 2nd 2 out: kpt on same pce* 6/1[3]	124
22-	5	2 ¼	**Mission Control (IRE)**[202] 2028 5-11-0 **128**........ DeanColeman(5) (Tim Vaughan) *mid-div: hdwy 6th: rdn to chse ldrs bef 2 out: kpt on same pce* 16/1	125
301-	6	nk	**Pemberton**[81] 4877 5-11-5 **128**........(p) TomScudamore (David Pipe) *prom: rdn to ld after 3 out: narrowly hdd bef next: kpt pressing ldr: no ex appr last* 14/1	124
51-0	7	5	**Overclear**[17] 524 8-11-7 **130**........ TomO'Brien (Victor Dartnall) *in tch: lft cl 6th after 3 out: sn rdn: one pce fr next: mstke last* 14/1	124
/61-	8	19	**National Trust**[87] 4725 8-11-0 **130**........ DavidBass(7) (Nicky Henderson) *mid-div: rdn after 3 out: sn wknd* 7/1	106
30-6	9	1 ¾	**Come Out Firing (IRE)**[12] 606 8-10-8 **117**........ TimmyMurphy (Michael Blake) *hld up towards rr: hdwy 6th: effrt after 3 out: wknd bef next* 14/1	93
2-62	10	1 ¼	**Ring For Time**[19] 494 7-10-9 **118**........ WillKennedy (Dai Burchell) *mid-div: rdn after 6th: hmpd after 3 out: wknd* 20/1	90
-000	11	1 ¾	**Raslan**[10] 633 7-11-5 **131**........(tp) DannyCook(3) (David Pipe) *prom: rdn after 5th: bhd fr next* 50/1	101
1-00	12	24	**Acambo (GER)**[10] 627 9-11-9 **135**........ HaddenFrost(3) (David Pipe) *mstke 6th: a towards rr: t.o fr after 3 out* 33/1	84
-000	P		**Is It Me (USA)**[10] 633 7-10-11 **120**........(t) PaulMoloney (Sophie Leech) *racd wd: in tch tl wknd after 6th: t.o whn p.u bef 2 out* 50/1	—
331-	B		**Tzora**[40] 5260 5-10-3 **112**........ RichardJohnson (Philip Hobbs) *mid-div whn blnd bdly 3rd and dropped to rr: mstke 6th: hdwy sn after: travelling wl in v cl 6th whn clipped heels and b.d after 3 out* 10/1	—

4m 22.0s (-11.90) **Going Correction** -0.45s/f (Good)
WFA 4 from 5yo+ 17lb 14 Ran SP% **125.8**
Speed ratings (Par 107): **107,106,106,105,104 104,102,94,93,93 92,82,—,—**
Tote Swingers: 1&2 £32.40, 1&3 £32.40, 2&3 £1.10 CSF £17.24 CT £126.20 TOTE £4.70: £2.00, £2.40, £4.10.
Owner BPD Ltd **Bred** Denis Duggan And Mrs Margaret Duggan **Trained** Coedkernew, Newport

FOCUS
A competitive handicap but the early pace was not strong so it produced a scramble to the line. Pretty solid form.

NOTEBOOK
Humbel Ben(IRE) was heavily supported but had quite a tussle to land the gamble. Prominent throughout, he got outpaced as the challengers jostled for position around the final turn, but his jockey was under orders to delay his run, and he had enough in reserve to come through quite convincingly at the finish. Having run well after a break in a good time over C&D last month, and getting into this race with a light weight, he was understandably popular in the market, and, as his trainer said afterwards, "job done". (op 13-2)
Dantari(IRE) disputed the lead until getting caught out as the pace lifted around the final bend, but he rallied well near the finish. Having been outpaced over shorter at Aintree last month, this trip looks more suitable, especially if the pace is stronger. (op 11-2 tchd 9-2)
Whenever did not stay when asked to go nearly 3m at Exeter in April but fared much better at this shorter trip, looking a threat as he took up the lead around the final turn before the lack of a recent run just made the difference. (op 16-1)
Forty Thirty(IRE), who had finished close behind Dantari at Aintree in May, settled better than he has on occasions, and made progress to challenge wide of the pack, but the 4yo was stepping up in trip and did not quite get home.
Mission Control(IRE) ran well for a long way but faded from the last. He was a dual winner over C&D last year but had been off the track since November and should come on for the run. (op 14-1)
Pemberton ran well on his debut for his new stable since leaving Howard Johnson's yard for £9,000 last month. Helping to set the pace in first-time cheekpieces, he was ultimately swamped but ran as if he would improve for the run and should soon be adding to his win tally. (op 16-1)
Ring For Time Official explanation: jockey said mare was hampered by faller

757 CHEAP AS CHIPS (S) H'CAP HURDLE (8 hdls) 2m 3f
7:45 (7:45) (Class 5) (0-95,93) 4-Y-O+ **£2,055** (£599; £299)

Form				RPR
606/	1		**Kopylova**[71] 7-11-3 **84**........ RichardJohnson (Tim Vaughan) *hld up towards rr: hdwy appr 6th: led bef 2 out: sn rdn and hrd pressed: r.o fr last: rdn out* 4/1[2]	95+
/0U2	2	2	**Amazing Request**[12] 593 6-10-5 **79**........(p) MissIsabelTompsett(7) (Bernard Llewellyn) *mid-div: mstke 4th: hdwy after 6th: rdn to chal 2 out: no ex fr last* 3/1[1]	89+
P0/5	3	12	**Award Winning (IRE)**[34] 272 9-10-6 **78**........ TomO'Connor(5) (John Berwick) *trckd ldrs: rdn to ld after 3 out: hdd bef next: sn one pce* 22/1	77
5-44	4	8	**Monty's Moon (IRE)**[9] 650 8-10-1 **68**........(b) AidanColeman (Rachel Hobbs) *trckd ldrs: rdn after 3 out: wknd next* 16/1	59
06-5	5	1 ¾	**Sheikhman (IRE)**[17] 522 9-11-2 **90**........(p) MrTJCannon(7) (Brett Johnson) *pckd 1st: mid-div tl rdn along fr after 4th: outpcd after 3 out: nvr on terms* 5/1[3]	80
6-24	6	16	**Masterpoint**[15] 557 10-10-3 **77**........ MrTomDavid(7) (Richard Harper) *hld up bhd: hdwy appr 6th: rdn and ev ch after 3 out: wknd bef next* 25/1	52
5-40	7	3 ¾	**Young Tot (IRE)**[12] 593 12-10-12 **79**........(p) HarrySkelton (Carroll Gray) *led tl after 5th: led next: rdn and hdd after 3 out: sn wknd* 50/1	51
P0-0	8	11	**Gainsborough's Art (IRE)**[23] 63 5-10-8 **82**........ MrRHawkins(7) (Chris Down) *a towards rr: t.o after 3 out* 50/1	44
U-64	P		**Killing Me Softly**[12] 593 9-10-13 **80**........(v) LiamTreadwell (Brian Forsey) *mid-div: nudged along to go prom after 3rd: wknd 6th: p.u bef 3 out* 8/1	—
33U/	P		**Starstruck Peter (IRE)**[337] 4722 6-11-12 **93**........(b) APMcCoy (Jim Best) *w ldr: led after 5th: sn rdn and hdd: wknd qckly: p.u after 3 out* 4/1[2]	—
50-4	F		**Welsh Jaunt**[33] 298 5-10-10 **77**........(p) WillKennedy (Dai Burchell) *mid-div: losing pl whn fell 6th* 14/1	—

4m 25.3s (-8.60) **Going Correction** -0.45s/f (Good) 11 Ran SP% **117.4**
Speed ratings (Par 103): **100,99,94,90,90 83,81,77,—,—,—**
Tote Swingers: 1&2 £6.30, 1&3 £25.70, 2&3 £16.10 CSF £16.23 CT £231.95 TOTE £6.60: £2.70, £2.10, £5.50.The winner was bought in for £4,500.
Owner optimumracing.co.uk **Bred** E M Peck And Sons **Trained** Aberthin, Vale of Glamorgan

FOCUS
Two pulled clear in a battle from the last in an average seller. It was run in a decent time for the grade and the winner produced a step up.

NOTEBOOK
Kopylova was held up early but made relentless progress down the back to strike the front at the right time. She still had to hold off a sustained challenge, but fought off that rival and ultimately stayed on best. Her previous form was mostly poor, including in a point two months ago, but she has been revitalised by the switch to the in-form Tim Vaughan yard and she looked very fit for this. Official explanation: trainer said, regarding apparent improvement in form, that it was the mare's first run for the yard and apperared to appreciate the drop in class. (op 7-2)
Amazing Request needed plenty of driving to challenge round the final turn, and was still responding to pressure to challenge the winner, but he was just outstayed in a strong bid for his first win. He finished clear of the rest and on this evidence looks capable of picking up a race in this grade. (op 5-1)
Award Winning(IRE) looked a threat around the final turn but he was soon outpaced in the straight. He is gradually coming back to form and previously has gone better at stiffer tracks.
Monty's Moon(IRE) was prominent to the home turn but he lacks the pace for hurdles, even at this level. (op 10-1)

Sheikhman(IRE) dropped himself out early and ran in snatches, so it was a surprise to see him carry on, albeit without threatening the leaders. (op 6-1 tchd 13-2)

758 RIVER TEIGN H'CAP CHASE (16 fncs) 2m 5f 110y
8:15 (8:15) (Class 5) (0-90,89) 5-Y-O+ **£2,945** (£858; £429)

Form RPR
50-1 **1** **Clifden Boy (IRE)**[9] 649 8-11-5 **82** 7ex..............................(b) APMcCoy 100+
(Jim Best) mde all: nt fluent 4th: blnd 12th: in command fr 3 out: sn rdn: comf **1/2**[1]
523- **2** 3 1/2 **Sir Bumble (IRE)**[65] 5151 10-11-0 **77**..............................(t) TimmyMurphy 86
(Michael Blake) trckd ldrs: wnt 2nd after 8th: j.lft fr 4 out: sn rdn: hld fr next: hit 2 out **10/1**[3]
05/P **3** 1 3/4 **Lord Lescribaa (FR)**[8] 665 7-11-6 **83**..............................(b) RhysFlint 89
(Philip Hobbs) trckd wnr tl 8th: remained in 3rd: rdn after 10th: styd on same pce fr 4 out **14/1**
-332 **4** 8 **Post It**[16] 533 9-11-7 **84**.............................. RichardJohnson 83
(Ron Hodges) mid-div: rdn into 4th after 4 out: nvr trbld ldrs **10/1**[3]
-461 **5** 3 1/2 **Classic Clover**[8] 665 10-11-7 **89**..............................(t) SamTwiston-Davies(5) 85
(Colin Tizzard) hld up towards rr: nvr gng pce to get on terms **6/1**[2]
00F- **6** 6 **Moon Bear**[287] 1372 9-11-2 **82**.............................. DannyCook(3) 73
(Linda Blackford) trckd ldrs: hit 6th: sn lost pl: rdn after 11th: sn btn **40/1**
60-4 **7** 1/2 **Beau Supreme (IRE)**[17] 13-11-1 **85**.............................. MrRHawkins(7) 75
(Kathleen Sanderson) hld up: hdwy fr 8th: rdn in 4th appr 11th: wknd 3 out **33/1**
0-P **8** dist **Tinalliat (FR)**[34] 283 7-11-0 **84**.............................. MrJFMathias(7) —
(David Rees) mid-div: rdn after 11th: wknd bef 4 out: t.o **80/1**
/P-0 **P** **Here To Eternity (IRE)**[34] 273 9-10-1 **64**.............................. RodiGreene —
(Sarah Robinson) sn drvn along in rr: lost tch 9th: p.u bef next **66/1**
4-5P **P** **Rash Moment (FR)**[9] 649 11-11-4 **84**..............................(v) CampbellGillies(3) —
(Michael Scudamore) a towards rr: t.o fr 12th: p.u bef 2 out **28/1**
534- **P** **Huntingford (IRE)**[51] 2 7-10-5 **75**.............................. MrRWoollacott(7) —
(Tracey Barfoot-Saunt) mid-div tl 9th: bhd whn p.u bef 11th **66/1**

5m 16.8s (-4.60) **Going Correction** -0.175s/f (Good) **11** Ran SP% **118.8**
Speed ratings: **101,99,99,96,94 92,92,—,—,— —**
Tote Swingers: 1&2 £1.40, 1&3 £5.30, 2&3 £30.80 CSF £6.41 CT £39.40 TOTE £1.40: £1.10, £1.50, £2.90; EX 8.50.
Owner The Jam Boys **Bred** Maurice Harrington **Trained** Lewes, E Sussex
■ Stewards' Enquiry : Danny Cook one-day ban: used whip when out of contention (Jun 29)

FOCUS
Few got into this as the in-form favourite turned this into a procession. He was value for further and is rated in line with his recent win.

NOTEBOOK
Clifden Boy(IRE) was well backed to follow up after gaining his first win in effortless fashion on his debut for his new yard last week. Given a positive ride, he did not jump fluently and so was a target for anything able to challenge, but he was well handicapped under a penalty on his old form and completely dominant in this grade. He had been able to get into a rhythm over the longer trip at Worcester but here, over a shorter trip and tighter track, he began to make errors, especially at the fences coming after a bend. He has returned in peak form and has been well placed by his astute connections. (op 4-7 after 8-11 and 4-6 in places, tchd 8-13 in places)
Sir Bumble(IRE) was the only one to offer up any sort of challenge to the winner, but he began to look reluctant going to the fences in the closing stages and did not quite see out the trip. (op 8-1 tchd 15-2)
Lord Lescribaa(FR) pulled up in the race won by Classic Clover last week but was much better here, racing prominently but only able to stay on at one pace. He has managed to win three points this year, but still needs to improve to feature under rules. (op 12-1)
Post It has been in good form since the spring but jumped out to the right at several fences and was never a threat. (op 9-1 tchd 12-1)
Classic Clover is usually better when racing prominently, but he did not travel that well and never got out of mid division. Considering he won here last week this was a bit disappointing, though he has not won over this short a trip before. (op 7-1 tchd 8-1)

759 PADDOCK RESTAURANT INTERMEDIATE OPEN NATIONAL HUNT FLAT RACE 2m 1f
8:45 (8:45) (Class 6) 4-6-Y-O **£1,747** (£509; £254)

Form RPR
2-51 **1** **Maggie Aron**[14] 568 4-10-13 0.............................. RichardJohnson 101+
(Tim Vaughan) hld up bhd: tk clsr order 5f out: wnt 2nd 3f out: rdn to ld wl over 1f out: styd on strly: rdn out **5/4**[1]
4-3 **2** 1 1/4 **Grandads Horse**[29] 375 4-10-13 0.............................. SamThomas 100+
(Alan Jones) mde most: rdn and hdd wl over 1f out: kpt on but no ex fnl f **4/1**[3]
3 20 **Ilewin Dundee** 4-10-13 0.............................. RodiGreene 80
(Gary Brown) hld up bhd: hdwy on inner fnl bnd: styd on fnl 2f but nvr any ch: bmpd over 1f out **80/1**
0/4 **4** 3 **Court Gamble (IRE)**[34] 277 6-10-9 0.............................. JoeTizzard 73
(Nerys Dutfield) t.k.h in mid-div: rdn over 4f out: wnt 4th nr fin: nvr trbld ldrs **50/1**
5 hd **Oscar Charlie (IRE)**[72] 5-11-2 0.............................. DarylJacob 80
(Jamie Snowden) trckd ldrs: rdn over 3f out: one pce fnl 2f: edgd rt over 1f out **28/1**
6 1 1/4 **Upper Deck (IRE)** 5-10-13 0.............................. SeanQuinlan(3) 78
(Richard Phillips) nvr bttr than mid-div **50/1**
7 1 1/4 **Stitchnick (IRE)**[38] 5-11-2 0.............................. TomScudamore 77
(Stuart Kittow) trckd ldrs: rdn over 3f out: sn one pce: wknd fnl f **20/1**
8 4 **Hamalac** 4-10-13 0.............................. RobertThornton 70
(Martin Keighley) mid-div: hdwy 5f out: effrt 4f out: one pce fr over 2f out: wknd fnl f **7/2**[2]
0 **9** 18 **Track Star (IRE)**[13] 589 5-11-2 0.............................. JamieMoore 55
(Luke Dace) trckd ldrs: rdn over 4f out: sn wknd **16/1**
10 1 1/4 **Loupy Loups** 4-10-6 0.............................. JimmyMcCarthy 44
(Brendan Powell) a towards rr **25/1**
0- **11** 1/2 **Kiristani**[228] 1991 5-10-9 0.............................. TomO'Brien 46
(Caroline Keevil) trckd ldrs tl 5f out **66/1**
00-3 **12** dist **Toxic Asset**[47] 60 5-11-2 0.............................. RhysFlint —
(John Flint) disp ld tl over 6f out: sn drvn in tch: wknd 4f out: t.o **9/1**
4-0 **13** 3/4 **Mini Shower**[10] 637 6-10-3 0 ow1.............................. MrSJO'Donovan(7) —
(Norma Twomey) mid-div tl 1/2-way: t.o **66/1**
P **Somerset Level** 6-10-9 0.............................. LiamTreadwell —
(James Payne) rn green in rr: wl bhd fnl 9f: t.o: p.u sn after **100/1**

3m 51.9s (-8.20) **Going Correction** -0.45s/f (Good)
WFA 4 from 5yo+ 3lb **14** Ran SP% **123.7**
Speed ratings: **101,100,91,89,89 88,88,86,77,77 77,—,—,—**
Tote Swingers: 1&2 £1.40, 1&3 £8.40, 2&3 £10.50 CSF £5.95 TOTE £2.00: £1.10, £2.20, £49.80; EX 7.00 Place 6: £11.20 Place 5:£4.75.
Owner J S Hughes **Bred** R J & S A Carter **Trained** Aberthin, Vale of Glamorgan

FOCUS
Just an ordinary bumper but some decent performances from the first two who pulled clear. The form is rated around them.

NOTEBOOK
Maggie Aron is just a small filly, so she had quite a task to defy a penalty following her smooth success at Ffos Las this month. Held up early, she made stylish progress in the back straight to challenge the leader, and had to dig deep to maintain her advantage. She obviously has a future, although she might find it easier tackling hurdles next rather than humping a double penalty. (tchd 6-4)
Grandads Horse set the pace and tried to fend off the winner's challenge but just got outbattled. He looks as if he will be a useful jumper given time to strengthen up. (op 11-2 tchd 3-1)
Ilewin Dundee was held up in rear and was caught behind traffic as the first two went for home. He got squeezed up when making a move over a furlong from home and looked green but will improve a lot for this.
Court Gamble(IRE) had hinted at more to come on her return from an absence at Exeter last month, so it was disappointing that she was never able to get involved. (op 33-1)
T/Plt: £55.50 to a £1 stake. Pool: £63,615.81 - 835.65 winning tickets T/Qpdt: £7.20 to a £1 stake. Pool: £6,226.67 - 638.61 winning tickets TM

645 WORCESTER (L-H)
Wednesday, June 16

OFFICIAL GOING: Good to firm (good in places) changing to good to firm after race 2 (2:45)
Chase and hurdle bends moved onto fresh ground but impact on distances not quantified.
Wind: Light behind Weather: Fine and sunny

760 LUNCH IN THE SEVERN RESTAURANT NOVICES' CLAIMING HURDLE (8 hdls) 2m
2:10 (2:10) (Class 5) 4-Y-O+ **£2,055** (£599; £299)

Form RPR
20-1 **1** **Players Please (USA)**[13] 607 6-11-10 112.............................. DenisO'Regan 126+
(Michael Blake) mde all: clr last: eased towards fin **3/1**[2]
1 **2** 9 **What A Riddle (IRE)**[35] 289 7-11-6 114.............................. APMcCoy 112+
(A J Martin, Ire) a.p: chsd wnr appr 3 out: rdn and mstke last: no ex **2/1**[1]
31 **3** hd **A Dream Come True**[16] 555 5-10-5 0.............................. JodieMogford 95
(Graeme McPherson) hld up in tch: rdn appr 3 out: styd on same pce fr next: j.rt last **10/1**
53P- **4** 10 **Rate Field (IRE)**[237] 1863 6-10-6 98.............................. MatthewClark(10) 96
(Emma Lavelle) bhd: hdwy appr 3 out: wkng whn j.rt last two **20/1**
3B3- **5** 15 **Grasscutter (IRE)**[190] 2763 6-10-12 100.............................. JasonMaguire 78
(Donald McCain) mid-div: hdwy u.p 5th: wknd next: t.o **15/2**[3]
11-3 **6** 1 3/4 **Brandy Butter**[24] 180 4-10-7 112..............................(bt) TomScudamore 70
(David Pipe) chsd wnr: j.rt 5th: sn rdn: wknd after next: t.o **3/1**[2]
P **7** 4 1/2 **Simone Martini (IRE)**[38] 215 5-10-7 0..............................(t) SeanQuinlan(3) 69
(Milton Harris) hld up: mstke 3rd: n.d: t.o **100/1**
0/20 **8** 17 **He's A Sheila**[34] 298 7-10-0 0.............................. JoshWall(10) 52
(Trevor Wall) prom tl rdn and wknd after 5th: t.o **80/1**
3-03 **9** 3 1/2 **Renege The Joker**[24] 439 7-10-3 92.............................. KyleJames(7) 48
(Sean Regan) hld up: rdn after 4th: sn lost tch: t.o **50/1**
00- **10** nse **Kemsley Lass**[251] 1674 5-10-5 0.............................. ColinBolger 43
(Milton Bradley) mid-div: bhd fr 4th: t.o **200/1**
11 24 **Spiders Tern**[160] 5-10-9 0.............................. ChrisDavies(7) 30
(Milton Bradley) a in rr: mstke 4th: t.o **200/1**
U **Bluebird Chariot**[35] 7-10-5 0.............................. MrTJCannon(7) —
(Milton Bradley) chsd ldrs tl rdn and wknd after 5th: bhd whn blnd and uns rdr next **200/1**
0/0 **P** **Poca A Poca (IRE)**[17] 535 6-10-3 0.............................. AidanColeman —
(Rachel Hobbs) hld up: a in rr: t.o whn p.u bef 3 out **100/1**

3m 36.3s (-11.00) **Going Correction** -0.55s/f (Firm)
WFA 4 from 5yo+ 17lb **13** Ran SP% **115.6**
Speed ratings (Par 103): **105,100,100,95,87 87,84,76,74,74 62,—,—**
toteswingers:1&2:£2.00, 1&3:£7.50, 2&3:£7.70 CSF £9.23 TOTE £4.10: £1.40, £2.00, £2.50; EX 9.90.
Owner Staverton Owners Group **Bred** 6 C Racing Limited **Trained** Trowbridge, Wilts

FOCUS
This claimer was run at a true gallop and few got seriously involved. The winner made a big step up, and the runner-up and fourth set the level.

NOTEBOOK
Players Please(USA) made all to supplement his Wetherby success in this grade 13 days earlier with another clear-cut success. He deserves credit as he was not granted an easy lead and there was a lot to like about his attitude in the home straight, so further success in this sort of class looks assured during the summer. (op 7-2 tchd 11-4)
What A Riddle(IRE) was a rare 16/1 winner for these connections at Perth last month and was entitled to start favourite this time, getting weight from the winner. He travelled nicely into contention, but Players Please held too many guns for him and he was well held prior to an error at the last. On this showing he wants a return to further. (op 13-8 tchd 6-4)
A Dream Come True, comfortably off the mark at Towcester 16 days previously, was another that travelled well through the race. She hit a flat spot at a crucial stage, however, and on this showing wants to return to a stiffer track. (op 11-1 tchd 9-1)
Rate Field(IRE) threatened to get involved after the fourth-last, but his response once asked for an effort was limited. He should come on nicely for the run. (op 25-1 tchd 28-1)
Brandy Butter isn't an easy ride, but came into this with a consistent profile. Looking at the way he folded, it may be that he would benefit from a little break. (op 7-2 tchd 4-1)

761 LEUKAEMIA CARE LEUKAEMIACARE.ORG.UK NOVICES' CHASE (14 fncs 1 omitted) 2m 4f 110y
2:45 (2:45) (Class 4) 5-Y-O+ **£3,252** (£955; £477; £238)

Form RPR
5-12 **1** **The Jigsaw Man (IRE)**[15] 565 6-10-12 0.............................. APMcCoy 124
(Rebecca Curtis) mde all: mstke 5 out: clr whn nt fluent next: shkn up appr last: styd on wl: eased nr fin **4/6**[1]
62-3 **2** 13 **Watch Out**[18] 518 6-10-12 96..............................(tp) ChristianWilliams 112+
(Dai Burchell) hld up: hdwy 8th: wnt 3rd after next: chsd wnr 4 out: rdn whn j.rt last: no ex **8/1**
P-21 **3** 16 **Cullahill (IRE)**[11] 631 8-11-5 0..............................(t) HarrySkelton 102
(Bob Buckler) chsd wnr tl rdn appr 4 out: wknd next **7/2**[2]
FP-2 **4** 10 **Vic's World (IRE)**[10] 647 8-10-2 92.............................. HaddenFrost(3) 78
(James Frost) hld up: rdn 7th: wknd next: t.o **16/1**
-P60 **5** 22 **Gilded Youth**[16] 554 6-10-12 0.............................. ColinBolger 63
(Simon Lewis) hld up: racd keenly: hdwy 5th: j. slowly and wknd 9th: t.o whn mstke last **100/1**

053/ **6** *14* **Cherokee Star**[16] 5-10-12 0 DenisO'Regan 49
(Mike Hammond) *chsd ldrs: lost pl 4th: wknd 7th: t.o* **33/1**

F **Thelobstercatcher**[167] 3203 6-10-7 0 DonalDevereux(5) —
(Peter Bowen) *fell 1st* **5/1**[3]

0P-0 **P** **Tribunel**[28] 410 6-10-12 0 DavidDennis —
(Nigel Hawke) *plld hrd and prom: lost pl 6th: sn p.u* **100/1**

4m 59.2s (-7.50) **Going Correction** -0.40s/f (Good) **8** Ran SP% **120.8**
Speed ratings: **98,93,86,83,74 69,—,—**
toteswingers:1&2:£2.60, 1&3:£1.10, 2&3:£4.20 CSF £7.94 TOTE £1.90: £1.02, £3.70, £1.10; EX 8.30.
Owner LL R P Racing **Bred** P J O'Connor **Trained** Newport, Dyfed

FOCUS
An uncompetitive event and the winner is rated to his chasing debut mark, although the race could go higher through the third and fourth..

NOTEBOOK
The Jigsaw Man(IRE) opened his account over fences at the second attempt and was well on top at the finish, but still didn't overly convince he is a natural for chasing. He was turned over on his debut in this sphere at Ffos Las, but is certainly not the biggest for jumping fences and was a ridiculously short price that day. These fences were more to his liking and it was an easier assignment, but again his jumping was unimpressive at times, especially when coming under some pressure. This will do his confidence a lot of good and he has the class to defy a penalty, but will likely struggle when the better novices emerge later in the season. (op 10-1, tchd Evens in places)
Watch Out took time to settle out the back. He emerged as the only real threat to the winner from four out, but it was apparent that rival was idling and he was beaten before going out to his right at the last. He helps to put the form into perspective and deserves to go one better. (tchd 10-1)
Cullahill(IRE) ultimately paid for trying to go with the winner through the race and is clearly vulnerable in this sphere now. A return to further should suit, though. (op 5-1)
Vic's World(IRE) began to feel the pinch on the far side and was well below her recent second over C&D. (op 12-1)
Thelobstercatcher looked a likely sort on his previous form in Ireland and has joined a decent yard for this time of year. He failed to take off at the first on this switch to chasing, however, and will clearly need some intensive schooling. (op 4-1 tchd 11-2)
Tribunel Official explanation: jockey said gelding hung right and its action (op 4-1 tchd 11-2)

762 BET US OPEN GOLF - BETDAQ (S) H'CAP HURDLE (8 hdls) 2m
3:20 (3:20) (Class 5) (0-90,90) 4-Y-O+ **£2,055** (£599; £299)

Form RPR
063- **1** **Domino Dancer (IRE)**[82] 4875 6-11-8 **86** APMcCoy 100+
(Jim Best) *chsd ldr tl led 5th: rdn and mstke next: styd on wl* **11/8**[1]

P0-3 **2** *4 1/2* **Art Man**[41] 171 7-11-9 **90** (b[1]) HaddenFrost(3) 95
(James Frost) *hld up: hdwy 4th: chsd wnr and mstke 3 out: rdn and hung lft flat: styd on same pce* **10/1**

00P/ **3** *15* **Sahara Prince (IRE)**[24] 10-11-3 **88** MrLRPayter(7) 78
(Matt Sheppard) *chsd ldrs: rdn appr 3 out: sn outpcd: wnt 3rd nr fin* **33/1**

6-04 **4** *1* **Golden Square**[22] 462 8-11-5 **88** LeeEdwards(5) 77
(Tony Carroll) *led to 5th: sn rdn: wknd appr last: lost 3rd nr fin* **8/1**

-425 **5** *9* **Bari Bay**[16] 557 4-11-5 **86** DenisO'Regan 63
(Michael Blake) *hld up: nvr on terms* **6/1**[3]

/BP- **6** *5* **Royal Master**[122] 4063 8-11-7 **85** AlanO'Keeffe 60
(Richard Ford) *hld up: hdwy appr 3 out: sn rdn and wknd: t.o* **66/1**

0-6F **7** *9* **Golden Smog (IRE)**[16] 554 4-11-0 **81** PaddyBrennan 44
(Ian Williams) *hld up: hdwy 5th: rdn and wknd next: t.o* **28/1**

/P3- **8** *10* **Monsieur (FR)**[365] 736 10-11-9 **87** HarrySkelton 43
(Carroll Gray) *hld up: a in rr: t.o* **22/1**

30-B **9** *4* **Ravine Rose**[31] 358 4-11-3 **84** (t) CharliePoste 33
(Ben Case) *hld up: a in rr: t.o* **66/1**

400- **10** *14* **Escardo (GER)**[10] 2031 7-11-2 **80** RodiGreene 18
(David Bridgwater) *chsd ldrs: rdn and wknd after 5th: t.o* **33/1**

P5-6 **11** *7* **We'Re Delighted**[22] 462 5-11-10 **88** (t) JasonMaguire 19
(Michael Blake) *hld up: a in rr: t.o* **12/1**

/PF- **P** **Tancredi (SWE)**[188] 2787 8-11-0 **85** KyleJames(7) —
(Gruffydd Jones) *hld up: bhd whn p.u 3rd* **100/1**

436- **P** **Etoile D'Or (IRE)**[106] 4370 6-10-11 **75** (t) RichardJohnson —
(Tim Vaughan) *chsd ldrs tl wknd qckly 3rd: t.o whn p.u bef 3 out* **9/2**[2]

3m 38.4s (-8.90) **Going Correction** -0.55s/f (Firm)
WFA 4 from 5yo+ 17lb **13** Ran SP% **120.1**
Speed ratings (Par 103): **100,97,90,89,85 82,78,73,71,64 60,—,—**
toteswingers:1&2:£6.30, 1&3:£46.00, 2&3:not won CSF £15.25 CT £330.66 TOTE £1.90: £1.10, £3.90, £7.50; EX 22.30.There was no bid for the winner.
Owner Derek Westley & Colin Pullen **Bred** D And Mrs D Veitch **Trained** Lewes, E Sussex

FOCUS
This selling handicap was another race where it paid to race on the front end. Big steps up from the first two but the time was reasonable for the grade.

NOTEBOOK
Domino Dancer(IRE) was making his debut for a new stable renowned for vastly improving horses it inherits from other yards and he came home a well-backed winner. He was never far away and took it up at the last leaving the back straight. He looked vulnerable three out as he hit that flight, but kept finding and was easily on top at the finish. He holds an entry at Hereford on Sunday and will probably be out again quickly. (op 2-1)
Art Man showed improved form when third on his previous outing and looked as though he was going to take some beating as he crept into things off the home turn here. He wasn't clever with the winner at the third-last, though, and ultimately found that rival far too strong. He seems the most sensible guide for the form. (op 15-2)
Sahara Prince(IRE), pulled up in two of his four outings between the flags, got outpaced and stayed on late in the day on this return to hurdling. It was his first run for the yard and he should enjoy stepping up in trip. (op 40-1 tchd 50-1)
Golden Square, whose yard won this last year, raced positively yet was a spent force before the third-last. (op 5-1)
Tancredi(SWE) Official explanation: jockey said gelding lost its action
Etoile D'Or(IRE) Official explanation: trainer said mare had breathing problem

763 BET IN RUNNING - BETDAQ MAIDEN HURDLE (DIV I) (12 hdls) 3m
4:00 (4:00) (Class 4) 4-Y-O+ **£2,397** (£698; £349)

Form RPR
00/ **1** **Genuine Pearl (IRE)**[770] 168 8-11-0 0 (t) ChristianWilliams 118+
(Lawney Hill) *chsd ldrs: led after 2nd: hdd 7th: led again after 9th: sn hdd: led 2 out: drvn out* **16/1**

24-2 **2** *1 1/4* **Chesapeake (IRE)**[17] 538 6-11-0 115 APMcCoy 117
(Jonjo O'Neill) *hld up: hdwy u.p after 3 out: styd on* **15/8**[2]

22/2 **3** *1* **Rith Bob (IRE)**[8] 684 7-10-7 102 PaulMoloney 109
(David Rees) *chsd ldrs: rdn appr 3 out: styd on u.p* **13/8**[1]

/P-5 **4** *nk* **Atlantic Coast (IRE)**[18] 514 6-10-9 110 (b) DonalDevereux(5) 116
(Peter Bowen) *hld up: hdwy 5th: led after 9th: hdd 2 out: styd on u.p* **9/1**

40-F **5** *15* **Bally Sands (IRE)**[11] 631 6-10-11 113 (p) SeanQuinlan(3) 101
(Robin Mathew) *led: nt fluent 2nd: sn hdd: chsd ldr tl led 7th: hdd 9th: rdn and wknd after next* **17/2**[3]

00-P **6** *3 3/4* **Nether Stream (IRE)**[28] 409 6-10-9 0 SamTwiston-Davies(5) 97
(Shaun Lycett) *hld up: hdwy 8th: rdn and wknd 3 out* **100/1**

7 *22* **Safe Catch (IRE)**[35] 8-10-11 0 BernieWharfe(3) 75
(Martin Hill) *prom: rdn after 9th: wknd bef next: t.o* **100/1**

3- **8** *6* **Micks Prospect (IRE)**[16] 7-11-0 0 (t) RichardJohnson 69
(Tim Vaughan) *mid-div: hdwy 7th: rdn and wknd appr 3 out* **12/1**

P/- **P** **Foxhill**[640] 1399 10-10-11 0 DannyCook(3) —
(Jacqueline Retter) *hld up: bhd fr 7th: t.o whn p.u after 9th* **100/1**

P **Court Oliver** 12-10-7 0 PeterHatton(7) —
(Peter Purdy) *hld up: drvn along 5th: bhd fr 7th: t.o whn p.u bef 3 out* **150/1**

U- **P** **Chestnut Lilly**[95] 4583 7-10-0 0 MrJFlook(7) —
(Pam Ford) *bhd and blnd 1st: nt fluent next: sn t.o: p.u bef 4th* **150/1**

P **P** **Hinton Luciana**[17] 538 7-10-7 0 AndrewTinkler —
(Nicky Henderson) *plld hrd and prom: rdn 7th: wknd next: t.o whn p.u bef 3 out* **40/1**

5m 28.4s (-16.20) **Going Correction** -0.55s/f (Firm) course record **12** Ran SP% **113.7**
Speed ratings (Par 105): **105,104,104,104,99 97,90,88,—,— —,—**
toteswingers:1&2:£8.10, 1&3:£7.80, 2&3:£1.70 CSF £46.41 TOTE £17.70: £5.70, £1.10, £1.30; EX 82.00.
Owner The Specials **Bred** William Shaughnessy **Trained** Aston Rowant, Oxon

FOCUS
The pace was ordinary in this maiden hurdle, but although the front four finished in a bit of a heap they still pulled clear of the others. The winner is rated in line with his Irish bumper form while the next three home are rated close to their pre-race marks.

NOTEBOOK
Genuine Pearl(IRE), a dual Irish bumper winner, was making his debut for his new yard having not been seen since finishing fourth on his hurdling debut more than two years ago, but the way he was ridden didn't suggest that fitness was thought to be a problem. Having helped to force the pace throughout, he faced some stern challenges over the last three flights, but he kept on finding up the run-in and ran out a convincing winner. A massive gelding that has had a breathing operation during his time off, he is still lightly raced for a horse of his age and there is more to come from him, though he may take a little time to get over this.
Chesapeake(IRE), placed a few times in novice/handicap company over hurdles, only finished as close as he did thanks to a bit of McCoy magic. The gelding was making hard work of it from some way out, but the champion jockey managed to force him into contention jumping the last before unable to find a telling turn of foot on the run-in. (op 7-4 tchd 13-8)
Rith Bob(IRE), unbeaten in four points earlier in the year and clear of the rest when just beaten on her return to hurdles at Southwell earlier this month after trying to make all, was happy to sit just behind the leaders over this longer trip. She was never far away and had every chance jumping the last, but couldn't quicken sufficiently and may be better off being ridden more aggressively. (op 15-8 tchd 2-1)
Atlantic Coast(IRE), who showed ability in his first couple of starts over hurdles, was entitled to need the run on his return from a year off at Cartmel last month and he stepped up on that effort here having been another to be up there from the start. He should be fully fit now. (op 17-2 tchd 8-1)
Bally Sands(IRE), back over hurdles after coming to grief on his chasing debut here earlier this month, ran well for a long way but he needs softer ground than this. (tchd 8-1 and 9-1)
Foxhill Official explanation: vet said mare pulled up lame
Chestnut Lilly Official explanation: jockey said mare was never travelling
Hinton Luciana Official explanation: vet said mare finished lame

764 BET SPAIN V SWITZERLAND - BETDAQ H'CAP CHASE (13 fncs 2 omitted) 2m 4f 110y
4:35 (4:35) (Class 3) (0-135,132) 5-Y-O+ **£5,703** (£1,684; £842; £421; £210)

Form RPR
4-P1 **1** **Neutrino**[8] 677 8-10-0 **105** 7ex (v) TomScudamore 120+
(David Bridgwater) *hld up in tch: led after 9th: sn clr: easily* **7/2**[2]

2-32 **2** *10* **Royal Kicks (FR)**[32] 330 9-9-9 **106** SamTwiston-Davies(5) 110+
(Suzy Smith) *hld up: mstke 6th: hit 8th: sn drvn along: hdwy to chse wnr 3 out: no imp* **6/4**[1]

1-15 **3** *7* **Warpath (IRE)**[28] 411 9-11-9 **129** PaulMoloney 123
(Evan Williams) *chsd ldrs: j.rt 3rd: hit 5th: rdn after 9th: outpcd appr next: styd on u.p to go 3rd post* **5/1**[3]

5-0F **4** *1/2* **Knight Legend (IRE)**[18] 523 11-11-12 **132** (t) TomO'Brien 130+
(Philip Hobbs) *led after 1st: j.rt thereafter: hdd after 9th: wknd bef 2 out* **11/1**

6F-3 **5** *26* **Line Ball (IRE)**[20] 493 9-11-4 **124** (p) APMcCoy 91
(Jonjo O'Neill) *in rr: reminders after 1st: mstke 4th: hdwy 9th: rdn and wknd bef next: t.o* **15/2**

PF-0 **P** **Osolomio (IRE)**[11] 636 7-10-11 **117** AlanO'Keeffe —
(Jennie Candlish) *led and mstke 1st: j.rt thereafter: hit 5th: wknd 8th: t.o whn p.u bef 4 out* **10/1**

1P-0 **P** **Nelson's Spice (IRE)**[18] 524 9-11-6 **129** RichieMcLernon(3) —
(Jonjo O'Neill) *a in rr: bhd fr 6th: t.o whn p.u bef 4 out* **20/1**

4m 54.2s (-12.50) **Going Correction** -0.40s/f (Good) course record **7** Ran SP% **112.8**
Speed ratings: **107,103,100,100,90 —,—**
toteswingers:1&2:£1.60, 1&3:£3.10, 2&3:£3.10 CSF £9.40 CT £24.32 TOTE £5.00: £4.50, £1.40; EX 10.50.
Owner Building Bridgies **Bred** D R Wellicome **Trained** Icomb, Gloucs

FOCUS
This feature handicap was notable for some errant jumping. The winner is in fine form while the runner-up sets the standard.

NOTEBOOK
Neutrino made his move on the far side and was going strongly five out. He skipped clear off the home turn and was never in any real danger thereafter. He was 1lb out of the handicap despite shouldering a penalty for his Bangor success eight days earlier and has clearly been rejuvenated by the recent application of a visor. He was already due to race off a 2lb higher future mark and the handicapper will hike him up again for this, so turning out under another penalty may be his best option. (op 4-1)
Royal Kicks(FR) finished a clear second-best and would have been a little closer had he jumped more fluently. He has been placed on his last four outings, so rates the benchmark. (op 9-4)
Warpath(IRE), back in trip, travelled okay through the race but couldn't find any extra when asked to close on the leaders. The handicapper probably has his measure. (op 4-1 tchd 7-2)
Knight Legend(IRE) got a positive ride, but constantly hampered his cause by jumping markedly out to his right. (op 17-2)

Line Ball(IRE) ran in snatches early on, but still looked a possible threat when making up ground on the back straight. It was an effort that proved short-lived, though, and he looks on the downgrade. (op 13-2 tchd 6-1)

765 SENIOR CITIZENS SPECIAL PACKAGE RACEDAY 23RD JUNE H'CAP HURDLE (DIV I) (10 hdls) 2m 4f

5:10 (5:10) (Class 4) (0-110,110) 4-Y-0+ **£2,602** (£764; £382; £190)

Form | | | | RPR
652/ **1** **Dakota Boy (IRE)**[60] 8-11-4 **102**....(t) RichardJohnson 103+
(Alex Hales) *hld up: hmpd bnd after 4th: hdwy and hmpd 6th: chsd ldr after 7th: rdn 3 out: styd on u.p to ld 1/2-way up the run-in: all out* **40/1**
-11F **2** *hd* **Cannon Fire (FR)**[6] 692 9-10-10 **94** 7ex.... PaulMoloney 94+
(Evan Williams) *chsd ldrs: reminder after 1st: hmpd bnd after 4th: rdn 3 out: styd on u.p to have ev ch run-in: jst hld* **11/10**[1]
-512 **3** *2 1/2* **Ton-Chee**[13] 595 11-10-10 **97**....(t) CharlieHuxley(3) 96+
(Arthur Whitehead) *hld up: racd keenly: hdwy 4th: lft in ld appr 7th: 6 l clr 3 out: j.lft last: rdn: hung lft: hdd and nrly hit rail 1/2-way up the run-in: styd on same pce* **14/1**
4-04 **4** *9* **Roisin's Prince (IRE)**[10] 651 8-10-11 **95**....(t) AidanColeman 83
(Matt Sheppard) *hld up: hdwy 7th: wknd appr 2 out* **14/1**
32-4 **S** **Wizard Of Odds**[35] 279 8-11-9 **110**.... MrDHDunsdon(3) —
(Nick Gifford) *trckd ldr: racd keenly: led 3rd tl after next: cl 2nd whn slipped up and uns rdr bnd bef 5th* **17/2**
4 **P** **Proform Native (IRE)**[38] 229 8-11-3 **101**.... DenisO'Regan —
(David Rees) *led to 2nd led after 4th tl p.u bef 7th* **5/2**[2]
00P- **P** **Arniecoco**[7] 1540 5-11-2 **100**....(p) TomO'Brien —
(Emma McWilliam) *chsd ldrs: lost pl 4th: wknd after next: t.o whn p.u after 7th* **50/1**
400- **P** **Shut The Bar**[30] 5255 5-11-7 **105**.... AndrewTinkler —
(George Baker) *hld up: hmpd 6th: hdwy next: sn wknd and p.u* **28/1**
0-00 **F** **Very Stylish (IRE)**[21] 479 6-11-7 **105**.... APMcCoy —
(Jonjo O'Neill) *chsd ldrs: lft 2nd bnd appr 5th: gng wl whn fell next* **7/1**[3]

4m 36.3s (-11.10) **Going Correction** -0.55s/f (Firm) **9** Ran SP% **120.4**
Speed ratings (Par 105): **100,99,98,95,— —,—,—,—**
toteswingers:1&2:£7.40, 1&3:£22.50, 2&3:£4.30 CSF £90.96 CT £737.51 TOTE £25.50: £5.20, £1.30, £3.80; EX 116.80.
Owner M J Tuckey **Bred** F R Jarvey **Trained** Wardington, Oxon
■ Stewards' Enquiry : Paul Moloney two-day ban: used whip with excessive frequency (Jun 30-Jul 1)

FOCUS
This ordinary handicap was run at an average gallop and it proved to be an eventful race with just four completing. There was still a cracking finish between the first three, with the winner back to his former best and the third the guide to the level.

NOTEBOOK
Dakota Boy(IRE), unsuccessful in three points this year, ran out a most game winner on this return to hurdling for his former stable. He was under pressure pretty much throughout the home straight, but refused to give in after the last as Richard Johnson threw the kitchen sink at him. This is his sort of ground and he has the scope to do better over regulation fences when making the switch. (op 50-1)
Cannon Fire(FR) turned in a moody looking effort in this quest to regain the winning thread. He was handed a reminder shortly after the tape went up and, considering his main market rivals departed, it can be deemed disappointing he didn't capitalise despite him only just losing out. He is probably feeling the affects of his recent busy spell and is due to race off an 11lb higher mark in this sphere from Saturday. (op 5-4 tchd 11-8)
Ton-Chee proved keen early on and that cost him after the last, though he would have been a little closer had his rider pulled him away from the elbow on the run-in earlier. He helps to set the standard. (op 20-1)
Roisin's Prince(IRE) proved very easy to back and was left behind by the principals in the home straight. (op 11-1)
Shut The Bar Official explanation: vet said gelding pulled up lame

766 BET IN RUNNING - BETDAQ MAIDEN HURDLE (DIV II) (12 hdls) 3m

5:40 (5:46) (Class 4) 4-Y-0+ **£2,397** (£698; £349)

Form | | | | RPR
22-4 **1** **Kilmore West (IRE)**[43] 137 5-11-0 0.... RichardJohnson 100+
(Tim Vaughan) *hld up: hdwy 7th: jnd ldr next: led after 9th: drvn out* **15/8**[1]
44-5 **2** *1 3/4* **Bled (FR)**[33] 318 5-11-0 85....(b) JasonMaguire 97
(Donald McCain) *led: mstke 3rd: blnd 9th: sn rdn and hdd: styd on u.p* **5/1**[3]
5 **3** *12* **Study Troubles (IRE)**[32] 327 6-10-7 0.... AodhaganConlon(7) 70
(Debra Hamer) *plld hrd and prom: rdn after 9th: wknd next* **11/1**
5 **4** *1 3/4* **Dawn Storm (IRE)**[11] 635 5-10-11 0....(b) SeanQuinlan(3) 69
(Rachel Hobbs) *hld up: hdwy 7th: rdn and wknd appr 3 out* **40/1**
5 *111* **The Buddy Mole** 9-10-7 0.... AnthonyFreeman(7) —
(Sean Curran) *prom: mstke 3rd: reminders after next: hung rt bnd appr 7th: wknd next: t.o* **33/1**
3 **D** *14* **Rimini (FR)**[17] 528 5-11-0 0.... PaulMoloney 84
(David Rees) *hld up: hdwy 8th: wknd 2 out* **5/2**[2]
6UP/ **P** **Iris Mary (IRE)**[53] 9-10-2 0.... SamTwiston-Davies(5) —
(Shaun Lycett) *hld up: nvr on terms: mstke 3 out: sn p.u* **66/1**
00/ **P** **Paperboy**[16] 6-11-0 0.... AndrewTinkler —
(Mike Hammond) *chsd ldr to 8th: wknd next: t.o whn p.u bef 2 out* **100/1**
0P/ **P** **Angus's Antics**[436] 4891 7-11-0 0.... LeightonAspell —
(Kevin Morgan) *hld up in tch: wknd 8th: t.o whn p.u bef last* **80/1**
/03- **P** **Marwan (IRE)**[84] 4826 6-11-0 100.... DougieCostello —
(Ian Williams) *hld up in tch: p.u after 7th* **13/2**
0-0 **P** **Time Legend**[28] 412 4-10-2 0.... GerardTumelty —
(Martin Keighley) *hld up: a in rr: bhd and rdn 6th: slipped bnd sn after: blnd 9th: t.o whn p.u bef next* **40/1**

5m 36.6s (-8.00) **Going Correction** -0.55s/f (Firm)
WFA 4 from 5yo+ 19lb **11** Ran SP% **113.2**
Speed ratings (Par 105): **91,90,81,81,— 85,—,—,—,— —**
toteswingers:1&2:£2.40, 1&3:£2.00, 2&3:£5.00 CSF £10.97 TOTE £2.10: £1.10, £1.60, £1.10; EX 8.60.
Owner Brian Jones **Bred** Tom Fitzgerald **Trained** Aberthin, Vale of Glamorgan

FOCUS
This second division of the maiden and they crawled through the early parts. The form still makes sense, though, rated through the winner and backed up by the placed horses.

NOTEBOOK
Kilmore West(IRE) jumped a lot better than had been the case on his hurdling debut at Fakenham and ran out a determined winner. His rider's decision to kick on three out proved to be a winning one and he evidently stays well. (op 2-1 tchd 6-4)
Bled(FR) set out to make all and looked in trouble when the winner loomed up around four out. He kept to his task under strong driving and came right back at him after the last, but it's not hard to see why he wears blinkers. (op 9-2)
Study Troubles(IRE) was in with a chance turning for home, but failed to really see out the longer trip in the end. He can find a race back over a sharper test. (op 16-1 tchd 18-1)
Rimini(FR) was somewhat surprisingly held up on this step up to what looked a more sensible trip. He looked a real danger when making up his ground, but found just the one pace for pressure and was held from the second-last. (op 10-3 tchd 9-4)
Iris Mary(IRE) Official explanation: trainer said mare bled from nose (op 7-2)
Marwan(IRE) was easy to back on this first run for 84 days and proved keen early on. Clearly something went amiss on the far side as he was quickly pulled up. (op 7-2)
Time Legend Official explanation: vet said filly lost a shoe (op 7-2)

767 SENIOR CITIZENS SPECIAL PACKAGE RACEDAY 23RD JUNE H'CAP HURDLE (DIV II) (10 hdls) 2m 4f

6:15 (6:15) (Class 4) (0-110,108) 4-Y-0+ **£2,602** (£764; £382; £190)

Form | | | | RPR
-014 **1** **Benmadigan (IRE)**[20] 494 8-11-9 **107**.... FearghalDavis(3) 115+
(Nicky Richards) *hld up: hdwy 7th: chsd ldr appr 3 out: sn rdn: led flat: styd on: eased nr fin* **14/1**
P-P0 **2** *1 1/4* **Paddleyourowncanoe (IRE)**[18] 522 9-10-13 **97**....(bt) TomMolloy(3) 101+
(Emma Baker) *hld up: bhd and rdn 4th: 15 l 6th at the last: fin wl u.p: nt rch wnr* **28/1**
B3-2 **3** *1/2* **Space Telescope (IRE)**[18] 527 4-11-3 **102**.... APMcCoy 103+
(Jonjo O'Neill) *chsd ldrs: outpcd after 7th: rallied next: styd on u.p: lost 2nd nr fin* **10/3**[2]
3-13 **4** *4* **Woodlark Island (IRE)**[15] 566 4-11-9 **108**....(bt[1]) TomScudamore 105
(David Pipe) *led: rdn and hung rt appr 2 out: mstke last: hdd and no ex flat* **9/2**[3]
0F-P **5** *10* **High Skies**[31] 354 7-11-3 **105**....(v[1]) MrTWeston(7) 94
(Dr Richard Newland) *chsd ldrs tl rdn and wknd appr 3 out* **10/1**
51-4 **6** *3* **Extreme Conviction (IRE)**[40] 196 6-11-10 **105**.... WillKennedy 91
(John Berry) *hld up: hdwy 4th: chsd ldr next: rdn appr 3 out: wknd next* **11/4**[1]
34-4 **P** **Sweet Seville (FR)**[26] 430 6-11-5 **100**....(p) AidanColeman —
(Michael Squance) *hld up: wknd 6th: t.o whn hmpd 2 out: sn p.u* **12/1**
64-P **P** **Coup De Tabac (FR)**[9] 663 6-11-7 **102**....(t) DavidDennis —
(Nigel Hawke) *chsd ldr to 5th: sn wknd: t.o whn p.u bef 7th* **40/1**
322- **F** **Penyfan Dawn (IRE)**[246] 1735 6-11-9 **104**.... RichardJohnson 105+
(Tim Vaughan) *hld up: hdwy and blnd 7th: sn eased: styd on into 10 l 4th whn fell 2 out* **5/1**

4m 38.6s (-8.80) **Going Correction** -0.55s/f (Firm)
WFA 4 from 5yo+ 18lb **9** Ran SP% **113.9**
Speed ratings (Par 105): **95,94,94,92,88 87,—,—,—**
toteswingers:1&2:£12.10, 1&3:£11.30, 2&3:£13.10 CSF £293.47 CT £1606.65 TOTE £13.90: £4.70, £7.20, £2.10; EX 277.30 Place 6 £5.31; Place 5 £3.56.
Owner Jimmy Dudgeon **Bred** Neilie O'Mahony **Trained** Greystoke, Cumbria

FOCUS
The second division of the moderate 2m4f handicap, and the first three are rated pretty much to their marks.

NOTEBOOK
Benmadigan(IRE) got a patient ride and was asked to improve around four out. He took time to get on top, but was always doing enough after the last and has now won two of his last three outings. He has also now won both his races over C&D and it was a decent effort under top weight, but he was racing against some less-than-genuine rivals here. (op 10-1)
Paddleyourowncanoe(IRE) flashed home on the run-in to get second, having looked like being one of the back numbers for most of the race as he ran in snatches. Perhaps a switch of headgear would help next time, as the engine is evidently still there. (tchd 33-1)
Space Telescope(IRE) came under pressure down the far side, but responded the further he went and held every chance at the last. He has become a disappointment since joining current connections for hurdling, but it would be a surprise were he not placed to open his account at some stage this summer. (op 9-2 tchd 11-4)
Woodlark Island(IRE) had first-time blinkers replacing the cheekpieces here. He was still the one to catch rounding the home turn, but hung markedly to his right when under maximum pressure and failed to see out the extra distance like the principals. (op 4-1 tchd 5-1)
Extreme Conviction(IRE) was laboured in the home straight and ran below his recent level. (op 3-1 tchd 7-2)
T/Plt: £5.00 to a £1 stake. Pool:£45,927.98 - 6,597.07 winning tickets T/Qpdt: £3.50 to a £1 stake. Pool:£3,387.33 - 703.83 winning tickets CR

563 FFOS LAS (L-H)

Thursday, June 17

OFFICIAL GOING: Good to firm
Wind: almost nil Weather: sunny and very warm

768 SINCLAIR GROUP NOVICES' HURDLE (8 hdls) 2m

5:50 (5:50) (Class 4) 4-Y-0+ **£3,252** (£955; £477; £238)

Form | | | | RPR
3-12 **1** **Praxiteles (IRE)**[16] 563 6-11-5 127....(t) APMcCoy 116+
(Rebecca Curtis) *pressed ldr: drew clr of rest home turn: led gng wl bef 2 out: rdn clr appr last: lft w big advantage and sn eased* **2/5**[1]
-235 **2** *10* **Apache Dawn**[17] 554 6-10-12 98....(t) JasonMaguire 97
(Aytach Sadik) *chsd ldng pair: 6 l 3rd: rdn and outpcd home turn: lft 15 l 2nd and impeded at last: v flattered by proximity to eased wnr* **18/1**
U **3** *6* **Carhue Princess (IRE)**[32] 358 4-10-2 0.... PaulMoloney 81
(Evan Williams) *t.k.h: hld up in rr: lost tch bef 2 out: plugged on and lft remote 3rd at last* **50/1**
050- **4D** *42* **Shadow Wood (IRE)**[219] 2213 6-10-12 92.... HarrySkelton 53
(Patrick Griffin, Ire) *bhd: 4th and outpcd wl bef 2 out where mstke: sn t.o subsequently disqualified: prohibited substance in sample* **50/1**
4 *7* **Carrowbehy Lad (IRE)**[245] 1774 6-10-12 0.... PaddyBrennan 47
(Paul John Gilligan, Ire) *blnd 2nd: nvr fluent: struggling 3 out: last bef next: sn t.o and eased* **7/1**[3]
3 **F** **Totoman**[14] 607 5-10-12 115.... RichardJohnson 103
(Tim Vaughan) *led: rdn bef 2 out: hdd appr last: nrly 3 l down and btn whn fell last* **4/1**[2]

3m 45.1s (-3.90) **Going Correction** -0.60s/f (Firm)
WFA 4 from 5yo+ 17lb **6** Ran SP% **113.1**
Speed ratings (Par 105): **98,93,90,69,65 —**
Tote Swingers: 1&2 £3.30, 1&3 £22.30 CSF £9.77 TOTE £1.50: £1.10, £5.80; EX 7.10.
Owner Walters Plant Hire Ltd **Bred** Ballymacoll Stud Farm Ltd **Trained** Newport, Dyfed

FOCUS
After problems with the hurdles being omitted due to low sun at the previous meeting, the last obstacle in the home straight was moved to the bend after the stands. This was a race that the favourite had to win, and the two market leaders had the race between them for most of the way. The winner is value for further and the placed horses are rated to their marks.

NOTEBOOK

Praxiteles(IRE) was a bit keen early but benefited from ideal tactics, tracking his market rival until challenging two out and, despite making his first mistake at the last, he ran out a clear winner. It helped that the long-time leader fell, but the winner was already comfortably on top. He had been unable to defy a penalty over course and distance at the beginning of the month - his third defeat at this track - but considering he was rated at least 12lb superior to his rivals here, he really needed to win this. He had Totoman's measure when that rival departed, which gives a hint as to the level of form, but other than that it was a weak race. (op 1-2)

Apache Dawn has been in reasonable form last month on his return from a winter break, but is still a longstanding maiden and, despite trying to chase down the leaders, he was soon under pressure on the home turn, though to his credit he kept on. (op 10-1)

Carhue Princess(IRE) had been hampered on her hurdling debut and took a long time to get any confidence over the flights this time, before staying on a bit at the end. She is likely to improve but probably at a lower level. (op 40-1)

Carrowbehy Lad(IRE) left Noel Meade's yard after finishing fifth in a bumper at Punchestown on his only previous outing. He may have been bred for jumping but his hurdling debut was anything but encouraging as he was never fluent. (op 15-2 tchd 13-2)

Totoman led to the second-last and as the winner went by he seemed to lose concentration and came down at the last. He could not get enough of an advantage in the lead so effectively set the race up for the higher-rated winner, and though he is 0-11 he is now with an in-form yard and could pick up a weak race. (op 9-2 tchd 5-1)

769 PIMMS H'CAP CHASE (18 fncs) 3m

6:20 (6:20) (Class 4) (0-115,114) 5-Y-0+ **£3,903** (£1,146; £573; £286)

Form				RPR
1-32	**1**		**Midnight Gold**[9] [680] 10-11-12 **114**.....(p) JasonMaguire (Peter Bowen) *cl up and racing keenly and gng wl: lft 3rd at 15th: chal 3 out: led last: galloped on strly* **4/1**[1]	126+
P00-	**2**	*3*	**Naughty By Nature**[12] 7-10-2 **97**..... AodhaganConlon(7) (Rebecca Curtis) *towards rr: hit 5th: prog 10th: j. awkwardly 11th: wnt 2nd at 14th: lft in ld next: rdn and hdd and mstke last: outpcd flat* **11/1**	107+
U6-3	**3**	*14*	**Moulin De La Croix**[15] [586] 6-10-10 **103**.....(t) SamTwiston-Davies(5) (Nigel Twiston-Davies) *hld up: hdwy 10th: chal after 14th: ev ch 3 out: rdn and btn next* **8/1**	100
1210	**4**	*3*	**Lord Gunnerslake (IRE)**[15] [587] 10-10-6 **94**.....(v) RichardJohnson (Tim Vaughan) *bhd: impeded 9th: effrt 11th: plugged on w ch but drvn bef 15th: sn btn* **5/1**[3]	88
-512	**5**	*10*	**Michigan Assassin (IRE)**[7] [694] 8-11-2 **109**..... DonalDevereux(5) (Debra Hamer) *t.k.h: led 8th tl blnd bdly 9th: mstke 12th: stl cl 3rd bef 15th: fdd tamely next* **9/2**[2]	99
0U0-	**6**	*4 ½*	**Quarry Town (IRE)**[235] [1925] 8-11-9 **111**.....(t) TomScudamore (David Pipe) *midfield: lost tch 14th: sn wl bhd* **14/1**	92
12-0	**7**	*30*	**Native City (IRE)**[14] [606] 8-11-11 **113**..... APMcCoy (Jonjo O'Neill) *bhd and nt a fluent: nvr gng wl: rdn 11th: lost tch 14th: sn wl bhd: eased last* **7/1**	87
PP-F	**8**	*38*	**Strong Coffee**[36] [274] 8-11-8 **110**.....(p) LeightonAspell (Oliver Sherwood) *prom: lost pl 6th: struggling in rr after 9th: t.o bef 15th: eased last* **25/1**	30
PP/3	**F**		**Portland Bill (IRE)**[35] [297] 10-10-8 **103**..... MarkQuinlan(7) (Bill Turner) *prom: lft in ld 9th: stl gng wl w slt advantage whn fell 15th* **12/1**	—
3P-3	**P**		**Turbulance (IRE)**[15] [588] 8-11-0 **102**.....(p) ChristianWilliams (Bernard Llewellyn) *sn last and detached: t.o 13th: p.u 3 out* **16/1**	—
3P-P	**U**		**Vial De Kerdec (FR)**[15] [586] 7-10-13 **101**.....(b1) FelixDeGiles (Mark Bradstock) *t.k.h: sn led: hdd 8th: in 2nd whn blnd bdly and uns rdr next* **33/1**	—
161-	**P**		**Backfromthecongo (IRE)**[52] [17] 9-11-2 **104**.....(bt) JohnnyFarrelly (Richard Lee) *prom: rdn 10th: wknd 14th: t.o and p.u next* **7/1**	—

5m 54.1s (-28.90) **Going Correction** -0.975s/f (Hard) **12** Ran SP% **126.3**
Speed ratings: **109,108,103,102,99 97,87,74,—,—,—,—**
toteswingers:1&2 £4.80, 2&3 £22.90, 1&3 £12.80 CSF £50.94 CT £352.02 TOTE £5.90: £2.20, £3.40, £4.20; EX 97.40.

Owner Blue Skyes **Bred** Barton Stallion Partnership **Trained** Little Newcastle, Pembrokes

FOCUS

A competitive handicap run at a good pace and two eventually pulled clear halfway up the straight. The winner ran a personal bet and the fourth sets the level.

NOTEBOOK

Midnight Gold did not travel as well as some, but he was always able to race near the head of affairs and, as stamina became an issue, he asserted in typically gritty fashion. He has been in good form since the spring and thoroughly deserved this success, especially after his brave attempt when just beaten at Southwell last week. Despite having to fend off a lightly weighted challenger, he came into this in the best recent form and that helped him justify the market faith. (tchd 9-2)

Naughty By Nature moved through to challenge in the home straight and pulled clear with the winner, but he could not make the weight advantage pay and was ultimately outclassed at the end. He had rather lost his way over hurdles last year, but managed to win a point 12 days ago. This was a tougher task for his handicap chasing debut but he acquitted himself well and should be up to winning over fences. (op 8-1)

Moulin De La Croix was produced to challenge holding every chance, but she did not see out the step up in trip as well as the first two. (op 7-1)

Lord Gunnerslake(IRE) has been progressing through low-grade handicaps for his in-form trainer but ran flat over hurdles two weeks ago and needed to find more to prove himself at this trip. He seemed to have regained his form and held every chance turning in but did not get home and the late market plunge proved unfounded. (op 9-1)

Michigan Assassin(IRE) was well backed to add to his course win gained earlier this month, but the step up in trip for his first chase outside novice company meant he needed to be at his best. Racing quite keenly in a prominent position, he was still with the leading quartet as they came to four out but made a mistake at the next and faded, and it may not have helped that this was his third run this month. (op 15-2)

Quarry Town(IRE), sporting a tongue-tie for his first race since October, was never in it.

Portland Bill(IRE) had regained the lead and was still going well enough when hitting the fourth-last and coming down. He has looked on the downgrade, but this was promising to be a better effort for his new yard. (op 16-1)

Backfromthecongo(IRE) Official explanation: jockey said gelding had been outpaced throughout (op 16-1)

770 TARMAC NOVICES' CHASE (13 fncs) 2m

6:50 (6:50) (Class 3) 5-Y-0+ **£6,124** (£2,106)

Form				RPR
1-21	**1**		**West With The Wind**[16] [565] 5-11-8 0..... PaulMoloney (Evan Williams) *mde all: rdn 3 out: kpt finding ex whn pressed fr next: a jst holding upper hand flat* **11/8**[1]	148
426-	**2**	*½*	**Lady Hillingdon**[14] [613] 7-10-5 134.....(t) PaddyBrennan (Paul John Gilligan, Ire) *racd keenly: lft 2nd at 2nd: effrt 3 out: rdn to chal and nt fluent next: kpt trying fr last: a jst hld* **5/2**[3]	131
1-01	**U**		**Noble Request (FR)**[23] [464] 9-11-8 138..... RichardJohnson (Philip Hobbs) *2nd whn mstke 2nd: j. sltly rt and uns rdr 4th* **7/4**[2]	—

3m 46.6s (-18.40) **Going Correction** -0.975s/f (Hard) **3** Ran SP% **107.0**
Speed ratings: **107,106,—**
CSF £4.67 TOTE £2.30; EX 5.90.

Owner Mrs Janet Davies **Bred** Newsells Park Stud **Trained** Llancarfan, Vale Of Glamorgan

FOCUS

An intriguing contest despite the low turnout that was depleted further at the fourth as Noble Request fell, leaving a good match to develop. This was a decent race for the time of year.

NOTEBOOK

West With The Wind soon got into his stride setting a comfortable pace, and despite getting low at a couple of fences he had enough in reserve to repel the repeated challenge of his sole rival. He looks a big chasing type who relishes lengthening at fences and is ideally suited by a galloping track, and those attributes helped offset the burden of a penalty. He has been in good form of late, most recently defeating odds-on The Jigsaw Man when they met at this track two weeks ago. That rival went on to success at Worcester yesterday, so the form looks sound for this promising fast-ground novice chaser. (op 6-4 tchd 13-8)

Lady Hillingdon, a capable hurdler last season, did not look as good over fences on her chasing debut last time, but is suited by fast ground and was getting 17lb from her two rivals. She mostly jumped well and had enough pace to remain competitive, but she is smaller and less experienced than the winner, which was a disadvantage on this track. She should be up to winning a novice chase, perhaps at a more speedy track. (op 3-1)

Noble Request(FR) was a late market drifter and that lack of confidence was prescient. He never looked up for competing, jumping slowly at the first, getting low at the second, skewing the third before departing at the next. He has only been tried in small fields over fences so far but looked to have transferred a lot of his old hurdling ability to chases. However, he needs to prove himself again now. (op 11-8)

771 MERCEDES BENZ SOUTH WALES H'CAP HURDLE (12 hdls) 3m

7:20 (7:20) (Class 3) (0-120,115) 4-Y-0+ **£5,529** (£1,623; £811; £405)

Form				RPR
41-1	**1**		**House Of Bourbon (IRE)**[39] [227] 7-11-12 **115**.....(vt) JasonMaguire (Tim Vaughan) *j. slowly: mde most: cajoled along 6th: drvn fr next: flat out over last two but jst hld rival: fine ride* **7/2**[3]	116
25-2	**2**	*shd*	**Bobble Hat Bob (FR)**[32] [351] 5-11-10 **113**.....(v1) APMcCoy (Jonjo O'Neill) *settled in rr but cl up: 5th and drvn and outpcd briefly bef 2 out: sn forced clsr: wavered whn chalng last: r.o u.p: jst hld* **10/3**[2]	114
61-5	**3**	*3 ½*	**Ripalong Lad (IRE)**[17] [553] 9-11-0 **108**.....(p) DonalDevereux(5) (Peter Bowen) *cl up: jnd ldrs 8th: rdn and ev ch 2 out: kpt on gamely: nt qckn fr last* **10/1**	106
F0-0	**4**	*9*	**Armenian Boy (FR)**[42] [170] 7-11-12 **115**.....(tp) TomScudamore (David Pipe) *settled trcking ldrs: gng wl bef 2 out: rdn wl bef last: little rsponse: btn last* **0/1**	107+
0/2-	**5**	*¾*	**Party Palace**[25] [767] 6-11-1 **104**..... RodiGreene (Stuart Howe) *prom and w wnr at times: rdn 3 out: btn next* **33/1**	93
06F-	**6**	*12*	**Orion Express**[55] [5365] 9-11-5 **108**..... AidanColeman (Susan Gardner) *towards rr but cl up: rdn wl bef 2 out: sn wknd* **18/1**	86
2-21	**7**	*1*	**Mac Halen (IRE)**[10] [660] 7-11-3 **109** 7ex..... DPFahy(3) (Evan Williams) *chsd ldrs: drvn wl bef 2 out: sn lost tch* **2/1**[1]	86
22/0	**F**		**Mad Moose (IRE)**[16] [566] 6-10-8 **102**..... SamTwiston-Davies(5) (Nigel Twiston-Davies) *hld up trcking ldrs: nt fluent 4th and 5th: disputing 4th and stl cl up and gng wl whn fell 3 out* **13/2**	—

5m 50.2s (3.20) **Going Correction** -0.60s/f (Firm) **8** Ran SP% **120.4**
Speed ratings (Par 107): **107,106,105,102,102 98,98,—**
toteswingers:1&2 £4.00, 2&3 £9.40, 1&3 £11.30 CSF £16.96 CT £109.04 TOTE £3.60: £1.10, £2.10, £3.00; EX 18.40.

Owner Mrs Gill Owens **Bred** Darley **Trained** Aberthin, Vale of Glamorgan

FOCUS

A competitive handicap run at a steady early pace, which helped the long-time leader cling on in a sustained duel to the line. The winner is rated to his mark but there is a case for rating the form higher.

NOTEBOOK

House Of Bourbon(IRE) is best when able to dominate, and though he could not get a soft lead the pace was not that strong until the back straight. By that stage he was under pressure to maintain his position, but he responded in gutsy fashion and had to draw on all his stamina and resilience to repel a prolonged challenge up the straight. He had only won a seller last time but that was in a decent time, and he goes well at this track. Things might be tougher once he is reassessed though. (tchd 4-1)

Bobble Hat Bob(FR) got in close to several flights but responded when driven up between horses to lay down a strong and sustained challenge and he very nearly succeeded. He seems to need to keep interested, and to that end a visor replaced the cheekpieces and blinkers worn previously. He looked well suited by the step up in trip. (op 4-1 tchd 11-4)

Ripalong Lad(IRE) held every chance but just lacked some strength at the finish. After getting well beaten on his reappearance at Cartmel last month this was an improved effort, and though he has yet to win over hurdles he is gradually coming into form and might be interesting back over fences. (op 12-1 tchd 14-1)

Armenian Boy(FR) lost his way over fences last autumn and was comprehensively beaten on his return from a winter break six weeks ago. Racing off a mark he won off last year, he travelled smoothly to loom up looking the most potent threat turning in, but was soon beaten and eventually eased. This was a better effort but he did not get home. (op 9-2)

Mac Halen(IRE) was well backed to follow up his first win gained ten days ago in a low-grade handicap at Newton Abbot under a penalty, but he was the first beaten on the home turn and may have found this coming too soon. (op 3-1)

772 SINCLAIR VOLKSWAGEN H'CAP CHASE (17 fncs) 2m 5f

7:50 (7:50) (Class 3) (0-125,122) 5-Y-0+ **£5,854** (£1,719; £859; £429)

Form				RPR
3211	**1**		**Putney Bridge**[4] [735] 8-11-11 **121** 14ex.....(tp) TomO'Brien (Keith Goldsworthy) *pressed ldr: led gng wl bef 14th: forged clr after 2 out: rdn flat: jst hld on to fast dwindling advantage* **5/4**[1]	135+
6/14	**2**	*hd*	**North Island (IRE)**[19] [524] 8-11-0 **115**..... DonalDevereux(5) (Peter Bowen) *prom: rdn 9th: nt fluent 10th: outpcd bef 14th: 7 l 3rd but rallying last: drvn and fin v strly: jst failed* **15/2**[3]	129+
-011	**3**	*6*	**Bankstair (FR)**[7] [689] 6-10-6 **102** 7ex.....(t) PaddyBrennan (Nigel Twiston-Davies) *hld up: 4th and effrt 9th: chsd wnr 14th: rdn 2 out: sn outpcd by wnr: lost 2nd after last* **9/4**[2]	110
1U-U	**4**	*32*	**Carrick Oscar (IRE)**[41] [195] 10-11-9 **119**..... JasonMaguire (Tim Vaughan) *j. slowly 1st: rdn 5th: nvr gng wl: lost tch 13th: t.o next: eased* **14/1**	98
4FF/	**P**		**Notre Cyborg (FR)**[566] [2479] 9-11-2 **115**.....(t) RichieMcLernon(3) (Jonjo O'Neill) *t.k.h: prom to 9th: dropped bk last and mstke 11th: p.u next* **33/1**	—
3-12	**P**		**Sir Bathwick (IRE)**[25] [446] 11-11-12 **122**.....(tp) TomScudamore (David Pipe) *led at brisk pce: rdn and hdd bef 14th: dropped out qckly: p.u 2 out* **8/1**	—

1-33 **P** **Whataboutya (IRE)**[19] 526 9-11-5 **115**..............................(p) APMcCoy —
(Jonjo O'Neill) *last mostly: pushed along 8th: nvr gng wl after: t.o and p.u 14th* **8/1**

5m 9.70s (-20.30) **Going Correction** -0.975s/f (Hard) **7** Ran SP% **118.8**
Speed ratings: **107,106,104,92,**— —,—
toteswingers:1&2 £2.90, 2&3 £4.60, 1&3 £1.10 CSF £12.14 TOTE £2.20: £1.10, £4.30; EX 14.40.
Owner Mrs L A Goldsworthy **Bred** I Norman **Trained** Yerbeston, Pembrokes

FOCUS
Several in-form horses fought out the finish and the form looks reliable, with the winner rated to his Stratford mark, backed up by the third to his pre-race rating.

NOTEBOOK
Putney Bridge had a 14lb penalty to anchor him owing to two wins within the last ten days, but he is at the top of his game and by virtue of jumping more cleanly than his rivals he was able to claim the hat-trick. He was taken on for the lead this time, where previously he had been able to dominate, and that might have contributed to the diminished winning margin, but he did not shirk the battle. This was canny planning by connections as his future might now be determined by the Handicapper. (op 7-4, tchd 15-8 in a place)
North Island(IRE) has won a couple of chases and evidently has ability, as seen by his storming late run to nearly catch the winner, but he was again hampered by some clumsy jumping and would probably have won if he had not lost momentum in the back straight. (op 8-1 tchd 7-1)
Bankstair(FR) was another in top form bidding for his third win this month. However, he made an early mistake then was beginning to make a move when losing momentum at the first in the back straight. Though he was still able to deliver a challenge, his jumping was not as fluent as the winner in the closing stages and he faded. (tchd 5-2 in a place)
Carrick Oscar(IRE) had failed to complete his last two hunter chases and was again let down by his jumping and could never get competitive. (tchd 12-1)
Sir Bathwick(IRE) won the battle for the early lead but once headed in the home straight he weakened quickly. He stays further than this so hopefully nothing is amiss. (op 7-1)

773 SINCLAIR AUDI "NATIONAL HUNT" NOVICES' HURDLE (10 hdls) 2m 4f
8:20 (8:20) (Class 4) 4-Y-0+ **£3,332** (£1,034; £557)

Form RPR
4-31 **1** **Pure Faith (IRE)**[14] 596 6-11-5 113.................................... TomO'Brien 126+
(Peter Bowen) *led 2nd tl 3rd: trckd ldr gng wl tl led over 5f out (wl bef 2 out): gng clr whn lft in long ld 2 out: unchal* **1/1**[1]
2- **2** *23* **One Cool Tornado (IRE)**[268] 1498 5-10-12 0...................... APMcCoy 95
(Paul John Gilligan, Ire) *t.k.h in rr: j. slowly 3rd: lost tch after slow jump 4th: clsd bef 3 out and blnd bdly: could nt rcvr: tk remote 2nd at last: given easy time flat* **2/1**[2]
51-4 **3** *8* **Quedillac (FR)**[42] 169 6-11-5 115.................................... JasonMaguire 98
(Tim Vaughan) *led at v slow pce tl 2nd: nt fluent 5th: rdn and struggling bef 3 out: lft hopeless 2nd at next tl mstke last* **9/2**[3]
40-1 **U** **U B Carefull**[16] 563 7-10-12 118.................................... MrPJTolman(7) 109
(Sirrell Griffiths) *taken down early: plld hrd: clsd to ld 3rd: rdn and hdd over 5f out: 6 l 2nd and btn whn pckd bdly and uns rdr 2 out* **5/1**

4m 47.3s (-1.70) **Going Correction** -0.60s/f (Firm) **4** Ran SP% **118.2**
Speed ratings (Par 105): **85,75,72,**—
CSF £3.87 TOTE £2.00; EX 6.00 Place 6: £41.48 Place 5: £30.60 .
Owner P Bowling,S Scott,R Harvey & K Bowen **Bred** P J Carmody **Trained** Little Newcastle, Pembrokes

FOCUS
Despite the small field this looked a closely-matched contest from a ratings perspective between three previous winners, though it did not pan out like that. The winner made a big step up with the beaten horses rated some way off their marks.

NOTEBOOK
Pure Faith(IRE) was never under any pressure and, after getting the better of a battle round the home turn, he was able to come home a long way clear. He did not make an impact over hurdles last autumn, but that has been a blessing as he has strengthened up, goes well on fast ground and looks dominant in these weaker summer contests. (op 13-8)
One Cool Tornado(IRE) had not been seen since finishing second in a bumper at Stratford last September. He took a while to get the hang of hurdling, dropping out at an early stage, but he finally began to get into gear until fluffing the third-last. He was well beaten and still needs to improve over hurdles, but it was a respectable reappearance. (op 11-4)
Quedillac(FR) won over this trip at Wincanton in April but has been chasing since, and that seemed to have had an effect, as he was never going that well and had to be niggled to stay in touch on the final circuit. (op 3-1)
U B Carefull had beaten Praxiteles, who scored earlier on the card, at this track last time but still had to prove himself at this trip. He was sweating beforehand and was too keen in the race, pulling himself to the front and refusing to settle, but would have finished second had he not blundered two out. (op 7-2)
T/Plt: £32.90 to a £1 stake. Pool:£37,275.35 - 824.84 winning tickets. T/Qpdt: £15.60 to a £1 stake. Pool:£3,150.60 - 148.81 winning tickets. IM

774 - 791a (Foreign Racing) - See Raceform Interactive

54 HEREFORD (R-H)
Sunday, June 20

OFFICIAL GOING: Good to firm (good in places; chs 8.1 hdl 7.8)
Wind: nil Weather: very hot and sunny

792 TOTEPLACEPOT CONDITIONAL JOCKEYS' NOVICES' HURDLE (8 hdls) 2m 1f
2:20 (2:20) (Class 4) 4-Y-0+ **£3,252** (£955; £477; £238)

Form RPR
0-11 **1** **Players Please (USA)**[4] 760 6-11-12 112........................... PeterToole 126+
(Michael Blake) *mde all: jnd and rdn between last 2: styd on wl u.p to assert flat* **5/2**[2]
5P-1 **2** *3 1/2* **Freedom Fire (IRE)**[26] 465 4-10-8 114.................... JosephAkehurst(8) 114+
(Gary Moore) *t.k.h: chsd ldrs: mstke 3rd: chsd wnr bef 2 out: rdn to chal between last 2: stl ev ch whn hit last: wknd flat* **5/1**[3]
6-6 **3** *3* **Whenwehadmoney (IRE)**[45] 180 6-10-9 0.......................... DPFahy(3) 106
(Evan Williams) *t.k.h: j.rt 1st: nt fluent 2nd: hld up in midfield: clsd on ldrs bef 3 out: pushed along to chse ldng pair between last 2: kpt on same pce after* **33/1**
12-2 **4** *6* **Monetary Fund (USA)**[23] 500 4-10-13 121.............. RichardKilloran(3) 105
(Nicky Henderson) *t.k.h: mstke 3rd: chsd wnr tl 3 out: drvn and nt qckn bef next: wknd after 2 out* **5/6**[1]
02-1 **5** *1 3/4* **Dirty Deal**[42] 222 6-10-5 0.. RichieMcLernon 93+
(John Flint) *t.k.h: chsd ldrs: wnt 2nd 3 out tl bef next: wknd sn after 2 out: wl hld whn mstke last* **14/1**
0- **6** *1 1/2* **Altos Reales**[61] 5294 6-10-5 0................................... SamJones 89
(Michael Scudamore) *in tch: rdn and unable qck after 3 out: wknd sn after next* **66/1**
45 **7** *20* **Iron Man Of Mersey (FR)**[26] 465 4-10-6 0.................. LeeEdwards(3) 73
(Tony Carroll) *hld up wl off the pce in rr: hdwy into midfield but stl plenty to do whn mstke 5th: lost tch w ldrs bef next* **50/1**
/45- **8** *30* **Bingo Des Mottes (FR)**[381] 586 5-10-12 100.................. HarrySkelton 46
(Patrick Griffin, Ire) *a wl off the pce towards rr: j.rt 1st: lost tch 5th: t.o bef 2 out: blnd last* **33/1**
00/ **9** *6* **Naledi**[11] 3031 6-10-12 0... GerardTumelty 40
(Richard Price) *t.k.h early: hld up wl in rr: j.rt 1st and 2nd: lost tch after 4th: t.o bef 2 out* **100/1**
0 **10** *1 1/2* **Frame And Cover**[23] 500 4-10-2 0.............................. JimmyDerham 29
(Joanna Davis) *chsd ldrs: rdn and wkng whn mstke 5th: t.o 2 out* **150/1**
P **11** *59* **Appeal To Paddy (IRE)**[10] 693 6-10-12 0...................(t) CharlieHuxley —
(Matt Sheppard) *a wl off the pce in rr: j.rt 1st: mstke 2nd: lost tch 5th: wl t.o bef 2 out* **150/1**
000- **12** *nk* **Babe Maccool (IRE)**[306] 1247 8-10-9 71....................... HaddenFrost(3) —
(David Pipe) *a wl off the pce in rr: mstke and rdn 3rd: lost tch after next: wl t.o bef 2 out* **80/1**
P **High Dee Jay (IRE)**[696] 5-10-9 0............................... BrianToomey(3) —
(Dai Burchell) *a wl off the pce towards rr: lost tch 5th: wl t.o whn p.u 2 out* **100/1**
30-0 **U** **The Wee Midget**[35] 355 5-10-12 0.................................. IanPopham —
(Arthur Whiting) *in rr whn stmbld and uns rdr 1st* **100/1**

3m 46.8s (-12.60) **Going Correction** -0.725s/f (Firm)
WFA 4 from 5yo+ 17lb **14** Ran SP% **121.3**
Speed ratings (Par 105): **100,98,96,94,93 92,83,69,66,65 37,37,**—,—
Tote Swingers: 1&2 £2.80, 1&3 £17.80, 2&3 £34.20 CSF £15.61 TOTE £2.90: £1.10, £2.40, £7.00; EX 19.60.
Owner Staverton Owners Group **Bred** 6 C Racing Limited **Trained** Trowbridge, Wilts

FOCUS
This was probably a fair race of its type for the time of year, even though only three appeared to matter, according to the market.

NOTEBOOK
Players Please(USA) was attempting a hat-trick after winning a couple of claimers and seemed to be up against it under his double penalty, but he again responded well to another positive ride. He faced a stern challenge from the runner-up from two out but, though untidy at the last, his nearest danger was even worse and he was well on top on the run-in. This was a decent effort on adjusted official ratings and he is likely to be kept on the go. (tchd 11-4)
Freedom Fire(IRE), who defeated a 128-rated odds-on shot at Huntingdon last month, was always up there and had every chance between the last two, but he just seemed to be getting the worst of it when making a mistake at the last. There will be other days for him. (tchd 9-2 and 11-2)
Whenwehadmoney(IRE) ◆, beaten a long way in his first two starts over hurdles, was nibbled at in the market and put up a much-improved effort. Having moved into contention before three out, he could plug on only at one pace from the next but he does seem to be getting his act together. (op 50-1 tchd 28-1)
Monetary Fund(USA), the highest-rated of those with a mark, was disappointing as he became outpaced after three out before staying on again. He looks to need a stiffer test. (op 10-11 tchd Evens)
Dirty Deal, making her hurdles debut after winning a 2m2f Plumpton bumper last month, ran as though she is going to need a stiffer test than this over hurdles. (tchd 12-1)
Altos Reales, rated just 51 on the Flat, ran better than when last of eight on her hurdles debut. (op 80-1)

793 TOTESUPER7 NOVICES' H'CAP HURDLE (8 hdls) 2m 1f
2:50 (2:50) (Class 5) (0-95,95) 4-Y-0+ **£2,602** (£764; £382; £190)

Form RPR
040- **1** **Mauritino (GER)**[61] 5295 6-11-4 **90**........................ RichieMcLernon(3) 99+
(Jonjo O'Neill) *hld up and bhd: hdwy 5th: wnt 2nd after 2 out: led last: sn clr: v easily* **7/2**[2]
/6-4 **2** *4* **Sparkling Brook (IRE)**[25] 480 7-10-8 **82**.......... SamTwiston-Davies(5) 83
(Nigel Twiston-Davies) *led after 1st: rdn and hdd and hit last: no ch w wnr after: nt pushed whn btn* **7/1**[3]
00/3 **3** *2* **Mulaazem**[26] 465 7-10-10 **86**.. DavidBass(7) 84
(Derek Frankland) *prom: hrd drvn in 3rd between last two: plugged on flat: n.d to ldrs* **14/1**
3-5P **4** *2 1/4* **Timoca (IRE)**[17] 600 5-11-6 **92**.. DPFahy(3) 88
(Evan Williams) *chsd ldrs: effrt 3 out: 4th and rdn between last two: one pce* **12/1**
040 **5** *10* **The Grey One (IRE)**[17] 590 7-11-3 **93**......................(p) ChrisDavies(7) 79
(Milton Bradley) *plld hrd: chsd ldrs: sme ungainly jumps: drvn and wknd between last two* **33/1**
2311 **6** *3* **Monkhair (IRE)**[10] 697 5-11-0 **88**.................................... LeeEdwards(5) 71
(Tony Carroll) *t.k.h: trckd ldrs: rdn 3 out: sn little rspnse: btn next* **9/4**[1]
6414 **7** *3 3/4* **Risk Challenge (USA)**[18] 585 8-10-13 **82**.......................(t) CharliePoste 61
(Milton Harris) *midfield: lost tch 3 out: wl bhd next* **10/1**
-P4P **8** *3 1/4* **Tar (IRE)**[14] 652 6-11-9 **92**..(tp) AidanColeman 68
(Matt Sheppard) *led tl after 1st: chsd ldr tl lost pl tamely 3 out: fin lame* **25/1**
P-06 **9** *22* **Aughcarra (IRE)**[9] 711 5-10-12 **84**................................ SeanQuinlan(3) 38
(Harry Chisman) *t.k.h: in tch tl 5th: t.o whn hit 2 out and last* **100/1**
0-6 **10** *dist* **Poacher's Dream (IRE)**[41] 249 8-11-2 **85**........................ FelixDeGiles —
(Jonathen de Giles) *towards rr: lost tch 5th: sn bdly t.o* **40/1**
5-35 **11** *54* **Ask Archer**[19] 563 5-11-12 **95**... PaulMoloney —
(Evan Williams) *hld up detached last: lost tch 4th: bdly t.o after 3 out: coasted in* **12/1**
F0P/ **12** *1/2* **Barodine**[8] 2971 7-10-12 **86**.. IanPopham(5) —
(Ron Hodges) *in rr whn j. slowly 3rd and reminders: nt keen: lost tch u.p next: sn hopelessly t.o* **14/1**
50-F **P** **Scotsbrook Cloud**[14] 646 5-11-0 **88**.............................. DonalDevereux(5) —
(C Roberts) *chsd ldrs tl lost pl 4th: wl bhd whn p.u next* **16/1**

3m 52.1s (-7.30) **Going Correction** -0.725s/f (Firm) **13** Ran SP% **119.4**
Speed ratings (Par 103): **88,86,85,84,79 78,76,74,64,45 20,19,**—
Tote Swingers: 1&2 £18.30, 1&3 £15.80, 2&3 £22.70 CSF £27.89 CT £311.31 TOTE £6.40: £2.50, £1.30, £2.60; EX 32.80.
Owner P A Byrne **Bred** Werner Klein **Trained** Cheltenham, Gloucs

FOCUS
A modest novice handicap and the winning time was 5.3 seconds slower than the opening novice hurdle.

NOTEBOOK
Mauritino(GER), a four-time winner on the Flat in Germany, had yet to show much in four previous attempts over hurdles and pulled too hard last time. However, the market vibes were encouraging and he settled much better off the pace on this occasion before making smooth progress after jumping three out. He had to work in order to get to the leader jumping the last, but always looked like winning and forced his way to the front on the run-in. There should be more to come from him now that he has got his head in front. Official explanation: trainer said horse settled better by being held up (op 11-2)

Sparkling Brook(IRE), dropping in trip after showing some ability on her handicap debut at Southwell last time, tried to make all but found the winner too strong after the last and was unfortunate to run into one. There is a race like this in her off this sort of mark. (op 5-1)
Mulaazem, beaten a long way into third on his return from 15 months off at Huntingdon last month, performed better here and he kept on well having come off the bridle some way out.
Timoca(IRE), pulled up behind Monkhair at Uttoxeter last time, looked the stable's second string behind Ask Archer, but she emerged the best of the pair. She made a promising move up the inside after three from home, but couldn't find much more when ridden jumping the next. (tchd 14-1)
The Grey One(IRE), making his handicap debut and wearing cheekpieces for the first time over hurdles, pulled hard early which wasn't ideal for a horse with suspect stamina, so he did well to keep going and finish where he did. (op 25-1)
Monkhair(IRE), 5lb higher in her bid for a hat-trick, raced prominently early but the writing was on the wall when she came under pressure running to the second-last. (op 5-2 tchd 3-1)
Tar(IRE) was reported to be lame. Official explanation: jockey said gelding finished lame (tchd 22-1)

794 TOTEQUADPOT H'CAP CHASE (DIV I) (16 fncs) 2m 5f 110y
3:20 (3:20) (Class 5) (0-95,95) 5-Y-0+ **£2,927** (£859; £429; £214)

Form			Horse	RPR
6-4P	1		**Thenameescapesme**[12] 677 10-11-7 **93**........ SeanQuinlan(3) (Kim Bailey) *chsd ldrs tl led after 7th: mde rest: pushed clr bef 3 out: in n.d after: eased after last* **11/1**	110+
6PP-	2	16	**Scalini's (IRE)**[56] 5 10-10-9 **78**........(p) SeamusDurack (Christopher Nenadich) *in tch: j.lft 2nd: rdn to chse wnr bef 3 out: no imp and wl btn fr 3 out: plugged on* **33/1**	78
P2-3	3	3 3/4	**Sean Og (IRE)**[39] 278 8-10-0 **69** oh9........(t) FelixDeGiles (Jonathen de Giles) *hld up in last trio: hdwy 10th: rdn to go modest 3rd 3 out: no imp u.p bef next* **12/1**	63
3324	4	3 1/4	**Post It**[5] 758 9-11-1 **84**........ RichardJohnson (Ron Hodges) *hld up in rr: mstke 4th and 6th: rdn and struggling 12th: 7th and wl btn after next: plugged on to go 4th after last: nvr trbld ldrs: fin lame* **3/1**[1]	75
-066	5	1/2	**Regain Du Charbonneau (FR)**[18] 585 5-11-3 **86**.(tp) TomScudamore (David Pipe) *chsd ldrs: rdn 12th: drvn and wknd bef 3 out* **6/1**	77
F34/	6	24	**Jimmy Bedney (IRE)**[57] 9-9-13 **75** ow2........(p) MrPJTolman(7) (Sirrell Griffiths) *chsd ldr: j. slowly 6th: mstke and reminders 8th: wknd u.p 13th: t.o* **5/1**[3]	42
-P30	7	24	**Satindra (IRE)**[10] 698 6-10-12 **81**........(tp) DenisO'Regan (Carole Ikin) *a bhd: rdn and toiling bdly 11th: mstke next: sn t.o* **28/1**	24
50/6	8	hd	**Diego Velasquez (IRE)**[14] 646 6-11-7 **90**........(t) HarrySkelton (Patrick Griffin, Ire) *a in rr: rdn and lost tch after 10th: t.o bef 3 out* **14/1**	32
-043	P		**Sarobar (IRE)**[14] 649 10-10-10 **79**........(b) LiamTreadwell (John Spearing) *nt jump wl: led: j.lft and mstke 2nd: hdd after 7th: sn lost pl: losing tch whn mstke 11th: t.o and p.u 3 out* **8/1**	—
05-2	P		**Smart John**[36] 341 10-11-12 **95**........ ColinBolger (Simon Lewis) *in tch: mstke 7th: dropped to last and j. slowly 9th: losing tch whn p.u next* **20/1**	—
35-5	P		**My Pal Val (IRE)**[5] 755 10-11-5 **91**........(t) DannyCook(3) (John Panvert) *in tch: mstke 1st: hdwy to chse ldrs 7th: chsd wnr 11th: blnd next: rdn and btn 3 out: 5th and wkng whn eased and p.u bef 2 out* **9/2**[2]	—

5m 8.00s (-12.00) **Going Correction** -0.50s/f (Good) 11 Ran SP% **119.1**
Speed ratings: **101,95,93,92,92 83,75,74,—,— —**
Tote Swingers: 1&2 £30.90, 2&3 £14.00 CSF £305.37 CT £4368.18 TOTE £12.40: £3.20, £15.00, £3.20; EX 512.70.
Owner Mrs Tania D Yeomans **Bred** Horseshoe Agency Ltd **Trained** Andoversford, Gloucs
■ Stewards' Enquiry : Danny Cook one-day ban; careless riding (4th) July

FOCUS
A modest handicap chase in which recent winning form was very thin on the ground, under rules at least.

NOTEBOOK
Thenameescapesme ◆, who was apparently taken out by a loose horse on his return to chasing at Bangor earlier this month, had the ground in his favour this time. Having taken over in front from the free-running Sarobar with over a circuit left, he was left with a decisive advantage when his nearest pursuer made a mistake five out and he made the best of his way home from there. He was able to take things very easily from the final fence and, though he may not have beaten much, he would be interesting if turned out again quickly. Official explanation: trainers said gelding was nearly brought down by loose horse on last outing and was better suited by faster ground (op 15-2)
Scalini's(IRE), pulled up in three of four starts since returning from a layoff, stayed on over the last couple of fences if never a threat to the winner, but this was still a fair effort as he probably prefers softer ground. (op 25-1)
Sean Og(IRE), 9lb wrong and a maiden after 37 attempts under both codes, ran on from the back of the field to take a remote third but his record hardly makes him a betting proposition. (op 8-1)
Post It, whose two career successes have come here, one a bumper and one a chase, never made any impression from off the pace and was reported to have finished lame. Official explanation: vet said mare pulled up lame (op 9-2)
Regain Du Charbonneau(FR), making his chase debut, hasn't looked an easy ride over hurdles and didn't look a natural over fences either. (op 13-2 tchd 8-1)
Jimmy Bedney(IRE), having his first start under rules since March of last year but winner of a point in April, paid the penalty for jumping poorly on the final circuit. (op 8-1 tchd 9-2)
My Pal Val(IRE), having his second start for the yard, was back up to a more suitable trip and looked a threat to the winner when a bad blunder five from home stopped him in his tracks. He was eventually pulled up, but is worth keeping an eye on if none the worse. (op 11-2 tchd 13-2)

795 TOTEQUADPOT H'CAP CHASE (DIV II) (16 fncs) 2m 5f 110y
3:50 (3:50) (Class 5) (0-95,94) 5-Y-0+ **£2,927** (£859; £429; £214)

Form			Horse	RPR
025-	1		**Fealing Real (IRE)**[15] 8-11-1 **90**........(t) AodhaganConlon(7) (Rebecca Curtis) *j. first two stickily but fine after: prom tl led 6th: gng much the best fr 3 out: 4 l clr next: nvr off the bridle* **9/4**[1]	111+
24-4	2	2 1/2	**Pipers Legend**[12] 677 11-11-6 **88**........(b) AidanColeman (Sarah Humphrey) *sn led: hdd 6th: prom: chsd wnr but drvn fr 13th: a wl hld and flattered by proximity* **9/1**	96
56-0	3	9	**Marked Man (IRE)**[36] 330 14-11-12 **94**........ CharliePoste (Richard Lee) *hdwy 7th: wnt 2nd at 9th tl rdn 13th: disp 8 l 3rd and btn 2 out: plodded on gamely* **12/1**	93
405-	4	3/4	**Le Forezien (FR)**[36] 11-10-11 **86**........ MrRHawkins(7) (Carroll Gray) *hld up: trckd ldrs fr 9th: rdn 13th: disp 3rd and btn 2 out: plugged on* **10/1**	84
	5	12	**Rumreelic (IRE)**[17] 615 8-10-8 **81**........ DonalDevereux(5) (Miss Elizabeth Doyle, Ire) *chsd ldrs: rdn 12th: sn struggling: wl btn 3 out* **8/1**	67
0-42	6	15	**Rudinero (IRE)**[21] 529 8-10-6 **77**........(p) PeterToole(3) (Barry Brennan) *nt jump wl and nvr looking keen: rdn and lost tch 12th: sn wl bhd* **4/1**[2]	48
3-05	7	65	**Delgany Gunner**[30] 429 6-10-11 **79**........(t) AndrewThornton (Ben Pollock) *prom tl lost pl 7th: t.o 11th: stl bumbling towards the last after wnr fin* **20/1**	—
00-6	P		**Wasntme (IRE)**[13] 665 7-10-9 **80**........(bt) HaddenFrost(3) (Colin Tizzard) *nt fluent: nvr enjoying himself in rr: t.o and p.u 9th* **20/1**	—
/0-5	P		**Zi Missile (IRE)**[13] 665 6-10-0 **68**........ PaulMoloney (Evan Williams) *mstkes in rr: struggling in last whn blnd 7th: stopped to nil: t.o and p.u after 8th* **9/2**[3]	—

5m 6.90s (-13.10) **Going Correction** -0.50s/f (Good) 9 Ran SP% **116.4**
Speed ratings: **103,102,98,98,94 88,65,—,—**
Tote Swingers: 1&2 £9.60, 1&3 £4.40, 2&3 £39.60 CSF £23.18 CT £194.76 TOTE £2.70: £1.10, £4.00, £6.00; EX 23.40.
Owner Miss Rebecca Curtis **Bred** James Maguire **Trained** Newport, Dyfed

FOCUS
Another modest event in which it paid to race handily, though the winning time was 1.1 seconds faster than the first division.

NOTEBOOK
Fealing Real(IRE) ◆, making his debut over regulation fences after winning a point-to-point a fortnight earlier, helped force the pace from the start and the race was his once he forged clear of his nearest rival after two out. He did appear to doss coming to the last fence with his head held a little high and he pricked his ears, but he was in no danger after jumping it and won with much more in hand than the margin would suggest. He can win again. (op 3-1)
Pipers Legendwas entitled to need his recent Bangor reappearance and stepped up from it. Another to be up there from the start, he did his best but was in vain pursuit of the winner from the second-last. This was a fair effort, but a career record of 1-41 isn't encouraging. (tchd 8-1)
Marked Man(IRE) has a fine record here, but he has been below his best of late. He tried to get into the race starting the final circuit and had his chance, but was in trouble on the run to three out. (tchd 11-1)
Le Forezien(FR), having his first start over regulation fences since October 2008, like the winner came into this after a point success. He ran well until coming under pressure before two out but could find an opportunity in a similarly modest event. (op 7-1)
Rumreelic(IRE), a good fourth of 18 at Tipperary on only her fourth start over regulation fences earlier this month, plugged on after coming off the bridle a long way out and may need further. (op 7-1)
Zi Missile(IRE) was reported to have never been travelling. Official explanation: jockey said mare was never travelling (op 7-2 tchd 3-1)

796 TOTESWINGER FLEXI BETTING MARES' H'CAP HURDLE (10 hdls) 2m 4f
4:20 (4:20) (Class 4) (0-115,111) 4-Y-0**£4,752** (£1,404; £702; £351; £175)

Form			Horse	RPR
-611	1		**Letham Island (IRE)**[17] 598 6-11-5 **109**........(vt) LeeEdwards(5) (Tony Carroll) *in tch in midfield: hdwy to chse ldr bef 2 out: led sn after and rdn clr: in command and idling bef last: rdn out* **10/1**	117+
-344	2	2 1/4	**Thehonourablelady**[21] 530 9-10-8 **93**........(tp) WillKennedy (John Flint) *in tch untl dropped to rr and rdn along after 4th: sme prog u.p 3 out: wnt 5th next: kpt on u.p flat to go 2nd towards fin: nvr threatened wnr* **8/1**[3]	93
2-43	3	3/4	**Kijivu**[14] 645 5-10-10 **95**........(bt) FelixDeGiles (Alastair Lidderdale) *led tl 2nd: chsd ldrs after tl led again 3 out: hdd sn after 2 out and immediately outpcd by wnr: kpt on same pce u.p after: lost 2nd towards fin* **6/1**[2]	95
-211	4	3 1/2	**Ruby Crown**[25] 472 8-11-8 **110**........ SeanQuinlan(3) (Kim Bailey) *t.k.h: hld up in tch in rr: mstke 4th: pushed along and hdwy bef 3 out: wnt 4th next: no real imp on wnr: pressing for 2nd last: wknd fnl 100yds* **12/1**	107
10-1	5	2 1/2	**Miss Saffron**[7] 737 7-10-7 **92** 7ex........ AidanColeman (Susan Gardner) *taken down early and mounted on crse: t.k.h: hld up in tch in rr: stdy prog 6th: trckd ldng pair 3 out: rdn and nt qckn bef next: wknd between last 2* **15/8**[1]	87
P0-P	6	13	**Chocolat (IRE)**[36] 340 5-11-6 **105**........(t) TomScudamore (Martin Keighley) *t.k.h: chsd ldrs: wnt 2nd after 4th tl led 7th: hdd next: wknd qckly bef 2 out* **25/1**	86
4030	7	1/2	**Enchanted Approach (IRE)**[7] 737 7-9-12 **90**........ MissLBrooke(7) (Lady Susan Brooke) *taken down early: in tch tl lost pl qckly 5th: bhd fr 3 out* **28/1**	70
356-	8	20	**Tesserae**[61] 5294 4-10-8 **100**........ CharlieHuxley(3) (Andrew Haynes) *hld up in tch in rr: hdwy 5th: pressed ldrs 7th tl rdn and wknd rapidly bef 2 out: t.o between last 2* **33/1**	56
44-P	9	56	**Garafena**[33] 384 7-9-9 **85** oh4........ GilesHawkins(5) (Richard Lee) *in tch in rr: hdwy into midfield 4th: mstke and pushed along 5th: wknd qckly 7th: wl t.o whn mstke 2 out* **22/1**	—
B-2U	P		**Topflight Wildbird**[9] 706 7-11-6 **105**........ RobertThornton (Alan King) *in tch in midfield: nt fluent 2nd: rdn and struggling after 6th: lost tch bef 3 out: t.o whn p.u 2 out* **8/1**[3]	—
014-	P		**Lady Jinks**[63] 5248 5-11-7 **111**........ JimmyDerham(5) (Joanna Davis) *mstke 1st: led 2nd tl 7th: sn dropped out: t.o whn p.u 2 out* **6/1**[2]	—

4m 40.4s (-15.10) **Going Correction** -0.725s/f (Firm)
WFA 4 from 5yo+ 18lb 11 Ran SP% **116.9**
Speed ratings (Par 105): **101,100,99,98,97 92,92,84,61,— —**
Tote Swingers: 1&2 £13.30, 1&3 £10.10, 2&3 £9.80 CSF £82.34 CT £527.57 TOTE £13.20: £3.80, £1.30, £1.70; EX 112.80.
Owner Joe Singh **Bred** Rathasker Stud **Trained** Cropthorne, Worcs

FOCUS
Quite a competitive mares' handicap hurdle run at a sound pace.

NOTEBOOK
Letham Island(IRE), making her debut for the yard and back up in trip after winning a couple of Uttoxeter sellers, proved herself well up to this better company. Held up early, she made her move jumping three out and responded to pressure to force her way to the front after the next. She gave her supporters a few anxious moments when she landed on all fours at the last and idled on the short run-in, but she was never going to be caught. (op 7-1)
Thehonourablelady, hard to win with in recent years but down to the same mark as for her last success in October, ran a strange race. Up there early, she dropped herself out at halfway and fell to the back of the field under pressure, but then got her second wind and ran on again to grab second, if never near the winner. (op 11-1 tchd 15-2)
Kijivu was in and out of the lead at various stages of the contest, but couldn't live with the winner from between the last two flights. She often makes the frame, but is without a win since successful here in September 2008. (op 7-1 tchd 5-1)
Ruby Crown, back up in trip and bidding for a hat-trick off an 8lb higher mark, looked a possible threat when moving into contention after three out, but then looked one paced under maximum pressure. (op 17-2)
Miss Saffron, carrying a 7lb penalty for her comfortable success at Stratford seven days earlier, moved smoothly into contention after three from home and looked sure to play a part in the finish, but she came off the bridle very quickly and could find only the one pace. (op 3-1)

Chocolat(IRE), twice a winner over hurdles in France, has been disappointing in three outings here. Making her debut for the yard in a first-time tongue tie, she didn't help herself by racing keenly early and, although in front jumping four from home, she didn't last there long and dropped away. (op 22-1)

Lady Jinks, a confirmed trailblazer, was dropping back down in trip. She didn't set off in front straight away and a blunder at the first flight didn't help her cause either. She was in front jumping the next, but it wasn't the start she needed and she stopped quickly once losing the advantage before jumping four out. She was later found to be in season. Official explanation: trainers said mare was in season (op 5-1)

797 TOTEEXACTA FLEXI BETTING BEGINNERS' CHASE (19 fncs) 3m 1f 110y
4:50 (4:50) (Class 3) 5-Y-O+ **£5,703** (£1,684; £842; £421; £210)

Form RPR

22-2 **1** **Acrai Rua (IRE)**[40] 266 7-11-0 0 PaulMoloney 108+
(Evan Williams) *trckd ldrs: shkn up 13th: wnt 2nd at 16th: sn rdn: chal and blnd 2 out: rcvrd u.p to ld after last: all out and unimpressive beating reluctant rival* **11/8**[1]

04-2 **2** *1 1/2* **Viper**[9] 714 8-11-0 0 SamThomas 104
(Dr Richard Newland) *wnt 2nd at 5th: lft in ld 13th tl 14th: led again next: pressed and rdn 2 out: sn hdd flat: put hd in air and nt run on* **9/4**[2]

-232 **3** *20* **Kanad**[10] 687 8-10-9 115 (tp) JimmyDerham[(5)] 84
(Milton Harris) *chsd ldrs: rdn and outpcd 15th: sn fnd nil: 15 l 3rd and struggling 3 out* **4/1**[3]

40-4 **4** *2 3/4* **Outclass**[34] 371 8-10-7 64 DavidEngland 77
(Harry Chisman) *led after 2nd tl mstke 13th: rdn to ld again next: hdd 15th: losing 2nd whn terrible mstke next: 17 l 4th and struggling 3 out* **18/1**

3-44 **5** *84* **Thyne Spirit (IRE)**[20] 556 11-11-0 58 (p) ColinBolger —
(Simon Lewis) *mstkes: last by 4th: rdn 6th: t.o by 9th: stl appr last after wnr fin* **33/1**

3-44 **P** **Little Girl**[18] 579 12-10-7 66 JamieMoore —
(Ray Peacock) *t.k.h: chsd ldr tl lost pl and j. slowly 6th: t.o 9th: p.u next* **33/1**

UP-6 **U** **The Hairy Mutt (IRE)**[7] 738 8-10-7 99 MissLBrooke[(7)] —
(Lady Susan Brooke) *chsd ldrs: 4th whn uns rdr 10th: horse b.d by fallen rdr* **10/1**

5P- **U** **Spiritonthemount (USA)**[13] 21 5-11-0 0 (b) LiamTreadwell —
(Peter Hiatt) *rdr unbalanced and uns at 1st* **50/1**

6m 14.5s (-17.30) **Going Correction** -0.50s/f (Good) **8** Ran SP% **115.1**
Speed ratings: **106,105,99,98,72 —,—,—**
Tote Swingers: 1&2 £1.20, 1&3 £1.20, 2&3 £1.70 CSF £4.98 TOTE £2.30: £1.20, £1.30, £1.40; EX 6.20.
Owner J Hutchinson **Bred** Miss Margaret Wall **Trained** Llancarfan, Vale Of Glamorgan
■ Stewards' Enquiry : Paul Moloney two-day ban; excessive use of whip (4th-5th) July

FOCUS
Only four mattered in this beginners' chase on the final circuit.

NOTEBOOK
Acrai Rua(IRE) had been placed four times over hurdles since unseating on his chase debut in a decent beginners' chase at Ludlow in February and made hard work of winning this. Off the bridle before three from home, he was pressing the leader when a blunder two out seemed to have ended his chance, but fortunately for him the leader was under pressure as well, and a big jump at the last was enough to take him into the lead. He seemed to win with a bit in hand at the line and, though this wasn't the most competitive race for the money, the fact he stayed this extended trip so well will be a big advantage in novice company at this time of year. (op 11-10 tchd 10-11)

Viper, formerly useful on the Flat and over hurdles, had run okay in two previous starts over fences without setting the world alight but looked the one to beat when jumping to the front five from home. The favourite's blunder two out seemed to have presented the race to him, but he looked very tired on the home turn and had little left when headed after the last. (op 7-2)

Kanad, who has faced a couple of stiff tasks since returning to fences recently, was trying beyond 2m4f for the first time. He had his chance on the final circuit, but lost touch with the front pair from four out and his stamina seemed to desert him. (op 7-2)

Outclass was given a positive ride, but she was already struggling when a blunder four out ended any chance she may still have had. She is yet to win a race of any sort and is rated just 64 over fences. (op 28-1 tchd 16-1)

798 TOTETRIFECTA FLEXI BETTING H'CAP HURDLE (8 hdls) 2m 1f
5:20 (5:20) (Class 3) (0-120,120) 4-Y-O+
£4,696 (£1,387; £693; £347; £173; £87)

Form RPR

-11U **1** **Ajman (IRE)**[12] 675 5-10-2 99 (t) DPFahy[(3)] 112+
(Evan Williams) *chsd ldrs and a gng wl: wnt 2nd bef 3 out: led 2 out: sn clr: idled flat: pushed out: v easily* **7/2**[2]

00-6 **2** *6* **Dark Energy**[13] 350 6-10-13 107 (t) TomScudamore 111
(Michael Scudamore) *t.k.h: hld up in tch in rr: hdwy 3 out: rdn to chse clr wnr between last 2: no imp* **12/1**

6014 **3** *3 1/2* **Cubism**[17] 595 4-10-6 103 (t) CharliePoste 101
(Milton Harris) *in tch: chsd ldrs and pushed along after 4th: styd on same pce u.p fr 2 out* **33/1**

11-2 **4** *6* **Exulto (IRE)**[7] 736 5-11-4 112 RichardJohnson 107
(Philip Hobbs) *t.k.h: hld up in tch towards rr: hdwy 5th: rdn and outpcd 2 out: plugged on flat: no ch w wnr* **2/1**[1]

-622 **5** *2 1/4* **Mister Benedictine**[9] 715 7-11-12 120 (t) MarkGrant 112
(Brendan Duke) *in tch: rdn and outpcd 2 out: v one pce and no ch w wnr after* **10/1**

6-2 **6** *2* **Two Left Boots (FR)**[31] 423 6-11-2 110 RobertThornton 100
(Tim Vaughan) *hld up in tch in rr: pushed along after 3 out: no prog and wl btn between last 2: mstke last* **10/1**

403- **7** *4 1/2* **Medicinal (IRE)**[80] 4970 9-11-10 118 (t) DenisO'Regan 105
(Michael Blake) *hld up wl in tch: hdwy to trck ldrs bef 2 out: rdn and fnd nil after 2 out: sn wl btn* **14/1**

0-6P **8** *3/4* **Nothing Is Forever (IRE)**[17] 595 6-9-12 95 (v[1]) SeanQuinlan[(3)] 81
(Liam Corcoran) *racd keenly: chsd ldr tl led 2nd: dived next: clr after 4th: hdd 2 out: sn drvn and wknd* **40/1**

P0-4 **9** *8* **Phoenix Eye**[12] 675 9-9-13 100 BrianToomey[(7)] 77
(Michael Mullineaux) *stdd s: hld up in rr: mstke 4th: rdn and lost tch bef 3 out* **40/1**

4 **10** *6* **Adare Manor (IRE)**[19] 566 6-11-0 111 RichieMcLernon[(3)] 82
(Jonjo O'Neill) *t.k.h: chsd ldrs: pushed along and struggling bef 3 out: wl bhd fr 2 out* **22/1**

1-13 **11** *48* **Barrel Of Fun (IRE)**[32] 400 4-11-9 120 (bt) JamieMoore 40
(Jim Best) *led tl 2nd: chsd ldr after tl bef 3 out: sn wknd u.p: t.o between last 2* **12/1**

04-0 **P** **Civil Servant**[44] 193 5-10-6 105 (t) SamTwiston-Davies[(5)] —
(Nigel Twiston-Davies) *chsd ldrs tl lost pl and rdn along after 4th: bhd and losing tch whn p.u 6th* **6/1**[3]

3m 44.0s (-15.40) **Going Correction** -0.725s/f (Firm)
WFA 4 from 5yo+ 17lb **12** Ran SP% **122.2**
Speed ratings (Par 107): **107,104,102,99,98 97,95,95,91,88 66,—**
Tote Swingers: 1&2 £19.60, 1&3 £48.30, 2&3 £59.40 CSF £44.42 CT £1209.14 TOTE £4.30: £1.70, £3.60, £4.60; EX 53.10 Trifecta £281.00 Part won. Pool: £379.76 - 0.10 winning units..
Owner R P R O'Neil **Bred** Pat McDonnell **Trained** Llancarfan, Vale Of Glamorgan

FOCUS
The classiest race on the card run at a decent pace, but it was a one-horse race from some way out. The winning time compared favourably with the two earlier novice hurdles.

NOTEBOOK
Ajman(IRE), who unseated when still in with a chance of completing the hat-trick at Bangor earlier this month, was 6lb above his last winning mark. He was keen enough in a handy position early, but it didn't stop him from moving smoothly to the front between the last two flights and quickly bounding clear. (tchd 3-1 and 4-1)

Dark Energy ◆, still 4lb above his last winning mark, seemed to be returning to form judging by his last two starts, including on the Flat last time, and ran well again here. He stayed on over the last couple of flights to finish a clear second-best and deserves to go one better before too long. (tchd 14-1)

Cubism stayed on after coming off the bridle after three out, but looks best when able to dominate. (tchd 40-1)

Exulto(IRE), narrowly thwarted in his hat-trick bid off this mark at Stratford seven days earlier, also ran on over the last couple of flights but could never get near the leaders. (tchd 15-8 and 9-4, after early 5-2)

Mister Benedictine, who hasn't won since landing a chase at Huntingdon in May 2008 and without a win over hurdles since October 2007, was up 3lb after a narrow defeat at Market Rasen nine days earlier and that seemed to anchor him. (tchd 9-1)

Two Left Boots(FR) was entitled to come on from last month's creditable debut for the yard at Wetherby when returning from eight months off, but this was a step backwards. (tchd 9-1 and 12-1)

Medicinal(IRE), making his debut for the yard, hasn't scored over hurdles since winning in France over four years ago and his last three wins have come over fences, the most recent in November 2008. He may have just needed this after a short break. (op 10-1)

Civil Servant was reported to have hung badly right. Official explanation: jockey said gelding hung badly right (op 11-1 tchd 12-1)

799 LEFT BANK HEREFORD H'CAP CHASE (12 fncs) 2m
5:50 (5:50) (Class 4) (0-105,103) 5-Y-O+ **£4,182** (£1,235; £617; £308; £154)

Form RPR

112/ **1** **Yellow Flag**[659] 1314 7-11-7 101 RichieMcLernon[(3)] 110+
(Jonjo O'Neill) *hld up: hdwy to midfield after 6th: clsd gng wl 3 out: 2nd next: sn rdn: led last: forged clr* **5/1**[3]

U3-P **2** *1 1/4* **One Of The Boys (IRE)**[39] 276 9-11-3 94 RichardJohnson 102
(Tim Vaughan) *pressed ldrs: led 8th: rdn and almost jnd whn sltly untidy jump last: sn hdd and one-pced* **8/1**

P-46 **3** *16* **Red Jester**[8] 728 9-11-3 99 DonalDevereux[(5)] 91
(Gerald Ham) *prom: led 5th tl 8th: rdn and lost 2nd 2 out: sn fdd* **16/1**

0P/3 **4** *15* **Sahara Prince (IRE)**[4] 762 10-10-4 88 (p) MrLRPayter[(7)] 65
(Matt Sheppard) *t.k.h in rr: outpcd 7th: mod prog 2 out: nvr anywhere nr ldrs but styd on* **33/1**

-231 **5** *5* **Ryeman**[23] 499 8-11-12 103 (vt) TomScudamore 77
(David Pipe) *j.lft: cl up tl drvn and outpcd 9th: poor 4th whn blnd bdly last: b.b.v* **13/8**[1]

05-2 **6** *13* **Weststern (GER)**[25] 477 7-11-6 97 JamieMoore 59
(Gary Moore) *nvr bttr than midfield: rdn and struggling 8th: hmpd last: t.o* **9/2**[2]

P510 **7** *41* **Glimmer Of Light (IRE)**[26] 460 10-11-8 99 (b) DenisO'Regan 17
(Dr Richard Newland) *t.k.h early: led: blnd 1st: hdd 5th: rapidly downed tools: hopelessly t.o* **10/1**

/6P- **8** *21* **Bythehokey (IRE)**[22] 9-10-0 82 (vt[1]) MichaelMurphy[(5)] —
(Brian Baugh) *bhd: mstke 6th and u.p: t.o 9th: fence bhd* **33/1**

U-30 **U** **Nawow**[26] 463 10-11-5 99 (tp) PeterToole[(3)] —
(Matt Hazell) *towards rr whn bmpd and uns rdr 5th* **28/1**

P3-4 **F** **Rapide Plaisir (IRE)**[42] 233 12-11-9 100 (t) CharliePoste 77
(Richard Lee) *prom: 4th whn blnd 9th: dropped out qckly: 27 l 5th whn fell last* **14/1**

3-5P **P** **Shanahan (IRE)**[28] 437 9-11-9 100 (p) JodieMogford —
(Nikki Evans) *j.big in detached last and ref to try: t.o and p.u 8th* **40/1**

00-F **P** **Overspin**[25] 477 7-10-12 89 WillKennedy —
(Paul Webber) *cl up: reminders 5th: lost pl 8th: t.o and p.u 3 out* **22/1**

3m 54.9s (-8.70) **Going Correction** -0.50s/f (Good) **12** Ran SP% **121.8**
Speed ratings: **101,100,92,84,82 75,55,44,—,— —,—**
Tote Swingers: 1&2 £11.10, 1&3 £38.20, 2&3 £33.20 CSF £43.08 CT £610.06 TOTE £7.40: £2.50, £2.50, £3.80; EX 54.50 Place 6: £573.77 Place 5: £248.88.
Owner John P McManus **Bred** Darley **Trained** Cheltenham, Gloucs

FOCUS
A fair handicap chase, run at a good pace.

NOTEBOOK
Yellow Flag hadn't been seen since being thwarted in his bid for a four-timer in August 2008, but proved fit enough to make a winning return. Held up early, he travelled into the race very smoothly jumping five out and kept on to hit the front after jumping the last. He can win again, but may need a little time to get over this. (op 9-2 tchd 13-2)

One Of The Boys(IRE), who bled at Exeter last month, joined in at the head of affairs jumping four from home and was in front on his own jumping the next. He did his best and kept battling away, but couldn't contain the winner after the last. He is 7lb higher than when winning at Fontwell in November, but this effort suggests this mark isn't beyond him. (op 7-1 tchd 13-2)

Red Jester, disappointing at Hexham last time but dropping back to a more reasonable mark, was up there from the start but had little left after three from home. (op 22-1)

Sahara Prince(IRE), third in a selling hurdle at Worcester four days earlier, was making his debut over regulation fences and made up a lot of late ground from the back of the field, but it may have been a case of running on past beaten horses. (op 25-1)

Ryeman, making his debut for the yard after winning a Stratford hunter chase last month, was still in touch when suddenly getting outpaced half a mile from home. He was found to have bled. Official explanation: vet said gelding finished distressed (op 9-4)

Glimmer Of Light(IRE), still 9lb higher than when winning at Uttoxeter last month, likes to go from the front but a bad blunder at the first did him few favours and he quickly lost his place after losing the advantage at the fifth.

Rapide Plaisir(IRE), without a win since September 2007, wasn't totally out of it when losing his back legs after jumping four out and was well behind when falling at the last. (tchd 16-1)

Shanahan(IRE) Official explanation: jockey said gelding was unsuited by good to firm (good in places) ground (tchd 16-1)

T/Jkpt: £17,759 to a £1 stake. Pool:£50,025.42 - 2 winning tickets T/Plt: £409.50 to a £1 stake. Pool:£78,902.45 - 140.65 winning tickets T/Qpdt: £59.70 to a £1 stake. Pool:£8,085.29 - 100.10 winning tickets IM

[726]HEXHAM (L-H)

Sunday, June 20

OFFICIAL GOING: Good to firm (good in places; 7.9)

Wind: light 1/2 against Weather: fine and sunny

800 ALL BETS ARE ON AT TOTESPORT.COM NOVICES' HURDLE (8 hdls) 2m 110y

2:30 (2:30) (Class 4) 4-Y-0+ **£3,425** (£998; £499)

Form RPR

40-3 **1** **Weetfromthechaff**[8] 727 5-10-9 98......(t) MichaelMcAlister(3) 100
(Maurice Barnes) *trckd ldrs: chal 2 out: led appr last: drvn out* **4/1**[3]

26 **2** *2 3/4* **Heart Of Dubai (USA)**[18] 576 5-10-12 0...... BarryKeniry 98
(Micky Hammond) *trckd ldrs: led after 3 out: hdd appr last: no ex* **7/2**[2]

0 **3** *19* **Mwaleshi**[37] 319 5-10-12 0...... JasonMaguire 81
(Donald McCain) *stdd s: t.k.h in last off pce: hdwy 3 out: rdn and tk modest 3rd appr last: one pce* **10/11**[1]

3-40 **4** *1 3/4* **Piccolo Pride**[35] 350 5-10-5 95......(t) MrDarylMillar(7) 79
(Maurice Barnes) *chsd ldrs: wnt 3rd between last 2: one pce* **12/1**

5 *3* **Rebel Swing**[390] 4-10-9 0...... HenryOliver 74
(Sue Smith) *chsd ldrs: lost pl between last 2* **14/1**

0 **6** *74* **Beano Boy**[8] 732 5-10-12 0......(t) PeterBuchanan 10
(Brian Storey) *chsd ldrs: lost pl 4th: bhd 3 out: t.o next* **100/1**

6BP- **P** **Daraybad (FR)**[195] 2752 8-10-12 0...... KeithMercer —
(Andrew Crook) *j. slowly and rt handed: led: drvn 3rd: hdd after 3 out: nt run on: sn bhd: t.o whn p.u bef last* **50/1**

4m 10.3s (-7.10) **Going Correction** -0.60s/f (Firm)
WFA 4 from 5yo+ 17lb 7 Ran SP% **111.9**
Speed ratings (Par 105): **92,90,81,80,79 44,—**
Tote Swingers: 1&2 £2.90, 2&3 £1.10 CSF £17.85 TOTE £3.80: £1.10, £2.60; EX 8.90.
Owner J M Carlyle **Bred** Ed Weetman (haulage And Storage) Ltd **Trained** Farlam, Cumbria

FOCUS
The jockeys reported that the ground was riding on the good side of good to firm. In the past this race has been won by a fair sort for the time of year but this looked a weak renewal.

NOTEBOOK
Weetfromthechaff, a longstanding maiden under both codes, he was held up off the pace but, once produced with his effort after two out, proved too strong for the second favourite. He will be kept on the go through the summer and might get further. (op 9-2 tchd 5-1)
Heart Of Dubai(USA), another without a previous success, travelled well for most of the way and went on approaching the penultimate flight. However, when headed approaching the last, there was nothing left in the tank. (op 5-2 tchd 9-4)
Mwaleshi, the well-backed favourite, was held up right out the back, as the intention was to get him to settle after pulling too hard in his sole previous start in a bumper. He had to make ground as those ahead of him were quickening, but in truth the response when asked was far less than might have been anticipated. Official explanation: vet said gelding finished distressed (op 7-4)
Piccolo Pride had shown only very moderate form in the past and, although he closed up to the leaders at the end of the back straight, he was beaten by the time they turned for home. (op 6-1)
Rebel Swing showed up for a fair way on this hurdling debut, and should be better for this first outing in over a year. (op 12-1)
Beano Boy Official explanation: jockeyv said gelding had breathing problem

801 40 LIVE FOOTBALL MARKETS AT TOTESPORT.COM CONDITIONAL JOCKEYS' (S) HURDLE (10 hdls) 2m 4f 110y

3:00 (3:00) (Class 5) 4-Y-0+ **£2,055** (£599; £299)

Form RPR

/63- **1** **Roznic (FR)**[20] 12-10-8 108...... MrTomDavid(6) 107+
(Tim Vaughan) *wnt prom 6th: led 3 out: styd on wl run-in* **5/4**[1]

P-00 **2** *5* **It's A Roofer (IRE)**[35] 353 10-11-0 0......(p) JamesHalliday 104
(Kate Walton) *hld up: wnt prom 7th: wnt handy 2nd appr last: kpt on same pce* **12/1**

/0U- **3** *1 1/2* **Hapthor**[43] 11-10-2 95......(p) PeterHatton(5) 94
(F Jestin) *chsd ldrs: led bef 6th: hdd 3 out: sn outpcd: rallied between last 2: kpt on to take 3rd nr fin* **40/1**

P-0P **4** *1/2* **Peters Star (IRE)**[9] 708 8-11-12 112......(b) RyanMania 113
(Donald McCain) *chsd ldrs: mstke 4th: rdn 3 out: one pce* **7/2**[2]

6-55 **5** *3* **Root Cause**[17] 601 7-11-0 95......(tp) JohnnyFarrelly 98
(Donald McCain) *wnt prom 7th: wknd between last 2* **5/1**[3]

36-5 **6** *88* **Ellandshe (IRE)**[15] 625 10-10-7 0......(b) StephenMulqueen(7) 19
(William Young) *bhd fr 4th: sn wl t.o: eventually completed* **66/1**

F6-0 **P** **Mr Midaz**[26] 459 11-11-2 70...... AlexanderVoy(3) —
(Donald Whillans) *in rr: t.o 5th: p.u bef 3 out* **28/1**

POP/ **P** **Delfinia**[35] 9-10-7 64...... FearghalDavis —
(David Thompson) *bhd and reminders after 4th: t.o 6th: p.u bef 2 out* **100/1**

/3- **P** **Tofta Tilly**[322] 1119 10-10-4 0...... KyleJames(3) —
(Lee James) *reluctant to go to post: t.k.h: led 2nd: hdd bef 6th: wknd rapidly: t.o whn p.u bef 7th* **66/1**

5-54 **F** **Follow On**[20] 553 8-11-0 90......(t) MrDarylMillar(5) —
(Maurice Barnes) *hld up in rr: fell 4th* **11/2**

P-P0 **P** **Rahood (IRE)**[15] 624 8-10-11 0...... OliverWilliams(3) —
(F Jestin) *led to 2nd: mstke 3rd: wknd after next: t.o 6th: p.u bef 7th* **125/1**

P **Gafferdy Lane**[28] 7-11-0 0...... CampbellGillies —
(Mike Sowersby) *chsd ldrs: lost pl after 4th: t.o 6th: p.u bef next* **66/1**

5m 2.90s (-9.60) **Going Correction** -0.60s/f (Firm) 12 Ran SP% **118.6**
Speed ratings (Par 103): **94,92,91,91,90 56,—,—,—,— —,—**
Tote Swingers: 1&2 £3.80, 1&3 £11.00, 2&3 £18.20 CSF £18.65 TOTE £2.40: £1.50, £2.10, £9.60; EX 22.20.No bid for the winner.
Owner Miss J Murphy **Bred** Francis Faure **Trained** Aberthin, Vale of Glamorgan
■ Stewards' Enquiry : Stephen Mulqueen nine-day ban; excessive use of whip (11th-18th) July

FOCUS
An uncompetitive seller with only two that could be seriously fancied judged on official ratings.

NOTEBOOK
Roznic(FR) is a veteran now but at least he knows how to win, having scored six times previously, and had won two of his three points this spring. Well backed, he gradually moved into contention on the second circuit and, going on after three out, found plenty for pressure when challenged by the runner-up. (tchd 6-5 and 6-4)
It's A Roofer(IRE), who like the winner has been chasing most recently, was held up out the back before joining the leaders after the third-last. He looked a serious threat to the winner approaching the final flight but the winner stayed on too strongly. (op 10-1)
Hapthor, a C&D winner two years ago, has been pointing recently. She went on when the too keen Tofta Tilly capitulated after the sixth but was headed after looking reluctant at the fourth last and looked set to drop away. However, she responded and came back into contention at the uphill flight, staying on to just get third. (op 33-1 tchd 28-1)
Peters Star(IRE) has been struggling for form this spring and is ideally better on a softer surface. He ran his race but was one paced in the straight. (op 11-2 tchd 10-3)
Root Cause, with a tongue-tie and cheekpieces combination replacing the blinkers, travelled well for a long way but tired from two out and might find this trip beyond him. (op 4-1 tchd 11-2)

802 GET LIVE FOOTBALL STATS AT TOTESPORT.COM NOVICES' CHASE (15 fncs) 2m 4f 110y

3:30 (3:30) (Class 4) 5-Y-0+ **£4,553** (£1,337; £668; £333)

Form RPR

1315 **1** **Flying Doctor**[9] 708 7-10-12 0...... JohnnyFarrelly 116+
(Elliott Cooper) *trckd ldrs: led 3 out: wnt clr appr last: eased towards fin* **9/2**[3]

0-21 **2** *11* **Diavoleria**[32] 394 7-10-5 0...... JakeGreenall(7) 101
(Michael Easterby) *trckd ldrs: j.lft and mstke 12th: hit next: kpt on to take 2nd run-in* **5/2**[2]

3-23 **3** *1 3/4* **Always Bold (IRE)**[17] 605 5-10-12 0......(p) JasonMaguire 99
(Donald McCain) *chsd ldr: led 3rd: reminders 10th: mstke 12th: hdd and hit next: kpt on same pce* **8/11**[1]

66/3 **4** *28* **Miss Sunflower**[15] 625 8-9-12 0......(p) MissTJackson(7) 63
(Tina Jackson) *in rr: hdwy and in tch 9th: lost pl 11th: sn bhd: detached last between last 2: styd on run-in to take remote 4th nr fin* **25/1**

5 *1 1/4* **Dougall (IRE)**[21] 7-10-12 0...... TjadeCollier 69
(Joanne Foster) *in tch: wl outpcd 11th: kpt on fr 3 out* **28/1**

0/P4 **6** *1* **Flag Hill**[17] 605 7-10-12 64......(t) PaddyAspell 68
(Peter Atkinson) *in rr: outpcd 9th: kpt on fr 3 out* **100/1**

00-0 **7** *8* **Short Straw (IRE)**[45] 176 7-10-9 0......(p) RyanMania(3) 60
(Barry Murtagh) *nt fluent: led to 3rd: outpcd 12th: wknd next* **100/1**

4-06 **8** *1* **Naughty Diesel**[20] 552 7-10-9 0......(t) MichaelMcAlister(3) 59
(Robert Johnson) *hld up: wnt prom and hit 9th: outpcd and lost pl whn hit 12th* **66/1**

P **Gunner Snow**[21] 9-10-7 0......(p) JamesHalliday(5) —
(Joanne Foster) *lost pl 7th: sn bhd: t.o 10th: p.u bef 3 out* **50/1**

5m 6.70s (-6.80) **Going Correction** -0.60s/f (Firm) 9 Ran SP% **117.4**
Speed ratings: **88,83,83,72,72 71,68,68,—**
Tote Swingers: 1&2 £1.90, 1&3 £1.20, 2&3 £1.10 CSF £16.17 TOTE £4.30: £1.40, £1.30, £1.10.
Owner Tom McNicholas **Bred** London Thoroughbred Services Ltd & J Gaines **Trained** Brigham, Cumbria

FOCUS
The market suggested this was a three-horse race and that's how it turned out, but the result was not quite as the betting indicated.

NOTEBOOK
Flying Doctor ◆ has had a busy and successful time of it of late, winning four of his seven starts since the beginning of May and being placed in two others. Making his chasing debut, he jumped and travelled better than his market rivals and, when asked to go for home after three out, soon had the race in safe keeping. This was a good effort considering connections though he might prefer a longer trip and a stiffer track. (op 11-2 tchd 7-2)
Diavoleria, a three-time hurdles winner earlier in the year, had won over further on her second chase start last time but she made a couple of errors this time and could not go with the winner when he quickened. (op 3-1 tchd 7-2)
Always Bold(IRE) had run reasonably in two previous chasing starts and had cheekpieces fitted for the first time. He was soon in front but was briefly headed by the winner early on the second circuit and his rider was soon at work. Although he responded to get back in front, he had nothing left when the winner committed on the climb to the straight. (tchd 4-6)

803 BET ON WORLD CUP AT TOTESPORT.COM H'CAP HURDLE (8 hdls) 2m 110y

4:00 (4:00) (Class 3) (0-135,113) 4-Y-0+ **£5,854** (£1,719; £859; £429)

Form RPR

63-6 **1** **Crosby Jemma**[20] 159 6-11-3 **104**...... BrianHughes 106+
(Mike Sowersby) *trckd ldrs: led between last 2: rdn rt out* **16/1**

53-4 **2** *1 1/2* **Celticello (IRE)**[50] 96 8-11-2 **110**...... OliverDayman(7) 111+
(Michael Quinlan) *hld up: hdwy 3 out: wnt 2nd appr last: styd on same pce* **4/1**[3]

2- **3** *9* **Daytime Dreamer (IRE)**[206] 2017 6-11-8 **109**...... GrahamLee 103
(Martin Todhunter) *trckd ldr: upsides 3 out: led appr next: hdd between last 2: wknd appr last* **14/1**

3-12 **4** *2 3/4* **Bucephalus (IRE)**[9] 712 6-11-9 **113**......(t) MichaelMcAlister(3) 104
(Maurice Barnes) *chsd ldrs: drvn 3 out: 6th whn hit next: wknd appr last* **5/2**[2]

4-0F **5** *7* **Word Of Warning**[17] 606 6-11-7 **113**...... JamesHalliday(5) 97
(Martin Todhunter) *hld up: wnt prom 3 out: wknd appr last* **11/2**

0 **6** *9* **King Benny (IRE)**[8] 727 6-10-8 **95**...... JohnnyFarrelly 71
(Elliott Cooper) *led: j.lft 2nd: jnd 3 out: hdd appr next: lost pl between last 2* **22/1**

-031 **7** *11* **Danny Zuko (IRE)**[12] 675 7-11-10 **111**......(b) JasonMaguire 77
(Donald McCain) *chsd ldrs: drvn and wl outpcd after 3 out: bhd fr next* **9/4**[1]

4m 7.20s (-10.20) **Going Correction** -0.60s/f (Firm) 7 Ran SP% **111.6**
Speed ratings (Par 107): **100,99,95,93,90 86,81**
Tote Swingers: 1&2 £6.50, 1&3 £9.70, 2&3 £5.90 CSF £75.02 CT £915.06 TOTE £9.60: £2.60, £2.30; EX 56.60.
Owner R D Seldon **Bred** Newsells Park Stud Limited **Trained** Goodmanham, E Yorks

FOCUS
A modest but fairly competitive-looking handicap and a surprise result.

NOTEBOOK
Crosby Jemma is suited by a sharp track and a sound surface and was always going well, perhaps too well early, before moving up to take the lead on the climb to the straight. When asked, she soon opened up a gap and, although having to be kept up to her work, was always holding on after the last. (op 11-1)
Celticello(IRE) was settled out the back before making steady headway from the third-last. He went after the winner in the straight and, although closing the gap, was not doing so quickly enough. All his wins have been on softer ground. (op 7-2)
Daytime Dreamer(IRE) was having his first start for the yard and first run since November. He acquitted himself well, although unable to stay with the first two from the home turn. He should be better for the outing.
Bucephalus(IRE) came into this in form but was never travelling that fluently, and was struggling after a mistake three out. He got to the heels of the leaders on the home turn but could only keep on at the one pace thereafter. (op 7-2)
Word Of Warning was held up early but moved up looking dangerous after three out. However, his effort petered out again before the final flight. (op 9-2)

Danny Zuko(IRE), 6lb higher for his recent success, was sent off favourite. He was held up out the back but was under pressure and making no impression before the penultimate flight. This was disappointing. Official explanation: trainer said gelding was unsuited by track (op 11-4 tchd 2-1)

804 BET ON LIVE GOLF AT TOTESPORT.COM H'CAP CHASE (19 fncs) 3m 1f

4:30 (4:30) (Class 4) (0-110,112) 5-Y-0+ **£5,204** (£1,528; £764; £381)

Form RPR

1P-6 **1** **Simply Smashing (IRE)**[12] 680 10-10-12 **103**..............(t) KyleJames(7) 116
(Philip Kirby) *in rr: wl bhd 11th: hdwy 4 out: wnt 2nd appr last: styd on wl to ld last 100yds* **14/1**

35-1 **2** *5* **Harry Flashman**[15] 626 9-11-9 **107**................................ PeterBuchanan 116
(Donald Whillans) *chsd ldrs: led 12th: hdd 4 out: led 2 out: hdd and no ex last 100yds* **4/1**[1]

5-26 **3** *11* **Von Galen (IRE)**[17] 597 9-10-4 **88**.................................. JohnnyFarrelly 87
(Michael Scudamore) *jnd ldrs 9th: led 4 out: hdd 2 out: wknd appr last* **9/1**

-443 **4** *13* **Sycho Fred (IRE)**[9] 716 9-9-11 **84** oh6..................(tp) CampbellGillies(3) 73
(Mike Sowersby) *chsd ldrs: wknd 2 out* **11/1**

P-44 **5** *11* **Executive's Hall (IRE)**[24] 491 6-10-0 **84** oh14................. BrianHughes 63
(Andrew Crook) *in rr: blnd and rdr briefly lost iron 7th: hdwy 13th: wknd 15th* **80/1**

P3-0 **6** *½* **Esme Rides A Gaine**[20] 549 8-10-2 **86**............................ KeithMercer 63
(Christopher Wilson) *lost pl 4th: bhd fr 10th* **7/1**

1-06 **7** *9* **Toulouse Express (IRE)**[6] 746 11-11-0 **103**..........(v) JamesHalliday(5) 71
(Robert Johnson) *in rr: sme hdwy 13th: sn wknd* **50/1**

3-55 **8** *24* **Teenando (IRE)**[12] 680 10-10-2 **86**.................................... TjadeCollier 33
(Sue Smith) *chsd ldrs: lost pl 10th: bhd fr 13th* **25/1**

-323 **P** **Nile Moon (IRE)**[6] 746 9-11-1 **99**....................................(b) PaddyAspell —
(Ann Hamilton) *w ldrs: led 7th: mstke and hdd 12th: wknd 4 out: bhd whn p.u bef 2 out* **9/2**[2]

3-P1 **P** **Tully Hill**[8] 730 9-10-0 **84** oh8.. GrahamLee —
(Kevin Hunter) *led 3rd: hdd 8th: w ldrs: wknd 3 out: 5th whn p.u bef last* **16/1**

-P44 **P** **The Green Hat (IRE)**[8] 730 10-10-0 **91** oh4 ow7..(p) MrJohnDawson(7) —
(Theresa Gibson) *chsd ldrs: lost pl 15th: sn bhd: t.o whn p.u bef last* **28/1**

10PP **U** **Lindseyfield Lodge (IRE)**[6] 749 9-10-5 **92**......(b[1]) MichaelMcAlister(3) —
(Robert Johnson) *swvd lft and uns rdr s* **40/1**

-4F2 **P** **Our Jim**[10] 695 8-12-0 **112**.. JasonMaguire —
(Donald McCain) *led to 3rd: lost pl 6th: bhd fr 10th: t.o whn p.u after 13th* **6/1**[3]

P3-3 **U** **Chernik (IRE)**[17] 608 9-11-11 **109**................................. WilsonRenwick —
(Micky Hammond) *in rr: hdwy 14th: 5th and styng on whn blnd and uns rdr 3 out* **9/1**

6m 13.5s (-18.70) **Going Correction** -0.60s/f (Firm) **14** Ran SP% **118.8**
Speed ratings: **105,103,99,95,92 92,89,81,—,— —,—,—,—**
Tote Swingers: 1&2 £16.70, 1&3 £23.50, 2&3 £12.10 CSF £68.04 CT £547.74 TOTE £17.10: £5.70, £1.40, £3.90; EX 79.90.

Owner P McMartin, M Mahon & C Fletcher **Bred** Thomas Heffernan **Trained** Castleton, N Yorks

FOCUS

A moderate staying chase but quite a competitive affair on paper and with plenty of front-runners a good gallop looked certain. It became a race of changing fortunes with the lead changing on several occasions and the winner coming from almost last at halfway.

NOTEBOOK

Simply Smashing(IRE) was a market drifter and looked well beaten at halfway. However, he gradually picked off rivals on the second circuit and proved too strong for the runner-up after the last. A stiffer test than this suits him ideally. (op 10-1)

Harry Flashman loves this track and ran his usual good race around here. He looked the winner on the climb to the straight, and his rider looked over the wrong shoulder for dangers turning in. However, it made no difference as he had no answer when challenged. (op 10-3)

Von Galen(IRE) has yet to win under rules but is suited by a test of stamina and ran well. He could win an ordinary staying novices' chase this summer. (op 8-1)

Sycho Fred(IRE) was held up off the pace before close up at the end of the back straight but could not pick up again on the climb to the straight. (op 10-1 tchd 12-1)

Executive's Hall(IRE) ran a fair race, especially as he was running from a stone out of the weights.

Esme Rides A Gaine was bidding to follow up her surprise success in 2009. However, she was beaten with a circuit to go. Official explanation: jockey said mare was never travelling (op 13-2 tchd 6-1)

Nile Moon(IRE) Official explanation: jockey said gelding lost its action (op 5-1 tchd 11-2)

Tully Hill helped make the running but was under pressure a good way from home. He was still not that far behind when being pulled up approaching the last. (op 5-1 tchd 11-2)

Our Jim ran a lacklustre race, was pulled up a long way from home and completed a disappointing day for the stable. (op 5-1 tchd 11-2)

Chernik(IRE) gradually crept into the race and appeared to still have a chance when jumping into the back of Nile Moon and unseating his rider. (op 5-1 tchd 11-2)

805 BET ON WIMBLEDON AT TOTESPORT.COM NOVICES' HURDLE (10 hdls) 2m 4f 110y

5:00 (5:00) (Class 4) 4-Y-0+ **£3,425** (£998; £499)

Form RPR

1 **1** **Majestic Mayhem (IRE)**[15] 624 7-11-5 0.......................... BarryKeniry 110+
(George Moore) *trckd ldrs: wnt cl 2nd 7th: led appr 2 out: rdn clr appr last: drvn out* **6/4**[1]

2-1U **2** *14* **Bow School (IRE)**[15] 628 9-10-12 107........................... PeterBuchanan 92+
(Mrs A C Hamilton) *shkn up 4th: prom whn nt fluent 6th: wnt 3rd 2 out: wnt 2nd between last 2: no ch w wnr* **11/1**

4-44 **3** *3½* **Fly Tipper**[31] 424 10-10-12 64.. GrahamLee 87
(Wilf Storey) *t.k.h: hit 5th: prom next: outpcd appr 2 out: styd on run-in* **50/1**

2 **4** *13* **Yeomanry**[17] 596 5-10-12 103... JasonMaguire 75
(Ian Williams) *chsd ldrs: rdn and wknd after 2 out* **4/1**[3]

0-05 **5** *7* **Searree**[20] 547 5-10-5 0... PaddyAspell 62
(James Turner) *hld up: hdwy 7th: wknd after next: lame* **50/1**

2-1 **6** *¾* **Mr Moonshine (IRE)**[31] 426 6-11-5 0............................. TjadeCollier 75
(Sue Smith) *t.k.h: led after 2nd: hdd after next: led after 5th: hdd 2 out: wknd appr last* **7/4**[2]

PP00 **P** **Danehill Silver**[17] 604 6-10-12 79..................................(p) BrianHughes —
(Brian Storey) *led tl after 2nd: led after next: hdd after 5th: wknd after next: wl bhd 3 out: t.o whn p.u bef 2 out* **100/1**

0-05 **P** **Magnushomesdotcom (IRE)**[15] 624 6-10-9 96(t) MichaelMcAlister(3) —
(Maurice Barnes) *chsd ldrs: drvn 4th: reminders and lost pl 6th: sn bhd: t.o whn p.u bef 2 out* **40/1**

4m 57.7s (-14.80) **Going Correction** -0.60s/f (Firm) **8** Ran SP% **112.0**
Speed ratings (Par 105): **104,98,97,92,89 89,—,—**
Tote Swingers: 1&2 £3.50, 1&3 £8.40, 2&3 £5.30 CSF £16.82 TOTE £2.50: £1.20, £2.50, £2.50; EX 20.90 Place 6: £138.98 Place 5: £37.48.

Owner J B Wallwin **Bred** D Hickey **Trained** Middleham Moor, N Yorks

FOCUS

A fair novice hurdle of its type, and a race in which six of the last nine winners had finished either first or second on their previous outing. The trend continued with an easy success for the well-backed favourite.

NOTEBOOK

Majestic Mayhem(IRE), a three-time point winner and successful in a bumper before joining his current yard, he had won easily over C&D on his hurdling debut and repeated the feat, going better as the race went on. He was ponderous at some of the early flights but warmed to his task and, when asked to go for home up the hill, soon had matters in control. He looks a fair sort for the time of year and chasing will obviously be his game eventually. (op 2-1 tchd 11-8)

Bow School(IRE) is better known as a chaser these days and was returning to hurdles after unseating last time. He was making ground when an error set him back, but he ran on again and was the only danger to the winner from the home turn. (op 13-2 tchd 12-1)

Fly Tipper, a longstanding maiden, had masses to find judged on official ratings and so ran pretty well, although beaten a long way in the end. (tchd 40-1)

Yeomanry, another Irish import, showed up for a fair way but gave the impression he did not stay on this step up in distance. (op 7-2)

Mr Moonshine(IRE), another Irish point winner, built on his debut for the yard when winning from the front at Wetherby last month. He helped make the running here but could not respond when the winner went past before the second-last flight and dropped right away. Official explanation: trainer was unable to offer any explanation for poor run (op 15-8 tchd 2-1)

T/Plt: £128.60 to a £1 stake. Pool:£60,899.14 - 345.52 winning tickets T/Qpdt: £22.80 to a £1 stake. Pool:£4,561.75 - 147.50 winning tickets WG

806 - 819a (Foreign Racing) - See Raceform Interactive

[754]NEWTON ABBOT (L-H)

Tuesday, June 22

OFFICIAL GOING: Good to firm (good in places; watered; 8.0)

All bends moved out since last fixture but impact on distances not quantified.
Third-last fence omitted on all circuits of the chase course.
Wind: mild breeze Weather: fine and sunny

820 BETTER LATE THAN NEVER MAIDEN HURDLE (10 hdls) 2m 6f

6:30 (6:30) (Class 5) 4-Y-0+ **£2,055** (£599; £299)

Form RPR

P-54 **1** **Atlantic Coast (IRE)**[6] 763 6-10-9 110..................(b) DonalDevereux(5) 116+
(Peter Bowen) *cl up: trckd ldrs 7th: rdn in cl 3rd after 3 out: led appr 2 out: kpt on but hung rt: rdn out* **5/6**[1]

30/3 **2** *2¾* **Prince Tom**[42] 266 6-11-0 0.................................. RobertThornton 114+
(Paul Nicholls) *trckd ldrs: led after 3 out: rdn and hdd but ev ch whn blnd 2 out: sn hld but kpt on for clr 2nd* **7/4**[2]

50/ **3** *18* **Flying Phento**[16] 8-10-7 0.. TomO'Brien 87
(Grant Cann) *mid-div: hdwy after 6th into 4th: rdn after 3 out: sn wknd: wnt modest 3rd last* **12/1**

0-60 **4** *2½* **Powerfullbeat**[36] 370 6-10-7 0.. MrRHawkins(7) 92
(Kathleen Sanderson) *trckd ldrs: led 5th: nt fluent next: rdn and hdd after 3 out: sn wknd: lost modest 3rd last* **20/1**

653 **5** *dist* **Sobre Tresor (FR)**[15] 662 4-10-10 98................................ DavidDennis —
(Nigel Hawke) *led tl 5th: chsd ldrs: rdn after next: wknd bef 3 out: t.o* **10/1**[3]

6 *19* **Magical Flight**[41] 8-10-2 0.. IanPopham(5) —
(Carroll Gray) *mid-div: rdn after 6th: wknd after next: t.o* **50/1**

6-0 **7** *2½* **Colour Trooper (IRE)**[7] 754 5-11-0 0.......................(t) TomScudamore —
(David Pipe) *in tch tl mstke 6th: sn wknd: t.o fr 3 out* **20/1**

P **P** **Platinum Bounty**[12] 690 4-9-10 0.................................. MarkQuinlan(7) —
(Neil Mulholland) *a in rr: t.o fr 7th: p.u bef 2 out* **66/1**

0-6 **P** **Hidden Pleasure**[44] 237 5-10-7 0..................................... LiamTreadwell —
(Nerys Dutfield) *a in rr: t.o after 6th: p.u bef 3 out* **50/1**

5-P **P** **Raise Your Hopes (IRE)**[47] 168 7-10-11 0.................... DannyCook(3) —
(Linda Blackford) *a in rr: t.o whn p.u bef 6th* **100/1**

5m 11.8s (-8.40) **Going Correction** -0.325s/f (Good)
WFA 4 from 5yo+ 18lb **10** Ran SP% **123.6**
Speed ratings (Par 103): **102,101,94,93,— —,—,—,—,—**
toteswingers:1&2:£1.30, 1&3:£3.20, 2&3:£5.20 CSF £2.64 TOTE £1.80: £1.10, £1.30, £2.10; EX 3.20.

Owner Mrs Karen Bowen **Bred** Gigginstown House **Trained** Little Newcastle, Pembrokes

■ Stewards' Enquiry : Donal Devereux five-day ban; used whip with excessive frequency (Jul 7th-15th)

FOCUS

The rails on the bends have been moved out adding a couple of metres to each circuit. A race that developed into a match from the home bend and the form looks solid enough, with the first two close to their marks, and the next two in line with their bumper form.

NOTEBOOK

Atlantic Coast(IRE) was placed over 3m at Worcester when last seen and this drop back in trip saw him break his duck over hurdles. He has not looked the most straightforward in the past, but he should be able to make his presence felt in similar company under a penalty. (op 10-11 tchd Evens)

Prince Tom ran well over C&D last time after a long absence and, if he hadn't made a mistake at the second last, he may well have been able to put up a stronger challenge to the winner. He has shown more than enough to suggest he will be winning over the summer. (tchd 13-8 and 9-4)

Flying Phento has been placed in her last three points and plugged on late to claim third. She will need to step up on this if she is to win a race of this nature. (op 16-1)

Powerfullbeat had shown good form at this track in bumpers and this was the first piece of form he has shown over hurdles. Low-grade handicaps are now an option for this chasing sort. (op 28-1)

Sobre Tresor(FR) ran poorly like most from his yard, and the fact the stable are without a winner since mid-March does not bode well for him in the future. (op 14-1)

Magical Flight Official explanation: vet said maye finished sore

Platinum Bounty Official explanation: jockey said filly was never travelling

821 CLARKS VILLAGE (S) HURDLE (8 hdls) 2m 3f

7:00 (7:00) (Class 5) 4-Y-0+ **£2,055** (£599; £299)

Form RPR

-320 **1** **Intac (IRE)**[16] 651 8-11-6 107.. PaddyBrennan 110+
(Colin Tizzard) *chsd ldrs: jnd ldr travelling wl 3 out: led next: enough in hand whn mstke last: pushed out* **7/1**[3]

0-52 **2** *nk* **Talenti (IRE)**[27] 478 7-11-6 115.............................(t) ChristianWilliams 107
(Lawney Hill) *chsd ldr: led appr 6th: rdn and hdd after 3 out: rallied whn wnr mde a mstke last: hld towards fin* **11/4**[2]

P-03 **3** *17* **Fongoli**[15] 661 4-10-12 97...(v) AidanColeman 83
(Brendan Powell) *chsd ldrs: wnt 2nd 4th tl 6th: rdn 3 out: wknd bef next* **8/1**

32-0 **4** 4½ **Heir To Be**[20] 581 11-11-12 113.......................(b) DenisO'Regan 93
(Michael Blake) *mid-div early: in rr and struggling 4th: jumping lft and wl bhd 6th: plugged on fr after 3 out: wnt 4th flat: nvr a danger* **8/1**

5/54 **5** 1 **Querido (USA)**[15] 661 8-10-9 83.......................(t) JimmyDerham(5) 81
(Simon Burrough) *hld up wl off pce: stdy prog after 5th: rdn to dispute 3rd after 3 out: wknd bef next* **20/1**

-225 **6** 16 **Bolton Hall (IRE)**[23] 530 8-11-9 108.......................(tp) APMcCoy 75
(Keith Goldsworthy) *led: set gd pce: rdn and hdd appr 6th: wknd after 3 out: t.o* **7/4**[1]

2-00 **7** 15 **Alrafid (IRE)**[23] 530 11-10-13 95.......................(b) JoshuaMoore(7) 59
(Gary Moore) *mid-div: rdn after 5th: wknd after next: t.o* **20/1**

065- **8** nk **Go Johnny Go (IRE)**[91] 4793 8-10-7 80....................... MrRGHenderson(7) 52
(Colin Tizzard) *nvr travelling: a in rr: t.o* **28/1**

00 **9** dist **Lean Burn (USA)**[7] 754 4-10-7 0.......................(t) DannyCook(3) —
(John Panvert) *t.o fr 3rd* **33/1**

P **Leoballero**[375] 10-10-7 0....................... MrDGPrichard(7) —
(Stephen Hughes) *slowly away: t.k.h: hdwy into mid-div whn awkward 3rd: wknd after 5th: t.o whn p.u bef 2 out* **66/1**

S-F **U** **Tobizzy**[7] 754 4-9-10 0....................... EdGlassonbury(7) —
(Linda Blackford) *sn outpcd in rr: mstke and uns rdr 5th* **66/1**

4m 23.7s (-10.20) **Going Correction** -0.325s/f (Good)
WFA 4 from 6yo+ 17lb **11** Ran SP% **116.7**
Speed ratings (Par 103): **108,107,100,98,98 91,85,85,—,— —**
toteswingers:1&2:£4.30, 1&3:£8.70, 2&3:£3.60 CSF £25.13 TOTE £12.20: £3.90, £1.20, £1.40; EX 35.00.There was no bid for the winner.
Owner Stranger, Mogridge, Romans **Bred** Patrick A Keogh **Trained** Milborne Port, Dorset

FOCUS
A moderate seller where the form amounts to little. It could be rated higher but the fifth looks the best guide for now.

NOTEBOOK
Intac(IRE) has not looked the most genuine in the past but was kidded to victory. He benefited from a good ride but he is unlikely to follow up in the future, unless things drop his way. (op 9-1)
Talenti(IRE) had run well in selling company when last seen but was unable to get his head in front here. He has not progressed since a winning debut for this yard and clearly has had his problems. (op 9-2)
Fongoli ran a similar race to when she was third at this venue last week. This is her level, but a victory is looking unlikely and her attitude is not what it should be. (op 17-2)
Heir To Be was making late progress having been under pressure from a long way out. He still looked in need of the run in the preliminaries and will be capable of better in time, possibly over a longer trip. (op 7-1)
Bolton Hall(IRE) was the form pick at a course he had run well at in the past but looked unwilling from an early stage and McCoy was unable to make him co-operate. He looks one to be wary of in future. (op 5-4)

822 LIMERICK RACECOURSE NOVICES' CHASE (11 fncs 2 omitted) 2m 110y
7:35 (7:35) (Class 3) 5-Y-O+ **£6,970** (£2,059; £1,029; £514; £257)

Form RPR

22-3 **1** **Blacktoft (USA)**[33] 422 7-10-12 0....................... PaulMoloney 132+
(Evan Williams) *mde all at brisk pce: qcknd clr after 2 out: v easily* **12/1**

34-1 **2** 8 **Gee Dee Nen**[19] 594 7-11-4 0....................... JamieMoore 125
(Gary Moore) *chsd wnr: rdn after 3 out: kpt on but nt pce of wnr fr after 2 out* **2/1**[2]

3/1 **3** 6 **Smack That (IRE)**[11] 709 8-11-1 135....................... PeterToole(3) 121
(Milton Harris) *hld up last but in tch: hdwy 7th: rdn to dispute cl 2nd after 3 out: nt pce of wnr fr after 2 out: sn lost 2nd* **10/11**[1]

P-00 **4** 19 **Paradise Regained (FR)**[19] 593 7-10-12 95....................... CharliePoste 94
(Sophie Leech) *trckd ldrs: rdn after 3 out: wknd bef next* **80/1**

/2-0 **5** shd **Conflictofinterest**[23] 528 8-10-12 0....................... HarrySkelton 94
(Paul Nicholls) *chsd ldrs: nudged along after 7th: rdn after 3 out: wknd bef next* **5/1**[3]

3m 58.5s (-8.00) **Going Correction** -0.325s/f (Good) **5** Ran SP% **111.3**
Speed ratings: **105,101,98,89,89**
CSF £37.21 TOTE £10.10: £2.60, £1.40; EX 23.30.
Owner C Watkins & Partner **Bred** Paradigm Thoroughbreds Inc **Trained** Llancarfan, Vale Of Glamorgan

FOCUS
The water jump was omitted in all chase races. The feature race on the card produced an easy winner, who made a big step uo, and the second is rated 6lb off recent course win.

NOTEBOOK
Blacktoft(USA) was well beaten over fences when last seen and prior to that had failed to win a claimer. The key to his rejuvenation was the removal of his usual headgear. It remains to be seen if he can reproduce this without the aids on. If he can, he will win more races over the summer. (op 10-1)
Gee Dee Nen had shown all his form over a longer trip and was outpaced at a crucial stage here. The form of his victory at this venue last time warrants him to plenty of respect in this company, and over a longer trip he ought to be able to win again over the summer. (op 11-4)
Smack That(IRE) travelled well and appeared to have plenty in hand when scoring at Aintree last time. He lacked the fluency and was clearly not travelling as well here. This was a disappointing effort from him and the form of his last win now looks questionable. (tchd 5-6)
Conflictofinterest was reported to have an irregular heartbeat when running poorly last time and this was another woeful effort. His physical problems are clearly stopping him from showing his true form and he is one to be wary of. Official explanation: trainers rep said gelding had breathing problem (op 9-2 tchd 11-2)

823 POINT 4 MARKETING NOVICES' H'CAP HURDLE (8 hdls) 2m 1f
8:10 (8:10) (Class 4) (0-110,109) 4-Y-O+ **£3,577** (£1,050; £525; £262)

Form RPR

6-04 **1** **Wilbury Star (IRE)**[21] 563 4-11-1 101....................... AndrewTinkler 102+
(Nicky Henderson) *trckd ldr: led 5th: rdn appr 2 out: kpt on wl: rdn out* **6/1**[3]

54-U **2** 1 **Erdeli (IRE)**[44] 233 6-11-5 102.......................(t) RichardJohnson 104
(Tim Vaughan) *hld up: sme hdwy appr 3 out: sn rdn: styd on to chse wnr appr 2 out: nt fluent and hld sn after last* **15/8**[1]

06-0 **3** 2¼ **Minneapolis**[25] 500 5-11-8 105....................... LeightonAspell 105
(Alison Batchelor) *hld up: rdn and stdy prog after 3 out: tk 3rd whn wnt lft last: styd on: nt rch ldrs* **9/1**

-442 **4** 9 **Navajo Nation (IRE)**[15] 661 4-11-0 105.......................(p) TomO'Connor(5) 94
(Bill Turner) *in tch: rdn after 3 out: sn one pce: lft 4th last* **12/1**

633- **5** 7 **Gunslinger (FR)**[15] 4804 5-11-8 105....................... TomScudamore 94+
(Michael Scudamore) *hld up: rchd for 3rd: hdwy appr 3 out: sn rdn: wknd next: lft 5th whn hmpd last* **5/1**[2]

42-4 **6** ¾ **Googoobarabajagal (IRE)**[18] 129 4-11-7 107.......................(p) TomO'Brien 89
(Stuart Kittow) *in tch: rdn after 3 out: wknd bef next* **10/1**

/2-0 **7** dist **Harlequinn Danseur (IRE)**[23] 534 5-10-12 95.......................(p) RhysFlint —
(John Flint) *in tch: rdn after 5th: wknd next: t.o* **14/1**

066- **P** **Raise Again (IRE)**[275] 1483 7-10-7 90....................... LiamTreadwell —
(Nerys Dutfield) *hld up towards rr: rdn after 3 out: sn wknd: mstke 2 out: p.u bef last* **14/1**

40-3 **F** **Al Amaan**[44] 216 5-11-7 109.......................(t) IanPopham(5) 101
(Paul Nicholls) *trckd ldr: jnd ldr after 4th: rdn after 3 out: rdn after 3 out: hld fr next: 9 l 4th whn fell last* **9/1**

F66/ **P** **Soviet Cat (IRE)**[450] 4784 5-10-6 89....................... DarylJacob —
(Miss C J Williams) *racd keenly: led tl 5th: sn rdn: wkng whn mstke 3 out: p.u bef next* **40/1**

3m 57.7s (-8.00) **Going Correction** -0.325s/f (Good)
WFA 4 from 5yo+ 17lb **10** Ran SP% **118.3**
Speed ratings (Par 105): **105,104,103,99,95 95,—,—,—,—**
toteswingers:1&2:£8.40, 1&3:£13.20, 2&3:£9.10 CSF £18.43 CT £103.51 TOTE £6.90: £2.10, £1.60, £2.10; EX 26.80.
Owner John Tobin, Ian Higginson & Fergus Carey **Bred** Rathasker Stud **Trained** Upper Lambourn, Berks

FOCUS
A modest novices' handicap and the second is rated as having run a small personal best and sets the level.

NOTEBOOK
Wilbury Star(IRE) made a winning handicap debut having only shown poor form over hurdles prior to this. He showed a willing attitude and the quick ground clearly helped his cause. This was not a good race and it is likely he has improvement in him, but he will need to have if he is to score again. (op 15-2 tchd 11-2)
Erdeli(IRE) was making his debut for Tim Vaughan and looked hard work, having come under pressure from a long way out. He did at least plug on late to challenge the winner but he will need to improve if he is to score. However, being with this yard that is not out of the question. (op 2-1 tchd 9-4 and 5-2 in a place)
Minneapolis was another making his handicap debut and on what he has achieved he looked a little high, but he ran creditably. However, he would need to drop a few pounds if he is to score but still being unexposed there could be improvement forthcoming. (op 8-1)
Navajo Nation(IRE) should have won a seller here last time out and he again ran well, but his proximity rather puts the form into context. Selling and claiming races will suit him better. (op 10-1)
Raise Again(IRE) Official explanation: jockey said gelding lost its action (op 8-1 tchd 15-2)
Al Amaan showed a little bit more on his handicap debut but was held when falling at the last. He may need a longer trip. (op 8-1 tchd 15-2)

824 TRITON GALLERIES H'CAP CHASE (14 fncs 2 omitted) 2m 5f 110y
8:40 (8:40) (Class 4) (0-115,112) 5-Y-O+ **£3,903** (£1,146; £573; £286)

Form RPR

05-4 **1** **William Butler (IRE)**[21] 567 10-11-8 111....................... DPFahy(3) 127+
(Evan Williams) *in tch: hit 6th: crept clsr fr 10th: shkn up to ld appr 2 out: in command whn nt fluent last: comf* **3/1**[1]

-P06 **2** 9 **Free Gift**[17] 636 12-11-12 112.......................(p) DarylJacob 117
(R H & Mrs S Alner) *chsd ldrs: rdn after 3 out: styd on same pce: wnt 2nd last: no ch w wnr* **12/1**

32-5 **3** 1¼ **Now Listen To Me**[47] 181 7-11-8 108.......................(t) RobertThornton 112
(Paul Nicholls) *trckd ldr: led 3 out: rdn and hdd bef next: sn no ch w wnr: nt fluent whn lost 2nd last* **9/2**[2]

4-02 **4** nk **Alroyal (GER)**[15] 663 11-11-0 107....................... MrDGPrichard(7) 112
(Phillip Dando) *hld up early: trckd ldrs fr 5th: rdn and ev ch after 3 out: styd on same pce fr next* **3/1**[1]

063- **5** 8 **Machu Picchu (FR)**[106] 4484 8-11-3 103....................... TomO'Brien 102
(Jamie Snowden) *hld up: effrt but unable to get on terms after 3 out: nvr trbld ldrs* **11/2**[3]

21-4 **P** **Tighe Caster**[38] 330 11-11-11 111....................... JodieMogford —
(Graeme McPherson) *untidy 1st: nvr travelling in last: lost tch fr 8th: p.u bef 10th* **7/1**

02-0 **P** **Mr Goofy (IRE)**[48] 148 9-10-12 98....................... TomScudamore —
(Michael Scudamore) *j. sltly rt: led tl 3 out: sn rdn and wknd: bhd whn p.u bef 2 out* **12/1**

-62P **P** **Tuscany Star (IRE)**[22] 556 7-10-9 98.......................(tp) PeterToole(3) —
(Edward Creighton) *trckd ldrs: slow jump 3rd: lost pl 8th: rdn after next: sn wknd: t.o whn p.u bef 2 out* **16/1**

5m 12.4s (-9.00) **Going Correction** -0.325s/f (Good) **8** Ran SP% **117.3**
Speed ratings: **103,99,99,99,96 —,—,—**
toteswingers:1&2:£8.40, 1&3:£3.90, 2&3:£19.90 CSF £37.29 CT £162.27 TOTE £5.90: £1.10, £6.60, £1.10; EX 26.70.
Owner J Swinnerton & Miss S Howell **Bred** John Lett **Trained** Llancarfan, Vale Of Glamorgan

FOCUS
An intriguing handicap chase which saw an easy winner who could progress from this. The fourth is rated to previous course form and sets the level.

NOTEBOOK
William Butler(IRE) had a successful summer for this yard two summers ago and poor runs since then, and had dropped to a generous mark. He travelled and on the whole jumped well to score easily. His mark remains workable, and he is sure to be a force throughout the summer for his in-form yard. (tchd 7-2)
Free Gift last won in July 09 off a 3lb higher mark and showed his first signs of a revival here. Quick ground suits him well and he will find a race over the summer. (tchd 11-1)
Now Listen To Me had failed to see the trip out in his last two starts but he also failed to see his race out over this shorter trip. He ought to be capable of winning from this mark but his weak finishing is holding him back. (op 4-1)
Machu Picchu(FR) has not progressed for his new yard and is one to tread carefully with now. (op 6-1 tchd 13-2)
Tighe Caster took no interest from an early stage and is clearly hard to predict. Official explanation: jockey said geling was never travelling (op 11-2)
Tuscany Star(IRE) Official explanation: jockey said gelding was never travelling (op 11-2)

825 NEWTON ABBOT RACES GB V IRELAND LADY AMATEUR RIDERS' H'CAP HURDLE (8 hdls) 2m 3f
9:10 (9:10) (Class 4) (0-105,101) 4-Y-O+ **£3,123** (£968; £484; £242)

Form RPR

00-4 **1** **Vintage Fabric (USA)**[16] 646 8-10-13 95.......................(t) MsLO'Neill(7) 101+
(Nigel Hawke) *mde most: rdn and narrowly hdd after 3 out: regained ld next: styd on wl* **5/1**[3]

4B31 **2** 3¾ **Bold Policy (IRE)**[12] 694 7-10-13 95.......................(p) L-BdrSallyRandell(7) 97
(Milton Harris) *hld up bhd ldrs in last: hdwy after 6th: led narrowly after 3 out: rdn and hdd whn hit and slipped 2 out: hld whn nt fluent last* **10/3**[1]

5P-2 **3** ¾ **Wisteria Lane (IRE)**[14] 678 7-9-12 80........ MissEvannaMcCutcheon(7) 80
(Anabel L M King) *trckd ldrs: rdn after 3 out: styd on same pce* **7/2**[2]

-4P3 **4** ¾ **Rock Me (IRE)**[19] 593 5-11-1 97.......................(tp) MissHLewis(7) 97+
(Lawney Hill) *trckd ldrs tl outpcd 3 out: wnt 4th next but nvr bk on terms* **10/3**[1]

2352 **5** 3½ **Apache Dawn**[5] 768 6-11-2 98.......................(t) MissSKMcCarthy(7) 94
(Aytach Sadik) *trckd ldrs: rdn after 3 out: sn one pce: hit last* **5/1**[3]

0-06 **6** 2 1/4 **Always Cruising (USA)**[23] 532 5-10-3 **85**........................ MissJBuck[(7)] 79
(Linda Blackford) *w wnr: rdn after 3 out: sn outpcd* **10/1**

4m 33.4s (-0.50) **Going Correction** -0.325s/f (Good) **6** Ran SP% **110.8**
Speed ratings (Par 105): **88,86,86,85,84 83**
toteswingers:1&2:£4.90, 1&3:£4.00, 2&3:£2.40 CSF £21.44 TOTE £6.20: £3.20, £2.10; EX 16.70 Place 6 £41.92; Place 5 £36.77.
Owner N J McMullan and S H Bryant **Bred** Juddmonte Farms Inc **Trained** Woolminstone, Somerset

FOCUS
A moderate lady riders' hurdle and the form is suspect, with the third the best guide.

NOTEBOOK
Vintage Fabric(USA) shaped well at Worcester last time and under his capable amateur rider he responded well to pressure to score. He goes well at this course and gave his trainer a much needed winner. He could be capable of winning again but would need to be well placed to do so. (op 9-2)
Bold Policy(IRE) won well at Uttoxeter over fences last time and off his lower hurdles mark looked to have a good chance, but his lack of fluency at the final two flights of hurdles possibly cost him victory. He will remain of interest off this mark when reunited with a stronger professional rider. (op 7-2)
Wisteria Lane(IRE) ran well at Bangor last time, but once he comes under pressure he puts his head up in the air and finds little. He also shaped as if this trip was the limit of his stamina.
Rock Me(IRE) ran well over C&D last time but never threatened to score here. He may find winning difficult but would benefit from a more positive ride. (op 4-1 tchd 3-1)
T/Plt: £79.20 to a £1 stake. Pool:£63,853.27 - 588.40 winning tickets T/Qpdt: £21.50 to a £1 stake. Pool:£5,009.42 - 171.82 winning tickets TM

760 WORCESTER (L-H)

Wednesday, June 23

OFFICIAL GOING: Good to firm (chs 7.8; hdl 7.4)
All bends on inside racing line.
Wind: Light against Weather: Fine

826 SENIOR CITIZENS SPECIAL PACKAGE DAY NOVICES' H'CAP HURDLE (10 hdls) 2m 4f

1:50 (1:50) (Class 4) (0-100,100) 4-Y-O+ **£2,927** (£859; £429; £214)

Form RPR
P-06 **1** **Occasionally Yours (IRE)**[24] 539 6-11-2 **90**...............(b[1]) DavidDennis 99
(Nigel Hawke) *hld up: hdwy 5th: led after 7th: hrd rdn flat: all out* **28/1**
U4-3 **2** *nk* **Lygon Legend**[33] 428 7-11-6 **94**.................................... LiamTreadwell 102
(Peter Hiatt) *mstke 1st: chsd ldr to 4th: remained handy: hrd rdn and ev ch fnl 100yds: styd on* **33/1**
P0 **3** *2* **Aisemma (IRE)**[18] 630 6-9-13 **80**.................................... MrMByrne[(7)] 87+
(Peter Bowen) *hld up: hdwy 5th: rdn and hung lft flat: styd on* **25/1**
6F/1 **4** *2 1/4* **Cash Back**[35] 410 10-10-9 **90**.. RachaelGreen[(7)] 94
(Anthony Honeyball) *hld up: styd on fr 3 out: rdn and hung lft flat: nt rch ldrs* **5/1**[1]
-21U **5** *10* **Basford Lass**[10] 737 5-11-10 **98**....................................(b) AlanO'Keeffe 93
(Jennie Candlish) *led: hdd appr 3 out: rallied and ev ch last: wknd flat* **6/1**[2]
-331 **6** *1 1/2* **Misamon (FR)**[8] 755 7-10-7 **81**..(v) PaulMoloney 75
(David Rees) *prom: chsd ldr 4th to 7th: sn rdn: wknd last* **5/1**[1]
-063 **7** *2 3/4* **Rien A Perdre (FR)**[15] 682 9-11-12 **100**...........................(v[1]) JodieMogford 90
(Graeme McPherson) *hld up in tch: rdn and outpcd 7th: n.d after* **16/1**
6/0 **8** *2 1/4* **Isle Of Inishmore (IRE)**[18] 630 7-11-7 **95**...............(t) RichardJohnson 83
(Tim Vaughan) *prom: rdn appr 3 out: wknd bef last* **6/1**[2]
40-2 **9** *4 1/2* **Appointment**[13] 688 5-11-6 **94**.................................(p) JamieGoldstein 77
(Sheena West) *hld up: a in rr* **12/1**
-52U **10** *3/4* **Abulharith**[13] 698 4-10-9 **87**.. TomScudamore 65
(Michael Scudamore) *chsd ldrs: rdn and wknd appr 3 out* **13/2**[3]
-11U **11** *1 1/2* **Nomad (FR)**[23] 557 9-10-6 **80**.. HarrySkelton 61
(Carroll Gray) *hld up: rdn after 6th: a in rr* **11/1**
U/0 **12** *40* **Ford Of Wells (IRE)**[9] 744 9-11-12 **100**.....................(tp) AidanColeman 41
(Patrick Griffin, Ire) *mid-div: rdn and wknd after 5th: bhd whn hmpd 7th: t.o* **66/1**
P545 **U** **A Haon A Do (IRE)**[16] 660 8-9-9 **74**............................ DonalDevereux[(5)] —
(Gerald Ham) *hld up: sme hdwy whn blnd and uns rdr 7th* **14/1**

4m 36.6s (-10.80) **Going Correction** -0.425s/f (Good)
WFA 4 from 5yo+ 18lb **13** Ran SP% **115.5**
Speed ratings (Par 105): **104,103,103,102,98 97,96,95,93,93 92,76,—**
toteswingers: 1&2 £37.40, 2&3 £55.00, 1&3 not won. CSF £676.72 CT £20908.89 TOTE £29.20: £10.10, £5.70, £6.60.
Owner Kay Russell **Bred** Gerard Connolly **Trained** Woolminstone, Somerset
■ Stewards' Enquiry : David Dennis four-day ban: used whip with excessive frequency and without giving gelding time to respond (Jul 7, 11, 14, 15)

FOCUS
This was far from a strong race, but the first three home were almost impossible to find on recent evidence. The winning time was decent, but most of the races on the card were quicker than standard. The fourth looks the best guide to the level.

NOTEBOOK
Occasionally Yours(IRE), blinkered for the first time, hadn't shown a thing on his two starts this season, so was not easy to find even though he put up a couple of fair efforts in 2009. He did fight on bravely when challenged, but unless the headgear has completely changed his outlook on life, he isn't one to be backing at a short price next time. Official explanation: trainer said, regarding the apparent improvement in form shown, gelding greatly benefited from having the blinkers fitted for the first time (op 25-1 tchd 33-1)
Lygon Legend, making his handicap debut, had been showing a bit of ability at a low level and took a strong hold for the majority of the race. However, he still found enough to get into contention again after losing his place for a while, and was only narrowly denied. (op 25-1)
Aisemma(IRE), beaten 177l last time, could not have been fancied on anything she had previously done on a racecourse, but could have played a bigger part in the finish had she not edged left under pressure. (op 33-1)
Cash Back, absent since beating Basford Lass after a huge 1312-day absence in May, confirmed form with that rival and, even though he was very one-paced under pressure, one couldn't help but think he would have gone closer had he been a little more prominent. (op 9-2)
Basford Lass failed to reverse recent form with Cash Back but was worse off at the weights. (tchd 5-1)
Misamon(FR), having his first run over hurdles since September 2008, won a low-grade handicap chase over about 2m recently but never got into this at the end after being prominent throughout. (op 4-1 tchd 11-2)
Isle Of Inishmore(IRE), fitted with a tongue-tie on this drop in trip, continues to show little under rules. (tchd 5-1)
Abulharith attracted market support and held a chance on turning in, but soon retreated. (op 8-1 tchd 6-1)
Nomad(FR), who unseated last time on his attempt to land a hat-trick, was very disappointing after being held up. (op 10-1)
Ford Of Wells(IRE) Official explanation: trainer said gelding was found to have suffered tendon injuries

827 WORLD CUP FREE BETS AT FREEBETTING.CO.UK NOVICES' HURDLE (8 hdls) 2m

2:20 (2:20) (Class 4) 4-Y-O+ **£2,927** (£859; £429; £214)

Form RPR
31 **1** **Clear Sailing**[26] 500 7-11-5 116.................................... DougieCostello 100+
(Ian Williams) *hld up: racd keenly: hdwy appr 3 out: shkn up to ld flat: r.o wl* **10/11**[1]
0/6- **2** *1 1/4* **Flichity (IRE)**[256] 1691 5-10-12 0...................................... JasonMaguire 91+
(Donald McCain) *hld up: hmpd after 2nd: racd keenly: hdwy fr 3 out: rdn and r.o flat: nt rch wnr* **18/1**
/0-P **3** *1/2* **Lago Verde (SWI)**[39] 327 5-10-12 0...............................(v[1]) WillKennedy 89
(Paul Webber) *led: rdn and hung lft after 3 out: hung rt last: drvn: hung lft and hdd flat: styd on same pce* **33/1**
4 *11* **Admiral Dundas (IRE)**[27] 5-10-9 0................................(t) SeanQuinlan[(3)] 80+
(Kim Bailey) *hld up: hdwy after 5th: n.m.r and mstke last: wknd flat* **3/1**[2]
5P-P **5** *6* **Tram Express (FR)**[18] 632 6-10-7 0..............(b[1]) SamTwiston-Davies[(5)] 71
(Shaun Lycett) *trckd ldr tl after 5th: wknd appr 2 out* **12/1**
5/2- **6** *3 1/4* **Dormouse**[406] 291 5-10-12 0.. TomScudamore 68
(Anabel L M King) *chsd ldrs: rdn after 5th: wknd appr 2 out* **5/1**[3]
500/ **7** *shd* **Lathyrus (FR)**[39] 10-10-5 0.. MrJFlook[(7)] 68
(John Needham) *prom: ev ch fr 3 out tl wknd last* **66/1**
6 **P** **First Watch**[20] 609 5-10-12 0.. RobertThornton —
(Martin Keighley) *hld up: p.u after 2nd: lame* **20/1**

3m 45.8s (-1.50) **Going Correction** -0.425s/f (Good) **8** Ran SP% **116.2**
Speed ratings (Par 105): **86,85,85,79,76 75,74,—**
toteswingers:1&2 £5.10, 2&3 £21.00, 1&3 £17.20 CSF £19.51 TOTE £2.90: £1.02, £6.30, £13.50; EX 22.00.
Owner C Owen **Bred** Juddmonte Farms Ltd **Trained** Portway, Worcs

FOCUS
An uncompetitive novice hurdle, in which the winner's time was disappointing compared with the rest of the races at the meeting. The form looks suspect otherwise could have been rated as much as a stone higher.

NOTEBOOK
Clear Sailing, running under a penalty, collected a second success despite looking a little tricky under pressure. This was a weak-looking affair and he'll need a similar contest to land a hat-trick in novice company. (op 4-7)
Flichity(IRE), a half-brother to the stable's Grand National winner Amberleigh House, was last of six on his hurdling debut back in October but did much better here after his early diversion by First Watch. He travelled strongly into the home straight and finished well once gathered together. The break has clearly done him good.
Lago Verde(SWI), fitted with a visor for the first time, didn't manage to finish on his first start over hurdles, so this was a lot better after making most of the running, although his attitude looked questionable on a couple of occasions, especially at the last in the back straight. (op 28-1)
Admiral Dundas(IRE), a useful sort at his best on the Flat, had not been handed the stiffest task on his hurdling debut, but connections fitted a tongue-tie for the first time and only a modicum of promise could be taken from this first effort. (op 4-1)
Tram Express(FR), blinkered for the first time, was dropping in trip after pulling up on his previous two outings and ran respectably until weakening after two out. (op 28-1)
Dormouse showed a glimpse of ability when last seen over a year ago but ran like a horse very much in need of this after his absence. (op 7-1)
First Watch was pulled up after jumping two hurdles. He was reported to have gone lame. Official explanation: vet said horse pulled up lame on the right-fore (op 25-1)

828 GREATWOOD NOVICES' CHASE (18 fncs) 2m 7f

2:55 (2:55) (Class 4) 5-Y-O+ **£3,252** (£955; £477; £238)

Form RPR
F-11 **1** **Baily Storm (IRE)**[18] 625 8-11-12 125.............................(p) DarylJacob 131+
(Tim Vaughan) *chsd ldr: led after 3 out: clr last: styd on wl* **7/2**[3]
3PP- **2** *14* **Pagan Sword**[129] 4058 8-10-12 90.. RodiGreene 105
(David Bridgwater) *led: blnd 3 out: sn hdd: hit next: wknd bef last* **18/1**
1-01 **3** *1/2* **Mous Of Men (FR)**[24] 536 7-11-5 126......................(tp) TomScudamore 111
(David Pipe) *hld up in tch: j.rt 4 out: rdn and wknd 2 out* **11/10**[1]
0-52 **4** *26* **Tucumcari (IRE)**[23] 559 5-10-12 0...................................... AidanColeman 93+
(Brendan Powell) *chsd ldrs tl wknd after 5 out: t.o whn slipped on landing 3 out* **10/1**
30/ **P** **Bricos Boy (IRE)**[39] 9-10-7 0..(t) IanPopham[(5)] —
(Miss C J Williams) *prom: lost pl 6th: hit 8th: wknd bef 10th: t.o whn blnd 13th: sn p.u* **66/1**
-0F4 **P** **Mumbles Pier (IRE)**[22] 565 5-10-12 0.................................. TomO'Brien —
(Peter Bowen) *blnd 1st: sn t.o: j.rt 4th: p.u bef next* **11/4**[2]

5m 37.3s (-5.30) **Going Correction** -0.425s/f (Good) course record **6** Ran SP% **112.4**
Speed ratings: **92,87,86,77,—,—**
toteswingers: 1&2 £1.60, 1&3 £1.40, 2&3 £6.60 CSF £47.07 TOTE £4.20: £1.90, £8.20.
Owner Chasing Gold Ltd **Bred** J Harold-Barry **Trained** Aberthin, Vale of Glamorgan

FOCUS
Probably just a fair novice chase, but it did feature a couple of in-form performers. Only four were left with any chance leaving the back straight for the final time. The form is rated around the first two.

NOTEBOOK
Baily Storm(IRE) has been in terrific form since joining Tim Vaughan, winning four of his six starts for him, including the last two, which were his only attempts over fences. It seemed a little surprising that connections opted to place cheekpieces on for the first time, but he showed by far the most resilience and was comfortably on top from the final fence. The plan is to head to the Summer Plate next. (op 11-4, tchd 4-1 in places)
Pagan Sword, officially rated well below the two horses who dominated the betting, seemed to really enjoy it left alone in front but one had the impression he would have still been beaten by Baily Storm even allowing for his blunder three out. (op 16-1)
Mous Of Men(FR) won on his first start over fences last time but connections still reached for cheekpieces this time. Up 3f in distance, he still looks like he needs more experience over fences but did finish badly dehydrated, which may explain why he looked a little reluctant under pressure. Official explanation: vet said gelding pulled up sore (op 10-11 tchd 5-6 and 6-5)
Tucumcari(IRE), well beaten on his three outings over hurdles, has the size to make it over fences (he is an ex-pointer) and there were a few positives to take from his run despite being well beaten. (op 16-1 tchd 9-1)
Mumbles Pier(IRE) made an horrendous error at the first and immediately got detached. (op 9-2 tchd 5-1)

829 SPONSOR A RACE BY CALLING 01905 25364 H'CAP HURDLE (8 hdls) 2m

3:25 (3:25) (Class 4) (0-105,106) 4-Y-O+ **£2,602** (£764; £382; £190)

Form RPR
1-45 **1** **Sadler's Star (GER)**[12] 712 7-11-12 **105**..........................(p) DenisO'Regan 113
(Michael Blake) *hld up: hdwy appr 2 out: rdn to ld nr fin* **14/1**

11U1 **2** *hd* **Ajman (IRE)**[3] 798 5-11-10 **106** 7ex (t) DPFahy(3) 114
(Evan Williams) *hld up: hdwy appr 3 out: led 150yds out: sn rdn: hdd nr fin* **5/6**[1]

3-65 **3** *1 1/2* **Petit Fleur**[17] 645 8-10-1 **85** SamTwiston-Davies(5) 91
(Julian Smith) *chsd ldrs: rdn to ld flat: hdd 150yds out: styd on same pce* **6/1**[3]

/-13 **4** *3* **Dereks (IRE)**[13] 697 8-11-11 **104** APMcCoy 107
(Jim Best) *led to 2nd: chsd ldr: led again 4th: rdn appr 3 out: hdd flat: styd on same pce* **7/2**[2]

/0-P **5** *6* **Welcome Stranger**[15] 682 10-11-0 **100** PeterHatton(7) 98
(Louise Davis) *hld up: hdwy appr 3 out: rdn and wknd flat* **66/1**

P14- **6** *4 1/2* **Le Brocquy**[371] 743 5-11-12 **105** (p) RobertThornton 98
(Martin Keighley) *chsd ldrs: rdn appr last: wknd flat* **18/1**

7 *1 1/4* **Topenhall (IRE)**[383] 612 9-11-10 **103** (t) CharliePoste 94
(Ben Case) *chsd ldrs tl rdn and wknd appr last* **66/1**

-F30 **8** *29* **Mayor Of Kilcock**[25] 522 7-11-4 **104** MrJMahot(7) 66
(James Danahar) *led 2nd to 4th: rdn and wknd appr 3 out: t.o* **25/1**

3m 38.5s (-8.80) **Going Correction** -0.425s/f (Good) **8** Ran SP% **109.8**
Speed ratings (Par 105): **105,104,104,102,99 97,96,82**
toteswingers:1&2 £3.40, 2&3 £1.90, 1&3 £8.30 CSF £25.32 CT £75.42 TOTE £11.10: £1.70, £1.20, £1.20; EX 39.60.
Owner Mrs J M Haines **Bred** R Haag And H Schniepp **Trained** Trowbridge, Wilts

FOCUS
This didn't look the strongest contest, even for the level, but it produced a close finish. The form is rated around those in the frame behind the winner.

NOTEBOOK
Sadler's Star(GER) didn't run too well at Market Rasen last time but did enough in the final 50 yards here to get his head in front. One got the impression that he may need things to fall right for him, which will not always be the case, and his rider deserves credit for getting him to the lead in the final stages. (op 12-1)
Ajman(IRE) was making a quick reappearance after winning at Hereford the previous Sunday, and has been in terrific heart since landing his first race over hurdles. 7lb higher than last time and well backed, he was produced to get to the front at the right time but was worn down close to the line. (op Evens tchd 4-5)
Petit Fleur, back down to 2m, is not the biggest but looks a game mare under pressure, and put up a good performance. This seemed a return to her best. (op 15-2)
Dereks(IRE) won easily on his first outing for this stable (well backed and returning from a long absence) but could not follow up next time. He ran a solid race here with no obvious excuses, and is a decent marker to the level of the form. (op 5-2)
Welcome Stranger had not run well since his return from a long layoff, but this was a little better, as he was running on quite well up the home straight after being behind.

830 BETFAIR H'CAP HURDLE (10 hdls) 3m
4:00 (4:00) (Class 2) (0-140,139) 4-Y-0+
£9,393 (£2,775; £1,387; £694; £346; £174)

Form RPR

1-S1 **1** **Tarvini (IRE)**[20] 606 5-10-4 **120** (p) RichieMcLernon(3) 127+
(Jonjo O'Neill) *hld up: hdwy 8th: rdn appr 3 out: led flat: styd on wl* **9/1**

5F/1 **2** *4* **Dont Call Me Derek**[28] 478 9-10-7 **120** SamThomas 123
(Dr Richard Newland) *hld up: hdwy 9th: chsd ldr bef next: led 2 out: j.lft last: hdd and unable qck flat* **12/1**

-121 **3** *6* **The Jigsaw Man (IRE)**[7] 761 6-11-5 **139** AodhaganConlon(7) 137
(Rebecca Curtis) *led: rdn and hdd 2 out: no ex last* **5/2**[1]

61-F **4** *3/4* **King Ar Aghaidh (IRE)**[50] 138 9-10-9 **122** JasonMaguire 118
(David Arbuthnot) *hld up: hdwy 9th: sn outpcd: styd on again fr 2 out* **20/1**

0-P0 **5** *3/4* **Tritonville Lodge (IRE)**[18] 633 8-10-11 **124** JackDoyle 120
(Emma Lavelle) *chsd ldr tl rdn appr last: wknd flat* **20/1**

-516 **6** *9* **Tabaran (FR)**[18] 633 7-10-6 **126** (tp) OliverDayman(7) 113
(Alison Thorpe) *hld up: hdwy appr 3 out: wknd after next* **16/1**

0-0F **7** *33* **Giovanna**[26] 503 9-10-7 **120** RobertThornton 74
(Richard Phillips) *mid-div: hdwy 8th: wknd after next: t.o* **16/1**

2-16 **8** *20* **Very Cool**[12] 708 8-10-7 **120** (bt) JohnnyFarrelly 54
(David Pipe) *prom: lost pl after 8th: sn wknd: t.o* **8/1**[3]

1-21 **9** *12* **Quo Video (FR)**[13] 690 6-11-3 **130** RichardJohnson 52
(Tim Vaughan) *mid-div: hdwy 8th: wknd next: t.o* **8/1**[3]

00-1 **10** *24* **Two Miles West (IRE)**[17] 651 9-10-10 **123** APMcCoy 21
(Jonjo O'Neill) *hld up: pushed along after 6th: effrt appr 9th: sn wknd: t.o* **7/1**[2]

U-02 **P** **The Real Deal (IRE)**[26] 503 9-10-11 **124** DarylJacob —
(Nick Williams) *chsd ldrs tl p.u bef 7th: fatally injured* **9/1**

01-6 **F** **Pemberton**[8] 756 5-11-1 **128** (p) TomScudamore —
(David Pipe) *prom tl wknd 3 out: fell next* **14/1**

5m 26.3s (-18.30) **Going Correction** -0.425s/f (Good) course record **12** Ran SP% **118.9**
Speed ratings (Par 109): **113,111,109,109,109 106,95,88,84,76 —,—**
toteswingers:1&2 £12.00, 2&3 £9.20, 1&3 £6.50 CSF £111.53 CT £350.40 TOTE £13.20: £3.60, £4.30, £1.90; EX 59.70.
Owner John P McManus **Bred** His Highness The Aga Khan's Studs S C **Trained** Cheltenham, Gloucs

FOCUS
The most competitive race on the card, and plenty of these could be given a chance on their best form. The winning time was decent, the winner is progressive and the third is the best guide, although the form could rate a little higher.

NOTEBOOK
Tarvini(IRE), chasing his fourth victory in his last five starts, was running off a 4lb higher mark than when winning at Wetherby (2m6f) but managed to gain another narrow victory after receiving a strong ride when it was needed. He was game under pressure and is progressive at this level, but collapsed after the race due to dehydration and was down a long time. (op 7-1)
Dont Call Me Derek bolted up on his first outing in 854 days when taking a seller at Southwell in late May for this trainer, easily beating a 120-rated rival. Patiently ridden, he moved through the pack as the pace increased and was a few lengths in front of Tarvini off the home bend. Once in front, he started to wander under pressure, which allowed the winner to grab him well after the final hurdle. (op 8-1)
The Jigsaw Man(IRE), back over hurdles after securing his first victory over fences at this course recently, didn't seem to quite get home after doing all the work in front. It was still a decent performance under a big weight. (op 4-1tchd 9-2 in places)
King Ar Aghaidh(IRE), returning to hurdles, looked unlucky not to get placed after making a move through the field, although he gave the impression that he may not be particularly straightforward under pressure. (op 18-1)
Tritonville Lodge(IRE) finished just behind Tabaran last time but comfortably reversed placings here.
Very Cool, disappointing at Aintree earlier this month, failed to get involved at any stage.\n\x\x Sadly, \bThe Real Deal\p sustained a fatal injury. (op 9-1 tchd 10-1)
Quo Video(FR) also failed to get involved at any point. (op 17-2 tchd 9-1)
Two Miles West(IRE), a C&D winner on his previous outing after a long layoff, failed to get involved and never seemed to be enjoying himself. (op 13-2 tchd 15-2)

The Real Deal(IRE) sadly sustained a fatal injury. Official explanation: vet said gelding pulled up lame (tchd 10-1)

831 WORCESTER-RACECOURSE.CO.UK H'CAP CHASE (12 fncs) 2m
4:30 (4:31) (Class 3) (0-135,135) 5-Y-0 **£5,703** (£1,684; £842; £421; £210)

Form RPR

0-2P **1** **Mibleu (FR)**[20] 592 10-9-10 **110** ow1 KeiranBurke(5) 125+
(R H & Mrs S Alner) *hld up: mstke 1st: hdwy 4th: led 7th: clr fr 3 out: eased flat* **9/1**

53U- **2** *11* **Ormello (FR)**[68] 5208 8-10-11 **120** PeterBuchanan 116
(Lucinda Russell) *chsd ldrs: outpcd 8th: rallied to go 2nd after 4 out: sn rdn and no imp* **7/1**

2-25 **3** *3/4* **Norborne Bandit (IRE)**[25] 523 9-10-0 **109** oh1 HarrySkelton 104
(Evan Williams) *chsd ldrs: outpcd 6th: rallied 2 out: styd on* **7/2**[2]

31-6 **4** *17* **Cortinas (GER)**[20] 592 8-10-9 **118** (tp) PaulMoloney 96
(Charlie Mann) *hld up: a in rr: bhd whn hmpd 4 out* **12/1**

1-10 **5** *4* **Marodima (FR)**[18] 627 7-11-5 **135** DavidBass(7) 113
(Jamie Snowden) *led: mstkes 1st and 4th: hdd 7th: nt fluent 4 out: wknd next* **6/1**

-234 **F** **Huguenot (IRE)**[20] 592 7-10-6 **115** TomO'Brien —
(Philip Hobbs) *hld up: hdwy whn fell 4 out: fatally injured* **11/4**[1]

12-4 **P** **Line Artic (FR)**[55] 57 6-11-4 **127** LiamHeard —
(Chris Down) *chsd ldr tl wknd appr 4 out: p.u bef next* **11/2**[3]

3m 43.0s (-8.60) **Going Correction** -0.425s/f (Good) course record **7** Ran SP% **108.8**
Speed ratings: **104,98,98,89,87 —,—**
toteswingers: 1&2 £10.60, 2&3 £4.50, 1&3 £4.80 CSF £60.53 CT £237.17 TOTE £12.30: £5.90, £6.50; EX 56.40.
Owner Chasing Gold Ltd **Bred** Haras De La Rousseliere S C E A **Trained** Droop, Dorset

FOCUS
The pace was always going to be good as a result of there being a couple of proven front-runners in the contest. The winner could be rated a lot higher but the third to fifth have all been below par recently, and the second was returning from a break.

NOTEBOOK
Mibleu(FR), winner of this race last year, pretty much carted his rider to the front a long way out and the pair were never troubled once establishing a lead, although his jumping wasn't always very fluent. He can surely expect a stiff rise in the weights for this. He has an entry at Uttoxeter and one would imagine he will take that up if showing no ill-effects from this. Official explanation: trainer's rep had no explanation for the apparent improvement in form shown (tchd 10-1)
Ormello(FR), not seen since unseating at the first at Cheltenham in April, plugged on for second but, like all of his rivals, never had a chance of success once the winner had gone to the front. (op 6-1)
Norborne Bandit(IRE) had an excuse for his last performance (blundered when still going well) but had his usual cheekpieces taken off this time, which did not seem to help him as he was struggling early. His rider didn't give up but he was never going to win. (op 4-1 tchd 3-1)
Cortinas(GER) pulled much too hard on his return to action earlier this month and looked held when hampered by the faller. (op 11-1 tchd 10-1 and 14-1)
Marodima(FR), who looked fairly treated on his best hurdling form, did not seem to go off too quickly. It was a little disappointing to see him run so moderately, although a blunder down the back straight may have knocked his confidence. (tchd 11-2)
Huguenot(IRE) was not completely done with when sadly taking a fatal fall four out. (op 7-2)
Line Artic(FR), given a break since a disappointing effort back in April, once again failed to get involved. He lost his back end after making a mistake at the fourth-last while looking comfortably held. (op 7-2)

832 GROUP GRANDSTAND VALUE PACKAGE JUST #15 STANDARD OPEN NATIONAL HUNT FLAT RACE (DIV I) 2m
5:05 (5:05) (Class 6) 4-6-Y-O **£1,370** (£399; £199)

Form RPR

1 **Eleven Fifty Nine** 4-10-0 0 RachaelGreen(7) 95+
(Anthony Honeyball) *hld up: swtchd rt and hdwy over 6f out: led on bit over 1f out: r.o wl* **7/1**[3]

2 *3 1/4* **Maid Of Silk (IRE)** 4-10-7 0 TomO'Brien 92
(Grant Cann) *hld up in tch: slipped on path after 3f: sn lost pl: hdwy over 7f out: n.m.r and lost pl over 6f out: hdwy over 2f out: nt clr run sn after: hung lft ins fnl f: r.o* **20/1**

3 *1/2* **Forcryingoutloud (IRE)**[256] 1713 6-11-0 0 RichieMcLernon(3) 101
(Andrew Haynes) *a.p: rdn to chse wnr ins fnl f: styd on same pce* **3/1**[2]

4 *4 1/2* **Sir Harry Cash** 4-10-7 0 BrianToomey(7) 94
(Michael Mullineaux) *chsd ldrs: rdn over 4f out: sn outpcd: styd on ins fnl f* **50/1**

5 *1/2* **Minella (IRE)**[53] 6-11-3 0 RodiGreene 97
(Michael Appleby) *led: rdn over 2f out: hdd over 1f out: hung lft and wknd ins fnl f* **16/1**

6 *hd* **Doubletoilntrouble (IRE)**[67] 4-11-0 0 APMcCoy 93
(Keith Goldsworthy) *hld up in tch: rdn over 4f out: wknd ins fnl f* **9/1**

00- **7** *8* **Love Love Me Do**[153] 3576 5-10-5 0 IanPopham(5) 81
(Carroll Gray) *hld up: rdn over 5f out: nvr on terms* **66/1**

2 **8** *2* **Rody (FR)**[20] 602 5-11-3 0 PaddyBrennan 91+
(Tom George) *prom: rdn over 2f out: wknd over 1f out: eased* **15/8**[1]

9 *9* **Westcoat Lad**[31] 5-10-10 0 MrDGPrichard(7) 77
(Kevin Tork) *plld hrd and prom: hmpd after 3f: rdn and wknd over 5f out* **25/1**

10 *8* **Silver Seraph** 6-10-10 0 PaddyAspell 62
(Patrick Holmes) *hld up: rdn and wknd over 5f out: t.o: fin lame* **40/1**

11 *3 1/4* **Sans Un Souci (FR)** 4-10-7 0 CharlieWallis(7) 63
(John O'Shea) *mid-div: wknd 6f out: t.o* **50/1**

12 *15* **Kalulushi (IRE)**[51] 5-11-3 0 JasonMaguire 51
(Donald McCain) *chsd ldr: rdn over 4f out: wknd over 2f out: t.o* **12/1**

U **Star Role** 6-11-0 0 (t) CharlieHuxley(3) —
(Richard Ford) *unruly to post: hld up: a in rr: bhd fr 1/2-way: swvd rt and uns rdr over 6f out* **33/1**

3m 37.5s (-4.20) **Going Correction** -0.425s/f (Good)
WFA 4 from 5yo+ 3lb **13** Ran SP% **115.3**
Speed ratings: **93,91,91,88,88 88,84,83,79,75 73,65,—**
toteswingers: 1&2 £12.90, 1&3 £6.60, 2&3 £17.10 CSF £138.12 TOTE £4.80: £1.40, £4.80, £2.70; EX 85.10.
Owner M Rowe & B Wright **Bred** M Rowe **Trained** Seaborough, Dorset

FOCUS
The winning time was much slower than the second division. Not an easy race to rate but the third is rated close to the best of his Irish form.

NOTEBOOK
Eleven Fifty Nine came from a stable that had a good record at this track in these events and, even though she lacked any racecourse form, was strong in the market. Held up early, she made a decisive move to the front on the home bend and did more than enough to stay there. Connections felt she needed a galloping track, as a sharper one would have been against her. (op 8-1)

Maid Of Silk(IRE) stumbled quite badly in the early stages and lost a bit of ground, but she made good headway in the final stages, despite hanging, and may have given Eleven Fifty Nine plenty to think about had she kept straight and not met traffic. (tchd 25-1)

Forcryingoutloud(IRE) showed some fair form for an Irish stable when last seen, and was strong in the market. He didn't always have the clearest of runs but stayed on well under pressure once in the clear. (op 11-4 tchd 9-4)

Sir Harry Cash, a good-sized individual, must have exceeded his connections' expectations judged on his starting price but may need more time.

Minella(IRE), who was placed on four occasions from six starts in Irish points, is another with plenty of scope and can do well in time. His stable is enjoying a good spell at the moment. (op 12-1)

Doubletoilntrouble(IRE), a brother to 2008 Grand Military Gold Cup Chase winner Bolachior, showed some promise in maiden points and plugged on here after getting warm. (op 9-2)

Love Love Me Do, having her first start since leaving Colin Tizzard, made a little bit of late ground after being behind. (tchd 50-1)

Rody(FR) shaped with loads of promise on his debut (started second favourite) at Uttoxeter recently and travelled well here for much of the race before finding less than expected off the bridle. The jockey was not hard on him in the final stages and he has a good frame to grow into. (op 9-4)

Silver Seraph, out of a winning hurdler, was struck into on this debut and reportedly finished lame. Official explanation: trainer later said gelding was struck into and found to be lame post-race

833 GROUP GRANDSTAND VALUE PACKAGE JUST #15 STANDARD OPEN NATIONAL HUNT FLAT RACE (DIV II) — 2m

5:35 (5:35) (Class 6) 4-6-Y-O — **£1,370** (£399; £199)

Form — RPR

1 **Cock Of The Rock (IRE)**[74] 5-11-3 0 .... APMcCoy 116+
(Keith Goldsworthy) *chsd ldrs: led over 3f out: rdn over 1f out: sn hung rt: all out* **9/1**

2 ½ **Victrix Gale (IRE)** 4-10-0 0 .... DavidBass(7) 104
(Nicky Henderson) *got loose on the way to post: hld up: pushed along and hdwy 10f out: rdn to chse wnr 2f out: styd on u.p* **11/2[3]**

22 3 1¾ **Arthur's Pass**[18] 637 6-10-7 0 .... CiaranMckee(10) 112
(Tom George) *chsd ldrs: outpcd over 5f out: rallied over 2f out: styd on* **5/2[1]**

2 4 3¼ **Whereveryougoigo (IRE)**[10] 739 4-10-9 0 .... DonalDevereux(5) 106
(Peter Bowen) *prom: rdn over 5f out: outpcd 4f out: rallied over 2f out: styd on same pce ins fnl f* **3/1[2]**

5 ½ **Spe Salvi (IRE)** 6-10-10 0 .... DarylJacob 102
(David Arbuthnot) *hld up: pushed along over 5f out: styd on fnl 2f: nt rch ldrs* **28/1**

6 16 **King's Lion (IRE)**[55] 74 6-11-0 0 .... (t) AdamPogson(3) 96+
(Charles Pogson) *led: rdn over 4f out: hdd over 3f out: wknd over 1f out* **9/1**

7 6 **Yu Tiger (IRE)** 4-11-0 0 .... TomScudamore 84
(David Pipe) *in rr: bhd and drvn along 1/2-way: nvr on terms:* **9/1**

05/ 8 2¼ **Dubrovnick (IRE)**[23] 5-11-3 0 .... RichardJohnson 84
(Tim Vaughan) *prom: lost pl 6f out: sme hdwy over 3f out: sn hung lft and wknd* **16/1**

9 1¼ **Drink Up**[51] 6-11-3 0 .... AndrewThornton 83
(John O'Neill) *mid-div: bhd fr 1/2-way* **66/1**

10 12 **Martin Scruff (IRE)** 4-11-0 0 .... JamieMoore 68
(Michael Quinlan) *hld up: bhd fr 1/2-way: t.o* **20/1**

11 8 **Vrondi (IRE)**[25] 6-10-10 0 .... MrBJPoste(7) 63
(William Davies) *hld up: bhd fr 1/2-way: t.o* **100/1**

12 54 **Theatrical Spirit** 5-10-10 0 .... CharliePoste —
(Robin Dickin) *mid-div: rdn 1/2-way: sn wknd: t.o* **66/1**

P **Papa Noel** 4-11-0 0 .... RodiGreene —
(Michael Mullineaux) *chsd ldrs: lost pl 10f out: bhd fr 1/2-way: p.u fnl 6f* **100/1**

P **Stonehenge Lad (AUS)** 5-10-10 0 .... LucyBarry(7) —
(Michael Appleby) *mid-div: dropped in rr 10f out: t.o fr 1/2-way: p.u fnl 6f* **28/1**

3m 32.6s (-9.10) **Going Correction** -0.425s/f (Good)
WFA 4 from 5yo+ 3lb — **14** Ran SP% **121.5**
Speed ratings: **105,104,103,102,102 94,91,89,89,83 79,52,—,—**
toteswingers:1&2 £17.70, 2&3 £5.40, 1&3 £10.40 CSF £56.04 TOTE £10.00: £2.70, £2.80, £1.70; EX 78.00 Place 6: £14548.67 Place 5: £389.07.

Owner The Rooster Partnership **Bred** Michael Forde **Trained** Yerbeston, Pembrokes

FOCUS

The second division of the bumper was run in a time much quicker than the preceding one, and the field came home at long intervals after the leading five finished. The time was good for the type of race and the form is rated positively through the third.

NOTEBOOK

Cock Of The Rock(IRE) had lots of experience in points, winning the last of his eight starts in that sphere. He wore cheekpieces then but not for his debut under rules, and they did not seem to be missed (although he did start to look at the paddock as he came alongside it inside the final furlong) as he stayed on well under pressure. (op 7-1)

Victrix Gale(IRE), a half-sister to a few winners, including the once useful but sadly deceased stayer Takagi, cost £18,500 as a foal but that price tag rose to £48,000 by the time she went through the sales last year at Cheltenham. Running off the lightest weight in this after her claimer reduced her burden by 7lb, she got loose before the start and looked green in the early stages. However, her rider managed to motivate her back into contention and she was only narrowly beaten. (op 9-2 tchd 6-1)

Arthur's Pass, runner-up on both his previous outings over this C&D, including under this 10lb claimer, was a little disappointing as he readily lost his place at one stage before staying on again. (op 3-1)

Whereveryougoigo(IRE), beaten 12l by an 80-1 shot on his debut, shaped like a stayer in this after running a similar race to the horse who finished one place in front of him. (op 7-2 tchd 5-2)

Spe Salvi(IRE), a half-sister to a few winners, caught the eye on her debut after looking a little green. (op 33-1)

King's Lion(IRE), who was having his first start for this trainer, was left well behind by the front quintet. (op 16-1 tchd 17-2)

Yu Tiger(IRE), a half-brother to the smart Champions Gallery, did not run without promise, despite being well behind, and will be better judged after his next effort. (op 10-1 tchd 11-1)

Papa Noel Official explanation: trainer said gelding pulled up distressed

T/Plt: £4,817.50 to a £1 stake. Pool:£47,515.16 - 7.20 winning tickets. T/Qpdt: £70.00 to a £1 stake. Pool: £5,414.29 - 57.22 winning ticket. CR

834 - (Foreign Racing) - See Raceform Interactive

[712]MARKET RASEN (R-H)

Friday, June 25

OFFICIAL GOING: Good to firm (good in places; hdl 7.8 chs 8.5)

Bungalow bend move din 2yds and Wood Bend moved out 2yds.
Wind: light 1/2 behind Weather: fine and sunny, very warm

835 ROWLINSON TIMBER (S) HURDLE (8 hdls) — 2m 1f

2:10 (2:11) (Class 4) 4-6-Y-O — **£2,740** (£798; £399)

Form — RPR

6- 1 **Bandanaman (IRE)**[79] 2513 4-10-9 0 .... BrianHughes 105+
(Alan Swinbank) *trckd ldrs: led appr 2 out: shkn up and wnt clr run-in: easily* **10/3[3]**

020- 2 8 **Treeko (IRE)**[126] 2347 5-10-5 100 .... (p) KyleJames(7) 97
(Philip Kirby) *j.lft 1st: sn chsng ldrs: wnt 2nd appr 2 out: no ch w wnr* **9/2**

14-3 3 10 **Calzaghe (IRE)**[22] 598 6-11-12 112 .... APMcCoy 106
(Jim Best) *chsd ldrs: drvn 5th: wnt 3rd 2 out: sn wknd* **2/1[1]**

P-40 4 dist **Camomile**[30] 470 4-10-0 69 ow5 .... MrJohnDawson(7) 52
(Tracy Waggott) *in rr: hdwy to chse ldrs 3 out: wknd appr next: sn bhd: mstke 2 out* **50/1**

0-P 5 32 **Pay The Russian**[15] 693 4-10-6 0 .... (t) AlexMerriam(3) 25
(Neil King) *hmpd 1st: t.k.h in rr: bhd fr 4th: t.o appr 2 out: blnd last* **66/1**

P **Remark (IRE)**[80] 6-10-12 0 .... TjadeCollier —
(Joanne Foster) *sn bhd: t.o and drvn 3rd: p.u bef 3 out* **66/1**

0-F F **Hannicean**[47] 224 6-10-12 0 .... DougieCostello 85
(Ian Williams) *led: sn clr: hdd appr 2 out: 5 l 4th and wkng whn fell last* **9/4[2]**

F-0 P **James Junior**[23] 349 4-10-9 0 .... WilsonRenwick —
(Peter Niven) *in rr: hung lft bnd after 3rd: sn bhd: t.o whn blnd 5th: sn p.u* **66/1**

4m 8.80s (2.10) **Going Correction** +0.10s/f (Yiel)
WFA 4 from 5yo+ 17lb — **8** Ran SP% **111.8**
Speed ratings: **99,95,90,74,59 —,—,—**
Tote Swingers: 1&2 £3.70, 1&3 £1.80, 2&3 £3.50 CSF £17.57 TOTE £3.60: £1.30, £1.30, £1.10; EX 13.20.Winner bought in for 10,000gns.

Owner Miss J S Peat **Bred** Carradale Ltd & T Stack **Trained** Melsonby, N Yorks

FOCUS

The ground had been well watered to maintain good to firm conditions. This was a typically weak seller but it was run at a sound pace. The easy winner improved to the level expected from his Flat form.

NOTEBOOK

Bandanaman(IRE)was the pick of the paddock beforehand and, despite a few careful jumps, travelled best through the race, moving to close down the leader in the back straight and striding on from the final turn for a comfortable victory. He had made little impression on his sole previous hurdle back in November, but had been well backed last time out on the Flat in April when his chance evaporated after the bit slipped through his mouth, and such was the level of this race that this gave him a shot for his shrewd yard. On this evidence there seems more to come at this level. (op 4-1 tchd 11-4)

Treeko(IRE) has been off the track since a moderate showing on the AW in February, and he was sweating beforehand. After a mistake at the first he held his position and, though he could not match the winner's pace, he stayed on near the finish to suggest that he should come on for this run. He had a couple of bits of form over hurdles last year and if he improves he could gain his first win in moderate company. (op 5-1)

Calzaghe(IRE) had to be scrubbed along to maintain his position, and though he responded he ran a bit scratchily and never looked happy on this fast ground. (op 15-8 tchd 7-4)

Camomile made some promising headway approaching the home turn but faded tamely in the straight. This was a bit of improvement on her previous form but she will need to prove she stays this far if she is to break her maiden. (op 80-1)

Pay The Russian

Remark(IRE) Official explanation: trainer said gelding had a breathing problem (op 2-1 tchd 11-4)

Hannicean took the field along at a good tempo but could not last home and, just as he had at Uttoxeter last month, he got tired, falling at the last. If he is able to settle in mid division he should be capable of a bit better. (op 2-1 tchd 11-4)

836 PD PORTS JUVENILE HURDLE (8 hdls) — 2m 1f

2:40 (2:41) (Class 4) 3-Y-O — **£2,740** (£798; £399)

Form — RPR

1 **Torran Sound**[31] 3-10-12 0 .... (b) FelixDeGiles 82+
(James Eustace) *trckd ldrs: chal last: led nr fin* **17/2**

2 hd **Lady Pacha**[16] 3-10-5 0 .... DougieCostello 74
(Tim Pitt) *w ldrs: led last 150yds: hdd nr fin* **25/1**

3 2¼ **Bring Sweets (IRE)**[17] 3-10-12 0 .... LiamHeard 80
(Brian Ellison) *hld up: prom whn blnd 3rd: upsides last: sn led: hdd 150yds out: no ex* **14/1**

4 nk **Destiny's Dancer**[9] 3-10-5 0 .... BarryKeniry 76+
(Ben Haslam) *chsd ldrs: chalng whn blnd and stmbld last: kpt on fnl 100yds* **11/2**

2 5 2¾ **Sansili**[20] 629 3-10-12 0 .... TomO'Brien 79+
(Peter Bowen) *chsd ldrs: led 2nd: hit last and sn hdd: sn fdd* **3/1[1]**

3 6 hd **Gulf Punch**[17] 674 3-10-2 0 .... PeterToole(3) 69
(Milton Harris) *prom: drvn 3 out: one pce fr next* **9/1**

U 7 ½ **Pobs Trophy**[11] 743 3-10-7 0 .... JamesHalliday(5) 76
(Richard Guest) *in rr: hdwy 3 out: kpt on between last 2* **66/1**

8 2 **Teela** 3-10-7 0 ow2 .... AndrewThornton 69
(Ben Haslam) *in rr: hdwy 4th: one pce fr 3 out* **20/1**

9 2 **Weekend Millionair (IRE)**[24] 3-10-9 0 .... LeeStephens(3) 72
(David Evans) *nt fluent: w ldrs: wknd appr last* **9/2[3]**

10 9 **All Moving Parts (USA)**[24] 3-10-12 0 .... PaddyAspell 64
(John Wainwright) *hld up in rr: hdwy whn nt fluent 2nd: bhd fr 3 out* **18/1**

11 2½ **A P Ling**[24] 3-10-5 0 .... TomMessenger 55
(Christopher Kellett) *stdd s: nt fluent 1st: a in rr* **100/1**

12 66 **Hannour (IRE)** 3-10-12 0 .... (t) PaulMoloney —
(Evan Williams) *led: hdd 2nd: wknd 5th: t.o next* **4/1[2]**

13 30 **Romeos Girl**[59] 3-10-5 0 .... AlanO'Keeffe —
(Jennie Candlish) *in rr: blnd and rdr briefly lost iron 5th: sn t.o* **40/1**

U **Lady Hetherington**[91] 3-9-9 0 .... QuintonJones(10) —
(Gary Brown) *in rr whn mstke and uns rdr 1st* **100/1**

4m 14.5s (7.80) **Going Correction** +0.10s/f (Yiel) — **14** Ran SP% **125.5**
Speed ratings: **85,84,83,83,82 82,82,81,80,75 74,43,29,—**
Tote Swingers: 1&2 £65.10, 1&3 £29.20, 2&3 £54.30 CSF £206.34 TOTE £10.90: £2.60, £9.30, £6.60; EX 254.60.

Owner The MacDougall Two **Bred** R E Crutchley **Trained** Newmarket, Suffolk

FOCUS

This was run at a slower pace than the earlier selling hurdle and it produced a three-way driving finish from the last. The form looks weak.

NOTEBOOK

Torran Sound was sporting blinkers for his hurdling debut reportedly to enable him to race handily, but he still had to fight his corner in the scrimmaging for position, and to his credit he kept finding more despite being carried to his left on the run from the last. He got a bit outpaced in the back straight and took a while to get into gear, but it looks as if he is more suited by the pace over hurdles and has improved on his Flat form. (op 10-1 tchd 11-1)

Lady Pacha avoided trouble by racing up with the pace, which was probably the best tactic given her lack of size, and she stuck to the task well despite drifting left after the last. This was an improvement on her Flat form and she could pick up a similar race. (op 16-1)

Bring Sweets(IRE) made gradual progress to move into a challenging position after the home turn but was just outpaced in a three-way drive to the line. He is a lowly-rated maiden on the Flat and will have to improve a bit to figure over hurdles. Official explanation: trainer's rep said gelding lost a shoe (op 12-1 tchd 16-1)

Destiny's Dancer was travelling well but met some trouble in the straight. First she jinked at the second last when poised to challenge and then caught the top of the final flight and sprawled on landing, before finishing with a rattle. This suggests there should be more to come, if the antics two out do not hint at a questionable attitude. (op 9-2 tchd 4-1)

Sansili had the best of the scant previous jumping form on offer but, despite holding a good position, he was soon outpaced when swamped at the last. (op 9-2)

Weekend Millionair(IRE) was too headstrong but was spooked by the early hurdles. He maintained his position for quite a way so might have more to come if his jumping improves. (op 4-1 tchd 5-1)

837 DFDS TOR LINE NOVICES' H'CAP HURDLE (8 hdls) 2m 1f

3:15 (3:18) (Class 4) (0-100,100) 4-Y-O+ **£2,740** (£798; £399)

Form				RPR
0-3P	1		**Aggravation**[11] 748 8-11-5 **98** MissLHorner[(5)] (Chris Grant) *hld up in rr: hdwy 5th: wnt 2nd 2 out: 3 l down last: styd on to ld towards fin* **14/1**	104
210U	2	*nk*	**Mountskip**[11] 748 6-11-10 **98** WilsonRenwick (Rose Dobbin) *w ldr: led appr 2 out: hdd nr fin* **12/1**	104
00-	3	*15*	**Savaronola (USA)**[46] 4460 5-10-1 **75** PaulMoloney (Barney Curley) *prom: reminders after 3rd: rdn to chse ldrs appr 2 out: kpt on same pce to take modest 3rd nr fin* **15/8**[1]	67+
0/-6	4	*3/4*	**Northern Lad (IRE)**[14] 713 8-11-6 **94** APMcCoy (Jim Best) *led tl after 1st: chsd ldr: led briefly appr 2 out: sn outpcd: lost 3rd nr fin* **5/1**[3]	87
600-	5	*6*	**Ibrox (IRE)**[115] 4368 5-11-11 **99** (p) KeithMercer (Alan Brown) *in rr: hit 3 out: kpt on appr next: nvr nr ldrs* **33/1**	85
0PP-	6	*1 1/2*	**National Heritage**[81] 5045 5-11-7 **95** BarryKeniry (Micky Hammond) *in rr: hdwy 3 out: nvr nr ldrs* **25/1**	80
405-	7	*2 1/2*	**Richo**[229] 2160 4-11-0 **94** AdamPogson[(3)] (Shaun Harris) *t.k.h: in tch: wknd appr 2 out* **40/1**	74
5-56	8	*3/4*	**Sphere (IRE)**[40] 349 5-11-9 **97** AndrewTinkler (John Mackie) *prom: rdn 3 out: sn wknd* **12/1**	79
-215	9	*8*	**J'Adhere (FR)**[14] 713 5-11-12 **100** RichardJohnson (Tim Vaughan) *in rr: wnt prom 3rd: hit 3 out: sn wknd* **9/4**[2]	75
/0-0	10	*12*	**Hollies Favourite (IRE)**[23] 582 7-11-4 **95** (t) AlexMerriam[(3)] (Neil King) *t.k.h in rr: bhd fr 3 out* **80/1**	59
0-66	11	*3 1/2*	**Bold Indian (IRE)**[22] 607 6-10-0 **74** oh7 BrianHughes (Mike Sowersby) *hld up in rr: bhd fr 3 out* **66/1**	35
/F-6	12	*2 3/4*	**Hair Of The Dog**[13] 727 6-10-2 **79** CampbellGillies[(3)] (William Amos) *led after 1st: hdd appr 2 out: wknd qckly* **33/1**	37
-03P	P		**Molesden Glen (IRE)**[11] 748 4-10-6 **90** (t) BrianToomey[(7)] (Simon Waugh) *reluctant to s: chsd ldrs: hit 3 out: wknd qckly: t.o whn p.u bef next* **66/1**	—
-00F	P		**Kashubian Quest**[14] 713 4-10-6 **83** TjadeCollier (Sue Smith) *lost pl 2nd: sn in rr: bhd whn j. bdly lft 2 out: t.o whn j.lft last: p.u run-in: fatally injured* **50/1**	—

4m 6.00s (-0.70) **Going Correction** +0.10s/f (Yiel)
WFA 4 from 5yo+ 17lb **14** Ran SP% **122.6**
Speed ratings (Par 105): **105,104,97,97,94 93,92,92,88,82 81,80,—,—**
Tote Swingers: 1&2 £9.70, 1&3 £18.70, 2&3 £14.80 CSF £159.53 CT £467.26 TOTE £13.50: £4.00, £3.10, £1.50; EX 48.30.
Owner Gareth Cheshire **Bred** John Khan **Trained** Newton Bewley, Co Durham

FOCUS

A competitive handicap with two near the top of the weights pulling clear in a driving finish. Both produced improved form, in the fastest of the three races over the trip.

NOTEBOOK

Aggravation showed good pace to move upsides the leader coming into the straight, and he had to dig deep to just get the better of a tough battle as the line approached. He had pulled up at Sedgefield earlier last month but that run could be forgiven as his saddle slipped. Judged on his good effort at this track back in May he held every chance and, with his amateur partner claiming a useful 5lb, he ran to a similar level of form. He was dismounted after the finish so might need some time to recuperate. (op 12-1)

Mountskip racing prominently, struck the front in the home straight and pulled clear of the field, but could not fight off the sustained challenge of the winner. His form had dipped following a win in a weaker race at Hexham in May, but he could be forgiven his last run at Sedgefield when hampered and unseating his jockey. He bounced back to form here and if anything improved. (op 10-1)

Savaronola(USA) was a little reluctant before the start but set off well enough, however he ran in snatches and never looked a potent threat, only staying on under some pressure to get up for third. He was well backed when winning on the AW last month and looked a possible handicap blot if able to leave his modest hurdling form behind. He did improve on those previous runs but it was not good enough. (tchd 7-4 and 9-4)

Northern Lad(IRE) attracted some market support to improve on his comeback run at this track a fortnight previously, and though he maintained a challenging position into the straight he got outpaced when the tempo quickened. He may need further than this but today he was outclassed. (op 7-1)

Ibrox(IRE) did not jump well enough in the early stages so could only stay on when it was too late, and he will need to improve to figure over hurdles, especially off his current mark. (op 28-1)

J'Adhere(FR) was well supported in the market but ultimately disappointing. (op 3-1 tchd 2-1)

838 GBA GROUP NOVICES' CHASE (14 fncs) 2m 4f

3:50 (3:50) (Class 4) 5-Y-O+ **£3,903** (£1,146; £573; £286)

Form				RPR
464-	1		**Invisible Man (FR)**[90] 4892 5-10-12 115 PaddyBrennan (Ian Williams) *led to 2nd: led 8th: nt fluent next: drew clr appr 2 out: 17 l ahd last: heavily eased* **5/2**[1]	139+
3/32	2	*13*	**Important Business (IRE)**[26] 536 7-10-12 0 SamJones (Renee Robeson) *chsd ldrs: wnt 2nd 9th: wknd 2 out* **3/1**[2]	117
5-2P	3	*1 1/4*	**Magical Legend**[43] 302 9-10-5 0 (t) PaulMoloney (Sophie Leech) *in rr: hdwy 4 out: kpt on to take modest 3rd run-in* **12/1**	109
1F-4	4	*9*	**Viable**[30] 479 8-10-12 116 MissGAndrews[(7)] (Pam Sly) *hld up in rr: hdwy 7th: 3rd and outpcd whn mstke 4 out: wknd run-in* **14/1**	116
F-12	5	*11*	**Baren De Doc (IRE)**[17] 681 7-11-5 118 (p) RichardJohnson (Tim Vaughan) *w ldr: led 2nd: hdd 8th: wknd 10th* **7/2**[3]	108+
0-03	6	*24*	**Moment Present (FR)**[22] 594 5-10-12 115 (p) TomScudamore (Charlie Mann) *chsd ldrs: reminders 8th: sn lost pl: t.o 3 out* **14/1**	72
3-20	7	*4 1/2*	**Tobago Bay**[20] 633 5-10-12 0 (p) JamieGoldstein (Sheena West) *reminders 7th: sn lost pl and bhd: t.o 9th* **5/1**	67

4m 45.5s (-20.20) **Going Correction** -0.70s/f (Firm) **7** Ran SP% **113.5**
Speed ratings: **112,106,106,102,98 88,86**
Tote Swingers: 1&2 £3.00, 1&3 £5.50, 2&3 £6.30 CSF £10.57 TOTE £3.80: £2.40, £1.80; EX 9.90.
Owner Power Panels Electrical Systems Ltd **Bred** J P J Dubois **Trained** Portway, Worcs

FOCUS

There was a battle for the lead for over a circuit and few really got into this, but the winner kept up the gallop to come clear in impressive fashion. This was a big step up on his previous chase form.

NOTEBOOK

Invisible Man(FR) responded well to a positive ride, in the main jumping well, and was never put off his stride despite a good pace, and he had plenty in reserve, flying the third last when fending off a nominal challenge. Last season he had a tendency to find less than expected at the finish, but the change of tactics on his first start for Ian Williams meant he had the race won without coming under pressure at the end. On this performance he should be capable of further success. (op 10-3)

Important Business(IRE) attempted to close down the leader in the back straight, but the effort of trying to make up ground on an uncatchable winner proved too much and he faded over the last two. He has not yet reached the level of his hurdles form, where he was rated 119 at his best, but should be able to win over fences. (op 7-2 tchd 11-4)

Magical Legend did not jump that fluently, and let the leaders get away when jumping slowly in the back straight, but she stayed on near the finish without ever looking a threat. She is a late recruit to chasing but will have to improve rapidly to feature in this sphere. (op 10-1)

Viable did not jump that fluently and was held up in a detached rear position. He settled better than he had last time at Southwell but could only plug on, and may be better when racing more prominently. (op 17-2)

Baren De Doc(IRE) duelled with the winner for over a circuit but eventually found the pace too much and gradually faded out of it. He jumped better than last time especially as he seems to need a stiffer test. (tchd 4-1)

Tobago Bay reportedly needs to lead but he did not jump fluently enough to get to the front on this chasing debut and was never able to get into it. (op 9-2 tchd 4-1)

839 ASSOCIATED BRITISH PORTS H'CAP CHASE (14 fncs) 2m 6f 110y

4:25 (4:25) (Class 3) (0-135,129) 5-Y-O+ **£7,806** (£2,292; £1,146; £572)

Form				RPR
241-	1		**Tempsford (USA)**[258] 1687 10-11-6 **123** (t) APMcCoy (Jonjo O'Neill) *hld up: hdy to trck ldrs 8th: reminders after 4 out: upsides next: rdr lost rt side iron last: styd on to ld towards fin* **9/2**[3]	131+
-051	2	*nk*	**Chorizo (IRE)**[14] 716 9-10-9 **112** PaddyAspell (Richard Guest) *chsd ldrs: hit 5th and 6th: chal 3 out: no ex nr fin* **7/2**[2]	120
14-P	3	*2*	**Silver Adonis (IRE)**[27] 525 9-11-7 **124** (p) DenisO'Regan (Dr Richard Newland) *led to 3rd: chsd ldr: led after 4 out: hdd and no ex fnl 50yds* **10/1**	129
U2-3	4	*3 1/2*	**Mizen Raven (IRE)**[37] 411 7-11-5 **122** (p) JasonMaguire (Peter Bowen) *in tch: chsng ldrs 4 out: outpcd appr next: kpt on fr 2 out* **9/2**[3]	123
-101	5	*3/4*	**Mhilu (IRE)**[4] 696 8-11-5 **129** (b) L-BdrSallyRandell[(7)] (John O'Shea) *t.k.h: sn trcking ldrs: led 3rd: j.rt: hdd after 4 out: one pce* **28/1**	131+
335-	6	*3 1/2*	**Description (IRE)**[59] 33 8-11-5 **122** TjadeCollier (Sue Smith) *chsd ldrs: outpcd appr 3 out* **7/1**	118
1-12	7	*21*	**Nothingbutthetruth (IRE)**[22] 608 6-11-0 **117** DougieCostello (Tim Pitt) *hld up in rr: mstke 5th: hdwy 4 out: lost pl and blnd next: sn bhd* **11/4**[1]	99
360-	P		**Run To Space**[64] 5334 9-10-5 **108** RobertThornton (Nicky Richards) *in rr and drvn 7th: bhd and nt fluent 9th: t.o whn p.u bef 3 out* **12/1**	—

5m 25.6s (-20.40) **Going Correction** -0.70s/f (Firm) **8** Ran SP% **118.0**
Speed ratings: **107,106,106,104,104 103,96,—**
Tote Swingers: 1&2 £4.40, 1&3 £7.20, 2&3 £7.10 CSF £22.01 CT £151.35 TOTE £4.80: £1.80, £1.50, £3.00; EX 22.50.
Owner John P McManus **Bred** Richard S Trontz, Et Al **Trained** Cheltenham, Gloucs
■ Stewards' Enquiry : Denis O'Regan caution: careless riding.

FOCUS

A reasonably competitive handicap that produced a stirring three-way battle from the last. Solid-looking form.

NOTEBOOK

Tempsford(USA), held up early, made some stealthy progress in the back straight but looked to be coming to the end of his tether as they turned for home. However, both horse and rider showed how game they are and they kept on driving to get up in a close battle. He was quietly progressive last season and still looked well treated resuming on a 7lb higher mark for this first run since October. If anything he might have just needed this but it should set him up for any bigger targets back at this course later in the summer. (op 4-1 tchd 7-2)

Chorizo(IRE) made a bold bid to repeat his C&D success of a fortnight previously, but he was just denied in a desperate fight to the line. It did not help that he made a few mistakes, so it suggests that he is still in top form and the 6lb rise for his latest success is well within his capabilities. (op 4-1 tchd 9-2)

Silver Adonis(IRE) was hassled for the lead throughout, which may have exposed his stamina limitations as he was the first to crack in the drive to the line. He was a surprise winner of the Aintree Fox Hunters' Chase over the National fences in April but is better on faster ground, though maybe at slightly shorter trips when the pace is strong. (tchd 12-1)

Mizen Raven(IRE) has been tried with a number of stables and was now running without the usual tongue tie, but he was never a threat. He runs to a consistent enough level that suggests he should win, but he is a frustrating sort for his supporters, though on this occasion the trip might have been a bit far. (op 5-1)

Mhilu(IRE) was keen disputing the lead with the winner but tended to jump out to the right and eventually weakened. He has changed stables several times following some selling hurdle success in the last couple of months, but looks to have regressed a little over fences on his previous form.

Nothingbutthetruth(IRE) could never get into a rhythm at this pace on a right-handed track and laboured along in rear. Official explanation: jockey said gelding never travelled (op 10-3 tchd 7-2 in a place)

840 GP SHIPPING NOVICES' H'CAP CHASE (14 fncs) 2m 6f 110y

4:55 (4:55) (Class 4) (0-105,105) 5-Y-O+ **£3,903** (£1,146; £573; £286)

Form				RPR
/-12	1		**Public Esteem (IRE)**[14] 716 9-10-10 **96** (p) MrsAlexDunn[(7)] (Dr Richard Newland) *mde all: reminders 2nd: kpt on gamely fr 3 out: hld on wl towards fin* **7/2**[1]	106+
0-P3	2	*3/4*	**Old Brigade (IRE)**[22] 597 6-11-0 **93** (t) APMcCoy (Jonjo O'Neill) *chsd ldrs: jnd wnr 8th: drvn 4 out: 3 l down sn after last: styd on u.str.p: a jst hld* **13/2**	101

-F13 **3** 7 **Ginger's Lad**[13] 730 6-10-0 79 (p) BrianHughes 82
(Michael Easterby) *trckd ldrs: t.k.h: 2 l 3rd whn mstke 2 out: keeping on same pce whn hit last* **4/1**[2]
P-05 **4** 3 **Sir Harry Cool**[28] 498 7-11-1 94 DavidEngland 92
(John Panvert) *chsd ldrs: one pce appr 3 out* **11/1**
-552 **5** 2 1/4 **Safe Investment (USA)**[22] 597 6-10-8 87 (p) AndrewThornton 84
(Ben Pollock) *in rr: hit 9th: hdwy 4 out: kpt on fr 2 out: nvr a threat* **12/1**
F1/2 **6** 11 **Tampa Boy (IRE)**[12] 734 8-11-11 104 CharliePoste 94+
(Milton Harris) *hld up: wnt prom 5th: drvn 4 out: 5th and one pce whn mstke 2 out: sn wknd* **6/1**[3]
0-45 **7** 8 **Western Palm (IRE)**[26] 528 7-11-0 96 PeterToole(3) 73
(Charlie Mann) *t.k.h: sn trcking ldrs: 5th and rdn whn hit 4 out: wknd appr next* **33/1**
3243 **8** 1 1/2 **King's Majesty (IRE)**[11] 747 8-10-5 84 (tp) DougieCostello 60
(Tim Pitt) *in rr: nvr a factor* **11/1**
00/0 **9** 1 **First Fought (IRE)**[11] 749 8-10-0 79 oh3 (tp) TjadeCollier 54
(Joanne Foster) *t.k.h: sn trcking ldrs: lost pl after 4 out* **18/1**
P/32 **10** 10 **Gothic Charm (IRE)**[25] 556 8-11-12 105 ChristianWilliams 70
(Rachel Hobbs) *prom: reminders 4th: lost pl 9th: sn bhd: t.o 3 out* **10/1**
PP/- **11** nk **The Masters Lesson**[26] 7-9-11 81 oh15 ow2 JamesHalliday(5) 45
(Keith Reveley) *in rr: bhd fr 8th: t.o 3 out* **14/1**

5m 34.0s (-12.00) **Going Correction** -0.70s/f (Firm) 11 Ran SP% **118.2**
Speed ratings: **92,91,89,88,87 83,80,80,80,76 76**
Tote Swingers: 1&2 £4.10, 1&3 £4.30, 2&3 £3.60 CSF £27.34 CT £95.76 TOTE £2.90: £1.10, £4.40, £1.90; EX 20.60.
Owner Mrs K R Smith-Maxwell **Bred** Neil R Tector **Trained** Claines, Worcs

FOCUS
The pace was only steady, with the finishing time around 8secs slower than the earlier handicap chase, and those racing prominently early on were still there at the finish, though none could get to the winner. He has been rated to his best.

NOTEBOOK
Public Esteem(IRE) was allowed to dictate affairs and was always just holding the challengers at bay. Having just been beaten by Chorizo (who finished a close second in the Class 3 handicap chase on this card) over C&D last time, he had every chance if able to repeat that form. This was a weaker race run at a slower pace, but he was always putting pressure on his rivals and still might be up to winning again even once reassessed. (tchd 3-1)
Old Brigade(IRE) raced on the heels of the winner throughout but, despite being driven up to challenge on the final circuit, he was always held by the winner. He seemed better with give in the ground over hurdles, and similar conditions might suit over fences, so that he is not so likely to get outpaced. (op 6-1)
Ginger's Lad held a prominent position but raced a bit too keenly and was one-paced near the finish. He is still on a feasible mark and could add to his Sedgefield success given a stronger gallop. (op 6-1)
Sir Harry Cool was up with the pace but did not jump that fluently when it mattered and, although just moderate over hurdles, does not look as good over fences. (op 12-1 tchd 10-1)
Safe Investment(USA) is usually held up, as he was again here, but those tactics put him at a disadvantage off a steady pace. He was staying on when losing momentum with a mistake at the second last, so in the circumstances ran better than the bare form suggests. (op 14-1)

841 SVITZER STANDARD OPEN NATIONAL HUNT FLAT RACE 2m 1f
5:25 (5:27) (Class 5) 4-6-Y-0 **£2,055** (£599; £299)

Form RPR
354- **1** **Black Annie (IRE)**[157] 3528 5-10-10 0 (t) APMcCoy 99+
(Paul Webber) *hld up towards rr: stdy hdwy 6f out: chal and hung lft over 2f out: swtchd rt over 1f out: styd on to ld towards fin* **7/2**[2]
00/ **2** 3/4 **Premier Kadam**[27] 5-10-10 0 JakeGreenall(7) 104+
(Michael Easterby) *led 3f: trckd ldrs: t.k.h: led 3f out: hdd and no ex towards fin* **10/1**
03-4 **3** 13 **Wicked Streak (IRE)**[22] 609 5-11-3 0 BarryKeniry 92
(Micky Hammond) *trckd ldrs: led over 4f out: hdd 3f out: wknd over 1f out* **11/2**[3]
66 **4** 1 1/2 **Weldone Honey**[24] 568 5-10-10 0 TomO'Brien 84
(Peter Bowen) *prom: outpcd over 3f out: kpt on fnl 2f* **11/2**[3]
5 4 **Winter Holly** 4-10-7 0 RobertWalford 78
(Tim Walford) *in rr: effrt over 6f out: hmpd bnd over 5f out: one pce fnl 3* **14/1**
3/ **6** 13 **Little Justice**[771] 298 6-10-10 0 CharliePoste 68
(Paul Cowley) *in rr: drvn 6f out: lost pl over 4f out* **20/1**
0 **7** 1/2 **Barnack**[46] 254 4-11-0 0 DavidEngland 72
(Pam Sly) *chsd ldrs drvn 6f out: lost pl over 4f out* **11/1**
8 3 1/2 **Peasant Law** 4-10-7 0 MrJohnDawson(7) 69
(Tracy Waggott) *mid-div: outpcd over 4f out: sn lost pl* **66/1**
9 19 **Alimure** 4-10-7 0 PaddyAspell 45
(C W Thornton) *mid-div: outpcd 7f out: sn lost pl: t.o 4f out* **25/1**
P **10** 3/4 **Monty's Fortune**[14] 718 5-11-3 0 AndrewThornton 54
(Mike Sowersby) *in rr: t.o 3f out* **100/1**
11 1 1/2 **Sir Cycroid Hawk (IRE)** 4-11-0 0 BrianHughes 50
(Alan Swinbank) *chsd ldrs: drvn 7f out: lost pl and hmpd bnd over 5f out: wl bhd and eased 3f out* **5/2**[1]
0 **12** 12 **Pocket Rocket Too**[17] 686 6-10-7 0 AlexMerriam(3) 35
(Neil King) *t.k.h: led after 3f: hdd over 4f out: sn lost pl* **80/1**
0 **13** dist **Silverwort**[22] 609 4-10-11 0 CampbellGillies(3) —
(Mike Sowersby) *t.k.h: hdwy after 4fr: lost pl 7f out: sn t.o: virtually p.u 3f out* **250/1**

4m 4.80s (3.70) **Going Correction** +0.10s/f (Yiel)
WFA 4 from 5yo+ 3lb 13 Ran SP% **118.4**
Speed ratings: **95,94,88,87,85 79,79,77,69,68 67,62,—**
Tote Swingers: 1&2 £13.80, 1&3 £3.50, 2&3 £11.60 CSF £36.39 TOTE £3.30: £1.10, £3.60, £1.70; EX 37.30 Place 6: £113.66 Place 5: £78.41 .
Owner Shully Liebermann **Bred** Mrs Lynne Lyons **Trained** Mollington, Oxon

FOCUS
This was a very modest contest in which three came clear from the home turn. The winner produced improved form.

NOTEBOOK
Black Annie(IRE) travelled best of the field and looked poised to go clear, but she looked awkward when asked and needed some persuasion before she finally knuckled down. However, once she got into a stride she was always going to get the better of the leader. She had disappointed previously in bumpers, but the tongue tie seemed to have an effect and she was the best in a weak race. (op 10-3 tchd 3-1)
Premier Kadam was given every chance, racing prominently and striking the front turning for home, but he had been in front for quite a while and was vulnerable to a faster finisher. After a couple of disappointing efforts in bumpers last year he had shown some improvement in points subsequently, and this run showed he has some prospects for his new stable when given a sterner test. (tchd 14-1)
Wicked Streak(IRE) pulled clear with the leaders from the home turn but could only finish at one pace. His previous bumper runs suggested he lacks a bit of pace for this discipline, and that again seemed the case, but he might do better over jumps. (op 6-1 tchd 5-1)
Weldone Honey needed to bounce back from a disappointing run at Ffos Las earlier this month, but she never really got into it. (op 6-1 tchd 15-2)
Sir Cycroid Hawk(IRE) who, as his name suggests, has only one eye, was under pressure in the back straight and struggled home. Presumably the market support was on the strength of the stable in bumpers rather than this individual. (op 9-4 tchd 15-8)
T/Plt: £710.60 to a £1 stake. Pool: £50,184.58 - 51.55 winning tickets T/Qpdt: £25.60 to a £1 stake. Pool: £4,571.51 - 132.10 winning tickets WG

693 UTTOXETER (L-H)
Sunday, June 27

OFFICIAL GOING: Good to firm (good in places; watered; 7.3)
Shared bends. Penultimate fence omitted on all circuits of the chase course.
Weather: sunny and hot

842 SEVERN VALLEY CATERING NOVICES' HURDLE (10 hdls) 2m
1:40 (1:41) (Class 4) 4-Y-0+ **£2,862** (£840; £420; £209)

Form RPR
3 **1** **Russian George (IRE)**[16] 711 4-10-9 0 KeithMercer 104+
(Steve Gollings) *j.rt: chsd ldrs: clr 3rd whn mstke 7th: hdwy to ld 2 out: j.rt last: drvn out* **1/1**[1]
0-50 **2** 4 1/2 **Basford Tara**[17] 693 5-10-5 0 AlanO'Keeffe 90
(Jennie Candlish) *led: hdd 7th: styd on to take 2nd last: no imp* **40/1**
40 **3** 11 **Cool The Heels (IRE)**[22] 635 5-10-6 0 ow1 MrSJO'Donovan(7) 90+
(Emma Lavelle) *chsd ldr: led 7th: hdd 2 out: wkng whn hit last* **40/1**
0- **4** 7 **Sirjosh**[15] 4786 4-10-9 0 PaulMoloney 76
(Des Donovan) *in rr: kpt on fr 3 out: tk modest 4th run-in* **33/1**
S-4 **5** 3 **Society Venue**[14] 733 5-10-12 0 SamThomas 76
(Michael Scudamore) *t.k.h in rr: nt fluent: wnt modest 4th sn after 7th: eased fr 2 out: fin lame* **15/2**[3]
4-60 **6** 5 **Jobekani (IRE)**[29] 519 4-10-9 98 BrianHughes 68
(Lisa Williamson) *mid-div: rdn 7th: sn wknd* **25/1**
FP/ **7** 7 **Drum Major (IRE)**[8] 2617 5-10-7 0 MarcGoldstein(5) 64
(Jim Best) *mid-div: lost pl 6th: wl bhd fr 3 out* **16/1**
5 **8** 15 **Oh Right (IRE)**[15] 732 6-10-9 0 RyanMania(3) 49
(Dianne Sayer) *chsd ldrs: drvn 5th: rdn and lost pl 7th: t.o next* **33/1**
/5 **9** 8 **John Potts**[49] 224 5-10-12 0 JodieMogford 41
(Brian Baugh) *nt jump wl and j.rt: in rr: mstke 2nd: bhd fr 6th: t.o 3 out* **33/1**
6-11 **R** **Battle Group**[20] 664 5-11-12 116 TomScudamore —
(David Pipe) *ref to r: tk no part* **2/1**[2]

3m 43.3s (-11.90) **Going Correction** -0.925s/f (Hard)
WFA 4 from 5yo+ 17lb 10 Ran SP% **118.5**
Speed ratings (Par 105): **92,89,84,80,79 76,73,65,61,—**
toteswingers:1&2:£8.80, 1&3:£19.70, 2&3:not won CSF £56.31 TOTE £2.10: £1.20, £10.30, £8.00; EX 43.30.
Owner P J Martin **Bred** Martin Walsh **Trained** Scamblesby, Lincs

FOCUS
This was a weak novice hurdle and nothing got involved from off the pace. The winner was value for further but didn't need to improve.

NOTEBOOK
Russian George(IRE) was left with a golden opportunity to open his account over hurdles after his market rival declined to take part, and he obliged at the second attempt. The four-year-old's debut third at Aintree was good enough to ensure he started a short price in this field and he could have been called the winner coming to the penultimate flight. Rated 82 on the Flat, this proves he gets the trip well and defying a penalty at this time of year ought to be well within his compass. (op 11-10 tchd 10-11)
Basford Tara got an aggressive ride and, while he was no match for the winner, this was better from him back down in trip. He is now eligible for handicaps and ought to find his feet in that sphere. (op 50-1)
Cool The Heels(IRE) was another ridden positively and he showed vastly improved form. He too is now eligible for a mark and his shrewd yard can find him an opening during the summer.
Sirjosh was never seriously in the hunt on this return to hurdling and left the impression he would have been closer under a more positive ride.
Society Venue caught the eye somewhat travelling well in midfield, but he ultimately lacked the pace to get involved and likely paid for racing keenly early on. He now has the option of handicaps. Official explanation: vet said gelding finished lame right-fore (op 12-1)
Battle Group, who was on a hat-trick, declined to take part. (op 13-8 tchd 6-4 and 9-4)

843 BANNER MARQUEES MAIDEN HURDLE (DIV I) (12 hdls) 2m 4f 110y
2:10 (2:10) (Class 5) 4-Y-0+ **£1,756** (£515; £257; £128)

Form RPR
20-2 **1** **Benedict Spirit (IRE)**[17] 693 5-11-0 109 (p) RhysFlint 105+
(John Flint) *chsd ldr tl 3 out: n.m.r: swtchd rt and hit 2 out: drvn to chal and j.lft last: led flat: forged ahd fnl 50yds: all out* **2/1**[1]
20-3 **2** 1 **Our Guardian Angel (IRE)**[22] 632 6-10-7 0 (t) RichardJohnson 94
(Tim Vaughan) *in tch in midfeld: mstke 5th: wandered 9th: effrt to chal 3 out: rdn to ld next: jnd and bmpd last: hdd flat: kpt on tl no ex and btn fnl 50yds* **5/1**[2]
3 7 **Rebel Hunter (IRE)**[56] 5-11-0 0 KeithMercer 93+
(Steve Gollings) *chsd ldrs: rdn 3 out: j.rt next: styd on same pce between last 2: wnt 3rd nr fin* **14/1**
26-3 **4** 1/2 **Danimix (IRE)**[14] 733 5-11-0 0 APMcCoy 93
(Peter Bowen) *hld up towards rr: mstke 1st: hdwy after 6th: chsd ldrs and rdn 3 out: swtchd rt between last 2: wnt 3rd last: no imp on ldrs: lost 3rd nr fin* **2/1**[1]
40-P **5** 1 **Himitas (FR)**[19] 684 5-10-7 0 JodieMogford 87
(Graeme McPherson) *t.k.h: hld up wl in tch: mstke 2nd: hdwy to ld and hit 3 out: hdd next: 3rd and wkng whn mstke last* **40/1**
455- **6** 1/2 **Nautical Approach (IRE)**[65] 5359 7-11-0 101 WillKennedy 91
(Alex Hales) *t.k.h: hld up towards rr: hdwy 7th: in tch in midfield and rdn 9th: styd on same pce u.p fr 3 out* **8/1**[3]
7 27 **Honorable Endeavor**[17] 4-10-7 0 AlexMerriam(3) 60
(Edward Vaughan) *t.k.h: hld up in rr: mstke 5th: hdwy and rdn 8th: wknd bef 3 out* **40/1**
05 **8** 1 **Buckden (IRE)**[19] 683 6-11-0 0 TjadeCollier 63
(Sue Smith) *in tch in midfield: nt fluent 1st: mstke 3rd: lost pl and dropped to rr 8th: lost tch bef 3 out* **80/1**
4 **9** 7 **Up And Away (IRE)**[16] 718 5-11-0 0 AndrewThornton 56
(Caroline Bailey) *a towards rr: j. slowly 1st: nt fluent 2nd: rdn and lost tch wl bef 3 out: t.o* **33/1**
03-4 **10** 5 **Klampenborg**[24] 591 5-11-0 0 TomScudamore 51
(Michael Scudamore) *j.rt: led tl hdd and hit 3 out: sn wknd: eased between last 2: t.o* **33/1**

The Form Book, Raceform Ltd, Compton, RG20 6NL

6-24 **11** *6* **Douglas**[28] 538 5-11-0 96........................ MarkGrant 45
(Barry Brennan) *chsd ldrs: mstke 3rd: struggling u.p 9th: wl bhd fr next: t.o* **14/1**

0 **12** *12* **Heavenly Saint**[12] 754 5-10-0 0........................ PeterHatton(7) 26
(Lisa Day) *nt fluent: t.k.h: hld up in tch in rr: lost tch qckly wl bef 3 out: t.o* **100/1**

4m 46.3s (-17.70) **Going Correction** -0.925s/f (Hard)
WFA 4 from 5yo+ 18lb **12** Ran SP% **120.8**
Speed ratings (Par 103): **96,95,92,92,92 92,81,81,78,76 74,70**
toteswingers:1&2:£2.70, 1&3:£6.70, 2&3:£13.90 CSF £12.62 TOTE £2.70: £1.10, £1.90, £2.70; EX 11.80.
Owner Jason Tucker **Bred** Allevamento Pian Di Neve Srl **Trained** Kenfig Hill, Bridgend

FOCUS
An ordinary maiden that saw the first pair come clear. The winner is rated better than the bare result.

NOTEBOOK
Benedict Spirit(IRE) was never far away and showed a willing attitude in the home straight to come out on top. He was produced to go for everything coming to the last, but rather ballooned it and had to work hard to repel the runner-up on the run-in. He still has something to learn in the jumping department and probably didn't have to improve much on his recent second over course and distance, but is open to a little further progression. (op 9-4)
Our Guardian Angel(IRE) took it up at the third-last and made a bold bid to open her account. She just got outstayed by the winner over this longer trip, but finished a clear second-best and should soon be winning. (tchd 6-1)
Rebel Hunter(IRE),a winning Irish pointer, was making his hurdling debut for new connections and ran well. A longer trip ought to suit and this was a pleasing introduction. (tchd 12-1 and 16-1)
Danimix(IRE) was ridden to get the longer distance. He was under pressure turning for home and, on this evidence, wants dropping back to a sharper test. (op 15-8, touched 9-4 in a place)
Himitas(FR) was produced with every chance and posted by far her most encouraging effort to date. (op 33-1)
Nautical Approach(IRE) has had plenty of chances and helps to put this form into perspective. (tchd 12-1)

844 BRITANNIA ENGLISH SUMMER NATIONAL H'CAP CHASE (LISTED RACE) (18 fncs 3 omitted) 3m 4f
2:40 (2:42) (Class 1) 5-Y-0+

£28,505 (£10,695; £5,355; £2,670; £1,340; £670)

Form RPR

01-0 **1** **Ouzbeck (FR)**[30] 503 8-11-6 **142**........................ JackDoyle 153
(Emma Lavelle) *trckd ldrs: t.k.h: led appr last: jst hld on* **14/1**

3P1- **2** *hd* **Brooklyn Brownie (IRE)**[66] 5336 11-10-8 **135**........... JamesHalliday(5) 146
(Malcolm Jefferson) *hld up: stdy hdwy 4 out: chal last: jst denied* **28/1**

FP-1 **3** *2 1/2* **Valley Ride (IRE)**[19] 003 10-10-7 **129**........................(p) TomO'Brien 137
(Peter Bowen) *prom: lost pl 8th: hdwy 4 out: 7th 2 out: 11 l down on ldrs in 4th last: fin wl* **14/1**

P2F- **4** *nk* **Minella Four Star (IRE)**[61] 38 7-10-1 **123**.............(p) TomScudamore 133+
(David Pipe) *led: blnd 6th: hdd 8th: led 12th: hdd appr last: one pce* **9/1**

2-22 **5** *1 3/4* **Templer (IRE)**[29] 525 9-10-5 **127**........................ RichardJohnson 135
(Philip Hobbs) *chsd ldrs: one pce fr 4 out* **8/1**[3]

6 *9* **Classic Frontier (IRE)**[21] 658 8-10-5 **127**..................(t) RobertThornton 127+
(C Byrnes, Ire) *in rr: hdwy 8th: chsng ldrs 14th: wknd next: 6th whn hmpd 3 out* **6/1**[1]

3-12 **7** *13* **Ballycarney (IRE)**[14] 735 6-10-1 **123**........................ JohnnyFarrelly 107
(Emma Lavelle) *chsd ldrs: 3rd whn blnd 13th: wknd 4 out* **15/2**[2]

1132 **8** *5* **Take The Stand (IRE)**[22] 628 14-9-11 **126**...............(p) MrMByrne(7) 113
(Peter Bowen) *in rr-div: sme hdwy 4 out: 7th and wkng whn hmpd next* **16/1**

PF-3 **9** *30* **That's Rhythm (FR)**[57] 98 10-10-13 **135**..................(p) DenisO'Regan 84
(Martin Todhunter) *mid-div: outpcd and lost pl 13th: sn bhd: t.o* **14/1**

UP-0 **P** **Lothian Falcon**[35] 446 11-10-0 **122**........................ RobertWalford —
(Peter Maddison) *in rr: struggling whn p.u bef 10th* **16/1**

2F3- **P** **Knowhere (IRE)**[70] 5247 12-11-4 **140**........................(b) PaddyBrennan —
(Nigel Twiston-Davies) *mid-div whn hmpd 1st: blnd 6th: lost pl 14th: bhd whn p.u bef 3 out* **22/1**

P-0F **P** **Seymar Lad (IRE)**[30] 501 10-10-3 **125**........................ LeightonAspell —
(Emma Lavelle) *nt fluent in last: t.o 12th: p.u after 14th* **66/1**

PP-1 **P** **Victor Daly (IRE)**[44] 314 9-9-12 **125**........................ JimmyDerham(5) —
(Martin Keighley) *chsd ldrs: lost pl qckly and p.u bef 4 out* **10/1**

233- **F** **Mumbles Head (IRE)**[141] 3898 9-10-10 **137**............... DonalDevereux(5) 140+
(Peter Bowen) *hld up: hmpd 1st: hdwy to trck ldrs 14th: cl 3rd whn fell 3 out* **12/1**

U13- **P** **Leac An Scail (IRE)**[61] 33 9-9-8 **123**........................ DavidBass(7) —
(Sue Smith) *w ldr: led 8th tl 12th: wknd qckly 14th: bhd whn p.u bef 2 out* **12/1**

0F-1 **P** **Keepitsecret (IRE)**[43] 335 9-10-12 **134**........................ APMcCoy —
(Jonjo O'Neill) *in rr: bhd fr 12th: t.o whn p.u bef 2 out* **14/1**

2F-1 **P** **Auroras Encore (IRE)**[57] 98 8-11-7 **148**........................ ShaneByrne(5) —
(Sue Smith) *chsd ldrs: hit 14th: wknd next: sn bhd: t.o whn p.u bef last* **16/1**

F- **P** **Clifton Debut**[21] 658 7-9-11 **124**........................ SamTwiston-Davies(5) —
(Henry De Bromhead, Ire) *blnd 1st and rdr briefly lost iron: nt jump wl in rr: bhd fr 8th: t.o whn p.u bef 14th* **20/1**

7m 3.70s (-17.80) **Going Correction** -0.35s/f (Good) course record **18** Ran SP% **130.0**
Speed ratings: **111,110,110,110,109 107,103,101,93,— —,—,—,—,— —,—,—**
toteswingers:1&2:£67.90, 1&3:£54.30, 2&3:£60.50 CSF £373.45 CT £5530.02 TOTE £17.20: £3.00, £4.10, £4.30, £2.90; EX 586.50 TRIFECTA Not won..
Owner Axom VII **Bred** Francois-Xavier & Anne Douce Lefeuvre **Trained** Wildhern, Hants

FOCUS
A valuable prize and a fittingly competitive line-up for this marathon contest. There was a good gallop on and most were found out before the home turn. Very solid form.

NOTEBOOK
Ouzbeck(FR), whose stable won the race last season, dug deep after taking it up at the last and ran out a really game winner. He had been given a prep run over hurdles 30 days earlier, but had won off an 8lb lower mark at Cheltenham on his previous outing over fences and has been handled really well by his current yard. This will no doubt tempt connections into a possible bid at the big one at Aintree next April. (op 12-1 tchd 16-1)
Brooklyn Brownie(IRE) had resumed winning ways at Perth off a 6lb lower mark on his previous outing. He hit top gear turning for home and gave his all, but was always just being held on the run-in. He gives the form a good look. (op 33-1)
Valley Ride(IRE), another winner last time out, in his case over hurdles, had failed to complete on his last two outings in this sphere. He was always staying on too late, but this was a performance he could build on. (op 12-1 tchd 11-1 and 16-1 in a place)
Minella Four Star(IRE) was making his debut for new connections and was the only one in this line-up to have previously won over the trip. He was not surprisingly given an aggressive ride and posted a sound effort for one so inexperienced. (op 8-1)
Templer(IRE) is better known as a hunter chaser these days, but he stays very well and ran a decent race on ground he enjoys. (op 11-1)

Classic Frontier(IRE), a well-backed Irish raider, was awash with sweat during the race and he was held prior to being hampered. (tchd 13-2)
Lothian Falcon Official explanation: jockey said gelding never travelled (op 10-1)
Mumbles Head(IRE), who was making his returning from a 141-day break and had some decent novice form last season, was the hard-luck story He was given a lovely ride, creeping into things around the home turn, and looked the most likely winner prior to falling three out. Providing he is none the worse for this experience, there should be a decent pot in him at some stage. (op 10-1)

845 SUSAN FERGUSON 60TH BIRTHDAY H'CAP HURDLE (10 hdls) 2m
3:10 (3:12) (Class 5) (0-95,95) 4-Y-0+ **£2,081** (£611; £305; £152)

Form RPR

P4-2 **1** **Hoar Frost**[24] 600 5-11-9 **92**........................ APMcCoy 98+
(Jim Best) *led tl 3rd: chsd ldr tl led again 6th: rdn 3 out: drvn between last 2: styd on u.p flat* **15/8**[1]

-003 **2** *2* **Three Ships**[17] 698 9-11-5 **95**........................ AdamWedge(7) 99
(S Wynne) *t.k.h: in tch in midfield: j.rt 4th: chsd wnr after 6th: rdn bef 3 out: 1 l down and hit last: one pce u.p flat* **12/1**

60-0 **3** *5* **Boo**[18] 527 8-10-13 **87**........................ LeeEdwards(5) 85
(James Unett) *chsd ldrs: 3rd bef 3 out: kpt on same pce u.p between last 2* **14/1**

0-15 **4** *1 1/4* **Shipboard Romance (IRE)**[13] 527 5-11-5 **91**...............(t) PeterToole(3) 89
(Mark Rimell) *t.k.h: hld up in tch in rr: stdy hdwy bef 3 out: chsd ldng trio 2 out: rdn and no imp between last 2* **7/1**[3]

534- **5** *1/2* **Shannersburg (IRE)**[155] 830 5-11-6 **89**.....................(tp) PaddyBrennan 86
(Ian Williams) *hld up in rr: pushed along and modest hdwy bef 3 out: no prog fr 2 out: nvr trbld ldrs* **5/1**[2]

4-00 **6** *6* **Mix N Match**[39] 410 6-11-0 **90**........................ AodhaganConlon(7) 80
(Gerald Ham) *in tch in midfield: chsd ldng trio wl bef 3 out: wknd u.p 2 out* **10/1**

255- **7** *7* **Rince Donn (IRE)**[80] 5104 8-10-13 **85**........................ HaddenFrost(3) 68
(Roger Curtis) *t.k.h: hld up in tch in midfield: rdn and btn bef 3 out* **25/1**

0026 **8** *9* **Billy Beetroot (USA)**[17] 696 4-11-1 **90**........................ LeeStephens(3) 61
(Katie Stephens) *a towards rr: rdn and no hdwy wl bef 3 out: wl bhd next* **33/1**

P-34 **9** *26* **Mujamead**[17] 698 6-11-3 **86**........................ ChristianWilliams 34
(Sally-Anne Wheelwright) *hld up towards rr: rdn and wl btn after 7th: t.o fr next* **11/1**

0-00 **U** **Racingisdreaming (USA)**[24] 595 4-11-0 **86**...........(tp) TomScudamore —
(David Pipe) *chsd ldrs tl blnd and uns rdr 6th* **14/1**

0-FP **P** **Haling Park (UAE)**[40] 384 4-11-1 **87**........................ RichardJohnson —
(Tim Vaughan) *chsd ldr tl led 3rd tl 6th: dropped out rapidly and wl bhd next: t.o whn p.u 3 out* **12/1**

3m 41.10 (-14.10) **Going Correction** -0.925s/f (Hard)
WFA 4 from 5yo+ 17lb **11** Ran SP% **116.9**
Speed ratings (Par 103): **98,97,94,93,93 90,87,82,69,— —**
toteswingers:1&2:£4.40, 1&3:£7.70, 2&3:£35.30 CSF £25.20 CT £250.47 TOTE £2.50: £1.40, £2.70, £3.10; EX 24.20.
Owner M&R Refurbishments Ltd **Bred** Mike Channon Bloodstock Ltd **Trained** Lewes, E Sussex

FOCUS
An ordinary handicap, run at a solid gallop. The form is sound enough.

NOTEBOOK
Hoar Frost was given a no-nonsense ride on the front end and went one better than her second over C&D 24 days earlier. She was 4lb higher, but probably didn't have to improve to take this and another rise could just find her out next time. (op 11-8)
Three Ships was the only one to take a real race of it with the winner from three out, but was always being held. This was a sound effort under top weight and he helps to set the standard. (tchd 10-1 and 14-1)
Boo went without the visor and posted a much-improved display. He has failed to score since 2005, however, and his proximity sums up the strength of this contest. (op 18-1 tchd 12-1)
Shipboard Romance(IRE) ran her race and continues to look held by the handicapper. (op 13-2 tchd 8-1)
Shannersburg(IRE) was equipped with first-time cheekpieces on this debut for a new yard and was restrained early. He plugged on all too late down the home straight should improve for the outing. (op 8-1)

846 LADIES AT THE RACES H'CAP HURDLE (12 hdls) 2m 4f 110y
3:45 (3:45) (Class 4) (0-115,115) 4-Y-0+ **£2,992** (£878; £439; £219)

Form RPR

/1-0 **1** **Breaking Storm (IRE)**[22] 627 7-11-7 **115**........................ JamesHalliday(5) 120+
(Kate Walton) *hld up in rr: stdy hdwy 8th: rdn 3 out: str run to ld sn after 2 out: drvn out* **11/2**[2]

31P/ **2** *2 3/4* **Herne Bay (IRE)**[707] 992 10-11-3 **106**........................(t) PaddyBrennan 106
(Ian Williams) *hld up in rr: hdwy 9th: chsng ldrs 3 out: wnt 2nd last: styd on same pce out* **9/1**

5-P0 **3** *5* **Winsley Hill**[16] 708 8-11-5 **115**........................ MarkQuinlan(7) 112+
(Neil Mulholland) *chsd ldrs: wnt 2nd 8th: hit 3 out: sn led: hdd sn after 2 out: wknd towards fin* **20/1**

04-5 **4** *2 1/4* **Ovthenight (IRE)**[28] 351 5-11-0 **110**........................(p) MissGAndrews(7) 103
(Pam Sly) *trckd ldrs: outpcd and n.m.r on inner appr 2 out: kpt on run-in* **8/1**

13-2 **5** *hd* **Jimbatai (IRE)**[38] 420 7-11-4 **110**........................ DannyCook(3) 105
(Barry Leavy) *chsd ldrs: outpcd 2 out: modest 4th whn hit last: kpt on* **9/2**[1]

0-00 **6** *15* **Daurica**[22] 633 6-11-5 **115**........................ BrianToomey(7) 93
(Renee Robeson) *in rr: bhd and drvn after 6th: nvr on terms* **16/1**

022- **7** *hd* **Taffy Thomas**[65] 5358 6-11-10 **113**........................ TomO'Brien 91
(Peter Bowen) *in tch: drvn 7th: lost pl appr 3 out* **15/2**

-P20 **8** *2* **Downing Street (IRE)**[16] 708 9-11-10 **113**...................(bt) AlanO'Keeffe 89
(Jennie Candlish) *s.s and reluctant: in rr: bhd fr 7th* **12/1**

3P-3 **9** *shd* **O'Toole (IRE)**[20] 664 11-11-7 **115**........................ IanPopham(5) 91
(Caroline Keevil) *chsd ldrs: lost pl appr 3 out: eased run-in* **16/1**

10F/ **10** *3 3/4* **Quaddick Lake (IRE)**[426] 15 7-11-12 **115**........................ TomScudamore 89
(David Pipe) *led: hit 3 out: sn hdd & wknd: wl btn 6th whn eased last* **7/1**[3]

4-54 **11** *17* **Woody Valentine (USA)**[29] 515 9-11-5 **108**........................ TjadeCollier 63
(Evelyn Slack) *chsd ldrs: reminders 6th: lost pl 7th: sn bhd* **9/1**

20-P **12** *9* **Viva Colonia (IRE)**[28] 530 5-11-4 **107**........................(tp) PaulMoloney 53
(Charlie Mann) *hld up in rr: hdwy 8th: chsng ldrs after next: lost pl bef 3 out* **16/1**

2U6- **P** **Liberty Seeker (FR)**[223] 2332 11-10-10 **106**........................ JoeCornwall(7) —
(John Harris) *in rr: detached in last and drvn 6th: t.o whn p.u after next* **33/1**

4m 41.5s (-22.50) **Going Correction** -0.925s/f (Hard) **13** Ran SP% **122.0**
Speed ratings (Par 105): **105,103,102,101,101 95,95,94,94,93 86,83,—**
toteswingers:1&2:£15.50, 1&3:£44.70, 2&3:£54.10 CSF £55.95 CT £940.54 TOTE £5.60: £2.20, £4.40, £8.70; EX 66.90.
Owner Yarm Racing Partnership **Bred** Miss Marie Harding **Trained** Middleham Moor, N Yorks

FOCUS
A wide-open handicap and they went a good gallop in the fastest time of the races over the trip. The form could have been rated a few pounds higher.

NOTEBOOK
Breaking Storm(IRE) bounced back to winning ways under a well-judged ride. Ridden to get the longer trip, he got going down the home straight and it was apparent coming to the last he was going to get up. This was a career-best effort. (op 15-2 tchd 8-1)
Herne Bay(IRE) was making his debut for Ian Williams and having a first outing since 2008. Indeed he landed this race back in 2005 and was back down to his last winning mark, so it wasn't that surprising to see him run a big race. One will have to be very wary of the bounce factor next time, though. (op 8-1)
Winsley Hill was bang there three out and this was much more like it again from her. She is weighted to strike over hurdles and could find a race back up in distance.
Ovthenight(IRE) hit a flat spot before staying on again all too late. (op 10-1)
Jimbatai(IRE) was well held on this debut in handicap company over hurdles. (op 5-1 tchd 11-2)

847 HEXLEASE.COM MAIDEN HURDLE (DIV II) (12 hdls) 2m 4f 110y
4:20 (4:20) (Class 5) 4-Y-0+ **£1,756** (£515; £257; £128)

Form RPR
3-22 **1** **Hadron Collider (FR)**[22] 635 5-10-11 **114**........................ PeterToole[(3)] 109+
(Charlie Mann) *hld up in tch: hdwy to chse ldr and mstke 8th: rdn to ld after 3 out: hit 2 out: styd on gamely u.p flat and asserted fnl 150yds: all out* **7/2**[2]
45-2 **2** *1 ½* **Just Victor**[29] 522 5-11-0 **110**..(t) SamThomas 109+
(Paul Webber) *t.k.h: in tch: led 7th: rdn and hdd after 3 out: hit next: stl ev ch after tl btn fnl 150yds: eased towards fin* **9/4**[1]
02/4 **3** *1 ¼* **Last One Standing**[59] 62 6-11-0 **0**............................ JamieGoldstein 105
(Sheena West) *hld up in tch in midfield: chsd ldrs 7th: rdn and outpcd bef 3 out: kpt on gamely u.p flat: styng on at fin: lame* **9/1**[3]
4 *½* **Mariinsky (GER)**[57] 101 4-10-10 **0**............................ RichardJohnson 102+
(Tim Vaughan) *t.k.h: hld up in tch: hdwy to chse ldrs 7th: 3rd and rdn whn hit 3 out: outpcd and mstke next: styd on same pce after* **9/4**[1]
5 *42* **Cloudy Dawn**[55] 5-11-0 **0**.. BrianHughes 62
(Sue Smith) *t.k.h: chsd ldrs: nt fluent and rdn 9th: wkng whn hit 3 out: sn lost tch: t.o* **16/1**
63 **6** *14* **Burnthill (IRE)**[43] 337 5-11-0 **0**.................................. LiamTreadwell 48
(Claire Dyson) *chsd ldr tl after 6th: wknd bef 9th: t.o fr 3 out: j.rt last* **22/1**
000- **7** *1* **Master Cardor Visa (IRE)**[112] 4461 5-10-11 **0**................ TomMolloy[(3)] 47
(Emma Baker) *j. slowly 1st and 4th: a bhd: lost tch 7th: t.o bef 3 out* **66/1**
PPF- **8** *21* **Gladeemma**[66] 5328 5-10-7 **0**.. CharliePoste 19
(Paul Cowley) *in tch towards rr: mstke 5th and 6th: struggling whn blnd 8th: t.o bef 3 out* **100/1**
P46- **P** **Kirkum (IRE)**[57] 5050 5-10-7 **0**..............................(p) MattCrawley[(7)] —
(Diana Weeden) *nt fluent: a in rr: rdn and no rspnse 5th: t.o 7th tl p.u 2 out* **100/1**
0/ **P** **Tough Cookie (IRE)**[29] 7-10-7 **0**.................................. MrJEngland[(7)] —
(Michael Gates) *racd keenly: led tl 7th: wknd qckly next: t.o whn p.u 2 out* **20/1**
0- **P** **Alaskan Prince (IRE)**[196] 2862 5-11-0 **0**...................... TomScudamore —
(Charlie Longsdon) *t.k.h: chsd ldrs tl after 6th: wkng qckly and mstke 8th: wl t.o whn p.u 2 out* **33/1**

4m 44.0s (-20.00) **Going Correction** -0.925s/f (Hard)
WFA 4 from 5yo+ 18lb **11** Ran SP% **115.2**
Speed ratings (Par 103): **101,100,99,99,83 78,78,70,—,— —**
toteswingers:1&2:£2.50, 1&3:£3.70, 2&3:£3.40 CSF £11.23 TOTE £4.10: £1.50, £1.40, £2.20; EX 7.40.
Owner John & Peter Heron **Bred** Serpentine Bloodstock Et Al **Trained** Upper Lambourn, Berks

FOCUS
This second division of the maiden was another moderate affair. The form is sound.

NOTEBOOK
Hadron Collider(FR) took it up three from home and knuckled down gamely thereafter. He had been placed on his three previous outings, so this was much deserved and he is going the right way. However, he would look somewhat vulnerable under a penalty in this sphere. (op 3-1)
Just Victor, second at Stratford 29 days earlier, was given every chance on this return to novice company. He made a mistake at the third-last just as the winner was hitting top gear and was fighting a losing battle thereafter. (op 2-1, touched 5-2 in a place)
Last One Standing ◆ was doing all of his best work at the finish late on over this longer trip. He didn't get a good trip through the race, though, continually racing on the outer of runners, and is a little better than the bare form. Official explanation: vet said gelding returned lame (op 8-1)
Mariinsky(GER), making his British debut for new connections, was right in the thick of things prior to hitting three out. He was never really on terms from that point but ran on gamely for pressure and can be found an opening before too long. (op 5-2 tchd 11-4 and 2-1 and 3-1 in a place)

848 IAN SHIPTON CARS.CO.UK H'CAP CHASE (10 fncs 2 omitted) 2m
4:55 (4:55) (Class 4) (0-115,116) 5-Y-0 **£3,802** (£1,123; £561; £280; £140)

Form RPR
12/1 **1** **Yellow Flag**[7] 799 7-11-11 **108** 7ex.. APMcCoy 123+
(Jonjo O'Neill) *hld up: hdwy 4th: chal 2 out: hit last: styd on to ld last 100yds* **7/4**[1]
3-P2 **2** *1 ¼* **One Of The Boys (IRE)**[7] 799 9-10-11 **94**................. RichardJohnson 108
(Tim Vaughan) *mstke 1st: jnd ldrs 3rd: led appr 2 out: hdd and no ex last 100yds* **5/1**[2]
-32B **3** *6* **Kirkhammerton (IRE)**[32] 477 8-11-0 **100**.................. DannyCook[(3)] 107
(Barry Leavy) *in rr: hdwy appr 2 out: styd on to take modest 3rd clsng stages* **20/1**
-2P1 **4** *1 ¼* **Mibleu (FR)**[4] 831 10-12-0 **116** 7ex................................ KeiranBurke[(5)] 123
(R H & Mrs S Alner) *hld up in rr: gd hdwy to trck ldrs 3 out: rdn appr last: j.rt: sn fdd* **9/1**
1-23 **5** *16* **The Kealshore Kid (IRE)**[33] 460 6-11-5 **102**..................... BarryKeniry 92
(George Moore) *towards rr: drvn and sme hdwy appr 3 out: sn wknd* **8/1**[3]
5P-1 **6** *7* **Ormus**[15] 728 7-10-11 **94**...(p) PaddyAspell 77
(Christopher Wilson) *w ldrs: led 7th: hdd appr 2 out: sn wknd* **12/1**
1335 **7** *4 ½* **Coach Lane**[19] 676 9-11-9 **106**.. AidanColeman 84
(Venetia Williams) *mid-div: drvn 7th: wknd 3 out* **22/1**
-164 **8** *8* **Schinken Otto (IRE)**[13] 747 9-10-5 **93**.................. JamesHalliday[(5)] 63
(Malcolm Jefferson) *led: hdd 6th: wknd and blnd 3 out* **16/1**
36-0 **9** *13* **King Ozzy (IRE)**[16] 715 6-11-11 **108**............................ RobertThornton 65
(Martin Keighley) *hld up: hdwy 5th: chsng ldrs 3 out: sn wknd* **20/1**
43-5 **10** *17* **Indiana Gold (FR)**[13] 746 6-10-12 **95**............................ DarylJacob 35
(Alison Thorpe) *in rr: hdwy 6th: sn drvn: reminders and lost pl next: bhd whn mstke 3 out* **10/1**
4-41 **P** **Arumun (IRE)**[33] 460 9-11-0 **97**.................................... TomScudamore —
(Michael Scudamore) *chsd ldrs: led 6th: hdd next: 6th and wkng whn blnd 2 out: bhd whn p.u bef last* **16/1**
U-23 **P** **Chilbury Hill (IRE)**[22] 634 7-11-2 **99**.................................... LiamHeard —
(Kevin Bishop) *in rr: last whn blnd 3rd: wl bhd whn blnd next: sn p.u* **22/1**

3m 52.0s (-3.60) **Going Correction** -0.35s/f (Good) **12** Ran SP% **120.9**
Speed ratings: **95,94,91,90,82 79,77,73,66,58 —,—**
toteswingers:1&2:£3.30, 1&3:£12.60, 2&3:£18.10 CSF £10.95 CT £129.89 TOTE £3.00: £1.30, £1.70, £6.30; EX 11.80.
Owner John P McManus **Bred** Darley **Trained** Cheltenham, Gloucs

FOCUS
A modest, but competitive handicap. The form looks solid enough.

NOTEBOOK
Yellow Flag eventually came out on top and followed up his comeback win a week earlier under a typically never-say-die ride from the champion. He looked held at the second-last but kept finding for maximum pressure and probably had a little to spare at the line. This rates a fine training performance. (op 9-4)
One Of The Boys(IRE) had a 7lb pull with the winner on their last-time-out running and looked likely to reverse it at the last fence. He was unable to sustain his effort when it mattered but does deserve to go one better. (op 6-1 tchd 9-2)
Kirkhammerton(IRE) looked like being a back number around four out, but he was motoring home inside the home straight. Surely stepping up in trip can see him find a race in this sphere. (op 18-1)
Mibleu(FR), penalised for winning at Worcester four days earlier, again travelled up to the leaders going easily three out. He ultimately faded after the last, though, and shaped as though the run came a bit too soon. (op 8-1)
The Kealshore Kid(IRE) wasn't disgraced and helps to set the level.
Ormus had his chance on this quicker ground and looked to be found out by his 5lb higher mark. (op 10-1)

849 COME AND JOIN CHASING GOLD RACING CLUB NOVICES' H'CAP HURDLE (12 hdls) 2m 6f 110y
5:30 (5:30) (Class 5) (0-95,94) 4-Y-0+ **£2,341** (£687; £343; £171)

Form RPR
25-1 **1** **Fealing Real (IRE)**[7] 795 8-11-8 **90**....................................(t) APMcCoy 101+
(Rebecca Curtis) *mde all: clr fr 3rd: rdn bef 2 out: pressed and drvn last: styd on gamely flat* **5/4**[1]
002/ **2** *¾* **Corso Palladio (IRE)**[604] 1930 8-11-5 **87**.......................(p) TomO'Brien 94
(Peter Bowen) *chsd ldrs: chsd clr wnr after 7th: rdn and clsd between last 2: kpt on same pce u.p flat: hld towards fin* **14/1**
U2P- **3** *¾* **Norwest (IRE)**[96] 4798 7-11-11 **93**..............................(t) RichardJohnson 99
(Tim Vaughan) *in tch in midfield: chsd ldng pair 8th: rdn and hit 3 out: drvn and clsd on wnr between last 2: no ex and btn fnl 150yds* **3/1**[2]
1-34 **4** *13* **Richard The Third**[28] 539 6-11-12 **94**.......................... AndrewThornton 87
(John Harris) *racd in midfield: pushed and chsd ldng trio bef 9th: no prog u.p between last 2: wknd last: dismntd after fin* **16/1**
-443 **5** *8* **Cool Bob (IRE)**[14] 737 7-11-9 **91**.................................(t) PaddyBrennan 79
(Matt Sheppard) *hld up wl bhd: hdwy 7th: modest 5th 9th: no hdwy bef 2 out: wknd between last 2* **7/1**[3]
PU-0 **6** *28* **Fly Direct (IRE)**[58] 84 7-11-8 **90**............................(p) ChristianWilliams 47
(Lawney Hill) *chsd wnr tl after 6th: dropped out qckly after next: t.o bef 3 out* **25/1**
50-0 **7** *3 ¾* **Raisthorpe**[16] 713 6-11-0 **82**...(p) BrianHughes 36
(Tim Fitzgerald) *racd off the pce in midfield: nt fluent 2nd: j.rt next: rdn and lost tch 7th: t.o bef 3 out* **100/1**
4P-P **8** *66* **Dashing Bach (IRE)**[17] 698 6-10-2 **77**.....................(tp) OliverDayman[(7)] —
(Alison Thorpe) *a in rr: mstke 2nd: rdn and toiling bdly after 6th: wl t.o fr 9th* **25/1**
00/0 **9** *1 ½* **Weather Permitting (IRE)**[13] 749 7-11-9 **91**..........(tp) TomScudamore —
(David Pipe) *t.k.h: chsd ldrs tl 6th: lost pl qckly next: wl t.o bef 3 out* **20/1**
/43- **P** **Kingfisher Niamh**[385] 632 10-11-1 **83**..............................(t) CharliePoste —
(Paul Cowley) *chsd ldrs: struggling u.p after 7th: 6th and losing tch 9th: t.o whn p.u last* **40/1**
5533 **P** **Wee Ziggy**[16] 713 7-11-0 **82**... RodiGreene —
(Michael Mullineaux) *hld up wl in rr: mstke 5th: rdn and no rspnse 7th: wl t.o fr 9th tl p.u 2 out* **12/1**
0-6 **U** **Baltimore Patriot (IRE)**[32] 480 7-11-5 **94**........................ RyanRaftery[(7)] —
(Barry Brennan) *hld up in rr tl mstke and uns rdr 4th* **28/1**
0-06 **P** **Mrs Overall**[20] 660 5-10-11 **79**.. HarrySkelton —
(Bob Buckler) *chsd ldrs: rdn and hdwy to chse wnr after 6th tl bef 8th: sn drvn and dropped out: t.o whn p.u 2 out* **40/1**

5m 6.80s (-24.10) **Going Correction** -0.925s/f (Hard) course record **13** Ran SP% **124.0**
Speed ratings (Par 103): **104,103,103,98,96 86,85,62,61,— —,—,—**
toteswingers:1&2:£4.10, 1&3:£16.80, 2&3:£6.50 CSF £19.16 CT £50.88 TOTE £2.20: £1.10, £3.80, £1.30; EX 16.80 Place 6 £176.93; Place 5 £88.68.
Owner Miss Rebecca Curtis **Bred** James Maguire **Trained** Newport, Dyfed

FOCUS
There was no hanging about in this moderate novice handicap hurdle and the first three came clear. The winner is rated 10lb off his recent chase win, with the next two close to their marks.

NOTEBOOK
Fealing Real(IRE) made all under another very strong ride from Tony McCoy. He had won easily on his debut for connections over fences a week earlier and was able to race off the same mark on this return to hurdling. He had his rivals stretched turning for home but looked vulnerable coming to the last. He was clearly idling after being in front for so long, however, as he picked up again when the challengers came at him on the run-in. This was another fine advertisement of his trainer's skills with horses plucked out of the pointing field. (op 11-10, touched 11-8 in places)
Corso Palladio(IRE) was having his first outing for a new yard after a 604-day layoff and proved very easy to back. He travelled nicely into contention and kept on after coming under pressure jumping three out. This was a sterling effort in defeat considering his absence, but he will probably need time to recover from the run. (op 9-1)
Norwest(IRE) was another debutant for a new trainer and attracted support. He crept into things turning for home and appeared to give his all when asked for everything, but was always just being held. (op 7-2 tchd 4-1)
Richard The Third's effort proved shortlived, but he was dismounted after the line and may have had an excuse. He rates the best guide for this form. (tchd 18-1)
Cool Bob(IRE) was given an awful lot to do considering his main target in the race was out in front, and never looked like getting on terms. He is surely capable of better under more positive handling. (op 10-1)
T/Jkpt: £7,487.50 to a £1 stake. Pool:£58,001.83 - 5.50 winning tickets T/Plt: £153.30 to a £1 stake. Pool:£77,272.14 - 367.85 winning tickets T/Qpdt: £53.10 to a £1stake. Pool:£5,106.93 - 71.10 winning tickets SP

[733]STRATFORD (L-H)

Tuesday, June 29

OFFICIAL GOING: Good to firm (good in places)

Rail realignment increased hurdle races by 20yds per circuit and chases by 13yds each circuit.

Wind: Nil Weather: very hot and sunny

850 PRIOR PRODUCTS MAIDEN HURDLE (9 hdls) 2m 110y

6:40 (6:40) (Class 4) 4-Y-O+ £3,252 (£955; £477; £238)

Form RPR

U3-4 1 **Pool Of Knowledge (FR)**[22] 664 4-10-11 102 AidanColeman 101+
(Venetia Williams) *set v stdy pce: gng best after 3 out: slt mstke next: kpt on wl: readily* 9/2[2]

00- 2 2 3/4 **Carbon Print (USA)**[29] 2916 5-11-0 0 WillKennedy 99
(Paul Webber) *sn chsng wnr: rdn and ev ch bef 2 out: no imp between last two* 14/1

5-32 3 1 1/2 **Decision**[30] 541 4-10-4 100 (t) DavidBass(7) 95
(Lawney Hill) *pressed ldrs: cl 3rd but hrd drvn home turn: nt qckn between last two* 7/4[1]

4 9 **Mystic Touch**[8] 4-10-11 0 JackDoyle 85
(Andrew Haynes) *dropped out last early: kpt on steadily after 3 out: 6 l 5th bef 2 out: n.d after but wnt 4th nr fin and nt disgraced* 66/1

0 5 3/4 **Soggy Dollar**[19] 693 5-10-11 0 (p) AlexMerriam(3) 88
(Neil King) *pressed ldrs: cl 4th but drvn home turn: wknd after 2 out: mstke last: lost 4th nr fin* 50/1

00/ 6 4 **Southway Star**[559] 2842 5-10-0 0 MattGriffiths(7) 76
(Kevin Bishop) *midfield: rdn and wkng whn mstke 3 out* 125/1

7 4 **Raptor (GER)**[6] 7-10-7 0 MrRichardCollinson(7) 79
(Mark Rimmer) *j. bdly in midfield: struggling 6th: drvn out* 13/2[3]

8 nk **Motor Home**[14] 4-10-11 0 JimmyMcCarthy 76
(Charlie Morlock) *midfield: effrt after 5th: 6th and btn bef 2 out* 33/1

/00- 9 25 **Flyford Prince**[115] 4452 5-10-9 0 LeeEdwards(5) 54
(Tony Carroll) *disp last after 4th: t.o fr 6th* 125/1

10 6 **Coach And Four (USA)**[699] 5-10-7 0 MrJEngland(7) 48
(Michael Gates) *t.k.h: in rr whn j. bdly rt 3rd: t.o bef 6th* 100/1

11 3 **Expensive Problem**[13] 7-11-0 0 RichardJohnson 45
(Ralph Smith) *mstkes in last pair: t.o bef 6th* 8/1

P- 12 36 **Mr Fantozzi (IRE)**[17] 4786 5-11-0 0 PaulMoloney 9
(Des Donovan) *chsd ldrs tl wknd bef 6th: bdly t.o* 100/1

/03- 13 29 **Flying Squad (UAE)**[17] 2797 6-11-0 0 (t) CharliePoste —
(Milton Harris) *cl up: lost pl rapidly 6th: t.o and virtually p.u after 3 out* 9/2[2]

3m 55.2s (-0.80) **Going Correction** -0.225s/f (Good)
WFA 4 from 5yo+ 17lb 13 Ran SP% 113.8
Speed ratings (Par 105): **92,90,90,85,85 83,81,81,69,66 65,48,34**
toteswingers:1&2:£13.30, 1&3:£3.60, 2&3:£7.00 CSF £58.94 TOTE £7.20: £2.70, £5.30, £1.10; EX 59.50.
Owner Font Of Wisdom Partners **Bred** The Staple Fitzpaine Compagny **Trained** Kings Caple, H'fords

FOCUS
A very modest maiden hurdle. The winer did not need to improve and the form looks a bit suspect.

NOTEBOOK
Pool Of Knowledge(FR) scored readily having been up with the pace throughout. This was a marked improvement on his previous efforts and he can probably win again at some stage this summer. (op 4-1 tchd 7-2)
Carbon Print(USA), beaten a long way on both previous starts over hurdles, ran creditably on the Flat last time and he posed an improved effort on this return to hurdles. (tchd 16-1)
Decision, runner-up off 99 at Uttoxeter latest, looked vulnerable at the head of the market and was duly beaten again. (op 9-4 tchd 5-2)
Mystic Touch stayed on late having been held up, and he should definitely improve.
Mr Fantozzi(IRE) Official explanation: jockey said gelding had a breathing problem

851 BERNADETTE'S RESTAURANT STRATFORD-ON-AVON JUVENILE CLAIMING HURDLE (9 hdls) 2m 110y

7:10 (7:10) (Class 4) 3-Y-O £2,602 (£764; £382; £190)

Form RPR

36 1 **Gulf Punch**[4] 836 3-10-0 0 (p) PeterToole(3) 93+
(Milton Harris) *chsd ldrs: clsd 5th: led next: gng strly after: 12 l clr 2 out: romped home* 3/1[1]

3B 2 17 **Anchorage Boy (USA)**[15] 743 3-10-4 0 AlexMerriam(3) 77
(Amy Weaver) *j. slowly 1st and wl off pce early: hdwy 5th: drvn to chse ldr (who was clr) bef 2 out: no imp* 13/2

3 18 **Sunshine Buddy**[28] 3-10-6 0 ChrisHonour(3) 62
(Chris Down) *wl off pce early: rdn and prog 5th: chal ldr and mstke next: sn outpcd: poor 4th and plugging on whn mstke 2 out: wnt remote 3rd after last* 20/1

4 4 1 **Alphacino**[15] 743 3-10-7 0 BarryKeniry 59
(Ben Haslam) *prom: chsd wnr after 6th tl wknd bef 2 out where mstke whn mod 3rd: fin tired* 8/1

4 5 21 **Clayton Flick (IRE)**[21] 674 3-10-10 0 JackDoyle 40
(Andrew Haynes) *wl off pce whn pckd bdly 3rd: effrt to trck ldrs bef 6th: sn wknd: t.o bef 2 out* 8/1

P5 6 29 **Another Grand (IRE)**[15] 743 3-10-9 0 OliverWilliams(7) 17
(Ruth Carr) *poor last whn blnd 2nd: effrt after 4th: in tch bef 6th: sn fdd: hopelessly t.o* 18/1

7 11 **Tiger Hawk (USA)**[49] 3-10-13 0 (v[1]) LeeStephens(3) 6
(David Evans) *immediately outpcd: t.o whn j. slowly 4th: continued in hopeless pursuit* 11/1

43 8 2 1/2 **Mr Mohican (IRE)**[15] 743 3-10-7 0 (b[1]) KeithMercer —
(Ann Duffield) *set fast pce: hdd 6th: stopped to nil next: hopelessly t.o* 11/2[3]

P **Ant Music (IRE)**[35] 3-11-8 0 PaulMoloney —
(Evan Williams) *nt fluent trying to match tearaway ldr: stopped to nil after 5th: t.o and p.u after next* 9/2[2]

F **Superhoops**[29] 3-10-7 0 (v[1]) RodiGreene —
(Stuart Howe) *3rd whn j.rt and fell 4th* 125/1

3m 51.1s (-4.90) **Going Correction** -0.225s/f (Good) 10 Ran SP% 113.3
Speed ratings: **102,94,85,85,75 61,56,55,—,—**
toteswingers:1&2:£7.20, 1&3:£22.30, 2&3:£20.60 CSF £22.17 TOTE £4.50: £2.90, £1.60, £8.80; EX 17.60.Gulf Punch was the subject of a friendly claim.
Owner John Gwynne **Bred** Brook Stud Bloodstock Ltd **Trained** Herridge, Wiltshire

FOCUS
A fairly weak juvenile hurdle. A massive step up from the winner but just about in line with his Flat form. The form makes sense on time compared with the later handicap.

NOTEBOOK
Gulf Punch could be called the winner a long way from the finish, eventually drawing clear in the first-time cheekpieces. On this evidence she could win again, though it's worth noting she did return sore. (op 4-1 tchd 11-4)
Anchorage Boy(USA), brought down at Sedgefield latest, came through and drew well clear of the remainder, but was no match for the winner. (op 6-1 tchd 5-1)
Sunshine Buddy, unplaced in four Flat starts, was beaten a long way, but did show enough to suggest he will do better over hurdles. (op 18-1)
Alphacino failed to improve on his initial effort and looked a non-stayer at the distance. (op 13-2 tchd 9-1)
Mr Mohican(IRE) suffered for setting too strong a pace. (op 6-1 tchd 7-1)
Ant Music(IRE), who tried to chase the early leader, jumped poorly and was eventually pulled up. (op 100-30)

852 BERNADETTE'S RESTAURANT CHAMPAGNE & OYSTER BAR H'CAP CHASE (GAY, EVE & TIM SHEPPARD MEMORIAL CUP) (14 fncs) 2m 4f

7:40 (7:40) (Class 3) (0-125,125) 5-Y-O+ £6,337 (£1,872; £936; £468; £234)

Form RPR

P-2P 1 **Oscar Royal (IRE)**[19] 694 9-10-5 104 LiamTreadwell 120+
(Peter Hiatt) *j. really wl and racd enthusiastically: mde all at fast pce: drew clr 2 out where only one stl on bridle: 10 l ahd last: unchal* 11/1

P-21 2 8 **Presentandcorrect (IRE)**[22] 663 9-11-1 119 SamTwiston-Davies(5) 125
(Nigel Twiston-Davies) *hld up in midfield: mstke 9th: effrt 3 out: 3rd and rdn next: wnt 2nd bef last: no imp on ready wnr* 9/1

2115 3 2 1/4 **Pilgrims Lane (IRE)**[26] 592 6-11-9 125 PeterToole(3) 130
(Milton Harris) *dropped out last tl hdwy 10th: 5th and rdn 2 out: one pce between last two* 11/2[2]

5-41 4 6 **William Butler (IRE)**[7] 824 10-11-2 118 7ex DPFahy(3) 117
(Evan Williams) *trckd ldrs gng wl: wnt 2nd at 11th: rdn and outpcd by wnr bef 2 out: lost 2nd appr last: wknd and lft modest 4th at last* 2/1[1]

30-4 5 31 **Lidjo De Rouge (FR)**[27] 586 11-10-5 104 RichardJohnson 75
(Paul Henderson) *handy: hit 4th: wnt 2nd at 5th tl 11th: 6th and fading whn mstke 2 out: t.o* 8/1

-P11 6 20 **Neutrino**[13] 764 8-11-5 118 (v) TomScudamore 71
(David Bridgwater) *chsd wnr tl 5th: rdn and lost tch tamely 3 out: t.o* 13/2[3]

-603 7 3 1/4 **Good Company (IRE)**[18] 707 10-11-7 120 APMcCoy 70
(Jonjo O'Neill) *in rr mostly: dropped bk last 10th: struggling after next: t.o* 10/1

3-22 F **Misty Dancer**[18] 707 11-10-13 112 AidanColeman 113
(Venetia Williams) *rn in snatches: in rr 6th tl rallied 10th: 4th and rdn 2 out: no ex: 13 l 4th whn fell last* 15/2

4m 43.9s (-10.30) **Going Correction** -0.225s/f (Good) 8 Ran SP% 112.4
Speed ratings: **111,107,106,104,92 84,82,—**
toteswingers:1&2:£8.00, 1&3:£6.20 , 2&3:£7.60 CSF £96.81 CT £602.87 TOTE £13.10: £3.20, £4.00, £1.30; EX 163.00.
Owner Bob Coles **Bred** Joseph J O'Connor **Trained** Hook Norton, Oxon

FOCUS
A decent handicap chase. Pretty solid form rated through the runner-up, with the winner back to his autumn form.

NOTEBOOK
Oscar Royal(IRE), pulled up on his recent handicap debut, jumped with great relish out in front, setting a fast gallop in the process, and never looked in any danger, drawing right away to win with ease. This was a first win for the 9yo, whose aggressive run-style will mean he is always a threat. Official explanation: trainer's rep said, regarding apparent improvement in form, that the gelding had suffered from back problems before returning to him prior to its last run and was better suited by the fast ground. (op 14-1)
Presentandcorrect(IRE), up 4lb for his recent Newton Abbot victory, appeared to run his race but wasn't quite as effective over the shorter distance, even with a good pace. (op 8-1 tchd 15-2 and 10-1)
Pilgrims Lane(IRE), still 8lb higher than when winning at the course in May, has now failed to reproduce anything like that form in two subsequent outings. (op 7-1)
William Butler(IRE), shouldered with a 7lb penalty for his recent Newton Abbot win, appeared to have the race run to suit so there was no obvious reason why he produced such a tame finishing effort. (op 13-8)
Misty Dancer was well held when coming down at the last and it over three years now since his last chase victory. (op 11-1)

853 STOUT CONSTRUCTION H'CAP HURDLE (9 hdls) 2m 110y

8:10 (8:10) (Class 4) (0-115,115) 4-Y-O+ £4,553 (£1,337; £668; £333)

Form RPR

6-41 1 **Wheelavit (IRE)**[26] 595 7-11-8 111 (t) LiamTreadwell 121+
(Claire Dyson) *racd keenly and mde nrly all: qcknd clr bef 2 out: 12 l ahd last: unchal* 6/1[3]

61-5 2 8 **Alph**[31] 521 13-11-5 115 MrTJCannon(7) 113
(Roger Teal) *prom: led briefly 5th and again 3 out: drvn and outpcd by ldr bef next: kpt on steadily to remain clr of rest* 8/1

000P 3 5 **Is It Me (USA)**[14] 756 7-11-12 115 (t) PaulMoloney 108
(Sophie Leech) *bhd: stl 7th 3 out: drvn and r.o fr next: wnt modest 3rd at last: nvr able to chal* 12/1

66-P 4 4 **Raise Again (IRE)**[7] 823 7-9-10 90 KeiranBurke(5) 79
(Nerys Dutfield) *bhd: effrt bef 6th: 6th at next: kpt on and ev ch of modest 3rd at last: no ex* 14/1

0U-0 5 2 1/2 **First Bay (IRE)**[34] 279 4-11-0 106 (vt[1]) TomO'Brien 92
(Keith Goldsworthy) *nt a fluent: prom: hit 6th: outpcd and rdn in 12 l 3rd bef 2 out: n.d after: stl contesting 3rd whn blnd last* 16/1

034- 6 2 1/4 **Massams Lane**[251] 1846 6-10-11 103 SeanQuinlan(3) 89
(Carole Ikin) *nt a fluent: cl up: blnd 3rd: drvn and outpcd in 4th 3 out: fdd bef next* 14/1

50-4 7 22 **Shadow Wood (IRE)**[12] 768 6-10-0 89 HarrySkelton 54
(Patrick Griffin, Ire) *midfield: 5th and drvn 3 out: sn wknd* 20/1

0-54 8 11 **Recurring Dream**[30] 535 4-10-3 95 (t) RhysFlint 47
(John Flint) *towards rr: rdn and lost tch bef 6th: t.o after next* 11/1

60- 9 35 **Ardistan (IRE)**[190] 3006 6-11-6 109 APMcCoy 33
(Jonjo O'Neill) *a last: struggling bef 5th: t.o next: nrly a hurdle bhd* 17/2

14/3 P **Garrulous (UAE)**[21] 675 7-11-2 105 RichardJohnson —
(Tim Vaughan) *chsd ldrs tl rdn and qckly dropped bk last after 4th: p.u next: lost action* 10/3[1]

441- **P** **Kashmina**[15] 2250 5-10-10 **104** .... MarcGoldstein(5) —
(Sheena West) *p.u after 2nd: lame* **11/2**[2]

3m 49.9s (-6.10) **Going Correction** -0.225s/f (Good)
WFA 4 from 5yo+ 17lb **11** Ran SP% **114.4**
Speed ratings (Par 105): **105,101,98,97,95 94,84,79,62,— —**
toteswingers:1&2:£6.40, 1&3:£15.40, 2&3:£13.50 CSF £52.05 CT £556.33 TOTE £7.10: £2.40, £1.70, £5.70; EX 54.10.
Owner Team Arrow **Bred** John Bourke **Trained** Cleeve Prior, Worcs

FOCUS
Just a fair handicap hurdle. The winner showed surprise improvement and the next two are difficult to pin down these days.

NOTEBOOK
Wheelavit(IRE), raised 7lb for his Newton Abbot victory, again prospered under a front-running ride and quickly drew clear for an easy win. He is clearly in cracking form at present and may bid for the hat-trick at back at Newton Abbot next week. (op 5-1)
Alph bounced back to form under top weight, staying on valiantly without proving a match for the winner. (op 12-1)
Is It Me(USA) shaped much more encouragingly in finishing a staying on third and may soon be able to capitalise on his plummeting handicap mark. (op 11-1)
Raise Again(IRE) was another to run a bit better. (op 22-1)
First Bay(IRE) was never particularly fluent in the first-time visor. (op 14-1)
Garrulous(UAE) dropped out very quickly on this second run back from injury. Official explanation: jockey said gelding lost its action (op 11-4)

854 TIM COX ASSOCIATES BEGINNERS' CHASE (17 fncs) 2m 7f
8:40 (8:40) (Class 4) 5-Y-O+ **£4,553** (£1,337; £668; £333)

Form RPR
6UF- **1** **Job One (FR)**[239] 2037 7-10-11 106 .... HaddenFrost(3) 115+
(Henrietta Knight) *pressed ldrs: cl 4th 3 out: rdn next: chal to ld last and lft clr: kpt on stoutly* **16/1**
2323 **2** *12* **Kanad**[9] 797 8-10-9 115 ....(t) JimmyDerham(5) 103
(Milton Harris) *bhd: looked to be struggling 13th: str run after 2 out: snatched 2nd but no ch w wnr* **16/1**
0 **3** *½* **Safe Catch (IRE)**[13] 763 8-11-0 0 ....(p) JackDoyle 104
(Martin Hill) *bad mstke 4th: dropped to rr and mstke 7th: rdn 10th: looked to be struggling 13th: fin strly bef last to snatch 3rd: no ch w wnr* **66/1**
53/6 **4** *¾* **Cherokee Star**[13] 761 5-11-0 0 .... DenisO'Regan 102
(Mike Hammond) *hdwy to ld 6th: rdn and hdd bef last where mstke: wknd flat and lost two positions cl home* **50/1**
41-0 **5** *3 ¼* **Tribe**[53] 193 8-11-0 0 .... WillKennedy 100
(Paul Webber) *in rr early: progress to 2nd at 9th: disp 2nd 3 out: wknd qckly after next: lft disputing 4th and blnd last* **3/1**[2]
-235 **6** *18* **Indian Pipe Dream (IRE)**[18] 716 8-11-0 108 ....(tp) KeithMercer 81
(Steve Gollings) *w ldr to 7th: dropped to rr and nt keen 10th: t.o whn climbed last* **12/1**[3]
7 *70* **Gougane (IRE)**[54] 187 7-11-0 0 .... JohnnyFarrelly 11
(Hugh McWilliams) *led tl hdd and j. slowly 6th: lost pl and j. slowly 8th: struggling in last at 12th: hopelessly t.o* **12/1**[3]
5-22 **F** **Last Flight (IRE)**[16] 738 6-10-2 0 ....(p) DonalDevereux(5) 105
(Peter Bowen) *cl up: effrt to dispute 2nd 3 out: drvn next: led between last two: jst hdd whn fell heavily last: bdly injured* **4/6**[1]

5m 33.6s (-8.00) **Going Correction** -0.225s/f (Good) **8** Ran SP% **115.6**
Speed ratings: **104,99,99,99,98 92,67,—**
toteswingers:1&2:£20.10, 1&3:£30.50, 2&3:£27.60 CSF £213.67 TOTE £27.30: £3.80, £2.90, £11.70; EX 289.20.
Owner Pertemps Group Limited **Bred** Mme Henri Devin **Trained** West Lockinge, Oxon

FOCUS
Not the most competitive beginners' chase and not a race to get carried away with, but the form could have been rated up to 20lb higher.

NOTEBOOK
Job One(FR) had just started to master the favourite when being left clear at the last. Winless in four previous starts over fences for another trainer, he has clearly been helped by the change of stable and may do better still returned to handicaps. (op 20-1)
Kanad got up late on to grab a fortunate second, but was still well held. (op 14-1)
Safe Catch(IRE) finished off well having got himself a bit behind with a notable early blunder. (op 100-1)
Cherokee Star lost out on a place due a rather weak finishing effort.
Tribe was the obvious disappointment of the race, clearly not taking as well to fences as expected. (op 100-30)
Last Flight(IRE), already twice a runner-up to decent sorts over fences, deserved a win, but having got to the front she was soon pressured by the winner and had been headed when falling and appearing to badly injure herself at the last. (op 8-11 tchd 8-13)

855 FIRS GARAGE, HOOK NORTON STANDARD NATIONAL HUNT FLAT RACE (CONDITIONAL JOCKEYS' AND AMATEUR RIDERS) 2m 110y
9:10 (9:10) (Class 5) 4-6-Y-O **£1,951** (£573; £286; £143)

Form RPR
1 **Mercury Bay (IRE)**[52] 5-11-4 0 .... RhysFlint 105+
(Keith Goldsworthy) *mde nrly all at gd pce: forged clr over 2f out: pushed along and r.o strly* **9/4**[1]
34 **2** *7* **Sohappyharry**[16] 739 4-10-12 0 .... DPFahy(3) 93
(Jane Mathias) *on his toes: prom and t.k.h: chsd ldr over 2f out: drvn and no imp but kpt on gamely* **13/2**
1 **3** *5* **Kings Riches (IRE)**[48] 277 5-11-6 0 .... DonalDevereux(5) 98
(Peter Bowen) *sn prom: chsd ldr 4f out tl rdn and wknd over 2f out* **5/1**[2]
4 *11* **Full Ov Beans** 6-10-11 0 .... MrJEngland(7) 81
(Michael Gates) *wl in rr: picked off btn horses fr 1/2-way: wnt modest 4th on home turn: no imp after* **40/1**
0/3- **5** *4* **Midnight Fun**[107] 4620 5-10-4 0 .... LucyBarry(7) 71
(Michael Appleby) *t.k.h: chsd ldrs: rdn and outpcd 3f out* **15/2**
5 **6** *1 ½* **Minella (IRE)**[6] 832 6-10-13 0 .... SamTwiston-Davies(5) 76
(Michael Appleby) *w ldr 4f and at times: lost pl 4f out: sn btn* **11/2**[3]
0 **7** *shd* **Sheezatreasure (IRE)**[41] 412 5-10-4 0 .... MarkQuinlan(7) 69
(James Evans) *t.k.h: chsd ldrs: wknd 3f out* **20/1**
0- **8** *1 ½* **Moonshine Hall (IRE)**[99] 4792 6-10-4 0 ....(t) MrRobertHawker(7) 68
(Richard Hawker) *plld hrd in midfield: wknd 4f out* **66/1**
9 *1 ¼* **Two Mile Borris (IRE)** 4-10-8 0 .... MrJMQuinlan(7) 71
(Michael Quinlan) *n.d fnl 6f* **18/1**
10 *22* **Reg's Ruby** 4-10-3 0 .... MichaelMurphy(5) 44
(David Bridgwater) *chsd ldrs: racd awkwardly on bnd after 7f: struggling fnl 5f: t.o* **33/1**
11 *1 ¼* **Flyford Princess** 4-10-3 0 .... LeeEdwards(5) 43
(Tony Carroll) *in rr early: t.o fnl 3f* **25/1**
12 *53* **Silverini** 4-10-3 0 .... JimmyDerham(5) —
(Milton Harris) *last most of way: struggling 1/2-way: bdly t.o* **10/1**

3m 46.6s (-3.80) **Going Correction** -0.225s/f (Good)
WFA 4 from 5yo+ 3lb **12** Ran SP% **117.8**
Speed ratings: **99,95,93,88,86 85,85,84,84,73 73,48**
toteswingers:1&2:£4.40, 1&3:£6.00, 2&3:£9.40 CSF £15.74 TOTE £3.70: £1.90, £1.40, £1.20; EX 21.00 Place 6 £1,013.81, Place 5 £643.33..
Owner E C Jones **Bred** Sean Gorman **Trained** Yerbeston, Pembrokes

FOCUS
This was just a modest bumper, but the winner looks a fair recruit.

NOTEBOOK
Mercury Bay(IRE), twice a runner-up in points, made full use of his guaranteed stamina, making all at a decent clip, and staying on strongly to win with plenty in hand. He looks quite a promising sort with hurdles in mind. (op 7-2)
Sohappyharry didn't settle that well, but ran his best race yet and should do better over hurdles. (op 8-1)
Kings Riches(IRE), the only previous winner in the field, won a race run at a virtual crawl on his debut at Exeter and wasn't so effective in a more truly run race. (op 4-1)
Full Ov Beans stayed on late past tiring horses. (op 50-1)
Midnight Fun should do better over hurdles. (op 6-1 tchd 10-1)
Minella(IRE) should do better over hurdles. (op 5-1 tchd 9-2)
T/Jkpt: Not won. T/Plt: £612.80 to a £1 stake. Pool £79,531.12 - 94.74 winning tickets. T/Qpdt: £174.90 to a £1 stake. Pool £5,768.22 - 24.40 winning tickets. IM

[442]PERTH (R-H)
Wednesday, June 30

OFFICIAL GOING: Good to firm (firm in places; 9.3)
All rails back in on fresh ground.
Wind: Slight, across Weather: Cloudy, warm

856 JOHN (THE HORSE) MACDONALD MEMORIAL NOVICES' HURDLE (12 hdls) 3m 110y
2:20 (2:20) (Class 4) 4-Y-O+ **£3,168** (£936; £468; £234; £117)

Form RPR
1 **Abbey Lane (IRE)**[10] 806 5-11-5 0 .... PCarberry 120+
(Gordon Elliott, Ire) *prom: smooth hdwy to ld bef 2 out: rdn run-in: kpt on wl* **4/7**[1]
4-3 **2** *2* **Kembla Grange (IRE)**[16] 744 4-10-7 110 .... BrianHughes 104
(C A McBratney, Ire) *hld up: hdwy and prom 3 out: sn rdn: edgd rt and chsd wnr bef last: kpt on run-in* **9/1**[3]
-450 **3** *14* **Elusive Muse**[33] 503 4-10-7 114 .... OliverDayman(7) 98
(Alison Thorpe) *in tch: hdwy to chse ldrs 5th: led 3 out to bef next: wknd bef last* **11/4**[2]
4 *19* **Walkonabubble (IRE)**[23] 6-10-5 0 .... KielanWoods(7) 76
(D J Barry, Ire) *t.k.h: nt fluent on occasions: w ldr: ev ch tl wknd after 3 out* **50/1**
-520 **5** *4* **Stolen Moments (FR)**[32] 514 9-10-12 107 .... PaddyAspell 72
(James Moffatt) *led to 3 out: sn rdn and wknd* **14/1**
6 *26* **Lambertstown Lad (IRE)**[87] 8-10-5 0 .... KMDonoghue(7) 46
(Miss Clare Judith Macmahon, Ire) *hld up: nt fluent and rdn after 4 out: struggling fr next* **66/1**
7 *101* **Kiosk (FR)**[144] 3906 6-10-12 0 ....(t) DougieCostello —
(J T R Dreaper, Ire) *nt fluent: bhd: lost tch fr 8th: t.o* **25/1**

5m 46.3s (-23.60) **Going Correction** -0.975s/f (Hard)
WFA 4 from 5yo+ 19lb **7** Ran SP% **114.3**
Speed ratings (Par 105): **98,97,92,86,85 77,—**
toteswingers:1&2 £2.80, 2&3 £2.60, 1&3 £1.10 CSF £6.96 TOTE £1.70: £1.10, £2.10; EX 3.70.
Owner Martin Lynch **Bred** Robert McCarthy **Trained** Trim, Co Meath

FOCUS
A weak novice event. The first two were clear and are rated to their marks, with the progressive winner value for further.

NOTEBOOK
Abbey Lane(IRE) made it 2-2 since joining current connections and got the longer trip without any fuss. He moved up going easily turning for home and looked sure to win as he pleased two out, but began to idle thereafter and allowed the runner-up a chance. He confirmed his authority when Paul Carberry got serious with him on the run-in, though, and rates value for further. He is yet another big advertisement for his trainer's skills and there should be more to come from this winning pointer, but he will not peak until going chasing. (tchd 4-6)
Kembla Grange(IRE) ◆ came under pressure nearing three out, but kept responding and finished a clear second-best. On such quick ground he looked to need all of this longer trip and, although flattered by his proximity to the winner, can soon be found an opening. (op 7-1)
Elusive Muse, well backed, was again somewhat free early on and that didn't help his cause in the home straight. He helps to set the moderate standard. (op 4-1)
Walkonabubble(IRE) was placed in three of his four outings between the flags in Ireland. Keen up front early on, he confirmed he is going to need a real test in this sphere with a dour staying display and will be one to take note of when eligible for handicaps.
Stolen Moments(FR) Official explanation: trainer said gelding knocked itself behind but returned sound

857 WALLACE WHITTLE CONSULTING ENGINEERS NOVICES' CHASE (12 fncs) 2m
2:50 (2:52) (Class 4) 5-Y-O+ **£4,752** (£1,404; £702; £351; £175)

Form RPR
66- **1** **Red Kingdom (IRE)**[11] 613 6-10-12 126 .... DenisO'Regan 129+
(A J Martin, Ire) *hld up: stdy hdwy fr 8th: chsd clr ldr 2 out: 7 l down and hld whn lft 1 l in front last: drvn out* **15/2**[3]
0-22 **2** *1* **Stagecoach Pearl**[18] 728 6-10-12 115 .... KeithMercer 128
(Sue Smith) *led after 1st: hdd 4 out: sn drvn: outpcd after next: 8 l down and hld whn lft 1 l 2nd last: kpt on u.p* **10/3**[2]
/30- **3** *3 ¾* **Grand Opera (IRE)**[17] 740 7-11-5 131 ....(p) PCarberry 130
(Gordon Elliott, Ire) *chsd clr ldrs: drvn and outpcd after 4 out: no imp whn lft 4 l 3rd last: no imp* **2/1**[1]
4-3P **4** *25* **All For The Cause (IRE)**[38] 444 8-10-12 113 .... BarryKeniry 103
(Nicky Richards) *hld up: outpcd bef 4 out: sn no imp: lft modest 4th last* **10/1**
13P/ **5** *80* **Saltrash (IRE)**[200] 2853 9-10-12 92 .... PeterBuchanan 18
(B R Hamilton, Ire) *nt fluent: set slow pce tl hdd after 1st: dropped in rr next: lost tch fnl circ* **50/1**

0F-1 **F** **Treaty Flyer (IRE)**[38] 440 9-10-12 132 JohnnyFarrelly 134
(Alison Thorpe) *pressed ldr and clr of rest: led 4 out: drew clr fr next: 7 l in front and styng on strly whn fell last: fatally injured* **2/1**[1]

3m 56.6s (-6.10) **Going Correction** -0.975s/f (Hard) **6** Ran SP% **112.6**
Speed ratings: **76,75,73,61,21** —
toteswingers: 1&2 £4.40, 1&3 £4.60, 2&3 £1.50 CSF £32.81 TOTE £8.90: £4.50, £1.50; EX 27.60.
Owner We Must Be Mad Syndicate **Bred** C McEvoy **Trained** Summerhill, Co. Meath

FOCUS
There was drama late on in this good novice chase as Treaty Flyer came down at the final fence with the race at her mercy, sadly with tragic consequences. Red Kingdom is obviously a very lucky winner but is on the upgrade.

NOTEBOOK
Red Kingdom(IRE) came through to pick up the pieces after Treaty Flyer fell at the last, but he obviously rates a very lucky winner. Tony Martin's 6-y-o showed his true colours when second on his previous outing and the way he raced here would suggest a stiffer test would ideally suit. (op 13-2)
Stagecoach Pearl, well backed, was given a positive ride on this return to novice company but was left for dead when Treaty Flyer went on four out. He kept on bravely for pressure, though, and should get off the mark in this division when dropped in grade. (op 9-2 tchd 3-1)
Grand Opera(IRE) was very closely matched with the winner on a collateral line of form in Ireland and it wasn't that surprising to see him held by that rival. He helps to set the standard. (tchd 15-8)
All For The Cause(IRE) remains a very hard horse to win with. (op 12-1)
Saltrash(IRE) Official explanation: trainer said gelding bled from the nose
Treaty Flyer(IRE) came down at the final fence with the race at her mercy, sadly with tragic consequences. (tchd 15-8 and 9-4 and 5-2 in a place)

858 CONCERT EVENING JULY 27TH MARES' MAIDEN HURDLE (10 hdls) 2m 4f 110y
3:20 (3:21) (Class 4) 4-Y-O+ **£2,534** (£748; £374; £187; £93)

Form RPR

0P/ **1** **Niamh's Way (IRE)**[12] 782 9-10-11 94 JamesO'Farrell(3) 102
(Liam Lennon, Ire) *hld up: hdwy 4 out: rdn next: led between last 2: edgd rt and kpt on wl run-in* **28/1**

2 1 ½ **Millrock Lady (IRE)**[20] 699 5-11-0 0 PCarberry 102
(Gordon Elliott, Ire) *chsd ldrs: wnt 2nd 4 out: effrt appr 2 out: sn outpcd: rallied to chse wnr run-in: r.o u.p* **4/5**[1]

3 3 **Grace N' Favour (IRE)**[42] 419 7-11-0 0 GrahamLee 98
(B R Hamilton, Ire) *led: rdn and hdd between last 2: kpt on same pce run-in* **9/4**[2]

4 81 **Tear Drops (IRE)**[234] 6-10-9 0 APThornton(5) 17
(P E Collins, Ire) *in tch tl rdn and wknd after 4 out: t.o bef 2 out* **8/1**[3]

5 9 **Windmill Cross (IRE)**[52] 8-10-7 0 KielanWoods(7) 8
(D J Barry, Ire) *in tch: struggling 4 out: sn btn: t.o* **25/1**

6 34 **Lady Edina (IRE)**[85] 7-11-0 0 PeterBuchanan —
(I A Duncan, Ire) *mstkes in rr: struggling bef 4 out: t.o* **50/1**

0-4 **R** **Orpen Bid (IRE)**[18] 726 5-10-9 0 ow2 (t) MrGCrow(7) —
(A M Crow) *ref to r* **50/1**

00- **P** **Alwood Flora**[217] 2515 7-10-7 0 NathanMoscrop(7) —
(Andrew Crook) *a bhd: lost tch and p.u bef 4 out* **100/1**

6-50 **P** **Thorpey's Girl (IRE)**[15] 754 5-10-7 0 OliverDayman(7) —
(Alison Thorpe) *bhd: struggling 4 out: t.o whn p.u bef 2 out* **66/1**

0-PP **P** **Modestine**[28] 577 8-10-8 0 ow1 AlistairFindlay(7) —
(Jane Walton) *chsd ldr: hit 5th: wknd and p.u after 4 out* **100/1**

4m 47.4s (-19.50) **Going Correction** -0.975s/f (Hard) **10** Ran SP% **112.1**
Speed ratings (Par 105): **98,97,96,65,62 49,—,—,—,—**
toteswingers:1&2 £7.30, 2&3 £1.10, 1&3 £6.00 CSF £51.19 TOTE £28.00: £4.00, £1.10, £1.10; EX 133.60.
Owner Kevin McQuillan **Bred** Paul Carberry **Trained** Newry, Co. Down

FOCUS
A poor mares' only novice event, run at a sound gallop. There were six challengers from Ireland and they were the only finishers. Surprise improvement from the winner, and suspect form.

NOTEBOOK
Niamh's Way(IRE) ran out a surprise winner. She had shown little over hurdles previously, but had obviously come on a bundle for her seasonal return 12 days earlier and completed the task with a little more in hand than the bare margin indicates. This is also clearly her ideal trip, but it's hard to see her following up under a penalty and, with an official mark of 81, she sums up the strength of the race. (op 25-1)
Millrock Lady(IRE) set the standard on the level of her second at Clonmel. She was given every chance, but was under pressure before making a mess of the penultimate flight. She responded to have a chance again under maximum pressure, but was always being held by the winner. It may be that she found the ground quicker than she cares for and perhaps a stiffer test is required, but she still doesn't look that straightforward. (op 5-6 tchd 8-11)
Grace N' Favour(IRE) looked in need of a test when making all in her bumper in May and was understandably up in trip for this hurdling debut. She again went off from the front, but didn't settle and was made to pay the price before the final flight. (op 5-2, tched 11-4 in places)
Tear Drops(IRE), a clear-cut winner of her point in Ireland, also failed to settle and was left behind after the third-last. (op 11-2)
Thorpey's Girl(IRE) Official explanation: jockey said mare jumped right-handed throughout
Modestine Official explanation: jockey said mare hung badly left

859 WALLACE WHITTLE CONSULTING ENGINEERS H'CAP CHASE (18 fncs) 3m
3:50 (3:53) (Class 3) (0-130,130) 5-Y-O+ **£7,604** (£2,246; £1,123; £561; £280)

Form RPR

0-53 **1** **Bill's Echo**[22] 680 11-10-10 114 DougieCostello 124+
(Alistair Whillans) *hld up and bhd: smooth hdwy 4 out: led after last: drvn clr* **7/1**

5-12 **2** 4 ½ **Harry Flashman**[10] 804 9-10-3 107 GrahamLee 111
(Donald Whillans) *cl up: led 3rd: reminders 10th: lft clr bef 3 out: hdd after last: kpt on same pce u.p* **11/4**[1]

P-43 **3** shd **Western Gale (IRE)**[25] 626 7-10-8 112 (p) DenisO'Regan 118
(Martin Todhunter) *prom: blnd 4 out: lft 2nd bef next: sn drvn: kpt on u.p fr last* **7/1**

PP-2 **4** 17 **Bear Witness (IRE)**[48] 308 8-10-13 117 PeterBuchanan 106
(S R B Crawford, Ire) *cl up: nt fluent 5th: drvn 4 out: wknd bef 2 out* **9/2**[3]

3151 **5** 8 **Flying Doctor**[10] 802 7-11-9 127 7ex JohnnyFarrelly 109
(Elliott Cooper) *hld up: rdn 14th: no imp whn mstke 3 out: sn btn* **7/1**

5-12 **6** 9 **Sheriff Hutton (IRE)**[19] 708 7-11-12 130 RobertWalford 100
(Tim Walford) *in tch: drvn and outpcd 13th: n.d after* **4/1**[2]

02-5 **U** **Petite Margot**[33] 501 11-10-11 115 PaddyBrennan 119+
(Nigel Twiston-Davies) *led to 3rd: w ldr: drvn along 14th: cl 2nd whn rdr lost iron and uns rdr bnd bef 3 out* **9/1**

5m 49.7s (-30.70) **Going Correction** -0.975s/f (Hard) course record **7** Ran SP% **112.3**
Speed ratings: **112,110,110,104,102 99,—**
toteswingers:1&2 £8.00, 2&3 £7.60, 1&3 £15.40 CSF £26.41 CT £138.88 TOTE £10.00: £4.70, £1.50; EX 33.80.
Owner Burns Partnership **Bred** Miss Frances Baker **Trained** Newmill-On-Slitrig, Borders

FOCUS
A fair handicap, run at a decent gallop and the first three came clear in the home straight. The third helps set the level.

NOTEBOOK
Bill's Echo, with the blinkers left off, relished this return to quicker ground and ran out a ready winner. He got a lovely, patient ride through the race and was delivered at the last. The result was soon settled and this veteran should be high on confidence now. (op 13-2)
Harry Flashman, very well backed, tends to keep his best for Hexham, but he ran right up to his best here. He did need strong handling pretty much throughout though, and is a happier horse going left-handed. (op 4-1)
Western Gale(IRE) was never a serious player, but did his best work towards the finish and this was better again from him. (tchd 8-1)
Bear Witness(IRE), second over C&D last time out, was 3lb higher and ran below his recent level, possibly on account of the quicker surface. (op 13-2)
Flying Doctor was well beaten off under his penalty over this stiffer test and could now be in need of a break. (op 4-1)
Sheriff Hutton(IRE), who beat Bear Witness on 4lb worse terms here on his penultimate outing, was held from the fourth-last and is another that probably found the ground quicker than he wants it. (tchd 7-2 and 9-2)
Petite Margot was fully under the pump, but holding onto second place prior to unseating around the home turn. Considering she is a dour stayer there is every chance she would have been bang there at the death. (op 15-2)

860 BLACK WATCH, 3 SCOTS NOVICES' H'CAP CHASE (15 fncs) 2m 4f 110y
4:20 (4:24) (Class 4) (0-105,105) 5-Y-O+ **£3,485** (£1,029; £514; £257; £128)

Form RPR

3F3 **1** **King Roonah**[36] 459 6-11-12 105 (t) PCarberry 124+
(Gordon Elliott, Ire) *in tch: smooth hdwy to ld bef 2 out: edgd rt and rdn clr run-in: eased nr fin* **7/2**[1]

2423 **2** 4 ½ **Emotive**[18] 728 7-10-9 91 CampbellGillies(3) 103
(Barry Murtagh) *hld up: rdn and hdwy bef 2 out: styd on run-in: tk 2nd nr fin: nt rch wnr* **9/2**[3]

63-6 **3** nk **Stolen Light (IRE)**[42] 404 9-10-0 79 oh12 (b) KeithMercer 91
(Andrew Crook) *led to 7th: led 11th to bef 2 out: kpt on u.p run-in: lost 2nd cl home* **40/1**

4-26 **4** 12 **Storm Prospect**[36] 460 7-11-2 95 (b) PeterBuchanan 95
(Lucinda Russell) *bhd: outpcd bef 9th: styd on fr 2 out: nvr on terms* **4/1**[2]

-420 **5** shd **Ice Image (IRE)**[28] 578 8-10-8 94 ow3 AlistairFindlay(7) 94
(George Charlton) *cl up: led 7th to 11th: rdn and wknd fr 2 out* **10/1**

P040 **6** 7 **Clueless**[18] 730 8-10-1 80 (p) BrianHughes 73
(Carol Ferguson) *prom tl rdn and wknd bef 3 out* **12/1**

0P-3 **7** 2 ¾ **High Stand Lad**[42] 403 8-11-4 97 DenisO'Regan 87
(Martin Todhunter) *hld up: hdwy and in tch 4 out: wknd fr next* **14/1**

8 14 **Noble Commander (IRE)**[29] 573 7-11-10 103 GrahamLee 89
(James Halpin, Ire) *midfield: drvn 11th: wknd bef 3 out* **8/1**

00-4 **9** 5 **Broadway Star (FR)**[16] 746 7-11-5 98 WilsonRenwick 84
(Rose Dobbin) *nt fluent on occasions: prom tl wknd after 4 out* **6/1**

5320 **10** 99 **Athoss**[30] 551 8-11-3 103 MrMEnnis(7) —
(Robert Smith) *bhd: lost tch fnl circ* **16/1**

4m 54.6s (-19.40) **Going Correction** -0.975s/f (Hard) course record **10** Ran SP% **117.6**
Speed ratings: **97,95,95,90,90 87,86,81,79,41**
toteswingers:1&2 £5.70, 2&3 £35.70, 1&3 £35.70 CSF £20.51 CT £539.05 TOTE £3.20: £1.10, £2.80, £12.80; EX 22.60.
Owner Sean F Gallagher **Bred** Helshaw Grange Stud And E Kent **Trained** Trim, Co Meath

FOCUS
A wide-open handicap, run at a fair enough gallop and there was an easy winner, who rates a personal best.

NOTEBOOK
King Roonah would've won here on his penultimate outing in May had he not fallen at the final fence, and then found the race coming too soon when reverting to hurdles next time. He was 15lb higher this time, so the fact he won the race so well under top weight is an indication he is fast-improving. He didn't have too hard a race so is set to turn out quickly again at the track, as he is due for another hike. (op 3-1 tchd 4-1)
Emotive fared best of those coming from off the pace and probably ran close to his previous level, so rates a solid benchmark. He deserves to find another race. (tchd 5-1)
Stolen Light(IRE) came into this looking out of sorts and was 12lb out of the handicap. His proximity therefore doesn't do much for the form on paper, but he was suited by racing on the front end and was rated a good bit higher when previously trained in Ireland. (op 50-1)
Storm Prospect once more got himself behind early on and never looked like rewarding support. He was motoring home late in the day and a further step up in trip may help negate his lazy tendencies. (op 5-1)
Ice Image(IRE), whose rider put up 3lb overweight, ran okay under a positive ride yet wasn't able to confirm previous Hexham form with Storm Prospect on these worse terms. (op 11-1)

861 WALLACE WHITTLE STAFF DAY H'CAP HURDLE (8 hdls) 2m 110y
4:50 (4:54) (Class 3) (0-135,130) 4-Y-O+ **£7,604** (£2,246; £1,123; £561; £280)

Form RPR

/30- **1** **Wikaala (USA)**[16] 752 5-11-4 122 (b) PCarberry 124
(Gordon Elliott, Ire) *hld up: smooth hdwy bef 2 out: led last: drvn out run-in* **3/1**[1]

-141 **2** ½ **Dishdasha (IRE)**[17] 736 8-11-5 130 (t) OliverDayman(7) 131
(Alison Thorpe) *t.k.h: chsd ldrs: effrt 2 out: styd on wl fr last* **15/2**[3]

312- **3** 2 **Rampant Ronnie (USA)**[238] 2059 5-10-4 108 (t) JohnnyFarrelly 109+
(Alison Thorpe) *led: rdn whn hit and hdd last: kpt on same pce* **12/1**

/0P- **4** hd **Spa Wells (IRE)**[12] 784 9-10-3 107 (b) GrahamLee 106
(C A McBratney, Ire) *prom: effrt and rdn 2 out: hung rt last: kpt on same pce* **4/1**[2]

P-2P **5** 2 ½ **Annibale Caro**[12] 444 8-10-3 107 KeithMercer 103
(Jim Goldie) *hld up: hdwy bef 3 out: effrt next: no imp fr last* **8/1**

5-26 **6** 2 ¾ **Duty Free (IRE)**[25] 627 6-10-10 114 PaddyAspell 108
(James Moffatt) *chsd ldr tl rdn and wknd after 2 out* **8/1**

4-12 **7** 2 ¼ **Right Or Wrong (IRE)**[13] 779 6-10-4 115 (tp) KMDonoghue(7) 107
(Gordon Elliott, Ire) *hld up: rdn bef 2 out: nvr able to chal* **4/1**[2]

-046 **8** 5 **Ravati (IRE)**[19] 715 4-9-11 109 MissLHorner(5) 94
(Chris Grant) *hld up on outside: struggling after 4 out: n.d after* **10/1**

3-PU **9** 12 **Humourous (IRE)**[25] 424 8-9-7 104 oh33 MissJRRichards(7) 78
(Brian Storey) *prom to 4 out: sn rdn and wknd* **100/1**

3m 40.9s (-18.80) **Going Correction** -0.975s/f (Hard)
WFA 4 from 5yo+ 17lb **9** Ran SP% **116.8**
Speed ratings (Par 107): **105,104,103,103,102 101,100,97,92**
toteswingers:1&2 £1.50, 2&3 £6.50, 1&3 £2.00 CSF £26.26 CT £237.78 TOTE £3.20: £2.30, £1.30, £4.00; EX 18.10 Place 6: £55.26 Place 5: £44.00.
Owner Sean F Gallagher **Bred** Shadwell Farm LLC **Trained** Trim, Co Meath
■ Stewards' Enquiry : Oliver Dayman one-day ban: used whip with excessive frequency (Jul 14)

FOCUS
A modest and open handicap that saw a host of chances in the home straight. Solid form.

NOTEBOOK

Wikaala(USA) eventually came out best and handed his yard yet another winner at the track. He unsurprisingly travelled sweetly into contention and, despite taking time to settle the issue when asked for an effort, his jockey ensured he would not be denied. He is talented enough to win again this summer, but his profile suggests he is one to be opposing again next time out. (op 7-2 tchd 4-1)

Dishdasha(IRE), who won the novice chase on this card last season, was 6lb higher than when scoring again at Stratford. That put him up to a career-high mark in this sphere, but he ran a big race under top weight and remains in great form. (op 9-2)

Rampant Ronnie(USA) was returning from a 238-day layoff. He got to the front early as he prefers and didn't go down without a real fight nearing the business end, so this was obviously a very pleasing comeback. (op 8-1)

Spa Wells(IRE) travelled nicely along with the winner into contention, but his response when put under pressure was limited and it's not hard to see why he sports headgear. (op 11-2)

Annibale Caro didn't prove too fluent early on this return to hurdling, but still ran a fair race and would be entitled to get closer when dropped in grade. (op 7-1 tchd 6-1)

T/Plt: £29.40 to a £1 stake. Pool: £59,814.13 - 1,484.41 winning tickets. T/Qpdt: £4.60 to a £1 stake. Pool:£4,104.92 - 647.20 winning tickets. RY

826 WORCESTER (L-H)

Wednesday, June 30

OFFICIAL GOING: Good to firm (chs 8.1; hdl; 7.7)

All bends moved out 3metres from inside racing line but impact on distances not quantified.

Wind: Light against Weather: Cloudy with sunny spells

862 WINTERFOLD HOUSE SCHOOL 0-13 YEARS CONDITIONAL JOCKEYS' NOVICES' H'CAP HURDLE (10 hdls) 2m 4f

2:10 (2:10) (Class 4) (0-105,105) 4-Y-0+ **£2,927** (£859; £429; £214)

Form / RPR

3-23 **1** **Space Telescope (IRE)**[14] 767 4-11-7 **105**........(b1) RichieMcLernon(3) 115+
(Jonjo O'Neill) *hld up: hdwy to chse ldr after 6th tl rdn appr 3 out: led and hung lft flat: styd on wl* **8/1**

-061 **2** *6* **Occasionally Yours (IRE)**[7] 826 6-11-6 **97** 7ex........(b) JimmyDerham 103
(Nigel Hawke) *a.p: led appr 3 out: rdn and hdd flat: styd on same pce* **6/1**[2]

0-FP **3** *4½* **Scotsbrook Cloud**[10] 793 5-10-11 **88**........................ MichaelMurphy 89
(C Roberts) *hld up: reminders after 4th: hdwy 7th: outpcd bef next: rallied appr last: r.o* **66/1**

6-42 **4** *½* **Sparkling Brook (IRE)**[10] 793 7-10-2 **82**.......... SamTwiston-Davies(3) 83
(Nigel Twiston-Davies) *led: rdn and hdd appr 3 out: rallied to ld briefly flat: sn hdd & wknd* **7/2**[1]

4-00 **5** *nse* **Glan Lady (IRE)**[27] 600 4-10-0 **81** oh9........................(p) CharlieHuxley 80
(John Mackie) *hld up in tch: rdn appr 3 out: ev ch whn slipped on landing last: wknd flat* **100/1**

30-5 **6** *13* **Sagunt (GER)**[35] 480 7-11-7 **101**....................................(t) DavidBass(3) 90
(Sean Curran) *hld up: hdwy u.p after 7th: wknd after next* **8/1**

42-4 **7** *16* **Magnetic Pole**[35] 475 9-11-3 **94**....................................(p) GilesHawkins 65
(Richard Lee) *hld up: bdly hmpd appr 6th: n.d: t.o* **15/2**[3]

P254 **8** *24* **Grand Award**[20] 693 5-11-11 **102**.. RyanMania 49
(Donald McCain) *hld up: bhd fr 7th: t.o* **8/1**

-536 **9** *¾* **Rowan River**[20] 697 6-10-10 **87**....................................(bt1) HaddenFrost 34
(Alison Thorpe) *mid-div: rdn appr 5th: hdwy next: rdn and wknd 3 out: t.o* **16/1**

10 *45* **Golden Gem (IRE)**[164] 3501 8-11-3 **94**..............................(tp) RhysFlint —
(Rachel Hobbs) *chsd ldrs: wkng whn mstke 5th: t.o* **12/1**

45-0 **11** *1½* **Bingo Des Mottes (FR)**[10] 792 5-11-6 **100**............. AodhaganConlon(3) —
(Patrick Griffin, Ire) *chsd ldr tl after 6th: wknd next: t.o* **40/1**

P-23 **F** **Wisteria Lane (IRE)**[8] 825 7-10-3 **80**..........................(v1) HarrySkelton —
(Anabel L M King) *prom tl fell appr 6th* **8/1**

0-30 **B** **Points Of View**[22] 678 5-11-12 **103**.............................. RichardKilloran —
(Kim Bailey) *hld up: b.d appr 6th* **16/1**

4m 38.6s (-8.80) **Going Correction** -0.35s/f (Good)
WFA 4 from 5yo+ 18lb 13 Ran SP% **117.1**
Speed ratings (Par 105): **103,100,98,98,98 93,86,77,77,59 58,—,—**
toteswingers: 1&2 £4.50, 1&3 £13.00, 2&3 £31.50 CSF £54.75 CT £2952.02 TOTE £4.90: £1.70, £2.70, £13.00.
Owner John P McManus **Bred** Yukiko Hosokawa **Trained** Cheltenham, Gloucs

FOCUS

A modest conditional jockeys' handicap. A big step up from the winner in the blinkers.

NOTEBOOK

Space Telescope(IRE) was clearly helped by the first-time blinkers, though again looked far from straightforward. He had finished third off 3lb lower over C&D last time and should go in again if the headgear continues to have a positive effect. (op 9-2 tchd 9-1)

Occasionally Yours(IRE), shouldering a 7lb penalty for last week's narrow C&D win (wore first-time blinkers), appeared to run his race without proving a match for the winner. The headgear has clearly been a help to him. (op 11-2 tchd 5-1 and 8-1)

Scotsbrook Cloud kept plugging away for strong pressure and gives the impression he will be suited by 3m.

Sparkling Brook(IRE) emptied disappointingly on the run-in, considering she had battled back well to regain the lead. (tchd 11-4)

Glan Lady(IRE), having to race from 9lb 'wrong', was closing for strong pressure and held every chance when appearing to slip a stride or two after the last.

Golden Gem(IRE) Official explanation: jockey said gelding had a breathing problem

863 BET IN RUNNING - BETDAQ NOVICES' HURDLE (12 hdls) 3m

2:40 (2:41) (Class 4) 4-Y-0+ **£2,927** (£859; £429; £214)

Form / RPR

4-22 **1** **Chesapeake (IRE)**[14] 763 6-10-12 117..........................(b1) APMcCoy 119+
(Jonjo O'Neill) *a.p: led on bit last: sn clr: easily* **11/10**[1]

0-41 **2** *6* **Downward Spiral (IRE)**[30] 559 5-11-5 116...................... AlanO'Keeffe 109
(Jennie Candlish) *led: rdn and hdd whn stmbld last: wknd flat* **8/1**[3]

1-2P **3** *½* **Marblehead (IRE)**[32] 525 8-10-7 0.................... SamTwiston-Davies(5) 101
(Nigel Twiston-Davies) *chsd ldr: hld up: drvn along after 7th: wknd last* **9/4**[2]

1-6P **4** *6* **Triggernometry**[20] 691 9-10-12 0......................................(t) JoeTizzard 96
(Colin Tizzard) *prom: rdn appr 3 out: wknd next* **11/1**

PP-P **5** *3* **Stafford Charlie**[46] 336 4-10-0 68..............................(p) CharlieWallis(7) 88
(John O'Shea) *hld up: hdwy after 8th: rdn bef 3 out: wknd next* **150/1**

64-4 **6** *21* **Karzelle**[25] 635 6-10-12 0.. JamieMoore 74
(John Spearing) *hld up: hdwy u.p after 9th: wknd 3 out: t.o* **33/1**

0-06 **7** *1½* **Chouromanesco (FR)**[31] 538 7-10-12 0.................... MattieBatchelor 69
(Mark Bradstock) *hld up: mstke 1st: hdwy appr 9th: rdn and wknd bef next: t.o* **50/1**

0-06 **8** *46* **Nishnash**[38] 436 7-10-12 72.. AndrewThornton 23
(Jim Wilson) *hld up: bhd fr 8th: t.o* **100/1**

0211 **9** *1* **Knar Mardy**[27] 603 5-11-2 110.................................... AdamPogson(3) 29
(Charles Pogson) *hld up: hdwy 8th: rdn and wknd after next: t.o* **10/1**

10 *26* **Diddle'Em**[25] 9-10-12 0... ChristianWilliams —
(Bernard Llewellyn) *hld up: bhd fr 8th: t.o* **66/1**

00 **P** **Frame And Cover**[10] 792 4-9-9 0.............................. JimmyDerham(5) —
(Joanna Davis) *chsd ldrs to 7th: bhd fr next: t.o whn p.u bef 3 out* **150/1**

P **Lighting Larry (IRE)**[80] 5-10-12 0...................................... DarylJacob —
(Liam Corcoran) *hld up: bhd fr 7th: t.o whn p.u after next: fatally injured* **100/1**

5m 33.9s (-10.70) **Going Correction** -0.35s/f (Good)
WFA 4 from 5yo+ 19lb 12 Ran SP% **116.6**
Speed ratings (Par 105): **103,101,100,98,97 90,90,75,74,66 —,—**
toteswingers: 1&2 £4.90, 1&3 £1.40, 2&3 £6.30 CSF £11.08 TOTE £2.50: £1.30, £2.30, £1.10; EX 13.40.
Owner John P McManus **Bred** Western Bloodstock **Trained** Cheltenham, Gloucs

FOCUS

A relatively weak novices' hurdle. The easy winner was value for further and is rated to his mark.

NOTEBOOK

Chesapeake(IRE), like his stablemate in the opening contest, appeared to benefit from having blinkers on for the first time. Rated 117, he had shown more than enough to win a race such as this, and may be capable of going on now that he's got his head in front. He'll stick to novice events. (op Evens tchd 5-4)

Downward Spiral(IRE), one of two previous winners in the race, proved to be nothing more than a sitting duck for Chesapeake, who readily brushed him aside on the run-in. He remains capable of better and could win again switched to handicaps. (op 15-2)

Marblehead(IRE), a decent hunter chaser, wasn't up to much over hurdles in Ireland, but he made a satisfactory debut for his new yard and should win races. (op 7-2)

Triggernometry, who has lost his form over fences, had a nice spin round on this return to hurdles. This should have restored some confidence. (op 12-1 tchd 10-1)

Stafford Charlie, pulled up in his last three starts, fared much better this time.

Knar Mardy, who was chasing a hat-trick, only won a seller last time and it looked a big ask for her to defy a double penalty. She failed to run her race, stopping quickly and ending up well held. Official explanation: jockey said mare never travelled (op 8-1 tchd 11-1)

864 IRISH NIGHT 7TH JULY NOVICES' H'CAP CHASE (12 fncs) 2m

3:10 (3:10) (Class 5) (0-95,95) 5-Y-0+ **£2,397** (£698; £349)

Form / RPR

5-5P **1** **My Pal Val (IRE)**[10] 794 10-11-4 **90**..............................(tp) DannyCook(3) 104+
(John Panvert) *hld up: hdwy 8th: led last: drvn out* **11/1**

PP-2 **2** *¾* **Pagan Sword**[7] 828 8-11-7 **90**.. RodiGreene 103
(David Bridgwater) *a.p: chsd ldr 5th: led appr 4 out: mstke 2 out: hdd last: r.o* **4/1**[1]

-P15 **3** *18* **Khazar (FR)**[20] 689 7-11-8 **91**.. APMcCoy 91+
(Jonjo O'Neill) *hld up: hmpd 2nd: mstke 5th: hdwy next: rdn and swtchd rt whn nt fluent last: wknd flat* **5/1**[2]

P/34 **4** *25* **Sahara Prince (IRE)**[10] 799 10-10-12 **88**...................(p) MrLRPayter(7) 57
(Matt Sheppard) *hld up: hdwy 5th: wknd 8th: t.o* **10/1**

0-FP **5** *20* **Overspin**[10] 799 7-11-6 **89**.. WillKennedy 38
(Paul Webber) *chsd ldr to 5th: remianed handy: rdn and wknd 3 out: t.o* **20/1**

P0/0 **6** *shd* **Mustamad**[24] 652 7-10-0 **69** oh5..(t) ColinBolger 18
(Chris Gordon) *prom: drvn along 5th: wknd after next: t.o* **50/1**

-0F0 **7** *1* **Un Autre Espere**[15] 755 11-9-7 **72** oh11 ow3.................(b) JoshWall(10) 20
(Trevor Wall) *chsd ldrs tl rdn and wknd 7th: bhd whn hit next: t.o* **66/1**

600- **8** *41* **Uffa Fox (IRE)**[78] 5172 7-11-10 **93**..................................(b1) DarylJacob —
(Ben De Haan) *prom tl wknd appr 4 out: t.o* **11/2**[3]

P4-U **U** **Simiola**[30] 558 11-9-11 **69** oh16.. PeterToole(3) —
(Simon Lewis) *blnd and uns rdr 2nd* **50/1**

4-43 **P** **Ruby Valentine (FR)**[38] 440 7-10-6 **75** ow2............... AndrewThornton —
(Jim Wilson) *bhd fr 6th: t.o whn p.u bef 8th* **15/2**

-004 **P** **Paradise Regained (FR)**[8] 822 7-11-7 **95**................ DonalDevereux(5) —
(Sophie Leech) *prom: blnd 2nd: sn lost pl: hdwy 6th: wknd 8th: t.o whn p.u bef 4 out* **11/1**

25U/ **F** **Morning Sunshine (IRE)**[477] 4411 7-11-11 **94**............... JasonMaguire —
(Donald McCain) *led: rdn: hdd and wkng whn fell 4 out* **5/1**[2]

3m 49.8s (-1.80) **Going Correction** -0.05s/f (Good) 12 Ran SP% **116.4**
Speed ratings: **102,101,92,80,70 70,69,49,—,— —,—**
toteswingers: 1&2 £10.10, 1&3 £12.40, 2&3 £5.40 CSF £54.02 CT £252.66 TOTE £6.50: £1.60, £2.80, £3.20; EX 73.50.
Owner Miss Carolyn Woods **Bred** V I McCalla And Winton Bloodstock **Trained** Stoodleigh, Devon

FOCUS

A moderate handicap chase that concerned only three in the straight. A step forward from the winner, with the second to his mark.

NOTEBOOK

My Pal Val(IRE) was always travelling best, and he did only what was required once asked to go on and win the race. Previously disappointing over fences, the return to 2m was clearly a help, but it was probably the first-time cheekpieces that was the prime factor in his improvement. Official explanation: trainer said, regarding apparent improvement in form, that the gelding was suited by the shorter trip and being fitted with the first-time cheek pieces. (tchd 12-1)

Pagan Sword has found some form again and ran right up to his best back in trip, but the winner always looked to have him covered. He did battle back once headed and deserves to find a race. (op 7-2)

Khazar(FR), whose only previous chase win came off 6lb lower, bounced back from a dismal effort at Fontwell latest, but he was eased once it became apparent he wasn't going to win. (op 9-2 tchd 11-2)

Sahara Prince(IRE) was well beaten. (op 12-1)

Uffa Fox(IRE) fared no better in the first-time blinkers. (op 13-2)

Morning Sunshine(IRE), who fell at the first in the straight, would have needed this first outing in 477 days and should improve if none the worse for the spill. (tchd 6-1)

865 BETDAQ ON 0870 178 1221 (S) HURDLE (8 hdls) 2m

3:40 (3:40) (Class 5) 4-Y-0+ **£1,781** (£519; £259)

Form / RPR

F-P5 **1** **High Skies**[14] 767 7-10-5 97..(b1) DavidBass(7) 109+
(Dr Richard Newland) *hld up: hdwy and pushed along 4th: led 2 out: rdn clr flat* **6/1**[3]

0032 **2** *10* **Three Ships**[3] 845 9-10-12 95.. AdamWedge(7) 104
(S Wynne) *plld hrd and a.p: rdn appr 3 out: ev ch bef next: no ex last* **12/1**

-023 **3** *1* **Tora Petcha (IRE)**[20] 696 7-11-2 104........................ DannyCook(3) 102
(Barry Leavy) *led: racd keenly: rdn and hdd 2 out: styd on same pce* **8/1**

0121 **4** *½* **Seaquel**[8] 678 4-10-6 105..(v) CharlieHuxley(3) 92
(Andrew Haynes) *chsd ldrs: rdn and ev ch appr 2 out: styd on same pce* **11/4**[2]

3/0- **5** *hd* **Parazar (FR)**[241] 2026 5-10-12 0 .... LeightonAspell 94
(Oliver Sherwood) *hld up: hdwy appr 3 out: sn rdn: styd on same pce fr next* **40/1**

3-4F **6** *1 3/4* **Rapide Plaisir (IRE)**[10] 799 12-10-12 98 .... RobertThornton 93
(Richard Lee) *hld up: hdwy appr 3 out: styd on same pce fr next* **12/1**

60- **7** *shd* **Douchkette (FR)**[33] 4167 4-10-2 0 .... WillKennedy 82
(John Berry) *hld up: hdwy appr 3 out: wknd flat* **9/1**

63-1 **8** *5* **Roznic (FR)**[10] 801 12-10-12 108 .... RichardJohnson 87
(Tim Vaughan) *chsd ldrs: rdn and ev ch appr 2 out: wknd and eased flat* **5/2**[1]

00-0 **9** *2* **Frosty's Gift**[9] 384 6-10-2 71 .... (b) HaddenFrost(3) 78
(Jimmy Fox) *hld up: bhd 3rd: hdwy appr 3 out: wknd next* **100/1**

045- **10** *10* **Thistle**[307] 1118 9-10-12 98 .... (t) AndrewTinkler 75
(George Baker) *hld up: hdwy 4th: rdn and wknd after next: t.o* **50/1**

PP-U **11** *11* **Tarkesar (IRE)**[52] 234 8-10-9 71 .... (p) SeanQuinlan(3) 64
(Carole Ikin) *chsd ldrs tl rdn and wknd appr 3 out: t.o* **100/1**

02-0 **12** *14* **Mid Wicket (USA)**[42] 216 4-10-6 104 .... (t) RichardKilloran(3) 47
(Mouse Hamilton-Fairley) *chsd ldrs: rdn and wknd after 5th: t.o* **14/1**

3m 39.3s (-8.00) **Going Correction** -0.35s/f (Good)
WFA 4 from 5yo+ 17lb **12** Ran SP% **119.1**
Speed ratings (Par 103): **106,101,100,100,100 99,99,96,95,90 85,78**
toteswingers: 1&2 £17.70, 1&3 £17.60, 2&3 £9.20 CSF £73.80 TOTE £6.30: £2.20, £5.20, £2.20; EX 67.20.There was no bid for the winner. Seaquel was subject to a friendly claim.
Owner Prof D E Newland **Bred** Juddmonte Farms Ltd **Trained** Claines, Worcs

FOCUS
A competitive selling hurdle and the form has a solid look to it.

NOTEBOOK
High Skies, from a yard in form, travelled well on this drop in grade, clearly being perked up by the first-time blinkers, and he readily came clear to win with a bit in hand. There were no bids for him. (op 17-2 tchd 9-1)
Three Ships, runner-up off 95 at Uttoxeter just three days earlier, ideally prefers going the other way round, but he was entitled to run well, and duly did in finishing second. (op 8-1)
Tora Petcha(IRE) battled on well to register another decent effort. (op 17-2 tchd 9-1)
Seaquel, winner of two of her last three, had been disappointing back on the Flat the other day and failed to meet expectations here. (tchd 5-2)
Parazar(FR), having only his third race, showed enough to suggest he is up to winning at a lowly level once handicapped. (op 33-1)
Roznic(FR) was disappointing, considering he had won so readily at Hexham last time. (tchd 9-4 and 3-1 in places)

866 BET ONE DAY CRICKET - BETDAQ H'CAP HURDLE (10 hdls) 2m 4f
1:10 (1:10) (Class 3) (0-135,127) 4-Y-O+ **£4,878** (£1,432; £716; £357)

Form RPR
12-2 **1** **Now This Is It (IRE)**[24] 648 6-11-12 127 .... APMcCoy 128+
(S R B Crawford, Ire) *hld up: hdwy 6th: rdn appr 3 out: mstke last: hrd drvn to ld fnl 100yds: edgd rt: all out* **13/8**[1]

F-0P **2** *nk* **Osolomio (IRE)**[14] 764 7-10-11 112 .... AlanO'Keeffe 111
(Jennie Candlish) *led: rdn and hdd bef 3 out: rallied u.p and ev ch flat: styd on gamely* **22/1**

31-B **3** *1 1/2* **Tzora**[15] 756 5-10-11 112 .... RichardJohnson 110
(Philip Hobbs) *hld up: hdwy 6th: led appr 3 out: rdn and hdd bef last: styd on u.p* **9/2**[3]

24-3 **4** *nk* **Whenever**[15] 756 6-11-3 118 .... JasonMaguire 116
(Richard Phillips) *in rr and pushed along early: hdwy after 5th: led appr last: rdn and hdd fnl 100yds: unable qck* **4/1**[2]

-430 **5** *24* **Pepporoni Pete (IRE)**[25] 627 9-11-5 120 .... (tp) CharliePoste 93
(Milton Harris) *plld hrd: trckd ldr tl after 4th: remained handy tl rdn and wknd appr 3 out* **14/1**

/FP- **6** *23* **Porters War (IRE)**[235] 2125 8-11-0 115 .... RobertThornton 65
(Alan King) *hld up in tch: rdn and wknd after 3 out: eased: t.o* **16/1**

-023 **7** *5* **Corkage (IRE)**[19] 708 7-11-8 123 .... (p) TomScudamore 68
(Lucinda Russell) *prom: chsd ldr after 4th tl rdn 6th: wknd next: t.o* **4/1**[2]

PP6- **P** **Another Brother (IRE)**[78] 5176 8-11-6 121 .... LiamHeard —
(Gerald Ham) *chsd ldrs tl lost pl appr 5th: sn wl bhd: t.o whn p.u bef 3 out* **50/1**

4m 36.8s (-10.60) **Going Correction** -0.35s/f (Good) **8** Ran SP% **115.1**
Speed ratings (Par 107): **107,106,106,106,96 87,85,—**
toteswingers: 1&2 £3.50, 1&3 £3.30, 2&3 £7.60 CSF £34.11 CT £140.23 TOTE £3.60: £1.70, £4.20, £1.30; EX 61.10.
Owner Mrs M McCrudden **Bred** S McElroy **Trained** Larne, Co Antrim

FOCUS
A fair handicap hurdle and it produced a cracking finish, with three holding a chance inside the final 100 yards. Pretty solid form.

NOTEBOOK
Now This Is It(IRE)'s victory is owed in large to McCoy, as the horse looked unlikely to finish in the three having jumped the first in the straight. Unplaced in only one of his eight previous starts, he has a willing attitude, and that was certainly needed here. In the end both horse and rider simply wanted it more than the others. On this evidence he is ready for a step back up in trip, and he may head for a decent race at Market Rasen's Summer Plate meeting. (op 5-2)
Osolomio(IRE) made most of the running and battled back gamely once headed, reclaiming second and only going down narrowly to the winner. (op 20-1)
Tzora, still going well when brought down latest, looked interesting on this handicap debut and he came through to hold every chance in the straight, but couldn't quicken sufficiently. He rallied well after the last to get up for third, though, and remains capable of better. (op 7-2 tchd 5-1 in places)
Whenever was towards the back being niggled for much of the way, but he started to pick up leaving the back straight. He was driven into the lead before the last, but having got there, he found little and lost third close home, his rider appearing to take it a little easy. (tchd 7-2)
Porters War(IRE) was eased once beaten and failed to improve for the switch to handicaps. (op 9-1 tchd 17-2)
Corkage(IRE) was entitled to do much better and clearly failed to run his race. (op 11-2)

867 SUCKLING TRANSPORT H'CAP CHASE (DIV I) (18 fncs) 2m 7f
4:40 (4:40) (Class 4) (0-110,109) 5-Y-O+ **£2,927** (£859; £429; £214)

Form RPR
5-54 **1** **Alfadora**[31] 540 10-10-2 90 .... (t) JimmyDerham(5) 107+
(Milton Harris) *hld up: hdwy 13th: led last: rdn clr flat* **10/1**

0-33 **2** *14* **Kilshannig (IRE)**[19] 717 5-11-0 97 .... (t) APMcCoy 106+
(Jonjo O'Neill) *hld up: hdwy 9th: led 4 out: rdn and hdd whn blnd last: eased whn btn fnl 100yds* **13/2**[3]

00-2 **3** *5* **Naughty By Nature**[13] 769 7-10-11 101 .... AodhaganConlon(7) 100
(Rebecca Curtis) *hld up: hdwy 7th: rdn 12th: wknd 2 out* **4/1**[1]

5-33 **4** *7* **Swordsman (GER)**[20] 691 8-11-4 101 .... (tp) ColinBolger 92
(Chris Gordon) *chsd ldr tl hit 2nd: wnt 2nd again after 5th: led 9th to 11th: rdn 13th: led after 5 out: hdd next: wknd 3 out* **11/1**

1-F3 **5** *6* **Port Talbot (IRE)**[17] 738 9-11-9 106 .... LeightonAspell 96+
(Oliver Sherwood) *hld up: hdwy and mstke 14th: blnd and wknd 3 out: t.o* **14/1**

2104 **6** *25* **Lord Gunnerslake (IRE)**[13] 769 10-10-11 94 .... (v) RichardJohnson 64
(Tim Vaughan) *j.rt: led to 9th: led again 11th: hdd after 5 out: wkng whn hit next: t.o* **12/1**

P-55 **7** *55* **Skipper's Lad (IRE)**[20] 695 8-11-12 109 .... (bt) JoeTizzard 14
(Colin Tizzard) *hld up: hmpd 4th: bhd fr 12th: t.o* **9/1**

1-33 **8** *3 1/2* **Wizards Dust**[27] 599 8-11-5 102 .... (b) JasonMaguire 4
(Donald McCain) *chsd ldr 2nd tl after 5th: remained handy tl rdn and wknd 12th: t.o* **7/1**

30-4 **F** **Borora**[40] 427 11-11-3 100 .... CharliePoste —
(Richard Lee) *chsd ldrs: disputing cl 4th and rdn whn fell 5 out* **20/1**

-312 **P** **Hoof It Harry (IRE)**[20] 691 9-11-5 102 .... RobertThornton —
(Paul Henderson) *prom: j.rt 4th: rdn after 9th: wkng whn hit next: sn p.u* **5/1**[2]

2-35 **P** **Manadam (FR)**[22] 685 7-11-8 105 .... AidanColeman —
(Anthony Middleton) *hld up: rdn after 8th: bhd fr 10th: t.o whn p.u bef 13th* **10/1**

5m 38.5s (-4.10) **Going Correction** -0.05s/f (Good) **11** Ran SP% **118.1**
Speed ratings: **105,100,98,95,93 85,66,64,—,— —**
toteswingers:1&2 £11.30, 2&3 £4.30, 1&3 £10.90 CSF £74.85 CT £308.12 TOTE £13.60: £5.50, £1.30, £2.60; EX 127.80.
Owner The Virtual Partnership **Bred** R Olley **Trained** Herridge, Wiltshire

FOCUS
The first division of a modest, yet competitive staying handicap chase. The winner was very well in on the best of his form.

NOTEBOOK
Alfadora, a bit disappointing at Uttoxeter latest, is nicely treated on the pick of his form, and he returned to something like his best to win this, finding plenty for pressure having travelled strongly. He returned with an overreach on his off-fore, but will be out under a penalty if none the worse. (op 12-1 tchd 14-1)
Kilshannig(IRE)looked a potential improver switched to fences and he appeared the likeliest winner when taking over at the last in the back, but couldn't shake Alfadora and had just been headed when making a mess of the last, which ended his chance. He is capable of going one better. (op 6-1 tchd 11-2)
Naughty By Nature failed to improve on his reappearance effort when second at Ffos Las, though he was 4lb higher and having only his second start over fences. (op 10-3 tchd 3-1)
Swordsman(GER) did no better with the cheekpieces back on. (op 10-1 tchd 12-1)
Port Talbot(IRE)'s chance ended with a blunder three out. (op 12-1)

868 SUCKLING TRANSPORT H'CAP CHASE (DIV II) (18 fncs) 2m 7f
5:10 (5:10) (Class 4) (0-110,100) 5-Y-O+ **£2,927** (£859; £429; £214)

Form RPR
3-13 **1** **Rifleman (IRE)**[25] 630 10-10-7 89 .... (t) TomScudamore 104+
(Richard Lee) *chsd ldrs: led appr 4 out: rdn bef last: styd on wl* **11/4**[1]

50-5 **2** *8* **Good Harvest (IRE)**[31] 540 7-11-5 101 .... (v) APMcCoy 109+
(Jonjo O'Neill) *hld up: hdwy 10th: chsd wnr 4 out: rdn whn pckd last: no etxra* **5/1**[2]

-4P1 **3** *7* **Thenameescapesme**[10] 794 10-11-1 100 7ex .... SeanQuinlan(3) 99
(Kim Bailey) *chsd ldrs: rdn appr 4 out: styd on same pce fr next* **6/1**[3]

0-0P **4** *3/4* **Keltic Lord**[20] 695 14-10-13 95 .... LiamTreadwell 93
(Peter Hiatt) *hld up: bhd and rdn 9th: styd on flat: nvr nrr* **25/1**

1-31 **5** *1 1/2* **Petroupetrov (FR)**[20] 695 7-11-12 108 .... RobertThornton 105
(Richard Phillips) *hld up: hdwy 12th: rdn after 5 out: wknd bef 3 out* **6/1**[3]

61-4 **6** *7* **Sarahs Gift (IRE)**[36] 463 7-11-6 102 .... (t) ChristianWilliams 92
(Lawney Hill) *hld up: nt a fluent: a in rr* **8/1**

0-6P **7** *18* **Sula's Legend**[23] 663 9-11-2 105 .... (p) MarkQuinlan(7) 77
(Neil Mulholland) *chsd ldr tl rdn to ld 11th: hdd appr 4 out: wknd next: t.o* **14/1**

PP-0 **P** **Bernard**[31] 540 10-10-0 87 .... DonalDevereux(5) —
(Kevin Bishop) *a bhd: t.o whn p.u bef 10th* **16/1**

5P-P **P** **Tayman (IRE)**[27] 601 8-11-7 103 .... (b) DavidEngland —
(Nigel Twiston-Davies) *prom: drvn along 7th: wknd 10th: hit next: t.o whn p.u bef 12th* **22/1**

2P-3 **P** **Prince Noora (IRE)**[17] 734 9-11-4 100 .... (t) RichardJohnson —
(Tim Vaughan) *mid-div: rdn and wknd after 10th: t.o whn p.u bef 13th* **10/1**

P-PU **P** **Vial De Kerdec (FR)**[13] 769 7-11-5 101 .... (b) FelixDeGiles —
(Mark Bradstock) *led: rdn and hdd 11th: wknd 13th: t.o whn p.u bef 4 out* **22/1**

5m 38.9s (-3.70) **Going Correction** -0.05s/f (Good) **11** Ran SP% **117.2**
Speed ratings: **104,101,98,98,98 95,89,—,—,— —**
toteswingers:1&2 £3.00, 2&3 £7.00, 1&3 £5.20 CSF £16.93 CT £76.66 TOTE £3.90: £2.10, £1.10, £3.00; EX 13.70.
Owner John Jackson & Mike Bevan **Bred** James Hanly, Trevor Stewart & Anthony Stroud **Trained** Byton, H'fords

FOCUS
This was a workmanlike win from Rifleman, who is rated back to his chase best.

NOTEBOOK
Rifleman(IRE) always looked to be holding the runner-up down the straight and stayed on strongly for his second win of the year. Rated 6lb lower over fences compared with hurdles, he will go back up in the weights now, but should remain competitive. (op 9-2)
Good Harvest(IRE) closed up well and held his chance from the end of the back straight, but couldn't get past the determined winner, even in receipt of the full works from McCoy, and ended up well held. (op 6-1 tchd 7-2)
Thenameescapesme, 2lb well in under his penalty for winning with ease at Hereford, came under pressure rounding for home and was beaten at the first in the straight. (tchd 7-1)
Keltic Lord made up good ground in the straight and snatched fourth, but winning seems beyond the 14-y-o these days. (op 28-1)
Petroupetrov(FR) was unable to repeat the level of form shown when winning at Uttoxeter, the 7lb rise appearing to find him out. (tchd 13-2)
Sula's Legend slowly dropped away in the straight, having been up there from an early stage. (op 12-1 tchd 16-1)

869 WORCESTER RACECOURSE FOR CHRISTMAS PARTIES STANDARD OPEN NATIONAL HUNT FLAT RACE 2m
5:40 (5:40) (Class 6) 4-6-Y-O **£1,712** (£499; £249)

Form RPR
0 **1** **Thomas Bell (IRE)**[45] 362 6-10-9 0 .... CharlieWallis(7) 100+
(John O'Shea) *hld up: hdwy 1/2-way: chsd ldr over 1f out: rdn to ld ins fnl f: r.o* **50/1**

2-3 **2** *1/2* **Jump Up**[17] 739 4-10-13 0 .... APMcCoy 96
(Keith Goldsworthy) *led: rdn over 5f out: hung rt over 1f out: hdd ins fnl f: r.o* **1/1**[1]

5 **3** *5* **Robello**[19] 718 6-11-2 0 ...... JasonMaguire 94
(Richard Phillips) *chsd ldrs: lost pl over 8f out: sn bhd: rdn over 3f out: r.o ins fnl f* **20/1**

4 **4** *8* **Grey Gold (IRE)**[52] 238 5-11-2 0 ...... RobertThornton 86
(Richard Lee) *hld up in tch: chsd ldr 10f out: rdn over 2f out: wknd ins fnl f* **11/4**[2]

5 *1 1/4* **Limbunya (IRE)**[74] 5-10-2 0 ...... DavidBass(7) 78
(Ron Hodges) *chsd ldr 6f: remained handy: rdn over 4f out: wknd 2f out* **22/1**

6 *10* **Classicality** 5-10-9 0 ...... RodiGreene 68
(Michael Mullineaux) *hld up: rdn 1/2-way: bhd fnl 6f* **33/1**

U **Misstaysia (IRE)** 5-10-9 0 ...... RichardJohnson —
(Henry Daly) *unruly as the tapes wnt up and eventually bucked the rdr off sn after the s* **9/2**[3]

3m 45.7s (4.00) **Going Correction** -0.35s/f (Good)
WFA 4 from 5yo+ 3lb **7** Ran SP% **108.9**
Speed ratings: **76,75,73,69,68 63,—**
toteswingers:1&2 £10.60, 2&3 £2.90, 1&3 £17.60 CSF £93.48 TOTE £68.20: £19.80, £1.40; EX 41.00 Place 6: £98.76 Place 5: £18.86 .
Owner K W Bell **Bred** Patrick Carroll **Trained** Elton, Gloucs
■ Stewards' Enquiry : Charlie Wallis two-day ban: careless riding (Jul 14-15)

FOCUS
A weak bumper that produced a bit of a turn-up. The second sets the level.

NOTEBOOK
Thomas Bell(IRE) left his debut effort well behind and overcoming greenness to deny the favourite. It wasn't a surprise to connections, however, as he is viewed as a very bright prospect, and could be excused his debut run as he bled and was later found to have a cough. He should improve again and, though he will struggle to defy a penalty, he should make an impact over hurdles.
Jump Up held his chance and made the winner work for it, but again found one too good. Perhaps he will find a small race over hurdles. (op 10-11)
Robello improved on his initial effort at Market Rasen and appeals as the type to fare a good deal better over hurdles. (op 22-1 tchd 25-1)
Grey Gold(IRE) has plenty of size about him and, although ultimately well held, again showed enough to suggest he has a future over hurdles. (tchd 5-2 and 3-1)
Limbunya(IRE) may do better against her own sex. (op 28-1 tchd 33-1 and 20-1)
Misstaysia(IRE) proved unruly down at the start and was intent on getting rid of Richard Johnson, which she successfully managed to do. (tchd 4-1 and 5-1)
T/Jkpt: Not won. T/Plt: £82.80 to a £1 stake. Pool: £65,248.49 - 575.23 winning tickets. T/Qpdt: £27.90 to a £1 stake. Pool: £4,223.19 - 111.80 winning tickets. CR

[856] PERTH (R-H)

Thursday, July 1

OFFICIAL GOING: Good to firm changing to good (good to firm in places) after race 3 (3.20)
All rails back on fresh ground.
Wind: Breezy, across Weather: Overcast, dull

870 ISLE OF SKYE WHISKY NOVICES' HURDLE (8 hdls) 2m 110y
2:20 (2:21) (Class 4) 4-Y-O+ **£3,168** (£936; £468; £234; £117)

Form RPR

5- **1** **Riverscape (IRE)**[13] 782 5-10-12 112 ...... (t) PCarberry 116+
(Gordon Elliott, Ire) *in tch: smooth hdwy bef 3 out: effrt next: led run-in: drvn out* **5/2**[2]

52-1 **2** *1 1/4* **Wind Shuffle (GER)**[17] 445 7-11-5 115 ...... GrahamLee 122
(Jim Goldie) *t.k.h: led: rdn and hdd last: kpt on u.p run-in* **18/1**

-111 **3** *9* **Beidh Tine Anseo (IRE)**[31] 548 4-11-0 122 ...... CampbellGillies(3) 112
(Lucinda Russell) *chsd clr ldrs: effrt bef 2 out: sn outpcd* **1/1**[1]

4 *26* **Mr Nobody (IRE)**[102] 4772 5-10-12 108 ...... JohnnyFarrelly 80
(A J Martin, Ire) *hld up: pushed along bef 3 out: edgd lft fr next: nvr able to chal* **33/1**

6P/ **5** *1* **Zahara Joy**[1345] 1839 7-10-2 0 ...... (t) MichaelMcAlister(3) 72
(Maurice Barnes) *midfield: drvn and outpcd bef 3 out: n.d after* **150/1**

0F3- **6** *1 3/4* **Deise Dan (IRE)**[11] 810 7-10-12 119 ...... (t) BrianHughes 77
(C A McBratney, Ire) *chsd clr and clr of rest: rdn and wknd fr 2 out* **9/1**

0-00 **7** *nk* **Wellesley**[17] 748 4-10-0 78 ...... CallumWhillans(10) 75
(Donald Whillans) *midfield: struggling after 4 out: btn fr next* **150/1**

P00 **8** *1 1/4* **Daasij (IRE)**[29] 576 5-10-12 58 ...... PaddyAspell 75
(J Barclay) *sn towards rr: struggling 4 out: nvr on terms* **150/1**

0P0- **9** *35* **Shahramore**[306] 1338 5-10-5 69 ...... WilsonRenwick 33
(P Monteith) *a bhd: no ch fr 1/2-way* **100/1**

10 *13* **Dramatic Jewel (USA)**[271] 4-10-10 0 ...... (p) PeterBuchanan 25
(Lucinda Russell) *nt fluent: t.k.h in rr: no ch fr 1/2-way* **66/1**

11 *27* **Johnnycarpethead (IRE)**[21] 700 5-10-12 0 ...... JasonMaguire —
(A J Martin, Ire) *a bhd: no ch fr 1/2-way* **80/1**

P- **P** **Wilmington**[110] 4576 6-10-9 0 ...... RyanMania(3) —
(Jean McGregor) *a bhd: struggling 1/2-way: t.o whn p.u bef 2 out* **150/1**

12 **F** **What A Riddle (IRE)**[15] 760 7-11-5 112 ...... DenisO'Regan 86
(A J Martin, Ire) *hld up in tch: effrt after 3 out: 10 l down whn fell next* **7/1**[3]

3m 47.8s (-11.90) **Going Correction** -0.75s/f (Firm)
WFA 4 from 5yo+ 15lb **13** Ran SP% **115.6**
Speed ratings (Par 105): **98,97,93,80,80 79,79,78,62,56 43,—,—**
toteswingers: 1&2 £5.70, 1&3 £1.80, 2&3 £6.60 CSF £41.19 TOTE £3.70: £1.40, £2.50, £1.10; EX 31.30.
Owner Fresh By Nature Syndicate **Bred** Newberry Stud Farm Ltd **Trained** Trim, Co Meath

FOCUS
This looked a weak contest despite the numbers, but the pace was good with two runners clear by about 10l in the early stages. The winner is rated in line with her best Irish form.

NOTEBOOK
Riverscape(IRE) has appeared to improve since having a tongue-tie fitted and collected her first success at Down Royal on her previous outing. Held up in the chasing pack, she moved up going well but only did enough to stay in front once there. (tchd 9-4 and 11-4)
Wind Shuffle(GER), comfortably held in two outings on the Flat since winning over C&D in late May, set off in front and kept on resolutely once challenged. There ought to be another novice event in him if connections preserve in those types of contests. (op 12-1 tchd 20-1)
Beidh Tine Anseo(IRE), chasing a four-timer, who could not pick up after getting into contention after two out. (op 11-10 tchd 6-5 and 10-11 and 11-8 and 5-4 in places)
Mr Nobody(IRE), having his first start for Tony Martin, seemingly showed little for previous connections but did better here.
Zahara Joy, fitted with a tongue-tie for the first time, also ran a little better.
Deise Dan(IRE), readily held over C&D in April, was beaten just over 36l at Gowran Park last time and folded tamely here as soon as he was placed under pressure. (op 11-1 tchd 8-1)
What A Riddle(IRE), a winner over 2m41/2f at this course, was seemingly held in fourth when falling two out. He probably wants further than this. (tchd 8-1)

871 STANJAMES.COM H'CAP HURDLE (12 hdls) 3m 110y
2:50 (2:50) (Class 4) (0-105,105) 4-Y-O+ **£3,485** (£1,029; £514; £257; £128)

Form RPR

1 **Long Wait (IRE)**[27] 620 4-10-8 91 ...... (p) JasonMaguire 109+
(Gordon Elliott, Ire) *a cl up: led bef 2 out: sn clr: eased run-in* **9/1**

-564 **2** *14* **Tarkani (IRE)**[20] 708 7-11-5 105 ...... (tp) KMDonoghue(7) 107
(Valentine Donoghue) *in tch: effrt bef 3 out: kpt on fr next: wnt 2nd run-in: no ch w wnr* **9/1**

3-23 **3** *nk* **Maolisa (IRE)**[29] 577 8-10-8 90 ...... CampbellGillies(3) 92
(S R B Crawford, Ire) *led to 2nd: cl up: effrt bef 2 out: sn chsng wnr: kpt on same pce* **10/1**

-54F **4** *2 1/2* **Follow On**[11] 801 8-10-8 90 ...... (t) MichaelMcAlister(3) 90
(Maurice Barnes) *hld up: hdwy and prom 4 out: effrt bef 2 out: sn one pce* **20/1**

33 **5** *12* **Dark Halo (IRE)**[17] 749 5-10-13 92 ...... (p) BrianHughes 82
(C A McBratney, Ire) *cl up untl rdn and wknd bef 2 out* **8/1**

-623 **6** *15* **Birnies Boy**[26] 624 6-11-6 99 ...... (t) GrahamLee 72
(Brian Storey) *led 2nd: hdd 7th: lft in ld bef next: hdd bef 2 out: sn wknd* **28/1**

04P- **7** *22* **Moscow Mischief**[69] 5374 6-11-7 100 ...... PeterBuchanan 51
(Lucinda Russell) *nt fluent: towards rr: struggling 4 out: nvr on terms* **40/1**

2/06 **8** *35* **Hooky's Hope**[37] 461 7-10-0 79 oh12 ...... TomMessenger —
(Harriet Graham) *in tch: outpcd whn hit 4 out: sn btn: t.o* **33/1**

0-20 **P** **Solway Minstrel**[20] 708 13-11-5 105 ...... MarkQuinlan(7) —
(Lisa Harrison) *towards rr: struggling fnl circ: t.o whn p.u bef 3 out* **12/1**

-PU0 **P** **Humourous (IRE)**[1] 861 8-9-7 79 oh8 ...... MissJRRichards(7) —
(Brian Storey) *in tch tl wknd bef 4 out: t.o whn p.u bef 2 out* **25/1**

3-35 **P** **Auberge (IRE)**[17] 749 6-9-10 82 oh1 ow3 ...... BrianToomey(7) —
(A M Crow) *racd wd in midfield: struggling bef 4 out: t.o whn p.u bef 2 out* **5/1**[1]

0-5B **P** **Lady Wright (IRE)**[20] 717 7-11-2 95 ...... DenisO'Regan —
(Michael Easterby) *hld up: struggling 4 out: nvr on terms: t.o whn p.u bef 2 out* **9/1**

5- **P** **Entre Vous Et Moi (FR)**[250] 1897 5-11-6 99 ...... AELynch —
(Garvan Donnelly, Ire) *midfield: struggling bef 4 out: t.o whn p.u bef next* **50/1**

-414 **U** **Sparkling Zola**[19] 729 8-11-1 97 ...... RyanMania(3) —
(Alistair Whillans) *towards rr: hdwy 4 out: in tch and drvn whn tried to run out and uns rdr 3 out* **11/2**[2]

00-3 **P** **Hermoso (IRE)**[21] 693 5-11-7 105 ...... SamTwiston-Davies(5) —
(Nigel Twiston-Davies) *hld up in midfield: hdwy to ld 7th: rdr rode fin a circ too sn and p.u bef next* **13/2**[3]

0-34 **P** **Nearly Sunday**[26] 624 5-10-3 92 ...... CallumWhillans(10) —
(Donald Whillans) *a bhd: pushed along bef 1/2-way: nvr on terms: t.o whn p.u bef 2 out* **25/1**

5m 47.5s (-22.40) **Going Correction** -0.75s/f (Firm)
WFA 4 from 5yo+ 17lb **16** Ran SP% **126.5**
Speed ratings (Par 105): **105,100,100,99,95 90,83,72,—,— —,—,—,—,— —**
toteswingers:1&2 £52.40, 2&3 £22.90, 1&3 £43.90 CSF £84.49 CT £849.39 TOTE £12.70: £2.80, £3.00, £2.50, £5.70; EX 107.00.
Owner Doomore Syndicate **Bred** Noel Carter **Trained** Trim, Co Meath
■ Stewards' Enquiry : Jason Maguire three-day ban: weighed-in 2lb heavy (Jul 15,17-18)
Sam Twiston-Davies 12-day ban: rode finish, circuit too early (Jul 15-18,20-23,26-30)

FOCUS
Plenty of runners but a weak contest, as a lot of these has been thoroughly exposed in the past. A big step forward from the winner.

NOTEBOOK
Long Wait(IRE) showed his best bit of form for a long time on his previous outing over 2m4f at Tramore and duly built on it to gain a first win over hurdles. The return of the cheekpieces and longer distances appear to have made a difference to him. His jockey weighed in 2lb heavier than when he weighed out. (op 15-2)
Tarkani(IRE) travelled quite well in behind until turning into the home straight. He was one-paced under pressure. (tchd 11-1)
Maolisa(IRE) was one of the last to come off the bridle, but she could only plug on once asked to quicken. (op 12-1)
Follow On can be determined in the latter stages of a race when in the mood, and he responded to every urge of his jockey, but still wasn't good enough. (op 18-1)
Dark Halo(IRE) should have had no problems with this sort of distance judged on her effort at Sedgefield, but she failed to make any impression after turning in. (tchd 15-2)
Auberge(IRE), running from 1lb out of the handicap, was sent off favourite despite having been beaten 18l on her previous two starts. She was disappointing and beaten early. (op 7-1 tchd 9-2)
Hermoso(IRE)'s jockey rode a finish a circuit too early and picked up a lengthy ban. Had the rider looked to his right, he would have seen the field continuing and possibly been able to carry on, albeit with his winning chance gone. The jockey was given a 12-day ban. (op 7-1 tchd 9-2)

872 WALLACE WHITTLE CONSULTING ENGINEERS H'CAP CHASE (18 fncs) 3m
3:20 (3:23) (Class 5) (0-90,90) 4-Y-O+ **£2,558** (£772; £397; £210)

Form RPR

F5-2 **1** **Hurricane Jack**[50] 287 7-11-9 87 ...... (bt) PeterBuchanan 102+
(Lucinda Russell) *in tch: mstke 5th: hdwy and cl up 10th: led 12th: mde rest: clr bef 2 out: styd on strly* **5/2**[1]

-U40 **2** *7* **Gershwinner (IRE)**[31] 549 7-11-12 90 ...... (b) JasonMaguire 95
(Donald McCain) *hld up: hdwy to chse ldrs 14th: wnt 2nd next: rdn and no imp fr 3 out* **5/1**[2]

-445 **3** *5* **Executive's Hall (IRE)**[11] 804 6-10-6 70 ...... (p) KeithMercer 69
(Andrew Crook) *chsd ldrs: drvn and outpcd bef 4 out: n.d after* **6/1**[3]

5/P3 **4** *16* **Lord Lescribaa (FR)**[16] 758 7-11-5 83 ...... (b) RhysFlint 70
(Philip Hobbs) *led to 5th: cl up: rdn whn nt fluent 4 out: wknd bef next* **7/1**

-322 **U** **Hasper**[19] 730 12-11-4 89 ...... MrGCrow(7) —
(Sandy Forster) *chsd ldrs: lost pl 12th: in tch: outpcd whn hit and uns rdr 13th* **6/1**[3]

435U **P** **Janal (IRE)**[23] 677 7-10-5 69 ...... WilsonRenwick —
(Stuart Coltherd) *j.lft: cl up: led 5th to 12th: rdn and wknd after 14th: t.o whn p.u bef 3 out* **9/1**

0-00 **P** **Short Straw (IRE)**[11] 802 7-10-0 64 ...... (p) PaddyAspell —
(Barry Murtagh) *in tch: struggling fr 10th: t.o whn p.u bef 13th* **16/1**

0-64 **P** **Ash High (IRE)**[21] 694 7-11-1 84 ...... (b[1]) SamTwiston-Davies(5) —
(Nigel Twiston-Davies) *mstkes in rr: a bhd: struggling fr 12th: t.o whn p.u bef 4 out* **9/1**

6m 4.40s (-16.00) **Going Correction** -0.75s/f (Firm) **8** Ran SP% **112.2**
Speed ratings (Par 103): **96,93,92,86,— —,—,—**
toteswingers: 1&2 £3.90, 1&3 £4.70, 2&3 £7.30 CSF £15.19 CT £65.37 TOTE £2.70: £1.10, £3.00, £2.90; EX 19.00.

Owner G S Brown **Bred** G Brown **Trained** Arlary, Perth & Kinross

FOCUS

Only ordinary sorts in this. The idling winner was value for further.

NOTEBOOK

Hurricane Jack had shaped really well when the blinkers were applied for the first time on his previous outing over C&D. He took a bit of riding along in the early stages but, once he got to the front, he showed a pleasing attitude to stay there. One would imagine he can win again next time if given a realistic target and a stiffer course may suit this dour sort even better. (op 11-4 tchd 3-1 in a place)

Gershwinner(IRE) got reminders just after the start but was given a patient ride thereafter. He is seemingly not easy to win with and a hard ride. (op 7-1)

Executive's Hall(IRE), with cheekpieces on for the first time, kept plugging away and can win a low-grade contest now he's found his level. (op 8-1)

Lord Lescribaa(FR) put up a disappointing display and doesn't seem to find it easy under rules when considering his record in points. (op 5-1)

Hasper didn't look completely beaten when departing at the thirteenth, but it looked unlikely that he would have troubled the winner. (op 15-2)

Ash High(IRE), with blinkers on for the first time, had shown little before this under rules and once again failed to get competitive. (op 15-2)

873 TIMOTHY HARDIE JEWELLERS NOVICES' CHASE (18 fncs) 3m

3:50 (3:51) (Class 4) 5-Y-0+ **£4,752** (£1,404; £702; £351; £175)

Form RPR

0-F1 **1** **Billie Magern**[18] 738 6-11-0 0............................. SamTwiston-Davies(5) 135+
(Nigel Twiston-Davies) *mde all: qcknd bef 3 out: styd on strly fr next* **2/1**[1]

0/1 **2** *6* **Del Rio (IRE)**[49] 306 7-11-5 135...(p) AELynch 130
(J T R Dreaper, Ire) *prom: stmbld after 4 out: effrt and chsd wnr bef 2 out: kpt on same pce bef last* **4/1**[2]

305- **3** *23* **Chicago Grey (IRE)**[87] 5066 7-10-12 145.............................(t) PCarberry 100
(Gordon Elliott, Ire) *novicey on occasions: hld up: stdy hdwy 4 out: outpcd bef next: no imp fnl 2* **2/1**[1]

4/ **4** *1* **Corrick Bridge (IRE)**[237] 2111 8-10-12 127.................... JohnnyFarrelly 98
(A J Martin, Ire) *hld up: rdn and outpcd 4 out: plugged on fnl 2: n.d* **16/1**

5 *2* **Queen Court (IRE)**[25] 657 8-10-5 0.................................... BrianHughes 90
(R K Watson, Ire) *cl up: chsd wnr 1/2-way to bef 2 out: 3rd and btn whn mstke last* **100/1**

10P- **6** *½* **Dukeofchesterwood**[142] 3955 8-10-12 0............................ KeithMercer 97
(Sandy Forster) *chsd ldrs tl lost pl bef 14th: n.d after* **33/1**

P- **7** *29* **Aurifex (IRE)**[67] 13 6-10-12 0.. PaddyAspell 67
(Paul Murphy) *bhd: lost tch bef 13th: t.o* **100/1**

8 *2¾* **Having Nightmares (IRE)**[24] 6-10-12 0........................... DenisO'Regan 64
(A J Martin, Ire) *in tch: drvn fr 13th: wknd after 4 out: sddle slipped* **11/2**[3]

6m 2.80s (-17.60) **Going Correction** -0.75s/f (Firm) **8** Ran SP% **112.9**

Speed ratings: **99,97,89,89,88 88,78,77**

toteswingers:1&2:£2.60, 2&3:£2.80, 1&3:£1.90 CSF £10.48 TOTE £3.00: £1.20, £1.30, £1.10; EX 12.10.

Owner Roger Nicholls **Bred** Roger Nicholls **Trained** Naunton, Gloucs

FOCUS

This looked a decent contest but the winner was handed an easy lead and dominated his rivals throughout. He produced another step up, with the second to his mark.

NOTEBOOK

Billie Magern was handed an easy lead and dominated his rivals throughout. His stamina was proven and none of his rivals seemed to want to make his life difficult, so it was almost a bloodless success. (op 15-8 tchd 7-4)

Del Rio(IRE), who was wearing cheekpieces for the first time, stumbled slightly after taking the fourth from home. He was travelling strongly in behind and seemingly waiting to make a challenge, but that mistake almost saw him come down. The distance did not look a problem. (op 5-1)

Chicago Grey(IRE) was much the best of these over hurdles,but only made a satisfactory chasing debut on his return from a break. The ground may have been quick enough for him. (op 6-4)

Corrick Bridge(IRE), having his first outing since November, kept on after being held up. It remains to be seen whether he can build on it. (op 12-1)

Queen Court(IRE) ran better than her final position suggested, as she was a bit keen early and still looked dangerous before three out. She got a little tired in the latter stages, as a couple of minor mistakes showed.

Having Nightmares(IRE), an easy winner of an Irish point for another trainer last time, ran disappointingly on his first start for these connections judged by the amount of market support there was for him, although the jockey's saddle reportedly slipped. A good-sized sort, he should be winning under rules. Official explanation: jockey said saddle slipped (op 16-1)

874 NORTHERN MARINE UNDERWRITERS SCOTLAND H'CAP CHASE (15 fncs) 2m 4f 110y

4:20 (4:22) (Class 3) (0-135,130) 4-Y-£6,871 (£2,620; £1,310; £655; £327)

Form RPR

P0-6 **1** **Native Coral (IRE)**[49] 308 12-10-11 115........................ DougieCostello 125
(Nicky Richards) *hld up: drvn and effrt after 3 out: styd on to ld last 75yds: kpt on wl* **16/1**

3-13 **2** *2* **Quito Du Tresor (FR)**[20] 709 6-11-1 122................. CampbellGillies(3) 130
(Lucinda Russell) *a cl up: led gng wl 2 out: rdn run-in: hdd and no ex last 75yds* **7/2**[2]

5F-4 **3** *7* **Stagecoach Amber (USA)**[26] 636 8-11-0 118................. KeithMercer 123+
(Sue Smith) *pressed wnr: blnd 8th: lost 2nd next: rallied: drvn fr 4 out: plugged on fr 2 out: no imp run-in* **11/1**

-0F4 **4** *¾* **Knight Legend (IRE)**[15] 764 11-11-12 130..........................(t) RhysFlint 132+
(Philip Hobbs) *set decent gallop: led to 2 out: one pce whn blnd last* **10/1**

56/ **5** *1½* **Retrievethelegend (IRE)**[60] 110 11-11-5 123........................ AELynch 122
(J T R Dreaper, Ire) *hld up: effrt bef 3 out: no imp fr next* **25/1**

0-01 **6** *30* **Soubriquet (IRE)**[17] 746 7-10-6 113.....................(t) MichaelMcAlister(3) 82
(Maurice Barnes) *hld up in tch: outpcd after 11th: wknd fr next* **10/1**

3F31 **7** *nk* **King Roonah**[1] 860 6-10-8 112 7ex.......................................(t) PCarberry 87+
(Gordon Elliott, Ire) *in tch: effrt bef 4 out: outpcd whn blnd next: sn eased* **7/4**[1]

2-10 **8** *8* **Storymaker**[33] 524 9-11-7 128...................................... FearghalDavis(3) 88
(Sandy Forster) *hld up in tch: struggling 11th: btn bef 3 out* **9/1**[3]

/55- **P** **Another Ambition (IRE)**[70] 5346 9-11-10 128................. DenisO'Regan —
(A J Martin, Ire) *nt fluent in rr: reminders after 7th: struggling bef 10th: t.o whn p.u bef 3 out* **10/1**

4m 53.8s (-20.20) **Going Correction** -0.75s/f (Firm) course record **9** Ran SP% **113.9**

Speed ratings (Par 107): **108,107,104,104,103 92,92,89,—**

toteswingers:1&2 £13.00, 2&3 £8.20, 1&3 £22.80 CSF £72.55 CT £654.16 TOTE £25.10: £5.40, £1.10, £3.50; EX 113.10.

Owner Greystoke Stables Ltd **Bred** P Fitzgerald **Trained** Greystoke, Cumbria

FOCUS

Three horses set off at a good pace, which ensured this was a decent test, and it wasn't a big surprise to see a finisher catch a prominent racer. The winning time was very quick. The winner#s first form since April last year with the next two close to their marks.

NOTEBOOK

Native Coral(IRE) had not been signalling that he was about to win judged on recent efforts under claiming riders, but he stayed on strongly after the final fence to get to the front. He's lightly raced for his age and reasonably treated, but it's still difficult to predict what he will do next time with any certainty. Official explanation: trainer had no explanation for the apparent improvement in form. (tchd 14-1)

Quito Du Tresor(FR), up 4f in distance, looked to have been given a perfect ride once settled in behind the leaders and it almost paid off. He is in good form. (op 9-2)

Stagecoach Amber(USA) tracked the leader but was ridden along a little way out and lost his position. He rallied well under pressure, however, and kept on.

Knight Legend(IRE) set a decent gallop but weakened steadily up the home straight. It still looked a decent effort under top weight. A mistake at the last probably did not have a massive effect on his position. (op 8-1 tchd 11-1)

Retrievethelegend(IRE), who unseated his rider when slipping up before the first time the starter attempted to let them go, made headway from the rear and ran respectably on his return to fence. (op 22-1)

King Roonah, a winner the previous day in a novice chase and under a 7lb penalty, made good headway but could not pick up. One would have to conclude that his recent victory took the edge off him. (op 9-4)

875 TOTESUPER7 CONDITIONAL JOCKEYS' H'CAP HURDLE (10 hdls) 2m 4f 110y

4:50 (4:51) (Class 5) (0-90,90) 4-Y-0+ **£2,217** (£655; £327; £163; £81)

Form RPR

-P25 **1** *hd* **Can't Remember**[36] 470 5-10-11 78..........................(t) OliverDayman(3) 91+
(Alison Thorpe) *trckd ldrs: effrt and ev ch 2 out: carried lft appr last: kpt on u.p run-in: fin 2nd, hd: awrdd r* **20/1**

000/ **2** **Grand Art (IRE)**[290] 4804 6-11-1 82............................... DeanColeman(3) 94+
(Tim Vaughan) *trckd ldrs: led gng wl 2 out: rdn and hung lft appr last: drvn out run-in: fin 1st: disqualified and plcd 2nd* **15/8**[1]

0-34 **3** *14* **Knight Valliant**[33] 520 7-11-6 84...................................... JamesO'Farrell 81
(Barbara Butterworth) *hld up on ins: hdwy bef 3 out: kpt on fr next: no ch w first two* **10/1**

-012 **4** *½* **Papradon**[21] 697 6-11-5 86.................................. SamTwiston-Davies(3) 84
(Nigel Twiston-Davies) *led to 2 out: sn rdn and outpcd* **4/1**[2]

00-4 **5** *1¾* **Middlemarch (IRE)**[26] 286 10-11-4 90............................ PaulNorton(8) 85
(Jim Goldie) *bhd tl hdwy after 3 out: plugged on: nvr able to chal* **25/1**

F0 **6** *16* **Saddlers' Supreme (IRE)**[21] 697 8-11-7 85..............(t) JamesHalliday 64
(Martin Todhunter) *hld up: sme hdwy 3 out: sn no imp* **20/1**

PP/0 **7** *1¾* **Make It Blossom (IRE)**[31] 552 8-10-11 78.............. KMDonoghue(3) 62
(John G Carr, Ire) *t.k.h: trckd ldrs: blnd bdly 6th: nt fluent next: sn btn* **66/1**

8 *2½* **Bronx Boy (IRE)**[78] 5191 7-11-8 89.............................. AlexanderVoy(3) 64
(Martin Todhunter) *hld up: hdwy u.p bef 3 out: btn next* **28/1**

00/4 **9** *¾* **Troys Steps**[7] 527 6-10-5 72.. KyleJames(3) 46
(Sandy Forster) *cl up: ev ch 3 out: wknd bef next* **40/1**

6-04 **10** *¾* **Pay On (IRE)**[37] 459 7-10-5 74.................................(b) CallumWhillans(5) 47
(Alistair Whillans) *prom tl rdn and wknd after 3 out* **14/1**

5P0- **11** *14* **Always Best**[207] 2729 6-11-9 87... FearghalDavis 46
(Dick Allan) *bhd: hdwy u.p bef 4 out: wknd next* **33/1**

6-12 **12** *4½* **Pugnacity**[12] 473 6-11-3 81.. RhysFlint 36
(Dianne Sayer) *in tch tl rdn and wknd after 3 out* **13/2**[3]

P-P6 **P** **Witness Run (IRE)**[43] 393 10-11-2 80......................(p) CampbellGillies —
(Sandy Thomson) *midfield: lost pl whn nt fluent 6th: sn n.d: t.o whn p.u bef 2 out* **25/1**

6U46 **P** **Solway Blue**[36] 473 8-10-11 80.. MarkQuinlan(5) —
(Lisa Harrison) *a bhd: t.o whn p.u bef 2 out* **12/1**

3-64 **P** **Parisian Knight (IRE)**[37] 456 7-10-7 74..................... BrianToomey(3) —
(A M Crow) *in tch: lost pl 1/2-way: struggling fr 4 out: t.o whn p.u bef 2 out* **25/1**

0-50 **P** **The Sheepdipper**[33] 520 6-10-10 79............................ PaulGallagher(5) —
(Lucy Normile) *hld up: hdwy and in tch 1/2-way: wknd bef 4 out: t.o whn p.u bef last* **80/1**

4m 52.3s (-14.60) **Going Correction** -0.75s/f (Firm) **16** Ran SP% **124.2**

Speed ratings (Par 103): **96,97,91,91,90 84,83,83,82,82 77,75,—,—,— —**

toteswingers:1&2 £34.90, 2&3 £10.20, 1&3 £34.10 CSF £55.63 CT £434.57 TOTE £29.30: £4.70, £1.40, £3.00, £1.50; EX 118.10.

Owner Tristar **Bred** R C And Mrs A J Long **Trained** Bronwydd Arms, Carmarthens

FOCUS

Two Welsh-trained horses fought out this finish on their first starts for these trainers. They were well clear of the remainder of the field and can probably rate higher.

NOTEBOOK

Can't Remember only showed a modicum of ability for previous connections, so this was a fine piece of training by Alison Thorpe. He doesn't look the easiest ride but there ought to be more races to be won with him at a low level. (op 18-1 tchd 22-1)

Grand Art(IRE) passed the post first, but he was demoted to second after causing accidental interference to the runner-up at the final hurdle. On another day, it's fair to say he may have kept the race, but the winning margin was so narrow that the stewards probably had no option but to reverse the position. (op 7-4 tchd 13-8)

Knight Valliant travelled well in behind but got slightly outpaced as the tempo increased on the home bend. He kept on but the first two were gone by the time he was in the clear. (op 14-1)

Papradon, up 4f in trip, set off to make all but was readily claimed entering the home straight. (op 9-2)

Middlemarch(IRE) should be up to winning something over hurdles judged on his winning ability on the Flat, and he caught the eye with the way he stayed on from off the pace. (op 22-1)

Pugnacity weakened quite quickly after being in the first five turning in. (op 10-1)

876 NEW FIXTURE SATURDAY AUGUST 21ST INTERMEDIATE OPEN NATIONAL HUNT FLAT RACE 2m 110y

5:20 (5:20) (Class 5) 4-6-Y-O **£1,712** (£499; £249)

Form RPR

1 **Esporao (IRE)**[18] 742 4-11-0 0..(t) JasonMaguire 105+
(Gordon Elliott, Ire) *t.k.h: trckd ldrs: led on bit over 2f out: rdn over 1f out: styd on wl ins fnl f* **6/4**[1]

1-44 **2** *5* **Corky Dancer**[19] 731 5-11-2 0.. AlexanderVoy(7) 109
(P Monteith) *cl up: ev ch over 5f out to over 2f out: kpt on same pce* **7/1**

3 *1¾* **Inishargie (IRE)**[47] 6-10-11 0................................ MrStevenCrawford(5) 100
(S R B Crawford, Ire) *t.k.h: cl up: led 6f to over 2f out: kpt on same pce* **4/1**[3]

4 *34* **Blue Shirt Lily** 5-10-9 0.. PCarberry 59
(R K Watson, Ire) *hld up: outpcd over 5f out: no ch w first three after* **12/1**

0 **5** *13* **Hey There Tiger (IRE)**[49] 311 5-10-9 0............................ WilsonRenwick 46
(Alistair Whillans) *led to 6f out: rdn and wknd fr 4f out* **50/1**

6 *2* **Jabus (IRE)** 4-11-0 0.. AELynch 49
(B R Hamilton, Ire) *hld up in tch: struggling over 4f out: t.o* **5/2**[2]

7 78 **Fleur De Vallee** 5-10-2 0 CallumWhillans(7) —
(Alistair Whillans) *bhd: lost tch 1/2-way: t.o* **22/1**

3m 43.7s (-10.40) **Going Correction** -0.75s/f (Firm)
WFA 4 from 5yo+ 2lb 7 Ran SP% **115.1**
Speed ratings: **94,91,90,74,68 67,31**
toteswingers: 1&2 £2.60, 2&3 £2.00, 1&2 not won. CSF £13.19 TOTE £2.50: £1.10, £1.90; EX 8.50 Place 6: £29.45 Place 5: £23.78 .
Owner Brendan Scully **Bred** J Stan Cosgrove **Trained** Trim, Co Meath
■ Stewards' Enquiry : Alexander Voy one-day ban: used whip with excessive frequency (Jul 15)

FOCUS
A modest bumper but the first three are fair types for the time of year.

NOTEBOOK
Esporao(IRE) took a good grip during the race but found enough once asked to quicken to the front. This was not much of a race, but he does have the scope to keep improving. That said, he will be lucky to find such an easy opportunity next time. (tchd 11-8 and 13-8)
Corky Dancer, giving weight away, gave away whatever chance he had by hanging left under pressure under a left-handed drive. Once he got over towards the stands side, he kept on nicely. (op 9-2)
Inishargie(IRE), twice a runner-up in points, can win a bumper and is one to keep an eye on if coming back to this course considering his trainer's record at the track. (op 11-4)
Jabus(IRE) was the subject of strong support and did travel quite well for a long way before dropping right away on turning in. (op 7-1)
T/Jkpt: Not won T/Plt: £43.10 to £1 stake Pool: £72,064.91 - 1,218.45 w. tckts T/Qpdt: £7.70 Pool: £4,964.51 - 476.90 w. tckts RY 877a-885a (Foreign Racing) See Raceform Interactive

[835]MARKET RASEN (R-H)
Sunday, July 4

OFFICIAL GOING: Good to firm (good in places) changing to good to firm after race 1 (2.20)
Hurdle track rail moved out 2yd on home straight and bends.
Wind: strong 1/2 against Weather: fine and sunny but very breezy

886 DON NOBLE NOVICES' H'CAP HURDLE (8 hdls) 2m 1f
2:20 (2:21) (Class 4) (0-105,105) 4-Y-0+ **£2,740** (£798; £399)

Form RPR

60-4 **1** **Avanos (FR)**[24] 697 5-10-9 **95** KyleJames(7) 101+
(Philip Kirby) *trckd ldr: squeezed through and led appr 2 out: rdn clr run-in* **9/4**[1]

3113 **2** 6 **Ruby Isabel (IRE)**[19] 755 6-11-0 **93** RichardJohnson 94
(Tim Vaughan) *set stdy pce: j.lft: qcknd 4th: hdd appr 2 out: 2nd whn hit last: kpt on same pce* **11/4**[2]

-323 **3** hd **Decision**[5] 850 4-11-0 **100** (t) DavidBass(5) 98
(Lawney Hill) *trckd ldrs: drvn 3 out: hung lft and styd on same pce run-in* **7/2**[3]

04/1 **4** ½ **Blue Eyed Eloise**[56] 216 8-11-12 **105** LeightonAspell 105
(Brian McMath) *trckd ldrs: effrt on ins appr 2 out: styd on same pce between last 2* **15/2**

UP-6 **5** 4½ **Vogarth**[15] 135 6-9-12 **82** GemmaGracey-Davison(5) 77
(Michael Chapman) *in rr: sme hdwy appr 2 out: nvr trbld ldrs* **40/1**

-424 **6** ½ **Galley Slave (IRE)**[23] 713 5-9-8 **80** oh3 ow1 StevenGagan(7) 75
(Michael Chapman) *hld up in last: sme hdwy 3 out: nvr a threat* **9/1**

240- **7** 6 **Coeur Brule (FR)**[82] 5172 4-10-12 **100** MrDavidTurner(7) 89
(Sam Davison) *trckd ldrs: 4th and wkng whn hit 2 out: sn wknd: eased towards fin* **14/1**

-404 **U** **Piccolo Pride**[14] 800 5-10-10 **92** (t) MichaelMcAlister(3) 81
(Maurice Barnes) *trckd ldrs: jnd ldr 5th: bmpd and wknd appr 2 out: last whn mstke and uns rdr last* **16/1**

4m 21.8s (15.10) **Going Correction** +0.50s/f (Soft)
WFA 4 from 5yo+ 15lb 8 Ran SP% **116.4**
Speed ratings (Par 105): **84,81,81,80,78 78,75,—**
Tote Swingers: 1&2 £3.20, 1&3 £2.80, 2&3 £1.20 CSF £9.41 CT £20.44 TOTE £3.30: £1.70, £2.20, £1.10; EX 13.00.
Owner Keith Sivills **Bred** Earl Haras Du Camp Benard **Trained** Castleton, N Yorks

FOCUS
It took this lot a while to jump off, and even then there was very little pace until coming to five out. The jockey on the runner-up reported the going to be as stated, but pretty fast, and the hurdles track was out two yards.

NOTEBOOK
Avanos(FR) ran by far his best race over hurdles last time at Uttoxeter (after a break) and built on that with an authoritative success here. Well backed before the off, he's in good heart and can win again. Official explanation: vet said gelding finished lame (op 9-2)
Ruby Isabel(IRE), back over hurdles, had an easy time of it in front but tended to jump to her left. It's disappointing that she was not able to capitalise on such a free time of it at the head of affairs, as she became very one-paced off the bridle. (op 15-8 tchd 3-1 and 10-3 in a place)
Decision was held up in midfield and needed to be ridden quite strongly before running on after the final hurdle.
Blue Eyed Eloise, the winner of a maiden hurdle last time, came through to look a danger but found little after the last, losing two places in the final 50 yards. (op 6-1 tchd 8-1)
Vogarth stayed on but never looked dangerous at any stage.
Galley Slave(IRE) was held up well behind the last runner in the chasing bunch even when the pace was slow, which was never going to help as the tempo increased. (op 14-1)
Coeur Brule(FR) looked to pull very hard on his return from a layoff and did not get home.

887 DONNOBLE.CO.UK NOVICES' HURDLE (10 hdls) 2m 3f
2:50 (2:50) (Class 4) 4-Y-0+ **£2,602** (£764; £382; £190)

Form RPR

2-12 **1** **Calon Crwbin**[31] 591 5-11-5 120 (t) JohnnyFarrelly 126+
(Alison Thorpe) *led: clr 2nd: hit 5th: eased towards fin: unchal* **4/6**[1]

0-54 **2** 18 **Broadway Allstar (IRE)**[49] 358 5-10-5 88 BrianHughes 89
(Karen Tutty) *chsd wnr: 15 l down whn hit 2 out: no ch w wnr* **14/1**

-463 **3** 13 **Sunset Resort (IRE)**[38] 492 5-10-9 90 (t) MichaelMcAlister(3) 82
(Maurice Barnes) *hmpd 1st: hdwy 4th: wnt modest 3rd appr 2 out* **12/1**

05-0 **4** 3¼ **Santamina (IRE)**[29] 624 4-10-9 0 (p) TomO'Brien 76
(Peter Bowen) *chsd ldrs: one pce appr 2 out* **18/1**

00/3 **5** 14 **Devils And Dust (IRE)**[40] 456 9-10-5 73 (p) MissPhillipaTutty(7) 65
(Karen Tutty) *in rr: hit 2nd: nvr on terms* **20/1**

00-F **6** 20 **Morecambe Bay**[45] 426 5-10-9 0 TommyPhelan(3) 45
(David Thompson) *nt fluent in rr: bhd fr 6th* **50/1**

7 **7** 1¼ **Capable Guest (IRE)**[30] 8-10-12 0 BarryKeniry 44
(George Moore) *j. poorly: chsd ldrs: lost pl 7th: poor 5th whn j.lft 2 out: bhd whn j. violently lft last* **6/1**[2]

8 **8** 33 **Riqaab (IRE)**[8] 5-10-12 0 DenisO'Regan 11
(Michael Easterby) *in rr: sme hdwy 6th: sn wknd: t.o whn mstke 2 out* **22/1**

P0 **9** 10 **Simone Martini (IRE)**[18] 760 5-10-12 0 (t) CharliePoste 1
(Milton Harris) *mid-div: lost pl 6th: t.o 2 out* **50/1**

P **Moscow Oznick**[22] 5-10-12 0 AlanO'Keeffe —
(Des Donovan) *j. bdly: j. bdly lft and lost pl 5th: bhd whn blnd 7th: sn t.o: p.u bef 2 out* **9/1**[3]

4m 42.2s (2.80) **Going Correction** +0.50s/f (Soft)
WFA 4 from 5yo+ 15lb 10 Ran SP% **116.9**
Speed ratings (Par 105): **114,106,100,99,93 85,84,70,66,—**
Tote Swingers: 1&2 £4.00, 1&3 £2.40, 2&3 £18.70 CSF £11.13 TOTE £1.80: £1.02, £3.20, £4.00; EX 9.40.
Owner Hanford's Chemist Ltd **Bred** R W And Mrs B D Neale **Trained** Bronwydd Arms, Carmarthens

FOCUS
A dreadful contest. Whilst the other horses in this race were not up to a great deal, it's never a smart idea to give the clear form choice a huge lead from the off.

NOTEBOOK
Calon Crwbin, the form pick, was handed a huge advantage early and only needed to get over the hurdles to collect, which he did. (tchd 8-11)
Broadway Allstar(IRE) chased the winner in second place for a lot of the race. Well beaten in a seller last time, she was never good enough to get closer. (op 16-1)
Sunset Resort(IRE), taking a big drop in trip, kept on just better than Santamina to get third place. (op 14-1)
Santamina(IRE), who had cheekpieces on, was well beaten in fourth. (op 28-1)
Capable Guest(IRE) did not jump at all well on this hurdles debut. (op 9-2)
Moscow Oznick, who often wears cheekpieces on the Flat, jumped poorly, and will have no chance of doing well over hurdles unless their fluency over them gets much better. (tchd 10-1)

888 TOM HALLIDAY MEMORIAL CONDITIONAL JOCKEYS' H'CAP HURDLE (10 hdls) 2m 5f
3:20 (3:21) (Class 4) (0-115,114) 4-Y-0+ **£3,903** (£1,146; £573; £286)

Form RPR

14 **1** **Tout Regulier**[38] 488 6-11-2 **107** DonalDevereux(3) 120+
(Peter Bowen) *t.k.h: trckd clr ldr: led bef 3 out: wnt clr appr 2 out: drvn out* **12/1**

0141 **2** 13 **Benmadigan (IRE)**[18] 767 8-11-8 **113** FearghalDavis(3) 113
(Nicky Richards) *in rr-div: hdwy u.p 3 out: wnt modest 2nd sn after 2 out: kpt on same pce* **5/1**[3]

20-0 **3** 1 **Goldan Jess (IRE)**[60] 166 6-10-12 **103** KyleJames(3) 102
(Philip Kirby) *hld up towards rr: hdwy and 6th appr 2 out: tk 3rd between last 2: kpt on same pce* **7/1**

0-31 **4** 16 **Choctaw Nation**[17] 713 6-10-7 **98** JamesHalliday(3) 85
(Malcolm Jefferson) *hld up in rr: hdwy 7th: 6th whn blnd next: 8 l 2nd whn nt fluent 2 out: sn wknd: eased clsng stages* **10/3**[1]

523- **5** 18 **Deadline (UAE)**[195] 3004 6-11-5 **107** (b) JohnnyFarrelly 72
(Alison Thorpe) *nt fluent: led and sn clr: hdd appr 3 out: modest 6th whn mstke last* **10/1**

B312 **6** 1¼ **Bold Policy (IRE)**[12] 825 7-10-8 **96** (p) PeterToole 70
(Milton Harris) *chsd ldrs: wnt 2nd 3 out: lost pl appr next: fin lame* **7/1**

12-P **7** 10 **Muntami (IRE)**[49] 351 9-11-0 **105** MrTomDavid(3) 59
(John Harris) *in rr: rdn and outpcd 7th: sn bhd* **25/1**

6-03 **8** 6 **Sea Cliff (IRE)**[33] 564 6-11-5 **110** RichieMcLernon(3) 58
(Jonjo O'Neill) *blnd 1st: chsd ldrs: lost pl 7th: sn bhd* **14/1**

6/1- **P** **Darksideofthemoon (IRE)**[323] 1221 8-11-9 **114** (p) DeanColeman(3) —
(Tim Vaughan) *chsd ldrs: wknd appr 2 out: 6th whn p.u bef last* **4/1**[2]

05-6 **P** **Tifoso (FR)**[47] 382 5-11-0 **102** (e) SamJones —
(Richard Guest) *mid-div: lost pl after 6th: sn bhd: t.o whn p.u after 3 out* **16/1**

5m 16.2s (7.40) **Going Correction** +0.50s/f (Soft) 10 Ran SP% **117.9**
Speed ratings (Par 105): **105,100,99,93,86 86,82,80,—,—**
Tote Swingers: 1&2 £12.00, 1&3 £46.20, 2&3 £10.90 CSF £72.68 CT £461.94 TOTE £19.40: £5.20, £3.20, £2.30; EX 87.40.
Owner G A Moore **Bred** Miss M E Steele **Trained** Little Newcastle, Pembrokes

FOCUS
The fifth set a strong pace. Very few got into this.

NOTEBOOK
Tout Regulier didn't show a great deal at Wetherby on her previous run, but this time showed the sort of ability she displayed when winning at Exeter in May. She travelled strongly throughout while sitting in an ideal stalking position, and won with any amount in hand. Connections will want to get her out quite quickly before her handicap mark goes up significantly, and the trainer mentioned afterwards that she will go chasing before too long. (tchd 10-1)
Benmadigan(IRE), 6lb higher than when winning at Worcester, owed his position to Fearghal Davis's strength, as the horse came under pressure quite a way out and didn't seem to be going anywhere quickly. That said, he did show resilience when the third came up alongside after the final hurdle, as he battled on gamely. (op 7-1)
Goldan Jess(IRE) ran a fair race after a two-month break. (op 8-1 tchd 6-1)
Choctaw Nation might have had a problem with the extra two furlongs, as he capitulated quickly after the second-last. (op 5-1 tchd 3-1)
Deadline(UAE), after setting a strong pace, was caught and readily passed relatively early in the contest. (tchd 9-1)
Bold Policy(IRE) seemed to disappoint but was reportedly lame afterwards. Official explanation: vet said gelding finished lame and lost a shoe (op 8-1)
Darksideofthemoon(IRE), having his first run since winning over the course last August, and 14lb higher as a consequence, had every chance but was one-paced under pressure. (op 11-4)

889 MANNYBERNSTEIN.CO.UK BEGINNERS' CHASE (14 fncs) 2m 4f
3:50 (3:51) (Class 4) 5-Y-0+ **£3,252** (£955; £477; £238)

Form RPR

20-5 **1** **Walamo (GER)**[21] 738 6-11-0 0 (t) RichardJohnson 121+
(Tim Vaughan) *trckd ldrs: wnt 2nd 6th: upsides 4 out: led appr next: 11 l ahd last: eased towards fin* **5/1**

F **2** 10 **Thelobstercatcher**[18] 761 6-11-0 0 TomO'Brien 107
(Peter Bowen) *nt fluent: sn chsng ldrs: outpcd 4 out: modest 4th whn blnd 3 out: kpt on to take n.d 2nd clsng stages* **3/1**[3]

23-2 **3** 3¼ **Blossom King (FR)**[29] 634 6-11-0 110 SamThomas 103
(Tom George) *led: jnd 4 out: hdd appr next: wknd and lost 2nd last 75yds* **85/40**[1]

2-32 **4** 4 **Watch Out**[18] 761 6-11-0 103 (tp) ChristianWilliams 99
(Dai Burchell) *t.k.h in rr: hdwy to go modest 3rd 4 out: one pce fr next* **9/4**[2]

P **5** 7 **Sendeed (USA)**[29] 628 8-11-0 0 (tp) KeithMercer 92
(Peter Atkinson) *chsd ldr to 6th: lost pl 4 out* **66/1**

6 **6** hd **Diaco (IRE)**[24] 687 6-10-11 0 RichieMcLernon(3) 92
(Jonjo O'Neill) *in tch: outpcd 8th: lost pl 4 out* **16/1**

5 7 13 **Keenans Reserve (IRE)**[49] 9-10-9 0........................(p) MichaelMurphy[(5)] 86
(Brian Baugh) *unruly s: in rr: sme hdwy 8th: wknd 4 out: 6th whn blnd and j.rt last* **33/1**

4m 50.8s (-14.90) **Going Correction** -0.80s/f (Firm) 7 Ran SP% **114.8**
Speed ratings: **97,93,91,90,87 87,82**
Tote Swingers: 1&2 £2.40, 1&3 £2.40, 2&3 £2.00 CSF £21.11 TOTE £5.10: £2.70, £2.00; EX 11.90.
Owner M & S Clarke **Bred** Gestut Hof Vesterberg **Trained** Aberthin, Vale of Glamorgan

FOCUS
A fair-looking contest.

NOTEBOOK
Walamo(GER) had been well beaten on his chasing debut, albeit after a long layoff, but ran out an easy winner of this once assuming control. One would imagine he will be kept on the go during the summer now he has got his head in front again. (op 11-2 tchd 4-1)
Thelobstercatcher departed at the first last time on his chasing debut under rules, and was a little hesitant early in this, but he was guided around carefully by his jockey and ran on nicely in the final stages. One would imagine that being the winner of a point he'll get further. (op 7-2 tchd 4-1)
Blossom King(FR) got to the lead without too many problems and looked in command until joined. He was made to look one-paced under pressure. (op 6-4)
Watch Out probably isn't an easy ride and, much like last time, he arrived on the scene after being held up going fairly well before not going on again. He seemed highly likely to get second at one point but ended up held in fourth. (op 4-1)

890 DONALD NOBLE MEMORIAL H'CAP CHASE (14 fncs) 2m 6f 110y
4:20 (4:20) (Class 3) (0-120,120) 4-Y-O+ **£5,529** (£1,623; £811; £405)

Form RPR
133- **1** **No Panic (IRE)**[78] 5223 7-11-12 **120**..............................(p) TomO'Brien 127+
(Peter Bowen) *chsd ldrs: led appr 3 out: 3 l ahd last: jst hld on* **9/4**[2]
0512 **2** *nk* **Chorizo (IRE)**[9] 839 9-11-2 **115**.............................. JamesHalliday[(5)] 121+
(Richard Guest) *chsd ldr: led 2nd to 4th: drvn to chse ldr sn after 4 out: styd on run-in: jst hld* **13/8**[1]
4-22 **3** *4 1/2* **Viper**[14] 797 8-11-9 **117**..............................(b[1]) SamThomas 118
(Dr Richard Newland) *led to 2nd: led 4th: hdd appr 3 out: one pce fr next* **9/2**[3]
24-P **4** *14* **On You Go (IRE)**[27] 663 9-11-1 **112**.............................. RichieMcLernon[(3)] 100
(Jonjo O'Neill) *in rr: hdwy and in tch 9th: 4th whn hit 2 out: sn wknd* **9/1**
P-43 **5** *3/4* **I'm The Decider (IRE)**[39] 476 8-11-10 **118**................(p) DougieCostello 104
(Jonjo O'Neill) *nt jump wl in last: outpcd and detached 7th: kpt on run-in* **10/1**
PF/- **6** *56* **Kasthari (IRE)**[624] 4899 11-11-7 **115**.............................. DenisO'Regan 45
(Chris Grant) *chsd ldrs: blnd 6th: lost pl 9th: t.o whn j.lft last 3* **20/1**
U/44 **P** **Mighty Matters (IRE)**[23] 707 11-11-5 **118**..............(t) DavidBass[(5)] —
(Charlie Longsdon) *prom: drvn 3rd: sn lost pl: t.o 7th: p.u bef next* **20/1**

5m 27.2s (-18.80) **Going Correction** -0.80s/f (Firm) 7 Ran SP% **115.7**
Speed ratings (Par 107): **100,99,98,93,93 73,—**
Tote Swingers: 1&2 £1.30, 1&3 £2.40, 2&3 £3.00 CSF £6.85 CT £13.11 TOTE £2.80: £1.50, £1.40; EX 6.10.
Owner Roddy Owen & Paul Fullagar **Bred** John Ryan **Trained** Little Newcastle, Pembrokes

FOCUS
A fair handicap.

NOTEBOOK
No Panic(IRE), last seen when third in the Scottish National, tracked the pace in a good position before putting his stamina to use once in a challenging position before three out. He didn't win by very far as he idled in front, but this should have teed him up for the Summer Plate. (op 7-2)
Chorizo(IRE), bidding to win this for the second year in a row off a 15lb higher mark, sat just in behind Viper throughout and looked held until running on gamely in the final stages. He is in great heart and should be competitive next time, although vulnerable to a less-exposed type. (op 2-1)
Viper had blinkers on for the first time and was making his handicap debut over fences. His jockey managed to start and stop the pace while in front and he gained nice advantages at a couple of stages of the race, but the gelding gave the impression that as soon as he is asked for any proper effort, he doesn't really want to know. (op 4-1 tchd 7-2)
On You Go(IRE) didn't show much on his return to action last time, and again here. (op 17-2 tchd 8-1)
I'm The Decider(IRE) never got involved after being well behind, but stayed on quite nicely up the home straight. (op 9-1)
Kasthari(IRE) ran well for a while on his return from a mammoth layoff. (op 11-1)
Mighty Matters(IRE) got behind early and the tongue-tie seemed to make no obvious difference. Official explanation: jockey said gelding never travelled (op 12-1)

891 MANNY BERNSTEIN FREEPHONE 0800 821821 H'CAP CHASE (12 fncs) 2m 2f
4:50 (4:50) (Class 4) (0-105,102) 4-Y-O+ **£2,927** (£859; £429; £214)

Form RPR
-634 **1** **Turbo Shandy**[19] 755 7-11-0 **90**..............................(p) TomO'Brien 106+
(Dai Burchell) *hld up in tch: smooth hdwy 8th: led 3 out: wnt clr appr next: 12 l ahd last: eased last 100yds* **11/2**[3]
-656 **2** *11* **Nesnaas (USA)**[10] 689 9-11-4 **94**..............................(bt[1]) TomScudamore 95
(Mark Rimell) *chsd ldrs: outpcd 4 out: rallied to take 2nd sn after 2 out: kpt on: no ch w wnr* **4/1**[2]
P-16 **3** *5* **Ormus**[7] 848 7-11-4 **94**..............................(p) KeithMercer 90
(Christopher Wilson) *prom: outpcd 6th: hdwy appr 3 out: wnt modest 3rd between last 2* **13/2**
4-26 **4** *3* **Peak Seasons (IRE)**[36] 516 7-10-0 **76** oh3.............................. PaddyAspell 69
(Michael Chapman) *mid-div: hdwy 6th: outpcd 4 out: kpt on fr 2 out* **10/1**
0/05 **5** *3/4* **Skiddaw Jones**[20] 747 10-10-4 **83**..............................(t) MichaelMcAlister[(3)] 75
(Maurice Barnes) *led to 4 out: 6 l 2nd whn j.rt 2 out: sn wknd* **16/1**
6-25 **6** *7* **Morenito (FR)**[26] 677 7-11-5 **95**..............................(p) SamThomas 80
(Tom George) *chsd ldrs: reminders 8th: wknd appr 3 out* **8/1**
15-4 **7** *nk* **Silver Dollars (FR)**[21] 734 9-11-5 **100**.............................. MrPYork[(5)] 85
(David Arbuthnot) *chsd ldrs: j.rt 3rd: wknd 4 out* **10/1**
4642 **8** *2 1/2* **Wee Forbees (IRE)**[26] 677 8-11-10 **100**.............................. DenisO'Regan 82
(Michael Easterby) *chsd ldr: hmpd 3rd: led 4 out: hdd next: sn wknd: hit last* **7/2**[1]
6P-0 **9** *48* **Bythehokey (IRE)**[14] 799 9-9-9 **76** oh2..............................(tp) MichaelMurphy[(5)] 10
(Brian Baugh) *in rr: reminders 5th: t.o 8th* **33/1**
P **Power Of Attorney (IRE)**[167] 3521 6-11-9 **102**......... RichieMcLernon[(3)] —
(Jonjo O'Neill) *detached in last: reminders 7th: t.o 3 out: p.u bef last* **14/1**

4m 18.1s (-16.90) **Going Correction** -0.80s/f (Firm) 10 Ran SP% **115.7**
Speed ratings (Par 105): **105,100,97,96,96 93,92,91,70,—**
Tote Swingers: 1&2 £3.60, 1&3 £7.50, 2&3 £4.60 CSF £28.42 CT £146.65 TOTE £7.20: £2.20, £2.10, £2.20; EX 26.80.
Owner The Beefeaters **Bred** Giles W Pritchard-Gordon (farming) Ltd **Trained** Briery Hill, Blaenau Gwent

FOCUS
There was a good gallop set by a couple in this.

NOTEBOOK
Turbo Shandy, suited by the decent pace, tracked the leaders going well throughout. A mainly consistent sort, the return of cheekpieces may have made all the difference, as he won with loads in hand. The handicapper is sure to raise him a lot in the weights for this easy success. (op 5-1 tchd 9-2)
Nesnaas(USA), the winner of this race last season off a 3lb higher mark, had blinkers fitted for the first time and a tongue-tie back on. He had absolutely no chance with the winner but did enough to claim second after being niggled and pushed some way out. (op 9-2 tchd 5-1)
Ormus, well beaten last time, attracted market support but only made modest late progress. (op 9-1 tchd 6-1)
Peak Seasons(IRE) never threatened from out of the handicap to get involved but passed a few horses late on. (op 17-2)
Skiddaw Jones set off in front and battled on quite well for a while until weakening after two out. (op 14-1)
Morenito(FR) travelled well in spells but didn't pick up when asked for maximum effort. (op 13-2)
Wee Forbees(IRE) sat in just behind the leader but found nothing when asked to quicken. (tchd 4-1)

892 DON NOBLE YOUR LOCAL BOOKMAKER STANDARD OPEN NATIONAL HUNT FLAT RACE 2m 1f
5:20 (5:20) (Class 6) 4-6-Y-O **£1,370** (£399; £199)

Form RPR
4 **1** **Harsh But Fair**[39] 474 4-10-5 0.............................. JakeGreenall[(7)] 90+
(Michael Easterby) *chsd ldrs: drvn 7f out: lost pl over 5f out: modest 5th 3f out: hung rt: rapid hdwy to go 6 l 2nd 1f out: led nr fin* **5/2**[2]
2 *1* **High Hoylander** 4-10-12 0.............................. PaddyAspell 89+
(John Norton) *hdwy to trck ldrs 7f out: chal over 5f out: led 3f out: sn 6 l clr: hdd towards fin* **25/1**
50-5 **3** *6* **Instant Decision (IRE)**[31] 602 4-10-12 0........................(p) TomO'Brien 83
(Peter Bowen) *led tl 6f out: sn outpcd and drvn: one pce fnl 3f: tk modest 3rd 1f out* **17/2**
4 *4 1/2* **Bury The Hatchet (IRE)** 4-10-12 0.............................. BrianHughes 79
(Alan Swinbank) *w ldr: led 6f out: rdn over 3f out: sn hdd: wknd 1f out* **2/1**[1]
5 *15* **Punta Baluarte** 4-10-5 0.............................. DougieCostello 57
(Julie Camacho) *hld up: hdwy 7f out: drvn over 5f out: lost pl over 3f out: bhd whn stmbld bdly path 1f out* **5/1**
5P- **6** *4 1/2* **Rationing (IRE)**[71] 5391 4-10-12 0..............................(t) RobertThornton 59
(Tim Easterby) *chsd ldrs: drvn 5f out: wknd over 2f out* **10/3**[3]
0 **7** *79* **Captain Tee Gee**[23] 718 4-10-7 0.............................. PaulCallaghan[(5)] —
(Michael Chapman) *sn detached in last: t.o 6f out: eventually completed* **66/1**

4m 12.2s (11.10) **Going Correction** +0.50s/f (Soft) 7 Ran SP% **117.5**
Speed ratings: **93,92,89,87,80 78,41**
Tote Swingers: 1&2 £10.20, 1&3 £2.60, 2&3 £13.20 CSF £58.63 TOTE £3.60: £1.60, £7.40; EX 98.50 Place 6: £39.10 Place 5: £31.99.
Owner T Dewhirst & R Moore **Bred** G H Sparkes And M W Easterby **Trained** Sheriff Hutton, N Yorks

FOCUS
An ordinary bumper.

NOTEBOOK
Harsh But Fair was going nowhere in the back straight and sat last of those with any chance turning in off the final bend. However, even though still clearly green, he managed to reel in the runner-up and win comfortably. (op 11-4 tchd 2-1)
High Hoylander, a newcomer that changed hands for only £2,000 in May 2009, is a really imposing sort and travelled strongly throughout the race. He probably got to the front a little too soon, through no fault of his own, and possibly dossed once there. He is effectively a winner without a penalty. (op 16-1)
Instant Decision(IRE), with cheekpieces on, shapes like a horse that is going to need a much stiffer test with time. (tchd 15-2 and 9-1)
Bury The Hatchet(IRE), who cost 13,000 euros as a foal, is related to some winners but only showed a modicum of promise here after racing prominently. (op 9-4 tchd 15-8)
Punta Baluarte, a a half-sister to the useful hurdler/chaser Calatagan, didn't seem unfancied on her racecourse debut but couldn't get involved. (op 6-1 tchd 8-1)
Rationing(IRE) is regressing on quicker ground than when he made his debut over the course and distance in February. (op 4-1)
T/Jkpt: Not won. T/Plt: £149.80 to a £1 stake. Pool: £71,896.21. 350.35 winning tickets. T/Qpdt: £80.40 to a £1 stake. Pool: £4,077.49. 37.50 winning tickets. WG

893a - 907a (Foreign Racing) - See Raceform Interactive

820 NEWTON ABBOT (L-H)
Monday, July 5

OFFICIAL GOING: Good to firm (good in places; 8.0)
Wind: mild breeze Weather: sunny

908 NEWTONABBOTRACING.COM MAIDEN HURDLE (8 hdls) 2m 3f
2:15 (2:15) (Class 5) 4-Y-O+ **£2,055** (£599; £299)

Form RPR
05P- **1** **Opening Meet**[104] 4793 6-11-0 0.............................. HarrySkelton 107+
(Paul Nicholls) *mid-div: hdwy 3 out: chal 2 out: led sn after: mstke last: r.o* **33/1**
6-03 **2** *1 1/2* **Minneapolis**[13] 823 5-11-0 108.............................. LeightonAspell 105
(Alison Batchelor) *trckd clr ldr: led after 3 out: rdn and hdd appr last: kpt on but no ex* **2/1**[2]
-00U **3** *8* **Racingisdreaming (USA)**[8] 845 4-10-11 86..........(tp) TomScudamore 95
(David Pipe) *hld up: gd hdwy after 3 out: ev ch next: sn rdn: kpt on same pce* **40/1**
0-3 **4** *3 1/2* **Tuppenny Piece**[36] 535 4-10-4 0.............................. RobertThornton 86
(Alan King) *trckd ldrs: shkn up briefly after 5th: effrt after 3 out: one pce fr next* **11/1**
F-4 **5** *25* **Pegasus Lad (USA)**[20] 754 4-10-11 0.............................. JackDoyle 69
(Linda Blackford) *led: clr tl 4th: rdn and hdd 3 out: sn wknd: t.o* **33/1**
-511 **6** *11* **Maggie Aron**[20] 759 4-10-4 0.............................. RichardJohnson 52
(Tim Vaughan) *racd keenly: hld up: hdwy after 3rd to go 3rd: led 3 out: sn rdn and hdd: wknd qckly* **10/11**[1]
0-0 **7** *1/2* **Kiristani**[20] 759 5-10-2 0.............................. IanPopham[(5)] 55
(Caroline Keevil) *mid-div: struggling 6th: sn wknd: t.o* **100/1**
P **Orsini Conti (FR)**[65] 8-10-9 0..............................(t) TomO'Connor[(5)] —
(Bill Turner) *mid-div tl wknd 6th: t.o whn p.u bef 2 out* **66/1**

4 P **Unleashed (IRE)**[20] 632 5-10-11 0 (bt) PeterToole(3) —
(Charlie Mann) *mid-div: blnd bdly 2nd: rdn after 6th: wknd next: t.o whn p.u bef 2 out* **11/4**[3]

4m 28.7s (-5.20) **Going Correction** -0.25s/f (Good)
WFA 4 from 5yo+ 15lb **9** Ran SP% **131.5**
Speed ratings (Par 103): **100,99,96,94,84 79,79,—,—**
toteswingers: 1&2 £25.90, 1&3 £25.90, 2&3 £15.10 CSF £113.47 TOTE £37.20: £8.10, £1.10, £15.50; EX 135.50.

Owner Frosties Friends **Bred** G Chambers **Trained** Ditcheat, Somerset

FOCUS
The betting suggested this maiden hurdle concerned the three clear market leaders, but it looked more open than that and there was something of a turn up. A massive step up from the winner, with the second and fourth giving the form a bit of substance.

NOTEBOOK
Opening Meet had disappointed since winning his bumper, but had been handed a break since pulling up on his previous outing 104 days previously and looked a rejuvenated character here. His connections later put that down to a breathing operation during his time off the track and, looking at the way he travelled through the race, he rates as progressive. He has also found his ideal sort of trip now and is obviously versatile regarding underfoot conditions. Official explanation: trainer's rep said, regarding apparent improvement in form, that the gelding was better suited by the longer trip and faster ground.
Minneapolis, up in trip, raced somewhat keenly just off the early leader. He took it up full of running round the home turn, but held his head a bit high under pressure and was readily held from two out. He still finished a clear second-best and should pick up a small race during the summer. (op 10-3 tchd 7-2)
Racingisdreaming(USA) showed by far his most encouraging form since coming over from France and could well build on this back over a sharper test.
Tuppenny Piece looked interesting up in trip. She tended to run in snatches and required plenty of driving, but may have found the ground plenty quick enough. Low-grade handicaps should offer her more viable opportunities. (op 12-1)
Maggie Aron, a dual bumper winner, proved very disappointing. She wasn't fluent and proved keen under early restraint, so her rider allowed her to get closer going out onto the far side. She found very little when it mattered, possibly on account of doing much too early and now has something to prove. (tchd 5-6 and 6-4 in places and 13-8 in a place)
Unleashed(IRE) was also disappointing on his return to hurdling, although it later turned out he bled from the nose. Official explanation: vet said gelding bled from the nose (op 4-1)

909 NORTHTOWN SCHOOL OLD GIRLS BEGINNERS' CHASE (16 fncs) 2m 5f 110y
2:45 (2:45) (Class 4) 5-Y-O+ **£4,228** (£1,241; £620; £310)

Form RPR
20/- 1 **Swing Bill (FR)**[1164] 5143 9-11-0 113 TomScudamore 128+
(David Pipe) *racd keenly: hld up in last trio: hdwy 11th: rdn to chal after 3 out: lft wl clr next: comf* **4/1**[2]
5-50 2 25 **Ballyvesey (IRE)**[52] 318 5-11-0 0 (p) TomO'Brien 110+
(Peter Bowen) *trckd ldr: rdn after 4 out: wknd after next: lft in 2nd 2 out* **6/5**[1]
2-46 3 23 **Another Trump (NZ)**[24] 714 6-10-11 0 RichieMcLernon(3) 84
(Jonjo O'Neill) *hld up in last pair: wnt rt 10th: rdn after next: unable to get on terms: wknd after 4 out: lft poor 3rd 2 out* **12/1**
/4-F 4 22 **Apartman (CZE)**[29] 647 5-11-0 0 HarrySkelton 80
(Paul Nicholls) *hld up last: hdwy 11th: chalng whn nt fluent 4 out: sn rdn: wknd qckly next: lft poor 4th 2 out: t.o* **4/1**[2]
/P-6 R **Hell's Bay (FR)**[57] 234 8-11-0 0 RobertThornton 123
(Paul Nicholls) *trckd ldrs: disp fr 6th: clr ldr 10th: mstke 3 out (water): sn rdn: narrow advantage whn rn out next* **11/2**[3]
P-0P P **Tribunel**[19] 761 6-11-0 0 DavidDennis —
(Nigel Hawke) *led tl 10th: wknd qckly: bhd whn p.u bef 12th* **100/1**

5m 19.8s (-1.60) **Going Correction** -0.25s/f (Good) **6** Ran SP% **109.5**
Speed ratings: **92,82,74,66,— —**
toteswingers:1&2 £1.70, 2&3 £3.30, 1&3 £5.60 CSF £9.26 TOTE £4.90: £2.40, £1.10; EX 10.30.

Owner D A Johnson **Bred** Maurice Veron **Trained** Nicholashayne, Devon
■ Robert Thornton suffered a serious knee injury in this fall and could be out of action for a year.

FOCUS
This modest novice chase was run at an uneven gallop and it proved an eventful affair.

NOTEBOOK
Swing Bill(FR) had been absent for a long time so it was a cracking training performance by David Pipe to produce him to score readily. He must have had lots of problems to have been off the track since 2007, but he did have previous chasing experience and attracted support. Keen early, he responded strongly when asked for his effort nearing the turn for home and was on top prior to his only serious rival ducking out at the penultimate fence. This confirms him adaptable regards ground and he obviously retains his ability, so it is hoped he comes out of this sufficiently. However, the bounce factor will still be a real worry ahead of his next assignment. (tchd 5-1)
Ballyvesey(IRE) was surprisingly sent off a short price as he had a lot to find with the majority of his rivals on hurdle ratings. Having his first outing over fences since last October, he took time to warm to his task and was readily left behind as the race got serious after three out. He would also have been third had Hell's Bay not departed two out and, although he may need further in this sphere, it will likely be in handicaps that he gets off the mark. (op 7-4 tchd Evens and 15-8 and 2-1 in a place)
Another Trump(NZ) lost the plot on the back straight and was keeping on again all too late in the home straight. This was a bit more encouraging, though, and it will be interesting to see what mark he is allotted as a chaser. (op 10-1)
Apartman(CZE) looked to be remembering the effects of his heavy fall on his chasing debut a month earlier as he was ponderous early on. He moved up promisingly on the back straight, but was left behind from four out and looks anything but a natural chaser. (op 3-1)
Hell's Bay(FR) was running a much-improved race prior to blotting his copybook at the second-last and has become a very tricky customer. (op 5-1 tchd 6-1)

910 NEWTON ABBOT RACECOURSE MARES' NOVICES' HURDLE (10 hdls) 2m 6f
3:15 (3:15) (Class 4) 4-Y-O+ **£3,577** (£1,050; £525; £262)

Form RPR
4-43 1 **Detroit Red**[32] 591 4-10-4 90 HaddenFrost(3) 102
(Martin Hill) *led tl 2nd: styd prom: led 7th: styd on wl: rdn out* **5/1**[3]
1-02 2 3 **Romance Dance**[24] 706 7-10-12 108 DonalDevereux(5) 109
(Sophie Leech) *trckd ldr: led 2nd tl 7th: rdn whn lost 2nd briefly after 3 out: styd on same pce fr next* **2/1**[2]
3 12 **Daliarose (FR)**[61] 4-11-0 0 TomScudamore 95
(David Pipe) *trckd ldrs: wnt 2nd briefly after 3 out: sn rdn: wknd bef next* **1/1**[1]
0-P5 4 dist **Himitas (FR)**[8] 843 5-10-10 0 JodieMogford —
(Graeme McPherson) *in tch: rdn appr 7th: wknd after 3 out: t.o* **12/1**
5 16 **Armagnac Empress**[86] 6-10-5 0 JimmyDerham(5) —
(Seamus Mullins) *in tch: hit 1st: struggling after 6th: wknd next: t.o* **66/1**
00- P **Polson**[362] 906 7-10-10 0 SamJones —
(Norma Twomey) *racd keenly: hld up: struggling after 6th: wknd next: t.o whn p.u bef 2 out* **100/1**
0- P **Graceful Fifi**[105] 4792 4-10-7 0 DarylJacob —
(Liam Corcoran) *a towards rr: slow 3rd: reminders: wknd after 6th: p.u bef next* **80/1**

5m 14.0s (-6.20) **Going Correction** -0.25s/f (Good) **7** Ran SP% **111.4**
Speed ratings (Par 105): **101,99,95,—,— —,—**
toteswingers: 1&2 £2.50, 1&3 £3.50, 2&3 £1.10 CSF £15.04 TOTE £4.50: £1.40, £1.50; EX 13.90.

Owner Martin Hill **Bred** Martin Hill **Trained** Littlehempston, Devon

FOCUS
This was a weak mares' novice hurdle. There was a sound gallop and the form looks straightforward enough.

NOTEBOOK
Detroit Red was given a positive ride and deservedly shed her maiden tag. She had run with credit on each of her three previous outings as a hurdler and stepping up in distance made all the difference to her. She is now likely to be put away for an autumn campaign. (op 15-2)
Romance Dance was the first of the principals to come under pressure down the back straight. She rallied gamely from two out, but was always being held under her penalty. She rates the benchmark. (tchd 9-4)
Daliarose(FR) was making her British debut after being bought by her new connections having won a claimer in France two months earlier. Unsurprisingly popular in the market, things looked good for her supporters as she loomed up around three out. Her response under pressure was most limited, however, and it appeared she failed to stay the longer trip. It may also be that this much quicker ground was against her, though. (op 10-11tchd 11-10 in places)
Himitas(FR) jumped more encouragingly in the main this time, but was firmly put in her place on the back straight and needs switching to low-grade handicaps. (op 10-1)

911 SIS LIVE H'CAP CHASE (16 fncs 4 omitted) 3m 2f 110y
3:45 (3:45) (Class 3) (0-135,128) 4-Y-~~£6,970~~ (£2,059; £1,029; £514; £257)

Form RPR
-301 1 **Cold Mountain (IRE)**[25] 691 8-10-11 118 JimmyDerham(5) 123+
(Seamus Mullins) *j.w in tch: clsd on ldrs after 14th: sn rdn: led last: styd on strly* **9/1**
-213 2 2 **Cullahill (IRE)**[19] 761 8-11-4 120 (t) HarrySkelton 125+
(Bob Buckler) *mid-div: hdwy fr 12th: rdn into narrow ld whn hit 2 out: hdd last: styd on but no ex* **11/1**
1-43 3 7 **Allterrain (IRE)**[25] 695 7-10-0 102 oh2 SamJones 99
(Norma Twomey) *trckd ldrs: rdn after 12th: led briefly gng to 2 out: no ex appr last* **14/1**
6-20 4 5 **Sou'Wester**[22] 735 10-11-7 128 SamTwiston-Davies(5) 122
(Colin Tizzard) *mid-div: hdwy fr 12th: led after bypassed 4 out: sn rdn: hdd bef 2 out: sn one pce* **25/1**
2-P2 5 ¾ **Mr Ed (IRE)**[33] 579 12-10-8 115 DonalDevereux(5) 106
(Peter Bowen) *nudged along in rr for most of the way: prog to chse ldrs in 6th after 14th: nvr able to mount chal* **16/1**
2-20 6 dist **Our Hero (IRE)**[22] 735 7-10-12 114 (tp) RichardJohnson —
(Charlie Longsdon) *trckd ldrs: led 12th: rdn and hdd on long run bef 2 out: sn wknd: eased bef last* **13/2**[3]
P-P3 7 dist **Sea Wall**[34] 567 8-10-13 118 RichieMcLernon(3) —
(Jonjo O'Neill) *j.rt: prom: led 4th tl 12th: chsd ldr: rdn after 13th: wknd on long run bef 2 out* **18/1**
15-6 8 11 **Over The Creek**[60] 181 11-11-3 119 (bt) TomScudamore —
(David Pipe) *j.rt early: led tl after 4th: chsd ldrs: rdn after 7th: wknd after 11th: sn t.o* **14/1**
U2P- P **Beehawk**[348] 1032 11-10-0 102 oh1 WillKennedy —
(Bob Buckler) *lost action whn p.u after 3rd: dismntd* **33/1**
-34P P **Dennis The Legend**[37] 525 9-10-10 112 TomO'Brien —
(Grant Cann) *a towards rr: lost tch after 10th: p.u bef 12th* **6/1**[2]
P-51 P **Hemington**[38] 502 7-10-13 115 SamThomas —
(Michael Scudamore) *in tch whn awkward 1st: rdn after 10th: wknd after next: p.u bef 12th* **16/1**
F0-2 P **Winchester Red**[32] 599 8-10-10 115 DPFahy(3) —
(Evan Williams) *nvr travelling in rr fr 3rd: lost tch qckly after 6th: sn p.u* **11/4**[1]
-250 P **Ginolad (AUS)**[22] 735 10-11-1 117 AidanColeman —
(Venetia Williams) *mid-div tl nt fluent 4th (water): slow jump 6th: sn lost tch: p.u bef 8th* **15/2**

6m 32.7s (-11.90) **Going Correction** -0.25s/f (Good) **13** Ran SP% **121.5**
Speed ratings (Par 107): **107,106,104,102,102 —,—,—,—,— —,—,—**
toteswingers:1&2 £12.90, 2&3 £23.10, 1&3 £13.50 CSF £105.50 CT £1393.27 TOTE £9.70: £3.70, £2.80, £5.40; EX 113.00.

Owner Woodford Valley Racing **Bred** Skymarc Farm **Trained** Wilsford-Cum-Lake, Wilts

FOCUS
The last two fences in the back straight were bypassed in the last two circuits. The top weight in this marathon handicap was rated 7lb below the race ceiling. The strong early gallop found out plenty of the runners, but there were still a host of chances turning into the straight. Ordinary handicap form.

NOTEBOOK
Cold Mountain(IRE) eventually came through to win readily and follow up his Fontwell success last month despite racing off a 12lb higher mark. He looked to be feeling the pinch on the final circuit, but rallied strongly and was produced to lead at the final fence. It rates a career-best effort from this dour stayer. (op 7-1)
Cullahill(IRE) posted a brave effort in defeat back over this suitably longer trip and has evidently begun life in handicaps over fences on a workable mark. (op 10-1 tchd 17-2)
Allterrain(IRE) was competing from 2lb out of the handicap, but came into this on good form and his proven stamina was a notable advantage. A drop in grade should see him get closer again.
Sou'Wester travelled well into the race and took it up full of running on the final circuit. He was held prior to a messy leap two out, though, and ultimately found the trip too testing. (op 20-1)
Our Hero(IRE) was given a very positive ride but blatantly failed to stay under such tactics. (op 9-1)
Dennis The Legend came in for some support but he looked to put in a mulish display and has now pulled up the last twice. (op 13-2 tchd 7-1 and 11-2)
Winchester Red didn't go a yard early in the race and was pulled up, something clearly being amiss. Official explanation: jockey said gelding never travelled (op 13-2 tchd 7-1 and 11-2)
Ginolad(AUS) Official explanation: jockey said gelding never travelled (op 13-2 tchd 7-1 and 11-2)

912 SIS LIVE (S) HURDLE (8 hdls) 2m 3f
4:15 (4:15) (Class 5) 4-Y-O+ **£2,055** (£599; £299)

Form RPR
F0/0 1 **Crathorne (IRE)**[55] 267 10-10-5 110 (t) OliverDayman(7) 103
(Alison Thorpe) *cajoled along in rr fr 4th: hdwy u.p after 3 out: styd on wl to ld run-in: drvn out* **20/1**

F51- **2** 3/4 **Shore Thing (IRE)**[28] [21] 7-11-8 127........................(p) RichardJohnson 113
(Bernard Llewellyn) *trckd ldrs: led after 3 out: rdn whn hrd pressed next: hdd run-in: no ex* **9/4**[1]

P-46 **3** 1 3/4 **Knightsbridgelives (IRE)**[25] [692] 7-10-7 87..................(t) DavidBass(5) 102+
(Lawney Hill) *nvr fluent: hld up towards rr: hdwy after 6th: chalng u.p whn mstke 2 out: kpt on same pce* **40/1**

-522 **4** 7 **Talenti (IRE)**[13] [821] 7-11-4 112..................................(t) ChristianWilliams 101
(Lawney Hill) *chsd ldrs tl dropped in rr rapidly bef 6th: wl bhd 3 out: styd on again appr 2 out: wnt 4th bef last* **11/4**[2]

4R-4 **5** 10 **Zafar (IRE)**[25] [696] 7-11-10 123..(tp) RhysFlint 99
(John Flint) *trckd ldrs: led 3 out: sn rdn: hdd bef next: fdd* **11/2**[3]

3201 **6** nk **Intac (IRE)**[13] [821] 8-11-8 115.. JoeTizzard 96
(Colin Tizzard) *mid-div: rdn after 5th: nvr any imp* **6/1**

P-P0 **7** 9 **Dashing Bach (IRE)**[8] [849] 6-10-12 77........................(p) JohnnyFarrelly 77
(Alison Thorpe) *led tl rdn 3 out: sn wknd* **66/1**

4424 **8** 6 **Navajo Nation (IRE)**[13] [823] 4-10-4 105....................(p) TomO'Connor(5) 74
(Bill Turner) *trckd ldrs tl short of room and lost pl on bnd bef 2nd: mid-div: hdwy after 5th: effrt after 3 out: wknd bef next* **7/1**

400/ **9** dist **Ful Of Grace (IRE)**[748] [725] 6-10-2 0............................. HaddenFrost(3) —
(James Frost) *hld up towards rr: sme hdwy after 6th: wknd after next: t.o* **25/1**

4-PP **10** 7 **Coup De Tabac (FR)**[19] [767] 6-10-12 97.......................(tp) DavidDennis —
(Nigel Hawke) *prom: rdn appr 6th: wknd bef 3 out: t.o* **20/1**

4m 25.8s (-8.10) **Going Correction** -0.25s/f (Good)
WFA 4 from 6yo+ 15lb **10** Ran SP% **116.9**
Speed ratings (Par 103): **107,106,105,103,98 98,94,92,—,—**toteswingers: 1&2 £6.80, 1&3 £24.90, 2&3 £17.30 CSF £toteswingers: 1&2 £6.80, 1&3 £24.90, 2&3 £17.30 .There was no bid for the winner.
Owner Centaur Global Partnership I **Bred** Shirley Blue Syndicate **Trained** Bronwydd Arms, Carmarthens

FOCUS
This was run in a reasonable time for the grade and the winner produced his best run since 2008.

NOTEBOOK
Crathorne(IRE) ran out a surprise winner. He had been out of sorts for a spell coming into this, but it was just his second outing for the stable and this was a drop in class for him. He looked a hopeless cause going out onto the back straight, but picked up strongly turning for home to mow down rivals and get up near the line. He has now evidently found his level. (op 16-1)
Shore Thing(IRE) had a decent chance at the weights on this debut over hurdles for current connections and looked for most of the race like he would do the business. Having cruised into the lead turning for home, however, he proved very hard work for his rider when coming under pressure and really threw it away. Returning to a stiffer test could see him take another one of these, though. (op 2-1 tchd 15-8 and 11-4)
Knightsbridgelives(IRE) did plenty wrong early on, but the further he went the better he was and this was a lot more like it down in class. Connections will no doubt find him an opening during the summer. (tchd 50-1)
Talenti(IRE) went in snatches and didn't seem to enjoy being crowded on the inside. He got well behind in the back straight, but flashed home for fourth and is better than the bare form. (op 3-1)
Zafar(IRE), with the cheekpieces back on, went well until looking to down tools off the home turn and is best watched at present. (op 13-2 tchd 7-1)

913 SIS LIVE CONDITIONAL JOCKEYS' H'CAP CHASE (16 fncs) 2m 5f 110y
4:45 (4:45) (Class 5) (0-90,90) 4-Y-0+ **£2,797** (£821; £410; £205)

Form RPR

23-2 **1** **Sir Bumble (IRE)**[20] [758] 10-11-1 79....................................(t) PeterToole 94+
(Michael Blake) *trckd ldrs: chal 3 out: led next: styd on wl: rdn out* **9/2**[1]

2 **2** 2 1/4 **Behind The Scenes (IRE)**[53] [293] 8-11-8 86........................ RhysFlint 100+
(Tim McCarthy) *led tl after 2nd: chsd ldrs: hmpd 4 out: sn rdn: styd on fr 2 out: drifted lft bef last: wnt 2nd towards fin* **17/2**

-060 **3** 1 **Captain Marlon (IRE)**[20] [755] 9-11-12 90............(t) SamTwiston-Davies 101
(Colin Tizzard) *mid-div: hdwy after 10th: rdn after 3 out: chsng wnr whn nt fluent 2 out and last: styd on same pce: lost 2nd towards fin* **12/1**

4-12 **4** 3 1/2 **Moon Melody (GER)**[36] [531] 7-10-9 76................................. DPFahy(3) 84
(Evan Williams) *hld up towards rr: hdwy fr 11th: effrt after 4 out: one pce fr 2 out* **11/2**[3]

0F-6 **5** 5 **Moon Bear**[20] [758] 9-11-1 79...(v) DeanColeman 81
(Linda Blackford) *trckd ldr: led 11th tl next: rdn after 4 out: fdd fr 2 out* **16/1**

3244 **6** 3/4 **Post It**[15] [794] 9-11-2 83.. MattGriffiths(3) 87
(Ron Hodges) *j.rt: racd keenly: mid-div: hdwy 7th to trck ldrs: led 4 out: rdn and hdd bef 2 out: fdd* **12/1**

4/50 **7** 7 **Knightsbridge Hill (IRE)**[28] [665] 8-9-11 64................(p) KeiranBurke(3) 60
(Patrick Rodford) *in tch: nt fluent 7th (water): in rr fr 9th: nvr bk on terms* **16/1**

P-0P **8** 4 **Ilewin Tom**[29] [650] 7-10-7 71.. DonalDevereux 68
(Gary Brown) *racd keenly: hld up towards rr: hdwy into midfield 6th: rdn for effrt after 4 out: wknd 2 out* **8/1**

000/ **P** **Frazers Fortune**[37] 10-9-11 64...................................... JimmyDerham(3) —
(Seamus Mullins) *mstke 3rd: a towards rr: bhd whn p.u bef 2 out* **33/1**

05-4 **B** **Le Forezien (FR)**[15] [795] 11-11-3 81.................................... HarrySkelton —
(Carroll Gray) *mid-div: tk cl order in 9th: travelling ok and cl enough whn b.d 4 out* **5/1**[2]

4U3/ **P** **Shannon Lodge (IRE)**[23] 12-10-9 73................................(t) TomMolloy —
(Tracey Barfoot-Saunt) *mid-div tl dropped in rr 6th: t.o whn p.u bef 12th* **33/1**

P/44 **P** **Mandalay Bay (IRE)**[25] [689] 10-10-0 64 oh3................. GerardTumelty —
(Chris Gordon) *reminders after 4th: a towards rr: t.o whn p.u bef 11th* **10/1**

0-6P **F** **Games (IRE)**[29] [652] 9-11-4 82..(b) AlexMerriam —
(Christopher Kellett) *racd keenly: led after 2nd: hdd 11th tl next: hdd but stl prom whn fell 4 out* **40/1**

0P3/ **P** **Hazelbury**[774] [406] 9-10-0 64 oh2....................................... CharlieHuxley —
(Nigel Hawke) *a towards rr: t.o whn p.u bef 12th* **18/1**

5m 22.6s (1.20) **Going Correction** -0.25s/f (Good) **14** Ran SP% **121.7**
Speed ratings (Par 103): **87,86,85,84,82 82,79,78,—,— —,—,—,—**
toteswingers: 1&2 £8.90, 1&3 £11.70, 2&3 £19.30 CSF £43.11 CT £440.64 TOTE £5.10: £1.90, £2.10, £5.10; EX 28.70.
Owner Staverton Owners Group **Bred** B Stack **Trained** Trowbridge, Wilts

FOCUS
A very moderate, but wide-open handicap for conditional jockeys and it was run at a sound gallop. The third sets the level.

NOTEBOOK
Sir Bumble(IRE) finally shed his maiden tag at the 22nd time of asking. He has been consistent, albeit a weak finisher, but he was not to be denied under a well-judged ride this time. It could be this confidence booster now enables him to progress a little and he will escape a penalty if turning out quickly. (op 7-2)
Behind The Scenes(IRE) was making his handicap debut as a chaser and having his first run for a new yard. He got a positive ride and, a touch better than the bare form, left the impression he could go one better when upped in trip. (op 7-1)
Captain Marlon(IRE) travelled sweetly into contention turning for home, but got caught flat-footed when the winner kicked on and was not clever at the final two fences. He still rallied under maximum pressure and was conceding weight all round, so it has to rate a much better effort. (tchd 14-1)
Moon Melody(GER), not for the first time, lacked fluency early on and got behind. He crept into things from four out, but his effort rather flattened out and he looks held by the handicapper. (op 5-1)
Le Forezien(FR) had work to do, but was still in with a fighting chance prior to being brought down by the faller four from home. (op 7-1)
Mandalay Bay(IRE) Official explanation: jockey said gelding pulled up lame (op 7-1)

914 COLIN TURNER SUPPORTS RACING WELFARE H'CAP HURDLE (8 hdls) 2m 1f
5:15 (5:15) (Class 4) (0-115,115) 4-Y-0+ **£3,382** (£993; £496; £248)

Form RPR

0P-0 **1** **Dream Catcher (SWE)**[36] [534] 7-10-12 104............ RichieMcLernon(3) 112+
(Jonjo O'Neill) *mid-div: hdwy 5th: nt best of runs in cl 4th 2 out: qcknd up wl to ld gng to last: r.o wl: rdn out* **33/1**

-11R **2** 2 **Battle Group**[8] [842] 5-11-12 115.................................... TomScudamore 122
(David Pipe) *hld up: rdn in 5th after 3 out: sn hung lft: led 2 out: hdd bef last: drifted lft and no ex* **4/1**[2]

-041 **3** 2 1/4 **Wilbury Star (IRE)**[13] [823] 4-11-3 108............................. AndrewTinkler 110
(Nicky Henderson) *trckd ldrs: rdn along fr after 4th: styd on same pce* **3/1**[1]

-6P0 **4** 3 1/4 **Nothing Is Forever (IRE)**[15] [798] 6-9-11 89................. SeanQuinlan(3) 91
(Liam Corcoran) *led: rdn and hdd 2 out: kpt on same pce* **12/1**

-123 **5** 16 **Forest Rhythm (IRE)**[25] [690] 6-11-4 112..................... JimmyDerham(5) 99
(Seamus Mullins) *hld up: rdn and sme hdwy after 3 out: wknd next* **7/1**

-206 **6** 7 **Bazart**[34] [566] 8-9-10 92...................................(b[1]) MissIsabelTompsett(7) 72
(Bernard Llewellyn) *racd keenly: trckd ldr tl rdn after 3 out: sn wknd: t.o* **5/1**[3]

2-26 **7** 3 **Boogie Dancer**[24] [706] 6-10-11 103................................. HaddenFrost(3) 81
(Stuart Howe) *mid-div: rdn after 3 out: sn btn: t.o* **9/1**

03-0 **8** 1/2 **Medicinal (IRE)**[15] [798] 9-11-12 115................................ DenisO'Regan 92
(Michael Blake) *t.k.h early: a towards rr: wknd 3 out: t.o* **12/1**

33-6 **9** dist **Watergate (IRE)**[32] [595] 4-10-12 103...............................(t) HarrySkelton —
(Paul Nicholls) *a towards rr: wknd after 5th: t.o* **7/1**

6-00 **10** 26 **Colour Trooper (IRE)**[13] [820] 5-10-5 94.....................(t) JohnnyFarrelly —
(David Pipe) *a towards rr: t.o fr bef 3 out* **40/1**

3m 58.2s (-7.50) **Going Correction** -0.25s/f (Good)
WFA 4 from 5yo+ 15lb **10** Ran SP% **117.4**
Speed ratings (Par 105): **107,106,105,103,95 92,91,91,—,—**
toteswingers:1&2 £31.40, 2&3 £3.00, 1&3 £23.50 CSF £164.93 CT £532.47 TOTE £45.50: £10.20, £1.80, £1.60; EX 216.70 Place 6: £426.49 Place 5: £120.82.
Owner Ms Mary Miles **Bred** Anna-Lena Smeds **Trained** Cheltenham, Gloucs

FOCUS
A modest handicap, run at a solid enough gallop. This was the winner's best run since October 2008.

NOTEBOOK
Dream Catcher(SWE) stepped up vastly on his previous efforts for the stable and ran out a determined winner. He moved strongly into contention and looked all over the winner turning for home. He had to wait for his challenge nearing two out, but dug deep under pressure and found a great stride at the last. That won him the day and he is evidently now back at the top of his game, so there may be more to come. Official explanation: trainer had no explanation for the apparent improvement in form other than the gelding may have been suited by the faster run race.
Battle Group attracted support and was on his best behaviour down at the start, jumping off without fuss. He showed his quirky side when coming under a strong drive turning out of the back straight, but responded and held every chance from two out. There is a handicap in him off this mark. (op 11-2 tchd 7-2)
Wilbury Star(IRE) proved easy to back off this 7lb higher mark, but held every chance and rates a good benchmark as the handicapper now appears to have his measure. (op 9-4 tchd 7-2)
Nothing Is Forever(IRE) posted a much better effort under front-running tactics and could be worth chancing back down in class now he has shown more enthusiasm. (op 16-1 tchd 18-1)
Bazart, whose yard won this race last term, was backed in the first-time blinkers. He proved free, however, and completely downed tools once put under some pressure. A drop into plating-company now looks on the cards. (op 11-2 tchd 9-2)
T/Plt: £262.50 to a £1 stake. Pool: £74,627.78 - 207.46 winning tickets. T/Qpdt: £47.90 to a £1 stake. Pool: £6,721.51 - 103.77 winning tickets. TM

LES LANDES
Sunday, July 4

OFFICIAL GOING: Firm

915a JERSEY RACE CLUB H'CAP HURDLE 2m 1f
2:30 (2:30) 4-Y-0+ **£950** (£350; £200)

RPR

1 **King Of The Beers (USA)**[16] 6-11-9 .... RobertKirk —
(T J Bougourd, Guernsey) **5/4**[2]

2 shd **Buckie Massa**[34] 6-11-10 .... AntonyProcter —
(J S O Arthur, Jersey) **5/1**

3 5 **Tanikos (FR)**[16] 11-10-13 .... MattieBatchelor —
(Mrs A Malzard, Jersey) **4/1**[3]

4 12 **Nobby Kivambo (IRE)**[24] [688] 5-11-4 .... WilsonRenwick —
(Brendan Powell) **1/1**[1]

4m 1.00s (241.00) **4** Ran SP% **131.1**

Owner T J Bougourd **Bred** Liberation Farm, Oratis Thoroughbreds Et Al **Trained** Guernsey

842 UTTOXETER (L-H)

Tuesday, July 6

OFFICIAL GOING: Good to firm (good in places; 7.6)

Wind: Light, across. Weather: overcast and muggy

916 EXCLOOSIVE EVENT HIRE CONDITIONAL JOCKEYS NOVICES' HURDLE (9 hdls 1 omitted) 2m

6:50 (6:50) (Class 4) 4-Y-O+ **£2,471** (£725; £362; £181)

Form				RPR
6-31	1		**Sahrati**[26] 693 6-11-5 115 PeterToole (Michael Blake) *cl up: led 6th: rdn bef 3 out and hit flight: drew clr 2 out: eased flat* **2/1**[2]	123+
21	2	8	**Heron Bay**[25] 711 6-10-13 119 OliverDayman(6) (Peter Bowen) *prom: veered at 6th: chsd wnr after: rdn 3 out: wknd next: 8 l 2nd whn mstke last* **8/11**[1]	112+
52-P	3	1 1/2	**Desolait**[28] 684 5-10-2 0 (t) SamTwiston-Davies(3) (Nigel Twiston-Davies) *mstkes or slow jumps: effrt in 4th bef 3 out: wnt 13 l 3rd 2 out: kpt on for driving but unable to chal* **20/1**	94
262	4	17	**Heart Of Dubai (USA)**[16] 800 5-10-12 96 FearghalDavis (Micky Hammond) *chsd ldrs: nt fluent 5th and 6th: rdn and wknd 3 out: lost 3rd at next* **8/1**[3]	86
FP/0	5	14	**Drum Major (IRE)**[9] 842 5-10-12 0 MarcGoldstein (Jim Best) *plld hrd: led tl 2nd: sn restrained in rr: j. slowly 6th and lost tch: keeping on though no ch fr 2 out* **66/1**	70
0-0	6	2 1/4	**Carrifran (IRE)**[25] 718 5-10-2 0 JamesHalliday(3) (Malcolm Jefferson) *plld hrd: led 2nd: hit 5th: jinked at next and hdd: rdn and lost tch bef 3 out: sn wl bhd* **100/1**	61
	7	16	**Red Current**[103] 6-10-5 0 SamJones (Michael Scudamore) *bhd: rdn and lost tch after 6th: t.o next* **80/1**	45

3m 45.3s (-9.90) **Going Correction** -0.80s/f (Firm) **7** Ran SP% **110.8**

Speed ratings (Par 105): **92,88,87,78,71 70,62**

Tote Swingers:1&2:£1.10, 2&3:£3.30, 1&3:£5.20 CSF £3.70 TOTE £3.70: £3.10, £1.10; EX 4.40.

Owner Mrs Val Butcher **Bred** Darley **Trained** Trowbridge, Wilts

FOCUS

The jockeys reported the ground to be riding good after this opener, a potentially informative race which looked a match in the betting and so it proved from the home turn. The cosy winner was value for further and is rated to his best.

NOTEBOOK

Sahrati was a winner over 2m4f here last time but coped with the drop in trip well here under an intelligent ride. The rider put his mount's stamina to good use and he should be competitive again over the summer, possibly over a longer trip. Similar novice races are also open to him as he will not get a penalty for this win. (op 5-2)

Heron Bay beat two subsequent winners at Aintree last time and, under a penalty, this former Royal Ascot winner was found out here. He still showed signs of inexperience off the bridle, however, and ought to be able to win a similar contest if placed to good effect. (op 4-6 tchd 5-6 and Evens in places)

Desolait stopped quickly over a longer trip on her hurdling debut last time and she jumped poorly here before making modest late progress. She will be seen to better effect in low-grade handicaps. (op 16-1)

Heart Of Dubai(USA) is officially rated 96 and was a little disappointing here. He is likely to be seen to better effect on fast summer jumping ground. (tchd 7-1)

Drum Major(IRE) lost touch before the home turn (not under strong riding) but appeared to finish with plenty left in the tank. He is likely to be a force in low-grade handicaps.

Red Current, a hurdling debutant, was a low-grade Flat performer for Ron Harris and jumped poorly here.

917 SIGNS 2000 (S) HURDLE (9 hdls 1 omitted) 2m

7:20 (7:20) (Class 5) 4-7-Y-O **£1,561** (£458; £229; £114)

Form				RPR
64-	1		**Rio Gael (IRE)**[201] 2931 4-10-10 0 (p) TomO'Brien (Peter Bowen) *chsd ldr: led bef 3 out: drew clr next: 12l ahd last: heavily eased* **11/1**	116+
1-32	2	19	**Tri Nations (UAE)**[26] 696 5-11-8 110 (t) JasonMaguire (Donald McCain) *prom: ev ch 3 out: rdn whn hit next: immediately outpcd by wnr: lost further grnd flat despite wnr easing down* **9/4**[1]	107
0-00	3	3	**Hollies Favourite (IRE)**[11] 837 7-10-9 90 (t) AlexMerriam(3) (Neil King) *led: rdn and hdd bef 3 out: btn next: plodded on* **50/1**	93
14-6	4	5	**Le Brocquy**[13] 829 5-11-5 102 (b) SamThomas (Martin Keighley) *racd freely in midfield: effrt after 6th: jnd wnr briefly 3 out: nt keen and wnt lft: sn btn* **13/2**	95
4	5	nk	**Mystic Touch**[7] 850 4-10-10 0 JackDoyle (Andrew Haynes) *bhd: mstke 4th: rdn and struggling after 6th: nvr gng wl enough after* **4/1**[3]	87
65-6	6	20	**Monreale (GER)**[36] 554 6-10-12 0 (t) TomScudamore (David Pipe) *chsd ldrs: hit 5th and rdn: fnd nil fr next: no ch 3 out: t.o* **11/4**[2]	68
516-	7	18	**Baguenaud (FR)**[333] 1160 7-11-5 108 GrahamLee (Stephen Clark) *chsd ldrs: hit 5th: wknd bef 3 out: t.o next: eased last* **16/1**	57
0/0-	P		**Bond Cruz**[221] 2240 7-10-5 92 (t) OliverDayman(7) (Olivia Maylam) *dropped to rr 5th: t.o after next: p.u 2 out* **28/1**	—

3m 44.8s (-10.40) **Going Correction** -0.80s/f (Firm)

WFA 4 from 5yo+ 15lb **8** Ran SP% **110.4**

Speed ratings: **94,84,83,80,80 70,61,—**

Tote Swingers:1&2:£5.80, 2&3:£22.70, 1&3:£42.70 CSF £34.56 TOTE £16.00: £3.70, £1.10, £15.90; EX 33.60.

Owner Mrs Karen Bowen **Bred** Glending Bloodstock **Trained** Little Newcastle, Pembrokes

FOCUS

A run-of-the-mill seller which saw an impressive winner clock a marginally quicker time than the opening novice hurdle. This was a big step up on his previous form, but it is believable.

NOTEBOOK

Rio Gael(IRE), making his debut for Peter Bowen having finished fourth in a claimer for Rebecca Curtis when last seen, was always towards the head of affairs and comprehensively outclassed his rivals. He ought to be competitive in similar races throughout the summer and could be worth a go in handicap company. He was bought in for 8,200gns. (op 10-1)

Tri Nations(UAE) has been acquitting himself well in similar company throughout the summer and once again ran well, but he did not look the most resolute performer. He is likely to run well in similar races this season but would not be one to back with any confidence. (op 5-2 tchd 2-1)

Hollies Favourite(IRE) showed his first meaningful piece of form for his yard under a change of tactics. He will, however, need to improve to win races though. (op 66-1)

Le Brocquy ran in selling company three starts ago at Sedgefield and shaped as if in need of the run at Worcester last time. Dropping back in grade, he travelled well but found very little off the bridle. He is one to tread carefully with in the future. (op 11-2 tchd 5-1)

Mystic Touch showed promise last time but this was a disappointing effort. (op 13-2)

Monreale(GER) looked to be carrying condition in the preliminaries and he found nothing off the bridle. (op 5-2 tchd 10-3)

918 MATTHEW CLARK NOVICES' H'CAP CHASE (13 fncs 3 omitted) 2m 5f

7:50 (7:50) (Class 4) (0-100,100) 4-Y-O+ **£3,041** (£898; £449; £224; £112)

Form				RPR
343-	1		**Gabreselassie (IRE)**[162] 3656 7-11-9 100 RichieMcLernon(3) (Jonjo O'Neill) *chsd ldrs: effrt and rdn 11th: hrd drvn passing 3 out: wnt 2nd after next: galvanised fr last to ld nr fin: fine ride* **11/2**[3]	113
0/6-	2	nk	**Merry Terry**[30] 6-10-11 85 JoeTizzard (Colin Tizzard) *cl up: led gng wl 2 out: sn pushed along and looking idle: under 1l ahd last: ct cl home* **7/2**[2]	98
/05-	3	19	**San Deng**[39] 514 8-11-10 98 BarryKeniry (Micky Hammond) *led: rdn and hdd 2 out: sn lost 2nd: tiring qckly flat* **8/1**	95
-033	4	2	**Fongoli**[14] 821 4-10-6 97 (v) AidanColeman (Brendan Powell) *towards rr: hit 8th and rdn: struggling after 11th: snatched poor 4th* **15/2**	72
3-41	5	hd	**Red Dynamite**[40] 489 9-11-6 94 (p) PaddyAspell (Geoffrey Harker) *chsd ldrs: rdn and outpcd 3 out: nt keen after: lost poor 4th fnl strides* **10/3**[1]	86
62PP	6	33	**Tuscany Star (IRE)**[14] 824 7-11-4 92 (vt[1]) AndrewThornton (Edward Creighton) *prom: j. slowly 10th: drvn and wknd bef next: t.o passing 3 out* **33/1**	51
B3-5	P		**Grasscutter (IRE)**[20] 760 6-11-4 92 JasonMaguire (Donald McCain) *nt fluent in rr: last after mstke 4th: lost tch 6th: p.u after next* **7/1**	—
00-0	U		**General Simara**[47] 424 6-10-1 75 TomMessenger (Tony Carroll) *towards rr tl uns rdr 5th* **10/1**	—
0PP-	P		**Mr Logistics (IRE)**[124] 4401 7-11-12 100 (b[1]) JimmyMcCarthy (Charles Egerton) *j.v.slowly 2nd: prom tl rdn and nt fluent 7th: reluctant and tailed himself off by 9th: p.u 11th* **25/1**	—

5m 12.2s (-11.30) **Going Correction** -0.40s/f (Good)

WFA 4 from 6yo+ 3lb **9** Ran SP% **111.9**

Speed ratings (Par 105): **105,104,97,96,96 84,—,—,—**

Tote Swingers:1&2:£13.30, 2&3:£2.80, 1&3:£2.40 CSF £24.83 CT £150.46 TOTE £4.80: £1.40, £1.30, £2.70; EX 32.70.

Owner John P McManus **Bred** P J Fortune **Trained** Cheltenham, Gloucs

FOCUS

Not a very strong novice handicap chase with the nine runners having amassed only four wins from 88 starts. The winner is rated to his best.

NOTEBOOK

Gabreselassie(IRE) was racing without the blinkers he had sported in his last two chase starts. He looked less than straightforward off the bridle but was given a tremendous ride by McLernon to get up close home. In the past he has blotted his copybook with weak finishing efforts, so he would be one to treat with caution with next time out. (op 4-1)

Merry Terry has been placed in his last three point-to-points and he ran creditably reverting to handicap chasing here. It is likely he was in front for too long as he was idling on the run-in, but he clearly likes this quick summer ground and he ought to be competitive in similar races this season. (op 5-1 tchd 10-3)

San Deng was a winner over hurdles at Wetherby in April last year and he shaped as if in good form when last seen on the Flat at Newcastle in May. He finished tired here having set the pace for a long way. (op 6-1)

Fongoli, a dual hurdles winner, lacks the size and scope for chasing. (op 10-1 tchd 13-2)

Red Dynamite, raised 5lb for winning at Wetherby in cheekpieces last time, was unwilling to co-operate with his rider once coming under pressure here. (op 3-1 tchd 4-1)

Tuscany Star(IRE) was sporting yet another combination of headgear, but he appeared not to gel with Andrew Thornton and gave up from some way out.

Grasscutter(IRE) Official explanation: jockey said gelding jumped badly; vet said gelding finished distressed (op 22-1 tchd 20-1)

Mr Logistics(IRE) looked far from keen and gave up some way from home with the blinkers making no difference to his poor attitude. (op 22-1 tchd 20-1)

919 MORGAN SPICED H'CAP CHASE (11 fncs 1 omitted) 2m

8:20 (8:22) (Class 4) (0-110,110) 4-Y-O+ **£3,041** (£898; £449; £224; £112)

Form				RPR
-252	1		**Folie A Deux (IRE)**[26] 689 8-10-6 95 (t) SamTwiston-Davies(5) (Colin Tizzard) *t.k.h to post: mde nrly all at gd pce and j.w: 3l clr and looked to be gng best 3 out: rdn next: styd on wl* **3/1**[1]	104+
32B3	2	3	**Kirkhammerton (IRE)**[9] 848 8-10-13 100 DannyCook(3) (Barry Leavy) *dropped out last: 12l bhd after 3rd: kpt on wl fr 3 out: stl 8l 5th and rdn next: styd on to snatch 2nd: nvr looked like catching wnr* **9/2**[3]	106
-463	3	hd	**Red Jester**[16] 799 9-10-10 99 MarcGoldstein(5) (Gerald Ham) *cl up: rdn 3 out: styd on to go 2nd at last: one pce and lost 2nd nr fin* **12/1**	105
64-P	4	3 1/4	**Glengarra (IRE)**[23] 734 13-11-9 107 (tp) JasonMaguire (Liam Corcoran) *prom: chsd wnr fr 7th: kpt on v gamely tl wknd last: lost two pls flat* **33/1**	111
3316	5	7	**Misamon (FR)**[13] 826 7-10-8 92 (v) RichardJohnson (David Rees) *led briefly and nt fluent 3rd: prom tl rdn 3 out: eased and btn bef next: plugged on* **4/1**[2]	90
-41P	6	13	**Arumun (IRE)**[9] 848 9-10-13 97 TomScudamore (Michael Scudamore) *hld up in rr: effrt after 7th: 5th and btn 3 out* **11/1**	80
0-50	7	1 1/2	**Rokinhorsescience (FR)**[51] 353 6-10-10 97 (p) RichieMcLernon(3) (Jonjo O'Neill) *midfield: shkn up 5th: little rspnse: btn 3 out: mstke next* **8/1**	80
41-4	8	1/2	**Tempting Paradise (IRE)**[38] 523 7-11-12 110 PaulMoloney (Evan Williams) *rdn most of way: pressed ldrs tl 5th: in rr and btn 7th* **7/1**	91
3350	9	13	**Coach Lane**[9] 848 9-11-8 106 AidanColeman (Venetia Williams) *in rr and rdn 3rd: nvr gng wl after: last and struggling 7th* **12/1**	74

3m 48.0s (-7.60) **Going Correction** -0.40s/f (Good) **9** Ran SP% **113.5**

Speed ratings (Par 105): **103,101,101,99,96 89,89,88,82**

Tote Swingers:1&2:£1.20, 2&3:£15.60, 1&3:£3.30 CSF £17.13 CT £138.05 TOTE £3.60: £1.10, £1.60, £3.90; EX 11.00.

Owner G Carstairs **Bred** Lord James Beresford **Trained** Milborne Port, Dorset

FOCUS

A strongly-run handicap chase which saw some of the field struggling from an early stage. Solid form.

NOTEBOOK

Folie A Deux(IRE) posted a decent effort when sporting a tongue-tie at Fontwell last time and made virtually all the running, jumping boldly to score under his capable claiming rider. He could win again as long as the Handicapper is not too harsh. (tchd 11-4)

Kirkhammerton(IRE) fared best of those who came from off the pace, and has now made the frame in all his completed starts over fences. Although he lacks size he ought to remain a force in this grade.

Red Jester, a previous C&D winner, shaped as if coming back to form at Hereford last time and again ran creditably, but has yet to win from a mark this high. (op 10-1)

Glengarra(IRE) showed more on his second run after a break and could still be up to winning races over the summer, especially if he can get an uncontested lead. (tchd 40-1)
Misamon(FR) ran adequately but will need to find more to win off his current mark. (op 13-2)

920 MATTHEW CLARK MARES' H'CAP HURDLE (10 hdls 2 omitted) 2m 4f 110y
8:50 (8:50) (Class 4) (0-105,97) 4-Y-0+ **£2,471** (£725; £362; £181)

Form RPR
-034 **1** **Wensleydale Web**[24] 727 8-11-7 92 .... GrahamLee 95
(Martin Todhunter) *plld v hrd towards rr: rdn 7th and cajoled along after: 6th bef 3 out: 4l 3rd next: chal and sltly bmpd last: coaxed ahd fnl 50yds* **16/1**

06-3 **2** ½ **Zoenicibel**[24] 726 6-10-11 87 .... JamesHalliday(5) 92+
(Malcolm Jefferson) *trckd ldrs: wnt 3rd bef 3 out: led next: rdn and hdd and no ex fnl 50yds* **11/1**

21U5 **3** 2½ **Basford Lass**[13] 826 5-11-12 97 ....(b) AlanO'Keeffe 97
(Jennie Candlish) *led at fast pce tl 4th: led again 6th: rdn and hdd 2 out: ev ch whn j rt last: nt qckn* **8/1**

3442 **4** 1½ **Thehonourablelady**[16] 796 9-11-8 93 ....(tp) RhysFlint 92
(John Flint) *prom: 4th and rdn bef 3 out: one pce after but kpt plugging on* **7/2**[1]

6-02 **5** 3¾ **Freedom Flying**[22] 745 7-11-2 94 ....(p) KyleJames(7) 89
(Philip Kirby) *cl up tl drvn and lost pl after 5th: mod 10th after 7th: styd on wl fr 2 out: unable to chal* **15/2**

P4-6 **6** 10 **Saddlewood (IRE)**[37] 528 7-11-2 87 ....(tp) DarylJacob 72
(Jamie Snowden) *chsd ldrs: 5th and rdn bef 3 out: sn wknd* **33/1**

5PP- **7** 2 **Happy Fleet**[128] 2934 7-9-11 71 .... HaddenFrost(3) 57
(Roger Curtis) *reluctant to set off and drvn in last: hdwy after 5th: 7th and rdn bef 3 out where mstke: sn btn: fin weakly* **10/1**

60-3 **8** 8 **Artic Bliss**[33] 600 8-10-0 71 oh1 .... FelixDeGiles 46
(Charlie Longsdon) *led in s: pressed ldr: led 4th tl hdd 6th: drvn and fdd tamely bef 3 out* **16/1**

P03 **9** 3¾ **Aisemma (IRE)**[13] 826 6-10-6 84 .... OliverDayman(7) 55
(Peter Bowen) *bhd: struggling after 6th* **11/2**[2]

10 55 **Highheelsnhandbags**[29] 668 7-11-8 93 ....(p) PaulMoloney 9
(Michael P Hourigan, Ire) *nt fluent: struggling towards rr whn blnd bdly 7th: sn t.o* **16/1**

-560 **P** **Sphere (IRE)**[11] 837 5-11-10 95 .... AndrewTinkler —
(John Mackie) *sn drvn along and nt keen in rr: struggling 6th: t.o and p.u 2 out* **14/1**

2211 **P** **Play A Cord (IRE)**[26] 688 7-11-1 93 ....(b) MarkQuinlan(7) —
(Neil Mulholland) *midfield: downed tools and lost tch after mstke 7th: t.o and p.u 3 out* **13/2**[3]

4m 52.2s (-11.80) **Going Correction** -0.80s/f (Firm) 12 Ran SP% **118.5**
Speed ratings (Par 105): **90,89,88,88,86 83,82,79,77,56 —,—**
Tote Swingers:1&2:£10.90, 2&3:£10.50, 1&3:£5.10 CSF £179.74 CT £1524.62 TOTE £17.30: £5.20, £3.20, £1.80; EX 96.10.
Owner Javas Charvers **Bred** Andrew Jenkins **Trained** Orton, Cumbria

FOCUS
A moderate mares' handicap hurdle in which plenty were in with a chance at the second-last. The winner and third ran to their marks, with a step up from the second.

NOTEBOOK
Wensleydale Web had previously failed to win away from Cartmel but found enough off the bridle (she doesn't always find much for pressure) to score over this longer trip under a good ride. She may return to Cartmel in August, although she would need to improve to win again. (tchd 18-1)
Zoenicibel shaped well at Hexham last time and was on a fair mark for her handicap debut upped in trip. The Handicapper probably has got her on the right mark. (op 10-1 tchd 9-1)
Basford Lass set too strong a pace last time at Worcester but showed her true form here. She is another who the Handicapper appears to have about right. Further improvement would be needed if she is to win. (op 9-1 tchd 11-1)
Thehonourablelady is back on her last winning mark and ran with credit but all her wins have come on ground good or softer. She would be worth a go over a longer trip. (op 11-2)
Freedom Flying has been unable to make an impact in sellers recently and her proximity underlines how moderate this race was. (tchd 8-1)
Saddlewood(IRE) travelled well for some way but found little off the bridle. She will need to be stepped up in trip in time but in truth she will struggle to win races. (op 25-1)
Artic Bliss was led in by her trainer at the start (she always is) but ran poorly and will prove difficult to win with. (op 25-1)
Play A Cord(IRE) Official explanation: jockey said mare never travelled

921 MOBILES24.COM H'CAP HURDLE (12 hdls 2 omitted) 3m
9:20 (9:20) (Class 4) (0-110,108) 4-Y-0+ **£2,471** (£725; £362; £181)

Form RPR
-00F **1** **Very Stylish (IRE)**[20] 765 6-11-6 105 .... RichieMcLernon(3) 113+
(Jonjo O'Neill) *confidently rdn: hld up gng wl: prog fr midfield 9th: mstke 3 out: rdn to ld and stmbld last: forged away nr fin* **11/2**[3]

00-0 **2** ¾ **Aldiruos (IRE)**[33] 606 10-10-13 100 .... LeeEdwards(5) 104
(Tony Carroll) *bhd: effrt 9th: clsd on outside bef next: w wnr last: outpcd cl home* **16/1**

P0-P **3** 2¼ **Starlight Air**[30] 651 7-11-4 100 .... LiamTreadwell 102
(John Spearing) *towards rr: blnd 7th: gd prog 3 out: rdn and nt qckn last but snatched 3rd* **14/1**

3-PP **4** hd **No Greater Love (FR)**[26] 689 8-10-13 98 .... TomMolloy(3) 101
(Charlie Longsdon) *trckd ldrs: led gng wl after 9th: rdn and hit 2 out: hdd last: wknd and lost 3rd cl home* **50/1**

1-53 **5** nk **Ripalong Lad (IRE)**[19] 771 9-11-12 108 ....(p) TomO'Brien 111
(Peter Bowen) *chsd ldrs: j. slowly 3rd and 8th: rdn and styd on wl fr 2 out: unable to chal* **4/1**[2]

2-04 **6** 8 **Heir To Be**[14] 821 11-11-11 107 ....(b) DenisO'Regan 101
(Michael Blake) *hld up: in midfield and rdn bef 3 out: chsng ldrs whn taken rt bef last: eased flat* **10/1**

222 **7** ½ **The Fox's Decree**[23] 737 6-11-3 99 ....(t) RichardJohnson 93
(Martin Keighley) *prom: rdn 3 out: wknd qckly bef last* **7/2**[1]

-554 **8** 15 **Morestead (IRE)**[26] 691 5-11-2 98 ....(p) AidanColeman 78
(Brendan Powell) *chsd ldr: led 5th tl rdn and hdd after 9th: wknd next* **14/1**

0-43 **9** 1¼ **Mcqueen (IRE)**[33] 601 10-11-1 100 .... DannyCook(3) 77
(Barry Leavy) *hld up: effrt to trck ldrs 8th: rdn and wknd bef 3 out* **14/1**

0U/F **10** hd **Delightful Touch (FR)**[26] 698 9-9-9 82 oh18 .... MarcGoldstein(5) 59
(Gerald Ham) *a bhd: struggling bef 9th* **66/1**

-044 **11** 2¼ **Roisin's Prince (IRE)**[20] 765 8-10-10 92 ....(t) LeightonAspell 66
(Matt Sheppard) *bhd: rdn and struggling bef 9th* **14/1**

-F45 **12** 10 **Lord Brunello (IRE)**[34] 588 8-11-4 100 ....(p) ChristianWilliams 64
(Lawney Hill) *nt jump wl: in rr and bmpd along after 7th: t.o whn mstke 9th* **12/1**

60-5 **13** ½ **Bathwick Breeze**[38] 517 6-10-13 95 ....(b) TomScudamore 61
(David Pipe) *led tl mstke 5th: prom tl downed tools bef 9th: sn t.o* **11/1**

5m 42.6s (-22.60) **Going Correction** -0.80s/f (Firm) 13 Ran SP% **118.7**
Speed ratings (Par 105): **105,104,104,103,103 101,101,96,95,95 94,91,91**
Tote Swingers:1&2:£41.90, 2&3:£57.60, 1&3:£21.20 CSF £88.55 CT £1177.96 TOTE £7.90: £3.20, £6.70, £6.20; EX 245.80 Place 6 £206.81, Place 5 £191.74..
Owner Mrs Gay Smith **Bred** Kenneth Parkhill **Trained** Cheltenham, Gloucs

FOCUS
A moderate staying handicap hurdle and they finished quite closely bunched. The form looks pretty solid.

NOTEBOOK
Very Stylish(IRE) was travelling well before falling at Worcester last time and he scored here upped in trip once again. He was always travelling well but idled close home, and it would not be a surprise to see him win again. Chasing could also suit him as he has plenty of size and scope.
Official explanation: trainer's rep said, regarding apparent improvement in form, that the gelding had benefited from the step up in trip and a seemingly weaker contest. (op 8-1 tchd 5-1)
Aldiruos(IRE)'s seven wins have come left-handed and he further enhanced his good track record with another placed effort (his seventh from 11 starts here, with one win). It was a new trip for him but he saw it out well and it will not be long before the shrewd Tony Carroll finds a race for him. (tchd 20-1)
Starlight Air returned to form on this quicker surface. She is only small but she might be able to find a race in the summer. (op 16-1)
No Greater Love(FR)'s previous form had come on similar ground and this return to hurdling saw him show up better. However, it would be unwise to go overboard as he has not been the most consistent in the past.
Ripalong Lad(IRE), a good third over hurdles when last seen at Ffos Las, he ran on well over this longer trip. He can still be a force, maybe over a little further. (tchd 9-2)
Heir To Be has shown promise on his last two starts and was chasing the leaders when taken right at the final flight of hurdles and was eased on the run-in. He is clearly capable of better and ought to be getting more competitive soon. (op 9-1 tchd 12-1)
The Fox's Decree has been running consistently this summer but dropped away as if something was amiss in the closing stages. (op 3-1)
Mcqueen(IRE) has shown all his form going left-handed and appeared not to stay this longer trip, but showed enough to suggest he can win over a more suitable trip this summer.
T/Plt: £665.60 to a £1 stake. Pool:£78,565.74 - 86.18 winning tickets. T/Qpdt: £511.50 to a £1 stake. Pool:£5,322.63 - 7.70 winning tickets. IM

922 - 928a (Foreign Racing) - See Raceform Interactive

[862]WORCESTER (L-H)
Wednesday, July 7

OFFICIAL GOING: Good to firm (good in places; chs 8.4, hdl 8.6)
All bends moved out 6m from inside racing line impact on distances not quantified. Hurdles and the run in on inside half of track.
Wind: Light across Weather: Overcast

929 PARTEX MARKING SYSTEMS NOVICES' HURDLE (10 hdls) 2m 4f
6:10 (6:10) (Class 4) 4-Y-0+ **£2,740** (£798; £399)

Form RPR
5-1 **1** **Ghimaar**[22] 648 5-11-5 0 .... APMcCoy 140+
(Nicky Henderson) *trckd ldr tl led 3rd: in control fr 3 out: eased flat* **1/3**[1]

-312 **2** 2 **Lamboro Lad (IRE)**[26] 710 5-11-5 126 .... TomO'Brien 125+
(Peter Bowen) *led to 3rd: chsd ldr thereafter: pushed along 2 out: kpt on but no ch w easy wnr* **11/4**[2]

5 **3** 43 **Oscar Charlie (IRE)**[22] 759 5-10-12 0 .... DarylJacob 88
(Jamie Snowden) *hld up in tch: wknd appr 3 out: t.o* **40/1**[3]

0/UP **4** 24 **Silver Sonnet**[29] 684 7-10-5 0 .... CharliePoste 57
(Ben Case) *chsd ldrs: nt fluent 1st: wknd appr 3 out: t.o* **200/1**

2P0- **5** 38 **Chaser's War (IRE)**[79] 5285 6-10-5 0 .... JodieMogford 6
(Nikki Evans) *prom: pushed along and outpcd 5th: rdn and wknd after 7th: t.o* **150/1**

4m 40.4s (-7.00) **Going Correction** -0.45s/f (Good) 5 Ran SP% **105.3**
Speed ratings (Par 105): **96,95,78,68,53**
CSF £1.43 TOTE £1.50: £1.10, £1.10; EX 1.20.
Owner Martin George **Bred** Hunscote House Farm Stud **Trained** Upper Lambourn, Berks

FOCUS
All bends were moved out six metres off the inside line, adding about 24 yards to each circuit. The hurdles and the hurdles course run-in were positioned on the inside half of the track. The ground seemed to be riding as advertised. This novice hurdle seriously lacked depth and appeared to be only steadily The easy winner was value for further and can rate higher.

NOTEBOOK
Ghimaar is a useful sort for the time of year. Since winning over 2m here he has dead-heated for fourth in the Ascot Stakes over 2m4f, and that trip proved no problem for him back over hurdles. In front with a circuit to cover, he was never seriously threatened and scored eased down, value for a considerably wider margin. His jumping had been sketchy on his previous start but was much better this time, and he had no problem with the sounder surface. (op 4-11)
Lamboro Lad(IRE) chased the winner for much of the way and never stopped trying, but he was flattered by the eventual margin of defeat. He was dismounted after the finish and was reported lame. It is to be hoped this nice individual makes a full recovery, as he is the type to make a chaser in time. Official explanation: jockey said gelding finished lame (op 5-2)
Oscar Charlie(IRE), placed in five of his six runs in Irish points and fifth in a recent bumper, was no match for the two principals on this hurdling debut but may be worth keeping an eye on in a lesser grade, perhaps when handicapped.

930 TONBRIE CONSTRUCTION NOVICES' H'CAP HURDLE (12 hdls) 3m
6:40 (6:40) (Class 5) (0-95,94) 4-Y-0+ **£1,712** (£499; £249)

Form RPR
06/1 **1** **Kopylova**[22] 757 7-11-10 92 .... RichardJohnson 101+
(Tim Vaughan) *hld up: hdwy 8th: rdn after 3 out: chalng whn hmpd flat: swtchd lft: rallied to ld nr fin* **4/1**[1]

0P-0 **2** ½ **Filippo Lippi (IRE)**[38] 539 5-11-8 90 .... APMcCoy 97+
(Jonjo O'Neill) *hld up: hdwy u.p 7th: hrd drvn to chse wnr appr 3 out: led and hung rt flat: hdd towards fin* **8/1**

34-6 **3** 3½ **Eastwell Smiles**[35] 587 6-10-12 80 ....(bt[1]) JasonMaguire 83
(Richard Phillips) *led: nt fluent 4 out: rdn and hdd flat: no ex* **15/2**[3]

-U45 **4** 2¼ **Smiling Applause**[27] 698 11-10-0 68 oh4 ....(b) DavidEngland 68
(Harry Chisman) *in rr and drvn along fr 4th: styd on u.p fr 3 out: nrst fin* **66/1**

-6UP **5** 8 **Hampton Court**[27] 691 5-11-6 93 .... JimmyDerham(5) 88
(Seamus Mullins) *mid-div: hdwy 8th: rdn appr 3 out: wkng whn mstke next* **12/1**

0P/6 **6** 7 **The Boat (IRE)**[32] 632 8-10-9 77 .... ChristianWilliams 64
(Lawney Hill) *chsd ldrs: rdn appr 3 out: wkng whn blnd next* **11/1**

-FP3 **7** 3 **Scotsbrook Cloud**[7] 862 5-10-10 83 .... MichaelMurphy(5) 66
(C Roberts) *mid-div: hdwy 7th: rdn and wknd after 3 out* **17/2**

2-03 **8** *35* **Flag Flier**[30] 660 7-10-7 **82** NathanSweeney(7) 29
(Bob Buckler) *chsd ldrs: rdn after 7th: wknd next: t.o* **14/1**

P-P5 **9** *9* **Stafford Charlie**[7] 863 4-9-10 **75** oh4 ow3 (p) CharlieWallis(7) 9
(John O'Shea) *hld up: rdn after 7th: a in rr: t.o* **9/2**[2]

6P4/ **P** **Zaffarani's Star**[213] 9-9-7 **68** (p) MrJEngland(7) —
(Michael Gates) *nt jump wl and sn bhd: t.o whn j. bdly rt 8th: sn p.u* **33/1**

53-0 **P** **Lifes A Mystery (IRE)**[53] 341 7-10-0 **68** oh5 (b[1]) DougieCostello —
(Pauline Robson) *prom tl rdn and wknd after 8th: t.o whn p.u bef 3 out* **17/2**

P **Lonely Sky (IRE)**[30] 672 5-11-12 **94** SamThomas —
(W F Codd, Ire) *mid-div: wknd after 7th: t.o whn p.u bef 3 out* **33/1**

0-00 **P** **Lady Of Ashcott**[31] 645 4-9-7 **72** oh1 MarkQuinlan(7) —
(Neil Mulholland) *mid-div: hdwy 6th: wknd 8th: t.o whn p.u bef 3 out* **33/1**

5m 31.2s (-13.40) **Going Correction** -0.45s/f (Good)
WFA 4 from 5yo+ 17lb **13** Ran SP% **115.1**
Speed ratings (Par 103): **104,103,102,101,99 96,95,84,81,— —,—,—**
toteswingers: 1&2 £8.90, 1&3 £7.20, 2&3 £6.90 CSF £33.83 CT £230.44 TOTE £4.20: £2.10, £3.20, £3.10; EX 19.80.
Owner optimumracing.co.uk **Bred** E M Peck And Sons **Trained** Aberthin, Vale of Glamorgan

FOCUS
They were soon strung out in this very moderate event. The field had run a total of 128 races between them under rules and Kopylova's victory last time out was the sole win. She is progressive and the third and fourth help with the level.

NOTEBOOK
Kopylova was the only previous winner in the field, having won a Newton Abbot seller last month. The mare went up 8lb for that, but the five-furlong longer trip suited here and she got up to lead close home after briefly finding herself sandwiched between the second and third on the run-in. She had sweated up markedly before the start on a relatively cool evening, but it obviously didn't have a detrimental effect. (op 7-2 tchd 3-1)
Filippo Lippi(IRE) has been dropped 16lb since starting out in handicaps and it appeared as if he would cash in when striking the front on the flat, but he put his head in the air and was run out of it. He looks less than straightforward and it would be no surprise to see headgear back in place next time. (op 17-2 tchd 9-1 and 7-1)
Eastwell Smiles, fitted with first-time blinkers, made a bold bid to lead all the way, but he was worn down after the last. He is performing creditably and handled the quick ground well enough, but his jumping was not all it might have been. (op 7-1)
Smiling Applause, who was 4lb out of the weights, was under a drive from an early stage and only consented to run on when it was all over.
Hampton Court, reverting to hurdles, made a couple of errors in the closing stages and could never get on terms. (tchd 14-1)
Scotsbrook Cloud had run well here over 2m4f last time but he did not appear to see out this longer trip. He is due to be dropped another 2lb from the weekend. (op 10-1 tchd 11-1)
Stafford Charlie's better display at this track last time means he is due to be raised 16lb from the weekend, effectively 9lb higher than he ran off here. After this lacklustre effort he is surely going to struggle off his revised mark. (op 11-2 tchd 6-1)

931 PP BUSINESS IMPROVEMENTS H'CAP CHASE (18 fncs) 2m 7f
7:10 (7:11) (Class 5) (0-85,85) 4-Y-0+ **£2,055** (£599; £299)

Form RPR

P-50 **1** **Sam Cruise**[39] 517 9-11-6 **79** (t) AidanColeman 96+
(Steve Gollings) *mde all: j.rt: rdn appr last: clr flat: eased towards fin* **16/1**

3-21 **2** *10* **Sir Bumble (IRE)**[2] 913 10-11-3 **79** (t) PeterToole(3) 81
(Michael Blake) *hld up in tch: chsd wnr 13th: rdn after 2 out: hit last: wknd flat* **11/4**[1]

-426 **3** *2* **Rudinero (IRE)**[17] 795 8-10-6 **70** (tp) MichaelMurphy(5) 72
(Barry Brennan) *hld up: hdwy 9th: rdn appr 4 out: wknd after 2 out* **12/1**

-1U4 **4** *10* **Overton Lad**[30] 665 9-11-9 **82** (p) JackDoyle 74
(Peter Pritchard) *hld up: sme hdwy u.p appr 4 out: nvr on terms* **14/1**

4434 **5** *15* **Sycho Fred (IRE)**[17] 804 9-11-2 **78** (tp) CampbellGillies(3) 53
(Mike Sowersby) *chsd ldrs tl rdn and wknd after 5 out: t.o* **15/2**[2]

PP-2 **6** *11* **Scalini's (IRE)**[17] 794 10-11-2 **78** (p) DannyCook(3) 46
(Christopher Nenadich) *prom: mstke 14th: rdn and wknd bef next: t.o* **20/1**

0P0- **7** *7* **Outside Investor (IRE)**[133] 4240 10-10-13 **77** (b) KeiranBurke(5) 34
(Patrick Rodford) *prom tl wknd after 13th: t.o* **33/1**

P5-1 **8** *2 3/4* **Gaining Ground (IRE)**[38] 531 10-11-4 **77** (v) JodieMogford 31
(Graeme McPherson) *chsd ldrs: rdn after 12th: wknd 14th: t.o* **9/1**

6/34 **9** *28* **Miss Sunflower**[17] 802 8-10-12 **78** (p) MissTJackson(7) 4
(Tina Jackson) *hld up: bhd fr 11th: t.o* **25/1**

26-2 **P** **Classic Rock**[31] 649 11-11-12 **85** (p) JimmyMcCarthy —
(James Unett) *prom: hit 4th: lost pl after next: bhd fr 9th: t.o whn p.u bef 4 out* **9/1**

P-P6 **P** **Panthers Run**[25] 730 10-11-2 **75** (t) BrianHughes —
(Jonathan Haynes) *mid-div: sme hdwy 10th: wknd next: t.o whn p.u bef 4 out* **33/1**

4-34 **P** **Great Ocean Road (IRE)**[38] 529 7-11-7 **80** PaulMoloney —
(Charlie Mann) *hld up: sme hdwy after 10th: wknd next: t.o whn p.u bef 4 out* **14/1**

0-60 **P** **Poacher's Dream (IRE)**[17] 793 8-11-6 **79** FelixDeGiles —
(Jonathen de Giles) *hld up: mstke 6th: wknd 12th: t.o whn p.u bef 3 out* **50/1**

F0-P **P** **Ocheekobee (IRE)**[27] 695 7-11-4 **80** SeanQuinlan(3) —
(Richard Phillips) *mstkes and a in rr: t.o whn p.u bef 4 out* **40/1**

P **Kingston Queen (IRE)**[270] 1710 7-11-12 **85** JasonMaguire —
(Kim Bailey) *hld up: a in rr: t.o whn p.u bef 4 out* **20/1**

2-63 **P** **You Can Of Course (IRE)**[30] 665 7-11-6 **79** (v) DougieCostello —
(Neil Mulholland) *hld up: bhd fr 11th: t.o whn p.u bef 4 out* **17/2**[3]

5m 40.9s (-1.70) **Going Correction** +0.025s/f (Yiel) **16** Ran SP% **119.5**
Speed ratings (Par 103): **103,99,98,95,90 86,83,82,73,— —,—,—,—,— —**
toteswingers: 1&2 £32.10, 1&3 £52.30, 2&3 £12.10 CSF £56.14 CT £572.07 TOTE £23.50: £4.40, £1.10, £3.30, £2.40; EX 67.30.
Owner M F Strawson **Bred** J G And Mrs Thomas **Trained** Scamblesby, Lincs

FOCUS
A big field for this decidedly moderate handicap. Sir Cruise was once a 100 horse and can probably still match that.

NOTEBOOK
Sam Cruise held pole position all the way. A keen sort who went to post early, he jumped soundly, if a little out to his right, and stayed on very well. He was down to the mark off which he gained his only previous win, at Sedgefield last summer. Official explanation: trainer said, regarding apparent improvement in form, that the gelding was better suited to the galloping track and faster ground. (op 14-1)
Sir Bumble(IRE), who escaped a penalty for his win in a conditionals' event at Newton Abbot 48 hours earlier, ran a solid race over this longer trip but could not reel in the all-the-way winner. (op 9-4 tchd 2-1)
Rudinero(IRE) was tried in a combination of first-time tongue-tie and cheekpieces. He lacked the pace to effectively challenge the winner, but is running creditably and the handicapper is giving him a chance. (op 16-1)
Overton Lad stayed on from the rear over a trip a bit on the short side. He remains 8lb higher than when winning at Towcester in May. (tchd 12-1)
Sycho Fred(IRE) is down to a career low mark and probably gave his running again, but he is a very infrequent winner. (op 7-1 tchd 13-2)
Scalini's(IRE) showed a return to form at Hereford and he showed up well again here until fading over this longer trip.
Gaining Ground(IRE) was no less than 18lb higher than when making virtually all at Fontwell and could never get to the front in this much larger field. (op 11-1 tchd 12-1)

932 PP BUSINESS IMPROVEMENTS MAIDEN HURDLE (8 hdls) 2m
7:40 (7:40) (Class 5) 4-Y-0+ **£1,712** (£499; £249)

Form RPR

6- **1** **Dreamwalk (IRE)**[91] 3001 4-10-9 0 HaddenFrost(3) 100
(Roger Curtis) *hld up: hdwy 5th: led 2 out: drvn out* **10/1**

4 **2** *2 1/2* **Admiral Dundas (IRE)**[14] 827 5-11-0 0 (t) JasonMaguire 102+
(Kim Bailey) *trckd ldrs: ev ch whn blnd 2 out: styd on u.p* **12/1**

5 **3** *3/4* **Swiss Art (IRE)**[7] 693 4-10-5 0 OliverDayman(7) 97
(Alison Thorpe) *hld up: hdwy 5th: ev ch 2 out: sn rdn: no ex towards fin* **7/2**[2]

24 **4** *3 3/4* **Yeomanry**[17] 805 5-11-0 103 (b[1]) DenisO'Regan 96
(Ian Williams) *hld up: hdwy appr 3 out: rdn after next: styd on same pce* **11/4**[1]

F-6U **5** *1 1/2* **Day Time Run (IRE)**[29] 683 6-10-11 100 AlexMerriam(3) 94
(Diana Grissell) *chsd ldrs: led after 5th: hdd 2 out: no ex flat* **33/1**

06-4 **6** *3 1/4* **Princess Laila (IRE)**[29] 683 5-10-7 0 DougieCostello 84
(Ian Williams) *hld up: hdwy 3 out: rdn after next: wknd last* **33/1**

P-P5 **7** *3 1/4* **Tram Express (FR)**[14] 827 6-10-9 0 (b) SamTwiston-Davies(5) 87
(Shaun Lycett) *prom: rdn after 2 out: wknd last* **33/1**

0/33 **8** *10* **Mulaazem**[17] 793 7-10-9 88 DavidBass(5) 77
(Derek Frankland) *hld up: pushed along 4th: bhd and rdn next: nvr on terms* **7/1**

9 *1* **Follow The Sun (IRE)**[31] 655 6-11-0 99 TomO'Brien 76
(Ronald O'Leary, Ire) *led to 2nd: chsd ldrs: mstke 3 out: sn wknd* **16/1**

4 **10** *3/4* **Hi Wycombe (IRE)**[26] 711 6-10-9 92 (p) APHeskin(5) 76
(Michael Hourigan, Ire) *racd keenly: led 2nd: pckd 5th: sn hdd: wknd 2 out* **9/1**

2P-0 **11** *11* **Highland River**[50] 382 4-10-5 95 KyleJames(7) 63
(Aytach Sadik) *mid-div: drvn along and lost pl 3rd: bhd fr next: t.o* **33/1**

20 **12** *3 1/4* **Crimson Canyon (IRE)**[22] 754 4-10-12 0 APMcCoy 59
(Jonjo O'Neill) *hld up: j. slowly 3rd: a in rr: t.o* **6/1**[3]

0P-P **13** *3 1/2* **London Times (IRE)**[50] 380 5-11-0 82 (t) ColinBolger 58
(Simon Lewis) *chsd ldrs tl wknd after 5th: t.o* **125/1**

3m 39.4s (-7.90) **Going Correction** -0.45s/f (Good)
WFA 4 from 5yo+ 15lb **13** Ran SP% **120.9**
Speed ratings (Par 103): **101,99,99,97,96 95,93,88,88,87 82,80,78**
toteswingers: 1&2 £25.60, 1&3 £13.10, 2&3 £13.80 CSF £118.11 TOTE £8.00: £2.20, £2.70, £1.70; EX 83.20.
Owner R P Behan **Bred** Peter Savill **Trained** Lambourn, Berks

FOCUS
A very modest event but the first two are entitled to rate higher on their Flat form. It was steadily run and there were plenty still in contention as the field turned for home.

NOTEBOOK
Dreamwalk(IRE) had more in front of him than behind turning for home, but he came through to take a narrow lead two out and found plenty to assert. In action on the Flat since his one previous experience of hurdling, he had underfoot conditions more to his liking here. (op 7-1)
Admiral Dundas(IRE), in the firing line when blundering two out, rallied to claim second on the run-in. He appeared to see out the trip better than he had on his hurdles debut here, but this was not a truly run race. (op 11-1)
Swiss Art(IRE) has run a reasonable race on the Flat since his hurdles debut over 2m4f last month. He had every chance over this shorter trip, but gave the impression that his stamina was giving out late on. (op 9-2)
Yeomanry was back in trip after failing to see out 2m4f latest, but seemed to find this steadily run 2m too sharp. He was blinkered for the first time and his attitude might be suspect. (tchd 3-1and 100-30 in a place)
Day Time Run(IRE) gave no repeat of his Southwell misdemeanour and had a stint in the lead, but he gave the impression that he really needs further.
Tram Express(FR) was right in the mix early in the straight before fading, and has yet to prove his stamina. (op 40-1 tchd 28-1)
Crimson Canyon(IRE) has run two poor races since his second in a weak event at Fontwell. (op 5-1)

933 COTSWOLD SCAFFOLDING H'CAP HURDLE (8 hdls) 2m
8:10 (8:10) (Class 4) (0-110,108) 4-Y-0+ **£2,602** (£764; £382; £190)

Form RPR

-231 **1** **Space Telescope (IRE)**[7] 862 4-11-9 **105** (b) APMcCoy 108+
(Jonjo O'Neill) *hld up: hdwy appr 3 out: rdn to ld and hung lft flat: r.o* **9/4**[1]

154 **2** *1 1/4* **Shipboard Romance (IRE)**[10] 845 5-10-8 **91** (t) PeterToole(3) 95
(Mark Rimell) *hld up: hdwy after 5th: rdn to ld appr last: hung lft and hdd flat: styd on same pce* **16/1**

0322 **3** *2* **Three Ships**[7] 865 9-10-8 **95** MattGriffiths(7) 97
(S Wynne) *trckd ldrs: racd keenly: rdn and ev ch 2 out: hung lft and no ex flat* **7/1**[3]

-134 **4** *4 1/2* **Woodlark Island (IRE)**[21] 767 4-11-12 **108** (bt) TomScudamore 105
(David Pipe) *led to 2nd: chsd ldr tl led 5th: mstke 2 out: hdd bef last* **7/1**[3]

-653 **5** *3 1/2* **Petit Fleur**[14] 829 8-10-3 **88** SamTwiston-Davies(5) 82
(Julian Smith) *hld up: outpcd after 5th: r.o flat: nrst fin* **7/1**[3]

0-P5 **6** *1 1/4* **Welcome Stranger**[14] 829 10-10-10 **97** PeterHatton(7) 89
(Louise Davis) *hld up: hdwy appr 3 out: sn rdn: wknd after next* **33/1**

0-P6 **7** *3 1/2* **Chocolat (IRE)**[17] 796 5-11-6 **100** (t) JasonMaguire 89
(Martin Keighley) *led 2nd to 5th: wknd 3 out* **18/1**

5123 **8** *5* **Ton-Chee**[21] 765 11-11-2 **99** (t) CharlieHuxley(3) 83
(Arthur Whitehead) *mid-div: hdwy 5th: wknd 2 out* **10/1**

-P51 **9** *10* **High Skies**[7] 865 7-11-3 **104** 7ex (b) MrTWeston(7) 78
(Dr Richard Newland) *prom: chsd ldr appr 3 out: sn rdn: hung lft and wknd after next: t.o* **5/1**[2]

-044 **10** *14* **Golden Square**[21] 762 8-10-2 **87** LeeEdwards(5) 47
(Tony Carroll) *racd keenly: prom tl wknd after 5th: t.o* **16/1**

3m 38.1s (-9.20) **Going Correction** -0.45s/f (Good) **10** Ran SP% **114.0**
Speed ratings (Par 105): **105,104,103,101,99 98,97,94,89,82**
toteswingers: 1&2 £12.50, 1&3 £2.00, 2&3 £14.60 CSF £36.65 CT £218.79 TOTE £1.90: £1.70, £5.30, £3.00; EX 42.00.
Owner John P McManus **Bred** Yukiko Hosokawa **Trained** Cheltenham, Gloucs

FOCUS
An ordinary handicap hurdle, run in a time 1.3 seconds quicker than the earlier maiden. The winner should rate higher back over further.

NOTEBOOK
Space Telescope(IRE) got off the mark over 2m4f here last week and, unpenalised for that, was 10lb ahead of the handicapper. The drop in trip was all against him and he looked in trouble before the straight, but eventually began to stay on for Tony McCoy's driving and got to the front on the run-in. He is hard work but there could be more to come from him back over a more suitable trip. (op 15-8)
Shipboard Romance(IRE) showed briefly ahead in the straight and stuck on gamely without being able to repel the winner. She just looks held off a mark 6lb higher than when winning at Uttoxeter in May. (op 25-1)
Three Ships reached a place again, staying on for third, but is due a 6lb rise from the weekend which will make things tougher for him. (op 15-2)
Woodlark Island(IRE) had competition up front and did not look entirely straightforward, but still ran another creditable race, only relinquishing the lead between the last two flights. (op 6-1 tchd 11-2)
Petit Fleur was held off a 3lb higher mark than when third here latest, doing her best work late on. (op 9-1)
High Skies, who won a seller here last week and was 2lb well in under the penalty, stopped quickly after the second-last. He was reported to have finished distressed. Official explanation: vet said gelding finished distressed (op 6-1 tchd 13-2)

934 MAZAK & POWER PANELS TOGETHER SUCCESS NOVICES' CHASE (12 fncs) 2m
8:40 (8:40) (Class 4) 5-Y-0+ **£2,927** (£859; £429; £214)

Form				RPR
2P6-	**1**		**Novikov**[11] 4413 6-10-9 0.....(t) LeeStephens(3) *(David Evans) chsd ldrs: led after 3rd: clr last: comf* **5/1**[3]	111+
116-	**2**	1	**Kickahead (USA)**[58] 2002 8-10-12 0.....(t) DougieCostello *(Ian Williams) hld up: hdwy 7th: chsd ldr after 5 out: rdn appr last: styd on but a hld* **6/4**[1]	108+
P-22	**3**	5	**Pagan Sword**[7] 864 8-10-12 92..... RodiGreene *(David Bridgwater) led to 2nd: chsd ldr tl j. slowly 6th: pushed along next: outpcd fr 3 out* **5/2**[2]	105
-125	**4**	3 ¾	**Foreign King (USA)**[24] 734 6-11-0 108..... JimmyDerham(5) *(Seamus Mullins) prom: j.rt: rdn appr 4 out: outpcd fr next* **6/1**	106
4-UU	**P**		**Simiola**[7] 864 11-10-5 53..... ColinBolger *(Simon Lewis) led 2nd: hit next: sn hdd: chsd ldrs tl wknd and p.u bef 4 out* **150/1**	—
P5P-	**P**		**Thenford Duke (IRE)**[237] 2244 10-10-5 0.....(b1) MrJEngland(7) *(Ken Wingrove) sn wl bhd and nt fluent: t.o whn p.u after 4th* **100/1**	—
06-4	**P**		**Miss Nightshade**[37] 555 6-10-5 0.....(t) DarylJacob *(Jamie Snowden) prom: hit 2nd: wknd 4 out: bhd whn stmbld bdly 2 out: p.u and dismntd bef last* **10/1**	—

3m 51.7s (0.10) **Going Correction** +0.025s/f (Yiel) **7** Ran SP% **110.3**
Speed ratings: **100,99,97,95,**— —,—
toteswingers: 1&2 £3.10, 1&3 £4.10, 2&3 £1.70 CSF £12.63 TOTE £8.50: £3.90, £1.70; EX 14.30.
Owner Nick Shutts **Bred** The Duke Of Devonshire **Trained** Pandy, Monmouths
FOCUS
A reasonable novice chase but the third limits the rating for the race.
NOTEBOOK
Novikov had a good spell over hurdles last winter before losing his way, but a couple of recent spins on the Flat put him right for this chasing debut. Making virtually all and jumping safely enough, he quickened with two to go and won more easily than the margin suggests. He is well at home in easier ground and can add to this initial success. (op 13-2)
Kickahead(USA), another chasing debutant, has been in action on sand since his last appearance over hurdles back in the autumn. Held up as usual until improving before the straight, he looked a threat to the winner at that stage, but could never get to him despite running on after the last. A more strongly run race is what he requires and he can find a race over fences in the coming weeks. (op 7-4 tchd 15-8)
Pagan Sword had finished runner-up at this track on his last two starts, but was unable to lead for long this time and his jumping suffered. This was still a respectable effort but he is not one to rely on too much. (op 3-1 tchd 100-30)
Foreign King(USA), penalised for his win at Exeter, tended to jump out to his right and could not go with the principals in the latter stages. He may need a return to further and a right-handed track. (op 9-2)
Miss Nightshade weakened on the home turn on this chasing debut and was well adrift when pulled up and dismounted. She was reported to have lost her action. Official explanation: jockey said mare lost its action (op 13-2)

935 PP BUSINESS IMPROVEMENTS STANDARD OPEN NATIONAL HUNT FLAT RACE 2m
9:10 (9:10) (Class 6) 4-6-Y-0 **£1,370** (£299; £299)

Form				RPR
20-	**1**		**Osmosia (FR)**[123] 4429 5-10-7 0.....(t) WillKennedy *(Paul Webber) chsd ldrs: rdn to ld over 1f out: styd on wl* **10/1**	89
30	**2**	½	**Bachley Gale**[29] 686 5-10-7 0..... RhysFlint *(Keith Goldsworthy) led 1f: chsd ldr tl led again 4f out: rdn and hdd over 1f out: styd on* **9/1**	88
35	**2**	dht	**Landenstown Pearl (IRE)**[29] 686 4-10-0 0..... JimmyDerham(5) *(Seamus Mullins) hld up in tch: outpcd 6f out: rallied over 3f out: r.o* **14/1**	86
0-	**4**	3 ¾	**Cruise In Style (IRE)**[153] 3853 4-10-5 0..... DenisO'Regan *(Kevin Bishop) mid-div: hdwy and swtchd rt over 3f out: sn rdn: styd on same pce ins fnl f* **25/1**	82
0	**5**	nse	**Nonobu (UAE)**[29] 686 4-10-5 0..... AndrewTinkler *(George Baker) hld up: hdwy over 3f out: rdn over 1f out: styd on* **16/1**	82
13	**6**	2	**Kings Riches (IRE)**[8] 855 5-11-7 0..... TomO'Brien *(Peter Bowen) chsd ldr: rdn over 2f out: styd on same pce appr fnl f* **5/1**[3]	96
0	**7**	8	**Littledean Jimmy (IRE)**[51] 375 5-10-7 0..... CharlieWallis(7) *(John O'Shea) hld up: hdwy 6f out: rdn and ev ch whn swvd rt over 1f out: nt rcvr* **8/1**	89+
	8	nk	**Khalashan (FR)** 4-10-12 0..... APMcCoy *(Ronald O'Leary, Ire) hld up: racd keenly: hdwy 1/2-way: wknd over 2f out* **3/1**[1]	79
U	**9**	15	**Misstaysia (IRE)**[7] 869 5-10-7 0..... RichardJohnson *(Henry Daly) hld up: racd keenly: hdwy 1/2-way: 3rd and gng wl whn hung bdly rt over 4f out: nt rcvr* **7/2**[2]	79+
	10	9	**Kavatina**[395] 644 6-10-7 0..... ChristianWilliams *(Lawney Hill) chsd ldr: led after 1f: hdd 4f out: wknd over 2f out* **22/1**	50
	11	12	**Waypost** 4-10-12 0..... RodiGreene *(David Bridgwater) hld up: rdn over 6f out: a in rr: t.o* **40/1**	43
0	**12**	33	**Ice Boru (IRE)**[35] 589 4-10-0 0..... MichaelMurphy(5) *(Mike Hammond) hld up: a in rr: t.o fnl 4f* **66/1**	3
U	**13**	30	**Star Role**[14] 832 6-10-11 0.....(t) CharlieHuxley(3) *(Richard Ford) hld up: pushed along 1/2-way: t.o whn hung bdly rt over 4f out* **40/1**	—

3m 41.7s **Going Correction** -0.45s/f (Good)
WFA 4 from 5yo+ 2lb **13** Ran SP% **121.2**
Speed ratings: **82,81,81,79,79 78,74,74,67,62 56,40,25**
PL: £3.30, BG £4.20, LP £11.40; Ex: O/BG £45.00, O/LP £55.80; CSF: O/BG £46.86, O/LP £68.18; toteswingers:O/BG £18.40, O/LP £12.80, BG/LP £27.20 TOTE £14.00 Place 6 £26.50, Place 5 £26.49..
Owner Shully Liebermann **Bred** Olivier Tricot **Trained** Mollington, Oxon
FOCUS
A very moderate bumper which contained plenty of incident. It was dominated by fillies and mares and is easy to rate. The time was slow.
NOTEBOOK
Osmosia(FR) had run well on her debut but was found wanting in a valuable race at Doncaster on her next start. Having her first run for four months, and equipped with a tongue tie, she edged ahead in the straight and showed the right attitude to repel a pair of dead-heaters. (op 11-2)
Bachley Gale was prominent all the way and proved a tough nut to crack, but she could produce no extra late on and had to settle for a share of second. (tchd 16-1)
Landenstown Pearl(IRE), who was staying on well again at the death, had finished in front of her fellow dead-heater at Southwell last time. (tchd 16-1)
Cruise In Style(IRE) knew more than she had on her debut at Wincanton in February and she ran a better race on this very different surface. (op 16-1)
Nonobu(UAE) performed respectably but could not turn around Southwell form with either of the pair who dead-heated for second. (op 14-1)
Littledean Jimmy(IRE) was very much in the picture when he hung badly to his right in the direction of the paddock with over a furlong left, losing all chance. Official explanation: jockey said gelding hung badly right (op 12-1 tchd 7-1)
Khalashan(FR) an Aga Khan cast-off, was keen through the early stages and was beaten with two furlongs to run.\n (tchd 11-4 and 7-2)
Misstaysia(IRE) was well supported. Very keen early on, she did settle and was on the heels of the leaders when she all but ran off the course on the home turn. She had been extremely mulish on her recent debut here and is clearly temperamental, but she does have ability. Official explanation: jockey said gelding hung badly right on home bend (op 7-1)
Star Role Official explanation: jockey said gelding hung badly right on home bend
T/Plt: £26.80 to a £1 stake. Pool:£57,872.15 - 1,572.72 winning tickets. T/Qpdt: £29.40 to a £1 stake. Pool:£5,375.09 - 135.14 winning tickets. CR

936 - 942a (Foreign Racing) See Raceform Interactive

870 PERTH (R-H)
Sunday, July 11
OFFICIAL GOING: Good to firm (good in places; 8.4)
Wind: Strong, half behind Weather: Cloudy

943 TOTEPLACEPOT MAIDEN HURDLE (8 hdls) 2m 110y
2:10 (2:10) (Class 4) 4-Y-0+ **£2,602** (£764; £382; £190)

Form				RPR
-220	**1**		**Baaher (USA)**[49] 447 6-10-4 108..... PaulNorton(10) *(Jim Goldie) hld up: hdwy bef 3 out: effrt and ev ch next: led run-in: drvn out* **10/3**[3]	114
14-	**2**	1 ¼	**Definite All Star (IRE)**[7] 901 6-11-0 0.....(t) JasonMaguire *(Gordon Elliott, Ire) t.k.h: prom: hdwy to ld bef 2 out: sn rdn: hdd run-in: kpt on same pce towards fin* **7/4**[1]	113
13-3	**3**	15	**Nodforms Violet (IRE)**[30] 710 6-11-0 0..... GrahamLee *(Karen McLintock) led to 1st: chsd ldr: rdn and ev ch bef 2 out: wknd between last 2* **5/2**[2]	99
62-4	**4**	8	**Devotion To Duty (IRE)**[58] 315 4-10-12 114..... PeterBuchanan *(Lucinda Russell) hld up in tch: mstke 4 out: sn rdn: rallied: wknd fr 2 out* **9/2**	88
043-	**5**	15	**Desert Soul**[215] 2766 6-10-11 83.....(t) MichaelMcAlister(3) *(Maurice Barnes) led 1st: rdn and hdd bef 2 out: sn wknd* **22/1**	75
P0-0	**6**	29	**Shahramore**[10] 870 5-10-7 69..... WilsonRenwick *(P Monteith) t.k.h: chsd ldrs: drvn and outpcd bef 3 out: sn btn* **100/1**	39

3m 52.1s (-7.60) **Going Correction** -0.625s/f (Firm)
WFA 4 from 5yo+ 15lb **6** Ran SP% **111.5**
Speed ratings (Par 105): **92,91,84,80,73 59**
toteswingers: 1&2 £1.10, 1&3 £1.20, 2&3 £1.30 CSF £9.79 TOTE £3.80: £1.50, £2.60; EX 8.10.
Owner Alf Chadwick **Bred** Shadwell Farm LLC **Trained** Uplawmoor, E Renfrews
■ Paul Norton's first jumps winner, to go with three on the Flat.
FOCUS
An ordinary maiden in which the first pair came clear.
NOTEBOOK
Baaher(USA) handed his stable a four-timer in the race. He has taken an age to come good in this sphere, but has often knocked on the door and displayed a willing attitude under his 10lb conditional. A penalty in novice company would make him look vulnerable, though. (op 3-1)
Definite All Star(IRE) went for everything with the winner on landing after two out and had every chance, but found that rival too resolute on the run-in. This was better again from him with the tongue tie back on, but he has somewhat of a disappointing profile. (tchd 13-8 and 2-1)
Nodforms Violet(IRE) ran better again, but wasn't always fluent and found this drop back in trip too sharp. (op 11-4)
Devotion To Duty(IRE) spoilt his cause with too many errors on this return from a 58-day break. He'll fare better in low-grade handicaps. (op 5-1 tchd 4-1)

944 TOTESWINGER FLEXI BETTING NOVICES' CHASE (15 fncs) 2m 4f 110y
2:40 (2:40) (Class 3) 5-Y-0+ **£5,529** (£1,623; £811; £405)

Form				RPR
-F11	**1**		**Billie Magern**[10] 873 6-11-3 0..... SamTwiston-Davies(5) *(Nigel Twiston-Davies) led to 7th: regained ld 9th: mde rest: drew clr fr 3 out: easily* **1/3**[1]	143+
-120	**2**	28	**Right Or Wrong (IRE)**[11] 861 6-10-12 115.....(tp) JasonMaguire *(Gordon Elliott, Ire) pressed wnr: led 7th to 9th: cl up tl wknd fr 3 out* **3/1**[2]	108+
	3	33	**Adrianeo (IRE)**[116] 4688 7-10-12 0..... PeterBuchanan *(S R B Crawford, Ire) chsd ldrs: outpcd fr 4th: no ch fnl circ* **12/1**[3]	65
6-56	**4**	13	**Ellandshe (IRE)**[21] 801 10-10-9 50.....(b) RyanMania(3) *(William Young) a last: struggling fr 4th: nvr on terms* **66/1**	52

4m 58.4s (-15.60) **Going Correction** -0.625s/f (Firm) **4** Ran SP% **109.2**
Speed ratings: **104,93,80,75**
CSF £1.87 TOTE £1.30; EX 1.40.
Owner Roger Nicholls **Bred** Roger Nicholls **Trained** Naunton, Gloucs
FOCUS
The fast-improving Billie Magern took this uncompetitive novice chase with ease.

NOTEBOOK
Billie Magern took full advantage of a decent opportunity and made it three wins from four outings as a chaser. He was taken on for the lead going out onto the final circuit, but stamped his class on the race over the last five fences and ultimately scored under his double penalty with any amount left up his sleeve. Like his more illustrious brother, Ollie Magern, he's quickly climbing the ladder over fences and is versatile as regards distance. He looks up to taking on the better chasers in handicaps later in the season, but his preference for a sound surface would make things tricky on that front and connections are clearly keen to may hay while the sun shines. His trainer later said there could be something for him at Cheltenham's October meeting, while there is also a valuable race at Market Rasen in September. (op 4-11)
Right Or Wrong(IRE) posted a more encouraging effort on this return to chasing. He was the only danger to the winner on paper and tried to put it up to him passing the stands for the first time. He was unable to match that rival's jumping from five out, however, and was eventually well beaten off. (op 10-3 tchd 7-2)
Adrianeo(IRE) was returning from a lengthy break and, while predictably outclassed, should come on for it. (op 11-1)

945 EXCLUSIVE LODGES NOVICES' HURDLE (10 hdls) 2m 4f 110y
3:10 (3:10) (Class 4) 4-Y-0+ **£2,602** (£764; £382; £190)

Form RPR
-124 **1** **Bucephalus (IRE)**[21] [803] 6-11-2 112..................(t) MichaelMcAlister(3) 119
(Maurice Barnes) *sn trcking ldrs: effrt bef 2 out: led bef last: hld on gamely u.p run-in* **13/2**[2]
11-1 **2** *nk* **Nedzer's Return (IRE)**[35] [654] 8-11-5 145..........................(t) JPElliott 119
(Gordon Elliott, Ire) *cl up: led bef 3rd: rdn bef 2 out: hdd bef last: rallied and ev ch run-in: jst hld* **5/4**[1]
2-2 **3** *21* **Rose Street (IRE)**[42] [535] 6-10-5 104.............................. GrahamLee 90
(Pauline Robson) *trckd ldr: effrt bef 2 out: sn wknd* **5/4**[1]
PP-0 **4** *54* **Murphys Future**[64] [209] 5-10-9 0................................ RyanMania(3) 37
(George Foster) *bhd: struggling fr 6th: nvr on terms* **100/1**
P0-0 **5** *1* **Franklee**[46] [470] 7-10-5 59................................ GaryRutherford(7) 36
(Harriet Graham) *chsd ldrs: outpcd whn hit 4 out: sn btn* **80/1**
0 **P** **Riqaab (IRE)**[3] [887] 5-10-12 0................................ WilsonRenwick —
(Michael Easterby) *t.k.h: led to bef 3rd: sn lost pl: t.o whn p.u after 4 out* **66/1**
P **Mr Chamonick (IRE)**[225] 6-10-5 0.............................. KMDonoghue(7) —
(Valentine Donoghue) *mstkes in rr: struggling fr 1/2-way: no ch whn p.u after 3 out: fatally injured* **25/1**[3]

4m 52.3s (-14.60) **Going Correction** -0.625s/f (Firm) **7** Ran SP% **109.8**
Speed ratings (Par 105): **102,101,93,73,72** —,—
toteswingers: 1&2 £1.70, 1&3 £1.20, 2&3 £1.02 CSF £14.45 TOTE £7.60: £2.50, £1.10; EX 15.70.
Owner T A Barnes **Bred** Michael J Kinane **Trained** Farlam, Cumbria

FOCUS
The three market leaders dominated here and the form is straightforward.

NOTEBOOK
Bucephalus(IRE) got on top after the penultimate flight and dug deep near the business end to get up. He allowed his two big rivals to go on down the back straight, but was asked for his effort off the home turn after making up his ground and this was a good ride by his conditional jockey, whose 3lb claim probably made all the difference. (tchd 5-1)
Nedzer's Return(IRE) had a curious jockey booking in J P Elliot, considering the excellent Jason Maguire had ridden the stable's two previous runners on the card. He did plenty from the front and paid the price from two out, but still proved most game once headed. (op Evens)
Rose Street(IRE) was a little free early, but still had her chance and has been a disappointment since embarking on her hurdling career. However, this formerly very useful Flat handicapper will surely be better off on easy ground in this sphere and could prove very well handicapped during the autumn when the ground gets softer. (op 7-4)
Murphys Future ran just about his best race to date, but is going to struggle to win a race on this evidence of his career thus far.

946 TOTEEXACTA FLEXI BETTING H'CAP HURDLE (12 hdls) 3m 110y
3:40 (3:40) (Class 4) (0-115,113) 4-Y-0+ **£3,903** (£1,146; £573; £286)

Form RPR
0-3P **1** **Hermoso (IRE)**[10] [871] 5-10-13 105.................... SamTwiston-Davies(5) 112+
(Nigel Twiston-Davies) *hld up on outside: stdy hdwy bef 3 out: led gng wl appr 2 out: rdn out fr last* **4/1**[2]
414U **2** *3* **Sparkling Zola**[10] [871] 8-10-7 97.................................. EwanWhillans(3) 99
(Alistair Whillans) *cl up: effrt and ev ch bef 2 out: kpt on u.p last: nt pce of wnr* **10/1**
5642 **3** *shd* **Tarkani (IRE)**[10] [871] 7-10-11 105..........................(tp) KMDonoghue(7) 107
(Valentine Donoghue) *hld up: hdwy bef 3 out: drvn next: no imp tl styd on run-in: nrst fin* **11/2**[3]
1 **4** *1 1/4* **Long Wait (IRE)**[10] [871] 4-11-5 110.............................(p) JasonMaguire 109+
(Gordon Elliott, Ire) *nt fluent: chsd ldrs: pushed along fr 4th: drvn and one pce fr 2 out* **7/2**[1]
-443 **5** *1 1/4* **Fly Tipper**[21] [805] 10-10-1 88................................ PaddyAspell 87
(Wilf Storey) *t.k.h: hld up in tch: effrt bef 2 out: sn no imp* **25/1**
0 **6** *1/2* **Bronx Boy (IRE)**[10] [875] 7-9-11 89............................ JamesHalliday(5) 88
(Martin Todhunter) *hld up: rdn after 3 out: kpt on fr last: nvr able to chal* **20/1**
1-P6 **7** *5* **Catch The Perk (IRE)**[49] [446] 13-11-12 113................. PeterBuchanan 107
(Lucinda Russell) *cl up: lost pl 5th: struggling after 4 out: plugged on fr 2 out: nvr able to chal* **16/1**
54F4 **8** *2 1/4* **Follow On**[10] [871] 8-9-13 89..........................(t) MichaelMcAlister(3) 84
(Maurice Barnes) *hld up: drvn after 4 out: nvr on terms* **11/1**
U-41 **9** *73* **Strobe**[30] [717] 6-11-1 109...(p) AlexanderVoy(7) 28
(Lucy Normile) *led to bef 2 out: sn wknd: eased whn no ch* **20/1**
-312 **P** **Paddington Bob (IRE)**[29] [729] 6-10-1 88.......................... GrahamLee —
(Pauline Robson) *trckd ldrs: drvn after 3 out: wknd and p.u bef next: dismntd* **4/1**[2]

5m 51.9s (-18.00) **Going Correction** -0.625s/f (Firm)
WFA 4 from 5yo+ 17lb **10** Ran SP% **114.3**
Speed ratings (Par 105): **103,102,102,101,101 101,99,98,75,**—
toteswingers: 1&2 £12.30, 1&3 £7.90, 2&3 £11.20 CSF £40.62 CT £219.69 TOTE £4.20: £1.10, £3.50, £2.20; EX 49.10.
Owner Walters Plant Hire Ltd **Bred** Cornelius Hays **Trained** Naunton, Gloucs

FOCUS
A competitive staying handicap for the class.

NOTEBOOK
Hermoso(IRE) showed his true colours and ran out a ready winner. Sam Twiston-Davies had to pull him up after prematurely riding a finish too early on him over the course and distance ten days earlier, but he was well backed to make amends and it wasn't at all surprising to see him ridden out the back this time. He was produced nearing the home turn full of running and hit the front easily two out. He didn't do a tap out in front, though, which allowed the others another chance and rates value for a good bit further. It wouldn't be at all surprising to see this former dual point winner defy a likely rise. (tchd 7-2 and 5-1 in a place)
Sparkling Zola was always near the front end and showed her true colours with a brave effort. (op 9-1)
Tarkani(IRE) finished a distant second over the course and distance ten days earlier to Long Wait and reversed that from on 19lb better terms. He sets the level, but is hard to win with. (op 6-1 tchd 7-1)
Long Wait(IRE) came under pressure before his new mark came into play and it's not hard to see why he wears cheekpieces. There could still be another race in him from this sort of rating. (tchd 10-3)
Fly Tipper, still a maiden, plugged on late in the day without ever seriously threatening and probably need more positive handling.
Paddington Bob(IRE) pulled up sharply nearing the penultimate flight with something visibly amiss. (tchd 7-2)

947 TOTETRIFECTA FLEXI BETTING H'CAP CHASE (15 fncs) 2m 4f 110y
4:10 (4:11) (Class 3) (0-130,124) 4-Y-0+ **£5,854** (£1,719; £859; £429)

Form RPR
56/5 **1** **Retrievethelegend (IRE)**[10] [874] 11-11-8 120....................... AELynch 131+
(J T R Dreaper, Ire) *cl up: led 5 out: drew clr fr 3 out: easily* **9/2**[3]
60-P **2** *16* **Run To Space**[16] [839] 9-10-2 103..........................(b[1]) FearghalDavis(3) 94
(Nicky Richards) *t.k.h: prom: effrt 4 out: wnt 2nd bef 2 out: no ch w wnr* **11/2**
2FP- **3** *13* **Island Flyer (IRE)**[80] [5335] 8-11-12 124............................ SamThomas 101
(Tom George) *led to 5 out: outpcd and lost 2nd bef 2 out: sn btn* **6/1**
42-3 **4** *2 1/2* **Go Silver Bullet (FR)**[49] [446] 9-11-8 120..................... PeterBuchanan 96
(Lucinda Russell) *chsd ldrs: drvn and outpcd bef 4 out: sn btn* **2/1**[1]
4316 **5** *hd* **Crofton Arch**[27] [747] 10-10-0 98 oh25..........................(p) PaddyAspell 72
(John Dixon) *hld up in tch: pushed along 10th: wknd fr 4 out* **33/1**
-1U2 **P** **Bow School (IRE)**[21] [805] 9-11-5 117.............................. GrahamLee —
(Mrs A C Hamilton) *hld up: struggling 5 out: t.o whn p.u bef 3 out* **3/1**[2]

4m 57.0s (-17.00) **Going Correction** -0.625s/f (Firm) **6** Ran SP% **109.1**
Speed ratings (Par 107): **107,100,95,95,94** —
toteswingers: 1&2 £6.00, 1&3 £7.90, 2&3 £6.50 CSF £26.46 TOTE £5.70: £2.10, £2.40; EX 29.60.
Owner Declan O'Farrell **Bred** J Walker **Trained** Kilsallaghan, Co Dublin

FOCUS
Unsurprisingly this modest handicap was run at a sound gallop and the winner hosed up.

NOTEBOOK
Retrievethelegend(IRE) was 3lb lower than when fifth over C&D last time out and he bolted up. Ridden a lot more positively this time, he jumped for fun and had the race sewn up shortly after skipping clear off the final turn. He has shown a liking for soft ground in the past, but is clearly versatile and would have to be of serious interest if found an opportunity under a penalty. (op 7-2)
Run To Space is another that has shown a preference for soft ground before, so it was interesting he was allowed to take his chance after the stable pulled out both its runners in the novice hurdle earlier on the card. He ran a lot better in first-time blinkers, but still proved hard work. (op 6-1)
Island Flyer(IRE) had pretty much his own way out in front and this was more like it on his return from an 80-day break. However, he needs further and now looks well flattered by his current mark. (op 5-1 tchd 13-2)
Go Silver Bullet(FR) was disappointing back down in trip, even allowing for the fact he is the sort that needs to dominate. At no stage was he asked to get to the front. Official explanation: jockey said gelding lost left-fore shoe (op 7-4)
Crofton Arch was held from five out, but he was fully 25lb out of the handicap. (op 40-1)
Bow School(IRE), well backed, was never really going under a restrained ride on this return to fences, eventually pulling up. Official explanation: jockey said gelding was found to have a nasal discharge following post rasce examination (op 9-2)

948 QUEEN TRIBUTE BAND JULY 27TH CONDITIONAL JOCKEYS' H'CAP HURDLE (8 hdls) 2m 110y
4:40 (4:40) (Class 4) (0-100,97) 4-Y-0+ **£2,927** (£859; £429; £214)

Form RPR
P-53 **1** **Shopfrontspecialst (IRE)**[5] [926] 7-10-8 85................ KMDonoghue(6) 102+
(Gordon Elliott, Ire) *trckd ldrs gng wl: led on bit 2 out: clr last: v easily* **13/8**[1]
5-04 **2** *5* **Front Rank (IRE)**[24] [582] 10-11-10 95............................ EwanWhillans 101
(Dianne Sayer) *led: rdn and hdd 2 out: kpt on run-in: no ch w easy wnr* **14/1**
000/ **3** *5* **Tiger King (GER)**[32] [4235] 9-11-0 88................................ RyanMania(3) 89
(P Monteith) *hld up in midfield: rdn after 3 out: kpt on fr last: no ch w first two* **14/1**
06-5 **4** *3* **Lady Rusty (IRE)**[39] [582] 4-11-0 90........................ CampbellGillies(3) 86
(Lucinda Russell) *in tch: nt fluent and outpcd 3 out: plugged on fr last: n.d* **16/1**
24-5 **5** *3* **Harcas (IRE)**[22] [459] 8-10-10 81.................................(b) JamesHalliday 77
(Martin Todhunter) *cl up tl rdn and wknd bef 2 out* **10/1**
0005 **6** *1 1/4* **Sea Cove**[8] [748] 10-10-6 82... PaulNorton(5) 76
(Dianne Sayer) *bhd: outpcd after 4 out: kpt on u.p fr 2 out: nvr rchd ldrs* **33/1**
U-00 **7** *3 3/4* **Perez (IRE)**[17] [604] 8-9-11 73....................................(vt) PaulGallagher(5) 63
(Wilf Storey) *midfield: hdwy bef 3 out: wknd bef next* **14/1**
-343 **8** *2* **Knight Valliant**[10] [875] 7-10-13 84................................ JamesO'Farrell 72
(Barbara Butterworth) *midfield: drvn along 3 out: wknd bef next* **6/1**[3]
-000 **9** *7* **Wellesley**[10] [870] 4-9-11 78.. CallumWhillans(8) 57
(Donald Whillans) *trckd ldrs tl rdn and wknd bef 3 out* **28/1**
-534 **10** *2* **King's Chorister**[38] [604] 4-10-0 73 oh1................(t) SamTwiston-Davies 50
(Barry Murtagh) *hld up: drvn after 3 out: nvr on terms* **5/1**[2]
30-P **11** *17* **Guerilla (AUS)**[36] [626] 10-10-12 89..........................(p) AlexanderVoy(6) 51
(Lucy Normile) *hld up on outside: stdy hdwy 4 out: wknd after next* **14/1**
PPF/ **12** *29* **Lofty Leader (IRE)**[461] [4888] 11-10-9 85..................(p) GaryRutherford(5) 18
(Harriet Graham) *bhd: struggling bef 4 out: nvr on terms* **50/1**
F-60 **P** **Hair Of The Dog**[16] [837] 6-10-2 73.................................. FearghalDavis —
(William Amos) *bhd: rn wd bnd after 3rd: sn struggling: p.u after next* **25/1**

3m 47.8s (-11.90) **Going Correction** -0.625s/f (Firm)
WFA 4 from 5yo+ 15lb **13** Ran SP% **122.9**
Speed ratings (Par 105): **103,100,98,96,95 94,93,92,88,87 79,66,**—
toteswingers: 1&2 £7.20, 1&3 £8.40, 2&3 £19.40 CSF £25.62 CT £258.84 TOTE £2.90: £1.50, £4.10, £6.50; EX 36.40 TRIFECTA Not won..
Owner Ms Annie Flora Joan Bowles **Bred** Martin C Fleming **Trained** Trim, Co Meath

FOCUS
A weak, but open handicap which saw a very easy winner.

NOTEBOOK
Shopfrontspecialst(IRE) could hardly have won much easier in the end and finally got off the mark. He was having just his second outing for Gordon Elliott and looked to have a decent chance on the strength of his previous outing at Roscommon, but stepped up a lot on that effort in winning this. He didn't have to come out of third gear and would surely be able to follow up if turning out quickly, as he escapes a penalty for this. (tchd 7-4)
Front Rank(IRE) set out to make all. He was a sitting duck for the winner turning for home, but kept on bravely thereafter and this was a fair effort under top weight. (op 10-1)

Tiger King(GER) is well handicapped over hurdles on his form back in 2007, which including success over C&D. Having his first outing in this sphere since last March, he got outpaced when things became serious, but may come on again for the run and would appreciate some easier ground. (op 9-1)
Lady Rusty(IRE) was another outpaced when it mattered, but this was better and she ought to enjoy stepping up in distance. (op 14-1)
King's Chorister, well backed, was never seriously in the hunt from off the pace may benefit for some form of headgear (worn on the Flat). Official explanation: jockey said gelding lost its left-fore shoe (op 15-2)

949 TOTEPOOL A BETTER WAY TO BET STANDARD OPEN NATIONAL HUNT FLAT RACE 2m 110y
5:10 (5:11) (Class 5) 4-6-Y-O **£1,712** (£499; £249)

Form				RPR
3-3	1		**Ciannte (IRE)**29 [731] 5-10-4 0 MrStevenCrawford(5)	87
			(S R B Crawford, Ire) *mde all: hrd pressed fr 3f out: edgd rt ins fnl f: hld on wl* **6/4**1	
0-	2	hd	**Hallmark Harry**179 [3419] 4-10-7 0 JakeGreenall(7)	92
			(Michael Easterby) *trckd ldr: effrt and ev ch fr 3f out: kpt on fnl f: jst hld* **11/2**	
6-3	3	7	**Float My Boat**23 [788] 4-11-0 0 JasonMaguire	85
			(S R B Crawford, Ire) *trckd ldrs: rdn and outpcd over 2f out: no imp fr over 1f out* **7/4**2	
0-	4	2 1/4	**Buraimi Oasis**216 [2753] 5-11-2 0 GrahamLee	85
			(Karen McLintock) *t.k.h: in tch: effrt over 2f out: sn outpcd: n.d after* **5/1**3	

3m 49.6s (-4.50) **Going Correction** -0.625s/f (Firm)
WFA 4 from 5yo 2lb 4 Ran SP% **108.4**
Speed ratings: **85,84,81,80**
CSF £9.29 TOTE £2.00; EX 8.90 Place 6 £63.29, Place 5 £41.72.
Owner Mrs Linda Gault **Bred** Mrs Linda Gault **Trained** Larne, Co Antrim
■ Stewards' Enquiry : Mr Steven Crawford five-day ban: used whip with excessive frequency (tbn)

FOCUS
A moderate little bumper, run at a routine gallop. It paid to race handily here and the first pair came clear in a tight finish.

NOTEBOOK
Ciannte(IRE) made just about all to open her account in this sphere at the third time of asking. She was just about the form pick on her previous third at Hexham and showed real guts to get the better off the runner-up from three furlongs out. While she is not the biggest, she has won a point and jumping hurdles will be no problem for her. (tchd 11-8 and 7-4)
Hallmark Harry ◆ pulled too hard when disappointing on his debut in a Fibresand bumper six months previously. He has plenty of scope, so it wasn't surprising to see him go close after settling better through the early parts this time. Things may well have been different had his rider gone for everything a little further out, but he should repay that kindness before too long. (op 5-1)
Float My Boat, the winner's stablemate, probably ran close enough to his recent level and helps to set the standard. (op 9-4 tchd 13-8)
Buraimi Oasis was beaten a long way on debut late on last year, but was short in the market that day and his yard know how to get winners in this sphere. He got outpaced, though, and the run may have been needed. (op 9-2 tchd 4-1)
T/Plt: £76.50 to a £1 stake. Pool: £61,819.61. 589.68 winning tickets. T/Qpdt: £26.80 to a £1 stake. Pool: £4,301.10. 118.70 winning tickets. RY

680 SOUTHWELL (L-H)
Sunday, July 11

OFFICIAL GOING: Good to firm (good in places; 8.7)
Fences 7yds and Golf Club Bend 5yds inside with the home bend 5yds outside the line raced on 8th June.
Wind: Fresh, half behind Weather: Fine and sunny, very warm but breezy

950 STEVE AND DAWN GOODINGS WEDDING DAY H'CAP CHASE (13 fncs) 2m
2:20 (2:20) (Class 4) (0-100,100) 4-Y-0+ **£4,553** (£1,337; £668; £333)

Form				RPR
3165	1		**Misamon (FR)**5 [919] 7-10-11 **92** (v) MrJFMathias(7)	102+
			(David Rees) *sn chsng ldr: led 2 out: styd on wl* **8/1**	
-P22	2	1 1/4	**One Of The Boys (IRE)**14 [848] 9-11-7 **100** DeanColeman(5)	108
			(Tim Vaughan) *hld up: wnt prom 7th: rdn 4 out: wnt 2nd 2 out: kpt on: no real imp* **6/4**1	
F133	3	1	**Ginger's Lad**16 [840] 6-10-5 **79** KeithMercer	85
			(Michael Easterby) *chsd ldrs: pushed along 6th: drvn and outpcd 9th: styd on wl fr 2 out* **4/1**2	
-1F3	4	1 3/4	**My Condor (IRE)**35 [652] 9-11-3 **91** (p) TomScudamore	96
			(Donald McCain) *set stdy pce: qcknd 8th: hdd 2 out: one pce* **13/2**	
64-0	5	3 1/4	**Lukie Victor (IRE)**35 [646] 9-11-4 **92** PaulMoloney	99+
			(Evan Williams) *nt fluent: chsd ldrs: mstke 7th: 4th and one pce whn hung bdly rt and blnd 2 out* **9/1**	
00B-	6	12	**Tropical Bachelor (IRE)**18 [5074] 4-10-5 **95** (p) DougieCostello	68
			(Tim Pitt) *nt fluent in rr: outpcd 9th: sn btn* **5/1**3	
/55-	7	21	**Cadwell**261 [1875] 6-10-2 **76** RodiGreene	44
			(Tim Pitt) *chsd ldrs: drvn 8th: lost pl 3 out: sn bhd* **33/1**	

4m 2.40s (-7.60) **Going Correction** -0.35s/f (Good)
WFA 4 from 6yo+ 2lb 7 Ran SP% **114.1**
Speed ratings (Par 105): **105,104,103,103,101 95,84**
toteswingers: 1&2 £4.00, 1&3 £4.30, 2&3 £1.80 CSF £21.41 TOTE £7.20: £3.00, £1.50; EX 29.70.
Owner The Supreme Racing Club **Bred** Alain Ranson **Trained** Clarbeston, Pembrokes

FOCUS
The course configuration had been altered since the previous meeting on 8 June, with the fences moved seven yards, the golf club bend moved 5 yards inside, and the home bend moved 5 yards outside. A steadily-run handicap with the field finishing closely grouped.

NOTEBOOK
Misamon(FR) gained his sole previous victory over fences last month when dictating the pace, but with My Condor in the field he was not going to have his own way in front this time. Tracking the leader, he lost some momentum when making a mistake in the back straight and had to be driven to get back on terms, but he rallied well and showed some tenacity to get on top near the finish. He is not the most reliable but seems to go well when kept busy and able to race at least near the lead. (tchd 7-1)
One Of The Boys(IRE) returned to form last month, albeit finding Yellow Flag too good on both occasions and, with his jockey's 5lb claim offsetting a 6lb rise, he held every chance in a weaker race and was backed accordingly. However, his jumping was occasionally on the low side, and he looked to be struggling in the back straight, before rallying again after turning for home to finish a respectable, though never-nearer, second. (tchd 7-4)
Ginger's Lad got outpaced in the back straight which effectively put paid to any winning chance, but he stayed on well from the turn to be closing at the line. His previous form suggests he needs further, and that was borne out here. (op 7-2 tchd 9-2)
My Condor(IRE) adopted his usual front-running role, but he lacks pace at the finish even off a modest gallop, which makes him difficult to win with. (op 7-1)
Lukie Victor(IRE) was running a respectable race but was beginning to weaken when a bad mistake two out cost him valuable momentum. He has dropped 10lb over fences to a level commensurate with his recent poor hurdling form, but might be better on easier ground. (op 11-1)
Tropical Bachelor(IRE) has been in good form on the Flat of late, but his previous hurdling form had been indifferent and he did not take to the fences on his chasing debut. (op 8-1 tchd 9-2)
Cadwell was too keen on his first run since October and ran well enough on his chasing debut before eventually fading.

951 BET WORLD CUP FINAL - BETDAQ NOVICES' CHASE (19 fncs) 3m 110y
2:50 (2:50) (Class 4) 5-Y-0+ **£3,665** (£1,137; £612)

Form				RPR
-212	1		**The Ferbane Man (IRE)**38 [605] 6-11-5 118 (p) TomScudamore	122
			(Tim Vaughan) *trckd ldr: hit 8th: styd on fr 4 out: chal last: sn led: all out* **10/11**1	
45-3	2	hd	**Chevy To The Levy (IRE)**35 [647] 8-10-12 107 AndrewThornton	114
			(John O'Shea) *led: rdn 4 out: jnd last: sn hdd: rallied towards fin* **6/1**3	
	3	49	**Canon's Corner (IRE)**413 7-10-9 0 SeanQuinlan(3)	72
			(Rachel Hobbs) *t.k.h: trckd ldrs: pckd 5th: outpcd 9th: lft 10 l 3rd 15th: sn lost tch: t.o* **12/1**	
1515	F		**Flying Doctor**8 [859] 7-11-5 128 JohnnyFarrelly	—
			(Elliott Cooper) *chsd ldrs: shkn up after 13th: rdn next: 3 l 3rd and struggling whn fell 15th* **9/4**2	
/P46	U		**Flag Hill**21 [802] 7-10-12 64 (t) KeithMercer	—
			(Peter Atkinson) *prom: lost pl 6th: bhd fr 9th: t.o 14th: uns rdr next* **66/1**	
5	P		**Dougall (IRE)**21 [802] 7-10-12 0 TjadeCollier	—
			(Joanne Foster) *in rr: bhd fr 9th: t.o whn mstke 9th: p.u bef last* **33/1**	

6m 20.4s (-5.60) **Going Correction** -0.35s/f (Good) 6 Ran SP% **109.6**
Speed ratings: **94,93,78,—,—, —**
toteswingers: 1&2 £1.60, 1&3 £3.40, 2&3 £3.00 CSF £6.74 TOTE £2.00: £1.10, £1.50; EX 6.80.
Owner Aidan & Gerard Flynn **Bred** Oliver Loughlin **Trained** Aberthin, Vale of Glamorgan

FOCUS
Little strength in depth with the first three in the market dominating with a circuit to go, and it produced a gritty driving finish between the first two.

NOTEBOOK
The Ferbane Man(IRE), who was the pick of the paddock, is a fast-ground stayer who held the strongest chance on form, and that was reflected in the market. However, he needed every yard to get on terms with the long-time leader, and he had to dig deep in a protracted battle for supremacy. Although he has now won twice over fences, his jumping lacks fluency and that might account for his difficulty in getting the better of a rival rated 11lb inferior. (op Evens tchd 11-10 and 5-6)
Chevy To The Levy(IRE) has also had problems with his jumping, but he showed a little more on his return from an 11-month break last month and continued the improvement. Setting the pace, he jumped adequately in the main but had been in front a long time and was there for the taking, although to his credit he went down fighting. He looks up to winning a race if he maintains this improvement in his jumping. (op 8-1)
Canon's Corner(IRE) had placed in his final start in a reasonably strong Irish point in May last year but struggled to cope with the fences on his rules debut. Official explanation: trainer said gelding finished distressed (op 16-1)
Flying Doctor had been in good form recently, but this was his 11th race since the beginning of May and the busy spell seemed to be taking its toll as he took a tired fall at the third in the back straight. (op 7-4)

952 BET IN RUNNING - BETDAQ CONDITIONAL JOCKEYS' H'CAP CHASE (16 fncs) 2m 4f 110y
3:20 (3:20) (Class 4) (0-105,105) 4-Y-0+ **£3,577** (£1,050; £525; £262)

Form				RPR
3134	1		**Mutual Respect (IRE)**33 [680] 8-11-2 **103** AdamWedge(8)	122+
			(Evan Williams) *w ldr: led 12th: drew clr appr 3 out: drvn out* **9/4**1	
-004	2	28	**More Like It (IRE)**30 [716] 10-10-12 **91** (p) TomMolloy	83
			(Peter Niven) *hit 7th: bhd and drvn 9th: kpt on fr 3 out: tk distant 2nd run-in* **9/2**	
-236	3	12	**Dancewiththedevil (IRE)**43 [521] 9-11-4 **105** MichaelByrne(8)	87
			(Peter Bowen) *hld up: hdwy and 3rd 9th: hit 11th: chsd wnr 4 out: 15 l down whn hit 2 out: wknd bdly run-in* **5/2**2	
/04-	4	2 1/2	**Space Star**144 [4097] 10-11-8 **101** JohnnyFarrelly	77
			(Paul Webber) *led to 12th: wknd next* **10/3**3	
5-6P	5	nk	**Dasher Reilly (USA)**35 [649] 9-10-0 **79** oh13 MichaelMurphy	54
			(Aytach Sadik) *drvn 7th: bhd fr 9th: t.o 4 out* **12/1**	

5m 16.8s (1.80) **Going Correction** -0.35s/f (Good) 5 Ran SP% **108.3**
Speed ratings (Par 105): **82,71,66,65,65**
CSF £11.85 TOTE £3.40: £1.50, £3.60; EX 7.30.
Owner R E R Williams **Bred** Highfort Stud **Trained** Llancarfan, Vale Of Glamorgan
■ A winner for Adam Wedge on his first ride since turning professional.

FOCUS
An open-looking handicap despite the small field, though a mid-race pace surge stretched the field producing elongated finishing distances.

NOTEBOOK
Mutual Respect(IRE) gave his jockey a debut professional success in emphatic style. Disputing the lead with his tongue lolling over the bit throughout, he was as asked by his jockey to subtly raise the pace in the back straight and soon had his rivals struggling, and though he was bound to tire a little near the finish the damage had been done. He is also effective at 3m, and when he is on-song he can stretch a field from some way out, so this combination means he should be up to winning another small-field race this summer. (op 11-4)
More Like It(IRE) got in close to several and his jumping was generally not that fluent. Consequently he got outpaced in the back straight and, although he stayed on towards the end, he was never able to pose a threat. (op 5-1 tchd 4-1)
Dancewiththedevil(IRE) was a late drifter on his first start for Peter Bowen, and that lack of confidence proved prescient. Ridden patiently, he did move into second mid-race but was never going that well and eventually weakened tamely. His chase rating is 15lb lower than that over hurdles, but on this showing he will need to improve to capitalise on that fences mark. (op 15-8)
Space Star helped set the pace but weakened quickly once headed. He may have needed this first run since February, but might also need a drop in trip. (op 3-1 tchd 11-4)

953 BETDAQ.CO.UK NOVICES' (S) HURDLE (11 hdls) 2m 4f 110y
3:50 (3:50) (Class 5) 4-Y-0+ **£2,397** (£698; £349)

Form				RPR
-134	1		**Dereks (IRE)**18 [829] 8-11-3 104 TomScudamore	115+
			(Jim Best) *mde all: drew clr appr 2 out: 6 l ahd whn mstke last: eased towards fin* **7/4**2	
-212	2	7	**King Of Castile**38 [603] 6-11-3 111 (vt) PaulMoloney	105
			(Evan Williams) *chsd wnr: reminders 6th: outpcd 8th: modest 4th 2 out: kpt on to take n.d 2nd clsng stages* **11/8**1	
0	3	1/2	**Golden Gem (IRE)**11 [862] 8-10-9 94 (b) SeanQuinlan(3)	101
			(Rachel Hobbs) *t.k.h: trckd ldrs: wnt handy 2nd 3 out: 5 l down whn hung bdly rt after 2 out: lost 2nd towards fin* **12/1**	

05/0 **4** *8* **Dubrovnick (IRE)**^{18} [833] 5-10-7 0 DeanColeman(5) 94+
(Tim Vaughan) *hld up in rr: hdwy 3 out: modest 3rd appr next: one pce* **16/1**

5 *37* **Media Stars**^{13} 5-10-12 0 KeithMercer 55
(Robert Johnson) *trckd ldrs: wknd 7th: bhd fr 3 out: t.o* **33/1**

0-55 **6** *14* **Pursuit Of Purpose**^{52} [421] 4-9-13 84 CharlieStudd(3) 31
(Philip Sharp) *hld up in rr: wnt prom 6th: rdn and lost pl 3 out: sn bhd: t.o* **50/1**

7 *42* **Kapellmeister (IRE)**^{678} 7-10-12 0 RodiGreene —
(Philip Sharp) *in rr: bhd fr 5th: t.o 7th: eventually completed* **66/1**

20-2 **P** **Treeko (IRE)**^{16} [835] 5-10-5 100 (p) KyleJames(7) —
(Philip Kirby) *trckd ldrs: 2nd and drvn 6th: hung lft and wknd qckly 8th: sn bhd: t.o whn p.u bef 2 out* **5/1**^{3}

0-P **P** **Autumn's Quest**^{36} [635] 7-10-5 0 WillKennedy —
(Teresa Spearing) *nt fluent: chsd ldrs: reminders 2nd and 4th: bhd fr 7th: t.o whn p.u bef 2 out* **66/1**

5m 8.10s (-2.60) **Going Correction** -0.10s/f (Good)
WFA 4 from 5yo+ 16lb **9** Ran SP% **116.6**
Speed ratings (Par 103): **100,97,97,94,80 74,58,—,—**
toteswingers: 1&2 £1.50, 1&3 £4.90, 2&3 £3.90 CSF £4.70 TOTE £3.00: £1.10, £1.10, £4.90; EX 5.10.The winner wae sold to Mr C Leech for 7,000gns.

Owner Miss J S Dollan **Bred** D Wall **Trained** Lewes, E Sussex

FOCUS
Little strength in depth in the seller, with the only two recent winners dominating.

NOTEBOOK
Dereks(IRE) was given a perfect pace-setting ride, setting a moderate early pace before stretching the field in the back straight and, despite a mistake at the last, finishing clear of the rest. After winning on his first start for Jim Best last month, his rating may have crept too high for handicaps at the moment, but he readily outclassed this opposition. (op 2-1 tchd 9-4)

King Of Castile was outpaced as the tempo increased in the back straight. He rallied towards the finish but was never a serious threat. He tends to need strong handling but does eventually respond, and has flourished since being dropped to selling class, but he just came up against a classier rival. (op 6-4 tchd 13-8 and 5-4)

Golden Gem(IRE) made some good progress to track the winner going to the final turn, but that was the extent of his threat and he eventually weakened. This was nevertheless an improvement on his return from a break last month, and he might have some improvement to come on easier ground, but that might still not be enough. (op 18-1 tchd 20-1)

Dubrovnick(IRE) plugged on from the home turn but could never get involved. This was a lowly introduction to hurdling but his astute trainer will still need to elicit more improvement for this grade. (op 14-1 tchd 11-1)

Treeko(IRE) Official explanation: jockey said gelding hung left

954 WORLD CUP FREE BETS AT FREEBETTING.CO.UK H'CAP HURDLE (11 hdls) 2m 4f 110y

4:20 (4:20) (Class 3) (0-130,129) 4-Y-0+ **£5,204** (£1,528; £764; £381)

Form RPR

32-0 **1** **To Arms**^{65} [196] 8-11-2 124 (t) DavidBass(5) 131+
(Lawney Hill) *hld up in rr: hdwy to chse ldrs 3 out: led between last 2: drvn and styd on wl: readily* **11/4**^{1}

P1-1 **2** *4* **Restart (IRE)**^{46} [480] 9-9-12 104 TommyPhelan(3) 109+
(Lucinda Featherstone) *t.k.h: trckd ldrs: wnt 2nd 8th: led on bit appr 2 out: 1 l ahd whn blnd 2 out: hung lft and hdd between last 2: no ex* **13/2**^{3}

6225 **3** *9* **Mister Benedictine**^{21} [798] 7-11-1 118 (tp) MarkGrant 114
(Brendan Duke) *hld up in rr: hdwy to trck ldrs 3 out: 3 l 3rd and wkng whn mstke last* **8/1**

21-P **4** *9* **Postmaster**^{43} [524] 8-11-12 129 PaulMoloney 116
(Evan Williams) *chsd ldrs: wknd appr 2 out* **11/1**

55-U **5** *5* **Cruchain (IRE)**^{28} [735] 7-11-3 120 DougieCostello 100
(Jonjo O'Neill) *led: hdd appr 2 out: sn wknd* **8/1**

6F-6 **6** *½* **Orion Express**^{24} [771] 9-9-9 105 MarkQuinlan(7) 85
(Susan Gardner) *hld up: wnt prom 6th: rdn 3 out: sn wknd* **8/1**

11 **7** *19* **Majestic Mayhem (IRE)**^{21} [805] 7-11-3 120 BarryKeniry 81
(George Moore) *nt fluent: chsd ldrs: lost pl sn after 3 out* **7/2**^{2}

/PP- **8** *¾* **Donovan (NZ)**^{77} [6] 11-9-6 105 oh5 ow2 (p) CraigGallagher(10) 65
(Richard Guest) *detached in last: bhd fr 6th: t.o 3 out* **40/1**

6-00 **9** *1 ½* **Englishtown (FR)**^{30} [708] 10-11-0 120 (p) MrAJBerry(3) 78
(Jonjo O'Neill) *chsd ldrs: drvn 6th: lost pl 8th: bhd and j.lft last 3* **12/1**

5m 4.50s (-6.20) **Going Correction** -0.10s/f (Good) **9** Ran SP% **114.0**
Speed ratings (Par 107): **107,105,102,98,96 96,89,89,88**
toteswingers: 1&2 £6.40, 1&3 £5.40, 2&3 £9.30 CSF £20.99 CT £125.84 TOTE £5.50: £2.10, £3.50, £1.20; EX 19.50.

Owner Carl Pyne **Bred** Mrs M Chaworth Musters **Trained** Aston Rowant, Oxon

FOCUS
A competitive handicap with three challenging up the home straight.

NOTEBOOK
To Arms needed some driving to progress into a challenging position round the final turn and had to fight off two challengers, but he found enough to extend his lead on the long run before the last. He had been without a win in nine attempts since his debut hurdling success, but has shown glimmers of form for a variety of yards. His current stable has proceeded steadily and, with a two-month break to freshen him up, he justified the market support in gritty style. The Handicapper may make life difficult now, but he is best off a strong pace so will never win by a wide margin and can act on easier ground so is not just a summer horse. (op 4-1)

Restart(IRE) swept into the lead on the home turn and looked set to go clear, but a juddering error two out halted his momentum. His form last year was woeful, but he took a long time to get his confidence back on the long return from a tendon injury, and has looked a different horse since reappearing this spring, gaining two C&D successes. He has been climbing up the weights but continues to progress at a similar rate and did not look outclassed by the step up in grade. He could gain compensation, especially if able to race off a light weight again. (op 9-2 tchd 7-1)

Mister Benedictine made steady progress to hold every chance entering the home straight, but he tends not to find much under pressure, even with cheekpieces fitted this time, and he weakened again. He has generally been consistent over the past couple of months but has not won over jumps for two years. (op 7-1)

Postmaster was a bit keen following a six-week break but still travelled quite well for a long way although he could not sustain it to the business end. He has some good previous form over hurdles and, with a more favourable mark compared to his chase rating, there should be more to come. (op 9-1 tchd 12-1)

Cruchain(IRE) led until midway down the back straight, but could find no extra once headed. He has been struggling over fences this year so this will have helped boost his confidence a bit. (op 7-1)

Orion Express ideally needs further and was outclassed here. (op 12-1)

Majestic Mayhem(IRE) won two novice hurdles last month but still needed to improve again for his handicap debut,and although he raced up with the pace his jumping was not that fluent and he weakened tamely. Official explanation: jockey said gelding jumped poorly throughout (op 4-1)

955 BRITISH OPEN GOLF FREE BETS FREEBETTING.CO.UK H'CAP HURDLE (13 hdls) 3m 110y

4:50 (4:53) (Class 5) (0-90,90) 4-Y-0+ **£2,397** (£698; £349)

Form RPR

0-0 **1** **Makena (FR)**^{35} [645] 8-11-5 90 (p) MrJFMathias(7) 107+
(David Rees) *hld up: smooth hdwy to trck ldrs 8th: led on bit after 3 out: 6 l ahd last: eased fnl 50yds* **10/1**

00P- **2** *7* **Treasury Counsel (IRE)**^{102} [4960] 8-11-7 85 PaulMoloney 92
(Evan Williams) *mid-div: drvn 8th: hdwy to chse ldrs 3 out: wnt 2nd appr next: hung lft between last 2: no ch w wnr* **7/2**^{1}

5-60 **3** *4 ½* **Barlin Bay**^{30} [708] 6-9-12 65 ow1 TommyPhelan(3) 67
(Harry Chisman) *in rr: drvn and outpcd 9th: hdwy to chse ldrs 3 out: tk modest 3rd appr next* **14/1**

U454 **4** *20* **Smiling Applause**^{4} [930] 11-9-11 64 (b) SeanQuinlan(3) 46
(Harry Chisman) *w ldrs: mstke and led 7th: hdd after 3 out: wknd appr next* **5/1**^{2}

043P **5** *5* **Sarobar (IRE)**^{21} [794] 10-10-10 74 WillKennedy 51
(John Spearing) *chsd ldrs 5th: outpcd and rdn 10th: tk remote 5th 2 out* **11/1**

PPP- **6** *25* **Artist's Return (IRE)**^{329} [1229] 8-10-3 70 AlexMerriam(3) 22
(William Stone) *in rr: bhd fr 9th* **28/1**

-060 **7** *3 ¾* **Naughty Diesel**^{21} [802] 7-10-8 72 JimmyMcCarthy 20
(Robert Johnson) *hld up in rr: nvr on terms* **11/1**

0-P0 **8** *6* **Vicentio**^{47} [461] 11-10-0 64 (b^{1}) KeithMercer 6
(Tim Fitzgerald) *in rr-div: bhd fr 9th* **22/1**

00-5 **9** *1 ¾* **Apache Brave (IRE)**^{41} [552] 7-10-0 64 (b^{1}) TjadeCollier —
(Henry Hogarth) *chsd ldrs: lost pl 10th: sn bhd* **7/1**^{3}

P0-0 **10** *6* **The Boat Shed (IRE)**^{41} [557] 4-11-3 85 (bt) MarkGrant 16
(Brendan Duke) *led to 4th: w ldrs: wknd 3 out* **18/1**

11 *17* **Free Speech**^{35} 7-10-13 87 (t) MissCareyWilliamson(10) —
(Sarah Humphrey) *prom: lost pl 9th: t.o 2 out* **9/1**

0-P0 **P** **Dancing Hill**^{35} [646] 11-11-2 80 JohnnyFarrelly —
(Kevin Bishop) *in rr: drvn 6th: sn lost pl and bhd: t.o whn p.u bef next* **33/1**

PP-4 **P** **Rahy's Crown (USA)**^{52} [420] 7-9-12 65 CharlieStudd(3) —
(Philip Sharp) *in rr: bhd fr 8th: t.o whn p.u bef next* **20/1**

0PPU **F** **Lindseyfield Lodge (IRE)**^{21} [804] 9-11-3 88 (p) KyleJames(7) —
(Robert Johnson) *sn w ldr: led 4th: hdd 7th: lost pl and towards rr whn fell 10th* **16/1**

P-05 **P** **Simbamead**^{38} [596] 5-10-0 64 oh2 RodiGreene —
(Michael Mullineaux) *t.k.h: w ldrs: reminders 8th: wknd rapidly after 3 out: t.o last whn p.u bef last* **25/1**

6m 7.50s **Going Correction** -0.10s/f (Good)
WFA 4 from 5yo+ 17lb **15** Ran SP% **124.3**
Speed ratings (Par 103): **96,93,92,85,84 76,75,73,72,70 65,—,—,—,—**
toteswingers: 1&2 £12.60, 1&3 £35.10, 2&3 £13.10 CSF £43.78 CT £513.69 TOTE £14.60: £3.70, £1.70, £5.40; EX 66.90 Place 6 £16.45, Place 5 £8.51.

Owner D L Evans **Bred** Roland Lacrampe Cuyaubere **Trained** Clarbeston, Pembrokes

FOCUS
The field was bunched until the final circuit but in the end four came clear from the home turn and the field finished strung out.

NOTEBOOK
Makena(FR) ◆ travelled up strongly to lead going into the final turn, and she stretched clear from the field, giving her trainer and jockey a double on the day. Her two runs under rules in Britain were not that encouraging, despite a glimmer of hope in her last race when making some progress before finishing well beaten. However, the clues to her potential lay in her multiple wins in France and latterly in points and she has soon converted that latent ability to hurdles. Even allowing for the Handicapper's reaction, there looks to be more leeway in her mark and there should be more to come. (op 8-1)

Treasury Counsel(IRE) has been out of form since last autumn but had a wind operation in the spring and that seems to have brought about some improvement. Ridden patiently, he made steady progress but was never really a threat to the well-handicapped winner. However, he should be up to winning a modest race if he can maintain this level of form. (tchd 3-1 and 4-1)

Barlin Bay tagged onto the leaders leaving the home turn but could only plug on at one pace. This was an easier test than she has faced of late and she responded accordingly, but still looks some way off gaining that elusive first win. (op 12-1)

Smiling Applause has been held up with little effect in recent months, but was ridden much more prominently this time. Unfortunately the change of tactics did not do the trick as he was too keen, hassling for the lead, and as a consequence he faded tamely in the home straight. (op 13-2)

Sarobar(IRE), running over hurdles for the first time in more than four years, began to feel the pace on the final circuit and could only plug on. (op 10-1)

Dancing Hill Official explanation: jockey said mare never travelled

T/Plt: £14.70 to a £1 stake. Pool: £57,888.72. 2,869.91 winning tickets. T/Qpdt: £6.60 to a £1 stake. Pool: £4,072.98. 454.06 winning tickets. WG

850 STRATFORD (L-H)

Sunday, July 11

OFFICIAL GOING: Good to firm (10.0)
Rail realignment increased advertised distances by about 25yds per circuit.
Wind: Light, against Weather: Fine and sunny

956 BIRMINGHAM MAIL "NATIONAL HUNT" NOVICES' HURDLE (9 hdls) 2m 110y

2:00 (2:00) (Class 3) 4-Y-0+ **£4,553** (£1,337; £668; £333)

Form RPR

-311 **1** **Pure Faith (IRE)**^{24} [773] 6-11-12 124 TomO'Brien 126+
(Peter Bowen) *led and nt fluent 1st: hdd next: led 4th: clr after 3 out: easily* **10/11**^{1}

0-P6 **2** *5* **Nether Stream (IRE)**^{25} [763] 6-10-12 0 DenisO'Regan 100
(Shaun Lycett) *hld up and bhd: styd on to go 2nd bef last: nvr nr to chal* **50/1**

3-66 **3** *13* **Quidam Blue (FR)**^{28} [739] 6-10-5 0 MrTomDavid(7) 87
(Tim Vaughan) *prom: chsd wnr and hit 3 out: rdn and wknd bef next: lost 2nd gng to the last* **40/1**

0/P- **4** *2 ¾* **Maderson Blue (IRE)**^{383} [797] 8-10-9 0 HaddenFrost(3) 85
(Roger Curtis) *hld up: hdwy 5th: wknd 3 out: blnd last* **33/1**

335P **5** *11* **Midnight Spirit**^{35} [648] 10-10-12 105 (bt) AnthonyFreeman(7) 88+
(Frederick Sutherland) *w ldrs to 5th: sn rdn: mstke and wknd next: bhd whn hit 2 out: t.o* **18/1**

3-0 **6** *37* **Micks Prospect (IRE)**[25] 763 7-10-12 0 (t) RichardJohnson 36
(Tim Vaughan) *prom tl wknd after 5th: t.o* **13/2**[3]
1-21 **P** **Dorabelle (IRE)**[29] 726 5-10-12 0 APMcCoy —
(Donald McCain) *led 2nd to 4th: chsd wnr: rdn and nt fluent 6th: wknd 3 out: t.o whn p.u bef next* **9/4**[2]
3m 53.1s (-2.90) **Going Correction** -0.325s/f (Good) **7** Ran SP% **109.1**
Speed ratings (Par 107): **93,90,84,83,78 60,—**
toteswingers: 1&2 £17.30, 1&3 £9.70, 2&3 £102.30 CSF £43.64 TOTE £2.10: £1.90, £5.80; EX 46.60.
Owner P Bowling,S Scott,R Harvey & K Bowen **Bred** P J Carmody **Trained** Little Newcastle, Pembrokes

FOCUS
The running rails were moved out by six yards on both the hurdles and chase tracks, meaning an increase in the distance of all races by about 25 yards. Almost 100mm of water had been put on to the track in the previous week and the ground, although fast, had a good covering of grass. This was not the most competitive of novice hurdles, but it was run at a brisk pace. The easy winner was value for further and can probably rate higher.

NOTEBOOK
Pure Faith(IRE) was not left with much to beat, with his main market rivals disappointing, and he accomplished the task in very easy style. Completing a hat-trick, he was not at all inconvenienced by the drop back in trip and he had seen off his pursuers before the home turn. Value for a considerably greater margin of victory, he has the scope to make a chaser in time. (op 11-8)
Nether Stream(IRE) trailed the field for much of the way but eventually stayed on in quite taking fashion to go second between the last two flights, if never a threat to the easy winner. A step back up in trip will surely suit him but he may have been flattered by running past beaten rivals.
Quidam Blue(FR) did not shape badly on this hurdles debut but he flattened the third-last when in pursuit of the winner and was soon labouring.
Maderson Blue(IRE), a one-time bumper winner, had not run for over a year and he did not show a whole lot, but he is entitled to come on for the outing.
Midnight Spirit, in a changed combination of headgear, paid for racing up with the fast pace and was again below his best despite having had a short break.
Micks Prospect(IRE), a winning pointer, was backed, but his supporters knew they had done their money early on the final circuit. He had finished behind today's runner-up on his return to rules action at Worcester last month. (op 11-1 tchd 6-1)
Dorabelle(IRE) had made a winning hurdles debut at Hexham and looked the principal threat to the favourite, but she ran a lacklustre race. Racing keenly up with the pace, carrying her head a little high, she was quickly in trouble after an untidy jump four out and was soon eased and pulled up. Tony McCoy reported that she had lost her action. Official explanation: jockey said mare lost its action (op 5-4)

957 BIRMINGHAM MAIL NOVICES' H'CAP CHASE (15 fncs) 2m 5f 110y
2:30 (2:30) (Class 3) (0-120,119) 5-Y-O+ **£5,529** (£1,623; £811; £405)

Form RPR
11-0 **1** **City Heights (IRE)**[28] 738 8-11-9 **116** DarylJacob 131+
(David Arbuthnot) *a.p: hmpd bnd and lft 2nd appr 12th: jnd ldr whn blnd 3 out: hmpd by loose horse and lost grnd bef next: rallied to ld bef last: styd on wl* **9/1**
-2P1 **2** *6* **Oscar Royal (IRE)**[12] 852 9-11-7 **114** LiamTreadwell 120
(Peter Hiatt) *led: blnd 3rd: nt fluent 5th: hdd 7th: led 9th to 11th: led again bef next: rdn and hdd appr last: styd on same pce flat* **5/2**[1]
3-22 **3** *12* **Maxwil**[39] 584 5-11-2 **109** ColinBolger 102
(Pat Phelan) *hld up in tch: nt fluent 8th (water): rdn 12th: 4 l 3rd whn hit 3 out: wknd next* **5/1**[3]
34-3 **4** *2 ½* **Rockiteer (IRE)**[51] 427 7-11-6 **113** RichardJohnson 104
(Henry Daly) *hld up in tch: rdn and wknd 13th* **10/3**[2]
-135 **5** *11* **Pheidias (IRE)**[28] 735 6-11-12 **119** (p) DavidEngland 103
(Pam Sly) *nt fluent in rr: hmpd bnd appr 12th: drvn along after 6th: hdwy 9th: rdn and wknd after 11th* **6/1**
F-14 **S** **Take A Mile (IRE)**[44] 498 8-10-7 **105** JimmyDerham[(5)] —
(Seamus Mullins) *prom whn slipped up bnd appr 4th* **7/1**
3/64 **S** **Cherokee Star**[12] 854 5-10-8 **101** (p) DenisO'Regan —
(Mike Hammond) *chsd ldr tl led 7th: hdd 9th: led 11th: jst hdd whn slipped up bnd bef next* **12/1**
5m 8.20s (-6.80) **Going Correction** -0.075s/f (Good) **7** Ran SP% **112.8**
Speed ratings: **109,106,102,101,97 —,—**
toteswingers: 1&2 £4.90, 1&3 £7.40, 2&3 £2.30 CSF £31.97 TOTE £12.90: £4.70, £1.90; EX 30.50.
Owner George Ward **Bred** Joe Barry And Joe Kinahan **Trained** Compton, Berks

FOCUS
A fair novice handicap run at a sound pace. The winner was value for further and should rate higher. Two horses slipped up at the same point on separate circuits.

NOTEBOOK
City Heights(IRE), who disappointed here last time after his chase debut victory at Fontwell, resumed winning ways with what was a fairly comfortable win in the end. About to challenge for the lead when blundering badly three out, and hampered by a loose horse at the next, he nonetheless got to the front on the home turn and came clear. The mistake apart, his jumping was reasonably good. (op 10-1)
Oscar Royal(IRE) went up 10lb for his recent win over 2m4f here and once again adopted trailblazing tactics. He took off a little soon at a couple of fences, notably the first ditch, but only relinquished his lead on the turn into the straight, from which point he had nothing left in the locker. (tchd 11-4)
Maxwil continues to edge up the weights without winning. He ran another respectable race but was left behind by the two leaders from the second-last and failed to prove his stamina for this trip. (op 11-2 tchd 9-2)
Rockiteer(IRE) did not do a whole lot wrong but seemed to find this a bit sharp and could not go with the leaders from the fourth-last. (op 9-2 tchd 5-1)
Pheidias(IRE), a quirky sort, was never really going and always in rear, although he may not have fancied it after being hampered when Take A Mile came down on the bend into the back straight early on. (op 11-2 tchd 13-2)
Cherokee Star slipped up while disputing the lead turning into the back straight on the second circuit. He was going well at the time and is capable of making his mark over fences if none the worse. (tchd 14-1)

958 BIRMINGHAM MAIL H'CAP HURDLE (FOR THE STRATFORD SUMMER SALVER) (9 hdls) 2m 110y
3:00 (3:25) (Class 3) (0-130,129) 4-Y-O **£6,337** (£1,872; £936; £468; £234)

Form RPR
141 **1** **Tout Regulier**[7] 888 6-10-6 **107** TomO'Brien 119+
(Peter Bowen) *chsd ldr tl led after 4th: clr appr 2 out: comf* **3/1**[1]
04-6 **2** *2 ½* **Nordwind (IRE)**[28] 736 9-11-0 **118** DPFahy[(3)] 124+
(Evan Williams) *a.p: rdn to chse wnr appr 2 out: no imp* **33/1**
3-42 **3** *3* **Celticello (IRE)**[21] 803 8-10-12 **113** APMcCoy 115
(Michael Quinlan) *hld up in tch: rdn after 3 out: mstke next: wnt 3rd bef last: nt trble ldrs* **9/1**
0135 **4** *2* **Murcar**[27] 744 5-10-7 **115** OliverDayman[(7)] 116
(Alison Thorpe) *hld up: hdwy appr 6th: rdn after 3 out: styng on same pce whn mstke last* **10/1**
3-23 **5** *1* **Aohna (FR)**[28] 736 5-10-9 **113** CharlieHuxley[(3)] 112
(Alan King) *hld up: drvn along after 3 out: styd on flat: nvr trbld ldrs* **5/1**[2]
1-24 **6** *1 ¾* **Exulto (IRE)**[21] 798 5-10-13 **114** RichardJohnson 111
(Philip Hobbs) *hld up: hdwy u.p after 3 out: no imp fr next* **15/2**[3]
0124 **7** *nk* **Stumped**[28] 736 7-10-7 **108** (t) DarylJacob 106
(Milton Harris) *hld up: rdn after 3 out: nvr nrr* **16/1**
-324 **8** *¾* **Forty Thirty (IRE)**[6] 756 4-11-12 **129** JamieGoldstein 123
(Sheena West) *hld up: rdn after 3 out: nvr on terms* **10/1**
-222 **9** *½* **Peaceful Means (IRE)**[18] 479 7-10-6 **112** LeeEdwards[(5)] 108
(Tony Carroll) *prom: rdn after 6th: wknd next* **11/1**
3-61 **10** *4 ½* **Crosby Jemma**[21] 803 6-10-10 **111** BrianHughes 102
(Mike Sowersby) *hld up: in tch: rdn after 3 out: wknd next* **28/1**
-411 **11** *15* **Wheelavit (IRE)**[12] 853 7-11-5 **120** (t) LiamTreadwell 99
(Claire Dyson) *led: hdd after 4th: chsd wnr tl rdn and wknd appr 2 out* **10/1**
2-3 **12** *7* **Daytime Dreamer (IRE)**[21] 803 6-10-7 **108** DenisO'Regan 77
(Martin Todhunter) *mid-div: nt a fluent: bhd fr 6th* **25/1**
3m 47.4s (-8.60) **Going Correction** -0.325s/f (Good) **12** Ran SP% **115.2**
Speed ratings (Par 107): **107,105,104,103,103 102,102,101,101,99 92,88**
toteswingers: 1&2 £29.30, 1&3 £9.40, 2&3 £47.30 CSF £100.16 CT £803.90 TOTE £4.40: £1.70, £7.30, £3.00; EX 110.30.
Owner G A Moore **Bred** Miss M E Steele **Trained** Little Newcastle, Pembrokes

FOCUS
Racing was delayed by 25 minutes before this event while the track was inspected following two fallers on the bend in the 2.30. A good, competitive handicap hurdle for the time of year, this was run at a sound pace and in a time 0.6 secs under the RP standard despite the slight increase in the race distance. The easy winner was well in and the second is rated to his 2009 best. The form should stand up.

NOTEBOOK
Tout Regulier made it three wins from four starts for the Bowen yard with a comfortable success. Able to run off the same mark as when taking a conditionals' race over 2m5f at Market Rasen a week earlier, she was never out of the first two and came clear from the home turn. The drop in trip was not ideal, but this progressive mare had no problem getting away with it. She may go over fences sooner rather than later. (tchd 7-2, 4-1 in places)
Nordwind(IRE) was always prominent in the main pack and he stuck on well for second, albeit holding no chance with the winner. He had been dropped 6lb since his recent return to action here after a nine-month break, and was able to turn around the form with three who had finished in front of him that day. (op 28-1)
Celticello(IRE) stuck on for third after racing a shade keenly. He managed to overturn Hexham form with Crosby Jemma but another win continues to elude him while the placings are mounting up. (op 8-1 tchd 10-1)
Murcar, still a novice, ran a creditable race on this handicap debut and might have been third had he not pecked at the last. He stays further but took the drop in trip in his stride. (op 14-1 tchd 9-1)
Aohna(FR) had been unlucky on her two most recent starts but had no obvious excuse here. She plugged on after coming under pressure down the far side. (tchd 4-1)
Exulto(IRE), one of those who finished in front of today's runner-up last time, made a forward move in the back straight but the progress soon flattened out. (op 8-1 tchd 7-1)
Wheelavit(IRE) became restless and on his toes during the delay. He was unable to dominate on this hat-trick bid but shared the lead with the winner, racing keenly and kept a little wide of his rivals. Beaten by the home turn, he was eased down to finish second-last. A couple of hefty rises have left him on a career-high mark. (op 8-1)

959 BIRMINGHAM MAIL SUMMER H'CAP CHASE (FOR THE STRATFORD SUMMER CUP) (12 fncs) 2m 1f 110y
3:30 (4:00) (Class 2) (0-145,138) 4-Y-O+
£9,393 (£2,775; £1,387; £694; £346; £174)

Form RPR
0-11 **1** **Passato (GER)**[43] 523 6-10-12 **124** (t) APMcCoy 136+
(Joanna Davis) *chsd ldr 2nd tl rdn to ld 3 out: styd on wl* **7/4**[1]
2P14 **2** *6* **Mibleu (FR)**[14] 848 10-10-5 **122** KeiranBurke[(5)] 126
(R H & Mrs S Alner) *hld up: mstke 2nd: hdwy 8th: chsd wnr 3 out: rdn after next: styd on same pce last* **20/1**
1412 **3** *5* **Dishdasha (IRE)**[11] 861 8-10-10 **129** (t) OliverDayman[(7)] 128
(Alison Thorpe) *chsd ldrs: rdn 9th: outpcd appr 2 out: styd on to go 3rd flat* **6/1**[3]
1-U2 **4** *2 ½* **Kikos (FR)**[30] 709 8-10-9 **121** SamJones 118
(Renee Robeson) *chsd ldr to 2nd: remained handy: rdn after 3 out: wknd appr last: lost 3rd flat* **14/1**
413- **5** *nk* **Storm Of Applause (IRE)**[211] 2839 9-10-9 **121** RichardJohnson 120+
(Philip Hobbs) *hld up in tch: cl 5th whn blnd 5th (water): sn lost pl: rdn after 9th: nvr on terms after* **9/2**[2]
-253 **6** *nk* **Norborne Bandit (IRE)**[18] 831 9-10-0 **112** oh4 (p) HarrySkelton 108
(Evan Williams) *hld up: pushed along 8th: nvr trbld ldrs* **10/1**
0P-0 **7** *45* **Lord Jay Jay (IRE)**[43] 524 10-11-4 **133** LeeStephens[(3)] 99
(David Evans) *led to 3 out: wknd next: t.o* **12/1**
42-3 **P** **Stan (NZ)**[65] 194 11-11-12 **138** AidanColeman —
(Venetia Williams) *prom: lost pl 3rd: bhd whn p.u bef 7th* **17/2**
3/13 **U** **Smack That (IRE)**[19] 822 8-11-4 **135** JimmyDerham[(5)] —
(Milton Harris) *hld up: plld hrd: hdwy 8th: cl 6th whn blnd and uns rdr next* **11/1**
4m 3.40s (-3.70) **Going Correction** -0.075s/f (Good) **9** Ran SP% **115.9**
Speed ratings (Par 109): **105,102,100,99,98 98,78,—,—**
toteswingers: 1&2 £9.20, 1&3 £2.30, 2&3 £11.80 CSF £34.29 CT £178.89 TOTE £2.30: £1.40, £5.90, £1.80; EX 38.20.
Owner P Ponting **Bred** Gestut Hof Ittlingen **Trained** East Garston, Berks

FOCUS
The rails were moved in order to avoid the area where two horses slipped up in the first chase, and there were no problems this time. A competitive handicap chase and a valuable prize for the time of year, it was run at a good tempo and the form has a sound look to it. Another step up from Passato and the race could have been rated a few pounds higher.

NOTEBOOK
Passato(GER) shadowed the leader until showing ahead in the back straight and stayed on strongly to complete a hat-trick. He was raised 11lb for his win here last month but is a likeable and progressive young chaser who should continue on the upgrade. He is only small though, and isn't built to carry big weights. The winner of three of his four starts at Stratford and third in the other, he stays further than this. (op 13-8 tchd 6-4, 15-8 in places)
Mibleu(FR), held up off the brisk pace, cut through the field down the far side to pose a real threat, but the younger horse proved too strong from the home turn. This was a solid effort from a career-high mark. (op 22-1)
Dishdasha(IRE) had not run over fences since finishing last in this event 12 months ago, when five places behind Mibleu. He has been in good heart over hurdles and transferred his form to fences, keeping on for third without ever seriously threatening to win. (op 7-1 tchd 15-2)

Kikos(FR) is by nature a front runner but he had competion for that role and had to be content with tracking the leaders. This consistent chestnut still ran well but faded from the home turn and lost third on the run-in. (tchd 16-1)
Storm Of Applause(IRE), running for the first time since December, blundered badly at the water jump with a lap to go and dropped to the back of the field. In the circumstances he did well to reach his final position. (op 5-1 tchd 11-2)
Norborne Bandit(IRE) was never a real threat, unsurprisingly as he had ground to make up on a number of these and was 4lb out of the weights. (op 12-1)
Lord Jay Jay(IRE) came in for support, despite not showing much in three starts since winning off this mark over course and distance for Venetia Williams in May 2009. Minus the cheekpieces, he bowled along in front to the third-last but ended up well beaten. (op 14-1)
Smack That(IRE) who was unruly in the preliminaries, was in touch in sixth place when coming down. (tchd 12-1)

960 BIRMINGHAM MAIL JUVENILE HURDLE (9 hdls) 2m 110y
4:00 (4:30) (Class 3) 3-Y-O **£5,204** (£1,528; £764; £381)

Form				RPR
1	**1**		**Beyond (IRE)**[33] [674] 3-11-4 0 APMcCoy (Evan Williams) *mde all: hung rt 5th: rdn appr last: styd on* **4/6**[1]	113+
	2	*1 ¾*	**Two Kisses (IRE)**[14] 3-10-5 0 AidanColeman (Brendan Powell) *hld up in tch: rdn to chse wnr 2 out: styd on* **16/1**	95
4	**3**	*6*	**Destiny's Dancer**[16] [836] 3-10-0 0 GilesHawkins(5) (Ben Haslam) *hld up: hdwy appr 5th: chsd wnr 3 out to next: styd on same pce* **11/2**[2]	90
361	**4**	*25*	**Gulf Punch**[12] [851] 3-10-8 0 (p) PeterToole(3) (Milton Harris) *chsd ldrs: disp 2nd 3 out: sn rdn and wknd: t.o* **6/1**[3]	70
	5	*1 ¾*	**Joe Rua (USA)**[20] 3-10-12 0 ColinBolger (John Ryan) *hld up: hdwy 6th: wknd bef next: t.o* **100/1**	70
	6	*2 ¾*	**Ariel Bender**[351] 3-10-12 0 BrianHughes (Donald McCain) *chsd ldrs: rdn and wknd after 3 out: t.o* **50/1**	67
	7	*21*	**Storm Command (IRE)**[38] 3-10-12 0 RichardJohnson (Tim Vaughan) *prom: chsd wnr 4th: mstke 6th: wknd after next: eased: t.o* **10/1**	52
2	**P**		**Glen Lass**[33] [674] 3-10-5 0 (p) DarylJacob (Jamie Snowden) *chsd wnr to 4th: rdn and wknd appr 6th: t.o whn p.u bef 2 out* **10/1**	—
	P		**Argyll**[216] 3-10-12 0 GerardTumelty (Jeff Pearce) *hld up: a in rr: bhd fr 5th: t.o whn p.u bef 2 out* **80/1**	—
0	**P**		**A P Ling**[16] [836] 3-10-0 0 LeeEdwards(5) (Christopher Kellett) *nt jump wl and sn bhd: t.o whn p.u after 6th* **100/1**	—

3m 55.4s (-0.60) **Going Correction** -0.325s/f (Good) **10** Ran SP% **118.9**
Speed ratings (Par 104): **88,87,84,72,71 70,60,—,—,—**
toteswingers: 1&2 £5.20, 1&3 £1.80, 2&3 £6.60 CSF £14.52 TOTE £1.80: £1.40, £3.90, £1.50; EX 21.40.
Owner R J H Geffen **Bred** Pat Fullam **Trained** Llancarfan, Vale Of Glamorgan

FOCUS
Not a bad early-season juvenile contest and the winner should go on to rate higher.

NOTEBOOK
Beyond(IRE) was a decent Polytrack performer for Jeremy Noseda and he had two of these rivals behind when making a winning hurdles debut at Bangor a month ago. Making all and scoring with a bit to spare, he hurdled pretty well but showed a tendency to jump out to his right. He is a reasonable type for the time of year and may be up to defying a double penalty. (op 8-13)
Two Kisses(IRE), a 6f winner on the AW, represented the yard successful in this race a year ago. Held up racing a little keenly, she survived a stumble turning into the back straight to emerge as the chief threat to the winner, but although staying on she was always being held. (op 40-1)
Destiny's Dancer's yard won this event three times in the previous six runnings, when the trainer's father Pat held the licence. She showed ability on her hurdle debut at Market Rasen and ran creditably again, but still looked novicey and lacked the pace to seriously challenge the winner. (op 7-1)
Gulf Punch easily won a claimer over course and distance last time but was unable to reverse earlier form with either Beyond or Destiny's Dancer. (op 11-2 tchd 5-1)
Joe Rua(USA) was a poor maiden on the Flat and he finished well adrift on this hurdles debut, but there was just a glimmer of promise in this performance.
Storm Command(IRE), a 56-rated maiden on the Flat who was placed over 1m3f last month, dropped away tamely after racing keenly close to the pace. (op 9-1)
Glen Lass split Beyond and Gulf Punch first time out at Bangor but failed to run her race here and was eventually pulled up. (op 9-1)

961 BIRMINGHAM MAIL H'CAP CHASE (12 fncs) 2m 1f 110y
4:30 (5:00) (Class 5) (0-95,98) 4-Y-0+ **£2,927** (£859; £429; £214)

Form				RPR
460-	**1**		**Barton Sun (IRE)**[80] [5331] 11-9-11 73 MrSHanson(7) (Alison Batchelor) *hld up: hdwy to ld last: styd on wl* **7/1**	80
-5P1	**2**	*1 ¼*	**My Pal Val (IRE)**[11] [864] 10-11-12 98 (tp) DannyCook(3) (John Panvert) *prom: lost pl 6th: hdwy 9th: rdn and ev ch last: styd on same pce flat* **11/4**[2]	104
3-50	**3**	*½*	**Indiana Gold (FR)**[14] [848] 6-11-2 92 OliverDayman(7) (Alison Thorpe) *a.p: mstke 4th: rdn appr last: hung lft and styd on same pce flat* **7/1**	99
/344	**4**	*2 ½*	**Sahara Prince (IRE)**[11] [864] 10-10-4 80 (p) MrLRPayter(7) (Matt Sheppard) *chsd ldr tl led appr last: hdd last: no ex flat* **11/1**	84
303-	**5**	*7*	**Cloonavery (IRE)**[312] [1375] 8-9-11 73 AnthonyFreeman(7) (Tony Carroll) *hld up: hdwy 6th: mstke 2 out: rdn and wknd bef last* **9/4**[1]	70
-43P	**6**	*2 ¼*	**Bid Art (IRE)**[42] [533] 5-11-5 88 (t) DarylJacob (Jamie Snowden) *led: rdn and hdd whn blnd last: wknd flat* **9/2**[3]	87+
-246	**7**	*13*	**Masterpoint**[26] [757] 10-10-13 82 CharliePoste (Richard Harper) *chsd ldrs: lost pl 8th: rdn and wknd after 2 out* **12/1**	67

4m 13.6s (6.50) **Going Correction** -0.075s/f (Good) **7** Ran SP% **116.6**
Speed ratings (Par 103): **82,81,81,80,77 76,70**
toteswingers: 1&2 £5.60, 1&3 £13.90, 2&3 £5.30 CSF £28.29 TOTE £10.20: £4.10, £2.20; EX 40.90.
Owner Mrs Alison Batchelor **Bred** T J Rooney **Trained** Petworth, W Sussex

FOCUS
A low-grade handicap run over ten seconds slower than the earlier 0-145 chase, and there were five abreast heading down to the last. Very moderate form, but solid with the first three all pretty much to their marks.

NOTEBOOK
Barton Sun(IRE), who had been held up, nipped through on the inner to lead at the last. He idled when in front and is value for a larger winning margin. This was his first run since April and only his second start since leaving Ferdy Murphy. (op 12-1)
My Pal Val(IRE), raised 8lb for his Worcester win, ran a solid race off his big weight and was coming back for more on the short run-in.
Indiana Gold(FR) continues to fall in the weights. He ran a respectable race, staying on after being crowded out going to the last, but gave the impression he might benefit from some headgear. (op 6-1 tchd 11-2)
Sahara Prince(IRE) had been dropped 8lb since finishing behind My Pal Val last time. He showed narrowly in front on the home turn but could not repel the challengers. (op 12-1)
Cloonavery(IRE), runner-up off 3lb lower in this race last year, ran over hurdles last time. He was close enough when a mistake two out effectively ended his chance. (op 11-4)
Bid Art(IRE) ran better than he had been of late, making a lot of the running and only conceding defeat after a mistake at the final fence. (op 5-1)

962 BIRMINGHAM MAIL CONDITIONAL JOCKEYS' H'CAP HURDLE (10 hdls) 2m 3f
5:00 (5:32) (Class 4) (0-115,118) 4-Y-0+ **£2,927** (£859; £429; £214)

Form				RPR
0-40	**1**		**Kristallo (GER)**[57] [328] 5-10-13 102 (v1) SamJones (Paul Webber) *mde virtually all: rdn whn pckd last: styd on u.p* **16/1**	105+
4-PP	**2**	*nk*	**Edgefour (IRE)**[33] [682] 6-11-0 103 (v1) GilesHawkins (Ben Case) *hld up: hdwy 6th: rdn and ev ch flat: styd on* **28/1**	106
1-35	**3**	*3*	**Shropshirelass**[30] [706] 7-10-7 99 GemmaGracey-Davison(3) (Zoe Davison) *hld up: blnd 5th: hdwy appr 7th: rdn after 3 out: r.o: nt rch ldrs* **14/1**	100+
4P34	**4**	*½*	**Rock Me (IRE)**[19] [825] 5-10-8 97 (tp) HaddenFrost (Lawney Hill) *chsd ldrs: rdn 2f out: mstke and no ex last* **9/1**	97
00-0	**5**	*1 ½*	**Blue Express (IRE)**[40] [566] 11-10-1 93 DPFahy(3) (Evan Williams) *hld up: hmpd bnd after 6th: hdwy 2 out: nt rch ldrs* **20/1**	90
0-31	**6**	*hd*	**Spate River**[31] [698] 5-10-8 100 RichieMcLernon(3) (Jonjo O'Neill) *prom: rdn after 3 out: styd on same pce appr last* **6/4**[1]	97
0-41	**7**	*7*	**Vintage Fabric (USA)**[19] [825] 8-10-13 102 (t) CharlieHuxley (Nigel Hawke) *chsd ldrs: rdn after 3 out: wknd bef next* **16/1**	92
U-46	**8**	*16*	**Tartan Tie**[27] [744] 6-10-6 98 (t) OliverDayman(3) (Alison Thorpe) *chsd ldrs: rdn appr 6th: wknd bef 3 out* **8/1**[3]	72
-451	**9**	*nk*	**Sadler's Star (GER)**[18] [829] 7-11-9 112 (p) PeterToole (Michael Blake) *hld up: rdn after 7th: nvr on terms* **8/1**[3]	91
4-54	**10**	*hd*	**Ovthenight (IRE)**[14] [846] 5-11-6 109 (p) LeeEdwards (Pam Sly) *prom: pushed along 3rd: grad lost pl: bhd fr 7th* **7/1**[2]	82
0-60	**11**	*12*	**Come Out Firing (IRE)**[26] [756] 8-11-11 114 HarrySkelton (Michael Blake) *w ldr: hit 7th: hrd drvn and ev ch after 3 out: wknd bef next: t.o* **16/1**	77
13F-	**P**		**Mouseen (IRE)**[289] [1528] 7-11-4 112 PeterHatton(5) (Lisa Day) *hld up: nt fluent 2nd: bhd fr 6th: t.o whn p.u bef next* **40/1**	—

4m 25.9s (-5.60) **Going Correction** -0.325s/f (Good) **12** Ran SP% **119.7**
Speed ratings (Par 105): **107,106,105,105,104 104,101,95,94,94 89,—**
toteswingers: 1&2 £30.00, 1&3 £28.00, 2&3 £68.30 CSF £363.38 CT £5435.81 TOTE £15.80: £4.70, £8.70, £3.80; EX 483.70 Place 6 £37.57, Place 5 £21.51.
Owner Iain Russell Watters **Bred** Gestut Hof Ittlingen **Trained** Mollington, Oxon

FOCUS
This ordinary handicap for conditionals was run at a good pace. The form reads sound enough.

NOTEBOOK
Kristallo(GER) made just about all the running and survived overjumping at the last to record his first hurdles win. The first-time visor, replacing blinkers, clearly had an effect. He escapes a penalty for this win. (tchd 18-1)
Edgefour(IRE), in common with the winner, wore a visor for the first time. After rather running in snatches she chased the winner hard from the second-last and momentarily looked like capitalising on his last-flight error, but was just held. (op 33-1)
Shropshirelass was almost out of the race with a circuit to cover but her rider made a fine recovery. The mare was under pressure for the rest of the way, but rewarded her jockey's persistence by staying on for third.
Rock Me(IRE) ran a sound race and might have been third had he not stumbled a stride or two after the last. He is capable of finding a small race over the coming weeks. (op 11-1)
Blue Express(IRE) was towards the rear when colliding with the rail early on the final circuit. He stayed on in the latter stages without posing a threat and has become well handicapped on his best form. (op 25-1)
Spate River was raised 13lb for his win in a weaker race at Uttoxeter and he could not race on with the leaders from the third-last. (tchd 11-8 and 7-4)
Vintage Fabric(USA) made all at Newton Abbot but was 7lb higher here and was taken on for the lead. (op 20-1)
T/Jkpt: £10,569.00 to a £1 stake. Pool: £104,202.39. 7.00 winning tickets. T/Plt: £23.10 to a £1 stake. Pool: £84,106.78. 2,650.41 winning tickets. T/Qpdt: £9.60 to a £1 stake. Pool: £6,371.28. 486.82 winning tickets. CR

963 - 982a (Foreign Racing) - See Raceform Interactive

[916]UTTOXETER (L-H)
Wednesday, July 14

OFFICIAL GOING: Good (good to firm in places on hurdle course; chs 6.8, hdl 7.1)
Second last fence omitted in all chases and last flight in back straight omitted in all hurdle races.
Wind: Fresh, behind Weather: Overcast

983 ODDSCHECKER.COM NOVICES' HURDLE (9 hdls 1 omitted) 2m
2:10 (2:10) (Class 4) 4-Y-0+ **£2,471** (£725; £362; £181)

Form				RPR
	1		**Paddy Partridge**[48] 4-10-10 0 RichardJohnson (Tim Vaughan) *a.p: led 3 out: nt fluent next: drvn out* **15/2**	103+
P-12	**2**	*6*	**Freedom Fire (IRE)**[24] [792] 4-11-3 120 JamieMoore (Gary Moore) *hld up: racd keenly: nt a fluent: hdwy 6th: rdn to chse wnr 2 out: no ex flat* **7/4**[1]	102
3525	**3**	*hd*	**Apache Dawn**[22] [825] 6-10-12 97 (t) JasonMaguire (Aytach Sadik) *led tl after 1st: chsd ldr tl rdn appr 3 out: no ex flat* **6/1**	97
P2P-	**4**	*3*	**Bedarra Boy**[23] [2815] 4-10-10 0 DarylJacob (David Arbuthnot) *led after 1st: hdd and mstke 3 out: styd on same pce appr last* **5/1**[3]	93
43	**5**	*13*	**Hypnotic Gaze (IRE)**[33] [712] 4-10-10 106 AndrewTinkler (John Mackie) *trckd ldrs: plld hrd: mstke and lost pl 6th: wknd appr 3 out* **9/4**[2]	81
/00-	**6**	*65*	**Yes Minister (IRE)**[240] [2339] 6-10-12 0 PaulMoloney (Sophie Leech) *hld up: a in last pl: wknd 6th: t.o* **50/1**	24

3m 51.1s (-4.10) **Going Correction** -0.675s/f (Firm) **6** Ran SP% **111.8**
Speed ratings (Par 105): **83,80,79,78,71 39**
toteswingers: 1&2 £3.70, 1&3 £5.50, 2&3 £3.40 CSF £21.55 TOTE £7.90: £3.40, £1.20; EX 18.50.
Owner Owen Promotions Limited **Bred** Owen Promotions Ltd **Trained** Aberthin, Vale of Glamorgan

FOCUS
Rain had eased the ground, with it appearing to ride slower than the official descriptions suggested. A moderate novices' hurdle and the third and fourth set the level.

NOTEBOOK
Paddy Partridge, unplaced in seven starts on the level, is bred to be a jumper, his brother Holoko Heights capping a memorable day for the family by winning the following selling hurdle, and he stayed on strongly having got to the front three out, winning with a bit to spare. It will be interesting to see how he fares under a penalty. (op 10-1 tchd 11-1 and 7-1)

Freedom Fire(IRE), a marked drifter beforehand, could have done without the rain and it's safe to assume he hasn't run up to his best. He can win again at some point during the summer. (op 10-11)
Apache Dawn, unplaced off 98 at Newton Abbot latest, fared a bit better returned to novice-only company, just missing out on second. (op 14-1)
Bedarra Boy will fare better in handicaps. (op 8-1)
Hypnotic Gaze(IRE), though disappointing here, did pull hard, so deserves another chance. Official explanation: jockey said gelding jumped poorly (op 11-4)

984 BYRKLEY GARDEN CENTRE (S) HURDLE (9 hdls 1 omitted) 2m
2:40 (2:40) (Class 5) 4-8-Y-O **£1,561** (£458; £229; £114)

Form				RPR
P6-0	1		**Holoko Heights**[33] [715] 5-11-3 115 (v) RichardJohnson (Tim Vaughan) *trckd ldrs: led appr 3 out: edgd lft bef next: drvn out* **9/2**[2]	110+
-322	2	2 3/4	**Tri Nations (UAE)**[8] [917] 5-11-6 110 (t) JasonMaguire (Donald McCain) *a.p: rdn to chse wnr 2 out: styd on u.p* **9/2**[2]	109
4-64	3	3/4	**Le Brocquy**[8] [917] 5-10-12 102 (p) JimmyDerham(5) (Martin Keighley) *hld up: hdwy after 6th: rdn bef next: styd on to go 3rd nr fin: nt rch ldrs* **22/1**	105
4-21	4	2	**Hoar Frost**[17] [845] 5-10-10 101 APMcCoy (Jim Best) *led: mstke 2nd: hdd next: chsd ldr: hit 5th: led next: rdn and hdd appr 3 out: n.m.r and swtchd rt bef 2 out: no ex flat: lost 3rd nr fin* **15/8**[1]	98
05	5	4	**Soggy Dollar**[15] [850] 5-10-9 0 (p) AlexMerriam(3) (Neil King) *hld up: hdwy after 6th: mstke 3 out: sn rdn: styd on same pce fr next* **40/1**	96
4420	6	3/4	**Mr Melodious**[31] [737] 4-10-5 100 (b) SamTwiston-Davies(5) (Nigel Twiston-Davies) *hld up: drvn along after 5th: styd on flat: nvr trbld ldrs* **17/2**	92
0233	7	6	**Tora Petcha (IRE)**[14] [865] 7-11-0 100 DannyCook(3) (Barry Leavy) *w ldr tl led 3rd: hdd 6th: wknd 3 out* **12/1**	94
134/	8	28	**Quiny Boy (FR)**[446] [5205] 6-10-12 0 (vt) TomScudamore (David Pipe) *hld up: bhd fr 6th: t.o* **11/2**[3]	64
3PP/	9	10	**Standing Order**[604] [2267] 7-10-12 0 BrianHughes (Richard Ford) *hld up: bhd fr 6th: t.o* **80/1**	55

3m 47.2s (-8.00) **Going Correction** -0.675s/f (Firm)
WFA 4 from 5yo+ 15lb **9** Ran SP% **112.8**
Speed ratings: **93,91,91,90,88 87,84,70,65**
toteswingers: 1&2 £4.10, 1&3 £19.70, 2&3 £11.20 CSF £24.38 TOTE £4.70: £1.60, £1.10, £7.10; EX 26.10.The winner was bought in for 3,000gns.
Owner Owen Promotions Limited **Bred** Owen Promotions Ltd **Trained** Aberthin, Vale of Glamorgan

FOCUS
The form of this seller looks reasonably solid, with the consistent Tri Nations again running his race in second. The form is rated through the first three.

NOTEBOOK
Holoko Heights, taking a marked drop in grade, had won on his hurdles debut late last year, and despite the ease in the going, he was more than good enough, like his brother in the opener striking on three out and keeping on well. He was bought in by connections and can probably win again at this level. (tchd 4-1 and 5-1)
Tri Nations(UAE) held every chance and again ran his race. He was conceding 3lb to the winner and can pick up another one of these at some point. (op 7-1)
Le Brocquy put in an improved effort, getting significantly closer to the runner-up than he had done at the course last time. (op 25-1)
Hoar Frost, a winner off 92 over C&D last time, failed to reproduce anything like that form, being headed before the third-last and slowly fading, being run out of the places on the run-in. (op 7-4 tchd 2-1)
Soggy Dollar showed a bit of improvement and should fare better in low-grade handicaps.
Quiny Boy(FR) never figured on this first start in 446 days, ending up well beaten. (op 9-2 tchd 4-1)

985 SIMPLY BLUETOOTH H'CAP CHASE (15 fncs 1 omitted) 2m 5f
3:10 (3:10) (Class 4) (0-115,113) 4-Y-0+ **£3,295** (£973; £486; £243; £121)

Form				RPR
P/4-	1		**Mad Jack Duncan (IRE)**[88] 8-10-3 90 AidanColeman (Lawney Hill) *chsd ldr tl led 11th: rdn appr last: styd on gamely* **2/1**[1]	97
-260	2	nk	**The Duke's Speech (IRE)**[31] [735] 9-11-12 113 PaulMoloney (Sophie Leech) *hld up: hdwy after 11th: hung lft fr 3 out: rdn and ev ch fr last: styd on* **16/1**	120
4633	3	1	**Red Jester**[8] [919] 9-10-7 99 MarcGoldstein(5) (Gerald Ham) *mid-div: hdwy appr 9th: rdn after 2 out: styd on* **8/1**	105
3-U1	4	19	**Silver Story**[38] [647] 7-11-12 113 RichardJohnson (Tim Vaughan) *hld up: hdwy 10th: ev ch 3 out: rdn and wknd appr last* **6/1**[3]	102
330-	5	10	**Bermuda Pointe (IRE)**[198] [3128] 8-11-4 110 SamTwiston-Davies(5) (Nigel Twiston-Davies) *chsd ldrs: rdn 11th: wknd 3 out: t.o* **11/2**[2]	90
3-64	6	25	**Hold The Bid (IRE)**[41] [608] 10-11-4 105 KeithMercer (Sue Smith) *hld up: pushed along 8th: rdn and wknd bef 3 out: t.o* **6/1**[3]	62
/PF-	P		**Funny Fellow**[210] [2920] 8-10-8 95 LeightonAspell (Richard Rowe) *chsd ldrs tl wknd 9th: t.o whn p.u bef 11th* **33/1**	—
434	P		**The Randy Bishop**[52] [437] 10-10-6 98 (v) LeeEdwards(5) (Tony Carroll) *racd keenly: led: hit 6th: hdd 11th: wknd bef next: t.o whn p.u bef last* **14/1**	—
/U0-	P		**Cadoulitique (FR)**[396] [700] 7-10-8 95 BrianHughes (Tina Jackson) *hld up: a in rr: bhd fr 9th: t.o whn p.u bef last* **50/1**	—
	P		**Tell Me The Story (IRE)**[565] [2992] 6-11-9 110 APMcCoy (Jonjo O'Neill) *hld up: bhd and rdn 10th: t.o whn p.u bef 2 out* **11/1**	—

5m 15.4s (-8.10) **Going Correction** -0.25s/f (Good) **10** Ran SP% **114.2**
Speed ratings (Par 105): **105,104,104,97,93 83,—,—,—,—**
toteswingers: 1&2 £10.70, 1&3 £6.60, 2&3 £19.30 CSF £32.46 CT £213.24 TOTE £3.20: £1.60, £3.70, £1.40; EX 46.80.
Owner Alan Hill **Bred** Paul Cashman **Trained** Aston Rowant, Oxon

FOCUS
Just a modest handicap chase, though it did at least produce a decent finish. The winner is rated in line with his best hurdles form.

NOTEBOOK
Mad Jack Duncan(IRE), well backed beforehand, just managed to prevail. A previously disappointing sort over hurdles for Alan King, he has really turned his fortunes around in points since joining current connections, and was up to taking this off a mark of 90. He remains capable of better at the right level over fences, with a longer trip and fast ground likely to help. (op 15-8 tchd 5-2 in places)
The Duke's Speech(IRE) has been shown some leniency by the handicapper following a couple of moderate efforts, and he came right back to form, challenging at the last and just missing out under top weight. (op 22-1 tchd 25-1)
Red Jester gave another good account on this step back up in trip, keeping on and just lacking a bit of acceleration towards the finish. (op 11-1)
Silver Story could have been expected to do better switched to handicaps. (op 9-2)
Tell Me The Story(IRE) Official explanation: jockey said gelding stopped very quickly

986 WEATHERBYS BANK H'CAP HURDLE (12 hdls 2 omitted) 3m
3:40 (3:40) (Class 4) (0-115,115) 4-Y-0+ **£2,471** (£725; £362; £181)

Form				RPR
-535	1		**Ripalong Lad (IRE)**[8] [921] 9-11-5 108 (p) TomO'Brien (Peter Bowen) *chsd ldr tl hit 2nd: remained handy: rdn to chse ldr appr 2 out: led last: edgd lft flat: styd on* **10/3**[1]	114+
/F6-	2	2 1/2	**Balladeer (IRE)**[45] 12-10-8 104 MrJFMathias(7) (Lawney Hill) *mid-div: hdwy 7th: led 3 out: rdn and hdd last: styd on same pce flat* **25/1**	107
U-51	3	7	**Grand Bay (USA)**[38] [646] 9-10-13 105 (t) RichieMcLernon(3) (Jonjo O'Neill) *hld up: mstke 4th: hdwy 9th: nt fluent 3 out: 3rd whn blnd 2 out: no ex last* **9/1**	102
P03-	4	8	**Mister Watzisname (IRE)**[122] [4608] 8-11-12 115 (t) JasonMaguire (Charlie Longsdon) *prom: chsd ldr 6th tl led 9th: hdd 3 out: rdn and wknd bef last* **16/1**	104
-121	5	8	**Public Esteem (IRE)**[19] [840] 9-10-9 105 (p) MrsAlexDunn(7) (Dr Richard Newland) *led: hit 8th: hdd next: wknd bef 2 out* **9/2**[2]	87
-126	6	36	**Haldibari (IRE)**[6] [651] 6-11-3 111 SamTwiston-Davies(5) (Shaun Lycett) *hld up: hdwy 8th: rdn and wknd after 3 out: t.o* **6/1**[3]	61
-006	7	9	**Daurica**[17] [846] 6-11-7 110 JimmyMcCarthy (Renee Robeson) *hld up: hdwy 4th: rdn after 9th: wknd bef next: t.o* **12/1**	52
-6P4	8	41	**Triggernometry**[14] [863] 9-10-13 102 (bt) JoeTizzard (Colin Tizzard) *prom: lost pl 6th: bhd fr 8th: t.o* **9/1**	7
-P03	9	4 1/2	**Winsley Hill**[17] [846] 8-11-12 115 DougieCostello (Neil Mulholland) *hld up in tch: dropped to rr 7th: bhd fr next: t.o* **8/1**	16
4503	10	78	**Elusive Muse**[14] [856] 4-11-7 114 JohnnyFarrelly (Alison Thorpe) *prom: chsd ldr 3rd: mstke 5th: lost 2nd next: wknd appr 9th: t.o* **8/1**	—

5m 45.5s (-19.70) **Going Correction** -0.675s/f (Firm)
WFA 4 from 6yo+ 17lb **10** Ran SP% **115.2**
Speed ratings (Par 105): **105,104,101,99,96 84,81,67,66,40**
toteswingers: 1&2 £50.60, 1&3 £3.10, 2&3 £36.10 CSF £75.85 CT £688.51 TOTE £4.80: £1.80, £8.20, £2.50; EX 142.50.
Owner A P Davies **Bred** Sean Murtagh **Trained** Little Newcastle, Pembrokes

FOCUS
A moderate handicap hurdle. The winner improved to his best chase mark.

NOTEBOOK
Ripalong Lad(IRE) is a strong stayer and he got well on top having taken over at the last, continuing the fine form of the Peter Bowen stable. He's lightly raced for a 9-y-o and it would be no surprise to see him returned to fences at some stage this summer, having won on two of his three previous attempts. (op 4-1 tchd 3-1)
Balladeer(IRE) has been out of luck in hunter chases and points of late, but really enjoyed himself returned to hurdles, in the end just getting outstayed by the winner. (op 20-1)
Grand Bay(USA), 7lb higher this time, couldn't race on with the front pair and was already looking held when hitting two out. (op 7-1)
Mister Watzisname(IRE), off since finishing well beaten over fences four months ago, was readily brushed aside from three out.
Public Esteem(IRE), a winner off 9lb lower over fences last time, proved most disappointing, dropping out rather tamely in the end. (op 5-1 tchd 11-2)
Winsley Hill Official explanation: jockey said mare never travelled

987 BYRKLEY GARDEN CENTRE NOVICES' H'CAP CHASE (16 fncs 2 omitted) 3m
4:10 (4:15) (Class 5) (0-95,95) 4-Y-0+ **£2,602** (£764; £382; £190)

Form				RPR
4F5/	1		**Bynack Mhor (IRE)**[45] 9-10-0 69 oh2 (p) AidanColeman (Lawney Hill) *prom: chsd ldr 5th to 10th: sn pushed along: wnt 9 l 2nd again 3 out: rdn bef last: styd on u.p to ld last stride* **3/1**[2]	82
45-5	2	hd	**Cinaman (IRE)**[67] [211] 6-9-10 70 MichaelMurphy(5) (Tim Vaughan) *unruly prior to s: hld up: hdwy 8th: chsd ldr 10th: led appr 4 out: sn clr: rdn bef last: hung lft flat: hdd last stride* **7/2**[3]	84+
0-11	3	53	**Clifden Boy (IRE)**[29] [758] 8-11-12 95 (b) APMcCoy (Jim Best) *led: hmpd 1st: hdd & wknd appr 3 out: t.o* **7/4**[1]	60
5525	4	13	**Safe Investment (USA)**[19] [840] 6-11-3 86 (p) AndrewThornton (Ben Pollock) *hld up: mstke 5th: drvn along and wknd after 10th: t.o* **12/1**	39
/431	5	11	**Justabout**[38] [650] 7-11-5 88 (t) JoeTizzard (Colin Tizzard) *w ldr whn j.lft and hmpd rival 1st: lost 2nd 5th: remained handy tl rdn and wknd after 10th: t.o* **6/1**	32
6-05	6	18	**Harvey May (IRE)**[44] [556] 8-9-7 69 oh12 (b) AnthonyFreeman(7) (John Upson) *chsd ldrs tl wknd 10th: t.o* **66/1**	—
P-0P	P		**Here To Eternity (IRE)**[29] [758] 9-10-0 69 oh10 (b) RodiGreene (Sarah Robinson) *prom: pushed along after 2nd: drvn along 6th: bhd and hit 8th: t.o whn p.u bef 2 out* **100/1**	—
0-53	P		**Maybe A Malt (IRE)**[45] [529] 8-10-6 75 LeightonAspell (Richard Rowe) *hld up: blnd 7th: t.o whn p.u bef last* **11/1**	—
/340	P		**Miss Sunflower**[7] [931] 8-10-2 78 (p) MissTJackson(7) (Tina Jackson) *a bhd: t.o whn p.u bef 11th* **28/1**	—

6m 13.8s (-1.30) **Going Correction** -0.25s/f (Good) **9** Ran SP% **119.8**
Speed ratings (Par 103): **92,91,74,69,66 60,—,—,—**
toteswingers: 1&2 £4.50, 1&3 £3.10, 2&3 £2.60 CSF £15.01 CT £23.73 TOTE £4.30: £1.20, £1.90, £1.10; EX 19.20.
Owner Alan Hill **Bred** Jay Kavanagh **Trained** Aston Rowant, Oxon
■ Stewards' Enquiry : Aidan Coleman one-day ban: used whip with excessive frequency (Aug 6)

FOCUS
The front two pulled a mile clear in this modest novices' handicap chase. The winner ran to the best of his hurdles form.

NOTEBOOK
Bynack Mhor(IRE) received a fine ride to get up in the final strides. Racing from 2lb out of the weights, he doesn't look the quickest, but has been in good form in points and was certainly helped again by the cheekpieces. He remains capable of better and gives the impression he will be suited by the test provided in marathon chases. (tchd 11-4 and 7-2)
Cinaman(IRE), a winner off 2lb higher over hurdles, gave trouble at the start on this debut for Tim Vaughan, but he travelled sweetly in the race and was sent clear turning in. However, his rider may have committed too soon, as he started to idle before the last and looked weary on the run-in. It's easy to say he should go one better next time, but he can expect a rise for this and clearly isn't the most straightforward. (op 11-4 tchd 9-4 and 4-1)
Clifden Boy(IRE), up another 13lb, took up his customary front-running role, but was beaten by the time they reached the straight, proving most disappointing. He is now left with plenty to prove. (op 11-4)
Justabout failed to build on his Worcester victory off this 6lb higher mark, the tongue tie seemingly not having the same effect a second time. (op 13-2 tchd 8-1)

Maybe A Malt(IRE) never recovered from an early blunder. (op 14-1 tchd 16-1)

988 SIGNS 2000 CONDITIONAL JOCKEYS' MAIDEN HURDLE (10 hdls 2 omitted) 2m 4f 110y
4:40 (4:40) (Class 4) 4-Y-0+ **£2,471** (£725; £362; £181)

Form				RPR
6-34	**1**		**Danimix (IRE)**[17] 843 5-11-0 105 RhysFlint (Peter Bowen) *chsd ldrs: led appr 2 out: clr last: styd on wl* **3/1**[2]	122+
5-24	**2**	*15*	**Favours Brave**[11] 468 4-10-11 108 JamesHalliday (Tim Easterby) *led: rdn and hdd appr 2 out: wknd bef last* **5/1**	107+
336-	**3**	*4 ½*	**Call At Midnight**[124] 4569 5-10-7 104 CharlieHuxley (Sarah Humphrey) *hld up in tch: racd keenly: mstke 3 out: sn rdn: wknd next* **9/2**[3]	99
4-U2	**4**	*13*	**Erdeli (IRE)**[22] 823 6-10-8 107 (t) MrTomDavid(6) (Tim Vaughan) *hld up in tch: chsd ldr whn blnd 7th: sn rdn: wknd 3 out: t.o* **15/8**[1]	97
5	**5**	*46*	**Cloudy Dawn**[17] 847 5-11-0 0 RyanMania (Sue Smith) *chsd ldrs: hmpd 7th: sn wknd: t.o* **25/1**	51
-50P	**6**	*107*	**Thorpey's Girl (IRE)**[14] 858 5-10-7 0 JohnnyFarrelly (Alison Thorpe) *j.rt: sn wl bhd: t.o fr 5th* **66/1**	—
-F05	**P**		**Kelly Manor (IRE)**[34] 697 6-10-4 83 LeeEdwards(3) (Tony Carroll) *hld up: hld up: sme hdwy after 5th: wknd 7th: t.o whn p.u bef 2 out* **14/1**	—
0	**P**		**Honorable Endeavor**[17] 843 4-10-11 0 (b) AlexMerriam (Edward Vaughan) *prom: mstke 3rd: rdn and dropped to rr 5th: bhd fr next: t.o whn p.u bef 3 out* **25/1**	—

4m 53.9s (-10.10) **Going Correction** -0.675s/f (Firm)
WFA 4 from 5yo+ 16lb **8** Ran SP% **110.5**
Speed ratings (Par 105): **92,86,84,79,62 —,—,—**
toteswingers: 1&2 £2.40, 1&3 £2.40, 2&3 £3.90 CSF £17.04 TOTE £2.70: £1.40, £1.30, £1.70; EX 11.60 Place 6 £62.00, Place 5 £27.10.
Owner Steve & Jackie Fleetham **Bred** Brendan Corbett **Trained** Little Newcastle, Pembrokes

FOCUS
This didn't take much winning and the winner produced a big step forward.

NOTEBOOK
Danimix(IRE) improved on his latest course effort to take this rather easily in the end, leading before the second-last and gradually drawing clear. His stable can do little wrong at present and he may well be up to defying a penalty at some stage. (tchd 11-4)
Favours Brave was expected to prove suited by the step up in trip, but he got warm beforehand and was readily left trailing by the winner. (op 15-2)
Call At Midnight, formerly with Alan King, didn't get home in the end, but showed enough to suggest she can pick up a small race at some point. (op 4-1)
Erdeli(IRE), runner-up in a handicap at Newton Abbot latest, lost his chance with a notable blunder towards the end of the back straight. He deserves another chance. (op 6-4)
T/Jkpt: £7,787.70 to a £1 stake. Pool: £16,453.05. 1.50 winning tickets. T/Plt: £43.80 to a £1 stake. Pool: £74,354.66. 1,236.77 winning tickets. T/Qpdt: £8.20 to a £1 stake. Pool: £4,669.09. 416.70 winning tickets. CR

[929]WORCESTER (L-H)
Wednesday, July 14

OFFICIAL GOING: Good (good to soft in places; chs 8.0; hdl 7.8)
All bends moved out 9metres from inside racing line but impact on distances not quantified. Hurdles and the run in positioned on inside half of track.
Wind: Moderate across Weather: Cloudy

989 BET ON LIVE GOLF AT TOTESPORT.COM MARES' MAIDEN HURDLE (8 hdls) 2m
6:40 (6:41) (Class 5) 4-Y-0+ **£2,055** (£599; £299)

Form				RPR
263	**1**		**Frosted Grape (IRE)**[29] 754 4-10-10 97 (b) TomScudamore (David Pipe) *w ldr: bmpd 2nd: upsides whn lft in ld next: jnd again fr 4 out: rdn and styd on to go clr 2 out: idled run-in: comf* **3/1**[2]	97+
54-1	**2**	*9*	**Black Annie (IRE)**[19] 841 5-10-12 0 (t) APMcCoy (Paul Webber) *in rr: drvn and hdwy appr 3 out: chsd wnr u.p after 2 out: nvr a threat and no ch whn hung lft after last* **6/4**[1]	91+
6-46	**3**	*½*	**Princess Laila (IRE)**[7] 932 5-10-12 0 DougieCostello (Ian Williams) *chsd ldrs: rdn 3 out: one pce in 3rd fr 2 out tl styd on u.p run-in to press for 2nd cl home but no ch w wnr* **9/1**[3]	90
0-6	**4**	*21*	**Singapore Harbour (IRE)**[62] 304 4-10-10 0 LeightonAspell (Oliver Sherwood) *in rr: styd on for poor 4th fr 2 out* **25/1**	67
0-06	**5**	*½*	**Spring Haze**[41] 590 5-10-6 74 ow1 MrJFMathias(7) (Phillip Dando) *chsd ldrs: chal 4th tl appr 3 out: sn wknd* **28/1**	69
0/5U	**6**	*20*	**Berry Hill Lass (IRE)**[14] 632 6-10-9 0 (v) PeterToole(3) (John O'Shea) *in rr: sme hdwy appr 3 out: nvr in contention and sn btn* **50/1**	48
	7	*11*	**Heart Of Tuscany**[27] 4-10-10 0 FelixDeGiles (Jonathen de Giles) *chsd ldrs to 4th: sn btn* **100/1**	35
/UP4	**8**	*8*	**Silver Sonnet**[7] 929 7-10-12 0 CharliePoste (Ben Case) *chsd ldrs tl nt fluent 4th: wknd sn after* **66/1**	29
000-	**9**	*2 ¾*	**Fenella Mere**[325] 1295 7-10-5 0 PeterHatton(7) (Patricia Rigby) *t.o fr 4th* **150/1**	26
-502	**P**		**Basford Tara**[17] 842 5-10-12 0 AlanO'Keeffe (Jennie Candlish) *slt ld tl tried to run out and dropped to rr 3rd: t.o sn after and p.u bef 3 out* **3/1**[2]	—

3m 48.2s (0.90) **Going Correction** +0.125s/f (Yiel)
WFA 4 from 5yo+ 15lb **10** Ran SP% **112.4**
Speed ratings (Par 103): **102,97,97,86,86 76,71,67,65,—**
toteswingers: 1&2:£1.40, 1&3:£5.00, 2&3:£4.70 CSF £7.61 TOTE £3.20: £1.10, £1.02, £3.80; EX 8.90.
Owner The Wise Partners **Bred** Austin Curran **Trained** Nicholashayne, Devon

FOCUS
After 7mm of rain overnight the ground was changed to good, good to soft in places. All bends were moved out nine metres and the hurdles were positioned on the inside half of the track. A weak mares' maiden hurdle event run at a steady pace. The winner has done bigger figures in Ireland.

NOTEBOOK
Frosted Grape(IRE) had finished placed in seven of her eight hurdle starts this year. She had another decent form chance and this time the ex-Irish performer got it right to get off the mark in decisive style under a positive ride on her 23rd career start. Her confidence should be boosted by this win and she could be a major force back in handicaps off a current mark of 97. (op 7-2)
Black Annie(IRE) put in a gritty display with a tongue-tie applied when winning a bumper at Market Rasen last time. She was a strong favourite for her hurdle debut but was a bit careful at several hurdles and couldn't land a blow on the enterprisingly ridden winner. This was a bit of a laboured start to her career at this discipline but she should have learned a lot and, being out of a dam from the family of Silver Birch and Alexander Banquet, she should appreciate a stiffer test. (tchd 11-8)
Princess Laila(IRE) was never a threat but produced a more sustained effort on her third hurdle run. She should find a stronger competitive edge in handicaps. (op 11-1)
Singapore Harbour(IRE) put in some ponderous jumps and didn't show a great deal of promise on hurdle debut.
Spring Haze put in another weak finishing effort and is now 0-10. (op 33-1)
Basford Tara ran much better than market expectations when a clear second to a promising winner at Uttoxeter last month, but she stuck her head up and virtually stopped when leading at a flight on the far side here and then dropped right out of it before being pulled up. (op 9-4)

990 PLAY BINGO AT TOTESPORT.COM (S) H'CAP HURDLE (10 hdls) 2m 4f
7:10 (7:10) (Class 5) (0-90,90) 4-Y-0+ **£1,712** (£499; £249)

Form				RPR
0P0-	**1**		**Devito (FR)**[141] 4220 9-10-13 80 DannyCook(3) (John Panvert) *chsd ldrs: led 6th: mstke 3 out: hdd last: rallied u.p run-in to ld again fnl 75yds: styd on wl* **12/1**	90+
140	**2**	*½*	**Risk Challenge (USA)**[24] 793 8-11-2 80 (t) CharliePoste (Milton Harris) *in rr tl hdwy fr 6th: chsd ldrs 4 out: chsd ldr fr next: nt fluent 2 out: led last and sn rdn: hdd and no ex fnl 75yds* **16/1**	88
00-0	**3**	*6*	**Low Delta (IRE)**[41] 593 10-11-12 90 AidanColeman (Michael Blake) *in rr tl gd prog fr 4 out: chsd ldrs: 3 out: rdn and one pce fr next* **8/1**[3]	92
-605	**4**	*2*	**Be Ashored**[33] 710 5-11-6 84 DenisO'Regan (Nicky Vaughan) *in rr tl stdy hdwy appr 3 out: sn rdn: styd on same pce after 2 out* **20/1**	84
5-0P	**5**	*16*	**Kaliski (IRE)**[56] 410 6-11-7 85 RhysFlint (John Flint) *chsd ldrs: nt fluent 3rd: rdn after 4 out: wknd next* **16/1**	69
0U22	**6**	*1 ¼*	**Amazing Request**[29] 757 6-10-12 83 (tp) MissIsabelTompsett(7) (Bernard Llewellyn) *in rr: hdwy fr 5th: chsd ldrs 3 out: sn rdn: wknd fr 2 out and no ch whn hit last* **4/1**[2]	67
	7	*4 ½*	**Spice Bar**[15] 2019 6-11-2 80 WillKennedy (John G Carr, Ire) *in rr tl stdy hdwy fr 4 out to chse ldrs 3 out: sn rdn: wknd next* **40/1**	58
-4P0	**8**	*6*	**Go Free**[41] 593 9-11-0 81 (v) PeterToole(3) (John O'Shea) *led tl hdd 3rd: styd chsng ldrs tl wknd qckly 4 out* **12/1**	53
32/6	**9**	*27*	**Penric**[56] 410 10-10-12 83 LucyBarry(7) (Martin Bosley) *chsd ldrs to 4 out: wl bhd whn blnd 2 out* **16/1**	28
/0-0	**10**	*1 ¼*	**Dr Dream (IRE)**[59] 359 6-11-3 81 (b) AndrewThornton (John O'Shea) *chsd ldrs: rdn after 4 out: wknd next* **33/1**	25
0-0P	**11**	*2 ¼*	**Zizou (IRE)**[50] 462 7-11-5 90 MrJFMathias(7) (Sean Curran) *a towards rr* **33/1**	32
-463	**12**	*1 ½*	**Knightsbridgelives (IRE)**[9] 912 7-11-4 87 (t) DavidBass(5) (Lawney Hill) *plld hrd: led 3rd: hdd 6th: wknd qckly appr 3 out* **11/4**[1]	27
	13	*13*	**Alchester (IRE)**[38] 10-11-6 84 (tp) PaulMoloney (Seamus G O'Donnell, Ire) *bhd most of way* **25/1**	11
440-	**P**		**Samurai Warrior**[297] 1473 5-11-11 89 DarylJacob (Jamie Snowden) *sn bhd: t.o whn p.u after 4 out* **40/1**	—
-60P	**P**		**Poacher's Dream (IRE)**[7] 931 8-11-1 79 (bt[1]) FelixDeGiles (Jonathen de Giles) *chsd ldrs to 5th: t.o whn p.u bef 3 out* **66/1**	—
34-0	**P**		**Pavanne (IRE)**[74] 100 5-11-9 87 (b[1]) JasonMaguire (Martin Keighley) *in tch 4th: j. slowly 6th and sn wknd: t.o whn p.u bef 3 out* **9/1**	—
P-P0	**P**		**London Times (IRE)**[7] 932 5-11-4 82 (t) ColinBolger (Simon Lewis) *chsd ldrs tl rdn and wknd qckly 4 out: t.o whn p.u bef next* **66/1**	—

4m 46.68s (-0.72) **Going Correction** +0.125s/f (Yiel)
WFA 4 from 5yo+ 16lb **17** Ran SP% **123.2**
Speed ratings (Par 103): **106,105,103,102,96 95,93,91,80,80 79,78,73,—,— —,—**
toteswingers: 1&2:£59.20, 1&3:£18.30, 2&3:£40.70 CSF £173.93 CT £1642.19 TOTE £15.30: £4.00, £5.50, £3.40, £8.70; EX 241.80.There was no bid for the winner.
Owner The Pinewoods Five **Bred** Patrick Chedeville **Trained** Stoodleigh, Devon

FOCUS
A modest selling handicap. The majority of runners were still maidens and most of the others were on long losing runs. The winner was 7lb off his 2009 best.

NOTEBOOK
Devito(FR) had tumbled 25lb in the weights since last February and put in a feisty front-running display to cash in on a lenient mark on return from 141 days off. This was his first success since November 2008, but it is a worry that he was reported to have finished lame and was taken off the course in a horse ambulance. (op 11-1)
Risk Challenge(USA) moved ominously alongside the leader in the straight but didn't find quite as much as expected and was out battled in the closing stages. However, he did run into a very well handicapped rival and deserves some credit for a big run off a mark 13lb higher than when a comfortable winner of a Huntingdon selling handicap in May. (op 25-1)
Low Delta(IRE) kept plugging away and has stepped up a bit on his staying-on seventh in a similar race at Newton Abbot last time. The return to a more galloping track should suit but he has a modest record of 1-30. (op 7-1)
Be Ashored, soundly beaten at big prices in five previous bumper/hurdle runs, showed some signs of life off a tough-looking mark on handicap debut. (op 16-1)
Kaliski(IRE) went a bit in snatches and could only plug on at the one pace.
Amazing Request looked poised to challenge around the final turn but found a limited response, which was disappointing from a runner who had finished runner-up in similar events the last two times. (op 11-2)
Knightsbridgelives(IRE) was surrounded by horses with much higher ratings when a close 40-1 third in a selling hurdle last time. Due to go up 18lb in future, this looked his opportunity to strike but he was a bit keen and was quickly beaten after coming off the bridle approaching the final turn. Official explanation: jockey said gelding ran too free (op 9-4)
London Times(IRE) Official explanation: jockey said gelding lost its action

991 PLAY BLACKJACK AT TOTESPORT.COM NOVICES' H'CAP CHASE (10 fncs 2 omitted) 2m
7:40 (7:40) (Class 5) (0-95,95) 4-Y-0+ **£2,276** (£668; £334; £166)

Form				RPR
0/06	**1**		**Mustamad**[14] 864 7-9-11 69 oh8 (vt) CharlieStudd(3) (Chris Gordon) *chsd ldrs: slt ld fr 5th and tendency to jump rt after: rdn 2 out: 1 l ahd but u.p whn wnt rt and lft w 3 l ld last: drvn clr fr bypassed fnl fence* **50/1**	80+
0124	**2**	*7*	**Papradon**[13] 875 6-10-12 86 SamTwiston-Davies(5) (Nigel Twiston-Davies) *chsd ldrs: rdn 3 out: disp 1 l 2nd but no imp on wnr whn bmpd last: wknd fr bypassed fnl fence* **9/4**[1]	90+

F-65 **3** *5* **Moon Bear**[9] 913 9-10-5 **79**..(v) DeanColeman(5) 77
(Linda Blackford) *led to 2nd: styd chsng ldrs to 4 out: sn rdn and bhd next: styd on again fr last to take 3rd at bypassed fnl fence but nvr a threat to ldng duo* **4/1**3

03-5 **4** *2 3/4* **Cloonavery (IRE)**[3] 961 8-9-11 **73**.......................... AnthonyFreeman(7) 69
(Tony Carroll) *in rr: j. slowly 5th: hdwy to chse ldrs 3 out: styng on same pce whn lft 3rd last: wknd into 4th at bypassed fnl fence* **7/2**2

-UUP **5** *29* **Simiola**[7] 934 11-10-1 **70** oh16 ow1...................................... ColinBolger 36
(Simon Lewis) *t.k.h: bhd fr 5th* **66/1**

0F00 **6** *1 1/2* **Un Autre Espere**[14] 864 11-9-7 **72** oh11 ow3................(b) JoshWall(10) 37
(Trevor Wall) *led 2nd: hdd 5th: hit 6th: wknd next* **66/1**

-450 **P** **Western Palm (IRE)**[19] 840 7-11-9 **95**............................ PeterToole(3) —
(Charlie Mann) *bdly hmpd 2nd: t.o fr 4th: t.o wen p.u bef 3 out* **8/1**

5U/F **U** **Morning Sunshine (IRE)**[14] 864 7-11-11 **94**................. JasonMaguire 98+
(Donald McCain) *t.k.h: in tch: stdy hdwy to trckd ldrs 3 out: 1 l down and stl travelling wl whn hmpd, wnt lft and uns rdr last* **8/1**

5-50 **P** **Gratification**[33] 716 7-11-11 **94**...................................(v1) LeightonAspell —
(Oliver Sherwood) *j. bdly rt in rr tl p.u bef 4th* **15/2**

3m 55.97s (4.37) **Going Correction** +0.35s/f (Yiel) **9** Ran SP% **111.9**
Speed ratings (Par 103): **103,99,97,95,81 80,—,—,—**
toteswingers:1&2:£24.40, 1&3:£27.40, 2&3:£1.30 CSF £161.73 CT £573.98 TOTE £48.00: £8.90, £2.20, £2.40; EX 247.60.
Owner The MustBMad Partnership **Bred** Shadwell Estate Company Limited **Trained** Morestead, Hants

FOCUS
A modest novice handicap chase, in which the last fence in the home straight was omitted. Most of the runners were in serious trouble a long way out and there was a shock winner. He was rated 90+ over hurdles at his best.

NOTEBOOK
Mustamad arrived here with a record of 0-18 with several blowouts and pulled-up efforts in his recent runs. He had plenty to do from out of the weights but a reapplied visor helped spark him back to action and he ran out a decisive winner under an positive ride, despite jumping to the right on occasions. The downside is that he will get hit hard for this first win and his rollercoaster profile suggests he may not repeat the form next time. Official explanation: trainer said, regarding apparent improvement in form, that the gelding was better suited by the re-application of a visor and being able to dominate. (op 66-1)
Papradon got off the mark over hurdles with a game win over course and distance last month and was fourth in a competitive race at Perth last time. He had solid claims if translating his ability to fences and gave it a fair try in a race where he could never quite adopt his favoured front-running role. (op 7-4)
Moon Bear put in a number of sloppy jumps and got outpaced at a crucial stage before plugging on again. (op 11-2)
Cloonavery(IRE) ran well until a mistake late on ruined his chance on comeback at Stratford on Sunday. He was prominent in the betting again but made several mistakes along the way and was never a serious threat. He is proving expensive to follow and has been beaten at 5-1 or shorter in his last five runs. (tchd 3-1)
Morning Sunshine(IRE) took a keen hold, but he managed to work his way into a position not far off the leader when swerving left and unseating his rider at the last. (op 13-2)
Gratification Official explanation: jockey said gelding jumped badly right-handed (op 13-2)

992 MUSIC NIGHT MAIDEN HURDLE (12 hdls) 3m
8:10 (8:11) (Class 5) 4-Y-0+ **£2,055** (£599; £299)

Form RPR

5-22 **1** **Bobble Hat Bob (FR)**[27] 771 5-11-0 116.............................(v) APMcCoy 99+
(Jonjo O'Neill) *a gng wl trcking ldrs: chal fr 3 out tl led sn after 2 out: won hrd hld* **1/3**1

00-0 **2** *5* **Master Cardor Visa (IRE)**[17] 847 5-10-11 0................. TomMolloy(3) 79+
(Emma Baker) *in rr tl hdwy fr 5th: pressed ldrs 3 out: rdn to take narrow ld whn blnd 2 out and sn hdd: no ch w hrd hld wnr but kpt on for clr 2nd* **50/1**

665- **3** *4* **Heezagrey (IRE)**[94] 5152 7-11-0 0... TomO'Brien 70
(James Evans) *in tch tl lost pl and bhd 4 out: plenty to do 3 out: styd on again appr last and fin wl to take 3rd run-in: gng on cl home but nvr any ch w hrd hld wnr* **16/1**

4-46 **4** *12* **Karzelle**[14] 863 6-11-0 0.. JamieMoore 62
(John Spearing) *chsd ldrs: chal fr 4 out and upsides whn nt fluent 3 out: wknd fr 2 out: no ch whn mstke last* **12/1**3

5 *3 3/4* **All Thyne Greats (IRE)**[115] 8-11-0 0............................... AidanColeman 54
(Rachel Hobbs) *led tl hdd 3 out: wknd fr 2 out: no ch whn hmpd last* **8/1**2

/ **6** *29* **Doheny Bar (IRE)**[259] 1963 7-11-0 0.............................(p) JodieMogford 25
(Nikki Evans) *t.k.h: chsd ldrs: hit 7th: wknd fr 3 out* **14/1**

7 *27* **Alittlebitmore**[60] 7-10-11 0.......................................(v1) TommyPhelan(3) —
(Tom Gretton) *chsd ldrs: rdn and wknd 4 out: no ch whn hit next* **66/1**

P03/ **8** *15* **She's Little Don**[849] 4543 10-10-4 0................................ LeeStephens(3) —
(Stephen Hughes) *bhd fr 1/2-way* **40/1**

4/ **P** **The Mighty Bard (IRE)**[81] 7-10-7 0...................................... MissLBrooke(7) —
(Tracey Watkins) *sn bhd: t.o whn p.u bef 3 out* **33/1**

5-40 **F** **Glacial Harry**[31] 739 4-10-3 0... PeterHatton(7) 66
(Reg Hollinshead) *in rr tl pushed along and hdwy fr 4 out: styng on whn hung lft fr 2 out: 9 l 3rd and no ch w hrd hld wnr whn fell last* **16/1**

6 **P** **The Buddy Mole**[28] 766 9-10-7 0........................... AnthonyFreeman(7) —
(Sean Curran) *chsd ldrs to 7th: t.o after 4 out: p.u bef 2 out* **66/1**

5m 53.3s (8.70) **Going Correction** +0.125s/f (Yiel)
WFA 4 from 5yo+ 17lb **11** Ran SP% **122.6**
Speed ratings (Par 103): **90,88,87,83,81 72,63,58,—,— —**
toteswingers:1&2:£52.20, 1&3:£4.00, 2&3:£67.80 CSF £40.19 TOTE £1.30: £1.10, £10.70, £3.90; EX 37.00.
Owner Dominic Burke & Andrew L Cohen **Bred** Mme M Aubree, D Hanin & Mme G Bozon **Trained** Cheltenham, Gloucs

FOCUS
An uncompetitive maiden hurdle run at a slow pace. The easy winner was value for a lot further.

NOTEBOOK
Bobble Hat Bob(FR) had been knocking on the door in handicaps recently and set a clear standard on his near-miss off 113 when upped to 3m at Ffos Las last time. Sent off a hot favourite, he cruised round and eased his way clear to get off the mark on the 11th attempt. The form is fairly worthless but it could be a valuable confidence-booster for the 5yo who may be able to win more races. (tchd 2-7)
Master Cardor Visa(IRE) finished tailed-off in two previous hurdle runs. He showed a bit more this time and did well to stay on his feet after crashing through the second-last. A runner-up in an Irish point last May, this was the first sign of him translating some of that ability to hurdles. (op 66-1)
Heezagrey(IRE) plugged on to snatch third from some way back, but he is 0-19 and the highlight of his career was a close call off a mark of 75 at Hereford last February. (op 20-1)
Karzelle showed a little bit more than he had in two previous hurdle runs, but was still ultimately well beaten. (op 16-1)
All Thyne Greats(IRE) was in fair form in points in the spring. A late recruit to this discipline, he was prominent for a long way but weakened into a remote fifth. (tchd 9-1)

993 PLAY ROULETTE AT TOTESPORT.COM H'CAP CHASE (16 fncs 2 omitted) 2m 7f
8:40 (8:40) (Class 4) (0-110,109) 4-Y-0+ **£3,252** (£955; £477; £238)

Form RPR

314 **1** **Prophete De Guye (FR)**[34] 695 7-11-2 **99**........................ FelixDeGiles 112+
(James Evans) *in rr but wl in tch: impr to trck ldrs 13th: pressed ldrs 3 out: chal fr next and stl upsides at bypassed fnl fence: rdn to ld fnl 75yds: pushed out* **2/1**1

-541 **2** *1 3/4* **Alfadora**[14] 867 10-10-13 **101**.......................................(t) JimmyDerham(5) 111
(Milton Harris) *in rr but wl in tch: hit 8th: hdwy 12th: qcknd to ld 3 out: jnd last: kpt slt advantage but u.p bypassed fnl fence: hdd and outpcd fnl 75yds* **9/4**2

4-35 **3** *11* **Distiller (IRE)**[34] 691 6-11-3 **105**......................... SamTwiston-Davies(5) 104
(Nigel Twiston-Davies) *trckd ldrs tl blnd and lost pl 10th: rcvrd to press ldrs 3 out: wknd fr next but kpt on to take 3rd run-in* **9/2**3

25P- **4** *3 1/2* **Milton Des Bieffes (FR)**[144] 4172 10-11-6 **106**............. LeeStephens(3) 104
(David Evans) *led tl hdd 8th: stl pressing ldrs u.p 3 out: btn next: blnd last and lost mod 3rd at bypassed fnl fence* **5/1**

U0-6 **5** *22* **Quarry Town (IRE)**[27] 769 8-11-12 **109**..................(bt1) TomScudamore 95
(David Pipe) *trckd ldrs: chal 7th: led next: hdd 3 out and sn wknd* **8/1**

5m 52.76s (10.16) **Going Correction** +0.35s/f (Yiel) **5** Ran SP% **110.1**
Speed ratings (Par 105): **96,95,91,90,82**
CSF £7.14 TOTE £3.30: £2.10, £2.40; EX 6.40.
Owner Elegant Clutter Ltd **Bred** G A E C Delorme Gerard & Vincent **Trained** Broadwas, Worcs

FOCUS
There were not many runners but this was a fairly competitive handicap chase. The first two pulled clear of the rest and the form looks solid with a small personal best from the winner.

NOTEBOOK
Prophete De Guye(FR) travelled well out wide for a long way and showed plenty of resolution to overhaul the runner-up. He managed just one win in his first 27 runs but has found a winning mentality to score on two of his last three starts. Versatile regarding trip, ground and tactics, he should continue to be a powerful force at this sort of level. (op 5-2)
Alfadora put in a much more polished display when storming clear over C&D two weeks earlier. He travelled smoothly in his bid to follow up and it looked like he was going to defy an 11lb rise when hitting the front but he may have gone for home a bit too soon and was just pegged back. Another impending rise will put him close to his previous career-high mark but he should be able to gain compensation and would be of strong interest in a similar race next time. (op 5-2)
Distiller(IRE) made some errors and was caught out when the pace increased. He is potentially thrown in on his highs as a hurdler, including a 3m win off 122 at Ayr last spring, but is beginning to frustrate over fences. (op 11-2)
Milton Des Bieffes(FR) was weak in the market and shaped like he needed the run on return form 144 days off. The likeable front-runner should be sharper next time. He has a decent chase strike-rate of 6-22 and has managed a few placed efforts off this sort of mark in six runs since his commanding performance at Ludlow last November. (op 3-1)
Quarry Town(IRE) raced prominently, but he was under pressure a long way out and dropped away with blinkers tried. (tchd 11-1)

994 C.R.U.K. WORCESTER RELAY FOR LIFE H'CAP HURDLE (10 hdls) 2m 4f
9:10 (9:10) (Class 4) (0-115,115) 4-Y-0+ **£2,602** (£764; £382; £190)

Form RPR

-P02 **1** **Paddleyourowncanoe (IRE)**[28] 767 9-10-10 **102**.....(bt) TomMolloy(3) 104
(Emma Baker) *in rr: drvn along fr 6th: rdn and styd on fr 4 out: j. slowly next and kpt on to chse ldr last: r.o u.p to ld fnl 100yds: rdn out* **10/1**

-330 **2** *2* **Consulate (IRE)**[33] 715 6-11-3 **113**................................. MrDEdwards(7) 114
(Gordon Edwards) *in tch: pressed ldrs 3 out: rdn to ld next: hdd u.p fnl 100yds: one pce* **20/1**

4-4P **3** *11* **Sweet Seville (FR)**[28] 767 6-10-6 **95**............................... DenisO'Regan 84
(Michael Squance) *hld up in rr: stdy hdwy fr 4 out to chse ldrs 3 out: rdn and tk 3rd last but nvr any ch w ldng duo* **20/1**

F55- **4** *8* **Major Miller**[356] 1038 9-10-11 **105**.. DavidBass(5) 86
(Nicky Henderson) *in tch: rdn: j. slowly and lost pl 4 out: mod prog u.p fr 2 out* **7/2**2

U10/ **5** *hd* **Fade To Grey (IRE)**[450] 5119 6-11-2 **110**..........(t) SamTwiston-Davies(5) 91
(Shaun Lycett) *chsd ldrs: chal 4 out to next: wknd 2 out* **11/1**

0612 **6** *3* **Occasionally Yours (IRE)**[14] 862 6-10-10 **99**...................(b) APMcCoy 80
(Nigel Hawke) *trckd ldrs: chal 4 out: slt ld appr 3 out: hdd next and wknd sn after* **11/4**1

1-60 **7** *4 1/2* **The Good Guy (IRE)**[33] 715 7-11-12 **115**........................ JodieMogford 88
(Graeme McPherson) *led after 1st: blnd 4th: rdn 4 out: hdd appr 3 out: wknd sn after* **12/1**

-0P2 **8** *3 3/4* **Osolomio (IRE)**[14] 866 7-11-12 **115**.................................. AlanO'Keeffe 85
(Jennie Candlish) *led tl after 1st: wknd 4 out* **11/1**

0-04 **9** *12* **Armenian Boy (FR)**[27] 771 7-11-10 **113**..................(tp) TomScudamore 71
(David Pipe) *in tch tl wknd 4 out* **13/2**3

-64P **10** *1* **Ash High (IRE)**[13] 872 7-10-3 **92**.. DavidEngland 49
(Nigel Twiston-Davies) *mstke 5th and bhd* **33/1**

F-06 **11** *11* **Like A Duke (FR)**[37] 664 7-11-0 **103**..................................... JoeTizzard 49
(Colin Tizzard) *t.k.h: hit 5th: a in rr* **16/1**

F-0P **12** *24* **Ouste (FR)**[54] 430 8-10-11 **100**.......................................(t) JohnnyFarrelly 22
(Alison Thorpe) *in rr: sme hdwy and in tch after 4 out: wknd qckly next* **25/1**

4m 47.14s (-0.26) **Going Correction** +0.125s/f (Yiel) **12** Ran SP% **117.9**
Speed ratings (Par 105): **105,104,99,96,96 95,93,92,87,86 82,72**
toteswingers:1&2:£15.20, 1&3:£23.00, 2&3:£61.60 CSF £190.06 CT £3874.71 TOTE £14.00: £2.90, £6.90, £4.60; EX 131.20 Place 6 £115.28, Place 5 £84.78..
Owner Miss E J Baker & Mrs M J Arnold **Bred** Seamus O'Farrell **Trained** Naunton, Gloucs
■ Emma Baker's first winner under rules.
■ Stewards' Enquiry : Tom Molloy six-day ban: used whip with excessive frequency (Jul 28-30, Aug 1-3)

FOCUS
They went a fair pace in this handicap hurdle and it was a race of changing fortunes. The second is probably the best guide to the level.

NOTEBOOK
Paddleyourowncanoe(IRE) got back to form from out of the blue when second over course and distance last time. He needed plenty of driving off 5lb higher here but kept grinding away and found a decent finishing effort to get on top close home. He may be able to rise to the challenge off a higher mark next time, but his slow-burning style makes him a bit risky and he may be one to concentrate on in-running. (op 9-1)
Consulate(IRE) gave it a good shot and put in a more fluent round than he did at Market Rasen last time. He is very capable off this sort of mark and will be suited by a switch back to faster ground. (op 33-1)
Sweet Seville(FR) gave a hint of a revival with cheekpieces removed, but she has been very in and out since winning a course and distance maiden hurdle at 33-1 last June. (op 25-1)

Major Miller was prominent in the betting but looked rusty and put in some sketchy jumps on his return from almost a year off. He has been a bit expensive to follow in some abbreviated campaigns over the years but is entitled to benefit from this run and is well treated off the same mark as when a decisive winner of a handicap chase at Perth in April last year. (op 4-1 tchd 9-2)
Fade To Grey(IRE) showed up well for a long way on return from 450 days off. The lightly raced sort was an easy winner of a Newton Abbot maiden hurdle on his penultimate start last spring and could step up quite a bit on this comeback run next time. (tchd 10-1 and 12-1)
Occasionally Yours(IRE) got off the mark in first-time blinkers on fast ground here before chasing home a subsequent winner under a penalty over course and distance last time. He was interesting off 2lb higher and things looked to be going smoothly for a long way, but he floundered after hitting the front at the third-last and the slow ground may have caused his downfall. (tchd 5-2)
Armenian Boy(FR) didn't find as much as expected at Ffos Las last time and he put in a very laboured effort here. (op 8-1)
T/Plt: £145.70 to a £1 stake. Pool: £73,562.89. 368.54 winning tickets. T/Qpdt: £17.30 to a £1 stake. Pool: £5,944.23. 254.00 winning tickets. ST

995 - 998a (Foreign Racing) - See Raceform Interactive

[576]CARTMEL (L-H)
Thursday, July 15

OFFICIAL GOING: Good to soft (soft by the woodside; 8.2)
Wind: fresh 1/2 behind Weather: overcast, heavy showers

999 JOHN SMITH'S NOVICES' HURDLE (11 hdls) 2m 6f
2:00 (2:00) (Class 4) 4-Y-0+ **£2,927** (£859; £429; £214)

Form RPR
62 **1** **Oursininlaw (IRE)**[37] 683 6-10-9 110 AdamWedge(10) 101+
(Evan Williams) *chsd ldrs 5th: chal last: sn led: rdn clr* **2/1**[2]
0-32 **2** *7* **Our Guardian Angel (IRE)**[18] 843 6-10-5 102 (t) RichardJohnson 80
(Tim Vaughan) *chsd ldrs: wnt 2nd 6th: styd on same pce run-in: tk 2nd last 200yds* **6/4**[1]
0P/5 **3** *nk* **Mulligan's Pride (IRE)**[42] 604 9-10-12 66 (v) PaddyAspell 86
(James Moffatt) *led: hdd sn after last: one pce* **66/1**
4633 **4** *18* **Sunset Resort (IRE)**[11] 887 5-10-9 90 (t) MichaelMcAlister(3) 72
(Maurice Barnes) *nt fluent in rr: sme hdwy 7th: tk poor 4th between last 2* **12/1**
4435 **5** *1* **Fly Tipper**[4] 946 10-10-12 88 GrahamLee 69
(Wilf Storey) *trckd ldrs: wknd 3 out* **5/1**[3]
0050 **6** *28* **Daniel's Dream**[47] 519 10-10-12 70 (b) BrianHughes 44
(John Dixon) *t.k.h: wnt prom 6th: modest 4th whn mstke 2 out: sn wknd: eased run-in* **66/1**
030- **7** *9* **Hathamore**[95] 5140 6-10-2 83 RyanMania(3) 29
(Allie Tullie) *in rr: bhd fr 8th* **40/1**
0-F6 **8** *39* **Morecambe Bay**[11] 887 5-10-9 0 TommyPhelan(3) —
(David Thompson) *nt fluent: t.k.h: trckd ldrs: lost pl 6th: bhd and rdn 8th: t.o* **66/1**
P04 **P** **Osbaldeston (IRE)**[31] 744 7-10-12 100 WilsonRenwick —
(Rose Dobbin) *hld up: hdwy to chse ldrs 7th: wknd appr 2 out: sn eased: distant 7th whn p.u bef last* **9/1**
P-0 **P** **Aurifex (IRE)**[14] 873 6-10-9 0 FearghalDavis(3) —
(Paul Murphy) *in rr: mstke 5th: rdn and lost tch 8th: t.o whn p.u bef next* **80/1**

5m 41.9s (12.60) **Going Correction** +0.70s/f (Soft) **10** Ran SP% **115.8**
Speed ratings (Par 105): **105,102,102,95,95 85,81,67,—,—**
toteswingers:1&2:£1.10, 1&3:£15.60, 2&3:£20.00 CSF £5.49 TOTE £2.00: £1.10, £1.10, £17.90; EX 5.20.
Owner R E R Williams **Bred** P And B Turley **Trained** Llancarfan, Vale Of Glamorgan

FOCUS
After a night of heavy showers which saw 20mm rain fall on the course the going was changed from the forecast good, good to firm in places, to good, good to soft in places, soft by the woodside (which always rides softer than the other stretch of the track). A race run at a slow pace in the rain-softened ground, being 30 secs outside the standard. A modest novice hurdle and fairly sound form.

NOTEBOOK
Oursininlaw(IRE), rated 110 and appreciating every yard of this 2m6f trip, had scored at Fakenham over a comparable distance in April and four winners have already come out of that race. He was given a fine ride by Adam Wedge, now two out of two since joining the Evan Williams' yard, and for whom he can claim an invaluable 10lb. This is a horse who can take a bit of cajoling, but against this rather plodding opposition he was firmly in command by the last. (tchd 15-8 and 9-4)
Our Guardian Angel(IRE) is a model of consistency, and she seemed to get the trip, but she has now been placed in three bumpers and three hurdles and still awaits that elusive first success. Her turn will probably come eventually. (op Evens)
Mulligan's Pride(IRE) has not won for four years, and that was on the Flat. Equipped with a second-time visor, he set a modest pace but was soon beaten when passed, and at nine time is running out for him. Far worse though, he is only rated 66 and, after this placing behind 100 plus performers, has now almost certainly scuppered any very slim future hopes. (op 80-1)
Sunset Resort(IRE) lacked early fluency and never threatened to get involved. There was no substantial hope for imminent improvement here. (op 18-1)
Daniel's Dream, who always runs left-handed, pulled too hard as usual. (op 80-1)
Hathamore ran as if she needed the run on her return from a three-month absence. (op 66-1)
Osbaldeston(IRE) Official explanation: jockey said gelding lost its action

1000 EUROPEAN BREEDERS' FUND BEGINNERS' CHASE (12 fncs) 2m 1f 110y
2:30 (2:30) (Class 4) 4-Y-0+ **£3,252** (£955; £477; £238)

Form RPR
-222 **1** **Stagecoach Pearl**[15] 857 6-11-9 115 APMcCoy 130+
(Sue Smith) *trckd ldr: led 8th: wnt clr sn after last: eased fnl f* **1/1**[1]
0-F4 **2** *21* **Kind Heart**[6] 648 4-10-0 0 GrahamLee 85+
(Donald McCain) *trckd ldrs: wnt 2nd after 8th: hit next: 3 l down whn blnd 2 out: no ch w wnr* **5/2**[2]
6B0- **3** *7* **Risk Runner (IRE)**[250] 2117 7-11-9 0 (v) PaddyAspell 99
(James Moffatt) *hdwy 6th: modest 4th whn mstke 2 out: tk 3rd last* **13/2**[3]
0 **4** *23* **Gougane (IRE)**[16] 854 7-11-9 0 AndrewThornton 78
(Hugh McWilliams) *in tch: outpcd 8th: sn bhd: tk distant 4th run-in* **25/1**
/0-2 **5** *17* **El Presidente (IRE)**[53] 440 5-11-6 110 (b) AlexMerriam(3) 63
(Neil King) *led: j. slowly 5th: hdd 8th: wknd rapidly last: sn bhd* **15/2**
6 *17* **Overquest**[53] 8-11-9 0 JohnnyFarrelly 48
(Elliott Cooper) *nt j.w in rr: sme hdwy 7th: sn wknd: mstke 4 out: sn t.o* **25/1**
P5 **7** *7* **Sendeed (USA)**[11] 889 8-11-9 0 (tp) KeithMercer 41
(Peter Atkinson) *in rr: bhd fr 6th: t.o 9th* **50/1**
0P/ **P** **Lisglynn Jim (IRE)**[27] 784 6-11-9 0 (t) PeterBuchanan —
(Mayne Kidd, Ire) *nt fluent: reminders and lost pl 6th: sn bhd: t.o whn p.u bef 8th* **80/1**

4m 24.0s (5.10) **Going Correction** +0.475s/f (Soft)
WFA 4 from 5yo+ 2lb **8** Ran SP% **114.6**
Speed ratings (Par 105): **107,97,94,84,76 69,66,—**
toteswingers:1&2:£1.40, 1&3:£2.00, 2&3:£1.70 CSF £3.84 TOTE £2.40: £1.10, £1.30, £2.00; EX 4.70.
Owner John Conroy Jaqueline Conroy **Bred** R F Broad **Trained** High Eldwick, W Yorks

FOCUS
This race was run at a good tempo throughout, and the ground appeared to be riding little worse than good on the chase course. The winner was the clear form pick but this still rates a personal best.

NOTEBOOK
Stagecoach Pearl had finished second in his three previous chases and had done nothing wrong in them except pull too hard, but A P McCoy, having only his second ride for the Sue Smith stable, had no difficulty getting him settled and ended a losing run of 38 for the trainer. He is a dual hurdling winner already, and although this was an easy opportunity he came home 21l clear, and this consistent sort will surely find similar chances, particularly as his self-confidence over fences should have been bolstered. (tchd 6-5)
Kind Heart has won twice on the Flat and was trying to emulate her feat of scoring in her first hurdle on this chasing debut. She was rather keen and absolutely no match for the winner, but as she is only four some progress might be expected. (op 3-1)
Risk Runner(IRE) did not jump well enough in the early stages and this trip is probably too short for him. Jimmy Moffatt, who trains within a mile of the racecourse, has now had 36 runners at Cartmel spread over 1092 days, but no winners, although he does well enough elsewhere. (op 6-1)
Gougane(IRE) is not firing at present for his new yard.
El Presidente(IRE) went off quickly but certainly did not finish with the same degree of enthusiasm and is one to be wary of. (op 7-1 tchd 13-2)
Overquest won at the Lisronagh point in Ireland 2009/10 but never looked happy with the regulation fences and was soon labouring. (op 20-1)

1001 TEMPLE HEELIS COMMERCIAL LLP H'CAP CHASE (12 fncs) 2m 1f 110y
3:05 (3:05) (Class 5) (0-95,92) 4-Y-0+ **£2,927** (£859; £429; £214)

Form RPR
P-30 **1** **High Stand Lad**[15] 860 8-11-12 **92** (t) DenisO'Regan 108+
(Martin Todhunter) *trckd ldrs: led 7th: wnt wl clr run-in: heavily eased last 100yds* **12/1**
-264 **2** *14* **Peak Seasons (IRE)**[11] 891 7-10-0 **73** StevenGagan(7) 69
(Michael Chapman) *w ldr: led 4th: hdd 7th: modest 2nd whn hit last: struggled to hang on to 2nd clsng stages* **11/1**
4205 **3** *1/2* **Ice Image (IRE)**[15] 860 8-11-3 **90** AlistairFindlay(7) 86
(George Charlton) *mid-div: hdwy 4 out: styd on to take modest 3rd 2f out: kpt on* **10/1**
0U-3 **4** *3/4* **Hapthor**[25] 801 11-11-3 **90** (p) PeterHatton(7) 87
(F Jestin) *stdd s: in rr: hit 4th: bhd fr 8th: poor 7th last: styd on wl to take 4th clsng stages: hmpd and fell sn after line* **40/1**
33-0 **5** *3 3/4* **Pinewood Legend (IRE)**[47] 520 8-11-10 **90** (bt) PeterBuchanan 84
(Peter Niven) *in rr: sme hdwy whn hit 3 out: tk modest 4th 1f out: one pce* **11/1**
3165 **6** *10* **Crofton Arch**[4] 947 10-10-7 **73** (p) PaddyAspell 56
(John Dixon) *led to 4th: modest 3rd and wkng whn mstke 2 out* **5/1**[2]
4-05 **7** *26* **Lukie Victor (IRE)**[4] 950 9-11-2 **92** AdamWedge(10) 52
(Evan Williams) *mstke 1st: prom: outpcd 8th: wknd last* **5/1**[2]
P-44 **8** *4 1/2* **Well Oiled (IRE)**[33] 728 9-11-5 **85** (tp) AndrewThornton 40
(Sandy Forster) *in rr-div: outpcd and bhd whn mstke 7th* **12/1**
0341 **9** *6* **Wensleydale Web**[9] 920 8-11-9 **89** GrahamLee 39
(Martin Todhunter) *stdd s: nt fluent in rr: hit 5th: bhd whn mstke 7th* **7/1**[3]
3252 **F** **Troodos Jet**[31] 747 9-10-11 **77** (p) BrianHughes —
(Dianne Sayer) *prom: handy 6th whn fell 8th* **8/1**
4232 **F** **Emotive**[15] 860 7-11-8 **91** CampbellGillies(3) —
(Barry Murtagh) *hld up: wnt prom 6th: handy 3rd and travelling strly whn fell 4 out* **4/1**[1]

4m 30.1s (11.20) **Going Correction** +0.75s/f (Soft) **11** Ran SP% **120.5**
Speed ratings (Par 103): **105,98,98,98,96 92,80,78,75,— —**
toteswingers:1&2:£32.80, 1&3:£26.80, 2&3:£22.30 CSF £137.38 CT £1383.68 TOTE £18.00: £4.30, £3.70, £4.70; EX 176.10.
Owner D Graves D Gillespie G Mitchell **Bred** A Slack **Trained** Orton, Cumbria

FOCUS
A low-grade handicap. The easy winner produced a big step up on his previous chase form and there is a case for rating the race a bit higher.

NOTEBOOK
High Stand Lad has the size and shape of a chaser but had previously been very disappointing over fences and was beaten over 25l in two previous races this spring. He turned this into a procession in the first time tongue-tie, and went well for Denis O'Regan, who has a good record for this yard. Given the weakness of this opposition and his previous record he would be no good thing to follow up. (op 14-1)
Peak Seasons(IRE) is 3-71 over jumps but this was one of his better efforts, and he gallantly held second but was struggling to keep up with the winner from a long way out. (op 10-1 tchd 12-1)
Ice Image(IRE) is a 26-time loser and this effort did not suggest that he will be winning soon. (tchd 9-1)
Hapthor got totally outpaced early and made one spectacular blunder, but this ex-pointer (who has her share of temperament) finished faster than anything with the rider working furiously, only to crash into the back of the easing winner and take a fall just after the line. Luckily she was soon on her feet. (op 33-1)
Pinewood Legend(IRE) was off the bridle before halfway and has an attitude problem. (op 8-1)
Lukie Victor(IRE) is struggling with his jumping and market support never looked likely to be justified. He is probably a bit better than he showed today, if he could get his act together. (op 8-1)
Wensleydale Web has won two hurdles here but this normally hard puller seemed flummoxed by the fences and made an inauspicious start to her chasing career for this stable (four miserable efforts for another trainer three years ago). Official explanation: jockey said mare did not take to fences (op 9-2)
Emotive finds this trip too short and, although falling four out, would not have troubled the winner in any case. (op 9-2 tchd 5-1)

1002 WEATHERBYS BANK H'CAP CHASE (18 fncs) 3m 2f
3:40 (3:40) (Class 3) (0-120,120) 4-Y-0+ **£6,505** (£1,910; £955; £477)

Form RPR
2-34 **1** **Mizen Raven (IRE)**[20] 839 7-11-12 **120** (tp) TomO'Brien 130+
(Peter Bowen) *chsd ldrs: wnt 2nd 13th: led 2 out: hung lft over 1f out: hung lft towards fin: all out* **15/2**
0P-6 **2** *1 1/4* **Dukeofchesterwood**[14] 873 8-10-6 **100** KeithMercer 107+
(Sandy Forster) *chsd ldrs: led 3 out: haded next: hmpd on ins over 2f out: keeping on whn short of room and swtchd rt nr fin* **11/1**

1-P5 **3** 3/4 **Dallas Bell**[33] 730 8-9-13 **96** EwanWhillans(3) 102
(Alistair Whillans) *in rr: hdwy 12th: hit 14th: chsng ldrs next: wnt 3rd over 3f out: styd on same pce last 100yds* **8/1**

2-5U **4** *nk* **Petite Margot**[15] 859 11-11-7 **115** APMcCoy 120
(Nigel Twiston-Davies) *nt fluent: chsd ldrs: drvn 13th: dropped bk 6th last: rallied over 2f out: styd on same pce fnl f* **7/2**[1]

-631 **5** *41* **The Artful Fox**[37] 680 9-9-11 **94** oh1 CampbellGillies(3) 62
(Mike Sowersby) *chsd ldrs: led 5th: hdd 2 out: wknd qckly last: sn bhd: t.o* **10/1**

-433 **6** *31* **Western Gale (IRE)**[15] 859 7-11-5 **113** (p) DenisO'Regan 53
(Martin Todhunter) *in rr: reminders 12th: hdwy 4 out: chsng ldrs appr last: sn wknd and eased: t.o* **9/2**[3]

1P-2 **7** *22* **Onthegoagain (IRE)**[47] 517 9-10-1 **95** TomScudamore 15
(J J Lambe, Ire) *chsd ldrs: outpcd 14th: sn lost pl and bhd: t.o* **4/1**[2]

4-41 **P** **Thunder Hawk (IRE)**[43] 580 10-10-3 **97** (p) PeterBuchanan —
(Stuart Coltherd) *led to 5th: lost pl 7th: sn bhd: t.o whn p.u bef 9th* **11/2**

6m 49.6s (14.70) **Going Correction** +0.75s/f (Soft) **8** Ran SP% **116.1**
Speed ratings (Par 107): **107,106,106,106,93 84,77,—**
toteswingers:1&2:£6.80, 1&3:£6.80, 2&3:£14.90 CSF £81.25 CT £680.17 TOTE £4.80: £1.10, £3.90, £3.70; EX 96.80.

Owner Steve & Jackie Fleetham **Bred** Con Collins **Trained** Little Newcastle, Pembrokes

■ Stewards' Enquiry : Tom O'Brien three-day ban: careless riding (Jul 29-30,Aug 1)

FOCUS
A modest staying handicap and a controversial finish. The winner is rated back to his best with a step forward from the second.

NOTEBOOK
Mizen Raven(IRE) has had several changes of stable in this ownership (two previous wins in this country for Alison Thorpe and one for Tim Vaughan), and is now back in the care of Peter Bowen, whose team is flying. He had not scored over further than 2m4f previously but saw the trip out in game fashion, although he was coming to the end of his tether at the end of 3m2f and lugged into the runner-up. He gave the impression of being rather dehydrated afterwards. (op 9-2 tchd 8-1)

Dukeofchesterwood is only small but has given some gutsy displays in the past, although not since winning a decent Newcastle hurdle in November 2009. This was only his second try over fences and he coped well, and would certainly have gone closer (although perhaps not won) had he not been left short of room in the final 100 yards. He has no stamina worries and may find compensation. (op 12-1 tchd 14-1)

Dallas Bell has broken blood-vessels in the past. He was going on well at the end and stays this trip but never looked like winning.\n (op 17-2)

Petite Margot was quite disappointing and McCoy could never get her fully motivated. After running in snatches and making the odd slow jump, she ultimately left a late spurt all too late. She is very unpredictable these days. (tchd 10-3)

The Artful Fox won a Southwell chase from which four subsequent winners have emerged (including Midnight Gold who picked up a good prize at Ffos Las), and he tried to run the opposition into the ground, but was unable to prove that his success was not a fluke, as it had seemed to be on the day. (op 11-1 tchd 12-1)

Western Gale(IRE) is not seeing his races out at the moment and cheekpieces have not appeared to be helpful. (op 5-1 tchd 4-1)

1003 BIRTHDAY GIRLS' MAIDEN HURDLE (7 hdls 1 omitted) 2m 1f 110y
4:15 (4:15) (Class 4) 4-Y-0+ **£2,602** (£764; £382; £190)

Form RPR

50-0 **1** **Bold Exit (IRE)**[70] 167 5-10-11 0 (t) MichaelMcAlister(3) 106+
(Maurice Barnes) *trckd ldrs: hit 1st: hmpd and lft cl 2nd 4th: led sn after normal 2 out: drew rt away fnl 2f* **25/1**

2-3P **2** *24* **Ace High Blue (IRE)**[44] 564 8-10-4 102 (t) AdamWedge(10) 86+
(Evan Williams) *chsd ldr: lft in ld 4th: hdd sn after normal 2 out: wknd fnl f* **9/4**[2]

P **3** *1 1/4* **Le Petit Vigier**[37] 684 4-10-5 0 (tp) DougieCostello 74
(Patrick Holmes) *towards rr: outpcd 5th: kpt on fr normal 2 out: tk n.d 3rd last 100yds* **125/1**

4U **4** *8* **Grethel (IRE)**[21] 577 6-10-7 0 BrianHughes 71
(Alan Berry) *prom: clr 3rd after 5th: wknd fnl f* **16/1**

00 **5** *32* **Miss Markham (IRE)**[34] 711 5-10-0 0 PeterHatton(7) 40
(Patricia Rigby) *in rr: hmpd 4th: prom next: sn wknd: t.o* **125/1**

/6-2 **6** *30* **Flichity (IRE)**[22] 827 5-11-0 0 GrahamLee 20
(Donald McCain) *unruly leaving paddock: t.k.h and overshot s: hld up in rr: blnd 1st: hmpd 4th: wnt prom next: sn wknd: t.o after normal 2 out: virtually p.u: hopelessly t.o: eventually completed* **2/1**[1]

-266 **F** **Duty Free (IRE)**[15] 861 6-11-0 113 PaddyAspell —
(James Moffatt) *racd wd: led: fell 4th* **11/4**[3]

00/ **P** **Tek A Deek**[14] 315 6-11-0 0 (v[1]) DenisO'Regan —
(James Moffatt) *nt fluent in rr: drvn 2nd: t.o whn p.u after 4th* **40/1**

5 **B** **Rebel Swing**[25] 800 4-10-12 0 HenryOliver —
(Sue Smith) *chsd ldrs: b.d 4th* **10/1**

0 **P** **Balwyllo (IRE)**[33] 731 5-11-0 0 BarryKeniry —
(Ben Haslam) *chsd ldrs: wknd 5th: t.o whn blnd next: sn p.u* **40/1**

4m 24.9s (11.70) **Going Correction** +0.70s/f (Soft)
WFA 4 from 5yo+ 15lb **10** Ran SP% **116.1**
Speed ratings (Par 105): **102,91,90,87,73 59,—,—,—,—**
toteswingers:1&2:£8.10, 1&3:£66.70, 2&3:£35.90 CSF £82.26 TOTE £37.30: £7.60, £1.10, £21.60; EX 111.90.

Owner Miss Alison P Lee **Bred** James Kinsella **Trained** Farlam, Cumbria

FOCUS
A truly dreadful race, but a worthy winner. He produced a massive step up with the second 20lb off his best. The final flight was bypassed.

NOTEBOOK
Bold Exit(IRE) was beaten 39l and 104l in two hurdles for Tom George but the new trainer slapped on a tongue-strap and the effects can only have been positive. Narrowly avoiding the skirmishing at the fourth where two rivals departed, he was in full command from two out. His next outing will be a lot more revealing. He cost just £1,100 last month (was sold for £18,000 before his racecourse debut), so is already a bargain as this effort earned him £2,600. (op 33-1 tchd 22-1)

Ace High Blue(IRE) has just one possible excuse, in that he might be better going right-handed (jumped violently right on his chasing debut last time). (op 11-4 tchd 3-1 in a place)

Le Petit Vigier was hopelessly tailed off when pulling up on her hurdling debut but gained third by default. (op 100-1)

Grethel(IRE) has made all her three appearances over hurdles at Cartmel and two fourths amount to nothing. She is moderate. (op 18-1 tchd 20-1)

Flichity(IRE) was badly hampered at the first (was also nearly taken out of the race by an early puller up last time), having looked mulish in the preliminaries. He ran a shocker, and this well-related sort now has a big question mark hanging over him. Official explanation: jockey said gelding was unsuited by the good to soft (soft in places) ground (tchd 15-8 and 9-4 in a place)

Tek A Deek was backed at big prices and wore a first time visor but virtually refused to race properly. (op 100-1)

1004 BETFAIR H'CAP HURDLE (11 hdls) 2m 6f
4:50 (4:50) (Class 4) (0-110,110) 4-Y-0+ **£3,903** (£1,146; £573; £286)

Form RPR

35-0 **1** **Rare Coincidence**[43] 581 9-11-2 **100** (p) KeithMercer 105
(Roger Fisher) *led to 6th: chsd ldrs: outpcd 2 out: 5th last: styd on wl to ld nr fin* **10/1**

11F2 **2** *3/4* **Cannon Fire (FR)**[29] 765 9-10-11 **105** AdamWedge(10) 109
(Evan Williams) *trckd ldrs: led after 2 out: hdd nr fin* **4/1**[2]

-016 **3** *1 3/4* **Soubriquet (IRE)**[14] 874 7-11-4 **105** (t) MichaelMcAlister(3) 107
(Maurice Barnes) *chsd ldrs: reminders 8th: wnt 2nd 2f out: kpt on same pce last 200yds* **11/1**

0-03 **4** *7* **Goldan Jess (IRE)**[11] 888 6-10-12 **103** KyleJames(7) 100
(Philip Kirby) *trckd ldrs: t.k.h: wnt 2nd after 6th: led 3 out: hdd after next: wknd fnl 2f* **7/2**[1]

2/0F **5** *2 1/4* **Mad Moose (IRE)**[28] 771 6-11-4 **102** DavidEngland 96
(Nigel Twiston-Davies) *nt fluent in rr: hdwy 5th: wknd appr 2 out* **7/2**[1]

-0F5 **6** *3* **Word Of Warning**[12] 803 6-11-6 **109** JamesHalliday(5) 100
(Martin Todhunter) *in rr: hdwy 8th: chsng ldrs next: wknd last 2f* **8/1**

5/0- **7** *14* **Inner Voice (USA)**[57] 417 7-11-5 **110** BrianToomey(7) 93
(J J Lambe, Ire) *nt fluent in rr: hmpd bnd and dropped last 8th: blnd 2 out: sn bhd: t.o* **14/1**

0-24 **8** *18* **Lets Go Girls**[31] 748 6-11-1 **99** PaddyAspell 62
(James Moffatt) *w ldr: led 6th: hdd 3 out: wknd qckly: t.o last* **7/1**[3]

5m 52.0s (22.70) **Going Correction** +0.975s/f (Soft) **8** Ran SP% **112.1**
Speed ratings (Par 105): **97,96,96,93,92 91,86,80**
toteswingers:1&2:£6.70, 1&3:£8.20, 2&3:£8.00 CSF £48.43 CT £448.42 TOTE £11.80: £3.10, £2.10, £4.40; EX 62.90.

Owner Des Johnston **Bred** D R Tucker **Trained** Ulverston, Cumbria

FOCUS
A modest handicap. The winner was 3lb off the best of his 2009 form.

NOTEBOOK
Rare Coincidence has been a wonderful servant to Roger Fisher, who paid 12,000gns for him in 2002. Since then he has won at least once in all of the last seven years and has now accumulated 17 victories and 32 placings from no less than 134 outings. He had not scored over jumps for four years and looked unlikely to do so when jumping the last in fifth place, but staying on with grim determination he forced his head in front near the line. He takes a long time to find his stride these days but all credit to him for this performance, on his local track. Official explanation: trainer said, regarding apparent improvement in form, that the gelding was better suited by the softer ground. (op 17-2 tchd 8-1)

Cannon Fire(FR) won twice in June and may have been unlucky when falling next time. He was less interested at Worcester subsequently but with a claimer offsetting some of his weight rise he looked all set to regain the winning thread here. However, his stride began to shorten dramatically inside the final furlong and he was just caught. He remains in good heart but the handicapper is having his say. (op 7-2 tchd 3-1)

Soubriquet(IRE) mixes hurdling with chasing and lacks consistency but ran as well as could have been expected, and his stable remains in good form. (op 10-1 tchd 12-1)

Goldan Jess(IRE) has never won off a mark this high and did himself no favours by pulling hard. (op 4-1)

Mad Moose(IRE) had looked like taking a hand in the finish until he fell at the last in the back straight at Ffos Las, but that tumble may have unnerved him, as his jumping was erratic throughout and cost him dear. Official explanation: jockey said gelding never travelled (op 4-1 tchd 9-2)

Word Of Warning travelled into the race going well enough two out, but the effort petered out tamely and he has never proved his stamina at beyond 2m4f. (op 10-1 tchd 7-1)

Lets Go Girls patently failed to stay.

1005 JOHN SMITH'S EXTRA SMOOTH NOVICES' H'CAP HURDLE (8 hdls) 2m 1f 110y
5:20 (5:20) (Class 4) (0-100,97) 4-Y-0+ **£3,252** (£955; £477; £238)

Form RPR

3116 **1** **Monkhair (IRE)**[25] 793 5-10-11 **87** LeeEdwards(5) 102+
(Tony Carroll) *trckd ldrs: led 2 out: sn clr: faltered: stmbld and rdr lost iron and almost uns 50yds fr line* **7/2**[2]

5-13 **2** *13* **Bonzeno Queen (IRE)**[45] 547 5-11-0 **95** AdamWedge(10) 94
(Evan Williams) *w ldrs: led 3 out: hdd next: kpt on same pce: no ch w inner* **5/1**

05-0 **3** *3 3/4* **Richo**[20] 837 4-11-2 **92** AdamPogson(3) 87
(Shaun Harris) *in rr: hdwy 5th: chsng ldrs next: styd on one pce fr 2 out: tk 3rd last* **16/1**

4246 **4** *15* **Galley Slave (IRE)**[11] 886 5-9-12 **76** StevenGagan(7) 61
(Michael Chapman) *w ldrs: led 5th: sn rdn: hdd 3 out: wknd next* **4/1**[3]

4-13 **5** *1/2* **Authentic Act (IRE)**[49] 490 6-10-9 **80** GrahamLee 62
(Martin Todhunter) *in rr: hdwy 5th: sn chsng ldrs: wknd last* **3/1**[1]

03P- **6** *30* **Bocciani (GER)**[216] 2818 5-11-9 **97** (p) JamesO'Farrell(3) 52
(Dianne Sayer) *led 2nd: hdd 4th: wknd after 2 out: eased and sn bhd* **22/1**

/2-P **7** *22* **Rolecarr (IRE)**[31] 748 7-11-2 **87** PaddyAspell 22
(Ann Hamilton) *led to 2nd: reminders 4th: sn lost pl: t.o 2 out* **16/1**

06P- **P** **Jumeirah Jane**[286] 1588 7-11-1 **86** HenryOliver —
(Sue Smith) *lost pl 3rd: reminders and sn bhd: t.o whn p.u bef 5th* **14/1**

06-F **P** **Strevelyn**[12] 748 4-11-1 **88** (e) KeithMercer —
(Ann Duffield) *prom: lost pl 5th: sn bhd: t.o whn p.u bef 2 out* **10/1**

4m 28.1s (14.90) **Going Correction** +0.975s/f (Soft)
WFA 4 from 5yo+ 15lb **9** Ran SP% **115.8**
Speed ratings (Par 105): **105,99,97,90,90 77,67,—,—**
toteswingers:1&2:£5.40, 1&3:£10.90, 2&3:£12.40 CSF £21.81 CT £246.07 TOTE £4.50: £3.00, £3.40, £5.90; EX 31.40 Place 6 £821.82; Place 5 £599.32.

Owner Group 1 Racing (1994) Ltd **Bred** James J Monaghan **Trained** Cropthorne, Worcs

FOCUS
A modest event. Another step forward from the easy winner with the next two to their marks.

NOTEBOOK
Monkhair(IRE) is a strong-travelling mare with a tendency to doss in the closing stages, as she showed at Uttoxeter when gaining her first win only six weeks ago. This was her third success and trainer and rider have done extremely well with her, but there was almost an awful conclusion here as she began to stop and Lee Edwards lost his balance and an iron, and almost fell off strides before the post. Another weight hike would make matters difficult. (op 4-1)

Bonzeno Queen(IRE) had gained her previous win in a mares' novices' seller and this was more competitive. She is very small and, although she did her best, there will not be many opportunities for her off this sort of mark, especially as she ended up getting far closer to the easy winner than was ideal. (op 9-2 tchd 6-1)

Richo is starting to find a bit of form, but he had looked to be struggling at halfway and may have been flattered by his final position, which was his first-ever placing. (op 14-1 tchd 12-1)

Galley Slave(IRE) was surprisingly well backed despite 35 previous jumping defeats. He pulled too hard, as is so often the case with him, and galloped himself into the ground. (op 6-1 tchd 10-3)

Authentic Act(IRE) gained the assistance of Graham Lee but he was off the bridle by halfway, and was clearly unwilling to put his best foot forward in the final half mile. His easy Sedgefield win came in a seller. Official explanation: jockey said gelding was unsuited by the track (op 11-4 tchd 10-3)
Bocciani(GER) is becoming a nuisance in the preliminaries these days. He had run well here in May but this was far less convincing. (op 18-1 tchd 16-1)
T/Jkpt: Not won. T/Plt: £236.70 to a £1 stake. Pool:£54,355.30 - 167.62 winning tickets T/Qpdt: £517.10 to a £1 stake. Pool:£3,284.61 - 4.70 winning tickets WG

1006 - 1016a (Foreign Racing) - See Raceform Interactive

[886] MARKET RASEN (R-H)
Saturday, July 17

OFFICIAL GOING: Good (hdl 7.2; chs 7.4)
All bends moved in 4yds to provide fresh ground.
Wind: Moderate half against Weather: Fine

1017 TOTESCOOP6 SUMMER HURDLE H'CAP (LISTED RACE) (8 hdls) 2m 1f
2:00 (2:02) (Class 1) (0-150,142) 4-Y-0+
£22,804 (£8,556; £4,284; £2,136; £1,072; £536)

Form — RPR
/1F- **1** **Australia Day (IRE)**[15] 1817 7-11-5 **135** DenisO'Regan 156+
(Paul Webber) *mde all: wnt clr 2 out: eased towards fin* **7/1**[2]
62-0 **2** 19 **Gloucester**[16] 207 7-11-1 **131** RhysFlint 134
(Michael Scudamore) *hld up in rr: hdwy 3 out: wnt 2nd and j.lft 2 out: j.lft last: hung bdly lft run-in* **33/1**
4-15 **3** hd **Stage Acclaim (IRE)**[24] 715 5-9-12 **119** GilesHawkins(5) 122
(Dr Richard Newland) *hld up in rr: hdwy 5th: styd on run-in* **25/1**
0-31 **4** 4 **Alazan (IRE)**[63] 331 4-10-4 **122** RichardJohnson 119
(Philip Hobbs) *in rr: hdwy 3 out: kpt on fr next: nvr nrr* **14/1**
4-43 **5** 1 **Mohanad (IRE)**[23] 648 4-10-5 **123** JamieGoldstein 119
(Sheena West) *mid-div: hdwy 3 out: 3rd next: one pce* **18/1**
3-11 **6** 2 3/4 **Tiger O'Toole (IRE)**[49] 521 5-11-1 **131** PaulMoloney 127
(Evan Williams) *mstke and hmpd 1st: mid-div: hdwy whn hit 3 out: kpt on same pce: nvr a threat* **8/1**[3]
11-5 **7** 6 **Conquisto**[35] 207 5-11-3 **133** KeithMercer 124
(Steve Gollings) *chsd wnr: wknd 2 out* **10/1**
-000 **8** 3/4 **Acambo (GER)**[32] 756 9-11-0 **130** (b[1]) TomScudamore 120
(David Pipe) *chsd ldrs: wknd appr 2 out* **14/1**
212 **9** shd **Heron Bay**[11] 916 6-9-11 **118** DonalDevereux(5) 108
(Peter Bowen) *towards rr: sme hdwy appr 2 out: nvr a factor* **11/1**
3111 **10** 2 **Pure Faith (IRE)**[6] 956 6-10-13 **129** 5ex TomO'Brien 119
(Peter Bowen) *trckd ldrs: wkng whn hmpd 2 out* **8/1**[3]
4-11 **11** 3 1/4 **Dunaskin (IRE)**[37] 515 10-10-4 **120** (b) PaddyAspell 105
(Richard Guest) *chsd ldrs: pushed along 3rd: lost pl after 5th: in rr whn hmpd 2 out* **50/1**
6-22 **12** nk **Santa's Son (IRE)**[42] 627 10-10-8 **127** (t) AdamPogson(3) 112
(Charles Pogson) *t.k.h: in rr: hdwy on outside 5th: lost pl after next* **14/1**
31-1 **13** nk **Inventor (IRE)**[42] 627 5-11-12 **142** APMcCoy 128
(Donald McCain) *chsd ldrs: 5th whn nt fluent 5th: lost pl next* **4/1**[1]
2-12 **14** 47 **Astrolibra**[51] 488 6-10-1 **117** MattieBatchelor 59
(Mark H Tompkins) *j. poorly detached in last: t.o 5th* **50/1**
4-62 **P** **Nordwind (IRE)**[6] 958 9-9-6 **118** AdamWedge(10) —
(Evan Williams) *mid-div: j. slowly and lost pl 4th: reminders next: sn bhd: t.o whn p.u bef 2 out* **10/1**
600- **P** **Secret Tune**[147] 4154 6-11-3 **133** SamThomas —
(Tom George) *prom: j.rt 1st: lost pl and bhd 4th: p.u bef next* **28/1**
124- **F** **Trumpstoo (USA)**[17] 2266 4-10-0 **118** oh3 BrianHughes 107
(Richard Fahey) *mid-div: 8th whn fell 2 out* **28/1**

3m 57.4s (-9.30) **Going Correction** -0.25s/f (Good)
WFA 4 from 5yo+ 15lb **17 Ran SP% 124.1**
Speed ratings (Par 111): **111,102,101,100,99 98,95,95,95,94 92,92,92,70,— —,—**
toteswingers: 1&2 £27.20, 1&3 £78.90, 2&3 £105.00 CSF £233.53 CT £5391.96 TOTE £7.30: £2.10, £5.40, £5.00, £3.30; EX 157.70 TRIFECTA Not won..
Owner Skippy & The Partners **Bred** Kenilworth House Stud **Trained** Mollington, Oxon

FOCUS
After 6mm of overnight rain, the going was changed slightly to good all round. A hugely competitive handicap, where the pace seemed guaranteed to be strong with at least two strong-travelling front-runners taking part, and one of them made all. The remainder virtually never got involved at any stage, and many were labouring quite a way out.

NOTEBOOK
Australia Day(IRE) ◆, one of the habitual front-runners, who had been performing with credit on the Flat recently, including at Royal Ascot, was more or less left alone in front and sauntered home for an easy success. The only downside to this impressive performance will be the stiff rise in the weights he will probably get. (op 13-2 tchd 6-1)
Gloucester has run some fine races in competitive handicaps, but was beaten over 87 lengths on the Flat on his previous outing. Tucked away early as usual, he came through when rivals around him faltered, but the winner was long gone by then.
Stage Acclaim(IRE), beaten a neck over 2m on the Flat at Kempton most recently, kept plugging away and was bearing down on the runner-up after the final flight. (op 33-1)
Alazan(IRE), 5lb higher than when winning at Bangor in May, was towards the rear of the chasing bunch coming to the final bend, and was never going to get to Australia Day from that position.
Mohanad(IRE) ran two fair races on the Flat before coming to this, and appeared to run up to his best over hurdles. (op 28-1)
Tiger O'Toole(IRE), 9lb higher than his last win, his fourth victory in his sixth starts, travelled strongly under restraint but found little off the bridle. (op 7-1)
Conquisto had hardly done a thing wrong since going hurdling, but came into this contest off the back of a poor effort under a leading rider in a prestigious lady amateur riders' Flat handicap. He sat closest to Australia Day early without bothering him, but faded quickly coming to the second-last hurdle. (op 11-1 tchd 12-1)
Acambo(GER), blinkered for the first time, had plummeted 10lb since his return from a lengthy layoff due to some desperate efforts, and didn't do any better in this. (op 10-1)
Heron Bay looked interesting off a low weight when considering the best of his Flat form at the height of his powers. Making his handicap debut over hurdles, he was niggled along early and gave the impression he was not enjoying it for some reason. He had been reported to have had a breathing operation before his previous outing. (op 10-1 tchd 12-1)
Pure Faith(IRE), carrying a 5lb penalty, was taking a major step up in class for this and did not appear up to it, as he raced kindly on the heels of the leaders but failed to quicken when his jockey needed more.
Dunaskin(IRE) had found his niche in selling grade, Flat and jumps, so wasn't really entitled to be getting that close in this. (op 66-1)
Santa's Son(IRE) made a brief effort down the back straight after being held up that came to little. (tchd 16-1)
Inventor(IRE) has taken well to hurdling but was most disappointing here under top weight. His hurdling didn't seem fluent on occasions. Official explanation: trainer had no explanation for the poor form shown (op 5-1 tchd 7-2)
Astrolibra, making her handicap debut over hurdles, and back down in trip after her second at Wetherby, showed little interest and got detached after jumping sloppily.
Nordwind(IRE) shaped nicely at a long price at Stratford the previous weekend, but steadily lost ground down the back straight as the tempo lifted. Official explanation: trainer had no explanation for the poor form shown (tchd 9-1)
Secret Tune, off the track since late February and down in trip, has mainly struggled since a good spell of form in the spring of 2009 and was being pushed along here passing the winning post for the first time. He did not get much further before being pulled up. Official explanation: jockey said gelding never travelled (tchd 9-1)
Trumpstoo(USA) ran with plenty of credit in some juvenile hurdles before being found out in Grade 2 company. Given a break after that, he had been running on the Flat recently, without showing a great deal, but was staying on here when coming down two out. (tchd 9-1)

1018 TOTEEXACTA FLEXI BETTING JUVENILE HURDLE (8 hdls) 2m 1f
2:35 (2:36) (Class 3) 3-Y-O **£4,553** (£1,337; £668; £333)

Form — RPR
1 **Dance For Julie (IRE)**[34] 3-10-5 0 BarryKeniry 90+
(Ben Haslam) *t.k.h: trckd ldrs: led 4th: wnt wl clr appr 2 out: 17 l ahd whn mstke last: eased fnl 100yds* **2/1**[1]
25 **2** 14 **Sansili**[22] 836 3-10-7 0 DonalDevereux(5) 82
(Peter Bowen) *trckd ldrs: j. slowly 4th: outpcd 3 out: styd on fr 2 out: 4th last: tk modest 2nd towards fin* **15/2**
3 **3** 3/4 **Bring Sweets (IRE)**[22] 836 3-10-12 0 KeithMercer 80
(Brian Ellison) *hld up in rr: gd hdwy 3 out: 3rd whn hmpd appr next: wnt mod 2nd last: kpt on same pce* **12/1**
1 **4** 6 **Torran Sound**[22] 836 3-11-4 0 (b) FelixDeGiles 82
(James Eustace) *t.k.h: chsd ldr: wknd last* **8/1**
U0 **5** 3/4 **Pobs Trophy**[12] 836 3-10-12 0 (p) PaddyAspell 74
(Richard Guest) *prom: rdn 3 out: wknd appr last* **66/1**
6 6 **Septemberintherain**[89] 3-10-12 0 (v) JamieMoore 69
(Robert Mills) *w ldrs: 2nd whn hung rt appr 2 out: wknd last* **4/1**[2]
0P **7** 4 1/2 **A P Ling**[6] 960 3-10-5 0 PeterBuchanan 58
(Christopher Kellett) *in rr: sme hdwy appr 2 out: nvr on terms* **250/1**
0 **8** 6 **Teela**[22] 836 3-10-6 0 ow1 AndrewThornton 53
(Ben Haslam) *s.s: in rr: sme hdwy 2 out: nvr on terms* **33/1**
2 **9** 6 **Lady Pacha**[22] 836 3-10-5 0 (p) DougieCostello 47
(Tim Pitt) *sn pushed along: prom: lost pl 4th: n.d after* **6/1**[3]
10 6 **Urban Clubber**[14] 3-10-12 0 BrianHughes 48
(Howard Johnson) *chsd ldrs: hit 3rd: rdn 3 out: wknd appr next* **14/1**
11 19 **Securitisation (IRE)**[53] 3-10-12 0 PaulMoloney 31
(Barney Curley) *led: hdd 4th: lost pl appr 2 out* **16/1**
12 37 **Mini Max**[13] 3-10-5 0 MarkGrant —
(Brendan Duke) *nt jump wl in rr: bhd fr 4th: t.o 3 out* **33/1**
0 **13** 28 **High Holborn (IRE)**[17] 674 3-10-12 0 (v) TomScudamore —
(David Pipe) *nt jump wl in rr: bhd fr 4th: t.o 3 out* **16/1**
0 **P** **Romeos Girl**[22] 836 3-10-5 0 AlanO'Keeffe —
(Jennie Candlish) *s.s: in rr: bhd fr 4th: t.o whn p.u bef 2 out* **100/1**
P **Dance With Chance (IRE)**[37] 3-10-2 0 CharlieHuxley(3) —
(Alan King) *towards rr: blnd and rdr lost irons 5th: sn t.o: p.u bef 2 out* **20/1**

4m 9.30s (2.60) **Going Correction** -0.25s/f (Good) **15 Ran SP% 130.1**
Speed ratings (Par 104): **83,76,76,73,72 70,67,65,62,59 50,33,19,—,—**
toteswingers: 1&2 £6.40, 1&3 £6.50, 2&3 £18.00 CSF £18.63 TOTE £3.90: £1.60, £2.50, £3.20; EX 28.20.
Owner Mark James **Bred** Lynn Lodge Stud **Trained** Middleham Moor, N Yorks

FOCUS
Lots of runners for this juvenile hurdle but only one mattered from a long way out. The form is modest but the easy winner should go on to rate higher.

NOTEBOOK
Dance For Julie(IRE) ◆ held her form quite well at a low level on the Flat and was far too good for these on her hurdling debut. She travelled strongly and came well clear once her jockey asked for her to edge away. It will take a decent horse to lower her colours if she is kept on the go during the summer, and connections nominated a mares' race at Hereford in a couple of weeks as a possible target. (op 4-1 tchd 9-2 in a place)
Sansili did keep on quite well to deny Bring Sweets the runner-up spot. He will probably need a stiffer test of stamina considering the way he was off the bridle a long way out before making ground. (op 13-2)
Bring Sweets(IRE) made good progress from a rear position and looks sure to find a race of this nature in due course. (op 8-1)
Torran Sound, a winner over C&D on his hurdling debut, and in front of Bring Sweets and Sansili then, pulled much too hard early, so did well to finish where he did. (tchd 13-2)
Pobs Trophy probably ran to at least the mark he did last time behind Torran Sound but, as with that rival, was not in the same league as the winner. (op 50-1)
Septemberintherain is fair on the Flat and came from a stable well capable of getting a decent hurdler. He had his chance after racing prominently but did not look the easiest of rides once under pressure. (op 11-2 tchd 6-1)
Teela Official explanation: jockey said filly lost a shoe
Lady Pacha got mugged late on by Torran Sound last time but showed little enthusiasm in this from an early stage and was always behind. Official explanation: jockey said filly never travelled (op 5-1 tchd 9-2)
Securitisation(IRE) represented respected connections and enjoyed an easy lead until joined. He was not given a hard time then. (op 12-1)
Dance With Chance(IRE) seemed to be disappointing when in the care of Walter Swinburn for her Flat campaign and did not improve from a move to Alan King and hurdling. She showed nothing. (op 16-1)

1019 TOTETRIFECTA FLEXI BETTING H'CAP HURDLE (10 hdls) 2m 5f
3:05 (3:09) (Class 2) (0-140,138) 4-Y-0+ **£8,131** (£2,387; £1,193; £596)

Form — RPR
0F4P **1** **Mumbles Pier (IRE)**[24] 828 5-9-9 **112** oh2 DonalDevereux(5) 115+
(Peter Bowen) *chsd ldrs: led after 3 out: hld on gamely* **28/1**
2-01 **2** 1 1/2 **To Arms**[6] 954 8-11-0 **131** 7ex (t) DavidBass(5) 132
(Lawney Hill) *hld up in mid-div: hdwy to chse ldrs 3 out: wnt cl 2nd appr 2 out: no ex last 100yds* **11/2**[2]
0-33 **3** 1 1/4 **Akarshan (IRE)**[42] 627 5-10-2 **124** AdamWedge(10) 123
(Evan Williams) *in tch: chsng ldrs whn hit 3 out: styd on same pce run-in* **8/1**[3]
1-01 **4** 1 3/4 **Breaking Storm (IRE)**[20] 846 7-10-6 **123** JamesHalliday(5) 120
(Kate Walton) *in rr: hdwy 3 out: styd on wl fr next: nt rch ldrs* **14/1**
00-2 **5** 1/2 **Rajeh (IRE)**[29] 633 7-11-8 **134** TomO'Brien 131
(John Spearing) *chsd ldrs: styd on same pce appr last* **9/1**
4/21 **6** 3 **Ring Bo Ree (IRE)**[44] 601 7-10-3 **115** RichardJohnson 111+
(Tom George) *hld up in rr: mstke 5th: hdwy to trck ldrs 3 out: wknd run-in* **5/2**[1]
1-45 **7** 3 1/4 **Agente Romano (USA)**[34] 736 5-10-1 **116** DPFahy(3) 109+
(Evan Williams) *chsd ldrs: mstke 5th: wknd last* **11/1**

The Form Book, Raceform Ltd, Compton, RG20 6NL

-101 **8** *7* **Son Of Flicka**[42] 633 6-11-12 **138** .... GrahamLee 123
(Donald McCain) *mid-div: drvn 5th: outpcd 7th: sn lost pl* **11/1**

0230 **9** *2 1/2* **Corkage (IRE)**[17] 866 7-10-11 **123** ....(p) PeterBuchanan 105
(Lucinda Russell) *in rr: sn pushed along: bhd fr 5th* **25/1**

1/0- **10** *3* **Ursis (FR)**[45] 5113 9-11-4 **130** .... KeithMercer 110
(Steve Gollings) *led tl after 3 out: wknd next* **20/1**

P40- **11** *9* **Tilt**[94] 5182 8-10-13 **125** .... JamieMoore 97
(Brian Ellison) *in rr: hdwy 3 out: sn chsng ldrs: wknd appr next* **14/1**

0000 **12** *6* **Raslan**[32] 756 7-11-0 **129** ....(v) DannyCook(3) 95
(David Pipe) *w ldr: drvn 6th: lost pl after next* **11/1**

0-10 **13** *91* **Two Miles West (IRE)**[24] 830 9-10-11 **123** .... APMcCoy 7
(Jonjo O'Neill) *in rr: sn pushed along: bhd fr 5th: t.o 3 out* **14/1**

20-0 **P** **Special Envoy (FR)**[42] 633 8-11-0 **129** .... RichardKilloran(3) —
(Nicky Henderson) *chsd ldrs: mstke 4th: sn p.u: fatally injured* **20/1**

5m 9.20s (0.40) **Going Correction** -0.25s/f (Good) **14** Ran SP% **126.9**
Speed ratings (Par 109): **89,88,87,87,87 85,84,82,81,79 76,74,39,—**
toteswingers: 1&2 £25.90, 1&3 £53.90, 2&3 £32.00 CSF £179.89 CT £1395.93 TOTE £33.60: £7.90, £2.30, £2.70; EX 201.30 TRIFECTA Not won..
Owner Gwilym J Morris **Bred** Miss Carmel Whelan **Trained** Little Newcastle, Pembrokes

FOCUS
The early pace did not seem too strong, which is probably why a whole host of horses had a chance coming round the final bend. The form is nothing special but the winner is rated back to his novice level.

NOTEBOOK
Mumbles Pier(IRE), back over hurdles after moderate jumping over fences had halted his progress in that sphere, was never far away and showed plenty of determination under pressure off a low weight. His stable is in cracking form, but there was little to point you his way for this on all of his efforts since taking a novice hurdle last September. (op 25-1)
To Arms, carrying a 7lb penalty for his Southwell success, a first victory since landing a novice hurdle for another stable at this course in June 2007, moved up going quite well but hit two out. He kept on but was readily held. (op 6-1 tchd 13-2)
Akarshan(IRE), a dual course winner, has never really promised to stay this far in the past but kept on respectably. (op 9-1)
Breaking Storm(IRE), the winner of two of his last three starts, and 8lb higher than his success at Uttoxeter, got badly outpaced heading to the home bend but kept on quite well once in the home straight. (op 12-1)
Rajeh(IRE), beaten a narrow margin by Son Of Flicka when last seen over hurdles, ran his race and is the solid form marker. (op 15-2)
Ring Bo Ree(IRE), 12lb higher after winning by a couple of lengths from an 110-rated horse, was forced to sit in behind a wall of horses once he started to make up ground from the rear. It may have been a different story had the rider been able to kick on and get an advantage entering the home straight, but he did have plenty of room coming to two out, which he hit, and one got the impression that the rise in the weights caught him out. (op 4-1)

1020 TOTESPORT.COM SUMMER PLATE H'CAP CHASE (LISTED RACE) (13 fncs 1 omitted) 2m 6f 110y
3:35 (3:41) (Class 1) (0-150,146) 4-Y-0+
£34,206 (£12,834; £6,426; £3,204; £1,608; £804)

Form RPR

3-11 **1** **Grand Slam Hero (IRE)**[46] 567 9-10-9 **129** ....(t) GrahamLee 141+
(Nigel Twiston-Davies) *hld up: hmpd 4th: stdy hdwy 10th: chsng ldrs and shkn up appr 3 out: led appr last: rdn rt out* **9/1**

2111 **2** *1 1/4* **Putney Bridge**[30] 772 8-10-11 **131** ....(tp) TomO'Brien 140
(Keith Goldsworthy) *chsd ldr: led omitted 4 out: hdd appr last: kpt on wl: no ex last 100yds* **10/1**

1F-1 **3** *6* **King Troy (IRE)**[49] 524 8-11-12 **146** .... JackDoyle 153+
(Alan King) *chsd ldrs 5th: 3rd whn hit 3 out: kpt on same pce run-in* **9/1**

-2F4 **4** *2 1/2* **Silverburn (IRE)**[39] 685 9-10-8 **128** .... PaulMoloney 130
(Evan Williams) *mid-div: hmpd 4th: hdwy to chse ldrs 3 out: outpcd between last 2: styd on wl last 150yds* **18/1**

41-1 **5** *1/2* **Tempsford (USA)**[22] 839 10-10-10 **130** ....(t) APMcCoy 131
(Jonjo O'Neill) *in rr: pushed along 8th: hdwy 10th: chsng ldrs 3 out: one pce fr next* **5/1**[1]

FF-0 **6** *4* **Pablo Du Charmil (FR)**[77] 98 9-11-11 **145** ....(t) TomScudamore 143
(David Pipe) *chsd ldrs: chal 3 out: wknd run-in* **7/1**[3]

PP-0 **7** *20* **Nostringsattached (IRE)**[34] 735 9-10-12 **132** ....(t) SamThomas 111
(Jonjo O'Neill) *in rr: hmpd 4th: hdwy 10th: lost pl appr 3 out: sn bhd* **40/1**

P-13 **8** *3* **Valley Ride (IRE)**[20] 844 10-10-7 **132** ....(p) DonalDevereux(5) 109
(Peter Bowen) *prom: hit 5th: lost pl 10th* **6/1**[2]

2-3P **9** *12* **Stan (NZ)**[6] 959 11-11-4 **138** .... AidanColeman 104
(Venetia Williams) *chsd ldrs: lost pl 10th: sn bhd* **28/1**

F-1P **10** *17* **Keepitsecret (IRE)**[20] 844 9-10-9 **132** ....(p) RichieMcLernon(3) 83
(Jonjo O'Neill) *mid-div: hdwy 10th: sn chsng ldrs: lost pl appr 3 out: sn bhd* **33/1**

050/ **11** *21* **Ballyagran (IRE)**[658] 1512 10-10-3 **130** .... MrTomDavid(7) 62
(Tim Vaughan) *mstkes: in tch: lost pl 8th: sn bhd* **20/1**

P1-2 **P** **Brooklyn Brownie (IRE)**[20] 844 11-11-1 **140** .... JamesHalliday(5) —
(Malcolm Jefferson) *last away: in rr: struggling fr 5th: bhd fr 8th: t.o whn p.u after 10th* **16/1**

FP0- **P** **Seymour Weld**[238] 2426 10-10-11 **134** .... AdamPogson(3) —
(Charles Pogson) *led: hdd omitted 4 out: sn wknd: p.u bef 3 out* **50/1**

12F- **P** **War Of The World (IRE)**[273] 1784 8-11-4 **138** .... RichardJohnson —
(Tim Vaughan) *in rr: bhd fr 5th: t.o whn p.u after 10th* **5/1**[1]

42-1 **P** **Polyfast (FR)**[42] 636 7-10-9 **129** .... AndrewTinkler —
(Nicky Henderson) *hdwy to chse ldrs 7th: 3rd whn hmpd and mstke 9th: sn lost pl: t.o whn p.u bef 3 out* **8/1**

21 **U** **Picaroon**[51] 491 6-10-13 **138** .... DeanColeman(5) —
(Tim Vaughan) *chsd ldrs: blnd and uns rdr 4th* **14/1**

5m 20.7s (-25.30) **Going Correction** -0.825s/f (Firm) course record **16** Ran SP% **133.7**
Speed ratings (Par 111): **111,110,108,107,107 106,99,98,93,87 80,—,—,—,— —**
toteswingers: 1&2 £25.30, 1&3 £24.30, 2&3 £26.10 CSF £100.47 CT £868.42 TOTE £12.30: £3.60, £2.90, £2.60, £5.00; EX 88.70 Trifecta £1046.50 Part won. Pool: £1,414.27 - 0.20 winning units..
Owner Walters Plant Hire Ltd **Bred** Lady Rathdonnell **Trained** Naunton, Gloucs

FOCUS
As is always the case, this showpiece event was fiercely contested by a lot of seemingly in-form horses and the winning time smashed a course record that had stood for over 30 years - although it has to be noted that the fourth-last fence on the final circuit was omitted due to an injured jockey on the landing side. Rock-solid form and the first two are progressive.

NOTEBOOK
Grand Slam Hero(IRE) ◆ was winning his third race in a row since rejoining Nigel Twiston-Davies - he is now unbeaten in five starts for that trainer. Another 4lb higher, he was slightly hampered early by a faller but arrived on the scene going ominously well before finding enough once in front to win tidily. He is certainly in the right hands to keep the momentum going and he may head to the Galway Plate. (op 8-1)
Putney Bridge has risen considerably through the weights for his progressive form and he ran a belter after being close up throughout. He is bound to get raised again for this, but has a fine attitude and should hold his own in good handicaps. (op 11-1 tchd 12-1)
King Troy(IRE) ◆, fourth in this race last season off a 12lb lower mark, made a good comeback after a lengthy absence at Stratford recently, winning by almost two lengths once getting to the front. He moved well just in behind but looked anchored by his weight as the first two pressed on. This was a decent performance and he has plenty of time to keep improving. (op 8-1)
Silverburn(IRE), back over fences after a few runs over hurdles, was undeniably well treated on his best form with Paul Nicholls and kept on in good style. (op 22-1 tchd 16-1)
Tempsford(USA), as is becoming usual, made the champion jockey work from a long way out. He was denied fourth close home. (op 13-2 tchd 7-1)
Pablo Du Charmil(FR) has some classy form when at his best, and shaped well in this before a combination of weight and distance got the better of him. (op 8-1)
Nostringsattached(IRE), last year's winner, had his chance but got outpaced off the final bend.
Valley Ride(IRE) didn't always look too happy on the outside of the field and lost ground quickly down the back straight on the final circuit. He may not be a completely straightforward character. (op 13-2)
Keepitsecret(IRE), runner-up a year ago, was held up and never got on terms.
Brooklyn Brownie(IRE), runner-up in the Summer National in late June, jumped away slowly and was never a factor. Official explanation: jockey said gelding never travelled (op 17-2)
War Of The World(IRE), described as a class act with a hell of an engine by his trainer, was returning from a long break after injuring himself at Cheltenham - he had also reportedly suffered from stomach ulcers this summer. Tim Vaughan had said prior to the race that he would have preferred another month to get him ready for this, so he can be given another chance. (op 17-2)
Polyfast(FR) seemed to be going well but dropped away alarmingly after hitting the ninth. (op 17-2)

1021 B EYRE & SON LTD FORD NOVICES' HURDLE (8 hdls) 2m 1f
4:10 (4:12) (Class 4) 4-Y-0+ **£3,252** (£955; £477; £238)

Form RPR

1-12 **1** **Sir Frank (IRE)**[42] 624 5-11-5 115 .... BrianHughes 112
(Alan Swinbank) *led: narrowly hdd last: styd on gamely to ld last 50yds: all out* **11/8**[1]

S-45 **2** *nk* **Society Venue**[20] 842 5-10-12 0 .... TomScudamore 104
(Michael Scudamore) *hld up wl in tch: hdwy to trck ldrs 3 out: chal next: slt ld whn hit last: hdd and no ex clsng stages* **7/1**[3]

31 **3** *hd* **Russian George (IRE)**[20] 842 4-11-3 115 .... KeithMercer 109
(Steve Gollings) *trckd ldrs: 1 l down whn n.m.r last: swtchd lft and styd on: no ex last 50yds* **6/4**[2]

U **4** *18* **Royal Entourage**[36] 712 5-10-5 0 .... KyleJames(7) 86
(Philip Kirby) *t.k.h: trckd ldrs: outpcd 3 out: lost pl appr 2 out: hung lft run-in* **16/1**

5 *3 3/4* **Play To Win (IRE)**[19] 4-10-7 0 .... TommyPhelan(3) 80
(Paul Midgley) *j.rt 1st: j. slowly 3rd: in tch: outpcd 3 out: lost pl appr next out* **33/1**

6 *1/2* **Loyal Knight (IRE)**[23] 5-10-12 0 .... AndrewThornton 82
(Paul Midgley) *nt fluent: trckd ldrs: lost pl appr 2 out* **40/1**

60-6 **7** *3* **Not A Bob (IRE)**[79] 62 5-10-12 0 .... APMcCoy 79
(Jonjo O'Neill) *chsd wnr: lost pl appr 2 out* **7/1**[3]

0-06 **8** *1 1/4* **Carrifran (IRE)**[11] 916 5-10-0 0 .... JamesHalliday(5) 71
(Malcolm Jefferson) *t.k.h in rr: hdwy and prom 3 out: outpcd and lost pl appr next* **40/1**

4m 16.3s (9.60) **Going Correction** -0.25s/f (Good)
WFA 4 from 5yo+ 15lb **8** Ran SP% **120.8**
Speed ratings (Par 105): **67,66,66,58,56 56,54,54**
toteswingers: 1&2 £3.70, 1&3 £1.10, 2&3 £2.70 CSF £12.63 TOTE £2.70: £1.10, £1.80, £1.10; EX 13.70.
Owner Frank Hanson **Bred** Mrs G Galvin **Trained** Melsonby, N Yorks

FOCUS
Form wise, this result means very little, as they went no pace early and sprinted up the home straight. The form is rated around the winner and third.

NOTEBOOK
Sir Frank(IRE) struggled to get home at Hexham last time after travelling well (the horse who beat him that day has won since) but, after making the running here, he responded well to pressure and regained the lead in the latter stages. His future is surely now in handicaps. (op 13-8 tchd 9-4)
Society Venue finished well behind Russian George last time but reversed that form here. It was a decent ride by Tom Scudamore to have him well positioned, and the horse appeared certain to win before tiring in the latter stages. This is not a result to be trusted but he can win a minor novice somewhere if running to this sort of level again. (op 12-1)
Russian George(IRE) was very useful on the Flat and, after showing promise on his hurdling debut, got off the mark at Uttoxeter. He seemed to get outpaced the most of the leading three when the tempo increased but was staying on well in the final 50 yards. (op 6-5 tchd 11-10)
Royal Entourage showed good form when trained in Ireland, but there has been little sign of that ability since being sold out of the Ger Lyons stable. (op 18-1)

1022 GEOFFREY & MOLLIE BOOTH MEMORIAL NOVICES' H'CAP CHASE (14 fncs) 2m 6f 110y
4:45 (4:45) (Class 4) (0-110,108) 4-Y-0+ **£3,252** (£955; £477; £238)

Form RPR

-502 **1** **Ballyvesey (IRE)**[12] 909 5-11-9 **105** ....(p) TomO'Brien 118+
(Peter Bowen) *trckd ldrs: wnt 2nd 10th: drvn next: led appr 2 out: rdn out: sddle slipped* **2/1**[2]

-500 **2** *7* **Rokinhorsescience (FR)**[11] 919 6-10-12 **94** ....(b) APMcCoy 102+
(Jonjo O'Neill) *led: qcknd 8th: hdd appr 2 out: kpt on one pce* **9/2**[3]

-420 **3** *5* **Feeling Peckish (USA)**[47] 549 6-9-7 **82** oh10 ....(t) PeterHatton(7) 85
(Michael Chapman) *chsd ldrs: outpcd 9th: rallied and modest 4th whn bmpd 3 out: one pce and j.rt last 2* **16/1**

1341 **4** *7* **Mutual Respect (IRE)**[6] 952 8-10-11 **103** .... AdamWedge(10) 101
(Evan Williams) *w ldr: drvn 8th: 3rd and wl btn whn j.lft 3 out: wknd run-in: eased towards fin: fatally injured* **11/8**[1]

2356 **5** *79* **Indian Pipe Dream (IRE)**[18] 854 8-11-12 **108** ....(tp) KeithMercer 33
(Steve Gollings) *nt jump wl: chsd ldrs: reminders 3rd and sn losing tch: sn drvn along: prom 5th: dropped out 7th and reluctant: t.o 4 out* **7/1**

5m 33.7s (-12.30) **Going Correction** -0.825s/f (Firm) **5** Ran SP% **112.0**
Speed ratings (Par 105): **88,85,83,81,53**
CSF £11.26 TOTE £2.70: £1.40, £2.90; EX 10.50.
Owner Roddy Owen & Paul Fullagar **Bred** Kevin Neville **Trained** Little Newcastle, Pembrokes

FOCUS
A dire contest which took little winning and has been rated through the third.

NOTEBOOK
Ballyvesey(IRE) was well beaten on his return to chasing at Newton Abbot last time, but almost couldn't fail to win this once handed a winning opportunity. He shapes like and out-and-out stayer in the making. (op 9-4 tchd 15-8 and 5-2 in a place)
Rokinhorsescience(FR), back up in trip and with blinkers back on, has been disappointing judged on his pedigree but was given a good chance to get things going here after being allowed to lead. However, he was already starting to falter when mistakes at the fences up the home straight started to creep in. (op 11-2 tchd 6-1)

Feeling Peckish(USA), who was running from well out of the weights, plugged on at the one pace from the home bend. (tchd 18-1)
Mutual Respect(IRE) looked thrown in here after winning a conditionals' chase last time, as he was unpenalised for winning by 28 lengths. However, he came under strong pressure in the back straight on their final circuit before suffering a sadly fatal injury late on. (op 6-5 tchd 11-10)
Indian Pipe Dream(IRE) had been disappointing on his last two outings, but was still rated high enough to be top weight. He lost interest early and made no impression at any stage. (tchd 15-2)

1023 TOTESWINGER FLEXI BETTING H'CAP CHASE (12 fncs) 2m 2f
5:20 (5:20) (Class 3) (0-120,120) 4-Y-0+ **£5,854** (£1,719; £859; £429)

Form RPR
F-44 **1** **Viable**22 838 8-11-1 **116** MissGAndrews(7) 125
(Pam Sly) *hdwy to chse ldrs 5th: led after 4 out: styd on wl run-in* **14/1**
U0-6 **2** *3 ¼* **High Bird Humphrey**64 316 11-11-2 **117** (p) MrSFMagee(7) 124
(Simon West) *slowly away in ragged s: hdwy 5th: chal 3 out: styd on same pce run-in* **12/1**
5-12 **3** *5* **Seeyaaj**39 676 10-11-5 **113** (t) PeterBuchanan 115
(Lucinda Russell) *mid-div: hdwy 4 out: wnt modest 3rd next: one pce* **9/1**
14-1 **4** *1 ½* **Elite Land**42 634 7-11-12 **120** KeithMercer 120
(Brian Ellison) *last away in v ragged s: bhd: hdwy 4 out: kpt on: nrst fin* **5/1**3
20P- **5** *1 ¼* **Blast The Past**89 5275 8-10-11 **105** ChristianWilliams 104
(Dai Burchell) *chsd ldng pair: one pce fr 3 out* **18/1**
6420 **6** *¾* **Wee Forbees (IRE)**13 891 8-10-4 **98** DenisO'Regan 98
(Michael Easterby) *mstke 5th: in rr: hdwy appr 3 out: hit 2 out: one pce* **8/1**
6562 **7** *18* **Nesnaas (USA)**13 891 9-10-0 **94** (bt) GrahamLee 78
(Mark Rimell) *in rr: j. slowly and bhd 6th: last whn blnd last* **4/1**2
2253 **8** *4 ½* **Mister Benedictine**6 954 7-11-10 **118** (t) MarkGrant 96
(Brendan Duke) *in rr: sme hdwy 5th: wknd 4 out* **10/1**
3 **9** *8* **Daliarose (FR)**12 910 4-10-3 **112** TomScudamore 75
(David Pipe) *w ldr: j.lft: led and mstke 7th: hdd after 4 out: sn wknd* **7/1**
-223 **P** **Viper**13 890 8-11-9 **117** (b) SamThomas —
(Dr Richard Newland) *led: hdd 7th: nt run on and sn lost pl: t.o 4 out: p.u bef next* **3/1**1

4m 17.2s (-17.80) **Going Correction** -0.825s/f (Firm)
WFA 4 from 7yo+ 2lb 10 Ran SP% **124.0**
Speed ratings (Par 107): **106,104,102,101,101 100,92,90,87,—**
toteswingers: 1&2 £55.40, 1&3 £46.90, 2&3 £35.70 CSF £172.54 CT £1618.32 TOTE £22.00: £5.20, £3.80, £4.00; EX 110.10 Place 6 £247.91, Place 5 £50.75.
Owner Thorney Racing Club **Bred** Mrs H B Raw **Trained** Thorney, Cambs

FOCUS
This was run at a scorching pace and the form looks solid enough, with the second setting the level. The winning time was a new course record.

NOTEBOOK
Viable, down 2f in trip, was settled off the pace and went a gallop that suited him, rather than getting involved in the speed duel in front. He got to the front coming to the final bend and kept on going to win off a career-high jumps mark.
High Bird Humphrey, absent since May, came away with the winner but didn't seem to show the same heart under pressure as Viable when the chips were down. (op 16-1)
Seeyaaj won this race in 2008 off a 1lb higher mark but was never within striking distance here. (op 7-1)
Elite Land, raised 9lb for winning over 2m at Worcester, is usually much better going left-handed and gave himself no chance of being involved at the end here after being well off the pace which, admittedly, is his usual racing style. (op 4-1)
Blast The Past, having her first start for this trainer after changing hands for 800gns, appeared to run a bit better than her final position suggests and is one to keep a close eye on. (op 20-1 tchd 16-1)
Nesnaas(USA), who won this race off a 10lb higher mark last season, appeared to lose interest at an early stage. Official explanation: jockey said gelding never travelled (op 9-2 tchd 7-2)
Daliarose(FR), a diminutive filly who had been well beaten over 2m6f on her first start for this stable over hurdles, pais for disputing a fast pace. (op 9-2)
Viper, taking a big drop in distance, was continually harried by Daliarose, almost certainly resulting in the pair going off a stride too quickly. (op 9-2)
T/Plt: £407.90 to a £1 stake. Pool: £90,147.27. 161.30 winning tickets. T/Qpdt: £29.10 to a £1 stake. Pool: £5,839.18. 148.35 winning tickets. WG

908 NEWTON ABBOT (L-H)
Sunday, July 18

OFFICIAL GOING: Good (good to firm in places; 8.0)
Wind: virtually nil Weather: sunny

1024 NEWTONABBOTRACING.COM JUVENILE HURDLE (8 hdls) 2m 1f
2:30 (2:30) (Class 4) 3-Y-0 **£3,382** (£993; £496; £248)

Form RPR
3614 **1** **Gulf Punch**7 960 3-10-9 0 (p) PeterToole(3) 90+
(Milton Harris) *chsd ldrs: trckd ldr after 3 out: led gng wl bef next: j.lft 2 out: drvn between last 2: styd on flat* **5/1**3
2 *1 ½* **Sassanian (IRE)**29 3-10-12 0 APMcCoy 90+
(Tim Vaughan) *j.lft and many mstkes: chsd ldr tl j.v.slowly and lost pl 4th: rdn and hdwy after next: chsd wnr and n.m.r 2 out: swtchd rt and out-j. last: one pce flat* **7/4**1
5 **3** *3 ¾* **Joe Rua (USA)**7 960 3-10-12 0 ColinBolger 83
(John Ryan) *j.lft: in tch in midfield: hdwy to chse ldrs after 4th: chsd ldng pair and drvn whn j.lft 2 out: btn bef last* **25/1**
U **4** *2 ¾* **Sefton Park**40 674 3-10-12 0 (p) JimmyMcCarthy 79
(Charles Egerton) *in tch in midfield: mstke and reminders 3rd: chsd ldrs after next: drvn and btn bef 2 out* **14/1**
12 **5** *17* **Lucky Quay (IRE)**34 743 3-11-5 0 (b) TomScudamore 71
(David Pipe) *led: pushed along after: j. slowly next: drvn and hdd after 3 out: fdd tamely bef next* **3/1**2
6 *5* **Brave Talk**57 3-10-12 0 DavidDennis 57
(Nigel Hawke) *hld up in rr: hdwy bef 5th: chsd ldrs and rdn after 3 out: wknd rapidly bef next* **50/1**
U **7** *62* **Dinkie Short**40 674 3-10-12 0 (p) DarylJacob —
(Ben De Haan) *t.k.h: chsd ldr 2nd tl after 3 out: dropped out rapidly and t.o fr next* **15/2**
P **Midnight Uno**370 3-10-7 0 (p) TomO'Connor(5) —
(Bill Turner) *nt jump wl: bhd: rdn and lost tch rapidly after 4th: t.o whn j. slowly 5th and 3 out: p.u 2 out* **66/1**
P **Rainsborough**18 3-10-5 0 AnthonyFreeman(7) —
(Sean Curran) *a in rr: rdn and lost tch after 4th: j. slowly next: t.o whn p.u 2 out* **16/1**
P **Miracle Wish (IRE)**74 3-9-12 0 MarkQuinlan(7) —
(Bernard Scriven) *a bhd: hmpd 4th: lost tch rapidly bef next: wl t.o whn p.u 2 out* **80/1**
U **P** **Lady Hetherington**23 836 3-10-2 0 EamonDehdashti(3) —
(Gary Brown) *t.k.h: in tch in midfield: rdn along and struggling after 4th: t.o whn p.u 2 out* **50/1**
F **P** **Superhoops**19 851 3-10-9 0 CharlieStudd(3) —
(Stuart Howe) *plld v hrd: hld up in tch tl stopped to nil after 3rd: t.o whn p.u after next* **100/1**

4m 3.30s (-2.40) **Going Correction** -0.725s/f (Firm) **12** Ran SP% **113.8**
Speed ratings (Par 102): **76,75,73,72,64 61,32,—,—,— —,—**
toteswingers:1&2:£1.10, 1&3:£10.30, 2&3:£13.70 CSF £13.61 TOTE £5.10: £2.10, £1.30, £4.10; EX 14.30.
Owner John Gwynne **Bred** Brook Stud Bloodstock Ltd **Trained** Herridge, Wiltshire

FOCUS
A typically low-grade juvenile novice hurdle which is unlikely to produce many winners. The winner was back to something like her best.

NOTEBOOK
Gulf Punch won a claimer at Stratford two starts ago and was the most experienced runner in the field. She put that to good use here and showed a willing attitude to score. She, however, has now won two races so following up under a double penalty would be difficult. (op 11-2 tchd 6-1)
Sassanian(IRE) had been placed in his last three starts in sellers and claimers on the Flat but gave the impression that he was not enjoying his hurdling debut. It was only the persistence of his rider that got him so close. He is likely to need to drop into plating class to win over hurdles though. (op 6-4)
Joe Rua(USA) jumped poorly when well beaten on debut and his jumping again was not up to standard. He is likely to struggle over hurdles in future. (tchd 20-1)
Sefton Park unseated his rider on hurdling debut and again his jumping looked poor. The fact he has worn headgear in his two hurdling starts to date is not encouraging either. (tchd 16-1)
Lucky Quay(IRE) won on his hurdling debut but as he did at Sedgefield last time looked less than willing. He also sports headgear and is one to be wary of. (op 11-4 tchd 7-2)
Dinkie Short came in for support beforehand but he was a clear non-stayer. (op 11-1)
Superhoops Official explanation: jockey said saddle slipped

1025 HAPPY BIRTHDAY CATH KING BEGINNERS' CHASE (13 fncs) 2m 110y
3:00 (3:00) (Class 5) 4-Y-0+ **£2,862** (£840; £420; £209)

Form RPR
0-22 **1** **Classic Swain (USA)**45 594 5-11-8 0 (bt) APMcCoy 122+
(Paul Nicholls) *nt fluent: chsd ldr: pushed along 7th: upsides ldr and mstke 10th: rdn to ld narrowly bef 2 out: mstke last: a jst doing enough flat* **8/11**1
2016 **2** *½* **Intac (IRE)**13 912 8-11-8 0 JoeTizzard 118
(Colin Tizzard) *led: rdn along and hdd bef 2 out: ev ch whn mstke last: unable qck and hld whn n.m.r towards fin* **6/1**3
66 **3** *19* **Diaco (IRE)**14 889 6-11-8 0 WillKennedy 99
(Jonjo O'Neill) *t.k.h: hld up in tch tl lost tch qckly on ldrs 7th: no ch fr next: wnt modest 3rd 10th: nvr threatened ldng pair* **22/1**
16-2 **4** *5* **Kickahead (USA)**11 934 8-11-8 0 (t) DougieCostello 99+
(Ian Williams) *t.k.h: hld up in tch: trckd ldng pair 5th tl blnd bdly 7th: sn lost tch w ldrs and j. slowly next: no ch after* **5/2**2
1P/0 **P** **King Gabriel (IRE)**49 534 8-11-5 0 (t) PeterToole(3) —
(Barry Brennan) *t.k.h: hld up in tch: nt fluent 5th: lost tch rapidly 7th: t.o whn j.lft and hit rail 9th: p.u next* **25/1**

3m 58.4s (-8.10) **Going Correction** -0.525s/f (Firm) **5** Ran SP% **109.0**
Speed ratings (Par 103): **98,97,88,86,—**
CSF £5.54 TOTE £1.60: £1.10, £2.80; EX 5.20.
Owner The Stewart Family **Bred** Ecurie Du Haras De Meautry **Trained** Ditcheat, Somerset

FOCUS
An ordinary novice chase. The winner is rated 12lb off his best.

NOTEBOOK
Classic Swain(USA) had finished runner-up on his last two chasing starts but was forced home by McCoy. He is not the most resolute but he clearly has plenty of ability and is capable of better than what he showed today. He is likely to be better in a big-field handicap and is now likely to come back to this venue for a novice handicap chase in two weeks' time. (op 10-11 tchd Evens)
Intac(IRE) had previously only shown form in selling company over hurdles. In his previous chasing attempts he had jumped poorly but he was more fluent today. He still has a questionable attitude and the form should be read with a degree of caution. (op 8-1)
Diaco(IRE) was having his third run back after a long absence and was not given a hard time once his chance had gone. He is capable of better and it is likely he will show his true colours in handicap company. (op 14-1)
Kickahead(USA) was second on his chasing debut last time but made a bad blunder at the seventh when nearly unseating his rider. He was not given a hard time though and is clearly capable of better. (tchd 2-1)

1026 EMMA'S HEN PARTY H'CAP HURDLE (8 hdls) 2m 3f
3:30 (3:30) (Class 3) (0-135,131) 4-Y-0+ **£6,395** (£1,930; £994; £526)

Form RPR
6-12 **1** **There's No Panic (IRE)**49 530 5-10-1 **111** MrRMahon(5) 129+
(Paul Nicholls) *chsd ldng pair tl wnt 2nd 5th: led on bit after 3 out: drew clr bef next: easily* **5/2**2
-216 **2** *18* **Saltagioo (ITY)**35 733 6-10-9 **117** (t) PeterToole(3) 118+
(Milton Harris) *racd keenly: chsd ldr tl led 5th: hdd after 3 out: sn rdn and wl btn whn hit 2 out* **7/1**
1-B3 **3** *21* **Tzora**18 866 5-10-9 **114** (t) RhysFlint 93
(Philip Hobbs) *hld up in last pair: hdwy and trckd ldrs after 5th: pushed along and racd awkwardly after 6th: sn lost tch w ldng pair and wl btn fr 3 out* **85/40**1
0F/0 **4** *29* **Quaddick Lake (IRE)**21 846 7-10-6 **111** TomScudamore 61
(David Pipe) *led tl 5th: rdn and dropped out tamely bef 6th: no ch fr 3 out* **5/1**3
23-5 **R** **Deadline (UAE)**14 888 6-10-2 **107** (b) JohnnyFarrelly —
(Alison Thorpe) *ref to r: tk no part* **5/1**3
524- **P** **Procas De Thaix (FR)**96 5176 7-10-6 **116** TomO'Connor(5) —
(James Frost) *a in rr: nt fluent 3rd: lost tch qckly after 5th: wl bhd whn p.u and dismntd last* **14/1**

4m 16.4s (-17.50) **Going Correction** -0.725s/f (Firm) **6** Ran SP% **113.1**
Speed ratings (Par 107): **107,99,90,78,—,—**
toteswingers:1&2:£5.10, 1&3:£1.10, 2&3:£4.40 CSF £19.58 TOTE £3.00: £1.70, £3.70; EX 17.90.
Owner The Stewart Family **Bred** J R Weston **Trained** Ditcheat, Somerset

FOCUS
Another moderate summer handicap hurdle where the form is not strong. The winner produced a big step forward.

NOTEBOOK
There's No Panic(IRE) scored at Plumpton in May and followed up that victory here in easy style under the capable Ryan Mahon. He is likely to be met with a stiff rise for this and would not be a certain winner next time out as everything fell his way here. (op 3-1)

Saltagioo(ITY) was a winner two starts ago over hurdles but he raced too keenly over this longer trip here. Dropped back in trip he could be a force, possibly back in novice company. (tchd 6-1)
Tzora finished weakly at Worcester last time and he gave up as soon as he came under pressure here. The tongue-tie made little difference and he never looked at ease and is one to treat with caution. (op 5-2 tchd 11-4)
Quaddick Lake(IRE) gave up as soon as he was taken on for the lead and although in the past he has shown ability he looks one to be wary of. (op 7-2 tchd 6-1)
Deadline(UAE) was withdrawn at Stratford last time because he did not line up and he planted himself today and refused to race. His temperament is clearly getting the better of him. (op 13-2)
Procas De Thaix(FR) never looked at ease and was dismounted before jumping the last and removed by horse ambulance. Official explanation: jockey said gelding was lame (tchd 12-1)

1027 KINGSCLERE RACING CLUB H'CAP CHASE (20 fncs) 3m 2f 110y
4:05 (4:05) (Class 4) (0-110,106) 4-Y-O+ **£3,802** (£1,123; £561; £280; £140)

Form RPR
P-F0 **1** **Strong Coffee**[31] 769 8-11-6 **100**..........(b[1]) LeightonAspell 114+
(Oliver Sherwood) *led tl mstke and hdd 2nd: led again 4th: mde rest and j.w after: rdn and jnd between last 2: styd on wl u.p flat: drvn out* **25/1**

-131 **2** *1 3/4* **Rifleman (IRE)**[18] 868 10-10-13 **98**..........(t) GilesHawkins[(5)] 109
(Richard Lee) *in tch: hdwy to chse wnr 14th: drvn bef 2 out: ev ch between last 2: no ex and btn fnl 75yds* **6/1**[2]

F2-3 **3** *7* **Back In Business (IRE)**[48] 549 10-10-10 **90**..........(p) PaulMoloney 94
(Evan Williams) *in tch: chsd ldrs 11th: chsd ldng pair 15th: rdn and outpcd 3 out: plugged on same pce fr next* **8/1**

P/5- **4** *4 1/2* **Dun Drinan (IRE)**[70] 11-11-12 **106**.......... DarylJacob 105
(Eamonn Fehily, Ire) *hld up in rr: stdy prog fr 9th: chsd ldng trio after 16th: rdn to chse ldng pair 3 out: btn next: lost 3rd last* **33/1**

-263 **5** *12* **Von Galen (IRE)**[28] 804 9-10-7 **87**..........(p) RhysFlint 74
(Michael Scudamore) *j.rt: chsd ldrs: rdn and struggling 14th: wknd and j.rt 16th: wl btn fr next* **9/1**

0-22 **6** *6* **Oamaru Stone (IRE)**[46] 588 7-11-4 **103**.......... MrRMahon[(5)] 84
(Paul Nicholls) *rdn along thrght: bhd: reminders after 6th: sme hdwy into midfield but stl wl off the pce 15th: no prog fr next: nvr trbld ldrs* **7/1**[3]

4615 **7** *22* **Classic Clover**[33] 758 10-11-7 **101**..........(t) AidanColeman 60
(Colin Tizzard) *chsd ldrs: lost pl and mstke 9th: drvn and struggling after 13th: wl bhd fr 15th: t.o* **12/1**

P0-0 **8** *13* **Outside Investor (IRE)**[11] 931 10-9-12 **83** oh6 ow3..(b) KeiranBurke[(5)] 29
(Patrick Rodford) *chsd wnr tl led 2nd: hdd 4th: chsd wnr after tl 14th: sn drvn: wknd qckly 16th: t.o bef 2 out* **33/1**

3-P2 **9** *3 1/4* **Pauillac (FR)**[48] 549 7-11-7 **101**.......... TomScudamore 44
(David Pipe) *nvr gng or jumping wl: a in rr: lost tch 14th: t.o bef 3 out* **14/1**

U31- **P** **Chico Time (IRE)**[104] 5060 9-10-4 **84**..........(p) WillKennedy —
(Norma Twomey) *j.rt: nt jump wl: in tch in midfield: losing tch whn blnd 14th: j.v.slowly next and immediately p.u* **16/1**

-433 **P** **Allterrain (IRE)**[13] 911 7-11-6 **100**.......... JohnnyFarrelly —
(Norma Twomey) *in tch in midfield tl dropped to rr and pushed along 7th: bhd whn blnd 11th: losing tch whn p.u after 13th* **9/1**

-P32 **P** **Old Brigade (IRE)**[23] 840 6-11-3 **97**..........(t) APMcCoy —
(Jonjo O'Neill) *towards rr and j. slowly 2nd: racd in midfield: rdn and dropped towards rr after 13th: 6th and wl btn whn j. slowly 17th: t.o whn p.u 2 out* **9/4**[1]

6m 26.6s (-18.00) **Going Correction** -0.525s/f (Firm) 12 Ran SP% **118.6**
Speed ratings (Par 105): **105,104,102,101,97 95,89,85,84,— —,—**
toteswingers:1&2:£36.60, 1&3:£36.60, 2&3:£7.80 CSF £169.38 CT £1327.71 TOTE £24.80: £6.30, £1.60, £3.40; EX 260.20.
Owner David Knox & John Rathbone **Bred** David Knox **Trained** Upper Lambourn, Berks

FOCUS
A moderate handicap chase and a surprise winner, who returned to form

NOTEBOOK
Strong Coffee's form had regressed, but the blinkers appeared to make all the difference and he found plenty when strongly challenged by the runner-up. He is a strong stayer, and as a result of his recent poor performances his chase rating is significantly lower than his hurdles rating. However, he might not be one to back with great confidence next time. Official explanation: trainer's rep said, regarding apparent improvement in form, that the gelding benfitted for the first-time blinkers.
Rifleman(IRE) has been running consistently of late and has won twice at Worcester this summer. He ran well again here, but it is likely to be tough for him off this sort of mark. (op 5-1)
Back In Business(IRE) is a dour stayer who possibly found this sharp track against him. He is likely to need extreme distances in order to win, but he has dropped to a tempting mark. (op 9-1)
Dun Drinan(IRE) travelled well before weakening after the home turn. It is likely age has now caught up with him. (tchd 28-1)
Oamaru Stone(IRE) was never travelling and is not reliable. (op 13-2 tchd 6-1)

1028 ACTION DUCHENNE CHARITY MAIDEN HURDLE (10 hdls) 2m 6f
4:35 (4:35) (Class 4) 4-Y-O+ **£3,382** (£993; £496; £248)

Form RPR
/0P- **1** **Lomitaar**[101] 5103 5-11-0 0.......... AndrewTinkler 103+
(Tony Newcombe) *t.k.h: hld up in rr: hdwy to trck ldrs and hit 7th: led gng wl bef 2 out: sn in command: wandered last: easily* **33/1**

5-04 **2** *11* **Santamina (IRE)**[14] 887 4-10-4 0..........(p) MichaelByrne[(7)] 89
(Peter Bowen) *racd in midfield: hdwy to chse ldrs 6th: led 7th: rdn and hdd bef 2 out: sn no ch w wnr: plugged on u.p* **9/1**[3]

6-33 **3** *6* **Magical Treasure**[61] 379 6-11-0 98.......... PaulMoloney 88
(Sophie Leech) *hmpd 1st: in rr: pushed along and effrt after 6th: wl outpcd next: wnt modest 4th after 3 out: plugged on to go 3rd last: no ch w wnr* **11/4**[2]

4 *6* **Kavegirl**[43] 7-10-7 0.......... DavidEngland 74
(John Panvert) *hld up in main gp: hdwy to press ldrs bef 7th: ev ch 3 out: rdn and btn bef next: wkng whn mstke 2 out: lost 3rd last* **14/1**

0-0 **5** *48* **Moonshine Hall (IRE)**[19] 855 6-10-1 0 ow1..........(t) MattGriffiths[(7)] 26
(Richard Hawker) *t.k.h: hld up in rr: hdwy and clsd 5th: rdn and btn 7th: t.o bef 2 out* **50/1**

0/53 **P** **Award Winning (IRE)**[33] 757 9-10-9 78.......... TomO'Connor[(5)] —
(John Berwick) *prom in main gp tl rdn and lost pl after 6th: wl t.o whn p.u 2 out* **10/1**

0P- **P** **Fusilade (FR)**[183] 3460 7-11-0 0.......... TomScudamore —
(Warren Greatrex) *led: j. bdly lft 1st and sn hdd: chsd clr ldr tl after 4th: lost pl qckly next and wl bhd whn p.u after 6th* **20/1**

4 **R** **Leitra House (IRE)**[46] 583 7-11-0 0.......... NickScholfield —
(Jeremy Scott) *plld hrd: hld up towards rr whn rn out 1st* **12/1**

F **Top Tide (IRE)**[43] 9-10-9 0.......... IanPopham[(5)] —
(Martin Hill) *t.k.h: hld up towards rr: clsd on ldrs 5th: rdn and struggling bef 7th: disputing modest 4th whn fell 3 out* **66/1**

P **Rocklandslad (IRE)**[71] 7-11-0 0.......... APMcCoy —
(Rebecca Curtis) *t.k.h: prom in main gp: chsd ldr 5th tl led after 6th: rdn and hdd next: wknd rapidly and wl btn next: t.o whn p.u 2 out* **7/4**[1]

66/P **P** **Soviet Cat (IRE)**[26] 823 5-10-11 85.......... PeterToole[(3)] —
(Miss C J Williams) *plld hrd: led 1st and sn clr: hdd after 6th and dropped out rapidly: wl t.o whn p.u 3 out* **22/1**

0-0U **P** **The Wee Midget**[28] 792 5-10-11 0.......... CharlieStudd[(3)] —
(Arthur Whiting) *in rr: nt fluent 1st: j. slowly next and immediately lost tch: wl t.o whn p.u 4th* **33/1**

5m 8.60s (-11.60) **Going Correction** -0.725s/f (Firm)
WFA 4 from 5yo+ 16lb 12 Ran SP% **114.9**
Speed ratings (Par 105): **92,88,85,83,66 —,—,—,—,— —,—**
toteswingers:1&2:£42.40, 1&3:£17.00, 2&3:£3.50 CSF £278.00 TOTE £44.80: £6.70, £1.80, £1.60; EX 448.00.
Owner Paul Nicholas **Bred** M K F Seymour **Trained** Yarnscombe, Devon

FOCUS
A weak novice hurdle even for the time of year, and the form should be taken with a pinch of salt.The first two are rated in line with their best bumper form.

NOTEBOOK
Lomitaar had some fair form in bumpers but had not shown any form over hurdles until winning with ease here. He went well for his new rider and could be a force in similar low-grade races. (op 40-1)
Santamina(IRE) benefited from the step up in trip and showed his first piece of worthwhile but he will have to step up on this to win over hurdles. (op 15-2)
Magical Treasure was stepping up in trip after disappointing last time but she showed limited promise. Official explanation: jockey said gelding hung left-handed (op 10-3 tchd 5-2)
Kavegirl was a non-stayer in point-to-points but she ran well for a long way here. She is, however, moderate. (op 10-1)
Leitra House(IRE) Official explanation: jockey said bridle broke
The Wee Midget Official explanation: jockey said gelding never travelled

1029 TROPICAL BUBBLICIOUS MAIDEN OPEN NATIONAL HUNT FLAT RACE 2m 1f
5:05 (5:05) (Class 5) 4-6-Y-O **£1,747** (£509; £254)

Form RPR
5 **1** **Spe Salvi (IRE)**[25] 833 6-10-7 0.......... DarylJacob 100+
(David Arbuthnot) *in tch in midfield: hdwy to trck ldrs 4f out: pushed along to ld wl over 1f out: rn green: hung rt and hdd over 1f out: pushed along and led again towards fin* **9/2**[2]

2 **2** *1/2* **Maid Of Silk (IRE)**[25] 832 4-10-5 0.......... NickScholfield 94+
(Grant Cann) *chsd ldrs on outer tl led ent fnl 2f: hdd and hung lft u.p wl over 1f out: lft in ld again over 1f out tl hdd and no ex towards fin* **6/1**[3]

6 **3** *6* **Doubletoilntrouble (IRE)**[25] 832 4-10-12 0.......... RhysFlint 93
(Keith Goldsworthy) *led: pushed along wl over 3f out: rdn and hdd ent 2f out: kpt on same pce after* **9/2**[2]

0- **4** *3 1/4* **All But Beat**[329] 1295 5-11-0 0.......... AidanColeman 92
(Ron Hodges) *in tch in midfield: rdn: rn green and rdr dropped whip over 5f out: outpcd by ldrs 4f out: kpt on wl under hands and heels fnl 2f: unable to chal* **33/1**

5 **5** *1 1/4* **Limbunya (IRE)**[18] 869 5-10-2 0..........(t) DavidBass[(5)] 84
(Ron Hodges) *hld up towards rr: pushed along 8f out: outpcd 5f out: rallied and styd on wl fr over 2f out: nvr trbld ldrs* **50/1**

6 *2 3/4* **Bach Protector (IRE)** 4-10-12 0.......... APMcCoy 86
(Rebecca Curtis) *in tch: hdwy to join ldrs over 4f out: rdn and btn ent fnl 2f: eased ins fnl f* **7/4**[1]

7 *nk* **July The Firth (IRE)**[104] 4-10-12 0.......... HarrySkelton 85
(Alan Jones) *in tch: hdwy to chse ldrs 6f out: rdn and outpcd 4f out: wknd 3f out: dismntd after fin* **12/1**

0 **8** *3 1/4* **Yu Tiger (IRE)**[25] 833 4-10-12 0..........(b[1]) TomScudamore 82
(David Pipe) *chsd ldrs: drvn 6f out: wknd u.p over 4f out: wl btn fnl 3f* **11/1**

9 *23* **Redgrave Dancer** 4-10-0 0.......... IanPopham[(5)] 52
(Kevin Bishop) *sn rdn along in rr: lost tch over 5f out: t.o fnl 3f* **25/1**

10 *nk* **Leomode (USA)** 4-10-9 0.......... SeanQuinlan[(3)] 59
(Liam Corcoran) *t.k.h: hld up in tch in rr: struggling over 5f out: no ch fnl 4f: t.o* **25/1**

11 *17* **Canny Lad** 4-10-12 0.......... ColinBolger 42
(John Ryan) *chsd ldr tl 5f out: wknd rapidly and sn wl bhd: t.o and eased fnl 2f* **14/1**

0- **12** *31* **Victory Bay**[364] 999 5-11-0 0.......... DavidDennis 13
(Nigel Hawke) *plld hrd: hld up in rr: lost tch rapidly 5f out: wl t.o fnl 3f* **40/1**

3m 54.5s (-5.60) **Going Correction** -0.725s/f (Firm)
WFA 4 from 5yo+ 2lb 12 Ran SP% **124.7**
Speed ratings: **84,83,80,79,78 77,77,75,65,64 56,42**
toteswingers:1&2:£5.00, 1&3:£4.20, 2&3:£8.50 CSF £31.89 TOTE £5.60: £1.90, £3.20, £1.60; EX 26.30 Place 6 £106.02; Place 5 £61.70.
Owner George Ward **Bred** Sandwell Old Manor Syndicate **Trained** Compton, Berks

FOCUS
An ordinary bumper but the first two are better than the bare result.

NOTEBOOK
Spe Salvi(IRE) was too green to do herself justice on debut and she nearly threw the race away after hanging close home. She clearly has plenty to learn but she could develop into a nice sort for the future. (tchd 4-1 and 5-1)
Maid Of Silk(IRE) shaped as though she would be up to winning a bumper over the summer. She showed promise on her debut and confirmed the form with Doubletoilntrouble. (op 5-1)
Doubletoilntrouble(IRE) who had shown little in point-to-points but is slowly getting the hang of things under rules and in time could be up to winning a small race. (op 8-1)
All But Beat was well beaten on debut but showed improved form here. His rider dropped his whip in the back straight and the horse ran as if this experience would bring him on again. (op 66-1)
Limbunya(IRE) was a moderate pointer who made late progress. She is unlikely to be up to winning races under rules. A step up in trip could help her though. (op 66-1)
Bach Protector(IRE) was sent off favourite but weakened tamely from the home turn. His relatives had only shown moderate form and it remains to be seen weather his excellent trainer can find a race for him. (op 6-4 tchd 11-8 and 15-8)
July The Firth(IRE) was dismounted and removed by the horse ambulance following a run which hinted at ability. Official explanation: jockey said gelding pulled up lame
Canny Lad did not look at ease on this quick ground but was well backed so is clearly thought to have some ability. (tchd 10-1)
T/Plt: £104.20 to a £1 stake. Pool:£66,279.57 - 464.13 winning tickets T/Qpdt: £13.70 to a £1 stake. Pool:£4,270.37 - 230.08 winning tickets SP

[956]STRATFORD (L-H)

Sunday, July 18

OFFICIAL GOING: Good to firm (good in places on chase course; watered; 9.5)

Wind: Light half-against Weather: Overcast

1030 CLAYDON HORSE EXERCISERS NOVICES' HURDLE (9 hdls) 2m 110y

2:20 (2:20) (Class 3) 4-Y-0+ **£4,435** (£1,310; £655; £327; £163)

Form RPR

1411 **1** **Tout Regulier**[7] 958 6-10-10 120................................ DonalDevereux(5) 111+
(Peter Bowen) *mde all: qcknd clr appr 2 out: easily* **1/4**[1]

-663 **2** 7 **Quidam Blue (FR)**[7] 956 6-10-12 0........................... RichardJohnson 96
(Tim Vaughan) *hld up: hdwy 3 out: sn rdn: wnt 2nd flat: no ch w wnr* **10/1**[3]

U3 **3** 2 ½ **Carhue Princess (IRE)**[31] 768 4-9-7 0........................ AdamWedge(10) 88+
(Evan Williams) *chsd wnr: hit 4th: rdn whn hit 2 out: wkng whn mstke last: lost 2nd flat* **25/1**

4 19 **Wind Star**[69] 7-10-7 0.. JimmyDerham(5) 81+
(Milton Harris) *hld up in tch: mstke 3rd: hit 3 out: rdn and wkng whn hit next* **7/1**[2]

00/6 **5** 9 **Southway Star**[19] 850 5-10-5 0.. CharliePoste 62
(Kevin Bishop) *chsd ldrs tl rdn and wknd after 3 out* **66/1**

6 3 **Rafta (IRE)**[20] 4-10-0 0... TommyPhelan(3) 57
(W G Harrison) *sn bhd: effrt after 5th: wknd bef next* **50/1**

7 33 **Cheekyrun (IRE)**[113] 7-10-5 0... MrTJCannon(7) 36
(Paul Henderson) *nt fluent: prom tl wknd 6th: t.o* **66/1**

3m 52.6s (-3.40) **Going Correction** -0.25s/f (Good)
WFA 4 from 5yo+ 15lb 7 Ran SP% **110.4**
Speed ratings (Par 107): **98,94,93,84,80 78,63**
toteswingers:1&2:£1.50, 1&3:£2.00, 2&3:£5.50 CSF £3.19 TOTE £1.30: £1.10, £2.70; EX 3.30.
Owner G A Moore **Bred** Miss M E Steele **Trained** Little Newcastle, Pembrokes

FOCUS

The track had been watered (8mm) and the ground was given as good to firm on the hurdle course and good to firm, good in places on the chase course. An uncompetitive novice hurdle in which the winner is rated 10lb off his best.

NOTEBOOK

Tout Regulier faced limited opposition and got the job done in a professional manner, making most of the running and winning without having to be asked for maximum effort. This taught us nothing we did not already know but connections have done well to get three wins out of her in the space of 15 days. She will apparently have another run in a novice before going chasing. (op 3-10)

Quidam Blue(FR) improved on his debut effort over hurdles and picked up second place when Carhue Princess fluffed the last. He looks more of a handicap prospect after one more run, and will appreciate a longer trip in time.

Carhue Princess(IRE), ridden more prominently this time, was again a bit keen and mistakes at the final two flights cost her second place, but it was still a step in the right direction.

Wind Star, a useful five-time winner at up to 1m2f on the Flat, was friendless in the market on his hurdling debut and didn't jump particularly well. Official explanation: vet said gelding lost its near-fore shoe (op 6-1)

1031 CLAYDON HORSE EXERCISERS (S) HURDLE (9 hdls) 2m 110y

2:50 (2:50) (Class 5) 4-6-Y-0 **£1,951** (£573; £286; £143)

Form RPR

60-0 **1** **Douchkette (FR)**[18] 865 4-10-3 88 ow1.......................... DannyCook(3) 98+
(John Berry) *a.p: shkn up to ld flat: r.o wl* **5/1**[3]

53 **2** 1 ¾ **Swiss Art (IRE)**[11] 932 4-10-5 0.................................(p) OliverDayman(7) 102+
(Alison Thorpe) *hld up in tch: mstke 3 out: led appr next: hdd and unable qck flat* **5/4**[1]

3 2 **Tigh Bhruadair (IRE)**[295] 1544 6-10-4 0..................(tp) JSMcGarvey(10) 100
(Evan Williams) *chsd ldr: led 3rd to 4th: led 5th: hdd appr 2 out: no ex flat* **16/1**

0- **4** 18 **Guga (IRE)**[8] 1537 4-10-12 0..(p) DenisO'Regan 80
(Dr Richard Newland) *hld up: bhd 5th: nvr on terms* **7/2**[2]

-P0P **5** 2 ½ **London Times (IRE)**[4] 990 5-10-7 74..................................(t) KyleJames(7) 80
(Simon Lewis) *prom: led 4th: hdd whn hit next: wknd after 3 out* **66/1**

45 **6** 21 **Mystic Touch**[12] 917 4-10-12 0... JackDoyle 64
(Andrew Haynes) *hld up: a in rr: wl bhd whn blnd 2 out* **5/1**[3]

0- **7** 3 ¾ **Fluters House**[320] 1371 6-11-0 0............................. ChristianWilliams 55
(Gerald Ham) *hld up: sme hdwy after 3 out: sn wknd* **33/1**

P- **8** 16 **Duke Of Normandy (IRE)**[6] 1421 4-10-12 0..................(p) JodieMogford 37
(Brian Baugh) *led and j. slowly 1st: hdd 3rd: wknd appr 7th* **18/1**

3m 58.5s (2.50) **Going Correction** -0.25s/f (Good)
WFA 4 from 5yo+ 15lb 8 Ran SP% **115.6**
Speed ratings: **84,83,82,73,72 62,60,53**
toteswingers:1&2:£1.30, 1&3:£15.70, 2&3:£7.60 CSF £12.24 TOTE £6.80: £1.70, £1.10, £4.50; EX 13.90.There was no bid for the winner.
Owner C And C Partnership **Bred** Henrietta Charlet & Danny Charlesworth **Trained** Newmarket, Suffolk

FOCUS

The early pace wasn't that strong and a few of these raced quite keenly. A weak seller.

NOTEBOOK

Douchkette(FR) won this quite readily in the end, but was clearly suited by the way the race developed, as she barely gets this trip and needs fast ground and a sharp track to be seen at her best. (op 4-1 tchd 11-2)

Swiss Art(IRE) was always keen to go faster than his rider would allow him. Although he turned into the straight seemingly going well it was noticeable that in behind the winner was travelling just as strongly, and when it came down to a battle heading to the final flight, his rival had more left in the tank. (op 6-4 tchd 6-5)

Tigh Bhruadair(IRE) showed little in six starts in Ireland but had cheekpieces and a tongue-tie on for the first time on his debut for his new yard, and ran a fairly promising race. He was done for a bit of toe in the closing stages but is bred to need further. (op 12-1)

Guga(IRE), tailed off on his only previous try over hurdles, was out the back for much of the race and didn't jump very well. It was only his Flat speed that allowed him to pass beaten rivals in the closing stages. (op 4-1 tchd 9-2)

1032 CLAYDON HORSE EXERCISERS H'CAP CHASE (17 fncs) 2m 7f

3:20 (3:20) (Class 3) (0-125,123) 4-Y-0+

£7,514 (£2,220; £1,110; £555; £277; £139)

Form RPR

-P30 **1** **Sea Wall**[13] 911 8-11-1 115... MrAJBerry(3) 122
(Jonjo O'Neill) *chsd ldr: led 6th to 7th: led 9th to 10th: led 14th: all out* **20/1**

54-1 **2** hd **Dead Or Alive (IRE)**[56] 438 7-11-12 123..................(t) RichardJohnson 130
(Tim Vaughan) *hld up: hdwy 9th: chsd wnr 2 out: rdn and ev ch last: styd on* **7/1**[3]

-33P **3** 3 ¾ **Whataboutya (IRE)**[31] 772 9-10-13 113..............(p) RichieMcLernon(3) 118
(Jonjo O'Neill) *hld up: hdwy 14th: rdn and ev ch appr last: no ex flat* **14/1**

-224 **4** 9 **Pairc Na Gcapall (IRE)**[51] 501 8-11-0 114..............(tp) AlexMerriam(3) 110
(Neil King) *led to 6th: led 7th to 9th: led 10th to 14th: wknd 2 out* **7/1**[3]

0-12 **5** ½ **Shammy Buskins**[51] 501 8-11-4 115......................(p) ChristianWilliams 111
(Lawney Hill) *sn pushed along in rr: hit 5th: nvr nrr* **5/1**[2]

250- **6** 5 **Some Craic (IRE)**[98] 10-11-0 118................................. MrTJCannon(7) 109
(Paul Henderson) *chsd ldrs tl wknd appr last* **40/1**

-0FP **7** 2 ¾ **Seymar Lad (IRE)**[21] 844 10-11-2 120..................... MrSJO'Donovan(7) 108
(Emma Lavelle) *chsd ldrs: rdn after 13th: wknd next* **18/1**

3232 **8** 6 **Kanad**[19] 854 8-10-10 112..(t) JimmyDerham(5) 95
(Milton Harris) *hld up: rdn after 13th: nvr on terms* **14/1**

-321 **9** ½ **Midnight Gold**[31] 769 10-11-11 122.................................(p) TomO'Brien 104
(Peter Bowen) *sn pushed along in mid-div: j. slowly 4th* **3/1**[1]

-206 **10** nk **Our Hero (IRE)**[13] 911 7-10-13 113..............................(tp) TomMolloy(3) 95
(Charlie Longsdon) *chsd ldrs: cl up whn blnd 13th: wknd next* **9/1**

-212 **11** 58 **Presentandcorrect (IRE)**[19] 852 9-11-8 119.................... SamThomas 49
(Nigel Twiston-Davies) *hld up: mstke 11th: sn rdn and lost tch: t.o* **15/2**

5m 31.2s (-10.40) **Going Correction** -0.25s/f (Good) 11 Ran SP% **114.2**
Speed ratings (Par 107): **108,107,106,103,103 101,100,98,98,98 78**
toteswingers:1&2:not won, 2&3:not won, 1&3:not won CSF £150.78 CT £2031.21 TOTE £27.50: £5.90, £2.60, £4.70; EX 261.80.
Owner John P McManus **Bred** Lord Rothschild **Trained** Cheltenham, Gloucs

■ Stewards' Enquiry : Richard Johnson three-day ban: used whip with excessive frequency without giving gelding time to respond (Aug 1-3)

FOCUS

A competitive handicap run at a good pace. The form looks solid with the winner back to something like his 2yo best.

NOTEBOOK

Sea Wall was up there all the way, disputing the lead for much of the race with Pairc Na Gcapall, but he saw him off, kept the stalking Some Craic at bay and finally fought off the strong challenge of Dead Or Alive in a titanic tussle up the straight. It was a fine, battling display, and his rider deserves plenty of credit, too. He had dropped to a fair mark after three ordinary efforts this term but had ground conditions to suit and is at his best when given a positive front-running ride. (tchd 22-1)

Dead Or Alive(IRE), 5lb higher for winning a small-field affair at Fakenham last time, enjoyed a nice run through the race and looked poised to take the winner's measure on the turn in, but he found Sea Wall a determined rival. This was a good effort off what looked a stiff mark. (op 5-1)

Whataboutya(IRE), whose jockey wore the winning owner's first colours, came through to have his chance in the straight but was just outstayed by the first two from the last.

Pairc Na Gcapall(IRE)'s two wins under rules have come when making all the running, so being harried in front by the winner the whole way round did him no favours at all. (op 9-1)

Shammy Buskins raced lazily in the early stages and was detached in last at halfway, but he stayed on past beaten rivals in the closing stages to be nearest at the finish. (op 9-2)

Midnight Gold was the disappointment of the race as he came here after a convincing success at Ffos Las and was representing a stable in cracking form. (op 7-2 tchd 11-4)

1033 CLAYDON HORSE EXERCISERS H'CAP HURDLE (12 hdls) 2m 6f 110y

3:55 (3:55) (Class 4) (0-115,115) 4-Y-0+ **£3,903** (£1,146; £573; £286)

Form RPR

-324 **1** **Mzuri Bay**[48] 559 5-11-4 107...(t) MarkGrant 110+
(Brendan Duke) *chsd ldr tl led 3 out: rdn clr whn nt fluent 2 out: kpt on* **9/1**

0143 **2** 3 ¼ **Cubism**[28] 798 4-10-6 104...(t) JimmyDerham(5) 100+
(Milton Harris) *hld up: hdwy 8th: rdn to chse wnr 2 out: sn hung lft: nt fluent last: styd on* **5/2**[2]

P030 **3** 4 ½ **Winsley Hill**[4] 986 8-11-12 115.. RodiGreene 110
(Neil Mulholland) *chsd ldrs: pushed along 6th: led after 9th: hdd next: styd on same pce fr 2 out* **14/1**

-430 **4** 13 **Mcqueen (IRE)**[12] 921 10-10-6 98..................................... DannyCook(3) 81
(Barry Leavy) *led tl after 9th: wknd appr 2 out* **5/1**[3]

1P/2 **5** 73 **Herne Bay (IRE)**[21] 846 10-11-8 111...............................(t) DenisO'Regan 29
(Ian Williams) *hld up: rdn and lost tch appr 8th: t.o* **7/4**[1]

-030 **6** 13 **Sea Cliff (IRE)**[14] 888 6-10-13 105.............................. RichieMcLernon(3) 11
(Jonjo O'Neill) *prom tl rdn and wknd 8th: t.o:* **8/1**

5m 20.1s (-8.00) **Going Correction** -0.25s/f (Good)
WFA 4 from 5yo+ 16lb 6 Ran SP% **109.4**
Speed ratings (Par 105): **103,101,100,95,70 65**
toteswingers:1&2:£4.60, 1&3:£5.30, 2&3:£7.50 CSF £30.62 CT £287.35 TOTE £10.80: £3.30, £1.60; EX 35.30.
Owner Ruth Tupper & Tom Fletcher **Bred** B W Duke **Trained** Lambourn, Berks

FOCUS

Quite a competitive race despite the small field. Ordinary handicap form.

NOTEBOOK

Mzuri Bay, a half-brother to the stable's multiple winner Openide, ran flat last time but was back to form here and ended a bit of a losing run for the yard. Running in a handicap for the first time, he tracked the leader on the rail for most of the race before taking things up heading to the turn into the straight. He got a bit tired in the closing stages but he was being chased by a horse with unproven stamina and always had enough in hand. (op 8-1 tchd 11-1)

Cubism made all to win here over 2m½f in May but faced a greater test of stamina this time and was ridden very much to get the trip. He had his chance if good enough but the impression left was that it just stretched him a little. (op 3-1 tchd 9-4)

Winsley Hill was being nudged along from some way out but she did respond and briefly hit the front before being seen off by the winner. The handicapper looks to have her measure both over hurdles and fences for the time being. (op 12-1)

Mcqueen(IRE) was allowed to take up his favoured front-running role, but he hasn't been at his best this term and he dropped out tamely after being headed. (op 7-2)

Herne Bay(IRE) never went a yard and the conclusion must be that he bounced after a good effort on his return from almost two years off at Uttoxeter three weeks earlier. Official explanation: trainer had no explanation for the poor form shown; vet said gelding lost its left-hind shoe (op 15-8 tchd 2-1 and 13-8)

1034 CLAYDON HORSE EXERCISERS NOVICES' H'CAP CHASE (17 fncs) 2m 7f

4:25 (4:25) (Class 4) (0-110,109) 5-Y-0+ **£4,553** (£1,337; £668; £333)

Form RPR

1/26 **1** **Tampa Boy (IRE)**[23] 840 8-11-12 109..............................(t) CharliePoste 117
(Milton Harris) *chsd ldr to 8th: wnt 2nd again next: rdn to ld appr last: styd on wl* **11/2**

6-21 **2** 3 ¼ **Local Present (IRE)**[46] 588 7-11-5 102........................ RichardJohnson 107
(Ron Hodges) *a.p: chsd ldr 8th to 9th: remained handy: rdn to chse wnr last: no ex flat* **3/1**[2]

/64S **3** 6 **Cherokee Star**[7] 957 5-11-4 101.......................................(p) DenisO'Regan 102
(Mike Hammond) *led: rdn and hdd appr last: styd on same pce* **7/1**

-332 **4** 38 **Kilshannig (IRE)**[18] 867 5-11-2 102.........................(t) RichieMcLernon(3) 67
(Jonjo O'Neill) *prom tl wknd 14th: t.o* **5/2**[1]

5-32 **P** **Chevy To The Levy (IRE)**7 [951] 8-11-10 **107**........... AndrewThornton —
(John O'Shea) *prom: reminders after 4th: wknd appr 14th: t.o whn p.u bef next* **7/2**3

0-0U **P** **General Simara**12 [918] 6-9-9 **83** oh8.............................. LeeEdwards(5) —
(Tony Carroll) *sn wl bhd: t.o whn p.u bef 14th* **14/1**

5m 39.2s (-2.40) **Going Correction** -0.25s/f (Good) **6** Ran SP% **110.3**
Speed ratings: **94,92,90,77,**— —
toteswingers:1&2:£2.90, 1&3:£6.40, 2&3:£33.40 CSF £21.85 TOTE £5.00: £3.30, £3.00; EX 27.10.

Owner G D Building Ltd J Parsons **Bred** Sig M Parola **Trained** Herridge, Wiltshire

FOCUS
They finished tired in this novices' handicap. The form is rated through the second.

NOTEBOOK
Tampa Boy(IRE), although tired, dug deepest and saw it out best from the last. The first-time tongue-tie possibly contributed to that and this was a fine run off what had looked to be a fairly stiff mark. There are two possible explanations for his disappointing effort at Market Rasen last time, as he apparently lost a shoe during the race, and might well have also bounced. (op 5-1)

Local Present(IRE), put up 9lb for last month's Fontwell success, ran right up to his best in defeat and had no excuses. (op 7-2)

Cherokee Star ran a good race from the front, showing no ill effects from his unfortunate experience here a week earlier. Having made most of the running he simply got very tired from the turn in, and it does look as if a drop back to 2m4f will help him.

Kilshannig(IRE) disappointed, although he didn't look to have been done any favours by the handicapper, who'd put him up 5lb for being beaten on his chasing debut. (tchd 9-4)

Chevy To The Levy(IRE), making his handicap debut, failed to build on the promise he showed at Southwell, tending to run in snatches for much of the race. His trainer suggested that the track didn't suit the gelding, although it's also worth noting that the vet reported that he'd lost his left hind shoe. Official explanation: trainer said gelding was unsuited by the track; vet said gelding lost its left-hind shoe (op 10-3)

1035 CLAYDON HORSE EXERCISERS NOVICES' H'CAP HURDLE (9 hdls 1 omitted) 2m 3f

4:55 (4:55) (Class 4) (0-105,104) 4-Y-0+ **£3,903** (£1,146; £429; £429)

Form RPR

22-F **1** **Penyfan Dawn (IRE)**32 [767] 6-11-12 **104**.................. RichardJohnson 113+
(Tim Vaughan) *hld up: hdwy appr 2 out: rdn to ld flat: styd on wl* **9/1**

4435 **2** *3* **Cool Bob (IRE)**21 [849] 7-10-5 **90**...............................(t) MrLRPayter(7) 95
(Matt Sheppard) *hld up: bhd and rdn 7th: r.o appr last: wnt 2nd towards fin: nt rch wnr* **5/1**0

600- **3** *½* **Elegant Olive**123 [4680] 7-9-11 **78** oh5.............................. HaddenFrost(3) 83
(Roger Curtis) *chsd ldrs: rdn and ev ch appr last: styd on same pce flat* **22/1**

-401 **3** *dht* **Kristallo (GER)**7 [962] 5-11-10 **102**....................................(v) SamJones 107
(Paul Webber) *chsd clr ldr tl led after 2 out: rdn and hdd flat: styd on same pce* **5/1**3

402 **5** *2¾* **Risk Challenge (USA)**4 [990] 8-10-2 **80**..........................(t) CharliePoste 83
(Milton Harris) *hld up: hdwy 6th: styd on same pce appr last* **9/2**2

-5P4 **6** *8* **Timoca (IRE)**28 [793] 5-10-4 **92**..................................... AdamWedge(10) 88
(Evan Williams) *mid-div: hdwy 6th: rdn and wknd appr last* **11/2**

-003 **7** *10* **Hollies Favourite (IRE)**12 [917] 7-10-9 **90**...................(t) AlexMerriam(3) 76
(Neil King) *led and sn clr: hdd after 2 out: sn wknd* **28/1**

0405 **8** *30* **The Grey One (IRE)**28 [793] 7-10-6 **91**........................(p) ChrisDavies(7) 50
(Milton Bradley) *mid-div: drvn along 3 out: sn wknd: t.o* **33/1**

-P50 **9** *14* **Tram Express (FR)**11 [932] 6-11-0 **92**..........................(b) DenisO'Regan 39
(Shaun Lycett) *chsd ldrs tl wknd 7th: t.o* **18/1**

660- **10** *36* **Strong Market**390 [802] 5-11-2 **94**....................................... SamThomas 8
(Jeremy Scott) *hld up: mstke 4th: bhd fr next: t.o* **40/1**

242/ **P** **Rescindo (IRE)**48 11-10-10 **88**.................................... ChristianWilliams —
(C Roberts) *chsd ldrs: lost pl after 3rd: bhd fr 5th: t.o whn p.u bef last* **66/1**

P-40 **F** **Aint She The Lady (IRE)**37 [713] 6-11-0 **99**................. MrTomDavid(7) —
(Tim Vaughan) *chsd ldrs: disputing 4th whn fell 5th* **7/2**1

4m 28.0s (-3.50) **Going Correction** -0.25s/f (Good) **12** Ran SP% **119.1**
Speed ratings (Par 105): **105,103,103,103,102 99,94,82,76,61** —,—
PL; Kristallo £1.00 Eligant Olive £3.90. Tricast; PD, CB, KL £112.08; PD, CB, OE £425.59. toteswingers:PD&CB:£12.40, CB&KL:£2.70, PD&KL:£4.70, CB&EO:£15.50, CB&EO:£15.50 CSF £49.58 TOTE £8.70: £2.90, £2.10; EX 70.70 Place 6 £129.42; Place 5 £112.31.

Owner D J Wallis **Bred** John Coleman And Alex Heskin **Trained** Aberthin, Vale of Glamorgan
■ Apache Dawn (5/1) was withdrawn on vet's advice. R4 applies, deduct 5p in the £.

FOCUS
This was run at a good gallop and it played into the hands of those held up off the pace. The form looks pretty solid for the grade.

NOTEBOOK
Penyfan Dawn(IRE) has been let down by his jumping in the past, including on his reappearance last month, and he wasn't always the slickest here, but he got round okay and, in a race run to suit those ridden patiently out the back, he came through to land the spoils in the straight. He still needs to get better over his obstacles if he's to progress. (tchd 8-1)

Cool Bob(IRE), a longstanding maiden, appeared very late on the scene having been well off the pace for most of the race. The race was run to suit him and he isn't one to be following. (op 11-2)

Elegant Olive, having mastered Hollies Favourite, took on Kristallo from quite far out and both paid for that up the run-in. It was still a good effort though considering she was 5lb out of the handicap. (op 4-1)

Kristallo(GER), who escaped a penalty for his win over the C&D a week earlier, was being shoved along from some way out but kept responding and deserves plenty of credit. (op 4-1)

Risk Challenge(USA) didn't run badly considering that he was hampered by the fall of Aint She The Lady early on. (op 5-1 tchd 11-2)

Timoca(IRE) ran as though she will appreciate dropping back to 2m. (op 7-1)

Hollies Favourite(IRE) went off far too fast in front and fell in a hole from the second last. (op 33-1)

Aint She The Lady(IRE) had to be put down as a result of her fall. (op 9-2)

T/Plt: £265.80 to a £1 stake. Pool: £67,073.29. 184.19 winning tickets. T/Qpdt: £134.20 to a £1 stake. Pool: £4,173.85. 23 winning tickets. CR

1036 - 1037a (Foreign Racing) - See Raceform Interactive

774 TIPPERARY (L-H)

Sunday, July 18

OFFICIAL GOING: Good (good to yielding in places)

1038a KEVIN MCMANUS BOOKMAKER GRIMES HURDLE (GRADE 3) (9 hdls) 2m

4:00 (4:00) 4-Y-0+ **£37,389** (£10,929; £5,176; £1,725)

RPR

1 **Bahrain Storm (IRE)**22 [5401] 7-11-4 147...............................(b) JRBarry 146+
(Patrick J Flynn, Ire) *chsd ldrs travelling wl: clsd bef 4 out: 3rd next: 2nd into st: chal and led fr 2 out: sn clr: styd on wl: comf* **3/1**2

2 *5* **Cuan Na Grai (IRE)**63 [365] 9-11-4 137................................. APCawley 138
(Paul Nolan, Ire) *chsd ldrs: wnt 2nd appr 4 out: led after 3 out: strly pressed and hdd fr next: sn no imp and kpt on same pce* **11/4**1

3 *2½* **Cooper's Crest (IRE)**71 [207] 7-10-9 124................................. MDarcy 127
(Sabrina J Harty, Ire) *hld up: clsr in 6th bef 4 out: 5th after next: kpt on same pce u.p in mod 3rd appr last* **10/1**

4 *5½* **Now This Is It (IRE)**18 [866] 6-11-4 .... DJCondon 130
(S R B Crawford, Ire) *mid-div: clsd into 3rd bef 4 out: 5th next: 4th after 3 out: no ex into st* **12/1**

5 *8* **Nicanor (FR)**86 [5379] 9-11-0 .... PCarberry 118
(Noel Meade, Ire) *in rr of mid-div: wnt mod 7th after 3 out: sn no imp and kpt on* **8/1**3

6 *3½* **Loch Long (IRE)**29 [789] 4-10-8 129.. APCrowe 109
(Tracey Collins, Ire) *chsd ldrs: rdn in 5th appr 5 out: 4th 3 out: sn dropped to 6th and no imp* **14/1**

7 *½* **Norther Bay (FR)**14 [904] 7-11-0 .... PTownend 114
(Eoin Griffin, Ire) *led and disp: clr of remainder: led 4th: hdd after 3 out: sn no ex* **25/1**

8 *8* **Kotkidy (FR)**68 [269] 4-10-8 128... AELynch 100
(Henry De Bromhead, Ire) *towards rr: 9th bef 4 out: sn no imp* **8/1**3

9 *13* **Essex (IRE)**22 [2539] 10-11-0 .... BarryGeraghty 93
(Denis W Cullen, Ire) *towards rr: no imp fr bef 3 out* **8/1**3

10 *8* **Powerstation (IRE)**69 [260] 10-11-9 151......................... SGMcDermott 94
(Eamonn O'Connell, Ire) *a towards rr* **10/1**

P **Takestan (IRE)**7 [966] 7-11-0 117... SWJackson —
(Patrick O Brady, Ire) *mid-div: 7th bef 4 out: sn wknd and p.u bef 2 out* **33/1**

P **Broom Battalion (IRE)**5 [981] 9-11-0 ....(p) RCColgan —
(Henry De Bromhead, Ire) *sn disp ld: 2nd at 4th: rdn appr 4 out: sn wknd and p.u bef 2 out* **50/1**

3m 44.8s (224.80)
WFA 4 from 6yo+ 15lb **12** Ran SP% **126.3**
CSF £12.75 TOTE £4.30: £1.70, £1.90, £3.00; DF 7.00.
Owner Patrick T Sweeney **Bred** Christopher Maye **Trained** Carrick-On-Suir, Co Waterford

FOCUS
Two horses stood out here and they finished first and second. The placed horses have all been rated close to their best hurdles form.

NOTEBOOK
Bahrain Storm(IRE), last year's Galway Hurdle hero, had shaped very well on the Flat at the Curragh last time and Pat Flynn said that he was in "savage order" going into this race. Benefiting from the good gallop, he travelled really well and the only question was what he would find when he joined Cuan Na Grai. He answered that in no uncertain fashion though, and was well in command at the end. Flynn said afterwards that he may use a 7lb claimer in his bid to win the Galway Hurdle again, and it is possible that this horse is still improving. He would have a chance in Ballybrit, though it is up to the handicapper now what penalty he gets. (op 3/1 tchd 7/2)
Cuan Na Grai(IRE) has been in fine form over fences and did nothing wrong. Though he had no answer to the winner, there was no shame in finishing a clear second. It seems doubtful that he will stay the Plate trip if going in that race. (op 11/4 tchd 9/4)
Cooper's Crest(IRE) had her chance on the ratings and travelled well. She was outpaced when the race hotted up but this was far better than her Swinton Hurdle effort and she will clearly be of interest in the Galway Hurdle if she runs. (op 14/1)
Now This Is It(IRE) had plenty on his plate on his first run in Ireland and probably exceeded expectations. He seems to be improving.
Nicanor(FR) will likely never be the horse he could have been and this trip is short for him, but he travelled well and this was a nice prep race for Galway.
Essex(IRE) was disappointing but is hard to place. (op 8/1 tchd 7/1)
Powerstation(IRE) was the disappointment of the race and was in trouble a long way out, even allowing for this trip being too sharp. (op 8/1)

1039 - 1042a (Foreign Racing) - See Raceform Interactive

674 BANGOR-ON-DEE (L-H)

Tuesday, July 20

OFFICIAL GOING: Good to soft changing to soft after race 2 (6.40)
Shared bends and hurdle rail on summer line.
Wind: Nil Weather: Heavy rain

1043 SUMMER SEASON CONDITIONAL JOCKEYS' H'CAP HURDLE (11 hdls) 2m 4f

6:10 (6:10) (Class 4) (0-115,114) 4-Y-0+ **£3,252** (£955; £477; £238)

Form RPR

1-46 **1** **Extreme Conviction (IRE)**34 [767] 6-11-3 **105**...................... RhysFlint 121+
(John Berry) *trckd ldrs: wnt 2nd appr 7th: led bef 3 out: a in command: clr 2 out: v easily* **9/4**1

200- **2** *7* **Dunkelly Castle (IRE)**103 [5107] 6-11-3 **105**...................(p) HaddenFrost 108
(Roger Curtis) *prom: pushed along and outpcd appr 3 out: u.p and hld whn nt fluent last: kpt on to take 2nd run-in: no ch w wnr* **5/2**2

0310 **3** *½* **Danny Zuko (IRE)**30 [803] 7-11-8 **110**..........................(b) JohnnyFarrelly 112
(Donald McCain) *hld up: clsd whn nt fluent 3 out: sn wnt 2nd: rdn and no imp on wnr appr 2 out: hld whn nt fluent last: lost 2nd run-in* **5/2**2

4 *22* **Murphys Appeal (IRE)**371 [946] 6-10-1 **92**................ DonalDevereux(3) 74
(Peter Bowen) *led: hdd appr 3 out: wknd sn after 3 out* **9/2**3

PP-0 **5** *22* **Donovan (NZ)**9 [954] 11-10-1 **99** ow1.......................(p) CraigGallagher(10) 62
(Richard Guest) *in rr: niggled along appr 5th: struggling 3 out: wl bhd after* **25/1**

5m 3.30s (5.90) **Going Correction** +0.425s/f (Soft) **5** Ran SP% **109.9**
Speed ratings (Par 105): **105,102,102,93,84**
toteswingers: 1&2 £2.40 CSF £8.39 TOTE £3.20: £1.40, £1.90; EX 8.20.
Owner All Points West Partnership **Bred** Mrs A S O'Brien And Lars Pearson **Trained** Newmarket, Suffolk

FOCUS
A handicap for conditional riders and the form is ordinary. A step up from the winner.

NOTEBOOK
Extreme Conviction(IRE) won without having to be anything like fully extended. The easing ground was of some concern for him, but he acted on it without fuss and could have been called the winner after jumping four out. He will go unpenalised if turning out before the handicapper can reassess him for this success. (op 2-1)
Dunkelly Castle(IRE) has raced mainly on quick ground since coming over from Ireland, but did win his point on soft ground and has twice been withdrawn of late on account of good to firm ground. The fact connections opted for first-time cheekpieces here is an indication he is not the most straightforward, but he could have done with more of a test and is entitled to improve for the run. (op 9-2)
Danny Zuko(IRE) saw the winner get first run on him leaving the back straight, but it made no difference to the result and he is happier on a sounder surface. (tchd 9-4)
Murphys Appeal(IRE) had shown very little when previously trained in Ireland, but was of some interest as she had joined a bang-in-form stable for her British debut and is related to winners on soft ground. She proved free out in front and was done with four out, but should come on nicely for the outing. (op 7-2)
Donovan(NZ) was left behind after the third-last and remains out of form. (op 20-1)

1044 BETFAIR H'CAP CHASE (15 fncs) 2m 4f 110y
6:40 (6:40) (Class 3) (0-130,130) 4-Y-0+ **£6,505** (£1,910; £955; £477)

Form RPR
P1-5 **1** **Radetsky March (IRE)**[67] 314 7-11-2 **120**........................ SamThomas 132+
(Mark Bradstock) *bmpd 2nd: prom in chsng gp after: j. slowly 9th: led after 3 out: clr last: styd on wl* **4/1**[1]
146- **2** *8* **Nudge And Nurdle (IRE)**[168] 3812 9-11-1 **122**................ TomMolloy(3) 126
(Nigel Twiston-Davies) *hld up: effrt 4 out: chsd front pair u.p appr 2 out: kpt on to take 2nd towards fin: no ch w wnr* **8/1**[3]
2-40 **3** *¾* **Magnetic Pole**[20] 862 9-9-9 **104** oh2..........................(v[1]) GilesHawkins(5) 107
(Richard Lee) *bmpd 2nd: chsd clr ldr fr 5th: hit 8th: clsd 10th: led 11th: hdd after 3 out: btn last: lost 2nd towards fin* **4/1**[1]
6030 **4** *5* **Good Company (IRE)**[21] 852 10-10-8 **115**............. RichieMcLernon(3) 114
(Jonjo O'Neill) *hld up: nt fluent 10th: struggling bef 3 out: plugged on at one pce bef 2 out: no imp* **9/2**[2]
-105 **5** *19* **Marodima (FR)**[27] 831 7-11-7 **130**...................................... DavidBass(5) 112
(Jamie Snowden) *led: clr appr 5th to 10th: hdd 11th: wknd after 3 out* **9/1**
P116 **6** *43* **Neutrino**[21] 852 8-10-13 **117**..(v) TomScudamore 60
(David Bridgwater) *hld up: pushed along appr 11th: lft wl bhd 4 out: t.o* **12/1**
0-3P **U** **Sunday City (JPN)**[66] 330 9-10-3 **107**......................... RichardJohnson —
(Peter Bowen) *cl up tl mstke and uns rdr 3rd* **9/2**[2]
1015 **P** **Mhilu (IRE)**[25] 839 8-11-9 **127**...................................(b) ChristianWilliams —
(John O'Shea) *j.rt thrght: prom: bhd fr 5th: t.o wh p.u bef 10th* **14/1**

5m 13.0s (3.90) **Going Correction** +0.375s/f (Yiel) **8** Ran SP% **111.8**
Speed ratings (Par 107): **107,103,103,101,94 78,—,—**
toteswingers: 1&2 £9.50, 1&3 £5.10, 2&3 £8.10 CSF £33.49 CT £132.72 TOTE £3.10: £1.10, £2.40, £3.00; EX 52.40.
Owner P J D Pottinger **Bred** Ms J Finn **Trained** Letcombe Bassett, Oxon

FOCUS
This was run at a good early gallop thanks to the front-running Marodima, who paid the price for that from six out. The ground appeared that bit better on the chase course. The form is sound rated around the second and third.

NOTEBOOK
Radetsky March(IRE) took full advantage of this easier assignment with a clear-cut success. He can be a headstrong performer, but with Marodima in attendance he was never going to gain a clear lead and a slow leap at the first fence put paid to any such aspirations. In fact he was slow at the majority of his fences, but that probably helped his cause as things transpired as it delayed his challenge until the race fell into his lap three from home. He came right away down the home straight and will be high on confidence after this, so a likely rise in the weights should ensure he can now have a deserved crack at something more valuable again later in the year. Indeed he looks the sort who may be nearing his peak, being still just a 7-y-o, and better things may await him. (op 9-2)
Nudge And Nurdle(IRE) was doing his best work late in the day on this return to action having taken an age to find his full stride from off the pace. He looks on a fair mark and should come on a deal for the outing. (op 7-1)
Magnetic Pole had a first-time visor replacing cheekpieces for his return to chasing and is a previous C&D winner on heavy ground. Well backed, he got a positive ride and hit the front four out, but was a sitting duck for the winner. He tired on the run-in and really needs his sights lowered again. (op 6-1)
Good Company(IRE) was creeping into things prior to hitting six from home and that hampered his cause. He didn't look the most willing for his rider thereafter, though. (op 11-2)

1045 IRVING SOLICITORS NOVICES' CHASE (15 fncs) 2m 4f 110y
7:10 (7:12) (Class 4) 5-Y-0+ **£3,577** (£1,050; £525; £262)

Form RPR
3-25 **1** **Jimbatai (IRE)**[23] 846 7-11-2 115...................................... DannyCook(3) 124+
(Barry Leavy) *in tch: wnt 2nd 9th: clsd on ldr 2 out: led last: rdn out and kpt on wl towards fin* **15/2**
2 *1½* **Ogre D'Estruval (FR)**[422] 455 8-10-12 106.................(b) JohnnyFarrelly 114+
(Paul John Gilligan, Ire) *led: c steadily clr fr 10th: mstke 11th: reduced advantage 2 out: rdn and hdd last: tried to rally run-in: no ex cl home* **50/1**
-2P3 **3** *15* **Magical Legend**[25] 838 9-10-5 0.....................................(t) PaulMoloney 95
(Sophie Leech) *in tch: chsd ldrs 6th: rdn appr 2 out: sn no imp* **9/4**[1]
250- **4** *7* **Call Me Mulligan (IRE)**[134] 4486 6-10-5 0...........(p) AodhaganConlon(7) 92
(Rebecca Curtis) *hld up: hdwy 7th: sn chsd ldrs: mstke 4 out: sn wknd* **9/2**[3]
0-51 **5** *2¼* **Walamo (GER)**[16] 889 6-11-5 0..................................(t) RichardJohnson 97
(Tim Vaughan) *hld up: pushed along 11th: mstke 4 out: 4th but no imp whn blnd 3 out: n.d after* **7/2**[2]
-463 **6** *82* **Another Trump (NZ)**[15] 909 6-10-12 0.................................. APMcCoy 6
(Jonjo O'Neill) *in tch: lost pl bef 9th: t.o* **11/2**
0/4- **P** **Massini Man (IRE)**[69] 9-10-12 0................................(b) JimmyMcCarthy —
(Brendan Powell) *racd keenly: prom: hit 8th: wknd 10th: t.o whn p.u bef 2 out* **28/1**
P-UU **U** **King Caine (IRE)**[66] 329 8-10-12 115......................... ChristianWilliams —
(Alan Jones) *in rr: mstke whn struggling 10th: no imp whn hmpd and uns rdr 11th* **14/1**
56 **P** **Minella (IRE)**[21] 855 6-10-12 0.. RodiGreene —
(Michael Appleby) *prom: mstke 9th: sn lost pl and wknd: t.o whn p.u bef 4 out* **50/1**

5m 13.9s (4.80) **Going Correction** +0.375s/f (Yiel) **9** Ran SP% **112.4**
Speed ratings: **105,104,98,96,95 63,—,—,—**
toteswingers: 1&2 £29.50, 1&3 £4.40, 2&3 £24.90 CSF £254.33 TOTE £4.30: £1.80, £14.20, £2.40; EX 321.20.
Owner Cops & Robbers **Bred** Mrs Cora Cronin **Trained** Forsbrook, Staffs

FOCUS
This wasn't much of a novice chase and the first pair came well clear. Ordinary form.

NOTEBOOK
Jimbatai(IRE) looked vulnerable under his penalty on this return to fences, but the rain was no doubt in his favour and he landed his first win for current connections with a game effort. He was idling once in front so is value for a touch further, but a double penalty in this sphere will most likely find him out again and a return to handicaps is now on the cards. (tchd 8-1)
Ogre D'Estruval(FR) was making his debut for new connections after a 422-day layoff and had plenty to prove. He ran a big race under an aggressive ride and only paid the price for his early exertions late on, so emerges with a lot of credit. His new yard can improve such characters, but the bounce factor will be a worry next time. (op 33-1)
Magical Legend jumped better than had been the case on her chasing debut last month, but still could've been more fluent on that front and she was a spent force soon after turning into the home straight. (op 10-3 tchd 2-1)
Call Me Mulligan(IRE), a 110-rated hurdler, looked in need of this initial experience over fences and may want further in this sphere. (op 6-1)
Walamo(GER) looked a shadow of the horse that won well at Market Rasen 16 days earlier, on account of the softer ground, but he would've had more of a say at the finish had his jumping kept together over the last four fences. (op 9-4 tchd 4-1)

1046 ENVIROSIPS NOVICES' HURDLE (9 hdls) 2m 1f
7:40 (7:45) (Class 4) 4-Y-0+ **£3,089** (£907; £453; £226)

Form RPR
3F **1** **Totoman**[33] 768 5-10-12 113..(t) RichardJohnson 113+
(Tim Vaughan) *mde all: mstke 2 out: clr last: eased down towards fin* **2/1**[2]
2 *5* **Stormyisland Ahead**[75] 189 5-11-2 0.................................(t) DPFahy(3) 113+
(Evan Williams) *chsd ldr: chalng 3 out: rdn and hung lft after 2 out: hld whn nt fluent last* **8/11**[1]
/2-6 **3** *12* **Dormouse**[27] 827 5-10-12 0... TomScudamore 93
(Anabel L M King) *in tch: effrt to chse ldrs 3 out: no imp on front 2 bef 2 out: eased whn wl hld bef last* **20/1**
/3-5 **4** *9* **Midnight Fun**[21] 855 5-10-5 0... RodiGreene 76
(Michael Appleby) *hld up: struggling 4 out: plodded on: nvr a danger* **25/1**
03 **5** *2½* **I Can Run Can You (IRE)**[72] 224 4-10-10 0.......................... APMcCoy 81
(Jonjo O'Neill) *handy: j.lft 1st and rdr lost iron briefly: nt fluent 3 out: sn wknd* **10/1**[3]
PP/0 **6** *6* **Standing Order**[6] 984 7-10-12 0... BrianHughes 75
(Richard Ford) *hld up: pushed along and struggling after 4 out: nvr a danger* **50/1**
0 **7** *12* **Motor Home**[21] 850 4-10-10 0.. JimmyMcCarthy 61
(Charlie Morlock) *hld up: nt fluent 5th: struggling whn nt fluent 3 out: nvr on terms* **25/1**
00- **8** *21* **Pergamon (IRE)**[41] 3701 4-10-10 0................................(t) LiamTreadwell 40
(Claire Dyson) *midfield: lost pl 5th: bhd 4 out* **80/1**

4m 17.0s (6.10) **Going Correction** +0.50s/f (Soft)
WFA 4 from 5yo+ 15lb **8** Ran SP% **116.0**
Speed ratings (Par 105): **105,102,97,92,91 88,83,73**
toteswingers: 1&2 £1.10, 1&3 £3.10, 2&3 £3.40 CSF £3.84 TOTE £4.00: £1.40, £1.02, £2.70; EX 4.80.
Owner Treoes Racing Club **Bred** Norcroft Park Stud **Trained** Aberthin, Vale of Glamorgan

FOCUS
A modest novices' hurdle. The easy winner closed in on the level of the best of his Irish form.

NOTEBOOK
Totoman made all for a deserved first success as a hurdler and obviously had no trouble with this easier surface. As a horse that had previously had plenty of chances, his attitude had come under question, but getting out in front here made the difference to him and he responded well to shake off his main market rival off the home turn. The winner will be vulnerable under a penalty unless this confidence-boost sees him improve a good deal, but connections could switch him to fences at the end of the summer. (op 15-8)
Stormyisland Ahead joined his new connections for £18,000 after winning at Clonmel in May and the money really came for him on this British debut. He travelled strongly just off Totoman through the race but got in too low at most of his hurdles, and the lack of fluency mounted up as he found little for pressure. He should be making amends providing his trainer can get him jumping more accurately. (op Evens)
Dormouse proved very easy to back. He couldn't live with the first pair after making up ground on the back straight, but has some scope and is one to look out for when switching to handicaps back on a quicker surface. (op 14-1)
Midnight Fun was never in the hunt from off the pace on this switch to hurdling and is more of one for handicaps over a stiffer test in due course. (op 22-1)
I Can Run Can You(IRE), returning from a 72-day break, still looked raw and was unable to raise his game for the softer surface. He will surely find his feet in handicaps down the line. (op 11-1)

1047 PADDOCK RESTAURANT H'CAP CHASE (12 fncs) 2m 1f 110y
8:10 (8:13) (Class 4) (0-105,105) 4-Y-0+ **£3,740** (£1,098; £549; £274)

Form RPR
6-00 **1** **King Ozzy (IRE)**[23] 848 6-11-12 **105**............................ RichardJohnson 116+
(Martin Keighley) *a.p: led 4th: clr appr 2 out: styd on wl: eased down run-in* **11/2**
1651 **2** *11* **Misamon (FR)**[9] 950 7-10-13 **99** 7ex...........................(v) MrJFMathias(7) 93
(David Rees) *led: hdd 4th: remained prom: rdn and wl outpcd appr 3 out: rallied bef last: kpt on to take 2nd run-in: no ch w wnr* **4/1**[3]
-643 **3** *3½* **Le Brocquy**[6] 984 5-10-11 **95**..............................(p) JimmyDerham(5) 86
(Martin Keighley) *hld up: hdwy to chse wnr 3 out: effrt 2 out: no imp bef last: lost 2nd run-in: wknd* **6/1**
F06- **4** *nse* **Whimper (FR)**[136] 4451 5-11-10 **103**................................ DavidEngland 94
(Nigel Twiston-Davies) *trckd ldrs tl lost pl and struggling appr 3 out: kpt on u.p but no ch run-in* **11/1**
-503 **5** *7* **Indiana Gold (FR)**[9] 961 6-10-13 **92**...................................(p) APMcCoy 75
(Alison Thorpe) *prom: rdn after 4 out: wknd after 3 out* **9/4**[1]
252F **6** *42* **Troodos Jet**[5] 1001 9-10-0 **79** oh2..(p) BrianHughes 20
(Dianne Sayer) *hld up: effrt and hdwy after 4 out: wknd after 3 out: eased whn wl btn run-in: t.o* **7/2**[2]

4m 31.7s (9.60) **Going Correction** +0.45s/f (Soft) **6** Ran SP% **111.0**
Speed ratings (Par 105): **96,91,89,89,86 67**
toteswingers: 1&2 £2.80, 1&3 £3.70, 2&3 £4.50 CSF £26.72 CT £129.88 TOTE £7.40: £4.80, £2.10; EX 24.80.
Owner The Black Pearl Racing Club **Bred** Edmond Kent **Trained** Condicote, Gloucs

FOCUS
A tricky looking handicap that was further muddled by the steady gallop. A step up from the winner on his hurdles best, but this is not strong form.

NOTEBOOK

King Ozzy(IRE) eventually went clear and ultimately defied top weight pretty much as he pleased. The subject of good support, this was a drop in class for him and the softer ground was a help, but it was still a vast improvement. He could be in trouble if the handicapper takes this form literally and perhaps turning out under a penalty is his best option. Official explanation: trainer's rep said, regarding apparent improvement in form, that the gelding appeared to benefit from the soft ground. (op 13-2)

Misamon(FR) was surprisingly taking his chance under a 7lb penalty considering the handicapper raised him 4lb for his Southwell win last week, and he is unproven on this contrasting ground. He hit a flat spot when the race got serious before rallying off the home turn. He will be more at home back on a sounder surface. (op 7-2 tchd 10-3)

Le Brocquy, making his chasing debut, travelled up nicely into contention in the back straight but lacked the required gear change to go with the winner when he asserted. He can win one of these when reverting to a quicker surface. (op 5-1 tchd 9-2)

Whimper(FR) showed very little for David Pipe and was making his debut for a new stable without the headgear. Easy to back, he showed his quirks by downing tools when first asked for an effort and then rallying strongly all too late in the home straight. Surely some headgear will be back on again next time, and he will likely appreciate going back up in distance. (op 7-1 tchd 12-1)

Indiana Gold(FR) failed to up his game for first-time cheekpieces, but probably found the ground against him. (op 11-4)

Troodos Jet, a faller at Cartmel five days earlier, looked a possible danger four out, but he stopped to nothing shortly afterwards. (op 5-1 tchd 3-1)

1048 ROSE HILL H'CAP HURDLE (DIV I) (10 hdls 1 omitted) 2m 4f

8:40 (8:40) (Class 5) (0-85,84) 4-Y-0+ **£2,500** (£728; £364)

Form RPR

4-63 **1** **Eastwell Smiles**[13] 930 6-11-10 **82**........................(bt) RichardJohnson 92
(Richard Phillips) *mde all: clr fr 3rd: hit 5th: rdn appr last: kpt on wl* **11/4**[1]

P3-0 **2** *5* **Magical Island**[67] 318 7-11-7 **79**.................................(b) PaulMoloney 84
(Sophie Leech) *chsd clr wnr thrght: mstke 6th: rdn and clsd appr last: no further imp run-in* **11/1**

54/5 **3** *16* **Miss Molly Be Rude (IRE)**[47] 600 8-10-10 **68**............. RobertWalford 61+
(Tim Walford) *hld up: hdwy into midfield after 5th: rdn whn chsd ldrs 8th: no further imp bef last* **9/1**

6-00 **4** *13* **Strumble Head (IRE)**[37] 737 5-11-9 **81**.......................(p) TomO'Brien 57
(Peter Bowen) *midfield: reminders and lost pl after 4th: plugged on u.p but no imp on ldrs fr 8th* **9/1**

05-0 **5** *32* **Robbmaa (FR)**[11] 698 5-10-9 **67**.............................(b) MattieBatchelor 11
(Tony Carroll) *chsd ldrs tl wknd bef 7th* **16/1**

4/- **6** *½* **Super Kay (IRE)**[93] 9-11-7 **84**................................ DavidBass(5) 28
(Lawney Hill) *chsd ldrs: lost pl and struggling 6th: n.d after* **6/1**[2]

P-U0 **7** *3 ¼* **Tarkesar (IRE)**[20] 865 8-10-10 **71**.............................(p) SeanQuinlan(3) 11
(Carole Ikin) *chsd ldrs: lost pl bef 5th: n.d after* **22/1**

-120 **8** *3* **Pugnacity**[19] 875 6-11-6 **81**.. RyanMania(3) 18
(Dianne Sayer) *hld up: struggling 6th: nvr on terms* **16/1**

F006 **P** **Un Autre Espere**[6] 991 11-10-4 **72**.............................(b) JoshWall(10) —
(Trevor Wall) *sn rdn along and bhd: t.o 6th: p.u bef 9th* **50/1**

P **One Shot Sheehan (IRE)**[553] 3348 14-11-1 **73**...........(t) JohnnyFarrelly —
(F M Hanley, Ire) *a in rr: t.o whn p.u bef 8th* **50/1**

-124 **P** **Moon Melody (GER)**[15] 913 7-11-5 **80**..........................(vt) DPFahy(3) —
(Evan Williams) *chsd ldrs: wknd bef 8th: t.o whn p.u bef 9th* **7/1**[3]

2P-2 **F** **Colonial Jim (IRE)**[40] 692 7-11-6 **78**........................(b) DougieCostello —
(Neil Mulholland) *midfield: niggled along whn fell 4th* **6/1**[2]

5m 5.70s (8.30) **Going Correction** +0.50s/f (Soft) **12** Ran SP% **116.1**
Speed ratings (Par 103): **103,101,94,89,76 76,75,73,—,— —,—**
toteswingers: 1&2 £6.60, 1&3 £6.80, 2&3 £11.70 CSF £32.20 CT £238.93 TOTE £2.70: £1.10, £3.60, £3.60; EX 41.70.
Owner Mrs S J Harvey **Bred** Old Mill Stud **Trained** Adlestrop, Gloucs
■ Stewards' Enquiry : Josh Wall two-day ban: used whip when out of contention (Aug 3,6)

FOCUS

This was a moderate handicap but the time was reasonable. The first two are on the upgrade.

NOTEBOOK

Eastwell Smiles was able to open up a clear early lead without having to over-exert himself, and nothing ever threatened to land a blow from out the back. The winner was 2lb higher than when attempting to make all on his previous outing, but the easier ground clearly suited this time and the recent application of blinkers has helped his cause. (op 9-2)

Magical Island, having his first outing for 57 days, was the one that kept closest tabs on Eastwell Smiles through the race and that saw him finish a clear second best. (op 8-1)

Miss Molly Be Rude(IRE), up in trip, did her best to close on the first two coming out of the back straight, but underfoot conditions eventually told on her. (op 17-2 tchd 8-1)

Strumble Head(IRE), ridden out the back, was hampered by the fall of Colonial Jim entering the home straight for the first time. He plugged on without landing a blow and more positive handling over this trip is required. (op 12-1)

1049 ROSE HILL H'CAP HURDLE (DIV II) (11 hdls) 2m 4f

9:10 (9:10) (Class 5) (0-85,84) 4-Y-0+ **£2,500** (£728; £364)

Form RPR

0/4- **1** **Optimum (IRE)**[275] 1812 8-11-9 **81**....................................... GrahamLee 97+
(Richard Ford) *hld up: hdwy after 6th: led after 3 out: in command whn j.lft last: eased down towards fin* **7/2**[1]

6054 **2** *3* **Be Ashored**[6] 990 5-11-12 **84**.. DenisO'Regan 95
(Nicky Vaughan) *in tch: wnt 2nd after 4 out: chalng 3 out: sn rdn: one pce fr last* **11/2**[3]

-340 **3** *35* **Mujamead**[23] 845 6-11-6 **83**.......................................(p) LeeEdwards(5) 64
(Sally-Anne Wheelwright) *led: rdn and hdd after 3 out: wknd 2 out* **8/1**

0406 **4** *6* **Clueless**[20] 860 8-11-4 **76**..(tp) PeterBuchanan 46
(Carol Ferguson) *midfield: rdn and struggling 7th: plugged on fr bef 2 out: nvr a danger* **14/1**

-43P **5** *2 ¾* **Ruby Valentine (FR)**[20] 864 7-10-13 **78**.................. MissGAndrews(7) 45
(Jim Wilson) *chsd ldrs: effrt 3 out: wknd sn after* **12/1**

U32- **6** *10* **Form And Beauty (IRE)**[219] 2861 8-11-3 **75**............... RichardJohnson 32
(Bernard Llewellyn) *hld up: u.p in midfield 6th: no imp whn mstke 4 out: n.d* **4/1**[2]

-00P **7** *13* **Lady Of Ashcott**[13] 930 4-9-10 **64**...............................(b[1]) MarkQuinlan(7) —
(Neil Mulholland) *chsd ldr tl after 4 out: sn rdn and wknd: eased whn wl btn bef 2 out* **25/1**

-P00 **8** *6* **Dashing Bach (IRE)**[15] 912 6-10-5 **70**....................(tp) OliverDayman(7) —
(Alison Thorpe) *midfield: rdn and wknd 7th* **6/1**

0-04 **9** *81* **Kalatime (IRE)**[47] 603 7-10-9 **72**.............................(p) JamesHalliday(5) —
(William Young) *a bhd: t.o* **14/1**

23-5 **P** **Magic Merlin**[51] 532 9-11-10 **82**..................................... JimmyMcCarthy —
(Charlie Morlock) *midfield: lost pl after 5th: t.o whn p.u bef 2 out* **12/1**

436- **F** **Diamanpeg (IRE)**[275] 1808 6-11-2 **81**........................(vt[1]) MrJFMathias(7) —
(David Rees) *bhd: struggling after 6th: fell 7th* **11/1**

-U66 **P** **Danzig Fox**[33] 678 5-11-7 **79**.. RodiGreene —
(Michael Mullineaux) *midfield: niggled along appr 6th: wknd 7th: t.o whn p.u bef 2 out* **33/1**

PP5- **P** **One More Cent**[84] 30 5-10-3 **64**................................. JamesO'Farrell(3) —
(Dianne Sayer) *chsd ldrs: mstke and lost pl 5th: t.o whn p.u bef 4 out* **33/1**

5m 11.1s (13.70) **Going Correction** +0.50s/f (Soft)
WFA 4 from 5yo+ 16lb **13** Ran SP% **129.8**
Speed ratings (Par 103): **92,90,76,74,73 69,64,61,29,— —,—,—**
toteswingers: 1&2 £6.90, 1&3 £13.90, 2&3 £13.20 CSF £25.34 CT £152.66 TOTE £5.30: £2.20, £1.20, £4.40; EX 25.60 Place 6 £37.20, Place 5 £22.77.
Owner J T Stimpson **Bred** Mrs Brid Cosgrove **Trained** Butterton, Staffs

FOCUS

This second division of the 2m4f handicap was another moderate and open-looking affair. The first two came clear and are rated to their marks. The time was slow.

NOTEBOOK

Optimum(IRE) was well backed on this first run for 274 days and ran out a ready winner. He was patiently ridden and made smooth headway to join the leaders turning out of the back straight. It was apparent before the penultimate flight he was in control and he clearly proved well suited by the easing ground. This was his first win since 2006. (tchd 4-1)

Be Ashored also crept into the race going strongly nearing the home bend. He couldn't match the winner from the top of the home straight, but was still a clear second-best and this was better from him on softer ground. The problem is the handicapper will put him up for this. (op 5-1 tchd 9-2)

Mujamead, with cheekpieces back on, ensured this was a fair test but was a sitting duck for the first pair after the third-last. It was a more encouraging display and he really needs better ground over this trip. (op 10-1 tchd 11-1)

Clueless got behind on the back straight before plugging on without posing any sort of threat from three out. (tchd 10-1)

T/Plt: £41.90 to a £1 stake. Pool: £65,206.23. 1,133.68 winning tickets. T/Qpdt: £19.00 to a £1 stake. Pool: £5,935.75. 230.10 winning tickets. DO

1050 - 1056a (Foreign Racing) - See Raceform Interactive

[989]WORCESTER (L-H)

Wednesday, July 21

OFFICIAL GOING: Good to firm (good in places; watered: chs 7.9, hde 7.8)

In the 4.20, the first and last fences in the back st were omitted on both circuits, plus the open ditch in the back st on the first circuit.

Wind: almost nil Weather: cloudy but very ward

1057 3663 FIRST FOR FOODSERVICE AMATEUR RIDERS' H'CAP HURDLE (DIV I) (12 hdls) 3m

2:20 (2:21) (Class 5) (0-95,97) 4-Y-0+ **£1,648** (£507; £253)

Form RPR

0-01 **1** **Makena (FR)**[10] 955 8-11-10 **97** 7ex.............................(p) MrJFMathias(5) 110+
(David Rees) *bhd: smooth prog 8th: led on bit 3 out: clr next: hrd hld* **5/2**[1]

P030 **2** *9* **Aisemma (IRE)**[15] 920 6-11-2 **84**... MrRMahon 82
(Peter Bowen) *cl up: led 8th: rdn and hdd 3 out: chsd wnr vainly after: flattered by proximity* **12/1**

P-6U **3** *1 ¼* **The Hairy Mutt (IRE)**[31] 797 8-11-0 **89**........................ MissLBrooke(7) 87+
(Lady Susan Brooke) *bhd: hdwy 8th: wnt 3rd and ev ch 3 out: wl hld by wnr fr next: j.rt last and hung rt after* **33/1**

4424 **4** *8* **Thehonourablelady**[15] 920 9-11-4 **93**.......................(tp) ThomasFlint(7) 82
(John Flint) *chsd ldr tl after 6th: remained handy: 6th and rdn bef 3 out: plugged on same pce* **5/1**[2]

0-50 **5** *2 ¾* **Bathwick Breeze**[15] 921 6-11-1 **90**.................................. MissJBuck(7) 76
(David Pipe) *last and rdn after 3rd: nvr gng willingly: plugged past btn horses after 9th: nvr nr ldrs* **16/1**

-51P **6** *6* **Hemington**[16] 911 7-11-9 **94**... MrTWeston(3) 75
(Michael Scudamore) *towards rr early: chsd ldrs fr 6th: rdn 8th: one pce and btn bef 3 out* **10/1**

5-4B **7** *9* **Le Forezien (FR)**[16] 913 11-10-7 **82**.............................. MrRHawkins(7) 53
(Carroll Gray) *chsd ldrs to 7th: struggling bef 3 out* **11/1**

4PP- **8** *1 ¾* **Mysaynoway**[46] 8-10-5 **80**............................ MissEmily-JaneHarbour(7) 49
(Lawney Hill) *midfield: lost tch after 9th* **16/1**

0-50 **9** *48* **Itzacliche (IRE)**[37] 749 10-10-4 **79**...................(b) MissJRRichards(7) —
(Nicky Richards) *prom: slt ld 7th tl 8th: fdd rapidly after 9th: wl t.o but rdn out* **12/1**

5P-4 **10** *2 ¾* **Milton Des Bieffes (FR)**[7] 993 10-11-3 **90**................... MrPJTolman(5) 9
(David Evans) *led tl hrd drvn and hdd 7th: t.o bef 3 out: eased last* **6/1**[3]

-603 **P** **Barlin Bay**[10] 955 6-9-9 **68** oh4................................. MrRGHenderson(5) —
(Harry Chisman) *pushed along in rr after 6th: sn looking distressed: t.o after 7th: p.u 9th: b.b.v* **9/1**

050 **P** **Rosie Larkin (IRE)**[57] 461 6-10-0 **75** oh8 ow7...............(t) MrMMarris(7) —
(Joss Saville) *dropped to rr and rdn 6th: t.o and p.u after next: sddle slipped* **40/1**

5m 36.6s (-8.00) **Going Correction** -0.05s/f (Good) **12** Ran SP% **119.5**
Speed ratings (Par 103): **111,108,107,104,104 102,99,98,82,81 —,—**
toteswingers:1&2:£8.30, 1&3:£29.70, 2&3:£29.70 CSF £33.65 CT £817.11 TOTE £4.40: £1.50, £4.30, £6.20; EX 47.00.
Owner D L Evans **Bred** Roland Lacrampe Cuyaubere **Trained** Clarbeston, Pembrokes

FOCUS

There was 1mm of rain overnight following 4mm of watering on Tuesday. One of the riders in the opener described the ground as "goodish with one or two good to soft patches", rather at odds with the official description. The bend on the hurdles course was 12m off the inside line, and the run-in on the hurdles track was dolled off with the horses finishing on the chase run-in. This very moderate handicap for amateurs was run at a solid pace, and in a time 9.4 seconds quicker than the second division. It was the better of the divisions and the winner is progressing quickly.

NOTEBOOK

Makena(FR) shrugged off a slight mistake two from home to saunter clear. The mare was 3lb well in under the penalty she picked up under this jockey at Southwell on her previous outing, and could turn out over fences at Southwell on Friday. (op 11-4 tchd 3-1)

Aisemma(IRE) found the winner laughing at her all the way up the straight, but this was still a better effort than the one she put in at Uttoxeter. The return to 3m probably helped but she gave the impression that some headgear would not come amiss.

The Hairy Mutt(IRE) ran well on this first foray over hurdles since 2008 but could make no inroads on the first two after latching on to the leaders' heels on the home turn. He has an unattractive action. (op 28-1)

Thehonourablelady is back on the mark off which she gained her last win, at this venue back in October, but has now made the frame nine times since that victory. This trip stretches her stamina.

Bathwick Breeze was being pushed along in rear with over a circuit left and eventually plugged on for fifth. The regular blinkers might well be back next time. (op 28-1)

Hemington landed the John Corbet Cup two runs back, but that prestigious hunter chase is over 3m4f and he found this an insufficient test of stamina. (op 11-1 tchd 12-1)

Milton Des Bieffes(FR), who made a fair bit of the running, is not as good over hurdles and found the ground a bit quick. (op 13-2 tchd 11-2)

1058 BET TEST MATCH CRICKET - BETDAQ NOVICES' HURDLE (8 hdls) 2m
2:50 (2:50) (Class 4) 4-Y-0+ **£2,602** (£764; £382; £190)

Form RPR
6-1 **1** **Dreamwalk (IRE)**[14] 932 4-11-0 0 HaddenFrost(3) 110+
(Roger Curtis) *trckd ldrs: pushed along bef 3 out: sn wnt 2nd: chal 3 out: tk slt ld and gng best whn lft clr next: 8 l ahd last: unchal* **6/4**[2]
12-1 **2** *4* **Five Out Of Five (IRE)**[44] 662 6-11-12 131 (t) PaulMoloney 114+
(Evan Williams) *led tl after 2nd: lft in ld 3rd: nt fluent 4th: pressed 3 out: jst hdd and looking 2nd best whn blnd next and landed v awkwardly: no ch after* **4/6**[1]
P **3** *25* **Whos Counting**[36] 754 6-9-12 0 MrRGHenderson(7) 63
(Kevin Bishop) *chsd ldrs: blnd 5th and rdn: btn next: poor 3rd fr 2 out: nt fluent last* **66/1**
U **4** *11* **Echo Dancer**[40] 711 4-10-0 0 JoshWall(10) 58
(Trevor Wall) *t.k.h: lft 2nd at 3rd tl rdn bef 3 out: dropped out rapidly* **40/1**[3]
0 **5** *24* **Roc De Guye (FR)**[46] 635 5-10-12 0 DavidDennis 35
(James Evans) *hld up in last pair: lost tch 5th: t.o next* **50/1**
PFP- **6** *22* **Heroic Lad**[132] 4541 5-10-12 0 (t) JackDoyle 13
(Andrew Haynes) *led after 2nd tl blnd 3rd: struggling 5th: t.o next: sn eased* **50/1**

3m 46.6s (-0.70) **Going Correction** -0.05s/f (Good)
WFA 4 from 5yo+ 15lb **6** Ran SP% **107.8**
Speed ratings (Par 105): **99,97,84,79,67 56**
toteswingers:1&2:£1.02, 1&3:£10.50, 2&3:£8.10 CSF £2.71 TOTE £1.90: £1.40, £1.10; EX 3.30.
Owner R P Behan **Bred** Peter Savill **Trained** Lambourn, Berks

FOCUS
Half the declared runners were absentees in this novice hurdle, which duly turned out to be the two-horse race it had looked on paper. The pace was ordinary. A big step up from the winner with the second 8lb off.

NOTEBOOK
Dreamwalk(IRE) followed up his C&D win a fortnight ago with a pretty easy success in the end, already looking about to get on top when his market rival blundered two out. There may be a bit more improvement in him granted a stiffer gallop. (tchd 11-8)
Five Out Of Five(IRE) had to be picked up off the ground two from home, and the blunder ended his winning chance. The drop in trip was against the doubly penalised gelding, whose jumping has given cause for concern before. (tchd 8-11)
Whos Counting plugged on for a modest third. She is very moderate on the Flat and it may prove a similar story over hurdles.
Echo Dancer, a fair performer on sand, was out of the race at the first on his hurdles bow and failed to get home here after taking a keen hold.

1059 3663 FIRST FOR FOODSERVICE AMATEUR RIDERS' H'CAP HURDLE (DIV II) (12 hdls) 3m
3:20 (3:21) (Class 5) (0-95,94) 4-Y-0+ **£1,648** (£507; £253)

Form RPR
-65P **1** **Shergill (IRE)**[57] 467 9-9-10 71 (b) MrOGarner(7) 77+
(Shaun Lycett) *prom: led 7th: 4 l clr but rdn bef 3 out: pressed briefly last but kpt plugging on flat* **9/1**
65-3 **2** *3 ¼* **Heezagrey (IRE)**[7] 992 7-9-11 68 oh3 RobertKirk(3) 68
(James Evans) *bhd: last and rdn after 6th: 15 l 6th 3 out: stl 12 l 5th at last: styd on stoutly to snatch 2nd: gave himself too much to do* **7/2**[2]
P **3** *¾* **Kingston Queen (IRE)**[14] 931 7-11-0 82 (p) MrRPQuinlan 81
(Kim Bailey) *pckd 1st: bhd: hmpd 7th: hdwy 9th: rdn and racd awkwardly and edging lft fr 2 out: wnt 2nd but nt rch wnr after last: lost 2nd nr fin* **33/1**
40-0 **4** *½* **Coeur Brule (FR)**[17] 886 4-11-3 94 MrDavidTurner(5) 90
(Sam Davison) *s.s: sn in tch in rr: effrt 8th: wnt 2nd bef 3 out: tried to chal last where j.lft: bmpd along and hung lft: one pce and lost two pls flat* **10/1**
5412 **5** *4 ½* **Alfadora**[7] 993 10-11-11 93 (t) MrRMahon 87
(Milton Harris) *towards rr: effrt 8th: sn rdn: 5th and outpcd bef 3 out: plugged on between last two and wnt 4th tl after last: no ex flat* **11/8**[1]
236- **6** *49* **Dan Maguire (IRE)**[53] 9-11-8 93 (p) MrTWeston(3) 38
(Peter Pritchard) *midfield: lost tch after 9th: t.o and eased next* **12/1**
-066 **7** *8* **Always Cruising (USA)**[29] 825 5-10-6 79 MrRGHenderson(5) 16
(Linda Blackford) *led tl after 3rd: w wnr but rdn whn nt fluent 9th: dropped out rapidly: t.o and fin v weakly* **14/1**
-025 **8** *3* **Freedom Flying**[15] 920 7-11-9 94 (p) MrMSeston(3) 28
(Philip Kirby) *on and off bridle and nvr looking keen: midfield: drvn 6th: no ch 8th: t.o 3 out* **8/1**[3]
P- **9** *42* **Carroll Grey (IRE)**[128] 4636 9-9-9 70 oh4 ow2 MissGSwan(7) —
(John Upson) *led after 3rd tl 7th: t.o and wd whn hmpd by loose horse 9th* **40/1**
2/60 **U** **Penric**[7] 990 10-10-8 83 MrJBanks(7) —
(Martin Bosley) *chsng ldrs on inner: hit 7th and uns rdr* **28/1**

5m 46.0s (1.40) **Going Correction** -0.05s/f (Good)
WFA 4 from 5yo+ 17lb **10** Ran SP% **117.7**
Speed ratings (Par 103): **95,93,93,93,92 75,73,72,58,—**
toteswingers:1&2:£5.60, 1&3:£26.80, 2&3:£21.30 CSF £41.23 CT £1012.55 TOTE £12.60: £3.00, £1.80, £7.80; EX 46.20.
Owner Xperience Racing **Bred** Edmond Vaughan **Trained** Clapton-on-the-Hill, Gloucs
■ Ollie Garner's first winner under rules.

FOCUS
This poor race was run in a time the best part of ten seconds slower than the first division. The race is rated around the second to fourth.

NOTEBOOK
Shergill(IRE) did not arrive here in any sort of form, but he had been dropped a further 7lb to a career-low mark and had the blinkers back on. He kept up the gallop down the straight to maintain his advantage and his retirement has been deferred for now. This did not take much winning and he may well struggle to follow this up. (tchd 10-1)
Heezagrey(IRE)'s improved third here on his recent debut for the yard did not go unnoticed and he will be racing off no less than 24lb higher in future. Not looking to be on a going day, he was in rear for much of the way and was still only fifth jumping the last before he flew home for second. Connections might be rueing this missed chance. (op 4-1 tchd 9-2)
Kingston Queen(IRE), an ex-Irish mare, was pulled up over fences here on her recent debut for the yard and had the cheekpieces back on. She began to stay on for pressure from the home turn and briefly reached second place on the run-in. (op 25-1)
Coeur Brule(FR), 6lb lower, travelled quite well after needing reminders to jump off at the start. He went in pursuit of the winner on the home turn, but jumped out to the left over the final flight as his stamina started to wane over this longer trip. (op 16-1)
Alfadora has been running well over fences at this track but despite being 10lb lower over hurdles he lacked the pace to get involved. (op 7-4)
Always Cruising(USA) failed to get home on this step back up in trip. (op 16-1)

Freedom Flying ran in snatches and looked hard work for her jockey. (op 5-1)

1060 BETDAQ.CO.UK H'CAP HURDLE (DIV I) (8 hdls) 2m
3:50 (3:50) (Class 5) (0-85,84) 4-Y-0+ **£1,712** (£499; £249)

Form RPR
6512 **1** **Misamon (FR)**[1] 1047 7-11-5 84 (v) MrJFMathias(7) 92+
(David Rees) *prom: rdn bef 4th: led and bmpd by rival between last two: kpt on wl flat: all out* **9/4**[1]
0P0- **2** *1 ½* **Princess Tahoe**[241] 2441 6-10-4 69 KyleJames(7) 74+
(Philip Kirby) *t.k.h and nt fluent: prom: led 5th: 3 l clr bef next: hdd and wnt lft between last two: drvn and kpt on flat: a hld* **11/1**
5-60 **3** *3 ¾* **We'Re Delighted**[9] 762 5-11-12 84 (t) DenisO'Regan 83
(Michael Blake) *bhd and keen: hdwy after 5th: chsd ldrs but hanging rt fr 3 out: no imp between last two* **11/2**[3]
-065 **4** *1 ¼* **Spring Haze**[7] 989 5-10-9 74 (t) MrDGPrichard(7) 72
(Phillip Dando) *prom: rdn after 5th: one pce and no imp fr two out* **8/1**
03P/ **5** *11* **Indigo Dancer**[615] 2176 7-10-8 73 OliverDayman(7) 60
(J D J Davies) *midfield: drvn 4th: wknd after next* **25/1**
55-0 **6** *2 ½* **Rince Donn (IRE)**[24] 845 8-11-3 78 HaddenFrost(3) 63
(Roger Curtis) *midfield: rdn after 5th: wknd next* **9/2**[2]
0440 **7** *10* **Golden Square**[14] 933 8-11-6 83 (b) LeeEdwards(5) 58
(Tony Carroll) *rdn to ld: drvn and hdd 5th: gave up rapidly* **15/2**
-066 **8** *11* **Kapborg (FR)**[36] 754 4-11-8 82 (t) TomScudamore 44
(David Pipe) *hld up in last trio: rdn and lost tch after 5th: coasting along whn blnd last* **8/1**
P00 **9** *57* **Special Bond**[36] 754 4-10-13 73 (b) RodiGreene —
(Kevin Bishop) *nt jump wl in rr: rdr lost iron briefly 2nd: rdn 4th: t.o 3 out* **16/1**

3m 48.1s (0.80) **Going Correction** -0.05s/f (Good)
WFA 4 from 5yo+ 15lb **9** Ran SP% **116.4**
Speed ratings (Par 103): **96,95,93,92,87 86,81,75,47**
toteswingers:1&2:£7.30, 1&3:£2.60, 2&3:£24.90 CSF £27.34 CT £123.78 TOTE £3.30: £1.30, £3.20, £2.40; EX 36.50.
Owner The Supreme Racing Club **Bred** Alain Ranson **Trained** Clarbeston, Pembrokes

FOCUS
A weak handicap hurdle run in a time 1.5 seconds slower than the earlier novice race, and not form to treat positively. The winner produced a big step up on his previous hurdles form.

NOTEBOOK
Misamon(FR) had been runner-up over fences at Bangor the previous night, but he showed no ill effects and was racing off a 15lb lower hurdles mark here, officially 4lb ahead of the handicapper. After coming under pressure some way out he showed ahead going to the last, idling once in front. He will be given a short break now. (op 7-2)
Princess Tahoe, a lightly raced maiden, had shown very little previously and was having her first outing since November. Racing off a lowly mark on this handicap debut, she went several lengths clear off the home turn but looked inexperienced in front and was worn down by the winner, after bumping him between the last two flights. She did rally after the last and will have learned from this. (op 14-1 tchd 10-1)
We'Re Delighted has been running moderately on the Flat since his last hurdles venture. He improved from the rear off the home turn but was no threat to the first two from the second-last. Stamina looks to be a problem. (op 6-1 tchd 5-1)
Spring Haze, tried in a first-time tongue tie, plugged on for fourth and probably needs further. (op 10-1)
Rince Donn(IRE) was 7lb lower but again finished weakly. (op 11-2 tchd 4-1)
Kapborg(FR) was always towards the rear on this handicap debut and looks very moderate on this evidence, but she is in good hands and it may be early days to be writing her off. (op 5-1)

1061 WEATHERBYS BLOODSTOCK INSURANCE H'CAP CHASE (13 fncs 5 omitted) 2m 7f
4:20 (4:20) (Class 4) (0-100,100) 4-Y-0+ **£3,252** (£955; £477; £238)

Form RPR
6-03 **1** **Marked Man (IRE)**[31] 795 14-11-2 90 CharliePoste 104+
(Richard Lee) *chsd ldrs: lft 2nd at 9th: led 2 out: 3 l clr last: pushed along and kpt gng gamely to increase advantage* **12/1**
-0P4 **2** *8* **Keltic Lord**[21] 868 14-11-4 92 NickScholfield 96
(Peter Hiatt) *prom: lft in ld 9th: rdn bef 3 out: hdd and mstke next: wknd last* **16/1**
-445 **3** *19* **Thyne Spirit (IRE)**[31] 797 11-10-0 74 oh16 ColinBolger 59
(Simon Lewis) *mstkes in rr: lost tch and mstke 6th: sn t.o: 45 l last at last: plugged on to go 3rd nr fin* **33/1**
/P34 **4** *2 ½* **Lord Lescribaa (FR)**[20] 872 7-10-7 81 (b) RhysFlint 63
(Philip Hobbs) *chsd ldrs: hmpd 9th: sn struggling: lft poor 3rd and hmpd 3 out: lost 3rd cl home* **9/1**
-400 **5** *25* **Young Tot (IRE)**[36] 757 12-10-6 85 IanPopham(5) 42
(Carroll Gray) *bhd fr 6th: t.o after 10th* **33/1**
6-2P **P** **Classic Rock**[14] 931 11-10-9 83 (p) JimmyMcCarthy —
(James Unett) *mstkes and nvr gng wl: lost tch 6th: t.o and p.u 3 out* **17/2**
43-P **P** **Kingfisher Niamh**[24] 849 10-10-4 85 (t) AdamWedge(7) —
(Paul Cowley) *in rr and rdn after 6th: sn lost tch: t.o and p.u 8th: dismntd* **12/1**
-256 **F** **Morenito (FR)**[17] 891 7-11-5 93 (p) SamThomas —
(Tom George) *pressed ldr tl fell heavily 9th* **12/1**
-501 **U** **Sam Cruise**[14] 931 9-11-2 90 (t) AidanColeman —
(Steve Gollings) *led and j.rt: hdd 9th: sn fdd: 17 l 3rd whn blnd and uns rdr 3 out* **9/2**[2]
10-2 **P** **Victory Surge (IRE)**[83] 55 6-11-12 100 APMcCoy —
(Jonjo O'Neill) *j.rt and nvr gng wl in rr: t.o whn hmpd 9th: p.u next* **6/1**[3]
/6-2 **B** **Merry Terry**[15] 918 6-11-3 91 JoeTizzard —
(Colin Tizzard) *trckd ldrs: nt fluent 8th: b.d next* **11/4**[1]

5m 43.8s (1.20) **Going Correction** -0.05s/f (Good) **11** Ran SP% **114.5**
Speed ratings (Par 105): **95,92,85,84,76 —,—,—,—,— —**
toteswingers:1&2:£31.70, 1&3:£51.50, 2&3:£28.40 CSF £175.21 CT £5974.35 TOTE £18.20: £4.90, £4.40, £7.00; EX 172.00.
Owner Mr & Mrs C R Elliott **Bred** Patrick Hogan **Trained** Byton, H'fords

FOCUS
A modest handicap and the only steeplechase on an eight-race card. The complexion of the race changed at the ninth. Only five finished and the first two were both 14yos. Marked Man is rated 3lb off his best form of 2009.

NOTEBOOK
Marked Man(IRE) led two from home and ground it out well enough up the extended run-in. Now 40lb below his peak rating, he was notching the tenth success of his long career, but his first away from his local Hereford track since late 2005. (op 11-1)
Keltic Lord reverted to more prominent tactics and ran a gallant race in second, but was held by his fellow veteran once headed. (tchd 20-1)
Thyne Spirit(IRE) was no less than 16lb out of the weights and was tailed off from an early stage, but a combination of his rider's persistence and others' misfortunes saw him pick up third prize. (op 40-1)

Sam Cruise lost his lead after a mistake at the ninth and was a poor third when exiting the race three out. He had been raised 11lb after his recent C&D win. (op 9-2)
Victory Surge(IRE) looked less than a natural on this chasing debut and was well adrift when pulling up. (op 9-2)
Merry Terry, 6lb higher, was right in the firing line when he was brought down. (op 9-2)

1062 3663 FIRST FOR FOODSERVICE H'CAP HURDLE (10 hdls) 2m 4f
4:50 (4:51) (Class 4) (0-100,100) 4-Y-O+ **£2,602** (£764; £382; £190)

Form RPR
40-5 **1** **Deep Reflection**[45] [651] 10-11-7 **100**........................(v) JimmyDerham(5) 104
(Martin Keighley) *chsd ldrs: effrt to go 3rd bef 3 out: rdn and styd on to surge past stopping ldr after last: sn clr* **8/1**
0 **2** *3 ¾* **Topenhall (IRE)**[28] [829] 9-11-10 **98**..................................(t) CharliePoste 100+
(Ben Case) *plld hrd and prom: led 6th: 5 l clr bef 3 out: stl 2 l up and rdn last: downed tools and hdd after last: kpt gng again once passed* **20/1**
54-6 **3** *14* **Shindig**[36] [755] 8-11-7 **95**...(tp) RhysFlint 83
(John Flint) *chsd ldrs: last of four w ch but rdn bef 3 out: btn next* **14/1**
-054 **4** *16* **Sir Harry Cool**[26] [840] 7-11-11 **99**.................................... DavidEngland 73
(John Panvert) *towards rr: rdn bef 5th: struggling wl bef 3 out* **8/1**
45-0 **5** *3 ¼* **Thistle**[21] [865] 9-11-7 **95**...(t) AndrewTinkler 66
(George Baker) *t.k.h towards rr: sme prog after 7th: lost tch bef next* **33/1**
F0- **6** *1 ½* **Pistol At Dawn (IRE)**[318] [1395] 6-10-9 **90**..................... TrevorWhelan(7) 59
(Ian Williams) *prom: 2nd after 7th: 4th and wkng whn mstke 3 out* **25/1**
200 **7** *8* **Crimson Canyon (IRE)**[14] [932] 4-11-4 **95**........................(t) APMcCoy 54
(Jonjo O'Neill) *t.k.h: nt fluent in rr: hmpd after 5th: mstke next: lost tch in 5th bef 3 out* **4/1**[2]
0440 **8** *4 ½* **Roisin's Prince (IRE)**[15] [921] 8-11-2 **90**.......................(t) AidanColeman 48
(Matt Sheppard) *handy tl reminders 5th: in rr and labouring 7th: t.o* **14/1**
FP30 **9** *¾* **Scotsbrook Cloud**[14] [930] 5-10-6 **85**......................(p) MichaelMurphy(5) 42
(C Roberts) *rn in snatches: reminders 4th: effrt 6th: sn drvn: lost tch after next: t.o* **7/1**[3]
P252 **10** *1 ¾* **Can't Remember**[20] [875] 5-10-10 **91**..........................(t) OliverDayman(7) 47
(Alison Thorpe) *chsd ldrs tl rdn and wknd 7th: t.o* **7/2**[1]
4-65 **11** *3 ¼* **Cadeaux Cerise (IRE)**[64] [384] 6-11-5 **93**............................. JackDoyle 46
(Andrew Haynes) *sn last: lost tch 5th: t.o bef 3 out: blnd last* **22/1**
6236 **12** *29* **Birnies Boy**[20] [871] 6-11-7 **95**..(t) DenisO'Regan 22
(Brian Storey) *t.k.h in ld: mstke 5th: hdd next: dropped out v rapidly: hopelessly t.o* **11/1**
0 **F** **Follow The Sun (IRE)**[14] [932] 6-11-5 **93**..........................(p) TomO'Brien —
(Ronald O'Leary, Ire) *t.k.h: prom tl wknd bdly after 7th: 25 l 8th whn fell 2 out* **14/1**

4m 43.7s (-3.70) **Going Correction** -0.05s/f (Good)
WFA 4 from 5yo+ 10lb **13** Ran SP% **121.2**
Speed ratings (Par 105): **105,103,97,91,90 89,86,84,84,83 82,70,—**
toteswingers:1&2:£2.40, 1&3:£1.80, 2&3:£5.10 CSF £159.22 CT £2213.31 TOTE £9.40: £4.10, £9.70, £4.70; EX 200.20.
Owner M Keighley **Bred** Mrs C J C Bailey **Trained** Condicote, Gloucs

FOCUS
A modest handicap hurdle run in a heavy shower. They finished strung out. The winner was back to the form of his Market Rasen win.

NOTEBOOK
Deep Reflection chased the runner-up from the third-last and swept past to win comfortably in the end. He had been given a chance by the handicapper and the drop back in trip helped. (tchd 10-1)
Topenhall(IRE) looked to have made a race-winning move when going clear on the home turn, but did not find much when tackled on the run-in. He had been dropped 5lb since an encouraging return to action recently but ultimately this longer trip found him out. (op 16-1)
Shindig was comfortably held in third but this was a respectable effort on his first start over hurdles since September 2008. This was only his second start for the Flint yard. (op 11-1)
Sir Harry Cool was a well beaten fourth on this return to hurdles. (op 17-2 tchd 9-1)
Pistol At Dawn(IRE) faded out of the picture on this first run since September. (op 20-1)
Can't Remember was disappointing off nearly a stone higher than when awarded the race at Perth last time. (op 5-1)

1063 BET IN RUNNING - BETDAQ NOVICES' HURDLE (10 hdls) 2m 4f
5:20 (5:20) (Class 4) 4-Y-O+ **£2,602** (£764; £382; £190)

Form RPR
-311 **1** **Sahrati**[15] [916] 6-11-5 130... DenisO'Regan 108+
(Michael Blake) *a gng wl: wnt 2nd at 4th: led 7th: lft clr 3 out: v easily* **1/2**[1]
2 *7* **Sir Ronan**[46] 7-10-5 0..(t) MrJFMathias(7) 91
(Lawney Hill) *chsd ldr tl 4th: rdn and j. slowly 5th: outpcd in mod 4th after 7th: lft 3rd bef next: wnt 2nd and mstke last: no ch w wnr* **9/1**[3]
/330 **3** *11* **Mulaazem**[14] [932] 7-10-7 86.. DavidBass(5) 80
(Derek Frankland) *cl up: rdn 5th: ev ch 7th: outpcd bef next where lft 2nd: plodded on: lost 2nd at last* **11/1**
0-00 **4** *48* **Kiristani**[16] [908] 5-10-0 0.. IanPopham(5) 30
(Caroline Keevil) *towards rr: mstke 3rd: t.o 6th: lft remote 4th bef 3 out* **66/1**
4/P **5** *14* **The Mighty Bard (IRE)**[7] [992] 7-10-5 0......................... MissLBrooke(7) 24
(Tracey Watkins) *a bhd: t.o fr 6th* **66/1**
0F-0 **6** *5* **Blazing Tommy**[67] [341] 7-10-9 64...............................(b) SeanQuinlan(3) 20
(Kim Bailey) *led at modest pce: nt fluent 5th: hdd and mstke 7th: hopelessly t.o next* **50/1**
5-51 **P** **Off Gallivanting**[46] [635] 5-11-5 0.. APMcCoy —
(Jonjo O'Neill) *trckd ldrs: effrt after 7th: pushed along in cl 2nd whn broke down and p.u 3 out: fatally injured* **11/4**[2]
0- **R** **Moonset**[253] [2217] 6-10-7 0.............................. GemmaGracey-Davison(5) —
(Sean Regan) *a last: rdn 2nd: swvd bdly 3rd and sn a f bhd: veered violently lft and rn out 5th* **33/1**

4m 49.9s (2.50) **Going Correction** -0.05s/f (Good) **8** Ran SP% **119.6**
Speed ratings (Par 105): **93,90,85,66,61 59,—,—**
toteswingers:1&2:£2.40, 1&3:£1.80, 2&3:£5.10 CSF £6.84 TOTE £1.70: £1.02, £2.20, £1.60; EX 6.30.
Owner Mrs Val Butcher **Bred** Darley **Trained** Trowbridge, Wilts

FOCUS
Not the most competitive of races and the winner is rated a stone off his best.

NOTEBOOK
Sahrati, who was unpenalised for his win last time in a conditional jockeys' novice hurdle, had his task made a lot easier when his market rival went lame. The further the winner went, the better he looked and he could easily collect a fourth novice event during the summer whilst in such good heart. He might well struggle in handicaps off his current mark. (op 8-13 tchd 4-6 in a place)
Sir Ronan, who had been running respectably in points, and was wearing a tongue-tie for the first time, lost his place for a while down the back straight but rallied under a jockey enjoying a good day, staying on resolutely. However, awkward leaps at the final two hurdles did not help his cause of getting any closer than he did to Sahrati. (op 11-1 tchd 8-1)
Mulaazem, officially rated over 40lb lower than the winner, didn't look an easy ride but plugged on respectably under pressure over this longer trip. (tchd 10-1)

Off Gallivanting, a winner over C&D latest, was quickly pulled up rounding the final bend, sadly with fatal consequences. (op 5-2 tchd 3-1)

1064 BETDAQ.CO.UK H'CAP HURDLE (DIV II) (8 hdls) 2m
5:50 (5:51) (Class 5) (0-85,85) 4-Y-O+ **£1,712** (£499; £249)

Form RPR
052- **1** **Mycenean Prince (USA)**[107] [5047] 7-11-2 **74**......................... APMcCoy 87+
(Jim Best) *mde all: racing idly w ears pricked: rdn bef 3 out: 6 l clr last: sn eased* **10/11**[1]
2-26 **2** *4 ½* **Nobel (FR)**[41] [698] 9-10-11 **76**...................................(p) MissJCoward(7) 80
(Brian Storey) *chsd wnr tl 2 out: rdn and kpt on same pce: no ch w wnr bef last but regained 2nd fnl stride* **10/1**
0-00 **3** *nse* **Frosty's Gift**[21] [865] 6-10-10 **71**.....................................(p) HaddenFrost(3) 75
(Jimmy Fox) *hld up in midfield: effrt bef 3 out: chsd wnr vainly fr next tl fnl stride* **16/1**
2-26 **4** *6* **Present**[19] [749] 6-10-5 **70**.. MattCrawley(7) 70
(Diana Weeden) *settled midfield: drvn bef 3 out: 4th and wl hld 2 out* **7/2**[2]
P3-0 **5** *3 ½* **Monsieur (FR)**[35] [762] 10-11-12 **84**.................................... HarrySkelton 79
(Carroll Gray) *taken down early: cl up: rdn after 5th: no rspnse: btn whn mstke 2 out* **28/1**
-P0P **6** *¾* **Dancing Hill**[10] [955] 11-11-8 **80**... JohnnyFarrelly 75
(Kevin Bishop) *chsd ldrs: rdn and fdd bef 3 out* **40/1**
0-B0 **7** *1 ¼* **Ravine Rose**[35] [762] 4-11-5 **79**...(tp) CharliePoste 71
(Ben Case) *nt fluent 2nd: in rr and nt gng wl whn mstke 5th: no ch after* **40/1**
533P **8** *18* **Wee Ziggy**[24] [849] 7-11-3 **82**... BrianToomey(7) 59
(Michael Mullineaux) *dropped out last and nt a fluent: struggling after 5th: hanging rt and finding nthing fr next* **8/1**[3]
UUP5 **9** *27* **Simiola**[7] [991] 11-10-3 **61**.. ColinBolger 14
(Simon Lewis) *t.k.h: handy but nt a fluent: lost tch bef 3 out: eased and t.o* **50/1**
0260 **10** *20* **Billy Beetroot (USA)**[24] [845] 4-11-8 **85**.......................(t) LeeStephens(3) 18
(Katie Stephens) *reminders 2nd: mstkes in rr: last whn blnd 5th: t.o whn blnd next* **33/1**

3m 47.7s (0.40) **Going Correction** -0.05s/f (Good)
WFA 4 from 6yo+ 15lb **10** Ran SP% **113.9**
Speed ratings (Par 103): **97,94,94,91,89 89,88,79,66,56**
toteswingers:1&2:£3.90, 1&3:£5.30, 2&3:£15.80 CSF £9.78 CT £88.76 TOTE £1.90: £1.10, £3.20, £3.70; EX 13.10 Place 6 £1,543.06; Place 5 £569.05.
Owner Con Harrington **Bred** Benjamin W Berger And Shadwell Farm Llc **Trained** Lewes, E Sussex

FOCUS
A very moderate handicap hurdle run at a fair pace. The winner was value for further and should win again.

NOTEBOOK
Mycenean Prince(USA) went off at odds-on despite having never won in a 64-race career, 43 of them over hurdles. Given a positive ride on his first run for the Best yard, he stayed on well to score in decisive fashion. He may be brought out under a penalty at Uttoxeter on Monday and now that he has broken his duck he could double his tally. (op Evens tchd 6-5)
Nobel(FR), back down in trip, chased the winner for much of the way. He hit a flat spot two from home but stayed on again after the last to salvage second. (op 15-2 tchd 7-1)
Frosty's Gift, just pipped for second, ran her best race so far over hurdles, but that is not saying much. (op 12-1)
Present had been dropped 4lb since a lacklustre effort last time. She was keeping on again in the latter stages and probably needs a return to further (op 11-2)
T/Plt: £1,899.10 to a £1 stake. Pool:£67,122.32 - 25.80 winning tickets T/Qpdt: £675.00 to a £1 stake. Pool:£4,652.25 - 5.10 winning tickets IM

983 UTTOXETER (L-H)
Thursday, July 22

OFFICIAL GOING: Good (6.8)
Last hurdle in back straight omitted in all hurdles races; 2nd last fence omitted in both chase races. Common bends with hurdles dolled right out.
Wind: Light behind Weather: Black clouds and cool

1065 IAN SHIPTON CARS NOVICES' HURDLE (10 hdls 2 omitted) 2m 6f 110y
2:00 (2:00) (Class 4) 4-Y-O+ **£2,471** (£725; £362; £181)

Form RPR
2-62 **1** **E Major**[49] [601] 5-10-12 116.. JimmyMcCarthy 124+
(Renee Robeson) *set modest pce tl 3rd: slt ld 7th tl forged on 3 out: 5 l clr and in command next: pushed out* **5/4**[2]
-221 **2** *20* **Chesapeake (IRE)**[22] [863] 6-11-5 125.................................(b) APMcCoy 119+
(Jonjo O'Neill) *led 3rd tl 7th: w wnr tl cajoled along 3 out: sn gave up: btn next: eased flat* **11/10**[1]
-221 **3** *10* **Hadron Collider (FR)**[25] [847] 5-11-2 115......................... PeterToole(3) 106+
(Charlie Mann) *nt fluent 1st: settled cl up: rdn 6th: ev ch bef 3 out: rdn and easily outpcd bef next: hit 2 out: 15 l 3rd last: sn eased* **8/1**[3]
3 **4** *7* **Rebel Hunter (IRE)**[25] [843] 5-10-12 0................................ KeithMercer 87
(Steve Gollings) *settled cl up: nt fluent 7th: rdn and ev ch bef 3 out where nt fluent: dropped out rapidly: hit next* **16/1**
050 **5** *48* **Buckden (IRE)**[25] [843] 6-10-12 0.. TjadeCollier 39
(Sue Smith) *cl up tl last and struggling 6th: t.o next* **100/1**

5m 27.3s (-3.60) **Going Correction** -0.225s/f (Good)
WFA 4 from 5yo+ 16lb **5** Ran SP% **110.0**
Speed ratings (Par 105): **97,90,86,84,67**
toteswinger: 1&2 £1.40. CSF £3.10 TOTE £2.40: £1.60, £1.10; EX 4.80.
Owner Sir Evelyn De Rothschild **Bred** Southcourt Stud **Trained** Tyringham, Bucks

FOCUS
The race was run at a mainly ordinary gallop, which almost certainly didn't suit the runner-up and fourth. The winner is on the upgrade.

NOTEBOOK
E Major, back in novice company, collected his first victory over hurdles after outpacing his market rival from three out. He can develop into solid handicapper at a fair level. (op 11-8 tchd 6-4 and 6-5)
Chesapeake(IRE), slightly down in trip but with the blinkers retained, was prominent throughout and kept on respectably after E Major gained an advantage. He can be given another chance. (op 11-8 tchd 6-4)
Hadron Collider(FR), a winner over 2m4f at this course last time, was niggled on occasions and never threatened. (op 6-1 tchd 11-2)
Rebel Hunter(IRE) made his debut under Rules in a maiden hurdle that had been working out at this course. He will no doubt be better over further in time considering his background in points. (op 14-1 tchd 11-1)

Buckden(IRE) has plenty of size and scope about him but looks to need plenty more time.

1066 CRABBIE'S ALCOHOLIC GINGER BEER NOVICES' H'CAP HURDLE (9 hdls 1 omitted) 2m
2:35 (2:36) (Class 5) (0-95,94) 4-Y-0+ **£1,951** (£573; £286; £143)

Form RPR

U6/3 **1** **Maizy Missile (IRE)**[68] [341] 8-10-10 **75**............................ PaulMoloney 85+
(Mary Evans) *led tl 2nd: pressed ldr tl led again bef 3 out: clr w one rival between last two: rdn and hung on gamely flat* **8/1**[3]

5P0- **2** *3/4* **Marie De Laufon (FR)**[149] [4210] 5-11-0 **86**..................... AdamWedge(7) 96
(Chris Bealby) *hld up in midfield: effrt after 6th: rdn and chsd wnr sn after 3 out: kpt on after last: a jst hld* **12/1**

000 **3** *13* **Lean Burn (USA)**[30] [821] 4-10-6 **76**.............................(tp) DannyCook(3) 72
(John Panvert) *midfield: effrt 3 out: sn outpcd by ldng pair: swtchd rt and disp 10 l 3rd at last: nvr able to chal* **25/1**

0-03 **4** *4 1/2* **Boo**[25] [845] 8-11-9 **88**... JimmyMcCarthy 82
(James Unett) *pressed ldrs: rdn 3 out: one pce and no imp after: mstke 2 out: disp 10 l 3rd at last* **7/1**[2]

1161 **5** *2 3/4* **Monkhair (IRE)**[7] [1005] 5-11-10 **94** 7ex............................ LeeEdwards(5) 88
(Tony Carroll) *t.k.h trcking ldrs: nt fluent 6th and rdn: chal to go 2nd briefly 3 out: sn outpcd: disp 10 l 3rd at last* **5/4**[1]

5-03 **6** *2 1/2* **Richo**[7] [1005] 4-11-8 **92**... AdamPogson(3) 82
(Shaun Harris) *mstkes: effrt to trck ldrs and mstke 3 out: wknd qckly next: blnd last* **9/1**

06 **7** *1/2* **King Benny (IRE)**[32] [803] 6-11-12 **91**.........................(tp) JohnnyFarrelly 80
(Elliott Cooper) *nvr bttr than midfield and on outside: lost tch 3 out: coasted on* **18/1**

450 **8** *2* **Iron Man Of Mersey (FR)**[32] [792] 4-11-2 **90**......... AnthonyFreeman(7) 75
(Tony Carroll) *reluctant to s and reminders: hit 3rd: bhd: struggling bef 3 out* **12/1**

00U3 **9** *1* **Racingisdreaming (USA)**[17] [908] 4-11-12 **93**........(tp) TomScudamore 77
(David Pipe) *led rnd s: towards rr: rdn and no rspnse 5th: struggling bef 3 out* **12/1**

U/F0 **10** *6* **Delightful Touch (FR)**[16] [921] 9-9-9 **65** oh1.............. MarcGoldstein(5) 46
(Gerald Ham) *prom: 3rd and rdn at 6th: fdd bef 3 out* **25/1**

F-45 **11** *nse* **Pegasus Lad (USA)**[17] [908] 4-11-9 **90**...............................(t) JackDoyle 69
(Linda Blackford) *t.k.h: led fr 2nd: hit 4th: 5 l clr next: rdn and hdd bef 3 out: dropped out rapidly* **40/1**

P-00 **P** **Highland River**[15] [932] 4-11-2 **90**.. KyleJames(7) —
(Aytach Sadik) *blnd 2nd and reminders: rdn 4th: last whn j.v.slowly 5th: t.o next: p.u 3 out* **50/1**

3m 50.3s (-4.90) **Going Correction** -0.225s/f (Good)
WFA 4 from 5yo+ 15lb **12 Ran SP% 118.5**
Speed ratings (Par 103): **103,102,96,93,92 91,91,90,89,86 86,—**
toteswingers: 1&2 £60.10, 1&3 £52.20, 2&3 £60.10. CSF £94.32 CT £2293.77 TOTE £6.10: £1.60, £3.60, £7.70; EX 222.20.
Owner Mary And Billy Evans **Bred** Mrs M Evans **Trained** Clarbeston Road, Pembrokeshire

FOCUS
A ordinary contest and the short-priced favourite disappointed. The form is rated through the third.

NOTEBOOK
Maizy Missile(IRE), the only horse in training for Evan Williams' mother, shaped really well last time on her return from a long absence over 4f further at this course, and duly built on it to take this. She is at the right end of the handicap to follow up in a low-grade event. (op 9-1 tchd 10-1)
Marie De Laufon(FR), making her handicap debut, must have benefited from her long layoff as this was much the best she has ever run, albeit in a short career. She travelled nicely and appeared to have no problem with the distance. (op 14-1 tchd 16-1)
Lean Burn(USA), thrashed in a seller on his last start, helps to confirm the form as being moderate, although first-time cheekpieces may have made a bit of a difference. (tchd 22-1 and 28-1)
Boo was never far away and plugged on for pressure. (op 8-1 tchd 11-2)
Monkhair(IRE) looked to be going well when diving at a hurdle in the back straight, which cost her momentum. However, she was still able to get back into the argument and had a chance three out before steadily weakening. (op 11-8 tchd 6-4)
King Benny(IRE) really caught the eye in a moderate race. Considering he was wearing headgear and a tongue-tie for the first time, it may be that he's not straightforward, but one gets the impression that he has a bit of ability when and if he chooses to use it. Official explanation: jockey said, regarding running and riding, that his orders were to drop in as the gelding hasn't been finishing, being keen in front, decided to go wide to find better ground, being keen over first two settled, although it hung left-handed and struggled with its breathing on and off throughout, he was happy with its position round final bend but when they hit the straight it found nothing. (op 12-1)

1067 SIS LIVE H'CAP HURDLE (FOR THE KEN BOULTON TROPHY) (10 hdls 2 omitted) 2m 4f 110y
3:10 (3:10) (Class 4) (0-115,115) 4-Y-0+ **£2,602** (£764; £382; £190)

Form RPR

3223 **1** **Three Ships**[15] [933] 9-10-5 **101**... MattGriffiths(7) 111+
(S Wynne) *settled in 3rd pl: wnt 2nd at 5th: led bef 3 out: 4 l clr next: r.o wl* **9/1**

-PP2 **2** *7* **Edgefour (IRE)**[11] [962] 6-10-9 **103**.............................(v) GilesHawkins(5) 104
(Ben Case) *hld up trcking ldrs: wnt 3rd at 7th: mstke next: sn rdn: wnt 2nd at last: fnd nil and no ch w wnr* **4/1**[3]

/24- **3** *1/2* **Beshairt**[403] [713] 6-11-7 **110**... ChristianWilliams 112
(Dai Burchell) *hmpd 1st: hit majority of flights: last tl after 7th: no real imp fr 3 out: blnd last: wnt modest 3rd flat* **22/1**

6111 **4** *5* **Letham Island (IRE)**[32] [796] 6-11-5 **113**....................(vt) LeeEdwards(5) 114
(Tony Carroll) *hmpd 1st: hld up: cajoled along and effrt to chse wnr bef 3 out: hld next: 6 l 2nd whn blnd last: nt keen* **3/1**[2]

451- **5** *12* **Hayes Princess (IRE)**[93] [5294] 6-11-10 **113**..............(t) RichardJohnson 99
(Tim Vaughan) *set stdy pce: rdn and hdd bef 3 out: sn dropped out and eased* **7/1**

21- **6** *5* **Hassadin**[29] [3867] 4-11-2 **108**... JackDoyle 86
(Andrew Haynes) *chsd ldr tl 5th: rdn and dropped bk last bef 3 out* **8/1**

1-13 **F** **Flower Haven**[41] [706] 8-11-5 **115**................................ EdGlassonbury(7) —
(Victor Dartnall) *fell 1st* **5/2**[1]

4m 56.2s (-7.80) **Going Correction** -0.225s/f (Good)
WFA 4 from 6yo+ 16lb **7 Ran SP% 111.5**
Speed ratings (Par 105): **105,102,102,100,95 93,—**
toteswingers: 1&2 £14.30, 1&3 £29.10, 2&3 £18.20. CSF £42.69 TOTE £7.90: £3.00, £2.40; EX 38.30.
Owner W B Probin **Bred** Juddmonte Farms **Trained** Malpas, Cheshire

FOCUS
The complexion of this race changed when Flower Haven came down at the first, hampering a couple of her rivals quite badly, albeit they had plenty of time to get back into things. The winner is rated back to his very best.

NOTEBOOK
Three Ships, 6lb higher than when finishing third over 2m at Worcester last time, seemed to be pulling hard at the head of affairs, but still had plenty in reserve when his jockey asked him to quicken to get right away. He could go back to Worcester next Tuesday. (op 8-1 tchd 10-1)
Edgefour(IRE), who is due to go up 4lb, travelled strongly but got outpaced and made a mistake before staying on again. (op 9-2)
Beshairt, already settled behind the main body of runners when meeting interference at the first hurdle, didn't always jump fluently but one got the strong impression that she was the second-best horse in the race, even though she was returning from a lengthy absence. (op 16-1)
Letham Island(IRE), 4lb higher than last time, got the worst of the interference at the first hurdle and was entitled to lose her position, as well as her concentration. Soon back in a challenging position, she was hard ridden at the top of the home straight and could only find the one pace thereafter. (op 10-3 tchd 9-4)
Hayes Princess(IRE) enjoyed an easy lead at a slow pace, so it was disappointing how easily she was brushed aside when the tempo increased, even though she was unproven at the distance. (op 9-2 tchd 8-1)
Hassadin ran badly on his recent start on the Flat, and was another easily outpaced when the leaders pressed on. (op 10-1)
Flower Haven came down at the first, hampering a couple of her rivals quite badly. (op 3-1 tchd 7-2)

1068 BRASKEM STKS BEGINNERS' CHASE (14 fncs 2 omitted) 2m 6f 110y
3:45 (3:45) (Class 4) 5-Y-0+ **£3,197** (£965; £497; £263)

Form RPR

0/0- **1** **The Shoe (NZ)**[446] [117] 8-11-0 0.. APMcCoy 124+
(Nicky Henderson) *cl 2nd tl led 9th: drvn after 2 out: rdn to go clr after last* **10/11**[1]

4-13 **2** *10* **I Need A Hero (IRE)**[42] [687] 5-11-0 112..............................(t) JackDoyle 117+
(Sarah Humphrey) *trckd ldrs: chal 8th: chsd wnr bef 11th: drvn and tried to chal and 1 l down last: wknd flat* **11/4**[2]

6 **3** *33* **Overquest**[7] [1000] 8-11-0 0.. JohnnyFarrelly 85
(Elliott Cooper) *trckd ldrs: rdn and lost tch and nt fluent 11th: wnt 15 l 3rd 3 out: t.o whn nt fluent last* **22/1**

3 **4** *24* **Adrianeo (IRE)**[11] [944] 7-11-0 0...................................... PeterBuchanan 64
(S R B Crawford, Ire) *slt ld tl 9th: 3rd and wkng whn hit 11th: t.o bef 2 out* **8/1**

324- **P** **Vasodilator (IRE)**[129] [4651] 7-11-0 115............................ LeightonAspell —
(Pat Murphy) *t.k.h in last: j. slowly 1st: hit 8th: lost tch 11th: t.o whn heavily eased 2 out: p.u last* **13/2**[3]

5m 38.4s (-10.10) **Going Correction** -0.225s/f (Good) **5 Ran SP% 107.8**
Speed ratings: **108,104,93,84,—**
CSF £3.73 TOTE £1.80: £1.10, £1.30; EX 3.50.
Owner Gerard Peterson **Bred** Bloomsbury Stud **Trained** Upper Lambourn, Berks

FOCUS
No pace early but only two had any chance from some way out. Ordinary novice form.

NOTEBOOK
The Shoe(NZ), returning from a long layoff and trying fences for the first time, gained his first victory since coming over from New Zealand and shapes like a horse who will enjoy a decent test of stamina, as although he always appeared to be holding the runner-up from three out, he was far from impressive. (tchd 5-6 and Evens)
I Need A Hero(IRE), a hurdles winner over about 2m2f, arguably travelled better than the winner but just lacked a little bit of toe when the tempo increased. The trip didn't seem a problem, which it shouldn't have been for a former point winner, but it should be noted that there was little pace on early, and his stamina will need to be tested again before it's conclusive that he stays. (tchd 5-2 and 3-1)
Overquest, up 5f in trip, moved well while the gallop was slow but soon lost his position (op 16-1)
Adrianeo(IRE) steadily dropped away after racing prominently. (op 11-1)
Vasodilator(IRE), making his debut for this stable, took a keen grip in rear and made a couple of jumping mistakes before getting well behind. (op 6-1 tchd 11-2)

1069 NMU BIRMINGHAM STANDARD OPEN NATIONAL HUNT FLAT RACE (DIV I) 2m
4:20 (4:21) (Class 6) 4-6-Y-0 **£1,301** (£382; £191; £95)

Form RPR

1 **Vesey Lodge (IRE)**[46] 4-11-0 0.. APMcCoy 108+
(S R B Crawford, Ire) *cl up: led gng best over 3f out: rdn and wl in command ent fnl f: unchal* **5/2**[1]

2 *10* **Unwanted Gift (IRE)**[60] 5-10-11 0.................................... MrDMurphy(5) 96
(L J Archdeacon, Ire) *towards rr: prog over 3f out: rdn to chse wnr wl over 1f out: in vain pursuit after* **11/2**[3]

4 **3** *2* **Sir Harry Cash**[29] [832] 4-10-7 0.. BrianToomey(7) 91
(Michael Mullineaux) *cl up tl lost pl over 4f out: hanging rt 3f out and lost pl to midfield: rallied over 1f out: styd on wl* **10/1**

5 **4** *1 1/2* **Superior Knight**[39] [739] 6-11-2 0.. DavidDennis 91
(James Evans) *on his toes: chsd ldrs: drvn over 3f out: one pce and n.d after* **10/1**

5 *1 1/4* **Gwendraeth Girl (IRE)** 5-10-4 0..................................... LeeEdwards(5) 83
(Tony Carroll) *t.k.h: chsd ldrs: wnt 2nd 3f out tl wl over 1f out: wknd* **14/1**

0- **6** *2* **Articulate (IRE)**[124] [4744] 5-11-2 0.................................... RichardJohnson 88
(Henry Daly) *plld hrd: sn prom: led over 4f out tl rdn and hdd over 3f out: grad lost pl* **7/2**[2]

06-4 **7** *1 3/4* **My Viking Bay (IRE)**[51] [568] 6-10-2 0............................ CharlieWallis(7) 79
(John O'Shea) *chsd ldrs: rdn 3f out: sn btn* **11/1**

0 **8** *1 3/4* **Waypost**[15] [935] 4-11-0 0.. RodiGreene 82
(David Bridgwater) *led at v slow pce: rdn and hdd over 4f out: looked reluctant whn struggling fnl 3f* **100/1**

9 *1/2* **Shuttle Diplomacy (IRE)** 5-10-9 0..................................... JohnnyFarrelly 77
(Elliott Cooper) *hld up in last: lost tch over 3f out* **16/1**

0 **10** *4* **Kingston Orla**[64] [412] 5-10-9 0.. NickScholfield 73
(Andrew Haynes) *a bhd: struggling over 3f out* **66/1**

11 *7* **Talk Up Trouble** 4-10-7 0.. LiamTreadwell 64
(Mark Brisbourne) *chsd ldrs: rdn and lost pl 5f out: t.o* **14/1**

12 *13* **Alfinski** 5-11-2 0.. PaddyAspell 60
(C W Thornton) *in tch: rdn 6f out: sn struggling: t.o fnl 3f* **25/1**

3m 55.7s (6.10) **Going Correction** -0.225s/f (Good)
WFA 4 from 5yo+ 2lb **12 Ran SP% 118.2**
Speed ratings: **75,70,69,68,67 66,65,64,64,62 59,52**
toteswingers: 1&2 £3.90, 1&3 £5.20, 2&3 £7.80. CSF £15.98 TOTE £4.00: £1.60, £2.20, £2.50; EX 14.60.
Owner G Wilson **Bred** Joe Brennan **Trained**

FOCUS
The runners for the first division of the bumper hung around at the start for a few seconds before jumping off, but even when they got going the pace was moderate. The easy winner is the type to rate higher.

NOTEBOOK

Vesey Lodge(IRE) was in the right position to kick on when the chance was offered to him, and gain an advantage that was never going to be eroded significantly. The winner of an Irish point the previous month, his third start in that sphere, he may find it difficult to follow up if faced with a solid challenger next time.

Unwanted Gift(IRE) was one of many pulling for his head in rear early, and had no chance of getting to the winner from his starting point. The winner of an Irish point on his previous outing in May, the fourth of his career, he should do better in a more strongly run contest.

Sir Harry Cash proved his debut effort was no fluke with another solid display. He's a big sort, he'll get better with time.

Superior Knight was very keen early but stayed on well to pass the fourth horse inside the final furlong.

Gwendraeth Girl(IRE) went well to a point.

Articulate(IRE) still looked green under pressure, but this big, scopey sort ought to improve with time

Shuttle Diplomacy(IRE) shaped with some promise after being held up.

1070 WILLIAM HILL H'CAP CHASE (10 fncs 2 omitted) 2m

4:50 (4:50) (Class 4) (0-115,113) 4-Y-0+ **£3,168** (£936; £468; £234; £117)

Form / RPR

2521 **1** **Folie A Deux (IRE)**[16] 919 8-11-0 **101**................(t) JoeTizzard 116+
(Colin Tizzard) *j.w: mde all: at least 5 l clr fr 7th: sn eased flat* **9/4**[1]

6333 **2** *9* **Red Jester**[8] 985 9-10-7 **99**................ MarcGoldstein(5) 104
(Gerald Ham) *chsd wnr: pushed along 6th: rdn and wl hld fr 3 out but plugged on gamely* **10/3**[2]

6341 **3** *2 1/2* **Turbo Shandy**[18] 891 7-11-2 **103**................ TomO'Brien 106
(Dai Burchell) *hld up: effrt and nt fluent 7th: wnt 3rd bef 3 out: drvn and chal for 8 l 2nd at last: nvr on terms w wnr* **4/1**[3]

5P12 **4** *15* **My Pal Val (IRE)**[11] 961 10-10-10 **100**................(tp) DannyCook(3) 89
(John Panvert) *trckd ldrs: mstke 6th: rdn bef 3 out: no rspnse and sn wknd* **11/2**

523- **5** *12* **Quincy Des Pictons (FR)**[128] 4667 6-11-1 **102**................ JodieMogford 80
(M S Tuck) *j. modly in last: t.o after mstke 5th* **13/2**

P510 **P** **High Skies**[15] 933 7-11-5 **113**................(b) MrTWeston(7) —
(Dr Richard Newland) *wnt 3rd at 4th: drvn and fdd bef 3 out: t.o and p.u last* **9/1**

3m 49.8s (-5.80) **Going Correction** -0.225s/f (Good) **6** Ran SP% **112.6**

Speed ratings (Par 105): **105,100,99,91,85** —

toteswingers: 1&2 £2.60, 1&3 £2.70, 2&3 £4.10. CSF £10.51 TOTE £2.90: £1.10, £3.10; EX 6.60.

Owner G Carstairs **Bred** Lord James Beresford **Trained** Milborne Port, Dorset

FOCUS

Nothing got into this. A big step forward from the winner but the form seems sound.

NOTEBOOK

Folie A Deux(IRE) adopted his usual tactics and led from start to finish. Racing off a mark 6lb higher than when winning last time, the fitting on a tongue-tie has appeared to help him back to his best and he's likely to be hard to beat in the short-term when allowed an uncontested lead. (op 5-2)

Red Jester, runner-up in this race last year, and a horse with a good record at this track, kept on but was readily held. (op 7-2 tchd 3-1)

Turbo Shandy, raised 13lb for his Market Rasen success but surprisingly without the cheekpieces he wore there, seemed sure to get into second after two from home, but for some reason couldn't get past Red Jester. (op 9-2)

My Pal Val(IRE) came into this in good heart but could never get on terms. (op 5-1 tchd 6-1)

Quincy Des Pictons(FR), having his first start for this trainer, and absent since March, took a good grip and steadily settled off the backmarker of the main bunch. He didn't always jump with much fluency and failed to get involved. (op 6-1)

High Skies was pushed along on the final bend and didn't look too enthusiastic once under strong pressure. He was soon pulled up. (op 11-1 tchd 12-1)

1071 NMU BIRMINGHAM STANDARD OPEN NATIONAL HUNT FLAT RACE (DIV II) 2m

5:20 (5:20) (Class 6) 4-6-Y-0 **£1,301** (£382; £191; £95)

Form / RPR

0-2 **1** **Hallmark Harry**[11] 949 4-11-0 0................ DenisO'Regan 92+
(Michael Easterby) *cl 2nd tl led gng best over 3f out: wl in command fnl f: pushed out* **4/1**[3]

0- **2** *3 1/2* **Great Hero**[432] 344 5-11-2 0................ RichardJohnson 89
(Richard Phillips) *t.k.h in rr: effrt on ins 3f out: chsd wnr wl over 1f out: one pce and nvr got in a blow* **11/1**

3 *2* **Mckyla (IRE)** 5-10-4 0................ LeeEdwards(5) 80
(Tony Carroll) *midfield: effrt to go 3rd home turn: rdn over 2f out: rn green and no imp after* **7/2**[2]

4 *2 1/2* **Mulranny (IRE)** 5-11-2 0................ DavidEngland 84
(Nigel Twiston-Davies) *chsd ldrs: rdn 5f out: plugged on but wl hld fnl 3f: edging lft over 1f out* **5/2**[1]

0 **5** *4 1/2* **Reg's Ruby**[23] 855 4-10-7 0................ RodiGreene 71
(David Bridgwater) *led at stdy pce tl rdn and hdd over 3f out: sn lost pl* **66/1**

0/ **6** *nk* **Gutter Lane**[538] 3650 6-10-11 0................ JamesHalliday(5) 79
(Malcolm Jefferson) *cl up tl rdn and fdd grad fnl 3f* **8/1**

7 *14* **Sir Tamburlane (IRE)**[68] 5-10-6 0................ BenjaminStephens(10) 65
(Sue Smith) *towards rr: lost tch 4f out* **9/1**

8 *33* **Paxford Junior** 4-11-0 0................(t) CharliePoste 30
(Milton Harris) *last pair: rdn and struggling 6f out: t.o fnl 3f* **20/1**

0-0 **9** *4* **Floating Cloud**[84] 60 6-10-6 0................(t) AdamPogson(3) 21
(Trevor Wall) *t.k.h: cl up for 10f: t.o fnl 3f* **66/1**

10 *29* **Beat All Odds** 4-10-7 0................ LeightonAspell —
(William Clay) *last pair: rdn 6f out: t.o fnl 3f* **20/1**

P **Miss Galross (IRE)** 6-10-6 0................ FearghalDavis(3) —
(Nicky Richards) *midfield: sn hanging rt: virtually unrideable and lost pl fr 1/2-way: t.o and p.u over 4f out* **10/1**

3m 49.3s (-0.30) **Going Correction** -0.225s/f (Good)

WFA 4 from 5yo+ 2lb **11** Ran SP% **121.8**

Speed ratings: **91,89,88,87,84 84,77,61,59,44** —

toteswingers: 1&2 £8.50, 1&3 £3.80, 2&3 £5.90. CSF £47.30 TOTE £2.40: £1.10, £4.10, £3.10; EX 45.00 Place 6: £65.02, Place 5: £59.56..

Owner N W A Bannister **Bred** Gyles Llewellyn **Trained** Sheriff Hutton, N Yorks

FOCUS

They went steady through the early stages, resulting in several of these racing keenly, but the time was still 6.40 seconds quicker than the first division. Modest form, but the cosy winner was value for a bit further.

NOTEBOOK

Hallmark Harry, given a forward ride, confirmed the promise he showed when a close second in a four-runner event at Perth last time. He was idling for much of the closing stages, so is probably better than the bare form indicates, and he has the scope to progress into a useful sort over obstacles.

Great Hero, tailed off over C&D on his only previous start last May, shaped nicely on his return. Having made good headway from off the pace to move into a challenging position, he was always being held by the winner, but still showed plenty of ability.

Mckyla(IRE), a 2,500euros half-sister to useful hunter chaser Monty's Quest, fared best of the newcomers and this was a pleasing introduction. She ran green off the bridle and there should be better to come, particularly when she tackles obstacles.

Mulranny(IRE), a 19,000euros half-brother to fairly useful 2m hurdle winner Jake Black, posted an encouraging effort on debut and should come on for the run.

Reg's Ruby was a little keen early on but still improved significantly on her first effort.

Miss Galross(IRE) Official explanation: jockey said mare hung right-handed and the bit slipped through its mouth

T/Plt: £295.40 to a £1 stake. Pool £55,105.00 - 136.14 winning units. T/Qpdt: £11.60 to a £1 stake. Pool £5,684.00 - 361.69 winning units. IM

1072a - 1079a (Foreign Racing) - See Raceform Interactive

950 SOUTHWELL (L-H)

Friday, July 23

OFFICIAL GOING: Good (good to firm in places) changing to good after race 1 (2.20)

Golf Club bend 5yds inside and bend into home straight 5yds outside line raced on July 11th.

Wind: light 1/2 behind Weather: overcast

1080 C J PETTITT TRANSPORT LTD H'CAP CHASE (16 fncs) 2m 4f 110y

2:20 (2:20) (Class 5) (0-90,90) 4-Y-0+ **£3,151** (£918; £459)

Form / RPR

-011 **1** *hd* **Makena (FR)**[2] 1057 8-11-5 **90**................(p) MrJFMathias(7) 105+
(David Rees) *in tch: prom whn hit 10th: chsng ldrs 4 out: sn rdn: styng on strly whn carried rt towards fin: fin 2nd, hd: awrdd r* **4/6**[1]

1-54 **2** **Ponchatrain (IRE)**[47] 649 10-11-9 **87**................ TomScudamore 101+
(Martin Keighley) *j.rt: chsd ldrs: led sn after 4 out: narrowly hdd and hit next: slt ld 2 out: veered bdly rt fnl 50yds: jst hld on: disqualified and plcd 2nd* **12/1**

-212 **3** *1* **Sir Bumble (IRE)**[16] 931 10-11-4 **85**................(t) PeterToole(3) 95
(Michael Blake) *chsd ldrs: narrow ld 3 out: hdd next: hung rt sn after last: no ex fnl 75yds* **15/2**[3]

-444 **4** *16* **Monty's Moon (IRE)**[38] 757 8-10-3 **67**................(b) AidanColeman 69
(Rachel Hobbs) *prom: mstke 11th: blnd and rdr briefly lost irons 4 out: 4th and wkng whn mstke next* **14/1**

2642 **5** *8* **Peak Seasons (IRE)**[8] 1001 7-10-2 **73**................ StevenGagan(7) 61
(Michael Chapman) *led to 2nd: racd keenly: w ldr: led 10th: hdd sn after 4 out: sn wknd* **25/1**

P300 **6** *21* **Satindra (IRE)**[33] 794 6-10-10 **74**................(tp) DenisO'Regan 44
(Carole Ikin) *nt fluent in rr: bhd fr 10th* **66/1**

35UP **7** *9* **Janal (IRE)**[22] 872 7-10-1 **65**................(p) WilsonRenwick 26
(Stuart Coltherd) *led 2nd: hdd 10th: wknd 4 out* **22/1**

2PP6 **8** *47* **Tuscany Star (IRE)**[17] 918 7-11-7 **85**................(tp) AndrewThornton —
(Edward Creighton) *in rr: mstke 2nd: sn reminders and bhd: t.o 9th* **66/1**

-6P5 **9** *nk* **Dasher Reilly (USA)**[12] 952 9-9-13 **66**................ EamonDehdashti(3) —
(Aytach Sadik) *prom: lost pl after 9th: sn bhd: t.o 13th* **66/1**

3444 **P** **Sahara Prince (IRE)**[12] 961 10-10-9 **80**................(p) MrLRPayter(7) —
(Matt Sheppard) *nt fluent in rr: bhd fr 10th: t.o whn p.u bef 3 out* **40/1**

P-26 **P** **Scalini's (IRE)**[16] 931 10-10-8 **75**................(p) SeanQuinlan(3) —
(Christopher Nenadich) *mid-div: blnd 8th: reminders after 9th: sn bhd: t.o whn p.u bef 3 out* **18/1**

1333 **P** **Ginger's Lad**[12] 950 6-11-1 **79**................ BrianHughes —
(Michael Easterby) *in tch: dropped in rr 5th: sn bhd: t.o whn p.u after 9th* **13/2**[2]

5m 14.3s (-0.70) **Going Correction** -0.425s/f (Good) **12** Ran SP% **119.8**

Speed ratings (Par 103): **83,84,83,77,74 66,62,45,44,— —,—**

Tote Swingers: 1&2 £4.00, 1&3 £2.30, 2&3 £13.50 CSF £9.33 CT £37.69 TOTE £1.70: £1.10, £3.60, £1.40; EX 14.50.

Owner D L Evans **Bred** Roland Lacrampe Cuyaubere **Trained** Clarbeston, Pembrokes

■ Stewards' Enquiry : Tom Scudamore three-day ban: careless riding (Aug 6,10,12)

FOCUS

There was a dramatic finish to this handicap chase, with Ponchatrain crossing the line first and appearing to have denied Makena the hat-trick, but the replay confirmed he had veered across the mare in the final half-furlong and the outcome was reversed. The first two are both better than the bare result.

NOTEBOOK

Makena(FR) escaped a penalty for winning an amateur riders' handicap hurdle at Worcester two days earlier, and looked the one to beat, having twice won over fences in France. The drop in trip didn't really suit, but it's likely she would have got up with an uninterrupted run close home. She gets on well with her rider, but things will obviously be tougher in future. (op 10-11 tchd Evens and 11-10 in a aplc)

Ponchatrain(IRE), just 2lb above his last winning mark, kept finding for pressure and showed a good attitude, but was judged to have cost Makena enough ground for the stewards to reverse the form. (op 10-1)

Sir Bumble(IRE), up 6lb from his latest second, again ran his race without quite matching the front pair. (op 7-1 tchd 13-2)

Monty's Moon(IRE)'s jumping wasn't the best. (op 20-1)

Ginger's Lad failed to run his race and was particularly disappointing. Official explanation: jockey said gelding never travelled (op 5-1)

1081 LINCOLNSHIRE DEVELOPMENTS LTD NOVICES' H'CAP CHASE (19 fncs) 3m 110y

2:55 (2:55) (Class 4) (0-110,108) 4-Y-0+ **£3,903** (£1,146; £573; £286)

Form / RPR

43-1 **1** **Gabreselassie (IRE)**[17] 918 7-11-12 **108**................ APMcCoy 115+
(Jonjo O'Neill) *hld up: jnd ldrs 12th: pushed along 14th: upsides whn hit 2 out: styd on to ld last 75yds* **11/10**[1]

0 **2** *1 1/2* **Free Speech**[12] 955 7-10-5 **87**................(t) JackDoyle 89
(Sarah Humphrey) *trckd ldrs: shkn up 12th: slt ld 4 out: hdd and no ex clsng* **8/1**

-524 **3** *13* **Tucumcari (IRE)**[30] 828 5-11-4 **100**................ AidanColeman 91
(Brendan Powell) *j.rt: w ldrs: led 7th tl after 9th: led 12th to 4 out: wknd appr next* **9/1**

6315 **4** *19* **The Artful Fox**[8] 1002 9-10-8 **93**................ CampbellGillies(3) 66
(Mike Sowersby) *chsd ldrs: struggling 11th: wknd 15th: poor 4th next* **13/2**[3]

P-P3 **5** *10* **Cute N You Know It**[64] 424 7-10-0 **82** oh4................(b) KeithMercer 46
(Andrew Crook) *j. bdly rt: led to 7th: led after 9th: hdd 12th: outpcd next: wknd 15th* **4/1**[2]

4203 **P** **Feeling Peckish (USA)**[6] 1022 6-9-7 82 oh10...............(t) PeterHatton(7) —
(Michael Chapman) *chsd ldrs: reminders and outpcd 12th: wknd 15th: last and bhd whn blnd 3 out: p.u bef next* **7/1**

6m 23.7s (-2.30) **Going Correction** -0.425s/f (Good) **6** Ran SP% **114.6**
Speed ratings (Par 105): **86,85,81,75,72** —
CSF £10.65 TOTE £1.40: £1.10, £3.70; EX 13.50.

Owner John P McManus **Bred** P J Fortune **Trained** Cheltenham, Gloucs

FOCUS
Just a modest handicap chase. The first three were all close to their marks and the winner looked to have a bit in hand.

NOTEBOOK
Gabreselassie(IRE) finally got his head in front at Uttoxeter last time and he seems to have taken heart from that success, as he kept finding under pressure from McCoy and got up close home to defy an 8lb rise. Stamina is clearly his strong suit and it would be no surprise to see him complete a hat-trick. (op 6-4)

Free Speech proved a tough rival to pass, jumping well and finding plenty for strong pressure, but he was eventually worn down. He will be of interest for something similar. (op 7-1 tchd 17-2)

Tucumcari(IRE) ended up comfortably held, but still improved on his initial effort over fences, shaping as though going the other way round would help too. (op 8-1 tchd 10-1)

The Artful Fox was again well held. (op 5-1)

Cute N You Know It jumped to her right and had little left at the business end. (tchd 7-2 and 9-2)

1082 ROSEMARY HERON MEMORIAL NOVICES' CHASE (13 fncs) 2m
3:30 (3:30) (Class 4) 5-Y-0+ **£3,577** (£1,050; £525; £262)

Form				RPR
1F-1	**1**		**What's Up Doc (IRE)**[15] 135 9-10-12 0..................... ChristianWilliams (Lawney Hill) *trckd ldrs: led on bit 7th: eased clr fr 3 out: 6 l ahd last: eased: v easily* **9/4**[2]	118+
1-43	**2**	4 ½	**Quedillac (FR)**[36] 773 6-10-12 107.............................. RichardJohnson (Tim Vaughan) *chsd ldrs: wnt cl 2nd 8th: drvn 4 out: kpt on: no ch w wnr* **11/8**[1]	107+
20-P	**3**	14	**Haka Dancer (USA)**[25] 472 7-10-5 0............................... KyleJames(7) (Philip Kirby) *j.rt: led to 7th: hit next: outpcd 9th: tk modest 3rd last* **8/1**	93
5-26	**4**	7	**Weststern (GER)**[33] 799 7-10-12 97.................................. JamieMoore (Gary Moore) *trckd ldrs: drvn 8th: sn outpcd and lost pl: wknd last* **7/1**[3]	87
-033	**5**	12	**Midnite Blews (IRE)**[39] 748 5-10-9 0...................(t) MichaelMcAlister(3) (Maurice Barnes) *in tch: drvn 8th: sn lost pl and bhd* **7/1**[3]	74

4m 0.90s (-9.10) **Going Correction** -0.425s/f (Good) **5** Ran SP% **109.0**
Speed ratings: **105,102,95,92,86**
CSF £5.91 TOTE £4.10: £2.60, £1.10; EX 5.60.

Owner M B Clarke **Bred** James J Monaghan **Trained** Aston Rowant, Oxon

FOCUS
Not a race that took much winning. The easy winner is rated in line with his recent Flat form.

NOTEBOOK
What's Up Doc(IRE), who has been a real money-spinner both on the Flat and over hurdles since joining current connections, was a bit free early on this chase debut, but his jumping was sound, and he proved much too good. On this evidence he will be capable of defying a penalty. (op 11-4)

Quedillac(FR), below-par over hurdles latest, had earlier run well on his chase debut and this was more like his true form. He was no match for the winner, but can find a small race at some stage. (op 6-4 tchd 6-5)

Haka Dancer(USA) was quickly brushed aside and ended up well held. (op 15-2 tchd 9-1)

Weststern(GER) hasn't yet gone on from a promising first start over fences. (op 9-2 tchd 15-2)

1083 JACKIE & JEANETTE NOVICES' HURDLE (9 hdls) 2m
4:05 (4:05) (Class 4) 4-Y-0+ **£2,740** (£798; £399)

Form				RPR
42	**1**		**Admiral Dundas (IRE)**[16] 932 5-10-9 105...................(t) SeanQuinlan(3) (Kim Bailey) *trckd ldrs: bmpd 1st: led 5th: briefly narrowly hdd appr last: hung rt and styd on run-in: all out* **11/4**[2]	105+
4/14	**2**	½	**Blue Eyed Eloise**[19] 886 8-10-12 105............................ LeightonAspell (Brian McMath) *trckd ldrs: wnt cl 2nd appr 2 out: narow ld appr last: nt fluent: no ex towards fin* **9/4**[1]	105+
253	**3**	17	**Apache Dawn**[9] 983 6-10-12 97.. APMcCoy (Aytach Sadik) *led to 5th: rdn and hung rt appr 2 out: wknd between last 2* **6/1**	90
6P/5	**4**	5	**Zahara Joy**[22] 870 7-10-2 73...................................(t) MichaelMcAlister(3) (Maurice Barnes) *bmpd 1st: chsd ldrs: outpcd fr 3 out* **40/1**	78
5B	**5**	22	**Rebel Swing**[8] 1003 4-10-10 0.. HenryOliver (Sue Smith) *reluctant and reminders sn after s: bhd fr 4th: t.o 2 out* **33/1**	63
-122	**6**	28	**Freedom Fire (IRE)**[9] 983 4-11-3 120..............................(b[1]) JamieMoore (Gary Moore) *t.k.h: prom: hit 6th: sn lost pl: t.o 2 out: eased* **3/1**[3]	45
	P		**King Of The Moors (USA)**[7] 7-10-12 0...........................(p) SamJones (Richard Guest) *j. bdly lft 1st: t.k.h: w ldrs: nt fluent 5th: lost pl after next: sn bhd: t.o whn p.u bef 2 out* **12/1**	—
	P		**Billys Flyer (IRE)**[73] 5-10-12 0.. PaulMoloney (Evan Williams) *nt fluent in rr: t.o 4th: p.u after next* **25/1**	—

3m 54.3s (-2.80) **Going Correction** -0.15s/f (Good)
WFA 4 from 5yo+ 15lb **8** Ran SP% **113.6**
Speed ratings (Par 105): **101,100,92,89,78 64,—,—**
Tote Swingers: 1&2 £2.10, 1&3 £3.70, 2&3 £4.20 CSF £9.44 TOTE £4.40: £2.40, £1.10, £1.20; EX 12.20.

Owner The Fun & Frolics Partnership **Bred** John Hussey And Stephen Hillen **Trained** Andoversford, Gloucs

FOCUS
The front two drew clear in what was an uncompetitive novices' hurdle. The winner continues to improve and the fourth limits the rating.

NOTEBOOK
Admiral Dundas(IRE) looked a sitting duck to the runner-up straightening for home, but he pulled out a bit more once joined and, having got a good jump at the last, edged ahead once more on the run-in. This was only his third start over hurdles and he looks the sort connections will enjoy further success with, especially once sent handicapping. (tchd 5-2 and 3-1)

Blue Eyed Eloise, fourth off a mark of 105 at Market Rasen earlier in the month, travelled well, but she has never looked the best of stayers and the winner proved too strong for her after the last. She could probably have done without the rain as a genuine fast surface seems to suit best. (op 3-1)

Apache Dawn ran his race and simply wasn't good enough. (op 5-1)

Freedom Fire(IRE) failed to run to anything like the form he had shown previously, the first-time blinkers not having the desired effect. He's another for whom a fast surface is required. Official explanation: trainer's rep had no explanation for the poor form shown (tchd 11-4)

King Of The Moors(USA) was too keen and didn't last home, eventually pulling up. (op 9-1)

1084 GARDEN CARE FISHTOFT H'CAP HURDLE (9 hdls) 2m
4:40 (4:40) (Class 4) (0-115,115) 4-Y-0+ **£3,577** (£1,050; £525; £262)

Form				RPR
1-52	**1**		**Alph**[24] 853 13-11-4 114.. MrTJCannon(7) (Roger Teal) *hld up in rr: smooth hdwy 5th: slt ld 2 out: gd jump last: hld on gamely* **7/1**	117+
-423	**2**	1	**Celticello (IRE)**[12] 958 8-11-10 113.............................. TomO'Brien (Michael Quinlan) *trckd ldrs: wnt cl 2nd appr last: styd on same pce last 100yds* **7/2**[1]	115+
00P3	**3**	1	**Is It Me (USA)**[24] 853 7-11-10 113.................................(t) PaulMoloney (Sophie Leech) *led: reminders appr 5th: hdd 2 out: styd on same pce appr last* **7/1**	114
P-01	**4**	nk	**Dream Catcher (SWE)**[18] 914 7-11-6 112.............. RichieMcLernon(3) (Jonjo O'Neill) *hdwy to chse ldrs 5th: styd on same pce appr last* **8/1**	112
6P-0	**5**	15	**Royal Max (IRE)**[58] 479 4-11-3 108..............................(t) DenisO'Regan (Ian Williams) *hld up: hdwy 6th: drvn and out;pced after next: modest 7th 2 out: kpt on appr last* **5/1**[3]	92
21-0	**6**	8	**Alfloramoor**[85] 64 8-10-13 105.....................................(p) AdamPogson(3) (Charles Pogson) *chsd ldrs: wknd and eased appr last* **8/1**	91
1-64	**7**	6	**Cortinas (GER)**[30] 831 8-11-12 115..................................(t) NoelFehily (Charlie Mann) *in rr: hdwy 3 out: sn chsng ldrs: wknd after 2 out* **14/1**	101
534-	**8**	23	**Hi Tide (IRE)**[256] 2195 6-11-9 112...................................... GrahamLee (J R Jenkins) *t.k.h in rr: hdwy 6th: sn chsng ldrs: lost pl appr 2 out* **33/1**	65
60-0	**9**	8	**Ardistan (IRE)**[24] 853 6-11-1 104...................................... APMcCoy (Jonjo O'Neill) *prom: drvn to chse ldrs 5th: lost pl after 3 out* **18/1**	50
3-41	**10**	3 ¼	**Pool Of Knowledge (FR)**[24] 850 4-10-13 104.............. AidanColeman (Venetia Williams) *t.k.h: trckd ldrs: upsides whn nt fluent 5th: wknd after 3 out* **9/2**[2]	45
00-P	**11**	16	**Classic Fly (FR)**[68] 350 7-10-6 95.................................. NickScholfield (Arthur Whiting) *chsd ldrs: reminders 4th: lost pl 6th: sn bhd* **33/1**	24
3F-P	**12**	27	**Mouseen (IRE)**[12] 962 7-11-2 112.................................. PeterHatton(7) (Lisa Day) *reminders and lost pl 4th: bhd fr 6th: sn t.o* **50/1**	16

3m 52.6s (-4.50) **Going Correction** -0.15s/f (Good)
WFA 4 from 6yo+ 15lb **12** Ran SP% **124.1**
Speed ratings (Par 105): **105,104,104,103,96 92,89,77,73,72 64,50**
Tote Swingers: 1&2 £8.10, 1&3 £13.50, 2&3 £10.20 CSF £33.58 CT £186.37 TOTE £12.00: £3.80, £1.10, £3.40; EX 49.30.

Owner Andy Chard **Bred** G A And Mrs Antill **Trained** Ashtead, Surrey

FOCUS
A most competitive handicap hurdle and solid form. The winner is rated back to the level of his Towcester win.

NOTEBOOK
Alph has found some form again and was only 4lb higher than when winning at Towcester in April. Always travelling strongly, he moved up to hold every chance in the straight and, having taken a narrow lead two out, a great jump at the last swung the momentum very much in his favour. He was rated 149 at his peak, but it's doubtful whether he would be up to defying much of a rise. (op 9-1)

Celticello(IRE) hugged the inside throughout and was produced to hold every chance, but he has never found it easy winning handicaps and the winner proved too determined. (tchd 9-2)

Is It Me(USA) kept boxing on for third and ran right up to form. (op 6-1 tchd 11-2)

Dream Catcher(SWE) was up 8lb from his Newton Abbot win and couldn't find any extra after the last.

Royal Max(IRE), making his debut for the yard, did well in the end considering he looked more likely to finish tailed off at one stage. (op 12-1)

Cortinas(GER) got on to the heels of the leaders leaving the back, but then couldn't race on in the straight. (op 9-1)

Pool Of Knowledge(FR), who very much had the run of things when winning a maiden hurdle at Stratford, was up 2lb and failed to reproduce his form on this return to handicaps. Official explanation: trainer's rep had no explanation for the poor form shown (tchd 5-1)

1085 CARTWRIGHT KING (S) HURDLE (9 hdls) 2m
5:15 (5:15) (Class 5) 4-Y-0+ **£2,055** (£599; £299)

Form				RPR
6-01	**1**		**Holoko Heights**[9] 984 5-11-8 115..............................(v) RichardJohnson (Tim Vaughan) *chsd ldrs: cl 2nd and hit 3 out: led appr next: sn sent clr: 14 l ahd last: eased* **4/6**[1]	116+
/F4-	**2**	9	**Mossmann Gorge**[39] 1337 8-10-9 104.............................. TomMolloy(3) (Anthony Middleton) *in rr: reminders 4th: hdwy 3 out: styd on to take modest 2nd between last 2* **8/1**[3]	91
0/03	**3**	5	**Reel Missile**[42] 714 11-10-9 98.................................... AdamPogson(3) (Charles Pogson) *led: j.rt: hdd appr 2 out: fdd appr last* **9/4**[2]	86
BP-P	**4**	1	**Daraybad (FR)**[33] 800 8-10-12 78..................................(p) KeithMercer (Andrew Crook) *drvn 5th: hdwy to chse ldrs 3 out: 3rd and one pce whn hit next* **50/1**	86
03-F	**5**	30	**Adjami (IRE)**[42] 717 9-10-12 78......................................(p) HarrySkelton (John Harris) *stmbld sn after 1st: drvn 5th: chsd ldrs next: hit 3 out: sn lost pl: eased whn t.o next* **20/1**	58
0/5-	**6**	1	**Bilbo Boggart (IRE)**[129] 4669 6-10-9 0........................ CampbellGillies(3) (Ian McInnes) *t.k.h: chsd ldr: mstke 5th: lost pl after 3 out: t.o next* **66/1**	57
010/	**P**		**Devilfishpoker Com**[25] 3534 6-10-7 92.......................... JamesHalliday(5) (Shaun Harris) *towards rr: mstke 5th: sn bhd: t.o whn p.u bef 2 out* **40/1**	—

3m 55.8s (-1.30) **Going Correction** -0.15s/f (Good)
WFA 4 from 5yo+ 15lb **7** Ran SP% **112.5**
Speed ratings (Par 103): **97,92,90,89,74 74,—**
Tote Swingers: 1&2 £2.00, 1&3 £1.40, 2&3 £2.40 CSF £6.57 TOTE £2.00: £1.30, £1.60; EX 5.10.Winner bought in for 4,250gns.

Owner Owen Promotions Limited **Bred** Owen Promotions Ltd **Trained** Aberthin, Vale of Glamorgan

FOCUS
A weak selling hurdle that was won in authoritative fashion by Holoko Heights who is decent in this grade and was value for further.

NOTEBOOK
Holoko Heights cleared right away in the straight before being eased. This was much easier than when winning in the same grade at Uttoxeter last time, and he looks sure to take the beating when bidding for a hat-trick, assuming he sticks to this sort of level. (tchd 8-13 and 8-11 in a place)

Mossmann Gorge came through in the end for second and looks capable of picking up a minor race at this level. (op 6-1 tchd 9-1)

Reel Missile was readily swept aside by the winner on this drop in grade. (op 7-2)

1086 EVENBROOK QUALITY HOMES FOR RENT STANDARD OPEN NATIONAL HUNT FLAT RACE 2m

5:45 (5:47) (Class 6) 4-6-Y-0 **£1,507** (£439; £219)

Form RPR

23-3 **1** **Mr Jay Dee (IRE)**[65] 399 5-11-2 0 BrianHughes 105+
(Alan Swinbank) *mde all: shkn up and qcknd clr over 3f out: rdn out: hung bdly rt nr fin* **1/1**[1]

6 **2** *8* **Helena Of Troy**[45] 686 4-10-7 0 TjadeCollier 89
(Sue Smith) *chsd ldrs: wnt modest 2nd over 3f out: kpt on same pce* **40/1**

05 **3** *8* **Nonobu (UAE)**[16] 935 4-10-7 0 AndrewTinkler 82
(George Baker) *hld up in rr: hdwy on ins to take modest 3rd over 3f out: one pce* **6/1**[3]

4 *1* **Teals Star** 6-10-10 0 ow1 MrMSeston(7) 91
(G P Kelly) *stdd s: in rr: outpcd over 2f out: kpt on fnl 2f* **11/1**

0- **5** *½* **Bullring (FR)**[254] 2238 4-11-0 0 (t) DougieCostello 89+
(Ollie Pears) *prom: drvn 6f out: outpcd whn hmpd over 3f out: kpt on fnl f* **3/1**[2]

5 **6** *6* **St Enoder**[51] 589 5-10-9 0 JimmyMcCarthy 78
(Brendan Powell) *t.k.h: hld up in rr: hdwy 6f out: wnt modest 4th 3f out: wknd over 1f out* **16/1**

3/6 **7** *11* **Little Justice**[28] 841 6-10-9 0 CharliePoste 69
(Paul Cowley) *chsd ldrs: pushed along 6f out: wkng whn hmpd over 3f out* **25/1**

0 **8** *2* **Two Mile Borris (IRE)**[24] 855 4-10-7 0 MrJMQuinlan(7) 71
(Michael Quinlan) *chsd ldrs: drvn 5f out: lost pl over 3f out* **33/1**

01 **9** *6* **Thomas Bell (IRE)**[23] 869 6-11-2 0 CharlieWallis(7) 78+
(John O'Shea) *t.k.h in rr: hdwy 6f out: chsng ldrs whn hung rt bnd over 4f out: lost pl over 2f out* **12/1**

3m 52.7s (1.20) **Going Correction** -0.15s/f (Good)
WFA 4 from 5yo+ 2lb **9** Ran SP% **120.4**
Speed ratings: **91,87,83,82,82 79,73,72,69**
Tote Swingers: 1&2 £10.00, 1&3 £1.80, 2&3 £24.50 CSF £63.33 TOTE £2.10: £1.10, £7.20, £2.10; EX 38.80 Place 6: £5.01 Place 5: £4.08 .Treasure's Girl was withdrawn, price at time of withdrawal 80/1. Rule 4 does not apply.
Owner R Dooly **Bred** Noel Dooly **Trained** Melsonby, N Yorks

FOCUS

This moderate bumper was won with ease by Mr Jay Dee. He and the third are rated to their marks.

NOTEBOOK

Mr Jay Dee(IRE) made all the running and cleared away in the straight for an easy success. He will stay further over hurdles and looks to have a bright future. (tchd 5-4)
Helena Of Troy stepped up on her initial effort and is another set to be suited by a stiffer test once sent hurdling. (op 33-1)
Nonobu(UAE) again showed ability without suggesting she's up to winning a bumper. (op 7-1 tchd 11-2)
Teals Star, gambled on beforehand, did his best work towards the finish and should improve. (op 33-1 tchd 10-1)
Bullring(FR), wearing a first-time tongue tie, fared better than he had done on his debut 254 days earlier. He was short of room from the end of the back straight, did get hampered before the final turn, and looks in need of further. (op 5-1)
Thomas Bell(IRE) hung badly right off the final bend and probably deserves another chance. Official explanation: jockey said gelding hung right (op 9-1)
T/Plt: £6.90 to a £1 stake. Pool:£55,722.42 - 5,827.69 winning tickets T/Qpdt: £3.90 to a £1 stake. Pool:£4,243.98 - 795.10 winning tickets WG

1087 - 1089a (Foreign Racing) - See Raceform Interactive

[1065] UTTOXETER (L-H)

Monday, July 26

OFFICIAL GOING: Good (good to firm in places)

Common bends with hurdles dolled out but 3m inside line used on July 22nd. 2nd last fence omitted all chases, last hurdle back str omitted all hurdles.
Wind: almost nil Weather: Overcast with black clouds

1090 ANNUAL BOXHOLDERS AT UTTOXETER RACECOURSE MARES' NOVICES' HURDLE (9 hdls 1 omitted) 2m

6:25 (6:25) (Class 4) 4-Y-0+ **£2,602** (£764; £382; £190)

Form RPR

5-1 **1** **Riverscape (IRE)**[15] 965 5-11-10 120 (t) APMcCoy 125+
(Gordon Elliott, Ire) *settled gng easily towards rr: effrt after 6th: led on bit next: 3 l clr 2 out: hit last: canter* **8/13**[1]

6 **2** *5* **Rafta (IRE)**[8] 1030 4-10-8 0 BarryKeniry 97+
(W G Harrison) *racd keenly and cl up: effrt 6th: led briefly bef 3 out: chsd wnr vainly after: flattered by proximity* **40/1**

146- **3** *13* **Halling Gal**[91] 19 4-11-1 111 PaulMoloney 90
(Evan Williams) *led: rdn and hdd nring 3 out: sn wknd: 16 l 3rd at last* **4/1**[2]

0 **4** *2½* **Red Current**[20] 916 6-10-10 0 TomScudamore 85
(Michael Scudamore) *t.k.h in rr: blnd 6th: brief effrt bef next: sn eased and lost tch: pushed along and kpt gng steadily after* **33/1**

00/1 **5** *12* **Washango (IRE)**[68] 407 8-11-3 0 RichardJohnson 87+
(Shaun Lycett) *trckd ldrs: rdn and effrt after 6th: ch next: sn wknd: mstke last* **5/1**[3]

502P **6** *8* **Basford Tara**[12] 989 5-10-10 0 (p) AlanO'Keeffe 65
(Jennie Candlish) *j.rt and prom: reminders 5th: wnt 2nd and rdn after next: lost pl tamely bef next* **10/1**

-060 **7** *8* **Carrifran (IRE)**[9] 1021 5-10-5 0 JamesHalliday(5) 57
(Malcolm Jefferson) *v free to post: plld hrd in rr tl lost tch qckly 6th: t.o 2 out* **50/1**

005 **8** *5* **Miss Markham (IRE)**[11] 1003 5-10-3 0 PeterHatton(7) 53
(Patricia Rigby) *v keen to post: t.k.h: chsd ldr tl hit 6th and wknd: t.o whn mstke 2 out* **150/1**

U **Aura**[564] 5-10-10 0 RhysFlint —
(John Flint) *j.lft and blnd 2nd: in rr whn j. bdly lft and uns rdr 5th* **40/1**

00-0 **P** **Kemsley Lass**[40] 760 5-10-3 0 MrTJCannon(7) —
(Milton Bradley) *mstke 5th: in tch tl mstke 6th and drvn: t.o and p.u next: dismntd: lame* **150/1**

3m 51.0s (-4.20) **Going Correction** -0.55s/f (Firm)
WFA 4 from 5yo+ 15lb **10** Ran SP% **118.8**
Speed ratings (Par 105): **88,85,79,77,71 67,63,61,—,—**
toteswingers: 1&2 £7.80, 1&3 £1.10, 2&3 £18.90. CSF £37.66 TOTE £2.00: £1.02, £15.90, £1.30; EX 35.40.
Owner Fresh By Nature Syndicate **Bred** Newberry Stud Farm Ltd **Trained** Trim, Co Meath

FOCUS

The third-last hurdle in the back straight was omitted on all circuits and the bends had been moved in by 3m on to fresh ground. The easy winner is value for further in this uncompetitive event.

NOTEBOOK

Riverscape(IRE) had disappointed on slightly easier ground at Sligo a fortnight ago but prior to that had shown ability on fast ground and, as a dual winner, was the one to beat. She jumped steadily and a bit clumsily early on, but was never under any pressure and had too much power for these rivals, coming clear with her ears pricked to make light of her double penalty. (op 4-6 tchd 8-11 and 4-5 in a place)
Rafta(IRE) improved markedly on her debut run at Stratford last week. Settling to track the leaders, her jumping was hesitant early on, but she came through well enough to pose a brief challenge to the winner. She could be up to winning once her jumping improves with more experience. (op 50-1)
Halling Gal was keen on her return from a three-month break and was hassled for the lead throughout, eventually capitulating as the field straightened up for home. She has not progressed from winning a juvenile hurdle in March and will need to find improvement to win again. (op 6-1)
Red Current did not jump fluently, especially in the back straight where she tended to jump low, and so could only plug on for a well-beaten fourth.
Washango(IRE) returned from lengthy absence to record a comfortable success in May, but has been absent again since then. She was beginning to feel the pace when driven to stay in touch three-wide around the final turn, and the lack of a recent run told as the leaders got away, after which she was eased. If she comes on for this run and can remain sound she evidently has ability. (op 7-2)
Basford Tara resumed her tendency to jump right, which the addition of cheekpieces could not correct. (op 8-1)

1091 RWH CONSTRUCTION BEGINNERS' CHASE (13 fncs 2 omitted) 2m 4f

6:55 (6:55) (Class 4) 4-Y-0+ **£3,168** (£936; £468; £234; £117)

Form RPR

0162 **1** **Intac (IRE)**[8] 1025 8-11-9 0 JoeTizzard 111+
(Colin Tizzard) *mde all: rdn fr 3 out: hung on gamely flat* **15/8**[1]

-P05 **2** *½* **Tritonville Lodge (IRE)**[33] 830 8-11-9 0 JackDoyle 111+
(Emma Lavelle) *pressed wnr: hit 5th: rdn and ev ch fr 3 out: jst hld by battling wnr fr last* **85/40**[2]

-223 **3** *6* **Pagan Sword**[19] 934 8-11-9 97 RodiGreene 105
(David Bridgwater) *trckd ldng pair: rdn bef 9th: abt 6 l down and no imp fr 3 out* **7/1**

4 *60* **Canal Bank (IRE)**[272] 1949 6-11-9 0 APMcCoy 51
(Jonjo O'Neill) *t.k.h: lost tch and rdn 8th: poor 4th at 10th: t.o next* **12/1**

/6 **5** *25* **Doheny Bar (IRE)**[12] 992 7-11-9 0 (b) JodieMogford 29
(Nikki Evans) *t.k.h: j. slowly 5th and rdn: reminders 6th: mstke 7th: lost tch 8th: t.o 10th* **33/1**

00-0 **U** **Jocheski (IRE)**[40] 170 6-11-9 0 AndrewThornton —
(Tony Newcombe) *cl up tl j. sltly lft: nrly fell and uns rdr 3rd* **9/2**[3]

4m 57.1s (-8.40) **Going Correction** -0.475s/f (Good) **6** Ran SP% **108.1**
Speed ratings (Par 105): **97,96,94,70,60** —
toteswingers: 1&2 £1.02, 1&3 £2.50, 2&3 £3.10. CSF £5.99 TOTE £1.90: £1.10, £2.40; EX 6.30.
Owner Stranger, Mogridge, Romans **Bred** Patrick A Keogh **Trained** Milborne Port, Dorset

FOCUS

Not a strong contest, but it was run at a sound pace with the two market leaders battling for supremacy throughout and they consequently dominated. The first three are rated in line with previous chase form.

NOTEBOOK

Intac(IRE) ran the enigmatic Classic Swain to half a length last week and, with the extra distance seemingly in his favour, he just had the edge. He was unable to get an uncontested lead, but overall jumped more efficiently, lengthening and using less energy than his market rival, and that seemed to prove the deciding factor. He has been competing in selling hurdles this summer, but looks better over fences. (op 2-1 tchd 7-4 and 5-2 in a place)
Tritonville Lodge(IRE) had the best rating of these over hurdles, but was now resuming a chasing career that had an inauspicious start in three runs two years ago. He has been well schooled in the interim, but still did not look a natural, not able to lengthen over the fences as well as the winner, and ultimately had to find too much on the flat and was just beaten. He actually gained some ground when launching himself at a couple of fences, so is not a forlorn hope for winning a moderate contest on fastish ground over easy fences. (op 11-4)
Pagan Sword jumped a bit better than he has of late, but he was always struggling to keep tabs on the leaders and that battle proved too much. He is 0-14 over fences. (op 11-2 tchd 15-2)
Canal Bank(IRE), making his debut for Jonjo O'Neill after two lacklustre runs for Christy Roche, jumped soundly, but was just too slow in the air and began to lose touch on the final circuit, after which he was allowed to complete in his own time. (op 7-1)
Jocheski(IRE), making his chasing debut, slithered on landing at the third and gave his jockey no chance of staying in situ. (tchd 5-1)

1092 INJURED JOCKEYS FUND (S) HURDLE (10 hdls 2 omitted) 2m 6f 110y

7:25 (7:26) (Class 5) 4-7-Y-0 **£1,561** (£458; £229; £114)

Form RPR

0 **1** **Cape Secret (IRE)**[50] 656 7-10-12 0 APMcCoy 88+
(Gordon Elliott, Ire) *hld up in rr in slow r: effrt and blnd 3 out: led next: clr whn hit last: idled and rdn out* **9/2**[3]

34/0 **2** *6* **Quiny Boy (FR)**[12] 984 6-10-9 100 (vt) DannyCook(3) 80
(David Pipe) *hld up in rr: clsd ent st: led sn after 3 out: hdd next: rdn and fnd nil: btn last* **8/1**

-35P **3** *1* **Manadam (FR)**[26] 867 7-10-12 110 (p) AidanColeman 80
(Anthony Middleton) *trckd ldrs: wnt 2nd at 7th tl rdn bef 3 out: sn outpcd: plugged on again after last: wnt 3rd fnl 100yds* **7/2**[2]

-0UP **4** *5* **General Simara**[8] 1034 6-10-12 75 (v[1]) NoelFehily 76
(Tony Carroll) *t.k.h: led 3rd tl after 3 out: sn lost pl: nt keen and lost 3rd flat* **33/1**

4-33 **5** *8* **Calzaghe (IRE)**[18] 835 6-11-12 110 TomScudamore 84
(Jim Best) *bhd: hit 7th and drvn: qckly lost tch* **11/2**

2122 **F** **King Of Castile**[15] 953 6-11-2 110 (bt) DPFahy —
(Evan Williams) *led at modest pce tl stmbld and fell after 2nd* **6/4**[1]

\- **P** **Woodfield Queen (IRE)**[61] 485 6-10-5 0 (p) JohnnyFarrelly —
(Joseph Fox, Ire) *j.rt: lft in ld after 2nd: hdd 3rd: lost pl 6th: sn last and rdn: t.o and p.u 3 out* **50/1**

5m 30.5s (-0.40) **Going Correction** -0.55s/f (Firm) **7** Ran SP% **111.8**
Speed ratings: **78,75,75,73,71** —,—
toteswingers: 1&2 £17.40, 1&3 £3.20, 2&3 £8.70. CSF £36.55 TOTE £9.10: £4.90, £8.60; EX 53.80.The winner was bought in for 4,600gns.
Owner Ms Annie Flora Joan Bowles **Bred** Declan And Catherine Macpartlin **Trained** Trim, Co Meath

FOCUS

A weak contest, even for a seller, run at just a steady pace. The race could be rated higher but the time was modest and the fourth is probably the best guide.

NOTEBOOK

Cape Secret(IRE) got warm beforehand but travelled well through the race, ridden confidently wide of the pack until produced to challenge when the pace lifted in the home straight, and he soon stretched clear. He had won four times on the Flat so evidently had some ability, however that was three years ago, and his form subsequently tailed off, leading to more than two years off the track. He evidently has had his problems, but his three recent outings over hurdles offered little encouragement. But the trainer and jockey combination are a potent force, and so it proved again here. (op 4-1)

Quiny Boy(FR) did not make much impact on his return from a lengthy absence this month, but was entitled to improve on that, and previously he had progressing quite nicely last season, admittedly in moderate contests. Moving through to briefly take up the running in the home straight, he ran a sound race but was just outpaced by a speedier rival, but at least he is coming into form. (op 9-1)

Manadam(FR) made some late progress, but is better on easier ground and is a bit of a plodder. (op 9-2 tchd 10-3)

General Simara responded to the first-time visor, racing prominently and holding a two-length lead turning for home. He was unable to sustain it but this was an improvement on his previous moderate form.

Calzaghe(IRE) came into this race in good form, having won on the Flat this month, but although he was a multiple winner of low-grade hurdles last year he has not been able to match that on faster ground this season. (op 7-2 tchd 6-1)

King Of Castile set the steady early pace but seemed to lose his footing after the second and came down. (op 15-8 tchd 2-1 and 11-8)

1093 MEYNELL & SOUTH STAFFORDSHIRE HUNT H'CAP CHASE (15 fncs 3 omitted) 3m

7:55 (7:55) (Class 4) (0-105,107) 4-Y-0+ **£3,168** (£936; £468; £234; £117)

Form RPR

4P13 **1** **Thenameescapesme**[26] 868 10-11-7 **102**.................... SeanQuinlan(3) 114+
(Kim Bailey) *t.k.h and trckd ldrs: led 11th: only one nt being pushed next: 5 l clr 3 out: rdn between last two: kpt on wl* **16/1**

0-03 **2** *6* **Browneyes Blue (IRE)**[60] 491 12-11-3 **95**....................... BrianHughes 102
(James Moffatt) *bhd: lost tch in 12 l 10th whn mstke 9th: styd on wl fr 3 out: wnt 2nd flat: nt rch wnr* **33/1**

-F01 **3** *2 1/2* **Strong Coffee**[8] 1027 8-12-1 **107** 7ex.............................(b) LeightonAspell 113+
(Oliver Sherwood) *led tl 11th: hit 12th: chsd wnr after: hld fr 3 out: pckd last and wknd to lose 2nd flat* **13/2**

F5/1 **4** *2 1/2* **Bynack Mhor (IRE)**[12] 987 9-10-0 **78** oh1..................(tp) AidanColeman 83+
(Lawney Hill) *midfield: n.m.r on bnd after 8th and rdn: outpcd 11th: btn 3 out: 12 l 5th whn mstke next: styd on after last* **3/1**[1]

5/P0 **5** *16* **What A Scientist (IRE)**[46] 695 10-11-6 **101**................(b) TomMolloy(3) 88
(Nigel Twiston-Davies) *mstke 3rd: towards rr: reminders 4th and 8th: mstke and lost tch 9th: wl bhd 3 out* **14/1**

141 **6** *6* **Prophete De Guye (FR)**[12] 993 7-11-12 **104**.................... FelixDeGiles 85
(James Evans) *taken down early: plld hrd and chsd ldrs: outpcd whn blnd 11th: wl bhd 3 out* **9/2**[2]

0-45 **7** *6* **Lidjo De Rouge (FR)**[27] 852 11-11-9 **101**.................... RichardJohnson 77
(Paul Henderson) *chsd ldrs: rdn 11th: sn wknd: blnd 3 out* **16/1**

0-52 **8** *5* **Good Harvest (IRE)**[26] 868 7-11-10 **102**.............................. APMcCoy 78
(Jonjo O'Neill) *blnd 2nd: pressed ldrs: mstke 5th: reminders 8th: 3rd and drvn bef 3 out: sn wknd: lost five pls after next* **5/1**[3]

6150 **9** *47* **Classic Clover**[8] 1027 10-11-9 **101**...................................(bt) JoeTizzard 30
(Colin Tizzard) *prom to 5th: dropped to rr 7th: last next: t.o and reluctant fr 9th: fin eventually* **33/1**

433P **P** **Allterrain (IRE)**[8] 1027 7-11-1 **100**................................ MrSO'Donovan(7) —
(Norma Twomey) *chsd ldr tl 11th: wkng whn mstke 3 out: t.o and p.u last* **10/1**

0/00 **P** **Weather Permitting (IRE)**[29] 849 7-10-0 **78** oh1...(tp) TomScudamore —
(David Pipe) *drvn along and nvr gng wl: t.o 6th: p.u 7th* **12/1**

6m 0.50s (-14.60) **Going Correction** -0.475s/f (Good) course record **11** Ran SP% **114.3**

Speed ratings (Par 105): **105,103,102,101,96 94,92,90,74,— —**

toteswingers: 1&2 £59.20, 1&3 £20.60, 2&3 £62.80. CSF £380.11 CT £3720.50 TOTE £22.10: £5.50, £8.30, £2.60; EX 277.70.

Owner Mrs Tania D Yeomans **Bred** Horseshoe Agency Ltd **Trained** Andoversford, Gloucs

FOCUS

Several recent winners made for a competitive handicap and the form should prove reliable. The third is rated to his recent form.

NOTEBOOK

Thenameescapesme raced handily, poised to make a challenge when required, and when asked he readily galloped several lengths clear. He began to tire coming to the last and the field closed up a bit, but the damage had already been done. He has sometimes looked a weak finisher over similar trips, such as last time at Worcester, but he has hit form this summer and the move in the back straight overcame that tendency to weaken, enabling him to register his first win at 3m. (op 12-1)

Browneyes Blue(IRE) was having only his third start over fences, but the veteran ran with credit, keeping on near the finish. He was well treated for his handicap chase debut compared to his hurdling mark, so on similar terms he could gain a belated victory over fences. (op 28-1 tchd 40-1)

Strong Coffee had a welter burden following his Newton Abbot success last week, but he ran a game race, leading for much of the way and keeping on once headed. He is in good heart and it will be a shame if the handicapper puts a stop to his run of form. (op 7-1 tchd 15-2 and 11-2)

Bynack Mhor(IRE) was still well treated and able to race off a low weight, so consequently was went off favourite. However, he lost position mid-race and, after getting bumped in the back straight, lost confidence at the fences. In the circumstances he did well to finish as close as he did, suggesting there is still more to come. (op 9-4)

Prophete De Guye(FR) still looked fairly treated, but he was free to post and raced too freely to have any chance of adding to his recent C&D success. (op 13-2 tchd 4-1)

1094 JAMES DEREK JOYNES H'CAP HURDLE (11 hdls 3 omitted) 3m

8:25 (8:25) (Class 4) (0-105,105) 4-Y-0+ **£2,602** (£764; £382; £190)

Form RPR

153- **1** **Changing Lanes**[309] 1474 7-11-10 **103**...................................(p) RhysFlint 114+
(John Flint) *trckd ldrs gng wl: wnt 2nd after 7th: rdn to ld bef 2 out: kpt on wl: pushed out* **6/1**[2]

P-02 **2** *5* **Filippo Lippi (IRE)**[19] 930 5-11-2 **95**.................................... APMcCoy 102+
(Jonjo O'Neill) *midfield: effrt in 4th and cajoled along bef 3 out: chsd wnr and hit last: fnd little and a hld* **7/2**[1]

-046 **3** *9* **Heir To Be**[20] 921 11-11-12 **105**....................................(b) NickScholfield 102
(Michael Blake) *prom: 3rd and rdn bef 3 out: one pce and wl hld fr next* **9/1**

24-0 **4** *5* **Converti**[76] 267 6-11-9 **105**.. RyanMania(3) 98
(Simon Burrough) *midfield: 7th and drvn bef 3 out: plodded on and no ch after* **11/1**

1F5- **5** *7* **Kisha King (IRE)**[247] 2434 9-11-4 **104**.........................(v) MrJFMathias(7) 90
(David Rees) *midfield: effrt 9th: 6th and rdn bef 3 out: sn btn* **10/1**

3P-4 **6** *2 1/4* **Rate Field (IRE)**[40] 760 6-10-6 **95**.............................. MatthewClark(10) 87+
(Emma Lavelle) *last whn j.rt 2nd: wl bhd whn mstke 3rd: prog whn crashed into rail bef 9th: 5th whn rdr nrly fell off next: sn lost an iron and nvr regained balance: no ch after but plugged on gamely in circumstances* **14/1**

0-02 **7** *5* **Aldiruos (IRE)**[20] 921 10-11-6 **104**.............................. LeeEdwards(5) 84
(Tony Carroll) *bhd: drvn 9th: no rspnse and sn wl bhd* **13/2**[3]

1U53 **8** *3/4* **Basford Lass**[20] 920 5-11-5 **98**..(b) AlanO'Keeffe 78
(Jennie Candlish) *led: rdn and hdd and hit 2 out: lost pl qckly* **7/1**

31-P **9** *1/2* **Chico Time (IRE)**[8] 1027 9-11-2 **102**........................(p) MrSO'Donovan(7) 81
(Norma Twomey) *bhd: rdn and lost tch after 9th* **33/1**

F450 **10** *7* **Lord Brunello (IRE)**[20] 921 8-10-11 **95**.......................(tp) DavidBass(5) 67
(Lawney Hill) *towards rr and rdn 6th: nvr looked to be gng wl: lost tch after 9th: mstke next* **11/1**

/PF- **11** *72* **Cunning Pursuit**[108] 5120 9-10-11 **90**........................(p) AndrewThornton —
(Robin Mathew) *j. slowly 5th: in rr and mstke 7th: rdn after 8th: t.o after next: virtually p.u fr 3 out* **66/1**

-PP4 **12** *4* **No Greater Love (FR)**[20] 921 8-11-4 **100**...................... TomMolloy(3) 4
(Charlie Longsdon) *plld hrd and pressed ldrs: lost pl qckly after 9th: t.o and virtually p.u fr 2 out* **12/1**

P-55 **P** **Cave Of The Giant (IRE)**[46] 692 8-10-9 **88**........................ JoeTizzard —
(Tim McCarthy) *bad mstke 3rd: continued t.o tl p.u 9th* **33/1**

5m 48.7s (-16.50) **Going Correction** -0.55s/f (Firm) **13** Ran SP% **119.8**

Speed ratings (Par 105): **105,103,100,98,96 95,93,93,93,91 67,65,—**

toteswingers: 1&2 £3.60, 1&3 £11.20, 2&3 £14.10. CSF £27.58 CT £192.78 TOTE £4.70: £1.40, £1.50, £4.50; EX 32.60.

Owner Terry Reffell **Bred** Mrs P And Miss Jane Starkey **Trained** Kenfig Hill, Bridgend

FOCUS

A moderate handicap with the third rated to recent form.

NOTEBOOK

Changing Lanes, returning from a ten-month absence for a new stable, was given the ideal ride, chasing down the leader and pouncing at the second-last, so when that rival capitulated he effectively had a break on the field, which proved decisive. He was a reasonable performer over hurdles and then fences last year, and though he was 10lb higher than his last hurdles win, he had continued the progression over fences to a 5lb higher mark than here, so could be said to be well treated. (op 13-2 tchd 7-1)

Filippo Lippi(IRE) was just beaten over this trip at Worcester this month, and, with a 5lb rise still leaving him reasonably treated, he was well backed. He held every chance in the chasing group but just lacked a bit of pace when needed and could not pick up as well as the winner, though he did stay on. (tchd 11-4 and 4-1)

Heir To Be held a prominent position in the chasing group but was beginning to feel the pace approaching the final turn before plugging on again. He hit a rich vein of form last year but has been struggling to finish his races since returning from a winter break, though this was a better effort and suggests he could be coming into form. (tchd 12-1)

Converti, reappearing after an 11-week break having changed stables in the interim, has gradually been dropping in the weights and could capitalise for his new stable if coming on for this run. (tchd 12-1)

Kisha King(IRE) hit form last autumn but has been off the track since November and may have needed the run as he was never really a factor here. (op 8-1)

Basford Lass attempted to make all, and turning in looked to have been given a finely judged ride, but her stride shortened two out and she faded rapidly. (op 8-1)

Cave Of The Giant(IRE) Official explanation: jockey said gelding made a mistake third and never travelled

1095 JENKINSONS CATERERS H'CAP HURDLE (9 hdls 1 omitted) 2m

8:55 (8:55) (Class 5) (0-95,95) 4-Y-0+ **£1,691** (£496; £248; £124)

Form RPR

3403 **1** **Mujamead**[6] 1049 6-10-10 **83**...(p) LeeEdwards(5) 92+
(Sally-Anne Wheelwright) *chsd ldrs: rdn to go 2nd bef 3 out: led bef next: 5 l clr last drvn and looked to be idling but nvr gng to be ct* **11/1**

/-64 **2** *5* **Northern Lad (IRE)**[31] 837 8-11-11 **93**........................ TomScudamore 98+
(Jim Best) *plld hrd: chsd ldrs: rdn and hit 3 out: 4th next: wnt 2nd at last: one pce and no ch w wnr* **7/1**

-424 **3** *5* **Sparkling Brook (IRE)**[26] 862 7-10-13 **84**...................... TomMolloy(3) 83
(Nigel Twiston-Davies) *racd keenly: led tl 2nd: hit 3rd: led again after 4th: rdn and hdd bef 2 out: no ex: lost 2nd at last* **9/2**[2]

56P- **4** *4* **Takelli (IRE)**[221] 2931 4-11-4 **95**...................................(t) AdamWedge(7) 89
(Evan Williams) *chsd ldrs: drvn 3 out: sn no imp and wl hld: mstke last* **14/1**

1640 **5** *2* **Schinken Otto (IRE)**[29] 848 9-10-5 **80**...................... MissRJefferson(7) 74
(Malcolm Jefferson) *racd keenly: led 2nd tl after 4th: 2nd but outpcd by wnr 2 out: grad wknd* **12/1**

4050 **6** *3 3/4* **The Grey One (IRE)**[8] 1035 7-11-2 **91**............................. ChrisDavies(7) 81
(Milton Bradley) *plld hrd in rr: effrt after 6th: rdn and wknd 3 out* **50/1**

-6PF **7** *19* **Games (IRE)**[21] 913 9-11-3 **85**.......................................(b) RodiGreene 58
(Christopher Kellett) *taken down early: hit 2nd: dropped to rr and drvn 5th: t.o after next* **20/1**

/0-P **8** *2 1/2* **Bond Cruz**[20] 917 7-10-10 **85**.. OliverDayman(7) 55
(Olivia Maylam) *bhd: mstkes 4th and 5th: t.o after next* **66/1**

/3-5 **9** *18* **Jose Bove**[69] 381 8-10-7 **75**..(t) HaddenFrost 29
(Henrietta Knight) *cl up tl 6th: drvn and fdd bdly bef next: t.o* **14/1**

600- **10** *4* **Wujood**[225] 2860 8-11-4 **86**....................................(b) AndrewGlassonbury 37
(Gerald Ham) *prom tl 4th: t.o fr 6th* **12/1**

6/3- **11** *17* **Chord**[274] 1921 6-11-12 **94**..................................... AndrewThornton 29
(Simon Earle) *midfield early: t.o after 6th: fin eventually* **5/1**[3]

0-6 **P** **Song In My Heart (IRE)**[60] 490 5-11-1 **83**........................... APMcCoy —
(Jonjo O'Neill) *last and rdn and labouring after 4th: t.o and p.u 6th* **5/2**[1]

3m 50.1s (-5.10) **Going Correction** -0.55s/f (Firm)

WFA 4 from 5yo+ 15lb **12** Ran SP% **121.2**

Speed ratings (Par 103): **90,87,85,83,82 80,70,69,60,58 49,—**

toteswingers: 1&2 £13.40, 1&3 £6.10, 2&3 £4.10. CSF £87.23 CT £406.48 TOTE £16.20: £4.60, £2.90, £1.40; EX 107.00 Place 6: £263.30, Place 5: £205.74..

Owner M Webb **Bred** D R Tucker **Trained** Alvechurch, Worcs

FOCUS

A moderate contest run at a sound gallop but sound enough rated through those in the frame behind the winner.

NOTEBOOK

Mujamead did not make his move until they had turned for home, but by that stage there were few with much left in the tank, so once he got to the lead at the second-last he was soon clear. He had looked to be on the downgrade with a number of trainers and had not won since November 2008, but that victory had been off a 28lb higher mark. Although he had done little to hint at an imminent resurgence of late, he had almost dropped so far he had to win, and with a return to his favoured fast ground, that proved enough here. (op 14-1)

Northern Lad(IRE) made an eyecatching forward move entering the home straight, but was rather clumsy at the third last and could make no further impression. He had a tendency to pull too hard last year, and while he settled better, he still does not look that straightforward, especially in the closing stages. (op 6-1)

Sparkling Brook(IRE) had a bit of a tussle for the early lead before making her claim for victory in the back straight. However, she had been too keen early on and could not sustain the run beyond the second last. (op 7-2 tchd 10-3)
Takelli(IRE), having his first run since December, ran respectably without making much impact, and he will need to improve on this if he is to be competitive in handicaps. (op 16-1)
Chord did not jump well enough on his first run since October 2009. Official explanation: trainer said jockey reported gelding made a noise (op 9-2)
Song In My Heart(IRE) attracted some late support but did not look to be on a going day and, never travelling, was pulled up mid-race. Official explanation: jockey said gelding lost its action but returned sound (op 11-2)
T/Plt: £157.70 to a £1 stake. Pool:£79,145.89 - 366.28 winning tickets. T/Qpdt: £92.00 to a £1 stake. Pool:£6,677.08 - 53.70 winning tickets. IM

1096 - 1098a (Foreign Racing) - See Raceform Interactive

943 PERTH (R-H)
Tuesday, July 27

OFFICIAL GOING: Good to firm (good in places; 8.4)
Wind: Breezy, half behind Weather: Fine

1099 JOHN SMITH'S EXTRA SMOOTH MAIDEN HURDLE (10 hdls) 2m 4f 110y
6:40 (6:40) (Class 5) 4-Y-O+ £2,276 (£668; £334; £166)

Form RPR
2-24 **1** **Gulf President**[27] [554] 4-10-11 110 .... RichardJohnson 114+
(Tim Vaughan) *chsd ldr: led after 3 out: sn rdn: drew clr fr last* **9/4**[2]
-2 **2** *13* **Symphonica (IRE)**[25] [877] 7-10-0 104 .... KMDonoghue(7) 99+
(Gordon Elliott, Ire) *t.k.h: led to after 3 out: sn drvn: hit and wknd 2 out* **5/4**[1]
P04P **3** *16* **Osbaldeston (IRE)**[12] [999] 7-11-0 100 .... WilsonRenwick 91
(Rose Dobbin) *prom: outpcd whn nt fluent 4 out: sn drvn: no ch after* **33/1**
5- **4** *18* **Jack Apple (IRE)**[37] [810] 8-11-0 96 .... GrahamLee 69
(C A McBratney, Ire) *towards rr: drvn and hdwy 4 out: wknd fr next* **7/1**[3]
6-33 **5** *26* **Float My Boat**[16] [949] 4-10-11 0 .... (t) BrianHughes 40
(S R B Crawford, Ire) *prom: drvn 4 out: wknd bef next* **14/1**
0- **6** *6* **Mersey**[14] [976] 6-11-0 95 .... PeterBuchanan 37
(S R B Crawford, Ire) *hld up: outpcd whn nt fluent 6th: sn lost tch* **33/1**
P **Be Bapalupa (IRE)**[142] 7-11-0 0 .... BarryKeniry —
(Gordon Elliott, Ire) *hld up: hung rt bnd after 5th: p.u bef next* **12/1**
P **Go Go Simon (IRE)** 6-10-7 0 .... (p) BrianToomey(7) —
(Noel G Hynds, Ire) *nt fluent: in tch: blnd 5th: sn struggling: p.u bef next* **66/1**

4m 53.3s (-13.60) **Going Correction** -0.725s/f (Firm)
WFA 4 from 6yo+ 10lb **8** Ran SP% **100.4**
Speed ratings (Par 103): **96,91,84,78,68 65,—,—**
toteswingers:1&2:£1.10, 1&3:£25.00, 2&3:£7.10 CSF £5.07 TOTE £2.10: £1.02, £1.10, £7.30; EX 4.60.
Owner Diamond Racing Ltd **Bred** Mrs J Gittins **Trained** Aberthin, Vale of Glamorgan

FOCUS
The 'big' two drew clear in what was a moderate maiden hurdle. The form is rated around that pair.

NOTEBOOK
Gulf President had shown enough in three previous starts to suggest he could win a race such as this, and he duly improved for the step up in trip, leading before the straight and staying on well to win comfortably. He's also a recent winner on the Flat, so this versatile sort remains capable of winning more races. (op 2-1, tchd 5-2 in a place)
Symphonica(IRE) again ran her race, but it was no surprise to see her find one too good. She's had plenty of chances and will find a race eventually, but is hardly one to follow. (op 13-8, tchd 7-4 in a place)
Osbaldeston(IRE) didn't shape too badly, but isn't going to be winning until he's handicapping. (op 28-1)
Jack Apple(IRE) didn't improve as much as anticipated for the step back up in trip, readily getting left behind by the front two before fading. (tchd 15-2)
Be Bapalupa(IRE), a former point winner, showed disappointingly little on this hurdles debut. (op 8-1)

1100 SHEEP DIP WHISKY NOVICES' H'CAP CHASE (15 fncs) 2m 4f 110y
7:10 (7:10) (Class 4) (0-100,93) 4-Y-O+ £2,851 (£842; £421; £210; £105)

Form RPR
-410 **1** **Strobe**[16] [946] 6-11-4 85 .... (p) JimmyMcCarthy 98+
(Lucy Normile) *led: qcknd 3 out: drvn and hdd briefly last: styd on wl u.p run-in* **11/2**[3]
232F **2** *3* **Emotive**[12] [1001] 7-11-7 91 .... CampbellGillies(3) 101
(Barry Murtagh) *prom: effrt and chsd wnr bef 3 out: led last: hung rt u.p and sn hdd: kpt on same pce* **7/2**[2]
5UP0 **3** *18* **Janal (IRE)**[4] [1080] 7-10-0 67 oh2 .... WilsonRenwick 59
(Stuart Coltherd) *hld up in tch: effrt 3 out: sn outpcd: no imp fr next* **12/1**
-564 **4** *hd* **Ellandshe (IRE)**[16] [944] 10-9-12 68 oh17 ow1 .... (b) RyanMania(3) 60
(William Young) *hld up in tch: outpcd 5 out: rallied to chse clr ldng pair bef 2 out: no imp whn hit last* **33/1**
52 **5** *25* **Cinaman (IRE)**[13] [987] 6-10-9 76 .... RichardJohnson 43
(Tim Vaughan) *chsd ldrs: hit 8th: bmpd 4 out: rdn bef next: sn wknd: btn whn mstke 2 out* **5/6**[1]
P- **6** *16* **Greengables (IRE)**[14] [981] 9-11-9 93 .... (tp) SGMcDermott(3) 44
(Aidan Anthony Howard, Ire) *cl up: bmpd: stmbld bdly and lost pl 4 out: lost tch fr next* **14/1**

5m 0.70s (-13.30) **Going Correction** -0.725s/f (Firm) **6** Ran SP% **109.5**
Speed ratings (Par 105): **96,94,88,87,78 72**
toteswingers:1&2:£2.70, 1&3:£7.00, 2&3:£4.70 CSF £23.78 CT £200.08 TOTE £7.50: £3.10, £1.10; EX 17.80.
Owner Miss P A & P J Carnaby **Bred** Old Mill Stud **Trained** Duncrievie, Perth & Kinross

FOCUS
A modest novices' handicap chase with the in-form runner-up the best guide.

NOTEBOOK
Strobe looked dangerously well treated on this return to fences (rated 22lb higher over hurdles), and he galloped on relentlessly to a well-deserved win. Soon in front, he was headed coming to the last, but battled back doggedly on the run-in. He's declared to run over hurdles at the course today, but connections are best advised sticking to fences for the time being. (op 4-1)
Emotive, still travelling well when falling at Carlisle latest, was clearly none the worse and took over before the last, but he couldn't stay on as strongly as the winner. He has still to win over fences, but can surely put that right at some stage. (op 4-1)
Janal(IRE)'s poor run of form continued at Stratford the other day, but she was making a quick reappearance and shaped much better.
Ellandshe(IRE), rated just 50 and racing from 17lb out of the handicap, did surprisingly well, just getting run out of third late on. (tchd 40-1)
Cinaman(IRE) had been narrowly denied on his recent debut for the yard and had only to the repeat that form to go close, but he proved bitterly disappointing. The 6lb rise cannot be put forward as an excuse, and neither can the bump he received four out, as he was already beginning to struggle. (op Evens tchd 11-10 and 4-5 and 6-5 in a place)
Greengables(IRE) stumbled badly four out and was soon beaten. (tchd 11-1)

1101 BET WITH THE DEWHURST RING (S) H'CAP HURDLE (10 hdls) 2m 4f 110y
7:40 (7:40) (Class 5) (0-90,88) 4-Y-O+ £2,276 (£668; £334; £166)

Form RPR
006/ **1** **Lords Bridge**[73] 9-10-9 70 .... RichardJohnson 97+
(Tim Vaughan) *cl up: led after 4 out: drew clr bef 2 out: v easily* **4/7**[1]
1-P0 **2** *20* **Zelos Diktator**[14] [552] 4-11-10 88 .... (p) WilsonRenwick 85
(Rose Dobbin) *a cl up: lft 2nd bnd bef 2 out: sn no ch w wnr* **14/1**[3]
600- **3** *1* **Supply And Fix (IRE)**[65] [450] 12-11-5 87 .... MissJAKidd(7) 87
(J J Lambe, Ire) *led to after 4 out: kpt on same pce bef 2 out* **14/1**[3]
6-0P **4** *10* **Mr Midaz**[37] [801] 11-10-2 63 .... PeterBuchanan 56
(Donald Whillans) *bhd and sn outpcd: sme hdwy u.p bef 3 out: nvr on terms* **14/1**[3]
-040 **5** *25* **Kalatime (IRE)**[7] [1049] 7-10-6 72 .... (p) JamesHalliday(5) 36
(William Young) *in tch tl outpcd bef 4 out: sn struggling: t.o* **50/1**
0-P0 **6** *25* **Guerilla (AUS)**[16] [948] 10-11-10 85 .... (p) JimmyMcCarthy 24
(Lucy Normile) *hld up in tch: outpcd 6th: lost tch fr next: t.o* **20/1**
06 **P** **Bronx Boy (IRE)**[16] [946] 7-11-12 87 .... GrahamLee —
(Martin Todhunter) *prom: hit 4 out: rdn to chse ldr whn p.u and dismntd bnd bef 2 out: fatally injured* **7/2**[2]
-64P **P** **Parisian Knight (IRE)**[26] [875] 7-10-4 72 .... BrianToomey(7) —
(A M Crow) *mstkes in rr: hmpd bnd after 5th: sn struggling: t.o whn p.u bef 2 out* **25/1**
P5-P **P** **One More Cent**[7] [1049] 5-10-3 67 ow3 .... JamesO'Farrell(3) —
(Dianne Sayer) *nt fluent: a bhd: t.o whn p.u bef 4 out* **66/1**

4m 50.0s (-16.90) **Going Correction** -0.725s/f (Firm)
WFA 4 from 5yo+ 16lb **9** Ran SP% **117.9**
Speed ratings (Par 103): **103,95,95,91,81 72,—,—,—**
toteswingers:1&2:£4.10, 1&3:£9.80, 2&3:£14.40 CSF £9.58 CT £65.72 TOTE £1.90: £1.10, £3.80, £4.70; EX 15.70.There was no bid for the winner. Zelos Diktator was claimed by G. L. Moore for £6,000.
Owner Miss J Murphy **Bred** J K S And Mrs Cresswell **Trained** Aberthin, Vale of Glamorgan

FOCUS
This couldn't have been more straightforward for Lords Bridge. The winner is value for further and the placed horses are rated to their marks.

NOTEBOOK
Lords Bridge was in full control before the straight and stayed on strongly to draw well clear, in the end winning eased down. His improved point form made him the one to beat, and it would be a surprise were Tim Vaughan not to get at least another win out of his new recruit, despite a hefty rise looking certain. (tchd 4-6)
Zelos Diktator went well to a point, but was quickly dropped by the winner. He's been running okay on the Flat and can surely find another lowly race over hurdles. (op 11-1)
Supply And Fix(IRE) was far from disgraced, for all that he was well held.
Kalatime(IRE) Official explanation: trainers rep said mare finished lame
Bronx Boy(IRE) was staying on for pressure and had just taken second when breaking down rounding the bend into the home straight. He had to be put down. (op 4-1)

1102 ORION GROUP ALL STARS H'CAP HURDLE (12 hdls) 3m 110y
8:10 (8:10) (Class 4) (0-100,98) 4-Y-O+ £2,851 (£842; £421; £210; £105)

Form RPR
1 **Supercede (IRE)**[210] [3169] 8-11-5 98 .... (bt) KMDonoghue(7) 122+
(Gordon Elliott, Ire) *trckd ldrs gng wl: led on bit bef 2 out: drew clr: v easily* **9/4**[1]
5P3/ **2** *14* **Uncommited (IRE)**[122] [4904] 10-10-11 90 .... (p) BrianToomey(7) 96
(Noel G Hynds, Ire) *hmpd 1st: sn chsng ldrs: effrt bef 2 out: sn chsng wnr: no imp* **16/1**
34F- **3** *3 1/4* **Gift Of The Gods (IRE)**[108] [5133] 7-10-11 83 .... (p) RichardJohnson 86
(Tim Vaughan) *cl up: led 3rd to 5th: ev ch tl outpcd bef 2 out* **9/4**[1]
U46P **4** *2 3/4* **Solway Blue**[26] [875] 8-10-0 75 .... (tp) EwanWhillans(3) 75
(Lisa Harrison) *t.k.h: hld up in tch: effrt whn n.m.r briefly bnd bef 2 out: sn outpcd* **10/1**
4355 **5** *hd* **Fly Tipper**[12] [999] 10-10-7 86 .... PaulGallagher(7) 87
(Wilf Storey) *hmpd 1st: sn led: hdd 3rd: led 5th to bef 2 out: sn btn* **8/1**[3]
P **6** *24* **De Danu (IRE)**[18] [940] 7-11-1 90 .... (tp) SGMcDermott(3) 66
(Aidan Anthony Howard, Ire) *hld up in tch: rdn bef 3 out: sn wknd* **20/1**
335 **P** **Dark Halo (IRE)**[26] [871] 5-11-6 92 .... (p) GrahamLee —
(C A McBratney, Ire) *led tl j.rt and hdd 1st: cl up: outpcd 1/2-way: t.o whn p.u after 8th* **4/1**[2]

5m 58.0s (-11.90) **Going Correction** -0.725s/f (Firm) **7** Ran SP% **112.4**
Speed ratings (Par 105): **90,85,84,83,83 75,—**
toteswingers:1&2:£9.20, 1&3:£2.00, 2&3:£18.30 CSF £32.41 TOTE £2.30: £1.10, £11.00; EX 72.20.
Owner T D Howley Jnr **Bred** Paul Starr **Trained** Trim, Co Meath

FOCUS
A rout for Supercede, who was making his debut for Gordon Elliott. The placed horses set the level of the form.

NOTEBOOK
Supercede(IRE) was making his debut for Gordon Elliot and routed his rivals. The return to hurdles, step up to 3m and application of a first-time tongue-tie were all decisive factors in his improvement, as well as a chance to race on a sounder surface, and his victory was never in doubt having taken over turning in. He will surely take the beating if turning out again, as he barely broke a sweat. (op 5-2)
Uncommited(IRE) recorded an improved effort, with the faster ground and return of cheekpieces making a difference. (op 20-1)
Gift Of The Gods(IRE) was expected to be another immediate success story for Tim Vaughan, but she was under pressure some way out and beaten by the time they hit two out. She's nicely weighted on old form, but needs to leave this form well behind. (op 15-8 tchd 5-2)
Dark Halo(IRE) failed to run her race, slowly losing touch and eventually pulling up. (tchd 7-2 and 9-2)

1103 JOHN SMITH'S H'CAP CHASE (18 fncs) 3m
8:40 (8:41) (Class 3) (0-130,125) 4-Y-O£5,386 (£1,591; £795; £397; £198)

Form RPR
2-20 **1** **Seize**[54] [608] 8-10-8 107 .... GrahamLee 112
(Ferdy Murphy) *trckd ldrs: rdn and outpcd after 4 out: rallied to chse ldr 2 out: 4 l down last: styd on strly to ld last 50yds* **5/1**
4-12 **2** *1 1/2* **Dead Or Alive (IRE)**[9] [1032] 7-11-10 123 .... (t) RichardJohnson 128+
(Tim Vaughan) *prom: hdwy to ld after 12th: sn jnd: asserted bef 2 out: 4 l clr last: hdd and no ex last 50yds* **2/1**[1]
-41P **3** *15* **Thunder Hawk (IRE)**[12] [1002] 10-9-11 99 oh2 .... (p) CampbellGillies(3) 88
(Stuart Coltherd) *led to after 12th: outpcd after 14th: plugged on fnl 2: no ch w first two* **11/1**
5122 **4** *7* **Chorizo (IRE)**[23] [890] 9-11-0 118 .... JamesHalliday(5) 100
(Richard Guest) *cl up tl outpcd 14th: wknd fr next* **3/1**[3]

-341 5 ¾ **Mizen Raven (IRE)**[12] 1002 7-11-9 **125**..................(tp) DonalDevereux(3) 106
(Peter Bowen) *t.k.h: cl up: hdwy to dispute ld 13th to bef 2 out: sn wknd* **11/4**[2]

6m 1.60s (-18.80) **Going Correction** -0.725s/f (Firm) **5** Ran SP% **110.0**
Speed ratings (Par 107): **102,101,96,94,93**
CSF £15.74 TOTE £8.20: £3.70, £1.10; EX 10.20.
Owner Mrs Sylvia Mizel **Bred** G Z Mizel **Trained** West Witton, N Yorks

FOCUS
A decent little handicap chase with the winner rated to his best.

NOTEBOOK
Seize, below form last time, had earlier gone well off this mark and he received a fine ride from Graham Lee, hunting up the leaders turning in and then staying on strongly after the last to run down Dead Of Alive. Stamina is his strong suit, but he's hardly the most prolific of winners, so it may be unwise to support him when he goes for a follow up. (op 6-1)
Dead Or Alive(IRE), narrowly denied off this mark at Stratford latest, had earlier won at Fakenham and he looked set to score when asserting before two out, but he wavered a bit after the last and was run down in the final 50 yards. (op 7-4 tchd 13-8)
Thunder Hawk(IRE), pulled up latest, was well held but didn't run too badly from 2lb out of the weights. (op 16-1)
Chorizo(IRE) has been in good form, but his best efforts have come at Market Rasen, and he had gone up a further 3lb. He was one of the first beaten, in the end dropping right out. (tchd 100-30)
Mizen Raven(IRE), up 5lb for his Cartmel win, ran too freely for much of the way and it was no surprise to see him finish weakly. He's better than this. Official explanation: trainers rep said gelding finished lame (op 3-1 tchd 7-2)

1104 DAILY RECORD H'CAP HURDLE (8 hdls) 2m 110y
9:10 (9:11) (Class 4) (0-115,109) 4-Y-0+ **£3,168** (£936; £468; £234; £117)

Form RPR
-531 1 **Shopfrontspecialst (IRE)**[9] 1040 7-10-12 **100**............ KMDonoghue(7) 115+
(Gordon Elliott, Ire) *t.k.h: hld up: smooth hdwy bef 2 out: led between last 2: kpt on strly run-in: readily* **4/6**[1]
-042 2 3¾ **Front Rank (IRE)**[16] 948 10-10-9 **97**.......................... MissECSayer(7) 105
(Dianne Sayer) *w ldr: led briefly 2 out: kpt on run-in: no ch w wnr* **12/1**
605- 3 *nse* **Jewelled Dagger (IRE)**[14] 4030 6-11-3 **98**........................ GrahamLee 106
(Jim Goldie) *t.k.h: prom: effrt and rdn bef 2 out: kpt on u.p run-in* **13/2**[2]
0/- 4 4 **Mister Castlefield (IRE)**[149] 4340 6-11-0 **95**............... RichardJohnson 99
(John J Maguire, Ire) *t.k.h: hld up: effrt bef 2 out: kpt on: nvr able to chal* **20/1**
P- 5 4½ **Lightening Sky (IRE)**[51] 655 7-11-7 **105**.................... SGMcDermott(3) 104
(Joseph Fox, Ire) *led to 2 out: sn rdn and wknd* **50/1**
10U2 6 *nk* **Mountskip**[32] 837 6-11-0 **105**....................................... MrAdamNicol(10) 104
(Rose Dobbin) *chsd ldrs: effrt and ev ch 2 out: sn wknd* **9/1**
/0-0 7 3½ **Inner Voice (USA)**[12] 1004 7-11-5 **107**......................... MissJAKidd(7) 106+
(J J Lambe, Ire) *hld up: shkn up bef 2 out: btn whn hit last* **40/1**
3P-6 8 3½ **Bocciani (GER)**[12] 1005 5-10-9 **93**.............................. JamesO'Farrell(3) 85
(Dianne Sayer) *hld up in tch: rdn bef 2 out: sn btn* **50/1**
0- 9 13 **Morning Time (IRE)**[74] 5320 4-11-12 **109**.................... PeterBuchanan 86
(Lucinda Russell) *plld hrd: chsd ldrs tl wknd bef 2 out* **7/1**[3]

3m 50.8s (-8.90) **Going Correction** -0.725s/f (Firm) **9** Ran SP% **114.6**
Speed ratings (Par 105): **91,89,89,87,85 85,83,81,75**
toteswingers:1&2:£2.20, 1&3:£1.10, 2&3:£13.80 CSF £9.12 CT £30.34 TOTE £1.80: £1.20, £2.80, £1.80; EX 6.60 Place 6 £20.15, Place 5 £15.78.
Owner Sean F Gallagher **Bred** Martin C Fleming **Trained** Trim, Co Meath

FOCUS
A low-grade handicap hurdle that turned into a bit of a sprint in the straight. The winner did not need to run to his best Irish form and the second is rated to his latest course mark.

NOTEBOOK
Shopfrontspecialst(IRE), 15lb higher than when winning over C&D two starts back, had to work hard enough to score, but he was well on top in the end, having stayed on well after the last. This consistent sort is progressing well. (tchd 8-11 and 4-5 in a place)
Front Rank(IRE) ran pretty much to form with the winner, having also finished second at the course to him last time. (op 10-1)
Jewelled Dagger(IRE) was a bit keen and ultimately lost out on second, but he does stay the trip and can break his duck over hurdles before long. (op 7-1 tchd 11-2)
Mister Castlefield(IRE) shaped well on this return from an absence and may be in need of a slightly stiffer test. (op 25-1)
Mountskip, up 7lb from last time, was disappointing, finishing weakly having held every chance. (op 10-1)
T/Plt: £43.60 to a £1 stake. Pool £66,940.77 - 1,120.44 winning tickets. T/Qpdt: £9.80 to a 31 stake. Pool £5,618.72 - 423.54 winning tickets. RY

1057 WORCESTER (L-H)
Tuesday, July 27

OFFICIAL GOING: Good (chs 7.9; hdl 8.0)
All bends back on inside and run-in switched to stands' side.
Wind: Light behind Weather: Overcast

1105 ST RICHARDS HOSPICE NOVICES' HURDLE (12 hdls) 3m
5:55 (5:55) (Class 4) 4-Y-0+ **£2,602** (£764; £382; £190)

Form RPR
-2P3 1 **Marblehead (IRE)**[27] 863 8-10-9 115............................ TomMolloy(3) 100+
(Nigel Twiston-Davies) *chsd ldr to 2nd: remained handy: shkn up 5th: drvn along fr 7th: wnt 2nd again 2 out: led last: all out* **9/4**[2]
000- 2 1¼ **King Rocky**[282] 1812 9-10-12 74.................................... DavidEngland 97
(Shaun Lycett) *chsd ldr 2nd: drvn along after 8th: lost 2nd 2 out: rallied flat: styd on* **40/1**
-412 3 2¼ **Downward Spiral (IRE)**[27] 863 5-11-5 116.................... AlanO'Keeffe 102
(Jennie Candlish) *led: rdn appr 3 out: hdd last: hung rt and no ex flat* **4/1**[3]
PP-6 4 66 **Artist's Return (IRE)**[16] 955 8-10-9 64.......................... AlexMerriam(3) 29
(William Stone) *hld up: hdwy 5th: drvn along bef 7th: wknd 9th: t.o* **100/1**
/142 F **North Island (IRE)**[40] 772 8-10-12 0................................. TomO'Brien —
(Peter Bowen) *fell 1st* **5/6**[1]

5m 43.3s (-1.30) **Going Correction** -0.05s/f (Good) **5** Ran SP% **108.8**
Speed ratings (Par 105): **100,99,98,76,—**
CSF £39.86 TOTE £3.20: £2.10, £5.80; EX 17.50.
Owner J C Collett **Bred** Thistletown Stud **Trained** Naunton, Gloucs
■ Stewards' Enquiry : Tom Molloy three-day ban; used whip with excessive frequency (10th-14th Aug)

FOCUS
The favourite's exit at the first left this wide-open and it was run at a muddling gallop. The runner-up clouds the form, although the winner is rated in line with recent course form.

NOTEBOOK
Marblehead(IRE) eventually came out on top and landed his first win as a hurdler at the fifth attempt. This was only his second outing over these obstacles for his current stable and he has improved as a hunter chaser since coming over from Ireland in 2008, however. As a horse that likes to dominate he did tend to travel somewhat in snatches just off the early leader, but the further he went the better he was and he ultimately outstayed his rivals from the last. He can win a handicap in this sphere or back over fences when ridden from the front again.
King Rocky, back from a 282-day absence, is a maiden and has an official mark of just 74, so puts this form into some perspective. He is entitled to improve for the run, though, and may be able to build on this back in a low-grade handicap providing his mark doesn't suffer. Official explanation: trainer said gelding lost a off-fore shoe (op 33-1)
Downward Spiral(IRE), by some way the youngest horse in the race, travelled all over his rivals from the front for most of the way. He felt the pinch nearing the second-last, however, and failed to confirm last-time-out C&D form with the winner on this easier surface. (op 7-2 tchd 100-30 and 9-2)
Artist's Return(IRE) remains out of sorts. (op 80-1)
North Island(IRE) had been keeping better company over fences of late, so it was no surprise to see him sent off at a short price on this return to hurdling. He got no further than the first as he over-jumped it, though. (op Evens)

1106 SWANSEA BAY H'CAP CHASE (12 fncs) 2m
6:25 (6:25) (Class 5) (0-90,90) 4-Y-0+ **£2,055** (£599; £299)

Form RPR
1F34 1 **My Condor (IRE)**[16] 950 9-11-5 **90**.................................(p) MrJHamer(7) 100
(Donald McCain) *w ldr: led 3rd: jnd 4 out: rdn flat: all out* **3/1**[1]
0603 2 *hd* **Captain Marlon (IRE)**[22] 913 9-11-12 **90**..........................(t) JoeTizzard 101+
(Colin Tizzard) *a.p: chsd wnr 8th: ev ch fr 4 out: hrd rdn flat: styd on* **4/1**[2]
3-54 3 9 **Cloonavery (IRE)**[13] 991 8-10-6 **70**................................ LiamTreadwell 71
(Tony Carroll) *hld up: hdwy 5th: rdn 3 out: styd on same pce* **4/1**[2]
34U- 4 6 **Past Heritage**[343] 1242 11-11-0 **78**...................................... SamThomas 73
(Alan Jones) *hld up: hdwy appr 4 out: wknd 2 out* **11/1**
/061 5 14 **Mustamad**[13] 991 7-10-10 **77**.......................................(vt) CharlieStudd(3) 58
(Chris Gordon) *chsd ldrs: drvn along after 8th: wkng whn j.rt 3 out* **8/1**
PP5- 6 12 **Western Pride**[108] 5131 7-10-0 **64** oh1.........................(t) GerardTumelty 33
(Richard Price) *hld up: hdwy appr 4 out: sn wknd: t.o* **25/1**
444P 7 2¼ **Sahara Prince (IRE)**[4] 1080 10-10-8 **79**.......................(b) MrLRPayter(7) 46
(Matt Sheppard) *chsd ldrs: rdn after 8th: wkng whn hmpd 3 out: t.o* **12/1**
32-6 8 6 **Form And Beauty (IRE)**[7] 1049 8-10-11 **75**............... ChristianWilliams 36
(Bernard Llewellyn) *prom: blnd 1st: lost pl next: pushed along appr 4th: wknd bef 4 out: t.o* **7/1**[3]
60F- 9 16 **Auditor**[261] 2156 11-10-9 **73**..(v) ColinBolger 18
(Simon Lewis) *led: j.rt: hdd 3rd: chsd ldr to 8th: sn wknd: t.o* **40/1**
U3/P P **Shannon Lodge (IRE)**[22] 913 12-10-1 **68**...........(t) EamonDehdashti(3) —
(Tracey Barfoot-Saunt) *sn pushed along in rr: bhd fr 4th: j. slowly next 5th: nt fluent next: t.o whn p.u bef 4 out* **33/1**
6P-P P **Marado (IRE)**[83] 148 9-9-11 **64** oh9................................ PeterToole(3) —
(Simon Lewis) *mid-div: dropped to rr 4th: bhd fr 6th: t.o whn p.u bef 4 out* **33/1**

3m 51.8s (0.20) **Going Correction** -0.125s/f (Good) **11** Ran SP% **116.8**
Speed ratings (Par 103): **94,93,89,86,79 73,72,69,61,—,—**
toteswingers:1&2:£3.60, 1&3:£4.90, 2&3:£4.40 CSF £15.29 CT £48.31 TOTE £4.50: £1.80, £2.00, £1.40; EX 8.40.
Owner Deva Racing Overbury Partnership **Bred** Mrs Claire Lonergan **Trained** Cholmondeley, Cheshire

FOCUS
A weak handicap, run at a routine gallop and the joint top weights came clear in a driving finish. The placed horses set the level.

NOTEBOOK
My Condor(IRE) has been called many names in the past for ducking out of a battle in his races, but he displayed a cracking attitude here and gamely resumed winning ways. Considering didn't get an easy lead and was continually pressed by the runner-up after the third-last, he a lot of deserves credit. His form figures at the course now read 2131. (op 7-2)
Captain Marlon(IRE) again travelled sweetly and looked the most likely winner two out. He couldn't get past My Condor try as he might, though, and he is clearly not the most resolute as his record of 1-30 indicates. He is happier over a bit further these days, however, and finished well clear in second. (tchd 7-2)
Cloonavery(IRE) was given a patient ride and looked a possible threat around five out, but his effort petered out. His sole win came on the level in 2004. (op 11-2 tchd 13-2)
Past Heritage was returning from a 343-day layoff and proved easy to back despite having run well when fresh in the past. He crept his way round out the back and made smooth headway turning for home, but was unable to find an extra gear. (op 8-1 tchd 15-2)
Mustamad was never a serious player off his 8lb higher mark for winning over C&D 13 days previously. (op 7-1)

1107 LADBROKES (S) HURDLE (10 hdls) 2m 4f
6:55 (6:55) (Class 5) 4-Y-0+ **£1,712** (£499; £249)

Form RPR
2231 1 **Three Ships**[5] 1067 9-11-1 101.. MattGriffiths(7) 115+
(S Wynne) *hld up: hdwy to chse clr ldr 3rd: led after 6th: rdn clr fr 2 out: eased nr fin* **15/8**[1]
-4F6 2 21 **Rapide Plaisir (IRE)**[27] 865 12-10-12 95......................... CharliePoste 82
(Richard Lee) *hld up: hdwy 7th: sn chsng wnr: wknd 2 out* **16/1**
/0-5 3 3¾ **Parazar (FR)**[27] 865 5-10-12 0... LeightonAspell 77
(Oliver Sherwood) *hld up: hdwy 7th: nt fluent 3 out: hung lft and wknd bef next* **8/1**
5-05 4 ½ **Thistle**[6] 1062 9-10-12 95..(t) AndrewTinkler 77
(George Baker) *hld up: hdwy 7th: wknd after next* **33/1**
03 5 1¼ **Golden Gem (IRE)**[16] 953 8-10-9 95........................(b) SeanQuinlan(3) 76
(Rachel Hobbs) *chsd ldrs tl wknd 7th* **6/1**[3]
P00/ 6 3½ **Sarin**[774] 677 12-10-12 0... AidanColeman 72
(Venetia Williams) *chsd ldrs: wnt 2nd briefly bef 5th: rdn and wknd appr 3 out* **16/1**
-6P0 7 90 **Sula's Legend**[27] 868 9-10-5 0...................................(b[1]) MarkQuinlan(7) —
(Neil Mulholland) *led and sn clr: hdd after 6th: wknd next: t.o* **12/1**
104- P **Dee Cee Elle**[15] 1403 6-11-1 96..................................(v[1]) ChristianWilliams —
(Dai Burchell) *hld up and a in rr: bhd fr 5th: t.o whn p.u bef 3 out* **15/2**
-0P4 P **Peters Star (IRE)**[37] 801 8-11-5 112.............................(b) AdrianLane(3) —
(Donald McCain) *j.lft 1st: chsd clr ldr to 3rd: sn lost pl: bhd fr 5th: t.o whn p.u bef 3 out* **4/1**[2]
P **Kassjan (IRE)**[59] 7-10-5 0... DavidDennis —
(Nigel Hawke) *chsd ldrs: nt fluent 1st: pushed along and lost pl after 4th: bhd fr next: t.o whn p.u bef 7th* **50/1**

4m 47.6s (0.20) **Going Correction** -0.05s/f (Good) **10** Ran SP% **116.3**
Speed ratings (Par 103): **97,88,87,86,86 85,49,—,—,—**
toteswingers:1&2:£10.70, 1&3:£4.00, 2&3:£40.90 CSF £34.92 TOTE £3.40: £1.20, £7.80, £2.60; EX 52.30.The winner was sold to Richard Lee for 5,000gns.
Owner W B Probin **Bred** Juddmonte Farms **Trained** Malpas, Cheshire

The Form Book, Raceform Ltd, Compton, RG20 6NL

FOCUS
A typically very weak seller with the winner rated to his recent course success.

NOTEBOOK
Three Ships took up a clear lead coming out of the back straight and it was a question of how much he had left in the reserve as he had pulled his way into a prominent position after halfway. He is a game sort, though, and kept finding from three out as his rivals downed tools. He was able to ease down near the finish and is a consistent performer in this grade, which always helps. He was later bought by Richard Lee for 5,000gns. (op 9-4 tchd 7-4)

Rapide Plaisir(IRE) made his way into contention turning for home, but his effort under pressure was limited and he was beaten a lot further than had been the case behind the winner here over 2m last time out. (op 10-1 tchd 20-1)

Parazar(FR) ran a similar sort of race as that to the runner-up, who had finished one place behind him at the track on his previous outing. A return to a sharper test now looks on the cards. (op 7-1 tchd 11-2)

Thistle did little for pressure, but was later found to have finished distressed. Official explanation: vet said gelding finished distressed (op 22-1)

Sarin looked interesting in this field, but the market strongly suggested he would need this first outing since June 2008. He ran accordingly. (op 12-1)

1108 LADBROKES H'CAP HURDLE (12 hdls) 3m
7:25 (7:25) (Class 3) (0-125,125) 4-Y-0+ **£4,553** (£1,337; £668; £333)

Form RPR

0633 **1** **Barnhill Brownie (IRE)**[49] 685 7-10-11 **115**..............(t) GilesHawkins(5) 126+
(Philip Hobbs) *hld up: hdwy 7th: jnd ldr next: led 3 out: rdn and hung lft flat: styd on wl* **4/1**[2]

P-11 **2** 3 ¾ **American World (FR)**[69] 409 6-10-10 **109**..........................(t) APMcCoy 117+
(Brendan Powell) *hld up: hdwy to chse ldr 3 out: rdn and swtchd lft after next: mstke last: rdn and ev ch flat: swtchd rt: styd on same pce* **11/4**[1]

2-32 **3** 8 **De Soto**[56] 567 9-11-7 **120**...(t) WillKennedy 118
(Paul Webber) *chsd ldrs: outpcd appr 3 out: rallied bef next: wnt 3rd and wknd flat* **4/1**[2]

33-1 **4** 1 ¼ **No Panic (IRE)**[23] 890 7-11-12 **125**..................................(p) TomO'Brien 122
(Peter Bowen) *chsd ldrs: rdn appr 3 out: wknd and lost 3rd flat* **11/4**[1]

FP-6 **5** 20 **Porters War (IRE)**[27] 866 8-10-11 **110**............................. SamThomas 87
(Alan King) *chsd ldr tl led 9th: hdd next: rdn and wknd 2 out: t.o* **25/1**

-000 **6** 11 **Englishtown (FR)**[16] 954 10-11-0 **116**..................(p) RichieMcLernon(3) 82
(Jonjo O'Neill) *hld up: nt fluent 3rd: hdwy 7th: rdn and wknd appr 3 out: t.o* **25/1**

0P20 **7** 1 ¼ **Osolomio (IRE)**[13] 994 7-11-2 **115**.................................... AlanO'Keeffe 80
(Jennie Candlish) *led to 9th: rdn and wknd bef next: t.o* **20/1**[3]

-100 **P** **Two Miles West (IRE)**[10] 1019 9-11-4 **120**.......................... MrAJBerry(3) —
(Jonjo O'Neill) *chsd ldrs: pushed along 5th: wknd 7th: sn t.o: p.u bef 3 out* **20/1**[3]

5m 39.2s (-5.40) **Going Correction** -0.05s/f (Good) 8 Ran SP% **110.5**
Speed ratings (Par 107): **107,105,103,102,96 92,91,—**
toteswingers:1&2:£2.00, 1&3:£3.50, 2&3:£3.80 CSF £14.22 CT £42.67 TOTE £3.40: £1.50, £2.40, £1.02; EX 14.30.

Owner Alex & Salvo Giannini **Bred** John P A Kenny **Trained** Withycombe, Somerset

FOCUS
A modest handicap, run at an average gallop and the first four came well clear. The runner -up sets the standard.

NOTEBOOK
Barnhill Brownie(IRE) attracted support and finally got his head back in front, registering a first success since winning a novice handicap at Ascot in 2008. He proved more relaxed than when previously third at Southwell and that helped him find extra when pressed by the runner-up from two out. He's not that straightforward and his overall profile suggests he is one to oppose next time, but there is a chance this confidence boost will see him progress. (op 11-2)

American World(FR) was patiently ridden on this return from a 69-day break. He began to feel the pinch around four out, but responded and held every chance. The winner proved the stronger stayer, but he was a clear second-best and can win over this trip again mark when reverting to a quicker surface. (op 15-8)

De Soto, back over hurdles, came under pressure nearing the home turn and was left behind by the first two but battled on for pressure. He has now been placed on his last four outings and rates the benchmark. (op 9-2 tchd 7-2)

No Panic(IRE) was 5lb higher than when winning over fences 23 days earlier. This was his first outing over hurdles since 2008 and, although he ran a fair race under top weight, he is more effective as a chaser. (op 7-2)

Porters War(IRE) paid for running freely on the front end from the third-last, but this was a step back in the right direction and he should enjoy dropping back in distance. (op 20-1)

1109 LADBROKES BEGINNERS' CHASE (18 fncs) 2m 7f
7:55 (7:55) (Class 4) 5-Y-0+ **£3,252** (£955; £477; £238)

Form RPR

50-4 **1** **Call Me Mulligan (IRE)**[7] 1045 6-11-0 0..............................(p) APMcCoy 105
(Rebecca Curtis) *chsd ldr tl led 7th: hdd 10th: remained w ldr tl rdn to ld after 14th: hdd 3 out: styd on u.p to ld nr fin* **11/4**[2]

/4-P **2** ¾ **Massini Man (IRE)**[7] 1045 9-10-7 0................................ MissCLWills(7) 105+
(Brendan Powell) *prom: rdn after 14th: lft 2nd 4 out: led next: j.lft and mstke 2 out: drvn flat: hdd nr fin* **50/1**

1-05 **3** 25 **Tribe**[28] 854 8-11-0 0.. WillKennedy 81
(Paul Webber) *hld up: mstke 2nd: hdwy 10th: rdn appr 4 out: blnd and wknd next* **7/2**[3]

2/1- **4** 10 **Boomtown Kat**[27] 200 6-11-0 0................................... AndrewThornton 68
(Karen George) *hld up: a in rr: bhd fr 10th: j.rt 13th: t.o* **7/1**

3 **5** 39 **Canon's Corner (IRE)**[16] 951 7-10-11 0........................ SeanQuinlan(3) 29
(Rachel Hobbs) *hld up: hdwy 8th: wknd 11th: t.o* **40/1**

223P **P** **Viper**[10] 1023 8-11-0 115..(b) SamThomas —
(Dr Richard Newland) *chsd ldrs: pushed along and reluctant appr 10th: nt run on and sn t.o: p.u bef 13th: b.b.v* **9/4**[1]

22P- **F** **Will If I Want (IRE)**[324] 1399 9-11-0 0............................... JohnnyFarrelly —
(Sophie Leech) *led to 7th: led again 10th: hdd after 14th: rdn and ev ch whn fell next* **8/1**

4P/0 **P** **Thumbprint (IRE)**[77] 267 8-11-0 0......................................(t) JoeTizzard —
(Colin Tizzard) *prom: plld hrd: mstke 7th: lost pl next: wknd appr 10th: sn t.o: p.u bef 13th* **14/1**

5m 43.9s (1.30) **Going Correction** -0.125s/f (Good) 8 Ran SP% **114.3**
Speed ratings: **92,91,83,79,66 —,—,—**
toteswingers:1&2:£14.90, 1&3:£2.60, 2&3:£56.40 CSF £83.54 TOTE £4.60: £2.40, £14.30, £2.30; EX 112.80.

Owner Chris McDonnell **Bred** Chris McDonnell **Trained** Newport, Dyfed

FOCUS
An ordinary beginners' chase and the form looks weak.

NOTEBOOK
Call Me Mulligan(IRE) looked in need of a stiffer test over fences when making his chase debut on softer ground at Bangor a week earlier and he relished this step up in trip. However, he had to work very hard to master the runner-up and was only on top near the line, needing all of his jockey's unparalleled strength to prevail. This extra experience could see him go forward again as a chaser and he is a game little horse. (op 2-1)

Massini Man(IRE) posted a very pleasing effort considering he had been pulled up on his last three outings, including on debut for the stable in the same race the winner contested at Bangor on his previous start. Current connections are clearly doing something right at home with him now so this triple-winning pointer could well find compensation in the coming weeks. He was later reported to have been struck into. (op 40-1)

Tribe's jumping again left something to be desired and he is something of an in-and-out performer. (op 3-1)

Boomtown Kat, who had a recent spin on the Flat, was making his chase debut having got off the mark on his last outing as a hurdler in May. He shaped as though this experience was needed and may come on again for the run. (op 6-1 tchd 15-2)

Viper was unsurprisingly ridden with greater restraint. However, he looked to down tools on the back straight and has now pulled up the last twice. He was later reported to have bled. Official explanation: vet said gelding bled from nose (tchd 9-1)

Will If I Want(IRE) attracted support on this switch to chasing and first run since pulling up on his debut for the stable at this venue last September. He was positively ridden and the jockey looked confident coming out of the back straight. He almost immediately came under pressure thereafter, however, and looked held before departing. It's hoped this experience doesn't dent his confidence as he had jumped nicely for a debutant until that point. (tchd 9-1)

1110 LADBROKES H'CAP CHASE (12 fncs) 2m
8:25 (8:25) (Class 3) (0-135,135) 4-Y-0**£5,386** (£1,591; £795; £397; £198)

Form RPR

2221 **1** **Stagecoach Pearl**[12] 1000 6-10-9 **118**.................................... APMcCoy 130+
(Sue Smith) *chsd ldrs: led 7th: clr fr 2 out: easily* **8/11**[1]

0F44 **2** 4 **Knight Legend (IRE)**[26] 874 11-11-5 **128**.............................(t) RhysFlint 132
(Philip Hobbs) *chsd ldr tl led bef 4th: j.rt 5th and 6th: hdd next: chsd ldr tl lost 2nd appr 4 out: styng on same pce whn wnt 2nd again 2 out* **15/2**[3]

0-62 **3** 5 **High Bird Humphrey**[10] 1023 11-10-4 **120**..................(p) MrSFMagee(7) 121+
(Simon West) *hld up: hdwy appr 4 out: styd on same pce fr 2 out* **8/1**

1-P4 **4** 4 ½ **Postmaster**[16] 954 8-11-5 **135**................................... AdamWedge(7) 129
(Evan Williams) *hld up: stmbld bnd after 3rd: hdwy 7th: rdn after 4 out: wknd next* **12/1**

P142 **5** 4 ½ **Mibleu (FR)**[16] 959 10-10-9 **123**.. KeiranBurke(5) 115+
(R H & Mrs S Alner) *hld up: hdwy 6th: chsd ldr appr and mstke 4 out: j.rt thereafter: wknd and lost 2nd 2 out* **12/1**

-204 **6** 40 **Sou'Wester**[22] 911 10-11-4 **127**...(p) JoeTizzard 76
(Colin Tizzard) *hld up: bhd fr 7th: t.o* **5/1**[2]

FP2- **P** **Beherayn**[98] 5293 7-10-10 **122**.................................... EamonDehdashti(3) —
(Carroll Gray) *plld hrd: led tl appr 4th: wknd 7th: t.o whn p.u bef 4 out* **28/1**

3m 46.7s (-4.90) **Going Correction** -0.125s/f (Good) 7 Ran SP% **116.3**
Speed ratings (Par 107): **107,105,102,100,98 78,—**
toteswingers:1&2:£2.90, 1&3:£3.20, 2&3:£3.20 CSF £7.57 TOTE £1.60: £1.10, £4.00; EX 4.90.

Owner John Conroy Jaqueline Conroy **Bred** R F Broad **Trained** High Eldwick, W Yorks

FOCUS
Not a bad handicap, run at a decent gallop and there was an easy winner. The runner-up is rated to his previous course mark.

NOTEBOOK
Stagecoach Pearl ran out a most decisive winner. He had come good over fences under McCoy at Cartmel 12 days previously and had obviously got in very lightly on this return to handicap company off just a 3lb higher mark. The handicapper will exact revenge on this progressive novice now, though, so his best option is surely to look for something under a penalty. If one can be found he ought to land the hat-trick. (op 10-11)

Knight Legend(IRE) emerges with credit for keeping on for second after doing plenty through the first half of the race, over a trip short of his best. He really does deserve to win another race. (op 13-2 tchd 6-1)

High Bird Humphrey's jumping went to pot down the back straight and, while he rallied well for pressure off the home turn, he nearly always seems to find a way of getting beat. (op 10-1)

Postmaster would've enjoyed the strong early gallop, but was laboured once push came to shove and is probably handicapped to the hilt over fences. It could prove he is more effective again when returned to further, though. (tchd 14-1)

Mibleu(FR) was the only real threat to the winner nearing the final bend, but he got the third-last wrong and was soon beaten. (tchd 11-1)

Sou'Wester ran too badly to be true. (op 11-2 tchd 7-1)

1111 LADBROKES MAIDEN HURDLE (8 hdls) 2m
8:55 (8:55) (Class 5) 4-Y-0+ **£2,055** (£599; £299)

Form RPR

23U- **1** **Comehomequietly (IRE)**[180] 3695 6-10-7 112.............. MrJFMathias(7) 114+
(David Rees) *hld up: hdwy 4th: led 3 out: drvn out* **6/1**[3]

2 **2** 1 **Scene Two**[57] 554 4-10-12 0.. TomO'Brien 111
(Philip Hobbs) *hld up in tch: rdn appr last: r.o* **6/1**[3]

/40- **3** nk **Raincoat**[59] 4492 6-11-0 106.. NoelFehily 114
(Barry Brennan) *a.p: chsd wnr 3 out: r.o u.p* **4/1**[2]

F-2 **4** 6 **Phoenix Flight (IRE)**[14] 711 5-11-0 0................................... APMcCoy 109+
(James Evans) *hld up: nt fluent 4th: hdwy u.p appr 3 out: mstke last: nt rch ldrs* **10/11**[1]

P **5** nse **Rocklandslad (IRE)**[9] 1028 7-11-0 0............................ TomScudamore 108
(Rebecca Curtis) *led 2nd: rdn and hdd 3 out: no ex flat* **33/1**

6 18 **Integria**[26] 4-10-12 0.. AidanColeman 87
(Venetia Williams) *chsd ldrs: rdn after 5th: wknd appr 2 out* **33/1**

00-2 **7** 6 **Carbon Print (USA)**[28] 850 5-11-0 100............................ WillKennedy 83
(Paul Webber) *led to 2nd: chsd ldrs: rdn appr 3 out: wknd next* **20/1**

8 ¾ **Munich (IRE)**[24] 6-11-0 0... HaddenFrost 82
(Roger Curtis) *hld up: sme hdwy appr 3 out: nvr on terms* **50/1**

-P62 **9** 3 ½ **Nether Stream (IRE)**[16] 956 6-11-0 101................................. RhysFlint 78
(Shaun Lycett) *hld up: hdwy appr 3 out: hung lft and wknd bef next* **20/1**

10 10 **The Mouse Carroll (IRE)**[28] 889 6-10-7 0............ AnthonyFreeman(7) 68
(Sean Curran) *hld up: a in rr: wknd after 5th: t.o* **100/1**

-06 **11** 8 **Calypso Bay (IRE)**[72] 356 4-10-9 0..................... RichieMcLernon(3) 58
(Jonjo O'Neill) *mid-div: hdwy 4th: rdn and wknd after next: t.o* **50/1**

12 29 **King Canute (IRE)**[104] 6-11-0 0... RodiGreene 31
(Neil Mulholland) *hld up: bhd fr 4th: t.o* **66/1**

40-P **13** 40 **Commanche Luke**[82] 168 7-11-0 0........................... ChristianWilliams —
(C Roberts) *hld up: bhd fr 3rd: t.o* **100/1**

14 *hd* **Carrigleade (IRE)**[877] 10-10-7 0.......................(t) MrLRPayter(7) —
(Matt Sheppard) *reluctant to s: a wl bhd: t.o* **100/1**

3m 48.4s (1.10) **Going Correction** -0.05s/f (Good)
WFA 4 from 5yo+ 15lb **14** Ran SP% **124.7**
Speed ratings (Par 103): **95,94,94,91,91 82,79,78,77,72 68,53,33,33**
toteswingers:1&2:£5.20, 1&3:£4.00, 2&3:£3.50 CSF £40.65 TOTE £7.70: £1.90, £1.10, £2.20; EX 42.00 Place6 £27.79, Place 5 £6.24..
Owner IWEC International Ltd **Bred** J F Mernagh **Trained** Clarbeston, Pembrokes

FOCUS
There was a muddling gallop on in this ordinary novice event. The winner is value for a little further and the third sets the level.

NOTEBOOK
Comehomequietly(IRE) belatedly opened his account over hurdles and rates value for further than his winning margin indicates. He was returning from a six-month absence with a consistent, but frustrating profile and was ridden with more restraint than has often been the case. His rider made his move down the back straight at just the right time and he looked like winning easily nearing the last, but he idled badly on the run-in and handed the placed horses another chance. This should do his confidence a lot of good and he ought to improve for the run, so may well be up to defying a penalty. (op 11-2)
Scene Two ◆ was having his first outing since finishing second on his hurdling debut 57 days earlier and proved easy to back. He was doing some decent late work, not surprisingly for a horse who enjoyed 1m4f on the Flat, and should soon be found an opening. (op 9-2 tchd 7-1)
Raincoat kept on to post his best effort as a hurdler on this return to action and he too can be found a winning turn before long, but really needs a stiffer test. (op 13-2)
Phoenix Flight(IRE) was sent off a short price on this return to hurdling. Tony McCoy tried to switch him off out the back early on, but he still ran free and got well behind. He did his best to close from four out, but was always fighting a losing battle due to the way the race was run. Surely a step up in trip would help in this sphere. (op 5-4)
Rocklandslad(IRE) settled better and ran much more encouragingly as a result, but still needs practice in the jumping department. (op 28-1)
T/Plt: £37.80 to a £1 stake. Pool £61,894.05 - 1,193.77 winning tickets. T/Qpdt: £5.00 to a £1 stake. Pool £6,931.90 - 1,016.70 winning tickets. CR

1112 - (Foreign Racing) - See Raceform Interactive

1096 GALWAY (R-H)
Tuesday, July 27

OFFICIAL GOING: Good

1113a LATIN QUARTER CHASE 2m 6f
5:45 (5:46) 5-Y-O+ **£14,380** (£4,203; £1,991; £663)

RPR

1 **Invisible Man (FR)**[32] 838 5-10-8 135.......................... BarryGeraghty 124+
(Ian Williams) *trckd ldrs: on terms fr 4 out: led bef 2 out where j.lft: sn clr: styd on wl: easily* **3/1**[1]

2 *11* **Tory Hill Lad (IRE)**[262] 2116 11-11-3 97.......................(b) JRBarry 113
(Mrs Hannah Lee, Ire) *led: j.lft 6th: jnd 4 out: hdd bef 2 out: dropped to 3rd ins fnl f tl rallied to go 2nd nr fin* **100/1**

3 *2* **Barna Bay (IRE)**[94] 5400 11-11-10 129.......................... JLCullen 118
(V T O'Brien, Ire) *sn mid-div: mod 5th appr 2 out: sn no imp u.p: styd on into 2nd ins fnl f tl dropped to 3rd nr fin* **25/1**

4 *2* **Decoy Daddy (IRE)**[11] 1014 8-11-0 127.......................... EMullins(3) 109
(Anthony Mullins, Ire) *chsd ldrs: mod 4th appr 2 out: sn no imp u.p and kpt on same pce* **11/2**[3]

5 *16* **Natal (FR)**[79] 243 9-11-7 147.......................(t) DenisO'Regan 97
(J J Lambe, Ire) *sn mid-div: prog bef 8th: 8th 4 out: mod 7th appr 2 out: sn no imp: 6th and kpt on same pce u.p fr last* **5/1**[2]

6 *hd* **Tasman (IRE)**[142] 4476 10-11-7 129.......................... MDarcy 97
(Liam McAteer, Ire) *prom: on terms 4 out: hdd bef 2 out: wknd fr last* **9/1**

7 *dist* **Knock On The Head (IRE)**[9] 1041 8-11-3 127.................(b) RMMoran —
(A L T Moore, Ire) *slow jump 1st: sn towards rr: nt a fluent: 9th 4 out: sn no ex: t.o* **33/1**

8 *dist* **Killenaule Boy**[15] 970 8-11-10 132.......................... AndrewJMcNamara —
(E J O'Grady, Ire) *mstke 2nd: prom: dropped to 6th appr 2 out: sn wknd: t.o* **20/1**

9 *dist* **Rathmore Castle (IRE)**[9] 1041 8-11-0 123.................(b) LPFlynn(3) —
(Mrs Maureen Danagher, Ire) *sn towards rr: no imp u.p fr 6 out: bhd fr 3 out: completely t.o* **50/1**

P **Oodachee**[15] 611 11-11-3 126.......................(tp) DJCasey —
(C F Swan, Ire) *sn towards rr: no ex u.p fr bef 8th: dropped bhd and p.u bef 6 out* **20/1**

P **Tawnies (IRE)**[60] 505 10-11-4 125.......................... PTEnright(3) —
(Thomas Gerard O'Leary, Ire) *chsd ldrs: 5th 4 out: no imp fr bef 2 out: p.u after last: dismntd* **16/1**

S **Battle Axe (IRE)**[71] 378 10-10-10 110.......................... BryanJCooper(7) —
(J J Lennon, Ire) *mid-div: slipped up appr 8th: broke leg: fatally injured* **66/1**

U **Nintytwo Team (IRE)**[47] 687 8-10-13 128.......................... AELynch —
(Paul John Gilligan, Ire) *towards rr: bdly hmpd and uns rdr 6th* **5/1**[2]

F **Classic Frontier (IRE)**[11] 1014 8-10-13 124.......................(t) DNRussell —
(C Byrnes, Ire) *towards rr: fell 6th* **6/1**

5m 25.5s (-14.50) **14** Ran SP% **124.6**
CSF £371.51 TOTE £3.30: £1.50, £22.10, £6.80; DF 713.30.
Owner Power Panels Electrical Systems Ltd **Bred** J P J Dubois **Trained** Portway, Worcs

FOCUS
The front-running runner-up sets the standard, rated to his best.

NOTEBOOK
Invisible Man(FR) ◆ went right away form his rivals after getting to the front on the approach to the two fences in the dip. One could quibble with the form of a race in which there was plenty of incident, but this confirms the French-bred as a progressive young chaser. (op 7/2)
Tory Hill Lad(IRE) was the surprise package of the race. He made a lot of the running and stuck to his task when he might have been expected to drop out of contention on the climb to the finish. As an 11-year-old with an official rating of just 97, and off the track since pulled up at Kelso last November, he had looked a forlorn hope in this company. He seems sure to take a rise in the ratings for this, and on the basis of his overall record it is almost inevitable that will make it hard for him to add to his tally when he goes back into handicaps.
Barna Bay(IRE), a C&D winner of a novice event on good ground last September, is almost a veteran at this stage, but his trainer has a great record with older horses, and this one can continue to pay his way.
Decoy Daddy(IRE), second in the Midlands National at Kilbeggan, ran a solid race, though overall form suggests that he should really have finished in front of the placed horses. (op 7/1)
Natal(FR), winner of this race last year and formerly a high-class sort in Britain, never looked likely to make a significant impression. (op 4/1 tchd 11/2)
Tasman(IRE) managed to show with a chance until running out of steam from two out.
Rathmore Castle(IRE) was reported to have burst a blood vessel. Official explanation: jockey said gelding was found to have a burst blood vessel post-race
Tawnies(IRE) was pulled up lame. Official explanation: jockey said gelding pulled up lame (op 5/1 tchd 9/2)
Battle Axe(IRE) suffered a fatal injury. (op 5/1 tchd 9/2)
Nintytwo Team(IRE) was brought down when Classic Frontier, also a faller at Kilbeggan on his previous start, made his exit at the sixth. (op 5/1 tchd 9/2)

1099 PERTH (R-H)
Wednesday, July 28

OFFICIAL GOING: Good to firm (good in places) changing to good to firm after race 2 (2.55)
Wind: Fresh, across Weather: Cloudy

1114 GLENGOYNE SINGLE MALT NOVICES' HURDLE (8 hdls) 2m 110y
2:25 (2:25) (Class 4) 4-Y-O+ **£2,602** (£764; £382; £190)

Form RPR

2-12 1 **Wind Shuffle (GER)**[12] 870 7-11-5 123.......................... KeithMercer 121+
(Jim Goldie) *mde all: rdn whn blnd bdly 2 out: hld on gamely u.p fr last* **4/5**[1]

266F 2 *2 ¼* **Duty Free (IRE)**[13] 1003 6-10-12 113.......................... BrianHughes 110
(James Moffatt) *pressed wnr: rdn and ev ch 2 out: kpt on same pce run-in* **9/2**[3]

3 *23* **Sir Boss (IRE)**[298] 5-10-12 0.......................(t) LeightonAspell 87
(Don Cantillon) *hld up: hdwy to chse ldrs 1/2-way: rdn appr 2 out: sn wknd* **3/1**[2]

4 *21* **Via Archimede (USA)**[27] 5-10-12 0.......................... PeterBuchanan 66
(Lucinda Russell) *prom tl rdn and wknd after 3 out* **8/1**

00-6 5 *33* **Yes Minister (IRE)**[14] 983 6-10-12 0.......................... PaulMoloney 33
(Sophie Leech) *nt fluent: prom to 3rd: lost tch fr next* **66/1**

3m 47.7s (-12.00) **Going Correction** -0.725s/f (Firm) **5** Ran SP% **111.3**
Speed ratings (Par 105): **99,97,87,77,61**
toteswinger: 1&2 £4.50. CSF £5.08 TOTE £1.60: £1.10, £2.10; EX 4.10.
Owner Mrs S Bruce & Mrs L Mackay **Bred** Gestut Elsetal **Trained** Uplawmoor, E Renfrews

FOCUS
The front pair drew clear in what was a weak novices' hurdle and are rated close to their marks.

NOTEBOOK
Wind Shuffle(GER), the only penalised runner, made a complete mess of two out, but he got away with it and stayed on well to recover the situation after the last. He is going to find defying a double penalty much tougher, but could do okay in handicaps. (tchd Evens)
Duty Free(IRE), a faller last time, was clearly none the worse and ran right up to his best. A race will fall his way eventually. (op 4-1)
Sir Boss(IRE) ran well to a point on his hurdling debut, although in the end looked a non-stayer. (op 7-2)
Via Archimede(USA), a moderate 1m4f winner on the Flat in Ireland, showed disappointingly little on this hurdles debut. (op 10-1 tchd 7-1)

1115 TRAWLER DARK RUM CLAIMING HURDLE (8 hdls) 2m 110y
2:55 (2:55) (Class 5) 4-Y-O+ **£2,217** (£655; £327; £163; £81)

Form RPR

4-10 1 **Dream Risk (FR)**[22] 706 4-9-10 108.......................(t) JamesHalliday(5) 95+
(Kate Walton) *trckd ldrs: led appr 2 out: sn hrd pressed: hld on wl u.p fr last* **5/1**[3]

-2P5 2 *1 ¼* **Annibale Caro**[28] 861 8-11-0 106.......................... KeithMercer 106
(Jim Goldie) *bhd: niggled along after 3rd: hdwy u.p bef 2 out: chsd wnr last 50yds: r.o* **7/2**[2]

0/-4 3 *1 ¾* **Mister Castlefield (IRE)**[1] 1104 6-11-0 95.......................... RichardJohnson 104
(John J Maguire, Ire) *hld up: hdwy and ev ch 2 out to last: one pce u.p run-in* **12/1**

000/ 4 *1 ¼* **Apt To Run (USA)**[359] 1692 7-10-7 115.......................(bt) KMDonoghue(7) 103
(Gordon Elliott, Ire) *hld up: smooth hdwy to chse ldrs bef 2 out: rdn: hung lft and outpcd after 2 out: rallied last: one pce run-in* **10/11**[1]

00-1 5 *10* **Planetarium**[15] 745 5-11-4 99.......................(p) WilsonRenwick 97
(P Monteith) *prom tl rdn and outpcd bef 2 out: n.d after* **16/1**

-240 6 *¾* **Lets Go Girls**[13] 1004 6-10-7 95.......................... BrianHughes 85
(James Moffatt) *w ldr: led after 3 out to appr next: sn wknd* **12/1**

5-0P 7 *2 ½* **Claude Carter**[18] 582 6-10-7 95.......................(b[1]) EwanWhillans(3) 86
(Alistair Whillans) *mde most to after 3 out: rdn and wknd bef next* **33/1**

404U 8 *10* **Piccolo Pride**[24] 886 5-10-10 86.......................(t) MichaelMcAlister 76
(Maurice Barnes) *midfield: rdn and outpcd 3 out: sn wknd* **22/1**

9 *14* **Shantour (IRE)**[25] 884 6-10-10 0.......................(t) JohnnyFarrelly 62
(Joseph Fox, Ire) *hld up: struggling after 4 out: no ch fr next* **100/1**

P-04 10 *¾* **Murphys Future**[17] 945 5-10-7 0.......................... RyanMania(3) 61
(George Foster) *in tch: mstke and struggling 3 out: sn btn* **100/1**

3m 48.9s (-10.80) **Going Correction** -0.725s/f (Firm)
WFA 4 from 5yo+ 15lb **10** Ran SP% **121.8**
Speed ratings (Par 103): **96,95,94,94,89 88,87,83,76,76**
toteswingers: 1&2 £1.90, 1&3 £40.10, 2&3 £12.60. CSF £24.03 TOTE £6.90: £2.00, £1.40, £3.60; EX 18.10.
Owner Keep The Faith Partnership **Bred** Trainers House Enterprises Ltd **Trained** Middleham Moor, N Yorks

FOCUS
A competitive claiming hurdle with the placed horses rated to their marks.

NOTEBOOK
Dream Risk(FR), well held in a competitive handicap hurdle at Aintree latest, had earlier won a novices' selling hurdle and she returned to that sort of form to take this, the first-time tongue-tie clearly enabling her to improve. She remains capable of further success in low-grade handicaps. (op 11-2)
Annibale Caro, dropping in grade, didn't travel all that well, but he kept responding to pressure and stayed on to take second. (tchd 4-1)
Mister Castlefield(IRE), fourth off a mark of 95 at the course the previous evening, had his chance and ran every bit as well dropped in grade. (op 16-1 tchd 20-1)
Apt To Run(USA) travelled well, but then started to hang under pressure and could only plug on at the one pace. (op 5-4 tchd 5-6)

1116 LONDON HILL DRY GIN NOVICES' CHASE (12 fncs) 2m
3:30 (3:30) (Class 4) 4-Y-O+ **£3,252** (£955; £477; £238)

Form RPR

1202 1 **Right Or Wrong (IRE)**[17] 944 6-10-8 114.......................(tp) KMDonoghue(7) 106+
(Gordon Elliott, Ire) *chsd clr ldr: clsd 7th: nt fluent and rdn 4 out: rallied and led 2 out: hrd pressed fr last: edgd rt: hld on wl* **9/4**[2]

1U 2 *nk* **Picaroon**[11] 1020 6-12-0 138.......................... DeanColeman(5) 122
(Tim Vaughan) *led and clr to 7th: qcknd bef 3 out: rdn and hdd next: rallied and chal fr last: edgd rt: kpt on: jst hld* **11/10**[1]

2201 **3** *10* **Baaher (USA)**[17] [943] 6-11-1 0 KeithMercer 94
(Jim Goldie) *hld up: hdwy to chse ldrs 3 out: effrt and ev ch next: sn outpcd* **3/1**[3]

/055 **4** *1 ¼* **Skiddaw Jones**[24] [891] 10-11-1 79 (t) MichaelMcAlister 95
(Maurice Barnes) *prom: effrt bef 3 out: mstke next: sn btn* **25/1**

P **Figairy (IRE)**[192] [3491] 6-10-8 0 (tp) MrDRFox(7) —
(Noel C Kelly, Ire) *bhd and sn struggling: no ch fnl circ: p.u after 3 out* **33/1**

3m 50.9s (-11.80) **Going Correction** -0.725s/f (Firm) **5** Ran SP% **110.2**
Speed ratings (Par 105): **100,99,94,94,—**
toteswinger: 1&2 £2.60. CSF £5.42 TOTE £3.20: £1.50, £1.20; EX 6.40.
Owner A M Egan/Ms Annie Flora Joan Bowles **Bred** Castlemartin Stud And Skymarc Farm **Trained** Trim, Co Meath

FOCUS
The front pair drew clear in this novices' chase. The winner is rated to recent course form.

NOTEBOOK
Right Or Wrong(IRE), well held on three previous starts over fences, including when second last time, really dig in after the last, but just proved good enough. (tchd 5-2)
Picaroon had plenty of weight to carry and could have been expected to fade once headed 2f out, but he rallied bravely and briefly looked like getting back up, but it wasn't to be. (tchd 5-4)
Baaher(USA), winner of a maiden hurdle at the course latest, made a satisfactory debut over fences. (op 10-3 tchd 11-4)
Skiddaw Jones, rated just 79, finished closer than he was entitled to. (op 33-1 tchd 40-1)

1117 BOTT LTD H'CAP CHASE (15 fncs) 2m 4f 110y

4:05 (4:05) (Class 3) (0-120,120) 4-Y-0 **£5,386** (£1,591; £795; £397; £198)

Form RPR

-3PU **1** **Sunday City (JPN)**[8] [1044] 9-10-13 107 TomO'Brien 128+
(Peter Bowen) *chsd ldrs: hit 11th: led appr 3 out: drew clr fr next: v easily* **8/1**

3U-2 **2** *14* **Ormello (FR)**[35] [831] 8-11-12 120 PeterBuchanan 122
(Lucinda Russell) *prom: nt fluent and outpcd 4 out: rallied 2 out: chsd wnr run-in: no imp* **12/1**

3 *1 ¼* **Grand Lahou (FR)**[85] [146] 7-11-11 119 (t) RichardJohnson 122+
(Tim Vaughan) *cl up: chal 4th: led 6th: hit 10th: hdd appr 3 out where nt fluent: sn one pce: lost 2nd run-in* **6/1**[2]

2602 **4** *¾* **The Duke's Speech (IRE)**[14] [985] 9-11-9 117 PaulMoloney 117
(Sophie Leech) *bhd: pushed along 1/2-way: effrt whn nt fluent 5 out: plugged on fr 2 out: n.d* **6/1**[2]

134/ **5** *nk* **Ohana**[9] [1849] 7-11-6 117 EwanWhillans(3) 117
(Alistair Whillans) *bhd: mstke 10th: effrt after 4 out: kpt on fnl 2: nvr rchd ldrs* **28/1**

0UP/ **6** *22* **Mon Oiseau (FR)**[40] [786] 10-11-7 115 BrianHughes 102+
(C A McBratney, Ire) *led to 6th: cl up tl wknd fr 3 out* **7/1**[3]

0-P2 **7** *33* **Run To Space**[17] [947] 9-10-5 102 (b) FearghalDavis(3) 46
(Nicky Richards) *hld up: struggling 1/2-way: eased whn no ch fnl 3* **6/1**[2]

F310 **U** **King Roonah**[27] [874] 6-10-13 114 (t) KMDonoghue(7) —
(Gordon Elliott, Ire) *hld up in tch: blnd and uns rdr 6th* **2/1**[1]

4m 54.6s (-19.40) **Going Correction** -0.725s/f (Firm) course record **8** Ran SP% **110.9**
Speed ratings (Par 107): **107,101,101,100,100 92,79,—**
toteswingers: 1&2 £10.10, 1&3 £9.50, 2&3 £8.60. CSF £85.76 CT £593.50 TOTE £9.50: £3.10, £2.10, £2.20; EX 86.80.
Owner R Greenway **Bred** Shiraoi Farm **Trained** Little Newcastle, Pembrokes

FOCUS
A decent little handicap chase rated around the first three.

NOTEBOOK
Sunday City(JPN) was always travelling well and came right away in the straight. Peter Bowen's horses can do little wrong at present, and this one could take some stopping if turned out under a penalty. (tchd 9-1)
Ormello(FR) again ran his race, boxing on well for second. He's not on a bad mark, but it's been over two years since his last win. (tchd 11-1)
Grand Lahou(FR), ex-Irish, showed improved form on this debut for Tim Vaughan, doing well considering he made several mistakes. He should prove up to winning an ordinary race. (op 5-1)
The Duke's Speech(IRE), up 4lb, failed to reproduce his Uttoxeter form, coming under pressure quite a way out and just plodding on at the one pace. (op 9-2 tchd 13-2)
Ohana had a spin on the Flat the other day but still shaped as though he would come on for this. (op 25-1 tchd 33-1)
King Roonah got no further than the sixth, blundering and unseating. (op 9-4 tchd 15-8)

1118 NEW FIXTURE SATURDAY AUGUST 21ST CONDITIONAL JOCKEYS' H'CAP HURDLE (10 hdls) 2m 4f 110y

4:40 (4:40) (Class 4) (0-115,115) 4-Y-0+ **£2,851** (£842; £421; £210; £105)

Form RPR

0F56 **1** **Word Of Warning**[13] [1004] 6-11-2 105 JamesHalliday 113+
(Martin Todhunter) *hld up: hdwy bef 2 out: ev ch last: led last 25yds: styd on wl* **11/1**

-341 **2** *hd* **Danimix (IRE)**[14] [988] 5-11-12 115 RhysFlint 122
(Peter Bowen) *cl up: rdn to ld after 2 out: hdd last 25yds: kpt on u.p* **5/1**[3]

6423 **3** *8* **Tarkani (IRE)**[17] [946] 7-11-2 105 (tp) JamesO'Farrell 104
(Valentine Donoghue) *t.k.h: trckd ldrs: effrt and ev ch 2 out: sn outpcd: kpt on fr last: no ch w first two* **8/1**

-264 **4** *3 ½* **Storm Prospect**[28] [860] 7-10-11 103 (b) CampbellGillies(3) 98
(Lucinda Russell) *cl up: led appr to jst after 2 out: sn outpcd* **12/1**

3- **5** *½* **The Shepherd (IRE)**[12] [1013] 6-11-3 112 KMDonoghue(6) 107
(Gordon Elliott, Ire) *in tch: effrt and rdn bef 2 out: sn one pce* **2/1**[1]

1412 **6** *3* **Benmadigan (IRE)**[24] [888] 8-11-8 114 FearghalDavis(3) 106
(Nicky Richards) *hld up in tch on ins: rdn bef 3 out: no imp fr next* **4/1**[2]

4/4- **7** *3 ¾* **Kyber**[15] [1505] 9-10-7 104 PaulNorton(8) 92
(Jim Goldie) *nt fluent in rr: hit and outpcd 4 out: n.d after* **11/1**

12-0 **8** *11* **Flemross (IRE)**[40] [786] 7-11-11 114 JohnnyFarrelly 91
(R T J Wilson, Ire) *led to bef 2 out: sn rdn and wknd* **14/1**

31-P **9** *7* **Bewery Man (IRE)**[44] [745] 9-10-7 104 PaulGallagher(8) 74
(Ferdy Murphy) *hld up: shortlived effrt bef 2 out: sn wknd* **25/1**

4m 55.2s (-11.70) **Going Correction** -0.725s/f (Firm) **9** Ran SP% **116.0**
Speed ratings (Par 105): **93,92,89,88,88 87,85,81,78**
toteswingers: 1&2 £6.70, 1&3 £15.90, 2&3 £5.50. CSF £65.98 CT £470.91 TOTE £16.40: £4.50, £1.10, £3.40; EX 82.30.
Owner Twelve Go Racing **Bred** Miss K Rausing **Trained** Orton, Cumbria
■ Stewards' Enquiry : Rhys Flint one-day ban: used whip with excessive frequency without giving gelding time to respond (Aug 12); caution: careless riding.

FOCUS
They didn't go much of a gallop in this handicap hurdle, so there were plenty in with a chance turning for home. The second is rated to his recent winning mark.

NOTEBOOK
Word Of Warning, challenging towards the inside, got the verdict, joining the runner-up at the last and staying on well under a strong ride. He had looked a promising sort last year and may begin to fulfil that potential again now he's got his head back in front. (op 12-1 tchd 14-1)
Danimix(IRE), up 10lb having easily won a maiden hurdle at Uttoxeter, improved again on this handicap debut, just finding the one too good. He's only five and remains capable of better. (op 4-1)
Tarkani(IRE) needs further than this and could only keep on at the one pace behind the front two.
Storm Prospect isn't badly weighted, but doesn't look like winning anytime soon. (op 10-1 tchd 14-1)
The Shepherd(IRE) was a little disappointing, being unable to quicken on from two out. (op 3-1tchd 7-2 in a place)
Benmadigan(IRE) was another who failed to meet with expectations. (op 9-2)

1119 ISLE OF SKYE BLENDED SCOTCH WHISKY NOVICES' H'CAP HURDLE (12 hdls) 3m 110y

5:15 (5:15) (Class 4) (0-105,105) 4-Y-0+ **£2,851** (£842; £421; £210; £105)

Form RPR

-233 **1** **Maolisa (IRE)**[27] [871] 8-10-11 90 CampbellGillies(3) 96
(S R B Crawford, Ire) *mde all: hrd pressed fr 2 out: edgd rt u.p run-in: hld on gamely* **11/2**[3]

1 **2** *shd* **Supercede (IRE)**[1] [1102] 8-11-8 105 7ex (bt) KMDonoghue(7) 111
(Gordon Elliott, Ire) *chsd ldrs: wnt 2nd 4 out: chal 2 out: sn rdn: kpt on u.p run-in: jst hld* **10/11**[1]

3 *3 ¼* **Banellie (IRE)**[15] [974] 6-11-5 102 (t[1]) MrDRFox(7) 105
(Noel C Kelly, Ire) *bhd: rdn bef 3 out: hdwy 2 out: kpt on: nt pce of first two* **16/1**

-35P **4** *5* **Auberge (IRE)**[27] [871] 6-10-2 78 FelixDeGiles 76
(A M Crow) *in tch: hdwy bef 3 out: rdn and outpcd fr next* **10/1**

4P-0 **5** *2 ½* **Moscow Mischief**[27] [871] 6-11-5 95 PeterBuchanan 91
(Lucinda Russell) *in tch: rdn and hung lft 2 out: sn outpcd* **33/1**

2P-3 **6** *31* **Norwest (IRE)**[31] [849] 7-11-8 98 (t) RichardJohnson 62
(Tim Vaughan) *nt fluent: chsd wnr to 4 out: wknd fr next: t.o* **9/4**[2]

5m 58.2s (-11.70) **Going Correction** -0.725s/f (Firm) **6** Ran SP% **116.5**
Speed ratings (Par 105): **89,88,87,86,85 75**
toteswingers: 1&2 £3.70, 1&3 £7.40, 2&3 £4.30. CSF £12.00 CT £76.53 TOTE £5.10: £2.10, £2.30; EX 17.30 Place 6: £76.29, Place 5: £52.55..
Owner Miss Patricia Duffin **Bred** Miss Patricia Duffin **Trained** Larne, Co Antrim
■ Stewards' Enquiry : Mr D R Fox nine-day ban: used whip with excessive frequency without giving gelding time to respond (tbn)

FOCUS
There was thrilling finish to this novices' handicap hurdle. The third, fourth and fifth set the level of the form.

NOTEBOOK
Maolisa(IRE) couldn't be begrudged this victory, having run several good races in defeat of late, and although a rise will follow, she seems sure to continue to pay her way. (op 9-2 tchd 6-1)
Supercede(IRE) was favourite to follow up his easy win from the previous evening, and he travelled like the winner for much of the way, but didn't find as much as expected once coming off the bridle. Things are only going to get tougher, but connections may try and capitalise on a lower chase rating. (op 6-5)
Banellie(IRE) stayed on well in first-time eyeshield without ever looking likely to reach the front pair. (op 11-1)
Auberge(IRE) bounced back from a dismal effort last time. (op 9-1 tchd 11-1)
Norwest(IRE) ran an absolute stinker, being one of the first beaten and dropping right out in worrying fashion. He has it to prove now. Official explanation: jockey said gelding never travelled (op 3-1)
T/Plt: £45.50 to a £1 stake. Pool £51,530.76 - 825.59 winning tickets. T/Qpdt: £20.20 to a £1 stake. Pool £3,580.80 - 130.70 winning tickets. RY

1112 GALWAY (R-H)

Wednesday, July 28

OFFICIAL GOING: Hurdle/flat course - good to firm (good in places); chase course - good (good to firm in places)

1121a TOTE TELEBET 1850 238 669 H'CAP HURDLE 2m 4f

3:35 (3:35) (81-123,120) 4-Y-0+ **£10,380** (£2,407; £1,053; £601)

RPR

1 **Novel Investment (IRE)**[24] [903] 9-11-1 108 TJDoyle 131
(John Brassil, Ire) *in rr of mid-div: prog 6th: 9th appr 5 out: trckd ldrs fr 3 out: on terms next: sn led and rdn clr: styd on wl: eased fr over 50yds out* **10/1**

2 *3 ½* **Mr Bones (IRE)**[22] [926] 8-10-8 108 KielanWoods(7) 127
(J G Coogan, Ire) *sn trckd ldrs: rdn to chse wnr fr bef st: no imp and kpt on same pce run-in* **13/2**[1]

3 *4 ½* **Dashing Ruby (IRE)**[41] [777] 6-10-13 106 (tp) MDarcy 121
(Paul W Flynn, Ire) *chsd ldrs: impr into 4th after 2 out: rdn into mod 3rd bef st: sn no imp and kpt on same pce* **10/1**

4 *5 ½* **Miss Pepperpot (IRE)**[19] [939] 6-10-9 102 MPWalsh 111
(F Flood, Ire) *chsd ldrs: 10th appr 5 out: rdn to chse ldrs and no imp appr st: kpt on* **20/1**

5 *1* **Hollywood Law (IRE)**[52] [654] 9-11-5 112 ADLeigh 120
(D M Leigh, Ire) *prom: 3rd 4 out: lost pl bef 2 out: sn no imp and kpt on* **33/1**

6 *shd* **Capall Eile (IRE)**[12] [1012] 7-10-0 98 RJMcCarth(5) 106
(Paul John Gilligan, Ire) *towards rr: prog to chse ldrs fr 2 out: sn no imp u.p and kpt on same pce* **20/1**

7 *3* **Guzzle An Go (IRE)**[38] [809] 5-11-9 116 AndrewJMcNamara 121
(E J O'Grady, Ire) *mstke 1st: cl up: slt mstke 4 out: sn on terms: hdd and no imp fr 2 out: kpt on same pce* **12/1**

8 *1 ¼* **False Evidence (IRE)**[97] [5345] 8-11-5 112 BarryGeraghty 116
(Mrs John Harrington, Ire) *in rr of mid-div: prog fr bef 5 out: cl up 3 out: no ex and kpt on same pce u.p fr 2 out* **12/1**

9 *4* **Waterloo Chateau (IRE)**[8] [1054] 7-11-4 111 PCarberry 111
(Noel Meade, Ire) *mid-div: 10th early: no imp and kpt on same pce fr bef 2 out* **10/1**

10 *½* **First Beauty (IRE)**[22] [923] 6-11-2 116 BryanJCooper(7) 115
(D T Hughes, Ire) *trckd ldrs: 7th after 3 out: no imp u.p and kpt on same pce fr next* **17/2**[3]

11 *2* **Arkendale (IRE)**[10] [1041] 8-10-8 101 (b) AELynch 98
(J P Fogarty, Ire) *chsd ldrs: no imp and kpt on same pce fr after 3 out* **20/1**

12 *1 ¾* **Cnoc An Einn (IRE)**[495] [4614] 11-10-12 105 DenisO'Regan 100
(W J Burke, Ire) *mid-div: 11th appr 5 out: no imp appr 2 out* **12/1**

13 *1* **Moonlight Sapphire**[51] [670] 5-10-12 105 (b) SGMcDermott 99
(J F O'Shea, Ire) *trckd ldrs: 5th appr 5 out: no ex fr bef 2 out* **16/1**

14 14 **Ikidunot (IRE)**[14] 996 6-11-7 114 (t) DJCasey 94
(Mrs Maureen Danagher, Ire) *sn trckd ldrs: on terms travelling wl after 3 out: 3rd bef next: sn wknd* 9/1
15 2 1/2 **Melon Delta (IRE)**[15] 975 9-11-0 107 (b) JLCullen 85
(John Joseph Hanlon, Ire) *towards rr for most: no imp appr 2 out* 20/1
16 3 1/2 **Black Jacari (IRE)**[33] 715 5-11-7 119 KyleJames(5) 93
(Philip Kirby) *nvr bttr than mid-div* 14/1
17 dist **Amarjit (IRE)**[656] 1293 9-10-11 107 (bt1) IJMcCarthy(3) —
(James McAuley, Ire) *towards rr: mstke 4 out: sn no ex: t.o* 40/1
P **No Stopping Sarah (IRE)**[19] 939 6-10-9 102 PTownend —
(P A Fahy, Ire) *led: jnd after 3 out: hdd & wknd fr bef next: p.u bef last* 16/1
P **King High (IRE)**[38] 811 6-11-2 109 JRBarry —
(Eoin Doyle, Ire) *p.u qckly bef 4th* 8/1[2]

4m 56.1s (-15.10) 19 Ran SP% 138.2
CSF £75.41 CT £707.53 TOTE £11.50: £2.40, £1.90, £2.60, £6.60; DF 86.10.
Owner Ten Men & A Lady Syndicate **Bred** Robert Finnegan **Trained** Newmarket-On-Fergus, Co Clare

FOCUS
The sixth has been rated to his mark, with the third, fourth and fifth all below their best.

NOTEBOOK
Novel Investment(IRE) won this well under a patient ride from Tom Doyle. Held up in mid-division, for a stride or two he just got caught on the heels of a couple of horses after the third-last. But when a split appeared before the second-last his rider sent him through and he got a vital few lengths. He's probably a horse that doesn't do a huge amount in front but he did more than enough to hold off these challengers. He's consistent and could well win another. (op 10/1 tchd 12/1)
Mr Bones(IRE) travelled well on the inside but was just caught for speed when the winner went on. It seemed to make little difference, however, as he was unable to make any impression on the winner, who went away from him in the end. A penalty for his two recent wins was probably just enough to anchor him. (op 7/1)
Dashing Ruby(IRE) raced towards mid-division but wasn't really travelling from some way out. He's quite a tough horse at his best, though, and stayed on well at the finish without really making an impression.
Miss Pepperpot(IRE) ran a very sound race. She raced close to the pace most of the way and looked as though she was going to weaken when coming off the bridle in the dip. While she lost her place to an extent, she did stay on well again at the finish.
Hollywood Law(IRE) ran well on the ground. He raced up with the pace for most of the journey and kept on well having lost his place coming out of the back straight. He looks a horse for whom a step up in trip would do no harm.
Capall Eile(IRE) got in as a reserve and kept on towards the outside in the final half-mile without making an impression. (op 25/1)
Guzzle An Go(IRE) took too much out of herself in front and faded once coming under pressure after the second-last.
King High(IRE) Official explanation: jockey said gelding got injured after a bad mistake at the 1st and was pulled up

1123a WWW.THETOTE.COM GALWAY PLATE (GRADE A) (HANDICAP CHASE) 2m 6f
5:25 (5:27) 4-Y-0+
£106,548 (£33,982; £16,283; £5,663; £3,893; £2,123)

RPR
1 **Finger Onthe Pulse (IRE)**[98] 5324 9-10-12 138 (t) APMcCoy 151
(T J Taaffe, Ire) *cl up and disp ld for much: strly pressed and j.lft 2 out: hdd bef st: rallied to regain ld 1f out: styd on wl: all out* 22/1
2 1/2 **Themoonandsixpence (IRE)**[95] 5398 7-10-6 132 (t) PTownend 144
(W P Mullins, Ire) *mstke 1st: hld up: gd prog appr 6 out: trckd ldrs fr bef 3 out: chal u.p and led bef st: sn jnd and narrowly hdd: kpt on wl wout matching wnr* 7/1[2]
3 2 **Majestic Concorde (IRE)**[84] 1584 7-10-12 138 DNRussell 148+
(D K Weld, Ire) *sn settled in mid-div: clsr in 5th after 3 out: 3rd bef st: no imp u.p and kpt on same pce fnl f* 3/1[1]
4 1 1/4 **The Fonze (IRE)**[24] 902 9-11-8 148 (p) JRBarry 157+
(Eoin Doyle, Ire) *mid-div: 10th after 3 out: rdn into 5th and no imp fr bef st: kpt on wout getting to ldrs* 33/1
5 2 **Northern Alliance (IRE)**[14] 2269 9-11-7 147 MrDerekO'Connor 154
(A J Martin, Ire) *mid-div: 14th appr 6 out: 9th after 3 out: rdn into 6th and no imp fr bef st: kpt on same pce wout threatening* 25/1
6 1/2 **Five Dream (FR)**[96] 5366 6-10-6 132 (b) HarrySkelton 138
(Paul Nicholls) *chsd ldrs: 7th after 3 out: rdn into 4th bef st: sn no imp* 16/1
7 11 **Sarteano (FR)**[40] 784 7-10-7 133 RLoughran 128
(D T Hughes, Ire) *chsd ldrs: 10th appr 6 out: kpt on u.p wout threatening fr bef 2 out* 20/1
8 5 **The Last Derby (FR)**[19] 938 6-10-6 132 BarryGeraghty 122
(Eoin Griffin, Ire) *sn trckd ldrs: 3rd after 3 out: no ex fr last* 8/1[3]
9 24 **Holly Tree (IRE)**[16] 970 10-10-6 132 (b) JLCullen 98
(E Sheehy, Ire) *mid-div at best: nvr a factor* 50/1
10 10 **Backstage (FR)**[24] 896 8-11-5 145 (tp) DJCondon 101
(Gordon Elliott, Ire) *sn trckd ldrs: 2nd appr 3 out: sn lost pl and no ex* 50/1
11 10 **Cuan Na Grai (IRE)**[10] 1038 9-10-13 139 APCawley 85
(Paul Nolan, Ire) *led early: prom: 4th appr 3 out: sn lost pl and wknd* 14/1
12 19 **Nicanor (FR)**[10] 1038 9-10-9 135 PCarberry 62
(Noel Meade, Ire) *mid-div: nt fluent 2nd: 12th appr 6 out: no ex fr 3 out* 16/1
13 dist **Bringbackthebiff (NZ)**[101] 5267 8-10-4 130 (b) AndrewJMcNamara —
(E J O'Grady, Ire) *trckd ldrs: 5th appr 6 out: lost pl fr bef 3 out: sn wknd: completely t.o* 10/1
R **Hampstead Heath (IRE)**[20] 271 5-10-5 136 KTColeman —
(David Marnane, Ire) *ref to r* 25/1
F **Lucky Wish**[71] 391 7-10-3 134 (b1) EJO'Connell(5) —
(Eoin Griffin, Ire) *prom: sn disp ld: 2nd after 3 out: rdn to hold pl whn fell last* 16/1
F **Don't Be Bitin (IRE)**[41] 778 9-10-10 141 MrMPFogarty(5) —
(C A Murphy, Ire) *fell 4th: fatally injured* 33/1
F **Bobs Pride (IRE)**[41] 778 8-11-0 140 RMPower 151+
(D K Weld, Ire) *towards rr: prog and travelling wl fr bef 2 out: cl up whn fell last* 20/1
P **Deutschland (USA)**[39] 546 7-11-5 145 DJCasey —
(W P Mullins, Ire) *hmpd 1st: a bhd: p.u bef 2 out* 16/1
F **Grand Slam Hero (IRE)**[11] 1020 9-10-10 136 7ex (t) GrahamLee —
(Nigel Twiston-Davies) *fell 1st* 11/1
U **Paco Jack (IRE)**[87] 110 6-10-6 132 (t) AELynch —
(P J Rothwell, Ire) *towards rr: mstke and uns rdr 8th* 25/1
F **Montero (IRE)**[14] 670 8-10-4 137 BryanJCooper(7) —
(D T Hughes, Ire) *a.p: slt mstke 3 out: sn struggling: fell 2 out* 20/1
B **Nedzer's Return (IRE)**[17] 945 8-11-1 141 (t) DenisO'Regan —
(Gordon Elliott, Ire) *hld up: prog into 11th after 3 out: chsng ldrs whn b.d last* 25/1

5m 21.2s (-18.80) 22 Ran SP% 140.1
CSF £166.48 CT £623.98 TOTE £29.40: £5.20, £1.80, £1.40, £9.70; DF 1070.40.
Owner John P McManus **Bred** Mary Fanning McCormack **Trained** Straffan, Co Kildare
■ Stewards' Enquiry : A P McCoy severe caution: used whip with excessive frequency
D N Russell one-day ban: used whip with excessive frequency (Aug 12)

FOCUS
A tremendous ride from Tony McCoy won this race. The form looks sound rated around the fifth and sixth, with the front-running winner rated back to his best form from 2009.

NOTEBOOK
Finger Onthe Pulse(IRE) dictated a mostly steady pace. The horse took control of the race early on the final circuit and his rider kept plenty in reserve for the hill, which he might not have been certain to find had there been the usual frantic Galway Plate gallop. He found plenty when the runner-up came to challenge and stayed on really strongly. It was a great training performance from Tom Taaffe after a year where very little has gone right. (op 25/1)
Themoonandsixpence(IRE) came into this hot handicap as a very inexperienced chaser. Held up and settled well off the steady pace, he began to make his ground coming out of the back straight and got there after the last looking the more likely. The winner was just that bit speedier when they hit the rising ground, though, and he couldn't get back at him. It was still a very good effort and connections can look forward to coming back next year. (op 7/1 tchd 8/1)
Majestic Concorde(IRE) was an almost unbackable price in such a competitive contest but he did run his race. Always keeping the leaders well in his sights, he may have been a fraction keen, but was still close enough if good enough in the dip. (op 3/1 tchd 10/3)
The Fonze(IRE) ran a gallant race, making up his ground from off the pace to have a chance from the home bend and staying on well at the same pace in the straight.
Northern Alliance(IRE) was given a typically patient ride by Derek O'Connor to come from well back and be on the heels of the leaders at the second-last. He could only keep on at the same pace but it was very encouraging in terms of a return to Listowel in September.
Five Dream(FR) kept on at the same pace having raced up with the pace most of the way, giving the impression that a stronger gallop would have suited.
The Last Derby(FR) was well off the bridle when Barry Geraghty threw him at the last two fences. The horse responded but was running on empty from there. (op 8/1 tchd 9/1)
Cuan Na Grai(IRE) ran disappointingly and lost touch from the second-last. (op 12/1)
Don't Be Bitin(IRE) was put down after breaking a shoulder in a fall at the seventh. (op 10/1 tchd 12/1)
Bobs Pride(IRE) ◆ had made good headway and was still travelling when falling at the last. The race had been run at a pace to suit him and it's not hard to have imagined him involved at the finish. (op 10/1 tchd 12/1)
Grand Slam Hero(IRE) unseated at the first. (op 10/1 tchd 12/1)
Nedzer's Return(IRE) was just starting to stay on when brought down by the fall of Bob's Pride. (op 10/1 tchd 12/1)

1120a, 1122a (Foreign Racing) - See Raceform Interactive

1030 STRATFORD (L-H)
Thursday, July 29

OFFICIAL GOING: Good to firm (good in places; watered; 10.1)
Wind: almost nil Weather: overcast but very warm

1124 IAN AND JUNE MAIDEN HURDLE (10 hdls) 2m 3f
2:20 (2:19) (Class 4) 4-Y-0+ **£3,903** (£1,146; £573; £286)

Form RPR
36-3 1 **Call At Midnight**[15] 988 5-10-7 102 AidanColeman 105+
(Sarah Humphrey) *plld hrd in last pair: effrt 7th: shkn up after 3 out: led next: qcknd 4 l clr last: eased flat* 4/1[3]
3 2 5 **Forcryingoutloud (IRE)**[36] 832 6-10-11 0 RichieMcLernon(3) 106+
(Andrew Haynes) *prom: mstke 7th: led 3 out and gng wl: rdn and hdd next: wl hld whn j. awkwardly last* 10/3[1]
440- 3 5 **Ladies Best**[172] 3917 6-10-11 107 DannyCook(3) 99
(Gordon Edwards) *j. modly: dropped bk last at 6th: plugged on bef 2 out: nvr able to rch ldrs: lft 3rd at last* 5/1
0-32 4 2 3/4 **Art Man**[43] 762 7-11-0 95 (b) HaddenFrost 98+
(James Frost) *last pair tl rdn and effrt bef 7th: wnt 4th bef 2 out: rdn and sn wknd and fnd little: lft 4th and impeded at last* 4/1[3]
5 7 **Sieglinde (FR)**[95] 4-10-4 0 LeightonAspell 79
(Alison Batchelor) *wnt 2nd bef 3rd tl ev ch 3 out: rdn and sn lost pl* 28/1
136 6 3 **Kings Riches (IRE)**[22] 935 5-11-0 0 RichardJohnson 86
(Peter Bowen) *handy: rdn bef 7th: struggling 3 out* 7/2[2]
53 7 20 **Oscar Charlie (IRE)**[22] 929 5-11-0 0 DarylJacob 66
(Jamie Snowden) *led: mstke 7th: sn hdd and dropped out rapidly* 20/1
40 U **Hi Wycombe (IRE)**[22] 932 6-11-0 0 RodiGreene 98
(David Bridgwater) *racd freely: prom tl rdn and lost pl bef 7th: rallied and mstke 3 out: ev ch bef next: 7 l 3rd and fading whn mstke: pckd and uns rdr last* 40/1

4m 23.1s (-8.40) **Going Correction** -0.525s/f (Firm)
WFA 4 from 5yo+ 15lb 8 Ran SP% 112.6
Speed ratings (Par 105): **104,101,99,98,95 94,86,—**
toteswingers:1&2:£9.50, 1&3:£6.80, 2&3:£9.30 CSF £17.38 TOTE £4.20: £1.30, £1.70, £1.20; EX 17.80.
Owner Mrs K Holmes **Bred** D And Mrs Holmes **Trained** West Wratting, Cambs
■ This race went off 47 seconds before the advertised off time.

FOCUS
This was a fairly moderate yet open-looking contest, and it did not unfold until the home straight. The winner was the form pick and is rated back to his best.

NOTEBOOK
Call At Midnight was ridden patiently, needing a bit of rousting to hold position around the final bend, but she had more stamina than her rivals and did it comfortably in the end. She won on her bumper debut last autumn when with Alan King, but has taken a while to flourish over hurdles, although there were encouraging signs last earlier this month when she perhaps just needed the outing on her first run for current connections. She has progressed from that warm-up and looks capable of winning again in a handicap at a similar level. (op 7-2 tchd 3-1)
Forcryingoutloud(IRE) was a bit keen early on, yet he travelled well to take up the running around the final turn, but he did not find much as his stamina bottomed out and he was eventually outstayed. This was a good hurdling debut however, and he showed enough pace to suggest he could win a race, perhaps at a shorter trip to start with. (op 7-2)
Ladies Best, off the track for nearly six months and now with a new yard, lacked pace near the finish and could only plug on. He may come on for the run, but might need a stiffer test and softer ground than this. (tchd 13-2)
Art Man was dropped into a seller for his latest run and looked a bit outclassed but did well to stay on considering he made several jumping errors that checked his momentum. (op 9-2)
Sieglinde(FR) was up with the early pace and perhaps too fresh on his first start for three months since moving to Britain. He was 0-10 over hurdles in France so would need to improve on this effort. (op 20-1)

Kings Riches(IRE) showed some ability in bumpers, but was under pressure as early as the third last and, with fitness not an issue, this was a disappointing hurdling debut. (op 4-1)

1125 GEOFF AND JACKIE (S) HURDLE (9 hdls) 2m 110y
2:55 (2:55) (Class 4) 4-7-Y-O **£2,602** (£764; £382; £190)

Form RPR

14- **1** **Herschel (IRE)**[14] 5355 4-11-2 109 JamieMoore 99+
(Gary Moore) *mde all: nt fluent 3 out: rdn next: 2 l clr last: kpt on* **7/2**[2]

0-01 **2** *2 1/4* **Douchkette (FR)**[11] 1031 4-10-6 88 DannyCook(3) 87
(John Berry) *hld up: j.rt 2nd: effrt after 3 out: chsd wnr after next: rdn and no imp* **9/2**[3]

11-P **3** *1 3/4* **Santera (IRE)**[84] 170 6-11-3 110 DenisO'Regan 95
(Michael Blake) *pressed wnr: nt fluent 6th: rdn bef 2 out: relegated 3rd after 2 out and one pce* **7/4**[1]

4630 **4** *nk* **Knightsbridgelives (IRE)**[15] 990 7-10-7 100 (t) DavidBass(5) 88
(Lawney Hill) *heavily restrained early: last but in tch whn mstke 4th: chal ldrs 6th: rdn and little rspnse bef 2 out* **11/2**

4240 **5** *1 1/4* **Navajo Nation (IRE)**[24] 912 4-10-6 99 ow1 (p) TomO'Connor(5) 87
(Bill Turner) *prom: rdn bef 2 out: ev ch of 3rd at last: wknd* **7/1**

00 **6** *9* **Motor Home**[9] 1046 4-10-10 0 JimmyMcCarthy 76
(Charlie Morlock) *heavily restrained s: in tch by 4th: rdn 3 out: sn struggling* **50/1**

7 *37* **Mocha Java**[73] 7-10-7 0 JimmyDerham(5) 41
(Seamus Mullins) *plld hrd to 4th: a jumping v modly: 7 l last bef 6th: t.o after next* **33/1**

4500 **U** **Iron Man Of Mersey (FR)**[7] 1066 4-10-5 90 LeeEdwards(5) —
(Tony Carroll) *planted on infield and fnlly dragged out to be mounted on crse: reluctant to set off and lost several l: clsng whn hmpd and uns rdr 2nd* **16/1**

3m 50.8s (-5.20) **Going Correction** -0.525s/f (Firm)
WFA 4 from 5yo+ 15lb 8 Ran SP% **115.4**
Speed ratings: **91,89,89,88,88 84,66,—**
toteswingers:1&2:£1.70, 1&3:£2.10, 2&3:£3.50 CSF £20.17 TOTE £3.90: £1.90, £2.00, £1.10; EX 21.10.The winner was bought in for 7,000gns.
Owner S E Sangster **Bred** Mount Coote Stud And M Johnston **Trained** Lower Beeding, W Sussex

FOCUS
An ordinary seller, dominated throughout by an easy winner. He is rated to form.

NOTEBOOK
Herschel(IRE) dictated the pace throughout, subtly increasing the tempo leaving the back straight, and soon had his rivals floundering as he strode on for a facile success. The winner of a juvenile hurdle on his jumping debut a year previously, his indifferent form since the spring both on the Flat and in another hurdle made a handicap mark of 109 look somewhat harsh. However, connections found an ideal opportunity as he is certainly better than selling class. (tchd 10-3)
Douchkette(FR) stayed on well but the winner had got first run and she was unable to bridge the gap. A C&D winner of a seller 11 days ago, she may have improved on that form a little as this was a stronger contest. (op 5-1)
Santera(IRE) has had some success in low-grade hurdles for a number of yards, but just could not sustain the pace on her debut for her current yard. She was disappointing when last seen out in May, but this represented a better effort and she should come on for this. (tchd 15-8)
Knightsbridgelives(IRE) was keen at the rear of the field until making some progress wide of the pack on the home turn, but once again he was unable to sustain the run. (op 6-1 tchd 7-1 and 5-1)
Navajo Nation(IRE) was staying on a bit until hitting the last, after which he showed little resilience to recover lost momentum. (op 8-1 tchd 10-1)

1126 JOHN DUNBAR MEMORIAL NOVICES' H'CAP CHASE (17 fncs) 2m 7f
3:30 (3:30) (Class 4) (0-100,96) 4-Y-O+ **£4,553** (£1,337; £668; £333)

Form RPR

0P-F **1** **Buailteoir (IRE)**[67] 436 8-10-0 77 AdamWedge(7) 100+
(Evan Williams) *prom: wnt 2nd at 12th: led next: 6 l clr 2 out: rdn and edgd rt bef last: unchal* **12/1**

/4-1 **2** *11* **Mad Jack Duncan (IRE)**[15] 985 8-11-5 96 MrJFMathias(7) 108
(Lawney Hill) *racd keenly: prom: nt fluent 12th: outpcd in 4th bef 14th: lft 2nd next: wl hld by wnr fr 2 out but kpt on to fin a dist clr of rest* **7/2**[2]

0334 **3** *35* **Fongoli**[23] 918 4-10-8 95 (v) AidanColeman 55
(Brendan Powell) *chsd ldrs: rdn 10th: outpcd 12th: nt fluent 14th: laboured on: wnt 43 l 3rd and mstke last* **16/1**

-53P **4** *6* **Maybe A Malt (IRE)**[15] 987 8-10-0 70 oh3 JamieMoore 41
(Richard Rowe) *towards rr: mstke 13th and rdn: struggling whn mstke 3 out: t.o after next* **40/1**

0UF- **5** *8* **Intense Suspense (IRE)**[127] 4829 7-10-0 70 oh8 CharliePoste 33
(Robin Dickin) *t.k.h in ld: hmpd by loose horse bef 12th: hdd next: wkng whn hit 3 out: t.o between last two* **20/1**

2-05 **6** *4 1/2* **Konigsbote (GER)**[60] 529 8-11-8 92 (b) JohnnyFarrelly 51
(Sophie Leech) *nt jump wl: sn drvn in rr and nvr gng wl: lost tch after 11th: t.o 3 out* **33/1**

4453 **P** **Thyne Spirit (IRE)**[8] 1061 11-10-1 70 oh12 ow1 ColinBolger —
(Simon Lewis) *clambering fences in last: t.o fr 5th tl p.u 14th* **50/1**

22 **F** **Behind The Scenes (IRE)**[24] 913 8-11-3 87 RhysFlint —
(Tim McCarthy) *prom: cl 2nd and gng wl whn fell 3 out* **7/1**[3]

06/1 **U** **Lords Bridge**[2] 1101 9-9-9 70 DeanColeman(5) —
(Tim Vaughan) *lunged at 2nd (water) and rdr fell off* **8/11**[1]

5m 33.3s (-8.30) **Going Correction** -0.525s/f (Firm)
WFA 4 from 7yo+ 3lb 9 Ran SP% **118.3**
Speed ratings (Par 105): **93,89,77,74,72 70,—,—,—**
toteswingers:1&2:£7.50, 1&3:£16.20, 2&3:£9.50 CSF £54.38 CT £692.71 TOTE £17.70: £3.80, £1.90, £3.20; EX 89.20.
Owner Tony Cromwell **Bred** R Lynch **Trained** Llancarfan, Vale Of Glamorgan

FOCUS
A good pace turned this into a thorough test, though it was rendered less competitive after the early departure of the favourite and they finished strung out. The winner had slipped to a very good mark.

NOTEBOOK
Buailteoir(IRE) bided his time until the leader cracked, seizing the initiative to move clear before the home straight, so although he was tiring near the finish he held enough of an advantage. He had to improve on his previous dismal form, including falling in a hurdle on his last start back in May, and as such he might have benefited from seemingly better rivals failing to complete. The bulk of his form had been on soft ground, which he patently does not like, though it has done no harm to his handicap mark, so on more suitable summer jumping ground he was able to put that to good use here. (tchd 16-1)
Mad Jack Duncan(IRE) tried to chase the winner from the home turn and gained a little ground, but ultimately the concession of 19lb proved beyond him. He continued his winning pointing form into rules when successful at Uttoxeter last time, but he may need to be dropped in trip again to cope with the rise in his handicap mark. (op 3-1)
Fongoli began to lose touch at a crucial stage in the back straight, but plugged on for a remote third. She guessed a bit at several fences and will need to jump with more aplomb if she is to make the transition as a chaser. (op 20-1 tchd 22-1)
Maybe A Malt(IRE) seems to lack scope and will struggle over anything other than easy fences. (op 33-1)
Intense Suspense(IRE) looked to have been well schooled since his failing to complete when last seen in March and jumped better as a consequence, managing to avoid the attentions of the loose horse, as he strode clear of the field. However, the absence told in the back straight and he faded tamely, but he should come on for this. (tchd 16-1)
Behind The Scenes(IRE) was travelling well enough and about to deliver a challenge when falling three out. (op 8-1)
Lords Bridge parted company with his jockey at the water jump first time round, but he remained involved, jumping intermittent fences and causing minor interference. (op 8-1)

1127 TONY AND JOSIE H'CAP HURDLE (9 hdls) 2m 110y
4:05 (4:05) (Class 3) (0-135,127) 4-Y-O+ **£6,337** (£1,872; £936; £468; £234)

Form RPR

020- **1** **Le Corvee (IRE)**[6] 2756 8-10-8 112 LeeEdwards(5) 116+
(Tony Carroll) *prom and t.k.h tl rdn and lost pl briefly 5th: rallied 3 out: led on inner nring next: rdn and r.o gamely flat: a holding rival* **7/1**

440- **2** *2 1/4* **Sweet World**[156] 4218 6-10-4 110 MissIsabelTompsett(7) 112
(Bernard Llewellyn) *plld hrd in last: effrt on inner fr 6th: no gap whn looking for room bef 2 out: wnt 2nd after 2 out: urged and nt qckn last: wnr got first run* **12/1**

3240 **3** *3/4* **Forty Thirty (IRE)**[18] 958 4-11-12 127 JamieGoldstein 126
(Sheena West) *settled in tch: effrt after 3 out: ev ch next: one pce and no imp after but kpt trying flat* **7/1**

0P33 **4** *1 3/4* **Is It Me (USA)**[6] 1084 7-11-0 113 (t) RichardJohnson 113
(Sophie Leech) *racd keenly and prom: mstke 5th: rdn and w ldr 6th: ev ch tl no ex 2 out* **2/1**[1]

-610 **5** *3 1/4* **Crosby Jemma**[18] 958 6-10-11 110 BrianHughes 106
(Mike Sowersby) *set modest pce: rdn and hdd nring 2 out: sn lost pl: wknd flat and eased* **16/1**

2363 **6** *29* **Dancewiththedevil (IRE)**[18] 952 9-11-3 119 DonalDevereux(3) 93
(Peter Bowen) *cl up in slow r tl bef 6th: last and fading whn mstke 3 out: sn wl bhd* **6/1**[3]

1U12 **F** **Ajman (IRE)**[36] 829 5-10-4 110 (t) AdamWedge(7) 96
(Evan Williams) *trckd ldrs: effrt 6th: ev ch whn blnd next: sn drvn: 5 l 6th and wkng whn fell 2 out* **3/1**[2]

3m 51.2s (-4.80) **Going Correction** -0.525s/f (Firm) 7 Ran SP% **111.2**
Speed ratings (Par 107): **90,88,88,87,86 72,—**
toteswingers:1&2:£18.10, 1&3:£4.80, 2&3:£12.00 CSF £73.71 TOTE £9.90: £3.30, £3.20; EX 60.50.
Owner A W Carroll **Bred** Forenaghts Stud And David O'Reilly **Trained** Cropthorne, Worcs

FOCUS
A competitive but tactical affair with the pace increasing on the final circuit leading to the field finishing close up. A personal best from the winner, but the steady pace makes the form suspect.

NOTEBOOK
Le Corvee(IRE) got a bit outpaced as the pace lifted on the final circuit, but he never lost the inside position and stayed with it to emerge the stronger at the end. He had inauspiciously been dropped into sellers when last seen over hurdles last December, but is not effective on deep winter ground. Since then he has been in good form on the Flat and, with the stable in form and back down to his last winning mark of last autumn, the threads came together here. (op 13-2 tchd 6-1)
Sweet World was restrained at the rear of the field before making an eye-catching move to challenge up the straight, but he was a bit squeezed for room and once again did not find as much as expected. He has just one win from 24 attempts over hurdles, but his style of racing does not help matters, as he needs to be delivered late but does not always find much, though he might come on for this first run since February. (tchd 14-1)
Forty Thirty(IRE) made some late progress but could never get there. This was another good run from this generally consistent performer, but he has paid for it with a tough enough mark and might be better off a stronger pace. (op 15-2 tchd 13-2)
Is It Me(USA) enjoyed a resurgence in form last year before ending up in a seller, the result of which was a move to his current yard. It has taken a while for him to emerge from the doldrums but there were signs of a revival over the past month. Though he was a bit short of pace near the finish he responded to pressure to post another reasonable performance. (op 3-1)
Crosby Jemma led for much of the way but was soon put in her place and might be better when relatively fresh in any case. (op 12-1)
Dancewiththedevil(IRE) was the first beaten and, though he may be getting on a bit in hurdling terms, this was still disappointing. He is not so good over fences, so connections have a conundrum to solve with him. (op 5-1)
Ajman(IRE) is effective on fast ground and looked on a fair mark for an improving horse, and was well supported but, though he loomed up travelling well around the home turn, he had already been beaten off when falling two out. (op 5-2)

1128 MR AND MRS PHILIP CONRAN H'CAP CHASE (14 fncs) 2m 4f
4:40 (4:40) (Class 4) (0-110,110) 4-Y-O+ **£4,553** (£1,337; £668; £333)

Form RPR

20-2 **1** **Inmate (IRE)**[44] 755 9-10-7 91 CharliePoste 115+
(Robin Dickin) *racd enthusiastically: led tl after 2nd: cl 2nd tl led again 9th: 5 l up and gng strly 2 out: 20 l ahd last: sn eased* **11/2**

4-P4 **2** *22* **Glengarra (IRE)**[23] 919 13-11-7 105 (tp) NoelFehily 104
(Liam Corcoran) *led after 2nd tl 9th: chsd wnr tl 11th: no ch fr 2 out but plugged on gamely to regain poor 2nd flat* **17/2**

5540 **3** *3 1/4* **Morestead (IRE)**[23] 921 5-10-9 93 (p) AidanColeman 90
(Brendan Powell) *prom: rdn 9th: wkng whn nt fluent 3 out* **7/2**[2]

-5PP **4** *nk* **Rash Moment (FR)**[44] 758 11-10-0 84 oh5 (p) SamJones 80
(Michael Scudamore) *bhd and tended to lack fluency: last and rdn 8th: hit 9th: sn outpcd: 20 l 6th whn j. slowly 2 out: rdn and styd on to snatch poor 4th: nrly grabbed 3rd* **20/1**

2233 **5** *nk* **Pagan Sword**[3] 1091 8-10-13 97 RodiGreene 95
(David Bridgwater) *bhd: nt fluent 7th (water) and 8th: sn drvn in last: wnt 2nd at 11th: chsd wnr hopelessly fr 2 out tl hit last: fdd and lost three pls flat* **5/2**[1]

-434 **6** *7* **Hereweareagain (IRE)**[52] 663 7-11-12 110 (b) RhysFlint 98
(Philip Hobbs) *settled handy: effrt 9th: 4th and rdn after next: no ch fr 11th* **9/2**[3]

5-40 **7** *4 1/2* **Silver Dollars (FR)**[25] 891 9-11-0 98 DarylJacob 82
(David Arbuthnot) *j. sltly rt at times: chsd ldrs: rdn 9th: struggling bef 11th* **7/1**

4m 41.0s (-13.20) **Going Correction** -0.525s/f (Firm) course record 7 Ran SP% **112.1**
Speed ratings (Par 105): **105,96,94,94,94 91,90**
toteswingers:1&2:£7.70, 1&3:£5.00, 2&3:£6.40 CSF £45.94 CT £184.25 TOTE £3.40: £1.60, £7.10; EX 35.40.
Owner John Rogers **Bred** B And Q Syndicate **Trained** Atherstone on Stour, Warwicks

FOCUS
Several horses fighting for the lead made for a good pace that only the winner could maintain. He produced a big step up but the second was 7lb off.

NOTEBOOK

Inmate(IRE) was not going to get his own way in front with several other pace-setters in the field, but as they embarked on their final circuit he proved the stronger and began to stretch clear, opening up a yawning gap that he maintained to the finish. The step up in trip may have helped this habitual front-runner, in that despite several jostling for the lead the pace was not as strong as he was used to, so it was a relatively easy task in the end. He was in good form, having run well on his first start for nearly a year making his debut for his current stable, and with six weeks to recover from that effort the bounce was not a factor. The handicapper might be the biggest threat now. (op 4-1)

Glengarra(IRE) may be a veteran but he is still capable on his day, although he could not concede 14lb and four years to the winner. Although he was back down to his last winning mark of a year ago he faced a stiff task trying to capitalise. (op 7-1)

Moresteád(IRE) raced prominently as he likes to do, but was beaten off in the back straight before staying on again for some modest late gains. He is back down to a similar mark to that of his sole previous chase victory but is better over further. (op 9-2)

Rash Moment(FR) had been dropped to a useful mark and was able to race off a light weight, which has proved beneficial in the past, but he still needed to recapture his form. He jumped ponderously in rear before making a late run, but still does not look to be firing as yet. (op 18-1 tchd 25-1)

Pagan Sword headed the market following his respectable run at Uttoxeter earlier in the week but he again ran in snatches, dropping to the rear early before staging a strong rally to briefly challenge the winner, before fading again. He has the heart for it but does not impress as a natural jumper, which limits his prospects. (op 3-1)

Hereweareagain(IRE) looked harshly treated on his achievements so far and was never a threat. (op 5-1 tchd 4-1)

1129 TONY AND ANDREA NOVICES' H'CAP HURDLE (12 hdls) 2m 6f 110y

5:15 (5:15) (Class 4) (0-105,105) 4-Y-O+ £3,903 (£1,146; £573; £286)

Form RPR

-461 **1** **Extreme Conviction (IRE)**[9] 1043 6-11-12 **105**................. WillKennedy 114+
(John Berry) *2nd or 3rd and gng wl: led bef 3 out: 5 l clr and in command whn stmbld last: comf* **10/11**[1]

2-46 **2** *5* **Googoobarabajagal (IRE)**[37] 823 4-11-6 **103**.......... RichardJohnson 98
(Stuart Kittow) *nvr jumping w any fluency: trckd ldrs: rdn after 3 out: duelled for 2nd fr next: a wl hld by wnr* **13/2**[3]

55-4 **3** *2 1/2* **Major Miller**[15] 994 9-11-3 **101**.................................... DavidBass(5) 100
(Nicky Henderson) *2nd or 3rd: pushed along bef 8th: mstke next and drvn: outpcd by wnr 2 out: j. slowly last whn disputing 2nd: fin weakly* **7/2**[2]

P620 **4** *3 1/2* **Nether Stream (IRE)**[2] 1111 6-11-8 **101**......................... DenisO'Regan 95
(Shaun Lycett) *bhd and hld up: last at 8th: effrt after 3 out: drvn and wnt 4th bef next: n.m.r bef 2 out where swtchd rt and mstke: hanging lft and n.d after* **14/1**

36-6 **5** *10* **Dan Maguire (IRE)**[8] 1059 9-11-0 **93**.................................(v[1]) JackDoyle 76
(Peter Pritchard) *led: hit 8th: rdn and hdd bef 3 out: fdd tamely bef next* **25/1**

6110 **6** *2* **Ashmolian (IRE)**[48] 708 7-11-4 **100**............................(p) DannyCook(3) 81
(Zoe Davison) *last tl 8th: drvn and brief effrt next: dropped out qckly after 3 out* **7/1**

5m 16.9s (-11.20) **Going Correction** -0.525s/f (Firm)
WFA 4 from 6yo+ 16lb **6** Ran SP% **111.0**
Speed ratings (Par 105): **98,96,95,94,90 90**
toteswingers:1&2:£2.30, 1&3:£1.40, 2&3:£2.20 CSF £7.30 TOTE £1.80: £2.00, £1.50; EX 5.90 Place 6 £658.74; Place 5 £361.16.
Owner All Points West Partnership **Bred** Mrs A S O'Brien And Lars Pearson **Trained** Newmarket, Suffolk

FOCUS

A modest handicap hurdle but the form is sound. The easy winner ran to a similar level as Bangor.

NOTEBOOK

Extreme Conviction(IRE) completed the task in style, despite a stumble at the last. He was able to get in here without a penalty for winning a Bangor conditionals' handicap, so it would have been mightily disappointing if he could not follow up having been dropped into novice company. The handicapper can reaction now, and unfortunately it could be enough to put a halt to things for a while. (op 11-10 tchd 5-4)

Googoobarabajagal(IRE) kept on well enough but he was readily outpointed by the winner. He goes well on tight flattish tracks such as this and, though he is still a maiden, he has enough raw ability to win. However, his jumping lacked fluency here and it needs to improve if it is not to scupper his future chances. (op 8-1 tchd 6-1)

Major Miller remained close up despite a mistake at the first in the back straight on the final circuit, but he did not pick up as well as his rivals and ran a bit flat in the end, suggesting he is still some way off hitting top form. (op 3-1 tchd 11-4)

Nether Stream(IRE) was ridden quietly at the rear of the field before making a promising forward move coming into the straight. He was squeezed out at the second last and showed little resilience from then on, thus tarnishing his previous good work.

Dan Maguire(IRE) set the pace in a first-time visor, but soon capitulated once headed at the last in the back straight. He won a point in March and might need further than this, but has largely been out of form since and will need to improve. (op 33-1)

Ashmolian(IRE) managed two wins off lower marks in May, but was never a factor at any stage. (op 11-2 tchd 5-1)

T/Plt: £254.40 to a £1 stake. Pool:£49,341.76 - 141.55 winning tickets T/Qpdt: £162.00 to a £1 stake. Pool:£3,570.51 - 16.30 winning tickets IM

1120 GALWAY (R-H)

Thursday, July 29

OFFICIAL GOING: Good to firm

1131a ST.JAMES'S GATE NOVICE CHASE (12 fncs) 2m 1f

2:25 (2:25) 5-Y-O+ £14,955 (£4,371; £2,070; £690)

RPR

1 **Beau Michael**[10] 938 6-11-6 ....(tp) BarryGeraghty 127
(Adrian McGuinness, Ire) *chsd ldrs in 3rd: impr to ld and dispute bef 4 out: led appr 2 out: rdn after last: chal ent st: disp clsng stages: prevailed cl home* **4/1**[1]

2 *nk* **Armaramak (IRE)**[25] 904 6-11-6 .... AndrewJMcNamara 127
(E J O'Grady, Ire) *settled bhd ldrs: 5th 1/2-way: pushed along appr 2 out: styd on in 3rd ent st: sn chal: disp clsng stages: jst hld cl home* **9/2**[2]

3 *3 1/2* **Adajal (IRE)**[48] 724 7-11-12 126......................................(t) APMcCoy 130
(C F Swan, Ire) *hld up towards rr early: 6th 1/2-way: hdwy into 4th 3 out: rdn into 2nd after last: chal ent st: no ex in 3rd clsng stages* **11/2**[3]

4 *1 3/4* **Coscorrig (IRE)**[25] 905 8-11-4 123.................................... PCarberry 120
(Andrew Lynch, Ire) *disp early: sn chsd ldr in 2nd: 3rd bef 4 out: rdn in 4th last: no ex ent st: kpt on same pce* **7/1**

5 *20* **Blacktoft (USA)**[37] 822 7-11-6 .... PaulMoloney 104
(Evan Williams) *led: slt mstke 4th: disp bef 4 out: rdn in 2nd and mstke 2 out: no ex after last: wknd* **12/1**

P **Who's Deal (IRE)**[42] 778 8-11-6 118...................................(t) PTownend —
(Gerard J O'Keeffe, Ire) *hld up bhd ldrs early: 7th 1/2-way: dropped towards rr bef 5 out: wknd and p.u bef 2 out* **14/1**

F **Cruising Katie (IRE)**[25] 905 8-10-13 121.......................... PFMangan(5) —
(R A Cotter, Ire) *chsd ldrs: 4th 1/2-way: fell 4 out* **4/1**[1]

F **Tribes And Banner (IRE)**[17] 970 6-11-9 ....(t) DJCasey —
(C F Swan, Ire) *hld up towards rr: fell 4 out* **11/2**[3]

4m 26.1s (-9.40) **8** Ran SP% **115.8**
CSF £22.98 TOTE £4.40: £1.60, £1.90, £1.50; DF 27.90.
Owner Total Recall Racing Club **Bred** Berkshire Equestrian Services Ltd **Trained** Lusk, Co Dublin
■ Stewards' Enquiry : Barry Geraghty one-day ban: used whip with excessive frequency (Aug 12); caution: careless riding

FOCUS

The winner is rated below his best, with the next two rated to their chase marks.

NOTEBOOK

Beau Michael ◆ came back to win this and showed depths of resolution in doing so. He was given a positive ride by Barry Geraghty, who drove him up between horses to dispute the lead five out, and, despite a mistake at the next fence, stayed there. When Geraghty kicked at the final fence he must have hoped that he would be able to steal an unassailable advantage, but he wasn't able to do that. However, his strengths came fully into play when the runner-up headed him and he responded generously to Geraghty's full-on drive. Apart from one mistake, his jumping stood up well and, while the ground remains good, one would imagine that some more hay will be made. (op 4/1 tchd 9/2)

Armaramak(IRE) ◆ retained the impression given at Limerick last time that he is very much an improving novice. The first of the leading group to come off the bridle, even marginally so, he kept in there and stayed in touch running into the dip, and it was from the last that he really began to stay on. In the end he was outbattled but there was little wrong with the performance. (op 4/1)

Adajal(IRE) came back to form after a poor effort last time, but just found the weight he was giving to the first two too much to cope with in the end. He was on the winner's heels turning in and looked the most likely winner for a stride or two but just ran out of steam in the last furlong. (op 6/1)

Coscorrig(IRE) has always shown herself to be best on a flatter track but didn't run badly here. She raced prominently without being able to dominate and was still travelling after the third-last but just couldn't find any extra once asked.

Blacktoft(USA) helped set the pace and jumped really well but just looked as though he was starting to flag when making a bad mistake at the second-last. He was soon beaten. (op 8/1)

Cruising Katie(IRE) was probably the most unlucky as she was well in touch when coming down at the fourth-last. (op 6/1)

1133a GUINNESS GALWAY HURDLE H'CAP (GRADE A) (9 hdls) 2m

4:50 (4:50) 4-Y-O+

£133,185 (£42,477; £20,353; £7,079; £4,867; £2,654)

RPR

1 **Overturn (IRE)**[33] 207 6-11-6 145.. GrahamLee 163
(Donald McCain) *sn led: rdn to assert ent st: kpt on strly: comf* **6/1**[2]

2 *5 1/2* **Bahrain Storm (IRE)**[11] 1038 7-11-8 147...............................(b) JRBarry 159
(Patrick J Flynn, Ire) *chsd ldrs: 4th 1/2-way: 5th 4 out: rdn into 3rd 2 out: kpt on into 2nd run-in: no ch w wnr* **8/1**

3 *1/2* **Dirar (IRE)**[40] 667 5-10-4 129.. BarryGeraghty 141
(Gordon Elliott, Ire) *chsd ldrs: 6th 1/2-way: hdwy into 2nd 3 out: rdn 2 out: no imp on ldr bef last: kpt on same pce* **4/1**[1]

4 *3* **Slieveardagh (IRE)**[81] 241 6-9-7 123.............................. PFMangan(5) 132
(E J O'Grady, Ire) *mid-div: hdwy into 6th 4 out: rdn into 4th 2 out: no ex ent st: kpt on same pce* **9/1**

5 *7* **No One Tells Me**[96] 5397 5-10-2 127...................................(p) RMPower 129
(Mrs John Harrington, Ire) *chsd ldrs: 8th 1/2-way: lost pl bef 4 out where pushed along in 13th: rdn into 11th 2 out: 8th ent st: kpt on same pce* **20/1**

6 *3/4* **Fisher Bridge (IRE)**[33] 5379 7-10-2 127...............................(b) PCarberry 128
(Noel Meade, Ire) *mid-div early: 7th 1/2-way: rdn into 5th 2 out: no ex in 6th ent st: kpt on same pce* **9/1**

7 *hd* **Gloucester**[12] 1017 7-10-5 130.................................... TomScudamore 131
(Michael Scudamore) *mid-div: hdwy in 9th 4 out: rdn in 8th appr 2 out: 5th ent st: no imp and kpt on one pce* **25/1**

8 *4* **Dantari (IRE)**[44] 756 5-10-4 129.. DPFahy 126
(Evan Williams) *chsd ldrs: 9th 1/2-way: 11th 4 out: rdn next: no imp in 9th 2 out: kpt on one pce* **33/1**

9 *5 1/2* **Tiger O'Toole (IRE)**[12] 1017 5-10-5 130............................. PaulMoloney 121
(Evan Williams) *hld up towards rr: rdn into mod 12th ent st: kpt on one pce* **28/1**

10 *6* **Lady Hillingdon**[25] 905 7-10-1 126.......................................(t) AELynch 111
(Paul John Gilligan, Ire) *chsd ldrs: 2nd 1/2-way: rdn in 3rd after 3 out: no ex in 7th 2 out: kpt on one pce* **25/1**

11 *1/2* **Tilabay (IRE)**[16] 975 5-9-9 127...................................... TCCarroll(7) 112
(S Buggy, Ire) *towards rr for most: nvr a factor* **40/1**

12 *1 1/4* **New Phase (IRE)**[25] 902 6-10-5 130....................... AndrewJMcNamara 113
(D K Weld, Ire) *mid-div: 12th 4 out: rdn and no imp next* **9/1**

13 *1 3/4* **Alpine Glade (IRE)**[28] 258 8-10-0 125.................................... DJCasey 107
(W McCreery, Ire) *towards rr for most: nvr a factor* **14/1**

14 *3/4* **Grand Opera (IRE)**[29] 857 7-9-7 123.......................(b) KMDonoghue(5) 104
(Gordon Elliott, Ire) *towards rr for most: nvr a factor* **33/1**

15 *7* **Fosters Cross (IRE)**[98] 5350 8-10-12 137............................. PTownend 111
(Thomas Mullins, Ire) *disp early: sn chsd ldrs: 3rd 1/2-way: rdn and no ex appr 2 out: wknd bef st* **16/1**

16 *3/4* **Magnum Force (IRE)**[26] 750 6-10-1 126..........................(p) RLoughran 99
(C A McBratney, Ire) *mid-div: rdn in 9th 3 out: 10th and no imp bef 2 out: wknd* **20/1**

17 *22* **Jigalo (IRE)**[10] 146 9-10-0 125...(p) DJCondon 76
(Ms Joanna Morgan, Ire) *mid-div best: rdn in 10th 4 out: sn no ex and wknd* **12/1**

18 *2* **Amazing King (IRE)**[34] 2444 6-9-12 123........................ JamesReveley 72
(Philip Kirby) *a towards rr* **20/1**

F **Lethal Weapon (IRE)**[11] 241 5-10-7 132................................. APMcCoy —
(C Roche, Ire) *chsd ldrs: fell 4th* **7/1**[3]

3m 33.7s (-23.00)
WFA 4 from 5yo+ 15lb **19** Ran SP% **141.9**
CSF £54.42 CT £232.32 TOTE £7.00: £2.00, £2.00, £1.80, £3.10; DF 48.40.
Owner T G Leslie **Bred** Pendley Farm **Trained** Cholmondeley, Cheshire
■ The first British-trained winner since Sagaman in 1991.

FOCUS

The winner is progressive under both codes and, although he had the run of the race from the front, the third had every chance if good enough and the form is rock solid rated around the placed horses.

NOTEBOOK

Overturn(IRE) ◆ could have gone round again, and if continuing his rate of progression could well develop into a Champion Hurdle horse. He made all, had almost everything off the bridle coming down the hill, and kept up that gallop all the way to the line. Nothing could live with him once he kicked after the second-last and this would have to be considered a career-best performance from a horse that has been on the go for a while. It was a display which makes one wonder where this horse could end up in six or seven months' time. (op 6/1 tchd 7/1)

Bahrain Storm(IRE) was a stone higher and giving 2lb to the winner. This could even be a better performance than his winning effort of 12 months ago. Tracking the pace on the inside, he wasn't that fluent at one or two of his flights but was pacy enough to keep his place. Niggled coming down the hill, he wasn't able to go immediately with the winner and the favourite when they went on, but he did stay on well in the straight and deservedly got up for second place close home. He would seem to be highly enough handicapped now over hurdles and what they do with him now is something to think about. (op 8/1 tchd 9/1)

Dirar(IRE) raced very handily indeed and attempted to take the winner on from the second-last, but once Overturn kicked again he just couldn't match him. In the end, the energy he had used up in doing that led to his effort flattening out from the last. (op 5/1)

Slieveardagh(IRE) ◆ was a lightly raced horse coming into this race and, as a horse that handles any ground, could well be an individual that will be a regular in this sort of race for a while. Racing just off the pace, he didn't have the speed to get involved when proceedings heated up, but what he did do was stay on well from the last, an attribute he had shown when winning at Killarney. It was a very good run from a progressive horse. (op 11/1)

No One Tells Me seemed to lose her place before staying on again for pressure late on. (op 25/1)

Fisher Bridge(IRE), the winner of two races on the Flat this summer, was travelling well in pursuit of the leaders as they began the descent into the dip but found little once off the bridle. (op 10/1 tchd 8/1)

Gloucester battled his way into some sort of contention at the second-last but ran out of steam in the straight.

Dantari(IRE) never really got into the race.

Tiger O'Toole(IRE) made some late headway.

1130a, 1132a, 1134a (Foreign Racing) - See Raceform Interactive

[1043]BANGOR-ON-DEE (L-H)

Friday, July 30

OFFICIAL GOING: Good (7.8)

Wind: almost nil Weather: overcast and cool with light showers

1135 BAGNALL & MORRIS JUVENILE HURDLE (9 hdls) 2m 1f

2:00 (2:00) (Class 4) 3-Y-O **£2,569** (£748; £374)

Form RPR

2 **1** **Two Kisses (IRE)**[19] [960] 3-10-5 0 ... AidanColeman 104+
(Brendan Powell) *cl up: led on bit bef 2 out: cruised 10 l clr last: canter* **3/1**[2]

2 **2** *13* **Sassanian (IRE)**[12] [1024] 3-10-12 0 ... APMcCoy 96+
(Tim Vaughan) *t.k.h: 2nd tl lft in ld 6th: hdd and rdn bef 2 out: sn no ch w wnr* **7/2**[3]

3 *13* **Baraathen (USA)** 3-10-9 0 ... AdrianLane(3) 83
(Donald McCain) *novicey in last pair: rdn 4th: 6th whn mstke 3 out: plugged on into modest 3rd bef next: no ch w ldrs* **33/1**

4 *17* **Forsyth**[15] 3-10-12 0 ... BrianHughes 69
(Alan Swinbank) *t.k.h: led: wandering into flights and looking awkward: tried to run out 5th: hdd and hit next: lost tch sn after 3 out* **11/2**

U0 **5** *3/4* **Dinkie Short**[12] [1024] 3-10-12 0 ... (p) DarylJacob 67
(Ben De Haan) *hld up towards rr: nt fluent 5th: rdn and outpcd next: modest 5th 3 out* **80/1**

U4 **6** *3 3/4* **Sefton Park**[12] [1024] 3-10-12 0 ... (b) JimmyMcCarthy 63
(Charles Egerton) *mstkes: in tch tl rdn after 5th: nt keen: wl bhd after mstke 3 out* **33/1**

7 *14* **Charmeur (USA)**[35] 3-10-12 0 ... RichardJohnson 59+
(Philip Hobbs) *trckd ldrs: chal and mstke 3 out: immediately struggling: lost modest 3rd bef 2 out and sn eased: t.o* **2/1**[1]

6 **P** **Ariel Bender**[19] [960] 3-10-12 0 ... GrahamLee —
(Donald McCain) *t.k.h: hit 2nd: cl up tl rdn 5th: lost pl u.p next: t.o and p.u 2 out* **50/1**

P **Moonlight Blaze**[54] 3-10-12 0 ... BarryKeniry —
(Chris Fairhurst) *in rr after mstke 3rd: t.o after mstke 4th: p.u 2 out* **40/1**

P **Thundering Home**[29] 3-10-12 0 ... (t) JamieMoore —
(Michael Attwater) *t.k.h in rr: wknd 5th: mstke 3 out: t.o and p.u 2 out* **16/1**

4m 6.80s (-4.10) **Going Correction** -0.275s/f (Good) **10** Ran SP% **113.3**

Speed ratings (Par 102): **98,91,85,77,77 75,69,—,—,—**

toteswingers:1&2:£2.20, 1&3:£20.20, 2&3:£28.10 CSF £13.31 TOTE £4.70: £1.40, £1.50, £9.20; EX 10.80.

Owner Brian McNamee & Jeff Mould **Bred** Jim Cockburn **Trained** Upper Lambourn, Berks

FOCUS

A modest juvenile hurdle that was run at a just an ordinary gallop, but it produced a winner that might be quite handy for this time of year. She stepped up on her debut form.

NOTEBOOK

Two Kisses(IRE) showed enough promise when chasing home Beyond (fourth has scored since) on her hurdling debut to suggest that a race of this nature was well within her compass and ran out a very easy winner. She had a handy sex allowance, but the manner in which she disposed of this field, albeit a modest one, suggests she should be capable of following up under a penalty. (tchd 11-4)

Sassanian(IRE) had been supported beforehand but had to sharpen up on his jumping after recent hurdling debut. His jumping was far more fluent this time, but he was readily brushed aside by the winner after the second last and didn't look at all keen. (op 9-4)

Baraathen(USA), out of an unraced dam by the top-class Sakhee, had joined connections for 4,500gns from Doncaster in April and, on jockey bookings, looked to be the stables' second-string. She made a satisfactory racecourse debut but, after staying on past beaten horses, never look like reeling in the principals.

Forsyth, a fair maiden on the Flat, who was switching his attention to hurdles after failing to build on an encouraging effort when just touched off at Pontefract in April but there were encouraging reports for him on the course beforehand. He was very green at his hurdles and after being headed was soon a spent force. Too early to write him off but this was a little disappointing from a yard in good form. (op 13-2 tchd 5-1)

Charmeur(USA) had joined Philip Hobbs since landing a 1m3f handicap last month and there was market support for him on this hurdling debut. He was not that fluent at his hurdles but warmed to the task as the race progressed and held every chance. He had reportedly schooled very well and he looked fit so, something has to prove now. Official explanation: vet said colt lost an off-fore shoe (op 11-4)

1136 MEADE KING ROBINSON NOVICES' H'CAP CHASE (15 fncs) 2m 4f 110y

2:35 (2:35) (Class 4) (0-110,112) 4-Y-0+ **£3,577** (£1,050; £525; £262)

Form RPR

P32P **1** **Old Brigade (IRE)**[12] [1027] 6-11-1 97 ... (t) APMcCoy 105
(Jonjo O'Neill) *j. slowly 1st: chsd ldr tl 8th and bef 10th: rdn and cajoled along rest of way: chal 2 out: wore down rival nr fin: all out: fine ride* **7/2**[3]

5-11 **2** *nk* **Fealing Real (IRE)**[33] [849] 8-11-7 103 ... (t) TomScudamore 111
(Rebecca Curtis) *led: nt fluent 6th: drvn bef 2 out and hrd pressed after: gamely fended off rival tl overwhelmed fnl strides* **5/4**[1]

04 **3** *15* **Gougane (IRE)**[15] [1000] 7-11-10 106 ... AndrewThornton 101
(Hugh McWilliams) *nt a fluent: j. slowly 3rd and 10th: chsd ldrs: outpcd 12th: plugged on into 3rd between last two: no ch w ldrs* **18/1**

-001 **4** *7* **King Ozzy (IRE)**[10] [1047] 6-11-11 112 7ex ... JimmyDerham(5) 103
(Martin Keighley) *3rd tl wnt 2nd 8th tl bef 10th: rdn 3 out: btn next: lost 3rd between last two* **3/1**[2]

5 *2 1/2* **In The Zone (IRE)**[82] [244] 6-11-3 102 ... RichieMcLernon(3) 91
(Jonjo O'Neill) *towards rr: lost tch 12th: j. bdly rt 3 out: wl bhd whn tired jumps 2 out and last* **15/2**

P **No Reception (IRE)**[132] [4751] 9-11-5 108 ... MissLBrooke(7) —
(Lady Susan Brooke) *a last: struggling 5th: reminders 7th: t.o 9th: plunged over 12th and p.u* **33/1**

5m 2.80s (-6.30) **Going Correction** -0.55s/f (Firm) **6** Ran SP% **111.6**

Speed ratings (Par 105): **90,89,84,81,80** —

toteswingers:1&2:£2.10, 1&3:£7.20, 2&3:£5.70 CSF £8.67 TOTE £3.80: £1.90, £1.50; EX 7.40.

Owner John P McManus **Bred** Gerry O'Sullivan **Trained** Cheltenham, Gloucs

FOCUS

An ordinary novice handicap chase that produced a real good tussle between the front pair, who sat prominently throughout. A step up from the winner.

NOTEBOOK

Old Brigade(IRE) looked potentially well-treated if repeating his effort when runner-up at Market Rasen, which he duly did under a typically strong drive under McCoy to get on top as the post neared. He was stepping back in trip after being pulled up over 3m2f, but jumped well and dug deep to come out on top here. A rise in the weights will make life difficult in the future which overall profile suggests. Official explanation: trainer's rep said, regarding apparent improvement in form, that the gelding was better suited by the shorter trip and being ridden more prominently. (tchd 3-1)

Fealing Real(IRE), an ex-pointer, has made a promising start to chasing career when scoring off 13lbs lower mark at Hereford (good for a bit more as idled) and duly followed up off same mark back over hurdles, again idling. He ran a solid race from the front and only narrowly gave best but does look hard work. He can make his presence felt again especially when the ground is on the quicker side. (op 7-4)

Gougane(IRE) produced his best effort since joining connections but was feeling the pinch from three out and could only stay on at the same pace. This is probably his optimum trip but at present he is rated up to his best. (op 22-1)

King Ozzy(IRE) had bounced back to form with a vengeance to impress on chasing debut, beating subsequent winner Misamon, and had to defy a penalty here. He held his chance at the third last but could not sustain his effort and was a shade disappointing. (op 9-4)

In The Zone(IRE), a winning hurdler in Ireland when with Mouse Morris, was having his first outing since joining Jonjo O'Neill. He had got soundly beaten off a mark off 89 when last seen at Killarney in May and will be up against it now as he has been risen to 103 since crossing the channel. He will come on for the run. (op 8-1 tchd 7-1)

1137 RON HICKMAN MEMORIAL H'CAP HURDLE (11 hdls) 2m 4f

3:10 (3:10) (Class 4) (0-100,107) 4-Y-0+ **£3,415** (£1,002; £501; £250)

Form RPR

4/53 **1** **Miss Molly Be Rude (IRE)**[10] [1048] 8-10-0 74 oh6 ... RobertWalford 83+
(Tim Walford) *lft in ld 1st: mde rest: gng best fr 2 out: 4 l clr whn hit last: pushed out* **11/2**

00/1 **2** *4 1/2* **Grand Art (IRE)**[29] [875] 6-11-7 95 ... RichardJohnson 100
(Tim Vaughan) *hld up in midfield: effrt 7th: wnt 2nd next: rdn after 3 out: kpt on steadily but wl hld by wnr fr 2 out* **11/4**[1]

4031 **3** *15* **Mujamead**[4] [1095] 6-10-11 90 7ex ... (p) LeeEdwards(5) 81
(Sally-Anne Wheelwright) *settled midfield: hit 6th: drvn and effrt after 8th: disp 2nd after 3 out: wknd tamely next* **7/2**[2]

4034 **4** *3 1/2* **Nobby Kivambo (IRE)**[26] [915] 5-10-7 88 ... GaryDerwin(7) 73
(Brendan Powell) *bhd: prog 6th: rdn and hanging lft whn mstke 8th: btn whn mstke 3 out: hit last* **12/1**

006/ **5** *7* **Panzer (GER)**[973] [2514] 9-10-4 85 ... MrJHamer(7) 65
(Donald McCain) *rn in snatches and nt a fluent: lost tch and j. slowly 7th: rallied next: rdn and lost tch after 3 out* **16/1**

6 *22* **Ardilaun (IRE)**[59] [573] 7-11-1 89 ... (p) HaddenFrost 45
(John W Nicholson, Ire) *cl up: nt fluent 5th: rdn and fdd bef 3 out: t.o* **25/1**

-005 **7** *1* **Glan Lady (IRE)**[30] [862] 4-10-1 81 ... (p) CharlieHuxley(3) 33
(John Mackie) *t.k.h and prom: rdn 8th: wknd next: t.o* **11/1**

/200 **8** *3* **He's A Sheila**[44] [760] 7-10-13 97 ... JoshWall(10) 49
(Trevor Wall) *bhd: last and rdn bef 6th: wl bhd whn mstke 3 out: t.o* **66/1**

P605 **9** *75* **Gilded Youth**[44] [761] 6-10-11 85 ... ColinBolger —
(Simon Lewis) *mstkes: in tch tl 6th: sn fdd: hurdle bhd fr 2 out* **66/1**

-5PP **10** *1/2* **Shanahan (IRE)**[40] [799] 9-11-11 99 ... (p) JodieMogford —
(Nikki Evans) *led tl j.v.slowly 1st: prom tl rdn after 6th: nt run on: hurdle bhd two out* **50/1**

0-51 **P** **Deep Reflection**[9] [1062] 10-12-0 107 7ex ... (v) JimmyDerham(5) 91
(Martin Keighley) *cl up: rdn to chal 3 out: wknd bef next: mod 5th whn p.u last* **4/1**[3]

4m 49.2s (-8.20) **Going Correction** -0.275s/f (Good)

WFA 4 from 5yo+ 16lb **11** Ran SP% **115.0**

Speed ratings (Par 105): **105,103,97,95,93 84,83,82,52,52** —

toteswingers:1&2:£2.60, 1&3:£3.40, 2&3:£2.80 CSF £20.65 CT £59.67 TOTE £6.20: £1.90, £1.40, £1.50; EX 19.50.

Owner Be Rude Not To Syndicate **Bred** William J White **Trained** Sheriff Hutton, N Yorks

FOCUS

A modest handicap hurdle that was run at a fair pace. A personal best from the winner.

NOTEBOOK

Miss Molly Be Rude(IRE) was racing from 6lb out of the handicap, but had shown a little more last time over this trip after returning from an long absence and put in a game display to record her first success. She had the race in safe keeping before two out, even after getting the last wrong she always held enough in hand to comfortably hold the runner up. The change to more forceful tactics worked well here and it will remain to be seen if connections can keep her sound as she has had more than her fair share of problems. (op 7-1)

Grand Art(IRE) was well-backed off an attractive mark when subsequently disqualified from finishing first at Perth on debut for TimVaughan, also suffering a further blow when receiving a 13lb hike for his efforts (winner well-held by Deep Reflection next time). He moved through to chase the winner from two out, but was always fighting a losing battle and his current mark might well be his undoing. He would be of interest again when connections switch his attention to chasing. (op 7-2)
Mujamead got his head back in front over 2m at Uttoxeter and if reproducing that effort looked sure to figure under his penalty back up in distance. He ran respectably but had no more to offer after holding every chance after three out, ultimately soundly beaten. (tchd 4-1)
Nobby Kivambo(IRE) was a beaten favourite when finishing last of four in Jersey last time, but did himself no favours here by hanging and making some clumsy mistakes. (op 17-2)
Panzer(GER) was returning here off a low mark after a lengthy 973 days on the sidelines, although the stable are very capable of readying one. He ran in snatches and was under pressure in the rear from three out, never getting competitive. (tchd 14-1)
Deep Reflection, a six-time winner, stepped up on previous efforts this season when landing similar affair at Worcester recently for which he now had to defy a 7lb penalty. He had his chance but was well held when pulled up before the last. Official explanation: jockey said gelding lost its action between last two; vet said gelding lost its off-hind shoe and suffered an over-reach (op 10-3)

1138 CHESHIRE LIFE NOVICES' HURDLE (9 hdls) 2m 1f
3:45 (3:45) (Class 4) 4-Y-0+ **£3,415** (£1,002; £501; £250)

Form RPR
2162 **1** **Saltagioo (ITY)**[12] 1026 6-11-5 117................................(t) WarrenMarston 120+
(Milton Harris) *t.k.h chsng clr ldng pair and wl ahd of rest: clsd bef 5th: led appr 3 out: hit next: sn rdn: 2 l clr last: kpt on* **7/2**[3]
1354 **2** *2 ¾* **Murcar**[19] 958 5-10-12 114................................ OliverDayman(7) 116
(Alison Thorpe) *t.k.h pressing ldr: wandered 4th and rdn: led 5th: hdd bef 3 out: rdn and ev ch next: no imp after: wavering lft and nt looking easy* **5/2**[2]
P0- **3** *14* **Art Deco (IRE)**[232] 2797 7-10-12 0................................(t) JimmyMcCarthy 97
(Charles Egerton) *mstkes and nvr nr ldrs: plugged on into 15 l 3rd bef 2 out: no imp after: mstke last* **28/1**
2- **4** *19* **Arcadia Boy (IRE)**[380] 955 7-10-9 103................................ AdrianLane(3) 79
(Donald McCain) *16 l 4th at 4th: nvr anywhere nr ldrs* **20/1**
2-63 **5** *9* **Dormouse**[10] 1046 5-10-12 0................................ TomScudamore 71
(Anabel L M King) *wl off pce in midfield: struggling fr 4th* **16/1**
3F1 **6** *13* **Totoman**[10] 1046 5-11-5 113................................(t) RichardJohnson 69
(Tim Vaughan) *led at brisk pce: hdd 5th: wkng whn mstke 3 out: fdd v bdly bef next: t.o* **6/4**[1]
7 *51* **Jockies Burn (IRE)** 4-10-10 0................................ APMcCoy 11
(Jonjo O'Neill) *v novicey jumping in last pair and immediately lost tch: bdly t.o fr 4th* **9/1**
00-0 **P** **Pergamon (IRE)**[10] 1046 4-10-10 0................................(t) LiamTreadwell —
(Claire Dyson) *20 l 4th at 3rd: nvr on terms: t.o 6th: p.u 2 out* **200/1**
U0 **R** **Star Role**[23] 935 6-10-12 0................................ BrianHughes —
(Richard Ford) *mstkes and immediately lost tch: bdly t.o 4th: j. 3 out and then swvd violently rt and dumped the rdr* **100/1**

4m 4.20s (-6.70) **Going Correction** -0.275s/f (Good)
WFA 4 from 5yo+ 15lb **9** Ran SP% **116.4**
Speed ratings (Par 105): **104,102,96,87,82 76,52,—,—**
toteswingers:1&2:£1.30, 1&3:£40.60, 2&3:£39.40 CSF £12.90 TOTE £4.40: £1.40, £1.30, £4.30; EX 9.00.
Owner J Zambuni **Bred** Az Ag Francesca **Trained** Herridge, Wiltshire

FOCUS
An ordinary novices' hurdle that was run at a good clip. Improvement from the winner with the second to his mark.

NOTEBOOK
Saltagioo(ITY) benefited from sitting behind the leading pair, although did take a good grip himself off the pace. He had the race run to suit, but can continue make his presence felt in handicaps and has been well handled by current connections. (op 10-3)
Murcar had probably shown better form in his placed efforts since getting off the mark in May but had struggled with his penalty. To his credit after doing his share of making this a true test he stuck to his task well and deserves a lot of credit. He looks to be better suited to handicaps where he can remain competitive off his mark of 115. (op 11-4)
Art Deco(IRE) has some classy Flat form to his name, notably winning the Dee Stakes, but has failed to show anywhere near that in this sphere. Although a little more encouraging this time, he remains a risky proposition until he shows anything better, and in the jumping department. (op 25-1)
Arcadia Boy(IRE) was runner-up in a seller last July when well fancied and last seen. He had it all to do coming from well off the pace that day which was also the case here. (op 18-1)
Dormouse was comfortably put in his place by Totoman last time and remained up against it at the revised weights, but was well beaten here. He could be of interest when tackling handicaps for which he is now qualified.
Totoman looked to have a good opportunity to follow up recent confidence-boosting C&D success but he was to keen with the runner up and ultimately paid the price. He is better than this. Official explanation: jockey said gelding stopped quickly (op 7-4 tchd 9-4 in a place)

1139 DEBENHAMS OF WREXHAM H'CAP CHASE (12 fncs) 2m 1f 110y
4:20 (4:21) (Class 4) (0-115,114) 4-Y-0+ **£5,204** (£1,528; £764; £381)

Form RPR
2B32 **1** **Kirkhammerton (IRE)**[24] 919 8-10-10 **101**................................ DannyCook(3) 110+
(Barry Leavy) *wl in tch: rdn fr bef 8th: cl 4th and effrt 2 out: led bef last: clr flat: kpt on wl* **5/1**[2]
F-05 **2** *6* **Silmi**[58] 581 6-11-12 **114**................................ PaulMoloney 118+
(Sophie Leech) *last whn mstke 6th: lost tch and j. slowly 9th: 12 l 6th and rallying 2 out: stl 4th at last: rdn and fin stoutly but nvr nr wnr* **6/1**[3]
0-30 **3** *4 ½* **Shinnecock Bay**[79] 272 6-11-2 **104**................................(b) LeightonAspell 105
(Oliver Sherwood) *racd keenly and cl up: chal after 3 out: rdn and ev ch next: plodded on: mstke last but lft 2nd tl cl home* **16/1**
5211 **4** *2 ½* **Folie A Deux (IRE)**[8] 1070 8-11-7 **109** 7ex................................(t) JoeTizzard 111+
(Colin Tizzard) *led: hrd pressed fr 9th: rdn 2 out: hdd bef last where blnd and fdd qckly* **13/8**[1]
3-23 **5** *8* **Blossom King (FR)**[26] 889 6-11-8 **110**................................ SamThomas 101
(Tom George) *pressed ldr: upsides fr 9th: nt fluent next: 3rd ev ch 2 out: sn floundering and fin v weakly* **8/1**
U/FU **6** *¾* **Morning Sunshine (IRE)**[16] 991 7-10-6 **94**................................ GrahamLee 84
(Donald McCain) *plld hrd in rr: rdn after mstke whn 5th 3 out: sn struggling* **5/1**[2]
41P6 **7** *24* **Arumun (IRE)**[24] 919 9-10-8 **96**................................(p) TomScudamore 70
(Michael Scudamore) *t.k.h early: chsd ldrs: rdn 8th: mstke 9th and lost tch: remote after 3 out* **16/1**

4m 9.80s (-12.30) **Going Correction** -0.55s/f (Firm) **7** Ran SP% **108.6**
Speed ratings (Par 105): **105,102,100,99,95 95,84**
toteswingers:1&2:£2.70, 1&3:£16.80, 2&3:£14.80 CSF £30.73 TOTE £6.00: £2.30, £2.60; EX 32.30.
Owner Valentino Racing **Bred** Barronstown Stud And Orpendale **Trained** Forsbrook, Staffs

FOCUS
A modest handicap chase that was run at fair pace. The winner improved to the best of his hurdles form.

NOTEBOOK
Kirkhammerton(IRE) was entitled to finish much closer to the Folie A Deux on revised terms after chasing him home last time, but went one better and recorded his first success since 2008. He holds few secrets from the handicapper and usually runs his race but his turn does not come that often. (op 4-1)
Silmi had failed to shine in four previous outings this year, but had strong claims on his fourth to Rivaliste at Newbury in November last year off 120 and had come in for some early support. A tumbling mark of 114 also looked attractive, but although coming through very late to snatch second he was never really flowing. This was a step back in the right direction with his confidence steadily being restored after a heavy fall back in February. (op 13-2)
Shinnecock Bay had shown glimmers of ability over hurdles but often failed to deliver. He looked the type to better over fences and duly did so. He should be capable of finding a little opportunity in this sphere. (tchd 20-1)
Folie A Deux(IRE) was off a career high mark here and trying to complete his hat-trick. He was not allowed an uncontested lead this time and was third and looked held when blundering at the last. (op 7-4 tchd 11-8)
Blossom King(FR) has been placed in all five starts over fences until now and looks to be struggling off his mark. (op 7-1)

1140 GOLDFORD STUD MARES' NOVICES' HURDLE (11 hdls) 2m 4f
4:55 (4:55) (Class 4) 4-Y-0+ **£3,252** (£955; £477; £238)

Form RPR
1 **Redunderthebed (IRE)** 5-10-10 0................................ RhysFlint 96+
(Philip Hobbs) *j. slowly 2nd: midfield: pushed along 8th: effrt after next: wnt 2nd bef 2 out: rdn to ld and mstke last: asserted gamely flat* **8/1**
-322 **2** *2* **Our Guardian Angel (IRE)**[15] 999 6-10-10 102.......(t) RichardJohnson 94
(Tim Vaughan) *trckd ldrs on ins: nt fluent 5th: mstke 3 out: cl 5th whn ct on heels after 3 out: disp 5 l 3rd and outpcd next: r.o wl bef last: wnt 2nd cl home: rather unlucky* **8/11**[1]
31- **3** *½* **Martha Elizabeth (IRE)**[17] 975 5-11-3 101................................(b) BrianHughes 101
(Liam Lennon, Ire) *cl up: wnt 2nd at 7th: led 3 out: drvn next: reluctant and hdd whn mstke last: nt run on: lost 2nd cl home* **13/2**[3]
4 **4** *1 ¼* **Kavegirl**[12] 1028 7-10-10 0................................ DavidEngland 91
(John Panvert) *hld up in rr: effrt to trck ldrs and nt fluent 3 out: plugged on same pce fr next* **9/2**[2]
OP/1 **5** *5* **Niamh's Way (IRE)**[19] 967 9-11-0 94................................ JamesO'Farrell(3) 94
(Liam Lennon, Ire) *nt fluent in rr: mod 8th after 3 out: nvr on terms* **8/1**
0-64 **6** *4* **Singapore Harbour (IRE)**[16] 989 4-10-7 0................................ LeightonAspell 80
(Oliver Sherwood) *cl up: effrt on outside and mstke 3 out: dropped out tamely bef next* **16/1**
0/6- **7** *3 ¼* **Star Of Raven**[118] 13-10-10 0................................ BarryKeniry 79
(Joss Saville) *mstke 1st: pressed ldr tl 7th: sn lost pl* **66/1**
00-0 **8** *98* **Fenella Mere**[16] 989 7-10-3 0................................ PeterHatton(7) —
(Patricia Rigby) *j. modly in last: rdn and mstke 7th: sn t.o: stl bumbling to last after wnr had fin* **150/1**
5 **P** **Winter Holly**[35] 841 4-10-7 0................................ RobertWalford —
(Tim Walford) *plld hrd: led and mod pce and sn 8 l clr: pressed fr 7th: hdd 3 out: sn eased: t.o and p.u 2 out* **16/1**

4m 56.4s (-1.00) **Going Correction** -0.275s/f (Good)
WFA 4 from 5yo+ 16lb **9** Ran SP% **125.6**
Speed ratings (Par 105): **91,90,90,89,87 85,84,45,—**
toteswingers:1&2:£2.50, 1&3:£3.70, 2&3:£2.20 CSF £16.10 TOTE £7.60: £2.50, £1.10, £1.90; EX 22.10.
Owner Frank Jarvey **Bred** Fintan Kealy **Trained** Withycombe, Somerset

FOCUS
A moderate and slowly run contest. It has been given a token rating through the second and third.

NOTEBOOK
Redunderthebed(IRE) is a half-sister to the useful hurdler Dromlease Express and hails from a top yard. Despite being the apparent second string, though, she ran out a deserved winner. This was a modest introduction and she did it all well, apart from clattering the last, and looks a very likeable type. In very capable hands, she can only build on this. (op 6-1)
Our Guardian Angel(IRE) has been knocking on the door in recent outings over hurdles, after some respectable efforts in bumpers, and again posted a satisfactory run in defeat. She got a little worked up beforehand but the drop back in trip was probably against her as she was doing all her best work in the latter stages. She should go one better when stepped back up in distance.
Martha Elizabeth(IRE) got off the mark over hurdles in April despite not looking the most straightforward but has been well held since. She had a good chance at this level against her own sex and looked to have snatched it before being run out of it after the last. A respectable effort with the blinkers back on. (op 15-2)
Kavegirl had twice been placed in points and made a satisfactory start to her hurdling career when fading back into fourth over 2m6f. The drop back in trip appeared to aid her cause and ran to a similar level again. She could find a small opportunity. (op 14-1)
Winter Holly Official explanation: jockey said filly ran too free early

1141 R W HOUGH MEMORIAL CONDITIONAL JOCKEYS' H'CAP HURDLE (12 hdls) 3m
5:30 (5:30) (Class 5) (0-95,95) 4-Y-0+ **£2,569** (£748; £374)

Form RPR
-0F4 **1** **Albert Park (IRE)**[58] 587 9-9-11 69 oh7................(p) AnthonyFreeman(3) 73+
(John Upson) *cajoled along 2nd: bhd: rdn in 3rd and prog 8th: lft in ld 3 out: sn 5 l clr: idled bdly and hdd bef next: rallied under heavy press to ld again nr fin: slowing again fnl strides* **14/1**
/14- **2** *hd* **Spare Change (IRE)**[47] 741 9-11-3 94................................(b) DJBates(8) 98
(P J Rothwell, Ire) *led tl after 6th: lft 2nd sn after 3 out: led whn rival idled bef next and 2 l clr: r.o under heavy press: hdd cl home* **8/1**
500- **3** *2 ¼* **Ridley Taylor**[116] 5048 7-10-9 83................................ MattCrawley(5) 85
(Sean Regan) *towards rr: nt fluent 3rd: rdn and hdwy 8th: chsd ldng pair bef 2 out: nt qckn bef last* **66/1**
P-3P **4** *4* **Prince Noora (IRE)**[30] 868 9-11-10 93................................(tp) RichardKilloran 91
(Tim Vaughan) *t.k.h: chsd ldrs: 5th and rdn after 3 out: one pce and edging lft fr next* **16/1**
4P-3 **5** *4* **Bring It On Home**[79] 273 6-11-8 91................................ JohnnyFarrelly 86
(Sophie Leech) *towards rr: nt fluent 3rd: struggling whn blnd 8th: mstke 3 out: 12 l 6th whn mstke next: no ch* **10/1**
P/53 **6** *19* **Mulligan's Pride (IRE)**[15] 999 9-10-5 82................................(v) JamesSmith(8) 59
(James Moffatt) *bhd: last and struggling bef 7th* **6/1**[3]
6/1U **7** *9* **Lords Bridge**[1] 1126 9-10-5 77 7ex................................ DeanColeman(3) 66+
(Tim Vaughan) *plld hrd: prom: led after 6th: slt advantage and stl gng wl whn sprawled bdly on landing 3 out and lost all ch: eased next* **5/6**[1]
00/6 **8** *2* **Stowford Press (IRE)**[55] 630 7-10-13 85................................ KyleJames(3) 53
(Nikki Evans) *slowly away: mstkes in rr: reminders 6th: no ch fr 8th: remote 3 out* **33/1**

5-2P **9** *27* **Smart John**[40] 794 10-11-12 **95**........ PeterToole 38
(Simon Lewis) *pressed ldr tl 6th: labouring in rr and drvn 8th: bdly t.o* **20/1**

-004 **P** **Strumble Head (IRE)**[10] 1048 5-10-9 **81**........(b[1]) DonalDevereux[(3)] —
(Peter Bowen) *t.k.h: nt fluent 2nd: prom: 2nd after 6th where reminders: lost action and p.u after next* **5/1**[2]

5m 51.2s (0.20) **Going Correction** -0.275s/f (Good) **10** Ran SP% **127.5**
Speed ratings (Par 103): **88,87,87,85,84 78,75,74,65,—**
toteswingers:1&2:£17.10, 1&3:£42.80, 2&3:£38.50 CSF £127.79 CT £7093.15 TOTE £21.80: £3.60, £2.40, £8.00; EX 183.50 Place 6 £40.51; Place 5 £19.24.
Owner The Peter Partnership **Bred** Frances Buttimer **Trained** Maidford, Northants
■ Stewards' Enquiry : D J Bates seven-day ban: used whip with excessive frequency (Aug 14,15, 17-21)
Anthony Freeman 25-day ban: used whip with excessive frequency without giving gelding time to respond, without regard to stride pattern, and down shoulder in the forehand position causing wealing (Aug 14-15,17-22,24-28, Aug 30-Sep1,4-8,19,21-23)

FOCUS
A weak conditional jockeys' handicap. The firsft two are rated close to their marks.

NOTEBOOK
Albert Park(IRE) had been runner-up off a lowly mark in September and had not been disgraced latest, but was running from out of the handicap here. He took over when the favourite dropped away but looked to have surrendered the lead going to the last before getting back up in the closing stages. This was his first success at the 16th attempt so he does not hold the most convincing of profiles to reproduce the performance. (op 16-1 tchd 20-1)
Spare Change(IRE) looked to have snatched it at the last only to be run out of it as the post neared. This was a better effort than of late after being largely campaigned over fences. (op 9-1)
Ridley Taylor has done very little to recommend himself since finishing second in a bumper. He plugged on from three out and momentarily looked as though he would figure.
Prince Noora(IRE) posted a better effort returning to hurdles but could only stay on at the same pace. (op 25-1)
Lords Bridge looked to have a good opportunity to gain immediate compensation for his early demise over fences the previous day. A winner at Perth earlier in the week, connections were hopeful that the exertions of the last few days had not taken their toll. They had appeared not to as he was travelling well enough before slipping badly on landing when holding a narrow advantage and immediately dropping away three out. Hopefully he will come out of this in good order. Official explanation: jockey said gelding ran too free (op 8-11 tchd 10-11)
Strumble Head(IRE) unfortunately pulled up with something amiss. Official explanation: jockey said gelding lost its action but returned sound (op 15-2)
T/Plt: £21.30 to a £1 stake. Pool:£42,814.89 - 1,466.81 winning tickets T/Qpdt: £7.00 to a £1 stake. Pool:£3,766.22 - 395.80 winning tickets IM

1142 - 1145a (Foreign Racing) - See Raceform Interactive

1142 GALWAY (R-H)
Saturday, July 31

OFFICIAL GOING: Good to firm

1146a KERRYMAID FESTIVAL INH FLAT RACE 2m
5:30 (5:30) 4-7-Y-O **£7,632** (£1,769; £774; £442)

RPR

1 **Masdar (IRE)** 4-11-8 .... MrRPMcNamara 109+
(D K Weld, Ire) *hld up towards rr: hdwy in 10th 4f out: 7th 3f out: rdn in 5th 2f out: styd on to chal ent st: led last 150yds: kpt on wl* **6/1**[3]

2 *2* **Somethingdifferent (IRE)**[16] 1009 4-11-3 .... MrMFahey[(5)] 106
(Mrs John Harrington, Ire) *mid-div: hdwy in 8th 4f out: 2nd 3f out: rdn to ld ent st: strly pressed: hdd last 150yds: no ex* **8/1**

3 *2 ½* **Mister Music Man (IRE)** 6-11-9 .... MrRO'Sullivan[(5)] 109
(Patrick J Flynn, Ire) *chsd ldrs: 8th 1/2-way: hdwy into 4th 3f out: rdn 2f out: 3rd 1f out: no ex fnl f and kpt on same pce* **5/1**[2]

4 *10* **Matilda Highway (IRE)**[43] 782 4-10-10 .... MrJoshHalley[(7)] 90
(John Halley, Ire) *chsd ldrs: 5th 1/2-way: hdwy to ld under 4f out: rdn and hdd ent st: no ex in 4th 1f out: kpt on one pce* **14/1**

5 *2 ½* **Maddoxtown (IRE)**[16] 1009 4-11-8 .... MsKWalsh 91
(Robert Alan Hennessy, Ire) *chsd ldrs: 5th 1/2-way: rdn in 6th 2f out: no ex in 5th 1f out: kpt on same pce* **7/1**

6 *10* **Anderson McAuley (IRE)**[25] 928 6-12-0 .... MrPWMullins 87
(W P Mullins, Ire) *led: hdd under 4f out: rdn in 3rd 2f out: no ex in 6th ent st: kpt on one pce* **7/2**[1]

7 *2* **Bailey Street (IRE)** 4-11-1 .... MrWASlattery[(7)] 79
(Andrew Slattery, Ire) *chsd ldrs: 9th 1/2-way: rdn in 11th 3f out: kpt on one pce: mod 7th over 1f out: kpt on one pce* **40/1**

8 *shd* **Macklycuddy (USA)** 4-11-1 .... MrSDolan[(7)] 78
(Patrick G Kelly, Ire) *hld up towards rr: rdn in 12th and no imp 3f out: kpt on one pce fr bef st* **33/1**

9 *1 ¼* **Copsehill Girl (IRE)**[118] 5-11-9 .... MrDerekO'Connor 78
(Ian Williams) *hld up towards rr: rdn into 9th and no imp 3f out: kpt on one pce* **8/1**

10 *7* **Spirit Diamond (IRE)**[16] 1009 4-10-10 .... MrPBRoche[(7)] 65
(P A Fahy, Ire) *chsd ldrs: 4th 1/2-way: rdn in 5th and no ex 3f out: wknd over 2f out* **20/1**

11 *1* **Gurteen Lass (IRE)**[40] 819 4-11-0 .... MrRPQuinlan[(3)] 64
(Miss G Lee, Ire) *chsd ldrs: 3rd 1/2-way: rdn in 6th 3f out: sn no ex and wknd* **20/1**

12 *4* **Fiachrua Lad (IRE)**[615] 6-11-7 .... MrPAKing[(7)] 71
(Donal Hassett, Ire) *a towards rr* **50/1**

13 *20* **Just Sandy (IRE)**[22] 936 7-11-2 .... MrDJByrne[(7)] 46
(Denis P Quinn, Ire) *mid-div: 10th 1/2-way: wknd 5f out* **50/1**

14 *dist* **Moonslit (IRE)**[16] 1009 4-11-3 .... MrJTCarroll[(5)] —
(Miss G Lee, Ire) *chsd ldr: 2nd 1/2-way: rdn and wknd 3 1/2f out: completely t.o* **40/1**

U **Castletown Lass (IRE)**[11] 1056 5-11-2 .... MrTDGeoghegan[(7)] —
(J M Kiernan, Ire) *towards rr: stmbld and uns rdr 3f out* **40/1**

S **Kick Start** 5-11-9 .... MrMPFogarty[(5)] —
(V C Ward, Ire) *chsd ldrs: 6th 1/2-way: rdn in 9th 4f out: no ex whn clipped heels and slipped up 3 1/2f out* **7/1**

3m 36.4s (216.40)
WFA 4 from 5yo+ 2lb **16** Ran SP% **130.8**
CSF £53.16 TOTE £4.90: £2.10, £2.10, £2.30; DF 67.00.
Owner Glen Devlin **Bred** Shadwell Estate Company Limited **Trained** The Curragh, Co Kildare
■ Stewards' Enquiry : Mr R P Quinlan one-day ban: careless riding
Mr M P Fogarty one-day ban: careless riding (Aug 15)

FOCUS
The runner-up travelled well but was no match for the winner.

NOTEBOOK
Masdar(IRE), patiently ridden, made very good headway before the straight and sustained that momentum to lead a furlong out before holding off the determined challenge of the game runner-up. He looks a good horse who could easily revert back to the Flat and win a staying maiden. (op 11/2)
Somethingdifferent(IRE) was close enough to the pace most of the way and made what was a potent looking challenge before the straight. He kept going well but the momentum built up by what was probably a better horse was just too much for him. There's little doubt that he'll win a bumper.
Mister Music Man(IRE), a half-brother to Cloone River, came here with a reasonable reputation and ran a very good race. He made up his ground to be on the heels of the leaders turning into the straight and was close enough to have every chance, but was just a bit one-paced inside the last. It was a very fair effort and he looks good enough to win a bumper. (op 7/2)
Matilda Highway(IRE), a previous point-to-point winner, looks quite a nice horse and might benefit from having slightly more use made of him over this trip. He went for his race half a mile out only set it up for the speed horses behind, and they left him behind inside the last. (op 25/1)
Maddoxtown(IRE) ran an okay sort of race, chasing the leaders for most of it and keeping on for pressure in the straight without managing to improve his position. (op 7/1 tchd 6/1)
Anderson McAuley(IRE) raced keenly in front until weakening inside the final half mile. (op 7/2 tchd 3/1)
T/Jkpt: Not won. T/Plt: @717.50. Pool of @25,637.64 - 27 winning units. II

1017 MARKET RASEN (R-H)
Sunday, August 1

OFFICIAL GOING: Good (good to firm in places; chs 7.5 hdl 7.9)
Bends moved out 2-3 yards.
Wind: almost nil Weather: overcast, occasional showers

1147 JACK SOUTH MEMORIAL H'CAP HURDLE (8 hdls) 2m 1f
2:00 (2:01) (Class 4) (0-105,105) 4-Y-0+ **£2,740** (£798; £399)

Form RPR

425 **1** **General Smith**[63] 541 11-10-8 **94**........ MarkQuinlan[(7)] 99
(James Evans) *hld up in rr: stdy hdwy 3 out: styd on to ld run-in: drvn out* **12/1**

02 **2** *1 ¼* **Topenhall (IRE)**[11] 1062 9-11-10 **103**........(t) CharliePoste 108+
(Ben Case) *chsd ldrs: led appr 2 out: hit last: hdd run-in: no ex* **9/1**

-314 **3** *2 ¾* **Choctaw Nation**[28] 888 6-11-0 **98**........ JamesHalliday[(5)] 99
(Malcolm Jefferson) *chsd ldrs: kpt on same pce fr 2 out* **4/1**[1]

-214 **4** *2 ½* **Hoar Frost**[18] 984 5-11-7 **100**........ APMcCoy 99
(Jim Best) *chsd ldrs: pushed along 3rd: one pce fr 2 out* **9/2**[2]

0-10 **5** *2 ¼* **Phoenix Eye**[42] 798 9-10-9 **95**........ BrianToomey[(7)] 95+
(Michael Mullineaux) *hld up in rr: hdwy appr 2 out: styd on run-in* **20/1**

-5BP **6** *3* **Lady Wright (IRE)**[31] 871 7-10-12 **91**........ DenisO'Regan 86
(Michael Easterby) *mid-div: effrt appr 2 out: hit last: nvr trbld ldrs* **11/2**[3]

-115 **7** *shd* **Ardesia (IRE)**[50] 727 6-11-2 **95**........ BrianHughes 89
(Tina Jackson) *chsd ldrs: drvn 3 out: wknd appr last* **7/1**

-542 **8** *¾* **Broadway Allstar (IRE)**[28] 887 5-10-1 **87**........ KyleJames[(7)] 81
(Karen Tutty) *chsd ldrs: one pce fr 3 out* **8/1**

34-6 **9** *7* **Massams Lane**[33] 853 6-11-4 **100**........ SeanQuinlan[(3)] 87
(Carole Ikin) *chsd ldrs: reminders 3 out: sn wknd* **20/1**

205- **10** *shd* **Toss The Caber (IRE)**[335] 1356 8-11-4 **100**........ CampbellGillies[(3)] 87
(Stephen Clark) *in rr: nvr on terms* **40/1**

P-65 **11** *3 ¼* **Vogarth**[28] 886 6-9-7 **79**........ JoeCornwall[(7)] 63
(Michael Chapman) *in rr: hit 5th: sn bhd* **40/1**

055 **12** *2 ½* **Soggy Dollar**[18] 984 5-10-13 **95**........(tp) AlexMerriam[(3)] 77
(Neil King) *hld up in rr: hdwy 3 out: sn rdn and wknd* **22/1**

/033 **13** *hd* **Reel Missile**[9] 1085 11-10-12 **94**........(p) AdamPogson[(3)] 76
(Charles Pogson) *led: hdd appr 2 out: sn wknd: heavily eased run-in: fatally injured* **22/1**

16-0 **14** *15* **Baguenaud (FR)**[26] 917 7-11-11 **104**........(t) GrahamLee 72
(Stephen Clark) *a in rr: bhd whn hit 5th* **50/1**

- **P** **Baltrap (FR)**[672] 5-11-5 **105**........ MissCareyWilliamson[(7)] —
(Clarissa Caroe) *unruly in paddock: prom: lost pl after 3rd: sn bhd: t.o 3 out: p.u bef next* **100/1**

4m 9.30s (2.60) **Going Correction** +0.225s/f (Yiel) **15** Ran SP% **120.9**
Speed ratings (Par 105): **102,101,100,98,97 96,96,96,92,92 91,90,89,82,—**
Tote Swingers: 1&2 £38.70, 1&3 £12.20, 2&3 £6.80 CSF £104.29 CT £518.47 TOTE £15.70: £4.30, £4.20, £1.80; EX 155.80.
Owner Mrs J Evans **Bred** D And Mrs Holmes **Trained** Broadwas, Worcs

FOCUS
The breeze, such as it was, was against the runners up the straight and the going remained good, good to firm in places. However, both Graham Lee and Tony McCoy described the going as good after riding in this. This didn't look much better than a seller, and the early gallop set by the ill-fated Reel Missile was far from quick.

NOTEBOOK
General Smith took a good grip in the early stages (as he can do) but manoeuvred his way stylishly through the field during the latter stages before joining the runner-up at the final hurdle. He kept on strongly from that point and secured his first victory since May 2007.
Topenhall(IRE) ◆, down 3f in distance, was never far away going strongly and hit the front heading to two out. A mistake there didn't help but he kept going and was still at least upsides the winner jumping the final flight. He seems to be in good heart. (op 8-1)
Choctaw Nation was always likely to be suited by a big field. He travelled nicely in a good position but did not run on as strongly as those in front of him. Ideally, he would have liked an even stronger pace to chase. (op 6-1)
Hoar Frost, beaten in a seller last time, needed all of her rider's strength to get her placed, as she was being niggled along with almost a circuit to go and was under strong pressure quite a way out. (op 7-2)
Phoenix Eye ◆ travelled strongly towards the rear and was going at least as well as the winner when squeezed up a little leaving the back straight. He then got short of space again down the home straight.
Lady Wright(IRE) ◆ showed enough to suggest an ordinary contest can come her way. (op 9-1)
Ardesia(IRE), given a break since his last outing, ran like a horse in the grip of the handicapper - he did win off 105, but that was in a juvenile seller. (op 6-1 tchd 11-2)
Baltrap(FR), having her first outing since September 2008, showed a bit of form in France but was said to be on her toes when throwing her rider off when she was getting on. Carey Williamson did manage to get on again but her mount got very worked up. (op 80-1)

1148 WATERLOO HOUSING GROUP NOVICES' HURDLE (8 hdls) 2m 1f
2:30 (2:30) (Class 4) 4-Y-0+ **£2,602** (£764; £382; £190)

Form RPR

-121 **1** **Sir Frank (IRE)**[15] 1021 5-11-12 115........ BrianHughes 117+
(Alan Swinbank) *w ldr: led after 3 out: styd on strly run-in: readily* **11/4**[2]

-452 **2** *2 ¾* **Society Venue**[15] 1021 5-10-12 106........ TomScudamore 101
(Michael Scudamore) *trckd ldrs: mstke 5th: chsd wnr appr 2 out: kpt on same pce run-in* **3/1**[3]

22-3 **3** *8* **Classic Contours (USA)**[11] 548 4-10-11 112 DougieCostello 92
(John Quinn) *t.k.h: set stdy pce: hdd after 3 out: one pce appr next* **5/2**[1]
34 **4** *3/4* **Rebel Hunter (IRE)**[10] 1065 5-10-12 103 KeithMercer 92
(Steve Gollings) *chsd ldrs: nt fluent: rdr lost irons and lost pl 3rd: regained them after next: chsng ldrs 5th: outpcd appr 2 out: kpt on run-in* **5/1**
346/ **5** *hd* **Isitcozimcool (IRE)**[157] 5223 5-10-12 0 DenisO'Regan 93
(Don Cantillon) *stdd s: hld up in rr: hdwy 3 out: nt fluent last 2: one pce* **16/1**
5 **6** *3 1/4* **Play To Win (IRE)**[15] 1021 4-10-8 0 TommyPhelan(3) 88
(Paul Midgley) *t.k.h: trckd ldrs: wl outpcd 5th: kpt on fr 2 out* **66/1**
6 **7** *20* **Loyal Knight (IRE)**[15] 1021 5-10-12 0 AndrewThornton 71
(Paul Midgley) *chsd ldrs: hit 5th: lost pl appr 2 out* **100/1**
8 *9* **Natures Way (IRE)** 4-10-11 0 APMcCoy 62
(Jonjo O'Neill) *in rr: pushed along and nt fluent 4th: bhd fr 3 out* **10/1**
00-0 **9** *shd* **Driving Seat**[77] 349 6-10-12 0 RodiGreene 63
(Michael Mullineaux) *stdd s: t.k.h in rr: bhd fr 4th* **100/1**

4m 18.2s (11.50) **Going Correction** +0.225s/f (Yiel)
WFA 4 from 5yo+ 13lb 9 Ran SP% **115.4**
Speed ratings (Par 105): **81,79,75,75,75 73,64,60,60**
Tote Swingers: 1&2 £1.20, 1&3 £2.30, 2&3 £1.80 CSF £11.80 TOTE £4.80: £1.10, £1.80, £1.30.

Owner Frank Hanson **Bred** Mrs G Galvin **Trained** Melsonby, N Yorks

FOCUS
A fair novices' hurdle.

NOTEBOOK
Sir Frank(IRE) raced prominently when the pace was virtually non-existent and then showed plenty of resolution to win under a double penalty. He can do no more than win and clearly has lots of ability, but once again the form could be suspect. (tchd 5-2)
Society Venue was narrowly edged out by Sir Frank over C&D last time but was 7lb better off with the him this time. He travelled strongly until smashing his way through the fifth, but even that error did not stop him looking a potential winner heading to two out. However, he didn't pick up for pressure and was readily held. (op 5-2)
Classic Contours(USA), who proved to be a right handful on the way to the start, helped to share the work out in front but didn't seem to be enjoying himself for some reason. He looked a beaten horse even before turning into the home straight. (op 3-1 tchd 10-3)
Rebel Hunter(IRE), taking a 5f drop in trip, effectively ended his winning chance when his jockey lost his equilibrium after the second hurdle (Keith Mercer was hanging around his mount's neck for a few strides before getting back in the saddle in time for the next hurdle, but still without both of his stirrups, which he regained well after it). He is obviously better than his final position suggests. (op 15-2)
Isitcozimcool(IRE) ◆, who won a couple of 1m all-weather handicaps after running in three bumpers, but had not been seen on a racecourse since February. In rear early, he went nicely for the majority of the contest and shaped with a lot of promise. (op 12-1 tchd 11-1)
Natures Way(IRE) looked an interesting prospect for respected connections but showed nothing on his debut. (op 11-1 tchd 9-1)

1149 GEORDIE LAD PADDY MCKENNA'S 80TH BIRTHDAY NOVICES' HURDLE (10 hdls) 2m 5f
3:05 (3:06) (Class 4) 4-Y-O+ **£2,602** (£764; £382; £190)

Form RPR
00/- **1** **Dowd's Destiny (IRE)**[899] 3903 7-10-12 0 BrianHarding 111+
(Nicky Richards) *hld up: hdwy 7th: wnt 2nd next: chal last: styd on strly to ld last 150yds* **10/1**[3]
1-32 **2** *2 1/4* **Cailin Na Ri (IRE)**[48] 744 7-10-12 115 DenisO'Regan 110+
(Martin Todhunter) *led: hit 7th: jnd last: hdd and no ex last 150yds* **1/3**[1]
3 *31* **Treason Trial**[11] 9-10-12 0 BarryKeniry 83
(Joss Saville) *reluctant to line-up; stdd s: hit 2nd: hdwy to trck ldrs next: wnt modest 3rd appr 2 out: one pce* **33/1**
0/35 **4** *7* **Devils And Dust (IRE)**[28] 887 9-10-5 73 (p) MissPhillipaTutty(7) 75
(Karen Tutty) *chsd ldrs: wl outpcd appr 2 out* **12/1**
55 **5** *1 1/2* **Cloudy Dawn**[18] 988 5-10-12 0 TjadeCollier 74
(Sue Smith) *chsd ldr: hit 7th: wl outpcd appr 2 out: hit last* **12/1**
-F60 **6** *1 1/2* **Morecambe Bay**[17] 999 5-10-9 0 TommyPhelan(3) 72
(David Thompson) *chsd ldrs: reminders 7th: wl outpcd appr 2 out* **100/1**
6/5- **7** *43* **Triton**[441] 353 7-10-12 95 GrahamLee 34
(Michael Easterby) *towards rr: sme hdwy 7th: wknd next: bhd whn hit 2 out: sn t.o* **6/1**[2]
00/- **P** **Topping The Bill**[589] 2881 7-10-5 0 MrRichardCollinson(7) —
(Michael Wigham) *j. poorly: detached in rr whn j. violently lft 3rd: t.o 7th: p.u bef 2 out* **40/1**
0-0 **R** **Moonset**[11] 1063 6-10-5 0 (v1) MattCrawley(7) —
(Sean Regan) *towards rr whn ref and uns rdr 1st* **66/1**

5m 19.3s (10.50) **Going Correction** +0.225s/f (Yiel) 9 Ran SP% **121.6**
Speed ratings (Par 105): **89,88,76,73,73 72,56,—,—**
Tote Swingers: 1&2 £3.40, 1&3 £45.90, 2&3 £8.90 CSF £15.22 TOTE £18.60: £2.70, £1.10, £7.70.
Owner Craig Bennett **Bred** Joseph Smiddy **Trained** Greystoke, Cumbria

FOCUS
An ordinary event.

NOTEBOOK
Dowd's Destiny(IRE) ◆, absent since February 2008, but entered recently before being declared a non-runner due to quick ground, was weak in the market but looks to have a serious engine, as he closed down the favourite easily before going on to win. One would imagine his future will be ground dependant, so he ought to be seen a few times during the winter if staying sound. (op 7-1)
Cailin Na Ri(IRE) set off in front and was unlucky to bump into a potentially decent sort returning from a long layoff. (op 2-5 tchd 4-9 in places)
Treason Trial, a modest stayer on the Flat, looked slightly reluctant to go out on the course at one stage. However, he shaped nicely once going and should build on this first start over hurdles.
Devils And Dust(IRE) sat close to the pace but was a bit too easily brushed aside by the third turning in before staying on.
Triton, having his first start for this stable, was relatively short in the betting almost by default, but he never got involved after being held up on his first outing since May 2009. (op 13-2)
Topping The Bill hardly looked the most straightforward of characters on his return to the course after a lengthy break. (op 50-1)
Moonset, fitted with a visor after looking an awkward ride last time, travelled sweetly until catching a glimpse of the first flight. He decided jumping it wasn't for him and slammed on the brakes. (op 50-1)

1150 LADIES NIGHT IS NEXT 14TH AUGUST H'CAP HURDLE (10 hdls) 2m 3f
3:40 (3:40) (Class 3) (0-130,128) 4-Y-O+ **£5,204** (£1,528; £764; £381)

Form RPR
11R2 **1** **Battle Group**[27] 914 5-11-4 120 TomScudamore 122+
(David Pipe) *hld up in tch: hrd drvn and hdwy to chse ldrs 3 out: jnd ldr next: led last: in command whn swvd lft 75yds out* **13/2**
-435 **2** *2 3/4* **Mohanad (IRE)**[15] 1017 4-11-5 123 JamieGoldstein 121
(Sheena West) *trckd ldrs: hit 3 out: led appr next: hdd last: hld whn edgd rt last 75yds* **4/1**[2]
0-25 **3** *11* **El Presidente (IRE)**[17] 1000 5-10-5 110 (b) AlexMerriam(3) 101
(Neil King) *chsd ldr: led and qcknd 6th: hdd appr 2 out: wknd between last 2* **25/1**
2311 **4** *1 3/4* **Space Telescope (IRE)**[25] 933 4-10-11 115 (b) APMcCoy 104
(Jonjo O'Neill) *chsd ldrs: cl 3rd whn hit 2 out: sn wknd* **7/2**[1]
1432 **5** *hd* **Cubism**[14] 1033 4-10-1 105 (t) CharliePoste 92
(Milton Harris) *chsd ldrs: 5th and wl outpcd whn mstke 2 out: hit last: kpt on* **9/2**[3]
/0-0 **6** *3 1/2* **Ursis (FR)**[15] 1019 9-11-12 128 KeithMercer 113
(Steve Gollings) *led: hdd 6th: sn rdn: lost pl appr 3 out* **14/1**
PP22 **7** *12* **Edgefour (IRE)**[10] 1067 6-9-13 106 (v) GilesHawkins(5) 86+
(Ben Case) *in rr: hdwy to chse ldrs 3 out: wknd and wl btn whn hit next: eased run-in* **6/1**
40-0 **R** **Tilt**[15] 1019 8-11-6 122 GrahamLee —
(Brian Ellison) *wnt lft and j. slowly 1st: rn out next* **6/1**

4m 40.3s (0.90) **Going Correction** +0.225s/f (Yiel)
WFA 4 from 5yo+ 13lb 8 Ran SP% **112.8**
Speed ratings (Par 107): **107,105,101,100,100 98,93,—**
Tote Swingers: 1&2 £2.50, 1&3 £27.20, 2&3 £11.90 CSF £32.21 CT £604.37 TOTE £5.80: £1.40, £1.30, £5.70.

Owner Jolly Boys Outing **Bred** Juddmonte Farms Ltd **Trained** Nicholashayne, Devon

FOCUS
This looked a competitive contest and it produced a good finish.\n

NOTEBOOK
Battle Group disgraced himself two starts previously, but has shown no such moody tendencies since. He fought on well once getting to the front after being held up, and the step up in trip proved to be no problem. (op 6-1 tchd 7-1, 15-2 and 8-1 in a place)
Mohanad(IRE), not disgraced in the valuable Summer Hurdle over this course last time, once again ran in his usual honest manner. He is the marker to the level of the form, as he seemed to run up to his recent best. (tchd 7-2)
El Presidente(IRE), back over hurdles, travelled nicely for a long way but seemed a little fortunate to get third, as Space Telescope hit the second-last hurdle quite hard when plugging on. (op 20-1)
Space Telescope(IRE), who had hit form since blinkers were applied, but was 10lb higher here than his last run, was plugging on when hitting the second-last hurdle quite hard. Tony McCoy's mount had proved to be hard work from some way out, and looked an unlikely winner when making that mistake, but probably would have been third without that error. (op 3-1)
Cubism, down just over 3f in trip, lost his place when the pace lifted but kept going under pressure to be staying on down the home straight. (op 6-1)
Ursis(FR), back down to his last winning handicap mark, completely lost his place down the back straight when El Presidente assumed command in front.
Edgefour(IRE), beaten by a horse last time that has gone on to win again, was 3lb higher for this and weakened quickly after making a brief effort from the rear. (op 8-1)
Tilt didn't look too enthusiastic at the first hurdle and then took evasive action at the next.

1151 WATCH RACING UK ON SKY CHANNEL 432 H'CAP CHASE (14 fncs) 2m 4f
4:15 (4:15) (Class 3) (0-135,130) 4-Y-O+ **£6,505** (£1,910; £955; £477)

Form RPR
4-34 **1** **Rockiteer (IRE)**[21] 957 7-10-6 110 (p) AndrewTinkler 119
(Henry Daly) *chsd ldrs: led 4 out: jnd next: styd on wl run-in* **14/1**
2/11 **2** *1 1/2* **Yellow Flag**[35] 848 7-11-1 119 APMcCoy 128+
(Jonjo O'Neill) *trckd ldrs: chal 3 out: upsides whn hit last: styd on last 100yds* **7/4**[1]
46-2 **3** *2* **Nudge And Nurdle (IRE)**[12] 1044 9-10-13 122 SamTwiston-Davies(5) 128
(Nigel Twiston-Davies) *in tch: hdwy to chse ldrs 10th: styd on same pce fr 2 out* **4/1**[2]
P23- **4** *4* **Frankie Anson (IRE)**[130] 4815 6-10-11 115 BrianHughes 117
(Alan Swinbank) *in rr: hdwy 9th: chsng ldrs whn hmpd appr 3 out: styd on same pce fr 2 out* **6/1**[3]
F-43 **5** *hd* **Stagecoach Amber (USA)**[31] 874 8-10-13 117 KeithMercer 119
(Sue Smith) *chsd ldrs: drvn along 8th: one pce fr 3 out* **8/1**
4-P3 **6** *15* **Silver Adonis (IRE)**[37] 839 9-11-7 125 (b) DenisO'Regan 117
(Dr Richard Newland) *chsd ldrs: j. slowly and lost pl 8th: bhd fr 4 out* **8/1**
P0-P **7** *19* **Seymour Weld**[15] 1020 10-11-9 130 AdamPogson(3) 102
(Charles Pogson) *led to 4 out: sn wknd: bhd whn eased bef 2 out* **18/1**
1153 **8** *26* **Pilgrims Lane (IRE)**[33] 852 6-11-3 124 PeterToole(3) 72
(Milton Harris) *in tch: stmbld bnd after 7th: lost pl 9th: sn bhd: t.o 3 out* **10/1**

4m 47.5s (-18.20) **Going Correction** -0.725s/f (Firm) 8 Ran SP% **113.9**
Speed ratings (Par 107): **107,106,105,104,103 97,90,79**
Tote Swingers: 1&2 £6.00, 1&3 £3.00, 2&3 £6.80 CSF £40.51 CT £120.78 TOTE £19.00: £4.90, £2.10, £1.10; EX 39.60.

Owner Michael O'Flynn & John Nesbitt **Bred** R C A Latta **Trained** Stanton Lacy, Shropshire

FOCUS
With a few proven front-runners in the race, this was always likely to be run at a good gallop.

NOTEBOOK
Rockiteer(IRE), wearing cheekpieces for the first time, was one of a few who could race prominently, but while he was never far away, he sat in a settled third. Leading into the final bend, he determinedly held off all challengers over the final two fences after appearing to be headed by the runner-up briefly approaching two out. The headgear possibly made all the difference and he can win again. (op 10-1)
Yellow Flag has been in terrific form since being sent over fences, and has risen from an opening mark of 81 when first winning over them to 119 today. Running over almost 3f further than he'd won over in the past, he ranged up to lead briefly after three out but tended to idle once there, allowing the winner an opportunity to get past him again. His head was a shade high under pressure and, ideally, one would imagine he'd be best placed in front as late as possible. (op 15-8 tchd 6-4 and 2-1 in places)
Nudge And Nurdle(IRE) is a shade high in the handicap on his win over fences (he won a novice event when rated 132) but battled on bravely after the final fence to get third. (op 5-1)
Frankie Anson(IRE) ◆, absent since March, was relatively lightly raced in comparison to his rivals and ran a race full of promise. He made good ground from the rear and was getting into the contest on the final bend when getting hampered. He then held a couple of positions down the home straight before keeping on. (op 11-2)

Stagecoach Amber(USA), 6lb higher than his highest winning mark over fences, came under strong pressure leaving the back straight, so did well to keep going to finish a fairly close-up fifth. (op 7-1)

1152 X FACTOR FINALISTS HERE 21ST AUGUST H'CAP CHASE (17 fncs) 3m 1f

4:50 (4:51) (Class 4) (0-105,103) 4-Y-O+ £2,927 (£859; £429; £214)

Form				RPR
5002	1		**Rokinhorsescience (FR)**[15] 1022 6-11-3 94 ....(bt) APMcCoy (Jonjo O'Neill) *trckd ldrs: wnt 2nd 11th: led 4 out: wnt clr appr 2 out: eased clsng stages* 3/1[1]	109+
5620	2	8	**Nesnaas (USA)**[15] 1023 9-11-3 94 ....(t) GrahamLee (Mark Rimell) *in rr: wnt modest 4th 13th: hit next: wnt 15 l 2nd 2 out* 12/1	96
02	3	13	**Free Speech**[9] 1081 7-10-10 87 ....(t) JackDoyle (Sarah Humphrey) *in tch: chsng ldrs whn stmbld landing 12th: wnt 2nd after 4 out: wknd 2 out* 9/2[2]	81
0P42	4	23	**Keltic Lord**[11] 1061 14-11-1 92 .... NickScholfield (Peter Hiatt) *in tch: chsng ldrs 12th: outpcd next: poor 4th whn blnd 2 out* 17/2	71
501U	5	22	**Sam Cruise**[11] 1061 9-10-13 90 ....(t) AidanColeman (Steve Gollings) *reluctant to go to s: led: hdd after 7th: lft in ld 9th: hdd 4 out: wknd rapidly: t.o 2 out* 7/1[3]	39
-330	6	31	**Wizards Dust**[32] 867 8-11-7 101 ....(b) AdrianLane(3) (Donald McCain) *chsd ldrs: reminders 7th and 11th: wknd 12th: t.o 3 out* 11/1	22
4345	P		**Sycho Fred (IRE)**[25] 931 9-9-11 77 oh1 ....(b) CampbellGillies(3) (Mike Sowersby) *in rr: reminders 7th: outpcd 11th: in rr whn blnd and p.u next* 9/2[2]	—
U0-P	P		**Cadoulitique (FR)**[18] 985 7-11-0 91 .... BrianHughes (Tina Jackson) *in rr: bhd and reminders 5th: t.o 8th: p.u bef 11th* 50/1	—
4453	P		**Executive's Hall (IRE)**[31] 872 6-10-0 77 oh8 ....(p) KeithMercer (Andrew Crook) *chsd ldr: led after 7th: blnd bdly: sddle slipped and rdr lost irons 9th: p.u after next* 11/1	—
06-4	F		**Whimper (FR)**[12] 1047 5-11-7 103 .... SamTwiston-Davies(5) (Nigel Twiston-Davies) *hld up in rr: sme hdwy whn fell 8th* 16/1	—

6m 12.3s (-19.00) **Going Correction** -0.725s/f (Firm) **10** Ran SP% **116.6**

Speed ratings (Par 105): **101,98,94,86,79 69,—,—,—,—**

Tote Swingers: 1&2 £11.70, 1&3 £3.30, 2&3 £14.10 CSF £38.21 CT £161.59 TOTE £3.00: £1.10, £5.10, £2.40; EX 39.00.

Owner S Burke, M Burke & Miss H Burke **Bred** Marius Bertella & Michel Coencas **Trained** Cheltenham, Gloucs

FOCUS

A modest event.

NOTEBOOK

Rokinhorsescience(FR) ◆, with a tongue-tie added to the blinkers he has been wearing, looked legless in a woeful contest at this course last time (2m6f) but travelled extremely well in this, and duly bolted up once stretching away. He didn't beat much but this was a visually pleasing effort, and it seems highly likely that the tongue-tie had a positive effect. (op 11-4 tchd 5-2)

Nesnaas(USA), without blinkers this time, has been running over much shorter trips recently, and ran on past some weakening/disappointing sorts to claim second. It's debatable what he achieved in this.

Free Speech came with a promising effort before failing to get home. (op 11-2)

Keltic Lord never really got involved but stayed on. He made a bad error two out but it cost him nothing in terms of places. (op 9-1 tchd 10-1)

Sam Cruise, who was reluctant to go to the start, helped to set a good pace but was readily brushed aside soon after jumping the fourth-last. One would imagine, judged on this run, he would be as effective over half a mile shorter on a tight course.

Sycho Fred(IRE), wearing blinkers for the first time since May 2008, was starting to get behind when hitting the 12th really hard. Official explanation: jockey said gelding never travelled (op 6-1)

Executive's Hall(IRE) was close up when his jockey lost his stirrups in front of the stands' - his saddle was reported to have slipped. He was quickly pulled up. Official explanation: jockey said saddle slipped (op 6-1)

1153 TURFTV INTERMEDIATE OPEN NATIONAL HUNT FLAT RACE 2m 1f

5:20 (5:20) (Class 6) 4-6-Y-O £1,370 (£399; £199)

Form				RPR
0-	1		**Cheatingsideoftown (IRE)**[148] 4429 4-10-13 0 .... APMcCoy (Paul Webber) *chsd ldrs: led 6f out: 4 l clr 2f out: drvn out* 3/1[2]	104+
0-	2	8	**The Wayward Lord**[229] 2896 5-11-0 0 .... DenisO'Regan (Michael Easterby) *hld up in midfield: hdwy 7f out: sn pushed along: wnt 2nd over 3f out: kpt on: no imp* 11/4[1]	96+
6	3	8	**Alta Rock (IRE)**[50] 731 5-11-0 0 .... TjadeCollier (Sue Smith) *chsd ldrs: wnt modest 3rd over 3f out: one pce* 33/1	87
4-0	4	5	**Jingoism (USA)**[50] 732 4-10-13 0 .... LiamHeard (Brian Ellison) *trckd ldrs: modest 4th and drvn over 3f out: one pce* 9/1	81
4	5	1 1/2	**Bury The Hatchet (IRE)**[28] 892 4-10-13 0 .... BrianHughes (Alan Swinbank) *chsd ldrs: drvn 6f out: lost pl over 3f out* 11/2	79
	6	6	**Lamb's Cross** 4-10-8 0 .... MrBConnell(5) (Nigel Twiston-Davies) *led: hung lft thrght: hdd 6f out: lost pl 3f out: eased over 1f out* 7/2[3]	78+
	7	19	**Lola Jay** 4-9-13 0 .... KyleJames(7) (Malcolm Jefferson) *in rr: lost pl after 6f: t.o over 4f out* 7/1	47
0-	8	112	**Quilip (IRE)**[172] 3979 4-10-13 0 .... AndrewTinkler (Nigel Tinkler) *hld up in rr: hdwy after 6f: sn chsng ldrs: lost pl 6f out: bhd and eased over 3f out: sn t.o: virtually p.u* 50/1	—
	9	dist	**Now Then Sam** 4-10-13 0 .... KeithMercer (Sharon Watt) *in rr: drvn 7f out: sn bhd: t.o over 3f out: sn virtually p.u: eventually completed* 33/1	—
	P		**Treasure's Girl** 5-10-0 0 ....(b1) JoeCornwall(7) (Michael Chapman) *reluctant and sn detached in last: sn hopelessly t.o: p.u after 6f* 66/1	—

4m 9.00s (7.90) **Going Correction** +0.225s/f (Yiel)

WFA 4 from 5yo 1lb **10** Ran SP% **121.1**

Speed ratings: **90,86,82,80,79 76,67,—,—,—**

Tote Swingers: 1&2 £4.70, 1&3 £13.80, 2&3 £6.60 CSF £12.02 TOTE £5.40: £1.40, £1.40, £5.00; EX 18.50 Place 6: £26.30 Place 5: £9.10.

Owner R C Moody **Bred** Michael Doyle **Trained** Mollington, Oxon

FOCUS

Probably only an ordinary bumper, but the first two could be better than average.

NOTEBOOK

Cheatingsideoftown(IRE), beaten over 33 lengths on his first run in March, showed a little bit of ability on his debut, and more than confirmed that here under a positive ride. Well positioned, he eased to the front when his jockey wanted him to quicken and gained enough of an advantage at that point to readily hold off any challenge that might come from behind. (op 4-1 tchd 9-2)

The Wayward Lord, beaten over 79 lengths on debut at Catterick last December, was the subject of a morning gamble but had no chance of catching the winner once he had struck for home. A horse with plenty of size, he was well clear of the third, and will surely win something similar soon. (tchd 5-2)

Alta Rock(IRE) appeared to improve on what he had achieved on his debut in June despite being keen early, so is making progress in the right direction. (op 25-1)

Jingoism(USA) looked a threat heading to the final bend but soon came under pressure and made no more progress. (op 14-1 tchd 8-1)

Bury The Hatchet(IRE) was making a forward move when he seemed to be squeezed up a little by Lamb's Cross. He lost a couple of places at that point, and never got back into the firing line. (op 9-2)

Lamb's Cross ran green throughout, and dropped right away once joined and headed. It appeared on some occasions that the jockey's saddle may have slipped forward a bit, but that proved to not be the case. Official explanation: jockey said, regarding running and riding, that his orders were to sit handy and then make the best of his way home adding that the gelding hung badly left throughout (op 10-3 tchd 4-1)

Lola Jay attracted some market support but didn't do a lot in the race to justify it. (op 9-1 tchd 13-2)

Quilip(IRE) Official explanation: jockey said gelding had a breathing problem

Treasure's Girl wore blinkers on her debut, and she soon showed little interest after jumping off. Her jockey pulled her up when it was a totally lost cause. (op 50-1)

T/Plt: £21.50 to a £1 stake. Pool:£65,982.43 - 2,236.32 winning tickets T/Qpdt: £9.70 to a £1 stake. Pool:£4,865.34 - 370.50 winning tickets WG

1154 - 1157a (Foreign Racing) - See Raceform Interactive

1144 GALWAY (R-H)

Sunday, August 1

OFFICIAL GOING: Good to firm

1155a EASYFIX H'CAP HURDLE (11 hdls) 2m 2f

2:50 (2:50) (88-116,115) 4-Y-O+ £9,159 (£2,123; £929; £530)

			RPR
1		**Impersonator**[12] 1053 10-10-3 96 .... EMullins(3) (Anthony Mullins, Ire) *hld up towards rr: hdwy into 5th 3 out: impr to ld 2 out: chal last: rdn and kpt on wl run-in* 11/2[3]	119+
2	1 1/4	**Acclaimed (IRE)**[6] 1097 5-10-13 103 ....(b1) JLCullen (John Joseph Hanlon, Ire) *hld up towards rr: hdwy in 7th 3 out: 4th 2 out: rdn into 2nd ent st: chal last: no ex run-in and kpt on same pce* 9/1	125
3	2	**Quai Du Roi (IRE)**[2] 1142 8-10-11 101 .... PTownend (T G McCourt, Ire) *mid-div: 8th 1/2-way: hdwy into 4th 2 out: 3rd bef 2 out: rdn in 5th 2 out: 3rd ent st: no ex last: kpt on same pce run-in* 5/1[2]	121
4	9	**Jack Cool (IRE)**[17] 1062 4-10-2 97 .... NPMadden (C Byrnes, Ire) *chsd ldrs early: 7th 1/2-way: rdn in 6th 2 out: no ex in 5th ent st: mod 4th last: kpt on one pce* 9/2[1]	103
5	4	**Ever Dreaming (USA)**[12] 1052 5-9-11 92 .... PFMangan(5) (J Morrison, Ire) *chsd ldrs: 4th 1/2-way: rdn and dropped towards rr 3 out: no imp in mod 6th ent st: kpt on one pce* 10/1	101
6	8	**Muzak (IRE)**[12] 1055 7-10-5 95 ....(p) TJDoyle (John Monroe, Ire) *sn chsd ldrs: 2nd 1/2-way: impr to ld 3 out: sn strly pressed: rdn and hdd 2 out: no ex in 4th ent st: kpt on one pce* 14/1	94
7	2 1/2	**Agglestone Rock**[99] 5398 5-11-7 111 .... AndrewJMcNamara (Philip Kirby) *chsd ldrs: 3rd 1/2-way: 6th 3 out: rdn in 8th bef 2 out: no ex and kpt on one pce* 5/1[2]	108
8	20	**Hepahepa Naeney (IRE)**[26] 923 6-10-9 102 .... IJMcCarthy(3) (D M Fogarty, Ire) *mid-div: 6th 1/2-way: hdwy into 3rd 4 out: impr to chal after 3 out: rdn in 3rd 2 out: no ex and wknd* 12/1	79
9	dist	**Millrock Lady (IRE)**[16] 1011 5-10-8 98 .... PCarberry (Gordon Elliott, Ire) *chsd ldrs: 5th 1/2-way: dropped towards rr 4 out: rdn and wknd next: t.o* 9/2[1]	—
10	1 3/4	**Fearless Warrior**[44] 783 5-10-8 103 .... EJO'Connell(5) (John Joseph Hanlon, Ire) *led: hdd 3 out: rdn and wknd bef next: t.o* 16/1	—

4m 9.50s (-6.40)

WFA 4 from 5yo+ 13lb **10** Ran SP% **124.4**

CSF £57.58 CT £271.74 TOTE £4.60: £1.60, £3.70, £2.00; DF 48.10.

Owner Nurney Racing Syndicate **Bred** The Earl Cadogan **Trained** Gowran, Co Kilkenny

FOCUS

No fewer than eight non-runners. The progressive winner has been rated to a personal best in line with his Flat form. The third and fourth set the standard.

NOTEBOOK

Impersonator completed a hat-trick following victories at Tipperary and Ballinrobe last month. He had gone up 12lb for those two wins but appeared to win quite comfortably here. Held up, he made headway three out and led, travelling well, two out. Pressed going to the last, he was well on top at the finish. (op 5/1)

Acclaimed(IRE), well beaten over 2m here on his handicap debut six days previously having finished in the frame on all three of his attempts in maiden hurdles, had first-time blinkers on here and produced a much better effort. Held up towards the back of the field, he began to make headway three out and went second on the climb after two out. He looked a threat to the winner nearing the last but found little enough in the closing stages. Official explanation: jockey said saddle slipped (op 10/1)

Quai Du Roi(IRE) hasn't won for just over two years but he had put together a few creditable efforts leading up to this and was sixth behind Kalellshan over the course and trip on Friday night. He got a run through on the inside to go third on the climb after two out and kept on without threatening the first two. (op 7/1)

Jack Cool(IRE), unplaced at Ballinrobe since winning off a 7lb lower mark than this on soft ground at last month's Killarney festival, stayed on to go fourth nearing the final hurdle but was never close enough to mount a serious challenge.

Ever Dreaming(USA), up 3lb since finishing in front of Jack Cool when third at Ballinrobe, lost her place three out before plugging on from two out without making any impression. (op 8/1)

Agglestone Rock, reverting from fences on his first start since the Punchestown festival in April, proved disappointing and was done with before two out. (op 4/1)

Hepahepa Naeney(IRE) Official explanation: trainer said mare scoped badly post race

Millrock Lady(IRE), dropping in trip for her first handicap following her win in a 2m6f maiden at Kilbeggan, dropped away after four out and was soon out of contention, finishing tailed off. Official explanation: jockey said mare made a bad mistake at the hurdle past the stands (op 5/1)

1024 NEWTON ABBOT (L-H)

Monday, August 2

OFFICIAL GOING: Good (good to firm in places; watered; 7.9)

Wind: mild breeze Weather: sunny

1158 NEWTONABBOTRACING.COM NOVICES' HURDLE (8 hdls) 2m 3f
2:30 (2:30) (Class 4) 4-Y-0+ £3,382 (£993; £496; £248)

Form RPR
03 1 **Safe Catch (IRE)**34 854 8-10-12 0 JackDoyle 103
(Martin Hill) *led tl 3rd: in tch: outpcd appr 3 out: styd on appr 2 out: led bef last: rdn out* **9/1**
4510 2 3 **Sadler's Star (GER)**22 962 7-11-12 109 (p) DenisO'Regan 115
(Michael Blake) *mid-div: hdwy after 5th: ev ch 2 out: sn rdn: styd on same pce* **11/2**
63 3 shd **Doubletoilntrouble (IRE)**15 1029 4-10-10 0 RhysFlint 98
(Keith Goldsworthy) *trckd ldr: led 3rd: rdn whn narrowly hdd after 3 out: remained w ev ch next: styd on same pce* **9/2**3
0413 4 2 1/4 **Wilbury Star (IRE)**28 914 4-11-3 111 (p) AndrewTinkler 103
(Nicky Henderson) *trckd ldrs: jnd ldr 5th: led after 3 out: sn rdn: hdd sn after next: styd on same pce* **2/1**1
5P-1 5 2 1/2 **Opening Meet**28 908 6-11-0 111 MrRMahon(5) 103
(Paul Nicholls) *in tch: tk clsr order after 5th: rdn after 3 out: cl 5th 2 out: styng on at same pce whn mstke last* **3/1**2
1366 6 13 **Kings Riches (IRE)**4 1124 5-10-5 0 MichaelByrne(7) 84
(Peter Bowen) *a towards rr* **16/1**
00- 7 1 1/4 **Catholic Hill (USA)**36 2563 5-10-9 0 TommyPhelan(3) 83
(Mark Gillard) *a towards rr* **100/1**
0/65 8 hd **Southway Star**15 1030 5-9-12 0 MattGriffiths(7) 76
(Kevin Bishop) *mid-div: reminders after 5th: wknd 3 out* **40/1**
55 9 nk **Limbunya (IRE)**15 1029 5-10-0 0 DavidBass(5) 75
(Ron Hodges) *mid-div: rdn after 3 out: wknd bef next* **50/1**
-0UP 10 22 **The Wee Midget**15 1028 5-10-12 0 NickScholfield 63
(Arthur Whiting) *t.k.h: trckd ldrs: slow 2nd: rdn after 5th: sn wknd: t.o* **100/1**
-004 11 1/2 **Kiristani**12 1063 5-10-0 0 IanPopham(5) 55
(Caroline Keevil) *trckd ldrs tl wknd appr 6th: t.o* **100/1**
P **Fleetwood Daughter**828 8-10-2 0 LeeStephens(3) —
(Dai Burchell) *nvr fluent: a towards rr: lost tch after 5th: p.u after 3 out* **150/1**

4m 27.6s (-6.30) **Going Correction** -0.45s/f (Good)
WFA 4 from 5yo+ 13lb 12 Ran SP% **115.8**
Speed ratings (Par 105): **95,93,93,92,91 86,85,85,85,76 76,—**
toteswingers:1&2:£32.50, 1&3:£14.00, 2&3:£6.70 CSF £56.26 TOTE £11.60: £3.10, £2.30, £1.40; EX 64.00.
Owner Eddie Rice **Bred** James Flood Jnr **Trained** Littlehempston, Devon

FOCUS
A very ordinary novice hurdle, run at an average gallop. The first five all held a chance of sorts in the home straight. The time was relatively slow and the form is suspect.

NOTEBOOK
Safe Catch(IRE) came home a ready winner. Martin Hill's 8-y-o didn't jump well when running on late over fences on his second outing under rules last time and this drop back in trip seemed sure to be against him. He also went without the cheekpieces and things didn't look good as he got left behind on the back straight when the tempo got serious. However, the further he went the better he was and he stayed on strongly to lead with a big jump at the last. There's no doubt he has improved for joining this yard and should relish getting back over further, but he failed to score in ten outings between the flags and the fact he won here sums up the strength of the race. (op 12-1)
Sadler's Star(GER) rates the benchmark. He travelled nicely into contention and held every chance, but ultimately his big weight told. (op 4-1)
Doubletoilntrouble(IRE), making his hurdling debut over a longer trip, attracted support. He ran a solid enough race from the front, but getting so warm beforehand cannot have helped his cause. (op 15-2)
Wilbury Star(IRE) looked by far the most likely winner turning into the home straight, but his rider was sending out distress signals before the last and he clearly failed to stay the longer trip sufficiently. He is one to be interested in again when getting back over his right trip. (op 9-4)
Opening Meet lacked the pace to land a telling blow, but was game under pressure and probably ran close to the form of his C&D success last month. (op 5-2 tchd 10-3)

1159 TEIGNMOUTH CONDITIONAL JOCKEYS' H'CAP CHASE (20 fncs) 3m 2f 110y
3:00 (3:00) (Class 5) (0-90,90) 4-Y-0+ £2,877 (£838; £419)

Form RPR
4315 1 **Justabout**19 987 7-11-9 87 (t) SamTwiston-Davies 96
(Colin Tizzard) *trckd ldrs: rdn after 16th: chsd ldr 3 out: led sn after last: styd on wl: rdn out* **8/1**
P344 2 3 1/4 **Lord Lescribaa (FR)**12 1061 7-10-10 77 (tp) RhysFlint(3) 85+
(Philip Hobbs) *disp ld: rdn into clr advantage after 4 out: veered rt sn after last and hdd: drifted rt: no ex* **11/2**2
-4B0 3 hd **Le Forezien (FR)**12 1057 11-11-3 81 IanPopham 87
(Carroll Gray) *hld up: hdwy fr 15th: rdn to chse ldrs after 4 out: styd on fr 2 out: jst failed to snatch 2nd* **7/1**
2635 4 7 **Von Galen (IRE)**15 1027 9-11-7 85 (p) SamJones 86
(Michael Scudamore) *disp ld tl rdn after 4 out: styd on same pce fr after next* **17/2**
4263 5 4 1/2 **Rudinero (IRE)**26 931 8-10-6 70 (tp) PeterToole 68
(Barry Brennan) *hld up towards rr of mid-div: in last pair whn hit 14th: rdn and hdwy 16th: styd on same pce fr 3 out* **9/2**1
440- 6 1 3/4 **Lough Rynn (IRE)**166 4102 12-10-11 75 (p) GilesHawkins 69
(Richard Lee) *hld up: hdwy after 13th: rdn to chse ldrs after 4 out: wknd 2 out* **14/1**
/12- 7 14 **Kavi (IRE)**295 1719 10-11-12 90 GerardTumelty 71
(Simon Earle) *hld up: hdwy after 13th: effrt after 15th: wknd after 4 out* **16/1**
1U44 8 19 **Overton Lad**26 931 9-11-3 81 (p) HarrySkelton 45
(Peter Pritchard) *trckd ldrs: reminders after 12th: rdn whn hit 14th: sn wknd* **6/1**3
-532 P **El Batal (IRE)**56 665 9-11-0 84 (p) AnthonyFreeman(6) —
(Sean Curran) *mid-div: rdn after 14th: wknd 16th: bhd whn p.u after 3 out* **7/1**
6P50 P **Dasher Reilly (USA)**10 1080 9-10-0 64 oh7.(bt) GemmaGracey-Davison —
(Aytach Sadik) *mid-div: mstke 11th (water) and lost pl: rdn whn hit 14th: wknd next: t.o whn p.u after 3 out* **33/1**
P3/P P **Hazelbury**28 913 9-10-0 64 oh6 CharlieHuxley —
(Nigel Hawke) *a towards rr: nudged along fr 10th: wknd 15th: p.u bef 4 out* **33/1**

6m 35.3s (-9.30) **Going Correction** -0.20s/f (Good) 11 Ran SP% **112.9**
Speed ratings (Par 103): **105,104,103,101,100 100,95,90,—,— —**
toteswingers:1&2:£10.10, 1&3:£17.00, 2&3:£2.80 CSF £50.53 CT £321.46 TOTE £8.00: £3.10, £1.90, £2.80; EX 44.40.
Owner Brocade Racing **Bred** H T Cole **Trained** Milborne Port, Dorset

FOCUS
Despite there being just a routine gallop in this weak marathon handicap few got into it from off the pace. The first three came clear and the form is rated through the winner.

NOTEBOOK
Justabout got on top after the last fence and resumed winning ways with a game display. He has won two of his last three outings and clearly stays all day, but he bombed out at Uttoxeter on his previous outing so consistency isn't his strong suit. Official explanation: trainer had no explanation regarding the apparent improvement in form
Lord Lescribaa(FR) looked as if he was about to break his duck for current connections, but he threw it away coming to the last by downing tools. He was even worse when badly hanging on the run-in, nearly taking the wrong course at one point, and is obviously a quirky customer. (tchd 6-1)
Le Forezien(FR) ran better on this return to chasing and was doing all of his best work late on, so the veteran is worth persevering with over 3m-plus. (op 6-1)
Von Galen(IRE) posted a sound effort under a positive ride, but failed to see it out like the principles. (op 8-1 tchd 9-1)
Rudinero(IRE) met support, and not for the first time, but was beaten well before stamina became an issue and is one to swerve. (op 11-2)

1160 WELCOME BACK SEAN DOONER NOVICES' H'CAP HURDLE (8 hdls) 2m 1f
3:30 (3:30) (Class 3) (0-120,124) 4-Y-O+ £5,703 (£1,684; £842; £421; £210)

Form RPR
1341 1 **Dereks (IRE)**22 953 8-11-4 110 PaulMoloney 114+
(Sophie Leech) *mde all: kpt on wl fr 2 out: readily* **6/1**3
1621 2 5 **Saltagioo (ITY)**3 1138 6-11-13 124 7ex (t) JimmyDerham(5) 124
(Milton Harris) *racd keenly: cl up: wnt 3rd after 5th: rdn to chse wnr bef 2 out: kpt on but readily hld* **13/2**
01-2 3 6 **Marc Aurele (IRE)**55 675 5-11-2 113 (t) MrRMahon(5) 109
(Paul Nicholls) *trckd ldrs: rdn after 5th: styd on same pce fr after next: regained 3rd run-in* **9/2**2
2P-4 4 1/2 **Bedarra Boy**19 983 4-10-5 98 DarylJacob 91
(David Arbuthnot) *trckd ldrs: rdn to chse wnr after 3 out tl next: kpt on same pce* **8/1**
3233 5 4 1/2 **Decision**29 886 4-10-3 101 (t) DavidBass(5) 90
(Lawney Hill) *hld up but cl enough: rdn after 5th: nvr gng pce to get on terms:* **6/1**3
64-1 6 4 1/2 **Rio Gael (IRE)**27 917 4-11-5 115 (p) DonalDevereux(3) 103+
(Peter Bowen) *v awkward 1st: cl up: rdn after 5th: c bk on bit briefly after 3 out: wknd bef next* **7/2**1
600- 7 4 **Kensington Oval**186 3694 5-11-4 110 APMcCoy 92
(Jonjo O'Neill) *racd wd: trckd ldrs: outpcd whn wnt lft 3 out* **18/1**
6-11 P **Dreamwalk (IRE)**12 1058 4-11-12 119 HaddenFrost —
(Roger Curtis) *cl up: rdn after 3 out: cl 6th whn stmbld on bnd bef 2 out: immediately p.u: lame* **9/2**2

3m 59.4s (-6.30) **Going Correction** -0.45s/f (Good)
WFA 4 from 5yo+ 13lb 8 Ran SP% **116.9**
Speed ratings (Par 107): **96,93,90,90,88 86,84,—**
toteswingers:1&2:£7.70, 1&3:£5.60, 2&3:£7.00 CSF £45.14 CT £193.42 TOTE £8.60: £2.10, £2.90, £1.60; EX 46.70.
Owner J Cocks & C J Leech **Bred** D Wall **Trained** Kingsbridge, Devon

FOCUS
A competitive novice handicap with four last-time-out winners lining up. It was run at a steady gallop early on and the field raced in a tight group, with most taking a pull. The winner is rated to the level of his recent win over further.

NOTEBOOK
Dereks(IRE) made all on this first start for a new stable and landed his third win from five outings since resuming this term. He only won a seller last time, but is better than that class on his day and being allowed to dictate again over this sharper test was much to his liking. It's most probable a likely rise would find him out again, so perhaps he would be better off looking for something under a penalty. (op 8-1)
Saltagioo(ITY) was penalised for his game win at Bangor last week and racing under a big weight on this return to handicap company. He probably didn't enjoy the way the race unfolded, pulling under early restraint, so clearly remains in good heart and helps to set the level. (op 6-1 tchd 7-1)
Marc Aurele(IRE) returning from a 55-day break, is probably better off when able to dominate his races and is entitled to come on a little for the run. The handicapper still probably has him about right, though (tchd 5-1)
Bedarra Boy ◆ showed improved form on this handicap debut as a hurdler and would've enjoyed more of a test, so is clearly on a workable mark. (op 12-1)
Decision came under heavy pressure on the back straight and is proving hard to get right. However, his Flat form suggests he may enjoy racing on softer ground and he is one to bear in mind when the rains come. (op 8-1)
Rio Gael(IRE) hacked up in a seller on debut for Peter Bowen and was well backed for this switch to handicap company. He looked a threat turning for home, but ultimately looked to pay for his reluctance to settle through the early parts. (op 10-3 tchd 3-1)
Kensington Oval has been massively disappointing since going over hurdles and there wasn't much encouragement to be taken from this comeback effort. He is another that probably needs easier ground and a longer trip, though, so he is not one to fully write off just yet. (op 14-1 tchd 20-1)
Dreamwalk(IRE) was under the pump prior to sadly going wrong on the home bend. Official explanation: vet said gelding had been struck into (tchd 4-1)

1161 ROYAL NATIONAL MISSION TO DEEP SEA FISHERMAN H'CAP CHASE (13 fncs) 2m 110y
4:00 (4:00) (Class 4) (0-115,110) 4-Y-0+ £3,252 (£955; £477; £238)

Form RPR
5035 1 **Indiana Gold (FR)**13 1047 6-10-1 92 (p) OliverDayman(7) 106
(Alison Thorpe) *hld up in cl 5th: rdn and stdy prog fr 4 out: led last: kpt on: rdn out* **5/1**3
6032 2 4 **Captain Marlon (IRE)**6 1106 9-10-1 90 (t) SamTwiston-Davies(5) 101
(Colin Tizzard) *trckd ldrs: rdn whn short of room sn after 4 out: nt fluent 3 out (water): styd on same pce fr next: lft cl 2nd last but hld* **7/4**1
0P-5 3 1 3/4 **Blast The Past**16 1023 8-11-6 104 ChristianWilliams 114
(Dai Burchell) *led tl 9th: rdn after 4 out: ev ch after 3 out: styd on same pce fr next: lft cl 3rd last* **8/1**
P-30 4 22 **O'Toole (IRE)**36 846 11-11-12 110 TomO'Brien 101
(Caroline Keevil) *tracled ldrs fr 2nd: rdn after 8th: wknd 4 out* **10/1**

1240 **5** *25* **Stumped**[22] 958 7-11-4 **102**....(t) APMcCoy 84
(Milton Harris) *nvr really travelling or particularly fluent: a last but cl enough: wknd 4 out* **10/3**[2]

U21P **F** **Bushwacker (IRE)**[55] 681 6-11-3 **106**....(t) JimmyDerham(5) 119
(Seamus Mullins) *prom fr 2nd: led 9th: j. sltly rt fr next: nt fluent 3 out (water): sn rdn: narrowly hdd whn fell last* **13/2**

4m 0.60s (-5.90) **Going Correction** -0.20s/f (Good) **6** Ran SP% **109.6**
Speed ratings (Par 105): **105,103,102,91,80** —
toteswingers:1&2:£3.10, 1&3:£2.40, 2&3:£4.00 CSF £14.13 TOTE £8.90: £5.00, £1.10; EX 12.80.
Owner A T Powell **Bred** Mlle Laure Godet **Trained** Bronwydd Arms, Carmarthens

FOCUS
A moderate handicap chase, run at a sound pace and the form is straightforward enough, although it could be rated up to 3lb higher.

NOTEBOOK
Indiana Gold(FR) bounced back to his best on this return to suitably quicker ground. He was given a patient ride, but still had to master Bushwacker before that one fell at the last. He would've probably won even if that one had stayed on his feet, but obviously he rates a bit flattered by his winning margin. (op 6-1)
Captain Marlon(IRE), just held at Worcester six days earlier, was very well backed off the same mark here. Not that surprisingly he lacked the tactical pace required when things got really serious, though, and looks to be crying out for a return to further. (op 5-2)
Blast The Past, a big market drifter, was ridden more aggressively on this second outing for her current connections and ran more encouragingly. She remains on a losing run and her last win came off a 5lb higher mark. (op 9-2)
O'Toole(IRE) was beaten a long way out and has it to prove at present. (op 15-2 tchd 7-1)
Stumped jumped too deliberately to get involved. (op 3-1 tchd 11-4)
Bushwacker(IRE), pulled up last time out, was still on the front end prior to his rider standing up in the saddle and going easy on him coming to the last. It may have been he was coming to the end of his tether, but that action did appear to contribute to his departure. (op 8-1)

1162 NEWTON ABBOT RACECOURSE H'CAP HURDLE (8 hdls) 2m 3f
4:30 (4:30) (Class 4) (0-110,105) 4-Y-0+ **£3,382** (£993; £496; £248)

Form RPR

P344 **1** **Rock Me (IRE)**[22] 962 5-10-13 **97**....(tp) DavidBass(5) 103
(Lawney Hill) *slowly away: hdwy into mid-div 3rd: rdn after 5th: clsd on ldrs after 3 out: led last: r.o strly to assert run-in: drvn out* **7/2**[2]

43-3 **2** *1 3/4* **Olivino (GER)**[10] 595 9-11-5 **105**.... MissIsabelTompsett(7) 109
(Bernard Llewellyn) *hld up: hdwy after 6th: led appr 2 out: sn rdn: hdd last: no ex* **13/2**

/2-5 **3** *5* **Party Palace**[18] 771 6-11-9 **102**.... RodiGreene 102
(Stuart Howe) *chsd ldrs: rdn along fr after 5th: styd on fr 3 out but nvr gng pce to chal* **14/1**

2631 **4** *8* **Frosted Grape (IRE)**[19] 989 4-11-7 **102**....(b) TomScudamore 92
(David Pipe) *slowly away: sn pushed along to sit promly: led 3rd: rdn and hdd after 3 out: wknd next* **5/1**[3]

0-65 **5** *15* **Vacario (GER)**[14] 478 6-11-9 **105**....(t) TommyPhelan(3) 84
(Mark Gillard) *sn pushed along: a towards rr* **40/1**

-410 **6** *2* **Vintage Fabric (USA)**[22] 962 8-11-8 **101**....(t) DavidDennis 78
(Nigel Hawke) *led tl 3rd: chsd ldrs: rdn after 6th: wknd after 3 out* **12/1**

0306 **7** *dist* **Sea Cliff (IRE)**[15] 1033 6-11-4 **100**.... RichieMcLernon(3) —
(Jonjo O'Neill) *hld up in tch: effrt after 3 out: sn wknd: eased whn btn* **25/1**

F-P0 **P** **Mouseen (IRE)**[10] 1084 7-11-3 **103**....(p) PeterHatton(7) —
(Lisa Day) *prom fr 3rd tl wknd qckly bef 6th: p.u after 3 out* **40/1**

-316 **P** **Spate River**[22] 962 5-11-7 **100**.... APMcCoy —
(Jonjo O'Neill) *trckd ldrs: rdn to ld briefly sn after 3 out: cl 3rd whn smething amiss and eased sn after: p.u bef next* **9/4**[1]

P **Davis Street (IRE)**[160] 4223 6-11-12 **105**.... NoelFehily —
(Jonjo O'Neill) *hld up: reminders after 4th: rdn after next: sn btn: t.o whn p.u after 3 out* **17/2**

4m 22.9s (-11.00) **Going Correction** -0.45s/f (Good)
WFA 4 from 5yo+ 13lb **10** Ran SP% **116.6**
Speed ratings (Par 105): **105,104,102,98,92 91**,—,—,—,—
toteswingers:1&2:£6.20, 1&3:£6.20, 2&3:£12.60 CSF £26.31 CT £280.44 TOTE £4.10: £1.80, £2.10, £2.90; EX 17.50.
Owner For Fun Partnership **Bred** Quay Bloodstock **Trained** Aston Rowant, Oxon

FOCUS
A weak handicap hurdle, run at an average gallop and the first pair came clear. The first three all ran pretty much to their marks.

NOTEBOOK
Rock Me(IRE) landed good support and won his first race since scoring off a 3lb higher mark at Fontwell last October on his debut for connections. He took it up at the last and was nicely on top near the line, but did require all of his talented conditional rider's strength to prevail. (op 4-1 tchd 9-2)
Olivino(GER) got his usual patient ride on this return to hurdling and emerged with every chance, but got outstayed by the winner on the run-in. This was just his second outing as a hurdler this year and, while weighted around his best, may just find another race when reverting to 2m. (op 11-2 tchd 7-1)
Party Palace, another returning from the Flat, lacked the pace to land a telling blow and needs a stiffer test these days. (op 12-1)
Frosted Grape(IRE), 5lb higher, appeared to give her all under a positive ride yet was done with after the last and didn't look to get this longer trip. (op 9-2 tchd 4-1)
Spate River was given his chance, but was sharply pulled up rounding the home turn with something presumably amiss. McCoy later reported him to have lost his action. Official explanation: jockey said gelding lost its action (op 5-2 tchd 2-1and 3-1 in a place)

1163 EMMA NOVICES' CHASE (13 fncs) 2m 110y
5:00 (5:00) (Class 4) 4-Y-0+ **£4,228** (£1,241; £620; £310)

Form RPR

42P- **1** **Quell The Storm (FR)**[364] 1132 6-11-0 0....(t) HarrySkelton 121+
(Paul Nicholls) *j.w: racd keenly most of way: trckd ldrs: jnd ldr 4 out: led after next: kpt on wl: comf* **7/4**[1]

P6-1 **2** *12* **Novikov**[26] 934 6-11-3 0....(t) LeeStephens(3) 114
(David Evans) *disp ld tl outrt ldr 8th: pressed fr 4 out: rdn and hdd after 3 out: kpt on but hld fr next* **7/2**[2]

F-11 **3** *6* **What's Up Doc (IRE)**[10] 1082 9-11-6 0.... ChristianWilliams 110+
(Lawney Hill) *disp ld: wnt lft 1st: hdd 8th: hit next: rdn after 4 out: hld fr next* **7/4**[1]

P124 **4** *15* **My Pal Val (IRE)**[11] 1070 10-11-3 99....(tp) DannyCook(3) 104+
(John Panvert) *trckd ldrs: rdn after 4 out: nt pce to chal: wknd after 2 out: virtually p.u run-in* **7/1**[3]

4m 2.00s (-4.50) **Going Correction** -0.20s/f (Good) **4** Ran SP% **107.4**
Speed ratings (Par 105): **102,96,93,86**
CSF £7.74 TOTE £2.70; EX 8.20.
Owner Sir Alex Ferguson & Ged Mason **Bred** Gilles Chaignon **Trained** Ditcheat, Somerset

FOCUS
A moderate novice chase and a clear-cut debut winner, who has been rated in line with his hurdles form and who could rate higher over fences.

NOTEBOOK
Quell The Storm(FR) ◆ was last seen pulling up over hurdles at this venue just over a year previously, when reportedly losing his action. He has always been regarded as a future chasing type and made a winning introduction to fences with a most decisive display. He was plenty keen enough early on and proved hard work for his rider, but all considered his jumping was particularly good for a debutant. He was well in command prior to badly idling and making a hash of the last, so providing such errant traits can be ironed out by his leading trainer than it's a good bet he will rate plenty higher in this sphere. His two wins have been at this venue, but he should be up to competing on the bigger tracks this season and it wouldn't be surprising to see him turn up for something at Cheltenham's October meeting. The only worry with him being the sort that only goes well when fresh, having won on his comeback last term. (op 2-1 tchd 9-4 and 5-2 in a place)
Novikov made a good fist of it under his penalty, but found the winner in a different league even allowing for the fact he was giving that rival weight. He sets the level. (op 3-1)
What's Up Doc(IRE) won really well at Southwell ten days earlier, but he didn't get so much the run of things here and his jumping wasn't as fluent. Looking at the way he folded from four out perhaps the run came a bit too soon. (op 6-4)
My Pal Val(IRE), rated 99, was never seriously involved and needs to revert to low-grade handicaps. Official explanation: vet said gelding lost a right-fore shoe (op 9-1 tchd 6-1)

1164 NEWTON ABBOT RACECOURSE H'CAP HURDLE (8 hdls) 2m 1f
5:30 (5:30) (Class 5) (0-95,95) 4-Y-0+ **£2,055** (£599; £299)

Form RPR

6P04 **1** **Nothing Is Forever (IRE)**[28] 914 6-11-7 **89**....(p) DarylJacob 93
(Liam Corcoran) *trckd ldrs: led 3 out: rdn whn jnd briefly 2 out: sn lft in command: kpt on wl: rdn out* **4/1**[2]

05-6 **2** *2 3/4* **Temple Place (IRE)**[65] 520 9-11-1 **83**.... DenisO'Regan 87+
(Alan Jones) *mid-div: smooth hdwy 3 out: travelling wl upsides wnr whn mstke and stmbld 2 out: nt rcvr and sn hld: mstke last* **16/1**

3-05 **3** *3 1/4* **Monsieur (FR)**[12] 1064 10-11-0 **82**.... HarrySkelton 81
(Carroll Gray) *hld up towards rr: hdwy fr 5th: rdn after 3 out: wnt 3rd bef last: styd on* **20/1**

/60- **4** *4 1/2* **Byblos**[24] 3808 5-11-10 **92**....(v) NoelFehily 88
(Warren Greatrex) *trckd ldrs: rdn after 3 out: nvr quite pce to chal: fdd appr last* **22/1**

U226 **5** *1* **Amazing Request**[19] 990 6-10-8 **83**....(p) MissIsabelTompsett(7) 77
(Bernard Llewellyn) *hld up towards rr: rdn and stdy prog fr after 3 out: styd on but nvr trbld ldrs* **7/2**[1]

-006 **6** *6* **Mix N Match**[36] 845 6-10-13 **88**.... AodhaganConlon(7) 76
(Gerald Ham) *mid-div: hdwy to chse ldrs 3 out: sn rdn: wknd after 2 out* **12/1**

0F0- **7** *8* **Cote D'Argent**[9] 5210 7-11-5 **87**....(t) AidanColeman 70
(Chris Down) *led 2nd tl 3 out: rdn appr 2 out: wknd bef last* **8/1**

-450 **8** *12* **Pegasus Lad (USA)**[11] 1066 4-11-1 **84**....(p) JackDoyle 53
(Linda Blackford) *a towards rr* **33/1**

0003 **9** *17* **Lean Burn (USA)**[11] 1066 4-10-0 **76**....(tp) AnthonyFreeman(7) 30
(John Panvert) *a towards rr: t.o* **5/1**[3]

53-0 **10** *20* **Am I Blue**[57] 646 4-11-12 **95**.... ChristianWilliams 31
(Mrs D Thomas) *a struggling in rr: t.o* **28/1**

00/0 **P** **Ful Of Grace (IRE)**[28] 912 6-10-8 **76**.... HaddenFrost —
(James Frost) *mid-div tl wknd 3 out: p.u bef next* **33/1**

66-5 **P** **Mangonel**[83] 263 6-10-11 **79**.... RodiGreene —
(Stuart Howe) *in tch: rdn appr 5th: wknd 3 out: bhd whn p.u bef 2 out* **14/1**

6/PP **P** **Soviet Cat (IRE)**[15] 1028 5-10-9 **80**.... PeterToole(3) —
(Miss C J Williams) *racd keenly: led tl 2nd: trckd ldrs tl wknd 5th: p.u bef 2 out* **50/1**

2000 **P** **Crimson Canyon (IRE)**[12] 1062 4-11-12 **95**....(t[1]) APMcCoy —
(Jonjo O'Neill) *hld up towards rr of midfield: rdn after 5th: wknd next: bhd whn p.u bef 2 out* **9/1**

3m 58.7s (-7.00) **Going Correction** -0.45s/f (Good) **14** Ran SP% **120.6**
Speed ratings (Par 103): **98,96,95,93,92 89,86,80,72,62** —,—,—,—
toteswingers:1&2:£9.20, 1&3:£16.50, 2&3:£14.70 CSF £58.61 CT £1163.50 TOTE £5.20: £1.90, £3.90, £6.00; EX 39.50 Place 6 £213.01; Place 5 £75.91.
Owner The Globe Partnership **Bred** Reg Griffin And Jim McGrath **Trained** Charlton Adam, Somerset

FOCUS
A wide-open handicap. The winner is rated in line with his best recent runs.

NOTEBOOK
Nothing Is Forever(IRE) was ridden with greater restraint this time and, taking it up off the home turn, battled on most gamely to end his losing run. This also represented a drop in class and he was well handicapped on his previous best efforts. He was a first winner this year for his stable. (op 5-1)
Temple Place(IRE), having his first outing for 65 days, made stylish headway to join the winner nearing the penultimate flight and looked to be going much the better of the pair. He hit it, however, and immediately came unstuck. It's not certain he would've prevailed even with a better jump, but it was still a lot more encouraging from this dangerously well handicapped horse and he was a clear second-best. (op 8-1)
Monsieur(FR) plugged on without ever threatening and his losing run dates back to 2006. (tchd 22-1)
Byblos, a handicap debutant, showed his best form to date as a hurdler and left the impression he may benefit for a longer trip. (op 20-1)
Amazing Request was very well backed on his return to this course, but was never seriously sighted from off the pace and again disappointed. (op 9-2)
Ful Of Grace(IRE) Official explanation: jockey said mare lost its action
T/Plt: £528.70 to a £1 stake. Pool:£69,582.80 - 96.06 winning tickets T/Qpdt: £30.00 to a £1 stake. Pool:£6,440.00 - 158.50 winning tickets TM

1165 - 1174a (Foreign Racing) - See Raceform Interactive

768 FFOS LAS (L-H)
Tuesday, August 3

OFFICIAL GOING: Good to firm (8.2)
Wind: Light, against Weather: Fine but cloudy

1175 ASPINALL FOUNDATION NOVICES' HURDLE (8 hdls) 2m
6:05 (6:05) (Class 4) 4-Y-0+ **£2,602** (£764; £382; £190)

Form RPR

22- **1** **Island Oscar (IRE)**[33] 240 6-11-5 119.... APMcCoy 113+
(Paul A Roche, Ire) *nt fluent: t.k.h: trckd ldrs: led and j. bdly lft 2 out: drvn out* **8/13**[1]

2-F1 **2** *1* **Penyfan Dawn (IRE)**[16] 1035 6-11-5 113.... TomScudamore 110
(Tim Vaughan) *trckd ldrs: led 4th to 3 out: bmpd 2 out: w wnr last: nt qckn* **7/2**[2]

323- **3** 3 3/4 **Supernoverre (IRE)**[45] 4302 4-10-11 110 NoelFehily 101+
(Liam Corcoran) *trckd ldrs: led 3 out: hdd and bmpd 2 out: n.m.r last: one pce* **9/1**

2 **4** 16 **Stormyisland Ahead**[14] 1046 5-11-2 115 (t) DPFahy(3) 92
(Evan Williams) *led tl 4th: wknd 3 out: mstke last* **6/1**[3]

5 60 **One Of A Kind (FR)**[18] 1011 6-10-12 0 AndrewThornton 31
(John Daniel Moore, Ire) *nt jump wl: a last: t.o fr 4th* **25/1**

3m 43.5s (-5.50) **Going Correction** -0.425s/f (Good)
WFA 4 from 5yo+ 13lb **5** Ran SP% **112.3**
Speed ratings (Par 105): **109,108,106,98,68**
CSF £3.35 TOTE £1.50: £1.50, £2.30; EX 3.50.
Owner Mrs Ann Roche **Bred** Cornelius Ahern **Trained** Tramore, Co. Waterford

FOCUS
A modest little novice hurdle. They went no gallop early on and that caused most of the runners to take a keen pull. The first three are all rated within 3lb of their pre-race marks.

NOTEBOOK
Island Oscar(IRE) got off the mark at Killarney in May and had run well on his sole outing on the level since then. Very well backed under his penalty for this fourth run as a hurdler, he completed the task with more in hand than the bare margin suggests, but was still workmanlike. He also failed to jump with the same fluency as when previously successful, going badly left over two out and then again not clever at the last despite the champion jockey doing his best to correct him. He did get warm beforehand, though, and would've been better off in a more truly run race, so is given the benefit of doubt. Things would be much harder for him off a double penalty in this division. (op 5-6 tchd 10-11 in a place)
Penyfan Dawn(IRE), a winner off 104 in a handicap at Stratford 16 days earlier, proved keen early on due to the lack of early pace. This also represented a drop back in trip, so it wasn't surprising to see him go on down the far side and he ultimately posted a solid effort considering he wasn't helped by the winner over the final two flights. He could well win one of these granted more of a test. (tchd 3-1)

1176 ASPINALL FOUNDATION H'CAP CHASE (15 fncs) 2m 3f 110y
6:35 (6:35) (Class 4) (0-115,115) 4-Y-0+ **£3,998** (£1,241; £668)

Form RPR
-112 **1** **Fealing Real (IRE)**[4] 1136 8-10-7 103 (tp) AodhaganConlon(7) 125+
(Rebecca Curtis) *mde all: clr 9th: unchal* **2/1**[1]

3PU1 **2** 10 **Sunday City (JPN)**[6] 1117 9-11-11 114 7ex TomO'Brien 127
(Peter Bowen) *mstke 4th: lost pl and last after 6th: hdwy and mstke 7th: chsd wnr after 11th: no imp* **9/4**[2]

P4 **3** 64 **Romping Home (IRE)**[61] 601 7-11-9 112 (p) PaulMoloney 67
(Evan Williams) *in tch: j.rt 3rd: bhd after mstke 9th: lft poor 3rd 3 out* **16/1**

P- **P** **Rathnaskillogue (IRE)**[59] 643 9-10-0 89 oh4 (t) TomScudamore —
(Paul A Roche, Ire) *in tch: mstke 6th: p.u after next: dismntd* **4/1**[3]

-435 **P** **I'm The Decider (IRE)**[30] 890 8-11-12 115 (p) APMcCoy —
(Jonjo O'Neill) *j. slowly 1st and 2nd: a in rr: t.o and p.u 4 out* **8/1**

5125 **P** **Michigan Assassin (IRE)**[47] 769 8-11-6 112 DonalDevereux(3) —
(Debra Hamer) *trckd wnr: slipped bdly 3rd: lost 2nd after 11th: btn whn mstke 4 out: p.u next* **8/1**

4m 45.6s (-20.40) **Going Correction** -1.075s/f (Hard) **6** Ran SP% **112.2**
Speed ratings (Par 105): **105,101,75,—,— —**
toteswingers:1&2:£1.10 CSF £7.25 TOTE £3.30: £1.30, £1.60; EX 8.00.
Owner Miss Rebecca Curtis **Bred** James Maguire **Trained** Newport, Dyfed

FOCUS
A moderate handicap which turned out to be an eventful race with only three completing, but it was still a decent effort by the winner.

NOTEBOOK
Fealing Real(IRE) made all to resume winning ways and took nearly two seconds off the existing course record. Equipped with first-time cheekpieces, the key to him being allowed a clear lead was Michigan Assassin's blunder at the third as that meant he was no longer hassled, and therefore able to dictate. The remainder of his rivals probably still allowed him too much rope, but he jumped well bar the fourth-last and is clearly still improving. The handicapper will now hike him up, however. (op 9-4 tchd 15-8)
Sunday City(JPN) was penalised for winning easily at Perth six days earlier. He really had too much to do when turning into the home straight, but the run probably came soon enough all the same. (op 15-8 tchd 5-2 in places)
Romping Home(IRE), another equipped with first-time cheekpieces, was never seriously in the hunt and her rider had accepted the situation from three out. She is at least entitled to come on for the run. (op 14-1)
Rathnaskillogue(IRE) was sharply pulled up on the back straight with something amiss. (op 11-2 tchd 6-1)
I'm The Decider(IRE)'s jumping was messy from the off and he was tailing off prior to pulling up. (op 11-2 tchd 6-1)
Michigan Assassin(IRE) was booked for third place prior to quickly pulling up after another mistake at the fourth-last, with something clearly going wrong. (op 11-2 tchd 6-1)

1177 WEATHERBYS BANK NOVICES' CHASE (18 fncs) 3m
7:10 (7:11) (Class 4) 4-Y-0+ **£3,998** (£1,241; £668)

Form RPR
-012 **1** **To Arms**[17] 1019 8-11-2 0 (t) APMcCoy 135+
(Lawney Hill) *in tch: wnt 2nd 12th: led 3 out: easily* **10/11**[1]

/261 **2** 21 **Tampa Boy (IRE)**[16] 1034 8-11-9 114 (t) CharliePoste 113
(Milton Harris) *in tch: led after 9th: hdd 3 out: no ch w wnr* **5/1**[3]

3 21 **Tiger Run (IRE)**[21] 980 7-11-2 0 NoelFehily 88
(John Queally, Ire) *in tch: mstke 14th: wknd next* **14/1**

0 **P** **Diddle'Em**[34] 863 9-10-9 0 (tp) MichaelByrne(7) —
(Bernard Llewellyn) *led to 9th: last fr 10th after mstke: t.o whn nrly ref 14th: p.u next* **66/1**

-U14 **P** **Silver Story**[20] 985 7-11-9 113 TomScudamore —
(Tim Vaughan) *hmpd 3rd: hdwy after 8th: j. slowly 10th and lost tch: blnd 4 out and p.u next* **12/1**

F2 **F** **Thelobstercatcher**[30] 889 6-11-2 0 TomO'Brien —
(Peter Bowen) *fell 3rd* **11/4**[2]

5m 59.5s (-23.50) **Going Correction** -1.075s/f (Hard) **6** Ran SP% **111.6**
Speed ratings (Par 105): **96,89,82,—,— —**
toteswingers:1&2:£1.50, 1&3:£4.20, 2&3:£8.80 CSF £6.12 TOTE £2.00: £1.10, £1.90; EX 6.20.
Owner Carl Pyne **Bred** Mrs M Chaworth Musters **Trained** Aston Rowant, Oxon

FOCUS
This was weakened by the early departure of Thelobstercatcher, but it was hard not to have been impressed with the ease in which the winner went about his business. He is rated value for further.

NOTEBOOK
To Arms ◆ ran poorly in two outings over fences for his previous yard, but was only just held on his chasing debut when with Tim Vaughan. He also had stamina to prove for this return to fences, but his current stable has improved him of late and he was entitled to be a short price if translating his hurdling form. He did just that, jumping neatly in the main, and not having to come out of third gear to master the runner-up from three out. This should do his confidence the world of good and this somewhat enigmatic character should really prove hard to stop again under a penalty. (op 6-5)
Tampa Boy(IRE) was officially upped 5lb for winning a handicap at Stratford 16 days previously. He put some pace into the race when taking control going out onto the final circuit, but came under heavy pressure nearing six out. He responded gamely, but was a sitting duck for the winner, who was in a different league. Returning to handicap company should be more to his liking, but a mark of 114 looks to have him about right all the same. (op 13-2 tchd 7-1)
Tiger Run(IRE) was well beaten on his return to rules last time and it was the same again on this British debut. (op 10-1)
Thelobstercatcher has now fallen in two of his three outings as a chaser and returning to hurdles looks on the cards. (op 2-1)

1178 WEATHERBYS BLOODSTOCK INSURANCE H'CAP CHASE (19 fncs) 3m 1f 110y
7:45 (7:45) (Class 3) (0-135,126) 4-Y-0 **£6,337** (£1,872; £936; £468; £234)

Form RPR
P301 **1** **Sea Wall**[16] 1032 8-11-4 121 MrAJBerry(3) 129+
(Jonjo O'Neill) *prog to press ldr 6th: led 14th: jnd and lft 2 l clr 2 out: all out* **9/1**

3210 **2** 3/4 **Midnight Gold**[16] 1032 10-11-5 122 (p) DonalDevereux(3) 129
(Peter Bowen) *trckd ldrs: chsd ldr 15th to 3 out: lft 2nd and hmpd 2 out: styd on wl flat* **11/1**

2P31 **3** 1 1/2 **Marblehead (IRE)**[7] 1105 8-11-7 126 (b) SamTwiston-Davies(5) 131
(Nigel Twiston-Davies) *led 4th to 14th: hrd rdn next: kpt on same pce fr 4 out* **7/1**

3P0- **4** 8 **Quattrocento (FR)**[98] 33 6-11-3 117 (p) TomO'Brien 114
(Peter Bowen) *hld up in last pair: hdwy 12th: chsd ldrs 15th: wknd 2 out* **5/1**

-120 **5** 7 **Ballycarney (IRE)**[37] 844 6-11-9 123 JackDoyle 116
(Emma Lavelle) *trckd ldrs: mstke 14th and lost tch: nvr on terms after* **11/4**[1]

6 26 **Defying Gravity (IRE)**[16] 1041 7-10-4 104 PaulMoloney 72
(Trevor Horgan, Ire) *led to 4th: wknd 12th: t.o* **9/2**[3]

50-6 **7** 9 **Some Craic (IRE)**[16] 1032 10-10-8 115 MrTJCannon(7) 75
(Paul Henderson) *mstke 2nd: chsd ldrs tl lost tch 13th: mstke 15th: t.o* **28/1**

33P3 **F** **Whataboutya (IRE)**[16] 1032 9-10-13 113 (p) APMcCoy 121+
(Jonjo O'Neill) *hld up in last pair: hdwy 12th: wnt 2nd 3 out: chalng whn fell 2 out* **4/1**[2]

6m 19.1s (-27.90) **Going Correction** -1.075s/f (Hard) **8** Ran SP% **115.8**
Speed ratings (Par 107): **99,98,98,95,93 85,82,—**
toteswingers:1&2:£14.70, 1&3:£7.30, 2&3:£8.00 CSF £96.38 CT £735.92 TOTE £13.30: £3.40, £2.80, £1.30; EX 77.60.
Owner John P McManus **Bred** Lord Rothschild **Trained** Cheltenham, Gloucs

FOCUS
A modest staying handicap with the top weight being rated 9lb below the race celing. The winner is rated back to last year's course win with the faller as a dead-heater.

NOTEBOOK
Sea Wall was given another positive ride and followed up his Stratford win from a 6lb higher mark. He took it up around five out and battled on gamely thereafter, under a rider who evidently gets the best out of him. It's not certain he would have held off Whataboutya had that one not come down two out, but his new-found attitude should continue to hold him in good stead and he ought to make a good fist of landing the hat-trick after another rise. (tchd 10-1)
Midnight Gold flopped behind the winner on his previous outing, but has shown a liking for this course before and the return brought about a much better effort. He just looks handicapped to his best now. (op 9-1)
Marblehead(IRE) stays all day long, as he showed when winning a maiden hurdle on his previous start. The blinkers were back on for this return to fences, but he still proved hard work for his rider. That was likely down to not being able to dominate from the start as he seems to prefer, and, on this evidence, a mark of 126 has him about right. (tchd 13-2)
Quattrocento(FR) is a dual winner at this venue and was back down to his last winning mark, but his effort was short-lived. Perhaps this first outing for 98 days was needed. (tchd 11-2 in a place)
Ballycarney(IRE) was having his first outing since failing to get home in the Summer National. He was going well enough until an error six from home saw him come under heavy pressure, and he disappointed. (tchd 5-2)
Defying Gravity(IRE), well backed, set off from the front but gradually lost his position and has questions to answer after this. Official explanation: jockey said gelding had a breathing problem (op 13-2 tchd 7-1)
Whataboutya(IRE) was weighted to gain revenge on his winning stablemate on their last-time-out form and it appeared as though he was just about to get on top prior to coming down. Looking at the way the winner kept finding, though, he may well still have been second-best with a clear round. (op 7-2 tchd 3-1)

1179 ASPINALL FOUNDATION H'CAP HURDLE (10 hdls) 2m 4f
8:20 (8:20) (Class 5) (0-90,90) 4-Y-0+ **£1,951** (£573; £286; £143)

Form RPR
025 **1** **Risk Challenge (USA)**[16] 1035 8-11-7 85 (t) CharliePoste 100+
(Milton Harris) *hld up last: smooth prog 7th: led bef 2 out: sn clr: easily* **9/2**[2]

0U30 **2** 7 **Racingisdreaming (USA)**[12] 1066 4-11-10 90 (vt[1]) TomScudamore 91
(David Pipe) *hld up in last trio: prog to chse ldrs 7th: rdn 2 out: kpt on to take 2nd nr fin* **14/1**

000- **3** 1 1/2 **Goat Castle (IRE)**[131] 4847 6-11-3 86 (t) SamTwiston-Davies(5) 87
(Nigel Twiston-Davies) *prom: mstke 4th: chsd ldr after 7th: led briefly after 3 out: no ch w wnr* **25/1**

P300 **4** 2 1/2 **Scotsbrook Cloud**[13] 1062 5-11-5 83 RhysFlint 83+
(C Roberts) *led: blnd 3rd: hdd 5th: led again 7th tl after 3 out: fdd* **18/1**

3PP- **5** nk **Plenty Of Chat (IRE)**[136] 4728 6-11-12 90 (t) APMcCoy 90
(Tim Vaughan) *hld up: mstkes 5th and 6th: rdn to chse ldrs 3 out: no imp next* **15/8**[1]

PP-0 **6** 2 **Happy Fleet**[28] 920 7-10-0 64 HaddenFrost 62
(Roger Curtis) *mstke 3rd: towards rr: hdwy to chse ldrs 7th: no imp whn mstke 2 out* **9/2**[2]

6535 **7** 6 **Petit Fleur**[27] 933 8-11-1 86 AnthonyFreeman(7) 78
(Julian Smith) *hld up towards rr: chsd ldrs after 7th: rdn and no imp fr next* **7/1**[3]

450P **8** 33 **Western Palm (IRE)**[20] 991 7-11-12 90 (t) NoelFehily 52
(Charlie Mann) *hld up in rr: wknd after 7th: t.o fr next* **33/1**

-050 **9** 5 **Lukie Victor (IRE)**[19] 1001 9-10-9 80 AdamWedge(7) 37
(Evan Williams) *prom tl wknd rapidly bef 7th: t.o* **9/1**

60P- **10** 2 1/2 **Tegan Lee**[133] 4811 7-10-13 80 SeanQuinlan(3) 35
(Liam Corcoran) *trckd ldrs tl wknd rapidly after 7th: t.o* **33/1**

-000 **11** 42 **Colour Trooper (IRE)**[29] 914 5-11-9 87 (vt[1]) JohnnyFarrelly 4
(David Pipe) *pressed ldr: led 5th to 7th: wknd v rapidly: t.o* **50/1**

P0P6 **P** **Dancing Hill**[13] 1064 11-11-0 78 PaulMoloney —
(Kevin Bishop) *in tch to 1/2-way: sn wknd and t.o: p.u bef 3 out* **16/1**

4m 41.9s (-7.10) **Going Correction** -0.425s/f (Good)
WFA 4 from 5yo+ 14lb **12** Ran SP% **123.1**
Speed ratings (Par 103): **103,100,99,98,98 97,95,82,80,79 62,—**
toteswingers:1&2:£12.20, 1&3:£38.00, 2&3:£62.90 CSF £64.40 CT £1449.41 TOTE £3.90: £1.40, £4.40, £4.90; EX 95.40.
Owner Gary Doel, Jim Parsons & Adam Howard **Bred** Juddmonte Farms Inc **Trained** Herridge, Wiltshire

FOCUS
A weak handicap run at a fair enough gallop. The easy winner was value for further.

NOTEBOOK
Risk Challenge(USA), 5lb higher than when coming fifth on his previous outing, bounced back to winning ways and did the job comfortably. He really caught the eye creeping into the race under a patient ride and it was clear nearing the penultimate flight that he was the one to be on. He came right away when asked for an effort and turning out under a penalty looks his best option, but consistency has never been his strong suit. (op 5-1)
Racingisdreaming(USA) made up good ground to get involved rounding the home turn, but lacked anything like the turn of gear required to match the winner. He appeared to give his all when under pressure, but had new headgear on this time and looks handicapped about right.
Goat Castle(IRE) made a bold bid on this return from a 131-day break, but was a sitting duck for the winner and eventually lost second as a result of trying to keep with that rival from the second-last. This was a lot more encouraging, the addition of a tongue-tie looked to help, and he should improve for the outing.
Scotsbrook Cloud performed better with the cheekpieces abandoned, but doesn't look an imminent winner. (op 16-1 tchd 20-1)
Plenty Of Chat(IRE) went astray as he failed to jump fluently and laboured. (op 5-2)

1180 ASPINALL FOUNDATION STANDARD OPEN NATIONAL HUNT FLAT RACE 2m
8:50 (8:50) (Class 6) 4-6-Y-O **£1,431** (£420; £210; £104)

Form RPR

2-32 **1** **Jump Up**[34] 869 4-11-0 0 TomO'Brien 96
(Keith Goldsworthy) *trckd ldr: rdn 4f out: styd on to ld over 1f out: drvn out* **7/4**[2]

2 *1 1/4* **Romeo Desbois (FR)**[157] 5-11-1 0 APMcCoy 96
(Rebecca Curtis) *cl up: rdn 4f out: hanging lft and nt qckn: kpt on to take 2nd fnl f* **11/8**[1]

3 *1 1/2* **Shadow's Gold (IRE)** 6-11-1 0 RhysFlint 95
(Keith Goldsworthy) *led tl over 1f out: fdd* **9/2**[3]

4 *30* **Floridahall (IRE)**[73] 6-10-12 0 RichardKilloran(3) 68
(Tim Vaughan) *cl up tl wknd 5f out: t.o* **15/2**

U **Salford Rose (IRE)** 4-10-4 0 LeeStephens(3) —
(David Evans) *veered and uns rdr s* **20/1**

3m 42.1s (-1.30) **Going Correction** -0.425s/f (Good)
WFA 4 from 5yo+ 1lb **5** Ran SP% **113.2**
Speed ratings: **98,97,96,81,—**
totesuper7: Win: Not won. Place: £398.60 CSF £4.72 TOTE £3.20: £1.40, £1.40; EX 5.40 Place 6 £61.46, Place 5 £47.90..
Owner Ashley Hart **Bred** D J And Mrs Deer **Trained** Yerbeston, Pembrokes

FOCUS
A moderate bumper.

NOTEBOOK
Jump Up ran out a game winner. His trainer saddled two here, but he was the more experienced of the pair and was well backed. It looked around 3f out as though he may have to play second fiddle to his stablemate, but the further he went the better he was and he was nicely on top at the finish. It was a deserved win and he is going to want further once sent over hurdles. (op 11-4 tchd 3-1)
Romeo Desbois(FR) hails from a yard that has a decent record at the track and has made a name for itself by winning bumpers with such types. He proved a little free under early restraint, but was produced with every chance off the home turn and, if anything, it was a lack of experience that caught him out. He is no great shakes, but should come on for the run and find a small bumper before going jumping. (op 10-11)
Shadow's Gold(IRE), the winner's stablemate, is a half-brother to an Irish point/bumper winner. He set out to make all and stretched the first pair in the home straight, but eventually tired out of it. The experience should see him improve nicely. (op 5-1)
Floridahall(IRE), a moderate winning pointer, was easy to back on this debut for Tim Vaughan and ran accordingly. Official explanation: jockey said gelding bled from the nose (op 8-1)
T/Plt: £21.50 to a £1 stake. Pool £65,592.36 - 2,221.40 winning tickets T/Qpdt: £14.40 to a £1 stake. Pool £5,167.84 - 264.55 winning tickets MD

1181 - 1194a (Foreign Racing) - See Raceform Interactive

1105 WORCESTER (L-H)
Friday, August 6

OFFICIAL GOING: Good (good to firm in places; watered; chs 7.5, hdl 7.9)
All bends moved out 3m from inside increasing race distances by about 18yards per circuit.
Wind: Virtually nil Weather: Overcast, rain

1195 PLEASE SUPPORT RACING WELFARE HERE TODAY CLAIMING HURDLE (10 hdls) 2m 4f
2:20 (2:22) (Class 5) 4-Y-O+ **£2,055** (£599; £299)

Form RPR

035 **1** **Golden Gem (IRE)**[10] 1107 8-10-9 95 (p) HarrySkelton 100
(Rachel Hobbs) *in rr 4th: stdy hdwy 4 out: chsd ldrs 3 out: chal after 2 out: upsides last: veered rt to stands' rail and hrd rdn: led fnl 100yds: all out* **14/1**

0463 **2** *1* **Heir To Be**[11] 1094 11-10-12 105 (b) NickScholfield 102
(Michael Blake) *prom early: in rr 5th: stdy hdwy after 3 out: styd on u.p run to take 2nd nr fin: nt rch wnr* **7/2**[1]

-600 **3** *1 3/4* **The Good Guy (IRE)**[23] 994 7-11-4 110 JodieMogford 106
(Graeme McPherson) *led tl appr 2nd: styd chsng ldr: led 6th: rdn and jnd fr 3 out: stl slt ld last: hdd and one pce fnl 100yds: wknd and lost 2nd nr fin* **13/2**

-2P0 **4** *3 1/4* **Smart John**[7] 1141 10-10-12 95 ColinBolger 97
(Simon Lewis) *in tch: rdn and hdwy to chse ldrs appr 3 out: styd on same pce fr next* **66/1**

1055 **5** *8* **Marodima (FR)**[17] 1044 7-11-8 134 DavidBass(5) 105
(Jamie Snowden) *v keen 5f bef s: led appr 2nd: hdd 6th: styd chsng ldr and upsides u.p 3 out: wknd fr 2 out* **5/1**

0FB- **6** *5* **Eljay's Boy**[272] 2130 12-10-9 0 (t) JoeTizzard 82+
(Colin Tizzard) *in rr: hdwy fr 6th: rdn 3 out: wknd next* **25/1**

4F62 **7** *11* **Rapide Plaisir (IRE)**[10] 1107 12-10-9 95 CharliePoste 70
(Richard Lee) *j. slowly 6th: a towards rr* **20/1**

3-10 **8** *1/2* **Roznic (FR)**[37] 865 12-10-9 105 APMcCoy 74
(Tim Vaughan) *in rr: hdwy 5th: rdn 4 out and nvr rchd ldrs: wknd 2 out* **4/1**[2]

00/6 **9** *18* **Sarin**[10] 1107 12-11-4 0 SamThomas 61
(Venetia Williams) *in rr: rdn and hdwy 6th: nvr rchd ldrs and wknd appr 3 out* **33/1**

20P- **10** *33* **Red Lancer**[3] 964 9-11-1 110 (p) FelixDeGiles 25
(Jonathen de Giles) *chsd ldrs: rdn and wknd 4 out: t.o* **16/1**

51P **11** *11* **Deep Reflection**[7] 1137 10-11-4 109 (v) WarrenMarston 17
(Martin Keighley) *in tch: rdn and wknd 5th: t.o* **9/2**[3]

4/P5 **P** **The Mighty Bard (IRE)**[16] 1063 7-10-2 0 MissLBrooke(7) —
(Tracey Watkins) *a in rr: t.o whn p.u bef 3 out* **200/1**

P **Final Flyer (IRE)**[459] 6-11-3 0 OliverDayman(7) —
(Alison Thorpe) *in tch to 5th: t.o whn p.u bef 3 out* **40/1**

4m 42.14s (-5.26) **Going Correction** -0.325s/f (Good) **13** Ran SP% **118.9**
Speed ratings (Par 103): **97,96,95,94,91 89,85,84,77,64 60,—,—**
toteswingers:1&2:£12.20, 1&3:£18.00, 2&3:£6.60 CSF £60.60 TOTE £22.10: £5.10, £1.50, £2.30; EX 99.00.
Owner The Vin de Roy Racing Syndicate **Bred** Seamus Byrne **Trained** Hanley Swan, Worcs

FOCUS
All bends were moved out 3 metres from the inside, increasing the distance of a 2m race by about 17 metres. There was rain before racing and jockeys' opinion of the ground was that it was generally good, but on the easy side in places. A fair claimer in which a pair of pacesetters set a sound pace, and the first two both came through from the rear. The form, rated through the second, does not look all that solid.

NOTEBOOK
Golden Gem(IRE) had something to find with most of his rivals at these weights. Beginning to pick up the leaders on the long home turn, he held on to his advantage after hanging over to the rail on the flat. He had looked in fine shape beforehand, and had cheekpieces back on in place of blinkers. (op 20-1)
Heir To Be lost his pitch with a circuit left and was under pressure and going nowhere turning out of the back. He was still only sixth over the last, but was staying on well from there and things would have been interesting with a little further to travel. (op 5-1)
The Good Guy(IRE), dropped in grade, had to concede the early lead to fellow front-runner Marodima. He did get to the front four out and deserves credit for sticking on in there for a long as he did. (op 12-1 tchd 6-1)
Smart John had a good deal on at these weights and ran a sound race in the circumstances. (op 50-1)
Marodima(FR), returning to hurdles, was 9lb clear on adjusted official figures, but after making the running as usual he had no more to offer from the second-last. This keen sort had run away with his rider going to the start and it is debatable if he should have been permitted to take part. (op 3-1)
Eljay's Boy, off the track since taking two tumbles over fences back in the autumn, ran well for a long way before his lack of race-fitness told. (op 20-1)
Roznic(FR), back up in trip, was under pressure behind the leaders when a stumble three from home ended any lingering chances he had. (op 3-1)

1196 SALLY PARKER'S BIRTHDAY CELEBRATION NOVICES' HURDLE (10 hdls) 2m 4f
2:50 (2:51) (Class 4) 4-Y-O+ **£2,602** (£764; £382; £190)

Form RPR

5-61 **1** **Great Mates (IRE)**[62] 632 6-11-5 0 HarrySkelton 119+
(Paul Nicholls) *trckd ldrs: wnt 2nd after 3 out: chal next: nt fluent and upsides last whn wnt rt to take stands' rail and led sn after: drvn out* **4/1**[2]

40 **2** *4 1/2* **Leitra House (IRE)**[19] 1028 7-10-12 0 NickScholfield 104
(Jeremy Scott) *hld up in rr: hdwy but stl plenty to do 3 out: styng on whn nt fluent next: kpt on wl to take 2nd nr fin but no imp on wnr* **25/1**

031/ **3** *1* **Didbrook**[1500] 762 8-10-0 0 SamTwiston-Davies(5) 96
(Nigel Twiston-Davies) *t.k.h: hit 4th: chsd ldrs: slt ld 6th: rdn 2 out: stl slt ld but u.p whn bmpd sn after last: sn no ch w wnr: lost 2nd nr fin* **8/1**

0-56 **4** *4* **Sagunt (GER)**[37] 862 7-10-5 101 AnthonyFreeman(7) 99
(Sean Curran) *chsd ldrs: outpcd appr 3 out: hrd rdn fr next and kpt on again fr 2 out but no ch w ldng trio* **15/2**

3241 **5** *19* **Mzuri Bay**[19] 1033 5-11-5 112 (t) MarkGrant 90
(Brendan Duke) *w ldr: led 2nd to 3rd: chal 6th tl approaching 3 out: wknd after 2 out* **6/1**[3]

5-22 **6** *6* **Just Victor**[40] 847 5-10-12 114 (t) SamThomas 80
(Paul Webber) *chsd ldrs: rdn appr 3 out: wknd bef next* **6/4**[1]

60/ **7** *80* **Nowzdetime (IRE)**[506] 4573 5-10-12 0 AndrewThornton —
(Caroline Bailey) *plld hrd early: chsd ldrs to 5th: t.o* **50/1**

0 **8** *6* **Alittlebitmore**[23] 992 7-10-9 0 (v) TommyPhelan(3) —
(Tom Gretton) *led to 2nd: led 3rd tl hdd 6th and wknd qckly: t.o* **100/1**

0-0 **9** *12* **Muzey's Princess**[56] 718 4-10-0 0 SeanQuinlan(3) —
(Michael Mullineaux) *in tch to 5th: t.o* **100/1**

005/ **P** **Another Flint (IRE)**[104] 10-10-5 0 MissLBrooke(7) —
(Lady Susan Brooke) *a in rr: t.o whn p.u and dismntd after 4 out* **100/1**

0 **U** **Cheekyrun (IRE)**[19] 1030 7-10-5 0 MrTJCannon(7) —
(Paul Henderson) *j. poorly in rr tl tried to run out: j.v.slowly and uns rdr 6th* **100/1**

0-01 **P** **Bold Exit (IRE)**[22] 1003 5-11-5 0 (t) MichaelMcAlister —
(Maurice Barnes) *chsd ldrs tl wknd qckly fr 3 out: t.o whn p.u bef last* **16/1**

6 **U** **Classicality**[37] 869 5-10-5 0 KeithMercer —
(Michael Mullineaux) *in rr: rdn 4th: t.o whn tried to refuse and uns rdr 6th* **100/1**

P **Pitton General** 9-10-5 0 MattGriffiths(7) —
(Kevin Bishop) *in tch: chal 6th: wknd sn after t.o whn p.u bef 3 out* **100/1**

4m 43.31s (-4.09) **Going Correction** -0.325s/f (Good)
WFA 4 from 5yo+ 14lb **14** Ran SP% **114.8**
Speed ratings (Par 105): **95,93,92,91,83 81,49,46,42,— —,—,—,—**
toteswingers:1&2:£15.30, 1&3:£9.40, 2&3:£11.90 CSF £91.18 TOTE £5.20: £2.20, £5.20, £3.00; EX 59.20.
Owner Jim Lewis **Bred** Con O'Keeffe **Trained** Ditcheat, Somerset

FOCUS
A reasonable novices' hurdle for the time of year, but the pace was steady and a number were keen through the first part of the race. Not form to be confident about with the fourth the best guide.

NOTEBOOK
Great Mates(IRE) gained his initial hurdling win over C&D two months ago and followed up in decent style in the end, running on well once securing the stands' rail after the last. The type to need time between his races, he has had his problems and has not always found much, but is getting his act together now. (op 3-1)
Leitra House(IRE) ran a promising race. Anchored at the back, this hard-pulling sort was still a good way off the pace turning into the straight but he stayed on well from that point. He has plenty of ability and it will be interesting to see if he is ridden more prominently in future. (op 28-1)
Didbrook had not run since winning a bumper in June 2006 - 1,500 days earlier to be precise. After racing keenly she challenged on the home turn, only fading from the final flight after coming close together with the winner soon after the last. This was a very pleasing return and she is well up to winning an ordinary race, provided she doesn't 'bounce'. (op 10-1)

Sagunt(GER) ran respectably back in novice company. He could not race on with the leaders on the home turn, but was staying on again for pressure late on. (op 7-1)

Mzuri Bay helped cut out the pace, but was ultimately found out under his penalty, weakening two from home. (tchd 13-2)

Just Victor brought sound form to this having finished second on his previous two starts. He attempted to latch on to the leaders turning in, but weakened two from home. The stewards considered his running, but decided not to hold an enquiry after the jockey reported that the gelding had stopped quickly. Official explanation: jockey said the gelding stopped quickly (op 7-4)

Bold Exit(IRE) won a poor race easily at Cartmel, but was found out in this better company. The longer trip told and he was eventually pulled up. (op 14-1)

1197 BOB LOVE "KING OF THE DIRT" MEMORIAL NOVICES' CHASE (15 fncs) 2m 4f 110y

3:20 (3:21) (Class 4) 4-Y-0+ **£2,927** (£859; £429; £214)

Form				RPR
1213	**1**		**The Jigsaw Man (IRE)**[44] [830] 6-11-7 0 .... APMcCoy (Rebecca Curtis) *mde virtually all: clr 7th: j. slowly 8th: nt fluent 3 out: pushed out run-in* **4/7**[1]	135+
2P33	**2**	*3 ¾*	**Magical Legend**[17] [1045] 9-10-8 0 .... (t) PaulMoloney (Sophie Leech) *in rr: sme hdwy 6th: lost position 9th: styd on again fr 4 out to chse wnr fr 3 out: hit last: kpt on run-in but a hld* **4/1**[2]	115
2F5-	**3**	*22*	**Venir Rouge**[109] [5282] 6-11-1 0 .... TomO'Brien (Matthew Salaman) *chsd ldrs: wnt 2nd bef 4 out: rdn and wknd 3 out* **11/1**	102
1621	**4**	*22*	**Intac (IRE)**[11] [1091] 8-11-7 0 .... JoeTizzard (Colin Tizzard) *w wnr to 2nd: racd in 2nd: hit 6th: wknd bef 4 out* **11/2**[3]	93
4	**5**	*45*	**Canal Bank (IRE)**[11] [1091] 6-11-1 0 .... NoelFehily (Jonjo O'Neill) *a bhd: t.o* **40/1**	33

4m 57.68s (-9.02) **Going Correction** -0.325s/f (Good) **5** Ran SP% **109.8**
Speed ratings (Par 105): **104,102,94,85,68**
CSF £3.44 TOTE £2.00: £1.30, £3.00; EX 3.30.

Owner LL R P Racing **Bred** P J O'Connor **Trained** Newport, Dyfed

FOCUS
An ordinary novice chase in which the winner set a reasonable gallop. The winner is rated to his best hurdle form backed up by the third.

NOTEBOOK
The Jigsaw Man(IRE), whose previous chase win came over C&D, made just about all the running and, although the runner-up was eroding his lead late on, he was always in control. His jumping was safe, if a little untidy at times. He is not matching his hurdles form at present and could revert to hurdling at Newton Abbot later this month. (op 4-6)

Magical Legend was a good way off the pace at one stage but she stayed on steadily from the third-last, just losing a bit of momentum when hitting the final fence. This was her best effort over fences so far and she might be suited by a little further. (tchd 7-2 and 9-2)

Venir Rouge, off the track since April, was ultimately well beaten on this chasing debut. (op 12-1 tchd 10-1)

Intac(IRE) eventually paid for chasing the winner and failed to run up to his previous form. (op 6-1 tchd 5-1)

Canal Bank(IRE) Official explanation: vet said gelding had been struck into

1198 TIDDESLEY WOOD YELLOW EGG PLUM H'CAP HURDLE (12 hdls) 3m

3:50 (3:50) (Class 3) (0-135,134) 4-Y-0+ **£4,228** (£1,241; £620; £310)

Form				RPR
6331	**1**		**Barnhill Brownie (IRE)**[10] [1108] 7-10-9 122 7ex .... (t) GilesHawkins[(5)] (Philip Hobbs) *chsd ldrs: chal fr 8th: stl upsides u.p fr last: led fnl 75yds: gamely* **10/3**[2]	132+
53-1	**2**	*2 ½*	**Changing Lanes**[11] [1094] 7-10-2 110 7ex .... (p) RhysFlint (John Flint) *chsd ldrs: chal fr 7th tl slt ld 3 out: rdn fr 2 out: hdd and no ex fnl 75yds* **2/1**[1]	118+
0163	**3**	*13*	**Soubriquet (IRE)**[22] [1004] 7-10-2 110 oh1 ow2 .... (t) MichaelMcAlister (Maurice Barnes) *chsd ldrs: rdn and outpcd by ldng duo after 3 out* **11/1**	105
2P1/	**4**	*5*	**Lyes Green**[30] [4634] 9-11-5 127 .... (p) LeightonAspell (Oliver Sherwood) *chsd ldrs: hit 6th: wknd appr 3 out: no ch whn hit 2 out* **14/1**	117
0-25	**5**	*3 ½*	**Rajeh (IRE)**[20] [1019] 7-11-12 134 .... WarrenMarston (John Spearing) *t.k.h in rr: rdn and sme prog 3 out: wknd next* **8/1**	119
/6P-	**6**	*shd*	**Inghwung**[174] [4040] 8-10-7 115 .... SamJones (Oliver Sherwood) *in tch to 6th* **20/1**	100
1266	**7**	*1 ¾*	**Haldibari (IRE)**[13] [986] 6-9-11 110 .... SamTwiston-Davies[(5)] (Shaun Lycett) *led tl hdd & wknd 3 out* **7/1**[3]	94
61	**8**	*19*	**Native Coral (IRE)**[36] [874] 12-10-11 122 .... FearghalDavis[(3)] (Nicky Richards) *bhd most of way: lost tch fr 4 out* **14/1**	86
515F	**9**	*10*	**Flying Doctor**[26] [951] 7-10-12 120 .... JohnnyFarrelly (Elliott Cooper) *in tch to 6th* **16/1**	74
1/0-	**P**		**Present Glory (IRE)**[62] 11-10-7 115 .... (p) AndrewThornton (Caroline Bailey) *chsd ldrs: reminders and wknd after 5th: t.o whn p.u bef 4 out* **16/1**	—

5m 32.2s (-12.40) **Going Correction** -0.325s/f (Good) **10** Ran SP% **118.2**
Speed ratings (Par 107): **107,106,101,100,99 98,98,92,88,—**
toteswingers:1&2:£3.00, 1&3:£5.10, 2&3:£9.50 CSF £10.89 CT £65.63 TOTE £4.50: £2.00, £1.80, £3.20; EX 8.10.

Owner Alex & Salvo Giannini **Bred** John P A Kenny **Trained** Withycombe, Somerset

FOCUS
A fair handicap hurdle with the third the best guide and steps up from the first two. The pair finished clear, were both well in at the weights, and the form has a sound look to it.

NOTEBOOK
Barnhill Brownie(IRE) stuck his neck out willingly to assert on the lengthy run-in. Following up his recent C&D win, he was 3lb ahead of the handicapper under the penalty. There has not been much wrong with his application on his last two starts, but he did jump out to his right a couple of times here. (tchd 7-2)

Changing Lanes was 2lb well in under the penalty for his Uttoxeter win. He travelled well into contention and lost little in defeat after a sustained duel. His new mark should not prove insurmountable. (op 11-4)

Soubriquet(IRE) ran respectably from a 3lb wrong at the weights. He saw out the longer trip well enough. (tchd 12-1)

Lyes Green had a run on the AW last month, his first start since winning over hurdles in March 2009. He could not go with the leaders up the straight and lost third place after hitting the final obstacle. (op 9-1)

Rajeh(IRE) was plugging on at the end on this first try over 3m. (op 9-1)

Inghwung has been dropped 4lb since her last appearance in February and she is entitled to come on for this run. (op 16-1)

Haldibari(IRE), who made the running, ran better than his finishing position suggests. (op 10-1)

1199 CARIBBEAN NIGHT TUESDAY 17TH AUGUST (S) H'CAP HURDLE (8 hdls) 2m

4:20 (4:20) (Class 5) (0-85,85) 4-Y-0+ **£1,541** (£449; £224)

Form				RPR
5-05	**1**		**Robbmaa (FR)**[7] [1048] 5-9-13 61 .... (b) EamonDehdashti[(3)] (Tony Carroll) *trckd ldrs: led travelling wl appr 3 out: sn jnd and persistently chal tl asserted fnl 100yds* **16/1**	71+
P0P5	**2**	*1 ¾*	**London Times (IRE)**[19] [1031] 5-11-1 74 .... (t) ColinBolger (Simon Lewis) *prom: slt ld 4 out: narrowly hdd next: styd pressing wnr and upsides tl outpcd fnl 100yds* **50/1**	82
-003	**3**	*5*	**Frosty's Gift**[16] [1064] 6-10-13 72 .... (p) HaddenFrost (Jimmy Fox) *in tch: rdn and kpt in fr 3 out: styd on run-in but nt trble ldng duo* **7/1**[2]	75
0050	**4**	*3*	**Glan Lady (IRE)**[7] [1137] 4-11-4 81 .... (p) CharlieHuxley[(3)] (John Mackie) *in tch: hrd drvn to chse ldrs after 4 out: kpt on fr next but no imp on ldrs fr 2 out* **16/1**	80
4005	**5**	*5*	**Young Tot (IRE)**[16] [1061] 12-10-6 70 .... (t) IanPopham[(5)] (Carroll Gray) *in rr: pushed along 4 out: kpt on fr 3 out but nvr gng pce to rch ldrs* **33/1**	65
40-0	**6**	*1 ¾*	**Airedale Lad (IRE)**[92] [176] 9-10-10 76 .... KyleJames[(7)] (Karen Tutty) *in rr: rdn and stl plenty to do after 3 out: styd on fr next but nvr any threat* **25/1**	69
52-1	**7**	*2 ¼*	**Mycenean Prince (USA)**[16] [1064] 7-11-11 84 .... (b) APMcCoy (Jim Best) *led tl rdn and hdd 5th: nvr travelling u.p after and no ch fr 4 out* **1/1**[1]	75
0/30	**8**	*½*	**Looks The Business (IRE)**[15] [490] 9-11-11 84 .... JamesDavies (Andrew Haynes) *chsd ldrs: led 5th: hdd 4 out: wknd appr next* **12/1**	75+
0	**9**	*½*	**Spice Bar**[23] [990] 6-11-2 75 .... (p) WillKennedy (John G Carr, Ire) *chsd ldrs tl wknd after 4 out* **8/1**[3]	65
00-0	**10**	*4 ½*	**Babe Maccool (IRE)**[47] [792] 8-10-6 68 .... (v[1]) DannyCook[(3)] (David Pipe) *chsd ldrs to 4 out* **20/1**	54
36-F	**11**	*3 ¼*	**Diamanpeg (IRE)**[17] [1049] 6-11-2 75 .... (vt) PaulMoloney (David Rees) *chsd ldrs tl wknd u.p after 4 out* **8/1**[3]	57
-0P0	**12**	*14*	**Zizou (IRE)**[23] [990] 7-11-5 85 .... AnthonyFreeman[(7)] (Sean Curran) *chsd ldrs to 3 out: wkng whn mstke next* **16/1**	53
-B00	**13**	*3 ¾*	**Ravine Rose**[16] [1064] 4-11-3 77 .... (tp) CharliePoste (Ben Case) *j. slowly 2nd: a in rr* **50/1**	41
46P-	**P**		**Jug Of Punch (IRE)**[105] [5359] 11-10-11 70 .... GerardTumelty (Simon Lewis) *sn wl bhd: t.o whn p.u bef 4 out* **50/1**	—

3m 46.95s (-0.35) **Going Correction** -0.325s/f (Good)
WFA 4 from 5yo+ 13lb **14** Ran SP% **127.5**
Speed ratings (Par 103): **87,86,83,82,79 78,77,77,77,74 73,66,64,—**
toteswingers:1&2:£40.20, 1&3:£12.50, 2&3:£34.30 CSF £659.78 CT £5995.12 TOTE £21.60: £5.40, £16.20, £2.40; EX 931.40.there was no bid for the winner.

Owner Group 1 Racing (1994) Ltd **Bred** Elevage De Bois Carrouges **Trained** Cropthorne, Worcs

FOCUS
An ordinary seller which concerned the first two from a good way out. Neither of them had made the frame over hurdles before but the third and fourth give the race some substance.

NOTEBOOK
Robbmaa(FR) did not have as much hurdling experience as some of these and was descending into selling company for the first time. He had been dropped 6lb too and took advantage, finding a bit more than the runner-up on the flat. The stewards considered his improved form and, having heard the trainer's explanation that the gelding was better suited by the faster ground and shorter trip, decided not to hold an enquiry. Official explanation: trainer said, regarding apparent improvement in form, that the gelding was better suited by the faster ground and shorter trip. (op 18-1 tchd 20-1)

London Times(IRE) had come down the weights after some uninspiring performances. He looked to be going better than the winner on the home turn, but did not find a great deal when it came to the crunch.

Frosty's Gift stayed on determinedly late in the day and turned around C&D running with Mycenean Prince. She is finding her feet now, and a seller should come her way. (op 9-1)

Glan Lady(IRE) ran respectably back over this shorter trip. (op 18-1)

Young Tot(IRE) ran over fences last time and had the tongue tie back on.

Airedale Lad(IRE), back from three months' absence, found this too sharp.

Mycenean Prince(USA) was raised 10lb for winning over the C&D last time. Back in the blinkers, he relinquished his lead rather tamely in the back straight. Last month's win was his only victory in 30 tries over hurdles. (op 5-4)

Looks The Business(IRE) Official explanation: vet said gelding was struck into

1200 PERSHORE PLUM FESTIVAL LAND O' PLUMS H'CAP CHASE (18 fncs) 2m 7f

4:50 (4:50) (Class 3) (0-120,117) 4-Y-O + **£5,069** (£1,497; £748; £374; £187)

Form				RPR
1312	**1**		**Rifleman (IRE)**[19] [1027] 10-10-7 103 .... (t) GilesHawkins[(5)] (Richard Lee) *in rr: 6th: hdwy fr 10th: chsd ldrs 4 out: styd on to chse ldr last: str chal u.p run-in: led last strides* **7/2**[1]	114+
5021	**2**	*hd*	**Ballyvesey (IRE)**[20] [1022] 5-11-7 112 .... (p) TomO'Brien (Peter Bowen) *chsd ldrs: chal 3 out and led sn after: rdn and jnd after last: kpt on u.p tl hdd last strides* **11/2**[3]	122
U-U4	**3**	*6*	**Carrick Oscar (IRE)**[50] [772] 10-11-9 117 .... RichardKilloran[(3)] (Tim Vaughan) *in tch 9th: chsd ldrs fr 14th: wnt 2nd u.p 2 out: wknd after last* **14/1**	121
-5U4	**4**	*nse*	**Petite Margot**[22] [1002] 11-11-5 115 .... SamTwiston-Davies[(5)] (Nigel Twiston-Davies) *chsd ldrs tl rdn and outpcd fr 4 out: styd on again fr last but no ch* **8/1**	119
P-F1	**5**	*4 ½*	**Builteoir (IRE)**[8] [1126] 8-9-7 84 7ex .... AdamWedge[(7)] (Evan Williams) *blnd 2nd: in rr: in tch 6th: chsd ldr 12th: chal 14th and led sn after: wnt rt and blnd 3 out: hdd sn after: btn after next* **4/1**[2]	93+
202/	**6**	*24*	**Rare Society (IRE)**[510] [4470] 12-11-5 110 .... TjadeCollier (Sue Smith) *led tl hdd u.p after 14th: awkward and wkng whn blnd 4 out* **14/1**	89
0P0/	**P**		**Team Allstar (IRE)**[650] [1847] 11-11-8 116 .... MrAJBerry[(3)] (Jonjo O'Neill) *in rr tl sme hdwy 10th: sn wknd: t.o whn p.u bef 4 out* **40/1**	—
3P-P	**P**		**Bubble Boy (IRE)**[77] [431] 11-11-5 110 .... (t) NoelFehily (Brendan Powell) *w ldr 1st: in rr 9th: t.o whn p.u bef 11th* **25/1**	—
00P-	**P**		**Prestbury Knight**[257] [2439] 10-11-12 117 .... (t) PaulMoloney (Sophie Leech) *reluctant to go to post: a bhd: j. slowly 11th: t.o whn p.u bef 4 out* **33/1**	—
-0P0	**P**		**Ouste (FR)**[23] [994] 8-11-5 117 .... (bt) OliverDayman[(7)] (Alison Thorpe) *hit 8th: blnd 11th: t.o whn p.u bef 4 out* **28/1**	—
F5-5	**U**		**Kisha King (IRE)**[11] [1094] 9-11-2 107 .... (v) AndrewThornton (David Rees) *trckd ldrs: stl gng wl whn blnd and uns rdr 13th* **15/2**	—
2-00	**P**		**Native City (IRE)**[50] [769] 8-11-5 110 .... APMcCoy (Jonjo O'Neill) *blnd 2nd and 3rd: nvr really jumping after and styd in rr tl t.o and p.u bef 4 out* **11/1**	—

14P- **P** **I'm A Legend**[148] 4538 8-11-4 **109**.................................(p) DougieCostello —
(Neil Mulholland) *hit 10th: a in rr: t.o whn p.u bef 4 out* **25/1**
5m 41.64s (-0.96) **Going Correction** -0.325s/f (Good) 13 Ran SP% **118.7**
Speed ratings (Par 107): **88,87,85,85,84 75,—,—,—,— —,—,—**
toteswingers:1&2:£5.30, 1&3:£12.50, 2&3:£13.20 CSF £22.03 CT £243.36 TOTE £4.90: £1.70, £2.50, £4.70; EX 19.50.

Owner John Jackson & Mike Bevan **Bred** James Hanly, Trevor Stewart & Anthony Stroud **Trained** Byton, H'fords

FOCUS

A reasonable handicap chase, run at a sound pace, and fairly solid form with the winner in form and the second on the upgrade.

NOTEBOOK

Rifleman(IRE) has a fine record at Worcester and he gained his third win here of the summer, the first of which came over hurdles. Now a stone higher, he had a bit of work to do up the straight but stayed on grittily to edge ahead near the line. (op 9-2)

Ballyvesey(IRE) won a lesser race at Market Rasen but he is on the upgrade and almost defied a 7lb rise, only missing out near the line. This was only his fifth run over fences so it is reasonable to assume he has more to offer. (op 9-2)

Carrick Oscar(IRE) jumped better than he had been doing of late and came to have his chance, but the longer trip just found him out in the end.

Petite Margot ran another decent race but this trip is shorter than ideal for her. (tchd 10-1 in a place)

Buailteoir(IRE) was 7lb out of the weights even with the penalty for his Stratford win, but was effectively still 2lb ahead of the handicapper. He took it up travelling strongly, but had tended to jump right and he weakened out of it after a mistake three from home.

Rare Society(IRE) showed up well for a long time on this first run since March last year. (op 16-1)

Kisha King(IRE) was on the heels of the leaders when departing six from home. (op 17-2)

1201 ROY AND CAROLINE HIRONS "PROLIFIC" STANDARD OPEN NATIONAL HUNT FLAT RACE 2m

5:20 (5:21) (Class 6) 4-6-Y-O **£1,370** (£399; £199)

Form RPR

1 **Vertige Dore (FR)**[264] 2319 5-11-1 0.................................. HarrySkelton 120+
(Paul Nicholls) *hld up in rr tl stdy hdwy fr 7f out: trckd ldrs 5f out: travelleing wl whn led appr fnl 2f but hung bdly rt to stands' rail whn shkn up: drvn and styd on wl fnl f* **4/9[1]**

4 **2** *6* **Point Blank (IRE)**[82] 362 4-11-0 0.......................................(t) APMcCoy 110
(Jonjo O'Neill) *disp ld tl led 7f out: rdn and hdd over 2f out: styd on wl for 2nd but no ch w wnr* **6/1[2]**

U **3** *2 1/4* **Salford Rose (IRE)**[3] 1180 4-10-4 0................................ LeeStephens(3) 100+
(David Evans) *in rr tl sme hdwy 6f out: rdn and styd on wl fr over 2f out: hung lft and r.o wl fnl f to take 3rd but nt trble ldng duo* **66/1**

4 *3 1/4* **Dancing Primo** 4-10-7 0.. LiamTreadwell 97
(Mark Brisbourne) *in tch 1/2-way: drvn to chse ldrs fr 4f out: no imp and one pce fnl 2f: lost 3rd ins fnl f* **50/1**

5 *12* **The Lollygagger (IRE)** 6-10-10 0.................................... DavidBass(5) 93
(Alex Hales) *in rr: pushed along 5f out: styd on fnl 2f but nvr any threat: rn wout declared tongue tie* **33/1**

0-4 **6** *3* **Cruise In Style (IRE)**[30] 935 4-10-2 0......................... GilesHawkins(5) 84+
(Kevin Bishop) *chsd ldrs: wnt 2nd 5f out: rdn: hung lft and wknd over 2f out* **16/1**

U0 **7** *3 3/4* **Misstaysia (IRE)**[30] 935 5-10-8 0.................................... AndrewTinkler 79
(Henry Daly) *t.k.h in rr: sme hdwy to get in tch over 4f out: sn dropped away* **25/1**

0-5 **8** *nse* **Bullring (FR)**[14] 1086 4-11-0 0...(tp) DougieCostello 85
(Ollie Pears) *chsd ldrs tl wknd over 4f out* **25/1**

9 *15* **Amazingreyce** 5-9-12 0.. AndrewYoxall(10) 64
(Owen Brennan) *in tch 1/2-way: rdn and wknd 5f out* **50/1**

10 *1 3/4* **Tuckers Treasure** 4-11-0 0.. TjadeCollier 68
(Sue Smith) *chsd ldrs tl wknd qckly over 3f out* **12/1[3]**

0/6 **11** *1/2* **Gutter Lane**[15] 1071 6-10-10 0....................................... JamesHalliday(5) 69
(Malcolm Jefferson) *chsd ldrs 11f: wknd 3f out* **28/1**

12 *3/4* **Mi Man Sam (IRE)**[96] 5-10-8 0.. MrJMahot(7) 68
(George Jones) *a in rr* **66/1**

00 **13** *hd* **Waypost**[15] 1069 4-10-7 0.. MrSWDrinkwater(7) 67
(David Bridgwater) *slt ld tl hdd & wknd rapidly 7f out* **66/1**

14 *80* **Hopeful Dream (IRE)** 5-10-5 0.................................... WayneKavanagh(3) —
(Seamus Mullins) *a in rr: t.o* **40/1**

3m 39.32s (-2.38) **Going Correction** -0.325s/f (Good)
WFA 4 from 5yo+ 1lb 14 Ran SP% **122.0**
Speed ratings: **92,89,87,86,80 78,76,76,69,68 68,67,67,27**
toteswingers:1&2:£1.70, 1&3:£28.30, 2&3:£46.40 CSF £2.86 TOTE £1.30: £1.10, £2.50, £17.80; EX 3.70 Place 6 £150.50; Place 5 £56.87.

Owner Cathal McCarthy **Bred** Chantal Becq **Trained** Ditcheat, Somerset

FOCUS

An ordinary bumper with the winner rated close to his mark, backed up by the seventh and eighth.

NOTEBOOK

Vertige Dore(FR) looks a reasonable recruit. Placed in two of his three bumpers for Willie Mullins back in the autumn, both in soft ground, he won easily despite hanging over to the stands' side as a lot of horses do at Worcester. He will switch to hurdling now and should pay his way. (op 1-2 tchd 8-15 and 4-7 in places)

Point Blank(IRE) built on his Stratford debut but ran into a a decent sort. He stuck on reasonably well for second this time. (op 7-1)

Salford Rose(IRE) unshipped her jockey at the start on her debut at Ffos Las on Tuesday and she hung both turning out of the back straight and in the final furlong here. She showed that she has ability too, but might have more chance against her own sex. (op 80-1)

Dancing Primo is a sister to a 1m4f winner out of a middle-distance mare and she showed enough to suggest she will not let the family down. (op 66-1)

Cruise In Style(IRE) floundered badly in the latter stages after turning for home in second. (tchd 14-1)

T/Plt: £175.90 to a £1 stake. Pool:£69,426.99 - 287.98 winning tickets T/Qpdt: £15.20 to a £1 stake. Pool:£5,367.66 - 260.50 winning tickets ST

1202a - 1225a (Foreign Racing) - See Raceform Interactive

[1158]NEWTON ABBOT (L-H)

Tuesday, August 10

OFFICIAL GOING: Good

All bends moved out about 2m but impact on distances not quantified.
Wind: Strong, across Weather: Overcast with light rain at times

1226 NEWTON ABBOT RACECOURSE JUVENILE HURDLE (8 hdls) 2m 1f

2:15 (2:16) (Class 4) 3-Y-O **£3,082** (£898; £449)

Form RPR

21 **1** **Two Kisses (IRE)**[11] 1135 3-10-12 0................................ AidanColeman 107+
(Brendan Powell) *travelled wl: trckd ldrs: disp fr 3rd: drew clr after 3 out: nt fluent next: v easily* **1/2[1]**

2 *22* **Parhelion**[43] 3-10-12 0...(vt[1]) APMcCoy 84
(Evan Williams) *trckd ldrs: shkn up briefly after 3rd: rdn after 3 out: wnt 2nd whn nt fluent 2 out but no ch w wnr* **5/1[2]**

252 **3** *1 1/4* **Sansili**[24] 1018 3-10-9 0.. DonalDevereux(3) 82
(Peter Bowen) *led: slow 1st: jnd by wnr 3rd: rdn and hdd after 3 out: sn one pce* **7/1[3]**

0 **4** *19* **Storm Command (IRE)**[30] 960 3-10-12 0.................. RichardJohnson 64
(Tim Vaughan) *w ldr early: trckd ldng pair fr 3rd: rdn after 3 out: sn wknd: t.o* **14/1**

2P **5** *5* **Glen Lass**[30] 960 3-10-5 0..(b) DarylJacob 52
(Jamie Snowden) *racd in 5th: reminders fr after 2nd: struggling fr after 4th: nvr any danger: t.o* **14/1**

4m 6.00s (0.30) **Going Correction** +0.125s/f (Yiel) 5 Ran SP% **109.2**
Speed ratings (Par 102): **104,93,93,84,81**
toteswingers: 1&2 £2.30 CSF £3.44 TOTE £1.40: £1.10, £2.00; EX 3.60.

Owner B McNamee, J Mould & J Warner **Bred** Jim Cockburn **Trained** Upper Lambourn, Berks

FOCUS

This was an ordinary race which saw an easy winner. Jockeys afterwards reported the ground to be riding good with a few softer patches.

NOTEBOOK

Two Kisses(IRE) was an easy winner at Bangor last time and doubled her tally over hurdles with the minimum of fuss. She showed a good attitude and her jumping was fluent throughout. This extra experience should hold her in good stead and she now heads to Market Rasen for a valuable contest later this month. (op 8-13 tchd 4-6 in places)

Parhelion, who won a 1m4f maiden for Mark Johnson earlier this year, was making his his hurdling debut for another new stable and raced in a first-time visor. The headgear combined with Tony McCoy failed to get him motivated and he looks a horse with problems, both physically and mentally. (op 7-2)

Sansili's jumping was still less than fluent and he came home well beaten. A step up in trip should suit him but he is beginning to look moderate. (tchd 15-2)

Storm Command(IRE) is a brother to Amir Pasha (low-grade hurdler) and came home well beaten behind the winner at Bangor on his hurdling debut. He well beaten again here and could well prove challenging to win with over hurdles. (op 16-1)

Glen Lass looked uwilling from an early stage. (op 22-1)

1227 NEWTON ABBOT RACECOURSE NOVICES' H'CAP CHASE (16 fncs) 2m 5f 110y

2:45 (2:45) (Class 4) (0-110,108) 4-Y-0+ **£3,577** (£1,050; £525; £262)

Form RPR

4-P2 **1** **Massini Man (IRE)**[14] 1109 9-11-5 **108**.......................... MissCLWills(7) 113+
(Brendan Powell) *led: nt fluent 4th and 5th: hdd next tl 7th: mstke and rdr lost whip 12th: sn hdd: chal 2 out: led sn after last: styd on* **13/2[3]**

52/ **2** *nk* **Ice Warrior (IRE)**[327] 1459 8-11-8 **104**..............................(t) CharliePoste 108
(Milton Harris) *hld up but in tch: rdn and hdwy after 4 out: led sn after 2 out: hdd sn after last: no ex* **9/1**

6-2B **3** *6* **Merry Terry**[20] 1061 6-10-11 **93**... JoeTizzard 95+
(Colin Tizzard) *trckd ldrs: nudged along after 10th: led after 12th: sn rdn whn idling: hdd sn after 2 out: no ex* **13/8[1]**

32P1 **4** *28* **Old Brigade (IRE)**[11] 1136 6-11-8 **104**..................................(t) APMcCoy 90+
(Jonjo O'Neill) *prom: led 6th tl next: w wnr: rdn after 11th: wknd after 3 out: eased flat* **5/2[2]**

23-5 **5** *42* **Quincy Des Pictons (FR)**[19] 1070 6-11-6 **102**................ JodieMogford 38
(M S Tuck) *nvr fluent: mstkes: a last: wknd 11th: t.o* **8/1**

2256 **P** **Bolton Hall (IRE)**[49] 821 8-11-11 **107**...............................(tp) RhysFlint —
(Keith Goldsworthy) *trckd ldrs: hit 5th: pushed along and reminders after 7th: wknd 10th: p.u bef 12th* **12/1**

5m 27.9s (6.50) **Going Correction** +0.225s/f (Yiel) 6 Ran SP% **108.8**
Speed ratings (Par 105): **97,96,94,84,69** —
toteswingers: 1&2 £7.20, 1&3 £3.20, 2&3 £8.30 CSF £51.68 TOTE £11.40: £6.50, £14.00; EX 55.90.

Owner Steven Astaire **Bred** Patrick O'Donnell **Trained** Upper Lambourn, Berks

FOCUS

A low grade race where it would be unwise to go over board about the form.

NOTEBOOK

Massini Man(IRE), switched to a handicap, ran creditably at Worcester when second last time and plugged on the best to score a first win under rules. His rider dropped her whip after the horse made a bad mistake at the 12th fence, but she kept him motivated to score. However, he doesn't appeal as one to follow-up. (tchd 6-1 and 7-1)

Ice Warrior(IRE) was having his first run for 11 months for his new yard and sporting a tongue tie. He is a good-looking sort who plugged on having looked beaten four from home and is entitled to come on for the outing. (op 8-1 tchd 15-2)

Merry Terry failed to win a maiden point, but travelled like the best horse here before finding nothing for pressure. He needs to be covered up until the last possible moment as he idles when he hits the front, but is beginning to look a little exposed. (op 9-4)

Old Brigade(IRE) was given a good ride to score last time, but was unable to follow up and has a cloud hanging over him now. (op 9-4)

Quincy Des Pictons(FR) jumped poorly. Official explanation: jockey said gelding pulled off fore-shoe and jumped poorly (op 7-1)

Bolton Hall(IRE)'s attitude seems to be getting the better of him. (op 10-1)

1228 NEWTON ABBOT RACECOURSE NOVICES' HURDLE (8 hdls) 2m 3f

3:15 (3:15) (Class 4) 4-Y-0+ **£3,903** (£1,146; £573; £286)

Form RPR

-121 **1** **There's No Panic (IRE)**[23] 1026 5-11-7 123...................... MrRMahon(5) 116+
(Paul Nicholls) *mid-div: tk clsr order after 4th: led 6th: rdn whn idled appr 2 out: in command whn nt fluent last: drvn out* **4/11[1]**

3666 **2** *2 1/2* **Kings Riches (IRE)**[8] 1158 5-10-9 0................................ DonalDevereux(3) 98+
(Peter Bowen) *mid-div: nt fluent 1st: hdwy 6th: outpcd after 3 out: styd on fr next: wnt 2nd bef last: nt rch wnr* **20/1**

031 **3** *1* **Safe Catch (IRE)**[8] 1158 8-11-5 104.. JackDoyle 103
(Martin Hill) *led tl 6th: pressed wnr: rdn after 3 out: ch whn nt fluent next: lost 2nd and no ex appr last: b.b.v* **9/2[2]**

0UPO **4** *11* **The Wee Midget**[8] 1158 5-10-12 0 NickScholfield 86
(Arthur Whiting) *hld up: nudged along after 5th: hdwy next: rdn after 3 out: wknd 2 out* **50/1**

-604 **5** *8* **Powerfullbeat**[49] 820 6-10-5 100 MrRHawkins(7) 79
(Kathleen Sanderson) *mid-div: hit 5th: in tch whn rdn after 3 out: wkng whn hit 2 out* **16/1**

4/ **6** *3* **Runaway Harry (IRE)**[869] 4699 7-10-12 0 TomO'Brien 77
(Peter Bowen) *trckd ldrs: hit 3 out: sn rdn: wknd bef next* **20/1**

302 **7** *100* **Bachley Gale**[34] 935 5-10-5 0 RhysFlint —
(Keith Goldsworthy) *disp ld tl wknd appr 6th: t.o* **7/1**[3]

346- **P** **Wadham Hill**[352] 1294 8-9-12 97 BrianToomey(7) —
(William Reed) *a towards rr: t.o whn p.u bef 2 out* **40/1**

0-65 **F** **Yes Minister (IRE)**[13] 1114 6-10-12 0 PaulMoloney —
(Sophie Leech) *hld up towards rr: fell 5th* **66/1**

4m 32.5s (-1.40) **Going Correction** +0.125s/f (Yiel) **9** Ran SP% **125.3**
Speed ratings (Par 105): **107,105,105,100,97 96,—,—,—**
toteswingers: 1&2 £3.90, 1&3 £1.20, 2&3 £7.10 CSF £15.33 TOTE £1.40: £1.02, £4.30, £1.60; EX 11.90.
Owner The Stewart Family **Bred** J R Weston **Trained** Ditcheat, Somerset

NOTEBOOK
There's No Panic(IRE) was a short-priced favourite and entitled to win this. He got the job done, but was workmanlike in doing so. His trainer is of the opinion he would appreciate better ground and idles when he hits the front. He will be kept going over the summer until the ground softens up. He also has the option of going chasing. (op 2-5 tchd 4-9 in a place)
Kings Riches(IRE) has taken his time to warm to hurdling and made good late progress here. This chasing sort could improve again with the added experience under his belt, possibly in handicaps.
Safe Catch(IRE) was outclassed by the winner on this occasion and paid late on for trying to keep with him turning for home. He was clumsy at more than one flight of hurdles and may now find life difficult under a penalty. Official explanation: vet said gelding bled from the nose (op 5-1)
The Wee Midget would be of interest in a low-grade handicap if he learns to settle.
Bachley Gale was disappointing and looked slow, so perhaps a longer trip would help. (op 8-1)

1229 HAPPY 80TH BIRTHDAY COLIN WILLCOCKS H'CAP CHASE (13 fncs) 2m 110y
3:45 (3:45) (Class 2) (0-145,129) 4-Y-0+ **£10,139** (£2,995; £1,497; £748; £374)

Form RPR

-221 **1** **Classic Swain (USA)**[23] 1025 5-11-10 127 (bt) APMcCoy 140+
(Paul Nicholls) *trckd ldrs: j.lft on occasions: led after 3 out: sn rdn whn idled: in command appr last: comf* **3/1**[1]

2536 **2** *3 ¾* **Norborne Bandit (IRE)**[30] 959 9-10-5 108 (p) HarrySkelton 114
(Evan Williams) *trckd ldr: led 7th: rdn after 4 out: hdd after next: kpt on but a being hld by wnr* **7/1**

3413 **3** *8* **Turbo Shandy**[19] 1070 7-9-7 103 (p) BrianToomey(7) 103
(Dai Burchell) *hld up: pckd 3rd: smooth hdwy 4 out: ev ch next: sn rdn: one pce fr next* **17/2**

4-14 **4** *3* **Elite Land**[24] 1023 7-11-3 120 LiamHeard 117
(Brian Ellison) *hld up: nt fluent 9th: sn rdn: styd on same pce fr after 4 out: nvr able to chal* **7/1**

13-5 **5** *3* **Storm Of Applause (IRE)**[30] 959 9-11-4 121 RichardJohnson 116
(Philip Hobbs) *in tch: nt a fluent: nudged along afer 7th: rdn after 4 out: nvr gng pce to get on terms* **10/3**[2]

4123 **6** *3* **Dishdasha (IRE)**[16] 959 8-11-5 129 (t) OliverDayman(7) 120
(Alison Thorpe) *trckd ldrs: rdn after 4 out: styd on same pce fr next: no ex appr last* **8/1**

3011 **P** **De Luain Gorm (IRE)**[58] 734 12-11-10 127 AidanColeman —
(Chris Down) *led tl 7th: chsd ldr tl wknd qckly 4 out: p.u bef next* **9/2**[3]

4m 6.30s (-0.20) **Going Correction** +0.225s/f (Yiel) **7** Ran SP% **112.9**
Speed ratings (Par 109): **109,107,103,102,100 99,—**
toteswingers: 1&2 £5.70, 1&3 £9.90, 2&3 £12.40 CSF £22.97 CT £157.98 TOTE £2.60: £1.10, £5.30; EX 32.00.
Owner The Stewart Family **Bred** Ecurie Du Haras De Meautry **Trained** Ditcheat, Somerset

FOCUS
This modest handicap was run at a solid gallop and the form looks sound enough.

NOTEBOOK
Classic Swain(USA) benefited from the stronger pace on his handicap debut as a chaser and ultimately scored with something in hand. His jumping was not always fluent, but he would also benefit from quicker ground and could return to this venue a week on Sunday for a valuable race over 2m5f, a trip his trainer does expect him to stay. (tchd 4-1)
Norborne Bandit(IRE) ran a creditable race after reverting to his usual prominent style of racing. He often runs his race and should continue to acquit himself well over the summer. However, he now has an overall record of 3-69 and a further 22 placed efforts to add to that, which would not make him appealing for win-only purposes next time. (op 8-1 tchd 9-1 and 13-2)
Turbo Shandy travelled well and finished weakly, as he often does. His trainer has done a tremendous job to win a race with him and he can continue to pay his way with place money for connections. (op 10-1 tchd 11-1)
Elite Land made the long journey from Brian Ellison's Malton base to contest this race, but he never threatened and only plugged on at the one pace from three out to claim minor honours. He lacks the size for fences and could be better returned to hurdles. (op 5-1 tchd 9-2)
Storm Of Applause(IRE) was not always fluent, but this slower ground would have hindered his chances in any case. He would still be of interst on quick summer ground off his current mark. (op 9-2 tchd 3-1)

1230 ST AUSTELL BREWERY H'CAP HURDLE (12 hdls) 3m 3f
4:15 (4:15) (Class 4) (0-115,114) 4-Y-0+ **£3,577** (£1,050; £525; £262)

Form RPR

/P05 **1** **What A Scientist (IRE)**[15] 1093 10-10-12 105 SamTwiston-Davies(5) 111+
(Nigel Twiston-Davies) *mde all: styd on dourly fr 3 out: rdn out* **12/1**

0-2 **2** *3* **Dunkelly Castle (IRE)**[21] 1043 6-11-3 105 HaddenFrost 106
(Roger Curtis) *trckd wnr tl 9th: rdn to regain 2nd after 3 out: styd on but a being hld by wnr* **7/2**[1]

-550 **3** *6* **Skipper's Lad (IRE)**[41] 867 8-10-13 101 (bt) JoeTizzard 97
(Colin Tizzard) *racd wd: in tch: wnt 2nd 9th tl 3 out: sn rdn: styd on same pce* **17/2**

P334 **4** *8* **Is It Me (USA)**[12] 1127 7-11-12 114 (t) PaulMoloney 103
(Sophie Leech) *hld up: short of room on bnd after 8th: sn struggling: styd on past btn horses fr after 3 out: wnt 4th run-in* **14/1**

-655 **5** *1 ½* **Vacario (GER)**[8] 1162 6-11-0 105 (t) TommyPhelan(3) 92
(Mark Gillard) *mid-div: rdn appr 9th: styd on same pce in 4th fr after 3 out: lost 4th run-in* **66/1**

F-66 **6** *16* **Orion Express**[30] 954 9-10-12 100 AidanColeman 79+
(Susan Gardner) *hld up towards rr: hdwy appr 9th: wknd after 3 out: t.o* **9/2**[2]

F6-2 **7** *6* **Balladeer (IRE)**[27] 986 12-11-3 110 DavidBass(5) 78
(Lawney Hill) *in tch: rdn after 8th: sn towards rr: wknd bef 3 out: t.o* **15/2**[3]

P-42 **8** *3* **Casual Garcia**[21] 467 5-11-3 105 (bt) NoelFehily 70
(Mark Gillard) *trckd ldrs: rdn appr 9th: wknd after 3 out: t.o* **11/1**

-210 **9** *7* **Mac Halen (IRE)**[54] 771 7-11-8 113 DPFahy(3) 72
(Evan Williams) *mid-div tl wknd after 9th: t.o* **7/2**[1]

040- **10** *1 ½* **Strikemaster (IRE)**[7] 4783 4-11-1 106 (b) LiamHeard 60
(Brian Ellison) *struggling fr after 8th: a towards rr: wknd 3 out: t.o* **12/1**

6m 45.3s (4.30) **Going Correction** +0.125s/f (Yiel)
WFA 4 from 5yo+ 15lb **10** Ran SP% **116.8**
Speed ratings (Par 105): **98,97,95,92,92 87,86,85,83,82**
toteswingers: 1&2 £4.30, 1&3 £28.80, 2&3 £10.10 CSF £55.03 CT £385.61 TOTE £20.50: £4.90, £1.60, £3.80; EX 82.30.
Owner Mr & Mrs Gordon Pink **Bred** A W Buller **Trained** Naunton, Gloucs

NOTEBOOK
What A Scientist(IRE) looked a reformed performer switched to hurdling under an enterprising ride from Sam Twiston-Davies. He plugged on to get the better of his rivals and ultimately his extra stamina reserves won him the day. He would not be one to back with confidence next time, though. (op 16-1)
Dunkelly Castle(IRE) was runner-up to a subsequent winner at Bangor last month and again ran creditably. He should remain a force in low-grade races, but might only be capable of picking up place money. (op 5-1)
Skipper's Lad(IRE) ran a poor race last time and achieved little in finishing third here. He could prove hard to win with. (op 15-2 tchd 7-1)
Is It Me(USA) would be seen to better effect over shorter trip when able to get an uncontested lead. (op 12-1 tchd 16-1)
Vacario(GER) has been sporting various types of headgear in his recent starts, but he is best left alone for punting purposes. (op 50-1)
Orion Express could be seen to better effect on quicker ground as he is well handicapped. (op 7-2)
Mac Halen(IRE) won on his previous outing over C&D, but disappointed this time out. Official explanation: vet said gelding returned with cut right-hind. (op 6-1)

1231 NEWTON ABBOT RACECOURSE H'CAP CHASE (13 fncs) 2m 110y
4:45 (4:45) (Class 5) (0-90,86) 4-Y-0+ **£2,797** (£821; £410; £205)

Form RPR

1242 **1** **Papradon**[27] 991 6-11-7 86 SamTwiston-Davies(5) 100+
(Nigel Twiston-Davies) *led tl 1st: trckd ldr: led after 4 out: sn rdn: kpt on wl: eased nr fin* **10/3**[1]

4U-4 **2** *6* **Past Heritage**[14] 1106 11-10-12 72 SamThomas 76
(Alan Jones) *hld up: hit 1st: hdwy after 4 out: rdn to chse wnr after 3 out: a being hld fr next* **7/1**

-653 **3** *shd* **Moon Bear**[27] 991 9-10-12 75 (v) DannyCook(3) 79
(Linda Blackford) *cl up: wnt rt 2nd: reminders after 7th: rdn after next: styd on same pce fr 3 out* **6/1**

60-1 **4** *1 ¼* **Barton Sun (IRE)**[30] 961 11-10-11 78 MrSHanson(7) 83+
(Alison Batchelor) *hld up: hdwy 10th: wnt 4th u.p after 4 out: styd on same pce fr next* **8/1**

43P6 **5** *22* **Bid Art (IRE)**[30] 961 5-11-7 86 (t) MrRMahon(5) 71
(Jamie Snowden) *led 1st: mstke 4 out: sn rdn and hdd: nt fluent next (water): wknd bef 2 out* **12/1**

466- **U** **Wild Power (GER)**[240] 2861 12-11-0 74 OwynNelmes —
(Helen Nelmes) *hld up: disputing cl 4th whn blnd and uns rdr 8th* **25/1**

2446 **P** **Post It**[36] 913 9-11-8 82 APMcCoy —
(Ron Hodges) *trckd ldrs tl wknd appr 4 out: bhd whn p.u bef 2 out* **9/2**[3]

34-0 **P** **Louis Ludwig (IRE)**[87] 338 5-11-11 85 (t) RichardJohnson —
(Tim Vaughan) *nt a fluent: cl up tl wknd 10th: t.o whn p.u bef 2 out* **4/1**[2]

4m 13.4s (6.90) **Going Correction** +0.225s/f (Yiel) **8** Ran SP% **110.7**
Speed ratings (Par 103): **92,89,89,88,78 —,—,—**
toteswingers: 1&2 £5.10, 1&3 £4.30, 2&3 £6.60 CSF £24.96 CT £125.79 TOTE £3.20: £1.10, £3.60, £2.90; EX 27.30.
Owner N A Twiston-Davies **Bred** B Whitehouse **Trained** Naunton, Gloucs

FOCUS
A weak handicap.

NOTEBOOK
Papradon, second off this mark at Worcester 27 days earlier, went one place better under another decent ride from his jockey. He appeared to idle once hitting the front and might be able to score again if the handicapper allows. (op 7-2 tchd 4-1 in a place)
Past Heritage ran with promise at Worcester last time and again he ran his race here. However, this does show how good he is. (op 6-1)
Moon Bear was closely matched with the winner on previous Worcester running and he once again ran his race, but his trainer has gone well over a year without a winner. (op 13-2 tchd 7-1)
Barton Sun(IRE) scored at Stratford last month under the same rider, but he was unable to run the same race again. He remains well handicapped on old form, but is becoming hard to predict.
Bid Art(IRE) is best when getting an easy lead and as usual as soon as he was headed he stopped. He is hard to predict and would not be one to back with any confidence. (op 9-1)
Post It failed to run her recent level. (op 11-2)
Louis Ludwig(IRE)'s jumping was not up to scratch. (op 11-2)

1232 NEWTON ABBOT RACECOURSE H'CAP HURDLE (10 hdls) 2m 6f
5:15 (5:18) (Class 5) (0-90,92) 4-Y-0+ **£2,055** (£599; £299)

Form RPR

4PP- **1** **Caheerloch (IRE)**[155] 4492 8-11-2 85 SamTwiston-Davies(5) 95
(Nigel Twiston-Davies) *mid-div: hdwy after 7th: rdn to ld appr 2 out: hld on wl: all out* **10/1**

-505 **2** *nk* **Bathwick Breeze**[20] 1057 6-11-7 85 (v) JohnnyFarrelly 95
(David Pipe) *mid-div: hdwy 7th: rdn to chal appr 2 out: ev ch fr last: kpt on: hld nr fin* **14/1**

0-04 **3** *3 ¼* **Mista Rossa**[79] 441 5-10-12 81 MissLHorner(5) 88
(Jamie Snowden) *hld up towards rr: hdwy after 7th: 6th whn nt clr run appr 2 out: sn rdn: styng on at same pce whn lft 4th last: wnt 3rd sn after* **14/1**

0251 **4** *nk* **Risk Challenge (USA)**[7] 1179 8-11-9 92 7ex (t) JimmyDerham(5) 99
(Milton Harris) *hld up bhd: stdy prog fr 7th: rdn to chse ldng quartet appr 2 out: nt pce to chal: lft 3rd briefly last* **7/2**[1]

03 **5** *11* **Low Delta (IRE)**[27] 990 10-11-12 90 NickScholfield 87
(Michael Blake) *hld up towards rr: rdn and stdy hdwy fr after 7th: styd on same pce fr 2 out: nvr rchd ldrs* **11/1**

P-35 **6** *12* **Bring It On Home**[11] 1141 6-11-12 90 PaulMoloney 76
(Sophie Leech) *trckd ldrs tl lost pl after 4th: sn rdn: nvr bk on terms* **14/1**

4 **7** *1* **Murphys Appeal (IRE)**[21] 1043 6-11-7 85 TomO'Brien 70
(Peter Bowen) *trckd ldr: led after 6th: rdn and hdd bef 2 out: wknd* **25/1**

PP0- **8** *8* **Lennox Gardens**[182] 3948 6-11-12 90 NoelFehily 68
(Warren Greatrex) *mid-div: hdwy 7th: effrt after 3 out: wknd bef next* **11/1**

00P- **9** *5* **Kyoto (GER)**[114] 5258 6-11-7 85 DavidDennis 58
(Nigel Hawke) *mid-div: hdwy 7th: effrt after 3 out: wknd bef next* **28/1**

-55P **10** *14* **Cave Of The Giant (IRE)**[15] 1094 8-11-10 88 JoeTizzard 49
(Tim McCarthy) *mid-div tl 6th: sn rdn and bhd: t.o* **33/1**

The Form Book, Raceform Ltd, Compton, RG20 6NL

0-02 **11** *15* **Bubbs**[64] 660 8-11-3 **86**...............(p) GilesHawkins(5) 33
(Nick Ayliffe) *led tl after 6th: sn rdn: wknd after next: t.o* **6/1**[2]

0P6P **P** **Dancing Hill**[7] 1179 11-11-0 **78**...............(t) ColinBolger —
(Kevin Bishop) *trckd ldrs: hit 5th: sn rdn and dropped to rr: p.u bef next: dismntd* **50/1**

/4P- **P** **Munching Mike (IRE)**[150] 4584 7-11-4 **82**...............(p) RhysFlint —
(Michael Scudamore) *blnd 1st: a towards rr: t.o whn p.u bef 2 out* **33/1**

P3 **P** **Kingston Queen (IRE)**[20] 1059 7-11-1 **82**...............(v1) SeanQuinlan(3) —
(Kim Bailey) *in tch: struggling whn hit 3 out: sn wknd: p.u bef next* **14/1**

U302 **F** **Racingisdreaming (USA)**[7] 1179 4-11-7 **90**...............(vt) DannyCook(3) 95
(David Pipe) *in tch: wnt 2nd 9th: rdn and ev ch appr 2 out: cl 3rd whn fell last: fatally injured* **13/2**[3]

00-3 **P** **Elegant Olive**[23] 1035 7-11-4 **82**............... HaddenFrost —
(Roger Curtis) *trckd ldrs: rdn after 3 out: wknd qckly: p.u bef next* **12/1**

5m 27.6s (7.40) **Going Correction** +0.125s/f (Yiel)
WFA 4 from 5yo+ 14lb **16** Ran SP% **125.1**
Speed ratings (Par 103): **91,90,89,89,85 81,80,77,76,71 65,—,—,—,— —**
toteswingers: 1&2 £33.30, 1&3 £57.90, 2&3 £54.80. totesuper7: Win: Not won. Place: £140.60. CSF £137.79 CT £1985.58 TOTE £19.70: £4.60, £5.60, £4.80, £1.10; EX 285.50 Place 6 £96.20, Place 5 £84.79.
Owner One For The Road Partnership **Bred** Ballylinch Stud **Trained** Naunton, Gloucs
■ Stewards' Enquiry : Joe Tizzard five-day ban: used whip with excessive force (Aug 24-28)

FOCUS
A big-field handicap where the overall form would be worth very little.

NOTEBOOK
Caheerloch(IRE) had been pulled up in both starts this year, but he responded well to this longer trip on this return from a 155-day break, handing his rider a treble in the process. He has turned over a new leaf form-wise here, but might find it hard to win again once reassessed. (op 9-1)
Bathwick Breeze has been tumbling down the weights of late and this was his first sign of a return to form. However, his inconsistent nature would make him hard to back with any real confidence next time.
Mista Rossa was a moderate fourth at Fakenham when last seen over hurdles and this form is not much better. Winning races over hurdles could proved challenging for him. Official explanation: jockey said gelding hung right-handed
Risk Challenge(USA) was an easy winner at Ffos Las last time, but the 7lb penalty left him on a career-high mark. In the circumstances, he ran respectably. (op 4-1)
Low Delta(IRE) has a poor strike-rate and never looked like landing a telling blow here. He would appreciate softer ground, but is another who probably needs to drop to plating class to register a win. (op 9-1)
Bubbs was well fancied at a course she goes well at, but this big field may have played against her. In a smaller field she could do better again. (tchd 13-2)
Dancing Hill was pulled up and later removed by horse ambulance. (op 9-1)
Racingisdreaming(USA) sadly took a fatal fall at the final flight. (op 9-1)
T/Plt: £217.60 to a £1 stake. Pool: £73,797.10. 247.56 winning tickets. T/Qpdt: £12.80 to a £1 stake. Pool: £6,360.91. 367.17 winning tickets. TM

1124 STRATFORD (L-H)

Thursday, August 12

OFFICIAL GOING: Good to firm (watered; 10.1)
Rails moved out by at least 1m on all bends.
Wind: almost nil Weather: showery but warm

1233 MID WARWICKSHIRE MARES' NOVICES' HURDLE (10 hdls) 2m 3f

5:35 (5:35) (Class 4) 4-Y-0+ **£3,252** (£955; £477; £238)

Form RPR

4-12 **1** **Black Annie (IRE)**[29] 989 5-10-10 0...............(t) APMcCoy 108+
(Paul Webber) *mde all: set slow gallop: blnd 5th: rdn 2 l clr after 3 out: styng on same pce but in command whn nt fluent last* **7/2**[3]

-120 **2** *3* **Astrolibra**[26] 1017 6-11-3 115............... ColinBolger 110
(Mark H Tompkins) *t.k.h in slow r: trckd ldrs: wnt 2nd after 6th: rdn after 3 out: no imp next: fin w tongue lolling* **11/4**[2]

6-31 **3** *11* **Call At Midnight**[14] 1124 5-11-3 104............... AidanColeman 102+
(Sarah Humphrey) *plld hrd in last: effrt bef 7th but sn rdn and outpcd: wnt 7 l 3rd bef 2 out: no imp after* **11/10**[1]

3-54 **4** *8* **Midnight Fun**[23] 1046 5-10-3 0............... RobertKirk(7) 84
(Michael Appleby) *w wnr tl hit 2nd: lost 2nd after 6th: mstke next: rdn and btn wl bef 2 out: wnt poor 4th nr fin* **50/1**

30 **5** *½* **Daliarose (FR)**[26] 1023 4-11-1 112............... JohnnyFarrelly 89
(David Pipe) *t.k.h in rr: nt fluent 6th: effrt bef next: drvn and fdd v tamely after 3 out* **10/1**

0-6 **6** *32* **Altos Reales**[53] 792 6-10-10 0............... SamJones 52
(Michael Scudamore) *settled trcking ldrs: stl in tch but rdn whn blnd 3 out and lost all ch: t.o whn blnd next* **20/1**

05 **7** *4 ½* **Reg's Ruby**[21] 1071 4-10-5 0............... SeanQuinlan(3) 45
(David Bridgwater) *numerous mstkes: lost tch and j. slowly 7th: t.o after next: blnd 2 out* **150/1**

4m 31.5s **Going Correction** -0.30s/f (Good)
WFA 4 from 5yo+ 13lb **7** Ran SP% **113.0**
Speed ratings (Par 105): **96,94,90,86,86 73,71**
toteswingers:1&2:£3.20, 1&3:£1.50, 2&3:£1.10 CSF £13.43 TOTE £3.70: £2.20, £2.00; EX 14.10.
Owner Shully Liebermann **Bred** Mrs Lynne Lyons **Trained** Mollington, Oxon

FOCUS
A steadily run mares' novice event, rated around the runner-up.

NOTEBOOK
Black Annie(IRE) was up in trip and got off the mark at the second attempt as a hurdler, but anyone who backed her has Tony McCoy to thank, as he gave her an excellent tactical ride that caught out most of the runners. She cut out most of the early running at an ordinary gallop, but McCoy sent her into a clear lead around four out and that saw most of the field become outpaced. She was in no real danger coming to the last and, although she was gifted the run of things, was comfortably on top at the finish. A penalty would make her look vulnerable in novice company, but she isn't fully exposed and could well defy one if kept to racing against her own sex. (op 11-4 tchd 4-1)
Astrolibra was the only one to get close to the winner after that one suddenly increased the tempo and performed a lot better than had been the case in a handicap on her previous outing. She helps to set the level (op 7-2 tchd 5-2)
Call At Midnight has improved since joining her current trainer and shouldn't be judged too harshly here as she was the chief sufferer when the winner kicked for home. Granted more of a test again, she ought to be seen back in a better light. (op 13-8)
Midnight Fun disputed a lot of the early running with the winner, but was left behind when the race got serious. She ought to fare better when faced with a stiffer test in low-grade handicaps. (op 40-1)
Daliarose(FR) failed to raise her game on this return to novice hurdling and has a disappointing profile. (op 15-2)

1234 GREENHILL JUVENILE (S) HURDLE (9 hdls) 2m 110y

6:05 (6:05) (Class 5) 3-Y-0 **£1,951** (£573; £286; £143)

Form RPR

U05 **1** **Pobs Trophy**[4] 1018 3-10-12 0...............(p) DougieCostello 85+
(Richard Guest) *w ldr tl led 5th: rdn bef 2 out: forged clr between last two: pushed out: comf* **3/1**[2]

2 *7* **Star Of Kalani (IRE)**[27] 3-10-12 0............... JackDoyle 81+
(Robert Wylie) *mstke 1st: bhd tl prog after 5th: wnt 2nd wl bef 2 out: 2 l down and looking tired whn mstke 2 out: wl hld after: mstke last* **20/1**

3 *6* **Massachusetts**[21] 3-10-12 0............... JohnnyFarrelly 75
(Brendan Powell) *midfield: rdn bef 5th: wnt 2nd and blnd 3 out: lost 2nd bef home turn: 9 l 3rd and tiring 2 out* **8/1**

U05 **4** *7* **Dinkie Short**[13] 1135 3-10-12 0...............(p) DarylJacob 67
(Ben De Haan) *hld up and nvr bttr than midfield: mstke 5th: rdn and wknd after 3 out: 15 l 4th next* **11/1**

U46 **5** *7* **Sefton Park**[13] 1135 3-10-12 0...............(p) JimmyMcCarthy 61
(Charles Egerton) *nt jump wl: chsd ldrs tl drvn and nt keen 6th: wl bhd after next: mstke last* **9/2**[3]

6P **6** *17* **Ariel Bender**[13] 1135 3-10-9 0...............(b) AdrianLane(3) 45
(Donald McCain) *plld hrd: mde most tl hit 5th: mstke 6th: drvn and looked v awkward after: sn t.o* **14/1**

7 *8* **Baltic Ben (USA)**[89] 3-10-12 0............... RichardJohnson 38
(Tim Vaughan) *nt jump wl towards rr: mstke 4th: rdn and stuggling bef 6th: sn t.o* **5/2**[1]

6 **8** *8* **Brave Talk**[25] 1024 3-10-12 0............... DavidDennis 31
(Nigel Hawke) *mstkes: in tch tl rdn and struggling bef 6th where blnd bdly: continued t.o* **33/1**

P **Labretella (IRE)**[8] 3-10-0 0............... JamesHalliday(5) —
(Shaun Harris) *bhd: rdn and struggling after 5th: bdly t.o whn p.u 2 out* **18/1**

P **Jonny No Eyebrows**[15] 3-10-5 0............... MrRichardCollinson(7) —
(Patrick Leech) *awkward to s: hld up in rr: pushed along after 4th: stopped to nil after next and p.u 6th* **80/1**

R **Wee Ginge** 3-10-12 0............... NickScholfield —
(Emma McWilliam) *clueless and climbed over 1st and 2nd: sn t.o: tk frt at sight of 3rd and threw rdr off on the approach* **20/1**

3m 53.4s (-2.60) **Going Correction** -0.30s/f (Good) **11** Ran SP% **116.8**
Speed ratings (Par 100): **94,90,87,84,81 73,69,65,—,— —**
toteswingers:1&2:£9.70, 1&3:£7.40, 2&3:£19.50 CSF £62.89 TOTE £3.90: £1.60, £11.40, £6.60; EX 76.00.There was no bid for the winner.
Owner Future Racing (Notts) Limited **Bred** Mrs S Joint **Trained** Stainforth, S Yorks

FOCUS
This was a desperately weak juvenile event.

NOTEBOOK
Pobs Trophy readily won his first race of any description at the seventh time of asking. He had shown little previously, including in three previous outings over hurdles, but the drop in class obviously did the trick and he has now found his level. (op 4-1)
Star Of Kalani(IRE), a 38-rated maiden on the level, stayed on best of the rest and this switch to hurdling brought about his best effort so far. This is his class, but he is entitled to improve for the initial experience. (op 16-1)
Massachusetts is a 45-rated maiden on the Flat. He never seriously threatened, but he too is entitled to come on for the experience and it wouldn't be surprising to see blinkers back on before too long in this sphere. (op 7-1 tchd 6-1)
Dinkie Short, dropped in class, was having his fourth outing as a hurdler and could only plod on at the same pace when it mattered. (op 12-1 tchd 10-1)
Baltic Ben(USA), making his debut for Tim Vaughan, didn't jump well but really performed too badly to be true and it later transpired he had sustained a cut to his near fore. Official explanation: vet said gelding was found to have a cut to its near-fore (tchd 9-4)

1235 AMBER SECURITY H'CAP CHASE (17 fncs) 2m 7f

6:40 (6:40) (Class 4) (0-110,109) 4-Y-0+ **£4,358** (£1,279; £639; £319)

Form RPR

P424 **1** **Keltic Lord**[11] 1152 14-10-9 **92**............... NickScholfield 101
(Peter Hiatt) *led after 1st and sn 15 l clr: stl 7 l up and gng best 14th: styd on v gamely flat* **9/1**

5PP4 **2** *3* **Rash Moment (FR)**[14] 1128 11-10-0 **83** oh4...............(p) SamJones 88
(Michael Scudamore) *led tl after 2nd: chsd clr ldr tl 11th: rdn 14th: regained 2nd 2 out: 5 l down last: kpt on under heavy press but a hld* **8/1**[3]

-432 **3** *23* **Quedillac (FR)**[20] 1082 6-11-10 **107**............... RichardJohnson 92
(Tim Vaughan) *mstke 2nd (water): hld up: wnt 3rd at 10th and modest 2nd at 11th: rdn 14th and nvr win 7 l of wnr: tired whn lost 2nd 2 out* **7/2**[2]

0021 **4** *5* **Rokinhorsescience (FR)**[11] 1152 6-11-4 **101** 7ex...............(bt) APMcCoy 81
(Jonjo O'Neill) *settled 3rd or 4th: rdn after 11th and immediately downed tools and lost tch: 25 l 4th at 14th* **5/6**[1]

2460 **5** *33* **Masterpoint**[32] 961 10-9-7 **83** oh4............... MrJBanks(7) 33
(Richard Harper) *chsd ldrs but wl off the pce of wnr: struggling fr 12th: bdly t.o* **33/1**

2320 **P** **Kanad**[25] 1032 8-11-12 **109**...............(tp) WarrenMarston —
(Milton Harris) *disputing poor last and reminders 10th: nvr gng wl after: t.o and p.u 13th: lame* **12/1**

624/ **P** **Sternenzelt (GER)**[75] 7-11-5 **109**............... MrJEngland(7) —
(Michael Gates) *last pair fr 5th and nvr gng wl after: t.o 12th: p.u 2 out* **16/1**

5m 36.9s (-4.70) **Going Correction** -0.075s/f (Good) **7** Ran SP% **114.4**
Speed ratings (Par 105): **105,103,95,94,82 —,—**
toteswingers:1&2:£5.10, 1&3:£6.60, 2&3:£3.40 CSF £73.00 TOTE £15.80: £4.20, £2.30; EX 57.10.
Owner Paul Porter **Bred** Miss H Day **Trained** Hook Norton, Oxon
■ Stewards' Enquiry : Sam Jones three-day ban: used whip with excessive frequency (Aug 26-28)

FOCUS
The heavens opened prior to this moderate handicap, but it wouldn't have affected the ground. It was run at a solid gallop and dominated by a pair of veteran course specialists.

NOTEBOOK
Keltic Lord was 3lb lower than when winning the race last season and he repeated the feat with a gallant round from the front, gaining a fourth success at the course. He set off at a decent pace and opened up the clear early lead. It was apparent on the final circuit he had most of his rivals in trouble, but he began to tire from the third-last and showed a most willing attitude to keep going in the home straight. This was his first win since and obviously his profile dictates he is not one for a follow up. (op 10-1 tchd 11-1)
Rash Moment(FR) came into this boasting four previous wins over C&D. He allowed the winner to go on early and never really looked like reeling him back, despite eating into his advantage from two out. He finished a clear second-best and it was a much more encouraging effort in defeat. (op 17-2)

Quedillac(FR), second over 2m last time, tried his best to get seriously involved on the final circuit but ultimately his stamina gave way before the home turn. He has scored over 2m4f as a hurdler and dropping back to that trip should help. (tchd 10-3 tchd 4-1 in places)

Rokinhorsescience(FR) belatedly showed his true colours when bolting up at Market Rasen 11 days earlier, when he had Keltic Lord well behind. He never looked that happy here, though, possibly on account of the stronger early gallop and it's not hard to see why he sports headgear. (op 10-11 after early evens in places)

Kanad never looked happy and was later found to have been lame. Official explanation: jockey said gelding finished lame (op 14-1)

1236 EDWARD BRAIN PLANT HIRE H'CAP HURDLE (9 hdls) 2m 110y

7:10 (7:10) (Class 4) (0-100,100) 4-Y-0+ **£3,903** (£1,146; £573; £286)

Form				RPR
34P-	1		**Lodgician (IRE)**[380] 1072 8-10-12 **91**.................. SamTwiston-Davies(5)	103+
(Nigel Twiston-Davies) *trckd ldrs gng wl: pushed ahd after 3 out: rdn and 4 l clr 2 out: styd on wl* **9/2**[3]

3-55 **2** *8* **Josephine Malines**[75] 515 6-11-10 **98**..................... (t) RichardJohnson 103+
(Tim Vaughan) *t.k.h towards rr: effrt bef 6th: chsd ldrs next: wnt 2nd bef 2 out where mstke whn drvn and no imp* **15/2**

63-1 **3** *9* **Domino Dancer (IRE)**[26] 762 6-11-12 **100**.......................(b) APMcCoy 98
(Jim Best) *set brisk pce: reminders after 5th: hdd briefly next: hdd again after 3 out: nt run on and lost 2nd bef next where nt fluent* **9/4**[1]

P041 **4** *10* **Nothing Is Forever (IRE)**[10] 1164 6-11-8 **96** 7ex.............(p) DarylJacob 84
(Liam Corcoran) *prom: led briefly 6th: blnd next: wknd tamely whn drvn wl bef 2 out: sn hanging lft: hit 2 out* **3/1**[2]

6-P4 **5** *1 1/2* **Raise Again (IRE)**[12] 853 7-10-13 **87**............................ AidanColeman 72
(Nerys Dutfield) *bhd tl sme prog after 5th: modest 5th and no ch after 3 out* **9/1**

3P-4 **6** *hd* **Just Beware**[74] 534 8-11-1 **92**....................................(p) CharlieStudd(3) 77
(Zoe Davison) *bhd: str reminders after 4th: outpcd after next: plugging on after last* **25/1**

0-P0 **7** *3 3/4* **Bond Cruz**[17] 1095 7-10-1 **82**... RobertKirk(7) 64
(Olivia Maylam) *towards rr: rdn and struggling bef 6th: blnd next* **33/1**

4-60 **8** *21* **Massams Lane**[11] 1147 6-11-7 **100**...................................... DavidBass(5) 63
(Carole Ikin) *pressed ldrs tl rdn bef 5th: little rspnse: btn next: t.o* **12/1**

10/P **9** *10* **Devilfishpoker Com**[20] 1085 6-10-10 **89**..................... JamesHalliday(5) 43
(Shaun Harris) *a last: nt gng wl after 4th: mstke 6th: t.o after* **100/1**

02P6 **P** **Basford Tara**[17] 1090 5-11-9 **97**.....................................(b[1]) AlanO'Keeffe —
(Jennie Candlish) *pressed ldr tl hit 4th and c u.p: nt run on fr next: t.o and p.u 3 out* **33/1**

3m 48.7s (-7.30) **Going Correction** -0.30s/f (Good) **10** Ran SP% **114.1**
Speed ratings (Par 105): **105,101,97,92,91 91,89,79,75,—**
toteswingers:1&2:£3.60, 1&3:£4.60, 2&3:£4.40 CSF £35.69 CT £94.19 TOTE £3.40: £1.10, £2.00, £1.20; EX 25.60.
Owner The Yes No Wait Sorries **Bred** Sir Eric Parker **Trained** Naunton, Gloucs

FOCUS
An ordinary handicap, run at a fair gallop.

NOTEBOOK
Lodgician(IRE) attracted plenty of support on this seasonal return and rewarded his supporters with an easy success. He travelled well through the race and took it up turning into the home straight. He had to be urged on before the second-last, but pinged it and was able to coast home near the finish, under a conditional rider who can do little wrong at present. It was his first win since he scored his only previous success in this sphere 2006, but he missed all of 2007 and most of 2008. He also hasn't been with this yard for all that long and has clearly done well for his time away from the track. The bounce factor would be of some concern if he turns out under a penalty, but he is worth treating as an improver nevertheless and this does look his optimum trip now. (op 7-2)

Josephine Malines was having her first run for Tim Vaughan after a 75-day break. She proved free early on and wasn't that fluent, but kept on for pressure and finished nicely clear in second. She probably wants more of a test and the market suggested the run would bring her on, so she is one to look out for next time. (op 7-1 tchd 13-2)

Domino Dancer(IRE) has been in good form the last twice on the level since winning comfortably over hurdles on debut for connections in June on his previous outing over hurdles. With the blinkers retained, he set out to make all but was in trouble from the third-last and his stone higher mark probably found him out. (op 15-8 tchd 5-2 in places)

Nothing Is Forever(IRE) was up 7lb for resuming winning ways at Newton Abbot ten days earlier. He was going as well as any three out, but wasn't clever at it and immediately began to feel the pinch. (op 4-1 tchd 9-2)

Raise Again(IRE), who met support, made laboured headway from off the pace and continues to look out of sorts. (op 12-1)

Massams Lane Official explanation: trainer said on return gelding was found to have burst a blood vessel

1237 STOUT CONSTRUCTION NOVICES' H'CAP CHASE (15 fncs) 2m 5f 110y

7:45 (7:45) (Class 5) (0-95,93) 4-Y-0+ **£2,797** (£821; £410; £205)

Form RPR

2123 **1** **Sir Bumble (IRE)**[20] 1080 10-11-3 **87**..............................(t) PeterToole(3) 97
(Michael Blake) *settled trcking ldrs: effrt 3 out: led nring next and decisive move to forge clr: 3 l ahd last: all out but hld on gallantly* **3/1**[1]

4444 **2** *1 1/4* **Monty's Moon (IRE)**[20] 1080 8-10-0 **67** oh1.................(b) AidanColeman 75
(Rachel Hobbs) *trckd ldrs: effrt and cl up whn mstke 3 out: chsd wnr but outpcd fr next where lft 5 l 3rd: drvn and tending to edge lft after: wnt 2nd between last 2: kpt on after last but a jst hld* **5/1**[3]

P153 **3** *1 3/4* **Khazar (FR)**[43] 864 7-11-10 **91**..................................... APMcCoy 97
(Jonjo O'Neill) *j. slowly 2nd: trckd ldrs: j.v.slowly 6th: one of six in tight huddle whn nt fluent 12th: drvn and w little rspnse 2 out and bec outpcd: wnt 3rd and kpt on after last: nvr helping rdr* **6/1**

/65 **4** *8* **Doheny Bar (IRE)**[17] 1091 7-11-12 **93**.........................(p) JodieMogford 94
(Nikki Evans) *racd keenly: w ldr: mstke 3rd: led 11th: rdn and hdd nring 2 out: wknd and lost 2nd between last two: lost 3rd at last* **50/1**

-543 **U** **Cloonavery (IRE)**[16] 1106 8-10-0 **67** oh2......................... LiamTreadwell 77
(Tony Carroll) *settled towards rr: effrt and cl up in 12th: half l 2nd and gng wl: whn blnd bdly 2 out and rdr thrown off* **11/2**

2514 **P** **Risk Challenge (USA)**[2] 1232 8-10-13 **80**.......................(t) CharliePoste —
(Milton Harris) *t.k.h in rr: effrt and cl up 12th: blnd and almost fell 3 out: lost all ch and sn p.u* **4/1**[2]

UF-5 **P** **Intense Suspense (IRE)**[14] 1126 7-9-11 **67** oh14... WayneKavanagh(3) —
(Robin Dickin) *hd str on outside: mde most w slt advantage tl 11th: stopped to nil bef next where mstke: t.o and p.u 3 out* **12/1**

060- **P** **Estrica (IRE)**[110] 5389 7-9-11 **69**...............................(t) MichaelMurphy(5) —
(Tim Vaughan) *midfield and pushed along 7th: rapidly lost tch u.p 9th: t.o and p.u 11th: b.b.v* **9/1**

0660 **P** **Always Cruising (USA)**[22] 1059 5-10-12 **79**.................... NickScholfield —
(Linda Blackford) *mstkes: last fr 5th: t.o 9th: p.u 11th* **33/1**

5m 11.6s (-3.40) **Going Correction** -0.075s/f (Good) **9** Ran SP% **113.9**
Speed ratings (Par 103): **103,102,101,99,— —,—,—,—**
toteswingers:1&2:£2.70, 1&3:£2.70, 2&3:£8.50 CSF £18.66 CT £83.16 TOTE £2.30: £1.02, £2.50, £3.00; EX 23.10.
Owner Staverton Owners Group **Bred** B Stack **Trained** Trowbridge, Wilts

FOCUS
This moderate novice handicap was run at a sound gallop and it proved a fairly eventful contest with only four getting home.

NOTEBOOK
Sir Bumble(IRE) dug deep on the run-in to repel the runner-up and gain a second career success. He came under pressure three out, but rallied and was in the firing line prior to be left in a clear lead at the penultimate fence. It's debatable what would've happened had Cloonavery not departed there, but this ultra-consistent performer's attitude cannot be questioned and it was another deserved win. (op 11-4 tchd 10-3 in places)

Monty's Moon(IRE) put in a more assured round of jumping and as a result finished an awful lot closer to the winner than was the case at Southwell last time. He will go up for this, but surely has a race in him providing his jumping holds up in future. (op 8-1)

Khazar(FR), back from a 43-day break, hit a marked flat spot two out before rallying late in the day. It may be that some headgear will be reapplied after this as he clearly gets the trip. (op 11-2 tchd 5-1)

Doheny Bar(IRE) did a lot of the donkey work and this was more respectable, but further respite in the weights is probably required. (tchd 66-1)

Cloonavery(IRE) ◆, ridden to get the trip, had crept into things going strongly prior to his exit at the second-last. He could well make amends next time if none the worse. (tchd 7-2)

Risk Challenge(USA), laboured over hurdles two days previously, is well handicapped over fences and things looked good for his supporters as he began to get involved nearing the third-last. He agonisingly clouted it, though, bringing and end to his chances and is now due to race off a 15lb higher mark due to his recent improvement over hurdles. (tchd 7-2)

Estrica(IRE) Official explanation: vet said mare bled from the nose (tchd 7-2)

Always Cruising(USA) Official explanation: trainer said gelding had a breathing problem (tchd 7-2)

1238 ORCHARD HILL NOVICES' HURDLE (9 hdls) 2m 110y

8:15 (8:16) (Class 4) 4-Y-0+ **£3,252** (£955; £477; £238)

Form RPR

4-16 **1** **Rio Gael (IRE)**[10] 1160 4-11-4 115.........................(p) TomO'Brien 116+
(Peter Bowen) *mde all: rdn bef 2 out: kpt on gamely flat* **11/4**[2]

2 *1 1/4* **Tara Warrior (IRE)**[62] 719 4-10-11 109....................... RichardJohnson 109+
(Tim Vaughan) *settled 3rd: drvn 3 out: wnt 2nd and blnd 2 out: no imp whn mstke last but kpt on* **15/8**[1]

62 **3** *8* **Rafta (IRE)**[17] 1090 4-9-11 0................................ MissIsabelTompsett(7) 94
(W G Harrison) *on her toes: sddle slipped 1st: towards rr: effrt 6th: kpt on after 3 out: bmpd along to go 3rd bef last: no ch w ldrs but gallant effrt fr horse and rdr* **13/2**[3]

030- **4** *4 1/2* **Crystal Rock (IRE)**[205] 3531 5-10-12 109.............................. APMcCoy 101+
(Nicky Henderson) *mstkes: pressed wnr: rdn after blunder 3 out: lost 2nd bef next and hanging lft: fin v weakly* **11/4**[2]

/0-0 **5** *35* **Bolanderi (USA)**[23] 182 5-10-12 0.............................(p) NickScholfield 66
(Andy Turnell) *t.k.h in rr: effrt 5th: rdn next: sn fdd: t.o* **20/1**

6 *61* **Pedasus (USA)**[27] 4-10-11 0.. PaulMoloney 10
(Tom Keddy) *mstke 2nd and drvn along: chsd ldrs tl lost pl 5th: sn hopelessly t.o* **28/1**

U **P** **Bluebird Chariot**[57] 760 7-10-5 0................................ MrTJCannon(7) —
(Milton Bradley) *j. most erratically in rr: t.o whn veered bdly lft 5th and qckly p.u* **150/1**

P **Trading Nation (USA)**[45] 4-10-11 0................................. LiamTreadwell —
(Peter Hiatt) *s.s: way adrift whn climbed 1st: v hdstr and in tch briefly 3rd: t.o after next: p.u after 5th* **66/1**

3m 51.2s (-4.80) **Going Correction** -0.30s/f (Good) **8** Ran SP% **111.8**
Speed ratings (Par 105): **99,98,94,92,76 47,—,—**
toteswingers:1&2:£1.70, 1&3:£3.30, 2&3:£2.30 CSF £8.14 TOTE £3.40: £1.30, £1.10, £2.00; EX 9.70 Place 6: £186.72 Place 5: £71.80.
Owner Mrs Karen Bowen **Bred** Glending Bloodstock **Trained** Little Newcastle, Pembrokes

FOCUS
An ordinary novice event.

NOTEBOOK
Rio Gael(IRE) made it 2-3 since joining Peter Bowen. Having bolted up in a seller on his debut for the yard, he failed to meet market expectation when switched to a handicap on his previous outing and came here with a bit to prove. The return to more positive tactics suited as he settled better, though, and he deserves credit for giving the runner-up 7lb. (op 7-2 tchd 4-1)

Tara Warrior(IRE), a maiden in Ireland, was having his 11th outing over hurdles on this British debut for Tim Vaughan and got well backed. He felt the pinch around three out, but kept on for pressure and this was certainly a run he can build on back over a stiffer test. (op 7-4 tchd 13-8 and 2-1)

Rafta(IRE), a maiden in Ireland, was having his 11th outing over hurdles on this British debut for Tim Vaughan and got well backed. He felt the pinch around three out, but kept on for pressure and this was certainly a run he can build on back over a stiffer test. Official explanation: jockey said saddle slipped (op 6-1 tchd 7-1)

Crystal Rock(IRE) failed to up his game on this return from a 205-day absence and jumped moderately. Connections will be praying he come on a bundle for the run and a return to the level could be on the cards. (tchd 9-4)

T/Plt: £234.90 to a £1 stake. Pool of £51,342.84 - 159.50 winning tickets. T/Qpdt: £38.20 to a £1 stake. Pool of £6,895.23 - 133.50 winning tickets. IM

1239 - 1248a (Foreign Racing) - See Raceform Interactive

[1147] MARKET RASEN (R-H)

Saturday, August 14

OFFICIAL GOING: Good (hdl: 6.6 chs: 7.1)
All rails moved out 3-4 yards to provide fresh ground.
Wind: moderate 1/2 behind Weather: fine and sunny

1249 HENDOO "HANDS AND HEELS" (S) HURDLE (THE RACING EXCELLENCE INITIATIVE) (CONDITIONALS/AMATEURS) (8 hdls) 2m 1f

5:40 (5:40) (Class 4) 4-Y-0+ **£2,276** (£668; £334; £166)

Form RPR

U6-P **1** **Liberty Seeker (FR)**[48] 846 11-11-5 100........................... MattCrawley 102+
(John Harris) *hld up: hdwy to chse ldrs 3 out: led last: drvn clr* **7/1**

40U **2** *5* **Hi Wycombe (IRE)**[16] 1124 6-10-9 99.......................... MrSWDrinkwater(3) 91
(David Bridgwater) *chsd ldrs: drvn to ld 3 out: hdd last: styd on same pce* **10/1**

-640 **3** *nse* **Cortinas (GER)**[22] 1084 8-10-7 113.................(t) MrCharlieDuckworth(5) 91
(Charlie Mann) *hld up wl off pce: hdwy 3 out: 7th next: 5th last: styd on wl* **5/1**[3]

/354 **4** *1* **Devils And Dust (IRE)**13 1149 9-10-7 75....................(p) MissGTutty(5) 90
(Karen Tutty) *w ldr: led after 1st: hdd 3rd: kpt on same pce fr 2 out* **25/1**
3222 **5** *1 1/2* **Tri Nations (UAE)**31 984 5-11-8 109..............................(tp) MrJHamer 101+
(Donald McCain) *trckd ldrs: chal 3 out: upsides and gng easily whn blnd next: wknd fnl 75yds* **6/4**1
-110 **6** *1 1/4* **Dunaskin (IRE)**5 1017 10-11-7 116.........................(b) CraigGallagher(5) 102
(Richard Guest) *t.k.h: led tl after 1st: led 3rd: hdd 3 out: outpcd appr next: 7th last: kpt on* **3/1**2
6- **7** *16* **Sea Land (FR)**14 5352 6-10-12 0.. PaulGallagher 73
(Brian Ellison) *mid-div: hdwy to chse ldrs 3 out: outpcd whn nt fluent next: wknd appr last* **14/1**
-650 **8** *17* **Vogarth**5 1147 6-10-7 78.. MrMMarris(5) 58
(Michael Chapman) *sn bhd: sme hdwy after 5th: wknd next* **66/1**
5-F6 **9** *65* **Simplified**75 547 7-10-2 65.. GaryRutherford(3) —
(Michael Chapman) *bhd: t.o 3 out* **100/1**

4m 16.4s (9.70) **Going Correction** +0.70s/f (Soft) 9 Ran SP% **116.3**
Speed ratings (Par 105): **105,102,102,102,101 100,93,85,54**
Tote Swingers: 1&2 £11.90, 1&3 £10.40, 2&3 £8.40 CSF £71.14 TOTE £17.10: £4.10, £5.60, £1.40; EX 97.00.No bid for the winner.
Owner Mrs A E Harris **Bred** Aylesfield Farms Stud Ltd **Trained** Eastwell, Leics

FOCUS
A very modest seller with hands and heels only allowed.

NOTEBOOK
Liberty Seeker(FR) is game on his day and likes the course, as he proved with a third win here (the first of them dating back six years). His record in the bottom grade is also good, and now stands at 421221. His partner cajoled him to the front at the right time and his mount displayed the right attitude. (op 8-1)
Hi Wycombe(IRE) had pulled too hard in previous efforts, but settled better here. He stuck to the task well but the form is obviously extremely weak, as the winner is only months away from his 12th birthday. (op 15-2)
Cortinas(GER) was partnered by an amateur having his first ride. Tailed off early, his late run was never going to succeed. This run can be disregarded, but the horse has been badly out of form lately in any case. (op 9-2)
Devils And Dust(IRE) has never managed to win. (op 20-1)
Tri Nations(UAE) was exceedingly disappointing. He travelled like the winner until blundering two out, but has a run of seconditis in this company behind him and can't be trusted. (op 9-4)
Dunaskin(IRE) is a multiple scorer, but he is only small and may have found this weight too much. (op 11-4 tchd 5-2 and 7-2 in a place)
Simplified Official explanation: trainer said mare had a breathing problem

1250 CHAMPAGNE LANSON BLACK LABEL N.V. NOVICES' HURDLE (8 hdls) 2m 1f
6:10 (6:11) (Class 4) 4-Y-0+ **£2,740** (£798; £399)

Form RPR
313 **1** **Russian George (IRE)**28 1021 4-11-4 117............................. APMcCoy 115+
(Steve Gollings) *trckd ldrs: jnd ldr 5th: slt ld 2 out: hung rt run-in: drvn rt out* **8/11**1
2120 **2** *3/4* **Heron Bay**7 1017 6-11-2 116.......................................(p) DonalDevereux(3) 115+
(Peter Bowen) *led: narrowly hdd 2 out: styd on same pce last 50yds* **7/4**2
U4 **3** *21* **Royal Entourage**28 1021 5-10-5 0...................................... KyleJames(7) 89
(Philip Kirby) *chsd ldrs: outpcd 4th: mod 3rd fr 3 out* **14/1**3
0 **4** *14* **Martin Scruff (IRE)**52 833 4-10-8 0........................... RichardKilloran(3) 75
(Michael Quinlan) *in rr: mstke 3rd: kpt on fr 3 out: tk modest 4th appr 2 out* **50/1**
4-04 **5** *13* **Jingoism (USA)**13 1153 4-10-11 0.. LiamHeard 64
(Brian Ellison) *prom: outpcd and drvn 3rd: tk modest 4thsn after 3 out: wknd appr next* **20/1**
6 *18* **Galileo Figaro (AUS)**201 6-10-12 0...................................... BarryKeniry 49
(Joss Saville) *t.k.h: trckd ldrs: upsides 3rd: wknd 5th: t.o 2 out* **25/1**
0/-P **7** *48* **Topping The Bill**13 1149 7-10-5 0......................... MrRichardCollinson(7) —
(Michael Wigham) *in rr: nt fluent: bhd fr 5th: sn t.o* **100/1**

4m 16.7s (10.00) **Going Correction** +0.70s/f (Soft) 7 Ran SP% **112.5**
Speed ratings (Par 105): **104,103,93,87,81 72,50**
Tote Swingers: 1&2 £1.02, 1&3 £2.40, 2&3 £2.70 CSF £2.20 TOTE £2.30: £2.30, £1.10; EX 2.70.

Owner P J Martin **Bred** Martin Walsh **Trained** Scamblesby, Lincs

FOCUS
Only two serious contestants here, and they duly fought out a decent finish.

NOTEBOOK
Russian George(IRE) is not the greatest of jumpers, but he was given the expected strong ride on his first attempt for A P McCoy, who drove him out vigorously in the final 50 yards. The plan is to run him again under a double penalty, and it might be worth taking him on as a betting proposition, as the time of this race was virtually identical to that of the seller. (op 5-6 tchd 11-10 in a place and evens in places)
Heron Bay had been biting off more than he could chew in his two previous outings, but fared better here in second-time cheekpeices. However, he could not confirm previous running with Russian George and looks rather limited, although his astute trainer can probably find other opportunities in the right grade. (op 13-8 tchd 15-8)
Royal Entourage had no hope with the winner after a previous drubbing, so did as well as might have been expected, although this Flat winner at up to 2m finished over 20l adrift and never looked like being any closer.
Martin Scruff(IRE) had struggled badly in his only bumper and this effort did not tell us a great deal, although he did keep plugging on. (op 33-1)
Galileo Figaro(AUS) managed a modest win at Colac (Melbourne, Australia), but he is small, pulls hard, and gives the impression that he will not stay more than a mile.

1251 JANE CLUGSTON PERPETUAL CHALLENGE CUP NOVICES' CHASE (14 fncs) 2m 4f
6:40 (6:40) (Class 4) 4-Y-0+ **£3,491** (£1,193)

Form RPR
2-5 **1** **Mission Control (IRE)**17 756 5-11-1 0......................... RichardJohnson 118+
(Tim Vaughan) *hit 4th: outpcd: nt fluent and lost pl 8th: drvn next: rallied appr 3 out: hit last: mde up 3 l to ld towards fin and win gng away* **5/4**1
-515 **2** *2* **Walamo (GER)**25 1045 6-11-0 0...................................(t) MrTomDavid(7) 121
(Tim Vaughan) *led: nt fluent 2nd: qcknd 8th: jnd 4 out: hdd appr next: wl btn whn lft in 2 l ld last: hdd and no ex fnl 75yds* **5/1**2
23-4 **F** **Frankie Anson (IRE)**13 1151 6-11-1 115............................... BrianHughes 124+
(Alan Swinbank) *trckd ldr: upsides 4 out: led appr next: shkn up 2 out: 5 l in front and in command whn fell last* **5/4**1

5m 1.30s (-4.40) **Going Correction** -0.60s/f (Firm) 3 Ran SP% **105.6**
Speed ratings (Par 105): **84,83,—**
CSF £5.84 TOTE £2.00.
Owner M Khan X2 **Bred** Darley **Trained** Aberthin, Vale of Glamorgan

FOCUS
A small field, but a dramatic race.

NOTEBOOK
Mission Control(IRE) was a competent hurdler who completed a hat-trick last summer. His jumping was extremely sketchy on this chasing debut and he hardly met a fence on the correct stride, but Richard Johnson seized the opportunity after the last (matters having looked hopeless four out) and his strength in the saddle won the day. He will have to brush up his jumping if he is to progress from this very lucky win. (op 11-8)
Walamo(GER) jumped economically and seemed happier on this good ground than he had in the soft last time (when Johnson rode him). He has scored only twice from 18 attempts and will always be vulnerable in anything competitive. (tchd 9-2 in places)
Frankie Anson(IRE) has the look of a chaser and seemed to have found the ideal opportunity here. He travelled and jumped well but seemed to lose concentration coming to the last and tipped up when 5l clear and in full command. Apparently none the worse for the experience, he should find compensation. He has a relaxed attitude and should stay further. (op 11-10)

1252 LINDUM FIRE H'CAP CHASE (12 fncs) 2m 2f
7:10 (7:11) (Class 4) (0-115,114) 4-Y-0+ **£3,252** (£955; £477; £238)

Form RPR
B321 **1** **Kirkhammerton (IRE)**15 1139 8-11-3 108........................ DannyCook(3) 116
(Barry Leavy) *hld up: hdwy to chse ldrs 8th: wnt 2nd 2 out: styd on wl to ld last 75yds* **4/1**2
0351 **2** *1* **Indiana Gold (FR)**12 1161 6-10-4 99..........................(p) OliverDayman(7) 106
(Alison Thorpe) *trckd ldrs: wnt handy 2nd 4 out: led appr next: over 2 l ahd last: hdd and no ex clsng stages* **8/1**
-052 **3** *5* **Silmi**15 1139 6-11-12 114... PaulMoloney 117
(Sophie Leech) *chsd ldrs: drvn 8th: upsides 3 out: kpt on same pce appr last* **9/2**3
2244 **4** *6* **Pairc Na Gcapall (IRE)**27 1032 8-11-7 112...............(b1) AlexMerriam(3) 109
(Neil King) *led: qcknd clr 5th: drvn 4 out: hdd appr next: wl outpcd 2 out: kpt on run-in* **17/2**
3332 **5** *29* **Red Jester**23 1070 9-10-8 101...................................... MarcGoldstein(5) 72
(Gerald Ham) *chsd ldr: hit 1st: lost pl appr 3 out: sn bhd* **6/1**
663 **6** *29* **Diaco (IRE)**27 1025 6-11-4 106.. APMcCoy 51
(Jonjo O'Neill) *chsd ldrs: drvn and outpcd 6th: bhd fr 8th: sn t.o* **7/2**1
-F42 **F** **Kind Heart**30 1000 4-10-7 109... GrahamLee —
(Donald McCain) *t.k.h in rr: last but wl in tch whn fell 7th* **9/2**3

4m 21.8s (-13.20) **Going Correction** -0.60s/f (Firm)
WFA 4 from 6yo+ 1lb 7 Ran SP% **114.5**
Speed ratings (Par 105): **105,104,102,99,86 73,—**
Tote Swingers: 1&2 £6.50, 1&3 £1.30, 2&3 £8.20 CSF £33.98 CT £148.70 TOTE £3.50: £1.60, £15.70.
Owner Valentino Racing **Bred** Barronstown Stud And Orpendale **Trained** Forsbrook, Staffs

FOCUS
A fair handicap chase.

NOTEBOOK
Kirkhammerton(IRE) is an improving sort who can finish stoutly, but he may have suffered from being dropped out too much in the past, and he has now completed a double since sitting a bit closer to the pace. He was given a strong ride from Danny Cook, who gets on well with him.
Indiana Gold(FR) seems to need everything to fall into place, as it did when he won a poor contest at Newton Abbot last time. He does not look very straightforward and is not one to have a huge amount of faith in. (op 17-2 tchd 10-1)
Silmi was beaten 6l by Kirkhammerton at Bangor two weeks ago and suffered an identical defeat here. He is a trier, but only small, and this counts against him now that he is at the top of the handicap. He might do better in a more competitive race off a lighter weight. (op 4-1)
Pairc Na Gcapall(IRE) has now run the gamut of headgear, but first-time blinkers did little for him. He has more ability than he is usually willing to show. (op 8-1 tchd 9-1)
Red Jester is having a busy summer and did not fire.
Diaco(IRE) is a tall, rangy sort and was not hard pushed when beaten last time, but this was a really poor display, and he had begun to toil soon after halfway, and was eventually beaten out of sight. (op 10-3 tchd 3-1)
Kind Heart, who pulls hard, took a heavy fall. This 4-y-o will need treating with caution next time. (op 13-2)

1253 2010 MISS MARKET RASEN RACECOURSE NOVICES' H'CAP HURDLE (10 hdls) 2m 3f
7:40 (7:41) (Class 4) (0-100,100) 4-Y-0+ **£2,740** (£798; £399)

Form RPR
6/00 **1** **Isle Of Inishmore (IRE)**52 826 7-11-2 90................(t) RichardJohnson 98
(Tim Vaughan) *hld up in rr: smooth hdwy 7th: led appr 2 out: rdn rt out: styd on wl towards fin* **13/2**3
2464 **2** *1 1/2* **Galley Slave (IRE)**30 1005 5-9-8 75................................. JoeCornwall(7) 82
(Michael Chapman) *chsd ldrs: pushed along 6th: rallied and cl 3rd 2 out: kpt on same pce last 150yds* **7/1**
24-1 **3** *1 3/4* **Maska Pony (IRE)**101 166 6-11-12 100............................. GrahamLee 106
(George Moore) *j.lft: led: mstke 3 out: hdd appr next: kpt on wl run-in: no ex* **7/2**2
0PP- **4** *15* **Vin Rose**153 4618 5-10-8 85.. PeterToole(3) 77
(Mark Rimell) *hld up in rr: hdwy 7th: chsng ldrs appr 2 out: wknd between last 2* **14/1**
-132 **5** *8* **Bonzeno Queen (IRE)**30 1005 5-11-0 95........................ AdamWedge(7) 80
(Evan Williams) *t.k.h: trckd ldrs: rdn 3 out: wknd next* **7/2**2
0-2P **6** *18* **Treeko (IRE)**34 953 5-11-2 97.......................................(tp) KyleJames(7) 66
(Philip Kirby) *chsd ldr: hrd drvn 7th: hung rt and lost pl appr 2 out: sn bhd* **8/1**
P0-2 **7** *4* **Princess Tahoe**24 1060 6-9-9 74......................... SamTwiston-Davies(5) 39
(Philip Kirby) *nt fluent: chsd ldrs: drvn 7th: lost pl next: last and bhd whn mstke last* **5/2**1

4m 52.8s (13.40) **Going Correction** +0.70s/f (Soft) 7 Ran SP% **116.6**
Speed ratings (Par 105): **99,98,97,91,87 80,78**
Tote Swingers: 1&2 £0.00, 1&3 £22.60, 2&3 £5.20 CSF £50.70 TOTE £8.30: £7.10, £7.70; EX 69.60.
Owner J H Frost **Bred** Garry Hadden **Trained** Aberthin, Vale of Glamorgan

FOCUS
Very modest fare, but Tim Vaughan maintained his stranglehold in the race, having now won three of the last four runnings.

NOTEBOOK
Isle Of Inishmore(IRE), who has been reported as having a breathing problem, won a Welsh maiden in the spring but has looked to struggle over longer trips than tonight's in two subsequent hurdles. He looked to be going best leaving the back straight but was not finding a lot after the last, so it would surprise if he had much scope for further improvement. (op 11-2 tchd 7-1)
Galley Slave(IRE), with 62 defeats behind him (25 of them on the Flat), was sixth in this race last year off 92, but has now been dropped to 75. He ran well when out of the handicap here earlier in the year and fought on well after the last, but he had expended plenty of energy by pulling keenly and was always just held. Perhaps he can exploit his really lowly mark if the handicapper does not overreact. (op 8-1 tchd 13-2)
Maska Pony(IRE) has been lightly raced and was returning from a three month absence. His jumping was modest in the closing stages and he might be better going left-handed (he gained his sole win at Kelso). (op 3-1 tchd 4-1)

Vin Rose was soundly beaten on her debut for a new yard.
Bonzeno Queen(IRE) lacks size and scope and probably needs to return to sellers if she is to score again. (op 9-2)
Treeko(IRE) was hanging, as he has done in the past. Official explanation: jockey said gelding hung right (op 15-2)
Princess Tahoe made errors and lost a shoe. Official explanation: jockey said mare never travelled or jumped and lost a front shoe (op 3-1)

1254 CHAMPAGNE LANSON ROSE LABEL N.V. H'CAP HURDLE (10 hdls) 2m 3f
8:10 (8:11) (Class 4) (0-115,115) 4-Y-0+ **£2,740** (£798; £399)

Form RPR
4232 **1** **Celticello (IRE)**[22] 1084 8-11-5 **115**................................ MrJMQuinlan(7) 120+
(Michael Quinlan) *t.k.h wl in tch: hdwy to chal 2 out: edgd rt and led last 200yds: hld on wl towards fin* **9/2**[3]
/1-P **2** *nk* **Darksideofthemoon (IRE)**[41] 888 8-11-11 **114**................(p) APMcCoy 118
(Tim Vaughan) *trckd ldrs: slt ld last: hdd run-in: crowded and no ex last 50yds* **4/1**[2]
3542 **3** *3¾* **Murcar**[15] 1138 5-11-4 **114**................................ OliverDayman(7) 116
(Alison Thorpe) *led 2nd: hdd last: kpt on same pce* **3/1**[1]
-405 **4** *¾* **Phoenix Eye**[13] 1147 9-9-12 **94**................................ BrianToomey(7) 94
(Michael Mullineaux) *hld up: stdy hdwy 6th: sn trcking ldrs: effrt 2 out: kpt on same pce appr last* **5/1**
253 **5** *1¼* **El Presidente (IRE)**[13] 1150 5-11-3 **109**......................(p) AlexMerriam(3) 108
(Neil King) *hld up in tch: effrt and chsng ldrs 3 out: outpcd whn nt fluent next: kpt on one pce* **8/1**
6/ **6** *1* **Ben's Folly (IRE)**[119] 5-10-13 **102**................................ RichardJohnson 100
(Tim Vaughan) *chsd ldrs: drvn 3 out: kpt on one pce fr next* **5/1**
5-6P **7** *6* **Tifoso (FR)**[14] 888 5-10-11 **100**................................(v) DougieCostello 93
(Richard Guest) *hld up: t.k.h: hdwy 7th: wknd appr 2 out* **25/1**
00-P **8** *73* **Petrus De Sormain (FR)**[90] 359 7-10-11 **100**.................. DavidDennis 27
(James Evans) *chsd ldrs: pushed along 5th: lost pl 3 out: sn bhd: t.o* **25/1**

4m 51.8s (12.40) **Going Correction** +0.70s/f (Soft) **8** Ran SP% **115.3**
Speed ratings (Par 105): **101,100,99,98,98 98,95,64**
CSF £23.44 CT £60.72 TOTE £7.80: £1.90, £1.10, £1.80; EX 27.70 Place 6: £248.72 Place 5: £75.81..
Owner Thomas Mann **Bred** P D Savill **Trained** Newmarket, Suffolk
■ Stewards' Enquiry : Mr J M Quinlan caution: careless riding.

FOCUS
Everything held a chance three out and just 7l separated the first five at the finish, and the form is muddling and not to be taken too seriously.

NOTEBOOK
Celticello(IRE) has now won six races (three apiece flat and hurdling) but had endured a losing sequence of 16 (placed in eight including for McCoy two outings back), so this effort was a real feather in the cap of the amateur Jack Quinlan, who previously caught the eye in pony races and points, and here pipped the 15-time champion. There was a stewards' inquiry regarding the possibility of hanging but the result remained unaltered, unsurprisingly as there was no contact. (tchd 4-1)
Darksideofthemoon(IRE) had been running under 7lb claimers in his last three runs and scored at this meeting two outings ago, but has evidently had some training difficulties since. He travelled strongly for McCoy and looked the winner at the last but was just outbattled. (op 9-2 tchd 5-1)
Murcar ran his race, but is a difficult ride and a mistake two out did not help. He is good at making the frame, but not at winning. (tchd 11-4 and 10-3)
Phoenix Eye is a funny little horse who travels strongly at the back of the field, but normally produces very little when it comes to a tussle. (op 11-2)
El Presidente(IRE) continues to flop.
Ben's Folly(IRE) blew a golden opportunity when unseating at the second in a three runner maiden in Wales, in which he erroneously ran as Piment d'Estruval. He has held a lot of entries lately, but on looks he seems the type who would be better at chasing than hurdling. (op 9-2)
T/Plt: £263.40 to a £1 stake. Pool of £56,491 - 156.55 winning tickets. T/Qpdt: £59.20 to a £1 stake. Pool of £5,072 - 63.30 winning tickets. WG

1080 SOUTHWELL (L-H)
Sunday, August 15

OFFICIAL GOING: Good (8.2)
Golf Club Bend 5yds inside and the bend into home straight 5yds outside the line raced on July 23rd.
Wind: light half across Weather: hot and sunny

1255 NEWARK ADVERTISER H'CAP CHASE (19 fncs) 3m 110y
2:20 (2:22) (Class 4) (0-115,118) 4-Y-0+ **£4,553** (£1,337; £668; £333)

Form RPR
-132 **1** **I Need A Hero (IRE)**[24] 1068 5-11-9 **112**..............................(t) JackDoyle 121+
(Sarah Humphrey) *settled towards rr: smooth prog 13th: led on bit sn after 16th: 8 l clr whn hit 3 out: in n.d after* **7/1**
0212 **2** *3* **Ballyvesey (IRE)**[9] 1200 5-12-1 **118**..................................(p) TomO'Brien 122
(Peter Bowen) *pressed ldrs: 3rd and rdn 13th: plugged on fr 3 out to go 2nd fnl 50yds: no match for wnr* **10/3**[2]
F013 **3** *1¾* **Strong Coffee**[20] 1093 8-11-5 **108**..................................(b) LeightonAspell 110
(Oliver Sherwood) *j. soundly: mde most tl hdd jst after 16th: drvn and v indolent and nt doing a tap in vain pursuit of wnr after: lost 2nd nr fin* **3/1**[1]
5-5U **4** *9* **Kisha King (IRE)**[9] 1200 9-11-4 **107**..................................(v) PaulMoloney 101
(David Rees) *towards rr: outpcd 14th: last next: nt fluent 16th: plugged on* **4/1**[3]
02/6 **5** *11* **Rare Society (IRE)**[9] 1200 12-11-5 **108**.................................. TjadeCollier 92
(Sue Smith) *chsd ldrs fr 5th tl rdn and lost pl 12th: struggling 16th: mstke 2 out* **16/1**
5-13 **6** *25* **Badger Foot (IRE)**[91] 352 5-11-9 **112**.................................. APMcCoy 74
(Jonjo O'Neill) *nt a fluent: cl 2nd tl led 5th tl 6th and 12th tl 13th: mstke 15th and wknd: mod 4th whn mstke 3 out* **4/1**[3]
P50 **P** **Sendeed (USA)**[31] 1000 8-10-9 **98**..................................(tp) BrianHughes —
(Peter Atkinson) *chsd ldrs tl hit 10th and 11th: sn given reminders: wknd and mstke 14th: t.o and p.u 3 out* **50/1**
0U04 **P** **Option Money (IRE)**[68] 682 8-10-3 **95**.............................. TomMolloy(3) —
(Peter Salmon) *nt jump wl in last and nvr gng wl: lost tch 9th: t.o and p.u after 12th: lame* **20/1**

6m 27.3s (1.30) **Going Correction** -0.275s/f (Good) **8** Ran SP% **113.2**
Speed ratings (Par 105): **86,85,84,81,78 70,—,—**
Tote Swingers: 1&2 £4.30, 1&3 £5.40, 2&3 £2.70 CSF £30.83 CT £84.56 TOTE £21.60: £6.00, £6.00, £1.02; EX 40.40.
Owner Mrs S J Humphrey **Bred** Martin Brickley **Trained** West Wratting, Cambs

FOCUS
An open handicap and a decisive winner.

NOTEBOOK
I Need A Hero(IRE) came home to score pretty much as he pleased in the end. He had improved in two outings over fences since winning his maiden hurdle, but had still been beaten a fair way in both of them. This step up in trip made all the difference, however, and he had the race sewn up coming to the third-last. He probably wasn't doing a lot out in front so rates value for further and remains open to improvement as a stayer as he is still only a 5-y-o. The handicapper will have his say now, though (op 8-1)
Ballyvesey(IRE) was another 6lb higher and carrying a big weight. He got a little caught out when the tempo increased down the back straight and, despite staying on stoutly after the last, didn't look to be helping his rider all that much under pressure. Perhaps switching to a stiffer track will see him back in a better light. (op 7-2 tchd 4-1)
Strong Coffee cut out a lot of the donkey work and looked set to make a bold bid when left in a clear lead nearing the home turn. He appeared to down tools shortly after, however, and was below his previous level. (tchd 11-4)
Kisha King(IRE) dropped himself out around the halfway stage before plugging on at the same pace in the home straight. (op 9-2)
Badger Foot(IRE) was returning from a three-month break over a longer trip and was ridden as though stamina wouldn't be a problem. He dropped out tamely on the final circuit, however, and it could have been that something went amiss as he didn't always convince with his fencing. (op 10-3)

1256 FLETCHERS CHARTERED SURVEYORS H'CAP CHASE (16 fncs) 2m 4f 110y
2:50 (2:50) (Class 4) (0-110,103) 4-Y-0+ **£4,331** (£1,344; £724)

Form RPR
0042 **1** **More Like It (IRE)**[35] 952 10-10-12 **89**.............................. BrianHughes 95
(Peter Niven) *lft in ld 5th: hdd 8th: led again wl bef 3 out: rdn and hrd pressed after: drew clr last: kpt on gamely: all out* **7/2**[3]
514P **2** *3¼* **Risk Challenge (USA)**[3] 1237 8-11-4 **95**..........................(t) CharliePoste 100+
(Milton Harris) *settled in rr and t.k.h: trckd ldrs gng wl fr 9th: wnt 2nd and pckd 3 out: hit next: swtchd rt bef last and nt fluent: edgd rt flat and fnd nil* **11/4**[2]
6-33 **3** *41* **Moulin De La Croix**[59] 769 6-11-7 **103**............(t) SamTwiston-Davies(5) 80
(Nigel Twiston-Davies) *lft 2nd at 4th: led 8th tl hdd wl bef 3 out: rdn and fdd tamely: sn wl bhd* **5/4**[1]
P50P **U** **Dasher Reilly (USA)**[13] 1159 9-9-11 **77** oh20.......(b) EamonDehdashti(3) —
(Aytach Sadik) *cl up tl hmpd and uns rdr 4th* **40/1**
3 **F** **Tigh Bhruadair (IRE)**[28] 1031 6-11-9 **100**......................(tp) PaulMoloney —
(Evan Williams) *set gd pce: j. crookedly and bmpd and fell 4th* **7/1**

5m 21.7s (6.70) **Going Correction** -0.275s/f (Good) **5** Ran SP% **108.3**
Speed ratings (Par 105): **76,74,59,—,—**
CSF £13.09 TOTE £8.30: £2.30, £1.20.
Owner Sandy Lodge Racing Club & P D Niven **Bred** Tom O'Connor **Trained** Barton-le-Street, N Yorks

FOCUS
This wasn't a strong race for the grade, but it still provided a decent finish.

NOTEBOOK
More Like It(IRE), not for the first time, didn't always look the most straightforward but still proved more resolute than his two rivals on the final circuit. His jumping was also a lot better under pressure this time and that also helped to get him home in front. He was 3lb lower than when landing his previous win over hurdles and it was his first success as a chaser since 2008. He doesn't appeal as one for a follow up. (op 11-2)
Risk Challenge(USA) was in the process of running a big race prior to whacking the third-last at Stratford three days earlier. He was well backed here despite having to compete off a 15lb higher mark, but that did still leave him 5lb lower than his current BHB rating over hurdles. He again raced enthusiastically under restraint and was produced with his challenge going well off the home turn. His jumping over the last three fences let him down, though, and he remains winless in this sphere after eight outings. (op 10-3 tchd 5-2)
Moulin De La Croix, returning from a 59-day break, was very popular to go in over this sharper test and things looked good for her coming out of the back straight for the final time. She folded tamely when the winner found his second wind, however, and has to rate as disappointing. Official explanation: trainer had no explanation for the poor form shown (op Evens tchd 11-8 in places)
Tigh Bhruadair(IRE) had set out to make all at a decent gallop prior to coming down at the fourth, and it's hoped this doesn't overly affect his confidence. (op 5-1)

1257 SOUTHWELL ADVERTISER NOVICES' CHASE (13 fncs) 2m
3:20 (3:20) (Class 4) 4-Y-0+ **£4,228** (£1,241; £620; £310)

Form RPR
6-12 **1** **Novikov**[13] 1163 6-11-3 0..................................(t) LeeStephens(3) 122+
(David Evans) *content to trck free gng ldrs: wnt 2nd at 9th: rdn 3 out: led 2 out: drew clr and j.lft last: readily* **15/2**[3]
1110 **2** *3½* **Pure Faith (IRE)**[29] 1017 6-11-0 0.................................. TomO'Brien 114+
(Peter Bowen) *lft 2nd after 6th: led next: rdn and nt fluent 3 out: hdd and nt fluent 2 out: nt qckn last* **6/4**[2]
2211 **3** *9* **Stagecoach Pearl**[19] 1110 6-11-12 132.................................. APMcCoy 118
(Sue Smith) *v keen to post: chsd clr ldr: lft in ld after 6th: hdd after mstke next and jumping modly after: relegated 3rd at 8th: wl btn bef 3 out* **10/11**[1]
0-P3 **4** *27* **Haka Dancer (USA)**[23] 1082 7-10-7 0..............................(p) KyleJames(7) 77
(Philip Kirby) *bhd: wnt poor 4th at 8th: hit 10th: nvr anywhere nr ldrs after* **25/1**
45 **5** *53* **Canal Bank (IRE)**[9] 1197 6-10-11 0.......................... RichieMcLernon(3) 24
(Jonjo O'Neill) *bhd: nt fluent 4th and 7th: lost tch and mstke 8th: t.o 10th: fin eventually* **40/1**
U0-P **P** **Border Fox**[73] 598 7-10-11 0..................................(t) TomMolloy(3) —
(Peter Salmon) *tried to bolt to s and again in r: sn wl clr: j. bdly rt: hdd after 6th and qckly p.u* **66/1**

4m 1.90s (-8.10) **Going Correction** -0.275s/f (Good) **6** Ran SP% **111.9**
Speed ratings (Par 105): **109,107,102,89,62 —**
CSF £19.86 TOTE £12.40: £5.30, £1.90; EX 28.40.
Owner Nick Shutts **Bred** The Duke Of Devonshire **Trained** Pandy, Monmouths

FOCUS
This novice chase was run at a fair gallop and the first pair came clear from four out.

NOTEBOOK
Novikov made it 2-3 since embarking on his chasing career with a very gutsy effort. He wasn't all that fluent early and looked to be feeling the pinch when the runner-up went clear around five out. He dug deep for his rider's urgings and, jumping the better in the home straight, was nicely on top at the finish. He's a likeable performer and will no doubt continue to pay his way, despite being vulnerable under a double penalty in this sphere. His success also a pays a compliment to his previous conqueror at Newton Abbot, Quell The Storm, who beat him easily there. (op 6-1)
Pure Faith(IRE) was well placed to win three novice hurdles this summer, but an official mark of 124 is probably the reason connections have switched him to fences. His hurdling form entitled him to go close here getting weight from the top two and he jumped professionally for a debutant for most of the race. Things looked good for him as he gained a clear advantage turning for home, but he came under pressure before the third-last and ultimately his jumping in the home straight cost him. It may be a stiffer test is what he needs as a chaser and he shouldn't be long in winning now he has this experience behind him. (op 2-1)

The Form Book, Raceform Ltd, Compton, RG20 6NL

Stagecoach Pearl was conceding upwards of 6lb all around under his double penalty, but still looked to have been found another fair opportunity if his new mark of 132 was to be believed. Tony McCoy was back on board again, but his fate was apparent soon after he hit one in the back straight and he wasn't on a going day here. It remains to be seen how he comes out of this now his confidence has been knocked and his official rating probably needs some looking at. (op 5-6 tchd Evens and 11-10 in places)
Border Fox Official explanation: jockey said bit slipped

1258 JORDAN SURFACING OF NEWARK (S) HURDLE (9 hdls) 2m
3:50 (3:50) (Class 5) 4-7-Y-O **£2,397** (£698; £349)

Form RPR
R-45 **1** **Zafar (IRE)**[41] [912] 7-11-12 118 (tp) ChristianWilliams 108+
(John Flint) *midfield: effrt 3 out: 2nd and 3 l clr of rest next: racd idly but rdn to ld bef last: sn outbattled rival* **7/2**[3]
0P- **2** *3* **Contrada**[12] [5278] 5-10-12 0 (b) RhysFlint 92
(Jim Old) *led tl 2nd: chsd ldr tl hit 3 out: sn led: clr w wnr next: drvn and reluctant and hdd bef last: sn btn* **12/1**
510P **3** *6* **High Skies**[24] [1070] 7-11-4 106 (b) APMcCoy 93
(Dr Richard Newland) *nt a fluent: midfield: dropped bk last and mstke 6th: nt keen after but cajoled into modest 3rd at last* **5/2**[2]
1-P3 **4** *3 ¼* **Santera (IRE)**[17] [1125] 6-11-5 106 DenisO'Regan 90
(Michael Blake) *pressed ldrs: j. slowly 5th: rdn and btn bef 2 out: wknd and lost 3rd at last* **2/1**[1]
/5-6 **5** *1 ¼* **Bilbo Boggart (IRE)**[23] [1085] 6-10-7 0 (t) JamesHalliday(5) 82
(Ian McInnes) *cl up: wnt 2nd after 3 out: rdn and wknd next* **50/1**
5FP- **6** *4 ½* **Bubses Boy**[110] [4810] 4-10-4 0 OliverDayman(7) 79+
(Alison Thorpe) *chsd ldrs: j. slowly 5th: rdn 6th: wknd bef 2 out: stmbld bdly last* **10/1**
7 *14* **Peter Tchaikovsky**[29] 4-10-4 0 (t) KyleJames(7) 64
(Brian Rothwell) *hld up last: blnd 3rd: effrt 5th: disp 3rd and looked to be gng wl after 3 out: fdd bdly next* **25/1**
6-00 **8** *45* **Baguenaud (FR)**[14] [1147] 7-11-4 95 (bt[1]) GrahamLee 31
(Stephen Clark) *led 2nd tl sn after 3 out: gave up immediately and sn t.o: eased 2 out* **12/1**

4m 0.40s (3.30) **Going Correction** -0.275s/f (Good)
WFA 4 from 5yo+ 13lb **8** Ran SP% **114.4**
Speed ratings: **80,78,75,73,73 71,64,41**
Tote Swingers: 1&2 £9.20, 1&3 £2.40, 2&3 £7.40 CSF £42.55 TOTE £3.60: £1.20, £2.90, £1.80; EX 55.50.There was no bid for the winner. Santera was claimed by J L Flint for £6,000.
Owner Terry Reffell **Bred** His Highness The Aga Khan's Studs S C **Trained** Kenfig Hill, Bridgend

FOCUS
The defection of Players Please obviously took a lot of interest out of this seller. Weak form.

NOTEBOOK
Zafar(IRE) had disappointed in this grade in two previous runs since joining the yard and his official mark had dropped 9lb in the process. It was the first time he has been ridden by Christian Williams, though, and he was reverting to a more suitable distance. He bounced back, despite still performing below his current mark, and it should help restore some of his confidence so another one of these could be within his compass before the summer is out. (op 4-1 tchd 9-2)
Contrada, whose pilot had been aboard the winner the last twice, ran a much more encouraging race back over hurdles and has evidently found his sort of level. He can win a seller providing he settles a little better. (op 14-1)
High Skies was representing the yard that won the race last season and got very well backed. He was returning to hurdling back in his winning class, but lost out by hitting a flat spot at a crucial stage on the far side and advertised his quirks. (op 7-2 tchd 9-4)
Santera(IRE) lacked the pace to land a telling blow and remains below her best. (op 13-8)

1259 OLLERTON ADVERTISER CLAIMING HURDLE (13 hdls) 3m 110y
4:20 (4:21) (Class 5) 4-Y-O+ **£2,397** (£698; £349)

Form RPR
1F22 **1** **Cannon Fire (FR)**[31] [1004] 9-11-2 109 (p) PaulMoloney 100+
(Evan Williams) *led 3rd: hit 3 out: pushed along and drew clr of only two in serious pursuit at next: v easily* **4/1**[3]
1215 **2** *10* **Public Esteem (IRE)**[32] [986] 9-10-3 102 (tp) MrsAlexDunn(7) 82
(Dr Richard Newland) *chsd clr ldng pair: clsd 8th: wnt 2nd at 10th: ev ch bef 2 out: pushed along and wl outpcd after* **5/2**[2]
603P **3** *6* **Barlin Bay**[25] [1057] 6-10-4 64 TommyPhelan(3) 72
(Harry Chisman) *s.i.s: bhd: 4th and prog 10th: chal ldng pair bef 2 out: rdn and sn btn: fading bdly flat* **50/1**
4632 **4** *4 ½* **Heir To Be**[9] [1195] 11-10-12 102 (b) NickScholfield 73
(Michael Blake) *trckd ldrs tl rdn and downed tools after 8th: poor last at 10th: plugged on again 2 out but no hope* **9/4**[1]
35P3 **5** *6* **Manadam (FR)**[20] [1092] 7-11-2 105 (p) AidanColeman 71
(Anthony Middleton) *chsd ldrs: rdn 9th: sn lost interest: wl btn 3 out* **13/2**
1-06 **6** *26* **Alfloramoor**[23] [1084] 8-11-3 104 AdamPogson(3) 49
(Charles Pogson) *midfield: hit 4th: nt fluent 9th: 4th and rdn and losing tch 3 out: eased next: t.o* **16/1**
4544 **P** **Smiling Applause**[35] [955] 11-10-7 68 (b) TomMolloy(3) —
(Harry Chisman) *sn last: t.o 4th: continued in pathetic fashion tl eventually p.u after 8th* **50/1**
3/PP **P** **Shannon Lodge (IRE)**[19] [1106] 12-11-1 0 (t) MrGBarfoot-Saunt(5) —
(Tracey Barfoot-Saunt) *s.i.s: lumbered rnd in rr: hopelessly t.o 6th tl p.u at 8th* **100/1**
U00 **P** **Tarkesar (IRE)**[26] [1048] 8-10-7 64 (p) SamTwiston-Davies(5) —
(Carole Ikin) *bhd: drvn and lost tch 8th: t.o and p.u next* **80/1**
0250 **P** **Freedom Flying**[25] [1059] 7-9-10 92 KyleJames(7) —
(Philip Kirby) *led tl 3rd: chsd ldr: rdn bef 9th: lost 2nd at next: t.o and p.u 2 out* **10/1**

6m 16.0s (8.50) **Going Correction** -0.275s/f (Good) **10** Ran SP% **113.8**
Speed ratings (Par 103): **75,71,69,68,66 58,—,—,—,—**
Tote Swingers: 1&2 £2.40, 1&3 £20.40, 2&3 £23.70 CSF £14.38 TOTE £4.30: £1.10, £1.50, £15.10; EX 16.00.Barlin Bay was claimed by D Pipe for £7,000. Public Esteem was subject to a friendly claim.
Owner R E R Williams **Bred** Gilles And Mrs Forien **Trained** Llancarfan, Vale Of Glamorgan

FOCUS
This was run at a good gallop and it produced an easy winner.

NOTEBOOK
Cannon Fire(FR) proved far too good for his rivals on this drop in class and ran out a clear-cut winner. He got a very positive ride but looked vulnerable as the placed horses came up to him turning for home. He kept finding under maximum pressure and was well on top from the penultimate flight. He obviously got the trip without fuss and has a good strike-rate for one of his ability. (op 11-4 tchd 5-2)
Public Esteem(IRE), well backed, looked a big threat when making his move four out but could only manage the same pace when push came to shove under his inexperienced rider. This was better again from him. (op 7-2 tchd 9-4)
Barlin Bay got a very patient ride and emerged going well nearing the final bend. She couldn't find any extra when put under some pressure, though, and was well held in the end. With an official mark of just 64 she helps to put the form into some perspective, but the suspicion is that she has a little more ability than she has shown to date and perhaps some headgear back over a shorter trip would help. (op 33-1)
Heir To Be was keeping on late in the day after losing ground on the final circuit and failed to up his game as might have been expected for the return to the longer trip. He looks one to have reservations about these days. (op 5-2 tchd 11-4)

1260 HORSE RACING FREE BETS AT FREEBETTING.CO.UK "NATIONAL HUNT" NOVICES' HURDLE (9 hdls) 2m
4:50 (4:51) (Class 4) 4-Y-O+ **£2,740** (£798; £399)

Form RPR
1 **Khorun (GER)**[37] [940] 5-10-12 0 RichardJohnson 114+
(Tim Vaughan) *wnt 2nd at 4th: led next: drew 7 l clr 2 out: sn rdn: in n.d whn blnd last* **10/11**[1]
3411 **2** *12* **Dereks (IRE)**[13] [1160] 8-12-5 122 PaulMoloney 120+
(Sophie Leech) *chsd ldr tl 4th: sn lost tch w ldng pair: wnt 12 l 2nd at last: nvr nr wnr* **13/8**[2]
/FU6 **3** *1* **Morning Sunshine (IRE)**[16] [1139] 7-10-9 0 AdrianLane(3) 98
(Donald McCain) *t.k.h in rr: outpcd 5th and rdn: poor 4th bef 2 out: plugged on into weak 3rd after last* **18/1**
6 **4** *4* **King's Lion (IRE)**[53] [833] 6-10-9 0 AdamPogson(3) 96
(Charles Pogson) *racd keenly: led tl 5th: lost tch w wnr bef 2 out: lost two pls fr last* **8/1**[3]
5P **5** *39* **Winter Holly**[16] [1140] 4-10-4 0 RobertWalford 51
(Tim Walford) *plld hrd in last pair: lost tch after 5th: t.o 3 out: eased next* **50/1**
6 *17* **Youandme (IRE)**[78] 8-10-9 0 PeterToole(3) 44
(Ray Peacock) *hld up in last trio: lost tch 5th: hopelessly t.o after 3 out* **80/1**

3m 58.6s (1.50) **Going Correction** -0.275s/f (Good)
WFA 4 from 5yo+ 13lb **6** Ran SP% **110.0**
Speed ratings (Par 105): **85,79,78,76,57 48**
Tote Swingers: 1&2 £1.10, 1&3 £2.60, 2&3 £4.30 CSF £2.61 TOTE £1.50: £1.10, £1.50; EX 2.50.
Owner Owen Promotions Limited **Bred** K Kaufmann U Dr H J Wiesner **Trained** Aberthin, Vale of Glamorgan

FOCUS
A weak novice event, run at a fair gallop.

NOTEBOOK
Khorun(GER) was making his British debut for new connections and proved all the rage. He got the job done easily, having the race fully sewn up prior to getting the last wrong, and has obviously improved for a change of scenery. He isn't the biggest, but did win on his only outing between the flags in Ireland and also clearly has a deal of speed. He shouldn't mind going back up in trip and should defy a penalty while this division remains weak. (op 8-11 tchd 4-6)
Dereks(IRE) had made all to win on his two previous outings and met support despite conceding a lot of weight all around, so it was surprising he wasn't asked to get to the front here. He was never a serious player and is better than this on his day. (op 5-2)
Morning Sunshine(IRE) proved free under restraint and never looked like getting seriously involved. This ought to help restore his confidence somewhat for a return to chasing should connections wish to return to that sphere with him. (op 9-1 tchd 8-1)
King's Lion(IRE), with the tongue tie left off, ran better than the bare form on this switch to hurdling. He ultimately paid for doing plenty on the front end, but has plenty of size about him and ought to be winning races down the line, most probably over a stiffer test. (op 10-1 tchd 11-1)

1261 ADVERTISER GROUP NEWSPAPERS H'CAP HURDLE (11 hdls) 2m 4f 110y
5:20 (5:26) (Class 4) (0-100,100) 4-Y-O+ **£2,740** (£798; £399)

Form RPR
5B5 **1** **Rebel Swing**[23] [1083] 4-10-3 **79** HenryOliver 83+
(Sue Smith) *hrd drvn to begin w: sn taking t.k.h and chsng ldrs: rdn bef 3 out where wnt 2nd: urged ahd bef last: edgd lft flat but hld on wl* **25/1**
0344 **2** *2 ¼* **Nobby Kivambo (IRE)**[16] [1137] 5-10-12 **86** JimmyMcCarthy 90+
(Brendan Powell) *a 2nd or 3rd: pushed along 3 out: kpt hanging lft fr bef next where mstke whn disputing 6 l 3rd: wnt 2nd at last but no match for wnr* **9/1**
4-63 **3** *4 ½* **Shindig**[25] [1062] 8-11-5 **93** (tp) RhysFlint 92
(John Flint) *mounted outside paddock: chsd ldrs: effrt after 3 out: led bef next: rdn and racd awkwardly and hdd bef last: fin weakly and sn btn: eased cl home* **15/2**[3]
4P-1 **4** *5* **Lodgician (IRE)**[3] [1236] 8-11-5 **98** 7ex SamTwiston-Davies(5) 94+
(Nigel Twiston-Davies) *towards rr: effrt 7th: chsd ldrs next: 6 l 3rd and hrd drvn whn mstke 2 out: sn btn: hung rt flat* **9/4**[1]
/531 **5** *16* **Miss Molly Be Rude (IRE)**[16] [1137] 8-10-8 **82** RobertWalford 62
(Tim Walford) *led: rdn and hdd bef 2 out: dropped out rapidly* **3/1**[2]
05-0 **6** *10* **Toss The Caber (IRE)**[14] [1147] 8-11-7 **95** BrianHughes 66
(Stephen Clark) *bhd: lost tch 7th: t.o 3 out* **33/1**
F4-2 **7** *½* **Mossmann Gorge**[23] [1085] 8-11-8 **99** (t) TomMolloy(3) 70
(Anthony Middleton) *last and nt fluent 4th: dashed up into midfield 6th: j. slowly 7th and nt run on: remote fr 3 out* **25/1**
0-0P **8** *3 ¾* **Free To Air**[82] [467] 7-10-2 **76** (p) SamJones 43
(Oliver Sherwood) *disp 2nd tl rdn after 4th: nt keen: dropped bk last bef 7th: t.o 3 out* **8/1**
P-05 **9** *16* **Donovan (NZ)**[26] [1043] 11-11-2 **90** (p) GrahamLee 43
(Richard Guest) *bhd: struggling 7th: t.o 3 out* **40/1**
3-06 **10** *¾* **Micks Prospect (IRE)**[35] [956] 7-11-12 **100** (t) RichardJohnson 52
(Tim Vaughan) *chsd ldrs: j. slowly 3rd: rdn and lost tch 3 out: t.o* **16/1**

5m 1.90s (-8.80) **Going Correction** -0.275s/f (Good)
WFA 4 from 5yo+ 14lb **10** Ran SP% **107.6**
Speed ratings (Par 105): **105,104,102,100,94 90,90,89,82,82**
Tote Swingers: 1&2 £23.20, 1&3 £21.80, 2&3 £5.10 CSF £185.15 CT £1380.74 TOTE £33.50: £5.80, £2.80, £2.60; EX 240.70 Place 6: £30.60 Place 5: £17.82.
Owner Broadway Racing Club 15 **Bred** Mrs D R Schreiber **Trained** High Eldwick, W Yorks
■ I Can't Remember was withdrawn (9/1, got loose in preliminaries). Deduct 10p in the £ under R4.

FOCUS
An ordinary handicap, run at a sound enough gallop.

NOTEBOOK
Rebel Swing, up in trip, showed his true colours and got off the mark with a determined effort on this handicap debut. He needed to be encouraged at the start, but was soon racing close enough to the pace. Despite coming under pressure around three out he kept finding and showed a nice attitude after the final flight. He should get a bit further and ought to have a little more to offer being only a 4-y-o. Official explanation: trainer said, regarding apparent improvement in form, that the gelding was reluctant to race last time and was suited by the step up in trip.
Nobby Kivambo(IRE) was never far away, but he too came under pressure from the third-last and didn't look to be helping his rider all that much. He also wasn't fluent two out, but to his credit rallied for maximum pressure and it was his best effort to date. (op 12-1)

Shindig found extra for pressure nearing the home turn, having travelled nicely until the third-last, and held every chance. This was more encouraging from him back over hurdles and he could just be worth trying over a longer trip. (op 9-1)
Lodgician(IRE) was an easy winner on his return three days earlier and connections must have felt confident enough to have allowed him to take his chance here. He moved sweetly into contention, so while some may point to the bounce factor being to blame for this backward step, it could also be that the return to further found him out. (op 7-4)
Miss Molly Be Rude(IRE) was up 8lb for her previous success at Bangor. She took them along at a fair gallop and was a sitting duck nearing the home turn. (op 7-2)
T/Plt: £62.00 to a £1 stake. Pool of £61,338 - 721.93 winning tickets. T/Qpdt: £13.10 to a £1 stake. Pool of £4,977 - 280.54 winning tickets. IM

1262 - 1271a (Foreign Racing) - See Raceform Interactive

1195 WORCESTER (L-H)
Tuesday, August 17

OFFICIAL GOING: Good
Cathedral and home bends moved out about 6yds adding circa 35yards per circuit to advertised distances.
Wind: Moderate behind Weather: Bright

1272 WORCESTER FESTIVAL CONDITIONAL JOCKEYS' H'CAP HURDLE (8 hdls) 2m
5:10 (5:15) (Class 5) (0-90,90) 4-Y-0+ **£2,055** (£599; £299)

Form				RPR
4-0P	1		**Louis Ludwig (IRE)**[7] 1231 5-11-2 **85** (t) MrTomDavid(6) (Tim Vaughan) *j. 1st flight after false s: hld up in rr: stdy hdwy after 4 out to ld 3 out gng smoothly: c clr fr next: v easily* **9/1**	108+
0P52	2	11	**London Times (IRE)**[11] 1199 5-10-13 **79** (t) KyleJames(3) (Simon Lewis) *j. 1st flight after false s: chsd ldrs: chal fr 4 out to next: chsd wnr fr 2 out: nvr any ch* **14/1**	85
0033	3	3 3/4	**Frosty's Gift**[11] 1199 6-10-4 **72** (p) NathanSweeney(5) (Jimmy Fox) *j. 1st flight after false s: hld up in rr: hdwy appr 3f out: styd on to cl on 2nd run-in: nvr any ch w v easy wnr* **15/2**	75
-051	4	5	**Robbmaa (FR)**[11] 1199 5-10-2 **68** (b) LeeEdwards(3) (Tony Carroll) *j. 1st 2 flight after false s: in rr tl hdwy 4 out: chsd ldrs 3 out: wknd and j. slowly next* **6/1**[3]	66
-23F	5	5	**Wisteria Lane (IRE)**[48] 862 7-10-12 **80** (p) AdamWedge(5) (Anabel L M King) *avoided jumping 1st flight after false s: chsd ldrs: rdn and wknd 3 out* **5/1**[2]	74
2421	6	2 1/2	**Papradon**[7] 1231 6-11-6 **86** SamTwiston-Davies(3) (Nigel Twiston-Davies) *j. 1st 2 flights after false s: pressed ldrs: chal 4 out to next: sn rdn: wknd after 2 out* **2/1**[1]	77
-053	7	4 1/2	**Monsieur (FR)**[15] 1164 10-11-5 **82** HarrySkelton (Carroll Gray) *j. 1st 2 flights after false s: t.k.h: led tl hdd & wknd after 4 out* **14/1**	69
0504	8	nk	**Glan Lady (IRE)**[11] 1199 4-11-2 **80** (p) CharlieHuxley (John Mackie) *j. 1st flight after false s: chsd ldrs tl wknd after 4 out* **25/1**	66
4500	9	1	**Pegasus Lad (USA)**[15] 1164 4-11-1 **79** AndrewGlassonbury (Linda Blackford) *j. 1st 2 flights after false s: chsd ldrs tl after 4 out* **50/1**	64
P500	10	30	**Tram Express (FR)**[30] 1035 6-11-10 **87** (b) PeterToole (Shaun Lycett) *j. 1st flight after false s: chsd ldrs tl led after 4 out: hdd next and wknd qckly: t.o* **40/1**	46
P0	11	4	**Ilewin Tom**[43] 913 7-10-1 **69** AshleyBird(5) (Gary Brown) *j. 1st 2 flights after false s: chsd ldrs tl wknd 4 out: t.o* **25/1**	25
3-00	12	21	**Am I Blue**[15] 1164 4-11-12 **90** DeanColeman (Mrs D Thomas) *j. 1st flight after false s: j. slowly in rr thrght: t.o* **40/1**	26

3m 43.55s (-3.75) **Going Correction** -0.15s/f (Good) 12 Ran SP% **113.9**
Speed ratings (Par 103): **103,97,95,93,90 89,87,86,86,71 69,58**
toteswingers:1&2 £24.00, 2&3 £13.40, 1&3 £13.10 CSF £111.15 CT £988.71 TOTE £10.60: £1.40, £5.60, £3.00; EX 185.70.
Owner Treoes Racing Club **Bred** John Osborne And Edgeridge Ltd **Trained** Aberthin, Vale of Glamorgan

FOCUS
There was a calamitous false start before they eventually jumped off in this weak handicap for conditional riders. They went a fair enough gallop. The winner produced a big step up.

NOTEBOOK
Louis Ludwig(IRE) could hardly have scored any easier in the end. He had pulled up on debut for new connections when sent chasing a week earlier, when lacking any fluency over his fences. He also came into this a maiden and had been well beaten in sellers for his previous stable, so it's hard to see just where this vast improvement came from. His current trainer has excelled with such characters in the past, though, and he obviously has more talent than originally thought. It's a good bet he will be turning out quickly as the handicapper will hike him up and he will go unpenalised until his new mark is published. (op 10-1)
London Times(IRE) again travelled nicely before finding just the same pace when push came to shove. However, he has found some form of late and reversed last-time-out C&D form with Robbmaa on 2lb better terms. (op 20-1)
Frosty's Gift didn't always jump that fluently, but was 7lb better off with Robbmaa and just did enough to reverse last-time-out form with her. She sets the level. (op 10-1 tchd 11-1)
Robbmaa(FR) had three of these behind when landing a course-and-distance seller recently but could not confirm the form of his 7lb higher mark. (op 7-1 tchd 11-2)
Wisteria Lane(IRE) met support and her rider was the first to notice the false start and take action. She ran in snatches after the third flight, though, and it's not hard to see why she sports headgear. (op 13-2)
Papradon won decisively over fences last time, in the same race in which the winner was pulled up, and was able to race off the same mark back over hurdles. He had no more to give from three out and may just have found the run coming a bit too soon. (op 6-4)
Monsieur(FR), who sweated up, was the chief sufferer in the false start. (op 12-1 tchd 16-1)
Am I Blue Official explanation: jockey said filly never travelled

1273 40 LIVE FOOTBALL MARKETS AT TOTESPORT.COM H'CAP CHASE (12 fncs) 2m
5:40 (5:41) (Class 5) (0-95,95) 4-Y-0+ **£1,884** (£549; £274)

Form				RPR
P5-6	1		**Western Pride**[21] 1106 7-10-0 **69** oh14 (t) GerardTumelty (Richard Price) *hit 1st: hld up in rr tl stdy hdwy appr 4 out: styd on to chse ldr appr last: kpt on u.p to ld fnl 100yds: all out* **66/1**	81+
53P-	2	1	**Red Birr (IRE)**[299] 1866 9-11-3 **86** SamThomas (Paul Webber) *hld up in tch: hdwy appr 4 out: qcknd to chal and gng wl whn chal and stmbld on landing 3 out: slt ld next: rdn after last: hdd and no ex fnl 100yds* **10/1**	98+
01U5	3	10	**Sam Cruise**[16] 1152 9-11-5 **88** (t) AidanColeman (Steve Gollings) *led to 4th: styd pressing ldrs: led again 3 out: narrowly hdd next: wknd fr last* **9/1**	89
0500	4	12	**Lukie Victor (IRE)**[14] 1179 9-11-4 **90** (v1) DPFahy(3) (Evan Williams) *chsd ldrs: led 7th: hdd 3 out: sn wknd* **20/1**	80
F341	5	3	**My Condor (IRE)**[21] 1106 9-11-5 **95** (p) MrJHamer(7) (Donald McCain) *chsd ldrs to 4 out: sn wknd* **4/1**[1]	83
6433	6	nk	**Le Brocquy**[28] 1047 5-11-7 **95** (p) JimmyDerham(5) (Martin Keighley) *in rr: stl bhd whn blnd 4 out: mod prog fr 2 out* **5/1**[3]	82
-445	7	1 3/4	**Lansdowne Princess**[65] 737 8-10-0 **74** DavidBass(5) (Gerald Ham) *in rr: rdn after 3rd: hit 4th: rdn 7th: mod prog fr 2 out* **8/1**	60
0F-0	8	6	**Auditor**[21] 1106 11-10-2 **70** oh5 ow2 ColinBolger (Simon Lewis) *chsd ldrs: hit 5th: wknd appr 4 out* **66/1**	51
FB-6	9	2	**Eljay's Boy**[11] 1195 12-11-12 **95** (t) JoeTizzard (Colin Tizzard) *blnd 1st: j. slowly 5th: blnd 8th: a in rr* **6/1**	76
6533	10	16	**Moon Bear**[7] 1231 9-10-3 **75** (v) DannyCook(3) (Linda Blackford) *hit 2nd and reminder: led 4th: rdn and hdd 7th: wknd rapidly appr 4 out* **9/2**[2]	39
-441	P		**New Rackheath (IRE)**[72] 652 7-11-1 **84** (v1) DenisO'Regan (Mark Shears) *j. modly in rr: t.o whn p.u bef 4 out* **14/1**	—

3m 52.69s (1.09) **Going Correction** +0.05s/f (Yiel) 11 Ran SP% **113.7**
Speed ratings (Par 103): **99,98,93,87,86 85,84,81,80,72 —**
CSF £603.13 CT £6393.40 TOTE £115.50: £18.90, £6.60, £4.50; EX 350.70.
Owner G E Amey **Bred** G E Amey **Trained** Ullingswick, H'fords

FOCUS
This moderate handicap was run at a decent gallop and the first pair, who pulled well clear after the last, were both given waiting rides. The winner was a surprise improver.

NOTEBOOK
Western Pride, a stone out of the handicap, got up under very strong handling near the finish and ran out a surprise winner. She arrived for this as a longstanding maiden and had finished miles behind My Condor over C&D on her previous outing. Things didn't look good for her early on here as she made errors, but the further she went the better she was and there appeared to be little fluke about it. It remains to be seen whether she can back this up, but her confidence will have been nicely boosted and her next outing should reveal as to whether she is an improver. Official explanation: trainer's rep said, regarding apparent improvement in form, that the mare had benefited from being held up and had come back after a long break before the previous run. (op 50-1)
Red Birr(IRE) finished fifth in this race last term off a 9lb higher mark and was returning from a 299-day absence here. He moved up stylishly in the home straight and overcame an error three out, but was ultimately mugged by the winner after hitting the front. He has a disappointing profile, but is clearly weighted to win and is entitled to improve for the run. (tchd 11-1)
Sam Cruise got a very positive ride and kept on gamely enough after being headed on the back straight. He rates the best guide for the form. (op 10-1 tchd 17-2)
Lukie Victor(IRE) was in a first-time visor and coming out of the back straight it looked as it might work the oracle, but he downed tools shortly after turning for home and continues to frustrate. (op 14-1)
My Condor(IRE) had today's winner a long way behind when scoring over course and distance last time, but was disappointing off his 5lb higher mark. (op 9-2 tchd 5-1)
Moon Bear was well backed, but after being ridden to the front on the back straight he quickly dropped the anchor and now has something to prove. (op 5-1 tchd 7-2)

1274 GET LIVE FOOTBALL STATS AT TOTESPORT.COM NOVICES' CHASE (18 fncs) 2m 7f
6:10 (6:11) (Class 4) 5-Y-0+ **£2,927** (£859; £429; £214)

Form				RPR
2120	1		**Presentandcorrect (IRE)**[30] 1032 9-11-0 119 (p) SamTwiston-Davies(5) (Nigel Twiston-Davies) *j. slowly 1st: trckd ldr 11th: rdn appr 4 out: chal 3 out: slt ld next: narrowly hdd after last: rallied u.p to ld again fnl 50yds: all out* **9/1**	128
20-1	2	1/2	**Baddam**[20] 408 8-11-5 0 APMcCoy (Ian Williams) *led: blnd 6th: hdd next: led again after 9th: drvn 4 out: narrowly hdd 2 out: styd chalng and slt ld after last: hdd and no ex fnl 50yds* **4/5**[1]	128
35	3	30	**Canon's Corner (IRE)**[21] 1109 7-10-12 0 AidanColeman (Rachel Hobbs) *in tch tl wknd bef 4 out: tk poor 3rd run-in: t.o* **66/1**	91
1321	4	27	**I Need A Hero (IRE)**[2] 1255 5-11-5 112 (t) JackDoyle (Sarah Humphrey) *in tch: hdwy and chsd ldng duo 14th: wknd qckly bef 4 out: no ch whn rdr lost iron briefly after 3 out: lost poor 3rd run-in* **11/4**[2]	86
1-01	P		**City Heights (IRE)**[37] 957 8-11-7 125 DavidBass(5) (Giles Smyly) *chsd ldr: hit 1st: led 7th: hdd after 9th: blnd and wknd 11th: mstke next: t.o whn p.u bef 4 out* **7/1**[3]	—
56P	P		**Minella (IRE)**[28] 1045 6-10-12 0 RodiGreene (Michael Appleby) *prom early: hit 8th: in rr and reminders: t.o after 9th and p.u bef next* **100/1**	—

5m 42.82s (0.22) **Going Correction** +0.05s/f (Yiel) 6 Ran SP% **107.2**
Speed ratings: **101,100,90,81,— —**
toteswingers:1&2 £2.20, 2&3 £9.50, 1&3 £8.50 CSF £16.26 TOTE £11.30: £2.60, £1.10; EX 20.60.
Owner Robroy Racing 2 **Bred** Daniel N O'Donovan **Trained** Naunton, Gloucs

FOCUS
There was a reasonable gallop on in this fair novice chase and the first pair came a long way clear in a battling finish. They both ran to their previous chase best.

NOTEBOOK
Presentandcorrect(IRE) got on top where it mattered and handed his bang in-form trainer/jockey combination another winner. He ran no sort of race at Stratford last time, but was equipped with first-time cheekpieces for this return to novice company and proved most game for his rider's urgings over the last two fences. Things will be trickier under a double penalty in this division and he is due a rise in the handicap now, but he is in good hands. Official explanation: trainer said, regarding apparent improvement in form, that the gelding had benefited from being fitted with first-time cheek pieces and being ridden by a jockey who it goes well for. (op 8-1 tchd 13-2 and 10-1)
Baddam has developed into a tricky veteran on the Flat, but has a decent strike-rate over jumps and came into this unbeaten in three previous runs at the course. Indeed he had slammed a subsequent winner on his chasing debut here when last seen in this sphere and was entitled to be favourite with Tony McCoy back aboard. He forfeited the lead after getting the open ditch wrong passing the stands for the first time, but was soon back on the front end and looked the one to be on turning for home. He came under pressure soon after, but McCoy threw the kitchen sink at him and he only just failed. He was later found to have finished distressed. Official explanation: vet said gelding finished distressed (op 10-11)
Canon's Corner(IRE) was never seriously in the hunt, but this was more encouraging and he should fare better when switching to low-grade handicaps.
I Need A Hero(IRE) looked good when upped in trip at Southwell two days earlier and connections must have felt confident to allow him to take his chance here. He did things nicely through the race under restraint, but found nothing when the first pair kicked for home and surely the outing came too soon for him. (op 5-2)

City Heights(IRE) had claims in this company despite being saddled with a double penalty. Back up in trip, his jumping didn't convince once he was left in front nearing the final circuit, but it went totally to pot on the back straight and he wasn't on a going day. His rider later reported him to have lost his action. Official explanation: jockey said gelding lost its action (op 8-1 tchd 10-1)

1275 BET ON LIVE TENNIS AT TOTESPORT.COM NOVICES' HURDLE (12 hdls) 3m

6:40 (6:41) (Class 4) 4-Y-0+ **£2,397** (£698; £349)

Form RPR

2 **1** **Sir Ronan**[27] 1063 7-10-12 0 (t) AidanColeman 101+
(Lawney Hill) *in tch: hdwy 8th: rdn appr 3 out: styd on to take slt ld 2 out: rdn and kpt on to go clr run-in* **8/1**

621 **2** 4 ½ **Oursininlaw (IRE)**[33] 999 6-11-5 110 AdamWedge(7) 111
(Evan Williams) *chsd ldrs: chal fr 8th: upsides wnr and u.p 2 out: stl ev ch last whn nt fluent: wknd run-in* **7/2**[3]

222 **3** 4 ½ **Our Guardian Angel (IRE)**[18] 1140 6-10-5 100 (t) RichardJohnson 85
(Tim Vaughan) *in rr tl hdwy to chse ldrs 4 out: rdn next: styd on to take 3rd run-in: no imp on ldng duo* **3/1**[2]

P-1P **4** 6 **Victor Daly (IRE)**[51] 844 9-10-12 0 WarrenMarston 87
(Martin Keighley) *trckd ldrs: j. slowly 2nd: chsd ldr 7th: chal next: slt ld 4 out: rdn next hdd 2 out and sn btn: lost 3rd run-in* **11/4**[1]

664 **5** 1 ¼ **Weldone Honey**[53] 841 5-10-2 0 DonalDevereux(3) 77
(Peter Bowen) *in rr: hit 5th: hdwy 7th: chsd ldrs and rdn 4 out: j. slowly 3 out: wknd next* **20/1**

-6U3 **6** 4 ½ **The Hairy Mutt (IRE)**[27] 1057 8-10-5 89 MissLBrooke(7) 85+
(Lady Susan Brooke) *towards rr: hdwy after 4 out: styng on one pce to dispute 4th whn veered bdly rt and tried to run out to stables after last: rcvrd and r.o again fnl 100yds* **9/1**

2415 **7** 1 ¼ **Mzuri Bay**[11] 1196 5-11-5 111 (t) MarkGrant 86
(Brendan Duke) *chsd ldrs: hit 8th: pressed ldrs after 4 out: wknd after 3 out* **9/1**

56-5 **8** ½ **Montevetro**[67] 717 5-10-12 78 (v) LeightonAspell 78
(William Clay) *chsd ldrs: rdn 7th: wknd 4 out* **50/1**

P0-5 **9** 30 **Chaser's War (IRE)**[41] 929 6-10-5 0 JodieMogford 41
(Nikki Evans) *t.k.h: hit 3rd: rdn 7th: wknd 8th: t.o* **80/1**

10 30 **Mr Johnson (IRE)**[128] 7-10-5 0 MrJEngland(7) 18
(Michael Gates) *led tl hdd & wknd 4 out: t.o* **40/1**

5m 40.93s (-3.67) **Going Correction** -0.15s/f (Good) **10** Ran SP% **115.4**
Speed ratings (Par 105): **100,98,97,95,94 93,92,92,82,72**
toteswingers:1&2 £3.90, 2&3 £2.90, 1&3 £5.40 CSF £35.59 TOTE £19.90: £5.60, £2.30, £1.10; EX 27.50.
Owner D Spearing **Bred** D C And Mrs M S Spearing **Trained** Aston Rowant, Oxon

FOCUS
An ordinary staying novice hurdle, run at an average gallop. The second sets the level.

NOTEBOOK
Sir Ronan relished this step up in trip and got off the mark as a hurdler at the second time of asking. He shaped as though in need of further when second here on his debut under rules last month, and his pointing exploits also showed he has the stamina for 3m. His form between the flags was just modest, but he has few miles on the clock and his decent connections ought to find a little further improvement in him. (op 7-1)
Oursininlaw(IRE) came under heavy pressure rounding the home turn and couldn't go with the winner late on, conceding that rival a stone (not taking into account his rider's claim). He still confirmed his last-time-out form with the third on these worse terms, though, and rates a solid enough benchmark. (op 9-2 tchd 5-1)
Our Guardian Angel(IRE) is a consistent mare, but it was somewhat disappointing she didn't reverse her Cartmel form with the runner-up and she is not going to prove simple to place successfully. (tchd 11-4)
Victor Daly(IRE), pulled up over fences last time, was having his first outing in this sphere since 2007. He wasn't disgraced and the experience ought to restore some confidence for a return to chasing. (op 5-2 tchd 9-4)

1276 PLAY BLACKJACK AT TOTESPORT.COM H'CAP CHASE (18 fncs) 2m 7f

7:10 (7:10) (Class 4) (0-115,111) 4-Y-0+ **£2,927** (£859; £429; £214)

Form RPR

4-12 **1** **Mad Jack Duncan (IRE)**[19] 1126 8-10-11 96 AidanColeman 111+
(Lawney Hill) *t.k.h: chsd ldrs: chal 3 out slt ld next: pushed out run-in: comf* **5/2**[1]

P052 **2** 2 **Tritonville Lodge (IRE)**[22] 1091 8-11-12 111 JackDoyle 122
(Emma Lavelle) *led 3rd to 7th: slt ld again 9th: rdn 4 out: narrowly hdd 2 out: kpt on run-in: no ch w wnr* **13/2**[3]

4-P4 **3** 11 **On You Go (IRE)**[44] 890 9-11-11 110 APMcCoy 113
(Jonjo O'Neill) *hld up in rr: in tch: improving whn bdly hmpd 11th: sn rcvrd and chsd ldrs 13th: rdn next: wknd after 4 out* **13/2**[3]

60U/ **4** 16 **Autumn Red (IRE)**[524] 4424 10-10-7 92 DenisO'Regan 76
(Paul Webber) *chsd ldrs: chal fr 13th tl rdn appr 4 out: wknd 3 out* **15/2**

-2B3 **5** 2 **Merry Terry**[7] 1227 6-10-8 93 (t) JoeTizzard 77
(Colin Tizzard) *in rr: j. slowly 8th and reminders: hdwy and rdn 14th: wknd 3 out: no ch whn hit 2 out* **10/3**[2]

-00P **6** 14 **Native City (IRE)**[11] 1200 8-11-5 107 RichieMcLernon(3) 75
(Jonjo O'Neill) *hdwy 9th: chsng ldrs whn hmpd 11th: wknd after next* **20/1**

P131 **F** **Thenameescapesme**[22] 1093 10-11-8 110 SeanQuinlan(3) —
(Kim Bailey) *led to 3rd: styd chalng: led again 7th to 9th: upsides whn fell 11th: fatally injured* **13/2**[3]

5m 50.0s (7.40) **Going Correction** +0.05s/f (Yiel) **7** Ran SP% **108.2**
Speed ratings (Par 105): **89,88,84,78,78 73,—**
toteswingers:1&2:£1.20, 2&3 £5.30, 1&3 £3.80 CSF £16.79 CT £79.95 TOTE £2.80: £1.50, £3.50; EX 17.20.
Owner Alan Hill **Bred** Paul Cashman **Trained** Aston Rowant, Oxon

FOCUS
Not a bad handicap for the class. A personal best from the winner and the second sets the level.

NOTEBOOK
Mad Jack Duncan(IRE) made it two from three since resuming under rules for current connections and completed the task readily, handing his trainer and jockey a quick-fire double. He was a well-held second when up to this trip at Stratford last time out and had stamina to prove, but he clearly stays well. The practice he gained between the flags earlier this year has stood him in decent stead for these regulation fences and he does jump well. There could still be a little more to come from this relation of Rhinestone Cowboy and Wichita Lineman. (tchd 9-4)
Tritonville Lodge(IRE) was given a positive ride and held every chance, but again managed to find one too good. It was still a pleasing effort in defeat as he was giving just over a stone to the progressive winner on ground slightly easier than he cares for. Connections believe he is best when fresh so won't rush him back. (op 7-1 tchd 6-1)
On You Go(IRE) did well to recover after being hampered by a faller in the back straight. However, he was soon under the pump after and, despite plugging on for pressure, never threatened to improve on his second in this race last term. (op 6-1 tchd 11-2 and 7-1 in places)
Autumn Red(IRE) made an encouraging enough comeback effort on this first outing since March last year. He has yet to win a race, but will surely be sharper for the run and is entitled to improve providing he comes out of the race without a hitch. (op 8-1 tchd 9-1)
Merry Terry, unsurprisingly, was more patiently ridden this time and he was also racing in a first-time tongue-tie. He was never really travelling with any fluency, however, and perhaps he wants dropping back in trip. He can also find less competitive assignments, so isn't one to abandon just yet. (op 7-2)
Native City(IRE), another hampered, was beaten before the home bend but at least completed again. (op 18-1)

1277 VICKY OWENS BIRTHDAY H'CAP CHASE (15 fncs) 2m 4f 110y

7:40 (7:40) (Class 4) (0-115,115) 4-Y-0+ **£2,927** (£859; £429; £214)

Form RPR

0304 **1** **Good Company (IRE)**[28] 1044 10-11-6 112 RichieMcLernon(3) 124+
(Jonjo O'Neill) *a travelling wl: trckd ldrs fr 7th: wnt 3rd 4 out: ht 2 out: stl gng wl after last: shkn up under hand riding: edgd lft and led fnl 100yds: v easily* **9/1**

125P **2** 2 ½ **Michigan Assassin (IRE)**[14] 1176 8-11-2 112 AodhaganConlon(7) 121+
(Debra Hamer) *t.k.h: led after 2nd: wnt rt 3rd: hdd 4th: hit 5th: led 7th: kpt narrow ld: jnd appr 4 out: rdn: blnd bdly and hdd 2 out: sn rcvrd and upsides last: led sn after: hdd and outpcd fnl 100yds* **5/1**[3]

1166 **3** 5 **Neutrino**[28] 1044 8-11-12 115 (v) TomScudamore 116
(David Bridgwater) *in rr and pushed along 6th: hrd drvn 10th: rapid hdwy u.p to chal fr 4 out and lft w slt ld 2 out: jnd last: sn hdd and edgd lft u.p and wknd run-in* **16/1**

-P42 **4** 30 **Glengarra (IRE)**[19] 1128 13-11-2 105 (tp) NoelFehily 79
(Liam Corcoran) *led tl after 2nd: bmpd 3rd: led 4th to 7th: styd pressing ldr: wknd bef 4 out: t.o* **13/2**

50PU **5** 24 **Dasher Reilly (USA)**[2] 1256 9-10-0 89 oh32 (b) LiamTreadwell 41
(Aytach Sadik) *nvr travelling: a bhd: t.o* **100/1**

-304 **P** **O'Toole (IRE)**[15] 1161 11-11-2 105 TomO'Brien —
(Caroline Keevil) *nvr trbld ldrs: t.o whn p.u bef 4 out* **10/1**

P-13 **P** **Good Old Days (IRE)**[84] 463 11-10-13 105 SeanQuinlan(3) —
(Kim Bailey) *t.k.h: in tch: chsd ldrs 8th: wknd and p.u bef 4 out* **8/1**

0322 **P** **Captain Marlon (IRE)**[15] 1161 9-10-0 94 (t) SamTwiston-Davies(5) —
(Colin Tizzard) *chsd ldrs: hit 4th: rdn 7th and 9th: wknd 11th: t.o whn p.u bef 4 out* **11/4**[1]

435P **P** **I'm The Decider (IRE)**[14] 1176 8-11-9 112 (p) APMcCoy —
(Jonjo O'Neill) *in rr and nvr really travelling: rdn 7th: j. slowly 11th: sn wknd: t.o whn p.u bef 4 out* **4/1**[2]

5m 4.95s (-1.75) **Going Correction** +0.05s/f (Yiel) **9** Ran SP% **113.7**
Speed ratings (Par 105): **105,104,102,90,81 —,—,—,—**
toteswingers:1&2 £8.20, 2&3 £12.30, 1&3 £29.00 CSF £53.51 CT £710.15 TOTE £10.70: £3.30, £1.60, £5.60; EX 75.20.
Owner John P McManus **Bred** County Down Bloodstock **Trained** Cheltenham, Gloucs

FOCUS
A moderate handicap, run at a fair gallop. The first three dominated in the home straight and, for differing reasons, each of the trio were given fine rides. The winner had slipped to a good mark.

NOTEBOOK
Good Company(IRE) finally exploited his falling handicap mark and did the job with a fair bit left in the tank. He had been laboured since resuming this year, including a spell hunter chasing, but had dropped to a mark 12lb lower than his last win back in 2008. He had run well at this venue in the past, though, and travelled here like by far the best horse in the race. Richie McLernon looked to have the leaders covered turning in, but he didn't count on a rallying Neutrino sweeping past and Good Company came under pressure two out. McLernon has shown a knack with similar characters in the past, however, and he soon had him back on the bridle, before cajoling him to the front on the run-in. (op 11-2)
Michigan Assassin(IRE) was held prior to being pulled up after a blunder late on at Ffos Las on his previous outing. Well backed here, he was given his usual aggressive ride and was still in with every chance prior to clouting the penultimate fence. His rider performed wonders to maintain the partnership and leave him in with a chance at the next, but the winner was always on top. He deserves to find another race. (op 8-1)
Neutrino was given an excellent ride in defeat by Tom Scudamore. He had to be ridden almost from the off, but Scudamore kept at him and he finally responded coming out of the back straight. He picked up so well that he nearly looked like winning, but eventually the burden of top weight told. (op 10-1)
Glengarra(IRE), last year's winner, raced off the same mark yet was done with on the back straight this time. (op 6-1 tchd 5-1)
Captain Marlon(IRE) looked ready for this return to further, but he stopped quickly turning out of the back straight and presumably something went amiss. (op 11-2 tchd 6-1 in places)
I'm The Decider(IRE) came in for support, but was another who ran in snatches from an early stage and has now been pulled up the last twice. (op 11-2 tchd 6-1 in places)

1278 PLAY ROULETTE AT TOTESPORT.COM MAIDEN HURDLE (8 hdls) 2m

8:10 (8:10) (Class 5) 4-Y-0+ **£1,712** (£499; £249)

Form RPR

-30B **1** **Points Of View**[48] 862 5-10-11 103 (t) SeanQuinlan(3) 108+
(Kim Bailey) *t.k.h: chsd ldrs: chal fr 3 out tl slt ld 2 out: shkn up and sn clr run-in: eased nr fin* **5/1**[3]

2 4 ½ **Mutadarrej (IRE)**[12] 414 6-11-0 0 DougieCostello 99
(Ian Williams) *t.k.h: in tch: hdwy 4 out: trckd ldrs and nt fluent 2 out: hung lft and outpcd after last: sn rcvrd and fin wl to cl on eased down wnr* **7/2**[2]

3 6 **Global**[35] 4-10-13 0 LiamHeard 93
(Brian Ellison) *t.k.h: chsd ldrs: styng on whn blnd last: kpt on: nvr any ch w easy wnr* **15/2**

500 **4** 1 **Swiss Guard**[65] 733 4-10-13 0 RichardJohnson 92
(Tim Vaughan) *blnd and detached after 2nd: rcvrd and in tch 4th: j. slowly 4 out: styng on one pce whn j. slowly 2 out: wnt lft and rallied last: sn one pce* **14/1**

0 **5** 1 **Coach And Four (USA)**[49] 850 5-10-7 0 MrJEngland(7) 92
(Michael Gates) *chsd ldrs: led appr 3 out: narrowly hdd 2 out: wknd last* **80/1**

2 **6** nk **Coeur De Lionne (IRE)**[63] 754 6-11-0 0 (t) APMcCoy 92
(Paul Nicholls) *t.k.h: trckd ldrs: drvn to chal and hung lft appr 2 out: fnd little u.p: btn whn nt fluent last and hung lft run-in* **1/1**[1]

60- **7** 19 **Whatdoyoucallit (IRE)**[116] 5363 5-10-11 0 (t) DPFahy(3) 72
(Evan Williams) *in rr but in tch: rdn: hdwy to chse ldrs and n.m.r bnd appr 3 out: wknd sn after* **20/1**

/50- **8** 23 **That Man Fox**[390] 1038 9-10-9 95 (b) LeeEdwards(5) 49
(Tony Carroll) *t.k.h: led tl hdd & wknd appr 3 out* **20/1**

UP0- **9** 3/4 **Okey Dokey**[116] 5363 4-10-3 0....(p) JSMcGarvey(10) 47
(Evan Williams) *in rr and j. slowly 4th: mod prog after 4 out: btn whn mstke next* **50/1**

3m 47.13s (-0.17) **Going Correction** -0.15s/f (Good)
WFA 4 from 5yo+ 13lb **9** Ran SP% **120.0**
Speed ratings (Par 103): **94,91,88,88,87 87,78,66,66**
toteswingers:1&2 £2.80, 2&3 £5.50, 1&3 £8.70 CSF £23.37 TOTE £9.20: £2.00, £1.30, £2.20 Place 6: £1249.90 Place 5: £229.80.
Owner W J Ives **Bred** Limestone And Tara Studs **Trained** Andoversford, Gloucs
■ Stewards' Enquiry : Mr J England one-day ban: used whip with excessive frequency (tbn)

FOCUS
A reasonable maiden hurdle, although the favourite disappointed. The winner is rated to his mark with a step forward from the second.

NOTEBOOK
Points Of View finally opened his account over hurdles at the tenth attempt. He had blighted his career in this sphere previously by refusing to settle, and again took a bit of a hold early here, but fairly sprinted away from his rivals when asked to win the race. The first-time tongue-tie has to go down as having had the desired effect and, formerly a useful handicapper on the Flat, it will be very interesting to see how he now copes with a penalty. (op 7-1 tchd 8-1)
Mutadarrej(IRE) has been rejuvenated on the level of late by his current trainer and arrived here on the back of consecutive wins in that sphere. Well backed on this return to hurdling, he got outpaced after an error two out and left the impression he needs more of a test, as his form on the level indicates. It shouldn't be long before he finds a moderate opening. (op 5-1)
Global, who defied a mark of 81 on the Flat when trained by Richard Hannon, had stamina to prove on this hurdling debut and was ridden accordingly. He posted a fair effort without truly proving he gets this far and ought to improve for the experience. (op 12-1)
Swiss Guard, who showed little in three runs over hurdles earlier this year, put in an odd performance. He looked like tailing off on the back straight, but rallied to bag fourth late on and clearly has some issues. (op 20-1)
Coach And Four(USA) got a positive ride and was still bang there two from home. He was held soon after, but this was a lot more encouraging and he will be of more interest when going handicapping in this sphere.
Coeur De Lionne(IRE) threw the race away when second on his hurdling debut two months earlier, but that form entitled him to collect here. He was keen early on, but still got produced with his chance only to down tools when put under maximum pressure. He now has it all to prove. (op 8-13 tchd 4-7)
T/Plt: £1,065.90 to a £1 stake. Pool of £73,450.53 - 50.30 winning tickets. T/Qpdt: £23.50 to a £1 stake. Pool of £7,947.79 - 250.10 winning tickets. ST

[792]HEREFORD (R-H)
Wednesday, August 18

OFFICIAL GOING: Good (good to firm in places)
Wind: almost nil Weather: overcast

1279 FREE RACING WITH ODDSCHECKER.COM WEDNESDAY JUVENILE FILLIES' HURDLE (8 hdls) 2m 1f
5:40 (5:40) (Class 4) 3-Y-O **£2,667** (£783; £391; £195)

Form RPR
43 **1** **Destiny's Dancer**[16] 960 3-10-10 0.... BarryKeniry 80+
(Ben Haslam) *t.k.h in rr: effrt in 4th and reminders 3 out: chal and hmpd 2 out: sn led: urged clr bef last* **2/5**[1]
0P0 **2** 6 **A P Ling**[32] 1018 3-10-3 0.... KyleJames(7) 65
(Christopher Kellett) *plld hrd: lft in ld briefly after 1st: prom: veered violently and j. bdly rt 2nd: lost pl and mstke 4th: outpcd in 8 l 5th after 3 out: rallied u.p to press wnr between last two: fnd nthing flat* **33/1**
3 2 **Doyenne Dream**[113] 3-10-10 0.... FelixDeGiles 65
(James Eustace) *j. bdly rt and mstkes: led after 1st: j.rt yet again 2 out and hmpd wnr: sn hdd: hanging rt and btn bef last* **17/2**[3]
6141 **4** 2 1/2 **Gulf Punch**[31] 1024 3-11-0 0....(p) RyanCrawford(10) 75
(Milton Harris) *sn detached in last: mstke 3rd: drvn along rest of way: stl 12 l last 2 out: plugged on: nvr on terms* **9/2**[2]
0 **5** 8 **Mini Max**[32] 1018 3-10-10 0.... MarkGrant 53
(Brendan Duke) *led tl nrly ref 1st: j. deliberately and chsd ldrs: u.p 5th: wknd after slow jump 3 out: j. slowly last* **40/1**
6 8 **Keep Silent**[60] 3-10-10 0.... WillKennedy 46
(John Berry) *prom: rdn and lost 2nd bef 2 out where lost 3rd: fin weakly* **50/1**
F **Banco Busto (IRE)**[85] 3-10-10 0.... RodiGreene —
(Stuart Howe) *last whn fell 1st* **100/1**

4m 3.60s (4.20) **Going Correction** -0.35s/f (Good) **7** Ran SP% **108.5**
Speed ratings (Par 99): **76,73,72,71,67 63,—**
toteswingers:1&2:£19.90, 2&3:£27.10, 1&3:£1.10 CSF £15.37 TOTE £1.50: £1.20, £13.60; EX 15.20.
Owner Mark James **Bred** Plantation Stud **Trained** Middleham Moor, N Yorks

FOCUS
Several showers before racing eased the going, and the ground was described as 'perfect' by a rider in the first. There was plenty of incident as some of these juvenile fillies betrayed their inexperience. The time was around 13 seconds slower than the following novice event and the form is really weak. The winner was value for further but still rated below her best.

NOTEBOOK
Destiny's Dancer had run creditably in defeat on her two previous tries over hurdles, against male opposition each time, and she comfortably landed the odds despite being seriously hindered by the errant third jumping the second-last. The penalty will not aid her cause and her jumping still has room for improvement. (op 4-9 tchd 4-11)
A P Ling suddenly improved to look a threat on the home turn, but was quickly put in her place by the winner. She had not shown much on her three previous tries, so this was a modest step up, but she is not straightforward. (op 28-1 tchd 40-1)
Doyenne Dream was making her hurdling debut but had been second in a Flat maiden in April on her latest start. She has more scope than most of these, but persisted in jumping markedly right while making the running and was no threat from two out. She was withdrawn after proving unruly on her most recent intended outing on the Flat and would appear to have temperament issues. (op 10-1 tchd 11-1 and 8-1)
Gulf Punch has two hurdle wins to her name - the first in a claimer - but had twice finished behind tonight's winner. Saddled with a double penalty, and partnered by a young jockey having his first ride under rules, she was struggling badly at halfway, but did make modest late gains. (op 4-1)

1280 SPIFFING CRABBIE'S ALCOHOLIC GINGER BEER NOVICES' HURDLE (8 hdls) 2m 1f
6:10 (6:10) (Class 4) 4-Y-O+ **£2,667** (£783; £391; £195)

Form RPR
F4 **1** **Tignello (IRE)**[76] 590 5-10-7 0....(t) IanPopham(5) 114+
(Paul Nicholls) *plld hrd: hld up chsng ldrs: wnt 2nd 2 out: led on bit between last two: clr last* **2/1**[2]
46-3 **2** 8 **Halling Gal**[23] 1090 4-10-11 107.... PaulMoloney 104
(Evan Williams) *set str gallop: mstke 1st: jnd by two rivals and rdn 2 out: hdd between last two: wl hld whn mstke last* **4/1**[3]
3 33 **Contradiktive (IRE)**[48] 4-10-11 0.... RichardJohnson 82
(Tim Vaughan) *prom: j.rt 5th: j.rt and hit next: chal and ev ch 2 out: immediately floundering in poor 3rd* **15/8**[1]
6 **4** 58 **Integria**[22] 1111 4-10-11 0....(b) AidanColeman 22
(Venetia Williams) *cl up: wknd bdly 5th: hopelessly t.o after 3 out* **5/1**
5 15 **Rowaad**[49] 5-10-9 0.... TomMolloy(3) 10
(Andrew Price) *a last: mstke 1st: mstke 3rd and lost tch: t.o 5th* **66/1**
P **Jinn And Tinick**[34] 4-9-13 0.... LeeEdwards(5) —
(Tony Carroll) *t.k.h early: prom tl mstke 2nd: j. slowly 3rd: wkng whn terrible mstke 4th and rdr lost irons and nrly uns: t.o next: f bhd whn climbed 2 out and p.u* **50/1**

3m 50.8s (-8.60) **Going Correction** -0.35s/f (Good)
WFA 4 from 5yo 13lb **6** Ran SP% **108.2**
Speed ratings (Par 105): **106,102,86,59,52 —**
toteswingers:1&2 £3.40, 2&3 £1.80, 1&3 £1.02 CSF £9.72 TOTE £3.00: £1.20, £2.80; EX 7.50.
Owner Mrs Mette Campbell-Andenaes **Bred** G Gorlsdorf **Trained** Ditcheat, Somerset

FOCUS
This ordinary novice event was run about 13 seconds quicker than the fillies' juvenile hurdle. The winner improved to the level you would expect from his Flat form.

NOTEBOOK
Tignello(IRE) was a fifth winner for Paul Nicholls from his last six runners. He had been given a break since finishing fourth on his latest start, form which has been boosted by a couple that finished in front of him. Equipped with a first-time tongue-tie, he was reluctant to settle but still won easily, although the opposition was limited. It will be interesting to see how he progresses from this, as he had been a disappointing type on the Flat for his previous yard. (tchd 9-4)
Halling Gal set a decent gallop, jumping fluently, but she was no match when Tignello made his move. She will remain vulnerable under her penalty. (op 3-1)
Contradiktive(IRE), a very moderate maiden at up to 1m4f on the Flat although he had been placed on his last three starts in that sphere, met support on this hurdles debut. After tending to jump out to his right, he was quickly left behind by the first pair from the second-last. It would not be a surprise to see headgear back on next time. (op 9-4 tchd 7-4)
Integria, who had the blinkers refitted, was cut adrift with three to jump and looks short of the required stamina. (op 7-1)

1281 BARRELS, HEREFORD'S LOCAL NOVICES' H'CAP CHASE (19 fncs) 3m 1f 110y
6:40 (6:40) (Class 4) (0-115,105) 4-Y-O+ **£3,057** (£897; £448; £224)

Form RPR
-212 **1** **Local Present (IRE)**[31] 1034 7-11-9 **102**.... APMcCoy 107
(Ron Hodges) *t.k.h and trckd ldrs: chal ldr 3 out: drvn and half l ahd next: racd lazily: edgd clr of rival fnl 50yds* **85/40**[1]
5243 **2** 1 **Tucumcari (IRE)**[26] 1081 5-11-2 **95**.... AidanColeman 98
(Brendan Powell) *led: 6 l clr 5th tl 9th: reminder 11th: hrd drvn and hdd 2 out: stl gng wl whn rdr dropped whip wl bef last: ev ch tl jst outpcd and eased fnl 50yds* **8/1**
22 **3** 12 **Dunkelly Castle (IRE)**[8] 1230 6-11-12 **105**.... HaddenFrost 97
(Roger Curtis) *racd keenly: pressed ldr: nt fluent 8th: rdn and lost 2nd bef 3 out where wkng in 4 l in 3rd* **7/2**[3]
312P **4** 9 **Hoof It Harry (IRE)**[49] 867 9-11-9 **102**.... RichardJohnson 88
(Paul Henderson) *hld up in tch: 4th whn hit 9th: rdn and wavered and lost tch 15th: struggling after* **11/2**
453P **5** 75 **Thyne Spirit (IRE)**[20] 1126 11-10-2 **81** oh27 ow2.... ColinBolger —
(Simon Lewis) *prom: lost pl 4th: last fr next: j.v.slowly 6th and continued t.o: several more ponderous jumps* **80/1**
-F15 **U** **Builteoir (IRE)**[12] 1200 8-10-7 **93**.... AdamWedge(7) 79
(Evan Williams) *chsd ldrs: 4th whn hit 3 out: sn wknd: 20 l 5th whn dived at last and uns rdr* **11/4**[2]

6m 26.6s (-5.20) **Going Correction** -0.475s/f (Good) **6** Ran SP% **108.6**
Speed ratings (Par 105): **89,88,85,82,59 —**
toteswingers:1&2 £2.90, 2&3 £2.20, 1&3 £1.80 CSF £16.94 TOTE £3.40: £2.10, £2.40; EX 14.00.
Owner Miss R Dobson, P Hart, R Hodges **Bred** John Quane **Trained** Charlton Mackrell, Somerset

FOCUS
No more than a fair novice handicap, it was run in a time over 25 seconds outside the standard. The winner is rated to his best.

NOTEBOOK
Local Present(IRE) challenged going best three from home, but he took plenty of urging to get past the runner-up late on. He is perhaps not straightforward, but McCoy evidently has the key to him. Good ground is what he needs.\n (op 2-1 tchd 15-8 and 9-4)
Tucumcari(IRE) ◆ made a bold bid from the front and battled on willingly, but his rider had dropped his whip on the home turn which certainly didn't help. Only a 5yo, the gelding had been lowered 5lb for this and he showed enough to suggest that he can win races over fences, particularly if he jumps as well as he did here. (op 7-1)
Dunkelly Castle(IRE) had been runner-up on his one previous try over fences, over a year ago, as well as in his last two runs over hurdles. He ran a solid enough race but could not go on with the front pair from the third-last. (op 4-1 tchd 5-1)
Hoof It Harry(IRE) was not fluent at times and his chance had slipped some way out. He remains 10lb higher than when winning at Fontwell in May. (op 15-2 tchd 9-2)
Builteoir(IRE) looks held by the handicapper, being 16lb higher than when winning at Stratford two runs back. He travelled quite well again but did not offer much off the bridle and was well beaten when departing at the last. (op 5-2 tchd 9-4)

1282 WYE VALLEY BREWERY CONDITIONAL JOCKEYS' H'CAP HURDLE (8 hdls) 2m 1f
7:10 (7:10) (Class 3) (0-125,119) 4-Y-O+ **£5,069** (£1,497; £748; £374; £187)

Form RPR
-260 **1** **Boogie Dancer**[44] 914 6-10-8 **101**.... HaddenFrost 106+
(Stuart Howe) *towards rr tl prog 3 out: 5 l 5th and rdn next: styd on gamely to ld last: forged clr fnl 75yds* **33/1**
24-F **2** 3 3/4 **Trumpstoo (USA)**[32] 1017 4-11-4 **115**.... BrianToomey(3) 115
(Richard Fahey) *prom: disp 2nd fr 4th: rdn and ev ch last: outpcd fnl 75yds* **11/1**
-014 **3** 3 3/4 **Dream Catcher (SWE)**[26] 1084 7-11-3 **113**.... RichieMcLernon(3) 112
(Jonjo O'Neill) *racd freely: led at brisk pce: rdn and hrd pressed fr 2 out: hdd last: sn wknd* **7/1**
421 **4** 6 **Admiral Dundas (IRE)**[26] 1083 5-11-0 **107**....(t) RichardKilloran 103+
(Kim Bailey) *nt a fluent: cl up: 4th and rdn whn mstke 2 out: immediately outpcd* **13/2**[3]
-246 **5** 2 1/2 **Exulto (IRE)**[38] 958 5-11-2 **112**.... RhysFlint(3) 104
(Philip Hobbs) *midfield: effrt 3 out: 2nd whn blnd next: rdn and sn lost pl* **9/2**[2]
3-32 **6** 3/4 **Olivino (GER)**[16] 1162 9-10-11 **109**.... MichaelByrne(5) 99
(Bernard Llewellyn) *towards rr: effrt bef 3 out: rdn and btn bef next* **16/1**

2220 **7** *3/4* **Peaceful Means (IRE)**[10] [958] 7-11-1 **108**........................ LeeEdwards 97
(Tony Carroll) *last tl 1/2-way: disp 10 l 6th 2 out: n.d* **12/1**

10/5 **8** *25* **Fade To Grey (IRE)**[35] [994] 6-11-2 **109**................(t) SamTwiston-Davies 76
(Shaun Lycett) *midfield: wknd after 5th: poor last bef 2 out* **14/1**

/22- **P** **Smoothly Does It**[148] [4794] 9-11-1 **108**.............................. HarrySkelton —
(Venetia Williams) *prom tl lost pl qckly after 4th: last whn mstke 5th and p.u: fatally injured* **9/1**

0-62 **F** **Dark Energy**[25] [798] 6-11-5 **112**..(t) SamJones —
(Michael Scudamore) *bhd: 10 l last whn fell 3 out* **12/1**

U12F **U** **Ajman (IRE)**[20] [1127] 5-10-13 **109**..(t) DPFahy(3) —
(Evan Williams) *mstke and uns rdr 1st* **4/1**[1]

3m 50.2s (-9.20) **Going Correction** -0.35s/f (Good)
WFA 4 from 5yo+ 13lb **11** Ran SP% **113.2**
Speed ratings (Par 107): **107,105,103,100,99 99,98,87,—,— —**
toteswingers:1&2 £27.40, 2&3 £13.30, 1&3 £20.20 CSF £343.41 CT £2826.45 TOTE £27.50: £7.60, £3.50, £3.60; EX 167.80.
Owner John Tackley **Bred** Millsec Limited **Trained** Oakford, Devon

FOCUS

A reasonably valuable race of its type and a suitably competitive affair, although it was weakened a little when favourite Ajman came down at the first, his third non-completion in his last five starts. The form still has a sound look to it though with the third helping to set the level. It was run at a solid pace.

NOTEBOOK

Boogie Dancer, suited by the sound pace, was held up and still only fifth jumping two out. The bottom weight, who had benefited from a break since running rather flat last time, won going away in the end. Her yard is back in form now. (op 28-1)

Trumpstoo(USA), a lightly raced 4yo, was staying on when coming down in a warm Listed event last time. He ran a thoroughly creditable race, but had no more to give on the run-in. (op 8-1)

Dream Catcher(SWE) was responsible for setting the generous gallop and he only gave way going to the last. He came here in good heart and is a decent guide to the form. (op 8-1 tchd 13-2)

Admiral Dundas(IRE) lacked the hurdles experience of most of these and ran well, but he was held following a mistake two from home. (op 6-1 tchd 15-2)

Exulto(IRE), who was hampered slightly going to the fourth-last, was in second place when blundering two out, which knocked the stuffing out of him. The handicapper still looks in charge. (op 5-1 tchd 4-1)

Olivino(GER) is on a career-high mark and threatened only briefly. (op 20-1)

Dark Energy, who was done no favours going into the fifth, was last but not entirely out of it when coming down at the next. (op 6-1)

Ajman(IRE), an impressive winner here in June, came down at the first, his third non-completion in his last five starts. (op 6-1)

1283 PERTEMPS PEOPLE DEVELOPMENT GROUP H'CAP CHASE (9 fncs 3 omitted) 2m

7:40 (7:43) (Class 4) (0-105,104) 4-Y-O+ **£2,667** (£783; £391; £195)

Form RPR

1 **January**[26] [1087] 7-11-2 **94**..(t) APMcCoy 104+
(Alan Fleming) *racd keenly and prom: wnt 2nd at 6th: chal and sltly bmpd 3 out: half l ld next: drvn and hld on wl cl home* **2/1**[1]

5121 **2** *nk* **Misamon (FR)**[28] [1060] 7-11-4 **96**................................(v) RichardJohnson 104
(David Rees) *led: rdn after 6th: jnd and j.lft 3 out: ev ch fr next: r.o u.p: jst hld* **7/2**[2]

-30U **3** *nk* **Nawow**[59] [799] 10-11-0 **99**..(tp) AdamWedge(7) 107
(Matt Hazell) *bhd: hit 2nd: prog on v long run to 3 out where 6 l 4th: sit 4 l 3rd: clsng whn rdr dropped whip last: styd on strly after: rather unlucky* **20/1**

446P **4** *8* **Post It**[8] [1231] 9-9-11 **82**.. MattGriffiths(7) 85
(Ron Hodges) *hld up: hdwy after 6th: 3rd and drvn bef 3 out: 4th and wkng whn nt fluent next: eased flat* **7/1**[3]

2330 **5** *7* **Tora Petcha (IRE)**[35] [984] 7-11-5 **100**.............................. DannyCook(3) 95
(Barry Leavy) *sn last: lost tch 4th: passed stragglers on v long run to 3 out: nvr nr ldrs* **16/1**

-3P2 **6** *1 1/4* **Ace High Blue (IRE)**[34] [1003] 8-11-9 **101**........................(t) PaulMoloney 94
(Evan Williams) *midfield: 5th after 6th: wknd bef 3 out* **9/1**

5-06 **7** *1 1/2* **Rince Donn (IRE)**[28] [1060] 8-11-1 **93**.................................. HaddenFrost 85
(Roger Curtis) *hld up towards rr: struggling bef 3 out* **25/1**

66-U **8** *39* **Wild Power (GER)**[8] [1231] 12-10-0 **78** oh4.......................... JamieMoore 35
(Helen Nelmes) *chsd ldrs tl after 6th: t.o bef 3 out* **28/1**

5 **9** *nk* **In The Zone (IRE)**[19] [1136] 6-11-3 **98**.......................... RichieMcLernon(3) 55
(Jonjo O'Neill) *cl up tl rdn and lost pl wl bef 3 out: t.o* **11/1**

F-00 **10** *11* **Auditor**[1] [1273] 11-10-2 **80** oh14 ow2..................................(b) ColinBolger 27
(Simon Lewis) *pressed ldrs tl reminders 5th: sn struggling: t.o bef 3 out* **100/1**

P-53 **P** **Blast The Past**[16] [1161] 8-11-5 **104**................................. BrianToomey(7) —
(Dai Burchell) *taken down early: plld hrd: chsd ldrs: 4th and outpcd whn p.u qckly 3 out* **17/2**

P- **P** **Your Night Out (FR)**[163] [4491] 5-11-0 **92**.......................(t) AidanColeman —
(Matt Sheppard) *bhd tl p.u 4th: dismntd: lost action briefly* **50/1**

3m 54.0s (-9.60) **Going Correction** -0.475s/f (Good) **12** Ran SP% **117.8**
Speed ratings (Par 105): **105,104,104,100,97 96,95,76,76,70 —,—**
CSF £9.23 CT £107.38 TOTE £3.30: £1.20, £1.20, £6.50; EX 9.40.
Owner BG Racing Partnership **Bred** Darley **Trained** Beare Green, Surrey

FOCUS

The three fences in the back straight were omitted in this moderate handicap chase due to the low sun. The pace was sound and the form looks fairly solid, the shortage of obstacles notwithstanding. The winner was well in on the best of his Irish form.

NOTEBOOK

January travelled well on this first start since leaving Ted Walsh's stable. He saw off a bump from the runner-up three out to move ahead, but his advantage was being eroded on the run-in. Although it is probably fair to say he is not straightforward, the ability is there and there could be more to come. (op 9-4, tchd 5-2 in places)

Misamon(FR) has enjoyed a fruitful summer and produced another good effort, rallying after making much of the running. He was 12lb higher than when winning over hurdles at Worcester last month, but 3lb lower than for his last run over fences. (op 9-2 tchd 3-1)

Nawow has reportedly undergone a wind operation since his last start two months ago. He ran well in the tongue-strap and was finishing to good effect after his jockey lost his stick at the last. (op 12-1)

Post It was not discredited, but her last win, over this course and distance, came more than three years ago. (op 10-1 tchd 13-2)

Tora Petcha(IRE), a selling hurdler, was never nearer than at the line on this chase debut. (tchd 20-1)

Ace High Blue(IRE)'s jumping still needs a bit of work, though he didn't shape badly. (op 12-1)

Blast The Past was held in fourth place when she pulled up sharply three from home. Official explanation: jockey said mare lost its action (op 6-1 tchd 9-1)

Your Night Out(FR) Official explanation: jockey said mare lost its action (op 6-1 tchd 9-1)

1284 HEREFORDSHIRE RIDING FOR DISABLED STANDARD OPEN NATIONAL HUNT FLAT RACE 2m 1f

8:10 (8:10) (Class 6) 4-6-Y-O **£1,370** (£399; £199)

Form RPR

341- **1** **Rudanphast (IRE)**[163] [4488] 5-11-8 0............................ RichardJohnson 119+
(Peter Bowen) *trckd ldrs and t.k.h in strly run r: led 3f out: rdn and styd on wl ins fnl f: eased nr fin* **4/1**[3]

U3 **2** *1 1/4* **Salford Rose (IRE)**[12] [1201] 4-10-4 0.............................. LeeStephens(3) 102+
(David Evans) *trckd ldrs: wnt 2nd 3f out: rdn and ev ch 1f out: hld after: kpt on gamely* **12/1**

3 *6* **Living Proof (IRE)** 5-10-4 0 ow3............................... MrSO'Donovan(7) 100
(Norma Twomey) *14th after 4f: prog to chse clr ldng pair 3f out: drvn and no imp after* **40/1**

4- **4** *10* **Good Tack (USA)**[325] [1556] 5-11-1 0............................. TomScudamore 95
(Richard Fahey) *chsd ldrs: rdn 3f out: little rspnse and sn btn* **11/4**[1]

2-64 **5** *4* **Spring Snow (USA)**[67] [732] 4-11-0 0..........................(b[1]) BrianHughes 90
(Alan Swinbank) *reminders to get gng: a abt same pl: rdn and wknd 3f out: t.o* **6/1**

2 **6** *8* **Romeo Desbois (FR)**[15] [1180] 5-11-1 0.................................. APMcCoy 84
(Rebecca Curtis) *racd freely: w ldr tl lost pl v tamely 4f out: t.o* **7/2**[2]

7 *3/4* **He's A Hawker (IRE)**[81] 5-10-8 0............................... BrianToomey(7) 84
(Michael Mullineaux) *t.k.h: nvr bttr than midfield: lost tch 3f out: sn eased: t.o* **50/1**

4 **8** *nk* **Mulranny (IRE)**[27] [1071] 5-10-8 0............................. MrSWDrinkwater(7) 83
(Nigel Twiston-Davies) *t.k.h: slt ld at str gallop tl drvn and hdd and fdd rapidly 3f out: t.o* **20/1**

0-2 **9** *1 1/2* **Great Hero**[27] [1071] 5-11-1 0... PaddyBrennan 82
(Richard Phillips) *t.k.h in rr: n.m.r bnd ent bk st: no ch fnl 3f: t.o* **11/1**

0 **10** *48* **Mi Man Sam (IRE)**[12] [1201] 5-10-8 0.............................. MrPJTolman(7) 39
(George Jones) *detached last early: hopelessly t.o fnl 4f* **80/1**

5 **11** *1* **Gwendraeth Girl (IRE)**[27] [1069] 5-10-3 0........................ LeeEdwards(5) 31
(Tony Carroll) *t.k.h and cl up: fdd over 3f out: hopelessly t.o* **33/1**

12 *4 1/2* **Henry's Hero** 4-11-0 0.. JamesDavies 33
(Gary Brown) *taken down early: t.k.h in rr: lost tch 4f out: hopelessly t.o: dismntd sn after fin* **33/1**

0 **13** *4* **Sans Un Souci (FR)**[56] [832] 4-10-7 0........................... CharlieWallis(7) 29
(John O'Shea) *towards rr: drvn 4f out: sn bdly t.o* **100/1**

14 *15* **Lavender Grey** 4-10-7 0.. DarylJacob 9
(Tony Carroll) *bhd: bdly t.o fnl 4f* **66/1**

0 **15** *8* **Talk Up Trouble**[27] [1069] 4-10-7 0.. LiamTreadwell 1
(Mark Brisbourne) *chsd ldrs tl 1/2-way: bdly t.o fnl 4f* **100/1**

3m 45.7s (-8.10) **Going Correction** -0.35s/f (Good)
WFA 4 from 5yo 1lb **15** Ran SP% **119.0**
Speed ratings: **105,104,101,96,95 91,90,90,90,67 66,64,62,55,52**
CSF £46.55 TOTE £3.50: £1.20, £3.90, £22.40; EX 61.80 Place 6: £199.33 Place 5: £150.07 .
Owner Mrs Tania Stepney **Bred** Kennedy O'Sullivan Syndicate **Trained** Little Newcastle, Pembrokes

FOCUS

A reasonable bumper. The pace was initially strong, before slowing up as they approached the back straight, and the overall time was not bad. The first two came clear before the home turn and the winner looks a decent prospect.

NOTEBOOK

Rudanphast(IRE) stayed on willingly for pressure to supplement his Ffos Las win in March. A big individual who has been given time to strengthen up since that success, he has the size to do well over obstacles. (op 11-2)

Salford Rose(IRE) stuck on in willing fashion, but she was always being held by her much bigger opponent. She has plenty of ability, but there were still signs of steering problems. (tchd 14-1)

Living Proof(IRE) ◆ is a half-sister to a bumper winner and she shaped with a good deal of promise on this debut. Mares' races could be the way forward with her. (op 50-1)

Good Tack(USA) was also fourth when favourite on his one previous start, at Market Rasen last September. He raced up with the pace but could not go with the first two when they kicked on three furlongs out. (op 10-3)

Spring Snow(USA) ran his race in the first-time blinkers, but once again he lacked a change of gear. He will have to switch to hurdles now. (tchd 11-2)

Romeo Desbois(FR) was unable to enhance his trainer's excellent record in bumpers at Hereford. (op 11-4 tchd 4-1)

He's A Hawker(IRE)

Henry's Hero Official explanation: jockey said gelding hung left-handed

T/Plt: £120.50 to a £1 stake. Pool: £52,414.20 - 317.41 winning tickets. T/Qpdt: £50.70 to a £1 stake. Pool: £5,482.86 - 79.90 winning tickets. IM

1285 - 1288a (Foreign Racing) - See Raceform Interactive

687 FONTWELL (L-H)

Thursday, August 19

OFFICIAL GOING: Good (good to firm in places)

Winning post moved back 26yds to original position after building work.

Wind: Light, across Weather: Fine

1289 888SPORT PREMIER GRANDSTAND NOVICES' HURDLE (9 hdls) 2m 2f 110y

5:20 (5:20) (Class 4) 4-Y-O+ **£3,122** (£916; £458; £228)

Form RPR

0- **1** **Brett Vale (IRE)**[6] [1765] 4-10-10 0....................................(t) LeightonAspell 108+
(Peter Hedger) *hld up: last to 1/2-way: stdy prog fr 3 out: chal next: upsides gng wl whn blnd last: pushed along and styd on wl to ld last 50yds* **5/1**[3]

-F12 **2** *1/2* **Penyfan Dawn (IRE)**[16] [1175] 6-11-5 120...................... TomScudamore 114
(Tim Vaughan) *led at modest pce: cajoled along bnd after 3 out: drvn and pressed 2 out: jnd and lft in ld last: hdd u.p last 50yds* **5/4**[1]

23-3 **3** *13* **Supernoverre (IRE)**[16] [1175] 4-10-10 110............................ DarylJacob 94+
(Liam Corcoran) *trckd ldr: rdn to chal 2 out: sn nt qckn: hld in 3rd whn flattened last: wknd* **2/1**[2]

-646 **4** *9* **Singapore Harbour (IRE)**[20] [1140] 4-10-3 0......................... SamJones 77
(Oliver Sherwood) *nt a fluent: trckd ldrs: rdn and wknd bef 2 out* **25/1**

5 *1 1/2* **Shamrogine (IRE)**[14] [1194] 4-10-3 0.............................. PaddyBrennan 76
(Paul John Gilligan, Ire) *trckd ldrs: nt fluent 6th: outpcd sn after 3 out: nvr on terms after* **10/1**

6 *26* **Aah Haa**[37] 5-10-12 0.. LiamTreadwell 61
(Nick Gifford) *in tch: wkng whn blnd 6th: sn wl bhd* **33/1**

00 7 40 **Two Mile Borris (IRE)**[27] 1086 4-10-10 0........................(p) JamieMoore 23
(Michael Quinlan) *chsd ldrs: wkng whn blnd 5th: t.o whn blnd 3 out* **66/1**

4m 23.8s (-10.50) **Going Correction** -0.75s/f (Firm)
WFA 4 from 5yo+ 13lb **7** Ran SP% **111.8**
Speed ratings (Par 105): **92,91,86,82,81 70,54**
toteswingers:1&2 £2.90, 2&3 £1.10, 1&3 £2.80 CSF £11.60 TOTE £7.10: £4.20, £1.10; EX 19.90.
Owner P C F Racing Ltd **Bred** Mrs O Murtagh **Trained** Dogmersfield, Hampshire

FOCUS
This was a reasonable contest run at a steady pace, but the three market leaders still managed to pull clear. The winner is better than the bare result.

NOTEBOOK
Brett Vale(IRE) was ridden with great confidence, biding his time despite the lack of early pace, and gradually improving to challenge in the home straight. He lost the lead when flattening the last, but showed a good turn of foot to get up again. He showed little promise on his hurdling debut back in October, but did win on the Flat off a mark of 80 in May and, though his form had dipped since, the addition of a tongue tie was a plus. Although he needs to brush up his jumping, his flat speed should enable him to win again, but it might not help his future options having beaten a rival rated 120 today. (op 8-1)
Penyfan Dawn(IRE) took ten attempts to gain his first victory over hurdles, but with a rating of 120 he was still the one to beat. He set only a modest pace but it was enough to shake off all challenges bar the winner's. This was a respectable run under a penalty, but his lack of pace might make him vulnerable in handicaps, especially off his current mark. (op Evens tchd 11-8)
Supernoverre(IRE) faced some stiff tests over hurdles last winter and showed some promise when less than four lengths behind Penyfan Dawn at Ffos Las on his return to action earlier this month. Tracking the favourite, he was poised to challenge but found little when asked and this was slightly disappointing. (op 9-4 tchd 15-8)
Singapore Harbour(IRE) made a bit of progress going to the third last before running out of steam. She has shown a modicum of promise but the stable has yet to hit form and she might be seen to better effect now she qualifies for handicaps. (op 20-1 tchd 14-1)
Shamrogine(IRE) showed little aptitude for hurdling in one previous attempt back in January but has been inching closer in each of three subsequent bumpers. That still left a chasm to bridge, and her jumping was not fluent enough to enable her to do that. (op 11-1 tchd 12-1 and 17-2)
Aah Haa is rated 48 on the Flat and looked up against it trying to add to his trainer's impressive record with hurdling debutants. He was keen early and showed his lack of experience, tending to hang to the right, but made some progress on the final circuit before weakening tamely from the fourth last. (tchd 25-1)

1290 PEPSI PURSUIT NOVICES' H'CAP CHASE (13 fncs) 2m 2f
5:50 (5:50) (Class 4) (0-105,104) 4-Y-0+ **£3,252** (£955; £477; £238)

Form RPR
1 **Courella (IRE)**[48] 882 6-11-12 **104**.................................... PaulMoloney 110+
(Evan Williams) *t.k.h early: hld up: nt fluent 9th: clsd on ldrs 3 out: rdn next: led last: hrd rdn and idled flat: hld on* **3/1**[1]

-303 2 1 ½ **Shinnecock Bay**[20] 1139 6-11-11 **103**...........................(b) LeightonAspell 108+
(Oliver Sherwood) *trckd ldrs: nt fluent 2nd and 3rd: poised to chal gng wl fr 10th: led 2 out: sn shkn up: hdd last: fnd nil* **3/1**[1]

3P65 3 6 **Bid Art (IRE)**[9] 1231 5-10-8 **86**..(t) DarylJacob 86
(Jamie Snowden) *led: nt fluent 2nd: mstke and hdd 10th: led again 3 out: hdd next: cl 3rd last: wknd* **4/1**[3]

0615 4 4 **Mustamad**[23] 1106 7-9-11 **78** oh1.................................(vt) CharlieStudd[(3)] 74
(Chris Gordon) *trckd ldr: led 10th: hdd and blnd 3 out: immediately btn* **6/1**

543U 5 12 **Cloonavery (IRE)**[7] 1237 8-10-0 **78** oh13........................ LiamTreadwell 61
(Tony Carroll) *hld up in tch: rdn 10th: lost tch bef next* **7/2**[2]

4-3P P **Randomer**[81] 532 7-9-12 **86**...(p) AshleyBird[(10)] —
(Paddy Butler) *mstke 2nd: last whn blnd 3rd and rdr lost iron: p.u bef next* **20/1**

4m 35.9s (1.20) **Going Correction** -0.075s/f (Good) **6** Ran SP% **111.3**
Speed ratings (Par 105): **94,93,90,88,83** —
toteswingers:1&2 £1.90, 2&3 £3.70, 1&3 £1.80 CSF £12.48 TOTE £4.20: £3.60, £3.30; EX 12.20.
Owner R E R Williams **Bred** Thomas Kinsella **Trained** Llancarfan, Vale Of Glamorgan

FOCUS
A tricky, open-looking contest run at a fair pace. Ordinary but sound form.

NOTEBOOK
Courella(IRE) was keen early on his British debut but his jockey was at pains to keep enough in hand for the finish. He did not travel that well but his jumping was fluent in the main and it enabled him to gain ground against his rivals. Emerging to challenge at the last, he hit a flat spot when meeting the rising ground on the run-in but without a strong threat to fight off, he was able to keep on top to the line. He had not been very consistent in Ireland, especially in heavy ground, but showed some improvement and looked likely to finish third when clipping heels and slipping up at Wexford last month. Jumping is his strong suit and thus stiffer fences play to his strengths, as his jockey noted he is not the most doughty in a finish. (tchd 10-3)
Shinnecock Bay showed little promise as a hurdler, but there was some encouragement to be gleaned from his chasing debut three weeks ago. He travelled well through the race and progressed to deliver a potentially winning challenge at the last, but he got in too close and could not take advantage of the faltering winner after the last. (op 11-4 tchd 10-3)
Bid Art(IRE) adopted his customary front-running position and despite getting in close and losing the lead four out he rallied to remain a threat up to the last. He dominated a lowly handicap over the course and distance back in April following a five-month break but had been well below that level subsequently, though this was a better effort and suggests he could go close if his 8lb higher mark does not get in the way. (op 6-1)
Mustamad sprung a surprise when capturing a novice handicap chase at Worcester last month at 50-1, and he was going well enough as he took up the running at the last in the back straight but soon weakened in the home straight when his stamina emptied. However, his jumping does seem to have improved on the whole. (op 13-2 tchd 7-1 and 11-2)
Cloonavery(IRE) was mounting a challenge when sprawling two out at Stratford last time, but overall is not very reliable, and after a mistake in the back straight he lost position and never recovered. He's still a maiden from 24 attempts. (tchd 10-3)
Randomer, on his chasing debut, made mistakes at the first two, causing his jockey to lose his irons and pull up. (op 16-1)

1291 NO.12 RESTAURANT AND BAR NOVICES' H'CAP HURDLE (11 hdls) 2m 6f 110y
6:25 (6:25) (Class 4) (0-110,104) 4-Y-0+ **£2,927** (£859; £429; £214)

Form RPR
02/2 1 **Corso Palladio (IRE)**[53] 849 8-11-2 **93**..........................(p) TomO'Brien 107+
(Peter Bowen) *cl up: led after 7th: pushed clr after 3 out: in n.d fr next: eased nr fin* **11/4**[2]

06-3 2 13 **Bon Spiel**[5] 82 6-11-12 **103**...(vt[1]) ColinBolger 103
(Chris Gordon) *trckd ldrs: wnt prom 7th: chsd wnr 3 out: outpcd bef next: no ch after: clung on to 2nd* **25/1**

1106 3 ¾ **Ashmolian (IRE)**[21] 1129 7-11-3 **99**...........(p) GemmaGracey-Davison[(5)] 98
(Zoe Davison) *hld up: prog and cl up 7th: outpcd after 3 out: modest 3rd next: kpt on to press runner-up fin* **25/1**

P-46 4 ½ **Rate Field (IRE)**[24] 1094 6-10-8 **95**.............................. MatthewClark[(10)] 96+
(Emma Lavelle) *j.rt: hld up in detached last: wnt modest 7th at 8th: latched on to bk of gp after 3 out gng easily: tk 4th whn slt mstke 2 out and rdr lost both irons: styd on under flapping to press for 3rd: capable of bttr* **17/2**

324- 5 13 **Court Red Handed (IRE)**[214] 3489 5-11-12 **103**.................. APMcCoy 93+
(Rebecca Curtis) *w.w in tch: mstkes 7th and next: rdn and struggling to stay w ldrs next: effrt to chal for btn 3rd 2 out: wknd* **11/8**[1]

4325 6 13 **Cubism**[7] 1150 4-11-10 **104**...(t) WarrenMarston 76
(Milton Harris) *tended to jump rt: pressed ldr: hit 3rd: led 5th: hdd after 7th: wknd after 3 out* **11/2**[3]

0-04 7 5 **Coeur Brule (FR)**[29] 1059 4-10-7 **94**........................(p) MrDavidTurner[(7)] 62
(Sam Davison) *hld up: blnd 4th: prog 8th: disputing 2nd whn mstke 3 out: hrd rdn and wkng whn mstke 2 out: blnd last* **12/1**

5 8 15 **Sieglinde (FR)**[21] 1124 4-11-6 **100**................................... LeightonAspell 54
(Alison Batchelor) *prom to 6th: struggling in rr after next: bhd fr 8th* **50/1**

0UP4 9 26 **General Simara**[24] 1092 6-10-11 **88**......................................(t) JoeTizzard 22
(Tony Carroll) *led to 4th: rdn after 7th: wknd next: t.o* **40/1**

5m 22.3s (-20.20) **Going Correction** -0.75s/f (Firm)
WFA 4 from 5yo+ 14lb **9** Ran SP% **114.5**
Speed ratings (Par 105): **105,100,100,100,95 91,89,84,75**
toteswingers:1&2 £9.20, 2&3 £40.30, 1&3 £10.40 CSF £64.16 CT £1418.02 TOTE £4.00: £1.40, £5.90, £6.60; EX 80.80.
Owner F Lloyd **Bred** Des De Vere Hunt **Trained** Little Newcastle, Pembrokes

FOCUS
A moderate contest and only a steady pace, but it produced an impressive winner who stepped up on his previous form.

NOTEBOOK
Corso Palladio(IRE) was having only his third run in two years, but he seems in rude health as he registered an authoritative success. Taking up the running on the final circuit, his jockey kicked for home from two out and his mount showed an impressive turn of foot to stride clear, leaving everything else looking one-paced. His return to action at the end of June was an encouraging second in a good time on his debut for his current stable, and if he can stay healthy there looks to be more to come.
Bon Spiel tracked the leader throughout on the inside, and kept on behind the winner but was outpaced. He has come on for his initial three hurdles in the spring, but may have blown his cover on his handicap debut. (op 16-1)
Ashmolian(IRE) gained his two wins to date in May with hold-up tactics, but was ridden more prominently this time. He plugged on but could not find an extra gear near the finish and looks in the grip of the handicapper. (op 28-1 tchd 33-1 and 22-1)
Rate Field(IRE) got detached from the field early and once again tended to jump right and looks an awkward ride. However, he does have some ability as he came home well from an unpromising position, despite his rider losing his irons for the second time on this horse. (op 10-1)
Court Red Handed(IRE) was well backed, presumably more in expectation of the in-form trainer and jockey combination eliciting some improvement on his previous moderate form. He was in position to deliver a challenge but began to feel the pace on the final circuit and, with this his first run since January, he may have needed this. (op 13-8 tchd 2-1 and 7-4 in a place)
Cubism is up to winning at this level off his current mark but he was unable to get an uncontested lead and did not get home. (op 6-1 tchd 5-1)

1292 PIMMS H'CAP HURDLE (9 hdls) 2m 2f 110y
6:55 (6:55) (Class 4) (0-110,110) 4-Y-0+ **£3,122** (£916; £458; £228)

Form RPR
-433 1 **Kijivu**[60] 796 5-10-11 **95**...(bt) FelixDeGiles 105
(Alastair Lidderdale) *w ldr at stdy pce: led 6th: drew clr fr next: rdn and 5 l up 2 out: styd on wl* **9/2**[2]

3441 2 6 **Rock Me (IRE)**[17] 1162 5-11-0 **103**................................(tp) DavidBass[(5)] 107
(Lawney Hill) *settled in midfield: j. slowly 6th and pushed along: outpcd next: styd on bef 2 out: wnt 2nd after last: no ch w wnr* **4/1**[1]

00P- 3 3 ¼ **Havenstone (IRE)**[173] 4298 9-10-0 **91**............................ AdamWedge[(7)] 95+
(Evan Williams) *hld up in tch: prog after 6th: wnt 3rd next: rdn to chse wnr bef 2 out: 5 l down and no imp whn blnd last* **5/1**[3]

0-53 4 1 ½ **Parazar (FR)**[23] 1107 5-10-10 **94**..................................... LeightonAspell 94
(Oliver Sherwood) *hld up in 8th in steadily run r: outpcd after 6th and pushed along: stl only 7th bef 2 out: styd on: nvr nrr* **12/1**

034- 5 3 **Emirates World (IRE)**[123] 5260 4-10-11 **97**.......................(t) TomO'Brien 93
(Alan Jessop) *trckd ldrs: outpcd 3 out: effrt bef next: 4th and wl btn last: fdd flat* **25/1**

-353 6 5 **Shropshirelass**[39] 962 7-10-10 **99**............... GemmaGracey-Davison[(5)] 92
(Zoe Davison) *hld up in last pair in steadily run r: prog fr 6th but sn outpcd by ldrs: kpt on fr 2 out: no ch* **10/1**

2405 7 3 ¾ **Stumped**[17] 1161 7-11-2 **105**...(t) JimmyDerham[(5)] 94
(Milton Harris) *hld up in last pair in steadily run r: outpcd and pushed along after 6th: plugged on fr 2 out: no ch* **11/2**

0-P0 8 33 **Viva Colonia (IRE)**[53] 846 5-11-4 **105**...........................(tp) PeterToole[(3)] 65
(Charlie Mann) *t.k.h: cl up: chsd wnr 3 out: wknd rapidly bef next: virtually p.u after last* **18/1**

01-0 9 35 **King Of The Titans (IRE)**[27] 534 7-11-5 **110**............... CharlieWallis[(7)] 38
(Patrick Gilligan) *trckd ldng pair: wknd and mstke 6th: wl t.o after next* **16/1**

004- 10 15 **Gamedor (FR)**[13] 4789 5-10-4 **88**....................................... JamieMoore 3
(Gary Moore) *led at stdy pce: hit 6th and hdd: wknd rapidly 3 out: t.o* **17/2**

4m 22.1s (-12.20) **Going Correction** -0.75s/f (Firm)
WFA 4 from 5yo+ 13lb **10** Ran SP% **112.5**
Speed ratings (Par 105): **95,92,91,90,89 87,85,71,56,50**
toteswingers:1&2 £3.40, 2&3 £4.00, 1&3 £2.90 CSF £22.44 CT £91.38 TOTE £4.90: £1.10, £2.30, £2.00; EX 21.80.
Owner KMC Partnership Three **Bred** M P Bishop **Trained** Eastbury, Berks

FOCUS
This was a competitive contest, although not quite at the 0-110 level, stolen by the winner kicking on from the home turn. She produced a personal best, and the form seems sound.

NOTEBOOK
Kijivu is generally consistent but lacks a finishing kick, and as a result had only a modest 1-15 record over hurdles coming into this. But with an enterprising change of tactics she kicked for home on the final bend and soon had the challengers scrubbing along, so even though the gap diminished a little near the end she still held an unassailable advantage. However, she might find it difficult to add to her tally once reassessed. (op 11-2)
Rock Me(IRE), despite a 6lb rise for winning at Newton Abbot earlier in the month, still looked well treated for the follow-up, but he found the winner's injection of pace too hot in the back straight. He did stay on for a gallant second to show that he remains in good heart. (op 7-2)
Havenstone(IRE) was beginning to make a move when getting caught out as the pace quickened, but he rallied and looked a small threat until pecking at the last and losing all chance. He failed to show much in soft ground over the winter but seems much better on faster going, and should come on for this first run since February. (op 8-1)
Parazar(FR) plugged on without ever threatening. He is gradually coming into form but needed to improve to figure here so ran as well as could be expected.

Emirates World(IRE) was close enough until getting outpaced from the home turn. He should improve on this first run since April but might need some easing of his mark if he is to make an impact in handicaps. (op 22-1 tchd 20-1)

Shropshirelass has been running well since her two wins in the spring, but looks to be in the grip of the handicapper now. (op 8-1)

Stumped was 5lb higher than for his course and distance success in May but still looked on a realistic mark, but he only managed to pass the stragglers. (op 5-1)

1293 BREEZE 107 H'CAP CHASE (16 fncs) 2m 6f

7:30 (7:30) (Class 5) (0-95,95) 4-Y-0+ **£2,602** (£764; £382; £190)

Form				RPR
256F	**1**		**Morenito (FR)**[29] 1061 7-11-10 **93**.....(p) PaddyBrennan (Tom George) *a gng wl: trckd ldrs: led 12th: drew clr fr next: eased flat* **10/1**	109+
015-	**2**	*15*	**Winning Show**[30] 2615 6-10-9 **78**.....(t) ColinBolger (Chris Gordon) *hld up in last pair: pushed along 11th: prog to chse wnr after 13th: no imp next* **8/1**	74
5403	**3**	*10*	**Morestead (IRE)**[21] 1128 5-11-8 **91**.....(p) AidanColeman (Brendan Powell) *led to 6th: reminder next: lost 2nd and drvn 11th: wl outpcd fr 13th* **3/1**[2]	78
PP40	**4**	*9*	**No Greater Love (FR)**[24] 1094 8-11-3 **86**..... TomScudamore (Charlie Longsdon) *trckd ldng pair to 7th: lost pl rapidly and toiling in last pair fr 9th: nvr on terms after* **7/1**[3]	64
P00	**5**	*7*	**Ilewin Tom**[2] 1272 7-10-0 **69**..... JamesDavies (Gary Brown) *hld up in last trio: cl enough 11th: rdn 13th: sn outpcd: wnt poor 3rd briefly bef 3 out: wknd* **18/1**	41
0-5P	**6**	*22*	**Zi Missile (IRE)**[60] 795 6-9-7 **69** oh4.....(p) AdamWedge[(7)] (Evan Williams) *mstke 1st: trckd ldr tl led 6th: hdd and mstke 12th: wknd rapidly after next* **7/1**[3]	21
/1U0	**P**		**Lords Bridge**[20] 1141 9-11-12 **95**..... APMcCoy (Tim Vaughan) *hld up in last trio: mstke 4th: rdn and wknd 8th: t.o whn p.u bef 11th* **7/4**[1]	—

5m 39.3s (-3.70) **Going Correction** -0.075s/f (Good) **7** Ran SP% **111.8**

Speed ratings (Par 103): **103,97,93,90,88 80,—**

toteswingers:1&2 £12.00, 2&3 £5.50, 1&3 £1.70 CSF £77.45 TOTE £11.10: £6.10, £4.20; EX 35.30.

Owner C B Compton B D Johnston **Bred** Francis Montauban **Trained** Slad, Gloucs

FOCUS

There was a three-way battle for the early lead and that opened the door for those ridden with more restraint. The easy winner produced a big step up on his previous best.

NOTEBOOK

Morenito(FR) was travelling best of all on the final circuit and, with everything else struggling, he was able to gain an easy victory on his jockey's return from injury. He showed no ill effects from his heavy fall at Worcester last month, but this will have given his confidence a boost nevertheless. He looked somewhat vulnerable off a 5lb higher mark than for his last win at Southwell a year ago, but the race effectively collapsed and, he was the only one to relish the strong early pace. (op 8-1)

Winning Show won on his chasing debut last winter but was switched to the all-weather after failing to build on that success on softer ground. He could only plug on behind the easy winner but finished clear of the third and showed that there is more to come from him over fences. (tchd 7-1)

Morestead(IRE) did not jump fluently enough to be able to dominate, but did well to stick on for third despite getting tired. Both his previous wins have come in the autumn and he looks on course for a similar target. (op 7-2)

No Greater Love(FR) held every chance if able to see out the trip and find some improvement on his previous attempts at this course, especially as he had shown a bit of form at Worcester last month. However, the Fontwell gremlins resurfaced and after a mistake in the back straight first time round he lost interest before making nominal gains when it was all too late. (op 9-1 tchd 10-1)

Ilewin Tom looked to be returning to a bit of form when making progress on the final circuit but his momentum was checked when making a mistake at the fourth last, and he tired thereafter. (op 14-1)

Lords Bridge won four point-to-points but has shown jumping frailties under rules and after another display of indifferent jumping he was pulled up. Official explanation: jockey said gelding was never travelling (op 6-4 tchd 5-4)

1294 TRY 888SPORT.COM MOBILE BETTING H'CAP HURDLE (10 hdls) 2m 4f

8:00 (8:00) (Class 5) (0-90,90) 4-Y-0+ **£2,211** (£649; £324; £162)

Form				RPR
0P-0	**1**		**Tegan Lee**[16] 1179 7-11-0 **78**..... DarylJacob (Liam Corcoran) *hld up last: gd prog after 7th to trck ldr sn after 3 out: led bef next: sn clr: v comf* **25/1**	96+
035	**2**	*8*	**I Can Run Can You (IRE)**[30] 1046 4-11-8 **88**..... APMcCoy (Jonjo O'Neill) *t.k.h: w ldr fr 2nd: led 3 out: hdd and j. awkwardly 2 out: no ch w wnr after* **6/4**[1]	90
-000	**3**	*9*	**Alrafid (IRE)**[31] 821 11-11-2 **90**.....(b) JosephAkehurst[(10)] (Gary Moore) *trckd ldrs: cl 3rd whn sltly hmpd 3 out: sn outpcd by ldng pair: kpt on* **8/1**[3]	88
PP0-	**4**	*6*	**Isintshelovely (IRE)**[162] 4519 7-11-4 **82**..... LeightonAspell (Chris Gordon) *hld up in tch: pushed along whn sltly hmpd 3 out: sn outpcd and struggling: lft modest 4th last* **9/1**	74
15/P	**5**	*¾*	**Native American**[14] 532 8-11-2 **80**.....(p) LiamTreadwell (Tim McCarthy) *cl up: shkn up after 6th: rdn and cl up 3 out: sn btn* **40/1**	70
00-0	**6**	*1*	**Wujood**[24] 1095 8-11-5 **83**.....(bt) AndrewGlassonbury (Gerald Ham) *wl in tch: rdn after 7th: lft bhd fr 3 out* **16/1**	72
55P0	**7**	*22*	**Cave Of The Giant (IRE)**[9] 1232 8-11-10 **88**..... JoeTizzard (Tim McCarthy) *hit 2nd: j. slowly next and reminders: bhd fr 7th: t.o whn hmpd 3 out* **12/1**	57
300/	**8**	*1 ½*	**Castle Craigs (IRE)**[683] 1593 8-10-5 **76**..... MrTomDavid[(7)] (Tim Vaughan) *prom: losing pl whn hmpd 3 out: sn tailed off* **9/2**[2]	44
0U0-	**F**		**Tootsie Too**[316] 1660 8-11-7 **90**.....(p) MichaelMurphy[(5)] (Mike Hammond) *led at modest pce: hdd and fell heavily 3 out* **14/1**	—
0660	**F**		**Kapborg (FR)**[29] 1060 4-10-11 **77**.....(t) TomScudamore (David Pipe) *hld up in tch: effrt fr 7th: rdn to go 4th 2 out: no imp and 15 l down whn fell last* **8/1**[3]	63

4m 54.2s (-5.20) **Going Correction** -0.75s/f (Firm)

WFA 4 from 6yo+ 14lb **10** Ran SP% **116.9**

Speed ratings (Par 103): **80,76,73,70,70 70,61,60,—,—**

CSF £65.16 CT £353.23 TOTE £27.80: £5.70, £1.60, £2.10; EX 117.50 Place 6: £288.18 Place 5: £169.63.

Owner GD Building Ltd **Bred** Mrs Helen Mobley **Trained** Charlton Adam, Somerset

FOCUS

A very moderate contest run at a steady pace that produced a surprise result. The easy winner produced a big step forward.

NOTEBOOK

Tegan Lee travelled supremely well to coast into the lead from the home turn to win with plenty in hand. She needed to improve markedly on her previous form, and though she may have needed her first run since March earlier this month, there was still little hint of what was to come. She evidently has taken time to find her form and may have improved for the faster ground, and on this evidence she has enough in hand to win again before the handicapper gets her measure. Official explanation: trainer said, regarding the apparent improvement in form shown, he used different tactics today, dropped her out and got her settled and jumping

I Can Run Can You(IRE) was well backed for his handicap debut and travelled well until the home turn, and though he stuck on well enough he had no answer as the winner cruised by.

Alrafid(IRE) has been on the downgrade for a while now but usually goes well here and ran another game race. He might have finished closer but for being hampered by the fall of Tootsie Too at the third last, but would not have won. His level is sellers and claimers nowadays, but this run shows there could still be some hope if a suitable opportunity can be found.

Isintshelovely(IRE) showed a bit better form than when last seen back in March, and the change of stables might have helped, though she is still a watching brief at present.

Castle Craigs(IRE) was a drifter on his first start for Tim Vaughan. He was badly hampered by the fall of Tootsie Too at the third last, but was beaten at the time to suggest he needed the run after his 683-day absence.

Tootsie Too broke a rib in the fall and may not race again.

T/Plt: £117.90 to a £1 stake. Pool of £46,126.59 - 285.54 winning tickets. T/Qpdt: £37.10 to a £1 stake. Pool of £5,483.03 - 109.35 winning tickets. JN

1233 STRATFORD (L-H)

Thursday, August 19

OFFICIAL GOING: Hurdle course: good to firm (good in places); chase course: good (good to firm in places)

Rail moved out 2m on bends to provide fresh ground.

Wind: almost nil Weather: cloudy but warm, raining last two races

1295 AJA INSURE THEIR MEMBERS AMATEUR RIDERS' H'CAP HURDLE (9 hdls) 2m 110y

2:05 (2:05) (Class 4) (0-105,105) 4-Y-0 **£3,646** (£1,138; £569; £284; £142)

Form				RPR
2-4	**1**		**Arcadia Boy (IRE)**[20] 1138 7-11-1 **99**..... MrJHamer[(5)] (Donald McCain) *prom: led bef 6th: rdn and hdd 2 out: pressed ldr tl drvn ahd nr fin: gd ride* **7/1**	101
4336	**2**	*hd*	**Le Brocquy**[2] 1273 5-11-5 **105**.....(p) MrDHiskett[(7)] (Martin Keighley) *j. slowly 1st: bhd: hdwy 6th: wnt 2nd after 3 out: led gng best 2 out: slt advantage and pushed along after: jst ct* **8/1**	107
0-P0	**3**	*2 ¾*	**Classic Fly (FR)**[27] 1084 7-10-6 **90**..... MrDGPrichard[(5)] (Arthur Whiting) *pressed ldr: rdn 6th: lost 2nd after 3 out: kpt on one pce fr next* **12/1**	90
0-05	**4**	*10*	**Blue Express (IRE)**[39] 962 11-10-7 **93**.....(t) MrJEngland[(7)] (Evan Williams) *midfield but off pce: rdn 5th: n.d fr 3 out: 12 l 4th next* **11/2**[3]	84
0-U0	**5**	*15*	**Lord Francois (FR)**[77] 595 5-10-13 **95**..... RobertKirk[(3)] (Tim Vaughan) *t.k.h in rr: lost tch 6th: hit last* **14/1**	72
2066	**6**	*12*	**Bazart**[45] 914 8-10-7 **89**.....(p) MissIsabelTompsett[(3)] (Bernard Llewellyn) *bhd: mstke 2nd: drvn hrd after 3 out: no rspnse: sn btn* **7/2**[1]	55
50P/	**7**	*10*	**Coral Shores**[14] 2501 5-11-1 **94**.....(v) MrRMahon (Peter Hiatt) *nt fluent 1st: prom tl fdd 6th: last whn blnd next: t.o bef 2 out* **22/1**	51
24/P	**8**	*8*	**Sternenzelt (GER)**[7] 1235 7-11-4 **104**.....(p) MrSWDrinkwater[(7)] (Michael Gates) *led tl hdd after 6th: wkng whn mstke next: t.o bef 2 out* **33/1**	54
6204	**U**		**Nether Stream (IRE)**[21] 1129 6-10-13 **99**..... MrOGarner[(7)] (Shaun Lycett) *6th whn rdr c off 4th* **7/1**	—
6632	**F**		**Quidam Blue (FR)**[32] 1030 6-10-11 **97**..... MrEDavid[(7)] (Tim Vaughan) *bhd: hit 3rd: rdn bef 5th: lost tch 6th: disputing 12l 4th whn fell heavily last* **4/1**[2]	91+

3m 52.9s (-3.10) **Going Correction** -0.275s/f (Good) **10** Ran SP% **115.4**

Speed ratings (Par 105): **96,95,94,89,82 77,72,68,—,—**

toteswingers:1&2:£8.70, 1&3:£20.50, 2&3:£20.50 CSF £61.09 CT £661.93 TOTE £7.30: £2.70, £2.30, £3.80; EX 71.40.

Owner Mr & Mrs Peter James Douglas **Bred** John Bernard O'Connor **Trained** Cholmondeley, Cheshire

FOCUS

An ordinary handicap for amateur riders that saw the first pair come clear late on in a very tight finish. They are rated to their best.

NOTEBOOK

Arcadia Boy(IRE) was having just his second outing for his current yard, who also won this race in 2007, and, under a decent rider in this sphere, was faced with a much more realistic task. It was his first win of any description, and there could be a little more to come despite a forthcoming rise in the handicap. (op 6-1 tchd 11-2)

Le Brocquy was laboured over fences at Worcester two days earlier. He is better as a hurdler as his 10lb higher mark highlights, and he went very close under top weight. He looked best kept to hurdling, but will go up in the weights for this. (tchd 9-1)

Classic Fly(FR), who met support, had looked out of sorts in three previous outings this term. He turned in a much more encouraging effort in defeat, but remains 4lb higher than his last winning mark. (op 18-1 tchd 20-1)

Blue Express(IRE) was also backed with a tongue tie back on. He wasn't disgraced and really wants a stiffer test. (op 13-2 tchd 5-1)

Bazart got well backed earlier in the day with cheekpieces replacing blinkers, but his losing run continues and he is one to swerve until showing more again. (op 9-2)

Quidam Blue(FR) proved easy to back for this handicap debut. He was given a lot to do and looked to be going well on the back straight, but his rider seemed reluctant to ask him for maximum effort as the principals stretched on. He was eventually put under pressure when well held coming to the last, but didn't produce a great deal and fell after a clumsy leap. More positive handling didn't help when he made his hurdling debut over C&D two runs back, and it remains to be seen how this fall affects his confidence, so he could well prove tricky to win with. (op 10-3)

1296 DRAYCOTTS ELECTRICIANS NOVICES' HURDLE (12 hdls) 2m 6f 110y

2:40 (2:40) (Class 3) 4-Y-0+ **£4,752** (£1,404; £702; £351; £175)

Form				RPR
2/0-	**1**		**Front Of House (IRE)**[165] 4461 8-10-12 0..... APMcCoy (Nicky Henderson) *quite keen towards rr: effrt in 5th bef 9th where nt fluent: chal and lft cl 2nd next: led and nodded on landing 2 out: rdn and in command whn idled flat* **5/1**[2]	122+
4111	**2**	*1 ½*	**Tout Regulier**[32] 1030 6-10-12 120..... DonalDevereux[(3)] (Peter Bowen) *pressed ldr tl led bef 9th: rdn and hdd 2 out: one pce and a hld after* **8/11**[1]	120

533 **3** *45* **Apache Dawn**[27] 1083 6-10-12 98..(t) GrahamLee 72
(Aytach Sadik) *nt fluent 2nd: cl up tl rdn and struggling bef 9th: wnt hopeless 3rd after defections next* **20/1**

3020 **4** *9* **Bachley Gale**[9] 1228 5-10-5 0.. RhysFlint 56
(Keith Goldsworthy) *j. modly: trckd ldrs: rdn 8th: fdd rapidly next: lft disputing remote 3rd and hmpd 3 out: continued t.o* **25/1**

/4P- **5** *29* **Holy Baloney**[148] 4823 7-10-12 0.................................. GerardTumelty 34
(Anabel L M King) *j. poorly and last mostly: j.rt 8th and reminders: t.o after next* **66/1**

6/P- **6** *hd* **Viking Affair (IRE)**[469] 200 6-10-5 0..................... AodhaganConlon[(7)] 34
(Rebecca Curtis) *racd keenly: led at modest pce: nt fluent 7th: hdd bef 9th and fdd rapidly: hmpd 3 out and continued t.o* **40/1**

2-41 **F** **Kilmore West (IRE)**[64] 766 5-11-4 102........................ RichardJohnson —
(Tim Vaughan) *hld up in rr: 4th and effrt bef 9th: cl 2nd whn fell 3 out* **7/1**[3]

32 **B** **Forcryingoutloud (IRE)**[21] 1124 6-10-9 0............... RichieMcLernon[(3)] —
(Andrew Haynes) *hld up: wnt 3rd bef 9th: sn hrd rdn: cl 4th but looked to be struggling whn b.d 3 out* **5/1**[2]

5m 18.5s (-9.60) **Going Correction** -0.275s/f (Good) **8** Ran SP% **116.3**
Speed ratings (Par 107): **105,104,88,85,75 75,—,—**
toteswingers:1&2:£1.80, 1&3:£9.90, 2&3:£5.90 CSF £9.39 TOTE £3.40: £1.40, £1.20, £5.70; EX 13.60.

Owner John P McManus **Bred** Newtownbarry House Stud **Trained** Upper Lambourn, Berks

FOCUS
A modest novice event. There was drama three out, but the form still makes sense. The winner has the potential to rate higher.

NOTEBOOK
Front Of House(IRE) showed his true colours again with a fairly ready success. He was highly thought as a bumper performer, but he was a beaten favourite on his hurdling debut, and ran miles below market expectations when returning from a two-year layoff at Huntingdon last season. He was reappearing here after a 165-day absence and has obviously has his problems, so this was a very pleasing display. He was getting weight from the 120-rated second so the handicapper will have to take that into account, and he may be better looking for something in that sphere when getting an official mark. He is also entitled to improve for the outing. (op 4-1 tchd 7-2)

Tout Regulier was bidding for a fifth win from her last six outings and made a bold show. She only gave way coming to the last and got the longer trip, but is probably at her very best given a slightly sharper test. She can still win one of these before the better novices emerge. (op 5-6 tchd 10-11)

Apache Dawn went in snatches nearing the final circuit and, performing below his recent level, remains winless. (op 28-1)

Bachley Gale, up in trip, was in trouble before the fourth-last and needs more practice. (op 28-1 tchd 20-1)

Viking Affair(IRE) Official explanation: jockey said gelding hung right-handed throughout

Kilmore West(IRE) had made his ground very nicely prior to falling, and it's hoped this doesn't dent his confidence too much. (op 13-2)

Forcryingoutloud(IRE) one was fully under the pump when brought down and looks to need dropping back in trip. (op 13-2)

1297 PADDOCK SUITE H'CAP CHASE (17 fncs) 2m 7f
3:15 (3:15) (Class 4) (0-110,105) 4-Y-O+ **£4,435** (£1,310; £655; £327; £163)

Form RPR

-334 **1** **Swordsman (GER)**[14] 867 8-10-11 **97**........................(vt) MrTJCannon[(7)] 111
(Chris Gordon) *nvr on the bridle and forced along thrght: 3rd tl wnt 2nd at 8th: reminder 10th: clsd u.str driving after 2 out to ld bef last: forged clr flat: splendid ride* **4/1**[2]

PP42 **2** *5* **Rash Moment (FR)**[7] 1235 11-10-0 **79**...........................(p) JohnnyFarrelly 89
(Michael Scudamore) *led 3rd and tended to jump wl: tried to get clr fr 12th and 5 l ahd whn j. slowly 3 out: drvn and hdd bef last: plodded on and sn outpcd* **11/4**[1]

52/2 **3** *26* **Ice Warrior (IRE)**[9] 1227 8-11-11 **104**..................................(t) CharliePoste 94
(Milton Harris) *mstke 3rd: chsd ldrs: j.rt and rdn 11th: j. slowly 12th: 12 l 3rd and labouring whn mstke 3 out* **6/1**[3]

-3P4 **4** *7* **Prince Noora (IRE)**[20] 1141 9-11-4 **97**......................(tp) RichardJohnson 76
(Tim Vaughan) *mstke 1st: j. poorly and nvr gng wl: struggling 13th: t.o whn mstke 2 out* **6/1**[3]

4241 **5** *15* **Keltic Lord**[7] 1235 14-11-3 **96** 7ex...................................... NickScholfield 62
(Peter Hiatt) *led tl 3rd: chsd ldr tl 8th: sn disheartened: lost tch and hit 12th: lft remote last at 14th: bdly t.o* **4/1**[2]

3565 **P** **Indian Pipe Dream (IRE)**[33] 1022 8-11-12 **105**...............(bt) GrahamLee —
(Aytach Sadik) *reluctant fr s: rdn and lost tch 4th: t.o 7th: hit 9th: p.u 14th* **20/1**

6-4F **P** **Whimper (FR)**[18] 1152 5-11-5 **103**........................ SamTwiston-Davies[(5)] —
(Nigel Twiston-Davies) *bhd and v unwilling: lost tch 4th: t.o after mstke 12th: p.u 14th* **7/1**

5m 32.2s (-9.40) **Going Correction** -0.275s/f (Good) **7** Ran SP% **112.5**
Speed ratings (Par 105): **105,103,94,91,86 —,—**
toteswingers:1&2:£1.80, 1&3:£2.40, 2&3:£2.50 CSF £15.44 CT £63.14 TOTE £4.30: £2.20, £2.40; EX 14.90.

Owner Mrs Kate Digweed **Bred** M Beining **Trained** Morestead, Hants

FOCUS
A moderate staying handicap, run at a decent gallop. The form is rated around the runner-up to the level of his recent course run.

NOTEBOOK
Swordsman(GER) got on top after the last and was given an outstanding ride by his young jockey. He had run two good races on the level since his previous outing in this sphere, but had yet to really convince as a chaser. Things didn't look good for him as he was on-and-off the bridle from the start, but he is a real dour stayer and his rider kept at him enough to keep him interested through the race. His stamina kicked in off the home turn, and a better leap at the final fence saw him master the runner-up. He is clearly tricky, but is currently rated 18lb higher over hurdles so it could be that he has more to offer after a likely rise, and his confidence should be nicely boosted now. (op 5-1)

Rash Moment(FR) didn't turn up last year, but was defending a hat-trick in the race having won it from 2006-08. He was also handed a chance by the handicapper after returning to form when second to off a 4lb higher mark here a week earlier. He was given a more aggressive ride this time and looked the most likely winner two out, but his early exertions told nearing the last. He does deserve a change of luck and obviously rates the benchmark. (tchd 3-1)

Ice Warrior(IRE), back up in trip, was left behind by the first pair on the final circuit, and ran some way below the level of his promising debut for connections nine days earlier. He still wasn't disgraced, though, and the percentage call is to think the run came a bit too soon, so his trainer could place him to effect before that long. (op 5-1)

Prince Noora(IRE) was never competitive on this return to fences and remains hard to get right. Official explanation: jockey said gelding finished distressed (op 8-1)

Keltic Lord, 4lb higher, was given plenty of rope when beating the runner-up over C&D last time. He was taken on early here, however, and his fate was sealed before the final circuit. (op 9-2 tchd 7-2)

1298 TIDDINGTON JUVENILE HURDLE (9 hdls) 2m 110y
3:50 (3:50) (Class 3) 3-Y-O **£4,752** (£1,404; £702; £351; £175)

Form RPR

1 **Architrave**[43] 3-10-12 0.. RichardJohnson 111+
(Tim Vaughan) *led at modest pce: pressed whn j.rt and blnd 3 out: drew 10 l clr and hit 2 out: mstke last: easily* **10/11**[1]

2 *15* **Bubbly Braveheart (IRE)**[24] 3-10-12 0............................ JamesDavies 89
(Alan Bailey) *settled trcking ldrs: effrt and disputing 2nd whn lft chsng wnr 3 out: sn 3 l down and drvn: 10 l bhd whn blnd 2 out* **16/1**

3 *15* **Valantino Oyster (IRE)**[23] 3-10-12 0.................................. BarryKeniry 71
(Ben Haslam) *j.big and reminder 4th: chsd ldrs: rdn after 5th: lft mod 3rd after mstke 3 out: 18 l 3rd next* **8/1**

0 **4** *1 3/4* **Hannour (IRE)**[55] 836 3-10-9 0...(t) DPFahy[(3)] 69
(Evan Williams) *j. slowly 1st: last whn j. slowly 2nd: rdn and struggling bef 3 out* **40/1**

5 *11* **Royal Etiquette (IRE)**[43] 3-10-12 0.. AidanColeman 73+
(Lawney Hill) *t.k.h: trckd ldrs: mstke 3 out and then bdly hmpd and lost all ch: eased fr last* **3/1**[2]

3 **F** **Baraathen (USA)**[20] 1135 3-10-9 0..................................... AdrianLane[(3)] —
(Donald McCain) *pressed ldr: hit 3rd: disputing cl 2nd whn fell 3 out* **5/1**[3]

3m 58.9s (2.90) **Going Correction** -0.275s/f (Good) **6** Ran SP% **113.5**
Speed ratings (Par 104): **82,74,67,67,61** —
toteswingers:1&2:£2.50, 1&3:£4.30, 2&3:£18.80 CSF £16.51 TOTE £1.80: £1.10, £4.20; EX 22.00.

Owner Pearn's Pharmacies Ltd **Bred** Cheveley Park Stud Ltd **Trained** Aberthin, Vale of Glamorgan

FOCUS
One of the more interesting juvenile events for the time of year and the debut winner is capable of rating higher, but overall the form may turn out weak.

NOTEBOOK
Architrave looked on top three out and he eventually ran out a decisive debut winner. This formerly Sir Mark Prescott-trained son of Hernando failed to win on the level, but had proven stamina and is lightly raced. He showed his inexperience throughout, tending to jump out to the right at his hurdles and when getting the last two all wrong. He does have scope, though, and represents the same connections that sent out Rupestrian to win his first four as a juvenile early on last season. All things considered he is open to a bundle of improvement, and looks one to keep on-side until his true level of ability becomes apparent. (op 11-8 tchd 6-4)

Bubbly Braveheart(IRE) is rated 9lb lower than the winner on the level, despite being a three-time winner on the AW. Very easy to back on this switch to hurdling, he made up his ground nicely from off the pace but was beginning to feel the pinch three out. Looking at the way in which he laboured thereafter, he still has stamina to prove for this game. (op 10-1)

Valantino Oyster(IRE) had won two of his three outings on the Flat since resuming as a 3-y-o, and was snapped up by his new connections after narrowly winning a selling handicap last month. He wasn't fluent at times and lost touch on the back straight, but is entitled to come on for the experience. (op 6-1)

Hannour(IRE) again disappointed and looks to need more time. (op 33-1)

Royal Etiquette(IRE), a 68-rated maiden on the Flat, has joined a decent new operation and should be given another chance to prove his worth. Official explanation: jockey said gelding finished distressed (op 4-1 tchd 11-4)

Baraathen(USA), a well-beaten third on debut last time, was the chief sufferer when the winner jumped out to his right. He was still in with every chance prior to guessing at the third-last, and will require plenty of schooling before his next assignment. (op 7-2)

1299 BETFAIR H'CAP CHASE (12 fncs) 2m 1f 110y
4:25 (4:25) (Class 3) (0-125,123) 4-Y-O+ **£6,337** (£1,872; £936; £468; £234)

Form RPR

3 **1** **Grand Lahou (FR)**[22] 1117 7-11-6 **117**.......................... RichardJohnson 138+
(Tim Vaughan) *enthusiatic in ld: 7 l ahd 3rd: in n.d fr 9th: 30 l ahd whn v awkward jump last: sn heavily eased* **5/2**[1]

5362 **2** *18* **Norborne Bandit (IRE)**[9] 1229 9-10-11 **108**..................(p) HarrySkelton 97
(Evan Williams) *nt fluent 3rd: chsd clr ldr tl 6th: drvn after mstke 8th: sn lost tch: stl 25 l 5th 2 out: styd on to go 2nd bhd v long ldr at last* **11/4**[2]

4133 **3** *3 1/4* **Turbo Shandy**[9] 1229 7-10-3 **103**..............................(p) DonalDevereux[(3)] 92+
(Dai Burchell) *hld up: lft 3rd at 8th: blnd bdly next: rdn to go 2nd 2 out: nvr nr wnr: lost remote 2nd at last* **5/1**[3]

23-4 **4** *1 3/4* **Silver Steel (FR)**[105] 177 7-10-13 **110**.................................. GrahamLee 95
(Richard Ford) *j.rt 1st: chsd ldrs but n.d: nt fluent 5th (water): struggling fr 9th: 20 l 4th 2 out* **6/1**

066- **5** *7* **Mango Catcher (IRE)**[261] 2624 10-11-1 **119**........... AodhaganConlon[(7)] 97
(Rebecca Curtis) *racd in last: rdn 5th: struggling bef 7th: t.o 9th* **8/1**

1425 **6** *8* **Mibleu (FR)**[23] 1110 10-11-7 **123**.. KeiranBurke[(5)] 94
(R H & Mrs S Alner) *nt fluent 4th: wnt 2nd at 6th: chsd wnr vainly tl 2 out: fin v weakly* **13/2**

4m 8.10s (1.00) **Going Correction** -0.275s/f (Good) **6** Ran SP% **110.6**
Speed ratings (Par 107): **86,78,76,75,72 69**
toteswingers:1&2:£1.60, 1&3:£2.50, 2&3:£1.80 CSF £9.82 TOTE £3.30: £2.00, £2.20; EX 8.90.

Owner Oceans Racing **Bred** Jean-Pierre Hebrard **Trained** Aberthin, Vale of Glamorgan

FOCUS
A modest handicap, run at a strong gallop. A seemingly massive step up from the winner but this isn't form to be confident about.

NOTEBOOK
Grand Lahou(FR) opened his account for connections at the second attempt and gave his trainer/rider a quick-fire double. He didn't jump all that well on his previous outing and wasn't always fluent here. It didn't stop him from running out a bloodless winner, however, and his error at the last was in fairness down to his jockey putting the brakes on as he approached it. He would surely follow up if turning out quickly under a penalty, as is expected, before the handicapper can reassess him. Connections will also likely return him to hurdling at some point as he remains a novice in that sphere. (op 10-3)

Norborne Bandit(IRE) kept on to win the race for second place and was some way below his previous level. This was the fourth time he has finished runner-up over C&D and is now on an 11-race losing run. (op 3-1)

Turbo Shandy still had plenty to do before a messy jump three from home saw him lose ground. He rallied, but didn't look particularly keen in the home straight, and failed to reverse last-time-out C&D form with the second.

Silver Steel(FR) got outpaced from an early stage and this return from a 106-day break was needed. (op 4-1)

Mango Catcher(IRE) was another that shaped as though his return from an absence was much needed. (op 10-1)

Mibleu(FR) proved keen and ran miles below expectations. (op 11-2 tchd 5-1 and 7-1)

1300 BROADWAY H'CAP HURDLE (10 hdls) 2m 3f
5:00 (5:00) (Class 5) (0-90,89) 4-Y-0+ **£2,276** (£668; £334; £166)

Form RPR

004P **1** **Strumble Head (IRE)**[20] 1141 5-10-13 77.................(b) DonalDevereux(3) 89+
(Peter Bowen) *led tl mstke 2nd: nt fluent 3rd: sn led again: blnd bdly 3 out: rdn and more resolute than only serious rival fr 2 out: drew clr bef last* **9/2**[1]

43P5 **2** *4* **Ruby Valentine (FR)**[30] 1049 7-10-9 70............................. HaddenFrost 74
(Jim Wilson) *midfield: wnt 2nd at 7th: rdn next: brief ch 2 out: fnd v little: 4 l down and btn last* **8/1**

456 **3** *4 ½* **Mystic Touch**[32] 1031 4-11-12 89.......................................(p) JackDoyle 87
(Andrew Haynes) *bhd tl prog bef 7th: wnt 3rd but outpcd by ldng pair after 3 out: 7 l 3rd and no imp next: plodded on* **12/1**

0055 **4** *5* **Young Tot (IRE)**[13] 1199 12-10-0 66..................................(t) IanPopham(5) 63
(Carroll Gray) *chsd ldrs: rdn and outpcd after 3 out: mod 4th whn hit next* **17/2**

3004 **5** *1* **Scotsbrook Cloud**[16] 1179 5-11-7 82....................................... RhysFlint 77
(C Roberts) *lft in ld 2nd tl 3rd: chsd wnr tl 7th: wknd after 3 out: plodded on* **5/1**[2]

-P00 **6** *½* **Bond Cruz**[7] 1236 7-11-0 82.. RobertKirk(7) 76
(Olivia Maylam) *bhd: modest effrt in 6th and rdn 3 out: struggling after* **28/1**

0P00 **7** *2* **Zizou (IRE)**[13] 1199 7-11-2 80... TomMolloy(3) 72
(Sean Curran) *mstke 3rd: nvr bttr than midfield: j. slowly 5th: rdn and lost tch tamely bef 7th* **20/1**

F-5P **8** *13* **Intense Suspense (IRE)**[7] 1237 7-9-12 69..........(t) ChristopherWard(10) 50
(Robin Dickin) *t.k.h: chsd ldrs tl pushed along and lost pl bef 6th: labouring after* **9/2**[1]

3-F5 **9** *48* **Adjami (IRE)**[27] 1085 9-10-13 74.......................................(p) HarrySkelton 11
(John Harris) *pressed ldrs: rdn bef 7th: wknd qckly: t.o and eased* **11/2**[3]

P/06 **P** **Standing Order**[30] 1046 7-11-7 82.. GrahamLee —
(Richard Ford) *j. slowly 2nd: in rr mostly: lost tch bef 7th: p.u 3 out* **16/1**

UP40 **P** **Silver Sonnet**[36] 989 7-10-9 70.......................................(b[1]) CharliePoste —
(Ben Case) *nt fluent 3rd: in tch tl rdn and reluctant after 6th: t.o and p.u after 3 out* **33/1**

4m 31.2s (-0.30) **Going Correction** -0.275s/f (Good) 11 Ran SP% **114.8**
Speed ratings (Par 103): **97,95,93,91,90 90,89,84,64,—** —
totswingers:1&2:£6.70, 1&3:£7.80, 2&3:£12.10. CSF £38.45 CT £402.72 TOTE £5.30: £2.00, £4.70, £2.30; EX 40.00 Place 6 £55.32; Place 5 £6.96.
Owner Jonathan Martin **Bred** Martin J Dibbs **Trained** Little Newcastle, Pembrokes

FOCUS
A weak handicap. It was run at an average gallop and the field were tightly grouped, but the first pair had it to themselves from three out. The winner probably didn't need to improve on his previous best.

NOTEBOOK
Strumble Head(IRE), despite meeting the third-last all wrong, got off the mark at the tenth time of asking by making most for a ready success. He had shaped when fourth on his penultimate outing as though he would be better off under more positive riding, but obviously had something to prove after being pulled up last time out (lost action). Connections have now evidently found the key to him and he could find a little further improvement as a result. (op 5-1 tchd 11-2)
Ruby Valentine(FR) was the only one to give the winner a serious race and enjoyed this return to quicker ground, but was always being held by that rival. She will go back up in the weights now, but her last win came off a stone higher mark so could just build on this. (op 13-2 tchd 11-2)
Mystic Touch, making his handicap debut, was given a very patient ride and kept on without threatening the first pair to post his most encouraging display over hurdles. The first-time cheekpieces helped, and more positive tactics could see him get a little closer now he has found his sort of level. (op 10-1 tchd 14-1)
Young Tot(IRE), whose last win came over fences in 2008, got markedly outpaced on the back straight before rallying gamely and surely needs a stiffer test these days. (op 8-1 tchd 10-1)
Scotsbrook Cloud raced in a share of the lead early, but was being niggled going out onto the back straight and it's not hard to see why he was tried in cheekpieces two runs back. He remains a maiden. (op 4-1)
Standing Order Official explanation: jockey said gelding lost its action but returned sound
Silver Sonnet Official explanation: jockey said mare bled from the nose
T/Plt: £90.50 to a £1 stake. Pool:£46,528.59 - 374.92 winning tickets T/Qpdt: £11.80 to a £1 stake. Pool:£3,733.50 - 232.30 winning tickets IM

1301 - 1307a (Foreign Racing) - See Raceform Interactive

[1135]BANGOR-ON-DEE (L-H)
Friday, August 20

OFFICIAL GOING: Good (good to soft in places on chase course; watered)
Wind: side wind, gathering srength Weather: sunny and humid

1308 MAELOR MAIDEN HURDLE (11 hdls) 2m 4f
1:55 (1:55) (Class 4) 4-Y-0+ **£2,740** (£798; £399)

Form RPR

1 **Miss Franklin (IRE)**[232] 3202 6-10-7 0................................ WillKennedy 91+
(Adrian Murray, Ire) *mde all: mstke 5th: plugging on gamely whn mstke last: all out* **100/1**

2 *7* **Butlers Glen (IRE)**[45] 927 7-10-7 0.................................... PaulMoloney 85
(Evan Williams) *t.k.h in midfield: effrt 3 out: 3rd and looking gng best bef 2 out where wnt 2nd: sn rdn and no rspnse: 3 l 2nd and hld last* **9/2**[3]

34-0 **3** *2 ½* **Himayna**[103] 230 6-10-7 0... RichardJohnson 84
(Tim Vaughan) *nt jump wl: keen early: j. slowly 1st: pressed wnr: drvn bef 2 out where lost 2nd: tired whn mstke last* **12/1**

402 **4** *4 ½* **Leitra House (IRE)**[14] 1196 7-11-0 0................................ NickScholfield 85
(Jeremy Scott) *t.k.h in rr: nvr fluent: slow 6th and 7th: wnt mod 4th after 3 out: nvr nr ldng trio: plugged on* **11/4**[2]

0- **5** *14* **Drop Anchor (IRE)**[47] 895 7-11-0 0................................ PaddyBrennan 77
(Edward Cawley, Ire) *hld up and bhd: pushed along bef 7th: brief effrt next: fdd tamely after 3 out* **50/1**

/0-0 **6** *22* **Flapjack Crumbly**[111] 92 7-11-0 0..................................... HenryOliver 57
(Sue Smith) *t.k.h chsng ldrs: mstke 4th: 5 l 4th and looking outpcd whn blnd bdly 3 out and lost all ch: t.o* **50/1**

7 *1* **Nouailhas**[10] 4-10-5 0.. PeterHatton(7) 54
(Reg Hollinshead) *mstke 1st: off pce in midfield: struggling bef 3 out: t.o bef next* **100/1**

P **8** *18* **Laurollie**[70] 711 8-10-4 0 ow7.. DerekSmith(10) 41
(Bill Moore) *set off 20 l last and plld hrd in rr: pushed along bef 7th where mstke and lost tch: t.o bef 3 out* **150/1**

P5 **9** *18* **Rocklandslad (IRE)**[24] 1111 7-10-7 0..................(p) AodhaganConlon(7) 27
(Rebecca Curtis) *prom: rdn after 7th: wkng whn mstke 8th: bdly t.o after 3 out* **5/1**

42-6 **U** **Pinerock (IRE)**[91] 431 6-11-0 110.......................................(v) APMcCoy —
(Jonjo O'Neill) *j.rt and uns rdr 1st* **15/8**[1]

U **Tenth Avenue (IRE)** 5-10-11 0.. AdrianLane(3) —
(Donald McCain) *uns rdr s* **25/1**

4m 57.9s (0.50) **Going Correction** -0.10s/f (Good)
WFA 4 from 5yo+ 14lb 11 Ran SP% **114.4**
Speed ratings (Par 105): **95,92,91,89,83 75,74,67,60,—** —
toteswingers:1&2:£30.90, 1&3:£30.90, 2&3:£7.90 CSF £498.05 TOTE £64.80: £22.80, £2.50, £2.60; EX 890.10.
Owner O B Syndicate **Bred** G J King **Trained** Rathowen, Co. Westmeath
■ Adrian Murray's first winner in Britain.

FOCUS
There had been 9mm of rain overnight and the rain set in again before the start of the meeting. Conditions were quite testing for the first, which was a poor contest. The 100/1 winner had no previous form.

NOTEBOOK
Miss Franklin(IRE), who has apparently had a breathing operation, set the pace throughout and had the field strung out early. She was tiring by the straight, but stuck to the task in gutsy fashion for a surprise win. After pulling up in two Irish points and tailing off on her bumper debut, she had little to recommend her, but she coped with the conditions better than the rest and that proved the difference. She can be a bit edgy - her trainer had to accompany her to the start - and she got progressively warmer throughout the race, but she has reportedly been working well at home, though connections were still as surprised that she won as everyone else.
Butlers Glen(IRE) had some reasonable form in Irish bumpers and had changed stables for her hurdling debut. She made good progress in the back straight to track the winner, but could not go on from there and eventually finished well beaten. She should learn from this experience and may be better on faster ground, but does not look too special. (op 7-2)
Himayna did not jump that fluently on her hurdling debut and got tired in the ground. After showing little promise in three bumpers, this was a bit better. (op 14-1)
Leitra House(IRE) is a headstrong sort and was again held up to help him settle. He made some late progress to suggest he has some ability, but could not get competitive in this ground. (op 3-1 tchd 5-2)
Drop Anchor(IRE) has yet to prove he has any discernible ability
Pinerock(IRE) did his tarnished reputation no favours by skewing markedly at the first and giving his jockey no chance. To redress the balance slightly he did then jump round loose and completed the course. (tchd 2-1)

1309 PERTEMPS H'CAP CHASE (15 fncs) 2m 4f 110y
2:30 (2:34) (Class 4) (0-105,105) 4-Y-0+ **£3,740** (£1,098; £549; £274)

Form RPR

-403 **1** **Magnetic Pole**[31] 1044 9-11-4 102...............................(v) GilesHawkins(5) 108
(Richard Lee) *trckd ldrs: nt fluent 7th: wnt 2nd after 3 out: rdn to ld bef next: nrly 3 l clr last: kpt finding on flat: jst hld on: gamely* **4/1**[3]

110/ **2** *shd* **Cebonne (FR)**[695] 1471 9-11-12 105................................... PaulMoloney 111
(Sophie Leech) *stdd s and set off 15 l last: stdy prog 12th: 5 l 3rd 2 out: drvn to chal last: edgd sltly lft: catching wnr nr fin* **12/1**

222 **3** *10* **One Of The Boys (IRE)**[40] 950 9-11-8 101................. RichardJohnson 101+
(Tim Vaughan) *racd keenly: chsd ldr 4th tl led 11th: dived at next: rdn and hdd bef 2 out: abt to lose 2nd whn mstke last* **10/3**[2]

4304 **4** *8* **Mcqueen (IRE)**[33] 1033 10-10-13 95................................... DannyCook(3) 85
(Barry Leavy) *led tl 11th: chsd ldr tl rdn and wknd after 3 out* **11/1**

-541 **5** *9* **Ponchatrain (IRE)**[28] 1080 10-10-11 90................................(p) TomO'Brien 72
(Martin Keighley) *chsd ldr tl 4th: remained cl up tl j.rt 9th and 10th: sn rdn and wknd* **3/1**[1]

0351 **6** *8* **Golden Gem (IRE)**[14] 1195 8-11-12 105..........................(p) HarrySkelton 79
(Rachel Hobbs) *lacked fluency towards rr: j. slowly 4th: rdn and struggling in 7 l 6th 3 out: fdd* **14/1**

4-PU **7** *45* **Benefit Game (IRE)**[68] 734 6-11-6 99.................................... APMcCoy 33
(Jonjo O'Neill) *midfield: nt fluent 7th: hit 8th: nvr looked to be gng wl after: lost tch bef 3 out and j. it slowly: sn eased and t.o* **5/1**

20- **P** **Some Magic (IRE)**[314] 1702 10-10-8 87..........................(t) PaddyBrennan —
(Edward Cawley, Ire) *towards rr: pushed along and struggling after 9th: j.v.slowly 10th: t.o and p.u next* **20/1**

5m 10.8s (1.70) **Going Correction** -0.325s/f (Good) 8 Ran SP% **112.2**
Speed ratings (Par 105): **83,82,79,76,72 69,52,—**
toteswingers:1&2:£7.00, 1&3:£3.10, 2&3:£9.70 CSF £45.59 CT £174.24 TOTE £4.40: £1.30, £4.10, £1.30; EX 51.80.
Owner D Pugh **Bred** The Queen **Trained** Byton, H'fords

FOCUS
An ordinary handicap in which the winner is rated to his best. Once again not all the runners could handle the easier conditions off a fair pace.

NOTEBOOK
Magnetic Pole sat just off the lead before making his move in the back straight and had to dig deep to repel the sustained challenge of the runner-up. Having tried to last home in a stronger contest over C&D last time, he was entitled to go well again off a 2lb lower mark, especially with the stable in such good form, and in this easier grade the go-for-home tactics prevailed, but only just. His trainer admitted he was not confident and had been leaning towards an alternative engagement at Worcester, but credited his jockey for an enterprising ride. (tchd 9-2)
Cebonne(FR) was held up early before making steady headway to emerge as a strong challenger in the straight. He just ducked in behind the winner momentarily, which was enough to hand away the advantage, although he made the winner work all the way to the line. He had not been seen since September 2008, so this was a fine performance and suggests he retains enough ability to go one better off a feasible mark. (op 17-2 tchd 14-1)
One Of The Boys(IRE) was always near the head of affairs and despite getting in too close to the final open ditch he stuck on. This trip on this ground may have been a bit far but he is game and consistent and as such a useful benchmark. (op 3-1)
Mcqueen(IRE) led to halfway but faded from the back straight and may not have appreciated the give in the ground. (op 16-1)
Ponchatrain(IRE) was late into the paddock and delayed proceedings, but after some fluent early jumps he got tired midway and his jumping became more ragged. Official explanation: trainer said the gelding had a breathing problem (op 7-2 tchd 11-4)
Benefit Game(IRE) attracted some market support, hopeful that his recent jumping problems had been sorted out, but although he did not make any palpable errors he just did not seem to relish the challenge and was beaten by halfway. (op 7-1)
Some Magic(IRE) Official explanation: trainer said the gelding had a breathing problem

1310 FRESHFIELD BOWLING CLUB "NATIONAL HUNT" NOVICES' HURDLE (9 hdls) 2m 1f
3:05 (3:06) (Class 4) 4-Y-0+ **£2,665** (£827; £445)

Form RPR

1 **1** **Vertige Dore (FR)**[14] 1201 5-10-12 0................................ HarrySkelton 123+
(Paul Nicholls) *settled 3rd tl wnt 2nd at 6th: wandering fr bef 2 out: led between last two: nrly 3 l clr and in command last* **7/4**[2]

2 *7* **Cass Bligh (IRE)**[119] 5382 6-11-5 130.................................. APMcCoy 125
(Adrian Murray, Ire) *led at v modest pce: nt fluent 3rd: 5th and 6th: rdn bef 2 out: hdd between last two: btn last: nt hrd pushed after* **8/13**[1]

0-00 **3** *67* **Fenella Mere**[21] 1140 7-9-12 0........................(p) PeterHatton(7) 42
(Patricia Rigby) *kpt up in 2nd in v slow r: wavered bdly 2nd: mstke 5th: lost 2nd at next and sn hopelessly t.o: inherited 3rd at last* **100/1**

6-26 **F** **Flichity (IRE)**[36] 1003 5-10-9 0........................ AdrianLane(3) 112
(Donald McCain) *on his toes and t.k.h: last tl wnt 3rd at 6th: disp 2nd 3 out: racd awkwardly whn rdn bef 2 out: sn btn: 8 l 3rd whn hit last: slipped bdly and fell* **11/1[3]**

4m 13.9s (3.00) **Going Correction** -0.10s/f (Good) **4** Ran SP% **107.6**
Speed ratings (Par 105): **88,84,53,—**
toteswingers:1&2:£15.50, 1&3:£13.80, 2&3:£2.60 CSF £3.31 TOTE £3.50; EX 3.10.
Owner Cathal McCarthy **Bred** Chantal Becq **Trained** Ditcheat, Somerset

FOCUS
Two above-average novices for the time of year fought out the honours. The race was steadily run though, and the form is suspect.

NOTEBOOK
Vertige Dore(FR) showed greenness on his hurdling debut, but despite wandering around approaching the second last he had enough speed to readily out-gun the favourite. After several respectable bumper runs in Ireland, he has now won on both starts for Paul Nicholls and looks to be a promising recruit. (op 11-8 tchd 15-8)
Cass Bligh(IRE) set a comfortable pace, but briefly looked in trouble around the home turn. He responded to pressure, but in the end was outpaced by the winner. He had put up some good performances in Ireland in the spring, but had reportedly been lame when withdrawn from his intended return to action 11 days ago and may have just lacked that extra edge. This was still a good performance under his penalty and he looks to have a future, especially if given a stiffer test. (op 5-6 tchd 10-11 in places)
Fenella Mere did not settle, her jumping was wayward and she again showed little aptitude for hurdles.
Flichity(IRE) was edgy before the start and keen during the race, but was still just about in touch when clattering the last and coming down. He possesses some ability but might need some time to develop.

1311 FREEBETS.CO.UK DEE HURDLE (H'CAP) (9 hdls) 2m 1f
3:40 (3:40) (Class 2) (0-150,141) 4-Y-0+ **£8,238** (£2,433; £1,216; £608; £304)

Form RPR

-314 **1** **Alazan (IRE)**[34] 1017 4-10-6 **122**........................ RichardJohnson 128+
(Philip Hobbs) *mde all: 10 l clr 3rd: given breather 6th: forged on again 2 out: 5 l ahd last: comf* **11/4[1]**

1010 **2** *5* **Son Of Flicka**[34] 1019 6-11-8 **137**........................ APMcCoy 137
(Donald McCain) *chsd clr ldr: mstke 4th: clsd 6th: 1 l down and rdn 3 out: outpcd fr 2 out* **9/2[3]**

40-2 **3** *2 1/2* **Sweet World**[22] 1127 6-9-7 **115** oh3........................ MissIsabelTompsett(7) 112
(Bernard Llewellyn) *t.k.h in last: hdwy after 4th: wnt 5 l 3rd at 6th: urged along and no imp after* **11/1**

1-10 **4** *1 1/4* **Inventor (IRE)**[34] 1017 5-11-5 **141**........................ MrJHamer(7) 139+
(Donald McCain) *prom bhd clr ldng pair tl lost pl bef 4th: tried to rally in 4th 3 out: 9 l 4th and rdn whn mstke 2 out: plugged on: mstke last* **7/2[2]**

-020 **5** *10* **Gloucester**[22] 1133 7-11-4 **133**........................ TomScudamore 121
(Michael Scudamore) *hld up towards rr: effrt after 4th: wnt 5 l 3rd and j. slowly 5th: rdn next and sn fnd nil: 5th and btn 3 out* **13/2**

-62P **6** *shd* **Nordwind (IRE)**[34] 1017 9-10-7 **122**........................ PaulMoloney 110
(Evan Williams) *prom bhd clr ldng pair: wnt 3rd after 4th: effrt next: 6th and fading 3 out* **25/1**

3636 **7** *dist* **Dancewiththedevil (IRE)**[22] 1127 9-9-11 **115** oh1..... DonalDevereux(3) 67
(Peter Bowen) *hld up and bhd: 7th and struggling 3 out: t.o and eased next* **10/1**

4636 **8** *11* **Another Trump (NZ)**[31] 1045 6-10-3 **121**........................ RichieMcLernon(3) 64
(Jonjo O'Neill) *a last trio: t.o 6th: eased after 3 out* **22/1**

P **Truxton King (IRE)**[122] 5300 5-10-4 **124**........................ IanPopham(5) —
(Paul Nicholls) *chsd ldrs but n.d: rdn 5th: sn fdd: t.o and p.u 2 out* **9/1**

4m 5.00s (-5.90) **Going Correction** -0.10s/f (Good)
WFA 4 from 5yo+ 13lb **9** Ran SP% **116.0**
Speed ratings (Par 109): **109,106,105,104,100 100,—,—,—**
toteswingers:1&2:£2.00, 1&3:£11.10, 2&3:£16.20 CSF £16.05 CT £116.89 TOTE £3.90: £1.40, £1.80, £3.80; EX 16.90.
Owner Mrs Caren Walsh & R J Budge **Bred** D G Iceton **Trained** Withycombe, Somerset

FOCUS
A competitive event turned into a procession by the wire-to-wire winner. This was a step up on his previous form.

NOTEBOOK
Alazan(IRE) was keen to get to the lead and soon had established a gap on the field. Given a breather on the final circuit and helped by some fluent jumping, he had the field floundering and retained enough in hand to readily dispense with the sole forlorn challenger. He was not disgraced when pitched into the Summer Hurdle at Market Rasen last month and was still on the same mark. He is versatile as to tactics, but can be devastating when being let loose in the lead, which might mean he still has something in reserve after the handicapper has his say. (op 7-2)
Son Of Flicka tracked the winner, but although he tried to peg back the gap he could never mount a serious challenge. He has been in good form since the spring and goes well here, but just looks to be in the handicapper's grip at the moment. (op 7-1)
Sweet World ran another consistent race, but he needs to be played late and though he tried to chase down the winner he had little chance of making up that much ground on a runaway leader who was not stopping. (op 17-2 tchd 12-1)
Inventor(IRE) hit a flat spot in the back straight before staying on again, but he was another who could make little impact. He was raised 8lb after winning at Hexham in June, which saw him struggle off top weight in the Summer Hurdle at Market Rasen next time and it was a similar story here, despite his jockey's 7lb allowance. (op 4-1)
Gloucester never got into it and began to labour in the back straight. He has put up some creditable performances in competitive hurdles and has maintained his form since the spring, but is still seeking a first win in handicap company. (op 6-1)
Nordwind(IRE) has not made the breakthrough in handicaps yet and is unlikely to do so off his current mark. (op 18-1)
Truxton King(IRE) sweated between his hind legs, was a drifter on course and ran as if he would come on for the run. He was no great shakes in handicap hurdles in Ireland, but looks on a reasonable mark if Paul Nicholls can elicit the necessary improvement. Official explanation: trainer's representative said that the gelding was unsuited by the good ground (op 7-1)

1312 GENESIS WEALTH MANAGEMENT H'CAP CHASE (18 fncs) 3m 110y
4:15 (4:15) (Class 3) (0-135,134) 5-Y-0+ **£7,480** (£2,196; £1,098; £548)

Form RPR

F-30 **1** **That's Rhythm (FR)**[54] 844 10-11-12 **134**........................(v[1]) GrahamLee 150+
(Martin Todhunter) *cl up: wnt 2nd at 11th: led 14th: gng wl whn mstke 3 out: 5 l clr next: styd on stoutly: eased flat* **8/1**

3/5- **2** *9* **Backbord (GER)**[23] 118 8-11-4 **126**........................(b) LeightonAspell 129
(Lucy Wadham) *shkn up 1st: j. indifferently: pushed along 8th: last tl 1/2-way: prog 13th: 3rd whn j.rt 3 out: sn disputing 2nd: nt rch wnr and outpcd by 3rd 2 out tl cajoled to pass him w reluctance fnl stride* **16/1**

3415 **3** *shd* **Mizen Raven (IRE)**[24] 1103 7-11-3 **125**........................(tp) TomO'Brien 128
(Peter Bowen) *trckd ldrs: effrt 14th: disp 2nd after 3 out: sn drvn: wl hld whn hit 2 out: 8 l 2nd at last: wknd to lose 2nd on line* **12/1**

11F- **4** *13* **Oscar Glory (IRE)**[5] 1265 10-10-2 **110**........................(tp) PaddyBrennan 100
(Edward Cawley, Ire) *bhd: nt fluent 6th: effrt in 4th at 14th: wknd after 3 out: 15 l 4th at next* **3/1[1]**

3121 **5** *3/4* **Rifleman (IRE)**[14] 1200 10-9-12 **111**........................(t) GilesHawkins(5) 100
(Richard Lee) *bhd: rdn and sme prog 14th: 11 l 5th 3 out: sn lost tch* **11/2[2]**

-435 **6** *36* **Stagecoach Amber (USA)**[19] 1151 8-10-8 **116**........................ HenryOliver 73
(Sue Smith) *mstke 5th: chsd ldr tl 11th: wkng whn j. slowly 13th: t.o bef 2 out* **12/1**

1121 **7** *1/2* **Fealing Real (IRE)**[17] 1176 8-10-2 **117**........................(tp) AodhaganConlon(7) 74+
(Rebecca Curtis) *led: bad mstke 12th: hdd 14th: rdn and wkng whn hmpd 3 out* **3/1[1]**

50/0 **P** **Ballyagran (IRE)**[34] 1020 10-11-7 **129**........................(t) RichardJohnson —
(Tim Vaughan) *midfield: mstke 2nd: nt a fluent: wknd 13th: t.o and p.u 3 out* **16/1**

-323 **P** **De Soto**[24] 1108 9-11-5 **127**........................(t) WillKennedy —
(Paul Webber) *prom: mstke 2nd: lost pl 8th: last after mstke 12th: hit 14th: t.o and j. slowly 15th: p.u next* **7/1[3]**

6m 7.10s (-12.70) **Going Correction** -0.325s/f (Good) **9** Ran SP% **116.1**
Speed ratings: **107,104,104,99,99 88,88,—,—**
toteswingers:1&2:£15.60, 1&3:£10.70, 2&3:£26.90 CSF £116.25 CT £1524.84 TOTE £9.50: £2.60, £5.50, £4.10; EX 111.50.
Owner Don't Tell Henry **Bred** Scea Du Haras Des Sablonets **Trained** Orton, Cumbria

FOCUS
A good early pace turned this competitive handicap into a fair test, and the time was relatively good. The winner produced a step up but the second was below his best.

NOTEBOOK
That's Rhythm(FR) travelled well to take up the running in the back straight and, despite diving at the third last, he stayed on well for his third C&D success. He is usually at his best when fresh and possesses plenty of stamina, so was able to handle the conditions and was further galvanised by the first-time visor. (op 7-1)
Backbord(GER) had not raced over jumps since May 2009 and had disappointed recently on the Flat. Jumping sketchily early on, he took a long while to warm to the task but began making steady progress throughout the final mile to suggest that he can still be a player over fences. (op 14-1 tchd 20-1)
Mizen Raven(IRE) tried to close on the winner, but was a tired horse by the home straight and was just caught for a repeat second place in this race. This was a reasonable performance considering the ground was possibly too soft, but he is beginning to look vulnerable off his current mark. (tchd 14-1 in places)
Oscar Glory(IRE) has been in good form in Ireland this summer and looked well treated in his bid for another C&D success, but although he tried to close down the leaders he needs faster ground to show his best. (tchd 7-2 in places)
Rifleman(IRE) is better on faster ground and a galloping track. (op 5-1)
Fealing Real(IRE) was going well and looked likely to shrug off the 14lb rise after his facile success in a small field at Ffos Las earlier in the month, but he clouted the open ditch in the back straight and that was the end of his challenge. (op 9-2 tchd 5-1 in places)
De Soto never looked happy and soon lost interest after a mistake midway. (op 13-2)

1313 ROSE HILL NOVICES' H'CAP HURDLE (9 hdls) 2m 1f
4:50 (4:50) (Class 4) (0-105,110) 4-Y-0+ **£3,425** (£998; £499)

Form RPR

30B1 **1** **Points Of View**[3] 1278 5-12-2 **110** 7ex........................(t) SeanQuinlan(3) 129+
(Kim Bailey) *hld up: clsd to ld 6th: clr after 3 out: 16 l ahd next: eased flat: v easily* **15/8[1]**

6314 **2** *14* **Frosted Grape (IRE)**[18] 1162 4-11-9 **101**........................(b) TomScudamore 98
(David Pipe) *t.k.h: cl 2nd tl j. slowly 5th and lost two pls and downed tools: 5th after 3 out: urged along and rallied to go 20 l 2nd at last* **5/2[2]**

54P- **3** *10* **Leulahleulahlay**[212] 2279 4-11-3 **95**........................ PaulMoloney 82
(Evan Williams) *dropped out last: nt fluent 3rd: effrt bef 3 out: wnt mod 2nd next: nvr nr wnr: lost 2nd and hit last* **9/1**

42- **4** *1 1/2* **Tae Kwon Do (USA)**[9] 1953 4-11-11 **103**........................ DougieCostello 88
(Julie Camacho) *cl up: rdn 3 out: one pce after: stl ev ch of 2nd bef last but 4th and wkng whn mstke* **6/1**

-034 **5** *25* **Boo**[10] 1066 8-10-5 **87**........................ LeeEdwards(5) 51
(James Unett) *drvn bef 2nd: u.p bef 4th: nvr looked keen: in tch tl 3 out: wl bhd whn blnd next: t.o* **11/2[3]**

60-0 **6** *16* **Strong Market**[33] 1035 5-10-13 **90**........................ NickScholfield 39
(Jeremy Scott) *led: j. v poorly: hdd and mstke 6th: 3rd and wkng whn mstke 3 out: t.o and nt fluent last: eased* **14/1**

4m 8.70s (-2.20) **Going Correction** -0.10s/f (Good)
WFA 4 from 5yo+ 13lb **6** Ran SP% **109.7**
Speed ratings (Par 105): **101,94,89,89,77 69**
toteswingers:1&2:£1.80, 1&3:£4.00, 2&3:£3.00 CSF £6.84 TOTE £3.10: £2.50, £1.10; EX 6.20 Place 6 £376.32; Place 5 £95.99.
Owner W J Ives **Bred** Limestone And Tara Studs **Trained** Andoversford, Gloucs

FOCUS
Not a strong race but a battle for the early lead between Frosted Grape and Strong Market meant the pace was decent. The winner produced a big step forward and is now approaching the level expected from his best Flat form.

NOTEBOOK
Points Of View took up the running in the back straight and soon scooted clear, easing down near the line having readily dispensed with the opposition. It has taken a while, but he finally seems to have learned how to preserve his energy throughout a race and now he is able to showcase his ability, he readily brushed aside the 7lb penalty for his win at Worcester on Wednesday. Both of his wins have come sporting a tongue tie and that has evidently made a significant difference. (tchd 2-1)
Frosted Grape(IRE) battled for the early lead before dropping out in the back straight only to rally again past toiling rivals to claim a remote second. The winner of a maiden hurdle at Worcester in July, she had things her own way in front on that occasion and might be better when not hassled for the lead as she was today. (op 9-4)
Leulahleulahlay made some late progress under pressure on his first run since January, but will need to improve if he is to be successful over jumps.
Tae Kwon Do(USA) looked on a stiff enough mark for his handicap debut and, after briefly challenging in the back straight, he did not fully see out the trip on this softer ground. (op 13-2)
Boo did not look that willing from halfway. (op 13-2)

T/Plt: £200.60 to a £1 stake. Pool:£40,873.32 - 148.72 winning tickets T/Qpdt: £32.10 to a £1 stake. Pool:£4,226.56 - 97.20 winning tickets IM

The Form Book, Raceform Ltd, Compton, RG20 6NL

1314 - 1323a (Foreign Racing) - See Raceform Interactive

1249 MARKET RASEN (R-H)

Saturday, August 21

OFFICIAL GOING: Good (good to soft in places; chase 6.6, hurdle 7.0)
All rails moved out 2yds to provide fresh ground.
Wind: light 1/2 against Weather: fine, light rain last 2

1324 GET X-CITED ABOUT X FACTOR JUVENILE MAIDEN HURDLE (8 hdls) 2m 1f

5:20 (5:20) (Class 4) 3-Y-O £2,740 (£798; £399)

Form RPR
53 1 **Joe Rua (USA)**[5] 1024 3-10-12 0 ColinBolger 83
(John Ryan) *chsd ldrs: nt fluent 2nd: joind ldr 3 out: led next: drvn clr run-in* **8/1**[3]
2 5 **Bateau Bleu**[10] 3-10-12 0 BarryKeniry 79
(Ben Haslam) *nt fluent: led: j. slowly 2nd: sn hdd: lft 3 l 2nd last: one pce* **2/1**[1]
3 40 **Desert Forest (IRE)**[45] 3-10-12 0 BrianHughes 43
(Howard Johnson) *t.k.h: trckd ldrs: handy 3rd and rdn whn mstke 3 out: sn wknd: lft distant 3rd whn mstke last* **6/1**[2]
4 64 **Kathindi (IRE)**[40] 3-10-9 0 AlexMerriam(3) —
(Neil King) *chsd ldrs: nt fluent 4th: reminders and lost pl next: t.o 3 out* **8/1**[3]
P **Woodhouse Mill (IRE)**[54] 3-10-5 0 AndrewTinkler —
(Nigel Tinkler) *in rr: drvn 4th: sn bhd: t.o whn p.u after 3 out* **40/1**
F **Frameit (IRE)**[40] 3-10-5 0 MrTomDavid(7) 83+
(Tim Vaughan) *j. slowly: w ldrs: led sn after 2nd: j. slowly and hdd 2 out: 2 l 2nd whn fell last* **2/1**[1]
U **Lynn's Lady** 3-10-5 0 BrianHarding —
(Michael Easterby) *last whn jinked rt and uns rdr 1st* **16/1**

4m 35.6s (28.90) **Going Correction** +1.225s/f (Heav) 7 Ran SP% **111.5**
Speed ratings (Par 102): **81,78,59,29,—,—,—**
toteswingers:1&2:£2.80, 1&3:£2.80, 2&3:£1.90 CSF £23.88 TOTE £9.80: £3.30, £1.30; EX 17.30.
Owner J Ryan **Bred** Martin Dunne **Trained** Newmarket, Suffolk

FOCUS
An ordinary juvenile maiden.

NOTEBOOK
Joe Rua(USA), the only one in the race with previous hurdling experience, obliged with the only halfway convincing round of jumping, despite needing stoking along from an early stage. Well held in two 1m6f Flat handicaps in the preceding week, he already looks a better hurdler, and according to connections could defy a step up in trip in due course. This looks very ordinary form, though, with victory owed much to both his rider's persistence and rivals' shortcomings.
Bateau Bleu, from a yard that does quite well with its juvenile hurdlers, is rated just 59 on the Flat. He proved deliberate at several flights, in particular on the first circuit, but in fairness he might have found them coming at him a bit too fast, having recorded his best work on the Flat around stiff courses. He can be given a chance to step up on this effort granted a more conducive test. (op 11-4)
Desert Forest(IRE) entered the race with the highest Flat rating, but also with little form beyond 7f and two comprehensive recent defeats to leave behind him. He coped with good to soft perfectly well on one try last year, so his early keenness and suspect stamina probably did for him rather than the changing conditions. (op 9-2)
Woodhouse Mill(IRE) Official explanation: jockey said filly had a breathing problem (op 9-4 tchd 15-8)
Frameit(IRE) was never likely to fail on stamina grounds as a 1m4f Flat winner, but the mistake that put him on the ground at the last when held was not his first of the race. The ability to win a poor heat is there, but there is a lot of room for improvement on the jumping front. (op 9-4 tchd 15-8)

1325 A.J. GLASSFIBRE NOVICES' HURDLE (8 hdls) 2m 1f

5:50 (5:50) (Class 4) 4-Y-0+ £2,740 (£798; £399)

Form RPR
-242 1 **Favours Brave**[38] 988 4-10-11 108 DougieCostello 111+
(Tim Easterby) *mde all: drvn clr appr 2 out: styd on strly: eased towards fin* **13/8**[1]
3 2 19 **Treason Trial**[20] 1149 9-10-12 0 BarryKeniry 92
(Joss Saville) *in rr: hit 3rd: hdwy to chse ldrs 3 out: sn outpcd: 5th last: styd on to take modest 2nd towards fin* **16/1**
344 3 3/4 **Rebel Hunter (IRE)**[20] 1148 5-10-12 103 AndrewGlassonbury 93+
(Steve Gollings) *chsd ldrs: drvn 3 out: one pce whn nt fluent next: 10 l 2nd whn mstke last: lost 2nd towards fin* **9/4**[2]
4 nk **Baltimore Jack (IRE)**[23] 6-10-12 0 RobertWalford 95+
(Tim Walford) *nt jump wl: chsd ldrs: mstke 1st: wknd appr 2 out: lost 3rd clsng stages* **4/1**[3]
5 nk **Chadwell Spring (IRE)**[21] 4-10-1 0 AdrianLane(3) 82
(Mike Sowersby) *in tch: 4th and wl outpcd 2 out: kpt on run-in* **20/1**
6 107 **Secret Palm (IRE)** 5-10-9 0 AdamPogson(3) —
(Caroline Bailey) *t.k.h: trckd ldrs: lost pl after 4th: t.o 3 out: eventually completed: btn 107 l in 6th* **25/1**
P **Paint The Town Red**[70] 5-10-5 0 MrJMQuinlan(7) —
(Hugh Collingridge) *in rr whn nt fluent 2nd: drvn 3rd: bhd next: t.o whn j. bdly lft 5th: p.u bef next* **9/1**

4m 25.4s (18.70) **Going Correction** +1.225s/f (Heav)
WFA 4 from 5yo+ 13lb 7 Ran SP% **113.4**
Speed ratings (Par 105): **105,96,95,95,95 —,—**
toteswingers:1&2:£5.50, 1&3:£2.50, 2&3:£4.50 CSF £26.41 TOTE £1.70: £1.10, £7.90; EX 27.50.
Owner Mrs J Bowser **Bred** Juddmonte Farms Ltd **Trained** Great Habton, N Yorks

FOCUS
A moderate novice event, run at a fair gallop.

NOTEBOOK
Favours Brave can sweat up and did so markedly here, but it doesn't tend to stop him running his races. Made a lot of use of, he looked to have the most left when his advantages was reduced to a length turning for home, and quickly put the matter beyond doubt with another injection of speed and a fine leap two out. He can be placed to advantage in another of these, with a step back up in trip unlikely to inconvenience, and connections suggest he should be able to jump a fence in time. (op 15-8)
Treason Trial, on his fourth run back from a three-year hiatus, ran creditably despite the trip being shorter than ideal. All of his Flat wins prior to the absence had been recorded around flat, galloping left-handers, and he could be the type to find a small race at Wetherby or Doncaster on that basis. (op 14-1)
Rebel Hunter(IRE) ◆ was arguably second best on merit, but paid for trying to keep tabs on the winner from an early stage and didn't land running at either of the last two flights, either. His capitulation over 2m6f at Uttoxeter two starts earlier owed far more to a stopping error than any stamina issues and this former Irish point winner can improve for a step back up in trip. (tchd 5-2)
Baltimore Jack(IRE) ran despite pre-race fears from connections that any significant rain would temper his chance, but the ground alone didn't beat him as he could never hold down the lead he might have preferred and his jumping was ragged. He can prove far better than this in future with more in his favour and a tidier round. (op 9-2 tchd 7-2)

1326 SINGLETON BIRCH H'CAP CHASE (17 fncs) 3m 1f

6:20 (6:20) (Class 4) (0-115,114) 4-Y-0+ £3,425 (£998; £499)

Form RPR
2444 1 **Pairc Na Gcapall (IRE)**[7] 1252 8-11-5 110 (b) AlexMerriam(3) 119
(Neil King) *mde all: drvn 4 out: jnd last: kpt on wl* **3/1**[1]
416 2 2 1/2 **Prophete De Guye (FR)**[26] 1093 7-11-2 104 FelixDeGiles 112
(James Evans) *trckd ldrs: t.k.h: wnt 2nd after 4 out: chalng whn nt fluent last: no ex* **3/1**[1]
4336 3 15 **Western Gale (IRE)**[37] 1002 7-11-10 112 BrianHarding 114+
(Martin Todhunter) *hld up detached in last: drvn along 8th: reminders and hdwy 11th: wnt 3rd 3 out: 3 l down last: eased whn no imp fnl 50yds* **9/2**[3]
3-3U 4 17 **Chernik (IRE)**[62] 804 9-11-7 109 BarryKeniry 90
(Micky Hammond) *j.rt: chsd wnr: wknd qckly bef 3 out: sn bhd* **4/1**[2]
203P 5 15 **Feeling Peckish (USA)**[29] 1081 6-9-7 88 oh15 JoeCornwall(7) 53
(Michael Chapman) *chsd ldrs: drvn and outpcd 10th: sn lost pl: t.o 3 out: j. bdly rt last 2* **12/1**
0P-P F **Prestbury Knight**[15] 1200 10-11-12 114 (p) CharliePoste —
(Sophie Leech) *last whn fell 1st: rn wout declared hood* **16/1**
00- R **Finzi Contini (FR)**[9] 4725 6-10-12 107 (p) MrTomDavid(7) —
(Tim Vaughan) *chsd ldrs: hmpd 7th: rn out and uns rdr bnd appr 11th* **12/1**

6m 25.5s (-5.80) **Going Correction** -0.10s/f (Good) 7 Ran SP% **109.4**
Speed ratings (Par 105): **105,104,99,93,89 —,—**
toteswingers:1&2:£1.20, 1&3:£3.90, 2&3:£2.70 CSF £11.73 TOTE £3.10: £2.40, £1.02; EX 13.50.
Owner So What Is Your Role In Life Partnership **Bred** Hugh Douglas **Trained** Newmarket, Suffolk

FOCUS
A decent gallop from the outset to this staying handicap chase, and very few got into it.

NOTEBOOK
Pairc Na Gcapall(IRE) needs a sharp, flat 2m7f-3m1f and no company up front to show his best form. He was granted all these, plus a mark 4lb below his last winning one, and duly ended a run of 14 straight losses dating back 15 months. A more resolute rival might have given him a bit more to think about from the last, though, and there's not certain to be too much more improvement to come from him after 22 chase starts. (tchd 11-4 and 7-2)
Prophete De Guye(FR), whose rider was at pains not to commit his mount fully until a good way up the straight, but the effort up the run-in was limited. Two wins this summer have taken him to a career-high mark, and either that or an untidy jump at the last (or both) could serve as mitigating circumstances, but he will still have questions to answer if finding himself equally well placed next time. (op 11-4 tchd 5-2)
Western Gale(IRE), dropped 9lb since set a huge task on his handicap debut in the Scottish National, couldn't live with the generous early pace and never looked like threatening the winner. His one chase win came when produced late over this trip around the more exacting Hexham, and his prospects should improve again once returned to that sort of venue. (tchd 4-1)
Chernik(IRE) has similarly put in his best work around stiffer 3m tests than this one, but a current mark 15lb above his highest winning one over fences is proving enough of an anchor in any event. (tchd 7-2)
Feeling Peckish(USA), for whom money came late, had a 75th career defeat from as many starts looking a certainty before the turn for home. (op 25-1)

1327 ST ANDREWS HOSPICE H'CAP CHASE (14 fncs) 2m 4f

6:50 (6:51) (Class 3) (0-125,124) 4-Y-0+ £5,204 (£1,528; £764; £381)

Form RPR
-446 1 **Ragador**[77] 634 9-10-0 98 TjadeCollier 105
(Sue Smith) *mde virtually all: hit 4 out: kpt on gamely fr 2 out: drvn rt out* **5/1**
34/5 2 2 1/4 **Ohana**[24] 1117 7-11-0 115 EwanWhillans(3) 120
(Alistair Whillans) *hld up in tch: hdwy to chse ldrs 8th: wnt 2nd 3 out: swtchd lft between last 2: styd on same pce run-in: no imp* **9/2**[3]
6-23 3 2 **Nudge And Nurdle (IRE)**[20] 1151 9-11-9 124 TomMolloy(3) 128
(Nigel Twiston-Davies) *trckd ldrs: nt fluent 8th: shkn up next: drvn 4 out: kpt on same pce fr 2 out* **5/4**[1]
4P-P 4 3 **I'm A Legend**[15] 1200 8-10-10 108 (p) DougieCostello 108
(Neil Mulholland) *w ldr: nt fluent 2nd: one pce fr 3 out: hit last* **12/1**
6202 5 3/4 **Nesnaas (USA)**[20] 1152 9-9-9 98 oh4 (t) DavidBass(5) 99
(Mark Rimell) *w ldrs: outpcd and lost pl after 4 out: kpt on fr 2 out* **3/1**[2]

5m 10.0s (4.30) **Going Correction** -0.10s/f (Good) 5 Ran SP% **112.0**
Speed ratings (Par 107): **87,86,85,84,83**
CSF £26.04 TOTE £13.90: £2.40, £5.60; EX 34.70.
Owner Widdop Wanderers **Bred** R W Isgar **Trained** High Eldwick, W Yorks

FOCUS
A contest weakened by the defection of leading fancy Rockiteer due to the ground, and then by a muddling gallop.

NOTEBOOK
Ragador travelled nicely at the head of affairs and an error at the final ditch didn't cost him enough energy to deal his finishing effort a critical blow. It's taken 16 career starts and a drop to a lowest-ever chase mark to get off the mark, but his attitude is good and he might have another of these in him if given enough time before his next race (frequently produces his best after a couple of months away). (op 4-1 tchd 11-2)
Ohana posted a solid effort on only his third run back after a 21-month absence, not least as the softening going wouldn't have rated an obvious plus. Winless beyond a sharp 2m2f, the moderate fractions here fudged the issue as to whether 2m4f is exactly what he needs now, and another outing at this trip may tell us more. (op 4-1)
Nudge And Nurdle(IRE) ran a moody race. Early restraint seemed to disappoint him this time and he could never quite be motivated to redouble his effort sufficiently on the final circuit despite his rider's best endeavours. He can prove better than this again in a more solidly run contest. (op 6-5 tchd 11-8)
I'm A Legend's strike-rate over fences pales next to that over hurdles, and both previous chase runs this season had been very poor. He revived a little here under what had turned out to be his optimum conditions (all career wins having been recorded around flat right-handed courses on good to soft), but more again is needed to resume winning ways. (op 10-1 tchd 9-1)
Nesnaas(USA), second over 3m1f here last time, duly found things happening too quickly for him when the tempo increased leaving the back straight. He remains tantalisingly well treated, but his losing run now stands at 15. (op 9-2)

1328 A.J. GLASSFIBRE H'CAP HURDLE (8 hdls) 2m 1f

7:20 (7:20) (Class 4) (0-110,110) 4-Y-0+ £2,740 (£798; £399)

Form RPR
022 1 **Topenhall (IRE)**[20] 1147 9-11-10 108 (t) CharliePoste 111
(Ben Case) *trckd ldr: led 2 out: hung lft run-in: styd on: drvn out* **9/2**[2]

-623 **2** 2 1/4 **High Bird Humphrey**[25] 1110 11-11-2 **107**...................(p) MrSFMagee(7) 108
(Simon West) *hld up: hdwy to trck ldrs 5th: handy 3rd 2 out: kpt on same pce run-in: tk 2nd towards fin* **3/1**[1]

4054 **3** hd **Phoenix Eye**[7] 1254 9-10-3 **94**.. BrianToomey(7) 95
(Michael Mullineaux) *stdd s: hld up in rr: hdwy 5th: chsng wnr 2 out: kpt on same pce run-in* **7/1**

6-P1 **4** 2 1/2 **Liberty Seeker (FR)**[7] 1249 11-11-5 **110**........................ MattCrawley(7) 109
(John Harris) *hld up in tch: outpcd 5th: styd on fr 2 out: 4th and one pce whn hit last* **8/1**

3/6- **5** 2 1/2 **Holiday Cocktail**[17] 2283 8-11-10 **108**..........................(p) DougieCostello 106
(John Quinn) *chsd ldrs: pushed along 4th: one pce appr 2 out* **7/1**

5BP6 **6** 2 **Lady Wright (IRE)**[20] 1147 7-10-5 **89**................................ BrianHarding 84
(Michael Easterby) *t.k.h: trckd ldrs: rdn and outpcd appr 2 out* **11/2**[3]

4642 **7** 1 1/4 **Galley Slave (IRE)**[7] 1253 5-9-7 **84** oh7.......................... JoeCornwall(7) 78
(Michael Chapman) *t.k.h: trckd ldrs: drvn 3 out: outpcd appr next* **11/1**

1150 **8** 3 1/4 **Ardesia (IRE)**[12] 1147 6-10-9 **93**.. BrianHughes 84
(Tina Jackson) *led: hdd appr 2 out: lost pl after last* **8/1**

4m 28.3s (21.60) **Going Correction** +1.225s/f (Heav) **8** Ran SP% **114.1**
Speed ratings (Par 105): **98,96,96,95,94 93,92,91**
toteswingers:1&2:£3.00, 1&3:£3.80, 2&3:£6.40 CSF £18.78 CT £91.95 TOTE £3.10: £1.10, £1.10, £5.90; EX 19.50.
Owner S F Cooper **Bred** J Mangan **Trained** Edgcote, Northants

FOCUS
An ordinary handicap, run at a steady gallop.

NOTEBOOK
Topenhall(IRE)'s winning time was nearly three seconds slower than that of the identically rated winner of the earlier novice hurdle. Absent for a year and in need of screws in a foreleg after acquisition from Ireland, the 9-y-o suffered no repeat of the last-flight error which killed off a possible winning opportunity over C&D last time, and despite edging over to his left close home stuck to the task willingly enough for a first ever handicap win. The form needs treating with a little caution, but his ability to produce some late tactical speed still appears to be there. (op 4-1 tchd 10-3)
High Bird Humphrey has now made the frame 14 times but only converted one of those into a victory. He may have preferred a truer test at the trip on this occasion but is best left alone for win purposes. (tchd 7-2)
Phoenix Eye ran a very similar race to his previous two, both around this course (one over C&D), in delivering an effort up the straight that quickly reached a plateau. His 36 hurdles starts have yielded just two wins, and the impression remains that plenty will need to fall his way to attain the third. (op 13-2)
Liberty Seeker(FR)'s recent C&D win came in a non-handicap seller. He last won a handicap hurdle in October 2004 and he never looked like putting that right even before clattering the last. (op 7-1 tchd 17-2)
Holiday Cocktail found a mark still 19lb above his sole winning mark in handicap hurdles a bit beyond him. (op 6-1 tchd 11-2)
Lady Wright(IRE) was unable to quicken and likely paid for running with a choke out. (op 7-1 tchd 5-1)

1329 TURFTV H'CAP HURDLE (10 hdls) 2m 5f
7:50 (7:51) (Class 4) (0-110,110) 4-Y-O+ **£2,740** (£798; £399)

Form RPR

-3P4 **1** **All For The Cause (IRE)**[52] 857 8-11-12 **110**.............(t) AndrewTinkler 114+
(John Davies) *hld up in last: gd hdwy appr 2 out: led after 2 out: hit last: drvn 3 l clr: all out* **16/1**

2/6- **2** 1 **Kanonkop**[386] 1110 6-10-10 **97**.. AdamPogson(3) 99
(Charles Pogson) *trckd ldrs: t.k.h: led briefly appr 2 out: styd on run-in: clsng at line* **9/2**[3]

2535 **3** 4 **El Presidente (IRE)**[7] 1254 5-11-7 **108**........................(p) AlexMerriam(3) 109+
(Neil King) *hld up: hdwy 3 out: hung rt: hmpd next: kpt on same pce: tk 3rd run-in* **7/2**[2]

PP-5 **4** 6 **Plenty Of Chat (IRE)**[18] 1179 6-9-12 **89**....................(v[1]) MrTomDavid(7) 86+
(Tim Vaughan) *trckd ldrs: t.k.h: nt fluent 5th: nt fluent and led 7th: hdd and 3rd whn mstke 2 out: wknd run-in* **7/4**[1]

220- **5** 8 **Hippodrome (IRE)**[76] 5015 8-10-11 **102**.......................(p) MattCrawley(7) 90
(John Harris) *in rr: outpcd after 3 out: n.d whn hung bdly lft between last 2* **10/1**

050- **6** 23 **Owls FC (IRE)**[119] 5389 4-9-7 **86** oh7.............................. JoeCornwall(7) 49
(Michael Chapman) *t.k.h: trckd ldrs: mstke 1st: lost pl after 3 out: sn bhd* **33/1**

PP-6 **7** 4 1/2 **National Heritage**[57] 837 5-10-9 **93**.................................... BarryKeniry 54
(Micky Hammond) *chsd ldr: drvn 3 out: wknd appr next: sn bhd* **9/1**

4-0P **8** 24 **Oniz Tiptoes (IRE)**[82] 553 9-10-11 **98**.........................(p) HarryHaynes(3) 38
(John Wainwright) *led: qcknd 6th: hdd next: lost pl after 3 out: sn bhd* **12/1**

5m 49.9s (41.10) **Going Correction** +1.225s/f (Heav)
WFA 4 from 5yo+ 14lb **8** Ran SP% **112.4**
Speed ratings (Par 105): **70,69,68,65,62 54,52,43**
toteswingers:1&2:£9.90, 1&3:£9.60, 2&3:£3.00 CSF £83.96 CT £313.02 TOTE £24.30: £4.40, £1.40, £1.10; EX 146.90 Place 6 £114.17; Place 5 £51.65.
Owner J J Davies **Bred** Michael O'Shea **Trained** Piercebridge, Durham
■ The first training success for permit holder John Davies, a former amateur rider.

FOCUS
A weak handicap, run at an uneven pace.

NOTEBOOK
All For The Cause(IRE) let his other more vaunted rivals make their forward moves first once the tempo increased, and had just enough left after his own surge to hold on. Winless and latterly inconsistent in 18 starts since his last hurdles win, it will be interesting to see whether the recent change of scenery (this was his first run for permit-holder John Davies) and the tongue-tie debuted here can continue to inspire a revival. His novice chaser status also remains intact after 15 unsuccessful tries over fences. (op 10-1)
Kanonkop ◆ was a touch keen on her first start in over a year, but still had enough in reserve to take the lead momentarily two from home and then bear down on the winner close home. Her strike-rate over hurdles is nothing special (albeit almost entirely compiled for another yard), but on this showing there is another race of this nature in her if she can remain sound. (op 11-2)
El Presidente(IRE) may not have been done many favours by some scrimmaging two from home, but it would be stretching things to say it cost him that much closer a finishing position. He remains tricky to win with this summer. (op 4-1)
Plenty Of Chat(IRE)'s jumping unravelled on his chasing debut back in March, and for the second race in succession since then (both over hurdles) he took his obstacles with little fluency or confidence. It's difficult to know if the first-time visor helped or hindered the problem. (tchd 13-8)
National Heritage raced more prominently than over 2m1f here last time, and didn't appear to stay. (op 16-1)
T/Plt: £138.10 to a £1 stake. Pool:£31,303.24 - 165.42 winning tickets T/Qpdt: £47.00 to a £1 stake. Pool:£4,205.66 - 66.12 winning tickets WG

[1226]NEWTON ABBOT (L-H)
Saturday, August 21

OFFICIAL GOING: Good (good to soft in places) changing to good to soft after race 2 (2.40)
All bends moved out since last meeting but impact on distances not notified.
Wind: Mild across Weather: Overcast but muggy

1330 BET ON TOTESCOOP6 AT TOTESPORT.COM JUVENILE HURDLE (8 hdls) 2m 1f
2:10 (2:10) (Class 4) 3-Y-O **£3,577** (£1,050; £525; £262)

Form RPR

1414 **1** **Gulf Punch**[3] 1279 3-11-0 0..(p) JimmyDerham(5) 103+
(Milton Harris) *trckd ldrs: rdn after 3 out: led bef 2 out: nt fluent last: kpt on: drvn out* **8/1**[3]

11 **2** 1/2 **Beyond (IRE)**[41] 960 3-11-12 0.. APMcCoy 108
(Evan Williams) *led: rdn after 5th: hdd wl after 3 out: swtchd rt after next: rallying and ev ch whn nt fluent last: kpt on but no ex* **4/11**[1]

04 **3** 36 **Storm Command (IRE)**[11] 1226 3-10-9 0.................. RichardKilloran(3) 62
(Tim Vaughan) *hmpd 1st: trckd ldr: rdn 5th: ev ch 3 out: wknd qckly: t.o* **33/1**

0 **4** 6 **Baltic Ben (USA)**[9] 1234 3-10-12 0.............................. TomScudamore 57
(Tim Vaughan) *hld up: hdwy bef 5th: sn rdn: wknd 3 out: t.o* **25/1**

5 4 **Othello (IRE)**[30] 3-10-9 0... RichieMcLernon(3) 53
(Jonjo O'Neill) *w ldr: hit 4th: rdn next: wknd 3 out: t.o* **20/1**

3 **6** 5 **Massachusetts**[9] 1234 3-10-12 0.................................(p) JohnnyFarrelly 49
(Brendan Powell) *trckd ldrs: rdn bef 5th: wknd 3 out: t.o* **22/1**

0 **7** 19 **Charmeur (USA)**[22] 1135 3-10-12 0...............................(t) TomO'Brien 31
(Philip Hobbs) *trckd ldrs rdn bef 5th: wknd 3 out: t.o* **8/1**[3]

P **Ocean Club**[47] 3-10-7 0... SamTwiston-Davies(5) —
(Nigel Twiston-Davies) *hmpd 1st: hld up: rdn after 5th: wknd 3 out: t.o whn p.u bef next* **7/1**[2]

4m 13.3s (7.60) **Going Correction** +0.05s/f (Yiel) **8** Ran SP% **123.9**
Speed ratings (Par 102): **84,83,66,64,62 59,50,—**
toteswingers: 1&2 £1.40, 1&3 £27.30, 2&3 £9.70. CSF £12.58 TOTE £10.20: £2.00, £1.02, £6.90; EX 22.50.
Owner John Gwynne **Bred** Brook Stud Bloodstock Ltd **Trained** Herridge, Wiltshire

FOCUS
Just a modest juvenile hurdle.

NOTEBOOK
Gulf Punch, already twice successful over hurdles, including over C&D, had no trouble with the cut in the ground and held on well having taken over before the first in the straight.
Beyond(IRE), another with a double penalty, having won both starts, had concerns regarding the ground, but gave it a good go and may still have won with slicker jumping. He can probably win again back on better ground, but will struggle once the better types emerge. (op 4-9)
Massachusetts Official explanation: jockey said gelding lost a shoe
Charmeur(USA) failed to improve for a first-time tongue-tie. (tchd 15-2)

1331 MORE LIVE FOOTBALL BETTING AT TOTESPORT.COM NOVICES' H'CAP CHASE (20 fncs) 3m 2f 110y
2:40 (2:47) (Class 5) (0-95,95) 4-Y-O+ **£2,797** (£821; £410; £205)

Form RPR

2635 **1** **Rudinero (IRE)**[19] 1159 8-9-11 **71** oh1 ow2.......(t) SamTwiston-Davies(5) 96+
(Barry Brennan) *disp ld: nt fluent 10th: outrt ldr 15th: styd on strly to draw clr fr after 4 out: eased run-in* **9/2**[1]

3151 **2** 6 **Justabout**[19] 1159 7-11-12 **95**..(t) JoeTizzard 108
(Colin Tizzard) *trckd ldrs: nt fluent 10th: chsd wnr fr after 15th: hld whn mstke 3 out (water): styd on same pce* **7/1**

124P **3** 3 3/4 **Moon Melody (GER)**[32] 1048 7-10-1 **73**................................ DPFahy(3) 84
(Evan Williams) *in tch: hdwy 4 out: rdn to dispute 2nd but no ch w wnr fr next: no ex fr last* **9/1**

5052 **4** 14 **Bathwick Breeze**[11] 1232 6-11-3 **86**............................(v) TomScudamore 83
(David Pipe) *mid-div: hdwy 14th: rdn after next: no ch fr 4 out* **6/1**[3]

3343 **5** 3 1/4 **Fongoli**[23] 1126 4-10-3 **87**..(v) AidanColeman 66
(Brendan Powell) *disp ld tl 15th: sn rdn: wknd after 4 out* **14/1**

3442 **6** 60 **Lord Lescribaa (FR)**[19] 1159 7-10-12 **81**..............................(tp) RhysFlint 21
(Philip Hobbs) *mid-div: rdn after 13th: wknd after 15th: t.o* **5/1**[2]

/60U **7** 4 1/2 **Penric**[31] 1059 10-10-9 **78**... WillKennedy 14
(Martin Bosley) *reminders after 13th: a towards rr: t.o fr 16th* **33/1**

-056 **P** **Konigsbote (GER)**[23] 1126 8-11-4 **87**.............................(p) PaulMoloney —
(Sophie Leech) *mid-div: nt fluent 4th (water): rdn in rr after 13th: t.o whn p.u bef 15th* **20/1**

25 **P** **Cinaman (IRE)**[25] 1100 6-10-7 **76**.................................. RichardJohnson —
(Tim Vaughan) *nt a fluent: hld up: hdwy after 14th: rdn after 16th: wknd after next: modest 5th whn p.u bef last* **5/1**[2]

6354 **P** **Von Galen (IRE)**[19] 1159 9-11-0 **83**...................................(p) SamJones —
(Michael Scudamore) *trckd ldrs: lost pl and drvn after 13th: sn bhd: t.o whn p.u bef 3 out* **15/2**

6m 43.3s (-1.30) **Going Correction** +0.05s/f (Yiel)
WFA 4 from 6yo+ 3lb **10** Ran SP% **114.4**
Speed ratings (Par 103): **103,101,100,95,95 77,75,—,—,—**
toteswingers: 1&2 £9.00, 1&3 £16.80, 2&3 £25.20. CSF £35.68 CT £270.59 TOTE £6.90: £2.10, £2.40, £2.60; EX 43.90.
Owner David Gibbons **Bred** A J Keane And Stephen Ryan **Trained** Lambourn, Berks

FOCUS
A low-grade handicap chase.

NOTEBOOK
Rudinero(IRE), a beaten favourite at the course last time, was 3lb 'wrong' at the weights, but that made no difference at all and he powered clear under a more positive ride this time to win with ease. Connections will no doubt want to get him out again soon as the handicapper is sure to have his say now. (op 6-1)
Justabout, winner of the race contested by Rudinero earlier in the month, had his chance and appeared to run every bit as well off this 8lb higher mark. (tchd 6-1)
Moon Melody(GER) didn't run badly, finishing clear of the remainder. (op 8-1)
Bathwick Breeze failed to reproduce his best form back over fences. (tchd 13-2 in a place)
Lord Lescribaa(FR) ran below par. (op 6-1)

The Form Book, Raceform Ltd, Compton, RG20 6NL

Cinaman(IRE) was again disappointing and looks to be going the wrong way. (tchd 9-2 and 11-2)

1332 LORD MILDMAY MEMORIAL H'CAP CHASE (LISTED RACE) (16 fncs) 2m 5f 110y

3:15 (3:16) (Class 1) (0-150,142) 4-Y-0+

£22,532 (£8,488; £4,248; £2,124; £1,064; £532)

Form RPR

-111 **1** **Passato (GER)**[41] 959 6-11-3 **133**.....(t) TomO'Brien 141+
(Joanna Davis) *travelled wl in tch: hdwy 4 out: led sn after 3 out: sn hrd pressed: rdn after last: kpt on gamely* **14/1**

2211 **2** ½ **Classic Swain (USA)**[11] 1229 5-11-6 **136**.....(bt) RWalsh 143+
(Paul Nicholls) *sltly hmpd 1st: mid-div: hdwy 11th: chal u.str.p fr 3 out: ev ch last: kpt on but no ex nr fin* **9/2**[1]

2F44 **3** 4 ½ **Silverburn (IRE)**[35] 1020 9-10-12 **128**..... PaulMoloney 132+
(Evan Williams) *bdly hmpd 1st: mid-div: rdn after 11th: plenty to do 4 out: styd on fr 2 out: wnt 3rd run-in but no ch w ldrs* **12/1**

0/-1 **4** 2 ¼ **Swing Bill (FR)**[47] 909 9-10-6 **125**..... DannyCook(3) 130+
(David Pipe) *hmpd 1st: hld up towards rr: hdwy whn mstke 12th: cl 4th but rdn whn mstke 3 out (water): styd on same pce fr next* **9/2**[1]

1P2- **5** 1 ½ **Quilinton (FR)**[151] 4795 6-10-11 **127**.....(p) HaddenFrost 126
(David Pipe) *trckd ldrs: led 10th tl rdn sn after 3 out: styd on same pce* **14/1**

F-06 **6** 2 ¼ **Pablo Du Charmil (FR)**[35] 1020 9-11-12 **142**.....(t) TomScudamore 140
(David Pipe) *sltly hmpd 1st: mid-div: rdn after 11th: nvr able to get on terms* **8/1**[3]

-P44 **7** 2 **Postmaster**[25] 1110 8-10-13 **132**..... DPFahy(3) 128
(Evan Williams) *hmpd 1st: hld up towards rr: rdn after 12th: sme late prog: wnt lft last: nvr a danger* **50/1**

4U- **8** 13 **Pallasmore (IRE)**[20] 1156 7-10-12 **128**.....(b) MDarcy 111
(Paul W Flynn, Ire) *wnt rt 1st and hmpd: trckd ldrs: rdn after 11th: pckd 4 out: wknd bef 2 out* **10/1**

-130 **9** 8 **Valley Ride (IRE)**[35] 1020 10-10-13 **132**.....(p) DonalDevereux(3) 108
(Peter Bowen) *prom tl 10th: sn rdn: wknd 4 out* **14/1**

430- **10** 50 **Au Courant (IRE)**[133] 5126 10-11-0 **130**.....(b) LeightonAspell 61
(Sophie Leech) *bdly hmpd 1st: nvr travelling in rr after: rdn after 9th: wknd after next: t.o* **22/1**

100- **P** **Star Of Germany (IRE)**[308] 1784 10-11-5 **135**..... DenisO'Regan —
(Ian Williams) *hld up in rr of mid-div: struggling after 9th: t.o whn p.u after 4 out* **16/1**

111F **P** **Grand Slam Hero (IRE)**[24] 1123 9-11-8 **138**.....(t) PaddyBrennan —
(Nigel Twiston-Davies) *v bdly hmpd 1st: nt rcvr: p.u after next* **7/1**[2]

6/0 **P** **Killenaule Boy**[25] 1113 8-11-2 **132**..... JohnnyFarrelly —
(David Pipe) *raced keenly: trckd ldrs: rdn after 10th: sn wknd: t.o whn p.u after 4 out* **40/1**

-1P0 **P** **Keepitsecret (IRE)**[35] 1020 9-11-0 **130**..... APMcCoy —
(Jonjo O'Neill) *led tl 10th: rdn after next: blnd 12th: wknd 4 out: t.o whn p.u bef 2 out* **25/1**

-122 **F** **Dead Or Alive (IRE)**[25] 1103 7-10-11 **127**.....(t) RichardJohnson —
(Tim Vaughan) *fell 1st* **20/1**

1-51 **B** **Radetsky March (IRE)**[32] 1044 7-10-12 **128**..... SamThomas —
(Mark Bradstock) *prom whn v bdly hmpd and b.d 1st (knocked over)* **10/1**

5m 22.5s (1.10) **Going Correction** +0.325s/f (Yiel) **16 Ran SP% 129.1**
Speed ratings (Par 111): **111,110,109,108,107 107,106,101,98,80 —,—,—,—,— —**
toteswingers: 1&2 £18.80, 1&3 not won, 2&3 £19.50. CSF £78.08 CT £818.08 TOTE £19.10: £3.00, £2.00, £2.50, £2.30; EX 112.80.
Owner P Ponting **Bred** Gestut Hof Ittlingen **Trained** East Garston, Berks

FOCUS
A competitive Listed chase that was dominated by two in-form sorts. Several of these had their chance compromised at the first fence, when Dead Or Alive fell, bringing down Radetsky March and interfering badly with a few others.

NOTEBOOK
Passato(GER), up another 9lb in his bid for a four-timer, moved well into contention and then stayed on pluckily for strong pressure, always just holding the favourite. This was a good effort considering the ground would have been slower than ideal, and he will now be forced to contest even stronger races.
Classic Swain(USA), a ready winner here on his recent handicap debut over fences, had gone up 9lb, but still looked a leading player and, despite not travelling that well, kept responding to pressure to hold every chance from the end of the back straight. He couldn't stay on quite as well as the winner, though, and was made to settle for second. (op 4-1)
Silverburn(IRE) may have been a bit unfortunate as he got well back having been hampered early. He stayed on strongly down the straight, taking third, but never looked like reaching the front pair.
Swing Bill(FR), another interfered with early, had won with ease at the course on his return from a lengthy absence, but went up 12lb ahead of this handicap debut and, for all that he ran well, he never looked the winner. (op 11-2)
Quilinton(FR) tried to kick on but was reeled in readily enough in the end. (op 12-1)
Pablo Du Charmil(FR) was done no favours early and never got close enough to challenge. (op 10-1 tchd 12-1)

1333 GET LIVE FOOTBALL STATS AT TOTESPORT.COM NOVICES' H'CAP HURDLE (8 hdls) 2m 1f

3:50 (3:50) (Class 4) (0-110,110) 4-Y-0+ **£3,577** (£1,050; £525; £262)

Form RPR

0542 **1** **Be Ashored**[32] 1049 5-10-6 **90**..... RichardJohnson 101+
(Tim Vaughan) *hld up: nt fluent 1st: hit 4th: sn nudged along: hdwy after next: led 2 out: sn in command: comf* **5/4**[1]

2405 **2** 10 **Navajo Nation (IRE)**[23] 1125 4-10-9 **99**.....(p) TomO'Connor(5) 98
(Bill Turner) *trckd ldrs: nudged along after 4th: jnd ldr after 3 out: ev ch 2 out: sn rdn: kpt on same pce* **9/1**

12FU **3** 1 ¼ **Ajman (IRE)**[3] 1282 5-11-11 **109**.....(t) PaulMoloney 110+
(Evan Williams) *trckd ldrs: led 5th: rdn after 3 out: hdd whn blnd 2 out: 3rd and hld whn mstke last* **5/2**[2]

465- **4** 41 **Goose Green (IRE)**[6] 2249 6-11-3 **106**..... IanPopham(5) 67
(Ron Hodges) *led tl 5th: sn rdn: wknd after next: t.o* **14/1**

0-05 **5** 4 ½ **Bolanderi (USA)**[9] 1238 5-10-1 **85**.....(p) NickScholfield 42
(Andy Turnell) *trckd ldr: rdn and ev ch after 3 out: sn wknd* **16/1**

00-0 **P** **Kensington Oval**[19] 1160 5-11-7 **105**..... APMcCoy —
(Jonjo O'Neill) *trckd ldr tl after 4th: rdn after next: wknd qckly 3 out: p.u bef next* **6/1**[3]

22U- **P** **Holden Caulfield (IRE)**[305] 1840 5-11-5 **103**..... RodiGreene —
(Nick Ayliffe) *hld up: lost tch 5th: t.o whn p.u bef 2 out* **20/1**

4m 12.8s (7.10) **Going Correction** +0.325s/f (Yiel)
WFA 4 from 5yo+ 13lb **7 Ran SP% 114.6**
Speed ratings (Par 105): **96,91,90,71,69 —,—**
toteswingers: 1&2 £3.30, 1&3 £1.10, 2&3 £3.70. CSF £13.17 CT £25.31 TOTE £2.20: £1.10, £5.70; EX 15.20.
Owner optimumracing.co.uk **Bred** R Gittins & Helshaw Grange Stud **Trained** Aberthin, Vale of Glamorgan

FOCUS
This was won in good fashion by well-backed favourite Be Ashored.

NOTEBOOK
Be Ashored took over at the second from home and readily came clear. Second over 2m4f at Bangor latest, this shorter trip seemed to suit and, although he can expect a significant rise for this, it's likely he'll win again. (op 15-8)
Navajo Nation(IRE) has been struggling in selling hurdles, so this has to go down as an improved effort. (op 7-1 tchd 13-2)
Ajman(IRE) was quickly brushed aside two out, where he also blundered, and he ended up well held. (op 11-4 tchd 10-3)
Goose Green(IRE) deserves another chance back on faster ground. (op 11-1)
Kensington Oval again disappointed, stopping quickly. Official explanation: jockey said gelding was unsuited by the good to soft ground (tchd 5-1)

1334 40 LIVE FOOTBALL MARKETS AT TOTESPORT.COM H'CAP CHASE (13 fncs) 2m 110y

4:20 (4:20) (Class 4) (0-115,112) 4-Y-0+ **£4,553** (£1,337; £668; £333)

Form RPR

30-5 **1** **Bermuda Pointe (IRE)**[38] 985 8-11-8 **108**..... PaddyBrennan 111+
(Nigel Twiston-Davies) *chsd ldrs: led 7th: rdn after 3 out: kpt on: rdn out* **7/1**

6636 **2** ½ **Diaco (IRE)**[7] 1252 6-11-1 **101**..... APMcCoy 103
(Jonjo O'Neill) *hld up: pushed along after 6th: no imp and 11 l down 2 out: clsng on ldrs appr last: kpt on: wnt 2nd run-in: nt quite rch wnr* **11/1**

3512 **3** 2 ¼ **Indiana Gold (FR)**[7] 1252 6-10-11 **104**.....(p) OliverDayman(7) 104
(Alison Thorpe) *in tch: rdn after 4 out: chsd wnr 2 out: kpt on same pce: lost 2nd run-in* **9/2**[3]

3622 **4** 4 **Norborne Bandit (IRE)**[2] 1299 9-11-9 **109**.....(p) HarrySkelton 105
(Evan Williams) *hld up: nudged along after 6th: hdwy u.p after 3 out: kpt on same pce fr next* **6/1**

2114 **5** ½ **Folie A Deux (IRE)**[22] 1139 8-11-7 **112**.....(t) SamTwiston-Davies(5) 108
(Colin Tizzard) *led tl 4th: trckd ldrs: pressed ldr 9th tl next: sn rdn: one pce fr next* **4/1**[2]

1212 **6** 60 **Misamon (FR)**[3] 1283 7-10-10 **96**.....(v) PaulMoloney 38
(David Rees) *prom: nt fluent 8th: sn struggling: wknd bef 4 out: t.o* **13/8**[1]

4m 13.7s (7.20) **Going Correction** +0.325s/f (Yiel) **6 Ran SP% 111.4**
Speed ratings (Par 105): **96,95,94,92,92 64**
toteswingers: 1&2 £16.20, 1&3 £1.10, 2&3 £16.20. CSF £65.50 CT £374.44 TOTE £6.20: £7.00, £6.70; EX 65.00.
Owner Mrs S A Goodman **Bred** Edward Sexton **Trained** Naunton, Gloucs

FOCUS
A competitive handicap chase.

NOTEBOOK
Bermuda Pointe(IRE) appreciated the return to this trip. He's been struggling off higher marks, but was just 2lb higher than when last winning and the ease in the going wasn't a problem. (op 13-2)
Diaco(IRE), disappointing last time, closed up from the rear to hold every chance and ran a much-improved race, but couldn't quite reach the winner. (op 9-1)
Indiana Gold(FR) again ran well considering the ground had probably turned softer than ideal. (op 4-1)
Norborne Bandit(IRE) kept on late but never got close enough to challenge (op 5-1)
Folie A Deux(IRE) didn't get home having made the early running.
Misamon(FR), although ideally suited by better ground, has form with some cut, and the way he dropped away was disappointing. Official explanation: jockey said gelding was unsuited by the good to soft ground (op 9-4)

1335 TOTESPORT.COM HOME OF POOL BETTING H'CAP HURDLE (8 hdls) 2m 3f

4:55 (4:55) (Class 5) (0-95,95) 4-Y-0+ **£2,055** (£599; £299)

Form RPR

5350 **1** **Petit Fleur**[18] 1179 8-10-10 **84**..... SamTwiston-Davies(5) 97+
(Julian Smith) *hld up towards rr: hdwy after 5th: led 3 out: drew clr fr 2 out: v easily* **6/1**[3]

2265 **2** 12 **Amazing Request**[19] 1164 6-10-5 **81**.....(p) MissIsabelTompsett(7) 83+
(Bernard Llewellyn) *chsd ldrs: ev ch 3 out: sn rdn: kpt on but hld fr bef next* **7/2**[2]

04P1 **3** 5 **Strumble Head (IRE)**[2] 1300 5-10-12 **84** 7ex.....(b) DonalDevereux(3) 82+
(Peter Bowen) *mid-div: hdwy 6th: sn rdn: ev ch briefly 3 out: styd on same pce* **5/2**[1]

0554 **4** 3 **Young Tot (IRE)**[2] 1300 12-9-9 **69** oh3.....(t) IanPopham(5) 62
(Carroll Gray) *in tch tl outpcd after 6th: styd on again fr 2 out: wnt 4th bef last* **16/1**

6-5P **5** 5 **Mangonel**[19] 1164 6-10-8 **77**.....(v) RodiGreene 66
(Stuart Howe) *led: hrd rdn after 6th: hdd next: grad fdd* **18/1**

3U/P **6** 12 **Starstruck Peter (IRE)**[67] 757 6-11-5 **93**.....(b) MarcGoldstein(5) 71
(Jim Best) *trckd ldrs: slow jump 2nd: rdn after 6th: wknd after 3 out* **12/1**

0P0P **P** **Ouste (FR)**[15] 1200 8-11-5 **95**.....(bt) OliverDayman(7) —
(Alison Thorpe) *mid-div: hit 5th: rdn after 6th: wknd next: bhd whn p.u bef 2 out* **16/1**

/53P **P** **Award Winning (IRE)**[34] 1028 9-10-5 **79** ow1.....(p) TomO'Connor(5) —
(John Berwick) *prom tl rdn after 5th: sn bhd: p.u after 3 out* **14/1**

441P **P** **New Rackheath (IRE)**[4] 1273 7-10-8 **84**.....(b) PeterHatton(7) —
(Mark Shears) *in tch: wnt 2nd tl rdn after 6th: wknd next: t.o whn p.u bef 2 out* **25/1**

6P **P** **Song In My Heart (IRE)**[26] 1095 5-11-0 **83**..... APMcCoy —
(Jonjo O'Neill) *a towards rr: t.o 6th: p.u after 3 out* **8/1**

660P **P** **Always Cruising (USA)**[9] 1237 5-10-10 **79**.....(t) NickScholfield —
(Linda Blackford) *mid-div tl 5th: lost tch qckly: p.u bef next* **28/1**

00-P **P** **Barton Alf**[96] 371 6-11-11 **94**..... RichardJohnson —
(Neil Mulholland) *a bhd: t.o 6th: p.u after 3 out* **14/1**

4m 38.4s (4.50) **Going Correction** +0.325s/f (Yiel)
WFA 4 from 5yo+ 13lb **12 Ran SP% 121.5**
Speed ratings (Par 103): **103,97,95,94,92 87,—,—,—,— —,—**
toteswingers: 1&2 £2.20, 1&3 £3.00, 2&3 £3.30. CSF £28.58 CT £68.05 TOTE £7.80: £2.30, £1.90, £1.90; EX 23.10.
Owner Exors Of The Late Donald Smith **Bred** Mrs W Smith **Trained** Tirley, Gloucs
■ Stewards' Enquiry : Miss Isabel Tompsett two-day ban: used whip with excessive frequency (tbn)

FOCUS
A moderate handicap hurdle.

NOTEBOOK
Petit Fleur made good headway to lead and then came right away in the straight. This was a first handicap win for the mare and connections will no doubt want to try to get her out under a penalty, as life will be much tougher once the handicapper has had a say. (op 11-2)
Amazing Request bounced back to form, sticking on well without proving a match for the winner. (op 6-1)

Strumble Head(IRE), penalised for his Stratford win just two days earlier, was faced with softer ground this time and didn't prove quite as effective.
Young Tot(IRE) didn't run badly from 3lb out of the handicap.

1336 BET ON LIVE TENNIS AT TOTESPORT.COM H'CAP HURDLE (12 hdls) 3m 3f
5:30 (5:31) (Class 4) (0-100,100) 4-Y-0+ **£3,252** (£955; £477; £238)

Form RPR
PP-1 **1** **Caheerloch (IRE)**[11] 1232 8-10-11 **90**................. SamTwiston-Davies(5) 95+
(Nigel Twiston-Davies) *hld up in last pair: hdwy 9th: rdn to ld whn pckd 2 out: hit last: styd on: rdn out* **7/2**[2]
1-P0 **2** *1 ½* **Chico Time (IRE)**[26] 1094 9-11-5 **100**......................(p) MrSO'Donovan(7) 103
(Norma Twomey) *led: j.rt thrght: rdn 5 l clr after 3 out: hdd 2 out: ev ch last: kpt on but no ex* **11/1**
6/11 **3** *9* **Kopylova**[45] 930 7-11-12 **100**................................ RichardJohnson 95
(Tim Vaughan) *trckd ldrs: hung rt after 8th: wnt 2nd whn carried rt next: rdn after 3 out: sn one pce* **11/4**[1]
5-32 **4** *2 ½* **Heezagrey (IRE)**[31] 1059 7-10-4 **78**................................. TomO'Brien 70
(James Evans) *trckd ldrs: rdn after 9th: one pce fr after 3 out* **6/1**
3060 **5** *8* **Sea Cliff (IRE)**[19] 1162 6-11-3 **91**.................................... APMcCoy 76
(Jonjo O'Neill) *hld up bhd ldrs: rdn after 3 out: no imp: wknd bef last* **10/1**
-666 **6** *10* **Orion Express**[11] 1230 9-11-7 **95**................................ AidanColeman 71
(Susan Gardner) *hld up last: tk clsr order after 8th: effrt 3 out: sn wknd* **15/2**
10-6 **7** *27* **Synonymy**[50] 232 7-10-12 **86**.....................................(b) NickScholfield 38
(Michael Blanshard) *trckd ldrs: hit 2nd: jnd ldr whn bmpd 4th: blnd 6th: rdn 9th: wknd after 3 out: t.o* **16/1**
0P-2 **P** **Treasury Counsel (IRE)**[41] 955 8-11-0 **88**...................... PaulMoloney —
(Evan Williams) *hld up in tch: rdn after 9th: wknd after 3 out: p.u bef next* **5/1**[3]

7m 3.60s (22.60) **Going Correction** +0.325s/f (Yiel) **8** Ran SP% **114.9**
Speed ratings (Par 105): **79,78,75,75,72 69,61,—**
toteswingers: 1&2 £10.50, 1&3 £3.00, 2&3 £14.00. CSF £39.98 CT £119.87 TOTE £4.90: £1.80, £4.80, £1.10; EX 71.70 Place 6 £204.30; Place 5 £154.59.
Owner One For The Road Partnership **Bred** Ballylinch Stud **Trained** Naunton, Gloucs

FOCUS
There wasn't much pace on in this low-grade staying handicap hurdle.

NOTEBOOK
Caheerloch(IRE), raised 5lb for his recent course success, managed to follow up despite hitting the last, staying on well for pressure and showing this longer trip not to be a problem. (tchd 3-1)
Chico Time(IRE) had the run of things and returned to something like her best. (op 14-1 tchd 10-1)
Kopylova, seeking the hat-trick, had much softer ground to contend with this time and came up short off her new 8lb higher mark. (op 7-2)
Heezagrey(IRE) was a little below par. (op 11-2 tchd 5-1)
Treasury Counsel(IRE) showed nothing like the form he did last time, appearing to dislike the ground. (tchd 13-2)
T/Plt: £151.40 to a £1 stake. Pool:£56,029.41- 270.15 winning tickets T/Qpdt: £25.60 to a £1 stake. Pool:£3,416.58 - 98.54 winning tickets TM

1114 PERTH (R-H)
Saturday, August 21
OFFICIAL GOING: Good (good to soft in places; 7.1)
All bends moved out but impact on distances not notified.
Weather: Cloudy

1337 NEW HOMES AT THE MILL BALGOWAN MAIDEN HURDLE (8 hdls) 2m 110y
3:00 (3:00) (Class 4) 4-Y-0+ **£3,082** (£898; £449)

Form RPR
05-3 **1** **Jewelled Dagger (IRE)**[14] 1104 6-10-12 101....................... GrahamLee 111+
(Jim Goldie) *mde all: rdn 2 out: pressed whn hit last: drvn and hld on wl* **5/2**[2]
66F2 **2** *1* **Duty Free (IRE)**[24] 1114 6-10-9 112................................... RyanMania(3) 110+
(James Moffatt) *sltly rel to r and lost 15 l at s: rcvrd to trck ldrs bef bef 3rd: chal whn hit last: sn drvn: no ex fnl 100yds* **13/8**[1]
0-0 **3** *6* **Morning Time (IRE)**[25] 1104 4-10-11 104...................... PeterBuchanan 103
(Lucinda Russell) *midfield: hdwy to chse ldr 2 out: kpt on same pce* **7/1**
P- **4** *4 ½* **Rain Stops Play (IRE)**[19] 320 8-10-9 0.................. FearghalDavis(3) 99
(Nicky Richards) *hld up: rdn bef 3 out: kpt on: nvr trbld ldrs* **20/1**
04U0 **5** *3 ¼* **Piccolo Pride**[24] 1115 5-10-12 82...............................(t) MichaelMcAlister 95
(Maurice Barnes) *prom: rdn bef 2 out: sn wknd* **20/1**
6 *1 ¾* **Makhaaleb (IRE)**[23] 808 4-10-11 0....................................... PCarberry 93
(Gordon Elliott, Ire) *midfield: rdn after 3 out: sn no imp* **9/2**[3]
7 *hd* **Latin Connection (IRE)**[48] 894 4-10-11 0............................ AELynch 93
(S R B Crawford, Ire) *hld up: mstke 3 out: sn btn* **40/1**
0 **8** *20* **Dramatic Jewel (USA)**[51] 870 4-10-8 0................... CampbellGillies(3) 72
(Lucinda Russell) *in tch: nt fluent 3 out: sn rdn: wknd after 2 out* **28/1**
-PPP **F** **Modestine**[52] 858 8-10-0 0...................................(p) JamesHalliday(5) —
(Jane Walton) *cl 2nd whn fell 2nd* **100/1**

(0.30) **Going Correction** -0.10s/f (Good)
WFA 4 from 5yo+ 13lb **9** Ran SP% **113.7**
Speed ratings (Par 105): **95,94,91,89,88 87,87,77,—**
toteswingers:1&2:£1.10, 1&3:£2.60, 2&3:£3.00 CSF £6.64 TOTE £2.90: £1.30, £1.10, £2.00; EX 5.60.
Owner A R M Galbraith, Billy Robinson **Bred** Ballyhane Stud **Trained** Uplawmoor, E Renfrews

FOCUS
A very ordinary maiden.

NOTEBOOK
Jewelled Dagger(IRE) made all in the end to open his account over hurdles at the sixth attempt. He was still going very well turning for home and, while he was gifted the run of the race, there was a fair bit to like about his attitude in completing the task. It was his first success since a prolific season on the level back in 2007, so while he will look vulnerable under a penalty, his confidence should be nicely boosted by this. (op 3-1 tchd 9-4)
Duty Free(IRE) finished second to a stablemate of the winner over course and distance last time out, and again managing to find one too good, remains winless over hurdles now after 11 attempts. After needing plenty of encouragement to adopt a handy position, he was badly hampered at the second and proved a little free after as a result, but still had every chance. The winner was just that bit more resolute, however. (tchd 15-8)
Morning Time(IRE) fared best of those coming from off the pace. He was going well three out, but lacked a change of gear to get seriously involved and may prefer a stiffer test. This was a much more encouraging display on just his second outing for connections. (op 8-1)
Rain Stops Play(IRE) was having his first outing over hurdles since pulling up on his debut in this sphere last May. He got going too late, suggesting a stronger gallop would've suited, and could build on this when switching to low-grade handicaps. (op 16-1)
Makhaaleb(IRE) didn't offer too much on this return to jumping. (op 7-2)
Dramatic Jewel(USA) was going as well as any when making up ground around three out, but dropped out from the home turn due to his reluctance to settle. Once consenting to relax as a hurdler, he ought to find improvement, and being faced with a better early gallop would also obviously help on that front.

1338 FEARLESS FREDDIE WILLIAMS NOVICES' H'CAP CHASE (15 fncs) 2m 4f 110y
3:30 (3:33) (Class 4) (0-115,114) 4-Y-0+ **£4,553** (£1,337; £668; £333)

Form RPR
32F2 **1** **Emotive**[25] 1100 7-10-0 **91**.. CampbellGillies(3) 101+
(Barry Murtagh) *prom: j. into ld 11th: rdn 3 out: kpt on wl* **11/4**[1]
310U **2** *5* **King Roonah**[24] 1117 6-11-12 **114**...(t) PCarberry 120+
(Gordon Elliott, Ire) *in tch: hit 10th: wnt 2nd 11th: rdn and kpt on one pce fr 3 out* **3/1**[2]
30- **3** *2 ¼* **More Equity**[153] 4756 8-11-2 **107**... RyanMania(3) 110
(P Monteith) *trckd ldrs: rdn and outpcd bef 11th: rallied to go 3rd after 4 out: kpt on same pce* **8/1**
4 *24* **Paint The Tape (IRE)**[16] 1190 7-10-0 **88**................................. AELynch 66
(J T R Dreaper, Ire) *hld up: rdn and wknd bef 3 out* **15/2**
4101 **5** *23* **Strobe**[25] 1100 6-10-3 **91**..(p) JimmyMcCarthy 46
(Lucy Normile) *led: j. slowly and hdd 11th: sn wknd* **3/1**[2]
2P52 **P** **Annibale Caro**[19] 1115 8-11-3 **105**.. GrahamLee —
(Jim Goldie) *hld up: j. slowly 3rd: p.u bef 7th* **7/1**[3]

5m 7.10s (-6.90) **Going Correction** -0.30s/f (Good) **6** Ran SP% **112.0**
Speed ratings (Par 105): **101,99,98,89,80 —**
toteswingers:1&2:£1.10, 1&3:£4.40, 2&3:£7.20 CSF £11.68 TOTE £3.90: £2.00, £1.40; EX 11.40.
Owner Hurst Farm Racing **Bred** Mrs J Mitchell **Trained** Low Braithwaite, Cumbria

FOCUS
A weak novice handicap chase, run at a fair gallop.

NOTEBOOK
Emotive gained belated reward for his consistency and did the job with something left up his sleeve. He was second off this mark over course and distance 25 days earlier and this easier ground proved more up his street. He is value for further as he was markedly idling on the run-in and this initial win over fences should boost his confidence plenty, but he does have a moderate strike-rate overall. Connections plan to run him next at Cartmel. (tchd 5-2)
King Roonah, who unseated here last time out, beat the winner comfortably when registering his only previous success in June. However, he was 9lb worse off this time and hampered his cause with some moderate jumping. (op 7-2 tchd 11-4)
More Equity probably blew up on the back straight as she rallied for pressure nearing the third-last. She was always being held by the first pair, though, and an error at the next fence didn't help. This first run for 153 days should put her spot on for her next assignment. (op 9-1)
Strobe was 6lb higher than when beating the winner over course and distance last month. He was still marginally ahead of that rival prior to blundering at the tenth and losing all chance. Official explanation: trainer said, regarding running, that the gelding made a mistake at the 5th and lost interest. (op 11-4 tchd 10-3)

1339 ECOSTEEL NOVICES' H'CAP HURDLE (10 hdls) 2m 4f 110y
4:00 (4:02) (Class 4) (0-115,107) 4-Y-0+ **£3,577** (£1,050; £525; £262)

Form RPR
3555 **1** **Fly Tipper**[25] 1102 10-10-4 **85**..(t) GrahamLee 87+
(Wilf Storey) *trckd ldrs: mstke 4 out: hit 3 out: rdn to ld 2 out: kpt on wl* **10/1**
01 **2** *2* **Cape Secret (IRE)**[8] 1247 7-11-12 **107**.................................. PCarberry 107+
(Gordon Elliott, Ire) *hld up in rr: hdwy after 3 out: rdn and ev ch last: one pce flat* **7/2**[2]
U-22 **3** *9* **Ormello (FR)**[24] 1117 8-11-3 **98**.. PeterBuchanan 88
(Lucinda Russell) *in tch: hdwy to chal 2 out: sn drvn: wknd appr last* **3/1**[1]
020/ **4** *9* **Soul Magic (IRE)**[486] 5143 8-9-7 **81** oh1...................... GaryRutherford(7) 62
(Harriet Graham) *trckd ldr: jnd ldr 4 out: stl ev ch 2 out: sn wknd* **28/1**
2331 **5** *2* **Maolisa (IRE)**[24] 1119 8-10-13 **97**.............................(p) CampbellGillies(3) 77
(S R B Crawford, Ire) *led: hdd appr 2 out: sn wknd* **4/1**[3]
602- **6** *26* **Hey Charlie (IRE)**[258] 2731 8-11-6 **104**.......................... FearghalDavis(3) 57
(Nicky Richards) *hld up: rdn and lost pl after 4 out: sn btn* **11/2**
6334 **7** *18* **Sunset Resort (IRE)**[37] 999 5-10-3 **82** ow2............(t) MichaelMcAlister 19
(Maurice Barnes) *awkward 1st: hld up: rdn and lost tch fr 4 out: wl bhd whn hit 3 out* **9/1**
8 *17* **Shiyrman (IRE)**[50] 879 4-10-12 **95**...(v1) AELynch 11
(J T R Dreaper, Ire) *hld up: hdwy to trck ldrs 4 out: rdn and wknd qckly after 3 out* **12/1**

5m 1.80s (-5.10) **Going Correction** -0.10s/f (Good)
WFA 4 from 5yo+ 14lb **8** Ran SP% **112.8**
Speed ratings (Par 105): **105,104,100,97,96 86,79,73**
toteswingers:1&2:£34.90, 1&3:£25.10, 2&3:£1.50 CSF £44.52 CT £131.48 TOTE £11.80: £2.60, £1.40, £1.90; EX 51.50.
Owner M D Townson **Bred** M D Townson **Trained** Muggleswick, Co Durham

FOCUS
A moderate novice handicap hurdle, run at a sound gallop.

NOTEBOOK
Fly Tipper, equipped with a first-time tongue-tie, dug deep when produced to lead from the penultimate flight and finally broke his duck, having taken five years to come good. He gets further than this and his jockey played his hand at just the right time here. Being a 10-y-o winning a novice event, though, dictates that this form is ordinary and he doesn't appeal as one to follow up. (op 11-1 tchd 9-1)
Cape Secret(IRE) was given a typical waiting ride by Paul Carberry and moved into contention going well turning into the home straight. He was given every chance from two out, but found the winner too strong. It must be noted he was conceding that rival 22lb, however, and he won't mind returning to a longer trip. (op 4-1 tchd 10-3)
Ormello(FR) had finished second on his last two outings over fences and was able to race off a 22lb lower mark on this return to hurdling, so this was obviously a big drop in class. He too had every chance, but failed to see it out like the first pair and looks well worth dropping back in trip in this sphere. (op 11-4)
Soul Magic(IRE) paid for his early exertions, but that wasn't surprising considering he was reappearing after a 486-day layoff. He looks to have begun life in handicaps on a workable mark and is entitled to come on a bundle for the run. (op 25-1)
Maolisa(IRE) was equipped with first-time cheekpieces despite having beaten a subsequent winner at this course on her previous outing. Racing off a 7lb higher mark, she set out to make all over this unsuitably sharper test and was done with before two out. (op 5-1)

1340 STANJAMES.COM (S) H'CAP HURDLE (8 hdls) 2m 110y
4:35 (4:35) (Class 5) (0-90,90) 4-Y-0+ **£2,055** (£599; £299)

Form RPR
-000 **1** **Perez (IRE)**[3] 948 8-9-13 **70**..(vt) PaulGallagher(7) 82+
(Wilf Storey) *in tch in chsng gp: wnt 3rd 4th: led 3 out: sn clr* **7/2**[3]
/0-0 **2** *21* **Arch**[74] 678 7-11-5 **90**.. MrGCrow(7) 81
(Sandy Forster) *hld up: hdwy after 3 out: tk 2nd after 2 out: nvr trbld wnr* **25/1**

43-5 **3** 2 ½ **Desert Soul**[41] 943 6-11-5 **83**........(t) MichaelMcAlister 73
(Maurice Barnes) *led: mstke 5th: hdd 3 out: lost 2nd after 2 out: plugged on* **6/1**

P-P4 **4** 3 ½ **Daraybad (FR)**[29] 1085 8-10-7 **78**........(v[1]) NathanMoscrop[(7)] 64
(Andrew Crook) *chsd clr ldrs: hdwy after 4th: rdn after 3 out: sn wknd* **12/1**

4255 **5** 30 **Bari Bay**[66] 762 4-10-13 **83**........ JamesHalliday[(5)] 37
(Michael Blake) *in tch in chsng gp: wknd after 5th* **5/2**[2]

-603 **6** 30 **We'Re Delighted**[31] 1060 5-11-7 **85**........(t) GrahamLee 10
(Michael Blake) *trckd ldr: nt fluent 5th: lost pl appr 3 out: sn wknd* **2/1**[1]

0-06 **P** **Shahramore**[41] 943 5-10-5 **69**........ WilsonRenwick —
(P Monteith) *hld up: reminders after 4th: t.o whn p.u bef 2 out* **20/1**

4m 0.30s (0.60) **Going Correction** -0.10s/f (Good)
WFA 4 from 5yo+ 13lb **7** Ran SP% **114.7**
Speed ratings (Par 103): **94,84,82,81,67 53,—**
toteswingers:1&2:£17.80, 1&3:£6.90, 2&3:£25.40 CSF £67.06 CT £509.31 TOTE £4.70: £2.20, £8.80; EX 74.60.The winner bought in for 5,200 guineas.
Owner H S Hutchinson **Bred** Calley House Syndicate **Trained** Muggleswick, Co Durham

FOCUS
A very weak affair and an effortless winner.

NOTEBOOK
Perez(IRE) ran out a very easy winner on his return to the smaller obstacles. It was the his first success over hurdles and a first since striking on the all-weather in 2006. The fact he scored so easily sums up the lowly form of this race and consistency is far from his strong suit, but he ought to be high on confidence now. He was bought in for 5,200gns. Official explanation: trainer said, regarding apparent improvement in form, that the gelding is quirky but decided to put its best foot forward in a poor race. (op 4-1)
Arch was given a patient ride and never threatened, but this was better on his debut for the stable after a 74-day break. (op 16-1)
Desert Soul set a sound gallop out in front and kept on for pressure once headed after four out, but he remains winless as a hurdler. (op 9-2)
Daraybad(FR), in a first-time visor, moved up going every bit as well as Perez on the inside nearing three out, but his response when push came to shove was disappointing. He too remains winless. (op 9-1)
We'Re Delighted eventually paid for refusing to settle and was eased off from the home turn. His long losing run continues. Official explanation: trainer had no explanation for the poor form shown (op 9-4 tchd 15-8)

1341 MURRAYSHALL HOUSE HOTEL H'CAP CHASE (18 fncs) 3m
5:10 (5:10) (Class 4) (0-110,101) 4-Y-0+ **£4,664** (£1,448; £779)

Form RPR

032/ **1** **Twelve Paces**[531] 4363 9-11-12 **101**........ WilsonRenwick 104+
(P Monteith) *hld up: hdwy to trck ldrs after 12th: chal fr 3 out: drvn to ld last: hung rt flat: all out* **11/2**[3]

/4-0 **2** nk **Kyber**[14] 1118 9-11-11 **100**........ GrahamLee 103+
(Jim Goldie) *hld up: hdwy after 12th: chal 3 out: rdr lost whip after 2 out: kpt on but a jst hld flat* **5/1**[2]

34 **3** 5 **Adrianeo (IRE)**[30] 1068 7-11-6 **95**........(p) PeterBuchanan 95
(S R B Crawford, Ire) *trckd ldrs: led 12th: rdn 3 out: hdd last: sn no ex flat* **8/1**

41P3 **P** **Thunder Hawk (IRE)**[25] 1103 10-10-11 **89**........(p) CampbellGillies[(3)] —
(Stuart Coltherd) *led: hdd 12th: wkng whn mstke 4 out: sn lost tch: p.u bef 3 out* **6/5**[1]

2P-4 **P** **Charming Knight (IRE)**[112] 91 9-10-8 **90**........ AlistairFindlay[(7)] —
(Jane Walton) *in tch: lost pl qckly after 4 out: p.u bef 3 out* **12/1**

-P35 **P** **Cute N You Know It**[29] 1081 7-9-12 **78**........(v[1]) JamesHalliday[(5)] —
(Andrew Crook) *disp ld tl slow 4th: nt fluent 6th: slow again 5 out and qckly lost tch: p.u bef 4 out* **5/1**[2]

6m 9.80s (-10.60) **Going Correction** -0.30s/f (Good) **6** Ran SP% **113.0**
Speed ratings (Par 105): **105,104,103,—,— —**
toteswingers:1&2:£5.40, 1&3:£4.20, 2&3:£15.60 CSF £32.10 TOTE £4.70: £2.10, £3.40; EX 10.80.
Owner D A Johnson **Bred** J W Haydon **Trained** Rosewell, Midlothian

FOCUS
Another moderate handicap chase and only three got home, but there was still a cracking finish.

NOTEBOOK
Twelve Paces was having his first outing since finishing a decent second on soft ground at Kelso in March 2009 and was carrying top weight, but his yard has shown in the past it can ready one after a layoff, and he just did enough to make a winning comeback, jumping really well in the main, and showed real guts considering his absence. He had been given a chance by the handicapper, but this rates a cracking training performance and he will still look feasibly treated after a likely rise. However, he will need sufficient time to recover from this. (op 5-1 tchd 13-2)
Kyber ◆ so nearly ended his losing run on this return to chasing. He came from a similar position from off the pace as Twelve Paces and travelled into contention just as well as that rival. His rider lost his whip, though, and looking at the margin of defeat that really has to go down as having made the difference. He certainly deserves a change of luck. (op 4-1 tchd 7-2)
Adrianeo(IRE) was up in trip for this handicap debut and turned in a much-improved performance, but he was outstayed by the first pair after the last. Slightly more patient tactics should see him find one of these. (op 7-1)
Thunder Hawk(IRE), a well-held third over C&D last time, was 3lb lower and proved popular. He got a positive ride, but was treading water approaching the home turn and his rider eventually called it a day. Official explanation: jockey said gelding was never travelling (op 7-4)
Charming Knight(IRE) Official explanation: jockey said gelding over-reached and lost a front shoe (op 7-4)

1342 PERTH BOOKMAKERS H'CAP HURDLE (8 hdls) 2m 110y
5:45 (5:45) (Class 3) (0-120,119) 4-Y-0+ **£4,878** (£1,432; £716; £357)

Form RPR

1 **Reportage (USA)**[16] 1189 4-10-12 **105**........ AELynch 109+
(Robert Alan Hennessy, Ire) *hdd after 1st: racd in 2nd: hdwy to trck ldr after 3 out: led 2 out: kpt on wl* **9/2**[3]

2013 **2** 3 ¼ **Baaher (USA)**[24] 1116 6-11-5 **118**........ PaulNorton[(7)] 118
(Jim Goldie) *hld up: stl 4th 2 out: rdn and kpt on to take 2nd on flat: nvr trbld wnr* **13/2**

0F1/ **3** 1 **Coolnaharan (IRE)**[48] 897 10-11-1 **110**........(p) CampbellGillies[(3)] 109
(S R B Crawford, Ire) *racd in 3rd: hdwy to hold ev ch after 3 out: rdn and one pce after 2 out: lost 2nd on flat* **18/1**

0/3 **4** 8 **Tiger King (GER)**[41] 948 9-9-9 **92** oh4........ JamesHalliday[(5)] 86
(P Monteith) *led after 1st: clr after 3rd: nt so far clr 3 out: hdd 2 out: sn wknd* **11/4**[2]

5311 **F** **Shopfrontspecialist (IRE)**[5] 1270 7-11-13 **119** 7ex........ PCarberry —
(Gordon Elliott, Ire) *in tch: fell 3rd* **11/10**[1]

3m 58.0s (-1.70) **Going Correction** -0.10s/f (Good)
WFA 4 from 6yo+ 13lb **5** Ran SP% **111.1**
Speed ratings (Par 107): **100,98,98,94,—**
CSF £29.70 TOTE £6.90: £3.10, £3.60; EX 42.60 Place 6 £337.58; Place 5 £259.32.
Owner Mrs S Hennessy **Bred** Gainsborough Farm Llc **Trained** Ratoath, Co Meath

FOCUS
The complexion of this modest handicap hurdle was completely changed when the favourite fell at the third flight. It was run at a good gallop and the second sets the level.

NOTEBOOK
Reportage(USA) eventually ran out a determined winner and landed his first success of any description at the 18th time of asking. He set off from the front, but his rider didn't panic when he was shortly headed by Tiger King. He took a little time to settle afterwards, but found what was required when produced to lead two out and, being a 4-y-o, is open to a little improvement now he has got his head in front. (op 11-2)
Baaher(USA) ran a fair race on his chasing debut last time and had got off the mark over C&D on his penultimate outing. He looked well held nearing two out, but rallied strongly for maximum pressure, albeit too late in the day. He rates a sound enough benchmark. (op 5-1 tchd 15-2)
Coolnaharan(IRE) came into this looking out of form and hadn't won over hurdles since 2008. He posted a much more encouraging effort in defeat, though. (op 16-1 tchd 20-1)
Tiger King(GER) was returning from a 41-day break and did plenty early on when gaining a clear lead. He was made to pay the price approaching the penultimate flight and is in need of a return to more patient tactics. (op 4-1)
Shopfrontspecialist(IRE) was expected to take all the beating in this, but got no further than the third. (op 10-11 tchd 5-6)
T/Plt: £178.30 to a £1 stake. Pool:£46,600.50 - 190.78 winning tickets T/Qpdt: £72.20 to a £1 stake. Pool:£2,743.71 - 28.10 winning tickets AS

[1330] NEWTON ABBOT (L-H)
Sunday, August 22

OFFICIAL GOING: Soft
All bends moved out since the previous day but impact on distances not notified.
Wind: Virtually nil Weather: Cloudy but dry

1343 TOTEPLACEPOT NOVICES' HURDLE (8 hdls) 2m 3f
2:00 (2:00) (Class 4) 4-Y-0+ **£3,577** (£1,050; £525; £262)

Form RPR

33- **1** **A Nun With A Gun (IRE)**[315] 1720 7-10-5 0........ TomO'Brien 112
(Alan Jones) *mid-div tl dropped towards rr 5th: shkn up and hdwy after 3 out: chal after 2 out: led run-in: pushed out* **16/1**

22 **2** nk **Scene Two**[26] 1111 4-10-10 114........ RichardJohnson 118+
(Philip Hobbs) *trckd ldrs: led after 3 out: rdn after 2 out: hdd run-in: kpt on but no ex* **15/8**[1]

-032 **3** 13 **Minneapolis**[48] 908 5-10-12 108........ LeightonAspell 106
(Alison Batchelor) *in tch: effrt after 3 out: no ch w ldng pair fr next: styd on same pce* **9/2**[3]

44 **4** 10 **Kavegirl**[23] 1140 7-10-5 92........ DavidEngland 90
(John Panvert) *trckd ldrs: rdn after 6th: wknd appr 2 out* **25/1**

2-12 **5** 1 ¼ **Five Out Of Five (IRE)**[32] 1058 6-11-12 125........(t) PaulMoloney 109
(Evan Williams) *led tl after 3 out: sn rdn: wknd bef next* **3/1**[2]

6045 **6** 2 ½ **Powerfullbeat**[12] 1228 6-10-5 96........(p) MrRHawkins[(7)] 92
(Kathleen Sanderson) *prom: rdn after 3 out: sn wknd* **40/1**

6212 **7** 9 **Saltagioo (ITY)**[20] 1160 6-11-7 128........(t) JimmyDerham[(5)] 97
(Milton Harris) *trckd ldrs: rdn after 3 out: wknd bef 2 out* **5/1**

F **8** 10 **Top Tide (IRE)**[35] 1028 9-10-9 0........ DannyCook[(3)] 73
(Martin Hill) *hld up towards rr: sme prog 3 out: wknd bef next* **40/1**

404- **9** ¾ **Miss Molly Moses**[154] 4767 6-10-5 0........ LiamHeard 65
(Gerald Ham) *struggling 5th: a towards rr* **66/1**

00/ **P** **Mr Tobias**[92] 13-10-12 0........ ChristianWilliams —
(C Roberts) *mid-div tl dropped to rr 4th: t.o whn p.u bef 6th* **150/1**

060- **P** **Just The Job (IRE)**[164] 4541 6-10-12 0........ DougieCostello —
(Neil Mulholland) *in tch tl wknd 5th: t.o whn p.u bef next* **40/1**

P **Rolanta (FR)**[154] 5-10-5 105........ HaddenFrost —
(James Frost) *a towards rr: wknd bef 3 out: p.u bef 2 out* **40/1**

4m 50.4s (16.50) **Going Correction** +0.725s/f (Soft)
WFA 4 from 5yo+ 13lb **12** Ran SP% **116.3**
Speed ratings (Par 105): **94,93,88,84,83 82,78,74,74,— —,—**
toteswingers: 1&2 £7.00, 1&3 £13.40, 2&3 £2.70. CSF £45.51 TOTE £16.10: £4.40, £1.80, £1.20; EX 57.40.
Owner BPD Ltd **Bred** James Barry **Trained** Coedkernew, Newport

FOCUS
All bends were moved after the previous day's card and the hurdles alignment was moved out by four metres, but impact on distances not notified. Following a wet afternoon on Saturday there were further showers before racing and the official going was officially amended to soft after the opener. That was an accurate description according to the jockeys.

NOTEBOOK
A Nun With A Gun(IRE) came from off the pace - she had seven in front of her jumping the third-last - to make a winning hurdles debut. Third in all four of her bumpers, she was suited by this greater test of stamina and leaving off the cheekpieces clearly had no adverse effect. (op 20-1)
Scene Two went on rounding the home turn but after diving at the penultimate flight he was edged out close home. He handled the ground well enough but has now found one to beat him on each of his three hurdling ventures, and there may be a question mark against his attitude. (op 2-1)
Minneapolis, placed on fast ground on his last two starts, could not go with the leaders from the home turn but did plug on for third. (op 5-1 tchd 11-2)
Kavegirl momentarily looked a threat when closing up turning out of the back straight but her effort soon flattened out. She was a little below the level of her previous efforts, which came on better ground.
Five Out Of Five(IRE), back over a more suitable trip, but doubly penalised, made the running before weakening tamely once headed. He jumped well enough this time, but the ground was an unknown and it has been reported that he has had breathing problems. (tchd 11-4)
Saltagioo(ITY), under a double penalty, was keen once again and he weakened badly on this rain-softened surface. He was reported to have lost his right-fore shoe. Official explanation: vet said gelding lost a right fore shoe (op 9-2 tchd 11-2)

1344 TOTEPOOL FLEXI BETTING CONDITIONAL JOCKEYS' MAIDEN HURDLE (8 hdls) 2m 1f
2:30 (2:31) (Class 5) 4-Y-0+ **£1,951** (£573; £286; £143)

Form RPR

532 **1** **Swiss Art (IRE)**[35] 1031 4-10-10 104........(p) OliverDayman[(3)] 102+
(Alison Thorpe) *mid-div: hdwy 3 out: led appr 2 out: sn in command: easily* **9/2**[3]

-321 **2** 9 **Jump Up**[19] 1180 4-10-13 0........ RhysFlint 93
(Keith Goldsworthy) *trckd ldrs: rdn to chse wnr appr 2 out: a being hld: styd on same pce* **9/2**[3]

3 2 ¼ **Mount Hadley (USA)**[60] 6-10-11 0........(t) HaddenFrost[(3)] 92
(David Pipe) *in tch: c wd for effrt ent st: styd on same pce fr 2 out* **13/2**

4 hd **Royial (FR)**[127] 5237 5-10-11 0........ JimmyDerham[(3)] 92
(Seamus Mullins) *hld up towards rr: rdn and hdwy after 3 out: styd on same pce fr next* **33/1**

5 2 3/4 **La Soie (IRE)**[369] 4-10-6 0 IanPopham 81
(James Frost) *hld up towards rr: mstke 2nd: rdn and hdwy after 3 out: styd on same pce fr next* **14/1**
03-0 **6** 7 **Flying Squad (UAE)**[54] 850 6-11-0 112 (t) PeterToole 84
(Milton Harris) *trckd ldr: led 3rd: rdn and hdd bef 2 out: sn wknd* **7/2**[2]
26 **7** 12 **Coeur De Lionne (IRE)**[5] 1278 6-10-11 0 (t) HarrySkelton(3) 74
(Paul Nicholls) *hld up towards rr: hdwy 3 out: rdn bef 2 out: sn btn* **11/4**[1]
4- **8** 48 **Operachy**[112] 4793 5-10-9 0 MarkQuinlan(5) 22
(James Frost) *trckd ldrs: rdn after 3 out: sn wknd: t.o* **25/1**
P **P** **Final Flyer (IRE)**[16] 1195 6-11-0 0 SamJones —
(Alison Thorpe) *awkward 1st: a towards rr: t.o whn p.u bef 2 out* **66/1**
PP- **P** **Saskatoon Lily (IRE)**[134] 5134 8-10-2 0 EdGlassonbury(5) —
(Malcolm Beck) *mid-div: blnd 4th: hdwy 5th: ev ch 3 out: sn rdn: wknd qckly: p.u bef next: b.b.v* **100/1**
P **Church Outing**[349] 1405 6-10-2 0 JeremiahMcGrath(5) —
(Susan Gardner) *led tl 3rd: chsd ldrs: rdn after 5th: sn wknd: t.o whn p.u bef 2 out* **66/1**

4m 30.5s (24.80) **Going Correction** +0.725s/f (Soft)
WFA 4 from 5yo+ 13lb 11 Ran SP% **116.0**
Speed ratings (Par 103): **70,65,64,64,63 60,54,31,—,— —**
toteswingers: 1&2 £3.20, 1&3 £2.80, 2&3 £10.40. CSF £24.35 TOTE £5.10: £1.60, £1.90, £3.00; EX 24.10.
Owner Phil Pye **Bred** John Yarr **Trained** Bronwydd Arms, Carmarthens

FOCUS
A decidedly modest maiden hurdle in which they took things very steadily for the first part of the race. The time was nearly 40 seconds outside the standard.

NOTEBOOK
Swiss Art(IRE) had stamina doubts, as his six wins on the Flat have all been at 7f-1m, but the sharp track helped. He acted well in the ground and ran out an easy winner, but was beaten in a seller last time and clearly has his limitations. There was evidence of his quirky side too as he wandered in front. (op 5-1)
Jump Up, winner of a Ffos Las bumper last time, made a pleasing hurdles debut but this represented an insufficient test of stamina for him. (op 7-2)
Mount Hadley(USA) was a fairly useful performer for Gerard Butler on the Flat but was another who had shown his best form at around a mile. Equipped with a tongue tie, but without the headgear he has been wearing, he ran a creditable race on this hurdles debut and handled the soft ground well enough. It was reported that he had lost his left-fore shoe. Official explanation: vet said gelding had lost a left fore shoe (op 7-1 tchd 9-1)
Royial(FR), who showed very little when trained in Ireland, was staying on at the end of this British debut and first start since April and nearly snatched third. (op 28-1)
La Soie(IRE) was placed in deep ground on two of her three starts in Ireland and she was not discredited on this hurdling debut, but she may need to jump better. (op 12-1)
Flying Squad(UAE) weakened tamely once headed and has now put in two moderate efforts since a promising run at Taunton last term. (op 4-1 tchd 10-3)
Coeur De Lionne(IRE) has now been a disappointing favourite twice in the space of six days. While the ground was probably a valid excuse here, he did back out of things pretty quickly and he does not look one to trust. (op 3-1 tchd 10-3)
Saskatoon Lily(IRE) Official explanation: jockey said that the mare bled from the nose

1345 TOTEPOOL A BETTER WAY TO BET NOVICES' CHASE (16 fncs) 2m 5f 110y
3:00 (3:00) (Class 3) 4-Y-0+ **£7,651** (£2,798)

Form RPR
3-13 **1** **Earth Dream (IRE)**[80] 592 7-11-3 120 MrRMahon(5) 132
(Paul Nicholls) *trckd ldrs: rdn after 4 out: wnt 2nd after 3 out: led bef last: styd on gamely: rdn out* **11/4**[3]
4-12 **2** 1 1/4 **Gee Dee Nen**[25] 822 7-11-8 130 JamieMoore 131
(Gary Moore) *j.w: prom: led after 4 out: rdn and hdd after 2 out: ev ch last: kpt on but no ex towards fin* **13/8**[1]
P1-1 **F** **Otage De Brion (FR)**[99] 329 8-11-7 142 MrSWaley-Cohen(5) 111
(Nigel Twiston-Davies) *led: rdn and hdd after 4 out: wknd after next: tired whn fell last* **7/4**[2]
0-0U **U** **Jocheski (IRE)**[27] 1091 6-11-2 0 AndrewTinkler —
(Tony Newcombe) *hld up: cl 4th whn slipped bdly and uns rdr 4 out* **12/1**

5m 39.9s (18.50) **Going Correction** +1.025s/f (Soft) 4 Ran SP% **108.8**
Speed ratings (Par 107): **107,106,—,—**
toteswinger: 1&2 £5.30. CSF £7.77 TOTE £2.30; EX 8.80.
Owner Mrs Catherine Penny **Bred** Gerald McStay **Trained** Ditcheat, Somerset

FOCUS
An interesting novice chase. Considering the conditions and the small field they went a reasonable gallop.

NOTEBOOK
Earth Dream(IRE) tracked the two market leaders and was temporarily outpaced by them, but he battled his way to the front between the last two fences. He jumped soundly and was suited by the return to a longer trip on this first run since June. Connections had been in two minds whether to run him in this ground, but he got through it well enough. (op 9-2)
Gee Dee Nen, another stepping back up from 2m, has run well in all three of his chases at this venue. After shadowing Otage De Brion he took it up after the fourth-last, but he could not hold off the winner in a good tussle. His sound jumping should see him back winning before long. (op 6-4 tchd 11-8)
Otage De Brion(FR) was sold out of Charlie Longsdon's yard for £66,000 after back-to-back wins at Bangor in the spring. Making the running again, but never given any peace by Gee Dee Nen, he was headed leaving the back and quickly beaten. He was tired when falling at the last and stayed down for about ten minutes, but had jumped pretty well otherwise. This was disappointing on the face of things, as he had 8lb in hand on official figures, but ground conditions had gone against him and he is worth another chance. (op 9-1)
Jocheski(IRE) was in touch, but had just started to be niggled along, when he slithered badly on landing over four out and lost the rider. It was unfortunate as he had jumped the fence well enough. (op 9-1)

1346 TOTESUPER7 H'CAP HURDLE (10 hdls) 2m 6f
3:30 (3:34) (Class 2) (0-140,139) 4-Y-0+
£18,666 (£5,523; £2,760; £1,380; £690; £348)

Form RPR
0000 **1** **Raslan**[36] 1019 7-10-9 125 (vt) DannyCook(3) 136+
(David Pipe) *disp ld: outrt ldr 3 out: in command fr 2 out: styd on strly: comf* **15/2**
1R21 **2** 3 3/4 **Battle Group**[21] 1150 5-11-2 129 TomScudamore 134
(David Pipe) *hld up towards rr: hdwy appr 6th: rdn after 3 out: styd on to chse wnr appr 2 out: a being hld* **8/1**
00-P **3** 10 **Secret Tune**[15] 1017 6-11-3 130 (b[1]) PaddyBrennan 128+
(Tom George) *hld up towards rr: racd wd: hdwy after 6th: rdn to chse wnr fr 3 out tl bef 2 out: styd on same pce* **12/1**
35/5 **4** 3 1/4 **Hollywood Law (IRE)**[15] 1211 9-10-9 122 ADLeigh 114
(D M Leigh, Ire) *towards rr: reminders after 2nd: hrd rdn fr after 6th: styd on after 3 out: wnt 4th last: nvr trbld ldrs* **12/1**
-S11 **5** 1/2 **Tarvini (IRE)**[60] 830 5-11-0 130 (p) RichieMcLernon(3) 122
(Jonjo O'Neill) *mid-div: hdwy to trck ldrs 4th: rdn bef 3 out: styd on same pce* **11/1**
3-12 **6** 1 3/4 **Changing Lanes**[16] 1198 7-10-5 118 (p) RhysFlint 108
(John Flint) *trckd ldrs: rdn after 7th: sn hld: styd on same pce fr after 3 out* **6/1**[2]
-333 **7** 6 **Akarshan (IRE)**[36] 1019 5-10-6 126 AdamWedge(7) 114
(Evan Williams) *in tch: rdn after 7th: hld fr next: wkng whn mstke 2 out* **7/1**[3]
-013 **8** hd **Mous Of Men (FR)**[60] 828 7-10-13 126 (tp) HaddenFrost 110
(David Pipe) *nvr bttr than mid-div* **14/1**
2131 **9** 6 **The Jigsaw Man (IRE)**[16] 1197 6-11-5 139 AodhaganConlon(7) 117
(Rebecca Curtis) *disp ld tl appr 3 out: sn rdn: wknd after next* **9/1**
0000 **10** 47 **Acambo (GER)**[25] 1017 9-10-7 127 MarkQuinlan(7) 58
(David Pipe) *towards rr of mid-div: rdn after 7th: sn wknd: t.o* **25/1**
PF1- **P** **Cracboumwiz (FR)**[144] 4961 10-11-4 131 DenisO'Regan —
(Mark Shears) *pckd 3rd: a towards rr: lost tch qckly after 6th: p.u bef next* **33/1**
-121 **P** **Calon Crwbin**[49] 887 5-10-11 124 (t) JohnnyFarrelly —
(Alison Thorpe) *mid-div: hdwy after 5th: rdn after 3 out: wknd qckly: p.u bef next* **12/1**
1112 **P** **Tout Regulier**[3] 1296 6-10-7 120 TomO'Brien —
(Peter Bowen) *trckd ldrs: rdn after 7th: sn wknd: bhd whn p.u bef 2 out* **5/1**[1]

5m 30.9s (10.70) **Going Correction** +0.725s/f (Soft) 13 Ran SP% **121.2**
Speed ratings (Par 109): **109,107,104,102,102 102,99,99,97,80 —,—,—**
toteswingers: 1&2 £17.30, 1&3 £27.50 , 2&3 £27.60. CSF £67.82 CT £726.07 TOTE £10.30: £4.00, £4.30, £6.10; EX 88.20.
Owner D J Reid **Bred** Darley **Trained** Nicholashayne, Devon

FOCUS
There were five non-runners in this valuable handicap hurdle, but the field was still suitably competitive. The pace was strong given the testing nature of the ground. David Pipe had won the previous two editions of this race and he sent out the first and second this time.

NOTEBOOK
Raslan added to last year's victory in this race. The gelding had shown little in the intervening 12 months and had finished in front of just three horses - and behind 47 - in his last four starts. He had been dropped to last year's winning mark though, and came in for support on this follow-up bid despite the soft ground being a concern for connections. After burning off The Jigsaw Man, with whom he had disputed the lead, he kept up the gallop for a comfortable win. The stewards decided not to hold an inquiry after hearing the trainer's explanation that the reapplication of a tongue tie had helped the gelding. Official explanation: trainer said, regarding the apparent improvement in form, that the gelding may have benefited from having a tongue strap re-fitted today (op 6-1)
Battle Group, a stablemate of the winner, is not straightforward but he has had a lucrative summer season and he ran another fine race off a 9lb higher mark than when winning at Market Rasen. He handled the conditions well enough. (tchd 15-2)
Secret Tune had been badly out of form but the first-time blinkers sparked something of a revival. It will be interesting to see if the headgear continues to have a positive effect. (tchd 10-1 and 14-1)
Hollywood Law(IRE), an Irish challenger who was a winner at Kilbeggan recently, was never really going and received reminders in rear at an early stage, but he kept going for fourth.
Tarvini(IRE) had won his last four completed starts, but he was another 10lb higher and the ground had gone against him. (op 10-1)
Changing Lanes, another who has taken a considerable hike in the weights, could have done without the rain but was not discredited. (tchd 11-2)
Akarshan(IRE) made a couple of errors and his stamina failed him in these conditions. (op 12-1)
The Jigsaw Man(IRE), back over hurdles, delayed the start after attempting to jump the tape and unseating the rider. Disputing a fast pace with the winner until fading three out, he is not the biggest to be carrying topweight in testing ground. (op 12-1)
Calon Crwbin was another for whom the soft ground was no good. (tchd 14-1)
Tout Regulier was disappointing, with the underfoot conditions and quick reappearance obvious excuses. (tchd 14-1)

1347 TOTEEXACTA FLEXI BETTING H'CAP HURDLE (10 hdls) 2m 6f
4:00 (4:00) (Class 4) (0-110,110) 4-Y-0+ **£3,252** (£955; £477; £238)

Form RPR
U530 **1** **Basford Lass**[27] 1094 5-11-0 98 (b) AlanO'Keeffe 106+
(Jennie Candlish) *chsd ldr in clr 2nd: led 3rd: mde rest: styd on v gamely: rdn out* **15/2**
0-21 **2** 3 1/4 **Benedict Spirit (IRE)**[15] 843 5-11-12 110 (p) RhysFlint 116+
(John Flint) *hld up towards rr: smooth hdwy after 6th: wnt 2nd 7th: rdn after 3 out: unable to get to wnr: nt fluent last: styd on* **7/2**[1]
524- **3** 21 **Pocket Too**[125] 4869 7-11-7 105 (p) TomO'Brien 90
(Matthew Salaman) *mid-div: rdn appr 7th: wnt modest 3rd appr 2 out: nvr a danger* **9/2**[2]
3256 **4** 2 **Cubism**[3] 1291 4-11-4 104 (tp) WarrenMarston 84
(Milton Harris) *trckd ldrs: rdn after 3 out but no ch w ldng pair: wknd next* **6/1**[3]
6003 **5** nk **The Good Guy (IRE)**[16] 1195 7-11-7 105 JodieMogford 88
(Graeme McPherson) *trckd ldrs: rdn to dispute 3rd after 3 out but no ch w ldng pair: wknd 2 out* **7/1**
0-S6 **6** 3 **Kristoffersen**[86] 503 10-11-7 105 OwynNelmes 84
(Helen Nelmes) *struggling 6th: a towards rr* **10/1**
P-15 **7** 9 **Opening Meet**[20] 1158 6-11-7 110 MrRMahon(5) 80
(Paul Nicholls) *mid-div: struggling in rr after 6th: sme prog fr 7th: wnt modest 3rd after 3 out: wknd bef 2 out* **9/1**
4106 **8** 19 **Vintage Fabric (USA)**[20] 1162 8-11-2 100 (t) DavidDennis 51
(Nigel Hawke) *trckd ldrs: rdn after 7th: wknd after 3 out: t.o* **14/1**
P0P- **9** 13 **Cashel Blue (USA)**[162] 4587 8-11-2 105 (p) KeiranBurke(5) 43
(Patrick Rodford) *led tl 3rd: chsd ldr in clr 2nd tl rdn after 6th: sn wknd: t.o* **16/1**
000- **P** **Princess Flame (GER)**[10] 4497 8-11-0 105 MissCLWills(7) —
(Brendan Powell) *mid-div: hdwy after 6th: rdn after 7th: wkng whn blnd 3 out: p.u bef next* **14/1**

5m 42.4s (22.20) **Going Correction** +0.725s/f (Soft)
WFA 4 from 5yo+ 14lb 10 Ran SP% **117.3**
Speed ratings (Par 105): **88,86,79,78,78 77,73,67,62,—**
toteswingers: 1&2 £9.10, 1&3 £8.10, 2&3 £4.30. CSF £34.87 CT £134.35 TOTE £12.10: £3.00, £1.10, £2.60; EX 48.50.
Owner Alan Baxter **Bred** L A C Ashby Newhall Estate Farm **Trained** Basford Green, Staffs

FOCUS
A modest handicap hurdle run around 12 seconds slower than the preceding 0-140 event.

NOTEBOOK
Basford Lass faced competition for the lead early on but soon had things her own way out in front. She began to tire between the last two flights but stayed on well enough. Unlike the majority of her rivals, she was at home in this ground. (op 9-1)

Benedict Spirit(IRE) emerged as the only danger to the winner in the latter stages, but a tired leap at the last ended his lingering hopes. He stays well enough and this was a pleasing handicap debut, especially given his maiden hurdle win last time came on fast ground. (op 4-1)
Pocket Too was in trouble with a circuit to run but plugged past toiling opponents late in the day. He was a well beaten third, but this was a satisfactory first run since the spring. (op 5-1 tchd 11-2)
Cubism, tried in cheekpieces, was not discredited on this quick reappearance but this trip stretches him. (op 8-1)
The Good Guy(IRE), third in a claimer last time, was 10lb lower than when in a handicap on his previous run but needs faster conditions. (op 6-1)
Opening Meet was ultimately well beaten on this handicap debut and has yet to fully prove his stamina for this sort of trip. He is rather small to be carrying big weights too. (op 6-1)

1348 TOTETRIFECTA FLEXI BETTING H'CAP CHASE (20 fncs) 3m 2f 110y

4:30 (4:31) (Class 4) (0-115,115) 4-Y-O **£4,119** (£1,216; £608; £304; £152)

Form				RPR
-520	1		**Good Harvest (IRE)**[27] [1093] 7-10-12 **101** ... APMcCoy (Jonjo O'Neill) *hld up: hdwy appr 15th: rdn to chse ldr after 4 out: chal after 2 out: led sn after last: styd on: rdn out* **5/1**[3]	111+
12F-	2	3/4	**Marufo (IRE)**[394] [1049] 8-11-12 **115** ... (t) RichardJohnson (Philip Hobbs) *hld up: hit 2nd: tk clsr order 10th: led 16th: rdn after 2 out: no ex whn hdd run-in* **4/1**[2]	123+
4B03	3	19	**Le Forezien (FR)**[20] [1159] 11-9-9 **89** oh5 ... (t) IanPopham[(5)] (Carroll Gray) *j.w: w ldr tl 4 out: sn rdn: styd on same pce fr next* **5/1**[3]	78
5503	4	22	**Skipper's Lad (IRE)**[12] [1230] 8-11-5 **108** ... (bt) JoeTizzard (Colin Tizzard) *trckd ldrs: rdn after 4 out: wknd after next* **13/2**	75
3-41	5	15	**Dusty Dane (IRE)**[86] [501] 8-11-3 **113** ... (t) MarkQuinlan[(7)] (Bill Turner) *hld up: trckd ldrs 12th: rdn after 14th: wknd 3 out* **14/1**	65
2-33	P		**Back In Business (IRE)**[35] [1027] 10-10-1 **90** ... (p) PaulMoloney (Evan Williams) *led tl 16th: sn rdn: wknd 4 out: bhd whn p.u bef 2 out* **10/3**[1]	—
-032	P		**Orchard King (IRE)**[78] [631] 9-10-11 **107** ... (p) OliverDayman[(7)] (Alison Thorpe) *trckd ldrs tl dropped to last but in tch 10th: rdn after 13th: lost tch fr next: p.u bef 4 out* **12/1**	—
2612	P		**Tampa Boy (IRE)**[19] [1177] 8-11-10 **113** ... (t) CharliePoste (Milton Harris) *trckd ldrs: pushed along after 13th: rdn after next: blnd bdly 3 out (water): p.u bef next* **10/1**	—

7m 8.90s (24.30) **Going Correction** +1.025s/f (Soft) **8** Ran SP% **113.2**
Speed ratings (Par 105): **105,104,99,92,88** —,—,—
toteswingers: 1&2 £3.70, 1&3 £5.80, 2&3 £5.20. CSF £25.35 CT £103.74 TOTE £4.70: £1.80, £1.20, £1.80; EX 18.20 Trifecta £173.00 Part won. Pool: £233.91 - 0.90 winning units..
Owner John P McManus **Bred** Pat Beirne **Trained** Cheltenham, Gloucs

FOCUS
The riders reported that the ground on the chase course was softer than on the hurdles track. The first two drew clear in this ordinary handicap chase.

NOTEBOOK
Good Harvest(IRE) got on top after the last following a lively tussle. Not the most consistent, he was running off the same mark as when gaining his most recent win, at Worcester last October, and that day was the last time he had encountered cut in the ground. Official explanation: trainer's representative said that the gelding appeared better suited by being settled in today (op 6-1 tchd 13-2)
Marufo(IRE) ◆, formerly with Heather Dalton, was debuting for the Hobbs team after more than a year off. He struck the front travelling easily, but could not shrug off the winner as lack of a recent run eventually told. He had previously shown a preference for better ground and this was a nice effort. (op 11-4)
Le Forezien(FR), who was runner-up in this two years ago, ran reasonably with the tongue tie reapplied from 5lb out of the handicap. (op 8-1)
Skipper's Lad(IRE) was second in this event a year ago but was 16lb higher this time round and did not come here in much form, including over hurdles on his most recent run. (op 7-1)
Dusty Dane(IRE) had been off the track since winning at Stratford in May and was well beaten off this 7lb higher mark. (op 10-1)
Back In Business(IRE) made the running in an attempt to make his stamina tell, but could offer no resistance when headed and was soon pulled up. (op 7-2 tchd 3-1, 4-1 in a place)

1349 TOTESWINGER FLEXI BETTING STANDARD OPEN NATIONAL HUNT FLAT RACE 2m 1f

5:00 (5:01) (Class 5) 4-6-Y-O **£1,644** (£479; £239)

Form				RPR
4-32	1		**Grandads Horse**[68] [759] 4-10-13 0 ... TomO'Brien (Alan Jones) *mde all: kpt on wl: rdn out* **9/4**[1]	100+
	2	2 1/2	**Youralltalk (IRE)**[76] 6-11-0 0 ... APMcCoy (Keith Goldsworthy) *chsd wnr thrght: rdn over 3f out: kpt on to draw wl clr of remainder but unable to mount chal* **9/4**[1]	98
	3	28	**Naughtyatiz (IRE)** 4-10-6 0 ... AodhaganConlon[(7)] (Debra Hamer) *cl up: effrt in 3rd over 3f out: wknd over 2f out* **11/1**	69
	4	3 3/4	**Glenseskin** 6-10-11 0 ... PeterToole[(3)] (Eamonn Fehily, Ire) *cl up: rdn over 5f out: wknd over 3f out* **7/2**[2]	66
	5	18	**Newyearsresolution (IRE)**[119] 6-11-0 0 ... DarylJacob (Nick Mitchell) *trckd ldrs: rdn 6f out: sn btn* **14/1**	48
	6	16	**John Sixteen (IRE)** 5-10-11 0 ... DonalDevereux[(3)] (Peter Bowen) *hld up: rdn 6f out: no imp: wknd 4f out* **6/1**[3]	32
0	7	dist	**Redgrave Dancer**[35] [1029] 4-10-1 0 ... GilesHawkins[(5)] (Kevin Bishop) *lost tch 1/2-way: wl t.o: btn 151 l* **50/1**	—

4m 13.9s (13.80) **Going Correction** +0.725s/f (Soft)
WFA 4 from 5yo+ 1lb **7** Ran SP% **115.0**
Speed ratings: **96,94,81,79,71 63**,—
toteswingers: 1&2 £2.30, 1&3 £5.20, 2&3 £6.60. CSF £7.50 TOTE £3.30: £2.00, £1.60; EX 6.50 Place 6: £164.27, Place 5: £99.33..
Owner Jim White **Bred** Wood Farm Stud **Trained** Coedkernew, Newport

FOCUS
A moderate bumper run at an ordinary pace in this bad ground. The first two finished a long way clear.

NOTEBOOK
Grandads Horse made all the running and held on well after picking out the better ground under the stands' rail in the straight. Described by his in-form trainer as a 3m chaser in the making, he had made the frame on his first three bumper starts, all on a sound surface. (op 5-2 tchd 11-4)
Youralltalk(IRE), an Irish maiden point winner on softish ground on his last start in June, stuck to his task commendably well and looks a staying type. (op 13-8)
Naughtyatiz(IRE) is only small and he joined his connections cheaply. He pulled clear with the first two before the conditions took their toll. (op 16-1)
Glenseskin, an Irish raider whose dam won a hunter chase at Newcastle, was a well beaten fourth on this debut. (op 13-2)
T/Jkpt: Not won. T/Plt: £368.20 to a £1 stake. Pool:£104,502.70 - 207.15 winning tickets T/Qpdt: £88.20 to a £1 stake. Pool:£6,180.42 - 51.80 winning tickets TM

1350 - 1356a (Foreign Racing) - See Raceform Interactive

743 SEDGEFIELD (L-H)

Tuesday, August 24

OFFICIAL GOING: Good to firm changing to good (good to firm in places) after race 1 (2.15)
Wind: fresh 1/2 behind Weather: fine

1357 SHEFFIELD INSULATIONS NOVICES' HURDLE (JOHN WADE HURDLE SERIES QUALIFIER) (10 hdls) 2m 4f

2:15 (2:15) (Class 4) 4-Y-O+ **£2,732** (£802; £401; £200)

Form				RPR
31-3	1		**Grand Zouki (FR)**[115] [92] 5-11-5 117 ... BarryKeniry (George Moore) *trckd ldr: led after 3 out: clr last: drvn out* **12/1**	124+
-322	2	13	**Cailin Na Ri (IRE)**[23] [1149] 7-10-7 114 ... JamesHalliday[(5)] (Martin Todhunter) *chsd ldrs: wnt 2nd sn after 3 out: styd on same pce between last 2* **11/4**[2]	106+
2110	3	3	**Knar Mardy**[55] [863] 5-11-2 110 ... AdamPogson[(3)] (Charles Pogson) *in tch: rdn and outpcd 3 out: styd on between last 2: tk modest 3rd towards fin* **28/1**	108
	4	nk	**Amical Risks (FR)**[18] 6-10-9 0 ... EwanWhillans[(3)] (Joss Saville) *in rr: hit 6th: pushed along next: hdwy appr 2 out: kpt on one pce run-in* **40/1**	101
3-31	5	1 1/4	**Mr Jay Dee (IRE)**[32] [1086] 5-10-12 0 ... BrianHughes (Alan Swinbank) *trckd ldrs: t.k.h: mstke 5th: nt fluent 7th: wnt 3rd after 3 out: hit last: wknd run-in* **7/2**[3]	104+
0-41	6	4 1/2	**Call Me Mulligan (IRE)**[28] [1109] 6-10-12 0 ... (p) GrahamLee (John Hellens) *led: hdd after 3 out: sn wknd: hit last* **8/1**	98
P/54	7	19	**Zahara Joy**[32] [1083] 7-10-5 76 ... (t) MichaelMcAlister (Maurice Barnes) *in tch: hdwy to chse ldrs 3 out: wknd appr next: heavily eased run-in* **150/1**	83+
3111	8	23	**Sahrati**[34] [1063] 6-11-12 128 ... DenisO'Regan (Michael Blake) *chsd ldrs: drvn 7th: lost pl and mstke 2 out: sn heavily eased* **15/8**[1]	72
0/60	9	2	**Gutter Lane**[18] [1201] 6-10-12 0 ... DougieCostello (Malcolm Jefferson) *in rr: blnd 3rd: pushed along 7th: sn bhd* **100/1**	56
	P		**Quo Vista (IRE)** 5-10-5 0 ... MrJohnDawson[(7)] (John Wade) *nt fluent in rr: drvn 7th: sn t.o: p.u after 3 out* **100/1**	—

4m 43.3s (-9.40) **Going Correction** -0.30s/f (Good) **10** Ran SP% **111.0**
Speed ratings (Par 105): **106,100,99,99,98 97,89,80,79**,—
toteswingers:1&2 £4.10, 2&3 £9.90, 1&3 £11.20 CSF £43.52 TOTE £15.30: £3.30, £1.50, £6.20.
Owner Mrs Mary Hatfield & Mrs Susan Kramer **Bred** Consev Holding S A **Trained** Middleham Moor, N Yorks

FOCUS
The first pair dominated off the home turn in this reasonable novice hurdle for the track and time of year. The winner arguably produced a stp up.

NOTEBOOK
Grand Zouki(FR) made light of a 115-day break and ran out a taking winner of this moderate novice event. Having improved for 3m in his two previous outings, this return to a sharper test was something of a worry, but he got a decent ride and showed a pleasing attitude. He will likely have to go handicapping to find further success now and is entitled to come on for the run. (op 14-1 tchd 10-1)
Cailin Na Ri(IRE) was well backed and moved nicely through the race, but couldn't go with the winner from the penultimate flight. She rates the benchmark.
Knar Mardy was staying on but failed to land a serious blow. She remains vulnerable in this division.
Amical Risks(FR), rated 58 on the Flat, took time to get the hang of things on this hurdling debut. He was keeping on late in the day, though, and ought to be wiser for the experience. A stiffer test may also suit in this sphere. (tchd 33-1)
Mr Jay Dee(IRE) looked one to be interested in on this switch to hurdling after finally showing his true colours when comfortably winning a bumper last month. He raced with enthusiasm, but made too many errors for his own good and was legless coming to the last. Perhaps dropping back in trip will help and he too is entitled to learn plenty for the experience. (tchd 10-3 and 4-1)
Zahara Joy Official explanation: jockey said mare lost its action but returned sound
Sahrati wasn't on a going day here and could well be feeling the effects of a busy summer. Dennis O'Regan later reported his mount was unsuited by the track. Official explanation: jockey said gelding did not handle the track (op 7-4 tchd 2-1)

1358 CLEM'S FISH RESTAURANTS H'CAP CHASE (11 fncs 2 omitted) 2m 110y

2:45 (2:45) (Class 4) (0-105,111) 4-Y-O+ **£3,285** (£1,053; £585)

Form				RPR
52F6	1		**Troodos Jet**[35] [1047] 9-9-11 **78** oh1 ... (p) RyanMania[(3)] (Dianne Sayer) *sn trcking ldrs: wnt 2nd 2 out: led between last 2: drvn rt out: hld on all out* **4/1**[3]	85+
6405	2	1	**Schinken Otto (IRE)**[29] [1095] 9-10-8 **91** ... JamesHalliday[(5)] (Malcolm Jefferson) *trckd ldrs: led 3rd: hdd 6th: nt fluent 2 out: chsd wnr appr last: sn 3 l down: styd on fnl 150yds* **4/1**[3]	97
-066	3	3	**Alfloramoor**[9] [1259] 8-10-13 **94** ... AdamPogson[(3)] (Charles Pogson) *t.k.h: led to 3rd: hit next: led 6th: hdd between last 2: kpt on same pce* **11/4**[1]	97
0554	U		**Skiddaw Jones**[27] [1116] 10-10-1 **79** ... (t) MichaelMcAlister (Maurice Barnes) *trckd ldrs: blnd and uns rdr 2nd* **7/2**[2]	—
05-3	U		**San Deng**[22] [918] 8-11-6 **98** ... BarryKeniry (Micky Hammond) *chsd ldrs: blnd and uns rdr 7th* **9/2**	—
500-	F		**Whatcanyasay**[134] [5167] 9-9-7 **78** oh7 ... (p) MissECSayer[(7)] (Evelyn Slack) *chsd ldrs: wknd and hit 7th: sn t.o: 30 l 4th whn fell heavily last* **28/1**	—

4m 2.30s (-6.30) **Going Correction** -0.475s/f (Good) **6** Ran SP% **110.5**
Speed ratings (Par 105): **95,94,93**,—,— —
toteswingers:1&2 £3.50, 2&3 £2.60, 1&3 £3.30 CSF £19.56 TOTE £4.50: £2.50, £4.60; EX 20.90.
Owner Anthony White **Bred** Auldyn Stud Ltd **Trained** Hackthorpe, Cumbria

FOCUS
The final fence was omitted in all chase races and that left a very long run-in. This weak handicap chase proved to be an eventful race, but the form makes some sense with the first two pretty much to their marks.

NOTEBOOK
Troodos Jet had been freshened up by a 35-day break and resumed winning ways at a track he likes. He bided his time until nearing the third-last and momentarily got outpaced after that fence, but came back onto the bridle turning for home. He kept finding for pressure once in front and was always holding the runner-up near the finish. This proves his versatility as regards underfoot conditions and he will continue to pay his way after a rise as he can hold his form well, but has never managed to follow up a previous win. (op 7-2)

Schinken Otto(IRE) took the race by the scruff of the neck early on and posted an improved effort for the return to chasing. He was 5lb higher than when beating the winner over C&D on his previous success back in May and so obviously helps to set the level.
Alfloramoor is able to race off a 7lb lower mark over fences and was well backed on this return over a suitably sharper test. He looked the one to be on two out, but didn't prove that willing when push came to shove and was ultimately well beaten. He is now 0-6 as a chaser. (op 4-1)
San Deng was still going well enough and had jumped soundly prior to getting the seventh all wrong and unseating. (op 4-1)

1359 JOHN WADE WASTE RECYCLING NOVICES' HURDLE (QUALIFIER) (8 hdls) 2m 1f

3:15 (3:15) (Class 4) 4-Y-0+ **£2,732** (£802; £401; £200)

Form / RPR

6-1 **1** **Bandanaman (IRE)**[9] 835 4-11-4 0 BrianHughes 112+
(Alan Swinbank) *trckd ldr: j.lft 1st: led between last 2: all out* **3/1**[2]

-161 **2** ½ **Rio Gael (IRE)**[12] 1238 4-11-11 118 (p) TomO'Brien 118
(Peter Bowen) *led: shkn up appr 2 out: hdd between last 2: 1 l down whn hit last: kpt on: a jst hld* **13/8**[1]

02-0 **3** 16 **The Magic Bishop**[110] 174 5-10-7 0 JamesHalliday(5) 101+
(Malcolm Jefferson) *chsd ldrs: outpcd appr 2 out: 6 l 3rd and wl hld last: heavily eased* **5/1**[3]

5102 **4** 15 **Sadler's Star (GER)**[22] 1158 7-11-12 115 (b1) DenisO'Regan 94+
(Michael Blake) *chsd ldrs: outpcd 3 out: sn btn: 17 l 4th whn mstke last* **3/1**[2]

6 **5** ½ **Galileo Figaro (AUS)**[10] 1250 6-10-12 0 BarryKeniry 77
(Joss Saville) *chsd ldrs: lost pl after 3 out: hit next* **50/1**

0/0- **6** 52 **Glen Vale**[319] 1685 7-10-5 0 MrJohnDawson(7) 30
(John Wade) *lost tch and drvn 5th: t.o 3 out* **100/1**

0 **P** **Peter Tchaikovsky**[9] 1258 4-10-4 0 (t) KyleJames(7) —
(Brian Rothwell) *in rr: bhd fr 3rd: t.o and reminders 5th: p.u bef 2 out* **50/1**

P **Train Spotter (IRE)** 5-10-9 0 CampbellGillies(3) —
(John Wade) *in rr: bhd fr 3rd: sn t.o: p.u bef 2 out* **50/1**

(-6.90) **Going Correction** -0.30s/f (Good)
WFA 4 from 5yo+ 13lb **8** Ran SP% **111.6**
Speed ratings (Par 105): **104,103,96,89,88 64,—,—**
toteswingers:1&2 £1.70, 2&3 £3.10, 1&3 £3.20 CSF £8.15 TOTE £3.80: £1.10, £1.10, £1.50; EX 7.40.
Owner Miss J S Peat **Bred** Carradale Ltd & T Stack **Trained** Melsonby, N Yorks

FOCUS
The first pair came well clear in this ordinary novice event and the form looks fair. The winner has the potential to rate a bit higher.

NOTEBOOK
Bandanaman(IRE) ground out success on this return from the Flat and is now 2-3 over hurdles. He is evidently more at home in this sphere than he is on the level and rates value for a little further here as he idled markedly nearing the finish. Things will be tougher under a double penalty, but he has the scope to rate a bit higher and may find further improvement for a stiffer test over hurdles. (op 7-2 tchd 4-1)
Rio Gael(IRE), gamely back to winning ways at Stratford 12 days earlier, unsurprisingly set out to make all and he turned in a brave effort. It must be remembered he was conceding 7lb to the winner, so emerges as the best horse at the weights and remains in decent heart. (tchd 6-4)
The Magic Bishop ◆ is definitely one to take from the race. He got outpaced from three out, but wasn't given at all a hard time off the home turn and was heavily eased after the last. He was returning from a 110-day absence here and it was a clear step back in the right direction. As a half-brother to his stable's smart stayer According To Pete, he will surely enjoy stepping up in trip and can soon find an opening. (op 11-2 tchd 7-2)
Sadler's Star(GER) had first-time blinkers replacing cheekpieces. He found little for pressure after travelling well until nearing three out. He was later reported to have lost a front shoe during the race. Official explanation: vet said gelding lost a near-fore shoe (tchd 7-2)
Galileo Figaro(AUS) showed improved form on this second outing for current connections and will find life easier when switching to low-grade handicaps. (op 40-1)

1360 CLASSIC EXCEL NOVICES' H'CAP CHASE (14 fncs 2 omitted) 2m 4f

3:45 (3:46) (Class 5) (0-95,91) 4-Y-0+ **£2,602** (£764; £382; £190)

Form / RPR

-P00 **1** **Archie's Wish**[82] 604 6-10-0 65 oh2 BarryKeniry 79+
(Micky Hammond) *trckd ldrs: effrt 3 out: styd on wl run-in: led and forged clr last 150yds* **16/1**

1200 **2** 3½ **Pugnacity**[35] 1048 6-10-5 73 RyanMania(3) 83+
(Dianne Sayer) *hld up in rr: hdwy 9th: w ldr 11th: led appr last: hdd and no ex last 100yds* **4/1**[1]

0/00 **3** 11 **First Fought (IRE)**[60] 840 8-10-3 68 (tp) TjadeCollier 67
(Joanne Foster) *prom: outpcd 10th: 6th last: hung lft and styd on to take modest 3rd clsng stages* **12/1**

1231 **4** 1½ **Sir Bumble (IRE)**[12] 1237 10-11-12 91 (t) GrahamLee 89
(Michael Blake) *chsd ldrs: led 10th: hdd appr last: wknd fnl 200yds* **5/1**[2]

453P **5** 7 **Executive's Hall (IRE)**[23] 1152 6-10-4 69 (p) BrianHughes 61
(Andrew Crook) *led: hit 9th: mstke and hdd next: wknd appr last* **8/1**

5644 **6** 10 **Ellandshe (IRE)**[28] 1100 10-9-10 66 oh15 ow1 (b) JamesHalliday(5) 51
(William Young) *chsd ldrs: wknd between last 2* **40/1**

UP03 **7** 16 **Janal (IRE)**[28] 1100 7-10-0 65 oh4 WilsonRenwick 33
(Stuart Coltherd) *in rr: bhd whn hmpd 10th* **11/1**

P-60 **8** 3 **Bocciani (GER)**[28] 1104 5-11-6 88 JamesO'Farrell(3) 53
(Dianne Sayer) *hld up in tch: wknd 10th* **33/1**

U-34 **R** **Hapthor**[40] 1001 11-11-4 90 (p) MrMGarnett(7) —
(F Jestin) *ref to r: lft s* **25/1**

5315 **P** **Miss Molly Be Rude (IRE)**[9] 1261 8-11-3 82 RobertWalford —
(Tim Walford) *in rr: mstke 2nd: lost tch 8th: t.o whn p.u bef 11th* **6/1**[3]

3442 **F** **Nobby Kivambo (IRE)**[9] 1261 5-11-7 86 JimmyMcCarthy —
(Brendan Powell) *chsd ldr: rdn and mstke 9th: wkng whn fell next* **4/1**[1]

4m 51.6s (-11.40) **Going Correction** -0.475s/f (Good) **11** Ran SP% **113.2**
Speed ratings (Par 103): **103,101,97,96,93 89,83,82,—,— —**
CSF £77.11 CT £805.46 TOTE £23.90: £6.70, £2.20, £3.90; EX 106.10.
Owner The Black Bull Partnership **Bred** Peter Cassidy **Trained** Middleham Moor, N Yorks

FOCUS
A wide-open looking handicap. It was run at an average gallop until they went out onto the final circuit and eventually the first two pulled well clear. The winner is rated up a stone on his best hurdles form.

NOTEBOOK
Archie's Wish crept into things nearing the home turn and, finding his full stride after the last, mowed down the runner-up to make a winning return from an 85-day break. He had shown little as a hurdler previously, but the switch to chasing clearly proved much more to his liking and he has come good for his recent time off the track. Well on top at the finish, there could be more to come. Official explanation: trainer said, regarding apparent improvement in form, that the gelding benefited by the switch to fences. (op 14-1)
Pugnacity, a course specialist, looked the most likely winner on jumping the last having scythed her way through the pack to lead, but ultimately the concession of 8lb to the winner proved beyond her. This was much better from her back at her favourite course and she rates a solid benchmark. (tchd 7-2)
First Fought(IRE) hit a marked flat spot before running on strongly down the home straight to bag third late on. It rates his most encouraging effort under rules for some time and returning to a stiffer test could see him build on this. (op 14-1)
Sir Bumble(IRE) was 4lb higher and ran his race again, but eventually his big weight told. (op 10-3 tchd 11-2)
Executive's Hall(IRE) who set out to make all, didn't go down lightly once headed yet was done with prior to the last.\n (op 10-1)
Miss Molly Be Rude(IRE) jumped too deliberately before pulling up. (op 11-2 tchd 7-2)
Nobby Kivambo(IRE) was well supported, but was beaten prior to departing on the back straight. (op 11-2 tchd 7-2)

1361 DONN DX3 MAIN RUNNERS AND RIDERS H'CAP HURDLE (9 hdls) 2m 2f 110y

4:15 (4:15) (Class 5) (0-90,89) 4-Y-0+ **£1,951** (£573; £286; £143)

Form / RPR

54P- **1** **Roman History (IRE)**[6] 1411 7-11-5 85 (p) CampbellGillies(3) 92+
(Tracy Waggott) *chsd ldrs: led after 3 out: 6 l clr whn j.lft last: lasted home* **66/1**

BP66 **2** 2¼ **Lady Wright (IRE)**[3] 1328 7-11-12 89 WilsonRenwick 93
(Michael Easterby) *hld up in rr: hdwy 6th: effrt after 3 out: wnt 2nd run-in: nt rch wnr* **12/1**

P000 **3** 3 **Daasij (IRE)**[54] 870 5-10-6 69 BrianHarding 71
(Nicky Richards) *mid-div: hdwy to chse ldrs 6th: chsd wnr appr 2 out: kpt on same pce* **4/1**[2]

4-00 **4** 1¼ **Cornish Castle (USA)**[91] 459 4-10-13 78 BarryKeniry 76
(Joss Saville) *in rr: reminders 4th: styd on wl appr last* **40/1**

4-55 **5** 7 **Harcas (IRE)**[17] 948 8-11-3 80 (b) GrahamLee 76
(Martin Todhunter) *nt fluent: chsd ldrs: outpcd 2 out: modest 3rd last: wknd* **7/1**[3]

-262 **6** 8 **Nobel (FR)**[34] 1064 9-10-7 77 (p) MissJCoward(7) 64
(Brian Storey) *chsd ldrs: wknd after 3 out* **16/1**

P40- **7** 4½ **Rivers Run Free (IRE)**[19] 1189 5-11-8 85 DougieCostello 68
(J J Lambe, Ire) *mid-div: hmpd 6th: nvr a factor* **66/1**

0-06 **8** 2¼ **Airedale Lad (IRE)**[11] 1199 9-10-3 73 MissPhillipaTutty(7) 54
(Karen Tutty) *in rr: bhd fr 5th* **40/1**

2555 **P** **Bari Bay**[3] 1340 4-11-4 83 (b) DenisO'Regan —
(Michael Blake) *led: nt fluent 5th: hdd after 3 out: wknd rapidly: t.o whn p.u bef 2 out* **22/1**

-0P1 **U** **Louis Ludwig (IRE)**[7] 1272 5-11-8 85 (t) RichardJohnson —
(Tim Vaughan) *stdd s: hld up in last: stmbld landing and uns rdr 2nd* **5/6**[1]

5-PP **P** **One More Cent**[28] 1101 5-9-12 64 oh4 ow1 RyanMania(3) —
(Dianne Sayer) *j.lft 1st: mid-div: hmpd and lost pl 6th: t.o whn p.u bef 2 out* **100/1**

0600 **P** **Carrifran (IRE)**[29] 1090 5-10-8 76 JamesHalliday(5) —
(Malcolm Jefferson) *chsd ldrs: outpcd whn blnd 6th: sn p.u* **66/1**

4m 20.8s (-7.90) **Going Correction** -0.30s/f (Good)
WFA 4 from 5yo+ 13lb **12** Ran SP% **115.3**
Speed ratings (Par 103): **104,103,101,101,98 94,93,92,—,— —,—**
toteswingers:1&2 £36.30, 2&3 £7.00, 1&3 £32.60 CSF £668.24 CT £3889.97 TOTE £44.80: £9.30, £3.10, £1.80; EX 344.00.
Owner Mrs J Waggott **Bred** Lodge Park Stud **Trained** Spennymoor, Co Durham

FOCUS
The early departure of the favourite took plenty of interest out of this weak handicap. The winner produced a personal best. It was run at a routine sort of gallop.

NOTEBOOK
Roman History(IRE) finally ended his losing run and registered a first win over hurdles at the seventh time of asking. He came here with something to prove, but has been in fair heart on the level of late and there was no fluke about this success. It remains to be seen whether he will follow this up, however.
Lady Wright(IRE), who didn't go unbacked, was ultimately undone by the very patient tactics over this sharper test. She can win one of these over a longer trip. (op 10-1)
Daasij(IRE) put in a more encouraging effort on his handicap debut and he too shaped as though there is a race for him over a stiffer test. (op 7-1 tchd 8-1 and 7-2)
Cornish Castle(USA) went in snatches from a very early stage. He plugged on for pressure, though, and this was a little better again on his first outing for three months.
Harcas(IRE) went well until fading in the home straight and seems better on the Flat these days. (op 11-2)
Louis Ludwig(IRE), who was unpenalised for his Worcester win, wasn't at all clever at the second, but it did appear something of a soft unseat. It wouldn't be surprising to see him back out again quickly. (op 4-5 tchd 4-6, 10-11 and evens in places)

1362 PHOENIX EYE CONDITIONAL JOCKEYS' H'CAP HURDLE (9 hdls 1 omitted) 2m 5f 110y

4:45 (4:45) (Class 4) (0-100,100) 4-Y-0+ **£2,602** (£764; £382; £190)

Form / RPR

-3FF **1** **Winged Farasi**[6] 516 6-11-4 92 GemmaGracey-Davison 99
(Joanne Foster) *chsd ldrs: narow ld normal 2 out: drvn rt out* **9/1**

35P4 **2** 1½ **Auberge (IRE)**[27] 1119 6-10-3 77 RyanMania 83
(Dianne Sayer) *w ldrs: lft in ld 5th: hdd normal 3 out: upsides omitted last: styd on same pce* **3/1**[1]

0-15 **3** 1¼ **Planetarium**[9] 1115 5-11-9 97 (p) CampbellGillies 102
(P Monteith) *chsd ldrs: styd on fr normal 2 out: upsides passing omitted last: no ex* **13/2**[3]

0-00 **4** 15 **Inner Voice (USA)**[28] 1104 7-11-9 100 (b) EJO'Connell(3) 95
(J J Lambe, Ire) *towards rr: pushed along 4th: sme hdwy normal 3 out: nvr on terms* **7/1**

0/12 **5** 5 **Grand Art (IRE)**[14] 1137 6-11-4 98 MrTomDavid(6) 89
(Tim Vaughan) *hld up: sltly hmpd 5th: outpcd 7th: no threat after* **4/1**[2]

04P3 **6** 1 **Osbaldeston (IRE)**[28] 1099 7-10-13 95 MrAdamNicol(8) 81
(Rose Dobbin) *mid-div: effrt 7th: outpcd next* **12/1**

1-P0 **7** 6 **Bewery Man (IRE)**[27] 1118 9-11-4 100 PaulGallagher(8) 83
(Ferdy Murphy) *hld up in rr: jnd ldrs 6th: led normal 3 out: hdd next: sn wknd* **7/1**

F606 **8** 7 **Morecambe Bay**[23] 1149 5-9-9 74 oh2 PeterHatton(5) 48
(David Thompson) *chsd ldrs: reminders 4th: wknd after normal 3 out* **50/1**

0P-5 **9** ½ **Amjad**[71] 745 13-9-11 74 oh1 (p) KyleJames(3) 48
(Simon West) *in rr: outpcd and bhd 4th* **40/1**

PU0P **10** 19 **Humourous (IRE)**[54] 871 8-10-0 74 oh3 JamesHalliday 31
(Brian Storey) *led tl after 1st: chsd ldrs: bdly hmpd 5th: sn lost pl: t.o normal 3 out* **12/1**

0-05 **F** **Franklee**[44] 945 7-9-6 **74** oh15.................................... GaryRutherford(8) —
(Harriet Graham) *led after 1st: fell 5th* **66/1**

5m 4.80s (-9.80) **Going Correction** -0.30s/f (Good) **11** Ran SP% **114.6**
Speed ratings (Par 105): **105,104,104,98,96 96,94,91,91,84** —
toteswingers:1&2 £5.90, 2&3 £4.20, 1&3 £10.70 CSF £35.84 CT £190.08 TOTE £11.20: £2.80, £1.30, £2.30; EX 37.70 Place 6: £215.38 Place 5: £69.65.
Owner The Smash Block Partnership **Bred** The National Stud **Trained** Menston, W Yorks

FOCUS
An ordinary handicap, confined to conditional riders. The final flight was bypassed on the final circuit. The first three came clear and all three are rated to their marks.

NOTEBOOK
Winged Farasi eventually came out on top in a tight three-way finish and was given a strong ride by his jockey. He had fallen on his previous two outings as a hurdler, but did go close on the Flat six days earlier and had finished third at this track on his only previous visit. He could have a bit more to offer over this sort of distance. (op 13-2)
Auberge(IRE) was well backed and held every chance yet ultimately got outstayed by the winner. She remains winless, but this was her debut for the yard and it was more encouraging. (op 9-2)
Planetarium, another returning from the Flat, was previously unbeaten in two outings at the course and shaped with a lot more encouragement. He isn't one for maximum faith, but looks worth trying over an even stiffer test now. (op 7-1 tchd 6-1)
Inner Voice(USA) had the blinkers back on and looked a possible threat turning for home. However, he produced a very limited finishing effort. (op 6-1)
Grand Art(IRE) was hampered by the faller passing the stands for the first time. He recovered, but came under heavy pressure before three out and was soon beaten. (tchd 3-1)
Osbaldeston(IRE), making his handicap debut, didn't appear an easy ride. (tchd 16-1)
T/Plt: £566.60 to a £1 stake. Pool of £81,072.33 - 104.45 winning tickets. T/Qpdt: £144.60 to a £1 stake. Pool of £6,441.61 - 32.95 winning tickets. WG

1308 BANGOR-ON-DEE (L-H)
Wednesday, August 25

OFFICIAL GOING: Good (good to firm in places; 8.2)
Wind: Half-against Weather: Overcast

1363 BANGORONDEERACES.CO.UK JUVENILE HURDLE (9 hdls) 2m 1f
5:30 (5:31) (Class 4) 3-Y-O **£2,397** (£698; £349)

Form RPR
1 **1** **Meetings Man (IRE)**[14] 743 3-11-5 0.................................. BarryKeniry 106+
(Micky Hammond) *mde all: nt fluent 4th: mstke 4 out: rdn clr appr last: styd on wl* **13/8**[1]
22 **2** *6* **Sassanian (IRE)**[26] 1135 3-10-5 0.................................. MrTomDavid(7) 96+
(Tim Vaughan) *w wnr: rdn whn mstke 3 out: unable to go w wnr 2 out: btn whn mstke last* **9/4**[3]
U054 **3** *77* **Dinkie Short**[13] 1234 3-10-7 0..(p) DavidBass(5) 32
(Ben De Haan) *nt fluent: a bhd: niggled along 2nd: nvr travelling after: lost tch after 5th: t.o but plugged on to take poor 3rd run-in* **40/1**
4 *1 ¾* **Rhyton (IRE)**[66] 3-10-12 0.................................. GrahamLee 31
(Donald McCain) *chsd front duo: rdn after 4th: j. slowly 5th: lost tch w ldrs after 4 out: t.o: lost 3rd run-in* **15/8**[2]

4m 11.4s (0.50) **Going Correction** -0.20s/f (Good) **4** Ran SP% **106.1**
Speed ratings (Par 102): **90,87,50,50**
CSF £5.47 TOTE £2.10; EX 5.10.
Owner Paul R Snook **Bred** Hakan Keles **Trained** Middleham Moor, N Yorks

FOCUS
A moderare juvenile event, rated around the second. The winner can rate higher.

NOTEBOOK
Meetings Man(IRE), who has a tendency to hang, at least shows the right attitude at the business end and gets the trip well. He defied the penalty he picked up at Sedgefield, since when he has scored over 1m4f on the Newmarket July course, and remains in good heart, but he had nothing to beat here. (op 5-2)
Sassanian(IRE) has twice defied McCoy over hurdles and has now finished runner-up in his last six attempts, including three on the Flat. His attitude has long been highly suspect and his desire to win is nil. (op 2-1)
Dinkie Short had twice been trounced by Sassanian and has since contested a seller. He never went a yard tonight. (op 33-1)
Rhyton(IRE) got home by a nose from a 57 rated rival over 1m4f at Pontefract for Sir Michael Stoute on just his second appearance, and was promptly sold. He lacked any fluency on this hurdling debut, was already struggling at halfway, and eventually laboured home many lengths behind. Surely there was some physical excuse for this awful display. Official explanation: jockey said gelding ran green (op 6-4)

1364 HYDRANT DIGITAL MEDIA H'CAP HURDLE (11 hdls) 2m 4f
6:00 (6:00) (Class 3) (0-125,119) 4-Y-0+ **£4,553** (£1,337; £668; £333)

Form RPR
0B11 **1** **Points Of View**[5] 1313 5-11-7 **117** 14ex..........................(t) SeanQuinlan(3) 132+
(Kim Bailey) *hld up: hdwy appr 4 out: led gng wl bef 2 out: clr bef last: eased down run-in* **11/4**[1]
F561 **2** *9* **Word Of Warning**[18] 1118 6-11-1 **113**.......................... JamesHalliday(5) 116+
(Martin Todhunter) *hld up: hdwy 3 out: chal appr 2 out: nt qckn between last 2 and sn unable to go w wnr: no ch after* **17/2**
506- **3** *9* **Callisto Moon**[31] 5213 6-11-12 **119**..............................(p) MarkGrant 114
(Barry Brennan) *led: clr fr bef 4th tl 7th: rdn and hdd appr 2 out where mstke: wl btn bef last* **16/1**
5423 **4** *2 ½* **Murcar**[11] 1254 5-11-0 **114**.. OliverDayman(7) 106
(Alison Thorpe) *midfield: impr to chse ldrs 6th: wnt 2nd 3 out and sn chalng tl appr 2 out: wknd between last 2* **5/1**[2]
4-34 **5** *5* **Whenever**[56] 866 6-11-11 **118**.......................................(b) SamThomas 106
(Richard Phillips) *trckd ldrs: pushed along 3 out: wknd appr 2 out* **8/1**
6 *2 ¼* **The Wifes Pet (IRE)**[293] 2087 6-11-7 **114**.......................... AidanColeman 100
(Lawney Hill) *racd keenly in midfield: niggled along appr 4 out: wknd bef 2 out* **9/1**
14-0 **7** *4 ½* **Parlesotho (FR)**[81] 633 7-11-6 **118**................................. MrRMahon(5) 101
(Ben Case) *chsd ldrs: j. slowly 4th: struggling whn mstke 7th: sn wknd* **13/2**[3]
2530 **8** *½* **Mister Benedictine**[24] 1023 7-11-7 **117**............(t) SamTwiston-Davies(3) 99
(Brendan Duke) *hld up: hdwy appr 3 out: effrt whn chsng ldrs sn after: nt fluent 2 out: sn wknd* **12/1**
U-34 **9** *26* **Bathwick Man**[75] 715 5-11-12 **119**..........................(tp) TomScudamore 80
(David Pipe) *chsd ldr tl mstke 3 out: sn wknd: eased bef 2 out: t.o* **10/1**
P/25 **10** *13* **Herne Bay (IRE)**[38] 1033 10-11-4 **111**..........................(t) DenisO'Regan 62
(Ian Williams) *in rr: struggling appr 7th: lost tch 4 out: t.o* **25/1**

4m 49.5s (-7.90) **Going Correction** -0.20s/f (Good) **10** Ran SP% **114.8**
Speed ratings (Par 107): **107,103,99,98,96 95,94,93,83,78**
toteswingers: 1&2 £4.60, 1&3 £14.70, 2&3 £11.90 CSF £26.23 CT £313.99 TOTE £2.90: £1.30, £3.10, £4.50; EX 15.50.
Owner W J Ives **Bred** Limestone And Tara Studs **Trained** Andoversford, Gloucs

FOCUS
A modest handicap. The easy winner stepped up again and rates a smart novice now.

NOTEBOOK
Points Of View ◆ completed his hat-trick (achieved in the space of nine days, including two at Bangor) with another most decisive win, and he has improved out of all recognition over hurdles since gaining a tongue strap and learning to settle. The 2m4f trip did not worry him in the slightest, but he did get in a stew in the preliminaries and was eventually mounted in the pre-parade ring. The handicapper will doubtless play his hand before long, but in the meantime he will attempt to strike again while the iron is hot at Cartmel on Saturday. (op 5-2 tchd 3-1 in places)
Word Of Warning looked particularly well and gave a solid display but was well beaten by a rapidly improving opponent. He stays 2m4f but the trip may be as far as he cares to go. Official explanation: vet said gelding was struck into (op 9-1)
Callisto Moon ran a good race considering that the handicapper has him in his grip, and he did not go down without a fight. (tchd 14-1)
Murcar made the frame yet again, but he remains a tricky ride and getting the most out of him in the closing stages is always difficult. (op 15-2 tchd 9-2)
Whenever has been a big disappointment since he won at Plumpton on his hurdling debut in the autumn and lack of enthusiasm looked a problem up the home straight. (op 17-2)
The Wifes Pet(IRE), a small mare who has come over from Ireland where she won twice, including in a point, ran encouragingly on her first appearance for 293 days and should be well worth keeping an eye on. (op 15-2 tchd 7-1)
Parlesotho(FR) has gone well fresh in the past, but she was struggling a long way out on this return from a three-month absence. Official explanation: vet said mare finished lame (op 8-1 tchd 6-1)

1365 WORTHENBURY NOVICES' CHASE (18 fncs) 3m 110y
6:30 (6:30) (Class 4) 4-Y-0+ **£3,577** (£1,050; £525)

Form RPR
1530 **1** **Pilgrims Lane (IRE)**[24] 1151 6-11-8 123..................(tp) JimmyDerham(5) 132+
(Milton Harris) *chsd ldr tl nt fluent 2nd: racd in last pl: hit 4 out: wnt 2nd 3 out: rdn appr last: r.o run-in to ld post* **17/2**[3]
/0-1 **2** *hd* **The Shoe (NZ)**[34] 1068 8-11-7 0.. AndrewTinkler 124
(Nicky Henderson) *racd in last pl: chsd ldr fr 2nd: led 4 out: nt fluent 2 out: rdn after last: sn strly pressed: worn down post* **1/1**[1]
01-5 **3** *42* **Diablo (IRE)**[112] 155 8-11-4 130........................... SamTwiston-Davies(3) 109+
(Nigel Twiston-Davies) *led: blnd 14th: hdd 4 out: sn rdn: dropped to last pl 3 out: losing tch whn j.rt 2 out: t.o* **6/5**[2]

6m 13.0s (-6.80) **Going Correction** -0.10s/f (Good) **3** Ran SP% **106.0**
Speed ratings (Par 105): **106,105,92**
CSF £16.64 TOTE £7.20; EX 9.50.
Owner Mrs D J Brown **Bred** J Mangan **Trained** Herridge, Wiltshire

FOCUS
Just the three runners, but a fair gallop, and a stirring finish. Fair form, the first two to their marks.

NOTEBOOK
Pilgrims Lane(IRE) was claimed for £8,000 out of Paul Nicholls' yard and has proved a bargain, and he was winning for the third time for current connections. He is not particularly consistent but does have a turn of foot on his day and nailed any doubts that he might not stay this slightly extended 3m under a good ride from the conditional Jimmy Derham. He was a late withdrawal from the big hurdle at Newton Abbot on Sunday, presumably because the ground there was thought to be too soft Official explanation: trainer said, regarding apparent improvement in form, that the gelding had lost interest previously but had benefited from the re-application of cheekpieces and first-time tongue-strap. (op 6-1 tchd 9-1)
The Shoe(NZ) won over fences at Uttoxeter (he had previously won Flat and hurdling in New Zealand), but was not especially convincing despite the ten-length margin. He seemed to have this race in the bag coming to the last, but was just pipped, and may not be one to have great faith in. (tchd 6-5)
Diablo(IRE), a real chaser on looks, dropped out rapidly in the final half mile and this seemed too bad to be true. He tended to jump slightly right at most of the fences and three of his five victories have been gained going right handed at Perth. Official explanation: vet said gelding finished lame (op 11-8 tchd Evens and 6-4 in a place)

1366 ECHO ARENA CLUB CHASE (H'CAP) (18 fncs) 3m 110y
7:00 (7:00) (Class 4) (0-105,102) 4-Y-0+ **£3,577** (£1,050; £525; £262)

Form RPR
0-2P **1** **Victory Surge (IRE)**[35] 1061 6-11-4 **97**..................(p) RichieMcLernon(3) 111+
(Jonjo O'Neill) *j.rt: chsd ldrs: wnt 2nd 13th: chalng 2 out: hit and led narrowly last: styd on for press: in command fnl strides* **4/1**[3]
1500 **2** *1 ¼* **Classic Clover**[30] 1093 10-11-8 **98**..............................(t) AidanColeman 107
(Colin Tizzard) *led: rdn appr 2 out: hdd narrowly last: styd on gamely: hld fnl strides* **5/1**
F/04 **3** *29* **Quaddick Lake (IRE)**[38] 1026 7-11-9 **102**.......................... DannyCook(3) 85
(David Pipe) *hld up: clsd 14th: effrt whn chsng ldrs appr 3 out: no imp on front duo fr 2 out: sn wl btn* **5/2**[2]
0PU5 **4** *½* **Dasher Reilly (USA)**[8] 1277 9-10-0 **76** oh19................(p) LiamTreadwell 58
(Aytach Sadik) *chsd ldr tl 13th: mstke 14th: dropped away after 4 out: chal for poor 3rd run-in* **14/1**
65P1 **P** **Shergill (IRE)**[35] 1059 9-9-11 **76** oh5................(b) SamTwiston-Davies(3) —
(Shaun Lycett) *hld up: mstke and hmpd 10th: struggling 12th: lost tch 13th: t.o whn p.u bef 2 out* **7/4**[1]

6m 13.8s (-6.00) **Going Correction** -0.10s/f (Good) **5** Ran SP% **108.3**
Speed ratings (Par 105): **105,104,95,95,**—
CSF £21.51 TOTE £7.20: £7.10, £3.30; EX 14.40.
Owner Mrs Gay Smith **Bred** Mary Fanning McCormack **Trained** Cheltenham, Gloucs

FOCUS
A weak staying handicap. The winner is rated up 10lb on his best hurdles form.

NOTEBOOK
Victory Surge(IRE) looks anything but an easy ride and again showed his tendency to jump right. He had to be cajoled along from a long way out, and he will do well to find another handicap as weak as this. (op 7-2 tchd 9-2)
Classic Clover has his good days, but he usually gets taken on and then sulks, so this bad contest could have been made to measure. In the end he was just outbattled, and he is normally one to take on as a betting proposition. (op 9-2 tchd 11-2)
Quaddick Lake(IRE), on his handicap debut, has been making the running and then stopping rapidly of late. This time hold-up tactics were used, but he again folded very tamely indeed, and is one to be wary of. (op 15-8 tchd 7-4)
Dasher Reilly(USA) at least went with a bit of purpose for a change, but he was 15lb out of the handicap and had an impossible task. (op 18-1 tchd 12-1)
Shergill(IRE) did not want to know after two miles, and there was never any hope of his repeating his surprise hurdling win at Worcester last time out. (op 5-2)

1367 DARLANDS NOVICES' HURDLE (12 hdls) 3m
7:30 (7:30) (Class 4) 4-Y-0+ **£2,911** (£848; £424)

Form RPR
142F **1** **North Island (IRE)**[29] 1105 8-10-12 0.......................... TomScudamore 112+
(Peter Bowen) *chsd ldrs: led appr 2 out: rdn bef last: styd on wl to draw away run-in* **7/4**[1]

110 **2** *2* **Majestic Mayhem (IRE)**45 954 7-11-12 120 BarryKeniry 123+
(George Moore) *a.p: chalng fr 3 out: rdn whn nt fluent last: kpt on but no imp on wnr run-in* **4/1**3
0/-1 **3** *nk* **Dowd's Destiny (IRE)**24 1149 7-11-5 0 BrianHarding 116+
(Nicky Richards) *hld up in rr: mstke 7th: clsd 4 out: rdn and outpcd after 3 out: rallied bhd ldrs appr last: kpt on u.p and chal for 2nd run-in but n.d to wnr* **7/2**2
4123 **4** *12* **Downward Spiral (IRE)**29 1105 5-11-5 115 AlanO'Keeffe 107
(Jennie Candlish) *led: hdd after 4th: chsd ldr tl lft in ld 8th: mstke 3 out: hdd appr 2 out: dropped away bef last* **5/1**
0- **5** *3 3/4* **What An Oscar (IRE)**291 2128 5-10-9 0 SamTwiston-Davies(3) 94
(Nigel Twiston-Davies) *in rr: pushed along appr 8th: struggling whn nt fluent 3 out: nvr a threat* **8/1**
6U36 **R** **The Hairy Mutt (IRE)**8 1275 8-10-5 89 MissLBrooke(7) —
(Lady Susan Brooke) *plld hrd: hung rt thrght: hdwy to ld after 4th: nt fluent 5th: hit 7th: rn out 8th* **20/1**

5m 51.7s (0.70) **Going Correction** -0.20s/f (Good) **6** Ran SP% **111.1**
Speed ratings (Par 105): **90,89,89,85,83** —
toteswingers: 1&2 £1.70, 1&3 £1.10, 2&3 £1.60 CSF £8.98 TOTE £2.90: £1.10, £2.70; EX 8.80.
Owner Steve & Jackie Fleetham **Bred** John Smyth **Trained** Little Newcastle, Pembrokes

FOCUS
A fair novice event. The winner is probably capable of rating higher than this over hurdles.

NOTEBOOK
North Island(IRE) is a versatile type, who was a multiple scorer in points and has won twice in chases, but this was his first success over hurdles. He achieved it in good style and came home with his ears pricked in a manner that suggests he can follow up in similar grade. He stays three miles really well and enjoys his racing. (op 2-1 tchd 85-40 in places)
Majestic Mayhem(IRE) is another who has done well pointing (in Ireland) and has the look of a chaser for the future. He already has a good record over hurdles and put a disappointing run last time (when he jumped poorly) behind him. (op 7-2)
Dowd's Destiny(IRE) was returning from a 32-month absence when he beat a consistent but moderate performer at Market Rasen. He was let down by his jumping tonight, but is speedy enough to do better if he can find a more consistent rhythm. (op 11-4)
Downward Spiral(IRE) looked to run up to his best, but he has not produced much in the closing stages in his last three outings. (op 11-2 tchd 9-2)
What An Oscar(IRE) is small and showed nothing on his hurdling debut. (op 11-1 tchd 15-2)
The Hairy Mutt(IRE) made a beeline for the River Severn at Worcester last time and again proved unrideable, finally ducking past the first on the far side and eventually decanting his hapless partner. He does have speed, and would be worth trying with a professional on board. (op 28-1)

1368 ERBISTOCK H'CAP HURDLE (12 hdls) 3m
8:00 (8:00) (Class 4) (0-115,114) 4-Y-0+ **£3,252** (£955; £477; £238)

Form RPR
P051 **1** **What A Scientist (IRE)**15 1230 10-11-7 **112** SamTwiston-Davies(3) 116+
(Nigel Twiston-Davies) *mde all: pushed along appr 3 out: pressed 2 out: styd on wl to draw clr after last: eased cl home* **5/2**1
0006 **2** *3 1/2* **Englishtown (FR)**29 1108 10-11-5 **110** (p) RichieMcLernon(3) 110+
(Jonjo O'Neill) *hld up: hdwy appr 8th: wnt 2nd after 3 out: chalng 2 out: nt qckn last: n.d to wnr run-in* **11/2**3
6P-6 **3** *3/4* **Inghwung**19 1198 8-11-8 **110** SamJones 109
(Oliver Sherwood) *chsd ldrs: rdn whn hit 3 out: keeping on same pce whn nt fluent last: no real imp after* **11/2**3
F2F **4** *2 3/4* **Thelobstercatcher**22 1177 6-11-5 **114** OliverDayman(7) 110
(Peter Bowen) *towards rr: rn in snatches: hdwy 4 out: chalng appr 2 out: no ex bef last* **4/1**2
5P35 **5** *17* **Manadam (FR)**10 1259 7-10-10 **105** MattGriffiths(7) 87
(Anthony Middleton) *chsd ldrs: wnt 2nd appr 7th: rdn 4 out: lost 2nd after 3 out: sn wknd* **12/1**
2660 **6** *6* **Haldibari (IRE)**19 1198 6-11-4 **106** DenisO'Regan 83
(Shaun Lycett) *chsd ldr tl appr 7th: lost pl 8th: struggling whn j.lft 4 out: n.d after* **9/1**
P0/P **7** *34* **Team Allstar (IRE)**19 1200 11-10-8 **103** MissJennyCarr(7) 53
(Jonjo O'Neill) *hld up: dropped tamely away 8th* **25/1**
0060 **8** *9* **Daurica**42 986 6-11-3 **105** (p) JimmyMcCarthy 48
(Renee Robeson) *chsd ldrs: niggled along after 7th: wknd bef 8th* **8/1**
3/P- **9** *59* **Wild Side Of Life (IRE)**268 2611 7-10-11 **106** MrTomDavid(7) 2
(Tim Vaughan) *bhd: struggling 8th: sn t.o: mstke last* **20/1**

5m 53.8s (2.80) **Going Correction** -0.20s/f (Good) **9** Ran SP% **116.8**
Speed ratings (Par 105): **87,85,85,84,79 77,65,62,43**
toteswingers: 1&2 £9.70, 1&3 £5.20, 2&3 £6.90 CSF £17.31 CT £69.62 TOTE £2.70: £1.10, £2.60, £2.50; EX 15.00 Place 6 £594.14, Place 5 £230.73.
Owner Mr & Mrs Gordon Pink **Bred** A W Buller **Trained** Naunton, Gloucs

FOCUS
A moderate handicap. The winner was value for further and in line with his old hurdles form.

NOTEBOOK
What A Scientist(IRE) has been revitalised by a change of yard and followed up his Newton Abbot win (over three furlongs further) by again making all the running and readily outstaying the opposition, who had nearly all been out of form. The hat-trick could be on the cards. He would also be worth noting if a return to chasing was envisaged. (op 2-1 tchd 15-8)
Englishtown(FR) has not recaptured the form he was showing last summer and he was readily brushed aside in the closing stages. (op 13-2 tchd 7-1)
Inghwung ran reasonably despite sweating up badly but she is still a long way from fulfilling the promise she showed two years ago. (op 6-1)
Thelobstercatcher had ended up on the floor in two of three chases (negotiating a total of two fences in two of them) so will at least have received a confidence booster on this return to hurdles. He might be better over slightly less than three miles and is not one to give up on yet. (op 9-2 tchd 5-1)
Wild Side Of Life(IRE), a strong sort, blew hard after his first outing since November (when he pulled too hard) and should strip fitter next time. He has been very lightly raced so far. Interestingly, his trainer is just one from 28 with handicap debutants in the last 12 months. (op 14-1)
T/Plt: £339.30 to a £1 stake. Pool: £38,433.16. 82.67 winning tickets. T/Qpdt: £48.40 to a £1 stake. Pool: £3,354.83. 51.22 winning tickets. DO

1175 FFOS LAS (L-H)
Wednesday, August 25

OFFICIAL GOING: Good to soft (7.5)
Wind: Fresh, behind Weather: Raining

1369 CASTELL HOWELL FOODS NOVICES' HURDLE (10 hdls) 2m 4f
5:20 (5:23) (Class 4) 4-Y-0+ **£3,252** (£955; £477; £238)

Form RPR
/P0- **1** **Russian War (IRE)**38 1039 7-11-5 119 (t) PCarberry 119+
(Gordon Elliott, Ire) *hld up: hdwy 3 out: led next: shkn up flat: r.o* **5/2**1
5-2 **2** *nk* **Gambo (IRE)**111 167 4-10-10 0 PaulMoloney 108+
(Evan Williams) *hld up: hdwy 3 out: chsd wnr last: rdn: hung lft and ev ch flat: r.o* **7/2**2
633 **3** *9* **Doubletoilntrouble (IRE)**23 1158 4-10-10 0 APMcCoy 101
(Keith Goldsworthy) *led to 2nd: chsd ldrs: mstke 6th: led appr 3 out: hdd next: wknd flat* **7/2**2
2 **4** *3* **Tara Warrior (IRE)**13 1238 4-10-10 109 RichardJohnson 97
(Tim Vaughan) *chsd ldrs: ev ch 2 out: wknd last* **5/2**1
0654 **5** *36* **Spring Haze**35 1060 5-9-12 74 (t) MrDGPrichard(7) 60
(Phillip Dando) *chsd ldrs: led 4th to appr next: rdn and wknd 3 out: t.o* **50/1**
4/6 **F** **Runaway Harry (IRE)**15 1228 7-10-12 0 TomO'Brien 92
(Peter Bowen) *chsd ldrs: ev ch 3 out: cl 4th and rdn whn fell next* **20/1**3
6645 **U** **Weldone Honey**8 1275 5-10-2 0 DonalDevereux(3) —
(Peter Bowen) *chsd ldr: led 2nd to 4th: led again bef next: rdn and hdd appr 3 out: sn wknd: t.o whn blnd and uns rdr next* **22/1**

5m 1.10s (12.10) **Going Correction** -0.20s/f (Good)
WFA 4 from 5yo+ 14lb **7** Ran SP% **112.7**
Speed ratings (Par 105): **73,72,69,68,53** —,—
toteswingers: 1&2 £2.20, 1&3 £2.50, 2&3 £1.60 CSF £11.35 TOTE £3.20: £1.60, £4.30; EX 11.90.
Owner T D Howley Jnr **Bred** Tommy Howley **Trained** Trim, Co Meath

FOCUS
Heavy rain had changed the going to good to soft on this free-draining course. Mindful of the conditions, jockeys took it very steadily in the opener, with the pace not lifting until midway in the back straight, eventually seeing four pull clear. The winner is rated below his best.

NOTEBOOK
Russian War(IRE), held up off the slow pace, refused to settle, but showed his superiority when cruising up to lead going to the second-last. He idled a bit on the run-in, but still had enough in hand to repel the late challenge of the runner-up. Previously, his best form had been on faster ground, but he was relatively unexposed on softer, and he proved here that he is versatile as to ground and possesses abundant stamina. He has had heart and muscle problems in the past, but when on song he possesses a bit of class. (op 2-1 tchd 11-4)
Gambo(IRE) was not that fluent in the early stages, but surged through under pressure to keep the winner on his toes on the run to the line. This was only his third race and he was still a bit green in the closing stages, but has potential given a test of stamina. (op 9-2)
Doubletoilntrouble(IRE) set the steady pace and looked to be coming to the end of his tether when making a mistake at the last in the back straight, but he was kept up to his work and responded well enough, though he could find no more from the last. This was softer ground than he had encountered before and it just made him struggle. (op 4-1 tchd 10-3)
Tara Warrior(IRE) tracked the leaders and was ideally placed to make a move but, when asked to pick up, he faded somewhat disappointingly considering he is rated just 4lb lower than the winner. He might be better on tighter tracks, but also might need a bit more time to strengthen up. (tchd 11-4)

1370 PLAY BLACKJACK AT TOTESPORT.COM CLAIMING HURDLE (8 hdls) 2m
5:50 (5:54) (Class 4) 4-Y-0+ **£3,577** (£1,050; £525; £262)

Form RPR
256P **1** **Bolton Hall (IRE)**15 1227 8-10-8 107 (bt1) RichardJohnson 111+
(Keith Goldsworthy) *chsd ldr: led after 2nd: clr fr 5th: wnt lft 2 out: easily* **12/1**
00/4 **2** *15* **Apt To Run (USA)**12 1115 7-10-8 112 (bt) PCarberry 101+
(Gordon Elliott, Ire) *hld up: hmpd and lft 3rd at the 3rd: chsd wnr appr 5th: rdn bef 2 out: fnd nil* **9/4**1
0555 **3** *15* **Marodima (FR)**19 1195 7-11-8 130 TomO'Brien 101
(Jamie Snowden) *led tl after 2nd: chsd wnr tl wknd appr 5th: wnt mod 3rd towards fin* **5/2**2
4/ **4** *6* **Cylindar Rattler (IRE)**30 1097 7-10-7 112 RichardKilloran(3) 84
(Tim Vaughan) *hld up: wnt 3rd appr 5th: rdn and wknd after 3 out: mstke last: lost 3rd towards fin: t.o* **6/1**3
2311 **F** **Three Ships**29 1107 9-10-11 120 GilesHawkins(5) —
(Richard Lee) *trckd ldrs: plld hrd: cl 3rd whn fell 3rd* **5/2**2

3m 49.5s (0.50) **Going Correction** -0.20s/f (Good) **5** Ran SP% **109.9**
Speed ratings (Par 105): **103,95,88,85,**—
CSF £39.06 TOTE £12.90: £6.80, £1.40; EX 23.80.
Owner Racing Coast **Bred** M Duffy **Trained** Yerbeston, Pembrokes

FOCUS
Despite the small field this was quite a competitive claimer, but some of the interest was lost when Three Ships fell in the back straight. There was a strong pace thanks to an early-pace duel. The winner is rated to his best but this is probably not form to get carried away with.

NOTEBOOK
Bolton Hall(IRE) likes to race up with the pace, but he was even more determined to do so in first-time blinkers. Such tactics looked sure to be his undoing but, after seeing off the early challenger, he was able to get a breather in the back straight and, to his credit, kept finding more, in the end running his rivals into the ground. He had the most to find on official ratings but the enterprising tactics allowed him to run above this. He ran in a chase last time and, although he did not perform well, connections thought the experience of fences had made him braver for this. (op 15-2)
Apt To Run(USA) looked to be travelling well and was held up until the last possible moment, but he was making no discernible inroads into the winner's lead and, when asked to pick up, he found very little. Since his promising return from a lengthy absence in July he has now disappointed both on the Flat and once again here. (op 7-2)
Marodima(FR) was taken on for the lead by the winner, but was the first to crack and tired in the back straight before staying on to claim a remote third. He seems better when able to dictate affairs on faster ground these days. (op 11-4 tchd 3-1)
Cylindar Rattler(IRE), a recent cheap purchase by the Tim Vaughan yard, was held up away from the early duel but never picked up once asked and needs to find improvement and his mark to drop to be competitive. (op 11-2 tchd 13-2)
Three Ships, making his debut for Richard Lee, was going well enough but the race had not begun to unfold when he clattered the third and came down. (op 9-4)

1371 PLAY ROULETTE AT TOTESPORT.COM NOVICES' CHASE (13 fncs) 2m
6:20 (6:20) (Class 4) 4-Y-0+ **£4,228** (£1,241)

Form RPR
506- **1** **Cootehill (IRE)**132 5194 6-11-0 0 PaddyBrennan 128+
(Nigel Twiston-Davies) *chsd ldr: mstke 9th: led appr and nt fluent 4 out: sn hdd: mstke 2 out: rallied to ld towards fin* **4/9**1
-315 **2** *1 1/4* **Blacktoft (USA)**27 1131 7-11-6 128 PaulMoloney 132
(Evan Williams) *led: hdd appr 4 out: led after 4 out: rdn and nt fluent last: hdd towards fin* **2/1**2

3m 57.8s (-7.20) **Going Correction** -0.375s/f (Good) **2** Ran SP% **102.6**
Speed ratings (Par 105): **103,102**
TOTE £1.40.
Owner Mrs Felicity Griffin **Bred** B And I McCelland **Trained** Naunton, Gloucs

FOCUS
Just a match after two withdrawals, but it was a close contest. The winner produced a decent debut and the second is rated to his mark.

NOTEBOOK
Cootehill(IRE) jumped low at several early fences, got in close to the second open ditch, and looked to be getting the worst of the argument in the home straight as he tired. He was still in touch coming to the last and, getting the better jump, had the better flat speed on the run to the line. This was a competent performance for his chasing debut, especially as his form and running style suggests he is more effective on faster ground. Given improvement and with this experience behind him, his connections should be able to take advantage of his attractive mark compared to his hurdles rating. (tchd 4-11)
Blacktoft(USA) got in close to several early fences, but found more fluency in the back straight and looked to be getting on top of the winner turning for home, but he could not shake off the pursuer and, after a hesitant jump at the last, he was outpaced on the run-in. He is already a winner over fences, but is really better on faster ground and that may have accounted for the early reticence in his jumping. However, he could struggle off a chase rating of 128 once tackling handicaps. (op 15-8)

1372 PLAY BINGO AT TOTESPORT.COM H'CAP HURDLE (10 hdls) 2m 4f
6:50 (6:50) (Class 3) (0-135,127) 4-Y-O+ **£6,505** (£1,910; £955; £477)

Form				RPR
3U-1 **1**		**Comehomequietly (IRE)**[29] 1111 6-11-1 **116**.................... PaulMoloney	121+
(David Rees) *hld up: hdwy 6th: led appr last: rdn out* **6/1**
3-14 **2** *4* **Hearthstead Dream**[28] 550 9-11-12 **127**............................ PCarberry 126
(Gordon Elliott, Ire) *hld up: hdwy 3 out: rdn appr last: r.o to go 2nd towards fin: nt rch wnr* **11/1**
1P3- **3** *1* **Alesandro Mantegna (IRE)**[129] 5252 5-10-8 **109**............... TomO'Brien 109+
(Keith Goldsworthy) *led: rdn and mstke 3 out: hdd whn nt fluent last: no ex flat* **9/1**
1202 **4** *1 1/2* **Heron Bay**[11] 1250 6-11-1 **116**..(b[1]) APMcCoy 114
(Peter Bowen) *chsd ldr: rdn appr 2 out: styng on same pce whn hit last* **9/2**[3]
3302 **5** *27* **Consulate (IRE)**[42] 994 6-11-4 **119**....................................... DarylJacob 91
(Gordon Edwards) *hld up in tch: rdn and wknd appr 3 out: bhd whn j.lft next: t.o* **16/1**
4611 **6** *5* **Extreme Conviction (IRE)**[27] 1129 6-11-0 **115**................. WillKennedy 83
(John Berry) *hld up: rdn and wknd after 7th: t.o* **3/1**[1]
-020 **7** *18* **Aldiruos (IRE)**[30] 1094 10-9-12 **104**.................................. LeeEdwards[(5)] 56
(Tony Carroll) *hld up: drvn along 5th: hdwy next: wknd 7th: t.o* **22/1**
1-P2 **8** *nk* **Darksideofthemoon (IRE)**[11] 1254 8-11-2 **117**........(p) RichardJohnson 68
(Tim Vaughan) *chsd ldrs tl rdn and wknd 3 out: t.o* **10/1**
3412 **P** **Danimix (IRE)**[28] 1118 5-11-7 **122**... RhysFlint —
(Peter Bowen) *chsd ldrs: rdn after 6th: sn p.u* **4/1**[2]

4m 51.5s (2.50) **Going Correction** -0.20s/f (Good) **9** Ran SP% **115.1**
Speed ratings (Par 107): **93,91,91,90,79 77,70,70,—**
toteswingers: 1&2 £16.50, 1&3 £10.80, 2&3 £6.30 CSF £67.51 CT £589.76 TOTE £7.30: £2.20, £4.30, £1.80; EX 93.10.
Owner IWEC International Ltd **Bred** J F Mernagh **Trained** Clarbeston, Pembrokes

FOCUS
A competitite handicap and sound form. Just a steady pace with the race developing from the back straight.

NOTEBOOK
Comehomequietly(IRE) was ridden patiently but not too far off the pace and so he was in a good position when making steady progress throughout the final half circuit. With just the two long-time leaders to take on, he ran out a comfortable winner. He had respectable form over the winter, including a couple of placed efforts at this course, but he just lacked the strength to see it out on winter ground. Connections gave him a break before he made a winning return at Worcester a month ago and the combination of freshness and relatively better ground seem to have made the difference. (op 5-1)
Hearthstead Dream did not jump that well early on and may have been held up too far off the early pace as a consequence. He made progress around the final turn, but never looked like getting there, although he gained a couple of lengths from halfway up the run-in. He is not that big and, given the ground he had to make up in the conditions, he did well really to finish as close as he did. (op 10-1 tchd 9-1)
Alesandro Mantegna(IRE) helped set the steady pace and stuck on well on his first run since April. He was sent chasing in the spring, but is still on an attractive mark over hurdles and, with this run under his belt, a return of headgear and drop in trip could make him interesting in the near future. (tchd 10-1)
Heron Bay is best when racing prominently, but the first-time blinkers may have made him do a bit too much too early, which did not help him see out the step up in trip. (op 6-1)
Consulate(IRE) has gone up in the weights again for finishing second in a 0-115 at Worcester last time, and that looks to have scuppered his chances in handicaps for the time being. (op 12-1 tchd 20-1)
Extreme Conviction(IRE) could not pick up in the rain-softened ground and faded out of it. Official explanation: trainer said gelding was unsuited by the good to soft ground (op 7-2 tchd 11-4)
Danimix(IRE) Official explanation: jockey said gelding lost its action

1373 PLAY SLOTS AT TOTESPORT.COM H'CAP CHASE (19 fncs) 3m 1f 110y
7:20 (7:22) (Class 2) (0-145,139) 4-Y-O+ **£12,674** (£3,744; £1,872; £936; £468)

Form RPR
11FP **1** **Grand Slam Hero (IRE)**[4] 1332 9-11-11 **138**.................(t) PaddyBrennan 157+
(Nigel Twiston-Davies) *hld up: hdwy 11th: led appr 3 out: clr whn nt fluent last: eased towards fin* **6/1**[3]
2102 **2** *5* **Midnight Gold**[22] 1178 10-10-11 **124**.......................................(p) RhysFlint 128
(Peter Bowen) *chsd ldr tl rdn 3 out: sn outpcd: styd on again to go 2nd towards fin* **16/1**
3011 **3** *shd* **Sea Wall**[22] 1178 8-10-9 **125**... MrAJBerry[(3)] 129
(Jonjo O'Neill) *sn chsng ldrs: ev ch fr 3 out tl rdn after next: no ex flat: lost 2nd towards fin* **16/1**
P-00 **4** *3 1/4* **Nostringsattached (IRE)**[39] 1020 9-11-1 **128**...................(tp) APMcCoy 130
(Jonjo O'Neill) *hld up: hit 10th: hdwy 4 out: nt fluent 2 out: styd on same pce appr last* **9/1**
-225 **5** *1 1/2* **Templer (IRE)**[59] 844 9-11-0 **127**.................................... RichardJohnson 128
(Philip Hobbs) *chsd ldrs: rdn 13th: styd on same pce fr 3 out* **8/1**
/11- **6** *1* **Valerius (IRE)**[42] 996 6-11-3 **130**......................................(bt) BrianHughes 130
(Gordon Elliott, Ire) *chsd ldrs: rdn after 15th: styd on same pce fr 3 out* **40/1**
P313 **7** *4* **Marblehead (IRE)**[22] 1178 8-10-10 **126**...........................(b) TomMolloy[(3)] 123+
(Nigel Twiston-Davies) *led: hit 15th: rdn and hdd bef 3 out: wknd next* **20/1**
1-P1 **8** *1/2* **Oscar Bay (IRE)**[98] 411 8-11-12 **139**...............................(b) HaddenFrost 134
(James Frost) *mid-div: mstke and lost pl 4th: n.d after* **25/1**
P0-4 **9** *2 1/4* **Quattrocento (FR)**[22] 1178 6-10-2 **115**..............................(p) TomO'Brien 116+
(Peter Bowen) *mid-div: stmbld after 8th and lost pl: hdwy 12th: wknd appr 4 out* **13/2**
P1/4 **10** *19* **Lyes Green**[19] 1198 9-11-0 **127**...(p) LeightonAspell 103
(Oliver Sherwood) *hld up: hdwy 6th: mstke and lost pl 9th: wknd 13th: t.o* **10/1**
12 **11** *8* **Supercede (IRE)**[5] 1319 8-10-10 **128** 12ex................(bt) KMDonoghue[(5)] 96
(Gordon Elliott, Ire) *hld up: hit 15th: hdwy appr 4 out: rdn and wknd after 3 out: t.o* **7/2**[1]
50-0 **P** **Hoopy (IRE)**[28] 1122 8-11-2 **129**..(tp) PCarberry —
(Gordon Elliott, Ire) *hld up in tch: mstke 5th wknd 13th: t.o whn p.u bef 4 out* **9/2**[2]

6m 31.4s (-15.60) **Going Correction** -0.375s/f (Good) **12** Ran SP% **121.0**
Speed ratings (Par 109): **109,107,107,106,105 105,104,104,103,97 95,—**
toteswingers: 1&2 £32.50, 1&3 £50.80, 2&3 £17.70 CSF £93.16 CT £1476.50 TOTE £6.90: £3.30, £2.50, £4.30; EX 77.10.
Owner Walters Plant Hire Ltd **Bred** Lady Rathdonnell **Trained** Naunton, Gloucs

FOCUS
A very competitive handicap for the time of year and the form should be reliable. The winner was value for a lot further.

NOTEBOOK
Grand Slam Hero(IRE) was keen to get on with things restrained in rear and when he was asked for his effort he cruised up effortlessly to win with his ears pricked. He has had a couple of blips recently, most recently when getting hampered in a valuable chase at Newton Abbot four days ago, and his jockey wisely pulled him up when his chance had gone to save him for today. This was a slightly easier opportunity for him to add to a summer tally that includes the Summer Plate at Market Rasen, and he remains in such good form that even a climb up the ratings and softer ground than ideal could not stop him. Even though he is nine connections feel there is still some improvement in him and long-term he might even make up into a Grand National prospect. (op 13-2 tchd 5-1 tchd 7-1 in a place)
Midnight Gold was near the pace until two out and rallied again to snatch second on the line. He goes well here (was second to Sea Wall earlier this month) and this was another game effort, although he might just be better over 3m when the going gets softer. (op 12-1)
Sea Wall had been raised 4lb for conquering three of these rivals over C&D earlier in the month, and ran another solid race, eventually weakening after the last, but he may have clung on for second if his jockey had been more punishing in the closing stages. However, since he really prefers faster ground, that may have been more detrimental in the long run. (op 11-1)
Nostringsattached(IRE) tried to close down the leaders in the home straight but was running on empty from the last. He has been out of form since his second in the equivalent race last year, but this was a step in the right direction. (op 11-1)
Templer(IRE) began to feel the pace down the back but responded to pressure until giving way in the home straight. He seems better over further these days. (op 7-1)
Supercede(IRE) has been the easy winner of some lower-grade events over fences and hurdles this summer and is progressive, but the combination of softer ground and a step up in class found him out here. (op 9-2)
Hoopy(IRE) was well backed for the switch back to fences but lost his position after a mid-race mistake and never recovered. (op 15-2 tchd 8-1)

1374 WALTERS UK CIVIL ENGINEERING & CONSTRUCTION STANDARD OPEN NATIONAL HUNT FLAT RACE 2m
7:50 (7:51) (Class 5) 4-6-Y-O **£1,626** (£477; £238; £119)

Form RPR
1 **Saint Luke (IRE)**[158] 5-11-2 0.. RichardJohnson 103+
(Peter Bowen) *led at stdy pce over 14f out: qcknd over 4f out: rdn clr fnl f* **9/4**[2]
2 *3 1/2* **Don Pooleoni (IRE)** 5-11-2 0... DarylJacob 99+
(David Arbuthnot) *hld up: hdwy 1/2-way: chsd wnr 2f out: sn rdn: styd on same pce fnl f* **4/1**[3]
U32 **3** *4* **Salford Rose (IRE)**[7] 1284 4-10-5 0.............................. LeeStephens[(3)] 87
(David Evans) *trckd ldrs: plld hrd: rdn over 2f out: wknd over 1f out* **9/2**
42 **4** *2 1/4* **Point Blank (IRE)**[19] 1201 4-11-1 0..(t) APMcCoy 92
(Jonjo O'Neill) *led at stdy pce tl hdd over 14f out: chsd ldrs: rdn over 2f out: wknd over 1f out* **13/8**[1]
54 **5** *1 3/4* **Superior Knight**[34] 1069 6-11-2 0.. DavidDennis 91
(James Evans) *hld up: hdwy 1/2-way: wknd over 2f out* **28/1**
6 *18* **Casper's Shadow (IRE)** 4-11-1 0... RhysFlint 72
(Keith Goldsworthy) *chsd ldrs: rdn over 3f out: wknd sn after* **12/1**

3m 58.4s (15.00) **Going Correction** -0.20s/f (Good)
WFA 4 from 5yo+ 1lb **6** Ran SP% **118.2**
Speed ratings: **67,65,63,62,61 52**
toteswingers: 1&2 £3.10, 1&3 £2.50, 2&3 £2.00 CSF £12.50 TOTE £3.10: £1.20, £1.90; EX 12.30 Place 6 £318.74, Place 5 £155.83.
Owner Miss R L Bryan **Bred** Joseph O'Dwyer **Trained** Little Newcastle, Pembrokes

FOCUS
No-one was keen to lead from the off which led to an early crawl, with a sprint developing off the home turn that opened up the field. The third and fourth were a stone or more off their best and the first two are capable of rating higher.

NOTEBOOK
Saint Luke(IRE) began duelling from the home turn and, along with Point Blank, got first run on the field. It was still a long way home from there but the former point winner relished the easy ground and had enough stamina to see out the trip well. (op 11-4 tchd 3-1 in a place)
Don Pooleoni(IRE) was caught just behind the leaders as the pace lifted, and so he had a bit more ground to make up. He gave it a good try and, despite looking a bit green, stayed on well. His stable does well with bumper runners, although not usually on their debuts, so he might be worth noting next time. (op 10-3 tchd 5-1)
Salford Rose(IRE) has taken a strong hold previously and was keen again here, but she stayed on to the line, although not posing a threat to the first two. She has a bit of ability and is slowly learning the game. (op 5-1 tchd 4-1)
Point Blank(IRE) matched strides with the winner as the race began in earnest round the final turn, but he was the first to crack and faded disappointingly. He has worn a tongue tie for each of his bumper runs and that might suggest he could not see it out on the rain-softened ground, and he has something to prove now. (op 15-8 tchd 2-1 in a place)
T/Plt: £529.30 to a £1 stake. Pool: £45,680.79. 63.00 winning tickets. T/Qpdt: £64.20 to a £1 stake. Pool: £4,951.60. 57.00 winning tickets. CR

999 CARTMEL (L-H)
Thursday, August 26

OFFICIAL GOING: Good (good to soft in places; 6.9)
Wind: light 1/2 against Weather: fine

1375 ROYAL OAK INN (S) HURDLE (8 hdls) 2m 1f 110y
5:25 (5:25) (Class 5) 4-Y-O+ **£1,951** (£573; £286; £143)

Form RPR
1106 **1** **Dunaskin (IRE)**[12] 1249 10-11-12 115..........................(b) DougieCostello 120+
(Richard Guest) *mde all: wnt clr sn after last: heavily eased clsng stages* **6/4**[2]

2225 **2** *15* **Tri Nations (UAE)**[12] 1249 5-11-7 109..........(t) AdrianLane(3) 104
(Donald McCain) *sn chsng wnr: j. slowly 1st: chal 2 out: kpt on same pce appr last* **5/4**[1]

0/P0 **3** *17* **Devilfishpoker Com**[14] 1236 6-10-5 80.......... KyleJames(7) 73
(Shaun Harris) *chsd ldrs: stmbld bnd after 3rd: one pce fr 3 out* **33/1**

-040 **4** *12* **Murphys Future**[29] 1115 5-10-9 61.......... CampbellGillies(3) 61
(Alan Berry) *in rr: hdwy 5th: wknd next* **66/1**

610/ **5** *40* **Dancing Partner (USA)**[853] 5192 9-10-12 0.......... DavidEngland 21
(Terry Caldwell) *chsd ldrs: lost pl 5th: t.o next* **25/1**

6 *18* **Papa's Princess**[8] 6-10-5 0.......... BrianHughes —
(James Moffatt) *j. slowly 1st: chsd ldrs 5th: sn drvn: wknd next: sn bhd: t.o* **11/2**[3]

7 *34* **Pitbull**[21] 7-10-12 0.......... CharliePoste —
(Alan Berry) *in rr: hit 4th: sn bhd: t.o 3 out: virtually p.u run-in* **40/1**

4m 7.70s (-5.50) **Going Correction** 0.0s/f (Good) **7** Ran SP% **110.5**
Speed ratings (Par 103): **112,105,97,92,74 66,51**
toteswingers:1&2:£1.60, 1&3:£8.70, 2&3:£5.60 CSF £3.56 TOTE £2.50: £1.90, £1.10; EX 3.50.There was no bid for the winner.
Owner Miss Alison Ibbotson **Bred** J P And Miss M Mangan **Trained** Stainforth, S Yorks
■ Stewards' Enquiry : Adrian Lane one-day ban: careless riding (Sep 19)

FOCUS
A bloodless success for Dunaskin, who is rated close to his best. The runner-up was a bit below par. The time was ok for the grade.

NOTEBOOK
Dunaskin(IRE) won a C&D seller in May and he put a poor run at Market Rasen behind him to make all the running and maintain his 100 per cent record at the track (now 3-3). His connections have done well to get three wins out of him this season (also won twice on the Flat for Brian Ellison) and he will go home with current connections having not attracted a bid in the subsequent auction. He is likely to continue to ply his trade at this level. (op 11-8)
Tri Nations(UAE) is a consistent but moderate sort whose jumping has let him down recently. This is clearly his grade but he finds winning races difficult at present. (op 11-8 tchd 6-4)
Devilfishpoker Com has finished well held on both starts since a long absence and this third placing amounts to nothing.
Murphys Future showed little on his debut for a new yard and will find winning races difficult. (tchd 80-1)
Dancing Partner(USA) jumped badly. Official explanation: jockey said gelding had a breathing problem (op 16-1)

1376 AGRILEK H'CAP CHASE (20 fncs) 3m 6f
5:55 (5:55) (Class 4) (0-115,115) 5-Y-0+ **£3,903** (£1,146; £573; £286)

Form RPR

56-1 **1** **Volcanic Rock (IRE)**[8] 1287 10-11-6 **109**.......... MrDerekO'Connor 119+
(John Anthony Staunton, Ire) *hld up: gd hdwy to chse ldrs 15th: upsides 2 out: led gng easily appr last: drvn out fnl f* **7/2**[3]

5U44 **2** *1 3/4* **Petite Margot**[20] 1200 11-11-9 **115**.......... SamTwiston-Davies(3) 122
(Nigel Twiston-Davies) *chsd wnr: nt fluent 10th: drvn along 12th: outpcd 2 out: tk 2nd sn after last: rallied and almost upsides over 1f out: no ex* **3/1**[2]

P-61 **3** *6* **Simply Smashing (IRE)**[67] 804 10-11-1 **111**..........(t) KyleJames(7) 113
(Philip Kirby) *chsd ldrs: hit 14th: outpcd 4 out: wnt modest 3rd run-in: styd on fnl 2f* **9/2**

1P3P **4** *27* **Thunder Hawk (IRE)**[5] 1341 10-10-0 **89**..........(v) BrianHughes 67+
(Stuart Coltherd) *led: hdd appr last: wknd sn after last: eased towards fin* **9/2**

-211 **5** *127* **Shulmin**[87] 549 10-10-2 **91**.......... PeterBuchanan —
(Carol Ferguson) *in rr: hdwy to chse ldrs 15th: wknd 4 out: t.o 2 out: virtually p.u* **11/4**[1]

7m 29.0s (-7.20) **Going Correction** -0.10s/f (Good) **5** Ran SP% **110.3**
Speed ratings: **105,104,102,95,—**
CSF £14.31 TOTE £6.30: £1.80, £2.30; EX 12.30.
Owner P T McNamara **Bred** Mrs Karen A Sinnott **Trained** Tubber, Co. Galway

FOCUS
A weak handicap in which the first pair came clear. The winner produced a big step up for this longer trip.

NOTEBOOK
Volcanic Rock(IRE) gained his first win here in May over 3m2f but has been unable to follow up over shorter trips in Ireland since. Back up in trip and returned to Cartmel, he scored well having travelled well throughout. He could return here on Saturday and could take some beating as he is a strong stayer who jumps well. (tchd 10-3)
Petite Margot is a hard ride who as usual was off the bridle from some way out. This 3m6f trip suited her along with the drop in class and she ran on well to make a race of it on the run-in. Her stable has been in good form recently and she is clearly well suited by marathon trips. (op 9-4)
Simply Smashing(IRE) had been given a rise of 8lb for a career-best performance at Hexham last time and she is another who needs a stern test of stamina. Her three wins have been gained on courses with uphill finishes so a similar course should suit her better. (tchd 11-2)
Thunder Hawk(IRE) won a 3m2f hunter chase here in June but has been unable to reproduce that form since and a change of headgear today did not seem to help as he stopped quickly once headed. He is one to have reservations about. (op 17-2)
Shulmin improved to win two handicaps here in the spring, but she was never really travelling on this return from a break and will need more to win off a mark this high. Official explanation: jockey said mare never travelled (tchd 3-1)

1377 CARTMEL THANKS NIGEL TAYLOR BEGINNERS' CHASE (18 fncs) 3m 2f
6:25 (6:25) (Class 5) 5-Y-0+ **£2,602** (£764; £382; £190)

Form RPR

P332 **1** **Magical Legend**[20] 1197 9-10-7 0..........(t) PaulMoloney 110+
(Sophie Leech) *chsd ldrs: hdwy to ld 7th: blnd 2 out: racd lazily run-in: 3 l clr 100yds out: drvn rt out* **4/5**[1]

120- **2** *3/4* **Amalfi Coast**[299] 2011 11-11-0 108.......... BrianHughes 111
(Karen Tutty) *trckd ldrs: wnt 2nd 4 out: upsides 2 out: styd on same pce fnl f* **17/2**[3]

B0-3 **3** *1/2* **Risk Runner (IRE)**[42] 1000 7-11-0 0..........(v) GrahamLee 112
(James Moffatt) *nt fluent 1st: hdwy to chse ldrs 13th: kpt on same pce fnl f* **7/4**[2]

-44P **4** *51* **Little Girl**[67] 797 12-10-4 66.......... PeterToole(3) 53
(Ray Peacock) *led to 3rd: drvn 12th: lost pl 13th: sn bhd: t.o 2 out* **33/1**

5P **U** **Dougall (IRE)**[46] 951 7-11-0 0..........(p) TjadeCollier —
(Joanne Foster) *chsd ldr: led 3rd: hdd 7th: mstke and lost pl 13th: sn bhd: last whn mstke and uns rdr 2 out* **40/1**

6m 35.0s (0.10) **Going Correction** -0.10s/f (Good) **5** Ran SP% **107.8**
Speed ratings: **95,94,94,78,—**
CSF £7.48 TOTE £2.20: £2.60, £1.10; EX 7.20.
Owner R H Kerswell **Bred** R H And Mrs Kerswell **Trained** Kingsbridge, Devon

FOCUS
A very modest beginners' chase. The winner is better than the bare result but is rated below her best.

NOTEBOOK
Magical Legend chased home a useful sort at Worcester last time and was given a positive ride to score here despite idling on the run-in. She has now reached the frame in there of her four chasing starts. She clearly stays well and should continue to run well for connections. (op 8-11)
Amalfi Coast ran a satisfactory race on this debut for a new yard and nearly gave them their first winner under rules. He can continue to run well over the summer and may even run in point-to points for the trainer's two daughters to ride. (op 10-1 tchd 12-1)
Risk Runner(IRE) ran fairly well over an inadequate trip but he never really jumped with much enthusiasm. This capable hurdler is clearly not as good over fences. (op 15-8 tchd 13-8)

1378 CLB COOPERS AHEAD OF THE FIELD H'CAP CHASE (12 fncs) 2m 1f 110y
6:55 (6:55) (Class 5) (0-90,89) 4-Y-0+ **£2,602** (£764; £382; £190)

Form RPR

00U- **1** **Colditz (IRE)**[89] 6-10-1 **64**..........(p) GrahamLee 76+
(Richard Ford) *hld up in tch: mstke 8th: chsng ldrs whn hmpd on ins sn after last: led on ins over 2f out: hung bdly rt: jst hld on* **7/2**[1]

6425 **2** *hd* **Peak Seasons (IRE)**[34] 1080 7-10-1 **71**.......... JoeCornwall(7) 80
(Michael Chapman) *chsd ldrs: pushed along 6th: chal 3 out: upsides over 2f out: styd on towards fin* **9/2**[3]

3-63 **3** *9* **Stolen Light (IRE)**[57] 860 9-10-12 **78**..........(b) FearghalDavis(3) 80
(Andrew Crook) *chsd ldrs: led 8th: mstke last: hdd and n.m.r over 2f out: sn wknd* **4/1**[2]

P030 **4** *3 1/4* **Janal (IRE)**[2] 1360 7-9-7 **63** oh2.......... GaryRutherford(7) 63+
(Stuart Coltherd) *t.k.h: led: mstke and rdr briefly lost iron 7th: hdd next: mstke and rdr lost irons last: wknd fnl 2f* **15/2**

45-2 **5** *5* **Devils Delight (IRE)**[89] 520 8-11-0 **77**.......... BrianHughes 72
(James Moffatt) *in tch: hdwy 6th: outpcd whn pckd 3 out: sn wknd* **4/1**[2]

2053 **6** *70* **Ice Image (IRE)**[42] 1001 8-11-5 **89**.......... AlistairFindlay(7) 11
(George Charlton) *chsd ldrs: hit 4th: lost pl 8th: sn bhd: t.o whn blnd 2 out* **9/2**[3]

4m 21.6s (2.70) **Going Correction** -0.10s/f (Good) **6** Ran SP% **110.4**
Speed ratings (Par 103): **90,89,85,84,82 51**
toteswingers:1&2:£2.20, 1&3:£4.60, 2&3:£4.00 CSF £18.62 TOTE £4.70: £3.50, £3.50; EX 18.10.
Owner R J Hewitt **Bred** Darley **Trained** Butterton, Staffs
■ Stewards' Enquiry : Joe Cornwall one-day ban: careless riding (Sep 19)

FOCUS
A desperately weak handicap. The winner was better than the bare result and is rated better than the bare form.

NOTEBOOK
Colditz(IRE) was a non-stayer in points so this shorter trip suited him well and he ran on gamely to score. Making his debut for this yard, for whom he has thrived since joining, he benefited from being ridden by a jockey who rides the course well and he went up the inside rail (suffered interference) on the home turn which proved crucial. He could turn out here later in the week but he may not be up to carrying a penalty to victory. (op 6-1)
Peak Seasons(IRE) has been running only passably in his recent starts but he kept trying for his young rider and ran with credit. A 4-93 career record would not inspire you to back him next time out. (op 4-1)
Stolen Light(IRE) was third at Perth last time when running from out of the weights and he once again ran creditably but an inconsistent profile would make him opposable next time. (op 7-2 tchd 9-2)
Janal(IRE) recorded her sole win in 2009 but has been in poor form recently and she remains one to be against. Official explanation: jockey said he lost his stirrups final fence (op 8-1)
Devils Delight(IRE) lacks scope for fences and this was a poor effort from a usually consistent mare.
Ice Image(IRE) ran a poor race and remains a maiden. (op 7-2)

1379 MARKETING CARTMEL MARES' MAIDEN HURDLE (11 hdls) 2m 6f
7:30 (7:31) (Class 5) 4-Y-0+ **£2,332** (£724; £389)

Form RPR

53-P **1** **Lucky Score (IRE)**[66] 140 4-10-5 100.......... MissLHorner(5) 97+
(Chris Grant) *hld up: hdwy 6th: prom next: led narrowly last: rdn and forged clr 2f out* **15/2**[3]

5420 **2** *13* **Broadway Allstar (IRE)**[25] 1147 5-10-12 87.......... BrianHughes 86
(Karen Tutty) *chsd ldr: led 3 out: hdd last: sn wknd: lame* **9/1**

-032 **3** *7* **Saintly Lady (IRE)**[85] 577 5-10-12 96.......... TomO'Brien 81
(Peter Bowen) *led: mstke 7th: hdd 3 out: wknd appr last* **2/5**[1]

204/ **F** **Lady Rapido (IRE)**[839] 203 8-10-12 0.......... DenisO'Regan 76
(J J Lambe, Ire) *trckd ldrs: pushed along 8th: 4th and btn whn fell heavily 2 out* **5/1**[2]

04-P **F** **Just Jennings (IRE)**[91] 488 5-10-5 0.......... AlexanderVoy(7) —
(John Norton) *nt jump wl: j.rt: outpcd 5th: fell next* **40/1**

5m 31.2s (1.90) **Going Correction** 0.0s/f (Good)
WFA 4 from 5yo+ 14lb **5** Ran SP% **112.3**
Speed ratings (Par 103): **96,91,88,—,—**
CSF £58.66 TOTE £6.20: £2.90, £2.80; EX 54.70.
Owner Gareth Cheshire **Bred** J Cullinan **Trained** Newton Bewley, Co Durham

FOCUS
A weak mares' maiden run at a modest pace. The form is rated around the first two.

NOTEBOOK
Lucky Score(IRE) was tailed off on the Flat last time but joined current connections for £4,000 and went some way to repaying that with a decisive victory here. She was well placed to find such a weak race and it will have to be a similarly weak race if she is to score again. (op 8-1 tchd 10-1)
Broadway Allstar(IRE) managed a moderate second at Market Rasen before her limitations were exposed in a handicap at that venue last time. She ran honourably and gave her all here, but she still remains a maiden. Her rider dismounted her after the finish, though. (op 11-1)
Saintly Lady(IRE) ran a lifeless race and was disappointing. Significant improvement would be needed if she is to score in the future. Official explanation: trainer's rep said he had no explanation for the poor form shown (op 4-9)
Lady Rapido(IRE) comes from the family of Cool Dawn and her future looks to be at stud after her crashing fall here. (tchd 6-1)

1380 ARMY BENEVOLENT CHALLENGE CUP H'CAP HURDLE (12 hdls) 3m 2f
8:00 (8:00) (Class 4) (0-105,103) 4-Y-0+ **£2,602** (£764; £382; £190)

Form RPR

/0F5 **1** **Mad Moose (IRE)**[42] 1004 6-11-8 **102**.......... SamTwiston-Davies(3) 115+
(Nigel Twiston-Davies) *trckd ldrs: chal 3 out: led between last 2: styd on strly: readily* **10/3**[2]

2/21 **2** *2 3/4* **Corso Palladio (IRE)**[7] 1291 8-11-9 **100** 7ex..........(p) TomO'Brien 113+
(Peter Bowen) *trckd ldrs: stmbld landing and lost pl 2 out: rallied to chse wnr over 1f out: no imp* **4/5**[1]

06/5 **3** *3 3/4* **Panzer (GER)**[27] 1137 9-9-12 **85**.......... HenryBrooke(10) 90
(Donald McCain) *w ldr 3rd: led next: hdd between last 2: one pce* **9/1**[3]

4-04 **4** *11* **Converti**[31] 1094 6-11-9 **103**.......... RyanMania(3) 97
(Simon Burrough) *wl away: led and clr to 2nd: hdd 4th: wknd 2 out* **10/1**

4064 **5** *21* **Clueless**[24] 1049 8-10-0 **77** oh5..............................(p) PeterBuchanan 50
(Carol Ferguson) *nt fluent towards rr: lost pl 7th: bhd fr 9th: tk poor 5th sn after last* **20/1**
4-60 **6** *18* **Night Knight (IRE)**[13] 604 4-10-0 **85**..............................(tp) MissLHorner(5) 37
(Chris Grant) *hld up in rr: effrt 9th: wknd 3 out: t.o last* **20/1**
6m 22.3s (-3.80) **Going Correction** 0.0s/f (Good)
WFA 4 from 6yo+ 15lb **6** Ran SP% **107.2**
Speed ratings (Par 105): **105,104,103,99,93 87**
toteswingers:1&2:£1.90, 1&3:£3.40, 2&3:£2.10 CSF £6.04 TOTE £4.90: £2.30, £1.10; EX 7.50 Place 6 £81.64; Place 5 £74.49.
Owner N A Twiston-Davies **Bred** Miss E And Miss M Murphy **Trained** Naunton, Gloucs

FOCUS
A modest handicap hurdle. The winner is rated back to the level of his best 2009 form.

NOTEBOOK
Mad Moose(IRE) was going well in a fair race when falling at Ffos Las two starts ago and was never travelling or jumping here last time. This step up in trip seemed to help and he kept galloping towards the line. He may be up to scoring again as his jumping seems to have improved.
Corso Palladio(IRE) has improved markedly since joining this yard and being fitted with cheekpieces. He stayed on resolutely after stumbling at the second from home. He may well have been unlucky but he is due for a rise in the weights now which could halt his progress.
Panzer(GER) scored at Wetherby in 2006 on quick ground but has shown little since then including on reappearance from a mammoth absence at Bangor when last seen. However, this was a better showing on his debut over this trip. His trainer will have to place him well if he is to score though.
Converti was making his second start for this yard and shaped as if he needs to drop in trip. He has dropped to a feasible mark but he is hard to win with.
T/Plt: £111.70 to a £1 stake. Pool:£48,962.21 - 319.93 winning tickets T/Qpdt: £36.80 to a £1 stake. Pool:£5,029.78 - 101.10 winning tickets WG

1381a -1388a - (Foreign Racing) - See Raceform Interactive

1369 FFOS LAS (L-H)
Friday, August 27

OFFICIAL GOING: Flat course - good to soft (7.7); jumps courses - good (good to soft in places; 7.9)
Wind: Fresh across Weather: Fine

1389 HM PLANT HITACHI NOVICES' CHASE (17 fncs) 2m 5f
4:15 (4:15) (Class 4) 4-Y-0+ **£4,423** (£1,521)

Form RPR
0121 **1** **To Arms**[24] 1177 8-11-7 134..............................(t) APMcCoy 135+
(Lawney Hill) *chsd ldr tl led after 11th: clr fr 4 out: easily* **2/5**[1]
2 *50* **Mythical Prince**[113] 4182 6-11-0 0.............................. PaulMoloney 103
(Evan Williams) *led: mstke 11th: sn hdd: rdn after 13th: outpcd fr next: nt fluent 2 out: t.o: fatally injured* **4/1**[2]
2-51 **P** **Mission Control (IRE)**[13] 1251 5-11-7 0.............................. RichardJohnson —
(Tim Vaughan) *hld up in tch: outpcd 9th: sn p.u: lame* **9/2**[3]
5m 21.2s (-8.80) **Going Correction** -0.65s/f (Firm) **3** Ran SP% **109.6**
Speed ratings (Par 105): **98,78,**—
CSF £2.46 TOTE £1.40; EX 2.40.
Owner Carl Pyne **Bred** Mrs M Chaworth Musters **Trained** Aston Rowant, Oxon

FOCUS
A dry night and sunny morning resulted in the ground drying out to Good, good to soft in places on the jumps track. A small field for this novices' chase. The winner is rated to his previous best.

NOTEBOOK
To Arms, an easy winner over C&D on his return to fences after a good spell over hurdles this spring and summer, jumped well throughout and, once left in front by his sole remaining rival's mistake at the 11th, he was always well in command.
Mythical Prince, making his chasing debut on his first run since joining current connections from Ireland, made the running and jumped pretty well until hitting the ditch on the far side on the second circuit. He was struggling from that point but sadly was found to have severed a tendon and had to be put down. Official explanation: jockey said gelding finished lame (op 5-1)
Mission Control(IRE), who was always in the rear, was pulled up quickly after the first fence on the second circuit. Official explanation: jockey said gelding pulled up lame (op 4-1)

1390 TOTEEXACTA FLEXI BETTING CHASE H'CAP CHASE (13 fncs) 2m
4:50 (4:50) (Class 2) 4-Y-0+ **£19,011** (£5,616; £2,808; £1,404; £702)

Form RPR
-211 **1** **West With The Wind**[71] 770 5-11-12 **140**.............................. PaulMoloney 150+
(Evan Williams) *chsd ldrs: lft 2nd 9th: sn led: wnt lft 2 out: styd on gamely* **7/1**
/112 **2** *1 ¼* **Yellow Flag**[26] 1151 7-10-9 **123**.............................. APMcCoy 130
(Jonjo O'Neill) *hld up: hdwy 4 out: rdn to chse wnr 2 out: unable qck towards fin* **7/2**[2]
-233 **3** *5* **Nudge And Nurdle (IRE)**[6] 1327 9-10-10 **124**.............................. PaddyBrennan 127
(Nigel Twiston-Davies) *sn pushed along in rr: stdy hdwy fr 4 out: edgd lft appr last: nt rch ldrs* **5/1**[3]
F442 **4** *5* **Knight Legend (IRE)**[31] 1110 11-10-13 **127**..............................(t) RhysFlint 127
(Philip Hobbs) *chsd ldr to 4th: remained handy: hmpd 9th: styd on same pce fr 3 out* **7/1**
024- **5** *½* **Enlightenment (IRE)**[141] 5097 10-10-13 **130**.............................. DPFahy(3) 128
(Evan Williams) *prom: chsd ldr 4th: lft in ld 9th: sn hdd: chsd wnr tl wnt lft 2 out: sn wknd* **14/1**
4256 **6** *1 ¼* **Mibleu (FR)**[8] 1299 10-10-4 **123**.............................. KeiranBurke(5) 120
(Colin Tizzard) *hld up: hdwy 8th: wknd appr last* **33/1**
6/0P **7** *46* **Killenaule Boy**[6] 1332 8-11-4 **132**..............................(t) TomScudamore 87
(David Pipe) *prom: hit 1st: sn lost pl: drvn along 5th: bhd fr next: t.o* **18/1**
31 **F** **Grand Lahou (FR)**[8] 1299 7-10-9 **123** 6ex.............................. RichardJohnson —
(Tim Vaughan) *led: mstkes 1st and 4th: slt ld whn fell 9th* **15/8**[1]
/13U **P** **Smack That (IRE)**[47] 959 8-11-3 **134**.............................. PeterToole(3) —
(Milton Harris) *sn bhd: t.o whn p.u bef 4 out* **14/1**
3m 50.7s (-14.30) **Going Correction** -0.65s/f (Firm) **9** Ran SP% **120.2**
Speed ratings (Par 109): **109,108,105,103,103 102,79,**—,—
Tote Swingers: 1&2 £6.00, 1&3 £8.10, 2&3 £5.10 CSF £34.11 CT £137.57 TOTE £8.10: £2.30, £1.20, £2.30; EX 33.00 Trifecta £99.80 Pool: £346.492 - 2.57 winning units..
Owner Mrs Janet Davies **Bred** Newsells Park Stud **Trained** Llancarfan, Vale Of Glamorgan

FOCUS
A valuable handicap chase for the time of year and it attracted a decent field. The pace was good from the start. The winner recorded a small personal best.

NOTEBOOK
West With The Wind has really got his act together over fences this summer and has proven well suited by a flat track and a sound surface. Making his handicap debut over fences, he looked to have a stiff task off a mark of 140. However, he settled in behind the leaders, and once left in front by the fall of the favourite, gradually drew away from his stable companion. He then had enough left to hold off the runner-up after the last and complete his hat-trick over C&D. He will not find things easy once reassessed, but this was a case of job done. (op 15-2)
Yellow Flag has returned this season from a near two-year absence better than ever. He was held up early but had a lot to do at around the halfway mark. However, he gradually began to eat into the leaders' advantage, and looked a real threat jumping the last before the winner found more. (op 4-1 tchd 9-2 and 3-1)
Nudge And Nurdle(IRE) is ideally suited by longer trips and found the pace too much for him early. His stamina came into play in the home straight and he kept on, but the principals had gone beyond recall. (op 6-1)
Knight Legend(IRE) has not won since coming to this country from Ireland. He tried to race up with the pace early but hit the first fence and then gradually lost his pitch from around the halfway mark. (op 15-2 tchd 8-1)
Enlightenment(IRE), a stable companion of the winner, was having his first start since April. He was left in second place after the last on the far side, but could not keep pace with his stablemate and tired once in line from home. The run should bring him on. (op 12-1)
Mibleu(FR) chased the leading group most of the way but could make no progress in the straight and probably needs faster ground. (op 28-1)
Grand Lahou(FR) set the pace and was beginning to get his rivals strung out when coming down at the last fence on the far side, five from home. (tchd 2-1)

1391 TOTETRIFECTA FLEXI BETTING H'CAP HURDLE (12 hdls) 3m
5:20 (5:20) (Class 3) (0-135,133) 4-Y-0 **£6,337** (£1,872; £936; £468; £234)

Form RPR
5351 **1** **Ripalong Lad (IRE)**[44] 986 9-10-10 **117**..............................(p) TomO'Brien 128+
(Peter Bowen) *chsd ldrs: led 2 out: clr last: easily* **5/1**[3]
5P-1 **2** *10* **Ambrose Princess (IRE)**[30] 340 5-10-13 **120**..........(p) TomScudamore 120
(Michael Scudamore) *led: mstke 6th: hdd 2 out: sn outpcd* **7/1**
-3P1 **3** *15* **Hermoso (IRE)**[47] 946 5-9-12 **108**.............................. SamTwiston-Davies(3) 94
(Nigel Twiston-Davies) *hld up: hdwy 9th: rdn after 3 out: wknd bef next: lame* **2/1**[1]
3311 **4** *22* **Barnhill Brownie (IRE)**[21] 1198 7-11-7 **133**..............................(t) GilesHawkins(5) 99
(Philip Hobbs) *chsd ldr to 9th: wknd bef next: t.o* **13/2**
1-1 **5** *21* **Thyne For Deploy (IRE)**[20] 1211 6-10-10 **117**..............................(p) APMcCoy 64
(Michael Hourigan, Ire) *prom tl rdn and wknd after 9th: t.o* **5/1**[3]
212 **U** **Oursininlaw (IRE)**[10] 1275 6-9-10 **110**.............................. AdamWedge(7) —
(Evan Williams) *hld up: hdwy and mstke 8th: cl 4th and gng wl whn n.m.r and uns rdr jst bef next* **7/2**[2]
5m 43.3s (-3.70) **Going Correction** -0.875s/f (Firm) **6** Ran SP% **114.7**
Speed ratings (Par 107): **107,103,98,91,84** —
Tote Swingers: 1&2 £4.60, 1&3 £1.50, 2&3 £4.10 CSF £37.71 TOTE £7.70: £2.80, £3.90; EX 48.20.
Owner A P Davies **Bred** Sean Murtagh **Trained** Little Newcastle, Pembrokes

FOCUS
A decent staying handicap hurdle with the majority of these coming into the race in good form. The winner seemingly produced a big step up, with the second to his mark.

NOTEBOOK
Ripalong Lad(IRE) has been running well back over hurdles this summer and, despite being 9lb higher than for his last success, he was always travelling well in this. He came right away once going to the front at the second last and the handicapper will have his say now, but connections always have the option of returning to fences, where he could be better handicapped. (tchd 11-2)
Ambrose Princess(IRE), fit from a successful spell on the Flat, made the running and jumped well, gradually shaking off most of her rivals. However, she could not get away from the winner, and had nothing more to give once he went on. This was still a creditable effort. (tchd 6-1 and 8-1)
Hermoso(IRE) was sent off favourite and was held up at the back. His jumping was not as fluent as some of his rivals but he responded to his rider's brief urgings to close up turning for home. He looked a big threat there but could offer disappointingly little once his rider went for everything. Official explanation: jockey said gelding finished lame (tchd 7-4 and 9-4 in a place)
Barnhill Brownie(IRE) came into this on a hat-trick but was being nudged along as early as the fourth flight. He was under serious pressure before the home turn and dropped away from that point. (op 5-1)
Thyne For Deploy(IRE), in first-time cheekpieces, tracked the leaders from the start but was quickly done with after the last on the far side. He seems to have lost his way for the time being. (op 6-1)
Oursininlaw(IRE) was held up early and was still close enough when unshipping his rider going into the last flight on the far side, four from home. (op 4-1)

1392 WALTERS UK CIVIL ENGINEERING & CONSTRUCTION NOVICES' HURDLE (8 hdls) 2m
5:50 (5:50) (Class 4) 4-Y-0+ **£2,927** (£859; £429; £214)

Form RPR
32-1 **1** **Lucaindubai (IRE)**[113] 168 4-11-4 114.............................. PaulMoloney 122+
(Evan Williams) *mde all: clr whn blnd last: easily* **11/8**[1]
1 **2** *4 ½* **Khorun (GER)**[12] 1260 5-11-5 0.............................. RichardJohnson 114
(Tim Vaughan) *a.p: chsd wnr 3 out: rdn appr last: styd on same pce* **6/4**[2]
623 **3** *1 ½* **Rafta (IRE)**[15] 1238 4-10-4 104.............................. BarryKeniry 98
(W G Harrison) *chsd ldrs: rdn appr 3 out: styd on same pce fr 2 out* **12/1**
3F16 **4** *11* **Totoman**[28] 1138 5-10-12 115..............................(t) MrTomDavid(7) 103
(Tim Vaughan) *chsd wnr to 3 out: sn rdn: wknd after next* **9/1**[3]
5 *22* **Granakey (IRE)**[143] 7-10-5 0.............................. TomO'Brien 69
(Peter Bowen) *mstke 1st: hld up: wknd 3 out* **14/1**
-060 **6** *28* **Calypso Bay (IRE)**[31] 1111 4-10-11 0.............................. APMcCoy 50
(Jonjo O'Neill) *sn trcking ldrs: nt fluent 4th: eased after 5th: t.o* **10/1**
3m 41.2s (-7.80) **Going Correction** -0.875s/f (Firm)
WFA 4 from 5yo+ 13lb **6** Ran SP% **115.6**
Speed ratings (Par 105): **97,94,94,88,77 63**
Tote Swingers: 1&2 £1.02 CSF £4.10 TOTE £2.40: £1.50, £1.20; EX 3.40 Place 6:£214.63 Place 5: £66.61..
Owner R J Gambarini **Bred** Martin Cullinane **Trained** Llancarfan, Vale Of Glamorgan

FOCUS
A fair novices' hurdle that looked to be dominated by local yards, the betting backed that up and that was how the race worked out. The easy winner produced another step up.

NOTEBOOK
Lucaindubai(IRE), who made all when scoring over 3f further on his previous start, adopted the same tactics and had this won from early in the straight. He made an error at the last flight but that did not stop him running on well, and the hat-trick looks a distinct possibility. (op 6-4 tchd 13-8)
Khorun(GER) got off the mark on his previous start and looked set to play a major role here. He was held up before being produced in the straight but the winner was always cantering over him. He can win again in ordinary company. (op 2-1)
Rafta(IRE) was useful last season before taking exception to racing on the Flat. However, she seems to enjoy hurdling and arguably ran her best race so far. She can win a small handicap or mares' hurdle on a sound surface. (op 8-1)
Totoman raced prominently early but was quite keen and paid for it at the business end. (op 8-1)
Granakey(IRE), a moderate AW performer at around 1m, was making her first appearance over hurdles and also her first on turf. She got around in her own time but will probably need to be contesting low-grade handicaps before making an impression. (op 8-1)
Calypso Bay(IRE) has been very disappointing and will need to improve a good deal to win any sort of race on this evidence. (op 5-1)
T/Plt: £195.40 to a £1 stake. Pool:£64,560.28 - 241.10 winning tickets T/Qpdt: £21.60 to a £1 stake. Pool:£5,717.59 - 195.42 winning tickets CR

[1375]CARTMEL (L-H)

Saturday, August 28

OFFICIAL GOING: Good (good to firm in places; 8.1)

Rail on both bends moved out 3m and roadside rail moved out 2m.

Wind: light 1/2 against Weather: overcast, changeable, light showers

1401 ROOFING CONSULTANTS LTD NOVICES' HURDLE (11 hdls) 2m 6f

1:35 (1:35) (Class 4) 4-Y-0+ **£2,602** (£764; £382; £190)

Form RPR

6/6 **1** **Ben's Folly (IRE)**[14] 1254 5-10-12 102 RichardJohnson 106+
(Tim Vaughan) *w ldr: led 6th: drvn clr run-in* **2/1**[2]

01-2 **2** *9* **Elevenses**[114] 180 6-11-5 0 BrianHughes 105
(James Moffatt) *trckd ldrs: wnt 2nd after 2 out: no imp* **6/1**[3]

32 **3** *2* **Treason Trial**[7] 1325 9-10-12 95 BarryKeniry 97
(Joss Saville) *t.k.h: trckd ldrs: hit 8th: nt fluent and outpcd next: styd on to take 3rd appr last* **18/1**

6662 **4** *14* **Kings Riches (IRE)**[18] 1228 5-10-9 102 DonalDevereux(3) 86
(Peter Bowen) *led: mstke 2nd: hdd 6th: nt fluent 8th: wknd sn after 2 out* **11/8**[1]

64 **5** *13* **King's Lion (IRE)**[13] 1260 6-10-9 0 AdamPogson(3) 77
(Charles Pogson) *t.k.h in last: gd hdwy to chse ldrs 8th: wnt cl 2nd 2 out: sn wknd: eased whn bhd clsng stages* **7/1**

U **6** *88* **Tenth Avenue (IRE)**[8] 1308 5-10-9 0 AdrianLane(3) —
(Donald McCain) *chsd ldrs: reminders 5th: lost pl 7th: sn wl bhd: t.o 3 out* **33/1**

5m 30.6s (1.30) **Going Correction** -0.15s/f (Good) **6** Ran SP% **110.4**
Speed ratings (Par 105): **91,87,87,81,77 45**
Tote Swingers: 1&2 £3.50, 1&3 £8.10, 2&3 £3.70 CSF £13.61 TOTE £3.60: £1.90, £3.30; EX 17.40.

Owner David Lovell **Bred** Mrs Kathleen Hennessy **Trained** Aberthin, Vale of Glamorgan

FOCUS

The rail on both bends was moved out three metres, and the roadside rail was moved out two metres to provide fresh ground. The ground had dried out a little overnight but was described as "good" by the winning jockey in the first, a very modest novice hurdle run at a steady pace. Improvement from the winner, with the next two setting the level.

NOTEBOOK

Ben's Folly(IRE) travelled best throughout and came clear off the final turn to win emphatically. Things will be harder under a penalty, but he promises to get further than this and handles soft ground too. (op 11-4)

Elevenses, a winner at Fontwell for Paul Nicholls in the spring, was making his debut for connections on this first run since May. He ran respectably under his penalty, but looked one-paced in the latter stages. (op 11-2)

Treason Trial, back up in trip, plugged on for a soundly beaten third. His hurdling lacked fluency. (op 14-1)

Kings Riches(IRE) jumped a little sketchily and was soon in trouble once headed by the winner. He did not appear to stay the trip, but should do in time. Official explanation: jockey said gelding ran flat (tchd 6-4)

King's Lion(IRE), ridden differently to Southwell, was held up in last place, taking a keen pull again. He made rapid progress into second place two from home, only to tie up badly on the long run to the final flight. He will have to settle a lot better if he is to see out this sort of trip under rules. (tchd 13-2 and 8-1)

1402 TOTEPOOL FLEXI BETTING BEGINNERS' CHASE (14 fncs) 2m 5f 110y

2:05 (2:06) (Class 4) 4-Y-0+ **£3,252** (£955; £477; £238)

Form RPR

3-4F **1** **Frankie Anson (IRE)**[14] 1251 6-11-7 117 BrianHughes 121+
(Alan Swinbank) *trckd ldrs: pushed along 10th: led last: drvn out* **4/5**[1]

4- **2** *3½* **Mister Two Fifty (IRE)**[181] 4342 7-11-7 114 APMcCoy 115
(John Anthony Staunton, Ire) *t.k.h: trckd ldrs: wnt 2nd 10th: led 2 out: hdd last: kpt on same pce* **3/1**[2]

221/ **3** *12* **Lockstown**[539] 4344 7-11-7 105 GrahamLee 108+
(Ann Hamilton) *chsd ldrs: 3rd whn hit 3 out: wknd last* **5/1**[3]

63 **4** *16* **Overquest**[37] 1068 8-11-7 0 JohnnyFarrelly 90
(Elliott Cooper) *chsd ldrs: outpcd 9th: lost pl next: sn bhd* **33/1**

00-0 **5** *32* **Finzi Contini (FR)**[7] 1326 6-11-7 107 (p) RichardJohnson 61
(Tim Vaughan) *reluctant to go to s: chsd ldrs: reluctant and lost pl after 9th: sn bhd: nt keen* **16/1**

5 **6** *15* **Queen Court (IRE)**[21] 1213 8-11-0 0 TomO'Brien 40
(R K Watson, Ire) *mstke 1st: wl in tch: outpcd 9th: bhd whn mstke 3 out* **28/1**

F **Wapiti Creek (IRE)**[82] 668 6-10-7 0 (t) MarkQuinlan(7) —
(John G Carr, Ire) *led: hdd and fell 2 out* **50/1**

5m 22.8s (-2.60) **Going Correction** +0.075s/f (Yiel) **7** Ran SP% **111.5**
Speed ratings (Par 105): **107,105,101,95,83 78,—**
Tote Swingers: 1&2 £1.02, 1&3 £1.60, 2&3 £1.90 CSF £3.46 TOTE £1.70: £1.10, £2.20; EX 4.10.

Owner Frank Hanson **Bred** Wendy Kochman **Trained** Melsonby, N Yorks

FOCUS

An ordinary beginners' chase, with the form rated around the first two.

NOTEBOOK

Frankie Anson(IRE) did not appear to be going that well at one stage, but came away on the long run-in to score comfortably enough, value for a bit further as he was idling in front. The form pick here, he had been very unfortunate to keel over at the last at Market Rasen with the race at his mercy last time. This win should have done his confidence a bit of good and he will be more effective on more galloping tracks. (op 10-11)

Mister Two Fifty(IRE), one of three Irish-trained runners, ran a decent race on this first start for six months but was perhaps flattered to have finished as close as he did to the winner. All his four previous chases had been in heavy conditions (second once), but he did win a point on good ground. (op 7-2 tchd 11-4)

Lockstown was well beaten in the end on this chase debut, but is fully entitled to improve for this first run since March last year. He won his sole point-to-point on good ground, but probably prefers softer conditions. (tchd 11-2)

Finzi Contini(FR) gave trouble before the start and is one to be very wary of. (op 10-1)

Wapiti Creek(IRE) was another having her first run over regulation fences. She made the running and attempted to get clear at one stage, but had been joined when falling two out. (op 40-1)

1403 GRANT THORNTON UK LLP NOVICES' H'CAP CHASE (12 fncs) 2m 1f 110y

2:35 (2:35) (Class 4) (0-105,102) 4-Y-0+ **£3,332** (£1,034; £557)

Form RPR

FU63 **1** **Morning Sunshine (IRE)**[13] 1260 7-10-13 92 AdrianLane(3) 100+
(Donald McCain) *hld up in last: hdwy to trck ldrs 9th: chal on ins sn after last: led over 1f out: drvn out* **3/1**[2]

4F-P **2** *1¼* **Tranos (USA)**[108] 290 7-11-1 91 BarryKeniry 98
(Micky Hammond) *chsd ldrs: hit 8th: sn outpcd: styd on wl run-in to go 2nd 1f out: kpt on same pce* **13/2**[3]

2F21 **3** *6* **Emotive**[7] 1338 7-11-6 99 CampbellGillies(3) 102+
(Barry Murtagh) *chsd ldr: pckd bdly 3rd (water): drvn 3 out: one pce: lft 3rd ins fnl f* **15/8**[1]

-301 **P** **High Stand Lad**[44] 1001 8-11-12 102 (t) DenisO'Regan 108
(Martin Todhunter) *nt fluent 8th: led: hdd over 1f out: 2 l down whn stmbld path: 3rd whn p.u jst ins fnl f: fatally injured* **15/8**[1]

4m 24.0s (5.10) **Going Correction** +0.075s/f (Yiel) **4** Ran SP% **107.9**
Speed ratings (Par 105): **91,90,87,—**
CSF £17.47 TOTE £3.00; EX 15.50.

Owner Jon Glews & Peter Knight **Bred** Peter Mc Manamy **Trained** Cholmondeley, Cheshire

FOCUS

An ordinary novices' handicap chase, but the pace was solid and the form should prove sound. The winner is rated to his mark.

NOTEBOOK

Morning Sunshine(IRE), back over fences, was held up in touch and somewhat keen again. Coming through to win fairly decisively, he could be capable of building on this although he isn't straightforward. (op 7-2)

Tranos(USA), off the track since May, looked set to finish last at one stage only to stage a determined finish once round the final bend. He is a limited performer, though, now without a win in 11 tries over fences. (op 8-1 tchd 6-1)

Emotive pitched on landing over the water jump on the first circuit but jumped soundly otherwise. He was held after the final fence, but despite the 8lb rise for his Perth win this consistent sort may be able to win again. (op 11-8)

High Stand Lad ran a brave race from the front only to break down on the run-in with fatal consequences. (op 2-1)

1404 HADWINS H'CAP CHASE (FOR CAVENDISH CUP) (18 fncs) 3m 2f

3:10 (3:10) (Class 3) (0-130,127) 4-Y-0+ **£6,505** (£1,910; £955; £477)

Form RPR

3-14 **1** **No Panic (IRE)**[32] 1108 7-11-10 125 (p) TomO'Brien 130
(Peter Bowen) *trckd ldrs: led 2 out: edgd rt fnl f: hld on gamely* **7/2**[2]

U3-4 **2** *½* **Cool Running (IRE)**[116] 139 10-11-9 124 APMcCoy 129
(Jonjo O'Neill) *hld up: hdwy and prom 13th: chsd wnr over 3f out: shkn up over 1f out: styd on: no ex clsng stages* **12/1**

6-11 **3** *3¼* **Volcanic Rock (IRE)**[2] 1376 10-11-1 116 7ex MrDerekO'Connor 118
(John Anthony Staunton, Ire) *in rr: hdwy and prom 13th: wnt 3rd over 2f out: kpt on same pce* **7/4**[1]

/5-2 **4** *6* **Backbord (GER)**[8] 1312 8-11-11 126 (bt) LeightonAspell 123
(Lucy Wadham) *wnt prom 7th: drvn 4 out: chsd wnr last: wknd over 1f out* **11/2**[3]

-201 **5** *32* **Seize**[32] 1103 8-10-13 114 GrahamLee 82
(Ferdy Murphy) *nt fluent in rr: outpcd 14th: bhd fr 3 out* **15/2**

122F **6** *3½* **Dead Or Alive (IRE)**[7] 1332 7-11-12 127 (t) RichardJohnson 92
(Tim Vaughan) *jnd ldrs and blnd 7th: drvn 12th: wknd 2 out* **8/1**

6- **7** *11* **Speedy Max (IRE)**[22] 1207 9-10-6 110 (t) PeterToole(3) 65
(George Stanley, Ire) *chsd ldr: led after 12th: hdd 2 out: wknd appr last* **25/1**

0-P0 **8** *28* **Seymour Weld**[27] 1151 10-11-7 125 AdamPogson(3) 55
(Charles Pogson) *led tl after 12th: wknd 14th: t.o last* **18/1**

6m 31.9s (-3.00) **Going Correction** +0.075s/f (Yiel) **8** Ran SP% **113.6**
Speed ratings (Par 107): **107,106,105,104,94 93,89,81**
Tote Swingers: 1&2 £3.80, 1&3 £2.00, 2&3 £4.80 CSF £41.32 CT £95.33 TOTE £3.30: £1.10, £2.30, £1.70; EX 24.40.

Owner Roddy Owen & Paul Fullagar **Bred** John Ryan **Trained** Little Newcastle, Pembrokes

■ Stewards' Enquiry : Mr Derek O'Connor two-day ban: used whip above shoulder height (tbn)
Tom O'Brien caution: careless riding.

FOCUS

A fair handicap chase run at a sound pace, and the form should stand up. The winner is rated back to his best. Four pulled well clear of the others in the latter stages.

NOTEBOOK

No Panic(IRE) appreciated the return to fences and stuck his neck out gamely in the final 100 yards to hold on to his advantage. This consistent gelding stays further than this and seems pretty versatile as regards ground conditions. (op 9-2)

Cool Running(IRE) was disappointing in three hunter chases in the spring, but was fresh from a break and had the assistance of the champion jockey for the first time since coming to Britain. Under a patient ride, the gelding momentarily looked like getting up but could produce no extra late on after the winner had carried him right. He had some useful form in Ireland for the Christy Roche yard and is obviously on a workable mark at present. (op 10-1)

Volcanic Rock(IRE), penalised for his comfortable win here two days earlier, gradually worked his way into contention but could not quicken late on over this half-mile shorter trip. (op 5-2)

Backbord(GER) tried in a combination of blinkers and a tongue tie, was the first of the leading quartet to cry enough, but this was still a respectable performance. He remains capable of winning again when the mood takes him. (op 6-1 tchd 13-2)

Seize went up 7lb to a career-high mark for his win at Perth a month ago and he was always towards the rear here, putting in more than one slow jump. (op 11-2 tchd 5-1)

Dead Or Alive(IRE), runner-up to the fifth horse at Perth, survived a seventh-fence blunder but remained in contention until weakening going to the last. (op 13-2)

Speedy Max(IRE), a tall challenger from Ireland, faded quickly after relinquishing his lead two from home. (tchd 20-1)

1405 MINSTER JAGUAR H'CAP HURDLE (11 hdls) 2m 6f

3:45 (3:45) (Class 3) (0-125,123) 4-Y-0+ **£5,204** (£1,528; £764; £381)

Form RPR

100P **1** **Two Miles West (IRE)**[32] 1108 9-11-5 116 APMcCoy 119+
(Jonjo O'Neill) *chsd ldrs: pushed along 6th: blnd and lost pl 8th: wnt 4th 2 out: chsd wnr over 1f out: styd on to ld towards fin* **3/1**[2]

15F0 **2** *nk* **Flying Doctor**[22] 1198 7-11-7 118 JohnnyFarrelly 117
(Elliott Cooper) *trckd ldrs: smooth hdwy to trake cl 2nd 3 out: led appr last: hdd and no ex nr fin* **7/1**

2644 **3** *3¼* **Storm Prospect**[31] 1118 7-10-5 102 (b) PeterBuchanan 98
(Lucinda Russell) *in tch: nt fluent 1st: pushed along 7th: hdwy to chse ldrs 3 out: kpt on same pce run-in: tk 3rd towards fin* **4/1**[3]

1633 **4** *½* **Soubriquet (IRE)**[22] 1198 7-10-10 107 MichaelMcAlister 104
(Maurice Barnes) *led to 2nd: led 5th tl appr last: kpt on one pce* **9/4**[1]

333 **5** *10* **Apache Dawn**[9] 1296 6-10-0 97 (t) LiamTreadwell 86
(Aytach Sadik) *w ldr: led 2nd to 5th: wknd appr 2 out* **6/1**

50P0 **6** *25* **Samizdat (FR)**[10] 745 7-10-1 101 RyanMania(3) 65
(Dianne Sayer) *in tch: drvn 8th: outpcd whn hit 3 out: sn lost pl and bhd* **11/1**

5m 29.1s (-0.20) **Going Correction** -0.15s/f (Good) **6** Ran SP% **110.9**
Speed ratings (Par 107): **94,93,92,92,88 79**
Tote Swingers: 1&2 £5.00, 1&3 £2.90, 2&3 £3.60 CSF £22.24 TOTE £3.80: £2.20, £3.60; EX 17.80.

Owner John P McManus **Bred** Tower Bloodstock **Trained** Cheltenham, Gloucs

FOCUS
A modest race for the grade, with the top-weight rated 7lb below the race maximum, and not form to treat positively. The winner returned to something like his best. The time was a second and a half quicker than the opening novice hurdle.

NOTEBOOK
Two Miles West(IRE) had been well beaten since winning at Worcester in June and was still 5lb higher here, but won a very competitive handicap at Aintree in 2007 off 9lb more. Already being niggled along when a blunder four out saw him drop to the rear, he remained in contention and inched his way to the front close home under another superlative Tony McCoy ride. The horse deserves credit too for battling as hard as he did. Official explanation: trainers rep said, regarding apparent improvement in form, that the gelding is inconsistent. (op 7-2)
Flying Doctor was 10lb higher than when winning here in May and had been below-par of late, but he bounced back to form. He was going best when taking it up, but was just run out of it. (op 6-1)
Storm Prospect did not get as far behind as he sometimes does, but although he plugged on up the long run-in he lacked the pace to trouble the principals. (op 9-2)
Soubriquet(IRE) was able to race off his correct mark here and he ran well for a long way. He was without the usual tongue tie. (tchd 5-2)
Apache Dawn, a first Cartmel ride for Liam Treadwell, was well held on this return to handicap company and remains a maiden after 25 tries over jumps now. (op 11-2)

1406 TOTEPOOL CARTMEL CUP (HANDICAP HURDLE) (8 hdls) 2m 1f 110y
4:20 (4:20) (Class 3) (0-130,126) 4-Y-0+ **£5,854** (£1,719; £859; £429)

Form — RPR
0422 **1** **Front Rank (IRE)**^{5} [1104] 10-9-10 **103**............ MissECSayer$^{(7)}$ 107+
(Dianne Sayer) *chsd ldrs: wnt 2nd 4th: led after 2 out: j.rt last: styd on strly* **5/1^{1}**
2601 **2** *4 1/2* **Boogie Dancer**^{10} [1282] 6-10-9 **109**............ HaddenFrost 109
(Stuart Howe) *in rr: hdwy 3 out: styd on to go 2nd 2f out: no imp* **8/1**
011 **3** *10* **Holoko Heights**^{36} [1085] 5-11-1 **115**............(v) RichardJohnson 107
(Tim Vaughan) *trckd ldrs: jnd ldrs 2 out: upsides last: one pce run-in* **13/2**
4-F2 **4** *2 1/2* **Trumpstoo (USA)**^{10} [1282] 4-11-3 **118**............ BrianHughes 106
(Richard Fahey) *hld up in tch: effrt 3 out: one pce fr next* **5/1^{1}**
-521 **5** *2 1/2* **Golden Future**^{6} [748] 7-10-7 **107**............ GrahamLee 94
(Peter Niven) *prom: chsd ldrs 3 out: one pce between last 2* **11/2^{2}**
/21- **6** *6* **Spirit Of The Mist (IRE)**^{412} [911] 6-10-7 **112**............ JamesHalliday$^{(5)}$ 93
(James Moffatt) *t.k.h: led 1st: hdd after 2 out: sn wknd* **11/1**
-220 **7** *29* **Santa's Son (IRE)**^{42} [1017] 10-11-9 **126**............(t) AdamPogson$^{(3)}$ 81
(Charles Pogson) *chsd ldrs: lost pl after 3 out: sn bhd* **6/1^{3}**
2-30 **8** *5* **Daytime Dreamer (IRE)**^{5} [958] 6-10-3 **103**............ BrianHarding 54
(Martin Todhunter) *nt fluent in rr: sme hdwy5th: lost pl after next: sn bhd* **8/1**
00P- **P** **Orpen Wide (IRE)**^{15} [1496] 8-10-5 **112**............(b) JoeCornwall$^{(7)}$ —
(Michael Chapman) *led to 1st: chsd ldrs: sn pushed along: lost pl 5th: sn bhd: t.o whn p.u bef next* **14/1**

4m 7.20s (-6.00) **Going Correction** -0.15s/f (Good)
WFA 4 from 5yo+ 13lb **9** Ran SP% **113.6**
Speed ratings (Par 107): **107,105,100,99,98 95,82,80,—**
Tote Swingers: 1&2 £19.70, 1&3 £15.50, 2&3 £6.50 CSF £43.48 CT £260.79 TOTE £6.30: £1.80, £1.70, £2.50; EX 61.20.
Owner Andrew Sayer **Bred** Ballymacoll Stud Farm Ltd **Trained** Hackthorpe, Cumbria

FOCUS
Quite a competitive handicap hurdle, and the pace was decent. The winner is rated back to the level of last season's win in this race. The time was approximately nine seconds quicker than the following lower-grade handicap.

NOTEBOOK
Front Rank(IRE) had been third in this race two years ago before winning it 12 months ago off 4lb higher than he was here, his most recent victory. Arriving here in good form in this sphere and third on the Flat earlier in the week, he asserted on the run-in for a pretty decisive win. (op 9-2)
Boogie Dancer was a surprise winner of a good little race at Hereford and she ran well off this 8lb higher mark, but after steadily picking off her rivals from the rear she could not trouble the winner. She is on a career-high mark now. (op 6-1)
Holoko Heights was attempting a hat-trick, having picked up a pair of sellers last month. His official mark wasn't raised for either win and he ran creditably in this better grade. He is likely to switch to fences before long. (op 7-1)
Trumpstoo(USA) was 5lb better off with Boogie Dancer on their Hereford meeting but could not turn the form around. He was ridden less prominently here and could never quite get in a blow at the leaders. (tchd 11-2)
Golden Future, raised 12lb for his win at Sedgefield in June, has been running well on the Flat since then. He looked a threat when moving into second but his effort quickly flattened out. (tchd 5-1)
Spirit Of The Mist(IRE), last seen winning a maiden hurdle for the Jim Goldie stable in July last year, was in front for a fair way and should strip fitter next time.
Santa's Son(IRE) has put in back-to-back lacklustre efforts now. (op 8-1)
Daytime Dreamer(IRE) won on the Flat last month and had been dropped 5lb since his last hurdles outing. He was always in rear and finished last, but was not given a hard time when held and may not be one to give up on yet.
Orpen Wide(IRE) Official explanation: jockey said gelding had a breathing problem

1407 A. F. CONNELL FAMILY AND FRIENDS "HANDS AND HEELS" H'CAP HURDLE (CONDITIONALS & AMATEURS) (8 hdls) 2m 1f 110y
4:55 (4:55) (Class 5) (0-90,89) 4-Y-0+ **£2,276** (£668; £334; £166)

Form — RPR
6420 **1** **Galley Slave (IRE)**^{7} [1328] 5-10-12 **77**............ MrOGarner$^{(3)}$ 92+
(Michael Chapman) *mde all: drew clr fr 5th: 25 l ahd run-in: eased last 100yds: unchal* **11/2**
63-3 **2** *16* **Royal Flynn**^{91} [520] 8-11-7 **86**............ HenryBrooke$^{(3)}$ 83
(Kate Walton) *chsd ldrs: wnt 2nd 5th: kpt on to regain modest 2nd towards fin* **5/1^{3}**
-036 **3** *1* **Richo**^{16} [1066] 4-11-12 **89**............(p) MattCrawley 84
(Shaun Harris) *stdd s: hld up in rr: rapid hdwy whn hit 2 out: sn illegally rdn: chsd wnr last: kpt on same pce* **12/1**
-004 **4** *2 3/4* **Cornish Castle (USA)**^{4} [1361] 4-11-1 **78**............(t) AodhaganConlon 70
(Joss Saville) *prom: nt fluent 5th: sn pushed along: one pce fr 2 out* **7/2^{1}**
0001 **5** *2 1/4* **Perez (IRE)**^{7} [1340] 8-11-8 **84**............(vt) PaulGallagher 75
(Wilf Storey) *prom: pushed along 5th: sn outpcd: one pce fr 2 out* **4/1^{2}**
P/00 **6** *2 3/4* **Make It Blossom (IRE)**^{58} [875] 8-11-2 **78**............ MarkQuinlan 67
(John G Carr, Ire) *chsd ldrs: wknd appr last* **6/1**
3544 **7** *5* **Devils And Dust (IRE)**^{14} [1249] 9-11-3 **84**............(p) MissGTutty$^{(5)}$ 68
(Karen Tutty) *chsd ldrs lost pl 3rd: no threat after* **10/1**
5340 **8** *7* **King's Chorister**^{26} [948] 4-10-9 **72**............(bt) NathanSweeney 49
(Barry Murtagh) *stdd s: in rr: bhd fr 3 out* **8/1**

4m 16.0s (2.80) **Going Correction** -0.15s/f (Good) **8** Ran SP% **116.5**
Speed ratings (Par 103): **87,79,79,78,77 76,73,70**
Tote Swingers: 1&2 £4.90, 1&3 £10.70, 2&3 £8.00 CSF £33.91 CT £318.52 TOTE £7.00: £1.70, £1.40, £3.50; EX 33.60 Place 6: £112.57 Place 5: £47.13.
Owner K D Blanch **Bred** Eddie O'Leary **Trained** Market Rasen, Lincs
■ Stewards' Enquiry : Matt Crawley seven-day ban: breach of conditions, used whip (tbn

FOCUS
A very weak handicap indeed, and form to treat with a pinch of salt. The eight runners had contested a total of 129 races over jumps between them, for the sum total of one victory. The time was around nine seconds slower than the preceding handicap.

NOTEBOOK
Galley Slave(IRE) had failed to get his head in front after no fewer than 38 attempts, but he got off the mark with ridiculous ease. Making all, he quickened things up on the final circuit and was never seriously challenged. This will have boosted his confidence, but his handicap rating will obviously suffer for this. (op 7-1 tchd 15-2)
Royal Flynn, third here when last seen in May, was minus the usual cheekpieces. He gave his running and got the best of the separate scrap for second. (op 6-1)
Richo, fitted with cheekpieces for the first time over hurdles, is edging down the weights and he came through from the rear for third. His rider broke the rules by giving him a smack with the whip after the second-last. (op 11-1 tchd 10-1)
Cornish Castle(USA), fourth at Sedgefield earlier in the week, ran his race in the first-time tongue tie but has yet to be placed after 11 hurdles outings now. (op 9-2)
Perez(IRE), wide-margin winner of a Perth selling handicap last time, was the only memeber of the field with a hurdling victory to his name. This quirky sort went up a stone for that and never really looked like following up. (op 7-2 tchd 10-3)
T/Plt: £235 to a £1 stake. Pool:£51,866 - 161.05 winning tickets T/Qpdt: £81.90 to a £1 stake. Pool:£3,113 - 28.10 winning tickets WG

1408 - 1421a (Foreign Racing) - See Raceform Interactive

1401 CARTMEL (L-H)
Monday, August 30

OFFICIAL GOING: Good (good to firm in places; 8.5)
Rail on both bends moved out a further 3m and roadside rail still 2m out to provide fresh ground.
Wind: Almost nil Weather: Fine

1422 STICKY TOFFEE PUDDING JUVENILE HURDLE (8 hdls) 2m 1f 110y
2:20 (2:20) (Class 5) 3-Y-O **£1,951** (£573; £286; £143)

Form — RPR
1 **Turf Trivia**^{33} 3-10-12 0............ BarryKeniry 86
(George Moore) *chsd ldrs: outpcd appr 3 out: clsd between last 2: led abt 1f out ent st: sn clr: styd on wl* **25/1**
4 **2** *7* **Forsyth**^{31} [1135] 3-10-12 0............ BrianHughes 79
(Alan Swinbank) *t.k.h: j. slowly 2nd and 3rd: mstke 3 out: hung rt whn chalng after last: sn outpcd by wnr and no ch* **7/2^{2}**
3 *1/2* **Leopard Hills (IRE)**^{11} 3-10-9 0............ RyanMania$^{(3)}$ 79
(Howard Johnson) *led to 1st: remained prom: led appr last: hdd after last abt 1f out: no ex fnl 150yds* **15/8^{1}**
4 *14* **Miereveld**^{5} 3-10-12 0............(v) LiamHeard 67
(Brian Ellison) *led 1st: mstke 4th: mstke 3 out: hdd appr last: sn wknd* **17/2**
5 *2 1/4* **On The Right Path**^{47} 3-10-5 0............ PaulGallagher$^{(7)}$ 68+
(Paul Murphy) *bhd: nt fluent at times: effrt to chse ldrs appr 2 out: no imp bef last: n.d whn hung bdly rt ent st abt 1f out* **40/1**
F **6** *8* **Frameit (IRE)**^{9} [1324] 3-10-12 0............(v^{1}) RichardJohnson 54
(Tim Vaughan) *towards rr: j. slowly most of way: mstke 4th: hdwy to go prom 5th: wknd 2 out and dropped away qckly: sn eased* **4/1^{3}**
P **P** **Labretella (IRE)**^{18} [1234] 3-10-0 0............ JamesHalliday$^{(5)}$ —
(Shaun Harris) *midfield: wknd 5th: t.o 2 out: p.u bef last* **100/1**
00 **P** **Teela**^{44} [1018] 3-10-0 0............ GilesHawkins$^{(5)}$ —
(Ben Haslam) *bhd: hmpd 1st: t.o whn p.u bef 3 out: sddle slipped* **8/1**
2 **P** **Star Of Kalani (IRE)**^{18} [1234] 3-10-12 0............ WillKennedy —
(Robert Wylie) *hld up: pushed along and struggling after 5th: t.o 2 out: p.u bef last* **8/1**

4m 18.6s (5.40) **Going Correction** +0.125s/f (Yiel) **9** Ran SP% **117.0**
Speed ratings (Par 100): **93,89,89,83,82 78,—,—,—**
Tote Swingers:1&2:£23.60, 1&3:£15.80, 2&3:£2.80 CSF £113.46 TOTE £19.60: £3.50, £1.70, £1.20; EX 80.30.
Owner Mrs Mary Hatfield & Mrs Susan Kramer **Bred** London Thoroughbred Services Ltd **Trained** Middleham Moor, N Yorks

FOCUS
The rails on both bends had been moved out a further 3 metres, and the roadside rail remained 2 metres out to provide fresh ground. A weak event, but he standard is tricky to pin down.

NOTEBOOK
Turf Trivia hit a flat spot and had about four lengths to find coming around the final turn but, as the others began to struggle, he was staying on and burst through on the run-in to stride clear. He had been struggling to stay middle distances on the Flat this year, but his jumping was reasonably assured and that helped him see out the trip over hurdles. However, this performance should be seen in context. (op 14-1)
Forsyth raced prominently and was poised to strike before the last, but once again he did not seem that willing when the pressure was on, although he might just need some time to strengthen up. (op 9-2)
Leopard Hills(IRE) was keen early so his jockey restrained him off the lead, but he was travelling best as they came round the final turn, only to run out of steam on the run-in. He has proved effective over 2m on the Flat and might need to put his stamina to use over jumps. (op 3-1)
Miereveld did not jump that fluently and was the first of the leaders beaten off. (op 8-1)
On The Right Path was given a quiet ride and made some late progress, but jumped awkwardly at the last when getting tired. (op 25-1)
Labretella(IRE) Official explanation: trauiner said filly was found to be in season
Teela Official explanation: jockey said saddle slipped

1423 CUBE247.CO.UK H'CAP CHASE (14 fncs) 2m 5f 110y
2:55 (2:55) (Class 5) (0-90,90) 4-Y-0+ **£2,602** (£764; £382; £190)

Form — RPR
P-5P **1** **Mischief Man**^{79} [730] 8-11-1 **84**............ ShaneByrne$^{(5)}$ 98+
(Sue Smith) *chsd ldrs: wnt 2nd at 5th: led 2 out: kicked on after last: styd on and rdn out fnl 100yds* **9/1**
4252 **2** *2 1/4* **Peak Seasons (IRE)**^{4} [1378] 7-10-0 **71**............ JoeCornwall$^{(7)}$ 82
(Michael Chapman) *led: hdd 2 out: rdn after last and nt qckn: kpt on u.p fnl 1f in st but a hld* **4/1^{3}**
PPP- **3** *31* **Murphys Beau (IRE)**^{332} [1591] 8-10-9 **73**............ GrahamLee 53
(Kate Walton) *in tch: niggled along 9th: outpcd 10th: tried to rally whn nt fluent 4 out (water): wknd 3 out* **7/2^{2}**
P-4P **4** *hd* **Charming Knight (IRE)**^{9} [1341] 9-11-5 **90**............ AlistairFindlay$^{(7)}$ 70
(Jane Walton) *hld up: struggling appr 9th: sme hdwy bef 4 out (water): no imp on ldrs bef last: wknd sn after* **8/1**
6446 **5** *6* **Ellandshe (IRE)**^{6} [1360] 10-9-9 **64** oh14............(b) JamesHalliday$^{(5)}$ 38
(William Young) *bhd: struggling fr 8th: nvr on terms: t.o after last* **22/1**

-63P **6** *44* **You Can Of Course (IRE)**[54] 931 7-11-0 **78**...........(v) RichardJohnson 8
(Neil Mulholland) *chsd ldr to 5th: stl prom whn hit 10th: wknd appr 4 out(water)* **11/2**

34R **R** **Hapthor**[6] 1360 11-11-5 **90**...(p) KyleJames(7) —
(F Jestin) *reluctant to go to post: ref to r: tk no part* **25/1**

P001 **F** **Archie's Wish**[6] 1360 6-10-6 **70** 7ex...................................... BarryKeniry 84+
(Micky Hammond) *hld up in tch: clsd appr 4 out (water): shkn up 3rd abt 4 l down whn fell last* **9/4**[1]

5m 18.9s (-6.50) **Going Correction** -0.10s/f (Good) **8** Ran SP% **111.3**
Speed ratings (Par 103): **107,106,94,94,92 76,—,—**
Tote Swingers: 1&2 £2.90, 1&3 £9.20, 2&3 £4.90 CSF £42.74 CT £146.88 TOTE £7.70: £2.00, £1.80, £1.60.

Owner Mrs S Smith **Bred** Mrs R S Huxley **Trained** High Eldwick, W Yorks

FOCUS
This was a weak race, with only three of them having actually completed the course in their previous race, but the pace was reasonable nonetheless. The first two finished clear and the form is pretty sound for the grade.

NOTEBOOK
Mischief Man was always well positioned and jumped well, so once the favourite had departed he had only to wait for the stamina of the leader to falter before going on to claim the race. He had only very modest form over shorter trips but handled this step up comfortably. Connections have had him for about a year now but it has taken a while for him to come into form, however he is not that robust so is unlikely to be making a quick reappearance. (op 7-1)

Peak Seasons(IRE) set a fair pace and gave it everything, but he was just outstayed on the run-in, although he rallied and closed a bit on the idling winner. He often goes well at this track and very nearly got up over a shorter trip here four days earlier. (op 3-1)

Murphys Beau(IRE) attracted some support on his first start for new connections and on the back of a ten-month break, but he was never really able to live with the pace and could only make late gains. He might come on for this and his best previous form came over shorter, but he will need to improve. (op 11-2)

Charming Knight(IRE) is generally inconsistent, and pulled up on his return from a break last time. He was due for a completion this time and obliged, but only at his own slow pace. (op 14-1)

Ellandshe(IRE) was languishing at the rear from an early stage and remains a very moderate maiden. (op 28-1)

You Can Of Course(IRE) began to struggle going up the hill for the second time and could not get back on terms, but he is generally better over further and might not come into his own until the autumn. (tchd 9-2)

Hapthor was reluctant on the way to the start and once again refused to go. (op 20-1)

Archie's Wish had a good opportunity to capitalise under a penalty following his winning chasing debut at Sedgefield six days previously. However, these fences proved trickier and he began to make mistakes at the line of four. Despite this he was still poised to pounce and may have got there on the long run-in had he negotiated the last. (op 5-2 tchd 11-4)

1424 CHAS KENDALL H'CAP CHASE (14 fncs) 2m 5f 110y
3:30 (3:30) (Class 3) (0-125,119) 4-Y-0+ **£6,505** (£1,910; £955; £477)

Form RPR

0523 **1** **Silmi**[16] 1252 6-11-7 **114**.. PaddyBrennan 125+
(Sophie Leech) *hld up in tch: impr to ld 4 out (water): drew clr fr last: r.o wl: eased down towards fin* **5/2**[1]

565P **2** *9* **Indian Pipe Dream (IRE)**[11] 1297 8-10-7 **100**................ LiamTreadwell 98
(Aytach Sadik) *in rr: hdwy appr 4 out (water): outpcd bef 3 out: styd on steadily fr 2 out: wnt 2nd on long run-in over 1f out: no ch w wnr* **20/1**

4/52 **3** *11* **Ohana**[9] 1327 7-11-7 **117**.. EwanWhillans(3) 105
(Alistair Whillans) *chsd ldrs: pushed along and outpcd appr 3 out: disputing 3rd whn mstke last: wnt 2nd on long run-in but no imp on wnr: lost 2nd 1f out: sn wknd* **17/2**

-251 **4** *4* **Jimbatai (IRE)**[41] 1045 7-11-9 **119**..................................... DannyCook(3) 102
(Barry Leavy) *trckd ldrs: pushed along 4 out: wknd 3 out* **5/1**[3]

4356 **5** *1 1/4* **Stagecoach Amber (USA)**[10] 1312 8-11-3 **115**............. ShaneByrne(5) 97
(Sue Smith) *led: hdd 4 out (water): u.p whn hit 3 out: wknd after last* **13/2**

0-3 **6** *3 1/4* **More Equity**[9] 1338 8-10-11 **107**.. RyanMania(3) 86
(P Monteith) *hld up: struggling after 8th: rdn to go pce bef 4 out (water): nvr on terms* **9/2**[2]

6-0 **7** *2 1/4* **Speedy Max (IRE)**[2] 1404 9-11-0 **110**............................(tp) PeterToole(3) 86
(George Stanley, Ire) *w ldr and continually outj. rival: stl ev ch 2 out: rdn after last: sn weakened: fatally injured* **9/1**

-656 **8** *91* **Player (FR)**[86] 624 7-11-0 **107**... GrahamLee —
(Ann Hamilton) *handy: hit 3rd: niggled along fr 6th: u.p and lost pl 9th: wknd aftter 10th: t.o 3 out* **12/1**

0-05 **R** **Finzi Contini (FR)**[2] 1402 6-11-0 **107**.........................(p) RichardJohnson —
(Tim Vaughan) *reluctant to go to post: ref to r: tk no part* **18/1**

5m 18.9s (-6.50) **Going Correction** -0.10s/f (Good) **9** Ran SP% **115.0**
Speed ratings (Par 107): **107,103,99,98,97 96,95,62,—**
Tote Swingers: 1&2 £11.80, 1&3 £2.40, 2&3 £15.70 CSF £46.45 CT £372.16 TOTE £3.50: £1.60, £4.60, £2.50; EX 107.80.

Owner J O'Brien & C J Leech **Bred** Shadwell Estate Company Limited **Trained** Kingsbridge, Devon

FOCUS
Quite a competitive handicap with a mid-race pace battle that saw the two leaders fading out of it, and the field eventually coming home in a slower time than the previous lower-grade handicap. The winner is rated in line with his previous best.

NOTEBOOK
Silmi has put up some decent efforts from similar marks this summer and, back on his favourite course, he converted that good form into a comprehensive win, despite getting in close to the last still scooting clear of the field. He found life tough outside of novice company last summer but has slipped down the weights and had looked reasonably treated, but had just been outpaced over shorter of late. He had won over 2m4f before but that was in a slow time, and on a tight track such as this he is able to see the trip out fully, and is becoming something of a course specialist with this his third win here. He is not that big and reportedly needs time between his races. (op 3-1)

Indian Pipe Dream(IRE)jumped sluggishly in rear early on and did not look to be on a going day, but by virtue of not getting involved in any pace battle he had enough in reserve at the finish and came home strongly. He has been in reasonable form this summer but is difficult to win with, although he looks on a reasonable mark. (op 16-1)

Ohanagot outpaced from the third-last but plugged on. He returned to action this summer following a lengthy layoff and seems to have retained ability, but may need to drop a couple of pounds and a slightly shorter trip to be fully effective.\n (op 11-2 tchd 9-1)

Jimbatai(IRE) raced prominently wide of the pack, which put him at something of a disadvantage, and he was outpaced on ground that would have been plenty fast enough, with a career-high mark to contend with as well. (op 6-1)

More Equityattracted some support but was never competitive, and the expected improvement on his second run back from a break did not materialise this time. (tchd 5-1 in places)

Speedy Max(IRE), who helped set the pace, collapsed and died after the race. (op 12-1)

1425 CENGIZ GUS SADIK MEMORIAL H'CAP CHASE (18 fncs) 3m 2f
4:05 (4:05) (Class 4) (0-100,91) 4-Y-0+ **£3,252** (£955; £477; £238)

Form RPR

1 **Ihaventabob (IRE)**[23] 1214 6-11-10 **89**.............................. JohnnyFarrelly 100+
(Aidan Anthony Howard, Ire) *hld up: wnt prom 7th: nt fluent 4 out (water): led after last: rdn and styd on all the way to the line* **11/2**[3]

4F-3 **2** *2 1/2* **Gift Of The Gods (IRE)**[34] 1102 7-11-4 **83**................(p) RichardJohnson 91
(Tim Vaughan) *prom: led appr 3rd (water): hdd after last: rdn after: kpt on u.p but no imp on wnr* **3/1**[2]

03P5 **3** *21* **Feeling Peckish (USA)**[9] 1326 6-10-1 **73**.....................(t) JoeCornwall(7) 60
(Michael Chapman) *prom: rdn after last: sn outpcd by front pair and wknd* **13/2**

PU54 **4** *3 1/2* **Dasher Reilly (USA)**[5] 1366 9-10-0 **65** oh8.................(tp) LiamTreadwell 49
(Aytach Sadik) *hld up: niggled along after 8th: hdwy 12th: outpcd bef 4 out (water): n.d after* **8/1**

6-0 **5** *1 1/2* **Star Of Raven**[31] 1140 13-10-0 **65** oh3.................................. BarryKeniry 47
(Joss Saville) *led: hdd appr 3rd (water): lost pl after 6th: struggling 12th: sme hdwy bef 4 out(water): no imp 2 out: n.d after* **16/1**

5/14 **6** *25* **Bynack Mhor (IRE)**[35] 1093 9-10-12 **77**........................(tp) AidanColeman 34
(Lawney Hill) *in tch: mstke 10th: struggling after 12th: wknd 4 out (water)* **6/4**[1]

6m 43.4s (8.50) **Going Correction** -0.10s/f (Good) **6** Ran SP% **110.7**
Speed ratings (Par 105): **82,81,74,73,73 65**
Tote Swingers: 1&2 £3.50, 1&3 £4.20, 2&3 £2.00 CSF £22.00 TOTE £6.50: £2.40, £1.90; EX 15.10.

Owner T Miley **Bred** L Whelan **Trained** The Curragh, Co Kildare

FOCUS
A very weak handicap chase. The form is rated around the runner-up.

NOTEBOOK
Ihaventabob(IRE) did not jump that fluently on occasions, but was still travelling best as the race began to unwind and, after a mistake at the last, had enough time to cement his superiority on the long run to the line. There were few previous clues in his form, but he had shown a tiny bit more on two runs in his native Ireland following a long layoff, and improved for the step up in trip. (op 5-1)

Gift Of The Gods(IRE) raced up with the pace until outpaced from the last, but she kept on despite flashing her tail on the run-in. She had little previous form on offer but improved on her second run for Tim Vaughan, despite changing her legs and not looking that happy on the track. (tchd 10-3)

Feeling Peckish(USA) raced near the pace for a way but he was readily beaten and looks no nearer breaking his maiden. (tchd 6-1)

Dasher Reilly(USA) made some progress late on, but he was never a serious threat to claim the race named after the trainer's late son. (tchd 15-2)

Bynack Mhor(IRE) was the only contender in any semblance of form, having won at Uttoxeter in July off an 8lb lower mark, but he did not cope with the tricky fences and turns and was struggling midway. Official explanation: jockey said gelding never travelled (op 7-4 tchd 15-8 in a place)

1426 MAHOOD MARQUEES NOVICES' HURDLE (8 hdls) 2m 1f 110y
4:40 (4:40) (Class 4) 4-Y-0+ **£2,602** (£764; £382; £190)

Form RPR

4-13 **1** **Maska Pony (IRE)**[16] 1253 6-11-5 100.................................. GrahamLee 120+
(George Moore) *chsd clr ldrs: clsd 3 out: led after 2 out: sn clr: eased down towards fin* **5/2**[2]

1612 **2** *8* **Rio Gael (IRE)**[6] 1359 4-11-11 118.......................................(p) TomO'Brien 116
(Peter Bowen) *chsd ldr: rdn after 2 out: outpcd by wnr after last: sn no ch* **5/2**[2]

0 **3** *10* **Red Skipper (IRE)**[4] 576 5-10-12 0.............................. WilsonRenwick 93
(Noel Wilson) *midfield: pushed along appr 5th to go pce: styd on steadily to take poor 3rd run-in: nvr a threat* **20/1**

6F22 **4** *14* **Duty Free (IRE)**[9] 1337 6-10-12 108................................(b[1]) BrianHughes 79
(James Moffatt) *racd keenly: led: rdn and hdd after 2 out: wknd appr last* **2/1**[1]

5 *35* **Pagan Lightning (USA)**[45] 1010 5-10-9 0.......................... RyanMania(3) 44
(Dianne Sayer) *midfield: struggling bef 3 out: nvr on terms* **20/1**

/06- **6** *11* **Best Horse (FR)**[276] 2547 8-10-5 97.............................. PaulGallagher(7) 33
(Ferdy Murphy) *bhd: struggling bef 5th: nvr on terms* **25/1**

0 **7** *3 1/4* **Tuckers Treasure**[24] 1201 4-10-11 0.................................. TjadeCollier 29
(Sue Smith) *midfield: lost pl 3rd: bhd and struggling bef 5th: nvr on terms* **33/1**

0 **8** *48* **Shuttle Diplomacy (IRE)**[39] 1069 5-10-5 0...................... JohnnyFarrelly —
(Elliott Cooper) *a bhd: t.o bef 3 out* **80/1**

P **Valdan (IRE)**[8] 6-10-12 0.. MichaelMcAlister —
(Maurice Barnes) *nt fluent: midfield: chsd clr ldrs bef 3 out: no imp: wknd 2 out: t.o whn p.u bef last* **16/1**[3]

00/ **P** **Sound Of Silver**[955] 3432 7-10-9 0................................. FearghalDavis(3) —
(Andrew Crook) *a bhd: t.o whn p.u bef 5th* **100/1**

F **P** **Wapiti Creek (IRE)**[2] 1402 6-9-12 0.............................(t) MarkQuinlan(7) —
(John G Carr, Ire) *midfield: mstke 1st: wknd 5th: t.o whn p.u bef 3 out* **40/1**

4m 11.5s (-1.70) **Going Correction** +0.125s/f (Yiel) **11** Ran SP% **117.3**
Speed ratings (Par 105): **108,104,100,93,78 73,71,50,—,—,—**
Tote Swingers: 1&2 £19.20, 1&3 £14.10, 2&3 £1.80 CSF £8.74 TOTE £3.70: £1.40, £1.30, £2.60; EX 9.80.

Owner Mrs J M Gray **Bred** Twelve Oaks Stud Establishment **Trained** Middleham Moor, N Yorks

FOCUS
The field was strung out from the start and few got into it. Improved form from the winner with the next two setting the level.

NOTEBOOK
Maska Pony(IRE) still had at least ten lengths to make up at halfway, but he patiently ate into the lead to strike just before the last and soon had the race won, giving his trainer a double on the card. He spent much of last winter slogging round over 3m, but he improved for a drop in trip and switch to faster ground to take a handicap at Kelso in May. The penalty for that win gave him a bit to find here, but the race was run to suit a horse with plenty of stamina and he has a bit of pace as well. (op 10-3 tchd 7-2 in places)

Rio Gael(IRE) kept tabs on the leader, rallied after getting a bit outpaced and then got squeezed out by the leader and the winner before the last, and from there could do no more than keep on. This was another commendable effort under his double penalty, but with such a burden to heave in novice events and a stiff-looking mark of 118 to contend with, connections have no easy task in placing him. (op 3-1 tchd 10-3)

Red Skipper(IRE) made some late gains without looking an imminent winner of a novice hurdle. (op 14-1)

Duty Free(IRE), a perennial placer, raced too freely in the lead in first-time blinkers, and paid for it when fading before the last. (op 5-2)

Shuttle Diplomacy(IRE) Official explanation: jockey said mare had a breathing problem

Wapiti Creek(IRE) Official explanation: jockey said mare never travelled

1427 THOMAS CHESTER LENNON MARES' H'CAP HURDLE (8 hdls) 2m 1f 110y

5:15 (5:15) (Class 4) (0-115,114) 4-Y-0+ **£3,252** (£955; £477; £238)

Form RPR

211P **1** **Play A Cord (IRE)**[55] 920 7-9-11 **92**............................(b) MarkQuinlan(7) 97
(Neil Mulholland) *hld up: hdwy appr 3 out: wnt 2nd between last 2: chalng last: stmbld on path sn after: nt qckn and abt 3 l down ent st: rallied towards fin: led fnl stride* **9/2**

-101 **2** *nk* **Dream Risk (FR)**[12] 1115 4-11-2 **105**............................(t) GrahamLee 109
(Kate Walton) *chsd ldr after 1st: led after 2 out: wnt abt 3 l clr after last: u.p towards fin: hdd fnl stride* **2/1**[1]

6233 **3** *25* **Rafta (IRE)**[3] 1392 4-11-1 **104**............................ BarryKeniry 85
(W G Harrison) *hld: pushed along 5th to go pce: no imp on ldrs: wnt poor 3rd run-in: n.d to front pair* **3/1**[3]

F42F **4** *7* **Kind Heart**[16] 1252 4-10-10 **109**............................ HenryBrooke(10) 81
(Donald McCain) *led: rdn and hdd after 2 out: wkng whn hit last: lost 3rd run-in* **11/4**[2]

4U4 **U** **Grethel (IRE)**[34] 1003 6-9-7 **88** oh9............................ JamesSmith(7) —
(Alan Berry) *t.k.h: stmbld and uns rdr 1st* **18/1**

50-6 **U** **Owls FC (IRE)**[9] 1329 4-9-7 **89** oh10............................ JoeCornwall(7) —
(Michael Chapman) *chsd ldr tl after 1st: remained prom: lost pl 4th: pushed along to keep up whn stmbld on road and uns rdr appr 5th* **33/1**

4m 16.6s (3.40) **Going Correction** +0.125s/f (Yiel)
WFA 4 from 6yo+ 13lb **6** Ran SP% **111.4**
Speed ratings (Par 105): **97,96,85,82,—** —
Tote Swingers: 1&2 £1.50, 1&3 £4.60, 2&3 £1.10 CSF £14.10 TOTE £6.20: £2.10, £2.10; EX 11.80.

Owner Neil Mulholland Racing Club **Bred** C J And Mrs D Hodgins **Trained** Burlescombe, Devon

FOCUS
The form horses fought it out from the last with the favourite idling on the long run-in and getting caught on the line. The first two are rated to their marks.

NOTEBOOK
Play A Cord(IRE) tended to run in snatches, but responded to pressure to move upsides the favourite at the last. She was still clinging on when slipping on the path at the start of the run-in and looked to have lost her chance, but to her credit she found more to just get up. She can be quirky and was never travelling last time at Uttoxeter, but the eight-week break seems to have freshened her up to regain the winning form she showed earlier in the summer. In this form she could win another small race off a similar mark. (op 5-1 tchd 6-1)

Dream Risk(FR) tracked the leader before making what looked like a winning move against the inside rail, and held the advantage on the run-in, only to idle a little and get caught by the rallying winner. However, if she can be found another contest off her current mark she could still add to her summer tally. (op 15-8 tchd 9-4)

Rafta(IRE) was taken down to the start early, but did not jump fluently and took an age to get going before moving into a remote third. She will need to settle and jump better if she is to figure over hurdles. (op 11-4 tchd 5-2)

Kind Heart has had jumping problems especially over fences this summer, and she was clumsy over many of the hurdles. She was also too free in the lead to have a chance of lasting home. (op 7-2)

1428 JEAN CONRON 60TH BIRTHDAY H'CAP HURDLE (11 hdls) 2m 6f

5:50 (6:17) (Class 5) (0-90,87) 4-Y-0+ **£2,276** (£668; £334; £166)

Form RPR

5P42 **1** **Auberge (IRE)**[6] 1362 6-10-13 **77**............................ RyanMania(3) 96+
(Dianne Sayer) *midfield: hdwy after 6th: lft chsng clr ldr after 7th: clsd 2 out: led appr last: sn clr: r.o wl: eased cl home* **9/4**[1]

5B51 **2** *7* **Rebel Swing**[15] 1261 4-11-9 **86**............................ HenryOliver 97+
(Sue Smith) *chsd ldrs: lost pl bef 5th: outpcd bef 3 out: styd on after 2 out: tk 2nd run-in: no ch w wnr* **4/1**[3]

4201 **3** *12* **Galley Slave (IRE)**[2] 1407 5-10-9 **77**............................ JoeCornwall(7) 76
(Michael Chapman) *led: clr after 2nd tl 2 out: hdd appr last: wknd run-in* **3/1**[2]

/536 **4** *11* **Mulligan's Pride (IRE)**[31] 1141 9-11-4 **79**............................(b) GrahamLee 67
(James Moffatt) *chsd clr ldr tl 6th: struggling fr 7th: no imp after* **5/1**

/006 **5** *5* **Make It Blossom (IRE)**[2] 1407 8-10-10 **78**............................ MarkQuinlan(7) 61
(John G Carr, Ire) *hld up: pushed along and hdwy to chse ldr 6th: nrly tk wrong crse after 7th and lost 2nd: wknd bef 3 out* **16/1**

4F40 **6** *9* **Follow On**[17] 946 8-11-5 **87**............................(t) MissAngelaBarnes(7) 61
(Maurice Barnes) *a bhd: strruggling bef 3 out: nvr on termsfr* **20/1**

/P03 **7** *158* **Devilfishpoker Com**[4] 1375 6-10-12 **80**............................ KyleJames(7) —
(Shaun Harris) *in tch in chsng gp: lost pl after 6th: wl bhd bef last: virtually p.u run-in* **16/1**

F40- **P** **Art Gallery**[165] 4709 6-11-8 **86**............................ CampbellGillies(3) —
(David Thompson) *in tch in chsng gp: mstke 6th: sn lost pl and struggling: t.o whn p.u bef 3 out* **33/1**

50P **P** **Rosie Larkin (IRE)**[40] 1057 6-10-0 **61** oh1............................(t) BarryKeniry —
(Joss Saville) *in rr: t.o 5th: p.u after 6th* **25/1**

5m 30.4s (1.10) **Going Correction** +0.125s/f (Yiel) **9** Ran SP% **115.7**
Speed ratings (Par 103): **103,100,96,92,90 87,—,—,—**
Tote Swingers: 1&2 £2.70, 1&3 £1.60, 2&3 £1.70 CSF £11.74 CT £26.79 TOTE £3.10: £1.30, £1.60, £1.30; EX 12.10 Place 6 £57.34; Place 5 £34.56.

Owner Ron Affleck **Bred** David Fenton **Trained** Hackthorpe, Cumbria

FOCUS
The third set a strong pace in this moderate handicap hurdle. The form is rated around the winner.

NOTEBOOK
Auberge(IRE) took her time to get on top and it was hard work, but she eventually picked off the leader before the last and kept on grimly to the line. Although still a maiden coming into this contest, she had some decent placed efforts to her name. She was well backed the previous week when just getting beaten in a battle at Sedgefield, but made no mistake for her supporters this time. (op 11-4 tchd 3-1 in places)

Rebel Swing made steady progress throughout the final circuit but never got any closer to the winner than near the line. His 7lb rise for his recent Southwell success does not look too harsh if he can get into the race. (tchd 10-3 and 9-2)

Galley Slave(IRE) was a runaway winner over 2m1f here two days previously and attempted to do repeat the trick off the same mark. He managed to stay clear until after the second-last but his stamina emptied soon after. (op 11-4 tchd 10-3)

T/Plt: £51.30 to a £1 stake. Pool:£46,767.45 - 665.35 winning tickets T/Qpdt: £10.90 to a £1 stake. Pool:£3,590.22 - 243.65 winning tickets DO

[462]HUNTINGDON (R-H)

Monday, August 30

OFFICIAL GOING: Good to firm (watered; 10.3)
Wind: Strong, half behind Weather: bright spells, partly cloudy

1429 HUNTINGDON RACECOURSE SUPPORTS RACING WELFARE H'CAP HURDLE (8 hdls) 2m 110y

2:30 (2:31) (Class 4) (0-110,110) 4-Y-0+ **£2,602** (£764; £382; £190)

Form RPR

3-4U **1** **Rebel Dancer (FR)**[105] 299 5-11-6 **104**............................(t) DougieCostello 118+
(Ian Williams) *hld up in rr: stdy hdwy after 3 out: j. into ld last: pushed clr flat: v easily* **13/2**

-552 **2** *4* **Josephine Malines**[18] 1236 6-10-9 **100**............................(t) MrTomDavid(7) 105
(Tim Vaughan) *chsd ldrs: wnt 2nd bef 3 out: chal and had bumping match w rival bef 2 out: rdn between last 2: nt pce of wnr flat: kpt on* **4/1**[1]

24/ **3** *nk* **Chrysander**[491] 1 8-11-12 **110**............................(p) PaulMoloney 115
(Evan Williams) *led: rdn and jnd bef 2 out: hdd last: nt pce of wnr flat: kpt on* **11/2**[2]

600/ **4** *6* **Laish Ya Hajar (IRE)**[22] 2458 6-11-6 **104**............................ DenisO'Regan 103
(Paul Webber) *hld up in midfield: blnd bdly bdly 5th: sn rcvrd and chsd ldrs bef next: chsd ldng pair and rdn bef 2 out: wknd between last 2* **4/1**[1]

0543 **5** *½* **Phoenix Eye**[9] 1328 9-10-4 **95**............................ BrianToomey(7) 95+
(Michael Mullineaux) *t.k.h: hld up in midfield: nt clr run on bnd bef 3 out: chsd ldrs after 3 out: mstke and btn next* **6/1**[3]

1214 **6** *14* **Seaquel**[61] 865 4-11-1 **103**............................ CharlieHuxley(3) 86
(Sally-Anne Wheelwright) *in tch towards rr: rdn and wknd bef 3 out: sn wl bhd* **10/1**

P-44 **7** *23* **Bedarra Boy**[28] 1160 4-10-12 **97**............................ DarylJacob 57
(David Arbuthnot) *chsd ldr tl bef 3 out: wknd rapidly bef 2 out: wl btn whn blnd 2 out: t.o* **13/2**

50-0 **8** *½* **That Man Fox**[13] 1278 9-9-13 **88**............................(b) LeeEdwards(5) 49
(Tony Carroll) *chsd ldrs tl after 5th: sn lost pl u.p: wl bhd bef 2 out: t.o* **16/1**

-3PP **9** *32* **Randomer**[11] 1290 7-9-6 **86**............................(p) AshleyBird(10) 15
(Paddy Butler) *a in rr: lost tch after mstke 4th: t.o fr 3 out* **40/1**

3m 34.5s (-20.40) **Going Correction** -1.075s/f (Hard) course record
WFA 4 from 5yo+ 13lb **9** Ran SP% **113.7**
Speed ratings (Par 105): **105,103,102,100,99 93,82,82,67**
Tote Swingers:1&2:£1.20, 1&3:£4.70, 2&3:£8.10 CSF £32.74 CT £152.05 TOTE £6.10: £1.60, £1.80, £2.40; EX 17.50.

Owner Michael H Watt **Bred** Paul Anthony Eugene Barthelemy **Trained** Portway, Worcs

FOCUS
A moderate handicap, run at a good gallop. Straightforward form with the winner value for further.

NOTEBOOK
Rebel Dancer(FR), making his debut for Ian Williams, had become slightly disappointing earlier in the year, refusing frequently to settle under hold-up tactics. The leaders went off fast enough for him from the outset, though, and he was content to bide his time before producing a strong run from the turn for home. Future prospects at this trip may always be reliant on finding such strongly run races, but this will have done his confidence no end of good, at least. (op 11-2 tchd 5-1)

Josephine Malines, keen early in defeat at Stratford last time, went about her business more calmly this time apart from the scrimmaging with Chrysander approaching two out, and was second best on merit without excuses. There is another small race to be had with her, with mares' handicaps remaining an untried option so far. (tchd 7-2)

Chrysander could never fully shake off the early attentions of Bedarra Boy, and may have been goaded into doing too much by that rival to have enough left to challenge the eventual winner late on. This was a fair effort after a 491-day absence all the same, and something similar could fall his way with the benefit of this outing. (op 5-1 tchd 6-1)

Laish Ya Hajar(IRE), unseen over hurdles since November 2008 but match-fit from the Flat, appeared to shrug off a jarring mistake at halfway. A mark of 104 for this handicap debut (which hadn't looked a gift beforehand) may therefore have been as much of a contributory factor to his tame finishing effort. (op 5-1)

Phoenix Eye refused to settle early on and remains tricky to win with. (tchd 13-2)

1430 WAGGON AND HORSES SUPPORTS RACING WELFARE H'CAP CHASE (12 fncs) 2m 110y

3:05 (3:05) (Class 4) (0-100,100) 4-Y-0+ **£3,252** (£955; £477; £238)

Form RPR

3P-2 **1** **Red Birr (IRE)**[13] 1273 9-11-4 **92**............................(t) SamThomas 106+
(Paul Webber) *hld up in last pair: mstke and pckd 2nd: mstke 5th: hdwy 6th: trckd ldr 3 out: led next: drew clr on bit bef last: easily* **4/1**[3]

3362 **2** *6* **Le Brocquy**[11] 1295 5-11-7 **95**............................(p) WarrenMarston 98
(Martin Keighley) *nt a fluent: racd off the pce in midfield: clsd and wl in tch 7th: chsd ldrs and rdn bef 2 out: outpcd between last 2: plugged on to go 2nd flat: no ch w wnr* **7/2**[2]

3P26 **3** *½* **Ace High Blue (IRE)**[12] 1283 8-11-12 **100**............................(tp) PaulMoloney 102
(Evan Williams) *chsd clr ldng pair: blnd 1st: mstke 4th: clsd and lft 2nd 7th: led next: hdd 2 out: sn rdn and outpcd by wnr and wl btn last: lost 2nd flat* **10/3**[1]

0-14 **4** *6* **Barton Sun (IRE)**[20] 1231 11-9-10 **77**............................ MrSHanson(7) 73
(Alison Batchelor) *hld up wl off the pce in last pair: j. slowly 5th: clsd and in tch 7th: 4th and rdn bef 2 out: wknd between last 2* **13/2**

4033 **5** *9* **Morestead (IRE)**[11] 1293 5-10-8 **89**............................ MissCLWills(7) 76
(Brendan Powell) *sn clr w rival: led after 1st: j. awkwardly 2nd: j.v.slowly 4th: hit next: tried to refuse and hdd 7th: u.p after but styd in tch tl wknd bef 2 out* **15/2**

0663 **6** *5* **Alfloramoor**[6] 1358 8-11-3 **94**............................(p) AdamPogson(3) 78
(Charles Pogson) *racd keenly: j.lft: led and sn clr w rival: hdd after 1st: lft in ld 7th: hdd next: j.lft and lost 2nd 3 out: wkng whn mstke 2 out: sn lost tch* **7/2**[2]

4m 4.40s (-5.80) **Going Correction** -0.525s/f (Firm) **6** Ran SP% **112.6**
Speed ratings (Par 105): **92,89,88,86,81 79**
Tote Swingers:1&2:£1.80, 1&3:£2.80, 2&3:£4.40 CSF £18.59 TOTE £4.00: £2.70, £2.30; EX 12.10.

Owner John Nicholls (Trading) Ltd **Bred** Mrs Ellen Lyons **Trained** Mollington, Oxon

■ Stewards' Enquiry : Miss C L Wills one-day ban: used whip when out of contention (Sep 15)

FOCUS
A weak handicap. Improved form from the winner with the standard set around the third.

NOTEBOOK
Red Birr(IRE), 6lb higher, travelled the best from some way out and was not hard pushed to record a first victory over jumps. Putting in an entirely spotless round remains a bit of a problem for him, but his gameness will continue to count for plenty. (op 10-3 tchd 3-1)

Le Brocquy, touched off by just a head returned to hurdles last time, looked to get caught flat-footed by the winner's move turning in, and never appeared likely to reel him back in. This still represents a best effort over fences to date, on the first occasion that he's had both a sharp 2m and a sound surface in the discipline. (op 4-1)
Ace High Blue(IRE) was on his nose at the first and wasn't entirely error-free after that, either. The raw material to win a poor heat is there, but jumping issues are limiting his progress this summer. (op 4-1)
Barton Sun(IRE), a winner off 73 two starts ago, hasn't defied a higher mark successfully since late 2007 and didn't threaten to do so here. (op 6-1)
Morestead(IRE) ran away with his rider early on before losing interest. He has only converted one of 17 attempts over fences now. (op 6-1 tchd 8-1)
Alfloramoor has run well here in the past but raced too wastefully this time, and also appeared to resent Morestead rivalling him for the early lead. (op 9-2)

1431 BECOME A RACING WELFARE VOLUNTEER CONDITIONAL JOCKEYS' (S) HURDLE (10 hdls) 2m 4f 110y
3:40 (3:41) (Class 5) 4-Y-0+ **£2,055** (£599; £299)

Form RPR
-U43 **1** **Carrick Oscar (IRE)**[24] 1200 10-10-12 0 RichardKilloran 110+
(Tim Vaughan) *chsd ldr tl led 3rd: hdd after 5th: ev ch and rdn 2 out: led and mstke last: styd on wl flat: rdn out* **9/4**[2]
-414 **2** *1* **William Butler (IRE)**[62] 852 10-10-9 125 (p) DPFahy[(3)] 108
(Evan Williams) *hld up in tch: hdwy to trck ldrs bef 3 out: ev ch 2 out: sn rdn: unable qck and a hld flat* **11/8**[1]
6304 **3** *4* **Knightsbridgelives (IRE)**[32] 1125 7-10-12 99 (t) DavidBass 107+
(Lawney Hill) *t.k.h: hld up in tch: hdwy to ld after 5th: rdn and wandered u.p bef 2 out: hdd and blnd bdly last: nt rcvr and styd on same pce flat* **7/1**[3]
10P3 **4** *20* **High Skies**[15] 1258 7-11-4 104 (b) SamJones 90
(Dr Richard Newland) *chsd ldrs: rdn and wknd qckly bef 3 out: sn wl btn* **9/1**
06U- **5** *10* **Lady Romanov (IRE)**[272] 2248 7-9-11 66 AshleyBird[(8)] 67
(Paddy Butler) *chsd ldrs: rdn bef 6th: lost tch after next* **100/1**
P000 **6** *3 ½* **Zizou (IRE)**[11] 1300 7-10-12 75 TomMolloy 71
(Sean Curran) *led tl 3rd: chsd ldrs after tl wknd qckly bef 3 out: wl bhd bef 2 out: t.o* **40/1**
40U2 **7** *19* **Hi Wycombe (IRE)**[16] 1249 6-10-12 99 SamTwiston-Davies 52
(David Bridgwater) *chsd ldrs tl lost pl and rdn after 6th: lost tch bef 3 out: t.o fr 2 out* **9/1**

4m 35.0s (-24.00) **Going Correction** -1.075s/f (Hard) **7 Ran SP% 108.8**
Speed ratings (Par 103): **102,101,100,92,88 87,80**
Tote Swingers: 1&2 £1.10, 1&3 £2.70, 2&3 £3.60 CSF £5.31 TOTE £2.70: £1.30, £1.60; EX 3.90.There was no bid for the winner.
Owner optimumracing.co.uk **Bred** Charles Clarke **Trained** Aberthin, Vale of Glamorgan

FOCUS
Not a bad seller, confined to conditional riders. Probably not form to take at face value, with the third a concern.

NOTEBOOK
Carrick Oscar(IRE), who hadn't contested a hurdle since the Martin Pipe at Cheltenham 17 months ago, was made more of than usual, which was entirely deliberate, with Tim Vaughan keen for Richard Killoran to draw the sting out of William Butler on his mount. An untidy leap at the last didn't scupper the plan, with the gelding already clearly on top by then, and this will have done plenty for a horse whose confidence has arguably looked a little low since a fall in the Fox Hunters' at Aintree. He was retained without a bid. (op 15-8 tchd 13-8)
William Butler(IRE)'s sole hurdling win came over this trip, but on a more testing surface. The manner in which he was run out of it from the last suggests he might require something a bit more taxing than today's assignment to add to his tally in this sphere. (op 6-4 tchd 7-4)
Knightsbridgelives(IRE)'s best effort in points last season came on good ground at nearby Cottenham, like Huntingdon a sharp, flat right-handed speed course. He might have had more left to throw at the winner late on but for proving too keen early and then bungling the last, and he'd be of interest again in an identical contest if getting more of the basics right. (op 9-1)
High Skies's effort on leaving the back straight was short-lived to say the least, and he's looking an increasingly faint-hearted competitor. (op 10-1 tchd 12-1)
Zizou(IRE) Official explanation: vet said gelding finished lame
Hi Wycombe(IRE) looked in trouble before this longer trip became an issue, and comprehensively failed to build on his second in this grade at Market Rasen last time. (op 8-1)

1432 SYNERGO SUPPORTS RACING WELFARE NOVICES' CHASE (14 fncs 2 omitted) 2m 4f 110y
4:15 (4:16) (Class 4) 4-Y-0+ **£3,332** (£1,034; £557)

Form RPR
5152 **1** **Walamo (GER)**[16] 1251 6-10-13 0 (t) MrTomDavid[(7)] 121+
(Tim Vaughan) *t.k.h: trckd ldrs: blnd 3rd: wnt 2nd 5th: lft in ld 11th: mde rest: jnd after 3 out: rdn and forged ahd 2 out: kpt on u.p flat: drvn out* **9/2**
-341 **2** *2 ¼* **Rockiteer (IRE)**[29] 1151 7-11-6 117 (p) AndrewTinkler 119
(Henry Daly) *t.k.h: trckd ldrs: lft 2nd 11th: chal after 3 out: rdn bef 2 out: one pce and btn between last 2* **5/4**[1]
4U5- **3** *51* **Night Orbit**[32] 4260 6-11-0 0 ColinBolger 62
(Julia Feilden) *chsd ldr tl dropped to last and mstke 5th: sn rdn and lost tch: rallied briefly after 8th: losing tch whn lft 3rd 11th: t.o bypassing 3 out* **7/2**[3]
-450 **F** **Agente Romano (USA)**[44] 1019 5-11-0 0 PaulMoloney —
(Evan Williams) *j. boldly: led tl fell 11th* **11/4**[2]

4m 51.5s (-13.80) **Going Correction** -0.525s/f (Firm) **4 Ran SP% 111.5**
Speed ratings (Par 105): **105,104,84,—**
CSF £11.15 TOTE £6.10; EX 7.10.
Owner M & S Clarke **Bred** Gestut Hof Vesterberg **Trained** Aberthin, Vale of Glamorgan

FOCUS
A modest novice chase. Straightforward novice form.

NOTEBOOK
Walamo(GER) had trip and track to suit once again, and also consented to settle better than the favourite, leaving him with enough left to assert up the run-in. He still doesn't convince entirely as a jumper, with one blunder on the first circuit followed by a guess at the final ditch, and however genuine he is it's hard to imagine him repelling the better novices under a double penalty when they start to appear. There are no hard and fast plans for him beyond "just chipping away", according to connections. (op 7-2 tchd 3-1)
Rockiteer(IRE) put in a tidier round of jumping than his rivals, as befits a horse with at least twice the chasing experience of all of them, but his effervescence has tempered his late effort on more than one occasion over fences now and did so again. He has to be treated with a degree of caution. (op 11-8 tchd 13-8)
Night Orbit got up to a mark as high as 130 over hurdles last season, but his propensity to make untimely errors limited him to just one victory at Market Rasen from nine starts in that sphere. The shuddering mistake at the fifth ended his meaningful involvement in this contest, his chasing debut, though he did at least complete without further alarm in a remote third and may have learned something from the experience. (op 10-3 tchd 3-1)
Agente Romano(USA) ◆, rated 118 at best over hurdles, had put in a sumptuous display of jumping out in front on this chasing debut. It is to be hoped the fall he took (with horse and rider both soon back on their feet) doesn't leave a mark, given the excellent impression created up to that point. (op 4-1 tchd 9-2)

1433 TIMEFORM RADIO SUPPORTS RACING WELFARE MAIDEN HURDLE (8 hdls) 2m 110y
4:50 (4:51) (Class 4) 4-Y-0+ **£2,602** (£764; £382; £190)

Form RPR
1 **Sircozy (IRE)**[26] 4-10-13 0 JamieMoore 99+
(Gary Moore) *t.k.h: hld up in tch towards rr: hdwy to chse ldrs and pushed along bef 2 out: rdn and ev ch between last 2: r.o wl u.p to ld flat* **4/1**[3]
2 *¾* **Get It On (IRE)**[41] 1052 5-11-0 0 PaulMoloney 100+
(Evan Williams) *t.k.h: hld up in tch: mstke 1st: chsd ldrs and mstke 3 out: rdn to chal 2 out: sn led: r.o wl u.p tl hdd and no ex flat* **15/8**[2]
2 **3** *4 ½* **Mutadarrej (IRE)**[13] 1278 6-11-0 112 DougieCostello 96+
(Ian Williams) *chsd ldrs: nt fluent 1st and 3rd: led 3 out: rdn and mstke next: sn hdd: drvn and outpcd bef last: styd on same pce flat* **7/4**[1]
4 *¾* **Hustle (IRE)**[11] 5-10-7 0 MrJBanks[(7)] 94
(Gay Kelleway) *t.k.h: hld up wl in tch: mstke 3rd: hmpd next: chsd ldrs and rdn bef 2 out: styd on same pce between last 2* **20/1**
5 *6* **Moonwolf (NZ)**[30] 6-11-0 0 JamieGoldstein 89+
(Sheena West) *hld up wl in tch towards rr: mstke 1st: hdwy to chse ldrs 3 out: wnt 2nd bef next tl hit 2 out: sn rdn and wknd bef last* **50/1**
3303 **6** *2 ¼* **Mulaazem**[40] 1063 7-10-9 86 DavidBass[(5)] 86
(Derek Frankland) *led at stdy gallop: hdd and rdn 3 out: wknd bef next* **20/1**
0 **7** *4* **Nouailhas**[10] 1308 4-10-6 0 PeterHatton[(7)] 81
(Reg Hollinshead) *plld v hrd: hld up wl in tch in midfield: rdn and outpcd bef 3 out: no ch w ldrs after* **80/1**
050 **8** *2 ¼* **Reg's Ruby**[18] 1233 4-10-6 0 RodiGreene 72
(David Bridgwater) *chsd ldr: mstke 3rd: lost 2nd after 5th and wknd next: wl btn next* **100/1**
3 **9** *shd* **Contradiktive (IRE)**[12] 1280 4-10-6 0 MrTomDavid[(7)] 79
(Tim Vaughan) *chsd ldrs: j. slowly and reminders 4th: wknd qckly u.p after 3 out* **14/1**
/-P0 **10** *2 ¼* **Topping The Bill**[16] 1250 7-10-7 0 MrRichardCollinson[(7)] 77
(Michael Wigham) *t.k.h: hld up in rr: hdwy after 4th: struggling and dropped to rr 5th: wl bhd after next* **100/1**
P **Burnbrake**[30] 5-11-0 0 LeightonAspell —
(Les Hall) *t.k.h: hld up in tch in rr tl lost tch qckly 4th: wl t.o and p.u 3 out* **33/1**

3m 43.1s (-11.80) **Going Correction** -1.075s/f (Hard)
WFA 4 from 5yo+ 13lb **11 Ran SP% 115.5**
Speed ratings (Par 105): **84,83,81,81,78 77,75,74,74,73 —**
Tote Swingers: 1&2 £1.30, 1&3 £1.50, 2&3 £2.00 CSF £11.47 TOTE £5.50: £2.10, £1.60, £1.10; EX 14.60.
Owner A E Dean **Bred** Allevamento Pian Di Neve Srl **Trained** Lower Beeding, W Sussex
■ Stewards' Enquiry : Peter Hatton two-day ban: used whip out of contention without giving gelding time to respond (Sep 19,21)

FOCUS
An ordinary maiden and tricky to pin down the form of the first three.

NOTEBOOK
Sircozy(IRE) was keen under restraint early on (arguably unusually so given that all four career Flat wins had also been gained dropped out the back), but no more so than the runner-up whom he was able to outstay up the run-in. His schooling had pleased connections and justifiably so, as his was the best round in the field by far, and while there are no grand plans for him, his professionalism over the flights should stand him in good stead in his bid to defy a penalty next time. (tchd 9-2)
Get It On(IRE), a recent acquisition from Fran Flood, couldn't make his comparative advantage of hurdling experience count, with keenness and two significant mistakes on the way round doing just enough cumulatively to cost him victory. It won't be a great novice he eventually wins, but the ability to land one is there, if he can keep unhelpful traits in check. (op 2-1 tchd 7-4)
Mutadarrej(IRE) has won two 2m1f Flat handicaps around Bath this summer, and although he raced more prominently than in either of those (or a 2m Worcester maiden since) just didn't find this run as enough of a test. A step up to 2m4f in this discipline may not go amiss. (op 15-8)
Hustle(IRE), winless beyond a galloping 7f on the level and rarely competitive over further, was ridden to see out the trip but was another to have his finishing effort dulled by early mistakes and keenness. He did finish clear of the remainder and may have something to offer over hurdles in due course, if translating enough of his Flat ability (rated 86 a year ago) to this discipline. (op 16-1)
Contradiktive(IRE), a beaten favourite at Hereford on his debut, jumped no better this time around and was quickly in trouble. (op 12-1)

1434 TICH KING, A LIFETIME IN RACING H'CAP HURDLE (12 hdls) 3m 2f
5:25 (5:27) (Class 5) (0-95,95) 4-Y-0+ **£2,055** (£599; £299)

Form RPR
-043 **1** **Mista Rossa**[20] 1232 5-10-8 **82** MissLHorner[(5)] 90+
(Jamie Snowden) *hld up in rr: stdy hdwy 9th: led 2 out: rdn and r.o wl to draw clr flat: comf* **13/2**
/62- **2** *6* **Brave Bugsy (IRE)**[5] 1229 7-10-10 **79** RodiGreene 82
(Michael Appleby) *prom in main gp: chsd clr ldr 7th: clsd next: led 9th: rdn and wandered u.p bef 2 out: hdd and hit 2 out: nt pce of wnr flat: kpt on* **14/1**
00-3 **3** *6* **Ridley Taylor**[31] 1141 7-10-8 **84** (p) MattCrawley[(7)] 81
(Sean Regan) *hld up towards rr: hdwy and in tch 8th: chsd ldrs 3 out: rdn and outpcd whn n.m.r next: kpt on u.p to go 3rd flat* **17/2**
0-3P **4** *4 ½* **Elegant Olive**[20] 1232 7-10-13 **82** HaddenFrost 75
(Roger Curtis) *hld up in main gp: clsd and in tch 8th: hdwy on inner bef 3 out: nt clr run bnd bef 2 out: rdn to chse clr ldng pair 2 out: no imp and btn whn edgd rt last: lost 3rd flat* **14/1**
1-46 **5** *1 ¾* **Sarahs Gift (IRE)**[61] 868 7-11-12 **95** (t) APMcCoy 85
(Lawney Hill) *prom in main gp: reminders after 7th: rdn to chse ldr after 9th tl bef 3 out: wknd bef 2 out: no ch whn swtchd lft last* **9/4**[1]
-33P **6** *1 ¾* **Back In Business (IRE)**[8] 1348 10-11-12 **95** (v[1]) PaulMoloney 83
(Evan Williams) *racd in midfield of main gp: mstke and lost pl 7th: lost tch after 9th and wl btn whn j. slowly 2 out: kpt on u.p flat* **5/1**[3]
4605 **7** *7* **Masterpoint**[18] 1235 10-9-13 **75** (v[1]) AdamWedge[(7)] 56
(Richard Harper) *prom in main gp: hdwy to chse ldrs 8th: hit 9th: rdn to chse ldr bef 3 out tl wl bef 2 out: wknd qckly 2 out* **28/1**
04F- **8** *12* **September Moon**[407] 996 12-10-13 **92** LucyBarry[(10)] 61
(Michael Appleby) *led and sn clr: c bk to field 8th: hdd and hit next: sn dropped out: wl bhd bef 2 out* **33/1**
0F41 **9** *24* **Albert Park (IRE)**[31] 1141 9-10-1 **73** (p) SamTwiston-Davies[(3)] 18
(John Upson) *hld up in rr: rdn and clsd after 7th: lost tch after 9th: t.o bef 2 out* **4/1**[2]

3P44 **P** **Prince Noora (IRE)**[11] 1297 9-11-7 **93**.....................(vt[1]) RichardKilloran(3) —
(Tim Vaughan) *chsd clr ldr: mstke 3rd: blnd 7th and lost pl: bhd next: t.o whn p.u 2 out* **16/1**

5m 56.4s (-26.50) **Going Correction** -1.075s/f (Hard) **10** Ran SP% **116.9**
Speed ratings (Par 103): **97,95,93,91,91 90,88,85,77,—**
Tote Swingers: 1&2 £19.60, 1&3 £7.80, 2&3 £21.50 CSF £90.44 CT £782.21 TOTE £8.50: £2.50, £3.40, £2.60; EX 111.90 Place 6 £195.76; Place 5 £100.96.
Owner The Mista Rossa Racing Partnership **Bred** The National Stud **Trained** Ebbesbourne Wake, Wilts

FOCUS
A weak staying handicap. The winner did it well and the form is rated around the runner-up.

NOTEBOOK
Mista Rossa looked in need of an even longer trip when stepped up to 2m6f at Newton Abbot last time, and duly came there swinging two out after a patient early ride to record an easy first hurdles win at the 11th attempt. This was just a modest contest, but there may be more to come from him over hurdles at what appears to be his ideal trip now. Alternatively, two entries this weekend suggest a switch to staying chases may be the offing soon. (op 7-1 tchd 6-1)
Brave Bugsy(IRE) also put up an improved effort stepped back up in trip on his first hurdling outing for a year, notwithstanding some untidy late jumps. The balance of his form both on the Flat and over hurdles suggests he is ground-dependent (does particularly well on firm at Bath), so connections will be hoping for a very dry autumn. (op 12-1)
Ridley Taylor, sporting first-time cheekpieces, proved too slow up the straight even stepped up to this trip. Second on her racecourse debut at Towcester in heavy 18 months earlier, a return to a more severe track might be needed to counter her lack of gears late on. (op 12-1)
Elegant Olive was ridden to see out this extra 4f, but didn't convince fully as having done so. (op 22-1)
Sarahs Gift(IRE) looked in trouble some way out on his first hurdles outing since January 2008, and remains winless over these obstacles, this long a trip and round a right-handed course. (op 13-8 tchd 6-4 and 5-2 in places)
Back In Business(IRE) found no improvement for the first-time visor and continues to prove extremely hard to win with. (op 6-1)
Albert Park(IRE) turned in a moody looking effort. (op 6-1)
Prince Noora(IRE) Official explanation: jockey said gelding hung left
T/Plt: £45.40 to a £1 stake. Pool:£37,163.14 - 597.16 winning tickets T/Qpdt: £11.90 to a £1 stake. Pool:£1,877.12 - 116.00 winning tickets SP

1435 - 1441a (Foreign Racing) - See Raceform Interactive

[1343]NEWTON ABBOT (L-H)

Tuesday, August 31

OFFICIAL GOING: Good to soft (soft in places) changing to good to soft after race 1 (2.20)
All bends moved but impact on distances not notified.
Wind: fresh across Weather: sunny

1442 EUROPEAN BREEDERS' FUND JUVENILE MAIDEN HURDLE (8 hdls) 2m 1f

2:20 (2:20) (Class 4) 3-Y-O **£3,447** (£1,012; £506; £252)

Form RPR
1 **Joan D'Arc (IRE)**[13] 3-9-12 0.......................... MrJMQuinlan(7) 91+
(Michael Quinlan) *hld up: hdwy 4th: led appr 2 out: sn rdn: kpt on: rdn out* **5/2**[2]
2 *1 1/4* **Royal And Ancient (IRE)**[69] 3-10-12 0.......................... WarrenMarston 95
(Milton Harris) *in tch: rdn in cl 3rd after 3 out: styng on whn nt fluent last: snatched 2nd fnl strides* **7/1**[3]
222 **3** *nse* **Sassanian (IRE)**[6] 1363 3-10-12 0..........................(v[1]) RichardJohnson 95
(Tim Vaughan) *led: rdn and hdd appr 2 out: kpt on: no ex fr last* **13/8**[1]
04 **4** *21* **Baltic Ben (USA)**[10] 1330 3-10-12 0..........................(p) TomScudamore 76
(Tim Vaughan) *trckd ldrs: rdn after 3 out: wknd bef next* **33/1**
05 **5** *6* **Mini Max**[7] 1279 3-10-5 0..........................(b) MarkGrant 64
(Brendan Duke) *hld up towards rr: rdn bef 5th: nvr any imp on ldrs* **66/1**
6 *5* **Celtic Intrigue (IRE)** 3-10-12 0.......................... PaddyBrennan 66
(Tom George) *hit 1st: towards rr whn pushed along after 2nd: rdn after 4th: nvr a threat* **15/2**
0P02 **7** *8* **A P Ling**[13] 1279 3-10-5 0.......................... DarylJacob 57
(Christopher Kellett) *in tch whn hmpd and stmbld after 4th: sn in rr: rdn next: wknd 3 out* **20/1**
465 **8** *17* **Sefton Park**[19] 1234 3-10-9 0..........................(vt[1]) SamTwiston-Davies(3) 44
(Charles Egerton) *trckd ldrs: j.rt: rdn after 5th: wknd next* **14/1**
5 **R** **Othello (IRE)**[10] 1330 3-10-9 0.......................... RichieMcLernon(3) —
(Jonjo O'Neill) *w ldr tl v reluctant and ref to continue on bnd after 4th* **28/1**
P **Freckle Face** 3-10-9 0.......................... PeterToole(3) —
(Bill Turner) *t.k.h: nt a fluent: hld up: hmpd on bnd after 4th: hdwy to dispute 2nd whn v slow next: bhd whn stmbld bdly 3 out: p.u bef next* **20/1**

4m 11.7s (6.00) **Going Correction** +0.40s/f (Soft) **10** Ran SP% **115.0**
Speed ratings (Par 102): **101,100,100,90,87 85,81,73,—,—**
toteswingers:1&2 £3.70, 2&3 £2.80, 1&3 £1.50 CSF £18.36 TOTE £3.30: £2.00, £2.40, £1.10; EX 18.20.
Owner Newtown Anner Stud Farm Ltd **Bred** Lynn Lodge Stud **Trained** Newmarket, Suffolk

FOCUS
A dry morning resulted in the going being changed to Good to soft, soft in places before the first race. The riders reported that it was riding "slow and a bit dead". A moderate-looking juvenile hurdle and it concerned just three from the last on the far side. The form is limited with the third helping with the level.

NOTEBOOK
Joan D'Arc(IRE) was the racecourse whisper in the morning having reportedly schooled better than any novice hurdler the trainer has had previously, and justified the support under a confident ride from her young jockey. Held up early, she picked her way through on the second circuit and, despite running green after hitting the front at the penultimate flight, she was always holding her rivals. Like her namesake she is not very big, but now she has scored she looks capable of winning again. (op 9-4 tchd 11-4)
Royal And Ancient(IRE), making his debut for his new trainer having been bought for 6,000gns after not fulfilling early promise, performed quite well on this hurdling debut but could not find a change of gear in the straight. (op 9-1 tchd 10-1 and 13-2)
Sassanian(IRE) had finished runner-up in his previous six starts, including three on the Flat. Fitted with a visor for the first time, he made the running and appeared to battle on under pressure but looks one to avoid for win purposes until he gets his head in front. (op 2-1tchd 9-4 in a place)
Baltic Ben(USA) has now been well beaten in all three hurdles starts, and the cheekpieces only brought about minor improvement. (op 28-1)
Celtic Intrigue(IRE) is related to a couple of winning hurdlers but had to be pushed along after a mistake at the first, and only made limited headway in the second half of the race. (op 7-1)

1443 COURTENAY PARK CONDITIONAL JOCKEYS' H'CAP HURDLE (8 hdls) 2m 3f

2:50 (2:50) (Class 4) (0-115,110) 4-Y-0+ **£3,082** (£898; £449)

Form RPR
-212 **1** **Benedict Spirit (IRE)**[9] 1347 5-11-12 **110**..........................(p) RhysFlint 118+
(John Flint) *led tl 5th: reminders: chsd ldrs: rdn after 6th: led after 3 out: j.lft last 2: a in command: rdn out* **4/5**[1]
0-00 **2** *8* **Ardistan (IRE)**[39] 1084 6-10-13 **100**.......................... RichieMcLernon(3) 101+
(Jonjo O'Neill) *trckd ldrs tl blnd bdly 5th: in tch: rdn after 3 out: wnt 2nd next: no ch w wnr* **14/1**
40-3 **3** *7* **Ladies Best**[33] 1124 6-11-1 **102**.......................... MattGriffiths(3) 96
(Gordon Edwards) *hld up: jnd ldrs 5th: rdn whn nt fluent 6th: ev ch after 3 out: wknd bef next* **7/1**[3]
600/ **4** *5* **Gold Ring**[42] 4566 10-10-11 **95**.......................... RichardKilloran 83
(Mark Gillard) *racd wd: prom: led 5th: rdn after 3 out: hdd bef next: fdd* **16/1**
4050 **5** *1 3/4* **Stumped**[12] 1292 7-11-5 **103**..........................(t) PeterToole 90
(Milton Harris) *hld up: hdwy after 5th: rdn after 6th: ch whn short of room after 3 out: one pce sn after* **5/1**[2]
-201 **6** *5* **Captain Becket**[85] 661 7-11-2 **100**.......................... HaddenFrost 82
(James Frost) *hld up: struggling fr after 5th: nvr any danger fr next* **8/1**

4m 38.8s (4.90) **Going Correction** +0.40s/f (Soft) **6** Ran SP% **108.4**
Speed ratings (Par 105): **105,101,98,96,95 93**
CSF £10.99 TOTE £1.40: £1.10, £9.50; EX 14.30.
Owner Jason Tucker **Bred** Allevamento Pian Di Neve Srl **Trained** Kenfig Hill, Bridgend

FOCUS
They went a sound gallop in this conditionals' handicap, which played into the hands of the favourite. The form is not the most solid but the winner can rate higher.

NOTEBOOK
Benedict Spirit(IRE) stays well and this drop in trip was not sure to suit but it was connections' only option before he goes up another 7lb at the weekend. After making the early running, he was headed at halfway but his rival's move played into his hands, as his stamina kicked in rounding the home turn and he was soon able to draw clear for a comfortable success. (op 11-8 tchd 6-4 in a place)
Ardistan(IRE) lost his good early pitch as the pace picked up at halfway, but he ran on again from the third-last to chase home the winner. This was his best effort since joining his current trainer, and the longer trip and soft ground clearly suited. (op 11-1)
Ladies Best was soon prominent and, despite being ridden along, helped push the pace from halfway. However, he could not respond when the winner went on. (op 5-1)
Gold Ring having his first run over hurdles since March 2008, has dropped a lot since his peak and did not perform badly, helping to force the pace until tiring from the home turn. Official explanation: jockey said gelding never travelled (tchd 14-1)
Stumped made a brief effort on the second circuit but was soon beaten. (op 4-1)
Captain Becket won a seller here last time but was always in the rear, and never looked to be travelling. (op 6-1)

1444 NEWTON ABBOT RACECOURSE NOVICES' CHASE (20 fncs) 3m 2f 110y

3:20 (3:20) (Class 3) 5-Y-0+ **£6,970** (£2,059; £1,029; £514)

Form RPR
P-60 **1** **Hell's Bay (FR)**[57] 909 8-10-12 0.......................... JoeTizzard 129+
(Colin Tizzard) *travelled wl: trckd ldr: hit 14th: led 4 out: sn wl in command: easily* **7/2**[2]
2122 **2** *8* **Ballyvesey (IRE)**[16] 1255 5-11-4 120..........................(p) TomO'Brien 125
(Peter Bowen) *led tl 4 out: sn rdn: styd on same pce fr next* **8/11**[1]
400/ **3** *26* **Openditch (FR)**[521] 4765 8-10-12 0.......................... TomScudamore 106
(David Pipe) *trckd ldng pair: effrt after 4 out: hld fr next: wknd bef 2 out* **7/2**[2]
65P2 **4** *29* **Indian Pipe Dream (IRE)**[1] 1424 8-10-12 100.......................... LiamTreadwell 70
(Aytach Sadik) *a in last of 4: blnd 7th: sn pushed along: no ch fr after 14th* **10/1**[3]

6m 49.9s (5.30) **Going Correction** +0.40s/f (Soft) **4** Ran SP% **111.4**
Speed ratings: **108,105,97,89**
CSF £7.06 TOTE £4.80; EX 7.30.
Owner A G Fear **Bred** James Patrick Kelly **Trained** Milborne Port, Dorset

FOCUS
A small field for this novices' chase despite the decent prizemoney. The winner scored with a bit of hand and the runner-up sets the level.

NOTEBOOK
Hell's Bay(FR), a useful but somewhat unreliable customer when with Paul Nicholls, was sold out of that yard for just £3,000 at the beginning of the month having run out here on his last appearance. Having just his fourth start over fences, he jumped well throughout and, going on at the last on the far side, he came right away in the straight. He already looks a bargain and, if this success helps his confidence, he could build on this during the autumn. (tchd 4-1)
Ballyvesey(IRE) has taken well to fences this summer and set off in front. He could not respond when the winner went past although he stayed on, and perhaps the ground was too soft for him. (op Evens)
Openditch(FR), making his first appearance since March 2009 and also making his chasing debut, ran pretty well until getting tired from the third last. He should be better for the outing but might need some time to recover to avoid the bounce. (op 11-4)
Indian Pipe Dream(IRE) had won on his only two previous visits here but looked to be feeling the effects of his run at Cartmel the day before, combined with the long journey to get to the track, and was tailed off for the last circuit. (tchd 9-1 and 11-1)

1445 NEWTON ABBOT RACECOURSE NOVICES' HURDLE (8 hdls) 2m 1f

3:50 (3:53) (Class 4) 4-Y-0+ **£3,447** (£1,012; £506; £252)

Form RPR
5321 **1** **Swiss Art (IRE)**[9] 1344 4-10-4 104..........................(p) OliverDayman(7) 100+
(Alison Thorpe) *trckd ldrs: shkn up to ld after 3 out: kpt on wl fr next: pushed out* **4/9**[1]
2 *5* **Django Reinhardt**[82] 4-10-4 0.......................... MrDavidTurner(7) 94
(Sam Davison) *mid-div: hdwy after 5th: nt clrest of runs but wnt 2nd bef 2 out: sn rdn: kpt on same pce* **16/1**
5 **3** *2 1/2* **La Soie (IRE)**[9] 1344 4-10-4 0.......................... HaddenFrost 84
(James Frost) *racd keenly: trckd ldrs: rdn and ev ch after 3 out: kpt on same pce fr next* **9/2**[2]
F0 **4** *4 1/2* **Top Tide (IRE)**[9] 1343 9-10-12 0.......................... JackDoyle 88
(Martin Hill) *led: rdn and hdd after 3 out: one pce fr next* **20/1**
5 *6* **Don Jose (USA)**[640] 7-10-12 0.......................... CharliePoste 83
(Richard Lee) *mid-div: hdwy 5th: rdn and ch after 3 out: wknd bef next* **33/1**

6 2 1/4 **Lilly Royal (IRE)**[45] 4-10-1 0 DPFahy(3) 73
(Bryn Palling) *hld up towards rr: rdn after 5th: sme late prog: nvr a factor* **28/1**

7 33 **Mr Demister**[108] 7-10-7 0 ow2 MissLGardner(7) 53
(Susan Gardner) *racd keenly: trckd ldr: wknd after 3 out: t.o* **66/1**

04-0 8 9 **Miss Molly Moses**[9] 1343 6-10-5 0 LiamHeard 36
(Gerald Ham) *a towards rr: t.o fr 5th* **33/1**

0 9 5 **Natures Way (IRE)**[30] 1148 4-10-11 0 APMcCoy 37
(Jonjo O'Neill) *mid-div tl after 4th: sn struggling: t.o fr next* **14/1**[3]

F **Hurst Park (IRE)** 8-10-12 0 AidanColeman —
(Susan Gardner) *mid-div: wnt rt 2nd: wknd bef 3 out: t.o whn fell last* **25/1**

4m 10.9s (5.20) **Going Correction** +0.40s/f (Soft)
WFA 4 from 6yo+ 13lb 10 Ran SP% **119.4**
Speed ratings (Par 105): **103,100,99,97,94 93,77,73,71,—**
toteswingers:1&2 £3.20, 2&3 £3.80, 1&3 £1.50 CSF £8.40 TOTE £1.40: £1.10, £2.10, £1.70; EX 9.30.
Owner Phil Pye **Bred** John Yarr **Trained** Bronwydd Arms, Carmarthens

FOCUS
Very little form to go on in this novices' hurdle apart from that shown by the favourite. He is rated a little below form in victory.

NOTEBOOK
Swiss Art(IRE), the form horse, ultimately ran out the winner, but not quite as easily as might have been expected. Connections feel he might need further but the soft ground helped him. (tchd 2-5 and 4-7 in places)
Django Reinhardt, making his hurdling debut, he settled well before coming through looking a big threat early in the straight. He had no more to offer under pressure but a sound surface might suit him better, and he could win a similar contest. (tchd 20-1)
La Soie(IRE) was a bit keen and raced wide of her field for most of the way. She had her chance in the straight before the effort flattened out. (op 4-1 tchd 5-1)
Top Tide(IRE) struggled to get round in points but managed to complete over hurdles last time and did so again, leading until fading in the straight. (op 33-1 tchd 40-1)
Natures Way(IRE) was held up at the back and never got competitive. (op 10-1)

1446 NEWTON ABBOT RACECOURSE H'CAP HURDLE (10 hdls) 2m 6f
4:20 (4:20) (Class 5) (0-95,95) 4-Y-O+ **£2,329** (£678; £339)

Form RPR

/001 1 **Isle Of Inishmore (IRE)**[17] 1253 7-11-11 **94** (t) RichardJohnson 102+
(Tim Vaughan) *mid-div: hdwy appr 7th: rdn after 3 out: led next: styd on: drvn out* **10/3**[2]

-040 2 4 **Coeur Brule (FR)**[12] 1291 4-11-2 **94** MrDavidTurner(7) 96
(Sam Davison) *hld up in last pair: hdwy 7th: led after 3 out: sn rdn: hdd next: wandered u.p: kpt on same pce* **10/1**

0-15 3 1 1/4 **Miss Saffron**[72] 796 7-11-9 **92** JackDoyle 95
(Susan Gardner) *hld up in last pair: hdwy 3 out: sn rdn: styd on: nt gng pce to chal* **7/2**[3]

UP04 4 nk **The Wee Midget**[21] 1228 5-11-7 **90** NickScholfield 93
(Arthur Whiting) *trckd ldrs: rdn and ev ch after 3 out: styng on same pce whn sltly hmpd after last* **16/1**

6555 5 1/2 **Vacario (GER)**[21] 1230 6-11-9 **95** (t) TommyPhelan(3) 97
(Mark Gillard) *racd wd in tch: rdn after 7th: ev ch after 3 out: kpt on same pce fr next* **11/1**

25P 6 17 **Cinaman (IRE)**[10] 1331 6-9-13 **75** MrTomDavid(7) 62
(Tim Vaughan) *led: rdn and hdd after 3 out: wknd next* **3/1**[1]

40 7 8 **Murphys Appeal (IRE)**[21] 1232 6-10-11 **80** TomO'Brien 60
(Peter Bowen) *trckd ldrs: rdn after 3 out: wknd bef next* **11/2**

0-06 8 2 **Wujood**[12] 1294 8-10-8 **77** (bt) AndrewGlassonbury 55
(Gerald Ham) *trckd ldr: rdn after 7th: wknd after 3 out* **16/1**

5m 30.7s (10.50) **Going Correction** +0.40s/f (Soft)
WFA 4 from 5yo+ 14lb 8 Ran SP% **114.9**
Speed ratings (Par 103): **96,94,94,93,93 87,84,83**
toteswingers:1&2 £7.50, 2&3 £8.50, 1&3 £2.10 CSF £35.48 CT £123.36 TOTE £2.60: £1.10, £3.40, £1.60; EX 28.20.
Owner J H Frost **Bred** Garry Hadden **Trained** Aberthin, Vale of Glamorgan
■ Stewards' Enquiry : Mr David Turner two-day ban: careless riding (tbn)

FOCUS
An ordinary handicap hurdle. The pace was pedestrian on the first circuit and didn't pick up until around a mile from home. The form should prove reliable.

NOTEBOOK
Isle Of Inishmore(IRE), raised 4lb for his Market Rasen win, had stamina doubts at the trip, especially on a slow surface, but the steady early pace would have been a big help. He became slightly outpaced after moving into a handy position rounding the home bend, but still managed to hit the front before two out and quickly established an unassailable lead. (op 7-2 tchd 3-1)
Coeur Brule(FR) was still to win a race after 18 previous attempts under both codes, but was nonetheless the subject of quite a plunge. The gamble looked like coming off when he went to the front on the home bend, but the winner had got to him before jumping two out and there was nothing he could do about it. At least the each-way money was saved. (op 25-1)
Miss Saffron may not have been helped by being dropped out in a steadily run race and, although she stayed on over the last couple of flights, it was never going to be enough. She looks best going this way around. (op 3-1)
The Wee Midget, making his handicap debut, was on ground softer than good for the first time. He had every chance turning for home, but was then done for pace. (op 22-1)
Vacario(GER) was down another 10lb and a change of stables hasn't halted his decline, but he wasn't totally disgraced here considering he gave the wide outside away to no-one. (op 12-1)
Cinaman(IRE), back over hurdles for the first time since March having become disappointing over fences, was very much on his toes beforehand. Although he settled well enough once under way and had the run of the race out in front, he was still well cooked once headed after jumping three out. (op 7-2)

1447 BAKERS PARK H'CAP CHASE (16 fncs) 2m 5f 110y
4:55 (4:55) (Class 5) (0-95,94) 4-Y-O+ **£2,797** (£821; £410; £205)

Form RPR

4450 1 **Lansdowne Princess**[14] 1273 8-9-13 **72** DavidBass(5) 79+
(Gerald Ham) *hld up last but in tch: rdn along after 10th: stdy prog after 4 out: wnt 2nd 2 out: chal last: styd on to ld sn after: rdn out* **11/2**

2314 2 nk **Sir Bumble (IRE)**[7] 1360 10-11-6 **91** (t) PeterToole(3) 97
(Michael Blake) *trckd ldrs: rdn appr 4 out: led appr 2 out: kpt on: no ex whn hdd run-in* **7/2**[2]

B033 3 3 1/4 **Le Forezien (FR)**[9] 1348 11-10-9 **84** (t) MrRHawkins(7) 87
(Carroll Gray) *trckd ldrs: rdn after 11th: swtchd rt bef 2 out: styd on same pce* **5/2**[1]

5544 4 10 **Young Tot (IRE)**[10] 1335 12-10-3 **76** (t) IanPopham(5) 70
(Carroll Gray) *led: rdn and hdd after 3 out: wknd bef last* **14/1**

322P 5 7 **Captain Marlon (IRE)**[14] 1277 9-11-12 **94** (t) JoeTizzard 82
(Colin Tizzard) *trckd ldr: led briefly after 3 out: sn rdn: wknd next* **9/2**

0665 6 24 **Regain Du Charbonneau (FR)**[72] 794 5-11-3 **85** (tp) TomScudamore 51
(David Pipe) *trckd ldrs: nudged along fr 8th: rdn after 10th: wkng whn mstke and stmbld bdly 4 out* **4/1**[3]

5m 30.2s (8.80) **Going Correction** +0.40s/f (Soft) 6 Ran SP% **111.0**
Speed ratings (Par 103): **100,99,98,95,92 83**
toteswingers:1&2 £6.60, 2&3 £1.50, 1&3 £3.60 CSF £24.47 TOTE £5.30: £1.90, £2.80; EX 32.00.
Owner The Lansdowners **Bred** D Malcolm Drury **Trained** Rooks Bridge, Somerset
■ Stewards' Enquiry : Mr R Hawkins four-day ban: used whip in incorrect place causing gelding to be wealed (Sep 19,21-23)

FOCUS
A low-grade handicap chase but it produced a good finish. The third and fourth limit the form.

NOTEBOOK
Lansdowne Princess has been running mainly over hurdles of late but likes some cut in the ground and, given a positive ride, she proved just good enough to record her first success at the 37th attempt. She was held up at the back but responded to pressure to get up near the line. (op 7-1 tchd 15-2)
Sir Bumble(IRE) likes this track, and when he took the lead off the home bend looked likely to score. He was run out of it on the flat, and might have found the ground softer than ideal. (op 3-1)
Le Forezien(FR), whose last success was over C&D just over two years ago, had dropped to just 2lb above that mark. Held up off the pace, he ran on in the straight but never looked able to close the gap on the principals.
Young Tot(IRE) made the running but had nothing left when headed on the home turn. (op 16-1)
Captain Marlon(IRE) travelled well from the start and looked sure to play a major part when taking the lead on the home turn. However, he was headed as soon as they straightened up and was quickly done with. He is another who was probably unsuited by the ground. (op 7-2)
Regain Du Charbonneau(FR), having just his second start over fences, was being pushed along some way out and was beaten when hitting the last ditch. (op 11-2)

1448 ALMAPA FATHER JOHN WRENN MEMORIAL INTERMEDIATE OPEN NATIONAL HUNT FLAT RACE 2m 1f
5:30 (5:30) (Class 6) 4-6-Y-O **£1,541** (£449; £224)

Form RPR

1 **Havingotascoobydo (IRE)**[157] 5-11-0 0 WarrenMarston 97+
(Martin Keighley) *t.k.h early: hld up: tk clsr order 7f out: led 3f out: rdn clr 2f out: kpt on: rdn out* **10/11**[1]

2 14 **Prairie Hero (GER)** 4-10-13 0 APMcCoy 84+
(Charles Egerton) *hld up: hdwy 7f out: rdn and ev ch 3f out: sn hld by wnr: kpt on same pce* **10/3**[2]

3 9 **Queen's Bay** 4-10-6 0 JoeTizzard 68+
(Colin Tizzard) *in tch: outpcd 7f out: styd on again fnl 2f: snatched 3rd towards fin: nt trble ldrs* **5/1**[3]

0- 4 1/2 **Pontyates**[164] 4729 5-10-11 0 DonalDevereux(3) 75
(Peter Bowen) *trckd ldrs tl outpcd 4f out: styd on again fnl 2f: nvr any danger* **12/1**

500- 5 1/2 **Double Or Quitz**[140] 5178 5-10-7 0 NathanSweeney(7) 75
(Bob Buckler) *led: rdn and hdd 3f out: grad fdd: lost 3rd nr fin* **14/1**

6 3/4 **Just Unique**[484] 6-11-0 0 TomScudamore 74
(Mark Rimell) *trckd ldrs tl outpcd over 4f out: styd on again fnl 2f: nvr a threat* **14/1**

7 dist **Brackenwood** 4-10-13 0 HaddenFrost —
(James Frost) *in tch tl wknd over 4f out: sn eased: virtually p.u* **20/1**

4m 5.30s (5.20) **Going Correction** +0.40s/f (Soft)
WFA 4 from 5yo+ 1lb 7 Ran SP% **117.9**
Speed ratings: **103,96,92,91,91 91,—**
toteswingers:1&2 £1.70, 2&3 £2.40, 1&3 £1.50 CSF £4.42 TOTE £1.90: £1.10, £2.40; EX 5.30 Place 6: £50.63 Place 5: £42.89.
Owner The League Of Gentlemen **Bred** Daniel Kenneally **Trained** Condicote, Gloucs

FOCUS
A very ordinary bumper which the betting suggested involved only three, and they filled the first three places. Weak, limited form, but the first two can do better.

NOTEBOOK
Havingotascoobydo(IRE) won a 3m point on heavy ground in Ireland, and was sent off favourite on the strength of that. He travelled well throughout and, when asked, came away to score despite rather idling and looking at the crowd in the closing stages and could be better than average. Having been with new connections just a short time, he will now have a month off. (op 11-8)
Prairie Hero(GER), a half-brother to a Flat and hurdles winner, was held up before making a quick forward move at the end of the back straight. He looked a threat to the winner on the home turn but could not respond to pressure and was well beaten. (op 5-2)
Queen's Bay, out of a pointer/staying chaser, was struggling in the back straight but stayed on in the closing stages. She will need further over hurdles. (op 6-1)
Pontyates raced up with the leaders but was left behind when the race began in earnest. (op 14-1 tchd 16-1)
Double Or Quitz, the most experienced of these in bumpers, made the running but got tired once headed on the home turn. (op 12-1)
T/Plt: £56.90 to a £1 stake. Pool of £56,744.27 - 726.86 winning tickets. T/Qpdt: £28.20 to a £1 stake. Pool of £3,236.31 - 84.80 winning tickets. TM

[1279]HEREFORD (R-H)
Wednesday, September 1

OFFICIAL GOING: Good (good to firm in places; chs 7.0, hdl 7.6))
Wind: Light against Weather: Fine

1449 LINDLEY CATERING NOVICES' HURDLE (10 hdls) 2m 4f
2:10 (2:10) (Class 4) 4-Y-O+ **£2,276** (£668; £334; £166)

Form RPR

4PP- 1 **Tiermore (IRE)**[170] 4648 6-10-5 110 MrPJTolman(7) 103+
(Sirrell Griffiths) *a.p: led 2nd to 3rd: led after 4th: mstke next: rdn appr 2 out: clr last: styd on* **10/3**[2]

220 2 6 **The Fox's Decree**[57] 921 6-10-12 99 (t) WarrenMarston 97
(Martin Keighley) *hld up: hdwy 6th: sn drvn along: chsd wnr last: no imp* **5/4**[1]

P4P- 3 2 **Brimley**[129] 3 7-10-9 105 LeeStephens(3) 95
(Ann Price) *led to 2nd: led 3rd tl after next: outpcd 3 out: rallied appr last: styd on same pce flat* **11/1**

54 4 1 1/2 **Himitas (FR)**[58] 910 5-10-5 0 JodieMogford 87+
(Graeme McPherson) *mid-div: hdwy 4th: rdn whn blnd 2 out: styd on same pce appr last* **12/1**

5 1 1/2 **Lindsay's Dream**[72] 4-10-4 0 JamesDavies 84
(Andrew Haynes) *prom: chsd wnr 7th: rdn after 2 out: wknd last* **40/1**

6/ 6 9 **Little Dibber**[804] 742 7-10-12 0 JackDoyle 84
(Peter Pritchard) *hld up: hdwy 5th: rdn and wknd after 3 out* **66/1**

4/6F 7 37 **Runaway Harry (IRE)**[7] 1369 7-10-12 0 TomO'Brien 51
(Peter Bowen) *hld up: hdwy 6th: wknd next: t.o* **7/2**[3]

6 **8** *13* **Youandme (IRE)**[17] 1260 8-10-9 0.................................... PeterToole(3) 39
(Ray Peacock) *hld up: hdwy 6th: rdn and wknd 3 out: t.o* **100/1**

0-00 **9** *88* **Muzey's Princess**[26] 1196 4-10-4 0.................................... RodiGreene —
(Michael Mullineaux) *in rr fr 3rd: bhd fr 5th: t.o* **100/1**

5 **10** *26* **One Of A Kind (FR)**[29] 1175 6-10-12 0.................................... FelixDeGiles —
(John Daniel Moore, Ire) *hld up: pushed along 4th: wknd 6th: t.o* **25/1**

6U **P** **Classicality**[26] 1196 5-10-2 0....................................(b[1]) SeanQuinlan(3) —
(Michael Mullineaux) *sn pushed along and prom: rdn after 4th: wknd next: t.o whn p.u bef 6th* **100/1**

4m 50.3s (-5.20) **Going Correction** -0.275s/f (Good)
WFA 4 from 5yo+ 12lb **11** Ran SP% **116.5**
Speed ratings (Par 105): **99,96,95,95,94 91,76,71,35,25** —
toteswingers:1&2 £1.50, 2&3 £2.30, 1&3 £5.20 CSF £7.95 TOTE £5.10: £2.00, £1.10, £1.90; EX 8.90.
Owner S G Griffiths **Bred** Michael Power **Trained** Nantgaredig, Carmarthenshire

FOCUS
Little strength in depth but a couple of reasonable performances. The form makes sense, with the first three close to their marks.

NOTEBOOK
Tiermore(IRE) had finished second in this race last year when trying to make up ground off a slow pace. This time he was leaving nothing to chance, racing prominently and taking it up down the back to run the finish out of his rivals. He shot up the weights after last year's run and failed to go on from that, and after pulling up in his final two starts of last season he was given a break. Evidently freshened up, he was spot on for this, and now he has to prove if he can go on from here off a revised future handicap mark. (op 7-2 tchd 11-4)
The Fox's Decree was well backed based on some consistent efforts on fast ground this summer since sporting a tongue tie, but although he made steady progress on the final circuit he was never getting there. He has been tried at a variety of trips without success, and is beginning to look slow. (op 7-4)
Brimley led at a reasonable pace and stuck on once headed by the winner. He did not take to fences last season but, while he might come on for this run, he needs to show a bit more pace to be effective in novice hurdles. (op 10-1 tchd 9-1 and 12-1)
Himitas(FR) was moving up to challenge when clouting the second-last and effectively losing all chance from there. However, she was in the process of putting up an improved effort up to that point. (op 9-1 tchd 16-1)
Lindsay's Dream was a bit keen but showed up for a long way before her stamina gave way in the straight. Pulled up twice over hurdles in France last December, she has shown little on the Flat this year but this was a bit better. (tchd 66-1)

1450 LINDLEY CATERING H'CAP HURDLE (8 hdls) 2m 1f
2:40 (2:40) (Class 5) (0-90,90) 4-Y-0+ **£1,821** (£534; £267; £133)

Form RPR

2-10 **1** **Mycenean Prince (USA)**[26] 1199 7-11-5 00.................................... APMcCoy 95+
(Jim Best) *led to 4th: sn drvn along: remained handy: led after 2 out: styd on wl* **9/2**[1]

0030 **2** *7* **Hollies Favourite (IRE)**[45] 1035 7-11-9 87.................................... DenisO'Regan 93
(Louise Davis) *hld up: hdwy after 3 out: rdn to chse wnr appr last: no ex flat* **18/1**

0506 **3** *5* **The Grey One (IRE)**[37] 1095 7-11-0 85.................................... ChrisDavies(7) 87
(Milton Bradley) *chsd wnr tl led 4th: rdn and hdd after 2 out: wknd last* **22/1**

00-0 **4** *2 3/4* **Catholic Hill (USA)**[20] 1158 5-11-8 89.................................... TommyPhelan(3) 88
(Mark Gillard) *hld up: hdwy 5th: rdn after 2 out: wkng whn mstke last* **12/1**

P522 **5** *1 3/4* **London Times (IRE)**[15] 1272 5-11-2 80....................................(t) ColinBolger 77
(Simon Lewis) *prom: rdn 6th: wknd after 2 out* **6/1**[2]

0/56 **6** *1/2* **Turkish Sultan (IRE)**[23] 593 7-10-11 82....................................(b) MrTJCannon(7) 79
(Milton Bradley) *chsd ldrs: mstke 3rd: sn rdn: outpcd bef 5th: n.d after* **16/1**

33P0 **7** *16* **Wee Ziggy**[42] 1064 7-11-2 80.................................... RodiGreene 63
(Michael Mullineaux) *in rr: bhd fr 4th: t.o* **16/1**

000- **8** *3* **Behest**[21] 4439 5-9-11 64 oh18.................................... SeanQuinlan(3) 44
(Robin Mathew) *chsd ldrs tl wknd appr 2 out: t.o* **100/1**

0666 **9** *2 3/4* **Bazart**[13] 1295 8-11-9 87.................................... DarylJacob 64
(Bernard Llewellyn) *nvr on terms: t.o* **9/1**

6545 **10** *1* **Spring Haze**[7] 1369 5-10-3 74.................................... MrDGPrichard(7) 51
(Phillip Dando) *mid-div: effrt 5th: wknd next: t.o* **14/1**

-00P **11** *17* **Gunnadoit (USA)**[99] 467 5-11-4 85....................................(p) LeeStephens(3) 46
(Ann Price) *sn drvn along and a in rr: t.o* **33/1**

130- **12** *1 1/4* **Tanmeya**[366] 1357 9-11-1 86.................................... MrTomDavid(7) 46
(Tim Vaughan) *prom: rdn after 5th: wknd next: t.o* **10/1**

012/ **13** *39* **Flamand (FR)**[1388] 2213 9-11-12 90.................................... JodieMogford 15
(Nikki Evans) *hld up: sme hdwy 5th: wknd next: t.o* **25/1**

U33 **14** *18* **Carhue Princess (IRE)**[45] 1030 4-11-9 87.................................... PaulMoloney —
(Evan Williams) *chsd ldrs to 5th: t.o* **7/1**[3]

005 **15** *4* **Ilewin Tom**[13] 1293 7-10-0 64 oh2.................................... JamesDavies —
(Gary Brown) *bhd fr 3rd: t.o* **33/1**

002/ **P** **Lerubis (FR)**[1766] 1957 11-10-7 71.................................... AidanColeman —
(Ken Wingrove) *a in rr: bhd fr 3rd: t.o whn p.u bef 2 out* **40/1**

04-4 **P** **Camino Real**[103] 432 7-11-5 83.................................... RhysFlint —
(Jim Old) *prom to 3rd: t.o whn p.u bef 2 out* **9/1**

3m 57.6s (-1.80) **Going Correction** -0.275s/f (Good)
WFA 4 from 5yo+ 11lb **17** Ran SP% **123.0**
Speed ratings (Par 103): **93,89,87,86,85 85,77,76,74,74 66,65,47,38,37** —,—
toteswingers:1&2 £4.70, 2&3 £31.30, 1&3 £46.00 CSF £78.34 CT £1644.56 TOTE £5.30: £2.10, £5.00, £6.30, £4.00; EX 84.20.
Owner Con Harrington **Bred** Benjamin W Berger And Shadwell Farm Llc **Trained** Lewes, E Sussex

FOCUS
This was run at a punishing pace but it still favoured those racing prominently as nothing was able to make up enough ground. The winner is rated back to his best.

NOTEBOOK
Mycenean Prince(USA), after leading early, looked to be under pressure after being headed in the back straight, but he kept in touch, and by just relaxing briefly he found a second wind to regain the lead and go on to the line. He is awkward and difficult to win with, but after many fruitless attempts for other yards he has now gained both wins for his current stable. The assistance of Tony McCoy is undoubtedly a key factor as he explained afterwards that the horse was off the bridle all the way but is best if he can be kept in contention despite this. (tchd 4-1)
Hollies Favourite(IRE) had around ten lengths to make up from the back straight and he steadily made up the ground until flattening out from the last. This was an encouraging run on his first start for his new yard, without it looking like a win is imminent. (op 20-1)
The Grey One(IRE) was very keen and raced with his ears back early on until wrestling the lead off the winner in the back straight. He opened up a few lengths' gap but was unable to sustain the effort after expending so much energy early in the race. If he learns to calm down there could be a small race in him. (op 33-1)
Catholic Hill(USA) attracted some support on his second hurdling start for his current yard despite not looking that well handicapped. He made some progress in the back straight but never looked like getting there. (op 10-1)
London Times(IRE) had the leaders in his sights despite coming under pressure from the fourth and plugged on but could do no more. He has found a bit of consistency over the past month without looking likely to break his maiden. (op 8-1)
Turkish Sultan(IRE) made a little progress without it amounting to much and he is struggling off his current mark.

1451 WYVERN ICES H'CAP HURDLE (10 hdls) 2m 4f
3:10 (3:10) (Class 5) (0-95,95) 4-Y-0+ **£1,821** (£534; £267; £133)

Form RPR

-000 **1** **Am I Blue**[15] 1272 4-10-13 83.................................... RichardJohnson 107+
(Mrs D Thomas) *led to 3rd: led again next: clr after 2 out: easily* **5/1**[3]

-642 **2** *19* **Northern Lad (IRE)**[37] 1095 8-11-12 95.................................... DougieCostello 103
(Jim Best) *hld up: hdwy 7th: wnt 2nd after 2 out: no ch w wnr* **7/1**

0605 **3** *16* **Sea Cliff (IRE)**[11] 1336 6-11-2 85....................................(p) APMcCoy 83+
(Jonjo O'Neill) *hld up in tch: chsd wnr 6th tl rdn and wknd after 2 out: t.o* **4/1**[1]

P006 **4** *4 1/2* **Bond Cruz**[13] 1300 7-9-11 73.................................... RobertKirk(7) 63
(Olivia Maylam) *prom tl rdn and wknd appr 2 out: t.o* **18/1**

-5P5 **5** *3 1/4* **Mangonel**[11] 1335 6-10-5 74....................................(v) RodiGreene 61
(Stuart Howe) *prom: racd keenly: rdn and wknd after 8th: t.o* **20/1**

F620 **6** *1* **Rapide Plaisir (IRE)**[26] 1195 12-11-2 90.................................... GilesHawkins(5) 76
(Richard Lee) *prom: pushedalong 7th: wknd after next: t.o* **16/1**

442F **7** *32* **Nobby Kivambo (IRE)**[8] 1360 5-11-7 90....................................(p) WarrenMarston 47
(Brendan Powell) *hld up in tch: rdn appr 7th: wknd bef next: t.o* **7/1**

4400 **8** *3 1/2* **Roisin's Prince (IRE)**[42] 1062 8-11-4 87....................................(t) AidanColeman 41
(Matt Sheppard) *hld up: nvr on terms: t.o* **16/1**

0-P0 **9** *25* **Petrus De Sormain (FR)**[18] 1254 7-11-7 90....................................(t) DavidDennis 21
(James Evans) *hld up: bhd fr 4th: t.o* **50/1**

2U0 **10** *12* **Abulharith**[20] 826 4-11-2 86....................................(p) TomScudamore 5
(Michael Scudamore) *hld up: sme hdwy 7th: sn wknd: t.o* **14/1**

/654 **11** *1/2* **Doheny Bar (IRE)**[20] 1237 7-11-7 90....................................(p) JodieMogford 10
(Nikki Evans) *racd keenly: w ldr tl led 3rd: hdd next: lost 2nd 6th: sn rdn and wknd: t.o* **40/1**

P-01 **12** *1 3/4* **Tegan Lee**[13] 1294 7-11-7 90.................................... DarylJacob 8
(Liam Corcoran) *hld up: sme hdwy 7th: wknd next: t.o* **9/2**[2]

04-P **13** *3/4* **Dee Cee Elle**[36] 1107 6-11-12 95....................................(p) RhysFlint 13
(John Flint) *in rr whn mstke 4th: drvn along and wknd after next: t.o* **8/1**

2P04 **P** **Smart John**[26] 1195 10-11-12 95.................................... ColinBolger —
(Simon Lewis) *chsd ldrs: drvn along after 5th: wknd next: t.o whn p.u bef 3 out* **33/1**

006 **P** **Motor Home**[34] 1125 4-11-5 89.................................... JimmyMcCarthy —
(Charlie Morlock) *hld up: sme hdwy 6th: wknd next: t.o whn p.u bef 2 out* **40/1**

4m 48.3s (-7.20) **Going Correction** -0.275s/f (Good)
WFA 4 from 5yo+ 12lb **15** Ran SP% **129.2**
Speed ratings (Par 103): **103,95,89,87,85 85,72,71,61,56 56,55,55,**—,—
toteswingers:1&2 £11.00, 2&3 £7.20, 1&3 £7.80 CSF £41.38 CT £161.74 TOTE £6.30: £1.90, £3.10, £2.10; EX 54.20.
Owner Mrs D Thomas **Bred** Bricklow Ltd **Trained** Aberkenfig, Bridgend

FOCUS
A moderate handicap livened up by a significant gamble. The gambled-on winner is rated up 10lb on her old form.

NOTEBOOK
Am I Blue had been tailed off in her previous two starts but was the subject of good money, having been as big as 25-1 in the morning. With Richard Johnson taking over in the saddle from a conditional rider, who was originally down to ride the filly but was apparently unwell, she was given a much more positive ride than of late and, at a track where such tactics often pay off, she came home an easy winner. On this evidence she has the ability to win off a higher mark, but whether she goes on from this is anyone's guess as this was clearly the day. Official explanation: trainer said, regarding apparent improvement in form, that the filly had benefited from some spinal therapy and a change in tactics. (op 15-2 tchd 4-1)
Northern Lad(IRE) stayed on from midfield to take second from Sea Cliff, but he had no chance with the gambled-on winner. (op 13-2)
Sea Cliff(IRE), who had the cheekpieces back on, went in pursuit of the winner and that effort probably cost him second place in the end. (op 9-2)
Bond Cruz, who's only ever won a selling hurdle in 31 starts under both codes, plugged on but was never a danger. (tchd 25-1)
Mangonel ran one of her better races, which isn't saying a lot. (op 22-1 tchd 25-1)
Rapide Plaisir(IRE) remains on a long losing run.
Tegan Lee Official explanation: jockey said mare was unsuited by the right-hand track; vet said mare finished distressed
Smart John Official explanation: jockey said gelding returned lame

1452 SUNSHINE RADIO NOVICES' CHASE (19 fncs) 3m 1f 110y
3:40 (3:40) (Class 4) 5-Y-0+ **£3,252** (£955; £477; £238)

Form RPR

-32P **1** **Chevy To The Levy (IRE)**[45] 1034 8-10-5 109....................................(p) CharlieWallis(7) 114
(John O'Shea) *a.p: led 15th: edgd rt flat: drvn out* **7/1**

UF-1 **2** *3/4* **Job One (FR)**[64] 854 7-11-5 114.................................... HaddenFrost 120
(Henrietta Knight) *chsd ldrs: lost pl 5th: hdwy 11th: ev ch fr 2 out: rdn and nt fluent last: n.m.r flat: styd on* **7/2**[3]

353 **3** *48* **Canon's Corner (IRE)**[15] 1274 7-10-12 0.................................... AidanColeman 70
(Rachel Hobbs) *led to 15th: rdn and wknd 2 out: t.o* **25/1**

-104 **4** *19* **Ethiopia**[91] 588 7-10-12 98.................................... NathanSweeney(7) 60
(Bob Buckler) *prom tl wknd 12th: t.o* **17/2**

P **Winter Star**[719] 1387 10-10-12 0.................................... APMcCoy —
(Evan Williams) *hld up: hdwy 5th: chsd ldr 9th: nt fluent next: mstke 13th: wknd 3 out: p.u bef next* **13/8**[1]

U **Flying Johnny M (IRE)**[14] 1287 10-10-12 105....................................(b) JohnnyFarrelly —
(Michael Hourigan, Ire) *hld up: blnd and uns rdr 9th* **10/3**[2]

P-PP **P** **Marado (IRE)**[36] 1106 9-10-12 46....................................(b) ColinBolger —
(Simon Lewis) *chsd ldr to 9th: wknd 11th: t.o whn p.u bef 15th* **100/1**

6m 23.7s (-8.10) **Going Correction** -0.35s/f (Good) **7** Ran SP% **111.3**
Speed ratings: **98,97,83,77,**— —,—
toteswingers:1&2 £9.10, 2&3 £4.70, 1&3 £10.30 CSF £30.47 TOTE £8.80: £3.50, £3.40; EX 33.60.
Owner K W Bell **Bred** John J M Power **Trained** Elton, Gloucs

FOCUS
An ordinary novice event with the two market leaders failing to complete. The form is rated around the first two.

NOTEBOOK
Chevy To The Levy(IRE) responded to the first-time cheekpieces to jump competently and was travelling best turning for home until coming under pressure in the straight, but he just had enough to see off the challenger. This continued the progress he had hinted at when narrowly beaten at Southwell in July, and although he flopped in a handicap next time this was a comparatively easier task. It will not help his future handicap options though. (tchd 9-1)

Job One(FR) had run away with a beginners' chase on his first start for his current yard in June, but he never attacked the fences on this occasion and gradually lost several lengths as a result. Credit to him for moving up to challenge at the last, which shows he is capable of winning again if he can find more fluency in his jumping. (op 10-3 tchd 11-4)
Canon's Corner(IRE) led and jumped well enough until hitting a wall on the long turn for home and once again he did not see out the trip. (tchd 28-1)
Ethiopia, a dual Plumpton winner, was struggling from the 11th on his first start for three months. (op 9-1 tchd 10-1)
Winter Star, a multiple hurdles winner, was well backed for his chasing debut after nearly two years off the track but he never looked happy facing the fences and was wisely pulled up. (op 7-2 tchd 4-1 and 3-1)
Flying Johnny M(IRE) jumped slowly and without any fluency, and after parting company with his jockey he also fell when loose. (op 7-2 tchd 4-1 and 3-1)

1453 DIGIBET.COM NOVICES' H'CAP HURDLE (8 hdls) 2m 1f
4:10 (4:10) (Class 4) (0-115,112) 3-Y-0+ **£2,602** (£764; £382; £190)

Form RPR
1226 **1** **Freedom Fire (IRE)**[40] 1083 4-11-12 **112**.......................... JamieMoore 116
(Gary Moore) *hld up: hdwy 6th: chal last: styd on u.p to ld last strides* **16/1**
F41 **2** *nse* **Tignello (IRE)**[14] 1280 5-11-3 **108**..............................(t) IanPopham(5) 112
(Paul Nicholls) *hld up: hmpd after 6th: hdwy bef next: led last: sn rdn: hdd last strides* **85/40**[1]
5P46 **3** *1 1/4* **Timoca (IRE)**[45] 1035 5-10-1 **90**..(p) DPFahy(3) 93
(Evan Williams) *hld up: hdwy appr 2 out: sn rdn: styd on* **10/3**[2]
006- **4** *shd* **Timocracy**[16] 5169 5-10-9 **95**.......................... ChristianWilliams 98
(Andrew Haynes) *chsd ldr tl led 2 out: hdd last: styd on* **4/1**[3]
4134 **5** *18* **Wilbury Star (IRE)**[30] 1158 4-11-11 **111**.......................(p) AndrewTinkler 98
(Nicky Henderson) *hld up: hdwy 5th: rdn after next: wknd 2 out* **11/2**
0P-2 **6** *1* **Contrada**[17] 1258 5-11-4 **104**...(b) RhysFlint 90
(Jim Old) *chsd ldrs tl rdn and wknd after 2 out* **16/1**
450- **7** *46* **Don't Think Twice (IRE)**[13] 1304 7-10-12 **98**................(b) PaulMoloney 42
(Michael Hourigan, Ire) *prom: lost pl 6th: wknd bef next: t.o* **14/1**
F-04 **P** **Strictly Business**[118] 168 5-10-9 **95**.............................. PaddyBrennan —
(Tom George) *led: mstke 4th: hdd 2 out: wknd and p.u bef last* **25/1**

3m 57.5s (-1.90) **Going Correction** -0.275s/f (Good) **8** Ran SP% **112.7**
Speed ratings (Par 105): **93,92,92,92,83 83,61,—**
CSF £50.31 CT £144.82 TOTE £10.90: £1.80, £1.80, £1.90; EX 48.00.
Owner The Horse Players Two **Bred** Ennistown Stud **Trained** Lower Beeding, W Sussex

FOCUS
Two of the top weights fought it out from the last producing a head bob on the line. Straightforward form, rated around the runner-up.

NOTEBOOK
Freedom Fire(IRE) received a perfectly judged ride, weaving his way through horses throughout the final circuit and produced at just the right time to make full use of his momentum. He had to fight up the home straight and, by getting the more fluent jump at the last, was able to stay on top. After winning at Huntingdon and recording a second place here earlier in the summer he looked on a stiff mark for handicaps, but a flop at Southwell six weeks ago led to a beneficial 8lb slide in the ratings and he was able to capitalise back on this right-handed track. (op 14-1 tchd 12-1)
Tignello(IRE) refused to settle and still had his head held high in the straight, but he progressed through to challenge and may have got up had he not hopped over the last. Despite pulling hard on each of his hurdling starts, he has demonstrated that he has plenty of ability that should come to fruition if he can race with more restraint. (op 5-2 tchd 11-4 and 2-1)
Timoca(IRE) travelled well wide of the pack down the back until he was outclassed before the last, but he is on a workable mark and could win a moderate handicap. (op 6-1)
Timocracy raced prominently until losing his position after hitting the second last, but he came again to lead turning for home before eventually capitulating. In good form on the Flat, he showed some improvement on his first start over hurdles for this stable. (op 3-1)
Wilbury Star(IRE) made a bit of headway but it did not amount to much and to date his best efforts have been round the tighter track of Newton Abbot. (op 6-1 tchd 5-1)
Strictly Business Official explanation: jockey said gelding ran too free

1454 SUNSHINE RADIO H'CAP CHASE (14 fncs) 2m 3f
4:40 (4:40) (Class 4) (0-115,114) 4-Y-0+ **£2,667** (£783; £391; £195)

Form RPR
3142 **1** **Frosted Grape (IRE)**[12] 1313 4-10-0 **101**..................(b) TomScudamore 115+
(David Pipe) *w ldr: hit 1st: led 9th: sn clr: easily* **4/1**[2]
1 **2** *19* **Courella (IRE)**[13] 1290 6-11-8 **110**...................................... PaulMoloney 118+
(Evan Williams) *hld up: hdwy 8th: chsd wnr appr 3 out: sn rdn: wknd next* **15/2**
223 **3** *2 1/4* **One Of The Boys (IRE)**[12] 1309 9-10-13 **101**.............. RichardJohnson 108+
(Tim Vaughan) *prom: rdn after 11th: wknd appr 2 out: blnd last* **7/2**[1]
6214 **4** *3 1/2* **Intac (IRE)**[26] 1197 8-11-11 **113**.. JoeTizzard 115
(Colin Tizzard) *led to 9th: wknd 3 out* **15/2**
4-0P **5** *25* **Civil Servant**[73] 798 5-11-0 **105**....................(bt[1]) SamTwiston-Davies(3) 84
(Nigel Twiston-Davies) *chsd ldrs: mstke 4th: wknd 10th: t.o* **6/1**[3]
5123 **6** *1/2* **Indiana Gold (FR)**[11] 1334 6-10-10 **105**....................(p) OliverDayman(7) 84
(Alison Thorpe) *hld up in tch: hit 7th: sn rdn: wknd after next: t.o* **4/1**[2]
-115 **7** *3* **Tyup Pompey (IRE)**[88] 636 9-11-9 **114**............................ LeeStephens(3) 90
(Ann Price) *chsd ldrs: mstke 9th: wknd next: t.o* **16/1**
35PP **8** *28* **I'm The Decider (IRE)**[15] 1277 8-11-8 **110**...............................(p) APMcCoy 61
(Jonjo O'Neill) *hld up: a in rr: drvn along after 5th: bhd fr 8th: t.o* **12/1**

4m 37.3s (-9.40) **Going Correction** -0.35s/f (Good)
WFA 4 from 5yo+ 11lb **8** Ran SP% **113.6**
Speed ratings (Par 105): **105,97,96,94,84 83,82,70**
toteswingers:1&2 £7.80, 2&3 £6.00, 1&3 £3.30 CSF £32.94 CT £113.49 TOTE £4.50: £1.20, £2.30, £2.60; EX 46.30.
Owner The Wise Partners **Bred** Austin Curran **Trained** Nicholashayne, Devon

FOCUS
A competitive handicap turned into a romp by a lightly weighted chasing debutante. She is rated up 3lb on her hurdles mark.

NOTEBOOK
Frosted Grape(IRE) blundered over the first and nearly unshipped her jockey, but Tom Scudamore was not about to let all the wasting down to ten stone be for nothing and stayed put. She was unsettled at the next few fences but was given time to get into a rhythm and by the closing stages was jumping quite fluently as she bounded clear of her flailing rivals. She proved over hurdles that she does not stop once she gets loose on the lead and, getting in here on a lenient mark for her chasing debut, she was able to do the same again. (op 5-1 tchd 11-2)
Courella(IRE) had to contend with a 6lb rise for winning at Fontwell two weeks ago where his fluent jumping proved decisive. That was not such an advantage over these easier obstacles and he needs to be kidded along, so although he made steady progress through the field he could never get on terms with the runaway winner, perhaps anchored by the burden and by having a lot of ground to make up. (op 5-1)
One Of The Boys(IRE) has been admirably consistent this summer and again ran his race but he lacks a bit of pace for 2m and did not get home over this longer trip. Official explanation: vet said gelding finished lame (op 4-1 tchd 10-3)
Intac(IRE) weakened tamely once headed down the back. He shot up the handicap after winning a reasonable beginners' chase at Uttoxeter in July and consequently had a lot to do. (op 8-1 tchd 7-1)
Indiana Gold(FR) blundered at the seventh and though there was still a circuit left to go he could never get back into it. (op 11-2)

1455 AMAZONS MAIDEN OPEN NATIONAL HUNT FLAT RACE 2m 1f
5:10 (5:10) (Class 6) 4-6-Y-0 **£1,301** (£382; £191; £95)

Form RPR
24 **1** **Whereveryougoigo (IRE)**[70] 833 4-11-0 0........................ TomO'Brien 106+
(Peter Bowen) *hld up in tch: chsd ldr over 4f out: led over 2f out: sn rdn: styd on wl* **11/10**[1]
2 *2* **Caravan Queen (IRE)**[88] 6-10-5 0 ow5...................... MrSO'Donovan(7) 102
(Norma Twomey) *chsd ldrs: led 5f out: rdn: hung lft and hdd over 2f out: kpt on* **11/4**[2]
3 *47* **Kilcommon Pride (IRE)** 5-11-0 0.................................... HaddenFrost 62
(Roger Curtis) *hld up: bhd fr 1/2-way: nvr on terms: t.o* **16/1**
00- **4** *1/2* **Silver Twilight**[139] 5200 5-10-7 0.. LiamTreadwell 54
(John Allen) *chsd ldrs: rdn 1/2-way: wknd 5f out: t.o* **66/1**
5 *3/4* **Lagan Katie** 4-10-7 0... DougieCostello 54
(Neil Mulholland) *plld hrd and prom: pushed along 10f out: wknd 1/2-way: t.o* **20/1**
3 **6** *22* **Naughtyatiz (IRE)**[10] 1349 4-10-7 0........................ AodhaganConlon(7) 41
(Debra Hamer) *led: hdd 5f out: wknd over 3f out: t.o* **10/1**
7 *4 1/2* **Crookshanks (IRE)** 4-11-0 0.. PaddyBrennan 37
(Tom George) *hld up: hdwy 1/2-way: wknd over 4f out: t.o* **9/1**[3]
00 **8** *65* **Kingston Orla**[41] 1069 5-10-7 0.. JamesDavies —
(Andrew Haynes) *chsd ldrs to 1/2-way: t.o* **40/1**
0-U **P** **Kirkton**[88] 637 5-10-4 0.. TommyPhelan(3) —
(Jim Wilson) *unruly and rel to r: sn p.u* **100/1**
00 **R** **Littledean Jimmy (IRE)**[56] 935 5-10-7 0........................ CharlieWallis(7) —
(John O'Shea) *hld up in tch: plld hrd: hung lft almost thrght: stl cl enough whn rn out and uns rdr over 4f out* **16/1**

3m 53.8s **Going Correction** -0.275s/f (Good)
WFA 4 from 5yo+ 11lb **10** Ran SP% **114.8**
Speed ratings: **89,88,65,65,65 55,52,22,—,—**
toteswingers:1&2 £1.70, 2&3 £8.60, 1&3 £5.70 CSF £3.81 TOTE £1.60: £1.02, £2.00, £5.20; EX 4.00 Place 6: £51.01 Place 5: £37.52.
Owner Roddy Owen & Paul Fullagar **Bred** Sean And Batt Leahy **Trained** Little Newcastle, Pembrokes

FOCUS
The two market leaders left the others trailing in their wake. The winner is the obvious guide to the form.

NOTEBOOK
Whereveryougoigo(IRE) demonstrated that stamina is his forte as it took a while to shake off his main rival, but he kept up the gallop to get on top. He had the best bumper form on offer and was a deserving winner, but is crying out for greater demands on his stamina. (op Evens tchd 10-11)
Caravan Queen(IRE) had won her sole point in Ireland and showed she has some ability, matching strides with the winner as the pair pulled clear, but the 88-day break just told in the end. This was a good run and she should be up to winning under rules. (op 4-1)
Kilcommon Pride(IRE) plugged on into third but was never a threat at any stage, although his stable is rarely successful in bumpers. (op 12-1)
Silver Twilight, who was sweating, raced up with the pace but was soon left floundering down the back on her first start in five months. Official explanation: jockey said mare hung badly left final 1/2m.
Crookshanks(IRE), a 2,500 euro purchase and half brother to winning jumper Uncle Max, was very green on his debut and will need to come on for this run. (tchd 11-1)
Littledean Jimmy(IRE) blew any chance when hanging right last time at Worcester, and this time he veered so far the other way he unseated his rider. However, he was still with the leaders at the time when the others were already beaten so if his steering problems can be sorted out there might be some hope. (op 14-1 tchd 12-1)
T/Jkpt: Not won. T/Plt: £37.90 to a £1 stake. Pool of £71,270.09 - 1,369.20 winning tickets.
T/Qpdt: £10.40 to a £1 stake. Pool of £5,224.67 - 369.82 winning tickets. CR

1456 - 1465a (Foreign Racing) - See Raceform Interactive

1295 STRATFORD (L-H)
Saturday, September 4

OFFICIAL GOING: Good to firm (good in places on chase course)
Hurdles track rail at inner position. Chase track 2m off inner position adding 20yds per circuit. Final hurdle omitted on all circuits of hurdle races.
Wind: almost nil Weather: hot and sunny

1466 LAFARGE GTEC PLASTERBOARD SOLUTIONS NOVICES' HURDLE 2m 110y
(7 hdls 2 omitted)
2:20 (2:20) (Class 3) 4-Y-0+ **£4,000** (£1,174; £587; £293)

Form RPR
3131 **1** **Russian George (IRE)**[21] 1250 4-11-8 117.............................. APMcCoy 124
(Steve Gollings) *j. carelessly and racd v idly in cl 2nd: rdn bef 4th: led over 2f out (wl bef last): r.o u.p: jst prevailed* **3/1**[2]
2120 **2** *shd* **Saltagioo (ITY)**[13] 1343 6-11-3 128..............................(t) JimmyDerham(5) 124
(Milton Harris) *trckd ldrs: 3rd and hrd drvn to cl after 2 out: w wnr last: battled on gamely: btn on nod* **9/2**[3]
112P **3** *6* **Tout Regulier**[13] 1346 6-10-12 124.............................. DonalDevereux(3) 111
(Peter Bowen) *led tl rdn and hdd 2f out: wknd sn after last* **7/4**[1]
0- **4** *nk* **Addwaitya**[14] 2382 5-10-12 0.. LeightonAspell 108+
(Laura Mongan) *trckd ldrs: rdn and effrt after 2 out: nrly 3 l 4th and hld whn mstke last* **14/1**
5 *hd* **Celtic Dragon**[20] 5-10-9 0.. LeeStephens(3) 108+
(David Evans) *last whn mstke 1st: j. v erratically but chsd ldrs after 4th: blnd next: drvn and tried to cl 2f out: 3 l 5th but hld whn mstke last: no ex* **33/1**
4P **6** *32* **Unleashed (IRE)**[61] 908 5-10-9 0.................................... PeterToole(3) 76
(Charlie Mann) *midfield: lost tch tamely 2 out (4f out): fin v weakly: t.o* **7/1**
5 **7** *12* **Chadwell Spring (IRE)**[14] 1325 4-10-5 0.......................... BrianHughes 57
(Mike Sowersby) *chsd ldrs: wkng whn mstke 2 out (4f out): fin v weakly* **40/1**
8 *4* **That's Some Milan (IRE)**[126] 5-10-12 0........................ WarrenMarston 60
(Milton Harris) *lost tch and j. slowly 2nd: v cumbersme in last: t.o whn j. violently rt 4th* **16/1**
0P- **9** *14* **Hector Spectre (IRE)**[26] 2931 4-10-12 0........................(t) JodieMogford 46
(Nikki Evans) *chsd ldrs tl fdd rapidly after 4th: t.o next* **66/1**

P 10 24 **High Dee Jay (IRE)**[26] 792 5-10-12 0 ....(b[1]) ChristianWilliams 22
(Dai Burchell) *t.k.h in rr: lost tch rapidly after 4th: t.o next* **125/1**

3m 45.0s (-11.00) **Going Correction** -0.625s/f (Firm) **10** Ran SP% **112.3**
Speed ratings (Par 107): **100,99,97,96,96 81,76,74,67,56**
Tote Swingers: 1&2 £1.50, 1&3 £1.20, 2&3 £1.90 CSF £16.25 TOTE £3.50: £1.70, £1.90, £1.10; EX 23.70.
Owner P J Martin **Bred** Martin Walsh **Trained** Scamblesby, Lincs

FOCUS
The hurdles track was at its minimum distance but the final flight was omitted, making the run-in longer than usual. This was a fair race for the time of year and the first three all carried double penalties. They went a brisk pace and the form looks pretty solid. The ground was riding on the quick side of good and the time, bearing in mind they jumped one flight fewer than usual, was three seconds inside the standard. The winner is rated up 10lb and can rate higher on his Flat form.

NOTEBOOK
Russian George(IRE) was always at the sharp end and, having seen off the mare, he just got the better of the runner-up in a close tussle from the last. He does not look the easiest ride and came under pressure turning into the back straight, but responded well to McCoy's handling. That's three wins from five hurdles runs now, despite his jumping not being the best. (op 11-4)
Saltagioo(ITY) was keen once again but it did not take much out of him and he ran a solid race on this faster ground, only missing out on the nod. Unfortunately he returned sore. (op 7-2)
Tout Regulier cut out a good gallop but was never able to get away and had nothing left approaching the final flight. This four-time hurdles winner is effective at this trip but may be best over further. (op 13-8)
Addwaitya, fit from the Flat, showed a lot more than he had on his one previous hurdles venture and might have been third had he taken the final flight cleanly. (op 22-1)
Celtic Dragon had lost his way on the Flat but there was mild encouragement to be gleaned from this hurdles debut and he would have been closer but for a last-flight error. A stiffer track at this sort of trip may help him, but he needs to jump better. (op 40-1)
Unleashed(IRE) made a brief forward move which soon evaporated. He is now eligible for handicaps and a return to further may benefit him in that sphere. (op 9-1)
Hector Spectre(IRE) Official explanation: jockey said gelding had a breathing problem

1467 WALLS AND CEILINGS INTERNATIONAL BEGINNERS' CHASE (14 fncs) 2m 4f
2:50 (2:50) (Class 4) 4-Y-0+ **£4,332** (£1,575)

Form RPR
53P- 1 **Mam Ratagan**[161] 4892 9-11-3 120 .... PeterToole(3) 114+
(Heather Main) *often j. boldly and racd enthusiastically: mde all: drvn bef last: a holding rival flat* **4/5[1]**
3443 2 9 **Rebel Hunter (IRE)**[14] 1325 5-11-6 101 .... AidanColeman 107
(Steve Gollings) *chsd wnr fr 4th: often less fluent than rival: rdn bef 3 out and hit fence: 4 l down and no imp whn hit last* **13/8[2]**
0 P **Mr Johnson (IRE)**[18] 1275 7-10-13 0 .... MrJEngland(7) —
(Michael Gates) *t.k.h: mstke 2nd: chsd ldr tl mstke 4th: lost tch 8th: t.o 10th: climbing fences after: p.u 2 out* **10/1[3]**
P **Rock The Soul (IRE)**[324] 1774 6-11-3 0 .... WayneKavanagh(3) —
(Seamus Mullins) *j. appallingly and to rt in last: sn drvn: lost tch after 5th: t.o whn tried to brake 8th: j. wildly rt and immediately p.u* **16/1**

4m 49.8s (-4.40) **Going Correction** -0.40s/f (Good) **4** Ran SP% **108.6**
Speed ratings (Par 105): **92,88,—,—**
CSF £2.57 TOTE £2.10; EX 2.10.
Owner Highnote Thoroughbreds **Bred** Cyril Humphris **Trained** Kingston Lisle, Oxon
■ Heather Main's first winner.

FOCUS
On the chase course the rails were 2m off the inside, adding 20 metres per circuit. This was an uncompetitive event, weakened considerably by three non-runners. The time was nearly seven seconds outside the standard.

NOTEBOOK
Mam Ratagan had made the frame seven times previously over fences without getting his head in front, but was faced with a relatively straightforward task on BHA figures on this first appearance since the spring. He jumped well once he had warmed up and saw off his only pursuer going to the final fence, with his stamina for this longer trip not fully put to the test. A penalty will make things harder, but this overdue win won't have harmed his confidence. (op 8-11 tchd 10-11)
Rebel Hunter(IRE) made the frame in a succession of novice hurdles after winning an Irish point. His jumping on this chase debut was generally sound, bar errors at the water and three from home, and it was only going to the final fence that he cried enough. (op 5-2)
Mr Johnson(IRE), a winning pointer, gave his fences plenty of air on this chase debut and was left trailing by the first two on the final circuit before eventually pulling up. (op 7-1)

1468 LAFARGE GTEC PLASTERBOARD CONDITIONAL JOCKEYS' (S) H'CAP HURDLE (9 hdls 3 omitted) 2m 6f 110y
3:25 (3:26) (Class 5) (0-95,95) 4-Y-0+ **£1,951** (£573; £286; £143)

Form RPR
-P50 1 **Stafford Charlie**[59] 930 4-9-12 75 .... (v[1]) CharlieWallis(6) 88+
(John O'Shea) *t.k.h: effrt to go prom and nt fluent 3 out (normal 4 out): led gng wl 3f out: sn clr: 9 l ahd whn hit last: eased flat* **12/1**
0045 2 9 **Scotsbrook Cloud**[16] 1300 5-10-7 81 .... PeterCarberry(5) 86
(C Roberts) *midfield: rdn after 5th: 6th and outpcd after 2 out: plugged on fnl 2f: wnt poor 2nd nr fin* **8/1**
4442 3 1 **Monty's Moon (IRE)**[23] 1237 8-10-0 69 oh1 .... (b) HarrySkelton 73
(Rachel Hobbs) *midfield: 7th whn mstke 3 out: sn outpcd: plodded into mod 2nd at last tl cl home* **7/2[1]**
-605 4 3 1/4 **Pearly Star**[93] 593 9-11-10 93 .... (b) MarcGoldstein 95
(Jim Best) *pressed ldr: led 3 out (normal 4 out): drvn and hdd after next: sn no ch w wnr: lost 3rd nring last* **6/1[2]**
00/0 5 7 **Castle Craigs (IRE)**[16] 1294 8-10-1 76 .... MrTomDavid(6) 74
(Tim Vaughan) *hld up towards rr: prog gng wl after 5th: ev ch 3 out: outpcd between last two: chsd wnr vainly tl fdd last and lost three pls after* **25/1**
3435 6 6 **Fongoli**[14] 1331 4-11-1 89 .... (v) SamJones(3) 75
(Brendan Powell) *led: rdn and hdd bef 6th: ev ch next: 4th and losing tch after 2 out* **9/1**
3P/5 7 8 **Indigo Dancer**[45] 1060 7-9-12 70 .... OliverDayman(3) 50
(J D J Davies) *t.k.h in rr: rdn and effrt bef 3 out: wknd tamely bef next* **25/1**
U/P6 8 1 3/4 **Starstruck Peter (IRE)**[14] 1335 6-11-1 89 .... AshleyBird(5) 67
(Jim Best) *mstke 3rd: midfield: struggling 3 out* **12/1**
0-00 9 1 1/2 **Monfils Monfils (USA)**[82] 745 8-10-3 75 .... KyleJames(3) 52
(Philip Kirby) *mstkes: last and u.p after 5th: wl adrift after mstke next* **10/1**
6P-P 10 10 **Jug Of Punch (IRE)**[29] 1199 11-10-0 69 oh5 .... (p) JohnKington 36
(Simon Lewis) *prom tl rdn 4th: nt keen after: t.o 6th* **40/1**
43U5 F **Cloonavery (IRE)**[16] 1290 8-9-11 69 .... (v[1]) LeeEdwards(3) —
(Tony Carroll) *hld up in rr tl fell 4th* **7/1[3]**
P44P P **Prince Noora (IRE)**[5] 1434 9-11-10 93 .... (tp) RichardKilloran —
(Tim Vaughan) *t.k.h: prom: mstke 2nd: led bef 6th: rdn and hdd 3 out: mstke next: wknd qckly: t.o and p.u last* **14/1**
1U0P B **Lords Bridge**[16] 1293 9-11-12 95 .... MichaelMurphy —
(Tim Vaughan) *hld up in rr tl b.d 4th* **12/1**

5m 11.6s (-16.50) **Going Correction** -0.625s/f (Firm)
WFA 4 from 5yo+ 12lb **13** Ran SP% **119.1**
Speed ratings (Par 103): **103,99,99,98,95 93,91,90,89,86 —,—,—**
Tote Swingers: 1&2 £21.50, 1&3 £5.00, 2&3 £10.50 CSF £102.94 CT £414.06 TOTE £16.60: £4.10, £3.00, £1.60; EX 142.00.The winner was bought in for 3,000gns. Scotsbrook Cloud was claimed by David Evans for £6,000.
Owner N G H Ayliffe **Bred** N G H Ayliffe **Trained** Elton, Gloucs

FOCUS
They went a sound pace in this very modest event,

NOTEBOOK
Stafford Charlie was suited by the good gallop and travelled strongly under restraint in the first-time visor (which replaced cheekpieces). Drawing well clear off the home turn for an easy victory, he avoids a penalty for this and would be hard to beat in the same mood if turned out again quickly. He had run no sort of race last time though, when two places behind today's runner-up, and might not be one to rely on overmuch. (tchd 14-1)
Scotsbrook Cloud was only fifth over the final flight before staying on well and may be ready for another try at 3m. David Evans claimed him. (op 17-2)
Monty's Moon(IRE), who was a pound out of the handicap, ran respectably returned to hurdles, plugging on after becoming outpaced by the leaders following a mistake three from home. (op 5-1)
Pearly Star has gone well fresh before and this was a fair effort from up with the pace after three months' absence. (op 5-1 tchd 13-2)
Castle Craigs(IRE) ◆, on his second run for the Vaughan yard, was another to travel well and looked a threat at one stage, but he could not go with the winner turning out of the back and weakened out of the frame on the run-in. He should be kept in mind if tackling slightly shorter. (op 20-1)

1469 MCMAHON (CONTRACTORS SERVICES) H'CAP CHASE (17 fncs) 2m 7f
3:55 (3:55) (Class 3) (0-125,125) 4-Y-0+ **£7,921** (£2,340; £1,170; £585; £292)

Form RPR
1205 1 **Ballycarney (IRE)**[32] 1178 6-11-9 122 .... JackDoyle 129
(Emma Lavelle) *trckd ldrs: wnt 3rd at 13th: rdn and sltly outpcd after 2 out: drvn and rallied last: got up cl home* **11/2[3]**
4153 2 nk **Mizen Raven (IRE)**[15] 1312 7-11-12 125 .... (tp) TomScudamore 133+
(Peter Bowen) *midfield: effrt bef 14th: led after 2 out: 2 l clr and nt fluent last: idled flat: ct nr fin* **10/1**
2F-2 3 3 3/4 **Marufo (IRE)**[13] 1348 8-11-7 120 .... (t) RichardJohnson 123
(Philip Hobbs) *bhd and hld up: nt fluent 9th: effrt bef 14th: rdn 2 out: wnt 2nd bef last: nt qckn flat and sn lost 2nd* **9/4[1]**
3P3F 4 5 **Whataboutya (IRE)**[32] 1178 9-11-3 116 .... (p) APMcCoy 114
(Jonjo O'Neill) *bhd: pushed along bef 9th: effrt 14th: nvr looking v keen: disp 4th between last two: edgd rt and fnd little bef last* **4/1[2]**
4441 5 8 **Pairc Na Gcapall (IRE)**[14] 1326 8-10-12 114 .... (b) AlexMerriam(3) 104
(Neil King) *pressed ldr: drvn after 13th: j.v.slowly next and lost several pls: continued wl bhd* **9/1**
1210 6 13 **Fealing Real (IRE)**[15] 1312 8-10-11 117 .... (tp) AodhaganConlon(7) 98
(Rebecca Curtis) *led at brisk gallop: rdn and hdd after 2 out: dropped out rapidly and eased* **8/1**
1P0P 7 28 **Keepitsecret (IRE)**[14] 1332 9-11-9 125 .... RichieMcLernon(3) 74
(Jonjo O'Neill) *towards rr: rdn 12th: struggling bef 14th: t.o* **28/1**
2046 P **Sou'Wester**[39] 1110 10-11-12 125 .... JoeTizzard —
(Colin Tizzard) *bhd tl p.u 8th: lame* **25/1**
323P F **De Soto**[15] 1312 9-11-12 125 .... (tp) SamThomas —
(Paul Webber) *cl up: disputing 3rd whn fell 11th* **12/1**
1-3P P **Grenoli (FR)**[99] 501 9-9-7 99 oh1 .... (bt) JoeCornwall(7) —
(John Cornwall) *bhd: rdn 7th: drvn into midfield and sltly impeded 11th: no ch after: t.o and p.u last* **33/1**
-01P P **City Heights (IRE)**[18] 1274 8-11-12 125 .... DarylJacob —
(Giles Smyly) *mstkes in rr: nvr gng wl: t.o after mstke 8th: p.u after 2 out* **28/1**

5m 28.1s (-13.50) **Going Correction** -0.40s/f (Good) **11** Ran SP% **117.7**
Speed ratings (Par 107): **107,106,105,103,101 96,86,—,—,— —**
Tote Swingers: 1&2 £15.90, 1&3 £4.00, 2&3 £1.70 CSF £55.33 CT £159.93 TOTE £6.90: £1.50, £2.70, £1.60; EX 67.20.
Owner Elite Racing Club **Bred** Aaron Metcalfe **Trained** Wildhern, Hants

FOCUS
A competitive handicap chase run at a decent pace, and the form looks solid.

NOTEBOOK
Ballycarney(IRE) chased the pace throughout and, after the leaders looked to have the legs of him on the home turn, staged a strong finish to get up near the line. Ideally served by a stiffer track than this, he is only six and there is more to come from him. (op 15-2 tchd 8-1)
Mizen Raven(IRE) got to the front soon after the second-last but idled a little on the run-in and was just caught. He is pretty consistent but perhaps one to take on for win-only purposes. (tchd 9-1)
Marufo(IRE) went up 5lb after a pleasing comeback run at Newton Abbot. He ran well on this quicker ground but just lacked a change of pace when he could have done with one. This was shade sharp for him. (op 5-2)
Whataboutya(IRE), raised 3lb after falling when in contention at Ffos Las, was under the pump for much of the final circuit but was still in there fighting between the last two. (op 7-2)
Pairc Na Gcapall(IRE) had things his own way up front at Market Rasen but faced competiton for the front-running role here and was feeling the heat on the final circuit. (op 10-1)
Fealing Real(IRE) set the pace and jumped boldly, but his stamina gave out in the latter stages. He should not be written off back at around 2m4f. (op 9-1)

1470 WALLS AND CEILINGS INTERNATIONAL H'CAP HURDLE (7 hdls 2 omitted) 2m 110y
4:25 (4:26) (Class 3) (0-125,125) 4-Y-0 **£6,337** (£1,872; £936; £468; £234)

Form RPR
204U 1 **Nether Stream (IRE)**[16] 1295 6-10-0 99 .... AidanColeman 104
(Shaun Lycett) *dropped out last tl prog 4th: pushed along on ins to cl after 2 out (normal 3 out): rdn to ld last: forged clr fnl 100yds* **33/1**
100- 2 1 1/2 **Oddshoes (IRE)**[7] 3574 8-11-12 125 .... RichardJohnson 128
(Philip Hobbs) *t.k.h: led tl 4th: led again after 2 out: drvn and hdd last: jst outpcd fnl 100yds* **16/1**
-4U1 3 1 **Rebel Dancer (FR)**[5] 1429 5-10-12 111 7ex .... (t) DougieCostello 113
(Ian Williams) *settled towards rr: 7th and prog after 2 out: tried to chal last: n.m.r and swtchd rt: no imp after* **7/2[1]**
B33 4 nk **Tzora**[48] 1026 5-10-6 112 .... MattGriffiths(7) 114
(Philip Hobbs) *midfield: nt fluent 3rd: chal 3 out: rdn after next: pressed ldrs tl nt qckn fr last* **8/1[3]**
P-14 5 3 **Lodgician (IRE)**[20] 1261 8-10-0 102 .... SamTwiston-Davies(3) 101
(Nigel Twiston-Davies) *cl up and t.k.h: rdn 2 out: one pce bef last* **7/2[1]**
0221 6 4 1/2 **Topenhall (IRE)**[14] 1328 9-11-0 113 .... (t) CharliePoste 107
(Ben Case) *plld hrd: pressed ldr tl led 4th: hdd after 2 out: btn bef last* **16/1**

2200 **7** *1* **Peaceful Means (IRE)**[4] 1282 7-10-2 **106**...................... LeeEdwards(5) 99
(Tony Carroll) *trckd ldrs: effrt 3 out: rdn and btn next* **12/1**

6105 **8** *shd* **Crosby Jemma**[37] 1127 6-10-10 **109**.................................. BrianHughes 102
(Mike Sowersby) *nvr bttr than midfield: outpcd after 3 out: plugged on flat* **40/1**

-521 **9** *5* **Alph**[43] 1084 13-10-13 **119**.. MrTJCannon(7) 107
(Roger Teal) *chsd ldrs: effrt 4th: 5th and rdn 2 out: sn wknd* **20/1**

6232 **10** *½* **High Bird Humphrey**[14] 1328 11-10-2 **108**......................(p) MrSFMagee(7) 96
(Simon West) *rn in snatches: nt fluent 3rd: mstke 3 out: rdn in rr whn mstke next* **7/1**[2]

001- **11** *21* **Gaspara (FR)**[134] 5365 7-11-6 **119**..............................(b) TomScudamore 86
(David Pipe) *dropped to rr after 4th: last and detached 3 out* **10/1**

010- **12** *7* **Superius (IRE)**[138] 5278 5-10-10 **109**...................................... JackDoyle 69
(Emma Lavelle) *cl up: 4th 2 out: sn rdn and lost pl* **7/1**[2]

3m 48.6s (-7.40) **Going Correction** -0.625s/f (Firm) **12 Ran SP% 119.2**
Speed ratings (Par 107): **92,91,90,90,89 87,86,86,84,84 74,70**
Tote Swingers: 1&2 £30.20, 1&3 £28.70, 2&3 £4.10 CSF £471.33 CT £2325.05 TOTE £38.60: £5.20, £3.50, £1.80; EX 558.70.
Owner The Berryman Lycett Experience **Bred** Miss Carmel Whelan **Trained** Clapton-on-the-Hill, Gloucs

FOCUS
A fair handicap hurdle but the pace was only ordinary and the time was 3.6 seconds slower than for the opening novice race.

NOTEBOOK
Nether Stream(IRE) hugged the inside all the way and came from the rear to win going away, despite a slight stumble on landing at the last. Still a novice, he looks to be on the upgrade now and he will be effective at a bit further than this.
Oddshoes(IRE), back down to his last winning mark, had been sharpened up by a run on the Flat last week. He ran a bold race from the front and gave best only on the run-in to a rival who was receiving 26lb. (op 14-1)
Rebel Dancer(FR) ran well under his penalty for his recent Huntingdon win, but after picking up ground from the rear he could not quicken up after the last. A stronger gallop would have suited him. (op 11-4 tchd 4-1 in a place)
Tzora ran a better race with the tongue tie discarded but lacked a change of gear late on. (op 10-1)
Lodgician(IRE) performed creditably back down in trip off 11lb higher than when winning here last month. (op 9-2 tchd 10-3)
Topenhall(IRE), raised a further 5lb for his Market Rasen win, raced keenly up with the pace and only dropped away from the final flight. (op 14-1)
Alph could never get into it off a 5lb higher mark than for his Southwell win. (op 22-1)
Gaspara(FR), who went up 12lb after passing the post first at Newton Abbot in April, ran poorly on this drop in trip. (op 9-1 tchd 11-1)
Superius(IRE) disappointed on this handicap debut, but he may be worth another chance with this run under his belt, perhaps on easier ground. (op 13-2 tchd 11-2)

1471 WALLS AND CEILINGS INTERNATIONAL H'CAP CHASE (12 fncs) 2m 1f 110y
5:00 (5:00) (Class 4) (0-115,113) 4-Y-0+ **£3,903** (£1,146; £573; £286)

Form RPR

-53P **1** **Blast The Past**[17] 1283 8-11-3 **104**............................... ChristianWilliams 117
(Dai Burchell) *taken down early: dismntd and led rnd: plld hrd in rr: smooth prog 3 out: wnt 2nd after next: led bef last: lft wl clr* **11/2**[3]

21PF **2** *17* **Bushwacker (IRE)**[33] 1161 6-11-9 **110**..........................(t) DenisO'Regan 104
(Seamus Mullins) *plentiful mstkes: midfield: 4th and rdn after blunder 3 out: btn next: 9 l 4th and being eased whn gained two pls at last* **7/1**

6403 **3** *1½* **Cortinas (GER)**[21] 1249 8-11-9 **113**..................................(t) PeterToole(3) 106
(Charlie Mann) *8 l 3rd at 3rd: clsd on clr ldrs 7th: wnt 2nd at 9th tl after 2 out: fin weakly: gained two pls at last* **11/1**

F5-3 **4** *6* **Venir Rouge**[29] 1197 6-11-6 **107**.. AndrewTinkler 94
(Matthew Salaman) *j. deliberately in last: lost tch 9th: lft poor 4th at last* **11/2**[3]

4216 **5** *7* **Papradon**[18] 1272 6-10-5 **95**.................................. SamTwiston-Davies(3) 75
(Nigel Twiston-Davies) *led: j. deliberately 2nd: hdd 4th: drvn 7th: lost 2nd at next: nt run on: wknd and j. slowly 2 out: eased bef last* **3/1**[1]

30U3 **F** **Nawow**[17] 1283 10-10-8 **102**..(tp) AdamWedge(7) 107
(Matt Hazell) *settled towards rr: drvn 3 out: stl 5th but prog after 2 out: 3 l 2nd and trying to cl whn fell last* **6/1**

0-21 **F** **Inmate (IRE)**[37] 1128 9-11-5 **106**.. CharliePoste 107
(Robin Dickin) *pressed ldr tl led 4th: rdn and hdd bef last: jst over 3 l 3rd and btn whn fell last* **10/3**[2]

4m 5.50s (-1.60) **Going Correction** -0.40s/f (Good) **7 Ran SP% 114.0**
Speed ratings (Par 105): **87,79,78,76,73 —,—**
Tote Swingers: 1&2 £7.30, 1&3 £8.30, 2&3 £15.10 CSF £41.30 TOTE £8.10: £3.30, £3.50; EX 53.80.
Owner Dan Kemp **Bred** A R And Mrs Dimmock **Trained** Briery Hill, Blaenau Gwent

FOCUS
A moderate handicap chase, and not form to treat too positively.

NOTEBOOK
Blast The Past had been racing prominently in recent outings but was ridden differently here. After making rapid headway to go after the winner on the home turn, she was already in the process of pulling away when left clear at the last. It was reported that she had lost her action when pulling up sharply in fourth place at Hereford last time. (op 7-1 tchd 15-2)
Bushwacker(IRE) had just been headed when falling at the last on his previous start and was 4lb higher here. He had a change of jockey but his jumping again left plenty to be desired, and he was fortunate to inherit a well-beaten second at the final fence. (op 13-2)
Cortinas(GER) ran his race on this return to fences but faded late on and was booked for fifth when a couple in front of him fell at the last. (op 10-1 tchd 12-1)
Papradon, reverting to fences, looked less than keen once he lost his lead and finished well adrift. (op 7-2)
Nawowwas raised 3lb for finishing third at Hereford in the race in which Blast The Past pulled up. He was staying on for pressure and looked set to finish second when he came down at the final fence. (op 7-2 tchd 11-4)
Inmate(IRE) was headed after the second-last and would probably have finished third had he not tipped up at the final fence. He was put up more than a stone for his wide-margin win over 2m4f here last month. (op 7-2 tchd 11-4)

1472 LAFARGE GTEC PLASTERBOARD SOLUTIONS STANDARD OPEN NATIONAL HUNT FLAT RACE 2m 110y
5:30 (5:30) (Class 5) 4-6-Y-0 **£1,626** (£477; £238; £119)

Form RPR

000 **1** **Littledean Jimmy (IRE)**[3] 1455 5-10-7 0....................... CharlieWallis(7) 100+
(John O'Shea) *covered up thrght: keen trcking ldrs: shkn up and looking dodgy 7f out: wnt 2 l 3rd and rdn 2f out: burst between ldng pair to ld and go clr fnl 75yds: canny ride* **6/1**[3]

3 **2** *1¼* **Music In The Air**[88] 686 6-10-7 0...................................... CharliePoste 92
(Robin Dickin) *cl 2nd in v slow r tl led 7f out: jnd and hrd drvn and hanging lft fr over 1f out: hdd and no ex fnl 75yds* **11/4**[2]

241 **3** *hd* **Whereveryougoigo (IRE)**[3] 1455 4-11-7 0................. RichardJohnson 106
(Peter Bowen) *set v sedate pce: hdd 7f out: sn drvn along: w ldr but hanging lft fr over 1f out tl overwhelmed cl home* **8/11**[1]

4 *37* **Avon Gale** 6-10-7 0.. LiamTreadwell 55
(John Allen) *v green: j. path after 6f: bdly t.o fnl 6f* **12/1**

0 **5** *15* **Lavender Grey**[17] 1284 4-10-2 0....................................... LeeEdwards(5) 40
(Tony Carroll) *plld hrd early: drvn and dropped bk last over 6f out: sn hopelessly t.o* **33/1**

3m 51.5s (1.10) **Going Correction** -0.625s/f (Firm) **5 Ran SP% 109.5**
Speed ratings: **72,71,71,53,46**
CSF £22.17 TOTE £8.70: £3.80, £1.10; EX 23.30 Place 6: £88.61 Place 5: £75.63 .
Owner K W Bell **Bred** John Lyons **Trained** Elton, Gloucs

FOCUS
A modest bumper. The pace was very steady early on before picking up with a circuit left, and the first three pulled a mile clear to fight out a good finish.

NOTEBOOK
Littledean Jimmy(IRE) had run off the course in Whereveryougoigo's race at Hereford earlier in the week and did much the same thing the time before at Worcester, but he was in contention both times and confirmed here that he has ability. His rider sensibly waited for a gap to appear between his two rivals rather than pull his mount to the outside and give him any chance to think about running out. (op 11-2 tchd 9-2 and 13-2)
Music In The Air, third on her debut nearly three months earlier, ran a solid race but lacked the pace of the winner late on. A mares' race could be the right option for her. (tchd 5-2 and 3-1)
Whereveryougoigo(IRE) had quite a hard race at Hereford three days earlier and was just found out under the penalty. This sharp track and fast ground were less than ideal for him and he can show his true colours when he switches to hurdling. (op 4-5 tchd 10-11)
Avon Gale was beaten a long way on this debut but is out of a decent racemare and should improve with time. (tchd 11-1 and 14-1)
Lavender Grey looks very short on ability. (op 20-1)
T/Plt: £142.90 to a £1 stake. Pool: £34,764.72 - 330.74 winning tickets T/Qpdt: £88.00 to a £1 stake. Pool:£4377.14 - 36.80 winning tickets IM

1289 FONTWELL (L-H)
Sunday, September 5

OFFICIAL GOING: Good (good to firm in places; watered; 7.3)
Rail realignment added 60yds per circuit on chase course and 30yds per circuit on hurdles course.
Wind: Moderate, half behind Weather: Fine

1473 WATCH THE 888SPORT SHOW AT 888SPORT.COM JUVENILE HURDLE (9 hdls) 2m 2f 110y
1:40 (1:40) (Class 4) 3-Y-0 **£2,602** (£764; £382; £190)

Form RPR

1 **1** **Architrave**[17] 1298 3-11-5 .... RichardJohnson 110+
(Tim Vaughan) *pressed ldr: led 2nd: nt fluent 5th: rdn clr 2 out: styd on wl* **4/9**[1]

2 *10* **Optimistic Duke (IRE)**[40] 3-10-12 .... JimmyMcCarthy 94
(William Muir) *in tch: trckd ldrs 1/2-way: wnt 2nd appr 2 out: sn outpcd by wnr* **40/1**

3 *8* **Dr Finley (IRE)**[37] 3-10-12 .... DarylJacob 87
(Jeff Pearce) *prom: j.lft 1st: mstke 2nd: chal 3 out: sn outpcd* **7/2**[2]

36 **4** *23* **Massachusetts**[15] 1330 3-10-12 .... JohnnyFarrelly 66
(Brendan Powell) *towards rr: hmpd 1st: effrt 6th: lft mod 4th appr 2 out: no ch whn mstke last* **66/1**

3 **5** *9* **Doyenne Dream**[18] 1279 3-10-5 .... FelixDeGiles 51
(James Eustace) *in rr: rdn 4th: sn wl bhd* **14/1**

6 *16* **Liberty Girl (IRE)**[17] 1301 3-9-12 .... PeterHatton(7) 37
(Linda Jewell) *plld hrd towards rr: lost tch 5th* **33/1**

4 **P** **Kathindi (IRE)**[15] 1324 3-10-9 ....(b) AlexMerriam(3) —
(Neil King) *prom tl wknd appr 6th: sn bhd: p.u bef 2 out* **66/1**

P **Captain Clint (IRE)**[31] 3-10-12 .... LeightonAspell —
(Mark H Tompkins) *nt fluent 1st: sn in midfield: wknd 5th: sn bhd: p.u bef 2 out* **66/1**

531 **U** **Joe Rua (USA)**[15] 1324 3-11-5 .... ColinBolger —
(John Ryan) *led tl 2nd: w wnr after: hit 5th: mstke and hrd rdn 3 out: 3 l 4th whn sddle slipped and uns rdr on bnd sn after* **10/1**[3]

00 **U** **Charmeur (USA)**[15] 1330 3-10-5 .... MattGriffiths(7) —
(Philip Hobbs) *mid-div: outpcd 3 out: mod 4th and btn whn sddle slipped and uns rdr bnd appr 2 out* **40/1**

4m 32.5s (-1.80) **Going Correction** -0.35s/f (Good) **10 Ran SP% 119.5**
Speed ratings (Par 103): **89,84,81,71,67 61,—,—,—,—**
toteswingers:1&2:£7.70, 1&3:£1.10, 2&3:£16.70 CSF £33.04 TOTE £1.50: £1.10, £9.10, £1.30; EX 23.80.
Owner Pearn's Pharmacies Ltd **Bred** Cheveley Park Stud Ltd **Trained** Aberthin, Vale of Glamorgan

FOCUS
The ground had been watered and it looked safe enough until two jockeys were independently unseated round the bends. However, their mounts did not slip and the state of the ground did not appear to be the cause, rather each jockey became unbalanced for different reasons in an otherwise straightforward juvenile contest. The time was slow and the winner probably didn't have to improve on his debut form.

NOTEBOOK
Architrave was all the rage to follow up his facile Stratford success last month. Racing prominently, he was keen and still looked a bit green when hitting the lead, but he stuck to the task and powered his rivals into submission. Saddled with a penalty for that previous win, he understandably got a little tired from the last, but still looks to have enough in hand for similar early-season contests. (op 8-15 tchd 4-7 and 4-5 in places)
Optimistic Duke(IRE) was a bit novicey on his hurdling debut and got tired in the closing stages, but overall this was a promising run. He was rated 52 on the Flat, and it certainly seems he can be better over hurdles. (op 33-1)
Dr Finley(IRE) jumped big at a couple of flights and, though making some headway down the back, he just lacked the pace to pose a threat. He did not win, but was consistent at distances up to 1m6f on the Flat, and could make an impact over hurdles once his jumping gains fluency. (op 4-1)
Massachusetts tended to jump left and ran out of steam before the second-last.
Joe Rua(USA) matched strides with the winner until the back straight, and was just beginning to struggle when the saddle slipped and his jockey came down on the flat. Official explanation: jockey said saddle slipped

Charmeur(USA) was being driven along in the chasing pack when his jockey got over-balanced and unseated around the final turn. Official explanation: jockey said saddle slipped slightly, vet said colt lost a near fore shoe

1474 CREATE A 3D AVATAR AT 888CASINO.COM H'CAP CHASE (13 fncs) 2m 2f

2:10 (2:10) (Class 5) (0-95,94) 4-Y-0+ **£1,951** (£573; £286; £143)

Form				RPR
0335	1		**Morestead (IRE)**[6] 1430 5-11-7 **89**.....(v) LeightonAspell (Brendan Powell) *mde all at gd pce: sn had field stretched out: slt mstke 6th: pressed by runner-up 9th: drvn clr again fr 3 out* **13/2**	111+
P653	2	19	**Bid Art (IRE)**[17] 1290 5-11-1 **83**.....(tp) DarylJacob (Jamie Snowden) *chsd wnr: wnt cl up and gng wl 9th: rdn 3 out: sn btn* **7/1**	88
3142	3	3 ¾	**Sir Bumble (IRE)**[5] 1447 10-11-6 **91**.....(t) PeterToole(3) (Michael Blake) *nvr gng wl: sn outpcd towards rr: sme hdwy 4 out: styd on to take 3rd run-in: nt trble ldrs* **11/4**[1]	93
1533	4	5	**Khazar (FR)**[24] 1237 7-11-6 **91**..... RichieMcLernon(3) (Jonjo O'Neill) *in tch: j. slowly 3rd and 4th: wnt 10 l 3rd appr 8th: nt fluent and rdn next: sn outpcd* **5/1**[3]	89
60PP	5	8	**Poacher's Dream (IRE)**[53] 990 8-10-2 **70**.....(t) FelixDeGiles (Jonathen de Giles) *a in mid-div: n.d fr 1/2-way* **28/1**	60
0003	6	3 ¾	**Alrafid (IRE)**[17] 1294 11-11-2 **94**.....(b) JosephAkehurst(10) (Gary Moore) *outpcd: sn bhd* **16/1**	80
-054	7	1 ¼	**Blue Express (IRE)**[17] 1295 11-11-8 **93**.....(t) DPFahy(3) (Evan Williams) *outpcd: sn bhd* **12/1**	78
423P	8	23	**Space Cowboy (IRE)**[87] 689 10-10-4 **72**.....(b) JamieMoore (Gary Moore) *hld up towards rr: mod hdwy 8th: sn wknd* **9/2**[2]	37
3-50	P		**Jose Bove**[41] 1095 8-10-12 **80**.....(t) HaddenFrost (Henrietta Knight) *chsd ldng pair tl wknd appr 8th: wl bhd whn p.u bef last* **16/1**	—
41PP	P		**New Rackheath (IRE)**[15] 1335 7-10-8 **83**.....(b) PeterHatton(7) (Mark Shears) *outpcd towards rr: mstke 1st: wl bhd whn mstke 8th: p.u bef 4 out* **50/1**	—

4m 36.4s (1.70) **Going Correction** +0.175s/f (Yiel) **10** Ran SP% **112.2**
Speed ratings (Par 103): **103,94,92,90,87 85,84,74,—,—**
toteswingers:1&2:£11.90, 1&3:£7.60, 2&3:£2.70 CSF £49.79 CT £152.55 TOTE £8.10: £2.20, £2.70, £1.10; EX 29.60.
Owner L Gilbert **Bred** Declan Hyland And Lillian Montgomery **Trained** Upper Lambourn, Berks

FOCUS
This was run at a searching pace from the outset with none of the chasers able to make up the ground on a tenacious all-the-way winner. Modest form with the winner rated back to his best.

NOTEBOOK
Morestead(IRE) is best when able to dominate and, lit up by the re-application of a visor, he set a gallop that no one could live with initially. His jumping got a bit ragged on the final circuit and that let his main challenger in, but to his credit he kept finding more and eventually wore the others down. He has gradually fallen in the weights to an exploitable mark and, back on a more favourable track after a disappointing show at Huntingdon earlier in the week, the added bonus of headgear and an astute ride did the trick. (op 7-1)
Bid Art(IRE) tracked the winner until looming up travelling ominously well on the home turn, but he could not go through with the effort and was eventually beaten out of sight. He was best of the rest but ideally needs to dominate from the front and was inconvenienced by chasing the strong pace set by the winner. (op 8-1 tchd 13-2)
Sir Bumble(IRE) was well fancied after his narrow defeat at Newton Abbot five days earlier, but he was struggling right from the first fence and it was only due to his jockey's persistence and his own consistency that he plugged on for a remote third. He has been busy over the last couple of months and looks in need of more of a break. (op 3-1)
Khazar(FR) had been beaten by Sir Bumble on their last meeting at Stratford in August and, with jockeys' allowances taken into account, were meeting on similar terms so give some handle on the form. He put in a few ponderous leaps but tried to chase down the runaway leaders in the back straight before running out of steam and losing third, and did not flourish off the strong pace. (op 7-2 tchd 11-2)
Space Cowboy(IRE) attracted some support on his first start since June, but could never get into it. (op 7-1)
Jose Bove Official explanation: jockey said gelding stopped quickly
New Rackheath(IRE) Official explanation: jockey said gelding was never travelling

1475 "WE RACE DIFFERENT" AT 888POKER.COM NOVICES' HURDLE (9 hdls) 2m 2f 110y

2:45 (2:45) (Class 4) 4-Y-0+ **£2,602** (£764; £382; £190)

Form				RPR
F-12	1		**Synthe Davis (FR)**[87] 690 5-10-12 115..... RichardJohnson (Laura Mongan) *mde all at gd pce: clr 3 out: unchal* **2/1**[2]	123+
1202	2	17	**Astrolibra**[24] 1233 6-10-12 115..... ColinBolger (Mark H Tompkins) *prom: lft 2nd at 5th: nt pce of wnr fr next* **4/1**[3]	110+
0-1	3	51	**Brett Vale (IRE)**[17] 1289 4-11-4.....(t) LeightonAspell (Peter Hedger) *bhd: hdwy into 3rd at 5th: rdn next: sn wknd* **15/8**[1]	68
5-	4	16	**Sommersturm (GER)**[118] 4461 6-10-12..... DenisO'Regan (Barney Curley) *in tch: outpcd 5th: sn bhd* **6/1**	48
0	5	38	**Westcoat Lad**[74] 832 5-10-5..... MrTJCannon(7) (Kevin Tork) *in tch to 4th: sn wl bhd* **50/1**	14
U	6	37	**Aura**[41] 1090 5-10-5..... ChristianWilliams (John Flint) *towards rr: rdn 4th: sn wl bhd* **66/1**	—
	F		**Great Bounder (CAN)**[55] 4-10-11..... NickScholfield (Michael Blake) *chsd wnr tl fell 5th* **25/1**	—
04	U		**Martin Scruff (IRE)**[22] 1250 4-10-8..... RichardKilloran(3) (Michael Quinlan) *in rr tl hmpd and uns rdr 5th* **50/1**	—

4m 21.2s (-13.10) **Going Correction** -0.35s/f (Good) **8** Ran SP% **111.7**
Speed ratings (Par 105): **113,105,84,77,61 46,—,—**
toteswingers:1&2:£1.70, 1&3:£1.10, 2&3:£1.60 CSF £9.94 TOTE £2.70: £1.10, £1.50, £1.50; EX 9.60.
Owner Mrs P J Sheen **Bred** Claude Quellier **Trained** Epsom, Surrey

FOCUS
A reasonable novice hurdle with the winner dictating the tactics for a runaway success.

NOTEBOOK
Synthe Davis(FR) was given a finely judged ride, able to set a comfortable pace, and gradually winding it up to go clear before the final turn to come home unchallenged. She had shown some ability for Nicky Henderson last season but looked too weak to cope with winter ground and did not gain her first win until May, when looking to have improved for a bit of time and faster ground. This new trainer-jockey combination learned from how to ride her when she just got collared over a longer trip here in June and they got the tactics just right this time. (op 5-2)
Astrolibra had every chance tracking the leader, but she began to feel the pressure from the sixth and could not reduce the winner's advantage. She is generally consistent but on this performance might be on a stiff mark when returned to handicaps. (op 7-2)
Brett Vale(IRE) was well backed to follow up his facile success over C&D last month. Held up early, he made steady progress on the final circuit but was making no inroads into the leaders and tired markedly before the last. (op 9-4)

Sommersturm(GER), a slight drifter in the market, never got into it. (op 11-2 tchd 5-1)

1476 888SPORT.COM NO LOSE £20 BET H'CAP CHASE (16 fncs) 2m 6f

3:20 (3:20) (Class 4) (0-110,110) 4-Y-0+ **£3,903** (£1,146; £573; £286)

Form				RPR
0112	1		**Makena (FR)**[44] 1080 8-11-4 **102**.....(p) RichardJohnson (David Rees) *t.k.h: hld up in tch: qcknd to ld 3 out: comf* **6/4**[1]	120+
00P6	2	8	**Native City (IRE)**[19] 1276 8-11-2 **103**..... RichieMcLernon(3) (Jonjo O'Neill) *trckd ldng pair: drvn to chse wnr 2 out: no imp* **4/1**[3]	112
3341	3	6	**Swordsman (GER)**[17] 1297 8-11-2 **107**.....(tp) MrTJCannon(7) (Chris Gordon) *on and off the bridle: w ldr: j. slowly 2nd: led 10th tl 3 out: nt pce of wnr* **9/4**[2]	111
24-P	4	9	**Vasodilator (IRE)**[45] 1068 7-11-9 **107**..... LeightonAspell (Pat Murphy) *t.k.h in rr: clsd up and in tch 11th: btn 3 out* **16/1**	103
-PUP	5	27	**Vial De Kerdec (FR)**[67] 868 7-10-11 **95**.....(t) FelixDeGiles (Mark Bradstock) *mde most tl 10th: wknd 3 out* **15/2**	76

5m 47.3s (4.30) **Going Correction** +0.175s/f (Yiel) **5** Ran SP% **108.4**
Speed ratings (Par 105): **99,96,93,90,80**
CSF £7.65 TOTE £2.30: £1.80, £1.70; EX 8.40.
Owner D L Evans **Bred** Roland Lacrampe Cuyaubere **Trained** Clarbeston, Pembrokes

FOCUS
A steady pace saw the field still bunched in the back straight, but the form still worked out in a tight handicap. The progressive winner is rated up 4lb.

NOTEBOOK
Makena(FR) ◆ was keen to get on with things early on and, once given some free rein in the back straight, she flew the fourth-last, only to be restrained before delivering the decisive blow after turning for home under another masterful ride from Johnson, gaining his third win on the card in the process. A multiple winner in points earlier this year, she has resumed the winning habit under Rules to gain her fourth win this summer. These were closely matched on handicap ratings and, if this is taken into account, there might still be some leeway even off her rising mark, as in this form she should be able to win again. (tchd 11-8 and 7-4 in a place and 13-8 in places)
Native City(IRE) was niggled with a circuit to go and did not always jump that fluently, but stuck on into a clear second. He has been none too consistent this summer but is back down to a workable mark and this suggests he might be coming into a bit of form at last. (op 7-2)
Swordsman(GER) as usual gave his jockey a thorough cardio workout and, though he stuck to it, he eventually capitulated. With cheekpieces replacing the visor he had worn to victory with this jockey at Stratford last month, it may have made the difference. (op 3-1)
Vasodilator(IRE) ran in snatches and, racing keenly early on, did not last home, but there was just enough encouragement to suggest he could improve now he is finally on a more realistic mark. (op 11-1)
Vial De Kerdec(FR) was admittedly the first beaten, but at least he managed to complete the race for the first time in five attempts, possibly aided by the application of a tongue tie. (tchd 8-1)

1477 888LADIES.COM "FINEST BREED OF BINGO" H'CAP HURDLE (11 hdls) 2m 6f 110y

3:55 (3:55) (Class 4) (0-110,110) 4-Y-0+ **£2,602** (£764; £382; £190)

Form				RPR
-313	1		**Call At Midnight**[24] 1233 5-11-6 **104**..... JackDoyle (Sarah Humphrey) *patiently rdn in rr: hdwy 3 out: drvn to ld fnl 50yds* **7/1**	109+
	2	1	**Felix Da Housecat (IRE)**[323] 1798 7-10-9 **100**..... TrevorWhelan(7) (Ian Williams) *chsd ldrs: disp ld appr 8th: blnd last: slt ld run-in: r.o u.p: hdd fnl 50yds* **7/4**[1]	105+
0/50	3	2	**Fade To Grey (IRE)**[18] 1282 6-11-2 **103**.....(t) RichardKilloran(3) (Shaun Lycett) *hld up in rr of midfield: hdwy to chse ldrs 3 out: hrd rdn 2 out: hung rt run-in: kpt on* **22/1**	104
-534	4	2	**Parazar (FR)**[17] 1292 5-10-8 **92**..... LeightonAspell (Oliver Sherwood) *chsd ldrs: disp ld appr 8th: ev ch whn blnd 2 out: no ex run-in* **11/2**[2]	93+
6-20	5	8	**Balladeer (IRE)**[26] 1230 12-11-7 **110**..... DavidBass(5) (Lawney Hill) *prom: rdn 7th: sn lost pl and struggling: styd on run-in* **25/1**	102
-462	6	¾	**Googoobarabajagal (IRE)**[38] 1129 4-11-3 **103**..... RichardJohnson (Stuart Kittow) *hld up towards rr: hdwy on outer 5th: wknd 2 out: 5th and btn whn j.lft and hit last* **13/2**[3]	93
6324	7	1 ½	**Heir To Be**[21] 1259 11-11-2 **100**.....(bt) NickScholfield (Michael Blake) *led tl appr 8th: sn rdn: wknd 3 out* **7/1**	90
P-P6	8	1 ¼	**Lucky Dancer**[98] 530 5-11-4 **105**..... DPFahy(3) (Evan Williams) *chsd ldrs: j.lft 1st: nt fluent 2nd: wknd after 3 out* **16/1**	94
0P-0	9	26	**Red Lancer**[30] 1195 9-11-7 **105**..... FelixDeGiles (Jonathen de Giles) *in tch on inner: hit 6th: wknd after next* **50/1**	71
503-	10	26	**Lost Glory (NZ)**[183] 4439 5-11-5 **106**..... RichieMcLernon(3) (Jonjo O'Neill) *hld up towards rr: rdn and lost tch 8th* **12/1**	48
35-3	11	31	**Hail The King (USA)**[66] 217 10-10-2 **84** oh8 ow2..... MarkGrant (Roger Curtis) *a bhd: no ch fr 8th* **33/1**	—

5m 31.2s (-11.30) **Going Correction** -0.35s/f (Good)
WFA 4 from 5yo+ 12lb **11** Ran SP% **116.8**
Speed ratings (Par 105): **105,104,103,103,100 100,99,99,90,81 70**
toteswingers:1&2:£2.60, 1&3:£9.30, 2&3:£23.20 CSF £19.36 CT £262.51 TOTE £8.40: £2.80, £1.30, £6.50; EX 31.30.
Owner Mrs K Holmes **Bred** D And Mrs Holmes **Trained** West Wratting, Cambs

FOCUS
A competitive handicap producing a prolonged four-way battle from the home turn. A 4lb personal best from the winner.

NOTEBOOK
Call At Midnight was restrained until gradually improving her position on the final circuit and travelled well to deliver her challenge on the home turn, but it was no easy task and she had to knuckle down to a battle before eventually emerging on top. On the form of her maiden hurdle win at the end of July she had been given a fair mark for her handicap debut, and seems to need a good pace to show her best. (op 13-2 tchd 15-2 in a place)
Felix Da Housecat(IRE) was well backed for his first run for 11 months having shown bits and pieces of form when trained in Ireland. Racing prominently, he was still right there when blundering at the last and surrendering his chance. This was a sound effort, especially as he finished best of the early pacesetters. (op 9-4)
Fade To Grey(IRE) made some good progress on the final circuit, but just got there a bit late to get to the leaders. He is still on a recovery mission this summer following a lengthy absence, but this looks a step in the right direction. (op 20-1 tchd 25-1)
Parazar(FR) looked to be going well and was well placed to deliver a challenge wide of the pack, but once again his effort flattened out near the finish. (op 6-1 tchd 13-2)
Balladeer(IRE) lost his prominent position down the back straight and the veteran looks vulnerable off his current mark. (op 18-1 tchd 16-1)

Googoobarabajagal(IRE) travelled as well as anything as he made headway leaving the back straight, but faded disappointingly afterwards and did not get home. (op 15-2)

1478 TRY THE ICARD AT 888SPORT.COM H'CAP CHASE (19 fncs) 3m 2f 110y

4:30 (4:30) (Class 4) (0-100,87) 4-Y-O+**£3,485** (£1,029; £514; £257; £128)

Form				RPR
24P3 **1**		**Moon Melody (GER)**[15] 1331 7-10-8 **72** ... DPFahy(3)		89+
			(Evan Williams) *in tch: led 4 out: sn clr: comf* 4/1[2]
22F **2**	*8*	**Behind The Scenes (IRE)**[38] 1126 8-11-12 **87** ... LiamTreadwell		95
			(Tim McCarthy) *cl up: ev ch 3 out: nt pce of wnr* 4/1[2]
F-32 **3**	*7*	**Gift Of The Gods (IRE)**[6] 1425 7-11-8 **83** ...(p) RichardJohnson		85
			(Tim Vaughan) *cl up tl outpcd 15th* 9/4[1]
1-3P **4**	*8*	**Siouxme (IRE)**[87] 691 8-11-8 **83** ... LeightonAspell		77
			(Alison Batchelor) *in tch: outpcd 15th: rallied to dispute 6 l 2nd 3 out: sn wknd* 13/2
5-10 **5**	*7*	**Gaining Ground (IRE)**[60] 931 10-10-13 **74** ...(v) JodieMogford		62
			(Graeme McPherson) *led: j. slowly 10th: rdn next: hdd 4 out: sn wknd* 5/1[3]
15-2 **P**		**Winning Show**[17] 1293 6-11-3 **78** ...(t) ColinBolger		—
			(Chris Gordon) *nt a fluent: in rr: rdn 9th: wl bhd fr 13th: p.u bef 15th* 9/1

7m 5.80s (4.70) **Going Correction** +0.175s/f (Yiel) **6** Ran SP% **110.8**
Speed ratings (Par 105): **100,97,95,93,91** —
toteswingers:1&2:£3.00, 1&3:£2.30, 2&3:£1.60 CSF £19.65 TOTE £4.30: £1.60, £2.20; EX 22.00.
Owner Bangor On Dee Racing Club Ltd **Bred** R Hartmann **Trained** Llancarfan, Vale Of Glamorgan

FOCUS
A moderate race with the runners struggling to last home.

NOTEBOOK
Moon Melody(GER) was gaining his first win over fences, but did it with some authority. His jumping was not that fluent in the early stages, but he gained confidence and a fluent jump at the last in the back straight took him into a winning lead. He got a bit tired from the last but had done enough and could not be caught. He has been tried at this trip with variable success in the past. While he does just get this trip, he is not overly big and seems better when carrying light weights. (tchd 9-2)
Behind The Scenes(IRE) has had jumping problems. He lurched at several early fences and consequently lost several lengths, and though he regained momentum he could never really threaten the winner. (op 7-2 tchd 10-3)
Gift Of The Gods(IRE) travelled well for two-thirds of the race but began to tire on the final circuit and her jumping became ragged. She plugged on, but really needed to cement her glimmers of recent form and capitalise on this mark here, so this was disappointing. (op 11-4)
Siouxme(IRE) was caught out when the pace eventually lifted on her first start for three months. (op 6-1tchd 3-1 in a place)
Gaining Ground(IRE) had his own way in front but was beaten by the home turn. He had beaten Moon Melody out of sight over C&D in May when fresh from a break, but shot up the weights as a result and has subsequently reverted to his usual indifferent form. (op 13-2)
Winning Show did not jump fluently and was eventually pulled up. Official explanation: jockey said gelding was never travelling (op 8-1)

1479 TRY 888SPORT.COM MOBILE BETTING MARES' H'CAP HURDLE (10 hdls) 2m 4f

5:00 (5:00) (Class 5) (0-95,99) 4-Y-O+ **£1,951** (£573; £286; £143)

Form				RPR
P-06 **1**		**Happy Fleet**[33] 1179 7-10-0 **68** oh6 ... HaddenFrost		70
			(Roger Curtis) *hld up in midfield: hdwy 3 out: drvn to chse ldr appr 2 out: led run-in: all out* 5/1[2]
11P1 **2**	*nk*	**Play A Cord (IRE)**[6] 1427 7-11-10 **99** 7ex ...(b) MattGriffiths(7)		101
			(Neil Mulholland) *hld up towards rr: mstke 6th: gd hdwy 7th: led and qcknd 6 l clr 3 out: hdd run-in: r.o* 11/2[3]
4-66 **3**	*8*	**Saddlewood (IRE)**[61] 920 7-11-3 **85** ...(tp) DarylJacob		80
			(Jamie Snowden) *chsd ldrs: rdn to briefly go 2nd after 3 out: one pce* 16/1
-650 **4**	*1 ¾*	**Atabaas Allure (FR)**[52] 585 4-10-5 **74** ... ColinBolger		66
			(Chris Gordon) *hld up and bhd: rdn and r.o fr 2 out: nvr nrr* 40/1
2520 **5**	*7*	**Can't Remember**[46] 1062 5-11-2 **91** ... OliverDayman(7)		78
			(Alison Thorpe) *bhd: sme hdwy and in tch 7th: outpcd fr 3 out* 9/1
500- **6**	*6*	**Buds Dilemma**[364] 1394 6-10-1 **72** ...(p) DonalDevereux(3)		53
			(Peter Bowen) *t.k.h: in tch: hrd rdn and wknd appr 2 out* 9/2[1]
-650 **7**	*10*	**Cadeaux Cerise (IRE)**[46] 1062 6-11-8 **90** ... JamesDavies		62
			(Andrew Haynes) *chsd ldrs: wknd 7th: bhd whn j.rt 3 out* 33/1
153- **8**	*5*	**Romney Marsh**[179] 4519 9-11-4 **93** ... DannyBurton(7)		61
			(Roger Curtis) *t.k.h: pressed ldr: led 6th tl wknd 3 out* 14/1
P0-4 **9**	*27*	**Isintshelovely (IRE)**[17] 1294 7-10-10 **78** ... LeightonAspell		22
			(Chris Gordon) *led tl 6th: wknd next* 17/2
50/ **P**		**Dora Explora**[43] 637 6-11-3 **85** ... JamieMoore		—
			(Linda Jewell) *a in rr: no ch 7th: wl bhd whn p.u bef 2 out* 22/1
313 **P**		**A Dream Come True**[81] 760 5-11-12 **94** ... JodieMogford		—
			(Graeme McPherson) *t.k.h: chsd ldrs: mstkes 2nd: 3rd and 4th: jnd ldr and hit 3 out: wknd qckly: p.u bef next: lame* 7/1
444 **U**		**Kavegirl**[14] 1343 7-11-10 **92** ... DavidEngland		—
			(John Panvert) *in tch: 6th whn n.m.r, stmbld and uns rdr appr 7th* 8/1

4m 53.6s (-5.80) **Going Correction** -0.35s/f (Good)
WFA 4 from 5yo+ 12lb **12** Ran SP% **116.6**
Speed ratings (Par 103): **97,96,93,92,90 87,83,81,70,—,—,—**
toteswingers:1&2:£5.60, 1&3:£17.80, 2&3:£19.70 CSF £31.94 CT £411.46 TOTE £6.50: £2.50, £2.40, £3.90; EX 50.00.
Owner London Racing Partnerships **Bred** Helshaw Grange Stud And B Ridge **Trained** Lambourn, Berks

FOCUS
Two of the market leaders at opposite ends of the weights came through to fight out the finish, with the bottom weight just gaining the advantage. Ordinary mares' form.

NOTEBOOK
Happy Fleet, always travelling well, was ridden with supreme confidence, allowing plenty of time to reel in the topweight, but in the end she had to dig deep to stay on top. She came into this race on a long losing run and was duly 6lb out of the handicap, but had shown a glimmer of ability at Ffos Las a month ago and improved here under a light weight. Official explanation: trainer said, regarding the apparent improvement in form shown, mare made a mistake last time at Ffos Las and was better suited by today's good, good to firm in places ground (op 8-1)
Play A Cord(IRE), in contrast to the winner, was attempting to defy a penalty to notch her third win at this track and fourth of the summer. She maintained her composure when stumbling after the last with a circuit to go and struck for home from the final turn, giving her all in a bid to repel the challenger, but in the end even her jockey's allowance was not enough to claw back the weight advantage of the winner. (op 5-1 tchd 9-2 and 6-1 in a place)
Saddlewood(IRE) held a chance straightening for home, but could only plug on and will need to improve to be competitive off her current mark.
Atabaas Allure(FR) made some late progress and improved on her recent dismal form.
Can't Remember could never get into it and looks to be in the grip of the handicapper. (op 15-2)
Buds Dilemma was well supported on her first start for a year, but in the end she may just have needed the run. She is a longstanding maiden but presumably was expected to improve for the switch to the Peter Bowen yard. (op 5-1)
A Dream Come True Official explanation: vet said mare finished lame on her left fore

1480 BET ON SWITZERLAND V ENGLAND AT 888SPORT.COM MARES' STANDARD OPEN NATIONAL HUNT FLAT RACE 1m 6f

5:30 (5:30) (Class 6) 4-6-Y-O **£1,301** (£382; £191; £95)

Form				RPR
1		**La Belle Au Bois (IRE)** 4-10-5 0 ... MrJBanks(7)		93
			(Nick Lampard) *t.k.h: chsd ldng pair: wnt 2nd 2f out: 1 l 2nd and rdn whn lft 7 l clr 150yds out* 14/1
2	*5*	**Dark Ruby** 5-10-12 0 ... LeightonAspell		87
			(Les Hall) *t.k.h in 4th: rdn to go 3rd 2f out: hld whn lft 7 l 2nd 150yds out* 13/2[2]
0 **3**	*13*	**Restless Harriet**[118] 254 4-10-2 0 ... ChristopherWard(10)		71
			(Robin Dickin) *t.k.h in rr: rn wd bnd 3f out: sn lost tch* 12/1
4	*shd*	**Karingabay Queen**[120] 5-10-5 0 ... MrTJCannon(7)		71
			(Kevin Tork) *led: rdn 4f out: hdd over 2f out: sn wknd* 8/1[3]
51 **R**		**Spe Salvi (IRE)**[49] 1029 6-10-9 0 ... RossWishart(10)		100+
			(David Arbuthnot) *t.k.h: hung rt thrght: trckd ldr: led over 2f out: 1 l ahd and shkn up whn veered rt: rn out and crashed through paddock exit 150yds out* 2/5[1]

3m 26.6s (-4.50) **5** Ran SP% **110.2**
CSF £90.41 TOTE £9.20: £3.50, £2.80; EX 73.50 Place 6 £9.92; Place 5 £8.65.
Owner The Outside Chance Racing Club **Bred** Barry Flannery **Trained** Clatford, Wilts

FOCUS
Drama in the bumper when the odds-on favourite veered out towards the paddock exit and crashed through the rail in an otherwise uninformative event. A slowly run race and weak form.

NOTEBOOK
La Belle Au Bois(IRE) tracked the leaders and had moved upsides the favourite when inheriting the race. It was too early to tell if she would have found much under pressure, but at the time she was just headed. She will find it more difficult under a winner's penalty next time.
Dark Ruby flashed her tail before the start but travelled well enough in the race and had a gentle introduction to racing. A cheap purchase as a yearling, this run did not tell us that much. (op 9-1)
Restless Harriet needed to improve on her debut run at Towcester in May and on this evidence still needs to find more. (op 10-1)
Karingabay Queen, a former pointer, led until the home turn but thereafter faded rapidly and does not look that good. (op 10-1)
Spe Salvi(IRE) had demonstrated steering problems at Newton Abbot in July, but had still managed to win. She was once again awkward during the race, veering towards the paddock exit on the first circuit and then ducking violently towards it second time round, giving her young jockey little chance as she crashed through the rail. She would most likely have won this uncompetitive contest, but now has to conquer her wayward tendencies. (op 1-3)
T/Plt: £11.60 to a £1 stake. Pool:£67,503.71 - 4,224.16 winning tickets T/Qpdt: £7.10 to a £1 stake. Pool:£4,826.59 - 498.70 winning tickets LM

1272 WORCESTER (L-H)

Sunday, September 5

OFFICIAL GOING: Good changing to good (good to soft in places) after race 2 (2:25)

Run in positioned on inside half of home straight, home turn bend out 9yds and Cathedral Bend on inside line increasing a 2m chase by about 26yds.
Wind: Light across Weather: Light rain

1481 JOHN BURKE MEMORIAL NOVICES' H'CAP CHASE (15 fncs) 2m 4f 110y

1:50 (1:50) (Class 4) (0-105,108) 4-Y-O+ **£3,903** (£1,146; £573; £286)

Form				RPR
6360 **1**		**Another Trump (NZ)**[16] 1311 6-11-8 **101** ... APMcCoy		118+
			(Jonjo O'Neill) *a.p: chsd ldr 11th: j.rt 2 out: hrd rdn to ld flat: all out* 3/1[2]
1421 **2**	*hd*	**Frosted Grape (IRE)**[4] 1454 4-11-2 **108** 7ex ...(b) TomScudamore		111
			(David Pipe) *chsd ldrs: led 3rd to 4th: led again 9th: j.rt 2 out: rdn and hdd flat: styd on u.p* 7/4[1]
3044 **3**	*12*	**Mcqueen (IRE)**[16] 1309 10-10-8 **90** ... DannyCook(3)		97+
			(Barry Leavy) *hld up: hdwy 11th: blnd 3 out: wknd next* 10/1
-14S **4**	*6*	**Take A Mile (IRE)**[56] 957 8-11-7 **105** ... JimmyDerham(5)		105
			(Seamus Mullins) *mid-div: hdwy 9th: rdn appr 3 out: j.rt 2 out: sn wknd* 14/1
2335 **5**	*15*	**Pagan Sword**[38] 1128 8-11-5 **105** ... MrSWDrinkwater(7)		91
			(David Bridgwater) *led to 3rd: chsd ldr: lft in ld 7th: hdd 9th: mstke 10th: wknd next: t.o* 20/1
-U63 **6**	*25*	**Mad Professor (IRE)**[102] 477 7-9-7 **79** oh3 ...(p) JoeCornwall(7)		43
			(John Cornwall) *hld up: a in rr: t.o* 22/1
3305 **7**	*2 ¼*	**Tora Petcha (IRE)**[18] 1283 7-10-13 **97** ... MichaelMurphy(5)		59
			(Barry Leavy) *hld up: hdwy 8th: wknd after 11th: t.o* 28/1
4/P0 **P**		**Sternenzelt (GER)**[17] 1295 7-11-0 **100** ...(p) MrJEngland(7)		—
			(Michael Gates) *prom tl wknd 9th: t.o whn p.u bef 4 out* 50/1
14P2 **P**		**Risk Challenge (USA)**[21] 1256 8-11-2 **95** ...(t) CharliePoste		—
			(Milton Harris) *a in rr: t.o whn p.u bef 4 out* 15/2[3]
5-61 **P**		**Western Pride**[19] 1273 7-10-0 **79** oh2 ...(t) GerardTumelty		—
			(Richard Price) *hld up: hdwy 11th: wknd bef next: t.o whn p.u bef 3 out* 9/1
-5P0 **F**		**Intense Suspense (IRE)**[17] 1300 7-10-0 **79** oh26 ...(vt) AidanColeman		—
			(Robin Dickin) *chsd ldrs: led 4th tl fell 7th* 50/1

5m 5.20s (-1.50) **Going Correction** +0.075s/f (Yiel)
WFA 4 from 6yo+ 1lb **11** Ran SP% **115.4**
Speed ratings (Par 105): **105,104,100,98,92 82,81,—,—,—,—**
toteswingers:1&2:£1.70, 1&3:£11.40, 2&3:£7.30 CSF £8.31 CT £43.28 TOTE £2.40: £1.20, £1.10, £3.50; EX 10.50.
Owner John P McManus **Bred** J E Schick **Trained** Cheltenham, Gloucs

FOCUS
Run-in positioned on inside half of home straight. The home turn bend was out by nine yards and the Cathedral bend was on its inside line, adding approximately 26 yards to a 2m race. Rain before racing saw good to firm in the official going description removed, and AP McCoy thought it was riding on the easy side of good in the opener. This was a modest race in which the first pair pulled clear. The winner is rated 8lb off his hurdles best.

NOTEBOOK
Another Trump(NZ) had not shown much in four chasing starts and was tailed off over hurdles last time, but he was very well handicapped on his best hurdling form and there was sustained support for him. Going after the favourite down the back straight, he was driven to the front after the last for a narrow win. He jumped soundly enough this time but it remains to be seen whether he can build on this improved effort. (op 8-1)

Frosted Grape(IRE) was a wide-margin winner on her chasing debut at Hereford four days earlier and looked very well treated under a penalty. Jumping out to her right on this left-handed track, she could never get her own way in front and was collared after the last by a determined rival. She was not the most straightforward over hurdles and this run may have come too soon for her. (op 5-4 tchd 15-8)
Mcqueen(IRE) could not get to the lead this time and he already looked held when blundering three from home. He is gradually getting his act together over fences. (op 11-1 tchd 12-1)
Take A Mile(IRE) could not go with the principals from the third-last but probably ran his race despite the easier underfoot conditions. (tchd 16-1)
Pagan Sword, racing off an 8lb higher mark, soon lost his pitch once headed for the second time and extended his losing run over fences to 16. (op 22-1 tchd 25-1)
Risk Challenge(USA) made a mistake on the first circuit and was always towards the rear before pulling up. (op 7-1 tchd 6-1 and 8-1)
Western Pride won here last month in a race that has worked out quite well but she was effectively 10lb higher now. She made a forward move down the back but soon weakened and was pulled up. This longer trip should not have been beyond her. Official explanation: trainer's rep said mare had a breathing problem (op 7-1 tchd 6-1 and 8-1)

1482 CORAL TV NOVICES' HURDLE (12 hdls) 3m

2:25 (2:25) (Class 4) 4-Y-O+ **£2,397** (£698; £349)

Form				RPR
2-6U	1		**Pinerock (IRE)**[16] 1308 6-10-12 110 APMcCoy (Jonjo O'Neill) *a.p: reminders after 9th: led 2 out: hung lft flat: drvn out* **3/1**[2]	107+
24	2	¾	**Stormyisland Ahead**[33] 1175 5-11-5 112 (t) PaulMoloney (Evan Williams) *a.p: pushed along 7th: nt fluent last: sn rdn and ev ch: nt qckn nr fin* **17/2**	113+
1215	3	1¾	**Rifleman (IRE)**[16] 1312 10-11-0 0 (t) GilesHawkins(5) (Richard Lee) *led at stdy pce fr 3rd: qcknd 7th: sn pushed along: hdd 2 out: rdn appr last: styd on same pce flat* **9/2**[3]	110
42F1	4	21	**North Island (IRE)**[11] 1367 8-11-5 115 TomScudamore (Peter Bowen) *led to 3rd: chsd ldr tl rdn appr 3 out: wknd last* **6/5**[1]	92
054-	5	1¾	**Easyfix (IRE)**[370] 1356 7-10-5 0 MissCLWills(7) (Brendan Powell) *hld up: hdwy 6th: mstkes 7th: 8th and 9th: sn rdn: wknd last* **50/1**	83
645U	F		**Weldone Honey**[11] 1369 5-10-5 0 TomO'Brien (Peter Bowen) *fell 1st* **12/1**	—

6m 2.60s (18.00) **Going Correction** +0.075s/f (Yiel) 6 Ran SP% **108.8**
Speed ratings (Par 105): **73,72,72,65,64** —
toteswingers:1&2:£2.60, 1&3:£2.00, 2&3:£5.50 CSF £24.55 TOTE £4.00: £1.80, £2.80; EX 18.80.
Owner Michael & John O'Flynn **Bred** Malachy Travers **Trained** Cheltenham, Gloucs

FOCUS
A very ordinary novice hurdle, run at a steady pace until the tempo picked up on the second circuit. The form is rated around the principals and is possibly not solid.

NOTEBOOK
Pinerock(IRE) finished second at Southwell three starts back, form which gave him a decent chance in this company, and he recorded a narrow win despite appearing reluctant to put his best foot forward. He was without the usual headgear but was fitted with earplugs. (op 11-4 tchd 5-2)
Stormyisland Ahead ran creditably upped to 3m for the first time, travelling best of the five turning into the straight but unable to quite force his head in front on the run-in. His jumping has not been the best and it was a similar story over these brush obstacles. (tchd 8-1)
Rifleman(IRE) ran a game race from the front on this return to hurdles but could not add to his three Worcester victories this term. (op 4-1)
North Island(IRE) was the first of the runners to come off the bridle turning for home and was not himself under the penalty for his Bangor win. (op 11-8 tchd 6-4 and 11-10)
Easyfix(IRE) made a succession of jumping errors. (op 33-1)

1483 2ND SKIN STORAGE KING BRA CHAIN CONDITIONAL JOCKEYS' H'CAP CHASE (18 fncs) 2m 7f

3:00 (3:00) (Class 5) (0-90,90) 4-Y-O+ **£2,740** (£798; £399)

Form				RPR
P422	1		**Rash Moment (FR)**[17] 1297 11-11-5 83 (p) JohnKington (Michael Scudamore) *chsd ldrs: led 10th to next: led appr 4 out: rdn and hung lft flat: all out* **7/1**[3]	94+
0P-3	2	½	**Havenstone (IRE)**[17] 1292 9-11-2 83 AodhaganConlon(3) (Evan Williams) *hld up: nt fluent 4th: mstke 9th: hdwy appr 4 out: r.o u.p: nt rch wnr* **9/2**[1]	93
0U/4	3	shd	**Autumn Red (IRE)**[19] 1276 10-11-12 90 (b) SamJones (Paul Webber) *led tl after 5th: led 7th: hdd next: led again 11th: hdd appr 4 out: j.rt next: r.o u.p* **9/1**	99
-324	4	2	**Heezagrey (IRE)**[15] 1336 7-10-0 67 BrianToomey(3) (James Evans) *hld up: plenty to do 2 out: r.o wl flat: nrst fin* **6/1**[2]	75
0524	5	3½	**Bathwick Breeze**[15] 1331 6-11-6 84 (v) CO'Farrell (David Pipe) *hld up: drvn along 10th: hdwy 2 out: rdn flat: no further imp* **8/1**	90
40-6	6	19	**Lough Rynn (IRE)**[34] 1159 12-10-7 71 (p) GilesHawkins (Richard Lee) *hld up: hdwy 10th: rdn 4 out: wknd 2 out* **8/1**	62
P-54	7	4½	**Plenty Of Chat (IRE)**[15] 1329 6-11-0 84 (p) MrTomDavid(6) (Tim Vaughan) *chsd ldrs: mstke 5 out: rdn and wknd 2 out* **10/1**	70
-000	8	4	**Auditor**[18] 1283 11-10-0 64 oh3 (v) MarcGoldstein (Simon Lewis) *mid-div: hdwy 8th: wknd 12th* **66/1**	44
U2-0	P		**Kercabellec (FR)**[123] 156 12-9-13 69 JoeCornwall(6) (John Cornwall) *prom tl rdn and wknd 10th: t.o whn p.u bef 4 out* **25/1**	—
U440	P		**Overton Lad**[34] 1159 9-10-13 77 (v) SamTwiston-Davies (Peter Pritchard) *prom: sn drvn along: lost pl after 3rd: bhd fr 7th: t.o whn p.u bef 4 out* **12/1**	—
1P3-	P		**R'Cam (IRE)**[174] 4653 8-11-4 90 StephenO'Donovan(8) (Emma Lavelle) *chsd ldr: led after 5th: hdd 7th: led again next: hdd 10th: wknd after 5 out: t.o whn p.u bef 2 out* **6/1**[2]	—

5m 55.9s (13.30) **Going Correction** +0.075s/f (Yiel) 11 Ran SP% **113.6**
Speed ratings (Par 103): **81,80,80,80,78 72,70,69,—,— —**
toteswingers:1&2:£14.00, 1&3:£15.60, 2&3:£9.30 CSF £38.21 CT £285.52 TOTE £6.60: £3.20, £2.40, £3.50; EX 30.10.
Owner M Scudamore **Bred** Ambroise Dupont & Alain Plainfosse **Trained** Bromsash, Herefordshire
■ Stewards' Enquiry : Sam Jones caution: careless riding; six-day ban: used whip with excessive frequency causing the gelding to be wealed (Sep 19, 21-25)

FOCUS
The going was amended to good, good to soft in places before this race. This was a weak handicap for conditional riders, but it produced a stirring finish. The winner is rated up 2lb on recent form.

NOTEBOOK
Rash Moment(FR) had shown a clear return to form on his last two starts, finishing second twice over this trip at Stratford, and he was racing off 15lb lower than when last winning in March 2009. After travelling well through the race he only scrambled home in the end, but he will be able to race off the same mark if brought out before he can be reassessed, so he would be of interest if running in similarly moderate company soon. (op 13-2 tchd 11-2)
Havenstone(IRE) was another who looked well handicapped and he ran his best race over fences. Sticking to the inner all the way, he lost his pitch on the home turn but rallied from the second-last to go down fighting. (op 7-2)
Autumn Red(IRE) had headgear back on for this second run after a long absence. Always up with the pace, he was coming back for more after the final fence but did have a hard race. (op 8-1)
Heezagrey(IRE), not for the first time, finished well but all too late. This frustrating sort remains a maiden. (op 8-1)
Bathwick Breeze was going nowhere for most of the race but was plugging on at the end. (op 15-2)
Plenty Of Chat(IRE) had cheekpieces back in place of a visor and showed more than on his one previous chasing start, but he was just beginning to backpedal when untidy two from home. (op 12-1 tchd 14-1)
R'Cam(IRE) shaped as if in need of this first run since March. (op 13-2)

1484 RIDING FOR DISABLED MALVERN HILLS GROUP H'CAP HURDLE (8 hdls) 2m

3:35 (3:36) (Class 4) (0-105,105) 4-Y-O+ **£3,425** (£998; £499)

Form				RPR
34-5	1		**Emirates World (IRE)**[17] 1292 4-11-2 95 (t) TomO'Brien (Alan Jessop) *hld up: hdwy appr 2 out: rdn to ld 100yds out: drvn out* **14/1**	100
P220	2	¾	**Edgefour (IRE)**[35] 1150 6-11-7 105 (v) GilesHawkins(5) (Ben Case) *hld up: hdwy after 2 out: rdn flat: r.o* **10/1**	109
5P0-	3	½	**War Party**[133] 5105 6-11-5 105 MrTWeston(7) (Dr Richard Newland) *hld up: hdwy 5th: led 2 out: rdn and hdd 100yds out: styd on same pce* **16/1**	109
-P03	4	¾	**Classic Fly (FR)**[17] 1295 7-10-6 92 MrDGPrichard(7) (Arthur Whiting) *chsd ldrs: rdn appr 3 out: styd on same pce flat* **11/1**	95
-P56	5	½	**Welcome Stranger**[60] 933 10-10-12 94 DannyCook(3) (Louise Davis) *hld up: blnd 2 out: rdn and r.o flat: nt rch ldrs* **20/1**	97
1P-6	6	2¾	**The Brimmer (IRE)**[113] 328 6-11-6 104 JimmyDerham(5) (Seamus Mullins) *led: clr whn mstke 3rd: hdd 2 out: no ex flat* **16/1**	105
-324	7	1	**Art Man**[38] 1124 7-10-13 95 (b) WayneKavanagh(3) (James Frost) *chsd ldrs: rdn appr 2 out: no ex flat* **8/1**[3]	95
00-0	8	7	**Long Distance (FR)**[123] 166 5-11-4 100 CampbellGillies(3) (Lucinda Russell) *chsd ldrs: rdn appr 3 out: wknd flat* **20/1**	93
-635	9	nk	**Dormouse**[37] 1138 5-11-0 93 TomScudamore (Anabel L M King) *hld up: hdwy 5th: mstke and wknd last* **16/1**	87
-633	10	2	**Shindig**[21] 1261 8-11-0 93 (tp) RhysFlint (John Flint) *hld up in tch: rdn after 5th: wknd appr last* **4/1**[1]	84
0-0P	11	nk	**Kensington Oval**[15] 1333 5-11-7 100 APMcCoy (Jonjo O'Neill) *hld up in tch: lost pl 4th: n.d after* **6/1**[2]	91
3516	12	hd	**Golden Gem (IRE)**[16] 1309 8-11-5 98 (p) AidanColeman (Rachel Hobbs) *hld up: effrt appr 3 out: sn wknd* **12/1**	89
2146	13	¾	**Seaquel**[6] 1429 4-11-5 103 LeeEdwards(5) (Sally-Anne Wheelwright) *chsd ldr tl rdn appr 3 out: wknd next* **22/1**	93
51	P		**General Smith**[35] 1147 11-11-1 101 RobertKirk(7) (James Evans) *bhd fr 4th: t.o whn p.u bef last* **6/1**[2]	—

3m 47.7s (0.40) **Going Correction** +0.075s/f (Yiel)
WFA 4 from 5yo+ 11lb 14 Ran SP% **123.0**
Speed ratings (Par 105): **102,101,101,101,100 99,98,95,95,94 94,93,93,—**
toteswingers:1&2:£19.50, 1&3:£73.90, 2&3:£17.70 CSF £146.09 CT £2286.24 TOTE £15.20: £4.40, £3.50, £7.60; EX 124.00.
Owner Mrs Gloria Jessop **Bred** Darley **Trained** South Hanningfield, Essex

FOCUS
A modest handicap hurdle and a good result for the official handicapper, with all bar General Smith still in with something of a chance between the last two flights. Straightforward form.

NOTEBOOK
Emirates World(IRE) was sharper for his recent run at Fontwell - a track which did not really suit him - and struck the front on the flat for his first hurdles win. Not for the first time, he carried his head rather high, and it may be asking a bit much for him to reproduce this sort of effort. (tchd 16-1)
Edgefour(IRE) disappointed last time in better company but threaded her way through from the rear to grab her third runner-up spot in her last four starts. She will not mind a return to further. (op 12-1 tchd 9-1)
War Party ran a big race on this first start since April. He travelled strongly before taking it up but was unable to fend off the challengers on the flat. His one hurdling win was here and he seems to like the place. (op 14-1)
Classic Fly(FR) showed more on his previous start and ran another creditable race. He remains 6lb above his most recent winning mark. (tchd 12-1)
Welcome Stranger has been eased another 3lb in the weights and he came home well after losing momentum with an error two from home. (op 18-1)
The Brimmer(IRE), down in trip, made the running and did well to last as long as he did.
Art Man jumped reasonably this time and ran a fair race on this drop in trip. (tchd 7-1)
Shindig probably needs further than this. (op 9-2 tchd 5-1)
Kensington Oval showed little once again but he is descending the weights and it would be no surprise if connections manage to squeeze a win out of him somewhere down the line. Official explanation: jockey said gelding had a breathing problem (op 8-1)
General Smith, put up 7lb for his Market Rasen win, was struggling by halfway. (op 9-1)

1485 CORAL TV NOVICES' CHASE (12 fncs) 2m

4:10 (4:10) (Class 4) 4-Y-O+ **£3,903** (£1,146; £573; £286)

Form				RPR
113	1		**Holoko Heights**[8] 1406 5-11-5 115 (v) TomScudamore (Tim Vaughan) *a.p: j. slowly 5th: chsd ldr appr 4 out: rdn to ld flat: styd on wl* **9/4**[1]	125+
3152	2	6	**Blacktoft (USA)**[11] 1371 7-11-12 128 PaulMoloney (Evan Williams) *led: rdn and hdd flat: styd on same pce: eased whn btn towards fin* **9/4**[1]	129+
62P6	3	4	**Nordwind (IRE)**[16] 1311 9-11-5 0 SamJones (Evan Williams) *hld up: tk clsr order bef 4 out: sn lost pl: lft 3rd 2 out: styd on but nvr a threat to the front pair* **9/2**[2]	116+
13UP	4	16	**Smack That (IRE)**[9] 1390 8-11-12 132 (t) WarrenMarston (Milton Harris) *chsd ldr tl rdn appr 4 out: wknd after next* **9/2**[2]	109
455	5	17	**Canal Bank (IRE)**[21] 1257 6-11-5 0 APMcCoy (Jonjo O'Neill) *hld up in tch: dropped in rr 4th: wknd appr 4 out: t.o* **20/1**	87
05	6	1¾	**Roc De Guye (FR)**[46] 1058 5-11-5 0 DavidDennis (James Evans) *hld up: hdwy 4th: wknd appr 4 out: t.o* **66/1**	85
34-0	F		**Hi Tide (IRE)**[44] 1084 6-11-5 0 AidanColeman (J R Jenkins) *hld up: hdwy 5th: jnd ldrs and gng wl whn fell 2 out* **12/1**[3]	119

3m 56.9s (5.30) **Going Correction** +0.075s/f (Yiel) 7 Ran SP% **111.8**
Speed ratings (Par 105): **89,86,84,76,67 66,—**
toteswingers:1&2:£1.30, 1&3:£1.60, 2&3:£4.90 CSF £7.50 TOTE £2.50: £1.60, £1.30; EX 8.50.
Owner Owen Promotions Limited **Bred** Owen Promotions Ltd **Trained** Aberthin, Vale of Glamorgan

FOCUS
A fair novice chase run at just a steady pace. Smack That was again way off his Aintree form but the race has been rated at face value. The winner is up 10lb on his hurdles form.

NOTEBOOK
Holoko Heights made a winning chasing debut, jumping soundly and running on nicely to assert after the last. He was a plater over hurdles, albeit a successful one, but promises to reach a higher level at this game. (op 7-2)
Blacktoft(USA) is proven on easy ground and ran a fair race from the front, but could not hold off the winner on the run-in. He jumps pretty well and more chases should come his way. (tchd 15-8 and 5-2 in a place)
Nordwind(IRE), the runner-up's stablemate, ran an eyecatching race on this return to chasing, coming home strongly after the leaders had got away from him. Better can be expected with this experience behind him, although he is not the most consistent. (op 11-2 tchd 6-1)
Smack That(IRE) set a fair standard on the pick of his form and had the tongue fitted after some lacklustre efforts in decent handicaps. He was ridden closer to the pace than usual but was held from the third-last. (op 7-2 tchd 5-1)
Hi Tide(IRE) was not as good as some of these over hurdles but was bang in contention when coming down two out. It was a heavy fall and he also came down on his one previous start over fences last October, so his confidence may need restoring. (tchd 11-1)

1486 TAYLORWIMPEY.CO.UK DIGLIS WATER RIVERSIDE APARTMENTS LAUNCH H'CAP CHASE (15 fncs) 2m 4f 110y
4:40 (4:40) (Class 3) (0-135,131) 4-Y-0 **£6,337** (£1,872; £936; £468; £234)

Form				RPR
-121	1		**Mad Jack Duncan (IRE)**[19] 1276 8-10-0 **105** .... AidanColeman (Lawney Hill) *a.p: mstke 6th: chsd ldr 4 out: led 2 out: clr whn j.rt last: styd on gamely* **2/1**[1]	113+
P440	2	*nk*	**Postmaster**[15] 1332 8-11-11 **130** .... PaulMoloney (Evan Williams) *hld up: hdwy 11th: chsd wnr appr last: sn rdn: styd on wl* **12/1**	136
P	3	*3 ¾*	**Tell Me The Story (IRE)**[53] 985 6-10-5 **110** .... DougieCostello (Jonjo O'Neill) *hld up: hdwy bef 4 out: rdn appr last: r.o* **28/1**	113
2-46	4	*5*	**Cossack Dancer (IRE)**[94] 608 12-10-13 **118** .... (p) MattieBatchelor (Mark Bradstock) *w ldr tl led 6th to 8th: led again 11th: rdn and hdd 2 out: wknd flat* **16/1**	116
5301	5	*12*	**Pilgrims Lane (IRE)**[11] 1365 6-11-6 **130** .... (tp) JimmyDerham(5) (Milton Harris) *hld up: hdwy 11th: wknd 3 out* **16/1**	117
PU12	6	*2 ½*	**Sunday City (JPN)**[33] 1176 9-11-3 **122** .... (p) TomO'Brien (Peter Bowen) *prom: rdn and wknd appr 2 out* **7/1**[2]	107
25P2	7	*29*	**Michigan Assassin (IRE)**[19] 1277 8-10-5 **117** .... AodhaganConlon(7) (Debra Hamer) *led to 6th: led 8th to 11th: wknd 3 out: t.o* **7/1**[2]	76
3211	P		**Kirkhammerton (IRE)**[22] 1252 8-10-7 **115** .... DannyCook(3) (Barry Leavy) *hld up: hit 8th: sn lost tch: t.o whn p.u bef 4 out* **8/1**[3]	—
0-51	P		**Bermuda Pointe (IRE)**[15] 1334 8-10-7 **115** .... SamTwiston-Davies(3) (Nigel Twiston-Davies) *chsd ldrs tl rdn and wknd 10th: t.o whn p.u bef 4 out* **7/1**[2]	—
30F-	P		**Mr Robert (IRE)**[171] 4703 9-11-5 **131** .... MrJEngland(7) (Evan Williams) *hld up: a in rr: bhd and pushed along 6th: t.o whn p.u bef last* **14/1**	—

5m 4.60s (-2.10) **Going Correction** +0.075s/f (Yiel) **10** Ran SP% **111.5**
Speed ratings (Par 107): **107,106,105,103,98 98,86,—,—,—**
toteswingers:1&2:£6.10, 1&3:£14.10, 2&3:£70.30 CSF £24.99 CT £493.93 TOTE £2.70: £1.30, £2.40, £11.90; EX 25.60.
Owner Alan Hill **Bred** Paul Cashman **Trained** Aston Rowant, Oxon

FOCUS
A competitive handicap chase run at a brisk pace, and the form looks solid. Another personal best from the winner who was value for a bit more.

NOTEBOOK
Mad Jack Duncan(IRE) made it three wins from four starts since returning to racing under rules, and even with a 9lb rise for his latest victory still got in here off 10st. The drop in trip was against him and he tended to jump out to his right, but after stuttering going into the last he showed a good attitude to hold off the runner-up. He handled the easier ground well and there is more to come from him back over 3m or so. (op 9-4 tchd 15-8)
Postmaster had been dropped 5lb over his last two runs and he came from off the pace to deliver a strong challenge on the run-in, but the winner had a bit more up his sleeve. He appeared to handle underfoot conditions well and this was a good effort conceding 25lb to a progressive rival. (op 10-1)
Tell Me The Story(IRE) ◆ was pulled up on his chase debut last month but this was far better, with the decent gallop suiting him. This was only the fifth run of his life and it is reasonable to expect further improvement. (op 25-1)
Cossack Dancer(IRE) ran a commendable race up with the gallop and could still be capable of getting his head in front if allowed an uncontested lead. (op 12-1)
Pilgrims Lane(IRE), on whom the tongue tie was retained, was close enough turning into the home straight but soon on the retreat again.
Sunday City(JPN), another to jump right, was raised 8lb for his Ffos Las second and he faded from the second-last.
Michigan Assassin(IRE) made a fair bit of the running but jumped sketchily. (op 10-1 tchd 13-2)
Kirkhammerton(IRE), seeking a hat-trick, was 7lb higher in a better race and could never get into the picture after a mistake at halfway. Official explanation: jockey said gelding was pulled up as rider had his foot against the running rail (op 18-1 tchd 20-1)
Bermuda Pointe(IRE), who has been tubed, was disappointing off a 7lb higher mark than when winning over half a mile less at Newton Abbot. (op 18-1 tchd 20-1)
Mr Robert(IRE), the runner-up's stablemate, was always trailing before pulling up on this first outing since the Cheltenham Festival. (op 18-1 tchd 20-1)

1487 BURSTING TO GO WITH ANDYLOOS MAIDEN HURDLE (8 hdls) 2m
5:10 (5:10) (Class 5) 4-Y-0+ **£1,712** (£499; £249)

Form				RPR
	1		**Drill Sergeant**[78] 5-11-0 0 .... APMcCoy (Donald McCain) *prom: chsd ldr 4th: led 3 out: nt fluent and j.lft last two flights: shkn up flat: styd on* **10/11**[1]	120+
60-0	2	*3 ¼*	**Whatdoyoucallit (IRE)**[19] 1278 5-11-0 0 .... (t) PaulMoloney (Evan Williams) *hld up: hdwy 5th: chsd wnr appr last: rdn flat: no imp* **25/1**	113+
30-4	3	*6*	**Crystal Rock (IRE)**[24] 1238 5-11-0 105 .... AndrewTinkler (Nicky Henderson) *hld up: hdwy 5th: rdn after 3 out: styd on same pce fr next* **15/2**[3]	108
3-06	4	*13*	**Flying Squad (UAE)**[14] 1344 6-11-0 104 .... (t) WarrenMarston (Milton Harris) *hld up: hdwy 5th: wkng whn mstke 2 out* **25/1**	98
06/	5	*7*	**Its Danny Boy (IRE)**[127] 7-11-0 0 .... RhysFlint (David Brace) *led to 3 out: wknd appr last* **25/1**	90
522	6	*3 ¼*	**Society Venue**[35] 1148 5-11-0 110 .... TomScudamore (Michael Scudamore) *prom: rdn appr 3 out: wknd next* **11/4**[2]	87
100-	7	*9*	**Amuse Me**[136] 5351 4-10-11 0 .... MrAJBerry(3) (Jonjo O'Neill) *prom tl wknd appr 3 out: t.o* **16/1**	79
42-	8	*27*	**Wise Princess**[388] 1195 4-10-0 0 .... AshleyBird(7) (Bill Turner) *hld up: a in rr: bhd fr 3rd: t.o* **100/1**	48
5	9	*15*	**Granakey (IRE)**[9] 1392 7-10-7 0 .... TomO'Brien (Peter Bowen) *hld up: a in rr: bhd fr 3rd: t.o* **33/1**	34
0-	10	*25*	**Madman (FR)**[330] 1354 6-10-7 105 .... JoeCornwall(7) (Christopher Kellett) *hld up: a in rr: bhd fr 3rd: t.o* **100/1**	19
	11	*10*	**Silvery Fox (IRE)**[90] 6-11-0 0 .... SamJones (Evan Williams) *hld up: plld hrd: hmpd 2nd: bhd fr next: t.o* **66/1**	10
05	U		**Coach And Four (USA)**[19] 1278 5-10-7 0 .... MrJEngland(7) (Michael Gates) *chsd ldr: disputing cl 2nd whn blnd and uns rdr 4th* **66/1**	—
0-46	U		**Cruise In Style (IRE)**[30] 1201 4-10-2 0 .... GilesHawkins(5) (Kevin Bishop) *hld up: j.lft 2nd: mstke next: tried to refuse and uns rdr 4th* **66/1**	—

3m 47.3s **Going Correction** +0.075s/f (Yiel)
WFA 4 from 5yo+ 11lb **13** Ran SP% **117.6**
Speed ratings (Par 103): **103,101,98,91,88 86,82,68,61,48 43,—,—**
toteswingers:1&2:£12.80, 1&3:£2.60, 2&3:£27.40 CSF £31.97 TOTE £1.50: £1.10, £7.40, £2.50; EX 35.70 Place 6 £214.78; Place 5 £160.70.
Owner T G Leslie **Bred** D G Hardisty Bloodstock **Trained** Cholmondeley, Cheshire

FOCUS
A reasonable maiden hurdle run just under half a second quicker than the earlier handicap. The winner can rate a lot higher on his Flat form.

NOTEBOOK
Drill Sergeant was a tough and smart perfomer for Mark Johnston on the Flat, placed in Group 2 company and effective at 1m4f-2m. Sold to current connections for 35,000gns, he landed the odds fairly comfortably on this hurdling debut despite an indifferent round of jumping. He is likely to be kept at a relatively low level for the time being as he builds experience, and will get further than this if required. (tchd 5-6)
Whatdoyoucallit(IRE) ◆ caught the stewards' attention first time out and he confirmed that he has plenty of ability with an improved run in second. He closed on the outside to give chase to the favourite and should be up to going one better before long. (op 50-1)
Crystal Rock(IRE) built on his reappearance effort and was keeping on for third. This half-brother to Jack The Giant may be suited by a step up in trip. (tchd 8-1)
Flying Squad(UAE) ran better than on his two most recent outings and may be the type for modest handicaps.
Its Danny Boy(IRE), a winning pointer, ran well for a long way on this return to hurdling and first start for four months. (op 33-1)
Society Venue, runner-up to Sir Frank at Market Rasen on his last two starts, was a little disappointing on this easier surface.
Amuse Me, highly tried in bumpers after his winning debut for another yard, had the tongue tie left off for this hurdling debut and didn't get home. (op 14-1)
T/Plt: £345.90 to a £1 stake. Pool:£68,504.57 - 144.57 winning tickets T/Qpdt: £81.40 to a £1 stake. Pool:£5,853.95 - 53.20 winning tickets CR

1442 NEWTON ABBOT (L-H)
Monday, September 6

OFFICIAL GOING: Soft changing to heavy after race 2 (3.00)
All bends moved but impact on distances not quantified.
Wind: quite strong across Weather: heavy rain until 5.00.

1488 SOUTH WEST RACING CLUB NOVICES' HURDLE (8 hdls) 2m 1f
2:30 (2:31) (Class 4) 4-Y-0+ **£3,577** (£1,050; £525; £262)

Form				RPR
41-1	1		**Rudanphast (IRE)**[19] 1284 5-10-12 0 .... RichardJohnson (Peter Bowen) *trckd ldr: led appr 3 out: styd on wl: pushed out* **15/8**[1]	116+
04	2	*9*	**Red Current**[25] 1090 6-10-5 0 .... TomScudamore (Michael Scudamore) *hld up towards rr: hdwy after 4th: rdn and ev ch after 3 out: sn hld: styd on same pce* **9/1**	97
4052	3	*20*	**Navajo Nation (IRE)**[16] 1333 4-10-7 99 .... (p) DavidBass(5) (Bill Turner) *trckd ldrs: rdn and ev ch sn after 3 out: wknd bef next* **4/1**[3]	84
1-23	4	*4*	**Marc Aurele (IRE)**[35] 1160 5-11-0 113 .... (t) MrRMahon(5) (Paul Nicholls) *led: hit 4th: rdn and hdd appr 3 out: sn btn* **85/40**[2]	87
2U-P	5	*20*	**Holden Caulfield (IRE)**[16] 1333 5-10-9 100 .... (t) ChrisHonour(3) (Nick Ayliffe) *mid-div tl wknd after 3 out: t.o* **12/1**	60
0	6	*8*	**Mr Demister**[6] 1445 7-10-7 0 ow2 .... MissLGardner(7) (Susan Gardner) *a towards rr: t.o* **80/1**	54
60-P	7	*21*	**Just The Job (IRE)**[15] 1343 6-10-12 0 .... RodiGreene (Neil Mulholland) *trckd ldrs tl after 4th: sn bhd: t.o* **25/1**	31
F	8	*14*	**Hurst Park (IRE)**[6] 1445 8-10-12 0 .... JackDoyle (Susan Gardner) *hit 2nd: a in rr: t.o* **100/1**	17
4-0	9	*21*	**Operachy**[15] 1344 5-10-12 0 .... HaddenFrost (James Frost) *mid-div tl wknd after 5th: t.o* **40/1**	—
0-6	10	*16*	**Jim Job Jones**[113] 362 6-10-12 0 .... DougieCostello (Neil Mulholland) *j.rt: hmpd and stmbld 1st: mid-div tl wknd after 4th: t.o* **50/1**	—

4m 22.5s (16.80) **Going Correction** +1.125s/f (Heav)
WFA 4 from 5yo+ 11lb **10** Ran SP% **114.9**
Speed ratings (Par 105): **105,100,91,89,80 76,66,59,49,42**
toteswingers:1&2:£7.10, 1&3:£2.50, 2&3:£10.40 CSF £18.41 TOTE £2.60: £1.10, £1.80, £1.80; EX 17.50.
Owner Mrs Tania Stepney **Bred** Kennedy O'Sullivan Syndicate **Trained** Little Newcastle, Pembrokes

FOCUS
A weak novices' hurdle in which very few handled the testing conditions. The winner is rated in line with his bumper form and can go on to rate higher.

NOTEBOOK
Rudanphast(IRE), a dual bumper winner, appeared to have no trouble with the ground as it turned out, travelling strongly and quickly putting daylight between himself and the others. This was a likable performance and he should have no trouble defying a penalty, with further expected to suit. (op 6-4 tchd 2-1)
Red Current, third back on the Flat earlier this month, made headway to challenge briefly, but she was no match for the winner. A return to better ground should help and she can pick up a small race at some stage. (op 11-1)
Navajo Nation(IRE) is now 0-13 over hurdles. (op 5-1)
Marc Aurele(IRE) simply failed to cope with the ground. His improvement has coincided with a sound surface, so he deserves another chance back on better going. Official explanation: trainer's rep said gelding had a breathing problem (op 9-4 tchd 15-8)
Operachy Official explanation: jockey said gelding was never travelling

1489 SOUTH WEST RACING NOVICES' H'CAP HURDLE (8 hdls) 2m 1f
3:00 (3:01) (Class 5) (0-90,89) 4-Y-0+ **£2,055** (£599; £299)

Form				RPR
000-	1		**Chestnut Ben (IRE)**[210] 3935 5-9-9 **63** oh25 .... DavidBass(5) (Gary Brown) *awkward 1st: in tch: jnd ldr 3 out: led bef next: sn in command: hit last: styd on wl: comf* **20/1**	78+
6/31	2	*9*	**Maizy Missile (IRE)**[46] 1066 8-11-7 **84** .... PaulMoloney (Mary Evans) *prom: lft in ld on bnd after 4th: rdn and hdd appr 2 out: styd on same pce* **6/1**	92

0-04 **3** *20* **Catholic Hill (USA)**[5] 1450 5-11-9 **89**.......... TommyPhelan(3) 75
(Mark Gillard) *trckd ldrs: rdn bef 3 out: wknd bef 2 out* **10/1**

2652 **4** *1 3/4* **Amazing Request**[16] 1335 6-10-13 **83**..........(p) MissIsabelTompsett(7) 67
(Bernard Llewellyn) *mid-div: struggling towards rr 4th: plugged on past btn horses fr 2 out: nvr a danger* **5/2**[1]

555P **5** *27* **Bari Bay**[13] 1361 4-11-1 **78**..........(bt) NickScholfield 35
(Michael Blake) *hld up towards rr: hdwy appr 3 out: sn rdn: wknd bef 2 out: t.o* **11/1**

/00- **6** *10* **Manathon (FR)**[298] 2247 7-11-2 **79**..........(p) PaddyBrennan 26
(Alan Jones) *hld up towards rr: hdwy 5th: rdn bef 3 out: wknd bef 2 out: t.o* **9/2**[3]

5063 **P** **The Grey One (IRE)**[5] 1450 7-11-1 **85**.......... ChrisDavies(7) —
(Milton Bradley) *mde most tl rn v wd on bnd after 4th: trckd ldr tl wknd 3 out: bhd whn p.u bef 2 out* **10/1**

60P/ **P** **Sunset Boulevard (IRE)**[72] 4099 7-11-7 **84**..........(b[1]) APMcCoy —
(Jim Best) *hld up towards rr: hdwy 5th: wknd qckly 3 out: sn p.u* **11/4**[2]

5000 **P** **Pegasus Lad (USA)**[20] 1272 4-10-13 **76**..........(v[1]) AndrewGlassonbury —
(Linda Blackford) *trckd ldrs tl rdn 5th: sn wknd: t.o whn p.u bef 2 out* **20/1**

4m 28.8s (23.10) **Going Correction** +1.125s/f (Heav)
WFA 4 from 5yo+ 11lb **9** Ran SP% **123.7**
Speed ratings (Par 103): **90,85,76,75,62 58,—,—,—**
toteswingers:1&2:£68.50, 1&3:£38.10, 2&3:£6.60 CSF £143.89 CT £1296.11 TOTE £39.10: £10.10, £2.30, £5.30; EX 598.80.
Owner John Bourke **Bred** Sean Deu Burca **Trained** East Garston, Berks

FOCUS
Although heavy ground sometimes lends itself to shock results, it was especially hard to predict victory for Chestnut Ben.

NOTEBOOK
Chestnut Ben(IRE) had beaten just four horses home in the same number of starts and had to race from no less than 25lb out of the handicap. He made it look straightforward, travelling kindly and readily asserting, but it remains to be seen whether he can repeat this form, and things are obviously going to be much tougher in future. The Stewards noted his trainers explanation for the improved showing, that the gelding had benefited from a knee operation and nice, long break over the summer. Official explanation: trainer said, regarding the apparent improvement in form shown, gelding benefited from a knee operation and a good summer break (op 25-1)
Maizy Missile(IRE), a winner at Uttoxeter latest, did well considering she was 9lb higher this time and the ground was completely different. (op 11-2 tchd 5-1)
Catholic Hill(USA), reappearing only five days after his handicap debut, was all out to hold on for third. (tchd 9-1 and 11-1)
Amazing Request is a tricky customer and he ran a strange race, dropping himself out before consenting to run on again once the race was all over. He's still a maiden and is evidently not one to take too short a price about. (op 7-2)
Manathon(FR) ended up well held but may do better on decent ground. (op 13-2)
Sunset Boulevard(IRE) didn't get home in the first-time blinkers and may prefer better ground. (op 9-4 tchd 4-1)
Pegasus Lad(USA) Official explanation: jockey said gelding had a breathing problem (op 9-4 tchd 4-1)

1490 JOAN PEARSON BIRTHDAY H'CAP HURDLE (12 hdls) 3m 3f
3:30 (3:31) (Class 4) (0-105,102) 4-Y-0+ **£2,764** (£811; £405; £202)

Form RPR

0P-0 **1** **Cashel Blue (USA)**[15] 1347 8-11-0 **95**..........(b) KeiranBurke(5) 110+
(Patrick Rodford) *mde all: hit 4th: clr 9th: mstke 3 out: styd on wl: unchal* **8/1**

P-11 **2** *12* **Caheerloch (IRE)**[16] 1336 8-11-3 **96**.......... SamTwiston-Davies(3) 100
(Nigel Twiston-Davies) *hld up: hdwy after 8th: chsd wnr appr 3 out: sn rdn: sme imp on wnr bef 2 out: no ex appr last* **9/4**[1]

-044 **3** *14* **Converti**[11] 1380 6-11-3 **100**.......... SClements(7) 88
(Simon Burrough) *trckd ldrs: rdn after 3 out: styd on same pce* **14/1**

/113 **4** *8* **Kopylova**[16] 1336 7-11-10 **100**.......... RichardJohnson 80
(Tim Vaughan) *hld up: n.m.r on inner on long run bef 9th: hdwy into modest 3rd 3 out but little ch: rdn and sn wknd* **4/1**[3]

-S66 **5** *3 1/4* **Kristoffersen**[15] 1347 10-11-12 **102**.......... OwynNelmes 79
(Helen Nelmes) *trckd ldrs: rdn appr 9th: sn wknd* **12/1**

0431 **6** *13* **Mista Rossa**[7] 1434 5-10-8 **89** 7ex.......... MissLHorner(5) 53
(Jamie Snowden) *hld up in rr: hung lft fr 9th: nvr making any imp: wknd after 3 out: t.o* **3/1**[2]

2016 **7** *31* **Captain Becket**[6] 1443 7-11-10 **100**.......... HaddenFrost 33
(James Frost) *trckd wnr tl 8th: wknd appr 9th: sn t.o* **14/1**

6P40 **P** **Triggernometry**[54] 986 9-11-12 **102**.......... JoeTizzard —
(Colin Tizzard) *trckd wnr tl 9th: sn rdn: wknd next: bhd whn p.u bef 2 out* **16/1**

7m 27.0s (46.00) **Going Correction** +1.525s/f (Heav) **8** Ran SP% **113.8**
Speed ratings (Par 105): **92,88,84,81,80 77,67,—**
toteswingers:1&2:£3.50, 1&3:£3.90, 2&3:£6.30 CSF £26.87 CT £249.99 TOTE £10.90: £4.20, £1.10, £4.60; EX 29.10.
Owner Monday Boys Partnership & Baggy **Bred** P J B Bloodstock **Trained** Ash, Somerset

FOCUS
They went a steady gallop for this staying handicap hurdle, understandably given the conditions, and the front-running Cashel Blue maintained his clear advantage all the way to the line. The runner-up sets the level.

NOTEBOOK
Cashel Blue(USA) kicked away under an enterprising ride and maintained his clear advantage all the way to the line, despite getting a little tired. Having only his second start for the yard, he had placed in similar ground to this in the past and was 18lb lower than when last successful, so it was no surprise to see him go in with the blinkers, which he wore with success on the Flat in his younger days, reapplied. (op 12-1)
Caheerloch(IRE), chasing the hat-trick, having won twice at this track last month, was the only one capable of going after the winner, but he never quite got close enough to challenge seriously. This was a decent effort considering the ground.
Converti, whose sole previous win over hurdles came on good to firm, was always prominent and kept on best he could. (op 11-1)
Kopylova, another to have done her winning on fast ground, never got close enough to challenge. (op 5-1)
Mista Rossa, penalised for his Huntingdon victory, found this ground too testing. (op 11-4)

1491 SOUTH WEST RACING CLUB H'CAP CHASE (16 fncs) 2m 5f 110y
4:00 (4:01) (Class 3) (0-120,117) 4-Y-0 **£6,337** (£1,872; £936; £468; £234)

Form RPR

-333 **1** **Moulin De La Croix**[22] 1256 6-10-7 **101**..........(t) SamTwiston-Davies(3) 111+
(Nigel Twiston-Davies) *trckd ldrs: led after 4 out: sn in command: easily* **8/1**

1P/5 **2** *2 3/4* **Sporting Rebel (IRE)**[96] 579 10-11-7 **112**.......... HaddenFrost 112
(James Frost) *in tch: rdn after 12th: wnt 3rd whn mstke 3 out (water): chal for 2nd fr 2 out: wnt 2nd sn after last: no ch w wnr* **11/1**

0-60 **3** *2* **Some Craic (IRE)**[34] 1178 10-11-5 **110**.......... RichardJohnson 109
(Paul Henderson) *led: rdn and hdd sn after 3 out: j.rt last 2: no ex run-in* **20/1**

12 **4** *20* **Courella (IRE)**[5] 1454 6-11-5 **110**.......... PaulMoloney 88
(Evan Williams) *hld up bhd: sme prog after 12th: sn rdn: wknd after 4 out* **13/2**[3]

612P **5** *7* **Tampa Boy (IRE)**[15] 1348 8-11-8 **113**..........(t) CharliePoste 84
(Milton Harris) *mid-div: tk clsr order 6th: rdn after 12th: wknd after 4 out* **10/1**

-P43 **6** *14* **On You Go (IRE)**[20] 1276 9-11-4 **109**.......... APMcCoy 66
(Jonjo O'Neill) *hld up: reminder after 9th: rdn and sme hdwy 11th: wknd 4 out* **5/2**[2]

2144 **7** *8* **Intac (IRE)**[5] 1454 8-11-8 **113**.......... JoeTizzard 62
(Colin Tizzard) *mid-div: tk clsr order 6th: struggling whn lost pl 11th: wknd 4 out* **17/2**

4346 **P** **Hereweareagain (IRE)**[39] 1128 7-11-0 **105**.......... TomO'Brien —
(Philip Hobbs) *disp 4th tl rdn appr 4 out: wknd after 3 out: tired 6th whn p.u bef last* **9/4**[1]

5m 50.9s (29.50) **Going Correction** +1.525s/f (Heav) **8** Ran SP% **116.5**
Speed ratings (Par 107): **107,106,105,98,95 90,87,—**
toteswingers:1&2:£8.90, 1&3:£12.10, 2&3:£24.10 CSF £86.63 CT £1695.87 TOTE £7.50: £1.80, £3.40, £5.30; EX 49.70.
Owner N A Twiston-Davies **Bred** Mrs Susan Orton **Trained** Naunton, Gloucs

FOCUS
The front three drew clear in this handicap chase.

NOTEBOOK
Moulin De La Croix won this with ease. Just 3lb higher than when scoring at Leicester earlier in the year, she always seemed to be travelling kindly and Sam Twiston-Davies had things under control from before the turn into the straight. She's only six and may still be improving, so could win again, with this sort of ground reportedly in her favour. Official explanation: trainer said, regarding the apparent improvement in form shown, mare appeared to appreciate today's heavy ground (op 13-2 tchd 6-1)
Sporting Rebel(IRE) goes well in testing ground and he kept on to do best of the remainder. (op 9-1)
Some Craic(IRE) ran a much more promising race. (tchd 16-1)
Courella(IRE), in good form and making a quick reappearance, seems suited by decent ground and he could never get into it. (op 5-1)
On You Go(IRE) was undone by several sloppy jumps, never travelling and ending up well held. (op 11-4 tchd 3-1)
Hereweareagain(IRE) stopped very quickly and was eventually pulled up. He was expected to be suited by the ground, but it didn't work out that way. (op 7-2)

1492 SOUTH WEST RACING CLUB H'CAP HURDLE (8 hdls) 2m 1f
4:30 (4:31) (Class 4) (0-115,113) 4-Y-0+ **£3,577** (£1,050; £525; £262)

Form RPR

4331 **1** **Kijivu**[18] 1292 5-11-2 **103**..........(bt) FelixDeGiles 110+
(Alastair Lidderdale) *racd wd: travelled wl thrght: trckd ldrs: led on bit after 2 out: easily* **3/1**[2]

-326 **2** *3* **Olivino (GER)**[19] 1282 9-11-0 **108**.......... MissIsabelTompsett(7) 105
(Bernard Llewellyn) *racd wd: hld up: hdwy after 3 out: effrt next: kpt on to go 2nd last but nt pce of wnr* **7/2**[3]

0414 **3** *1 1/2* **Nothing Is Forever (IRE)**[25] 1236 6-10-8 **95**..........(p) DarylJacob 91
(Liam Corcoran) *racd wd: led: rdn whn hung lft after 2 out: sn hdd: kpt on same pce* **9/4**[1]

P034 **4** *hd* **Classic Fly (FR)**[1] 1484 7-10-5 **92**.......... NickScholfield 88
(Arthur Whiting) *racd alone on inner: prom: rdn after 3 out: ev ch after 2 out: mstke last: no ex* **9/2**

3-33 **P** **Supernoverre (IRE)**[18] 1289 4-11-8 **109**..........(p) DenisO'Regan —
(Liam Corcoran) *racd wd: trckd ldrs: mstke 3 out: sn rdn and wknd: p.u bef next* **11/2**

4m 32.9s (27.20) **Going Correction** +1.525s/f (Heav)
WFA 4 from 5yo+ 11lb **5** Ran SP% **111.6**
Speed ratings (Par 105): **97,95,94,94,—**
CSF £13.80 TOTE £3.30: £2.50, £1.60; EX 18.80.
Owner KMC Partnership Three **Bred** M P Bishop **Trained** Eastbury, Berks

FOCUS
A modest handicap hurdle that was won with ease by Kijivu, who was value for further. The time was slow and the form is suspect.

NOTEBOOK
Kijivu looked the only one to handle the ground. Raised 8lb for winning on much quicker going at Fontwell latest, Felix De Giles always looked to have things under control aboard the mare, and she readily asserted going to the last. (tchd 7-2 and 4-1 in a place)
Olivino(GER) kept responding to pressure and stayed on late to take second. (op 10-3 tchd 3-1)
Nothing Is Forever(IRE) gave it his best shot without being able to quicken in the ground back in third. (op 10-3)
Classic Fly(FR), fourth at Worcester the previous day, stuck towards the inner throughout and gave it a right good go, but a mistake at the last pretty much ended his hopes of second. (op 11-2 tchd 6-1 and 4-1)
Supernoverre(IRE) was quickly beaten after a mistake three out. (op 7-2)

1493 SOUTH WEST RACING H'CAP CHASE (13 fncs) 2m 110y
5:00 (5:01) (Class 4) (0-110,101) 4-Y-0+ **£3,528** (£1,028; £514)

Form RPR

50 **1** **In The Zone (IRE)**[19] 1283 6-11-2 **94**.......... RichieMcLernon(3) 103+
(Jonjo O'Neill) *hld up bhd ldng trio: clsd on ldrs after 4 out: mounting chal whn hit 2 out: rdn and r.o wl after last: led fnl 75yds* **7/2**[2]

1 **2** *1 1/4* **January**[19] 1283 7-11-12 **101**..........(t) APMcCoy 108+
(Liam Corcoran) *racd freely: trckd ldrs: led after 2 out: sn rdn: hdd run-in: no ex* **11/8**[1]

2025 **3** *8* **Nesnaas (USA)**[16] 1327 9-11-5 **94**.......... TomScudamore 95
(Mark Rimell) *led: rdn after 4 out: hdd sn after 2 out: no ex* **4/1**[3]

6-U0 **4** *56* **Wild Power (GER)**[19] 1283 12-10-1 **76** oh1 ow1..........(p) OwynNelmes 19
(Helen Nelmes) *prom tl rdn after 9th: wknd after 4 out: t.o* **16/1**

3F **P** **Tigh Bhruadair (IRE)**[22] 1256 6-11-11 **100**..........(tp) PaulMoloney —
(Evan Williams) *rn in snatches: last but wl in tch: reminders after 1st: rdn after 7th: hit 9th: wknd 4 out: bhd whn p.u bef last* **7/2**[2]

4m 35.2s (28.70) **Going Correction** +1.525s/f (Heav) **5** Ran SP% **112.4**
Speed ratings (Par 105): **93,92,88,62,—**
CSF £9.38 TOTE £7.20: £3.90, £1.10; EX 11.10.
Owner John P McManus **Bred** Frank Motherway **Trained** Cheltenham, Gloucs

FOCUS
A competitive little race, made harder by the fact none of the runners had any noteworthy form on this sort of going. The winner is rated back to the best of his Irish form with the next two close to their marks.

NOTEBOOK

In The Zone(IRE), some 58l behind January at Hereford latest, was a completely different proposition this time, tracking his old rival through and staying on the stronger after the last. He won with a bit in hand and could follow up assuming the handicapper is fair. Official explanation: trainer said, regarding the apparent improvement in form shown, gelding was better suited by today's heavy ground (op 4-1 tchd 9-2)

January, who has changed stables again, displays a high head carriage, but it didn't stop him winning last time and he may have been thwarted by the much slower conditions here, as well as the 7lb rise. (op 6-4 tchd 5-4 and 13-8 in a place)

Nesnaas(USA) couldn't see it out in the ground. (tchd 5-1)

Wild Power(GER) was again well held. (op 10-1)

Tigh Bhruadair(IRE) jumped moderately and was another who struggled in the conditions. (op 4-1 tchd 10-3)

1494 SOUTH WEST RACING CLUB NOVICES' H'CAP HURDLE (8 hdls 2 omitted) 2m 6f

5:30 (5:30) (Class 5) (0-95,93) 4-Y-0+ **£2,055** (£599; £299)

Form | | | | RPR
0001 **1** **Am I Blue**[5] 1451 4-11-8 **90** 7ex ... RichardJohnson 107+
(Mrs D Thomas) *disp ld most of way: rdn clr appr 2 out: comf* **5/6**[1]
63P6 **2** *22* **You Can Of Course (IRE)**[7] 1423 7-10-11 **78** ... DougieCostello 74
(Neil Mulholland) *disp ld w wnr tl rdn appr 2 out: sn wknd* **9/1**
4 **3** *56* **Royial (FR)**[15] 1344 5-11-7 **93** ... JimmyDerham(5) 33
(Seamus Mullins) *hld up: wnt modest 3rd on long run to 3 out: nvr any danger to ldng pair* **7/2**[2]
5P5- **P** **Three Boars**[34] 2367 8-11-4 **85** ... (t) LiamTreadwell —
(Claire Dyson) *hld up: lost tch after 5th: t.o whn p.u bef 2 out* **11/1**
00F/ **P** **Hollandia (IRE)**[562] 9-9-11 **67** ... GilesHawkins(5) —
(Kathleen Sanderson) *trckd ldrs tl 5th: wknd qckly: p.u on long run to 3 out* **13/2**[3]
0/P- **P** **Roughing It (IRE)**[224] 3654 7-11-6 **87** ... TomScudamore —
(Michael Scudamore) *prom tl after 5th: sn bhd: t.o whn p.u bef 2 out* **16/1**

5m 52.9s (32.70) **Going Correction** +1.525s/f (Heav)
WFA 4 from 5yo+ 12lb **6** Ran SP% **114.3**
Speed ratings (Par 103): **101,93,72,—,—,—**
toteswingers:1&2:£2.40, 1&3:£1.40, 2&3:£2.90 CSF £9.28 CT £18.78 TOTE £1.70: £1.10, £3.60; EX 8.50 Place 6 £489.33; Place 5 £307.93.
Owner Mrs D Thomas **Bred** Bricklow Ltd **Trained** Aberkenfig, Bridgend

FOCUS

The first flight in the back straight was omitted on both circuit because of the ground. This was run at a fair enough clip considering the conditions. The easy winner confirmed the merit of her recent improved run and is rated to the level of her best Flat form.

NOTEBOOK

Am I Blue enjoyed a nice tow through the race, and then stayed on well for an easy success having taken over turning in. She had to win under a 7lb penalty if her Hereford win was to be believed, and at least she shows she handles all sorts of ground now. Things are obviously going to get a lot tougher in future, though. (op 10-11 tchd 11-10)

You Can Of Course(IRE), a scorer over fences last November, stays really well and he pushed the winner to a point, but in the end was left well behind. He remains capable of better over both hurdles and fences. (op 11-1 tchd 12-1)

Royial(FR), a promising fourth at the course on his debut for the yard, was ridden too far out of his ground on this step up in trip. (tchd 3-1)

Hollandia(IRE), returning from a lengthy absence, having last been seen running in points, fell on his last start in a hunter chase and he showed little on this return to hurdles. Official explanation: jockey said gelding was never travelling (op 17-2)

T/Plt: £411.90 to a £1 stake. Pool:£71,209.88 - 126.20 winning tickets T/Qpdt: £62.30 to a £1 stake. Pool:£6,896.50 - 81.90 winning tickets TM

1495 - 1497a (Foreign Racing) - See Raceform Interactive

1357 SEDGEFIELD (L-H)

Tuesday, September 7

OFFICIAL GOING: Chase course: good to soft (good in places) changing to good (good to soft in places) after race 3 (3.35) hurdle course: good (good to soft in plThe final fence was omitted in all chases due to ground being under repair.

Wind: Moderate 1/2 behind, Weather: Fine and sunny

1498 BET365 JUVENILE MAIDEN HURDLE (JOHN WADE HURDLE SERIES QUALIFIER) (8 hdls) 2m 1f

2:25 (2:26) (Class 4) 3-Y-0 **£2,732** (£802; £401; £200)

Form | | | | RPR
223 **1** **Sassanian (IRE)**[7] 1442 3-10-12 0 ... (v) RichardJohnson 91+
(Tim Vaughan) *chsd ldrs: hit 3 out: sn rdn: led between last 2: clr whn nt fluent last: rdn out* **11/10**[1]
3F **2** *7* **Baraathen (USA)**[19] 1298 3-10-9 0 ... AdrianLane(3) 83
(Donald McCain) *w ldr: led appr 2 out: hdd between last 2: kpt on same pce* **7/2**[2]
3 *7* **Bojangles Andrews**[30] 3-10-12 0 ... DougieCostello 76
(Tim Pitt) *hld up in tch: effrt 3 out: one pce whn j.lft last* **80/1**
00P **4** *2 1/2* **Teela**[8] 1422 3-10-5 0 ... AndrewTinkler 67
(Ben Haslam) *hld up in rr: hdwy 3 out: one pce fr next* **22/1**
3 **5** *5* **Valantino Oyster (IRE)**[19] 1298 3-10-12 0 ... (p) BarryKeniry 71
(Ben Haslam) *nt fluent: led tl hdd & wknd 2 out* **7/1**[3]
4 **6** *3 1/2* **Miereveld**[8] 1422 3-10-5 0 ... (v) KyleJames(7) 65
(Brian Ellison) *nt fluent: chsd ldrs: hmpd by loose horse after 3rd: rdn 3 out: wknd appr next* **9/1**
U **Dazeen**[7] 3-10-12 0 ... BrianHughes —
(Paul Midgley) *t.k.h in rr: dived lft and uns rdr 1st* **9/1**

4m 10.1s (3.20) **Going Correction** -0.225s/f (Good) **7** Ran SP% **107.9**
Speed ratings (Par 103): **83,79,76,75,72 71,—**
Tote Swingers: 1&2 £1.10, 1&3 £14.20, 2&3 £31.90 CSF £4.52 TOTE £1.90: £1.10, £3.10; EX 5.20.
Owner Malcolm Page **Bred** Rathasker Stud **Trained** Aberthin, Vale of Glamorgan

FOCUS

A weak juvenile novices' hurdle run in a slow time. The form reads sound.

NOTEBOOK

Sassanian(IRE) finally got off the mark over hurdles. Runner-up on three of his first four starts, he was only third in a first-time visor at Newton Abbot latest, but was ridden with more restraint this time and that seemed to suit, coming through to take it up after two out and winning with plenty in hand. This should do his confidence good and it will be no surprise to see him defy a penalty in a similarly moderate contest. (op 5-4 tchd Evens and 11-8 in a place)

Baraathen(USA), still very much in contention when falling three out at Stratford latest, probably failed to run up to his best, but this would have helped to restore some confidence and he should do better again next time. (op 3-1 tchd 11-4)

Bojangles Andrews, a 41-rated Flat performer at up to 1m, shaped surprisingly well on this hurdles debut, although will need to improve a considerable mount to win a race.

Valantino Oyster(IRE), wearing first-time cheekpieces, didn't get home having made a lot of the running. (op 15-2 tchd 8-1)

Miereveld Official explanation: jockey said gelding had a breathing problem

1499 JOHN WADE GROUP NOVICES' HURDLE (QUALIFIER) (10 hdls) 2m 4f

3:00 (3:00) (Class 4) 4-Y-0+ **£2,732** (£802; £401; £200)

Form | | | | RPR
222 **1** **Cailin Na Ri (IRE)**[14] 1357 7-10-12 114 ... GrahamLee 110
(Martin Todhunter) *led: hdd after 2 out: lft in ld last: styd on* **5/4**[2]
P-4 **2** *4* **Rain Stops Play (IRE)**[17] 1337 8-10-9 0 ... FearghalDavis(3) 106
(Nicky Richards) *hld up in rr: hdwy 5th: nt fluent next: wnt 3rd between last 2: lft 2nd and hit last* **12/1**[3]
1-31 **3** *2* **Grand Zouki (FR)**[14] 1357 5-11-12 128 ... BarryKeniry 118
(George Moore) *chsd ldr: rdn appr 2 out: one pce: lft 3rd last* **11/10**[1]
P **4** *73* **Quo Vista (IRE)**[14] 1357 5-10-12 0 ... BrianHughes 31
(John Wade) *mid-div: outpcd and lost pl 7th: sn bhd: t.o* **100/1**
/0-6 **5** *46* **Glen Vale**[14] 1359 7-10-5 0 ... MrJohnDawson(7) —
(John Wade) *mid-div: outpcd 7th: bhd whn blnd next: t.o next* **100/1**
P **6** *1 1/2* **Train Spotter (IRE)**[14] 1359 5-10-12 0 ... BrianHarding —
(John Wade) *mid-div: outpcd 6th: bhd and reminders next: sn wl t.o* **100/1**
P **That's All Right (IRE)**[93] 7-10-5 0 ... KyleJames(7) —
(Kevin M Prendergast) *w ldr whn mstke and rdr lost irons 1st: sddle slipped: p.u bef next* **33/1**
5FP- **U** **Glaced Over**[175] 4663 5-9-12 0 ... GaryRutherford(7) 105+
(Raymond Shiels) *chsd ldrs: led sn after 2 out: 1 1/2 l ahd whn hit last and uns rdr* **50/1**
5P5 **P** **Winter Holly**[23] 1260 4-10-4 0 ... RobertWalford —
(Tim Walford) *stdd s: hld up in rr: sddle slipped and p.u bef 3rd* **25/1**

4m 50.3s (-2.40) **Going Correction** -0.225s/f (Good)
WFA 4 from 5yo+ 12lb **9** Ran SP% **111.5**
Speed ratings (Par 105): **95,93,92,63,45 44,—,—,—**
Tote Swingers: 1&2 £1.02, 1&3 £3.00, 2&3 £3.80 CSF £13.17 TOTE £2.30: £1.10, £1.80, £1.10; EX 17.00.
Owner Barry Brown **Bred** Jim McDonald **Trained** Orton, Cumbria

FOCUS

This had looked a straight match on paper, but 50-1 shot Glaced Over was all set to spring a surprise when blundering and unseating her rider at the last. The form is rated through the fortunate winner to her best, with the unseater rated as a 2l winner.

NOTEBOOK

Cailin Na Ri(IRE) was left to pick up the pieces for a second course victory. A consistent sort, having three times been a runner-up since winning at the course back in April (including behind Grand Zouki over C&D), she should continue to give a good account at a lowly level. (op 13-8 tchd 7-4 and 15-8 in a place)

Rain Stops Play(IRE) travelled well enough and readily made his ground to challenge, but then couldn't quicken in the straight. His jumping should improve as he gains further experience. (op 17-2)

Grand Zouki(FR), already a dual winner over hurdles, was conceding weight all round, but he was entitled to confirm earlier course form with the winner, so it was disappointing to see him trail in well held in third. Perhaps a return to 3m is in order. (op 6-5, tchd 5-4 in places)

That's All Right(IRE) Official explanation: jockey said saddle slipped (op 33-1)

Glaced Over, off since pulling up at the course in March, her second run over hurdles, had fallen on her first start and this represented a dramatic step forward. Always travelling strongly, she readily went on and only needed to clear the last safely to score, but her rider couldn't stay aboard. It is hoped she can bounce back from this and pick up a race. (op 33-1)

Winter Holly Official explanation: jockey said saddle slipped (op 33-1)

1500 POKER @BET365 H'CAP CHASE (14 fncs 2 omitted) 2m 4f

3:35 (3:35) (Class 4) (0-105,105) 4-Y-0+ **£3,168** (£936; £468; £234; £117)

Form | | | | RPR
633 **1** **Stolen Light (IRE)**[12] 1378 9-10-0 **79** oh1 ... (b) BrianHughes 90+
(Andrew Crook) *j.rt: mde all: styd on gamely: rdn rt out* **6/1**
16U/ **2** *2 3/4* **Festival King (IRE)**[508] 5058 8-10-11 **90** ... BrianHarding 98
(Pauline Robson) *hld up in rr: hdwy 10th: chsng ldrs and drvn next: tk 2nd 2f out: no imp* **7/2**[2]
2F6- **3** *3 1/2* **Keoghs Bar (IRE)**[26] 1242 6-11-2 **95** ... (t) PaulMoloney 99
(Irene J Monaghan, Ire) *trckd ldrs: nt fluent 9th: kpt on same pce fr 3 out: tk 3rd nr fin* **11/2**
0011 **4** *1 1/4* **Isle Of Inishmore (IRE)**[7] 1446 7-11-1 **94** ... (t) RichardJohnson 97
(Tim Vaughan) *trckd ldrs: wnt 2nd appr 2 out: kpt on same pce:* **2/1**[1]
P- **5** *6* **Colours Of Autumn (IRE)**[26] 1242 9-10-6 **85** ... (t) JohnnyFarrelly 82
(D J Ryan, Ire) *in rr: mstke 9th: tk modest 5th last: nvr on terms* **16/1**
0FP- **6** *12* **Maidstone Mixture (FR)**[278] 2670 5-10-6 **92** ... PaulGallagher(7) 77
(Paul Murphy) *chsd ldrs: hmpd bnd after 7: rdn and lost pl 3 out* **9/2**[3]
P50P **P** **Sendeed (USA)**[23] 1255 8-10-4 **90** ... (t) MrJohnDawson(7) —
(Peter Atkinson) *w wnr: blnd 1st: reminders 8th: wknd appr 2 out: 7th whn stmbld last: sn p.u: lame* **33/1**

4m 59.0s (-4.00) **Going Correction** -0.225s/f (Good) **7** Ran SP% **112.2**
Speed ratings (Par 105): **99,97,96,96,93 88,—**
Tote Swingers: 1&2 £4.80, 1&3 £2.00, 2&3 £4.10 CSF £26.71 CT £120.52 TOTE £8.80: £3.30, £3.20; EX 25.20.
Owner John Sinclair (haulage) Ltd **Bred** Moyglare Stud Farm Ltd **Trained** Middleham Moor, N Yorks

■ Stewards' Enquiry : Mr John Dawson three-day ban: careless riding (TBA)

FOCUS

A moderate handicap chase but the form is solid enough. There may still be more to come from the winner.

NOTEBOOK

Stolen Light(IRE), racing from 1lb out of the handicap, had run well the last twice and, despite going to his right at fences, he stayed on well enough to record and all-the-way success. He'll return to the course in two weeks' time. (tchd 9-2)

Festival King(IRE), returning from a 508-day absence, was solid in the market and ran a race full of promise. This should put him straight for next time, although he may fall vulnerable to the dreaded 'bounce'. (op 4-1)

Keoghs Bar(IRE) could have done without the ease in the ground, but still ran well, keeping on to deny the favourite third. (op 6-1 tchd 5-1)

Isle Of Inishmore(IRE), chasing a hat-trick following wins over hurdles at Market Rasen and Newton Abbot, looked the one to beat switched to fences, off the same mark as when winning last time, but he didn't pick up as expected under pressure and had no apparent excuse. (op 13-8 tchd 9-4)

1501 CASINO @BET365 H'CAP HURDLE (10 hdls) 2m 4f
4:10 (4:10) (Class 4) (0-115,115) 4-Y-0+ £2,732 (£802; £401; £200)

Form				RPR
-131	1		**Maska Pony (IRE)**[8] 1426 6-11-4 107 7ex GrahamLee (George Moore) *hld up in rr: jnd ldrs 4th: led after 3 out: jnd between last 2: hld on gamely* 5/4[1]	119
3P41	2	¾	**All For The Cause (IRE)**[17] 1329 8-11-12 115 (t) BarryKeniry (John Davies) *hld up in rr: wnt prom 6th: chsd wnr 2 out: chal on bit between last 2: rdn and no ex fnl 50yds* 16/1	126
303-	3	21	**Helieorbea**[10] 3868 4-11-1 105 DougieCostello (Tim Easterby) *hld up: wnt prom 5th: one pce appr 2 out: tk modest 3rd last* 10/1	94
6334	4	½	**Soubriquet (IRE)**[10] 1405 7-11-4 107 (t) MichaelMcAlister (Maurice Barnes) *chsd ldrs: reminders 5th: one pce appr 2 out* 7/1[3]	97
P200	5	1	**Osolomio (IRE)**[18] 1108 7-11-9 112 (e) AlanO'Keeffe (Jennie Candlish) *led: hdd after 3 out: kpt on one pce fr next* 8/1	101
14-3	6	1	**Lawgiver (IRE)**[111] 396 9-11-2 112 (p) KyleJames(7) (Marjorie Fife) *in tch: drvn 5th: lost pl next: kpt on in own time fr 2 out* 12/1	100
F2F4	7	6	**Thelobstercatcher**[13] 1368 6-11-11 114 (p) RichardJohnson (Peter Bowen) *chsd ldrs: lost pl appr 2 out: eased run-in* 5/1[2]	96
-0P0	8	2¼	**Oniz Tiptoes (IRE)**[17] 1329 9-10-4 96 (v) HarryHaynes(3) (John Wainwright) *in tch: drvn 5th: sn lost pl: bhd fr next* 28/1	76
0P06	P		**Samizdat (FR)**[10] 1405 7-10-4 100 MissECSayer(7) (Dianne Sayer) *chsd ldrs: lost pl 6th: sn bhd: p.u bef 3 out* 28/1	—

4m 44.9s (-7.80) **Going Correction** -0.225s/f (Good)
WFA 4 from 5yo+ 12lb 9 Ran SP% **114.3**
Speed ratings (Par 105): **106,105,97,97,96 96,93,93,—**
Tote Swingers: 1&2 £6.00, 1&3 £6.40, 2&3 £39.50 CSF £21.52 CT £139.70 TOTE £2.10: £1.10, £5.00, £3.90; EX 27.60.
Owner Mrs J M Gray **Bred** Twelve Oaks Stud Establishment **Trained** Middleham Moor, N Yorks

FOCUS
Just a modest handicap hurdle. The winner was well in on his recent improved form and is rated to the same level. The second is rated in line with his best chase form.

NOTEBOOK
Maska Pony(IRE), already twice a winner this year, including a moderate novices' hurdle at Cartmel latest, looked the one to beat under a 7lb penalty and he showed a particularly good attitude, fending off the strong-travelling runner-up, who had looked all over the winner for most of the straight. He can continue to progress, but will be given a short break first. (op 13-8, tchd 7-4 in a place)
All For The Cause(IRE), raised 5lb for his recent Market Rasen success, travelled much the best under Andrew Tinkler, who could thought he could take the winner in the straight, but the response wasn't what he expected and in the end he was just held. (op 14-1 tchd 18-1)
Helieorbea, trying this trip for the first time, may not have stayed, but certainly ran well enough to suggest he can win again over hurdles. (op 11-1 tchd 14-1)
Soubriquet(IRE) was readily left behind. (op 9-1)
Thelobstercatcher failed to reproduce the form of his latest Bangor effort and was disappointing. Official explanation: jockey said that the trainer was unable to offer any explanation (tchd 4-1 and 11-2 in a place)

1502 BET365 BEST ODDS GUARRANTEED H'CAP CHASE (11 fncs 2 omitted) 2m 110y
4:45 (4:45) (Class 4) (0-115,112) 4-Y-0+ £3,285 (£1,053; £585)

Form				RPR
0-60	1		**Calculaite**[101] 515 9-11-12 112 GrahamLee (Martin Todhunter) *trckd ldrs: shkn up after 4th: wnt 2nd 8th: styd on run-in: led nr fin* 13/2	124
00/2	2	½	**Film Festival (USA)**[34] 748 7-11-1 108 KyleJames(7) (Brian Ellison) *led: quite keen: nt fluent 2nd: clr next: reminders between last 2: 5 l ahd whn untidy last last: hdd nr fin* 2/1[1]	119
4052	3	9	**Schinken Otto (IRE)**[14] 1358 9-10-0 91 JamesHalliday(5) (Malcolm Jefferson) *chsd ldrs: rdn 3 out: btn next* 7/2[2]	94
554U	P		**Skiddaw Jones**[14] 1358 10-10-0 86 oh7 (t) MichaelMcAlister (Maurice Barnes) *chsd ldr: j.rt: lost pl 7th: bhd whn mstke next: sn p.u* 9/2	—
34	P		**Tiger King (GER)**[17] 1342 9-10-2 88 WilsonRenwick (P Monteith) *in rr: blnd 1st: bhd whn reminders 5th: t.o whn j. slowly next: p.u bef next* 4/1[3]	—

4m 2.50s (-6.10) **Going Correction** -0.225s/f (Good) 5 Ran SP% **107.1**
Speed ratings (Par 105): **105,104,100,—,—**
CSF £19.22 TOTE £11.30: £5.90, £1.10; EX 21.30.
Owner The Hexham Handicappers **Bred** Capt J H Wilson **Trained** Orton, Cumbria

FOCUS
No hanging around here, with Film Festival shooting into the early lead and racing clear for much of the way, but he was eventually worn down by top weight Calculaite. Ordinary form, with the winner rating a 3lb personal best.

NOTEBOOK
Calculaite loves it at this course, and he got up in the dying strides under an excellent ride from Graham Lee. Although well beaten in a selling hurdle latest, he looked interesting on the pick of his form returned to fences, and jumped well throughout, suggesting he could go well again if the handicapper doesn't put him up much. (op 6-1 tchd 7-1)
Film Festival(USA), twice a winner on the Flat this summer, had shown fair form over fences without winning, and this looked his day, finding himself in a clear lead still turning for home. However, his lead was slowly being eroded with each stride and he couldn't quite hang on, a mistake at the last not helping. He jumped well in the main, though, and winning something similar shouldn't be too difficult. (op 15-8 tchd 7-4)
Schinken Otto(IRE) failed to back up his latest C&D second, although he didn't run badly. (op 11-4)
Skiddaw Jones was 7lb out of the handicap but should still have done better. (op 9-2 tchd 5-1)
Tiger King(GER) failed to jump on this first start over fences and was the first one pulled up. (op 9-2 tchd 5-1)

1503 BET365.COM H'CAP CHASE (18 fncs 3 omitted) 3m 3f
5:20 (5:22) (Class 5) (0-95,91) 5-Y-0+ £2,602 (£764; £382; £190)

Form				RPR
001F	1		**Archie's Wish**[8] 1423 6-10-7 72 BarryKeniry (Micky Hammond) *trckd ldr: drvn 2 out: upsides last: sn led: styd on to forge clr over 1f out: eased towards fin* 5/2[2]	89+
53P5	2	7	**Executive's Hall (IRE)**[14] 1360 6-10-0 65 (v[1]) BrianHughes (Andrew Crook) *led: qckند 13th: jnd last: sn hdd: kpt on same pce* 5/2[2]	71
4P31	3	6	**Moon Melody (GER)**[2] 1478 7-10-11 79 7ex DPFahy(3) (Evan Williams) *hld up wl in tch: chsng ldrs 3 out: sn drvn: one pce between last 2* 7/4[1]	80
115	4	30	**Shulmin**[12] 1376 10-11-7 91 JamesHalliday(5) (Carol Ferguson) *hld up wl in tch: drvn: outpcd and lost pl 3 out: bhd whn eased fnl 2f* 7/1[3]	73

6m 50.4s (1.40) **Going Correction** -0.225s/f (Good) 4 Ran SP% **106.0**
Speed ratings: **88,85,84,75**
CSF £8.59 TOTE £4.70; EX 7.70.
Owner The Black Bull Partnership **Bred** Peter Cassidy **Trained** Middleham Moor, N Yorks

FOCUS
A weak handicap chase. The winner improved and was value for further.

NOTEBOOK
Archie's Wish, a course winner off 7lb lower on his penultimate start, was held when falling at Cartmel less than a week later and he was trying this sort of trip for the first time, having never previously gone beyond 2m6f. He had no trouble with it, though, taking over soon after the last and staying on strongly to get well on top. There should be more to come from this 6-y-o and he looks one to keep on side. (op 9-4)
Executive's Hall(IRE) came back to life in the first-time visor, enjoying himself out in front, but in the end he was no match for the winner. (op 7-2 tchd 4-1)
Moon Melody(GER), shouldering a penalty for his comfy Fontwell victory just two days earlier, failed to reproduce the form and may have found the race coming too soon. (op 2-1 tchd 6-4)
Shulmin, whose winning run came to an end when returning from five months off at Cartmel latest, fared only a little better this time and has it all to prove at present. (op 7-2 tchd 8-1)

1504 FINANCIALS @BET365 H'CAP HURDLE (8 hdls) 2m 1f
5:50 (5:53) (Class 5) (0-95,95) 4-Y-0+ £1,821 (£534; £267; £133)

Form				RPR
/540	1		**Zahara Joy**[14] 1357 7-10-7 76 (t) MichaelMcAlister (Maurice Barnes) *hdwy to chse ldrs 3rd: led bef 2 out: drew clr between last 2: drvn out* 13/2[3]	83+
54P-	2	7	**World Of Events (USA)**[136] 5386 5-11-12 95 WilsonRenwick (Howard Johnson) *prom: chsd ldrs 3 out: 2nd whn hit 2 out: kpt on same pce* 5/1[2]	96
006-	3	2¼	**River Rhapsody (IRE)**[156] 5012 4-11-0 83 PaulMoloney (Evan Williams) *hld up in rr: hdwy 5th: chsng ldrs next: kpt on same pce fr 2 out* 14/1	81
-600	4	1¾	**Bocciani (GER)**[14] 1360 5-11-2 88 JamesO'Farrell(3) (Dianne Sayer) *led into s: sn chsng ldrs: led after 3rd: hdd bef 2 out: one pce* 10/1	84
0015	5	1¾	**Perez (IRE)**[10] 1407 8-10-6 82 (vt) PaulGallagher(7) (Wilf Storey) *in rr: hdwy 5th: chsng ldrs next: one pce appr 2 out* 9/2[1]	76
U0P0	6	4	**Humourous (IRE)**[14] 1362 8-10-2 71 BrianHughes (Brian Storey) *chsd ldrs: lost pl after 5th: no ch after* 11/1	61
-135	7	2½	**Authentic Act (IRE)**[54] 1005 6-10-11 80 BrianHarding (Martin Todhunter) *towards rr: hdwy 5th: chsng ldrs next: lost pl and hit 2 out: 6th whn eased run-in* 5/1[2]	70
PPUF	8	13	**Lindseyfield Lodge (IRE)**[58] 955 9-10-13 85 RyanMania(3) (Robert Johnson) *led: j.rt 1st: hdd after 3rd: hit 3 out: sn wknd* 10/1	60
005-	P		**Handsome Chap**[410] 1052 5-10-0 74 JamesHalliday(5) (Ian McInnes) *j.rt 1st: chsd ldrs: wkng whn mstke 5th: bhd whn p.u bef next* 25/1	—
-U05	P		**Lord Francois (FR)**[19] 1295 5-11-10 93 RichardJohnson (Tim Vaughan) *t.k.h in rr: hit 2nd and 4th: sme hdwy 5th: wknd next: last whn p.u bef last* 8/1	—

4m 3.30s (-3.60) **Going Correction** -0.225s/f (Good)
WFA 4 from 5yo+ 11lb 10 Ran SP% **113.0**
Speed ratings (Par 103): **99,95,94,93,93 91,89,83,—,—**
Tote Swingers: 1&2 £6.60, 1&3 £15.30, 2&3 £12.00. totesuper7: Win: Not won, Place: £47.00. CSF £38.28 CT £436.54 TOTE £10.20: £3.70, £1.50, £6.40; EX 54.60 Place 6: £45.84 Place 5: £38.06..
Owner Arthur B Graham **Bred** Arthur B Graham **Trained** Farlam, Cumbria

FOCUS
A low-grade handicap hurdle that was won in authoritative fashion by Zahara Joy. She rates a small step up, with the second to his mark.

NOTEBOOK
Zahara Joy, unplaced in five previous attempts over hurdles, including twice at this course, proved a different proposition switched to handicaps here, taking over before the straight and scooting clear from after the second-last. The handicapper is sure to make life much tougher for her in future, but there could be more to come and it will be interesting to see how she fares next time. (op 15-2 tchd 8-1)
World Of Events(USA), another making his handicap debut, travelled really well into the straight, but he made a slight mistake two out and was soon outpaced by the winner. He kept on well for second and can pick up a small race if building on this. (tchd 11-2)
River Rhapsody(IRE) ◆, making his handicap debut, certainly caught the eye back in third. Held up early on, he never really got close enough to challenge under Paul Moloney, who was certainly keen not to be overly hard on him down the straight, just nursing him into the places after the last. He would almost certainly have finished second under a more animated ride and he'll no doubt be a popular choice wherever he turns up next. (op 13-2)
Bocciani(GER) ran a bit better returned to hurdles. (tchd 11-1)
Perez(IRE) again gave the impression this sort of mark is beyond him. (op 13-2)
Authentic Act(IRE) was slow at a few of his hurdles and could never get involved. (op 9-2 tchd 4-1)
Lord Francois(FR) took a fierce hold in rear and gave himself little chance of competing. (op 9-1)
T/Plt: £54.70 to a £1 stake. Pool:£78,253 - 1,043.06 winning tickets T/Qpdt: £34.40 to a £1 stake. Pool:£4,306 - 92.45 winning tickets WG

1090 UTTOXETER (L-H)
Wednesday, September 8

OFFICIAL GOING: Chase course - good to soft; hurdle course - good (chs 6.4; hdl 6.9)
Final hurdle in the back straight omitted in all hurdle races; Final fence omitted in all chase races. Divided bends with chasers on outside and hurdlers on inside.
Wind: Nil Weather: Fine and sunny

1505 PETER & LINDA DOUGLAS WEDDING ANNIVERSARY NOVICES' HURDLE (10 hdls 2 omitted) 2m 4f 110y
2:20 (2:20) (Class 4) 4-Y-0+ £2,211 (£649; £324; £162)

Form				RPR
121P	1		**Calon Crwbin**[17] 1346 5-11-5 124 (t) OliverDayman(7) (Alison Thorpe) *a.p: led and mstke 3 out: sn clr: nt fluent last: easily* 6/4[1]	132+
-121	2	29	**Black Annie (IRE)**[27] 1233 5-10-12 115 (t) APMcCoy (Paul Webber) *w ldr to 7th: sn rdn: wknd 2 out* 9/4[2]	90

0 **3** *1 1/4* **Copsehill Girl (IRE)**[39] 1146 5-10-5 0 DougieCostello 81
(Ian Williams) *prom: blnd 2nd: rdn after 7th: wknd after 3 out* **16/1**

60 **4** *8* **Youandme (IRE)**[7] 1449 8-10-9 0 (p) PeterToole(3) 81
(Ray Peacock) *led to 3 out: sn wknd: t.o* **150/1**

0 **5** *3/4* **That's Some Milan (IRE)**[4] 1466 5-10-12 0 WarrenMarston 80
(Milton Harris) *mid-div: rdn 7th: nvr on terms: t.o* **50/1**

00-0 **6** *10* **Behest**[7] 1450 5-10-2 46 SeanQuinlan(3) 64
(Robin Mathew) *hld up: sme hdwy after 7th: sn wknd: t.o* **150/1**

0/0- **7** *48* **Middleton Red (IRE)**[133] 53 6-10-12 0 JodieMogford 28
(Graham Smith) *hld up: plld hrd: bhd fr 5th: t.o* **100/1**

00 **8** *1 3/4* **Shuttle Diplomacy (IRE)**[9] 1426 5-10-5 0 JohnnyFarrelly 19
(Elliott Cooper) *mid-div: rdn whn mstke 7th: sn lost tch: t.o* **100/1**

9 *8* **Womaniser (IRE)**[224] 6-10-5 0 MrRichardCollinson(7) 19
(Clive Drew) *hld up: sme hdwy after 7th: sn wknd: t.o* **80/1**

60/- **10** *24* **Lambrini Classic**[630] 2832 7-10-12 0 BrianHughes —
(Lisa Williamson) *hld up: stmbld 3rd: bhd fr 5th: t.o* **50/1**

0-00 **11** *2 1/4* **Sheriff Hall (IRE)**[112] 397 5-10-12 0 BrianHarding —
(George Charlton) *hld up: bhd fr 5th: t.o* **25/1**

2-41 **P** **Arcadia Boy (IRE)**[20] 1295 7-11-2 106 AdrianLane(3) —
(Donald McCain) *chsd ldrs: rdn after 6th: wknd next: t.o whn p.u bef 3 out* **7/1**

F164 **F** **Totoman**[12] 1392 5-11-5 112 (t) RichardJohnson —
(Tim Vaughan) *chsd ldrs: disputing cl 2nd whn fell 3 out* **5/1**[3]

4m 58.7s (-5.30) **Going Correction** -0.55s/f (Firm)
WFA 4 from 5yo+ 12lb 13 Ran SP% **118.1**
Speed ratings (Par 105): **88,76,76,73,73 69,51,50,47,38 37,—,—**
toteswingers:1&2:£1.10, 1&3:£8.80, 2&3:£12.60 CSF £4.90 TOTE £2.50: £1.10, £1.10, £3.00; EX 5.50.

Owner Hanford's Chemist Ltd **Bred** R W And Mrs B D Neale **Trained** Bronwydd Arms, Carmarthens

FOCUS
An uncompetitive novice event. The easy winner is rated to his mark with his main rivals all well below form. The form makes sense on time compared with other handicaps.

NOTEBOOK
Calon Crwbin was heavily backed and proved far too good for his rivals, running out a very easy winner. He travelled best throughout and didn't have to be extended to go clear from the third-last. The ground went against him in better company on his previous outing, but he previously had a likeable profile and his rider's 7lb claim was a definite advantage under his double penalty back against ordinary novices. It's hoped the handicapper doesn't take the form literally now, however. (op 9/4)

Black Annie(IRE) proved easy to back and was in trouble before the home straight. She looked to be racing somewhat awkwardly from three out and the fact she took time to master Youandme would suggest she had an off-day here. (op 15/8)

Copsehill Girl(IRE) took time to really get the hang of things on this hurdling bow. A former point winner, she looks as though an even longer trip is needed in this sphere and she is more one for handicaps down the line. (op 12/1)

Youandme(IRE) was always on the front end and turned in his most encouraging effort so far, probably as a result of cheekpieces being fitted. He can now go handicapping.

Shuttle Diplomacy(IRE) Official explanation: jockey said mare had a breathing problem

Arcadia Boy(IRE) Official explanation: trainer had no explanation for the poor form shown (op 7/1)

Totoman was just held prior to falling, but would've surely been second had he stayed on his feet. (op 7/1)

1506 DAVIDPARRYRACING.COM FOR SYNDICATES CONDITIONAL JOCKEYS' (S) HURDLE (9 hdls 1 omitted) 2m

2:55 (2:55) (Class 5) 4-7-Y-O **£1,561** (£458; £229; £114)

Form RPR

2252 **1** **Tri Nations (UAE)**[13] 1375 5-10-12 105 (bt[1]) HenryBrooke(8) 111
(Donald McCain) *hld up: hdwy 5th: led appr 2 out: sn rdn: mstke last: all out* **2/1**[1]

1024 **2** *nk* **Sadler's Star (GER)**[15] 1359 7-11-6 115 (p) HarrySkelton 111
(Michael Blake) *hld up: hdwy 6th: rdn after 3 out: chsd wnr next: styd on* **5/2**[2]

111- **3** *6* **Gamesters Lady**[58] 4841 7-11-1 115 (b) MarcGoldstein 101+
(Jim Best) *led: rdn and hdd appr 2 out: styd on same pce appr last* **3/1**[3]

P/ **4** *8* **Straight Face (IRE)**[36] 3087 6-10-12 0 TomMolloy 92
(David Evans) *prom: lost pl 3rd: handy again and reminder after 5th: rdn and wknd after 3 out* **14/1**

230- **5** *6* **Petrosian**[212] 2788 6-11-6 111 (p) DonalDevereux 95+
(Dai Burchell) *chsd ldr: hit 3rd: rdn and wknd after 3 out* **12/1**

00 **6** *17* **Nouailhas**[9] 1433 4-10-7 0 PeterHatton(5) 69
(Reg Hollinshead) *hld up: racd keenly: hdwy 3rd: rdn and wknd after 6th: t.o* **40/1**

0U20 **P** **Hi Wycombe (IRE)**[9] 1431 6-10-12 99 SamTwiston-Davies —
(David Bridgwater) *chsd ldrs tl rdn and wknd 5th: t.o whn p.u bef 3 out* **10/1**

3m 50.3s (-4.90) **Going Correction** -0.55s/f (Firm)
WFA 4 from 5yo+ 11lb 7 Ran SP% **112.8**
Speed ratings: **90,89,86,82,79 71,—**
toteswingers:1&2:£1.10, 1&3:£1.40, 2&3:£2.90 CSF £7.26 TOTE £2.40: £1.30, £1.20; EX 6.80.The winner was bought in for 5,000gns.

Owner Mr & Mrs Peter James Douglas **Bred** Darley **Trained** Cholmondeley, Cheshire
■ Henry Brooke's first winner since turning professional.

FOCUS
A fair seller, confined to conditional riders, and it was fought out by some real characters. The winner is rated to his best.

NOTEBOOK
Tri Nations(UAE) attracted solid support with first-time blinkers added to his tongue tie and scored under a strong ride. He had plenty to find at the weights, but rarely are BHA ratings a solid guide in these races and his recent level was as good as his main rivals. It was his first win since scoring in this grade in April and the fact he scored would suggest the ground was not riding that slow. He was bought back in for 5,000gns. (op 3/1 tchd 100/30)

Sadler's Star(GER) had cheekpieces back on and did his best work late in the day. He had 10lb in hand of the winner according to official figures, but rarely performs up to his mark of 115 and once again didn't look that willing under pressure. (op 3/1)

Gamesters Lady came into this bidding for the four-timer over hurdles and has been in good heart on the level. She wasn't able to get her own way out in front and was pretty much done with after being headed by the winner. (op 2/1)

Straight Face(IRE) went without headgear on this switch to hurdling and ran in snatches from an early stage. She kept on late, suggesting she gets the trip, and it wouldn't be at all surprising to see the headgear back on next time in this sphere. (op 20/1)

Petrosian left the impression this return from a 212-day break was needed. (op 11/1)

1507 BESWICKS SOLICITORS H'CAP HURDLE (12 hdls 2 omitted) 3m

3:30 (3:36) (Class 4) (0-110,110) 4-Y-0+ **£2,211** (£649; £324; £162)

Form RPR

6/61 **1** **Ben's Folly (IRE)**[11] 1401 5-11-10 108 RichardJohnson 121+
(Tim Vaughan) *chsd ldrs: led and j. slowly 4th: rdn after 2 out: styd on wl* **9/2**

P421 **2** *5* **Auberge (IRE)**[9] 1428 6-10-0 87 7ex RyanMania(3) 93
(Dianne Sayer) *led 2nd to 4th: remained w wnr tl mstke 3 out: sn rdn: no ex last* **3/1**[1]

0323 **3** *7* **Saintly Lady (IRE)**[13] 1379 5-10-9 96 DonalDevereux(3) 96
(Peter Bowen) *hld up: hdwy u.p 9th: styd on same pce fr 2 out* **14/1**

544P **4** *17* **Smiling Applause**[24] 1259 11-10-0 84 oh16 (p) DavidEngland 68
(Harry Chisman) *led tl j. slowly 2nd: remained handy tl rdn and wknd after 9th* **66/1**

040- **5** *11* **Whatdoidowiththat**[459] 621 7-10-2 96 BenjaminStephens(10) 70
(Sue Smith) *hld up: rdn and wknd appr 8th: t.o* **22/1**

202 **6** *12* **The Fox's Decree**[7] 1449 6-11-1 99 (t) WarrenMarston 66
(Martin Keighley) *chsd ldrs: rdn after 9th: wkng whn blnd 3 out: t.o* **4/1**[3]

F406 **7** *15* **Follow On**[9] 1428 8-10-3 87 (t) MichaelMcAlister 37
(Maurice Barnes) *hld up: hmpd 2nd: rdn and wknd after 8th: t.o* **16/1**

4150 **8** *42* **Mzuri Bay**[22] 1275 5-11-12 110 (t) MarkGrant 22
(Brendan Duke) *hld up: hdwy 4th: mstke 7th: sn rdn and wknd: t.o* **20/1**

/P-0 **P** **Wild Side Of Life (IRE)**[14] 1368 7-10-9 100 MrTomDavid(7) —
(Tim Vaughan) *hld up: hmpd 2nd: a in rr: t.o whn p.u bef 9th* **33/1**

0F51 **F** **Mad Moose (IRE)**[13] 1380 6-11-9 110 SamTwiston-Davies(3) —
(Nigel Twiston-Davies) *chsd ldrs: hmpd and fell 2nd* **7/2**[2]

4013 **P** **Kristallo (GER)**[52] 1035 5-11-8 106 (b) SamJones —
(Paul Webber) *hld up: hdwy 9th: rdn and wknd bef next: t.o whn p.u bef 3 out* **7/1**

5m 48.8s (-16.40) **Going Correction** -0.55s/f (Firm) 11 Ran SP% **124.0**
Speed ratings (Par 105): **105,103,101,95,91 87,82,68,—,— —**
toteswingers:1&2:£3.70, 1&3:£12.80, 2&3:£9.00 CSF £19.27 CT £183.42 TOTE £6.10: £2.20, £1.20, £3.20; EX 18.20.

Owner David Lovell **Bred** Mrs Kathleen Hennessy **Trained** Aberthin, Vale of Glamorgan
■ Eastwell Smiles (6/1) was withdrawn after unseating his rider and bolting before the start. Deduct 10p in the £ under R4.

FOCUS
An eventful race, but the form still looks sound enough. The cosy winner is on the upgrade.

NOTEBOOK
Ben's Folly(IRE) relished this further step up in distance and followed up his Cartmel success 11 days earlier. He comfortably went clear of the runner-up three out and wasn't helped by the loose horse late on, so rates value for a little further. There's likely more to come from him over this sort of distance, but the best of him probably will not be seen until he goes chasing in due course. (op 6/1 tchd 5/1)

Auberge(IRE) was penalised for success at Cartmel nine days previously and, never far away, posted a solid effort in defeat. She helps to set the standard. (op 7/2 tchd 4/1)

Saintly Lady(IRE) got caught out when the pace lifted on the final circuit and came under heavy pressure. She stayed on dourly, though, getting the trip and this was more like it in defeat. (op 12/1)

Smiling Applause plugged on and at least completed.

Whatdoidowiththat is sure to come on plenty for the run.

1508 STAFFORDSHIRE WEDDING SHOW H'CAP HURDLE (10 hdls 2 omitted) 2m 4f 110y

4:05 (4:05) (Class 3) (0-135,130) 4-Y-0 **£3,928** (£1,160; £580; £290; £145)

Form RPR

20-6 **1** **Working Title (IRE)**[114] 372 8-11-7 130 DavidBass(5) 141+
(Nicky Henderson) *hld up in tch: plld hrd: led 3 out: clr whn blnd last: comf* **11/2**[2]

214- **2** *6* **No Rules**[27] 4450 5-10-13 117 MattieBatchelor 118+
(Mark H Tompkins) *hld up: rdn after 7th: hdwy 3 out: chsd wnr appr last: no imp* **20/1**

3511 **3** *1 3/4* **Ripalong Lad (IRE)**[12] 1391 9-11-12 130 (p) TomO'Brien 130+
(Peter Bowen) *prom: lost pl 5th: hdwy 3 out: styd on to go 3rd flat* **6/1**[3]

12-0 **4** *1 3/4* **Pokanoket (IRE)**[123] 206 7-11-2 125 JamesHalliday(5) 121
(Malcolm Jefferson) *hld up: hdwy 6th: mstke 3 out: sn rdn to chse wnr tl no ex appr last* **10/1**

P-05 **5** *4 1/2* **Royal Max (IRE)**[47] 1084 4-10-3 108 (t) PaddyBrennan 99
(Ian Williams) *hld up: hdwy after 7th: rdn and wknd bef last* **7/1**

5612 **6** *19* **Word Of Warning**[14] 1364 6-10-11 115 GrahamLee 100+
(Martin Todhunter) *hld up: mstke 2nd: hdwy 3 out: rdn and wknd bef next: t.o* **7/2**[1]

2200 **7** *16* **Santa's Son (IRE)**[11] 1406 10-11-2 123 (t) AdamPogson(3) 84
(Charles Pogson) *led 2nd tl hdd & wknd 3 out: t.o* **28/1**

-340 **8** *13* **Bathwick Man**[14] 1364 5-10-13 117 (tp) TomScudamore 66
(David Pipe) *led to 2nd: remained w ldr: ev ch 3 out: sn rdn and wknd: t.o* **14/1**

5F02 **9** *23* **Flying Doctor**[11] 1405 7-11-3 121 (p) JohnnyFarrelly 49
(Elliott Cooper) *chsd ldrs tl rdn and wknd after 7th: t.o* **16/1**

-226 **10** *1 3/4* **Just Victor**[33] 1196 5-10-10 114 (t) SamThomas 41
(Paul Webber) *hld up: hit 5th: bhd fr 7th: t.o* **12/1**

S115 **11** *shd* **Tarvini (IRE)**[17] 1346 5-11-9 130 (p) RichieMcLernon(3) 57
(Jonjo O'Neill) *mid-div: rdn and lost pl after 6th: sn bhd: t.o* **8/1**

1300 **U** **Valley Ride (IRE)**[18] 1332 10-11-9 130 (p) DonalDevereux(3) 115
(Peter Bowen) *chsd ldrs: rdn and wkng whn stmbld and uns rdr after 2 out* **18/1**

4m 55.5s (-8.50) **Going Correction** -0.55s/f (Firm)
WFA 4 from 5yo+ 12lb 12 Ran SP% **118.3**
Speed ratings (Par 107): **94,91,91,90,88 81,75,70,61,60 60,—**
toteswingers:1&2:£29.10, 1&3:£7.50, 2&3:£18.20 CSF £105.99 CT £687.71 TOTE £7.50: £2.50, £7.90, £1.60; EX 186.00.

Owner Auld Hayes & Murphy **Bred** Mrs Caroline O'Driscoll **Trained** Upper Lambourn, Berks

FOCUS
Not the strongest race for the grade but still a decent handicap. It was run at a decent gallop and produced a clear-cut winner who rates a personal best.

NOTEBOOK
Working Title(IRE) again advertised his ability to go well when fresh and ran out a comfortable winner on this return to action. He was one of the top weights, but had a decent claimer aboard and simply proved in a different league to these rivals. It was actually his first win in handicap company and a hefty rise is forthcoming, but he is a likeable sort that could just have more to offer as a chaser this season. (op 5/1)

No Rules ◆, making his handicap debut, kept on to win the race for second and this was an encouraging return to hurdling. He wants more positive handling over this trip now and definitely has a handicap in him off this sort of mark. (op 14/1)

Ripalong Lad(IRE) was hiked up 13lb for his taking win at Ffos Las 12 days earlier. He found this too sharp and will still be of some interest when reverting to further. No doubt his trainer will have one eye on his much lower chase mark now, too. (op 5/1)
Pokanoket(IRE) proved suited by this drop back in trip and ran a fair race on her return from a four-month break. The handicapper probably just has her measure, though. (op 9/1)
Royal Max(IRE) threatened from the third-last, but his effort flattened out and he rates a non-stayer. This wasn't a bad effort for a 4-y-o, on just his second outing for the stable, and he can find less competitive assignments. (op 10/1)
Word Of Warning, well backed, never looked a serious player from off the pace and tended to run in snatches, so now has a touch to prove. Official explanation: trainer said, regarding running, that the gelding was unsuited by the good ground (op 5/1)

1509 TOTAL PEOPLE LTD H'CAP CHASE (13 fncs 2 omitted) 2m 4f

4:40 (4:40) (Class 4) (0-115,115) 4-Y-0+ **£2,661** (£786; £393; £196; £98)

Form RPR
4212 1 **Frosted Grape (IRE)**[3] 1481 4-10-6 **108** 7ex..............(b) TomScudamore 112+
(David Pipe) *chsd ldr tl led after 6th: chal fr 2 out: j.rt: hmpd rival and lft wl clr last* **13/8**[1]
F15U 2 *41* **Builteoir (IRE)**[21] 1281 8-10-2 **91**................................ PaulMoloney 76
(Evan Williams) *hld up: hdwy 9th: rdn and wknd 3 out: t.o* **16/1**
3324 3 *17* **Kilshannig (IRE)**[52] 1034 5-10-12 **101**................................(t) APMcCoy 64
(Jonjo O'Neill) *prom: lost pl 5th: sn drvn along: hit 9th: wknd bef next: t.o* **4/1**[2]
3-44 4 *1 1/4* **Silver Steel (FR)**[20] 1299 7-11-6 **109**................................ GrahamLee 71
(Richard Ford) *hld up: mstke 3rd: hdwy 9th: wknd 3 out: t.o* **16/1**
P424 5 *1 1/2* **Glengarra (IRE)**[22] 1277 13-10-13 **102**.....................(tp) RichardJohnson 62
(Liam Corcoran) *led tl after 6th: chsd wnr to 9th: sn rdn and wknd: t.o* **28/1**
3-55 6 *44* **Quincy Des Pictons (FR)**[29] 1227 6-10-10 **99**................ JodieMogford 20
(M S Tuck) *hld up and a bhd: t.o* **33/1**
P/1- P **Alfie's Sun**[416] 1006 11-11-12 **115**................................ LeightonAspell —
(Don Cantillon) *chsd ldrs: mstke 3rd: wknd 9th: t.o whn p.u bef 2 out* **16/1**
24-3 P **Beshairt**[13] 1067 6-11-7 **110**................................ ChristianWilliams —
(Dai Burchell) *hld up: a in rr: t.o whn p.u bef 2 out* **18/1**
3331 F **Moulin De La Croix**[2] 1491 6-11-2 **108** 7ex.......(t) SamTwiston-Davies(3) 120+
(Nigel Twiston-Davies) *prom: chsd wnr 9th: ev ch fr 2 out tl hmpd and fell last* **9/2**[3]
-136 P **Badger Foot (IRE)**[24] 1255 5-11-6 **112**.................... RichieMcLernon(3) —
(Jonjo O'Neill) *hld up in tch: drvn along 6th: wknd next: t.o whn p.u bef 8th* **12/1**

5m 1.30s (-4.20) **Going Correction** -0.075s/f (Good)
WFA 4 from 5yo+ 1lb **10** Ran SP% **113.3**
Speed ratings (Par 105): **105,88,81,81,80 63,—,—,—,—**
toteswingers:1&2:£7.30, 1&3:£2.70, 2&3:£11.80 CSF £26.71 CT £90.57 TOTE £2.50: £1.10, £4.60, £1.40; EX 29.20.
Owner The Wise Partners **Bred** Austin Curran **Trained** Nicholashayne, Devon

FOCUS
A moderate handicap that was run at a decent gallop and most were found out before turning for home. The in-form winner is flattered by her winning margin but is rated in line with her recent second. The faller was headed for another personal best.

NOTEBOOK
Frosted Grape(IRE) was held under her penalty at Worcester three days earlier, but she was again well backed on this quick turnout and made amends with a ready effort. She was given an aggressive ride and kept finding for her rider's urgings. She is flattered by her margin of success as she hadn't shaken off Moulin De La Croix prior to that one coming down at the last, but did just look on top at the time so rates a worthy winner. However, the handicapper was already due to put her up 7lb in the future and she could be in trouble if he takes this form literally, so her best option is perhaps to turn out under another penalty. (op 2/1)
Builteoir(IRE) caught the eye staying on late in the day on this drop in trip and would've very likely finished closer under more animated handling off the home turn, as he does stay further. He's one to look out for again when reverting to suitably quicker ground. (tchd 20/1)
Kilshannig(IRE) got well backed, but proved very hard work for his rider from an early stage and was well held prior to a bad mistake at the ninth. He plodded on in the home straight and now is surely the time to try out some form of headgear. (op 5/1 tchd 7/2)
Moulin De La Croix, like the winner, was also penalised for winning a few days earlier and has to rate as very unlucky not to have at least finished runner-up here. She was soon up on her feet. (op 7/2)

1510 HAGUE PRINT MANAGEMENT INTERMEDIATE OPEN NATIONAL HUNT FLAT RACE 2m

5:10 (5:15) (Class 6) 4-6-Y-O **£1,301** (£382; £191; £95)

Form RPR
1 **Sybarite (FR)** 4-11-0 0................................ PaddyBrennan 115+
(Nigel Twiston-Davies) *chsd ldrs: led 5f out: pushed clr fr over 1f out: easily* **6/4**[1]
1 2 *12* **Saint Luke (IRE)**[14] 1374 5-11-7 0................................ RichardJohnson 106+
(Peter Bowen) *led to 1/2-way: remained handy: rdn to chse wnr over 2f out: sn outpcd* **13/8**[2]
0 3 *6* **He's A Hawker (IRE)**[21] 1284 5-10-7 0.....................(b[1]) BrianToomey(7) 93
(Michael Mullineaux) *prom: rdn over 4f out: wknd 3f out: wnt 3rd nr fin* **33/1**
4 *hd* **Tribal Dance (IRE)** 4-11-0 0................................ CharliePoste 92
(Ben Case) *chsd ldrs: rdn over 3f out: hung lft and wknd over 1f out: lost 3rd nr fin* **12/1**
5 *14* **Sound Judgment (IRE)** 4-11-0 0................................ TomScudamore 80
(Mark Rimell) *hld up: wknd over 5f out: t.o* **22/1**
6 *4 1/2* **Search My Soul (IRE)**[108] 4-11-0 0................................ AlanO'Keeffe 76
(Jennie Candlish) *chsd ldr tl led 1/2-way: hdd 5f out: rdn and wknd over 2f out: t.o* **16/1**
7 *18* **Overpriced** 4-10-7 0................................ MichaelMcAlister 53
(Maurice Barnes) *hld up: wknd over 5f out: t.o* **66/1**
8 *7* **O'Er And Beyond** 4-11-0 0................................ BrianHarding 53
(Carol Ferguson) *hld up: a in rr: bhd fnl 6f: t.o* **100/1**
0- 9 *40* **Under A Spell (IRE)**[322] 1853 5-11-0 0................................ TjadeCollier 17
(Sue Smith) *chsd ldrs: rdn over 7f out: wknd over 5f out: t.o* **50/1**
10 *27* **One Last Tipple (IRE)** 4-10-7 0................................ MissRJefferson(7) —
(Malcolm Jefferson) *hld up: racd keenly early: pushed along 10f out: wknd 1/2-way: t.o* **6/1**[3]

3m 43.7s (-5.90) **Going Correction** -0.55s/f (Firm)
WFA 4 from 5yo 11lb **10** Ran SP% **117.7**
Speed ratings: **92,86,83,82,75 73,64,61,41,27**
toteswingers:1&2:£1.90, 1&3:£7.00, 2&3:£8.60 CSF £4.06 TOTE £2.70: £1.50, £1.10, £7.00; EX 4.30.
Owner H R Mould **Bred** Mme Andre Vagne And Bruno Vagne **Trained** Naunton, Gloucs

FOCUS
An uncompetitive bumper but an impressive debut winner who should rate much higher. The race is rated around the penalised runner-up.

NOTEBOOK
Sybarite(FR) ◆ attracted heavy support on this racecourse debut and ultimately scored pretty much as he pleased. He is certainly bred to make his mark in this sphere and is a lovely looking 4-y-o. The bit of cut in the ground helped and he should be well up to defying a penalty at this time of year, before embarking on a hurdling career. Connections may possibly take him to Cheltenham's opening October meeting next month and he would have to be respected there, despite the likely stronger opposition. (op 7/4 tchd 11/8)
Saint Luke(IRE) is well thought of, but held no chance with the winner under his penalty. He would've been better off making this more of a test and now is probably the time to go hurdling with him, where a longer trip will suit. (op 6/4 tchd 7/4)
He's A Hawker(IRE), in first-time blinkers, just got up for third and posted an improved effort despite again taking a keen early hold. He too will need further once sent hurdling.
Tribal Dance(IRE), out of a dam that scored in this sphere, didn't go unbacked for this debut and left the impression he would come on nicely for the outing. (tchd 9/1)

1511 SIMON AND SARAH AT FOINAVEN 20TH WEDDING ANNIVERSARY H'CAP CHASE (11 fncs 1 omitted) 2m

5:40 (5:41) (Class 4) (0-100,100) 4-Y-0+ **£2,732** (£802; £401; £200)

Form RPR
U-42 1 **Past Heritage**[29] 1231 11-10-0 **74** oh2................................ PaddyBrennan 85+
(Alan Jones) *hld up: hdwy 6th: led 2 out: mstke last: drvn out* **9/2**[2]
1U53 2 *1 1/2* **Sam Cruise**[22] 1273 9-11-0 **88**................................(t) AidanColeman 96
(Steve Gollings) *chsd ldr: led 7th: rdn and hdd 2 out: styd on u.p* **5/1**[3]
5522 3 *19* **Josephine Malines**[9] 1429 6-11-12 **100**.....................(t) RichardJohnson 93
(Tim Vaughan) *hld up and bhd: nt fluent 1st: j. slowly 4th: hdwy 7th: wknd 2 out* **7/2**[1]
-060 4 *9* **Rince Donn (IRE)**[21] 1283 8-11-3 **91**................................ LeightonAspell 73
(Roger Curtis) *hld up: hdwy 7th: rdn and wknd 2 out* **16/1**
0/- 5 *33* **Bajan Sunshine (IRE)**[792] 869 9-10-2 **76**........................ JamesDavies 29
(Gary Brown) *chsd ldrs tl wknd 7th: t.o* **14/1**
/043 P **Quaddick Lake (IRE)**[14] 1366 7-11-12 **100**............(bt[1]) TomScudamore —
(David Pipe) *led and hit 1st: sn clr: hit 5th: hdd and blnd 7th: wknd qckly: t.o whn p.u bef next* **7/1**
3622 P **Le Brocquy**[9] 1430 5-11-7 **95**................................(p) WarrenMarston —
(Martin Keighley) *mid-div: sn pushed along: hdwy 4th: wkng whn blunderd 2 out: sn p.u* **7/2**[1]
6P-4 P **Takelli (IRE)**[44] 1095 4-10-8 **94**................................(tp) PaulMoloney —
(Evan Williams) *mid-div: bhd fr 4th: t.o whn p.u bef 3 out* **7/1**

3m 58.8s (3.20) **Going Correction** -0.075s/f (Good)
WFA 4 from 5yo+ 11lb **8** Ran SP% **116.8**
Speed ratings (Par 105): **89,88,78,74,57 —,—,—**
toteswingers:1&2:£4.40, 1&3:£3.30, 2&3:£5.10. totesuper7: Win: Not won, Place: £91.40. CSF £28.20 CT £87.97 TOTE £6.40: £2.70, £1.30, £1.10; EX 26.40 Place 6 £12.38; Place 5 £9.26.
Owner BPD Ltd **Bred** Graham Brown **Trained** Coedkernew, Newport

FOCUS
A weak handicap, run at a strong gallop and the first pair dominated off the home turn. The idling winner is value for further and is rated in line with his 2yo best.

NOTEBOOK
Past Heritage was a market mover and got off the mark as a chaser under strong handling, giving his rider a quick-fire double. This was his first success since way back in 2005 and he is value for further, as he idled badly after hitting the final fence. However, he is a veteran and it would be a bit surprising to see him go in again next time. (op 6/1 tchd 7/2)
Sam Cruise fared best of those to race handily and posted a brave effort. He is flattered by his proximity to the winner, but was a clear second-best and deserves another winning turn. (op 11/2 tchd 9/2)
Josephine Malines, making her chasing debut, was taken off her feet early on and proved careful at her fences. She got going late, but was never going to get to the first pair and probably wants further in this sphere. (tchd 4/1)
Rince Donn(IRE) couldn't find an extra gear and remains hard to win with. (tchd 14/1)
Le Brocquy was well held prior to hitting the penultimate fence and sharply pulling up. Official explanation: jockey said gelding never travelled (op 3/1 tchd 4/1)
T/Plt: £19.90 to a £1 stake. Pool:£69,425.64 - 2,543.36 winning tickets T/Qpdt: £7.70 to a £1 satke. Pool:£5,336.75 - 510.50 winning tickets CR

1512 - 1525a (Foreign Racing) - See Raceform Interactive

[1523]LISTOWEL (L-H)

Wednesday, September 15

OFFICIAL GOING: Flat course - yielding to soft; jumps courses - good to yielding

1526a BALLYGARRY HOUSE HOTEL NOVICE HURDLE (12 hdls) 2m 4f

4:05 (4:05) 4-Y-0+ **£13,517** (£3,951; £1,871; £623)

RPR
1 **One Cool Tornado (IRE)**[17] 1416 5-11-7................................ RWalsh 134
(Paul John Gilligan, Ire) *trckd ldrs: rdn in 2nd appr 3 out: on terms fr bef 2 out: def ldr between last 2: styd on wl run-in* **9/2**[3]
2 *1 1/4* **Casey Top (IRE)**[27] 1302 7-10-13 122........................(t) BryanJCooper(5) 130
(Leonard Whitmore, Ire) *led: jnd st: hdd and kpt on wout matching wnr fr between last 2* **9/2**[3]
3 *2* **Battle Group**[24] 1346 5-11-10 132................................ TomScudamore 134
(David Pipe) *sn mid-div: prog to trck ldrs fr bef 6 out: dropped to mod 4th appr st: 3rd and kpt on wout threatening fr bef last* **7/1**
4 *1/2* **Bavard Court (IRE)**[41] 1192 4-10-4 102................................ APHeskin(5) 119
(Michael Hourigan, Ire) *in rr of mid-div: clsd fr bef 4 out: 6th fr bef next: no imp u.p and kpt on fr bef st* **33/1**
5 *5* **Our Gar (IRE)**[146] 5345 7-11-7 133................................(t) BarryGeraghty 126
(Mrs Prunella Dobbs, Ire) *chsd ldrs: clsr in 3rd travelling wl appr st: slt mstke 2 out: sn no ex and eased: slt mstke and kpt on same pce fr last* **5/2**[1]
6 *1/2* **He'Lliberemembered (IRE)**[17] 1415 7-10-11 .... MrJAFahey(7) 122
(P G Fahey, Ire) *in rr of mid-div: mstke 6th and pushed along: wnt 7th appr 3 out: sn no imp and kpt on same pce* **14/1**
7 *13* **Bruach Na Mara (IRE)**[18] 1412 7-11-4................................ RCColgan 109
(W Harney, Ire) *towards rr: sme hdwy and no imp fr bef 3 out: kpt on same pce* **50/1**
8 *1* **Carrigmartin (IRE)**[41] 1190 5-11-7 118................................ APMcCoy 111
(Edward P Harty, Ire) *t.k.h: sn trckd ldrs: mstke 6 out: rdn in 5th appr 3 out: sn no imp* **7/2**[2]
9 *16* **Imperial Shabra (IRE)**[16] 1437 6-11-0 110........................ MWBowes(7) 95
(Patrick O Brady, Ire) *prom: bad mstke 5 out: lost pl and no ex appr 3 out* **16/1**
10 *1 3/4* **Queiros Bleu (FR)**[27] 1302 6-11-7 122................................ AELynch 93
(Henry De Bromhead, Ire) *mid-div: mstke 4 out: sn btn* **10/1**

11 4 **Freneys Well**[144] 5396 10-11-0 95 MrJTMcNamara 82
(E Bolger, Ire) *a towards rr* **25/1**
12 5 **Russian War (IRE)**[21] 1369 7-11-7 119 (t) PCarberry 84
(Gordon Elliott, Ire) *a towards rr* **14/1**
13 2 **Rare Commodity (IRE)**[27] 1305 6-11-7 118 AndrewJMcNamara 82
(E J O'Grady, Ire) *trckd ldrs: slt mstke 6 out: 7th appr 4 out: wknd fr bef next* **25/1**
5m 12.3s (-12.70)
WFA 4 from 5yo+ 12lb **13** Ran SP% **140.6**
CSF £29.71 TOTE £4.60: £1.60, £2.70, £2.50; DF 53.70.
Owner Kings & Rovers Syndicate **Bred** Donal Brazil **Trained** Athenry, Co Galway

FOCUS
This looked a decent type of novice with seven dual hurdle winners, one three-time hurdles winner and three maiden hurdle winners in the line-up.

NOTEBOOK
One Cool Tornado(IRE) ◆ was ridden to go second nearing three out and was disputing the lead before the second-last. In front away from that hurdle, he stayed on under pressure. Trainer Paul Gilligan plans to send him for the same Cheltenham novices' event in November in which his subsequent Albert Bartlett winner, Berties Dream, finished third in last season, and it would be no surprise to see him tackling the Festival event in March. (op 5/1)
Casey Top(IRE) attempted to make all. Joined by the winner before two out, he was headed on landing over that hurdle and, although he stuck to his task quite well on the run-in, he was always being held. (op 5/1 tchd 6/1)
Battle Group was dropping back in trip having run second in a 2m6f handicap at Newton Abbot on his previous start. He closed on the inside to track the leaders from the eighth hurdle but came under pressure in fourth place three out. He made no impression approaching the second-last before staying on again from the final hurdle. (op 5/1)
Bavard Court(IRE), the only one in the race without a victory, was having only his seventh start and had been placed in two of his five previous attempts over hurdles. This was his most encouraging effort to date and, after beginning to make headway four out, he stayed on steadily.
Our Gar(IRE), twice a winner over the trip and having his first run since scoring at the Punchestown festival in April, was soon close up and appeared to be travelling best when closing in third after three out, However, he was a bit untidy at the second-last and had weakened and been eased before the last, where he was again not foot perfect. He should come on for the run. Official explanation: trainer said gelding scoped badly post-race (op 4/1)
He'Llberemembered(IRE), stepping up in trip following his maiden win over 2m at Galway last month, was held up. He fluffed the sixth before chasing the leaders from before three out and kept on. He was later reported to have suffered an over-reach to his near foreleg. Official explanation: trainer said gelding suffered an overreach to its near-fore in running (op 12/1)
Carrigmartin(IRE), on a hat-trick after wins on good ground over 2m Ballinrobe and over this distance at Sligo, was in mid-division when he made a mistake six out and was unable to make any impression on the leaders from three out. (op 9/2)

1527a GUINNESS KERRY NATIONAL H'CAP CHASE (GRADE A) (18 fncs) 3m
4:35 (4:35) 4-Y-0+
£85,309 (£27,256; £13,097; £4,601; £3,185; £1,769)

RPR
1 **Alfa Beat (IRE)**[17] 1420 6-10-10 137 (p) BarryGeraghty 146+
(C Byrnes, Ire) *racd wd: sn mid-div: hdwy to trck ldrs fr 7 out: led bef 3 out: sn hdd: on terms again 2 out: led last: styd on wl run-in* **6/1**[2]
2 3½ **Dancing Tornado (IRE)**[26] 1321 9-10-12 139 APMcCoy 144
(Michael Hourigan, Ire) *mid-div: mstke 6 out: 7th and hdwy fr bef 3 out: rdn into 5th bef st: mod 3rd 2 out: kpt on wout troubling wnr to go 2nd nr fin* **7/2**[1]
3 hd **Finger Onthe Pulse (IRE)**[49] 1123 9-11-5 146 (t) MPWalsh 151
(T J Taaffe, Ire) *sn disp ld: lft in ld 4 out: hdd bef next: bk in ld bef st: jnd 2 out: hdd last: dropped to 3rd nr fin* **14/1**
4 4 **Swift Counsel (IRE)**[27] 1306 9-10-0 127 AELynch 128
(John O'Callaghan, Ire) *mid-div: clsd into 6th after 5 out: 4th bef 3 out: 3rd bef st: sn no imp u.p and kpt on same pce* **16/1**
5 3½ **Northern Alliance (IRE)**[16] 1123 9-11-7 148 AndrewJMcNamara 145
(A J Martin, Ire) *sn mid-div: bad mstke 6th: prog 6 out: rdn into 6th bef st: sn no imp and kpt on same pce* **12/1**
6 3 **Will Jamie Run (IRE)**[61] 1014 9-9-12 128 CDMaxwell(3) 122
(Paul Stafford, Ire) *prom: 4th bef st: sn no imp u.p and kpt on same pce* **12/1**
7 12 **Montero (IRE)**[49] 1123 8-10-4 136 BryanJCooper(5) 118
(D T Hughes, Ire) *prom: 5th appr 6 out: lost pl after next: sn no imp* **28/1**
8 nk **Ponmeoath (IRE)**[17] 1417 10-10-9 136 PTownend 118
(E McNamara, Ire) *trckd ldrs: 7th after 5 out: 6th appr 3 out: sn no imp* **8/1**[3]
9 11 **Lucky Wish**[49] 1123 7-10-2 134 (b) EJO'Connell(5) 105
(Eoin Griffin, Ire) *chsd ldrs: hmpd 4 out: 5th appr 3 out: no ex fr bef st* **10/1**
10 9 **Golden Kite (IRE)**[46] 1145 8-10-3 130 BTO'Connell 92
(Adrian Maguire, Ire) *a towards rr* **12/1**
11 5 **Nedzer's Return (IRE)**[49] 1123 8-11-0 141 (t) DJCondon 98
(Gordon Elliott, Ire) *mid-div: prog 6 out: no ex appr 3 out* **12/1**
12 dist **Paco Jack (IRE)**[49] 1123 6-10-5 132 (t) RMPower —
(P J Rothwell, Ire) *a towards rr: t.o* **20/1**
P **Barna Bay (IRE)**[50] 1113 11-10-2 129 DJCasey —
(V T O'Brien, Ire) *mid-div tl wknd and p.u after 7 out* **25/1**
F **Deutschland (USA)**[28] 1123 7-11-4 145 (p) RWalsh —
(W P Mullins, Ire) *fell 1st* **12/1**
P **Footy Facts (IRE)**[174] 4854 10-10-2 132 PTEnright(3) —
(Robert Tyner, Ire) *mstke 1st: mid-div: no ex and p.u bef 4 out* **14/1**
F **Archie Boy (IRE)**[89] 786 8-11-1 147 (p) KMDonoghue(5) —
(Paul W Flynn, Ire) *sn disp ld: fell 4 out* **20/1**
P **Fosters Cross (IRE)**[19] 1354 8-10-6 133 NPMadden —
(Thomas Mullins, Ire) *sn towards rr: n.d whn p.u bef 3 out* **14/1**
F **Oscar Looby (IRE)**[220] 3926 7-10-11 138 (t) PCarberry —
(Noel Meade, Ire) *fell 2nd* **14/1**
5m 45.1s (-14.80) **18** Ran SP% **144.5**
CSF £31.51 CT £317.74 TOTE £7.80: £2.20, £1.40, £4.10, £4.90; DF 34.40.
Owner Barry Healy **Bred** Alex McCarthy **Trained** Ballingarry, Co Limerick

FOCUS
The meteoric rise through the ranks of Alfa Beat since joining Charles Byrnes reached what was almost an inevitable climax when he won this feature race, a performance which answered a lot of questions about him.

NOTEBOOK
Alfa Beat(IRE) ◆ came through to lead at the third last and Barry Geraghty didn't really push him until after the second last. With a Galway Plate winner upsides him on his inside, he was set for his biggest test, but he saw a good stride at the last and galloped on strongly to the line. It is unclear how far this horse can go or whether we have seen the best of him. (op 7/1 tchd 8/1)
Dancing Tornado(IRE) ◆ was a little unlucky but his method of jumping wasn't conducive to winning this. He must have a lot of ability to finish as close as he did. Held up on the inner, his jumping in general lacked the required fluency. A bad mistake six out dropped him back and jockey Tony McCoy ended up coming from further back than he would have liked. By the time he fully got back into the race early in the straight, it would have taken a herculean effort to trouble the winner. The intention is to go to Cheltenham for the Paddy Power Gold Cup in November, but surely the Galway Plate, over that trip and especially with the lack of a fence in the straight, is just made for this horse. (op 5/1)
Finger Onthe Pulse(IRE) ran tremendously well. He helped set the pace and jumped superbly, challenging the winner until his stamina probably just gave way in the straight. It was a highly creditable performance. (op 12/1)
Swift Counsel(IRE) got in as a reserve and ran a blinder. Brought into the race on the final circuit, he improved into a challenging position before the third last and kept going in the straight without threatening those in front of him. He just falls short of the standard of winning one of these but needs a trip. He may be the sort of horse that will hold an each-way chance in a race like the Munster National.
Northern Alliance(IRE) was lucky to stay in the race after a very bad early mistake which knocked him back through the field. He struggled to get into the race after that and ended up staying on from the third last. That was not a bad effort considering. (op 10/1)
Will Jamie Run(IRE) raced close to the pace and jumped boldly until running out of steam after the fourth last.
Ponmeoath(IRE) had a very nice position most of the way, jumped and travelled well for a lot of it but came under pressure before the third last and dropped away in the straight. (op 9/1)
Archie Boy(IRE) ◆ jumped boldly over the first two and still had a bit in the tank it would seem when he came a cropper at the fourth last.

1528a - 1544a (Foreign Racing) - See Raceform Interactive

[215]PLUMPTON (L-H)
Sunday, September 19

OFFICIAL GOING: Good to firm (8.9)
Single bends for all races.
Wind: Moderate, against Weather: Fine

1545 SIS LIVE JUVENILE HURDLE (9 hdls) 2m
2:00 (2:00) (Class 4) 3-Y-O **£2,927** (£859; £429; £214)

Form RPR
1 **Kahfre**[328] 3-10-12 0 JamieMoore 98+
(Gary Moore) *disp ld to 4th: styd cl up: rdn to dispute ld again 3 out: drvn to ld next: forged clr* **5/1**[3]
2 6 **Denton Ryal**[45] 3-10-5 0 JamieGoldstein 83
(Sheena West) *hld up in tch: trckd ldrs 6th: pushed along to go 3rd after 3 out but nt on terms: wnt 2nd last: kpt on but no ch* **7/2**[2]
F6 3 3¼ **Frameit (IRE)**[20] 1422 3-10-5 0 (vt) MrTomDavid(7) 87
(Tim Vaughan) *trckd ldrs: smooth prog to dispute ld 3 out and gng bttr than wnr: rdn and fnd nil 2 out: lost 2nd last* **13/2**
2 4 10 **Royal And Ancient (IRE)**[19] 1442 3-10-12 0 WarrenMarston 79
(Milton Harris) *w ldrs: rdn and nt qckn bef 3 out: steadily wknd bef next* **1/1**[1]
04 5 5 **Hannour (IRE)**[31] 1298 3-10-9 0 (t) DPFahy(3) 72
(Evan Williams) *hld up in rr: bmpd 3rd: outpcd in 7th bef 6th: rdn 3 out: modest late prog* **33/1**
055 6 ½ **Mini Max**[19] 1442 3-10-5 0 (b) MarkGrant 64
(Brendan Duke) *disp ld tl led 4th: hdd 3 out: wknd bef next* **40/1**
7 21 **Royal Torbo (ISR)**[34] 3-10-12 0 AndrewTinkler 50
(George Baker) *j.lft 2nd and rt 3rd: a in rr: wl outpcd in 8th bef 6th: t.o* **28/1**
8 1¼ **Shark Man (IRE)**[64] 3-10-5 0 MrJMQuinlan(7) 49
(Andrew Reid) *t.k.h: trckd ldrs: outpcd bef 6th: wknd next: t.o* **16/1**
5R 9 42 **Othello (IRE)**[19] 1442 3-10-5 0 MissJennyCarr(7) 7
(Jonjo O'Neill) *j. slowly 1st and 2nd: in tch to 5th: wl bhd whn mstke next: wl t.o* **40/1**
P **Vadition (IRE)**[33] 3-10-2 0 ow4 MrJackSalmon(7) —
(John Bridger) *bmpd 2nd and p.u sn after: sddle slipped* **100/1**
P **Tigers Charm**[15] 3-10-5 0 (t) ChrisDavies(7) —
(Milton Bradley) *hmpd 1st: a in rr: t.o after 5th: p.u bef 3 out* **150/1**
3m 39.3s (-21.50) **Going Correction** -1.50s/f (Hard) **11** Ran SP% **121.0**
Speed ratings (Par 103): **93,90,88,83,80 80,70,69,48,— —**
toteswingers: 1&2 £3.20, 1&3 £9.60, 2&3 £6.30 CSF £23.20 TOTE £6.30: £2.20, £1.30, £3.40; EX 26.90.
Owner SelectRacingClub.co.uk & Dr C A Barnett **Bred** Ballygallon Stud Limited **Trained** Lower Beeding, W Sussex

FOCUS
Good to firm ground for Plumpton's first fixture of the new season. Royal And Ancient comfortably set the standard from those with hurdles form having run well in defeat at Newton Abbot last time, but he was no match for a couple of the newcomers, who look to have decent futures. The form is rated around the third and sixth.

NOTEBOOK
Kahfre, a cheap purchase by Gary Moore after three modest runs on the Flat for Ed Dunlop, made an instant impact to his new career and already looks a brighter prospect in this sphere than on the level. Although he looked a sitting duck for the strong-travelling Frameit, he kept finding plenty for pressure and really saw his race out strongly, drawing away again after the last. Difficult to say how strong this form is, but he's a big sort open to plenty of progress and he looks a useful prospect. (op 7-2)
Denton Ryal, a dual winner on the level and a half-sister to two jumps winners, also making her hurdles debut, travelled kindly under a patient ride and, although she could never quite bridge the gap on the winner, she kept on stoutly to pass Frameit for second. On this evidence she's capable of winning one of these and she has the size and scope to do well at this game. (op 5-1)
Frameit(IRE) left his two previous hurdles starts miles behind and that may be attributed to the tongue-tie, which was on for the first time. He travelled powerfully and looked to be running all over the winner turning for home, but he didn't find as much for pressure as his rival and tired after the last. This was still a run full of promise and he's one to keep on side next time. (op 16-1)
Royal And Ancient(IRE) put in a laboured performance, jumping shabbily and struggling from some way out. This was clearly not the same level of performance as on debut, and maybe these much quicker conditions were not to his liking. He's got questions to answer now though. (tchd 11-10)
Hannour(IRE) Official explanation: vet said gelding lost a left-fore shoe

Vadition(IRE) Official explanation: jockey said saddle slipped

1546 JIMMY PARSONS MEMORIAL NOVICES' H'CAP CHASE (14 fncs) 2m 4f

2:30 (2:30) (Class 4) (0-105,104) 4-Y-O+

£3,131 (£925; £462; £231; £115; £58)

Form RPR

15U2 **1** **Buailteoir (IRE)**[11] 1509 8-10-9 **90**..........(p) DPFahy(3) 101+
(Evan Williams) *trckd clr ldng pair: wnt 2nd 9th to after 3 out: cl 3rd 2 out: plld out and drvn to chal last: sn led and styd on* **11/4**[1]

2 1 3/4 **Mister Micheau (IRE)**[432] 951 7-10-12 **90**..........(t) JamieMoore 98
(Joanna Davis) *mde most: hrd pressed fr 3 out: kpt on wl tl hdd and one pce sn after last* **9/1**

14S4 **3** 2 1/4 **Take A Mile (IRE)**[14] 1481 8-11-7 **104**.......... JimmyDerham(5) 112
(Seamus Mullins) *trckd ldrs: cl up fr 9th: nt fluent 4 out: wnt 2nd after next: chal and upsides whn nt fluent last: no ex* **5/1**

0P-F **4** 24 **Drombeg Pride (IRE)**[130] 283 6-9-9 **78** oh6.......... MarcGoldstein(5) 60
(Gerry Enright) *hld up in last: lost tch 10th: wl bhd 4 out: wnt remote 4th last* **40/1**

4P2P **5** 13 **Risk Challenge (USA)**[14] 1481 8-11-0 **92**..........(tp) CharliePoste 70
(Milton Harris) *hld up: pushed along after 8th: effrt 10th: disputing 3rd and wl in tch whn terrible blunder 4 out: nt rcvr: t.o* **17/2**

3/PP **6** 22 **Hazelbury**[48] 1159 9-9-11 **80** oh20 ow2.......... KeiranBurke(5) 27
(Nigel Hawke) *pressed ldr early: lost 2nd pl 9th: stl cl up 4 out: wknd rapidly: t.o* **40/1**

-513 **U** **Grand Bay (USA)**[38] 986 9-11-2 **97**..........(t) RichieMcLernon(3) —
(Jonjo O'Neill) *hld up: mstke 4th (ditch): cl 7th whn nt fluent and uns rdr 10th (ditch)* **4/1**[3]

2B35 **P** **Merry Terry**[33] 1276 6-11-0 **92**..........(p) JoeTizzard —
(Colin Tizzard) *nvr looked to be gng v sweetly: chsd ldrs: stl in tch whn p.u bef 4 out* **7/2**[2]

5m 0.60s (-6.70) **Going Correction** -0.475s/f (Good) **8** Ran SP% **111.0**
Speed ratings (Par 105): **94,93,92,82,77 68,—,—**
toteswingers: 1&2 £4.80, 1&3 £5.40, 2&3 £7.90 CSF £25.37 CT £111.25 TOTE £3.80: £1.10, £2.50, £1.90; EX 36.10.
Owner Tony Cromwell **Bred** R Lynch **Trained** Llancarfan, Vale Of Glamorgan

FOCUS
A strongly run handicap chase and a race littered with jumping errors. Ordinary form, the winner rated back to his Stratford level.

NOTEBOOK
Buailteoir(IRE) timed his challenge to perfection. At his best on a sound surface, he doesn't always jump with the greatest of fluency but, having been pulled wide, he pinged the last to score off a 13lb higher mark than when off the mark under rules at Stratford in July. (op 4-1)
Mister Micheau(IRE), off the track since being pulled up in Ireland in July 2009, was having his first start for new connections and ran a blinder. He and Hazelbury took each other on for the lead early but, having seen off that rival, Mister Micheau just kept on galloping out in front, jumping fluently and having most of his rivals in trouble some way out. This was his first start over fences and he looks nailed on to win races in this sphere. (op 6-1 tchd 10-1)
Take A Mile(IRE) looked a huge threat turning for home but his effort flattened out after the last. Still, this was a good effort and there are more races in him. (tchd 4-1)
Risk Challenge(USA) was still travelling okay when making a shuddering mistake four out, which effectively ended his hopes. (op 7-1 tchd 10-1)
Merry Terry Official explanation: jockey said gelding struck into itself

1547 FRONTRUNNERS IN PROPERTY - SAVILLS NOVICES' HURDLE (9 hdls) 2m

3:00 (3:00) (Class 4) 4-Y-O+ **£2,927** (£859; £429; £214)

Form RPR

-234 **1** **Marc Aurele (IRE)**[13] 1488 5-11-0 112..........(t) MrRMahon(5) 114+
(Paul Nicholls) *mde all: clr after 6th: hrd pressed and rdn 2 out: mstke last: styd on wl flat* **9/2**[2]

2261 **2** 3 3/4 **Freedom Fire (IRE)**[18] 1453 4-11-12 118.......... JamieMoore 116+
(Gary Moore) *hld up in last trio: prog 5th: sltly hmpd next: sn chsd wnr: clsd to chal 2 out: nt qckn u.p after last* **6/1**[3]

P- **3** 1 1/4 **Beaubrav**[5] 1601 4-10-7 0..........(t) MarcGoldstein(5) 101
(Michael Madgwick) *hld up in last trio: mstke 4th: prog after next: rdn to go 3rd after 3 out: clsd and mstke 2 out: mstke last: nt qckn flat* **25/1**

0523 **4** 7 **Navajo Nation (IRE)**[13] 1488 4-10-9 96..........(p) SamTwiston-Davies(3) 93
(Bill Turner) *prom: rdn to dispute 2nd bef 3 out: outpcd and btn bef next* **14/1**

2 **5** 11 **Django Reinhardt**[19] 1445 4-10-5 0.......... MrDavidTurner(7) 86
(Sam Davison) *t.k.h: hld up last: n.m.r after 5th: prog and sltly hmpd next: rchd 5th after 3 out: sme urging but no imp: eased flat* **12/1**

5-4 **6** 1 1/4 **Sommersturm (GER)**[14] 1475 6-10-12 0.......... DenisO'Regan 81
(Barney Curley) *racd wd: hld up: wnt prom briefly 4th: lost pl and last after next: sn bhd: poor 9th 3 out: kpt on after: couple of reminders after last* **16/1**

0 **7** 1/2 **Spiders Tern**[95] 760 5-10-5 0..........(t) MrTJCannon(7) 80
(Milton Bradley) *in tch to 6th: outpcd bef next: 6th and wl btn after 3 out* **150/1**

3- **8** 9 **Zuwaar**[8] 743 5-10-12 0..........(tp) AndrewGlassonbury 71
(Paddy Butler) *prom to 6th: sn lost pl: wl btn after 3 out* **66/1**

9 33 **Aragall (GER)**[69] 5-10-12 0.......... AndrewTinkler 38
(George Baker) *prom: chsd wnr 4th to 6th: wknd bef next: sn t.o* **9/2**[2]

35 **10** 15 **O'Callaghan Strand (AUS)**[96] 754 4-10-2 0.......... RichieMcLernon(3) 16
(Jonjo O'Neill) *in tch: pushed along 4th: sn dropped to rr and struggling: t.o* **40/1**

6 **11** 3/4 **Aah Haa**[31] 1289 5-10-12 0.......... LiamTreadwell 22
(Nick Gifford) *t.k.h: mostly chsd wnr to 4th: wknd rapidly next: sn wl t.o* **33/1**

U **Incy Wincy**[41] 4-10-5 0.......... ChrisDavies(7) —
(Milton Bradley) *in tch in midfield: rdn 5th: struggling whn hmpd and uns rdr next* **100/1**

0-02 **F** **Whatdoyoucallit (IRE)**[14] 1487 5-10-12 111..........(t) APMcCoy —
(Evan Williams) *trckd ldrs: wnt 2nd and fell 6th* **13/8**[1]

3m 37.7s (-23.10) **Going Correction** -1.50s/f (Hard) **13** Ran SP% **121.4**
Speed ratings (Par 105): **97,95,94,91,85 84,84,80,63,56 55,—,—**
toteswingers: 1&2 £3.10, 1&3 £26.40, 2&3 £27.30 CSF £31.43 TOTE £4.80: £1.10, £1.70, £6.80; EX 17.90.
Owner Ged Mason & Sir Alex Ferguson **Bred** Haras Du Mezeray And Ecurie Demgalop **Trained** Ditcheat, Somerset

FOCUS
Not a bad novice hurdle for the time of year, and easy form to rate.

NOTEBOOK
Marc Aurele(IRE) put up a game front-running effort. He set a good pace, had his rivals on the stretch some way out and kept galloping away to draw away again after the last. He was beaten a long way at Newton Abbot last time but that was on soft ground and he is a different animal on a sound surface. A breathing problem was also reported last time, so the application of a tongue-tie solved that problem and he's clearly decent when everything is right. Life is about to get much tougher though, as he'll have to shoulder a double penalty in this sphere as a result of this win. (op 11-2)
Freedom Fire(IRE) found the burden of the double penalty too much for he looked a major threat turning for home, but the weight told in the closing stages as he struggled to reel in Marc Aurele. This was a cracking effort though. (op 9-2)
Beaubrav was modest on the Flat (both wins on Polytrack) but, having been pulled up on his only previous try over hurdles (last year), this was a hugely encouraging effort and he's entitled to improve for this experience, which would make him an obvious player in similar company next time. (op 33-1)
Navajo Nation(IRE)'s tally now reads 0-24 under all codes (0-13 over hurdles).

1548 ANDY DAVIES MEMORIAL H'CAP HURDLE (9 hdls) 2m

3:30 (3:30) (Class 3) (0-125,123) 4-Y-O+

£6,262 (£1,850; £925; £463; £231; £116)

Form RPR

14-1 **1** **Herschel (IRE)**[52] 1125 4-11-0 **111**.......... JamieMoore 118+
(Gary Moore) *mde all: kicked on fr 3 out: styd on wl fr next* **8/1**

5210 **2** 3 1/2 **Alph**[15] 1470 13-11-0 **118**.......... MrTJCannon(7) 121
(Roger Teal) *trckd ldrs: wnt 2nd 3 out: drvn 2 out: kpt on but no imp on wnr* **25/1**

6012 **3** 3 **Boogie Dancer**[22] 1406 6-11-0 **111**.......... APMcCoy 111
(Stuart Howe) *hld up in tch: trapped bhd wall of rivals after 3 out in 8th: prog to go 3rd after 2 out: kpt on but no ch to chal* **3/1**[1]

1254 **4** 2 3/4 **Foreign King (USA)**[74] 934 6-10-1 **103**.......... JimmyDerham(5) 100
(Seamus Mullins) *chsd wnr to 2nd: remained prom: hrd rdn after 3 out: one pce fr next* **16/1**

2FU3 **5** 2 1/2 **Ajman (IRE)**[29] 1333 5-10-9 **109**..........(t) DPFahy(3) 104
(Evan Williams) *hld up in tch: effrt after 6th: rdn to dispute 3rd after 3 out: nt qckn bef next: wl hld whn blnd last* **4/1**[3]

F412 **6** 1 3/4 **Tignello (IRE)**[18] 1453 5-10-11 **113**..........(t) MrRMahon(5) 107
(Paul Nicholls) *t.k.h: pressed wnr fr 2nd: mstke 3 out: sn lost pl and btn* **7/2**[2]

0143 **7** 1 1/4 **Dream Catcher (SWE)**[32] 1282 7-10-13 **113**.......... RichieMcLernon(3) 104
(Jonjo O'Neill) *prom: hrd rdn and wknd after 3 out* **6/1**

0-23 **8** 4 **Sweet World**[30] 1311 6-10-9 **113**.......... MissIsabelTompsett(7) 102
(Bernard Llewellyn) *t.k.h: hld up in tch: cl enough whn mstke 3 out: no imp bef next: wknd* **10/1**

000- **9** 11 **The Lemonpie (GER)**[176] 4891 5-10-0 **97**.......... GerardTumelty 73
(Milton Harris) *hld up in last: lost tch w main gp fr 5th: nudged along and nvr remotely involved after* **33/1**

-451 **10** 13 **Zafar (IRE)**[35] 1258 7-11-12 **123**..........(tp) ChristianWilliams 86
(John Flint) *hld up in last pair: pushed along after 5th: sn lost tch: wl bhd fr 3 out* **33/1**

3m 33.9s (-26.90) **Going Correction** -1.50s/f (Hard)
WFA 4 from 5yo+ 11lb **10** Ran SP% **117.3**
Speed ratings (Par 107): **107,105,103,102,101 100,99,97,92,85**
toteswingers: 1&2 £58.20, 1&3 £2.50, 2&3 £18.00 CSF £173.57 CT £732.56 TOTE £9.00: £3.30, £9.00, £1.70; EX 167.80.
Owner S E Sangster **Bred** Mount Coote Stud And M Johnston **Trained** Lower Beeding, W Sussex

FOCUS
Another game front-running performance. Herschel has the potential to rate a bit higher on the best of his Flat form.

NOTEBOOK
Herschel(IRE) is now 3-4 over hurdles. This was a much stronger race than the selling hurdle he won at Stratford in July, so he's clearly going the right way and he seems well suited by fast ground. He is apparently held in quite high regard by Gary Moore and there may well be more to come. (op 15-2)
Alph is much more exposed and he's done his winning in a slightly lower grade than this, but he's a solid yardstick who ran his race, although the handicapper knows all about him. (op 20-1)
Boogie Dancer came here in good form and again ran well, but the handicapper looks to have her since her Hereford win in August. (op 4-1)
Foreign King(USA)'s sole success in this sphere came in 2007 and the handicapper has his measure over fences. He is slightly lower in this sphere but not enough to make him of interest in handicaps at the moment, and could only plug on at the one speed. (op 14-1 tchd 20-1)
Tignello(IRE) again raced too freely through the early stages and was struggling a long way out. He needs to learn to settle. (tchd 11-4)

1549 KC CARPET WAREHOUSE (S) H'CAP HURDLE (9 hdls) 2m

4:00 (4:00) (Class 5) (0-95,94) 4-Y-O+ **£1,541** (£449; £224)

Form RPR

405- **1** **Musashi (IRE)**[11] 2612 5-11-2 **84**.......... LeightonAspell 106+
(Laura Mongan) *hld up wl in rr: mstke 5th: stdy prog fr next: wnt 2nd after 3 out: clsd to ld 2 out: sn clr: easily* **11/2**[3]

6036 **2** 21 **We'Re Delighted**[29] 1340 5-11-3 **85**..........(t) DenisO'Regan 84
(Michael Blake) *hld up in last trio: stl only 8th 3 out and wl off the pce: gd prog bef next: mstke last: styd on to take 2nd flat: no ch* **16/1**

05- **3** 2 1/2 **Adage**[279] 1973 7-11-3 **85**..........(t) APMcCoy 82
(Jim Best) *led at str pce but harried fr the s: drvn clr after 6th: hdd 2 out: wknd rapidly: jst hld on for 3rd* **6/5**[1]

4P-3 **4** hd **Leulahleulahlay**[30] 1313 4-11-8 **93**.......... DPFahy(3) 89
(Evan Williams) *hld up in rr: nt fluent 4th: rdn and lost tch w ldrs after 6th: no ch after: kpt on fr 2 out: nrly snatched 3rd* **7/2**[2]

6050 **5** 9 **Masterpoint**[20] 1434 10-9-13 **70**..........(v) RichieMcLernon(3) 57
(Richard Harper) *chsd ldrs: rdn and struggling to hold pl fr 6th: n.d after 3 out* **12/1**

/566 **6** nk **Turkish Sultan (IRE)**[18] 1450 7-10-6 **81**..........(b) ChrisDavies(7) 70
(Milton Bradley) *chsd ldrs: outpcd fr 6th: wl btn whn mstke 3 out* **18/1**

04-0 **7** 1 3/4 **Gamedor (FR)**[31] 1292 5-11-0 **82**..........(be) JamieMoore 67
(Gary Moore) *trckd ldrs: rdn to dispute 3rd 3 out: wl btn but stl disputing 3rd 2 out: wknd* **10/1**

50/P **8** 1 1/2 **Dora Explora**[14] 1479 6-10-12 **80**..........(p) AndrewGlassonbury 63
(Linda Jewell) *pressed ldr: stl upsides whn mstke 6th: wknd rapidly 3 out* **50/1**

005- **9** 15 **Monaadi (IRE)**[33] 1258 5-10-11 **82**..........(b1) SamTwiston-Davies(3) 50
(Bernard Llewellyn) *chsd ldrs: rdn after 5th: dropped to rr and btn fr next* **25/1**

3PP0 **10** 15 **Randomer**[20] 1429 7-10-7 **80**..........(v1) MarcGoldstein(5) 33
(Paddy Butler) *chsd ldrs to 5th: wknd rapidly fr next: t.o* **66/1**

42-0 **P** **Wise Princess**[14] 1487 4-11-5 **94**.....(p) SClements(7) —
(Bill Turner) *j. bdly: t.o last after 3rd: p.u bef 3 out* **66/1**
3m 36.7s (-24.10) **Going Correction** -1.50s/f (Hard) **11** Ran SP% **119.8**
Speed ratings (Par 103): **100,89,88,88,83 83,82,81,74,66** —
toteswingers: 1&2 £13.40, 1&3 £2.30, 2&3 £9.50 CSF £83.74 CT £173.38 TOTE £7.20: £2.10, £6.00, £1.02; EX 43.10.The winner was bought in for £5,200.
Owner Mrs P J Sheen **Bred** Corduff Stud & J Corcorcan **Trained** Epsom, Surrey

FOCUS
A big step up from the winner but the form looks believable.

NOTEBOOK
Musashi(IRE) joined long-time leader Adage at the second-last and went clear readily after that. Previously 0-6 over hurdles, this was his first foray into selling grade and, having shaped encouragingly on the Flat on return earlier this month, he got off the mark in this sphere in emphatic style. (op 8-1 tchd 17-2 and 5-1)
We'Re Delighted is also winless in this sphere (0-15) but he stayed on late in the day to post one of his better efforts. (op 11-1 tchd 20-1)
Adage, making her debut for Jim Best, was running on empty turning for home and was all out to cling on to third in the end. This was her first start since December though, so she's entitled to strip fitter for it. (op 7-4)
Leulahleulahlay kept plugging away without threatening and looks to need a stiffer test of stamina. (op 9-2 tchd 11-2)

1550 PETE WALSH 60TH BIRTHDAY CELEBRATION H'CAP CHASE (18 fncs) 3m 2f
4:30 (4:31) (Class 4) (0-110,110) 4-Y-O **£3,771** (£1,123; £568; £291; £152)

Form RPR
-465 **1** **Sarahs Gift (IRE)**[20] 1434 7-10-12 **101**.....(t) DavidBass(5) 116+
(Lawney Hill) *settled in rr: prog and trckd ldr after 13th: led 4 out gng strly: clr 2 out: mstke last: rdn out* **7/1**
5201 **2** *9* **Good Harvest (IRE)**[28] 1348 7-11-10 **108**..... APMcCoy 115
(Jonjo O'Neill) *settled in rr: rdn to go 3rd at 14th: drvn to chse wnr 2 out: no imp whn nt fluent last* **7/2**[2]
5002 **3** *16* **Classic Clover**[25] 1366 10-10-11 **98**.....(t) SamTwiston-Davies(3) 91
(Colin Tizzard) *chsd ldng pair: wnt 2nd 10th: led after 13th: tried to kick on next: mstke and hdd 4 out: blnd next whn upsides: btn after* **8/1**
2415 **4** *1/2* **Keltic Lord**[31] 1297 14-10-12 **96**..... NickScholfield 85
(Peter Hiatt) *nt fluent 1st and 2nd: led to 3rd: lost 2nd 10th and a fighting losing battle after: outpcd fr 14th: plugged on flat* **25/1**
310- **5** *29* **Absolute Shambles**[235] 3682 6-10-8 **92**..... ColinBolger 52
(Chris Gordon) *chsd ldng pair: dropped to last pair and u.p 12th: no ch fr 14th* **6/1**
0133 **P** **Strong Coffee**[35] 1255 8-11-10 **108**.....(b) LeightonAspell —
(Oliver Sherwood) *led 3rd: j.w tl mstke and hdd 13th: dropped out qckly: t.o whn p.u bef 2 out* **5/1**[3]
-126 **P** **Changing Lanes**[28] 1346 7-11-12 **110**.....(p) ChristianWilliams —
(John Flint) *settled in rr: reminders after 7th: nvr gng wl after: mstkes 10th and 12th: t.o whn p.u bef 14th* **9/4**[1]
6m 34.7s (-16.00) **Going Correction** -0.475s/f (Good) **7** Ran SP% **111.4**
Speed ratings (Par 105): **105,102,97,97,88** —,—
toteswingers: 1&2 £3.90, 1&3 £9.70, 2&3 £4.00 CSF £30.55 CT £194.71 TOTE £8.30: £4.20, £3.30; EX 39.20.
Owner M B Clarke **Bred** The Trigger Syndicate **Trained** Aston Rowant, Oxon

FOCUS
A good gallop to this staying chase. A personal best from the winner, in a race rated through the second.

NOTEBOOK
Sarahs Gift(IRE) returned to winning ways despite never having won off a mark this high. He went clear leaving the back and was always keeping the staying-on Good Harvest at arm's length. The winner has improved markedly over fences over the last year and this effort suggests he's not finished yet. (op 13-2 tchd 6-1)
Good Harvest(IRE) kept chasing and ran well especially as he'd have preferred easier ground, but this mark has proved beyond him in the past.
Classic Clover is another in the grip of the assessor but he didn't run badly. (tchd 9-1)
Keltic Lord is too inconsistent nowadays. (op 16-1)
Changing Lanes was never having a cut at his fences and failed to fire. Official explanation: jockey said gelding never travelled (op 11-4)

1551 CREATE FOOD AND PARTY DESIGN H'CAP HURDLE (12 hdls) 2m 5f
5:00 (5:00) (Class 4) (0-105,104) 4-Y-O+ **£2,602** (£764; £382; £190)

Form RPR
4P13 **1** **Strumble Head (IRE)**[29] 1335 5-10-3 **84**.....(b) DonalDevereux(3) 88+
(Peter Bowen) *pressed ldr: led 9th: mstke 3 out and jnd: drvn 2 l clr 2 out: jst hld on* **5/2**[1]
0035 **2** *shd* **The Good Guy (IRE)**[28] 1347 7-11-12 **104**..... JodieMogford 106
(Graeme McPherson) *led: hdd and rdn 9th: upsides again 3 out: nt qckn 2 out: styd on flat: jst failed* **8/1**[2]
0402 **3** *1 3/4* **Coeur Brule (FR)**[19] 1446 4-10-9 **95**..... MrDavidTurner(7) 96+
(Sam Davison) *hld up in tch: prog to chse ldng pair after 7th: rdn bef 3 out: nt qckn and nvr bridged the gap: kpt on flat* **9/1**[3]
4412 **4** *6* **Rock Me (IRE)**[31] 1292 5-11-6 **103**.....(tp) DavidBass(5) 97
(Lawney Hill) *hld up in tch: outpcd and rdn 9th: effrt to go 4th bef next: one pce and no imp after* **5/2**[1]
5P55 **5** *2* **Mangonel**[18] 1451 6-10-0 **78** oh9.....(v) MattieBatchelor 71
(Stuart Howe) *hld up in last trio: sme prog after 8th: sn outpcd: kpt on fr 3 out: blnd last: hung lft flat: n.d* **33/1**
3240 **6** *1 3/4* **Heir To Be**[14] 1477 11-11-6 **98**.....(b) NickScholfield 88
(Michael Blake) *prom: lost pl after 5th: outpcd fr 9th and struggling: plugged on fr 2 out* **10/1**
3536 **7** *1 1/4* **Shropshirelass**[31] 1292 7-11-1 **98**..... GemmaGracey-Davison(5) 87
(Zoe Davison) *hld up in last trio: sme prog 8th: outpcd next: plugged on but nvr on terms after* **12/1**
P-2P **8** *10* **Treasury Counsel (IRE)**[29] 1336 8-10-3 **88**..... MrJEngland(7) 67
(Evan Williams) *hld up in last trio: lost tch 8th: wl bhd next: kpt on steadily fr 3 out: nvr nr ldrs* **14/1**
0064 **9** *nse* **Bond Cruz**[18] 1451 7-9-7 **78** oh5..... RobertKirk(7) 57
(Olivia Maylam) *chsd ldrs: outpcd after 8th: wknd bef 3 out* **33/1**
-330 **10** *4 1/2* **Ghaill Force**[119] 441 8-10-0 **78**..... LiamTreadwell 52
(Paddy Butler) *in tch: mstke 5th: sn dropped to rr: t.o fr 9th* **25/1**
3FP **11** *34* **Tigh Bhruadair (IRE)**[13] 1493 6-10-12 **100**.....(tp) JSMcGarvey(10) 40
(Evan Williams) *prom: mstke 7th: sn dropped out rapidly: t.o fr 9th* **50/1**
4563 **12** *11* **Mystic Touch**[31] 1300 4-10-10 **89**.....(p) JamesDavies 17
(Andrew Haynes) *in tch tl wknd u.p after 7th: wl bhd in last quartet 9th: t.o* **16/1**
4m 48.4s (-33.90) **Going Correction** -1.50s/f (Hard) course record
WFA 4 from 5yo+ 12lb **12** Ran SP% **119.3**
Speed ratings (Par 105): **104,103,103,101,100 99,99,95,95,93 80,76**
toteswingers: 1&2 £5.60, 1&3 £4.90, 2&3 £9.00 CSF £22.64 CT £159.76 TOTE £3.40: £2.00, £2.50, £2.30; EX 38.70 Place 6 £161.28, Place 5 £69.32.
Owner Jonathan Martin **Bred** Martin J Dibbs **Trained** Little Newcastle, Pembrokes

FOCUS
A moderate handicap but the form is sound.

NOTEBOOK
Strumble Head(IRE) locked horns with The Good Guy from a long way out and and the pair were separated by just a short head at the line. Strumble Head travelled the better of the pair but was all out to hold on after the last as The Good Guy rallied. This is probably something close to a career-best effort from the winner but this trip probably looks as far as he needs for now. He has probably got more to offer. (op 9-2)
The Good Guy(IRE) kept battling away and lost nothing in defeat. The return to a sound surface helped and, on this evidence, he is capable of winning a handicap of this sort of mark. (op 7-1 tchd 9-1)
Coeur Brule(FR) is still to break his duck (0-20 now) but this was his second solid effort in defeat on the spin and he looks good enough to find a race at some point, although he doesn't look totally straightforward (tended to hang under pressure). (op 11-1)
Rock Me(IRE), who was outpaced mid-race, picked up to latch on to the heels of the leading trio, but his effort flattened out in the straight. (op 10-3 tchd 7-2 and 9-4 and 4-1 in a place)
Mangonel's form is very poor on the whole but she finished her race in mildly encouraging style and may do better over marathon trips. (op 22-1)
Ghaill Force Official explanation: jockey said gelding made a mistake early and never travelled thereafter
T/Plt: £161.70 to a £1 stake. Pool: £71,044.75. 320.59 winning tickets. T/Qpdt: £21.10 to a £1 stake. Pool £6,470.59. 226.85 winning tickets. JN

1505 UTTOXETER (L-H)
Sunday, September 19

OFFICIAL GOING: Chase course - good to soft; hurdle course - good
Divided bends. Hurdle bend course dolled out 4m from inner line. Final fence home straight omitted all chases. Final flight back straight omitted all hdles.
Wind: Fresh, half against Weather: overcast

1552 MIRIAD PRODUCTS NOVICES' H'CAP HURDLE (DIV I) (9 hdls 1 omitted) 2m
1:50 (1:51) (Class 5) (0-95,95) 4-Y-O+ **£1,301** (£382; £191; £95)

Form RPR
-060 **1** **Aughcarra (IRE)**[8] 793 5-10-5 **77**..... TommyPhelan(3) 82
(Harry Chisman) *in rr-div: mstke 6th: hdwy appr 2 out: styd on to ld nr fin* **66/1**
300- **2** *nk* **Blackstone Vegas**[11] 1625 4-11-1 **87**..... SeanQuinlan(3) 92
(Derek Shaw) *hit 2nd: wnt prom 5th: led appr 2 out: edgd lft and bmpd between last 2: hdd nr fin* **9/1**
6004 **3** *1* **Bocciani (GER)**[12] 1504 5-11-0 **86**..... JamesO'Farrell(3) 90
(Dianne Sayer) *stdd s: hdwy to trck ldrs 3rd: led appr 3 out: hdd appr next: edgd rt and bmpd between last 2: no ex fnl 50yds* **5/1**[3]
3U5F **4** *4* **Cloonavery (IRE)**[15] 1468 8-9-7 **69**.....(v) MissGAndrews(7) 72+
(Tony Carroll) *chsd ldrs: hmpd and dropped bk after 3 out: styd on same pce between last 2* **9/4**[1]
0P- **5** *9* **Art Value**[115] 3857 5-10-3 **72**..... HarrySkelton 64
(Carroll Gray) *hld up in rr: hdwy 6th: chsng ldrs 2 out: sn wknd* **10/1**
63P- **6** *55* **Colliers Court**[314] 2192 13-10-2 **78**..... HarryChalloner(7) 20
(Lisa Williamson) *led: hdd appr 3 out: sn lost pl and bhd: t.o* **20/1**
2000 **7** *43* **He's A Sheila**[51] 1137 7-10-11 **90**..... JoshWall(10) —
(Trevor Wall) *in rr: drvn and detached 5th: sn t.o: eventually completed* **33/1**
P **Back To Paris (IRE)**[27] 1406 8-11-0 **90**.....(t) KyleJames(7) —
(Philip Kirby) *in rr: t.k.h: bhd fr 6th: t.o next: p.u bef last* **12/1**
0-00 **P** **Babe Maccool (IRE)**[44] 1199 8-10-0 **69** oh5.....(v) TomScudamore —
(David Pipe) *in rr: hit 1st: hdwy 6th: chsng ldrs next: wknd 2 out: 6th whn p.u bef last* **12/1**
P **Laureus (GER)**[1110] 1371 7-10-12 **81**..... AidanColeman —
(Rachel Hobbs) *chsd ldr to 6th: hung rt and lost pl appr next: t.o whn p.u bef 2 out* **33/1**
3335 **P** **Apache Dawn**[22] 1405 6-11-12 **95**.....(t) RichardJohnson —
(Aytach Sadik) *chsd ldrs: lost pl and p.u after 6th* **7/2**[2]
3m 55.7s (0.50) **Going Correction** -0.075s/f (Good)
WFA 4 from 5yo+ 11lb **11** Ran SP% **116.3**
Speed ratings (Par 103): **95,94,94,92,87 60,38**,—,—,—,—
toteswingers: 1&2 £67.10, 1&3 £70.80, 2&3 £6.00 CSF £559.22 CT £3520.68 TOTE £86.30: £15.40, £3.40, £2.20; EX 589.90.
Owner B Wilton **Bred** G Flannery Developments **Trained** Moreton-In-Marsh, Gloucs
■ The first winner for trainer Harry Chisman.
■ Stewards' Enquiry : James O'Farrell Caution: used whip with excessive frequency
Sean Quinlan Caution: used whip with excessive frequency
Tommy Phelan Caution: used whip with excessive frequency.

FOCUS
The hurdles course was dolled out 4m from the last meeting. This was a very weak race run at a steady pace, and it is not form to treat seriously.

NOTEBOOK
Aughcarra(IRE) had shown very little previously over hurdles and had been well beaten on the Flat too in recent starts, so this was a big surprise. He had looked a non-stayer in this discipline, but the steady pace helped and he wore down the two leaders close home. Official explanation: trainer said, regarding apparent improvement in form, that the gelding has been schooling better over hurdles and benefited from the slower ground
Blackstone Vegas won an amateurs' handicap on the Flat in the summer and improved on some very modest hurdling efforts from another yard last year. After challenging two out he eventually edged past the third, the pair having come close between the last two flights, only to be run out of it himself. (op 8-1 tchd 15-2)
Bocciani(GER)'s mark has been edging down and he ran another fair race, showing narrowly ahead on the home turn and only conceding defeat in the final 50 yards. (op 9-2 tchd 11-2)
Cloonavery(IRE), with the visor retained, was going well enough just behind the leaders when he was short of room three from home, forcing him into a costly mistake. (op 7-2)
Art Value, an ex-Irish maiden, looks to have stamina limitations. (op 14-1)
Babe Maccool(IRE) who was 5lb out of the weights, was still in the picture two out but then weakened rapidly and was pulled up. (op 4-1)
Laureus(GER) Official explanation: jockey said gelding hung right (op 4-1)

Apache Dawn was in touch when dropping behind and pulling up in the back straight, his rider clearly not happy with him. (op 4-1)

1553 ANOKI NOVICES' HURDLE (10 hdls 2 omitted) 2m 4f 110y

2:20 (2:20) (Class 4) 4-Y-0+ **£2,211** (£649; £324; £162)

Form RPR

622- **1** **Ackertac (IRE)**[196] 4461 5-10-12 118 PaddyBrennan 126+
(Nigel Twiston-Davies) *chsd ldrs: j.big 3rd: led 3 out: clr between last 2: 25 l clr 100yds out: heavily eased* **4/6**[1]

2 *10* **You Know Yourself (IRE)**[666] 7-10-12 0 HenryOliver 102
(Sue Smith) *chsd ldrs 5th: kpt on fr 3 out: tk remote 2nd run-in* **50/1**

6P3- **3** *1 3/4* **Icy Colt (ARG)**[147] 4 4-10-4 0 (v[1]) WillKennedy 91
(Paul Webber) *chsd ldrs: chsd wnr appr 2 out: rdr sn dropped whip: remote 2nd whn mstke last: one pce* **20/1**

5 **4** *3 3/4* **Newyearsresolution (IRE)**[28] 1349 6-10-12 0 DarylJacob 97
(Nick Mitchell) *led tl appr 3rd: one pce fr 3 out* **66/1**

20- **5** *2* **Grassfinch**[190] 4592 4-10-4 0 RodiGreene 86
(Renee Robeson) *hld up: hdwy to chse ldrs 7th: 6th whn nt fluent 3 out: one pce* **40/1**

4-03 **6** *6* **Himayna**[30] 1308 6-10-5 0 RichardJohnson 84+
(Tim Vaughan) *in rr: hit 2nd: sme hdwy appr 3 out: eased after next: nvr nr ldrs* **10/1**[3]

/600 **7** *14* **Gutter Lane**[26] 1357 6-10-7 0 JamesHalliday[(5)] 76
(Malcolm Jefferson) *in rr: sme hdwy 7th: nvr on terms: mstke last: fatally injured* **100/1**

PP-1 **8** *7* **Tiermore (IRE)**[18] 1449 6-10-12 110 MrPJTolman[(7)] 78
(Sirrell Griffiths) *t.k.h: trckd ldr: led appr 3rd: hdd 3 out: wknd qckly appr last* **12/1**

4 **9** *3 3/4* **Amical Risks (FR)**[26] 1357 6-10-12 0 BarryKeniry 66
(Joss Saville) *in rr-div: bhd fr 7th* **14/1**

2-21 **10** *10* **Call Me Bill (IRE)**[108] 609 4-10-11 0 TomO'Brien 56
(Peter Bowen) *chsd ldrs: lost pl appr 3 out: sn heavily eased* **7/2**[2]

0/-0 **11** *3* **Lambrini Classic**[11] 1505 7-10-12 0 BrianHughes 54
(Lisa Williamson) *in tch: outpcd 7th: sn wknd* **200/1**

4/ **12** *4* **Belmore Baron**[655] 2576 8-10-12 0 TjadeCollier 51
(Sue Smith) *in rr: blnd 6th: sn t.o* **40/1**

- **13** *12* **Mr Redwood**[127] 8-10-12 0 JackDoyle 40
(Susan Gardner) *in tch: lost pl 6th: sn bhd: eased 2 out* **66/1**

-P00 **14** *9* **Topping The Bill**[20] 1433 7-10-5 0 (p) MrRichardCollinson[(7)] 32
(Michael Wigham) *a in last: t.o after 7th* **40/1**

P **P** **Church Outing**[28] 1344 6-10-2 0 CharlieHuxley[(3)] —
(Susan Gardner) *prom: lost pl 6th: sn bhd: t.o whn p.u bef next* **150/1**

F0 **P** **Hurst Park (IRE)**[13] 1488 8-10-12 0 AidanColeman —
(Susan Gardner) *in rr: reminders after 5th: sn bhd: t.o whn p.u bef 7th* **150/1**

5m 1.50s (-2.50) **Going Correction** -0.075s/f (Good)
WFA 4 from 5yo+ 12lb **16** Ran SP% **125.5**
Speed ratings (Par 105): **101,97,96,95,94 92,86,84,82,78 77,76,71,68,— —**
toteswingers: 1&2 £60.30, 1&3 £60.30, 2&3 £8.70 CSF £63.19 TOTE £1.60: £1.10, £10.10, £5.80; EX 93.70.
Owner Mark Aspey & Steve Catton **Bred** Jerry Capliss **Trained** Naunton, Gloucs

FOCUS

Not much strength in depth to this novice hurdle.

NOTEBOOK

Ackertac(IRE), twice runner-up in similar events last season, was 15lb clear on adjusted official figures. He ran out a very easy winner, with the margin of victory not giving a true reflection of his dominance, and while he did not have a great deal to beat here he should be up to winning again. Connections reported that he had strengthened up since last season. (op 10-11)
You Know Yourself(IRE) ◆ off since running in a couple of Irish points in late 2008, ran with considerable promise on this hurdling debut. Held up and keen before making steady headway, he was not knocked about when the winner went clear two from home but kept on to go second on the run-in. It will be interesting to see whether he can build on this sympathetic introduction to hurdling.
Icy Colt(ARG), who ran an improved race in cheekpieces on his latest start back in April, had a change of headgear now. Upped in trip, he was in second place when his rider dropped his whip two from home and could only plug on at the same pace from there.
Newyearsresolution(IRE) made a good deal of the running and stuck on well enough for fourth, albeit a well-beaten one. This was a satisfactory hurdles debut from this ex-pointer. (tchd 80-1)
Grassfinch, whose connections won this race with the smart Ogee two years ago, showed ability on this hurdles debut and first start since March. She looks one to look out for in mares-only races.
Himayna again failed to jump fluently, but she was never nearer than at the finish and is far from a lost cause. (tchd 12-1)
Tiermore(IRE), a recent Hereford winner, was found out under his penalty. (tchd 14-1)
Call Me Bill(IRE) faded disappointingly on this first start since landing a bumper in June. (op 3-1)

1554 MIRIAD PRODUCTS NOVICES' H'CAP HURDLE (DIV II) (9 hdls 1 omitted) 2m

2:50 (2:50) (Class 5) (0-95,93) 4-Y-0+ **£1,301** (£382; £191; £95)

Form RPR

3-32 **1** **Royal Flynn**[22] 1407 8-10-11 **85** (tp) HenryBrooke[(7)] 92+
(Kate Walton) *hld up: hdwy to trck ldrs 6th: led appr last: all out* **6/1**[3]

50-P **2** *hd* **Douglas Julian**[117] 459 8-10-8 **75** HenryOliver 82+
(Sue Smith) *hld up: hdwy to chse ldrs 6th: sn outpcd: hdwy and cl 3rd whn blnd 2 out: styd on run-in: jst hld* **14/1**

P0-2 **3** *2 1/2* **Marie De Laufon (FR)**[59] 1066 5-11-9 **93** SeanQuinlan[(3)] 96
(Chris Bealby) *hld up: jnd ldrs 6th: lft in ld appr next: hdd appr last: no ex fnl 150yds* **7/1**

06-3 **4** *18* **River Rhapsody (IRE)**[12] 1504 4-11-2 **83** PaulMoloney 70
(Evan Williams) *chsd ldrs: lost pl appr 3 out* **9/2**[1]

2013 **5** *3 1/2* **Galley Slave (IRE)**[20] 1428 5-11-0 **88** KyleJames[(7)] 72
(Michael Chapman) *led to 2nd: led 4th tl sn after 6th: wknd 3 out* **5/1**[2]

0302 **6** *14* **Hollies Favourite (IRE)**[18] 1450 7-11-9 **90** RichardJohnson 66
(Louise Davis) *stdd s: hld up in rr: hdwy 6th: wknd after 2 out* **9/2**[1]

UP40 **7** *2 1/4* **General Simara**[31] 1291 6-10-13 **80** (v) WayneHutchinson 49
(Tony Carroll) *chsd ldrs: reminders 6th: wknd appr next* **25/1**

5U0/ **8** *83* **Always Baileys (IRE)**[19] 2956 7-9-7 **67** oh3 MissCBoxall[(7)] —
(Pam Ford) *nt jump wl in last: t.o 4th: eventually completed* **66/1**

3036 **9** *20* **Mulaazem**[20] 1433 7-11-5 **86** (p) FelixDeGiles —
(Derek Frankland) *prom: lost pl 6th: sn wl bhd: t.o next: eventually completed* **14/1**

0050 **U** **Miss Markham (IRE)**[55] 1090 5-9-11 **71** ow4 DerekSmith[(7)] —
(Patricia Rigby) *in rr: bhd whn blnd and uns rdr 5th* **66/1**

60/0 **P** **Nowzdetime (IRE)**[44] 1196 5-10-2 **69** TomScudamore —
(Caroline Bailey) *w ldr: led 2nd to 4th: led sn after 6th: p.u appr next: fatally injured* **8/1**

5040 **F** **Glan Lady (IRE)**[33] 1272 4-10-8 **78** (p) CharlieHuxley[(3)] —
(John Mackie) *prom whn fell 4th* **14/1**

3m 58.1s (2.90) **Going Correction** -0.075s/f (Good)
WFA 4 from 5yo+ 11lb **12** Ran SP% **117.8**
Speed ratings (Par 103): **89,88,87,78,76 69,68,27,17,— —,—**
toteswingers: 1&2 £21.40, 1&3 £3.60, 2&3 £20.00 CSF £83.59 CT £602.50 TOTE £8.50: £2.40, £3.70, £3.20; EX 135.60.
Owner Mr and Mrs Paul Chapman **Bred** Highclere Stud Ltd **Trained** Middleham Moor, N Yorks
■ Stewards' Enquiry : Henry Oliver caution: used whip with excessive frequency.

FOCUS

Division two of this low-grade race was run in a time two seconds slower than the first. The first three finished clear.

NOTEBOOK

Royal Flynn had been running creditably and he ground out a hard-fought win, seeing off rivals on either side of him after the last. The usual cheekpieces were back on, accompanied by a first-time tongue tie. (tchd 5-1)
Douglas Julian had not been seen since pulling up on his handicap debut in May. He received reminders as early as the fifth, but stayed on to go down fighting after walking through the second-last. A return to further will suit him. (op 16-1)
Marie De Laufon(FR) was 7lb higher than when runner-up over course and distance last time and the extra weight just told late on. (op 9-2)
River Rhapsody(IRE) was unable to build on his eyecatching display at Sedgefield, but it might pay not to write him off just yet. (op 4-1 tchd 7-2)
Galley Slave(IRE) beat today's winner at Cartmel two runs back but was well beaten off this 11lb higher mark. (tchd 9-2 and 11-2)
Hollies Favourite(IRE) was a little keen and could not race on with the leaders from the second-last. (op 6-1)
Mulaazem Official explanation: trainer said gelding coughed post-race
Nowzdetime(IRE), who was well backed, was in second place when sadly breaking down just after turning for home. (op 25-1)

1555 DIAL (S) HURDLE (10 hdls 2 omitted) 2m 6f 110y

3:20 (3:20) (Class 5) 4-8-Y-0 **£1,561** (£458; £229; £114)

Form RPR

5160 **1** **Golden Gem (IRE)**[14] 1484 8-10-11 98 (p) MrJMahot[(7)] 100
(Rachel Hobbs) *in rr: hdwy 4th: chsng ldrs 7th: narrow ld appr next: kpt on run-in: all out* **28/1**

235/ **2** *3/4* **Easement**[1077] 1342 7-10-12 0 (v[1]) JimmyMcCarthy 93
(Charlie Morlock) *chsd ldrs: styd on run-in: wnt 2nd last 150yds: no ex nr fin* **66/1**

P355 **3** *5* **Manadam (FR)**[25] 1368 7-10-5 100 MattGriffiths[(7)] 91+
(Anthony Middleton) *chsd ldrs: led 7th: hdd next: wknd run-in* **16/1**

24-3 **4** *1 1/4* **Pocket Too**[28] 1347 7-10-5 105 (p) CDTimmons[(7)] 88
(Matthew Salaman) *chsd ldrs: outpcd after 3 out: kpt on run-in* **4/1**[2]

20-5 **5** *1 3/4* **Hippodrome (IRE)**[21] 1329 8-10-11 100 (p) MattCrawley[(7)] 92
(John Harris) *in rr: t.o 6th: sme hdwy 3 out: kpt on fr last* **25/1**

3043 **6** *11* **Knightsbridgelives (IRE)**[20] 1431 7-10-12 105 (t) AidanColeman 76
(Lawney Hill) *hld up: stdy hdwy 6th: chsng ldrs 3 out: ev ch tl wknd last* **8/1**

6/6 **7** *3 1/4* **Little Dibber**[18] 1449 7-10-12 0 JackDoyle 73
(Peter Pritchard) *nt fluent 1st: in rr fr 7th* **25/1**

-150 **8** *12* **Opening Meet**[28] 1347 6-11-4 108 (t) HarrySkelton 69
(Paul Nicholls) *hld up in rr: sme hdwy u.p 7th: wknd appr next* **12/1**

0-6U **9** *45* **Owls FC (IRE)**[20] 1427 4-10-3 79 RodiGreene 13
(Michael Chapman) *in rr: reminders 4th: bhd fr next: t.o 6th* **100/1**

3050 **P** **Tora Petcha (IRE)**[14] 1481 7-10-11 97 HarryChalloner[(7)] —
(Barry Leavy) *in rr: bhd fr 5th: t.o 7th: p.u bef next* **28/1**

/0P0 **P** **Killenaule Boy**[23] 1390 8-10-12 0 RichardJohnson —
(Tim Vaughan) *nt fluent: prom: mstke 3rd: lost pl and p.u after 5th* **5/1**

0P34 **P** **High Skies**[20] 1431 7-11-4 104 (bt) SamThomas —
(Dr Richard Newland) *led to 7th: sn wknd: bhd whn p.u between last 2* **20/1**

122F **P** **King Of Castile**[55] 1092 6-11-4 110 (vt) PaulMoloney —
(Evan Williams) *chsd ldrs: sn constant reminders: lost pl after 5th: sn bhd: t.o whn p.u bef 3 out* **3/1**[1]

5353 **P** **El Presidente (IRE)**[29] 1329 5-10-9 108 (b) AlexMerriam[(3)] —
(Neil King) *prom: lost pl 6th: bhd whn p.u between last 2* **9/2**[3]

5m 29.5s (-1.40) **Going Correction** -0.075s/f (Good)
WFA 4 from 5yo+ 12lb **14** Ran SP% **126.4**
Speed ratings: **99,98,97,96,95 92,91,86,71,— —,—,—,—**
toteswingers: 1&2 £58.20, 1&3 £49.30, 2&3 £49.70 CSF £1198.22 TOTE £40.20: £13.00, £15.20, £6.30; EX 915.20.There was no bid for the winner.
Owner The Vin de Roy Racing Syndicate **Bred** Seamus Byrne **Trained** Hanley Swan, Worcs

FOCUS

A moderate seller in which several of the market leaders disappointed.

NOTEBOOK

Golden Gem(IRE), who landed a Worcester claimer last month, regained winning ways back in this more suitable grade. The step back up in trip suited and he won all out after idling in front. (op 25-1)
Easement, runner-up twice in bumpers for Charles Cyzer in 2007, was making his hurdling debut in the bottom grade after a long lay-off. Visored for the first time, he had the rail to race against after the last, but despite battling on he could not quite get to the winner in the centre of the track.
Manadam(FR) ran a better race than of late but this trip might be on the short side for him. (op 33-1)
Pocket Too, a well-beaten third in bad ground last time, ran his race on this drop in grade. (tchd 7-2 and 9-2 in places)
Hippodrome(IRE) was struggling with a circuit left and merely plugged on past beaten rivals. (op 50-1)
Knightsbridgelives(IRE) settled better and improved going well leaving the back straight. He looked a big threat jumping two out, but failed to get home.
Opening Meet, a rare runner in this grade for the champion trainer, was never really in the hunt. (op 8-1)
Killenaule Boyreverting to hurdles on his debut for the yard, was out of the race early. Official explanation: jockey said, regarding running and riding, that his orders were to jump off, get a prominent position and ride his race from there, adding that although the gelding travelled well between hurdles, it jumped the first two awkwardly, expecting it to get better as it warmed up but it continued to jump poorly and decided in its best interests to pull up; vet said: gelding returned lame behind. (op 4-1 tchd 11-2)
King Of Castilegave a very moody display and was well adrift by halfway.\n Official explanation: jockey said gelding never travelled (op 4-1 tchd 11-2)

El Presidente(IRE), best in at the weights on this descent into selling grade, was beaten before stamina became an issue. (op 4-1 tchd 11-2)

1556 RITCHIE & RITCHIE H'CAP HURDLE (10 hdls 2 omitted) 2m 4f 110y
3:50 (3:51) (Class 4) (0-115,115) 4-Y-0+ £2,211 (£649; £324; £162)

Form RPR
-P34 1 **Santera (IRE)**[35] 1258 6-11-1 104 ....(p) RhysFlint 117+
(John Flint) *in rr-div: hdwy to chse ldrs7th: led 3 out: wnt clr between last 2: 10 l ahd last: eased nr fin* 7/1[2]
-040 2 10 **Armenian Boy (FR)**[67] 994 7-11-6 109 ....(bt) TomScudamore 112
(David Pipe) *chsd ldrs: wnt 2nd between last 2: no ch w wnr* 10/1
444U 3 1 1/4 **Kavegirl**[14] 1479 7-10-3 92 .... DavidEngland 94
(John Panvert) *in rr: hdwy to chse ldrs 7th: kpt on same pce fr next* 22/1
24-5 4 5 **Court Red Handed (IRE)**[31] 1291 5-10-6 102 .... AodhaganConlon(7) 100
(Rebecca Curtis) *chsd ldr: led after 7th: hdd next: wknd between last 2* 5/2[1]
-540 5 hd **Ovthenight (IRE)**[70] 962 5-10-10 106 ....(b) MissGAndrews(7) 105
(Pam Sly) *chsd ldrs: drvn after 7th: outpcd appr 3 out: 5th and keeping on whn mstke last* 10/1
2000 6 18 **Peaceful Means (IRE)**[15] 1470 7-10-11 105 .... LeeEdwards(5) 86
(Tony Carroll) *in rr-div: hdwy to chse ldrs 7th: wknd 2 out* 14/1
0200 7 25 **Aldiruos (IRE)**[25] 1372 10-10-13 102 .... WayneHutchinson 61
(Tony Carroll) *in rr: reluctant: bhd and reminders 5th: t.o 7th* 16/1
5301 8 17 **Basford Lass**[28] 1347 5-11-7 110 ....(b) AlanO'Keeffe 53
(Jennie Candlish) *led: hdd sn after 7th: sn wknd* 9/1
0062 9 6 **Englishtown (FR)**[25] 1368 10-10-13 112 ....(p) GeraldQuinn(10) 50
(Jonjo O'Neill) *in rr-div: drvn 6th: sn bhd: eased fr 2 out* 8/1[3]
2-03 10 69 **The Magic Bishop**[26] 1359 5-10-9 103 .... JamesHalliday(5) —
(Malcolm Jefferson) *chsd ldrs: lost pl after 7th: sn bhd: virtually p.u run-in: wl t.o* 8/1[3]
63F/ P **Master Builder (FR)**[572] 4116 9-11-7 110 .... GrahamLee —
(Ferdy Murphy) *in rr: nvr gng wl and sn drvn along: t.o whn p.u bef 6th* 25/1
51F/ P **Krackatara**[906] 4753 8-11-12 115 .... JackDoyle —
(Susan Gardner) *hld up toward rr: sme hdwy 7th: sn wknd: bhd whn p.u bef 2 out* 9/1
0-06 P **Flapjack Crumbly**[30] 1308 7-10-0 89 oh4 .... HenryOliver —
(Sue Smith) *mstke 2nd: hdwy and prom whn mstke 6th: sn lost pl: wl bhd whn p.u after next* 33/1

4m 59.6s (-4.40) **Going Correction** -0.075s/f (Good) 13 Ran SP% 125.2
Speed ratings (Par 105): **105,101,100,98,98 91,82,75,73,47** —,—,—
toteswingers: 1&2 £14.10, 1&3 £25.00, 2&3 £58.70 CSF £77.09 CT £1496.38 TOTE £6.40: £2.10, £4.40, £6.10; EX 103.30.
Owner Jason Tucker **Bred** Pedro Rosas **Trained** Kenfig Hill, Bridgend

FOCUS
An ordinary handicap hurdle run at a decent clip and in a time over two seconds quicker than the earlier novice event.

NOTEBOOK
Santera(IRE) had been a beaten favourite in sellers on her last two starts for Michael Blake, but she bounced back on her debut for the John Flint stable. Scooting clear after jumping to the front three out, she had cheekpieces on for the first time over hurdles and the step back up in trip seemed to suit. (op 11-2)
Armenian Boy(FR) has dropped to a handy mark and he ran a better race, although he had no chance with the clear winner. He had blinkers back on in place of cheekpieces. (op 12-1 tchd 14-1)
Kavegirl has been performing creditably since switching to hurdles. She did not seem to stay 3m in point-to-points but might be worth a try over that trip again. (op 25-1)
Court Red Handed(IRE) went on going well but was soon headed by the winner and faded out of things. He has now been a beaten favourite on his last two starts, but this was only his fifth run over hurdles and he is probably worth another chance. (op 5-1)
Ovthenight(IRE) was blinkered for the first time over hurdles. He has become well handicapped but is not really performing well enough to take advantage. (op 12-1)
Aldiruos(IRE) Official explanation: jockey said gelding had been reluctant to race
Basford Lass, who set the pace, was found out by the 12lb rise for her win in testing ground at Newton Abbot.
Krackatara has been given a chance by the handicapper and should come on for this first run since March 2008. (op 7-1 tchd 10-1)

1557 A & S ENTERPRISES H'CAP CHASE (14 fncs 2 omitted) 2m 5f
4:20 (4:20) (Class 3) (0-130,130) 4-Y-0£4,816 (£1,422; £711; £355; £177)

Form RPR
2121 1 **Frosted Grape (IRE)**[11] 1509 4-10-4 120 ....(b) TomScudamore 126+
(David Pipe) *chsd ldr: led 6th: j. boldly: drew clr fr 3 out: shkn up between last 2: 15 l ahd whn eased last 100yds* 5/4[1]
2514 2 14 **Jimbatai (IRE)**[20] 1424 7-11-1 119 .... RichardJohnson 124
(Barry Leavy) *chsd ldrs: wnt 2nd 8th: kpt on same pce fr 3 out: 13 l bhd whn mstke last* 8/1
P/52 3 4 **Sporting Rebel (IRE)**[13] 1491 10-10-8 112 .... HaddenFrost 112
(James Frost) *chsd ldrs: drvn along 8th: one pce fr 3 out* 8/1
14P- 4 2 **Le Commencement (IRE)**[239] 3612 8-10-13 117 .... JackDoyle 115
(Emma Lavelle) *in rr: bhd fr 9th: kpt on fr 3 out: nvr on terms* 7/1[3]
3325 5 12 **Red Jester**[36] 1252 9-9-11 104 oh4 .... PeterToole(3) 91
(Gerald Ham) *trckd ldrs: drvn 9th: lost pl appr 3 out* 14/1
-51B 6 13 **Radetsky March (IRE)**[29] 1332 7-11-12 130 .... SamThomas 106
(Mark Bradstock) *nt fluent 3rd: hdwy and prom 8th: lost pl and j.lft 3 out* 6/1[2]
30-0 P **Au Courant (IRE)**[29] 1332 10-11-12 130 ....(b) PaulMoloney —
(Sophie Leech) *sn detached in last and drvn along: reminders 2nd: t.o 4th: p.u after 4 out* 16/1
4461 P **Ragador**[29] 1327 9-10-0 104 .... TjadeCollier —
(Sue Smith) *led: hdd 5th: hit next: lost pl 9th: sn bhd: t.o whn p.u bef 3 out* 10/1

5m 24.8s (1.30) **Going Correction** +0.25s/f (Yiel)
WFA 4 from 7yo+ 1lb 8 Ran SP% 115.1
Speed ratings (Par 107): **107,101,100,99,94 89**,—,—
toteswingers: 1&2 £3.40, 1&3 £2.30, 2&3 £6.20 CSF £12.31 CT £57.86 TOTE £2.10: £1.02, £2.60, £2.40; EX 11.40.
Owner The Wise Partners **Bred** Austin Curran **Trained** Nicholashayne, Devon

FOCUS
A fair handicap chase.

NOTEBOOK
Frosted Grape(IRE) has been a revelation since switching to fences and she made it three from four with a clear-cut victory. She defied a mark 19lb higher than when she scored at Hereford at the start of the month, with a her spring-heeled jumping again a feature. (op 2-1)
Jimbatai(IRE) was unlucky to run up against a progressive opponent. He did not do a lot wrong and can win more races in ordinary company.
Sporting Rebel(IRE) was at work some way out but kept going for third. He probably needs a stiffer test. (tchd 7-1)
Le Commencement(IRE) ◆, who had not been seen out since January, made a promising chasing debut. He was staying on in the latter stages without being given a hard time and improvement should follow. (tchd 6-1 and 8-1)
Red Jester usually runs well here and he performed respectably enough from 4lb out of the handicap. (tchd 12-1)
Radetsky March(IRE) was disappointing off 10lb higher than when scoring at Bangor two runs back. He recovered from a slow early jump but his effort fizzled out. (op 9-2)
Ragador made all at Market Rasen but could not dominate here and the writing was on the wall a good way out. Official explanation: trainer's rep said, regarding running, that the gelding was unable to dominate (op 8-1)

1558 HENRY MEIN ARCHITECTS NOVICES' CHASE (10 fncs 2 omitted) 2m
4:50 (4:50) (Class 4) 4-Y-0+ £2,862 (£840; £420; £209)

Form RPR
0/4- 1 **Pouvoir (FR)**[237] 3650 7-10-12 0 .... SamThomas 116+
(Alan King) *trckd ldrs: led on bit 3 out: shkn up between last 2: rdn out run-in* 7/2[3]
0344 2 4 1/2 **Classic Fly (FR)**[13] 1492 7-10-12 0 .... FelixDeGiles 109
(Arthur Whiting) *w ldrs: drvn along 6th: upsides 3 out: styd on same pce run-in* 20/1
2P63 3 19 **Nordwind (IRE)**[14] 1485 9-10-12 0 .... PaulMoloney 92
(Evan Williams) *led: hdd 3 out: one pce* 5/1
2P-1 4 nk **Quell The Storm (FR)**[48] 1163 6-11-5 0 ....(t) HarrySkelton 100
(Paul Nicholls) *trckd ldrs: effrt appr 3 out: one pce* 15/8[1]
-F50 5 31 **Adjami (IRE)**[31] 1300 9-10-12 0 ....(p) RodiGreene 64
(John Harris) *detached in last 3rd: t.o 3 out* 66/1
5P0F P **Intense Suspense (IRE)**[14] 1481 7-10-12 53 ....(vt) AidanColeman —
(Robin Dickin) *trckd ldrs: t.k.h: wknd 6th: t.o 3 out: p.u bef last* 66/1
131 P **Holoko Heights**[14] 1485 5-11-5 0 ....(v) RichardJohnson —
(Tim Vaughan) *chsd ldrs: blnd 2nd: reminders and lost pl 4th: wl bhd whn p.u bef 6th: b.b.v* 9/4[2]

4m 1.90s (6.30) **Going Correction** +0.25s/f (Yiel) 7 Ran SP% **112.2**
Speed ratings (Par 105): **94,91,82,82,66** —,—
toteswingers: 1&2 £4.10, 1&3 £2.70, 2&3 £3.70 CSF £44.71 TOTE £4.30: £2.80, £7.50; EX 71.90.
Owner Mr & Mrs R Scott **Bred** Count Edouard Decazes **Trained** Barbury Castle, Wilts

FOCUS
An interesting novice chase, but there are perhaps one or two doubts over the form.

NOTEBOOK
Pouvoir(FR) had previous experience over fences, finishing fourth at Fontwell back in January, but had not run since. The one-time smart hurdler jumped soundly and stayed on well after easing to the front three out. He will be kept low-key for the time being and is still young enough to do quite well at this game. Easy ground suits and he gets further than this. (op 3-1 tchd 9-4)
Classic Fly(FR) is officially rated no less than 38lb behind Pouvoir over hurdles but made a very pleasing chasing debut, jumping soundly and looking for a fleeting moment as if he might spring a shock. This won't help his rating but he should be up to winning in ordinary novice company. (op 16-1)
Nordwind(IRE), who adopted very different tactics to those at Worcester, had no answers once headed at the first in the home straight. He did rally for third after the last. (op 13-2)
Quell The Storm(FR), given a break since his Newton Abbot win, was a little disappointing, coming under pressure turning into the straight and soon left behind by the first two from there. This ground may have been a little softer than ideal. (op 13-8 tchd 9-4)
Holoko Heights won well on his chasing debut at Worcester, where he had Nordwind back in third, but looked less than happy after an early mistake here. Soon pulled up, it turned out that he had broken a blood vessel. Official explanation: trainer's rep said gelding bled from the nose (op 3-1)

1559 HOAR CROSS HALL GYM TEAM NOVICES' H'CAP HURDLE (12 hdls 2 omitted) 3m
5:20 (5:20) (Class 5) (0-95,94) 4-Y-0+ £1,520 (£449; £224; £112; £56)

Form RPR
B512 1 **Rebel Swing**[20] 1428 4-11-5 89 .... HenryOliver 97+
(Sue Smith) *chsd ldrs: outpcd appr 3 out: styd on: 4th last: hung lft and led last 100yds: kpt on wl* 4/1[2]
0606 2 3 1/2 **Calypso Bay (IRE)**[23] 1392 4-10-11 84 .... MrAJBerry(3) 87
(Jonjo O'Neill) *hld up in rr: hdwy to chse ldrs 6th: kpt on to ld sn after last: hdd and no ex last 100yds* 18/1
4212 3 3 1/2 **Auberge (IRE)**[11] 1507 6-11-4 89 .... RyanMania(3) 93+
(Dianne Sayer) *mid-div: hdwy to chse ldrs 8th: chal 3 out: hit last: kpt on same pce* 10/3[1]
44 4 8 **Himitas (FR)**[18] 1449 5-11-1 90 .... MattGriffiths(7) 87
(Graeme McPherson) *chsd ldrs: dropped bk to 7th: rallied and chsng ldrs next: led and hit 3 out: hdd sn after last: wknd* 16/1
P044 5 21 **The Wee Midget**[19] 1446 5-11-8 90 .... FelixDeGiles 70
(Arthur Whiting) *hdwy to chse ldrs 6th: outpcd 3 out: sn wknd: 5th and wl btn whn blnd last* 16/1
P3P 6 7 **Kingston Queen (IRE)**[40] 1232 7-11-0 82 ....(p) AidanColeman 52
(Rachel Hobbs) *in rr-div: hdwy to chse ldrs 8th: wknd appr 3 out* 25/1
5364 7 5 **Mulligan's Pride (IRE)**[20] 1428 9-10-7 75 ....(b) GrahamLee 47
(James Moffatt) *led: mstke 6th: hdd 3 out: sn wknd: eased between last 2* 11/1
44P4 8 1 1/2 **Smiling Applause**[11] 1507 11-10-0 68 ....(p) DavidEngland 32
(Harry Chisman) *chsd ldrs: lost pl 8th* 16/1
2P0- 9 1/2 **Russellstown Boy (IRE)**[243] 3530 10-10-11 79 .... PaulMoloney 42
(Evan Williams) *in rr: bhd fr 7th* 16/1
544 10 1 1/2 **Midnight Fun**[38] 1233 5-11-7 89 .... RodiGreene 51
(Graham Smith) *chsd ldrs: wknd appr 3 out* 22/1
6P6- F **Ordelia**[186] 4682 6-11-5 90 .... SeanQuinlan(3) —
(Chris Bealby) *prom: fell 5th* 25/1
00-6 F **Buds Dilemma**[14] 1479 6-10-1 69 ow1 ....(tp) TomO'Brien —
(Peter Bowen) *in rr whn fell 1st* 13/2[3]
5P-P P **Little Al**[101] 694 7-11-12 94 .... SamThomas —
(Oliver Sherwood) *chsd ldrs: lost pl 7th: sn bhd: t.o whn p.u bef 3 out* 20/1
0044 P **Cornish Castle (USA)**[22] 1407 4-10-8 78 ....(t) BarryKeniry —
(Joss Saville) *reluctant in last: drvn 5th: t.o 7th: p.u after next* 20/1
P501 P **Stafford Charlie**[15] 1468 4-10-13 90 ....(v) CharlieWallis(7) —
(John O'Shea) *in rr: bhd fr 8th: t.o whn p.u bef next* 8/1

5m 57.9s (-7.30) **Going Correction** -0.075s/f (Good)
WFA 4 from 5yo+ 13lb 15 Ran SP% **126.2**
Speed ratings (Par 103): **109,107,106,104,97 94,93,92,92,91** —,—,—,—,—
toteswingers: 1&2 £23.30, 1&3 £2.70, 2&3 £26.60 CSF £69.19 CT £273.01 TOTE £5.60: £2.80, £7.70, £1.80; EX 163.80 Place 6 £4,959.30, Place 5 £1,333.08.
Owner Broadway Racing Club 15 **Bred** Mrs D R Schreiber **Trained** High Eldwick, W Yorks

FOCUS
Just a modest novices' handicap, but the form looks sound enough for the grade with the first four pulling a long way clear.
NOTEBOOK
Rebel Swing ◆ had plenty to do turning into the straight and was still only fourth over the last, but picked up well from there to win readily. He is progressing nicely and there is more to come from him. If anything he will stay further. (op 9-2 tchd 5-1)
Calypso Bay(IRE) had shown very little previously, but the extra mile and switch to handicaps saw him in a much better light. He battled his way to the front after the last only for the winner to sweep past. (tchd 16-1 and 20-1)
Auberge(IRE) had beaten Rebel Swing at Cartmel two runs back but was 9lb worse off here. She ran a solid race but was just held after nodding over the last. (op 7-2 tchd 3-1)
Himitas(FR) ran well on this handicap debut, but after showing ahead three from home she could not hold on after the last. She seems worth persevering with over this trip. (tchd 18-1)
The Wee Midget was well beaten in the end but was probably not far off his Newton Abbot level.
Stafford Charlie, raised no less than 15lb after an easy win in a Stratford seller, was just about in touch when a mistake down the back straight ended any lingering hopes. (op 7-1)
T/Jkpt: Not won. T/Plt: £17,133.10 to a £1 stake. Pool: £78,624.64. 3.35 winning tickets. T/Qpdt: £1,798.30 to a £1 stake. Pool: £6,075.57. 2.50 winning tickets. WG

1560 - 1566a (Foreign Racing) - See Raceform Interactive

1466 STRATFORD (L-H)
Tuesday, September 21

OFFICIAL GOING: Good to firm (good in places on chase course; hdl 10.7; chs 9.9)
Water jump omitted on all circuits of the chase course; false ground. Hurdle rails moved out by 2m and chase rails moved in by 3m.
Wind: almost nil Weather: hot and sunny

1567 PADDY POWER REDDITCH CUSTOMERS "NATIONAL HUNT" NOVICES' HURDLE (9 hdls) 2m 110y
2:10 (2:10) (Class 4) 4-Y-0+ £2,602 (£764; £382; £190)

Form RPR
340- 1 **My Brother Sylvest**[215] 4123 4-10-12 0 .... RhysFlint 111+
(David Brace) *mde all at decent pce: j.rt 1st: mstke 2nd: 4 l clr and in command whn hit 2 out: j. sltly rt last: unchal* **5/1**
-26F 2 17 **Flichity (IRE)**[32] 1310 5-10-9 108 .... AdrianLane(3) 96+
(Donald McCain) *settled off pce in midfield: effrt 5th: chsd wnr after 3 out: sn rdn and finding little: hit 2 out: 8 l 2nd whn blnd last* **2/1**[1]
0500 3 7 **Reg's Ruby**[22] 1433 4-10-5 0 .... RodiGreene 79
(David Bridgwater) *chsd wnr fr 3rd tl rdn after 3 out: steadily fdd: 20 l 3rd whn tired jump last* **100/1**
0001 4 10 **Littledean Jimmy (IRE)**[17] 1472 5-10-5 0 .... CharlieWallis(7) 76
(John O'Shea) *off pce in midfield: mstkes 3rd and 4th: wknd 3 out: 20 l 4th st* **9/1**
403- 5 5 **Backfromthebrink (IRE)**[190] 4636 6-10-12 0 .... WillKennedy 71
(Paul Webber) *off pce in midfield: clsng whn bmpd 5th and drvn: sn toiling: t.o 3 out* **9/2**[3]
00- 6 38 **Alarming Alacrity (IRE)**[301] 2490 4-10-9 0 .... DPFahy(3) 33
(Evan Williams) *chsd ldrs: j.rt 5th: struggling next: t.o after 3 out* **33/1**
06 7 4 **Mr Demister**[15] 1488 7-10-7 0 ow2 .... MissLGardner(7) 31
(Susan Gardner) *taken v steadily in rr: impeded 2nd: t.o after mstke 3rd: plugging on at fin* **100/1**
000- 8 1 ½ **Magical Maybe (IRE)**[291] 2690 5-10-12 0 .... DavidDennis 28
(Matt Sheppard) *a bhd: t.o 3 out* **50/1**
/00- 9 2 ½ **Over The Hill**[336] 1840 6-10-12 0 .... PaddyBrennan 25
(Nigel Twiston-Davies) *t.k.h: nt jump wl: pressed wnr tl mstke 3rd: losing pl whn mstke 5th: t.o 3 out* **9/4**[2]
00 F **La Chemme**[108] 637 4-10-5 0 .... PaulMoloney —
(Reg Hollinshead) *sweating profusely: plld v hrd in rr tl fell 2nd* **50/1**

3m 45.2s (-10.80) **Going Correction** -0.45s/f (Good) 10 Ran SP% **117.8**
Speed ratings (Par 105): **107,99,95,91,88 70,68,68,67,—**
totewingers:1&2:£3.10, 1&3:£31.70, 2&3:£45.80 CSF £15.94 TOTE £7.30: £3.10, £2.30, £18.10; EX 19.30.
Owner David Brace **Bred** David Brace **Trained** Pyle, Bridgend

FOCUS
There was no strength-in-depth to this contest. The winner stepped up in his bumper form and looks a decent recruit.
NOTEBOOK
My Brother Sylvest made all for a stylish success. Twice placed in bumpers for another yard, he had his rivals burnt off some way from the finish and cleared even further away in the straight to win as he liked. This was a really pleasing start from the 4-y-o, and he remains capable of better on this sort of ground. (op 13-2 tchd 7-1)
Flichity(IRE), already held when slipping and falling at Bangor last month, couldn't match the winner, but this would have helped restore some confidence and he may fare better in handicaps. (op 3-1)
Reg's Ruby ran easily her best race so far over hurdles and she should have a future in low-grade handicaps.
Littledean Jimmy(IRE), winner of a course bumper earlier in the month, ended up well held, but should learn from the experience. Official explanation: vet said gelding lost a shoe (op 13-2)
Backfromthebrink(IRE) was always going to find this test on the sharp side, and he won't be seen at his best until faced with 3m in handicaps. (op 5-1)
Magical Maybe(IRE) Official explanation: vet said gelding was struck into
Over The Hill was supported throughout the day, but he stopped very quickly, having raced keenly, and needs to brush up his jumping. (tchd 2-1 and 5-2)

1568 PADDY POWER WOLVERHAMPTON CUSTOMERS NOVICES' CHASE (13 fncs 1 omitted) 2m 4f
2:40 (2:40) (Class 4) 4-Y-0+ £2,927 (£859; £429; £214)

Form RPR
06-1 1 **Cootehill (IRE)**[27] 1371 6-11-6 0 .... PaddyBrennan 131+
(Nigel Twiston-Davies) *settled 3rd: pressed ldr and hit 10th: led on bit bef last: v easily* **1/1**[1]
3P-1 2 4 **Mam Ratagan**[17] 1467 9-11-3 120 .... PeterToole(3) 115
(Heather Main) *t.k.h and sn led: drew clr w wnr after 2 out: rdn and hdd bef last: v flattered by proximity to wnr* **9/2**[3]
02/P 3 10 **Lerubis (FR)**[20] 1450 11-10-6 0 .... MrRGHenderson(7) 99
(Ken Wingrove) *nt fluent early: in tch tl rdn 9th: drvn and btn whn nt fluent 2 out: lft poor 3rd bef last where blnd bdly* **100/1**
1500 4 48 **Mzuri Bay**[13] 1507 5-10-13 0 .... (bt1) MarkGrant 50
(Brendan Duke) *last pair: rdn 8th: no rspnse: t.o whn mstke 3 out: lft 4th bef last* **28/1**
1521 P **Walamo (GER)**[22] 1432 6-11-13 0 .... (t) RichardJohnson —
(Tim Vaughan) *p.u lame 2nd: bdly wrong bhd: cut hind leg bdly* **12/1**
12- P **Ravenclaw (IRE)**[190] 4636 7-10-13 0 .... JackDoyle —
(Emma Lavelle) *chsd ldr tl 10th: wkng whn eased after 2 out: poor 4th whn p.u at last: b.b.v* **5/2**[2]

4m 46.7s (-7.50) **Going Correction** -0.45s/f (Good) 6 Ran SP% **108.9**
Speed ratings (Par 105): **97,95,91,72,— —**
toteswingers:1&2:£3.90, 1&3:£1.90, 2&3:£3.20 CSF £5.77 TOTE £2.00: £1.10, £1.90; EX 4.80.
Owner Mrs Felicity Griffin **Bred** B And I McCelland **Trained** Naunton, Gloucs

FOCUS
A fair novices' chase that was won in good style by Cootehill who was value for a lot further.
NOTEBOOK
Cootehill(IRE) made it 2-2 over fences. Successful in a match race on his debut at Ffos Las, this represented a stiffer test, but the quicker ground was in his favour and he always looked in control, cruising clear under Paddy Brennan. He looks capable of mixing it with a stronger calibre of opposition, and will probably turn up at next month's Cheltenham meeting. (op 6-4 tchd 10-11)
Mam Ratagan, finally off the mark over fences at the course last time, always races enthusiastically and he was the only one capable of troubling the winner, though in the end he was well and truly put in his place. (op 4-1 tchd 5-1)
Lerubis(FR) kept on steadily inside the final 4f despite jumping poorly.
Walamo(GER) Official explanation: vet said gelding suffered a cut leg (op 9-4 tchd 11-4)
Ravenclaw(IRE), a 123-rated hurdler, looked to get tired on this first start in 190 days and his rider wasted no time in pulling him up. This wasn't his true form, obviously, and he deserves another chance. Official explanation: jockey said gelding bled from the nose (op 9-4 tchd 11-4)

1569 BOTT H'CAP HURDLE (9 hdls) 2m 110y
3:10 (3:10) (Class 4) (0-115,115) 4-Y-0+ £2,602 (£764; £382; £190)

Form RPR
3262 1 **Olivino (GER)**[15] 1492 9-10-13 109 .... MissIsabelTompsett(7) 111+
(Bernard Llewellyn) *settled midfield: rdn to cl fr 3 out: led after next: r.o gamely* **7/1**
2465 2 1 ¼ **Exulto (IRE)**[34] 1282 5-11-9 112 .... RichardJohnson 114
(Philip Hobbs) *prom: mstke 4th: rdn to ld bef 2 out where mstke: sn hdd and outbattled* **4/1**[1]
515- 3 6 **Feeling (IRE)**[7] 2532 6-10-10 99 .... ChristianWilliams 95
(Dai Burchell) *pressed ldrs: rdn after 3 out: cl 3rd next: fnd little after* **14/1**
P565 4 5 **Welcome Stranger**[16] 1484 10-10-6 95 .... DenisO'Regan 85
(Louise Davis) *bhd: rdn to go 6th 3 out where chsng ldrs: nvr looked to be gng wl enough after: no imp fr 2 out* **5/1**[3]
2-34 5 5 **Sonic Anthem (USA)**[110] 598 8-10-7 96 .... RhysFlint 81
(John Mackie) *led & t.k.h: hdd 3 out: rdn & fdd bef next* **7/1**
P50 6 4 ½ **Rocklandslad (IRE)**[32] 1308 7-10-11 107 .... (b1) AodhaganConlon(7) 88
(Rebecca Curtis) *chsd ldr 3rd tl led 3 out: drvn and hdd bef 2 out: fin v weakly* **25/1**
3400 7 6 **Bathwick Man**[13] 1508 5-11-12 115 .... (tp) TomScudamore 90
(David Pipe) *bhd: rdn and lost tch after 4th* **11/1**
12 8 3 ½ **January**[15] 1493 7-11-9 112 .... (t) TimmyMurphy 83
(Liam Corcoran) *midfield: 5th bef 6th where j.v.slowly and lost all ch: wl bhd after next: put hd in air* **7/1**
0P-P 9 9 **Orpen Wide (IRE)**[24] 1406 8-10-11 107 .... (bt) JoeCornwall(7) 69
(Michael Chapman) *chsd ldr tl 3rd: drvn and struggling bef 5th: t.o 3 out* **33/1**
110/ P **Mister Right (IRE)**[750] 1835 9-10-11 103 .... PeterToole(3) —
(Dominic Ffrench Davis) *t.k.h in midfield: nt fluent 5th and rdn: sn lost pl: t.o and p.u 3 out* **50/1**
04U1 P **Nether Stream (IRE)**[17] 1470 6-11-1 104 .... AidanColeman —
(Shaun Lycett) *blnd 1st: nvr gng wl in last: nt fluent: u.p 4th: t.o and p.u 6th* **9/2**[2]

3m 47.8s (-8.20) **Going Correction** -0.45s/f (Good) 11 Ran SP% **116.1**
Speed ratings (Par 105): **101,100,97,95,92 90,87,86,82,— —**
toteswingers:1&2:£7.20, 1&3:£11.70, 2&3:£16.10 CSF £34.79 CT £384.95 TOTE £9.60: £3.40, £1.20, £7.00; EX 41.30.
Owner Alex James **Bred** A And R Monscheuer **Trained** Fochriw, Caerphilly

FOCUS
A competitive handicap hurdle. Ordinary but sound form.
NOTEBOOK
Olivino(GER) won his first race since the summer of last year. He has been running well of late, including when second at Newton Abbot earlier in the month, and he stayed on best for pressure, appreciating the return to a sound surface. Official explanation: vet said gelding finished distressed (op 15-2 tchd 13-2)
Exulto(IRE), narrowly denied off this mark over the C&D back in June, has not been running so well of late, but this signalled a return to something like his best, just not staying on as strongly as the winner. (op 9-2 tchd 7-2)
Feeling(IRE), who ran creditably considering the saddle had slipped back on the Flat the other day, didn't find as much as respected returned to hurdles and ended up comfortably held. (op 20-1)
Welcome Stranger never really got close enough to throw down a serious challenge and was a tad disappointing, failing to build on his recent Worcester effort. (op 13-2)
Sonic Anthem(USA) didn't last home having raced keenly. (op 13-2 tchd 6-1)
January made a costly mistake and didn't look keen under pressure. (op 5-1 tchd 8-1)
Nether Stream(IRE) was nevver going following a blunder at the first. Official explanation: jockey said gelding made a mistake first flight and never travelled (op 5-1 tchd 4-1)

1570 PADDY POWER NEW SMALL HEATH SHOP H'CAP CHASE (18 fncs 2 omitted) 3m 4f
3:40 (3:40) (Class 3) (0-135,126) 4-Y-0+ £4,943 (£1,451; £725; £362)

Form RPR
-613 1 **Simply Smashing (IRE)**[26] 1376 10-10-4 111 .... (t) KyleJames(7) 128
(Philip Kirby) *led fr 2nd: rdn and looked vulnerable fr bef 2 out: kpt pulling out ex: in command again last: styd on stoutly* **8/1**
2255 2 5 **Templer (IRE)**[27] 1373 9-11-4 125 .... MattGriffiths(7) 137
(Philip Hobbs) *pressed ldrs: mstke 9th: wnt 2nd after 12th: looked to be gng wl after: rdn and drew level briefly between last two: nt qckn fr last* **11/4**[1]
F-12 3 24 **Job One (FR)**[20] 1452 7-11-0 114 .... HaddenFrost 102
(Henrietta Knight) *bhd: hdwy 11th: wnt 3rd at 15th: 3 l 3rd 2 out: sn wknd and fin tired* **11/2**[2]
4415 4 4 ½ **Pairc Na Gcapall (IRE)**[17] 1469 8-10-11 114 .... (b) AlexMerriam(3) 98
(Neil King) *racd freely: chsd ldr mostly 5th tl after 12th: 7 l 3rd at 14th: struggling whn mstke next* **16/1**
P16- 5 20 **Mr Big (IRE)**[158] 5212 9-10-10 110 .... (p) NoelFehily 74+
(Charlie Mann) *t.k.h: midfield: hdwy 9th: prom 10th tl next: 10 l 5th and wkng 15th: bttr for r* **11/2**[2]
3011 6 ¾ **Cold Mountain (IRE)**[78] 911 8-11-7 126 .... JimmyDerham(5) 89
(Seamus Mullins) *sn last: rdn 13th: struggling after: t.o 3 out* **9/1**
1224 7 25 **Chorizo (IRE)**[56] 1103 9-11-4 118 .... APMcCoy 56
(Richard Guest) *chsd ldrs tl blnd 11th: nvr rcvrd: 6th and btn at 14th: t.o 3 out* **15/2**

3413 **8** *6* **Swordsman (GER)**[16] 1476 8-10-0 **107**........................(vt) MrTJCannon(7) 39
(Chris Gordon) *j. slowly 1st: drvn along vigorously most of way: nvr wnt a yard: lost tch 12th: t.o 3 out* **14/1**

1-11 **P** **House Of Bourbon (IRE)**[96] 771 7-11-3 **117**.........(vt) RichardJohnson —
(Tim Vaughan) *led tl 2nd: rdn and wknd after 11th: t.o whn climbed 3 out: p.u last* **7/1**[3]

12P5 **P** **Tampa Boy (IRE)**[15] 1491 8-10-13 **113**..............................(t) CharliePoste —
(Milton Harris) *midfield: rdn bef 11th: struggling 13th: t.o 3 out: p.u last* **28/1**

6m 43.8s (-19.20) **Going Correction** -0.45s/f (Good) course record **10** Ran SP% **118.8**
Speed ratings (Par 107): **109,107,100,99,93 93,86,84,—,—**
toteswingers:1&2:£12.20, 1&3:£10.10, 2&3:£5.70 CSF £32.09 CT £135.57 TOTE £9.80: £2.60, £1.10, £2.90; EX 36.90.
Owner P McMartin, M Mahon & C Fletcher **Bred** Thomas Heffernan **Trained** Castleton, N Yorks

FOCUS
The front two drew clear in what was a modest staying handicap chase. The winner posted a personal best.

NOTEBOOK
Simply Smashing(IRE) put up a particularly game effort to win his second race of the season. A certain stayer, he set off in front and jumped well throughout, then when challenged by the runner-up, kept pulling out more until he had the race in safe keeping at the last. A likeable sort, this was the highest mark he has ever won off and things will be tougher in future, but he's clearly still progressing. (tchd 9-1)
Templer(IRE) was never far away and looked the winner turning into the straight, but he found nowhere near as much as Simply Smashing and was always being held from the last. (tchd 5-2 and 10-3)
Job One(FR) looked interesting on this return to handicaps and he ran well for a long way, but stamina ultimately failed him. Official explanation: vet said gelding finished distressed (op 7-1)
Pairc Na Gcapall(IRE) was again comfortably held off this mark. (tchd 18-1)
Mr Big(IRE) showed enough before getting tired to suggest he's up to winning off this sort of mark. (op 8-1)
Swordsman(GER) Official explanation: vet said gelding lost a shoe
House Of Bourbon(IRE) was seeking a four-timer having won three straight over hurdles, but he didn't look overly happy and failed to run his race. (op 11-2 tchd 5-1)

1571 JOHN SMITHS MAIDEN HURDLE (12 hdls) 2m 6f 110y
4:10 (4:10) (Class 4) 4-Y-0+ **£2,276** (£668; £334; £166)

Form RPR
324- **1** **Theologist (IRE)**[156] 5243 4-10-12 111.................................. JamieMoore 107
(Dr Richard Newland) *hld up in bunch in v slow r: clsd 7th: w ldr briefly 9th: nt fluent next and drvn and outpcd: 5 l 3rd 2 out: styd on u.p to snatch verdict* **5/4**[1]

23 **2** *shd* **Mutadarrej (IRE)**[22] 1433 6-11-0 110... APMcCoy 111+
(Ian Williams) *nt fluent: hld up: clsd w bunch 7th: chal 9th: drvn ahd on ins bef 2 out: awkward again at last: jst ct* **5/4**[1]

4P6 **3** *5* **Unleashed (IRE)**[17] 1466 5-11-0 0.. NoelFehily 106+
(Charlie Mann) *hld up: effrt 7th: reminders next: led 9th tl edgd rt home turn: hdd and mstke 2 out: plodded on* **13/2**[2]

06/5 **4** *2 ½* **Its Danny Boy (IRE)**[16] 1487 7-11-0 0...................................... RhysFlint 101
(David Brace) *hld up: effrt 7th: rdn and outpcd after 3 out: plugged on* **20/1**[3]

F04 **5** *11* **Top Tide (IRE)**[21] 1445 9-11-0 0.. JackDoyle 90
(Martin Hill) *nt fluent: chsd clr ldr: clsd 7th: lost pl 9th: wkng whn mstke 3 out* **66/1**

F **6** *125* **Great Bounder (CAN)**[16] 1475 4-10-12 0........................ NickScholfield —
(Michael Blake) *led and wavering bdly at hurdles: up to 12 l clr tl 6th: hdd 8th: stopped to nil bef 3 out: sn hopelessly t.o* **50/1**

P **Winbury**[577] 7-10-7 0... MrRGHenderson(7) —
(Ken Wingrove) *last and u.p 6th: blnd next: continued although hopelessly t.o tl p.u 9th* **150/1**

5m 19.7s (-8.40) **Going Correction** -0.45s/f (Good)
WFA 4 from 5yo+ 12lb **7** Ran SP% **111.1**
Speed ratings (Par 105): **96,95,94,93,89 —,—**
toteswingers:1&2:£1.30, 1&3:£2.50, 2&3:£2.10 CSF £2.89 TOTE £3.00: £1.70, £1.10; EX 3.60.
Owner C E Stedman **Bred** Gestut Romerhof **Trained** Claines, Worcs

FOCUS
This looked a match between the front two in the market. It was steadily run and the winner is rated below his best. The second probably should have won.

NOTEBOOK
Theologist(IRE) got up in the final strides to deny the favourite. Although without a win in seven previous tries over hurdles, he kept some decent company last season, and this trip on decent ground was always likely to bring about improvement. He took an age to pick up having come under pressure, but showed a determined attitude and may have even more to offer at 3m. (op 13-8 tchd 15-8)
Mutadarrej(IRE), twice a winner on the Flat this summer, has been finding 2m on the sharp side since returned to hurdles, so this much longer trip looked in his favour. He looked all over the winner having got the better of Unleashed, but idled once in front and was worn down close home. He certainly stayed, but doesn't look straightforward and may need headgear. (tchd Evens and 11-8 in places)
Unleashed(IRE) rather ran in snatches, but he showed a lot more zest than in previous starts. His finishing effort was weak, however, which is a concern for a horse who's reportedly bled in the past. (op 5-1)
Its Danny Boy(IRE) kept grinding away and looks a likely sort for 3m handicaps. This point winner will probably be happiest once jumping fences. (op 14-1)

1572 JENKINSONS STANDARD OPEN NATIONAL HUNT FLAT RACE 2m 110y
4:40 (4:40) (Class 5) 4-6-Y-O **£1,626** (£477; £238; £119)

Form RPR
1 **Panache** 5-10-7 .... MrPJTolman(7) 99+
(C Roberts) *plld hrd in dawdle: led over 1f out: ran on* **13/2**[3]

010 **2** *2 ¾* **Thomas Bell (IRE)**[60] 1086 6-11-0 .... CharlieWallis(7) 100
(John O'Shea) *sn 2nd: rdn over 2f out: v one pce fnl f* **14/1**

32 **3** *2 ¾* **Alaska River (IRE)**[105] 686 4-10-7 .... APMcCoy 83
(Brendan Duke) *led at crawl: rdn 4f out: hdd over 1f out: gave up tamely* **10/11**[1]

4 *3* **La Milanaise** 4-10-0 .... RachaelGreen(7) 80
(Anthony Honeyball) *in tch: rn green fr 4f out: wkng whn j. path over 1f out* **2/1**[2]

5 *12* **Logan Rock** 6-11-0 .... JackDoyle 75
(Susan Gardner) *bucked rdr off leaving paddock: in last pair: lost tch 3f out* **33/1**

3m 55.1s (4.70) **Going Correction** -0.45s/f (Good)
WFA 4 from 5yo+ 11lb **5** Ran SP% **108.7**
Speed ratings: **70,68,67,66,60**
CSF £69.70 TOTE £8.50: £2.00, £4.30; EX 46.00 Place 6 £94.32; Place 5 £47.39.
Owner Dr Simon Clarke **Bred** Cheveley Park Stud Ltd **Trained** Coedkernew, Newport

FOCUS
A weak bumper run at a dawdle. The form is rated through the second, with the winner probably capable of better.

NOTEBOOK
Panache, a half-brother to Echelon and Chic, comes from a yard whose record in bumpers in recent years is 0-37, but he certainly didn't need to be anything out of the ordinary to score and he did so in style in the end, getting well on top inside the final furlong. Whether he'll be able to defy a penalty remains to be seen, though. (op 6-1 tchd 9-2 and 7-1)
Thomas Bell(IRE) has been finding life tough under the penalty, but this was a fair effort and he'll do well once sent hurdling. (op 9-1)
Alaska River(IRE) set off in front under McCoy, but it was clear from 4f out that she wasn't going to have things her own way and, having been strongly challenged in the straight, she ultimately backed out of the fight. This was disappointing. (op 8-11)
La Milanaise, from a yard capable of getting winners in this sphere, didn't show enough to suggest she'll be winning a bumper. (op 10-3)
T/Plt: £136.00 to a £1 stake. Pool:£66,373.99 - 356.04 winning tickets T/Qpdt: £52.00 to a £1 stake. Pool:£5,404.46 - 76.80 winning tickets IM

1337 PERTH (R-H)
Wednesday, September 22

OFFICIAL GOING: Soft (good to soft in places; 6.8)
All bends moved out to provide fresh ground but impact on distances not quantified.
Wind: Almost nil Weather: Overcast, drizzle

1573 SALUTATION HOTEL MAIDEN HURDLE (10 hdls) 2m 4f 110y
2:25 (2:25) (Class 4) 4-Y-0+ **£2,276** (£668; £334; £166)

Form RPR
22- **1** **Frontier Spirit (IRE)**[262] 3281 6-10-11 0.............. SamTwiston-Davies(3) 110+
(Nigel Twiston-Davies) *t.k.h: trckd ldrs: effrt and led 2 out: j.rt last: rdn and styd on strly* **6/1**[3]

2-44 **2** *1 ¾* **Devotion To Duty (IRE)**[73] 943 4-10-13 110................ PeterBuchanan 105
(Lucinda Russell) *hld up towards rr: hdwy 3 out: chal next: kpt on run-in: nt rch wnr* **14/1**

3 *1* **Traffic Article (IRE)**[33] 1315 6-11-0 0...................................(t) PCarberry 106
(Gordon Elliott, Ire) *hld up in midfield: stdy hdwy and cl up after 3 out: effrt next: cl 3rd whn pckd last: kpt on same pce* **5/1**[2]

424- **4** *8* **Present To You (IRE)**[192] 4615 5-11-0 124.................. RichardJohnson 98
(Philip Hobbs) *t.k.h: cl up: led 4 out to 2 out: sn rdn: wknd last* **5/6**[1]

4-05 **5** *3 ¾* **Rossini's Dancer**[122] 445 5-11-0 87....................................... PaddyAspell 94
(Sue Bradburne) *in tch: effrt after 3 out: rdn and wknd fr next* **100/1**

343- **6** *22* **Fightstar (FR)**[152] 5376 6-10-11 0................................ CampbellGillies(3) 71
(Lucinda Russell) *prom tl rdn and wknd after 3 out* **33/1**

323 **7** *11* **Treason Trial**[25] 1401 9-11-0 105.. BarryKeniry 60
(Joss Saville) *hld up: drvn 4 out: shortlived effrt after next: sn btn* **33/1**

0- **8** *55* **Solway Silver**[325] 2025 4-10-10 0.................................... HarryHaynes(3) 4
(Lisa Harrison) *bhd: drvn and outpcd 1/2-way: sn lost tch* **100/1**

54UP **P** **Skiddaw Jones**[15] 1502 10-10-11 0.................................(t) RyanMania(3) —
(Maurice Barnes) *led to 4 out: wknd after next: t.o whn p.u bef 2 out* **100/1**

P **Promising Times (IRE)**[6] 1536 7-11-0 0.. APMcCoy —
(John Joseph Hanlon, Ire) *prom: nt fluent 3 out: wknd qckly: p.u bef next* **6/1**[3]

P **Harley Road (IRE)**[635] 2980 7-11-0 0.................................. TimmyMurphy —
(Gordon Elliott, Ire) *hld up: rdn after 4 out: sn struggling: t.o whn p.u bef 2 out* **50/1**

0- **P** **Legbeforewicket**[210] 4235 4-10-6 0.. BrianHughes —
(James Bethell) *nt jump wl: a last: t.o whn p.u after 4 out* **150/1**

5m 17.6s (10.70) **Going Correction** +0.60s/f (Soft)
WFA 4 from 5yo+ 12lb **12** Ran SP% **117.9**
Speed ratings (Par 105): **103,102,101,98,97 89,84,63,—,— —,—**
Tote Swingers: 1&2 £14.70, 1&3 £3.70, 2&3 £33.50 CSF £77.89 TOTE £6.10: £1.90, £4.00, £2.30; EX 46.80.
Owner Jump For Fun Racing **Bred** Edward Ryan **Trained** Naunton, Gloucs

FOCUS
Rain fell before racing (5.5mm during the morning), which changed the going to soft, good to soft in places. A competitive event, as at least seven of these could be given some sort of chance on the ability they had shown, whether it be over hurdles or in bumpers. The winner is rated up 10lb on his bumper form with the next two close to form.

NOTEBOOK
Frontier Spirit(IRE), who finished runner-up on both his outings in bumpers, tracked the steady early pace and started to quicken up heading to two out, whilst still looking a little green. He kept on resolutely from that point and got his hurdling career off to a perfect start. (op 9-2)
Devotion To Duty(IRE), up in trip, made good ground from the rear and appeared to be narrowly in front jumping the second-last. He didn't give up under pressure, but found the winner in a determined mood and wasn't able to hang on once joined. (op 16-1 tchd 20-1)
Traffic Article(IRE), back up in trip and with a tongue-tie fitted, was a little keen under restraint but showed a good attitude down the home straight until making a slight mistake at the final hurdle. (op 6-1 tchd 7-1)
Present To You(IRE) officially rated 124 and down in trip after trying 3m1f last time, raced too enthusiastically at the head of affairs. His stamina gave way heading to two out and, with hindsight, his jockey would have been better to go on earlier while the combination were travelling so strongly. (op 6-5 tchd 11-8 in a place)
Rossini's Dancer went well for a long way on his return from a break but it remains to be seen whether he can build in this.
Promising Times(IRE), making a fairly quick reappearance after a good effort after a lengthy break, is a big sort and may have found this coming too soon after his outing in Ireland. (op 5-1)

1574 PERTH FM 106.6 CLAIMING HURDLE (7 hdls 1 omitted) 2m 110y
3:00 (3:01) (Class 4) 4-6-Y-O **£2,276** (£668; £334; £166)

Form RPR
5-11 **1** **Riverscape (IRE)**[28] 1090 5-10-5 132....................................(t) PCarberry 114+
(Gordon Elliott, Ire) *hld up: smooth hdwy 2 out (usual 3 out): led bef next: canter* **2/5**[1]

302- **2** *2 ½* **Grand Diamond (IRE)**[14] 2547 6-11-0 0...........................(p) GrahamLee 108
(Jim Goldie) *cl up: lft in ld 3rd: rdn and hdd bef last (usual 2 out): flattered by proximity to wnr* **9/2**[2]

65 **3** *19* **Galileo Figaro (AUS)**[29] 1359 6-10-10 0.............................. BarryKeniry 85
(Joss Saville) *prom: rdn 2 out (usual 3 out): wknd bef next* **80/1**

4 *8* **Holyrood**[23] 1435 4-10-12 0...(p) DenisO'Regan 79
(T G McCourt, Ire) *trckd ldrs tl rdn and wknd after 2 out (usual 3 out)* **8/1**[3]

3400 **5** *8* **King's Chorister**[25] 1407 4-10-7 66.........................(tp) CampbellGillies(3) 69
(Barry Murtagh) *cl up: lft cl 2nd 3rd: wknd 2 out (usual 3 out)* **100/1**

FU0- **B** **No Supper (IRE)**[290] [2735] 6-10-7 0.................................... MrJBewley(7) —
(George Bewley) *in tch tl b.d 3rd* **40/1**

F **Knockbaun Prince (IRE)**[51] [1169] 6-10-10 0................ RichardJohnson —
(John G Carr, Ire) *led tl fell 3rd* **16/1**

4m 6.00s (6.30) **Going Correction** +0.60s/f (Soft)
WFA 4 from 5yo+ 11lb 7 Ran SP% **111.3**
Speed ratings: **109,107,98,95,91** —,—
Tote Swingers: 1&2 £1.02, 1&3 £8.90, 2&3 £23.70 CSF £2.52 TOTE £1.40: £1.30, £1.10; EX 2.60.Riverscape was claimed by B. D. Haynes for £7,000.
Owner Fresh By Nature Syndicate **Bred** Newberry Stud Farm Ltd **Trained** Trim, Co Meath

FOCUS
The market suggested that this was going to be a one-sided affair as Riverscape stood out in a weak race. She is rated value for a lot further.

NOTEBOOK
Riverscape(IRE), apart from a minor worrying moment when she was hampered by a horse that was brought down, won as her odds implied. She didn't need to come off the bridle to gain victory and bolted up, so it wasn't a surprise that someone claimed her afterwards. (op 4-9 tchd 1-2)
Grand Diamond(IRE), who probably had no realistic chance giving a 132-rated hurdler weight, helped to share the work out in front in the early stages and was the only one to make the winner do any work from the home bend.
Galileo Figaro(AUS) was still going reasonably well turning in but looked thoroughly one-paced when asked to quicken. (op 100-1)
Holyrood doesn't look one to trust. (op 10-1)
King's Chorister Official explanation: trainer said gelding lost a hind shoe

1575 7TH EDWARD MASSIE BROWN CLASSIC NOVICES' H'CAP CHASE (12 fncs) 2m

3:35 (3:36) (Class 4) (0-115,105) 4-Y-0+ **£3,998** (£1,241; £668)

Form RPR
P-U1 **1** **Cappagh (IRE)**[133] [273] 5-11-12 **105**....................................... APMcCoy 123+
(Philip Hobbs) *nt fluent on occasions: hld up: stdy hdwy whn lft 4 l 3rd 3 out: sn chsng ldr: led gng wl run-in: nt extended* **4/1**[3]

22P- **2** *1 ¼* **Reland (FR)**[183] [4800] 5-11-6 **102**.......................... SamTwiston-Davies(3) 108
(Nigel Twiston-Davies) *chsd ldrs: led 8th: rdn bef 3 out: hdd run-in: no ch w wnr* **5/4**[1]

06-6 **3** *29* **Best Horse (FR)**[23] [1426] 8-10-13 **92**.................................. GrahamLee 83+
(Ferdy Murphy) *hld up in tch: effrt and lft 3 l 2nd 3 out: wknd fr next* **14/1**

0-55 **F** **Safin (GER)**[9] [405] 10-10-0 **79** oh5...............................(t) WilsonRenwick —
(Sue Bradburne) *cl up whn fell 1st* **50/1**

PUF0 **R** **Lindseyfield Lodge (IRE)**[15] [1504] 9-10-10 **92**........... FearghalDavis(3) —
(Robert Johnson) *led tl rn out paddock bnd after 5th* **16/1**

U **Silver Palm (IRE)**[4] [1541] 7-11-12 **105**...........................(t) JohnnyFarrelly —
(John Joseph Hanlon, Ire) *cl up: lft in ld paddock bnd after 5th: hdd 8th: rallied: rdn and 2 l 2nd whn awkward and uns rdr 3 out* **16/1**

2F-1 **R** **Kosta Brava (FR)**[139] [174] 6-11-7 **103**.............................. RyanMania(3) —
(Howard Johnson) *cl up: lft in ld whn rn out paddock bnd after 5th* **3/1**[2]

4m 13.2s (10.50) **Going Correction** +0.60s/f (Soft) 7 Ran SP% **109.8**
Speed ratings (Par 105): **97,96,81**,—,— —,—
Tote Swingers: 1&2 £1.20, 1&3 £4.30, 2&3 £4.80 CSF £9.13 TOTE £3.50: £2.50, £1.10; EX 6.80.
Owner John P McManus **Bred** Legends Stud **Trained** Withycombe, Somerset

FOCUS
Anotehr step forward from the easy winner, who was value for a lot further.

NOTEBOOK
Cappagh(IRE)who had been raised 15lb after winning over hurdles in May, won with a bit in hand after taking his time to get into the race. Taking a sharp drop in distance, his jumping was sometimes sloppy and not fluent on his chasing debut, but his rider never gave up and finessed his mount back into contention coming into the home straight. The jockey was possibly mindful of his mount's antics at Exeter two starts previous, so delayed his effort until as late as possible. The winning margin doesn't give a clear indication of his superiority and one would imagine that he can gain a hat-trick if his mind stays on the job. (op 5-2)
Reland(FR), absent since pulling up in a 2m4.5f novice handicap chase back in March, came clear of the other horse that completed but is still to get his head in front. (op 2-1)
Best Horse(FR) did at least finish but never held any serious chance when the tempo increased. (op 11-1)
Lindseyfield Lodge(IRE) decided that going out for a final circuit was not for him, and slammed the brakes on just before he was due to head away from the paddock bend. (op 14-1)
Silver Palm(IRE) did at least finish but never held any serious chance when the tempo increased. (op 14-1)
Kosta Brava(FR), who was sat in second when the leader ran out, also declined the opportunity to go round again and headed back towards the paddock. (op 14-1)

1576 A C MANAGEMENT CONSULTING JUVENILE HURDLE (8 hdls) 2m 110y

4:10 (4:10) (Class 4) 3-Y-O **£2,602** (£764; £382; £190)

Form RPR
1 **Al Dafa (USA)**[10] [1514] 3-10-12 0.. PCarberry 92+
(Gordon Elliott, Ire) *cl up: hit 3 out: led bef next: sn rdn: kpt on wl run-in* **11/8**[1]

2 *6* **Ancient Times (USA)**[33] 3-10-12 0..................................... BarryKeniry 84
(Joss Saville) *prom: hdwy after 3 out: chsd wnr after next: no imp run-in* **28/1**

3 **3** *5* **Leopard Hills (IRE)**[23] [1422] 3-10-9 0................................ RyanMania(3) 79
(Howard Johnson) *cl up: mstke 3 out: ev ch and rdn bef next: wknd bef last* **11/4**[2]

4 *30* **Master Performer (USA)**[67] 3-10-12 0............................. BrianHughes 54
(Barry Murtagh) *led to bef 2 out: sn wknd* **9/2**[3]

P **Weetentherty**[27] 3-10-12 0.. GrahamLee —
(Jim Goldie) *bhd: reminders 2nd: struggling after 4 out: t.o whn p.u bef 2 out* **28/1**

P **Quitao (GER)**[9] 3-10-12 0.. WilsonRenwick —
(P Monteith) *hld up: hmpd bnd after 3rd: sn rdn: wknd 3 out: t.o whn p.u bef next* **80/1**

P **Resolute Road**[43] 3-10-9 0.................................. SamTwiston-Davies(3) —
(Nigel Twiston-Davies) *prom: drvn 4 out: wknd next: t.o whn p.u bef 2 out* **9/2**[3]

4m 16.5s (16.80) **Going Correction** +0.875s/f (Soft) 7 Ran SP% **113.3**
Speed ratings (Par 103): **95,92,89,75**,— —,—
Tote Swingers: 1&2 £5.80, 1&3 £1.30, 2&3 £9.50 CSF £34.77 TOTE £2.30: £1.10, £16.50; EX 43.60.
Owner Sean F Gallagher **Bred** Darley **Trained** Trim, Co Meath

FOCUS
Not much hurdling form to go on in this juvenile contest, so it's not easy to know how good the winner is.

NOTEBOOK
Al Dafa(USA), a well-bred sort for the Flat, had run satisfactorily on his first outing over hurdles, his first start for Gordon Elliott, and duly built on it with a determined effort. Whether he can win again under a penalty is open to debate. It's unlikely that he'll be out during the winter on soft ground, and he could be heading for a run on Polytrack next. (tchd 6-4)
Ancient Times(USA), a modest maiden on the Flat, was an eyecatcher with the way he travelled into a challenging position. He wasn't quite good enough to get to the front, but shaped with enough promise to suggest a small race can come his way. (op 25-1)
Leopard Hills(IRE), a beaten-favourite on his hurdling debut, raced prominently but could only find the one pace when he needed more. (op 3-1 tchd 5-2)
Master Performer(USA), a fair-looking performer on limited evidence when trained in Ireland, was supported in the market but weakened before the home turn after leading. He looked to have sweated up. (op 8-1)
Resolute Road was extremely disappointing and didn't always jump fluently. (op 10-3 tchd 5-1)

1577 SODEXO PRESTIGE H'CAP CHASE (FOR THE DUKE OF ATHOLL CHALLENGE CUP) (18 fncs) 3m

4:45 (4:45) (Class 3) (0-130,130) 4-Y-0+ **£5,204** (£1,528; £764; £381)

Form RPR
3344 **1** **Soubriquet (IRE)**[15] [1501] 7-10-6 **113**..............................(t) RyanMania(3) 128+
(Maurice Barnes) *in tch: hdwy to ld 4 out: drew clr fr 2 out* **14/1**

32/1 **2** *23* **Twelve Paces**[32] [1341] 9-10-4 **108**..................................... TimmyMurphy 98
(P Monteith) *hld up: hdwy and prom 5 out: ev ch and rdn after next: no ex fr 2 out: hld on for 2nd but fin tired* **3/1**[1]

0-06 **3** *2* **Ursis (FR)**[52] [1150] 9-11-2 **120**.. RichardJohnson 108
(Steve Gollings) *cl up: led 5th: j.big next: hdd 4 out: wknd fr 2 out* **9/1**

-P60 **4** *hd* **Catch The Perk (IRE)**[73] [946] 13-10-11 **115**..............(p) PeterBuchanan 103
(Lucinda Russell) *in tch: lost pl after 7th: shortlived effrt bef 4 out: outpcd fr next* **16/1**

2333 **5** *5* **Nudge And Nurdle (IRE)**[26] [1390] 9-11-3 **124**.... SamTwiston-Davies(3) 107
(Nigel Twiston-Davies) *trckd ldrs: pushed along 12th: rallied and chsd ldr next to 4 out: hung rt and wknd 3 out* **11/2**

13P- **P** **Echo Point (IRE)**[211] [4211] 10-11-12 **130**............................ BrianHarding —
(Nicky Richards) *led to 5th: cl up: lost pl bef 8th: t.o whn p.u bef 5 out* **6/1**

11-6 **P** **Valerius (IRE)**[28] [1373] 6-11-10 **128**.....................................(bt) APMcCoy —
(Gordon Elliott, Ire) *cl up: chsd ldr 5th to 12th: wknd next: p.u bef 4 out* **9/2**[3]

P **Steel Magnate (IRE)**[19] [1464] 7-10-6 **110**.............................(t) PCarberry —
(Gordon Elliott, Ire) *hld up last: struggling 13th: t.o whn p.u bef 4 out* **4/1**[2]

6m 21.1s (0.70) **Going Correction** +0.60s/f (Soft) 8 Ran SP% **115.4**
Speed ratings (Par 107): **107,99,98,98,96** —,—,—
Tote Swingers: 1&2 £9.50, 1&3 £9.40, 2&3 £0.20 CSF £50.10 CT £409.59 TOTE £15.00: £5.10, £1.50, £4.20; EX 65.10.
Owner Minstrel's Double Racing **Bred** Stonethorn Stud Farms Ltd **Trained** Farlam, Cumbria

FOCUS
Most of the runners could be given a chance, although there was 22lb between top and bottom weights. The winner was nicely in on his best old form but this still rates a step up of around 7lb. There is a case for rating the form 10lb higher.

NOTEBOOK
Soubriquet(IRE), who had Ryan Mania taking over from Michael McAlister, was beaten a long way over hurdles last time, and had not been over fences since July, but he crept into contention steadily after racing in midfield and edged to the front just after four out. He was always going better than the runner-up at that point, and came home a comfortable winner. (op 25-1)
Twelve Paces, given plenty of time to get over his winning return after a long absence, was settled out that back and made ground up nicely while others faltered. However, he couldn't get the better of the winner as they tussled, and he looked tired after jumping the final fence. (tchd 7-2 and 4-1 in places)
Ursis(FR), back over fences, took the field along at a good pace from the fifth and stayed on fairly well once headed considering the gallop he went. He is possibly up to winning again soon, especially if allowed an uncontested lead. (op 11-1)
Catch The Perk(IRE), the winner of this race in 2004 and 2006, was a gallant fourth on his first outing since July, but may be heading into retirement fairly soon. (tchd 18-1)
Nudge And Nurdle(IRE) was never far away but had nothing extra when asked to quicken. (op 9-2 tchd 6-1 in a place)
Echo Point(IRE) held a narrow lead in the early stages but dropped away before the race started to develop. (tchd 9-2)
Valerius(IRE), who has a fine record at this course, raced close to the lead but couldn't go with the leading bunch as soon as his rider asked for maximum effort. He wouldn't have wanted the ground as soft as it was. (tchd 9-2)
Steel Magnate(IRE) was always detached and rarely suggested that he was going to get involved. Official explanation: jockey said gelding did not jump well (tchd 9-2)

1578 STANJAMES.COM H'CAP HURDLE (12 hdls) 3m 110y

5:20 (5:20) (Class 4) (0-115,112) 4-Y-0+ **£3,252** (£955; £477; £238)

Form RPR
15-0 **1** **Bescot Springs (IRE)**[138] [193] 5-11-12 **112**................. PeterBuchanan 119
(Lucinda Russell) *chsd ldr: rdn and no imp bef 2 out: 7 l down last: styd on to ld towards fin* **9/2**[3]

F51F **2** *2* **Mad Moose (IRE)**[14] [1507] 6-11-7 **110**................. SamTwiston-Davies(3) 115
(Nigel Twiston-Davies) *led: clr bef 2 out: 7 l clr and rdr looked rnd last: hrd rdn last 100yds: no ex and hdd towards fin* **7/4**[1]

20/4 **3** *24* **Soul Magic (IRE)**[32] [1339] 8-9-7 **86** oh6.................. GaryRutherford(7) 67
(Harriet Graham) *t.k.h: trckd ldrs tl wknd bef 2 out* **8/1**

4 *30* **Dickie Henderhoop (IRE)**[24] [1418] 5-10-3 **94**.................... CO'Farrell(5) 45
(John Long, Ire) *t.k.h: prom: hit and reminders 7th: wknd after 4 out* **8/1**

06 **P** **Guerilla (AUS)**[57] [1101] 10-9-9 **86** oh6........................(p) JamesHalliday(5) —
(Lucy Normile) *prom: struggling bef 3 out: p.u run-in* **25/1**

11-1 **P** **Liz's Dream**[144] [100] 10-11-3 **103**......................................(t) BrianHarding —
(Lisa Harrison) *hld up: struggling bef 4 out: p.u bef next* **5/2**[2]

6m 28.3s (18.40) **Going Correction** +0.875s/f (Soft) 6 Ran SP% **109.2**
Speed ratings (Par 105): **105,104,96,87**,— —
Tote Swingers: 1&2 £3.20, 1&3 £2.40, 2&3 £3.10 CSF £12.49 CT £52.60 TOTE £3.60: £1.70, £1.10; EX 13.60 Place 6: £33.08 Place 5:£8.07.
Owner Mrs Jo Tracey **Bred** Pat Tobin **Trained** Arlary, Perth & Kinross

FOCUS
Only the first two ever made an impact on the race. The winner is rated 3lb off his best for his new yard.

NOTEBOOK
Bescot Springs(IRE), who wasn't wearing cheekpieces this time, was on-and-off the bridle at various stages of the race. His rider persevered with his pushing and the pair got on top in the latter stages. This was a good start to the gelding's career with this trainer after leaving Phillip Hobbs, but he hasn't held his form in the past, so a follow-up is far from certain. Plenty of credit goes to Peter Buchanan. (op 11-2 tchd 4-1)

Mad Moose(IRE) looked almost certain to win bar a fall as he scooted clear after two out, but distress signals quickly started to show after the rider appeared to ease off a little after jumping the final hurdle. In hindsight, when considering the ground, the jockey would have been best advised to keep his mount going as vigorously as he could. That said, Mad Moose still held an advantage when his rider went for him again but the horse looked tired, which wasn't surprising, as he'd gone a good pace throughout. Official explanation: jockey said, regarding appearing to ease, that the gelding was tired and he was trying to hang on to it and keep it balanced on the soft ground, he was conscious of the winner and felt he wouldn't have finished in front, however ridden. (tchd 6-4)
Soul Magic(IRE), who was 6lb wrong, was well held back in third. (op 13-2)
Liz's Dream, chasing a four-timer after a long break, but for some reason without the cheekpieces he'd been wearing, was held up and made no impression. The 11lb rise since that last success was clearly too much for him. Official explanation: trainer had no explanation for the poor form shown (op 9-4 tchd 3-1)
T/Plt: £55.40 to a £1 stake. Pool:£66,681 - 903.98 winning tickets T/Qpdt: £8.90 to a £1 stake. Pool:£5,705 - 472.30 winning tickets RY

1579 - 1585a (Foreign Racing) - See Raceform Interactive

1473 FONTWELL (L-H)

Thursday, September 23

OFFICIAL GOING: Good (good to firm in places) changing to good after race 1 (2:10)
Rail realignment increased chases by 40yds and hurdles by 25yds each circuit.
Wind: mild breeze across Weather: overcast

1586 N G BAILEY JUVENILE MAIDEN HURDLE (9 hdls) 2m 2f 110y
2:10 (2:10) (Class 4) 3-Y-O **£3,903** (£1,146; £573; £286)

Form RPR
1 **Whipperway (IRE)**[169] 3-10-0 0 MarcGoldstein(5) 95+
(Sheena West) *trckd ldrs: hit 1st: led appr 2 out: pushed clr appr last: r.o wl* **16/1**
2 14 **Finch Flyer (IRE)**[10] 3-10-12 0 JamieMoore 89
(Gary Moore) *trckd ldrs: rdn after 3 out: styd on to go 2nd sn after last: no ch w wnr* **10/3**[2]
3 1 ¾ **Tallulah Mai**[176] 3-10-5 0 TomO'Brien 81
(Matthew Salaman) *trckd ldr: wnt 2nd appr 3 out: sn rdn: nt pce of wnr: no ex whn lost 2nd sn after last* **15/2**
4 8 **Plus Ultra (IRE)**[31] 3-10-5 0 KyleJames(7) 81
(Philip Kirby) *trckd ldrs: hit 3 out: sn rdn: one pce fr next* **5/2**[1]
5 6 **Red Barcelona (IRE)**[22] 3-10-12 0 MattieBatchelor 77+
(Mark H Tompkins) *racd keenly: nt a fluent: disp tl clr ldr after 3 out: sn rdn: hdd bef next: wkng whn awkward last* **5/1**[3]
4 6 35 **Rhyton (IRE)**[29] 1363 3-10-12 0 APMcCoy 44
(Donald McCain) *disp ld most of way tl rdn after 3 out: sn wknd: t.o* **11/2**
7 12 **Lady Willa (IRE)**[20] 3-10-2 0 TommyPhelan(3) 26
(Mark Gillard) *bhd fr 3rd: t.o fr after 6th* **50/1**
8 26 **Gilderoy**[13] 3-10-12 0 RhysFlint 10
(Dominic Ffrench Davis) *t.k.h early: a towards rr: t.o fr after 6th* **28/1**
00U 9 nk **Charmeur (USA)**[18] 1473 3-10-12 0 RichardJohnson 9
(Philip Hobbs) *trckd ldrs tl wknd qckly after 5th: t.o fr next* **14/1**
P 10 18 **Vadition (IRE)**[4] 1545 3-10-2 0 ow4 MrJackSalmon(7) —
(John Bridger) *cl up tl pushed along 5th: wknd appr 6th: sn t.o* **100/1**
4m 33.7s (-0.60) **Going Correction** -0.125s/f (Good) **10** Ran SP% **114.4**
Speed ratings (Par 103): **96,90,89,86,83 68,63,52,52,45**
toteswingers:1&2:£3.70, 1&3:£14.90, 2&3:£7.10 CSF £68.60 TOTE £17.20: £3.90, £1.80, £4.50; EX 50.70.
Owner Gerald West **Bred** Mesnil Investments Ltd And Deerpark Stud **Trained** Falmer, E Sussex

FOCUS
The rails had been moved, adding 40 yards per circuit on the chase course and 25 yards on the hurdles course. The pace did not begin to build until the final circuit, when the two leaders, Red Barcelona and Rhyton, started duelling, and they effectively set the race up for the chasing pack. Not much form to go on but probably an ordinary early-season juvenile hurdle.

NOTEBOOK
Whipperway(IRE), the only runner to cover the pace move without coming under pressure, cruised through on the inside to go clear up the straight. After blundering at the third, she guessed at several subsequent flights, but that did not stop her momentum and her jumping should improve for experience. Her stable do well with juvenile hurdlers and she seems destined to do better in this sphere.
Finch Flyer(IRE), fractious in the saddling boxes, was never travelling that well, getting outpaced on the final circuit, but he stuck to the task to finish best of the rest. He might be worth another chance, although at this stage he does not look that quick. (op 11-4 tchd 7-2)
Tallulah Mai held a good position but was unable to respond once the pace quickened. She had been off the track for almost six months so could well come on for this. (op 8-1 tchd 6-1)
Plus Ultra(IRE) was moving up to challenge when blundering at the third-last and was soon struggling afterwards. He was among the best of these on the Flat but still has it to prove over jumps. (op 9-4 tchd 11-4 in a place)
Red Barcelona(IRE), well supported, disputed the running but was legless from the second last. This was still an encouraging run and he could do better if getting an easier time of it. (op 9-1)
Rhyton(IRE), who disputed the lead, jumped more fluently than he had at Bangor and seemed to appreciate having his mind made up for him, but he does not look up to much. (op 5-1 tchd 6-1)

1587 BUCKINGHAM GROUP CONTRACTING LTD BEGINNERS' CHASE (13 fncs) 2m 2f
2:40 (2:40) (Class 4) 4-Y-0+ **£4,435** (£1,310; £655; £327; £163)

Form RPR
12F- 1 **Harry Tricker**[222] 4034 6-11-4 0 JamieMoore 114+
(Gary Moore) *hld up in 4th: trcking ldr whn hit 3 out: led next: rdn clr* **9/4**[2]
3355 2 4 ½ **Pagan Sword**[18] 1481 8-10-11 102 MrSWDrinkwater(7) 105
(David Bridgwater) *led: rdn after 4 out: hdd 2 out: kpt on but sn hld by wnr* **33/1**
4323 3 4 **Quedillac (FR)**[42] 1235 6-11-4 104 RichardJohnson 103+
(Tim Vaughan) *prom: mstke 2nd: nt fluent 4th: trckd ldrs fr 7th: rdn after 4 out: kpt on same pce fr next* **12/1**[3]
-P34 4 26 **Haka Dancer (USA)**[8] 1257 7-10-11 0 (p) KyleJames(7) 78
(Philip Kirby) *hld up last: awkward 3rd: cl up 4 out: effrt next: wknd bef 2 out* **66/1**
-026 5 1 ¾ **Bold Pioneer (USA)**[101] 745 7-10-13 71 GemmaGracey-Davison(5) 79
(Zoe Davison) *trckd ldrs: awkward 2nd: wnt 2nd after 7th tl mstke 4 out: sn rdn: wknd after next: mstke last* **100/1**
533- P **Pepe Simo (IRE)**[161] 5194 6-11-4 0 RWalsh —
(Paul Nicholls) *disp 4th: blnd bdly 1st and 5th: cl up 4 out: sn eased: p.u bef next* **8/15**[1]
4m 40.8s (6.10) **Going Correction** +0.025s/f (Yiel) **6** Ran SP% **109.1**
Speed ratings (Par 105): **87,85,83,71,70** —
toteswingers:1&2:£9.90, 1&3:£2.10, 2&3:£8.40 CSF £33.09 TOTE £3.20: £2.00, £8.00; EX 88.90.
Owner R A Green **Bred** Lawn Stud **Trained** Lower Beeding, W Sussex

FOCUS
An interesting early season beginners' chase featuring a couple of smart hurdlers making their chasing debuts. The race was peppered with jumping errors meaning the anticipated match did not develop. It was steadily run and the form is rated around the second and fifth.

NOTEBOOK
Harry Tricker jumped slowly at the fourth and again three out, but he was one of the few not to make any serious errors. Sent up to challenge in the back straight, it took a while but his superior Flat speed meant he was always going to win with some comfort. He was developing into a smart hurdler when his season was cut short after falling at Newbury in February and had been off the track since. This was a pleasing reappearance, especially as he may have just needed the run, but he will need to jump with more fluency to hold his own in stiffer company. (op 15-8)
Pagan Sword had no obvious chance against a much classier rival, but he ran his race and stuck to the task once passed. He is a long-standing maiden but it was encouraging that his jumping was more fluent than it has been.
Quedillac(FR) got in close to several fences and put in only one fluent leap, which meant he was unable to remain competitive. (op 11-1 tchd 10-1)
Haka Dancer(USA) made a mistake at the third and thereafter just plodded around at the rear of the field.
Bold Pioneer(USA)
Pepe Simo(IRE) developed into a decent novice hurdler last season and was not outmatched when thrown into competitive handicaps off a mark of 140, and was a hot favourite for his chasing debut. However, it all started to go wrong when he took a chunk out of the first fence, and worse was to follow when he made a dramatic error at the fifth, an open ditch, forcing Ruby Walsh to cling onto his neck to stay aboard - it was remarkable that the pair were still united. However, his jumping never recovered and, after failing to raise his hind legs over the fences in the back straight, he was wisely pulled up. He might need some time to recover. (op 4-6 tchd 8-11 in places and 4-5 in a place)

1588 AFL ARCHITECTS NOVICES' HURDLE (10 hdls) 2m 4f
3:10 (3:10) (Class 4) 4-Y-0+ **£3,903** (£1,146; £573; £286)

Form RPR
-121 1 **Synthe Davis (FR)**[18] 1475 5-11-5 130 RichardJohnson 132+
(Laura Mongan) *mde all: hit 2nd: drew wl clr fr 3 out: heavily eased run-in* **2/7**[1]
2 26 **Kasban**[421] 6-10-12 0 AndrewGlassonbury 92+
(Luke Dace) *hld up: wnt 3rd but plenty to do whn mstke 7th: rdn whn stmbld bdly 3 out: sn rdn: chalng for modest 2nd whn blunder 2 out: wnt 2nd run-in: nvr any ch w wnr* **12/1**[3]
22-2 3 2 ¼ **Spent**[142] 129 5-10-5 112 OliverDayman(7) 88
(Alison Thorpe) *chsd wnr: clr w wnr whn short of room 5th: rdn appr 7th: no ch w wnr fr 3 out: lost modest 2nd run-in* **9/2**[2]
000- 4 29 **Quatuor Collonges (FR)**[422] 1076 6-10-12 0 RodiGreene 61
(David Bridgwater) *trckd ldrs: hit 6th: sn no ch: wknd next: t.o* **66/1**
00- P **Bright Decision**[167] 5122 4-10-11 0 JamieMoore —
(Joanna Davis) *chsd ldrs tl rn v wd on bnd appr 5th: immediately t.o: nvr rcvrd: p.u bef 7th* **25/1**
4m 51.9s (-7.50) **Going Correction** -0.125s/f (Good)
WFA 4 from 5yo+ 12lb **5** Ran SP% **109.0**
Speed ratings (Par 105): **110,99,98,87,—**
CSF £4.72 TOTE £1.10: £1.10, £2.70; EX 3.20.
Owner Mrs P J Sheen **Bred** Claude Quellier **Trained** Epsom, Surrey

FOCUS
No strength in depth but the time was good and the easy winner may be capable of better.

NOTEBOOK
Synthe Davis(FR) gained her third win with the minimum of fuss. Setting the pace, she had the field strung out from an early stage and, after readily dispensing with a brief challenge heading out onto the final circuit, she was never troubled. She has come into her own this summer and has been placed to optimum effect to notch up three wins in novice company. That meant she had penalties to overcome, but in this field it was hardly an inconvenience, and was certainly an easier task than racing off her current mark in a handicap. (op 4-11tchd 2-5 in places)
Kasban gave reluctant chase to the front two and plugged on despite clattering two of the final three hurdles, and it eventually paid dividends as he got up for second. A winning stayer on the Flat, he was returning from a 421-day absence having changed stables in the interim, so he could improve on this. (op 14-1)
Spent tried to chase down the winner on the final circuit but paid for that effort as he tired to lose second in the straight. He is consistent but has a tendency to find at least one too good, indeed he's only 1-25 under all codes. (op 10-3)
Quatuor Collonges(FR) was quite keen on his first start in over a year and could only plug on at one pace.
Bright Decision Official explanation: jockey said gelding ran out

1589 ARCADIS UK H'CAP CHASE (15 fncs) 2m 4f
3:40 (3:40) (Class 4) (0-115,110) 4-Y-O **£5,069** (£1,497; £748; £374; £187)

Form RPR
24 1 **Courella (IRE)**[17] 1491 6-11-12 110 PaulMoloney 122
(Evan Williams) *hld up towards rr: stdy prog fr 9th: wnt 2nd after 4 out: hrd rdn 2 out: tk narrow advantage fnl 100yds: hld on: all out* **9/2**[1]
3351 2 nse **Morestead (IRE)**[18] 1474 5-11-2 100 (b[1]) LeightonAspell 112
(Brendan Powell) *sn prom: led 6th: clr 10th: rdn appr 4 out: kpt on: narrowly hdd fnl 100yds: rallied v gamely: jst hld* **6/1**[3]
1440 3 7 **Intac (IRE)**[17] 1491 8-11-12 110 JoeTizzard 116
(Colin Tizzard) *trckd clr ldrs: rdn whn ev ch sn after 4 out: kpt on same pce fr next* **16/1**
346P 4 8 **Hereweareagain (IRE)**[17] 1491 7-11-5 103 (tp) TomO'Brien 103
(Philip Hobbs) *mid-div: hdwy after 10th: rdn after 4 out: wnt 3rd briefly next: styd on same pce tl fdd fnl 120yds* **8/1**
1236 5 12 **Indiana Gold (FR)**[22] 1454 6-11-0 105 (p) OliverDayman(7) 93
(Alison Thorpe) *mid-div: hdwy whn mstke 11th: rdn after 4 out: wknd bef next* **12/1**
-603 6 1 **Some Craic (IRE)**[17] 1491 10-11-11 109 RichardJohnson 96
(Paul Henderson) *led tl 6th: chsd ldr tl rdn after 4 out: wknd next* **13/2**
0253 7 12 **Nesnaas (USA)**[17] 1493 9-10-10 94 TomScudamore 70
(Mark Rimell) *sn pushed along in midfield: dropped to rr 6th: nvr bk on terms* **11/2**[2]
P-4P 8 14 **Milesian King (IRE)**[113] 586 9-10-13 97 AidanColeman 60
(Lawney Hill) *trckd ldrs: hit 4th: nt fluent next: wknd bef 10th: t.o* **13/2**
0U3F 9 11 **Nawow**[19] 1471 10-11-1 102 (tp) PeterToole(3) 55
(Matt Hazell) *nvr travelling: sn in rr: t.o fnl circ* **10/1**

5PP0 **10** *38* **I'm The Decider (IRE)**[22] 1454 8-11-9 **107**..........................(p) APMcCoy 26
(Jonjo O'Neill) *nvr travelling in rr: t.o fnl circ* **10/1**
5m 5.30s (-2.00) **Going Correction** +0.025s/f (Yiel) **10** Ran SP% **117.4**
Speed ratings (Par 105): **105,104,102,98,94 93,88,83,78,63**
toteswingers:1&2:£4.90, 1&3:£24.80, 2&3:£52.30 CSF £32.48 CT £399.51 TOTE £5.10: £2.80, £1.30, £4.60; EX 41.70.

Owner R E R Williams **Bred** Thomas Kinsella **Trained** Llancarfan, Vale Of Glamorgan

FOCUS
An exciting conclusion to this tight handicap with a late finisher trying to overhaul a bold front-runner, and a head-bob on the line deciding the outcome. It was strongly run and the form looks solid.

NOTEBOOK
Courella(IRE), held up early, made steady progress throughout the final circuit, gaining ground with a particularly fluent leap at the last in the back straight, but he still had a tough battle to get on terms with the rallying front-runner, and he only just prevailed. He did not cope with the soft ground at Newton Abbot last time and could not reel in the runaway winner at Hereford before that, but prior to that had won at this course on his debut for his current trainer. His jumping was better this time and he was well backed for his return to this track. (op 9-1)

Morestead(IRE) needs to dominate and had quite a battle before wrestling the lead from Some Craic with a circuit to go. He looked to have paid for those early efforts half a mile out, but his astute jockey had given him a breather and he found more to give everything in a brave bid to fend off the winner. He had responded to the first-time visor when romping home in a lower grade at this track earlier in the month and the application of blinkers this time nearly produced the same effect, but in the end the 11lb rise in a better race just made the difference. (op 5-1 tchd 9-2)

Intac(IRE), who finished behind Courella when both were soundly beaten by the well-handicapped Frosted Grape at Hereford at the start of the month, ran a sound race but was unable to get to the lead and was perhaps inconvenienced by trying to chase the pace. He has winning form over hurdles and fences but is yet to land a handicap. (tchd 18-1)

Hereweareagain(IRE) hit a flat spot before making a little progress round the home turn, but his run flattened out again and the re-application of a tongue-tie did not have enough of an effect. (tchd 10-1)

Indiana Gold(FR) has been busy over the summer, including a win off 92 last month, but it looked as if the efforts of that campaign and the inevitable rise up the weights are beginning to take their toll. (op 10-1)

Some Craic(IRE) duelled for the early lead but was beaten off with a circuit to go and, though he rallied a bit afterwards, his race was run. He has been gradually sliding down the weights since a high of 121 last summer, and this may have helped in the quest for an exploitable mark. (op 11-2 tchd 5-1)

Nesnaas(USA) was quite well backed but was always struggling and is generally best on right-handed tracks. (op 7-1)

1590 KCCJ H'CAP HURDLE (11 hdls) 2m 6f 110y
4:10 (4:10) (Class 4) (0-115,113) 4-Y-0+ **£3,903** (£1,146; £573; £286)

Form RPR
0303 **1** **Winsley Hill**[67] 1033 8-11-12 **113**.......................... RodiGreene 123+
(Neil Mulholland) *mde all: pushed along after 8th: styd on strly fr 2 out: rdn out* **25/1**

3344 **2** *10* **Is It Me (USA)**[44] 1230 7-11-11 **112**..........................(t) PaulMoloney 114
(Sophie Leech) *trckd ldrs: hit 1st and 3 out: sn rdn: lft 3rd 2 out: styd on: wnt 2nd run-in: no ch w wnr* **12/1**

5205 **3** *2 1/4* **Can't Remember**[18] 1479 5-9-10 **90**.......................... OliverDayman(7) 89
(Alison Thorpe) *mid-div: mstke 1st: hdwy 8th: rdn whn lft 2nd 2 out: no ex whn lost 2nd run-in* **22/1**

5555 **4** *9* **Vacario (GER)**[23] 1446 6-10-5 **95**..........................(t) TommyPhelan(3) 85
(Mark Gillard) *mid-div tl after 7th: sn rdn in rr: styd on after 2 out: hit last: wnt 4th run-in* **16/1**

5-43 **5** *2 1/4* **Major Miller**[56] 1129 9-10-8 **100**.......................... DavidBass(5) 88
(Nicky Henderson) *sn niggled along towards rr: nt fluent 6th: hrd rdn after 8th: wnt 4th after 3 out: fdd run-in* **11/4[2]**

1-26 **6** *11* **Canni Thinkaar (IRE)**[112] 601 9-11-4 **110**(p) GemmaGracey-Davison(5) 88
(Zoe Davison) *trckd wnr tl rdn after 3 out: sn btn* **22/1**

1121 **7** *14* **Makena (FR)**[18] 1476 8-11-9 **110**..........................(p) RichardJohnson 82+
(David Rees) *hld up towards rr: v short lived effrt 3 out: eased bef next* **13/8[1]**

-33P **8** *49* **Supernoverre (IRE)**[17] 1492 4-11-5 **108**..........................(v[1]) TimmyMurphy 27
(Liam Corcoran) *hld up towards rr: sme prog u.p 8th: wknd bef next: t.o* **20/1**

/503 **F** **Fade To Grey (IRE)**[18] 1477 6-11-3 **104**..........................(t) APMcCoy 107
(Shaun Lycett) *hld up towards rr: hdwy after 4th to trck ldrs: wnt 2nd after 3 out: rdn and 3 l down whn fell 2 out* **9/2[3]**

5m 36.7s (-5.80) **Going Correction** -0.125s/f (Good)
WFA 4 from 5yo+ 12lb **9** Ran SP% **113.8**
Speed ratings (Par 105): **105,101,100,97,96 93,88,71,—**
toteswingers:1&2:£22.90, 1&3:£45.20, 2&3:£23.90 CSF £259.91 CT £6533.90 TOTE £32.60: £7.60, £4.30, £8.10; EX 159.50.

Owner Mrs H R Cross **Bred** Mrs H R Cross **Trained** Burlescombe, Devon

FOCUS
An enterprising ride saw the winner dominate from start to finish. A hurdles best from the winner with the next two and the faller close to their marks.

NOTEBOOK
Winsley Hill set a good pace, got a breather on the final circuit before kicking on again and stayed on well, hardly seeing a rival. She had put up a couple of decent efforts in hurdles this summer but overall did not look as good as she did over fences last year. However, she was on a tempting hurdles mark compared to her chase rating and, with more fancied rivals failing to run up to form, she was able to capitalise, despite the ground being as soft as she can handle. (tchd 20-1)

Is It Me(USA) dived at the first and was never able to get to the lead, but stuck on regardless. He has not won since being bought out of a seller for 12,000gns by current connections a year ago, but he is creeping towards a tempting mark and could be interesting on any remaining fast ground. (op 10-1)

Can't Remember was in a good position if able to mount a challenge from the final turn but her effort flattened out in the straight. This was the most competitive handicap she has tackled, and she ran as well as could be expected. (tchd 25-1)

Vacario(GER) did not help his cause with some iffy jumping, and he remains a frustrating sort. (tchd 20-1)

Major Miller was well backed but not for the first time let his supporters down as he ran in snatches, dropping to the rear with a circuit to go before struggling on. (op 4-1)

Makena(FR) has mixed chasing and hurdling to great effect this summer, winning four times, but the career-high mark seems to have put an end to her summer campaign. Official explanation: jockey said mare never travelled; trainer said, regarding running, that the mare was unsuited by the good ground, which he felt was riding on the slow side of good (op 11-8 tchd 7-4 in a place)

Fade To Grey(IRE) had made good progress and was making inroads into the winner's lead to look the biggest danger when taking the second-last too quickly and coming down. (op 5-1 tchd 4-1)

1591 DOUG BRADMORE MEMORIAL H'CAP CHASE (13 fncs) 2m 2f
4:40 (4:40) (Class 5) (0-95,97) 4-Y-0+ **£2,406** (£706; £353; £176)

Form RPR
P3-P **1** **R'Cam (IRE)**[18] 1483 8-11-6 **89**.......................... JackDoyle 104+
(Emma Lavelle) *trckd ldrs: led 2 out: sn in command: rdn clr: eased nr fin* **8/1**

U532 **2** *18* **Sam Cruise**[15] 1511 9-11-7 **90**..........................(t) AidanColeman 89
(Steve Gollings) *racd keenly: trckd ldr: led 3rd: rdn after 4 out: hit next: hdd 2 out: sn no ch w wnr* **4/1[2]**

5444 **3** *9* **Young Tot (IRE)**[23] 1447 12-9-12 **72**..........................(bt) GilesHawkins(5) 62
(Carroll Gray) *trckd ldrs: hit 5th: rdn and ev ch after 4 out: wknd appr last* **20/1**

46P4 **4** *2 1/4* **Post It**[36] 1283 9-10-5 **81**..........................(b) MattGriffiths(7) 71
(Ron Hodges) *hld up in tch: reminders after 6th: wnt 4th u.p 4 out: hld whn blnd 2 out: wkng whn wnt bdly rt last* **11/1**

0604 **5** *1/2* **Rince Donn (IRE)**[15] 1511 8-11-7 **90**.......................... HaddenFrost 76
(Roger Curtis) *hld up towards rr: rdn after 4 out: sme late prog past btn horses: nvr a factor* **28/1**

23P0 **6** *8* **Space Cowboy (IRE)**[18] 1474 10-10-1 **70**..........................(b) JamieMoore 49
(Gary Moore) *hld up: lost tch 4 out: styd on past btn horses fr next: nvr trbld ldrs* **9/1**

6532 **7** *16* **Bid Art (IRE)**[18] 1474 5-11-0 **83**..........................(tp) DarylJacob 48
(Jamie Snowden) *led tl 3rd: chsd ldrs: rdn appr 4 out: wknd 3 out* **6/1[3]**

5U21 **8** *7* **Builteoir (IRE)**[4] 1546 8-11-11 **97** 7ex..........................(p) DPFahy(3) 55
(Evan Williams) *in tch: rdn afer 8th: nvr any imp: btn whn stmbld bdly 2 out* **2/1[1]**

-146 **P** **Nono Le Sage (FR)**[101] 748 6-11-12 **95**..........................(t) TomScudamore —
(David Pipe) *in tch: blnd 7th: sn rdn: wknd qckly: p.u bef 9th* **17/2**

4m 41.9s (7.20) **Going Correction** +0.025s/f (Yiel) **9** Ran SP% **115.8**
Speed ratings (Par 103): **85,77,73,72,71 68,61,58,—**
toteswingers:1&2:£8.10, 1&3:Not won, 2&3:£22.10 CSF £41.18 CT £623.24 TOTE £8.70: £5.00, £1.60, £9.40; EX 45.30.

Owner The High Altitude Partnership **Bred** Mrs Bronagh Brady-Lawler **Trained** Wildhern, Hants

FOCUS
Just a moderate handicap with several of the summer campaigners running below form. The winner rates a chase best.

NOTEBOOK
R'Cam(IRE) was held off the early pace skirmishes but still within striking distance, and he moved up smoothly to come clear from the last. He is hardly a model of consistency and pulls up almost as often as he completes, but on his day he is a capable performer in this grade. He pulled up on his last start, which was his first run for six months, but his previous victory had also come on the second start after a break. Official explanation: trainer said, regarding apparent improvement in form, that the gelding was better suited by the quicker ground and shorter distance. (op 15-2 tchd 7-1)

Sam Cruise has been largely consistent this summer and ran another sound race, setting the pace and bravely trying to fend off the winner despite tiring over the final two fences. As such he is a useful benchmark for the form. (op 7-2 tchd 10-3)

Young Tot(IRE) moved into a challenging position and he would have finished closer but he did not cope with the open ditches and eventually tired. (op 16-1)

Post It was never really on terms and got tired over the final two fences. She has some reasonable form at this track and goes well fresh, but has not managed to win for three and a half years. (op 9-1)

Bid Art(IRE) soon surrendered the early lead and did not jump as fluently as he had here earlier in the month, and looks to be feeling the effects of a busy summer. (tchd 5-1)

Builteoir(IRE) was attempting to defy a penalty for winning at Plumpton four days earlier, but was under pressure with a circuit to go and found this race coming too soon. Official explanation: jockey said gelding never travelled (op 7-2)

1592 INLINE DESIGN CONDITIONAL JOCKEYS' NOVICES' H'CAP HURDLE (10 hdls) 2m 4f
5:10 (5:10) (Class 5) (0-95,92) 4-Y-0+ **£2,276** (£668; £334; £166)

Form RPR
5-2P **1** **Winning Show**[18] 1478 6-10-5 **74**..........................(tp) CharlieWallis(3) 83+
(Chris Gordon) *trckd ldr: led 3 out: sn rdn: nt fluent last: styd on wl: rdn out* **16/1**

-010 **2** *2 3/4* **Tegan Lee**[22] 1451 7-11-10 **90**.......................... DPFahy 96+
(Liam Corcoran) *mid-div: smooth hdwy 3 out: sn trcking ldr: rdn after 2 out: kpt on same pce* **16/1**

-65F **3** *20* **Yes Minister (IRE)**[44] 1228 6-10-3 **69**..........................(b[1]) RichardKilloran 56
(Sophie Leech) *led tl 3 out: sn rdn: wknd next* **20/1**

-061 **4** *7* **Happy Fleet**[18] 1479 7-10-9 **75**.......................... GilesHawkins 55
(Roger Curtis) *mid-div: rdn after 7th: wnt 4th after 3 out: wknd next* **15/2**

30-4 **5** *9* **Hawk Gold (IRE)**[105] 688 6-10-8 **74**..........................(b) DavidBass 46
(Michelle Bryant) *in tch: hit 4th: rdn appr 3 out: wknd bef 2 out* **28/1**

F31- **6** *1/2* **Bollywood (IRE)**[149] 36 7-10-11 **82**.......................... EdGlassonbury(5) 54
(Alison Batchelor) *mid-div: reminders after 4th: sn rdn in rr: no ch fr next* **11/1**

5344 **7** *4 1/2* **Parazar (FR)**[18] 1477 5-11-12 **92**.......................... CharlieHuxley 60
(Oliver Sherwood) *trckd ldrs: rdn after 3 out: wknd bef next* **4/1[2]**

03P3 **8** *2* **Barlin Bay**[39] 1259 6-10-7 **76**.......................... HaddenFrost(3) 42
(David Pipe) *a towards rr* **5/2[1]**

0/05 **9** *1 1/4* **Castle Craigs (IRE)**[19] 1468 8-10-2 **74**.......................... MrTomDavid(6) 39
(Tim Vaughan) *in tch: rdn appr 3 out: sn wknd* **11/2[3]**

P45 **10** *23* **Raise Again (IRE)**[21] 1236 7-11-2 **82**.......................... KeiranBurke 26
(Nerys Dutfield) *hld up towards rr: hdwy into midfield after 6th: sn rdn: wknd after 3 out: t.o* **22/1**

-U04 **11** *2* **Keckerrockernixes (IRE)**[105] 690 4-10-13 **90**.......... DonovanEldin(10) 31
(Richard Rowe) *a bhd: t.o* **40/1**

0352 **P** **I Can Run Can You (IRE)**[35] 1294 4-11-6 **90**........... RichieMcLernon(3) —
(Jonjo O'Neill) *hld up towards rr: rdn after 5th: lost tch after next: p.u bef 7th* **7/1**

4m 59.4s **Going Correction** -0.125s/f (Good)
WFA 4 from 5yo+ 12lb **12** Ran SP% **123.3**
Speed ratings (Par 103): **95,93,85,83,79 79,77,76,76,67 66,—**
toteswingers:1&2:£48.30, 1&3:£48.30, 2&3:£48.30 CSF £234.63 CT £5086.14 TOTE £14.30: £2.70, £6.10, £9.90; EX 197.10 Place 6 £927.05; Place 5 £330.49.

Owner Roger Alwen **Bred** Sir Gordon Brunton **Trained** Morestead, Hants

■ Stewards' Enquiry : Charlie Wallis caution: used whip with excessive frequency.
Richard Killoran caution: used whip with excessive frequency.

FOCUS
Several of these found it tough on the cut-up ground and the first two pulled clear. The race is rated through the second and could be rated quite a bit higher.

NOTEBOOK
Winning Show was given an enterprising ride, tracking the early leader before striking for home, and getting first run paid dividends as he desperately clung on to his lead near the finish. He had run well on his return from an absence over fences here last month, but his jumping went to pieces next time so he reverted to hurdles here off a similar mark and the tactic worked. He should be able to pick up another small race this autumn.
Tegan Lee was cutting down the winner's lead when getting stuck briefly behind the fading Yes Minister, so he effectively had more ground to make up from the home turn. He made a good fist of it but could not quite get there, and showed he can be competitive off his current mark. (op 14-1 tchd 12-1)
Yes Minister(IRE) led until headed in the back straight and though he plugged on he could find no more. He responded to the first-time blinkers to post his best effort to date, although a win does not look imminent.
Happy Fleet narrowly landed a gamble off a light weight over C&D earlier in the month, but was never able to get out of mid-division this time, presumably anchored by the 7lb rise with the edge taken off her freshness. (op 13-2)
Parazar(FR) attracted some support but he failed to cope with top weight and faded from the home turn. (op 9-2 tchd 7-2 and 5-1 in a place)
Barlin Bay was well backed on his first start for David Pipe but was never a factor and this long-standing maiden still needs to find some improvement. (op 5-1 tchd 11-2)
T/Plt: £995.20 to a £1 stake. Pool:£67,184.97 - 49.28 winning tickets T/Qpdt: £175.40 to a £1 stake. Pool:£5,192.10 - 21.90 winning tickets TM

1573 PERTH (R-H)
Thursday, September 23

OFFICIAL GOING: Soft (6.6)
All Bends moved out to provide fresh ground but impact on distances not quantified.
Wind: Breezy, half against Weather: Overcast

1593 SIS NOVICES' HURDLE (12 hdls) 3m 110y
2:20 (2:21) (Class 4) 4-Y-0+ **£2,527** (£919)

Form				RPR
120	1		**Supercede (IRE)**[29] 1373 8-11-4 115 ....(bt) PCarberry (Gordon Elliott, Ire) *hld up last but in tch: lft 3rd after 5th: lft in clr ld paddock bnd after 7th: unchal* **15/8**[2]	128+
42-	2	40	**Wood Yer (IRE)**[173] 4992 4-10-10 0 .... PaddyBrennan (Nigel Twiston-Davies) *trckd ldrs: lft 2nd after 3rd: lft in ld whn tried to run out and hdd paddock bnd after 7th: sn no ch w wnr* **3/1**[3]	95+
12-	R		**Monogram**[229] 3896 6-10-9 0 .... RyanMania(3) (Howard Johnson) *t.k.h: cl up: lft in ld whn tried to run out paddock bnd after 3rd: jst in front whn rn out same bnd after 7th* **7/4**[1]	—
FP-U	P		**Glaced Over**[16] 1499 5-9-12 0 .... GaryRutherford(7) (Raymond Shiels) *led: tried to run out and hdd paddock bnd after 3rd: chsd ldrs: sddle slipped and p.u after 5th* **9/1**	—

6m 48.9s (39.00) **Going Correction** +1.025s/f (Soft)
WFA 4 from 5yo+ 13lb **4** Ran SP% **106.1**
Speed ratings (Par 105): **78,65,—,—**
CSF £7.35 TOTE £2.90; EX 6.70.
Owner T D Howley Jnr **Bred** Paul Starr **Trained** Trim, Co Meath

FOCUS
This looked an interesting little novice event, but it developed into a complete farce and the form should be taken with a pinch of salt. There was no pace on early as nothing wanted to lead and three of the field took a good look at the paddock bend first time round, causing a change in the running order. The winner is rated to his mark.

NOTEBOOK
Supercede(IRE) eventually sauntered home for a bloodless success in this farcical contest. He failed to shine on easy ground over fences on his previous outing and the ground was of concern here, but as it turned out his credentials for it were not tested. This will boost his confidence no end and he may well have won whatever, but he is obviously grossly flattered. (op 9-4)
Wood Yer(IRE), unplaced in two bumpers last term, was representing a bang in-form stable that like to win this race and taking a big step up in trip. His chance went going out onto the final circuit, but he still looked distinctly inexperienced when his rider asked him to close and looks more of a long-term project. (op 2-1)
Monogram was popular for this seasonal return. He almost ran out on the first circuit, but gave his rider no chance of staying aboard second time round. He should be given another chance and it wouldn't be at all surprising to see him revert to a left-handed track next time. (op 9-4)
Glaced Over's saddle eventually slipped having earlier tried to run out. Official explanation: jockey said saddle slipped (op 9-4)

1594 ISLE OF SKYE BLENDED SCOTCH WHISKY NOVICES' HURDLE (8 hdls) 2m 110y
2:50 (2:59) (Class 4) 4-Y-0+ **£2,276** (£668; £334; £166)

Form				RPR
0-	1		**Time Machine (UAE)**[28] 1383 4-10-12 114 ....(t) AELynch (Robert Alan Hennessy, Ire) *hld up: hdwy on outside bef 3 out: led bef next: clr last: pushed out* **5/2**[1]	111+
6	2	3 ¾	**Makhaaleb (IRE)**[16] 1393 4-11-5 115 .... PCarberry (Gordon Elliott, Ire) *hld up towards rr: stdy hdwy bef 2 out: sn chsng wnr: kpt on u.p fr last* **9/2**[3]	112
5-31	3	¾	**Jewelled Dagger (IRE)**[28] 1337 6-11-5 107 .... GrahamLee (Jim Goldie) *trckd ldrs: effrt bef 2 out: one pce fr last* **7/1**	111
	4	½	**Ross Limestone (IRE)**[34] 1323 7-10-12 0 .... DenisO'Regan (T G McCourt, Ire) *hld up: hdwy bef 2 out: kpt on fr last: nvr rchd ldrs* **25/1**	104
	5	27	**The Cockney Squire (IRE)**[165] 5159 5-11-5 0 .... PeterBuchanan (Lucinda Russell) *led to bef 2 out: sn rdn and wknd* **11/4**[2]	84
0	6	1 ¾	**Le Roi Max (FR)**[129] 375 6-10-12 0 .... PaddyBrennan (Nigel Twiston-Davies) *nt fluent: trckd ldrs: hit 4 out: rdn and wknd bef 2 out* **14/1**	75
20-1	7	5	**Montoya's Son (IRE)**[138] 209 5-11-5 112 .... WilsonRenwick (Howard Johnson) *prom: drvn 3 out: wknd bef next* **7/1**	77
000-	8	11	**Lochore (IRE)**[165] 5140 4-10-5 0 .... AlexanderVoy(7) (Lucy Normile) *in tch tl rdn and wknd fr 3 out* **100/1**	59
000	9	54	**Shuttle Diplomacy (IRE)**[15] 1505 5-10-5 0 ....(t) JohnnyFarrelly (Elliott Cooper) *hld up: hdwy and prom bef 3rd: wknd fr next: t.o fnl 2* **100/1**	—
606-	U		**Educated Evans (IRE)**[183] 4819 5-10-9 0 .... SamTwiston-Davies(3) (Nigel Twiston-Davies) *bhd whn nt fluent and uns rdr 4 out* **33/1**	—

4m 14.5s (14.80) **Going Correction** +1.025s/f (Soft)
WFA 4 from 5yo+ 11lb **10** Ran SP% **113.9**
Speed ratings (Par 105): **106,104,103,103,90 90,87,82,57,—**
toteswingers:1&2:£3.60, 1&3:£4.10, 2&3:£4.20 CSF £13.70 TOTE £2.80: £1.10, £2.50, £2.60; EX 12.60.
Owner W Hennessy **Bred** Darley **Trained** Ratoath, Co Meath

FOCUS
Not a bad novice event for the grade with four last-time-out winners in attendance. There was an uneven gallop on and the first four eventually came clear. The first two are rated close to form.

NOTEBOOK
Time Machine(UAE), who cost connections 95,000gns, belatedly opened his account as a hurdler and got a good ride from Andrew Lynch, who was alive to the better ground being towards the outside. He took a little time to settle, but made smooth headway off the home turn and had the race in the bag jumping the last. He ideally wants quicker ground, but was getting weight from his main rivals here and that was a big help. This should do his confidence a lot of good. (op 7-2)
Makhaaleb(IRE) came good over hurdles on his previous outing in this sphere and has been in good form on the Flat since. The ground was a worry for him and, while he ran a sound race in defeat, it was that which looked to just find him out. He can no doubt win another one of these back on a sounder surface. (op 7-1 tchd 15-2 and 4-1)
Jewelled Dagger(IRE) was another returning from the Flat who had opened his account over hurdles on his previous start in this sphere, in his case over C&D last month. He wasn't able to dictate as he prefers and so this was a respectable effort under his penalty, on ground softer than he cares for. (op 8-1 tchd 9-1)
Ross Limestone(IRE) travelled kindly into contention, but lacked the required change of gear to get near the front. This was probably the easiest ground he has yet to encounter and he could build on this when it's less demanding underfoot again. (tchd 28-1)
The Cockney Squire(IRE), having his first outing for 183 days, had some fair form when previously trained in Ireland and had proven himself on soft ground. He is a headstrong character, but settled well enough due to getting his own way out in front. No doubt he would've been better off making this more of a test, but the manner in which he backed of things under pressure was very disappointing. (op 9-4 tchd 3-1)
Montoya's Son(IRE) offered little on this first run since winning at Hexham in May and has now posted two poor efforts at this venue. (op 6-1)

1595 GEORGE STUBBS INSURANCE SERVICES NOVICES' CHASE (FOR THE CENTENARY SILVER PLATE) (15 fncs) 2m 4f 110y
3:20 (3:25) (Class 3) 4-Y-0+ **£5,204** (£1,528; £764; £381)

Form				RPR
F5-6	1		**Frontier Dancer (IRE)**[145] 94 6-11-2 0 .... PaddyBrennan (Nigel Twiston-Davies) *cl up: led gng wl bef 3 out: drew clr fr next: easily* **4/9**[1]	123+
P	2	13	**Steel Magnate (IRE)**[1] 1577 7-11-2 110 ....(t) PCarberry (Gordon Elliott, Ire) *led tl rdn and hdd bef 3 out: lost 2nd bef next: rallied to chse (clr) wnr run-in: no imp* **4/1**[2]	107
0132	3	2 ½	**Baaher (USA)**[33] 1342 6-11-2 118 .... GrahamLee (Jim Goldie) *hld up in tch: hdwy to chse wnr bef 2 out: sn no imp: no ex and lost 2nd run-in* **11/2**[3]	105
4465	4	59	**Ellandshe (IRE)**[24] 1423 10-10-11 50 ....(b) JamesHalliday(5) (William Young) *cl up: rdn 10th: wknd fr next: t.o* **66/1**	46

5m 27.2s (13.20) **Going Correction** +0.675s/f (Soft) **4** Ran SP% **106.1**
Speed ratings (Par 107): **101,96,95,72**
CSF £2.60 TOTE £1.30; EX 2.30.
Owner Jump For Fun Racing **Bred** James P Linnane Mrcvs **Trained** Naunton, Gloucs

FOCUS
An uncompetitive novices' chase run in a slow time compared with the later handicap. The form is rated through the second.

NOTEBOOK
Frontier Dancer(IRE) made the perfect start to his chasing career and kept up the good recent work of his stable. The winner was very much entitled to win this on his hurdling form and got backed pretty much to the exclusion of his rivals. He was given a very confident ride and eventually came clear from the third-last without having to be fully extended. His jumping was very pleasing for a debutant and he went on the ground with a bother. It may be that he stays further as a chaser and there could well be a decent pot in him down the line. The Jewson Handicap at next year's Cheltenham Festival is not an unrealistic target at this early stage, and he is now due to head to the October meeting at that track for his next assignment. (op 8-15 tchd 4-7 in a place)
Steel Magnate(IRE), a former point winner, had been pulled up over 3m here the previous day. He was ridden a lot more aggressively over this sharper test and performed creditably, but really needs quicker ground. (op 9-2 tchd 7-2)
Baaher(USA) knows his way around this track very well and was back over fences after a fair effort in defeat over hurdles last month. Stepping up in distance, he took a keen hold for most of the race and that ultimately cost him the runner-up spot. He is another that ideally wants a faster surface, though. (op 4-1)
Ellandshe(IRE) was predictably outclassed, but still picked up the best part of £400 for finishing last of the four. (op 50-1)

1596 BREWIN DOLPHIN INVESTMENT MANAGEMENT NOVICES' H'CAP HURDLE (10 hdls) 2m 4f 110y
3:50 (3:50) (Class 4) (0-110,104) 4-Y-0+ **£2,602** (£764; £382; £190)

Form				RPR
600-	1		**De Bansha Man (IRE)**[205] 4377 5-11-2 97 .... SamTwiston-Davies(3) (Nigel Twiston-Davies) *cl up: led 3 out: hrd pressed next: styd on wl last* **7/2**[1]	105+
	2	9	**Coosan Belle (IRE)**[21] 1457 4-11-4 102 .... CO'Farrell(5) (John Joseph Hanlon, Ire) *hld up: hdwy 3 out: ev ch after next: outpcd fr last* **13/2**	102
	3	25	**On The Loose (IRE)**[49] 1189 6-11-10 102 .... AELynch (T G McCourt, Ire) *hld up: hdwy and in tch bef 3 out: wknd fr next* **11/1**	75
3-53	4	¾	**Desert Soul**[33] 1340 6-10-0 83 ....(t) JamesHalliday(5) (Maurice Barnes) *led and sn clr: hdd 3 out: wknd bef next* **6/1**[3]	55
02-6	5	1 ¾	**Hey Charlie (IRE)**[33] 1339 8-11-9 104 .... FearghalDavis(3) (Nicky Richards) *hld up: hdwy to chse ldrs whn hit 4 out: wknd fr next* **9/1**	75
3-10	P		**Balnagore**[104] 713 6-11-4 96 .... PeterBuchanan (Lucinda Russell) *midfield: struggling bef 4 out: sn btn: p.u after 3 out* **6/1**[3]	—
505-	P		**Regal Lyric (IRE)**[24] 1438 4-11-7 100 .... PCarberry (Gordon Elliott, Ire) *trckd ldrs: lost pl bef 4 out: sn struggling: t.o whn p.u after next* **9/2**[2]	—
3-23	P		**Proficiency**[10] 442 5-11-4 96 ....(v) PaddyAspell (Sue Bradburne) *chsd clr ldng trio to after 3rd: struggling next: p.u after 5th* **8/1**	—

5m 30.3s (23.40) **Going Correction** +1.025s/f (Soft)
WFA 4 from 5yo+ 12lb **8** Ran SP% **111.8**
Speed ratings (Par 105): **96,92,83,82,82 —,—,—**
toteswingers:1&2:£5.80, 1&3:£7.40, 2&3:£11.20 CSF £25.17 CT £219.61 TOTE £5.10: £1.80, £2.20, £3.20; EX 25.80.
Owner N A Twiston-Davies **Bred** Daniel O'Mahony **Trained** Naunton, Gloucs

FOCUS
A modest novice handicap, run at a sound gallop considering the demanding surface. The winner is rated up 10lb on his previous best.

NOTEBOOK
De Bansha Man(IRE) ran out a gutsy winner on this return to hurdling after a 205-day break and handed his yard another winner. The ground was of some concern for him, but that didn't stop him from being well backed and he showed a likeable attitude when under pressure in the home straight. He will get further when reverting to better ground and it will be interesting to see if he stays hurdling or has another go over fences now. (op 10-3)
Coosan Belle(IRE) emerged as the only danger to the winner from two out, but was always being held by that rival. She probably just found the ground that bit too soft for her and deserves to find a race. (op 8-1)
On The Loose(IRE) plugged on without threatening and didn't really prove he wants to go this far. (op 9-1)
Desert Soul ensured this was a good test but was done with after three out. (op 8-1 tchd 17-2)
Regal Lyric(IRE) shaped as though something went amiss on the back straight, but this ground wouldn't have been for him over the longer trip. (op 4-1 tchd 5-1)
Proficiency attracted support, but was beaten before passing the stands for the first time and clearly something went wrong with him. Official explanation: trainer had no explanation for the poor form shown; jockey said mare finished distressed (op 4-1 tchd 5-1)

1597 ANDERSON ANDERSON AND BROWN H'CAP HURDLE (8 hdls) 2m 110y
4:20 (4:21) (Class 3) (0-120,118) 4-Y-O+ **£4,228** (£1,241; £620; £310)

Form			Horse	RPR
00-3	1		**Regent's Secret (USA)**[4] 288 10-10-11 **103**....................(v) GrahamLee (Jim Goldie) *cl up: effrt bef 2 out: styd on wl run-in: led nr fin* **12/1**	111
-132	2	*nk*	**Quito Du Tresor (FR)**[84] 874 6-11-4 **113**................. CampbellGillies(3) (Lucinda Russell) *led: rdn bef 2 out: kpt on u.p run-in: hdd nr fin* **5/2**[2]	121
4-	3	*16*	**Vinnes Friend (IRE)**[10] 1521 6-11-3 **109**.................. PCarberry (Gordon Elliott, Ire) *hld up: stdy hdwy bef 3 out: rdn and chsd clr ldrs bef next: sn no imp* **7/4**[1]	101
-F24	4	*1*	**Trumpstoo (USA)**[26] 1406 4-11-12 **118**.............................. BrianHughes (Richard Fahey) *trckd ldrs tl rdn and wknd bef 2 out* **16/1**	110
-145	5	*15*	**Lodgician (IRE)**[19] 1470 8-10-6 **101**...................... SamTwiston-Davies(3) (Nigel Twiston-Davies) *prom: drvn 3 out: wknd bef next* **11/2**[3]	80+
P06P	6	*7*	**Samizdat (FR)**[16] 1501 7-9-12 **95**...............................(p) JamesHalliday(5) (Dianne Sayer) *cl up tl rdn and wknd fr 3 out* **16/1**	64
1	7	*8*	**Reportage (USA)**[33] 1342 4-11-5 **111**....................................... AELynch (Robert Alan Hennessy, Ire) *hld up: shortlived effrt on outside bef 3 out: sn btn* **16/1**	72
4221	8	*28*	**Front Rank (IRE)**[26] 1406 10-10-12 **111**......................... MissECSayer(7) (Dianne Sayer) *bhd: struggling after 3rd: t.o* **9/1**	44

4m 13.9s (14.20) **Going Correction** +1.025s/f (Soft) **8** Ran SP% **115.7**
Speed ratings (Par 107): **107,106,99,98,91 88,84,71**
toteswingers:1&2:£4.50, 1&3:£4.80, 2&3:£2.40 CSF £43.84 CT £80.17 TOTE £11.90: £2.80, £1.30, £1.80; EX 58.60.
Owner Mrs M Craig **Bred** Adena Springs **Trained** Uplawmoor, E Renfrews

FOCUS
A modest handicap, run at a fair gallop and the first pair came clear in a driving finish. The winner is rated in line with the best of his old hurdles form.

NOTEBOOK
Regent's Secret(USA) received a very strong ride from Graham Lee and just did enough to resume winning ways. This was his first outing over hurdles since May and he was ridden more positively than can often be the case. Getting the stands' rail after the last was a help and he proved game under maximum pressure. It would be surprising to see him follow up, though. (op 11-1 tchd 10-1)
Quito Du Tresor(FR) is better known as a chaser, but was able to race off a 12lb lower mark on this rare outing over hurdles. Returning from an 84-day break, he set out to make all and looked the most likely winner coming to the last. He didn't find a great deal when asked for maximum effort and allowed the winner another chance, though. He was always just being held by that rallying rival near the finish, but there was more than enough in this effort to suggest he can be found an opening over hurdles, probably when reverting to better ground. (op 4-1)
Vinnes Friend(IRE) was bidding to give her stable a third consecutive winner in this race. She raced well off the early pace, though, and, while faring by far the best of the trio that did so, such tactics failed to suit. (op 9-4)
Trumpstoo(USA) kept on under pressure from the home turn and ideally wants a less taxing surface in this sphere. (op 12-1)
Front Rank(IRE) Official explanation: trainer had no explanation for the poor form shown

1598 BREWIN DOLPHIN INVESTMENT MANAGEMENT H'CAP CHASE (15 fncs) 2m 4f 110y
4:50 (4:51) (Class 3) (0-120,120) 4-Y-O+ **£5,204** (£1,528; £764; £381)

Form			Horse	RPR
201-	1		**Swincombe Rock**[157] 5282 5-11-12 **120**.......................... PaddyBrennan (Nigel Twiston-Davies) *trckd ldrs: led 3 out: styd on strly fr next* **11/10**[1]	142+
10U2	2	*14*	**King Roonah**[33] 1338 6-11-7 **115**...(t) PCarberry (Gordon Elliott, Ire) *hld up: blnd 2nd: smooth hdwy and prom bef 4 out: effrt and chsd wnr next: 3 l down whn blnd 2 out: sn no ex* **9/2**[2]	125+
36	3	*27*	**More Equity**[24] 1424 8-10-11 **105**.................................. DenisO'Regan (P Monteith) *in tch: outpcd 5 out: lft poor 3rd run-in* **14/1**	83
-223	4	*4*	**Ormello (FR)**[33] 1339 8-11-11 **119**.................................. PeterBuchanan (Lucinda Russell) *prom: drvn and outpcd 5 out: lft poor 4th run-in* **10/1**[3]	93
01-4	5	*2 1/2*	**Top Dressing (IRE)**[133] 308 9-11-11 **119**.............................. BrianHughes (Howard Johnson) *hld up: nt fluent and outpcd 5 out: sn btn* **14/1**	91
015	6	*5*	**Strobe**[33] 1338 6-9-9 **94** oh3...(p) JamesHalliday(5) (Lucy Normile) *cl up tl rdn and wknd fr 3 out* **11/1**	61
4-02	P		**Kyber**[33] 1341 9-10-11 **105**.. GrahamLee (Jim Goldie) *cl up tl wknd 11th: t.o whn p.u bef 3 out* **12/1**	—
0-	U		**Master'n Commander**[42] 1244 8-10-4 **103**.......................(b) CO'Farrell(5) (John Joseph Hanlon, Ire) *hld up: blnd and uns rdr 10th* **25/1**	—
PP-3	U		**Or De Grugy (FR)**[133] 308 8-11-5 **120**.......................... AlexanderVoy(7) (Sue Bradburne) *led to 3 out: sn drvn and outpcd: 3rd and btn whn bdly hmpd by loose horse and uns rdr run-in* **22/1**	108+

5m 24.2s (10.20) **Going Correction** +0.675s/f (Soft) **9** Ran SP% **112.4**
Speed ratings (Par 107): **107,101,91,89,88 87,—,—,—**
toteswingers:1&2:£2.70, 1&3:£5.70, 2&3:£7.40 CSF £6.70 CT £41.43 TOTE £2.00: £1.10, £2.70, £5.20; EX 5.20.
Owner Mills & Mason Partnership **Bred** M C And Mrs Yeo **Trained** Naunton, Gloucs

FOCUS
This was a modest handicap. The easy winner is rated up over a stone on his best hurdles form and looks a useful novice.

NOTEBOOK
Swincombe Rock ran out a comfortable winner. This 5-y-o was having his first outing since winning a novice handicap over hurdles on his final run for Robert and Sally Alner back in April, and proved all the rage on this debut for his bang in-form stable. He was a stone higher for this switch to chasing, but the fact connections were starting him off as a chaser in a handicap was a good indication they believed he was well treated. So it proved as he completed the task with plenty left in the tank and he jumped nicely enough for a first-timer. He is clearly an improver and, while the handicapper will have his say, he could well follow up while in this sort of form. He also has the option of novice races. (tchd Evens and 6-5 and 5-4 in a place)
King Roonah's inconsistent jumping had hampered him on his last two outings and he wasn't always foot perfect here. He was held prior to another error two out, but this still rates a sound effort in defeat on ground soft enough for his liking, and he is a fair benchmark. (op 5-1 tchd 4-1)
More Equity shaped better again and really needs a sounder surface. (op 18-1)
Ormello(FR) also found this too testing back on his return to fences. (op 8-1 tchd 15-2)
Or De Grugy(FR) was booked for third place prior to being very badly hampered as the loose horse crashed into the wing near the finish and caused him to unseat. He ran a bold race from the front until tiring from the third-last on this return to action and should be sharper next time out. (op 20-1 tchd 25-1)

1599 PERTH FM 106.6 STANDARD OPEN NATIONAL HUNT FLAT RACE 2m 110y
5:20 (5:28) (Class 6) 4-6-Y-O **£1,712** (£499; £249)

Form			Horse	RPR
	1		**The Cockney Mackem (IRE)** 4-11-4 0......................... PaddyBrennan (Nigel Twiston-Davies) *mde virtually all: drew clr fr 2f out: shkn up and kpt on wl fnl f* **1/1**[1]	113+
1-	2	*7*	**Dr Flynn (IRE)**[185] 4785 5-11-11 0.................................. WilsonRenwick (Howard Johnson) *w ldr to 3f out: kpt on same pce fnl 2f* **5/2**[2]	108
	3	*21*	**Monroe Park (IRE)**[359] 1579 5-11-4 0...................................(t) PCarberry (John Joseph Hanlon, Ire) *t.k.h: hld up in tch: hdwy to chse clr ldrs over 4f out: sn outpcd* **7/1**	80
50-	4	*6*	**Tomzatackman (IRE)**[314] 2265 5-10-11 0................. GaryRutherford(7) (Raymond Shiels) *t.k.h: hld up: struggling over 4f out: sn btn* **40/1**	74
0-	5	*24*	**Farm Pixie (IRE)**[185] 4785 4-11-4 0..................................... PaddyAspell (Ann Hamilton) *bhd: pushed along over 5f out: sn btn* **33/1**	50
5	6	*44*	**Orraloon**[127] 399 4-11-4 0.. BrianHughes (Donald Whillans) *trckd ldrs tl rdn and wknd over 4f out* **6/1**[3]	6

4m 23.5s (29.40) **Going Correction** +1.025s/f (Soft)
WFA 4 from 5yo 11lb **6** Ran SP% **110.7**
Speed ratings: **71,67,57,55,43 23**
toteswingers:1&2:£1.50, 2&3:£2.20, 1&3:£2.00. totesuper7: Win: Not won. Place: Not won. CSF £3.56 TOTE £2.00: £1.40, £1.30; EX 3.40 Place 6 £20.91; Place 5 £5.01.
Owner Mills & Mason Partnership **Bred** Albert Sherwood **Trained** Naunton, Gloucs

FOCUS
A fair bumper, run at a moderate gallop. The easy winner should go on to rate a lot higher and the second sets a decent standard.

NOTEBOOK
The Cockney Mackem(IRE) was unsurprisingly a popular choice considering his stable had scored with three of its four runners earlier on the card and he comfortably provided them with further success. He is a half-brother to juvenile sprint winners, but his dam is a half-sister to Vinnie Roe and he has plenty of size about him. He cut out most of the running and it was clear with 3f to run he was going to do the business. There is good reason to think he can defy a penalty at this time of year, and he obviously stays well. (op 10-11 tchd 11-10)
Dr Flynn(IRE) was a game winner on debut at Kelso in March. He matched the winner into the home straight, but was in trouble soon after and time will likely tell he faced an impossible task conceding that one 7lb. He still finished well clear in second and now looks ready to go hurdling. (op 2-1)
Monroe Park(IRE), a half-brother to 2003 Triumph Hurdle winner Spectroscope, was having his first outing for a new stable and equipped with a first-time tongue-tie. He was labouring on the ground before the home turn and the run looked needed. (op 12-1 tchd 6-1)
Tomzatackman(IRE), who got warm beforehand, lacked the required pace to get seriously involved. He has some scope, though, and will find his level over jumps in due course. (tchd 33-1)
Orraloon showed some ability on his debut in May. He was beaten a long way out on this contrasting surface, however, and is surely capable of better again back on quicker ground. (op 9-1)
T/Plt: £53.00 to a £1 stake. Pool:£67,307.31 - 925.75 winning tickets T/Qpdt: £7.50 to a £1 stake. Pool:£5,373.18 - 525.34 winning tickets RY

1481 WORCESTER (L-H)
Friday, September 24

OFFICIAL GOING: Good (good to firm in places; good to soft in places in home straight; chs 8.3 hdl 8.2)
Home turn bends on inner racing line Cathedral bend out 3m increasing distances by about 9yds per circuit.
Wind: Strong behind Weather: Overcast

1600 LADBROKES MAIDEN HURDLE (DIV I) (10 hdls) 2m 4f
1:50 (1:50) (Class 4) 4-Y-O+ **£2,397** (£698; £349)

Form			Horse	RPR
6	1		**Lamb's Cross**[54] 1153 4-10-13 0...................................... PaddyBrennan (Nigel Twiston-Davies) *t.k.h: hld up in tch: hdwy fr 4 out to trck ldrs 3 out: led appr last: sn pushed clr: eased cl home* **11/4**[2]	110+
	2	*10*	**Try Cat**[208] 4-10-6 0.. RichardJohnson (Philip Hobbs) *t.k.h: chsd ldrs: styng on same pce whn hit 2 out: wnt 2nd last: kpt on but no ch w eased wnr* **9/1**	93+
36-5	3	*7*	**Sir Bere (FR)**[148] 58 4-10-6 0..............................(p) AodhaganConlon(7) (Rebecca Curtis) *led: drvn 6 l clr after 4 out: rdn and blnd 2 out: hdd appr last and sn wknd into 3rd* **4/1**[3]	94
2	4	*1 1/4*	**Butlers Glen (IRE)**[35] 1308 7-10-7 0.................................. PaulMoloney (Evan Williams) *in rr: j. slowly 4th: hdwy 5th: chsd ldrs appr 3 out: nvr quite on terms: no ch whn hung lft u.p run-in but kpt on* **6/4**[1]	85
600/	5	*5*	**Cilrhiwviv**[751] 1342 7-10-7 0.. MrMWall(7) (Sue Wilson) *in rr tl hdwy 5th: styd in tch tl outpcd fr 2 out* **25/1**	88
05U	6	*1 3/4*	**Coach And Four (USA)**[19] 1487 5-10-7 0........................ MrJEngland(7) (Michael Gates) *in rr: j. slowly 4 out: nvr nr ldrs* **16/1**	86
	7	*40*	**Quartz D'Anjou (FR)**[66] 861 6-10-7 0................................ ColinBolger (Pat Phelan) *sn chsng ldr: wknd 3 out: t.o* **33/1**	43
0-60	8	*1*	**Jim Job Jones**[18] 1488 6-10-7 0.................................... MarkQuinlan(7) (Neil Mulholland) *t.k.h: chsd ldrs: rdn 6th: sn wknd: t.o* **80/1**	49
60-0	9	*55*	**Knottage Hill (IRE)**[146] 93 5-11-0 0.................................. JohnnyFarrelly (Reg Hollinshead) *in tch tl dropped to rr 5th and no ch after: blnd 3 out: t.o* **66/1**	—

4m 50.11s (2.71) **Going Correction** -0.525s/f (Firm)
WFA 4 from 5yo+ 12lb **9** Ran SP% **112.1**
Speed ratings (Par 105): **73,69,66,65,63 63,47,46,24**
Tote Swingers: 1&2 £6.30, 1&3 £3.80, 2&3 £5.90 CSF £25.04 TOTE £4.10: £1.60, £1.80, £1.60; EX 38.70.
Owner Barry Connell **Bred** Shade Oak Stud **Trained** Naunton, Gloucs

FOCUS
The first division of a lowly maiden hurdle. Hard to be confident about the form.

NOTEBOOK
Lamb's Cross didn't get home having been made plenty of use of on his bumper debut at Market Rasen, but he was ridden with more restraint upped in trip over hurdles and always looked to be travelling strongly under Paddy Brennan. Having readily closed on the leader in the straight, he stayed on strongly once taking it up and won with plenty in hand. There should be more to come, with him expected to stay 3m in time, and he may well go on to defy a penalty. (op 5-2 tchd 9-4)
Try Cat, unplaced in four starts at up to 2m on the Flat, closed to hold every chance turning in, but couldn't stay on as strongly as the winner. There'll be other opportunities for her. (op 8-1)
Sir Bere(FR) pressed on a long way from home and held a handy advantage turning in, but he couldn't maintain the gallop and ended up a well-held third, a mistake two out not helping. This was better than his initial effort over hurdles and the cheekpieces were clearly a help. (op 13-2 tchd 7-1)
Butlers Glen(IRE), runner-up at Bangor on her debut for the yard, never got close enough to challenge having been held up and may find life easier again her own sex. (op 11-8 tchd 5-4)
Cilrhiwviv made some late headway and could be of interest once handicapping. (tchd 28-1)

1601 ENDLESS TOAST NOVICES' H'CAP HURDLE (8 hdls) 2m
2:20 (2:20) (Class 4) (0-105,105) 4-Y-O+ **£3,252** (£955; £477; £238)

Form				RPR
0-43	**1**		**Crystal Rock (IRE)**[19] 1487 5-11-7 **105** DavidBass(5) (Nicky Henderson) *in tch: hdwy 4th: chal 3 out and sn led: hung rt after last: drvn and styd on wl fnl 120yds* **9/2**[2]	115+
00-3	**2**	1 ¼	**Goat Castle (IRE)**[52] 1179 6-10-4 **86** (t) SamTwiston-Davies(3) (Nigel Twiston-Davies) *t.k.h: racked ldrs: hit 2nd and 4th: chsd wnr after 3 out: one pce after last tl rdn and styd on wl fnl 120yds but a hld* **11/4**[1]	91
P-66	**3**	2 ¾	**The Brimmer (IRE)**[19] 1484 6-11-6 **104** JimmyDerham(5) (Seamus Mullins) *led: hit 3rd: jnd 3 out and sn hdd: rdn and nt fluent last: one pce run-in tl styd on again fnl 50yds* **17/2**	107
4352	**4**	9	**Cool Bob (IRE)**[68] 1035 7-10-9 **95** (t) MrLRPayter(7) (Matt Sheppard) *mid-div: hdwy fr 4 out to chse ldrs 3 out: sn rdn: wknd after 2 out* **8/1**[3]	90
3240	**5**	8	**Art Man**[10] 1484 7-11-2 **95** (b) HaddenFrost (James Frost) *in rr tl hdwy and hmpd 3 out: kpt on again run-in but nvr any ch* **9/1**	83
0-2P	**6**	4 ½	**Naughty Naughty**[21] 684 5-11-7 **100** APMcCoy (Brendan Powell) *in tch: pushed along and hdwy to chse ldrs 3 out: sn rdn and btn* **9/1**	84
-0P0	**7**	3 ½	**Kensington Oval**[19] 1484 5-11-4 **100** (t) RichieMcLernon(3) (Jonjo O'Neill) *in rr: pushed along and rn in snatches fr 3rd: styng on same pce whn hmpd 3 out* **25/1**	83+
4-56	**8**	9	**Azulada Bay (IRE)**[120] 494 6-11-7 **100** (t) TomScudamore (Mark Rimell) *bhd most of way and little ch whn hmpd 3 out* **14/1**	72
P-26	**9**	22	**Contrada**[23] 1453 5-11-6 **99** (p) RhysFlint (Jim Old) *chsd ldrs: rdn 4th: wknd appr 3 out* **16/1**	52
P	**10**	29	**Rolanta (FR)**[33] 1343 5-11-0 **98** TomO'Connor(5) (James Frost) *in rr: rdn 4 out and no prog whn hmpd 3 out* **100/1**	25
30-0	**U**		**Tanmeya**[23] 1450 9-9-11 **83** MrTomDavid(7) (Tim Vaughan) *chsd ldrs: rdn 4 out: stl in tch but u.p whn bdly hmpd and uns rdr 3 out* **28/1**	—
5225	**F**		**London Times (IRE)**[23] 1450 5-10-2 **81** ow2 (t) ColinBolger (Simon Lewis) *chsd ldrs: u.p and disputing 3 l 3rd whn fell 3 out* **12/1**	—

3m 36.88s (-10.42) **Going Correction** -0.525s/f (Firm) 12 Ran SP% **115.0**
Speed ratings (Par 105): **105,104,103,98,94 92,90,86,75,60 —,—**
Tote Swingers: 1&2 £4.00, 1&3 £4.40, 2&3 £8.30 CSF £16.81 CT £100.61 TOTE £3.40: £2.20, £2.00, £2.60; EX 15.00.
Owner Mrs Christopher Hanbury **Bred** Triermore Stud **Trained** Upper Lambourn, Berks

FOCUS
Just a modest handicap hurdle. It was sound run and the form is pretty solid at face value.

NOTEBOOK
Crystal Rock(IRE), who ran his best race to date over hurdles when third at the course last time, looked feasibly weighted on this handicap debut and he duly showed improved form, taking a narrow lead after three out and staying on too strongly for the runner-up. He's clearly going the right way and may be able to defy a rise. (op 5-1)
Goat Castle(IRE) improved when third off this mark at Ffos Las on his handicap debut and, with his stable in such fine form, it was no surprise to see him step up again, holding every chance and just not being able to stay on as strongly as the winner. He should go one better before long. (op 5-2 tchd 9-4)
The Brimmer(IRE) looked vulnerable as the first two loomed turning in and he was duly outpaced once they came to challenge. (op 8-1 tchd 15-2 and 9-1)
Art Man, one of several hampered three out, did stay on again. (tchd 8-1)
Kensington Oval was interfered with when trying to keep on. (op 22-1 tchd 28-1)
London Times(IRE) was under pressure, but not far away when falling three out. (op 14-1 tchd 16-1)

1602 LADBROKES BEGINNERS' CHASE (18 fncs) 2m 7f
2:55 (2:55) (Class 4) 4-Y-O+ **£3,252** (£955; £477; £238)

Form				RPR
F06-	**1**		**Balthazar King (IRE)**[155] 5349 6-11-6 0 TomO'Brien (Philip Hobbs) *trckd ldrs: 1 l 2nd and travelling wl whn lft in ld 4 out: rdn and styd on strly run-in* **2/1**[2]	123+
210-	**2**	2 ¼	**Triggerman**[162] 5197 8-11-6 0 RichardJohnson (Philip Hobbs) *hld up in tch: j. slowly 3rd: hit 10th: hdwy 13th: chsd wnr after 4 out: styd on u.p but no imp run-in* **5/6**[1]	122+
U5-3	**3**	6	**Night Orbit**[25] 1432 6-11-6 0 MattieBatchelor (Julia Feilden) *chsd ldrs tl blnd 12th: rdn 14th: lost pl sn after: rdn 4 out: blnd 2 out: rallied to take 3rd run-in and kpt on but no ch w ldng duo* **25/1**	117
P	**4**	¾	**No Reception (IRE)**[56] 1136 9-10-13 104 MissLBrooke(7) (Lady Susan Brooke) *j. slowly 2nd: in rr: hit 12th: kpt on fr 3 out and styd on run-in but nvr a threat* **150/1**	115
055-	**5**	7	**Priors Glen (IRE)**[168] 5117 6-11-6 0 JackDoyle (Emma Lavelle) *tendency to jump rt: hit 4th: disp 2nd 11th tl appr 4 out: wnt rt and mstke 3 out: btn whn wnt bdly rt and mstke 2 out* **15/2**[3]	114+
5P24	**6**	32	**Indian Pipe Dream (IRE)**[24] 1444 8-11-6 100 LiamTreadwell (Aytach Sadik) *rdn 8th: a in rr* **33/1**	80
66/	**U**		**Brightwell**[1020] 9-11-3 0 CharlieStudd(3) (Chris Gordon) *led: tended to jump rt: stl 1 l ahd and goin ok whn j. bdly rt: mstke and uns rdr 4 out* **33/1**	—

5m 49.07s (6.47) **Going Correction** -0.375s/f (Good) 7 Ran SP% **110.0**
Speed ratings (Par 105): **78,77,75,74,72 61,—**
Tote Swingers: 1&2 £1.10, 1&3 £6.40, 2&3 £5.20 CSF £3.89 TOTE £2.50: £1.60, £1.50; EX 4.00.
Owner The Brushmakers **Bred** Sunnyhill Stud **Trained** Withycombe, Somerset

FOCUS
Philip Hobbs had a strong grip on this beginners' chase, with 132-rated hurdlers Triggerman and Balthazar King. It was steadily run and the form is limited by the fourth.

NOTEBOOK
Balthazar King(IRE), always travelling strongly under Tom O'Brien, he undoubtedly has more pace than his stablemate, jumped fluently throughout and, having taken over soon after three out, he found plenty in front to hold on well. He came to hand early last season and can probably defy a penalty. (tchd 7-4)
Triggerman, a more robust type than the winner, was going to come on plenty for this first run and he ran like a rusty horse. Tending to jump right, he closed to hold every chance off the final bend, but wasn't as slick as his stablemate at the fences in the straight and, despite staying on well, he was always booked for second. It looks as though he may prefer going the other way round and it surely won't take him long to get off the mark over fences. (op Evens tchd 11-10 in places)
Night Orbit stayed on again having lost his place with a few slow jumps. (op 22-1)
No Reception(IRE) kept grinding away. (op 100-1)
Priors Glen(IRE) travelled strongly before getting tired in the straight. Brought along steadily over hurdles, he has the look of a chaser and looks sure to make an impact at some stage, maybe once handicapped. (op 13-2)
Brightwell had been jumping to his right, but was still in front and going okay when blundering and unseating his rider four out. It's unlikely he'd have won, but this multiple winning pointer looks to have a future. (op 20-1)

1603 LADBROKES MAIDEN HURDLE (DIV II) (10 hdls) 2m 4f
3:30 (3:30) (Class 4) 4-Y-O+ **£2,397** (£698; £349)

Form				RPR
5-22	**1**		**Gambo (IRE)**[30] 1369 4-10-13 113 PaulMoloney (Evan Williams) *in tch: hdwy to chse ldrs and hit 3 out: drvn to chal last: drvn to ld run-in: styd on strly fnl 120yds* **11/8**[1]	116+
	2	2 ¾	**Foynes Island (IRE)**[109] 4-10-13 0 RichardJohnson (Philip Hobbs) *hld up in rr but in tch: hdwy 6th: disputing 2nd appr 3 out: rdn and pressing for ld last: outpcd sn after: rallied u.p to take 2nd cl home but no imp on wnr* **9/2**[3]	110+
232	**3**	nk	**Mutadarrej (IRE)**[3] 1571 6-11-0 110 (p) APMcCoy (Ian Williams) *hit 1st: in tch: hdwy 3 out: drvn to chse ldrs 2 out: hit last: kpt on u.p to dispute 2nd fnl 120yds but no imp on wnr: dropped to 3rd cl home* **5/2**[2]	111
P2-0	**4**	1	**Meet The Critics (IRE)**[140] 191 7-11-0 112 AidanColeman (Brendan Powell) *led: rdn 2 out: hdd after last: kpt on tl outpcd into 4th fnl 120yds* **11/1**	110
U323	**5**	27	**Salford Rose (IRE)**[30] 1374 4-10-3 0 LeeStephens(3) (David Evans) *plld hrd: chsd ldr and wandered at 2nd: 3rd and 4th: wknd fr 6th* **28/1**	78
	6	7	**Ezdiyaad (IRE)**[333] 6-11-0 0 LeightonAspell (Kevin Morgan) *hit 1st: in rr: sme hdwy appr 3 out: hit 2 out and wknd qckly* **10/1**	79+
40	**7**	29	**Mulranny (IRE)**[37] 1284 5-10-7 0 MrSWDrinkwater(7) (Nigel Twiston-Davies) *in rr 3rd: hdwy and j. slowly 5th: rcvrd next: styd wl there tl wknd 3 out* **66/1**	53

4m 41.27s (-6.13) **Going Correction** -0.525s/f (Firm)
WFA 4 from 5yo+ 12lb 7 Ran SP% **111.2**
Speed ratings (Par 105): **91,89,89,89,78 75,64**
Tote Swingers: 1&2 £2.60, 1&3 £1.80, 2&3 £2.20 CSF £7.72 TOTE £2.70: £1.30, £2.60; EX 7.20.
Owner R J Gambarini **Bred** Mrs M Fox **Trained** Llancarfan, Vale Of Glamorgan

FOCUS
This was certainly the more competitive of the two divisions, and it was much quicker. The form looks pretty sound.

NOTEBOOK
Gambo(IRE) ran out a ready winner, quickening well after the last to draw clear. Runner-up on each of his last two starts, this represented another step forward in his progression and it would be a surprise were he not to go on and defy a penalty. (tchd 6-5)
Foynes Island(IRE) looked an interesting contender and he very much shaped like a stayer, getting outpaced straightening for home before keeping on well after the last to grab second. This was a promising debut and he should have little trouble going one better, with the step up to 3m expected to suit. (tchd 7-2 and 5-1)
Mutadarrej(IRE) threw the race away at Stratford the other day and the cheekpieces were expected to help him concentrate. He isn't the quickest, however, and the drop in trip was against him this time, as he proved unable to quicken in the straight. He's sure to find a small race before long. (tchd 11-4)
Meet The Critics(IRE) ran well for a long way on this first start since May and should make an impact once handicapping. (op 14-1 tchd 16-1)
Ezdiyaad(IRE), rated 98 on the level, travelled well in rear, but stopped quickly having hit two out and may have either needed it or failed to stay. Official explanation: jockey said horse had no more to give (op 9-1 tchd 14-1)

1604 LADBROKES AT WORCESTER RACECOURSE H'CAP CHASE (15 fncs) 2m 4f 110y
4:05 (4:05) (Class 3) (0-120,126) 4-Y-O+ **£5,204** (£1,528; £764; £381)

Form				RPR
13F-	**1**		**Sir Ian (IRE)**[154] 5360 7-11-0 **108** FelixDeGiles (Charlie Longsdon) *t.k.h: trckd ldrs: chal fr 7th tl led 9th: c readily clr appr 4 out: in n.d after: eased run-in* **16/1**	122+
3-55	**2**	5	**Storm Of Applause (IRE)**[45] 1229 9-11-11 **119** RichardJohnson (Philip Hobbs) *chsd ldrs: rdn 4 out: styd on fr 2 out to chse wnr last but nvr any ch* **12/1**	121
1145	**3**	½	**Folie A Deux (IRE)**[34] 1334 8-11-3 **111** (t) JoeTizzard (Colin Tizzard) *led 2nd to 3rd: hit 6th: styd wl in tch tl blnd 3 out: styd on again appr last to press for 2nd cl home but nvr any ch w wnr* **20/1**	113
331F	**4**	9	**Moulin De La Croix**[16] 1509 6-11-4 **115** (t) SamTwiston-Davies(3) (Nigel Twiston-Davies) *chsd ldrs: chsd wnr after 11th but nvr any imp: wknd bef last* **10/3**[2]	108
1211	**5**	1 ¼	**Frosted Grape (IRE)**[5] 1557 4-11-6 **126** 6ex (b) TomScudamore (David Pipe) *led to 2nd: led 3rd: jnd fr 7th tl hdd 9th: blnd 11th: btn whn mstke 3 out* **11/4**[1]	107
3412	**6**	17	**Rockiteer (IRE)**[25] 1432 7-11-9 **117** (p) AndrewTinkler (Henry Daly) *in rr: mod prog fr 4 out: nvr any ch hit last* **16/1**	98+
4031	**7**	13	**Magnetic Pole**[35] 1309 9-10-10 **109** (v) GilesHawkins(5) (Richard Lee) *chsd ldrs: hit 7th: nvr any threat after and bhd fr 11th* **12/1**	74
106-	**8**	3 ¼	**Qianshan Leader (IRE)**[155] 5326 6-11-5 **113** JackDoyle (Emma Lavelle) *in rr and j. bdly rt 4th: styd in rr: hit 11th and no ch after* **12/1**	75
P0P0	**9**	50	**Keepitsecret (IRE)**[20] 1469 9-11-9 **120** RichieMcLernon(3) (Jonjo O'Neill) *hit 3rd: in rr: sme hdwy fr 6th: in tch 8th: sn bhd: t.o* **40/1**	37

P3 **P** **Tell Me The Story (IRE)**[19] 1486 6-11-2 **110**........................ APMcCoy —
(Jonjo O'Neill) *in rr: sme hdwy fr 6th: blnd 11th: wknd, p.u and dismntd bef 4 out* **7/2**[3]

4m 50.38s (-16.32) **Going Correction** -0.375s/f (Good) course record
WFA 4 from 6yo+ 1lb **10** Ran SP% **114.0**
Speed ratings (Par 107): **107,105,104,101,101 94,89,88,69,—**
Tote Swingers: 1&2 £21.70, 1&3 £39.50, 2&3 £22.90 CSF £182.51 CT £3806.85 TOTE £24.10: £5.50, £1.90, £5.40; EX 170.20.
Owner Mrs Phillip Stevenson **Bred** Mrs Valerie Hore **Trained** Over Norton, Oxon

FOCUS
A fair handicap chase. The winner walue for 12l and the next two ran to form.

NOTEBOOK
Sir Ian(IRE) took it up a long way from home and galloped on relentlessly to win as he liked. Off since falling at Chepstow back in April, he wasn't at all badly weighted on earlier efforts and has clearly improved over the summer. Winning from a mark of 108, he can expect a hefty rise, but could improve again and it will be interesting to see where he goes next. (op 20-1)
Storm Of Applause(IRE) stayed on well for second, but was flattered to get so close to the winner. He's still 4lb above his last winning mark, but is clearly in fair form. (op 11-1 tchd 10-1)
Folie A Deux(IRE) remains 10lb above his last winning mark but would probably have been second had he not blundered three out. (op 16-1)
Moulin De La Croix, off since falling at Uttoxeter, had her chance but didn't quite run up to her best. (tchd 11-4)
Frosted Grape(IRE), bidding for her fourth win over fences this month and second in five days, was taken on for the lead and never looked completely comfortable, being unable to race on with the winner and ending up well held having faded. (op 9-4 tchd 2-1)
Tell Me The Story(IRE) was just trying to stay on when appearing to go wrong and pulled up rounding for home. (op 5-1 tchd 11-2)

1605 LADBROKES H'CAP HURDLE (12 hdls) 3m
4:40 (4:40) (Class 4) (0-100,100) 4-Y-0+ **£2,927** (£859; £429; £214)

Form RPR
6053 **1** **Sea Cliff (IRE)**[23] 1451 6-10-9 **83**......................................(p) APMcCoy 89
(Jonjo O'Neill) *in rr but in tch: hdwy appr 3 out: styd on u.p run-in to ld last strides* **9/2**[3]
42F0 **2** *nk* **Nobby Kivambo (IRE)**[23] 1451 5-11-2 **90**.................... JimmyMcCarthy 96
(Brendan Powell) *led 3rd tl after 6th: led 7th tl after 4 out: styd pressing ldr but a tending to hang lft: led last: hung lft sn after and rdr lost whip: ct last strides* **16/1**
3233 **3** *2 1/4* **Saintly Lady (IRE)**[16] 1507 5-11-4 **95**......................(p) DonalDevereux(3) 99
(Peter Bowen) *led to 3rd: styd w ldr and led after 6th to 7th: styd chalng and led after 4 out: hdd last: one pce run-in* **15/2**
-321 **4** *3 3/4* **Silver Phoenix**[111] 630 6-11-12 **100**..............................(p) TomO'Brien 101
(Caroline Keevil) *t.k.h: chsd ldrs: rdn and rt there fr 3 out: wknd run-in* **8/1**
-112 **5** *1 3/4* **Caheerloch (IRE)**[18] 1490 8-11-5 **96**.................. SamTwiston-Davies(3) 95
(Nigel Twiston-Davies) *chsd ldrs: rdn after 4 out: styd on same pce fr 2 out* **5/2**[1]
P-P0 **6** *10* **Jug Of Punch (IRE)**[20] 1468 11-9-7 **74** oh10.................. MissCBoxall(7) 64
(Simon Lewis) *dropped to rr 3rd: rdn 6th: sme hdwy 7th: wknd u.p after 4 out* **100/1**
0-60 **7** *5* **Synonymy**[34] 1336 7-10-9 **83**..(b) NickScholfield 69
(Michael Blanshard) *chsd ldrs: rdn 4 out: wknd bef next* **22/1**
0-33 **8** *75* **Ladies Best**[24] 1443 6-11-8 **99**.............................. DannyCook(3) 17
(Gordon Edwards) *blnd 3 out: a in rr: t.o* **25/1**
1134 **P** **Kopylova**[18] 1490 7-11-10 **98**.............................. RichardJohnson —
(Tim Vaughan) *in rr: rdn 7th: wknd next: t.o whn p.u bef 4 out* **4/1**[2]
-464 **U** **Karzelle**[72] 992 6-11-1 **89**......................................(b1) WarrenMarston —
(John Spearing) *uns rdr 1st* **9/1**

5m 42.74s (-1.86) **Going Correction** -0.525s/f (Firm)
WFA 4 from 5yo+ 13lb **10** Ran SP% **114.7**
Speed ratings (Par 105): **82,81,81,79,79 75,74,49,—,—**
Tote Swingers: 1&2 £11.00, 1&3 £7.70, 2&3 £20.70 CSF £67.06 CT £527.35 TOTE £6.20: £1.80, £5.20, £2.20; EX 78.10.
Owner John P McManus **Bred** G W Robinson **Trained** Cheltenham, Gloucs

FOCUS
Little got into this low-grade staying handicap. The form looks sound.

NOTEBOOK
Sea Cliff(IRE) produced a stirring run after the last to get up close home. Far from straightforward, it was his first win since January 2009 (on the Flat) and it remains to be seen whether he can back the effort up next time. (op 11-2)
Nobby Kivambo(IRE), trying this trip for the first time, was soon on the speed and he battled on well for pressure, but carried his head awkwardly and his rider dropping his whip probably cost him. He's yet to win in 13 attempts and clearly isn't straightforward. (op 14-1)
Saintly Lady(IRE) disputed it with the runner-up for much of the way and showed improved form, just backing out of it after the last. She's only moderate, but can be found a small race eventually. (op 13-2 tchd 8-1)
Silver Phoenix travelled well under top weight but couldn't race on with the front trio. (tchd 17-2)
Caheerloch(IRE), bogged down by heavy ground latest, was again below his best and looks in the handicapper's grip now. (tchd 9-4)
Kopylova seems to have lost her form. Official explanation: vet said mare pulled up lame (op 5-1)

1606 LADBROKES H'CAP CHASE (12 fncs) 2m
5:15 (5:15) (Class 3) (0-135,125) 4-Y-0 **£6,337** (£1,872; £936; £468; £234)

Form RPR
U03- **1** **Oneway (IRE)**[297] 2630 13-11-7 **120**............................... TomScudamore 130+
(Mark Rimell) *hld up in tch: hdwy 4 out: qcknd to chal 2 out: led appr last: drvn and styd on strly run-in* **25/1**
04-0 **2** *1 1/4* **Nikola (FR)**[138] 236 9-11-11 **124**...................................... PaddyBrennan 132
(Nigel Twiston-Davies) *chsd ldrs: chal 4 out: led next: hdd 2 out: rdn and swtchd rt run-in: styd on wl but nt pce of wnr* **11/4**[1]
0/22 **3** *10* **Film Festival (USA)**[17] 1502 7-10-5 **111**........................ KyleJames(7) 110
(Brian Ellison) *trckd ldrs: chal fr 6th tl led after 8th: jnd 4 out: hdd next: lost pl u.p 2 out: rallied to take 3rd fnl fn* **4/1**[2]
2566 **4** *1* **Mibleu (FR)**[28] 1390 10-11-7 **120**.. JoeTizzard 118
(Colin Tizzard) *hld up in rr: stdy hdwy appr 4 out: drvn to ld 2 out: hdd appr last: wknd run-in* **12/1**
2132 **5** *11* **Cullahill (IRE)**[81] 911 8-11-5 **125**............................ NathanSweeney(7) 113
(Bob Buckler) *led tl hdd 5th: led again 7th: sn jnd: hdd after 8th: wknd after 4 out* **8/1**
-U24 **6** *2 1/4* **Kikos (FR)**[75] 959 8-11-7 **120**... APMcCoy 106
(Renee Robeson) *w ldr: led 5th to 7th: upsides 4 out tl rdn: next: wknd sn after* **6/1**[3]
53P1 **7** *4 1/2* **Blast The Past**[20] 1471 8-10-11 **110**............................ ChristianWilliams 92
(Dai Burchell) *hit 8th: a in rr* **17/2**
-121 **8** *19* **Novikov**[40] 1257 6-11-6 **122**...(t) LeeStephens(3) 112+
(David Evans) *chsd ldrs tl blnd and wknd 4 out* **4/1**[2]

3m 46.13s (-5.47) **Going Correction** -0.375s/f (Good) **8** Ran SP% **114.1**
Speed ratings (Par 107): **98,97,92,91,86 85,83,73**
Tote Swingers: 1&2 £9.50, 1&3 £12.20, 2&3 £3.00 CSF £95.83 CT £344.75 TOTE £27.50: £7.50, £2.60, £1.60; EX 76.60.
Owner Mark Rimell **Bred** Eamonn Garrett **Trained** Leafield, Oxon

FOCUS
A fair handicap chase. The runner-up sets the standard.

NOTEBOOK
Oneway(IRE) rolled back the years. A 157-rated chaser at his peak, when fourth to Moscow Flyer in the 2005 Champion Chase, he hadn't shown any worthwhile form over fences since late 2008, but ran creditably over hurdles when last seen and was clearly cherry-ripe to run a big race first time back. It remains to be seen how he gets on off a higher mark next time. (op 28-1)
Nikola(FR) travelled well on this return from a 138-day absence and looked the winner two out, but couldn't match the winner's acceleration late on, keeping on well but always looking held. (tchd 10-3)
Film Festival(USA), narrowly denied at Sedgefield latest, plugged on again having been outpaced. (op 5-1)
Mibleu(FR), dropped 3lb, bounced back from a few below-par efforts. (op 10-1)
Cullahill(IRE) was keen on this return and it should have set him up nicely for a return to further. (op 9-1)
Kikos(FR) didn't find much for strong pressure (tchd 11-2)
Novikov was beaten soon after a blunder four out. (op 7-2 tchd 3-1)

1607 IRIS BIRTHDAY INTERMEDIATE OPEN NATIONAL HUNT FLAT RACE 2m
5:50 (5:50) (Class 5) 4-6-Y-O **£1,781** (£519; £259)

Form RPR
1 **Kartanian (IRE)** 4-11-0 0.. TomO'Brien 103+
(Philip Hobbs) *trckd ldrs: led 2f out: sn rn green: hung rt: r.o wl: readily* **1/1**[1]
03/ **2** *2 3/4* **Representingceltic (IRE)**[550] 4680 5-11-0 0....................... ColinBolger 95
(Pat Phelan) *trckd ldr: led over 4f out: rdn whn hdd 2f out: carried rt: kpt on but readily hld fnl f* **3/1**[2]
0- **3** *1 1/2* **Father Probus**[207] 4358 4-11-0 0.................................. PaddyBrennan 94
(Nigel Twiston-Davies) *mid-div: rdn wl over 3f out: wnt 3rd over 1f out: styd on same pce* **8/1**
4 *5* **Jigsaw Financial (IRE)** 4-11-0 0.................................. LeightonAspell 89
(Roger Curtis) *hld up towards rr: hdwy on outer ent st: sn rdn to chse ldrs: styd on same pce fnl 2f* **33/1**
4- **5** *6* **Genny Wren**[217] 4145 4-10-7 0...................................... JimmyMcCarthy 76
(Renee Robeson) *hld up towards rr: hdwy on outer fr 5f out: rdn to chse ldrs 3f out: wknd over 1f out* **25/1**
3 **6** *6* **Kilcommon Pride (IRE)**[23] 1455 5-11-0 0......................... HaddenFrost 77
(Roger Curtis) *trckd ldrs: rdn 3f out: wknd 2f out* **20/1**
7 *10* **Fairwood Dante (IRE)**[556] 6-11-0 0................................ JoeTizzard 67
(Simon Earle) *t.k.h: led tl over 4f out: wknd 3f out* **28/1**
8 *dist* **Samtheman** 5-10-7 0... MrBJPoste(7) —
(Christopher Nenadich) *a towards rr: wknd 4f out: t.o* **40/1**
03 **9** *1 1/4* **Restless Harriet**[19] 1480 4-10-7 0.................................... CharliePoste —
(Robin Dickin) *mid-div tl wknd 5f out: t.o* **40/1**
0- **10** *1 3/4* **Head Of Chambers**[171] 5078 4-11-0 0..............................(t) APMcCoy —
(Lawney Hill) *mid-div: effrt to dispute 3rd 5f out: wknd 3f out: t.o* **7/1**[3]
P **Moorland Picture** 5-11-0 0.. JohnnyFarrelly —
(Mark Shears) *lost tch 1/2-way: t.o whn p.u over 6f out* **100/1**

3m 36.7s (-5.00) **Going Correction** -0.525s/f (Firm) **11** Ran SP% **119.5**
Speed ratings: **91,89,88,86,83 80,75,—,—,—**
Tote Swingers: 1&2 £1.50, 1&3 £2.60, 2&3 £6.30 CSF £3.66 TOTE £2.60: £2.00, £1.10, £3.10; EX 5.40 Place 6: £182.31 Place 5: £91.50..
Owner Louisville Syndicate III **Bred** His Highness The Aga Khan's Studs S C **Trained** Withycombe, Somerset

FOCUS
An ordinary bumper, weakened by the late defection of Sir Cool. The form is rated around the runner-up.

NOTEBOOK
Kartanian(IRE) ◆ justified the hype with a ready debut success. From a good Flat family, there was plenty of talk about him beforehand and, having travelled smoothly under Tom O'Brien, he found plenty to go on and score with a bit in hand, despite showing distinct signs of greenness. There should be plenty of improvement to come and he looks capable of handling a rise in grade.
Representingceltic(IRE), off for 550 days, showed useful form at Kempton on his latest outing and seemed straight enough, so can be used as a benchmark to the form. He's likely to stay further over hurdles and has more to offer. (op 11-2)
Father Probus stepped up markedly on his initial effort and has a definite future over hurdles. (op 7-1)
Jigsaw Financial(IRE), related to several winners, was weak in the market, but stayed on nicely in the straight and looks to have a future.
Genny Wren was another to leave her debut form behind. (op 18-1)
Kilcommon Pride(IRE) should come on for this initial outing. (op 18-1)
Head Of Chambers made a low-key debut for his new connections. (op 11-2 tchd 5-1)
T/Plt: £910.80 to a £1 stake. Pool:£61,965 - 49.66 winning tickets T/Qpdt: £85.70 to a £1 stake. Pool:£6,314 - 54.50 winning tickets ST

1324 MARKET RASEN (R-H)
Saturday, September 25

OFFICIAL GOING: Good (good to soft in places; hdl 6.5; chs 6.9)
Hurdle rail moved out 9yds since last fixture.
Wind: Light across Weather: Overcast and cool

1608 READ PAUL NICHOLLS EXCLUSIVELY ON BETFAIR H'CAP HURDLE (DIV I) (10 hdls) 2m 3f
1:45 (1:46) (Class 3) (0-120,120) 4-Y-0+ **£4,453** (£1,298; £649)

Form RPR
6116 **1** **Extreme Conviction (IRE)**[31] 1372 6-11-7 **115**................. WillKennedy 129+
(John Berry) *prom: chal 3 out: led on ins wl bef next where 2 l clr and nt fluent: jnd last: drvn and responded gamely to forge clr fnl 100yds* **13/2**
P341 **2** *2* **Santera (IRE)**[6] 1556 6-11-3 **111** 7ex...................................(p) RhysFlint 121
(John Flint) *hld up in midfield: j. deliberately 6th and rdn: clsd next: wnt 2nd bef 2 out and nt fluent: jnd last: outstyd fnl 100yds* **9/4**[1]
020- **3** *23* **Wester Ross (IRE)**[22] 5255 6-11-10 **118**.............................. FelixDeGiles 108
(James Eustace) *prom: rdn after 3 out: wknd bef next: tk poor 3rd at last* **5/1**[3]

045- **4** 1½ **Pollen Jock (IRE)**[179] 4942 6-10-9 **103**.......................... TomMessenger 91
(Chris Bealby) *set stdy pce tl 5th: pressed ldr tl led again 3 out: hdd wl bef 2 out: sn lost tch w ldng pair: lost modest 3rd at last* **40/1**

01-0 **5** 9 **Gaspara (FR)**[21] 1470 7-11-11 **119**............................(b) TomScudamore 99
(David Pipe) *hld up and bhd: plenty to do 6th: nvr on terms after* **14/1**

B12- **6** 2½ **Stopped Out**[155] 5374 5-11-12 **120**.......................... RichieMcGrath 98
(Kate Walton) *pressed ldr: led 5th tl 3 out: sn dropped out* **8/1**

40 **7** 22 **Adare Manor (IRE)**[97] 798 6-10-11 **105**.............................. APMcCoy 63
(Jonjo O'Neill) *hld up and bhd: plenty to do whn mstke 7th: awkward next: struggling after: t.o wl bef 2 out* **9/2**[2]

064 **8** 22 **Flying Squad (UAE)**[20] 1487 6-10-6 **100**.........................(t) CharliePoste 38
(Milton Harris) *last pair: nt fluent 3rd: wl bhd 6th: t.o 3 out* **12/1**

P **Tibetan Dragon (IRE)**[30] 1383 6-11-1 **109**......................... PaulMoloney —
(Evan Williams) *last pair: struggling whn blnd 4th: p.u and dismntd after next* **16/1**

4m 45.9s (6.50) **Going Correction** +0.20s/f (Yiel) **9** Ran SP% **112.7**
Speed ratings (Par 107): **94,93,83,82,79 78,68,59,—**
toteswingers: 1&2 £2.50, 1&3 £10.60, 2&3 £2.80. CSF £21.52 CT £78.49 TOTE £8.60: £2.00, £1.30, £2.50; EX 23.10.
Owner All Points West Partnership **Bred** Mrs A S O'Brien And Lars Pearson **Trained** Newmarket, Suffolk

FOCUS
Probably the slightly less competitive of the two divisions of the 0-120 handicap hurdle, but it produced a good tussle in the home straight between the two principals, who drew well clear.

NOTEBOOK
Extreme Conviction(IRE) had been in fine fettle before a disappointing effort when well beaten at Ffos Las recently - got bogged down - and he bounced back to form with a game success. He is a big, scopey sort whom connections are keen on going to the October Cheltenham meeting with for the two-and-a-half mile 0-140 handicap hurdle, with a sound surface being the key. (op 6-1 tchd 11-2)
Santera(IRE) showed improved form in first-time cheek pieces on her debut for John Flint when scooting up at Uttoxeter. She was a well-supported favourite under her 7lb penalty, which proved enough to anchor her, but she looked to have the measure of the winner soon after the last before relenting in the final 100 yards. It was a sound effort but, after being reassessed, life will only become tougher. (op 5-2, tchd 11-4 in places)
Wester Ross(IRE) had run well on the Flat recently and looked ready to do himself justice. He had his chance on the home bend but could stay on at only the same pace when the front pair kicked. His connections were slightly concerned with the ease in the ground, but he needs some respite from the handicapper. (op 4-1)
Pollen Jock(IRE) had shown some promise but was up against it here on his handicap debut. Although running respectably, there will be easier opportunities than this if he can build on it. (op 33-1)
Gaspara(FR) has plenty of ability and has done most of her winning when forcing the pace. This was another disappointing run since returning to action, although over trips on the sharp side, and she is best watched. (op 12-1)
Stopped Out will come on for the run after dictating an ordinary pace until tiring three out. (op 6-1)
Adare Manor(IRE) was well backed but showed little. (op 13-2)
Flying Squad(UAE) never got involved and was struggling from a fair way out, finishing well tailed off. (op 18-1)
Tibetan Dragon(IRE) Official explanation: jockey said gelding lost its action

1609 40% BETTER OFF ON BETFAIR SP "PRELUDE" HURDLE (A H'CAP) (8 hdls) 2m 1f

2:20 (2:20) (Class 2) (0-150,138) 4-Y-O+

£25,048 (£7,400; £3,700; £1,852; £924; £464)

Form RPR

300- **1** **Palomar (USA)**[20] 5222 8-10-10 **125**............................ FearghalDavis(3) 130
(Brian Ellison) *towards rr: j. rather deliberately 4th: rdn and prog after 3 out: led next: styd on stoutly after: a looked in command flat* **20/1**

0- **2** 2½ **Tarkari (IRE)**[158] 5300 5-11-2 **128**...................................... PaulMoloney 131
(Evan Williams) *bhd: gd prog bef 2 out: drvn to go 2nd after last: kpt on but nt rch wnr* **16/1**

0-11 **3** ½ **Astracad (FR)**[141] 196 4-10-13 **125**............................... PaddyBrennan 127
(Nigel Twiston-Davies) *chsd ldrs: effrt after 3 out: rdn to ld briefly bef next where mstke: hld bef last: edgd rt flat: kpt on cl home* **9/2**[1]

2321 **4** ¾ **Celticello (IRE)**[18] 1254 8-10-1 **120**.............................. MrJMQuinlan(7) 122
(Michael Quinlan) *hld up: effrt on ins ent st: chal 2 out: rdn and nt qckn bef last* **22/1**

0102 **5** 4 **Son Of Flicka**[36] 1311 6-11-9 **138**..................................... AdrianLane(3) 137
(Donald McCain) *towards rr whn nt fluent 3rd: rdn and effrt 3 out: last of 7 w ch st: one pce 2 out: mstke last* **25/1**

B111 **6** ½ **Points Of View**[31] 1364 5-11-3 **132**..............................(t) SeanQuinlan(3) 130
(Kim Bailey) *brought to paddock late: settled midfield: effrt 5th: led after 3 out: hdd bef next: rdn and mstke: btn bef last but plugged on* **15/2**[3]

00-0 **7** 3¼ **Amazing King (IRE)**[17] 1133 6-10-0 **119**........................ KyleJames(7) 114
(Philip Kirby) *prom: wnt 2nd at 5th tl lost pl bef 2 out* **10/1**

-214 **8** 18 **Now This Is It (IRE)**[30] 1384 6-11-11 **137**............................ APMcCoy 115
(S R B Crawford, Ire) *bhd: rdn and sme prog bef 3 out: sn btn: eased 2 out* **9/1**

203- **9** 1 **Diktalina**[14] 4933 4-10-1 **120**...(t) OliverDayman(7) 98
(Alison Thorpe) *last whn mstke 2nd: nvr on terms* **25/1**

-153 **10** 2½ **Stage Acclaim (IRE)**[29] 1017 5-10-2 **119**..................... GilesHawkins(5) 94
(Dr Richard Newland) *bhd: lost tch after 3 out* **9/1**

1236 **11** 4 **Dishdasha (IRE)**[23] 1229 8-10-13 **130**.............................(t) DavidBass(5) 102
(Alison Thorpe) *nvr bttr than midfield: mstke 5th: rdn and lost tch after next: poor 9th st* **28/1**

03-0 **12** 2¾ **Baccalaureate (FR)**[131] 372 4-10-10 **125**......... SamTwiston-Davies(3) 94
(Nigel Twiston-Davies) *bhd: sme prog 5th: sn drvn: fdd after 3 out* **20/1**

31F **13** 1½ **Grand Lahou (FR)**[29] 1390 7-10-13 **125**.......................... RichardJohnson 100
(Tim Vaughan) *led at fast pce: mstke 3rd: hdd after 3 out: dropped out qckly bef next: mstke last and eased* **12/1**

101/ **14** 5 **Higgy's Boy (IRE)**[547] 4742 5-11-6 **132**........................... BarryGeraghty 95
(Nicky Henderson) *midfield: effrt 5th: rdn next: sn btn: eased bef 2 out* **6/1**[2]

140- **15** 7 **Oceana Gold**[393] 1319 6-11-8 **134**.. JackDoyle 91
(Emma Lavelle) *chsd ldr tl bef 4th: sn lost pl: t.o bef 2 out* **11/1**

1061 **16** ½ **Dunaskin (IRE)**[7] 1375 10-10-8 **120**...................................(b) GrahamLee 77
(Richard Guest) *prom: wnt 2nd bef 4th tl lost pl next: t.o* **25/1**

1F-F **17** 36 **Master Nimbus**[23] 194 10-10-12 **124**............................. RichieMcGrath 48
(John Quinn) *t.k.h: prom tl 5th: sn dropped out: mstke next: t.o and eased* **20/1**

4m 5.90s (-0.80) **Going Correction** +0.20s/f (Yiel)
WFA 4 from 5yo+ 11lb **17** Ran SP% **128.9**
Speed ratings (Par 109): **109,107,107,107,105 105,103,95,94,93 91,90,89,87,83 83,66**
toteswingers: 1&2 £82.10, 1&3 £31.40, 2&3 £28.30. CSF £288.74 CT £1719.81 TOTE £32.40: £5.30, £4.90, £2.00, £5.60; EX 362.90 TRIFECTA Not won..
Owner Koo's Racing Club **Bred** Juddmonte Farms Inc **Trained** Norton, N Yorks

FOCUS
A valuable and competitive handicap hurdle run at a good pace, with nine holding chances turning in.

NOTEBOOK
Palomar(USA) showed a good turn of foot to hit the front and run out a deserved winner. Formerly a useful hurdler/chaser with Nicky Richards, he had shown little of the old spark on the Flat for new connections and came into this relatively unfancied. There's no doubt he retains all his old ability and he has already repaid the 14,000gns connections paid for him, but, after the handicapper has his say, he will become difficult to place. He holds an entry in the Cesarewitch, for which he is currently 50-1.

Tarkari(IRE) crept through the field after three out, travelling as well as the winner going to the next. He landed flat-footed at that flight and could not quicken when asked but stayed on well on the run-in. This was a good effort on his first run for Evan Williams and this former inmate of Willie Mullins' yard could make up into a decent novice chaser.

Astracad(FR) had been in fine fettle since switching to handicaps but had to defy a 15lb hike in the ratings and an absence since early May. He held his chance going to two out and kept on well enough to suggest he can remain competitive off this mark with the stable in good form. (op 5-1 tchd 4-1)

Celticello(IRE) ran respectably off a 5lb higher mark than when successful here in August and can continue to pay his way.

Son Of Flicka ran a fine race going right-handed and remains in good form but looks handicapped to the hilt.

Points Of View had rattled off a hat-trick but was racing off 29lb higher than when the winning streak began. A tongue-tie has worked the oracle and this was a fair effort. (op 7-1)

Amazing King(IRE) had been performing better on the Flat compared to his hurdling form of late, but this was one of his better efforts. (tchd 11-1)

Higgy's Boy(IRE) was soundly beaten, with connections believing he has a high enough mark, but he will come on for the race after a lengthy absence. (op 5-1)

1610 40% BETTER OFF ON BETFAIR SP JUVENILE HURDLE (8 hdls) 2m 1f

2:50 (2:53) (Class 2) 3-Y-O **£7,806** (£2,292; £1,146; £572)

Form RPR

11 **1** **Architrave**[20] 1473 3-11-6 126.. RichardJohnson 121+
(Tim Vaughan) *j. economically: mde all: rdn bef 2 out: kpt finding plenty: edgd lft flat* **10/3**[2]

211 **2** 5 **Two Kisses (IRE)**[46] 1226 3-10-13 130............................. AidanColeman 110
(Brendan Powell) *pressed ldrs: effrt bef 2 out where 1 l down and mstke: stl w ch whn nt fluent last: sn outpcd flat* **11/4**[1]

3 2¾ **Jubail (IRE)**[13] 3-10-12 0.. WayneHutchinson 107+
(Alan King) *t.k.h in midfield: effrt after 3 out: 4th and drvn st: mstke 2 out: no imp between last two* **13/2**

112 **4** 4 **Beyond (IRE)**[35] 1330 3-11-6 120.. APMcCoy 111
(Evan Williams) *prom: pushed along 5th: wnt 2nd after next tl bef 2 out: drvn and styd on same pce* **5/1**[3]

5 3¼ **Akula (IRE)**[9] 3-10-12 0.. ColinBolger 99
(Mark H Tompkins) *t.k.h in midfield: j. slowly 4th: btn bef 2 out* **40/1**

24 **6** 1 **Royal And Ancient (IRE)**[6] 1545 3-10-12 0...................... SeanQuinlan 98
(Milton Harris) *bhd: effrt after 3 out: nvr able to chal* **33/1**

4141 **7** 8 **Gulf Punch**[35] 1330 3-10-13 110....................................(p) JimmyDerham 93
(Milton Harris) *chsd ldrs to 3 out: 5th and rdn and btn next* **25/1**

3 **8** ¾ **Dr Finley (IRE)**[20] 1473 3-10-12 0.................................... GerardTumelty 90
(Jeff Pearce) *towards rr: lost tch wl bef 2 out* **33/1**

1 **9** 8 **Joan D'Arc (IRE)**[25] 1442 3-10-10 0.................................... TomO'Brien 81
(Michael Quinlan) *hld up towards rr: lost tch wl bef 2 out* **11/1**

11 **10** 3 **Meetings Man (IRE)**[10] 1363 3-11-6 119............................ BarryKeniry 88
(Micky Hammond) *nt jump wl: mstkes 3rd and 5th: pressed wnr tl after 3 out: fdd bef next* **8/1**

11 30 **Chain Of Events**[3] 3-10-12 0... AlexMerriam 53
(Neil King) *midfield: effrt and rdn after 3 out: sn wknd: wl t.o* **20/1**

531U **12** 52 **Joe Rua (USA)**[20] 1473 3-11-3 100................................... TimmyMurphy 11
(John Ryan) *midfield: j. slowly 4th and lost pl: t.o next* **50/1**

P **Baby Judge (IRE)**[51] 3-10-12 0... JoeCornwall —
(Michael Chapman) *plld hrd in rr: t.o 5th: p.u after next* **150/1**

U **P** **Lynn's Lady**[35] 1324 3-10-5 0.. DenisO'Regan —
(Michael Easterby) *ballooning jumps in last: t.o and p.u after blundering 4th* **100/1**

4m 16.4s (9.70) **Going Correction** +0.475s/f (Soft) **14** Ran SP% **119.7**
Speed ratings (Par 107): **96,93,92,90,88 88,84,84,80,79 65,40,—,—**
toteswingers: 1&2 £3.70, 1&3 £5.20, 2&3 £.40. CSF £12.25 TOTE £4.70: £2.10, £1.80, £2.30; EX 14.20 Trifecta £93.40 Pool: £381.19 - 3.02 winning units..
Owner Pearn's Pharmacies Ltd **Bred** Cheveley Park Stud Ltd **Trained** Aberthin, Vale of Glamorgan

FOCUS
An informative juvenile hurdle in the past, with the likes of Katchit and Franchoek - beaten in this - and Punchestown winner Barizan winning last year. This looked a particularly hot renewal, with plenty of decent form on offer.

NOTEBOOK
Architrave ran out an impressive victor under his penalties after making all the running before quickening clear when challenged briefly going to the last. He was still rather green but showed a really good attitude and stayed on well to assert on the run from the last. He can still brush up a little on his hurdling but, with an even stronger pace, can continue to progress. He is an out-and-out stayer who could be aimed at the Listed juvenile at Cheltenham next month, where the hill should play to his strengths. (op 9-2)

Two Kisses(IRE) did little wrong in defeat and remains the best of her sex in this division so far this season and sets a good standard. She threw down a serious challenge going to the last but blundered and was ultimately outstayed by the winner. (op 7-2)

Jubail(IRE) ◆, a former Flat winner earlier this summer who had continued to perform with credit in that sphere, had reportedly been schooling well and did best of the newcomers. He was just beginning to get involved when missing the second-last but looks as though he will be competitive in the better juveniles this season, as he can only build on this. (op 6-1 tchd 11-2)

Beyond(IRE), who had beaten Two Kisses earlier in the season, was beaten at short odds by Gulf Punch at Newton Abbot on soft ground last time. This was another fair effort, as he held every chance two out before having no more to give from the last. (tchd 9-2)

Akula(IRE) ◆ ran with credit on debut but never had the pace to lay down a challenge to the principals. This was a hot introduction but he looks capable of winning off the back of it. (tchd 33-1)

Royal And Ancient(IRE) had to bounce back after a disappointing effort last time. He ran well enough and should find an opening before long when dropped back in class. (op 25-1)

The Form Book, Raceform Ltd, Compton, RG20 6NL

Gulf Punch has had a busy season already but runs consistently and did so again. (op 18-1)

1611 READ PAUL NICHOLLS EXCLUSIVELY ON BETFAIR "PRELUDE" H'CAP CHASE (LISTED RACE) (14 fncs) 2m 6f 110y

3:20 (3:23) (Class 1) (0-150,150) 4-Y-0+

£28,505 (£10,695; £5,355; £2,670; £1,340; £670)

Form RPR

5231 **1** **Silmi**[26] 1424 6-9-11 **124** .... RichieMcLernon(3) 134+
(Sophie Leech) *settled towards rr: smooth prog after 11th: wnt 2nd 2 out: led w ears pricked bef last: styd on gamely* **16/1**

22-6 **2** *1 ¼* **Five Dream (FR)**[59] 1123 6-10-3 **132** .... (b) MrRMahon(5) 140
(Paul Nicholls) *mstke 1st: chsd ldrs: 5th and drvn bef 3 out: stl 4th whn j. awkwardly last: fin strly u.p: nt rch wnr* **15/2**

P2-5 **3** *1 ¾* **Qulinton (FR)**[35] 1332 6-10-3 **127** .... (p) TomScudamore 133
(David Pipe) *mstke 4th: pressed ldr tl led 9th: rdn whn j.lft 2 out: hdd bef last: one pce: lost 2nd after last* **7/1**[3]

/-14 **4** *nk* **Swing Bill (FR)**[35] 1332 9-10-1 **125** .... HaddenFrost 130
(David Pipe) *cl up: wnt 2nd after 11th: rdn to join ldr and hit 3 out: kpt on at same pce fr last* **6/1**[2]

300U **5** *4* **Valley Ride (IRE)**[17] 1508 10-10-3 **130** .... (p) DonalDevereux(3) 132
(Peter Bowen) *pressed ldrs: 5th and rdn after 11th: no imp fr 3 out* **28/1**

U126 **6** *¾* **Sunday City (JPN)**[20] 1486 9-10-0 **124** oh5 .... AidanColeman 125
(Peter Bowen) *prom: disp 2nd and rdn after 11th: outpcd fr 3 out* **33/1**

5-24 **7** *2 ½* **Backbord (GER)**[28] 1404 8-10-2 **126** ow1 .... (bt) LeightonAspell 125
(Lucy Wadham) *j. slowly in last: u.p 4th: sme prog after 10th: fnd little bef 3 out and plugged on: n.d* **14/1**

1FP1 **8** *3 ¼* **Grand Slam Hero (IRE)**[31] 1373 9-11-12 **150** .... (t) PaddyBrennan 146
(Nigel Twiston-Davies) *settled in midfield: rdn and effrt after 11th: btn 3 out* **7/1**[3]

-066 **9** *½* **Pablo Du Charmil (FR)**[35] 1332 9-11-2 **140** .... (bt) JohnnyFarrelly 135
(David Pipe) *bhd: effrt to chse ldrs after 11th: btn next* **20/1**

-301 **10** *11* **That's Rhythm (FR)**[36] 1312 10-11-7 **145** .... (v) GrahamLee 130
(Martin Todhunter) *rn in snatches: sn urged along: drvn 9th: struggling after* **20/1**

0P1- **11** *5* **Always Waining (IRE)**[169] 5111 9-11-2 **140** .... (p) BrianHughes 121
(Peter Bowen) *rdn 1st: midfield: mstke 7th: j. slowly 9th: lost tch 11th* **20/1**

24-5 **12** *9* **Enlightenment (IRE)**[29] 1390 10-10-4 **128** .... PaulMoloney 101
(Evan Williams) *led tl 9th: mstke next: disp 2nd after 11th: wknd wl bef 3 out: eased next* **33/1**

0UU- **13** *5* **Ellerslie George (IRE)**[154] 5400 10-10-7 **138** .... MrRGHenderson(7) 106
(Nick Mitchell) *i. slowly 2nd: reminders 4th: rdn in snatches: wnt cl up 8th: fdd u.p 11th* **8/1**

1532 **F** **Mizen Raven (IRE)**[21] 1469 7-10-5 **129** .... (tp) RhysFlint —
(Peter Bowen) *midfield and in tch whn fell 10th* **12/1**

-141 **P** **No Panic (IRE)**[28] 1404 7-10-6 **130** .... (p) TomO'Brien —
(Peter Bowen) *midfield: hmpd bnd bef 8th: j. slowly 9th and lost tch: t.o and p.u after 11th* **11/2**[1]

5m 38.9s (-7.10) **Going Correction** -0.025s/f (Good)
WFA 4 from 6yo+ 1lb 15 Ran SP% **121.4**
Speed ratings (Par 111): **111,110,109,109,108 108,107,106,106,102 100,97,95,—,—**
Tote Swingers: 1&2 £17.00, 1&3 £32.40, 2&3 £8.70 CSF £120.30 CT £931.10 TOTE £21.60: £5.80, £1.20, £3.40; EX 245.50 TRIFECTA Not won..
Owner J O'Brien & C J Leech **Bred** Shadwell Estate Company Limited **Trained** Kingsbridge, Devon

FOCUS
A competitive renewal of this valuable handicap chase, run at a decent pace.

NOTEBOOK
Silmi proved well up to the task on this big step up in class. He had been carrying enough weight in his regular grade, as he is only small, and a crack at a better race off a light weight had been mentioned before. It certainly paid dividends here. He is a game little fellow whom connections feel is due a break, but that may be put on hold if it is decided to go to Cheltenham's October meeting for a valuable two-and-a-half-mile chase. (tchd 18-1)
Five Dream(FR) had run with credit when last seen in the Galway Plate but connections felt he was handicapped to his best. This was a good performance, as he was staying on stoutly at the end, although not always fluent at the obstacles. He shaped as though he would get further. (op 17-2 tchd 7-1)
Qulinton(FR) did his best to make all and, but for a couple of novicey mistakes, could possibly have done so. (op 8-1)
Swing Bill(FR) was well supported and gave a good account of himself but could stay on at only the same pace. He is lightly raced over fences and can continue to pay his way. (tchd 11-2 and 13-2)
Valley Ride(IRE) did the best of the Peter Bowen-trained horses but could never get involved, doing all his best work too late.
Sunday City(JPN) was up there for a long way before fading in the straight but was always up against it from 5lb out of the handicap.
Grand Slam Hero(IRE), although running respectably, looks to be in the grip of the handicapper after, bar two unfortunate experiences, enjoying a good run over the summer. (op 11-2 tchd 9-2)
Ellerslie George(IRE) likes to be up with the pace but after a poor start was never really happy and finished soundly beaten after flattering in the back straight. (op 15-2)
No Panic(IRE) Official explanation: jockey said gelding made a mistake in back straight and lost confidence

1612 SINGLETON BIRCH H'CAP CHASE (14 fncs) 2m 6f 110y

3:55 (3:56) (Class 4) (0-110,110) 4-Y-0+ **£3,252** (£955; £477; £238)

Form RPR

52-P **1** **Thai Vango (IRE)**[143] 158 9-11-7 **105** .... PaddyBrennan 116+
(Nigel Twiston-Davies) *settled 3rd: relegated to 4th and mstke 9th: effrt 3 out: led next: clr last: racd idly and drvn rt out* **3/1**[2]

0214 **2** *4 ½* **Rokinhorsescience (FR)**[44] 1235 6-11-3 **101** .... (bt) APMcCoy 109+
(Jonjo O'Neill) *settled 4th: wnt 4th at 10th: sn rdn: jnd ldr and blnd 3 out: ev ch whn slt mstke next: fnd nil after: eased fnl 100yds* **5/2**[1]

140- **3** *14* **Persian Gates (IRE)**[173] 5038 6-10-11 **95** .... TomMessenger 94+
(Chris Bealby) *mstke 7th: cl 2nd tl led 9th: hrd pressed 3 out: rdn and hdd 2 out: 4th and fading qckly whn lft 3rd and bdly hmpd last* **7/1**

-050 **4** *2 ¼* **Donovan (NZ)**[41] 1261 11-11-2 **100** .... GrahamLee 90
(Richard Guest) *bhd: j. slowly 8th: sn lost tch: t.o 11th: plodded on fr 3 out* **40/1**

5254 **5** *40* **Safe Investment (USA)**[73] 987 6-10-2 **86** oh1 ow2 .... (p) DenisO'Regan 40
(Ben Pollock) *bhd: mstke 5th: struggling 8th: t.o 11th* **12/1**

142- **6** *16* **Phoenix Des Mottes (FR)**[154] 5387 7-10-4 **95** .... JoeCornwall(7) 35
(John Cornwall) *nt fluent: mstke 7th and rdn: lost tch next: t.o 11th* **7/1**

20P- **F** **Bobby Gee**[189] 4738 9-11-12 **110** .... AidanColeman 114
(Renee Robeson) *led tl 9th: rdn after 11th: 7 l 3rd and tiring whn fell last* **11/2**[3]

-3U4 **P** **Chernik (IRE)**[35] 1326 9-11-8 **106** .... WilsonRenwick —
(Micky Hammond) *towards rr: outpcd 8th: t.o and p.u 11th* **10/1**

P34P **P** **High Skies**[6] 1555 7-11-10 **108** .... (bt) SamThomas —
(Dr Richard Newland) *15 l last whn mstke 2nd: nvr looked keen or in tch: t.o and p.u 3 out* **33/1**

5m 42.0s (-4.00) **Going Correction** -0.025s/f (Good) 9 Ran SP% **116.1**
Speed ratings (Par 105): **105,103,98,97,83 78,—,—,—**
toteswingers: 1&2 £1.10, 1&3 £4.30, 2&3 £7.20. CSF £11.53 CT £47.33 TOTE £4.20: £1.10, £1.80, £2.20; EX 10.20.
Owner Mrs C Bance **Bred** Michael Dobbs **Trained** Naunton, Gloucs

FOCUS
A tricky handicap chase to work out.

NOTEBOOK
Thai Vango(IRE) broke blood vessels when last seen in May but won this race last year off a long lay-off and obviously performs well when fresh. He ran respectably in defeat after initial success last season so, with the yard flying, there is no reason why he can't do so again. (op 2-1)
Rokinhorsescience(FR) does not look the most straightforward after opening his account in a first-time tongue-tie with a laboured effort last time. He has been given a short break since then and put up a better effort returning to the scene of his success. On his day, he can remain competitive at this level. (op 3-1 tchd 9-4)
Persian Gates(IRE), making his chasing debut, had scored over hurdles last season and a return to a right-handed track was thought to be beneficial after jumping badly right last time out. He ran a sound enough race, jumping well, and did particularly well to avoid being brought down at the last. (op 8-1)
Bobby Gee, returning after an absence of six months, was running creditably before crashing out at the final fence. It looked a nasty fall and hopefully his confidence will not be too badly knocked. (op 7-1)
Chernik(IRE) Official explanation: trainer said gelding pulled up lame (op 7-1)

1613 BETFAIR IPHONE & ANDROID APP NOVICES' HURDLE (8 hdls) 2m 1f

4:30 (4:30) (Class 4) 4-Y-0+ **£3,425** (£998; £499)

Form RPR

522- **1** **Karasenir (IRE)**[203] 4452 4-10-12 0 .... RichardJohnson 127+
(Philip Hobbs) *racd exuberntly and mde all: 6 l clr 2nd: wl in command bef 2 out: nvr out of a canter* **10/11**[1]

660- **2** *26* **Altan Khan**[154] 5391 5-10-7 0 .... JamesHalliday(5) 110+
(Malcolm Jefferson) *settled midfield: wnt 5th after 3 out: tk 10 l 2nd and blnd next: nvr anywhere nr wnr: mstke last: do bttr* **25/1**

3 *14* **Union Island (IRE)**[55] 4-10-12 0 .... WayneHutchinson 86
(Alan King) *chsd ldrs: rdn and wnt modest 2nd after 3 out tl bef next: fdd tamely* **2/1**[2]

0/ **4** *3 ¾* **Wild Desert (FR)**[35] 4181 5-10-12 0 .... ChristianWilliams 83
(Alan King) *cl up: rdn and disp 2nd after 3 out: fdd tamely bef next* **7/1**[3]

60 **5** *1* **Loyal Knight (IRE)**[55] 1148 5-10-12 0 .... (t) TommyPhelan(3) 82
(Paul Midgley) *nt jump wl: chsd wnr tl lost pl qckly after 3 out* **66/1**

00-0 **6** *4 ½* **Amuse Me**[20] 1487 4-10-9 0 .... MrAJBerry(3) 78
(Jonjo O'Neill) *j. awkwardly in rr gp: no ch 3 out: t.o but plugging away after last* **12/1**

7 *5* **Are Olive** 7-10-5 0 .... RobertWalford 66
(Tim Walford) *hld up in rr: t.o after 3 out* **33/1**

50 **8** *hd* **Granakey (IRE)**[20] 1487 7-10-1 0 ow3 .... MichaelByrne(7) 69
(Peter Bowen) *chsd ldrs tl 5th: t.o after next* **50/1**

50 **9** *6* **Chadwell Spring (IRE)**[21] 1466 4-10-5 0 .... BrianHughes 61
(Mike Sowersby) *sn bhd: t.o 3 out* **20/1**

10 *4 ½* **Kheskianto (IRE)**[10] 4-9-12 0 .... JoeCornwall(7) 57
(Michael Chapman) *j. v erratically in rr: mstke 4th and drvn: blnd 5th: continued t.o* **80/1**

4m 15.8s (9.10) **Going Correction** +0.75s/f (Soft) 10 Ran SP% **122.1**
Speed ratings (Par 105): **108,95,89,87,86 84,82,82,79,77**
toteswingers: 1&2 £8.10, 1&3 £1.10, 2&3 £25.00. CSF £32.10 TOTE £2.10: £1.02, £5.90, £1.40; EX 18.90.
Owner Louisville Syndicate **Bred** His Highness The Aga Khan's Studs S C **Trained** Withycombe, Somerset

FOCUS
An ordinary novice hurdle won convincingly by the well-supported favourite.

NOTEBOOK
Karasenir(IRE) made all and won with his head in his chest. He failed to score but had fair placed bumper form last season and was entitled to win this as he did, although, he beat little. He will be kept to this distance for now, as he can be a little too free, and should be capable of following up with a penalty. (op 6-5 tchd 4-5)
Altan Khan, a strapping sort, had been well held in three bumpers last season. He ran with a degree of promise and gave chase to the winner before clattering the second-last but never had any chance. He looks a horse for the future. (op 20-1)
Union Island(IRE) was a maiden winner on the Flat who had been performing well enough in middle-distance handicaps this season. The ground might have been an issue but, after sitting on the heels of the winner turning in, he failed to get home. (op 11-4 tchd 7-2)
Wild Desert(FR) had a similar chance to his stable companion turning in but was another who appeared not to see out the trip. (op 11-2 tchd 15-2)

1614 READ PAUL NICHOLLS EXCLUSIVELY ON BETFAIR H'CAP HURDLE (DIV II) (10 hdls) 2m 3f

5:05 (5:05) (Class 3) (0-120,119) 4-Y-0+ **£4,453** (£1,298; £649)

Form RPR

2564 **1** **Cubism**[34] 1347 4-10-1 **100** .... (t) JimmyDerham(5) 101
(Milton Harris) *pressed ldr: led 7th: hrd pressed fr between last two: rdn and hld on gamely fr last* **9/1**

10-5 **2** *1* **Mickmacmagoole (IRE)**[148] 80 8-11-12 **119** .... PaulMoloney 120+
(Evan Williams) *shkn up after 5th: downed tools and dropped bk to last: drvn 6th: stl 10 l 5th at last: str run up inner to snatch 2nd: gave himself too much to do* **16/1**

2216 **3** *hd* **Topenhall (IRE)**[21] 1470 9-11-5 **112** .... (t) CharliePoste 113
(Ben Case) *t.k.h: prom: nt fluent 5th: wnt 2nd 3 out: ev ch and cajoled along fr next: declined to overtake wnr flat and lost 2nd cl home* **25/1**

-055 **4** *1 ½* **Royal Max (IRE)**[17] 1508 4-10-12 **106** .... (t) PaddyBrennan 106
(Ian Williams) *cl up: mstke 7th: 4th and rdn 2 out: no imp flat* **5/2**[1]

205/ **5** *½* **Ruthenoise (FR)**[548] 4730 5-11-8 **115** .... BarryGeraghty 114+
(Nicky Henderson) *v keen to s: plld hrd in rr: effrt bef 2 out: sn drvn: ev ch of 2nd tl nt qckn fr last* **4/1**[2]

3211 **6** *11* **Swiss Art (IRE)**[25] 1445 4-10-4 **105** .... OliverDayman(7) 96
(Alison Thorpe) *hld up towards rr: nt a fluent: sme prog whn mstke 3 out and rdn: btn between last two* **5/1**[3]

02-2 **7** *10* **Dontpaytheferryman (USA)**[129] 401 5-11-4 **118** .... KyleJames(7) 98
(Brian Ellison) *led tl 7th: rdn and wknd qckly after next* **13/2**

3143 **8** *72* **Choctaw Nation**[55] 1147 6-10-2 **100** .... JamesHalliday(5) 15
(Malcolm Jefferson) *last much of way: lost tch after 3 out: t.o and eased bef last* **6/1**

F1/3 **P** **Coolnaharan (IRE)**[35] 1342 10-11-2 **109**............................(p) APMcCoy —
(S R B Crawford, Ire) *midfield: wknd 7th: t.o and p.u 2 out* **14/1**

4m 52.9s (13.50) **Going Correction** +0.75s/f (Soft)
WFA 4 from 5yo+ 11lb **9** Ran SP% **119.3**
Speed ratings (Par 107): **101,100,100,99,99 95,90,60,—**
toteswingers: 1&2 £28.70, 1&3 £25.60, 2&3 £31.00. CSF £136.39 CT £3449.80 TOTE £15.30: £4.30, £4.20, £11.20; EX 181.20 Place 6: £28.94, Place 5: £18.63..
Owner Ms Barbara Woodcock **Bred** Darley **Trained** Herridge, Wiltshire
■ Stewards' Enquiry : Jimmy Derham one-day ban: used whip with excessive frequency (Oct 9)

FOCUS
Marginally the stronger division of the two divisions of the 0-120 handicap hurdle, run at a fair pace.

NOTEBOOK
Cubism was always sitting prominently before taking the lead 3 out and held on gamely in a driving finish. He failed to get home when tried at 2m6f the last twice and was much better suited to this drop back in trip. A good ride from Jimmy Derham and his 5lb allowance might just have been the key, and any significant rise in the ratings might just scupper his chances of repeating the success. (op 16-1)
Mickmacmagoole(IRE) ran in snatches and dropped well out of contention in the back straight before making steady progress from two out and finishing with a flourish to snatch second. He remains capable but holds few secrets. (op 14-1)
Topenhall(IRE) won a tactical affair here two runs back but pulled too hard last time. He was on 7lb worse terms with Choctaw Nation but reversed the placings comfortably. He took a keen hold, as usual, but had his chance after the last before emptying nearing the finish.
Royal Max(IRE) was potentially well-in if recapturing his form and had attracted support. He had his chance in the straight but could keep on at only the same pace. (op 9-2)
Ruthenoise(FR), having her first run for Nicky Henderson after an absence of 548 days, was keen to the start and pulled far too hard early on in the race itself. To her credit, she managed to get within striking distance of the winner going to the last but could stay on at only the same pace. (op 9-4)
Swiss Art(IRE) came here seeking his hat-trick on handicap debut but, after a mistake three out, was a spent force half-way up the straight. (op 13-2)
T/Plt: £40.20 to a £1 stake. Pool:£70,295.52 - 1,274.44 winning tickets T/Qpdt: £12.60 to a £1 stake. Pool:£3,913.83 - 229.30 winning tickets IM

1615 - 1622a (Foreign Racing) - See Raceform Interactive

1608 MARKET RASEN (R-H)

Sunday, September 26

OFFICIAL GOING: Good changing to good (good to soft in places) after race 1 (2.00)
Hurdle bends out 4yds and chase rail into Wood bend out 3yds.
Wind: Almost nil Weather: Cold and wet

1623 BETFAIR TELBET 0844 871 5555 "NATIONAL HUNT" NOVICES' HURDLE (10 hdls) 2m 3f
2:00 (2:00) (Class 4) 4-Y-0+ **£2,740** (£798; £399)

Form RPR
2 **1** **Get It On (IRE)**[27] 1433 5-10-12 112.................................. PaulMoloney 119+
(Evan Williams) *settled towards rr: effrt after 3 out: qcknd smoothly to ld nring 2 out and wnt rt and hit it: clr last: eased fnl 100yds* **5/1**[2]
2-11 **2** *8* **Rubipresent (IRE)**[107] 712 6-11-7 120....................... JamesHalliday(5) 124+
(Malcolm Jefferson) *chsd ldrs: rdn after 3 out: wnt 2nd next but qckly outpcd by wnr* **8/1**
1-11 **3** *9* **Rudanphast (IRE)**[20] 1488 5-11-5 0............................ RichardJohnson 111+
(Peter Bowen) *cl 2nd tl led bef 6th: mstke 3 out and hdd: led again wl bef next where repassed and hit it: sn btn: eased last* **10/11**[1]
331- **4** *3 3/4* **Skipper Robin (FR)**[156] 5376 4-10-11 0......................... PaddyBrennan 96+
(Nigel Twiston-Davies) *consistently j. poorly: chsd ldrs: pushed along after 3 out: one pce and btn next: mstke last* **6/1**
5P5P **5** *4* **Winter Holly**[19] 1499 4-10-4 0.. RobertWalford 84
(Tim Walford) *t.k.h in last: lost tch bef 2 out: passed two faders after* **150/1**
6 *12* **Panama Canal (IRE)**[135] 5-10-9 0................................ AdamPogson(3) 82
(Charles Pogson) *plld hrd in 3rd: chal and lft in ld 3 out: hdd wl bef next and sn dropped out* **40/1**
31/3 **7** *8* **Didbrook**[51] 1196 8-10-2 0..................................... SamTwiston-Davies(3) 67
(Mary Hambro) *led tl bef 6th: w ldr whn hit 7th: wknd qckly bef 2 out: j. slowly last* **11/2**[3]

4m 49.2s (9.80) **Going Correction** +0.125s/f (Yiel)
WFA 4 from 5yo+ 11lb **7** Ran SP% **112.9**
Speed ratings (Par 105): **84,80,76,75,73 68,65**
toteswingers: 1&2 £6.00, 1&3 £1.80, 2&3 £1.60 CSF £41.19 TOTE £6.80: £2.50, £4.50; EX 42.40.
Owner John Lee Jones **Bred** G Martin **Trained** Llancarfan, Vale Of Glamorgan

FOCUS
The ground, having started out as good, had good to soft patches added to it after the opener due to the drizzling rain that had been falling for most of the day. A competitive novice hurdle.

NOTEBOOK
Get It On(IRE), just run out of it late on at Huntingdon on his last outing, was always travelling strongly on this step up in trip and the race was over when he tanked into the lead two out. Suited by a decent surface, he looks a horse with more to offer on this evidence and should defy a penalty. (tchd 4-1)
Rubipresent(IRE), already a dual course winner over hurdles, looked vulnerable under his double penalty on this return from a 107-day absence, but ran really well, coming to have a chance two out but not being able to match the winner's kick. (op 6-1)
Rudanphast(IRE) completed the hat-trick when winning well on his hurdles debut at Newton Abbot and everything was going well here until he made a complete mess of the last in the back straight, which knocked him off his stride. He did get back into lead, but it took its toll in the closing stages. (op 5-4)
Skipper Robin(FR)'s inexperience was there for all to see on his hurdles debut. A bumper winner on his final start last season, he has the shape of a future chaser, but there are races to be won over hurdles first. His hurdling will improve with time. (op 4-1)
Didbrook, who ran well on her return from a lengthy absence, dropped right out in the end, but should find opportunities against her own sex at some stage. (op 10-1)

1624 RONNIE CROSS H'CAP HURDLE (8 hdls) 2m 1f
2:35 (2:35) (Class 4) (0-105,105) 4-Y-0+ **£2,602** (£764; £382; £190)

Form RPR
6350 **1** **Dormouse**[21] 1484 5-10-11 **90**....................................(p) TomScudamore 100+
(Anabel L M King) *prom: hmpd bnd after 3 out and relegated to 6th briefly: rallied to ld wl bef next and sn clr w one rival: upsides whn hit last: battled on to ld nr fin* **9/1**
P40/ **2** *nk* **Manshoor (IRE)**[12] 4191 5-10-4 **90**.................................... MattCrawley(7) 99
(Lucy Wadham) *trckd ldrs: effrt and n.m.r after 3 out: jnd wnr and mstke 2 out: upsides fr last: rdr changed whip hand twice ins fnl f: jst ct: rather unlucky* **13/2**
0135 **3** *8* **Galley Slave (IRE)**[7] 1554 5-10-2 **88**................................ JoeCornwall(7) 90
(Michael Chapman) *t.k.h in ld: hdd wl bef 2 out where 8 l 3rd: plugged on gamely but wl hld after* **10/1**
1P12 **4** *5* **Play A Cord (IRE)**[21] 1479 7-11-5 **105**........................(b) MarkQuinlan(7) 103
(Neil Mulholland) *midfield: cajoled along 5th: rdn and little rspnse after 3 out: sn no ch w ldng pair* **11/2**[2]
03-3 **5** *10* **Helieorbea**[19] 1501 4-11-12 **105**..................................... RichieMcGrath 93
(Tim Easterby) *hit 1st: bhd: rdn bef 4th: sn lost tch w ldng sextet: n.d* **6/1**[3]
500- **6** *8* **Railway Park (IRE)**[220] 3895 6-11-5 **98**...........................(v) PaddyAspell 79
(John Wainwright) *prom: rdn and edgd rt after 3 out: fdd wl bef next* **50/1**
6500 **7** *1 3/4* **Vogarth**[43] 1249 6-9-9 **79** oh1.......................... GemmaGracey-Davison(5) 59
(Michael Chapman) *bhd: struggling fr 4th* **40/1**
P-60 **8** *7* **National Heritage**[36] 1329 5-10-6 **85**.................................... BarryKeniry 58
(Micky Hammond) *towards rr: rdn 4th: struggling after* **12/1**
-410 **9** *2 1/2* **Pool Of Knowledge (FR)**[9] 1084 4-11-10 **103**..........(b[1]) AidanColeman 80+
(Venetia Williams) *t.k.h: j. modly in cl 2nd tl dropped out rapidly sn after 3 out: eased next* **7/2**[1]
632F **10** *34* **Quidam Blue (FR)**[38] 1295 6-11-4 **97**........................... RichardJohnson 37
(Tim Vaughan) *dropped out last and t.k.h: lost tch 4th: t.o bef 2 out* **6/1**[3]
414- **P** **Bromhead (USA)**[155] 5385 4-11-2 **95**................................. BrianHughes —
(Kevin Morgan) *wore a nosenet: bhd: lost tch 4th: bdly t.o after 3 out: p.u next* **25/1**

4m 18.7s (12.00) **Going Correction** +0.125s/f (Yiel) **11** Ran SP% **114.5**
Speed ratings (Par 105): **76,75,72,69,65 61,60,57,55,39** —
toteswingers: 1&2 £27.00, 1&3 £22.70, 2&3 £6.70 CSF £64.11 CT £598.11 TOTE £12.50: £4.90, £2.50, £3.70; EX 71.10.
Owner Aiden Murphy **Bred** Deerfield Farm **Trained** Wilmcote, Warwicks
■ Stewards' Enquiry : Matt Crawley three-day ban: used whip with excessive frequency without giving gelding time to resopond (Oct 12-14)

FOCUS
A modest handicap hurdle.

NOTEBOOK
Dormouse hadn't previously won a race, but the application of cheekpieces and a very strong ride from Tom Scudamore, who practically lifted him over the line following a mistake at the last, enabled him to finally get off the mark. The headgear clearly made a big difference, as he travelled sweetly, and he should continue to give a good account at this level. (op 10-1)
Manshoor(IRE), having his first run over hurdles since February 2009, has been running on the Flat and he looked the winner when asserting after the last, but was eventually worn down on the long run-in. There's clearly a small race to be won with him. (op 8-1 tchd 17-2)
Galley Slave(IRE) ran better than of late, although still ended up well held. (tchd 9-1)
Play A Cord(IRE) didn't find much under pressure. (op 5-1 tchd 4-1)
Pool Of Knowledge(FR) failed to settle in the first-time blinkers and a rather shoddy round of jumping didn't help either. Official explanation: trainer had no explanation for the poor form shown (op 4-1 tchd 10-3)

1625 F CROSS AND SON NOVICES' HURDLE (12 hdls) 3m
3:10 (3:10) (Class 4) 4-Y-0+ **£2,602** (£764; £382; £190)

Form RPR
31-P **1** **Penylan Star (IRE)**[141] 206 5-11-5 124.......................... RichardJohnson 121+
(Philip Hobbs) *trckd ldrs: mstke 8th: led next: mstke 3 out: rdn bef 2 out: nt fluent last: hung fr far side to stands' side and jnd: jst hung on: dismntd: cut a leg* **11/8**[1]
353- **2** *shd* **Bobbie Magern**[174] 5035 5-10-12 0................................. PaddyBrennan 114+
(Nigel Twiston-Davies) *nt fluent 2nd: hld up in midfield: 8 l 5th at 9th: stdy prog bef 2 out where nt fluent: 3 l 3rd at last: sn rdn to join bdly hanging wnr: nt qckn fnl strides* **8/1**
3130 **3** *2 1/4* **Marblehead (IRE)**[32] 1373 8-11-2 115.............(b) SamTwiston-Davies(3) 118
(Nigel Twiston-Davies) *pressed ldr: nt fluent 8th and under heavy press: ev ch tl relegated 3rd after last: styd on one pce* **4/1**[2]
1234 **4** *34* **Downward Spiral (IRE)**[32] 1367 5-11-5 115......................... AlanO'Keeffe 87
(Jennie Candlish) *sn led: hdd and mstke 9th: blnd next: bmpd along and qckly lost tch: t.o bef 2 out* **12/1**
1103 **5** *4 1/2* **Knar Mardy**[33] 1357 5-11-2 110.. AdamPogson(3) 83
(Charles Pogson) *sn last: struggling fr 8th: t.o bef 2 out* **20/1**
2024 **6** *18* **Heron Bay**[32] 1372 6-11-2 116...................................(tp) DonalDevereux(3) 67
(Peter Bowen) *settled in midfield: stdy prog 9th: rdn and pressed ldng pair after 3 out: fdd bdly wl bef next: t.o* **9/2**[3]
5440 **P** **Devils And Dust (IRE)**[29] 1407 9-10-5 79............(p) MissPhillipaTutty(7) —
(Karen Tutty) *blnd 2nd: pushed along bef 3rd: j. slowly 4th: midfield tl qckly dropped to rr 8th: t.o and p.u next* **100/1**
12U **P** **Oursininlaw (IRE)**[30] 1391 6-11-12 118................................... PaulMoloney —
(Evan Williams) *towards rr: bad mstke 5th: nt fluent next: sn pushed along and fnd nthing: struggling 8th: t.o and p.u 2 out* **17/2**

6m 14.0s (12.00) **Going Correction** +0.125s/f (Yiel) **8** Ran SP% **115.4**
Speed ratings (Par 105): **94,93,93,81,80 74,—,—**
toteswingers: 1&2 £1.90, 1&3 £2.00, 2&3 £8.30 CSF £13.75 TOTE £2.60: £1.50, £3.30, £1.10; EX 10.40.
Owner Alan Peterson **Bred** J R Weston **Trained** Withycombe, Somerset
■ Stewards' Enquiry : Sam Twiston-Davies one-day ban: used whip with excessive frequency (Oct 10)

FOCUS
An interesting novice hurdle that produced a thrilling finish between Penylan Star and Bobbie Magern.

NOTEBOOK
Penylan Star(IRE), off since pulling up in a decent handicap hurdle at Haydock back in May, was sent on plenty soon enough, probably too soon in fact, as he still looked clueless in front, running round all over the place, and only when joined on the run-in did he put his head down and rally, just getting back up. He had to be dismounted afterwards, having cut his leg, but is a likable sort who is very much a future chaser. It's hoped this doesn't take too much out of him and he may well embark on a chasing career sooner rather than later. (op 2-1)
Bobbie Magern, a brother to Ollie Magern and Billie Magern, the latter a winner later on this card, was always likely to improve for this sort of trip and he crept into it under a waiting ride from Paddy Brennan. However, having looked to have the momentum to go on and score after the last, the winner rallied, and he was just denied. This was a promising start and he should have no trouble winning something similar. (op 5-1)
Marblehead(IRE), returning from fences, stays really well and he was in the mix all the way up the straight, but couldn't quite match the front pair late on. (op 11-2)
Heron Bay faded right out in the end and proved most disappointing. (op 4-1 tchd 5-1)

The Form Book, Raceform Ltd, Compton, RG20 6NL

Oursininlaw(IRE) Official explanation: jockey said gelding never travelled

1626 READ PAUL NICHOLLS EXCLUSIVELY ON BETFAIR H'CAP HURDLE (12 hdls) 3m

3:45 (3:45) (Class 2) (0-145,137) 4-Y-0+ **£9,107** (£2,674; £1,337; £667)

Form					RPR
/611	1		**Ben's Folly (IRE)**[18] 1507 5-9-11 **115**	MrTomDavid(7)	124+
			(Tim Vaughan) *a gng wl: towards rr tl prog 8th: led after 3 out: clr w one rival next: nt fluent last: rdn and edgd sltly lft flat: fnd ex fnl 100yds* **7/2**[1]		
0001	2	1	**Raslan**[35] 1346 7-11-9 **137**	(vt) DannyCook(3)	142
			(David Pipe) *j. slowly 3rd: wnt 2nd at 5th: jnd ldr 7th: led 9th tl after next: drvn and sltly outpcd bef last where lft w ev ch: carried sltly lft: nt qckn fnl 100yds* **12/1**		
41P-	3	11	**Fairoak Lad (IRE)**[155] 5395 7-11-6 **131**	RichardJohnson	127
			(Philip Hobbs) *bhd: rdn in last pair and looked to be struggling 7th: clsd after 3 out: drvn into modest 3rd after 2 out: no ch w ldrs* **9/2**[2]		
5113	4	3	**Ripalong Lad (IRE)**[18] 1508 9-11-5 **130**	(p) TomO'Brien	123
			(Peter Bowen) *cl up: mstke 9th: rdn and outpcd in 3rd whn mstke 2 out: plugged on* **7/1**		
46-0	5	3 1/4	**Astarador (FR)**[136] 309 8-11-0 **125**	WilsonRenwick	114
			(Howard Johnson) *towards rr: effrt into 6th but drvn after 3 out: nvr rchd ldrs* **33/1**		
3015	6	23	**Pilgrims Lane (IRE)**[21] 1486 6-10-6 **122**	(tp) JimmyDerham(5)	91
			(Milton Harris) *bhd: mstke 1st: rdn and lost tch 3 out* **20/1**		
P-12	7	hd	**Ambrose Princess (IRE)**[30] 1391 5-10-9 **120**	(p) TomScudamore	91
			(Michael Scudamore) *led: mstke 7th and jnd: hdd 9th: sn lost pl: eased flat* **9/1**		
104-	8	2 1/2	**King's Forest (IRE)**[170] 5116 6-11-9 **134**	JackDoyle	100+
			(Emma Lavelle) *hld up in last pair tl 5th: effrt 8th: cl 3rd after 3 out: fdd bef next: bttr for r* **18/1**		
2-04	9	14	**Pokanoket (IRE)**[18] 1508 7-10-8 **124**	JamesHalliday(5)	78
			(Malcolm Jefferson) *bhd: hit 7th: j. slowly 8th: labouring after: t.o 2 out* **13/2**[3]		
3114	10	2 1/2	**Barnhill Brownie (IRE)**[30] 1391 7-11-0 **130**	(t) GilesHawkins(5)	81
			(Philip Hobbs) *drvn and lost pl 4th: nvr gng wl after: last at 7th: t.o after 3 out* **16/1**		
06-3	11	54	**Callisto Moon**[21] 1364 6-10-8 **119**	MarkGrant	22
			(Barry Brennan) *wnt cl up 5th tl 7th: sn lost pl: hopelessly t.o after 3 out* **16/1**		
0511	P		**What A Scientist (IRE)**[32] 1368 10-10-6 **120**	SamTwiston-Davies(3)	—
			(Nigel Twiston-Davies) *mstkes 1st and 2nd: chsd ldr tl 5th: wknd 8th: t.o and p.u 2 out* **10/1**		

6m 4.80s (2.80) **Going Correction** +0.125s/f (Yiel) **12** Ran SP% **117.8**

Speed ratings (Par 109): **109,108,105,104,102 95,95,94,89,88 70,—**

toteswingers: 1&2 £19.50, 1&3 £5.80, 2&3 £22.90 CSF £45.14 CT £194.58 TOTE £6.20: £3.30, £4.00, £2.90; EX 71.20.

Owner David Lovell **Bred** Mrs Kathleen Hennessy **Trained** Aberthin, Vale of Glamorgan

FOCUS

The front pair drew clear in what was a fair staying handicap hurdle.

NOTEBOOK

Ben's Folly(IRE), bidding for a hat-trick following wins at Cartmel and Uttoxeter, was up another 7lb, but it wasn't enough to stop him, leading soon after the last in the back straight and pulling out plenty when strongly pressed by the runner-up from the last. He's in again at Sedgefield and Hexham this week (both novice hurdles). (op 9-2)

Raslan, 12lb higher than when winning at Newton Abbot latest, was always travelling strongly and his rider seemed happy enough to let the winner stride on after three out. He came to challenge strongly again before the last, and briefly looked like going past, but in the end the massive weight differential between the pair told. A cracking effort none the less. (op 16-1)

Fairoak Lad(IRE) was in rear and struggling from quite a way out, but he kept responding to pressure and, despite a couple of slow jumps in the straight, managed to claim third. This should blow the cobwebs away for a return to fences. (op 7-2)

Ripalong Lad(IRE) has been in good form, but this mark looked beyond him last time and that was again the case here. (op 8-1 tchd 6-1)

Astarador(FR) was well held on this return.

King's Forest(IRE) travelled well before tiring and should come on appreciably for the run. (op 12-1)

Barnhill Brownie(IRE) Official explanation: trainer said gelding was unsuited by the good (good to soft places) ground

1627 40% BETTER OFF ON BETFAIR SP NOVICES' CHASE (14 fncs) 2m 6f 110y

4:20 (4:20) (Class 2) 4-Y-0+ **£9,757** (£2,865; £1,432; £715)

Form					RPR
F111	1		**Billie Magern**[77] 944 6-11-9 0	PaddyBrennan	138+
			(Nigel Twiston-Davies) *mde all: gng wl 11th: pushed along 3 out: rdn and kpt on wl and a looked like holding diminishing advantage flat* **11/4**[2]		
5U1-	2	3/4	**Pause And Clause (IRE)**[191] 4715 6-11-1 0	JackDoyle	131+
			(Emma Lavelle) *j. tentatively tl 1/2-way and off pce in 3rd: reminder 7th: mstke 10th: 15 l 3rd next: clsd to 2nd bef 3 out: rdn and styd on to be 2 l down at last: kpt trying but a hld* **7/4**[1]		
4-11	3	55	**Invisible Man (FR)**[61] 1113 5-11-9 132	APMcCoy	108+
			(Ian Williams) *press wnr: nt fluent 8th: blnd 11th and rdn: lost 2nd bef next where lft poor 3rd and hmpd: sn v tired: j.lft last: grinding to a halt flat* **7/4**[1]		
3P53	4	1 1/4	**Feeling Peckish (USA)**[27] 1425 6-11-1 73	(t) TjadeCollier	81
			(Michael Chapman) *outpcd in last after mstke 2nd: t.o 7th: fence bhd whn impeded 3 out* **100/1**		
056-	F		**Sheshali (IRE)**[173] 4054 6-11-1 0	PaulMoloney	—
			(Evan Williams) *mstke 1st: off pce in 4th: wnt modest 3rd after 11th: 8 l 3rd and looking tired whn fell heavily 3 out* **16/1**[3]		
0P0-	P		**That's The Deal (IRE)**[209] 4357 6-11-1 0	JoeCornwall	—
			(John Cornwall) *last pair: t.o whn mstke 7th: p.u 10th* **66/1**		

5m 45.1s (-0.90) **Going Correction** -0.20s/f (Good) **6** Ran SP% **107.8**

Speed ratings (Par 109): **93,92,73,73,—,—**

toteswingers: 1&2 £1.10, 1&3 £1.10, 2&3 £1.10 CSF £7.66 TOTE £3.20: £2.60, £2.40; EX 8.70.

Owner Roger Nicholls **Bred** Roger Nicholls **Trained** Naunton, Gloucs

FOCUS

A decent novice chase for the time of year.

NOTEBOOK

Billie Magern, a winner on all three completed starts over fences coming into this, set off in front, jumping well, and galloped on relentlessly to score, reminiscent of many a fine performance by his brother Ollie Magern. Although he looked vulnerable down the straight, and was visibly tired, he was in no mood to be denied and always looked to be holding on close home. He will presumably head to Cheltenham's October meeting now. (op 9-4)

Pause And Clause(IRE), winner of the Martin Pipe Hurdle at the Cheltenham Festival, had been schooled extensively at home, but couldn't keep tabs on his market leaders through the first two miles of the race, jumping slowly. However, as they began to tire, he closed right up to throw down a strong challenge, but became weary himself late on and couldn't get past. This was a promising start, but he did have a hard enough race. (op 2-1 tchd 13-8)

Invisible Man(FR), off since winning at Galway in July, is a fine, physical sort, but the ground would probably have been a bit dead for him and he stopped quickly following a bad nod on landing towards the end of the back straight. (op 15-8 tchd 2-1)

Sheshali(IRE) had run a fine race and was tired, but still had third in the bag when falling heavily three out.

That's The Deal(IRE) Official explanation: trainer said gelding lost a front shoe

1628 BETFAIR IPHONE & ANDROID APP H'CAP CHASE (12 fncs) 2m 2f

4:55 (4:56) (Class 4) (0-110,108) 4-Y-0+ **£3,082** (£898; £449)

Form					RPR
6362	1		**Diaco (IRE)**[36] 1334 6-11-10 **106**	APMcCoy	123
			(Jonjo O'Neill) *settled in midfield: effrt in last of five gng clr after 9th: wnt 2nd and nt fluent 3 out: drvn fr next: led cl home* **9/2**[2]		
3442	2	shd	**Classic Fly (FR)**[7] 1558 7-10-10 **92**	FelixDeGiles	109
			(Arthur Whiting) *cl up: wnt 2nd after 9th: led bef next: clr w rival and rdn 2 out: kpt trying hrd but jst pipped* **5/2**[1]		
P0-3	3	20	**War Party**[21] 1484 6-11-4 **107**	MrTWeston(7)	109
			(Dr Richard Newland) *hld up and bhd: hdwy 8th: cruised up to heels of ldrs bef 3 out: fnd little whn rdn: wknd 2 out* **8/1**		
-6P0	4	3 1/4	**Tifoso (FR)**[13] 1254 5-11-1 **97**	(v) BrianHughes	93
			(Richard Guest) *towards rr: effrt in 6th and rdn after 9th: fnd nthing bef next where blnd: sn btn* **20/1**		
2522	5	2 1/4	**Peak Seasons (IRE)**[27] 1423 7-9-9 **82** oh8	GemmaGracey-Davison(5)	76
			(Michael Chapman) *prom: mstke 5th: wknd 7th: wl bhd after 9th* **12/1**		
P-P4	6	6	**I'm A Legend**[36] 1327 8-11-9 **105**	(p) RichardJohnson	94
			(Neil Mulholland) *led: hit 8th and rdn: hdd bef 3 out: dropped out qckly* **6/1**[3]		
40P-	7	4 1/2	**First Boy**[380] 1423 8-11-1 **97**	TjadeCollier	82
			(Sue Smith) *pressed ldr: rdn 7th: hit next: lost 2nd after 9th: 6th and fading bef 3 out* **14/1**		
6224	8	2 1/2	**Norborne Bandit (IRE)**[36] 1334 9-11-12 **108**	(p) HarrySkelton	91
			(Evan Williams) *plld hrd: sn chsng ldrs: lost pl and j. slowly 6th: no ch after: blnd last* **7/1**		
P00-	9	37	**Corredor Sun (USA)**[127] 5245 4-10-8 **104**	SamTwiston-Davies(3)	42
			(Nigel Twiston-Davies) *rdr wobbled 3rd: towards rr after: struggling 8th: eased 2 out: t.o* **8/1**		
-6U0	P		**Owls FC (IRE)**[7] 1555 4-9-7 **93** oh14	JoeCornwall(7)	—
			(Michael Chapman) *led in and reluctant in detached last: nt jump wl: t.o 7th: p.u 3 out* **150/1**		

4m 28.8s (-6.20) **Going Correction** -0.20s/f (Good)

WFA 4 from 5yo+ 11lb **10** Ran SP% **115.5**

Speed ratings (Par 105): **105,104,96,94,93 90,88,87,71,—**

toteswingers: 1&2 £3.90, 1&3 £11.70, 2&3 £5.80 CSF £16.68 CT £86.89 TOTE £3.60: £2.30, £1.50, £3.10; EX 17.30.

Owner John P McManus **Bred** J Mangan **Trained** Cheltenham, Gloucs

FOCUS

Just a modest handicap chase.

NOTEBOOK

Diaco(IRE), narrowly denied off 5lb lower at Newton Abbot latest, received a vintage McCoy ride to go one better, just getting up in a desperately tight finish. Clearly progressive, the 6-y-o remains capable of better, with a bit further unlikely to hurt. (op 10-3)

Classic Fly(FR), runner-up to a useful sort in a novice chase at Uttoxeter latest, looked fairly treated on that form and he came clear with the winner, just losing out in a driving finish. He shouldn't be long in going one better. (op 7-2)

War Party found disappointingly little having travelled strongly and ended up being beaten a long way. (tchd 9-1)

Tifoso(FR) was another who didn't pick up as expected. (op 18-1)

I'm A Legend dropped away in the end having made the early running. (op 5-1 tchd 4-1)

1629 40% BETTER OFF ON BETFAIR SP STANDARD OPEN NATIONAL HUNT FLAT RACE 2m 1f

5:30 (5:30) (Class 6) 4-6-Y-O **£1,370** (£399; £199)

Form					RPR
356-	1		**Dipity Doo Dah**[400] 1280 6-10-0	MichaelByrne(7)	99+
			(Peter Bowen) *wl bhd: gd prog over 3f out: rdn to ld wl over 1f out: clr ins fnl f: pushed out* **5/1**[2]		
0-4	2	4 1/2	**Pontyates**[26] 1448 5-10-11	DonalDevereux(3)	98
			(Peter Bowen) *cl up: rdn 5f out: outpcd 4f out: 5th over 1f out: styd on for driving to go 2nd ins fnl f: nt rch wnr* **18/1**		
	3	2 1/4	**Dontupsettherhythm (IRE)**[140] 5-10-11	AdamPogson(3)	96
			(Charles Pogson) *plld hrd: 2nd tl led 1/2-way: rdn and hdd wl over 1f out: wknd to lose 2nd ins fnl f* **7/1**		
43-	4	3/4	**Big Knickers**[188] 4792 5-10-0	MarkQuinlan(7)	88
			(Neil Mulholland) *led tl 1/2-way: press ldr tl rdn and no ex wl over 1f out* **7/2**[1]		
22-	5	shd	**River Dragon (IRE)**[400] 1280 5-10-9	JamesHalliday(5)	95
			(Malcolm Jefferson) *towards rr: effrt over 3f out: 4th st: sn no imp* **7/2**[1]		
	6	4	**Bold Warning** 6-11-0	DenisO'Regan	93+
			(Alex Hales) *chsd ldrs: 3rd and rdn st: kpt on same pce: btn wl over 1f out* **25/1**		
0	7	27	**Alimure**[93] 841 4-10-7	PaddyAspell	57
			(C W Thornton) *nvr bttr than midfield: t.o fnl 2f* **66/1**		
	8	1 1/2	**Wicked Times** 5-11-0	HenryOliver	62
			(Sue Smith) *chsd ldrs tl 1/2-way: rdn 6f out: t.o fnl 2f* **6/1**[3]		
4	9	5	**Teals Star**[65] 1086 6-11-0	BrianHughes	57
			(G P Kelly) *chsd ldrs: drvn 6f out: sn struggling: t.o fnl 2f* **16/1**		
	10	8	**Furius** 4-11-0	TjadeCollier	49
			(Sue Smith) *bhd: struggling 6f out: t.o fnl 3f* **20/1**		
	F		**Take The Profit** 4-10-11	CampbellGillies(3)	—
			(Chris Grant) *wl bhd: hrd drvn 1/2-way: suffered fatal injury and fell 5f out* **8/1**		
	P		**Miss Kessie** 4-10-4	AdrianLane(3)	—
			(Alan Lockwood) *towards rr: hung bdly lft ent bk st: continued t.o tl p.u 5f out* **66/1**		

4m 17.7s (16.60) **Going Correction** +0.125s/f (Yiel) **12** Ran SP% **121.7**

Speed ratings: **65,62,61,61,61 59,46,46,43,40 —,—**

toteswingers: 1&2 £25.70, 1&3 Not won, 2&3 £36.30 CSF £89.82 TOTE £6.10: £1.80, £4.70, £3.40; EX 138.40 Place 6 £154.92, Place 5 £24.66.

Owner Colin G R Booth **Bred** R W Russell **Trained** Little Newcastle, Pembrokes

FOCUS

Just a moderate bumper.

NOTEBOOK
Dipity Doo Dah, returning from a 400-day absence, had run all her three previous bumpers here and she was clearly fit enough to win, staying on strongly down the straight and in the end going clear. She should stay further over hurdles. (tchd 11-2)
Pontyates, a stablemate of the winner, has got better with each start and she too will require a stiffer test over hurdles. (op 14-1)
Dontupsettherhythm(IRE) went well for a long way before tiring in the final furlong. (op 10-1)
Big Knickers went well up to a point before weakening. (op 9-2 tchd 10-3)
River Dragon(IRE) never really looked like winning but should improve on this first start in 400 days. (op 9-2 tchd 10-3)
Wicked Times is sure to improve for the experience. (op 7-1)
T/Plt: £220.60 to a £1 stake. Pool: £66,665.38. 220.60 winning tickets. T/Qpdt: £7.40 to a £1 stake. Pool: £5,765.75. 575.95 winning tickets. IM

1630 - 1640a (Foreign Racing) - See Raceform Interactive

[1498] SEDGEFIELD (L-H)
Tuesday, September 28

OFFICIAL GOING: Good (good to firm in places in home straight; 7.8)
Wind: light 1/2 against Weather: overcast

1641 DURHAM ARMY CADET FORCE NOVICES' HURDLE (JOHN WADE HURDLE SERIES QUALIFIER) (8 hdls) 2m 1f
2:25 (2:25) (Class 4) 4-Y-0+ **£2,602** (£764; £382; £190)

Form RPR
34P- **1** **Ashammar (FR)**[213] 4304 5-10-12 116 DenisO'Regan 122+
(Paul Webber) *trckd ldrs: t.k.h: led on bit after 3 out: pushed clr whn nt fluent last: eased towards fin* **2/1**[1]
112- **2** *11* **Fred Bojangals (IRE)**[164] 5225 8-10-12 0 (p) BrianHughes 107
(Ann Hamilton) *trckd ldrs: t.k.h: wnt 2nd appr 2 out: kpt on: no ch w wnr* **7/1**[3]
4FF- **3** *7* **Southerness**[191] 4765 6-10-9 120 ChrisHonour(3) 113+
(David Pipe) *chsd ldrs: blnd bdly and lost pl 3 out: sn detached in last: styd on to take modest 3rd last: hung bdly rt run-in* **11/4**[2]
P-42 **4** *nk* **Rain Stops Play (IRE)**[21] 1499 8-10-9 110 FearghalDavis(3) 100
(Nicky Richards) *in rr: drvn 3 out: chsng ldrs next: one pce whn carried rt towards fin* **16/1**
0-03 **5** *3 ½* **Morning Time (IRE)**[38] 1337 4-10-12 99 PeterBuchanan 97
(Lucinda Russell) *chsd ldrs: drvn appr 2 out: wknd last* **12/1**
050- **6** *2* **Veronicas Boy**[209] 4380 4-10-12 106 BarryKeniry 95
(George Moore) *mde most: hdd after 3 out: wknd between last 2* **7/1**[3]
1241 **7** *6* **Bucephalus (IRE)**[79] 945 6-11-5 123 (t) MissAngelaBarnes(7) 104
(Maurice Barnes) *w ldr: wknd 3 out* **11/1**
30 **8** *20* **Contradiktive (IRE)**[29] 1433 4-10-12 0 RichardJohnson 84
(Tim Vaughan) *chsd ldrs: drvn 5th: lost pl and hit next: sn bhd: eased run-in: t.o* **40/1**

4m 3.60s (-3.30) **Going Correction** -0.175s/f (Good)
WFA 4 from 5yo+ 11lb 8 Ran SP% **109.3**
Speed ratings (Par 105): **100,94,91,91,89 88,85,76**
toteswingers:1&2:£1.50, 1&3:£2.80, 2&3:£6.40 CSF £15.12 TOTE £2.80: £1.10, £1.80, £1.20; EX 16.20.
Owner G L Porter **Bred** H H The Aga Khan's Studs Sc **Trained** Mollington, Oxon
■ Stewards' Enquiry : Chris Honour caution: used whip with excessive frequency

FOCUS
An ordinary novice event. The easy winner is flattered by his winning margin with the form rated around the third, fourth and fifth.

NOTEBOOK
Ashammar(FR) opened his account over hurdles at the fourth time of asking on this seasonal return and won easily. His task was greatly aided by his main-market rival Southerness losing all chance at the last in the back straight, but looking at the way he coasted up the run-in, it would be pushing to think that rival would have beaten him with a clear round. He will need to learn to settle better if he is to progress in this sphere, but he clearly likes a sound surface and ought to be high on confidence. (op 9-4 tchd 7-4 and 5-2 in places)
Fred Bojangals(IRE), a 125-rated chaser, was returning from a 165-day break and having a rare outing over hurdles. Indeed this was just his fourth outing in this sphere and, while he ran as though the race would bring him on a good bit, connections probably missed a trick not starting off in a handicap, as he is officially rated just 85 as a hurdler. His rating will be reassessed after this, but he looks well up to winning over these smaller jumps and could still be well treated enough to land a handicap before going back over fences. (op 5-1 tchd 9-2 and 15-2)
Southerness ◆ failed to complete in three of his five outings as a novice last term, but he has always looked capable of winning a race of this nature on decent ground and this was his debut for David Pipe. He wasn't always foot-perfect, but was still going every bit as the winner prior to nearly coming down at the third-last. His rider was also lucky not to come off there and it looked a case of game over. However, he rallied gamely down the home straight and it was a decent effort to bag third. No doubt he would've finished at least second without that incident, and there ought to be one of these within his compass before the better novices emerge. A stiffer test may just suit ideally, though. (op 2-1)
Rain Stops Play(IRE) again wasn't disgraced despite finding this too sharp and will appreciate moving into handicaps. (tchd 18-1)

1642 CUMMINS DIESEL DASH BEGINNERS' CHASE (14 fncs 2 omitted) 2m 4f
3:00 (3:00) (Class 4) 4-Y-0+ **£3,168** (£936; £468; £234; £117)

Form RPR
311F **1** **Shopfrontspecialst (IRE)**[12] 1534 7-11-5 122 APMcCoy 101+
(Gordon Elliott, Ire) *hld up: trckd ldrs 6th: wnt 3rd 10th: chsng ldrs 2 out: pushed along to ld 1f out: comf* **7/4**[1]
U2-2 **2** *¾* **Lord Larsson**[142] 226 7-11-5 DenisO'Regan 98
(Malcolm Jefferson) *trckd ldrs: led after 8th: hdd 1f out: kpt on same pce* **7/2**[2]
000- **3** *15* **Harbour Way**[190] 4779 7-10-12 MrJohnDawson(7) 83
(John Wade) *hld up: wl outpcd and lost pl 10th: hdwy appr 2 out: tk modest 3rd cl home* **100/1**
-P20 **4** *1 ¾* **Darksideofthemoon (IRE)**[34] 1372 8-11-5 (p) RichardJohnson 82
(Tim Vaughan) *hld up: hdwy to chse ldrs 9th: wknd over 1f out: lost 3rd nr fin* **11/2**
003 **5** *4 ½* **First Fought (IRE)**[35] 1360 8-10-12 68 (vt) HenryBrooke(7) 77
(Joanne Foster) *chsd ldrs: outpcd and lost pl 11th: lost modest 4th appr last* **100/1**
2P2- **6** *61* **Greenbelt**[156] 13 9-11-5 118 BarryKeniry 16
(George Moore) *led: hdd after 8th: 3rd whn blnd and lost pl next: sn bhd: t.o 2 out* **14/1**
310- **P** **Kingsben**[290] 2835 7-11-0 JamesHalliday(5) —
(Malcolm Jefferson) *trckd ldrs: blnd 4th: rdr lost iron and sddle slipped: p.u after next* **6/1**
F02- **U** **Teenage Idol (IRE)**[184] 4909 6-11-5 TjadeCollier —
(Evelyn Slack) *last whn nt fluent 2nd: j slwly next and uns rdr* **5/1**[3]

4m 59.6s (-3.40) **Going Correction** -0.175s/f (Good) 8 Ran SP% **113.6**
Speed ratings (Par 105): **99,98,92,92,90 65,—,—**
toteswingers:1&2:£3.90, 1&3:£9.30, 2&3:£45.70 CSF £8.38 TOTE £2.70: £1.10, £1.60, £25.60; EX 9.10.
Owner Sean F Gallagher **Bred** Martin C Fleming **Trained** Trim, Co Meath

FOCUS
A moderate novice chase and straightforward enough form, rated through the runner-up.

NOTEBOOK
Shopfrontspecialst(IRE) was entitled to make a winning start over fences with an official rating over hurdles of 122, and he duly completed the task, but his backers have the champion jockey to thank as he gave him a masterful ride. Tony McCoy was at pains to settle out the back and his mount proved keen under restraint. He covered the pace as it increased around the ninth, though, and was travelling strongly off the home turn. His jumping hadn't been all that fluent and he wasn't that good at the last, but McCoy knew what he had up his sleeve and made up the horse's mind on the run-in. This 7-y-o doesn't have that much scope for chasing, but this experience should teach him plenty and he is in the right hands to defy a penalty. (op 2-1 tchd 9-4 in places)
Lord Larsson ◆ came into this return from a 142-day break with a frustrating profile and he again found one too good. O'Regan allowed him to go on down the far side as he refused to settle, but getting out in front suited and he was the only one to give the winner a serious race. It's not hard to see why connections tried him over further last time and there is surely one of these to be won with him, especially as he should come on for the run. (op 4-1 tchd 10-3)
Harbour Way, yet another that took a keen hold though the race, hit a flat spot when the pace began to get more serious. He stuck on well to grab third late on, though, and, on this evidence, chasing will be his game. Stepping up in trip should also help.
Darksideofthemoon(IRE) made a positive move nearing the ninth fence, but came under pressure off the final bend and failed to see it out. His jumping was okay for a debutant and perhaps dropping back in trip in this sphere will suit, but he did win nicely over this distance as a hurdler and isn't that straightforward. (op 5-1 tchd 9-2)
Greenbelt badly needed this run. (op 11-1)
Kingsben Official explanation: jockey said saddle slipped

1643 JOHN WADE SKIP HIRE NOVICES' HURDLE (QUALIFIER) (10 hdls) 2m 5f 110y
3:35 (3:35) (Class 4) 4-Y-0+ **£2,602** (£764; £382; £190)

Form RPR
0-10 **1** **Russian War (IRE)**[13] 1526 7-11-12 119 (t) APMcCoy 125+
(Gordon Elliott, Ire) *hld up: hdwy to trck ldrs 4th: led on bit appr 2 out: rdn between last 2: edgd lft run-in: all out* **9/2**[3]
221 **2** *½* **Cailin Na Ri (IRE)**[21] 1499 7-11-5 114 GrahamLee 117
(Martin Todhunter) *led to 3rd: chsd ldrs: upsides fr 2 out: carried lft run-in: no ex cl home* **4/1**[2]
3 *38* **Clarach (IRE)**[44] 1263 5-10-5 108 RichardJohnson 68
(Tim Vaughan) *led 3rd: hit 3 out: hdd appr next: sn wknd* **10/11**[1]
14-P **4** *3 ½* **Lady Jinks**[100] 796 5-10-9 111 RyanMania(3) 72
(Maurice Barnes) *trckd ldrs: reminders after 7th: wknd appr 2 out* **7/1**
24-4 **5** *14* **Brooklyn Bay**[141] 254 5-10-7 0 JamesHalliday(5) 60
(Malcolm Jefferson) *chsd ldrs: lost pl 4th: reminders after next: sn bhd* **33/1**
0/F- **6** *shd* **Ceasar's Return**[326] 2105 5-10-12 0 BarryKeniry 60
(George Moore) *chsd ldrs to 3rd: bhd fr 7th* **18/1**
7 *127* **Power Desert (IRE)**[15] 5-10-12 0 (v) PaddyAspell —
(Geoffrey Harker) *lost pl and reminders 4th: bhd fr 6th: wl t.o* **200/1**
P **P** **That's All Right (IRE)**[21] 1499 7-10-12 0 DenisO'Regan —
(Kevin M Prendergast) *hld up in rr: nt fluent 1st: sme hdwy 6th: wknd next: t.o 3 out: p.u bef next* **100/1**

5m 9.60s (-5.00) **Going Correction** -0.175s/f (Good) 8 Ran SP% **112.8**
Speed ratings (Par 105): **102,101,88,86,81 81,—,—**
toteswingers:1&2:£1.90, 1&3:£1.40, 2&3:£1.70 CSF £22.33 TOTE £3.70: £1.10, £1.90, £1.10; EX 15.50.
Owner T D Howley Jnr **Bred** Tommy Howley **Trained** Trim, Co Meath

FOCUS
An ordinary novice event where the first pair came well clear in a battling finish and they set the level.

NOTEBOOK
Russian War(IRE) handed his yard a quick-fire double. Gordon Elliot's enigmatic 7-y-o proved easy to back largely on account of having to concede 21lb to the strongly fancied Clarach, and also as he came here on the back of a tame effort at Listowel. He found the race run to suit, though, and McCoy again judged his timing just right as he powered into contention from three out. It was clear he was going best of all, but once push came to shove Russian War found less than expected and didn't help his rider at all by continually hanging left. He was always doing enough to repel the game runner-up, however, and this was a decent effort under his double penalty. Inconsistency seems to be his issue, but he does look fairly handicapped off a mark of 119, and always has the option of going chasing to find further success. (op 7-2)
Cailin Na Ri(IRE) went down fighting over this stiffer test and rates a rock-solid benchmark. She too was given a decent ride in defeat and it rates another improved effort under her double penalty. She will always be of interest around here. (op 13-2)
Clarach(IRE) produced a career-best in defeat at Tramore on her previous outing and was making her British debut for a new stable that is renowned for winning first time out with horses from other yards. She had very little weight on her back and the money poured in for her, but she ultimately spoilt her chance by refusing to settle. It's a decent bet her trainer will find the key to her before long. (op 5-4 tchd 11-8)
Lady Jinks was another making her debut for a new yard, and she too could've settled better. This was probably a bit too sharp for her and the run ought to bring her on. (op 5-1 tchd 8-1)
Ceasar's Return, who fell on his hurdling debut when last seen just over a year previously, shaped very much as though the run was needed and this experience should be to his benefit. (op 12-1 tchd 10-1)

1644 CUMMINS ENGINES SOLDIERS CHARITY H'CAP HURDLE (10 hdls) 2m 4f
4:10 (4:10) (Class 4) (0-110,110) 4-Y-0+ **£2,602** (£764; £382; £190)

Form RPR
0/12 **1** **Jeu De Roseau (IRE)**[32] 539 6-10-12 96 DenisO'Regan 112+
(Chris Grant) *chsd ldrs: wnt handy 2nd after 3 out: drvn appr next: led appr last: styd on strly to forge clr* **7/4**[1]
624 **2** *10* **Heart Of Dubai (USA)**[26] 916 5-10-12 96 (p) BarryKeniry 100
(Micky Hammond) *trckd ldrs: led 3 out: hdd appr last: no ex* **10/1**
3 *15* **Quel Ballistic**[800] 6-10-9 100 MrJohnDawson(7) 90
(John Wade) *prom: hdwy to chse ldrs 7th: kpt on to take modest 3rd run-in* **66/1**
5435 **4** *1* **Phoenix Eye**[29] 1429 9-10-3 94 BrianToomey(7) 83
(Michael Mullineaux) *hld up in rr: hdwy 3 out: modest 3rd 2 out: one pce* **14/1**
540- **5** *3* **Wheyaye**[225] 4074 8-10-8 92 BrianHughes 78
(Valerie Jackson) *chsd ldrs: one pce fr 3 out* **28/1**

-034 **6** 1/2 **Goldan Jess (IRE)**[75] 1004 6-10-12 **103**.............................. KyleJames(7) 88
(Philip Kirby) *hld up in rr: hdwy 7th: fdd 2 out* **11/2**[2]
-300 **7** 9 **Daytime Dreamer (IRE)**[31] 1406 6-11-2 **100**........................ GrahamLee 77
(Martin Todhunter) *chsd ldr: led 4th: hdd 3 out: wknd next* **18/1**
0P0- **8** 5 **Farmers Cross (IRE)**[182] 4941 6-11-6 **104**...................... RichieMcGrath 77
(Ferdy Murphy) *hld up in rr: racd wd: hdwy 7th: wknd next* **25/1**
P662 **9** 1 1/4 **Lady Wright (IRE)**[35] 1361 7-10-2 **93**.......................... JakeGreenall(7) 65
(Michael Easterby) *in rr: sme hdwy u.p 7th: sn wknd* **6/1**[3]
P06- **10** 14 **Dark Gentleman**[178] 4983 7-10-6 **90**.................................... TjadeCollier 49
(Evelyn Slack) *chsd ldrs: lost pl 7th: sn bhd* **33/1**
4P-1 **P** **Roman History (IRE)**[15] 1361 7-10-7 **94**.................(p) CampbellGillies(3) —
(Tracy Waggott) *chsd ldrs: nt fluent 3rd: lost pl 5th: bhd fr 7th: t.o whn p.u bef 2 out* **18/1**
2005 **P** **Osolomio (IRE)**[12] 1501 7-11-12 **110**................................(e) AlanO'Keeffe —
(Jennie Candlish) *led: hdd 4th: reminders 6th: lost pl next: sn bhd: t.o whn p.u bef 2 out* **8/1**

4m 49.2s (-3.50) **Going Correction** -0.175s/f (Good) **12** Ran SP% **115.2**
Speed ratings (Par 105): **100,96,90,89,88 88,84,82,82,76 —,—**
toteswingers:1&2:£5.70, 1&3:£35.70, 2&3:£16.20 CSF £18.60 CT £836.98 TOTE £2.40: £1.10, £4.00, £8.10; EX 21.60.
Owner W Raw **Bred** P Connolly **Trained** Newton Bewley, Co Durham

FOCUS
An ordinary handicap, run at a fair gallop and the first pair dominated from three out. The form is rated around the first two.

NOTEBOOK
Jeu De Roseau(IRE) ran out a clear-cut winner on this return to hurdling. He has been in good heart on the Flat since his last outing in this sphere, and was again the subject of decent support. He momentarily looked in trouble before two out as the runner-up was still swinging away in front, but his superior stamina kicked in soon after and he was able to coast home near the finish. No doubt he is an improving hurdler, but the handicapper will have his say and his best option is probably to turn out under a penalty. Should connections be able to find him such an opportunity, he would prove very hard to stop again. (op 15-8 after early 11-4 and 5-2 in places tchd 13-8)
Heart Of Dubai(USA) ◆ was something of an eye-catcher on his previous outing on the level, and he too came in for some support. Given a positive ride, he looked the most likely winner off the home turn. However, the winner is rated 16lb higher than him on the Flat, and he was racing on level weights with that rival here, so cannot be considered surprising that he eventually got put in his place by that rival. There should be a race for him in the coming weeks, despite him being raised in the weights for this, and a slight drop in trip could prove ideal. (op 16-1)
Quel Ballistic was making his British debut for new connections after a whopping 800-day layoff, and he turned in a promising run. A winner on his hurdling debut in France two runs back, he should improve a bundle for the outing and is one to look out for next time, providing he is given sufficient time to recover. (op 50-1)
Phoenix Eye didn't help his rider by pulling under restraint and was never a serious player. (op 10-1)
Wheyaye wasn't disgraced on her seasonal return and ought to appreciate returning to easier ground in due course. (op 33-1)
Goldan Jess(IRE) was having his first run at this track since finishing a well-beaten second off the same mark in the race last season. He proved laboured from three out on this return from a 75-day absence. (op 6-1)
Daytime Dreamer(IRE) Official explanation: jockey said gelding had a breathing problem
Lady Wright(IRE) was very disappointing over this longer trip. (tchd 5-1)

1645 C & A PUMPS H'CAP CHASE (14 fncs 2 omitted) 2m 4f
4:45 (4:45) (Class 4) (0-110,108) 4-Y-0+ **£3,168** (£936; £468; £234; £117)

Form RPR
20-2 **1** **Amalfi Coast**[33] 1377 11-11-12 **108**.. BrianHughes 115
(Karen Tutty) *led: hdd 7th: led 10th: hdd appr last: kpt on to ld last 150yds* **7/1**[3]
4432 **2** 1 1/2 **Rebel Hunter (IRE)**[24] 1467 5-11-5 **101**.................................. APMcCoy 107
(Steve Gollings) *w ldr: led 7th to 10th: led appr last: hdd last 150yds: kpt on same pce* **5/2**[1]
205- **3** hd **Ballabrook (IRE)**[209] 4383 8-11-2 **101**.............................. AdrianLane(3) 107
(Donald McCain) *chsd ldng pair: styd on run-in: keeping on at fin* **7/2**[2]
4-F5 **4** 17 **Poseidon (GER)**[132] 401 8-11-6 **102**................................ DenisO'Regan 93
(John Wade) *in tch: outpcd 10th: kpt on run-in: tk poor 4th fnl strides* **14/1**
U26 **5** shd **Mountskip**[63] 1104 6-11-9 **105**.. WilsonRenwick 95
(Rose Dobbin) *in tch: pushed along after 7th: outpcd 11th: lost poor 4th nr fin* **10/1**
51- **6** 2 1/4 **The Thirsty Bricky (IRE)**[236] 3841 8-11-9 **105**.................... FelixDeGiles 94
(John Daniel Moore, Ire) *t.k.h in tch: blnd 3rd: outpcd and lost pl 11th* **12/1**
-444 **7** 68 **Silver Steel (FR)**[20] 1509 7-11-10 **106**.................................. GrahamLee 33
(Richard Ford) *hld up towards rr: blnd 8th: bhd 10th: t.o 3 out* **7/1**[3]
F/P- **8** 23 **Got The Gift (IRE)**[464] 778 9-10-0 **82** oh2.......................... TjadeCollier —
(Sue Smith) *prom: nt fluent 2nd: reminders and lost pl 9th: sn bhd: t.o 3 out* **11/1**
346- **P** **New Shuil (IRE)**[235] 3870 6-10-6 **95**........................... MrJohnDawson(7) —
(John Wade) *in rr: blnd 1st: sddle slipped and p.u bef 5th* **10/1**

4m 56.7s (-6.30) **Going Correction** -0.175s/f (Good) **9** Ran SP% **116.7**
Speed ratings (Par 105): **105,104,104,97,97 96,69,60,—**
toteswingers:1&2:£7.60, 1&3:£10.70, 2&3:£3.10 CSF £26.18 CT £72.88 TOTE £8.50: £3.10, £1.30, £2.00; EX 25.00.
Owner N D Tutty **Bred** Devonia Stud **Trained** Osmotherley, N Yorks

FOCUS
An open-looking handicap in which the first three, who were always to the fore, totally dominated. The runner-up is rated close to his latest form.

NOTEBOOK
Amalfi Coast, who won the preceding handicap hurdle on this card last year, registered his first success since with a game effort under top weight. Despite being an 11-y-o this was just his second outing over fences, and the positive tactics over this sharper test suited. It's hard to envisage him following up in a higher grade, though, despite him being open to a little more improvement as a chaser (op 11-2 tchd 5-1)
Rebel Hunter(IRE) looked sure to make it 3-3 on the day for his rider, but having got to the front going easily near the last he came under heavy pressure on the run-in. McCoy did his best, but couldn't muster another effort from him and he was always being held near the finish. It was just his second outing over fences under rules and it may be that he needs to get there as late as possible, but his attitude will now be questioned. (op 3-1 tchd 7-2)
Ballabrook(IRE) ◆ attracted support on this seasonal debut and wasn't beaten at all far, but he would have surely prevailed had he proved more willing for his rider's urgings in the home straight. It was still a sound run on ground quick enough for him, and he shouldn't too long in winning over fences when reverting to an easier surface. (op 3-1 tchd 11-4)
Poseidon(GER) left the impression he would come on for this return to action and will be suited by further. (tchd 16-1)
Mountskip failed to land a serious blow and could've jumped more fluently on this switch to fences, but this was a little more encouraging on his first outing since July. (op 14-1)
The Thirsty Bricky(IRE) was seen winning at Towcester off a 10lb lower mark back in February. He too wasn't fluent, but probably found the ground quicker than he cares for all the same. (op 10-1)
New Shuil(IRE) Official explanation: jockey said saddle slipped

1646 SIMON ROBINSON CLASSIC CARS NOVICES' H'CAP CHASE (12 fncs 1 omitted) 2m 110y
5:15 (5:15) (Class 5) (0-95,92) 4-Y-0+ **£2,211** (£649; £324; £162)

Form RPR
430- **1** **Penny Queen**[210] 4370 5-11-10 **90**.................................(tp) DenisO'Regan 98+
(Paul Webber) *in rr: hdwy 8th: 5th whn blnd bdly last: styd on wl to ld last 150yds* **17/2**
331 **2** 2 1/2 **Stolen Light (IRE)**[21] 1500 9-11-6 **86**...............................(b) BrianHughes 91+
(Andrew Crook) *w ldr: led 3 out: hit next: j.rt last: hdd and no ex last 150yds* **6/1**[3]
F-P2 **3** nk **Tranos (USA)**[31] 1403 7-11-12 **92**...(p) BarryKeniry 95
(Micky Hammond) *hld up: hdwy to trck ldrs 4th: outpcd 3 out: styd on to take 3rd last 50yds* **8/1**
0-6F **4** 2 1/4 **Buds Dilemma**[9] 1559 6-9-12 **67**................................... DonalDevereux(3) 68
(Peter Bowen) *in tch: hit 4th: outpcd and lost pl 3 out: 7th last: styd on run-in: gng on at fin* **7/1**
2F61 **5** 2 3/4 **Troodos Jet**[35] 1358 9-10-12 **81**.......................................(p) RyanMania(3) 80
(Dianne Sayer) *hld up: hdwy to trck ldrs 7th: chal last: wknd fnl 50yds* **11/2**[2]
-440 **6** 1 3/4 **Well Oiled (IRE)**[75] 1001 9-10-11 **77**...............................(tp) PaddyAspell 74
(Sandy Forster) *in rr: outpcd 6th: blnd 8th: kpt on run-in: nvr trbld ldrs* **7/1**
6636 **7** 1 **Alfloramoor**[29] 1430 8-11-8 **91**... AdamPogson(3) 90
(Charles Pogson) *trckd ldrs: rallied and chsng ldr last: wknd and eased last 100yds* **9/1**
/-5 **8** 3 3/4 **Bajan Sunshine (IRE)**[20] 1511 9-10-8 **74**.......................... JamesDavies 66
(Gary Brown) *led: j.rt fr 4th: hdd 3 out: wknd appr fnl f* **22/1**
P06- **9** 5 **Fencote Mystery**[245] 3677 8-9-9 **66** oh6....................... JamesHalliday(5) 54
(Malcolm Jefferson) *chsd ldrs: drvn 6th: sn lost pl: wl bhd 3 out* **7/2**[1]

4m 8.60s **Going Correction** -0.175s/f (Good)
WFA 4 from 5yo+ 11lb **9** Ran SP% **112.9**
Speed ratings (Par 103): **93,91,91,90,89 88,88,86,83**
toteswingers:1&2:£7.60, 1&3:£10.70, 2&3:£3.10 CSF £57.60 CT £422.71 TOTE £9.70: £3.20, £3.20, £3.80; EX 49.70.
Owner The Bordeaux Bandits **Bred** Paramount Bloodstock **Trained** Mollington, Oxon

FOCUS
A pretty competitive for the class. It was run at a sound enough gallop and there were changing fortunes after the last. The form is rated around the placed horses.

NOTEBOOK
Penny Queen made a winning start over fences and gave her stable a second winner from as many runners on the card. She took time to pick up and hit the last, but got better the further she went and the long run-in no doubt helped. She probably wants a stiffer test and there should be more to come from her. (op 8-1 tchd 9-1)
Stolen Light(IRE) made all over 2m4f here on his previous outing. He didn't try to dictate over this sharper test, but still looked the most likely winner at the last. He jumped right at it, however, and then hung under maximum pressure. He was mugged late on, but this was still an improved display off a 7lb higher mark and returning to a stiffer test could see him go in again. (op 9-2)
Tranos(USA) was equipped with first-time cheekpieces and tended to go in snatches throughout. He is now 0-12 over fences, but helps to set the level all the same. (op 6-1)
Buds Dilemma ◆ again attracted some support on this first run over fences for her current yard. She looked well held turning for home, but stayed on after the last and should relish getting back over further in this sphere. (op 8-1)
Troodos Jet was given every chance to follow-up his C&D success off a 3lb higher mark, but his run petered out near the finish. (op 5-1)
Fencote Mystery was very well backed on this seasonal return for a new yard, but was beaten a long way out and remains a longstanding maiden. (op 11-2)

1647 ROFLOW ENVIRONMENTAL ENGINEERING SUPPORTS SSAFA CONDITIONAL JOCKEYS' NOVICES' H'CAP HURDLE (10 hdls) 2m 5f 110y
5:45 (5:45) (Class 5) (0-90,85) 4-Y-0+ **£1,691** (£496; £248; £124)

Form RPR
-534 **1** **Desert Soul**[5] 1596 6-11-10 **83**..(t) RyanMania 92+
(Maurice Barnes) *trckd ldrs: led appr 2 out: wnt 12 l clr last: wknd towards fin* **9/2**[3]
400 **2** 1 1/2 **Murphys Appeal (IRE)**[28] 1446 6-10-10 **75**................... OliverDayman(6) 80
(Peter Bowen) *in rr: reminders 4th: hdwy 3 out: hrd rdn and styd on to take modest 2nd between last 2: kpt on wl run-in* **13/2**
0065 **3** 16 **Make It Blossom (IRE)**[29] 1428 8-10-12 **74**................... MarkQuinlan(3) 65
(John G Carr, Ire) *in tch: outpcd 7th: 6th whn mstke 3 out: styd on appr next: tk poor 3rd last* **9/1**
315P **4** 11 **Miss Molly Be Rude (IRE)**[35] 1360 8-11-4 **82**..........(b1) HenryBrooke(5) 65
(Tim Walford) *t.k.h: trckd ldrs: led 7th: hdd appr 2 out: wknd and lost poor 3rd last* **7/2**[1]
0-0P **5** 21 **Besi**[120] 552 8-11-2 **75**... HarryHaynes 36
(Lisa Harrison) *prom: wknd 3 out* **20/1**
0P6/ **6** 106 **Bronze Dancer (IRE)**[41] 2575 8-10-5 **64**.....................(tp) JamesHalliday —
(Brian Storey) *led 1st: hdd 7th: wknd next: sn bhd: wl t.o* **40/1**
00-F **P** **Whatcanyasay**[35] 1358 9-10-9 **71**................................(p) AlexanderVoy(3) —
(Evelyn Slack) *led to 1st: chsd ldrs: reminders and lost pl 7th: t.o whn p.u bef next* **25/1**
3P00 **P** **Wee Ziggy**[12] 1450 7-11-2 **78**.. BrianToomey(3) —
(Michael Mullineaux) *t.k.h towards rr: hdwy 5th: lost pl 7th: sn bhd: t.o whn p.u bef 2 out* **8/1**
-06P **P** **Flapjack Crumbly**[9] 1556 7-11-9 **85**................................ ShaneByrne(3) —
(Sue Smith) *in rr: reminders 2nd: sn struggling in rr: t.o 6th: p.u bef next* **16/1**
06-0 **P** **Transact (IRE)**[143] 209 5-11-3 **81**.................................. PaulGallagher(5) —
(Andrew Wilson) *in rr: hdwy and in tch 5th: lost pl 7th: sn bhd: t.o whn p.u bef 2 out* **40/1**
00-1 **P** **Chestnut Ben (IRE)**[22] 1489 5-10-12 **71**......................... DonalDevereux —
(Gary Brown) *hld up: wnt prom 3rd: drvn 3 out: modest 4th whn stmbld bnd bef next: sn p.u* **4/1**[2]

5m 18.9s (4.30) **Going Correction** -0.175s/f (Good) **11** Ran SP% **114.2**
Speed ratings (Par 103): **85,84,78,74,67 —,—,—,—,— —**
toteswingers:1&2:£6.70, 1&3:£9.40, 2&3:£12.00 CSF £31.51 CT £248.09 TOTE £5.60: £1.20, £3.30, £5.10; EX 35.90 Place 6 £14.62; Place 5 £11.47.
Owner Neil Haughan **Bred** D A Yardy **Trained** Farlam, Cumbria
■ Stewards' Enquiry : Shane Byrne one-day ban: used whip with excessive force (Oct 12)
Oliver Dayman four-day ban: used whip with excessive frequency (Oct 12-15)

FOCUS
A weak handicap, confined to conditional riders and the placed horses set the level.

NOTEBOOK

Desert Soul relished this return to better ground and rates value for further than the bare margin as he was idling up the run-in. This was his first win of any description at the 29th attempt and a deserved success. He would escape a penalty if turning out before his new mark kicks in, but then there would be the worry with him having three runs in quick succession. Official explanation: trainer had no explanation for the apparent improvement in form shown (op 4-1)

Murphys Appeal(IRE) proved very hard work for her rider, but was closing all the way in the home straight and it was a much-improved effort. A stiffer test is probably what she wants and perhaps some cheekpieces would also be of benefit. (op 5-1 tchd 7-1)

Make It Blossom(IRE) is a longstanding maiden and, while this was better from her, she remains one to swerve for betting purposes. (op 12-1)

Miss Molly Be Rude(IRE) didn't take to chasing at this track on her previous outing and was well supported back over hurdles. She ultimately paid for refusing to settle, though. (op 6-1)

Chestnut Ben(IRE), 8lb higher, was starting to look a threat prior to clouting the fourth-last and coming under pressure. He was held prior to losing his action round the home bend and surely needs a return to softer ground, but may be set for another spell on the sidelines. Official explanation: jockey said gelding lost it's action but returned sound (tchd 3-1)

T/Plt: £10.70 to a£1 stake. Pool:£71,648.76 - 4,872.27 winning tickets T/Qpdt: £5.20 to a £1 stake. Pool:£5,905.95 - 838.50 winning tickets WG

1648 - 1657a (Foreign Racing) - See Raceform Interactive

1622 AUTEUIL (L-H)

Thursday, September 30

OFFICIAL GOING: Turf: heavy

1658a PRIX PRIDE OF KILDARE (HURDLE) (CONDITIONS) (3YO, UNRACED OVER HURDLES OR FENCES) (TURF) — 2m 2f

1:40 (12:00) 3-Y-O **£22,088** (£11,044; £6,442; £4,371; £2,070)

Pos	Dist	Horse	Jockey	SP	RPR
1		**Criqtonic (FR)** 3-10-4 0 ow1 (G Macaire, France)	DavidCottin	7/1³	—
2	5	**Sassenheim (FR)** 3-10-3 0 (G Macaire, France)	JacquesRicou	10/1	—
3	6	**Tout Ou Rien (FR)** 3-10-3 0 (M Rolland, France)	RegisSchmidlin	8/1	—
4	8	**Tou Fou (FR)** 3-10-3 0 (G Macaire, France)	AlexisMercurol	14/1	—
5	2 ½	**Terre De Grez (FR)** 3-10-3 0 (J Ortet, France)	JonathanPlouganou	33/1	—
6	8	**Triagoz (FR)**[46] 3-10-3 0 (F Belmont, France)	SylvainDupuis	53/10²	—
7	10	**Horatio Caine (FR)** 3-10-3 0 (Nick Williams) *hld up in rr tl making prog bk st fnl time: proged early in st: no ex fr 2nd last*	DarylJacob	31/1	—
8	snk	**Tarisandre Du Bosc (FR)** 3-10-3 0 (F-M Cottin, France)	PACarberry	21/1	—
9	15	**Summer Blues (FR)** 3-10-8 0 ow5 (J-C Baudoin, France)	YannickPruszko	91/1	—
P		**L'Ami Gaby (FR)**[38] 3-10-6 0 ow3 (R Chotard, France)	ChristophePieux	2/1¹	—
P		**Sasharzy (FR)**[75] 3-10-3 0 (B Barbier, France)	ElwisLequesne	39/1	—
P		**What Mix (FR)** 3-10-8 0 (F-X De Chevigny, France)	BenoitDelo	27/1	—
P		**Thomas O'Malley (FR)** 3-10-3 0 (Robert Collet, France)	CyrilleGombeau	10/1	—

4m 42.0s (282.00) **13** Ran SP% **115.4**

WIN (incl. 1 euro stake): 3.10 (Criqtonic combined with Sassenheim, Terre de Grez & Tou Fou). PLACES: 2.30, 3.80, 2.60. DF: 21.90. SF: 63.20.

Owner Gerald Laroche **Bred** Scea Haras Des Monts D'Arree **Trained** Les Mathes, France

1659a PRIX PATRICK LEC (HURDLE) (CONDITIONS) (4YO NON-THOROUGHBRED COLTS & GELDINGS) (TURF) — 2m 2f

3:45 (12:00) 4-Y-O **£18,690** (£9,345; £5,451; £3,699; £1,752)

Pos	Dist	Horse	Jockey	SP	RPR
1		**Saint Gratien (FR)**[21] 4-10-6 0 (E Leenders, France)	WilfridDenuault	2/1¹	—
2	10	**Shalimar Fromentro (FR)**[138] 4-10-6 0 (Nick Williams) *racd midfield on wd outside: a handy and mde prog down bk st fnl time: rdn and wnt 2nd 2 out: u.p to stay 2nd fr last fence: styd on wl*	DarylJacob	32/1	—
3	1 ½	**Steeple D'Or (FR)** 4-10-6 0 (G Chaignon, France)	RaphaelDelozier	23/1	—
4	2 ½	**Salto Royal (FR)** 4-10-6 0 (P Peltier, France)	DavidBerra	11/1	—
5	1 ½	**Sacre Toi (FR)**[179] 4-10-6 0 (E Leray, France)	StephanePaillard	5/1³	—
6	6	**Santal D'Alene (FR)** 4-10-6 0 (M Rolland, France)	RegisSchmidlin	5/1³	—
P		**Saint Des Fresnes (FR)**[200] 4-10-6 0 (P Lenogue, France)	ArnaudDuchene	28/1	—
P		**Soleil Du Mou (FR)** 4-10-6 0 (T Doumen, France)	ElwisLequesne	12/1	—
P		**Sherlock (FR)** 4-10-6 0 (E Clayeux, France)	ChristophePieux	19/5²	—
P		**Shamrock Bay (FR)** 4-10-6 0 (E Lecoiffier, France)	FabienDehez	59/1	—

4m 44.0s (284.00) **10** Ran SP% **115.8**

PARI-MUTUEL (all including 1 euro stakes): WIN 3.00; PLACE 1.90, 5.50, 4.40; DF 42.80; SF 58.70.

Owner Comte Antoine-Audoin Maggiar **Bred** J Cypres **Trained** France

800 HEXHAM (L-H)

Friday, October 1

OFFICIAL GOING: Good to soft changing to soft after race 4 (3.50)

Wind: strong behind Weather: persistent rain

1660 REGISTER @ SPORTPOOL.CO.UK (S) HURDLE (8 hdls) — 2m 110y

2:10 (2:10) (Class 5) 4-Y-0+ **£2,055** (£599; £299)

Form	Pos	Dist	Horse	Jockey	SP	RPR
/6-5	1		**Holiday Cocktail**[17] 1328 8-10-12 106 (John Quinn) *prom: hdwy to ld bef last: edgd rt after last: styd on wl*	(p) DougieCostello	5/1²	106
	2	nk	**Not Til Monday (IRE)**[61] 1343 4-10-9 0 (Ronald O'Leary, Ire) *chsd ldrs: outpcd appr 2 out: rallied and ev ch bef last: swtchd lft after last: styd on: hld towards fin*	DGHogan(3)	13/2	106
-004	3	9	**Inner Voice (USA)**[38] 1362 7-10-5 100 (J J Lambe, Ire) *chsd ldrs: rdn to ld briefly bef last: outpcd by 1st 2 run-in*	(p) BrianToomey(7)	5/1²	99
052-	4	12	**Yossi (IRE)**[17] 5385 6-11-3 109 (Richard Guest) *led to 3 out: led bef next tl bef last: sn wknd*	(b) PaddyAspell	11/2³	92
200-	5	8	**Hawksbury Heights**[32] 1438 8-10-12 97 (J J Lambe, Ire) *in tch: drvn and outpcd 3 out: n.d after*	DenisO'Regan	5/1²	80
5	6	1 ¾	**Media Stars**[9] 953 5-10-12 0 (Robert Johnson) *bhd: drvn and outpcd 4 out: nvr rchd ldrs*	KennyJohnson	33/1	78
0-	7	2 ½	**Maree Prince (IRE)**[210] 3128 9-10-5 0 (Ferdy Murphy) *bhd: struggling 4 out: nvr on terms*	MrJosephPalmowski(7)	33/1	76
164F	8	1 ½	**Totoman**[23] 1505 5-11-3 112 (Tim Vaughan) *cl up: led 3 out tl bef next: wknd qckly between last 2*	(t) APMcCoy	9/4¹	79
000-	9	27	**Its Bobkat (IRE)**[190] 4833 4-10-12 0 (Robert Smith) *a bhd: struggling 1/2-way: t.o*	RichieMcGrath	80/1	50
P030	P		**Devilfishpoker Com**[15] 1428 6-10-5 75 (Shaun Harris) *midfield: outpcd bef 3 out: wknd bef next: t.o whn p.u bef last*	(b) KyleJames(7)	100/1	—
U/P-	P		**Bulas Boy**[206] 4505 5-10-12 78 (Edwin Tuer) *towards rr: struggling 4 out: t.o whn p.u bef 2 out*	BrianHarding	50/1	—

4m 17.2s (-0.20) **Going Correction** +0.075s/f (Yiel)

WFA 4 from 5yo+ 9lb **11** Ran SP% **119.6**

Speed ratings (Par 103): **103,102,98,92,89 88,87,86,73,— —**

toteswingers:1&2 £9.90, 2&3 £9.20, 1&3 £7.40 CSF £37.04 TOTE £4.80: £2.20, £2.80, £2.40; EX 40.50.There was no bid for the winner. Not Til Monday was claimed by John Jenkins for £6,000.

Owner Estio Racing **Bred** Mrs W H Gibson Fleming **Trained** Settrington, N Yorks

FOCUS

A selling hurdle run at a sound pace and just five still in serious consideration at the second-last flight. The winner sets the standard.

NOTEBOOK

Holiday Cocktail, one of three with a leading chance on official ratings, put a poor effort on the Flat behind him. He had to battle hard and there was not an ounce to spare at the line. (op 7-2)

Not Til Monday(IRE), rated a stone ahead of the winner on the level, had finished a well-beaten third in a heavy ground maiden hurdle at Galway over a year ago. His claiming rider was having his first mount here and his lack of local knowledge probably cost his mount victory. He had work to do at the second-last flight and was asked to make up the leeway up the stiffest part of the track. Level and going better approaching the final flight, in the end he just missed out. He was claimed by John Jenkins. (op 7-1)

Inner Voice(USA), tried in cheekpieces this time rather than blinkers, hasn't won for over two years now and looks very vulnerable, even at the lowest level. (op 7-1)

Yossi(IRE), having his first start over hurdles since April, has struggled on the Flat this summer and, after setting the pace, stopped to nothing at the foot of the final hill. (op 9-2)

Hawksbury Heights did not jump fluently and was under pressure and failing to keep up at halfway. (op 11-2)

Totoman took on the leader three from home, but like him was legless at the next and in the end was allowed to complete in his own time. (op 11-4)

1661 SUPPORT GOOD CAUSES @ SPORTPOOL.CO.UK NOVICES' CHASE (19 fncs) — 3m 1f

2:40 (2:40) (Class 3) 5-Y-0+ **£6,337** (£1,872; £936; £468; £234)

Form	Pos	Dist	Horse	Jockey	SP	RPR
440-	1		**Cape Tribulation**[197] 4701 6-10-12 0 (Malcolm Jefferson) *hld up: hdwy to chse clr ldr 9th: slt mstke 4 out: effrt and led last: kpt on strly*	DenisO'Regan	4/7¹	130+
3321	2	4	**Magical Legend**[36] 1377 9-10-11 0 (Sophie Leech) *in tch: hdwy to ld after 13th: rdn and hdd last: kpt on same pce*	(t) PaulMoloney	6/1³	120
1222	3	1	**Ballyvesey (IRE)**[31] 1444 5-11-4 120 (Peter Bowen) *prom chsng gp: rdn bef 2 out: kpt on u.p fr last*	(p) TomO'Brien	4/1²	125
F020	4	20	**Flying Doctor**[23] 1508 7-10-11 0 (Elliott Cooper) *prom chsng gp: struggling 2 out: sn btn*	StevenGagan(7)	18/1	107
5PU	5	46	**Dougall (IRE)**[36] 1377 7-10-5 0 (Joanne Foster) *bhd: pushed along 1/2-way: rallied after 4 out: wknd fr next*	(p) HenryBrooke(7)	66/1	60
-416	6	24	**Call Me Mulligan (IRE)**[38] 1357 6-11-4 113 (John Hellens) *chsd clr ldr to 9th: lost pl 11th: sn struggling: t.o*	GrahamLee	20/1	44
0-33	P		**Risk Runner (IRE)**[36] 1377 7-10-12 0 (James Moffatt) *mstkes in rr: lost tch 10th: t.o whn p.u bef 14th*	(b) PaddyAspell	14/1	—
643-	F		**Luso's Lad (IRE)**[206] 4506 6-10-9 0 (Howard Johnson) *j.rt and several slow jumps: led and clr to 12th: hdd after next: lost pl whn fell 14th*	RyanMania(3)	10/1	—

6m 34.0s (1.80) **Going Correction** +0.075s/f (Yiel) **8** Ran SP% **125.2**

Speed ratings: **100,98,98,92,77 69,—,—**

toteswingers:1&2 £1.10, 2&3 £2.30, 1&3 £1.80 CSF £5.92 TOTE £1.80: £1.02, £2.30, £1.10; EX 4.60.

Owner J David Abell **Bred** Taker Bloodstock **Trained** Norton, N Yorks

FOCUS

Cape Tribulation was workmanlike, but the runner-up is a fair benchmark and he should rate higher in this sphere. The placed horses are rated in line with their recent best.

NOTEBOOK

Cape Tribulation ◆, rated 154 over hurdles, has always had the size and scope of a horse likely to make an even better chaser. Looking really well, he jumped soundly apart from the fourth last. He made quite hard work of it, but was right on top at the end. He is not short of speed and a drop back in trip will not bother him. He looks an exciting recruit who relishes soft ground, and he could come back here for another one of these under a penalty next month. (op 5-6)

Magical Legend, rated 125 over hurdles, was off the mark at the fourth attempt with a hard-fought victory at Cartmel. She went on six out, but in the end was very much second best, eased near the line. She deserves plenty of credit. (op 11-2)

Ballyvesey(IRE), rated 105 over hurdles, is a stone better chaser. He went third five from home and though never a threat, was staying on in good style at the end. This was his eighth start over fences and a return to handicaps looks the better option. (tchd 7-2)

Flying Doctor, rated 125 over fences, has had a good summer but the ground is starting to turn against him now. (op 16-1)

Luso's Lad(IRE) went off at a suicidal gallop, jumping erratically and badly right at times on his first try over fences. After holding a long lead, he came back with a full circuit to go and was out on his feet and losing touch when hitting the deck. A trip of around 2m looks a far better option. (op 12-1)

1662 WIN £10,000 FOR £2 @ SPORTPOOL.CO.UK NOVICES' HURDLE (12 hdls) 3m

3:15 (3:15) (Class 4) 4-Y-0+ **£2,945** (£858; £429)

Form RPR

322- **1** **Sunnyside**[173] [5144] 5-10-5 0 AlexanderVoy(7) 120+
(Lucy Normile) *mde all: drew clr fr 2 out: kpt on wl fr last: unchal* **7/1**

2 *5* **Moon Indigo**[44] 4-10-11 0 BrianHughes 110
(Howard Johnson) *prom: effrt and wnt 2nd whn pckd 2 out: sn outpcd: kpt on fr last: no ch w wnr* **7/4**[1]

\- **3** *47* **Bear Dancing (IRE)**[160] 6-10-12 0 PeterBuchanan 68
(Lucinda Russell) *chsd wnr tl bef 2 out: sn rdn and wknd* **7/1**

1102 **4** *45* **Majestic Mayhem (IRE)**[37] [1367] 7-11-12 123 BarryKeniry 42
(George Moore) *trckd ldrs: drvn and outpcd bef 4 out: struggling fr next* **5/2**[2]

P6/6 **P** **Bronze Dancer (IRE)**[3] [1647] 8-10-7 64 (tp) JamesHalliday(5) —
(Brian Storey) *hld up: struggling 4 out: t.o whn p.u 2 out* **66/1**

3P- **P** **Roll Over Rose (IRE)**[163] [5305] 5-10-2 0 CampbellGillies(3) —
(William Amos) *hld up in tch: effrt u.p 3 out: wknd bef next: t.o whn p.u bef last* **7/2**[3]

6m 8.30s (-4.90) **Going Correction** +0.075s/f (Yiel)
WFA 4 from 5yo+ 11lb **6 Ran SP% 113.6**
Speed ratings (Par 105): **111,109,93,78,—** —
toteswingers:1&2 £7.10, 2&3 £2.10, 1&3 £10.80 CSF £20.71 TOTE £3.20: £2.60, £1.50; EX 22.00.
Owner Gauld Lints Racing Partnership **Bred** Mrs M Morrison (camp Farm Racing) **Trained** Duncrievie, Perth & Kinross

FOCUS
A modest staying novice hurdle and not easy to rate, with the winner a big improver on his bumper form.

NOTEBOOK
Sunnyside ♦, an Irish bumper winner and runner-up on his final two starts in bumpers, made this a true test on his hurdling bow. He jumped soundly and, forging clear going to the final flight, in the end won easing down. He looks every inch a long-term chasing prospect and is clearly a real stayer. (op 6-1 tchd 5-1)
Moon Indigo, a 92-rated stayer on the Flat, looked fit and well on his first try over hurdles. He travelled strongly but, not fluent at the second last flight, had been beaten off before the last. A drop back in trip might suit and though this must go down as a let-down, he will surely find opportunities. (op 11-8)
Bear Dancing(IRE), a dual point winner, was shaken off two out and looked to finish leg-weary. He is surely better than he showed here, but will not be seen at his best until he switches to fences. (op 8-1)
Majestic Mayhem(IRE), another Irish point winner, took two modest fast ground novice hurdles here over shorter in the summer. He faced a very stiff task with his double penalty and, struggling to keep up early on the final circuit, he dropped right away three from home. Now may be the time to switch him to fences. (op 11-4 tchd 3-1 and 9-4)
Roll Over Rose(IRE), who came in for market support, had been pulled up when last seen at Perth in April, and suffered the same fate here. (op 5-1)

1663 YOUNGS CHARTERED SURVEYORS H'CAP CHASE (19 fncs) 3m 1f

3:50 (3:51) (Class 5) (0-95,95) 4-Y-0+ **£2,740** (£798; £399)

Form RPR

634 **1** **Overquest**[34] [1402] 8-11-3 86 JohnnyFarrelly 102+
(Elliott Cooper) *trckd ldrs: led bef 3 out: styd on strly fr next* **8/1**[3]

22-3 **2** *17* **Reckless Venture (IRE)**[149] [164] 9-11-3 89 (t) CampbellGillies(3) 94+
(Lucinda Russell) *led or disp ld tl after 4 out: wnt 2nd after next: no ch w wnr* **3/1**[1]

PP-3 **3** *24* **Murphys Beau (IRE)**[32] [1423] 8-10-2 71 ow1 RichieMcGrath 51
(Kate Walton) *led or disp ld: hdd whn hit and outpcd 3 out: no imp whn hit last* **5/1**[2]

52-3 **4** *½* **Pistol Basc (FR)**[153] [95] 6-10-13 89 PaulGallagher(7) 65
(Ferdy Murphy) *hld up: outpcd after 3 out: sn btn* **10/1**

060- **5** *10* **Braden Brook (IRE)**[157] [32] 7-10-1 77 (t) MrJohnDawson(7) 44
(John Wade) *hld up in tch: drvn and struggling bef 3 out: sn btn* **16/1**

-323 **P** **Gift Of The Gods (IRE)**[26] [1478] 7-11-4 87 (v) APMcCoy —
(Tim Vaughan) *prom: nt fluent: drvn and lost pl 8th: t.o whn p.u bef 13th* **5/1**[2]

F6-3 **U** **Keoghs Bar (IRE)**[24] [1500] 6-11-7 95 (t) ShaneByrne(5) —
(Irene J Monaghan, Ire) *in tch: outpcd whn blnd and uns rdr 3 out* **11/1**

01F1 **U** **Archie's Wish**[24] [1503] 6-10-12 81 BarryKeniry —
(Micky Hammond) *prom: blnd and uns rdr 14th* **3/1**[1]

6m 42.0s (9.80) **Going Correction** +0.475s/f (Soft) **8 Ran SP% 117.8**
Speed ratings (Par 103): **103,97,89,89,86** —,—,—
toteswingers:1&2 £6.20, 2&3 £5.70, 1&3 £4.80 CSF £34.33 CT £135.57 TOTE £12.50: £3.20, £1.40, £3.30; EX 58.30.
Owner Derrick Mossop **Bred** Mrs Joy Maund-Powell **Trained** Brigham, Cumbria

FOCUS
Conditions were pretty nasty during this handicap chase and they finished very tired. The runner-up sets the level.

NOTEBOOK
Overquest ♦, whose two wins in Irish points came with cut in the ground, was making his handicap debut. Never too far off the pace, he took over in front three from home and then outstayed his only serious rival. He looks a real stayer. (op 9-2)
Reckless Venture(IRE) had gained both of his career wins here over shorter, but he stays this trip. He was always up with the pace and tried to keep tabs on the winner up the final hill, but couldn't live with him and finished tired. He has rather more placings to his name than is ideal, but he should at least come on for this first start since May. (op 7-2)
Murphys Beau(IRE) was given a more positive ride on this second start for the yard, but had already been passed by the winner when blundering badly three from home. (op 9-1)
Pistol Basc(FR) again ran as though finding this trip too much of a test of stamina. (op 8-1)
Gift Of The Gods(IRE), who is yet to win under Rules, ran no sort of race and had dropped himself out before being pulled up with a circuit left. Official explanation: jockey said mare never travelled (op 9-2 tchd 11-2)
Archie's Wish, 9lb higher, was starting to feel the pinch prior to departing. He wants better ground. (op 9-2 tchd 11-2)

1664 FUND RAISING @ SPORTPOOL.CO.UK MAIDEN HURDLE (8 hdls) 2m 110y

4:25 (4:25) (Class 4) 4-Y-0+ **£2,945** (£858; £429)

Form RPR

52-3 **1** **Al Qeddaaf (IRE)**[138] [349] 4-11-0 117 APMcCoy 122+
(Donald McCain) *trckd ldrs: wnt 2nd 2 out: led appr last: pushed out* **4/5**[1]

2F4- **2** *3½* **Maggio (FR)**[117] [654] 5-11-0 120 (p) AndrewTinkler 113
(Patrick Griffin, Ire) *led tl hdd appr last: kpt on same pce run-in* **4/1**[2]

000/ **3** *10* **Dechiper (IRE)**[29] [2477] 8-11-0 0 (t) KennyJohnson 103
(Robert Johnson) *cl up: rdn and outpcd appr 2 out: rallied bef last: no ch w 1st 2* **20/1**

4-0 **4** *1¾* **Shooting Times**[141] [311] 5-10-9 0 JamesHalliday(5) 101
(Andrew Parker) *hld up: shkn up and sme hdwy after 2 out: nvr nr ldrs* **40/1**

063- **5** *10* **Quacity (FR)**[173] [5138] 6-11-0 0 PeterBuchanan 93+
(Lucinda Russell) *mid-div: hdwy and cl up after 3 out: wknd between last 2* **5/1**[3]

00- **6** *13* **Bunacurry**[173] [5144] 5-10-11 0 CampbellGillies(3) 78
(Barry Murtagh) *hld up: hdwy and prom after 3 out: rdn and wknd next* **100/1**

0-0 **7** *12* **Solway Silver**[9] [1573] 4-10-11 0 HarryHaynes(3) 66
(Lisa Harrison) *trckd ldrs tl wknd after 3 out* **80/1**

436- **8** *4* **Jersey Boys**[157] [35] 4-11-0 0 BrianHughes 62
(Howard Johnson) *hld up in midfield: stdy hdwy after 3 out: wknd fr next* **14/1**

46/5 **9** *17* **Isitcozimcool (IRE)**[61] [1148] 5-10-11 0 RyanMania(3) 45
(Barry Murtagh) *hld up: struggling bef 2 out: sn btn* **16/1**

00 **10** *1½* **Tuckers Treasure**[32] [1426] 4-11-0 0 TjadeCollier 44
(Sue Smith) *cl up: lost pl 1/2-way: no ch fr 3 out* **100/1**

P64- **11** *½* **Dollar Express (USA)**[321] [2279] 4-11-0 0 BrianHarding 43
(Edwin Tuer) *hld up: rdn and struggling bef 2 out: sn btn* **50/1**

4m 24.6s (7.20) **Going Correction** +0.475s/f (Soft) **11 Ran SP% 117.1**
Speed ratings (Par 105): **102,100,95,94,90 84,78,76,68,67 67**
toteswingers:1&2 £2.00, 2&3 £10.10, 1&3 £4.70 CSF £4.07 TOTE £1.70: £1.50, £1.10, £4.70; EX 5.30.
Owner T G Leslie **Bred** Gerrardstown House Stud **Trained** Cholmondeley, Cheshire

FOCUS
The going was changed to soft before this ordinary maiden in which the first pair came clear. The form is rated around the winner and third.

NOTEBOOK
Al Qeddaaf(IRE) ♦ had twice been turned over at odds-on since finishing fifth in the Grade 1 juvenile hurdle at the Aintree Grand National meeting, so wasn't an obvious betting opportunity at skinny prices again here. However, everything went right for him and a superb leap at the second last carried him right on to the heels of the leader. Sent to the front approaching the last, he had little trouble in pulling clear and, with his confidence now boosted, he ought to be able to go on from here. (op 4-6 tchd 5-6)
Maggio(FR), tailed off on his debut for his new yard having previously shown some ability for Nigel Hawke, had cheekpieces on for the first time and tried to make just about every yard, but he had no answer when the favourite was unleashed. He was 3lb well-in with the winner at the weights and is starting to look exposed. (op 7-1)
Dechiper(IRE), having his first start over hurdles in almost two years but fit from the Flat, ran much better than in his first three tries over the smaller obstacles, but he was still beaten a long way and is only rated 44 on the level.
Shooting Times showed a little ability on this hurdles debut and should come on for it. (op 50-1)
Quacity(FR) was close enough on the long run between the last two flights, but then blew up as though this first start since April was needed. (op 10-3 tchd 3-1)

1665 GRAEME CONLON H'CAP CHASE (12 fncs) 2m 110y

5:00 (5:00) (Class 5) (0-95,90) 4-Y-0+ **£2,740** (£798; £399)

Form RPR

0304 **1** **Janal (IRE)**[36] [1378] 7-9-7 64 oh3 GaryRutherford(7) 81+
(Stuart Coltherd) *trckd ldrs: rdn to ld bef last: kpt on strly run-in* **5/1**

03P- **2** *6* **Against The Wind**[173] [5139] 7-11-12 90 PeterBuchanan 101
(Lucinda Russell) *disp ld to bef last: kpt on u.p run-in: nt pce of wnr* **9/2**[3]

-P52 **3** *3* **More Shennanigans**[117] [652] 9-10-6 73 RyanMania(3) 81
(Jean McGregor) *prom: drvn and outpcd between last 2: styd on run-in: no imp* **4/1**[2]

5322 **4** *2* **Sam Cruise**[8] [1591] 9-11-12 90 (t) AidanColeman 97
(Steve Gollings) *led or disp to bef last: sn one pce* **9/4**[1]

-P6P **5** *14* **Panthers Run**[86] [931] 10-10-7 71 (t) DougieCostello 63
(Jonathan Haynes) *in tch: outpcd bef 3 out: sn btn* **9/2**[3]

/0P- **P** **Shara Like Magic**[226] [4103] 7-9-9 64 oh2 JamesHalliday(5) —
(Dianne Sayer) *hld up: blnd bdly 5th: sn p.u* **8/1**

4m 16.2s (6.40) **Going Correction** +0.475s/f (Soft) **6 Ran SP% 114.9**
Speed ratings (Par 103): **103,100,98,97,91** —
toteswingers:1&2 £4.30, 2&3 £2.60, 1&3 £4.20 CSF £27.79 CT £98.26 TOTE £6.20: £4.60, £2.20; EX 33.20.
Owner S Coltherd **Bred** Niall McGrady **Trained** Selkirk, Borders

FOCUS
A very weak handicap with the winner rated to his best.

NOTEBOOK
Janal(IRE), 1-32 over jumps and 0-15 over fences coming into this, was also 3lb wrong but it made no difference to her and, once sent to the front on the long run to the final fence, she fairly bounded clear. Her best previous form had come on quicker ground than this, but it's not hard to pick holes in this form and she would be no good thing to follow up. (op 7-1)
Against The Wind, racing for the first time since bursting at Kelso in April, took his turn in making the running before the mare collared him coming to the last. A return to further may be in order and he was entitled to need this. (tchd 4-1 and 5-1)
More Shennanigans was close enough between the last two fences before getting left behind, and he didn't run up to the form of his narrow defeat off this mark when last seen at Worcester in June. He is still to win a race over jumps after 25 attempts. (tchd 3-1 and 9-2)
Sam Cruise helped share pace-making duties and was still just about in second place jumping the last before folding. He doesn't want the ground this soft. (tchd 2-1)
Panthers Run was 4lb lower than when winning this race last year, but that was on much faster ground and he has been in no sort of form over further recently. He was beaten a good half mile from home. (op 4-1 tchd 5-1)
Shara Like Magic Official explanation: jockey said saddle slipped

1666 RIDING OFFICE H'CAP HURDLE (10 hdls) 2m 4f 110y

5:35 (5:35) (Class 5) (0-90,90) 4-Y-0+ **£2,397** (£698; £349)

Form RPR

0-P2 **1** **Douglas Julian**[12] [1554] 8-10-11 75 HenryOliver 85+
(Sue Smith) *hld up: hdwy and prom 4th: led bef 2 out: sn rdn clr: styd on wl run-in* **3/1**[1]

20-0 **2** *3* **Manoubi**[153] 88 11-10-13 **82** JamesHalliday(5) 88
(Martin Todhunter) *hld up: smooth hdwy and prom bef 2 out: chsd wnr bef last: kpt on* **9/1**

P/P- **3** *10* **With Speed (GER)**[78] 1006 7-11-4 **85** DGHogan(3) 82
(Ronald O'Leary, Ire) *hld up: hdwy bef 2 out: sn rdn: chsd ldrs bef last: no imp* **12/1**

40-0 **4** *27* **Rivers Run Free (IRE)**[38] 1361 5-11-3 **81** (tp) BrianHarding 50
(J J Lambe, Ire) *hld up: hdwy and prom whn nt fluent 3 out: wnt 2nd next: wknd qckly bef last* **8/1**[3]

4060 **5** *3 ½* **Follow On**[23] 1507 8-11-2 **83** (t) RyanMania(3) 49
(Maurice Barnes) *prom: lost pl after 6th: n.d after* **10/1**

000- **6** *8* **Queenstown Lad**[256] 3511 5-10-0 **64** oh36 JamesDavies 22
(Gary Brown) *trckd ldrs: outpcd after 6th: n.d after* **20/1**

/03- **7** *2* **Not Talking (IRE)**[206] 4503 7-10-0 **64** DougieCostello 20
(John Quinn) *hld up: rdn and hdwy after 3 out: wknd fr next* **7/2**[2]

500- **8** *3* **Sir Quigley (IRE)**[32] 1438 8-10-11 **82** BrianToomey(7) 35
(Mayne Kidd, Ire) *prom: stdy hdwy 1/2-way: rdn 2 out: sn btn* **28/1**

2-0F **9** *2 ¼* **Solway Bee**[128] 471 10-11-9 **90** HarryHaynes(3) 40
(Lisa Harrison) *trckd ldrs tl lost pl 6th: sn struggling* **14/1**

05F **10** *13* **Franklee**[38] 1362 7-9-7 **64** oh5 GaryRutherford(7) 1
(Harriet Graham) *led to 5th: rdn and outpcd whn hit 3 out: sn btn* **50/1**

3PP- **11** *28* **Oscar Trial (IRE)**[203] 4556 8-10-6 **73** (p) FearghalDavis(3) —
(Sharon Watt) *cl up: led 5th tl bef 2 out: sn wknd* **12/1**

P-50 **12** *7* **Amjad**[38] 1362 13-10-2 **73** (p) KyleJames(7) —
(Simon West) *a bhd: lost tch bef 4 out* **33/1**

-0P4 **P** **Mr Midaz**[66] 1101 11-9-4 **64** oh5 CallumWhillans(10) —
(Donald Whillans) *t.k.h: prom tl wknd bef 3 out: t.o whn p.u bef last* **17/2**

0/60 **P** **Diego Velasquez (IRE)**[103] 794 6-11-7 **88** JamesO'Farrell(3) —
(Patrick Griffin, Ire) *towards rr: struggling bef 4 out: t.o whn p.u bef 2 out* **22/1**

5m 22.1s (9.60) **Going Correction** +0.475s/f (Soft) **14 Ran SP% 127.5**
Speed ratings (Par 103): **100,98,95,84,83 80,79,78,77,72 62,59,—,—**
toteswingers:1&2:£7.00, 2&3 £31.10, 1&3 £14.20 CSF £30.59 CT £302.84 TOTE £4.60: £2.80, £1.10, £5.90; EX 31.40 Place 6: £60.20 Place 5: £16.45 .
Owner Mrs S Smith **Bred** A M Armitage **Trained** High Eldwick, W Yorks

FOCUS
Quite a competitive handicap hurdle on paper, but it became a war of attrition in the ground and they finished well strung out. The winner is rated an improver for the longer trip.

NOTEBOOK
Douglas Julian had plenty going for him as he was already due to go up 5lb following his narrow defeat at Uttoxeter 12 days earlier, and this step back up on trip was also expected to suit. He travelled into the race very smoothly before taking over in front before two out and even a sloppy jump at the final flight wasn't enough to stop him. Life will be tougher off his new mark, but he still has a bit of scope. (op 4-1 tchd 11-4)
Manoubi ◆ was making a rare appearance over hurdles on this return from a five-month absence, and he ran really well. He looked a possible winner when making smooth progress racing down the far side on the final circuit, but by the time he reached second place the winner had already gone for home, and he could make no impression on him. The outing should have done this three-time course winner over fences the power of good. (tchd 8-1)
With Speed(GER) made a move jumping two out, but lacked the pace to get to the front pair. His form up to now hasn't amounted to much, so it remains to be seen if he can build on this.
Rivers Run Free(IRE), another Irish challenger, also hadn't shown much up to now and had cheekpieces and a tongue tie on for the first time. He ran a bit better, but still finished a mile behind the front three, so he may not have achieved that much. (op 7-1)
Not Talking(IRE) ◆ ran much better than his finishing position would suggest. Having made some progress to latch on to the tails of the leading pack running to two out, he was still there until blowing up in the testing ground on the run to the final flight, which was perhaps not surprising considering this was his first start since March. Better can be expected.
T/Plt: £74.20 to a £1 stake. Pool of £58,416.99 - 574.31 winning tickets. T/Qpdt: £33.90 to a £1 stake. Pool of £4,988.92 - 108.80 winning tickets. RY

1667 - 1673a (Foreign Racing) - See Raceform Interactive

[1586]FONTWELL (L-H)
Saturday, October 2

OFFICIAL GOING: Good to soft (soft in places) changing to soft after race 1 (2.20)
Bottom bend divided and rail movement added 12yds per circuit on chase course and 35yds per circuit on hurdles track.
Wind: mild across Weather: light rain

1674 WIPRO SUPPORTING WATERAID JUVENILE MAIDEN HURDLE (9 hdls) 2m 2f 110y
2:20 (2:21) (Class 5) 3-Y-O £1,561 (£458; £229; £114)

Form RPR

1 **Zakeeta (IRE)**[169] 3-10-5 0 LeightonAspell 105+
(Oliver Sherwood) *hld up towards rr: pckd 2nd: rdn and hdwy after 3 out: chal next: led last: styd on wl* **20/1**

2 *6* **Kalamill (IRE)**[43] 3-10-12 0 AidanColeman 106
(Shaun Lycett) *mid-div: rdn and hdwy after 3 out: j. sltly lft last 2: led 2 out tl last: no ex* **15/8**[1]

3 *8* **Big Talk**[343] 3-10-12 0 (b[1]) RodiGreene 99
(David Bridgwater) *w ldr: stmbld whn awkward 3 out: sn rdn: ev ch next: kpt on same pce* **80/1**

P **4** *½* **Freckle Face**[32] 1442 3-10-7 0 TomO'Connor(5) 99
(Bill Turner) *hld up towards rr: hdwy to trck ldrs 5th: rdn and c wd on bnd after 3 out: one pce fr next* **40/1**

5 *23* **Electric City (IRE)**[31] 3-9-12 0 MrJMQuinlan(7) 71
(Michael Quinlan) *trckd ldrs: rdn after 3 out: sn wknd: t.o* **10/1**

2 **6** *22* **Finch Flyer (IRE)**[9] 1586 3-10-12 0 (b[1]) JamieMoore 58
(Gary Moore) *led: j.lft: rdn and hdd appr 2 out: hld in 4th last: wknd run-in: t.o* **9/4**[2]

0556 **7** *1* **Mini Max**[13] 1545 3-10-5 77 (b) MarkGrant 50
(Brendan Duke) *mid-div tl wknd appr 3 out: t.o* **40/1**

2 **8** *2 ½* **Optimistic Duke (IRE)**[27] 1473 3-10-12 0 JimmyMcCarthy 55
(William Muir) *trckd ldrs: rdn after 3 out: sn wknd: t.o* **3/1**[3]

P **Land Of Plenty (IRE)**[72] 3-10-5 0 MattieBatchelor —
(Jamie Poulton) *hld up towards rr: slow jump 4th: sn lost tch: t.o whn p.u bef 2 out* **50/1**

4m 49.0s (14.70) **Going Correction** +0.675s/f (Soft) **9 Ran SP% 112.5**
Speed ratings (Par 101): **96,93,90,89,80 70,70,69,—**
Tote Swingers: 1&2 £6.30, 1&3 £92.50, 2&3 £18.10 CSF £56.93 TOTE £17.70: £3.00, £1.40, £12.50.
Owner B G Fillery **Bred** Sean Collins **Trained** Upper Lambourn, Berks

FOCUS
This was run at a modest pace, but the majority of the runners still floundered home. The form is modest with the form ordinary.

NOTEBOOK
Zakeeta(IRE) was an inexpensive purchase who did not look straightforward when tried in a visor on just her second attempt on the Flat. Making her debut over hurdles, she was already under a fair amount of driving on the turn for home but simply outstayed the rest in the testing conditions. She has a bit of physical scope, but mud could be the key to her. (op 16-1)
Kalamill(IRE) has been second over 1m6f in the mud, but he has shown a tendency to hang right on the level, and went a bit left-handed at the final two flights here. He can probably score in this grade. (op 7-4 tchd 2-1)
Big Talk was in first-time blinkers for his debut over hurdles, having been of no account on the level for another yard in 2009. His jumping could have been better and he was fading from two out.
Freckle Face was the only one of the party who was unraced on the Flat, presumably because he is a big, gawky type who needs time. This was a distinct improvement on his debut, and he is worth another look. Official explanation: vet said gelding lost an off-fore shoe (op 66-1)
Finch Flyer(IRE) seemed lit up by his blinkers and, after making the running, he finished out on his feet. Soft ground looked very much against him. This Flat winner chased home the miniscule Whipperway here last time, and is surely a bit better than this showing. (op 2-1 tchd 5-2)
Optimistic Duke(IRE) was disappointing and is one to field against at present. (op 9-2)

1675 MORRISON UTILITY SERVICES SUPPORTING CANCER RESEARCH UK NOVICES' HURDLE (10 hdls) 2m 4f
2:55 (2:57) (Class 4) 4-Y-O+ £2,341 (£687; £343; £171)

Form RPR

5 **1** **Moonwolf (NZ)**[33] 1433 6-10-12 0 JamieGoldstein 103
(Sheena West) *hld up towards rr: hdwy after 3 out: lft in ld next: styd on: rdn out* **8/1**[3]

653- **2** *¾* **Hill Forts Gloria (IRE)**[159] 27 5-10-2 0 WayneKavanagh(3) 95
(Seamus Mullins) *trckd ldr: rdn after 3 out: lft 2nd whn hmpd next: styd on run-in: a being hld* **9/1**

3 *10* **The Clyda Rover (IRE)**[209] 6-10-12 0 OwynNelmes 92
(Helen Nelmes) *hld up towards rr: hdwy after 3 out: lft disputing 3rd next: hit last: styd on same pce* **50/1**

404- **4** *1* **Balustrade (IRE)**[163] 5332 4-10-12 0 ColinBolger 91
(Chris Gordon) *hld up towards rr: sme imp after 3 out: lft disputing 3rd next: sn rdn: fdd towards fin* **20/1**

5 *11* **Mtpockets (IRE)**[146] 5-10-5 0 DougieCostello 73
(Neil Mulholland) *trckd ldrs tl dropped in rr after 7th: nvr gng to trble ldrs: styd on past btn horses fr 2 out* **20/1**

/4P- **6** *1 ½* **Wild Bay**[163] 5326 7-10-12 0 LiamTreadwell 79
(Nick Gifford) *trckd ldrs: rdn after 3 out: wknd bef next* **25/1**

600/ **7** *1 ½* **Giollacca (IRE)**[565] 4530 6-10-5 0 JodieMogford 70
(Graeme McPherson) *trckd ldrs tl after 6th: rdn towards rr after next: nvr bk on terms* **100/1**

8 *1 ¾* **Jack The Soldier (IRE)**[152] 6-10-9 0 CharlieStudd(3) 76
(Chris Gordon) *a towards rr* **7/1**[2]

-600 **9** *18* **Jim Job Jones**[8] 1600 6-10-5 0 MarkQuinlan(7) 58
(Neil Mulholland) *mid-div tl wknd 3 out: t.o* **66/1**

10 *33* **El Diego (IRE)**[135] 6-10-12 0 DarylJacob 25
(Jamie Snowden) *mid-div tl wknd appr 7th: t.o* **8/1**[3]

205- **F** **Iona Days (IRE)**[174] 5146 5-10-12 0 HaddenFrost 102
(Henrietta Knight) *led: nt fluent 5th: 4l clr whn pckd 3 out: pushed along and jnd whn hmpd and fell 2 out* **11/4**[1]

03-1 **F** **Vincitore (FR)**[156] 62 4-10-9 117 PeterCarberry(10) 109
(Charlie Longsdon) *mid-div: hdwy 7th: mounting chal whn fell 2 out* **11/4**[1]

5m 14.6s (15.20) **Going Correction** +0.675s/f (Soft)
WFA 4 from 5yo+ 10lb **12 Ran SP% 115.9**
Speed ratings (Par 105): **96,95,91,91,86 86,85,85,77,64 —,—**
Tote Swingers: 1&2 £12.20, 1&3 £48.10, 2&3 £23.80 CSF £68.85 TOTE £9.70: £2.70, £2.90, £12.40; EX 109.40.
Owner The Kiwi Club **Bred** J Charlton **Trained** Falmer, E Sussex

FOCUS
A race run at a crawl. The two leaders came to grief two out, rapidly changing the complexion of the race. The runner-up is rated in line with his bumper.

NOTEBOOK
Moonwolf(NZ) is a strong sort but he could not win on the Flat in his native New Zealand (despite plentiful chances) or for his current yard here. Not unsupported and patiently ridden, he was getting into contention apparently going well when left in front two out, but after being left clear at the last his stamina began to ebb away and he was all out to hold on. He might prefer to revert 2m, at least when conditions are testing. (op 9-1 tchd 15-2)
Hill Forts Gloria(IRE) is only small but gave a plucky display and, despite being impeded two out and making a sloppy jump at the last, she kept the winner at full stretch and was catching him close home. She will certainly stay further. (op 17-2 tchd 10-1)
The Clyda Rover(IRE) is a chasing type who looked decidedly burly. He was a very lucky third, and if he is to do any good it will surely be over fences and a longer trip. (op 40-1)
Balustrade(IRE) is well-related and continues to show a modicum of promise, making it three fourths from four attempts, including on this hurdling debut. (op 16-1)
Mtpockets(IRE) was given a very easy time and this Irish pointing winner will benefit from the experience. (op 16-1 tchd 14-1)
Jack The Soldier(IRE) is a stablemate of Balustrade and is more of a chaser on looks. He was sweating up beforehand. (op 9-1)
El Diego(IRE) Official explanation: jockey said gelding ran green
Iona Days(IRE) had finished second here in a bumper on his debut and was in the process of running a fair race when he got tangled up with the narrow leader falling two from home. He is not over-big. (op 7-2)
Vincitore(FR) ◆ won a hurdle at Huntingdon (by a head) and would surely have followed up on this first appearance since had he not toppled two out. Evidently held in some regard by his trainer, he can gain deserved compensation. (op 7-2)

1676 COSTAIN SUPPORTING THE NSPCC H'CAP CHASE (13 fncs) 2m 2f
3:30 (3:30) (Class 3) (0-130,129) 4-Y-O £5,069 (£1,497; £748; £374; £187)

Form RPR

P3-3 **1** **Alesandro Mantegna (IRE)**[38] 1372 5-10-11 **114** TomO'Brien 121
(Keith Goldsworthy) *trckd ldr: rdn to chal 3 out: led 2 out: idled run-in: drvn out* **7/4**[1]

5553 **2** *¾* **Marodima (FR)**[38] 1370 7-11-2 **119** (p) DarylJacob 125
(Jamie Snowden) *led: hdd 2 out: sn swtchd rt and rdn: kpt on cl home* **7/1**

0/ **3** *26* **Mister Virginian (IRE)**[276] 11-9-7 **103** oh1 MrTJCannon(7) 83
(Chris Gordon) *trckd ldrs: reminders after 6th: no ch fr 4 out: wnt modest 3rd after 2 out* **28/1**

3 **4** *19* **Adajal (IRE)**[35] 1408 7-11-12 **129** (t) APMcCoy 90
(C F Swan, Ire) *hld up in tch: wknd 4 out: t.o* **6/1**

110- **5** *15* **Award Winner**169 5217 7-11-0 **120**............................ RichieMcLernon(3) 66
(Brendan Powell) *hld up in tch: stmbld 1st: wknd after 8th: t.o* **7/1**

-51P **6** *8* **Bermuda Pointe (IRE)**27 1486 8-10-9 **115**......... SamTwiston-Davies(3) 53
(Nigel Twiston-Davies) *trckd ldrs: mstke 4 out: sn rdn: wknd bef next: mstke 2 out* **11/2**3

0-21 **P** **Marc Of Brilliance (USA)**143 281 7-10-5 **118**....... JosephAkehurst(10) —
(Gary Moore) *lost tch tamely fr 4th: p.u after 7th* **5/1**2

4m 41.2s (6.50) **Going Correction** +0.55s/f (Soft) 7 Ran SP% **111.1**
Speed ratings (Par 107): **107,106,95,86,80 76,—**
Tote Swingers: 1&2 £8.90, 1&3 £18.20, 2&3 £100.80 CSF £13.58 CT £234.95 TOTE £2.20: £1.10, £4.50; EX 16.90.

Owner M Duthie,P Fisher,P Gough,Hughes,Barrack **Bred** Mount Coote Partnership **Trained** Yerbeston, Pembrokes

FOCUS
A better early pace than in the two preceding hurdles, and a two-horse race from the home turn. The winner is on the upgrade and the race could be rated higher.

NOTEBOOK
Alesandro Mantegna(IRE) has a better record over fences than he had over hurdles (0-15 in the latter, but now 2-6 in the former). This was arguably the best he has jumped to date in chases, and he held on well in closing stages, despite idling quite badly inside the final furlong. (op 3-1)
Marodima(FR) has won 12 times over jumps (four this year, all over hurdles), did his best to make it 13, and he responded generously to the cheekpieces. He loves to bowl along in front, and his winning may not be over yet. (tchd 8-1)
Mister Virginian(IRE) arrived here after a long losing sequence (including Irish points), so this tall, strong individual did not do badly in the circumstances, although he was eventually beaten out of sight. (op 20-1)
Adajal(IRE) was a four-time winner over fences on good or firmish ground in Ireland in May (on four different tracks) but the handicapper is now having his say. He was far from nimble at the fences and has yet to prove himself at beyond 2m1f, but the inestimable advantage of McCoy in the saddle may pay dividends eventually, especially as it looked too testing for him here. (op 5-1 tchd 9-2)
Award Winner can be clumsy, as he was here. McCoy won on him twice in the spring, and he could be a horse who takes plenty of knowing. (op 6-1 tchd 15-2)
Bermuda Pointe(IRE) has a wind problem and the beneficial effects of a tube (which had been inserted when he scored at Newton Abbot two outings previously) may already have worn off, as he has been tailed off since. (op 5-1 tchd 6-1)
Marc Of Brilliance(USA) has ability combined with plenty of temperament, and after being very apprehensive at the early fences he quickly tailed himself off. (op 4-1)

1677 MAYO WYNNE BAXTER SUPPORTING CHESTNUT TREE HOUSE H'CAP HURDLE (9 hdls) 2m 2f 110y

4:05 (4:05) (Class 4) (0-115,114) 4-Y-0+ **£2,341** (£687; £343; £171)

Form RPR

0352 **1** **The Good Guy (IRE)**13 1551 7-11-5 **107**.......................... JodieMogford 113+
(Graeme McPherson) *mde all: sn clr: rdn appr 6th: mstke last: styd on v gamely* **5/1**2

00-P **2** *1 1/2* **Princess Flame (GER)**11 1347 8-10-7 **95**.................... JimmyMcCarthy 98
(Brendan Powell) *led chsng gp thrght: clsd on wnr u.p after 3 out: styd on but a being hld fr last* **5/1**2

-431 **3** *2 1/4* **Crystal Rock (IRE)**8 1601 5-11-7 **114**............................... DavidBass(5) 115
(Nicky Henderson) *chsd ldr in main gp: rdn appr 2 out: styd on same pce* **11/4**1

4 *2 1/2* **Kylenoe Fairy (IRE)**72 1077 6-10-2 **97**.........................(t) MattGriffiths(7) 96
(Paul Henderson) *hld up towards rr: rdn and hdwy after 3 out: styd on same pce* **16/1**

55-0 **5** *30* **Lepido (ITY)**146 235 6-11-0 **102**... JamieMoore 71
(Gary Moore) *a towards rr: wknd 2 out: t.o* **15/2**3

P-46 **6** *hd* **Just Beware**51 1236 8-9-8 **88** oh1...............(p) GemmaGracey-Davison(5) 56
(Zoe Davison) *mid-div of main gp: rdn after 6th: wknd 2 out: t.o* **18/1**

F4U- **7** *24* **Princely Hero (IRE)**168 4937 6-11-9 **111**......................... LeightonAspell 55
(Chris Gordon) *chsd ldr in main gp tl wknd 3 out: t.o* **12/1**

400 **8** *20* **Adare Manor (IRE)**7 1608 6-11-0 **102**.................................... APMcCoy 26
(Jonjo O'Neill) *mid-div in main gp tl wknd after 3 out: t.o* **12/1**

0436 **P** **Knightsbridgelives (IRE)**13 1555 7-10-11 **99**............(t) AidanColeman —
(Lawney Hill) *hit 3 out: a towards rr: p.u bef 2 out* **5/1**2

4m 44.6s (10.30) **Going Correction** +0.675s/f (Soft)
WFA 4 from 5yo+ 9lb 9 Ran SP% **115.0**
Speed ratings (Par 105): **105,104,103,102,89 89,79,71,—**
Tote Swingers: 1&2 £4.50, 1&3 £1.70, 2&3 £1.80 CSF £30.44 CT £81.94 TOTE £5.10: £1.10, £3.10, £1.90; EX 39.90.

Owner S D Barling **Bred** Brian Slattery **Trained** Upper Oddington, Gloucs

FOCUS
A fair handicap hurdle in which the winner is rated to previous course form backed up by the placed horses.

NOTEBOOK
The Good Guy(IRE) is a gutsy front-runner who was pipped by a short head over further at Plumpton last time. He often competes at a lowly level, but likes Fontwell, and was winning for the third time here from just four visits. He showed ability pointing as a juvenile, but can put in the odd sticky jump (as he did at the last), which is perhaps why he does not go down the chasing route. (op 11-2 tchd 7-1)
Princess Flame(GER) is in good heart at the moment and after a Folkestone Flat win 11 days ago, she again did her best. Consistency is not always her strong suit however, and next time could be more competitive than this weak affair. (op 7-2)
Crystal Rock(IRE) got his in front for the first time over hurdles at the sixth attempt at Worcester, but he does not look the stoutest battler and never really looked likely to follow up on his second attempt in a handicap. The handicapper possibly over-rates him. (op 3-1 tchd 5-2)
Kylenoe Fairy(IRE) was running for the first time in England and showed improved form, looking a trier despite finishing quite weary. She had been off the bridle at halfway and may need a bit of time to get over this run. (op 14-1 tchd 18-1)
Just Beware has now been trounced in this race for the last three years. (op 16-1)
Adare Manor(IRE) never got involved but should continue to descend in the weights, and is surely better than he has shown so far in this country. (tchd 10-1)
Knightsbridgelives(IRE) has been easy to beat in sellers and was out of his depth, particularly in the soft ground. (op 8-1)

1678 CLANCY DOCWRA SUPPORTING RNLI H'CAP CHASE (16 fncs) 2m 6f

4:40 (4:40) (Class 5) (0-95,90) 4-Y-0+ **£1,691** (£496; £248; £124)

Form RPR

-34P **1** **Great Ocean Road (IRE)**87 931 7-10-10 **74**....................... NoelFehily 80
(Charlie Mann) *in tch: hit 2nd and 5th: rdn after 4 out: nt fluent in 7l 4th 3 out: styd on fr after 2 out: led sn after last: drvn out* **11/2**2

4221 **2** *1* **Rash Moment (FR)**27 1483 11-11-10 **88**...................(p) TomScudamore 92
(Michael Scudamore) *trckd ldrs: led after 10th: rdn after 3 out: hdd sn after last: kpt on but no ex* **11/2**2

5334 **3** *6* **Khazar (FR)**27 1474 7-11-12 **90**..(t) APMcCoy 88
(Jonjo O'Neill) *mid-div: nudged along fr 4th: nt fluent 6th: rdn after 10th: 1 l 2nd 3 out: no ex fr last* **9/2**1

4356 **4** *11* **Fongoli**28 1468 4-10-7 **82**...(v) AidanColeman 58
(Brendan Powell) *disp ld tl after 10th: sn rdn: nvr bk on terms: plugged on fr 3 out: lft 4th last* **15/2**3

-6F4 **P** **Buds Dilemma**4 1646 6-10-0 **67**.............................(p) DonalDevereux(3) —
(Peter Bowen) *pushed along fr 4th: nvr any imp fr rr: mstke 12th: wknd next: t.o whn p.u bef last* **9/2**1

/PP6 **P** **Hazelbury**13 1546 9-9-12 **67** oh6 ow3................................ KeiranBurke(5) —
(Nigel Hawke) *chsd ldrs tl 8th: sn bhd: p.u bef 11th* **33/1**

PUP5 **P** **Vial De Kerdec (FR)**27 1476 7-11-9 **87**...........................(b) FelixDeGiles —
(Mark Bradstock) *disp ld: reminders after 6th: drvn to chse ldrs after 9th: stopped qckly after 10th: p.u bef next* **14/1**

53P- **U** **Killfinnan Castle (IRE)**175 5133 7-10-10 **74**....................... WillKennedy 75
(F Jordan) *mid-div: hdwy 9th: prom fr after next: rdn after 4 out to chse ldng pair: 3 l down and styng on whn hmpd and uns rdr last* **10/1**

P32- **P** **Hobb's Dream (IRE)**181 5010 6-10-2 **73**......................... MarkQuinlan(7) —
(Neil Mulholland) *nvr travelling in rr: lost tch 10th: p.u after 12th* **11/2**2

5m 58.1s (15.10) **Going Correction** +0.55s/f (Soft)
WFA 4 from 6yo+ 10lb 9 Ran SP% **113.0**
Speed ratings (Par 103): **94,93,91,87,—,—,—,—,—**
Tote Swingers: 1&2 £8.00, 1&3 £7.80, 2&3 £1.50 CSF £35.45 CT £146.00 TOTE £5.70: £2.60, £1.80, £2.50; EX 33.10.

Owner Mrs J Maynard,Mrs D Mosley,P Docherty **Bred** Michael Conroy **Trained** Upper Lambourn, Berks

FOCUS
Several disinterested types here but the winner was well in on his spring form and the runner-up is in line with his recent win.

NOTEBOOK
Great Ocean Road(IRE) was second in an Irish point but had managed only a modest third (in a long-distance chase at Fontwell) from six previous attempts for this yard, who had been without a winner for 97 days. His ran in snatches and his cause looked hopeless three out, but he stuck to his guns while the opposition faltered, and Fehilly never let up and he led close home. It was a sterling effort from the rider, who was badly struck by injury and making a most welcome return to the winner's enclosure. Essentially, the horse looks slow but probably stays forever. Official explanation: trainer said, regarding apparent improvement in form, that the gelding was better suited by the easier soft ground. (op 15-2)
Rash Moment(FR) does not mind the mud and looked likely to follow up his Worcester win of last month, but he idled on that occasion and did the same here, thus presenting the race to his late-challenging rival. He is fully exposed but remains consistent despite entering the veteran stage. (op 7-2)
Khazar(FR) gave McCoy no help whatsoever, as is normally the case, and getting him to win is a real struggle (2-26 now). He was soon nudged along and his jumping typically lacked alacrity. (op 6-1 tchd 4-1)
Fongoli has been beaten in selling hurdles and faced a stiff task, despite her low weight. (op 17-2)
Killfinnan Castle(IRE) travelled well for a long way, but was fourth and quickly coming to the end of his tether when he got rid of the rider at the last. Both previous wins have come here, and he was not discredited on this comeback from a 175-day absence. (op 8-1)
Hobb's Dream(IRE) Official explanation: jockey said mare never travelled (op 8-1)

1679 4D SUPPORTING SUSSEX COMMUNITY FOUNDATION H'CAP HURDLE (11 hdls) 2m 6f 110y

5:15 (5:15) (Class 5) (0-95,95) 4-Y-0+ **£1,561** (£458; £229; £114)

Form RPR

0-40 **1** **Isintshelovely (IRE)**27 1479 7-10-5 **74**........................... LeightonAspell 84
(Chris Gordon) *hld up towards rr: hdwy 8th: sn rdn: wnt 2nd gng to 2 out: led last: styd on wl fnl 120yds: rdn out* **11/2**

3P62 **2** *2 1/2* **You Can Of Course (IRE)**26 1494 7-10-5 **74**............... DougieCostello 82
(Neil Mulholland) *led: hrd rdn appr 2 out: hdd last: no ex fnl 120yds* **7/2**2

0-6P **3** *4 1/2* **Galantos (GER)**124 557 9-10-13 **82**................................. OwynNelmes 85
(Helen Nelmes) *mid-div: hdwy after 3 out: wnt 3rd next: sn rdn: styd on same pce* **10/1**

62-3 **4** *17* **Pete The Feat (IRE)**155 84 6-11-2 **85**.................. MattieBatchelor 71
(Anna Newton-Smith) *mid-div: hdwy 8th: rdn after 3 out: wknd next* **10/3**1

00F- **5** *11* **All The Fashion (IRE)**163 5339 6-10-5 **74**........................ WillKennedy 49
(F Jordan) *hld up towards rr: effrt after 3 out: sn wknd: t.o* **8/1**

6504 **6** *12* **Atabaas Allure (FR)**27 1479 4-10-3 **73**................................ ColinBolger 35
(Chris Gordon) *hld up towards rr: hdwy 6th: hit 8th: rdn after 3 out: sn wknd: t.o* **5/1**3

/FF- **7** *10* **Toomuchinformation**195 4764 6-11-8 **91**........................... FelixDeGiles 44
(Anna Newton-Smith) *chsd ldrs tl wknd after 6th: sn bhd: t.o* **8/1**

U20P **8** *2 3/4* **Hi Wycombe (IRE)**24 1506 6-11-5 **95**...................... MrSWDrinkwater(7) 45
(David Bridgwater) *chsd ldr: hit 7th: rdn after 3 out: sn wknd: t.o* **20/1**

6m 1.90s (19.40) **Going Correction** +0.675s/f (Soft)
WFA 4 from 6yo+ 10lb 8 Ran SP% **113.4**
Speed ratings (Par 103): **93,92,90,84,80 76,73,72**
Tote Swingers: 1&2 £8.30, 1&3 £11.70, 2&3 £10.50 CSF £25.13 CT £185.79 TOTE £7.60: £1.80, £1.60, £3.60; EX 41.80.

Owner L Gilbert **Bred** Mrs Sheila O'Ryan **Trained** Morestead, Hants

FOCUS
An extremely modest staying hurdle rated around the placed horses.

NOTEBOOK
Isintshelovely(IRE) finished 55l behind stablemate Atabaas Allure when they were ninth and fourth respectively here last month, but over a longer trip and in the mud the placings were comprehensively reversed. The mare won her bumper here in January 2008 but had managed only one success since, and catching her right is very difficult. Official explanation: trainer said, regarding apparent improvement in form, that the mare was better suited by the easier soft ground. (op 8-1)
You Can Of Course(IRE) was no match for the handicap good thing Am I Blue at Newton Abbot last time but, although battling quite hard, he again had to settle for second, and he has only won one of 20 attempts. (op 4-1 tchd 3-1)
Galantos(GER) looked to be going best on the home turn but did not pick up and he is a 15-time loser over jumps (and been tried in a seller). His infrequent appearances suggest training training difficulties. (op 14-1)
Pete The Feat(IRE) has managed five placings but not won despite 18 chances so far. (op 11-4)
Atabaas Allure(FR) was taken wide in search of better ground and, after flattering three out, she did not get the trip in the ground. (tchd 9-2)

Hi Wycombe(IRE) pulls hard, usually runs in sellers, never wins, and looks badly handicapped. (op 16-1)

1680 SOUTHERN WATER SUPPORTING AAIR/AWAAIREBEAR INTERMEDIATE OPEN NATIONAL HUNT FLAT RACE 1m 6f

5:50 (5:50) (Class 6) 4-6-Y-O **£1,370** (£399; £199)

Form RPR

14- **1** **Fountains Flypast**[176] 5122 6-11-0 0..........................(t) RachaelGreen(7) 116+
(Anthony Honeyball) *hld up towards rr: stdy hdwy fr 6f out: jnd ldr on bit 2f out: led jst over 1f out: rdn and qcknd readily clr: easily* **9/4**[1]

352 **2** *13* **Landenstown Pearl (IRE)**[87] 935 4-10-2 0.............. JimmyDerham(5) 85
(Seamus Mullins) *led: rdn and hdd wl over 2f out: styd on to regain 2nd towards fin: no ch w wnr* **9/2**[2]

600- **3** *1* **Dark Dancer**[166] 5283 6-10-7 0....................................... RichardJohnson 83
(Laura Mongan) *in tch: led 3f out: sn rdn: hdd over 1f out: sn outpcd by wnr: lost 2nd towards fin* **6/1**[3]

1 **4** *6* **La Belle Au Bois (IRE)**[27] 1480 4-10-7 0........................... MrJBanks(7) 83
(Nick Lampard) *mid-div: effrt 4f out: sn one pce* **8/1**

6 **5** *7* **Casper's Shadow (IRE)**[38] 1374 4-11-0 0.................................. RhysFlint 75
(Keith Goldsworthy) *trckd ldr: rdn over 2f out: sn wknd* **12/1**

0 **6** *1 1/2* **Downe Payment (IRE)**[122] 589 5-10-4 0...................... AlexMerriam(3) 66
(Diana Grissell) *in tch tl outpcd over 5f out* **25/1**

00- **7** *25* **Padys Arkle (IRE)**[176] 5121 6-11-0 0.. JamieMoore 43
(Gary Moore) *t.k.h trcking ldr: rdn over 3f out: wknd over 1f out: eased* **6/1**[3]

00- **8** *5* **Hammerwood**[176] 5121 4-10-9 0.................... GemmaGracey-Davison(5) 37
(Zoe Davison) *a towards rr: t.o* **50/1**

00/ **9** *3 1/4* **My Only Boy**[577] 4287 5-10-9 0.. MarcGoldstein(5) 33
(Michael Madgwick) *a towards rr: t.o fr over 5f out* **14/1**

0- **10** *10* **Quahadi (IRE)**[325] 2238 4-10-11 0................................... CharlieStudd(3) 21
(Chris Gordon) *mid-div: hdwy to trck ldrs over 6f out: rdn 4f out: sn eased whn smething amiss* **12/1**

0-0 **11** *dist* **Poesmulligan (IRE)**[143] 284 4-11-0 0........................... LeightonAspell —
(Linda Jewell) *mid-div tl over 6f out: sn t.o* **40/1**

3m 34.7s (3.60) **11** Ran SP% **118.9**
CSF £11.90 TOTE £3.10: £1.20, £1.80, £2.20; EX 11.70 Place 6: £211.62 Place 5: £86.94 .
Owner The Fountains Partnership **Bred** Mrs M H Bowden **Trained** Seaborough, Dorset

FOCUS
A worthy winner, but exposed types and no strength in depth, although the form looks fairly sound with the placed horses and fifth and sixth pretty much to their marks.

NOTEBOOK
Fountains Flypast is a strong sort and looked very much the pick of the paddock. He won well at Stratford in March under a confident ride from Rachel Green before finishing a decent fourth behind a potentially useful type at Kempton, and had no trouble defying his penalty here. He has the scope to do well hurdling.
Landenstown Pearl(IRE) has been placed in three of four bumpers and now has to go jumping. She is quite small but may have found this 1m6f inadequate, as her pedigree suggests stamina. She may need to strengthen up. (op 4-1)
Dark Dancer is a half-sister to Diamond Harry but has only a fraction of his ability, and she finished a modest third after trying to assert up the straight. She too has contested her final bumper. (op 17-2)
La Belle Au Bois(IRE) is light-framed and a penalty incurred for her win here (over just four rivals) found her out.
Quahadi(IRE) Official explanation: jockey said gelding lost its action
T/Plt: £390.03 to a £1 stake. Pool of £64,512.18 - 120.66 winning tickets. T/Qpdt: £12.30 to a £1 stake. Pool of £5,460.69 - 327.60 winning tickets. TM

1681 - 1683a (Foreign Racing) - See Raceform Interactive

1667 GOWRAN PARK (R-H)
Saturday, October 2

OFFICIAL GOING: Yielding to soft

1684a GOWRAN PARK CHAMPION CHASE (GRADE 2) (14 fncs) 2m 4f

3:35 (3:36) 5-Y-O+ **£23,008** (£6,725; £3,185; £1,061)

RPR

1 **China Rock (IRE)**[165] 5303 7-11-3 142.. RWalsh 142
(M F Morris, Ire) *trckd ldrs: 3rd 1/2-way: mstke 8th: impr into 2nd appr 3 out: led bef 2 out where mstke: kpt on wl u.p fr last* **13/8**[1]

2 *1 1/2* **Coolcashin (IRE)**[137] 386 9-11-6 138.................................... DJCondon 143
(Michael J Bowe, Ire) *hld up: hdwy into 5th 1/2-way: wnt 4th appr 3 out: sn rdn: 3rd at last: kpt on wl run-in wout rching wnr* **12/1**

3 *1 1/2* **Oscar Looby (IRE)**[17] 1527 7-11-8 138..........................(t) PCarberry 144
(Noel Meade, Ire) *led: strly pressed appr 3 out: hdd bef next: kpt on u.p: no ex run-in* **6/1**[3]

4 *9* **Royal Choice (IRE)**[57] 1206 6-11-1 123................................. AELynch 128
(Henry De Bromhead, Ire) *in rr: rdn in 6th appr 3 out: no imp fr 2 out: kpt on one pce* **20/1**

5 *4 1/2* **Miss Mitch (IRE)**[252] 3602 9-10-12 .... PTownend 120
(P A Fahy, Ire) *trckd ldr in 2nd: rdn after 4 out and dropped to 5th bef next: no ex* **10/3**[2]

P **Glencove Marina (IRE)**[189] 4905 8-11-6 158................... BarryGeraghty —
(Eoin Griffin, Ire) *trckd ldrs: 4th 1/2-way: gd prog into 3rd 6 out: pushed along appr 3 out: no ex fr next: btn in 4th whn blnd at last: sn p.u* **10/3**[2]

P **Schelm (GER)**[15] 1537 8-11-6 137.. DJCasey —
(Ronald O'Leary, Ire) *a towards rr: trailing appr 3 out: bhd whn p.u bef next* **16/1**

4m 47.6s (-23.70) **7** Ran SP% **116.9**
CSF £21.72 TOTE £2.40: £1.70, £3.60; DF 15.30.
Owner Michael O'Flynn **Bred** Brian Griffin **Trained** Fethard, Co Tipperary

FOCUS
This Grade 2 event didn't look as strong on paper as some of the previous encounters. The runner-up and fourth set the standard.

NOTEBOOK
China Rock(IRE) was settled in third as Oscar Looby set a decent clip up front, given the ground, closely tracked by British import Miss Mitch. The winner, who got in close five out, took over on the run to the penultimate fence where he was untidy. To his credit, though, he kept up to his task and got the job done. (op 2/1)
Coolcashin(IRE) ran a cracker over this inadequate trip.
Oscar Looby(IRE) was off the track since February before he fell early in the Kerry National last month. He showed a return to the form that saw him win three times in testing ground including a Grade 2 event over 3m at Naas. He won't mind a step back up in trip on this evidence. (op 7/1)
Royal Choice(IRE) looked up against it on figures, but the 123-rated runner plugged on for a share of the minor honours. She proved successful before in a Cork Grade 3 event confined to mares last December, and it would come as no surprise if she's targeted for a similar event before the year's end.
Miss Mitch(IRE), last seen at Ascot back in January, showed the lack of a run since then here. The distress signals went up rounding the home turn, but she should come on a fair bit from this comeback effort. (op 4/1 tchd 11/4)
Glencove Marina(IRE) was easy to back on his first run since winning at Navan last March. He jumped a bit deliberate at times and the writing was on the wall turning for home. He landed awkwardly at the last and his rider was quick to pull him up, but reported afterwards all was well with the former Grade 1 winning novice hurdler. He probably lacked match-fitness for his comeback effort and might be sharper following this run next time. (op 9/4 tchd 7/2)
Schelm(GER) was another to pull up, and he never got competitive before he called it a day before the second-last. (op 9/4 tchd 7/2)

1685 - 1687a (Foreign Racing) - See Raceform Interactive

1429 HUNTINGDON (R-H)
Sunday, October 3

OFFICIAL GOING: Good (8.7)
Wind: moderate against Weather: wet and warm

1688 DOMINO'S PIZZA NOVICES' HURDLE (DIV I) (8 hdls) 2m 110y

2:10 (2:11) (Class 4) 4-Y-O+ **£2,276** (£668; £334; £166)

Form RPR

6126 **1** **Occasionally Yours (IRE)**[81] 994 6-11-0 99............ MarcGoldstein(5) 120+
(Alan Blackmore) *chsd ldr: rdn to ld bef 2 out: clr bef last: r.o stoutly* **9/1**[3]

2 *8* **Betabob (IRE)**[30] 1459 7-10-12 110.................................. RichardJohnson 106
(Tim Vaughan) *led at fair pce: hit 3rd: rdn and hdd bef 2 out: one pce between last two* **6/4**[1]

00- **3** *4 1/2* **Brother Bob (IRE)**[162] 5391 4-10-12 0.................................... PaddyBrennan 102
(Charlie Longsdon) *t.k.h towards rr: effrt but plenty to do bef 3 out: wnt modest 3rd bef last: kpt on steadily but nt rch ldrs* **40/1**

4-51 **4** *8* **Emirates World (IRE)**[28] 1484 4-11-5 98.....................(t) DougieCostello 103
(Alan Jessop) *t.k.h: 4th but out of tch w ldng trio after 5th: n.d after: 8 l 4th next: nt fluent last* **11/1**

5 *7* **Incendo**[21] 4-10-12 0.. PaulMoloney 89
(James Fanshawe) *pressed ldng pair: mstke 5th: hit next and sn outpcd: wnt lft bef 2 out: lost 3rd and fading last* **5/2**[2]

04U **6** *11* **Martin Scruff (IRE)**[28] 1475 4-10-12 0........................... MattieBatchelor 79
(Michael Quinlan) *plld hrd in rr: stl last but one at 4th: no ch fr 5th: styng on wl after last* **125/1**

055/ **7** *1/2* **Trachonitis (IRE)**[6] 4996 6-10-12 93.............................(t) LeightonAspell 78
(J R Jenkins) *midfield: outpcd 5th: 5th and no ch w ldng trio next* **9/1**[3]

5- **8** *2 3/4* **Graylyn Ruby (FR)**[40] 4828 5-10-9 0......................... WayneKavanagh(3) 76
(Robin Dickin) *chsd ldrs: mstke 5th: sn lost tch* **33/1**

9 *10* **Me Fein**[198] 6-10-12 0.. DenisO'Regan 67
(Barney Curley) *midfield: lost tch after 5th: t.o* **12/1**

10 *13* **Harley Fern**[59] 4-10-5 0.. RodiGreene 48
(Terry Clement) *blnd 1st: nt fluent and wl bhd: lost tch and mstke 4th: t.o 3 out* **200/1**

0/ **11** *17* **Parisian Dream**[9] 62 6-10-5 0..................................(t) BrianToomey(7) 40
(Tim Pitt) *prom tl 4th: no ch fr next: hopelessly t.o* **100/1**

00F **P** **La Chemme**[12] 1567 4-10-5 0... JamieGoldstein —
(Reg Hollinshead) *mstke 1st: plld v hrd and last early: dashed up to press ldrs 3rd tl 4th: fdd rapidly next: t.o and p.u 2 out* **125/1**

3m 47.3s (-7.60) **Going Correction** -0.55s/f (Firm) **12** Ran SP% **113.1**
Speed ratings (Par 105): **95,91,89,85,82 76,76,75,70,64 56,—**
Tote Swingers: 1&2 £4.00, 1&3 £28.50, 2&3 £4.40 CSF £22.52 TOTE £11.30: £5.50, £1.10, £13.20; EX 32.30.
Owner A G Blackmore **Bred** Gerard Connolly **Trained** Little Berkhamsted, Herts

FOCUS
The rain had arrived at the track before racing, but it wouldn't have affected this novice hurdle that much. It was a race where it paid to race handy as the pace only got serious nearing the fourth-last and the form looks ordinary. The fourth sets the level and the form should work out.

NOTEBOOK
Occasionally Yours(IRE) ran out a ready winner on his return from an 88-day break. He was never far from the early leader and went for everything off the final turn. It was clear as he lept to the front two out he was going to take some catching, and he was comfortably on top after the last. He likes quick ground, so his success is an indication that underfoot conditions were still fine for him, and he looked suited by the positive tactics back in trip. He will struggle under a double penalty, but is entitled to come on for the run and can hold his own in handicaps this term. (op 16-1)
Betabob(IRE) came into this British debut a longstanding maiden, but was having his first outing for Tim Vaughan and was the one to beat on previous form. He dictated as he pleased, but was in trouble coming to the penultimate flight and could prove a challenge for his new trainer to place successfully. (op 15-8 after early 9-4 in a place tchd 2-1)
Brother Bob(IRE) ◆, making his seasonal/hurdling debut, would have no doubt had more of a say had he raced closer to the ordinary early gallop. He stayed on very nicely in the home straight, may well prefer a longer trip, and shouldn't be long in opening his account. (op 25-1)
Emirates World(IRE) had more on his plate than when getting off the mark in a handicap off a mark of 95 28 days earlier, and never seriously threatened. He will look more interesting back in a handicap. (op 8-1 tchd 12-1)
Incendo is rated 80 on the Flat and stays well in that sphere. His trainer also does very well with his dual-purpose performers, so everything looked in place for a big run on this switch to hurdling. He raced close to the pace, but didn't look too keen nearing the home turn and was soon beaten. It may be that a return of some headgear is required, and he is surely capable of better. (tchd 2-1)

1689 DOMINO'S PIZZA NOVICES' HURDLE (DIV II) (8 hdls) 2m 110y

2:45 (2:45) (Class 4) 4-Y-O+ **£2,276** (£668; £334; £166)

Form RPR

1 **Dark Ranger**[33] 4-10-5 .... BrianToomey(7) 106+
(Tim Pitt) *t.k.h in rr: effrt on outside and mstke 3 out: tk 2nd bef next and nt fluent: on bit tl led last: rdn out cl home* **10/1**

2 *1* **Lucy's Perfect**[108] 4-10-5 ....(b) TomScudamore 96
(David Pipe) *prom: led after 5th: rdn 2 out: in front on suffernce tl hdd last: nt qckn flat* **9/2**[2]

1 **3** *6* **Sircozy (IRE)**[34] 1433 4-11-5 .... JamieMoore 106
(Gary Moore) *settled towards rr: nt fluent 5th: hdwy but drvn next: no imp in 3rd whn hit 2 out: 5 l 3rd whn blnd last* **5/4**[1]

20-5 **4** *11* **Keep Talking (IRE)**[157] 62 6-10-9 .... AlexMerriam(3) 88
(Neil King) *bhd: rdn 5th: hdwy after 3 out: rdn 5th: wnt 4th at last: nvr nr ldrs* **8/1**[3]

2/F- **5** *8* **Sail And Return**[298] 2774 6-10-5 .... JosephAkehurst(7) 82
(Philip Middleton) *plld hrd: jnd ldrs 3rd: rdn and wknd 3 out* **10/1**

5 **6** *6* **Lindsay's Dream**[32] 1449 4-10-5 .... JamesDavies 69
(Andrew Haynes) *t.k.h pressing ldr tl after 5th: wknd next* **11/1**

0- **7** *1/2* **Citrus Mark**[311] 2522 5-10-12 .... WillKennedy 75
(Paul Webber) *prom: drvn and wknd bef 2 out* **11/1**

0-0 **8** *43* **Madman (FR)**[28] 1487 6-10-12 95 RodiGreene 36
(Christopher Kellett) *v free to s: tore off in ld: hdd after 5th and rapidly lost pl: t.o whn bad mstke last* **125/1**

0-00 **9** *9* **Welcome Wonder**[112] 733 6-9-12 0-CdtJessicaLodge(7) 21
(John Allen) *prom early: wkng whn j. slowly 4th: t.o 3 out* **50/1**

0/F- **P** **Between Dreams**[177] 5117 7-10-5 NickScholfield —
(Andy Turnell) *mstke 1st: t.k.h pressing ldrs: rdn and struggling after 5th: t.o and p.u 2 out* **100/1**

00- **P** **Cherokee Story**[250] 3679 4-10-5 TomMessenger —
(Chris Bealby) *bhd whn j.lft 2nd: rdn and struggling after 3rd: bdly t.o next: p.u 3 out* **100/1**

3m 49.9s (-5.00) **Going Correction** -0.55s/f (Firm) **11** Ran SP% **113.3**
Speed ratings (Par 105): **89,88,85,80,76 73,73,53,49,— —**
Tote Swingers: 1&2 £5.80, 1&3 £3.30, 2&3 £2.90 CSF £53.42 TOTE £8.90: £2.60, £2.10, £1.10; EX 73.50.

Owner Recycled Products Limited **Bred** Thomas G N Burrage **Trained** Norton, N Yorks

FOCUS
The second division of the novice hurdle appeared less competitive than the first, but there was a better finish and the form is rated around the third.

NOTEBOOK
Dark Ranger bounced back to winning ways on the Flat last time out, and he showed himself to be in decent heart still with a ready debut success as a hurdler. He travelled sweetly through the race and, having made smooth headway nearing the home turn, his rider looked very confident two out. He ultimately had to work a bit harder for his win than looked likely at that stage, but he is most effective on the level when equipped with cheekpieces, and they were absent here. It wouldn't be that surprising to see them back on in future, though it may also prove that he is best when delivered as late as possible in his races. Whatever the case there should be some more to come. (op 17-2)

Lucy's Perfect, plating class on the Flat, was having her first run for David Pipe on this hurdling debut and attracted support. She went clear into the home turn, but began to idle nearing two out and proved hard work for her rider. She rallied under pressure and, while it's not hard to see why she wears headgear, connections ought to place her successfully before all that long. (op 6-1 tchd 4-1)

Sircozy(IRE) won on debut over C&D last month and that form has worked out nicely since. He came under pressure soon after making up his ground from off the pace, and lacked the pace to get seriously involved. It may be he needs a stiffer test, but his tail was swishing around under maximum pressure, and he now has a bit to prove. (tchd 6-5 and 6-4)

Keep Talking(IRE) was returning from a 157-day break and was backed earlier in the day. He proved laboured from three out and the run looked needed. (op 7-1 tchd 17-2)

1690 JOHN AND SUE GOLDEN WEDDING H'CAP CHASE (16 fncs) 2m 4f 110y
3:30 (3:30) (Class 3) (0-135,130) 4-Y-O+ **£5,529** (£1,623; £811; £405)

Form RPR

0-U2 **1** **Songe (FR)**[131] 464 6-11-4 122 RichardJohnson 143+
(Charlie Longsdon) *nt a fluent: dropped out last tl 9th: prog and blnd 12th: led gng wl 2 out: sn dashed clr: easily* **11/4**[1]

211P **2** *12* **Kirkhammerton (IRE)**[28] 1486 8-10-8 115 DannyCook(3) 119
(Barry Leavy) *cl up tl 5th: in rr and pushed along 8th: last and rdn next: stl 6th 3 out: kpt on wl after: snatched 2nd but no match for wnr* **14/1**

/F0- **3** *hd* **Picts Hill**[191] 4868 10-11-4 122 DenisO'Regan 128
(Anthony Honeyball) *j.w: prom: led 8th tl 3 out: rdn and kpt on gamely fr next: no ch w wnr* **14/1**

U246 **4** *3 3/4* **Kikos (FR)**[9] 1606 8-10-13 117 SamJones 118
(Renee Robeson) *prom: led 3 out tl rdn and nt fluent next: lost two pls in fnl 100yds* **12/1**

3P6- **5** *3/4* **Russian Flag (FR)**[170] 5208 7-11-9 130 AlexMerriam(3) 130
(Neil King) *hld up and bhd: prog 11th: tried to cl after 3 out: ch of 2nd at last: rdn and fnd little flat* **14/1**

-063 **6** *3 1/4* **Ursis (FR)**[11] 1577 9-11-0 118 TomScudamore 117
(Steve Gollings) *j. poorly: led tl 8th: remained prom tl mstke 3 out: btn whn j. bdly rt and blnd 2 out* **11/1**

-441 **7** *32* **Viable**[78] 1023 8-10-13 124 MissGAndrews(7) 92
(Pam Sly) *bhd: mstke 10th and lost tch: t.o whn j.rt and hit wing 2 out* **8/1**[3]

2P-P **P** **Leamington Lad (IRE)**[127] 523 7-11-7 125 (b) PaddyBrennan —
(Nigel Twiston-Davies) *j. slowly 1st: frequently lacked fluency: prom tl 8th: nt fluent 10th and dropped out rapidly: t.o and p.u 2 out* **4/1**[2]

0F3- **P** **Isn't That Lucky**[177] 5111 7-11-7 130 MrSWaley-Cohen(5) —
(Jonjo O'Neill) *taken v wd in rr: j. slowly 1st and 2nd: j.lft fr 9th: struggling whn j. bdly lft 12th: rdr lost iron and p.u* **4/1**[2]

4m 57.6s (-7.70) **Going Correction** -0.175s/f (Good) **9** Ran SP% **113.8**
Speed ratings (Par 107): **107,102,102,100,100 99,87,—,—**
Tote Swingers: 1&2 £8.00, 1&3 £7.00, 2&3 £17.30 CSF £38.31 CT £456.04 TOTE £3.70: £1.20, £5.50, £4.00; EX 45.10 Trifecta £282.50 Pool: £511.69 - 1.34 winning units..

Owner Alan Halsall **Bred** Alec Head And Mme Ghislaine Head **Trained** Over Norton, Oxon

FOCUS
An open-looking handicap and an easy winner. The placed horses are rated to their old form.

NOTEBOOK
Songe(FR), very well backed, eventually ran out an easy winner to finally open his account as a chaser. He was having his third consecutive outing at the track and his seventh over fences. Returning from a 131-day absence, he bided his time and began his move nearing the fourth-last. He wasn't brilliant when in the firing line two out, but was better again at the last when in control and this should boost his confidence no end. The handicapper will raise him, but he was a Grade 2 winner over hurdles and will still look well treated off his new mark if building on this. (op 4-1 tchd 5-2)

Kirkhammerton(IRE) was pulled up on his previous outing and things didn't look so good passing the stands for the first time, as he began to jump slowly. He then got outpaced on the final circuit, but rallied off the home bend and this was more encouraging again. He can find easier assignments. (op 12-1 tchd 11-1)

Picts Hill got a positive ride on this seasonal return and only began to feel the pinch at the top of the home straight. He can build on this. (op 11-1)

Kikos(FR), who attracted some support, took it up around three out yet was unable to raise his game when the winner challenged at the next. This was a step back in the right direction on ground easy enough for him, but he doesn't look an imminent winner. (op 10-1 tchd 9-1)

Russian Flag(FR) wasn't disgraced under top weight over a trip he finds stretching him, and ought to come on nicely for the run. (op 12-1 tchd 10-1)

Viable Official explanation: jockey said gelding was unsuited by the good ground

Leamington Lad(IRE) went in snatches and failed to jump with any fluency from an early stage, and has now been pulled up on his last three outings. (tchd 5-1)

Isn't That Lucky proved easy to back on this return to action, and was in trouble before he began jumping badly to his left on the final circuit. He ought to come on plenty for this, but it does leave him with a little to prove. (tchd 5-1)

1691 EVENTGUARD TILLEY JUVENILE HURDLE (8 hdls) 2m 110y
4:05 (4:05) (Class 4) 3-Y-O **£2,602** (£764; £382; £190)

Form RPR

10 **1** **Joan D'Arc (IRE)**[8] 1610 3-10-5 0 MrJMQuinlan(7) 91
(Michael Quinlan) *pressed ldrs: led bef 3 out: rdn and kpt finding ex after: hld on gamely* **5/1**[3]

1 **2** *nk* **Kahfre**[14] 1545 3-11-5 0 JamieMoore 98
(Gary Moore) *prom: w wnr fr 3 out: drvn bef next: ev ch after: outbattled cl home* **6/4**[1]

35 **3** *1 1/2* **Doyenne Dream**[28] 1473 3-10-5 0 FelixDeGiles 82
(James Eustace) *chsd ldrs: 5th and rdn bef 3 out: wavered lft bef next: 3rd at last: rdn and kpt on flat but a hld* **16/1**

2 **4** *5* **Bubbly Braveheart (IRE)**[20] 1298 3-10-12 0 JamesDavies 85
(Alan Bailey) *cl up and t.k.h: mstke 4th: 3rd and drvn bef 2 out: 4th at last: no ex flat* **9/2**[2]

5 *3 1/4* **Jinksy Minx**[78] 3-10-5 0 ColinBolger 75
(Suzy Smith) *hld up: effrt bef 3 out: sn rdn and no imp: 10 l 5th whn mstke last* **50/1**

6 *15* **Always Roses**[51] 3-10-5 0 TomMessenger 61
(Chris Bealby) *v green: j. slowly 1st: lost tch and j.v.slowly 4th* **33/1**

31U0 **7** *nk* **Joe Rua (USA)**[8] 1610 3-10-12 100 MissGAndrews(7) 75
(John Ryan) *j. slowly 1st: lost tch 4th: remote fr next* **20/1**

8 *4 1/2* **Baggsy (IRE)**[108] 3-10-5 0 MattieBatchelor 57
(Julia Feilden) *hld up: effrt bef 4th: rdn and looked wkng whn mstke 3 out: wl btn after* **40/1**

9 *2 3/4* **Motirani**[18] 3-10-12 0 GerardTumelty 62
(Jeff Pearce) *hrd rdn and lost tch 5th: hung lft bef 2 out* **7/1**

P020 **10** *1/2* **A P Ling**[33] 1442 3-10-5 82 DarylJacob 54
(Christopher Kellett) *led: nt fluent 5th: rdn and hdd bef 3 out: qckly lost pl bef next* **33/1**

11 *38* **Omaruru (IRE)**[67] 3-10-12 0 SamJones 27
(Renee Robeson) *plld hrd and prom tl mstke 4th: wknd bef 3 out: bdly t.o* **14/1**

P **Both Ends Burning (IRE)**[35] 3-10-2 0 HarryHaynes(3) —
(John Wainwright) *bhd: struggling 4th: t.o and p.u 3 out* **100/1**

3m 53.1s (-1.80) **Going Correction** -0.55s/f (Firm) **12** Ran SP% **115.9**
Speed ratings (Par 103): **82,81,81,78,77 70,70,67,66,66 48,—**
Tote Swingers: 1&2 £2.10, 1&3 £13.10, 2&3 £5.30 CSF £12.28 TOTE £5.80: £2.20, £1.10, £2.20; EX 13.20.

Owner Newtown Anner Stud Farm Ltd **Bred** Lynn Lodge Stud **Trained** Newmarket, Suffolk

FOCUS
A weak juvenile event in which few landed a serious blow. The form is easy to rate around the second and fourth.

NOTEBOOK
Joan D'Arc(IRE) resumed winning ways with a narrow success under her inexperienced rider, who is now 2-2 aboard her. She bombed out in a much better event at Market Rasen last time, but found this company a lot more to her liking, and her rider's 7lb claim no doubt made the difference. Things will be much tougher from now on. (op 9-2 tchd 11-2)

Kahfre held every chance to follow up his debut success at Plumpton a fortnight earlier, but was always just being held by the winner. He still emerges as the best horse at the weights, looked as though he would enjoy a stiffer test in time here, and still appears a bargain purchase for current connections. (op 7-4 tchd 15-8)

Doyenne Dream, in front of the winner when well beaten at Market Rasen 28 days earlier, got outpaced but rallied strongly after the second-last flight. This was her best effort so far, and she is surely capable of winning in this sphere, but looks to need a stiffer test all the same. (op 12-1)

Bubbly Braveheart(IRE) finished a well-beaten second on debut two runs back and didn't offer too much back on the level last time out. This was more like it from him considering he took time to settle, and he will find his level as a hurdler as he becomes more streetwise. (op 5-1)

1692 HUNTINGDON-RACECOURSE.CO.UK H'CAP HURDLE (10 hdls) 2m 4f 110y
4:45 (4:55) (Class 3) (0-120,122) 4-Y-O+ **£4,553** (£1,337; £668; £333)

Form RPR

5P3- **1** **Rathcor**[169] 5231 8-11-5 120 TrevorWhelan(7) 132+
(Ian Williams) *confidently rdn in rr: smooth prog 3 out: led bef next: 3 l clr whn wnt rt last: pushed out: readily* **4/1**[1]

-235 **2** *4* **Aohna (FR)**[84] 958 5-11-3 111 WayneHutchinson 120+
(Alan King) *settled towards rr: hdwy 5th: led on ins wl bef 2 out: sn hdd and rdn: no imp after: hit last* **5/1**[2]

3214 **3** *12* **Celticello (IRE)**[8] 1609 8-11-7 122 MrJMQuinlan(7) 119
(Michael Quinlan) *pressed ldrs: rdn bef 2 out: no ex: 14 l 4th whn mstke last: wnt mod 3rd flat* **7/1**[3]

4-23 **4** *nk* **Woodmore (IRE)**[127] 514 6-11-2 110 FelixDeGiles 107
(Charlie Longsdon) *prom: led 3 out: rdn and hdd wl bef next: stl 3rd at last: tied up bdly flat* **17/2**

1530 **5** *7* **Stage Acclaim (IRE)**[8] 1609 5-11-10 118 (v[1]) JamieMoore 109
(Dr Richard Newland) *bhd: effrt after 7th: sn drvn: btn bef 2 out: racd awkwardly flat* **7/1**[3]

5-U5 **6** *6* **Cruchain (IRE)**[84] 954 7-11-7 115 APMcCoy 100
(Jonjo O'Neill) *disp ld: hdd and nt fluent 3 out: fnd nthing bef next: nt hrd pressed whn btn* **9/1**

F-4F **7** *9* **Predateur (FR)**[128] 499 7-11-12 120 DavidEngland 97
(Giles Smyly) *cl up tl 5th: lost tch 7th* **40/1**

013P **8** *35* **Kristallo (GER)**[25] 1507 5-10-11 105 (v) SamJones 50
(Paul Webber) *t.k.h: w ldr tl rdn 3 out: lost pl tamely: eased after next: t.o* **9/1**

15F- **9** *40* **Vivarini**[188] 4930 6-11-2 113 AdamPogson(3) 22
(Caroline Bailey) *hung lft in last: detached whn nt fluent 3rd and 5th: t.o whn climbed 3 out: j. violently lft last* **10/1**

S26- **P** **The Rainbow Hunter**[190] 4891 6-11-3 118 EdCookson(7) —
(Andy Turnell) *t.k.h: pressed ldrs tl nt fluent 6th: lost tch next: t.o and eased after 3 out: p.u last* **10/1**

4m 43.4s (-15.60) **Going Correction** -0.55s/f (Firm)
WFA 4 from 5yo+ 10lb **10** Ran SP% **112.8**
Speed ratings (Par 107): **107,105,100,100,98 95,92,79,63,—**
Tote Swingers: 1&2 £4.90, 1&3 £4.80, 2&3 £3.90 CSF £23.84 CT £133.22 TOTE £6.20: £1.50, £1.20, £2.90; EX 22.00.

Owner Playboy Kennels **Bred** Helshaw Grange Stud Ltd **Trained** Portway, Worcs

FOCUS
A wide-open handicap. It was run at a fair gallop, but the majority raced in a tight bunch until things began to get more serious nearing the fourth-last. The form looks pretty solid.

NOTEBOOK

Rathcor, without his usual tongue-tie, was very well backed on this return to the track and he came home a ready winner. He was given a well-judged ride and could have been called the winner jumping two out. He didn't do a great deal out in front, but was always in control and has clearly done well for his time off the track. He ought to be competitive off a likely higher mark, but he has now been at his best first time out the last two seasons, and his profile suggests he is one to oppose again next time. (op 6-1 tchd 7-2)

Aohna(FR) was produced with every chance on this first run for 84 days. She finished a clear second-best and is a consistent performer, but the handicapper probably has her where he wants her. (tchd 9-2 and 11-2)

Celticello(IRE) proved easy to back on this drop in grade. He moved nicely though the race, but couldn't go with the leaders from three out. He rates a fair benchmark for the form. (op 11-2 tchd 5-1)

Woodmore(IRE), placed on his last two outings, was making his handicap debut for a new yard in good form and had his chance. He ultimately left the impression this return from a 127-day break would do him good, though. (op 9-1 tchd 10-1)

1693 EMMA AND MEGAN DEANUS NOVICES' CHASE (12 fncs) 2m 110y

5:20 (5:24) (Class 3) 4-Y-0+ **£5,529** (£1,623; £811; £405)

Form / RPR

2F-1 **1** **Cockney Trucker (IRE)**[145] 265 8-11-8 135............... RichardJohnson 146+
(Philip Hobbs) *v exubernt in ld: set fast pce: mstke 3rd: hrd pressed 3 out: crashed through next but sn drew clr: readily* **7/2**[3]

0- **2** *17* **Rock Noir (FR)**[198] 4711 5-11-2 0............................ APMcCoy 130+
(Jonjo O'Neill) *plld hrd and tended to pay scant regard to fences: a 2nd: mstke 2nd: effrt and hit 3 out: ev ch whn hit 2 out: sn outpcd: eased last* **8/11**[1]

6-11 **3** *11* **Cootehill (IRE)**[12] 1568 6-11-12 0.................................... PaddyBrennan 122
(Nigel Twiston-Davies) *several shoddy jumps: a 3rd or 4th: 3rd and struggling whn mstkes 8th and next: no ch after* **11/4**[2]

4-0F **4** *6* **Hi Tide (IRE)**[28] 1485 6-11-2 0.. DenisO'Regan 104
(J R Jenkins) *mstke 3rd: chsd ldng pair and nt a fluent: 4th and outpcd 8th: continued wl bhd* **66/1**

F-30 **5** *44* **Wade Farm Billy (IRE)**[115] 687 6-11-2 0........................... JamieMoore 65
(Gary Moore) *a 5th: t.o whn j. slowly 4th* **25/1**

500- **P** **Highland Storm**[333] 2061 4-10-6 0..............................(t) RodiGreene —
(Ben Pollock) *t.o 1st: appalling jump 4th: climbed 5th: p.u next* **150/1**

4m 5.20s (-5.00) **Going Correction** -0.175s/f (Good)
WFA 4 from 5yo+ 9lb **6 Ran SP% 112.8**
Speed ratings (Par 107): **104,96,90,88,67** —
Tote Swingers: 1&2 £1.50, 1&3 £1.50, 2&3 £1.20 CSF £6.95 TOTE £4.30: £1.70, £1.20; EX 8.30.
Owner Mrs Karola Vann **Bred** Gerald Monahan **Trained** Withycombe, Somerset

FOCUS

A very interesting little novice chase, run at a decent gallop. The form is rated around the first two.

NOTEBOOK

Cockney Trucker(IRE) was last seen belatedly opening his account over fences at Newton Abbot in May, and he followed up under his penalty by making all. He looked a sitting duck turning for home as Rock Noir loomed up and walked through the penultimate fence, but that rival soon fell in a hole and he had the race in the bag coming to the last. It's likely he is a touch flattered by this and he still has something to learn in the jumping department, but it was a likeable effort all the same. He likes a sound surface and can make his mark in handicap company this term. (op 9-2)

Rock Noir(FR), who bombed out under top weight in the County Hurdle on debut for connections back in March, was a Grade 1 winning hurdler in France and proved all the rage for this chasing debut. He was equipped with a cross-noseband and took a grip to post, though, so it wasn't that surprising to see him run with the choke out through the race. His fencing was somewhat mixed as he got in too low at times, but he still appeared the most likely winner coming out of the back straight. He found nothing when asked to get to the front nearing two out, however, and ultimately paid for doing too much early on. This experience should not be lost on him and softer ground should be more up his street, but he is evidently a headstrong character. (op 5-6)

Cootehill(IRE) arrived here unbeaten in two outings as a chaser and his yard remains in decent form. He did look better the further he went when upped to 2m4f last time out though, and he got badly outpaced on this return to the minimum, which affected his jumping. He faced a stiff task conceding weight all round in any case, and he should show his true colours back over a stiffer test, but may not be the easiest to place. (tchd 3-1)

Hi Tide(IRE) was faced with a very tough assignment, but he shaped fairly well and this should restore his confidence. (op 40-1)

1694 BOOK YOUR CHRISTMAS PARTY AT HUNTINGDON H'CAP HURDLE (12 hdls) 3m 2f

5:55 (5:55) (Class 5) (0-95,91) 4-Y-0+ **£1,951** (£573; £286; £143)

Form / RPR

004- **1** **Rey Nacarado (IRE)**[175] 5157 5-11-1 90...................... PeterCarberry(10) 104+
(Charlie Longsdon) *settled 3rd and gng wl: chal 3 out: sn led and drew clr: 10 l ahd whn blnd last: eased fnl 100yds* **10/3**[1]

3244 **2** *16* **Heezagrey (IRE)**[28] 1483 7-10-3 75.................................. MarkQuinlan(7) 71
(James Evans) *midfield: rdn 8th: sn outpcd: 17 l 3rd 2 out: drvn into poor 2nd cl home* **4/1**[2]

-663 **3** *½* **Saddlewood (IRE)**[28] 1479 7-11-6 85..............................(tp) DarylJacob 81
(Jamie Snowden) *led at gd pce and abt 6 l clr mostly: rdn and hdd 3 out: sn no ch w wnr: lost 2nd nr fin* **8/1**

P3P6 **4** *22* **Kingston Queen (IRE)**[14] 1559 7-11-1 80.............(b[1]) ChristianWilliams 56
(Rachel Hobbs) *racd wd in rr: effrt 9th: disputing 3rd whn mstke 3 out: nt keen after and plodded on* **12/1**

P35P **5** *14* **Cute N You Know It**[43] 1341 7-10-3 71.....................(v) FearghalDavis(3) 34
(Andrew Crook) *chsd ldr tl rdn bef 9th: dropped rt out after next: t.o* **10/1**

3P30 **6** *15* **Barlin Bay**[10] 1592 6-10-11 76....................................(b[1]) TomScudamore 26
(David Pipe) *in rr: rdn bef 9th: no rspnse: t.o bef 2 out* **6/1**[3]

0P00 **U** **Oniz Tiptoes (IRE)**[26] 1501 9-11-8 90.........................(v) HarryHaynes(3) —
(John Wainwright) *mstke 1st and uns rdr* **10/1**

4316 **P** **Mista Rossa**[27] 1490 5-11-7 91....................................... MissLHorner(5) —
(Jamie Snowden) *last pair: struggling 8th: t.o and p.u 3 out: dismntd* **6/1**[3]

-050 **P** **Delgany Gunner**[105] 795 6-10-6 71.................................(t) DenisO'Regan —
(Ben Pollock) *chsd ldrs tl wknd and mstke 8th: sn hopelessly t.o: hopped over 3 out and p.u* **25/1**

6m 15.6s (-7.30) **Going Correction** -0.55s/f (Firm) **9 Ran SP% 112.5**
Speed ratings (Par 103): **89,84,83,77,72 68,—,—,—**
Tote Swingers: 1&2 £3.80, 1&3 £4.80, 2&3 £4.00 CSF £16.89 CT £95.61 TOTE £4.10: £1.20, £1.90, £2.30; EX 19.40 Place 6: £10.21 Place 5: £5.52..
Owner Runthatbymeagainagain **Bred** Sweet Wall **Trained** Over Norton, Oxon

FOCUS

A moderate handicap, weakened by the non-runner. It was run at a sound gallop and the placed horses set the level.

NOTEBOOK

Rey Nacarado(IRE) shot clear when asked for his effort off the home turn and had the race fully in the bag prior to hitting the last. This former winning pointer didn't show a lot after joining connections last season, but did post his best effort when upped to 3m on his final outing, and his yard's horses are going well at present. The handicapper will make things tricky for him if taking this form too literally, but he should be treated as an improver and always has the option of going chasing this term. (op 4-1)

Heezagrey(IRE) failed to land a blow after being held up and only grabbed second place near the finish. He remains a longstanding maiden. (op 7-2)

Saddlewood(IRE) was given an aggressive ride on this big step up in trip and ran well, but failed to see it out under such tactics. He could well bag one of these when eased slightly in distance. (op 15-2 tchd 6-1)

Kingston Queen(IRE) had first-time blinkers replacing cheekpieces and, not for the first time, hit a flat spot before plugging on again towards the finish. (op 16-1)

Mista Rossa never looked that happy out the back and was eventually pulled up with something going amiss. (op 5-1)

T/Jkpt: Not won. T/Plt: £12.60 to a £1 stake. Pool of £50,998.29 - 2,946.47 winning tickets. T/Qpdt: £10.10 to a £1 stake. Pool of £3,896.61 - 283 winning tickets. IM

393 KELSO (L-H)

Sunday, October 3

OFFICIAL GOING: Good (6.8)
Wind: Almost nil Weather: Overcast, drizzling

1695 SUNDAY MAIL H'CAP HURDLE (8 hdls) 2m 110y

2:25 (2:25) (Class 4) (0-115,115) 4-Y-0+ **£3,903** (£1,146; £573; £286)

Form / RPR

0335 **1** **Midnite Blews (IRE)**[72] 1082 5-9-11 89..........................(t) RyanMania(3) 93
(Maurice Barnes) *cl up: led 2nd: mde rest: drvn and styd on strly fr last* **8/1**

062- **2** *2* **Sumak (FR)**[174] 5166 6-11-3 106.. GrahamLee 108
(Ferdy Murphy) *hld up in midfield: effrt on ins 2 out: chsd wnr fnl 200yds: r.o* **8/1**

02-2 **3** *1½* **Grand Diamond (IRE)**[11] 1574 6-10-10 102..............(p) EwanWhillans(3) 103
(Jim Goldie) *t.k.h: hld up on outside: hdwy and in tch 3 out: rdn and one pce after last* **4/1**[1]

344- **4** *¾* **Cast Iron Casey (IRE)**[167] 5274 8-11-12 115................ WilsonRenwick 115
(P Monteith) *hld up towards rr: drvn bef 2 out: kpt on run-in: nrst fin* **7/1**[3]

0-00 **5** *½* **Long Distance (FR)**[28] 1484 5-10-6 95........................(p) PeterBuchanan 94
(Lucinda Russell) *hld up: rdn and hdwy whn mstke 2 and outpcd 2 out: styd on fr last* **22/1**

1012 **6** *1½* **Dream Risk (FR)**[34] 1427 4-11-5 108.............................(t) RichieMcGrath 106
(Kate Walton) *t.k.h: chsd wnr: rdn 2 out: lost 2nd and no ex last 200yds* **7/1**[3]

2210 **7** *½* **Front Rank (IRE)**[10] 1597 10-11-0 110........................... MissECSayer(7) 107
(Dianne Sayer) *led to 2nd: cl up: rdn 2 out: no ex run-in* **22/1**

5215 **8** *3¼* **Golden Future**[15] 1406 7-11-3 106....................................... BrianHughes 100
(Peter Niven) *trckd ldrs: pushed along 2 out: no ex fr last* **12/1**

34P **9** *1¾* **Tiger King (GER)**[20] 1502 9-9-11 89 oh1.................(p) CampbellGillies(3) 81
(P Monteith) *hld up: rdn bef 2 out: nvr rchd ldrs* **12/1**

10 *5* **Eventide**[30] 1461 5-10-4 98.. CDMaxwell(5) 85
(Sean Thornton, Ire) *trckd ldrs: rdn 3 out: wknd after next* **13/2**[2]

PP0- **11** *¾* **Knock Three Times (IRE)**[31] 4752 4-10-9 105.......(t) MissLAlexander(7) 92
(Wilf Storey) *hld up: pushed along after 3 out: wknd fr next* **25/1**

P06/ **12** *3½* **Park's Prodigy**[20] 1952 6-11-5 108.. PaddyAspell 91
(Geoffrey Harker) *t.k.h: prom tl wknd fr 2 out* **11/1**

PF/0 **13** *64* **Lofty Leader (IRE)**[84] 948 11-9-7 89 oh7.................. GaryRutherford(7) 8
(Harriet Graham) *cl up: lost pl bef 4th: hit next: nt fluent 3 out: sn lost tch* **100/1**

3m 59.2s (-2.60) **Going Correction** -0.275s/f (Good)
WFA 4 from 5yo+ 9lb **13 Ran SP% 117.8**
Speed ratings (Par 105): **95,94,93,93,92 92,91,90,89,87 86,85,55**
Tote Swingers: 1&2 £31.10, 1&3 £9.50, 2&3 £22.20 CSF £67.01 TOTE £11.80: £2.80, £2.40, £1.10; EX 113.80.
Owner Minstrel's Double Racing **Bred** Lodge Park Stud **Trained** Farlam, Cumbria

FOCUS

A decent sized field for this handicap hurdle but the gallop was modest until three from home. The winner is rated close to his best with the second and fourth to their marks.

NOTEBOOK

Midnite Blews(IRE), who was backed beforehand, took the lead after the second flight and made the rest of the running, sticking on gamely on the flat. The ten-week break had clearly freshened him up. Official explanation: trainer said, regarding apparent improvement in form, that the gelding was better suited by reverting back to hurdles and a 72-day break after its last run. (op 12-1)

Sumak(FR) ♦, another returning from a break, finished well having still been at the rear turning in. This should bring him on and easier ground could enable him to get off the mark. (op 15-2)

Grand Diamond(IRE) has been on good form both on the Flat and over hurdles. He had his chance in the straight but could not quicken after the last. (tchd 5-1)

Cast Iron Casey(IRE) was another held up at the back of the field and only ran on after the last but too late to trouble the principals. (op 11-2 tchd 5-1)

Long Distance(FR) was also held up at the back of the field and ran on too late to trouble the principals. (tchd 20-1)

Dream Risk(FR), another who has been in good form, was always close up and had every chance. She jumped the last in third but weakened on the climb to the line. A flatter track seems to suit her better.

Eventide, the Irish challenger, tracked the leaders but weakened from the penultimate flight. (op 7-1 tchd 15-2)

1696 URWIN HALF CENTURY JUVENILE HURDLE (DIV I) (8 hdls) 2m 110y

2:55 (2:55) (Class 4) 3-Y-O **£2,471** (£725; £362; £181)

Form / RPR

1 **1** **Turf Trivia**[34] 1422 3-11-5 0.. BarryKeniry 94+
(George Moore) *trckd ldrs: effrt and led last: styd on strly to go clr last 200yds* **9/4**[1]

2 *4½* **Almutaham (USA)**[17] 3-10-12 0.. PaddyAspell 83
(James Moffatt) *prom: hdwy to chal after 3 out: rdn bef next: kpt on fr last tl no ex fnl 200yds* **9/1**[3]

5 **3** *4½* **Henry Havelock**[46] 629 3-10-12 0.. PeterBuchanan 79
(Chris Grant) *trckd ldrs: rdn and outpcd bef 4th: rallied and prom bef 3 out: kpt on same pce fr next* **16/1**

4 *nk* **Maison Brillet (IRE)**[41] 3-10-9 0................................ JamesO'Farrell(3) 79
(Howard Johnson) *nt fluent on occasions: hld up: rdn 3 out: kpt on fr last: n.m.r briefly run-in: nvr rchd ldrs* **6/1**[2]

P **5** *7* **Quitao (GER)**[11] 1576 3-10-9 0 ....(p) CampbellGillies(3) 75
(P Monteith) *t.k.h: w ldrs: led after 4 out to last: hrd rdn and hung rt run-in: wknd last 200yds* **100/1**

6 *25* **Acol**[30] 3-10-5 0 .... AlexanderVoy(7) 50
(George Foster) *trckd ldrs: lost pl bef 4th: rallied and prom bef 3 out: wknd next* **20/1**

46 **7** *1 1/4* **Rhyton (IRE)**[10] 1586 3-10-9 0 ....(t) AdrianLane(3) 49
(Donald McCain) *cl up: chal after 3rd: reminders 1/2-way: wknd bef 3 out* **10/1**

8 *1/2* **Capricornus (USA)**[186] 3-10-12 0 .... GrahamLee 49
(Ferdy Murphy) *hld up: stdy hdwy and in tch 3 out: rdn and wknd bef next* **9/4**[1]

P **9** *54* **Weetentherty**[11] 1576 3-10-12 0 ....(p) RichieMcGrath —
(Jim Goldie) *t.k.h: mde most to after 4 out: wknd fr next: eased whn no ch run-in* **33/1**

10 *5* **Elie Shore**[166] 3-10-2 0 ....(t) RyanMania(3) —
(Maurice Barnes) *nt fluent on occasions: bhd: hit and struggling 4 out: sn btn: eased whn no ch run-in* **22/1**

3m 59.7s (-2.10) **Going Correction** -0.275s/f (Good) **10** Ran SP% **113.8**
Speed ratings (Par 103): **93,90,88,88,85 73,72,72,47,44**
Tote Swingers: 1&2 £6.60, 1&3 £5.40, 2&3 £37.40 CSF £22.67 TOTE £2.90: £1.10, £4.20, £6.10; EX 29.10.
Owner Mrs Mary Hatfield & Mrs Susan Kramer **Bred** London Thoroughbred Services Ltd **Trained** Middleham Moor, N Yorks
■ Stewards' Enquiry : Campbell Gillies caution: careless riding.

FOCUS
The first division of this juvenile hurdle, few with experience and most of the runners were moderate performers on the Flat. In the end two came clear and the winner sets the standard.

NOTEBOOK
Turf Trivia, the only previous winner in the field, was never far away and, when he took the lead at the last, looked sure to score easily. However, he had to be driven out to hold off the runner-up, and a less stiff finish might suit him better. He may go for the Wensleydale Hurdle at the end of the month. (op 11-4)
Almutaham(USA) stayed 1m6f on the Flat and ran well on this hurdling debut. He battled back after the last and should be up to winning a similar event before the better performers come out. (op 12-1)
Henry Havelock lost a good early pitch and looked in trouble when ridden at the last on the far side. However, he ran on again at the finish and looks in need of a stiffer test or stronger gallop. (op 18-1 tchd 20-1)
Maison Brillet(IRE) was held up at the rear on this hurdling debut and looked to be making no headway until staying on after the last. He was a 6-7f winner on the Flat but appeared to get the trip well enough. (op 4-1)
Quitao(GER) improved considerably on his hurdling debut on soft and this better ground clearly helped. (op 125-1)
Capricornus(USA), an all-weather winner having his first start on turf and first over hurdles, was held up at the rear and made only limited headway from that position. (op 2-1 tchd 11-4)

1697 STARK MAIN ACCOUNTANTS H'CAP CHASE (19 fncs) 3m 1f
3:40 (3:42) (Class 4) (0-115,113) 4-Y-O+ **£3,577** (£1,050; £525; £262)

Form RPR

0/1- **1** **La Pantera Rosa (IRE)**[514] 194 7-10-7 **94** ....(p) BarryKeniry 106+
(Micky Hammond) *trckd ldrs: led 11th: mde rest: styd on strly u.p fr last* **8/1**

/5F- **2** *2 1/2* **Casadei (IRE)**[11] 1584 11-10-10 **97** ....(tp) BrianHughes 107
(T G McCourt, Ire) *trckd ldrs: wnt 2nd 14th: effrt between last 2: kpt on u.p run-in* **5/1**[2]

5PP- **3** *11* **Coldwells (IRE)**[167] 5271 10-10-1 **91** .... CampbellGillies(3) 92
(Martin Todhunter) *cl up: lft in ld 6th: hdd 11th: blnd next: rdn and outpcd 3 out: rallied and cl up last: wknd run-in* **11/2**[3]

6U/2 **4** *6* **Festival King (IRE)**[26] 1500 8-10-6 **93** .... TimmyMurphy 86
(Pauline Robson) *hld up: stdy hdwy on outside to trck ldrs 4 out: effrt 2 out: edgd lft and wknd run-in* **11/8**[1]

5P- **5** *15* **Not Left Yet (IRE)**[183] 4980 9-11-12 **113** .... WilsonRenwick 95
(P Monteith) *hld up: shkn up whn blnd bdly 4 out: sn n.d* **14/1**

2015 **6** *4* **Seize**[36] 1404 8-11-11 **112** .... GrahamLee 88
(Ferdy Murphy) *hld up: stdy hdwy and in tch 4 out: rdn and wknd fr next* **9/1**

PP-0 **7** *3 1/4* **Nelliedonethat (IRE)**[148] 213 10-10-10 **97** .... PeterBuchanan 73
(Lucinda Russell) *led tl blnd and hdd 6th: cl up: lost pl 10th: hit 12th: struggling fr 14th* **14/1**

-060 **8** *9* **Toulouse Express (IRE)**[105] 804 11-11-1 **102** ....(b) KennyJohnson 67
(Robert Johnson) *t.k.h: in tch: hit 8th: rdn and wknd after 15th* **25/1**

6m 28.0s (-3.50) **Going Correction** 0.0s/f (Good) **8** Ran SP% **112.4**
Speed ratings (Par 105): **105,104,100,98,93 92,91,88**
Tote Swingers: 1&2 £13.40, 1&3 £10.20, 2&3 £5.80 TOTE £8.70: £2.40, £2.00, £1.30; EX 69.10.
Owner Nick Rust **Bred** A W Buller **Trained** Middleham Moor, N Yorks

FOCUS
A run-of-the-mill handicap chase but a game winner. The form could be rated a little higher.

NOTEBOOK
La Pantera Rosa(IRE), having his first run since May 2009, took over with just over a circuit to go and galloped on gamely under pressure. He will need time to get over this, but handles any ground and appears on the upgrade. (op 11-1 tchd 12-1)
Casadei(IRE) has not won since June 2005 but came into this in reasonable form. He did not help himself by making a mistake at the second-last, but still had every chance after the final fence, only to find the winner refusing to be denied. (op 6-1 tchd 13-2 and 9-2)
Coldwells(IRE), having her first run since the spring, was left in the lead at the fifth and rallied after losing the lead at the 11th and making a mistake at the next. (op 8-1 tchd 17-2)
Festival King(IRE) was held up before making steady headway to track the leaders into the straight. He faded from the last though, and he may have bounced after his good effort after a long break last month. (tchd 11-10)
Not Left Yet(IRE) has not had much racing of late but did hint that some of his former ability remains. (op 12-1 tchd 11-1)
Seize made ground from the rear but the effort was short-lived and he seems to have lost his way since his success in July. (op 7-1 tchd 6-1)

1698 NSPCC SCHOOL SERVICE INTERMEDIATE HURDLE (11 hdls) 2m 6f 110y
4:15 (4:15) (Class 3) 4-Y-O+ **£4,553** (£1,337; £668; £333)

Form RPR

2140 **1** **Now This Is It (IRE)**[8] 1609 6-11-1 135 .... MrBGCrawford(7) 136
(S R B Crawford, Ire) *hld up: stdy hdwy bef 2 out: effrt and swtchd lft after last: edgd lft and led last 100yds: hld on wl* **11/4**[2]

500- **2** *nk* **Any Given Day (IRE)**[198] 4711 5-11-5 137 .... AdrianLane(3) 136
(Donald McCain) *trckd ldrs: shkn up to ld last: sn rdn: hdd last 100yds: kpt on* **11/8**[1]

31- **3** *4 1/2* **Strongpoint (IRE)**[73] 1075 6-10-12 127 ....(t) GrahamLee 122
(Patrick Griffin, Ire) *t.k.h: led: rdn 2 out: hdd last: rallied: flashed tail and no ex last 100yds* **3/1**[3]

P-UP **4** *12* **Glaced Over**[10] 1593 5-9-12 0 .... GaryRutherford(7) 104
(Raymond Shiels) *nt fluent: prom tl rdn and wknd last* **40/1**

-313 **5** *12* **Grand Zouki (FR)**[26] 1499 5-11-8 126 .... BarryKeniry 110
(George Moore) *trckd ldrs tl wknd bef 2 out* **8/1**

6 **6** *12* **Bertie Milan (IRE)**[143] 311 5-10-12 0 .... PaddyAspell 89
(Sue Bradburne) *trckd ldrs: rdn and outpcd 4 out: sn struggling* **33/1**

5m 29.1s (-11.90) **Going Correction** -0.275s/f (Good) **6** Ran SP% **110.3**
Speed ratings (Par 107): **109,108,107,103,98 94**
Tote Swingers: 1&2 £2.20, 1&3 £1.80, 2&3 £1.30 CSF £6.93 TOTE £3.20: £1.40, £1.10; EX 7.60.
Owner Mrs Margaret McCrudden **Bred** S McElroy **Trained** Larne, Co Antrim
■ Stewards' Enquiry : Adrian Lane one-day ban: used whip with excessive frequency (Oct 17)
Mr B G Crawford four-day ban: used whip with erxcessive frequency (tbn)

FOCUS
The best race on the card and a decent field for this intermediate hurdle. It produced a really good finish. The first two are rated below their best with the third and fourth setting the level.

NOTEBOOK
Now This Is It(IRE) is trained in Ireland but has gained all his wins in Britain. Held up at the rear, he made ground quietly before coming with a strong run up the centre of the track to snatch the race from the favourite near the line. (op 3-1)
Any Given Day(IRE), was settled early but after a brief tussle managed to get the better of the pacemaker jumping the final flight. He had to battle to hold of the renewed effort of that rival but, just as he looked to have got the upper hand, the winner swooped down the other side of the track. (op 6-5 tchd 11-10)
Strongpoint(IRE), twice a winner in four starts over fences this summer, was making his first start for the yard. He set off in front to ensure a sound gallop and refused to give in when challenged by the favourite. He could well win more hurdles over longer trips and a return to fences is his other option. (op 9-2, tchd 5-1 in a place)
Glaced Over had failed to complete over hurdles previously and ran a far better race than looked likely. (op 33-1)
Grand Zouki(FR) has been in good form but may have failed to stay over this longer trip on a stiffer track. (op 15-2 tchd 7-1 and 9-1)

1699 URWIN HALF CENTURY JUVENILE HURDLE (DIV II) (8 hdls) 2m 110y
4:55 (4:55) (Class 4) 3-Y-O **£2,471** (£725; £362; £181)

Form RPR

1 **Pena Dorada (IRE)**[20] 3-10-12 0 .... BarryKeniry 114+
(Mrs K Burke) *t.k.h: cl up: led after 3rd: mde rest: rdn and r.o strly to go clr run-in* **4/1**[2]

2 *11* **Fearless Falcon (IRE)**[7] 1630 3-10-12 0 .... GrahamLee 103
(Adrian McGuinness, Ire) *chsd ldrs: effrt and wnt 2nd bef 2 out: outpcd run-in* **9/4**[1]

3 *11* **Stags Leap (IRE)**[14] 3-10-12 0 ....(v) WilsonRenwick 94
(P Monteith) *hld up in tch: stdy hdwy after 3 out: 3rd and one pce whn hit last: wknd run-in* **14/1**

P **4** *10* **Petrocelli**[4] 743 3-10-12 0 .... PaddyAspell 86
(Wilf Storey) *hld up: rdn and sme hdwy whn hit 2 out: nvr on terms* **50/1**

3F2 **5** *5* **Baraathen (USA)**[26] 1498 3-10-9 95 .... AdrianLane(3) 83
(Donald McCain) *t.k.h: led to after 3rd: cl up tl wknd bef 2 out* **8/1**

6 *6* **Venture Girl (IRE)**[39] 3-10-5 0 .... RichieMcGrath 67
(Tim Easterby) *t.k.h: hld up: outpcd whn nt fluent 4 out: n.d after* **25/1**

42 **7** *2 1/4* **Forsyth**[34] 1422 3-10-12 0 ....(b[1]) BrianHughes 74
(Alan Swinbank) *t.k.h: trckd ldrs: hit 1st: rdn after 3 out: wknd bef next* **5/1**[3]

8 *3 1/4* **Vittachi**[17] 3-10-9 0 .... EwanWhillans(3) 69
(Alistair Whillans) *bhd: struggling 4 out: nvr on terms* **4/1**[2]

9 *3 1/2* **Decimus Meridius (IRE)**[46] 3-10-12 0 .... JohnnyFarrelly 66
(Howard Johnson) *hld up towards rr: outpcd bef 3 out: nvr on terms* **25/1**

10 *52* **Brisbane (IRE)**[27] 3-10-9 0 .... RyanMania(3) 19
(Dianne Sayer) *nt jump wl: bhd: struggling 1/2-way: t.o* **66/1**

3m 59.1s (-2.70) **Going Correction** -0.275s/f (Good) **10** Ran SP% **116.4**
Speed ratings (Par 103): **95,89,84,79,77 74,73,72,70,46**
Tote Swingers: 1&2 £3.60, 1&3 £12.30, 2&3 £7.60 CSF £13.41 TOTE £5.20: £1.80, £1.40, £4.20; EX 16.70.
Owner Mrs Elaine M Burke **Bred** J P Dwan **Trained** Middleham Moor, North Yorks

FOCUS
The second leg of the juvenile hurdle and run 0.6secs faster than the first. The form is ordinary with the runner-up setting the level.

NOTEBOOK
Pena Dorada(IRE) ◆, a modest maiden at up to 1m6f on the Flat, made a promising start to his hurdling career. Always in the front rank, he went on at the fourth and galloped on well for pressure. His hurdling was pretty good and he looks capable of winning again. (op 5-1, tchd 11-2 in a place)
Fearless Falcon(IRE) had run well on his second start over hurdles and arguably built on that, although no match for the winner over the last couple of flights. (tchd 5-2 in a place)
Stags Leap(IRE) won an extended 1m3f claimer on the Flat for Richard Hannon and was rated in the high-80s at one time in that sphere. With the visor back on for this hurdling debut, he travelled well enough and looked a big threat turning in, but was treading water going to the final flight. He might be ideally suited by an easier track. (op 11-1)
Petrocelli won over 5f on the Flat and was held up on this second start over hurdles. He could only run on past beaten rivals.
Baraathen(USA) made the running until losing the advantage following a mistake at the fourth. He rallied to have a chance two out but went left at that flight and was soon beaten. (op 5-1)
Forsyth, wearing blinkers for the first time, had finished runner-up to the winner of the first division of this race last time. He went well enough but was rather keen and was beginning to struggle when an error two out ended his chance. (op 9-2)

1700 SIS NOVICES' H'CAP HURDLE (10 hdls) 2m 2f
5:30 (5:30) (Class 5) (0-95,92) 3-Y-O+ **£2,276** (£668; £334; £166)

Form RPR

5401 **1** **Zahara Joy**[26] 1504 7-11-2 **85** ....(t) RyanMania(3) 97+
(Maurice Barnes) *cl up: led bef 2 out: styd on strly to draw clr run-in* **5/1**[2]

1350 **2** *9* **Authentic Act (IRE)**[15] 1504 6-10-8 **77** .... CampbellGillies(3) 82+
(Martin Todhunter) *midfield: hdwy to chse wnr between last 2: kpt on same pce run-in* **6/1**[3]

-600 **3** *5* **National Heritage**[7] 1624 5-11-5 **85** ....(p) BarryKeniry 85
(Micky Hammond) *hld up in tch: drvn and outpcd 3 out: rallied next: kpt on run-in: no imp* **18/1**

U43 **4** *1 3/4* **Royal Entourage**[50] 1250 5-11-5 **92** .... KyleJames(7) 89
(Philip Kirby) *hld up: rdn and outpcd after 4 out: rallied 2 out: nvr rchd ldrs* **13/2**

U051 **5** *3 3/4* **Pobs Trophy**[20] 1234 3-10-7 **90** ....(p) PaddyAspell 67
(Richard Guest) *cl up: drvn after 3 out: no ex after next* **4/1**[1]

0-40 **6** *2* **Shadow Wood (IRE)**[96] 853 6-11-5 **85**..........................(p) BrianHughes 78
(Patrick Griffin, Ire) *led to bef 2 out: rdn and wknd fr last* **28/1**

05P- **7** *3 1/4* **Bed Fellow (IRE)**[13] 2102 6-10-6 **72**.......................... WilsonRenwick 61
(P Monteith) *hld up in midfield: stdy hdwy 3 out: wknd fr next* **14/1**

0-02 **8** *1 3/4* **Arch**[43] 1340 7-11-3 **90**.......................... MrGCrow(7) 77
(Sandy Forster) *in tch: drvn and outpcd bef 2 out: sn btn* **28/1**

0043 **9** *nk* **Bocciani (GER)**[14] 1552 5-11-7 **90**.......................... JamesO'Farrell(3) 77
(Dianne Sayer) *hld up: rdn after 4 out: nvr rchd ldrs* **14/1**

/0P- **10** *1* **Sam Patch**[448] 916 7-11-1 **91**.......................... CallumWhillans(10) 77
(Donald Whillans) *towards rr: pushed along after 4 out: n.d after* **33/1**

5551 **11** *22* **Fly Tipper**[43] 1339 10-11-11 **91**..........................(t) GrahamLee 57
(Wilf Storey) *chsd ldrs: outpcd whn hit 4 out: sn wknd: t.o* **10/1**

-000 **12** *39* **Sheriff Hall (IRE)**[25] 1505 5-11-2 **82**.......................... TimmyMurphy 13
(George Charlton) *hld up: struggling after 4 out: t.o* **8/1**

0FP/ **13** *6* **King's Envoy (USA)**[581] 4237 11-9-11 **66** oh4.......................... AdrianLane(3) —
(Jean McGregor) *hld up: struggling after 4 out: sn btn: t.o* **66/1**

U30 **14** *61* **Humbel Lad (IRE)**[111] 744 6-11-2 **92**.......................... CraigGallagher(10) —
(Richard Guest) *bhd and sn detached: lost tch fnl circ* **50/1**

4m 26.8s (-0.20) **Going Correction** -0.275s/f (Good)
WFA 3 from 5yo+ 17lb **14** Ran SP% **116.4**
Speed ratings (Par 103): **89,85,82,82,80 79,78,77,77,76 66,49,46,19**
Tote Swingers: 1&2 £4.90, 1&3 £26.00, 2&3 £29.50 CSF £32.75 CT £500.86 TOTE £4.40: £1.90, £2.30, £4.00; EX 46.80.
Owner Arthur B Graham **Bred** Arthur B Graham **Trained** Farlam, Cumbria

FOCUS
A very moderate hurdle in which the second and fourth are the best guides to the level.

NOTEBOOK
Zahara Joy, raised 9lb for winning at Sedgefield last time, she has really got her act together and travelled well before going to the front two out. She had to be ridden out but in truth was in no danger afterwards. (tchd 9-2)
Authentic Act(IRE) had shown some reasonable form in the spring but had not built on it since a summer break. This was better but he could make no impression on the winner after the last. (op 9-1)
National Heritage was getting reminders as early as the fifth and was under pressure at the last on the far side. However, he rallied well up the hill, passing several rivals, and might have been second but for an untidy jump at the final flight. (op 25-1)
Royal Entourage was held up out the back and looked to be struggling before running on past a number of tiring rivals up the hill. (op 6-1)
Pobs Trophy, placed three times on the Flat since winning at Stratford in August, is only a 3-yo and he was in trouble turning for home. (op 9-2 tchd 7-2)
Shadow Wood(IRE), wearing cheekpieces for the first time, made the running but had nothing left when the winner went on.
Arch had his chance at the third last but could not sustain his effort up the hill.

1701 SNOWY'S FAREWELL RADIO BORDERS CLASSIFIED CHASE (17 fncs) 2m 6f 110y

6:00 (6:00) (Class 5) 5-Y-0+ **£2,797** (£821; £410; £205)

Form RPR

113- **1** **Desperate Dex (IRE)**[215] 4367 10-10-12 95.......................... GrahamLee 105
(Ferdy Murphy) *hld up: stdy hdwy and prom 12th: effrt whn lft 4 l 2nd and swvd to avoid faller last: styd on wl u.p to ld towards fin* **3/1**[1]

-415 **2** *nk* **Red Dynamite**[89] 918 9-10-12 94..........................(p) BrianHughes 106+
(Geoffrey Harker) *hld up: stdy hdwy to chse ldrs 4 out: cl 2nd whn blnd 2 out: sn rcvrd: chalng whn lft 4 l clr last: kpt on run-in: hdd towards fin* **9/2**[3]

156 **3** *16* **Strobe**[10] 1598 6-10-5 91..........................(p) AlexanderVoy(7) 92
(Lucy Normile) *cl up: wnt 2nd bef 12th: effrt 3 out: 8 l down and hld whn lft 3rd last* **8/1**

5PP- **4** *22* **Snowy (IRE)**[158] 46 12-10-12 94.......................... TimmyMurphy 70
(P Monteith) *prom: drvn and outpcd 12th: n.d after* **5/1**

UF00 **5** *hd* **Lindseyfield Lodge (IRE)**[11] 1575 9-10-12 92..........(p) KennyJohnson 69
(Robert Johnson) *led: hit 5th: hdd 10th: hit 12th: rallied and cl up bef 3 out: wknd fr next* **25/1**

11-6 **6** *3 1/2* **Copper's Gold (IRE)**[127] 517 6-10-12 95..........(b) PeterBuchanan 66
(Lucinda Russell) *trckd ldrs: slipped bnd bef 3rd: blnd bdly 13th: wknd fr next* **10/3**[2]

4654 **7** *29* **Ellandshe (IRE)**[10] 1595 10-10-9 50..........................(b) RyanMania(3) 40
(William Young) *in tch: blnd 4trh: rdn and struggling fr 12th* **100/1**

1/3P **F** **Coolnaharan (IRE)**[8] 1614 10-10-9 94..........(p) CampbellGillies(3) 106
(S R B Crawford, Ire) *cl up: bmpd bnd bef 3rd: chal next: led 10th: rdn and jnd whn fell last: fatally injured* **12/1**

-4P4 **P** **Charming Knight (IRE)**[34] 1423 9-10-5 87.......... AlistairFindlay(7) —
(Jane Walton) *midfield: pushed along 1/2-way: struggling fr 13th: t.o whn p.u bef last* **33/1**

F04- **U** **Seek The Truth (IRE)**[167] 5272 7-10-12 84.......................... PaddyAspell —
(Sue Bradburne) *blnd 1st: bhd: struggling whn blnd bdly and uns rdr 4 out* **14/1**

5m 44.5s **Going Correction** 0.0s/f (Good) **10** Ran SP% **116.2**
Speed ratings: **100,99,94,86,86 85,75,—,—,—**
Tote Swingers: 1&2 £4.30, 1&3 £10.80, 2&3 £6.30 CSF £17.02 TOTE £3.40: £1.70, £1.60, £2.70; EX 14.10.
Owner Crossed Fingers Partnership **Bred** Sir Anthony Scott **Trained** West Witton, N Yorks
■ Stewards' Enquiry : Graham Lee caution: used whip down shoulder in the forehand.

FOCUS
A plating-class classified chase that resulted in a very close finish. The winner is rated to form in an ordinary handicap.

NOTEBOOK
Desperate Dex(IRE) was in decent form when last seen in March and was sent off favourite despite that absence and the fact the ground was much faster than he had been winning on. He made steady headway from the back, and managed to get a run between the runner-up and the rail after the last, which enabled him to just prevail. He continues on the upgrade. (op 9-4)
Red Dynamite, returning from a break, had won over this trip before that. He overcame a mistake to join the leader at the last and was left clear in front when that rival fell. However, he started to struggle on the long run-in and, carrying his head awkwardly, was worn down near the line. (op 6-1)
Strobe was never far away, and overcame a mistake at the ditch going away from the stands to still have a chance on the home turn. However, he could only stay on at the one pace from there. (op 9-1 tchd 7-1)
Snowy(IRE), whose last race this was and had the race named in his honour, showed up for a circuit but lost his place going away from the stands. He ran on as usual up the hill and just snatched fourth place on the line. A winner four times on the track, he retires to the British Racing School. (op 9-2)
Lindseyfield Lodge(IRE), with the cheekpieces reapplied, made the running for over a circuit and kept trying, but was very tired up the hill and lost fourth place on the line. Official explanation: vet said gelding returned lame left-hind (op 22-1)
Copper's Gold(IRE) was never far away but was struggling after a mistake on the far side on the final circuit. (op 9-2)

Coolnaharan(IRE) travelled well throughout and took the lead on the second circuit. He was still in front but beginning to come under pressure when coming down at the last, sadly taking a fatal fall. (op 16-1)

1702 CITY ROOFING LTD STANDARD OPEN NATIONAL HUNT FLAT RACE 2m 110y

6:25 (6:28) (Class 5) 4-6-Y-0 **£1,626** (£477; £238; £119)

Form RPR

1 **Rocking Blues (FR)** 5-11-0 0.......................... GrahamLee 111+
(Rose Dobbin) *in tch: smooth hdwy to ld over 2f out: pushed clr fnl f* **12/1**[3]

20- **2** *8* **First Rock (IRE)**[176] 5129 4-11-0 0.......................... BrianHughes 101
(Alan Swinbank) *cl up: led over 3f to over 2f out: one pce fnl f* **11/4**[1]

3 **3** *nk* **Milano Supremo (IRE)**[113] 732 5-11-0 0..........(t) RichieMcGrath 101
(Chris Grant) *prom: lost pl 1/2-way: rallied over 3f out: plugged on fnl 2f: nrst fin* **9/2**[2]

60- **4** *7* **Ballet D'Anges (FR)**[195] 4785 4-10-7 0.......................... AlexanderVoy(7) 94
(Lucy Normile) *led 5f: cl up tl rdn and outpcd fr 2f out* **66/1**

5 *9* **Shanen (IRE)** 4-11-0 0.......................... TimmyMurphy 87
(George Charlton) *hld up: hdwy on outside and prom over 3f out: shkn up and wknd fr 2f out* **9/2**[2]

23- **6** *2 3/4* **Darna**[211] 4429 4-10-11 0.......................... RyanMania(3) 83
(William Amos) *hld up: pushed along over 3f out: sn outpcd* **11/4**[1]

54- **7** *13* **Exotic Man (FR)**[209] 4488 5-10-7 0.......................... MrJohnDawson(7) 69
(John Wade) *t.k.h: prom: led after 5f to over 3f out: sn wknd* **20/1**

8 *12* **Dancing Gizmo** 5-10-11 0.......................... EwanWhillans(3) 57
(Alistair Whillans) *hld up: stdy hdwy over 3f out: wknd over 2f out* **12/1**[3]

0- **9** *1 1/2* **Scotswell**[305] 2639 4-10-7 0.......................... GaryRutherford(7) 56
(Harriet Graham) *t.k.h: cl up tl wknd over 3f out* **100/1**

650- **10** *13* **Politelysed**[236] 3957 4-10-7 0.......................... KennyJohnson 36
(Robert Johnson) *hld up: hdwy and prom after 5f: wknd over 3f out* **66/1**

3m 53.5s (-2.70) **Going Correction** -0.275s/f (Good)
WFA 4 from 5yo 9lb **10** Ran SP% **113.8**
Speed ratings: **95,91,91,87,83 82,76,70,69,63**
Tote Swingers: 1&2 £13.60, 1&3 £12.30, 2&3 £9.60. totesuper7: Win: Not won. Place: Not won. CSF £43.46 TOTE £9.30: £2.60, £1.60, £1.90; EX 53.70 Place 6: £59.01 Place 5: £24.00..
Owner James Filmer-Wilson **Bred** Mme Genevieve Mongin **Trained** South Hazelrigg, Northumbria

FOCUS
A fair amount of experience amongst the runners in this bumper and it looked a better than average race of its type. The form could rate higher but is limited by the proximity of the fourth.

NOTEBOOK
Rocking Blues(FR), a French-bred making his debut, moved up to challenge off the home turn, and proved too good for the favourite up the hill. He looks to have a future and can win again and over hurdles. (op 8-1)
First Rock(IRE), placed in a Fibresand bumper last winter before being held in a Grade 2 at Aintree, was sent off favourite and looked the winner when going on turning for home, but the winner took his measure soon after and he had no response. (op 15-8)
Milano Supremo(IRE), the most experienced in the field, was never far away but looked in trouble on the home turn before staying on again. He looks likely to need further over hurdles. (op 15-2 tchd 4-1)
Ballet D'Anges(FR), well beaten on two previous bumper starts last winter, looks to have improved and ran a decent race from the front.
Shanen(IRE) ◆, from the family of a Grande Steeplechase de Paris winner, showed plenty of promise on this debut, making good ground leaving the back straight before tiring up the hill. A lot better can be expected in time. (op 5-1 tchd 11-2)
Darna, placed in two starts early in the year, was held up on this return but failed to get into contention and this was slightly disappointing. Official explanation: jockey said gelding was unsuited by the track (op 4-1 tchd 5-2)
T/Plt: £293.10 to a £1 stake. Pool of £59,940.85 - 149.25 winning tickets. T/Qpdt: £43.00 to a £1 stake. Pool of £4,866.09 - 83.60 winning tickets. RY

1552 UTTOXETER (L-H)

Sunday, October 3

OFFICIAL GOING: Heavy (chs 5.5, hdl 6.9)

Ttrack dolled out 4yds from last meeting. Final flight of hurdles in back straight and 2nd last flight omitted all circuits, final fence omitted all chases.
Wind: moderate 1/2 against Weather: overcast, heavy rain before racing, becoming dry

1703 MUSICMAGPIE.CO.UK CONDITIONAL JOCKEYS' "NH" NOVICES' HURDLE (STAFFORDSHIRE REGIMENT CHALLENGE CUP) (8 hdls 4 omitted) 2m 6f 110y

1:30 (1:30) (Class 4) 4-Y-0+ **£2,211** (£649; £324; £162)

Form RPR

66- **1** **Cotswold Charmer (IRE)**[306] 2621 5-10-9 0...... SamTwiston-Davies(3) 110+
(Nigel Twiston-Davies) *hdwy 5th: chsng ldrs next: wnt 2nd sn after 2 out: led bef last: forged clr: eased towards fin* **10/1**

-036 **2** *10* **Himayna**[14] 1553 6-9-13 0.......................... MrTomDavid(6) 93+
(Tim Vaughan) *j. poorly and rt-handed: led: reluctant and reminders bnd bef 5th: hdd between last 2: 4 l down whn blnd last* **8/1**

54 **3** *21* **Newyearsresolution (IRE)**[14] 1553 6-10-12 0.......................... GilesHawkins 76
(Nick Mitchell) *chsd ldr to 4th: sn drvn along: lost pl appr 2 out: tk distant 3rd appr last* **11/2**[3]

/-00 **4** *nk* **Lambrini Classic**[14] 1553 7-10-12 0.......................... JamesHalliday 76
(Lisa Williamson) *detached and drvn 4th: sn bhd: kpt on to take distant 4th last* **100/1**

5 *11* **Code Blue** 7-10-9 0.......................... JohnKington(3) 70
(Donald McCain) *wnt prom 4th: chsd ldr 3 out: hung rt bnd appr next: wknd qckly between last 2: last whn swvd rt and hit rail sn after last: fin v tired* **14/1**

/0-1 **P** **Front Of House (IRE)**[45] 1296 8-11-2 123.......................... RichardKilloran(3) —
(Nicky Henderson) *in tch: pushed along 3rd: chsng ldrs 3 out: wknd appr next: t.o last whn p.u between last 2* **10/11**[1]

/0-0 **P** **Middleton Red (IRE)**[25] 1505 6-10-9 0.......................... CharlieWallis(3) —
(Graham Smith) *chsd ldrs: wnt 2nd 4th: wknd next: sn t.o: p.u bef 2 out* **66/1**

-210 **P** **Call Me Bill (IRE)**[14] 1553 4-10-8 0.......................... DonalDevereux(3) —
(Peter Bowen) *chsd ldrs: nt fluent 2nd: lost pl 4th: sn bhd: t.o whn p.u bef 2 out* **5/1**[2]

5m 55.6s (24.70) **Going Correction** +1.275s/f (Heav)
WFA 4 from 5yo+ 10lb **8** Ran SP% **113.8**
Speed ratings (Par 105): **108,104,97,97,93 —,—,—**
Tote Swingers: 1&2 £10.10, 1&3 £3.90, 2&3 £6.60 CSF £83.71 TOTE £11.00: £2.30, £2.30, £1.30; EX 101.40.

Owner The Double Octagon Partnership **Bred** Raymond McDonnell **Trained** Naunton, Gloucs

FOCUS

The rails had been moved to provide fresh ground on the bends and the hurdles dolled out a further four metres from the last meeting. Persistent rain had changed the going to heavy, and there was some waterlogging after the final bend. Not surprisingly the ground was the decisive factor, with few able to act on it. The second and fourth set the level.

NOTEBOOK

Cotswold Charmer(IRE) moved well in the conditions, moving up to challenge the leader around the final bend before sluicing up the straight. He had a tendency to hang in both starts last year, but seems to have grown up during his ten months off and the Alderbrook gelding looks a potentially useful winter-ground performer. (op 11-1 tchd 12-1)

Himayna dived at a couple of flights but stayed up with the lead, and began to open up a gap until looking reluctant going out onto the final circuit. However, he stuck to the task and, despite tiring markedly after the last, he ran his race. He evidently has his quirks but showed a little ability and might do better over a shorter trip. (op 9-1)

Newyearsresolution(IRE) disputed the lead for a while, but gradually dropped further behind throughout the final circuit on ground that he found too testing. (op 13-2)

Lambrini Classic was a well-beaten fourth and ran to the moderate level he has established so far. (op 80-1)

Code Blue showed up promisingly on the final circuit before getting very tired in the straight and finishing legless. Nonetheless, there was some encouragement to be gleaned from his jumping debut.

Front Of House(IRE) had the best form on offer but did not act in the conditions and the penalty for his Stratford win in August did not help matters. Official explanation: jockey said gelding was unsuited by the heavy ground (op 8-11tchd Evens in places)

Call Me Bill(IRE) was arguably one of the least likely to be inconvenienced by the ground, but he was struggling on the first circuit and for the second time weakened tamely. (op 8-11tchd Evens in places)

1704 MUSICMAGPIE.CO.UK H'CAP HURDLE (DIV I) (7 hdls 3 omitted) 2m

2:00 (2:01) (Class 5) (0-90,92) 4-Y-O+ **£1,366** (£401; £200; £100)

Form RPR

P00 **1** **Simone Martini (IRE)**[91] 887 5-9-12 **67**................(tp) JimmyDerham(5) 84+
(Milton Harris) *trckd ldrs: cl 3rd and gioing wl whn swtchd lft between last 2: shkn up to ld appr last: pushed clr: v readily* **3/1**[1]

0-32 **2** *10* **Goat Castle (IRE)**[9] 1601 6-11-9 **90**..................(t) SamTwiston-Davies(3) 92
(Nigel Twiston-Davies) *in tch: nt fluent 3 out: hdwy to chse ldrs next: kpt on same pce run-in* **7/2**[2]

U5F4 **3** *1 1/2* **Cloonavery (IRE)**[14] 1552 8-10-5 **69**............................(v) LiamTreadwell 70
(Tony Carroll) *trckd ldrs: led appr 2 out: hdd appr last: kpt on one pce* **4/1**[3]

43-3 **4** *15* **Stravita**[143] 298 6-11-2 **80**....................................... AndrewGlassonbury 66
(Jim Best) *hld up: jnd ldrs 3 out: wknd appr 2 out* **4/1**[0]

0360 **5** *1 1/2* **Mulaazem**[14] 1554 7-11-1 **86**....................................(p) DavidDennis(7) 70
(Derek Frankland) *led: hdd 4th: lost pl appr 2 out* **12/1**

0601 **6** *hd* **Augharra (IRE)**[14] 1552 5-11-3 **84**.............................. TommyPhelan(3) 68
(Harry Chisman) *chsd ldrs: lost pl appr 2 out* **7/1**

U0/0 **7** *72* **Always Baileys (IRE)**[14] 1554 7-9-7 **64** oh4.................. MissCBoxall(7) —
(Pam Ford) *stdd s: jnd ldrs 3rd: led next: hdd appr 2 out: sn wknd: t.o last* **25/1**

4m 25.0s (29.80) **Going Correction** +1.275s/f (Heav) 7 Ran SP% **111.3**

Speed ratings (Par 103): **76,71,70,62,62 61,25**

Tote Swingers: 1&2 £2.40, 1&3 £6.20, 2&3 £2.90 CSF £13.40 CT £39.37 TOTE £4.20: £2.00, £2.60; EX 14.20.

Owner Miss J M Foran **Bred** Epona Bloodstock Ltd **Trained** Herridge, Wiltshire

FOCUS

Mindful of the conditions, they set off at a crawl, so many of them pulled hard early on in this weak affair. The pace picked up midway through the final circuit and three pulled clear in the home straight. The form appears sound rated around the placed horses.

NOTEBOOK

Simone Martini(IRE) made stealthy progress down the back, and was full of running turning for home, easing to the front to land quite a gamble. He had shown absolutely nothing in three previous runs over hurdles on much faster ground, but the consequent light weight was a bonus in these conditions, as were first-time cheekpieces and a wind operation, so improvement was clearly expected for his handicap debut. Official explanation: trainer said, regarding apparent improvement in form, that the gelding had benefitted from having a wind operation and from the heavy ground. (op 7-1)

Goat Castle(IRE) has improved since fitted with a tongue tie and ran another sound race, but he never looked that happy on the ground and, despite giving his all, could not concede 23lb to the winner. (op 2-1)

Cloonavery(IRE) raced prominently throughout and was still there turning for home, but he could not find the extra gear and the hunt for his long-awaited first success continues. (op 9-2 tchd 7-2)

Stravita made some late progress but was never competitive on her first start for her new stable since being claimed out of a Ludlow seller in May. (op 3-1)

Mulaazem got warm beforehand and led until his jumping lost fluency in mid-race and he dropped away. He reportedly coughed after the race when tailed off last month over C&D but needed to find improvement on his general form to feature even in this. (op 16-1 tchd 11-1)

Aughcarra(IRE), 7lb higher after just getting up on the line at big odds in a similar event over C&D a fortnight ago, got warm and pulled hard this time round, and never looked likely to continue the improvement. (op 13-2)

1705 MUSICMAGPIE.CO.UK MAIDEN HURDLE (7 hdls 3 omitted) 2m

2:35 (2:35) (Class 4) 4-Y-O+ **£2,211** (£649; £324; £162)

Form RPR

040- **1** **Rhum (FR)**[344] 1895 5-10-11 0.............................. SamTwiston-Davies(3) 117+
(Nigel Twiston-Davies) *chsd ldrs: wnt handy 3rd after 4th: led after 2 out: styd on wl run-in* **4/1**[2]

323- **2** *6* **Sagredo (USA)**[18] 1294 6-10-11 0.............................. RichieMcLernon(3) 112+
(Jonjo O'Neill) *hld up towards rr: smooth hdwy 4th: trcking ldrs next: wnt 2nd on bit between last 2: 2 l down last: sn shkn up and fnd nthing* **9/4**[1]

05 **3** *29* **That's Some Milan (IRE)**[25] 1505 5-11-0 0.................. WarrenMarston 85
(Milton Harris) *chsd ldrs: wnt modest 3rd appr last* **7/1**

0/P- **4** *6* **Kathleen Kennet**[122] 2664 10-10-0 0.............................. MrJBanks(7) 69
(Martin Bosley) *t.k.h: led: hdd after 2 out: wknd appr last* **50/1**

5 *nk* **Cygnet**[93] 4-11-0 0.. BrianHarding 76
(Donald McCain) *mid-div: hdwy 4th: chsng ldrs 2 out: wknd between last 2* **5/1**[3]

U4 **6** *4* **Echo Dancer**[74] 1058 4-10-4 0.. JoshWall(10) 72
(Trevor Wall) *chsd ldrs: wnt 2nd 4th: wknd after 2 out* **20/1**

00-P **7** *25* **Bright Decision**[10] 1588 4-10-7 0.................................. DannyBurton(7) 47
(Joanna Davis) *hit 3rd: mid-div: hdwy next: lost pl after next: sn bhd* **12/1**

460- **8** *8* **Smokey George**[181] 5048 5-10-11 0.............................. SeanQuinlan(3) 39
(Kim Bailey) *hld up: hdwy to trck ldrs 3rd: wknd 2 out* **11/1**

0-5 **9** *15* **Tocatchaprince (IRE)**[147] 238 4-11-0 0.............................. DaveCrosse 24
(Milton Harris) *in rr: drvn after 3rd: sn bhd: t.o 3 out* **7/1**

P **10** *30* **Winbury**[12] 1571 7-10-7 0.......................................(b[1]) MrRGHenderson(7) —
(Ken Wingrove) *t.k.h: trckd ldrs: nt fluent 3rd: wknd 5th: sn bhd: t.o (btn 140 l)* **66/1**

000/ **U** **Penny King**[777] 1207 9-10-7 0.. MrDGPrichard(7) —
(Ken Wingrove) *prom whn swvd rt and uns rdr 2nd* **50/1**

0- **P** **Idol Deputy (FR)**[134] 4023 4-11-0 0.. MarkGrant —
(James Bennett) *prom: lost pl 4th: t.o next: p.u bef 2 out* **80/1**

0 **P** **Beat All Odds**[73] 1071 4-10-7 0.. LiamTreadwell —
(William Clay) *sn bhd: t.o whn p.u bef 3 out* **40/1**

4m 12.6s (17.40) **Going Correction** +1.275s/f (Heav)

WFA 4 from 5yo+ 9lb 13 Ran SP% **122.3**

Speed ratings (Par 105): **107,104,89,86,86 84,71,67,60,45** —,—,—

Tote Swingers: 1&2 £2.00, 1&3 £4.20, 2&3 £3.00 CSF £13.60 TOTE £4.30: £1.10, £1.90, £2.90; EX 16.50.

Owner H R Mould **Bred** Thierry Cypres & Jean-Francois Naudin **Trained** Naunton, Gloucs

FOCUS

The two market leaders fought out the finish with the jumps-bred fending off the speedier Flat-bred favourite. The second looks the best guide.

NOTEBOOK

Rhum(FR) kept tabs on the leaders and so was in the ideal position to make his move first, and by staying on grittily he was able to maintain his advantage. He had weakened in a couple of hurdles over longer trips last season, but, like his stablemate who won the earlier novice hurdle, he has evidently strengthened up over the past year. A testing 2m looks ideal at this stage and he should be up to being competitive in handicaps. (op 9-2)

Sagredo(USA), who has run respectably on the Flat since last tried over hurdles, had the form to win this despite finding little near the finish in three hurdles last summer. He was ridden with supreme confidence and made eye-catching headway travelling best of all turning in, but again found nothing. (op 7-4, tchd 5-2 in places)

That's Some Milan(IRE)\n\x\x finished best of the Milton Harris pair, having always been in touch and rallying a bit once losing his place turning for home. The former Irish point winner had shown nothing in two previous hurdles but is probably better than that. (op 14-1)

Kathleen Kennet was keen in the lead on her return from a break and ran as well as could be expected.

Cygnet was ridden patiently and made up some ground before his run flattened out in the straight. Sold for 7,000gns after showing little on the Flat for Luca Cumani this season, given better ground he should improve for this effort. (op 9-2 tchd 11-2)

Bright Decision Official explanation: trainer said gelding lost a shoe

Tocatchaprince(IRE) left the Alan King yard after a couple of bumper runs and was well supported on his debut for Harris, but he will have to improve on this first try over hurdles. (op 10-1 tchd 11-2)

1706 MUSICMAGPIE.CO.UK NOVICES' CHASE (FOR THE ROYAL MERCIAN & LANCASTRIAN YEOMANRY CHALLENGE CUP) (14 fncs 2 omitted) 2m 5f

3:20 (3:20) (Class 3) 5-Y-O+ **£5,069** (£1,497; £748; £374; £187)

Form RPR

1U-P **1** **Darstardly Dick (IRE)**[114] 708 7-11-4 118.....................(b) HarrySkelton 127+
(Victor Dartnall) *trckd ldrs: edgd lft and led 2 out: sn drvn clr: hit last: rdn rt out* **3/1**[3]

0U-0 **2** *7* **Shadow Dancer (IRE)**[155] 94 5-10-9 0.................. RichieMcLernon(3) 113+
(Jonjo O'Neill) *trckd ldrs: n.m.r and wnt 2nd 2 out: 6 l down whn hit last: kpt on same pce* **9/4**[2]

00P/ **3** *1/2* **Kitley Hassle**[125] 8-10-12 0...(b[1]) HaddenFrost 112
(James Frost) *led: j.big 1st: sn clr: reminders 8th: hdd 2 out: kpt on one pce run-in* **14/1**

11-5 **4** *19* **Federstar (GER)**[155] 94 8-10-7 0.............................. JimmyDerham(5) 100+
(Milton Harris) *chsd ldr: hit 3rd: n.m.r: nt fluent and wknd 2 out* **11/8**[1]

P246 **5** *21* **Indian Pipe Dream (IRE)**[9] 1602 8-10-12 100.................. LiamTreadwell 72
(Aytach Sadik) *chsd ldrs: reminders 7th: drvn along next: hit 9th: outpcd and lost pl whn hit 3 out* **16/1**

5m 58.5s (35.00) **Going Correction** +1.575s/f (Heav) 5 Ran SP% **110.4**

Speed ratings: **96,93,93,85,77**

CSF £10.44 TOTE £4.50: £2.80, £2.80; EX 11.50.

Owner Cheltenham Or Bust **Bred** Mrs Rose Barry **Trained** Brayford, Devon

FOCUS

The three market leaders surged to the lead in a line straightening up for home in a reasonable novice chase. The winner is rated to his hurdles form.

NOTEBOOK

Darstardly Dick(IRE) was keen throughout the race and did not jump with particular fluency, but showed the greater acceleration to power away from his rivals and was clear when scrambling over the last. He achieved a similar rating to his market rivals over hurdles, even though he was not always that consistent, but had the benefit of experience over fences and that enabled him to defy a penalty here. He is versatile regarding ground conditions and seems better when given at least five weeks between races. (tchd 11-4 and 10-3)

Shadow Dancer(IRE), a winner off a mark of 119 over hurdles on testing ground last winter, jumped a little cautiously on his chasing debut, but acts on soft and showed enough to suggest he is up to winning over fences with more experience. (op 5-2 tchd 11-4)

Kitley Hassle raced keenly in first-time blinkers, setting the pace and sticking on once swamped in the straight. The winner of four British points, he looked likely to come on for this run so he might be up to winning a small race. (op 8-1)

Federstar(GER) was making his move when getting squeezed out as three came together at the second-last, but weakened from there and lost third place. He won on soft ground over hurdles and was sent off a well-backed favourite for his second chasing start, but tended to jump low and might not prove as good over fences. (op 13-8)

Indian Pipe Dream(IRE) has plenty of chasing experience but prefers faster ground and was outclassed. (op 11-1)

1707 MUSICMAGPIE.CO.UK H'CAP HURDLE (DIV II) (7 hdls 3 omitted) 2m

3:55 (3:56) (Class 5) (0-90,90) 4-Y-O+ **£1,366** (£401; £200; £100)

Form RPR

00P- **1** **Quam Celerrime**[164] 5340 5-10-0 **64** oh4.............................. HaddenFrost 80+
(Roger Curtis) *trckd ldrs: wnt 2nd appr 2 out: led between last 2: sn pushed wl clr: 23 l ahd last: eased towards fin* **6/1**

050U **2** *23* **Miss Markham (IRE)**[14] 1554 5-9-10 **67**.......................... PeterHatton(7) 58
(Patricia Rigby) *chsd ldrs: kpt on same pce between last 2: tk 2nd towards fin* **16/1**

P-0P **3** *3 1/4* **Wild Side Of Life (IRE)**[25] 1507 7-11-5 **90**.................... MrTomDavid(7) 78
(Tim Vaughan) *wl away: led and sn clr: hit 2nd: hdd after 2 out: wknd and lost 2nd clsng stages* **13/2**

5-62 **4** *5* **Temple Place (IRE)**[62] 1164 9-11-11 **89**.......................... SamThomas 72
(Alan Jones) *in rr: reminders 4th: hdwy next: one pce fr 2 out* **10/3**[2]

0P-0 **5** *1/2* **Kyoto (GER)**[54] 1232 6-11-2 **80**.. DavidDennis 62
(Nigel Hawke) *t.k.h: hdwy 5th: sn trcking ldrs: rdn between last 2: 4th and wkng whn mstke last* **11/4**[1]

0/0P **6** *1/2* **Ful Of Grace (IRE)**[62] 1164 6-10-7 **76**.......................(b) TomO'Connor(5) 58
(James Frost) *t.k.h: trckd ldrs: wkng whn hit 2 out* **10/1**

P4-0 **P** **Evelith Regent (IRE)**[129] 490 7-10-9 **73**........................(t) AndrewTinkler —
(John Davies) *stdd s: hld up in rr: effrt appr 2 out: wknd qckly between last 2: t.o whn p.u bef last* **4/1**[3]

4m 19.2s (24.00) **Going Correction** +1.275s/f (Heav) **7** Ran SP% **112.3**
Speed ratings (Par 103): **91,79,77,75,75 74,—**
Tote Swingers: 1&2 £10.80, 2&3 £4.00 CSF £79.18 CT £637.54 TOTE £8.20: £5.20, £9.30; EX 124.20.
Owner The Maderson Blue Partnership **Bred** Mrs C Regalado-Gonzalez **Trained** Lambourn, Berks

FOCUS
A weak contest run at a steady pace. The form is rated around the placed horses but could be a few pounds out either way.

NOTEBOOK
Quam Celerrime looked a bit hesitant jumping the flattened second hurdle, but he eventually got the hang of things to pounce two out and saunter clear of the field in some style. In three previous attempts over hurdles he had not managed to get within 50 lengths of the winner but was fresh from a break after breaking a blood-vessel over C&D in May. He had been tried on soft ground, and the light weight for his handicap debut was enough to inspire market confidence. He will be clobbered by the handicapper, but from a starting rating of 60 there might still be some leeway. Official explanation: trainer said, regarding apparent improvement in form, that the gelding had benefitted from having time off during the summer and the heavy ground. (op 9-1)
Miss Markham(IRE), who was sweating profusely, tracked the long-time leader and stuck on after losing her place in the straight to grab a distant second. She had also failed to get within 50 lengths of the winner in previous completed starts, but benefited from carrying a light weight in the conditions. (tchd 20-1)
Wild Side Of Life(IRE) set off at a good pace before settling down mid-race, and he gamely tried to stick to the task despite getting tired in the closing stages. Having failed to get home over 3m last time he was dropping in trip here so it was a little disappointing to see him tire once again even allowing for the weight concession to the first two. (op 6-1 tchd 5-1)
Temple Place(IRE) is not the force he was a couple of years ago, but had been in with a winning chance at Newton Abbot in August on his second start for this yard. He still can be competitive from his current mark, but was unable to pick up in this testing ground. (op 5-2 tchd 7-2)
Kyoto(GER) got very tired in the ground on this occasion, but he has dropped to a feasible mark and is coming into form. (op 7-2)
Evelith Regent(IRE) attracted some support, but it seems it will take more than the addition of a tongue tie to gain his first hurdling success. (op 9-2 tchd 7-2)

1708 DIGIBET.COM H'CAP CHASE (FOR THE QUEEN'S ROYAL LANCERS CHALLENGE CUP) (15 fncs 3 omitted) 3m
4:25 (4:29) (Class 4) (0-105,105) 4-Y-0+ **£2,862** (£840; £420; £209)

Form RPR
2P-3 **1** **Festival Dreams**[119] 646 5-10-4 **90**............................(p) DannyBurton(7) 100
(Joanna Davis) *t.k.h: w ldr: led 3rd: drvn and increased pce after 12th: styd on u.p run-in* **2/1**[1]
05P- **2** *2* **Aztec Treasure (NZ)**[225] 4172 6-10-11 **90**.............................. NoelFehily 98
(Jonjo O'Neill) *hld up in last: wnt 6 l 2nd 2 out: 3 l down last: styd on same pce: no imp* **2/1**[1]
00/ **3** *50* **Bellflower Boy (IRE)**[142] 323 7-11-11 **104**........................ SamThomas 62
(Dr Richard Newland) *led: blnd 1st: hdd 3rd: pckd 11th: 6 l 2nd whn blnd 2 out: 13 l 3rd whn mstke last: eased: t.o* **11/4**[2]
-PU0 **4** *105* **Benefit Game (IRE)**[44] 1309 6-11-0 **96**..................... RichieMcLernon(3) —
(Jonjo O'Neill) *chsd ldrs: pckd 9th: wknd 3 out: 8 l down in 4th whn j.v.slowly last: eased: wl t.o* **13/2**[3]

7m 13.2s (58.10) **Going Correction** +1.575s/f (Heav) **4** Ran SP% **106.7**
Speed ratings (Par 105): **66,65,48,—**
CSF £6.29 TOTE £2.20; EX 5.80.
Owner Oakhedge Racing **Bred** Mrs M Davis **Trained** East Garston, Berks

FOCUS
Six withdrawals left a depleted field that dawdled through the early stages, but still only two were able to keep up the gallop. The winner sets the level backed up by the runner-up.

NOTEBOOK
Festival Dreams, after an early mistake, jumped more fluently than the rest and was able to draw clear for an easy victory. His jumping had let him down on his sole previous attempt over fences, but he was fresh from a break, found this pace well within his comfort zone and was able to capitalise on a relatively light weight for his handicap debut. He looked quite good here, but might still need to prove his jumping in a more competitive event. (op 9-4 tchd 15-8)
Aztec Treasure(NZ) made progress from a rear position, but his jumping was a bit too ponderous and, as a consequence, he did not pose much of a threat. This was a reasonable chasing debut, but he does not look too well treated by the handicapper. (op 11-4, tchd 3-1 in places)
Bellflower Boy(IRE) nearly failed to take off at the first and, although he recovered, his jumping was inconsistent and he eventually faded out of it. Considering his previous winning form over hurdles in Ireland, this was somewhat disappointing, but he has had a wind operation since moving to his new stable and might do better for this run. (op 2-1)
Benefit Game(IRE) did not cope with the conditions and got so tired he only just managed to clamber over the last. (op 9-2)

1709 MCQUEEN 80 NOT OUT H'CAP HURDLE (6 hdls 6 omitted) 2m 6f 110y
5:10 (5:10) (Class 4) (0-115,111) 4-Y-0+ **£2,211** (£649; £324; £162)

Form RPR
56-4 **1** **Young Albert (IRE)**[145] 267 9-11-11 **110**........................ AndrewTinkler 118+
(Charlie Longsdon) *t.k.h: sn prom: effrt omitted 2 out: styd on to ld bef last: hit last: drvn out* **17/2**
20-0 **2** *6* **Feel The Force (IRE)**[147] 232 6-10-8 **100**................(b[1]) MrTJCannon(7) 102
(Alan Fleming) *hld up: hdwy 5th: chsng ldrs omitted 2 out: kpt on to take 2nd last 100yds* **8/1**
-41F **3** *5* **Kilmore West (IRE)**[45] 1296 5-10-10 **102**....................... MrTomDavid(7) 100
(Tim Vaughan) *hld up: wnt prom 5th: hrd rdn and chsd wnr between last 2: 5 l 2nd last: wknd run-in* **7/2**[1]
4-34 **4** *12* **Pocket Too**[14] 1555 7-10-11 **103**....................................(b) CDTimmons(7) 88
(Matthew Salaman) *chsd ldrs: wknd omitted 2 out* **5/1**[2]
4100 **5** *17* **Pool Of Knowledge (FR)**[7] 1624 4-11-3 **103**.............. AidanColeman 70
(Venetia Williams) *in rr: hdwy 5th: sn chsng ldrs: wknd between last 2* **5/1**[2]
135- **6** *18* **Stick Together**[169] 5231 7-11-5 **109**............................(b) JamesHalliday(5) 59
(Malcolm Jefferson) *led: hdd between last 2: wknd rapidly: t.o last: virtually p.u* **6/1**[3]
0- **7** *dist* **Golden Partner**[204] 4596 5-10-10 **95**.................................(t) DavidDennis —
(Matt Sheppard) *chsd ldrs: drvn 4th: sn lost pl: t.o after next: eventually completed* **20/1**
-6U1 **P** **Pinerock (IRE)**[28] 1482 6-11-8 **110**............................ RichieMcLernon(3) —
(Jonjo O'Neill) *in rr: nt fluent and drvn 5th: sn wknd: hopelessly t.o omitted 2 out: last whn p.u bef last* **6/1**[3]

6m 3.80s (32.90) **Going Correction** +1.275s/f (Heav)
WFA 4 from 5yo+ 10lb **8** Ran SP% **110.5**
Speed ratings (Par 105): **93,90,89,85,79 72,—,—**
Tote Swingers: 1&2 £25.50, 1&3 £25.50, 2&3 £16.00 CSF £67.68 CT £268.81 TOTE £8.00: £2.70, £3.00, £1.70; EX 86.90.
Owner Hither Green Syndicate **Bred** S G And W R Deacon **Trained** Over Norton, Oxon

■ Stewards' Enquiry : Andrew Tinkler one-day ban: used whip with excessive frequency (Oct 17)
Mr Tom David six-day ban: used whip with excessive frequency (Oct 17-22)

FOCUS
A moderate hurdle in which the winner is rated to his old form with the placed horses to their marks.

NOTEBOOK
Young Albert(IRE) was keen early on and looked to have run his race as he got outpaced around the final turn, but he found more and was able to keep up the gallop on an ever-shortening stride for a game success. He is not all that consistent overall, although he has won in all national hunt disciplines and he had previously seemed better on faster ground. He comes into his own in the spring and autumn so this was the ideal time to catch him. (op 9-1)
Feel The Force(IRE) was held up early and made some progress in the home straight, but struggled to peg back the leader in the conditions. (op 15-2)
Kilmore West(IRE) made gradual progress and was given every chance, but ultimately did not get home in the ground. (tchd 3-1)
Pocket Too finished best of those racing in the front rank despite not fully seeing out the trip. Although he has not won for two years, he is gradually being given a chance by the handicapper.
\n\x\x was ridden patiently, presumably to help him get the step up in trip, and he travelled well until the home straight. His jumping was better at this slower pace and he looks on a reasonable mark. (op 9-2)

1710 CHEMTECH H'CAP CHASE (16 fncs) 2m 5f
5:40 (5:40) (Class 5) (0-95,94) 4-Y-0+ **£2,211** (£649; £324; £162)

Form RPR
P0-0 **1** **Russellstown Boy (IRE)**[14] 1559 10-10-11 **79**................. PaulMoloney 95+
(Evan Williams) *chsd ldrs: wnt 2nd appr 3 out: led bef next: sn wl clr: eased fnl 100yds* **12/1**
62P- **2** *27* **Mister Wiseman**[162] 5390 8-11-12 **94**...............................(p) DavidDennis 80
(Nigel Hawke) *chsd ldr: led appr 3 out: hdd bef next: sn btn* **14/1**
2165 **3** *9* **Papradon**[29] 1471 6-11-9 **94**........................(b) SamTwiston-Davies(3) 71
(Nigel Twiston-Davies) *chsd ldrs 5th: mstke next: wknd appr 3 out* **7/1**[2]
0443 **4** *5* **Converti**[19] 1490 6-11-1 **90**.. SClements(7) 62
(Simon Burrough) *in tch: lost pl 9th: sn bhd: t.o 3 out: plugged on: lft 4th last* **8/1**
6045 **P** **Rince Donn (IRE)**[10] 1591 8-11-5 **87**................................... HaddenFrost —
(Roger Curtis) *wnt prom 4th: wknd 10th: sn bhd: t.o whn p.u bef 3 out* **12/1**
5-42 **P** **Whatcanisay**[119] 650 11-10-5 **76** ow3...........................(t) ChrisHonour(3) —
(James Frost) *in rr: bhd fr 7th: sn t.o: p.u bef 3 out* **4/1**[1]
F **Turn Up (IRE)**[150] 187 7-10-12 **87**.....................................(t) MrJMRidley(7) 59
(Matt Sheppard) *led: hit 8th: hdd appr 3 out: sn wknd: distant 4th whn fell last* **33/1**
4555 **P** **Canal Bank (IRE)**[28] 1485 6-11-8 **93**......................... RichieMcLernon(3) —
(Jonjo O'Neill) *nt jump wl: in rr: drvn and hdwy 8th: hit next: wknd 11th: bhd whn p.u bef 2 out* **4/1**[1]
000- **U** **Rossmill Lad (IRE)**[177] 5115 6-10-7 **82**........................(t) MrTomDavid(7) —
(Tim Vaughan) *in rr: hdwy 8th: modest 7th whn hit 10th: poor 5th whn blnd and uns rdr 2 out* **15/2**[3]
403- **P** **Macdougal (IRE)**[163] 5353 6-11-9 **91**................................. BrianHarding —
(Donald McCain) *chsd ldrs: hit 6th: lost pl after next: sn bhd: t.o whn p.u bef 11th* **4/1**[1]

5m 54.5s (31.00) **Going Correction** +1.575s/f (Heav) **10** Ran SP% **120.4**
Speed ratings (Par 103): **103,92,89,87,— —,—,—,—,—**
Tote Swingers: 1&2 £18.60, 1&3 £24.80, 2&3 £20.30 CSF £163.01 CT £1278.42 TOTE £11.10: £4.20, £3.80, £2.10; EX 221.70 Place 6: £404.36 Place 5: £112.10..
Owner R E R Williams **Bred** P Cleary **Trained** Llancarfan, Vale Of Glamorgan

FOCUS
Only four managed to complete in the ever-softening conditions. The form could be rated higher.

NOTEBOOK
Russellstown Boy(IRE) was one of the few to act in the conditions, and he jumped well to come through for an untroubled first success over fences. He had put up a couple of reasonable efforts in soft-ground chases last year but was well beaten two weeks ago in a 3m hurdle at this track on his return from an eight-month break. However, that run put him spot-on for this and it was the story of the handicaps at this meeting, namely capitalising on a light weight and an exploitable mark. (op 14-1)
Mister Wiseman raced prominently throughout and ran a game race but was just outdone by the lack of a recent outing. He is on a feasible mark and could handle a step up in trip in his quest for his first chasing success. (op 12-1 tchd 11-1)
Papradon, a winner over fences at Newton Abbot in August, did not jump with any fluency in these testing conditions and the reapplication of blinkers produced no better effect than the last time they were deployed in the spring. (op 8-1 tchd 13-2)
Converti needs a more testing track but less testing underfoot conditions to be effective. (op 11-1)
Rossmill Lad(IRE), despite jumping low at several fences, had made some headway and was in the process of running a reasonable race when dumping his jockey at the second-last. He would not have challenged the winner but nevertheless should come on for this first run for Tim Vaughan. (op 7-1 tchd 9-1)
T/Plt: £4,611.20 to a £1 stake. Pool of £56,220 - 8.90 winning tickets. T/Qpdt: £325.70 to a £1 stake. Pool of £5,987 - 13.60 winning tickets. WG

1036 TIPPERARY (L-H)
Sunday, October 3

OFFICIAL GOING: Flat course - soft (heavy in places); jumps courses - yielding (yielding to soft in places)

1711a FRIENDS OF TIPPERARY HURDLE (GRADE 2) (9 hdls) 2m
3:45 (3:45) 4-Y-0+ **£31,637** (£9,247; £4,380; £1,460)

RPR
1 **Donnas Palm (IRE)**[181] 5066 6-11-10 155.............................. PCarberry 150+
(Noel Meade, Ire) *trckd ldrs: hdwy to ld ent st: clr whn slow at last: hdd and rdn early run-in: rallied to regain ld cl home: cosily at line* **5/4**[1]
2 *1 1/4* **Aitmatov (GER)**[164] 5348 9-11-10 148.................................(bt) DJCondon 149
(Noel Meade, Ire) *led: rdn and hdd ent st: capitalised on wnr's mstke at last and led early run-in: hdd and no ex cl home* **12/1**
3 *1 1/4* **On The Way Out (IRE)**[17] 1929 7-11-7 .... RWalsh 145
(John E Kiely, Ire) *hld up in 5th: rdn fr 3 out: wnt mod 3rd fr 2 out: kpt on one pce* **12/1**
4 *13* **Grey Soldier (IRE)**[86] 938 5-11-4 133...........................(t) BarryGeraghty 129
(Gordon Elliott, Ire) *trckd ldrs: 4th 3 out: sn rdn: no imp st* **11/2**[3]
5 *2* **Bahrain Storm (IRE)**[23] 1133 7-11-7 153..............................(b) DJCasey 130
(Patrick J Flynn, Ire) *trckd ldr in 2nd: rdn in 3rd ent st: wknd* **7/4**[2]
6 *dist* **Takestan (IRE)**[62] 1038 7-11-4 117.. JLCullen —
(Patrick O Brady, Ire) *a last: wknd fr 4 out: t.o* **50/1**

3m 50.5s (230.50) **6** Ran SP% **113.5**
CSF £16.55 TOTE £2.00: £2.60, £6.60; DF 14.50.

Owner Grand Alliance Racing Club **Bred** Mrs J Brown **Trained** Castletown, Co Meath

FOCUS

A one-two for Noel Meade and a successful return for Donna's Palm, runner-up to Solwhit in last season's Irish Champion Hurdle. The race has been rated around the third to his best form.

NOTEBOOK

Donnas Palm(IRE), who also scored on his seasonal debut last year, maintained his record of running well when fresh, recovering from a clumsy jump at the last to regain the initiative from his stable companion Aitmatov. He should improve plenty from this as the trainer says he's only just come to himself at home. (op 4/5)

Aitmatov(GER) set out to make all, but Donnas Palm took command early in the straight and was well in command before his error at the last briefly changed the complexion of the race. This was encouraging and he will be suited by a return to further. (op 10/1 tchd 14/1)

On The Way Out(IRE) produced an encouraging display on only his second outing since returning from a spell on the sidelines. His run in a Flat handicap at Listowel had been inconclusive, but this provided clear evidence that he can re-establish a presence over hurdles, especially since he stays a good deal further than this. (op 12/1 tchd 14/1)

Grey Soldier(IRE) faced a tough task at the weights and is a better horse on good ground. (op 7/1)

Bahrain Storm(IRE), the 2009 Galway Hurdle winner who won a Grade 3 event over the course and trip in July prior to a fine second to Overturn at Galway, theoretically had much the same chance as Donnas Palm at the weights and had a potential edge in terms of race-fitness as well, but he managed no response when coming under pressure off the home turn. Official explanation: jockey said gelding stumbled on the bend past the stand (op 5/2 tchd 13/8)

1712a O'DWYER STEEL NOVICE CHASE (GRADE 3) (14 fncs) 2m 4f

4:20 (4:20) 4-Y-O+ **£17,256** (£5,044; £2,389; £796)

RPR

1 **Beau Michael**[6] 1637 6-11-5 ....(tp) BarryGeraghty 143
(Adrian McGuinness, Ire) *trckd ldrs: led fr 4 out: clr ent st: styd on wl fr last: easily* **7/1**

2 9 **Gonebeyondrecall (IRE)**[21] 1517 7-11-5 132....(b) RMPower 134
(N F Glynn, Ire) *trckd ldrs: j.w tl mstke 5 out: dropped to 4th: rdn in mod 2nd ent st: kpt on* **11/4**[2]

3 1 ½ **Glenstal Abbey (IRE)**[20] 1519 6-11-5 ....(t) DJCasey 133
(C F Swan, Ire) *trckd ldrs: 3rd 3 out: sn rdn: kpt on one pce st* **15/8**[1]

4 dist **Seeability (IRE)**[7] 1634 7-11-2 .... JLCullen —
(Patrick O Brady, Ire) *racd in last: mstke 2nd: 5th fr 8th: wknd fr 3 out: t.o whn j.rt 2 out and mstke last* **12/1**

5 dist **Essex (IRE)**[21] 1516 10-11-2 ....(b) AELynch —
(Denis W Cullen, Ire) *trckd ldrs: bad mstke 8th and dropped to last: trailing fr 5 out: completely t.o* **5/1**[3]

F **Pallasmore (IRE)**[21] 1517 7-11-8 128....(b) MDarcy —
(Paul W Flynn, Ire) *led: jnd whn fell 4 out* **6/1**

5m 6.00s (306.00) **6 Ran SP% 112.6**

CSF £27.15 TOTE £4.30: £2.50, £1.20; DF 34.60.

Owner Total Recall Racing Club **Bred** Berkshire Equestrian Services Ltd **Trained** Lusk, Co Dublin

FOCUS

The runner-up is the best guide to the form.

NOTEBOOK

Beau Michael came right back to his best here only six days after a Roscommon third that could have been used to question his chance. In front after Pallasmore fell at the fourth-last, he was in control before the straight on his way to a third win over fences. All told, he has won five of his eight races since May, proving a great credit to trainer Ado McGuinness. Though suited by ease in the ground, the winner is probably not really equipped for typical winter conditions. Having been on the go through the summer it would be no surprise if he gets a break fairly soon, though McGuinness indicated a few months back that he could go to Cheltenham in November.

Gonebeyondrecall(IRE) has been on a roll lately, having initially taken longer than might have been anticipated to make his mark over fences. He was in trouble after a mistake four out and failed to rally in what was a tame effort against the background of a decisive win in a handicap chase at Listowel. (op 2/1)

Glenstal Abbey(IRE), favourite to maintain an unbeaten record over fences, faced his stiffest task yet and found little when it mattered. It looks as if he will need to raise his game in order to be competitive in the better novice chases as the season gains momentum. (op 9/4)

Seeability(IRE) was set a tough task here on only his second run over fences. He would benefit from a drop in class, but needs to get his jumping act together on this evidence.

Essex(IRE) blew his chance with a bad error at the eighth, from which point he was tailed off. (op 5/1 tchd 9/2)

1713a DOLORES PURCELL MEMORIAL NOVICE HURDLE (GRADE 3) (9 hdls) 2m

4:50 (4:50) 4-Y-O+ **£16,393** (£4,792; £2,269; £756)

RPR

1 **Oilily (IRE)**[105] 810 7-10-10 .... ADLeigh 130
(Sean Byrne, Ire) *s.i.s and in rr: hdwy into 3rd after 3 out: rdn to ld after 2 out: styd on wl fr last* **5/1**[3]

2 2 ½ **Ballyadam Brook (IRE)**[16] 1538 6-11-8 .... PTownend 139
(Terence O'Brien, Ire) *attempted to make all: nt fluent 3rd: rdn and u.p whn nt fluent 2 out: sn hdd: kpt on same pce fr last* **3/1**[1]

3 5 **Oneeightofamile (IRE)**[8] 1615 5-11-1 .... DJCondon 127
(John E Kiely, Ire) *hld up: hdwy into 4th and rdn ent st: wnt 3rd fr last: kpt on same pce* **5/1**[3]

4 2 **Takeyourcapoff (IRE)**[16] 1538 5-10-10 .... RMPower 121
(Mrs John Harrington, Ire) *mid-div: hdwy fr 3 out: rdn in 3rd ent st: no ex and dropped to 4th fr last* **4/1**[2]

5 2 **False Economy (IRE)**[21] 1513 5-11-1 .... PCarberry 123
(Michael Hourigan, Ire) *mid-div: 6th 3 out: sn rdn: no imp st* **10/1**

6 9 **Hazeymm (IRE)**[16] 1538 7-11-5 125.... AndrewJMcNamara 118
(E J O'Grady, Ire) *trckd ldrs: rdn in 4th after 3 out: no imp* **16/1**

7 24 **Imperial Shabra (IRE)**[16] 1538 6-11-5 116.... SWJackson 94
(Patrick O Brady, Ire) *trckd ldr in 2nd: rdn and wknd fr 3 out* **33/1**

8 1 ½ **One Cool Tornado (IRE)**[18] 1526 5-11-8 .... AELynch 96
(Paul John Gilligan, Ire) *trckd ldrs: 4th 4 out: rdn and wknd fr next* **7/1**

9 3 **Golden Grimshaw (IRE)**[37] 1395 8-11-5 117.... BarryGeraghty 90
(J J Lambe, Ire) *mid-div: wknd fr 3 out* **16/1**

10 18 **Foildubh (IRE)**[153] 114 6-11-1 .... RCColgan 68
(John Patrick Ryan, Ire) *trckd ldrs: wknd fr 4 out* **50/1**

F **Dont Tell The Boys**[20] 1522 4-10-11 .... RWalsh —
(P J Rothwell, Ire) *in rr: fell 4th* **12/1**

3m 50.9s (230.90)

WFA 4 from 5yo+ 9lb **11 Ran SP% 124.3**

CSF £22.17 TOTE £7.10: £1.80, £1.30, £1.70; DF 35.00.

Owner Mrs Paula Murphy **Bred** Mrs Paula Murphy **Trained** Athy, Co Kildare

FOCUS

The runner-up has been rated to his mark and the third in line with his Flat form.

NOTEBOOK

Oilily(IRE) ◆ was produced in fine shape by Sean Byrne to account for a gelding who can be considered a very solid yardstick. Her overall record now reads three wins and six second places from nine starts, and there are not going to be many more of her calibre on the novice hurdling scene this winter. (op 6/1)

Ballyadam Brook(IRE) set out to make all. He was beginning to feel the strain when getting the second-last wrong, but this was another grand effort by a novice who has made sustained improvement since the spring. (op 11/4)

Oneeightofamile(IRE), reappearing only eight days after a winning hurdling debut at Navan, coped adequately with the rise in class, underlining the stables' current excellent form. He should continue to pay his way. (op 6/1)

Takeyourcapoff(IRE), who had looked a possible danger to Ballyadam Brook when unseating two out at Listowel, had her chance to make amends but failed to get to grips when trying to thrown down a challenge before the straight. (op 4/1 tchd 9/2)

Hazeymm(IRE) wasn't suited by the change in the ground. (op 14/1)

One Cool Tornado(IRE) has shown his best form on quick ground.

1718 - 1722a (Foreign Racing) - See Raceform Interactive

298 LUDLOW (R-H)

Wednesday, October 6

OFFICIAL GOING: Good (7.6)

Wind: nil Weather: showers

1723 WELCOME BACK TO LUDLOW (S) HURDLE (9 hdls) 2m

2:20 (2:20) (Class 5) 4-7-Y-O **£1,951** (£573; £286; £143)

Form RPR

-110 1 **Skye But N Ben**[146] 298 6-11-8 108....(b) JamieMoore 112
(Jim Best) *trckd ldrs: stmbld bef 3 out: sn led: drvn out and styd on wl after last* **11/1**

0/42 2 2 **Apt To Run (USA)**[42] 1370 7-10-12 0....(t) PaulMoloney 100
(David Rees) *hld up: hdwy after 6th: trckd ldrs 3 out: wnt 2nd last: no imp run-in* **11/2**[2]

4126 3 nk **Tignello (IRE)**[17] 1548 5-10-13 112....(t) IanPopham[(5)] 106
(Paul Nicholls) *midfield: hdwy after 6th: chalng 3 out: kpt on same pce fr last* **5/2**[1]

5234 4 5 **Navajo Nation (IRE)**[17] 1547 4-10-9 96....(p) SamTwiston-Davies[(3)] 95
(Bill Turner) *midfield: hdwy appr 3 out: one pce fr 2 out* **15/2**[3]

/6F0 5 1 **Runaway Harry (IRE)**[35] 1449 7-10-12 0.... TomO'Brien 94
(Peter Bowen) *in rr: rdn after 6th: hdwy 3 out: one pce and no further imp fr 2 out* **25/1**

0242 6 1 ¼ **Sadler's Star (GER)**[28] 1506 7-11-8 112....(p) TimmyMurphy 103
(Michael Blake) *in rr: j. slowly 6th: hdwy sn after: styd on same pce fr 3 out* **11/2**[2]

0P-5 7 9 **Art Value**[17] 1552 5-10-12 70.... HarrySkelton 85
(Carroll Gray) *in rr: hdwy to chse ldrs after 6th: wknd 3 out* **100/1**

20F/ 8 20 **Sumner (IRE)**[65] 1895 6-10-9 0....(v[1]) LeeStephens[(3)] 67
(David Evans) *trckd ldrs: blnd 5th: wknd next* **20/1**

P506 9 ¾ **Rocklandslad (IRE)**[15] 1569 7-10-12 105....(b) APMcCoy 69
(Rebecca Curtis) *led to 2nd: remained prom: regained ld briefly bef 3 out: mstke 3 out whn wkng* **8/1**

3 10 nk **Mount Hadley (USA)**[45] 1344 6-10-12 0....(t) TomScudamore 66
(David Pipe) *in tch: led bef 3 out where mstke and hdd: wknd bef 2 out* **8/1**

5/0- 11 7 **Zaif (IRE)**[15] 2158 7-10-12 0.... MarkGrant 60
(Dominic Ffrench Davis) *led 2nd tl appr 3 out: sn wknd* **40/1**

5000 12 nk **Vogarth**[10] 1624 6-10-5 78.... KyleJames[(7)] 59
(Michael Chapman) *midfield: reminders after 4th: wknd bef 3 out* **150/1**

00 13 2 ¼ **Spiders Tern**[17] 1547 5-10-5 0.... MrTJCannon[(7)] 57
(Milton Bradley) *in tch: hit 4th: rdn 5th: wknd 3 out: sn eased* **125/1**

P/ P **Millers Saphire**[783] 1176 5-9-12 0....(b[1]) MrRGHenderson[(7)] —
(Ken Wingrove) *a bhd: t.o 5th: p.u 6th* **200/1**

0 P **Kheskianto (IRE)**[11] 1613 4-10-5 0.... JamieGoldstein —
(Michael Chapman) *midfield: wknd bef 6th: t.o whn p.u bef 3 out* **200/1**

3m 43.0s (-6.50) **Going Correction** -0.25s/f (Good)

WFA 4 from 5yo+ 9lb **15 Ran SP% 116.1**

Speed ratings: **106,105,104,102,101 101,96,86,86,86 82,82,81,—,—**

toteswingers:1&2 £11.70, 2&3 £2.80, 1&3 £4.20 CSF £66.33 TOTE £9.90: £4.30, £2.30, £1.50.The winner was sold to D. Chapman for £5,000. Tignello was claimed by Miss E. J. Baker for £6,000.

Owner Sills Racing **Bred** Charles And David Hodge **Trained** Lewes, E Sussex

FOCUS

A decent selling hurdle with the winner rated in line with his best Flat form and those in the frame behind just a few pounds off their best.

NOTEBOOK

Skye But N Ben kept finding having gone on three out and was clearly fit on this return from a 108-day absence. He is better than this level, as his two handicap wins in the spring demonstrate, and he remains capable of further success for his new trainer Michael Chapman. (op 9-1)

Apt To Run(USA), runner-up in a claiming hurdle at Ffos Las latest, kept on to take second, but never looked like winning. (op 6-1 tchd 5-1)

Tignello(IRE), disappointing in a handicap at Plumpton latest, was expected by many to capitalise on the drop in grade, but he didn't find as much as had looked likely and was always being held from after two out. (op 11-4 tchd 3-1)

Navajo Nation(IRE) often runs well without winning and he's now winless in 25 attempts. (op 10-1)

Sadler's Star(GER) never got into it, just plodding on late. (tchd 13-2)

1724 UKFP MEMBERS DAY AT LUDLOW MARES' NOVICES' HURDLE (11 hdls) 2m 5f

2:50 (2:50) (Class 4) 4-Y-O+ **£3,252** (£955; £477; £238)

Form RPR

040- 1 **Miss Overdrive**[174] 5196 6-10-3 116.... MrBJPoste[(7)] 121+
(Andy Turnell) *trckd ldrs: travelled wl to ld appr 3 out: r.o wl to draw clr run-in* **7/2**[2]

3- 2 13 **Boragh Princess (IRE)**[33] 1460 6-11-3 112.... APMcCoy 119+
(Gordon Elliott, Ire) *midfield: hdwy appr 8th: 2nd and chalng bef 3 out: no ex run-in* **4/1**[3]

1212 3 14 **Black Annie (IRE)**[28] 1505 5-11-3 113....(t) SamThomas 103
(Paul Webber) *led: hdd appr 3 out: sn wknd* **8/1**

30P- 4 2 ¾ **Emmaslegend**[208] 4569 5-10-3 0.... MrTJCannon[(7)] 94
(Suzy Smith) *prom: rdn appr 3 out: sn wknd* **40/1**

35-3 5 3 ½ **Be My Light (IRE)**[148] 263 4-10-10 0.... AndrewTinkler 90
(Charlie Longsdon) *midfield: rdn bef 8th: hdwy 3 out: wknd bef next* **10/1**

2022 6 29 **Astrolibra**[31] 1475 6-11-3 115.... ColinBolger 71
(Mark H Tompkins) *hld up: hdwy bef 8th: wknd 3 out* **13/2**

2 **7** *68* **Try Cat**[12] 1600 4-10-10 0 RichardJohnson —
(Philip Hobbs) *a bhd: nt fluent 5th: t.o* **12/1**

323 **8** *dist* **Alaska River (IRE)**[15] 1572 4-10-10 0 MarkGrant —
(Brendan Duke) *midfield early: bhd 6th: t.o* **40/1**

2-14 **P** **Prescelli (IRE)**[146] 302 6-11-10 115 (b) TomO'Brien —
(Keith Goldsworthy) *cl up tl wknd 8th: t.o whn p.u bef 3 out* **11/4**[1]

0-00 **R** **Floating Cloud**[76] 1071 6-10-10 0 CharliePoste —
(Trevor Wall) *bhd: rn out bef 6th* **125/1**

-000 **P** **Muzey's Princess**[35] 1449 4-10-7 0 CharlieStudd(3) —
(Michael Mullineaux) *chsd ldrs early: struggling 7th: t.o whn p.u bef 3 out* **150/1**

5m 8.40s (-6.40) **Going Correction** -0.25s/f (Good)
WFA 4 from 5yo+ 10lb **11** Ran SP% **116.5**
Speed ratings (Par 105): **102,97,91,90,89 78,52,—,—,— —**
toteswingers:1&2 £4.10, 2&3 £7.50, 1&3 £17.40 CSF £18.00 TOTE £5.20: £1.90, £2.30, £1.60; EX 22.20.
Owner Partners In Wine **Bred** R And J Micklethwait **Trained** Broad Hinton, Wilts

FOCUS
An ordinary mares' novice hurdle with the first two close to their marks backed up by the fourth and fifth.

NOTEBOOK
Miss Overdrive looked the one to beat on the form of last season's fourth in the Listed mares' final at Newbury, and, despite disappointing next time, she returned to her best to take this. It was clear from well before the turn into the straight she was travelling best, and had the race won by the time she took the second-last. She will presumably be aimed towards the Newbury contest once again. (op 4-1)
Boragh Princess(IRE) was driven to challenge off the final bend, but she couldn't race on with the winner and ended up well held in second. (op 5-1)
Black Annie(IRE) went well to a point, but was quickly left trailing by the winner and finished well beaten. (op 9-1)
Emmaslegend showed improved form and could make her mark in low-grade handicaps. (op 33-1)
Be My Light(IRE) was under pressure well before the straight and eventually weakened. (op 8-1)
Astrolibra briefly threatened to stay on down the straight, but it didn't happen. (op 7-1 tchd 15-2)
Try Cat failed to build on a promising debut effort. (op 15-2)
Alaska River(IRE) Official explanation: vet said filly finished lame
Prescelli(IRE) failed by a long way to run her race and it would come as no surprise to learn something was amiss. Official explanation: jockey said mare never travelled; vet said mare lost left-fore shoe (op 7-2)
Floating Cloud Official explanation: jockey said mare ran out stables bend and saddle slipped (op 7-2)
Muzey's Princess Official explanation: jockey said filly never travelled (op 7-2)

1725 READ PAUL NICHOLLS EXCLUSIVELY ON BETFAIR H'CAP CHASE (19 fncs) 3m
3:20 (3:20) (Class 3) (0-120,120) 4-Y-0+
£7,514 (£2,220; £1,110; £555; £277; £139)

Form RPR

0U22 **1** **King Roonah**[13] 1598 6-11-7 115 (t) TimmyMurphy 131+
(Gordon Elliott, Ire) *hld up: smooth hdwy 15th: swtchd rt after 4 out: led last: drew clr and r.o wl* **15/2**

2/0- **2** *5* **Our Jasper**[390] 1426 10-11-4 119 MrJHamer(7) 131+
(Donald McCain) *chsd ldrs: led 3 out: hdd last: no ex run-in* **25/1**

454- **3** *4 ½* **Marleybow (IRE)**[173] 5206 7-11-4 112 TomScudamore 118
(Richard Lee) *midfield: nt fluent 14th: hdwy 15th: ev ch appr 4 out: one pce fr 3 out* **15/2**

10/2 **4** *1* **Cebonne (FR)**[47] 1309 9-11-2 110 PaulMoloney 115
(Sophie Leech) *hld up: hdwy to chse ldrs 4 out: rdn and btn 3 out* **5/1**[2]

/1-P **5** *19* **Alfie's Sun**[28] 1509 11-11-4 112 NoelFehily 103
(Don Cantillon) *led: hdd 3 out: sn wknd* **25/1**

P3F4 **6** *3 ¼* **Whataboutya (IRE)**[32] 1469 9-11-7 115 (p) APMcCoy 103
(Jonjo O'Neill) *midfield: brief effrt 4 out: btn bef 2 out* **8/1**

1150 **7** *7* **Tyup Pompey (IRE)**[35] 1454 9-11-2 113 LeeStephens(3) 96
(Ann Price) *prom: ev ch 4 out: wknd 3 out* **25/1**

5-3P **8** *2 ½* **Go West (IRE)**[125] 599 9-11-2 113 SamTwiston-Davies(3) 91
(Nigel Twiston-Davies) *nt fluent: midfield: wknd 4 out* **7/1**

P4 **9** *5* **No Reception (IRE)**[12] 1602 9-10-7 108 MissLBrooke(7) 80
(Lady Susan Brooke) *a bhd* **40/1**

031- **10** *5* **Estates Recovery (IRE)**[176] 5175 5-11-11 119 RichardJohnson 86
(Philip Hobbs) *nt jump wl: midfield early: sn bhd* **11/2**[3]

FP-3 **11** *19* **Island Flyer (IRE)**[87] 947 8-11-12 120 SamThomas 70
(Tom George) *midfield: wknd 13th: bhd and toiling 15th* **25/1**

0522 **P** **Tritonville Lodge (IRE)**[50] 1276 8-11-7 115 JackDoyle —
(Emma Lavelle) *prom: wknd qckly after 4 out: p.u bef next: dismntd: lame* **9/2**[1]

P-PF **P** **Prestbury Knight**[46] 1326 10-11-6 114 JohnnyFarrelly —
(Sophie Leech) *a bhd: t.o whn p.u bef 4 out* **40/1**

6m 6.80s (-1.50) **Going Correction** +0.125s/f (Yiel) **13** Ran SP% **117.6**
Speed ratings (Par 107): **107,105,103,103,97 96,93,92,91,89 83,—,—**
toteswingers:1&2 £38.50, 2&3 £18.80, 1&3 £26.30 CSF £177.35 CT £1448.81 TOTE £5.40: £3.20, £6.90, £2.60; EX 109.60.
Owner Sean F Gallagher **Bred** Helshaw Grange Stud And E Kent **Trained** Trim, Co Meath

FOCUS
A modest handicap hurdle rated around the placed horses.

NOTEBOOK
King Roonah was always travelling kindly under Timmy Murphy. Runner-up in his previous two starts, the better ground was to his liking and he can continue to give a good account, even after a rise. He may now head for an amateur riders' handicap chase at Cheltenham next week. (op 7-1)
Our Jasper, off for over a year but on a fair mark, was clearly straight enough to run a big race and he found only the in-form winner too good. (op 22-1 tchd 28-1)
Marleybow(IRE), making his debut for the yard, shaped promisingly and should improve. He's in good hands. (op 11-2)
Cebonne(FR), narrowly denied at Bangor on his return from almost two years off, didn't run as well off 5lb higher this time, but deserves another chance. (op 6-1)
Alfie's Sun ran better than he had done at Uttoxeter. (tchd 28-1)
Estates Recovery(IRE) failed to jump with any fluency on this first start over fences. (tchd 6-1)
Tritonville Lodge(IRE) was dismounted having been pulled up, suggesting something had gone amiss. Official explanation: jockey said gelding pulled up lame (op 11-2)

1726 JUBILEE RESTAURANT & BOXES H'CAP HURDLE (11 hdls) 2m 5f
3:50 (3:52) (Class 4) (0-115,112) 4-Y-0+ **£3,903** (£1,146; £573; £286)

Form RPR

4-54 **1** **Court Red Handed (IRE)**[17] 1556 5-11-2 102 (p) TomO'Brien 108+
(Rebecca Curtis) *trckd ldrs: led after 4 out: rdn bef last: styd on* **7/2**[1]

0402 **2** *1 ½* **Armenian Boy (FR)**[17] 1556 7-11-10 110 (bt) TomScudamore 114
(David Pipe) *in tch: rdn appr 7th: wnt 2nd bef 3 out: kpt on u.p run-in: a hld* **11/1**

03-0 **3** *1 ¾* **Lost Glory (NZ)**[31] 1477 5-11-6 106 APMcCoy 108
(Jonjo O'Neill) *midfield: hdwy to chse ldrs 3 out: rdn bef 2 out: swtchd lft after last: one pce* **20/1**

3131 **4** *shd* **Call At Midnight**[31] 1477 5-11-8 108 JackDoyle 109
(Sarah Humphrey) *hld up: hdwy after 4 out: chsd ldrs appr 3 out: rdn 2 out: one pce* **7/1**[3]

4214 **5** *2* **Admiral Dundas (IRE)**[49] 1282 5-11-3 106 (t) SamTwiston-Davies(3) 106
(Kim Bailey) *in tch: effrt appr 3 out: no imp fr 2 out* **8/1**

0-03 **6** *5* **Timpo (FR)**[122] 651 7-11-0 100 RichardJohnson 96
(Henry Daly) *trckd ldrs tl rdn and wknd 3 out* **9/1**

5641 **7** *½* **Cubism**[11] 1614 4-10-12 103 (t) JimmyDerham(5) 98
(Milton Harris) *trckd ldrs: rdn and outpcd bef 3 out* **11/1**

3-40 **8** *4 ½* **Fool's Wildcat (USA)**[94] 899 5-10-9 95 (bt) TimmyMurphy 88
(Gordon Elliott, Ire) *hld up: rdn bef 3 out: no imp* **9/1**

1-4P **9** *7* **Tighe Caster**[106] 824 11-11-10 110 JodieMogford 94
(Graeme McPherson) *hld up: hit 3 out: nvr able to get on terms* **33/1**

1601 **10** *9* **Golden Gem (IRE)**[17] 1555 8-11-2 109 (p) MrJMahot(7) 85
(Rachel Hobbs) *j. slowly 7th: a bhd* **28/1**

0-55 **11** *1 ½* **Hippodrome (IRE)**[17] 1555 8-10-7 100 (p) KyleJames(7) 75
(John Harris) *a bhd* **33/1**

P131 **12** *2* **Strumble Head (IRE)**[17] 1551 5-9-13 88 (b) DonalDevereux(3) 61
(Peter Bowen) *chsd ldr: led 7th: hdd after 4 out: sn wknd* **11/2**[2]

F300 **13** *13* **Mayor Of Kilcock**[105] 829 7-10-7 100 AnthonyFreeman(7) 61
(James Danahar) *led to 7th: wknd after 4 out* **33/1**

62F **14** *20* **Dark Energy**[33] 1282 6-11-12 112 (t) SamThomas 55
(Michael Scudamore) *hld up: rdn appr 3 out: no imp* **25/1**

4P-3 **15** *27* **Brimley**[35] 1449 7-10-11 100 LeeStephens(3) 19
(Ann Price) *chsd ldrs: lost pl 5th: sn struggling and bhd* **40/1**

500- **P** **Cosavita (FR)**[230] 4120 5-11-5 105 PaulMoloney —
(David Rees) *in tch: lost pl 7th: t.o whn p.u bef 3 out* **40/1**

33P0 **P** **Supernoverre (IRE)**[13] 1590 4-11-5 105 NoelFehily —
(Liam Corcoran) *midfield: wknd after 4 out: t.o whn p.u bef 3 out* **33/1**

5m 6.80s (-8.00) **Going Correction** -0.25s/f (Good)
WFA 4 from 5yo+ 10lb **17** Ran SP% **126.6**
Speed ratings (Par 105): **105,104,103,103,102 101,100,99,96,93 92,91,86,79,68 —,—**
toteswingers:1&2 £14.40, 2&3 £15.30, 1&3 £18.70 CSF £38.57 CT £699.68 TOTE £5.00: £2.00, £2.80, £4.90, £1.70; EX 67.00.
Owner G Costelloe **Bred** O Maguire **Trained** Newport, Dyfed

FOCUS
A modest handicap hurdle but the form looks solid rated around the runner-up, fourth and fifth.

NOTEBOOK
Court Red Handed(IRE), backed beforehand, took over quite a way out and galloped on relentlessly to get off the mark over hurdles. The first-time cheekpieces were clearly a big help and he will now go over fences. (op 5-1)
Armenian Boy(FR) made Tom Scudamore earn his riding fee, looking very hard work, but he kept responding and was always holding second. (tchd 14-1)
Lost Glory(NZ) had finished well held on his handicap debut at Fontwell, and showed enough here to suggest he won't be long in winning. (op 14-1)
Call At Midnight ran her race and gives the form a solid look. She's been in good form of late, winning twice, and can continue to give a good account. (tchd 6-1)
Admiral Dundas(IRE), up in trip for the first time, was ridden to hold a chance before the straight, but he couldn't stay on as strongly as the principals. (op 15-2)
Golden Gem(IRE) Official explanation: vet said gelding finished lame
Strumble Head(IRE) may have done a bit too much through the early stages looking at how quickly he dropped away. (op 7-1)

1727 LUDLOW FOOD CENTRE BEGINNERS' CHASE (17 fncs) 2m 4f
4:20 (4:20) (Class 4) 4-Y-0+
£3,757 (£1,110; £555; £277; £138; £69)

Form RPR

1P4- **1** **Golan Way**[220] 4328 6-11-4 0 JamieGoldstein 145+
(Sheena West) *mde all: sn clr: unchal* **5/6**[1]

620- **2** *29* **Key Cutter (FR)**[164] 3 6-11-4 118 (t) WillKennedy 116+
(Paul Webber) *chsd wnr thrght: hit 13th: no imp on wnr* **9/2**[2]

30 **3** *7* **Not So Sure Dick (IRE)**[115] 739 5-11-4 0 AndrewTinkler 100
(George Baker) *chsd ldrs: wnt mod 3rd 11th: hit 13th: no imp* **33/1**

6540 **4** *16* **Doheny Bar (IRE)**[35] 1451 7-11-4 85 (v[1]) JodieMogford 89
(Nikki Evans) *a bhd: toiling fnl circ: nvr on terms* **66/1**

-233 **5** *4 ½* **Always Bold (IRE)**[108] 802 5-11-4 0 BrianHarding 81
(Donald McCain) *chsd ldrs tl wknd 11th* **11/2**[3]

00P0 **6** *dist* **Gunnadoit (USA)**[35] 1450 5-11-1 0 (p) LeeStephens(3) 45
(Ann Price) *a bhd: toiling fnl circ: t.o* **125/1**

510- **F** **Corker**[175] 5184 8-11-4 0 (t) ColinBolger —
(Suzy Smith) *chsd ldrs tl fell 4th* **14/1**

P2 **F** **Steel Magnate (IRE)**[13] 1595 7-11-4 110 (t) APMcCoy —
(Gordon Elliott, Ire) *fell 1st* **7/1**

5m 4.10s (-0.30) **Going Correction** +0.125s/f (Yiel) **8** Ran SP% **112.5**
Speed ratings (Par 105): **105,93,90,84,82 66,—,—**
toteswingers:1&2 £2.70, 2&3 £10.00, 1&3 £6.30 CSF £5.01 TOTE £1.50: £1.02, £2.30, £7.20; EX 6.30.
Owner W R B Racing 58 **Bred** Lewis Caterers **Trained** Falmer, E Sussex

FOCUS
This was all about 147-rated hurdler Golan Way, who won easily, and the first two are rated in line with their hurdles form.

NOTEBOOK
Golan Way had plenty in hand on the rating, providing he could make the transition to fences, and he did so in style, jumping well in a clear lead and galloping on relentlessly to score with ease. A very useful recruit to chasing, he ought to defy the penalty before going up in grade, with his trainer nominating the Grade 1 Feltham Novices' Chase at Kempton on Boxing Day as the target. (op Evens tchd 11-10)
Key Cutter(FR), soon chasing the winner on this first start over fences, jumped well in the main before getting tired. This was a pleasing enough start and he seems sure to find easier opportunities. (op 11-2)
Not So Sure Dick(IRE), a former Irish point winner, has yet to run over hurdles, but he jumped soundly enough and looks to have a future in handicaps. (tchd 25-1)
Always Bold(IRE) was particularly disappointing, stopping very quickly. (op 9-2 tchd 6-1)

Steel Magnate(IRE) didn't get beyond the first. (op 11-2 tchd 5-1)

1728 LUDLOW RACING PARTNERSHIP JUVENILE MAIDEN HURDLE (9 hdls) 2m
4:50 (4:50) (Class 4) 3-Y-0 **£3,252** (£955; £477; £238)

Form RPR
5 **1** **Akula (IRE)**[11] 1610 3-10-12 0 ColinBolger 96+
(Mark H Tompkins) *prom: led 3rd: rdn appr 2 out: clr bef last: r.o wl* **9/4**[1]
2 *12* **Caracal**[17] 3-10-12 0 APMcCoy 85+
(Gordon Elliott, Ire) *a.p: swtchd lft to avoid loose horse whn chsng wnr after 3 out: no imp after* **4/1**[3]
3 *4 ½* **Jazz Age (IRE)**[261] 3-10-12 0 TomScudamore 80
(David Pipe) *hld up: mstke 5th: hdwy 6th: rdn and hung lft whn chsng ldrs appr 3 out: wknd bef 2 out* **12/1**
4 *1* **Until The Man (IRE)**[94] 3-10-12 0 JamieMoore 79
(Jim Best) *chsd ldrs: rdn appr 3 out: wknd bef 2 out* **11/2**
5 *24* **Pullyourfingerout (IRE)**[74] 3-10-12 0 NoelFehily 58
(Brendan Powell) *midfield: effrt after 6th: wknd appr 3 out* **7/2**[2]
6 *38* **Diamondgeezer Luke (IRE)**[16] 3-10-12 0 BarryKeniry 23
(Patrick Morris) *a bhd: struggling 6th: nvr on terms* **25/1**
P **7** *4 ½* **Resolute Road**[14] 1576 3-10-9 0 SamTwiston-Davies(3) 19
(Nigel Twiston-Davies) *chsd ldrs tl rdn and wknd after 6th: t.o* **16/1**
0 **P** **Shark Man (IRE)**[17] 1545 3-10-5 0 MrJMQuinlan(7) —
(Andrew Reid) *a bhd: t.o whn p.u bef 3 out* **50/1**
U **Tom Wade (IRE)**[26] 3-10-5 0 KyleJames(7) 89+
(John Harris) *hld up: hdwy after 6th: disputing 2nd abt 1 l down whn blnd and uns rdr 3 out* **66/1**
P **Moonbalej**[191] 3-10-12 0 CharliePoste —
(Milton Harris) *midfield: wknd after 6th: t.o whn p.u bef 3 out* **18/1**
0 **P** **Gilderoy**[13] 1586 3-10-12 0 (p) RhysFlint —
(Dominic Ffrench Davis) *led to 3rd: remained handy: mstke 6th: sn wknd: t.o whn p.u bef 3 out* **100/1**

3m 48.2s (-1.30) **Going Correction** -0.25s/f (Good) 11 Ran SP% **115.5**
Speed ratings (Par 103): **93,87,84,84,72 53,51,—,—,— —**
toteswingers:1&2 £2.30, 2&3 £8.70, 1&3 £7.00 CSF £11.04 TOTE £2.70: £1.60, £2.80, £3.60; EX 11.70.
Owner Jay Three Racing **Bred** Ballylinch Stud **Trained** Newmarket, Suffolk

FOCUS
Not a particularly competitive juvenile hurdle and the winner is rated close to his debut form.

NOTEBOOK
Akula(IRE), fifth behind Architrave on his hurdles debut at Market Rasen, put that experience to good use and, although left clear three out, still held a 1l advantage and did stay on strongly, so there's a good chance he'd have won anyway. He'll have more on under a penalty, but is clearly going the right way. (op 11-4 tchd 10-3)
Caracal, rated 62 on the level, was comfortably held but showed enough to suggest he will win races at the right level. (op 11-4 tchd 5-2)
Jazz Age(IRE), who wasn't up to much in a handful of starts on the Flat, has joined a top yard and he ran well for a long way on this first start over hurdles. (tchd 11-1)
Until The Man(IRE) had shown more than most of these on the Flat, so could be considered a little disappointing. (op 6-1)
Pullyourfingerout(IRE) was solid in the market but showed little on this first start over hurdles. (op 9-2 tchd 10-3)
Tom Wade(IRE), a moderate sort on the level, was a big outsider on this first start over hurdles, but he travelled strongly into contention and was challenging when blundering and unseating his rider three out. He would have been at least second and can probably gain compensation.

1729 LUDLOWRACECOURSE.CO.UK INTERMEDIATE OPEN NATIONAL HUNT FLAT RACE 2m
5:20 (5:20) (Class 5) 4-5-Y-0 **£1,951** (£573; £286; £143)

Form RPR
1 **Natureofthebeast (IRE)**[184] 5-11-2 0 PaulMoloney 109+
(Evan Williams) *a.p: led 3f out: rdn over 1f out: kpt on wl and in command ins fnl f* **13/8**[1]
2 *2* **Blue Signal (IRE)**[183] 5-10-6 0 CiaranMckee(10) 106
(Tom George) *led: hdd 3f out: rdn over 1f out: kpt on u.p: a looked hld* **16/1**
3 *11* **Egypt Mill Spirit (IRE)** 4-11-2 0 HarrySkelton 96+
(Paul Nicholls) *hld up: hdwy 4f out: wnt 3rd over 2f out: n.d to front pair* **6/1**
4 *1 ¾* **Kiss Me Twice** 4-10-11 0 JimmyDerham(5) 95
(Martin Keighley) *midfield: effrt 4f out: outpcd 3f out* **11/2**[3]
4 **5** *2 ½* **Tribal Dance (IRE)**[28] 1510 4-11-2 0 CharliePoste 92
(Ben Case) *towards rr: hdwy 6f out: wknd 3f out* **11/1**
4 **6** *6* **Jigsaw Financial (IRE)**[12] 1607 4-11-2 0 HaddenFrost 87
(Roger Curtis) *plld hrd: prom tl 4f out* **10/1**
7 *7* **Hidden Springs** 5-11-2 0 TomScudamore 83
(Brian Baugh) *chsd ldrs tl wknd 6f out* **20/1**
8 *2 ¾* **Mar Ocean (FR)** 4-11-2 0 AndrewTinkler 80
(Patrick Griffin, Ire) *hld up: hdwy 5f out: sn trckd ldrs: rdn over 3f out: wknd over 2f out* **5/1**[2]
6 **9** *14* **John Sixteen (IRE)**[45] 1349 5-10-13 0 DonalDevereux(3) 66
(Peter Bowen) *plld hrd: hld up: struggling over 5f out: nvr on terms* **25/1**
10 *1* **Hard To Tell (IRE)** 4-10-11 0 TomO'Connor(5) 65
(Bill Turner) *midfield tl wknd 5f out* **33/1**
0- **11** *12* **Sir Clad**[329] 2238 4-10-13 0 (t) TommyPhelan(3) 54
(Claire Dyson) *midfield: sme hdwy 5f out: wknd 4f out* **100/1**
- **12** *¾* **Wychwoods Kaddy** 4-11-2 0 (t) JodieMogford 53
(Graeme McPherson) *plld hrd: midfield tl wknd over 3f out* **33/1**

3m 43.6s (-0.30) **Going Correction** -0.25s/f (Good) 12 Ran SP% **123.2**
Speed ratings: **90,89,83,82,81 78,74,73,66,66 60,59**
toteswingers:1&2 £9.00, 2&3 £10.50, 1&3 £2.70 CSF £32.17 TOTE £2.90: £1.60, £4.70, £2.40; EX 28.20 Place 6: £64.38 Place 5: £41.07 .
Owner Mrs Janet Davies **Bred** Mr And Mrs R A St George **Trained** Llancarfan, Vale Of Glamorgan

FOCUS
An ordinary bumper in which two dual point winners came clear. The fifth and sixth help set the level.

NOTEBOOK
Natureofthebeast(IRE), twice successful in Yorkshire points in the spring, was bought for £32,000 and made a perfectly satisfactory start to his career under rules. Always travelling kindly, he found plenty when asked, despite running around a bit in front, and looks to have a bright future. Whatever he does in bumpers and over hurdles, it's over fences where he's expected to really shine. (op 9-4)
Blue Signal(IRE), successful in two Irish points, was ignored in the betting, but seemed to thrive under a positive ride and kept finding for pressure, just lacking the winner's acceleration late in the day. This was a promising start. (tchd 14-1)
Egypt Mill Spirit(IRE), related to several winners, is from a top yard and he travelled well until showing his inexperience once coming under pressure. He kept on well in third, though, and clearly has a future. (op 4-1)
Kiss Me Twice, whose dam is related to top-notch chaser Jair du Cochet, made some late headway and will have pleased connections with this debut effort. (op 9-1)
Jigsaw Financial(IRE) Official explanation: jockey said gelding hung left
Mar Ocean(FR), related to winners both on the Flat and over jumps, didn't live up to market expectations on debut. (op 13-2 tchd 9-2)
T/Jkpt: Not won. T/Plt: £78.00 to a £1 stake. Pool of £53,540.67 - 501.07 winning tickets. T/Qpdt: £23.00 to a £1 stake. Pool of £3,932.80 - 126.50 winning tickets. DO

[554]TOWCESTER (R-H)
Wednesday, October 6

OFFICIAL GOING: Good
All chase bends dolled out to furthest position and hurdle course on inside line.
Wind: Fresh half-against Weather: Cloudy with sunny spells

1730 TIPZONE @ GG.COM "NATIONAL HUNT" NOVICES' H'CAP HURDLE (11 hdls) 2m 5f
2:30 (2:31) (Class 4) (0-105,104) 3-Y-0+ **£2,927** (£859; £429; £214)

Form RPR
306- **1** **Red Rouble (IRE)**[213] 4460 5-11-5 **97** PaddyBrennan 104+
(Nigel Twiston-Davies) *hld up in tch: chsd ldr 8th: led after 3 out: blnd last: drvn out* **5/2**[1]
2F02 **2** *½* **Nobby Kivambo (IRE)**[12] 1605 5-11-3 **95** JimmyMcCarthy 100+
(Brendan Powell) *hld up in tch: rdn appr last: styd on* **7/1**
P-PP **3** *1 ¼* **Little Al**[17] 1559 7-10-13 **91** (b[1]) LeightonAspell 94
(Oliver Sherwood) *hld up: hdwy 8th: rdn appr 2 out: styd on u.p* **25/1**
5421 **4** *1* **Be Ashored**[46] 1333 5-11-5 **100** RichardKilloran(3) 102
(Tim Vaughan) *hld up: hdwy 8th: rdn appr last: styd on same pce flat* **3/1**[2]
45-4 **5** *31* **Pollen Jock (IRE)**[11] 1608 6-11-3 **102** OliverWilliams(7) 76
(Chris Bealby) *chsd ldr tl led 3rd: hdd next: led again 7th: hdd after 3 out: wknd bef next: t.o* **33/1**
6-56 **6** *¾* **Mauricetheathlete (IRE)**[130] 522 7-11-4 **103** MrNSlatter(7) 78
(Martin Keighley) *mid-div: mstke and lost pl 4th: hdwy 8th: rdn and wknd appr 2 out: t.o* **7/1**
00/5 **7** *shd* **Chilliwviv**[17] 1600 7-11-5 **104** MrMWall(7) 77
(Sue Wilson) *hld up: hdwy u.p 3 out: wknd bef next: t.o* **50/1**
026 **8** *16* **The Fox's Decree**[28] 1507 6-11-7 **99** (t) WarrenMarston 73
(Martin Keighley) *hld up: hdwy 3 out: rdn and wknd bef next: t.o* **14/1**
0-00 **9** *8* **That Man Fox**[37] 1429 9-9-13 **82** (b) LeeEdwards(5) 34
(Tony Carroll) *chsd ldrs tl wknd 3 out: t.o* **66/1**
0-1P **10** *13* **Glacial Call (IRE)**[131] 502 7-9-9 **78** (b) GilesHawkins(5) 18
(James Frost) *mid-div: dropped in rr 4th: bhd fr 6th: t.o* **6/1**[3]
604 **P** **Youandme (IRE)**[28] 1505 8-10-0 **81** (p) PeterToole(3) —
(Ray Peacock) *led to 3rd: led 4th to 7th: wknd appr 3 out: t.o whn p.u bef next* **66/1**
135- **P** **Me Julie**[293] 2929 7-10-9 **87** FelixDeGiles —
(Arthur Whiting) *prom: blnd 6th: wknd bef next: t.o whn p.u bef 2 out* **16/1**

5m 18.4s (-8.80) **Going Correction** -0.625s/f (Firm) 12 Ran SP% **117.1**
Speed ratings (Par 105): **91,90,90,89,78 77,77,71,68,63 —,—**
toteswingers:1&2 £7.90, 2&3 £22.60, 1&3 £13.90 CSF £19.64 CT £353.03 TOTE £4.00: £2.00, £2.60, £8.00; EX 23.40.
Owner Patrick Bancroft **Bred** Hugh F Williams **Trained** Naunton, Gloucs
■ Stewards' Enquiry : Richard Killoran two-day ban: careless riding (Oct 20-21)

FOCUS
A moderate novice handicap run at an average gallop and there was a cracking four-way finish. The runner-up and fourth set the level.

NOTEBOOK
Red Rouble(IRE) duly opened his account at the fifth time of asking. His best run in novice company last year came on his debut and, with his yard in decent form, the strong market support was ominous for the rest of his rivals. He raced enthusiastically just off the pace and took it up going strongly turning for home. He idled out in front from two out, and Brennan needed to get very serious with him. He was always just doing enough, though, and looks value for a bit further. A horse with scope, he evidently enjoys a sound surface and can build on this, but his long-term future lies over fences. (op 2-1)
Nobby Kivambo(IRE), 5lb higher, responded to pressure three out and went down fighting. He has now found one too strong on his last two outings, but does deserve a change of fortune. (op 9-1 tchd 10-1)
Little Al had been pulled up in five of his last six runs, but was equipped with first-time blinkers and he turned in a vastly improved effort as a result. He's well treated on his previous best efforts, but it remains to be seen whether the headgear continues to have the same effect. (op 20-1)
Be Ashored was 10lb higher than when getting off the mark in August. Ridden to get the trip back over this longer test, he held every chance off the front turn but his rider may have been better off pulling him to the outer of the front two thereafter as he did look to get a bit crowded. He still failed to see it out like the principals, though, and will be better off back over an easier test. (tchd 5-2 and 10-3, tchd 7-2 in places)

1731 GG.COM BEGINNERS' CHASE (12 fncs) 2m 110y
3:00 (3:00) (Class 4) 4-Y-0+ **£3,252** (£955; £477; £238)

Form RPR
1UP- **1** **Have You Seen Me (IRE)**[186] 4990 7-11-0 0 TomMolloy(3) 135+
(Nigel Twiston-Davies) *mde all: racd keenly: drvn out* **13/2**[2]
04F- **2** *¾* **Micheal Flips (IRE)**[172] 5222 6-11-3 0 NickScholfield 134+
(Andy Turnell) *hld up in tch: chsd wnr after 3 out: rdn appr last: styd on* **10/11**[1]
02-0 **3** *8* **Divers (FR)**[145] 316 6-11-3 0 GrahamLee 127+
(Ferdy Murphy) *hld up: hdwy 3 out: rdn to go 3rd last: styd on same pce* **9/1**
6 **4** *6* **The Wifes Pet (IRE)**[42] 1364 6-10-10 0 AidanColeman 116+
(Lawney Hill) *hld up: hdwy 6th: rdn after 2 out: wknd last* **14/1**
4422 **5** *21* **Classic Fly (FR)**[10] 1628 7-11-3 104 FelixDeGiles 104
(Arthur Whiting) *mid-div: pushed along 5th: hdwy next: chsd ldr 8th: rdn and wknd appr 2 out: t.o* **14/1**
20-1 **6** *3 ¾* **Le Corvee (IRE)**[27] 1127 8-10-12 0 LeeEdwards(5) 100
(Tony Carroll) *chsd ldr to 3rd: remained handy: rdn and wknd appr 2 out* **16/1**
30-5 **7** *4 ½* **Petrosian**[28] 1506 6-10-10 0 (p) MissIsabelTompsett(7) 97
(Dai Burchell) *prom: j.lft: chsd ldr 3rd tl mstke 6th: wknd after 3 out* **66/1**
10-P **8** *4* **Kingsben**[8] 1642 7-10-12 0 JamesHalliday(5) 92
(Malcolm Jefferson) *hld up: mstke 4th: sn bhd: nt fluent after: t.o* **25/1**

20P- **9** ¾ **Sonowyouno (IRE)**[207] 4589 6-11-0 0........................ RichieMcLernon(3) 91
(Jonjo O'Neill) *hld up: bhd fr 6th: t.o* **7/1**[3]

4m 6.90s (-9.20) **Going Correction** -0.20s/f (Good) **9** Ran SP% **112.8**
Speed ratings (Par 105): **113,112,108,106,96 94,92,90,90**
toteswingers:1&2 £1.80, 2&3 £5.00, 1&3 £10.50 CSF £13.14 TOTE £6.40: £2.00, £1.20, £2.90; EX 15.70.

Owner The Maple Hurst Partnership **Bred** Pat And Oliver McCarthy **Trained** Naunton, Gloucs

FOCUS

This was a very interesting beginners' chase and there was a sound gallop on. The third and fourth are the best guides to the form.

NOTEBOOK

Have You Seen Me(IRE) is a headstrong character and often blighted his cause over hurdles by refusing to settle. He again took a keen hold on this switch to chasing and looked vulnerable out in front nearing the home turn. Having pulled hard it seemed safe to assume the favourite would take his measure up the climbing straight, but he kept finding for pressure and was always doing enough on the run-in. This rates his best effort to date and it looks as though he will reach greater heights as a chaser, but the strong form of his stable counted for plenty here. (op 8-1)

Micheal Flips(IRE), who won his sole outing between the flags, was a smart novice hurdler two seasons back and his finest hour over hurdles last term came when he readily won the Lanzarote Hurdle at Kempton in January. His yard had been going through a quiet period, but it sent out a winner earlier in the afternoon at Ludlow and backing Andy Turnell's horses in October has also been profitable in the past decade, so everything looked in place for a big run. He jumped neatly enough until eventually coming under pressure nearing two out, when he got a little big and was always being held after the last. This experience and the outing should be to his benefit, but it has to be considered somewhat disappointing that he failed to get on top of a horse rated 27lb his inferior over hurdles. He also had a pretty hard race considering it was his first run back, but stepping up in trip could be what he wants as a chaser, and it wouldn't be surprising to see him make amends next time. (tchd 4-5)

Divers(FR) looked the chief danger to the winner on his hurdling form, but his stable is traditionally slow with its runners in October and he proved very easy to back. He tended to run in snatches on this return from a 145-day break, but got much better as the race developed and this was an encouraging introduction to chasing. (op 7-1)

The Wifes Pet(IRE) was making her chasing debut and having just her second outing for connections. She did things nicely until being outclassed when the first pair kicked for home, and should be well capable of winning races in this sphere. (tchd 16-1)

Classic Fly(FR) tended to go in snatches after an error at the third, but kept plugging away for pressure in the face of this stiff task. (tchd 16-1 in places)

Petrosian Official explanation: jockey said gelding jumped left

Sonowyouno(IRE), a dual novice winner over hurdles last term, looked very much in need of the experience and the outing on his seasonal debut. (op 10-1)

1732 MICK WHITE BIRTHDAY CELEBRATION H'CAP HURDLE (8 hdls) 2m

3:30 (3:34) (Class 4) (0-100,100) 4-Y-0+ **£3,252** (£955; £477; £238)

Form RPR

40/2 **1** **Manshoor (IRE)**[10] 1624 5-10-9 **90**.................................. MattCrawley(7) 105+
(Lucy Wadham) *trckd ldr: racd keenly: stmbld 3 out: sn led: clr whn mstke last: styd on wl* **7/2**[1]

3501 **2** 8 **Dormouse**[10] 1624 5-11-9 **97** 7ex..................................(p) AidanColeman 102+
(Anabel L M King) *a.p: chsd wnr and mstke 2 out: sn rdn: mstke and no ex last* **17/2**

53-0 **3** 3¾ **Romney Marsh**[31] 1479 9-10-11 **92**................................ DannyBurton(7) 93
(Roger Curtis) *chsd ldrs: rdn after 3 out: wknd appr last* **28/1**

-13P **4** 1¼ **Good Old Days (IRE)**[50] 1277 11-11-6 **97**..................... SeanQuinlan(3) 97
(Kim Bailey) *prom: rdn after 3 out: wknd appr last* **18/1**

4354 **5** 1¾ **Phoenix Eye**[8] 1644 9-10-13 **94**....................................... BrianToomey(7) 93
(Michael Mullineaux) *hld up: hdwy appr 2 out: wknd bef last* **20/1**

630- **6** 6 **Keyneema**[210] 4519 8-10-11 **88**.. DannyCook(3) 82
(Cathy Hamilton) *chsd ldrs: rdn after 3 out: wknd appr last* **20/1**

2530 **7** 2½ **Nesnaas (USA)**[13] 1589 9-11-1 **92**.................................. PeterToole(3) 83
(Mark Rimell) *chsd ldrs: j.lft 2nd: wknd after 3 out* **28/1**

050- **8** ¾ **Le Toto**[162] 36 7-11-2 **90**.. LeightonAspell 80
(Oliver Sherwood) *hld up: hdwy appr 2 out: sn wknd* **20/1**

040F **9** nk **Glan Lady (IRE)**[17] 1554 4-10-1 **78**..............................(p) CharlieHuxley(3) 68
(John Mackie) *hld up: nvr on terms* **25/1**

5-46 **10** 2 **Sommersturm (GER)**[17] 1547 6-11-7 **95**......................... DenisO'Regan 83
(Barney Curley) *hld up: nvr on terms* **10/1**

0-23 **11** 7 **Marie De Laufon (FR)**[17] 1554 5-11-7 **95**...................... TomMessenger 77
(Chris Bealby) *trckd ldrs: racd keenly: hmpd 2nd: rdn and wknd after 3 out: t.o* **8/1**[3]

P0-3 **12** 6 **Art Deco (IRE)**[68] 1138 7-11-12 **100**............................(t) JimmyMcCarthy 76
(Charles Egerton) *hld up: effrt and nt clr run after 3 out: sn wknd: t.o* **9/2**[2]

2144 **13** 12 **Hoar Frost**[66] 1147 5-11-7 **100**....................................... MarcGoldstein(5) 65
(Jim Best) *mid-div: rdn after 3 out: sn wknd: t.o* **8/1**[3]

P00P **14** 1 **Wee Ziggy**[8] 1647 7-10-4 **78**...(b) RodiGreene 43
(Michael Mullineaux) *led: rdn and hdd after 3 out: sn wknd: t.o* **40/1**

000/ **15** ½ **Mucho Loco (IRE)**[520] 4993 7-10-2 **76**.............................. DaveCrosse 40
(Roger Curtis) *prom: rdn appr 3 out: sn wknd: t.o* **33/1**

3m 55.6s (-12.30) **Going Correction** -0.625s/f (Firm)
WFA 4 from 5yo+ 9lb **15** Ran SP% **117.9**
Speed ratings (Par 105): **105,101,99,98,97 94,93,93,92,91 88,85,79,78,78**
toteswingers:1&2 £5.20, 2&3 £37.20, 1&3 £29.10 CSF £27.87 CT £724.53 TOTE £4.70: £1.90, £2.90, £7.10; EX 22.30.

Owner Tim Wood **Bred** Liberty Road Stables **Trained** Newmarket, Suffolk

■ Stewards' Enquiry : Sean Quinlan two-day ban: careless riding (Oct 20-21)

FOCUS

An ordinary handicap, run at an average gallop and it paid to race handily. The form looks straightforward rated around the third, fourth and fifth.

NOTEBOOK

Manshoor(IRE) gained revenge on Dormouse for a narrow defeat on his seasonal debut at Market Rasen ten days earlier, and completed the task with plenty left up his sleeve. He was never far away and was comfortably holding his old rival after the second-last flight. The handicapper had already elected to raise him 6lb for his previous run and will reassess that mark now, but he still remains open to improvement in this sphere. (tchd 4-1)

Dormouse ran a solid race in defeat under his penalty and was a clear second-best. (op 10-1)

Romney Marsh was another always to the fore and she showed the benefit of her seasonal return a month earlier, running a game race in defeat. The handicapper is still probably in charge of her, though. (op 22-1)

Good Old Days(IRE) was plugging on late in the day and this was much more encouraging again on his return from a 50-day break. (op 16-1 tchd 20-1)

Le Toto, having his first outing for 162 days, was keeping on from off the pace without threatening up the home straight. He is entitled to improve for the run and it was a step back in the right direction, but he still probably isn't one to completely trust. (op 16-1)

Art Deco(IRE) was making his handicap debut in this sphere after a 68-day absence. He used to be Group class on the Flat, but any supporters knew their fate before three out as he toiled out the back. (op 10-1)

1733 HAYGAIN HAY STEAMERS H'CAP CHASE (18 fncs) 3m 110y

4:00 (4:02) (Class 5) (0-90,84) 4-Y-0+ **£2,276** (£668; £334; £166)

Form RPR

354P **1** **Von Galen (IRE)**[46] 1331 9-11-9 **81**...(p) SamJones 95+
(Michael Scudamore) *chsd ldrs: rdn to ld last: all out* **11/1**

-105 **2** 8 **Gaining Ground (IRE)**[31] 1478 10-10-10 **71**.................(v) TomMolloy(3) 81+
(Graeme McPherson) *led to 2nd: led 3rd: j. slowly next: rdn appr 2 out: hdd & wknd last* **11/1**

60U0 **3** 37 **Penric**[46] 1331 10-10-12 **70**... JimmyMcCarthy 43
(Martin Bosley) *mid-div: hdwy 5th: chsd ldr 11th: mstke next: hit 3 out: sn wknd: t.o* **40/1**

2545 **4** 2¾ **Safe Investment (USA)**[11] 1612 6-11-7 **79**...................(p) DenisO'Regan 49
(Ben Pollock) *hld up: hmpd 10th: hdwy 14th: mstke 3 out: sn rdn and wknd: t.o* **18/1**

050P **5** 2¾ **Delgany Gunner**[3] 1694 6-10-13 **71**.........................(vt[1]) AndrewThornton 39
(Ben Pollock) *hld up: hdwy 8th: rdn and wknd after 3 out: t.o* **25/1**

-423 **6** 10 **Monsieur Georges (FR)**[129] 531 10-10-7 **68**............. JohnKington(3) 27
(F Jordan) *prom: hit 1st: wknd 11th: bhd whn hit 3 out: t.o* **14/1**

06-0 **7** 4½ **Fencote Mystery**[8] 1646 8-9-11 **60**................................. JamesHalliday(5) 15
(Malcolm Jefferson) *hld up: a in rr: bhd whn hmpd 10th: t.o* **11/2**[2]

1-40 **8** 64 **Arceye**[141] 383 13-11-7 **79**...(p) RodiGreene —
(William Davies) *sn pushed along in rr: bhd fr 7th: t.o* **20/1**

0333 **U** **Le Forezien (FR)**[36] 1447 11-11-5 **84**............................(t) MrRHawkins(7) —
(Carroll Gray) *hld up: hdwy 8th: cl up whn blnd and uns rdr 10th* **8/1**[3]

P4-5 **P** **Jacarado (IRE)**[149] 251 12-11-10 **82**.................................(v) HenryOliver —
(Robin Dickin) *mid-div: sn pushed along: bhd and rdn 8th: hmpd 10th: t.o whn p.u bef 13th* **9/1**

53P5 **P** **Thyne Spirit (IRE)**[49] 1281 11-10-0 **58** oh6.................(p) MattieBatchelor —
(Simon Lewis) *sn wl bhd: t.o whn p.u bef 10th* **20/1**

146 **F** **Bynack Mhor (IRE)**[37] 1425 9-11-5 **77**........................(tp) AidanColeman —
(Lawney Hill) *chsd ldrs: mstke 3rd: hmpd and fell 10th* **9/2**[1]

4501 **B** **Lansdowne Princess**[36] 1447 8-11-0 **77**........................... DavidBass(5) —
(Gerald Ham) *hld up: b.d 10th* **8/1**[3]

440P **P** **Overton Lad**[31] 1483 9-11-1 **76**...............................(b) RichieMcLernon(3) —
(Peter Pritchard) *drvn along early and mstke 1st: led 2nd to next: chsd ldr tl after 9th: wknd 13th: t.o whn p.u bef last* **12/1**

6m 35.8s (-1.10) **Going Correction** -0.20s/f (Good) **14** Ran SP% **117.9**
Speed ratings (Par 103): **93,90,78,77,76 73,72,51,—,— —,—,—,—**
CSF £117.00 CT £4603.83 TOTE £10.50: £3.10, £4.60, £13.70; EX 183.60.

Owner Mrs Bettine Evans **Bred** Donal Turner **Trained** Bromsash, Herefordshire

FOCUS

A very weak staying handicap. The first pair dominated from four out and are rated to their marks.

NOTEBOOK

Von Galen(IRE) proved most resolute nearing the final fence and kept on up the run-in to finally get his head in front under rules. He had been placed on one of his two previous outings here so the track obviously suits, and his confidence should be nicely boosted, but he doesn't appeal as one for a follow up. Official explanation: trainer said, regarding apparent improvement in form, that the gelding was unsuited by the rain-affected ground on its previous run. (tchd 12-1)

Gaining Ground(IRE) posted a bold effort from the front and only gave way to the winner after the last. He was legless at the finish so will need some time to recover, but this former point winner certainly deserves to go one better. (op 14-1)

Penric ran one of his better races but is likely to continue to struggle to get his head back in front.

Safe Investment(USA) looked a brief threat as he crept into things on the final circuit, but he was toiling before the home turn and remains a maiden over jumps.

Bynack Mhor(IRE) jumped into the back of Von Galen and fell, causing some carnage in the process. He had been tight for room after jumping the previous fence and this wasn't his fault. Looking at the way things panned out he would have surely had a say in the finish. (op 5-1 tchd 7-2)

1734 FREE TIPS @ GG.COM NOVICES' HURDLE (8 hdls) 2m

4:30 (4:31) (Class 3) 4-Y-0+ **£4,228** (£1,241; £620; £310)

Form RPR

212- **1** **Cinderella Rose**[174] 5200 4-10-2 0.................................... SeanQuinlan(3) 103+
(Kim Bailey) *trckd ldrs: hit 3 out: led 2 out: clr last styd on wl* **11/4**[1]

2 4½ **Causing Chaos (IRE)** 4-10-12 0.................................... PaddyBrennan 104
(Nigel Twiston-Davies) *chsd ldr tl led after 3 out: hdd next: styd on same pce appr last* **10/1**

400- **3** 12 **Quite The Man (IRE)**[167] 5333 5-10-12 109...................... DenisO'Regan 92
(Malcolm Jefferson) *hld up: hdwy 3 out: wknd appr last* **9/1**

25 **4** shd **Django Reinhardt**[17] 1547 4-10-5 0.............................. MrDavidTurner(7) 94+
(Sam Davison) *prom: rdn after 3 out: nt fluent next: sn wknd* **50/1**

U-05 **5** 2¼ **Kack Handed**[123] 634 7-10-12 0..................................... ChristianWilliams 92+
(Henry Daly) *led: hdd after 3 out: wknd appr last* **4/1**[3]

5-0 **6** 4½ **Graylyn Ruby (FR)**[3] 1688 5-10-9 0............................. WayneKavanagh(3) 85
(Robin Dickin) *hld up in tch: rdn after 3 out: wknd bef last* **50/1**

000- **7** 6 **Earl Of Thomond (IRE)**[261] 3505 5-10-12 0.................. AndrewThornton 79
(Caroline Bailey) *chsd ldrs tl wknd appr 2 out* **100/1**

8 1¼ **Alnwick**[24] 6-10-12 0... LeightonAspell 80
(Peter Cundell) *mid-div: hdwy 5th: wknd appr 2 out* **7/2**[2]

0-06 **9** 1 **Amuse Me**[11] 1613 4-10-9 0.. RichieMcLernon(3) 77
(Jonjo O'Neill) *hld up: hdwy 5th: wknd 3 out* **40/1**

4- **10** 8 **Dashing John**[179] 5134 8-10-5 0...................................... MrSParish(7) 69
(Audrey Manners) *a in rr: t.o* **33/1**

0 **11** 20 **Hamalac**[113] 759 4-10-12 0... WayneHutchinson 49
(Martin Keighley) *mid-div: hdwy 4th: wknd after next: t.o* **40/1**

0- **12** 11 **Monty's Revenge (IRE)**[282] 3124 5-10-12 0................... WarrenMarston 38
(Martin Keighley) *a in rr: bhd fr 5th: t.o* **66/1**

2-23 **F** **Spent**[13] 1588 5-10-5 108.. OliverDayman(7) —
(Alison Thorpe) *hld up: fell 4th* **7/1**

3/60 **P** **Little Justice**[75] 1086 6-10-5 0.. LiamTreadwell —
(Paul Cowley) *a in rr: hmpd 4th: t.o whn p.u bef next* **150/1**

3m 58.3s (-9.60) **Going Correction** -0.625s/f (Firm) **14** Ran SP% **115.8**
Speed ratings (Par 107): **99,96,90,90,89 87,84,83,83,79 69,63,—,—**
toteswingers:1&2 £7.70, 2&3 £15.30, 1&3 £9.80 CSF £28.84 TOTE £4.10: £1.10, £2.90, £2.90; EX 34.70.

Owner Mrs Nicholas Jones **Bred** Coln Valley Stud **Trained** Andoversford, Gloucs

FOCUS

An ordinary-looking novice hurdle with the winner to bumper form and the fourth and ninth to their marks.

NOTEBOOK

Cinderella Rose got her hurdling career off to a perfect start and completed the task in very ready fashion. She was never far away, but wasn't too clever at the third-last as the race began to get serious. Her response was most positive, though, as she swept to the front off the home turn and produced two fine leaps at the next two flights. This stiff 2m proved spot-on for this former bumper winner, a decent surface is what she wants and connections clearly have a decent mare on their hands. She should have little trouble defying a penalty if found an opportunity against her own sex, but should also improve for the run so going in against the boys again is also a distinct possibility. (op 3-1 tchd 9-4)

Causing Chaos(IRE) hails from a yard that can do little wrong at present, so it was surprising to see him prove so easy to back on this racecourse debut. He travelled every bit as well as the winner into the home straight, but was put in his place from two out. This was a decent introduction as he was nicely clear of the remainder, and he should be found an opening in the coming weeks. (op 8-1 tchd 7-1)

Quite The Man(IRE) failed to build on an encouraging debut over hurdles last term, but looked to have strengthened up for his time off the track and ran with a good deal more encouragement again. His ideal trip remains unknown, but this scopey 5-y-o should make his mark when switching to handicap company. (op 14-1 tchd 18-1)

Django Reinhardt wasn't always fluent and still has something to learn for this game, but he definitely has it in him to win races over hurdles, and is one to note when going handicapping.

Kack Handed was somewhat of a disappointment as a novice chaser last term, but his previous efforts over hurdles gave him every chance in this company. He did too much from the front after refusing to settle, however, and was done with two from home. (op 5-2)

Alnwick attracted money on his hurdling debut and his efforts on the level made him of definite interest. He got a very rough trip through the race after his rider elected to stick to the inside, though, and was in trouble a long way out. (op 7-1)

Little Justice Official explanation: jockey said mare was badly hampered by faller

1735 RACING FORUM @ GG.COM H'CAP HURDLE (10 hdls) 2m 3f 110y

5:00 (5:01) (Class 5) (0-95,95) 4-Y-0+ **£1,951** (£573; £286; £143)

Form | | | | RPR
0445 **1** **The Wee Midget**[17] [1559] 5-11-6 **89** NickScholfield 92
(Arthur Whiting) *hld up in tch: racd keenly: chsd ldr last: led flat: rdn out* **11/1**

03-0 **2** *3/4* **Crystal Prince**[154] [157] 6-11-2 **85** (tp) FelixDeGiles 90+
(Charlie Longsdon) *hld up: hdwy 5th: led 2 out: rdn and blnd last: sn hdd: styd on* **13/2**[1]

3006 **3** *1 3/4* **Satindra (IRE)**[75] [1080] 6-10-5 **74** (tp) TomMessenger 75
(Carole Ikin) *hld up: hdwy 3 out: rdn appr last: styd on* **33/1**

P5-P **4** *3 1/4* **Three Boars**[30] [1494] 8-10-11 **80** (tp) LiamTreadwell 79+
(Claire Dyson) *chsd ldrs: led after 6th: hdd and hit 2 out: mstke last: no ex* **8/1**[3]

31-6 **5** *4 1/2* **Bollywood (IRE)**[13] [1592] 7-10-11 **80** AndrewThornton 75
(Alison Batchelor) *mid-div: hdwy appr 2 out: sn rdn and no imp* **8/1**[2]

-P06 **6** *3* **Jug Of Punch (IRE)**[12] [1605] 11-9-7 **69** oh5 MissCBoxall(7) 60
(Simon Lewis) *sn pushed along in rr: nvr nrr* **33/1**

23F5 **7** *2* **Wisteria Lane (IRE)**[50] [1272] 7-10-9 **78** GerardTumelty 68
(Anabel L M King) *chsd ldrs: outpcd after 6th: rallied 3 out: wknd next* **13/2**[1]

-540 **8** *1* **Plenty Of Chat (IRE)**[31] [1483] 6-10-12 **88** (p) MrTomDavid(7) 77
(Tim Vaughan) *prom: rdn after 3 out: wknd next* **8/1**[2]

660- **9** *1 1/2* **Dancing Daffodil**[197] [4811] 5-9-5 **70** ChristopherWard(10) 57
(Robin Dickin) *prom: edgd rt and wknd appr 2 out* **12/1**

25-0 **10** *3 1/2* **Jerry Lee (IRE)**[144] [341] 7-9-12 **70** JohnKington(3) 54
(F Jordan) *hld up: hdwy 3 out: wknd bef next* **8/1**[2]

0640 **11** *5* **Bond Cruz**[17] [1551] 7-10-4 **73** MattieBatchelor 53
(Olivia Maylam) *hld up: hdwy 5th: wknd appr 2 out* **18/1**

5415 **12** *12* **Ponchatrain (IRE)**[47] [1309] 10-11-12 **95** (p) WarrenMarston 66
(Martin Keighley) *chsd ldrs: rdn and wknd after 3 out: t.o* **8/1**[2]

13 *8* **Curragh Dancer (FR)**[668] [2667] 7-10-4 **80** NathanSweeney(7) 42
(Paddy Butler) *hld up: a in rr: bhd fr 5th: t.o* **33/1**

-50P **14** *18* **Gratification**[84] [991] 7-11-6 **89** LeightonAspell 34
(Oliver Sherwood) *hld up: hdwy 4th: rdn and wknd after 7th: t.o* **14/1**

/3-0 **P** **Chord**[72] [1095] 6-11-7 **90** (b) DenisO'Regan —
(Simon Earle) *led: hdd after 6th: wknd next: t.o whn p.u bef 2 out* **10/1**[3]

4m 54.6s (-15.00) **Going Correction** -0.625s/f (Firm) **15** Ran SP% **119.9**

Speed ratings (Par 103): **105,104,104,102,100 99,98,98,97,96 94,89,86,79,—**

toteswingers:1&2 £9.30, 2&3 £71.20, 1&3 £70.40 CSF £78.39 CT £2261.82 TOTE £13.30: £4.10, £1.30, £9.30; EX 87.70 Place 6: £444.62 Place 5: £187.56 .

Owner A J Whiting **Bred** David Jenks **Trained** North Nibley, Gloucs

■ Stewards' Enquiry : Christopher Ward caution: careless riding.

FOCUS

Another very weak handicap in which the third, fourth and fifth help set the level.

NOTEBOOK

The Wee Midget got on top after the runner-up met the final flight all wrong, and he registered his first win at the tenth time of asking. Not for the first time he took time to settle, but he loved the decent ground, and the drop back in trip on this really stiff track was more up his street. He was obviously a somewhat fortunate winner, however. (op 12-1 tchd 14-1)

Crystal Prince was last seen running out when still going well enough at Huntingdon back in May. His stable is in cracking form at present and he came through going strongly nearing the second-last. Three Boars was in front at that stage but hit it and that looked to have handed him the race as he went clear. He clouted the last though, and that ultimately cost him. There is every chance he will make amends next time out. (op 9-2)

Satindra(IRE), who has scored at this track, hit something of a flat spot before staying on stoutly from the penultimate flight, and this was one of her better efforts in defeat. She should come on nicely for the run.

Three Boars, pulled up in two of his last three outings, was given a positive ride and would have been closer had he met the second-last on a decent stride. (op 40-1)

T/Plt: £607.50 to a £1 stake. Pool of £64,222.81 - 77.17 winning tickets. T/Qpdt: £240.10 to a £1 stake. Pool of £5,126.70 - 15.80 winning tickets. CR

[272] EXETER (R-H)

Thursday, October 7

OFFICIAL GOING: Good (good to soft in places)

Wind: mild across getting stronger Weather: overcast, light rain

1736 BATHWICK TYRES TAUNTON NOVICES' HURDLE (8 hdls) 2m 1f

2:25 (2:26) (Class 4) 4-Y-0+ **£2,602** (£764; £382; £190)

Form | | | | RPR
101- **1** **Dunraven Storm (IRE)**[177] [5178] 5-10-12 0 RichardJohnson 126+
(Philip Hobbs) *mde all: hung lft fr 3 out: shkn up after 2 out: wnt bdly lft last: kpt on wl* **2/5**[1]

31-0 **2** *11* **Dean's Grange**[151] [235] 5-11-5 112 JoeTizzard 115
(Colin Tizzard) *trckd ldrs: ev ch 2 out: sn rdn: kpt on: nt gng pce of wnr* **10/1**[3]

35- **3** *3 3/4* **Molanna View (IRE)**[322] [2389] 5-10-12 0 JackDoyle 104
(Emma Lavelle) *trckd ldrs: rdn appr 3 out: kpt on same pce* **11/1**

23- **4** *10* **Bally Legend**[177] [5178] 5-10-7 0 IanPopham(5) 94
(Caroline Keevil) *w wnr: mstke 1st: hit 4th: rdn appr 3 out: sn wknd* **25/1**

5 *2 1/2* **Ask The Oracle**[238] 4-10-5 0 MissIsabelTompsett(7) 94+
(John Price) *mid-div: rdn after 5th: one pce fr 3 out* **16/1**

6 *3/4* **Remember Now (IRE)**[566] 4-10-7 0 DavidBass(5) 92+
(Nicky Henderson) *hld up towards rr: sme prog into mid-div 5th: rdn next: no further imp* **15/2**[2]

000- **7** *13* **Blakeneys Pet (IRE)**[280] [2931] 4-10-5 0 AndrewGlassonbury 72
(John Berwick) *trckd ldrs: mstke 3rd: rdn after 5th: wknd next* **80/1**

/P4- **8** *1 1/4* **Canyouseeme**[194] [4894] 7-10-12 0 LiamTreadwell 77
(Claire Dyson) *a towards rr* **50/1**

9 *9* **Chase Gate**[157] 5-10-12 0 SamThomas 68
(James Frost) *a towards rr* **66/1**

-46U **10** *16* **Cruise In Style (IRE)**[32] [1487] 4-10-5 0 JohnnyFarrelly 45
(Kevin Bishop) *mstke 4th: a towards rr* **100/1**

0- **11** *3 1/4* **Benny The Swinger (IRE)**[201] [4744] 5-10-12 0 HaddenFrost 49
(Henrietta Knight) *trckd ldrs early: sn dropped to mid-div: wknd after 5th* **25/1**

0- **12** *1/2* **Gallimaufry**[173] [5235] 4-10-5 0 RodiGreene 41
(Neil Mulholland) *mid-div tl 4th: sn bhd* **100/1**

05/ **13** *13* **Tracy Road (FR)**[697] [2093] 6-9-12 0 MattGriffiths(7) 28
(Carroll Gray) *a towards rr* **100/1**

4m 9.00s (-6.50) **Going Correction** -0.675s/f (Firm)

WFA 4 from 5yo+ 9lb **13** Ran SP% **121.9**

Speed ratings (Par 105): **88,82,81,76,75 74,68,68,63,56 54,54,48**

toteswingers:1&2 £1.50, 2&3 £11.30, 1&3 £3.60 CSF £5.39 TOTE £1.30: £1.10, £2.40, £2.30; EX 5.90.

Owner Mrs Karola Vann **Bred** Miss Violet Sweeney **Trained** Withycombe, Somerset

FOCUS

A few fairly decent horses have taken this novice hurdle down the years, namely Albuhera, Boychuk and Deep Purple, so this may be an informative contest despite the early gallop being moderate. The winner is value for further and the placed horses help set the level.

NOTEBOOK

Dunraven Storm(IRE) ◆, a dual winning bumper performer, including once over this C&D, represented a stable with a good record in this race, so made appeal for obvious reasons. The market suggested that defeat wasn't envisaged, and apart from the odd novicey leap and looking a bit green in the latter stages, his supporters had little to worry about. He looks decent and connections feel another run at this distance, probably on a stiff course, is next for him as he doesn't look short of pace. The Sharp Novices' Hurdle on the 12th of November (a race won by some classy sorts in the past) at Cheltenham is possibly in their minds. (op 4-7 tchd 4-11and 8-13 in places after 4-6 in a place)

Dean's Grange won a maiden hurdle in April and was the only horse in the race with an official mark - 112. Carrying a 7lb penalty for that success, he went smoothly just behind the leaders for much of the contest but couldn't match the winner as he increased the tempo coming to the last hurdle. (op 9-1)

Molanna View(IRE) wasn't completely disgraced on his hurdling debut back in November (absent since) and threatened for a while in this before not quite having the pace to mount a challenge from two out. (op 12-1 tchd 14-1)

Bally Legend, over 13 lengths behind Dunraven Storm in a C&D bumper when last out, travelled alongside the winner for much of the race and will no doubt do even better over further in time. He hit a couple of hurdles quite hard, which would not have helped. (op 20-1)

Ask The Oracle ◆, a modest sort at up to 1m4f on the Flat, had been absent since February, and was having his first start for this trainer. Settled in midfield, he was making pleasing late progress before clouting two out, which stopped his momentum. This was a good start to his hurdling career. (op 20-1)

Remember Now(IRE), the Champion Hurdle winner Binocular's half-brother, was having his first outing since March 2009, the last of three outings for the Elie Lellouche stable in France, which was the same source for the aforementioned festival winner. Wearing a cross-noseband and a ring bit, he was said to be buzzy in the paddock prior to the off and travelled with too much exuberance while being held up at the back. It wasn't a surprise to see him not get home, but there was more than enough in the effort to suggest he can win something, especially if learning to settle. (op 5-1)

1737 CHAMPAGNE LANSON 250TH ANNIVERSARY NOVICES' H'CAP HURDLE (11 hdls) 2m 5f 110y

3:00 (3:00) (Class 4) (0-105,105) 3-Y-0+ **£2,602** (£764; £382; £190)

Form | | | | RPR
-153 **1** **Miss Saffron**[37] [1446] 7-10-13 **92** JackDoyle 97+
(Susan Gardner) *hld up towards rr: hdwy fr 7th: disp 3rd gng 3 out: hrd rdn after 2 out: chalng whn hit last: led run-in drvn out* **11/2**

42-6 **2** *3/4* **Restezen D'Armor (FR)**[148] [282] 5-11-6 **99** FelixDeGiles 102+
(Charlie Longsdon) *hld up towards rr: smooth hdwy fr 7th: led gng wl after 3 out: rdn after next: hdd run-in: kpt on: no ex* **9/2**[2]

-000 **3** *2 1/4* **Henry Hook (IRE)**[122] [664] 6-11-5 **98** (p) JamieMoore 100
(Victor Dartnall) *trckd clr ldr: pushed along 7th: led after 8th: sn rdn: hdd appr 2 out: styd on same pce* **5/1**[3]

4 *10* **Deuce**[144] [363] 4-11-0 **98** DavidBass(5) 90
(Lawney Hill) *mid-div: hdwy to trck ldng pair 6th: rdn appr 3 out: fdd fr 2 out* **9/1**

P-00 **5** *6* **Hot Tottie (IRE)**[116] [737] 6-10-12 **96** IanPopham(5) 83
(Jeremy Scott) *mid-div: rdn appr 3 out: wknd bef 2 out* **16/1**

P00- **6** *11* **Potemkin (USA)**[253] [3680] 5-11-4 **100** (t) SamTwiston-Davies(3) 77
(David Evans) *mid-div: hdwy 7th: rdn appr 3 out: wknd bef 2 out* **25/1**

-663 **7** *27* **The Brimmer (IRE)**[13] [1601] 6-11-7 **105** JimmyDerham(5) 57
(Seamus Mullins) *led: sn clr: rdn after 8th: sn hdd: wknd next: t.o* **4/1**[1]

4626 **8** *5* **Googoobarabajagal (IRE)**[32] [1477] 4-11-10 **103** (p) RichardJohnson 51
(Stuart Kittow) *hld up towards rr: hdwy 7th: rdn after next: sn wknd: t.o* **10/1**

F045 **P** **Top Tide (IRE)**[16] [1571] 9-11-0 **93** SamThomas —
(Martin Hill) *chsd ldng pair tl lost pl and pushed along after 5th: lost tch fr next: p.u after 8th* **25/1**

400- **P** **Celtic Ballad (IRE)**[172] [5260] 4-11-1 **94** JoeTizzard —
(Colin Tizzard) *mid-div tl wknd 7th: t.o whn p.u bef 3 out* **10/1**

000- **P** **Autumm Spirit**[300] [2813] 6-10-7 **89** WayneKavanagh(3) —
(Robin Dickin) *chsd ldrs tl 8th: sn wknd: p.u bef 3 out* **40/1**

5m 15.2s (-17.80) **Going Correction** -0.675s/f (Firm) **11** Ran SP% **114.4**

Speed ratings (Par 105): **105,104,103,100,98 94,84,82,—,— —**

toteswingers:1&2 £3.50, 2&3 £2.40, 1&3 £10.80 CSF £29.48 CT £131.14 TOTE £4.00: £1.20, £2.20, £3.10.

Owner P A Tylor & G N Noye **Bred** P A Tylor **Trained** Longdown, Devon

■ Stewards' Enquiry : Felix De Giles one-day ban: used whip with excessive frequency (Oct 21)

FOCUS
An ordinary-looking contest. This may not be reliable form considering that lots of these were returning from 100-day-plus absences. The third is the best guide to the level.

NOTEBOOK
Miss Saffron, who had at least proved she can win races, was a little keen in rear before making good progress down the home straight to win by a narrow margin. (op 9-2)
Restezen D'Armor(FR) had shown bits of ability in limited previous starts and looked set to collect this before not quite getting home under pressure. (tchd 4-1 and 11-2)
Henry Hook(IRE), with cheekpieces back on, was prominent in the chasing pack and kept plugging on to run respectably. (op 9-2 tchd 7-2)
Deuce, who showed little in three starts over hurdles in Ireland for another trainer after racing on the Flat for Eve Johnson Houghton, didn't get home after racing keenly. (op 10-1)
Hot Tottie(IRE), whose best previous performance came at this course over 2m3f in March 2009, was never really a threat but should be sharper for the outing. (op 25-1)
Potemkin(USA), having his first start for this stable and with a tongue-tie on for the first time, moved up going quite nicely but did not pick up strongly once under pressure. (tchd 33-1)
The Brimmer(IRE) has been running fairly well over 2m this season. Up over 5f in trip for this, he gained a good advantage from the start despite only going a fair pace, so one must conclude he just doesn't stay this far under any circumstances. (op 9-2)
Googoobarabajagal(IRE), with cheekpieces back on, never got into the race after being held up. (op 12-1)
Autumn Spirit Official explanation: jockey said mare had a breathing problem

1738 SOUTH WEST RACING CLUB H'CAP CHASE (18 fncs) 3m
3:35 (3:35) (Class 4) (0-115,115) 4-Y-0+ **£3,903** (£1,146; £573; £286)

Form RPR
546- **1** **Ammunition (IRE)**[255] 3656 10-10-8 **100**............ SamTwiston-Davies(3) 113
(Nigel Twiston-Davies) *chsd ldrs: rdn after 14th: styd on fr 3 out: chal last: led sn after: pushed out: rdr dropped whip* **4/1**[1]
41F- **2** *nk* **Vamizi (IRE)**[175] 5195 7-11-9 **112**............................ MattieBatchelor 126+
(Mark Bradstock) *mde most: mstke 4 out: sn rdn: kpt narrow advantage tl edgd lft and hdd sn after last: styd on* **11/2**[3]
162 **3** *5* **Prophete De Guye (FR)**[47] 1326 7-11-1 **104**...................... FelixDeGiles 112
(James Evans) *t.k.h: hld up: hdwy fr 8th: effrt 4 out: unable to chal: styd on same pce* **6/1**
6024 **4** *15* **The Duke's Speech (IRE)**[71] 1117 9-11-12 **115**............ LeightonAspell 108
(Sophie Leech) *hld up bhd: smooth hdwy 12th: rdn appr 4 out: wknd 2 out* **14/1**
041- **5** *2¼* **Son Histoire (FR)**[185] 5034 6-11-9 **112**......................(b) RichardJohnson 104
(Philip Hobbs) *mid-div: hdwy after 14th: rdn after 4 out: wknd 2 out* **6/1**
1512 **6** *10* **Justabout**[47] 1331 7-10-6 **95**...(t) JoeTizzard 79
(Colin Tizzard) *w ldr: rdn after 4 out: ev ch whn blnd bdly 2 out: nt rcvr: wknd* **9/2**[2]
P436 **7** *3½* **On You Go (IRE)**[31] 1491 9-11-1 **107**........................ RichieMcLernon(3) 84
(Jonjo O'Neill) *hld up towards rr: rdn appr 4 out: no imp: wknd 3 out* **9/1**
-160 **8** *36* **Very Cool**[106] 830 8-11-12 **115**.......................................(bt) JohnnyFarrelly 56
(David Pipe) *chsd ldrs tl 12th: wknd 14th: t.o* **12/1**
P40P **9** *16* **Triggernometry**[31] 1490 9-10-6 **102**.....................(bt) MrRGHenderson(7) 27
(Colin Tizzard) *mid-div tl 7th: lost tch fr 12th: t.o* **25/1**
P/0P **U** **Thumbprint (IRE)**[72] 1109 8-11-1 **104**..................................(t) LiamHeard —
(Chris Down) *in tch tl lost pl after 9th: in rr whn awkward and uns rdr 11th* **33/1**

5m 51.8s (-17.50) **Going Correction** -0.60s/f (Firm) **10** Ran SP% **113.3**
Speed ratings (Par 105): **105,104,103,98,97 94,92,80,75,—**
toteswingers:1&2:£4.40, 2&3:£4.40, 1&3:£4.30 CSF £26.08 CT £128.77 TOTE £4.20: £1.10, £3.90, £3.10.
Owner Miss Katharine J Holland **Bred** D Morrissey **Trained** Naunton, Gloucs

FOCUS
The gallop set seemed fair for the distance, which helped make it into a stiff test, although seven still held some sort of chance heading to four out. The third sets the level and the time was decent for the grade.

NOTEBOOK
Ammunition(IRE) had run well at this course in the past but usually wears cheekpieces nowadays, so it was reassuring to see him pull out plenty for pressure to win in a tight finish, especially as his rider dropped his whip inside the final 50 yards. It was a good, strong ride by Sam Twiston-Davies to keep his mount going, but whether the horse can follow this win up is open to debate. (op 5-1tchd 11-2 in a place)
Vamizi(IRE) ◆, a C&D winner in March off a 9lb lower mark, ran a cracker after sharing the lead and can gain compensation soon. He doesn't lack anything in bravery when considering how well he kept going. (op 6-1 tchd 5-1)
Prophete De Guye(FR) looks a little high in the handicap judged on his winning form, so it wasn't a huge surprise that he couldn't pick up after moving strongly. (op 11-2 tchd 5-1)
The Duke's Speech(IRE) hadn't looked a strong stayer in the past (all best performances are over 2m) and only made some modest late headway after being held up. (op 10-1 tchd 16-1)
Son Histoire(FR), without a tongue-tie on his reappearance, made a move on the side of the course but weakened steadily up the home straight. (tchd 11-2)
Justabout, who looked the stable first-string on jockey bookings, was just about in line with the runner-up, going much the same, when meeting two out all wrong. (op 4-1)
On You Go(IRE) had come down the weights and does stay well, but he couldn't or wouldn't quicken after looking to be going well. (op 8-1)

1739 GLOBE HOTEL TOPSHAM BEGINNERS' CHASE (18 fncs) 3m
4:10 (4:10) (Class 4) 4-Y-0+ **£4,553** (£1,337; £668; £333)

Form RPR
2F0- **1** **Dover's Hill**[198] 4802 8-11-2 124..........................(t) SamTwiston-Davies(3) 140+
(Mary Hambro) *tendency to jump rt: mde all: drew clr fr 4 out: comf* **3/1**[2]
10-2 **2** *11* **Triggerman**[13] 1602 8-11-5 0.. RichardJohnson 127
(Philip Hobbs) *hld up: hdwy to trck ldrs 12th: rdn to chse wnr 4 out: sn hld: styd on same pce* **1/1**[1]
55-5 **3** *2¾* **Priors Glen (IRE)**[13] 1602 6-10-9 115................(t) StephenO'Donovan(10) 123
(Emma Lavelle) *in tch: trckd ldrs 12th: disp 2nd 14th: rdn appr 4 out: styd on same pce* **20/1**
5/ **4** *1* **Keel Road (IRE)**[157] 8-10-12 0... DavidEngland 116
(Giles Smyly) *chsd ldr tl rdn after 14th: styd on same pce fr next* **66/1**
32-0 **5** *52* **Persian Run (IRE)**[159] 94 6-11-5 0....................................... JoeTizzard 70
(Colin Tizzard) *chsd ldrs: disp 2nd 10th tl 12th: wknd 14th: t.o* **7/1**
4P-4 **6** *15* **Le Commencement (IRE)**[18] 1557 8-11-5 117........................ JackDoyle 55
(Emma Lavelle) *in tch: dropped to last three 10th: wknd 14th: t.o* **5/1**[3]
2P-F **7** *30* **Will If I Want (IRE)**[72] 1109 9-11-5 0.............................. JohnnyFarrelly 25
(Sophie Leech) *in tch: rdn after 14th: sn wknd: t.o* **20/1**
P **Battle Bridge (IRE)**[193] 5-11-5 0.. SamThomas —
(Nick Mitchell) *a last of gp: rdn along fr 11th: nvr any imp: p.u bef last* **50/1**

5m 52.1s (-17.20) **Going Correction** -0.60s/f (Firm) **8** Ran SP% **117.1**
Speed ratings (Par 105): **104,100,99,99,81 76,66,—**
toteswingers:1&2 £1.60, 2&3 £5.10, 1&3 £7.40 CSF £6.74 TOTE £3.90: £1.40, £1.10, £5.70; EX 7.10.
Owner Mrs Richard Hambro **Bred** Cotswold Stud **Trained** Bourton-on-the-Hill, Gloucs

FOCUS
Three of these had a bit of chasing experience already behind them, and had BHA marks, the highest of which was 124. It remains to be seen how strong this contest turns out to be, but it promises to produce quite a few winners. The first three are all rated improvers, although the proximity of the fourth raised slight doubts.

NOTEBOOK
Dover's Hill, who may have won a couple of races last season had he managed to stay upright jumping the final fence, went off in front and stayed there after going well throughout. He was hardly winning out of turn and he should develop into a useful handicapper when allowed to dominate. (op 10-3)
Triggerman, a very useful hurdler at his best, was beaten by a stablemate on his first run over fences and filled the same position in this after being held up. He was unable to find any way past the winner when he got within range and then became one-paced. (op 11-10 tchd 5-4)
Priors Glen(IRE) ◆, a long way behind Triggerman on their first start over fences, had a tongue-tie fitted for the first time and went well for his 10lb claimer. He didn't quite have the acceleration to get to the front, but should be winning his first race before the end of the season. (op 16-1)
Keel Road(IRE) ◆, well beaten on her only start under rules for Donald McCain in March 2009 but a consistent type in points, raced prominently before getting outpaced, but strongly suggested she can win an ordinary contest at some stage considering the way she kept on again.
Persian Run(IRE) ◆, over seven lengths behind Triggerman in a novice hurdle in March, travelled strongly but failed to pick up. He is well worth giving another chance to, as this big sort may have needed the run. (tchd 15-2)
Le Commencement(IRE) showed promise on his chasing debut in September (2m5f) but never got in to contention here once the tempo lifted. (op 6-1 tchd 9-2)
Will If I Want(IRE) has seemed a bit fragile over the years but certainly has ability. He got himself into contention at one point but could not go on. (op 16-1)

1740 BATHWICK TYRES PLYMOUTH H'CAP HURDLE (10 hdls) 2m 3f
4:45 (4:45) (Class 4) (0-115,114) 4-Y-0+ **£3,252** (£955; £477; £238)

Form RPR
53-2 **1** **Cantabilly (IRE)**[149] 264 7-11-3 **112**.................................. MattGriffiths(7) 116+
(Ron Hodges) *towards rr of mid-div: pushed along after 4th: hdwy fr next: rdn to ld appr 3 out: styd on gamely* **14/1**
000- **2** *2¾* **Cardinal James (IRE)**[177] 5172 6-10-9 **100**........ SamTwiston-Davies(3) 104+
(Tor Sturgis) *hld up towards rr: hdwy 7th: sn rdn: wnt 2nd after 3 out: chalng whn mstke 2 out: hld whn mstke last: wandered run-in* **20/1**
/1-4 **3** *2* **Boomtown Kat**[72] 1109 6-11-4 **109**........................... EamonDehdashti(3) 108
(Karen George) *mid-div: rdn after 4th: styd on fr 3 out: wnt 3rd last: nt rch ldrs* **40/1**
1430 **4** *2¾* **Dream Catcher (SWE)**[18] 1548 7-11-6 **111**............. RichieMcLernon(3) 107
(Jonjo O'Neill) *chsd ldr: rdn to chse wnr appr 3 out tl 2 out: styd on same pce* **11/1**
2-53 **5** *1¼* **Party Palace**[10] 1162 6-10-9 **102**... IanPopham(5) 97
(Stuart Howe) *chsd ldrs: rdn after 7th: one pce fr next* **14/1**
2116 **6** *hd* **Swiss Art (IRE)**[12] 1614 4-10-8 **103**............................(p) OliverDayman(7) 98
(Alison Thorpe) *mid-div tl lost pl after 5th: styd on again fr 3 out: nvr trbld ldrs* **6/1**[2]
0160 **7** *4* **Captain Becket**[31] 1490 7-10-3 **96**................................ TomO'Connor(5) 87
(James Frost) *mid-div: rdn after 6th: styd on same pce fr 3 out: nvr trbld ldrs* **33/1**
001/ **8** *17* **De Welsh Wizzard**[551] 4853 7-11-8 **110**.................................. JackDoyle 93+
(Emma Lavelle) *in tch: trcking ldrs gng wl after 7th: rdn bef next: wknd 2 out* **14/1**
213- **9** *11* **Bathwick Quest (IRE)**[10] 2925 6-11-7 **114**................ MrMMO'Connor(5) 80
(Brendan Powell) *led at gd pce: rdn and hdd appr 3 out: sn wknd* **16/1**
30-0 **10** *25* **Lordsbridge (USA)**[156] 131 8-11-5 **114**.......................... EdCookson(7) 58
(Andy Turnell) *hld up towards rr: hdwy 7th: sn rdn: wknd next* **10/1**[3]
1PP- **P** **Organiz (FR)**[157] 8-10-1 **94**...................................... MrSWaley-Cohen(5) —
(Robin Dickin) *towards rr of mid-div tl wknd after 6th: t.o whn p.u bef 3 out* **22/1**
P2P5 **P** **Risk Challenge (USA)**[18] 1546 8-10-9 **97**........................(t) CharliePoste —
(Milton Harris) *a towards rr: t.o whn p.u bef 2 out* **14/1**
4000 **P** **Bathwick Man**[16] 1569 5-11-10 **112**...............................(tp) JohnnyFarrelly —
(David Pipe) *mid-div: rdn after 6th: wknd next: bhd whn p.u bef 3 out* **16/1**
1F/P **P** **Krackatara**[18] 1556 8-11-10 **112**...................................... SamThomas —
(Susan Gardner) *mstke 6th: a in rr: t.o whn p.u bef 3 out* **10/1**[3]
33- **P** **Ballycracken (IRE)**[249] 3763 6-11-5 **112**............................ DavidBass(5) —
(Nicky Henderson) *chsd ldrs: rdn after 7th: wknd next: p.u bef last* **5/2**[1]

4m 31.3s (-11.40) **Going Correction** -0.675s/f (Firm)
WFA 4 from 5yo+ 9lb **15** Ran SP% **122.3**
Speed ratings (Par 105): **97,95,95,93,93 93,91,84,79,69 —,—,—,—,—**
toteswingers:1&2 £72.80, 2&3 £133.20, 1&3 £39.40 CSF £269.74 CT £10443.10 TOTE £16.80: £5.80, £10.20, £12.40; EX 595.20.
Owner Mrs S G Clapp **Bred** W P Iceton **Trained** Charlton Mackrell, Somerset

FOCUS
A modest but competitive-looking handicap, in which the leaders appeared to set a good gallop, resulting in some tired-looking runners. The form is ordinary with the winner a small improver on his 2009 form.

NOTEBOOK
Cantabilly(IRE), without a win since October 2007, was settled out the back before making good progress to get him to the front quite a way from the finish. He had every chance to throw it away had he wanted to, but under a fine ride by Matt Griffiths, he displayed plenty of willing and kept on the best. (op 16-1)
Cardinal James(IRE), trying this sort of trip for the first time, was another to get a patient ride early. He became outpaced on the home turn but stayed on well to be almost upsides the winner two out, at which point he made a mistake and lost his back end. Gathered together, his rider got another run out of his mount before hitting the last hurdle hard as well. Those mistakes possibly cost him victory, although it was fair to say he didn't always look the most straightforward horse under pressure. (op 25-1)
Boomtown Kat, back over hurdles after one attempt over fences in late July, got behind but stayed on nicely through some tired rivals down the home straight.
Dream Catcher(SWE), up 3f in distance, looks a bit high in the weights on his winning form but ran well after being prominent throughout. (tchd 10-1 and 12-1)
Party Palace rallied and ran on again under pressure. (op 16-1)
Swiss Art(IRE), with the cheekpieces back on that looked to improve his form since mid-July, was one-paced when asked for maximum effort after two out. He did make a couple of jumping errors at a crucial stage, that didn't help. (op 17-2)
De Welsh Wizzard, absent since winning a 2m4f novice hurdle in April 2009, was keen under restraint and had little left at the end. With the freshness taken out of him, he should be of interest next time. (op 11-1)

Ballycracken(IRE), making his handicap debut for a powerful stable, sat close to the good early pace but was beaten at a relatively early stage. He has plenty to prove. (op 7-2)

1741 BATHWICK TYRES CONDITIONAL JOCKEYS' H'CAP HURDLE (10 hdls) 2m 3f

5:20 (5:20) (Class 5) (0-95,95) 4-Y-O+ **£1,626** (£477; £238; £119)

Form RPR

6422 **1** **Northern Lad (IRE)**[36] 1451 8-11-9 **95** MarcGoldstein(3) 107+
(Jim Best) *hld up towards rr: hdwy 7th: led 2 out: sn clr: readily* **9/2**[2]

P555 **2** *6* **Mangonel**[18] 1551 6-10-3 **72** (v) IanPopham 75
(Stuart Howe) *led: rdn appr 3 out: hdd whn hit 2 out: kpt on: sn hld by wnr* **6/1**[3]

P001 **3** *1 ½* **Simone Martini (IRE)**[4] 1704 5-10-5 **74** 7ex (tp) SamTwiston-Davies 77+
(Milton Harris) *mid-div: hdwy 7th: hung lft fr next: rdn to dispute 2nd whn stmbld 2 out: kpt on same pce: drifted lft run-in* **15/8**[1]

P-32 **4** *¾* **Havenstone (IRE)**[32] 1483 9-11-5 **91** DPFahy(3) 91
(Evan Williams) *trckd ldr: rdn appr 3 out: kpt on same pce* **9/2**[2]

6666 **5** *15* **Orion Express**[47] 1336 9-11-5 **91** MarkQuinlan(3) 77
(Susan Gardner) *mid-div: rdn and sme hdwy 3 out: wknd bef last* **14/1**

00F- **6** *nk* **Goodwill Phil**[210] 4537 6-10-6 **75** (t) CharlieHuxley 61
(Nigel Hawke) *mid-div: hdwy after 7th: sn rdn: wknd bef last* **33/1**

P-0P **7** *1 ½* **Bernard**[99] 868 10-10-11 **80** MichaelMurphy 65
(Kevin Bishop) *a towards rr* **40/1**

-060 **8** *3 ¼* **Wujood**[37] 1446 8-10-1 **70** (t) DonalDevereux 52
(Gerald Ham) *mid-div: rdn after 6th: sn wknd* **16/1**

-330 **9** *3 ½* **Ladies Best**[13] 1605 6-11-9 **95** (v[1]) MattGriffiths(3) 74
(Gordon Edwards) *trckd ldrs: rdn after 7th: sn wknd* **25/1**

0-P0 **10** *21* **Just The Job (IRE)**[31] 1488 6-11-8 **91** MrMMO'Connor 51
(Neil Mulholland) *mid-div: rdn after 7th: sn wknd: t.o* **50/1**

146P **P** **Nono Le Sage (FR)**[14] 1591 6-11-12 **95** (bt[1]) JohnKington —
(David Pipe) *hld up towards rr: rdn appr 3 out: sn wknd: t.o whn p.u bef last* **28/1**

060- **P** **Honourable Dreamer (IRE)**[195] 4867 5-11-2 **88** RichieMcLernon(3) —
(Jonjo O'Neill) *trckd ldrs: rdn after 7th: wknd 3 out: bhd whn p.u bef last* **20/1**

4m 33.1s (-9.60) **Going Correction** -0.675s/f (Firm) **12** Ran SP% **117.4**
Speed ratings (Par 103): **93,90,89,89,83 83,82,81,79,70 —,—**
toteswingers:1&2 £5.10, 2&3 £3.90, 1&3 £3.50. totesuper7: Win: Not won. Place: Not won. CSF £28.84 CT £67.66 TOTE £3.70: £1.20, £2.90, £1.10; EX 34.20 Place 6: £94.66 Place 5: £80.32.
Owner J D Sells **Bred** Oliver Loughlin **Trained** Lewes, E Sussex

FOCUS
A very moderate hurdle and the form is best rated through the runner-up, although the winner may have more to offer.

NOTEBOOK
Northern Lad(IRE) ◆, who ran into the gambled-on Am I Blue on his previous start, claimed his first success of any kind after travelling strongly throughout. Eased to the front after three out, he sauntered home under restraint to win with a bit in hand. He should gain plenty of confidence for this performance and should win again. (op 4-1 tchd 7-2)
Mangonel showed a fine attitude under pressure after holding a nice lead throughout. She could have easily capitulated once things got tough, but she kept on well and ran a brave race. (op 8-1 tchd 9-1)
Simone Martini(IRE) landed a gamble on his handicap debut on his previous start (2m Uttoxeter with cheekpieces for the first time) after showing virtually nothing in three other runs over hurdles. Raised 7lb for that ten-length success, he appeared to have ever chance until ploughing through two out and then hung badly left after the last. He had tended to edge that way earlier in the straight. (op 9-4 tchd 5-2 in a place)
Havenstone(IRE), runner-up over fences last time, was always thereabouts and stayed on under pressure. (op 11-2)
Orion Express stays much further than this trip and looked to be outpaced after making a positive move on the side of the course. (op 12-1)
T/Plt: £80.50 to a £1 stake. Pool of £54,082.90 - 489.90 winning tickets. T/Qpdt: £35.30 to a £1 stake. Pool of £4,578.35 - 95.90 winning tickets. TM

1600 WORCESTER (L-H)

Thursday, October 7

OFFICIAL GOING: Home straight - good to soft (good and soft in places); back straight - good
Cathedral Bend out 6yds and home turn bend out 3yds from innermost line adding 26yds to a 2m race. Run-in on inside half of straight.
Wind: Light against Weather: Cloudy with sunny spells

1742 LADBROKES NOVICES' HURDLE (12 hdls) 3m

2:00 (2:02) (Class 4) 4-Y-O+ **£2,740** (£798; £399)

Form RPR

0 **1** **Tullyraine (IRE)**[146] 319 6-10-12 0 PaddyBrennan 120+
(Nigel Twiston-Davies) *a.p: chsd ldr appr 7th: led 9th: clr fr 3 out: mstke next: sn hung lft: rdn and hung lft again flat: styd on* **16/1**

422- **2** *8* **Qroktou (FR)**[176] 5184 6-10-12 122 TomO'Brien 112
(Philip Hobbs) *prom: pushed along 8th: rdn to chse wnr flat: hung rt 110yds out: styd on: nt trble wnr* **4/9**[1]

242 **3** *8* **Stormyisland Ahead**[32] 1482 5-11-4 112 (t) PaulMoloney 113
(Evan Williams) *hld up in tch: chsd wnr appr 3 out: sn rdn: wknd flat* **7/1**[2]

330- **4** *3 ¼* **Lady Karinga**[180] 5137 5-10-2 0 LeeStephens(3) 94
(David Evans) *chsd ldr to appr 7th: wknd 9th* **25/1**

2213 **5** *2* **Hadron Collider (FR)**[77] 1065 5-11-1 114 DannyCook(3) 105
(Christopher Nenadich) *chsd ldrs: rdn appr 3 out: sn wknd* **9/1**[3]

440- **6** *25* **Landenstown Star (IRE)**[172] 5243 5-10-12 0 DenisO'Regan 80
(Seamus Mullins) *hld up: sme hdwy appr 3 out: nvr on terms: t.o* **40/1**

542/ **7** *18* **Bob Casey (IRE)**[742] 1483 8-10-12 0 RhysFlint 71+
(Keith Goldsworthy) *led to 9th: rdn and wknd bef next: t.o* **28/1**

00- **8** *32* **Shared Secret**[207] 4620 6-9-12 0 RachaelGreen(7) 25
(Anthony Honeyball) *hld up: hdwy 7th: wknd 9th: t.o* **33/1**

0- **9** *11* **Man Of Leisure**[507] 371 6-10-7 0 KeiranBurke(5) 22
(Nerys Dutfield) *hld up: effrt 7th: wknd after next: t.o* **100/1**

10 *1* **Inishrush (IRE)**[502] 9-10-5 0 MrRHawkins(7) 21
(Adrian Chamberlain) *unruly prior to the s: a in rr: t.o* **150/1**

2 **11** *shd* **Kasban**[14] 1588 6-10-12 0 TimmyMurphy 21
(Luke Dace) *hld up: a in rr: t.o* **14/1**

-060 **12** *1 ½* **Nishnash**[99] 863 7-10-12 72 AndrewThornton 20
(Jim Wilson) *hld up: pushed along and hung lft after 5th: bhd fr 7th: t.o* **200/1**

4-U0 **13** *11* **Commanche Dream**[141] 409 7-10-5 77 MissCBoxall(7) 10
(Simon Lewis) *mid-div: effrt 7th: sn wknd: t.o* **250/1**

0- **14** *45* **It's Molly**[470] 807 8-10-5 0 GerardTumelty —
(Simon Earle) *in rr and nt fluent: lost tch 7th: t.o* **250/1**

P **Harry Oscar (IRE)**[971] 9-10-5 0 MrPJTolman(7) —
(Ken Wingrove) *hld up: effrt appr 7th: wkng whn mstke next: t.o whn p.u bef 3 out* **100/1**

0PP/ **P** **Native Cherry**[602] 3858 9-10-5 0 JamesDavies —
(George Yardley) *mid-div: lost pl 6th: t.o whn p.u bef next* **250/1**

5m 49.4s (4.80) **Going Correction** +0.475s/f (Soft) **16** Ran SP% **121.3**
Speed ratings (Par 105): **111,108,105,104,103 95,89,78,75,74 74,74,70,55,— —**
toteswingers:1&2 £4.10, 2&3 £5.90, 1&3 £7.80 CSF £24.08 TOTE £25.00: £4.20, £1.10, £1.70; EX 39.30.
Owner Geoffrey & Donna Keeys **Bred** Mrs Judith Todd **Trained** Naunton, Gloucs
■ Stewards' Enquiry : Danny Cook two-day ban: careless riding (Oct 21-22)

FOCUS
The ground was good in the back straight and good to soft, good in places in the home straight, with the odd soft patch. This didn't go the way it was expected to but the winner looks a decent recruit. The second was 12lb off his best but the form has a fairly solid look.

NOTEBOOK
Tullyraine(IRE) took over four out and stayed on well to win with a fair bit in hand. Well beaten in a bumper back in May, he had previously placed in a point and the switch to hurdles was clearly the making of him. He looks a nice staying prospect. (op 14-1)
Qroktou(FR) had the form to take this and looked very fit in the paddock, so was understandably a short price, but not for the first time he was made to look rather slow, coming under pressure down the back and then plodding on despite carrying his head a tad high and hanging after the last. The sooner he's switched to fences the better and it's clear he needs a thorough test of stamina. (op 4-6)
Stormyisland Ahead, one of two previous winners over hurdles, has been coming up short under the penalty and he was again comfortably held back in third. (op 11-2)
Lady Karinga shaped with some promise on this hurdles debut and should improve.
Hadron Collider(FR) again struggled under the penalty. (tchd 10-1)
Bob Casey(IRE) ran well for a long way on this return from a 742-day absence. (op 22-1)

1743 E B F "NATIONAL HUNT" NOVICES' HURDLE (QUALIFIER) (8 hdls) 2m

2:35 (2:35) (Class 4) 4-6-Y-O **£3,252** (£955; £477; £238)

Form RPR

213- **1** **Owen Glendower (IRE)**[242] 3922 5-10-12 0 BarryGeraghty 121+
(Nicky Henderson) *trckd ldrs: led last: rdn out* **7/4**[1]

6/ **2** *3 ¼* **Gurtacrue (IRE)**[122] 673 5-10-12 0 PaulMoloney 118+
(Evan Williams) *w ldr: ev ch last: rdn and hung lft flat: no ex* **2/1**[2]

3 *14* **Dynaste (FR)**[341] 4-10-12 0 TomScudamore 108+
(David Pipe) *led: rdn and hdd whn mstke last: wknd flat* **5/1**[3]

2- **4** *13* **Royale's Charter**[165] 7 4-10-12 0 DarylJacob 99+
(Nick Williams) *prom: pckd 1st and 3rd: j. slowly next: sn lost pl: n.d after* **9/1**

406- **5** *2 ¾* **Jay J**[239] 3972 6-10-9 0 TomMolloy(3) 93
(Andrew Price) *hld up: mstke 2 out: nvr on terms* **20/1**

6 *16* **Sablazo (FR)**[169] 4-10-12 0 NickScholfield 77
(Andy Turnell) *hld up in tch: plld hrd: wknd appr 3 out: t.o* **20/1**

50P- **7** *15* **Jumpjack Flint**[251] 3727 4-10-12 0 PaddyBrennan 63
(Charlie Longsdon) *hld up: plld hrd: hdwy 3rd: rdn and wknd appr 3 out: t.o* **25/1**

00 **8** *7* **Track Star (IRE)**[114] 759 5-10-12 0 TimmyMurphy 57
(Luke Dace) *hld up: a in rr: bhd fr 4th: t.o* **100/1**

00 **9** *3 ½* **Sheezatreasure (IRE)**[100] 855 5-10-5 0 DavidDennis 47
(James Evans) *hld up in tch: wknd 5th: t.o* **100/1**

00- **10** *hd* **Prince Paolo (FR)**[226] 4213 5-10-12 0 AndrewTinkler 53
(George Baker) *hld up: a in rr: bhd fr 4th: t.o* **100/1**

3m 54.9s (7.60) **Going Correction** +0.475s/f (Soft) **10** Ran SP% **112.7**
Speed ratings: **100,98,91,84,83 75,68,64,62,62**
toteswingers:1&2 £1.50, 2&3 £2.70, 1&3:£2.60 CSF £5.04 TOTE £2.80: £1.80, £1.10, £1.10; EX 6.00.
Owner The Ten From Seven **Bred** Kenilworth House Stud **Trained** Upper Lambourn, Berks

FOCUS
A decent novices' hurdle for the track and the time of year. The first two should rate higher and the third is rated close to his mark.

NOTEBOOK
Owen Glendower(IRE), a half-brother to useful hurdler Dave's Dream, had reportedly strengthened up over the summer and he made a good start to his hurdles career, travelling and jumping well before staying on too strongly for the well-backed runner-up. There's plenty to like about this performance and it would be a surprise were he not able to defy a penalty. (op 11-8 tchd 2-1)
Gurtacrue(IRE), making his debut for the yard, hadn't run since winning a 2m4f bumper at Listowel in the summer, but he was solid in the market and he too travelled well. However, despite a valiant effort, he couldn't match the winner and it more than likely he'll benefit from a return to further. It shouldn't be long before he goes one better. (op 7-2)
Dynaste(FR), returning from 341 days off, was disputing it from an early stage but having been strongly challenged on both sides in the straight, he blundered three out and quickly dropped away. He should improve on this and will find easier opportunities. (op 7-2 tchd 10-3)
Royale's Charter, a promising second at Ludlow in his bumper, was outpaced following a mistake down the back, but did plug on again and looks in need of a stiffer test. He's bred to do better with time and should improve. (op 15-2 tchd 7-1)
Jumpjack Flint Official explanation: jockey said gelding ran too free
Prince Paolo(FR) Official explanation: jockey said gelding hung right throughout

1744 LADBROKES CONDITIONAL JOCKEYS' H'CAP CHASE (12 fncs) 2m

3:10 (3:10) (Class 4) (0-100,99) 4-Y-O+ **£3,252** (£955; £477; £238)

Form RPR

00-0 **1** **The Darling Boy**[142] 381 5-11-2 **89** (t) PeterToole 107+
(Tom George) *chsd clr ldr to appr 4th: wnt 2nd again 6th: clsd on ldr 8th: led 3 out: clr whn blnd last: eased towards fin* **8/1**

4245 **2** *18* **Glengarra (IRE)**[29] 1509 13-11-11 **98** (tp) GilesHawkins 101+
(Liam Corcoran) *led and sn clr: hdd 3 out: rdn and wknd bef last* **4/1**[1]

04-4 **3** *14* **Space Star**[88] 952 10-11-7 **99** PeterCarberry(5) 83
(Paul Webber) *hld up: rdn whn j.rt 4 out: wnt remote 3rd appr 2 out: nvr on terms: t.o* **9/2**[2]

U636 **4** *17* **Mad Professor (IRE)**[32] 1481 7-9-10 **75** (p) JoeCornwall(6) 44
(John Cornwall) *sn pushed along and a in rr: t.o* **7/1**

0-0U **P** **Tanmeya**[13] 1601 9-11-3 **96** MrTomDavid(6) —
(Tim Vaughan) *hld up: drvn along 5th: sn wknd: t.o whn p.u bef 7th* **13/2**

6P44 **R** **Post It**[14] 1591 9-10-3 **79** (b) CharlieWallis(3) —
(Ron Hodges) *j.rt: prom: chsd clr ldr appr 4th to 6th: wknd after 8th: 4th and t.o whn ref last* **5/1**[3]

-61P **P** **Western Pride**[32] 1481 7-10-1 **77** (t) KyleJames(3) —
(Richard Price) *j.rt and a bhd: t.o whn p.u bef 2 out* **9/2**[2]

3m 59.0s (7.40) **Going Correction** +0.475s/f (Soft) **7** Ran SP% **110.0**
Speed ratings (Par 105): **100,91,84,75,— —,—**
CSF £37.19 TOTE £8.20: £4.00, £1.80; EX 49.80.

Owner Hugo Rittson-Thomas **Bred** G Russell **Trained** Slad, Gloucs

FOCUS

A modest conditional jockeys' handicap chase, though the pace set by Glengarra was sound and only four of the seven runners managed to complete. A massive step up from the easy winner and there is a case for rating the form a few pounds higher.

NOTEBOOK

The Darling Boy had been placed in three bumpers, but was disappointing when sent over hurdles a year ago and ran poorly on his chase debut at Towcester back in May. He was tried in a tongue tie on this return to action, however, and what a difference it appeared to make. Always prominent in the chasing group, he moved smoothly alongside the leader rounding the home bend before being sent on jumping three out. Even a sloppy jump at the last wasn't enough to stop him and he won easily, but this was a weak race and it remains to be seen whether the tongue tie continues to have a similar effect. Official explanation: trainer said, regarding apparent improvement in form, that the gelding bled after its first run over fences and was always going to be a better chaser than hurdler. (op 17-2 tchd 9-1)

Glengarra(IRE) was down to a mark 7lb lower than for his last win which came over an extra half-mile here 14 months ago. Given his usual attacking ride, the likeable veteran soon held a clear lead and ran most of his rivals into the ground, but the winner was the exception and he couldn't match him from three out. (op 9-2)

Space Star, lightly raced since making a winning chase debut in April 2005, was down to a new career-low mark over fences but he could never make any impression on the front pair and on this evidence needs a return to further. (op 4-1 tchd 5-1)

Tanmeya, whose two career victories came over C&D in the summer of last year, had a couple of outings over hurdles last month following a lengthy absence to help put her straight, but she never looked happy on this return to fences and was pulled up at halfway. Official explanation: vet said mare bled from the nose (tchd 11-2)

Post It ruined her chance by jumping out to her right from the start, a trait which became worse as the race progressed until she decided not to jump the last. Unsurprisingly, her two career wins have come on the right-handed track at Hereford. (tchd 11-2)

1745 LADBROKES (S) H'CAP HURDLE (12 hdls) 3m

3:45 (3:45) (Class 5) (0-95,95) 4-Y-0+ **£1,712** (£499; £249)

Form RPR

6/53 **1** **Panzer (GER)**42 [1380] 9-10-6 **85** .... HenryBrooke(10) 98+
(Donald McCain) *hld up in tch: chsd ldr appr 3 out: led 2 out: rdn clr flat* **5/1**2

0P5- **2** *12* **Supreme Team (IRE)**339 [2042] 7-10-1 **77** .... PeterHatton(7) 78
(Louise Davis) *a.p: led 9th: rdn and hdd 2 out: wknd flat* **20/1**

3P64 **3** *4* **Kingston Queen (IRE)**4 [1694] 7-10-11 **80** ....(b) ChristianWilliams 77
(Rachel Hobbs) *hld up: reminders after 7th: hdwy 3 out: rdn and hung lft appr last: wkng whn hung rt flat* **9/1**

0/60 **4** *2* **Stowford Press (IRE)**69 [1141] 7-10-3 **79** .... KyleJames(7) 75
(Nikki Evans) *hld up: rdn and r.o flat: nvr nrr* **28/1**

5554 **5** *1 3/4* **Vacario (GER)**14 [1590] 6-11-8 **94** ....(t) TommyPhelan(3) 87
(Mark Gillard) *prom: rdn appr 3 out: sn outpcd* **7/1**3

/PP- **6** *1 1/4* **Supreme Piper (IRE)**198 [4811] 12-10-9 **78** .... NoelFehily 70
(Claire Dyson) *led: hdd after 1st: chsd ldrs: rdn appr 3 out: wknd after next* **22/1**

2406 **7** *1* **Heir To Be**18 [1551] 11-11-12 **95** ....(b) NickScholfield 86
(Michael Blake) *prom: lost pl 5th: hit wings of the next: bhd and rdn appr 7th: n.d after* **7/1**3

0531 **8** *1 3/4* **Sea Cliff (IRE)**13 [1605] 6-11-6 **89** ....(tp) APMcCoy 78
(Jonjo O'Neill) *hld up: hdwy 7th: rdn appr last: wknd flat* **10/3**1

P6-0 **9** *2 1/4* **Ticket To Ride (FR)**129 [557] 12-9-7 **69** oh5 .... CDTimmons(7) 56
(Jim Wilson) *hld up: hdwy 5th: rdn and wknd bef last* **50/1**

3564 **10** *4 1/2* **Fongoli**5 [1678] 4-10-10 **87** ....(b) MissCLWills(7) 69
(Brendan Powell) *reminders sn after s: led after 1st: hdd 9th: rdn and wknd bef next* **16/1**

P306 **11** *nk* **Barlin Bay**4 [1694] 6-10-7 **76** ....(b) TomScudamore 59
(David Pipe) *hld up: hdwy 3 out: sn rdn and wknd* **10/1**

/P-P **P** **Muraqeb**119 [697] 10-9-13 **71** oh8 ow2 .... SeanQuinlan(3) —
(Harry Chisman) *mid-div: blnd 5th: bhd whn p.u after next* **66/1**

006- **P** **The Walnut Tree (IRE)**167 [5361] 9-9-7 **69** oh3 ....(b) MissCBoxall(7) —
(Simon Lewis) *chsd ldrs tl wknd 8th: t.o whn p.u bef 3 out* **50/1**

P35/ **P** **Brilliant (GER)**551 [4852] 7-10-1 **70** ow1 ....(v) PaulMoloney —
(Debra Hamer) *sn pushed along in rr: hmpd 5th: t.o whn p.u bef last* **11/1**

00-4 **P** **Quatuor Collonges (FR)**14 [1588] 6-10-0 **76** ....(b) MrSWDrinkwater(7) —
(David Bridgwater) *chsd ldrs: lost pl 4th: sn looked reluctant: bhd whn p.u after 6th* **33/1**

5m 54.2s (9.60) **Going Correction** +0.475s/f (Soft)
WFA 4 from 6yo+ 11lb **15** Ran SP% **119.0**
Speed ratings (Par 103): **103,99,97,97,96 96,95,95,94,92 92,—,—,—,—**
toteswingers:1&2 £17.10, 2&3 £42.80, 1&3 £10.50 CSF £102.04 CT £884.87 TOTE £5.90: £2.20, £6.00, £2.60; EX 118.80.The winner was bought in for 7,500gns

Owner D McCain Jnr **Bred** Baron N C J Rothschild **Trained** Cholmondeley, Cheshire

FOCUS

A competitive selling handicap hurdle. The easy winner was back to the level of his 2005/6 form with the next three close to their marks.

NOTEBOOK

Panzer(GER), back to something like his best at Cartmel latest, was always going well under Henry Brooke, who was looking round in the straight, and the pair forged clear after the last to win with ease. The handicapper will have his say now, though, and it remains to be seen whether he can follow up. (op 9-2 tchd 7-2)

Supreme Team(IRE), making his debut for the yard, stays well and he took over leaving the back, but proved no match for the winner.

Kingston Queen(IRE), making a quick reappearance, made some late headway into third. (op 14-1 tchd 17-2)

Stowford Press(IRE) has taken a drop in the weights and shaped with a bit more promise in a never-nearer fourth. (op 33-1)

Sea Cliff(IRE), lifted home when winning off 6lb lower at the course last time, travelled more kindly on this occasion but he found nothing for strong pressure and dropped away in the end. (op 4-1 tchd 5-1)

Muraqeb Official explanation: jockey said gelding was struck into

1746 LADBROKES MARES' H'CAP HURDLE (10 hdls) 2m 4f

4:20 (4:20) (Class 3) (0-120,113) 4-Y-0 **£5,069** (£1,497; £748; £374; £187)

Form RPR

04P- **1** **Gan On**257 [3610] 6-11-5 **113** .... RachaelGreen(7) 121+
(Anthony Honeyball) *a.p: chsd ldr 6th: led 3 out: rdn out* **9/1**

251- **2** *4* **Je Ne Sais Plus (FR)**196 [4840] 6-11-9 **110** .... PaddyBrennan 115
(Tom George) *hld up: hdwy 7th: ev ch whn mstke 2 out: sn rdn: edgd lft and styd on same pce flat* **9/2**2

2202 **3** *7* **Edgefour (IRE)**32 [1484] 6-11-1 **107** ....(v) GilesHawkins(5) 106
(Ben Case) *hld up: hdwy 7th: rdn and wknd flat* **7/1**3

F13- **4** *4 1/2* **Bosamcliff (IRE)**3 [4416] 5-11-4 **105** .... APMcCoy 99
(David Evans) *hld up: hdwy 7th: rdn appr last: wknd flat* **11/4**1

1210 **5** *11* **Makena (FR)**14 [1590] 8-11-9 **110** ....(p) PaulMoloney 94
(David Rees) *mid-div: lost pl 5th: rdn appr 3 out: sn wknd* **7/1**3

16P- **6** *6* **Dawn At Sea**222 [4298] 8-11-5 **106** ....(p) RhysFlint 84
(John Flint) *chsd ldr to 6th: rdn and wknd appr 3 out* **9/1**

43-4 **7** *30* **Dot's Delight**24 [340] 6-11-3 **107** .... PeterToole(3) 58
(Mark Rimell) *hld up: hdwy 7th: rdn and wknd bef next: t.o* **8/1**

3-22 **8** *1 1/2* **Stir On The Sea (IRE)**129 [547] 4-11-0 **104** .... ChrisHonour(3) 54
(James Frost) *mid-div: rdn and wknd 7th: t.o* **25/1**

030- **9** *shd* **Jaunty Dove**201 [4741] 8-9-7 **87** oh2 .... MrJFlook(7) 37
(Andrew Price) *chsd ldrs tl rdn and wknd after 7th: t.o* **33/1**

3010 **P** **Basford Lass**18 [1556] 5-11-9 **110** ....(b) AlanO'Keeffe —
(Jennie Candlish) *led to 3 out: sn rdn: wknd after next: p.u flat* **16/1**

4m 58.4s (11.00) **Going Correction** +0.475s/f (Soft)
WFA 4 from 5yo+ 10lb **10** Ran SP% **113.6**
Speed ratings (Par 107): **97,95,92,90,86 84,72,71,71,—**
toteswingers:1&2 £7.20, 2&3 £6.80, 1&3 £16.00 CSF £48.75 CT £301.42 TOTE £7.70: £1.80, £1.10, £3.10; EX 53.20.

Owner Club Revive **Bred** Mrs Valerie Jackson **Trained** Seaborough, Dorset

FOCUS

An open-looking mares' handicap hurdle. A step up from the winner with the second rated to her mark.

NOTEBOOK

Gan On, who won first time out last season, had the assistance of a capable rider who was claiming 7lb and, having travelled well, she stayed on strongly to win with a bit in hand. It remains to be seen whether she can go on from this, as she struggled after her first win a year ago. (op 6-1)

Je Ne Sais Plus(FR), a three-time winner last season, was clearly straight enough to run well on this first start since March, but she should improve and can go one better before long. (op 5-1)

Edgefour(IRE) has been running well of late, but she was comfortably held in the end here. (op 8-1)

Bosamcliff(IRE), who's had a couple of pipe-openers on the Flat, was a bit disappointing and again gave the impression this mark is beyond her. (op 7-2 tchd 4-1)

Basford Lass Official explanation: jockey said mare finished lame

1747 RICHARD WRIGHT MEMORIAL NOVICES' H'CAP CHASE (18 fncs) 2m 7f

4:55 (4:55) (Class 4) (0-105,105) 4-Y-0+ **£3,252** (£955; £477; £238)

Form RPR

23 **1** **Dunkelly Castle (IRE)**50 [1281] 6-11-12 **105** .... HaddenFrost 113
(Roger Curtis) *hld up: hdwy 12th: chsd ldr 4 out: led 1ast: sn rdn: jst hld on* **13/2**

U/43 **2** *nk* **Autumn Red (IRE)**32 [1483] 10-11-0 **93** ....(bt) DenisO'Regan 101
(Paul Webber) *chsd ldr tl led 8th: rdn and hdd last: r.o wl* **11/2**2

345- **3** *nk* **Flemish Invader (IRE)**215 [4451] 7-11-11 **104** .... PaddyBrennan 112
(Nigel Twiston-Davies) *hld up: hdwy 14th: hung rt fr 3 out: rdn and r.o wl flat: nt quite get there* **3/1**1

3533 **4** *1* **Canon's Corner (IRE)**36 [1452] 7-11-2 **95** .... AidanColeman 102
(Rachel Hobbs) *prom: mstke 4 out: shkn up after next: rdn flat: r.o wl* **16/1**

4P6- **5** *11* **Qualypso D'Allier (FR)**181 [5120] 6-10-7 **86** .... NickScholfield 83
(Andy Turnell) *hld up: hdwy 14th: wknd 2 out* **7/1**

61-P **6** *68* **Backfromthecongo (IRE)**112 [769] 9-11-5 **103** ....(bt) GilesHawkins(5) 38
(Richard Lee) *hld up: a in rr: bhd fr 10th: t.o* **18/1**

30-5 **7** *11* **No More Whispers (IRE)**161 [59] 5-10-13 **92** .... PaulMoloney 18
(Evan Williams) *led to 8th: chsd ldr tl wknd 14th: t.o* **9/1**

44P4 **U** **Little Girl**42 [1377] 12-9-7 **79** oh21 ....(p) PeterHatton(7) —
(Ray Peacock) *w ldrs whn mstke 1st: blnd and uns rdr next* **100/1**

3243 **F** **Kilshannig (IRE)**29 [1509] 5-11-6 **99** ....(t) APMcCoy —
(Jonjo O'Neill) *prom: disputing cl 3rd whn fell 5 out* **6/1**3

3PU/ **P** **Byways Boy**159 7-10-6 **85** .... AndrewThornton —
(Caroline Bailey) *hld up: drvn along 10th: wknd next: t.o whn p.u bef 4 out* **28/1**

42-6 **U** **Phoenix Des Mottes (FR)**12 [1612] 7-10-9 **95** .... JoeCornwall(7) —
(John Cornwall) *hld up: blnd and uns rdr 4th* **25/1**

03-5 **P** **Backfromthebrink (IRE)**16 [1567] 6-11-11 **104** .... WillKennedy —
(Paul Webber) *chsd ldrs: drvn along appr 10th: wknd 12th: t.o whn p.u bef 4 out* **16/1**

5m 54.9s (12.30) **Going Correction** +0.475s/f (Soft) **12** Ran SP% **115.8**
Speed ratings (Par 105): **97,96,96,96,92 68,65,—,—,— —,—**
toteswingers:1&2 £6.00, 2&3 £4.80, 1&3 £4.80 CSF £41.43 CT £129.71 TOTE £7.60: £2.70, £2.50, £1.10; EX 36.20.

Owner R P Behan **Bred** Kieran Hanlon **Trained** Lambourn, Berks

■ Stewards' Enquiry : Denis O'Regan caution: used whip down shoulder in the forehand.

FOCUS

A modest novices' handicap chase. The winner improved to the level of his hurdles form.

NOTEBOOK

Dunkelly Castle(IRE) gained reward for a string of consistent efforts. Having only his second start over fences when third at Hereford latest, he was clinging on as they crossed the line, but is only six and may yet have more to offer. (op 9-1 tchd 6-1)

Autumn Red(IRE) was up there from an early stage and kept finding for strong pressure, closing again on the winner as they passed the line without quite being able to get back up. (op 15-2)

Flemish Invader(IRE) travelled like the best horse in the race, but Paddy Brennan seemed keen to keep him in behind runners and, having not picked up as expected, he rallied all too late to just miss out. He's clearly not straightforward. (op 5-2)

Canon's Corner(IRE) put up a better effort from on this first start in a handicap. He should be up to winning a small race.

Qualypso D'Allier(FR)'s jumping wasn't the sharpest, but he may be worth one last chance. (op 8-1 tchd 13-2)

Kilshannig(IRE) was in the process of running a big race and still sat a handy third when taking a heavy fall three out. (op 5-1)

Backfromthebrink(IRE) didn't improve as expected for the switch to handicaps. (op 5-1)

1748 LADBROKES INTERMEDIATE OPEN NATIONAL HUNT FLAT RACE (DIV I) 2m

5:30 (5:30) (Class 6) 4-6-Y-0 **£1,370** (£399; £199)

Form RPR

46- **1** **Laveroque (FR)**171 [5284] 4-10-11 0 .... PeterCarberry(7) 114+
(Charlie Longsdon) *hld up: hdwy over 5f out: led over 1f out: sn rdn and hung lft: r.o wl* **7/1**

2 **2** *7* **Youralltalk (IRE)**46 [1349] 6-11-4 0 .... APMcCoy 107
(Keith Goldsworthy) *chsd ldrs: led over 10f out: rdn and hdd over 1f out: no ex ins fnl f: wnt 2nd nr fin* **4/1**3

3 *1/2* **Hes Our Lad (IRE)** 4-10-11 0 .... RachaelGreen(7) 106
(Anthony Honeyball) *hld up: hdwy over 5f out: swtchd rt over 3f out: ev ch over 1f out: sn rdn: hung lft and wknd wl ins fnl f* **7/2**2

4 *2 1/4* **Cap Elorn (FR)** 4-11-4 0 .... HarrySkelton 104
(Paul Nicholls) *prom: rdn over 2f out: wknd over 1f out* **13/8**1

	5	15	**Driving Onwards (IRE)**[152] 6-10-11 0 SClements(7) (Ron Hodges) *sn led: hdd over 10f out: remained handy tl rdn and wknd over 2f out* **33/1**		91
	6	5	**Otis Tarda (IRE)** 4-11-4 0 TomO'Brien (Philip Hobbs) *prom: rdn over 3f out: wknd over 2f out* **7/1**		86
	7	11	**Withy Mills** 5-10-6 0 GilesHawkins(5) (Kevin Bishop) *hld up: drvn along 6f out: n.d: wknd wl over 3f out: t.o* **66/1**		69
0	8	36	**Samtheman**[13] 1607 5-10-11 0 MrBJPoste(7) (Christopher Nenadich) *hld up: hdwy over 5f out: wknd over 4f out: t.o* **100/1**		44
4	9	11	**Avon Gale**[33] 1472 6-10-11 0 LiamTreadwell (John Allen) *plld hrd: trckd ldr over 4f: wknd over 6f out: t.o* **66/1**		27
	10	88	**Spring A Suprise** 6-10-4 0 MrPJTolman(7) (Ken Wingrove) *hld up: drvn along 1/2-way: sn t.o* **100/1**		—

3m 51.2s (9.50) **Going Correction** +0.475s/f (Soft) **10** Ran SP% **113.2**
Speed ratings: **95,91,91,90,82 80,74,56,51,7**
toteswingers:1&2 £4.70, 2&3 £3.40, 1&3 £4.90 CSF £33.66 TOTE £7.20: £2.20, £1.50, £1.60; EX 37.00.
Owner The Saddleworth Players **Bred** Elevage Avicole Lozac'H-Leyan Et Al **Trained** Over Norton, Oxon

FOCUS
This looked much the stronger of the two divisions of the bumper. A big step up from the easy winner.

NOTEBOOK
Laveroque(FR) had shaped with promise on both his runs in bumpers last season and, under a cool ride from Peter Carberry, he was able to turn in a much-improved effort, staying on strongly to go clear inside the final furlong. On this evidence he will make a nice hurdler. (op 12-1)
Youralltalk(IRE), a point winner who finished second at Newton Abbot on his bumper debut, was ridden positively by McCoy and kept finding for pressure to re-take second, but the winner had too much in hand. (op 10-3)
Hes Our Lad(IRE), whose dam is an unraced half-sister to She's Out Mare, travelled like a dream for connections well adept at readying one to win a bumper first time, but he couldn't sustain his effort once coming under pressure and lost out on second. There were plenty of positives to take from this. (tchd 3-1)
Cap Elorn(FR), very much bred to stay, was going on again at the finish and looked in need of this experience. He should improve and can make his mark over hurdles. (tchd 6-4 and 15-8 and 2-1 in a place)
Driving Onwards(IRE) remained prominent once overtaken, but faded out of it in the end. (tchd 25-1)
Otis Tarda(IRE) was right there turning for home, but he got tired and will presumably come on for this debut outing. (tchd 13-2 and 15-2)

1749 LADBROKES INTERMEDIATE OPEN NATIONAL HUNT FLAT RACE (DIV II) 2m
6:00 (6:00) (Class 6) 4-6-Y-O **£1,370** (£399; £199)

Form				RPR
	1		**Eastlake (IRE)** 4-11-4 0 APMcCoy (Jonjo O'Neill) *hld up: hdwy 4f out: rdn to ld ins fnl f: r.o* **13/8**[1]	99+
	2	1 1/4	**Lord Kennedy (IRE)** 5-10-11 0 MrKevinJones(7) (Seamus Mullins) *hld up: hdwy 1/2-way: led over 5f out: rdn and hung rt fr over 1f out: hit rails ins fnl f: sn hdd: styd on same pce* **14/1**	99+
	3	1 1/2	**Shan Blue (IRE)**[242] 5-11-4 0 BarryGeraghty (Steve Gollings) *hld up: hdwy 7f out: chsd ldr 4f out: rdn over 1f out: styd on same pce ins fnl f* **7/4**[2]	97+
	4	10	**Brannoc (IRE)** 5-11-4 0 AndrewThornton (Tony Newcombe) *mid-div: rdn over 3f out: nvr trbld ldrs* **20/1**	88
0	5	2	**Fairwood Dante (IRE)**[13] 1607 6-11-4 0 DarylJacob (Simon Earle) *chsd ldr tl led 11f out: hdd 9f out: remained handy tl rdn and wknd over 2f out* **28/1**	86
	6	2	**Subtle Approach (IRE)** 5-11-1 0 TomMolloy(3) (Emma Baker) *hld up: pushed along 7f out: rdn over 3f out: hung rt and wknd over 2f out* **40/1**	84
6	7	3/4	**Just Unique**[37] 1448 6-11-4 0 (p) TomScudamore (Mark Rimell) *led 5f: led again 9f out: rdn and hdd over 5f out: wknd 3f out* **50/1**	83
506-	8	8	**Boosha**[207] 4620 5-10-8 0 SeanQuinlan(3) (Rachel Hobbs) *chsd ldrs: hmpd 6f out: rdn and wknd over 2f out* **16/1**	69
0-	9	4	**Flora King**[237] 4023 5-11-4 0 AidanColeman (Anthony Honeyball) *hld up in tch: rdn and wknd over 3f out* **11/2**[3]	72
	10	70	**Kidajo** 4-11-4 0 HaddenFrost (Roger Curtis) *chsd ldrs: drvn along 7f out: sn wknd: t.o* **40/1**	9

3m 52.5s (10.80) **Going Correction** +0.475s/f (Soft) **10** Ran SP% **117.4**
Speed ratings: **92,91,90,85,84 83,83,79,77,42**
toteswingers:1&2 £7.10, 2&3 £5.70, 1&3 £1.50 CSF £23.79 TOTE £5.00: £1.70, £3.00, £1.10; EX 33.30 Place 6: £56.28 Place 5: £47.77.
Owner John P McManus **Bred** Mrs Eleanor Hadden **Trained** Cheltenham, Gloucs

FOCUS
The front three drew clear in the this second division and are probably capable of rating higher. Ordinary form.

NOTEBOOK
Eastlake(IRE), a half-brother to several winners, including Santenay, was nursed into contention by McCoy and then picked up well for strong pressure inside the final furlong. A likeable debut effort, he may struggle to defy a penalty, but is sure to stay further over hurdles and remains capable of better. (op 6-4 tchd 11-8 and 7-4)
Lord Kennedy(IRE), very much bred to be a stayer over jumps, travelled nicely and struck on turning for home, but the winner had the legs of him late on and he was already held when his jockey became unbalanced and the pair bumped the rail. This was a very promising start. (op 16-1)
Shan Blue(IRE) moved well throughout and held his chance in the straight, but couldn't get the better of the runner-up and had to make do with third. He is obviously going to benefit from a stiffer test over hurdles and should have no trouble winning races. (tchd 6-4)
Brannoc(IRE), from a yard capable of getting the odd bumper winner, kept on late and looks in need of a stiffer test.
Flora King was disappointing considering he had shaped with some promise in a good bumper at Kempton back in February. (op 7-1)
Kidajo Official explanation: jockey said gelding made a noise
T/Plt: £47.70 to a £1 stake. Pool of £51,234.41 - 782.53 winning tickets. T/Qpdt: £44.40 to a £1 stake. Pool of £3,596.20 - 59.90 winning tickets. CR

1750 - 1756a (Foreign Racing) - See Raceform Interactive

CARLISLE (R-H)
Friday, October 8

OFFICIAL GOING: Chase course - good to soft (good in places); hurdle course - good (good to soft in places)
Wind: Almost nil Weather: Cloudy

1757 EDINBURGH WOOLLEN MILL NOVICES' HURDLE (DIV I) (9 hdls) 2m 1f
1:30 (1:31) (Class 4) 4-Y-0+ **£2,397** (£698; £349)

Form				RPR
	1		**Recession Proof (FR)**[34] 4-10-12 0 DougieCostello (John Quinn) *hld up in midfield: smooth hdwy 3 out: led last: rdn out* **7/4**[1]	114+
004-	2	2 3/4	**County Colours (IRE)**[172] 5273 5-10-12 107 TimmyMurphy (Howard Johnson) *t.k.h: hld up in tch: hdwy to ld 3 out: hdd last: kpt on same pce run-in* **9/2**[3]	106
3-	3	nk	**Flinty Bay (IRE)**[197] 4839 5-10-9 0 FearghalDavis(3) (Nicky Richards) *nt fluent on occasions: hld up: hdwy and prom 2 out: kpt on same pce run-in: bttr for r* **17/2**	106
3-	4	18	**Ebony River (IRE)**[211] 4536 4-10-12 0 APMcCoy (Donald McCain) *nt fluent on occasions: trckd ldrs: hit 4 out: rallied after next: wkng whn nt fluent last* **3/1**[2]	91+
	5	3	**Accordion To Paddy (IRE)**[138] 450 6-10-5 0 MissHollyCurran(7) (Michael O'Hare, Ire) *hld up: shkn up and outpcd bef 3 out: plugged on run-in: nvr on terms* **50/1**	85
1-22	6	14	**Elevenses**[41] 1401 6-11-5 0 PaddyAspell (James Moffatt) *led tl hdd 3 out: wknd bef next* **8/1**	78
0-P3	7	3 1/4	**Lago Verde (SWI)**[107] 827 5-10-12 0 PeterBuchanan (Lucinda Russell) *trckd ldrs tl rdn and wknd bef 2 out* **33/1**	67
0000	8	4 1/2	**Shuttle Diplomacy (IRE)**[15] 1594 5-9-12 0 StevenGagan(7) (Elliott Cooper) *in tch on outside: struggling after 4 out: wknd bef next* **200/1**	56
063-	9	1 1/4	**Bob Will (IRE)**[309] 2668 5-10-12 0 RichieMcGrath (Chris Grant) *t.k.h: stdd towards rr: struggling bef 3 out: sn btn* **40/1**	62
/00-	10	3 1/4	**Yes Mate**[304] 2762 6-10-9 0 RyanMania(3) (Dianne Sayer) *midfield on ins: rdn 3 out: sn wknd* **200/1**	58
0	F		**Roi's Last Runner**[142] 399 5-10-5 0 GarethThomas(7) (Barry Murtagh) *trckd ldrs tl wknd bef 2 out: wl btn whn fell run-in: fatally injured* **250/1**	—

4m 18.8s (-11.00) **Going Correction** -0.825s/f (Firm)
WFA 4 from 5yo+ 9lb **11** Ran SP% **109.9**
Speed ratings (Par 105): **92,90,90,82,80 74,72,70,69,68** —
toteswingers:1&2:£2.30, 1&3:£12.00, 2&3:£8.50 CSF £9.13 TOTE £2.40: £1.10, £1.80, £2.50; EX 10.10.
Owner Mrs Vanessa J Stone **Bred** N P Bloodstock Ltd & Morton Bloodstock **Trained** Settrington, N Yorks

FOCUS
An interesting novices' hurdle in which the early pace was steady until an increase just after halfway. Because of the early pace a lot of the horses took a keen hold. The first three pulled well clear and the winner looks a decent recruit. The second is rated to his mark.

NOTEBOOK
Recession Proof(FR), a useful performer up to 1m6f on the Flat, made a very pleasing start to his hurdling career, jumping well throughout. His trainer has done well with similar types in the past and can certainly progress up the ladder. A similar race with a penalty would be an obvious target for him next time. (op 2-1, after early 5-2 in a place, tchd 13-8)
County Colours(IRE), rated 107, is a good bench mark to the form. His yard have yet to hit top form but this was a pleasing first run after a break and can go one better at some point soon. (op 5-1)
Flinty Bay(IRE) ◆, sent off a short-priced favourite on in only start in a bumper, stayed on very well here and will have little trouble losing his maiden tag in similar company. (op 8-1 tchd 9-1)
Ebony River(IRE) ran well for a long time and wasn't suited the way the race panned out. He will be seen in a better light over further. (op 9-4)
Elevenses will always be vulnerable in this company and modest handicaps will be the way forward for him. (op 9-1)
Lago Verde(SWI) Official explanation: jockey said the gelding had a breathing problem

1758 EDINBURGH WOOLLEN MILL NOVICES' HURDLE (DIV II) (9 hdls) 2m 1f
2:00 (2:00) (Class 4) 4-Y-0+ **£2,397** (£698; £349)

Form				RPR
024-	1		**Bow Badger**[211] 4536 4-10-12 0 BrianHughes (Howard Johnson) *t.k.h: cl up: led 4th: clr fr next: styd on wl: unchal* **3/1**[2]	108+
5F-5	2	10	**Chapolimoss (FR)**[155] 180 6-10-12 0 GrahamLee (Martin Todhunter) *nt fluent on occasions: hld up: smooth hdwy after 4 out: chsd wnr 2 out: kpt on run-in: no imp* **9/1**	98
2	3	6	**You Know Yourself (IRE)**[19] 1553 7-10-12 0 HenryOliver (Sue Smith) *trckd ldrs: hit 4 out: rdn and outpcd 4 out: rallied to chse wnr next to 2 out: 3rd and no ex whn mstke last* **5/4**[1]	94
040-	4	9	**Ouest Eclair (FR)**[180] 5140 5-10-5 0 PaulGallagher(7) (Ferdy Murphy) *prom: effrt and disp 2nd pl 3 out: wknd after next: btn whn mstke last* **66/1**	87
000-	5	15	**Izzy Bella**[168] 5370 4-10-5 0 PaddyAspell (Sue Bradburne) *hld up: pushed along and hdwy after 4 out: wknd fr next* **100/1**	64
006-	6	nk	**Stormion (IRE)**[163] 42 5-10-12 0 PeterBuchanan (Lucinda Russell) *trckd ldrs tl wknd fr 4 out* **40/1**	71
6/50	7	17	**Isitcozimcool (IRE)**[7] 1664 5-10-9 0 RyanMania(3) (Barry Murtagh) *midfield: lost pl 1/2-way: sn n.d* **40/1**	55
0	8	4 1/2	**Orlittlebylittle**[127] 602 4-10-9 0 AdrianLane(3) (Donald McCain) *midfield: hit 4th: sn drvn along: struggling fr 4 out* **33/1**	51
6	9	2	**Sammy Pat (IRE)**[127] 603 6-10-5 0 MissHollyCurran(7) (Michael O'Hare, Ire) *nt fluent on occasions: hld up: struggling 1/2-way: nvr on terms* **25/1**	50
00P-	10	1/2	**Peachey Moment (USA)**[303] 2778 5-10-12 0 BrianHarding (Nicky Richards) *hld up on ins: shortlived effrt after 4 out: sn wknd* **12/1**	49
0/5-	P		**The Portonion (IRE)**[257] 3623 6-10-12 0 DenisO'Regan (Malcolm Jefferson) *led to 4th: chsd wnr tl wknd 3 out: p.u bef last* **17/2**[3]	—

4m 15.9s (-13.90) **Going Correction** -0.825s/f (Firm) **11** Ran SP% **111.8**
Speed ratings (Par 105): **99,94,91,87,80 80,72,69,68,68** —
toteswingers:1&2:£5.20, 1&3:£1.10, 2&3:£3.70 CSF £25.89 TOTE £3.30: £1.10, £2.40, £1.40; EX 27.70.
Owner Mrs S Johnson **Bred** Juddmonte Farms Ltd **Trained** Billy Row, Co Durham

FOCUS
On paper this looked much the weaker division. It was run at an ordinary gallop but, in the end, produced an impressive winner. The second sets the level.

NOTEBOOK

Bow Badger, who had shown clear ability in bumpers, jumped well and should be up to carrying a penalty in similar company next time out. (op 9-4)

Chapolimoss(FR) ◆, having his first start for this trainer, ran well. A little keen early, he stayed on from the back but never looked like catching the winner. He is now qualified for a handicap mark and should get plenty of opportunities to go one better, if able to build on this effort. (op 8-1)

You Know Yourself(IRE), who made a pleasing start for this yard last time out, was probably found out by the drop back in trip. He will also be one for handicaps later on, over fences and further. (op 15-8)

Ouest Eclair(FR) showed up well on his first start since April. There is room for improvement with his jumping. (op 50-1)

Peachey Moment(USA) never really threatened on his first start for this yard and the rest can only be watched for the short term. (op 14-1)

The Portonion(IRE) Official explanation: jockey said that the gelding stopped quickly

1759 CLARE BURNS 60TH BIRTHDAY NOVICES' CHASE (16 fncs) 2m 4f

2:30 (2:30) (Class 4) 4-Y-0+ **£3,577** (£1,050; £525; £262)

Form RPR

12P- **1** **Alvarado (IRE)**209 4589 5-11-4 0 TimmyMurphy 123+
(Howard Johnson) *trckd ldrs: nt fluent 9th: effrt and led bef 2 out: drvn and styd on wl run-in* **3/1**1

0204 **2** 1 1/4 **Flying Doctor**7 1661 7-11-4 0 StevenGagan(7) 128
(Elliott Cooper) *cl up: led 9th: hdd whn hit 2 out: kpt on u.p fr last* **20/1**

U30- **3** 3 1/4 **C'Monthehammers (IRE)**176 5197 7-11-4 0 PaddyBrennan 119
(Nigel Twiston-Davies) *j.rt and nt fluent on occasions: led to 9th: cl up: rdn 3 out: one pce after next* **11/2**

04-1 **4** hd **Alderley Rover (IRE)**154 193 6-11-4 0 NoelFehily 117
(Donald McCain) *hld up: hdwy and in tch bef 4 out: rdn and kpt on same pce fr 2 out: bttr for r* **5/1**3

120- **5** 11 **Born Again (IRE)**203 4715 5-11-4 0 APMcCoy 108
(Jonjo O'Neill) *hld up: pckd 8th: outpcd 10th: hdwy after 5 out: shkn up and no imp fr 3 out* **10/3**2

456- **6** 5 **Tyrone House (IRE)**200 4783 6-10-11 0 MrJohnDawson(7) 105
(John Wade) *t.k.h: hld up in midfield: hdwy and in tch 5 out: blnd next: wknd bef 3 out* **66/1**

011- **7** 24 **Mister Marker (IRE)**202 4733 6-11-1 0 FearghalDavis(3) 81
(Nicky Richards) *hld up: blnd 7th: outpcd 10th: n.d after* **9/1**

-055 **8** hd **Rossini's Dancer**16 1573 5-11-4 93 PaddyAspell 81
(Sue Bradburne) *midfield: lost pl 1/2-way: n.d after* **100/1**

0/ **9** 9 **Cockleshell Road (IRE)**258 3620 7-11-4 0 BrianHarding 73
(Martin Todhunter) *hld up: blnd 10th: sn struggling* **25/1**

10 14 **Seigneur Des Bois (FR)**163 4-10-7 0 GrahamLee 50
(Ferdy Murphy) *nt fluent on occasions: hld up: shortlived effrt after 5 out: sn btn* **16/1**

-024 **11** 3 3/4 **Terenzium (IRE)**19 717 8-11-4 0 (p) BarryKeniry 57
(Micky Hammond) *trckd ldrs tl lost pl 12th: sn struggling* **33/1**

4PP/ **P** **Steel Man (IRE)**533 5166 8-11-1 0 (t) RyanMania(3) —
(Bruce Mactaggart) *in tch: lost pl 1/2-way: t.o whn p.u bef 4 out* **200/1**

4P3- **U** **Sibenek (IRE)**168 5372 6-11-4 0 JamesReveley —
(Martin Todhunter) *hld up: blnd and uns rdr 4th* **25/1**

5m 16.4s (-11.00) **Going Correction** -0.60s/f (Firm)
WFA 4 from 5yo+ 10lb **13** Ran SP% **114.4**
Speed ratings (Par 105): **98,97,96,96,91 89,80,80,76,70 69,—,—**
toteswingers:1&2:£28.50, 1&3:£4.00, 2&3:Not won CSF £59.90 TOTE £4.50: £2.00, £3.60, £2.60; EX 69.10.

Owner Andrea & Graham Wylie **Bred** P R Joyce **Trained** Billy Row, Co Durham

FOCUS

An interesting novices' chase which should throw up plenty of future winners. It was run at a sound pace. The winner can match his hurdles form over fences and the second set the standard on chase form.

NOTEBOOK

Alvarado(IRE), a dual course winner over hurdles, jumped well on this chasing debut. Rated 134 over hurdles, he can go on to better things over fences. All of his wins have come at right-handed tracks. (op 9-2)

Flying Doctor has been a revelation since joining this yard and this run was bang up there with the best of him. Rated 125, he should remain competitive but won't be the easiest to place.

C'Monthehammers(IRE), coming from a stable in super form, tended to jump to the left. He might be better in a contest where he is given an early lead but can still win races. (op 5-1 tchd 6-1)

Alderley Rover(IRE), having his first start since May, jumped soundly on his first try over fences. A stiffer test of stamina will see him get his head in front. (tchd 9-2)

Born Again(IRE) didn't help his chances with a mistake at halfway. He can do better in due course. (tchd 3-1 and 7-2)

Seigneur Des Bois(FR) looks the type his trainer will win with later in the campaign. (op 14-1)

Steel Man(IRE) Official explanation: trainer said that the gelding had a breathing problem

1760 LLOYD MOTOR GROUP NOVICES' H'CAP HURDLE (11 hdls) 2m 4f

3:05 (3:05) (Class 5) (0-90,90) 3-Y-0+ **£1,712** (£499; £249)

Form RPR

3640 **1** **Mulligan's Pride (IRE)**19 1559 9-10-9 **73** (v) PaddyAspell 79
(James Moffatt) *prom: effrt 3 out: hung lft last: styd on wl run-in: led last stride* **6/1**3

43 **2** hd **Soul Magic (IRE)**16 1578 8-10-9 **80** GaryRutherford(7) 86
(Harriet Graham) *t.k.h early: hld up in tch: hdwy to chse ldr 1/2-way: led after 4 out: rdn next: kpt on wl run-in: hdd last stride* **6/1**3

601/ **3** 15 **Springaway**947 4289 11-10-3 **74** MrSFMagee(7) 67
(Simon West) *prom: effrt bef 3 out: wknd bef last* **15/2**

605- **4** 18 **The Rustlin Rhino**181 5135 5-11-2 **90** HenryBrooke(10) 66
(Donald McCain) *prom: outpcd 4 out: n.d after* **3/1**1

/06P **5** 11 **Standing Order**50 1300 7-11-4 **82** RichieMcGrath 48
(Richard Ford) *hld up: outpcd 7th: shortlived effrt bef 3 out: sn wknd* **25/1**

00/3 **6** 5 **Dechiper (IRE)**7 1664 8-11-9 **87** (tp) KennyJohnson 49
(Robert Johnson) *t.k.h: w ldr: led 4th to next: cl up tl wknd bef 3 out* **5/1**2

/0-0 **7** 6 **Whateverthe weather**135 470 6-10-0 **64** oh6 BrianHarding 20
(Sandy Forster) *in tch: drvn and outpcd bef 7th: sn struggling* **33/1**

U6-5 **8** 24 **Soldiers Tree (IRE)**149 289 5-11-8 **86** PeterBuchanan 21
(Sue Bradburne) *trckd ldrs: lost pl 6th: struggling fr next* **6/1**3

0P-P **P** **Shara Like Magic**7 1665 7-9-12 **64** oh2 ow1 RyanMania(3) —
(Dianne Sayer) *led to 4th: led next: hdd 4 out: wknd qckly: p.u bef next* **16/1**

030/ **P** **Brian's Journey**595 4036 8-11-1 **82** JamesO'Farrell(3) —
(Barbara Butterworth) *bolted bef s: hld up: lost tch and p.u after 6th* **40/1**

000- **P** **Archdale Lady (IRE)**208 4609 6-11-6 **84** GrahamLee —
(Ferdy Murphy) *bhd: reminders 4th: lost tch bef 7th: t.o whn p.u bef 3 out* **25/1**

5m 4.70s (-18.10) **Going Correction** -0.825s/f (Firm) **11** Ran SP% **115.2**
Speed ratings (Par 103): **103,102,96,89,85 83,80,71,—,— —**
toteswingers:1&2:£7.00, 1&3:£8.60, 2&3:£12.70 CSF £39.60 CT £274.13 TOTE £7.20: £1.90, £3.30, £1.50; EX 35.10.

Owner Jamie Latham & Gemma Walton **Bred** Mrs J Norris **Trained** Cartmel, Cumbria

■ Stewards' Enquiry : Paddy Aspell one-day ban: use of whip (22 Oct)

FOCUS

A 0-90 novices' handicap hurdle which was basically a seller all but in name. It was run at an even tempo but is highly unlikely to throw up many future winners. The winner is rated back to something like his best.

NOTEBOOK

Mulligan's Pride(IRE) managed to lose his maiden tag at the 23rd attempt, benefiting from a strong ride. The handicapper surely shouldn't be too harsh but he isn't one to take a short price about in a bid to follow up. (op 8-1 tchd 5-1)

Soul Magic(IRE) looked the most likely winner prior to getting caught close home. This was only his sixth career start under rules, so he could well improve and should find a small race. (op 5-1 tchd 4-1)

Springaway ◆ made a solid reappearance on his first start in two and a half years. (op 17-2 tchd 10-1)

The Rustlin Rhino, coming from a respected yard and with a very useful 10lb claimer on board, never really threatened and looks harshly handicapped on the evidence of this. (op 7-2 tchd 4-1)

Dechiper(IRE), third at Hexham recently, is due to race off a 14lb higher mark in future handicaps for that one run. After this tame effort, surely the handicapper will step in and help out. (op 4-1)

1761 PES-SECURITY.COM H'CAP CHASE (12 fncs) 2m

3:40 (3:40) (Class 3) (0-125,123) 4-Y-0+ **£5,529** (£1,623; £811; £405)

Form RPR

53-1 **1** **Sotovik (IRE)**138 443 9-10-7 **107** EwanWhillans(3) 112
(Alistair Whillans) *chsd clr ldr: effrt 3 out: styd on wl u.p fr last to ld nr fin* **8/1**

1/P- **2** 1 **Cantgeton (IRE)**518 212 10-11-4 **115** TimmyMurphy 119
(P Monteith) *hld up: hdwy and in tch chsng gp whn hit 5 out: effrt and cl up bef last: kpt on run-in: wnt 2nd cl home* **16/1**

2P-1 **3** shd **Carrietau**142 395 7-11-4 **118** (bt) RyanMania(3) 122
(Barry Murtagh) *led and sn clr: rdn 4 out: kpt on run-in: hdd towards fin* **8/1**

000- **4** 2 **Forty Five (IRE)**262 3529 8-10-13 **110** APMcCoy 113
(Jonjo O'Neill) *hld up: hdwy 5 out: effrt after 3 out: kpt on steadily fr last: nrst fin* **11/2**2

231/ **5** 4 1/2 **Cavers Glen**705 1966 8-10-6 **103** BrianHarding 102+
(Alistair Whillans) *hld up: effrt 4 out: rdn and no imp fr 2 out* **17/2**

2320 **6** 15 **High Bird Humphrey**34 1470 11-11-0 **118** (p) MrSFMagee(7) 110+
(Simon West) *bhd: rdn after 5th: hdwy 4 out: blnd next: nt rcvr* **8/1**

331- **7** 3/4 **Et Maintenant (FR)**188 4984 8-11-9 **120** PeterBuchanan 104
(Lucinda Russell) *prom tl outpcd after 5 out: n.d after* **5/1**1

3224 **8** 3 3/4 **Prioryjo**116 745 7-10-12 **109** JamesReveley 90
(Martin Todhunter) *bhd: pushed along 1/2-way: nvr on terms* **20/1**

F02- **9** 1 1/2 **Le Roi Rouge (FR)**185 5075 8-11-12 **123** GrahamLee 102
(Ferdy Murphy) *hld up: sme hdwy whn hit 7th: wknd after next* **17/2**

436- **10** 3 3/4 **Camden George (IRE)**185 5075 9-11-6 **117** HenryOliver 93
(Sue Smith) *in tch: drvn 5 out: wknd after next* **7/1**3

F/0- **11** 2 1/2 **Rayshan (IRE)**208 4605 10-11-12 **123** WilsonRenwick 97
(Rose Dobbin) *prom tl lost pl 5th: n.d after* **22/1**

0FU- **P** **Polar Gunner**169 5337 13-10-13 **115** JamesHalliday(5) —
(Malcolm Jefferson) *hld up: struggling and p.u bef 6th* **25/1**

4m 6.20s (-9.90) **Going Correction** -0.60s/f (Firm) **12** Ran SP% **117.8**
Speed ratings (Par 107): **100,99,99,98,96 88,88,86,85,83 82,—**
toteswingers:1&2:£16.90, 1&3:£16.50, 2&3:£44.10 CSF £118.54 CT £1062.07 TOTE £9.30: £3.80, £5.70, £3.00; EX 171.10.

Owner Jethart Justice **Bred** Timothy Fennessy **Trained** Newmill-On-Slitrig, Borders

FOCUS

A 0-125 handicap chase in which the top weight was 2lb below the ceiling rating. It was full of horses coming back from a break. It was run at a sound pace thanks to Carrietau and the first three are rated pretty much to their marks.

NOTEBOOK

Sotovik(IRE), a winner when last seen in May, loves it around here and gained his third win in determined style. He should remain competitive and is versatile regarding the ground. (op 9-1)

Cantgeton(IRE), also a C&D winner, ran a cracker on his first start in 17 months. There is race to be won with him if he is okay after this run. (op 14-1)

Carrietau led at a good pace and ran bang up to form, but is suited to easier tracks. (op 9-1)

Forty Five(IRE) is still a maiden over fences but should be able to find something in due course. (op 13-2)

High Bird Humphrey, who has never been the easiest to win with, would have finished closer if jumping better. (op 17-2 tchd 9-1)

Et Maintenant(FR) ran reasonably on his seasonal reappearance but is handicapped up to his very best form. (op 4-1)

Le Roi Rouge(FR) probably needs help from the handicapper. (op 11-1)

Polar Gunner Official explanation: jockey said that the gelding lost his action

1762 NORTHERN RACING CLUB 30TH ANNIVERSARY CONDITIONAL JOCKEYS' H'CAP HURDLE (9 hdls) 2m 1f

4:15 (4:16) (Class 4) (0-110,107) 4-Y-0+ **£2,740** (£798; £399)

Form RPR

U0-B **1** **No Supper (IRE)**16 1574 6-10-12 **93** HarryHaynes 97
(George Bewley) *hld up in tch on outside: hdwy to ld bef 3 out: kpt on wl fr next* **33/1**

4P-2 **2** 1 1/4 **World Of Events (USA)**31 1504 5-10-12 **96** JamesO'Farrell(3) 99
(Howard Johnson) *midfield: hdwy on outside 3 out: rdn and chsd wnr between last 2: kpt on run-in* **10/3**1

3430 **3** 9 **Knight Valliant**89 948 7-10-3 **84** CO'Farrell 81+
(Barbara Butterworth) *hld up: hdwy and prom bef 2 out: outpcd fr last* **9/1**

5-25 **4** 3 3/4 **Devils Delight (IRE)**43 1378 8-9-9 **81** oh4 HenryBrooke(5) 73
(James Moffatt) *trckd ldrs tl rdn and wknd between last 2* **10/1**

06P6 **5** 2 1/4 **Samizdat (FR)**15 1597 7-10-9 **90** RyanMania 80
(Dianne Sayer) *cl up: led 4th to bef 3 out: wknd after next* **14/1**

016/ **6** 6 **Banoge (IRE)**572 4492 8-11-12 **107** EwanWhillans 91
(Rose Dobbin) *t.k.h: trckd ldrs tl wknd fr 2 out: bttr for r* **12/1**

16-0 **7** 5 **Mister Pete (IRE)**160 89 7-11-0 **98** (p) AlexanderVoy(3) 78
(Chris Grant) *led to 4th: drvn and outpcd after 4 out: n.d after* **17/2**

-10P **8** 7 **Balnagore**15 1596 6-10-10 **94** CampbellGillies(3) 72
(Lucinda Russell) *prom tl rdn and hmpd bef 3 out: sn wknd* **9/1**

1430 **9** 1 3/4 **Choctaw Nation**13 1614 6-11-0 **98** JamesHalliday(3) 70
(Malcolm Jefferson) *hld up: drvn and outpcd after 4 out: btn next* **14/1**

00-0 **10** *1 ½* **Appeal Denied (IRE)**[142] 405 8-9-13 **85**...................... PaulGallagher(5) 55
(Sandy Forster) *prom tl rdn and wknd bef 3 out* **28/1**

2-65 **11** *50* **Hey Charlie (IRE)**[15] 1596 8-11-2 **100**......................... FearghalDavis(3) 25
(Nicky Richards) *hld up: struggling after 4 out: lost tch after next: t.o* **8/1**3

020- **P** **Top It All**[169] 5334 7-10-13 **97**.. BrianToomey(3) —
(Rose Dobbin) *hld up: rdn whn blnd 4 out: sn btn: p.u bef next* **7/1**2

4m 18.1s (-11.70) **Going Correction** -0.825s/f (Firm) **12** Ran SP% **113.7**
Speed ratings (Par 105): **94,93,89,87,86 83,81,77,77,76 52,—**
toteswingers:1&2:£16.80, 1&3:Not won, 2&3:£7.30 CSF £138.22 CT £1102.12 TOTE £44.50: £8.70, £1.70, £3.20; EX 188.20.
Owner Thomason & Jefferson **Bred** J C Condon **Trained** Bonchester Bridge, Borders
■ Stewards' Enquiry : James O'Farrell two-day ban: use of whip (22-24 Oct)

FOCUS
An ordinary gallop for this 0-110 handicap hurdle in which the top weight was 3lb below the ceiling rating. The winner was very well in on one run in 2009 and the second ran to his best.

NOTEBOOK
No Supper(IRE) ◆ was having only his second start for current connections, and if they have found the key to him, he could well win again judged on the way he took this. (op 28-1)
World Of Events(USA) would give the form some substance. This was only his fifth start over hurdles and he can go one better in similar company (op 7-2)
Knight Valliant ran another sound race and should pop up at some point in the coming months. (op 10-1 tchd 11-1)
Banoge(IRE) showed up well on his first start since March and should be straighter for this run. (op 8-1)
Balnagore ◆ was still going well when getting hampered and stumbling three from home. Official explanation: jockey said the gelding suffered interference on the bend leaving the back straight (tchd 10-1)
Top It All, who had shown clear ability in bumpers, continues to disappoint. (op 8-1)

1763 COMLONGON CASTLE H'CAP CHASE (18 fncs) 3m 110y
4:50 (4:50) (Class 4) (0-115,115) 4-Y-0+ **£2,927** (£859; £429; £214)

Form RPR

306- **1** **Newman Des Plages (FR)**[172] 5274 9-11-12 **115**........... JamesReveley 130+
(Martin Todhunter) *led to 11th: drvn and outpcd after 5 out: rallied to chse clr ldr after 3 out: led and hit last: styd on strly to go clr run-in* **28/1**

6341 **2** *5* **Overquest**[7] 1663 8-10-4 **93** 7ex.. JohnnyFarrelly 102
(Elliott Cooper) *cl up: led 11th: clr 3 out: hdd last: kpt on same pce run-in* **6/5**1

PPP- **3** *3 ½* **Star Player (IRE)**[168] 5373 8-11-1 **104**............................(t) DenisO'Regan 110
(Chris Grant) *in tch: effrt bef 3 out: kpt on same pce fr next* **7/1**2

3363 **4** *5* **Western Gale (IRE)**[48] 1326 7-11-7 **110**......................... GrahamLee 111
(Martin Todhunter) *hld up in tch: rdn along bef 5 out: effrt after next: edgd rt: no imp fr 3 out* **8/1**3

0P-3 **5** *7* **Master Sebastian**[128] 579 11-11-2 **105**......................... PeterBuchanan 100
(Lucinda Russell) *hld up in tch: outpcd 12th: drvn and effrt bef 3 out: nvr rchd ldrs* **22/1**

43F- **6** *¾* **Garleton (IRE)**[182] 5111 9-10-11 **107**............................(t) AlexanderVoy(7) 101
(Maurice Barnes) *cl up: rdn bef 4 out: wknd after next* **8/1**3

13F- **7** *23* **Blazing Diva (IRE)**[168] 5373 7-11-2 **108**......................... RyanMania(3) 82
(Sandy Thomson) *cl up: chal 11th: rdn after 5 out: wknd bef 3 out* **16/1**

2/12 **8** *26* **Twelve Paces**[16] 1577 9-11-5 **108**.. TimmyMurphy 58
(P Monteith) *hld up: struggling 5 out: btn fr next* **8/1**3

0P-5 **9** *1 ¾* **Foxesbow (IRE)**[127] 599 6-10-11 **100**.................................. APMcCoy 49
(Jonjo O'Neill) *hld up: outpcd bef 5 out: nvr on terms* **12/1**

342/ **P** **Julius Caesar**[621] 3551 10-11-7 **110**.................................. RichieMcGrath —
(Ferdy Murphy) *bhd: struggling 10th: t.o whn p.u bef 4 out* **40/1**

6m 24.1s (-18.50) **Going Correction** -0.60s/f (Firm) **10** Ran SP% **115.1**
Speed ratings (Par 105): **105,103,102,100,98 98,90,82,81,—**
toteswingers:1&2:£6.10, 1&3:£29.10, 2&3:£3.60 CSF £63.70 CT £284.53 TOTE £35.20: £5.90, £1.40, £2.10; EX 114.20.
Owner James Callow **Bred** Rene And Mrs Ricous **Trained** Orton, Cumbria

FOCUS
A competitive-looking handicap. The winner is rated to the level of his best French form and the second in line with his recent win.

NOTEBOOK
Newman Des Plages(FR) has good form in his native France on very soft ground. Not normally noted for back-to-back wins, it will be interesting to see how he gets on next time out. (op 22-1)
Overquest looked the most likely winner until getting caught close home. He is due to race off a 6lb higher mark in future handicaps, but this was only his fifth start over fences so there could well be more to come. (op 11-8 tchd 11-10 and 6-4 in places)
Star Player(IRE), well backed beforehand despite a string of Ps next to his name, ran well on his first start since April. Three times a course winner, he can win mores race if able to reproduce this effort. (op 13-2)
Western Gale(IRE) has been running consistent of late and deserves to land on a similar race. (op 17-2 tchd 9-1)
Twelve Paces was disappointing and will need to bounce back. (op 15-2 tchd 7-1)
Julius Caesar was entitled to need this after a long time off the track. (op 33-1)

1764 WEDDINGS AT CARLISLE RACECOURSE STANDARD OPEN NATIONAL HUNT FLAT RACE 2m 1f
5:20 (5:21) (Class 6) 4-6-Y-O **£1,370** (£399; £199)

Form RPR

0 **1** **Lively Baron (IRE)**[147] 319 5-10-11 0.............................. AdrianLane(3) 111+
(Donald McCain) *in tch: hdwy to ld over 2f out: drew clr fr over 1f out* **9/2**2

2 *17* **Middlebrook (IRE)** 5-11-0 0.. BrianHughes 96
(Peter Niven) *trckd ldr gng wl: led over 3f out to 2f out: no ch w wnr fr over 1f out* **7/2**1

1-2 **3** *2 ¼* **Dr Flynn (IRE)**[15] 1599 5-11-7 0...................................... WilsonRenwick 101
(Howard Johnson) *trckd ldrs: effrt and ev ch over 2f out: outpcd over 1f out* **9/2**2

0- **4** *½* **Harris Hawk**[311] 2632 5-10-7 0..................................... MrJohnDawson(7) 93
(John Wade) *hld up: hdwy whn nt clr run over 3f out: styd on wl fnl 2f: improve* **80/1**

5 *6* **Floraclock** 5-10-7 0... TjadeCollier 81
(Sue Smith) *hld up in midfield: effrt over 3f out: edgd rt and no imp fnl 2f* **28/1**

00 **6** *4* **Alimure**[12] 1629 4-10-7 0... PaddyAspell 77
(C W Thornton) *in tch: drvn along over 5f out: no ex fr wl over 2f out* **100/1**

4- **7** *hd* **Ballinasloe (IRE)**[188] 4992 6-10-11 0............................. JohnKington(3) 84
(Donald McCain) *led to over 3f out: wknd over 2f out* **25/1**

8 *31* **Howizee** 4-10-7 0.. MissAngelaBarnes(7) 56
(Maurice Barnes) *bhd: struggling 1/2-way: nvr on terms* **50/1**

6/ **9** *3 ½* **Fairlea Bob (IRE)**[568] 4584 6-11-0 0................................. GrahamLee 53
(Rose Dobbin) *midfield: drvn and outpcd over 4f out: sn btn* **16/1**

10 *1* **Allamonty (IRE)** 4-11-0 0.. BrianHarding 52
(Martin Todhunter) *hld up: rdn 6f out: nvr on terms* **40/1**

11 *¾* **Dirleton (IRE)** 4-11-0 0... TimmyMurphy 51
(George Charlton) *trckd ldrs tl wknd over 5f out* **7/2**1

0- **12** *½* **The Tiddly Tadpole**[297] 2896 5-10-7 0............................. MrSFMagee(7) 51
(Simon West) *bhd and sn pushed along: nvr on terms* **40/1**

13 *14* **Cawthorne** 4-10-7 0... JakeGreenall(7) 38
(Michael Easterby) *hld up: drvn over 5f out: wknd over 4f out* **25/1**

2- **14** *9* **Kvarner Riviera (IRE)**[163] 47 4-11-0 0............................. DenisO'Regan 30
(Malcolm Jefferson) *hld up: stdy hdwy and in tch 5f out: wknd over 3f out* **11/2**3

15 *24* **Beau D'Argent** 4-10-0 0.. PaulGallagher(7) 2
(Ferdy Murphy) *midfield: drvn and outpcd over 6f out: sn btn* **28/1**

4m 9.50s (-14.70) **Going Correction** -0.825s/f (Firm)
WFA 4 from 5yo+ 9lb **15** Ran SP% **125.7**
Speed ratings: **101,93,91,91,88 87,86,72,70,70 69,69,63,58,47**
toteswingers:1&2:£4.30, 1&3:£5.40, 2&3:£5.80 CSF £19.75 TOTE £5.60: £1.60, £2.30, £3.40; EX 31.60 Place 6 £111.49; Place 5 £73.10.
Owner Trevor Hemmings **Bred** Michael Gowen **Trained** Cholmondeley, Cheshire
■ Stewards' Enquiry : Adrian Lane caution: use of whip

FOCUS
Probably no more than an ordinary bumper, which was run at an even tempo. The winner looks a fair prospect and the form could be rated up to 7lb higher.

NOTEBOOK
Lively Baron(IRE) had showed ability in a similar race at Aintree in May and had clearly learned from that experience. Not lacking for size and scope, he can go on to better things over hurdles and fences in due course. (op 9-1)
Middlebrook(IRE), well backed beforehand, showed up well on this debut and time might prove he ran into an above-average recruit. He can go one better in similar company next time out. (op 4-1 tchd 5-1)
Dr Flynn(IRE), a winner of a bumper on his debut at Kelso last March, gives the form some substance. He will always be vulnerable with a penalty in this type of race but can make his mark over hurdles in due course. (op 7-2)
Harris Hawk ran well after a long time off the track. He can also make his mark over hurdles, probably over a little further. (op 66-1)
Ballinasloe(IRE) led early but lacked a gear in the straight. (tchd 22-1)
T/Plt: £208.90 to a £1 stake. Pool of £45,208.20 - 157.91 winning tickets T/Qpdt: £68.90 to a £1 stake. Pool of £4,325.45 - 46.40 winning tickets RY

[1363]BANGOR-ON-DEE (L-H)
Saturday, October 9

OFFICIAL GOING: Good (7.2)
Wind: Light, against Weather: Fine

1765 JANE WOODWARD 40TH BIRTHDAY NOVICES' HURDLE (11 hdls) 2m 4f
2:25 (2:25) (Class 3) 4-Y-0+ **£4,878** (£1,432; £716; £357)

Form RPR

1 **Kilcrea Kim (IRE)**[195] 5-10-12 0.. TomO'Brien 117+
(Philip Hobbs) *plld hrd: racd in 2nd pl tl led after 3rd: asserting whn mstke last: pushed clr run-in* **7/2**2

1 **2** *8* **Drill Sergeant**[34] 1487 5-11-4 0.. APMcCoy 117
(Donald McCain) *led: hdd after 3rd: mstke 4th: nt a fluent after: upsides wnr bef 7th: rdn after 3 out: nt qckn after 2 out: one pce and wl hld run-in* **4/7**1

0-5 **3** *14* **What An Oscar (IRE)**[45] 1367 5-10-9 0.............. SamTwiston-Davies(3) 100
(Nigel Twiston-Davies) *hld up: hit 1st: nt fluent 6th: outpcd after 4 out: rdn after 3 out whn tried to cl on ldrs but no imp: mstke 2 out: wl btn after* **9/1**

4 *22* **Three Chords (IRE)**[195] 6-10-12 0................................ AndrewThornton 77
(Caroline Bailey) *hld up: outpcd u.p and dropped away after 4 out: eased whn wl btn bef 2 out* **15/2**3

4m 50.2s (-7.20) **Going Correction** -0.375s/f (Good) **4** Ran SP% **107.6**
Speed ratings (Par 107): **99,95,90,81**
CSF £6.21 TOTE £3.60; EX 6.40.
Owner James and Jean Potter **Bred** Francis O'Brien **Trained** Withycombe, Somerset

FOCUS
A fair event, but the defection of two winning novices deprived the contest of much of its competitiveness. The early pace was slow until the two market leaders began to duel on the final circuit until the home turn. The winner looks a decent recruit.

NOTEBOOK
Kilcrea Kim(IRE) got a bit warm at the start and was keen to get on with things, so his jockey sensibly let him move into the lead which enabled him to settle much better. His jumping was neat and he travelled well, saw out the trip and in the end had too much for the favourite. The winner of an Irish point in the spring, he had changed hands for £42,000 in April and looks a decent recruit even if he sticks to hurdles for the time being. (op 9-2 tchd 5-1)
Drill Sergeant had won on his hurdling debut at Worcester and was a warm favourite with seemingly little to beat. He matched strides with the winner as the pace quickened but his jumping was sketchy at times and that took its toll as he was outpaced before they turned for home. His jumping will need to improve if he is to add to his tally as the competition begins to hot up at this time of year. (op 8-13 tchd 4-6)
What An Oscar(IRE) does not look a natural over hurdles but he did plug on after being outpaced in the back straight and may need a longer trip. (tchd 17-2 and 10-1)
Three Chords(IRE), a three-time winning British pointer making his rules debut, was readily outpaced when the tempo quickened and was eventually eased, but he will come on for this run. (op 11-2)

1766 VITTORIA HEALTHCARE H'CAP HURDLE (9 hdls) 2m 1f
2:55 (2:56) (Class 3) (0-130,130) 4-Y-0+ **£7,921** (£2,340; £1,170; £585; £292)

Form RPR

42-0 **1** **Nearby**[148] 316 6-11-0 **125**... ChrisDavies(7) 140+
(Philip Hobbs) *hld up: hdwy to trck ldrs after 3 out: led narrowly whn lft clr last: rdn out and r.o wl* **14/1**

2-23 **2** *9* **Grand Diamond (IRE)**[6] 1695 6-10-0 **104** oh2..................... BarryKeniry 112
(Jim Goldie) *hld up bhd: hdwy appr 2 out: lft abt 5 l 2nd whn blnd last: no imp on wnr* **17/2**

13-6 **3** *9* **Soft Spoken Guy (IRE)**[154] 206 7-11-11 **129**..........(t) AndrewThornton 128
(Maurice Barnes) *midfield: rdn and lost pl after 3 out: rallied to chse ldrs bef 2 out: wknd between last 2* **14/1**

02P- **4** *4* **Sambulando (FR)**[170] 5338 7-11-7 **125**............................ DenisO'Regan 121
(Tom George) *trckd ldrs: led after 3 out: hdd 2 out: wknd appr last* **9/1**

311F **5** *1* **Three Ships**[45] 1370 9-10-11 **120**...................................... GilesHawkins(5) 115
(Richard Lee) *hld up: rdn after 3 out: no imp whn mstke 2 out: nvr on terms* **16/1**

P60- **6** 3/4 **Blazing Desert**28 3627 6-10-3 **107** DougieCostello 101
(John Quinn) *midfield: hdwy 5th: shkn up and chalng 2 out: wknd sn after* **5/1**2

163- **7** 2 **Fiendish Flame (IRE)**175 5221 6-11-9 **130** AdrianLane(3) 122
(Donald McCain) *j.rt thrght: led: rdn after 4 out: hdd after 3 out: wknd after 2 out* **6/1**3

12-6 **8** 6 **Stopped Out**14 1608 5-11-2 **120** RichieMcGrath 106
(Kate Walton) *trckd ldrs: wnt 2nd 5th: stl chalng 3 out: wknd sn after* **22/1**

0014 **9** 9 **King Ozzy (IRE)**71 1136 6-10-1 **108** SamTwiston-Davies(3) 86
(Martin Keighley) *chsd ldrs: wnt 2nd briefly appr 5th: rdn and wknd bef 2 out* **10/1**

P2-P **F** **Beherayn**74 1110 7-10-9 **116** EamonDehdashti(3) —
(Carroll Gray) *racd keenly: w ldr whn carried rt and stmbld 2nd: wknd after 4th: bhd whn fell 5th* **33/1**

4U13 **F** **Rebel Dancer (FR)**35 1470 5-10-9 **113** (t) APMcCoy 126
(Ian Williams) *hld up: hdwy whn nt fluent 3 out: led 2 out: shkn up whn hdd narrowly and fell last* **5/2**1

P2-0 **F** **Playing With Fire (IRE)**153 235 6-10-6 **110** CharliePoste —
(Robin Dickin) *midfield: effrt 4 out: wknd after 3 out: in rr whn fell 2 out* **28/1**

4m 1.20s (-9.70) **Going Correction** -0.375s/f (Good) **12 Ran SP% 119.1**
Speed ratings (Par 107): **107,102,98,96,96 95,94,92,87,—,—,—**
toteswingers:1&2:£15.90, 1&3:£41.80, 2&3:£11.30 CSF £125.77 CT £1712.46 TOTE £16.30: £4.20, £1.50, £4.20; EX 141.50.
Owner Andy Ash **Bred** Juddmonte Farms Ltd **Trained** Withycombe, Somerset

FOCUS
A decent handicap, although in recent years it has not produced too many future winners, but it was run at a good early pace as a duel developed, until it slowed a bit midway. The winner produced a step forward and faller Rebel Dancer was heading for a new personal best.

NOTEBOOK
Nearby, a drifter in the betting, was held up off the pace before making quiet progress in the back straight travelling with ease, and when asked to challenge he was left clear at the last but galloped on strongly right away from the chasing pack. Despite not being able to win in eight attempts in handicaps last season, he had placed several times and had the form to win off his mark, especially on fast ground. He looked as if the race might bring him on, which may explain why he drifted in the betting, but the stable are flying at the moment, and so he might be interesting next time as well. (op 9-1)
Grand Diamond(IRE) was held up early and got a little outpaced in the back straight but made some good late progress. He continued the good form he has shown this autumn, placing in his last three contests, and just about coped with this step up in class. (op 10-1 tchd 8-1)
Soft Spoken Guy(IRE) was finding the pace a bit hot as they left the back straight but he stayed on. This was another good run for a yard that has been in excellent form over the past couple of weeks, especially as he ideally needs softer ground and a longer trip. (tchd 16-1)
Sambulando(FR) was keen on his first run since April but travelled well enough until fading in the straight. He might be better in a more tactical race and should come on for this run.
Three Ships has won several times in selling grade, and when he was finally on a reasonable mark to contest a handicap he got clobbered by the handicapper after winning at Uttoxeter in July. Once again he looks to need some easing in his mark. (tchd 14-1)
Blazing Desert has winning form over 1m6f on the Flat this summer but this was only his fourth hurdle run since his last win in March 2009, and he does not look as good in this sphere. (tchd 11-2)
Fiendish Flame(IRE) set the pace until capitulating as they turned for home and ran as well as could be expected on this switch back to hurdles after a six-month layoff. (op 5-1)
Rebel Dancer(FR) had moved up well and was about to battle it out with the comfortable winner when taking a heavy fall at the last, but thankfully he got to his feet, understandably looking a little sore. (op 7-2)

1767 MALISE NICOLSON H'CAP CHASE (12 fncs) 2m 1f 110y
3:30 (3:30) (Class 4) (0-115,113) 4-Y-0+ **£4,553** (£1,337; £668; £333)

Form RPR

U631 **1** **Morning Sunshine (IRE)**42 1403 7-10-8 **98** AdrianLane(3) 114+
(Donald McCain) *midfield: hdwy 8th: led 2 out: drvn clr and styd on wl after last* **11/2**3

1344 **2** 5 **Woodlark Island (IRE)**94 933 4-10-11 **108** (bt) TomScudamore 109
(David Pipe) *led: rdn and hdd 2 out: one pce and wl hld after last* **10/3**1

-235 **3** 17 **Blossom King (FR)**71 1139 6-11-8 **109** (t) DenisO'Regan 108+
(Tom George) *prom: blnd 1st: mstke 8th: ch and trying to chal appr 2 out: wknd bef last* **11/2**3

1323 **4** 4 1/2 **Baaher (USA)**16 1595 6-11-12 **113** BarryKeniry 105
(Jim Goldie) *hld up bhd: sme hdwy appr 3 out: nvr able to get to ldrs* **15/2**

3P10 **5** 8 **Blast The Past**15 1606 8-11-2 **110** MrJohnDawson(7) 95
(Dai Burchell) *racd keenly: hld up: sme hdwy whn nt fluent 3 out: no imp after* **14/1**

1-02 **6** 32 **Duke Of Malfi**143 395 7-10-13 **100** (p) RichieMcGrath 56
(Lucinda Russell) *prom: j. slowly 7th: lost pl 8th: wknd 4 out* **7/1**

U65- **7** 16 **Pelo Du Bief (FR)**200 4807 7-10-0 **94** JoeCornwall(7) 36
(John Cornwall) *chsd ldrs: mstke 5th: sn lost pl: mstke 6th: toiling 4 out: t.o* **16/1**

P-21 **8** 6 **Red Birr (IRE)**40 1430 9-11-0 **101** (t) SamThomas 37
(Paul Webber) *hld up: blnd 6th: struggling after: t.o bef 2 out* **4/1**2

4m 15.3s (-6.80) **Going Correction** -0.575s/f (Firm)
WFA 4 from 6yo+ 9lb **8 Ran SP% 110.7**
Speed ratings (Par 105): **92,89,82,80,76 62,55,52**
toteswingers:1&2:£4.10, 1&3:£4.60, 2&3:£2.70 CSF £23.29 CT £99.17 TOTE £5.00: £2.60, £1.80, £1.10; EX 28.10.
Owner Jon Glews & Peter Knight **Bred** Peter Mc Manamy **Trained** Cholmondeley, Cheshire

FOCUS
This was run at a strong early gallop and the field were soon strung out, and though it slowed a little late on few were able to get into this. Recent renewals of this handicap have frequently thrown up a next-time-out winner, often among those down the field that should improve for the run. Modest handicap form but a big step up from the winner.

NOTEBOOK
Morning Sunshine(IRE) had the ideal trip, not attempting to get embroiled in the early pace to reserve enough energy for a decisive move leaving the back straight, and he came home an easy winner. It took him a couple of attempts to get the hang of jumping fences, but he came good in a novice handicap chase at Cartmel in August and oozed confidence here, readily coping with the 8lb higher mark. (tchd 5-1 and 13-2)
Woodlark Island(IRE) looked to be in the handicapper's grip over hurdles and had not been given any leeway for his chasing debut, but he still made a bold bid to seize this race from the off, and it was a bold attempt just foiled by an in-form rival. As such he looks set to be a better chaser. (op 9-2)
Blossom King(FR) made an error at the first and that enabled his jockey to hold him back off the early lead. Despite hitting another in the back straight he travelled well enough to move up to challenge the first two around the final turn, but he found little from there and the application of a tongue tie was unable to help him see out his race. (op 6-1 tchd 13-2)
Baaher(USA) is generally better at Perth and did not look particularly well handicapped on his two previous runs in chases, so ran as well as could be expected. (op 8-1 tchd 7-1)
Blast The Past, returning to a more realistic grade after making no impact in a better race two weeks ago, is capable of running to her new mark but might need an easier contest to be competitive. (op 12-1)
Duke Of Malfi tracked the leader until crying enough midway down the back straight. He has won at Hexham in early November for the past couple of years and might be worth noting if he turns up there again. (op 11-2)
Pelo Du Bief(FR) jumped low at several fences and looked to need his first outing since March.
Red Birr(IRE) has been in good form this summer, but he made too many mistakes and could not get competitive. (op 7-2 tchd 3-1)

1768 TOTEEXACTA FLEXI BETTING "NATIONAL HUNT" NOVICES' HURDLE (9 hdls) 2m 1f
4:05 (4:07) (Class 3) 4-Y-0+ **£4,878** (£1,432; £716; £357)

Form RPR

1 **Silviniaco Conti (FR)**182 4-11-3 135 MrRMahon(5) 145+
(Paul Nicholls) *chsd clr ldrs: clsd to ld 4 out: effrtlessly wnt clr after 3 out: v easily* **2/1**2

340- **2** 29 **Grafite**208 4649 5-10-12 0 WarrenMarston 104
(Milton Harris) *hld up: pushed along and hdwy after 3 out: kpt on to take poor 2nd appr 2 out: plugged on: no ch w wnr* **33/1**

103- **3** 1 1/4 **Malindi Bay**176 5214 5-10-2 0 SeanQuinlan(3) 96
(Kim Bailey) *chsd clr ldrs: mstke whn u.p and outpcd 3 out: kpt on to take 3rd cl home: nvr any ch* **7/1**3

403- **4** 1/2 **Pie At Midnight**196 4881 4-10-9 0 AdrianLane(3) 103
(Donald McCain) *racd keenly in midfield a long way off ldrs: pushed along and hdwy after 3 out: kpt on u.p to chal for pls way bhd wnr* **9/1**

5 16 **Roper (IRE)** 5-10-12 0 DougieCostello 88
(Jonjo O'Neill) *bhd: kpt on modly fr 2 out: nvr in hunt* **25/1**

40-1 **6** 12 **My Brother Sylvest**18 1567 4-10-11 0 MattGriffiths(7) 88
(David Brace) *j.rt: led: sn clr: mstke and hdd 4 out: mstke 3 out: sn wknd* **15/8**1

7 3/4 **Barrie Burn (IRE)** 4-10-12 0 APMcCoy 77
(Jonjo O'Neill) *hld up bhd: nt fluent 3rd: nvr in contention* **17/2**

8 18 **Our Flora** 5-9-13 0 ow1 MrCGreene(7) 54
(Kim Bailey) *a wl bhd* **33/1**

000- **9** 3 3/4 **Roxane Bruere (FR)**174 5256 5-10-5 0 CharliePoste 50
(Robin Dickin) *midfield but long way off pce: nt fluent 5th: struggling whn nt fluent 3 out: t.o* **100/1**

06- **10** 15 **Kayfton Pete**181 5158 4-10-5 0 PeterHatton(7) 44
(Reg Hollinshead) *a wl bhd: t.o* **66/1**

4m 3.60s (-7.30) **Going Correction** -0.375s/f (Good) **10 Ran SP% 113.4**
Speed ratings (Par 107): **102,88,87,87,80 74,74,65,63,56**
toteswingers:1&2:£9.50, 1&3:£4.40, 2&3:£11.40 CSF £65.72 TOTE £3.10: £1.40, £5.60, £1.20; EX 53.90.
Owner Potensis Limited **Bred** Patrick Joubert **Trained** Ditcheat, Somerset

FOCUS
As a contest this was a frustrating affair, as the leader blasted off from the tapes and only two horses made any attempt to close him down. Eventually the hot favourite sauntered home a distance clear. He looks a decent recruit but this didn't take much winning.

NOTEBOOK
Silviniaco Conti(FR) kept tabs on the leader, and once that rival began to tire he still had enough in reserve to increase the already yawning gap back to the rest of the pack. He notched up two comfortable successes over hurdles in the French provinces last spring and won in similar style on his British debut. It is difficult to place this performance in context, but he coped with the pace effortlessly under his penalty, jumped well and stays well and is an exciting recruit to the Paul Nicholls yard. (op 9-4 tchd 15-8)
Grafite made a mistake at the third but eventually stayed on for a distant second. He placed on his bumper debut but his form deteriorated subsequently and he will do well to win over hurdles. (op 25-1)
Malindi Bay was a bit keen but at least tried to track the winner until finding the pace too much down the back straight, but plugged on to regain third. There is some encouragement to be gleaned from this run, for although she was well beaten in two hurdles in the spring since moving from the Oliver Sherwood yard, her earlier heavy-ground bumper win points to her needing a stiffer test than this. Official explanation: jockey said mare hung right-handed (op 10-1 tchd 13-2)
Pie At Midnight, who had already been beaten in a bumper and hurdle at this track, plugged on for a never-nearer fourth on his first start since March. (op 7-1)
Roper(IRE) was friendless in the market and was never competitive. (op 14-1)
My Brother Sylvest did not beat much on his hurdling debut at Stratford, but did it in good style in a good time and was the main danger to the winner. However, he set off at a blistering pace and the tank emptied midway down the back straight. Official explanation: jockey said gelding hung right-handed (op 11-4)

1769 TOTETRIFECTA FLEXI BETTING H'CAP CHASE (18 fncs) 3m 110y
4:40 (4:41) (Class 3) (0-130,130) 4-Y-£9,505 (£2,808; £1,404; £702; £351)

Form RPR

-322 **1** **Royal Kicks (FR)**115 764 9-9-9 **106** MrTJCannon(7) 116+
(Suzy Smith) *a.p: led 12th: wnt clr after 3 out to 2 out: hdd narrowly last: rallied to regain ld towards fin* **7/1**

1P0- **2** nk **I'moncloudnine (IRE)**196 4890 7-11-11 **129** DougieCostello 138
(Neil Mulholland) *midfield: hdwy 12th: pushed along appr 3 out: clsd to take 2nd 2 out: led narrowly last: hdd u.p towards fin* **16/1**

1022 **3** 4 **Midnight Gold**45 1373 10-11-6 **124** (p) TomScudamore 129
(Peter Bowen) *trckd ldrs: rdn appr 14th: hrd at work bef 3 out: clsd up 2 out: same pce u.p fr last* **6/1**2

U442 **4** 6 **Petite Margot**44 1376 11-10-10 **117** SamTwiston-Davies(3) 117
(Nigel Twiston-Davies) *prom: led 3rd: hdd 12th: pushed along bef 13th: sltly outpcd after 3 out: stl in contention 2 out: wknd appr last* **7/1**

32-P **5** 17 **Michigan D'Isop (FR)**129 579 10-10-3 **107** HarrySkelton 91
(John Ryall) *hld up: hdwy after 13th: no imp on ldrs fr 4 out* **9/1**

23F- **6** 31 **Ballydub (IRE)**203 4740 7-11-10 **128** TomO'Brien 84
(Philip Hobbs) *hld up: nt fluent 9th: blnd 12th: u.p after: nvr on terms* **11/2**1

155- **7** 1 **Doctor Pat (IRE)**231 4164 6-11-4 **122** APMcCoy 78
(Jonjo O'Neill) *hld up: stdy hdwy whn j. slowly 13th: wknd 4 out* **8/1**

1P1- **8** 18 **Fine By Me (IRE)**209 4619 11-10-12 **116** (p) GerardTumelty 55
(Julian Smith) *trckd ldrs tl rdn and wknd appr 13th* **20/1**

P/3- **9** 35 **Arnold Layne (IRE)**175 5232 11-10-11 **115** AndrewThornton 23
(Caroline Bailey) *prom: rdn and wknd after 12th* **20/1**

356- **10** dist **Out The Black (IRE)**175 5223 12-11-7 **130** IanPopham(5) 104+
(Caroline Keevil) *led: hdd 3rd: remained prom: lost pl after 12th: u.p and outpcd fr 4 out: 6th and n.d whn eased down to walk and virtually p.u run-in* **16/1**

23PF **P** **De Soto**35 1469 9-11-7 **125** (tp) SamThomas —
(Paul Webber) *hld up: j. slowly 3rd: blnd whn struggling 12th: t.o whn p.u bef 13th* **14/1**

-240 **P** **Backbord (GER)**[14] 1611 8-11-5 123............................(bt) LeightonAspell —
(Lucy Wadham) *bhd: blnd bdly 4th: t.o whn p.u bef 13th* **13/2**[3]
6m 1.00s (-18.80) **Going Correction** -0.575s/f (Firm) **12** Ran SP% **117.1**
Speed ratings (Par 107): **107,106,105,103,98 88,88,82,71,— —,—**
toteswingers:1&2:£41.30, 1&3:£7.30, 2&3:£26.70 CSF £108.21 CT £705.58 TOTE £7.20: £2.00, £6.40, £2.30; EX 194.90 TRIFECTA Not won..
Owner Four J's Partnership **Bred** Olivier Tricot **Trained** Lewes, E Sussex

FOCUS
A competitive handicap that should throw up some future winners. Solid form. The pace was ordinary, allowing those that raced prominently to feature at the finish, with a battle ensuing as the mid-race leader rallied to get up on the line.

NOTEBOOK
Royal Kicks(FR) travelled well as he opened up a clear lead around the home turn, but his legs began to tire soon after, and as he was challenged for the lead he showed great tenacity to dig deep and get up on the line. He had been in reasonable form earlier in the summer, but his jumping tended to prove his undoing at the pace of shorter trips on fast summer ground. He had been crying out for a step up to 3m and at this more comfortable tempo his jumping held together so he was able to capitalise on a light weight in a competitive event. (op 17-2 tchd 13-2)
I'moncloudnine(IRE) moved up under a bit of sufferance but stayed on well and was only just denied, partly due to the lack of a recent run and having to concede plenty of weight to the winner. This showed he is back to the sort of form of last autumn, especially as he really prefers softer ground, but he might be in the grip of the handicapper after this. (op 14-1)
Midnight Gold was always on the premises but just lacked the finishing kick in this stiffer contest. He has been in good form over the summer and is now on a career-high mark, but usually runs his race and is a reliable yardstick. (tchd 5-1)
Petite Margot disputed the early lead and stuck to the task once passed in the back straight to run a sound race, especially since she is handicapped up to her very best and the eleven-year-old is not exactly improving. (op 13-2)
Michigan D'Isop(FR) did not always travelling that well in rear and could never get competitive but should come on for the run if dropping in grade. (op 10-1 tchd 11-1)
Ballydub(IRE) is yet to win a chase and he made too many mistakes to suggest that he will be breaking his duck anytime soon. (op 6-1)
Doctor Pat(IRE) jumped indifferently on ground that was faster than ideal on his first run since leaving Francois Doumen. (op 7-1)
Out The Black(IRE) Official explanation: vet said gelding pulled up lame near-fore
Backbord(GER) jumped slowly and lost ground after a bad mistake at the fourth, from which he was unable to get back into it. (op 8-1)

1770 TOTEPOOL BRIGHT FUTURE NOVICES' CHASE (15 fncs) 2m 4f 110y
5:15 (5:15) (Class 3) 4-Y-0+ **£6,830** (£2,005; £1,002; £500)

Form RPR
1 **1** **Robinson Collonges (FR)**[253] 3727 5-11-2 0 HarrySkelton 139+
(Paul Nicholls) *hld up: hdwy to chse ldrs 5th: wnt 2nd appr 10th: led 4 out: clr bef last: easily* **3/1**[2]
/4-1 **2** *20* **Pouvoir (FR)**[20] 1558 7-11-8 0.. SamThomas 124
(Alan King) *trckd ldrs: lost pl 9th: clsd 10th: sltly outpcd 2 out: rdn bef last: kpt on to take 2nd cl home: no ch w wnr* **6/1**
31-3 **3** *hd* **Wessex King (IRE)**[147] 329 6-11-8 0.......................... TomScudamore 123
(Henry Daly) *hld up bhd: hdwy appr 10th: cl 4th whn blnd 4 out: rdn and nt qckn bef 2 out: kpt on to take 2nd last: no ch w wnr run-in: lost 2nd cl home* **12/1**
1-1F **4** *3 ½* **Otage De Brion (FR)**[48] 1345 8-11-7 142................ MrSWaley-Cohen(5) 125
(Nigel Twiston-Davies) *chsd ldr: led 5th: hdd 4 out: pushed along appr 2 out: lost 2nd last: kpt on same pce after* **5/1**[3]
033- **5** *50* **Marley Roca (IRE)**[197] 4871 6-11-2 0................................ DenisO'Regan 69
(Paul Webber) *hld up bhd: mstke 8th: struggling after: t.o* **17/2**
P0-P **6** *2 ½* **That's The Deal (IRE)**[13] 1627 6-10-9 0.......................... JoeCornwall(7) 67
(John Cornwall) *led: clr tl hdd 5th: wknd 10th: t.o* **150/1**
10-1 **U** **Tara Royal**[154] 208 5-11-8 0.. APMcCoy —
(Donald McCain) *hld up: blnd and uns rdr 3rd* **7/4**[1]
5m 2.30s (-6.80) **Going Correction** -0.575s/f (Firm) **7** Ran SP% **111.2**
Speed ratings (Par 107): **89,81,81,79,60 59,—**
toteswingers:1&2:£3.80, 1&3:£3.80, 2&3:£4.90 CSF £19.89 TOTE £3.80: £3.00, £4.70; EX 19.10.
Owner Mr & Mrs G Calder **Bred** Gaec Delorme Freres **Trained** Ditcheat, Somerset

FOCUS
A decent contest featuring four previous novice chase winners. The winner produced a big step up on his hurdles form and should go on to rate higher.

NOTEBOOK
Robinson Collonges(FR) was keen on his first start since January, but had enough in reserve to cruise to the front two from home and leave some fair rivals toiling as he sauntered clear. Despite two bumper wins and a hurdle win in the French provinces, he was something of an unknown quantity based on his previous outing in a novice hurdle at Newbury, but based on this performance he looks a very exciting prospect. (op 10-3 tchd 7-2)
Pouvoir(FR) was the first of the leading quartet to feel the pace, but he stuck to the task to emerge best of the chasing pack. He has had several lengthy layoffs since his hurdling heyday three years ago, but shows he retains enough ability over fences, but probably just below top level. (op 9-2)
Wessex King(IRE) made steady progress and travelled well until blundering four out and he could only continue at one pace afterwards. This trip might have stretched his stamina but he should come on for the run.
Otage De Brion(FR) was too anxious to chase down the clear early leader That's The Deal, and a slow jump at the final open ditch suggested the reserves were dwindling. He had been off since falling at Newton Abbot but that has not dented his confidence and the double C&D winner can win again in more modest company. (op 7-2 tchd 11-2)
Marley Roca(IRE) was bumped by the loose horse at halfway and seemed to lose confidence thereafter. (op 14-1)
Tara Royal got in too close to the third and gave his jockey no chance of staying aboard. (op 2-1)

1771 TOTESWINGER FLEXI BETTING MARES' STANDARD OPEN NATIONAL HUNT FLAT RACE 2m 1f
5:50 (5:50) (Class 5) 4-6-Y-0 **£2,055** (£599; £299)

Form RPR
1 **Dream Performance (IRE)** 5-10-10 0.......................... GerardTumelty 100
(G C Maundrell) *midfield: hdwy bef 1/2-way: effrt over 2f out: sn wnt 2nd: led 1f out: drvn out and styd on towards fin* **50/1**
2 *1 ¾* **Fiddlededee (IRE)**[163] 72 5-11-3 0.............................. SamThomas 105
(Jonjo O'Neill) *prom: led 6f out: rdn whn pressed 2f out: hdd 1f out: kpt on u.p: hld towards fin* **5/4**[1]
3 *4 ½* **Jaya Bella (IRE)** 5-10-10 0.. WarrenMarston 94
(Milton Harris) *hld up: u.p over 4f out: hdwy 2f out: styd on to take 3rd ins fnl f: nt trble front 2* **33/1**
4 **4** *1 ¾* **Native Breeze (IRE)**[148] 319 5-10-10 0.............................. TomO'Brien 93
(Philip Hobbs) *trckd ldrs: wnt 2nd over 3f out: chal over 2f out: sn lost 2nd: no ex fnl f* **3/1**[2]
50- **5** *2* **Pampelonne (IRE)**[169] 5383 4-10-10 0................................. FelixDeGiles 91
(Nicky Henderson) *midfield: hdwy 7f out: effrt to chse ldrs over 4f out: one pce fr wl over 1f out* **5/1**[3]
6 *¾* **Erin Vogue** 4-10-10 0.. DougieCostello 90
(Nicky Richards) *hld up: pushed along and effrt into midfield 6f out: one pce fr 2f out* **16/1**
20-6 **7** *1 ¾* **Definitley Lovely**[153] 230 5-10-7 0.................... SamTwiston-Davies(3) 90
(Nigel Twiston-Davies) *led: hdd 6f out: rdn and wknd 3f out* **10/1**
6 **8** *16* **Jessie Gwendoline (IRE)**[147] 333 4-10-0 0............... HenryBrooke(10) 74
(Donald McCain) *prom: reminder 7f out: wknd 5f out* **14/1**
9 *4 ½* **Valrene** 4-10-7 0.. CharlieStudd(3) 70
(George Jones) *hld up: outpcd 6f out: nvr on terms* **66/1**
10 *21* **Lulu's Gift (IRE)** 4-10-3 0.. BrianToomey(7) 51
(Michael Mullineaux) *midfield: pushed along 6f out: wknd over 4f out* **25/1**
0 **11** *71* **Theatrical Spirit**[108] 833 5-10-10 0.................................... CharliePoste —
(Robin Dickin) *a bhd: t.o* **66/1**
4m 3.30s (-2.00) **Going Correction** -0.375s/f (Good)
WFA 4 from 5yo 9lb **11** Ran SP% **119.5**
Speed ratings: **89,88,86,85,84 83,83,75,73,63 30**
toteswingers:1&2:£14.00, 1&3:£50.20, 2&3:£11.10 CSF £113.83 TOTE £91.90: £15.50, £1.10, £15.50; EX 155.40 Place 6 £687.62, Place 5 £152.34.
Owner G C Maundrell **Bred** Edmond Coleman **Trained** Marlborough, Wilts

FOCUS
Just a fair mares' bumper. The early pace was the customary crawl, but it picked up and from the home turn most of the field were under pressure.

NOTEBOOK
Dream Performance(IRE) was one of the first to receive reminders, and she looked a bit green and cumbersome negotiating the final turn, but she evidently has stamina to call on and stayed on best in a battle to the line. She is a big mare and looks booked for chasing in the future. (op 66-1)
Fiddlededee(IRE) has already won a point and a bumper, and she travelled among the best at the head of the field but was just outstayed near the finish. She may not have been fully wound up for her stable debut, but should be up to winning in time. (tchd 6-5 and 11-8)
Jaya Bella(IRE) was off the pace as the race got serious, but she made continuous good progress right to the line, without getting to the leaders. She is related to a French Flat and hurdle winner and made a favourable impression here.
Native Breeze(IRE) raced up with the pace but gradually faded, which was a little disappointing given the overall form of the stable at present. (op 5-1)
Pampelonne(IRE) tried to go with the leaders but got outpaced from the home turn and could make no further inroads. She is only four so has plenty of time to strengthen up, but does not look all that promising on evidence to date. (tchd 4-1)
T/Plt: £642.60 to a £1 stake. Pool of £43,443.20 - 49.35 winning tickets T/Qpdt: £31.70 to a £1 stake. Pool of £4,123.86 - 96.25 winning tickets DO

CHEPSTOW (L-H)
Saturday, October 9

OFFICIAL GOING: Good to soft (good in places; soft in places in back straight; chase 6.6, hurdle 6.7)
Wind: breezy at times, across Weather: overcast

1772 BETFAIR.COM/PAULNICHOLLS JUVENILE HURDLE (7 hdls 1 omitted) 2m 110y
2:20 (2:20) (Class 4) 3-Y-O **£2,764** (£811; £405; £202)

Form RPR
1 **Domtaline (FR)**[153] 3-10-12 0.. RWalsh 120+
(Paul Nicholls) *chsd ldr tl 2nd: wnt 2nd again next: drew wl clr w ldr bef 4th: led 3 out: nt fluent and wnt sltly lft next: cruised clr bef last: v easily* **30/100**[1]
2 *25* **Fine Lace (IRE)**[9] 3-10-5 0... PaulMoloney 90+
(Evan Williams) *t.k.h: led: wandered on approach to 2nd: clr w wnr bef 4th: hdd 3 out: wl btn between last 2* **7/1**[2]
3 *20* **Groove Master**[43] 3-10-12 0...................................... WayneHutchinson 76
(Alan King) *chsd ldrs: wnt 3rd on long run after 3rd: rdn and lost tch bef w ldng pair bef 4th: t.o whn mstke 2 out and last* **9/1**[3]
4 *1 ¾* **Highland Cadett**[58] 3-10-12 0.. HaddenFrost 73
(Rod Millman) *mstke and rdr lost iron 1st: in tch in midfield tl lost pl and rdn sn after 3rd: no ch w ldrs wl bef next: 4th and t.o fr 3 out* **40/1**
5 *5* **Fochabers**[152] 3-10-12 0.. ChristianWilliams 68
(Bernard Llewellyn) *in tch towards rr: sme hdwy and j. slowly 3rd: sn rdn along and lost tch w ldrs wl bef next: t.o whn j. slowly 3 out* **66/1**
P **6** *9* **Moonbalej**[3] 1728 3-10-12 0...(p) DaveCrosse 60
(Milton Harris) *hld up in tch in rr: sme prog 3rd: rdn and lost tch w ldrs on long run bef next: t.o bef 3 out* **40/1**
7 *17* **Whiepa Snappa (IRE)**[26] 3-10-12 0..................................... ColinBolger 45
(Pat Phelan) *hld up in rr: rdn and lost tch on long run between 3rd and 4th: t.o fr bef 3 out* **16/1**
8 *74* **Kingspark Boy (IRE)**[391] 3-10-12 0...................................... RodiGreene —
(David Rees) *t.k.h: chsd ldr 2nd tl 3rd: dropped out rapidly on long run between 3rd and 4th: wl t.o fr 3 out: blnd 2 out and last* **100/1**
P **Naseby (USA)**[24] 3-10-12 0.. JamesDavies —
(Sam Davison) *in tch in rr: mstke and rdn 2nd: sn struggling: lost tch sn after next: wl t.o and p.u 4th* **100/1**
4m 3.00s (-7.60) **Going Correction** -0.625s/f (Firm) **9** Ran SP% **113.7**
Speed ratings (Par 103): **92,80,70,70,67 63,55,20,—**
toteswingers:1&2:£1.02, 1&3:£1.60, 2&3:£6.70 CSF £2.91 TOTE £1.30: £1.02, £1.20, £1.80; EX 2.40.
Owner Mr And Mrs J D Cotton **Bred** Mme Marinette Avril & Mlle Marie Avril **Trained** Ditcheat, Somerset

FOCUS
This didn't look the most competitive juvenile hurdle, although it's gone to smart names such as Katchit and Franchoek in the recent past and Domtaline looks decent. The time was relatively slow.

NOTEBOOK
Domtaline(FR) cruised to victory on his first start for connections. Third in a Listed hurdle at Auteuil back in May, he was always travelling powerfully under Ruby Walsh and will now head to Wetherby's Charlie Hall meeting for a Listed event later in the month. (op 1-3 after 2-5 in places and 4-9 in a place)
Fine Lace(IRE), winner of a Warwick seller nine days earlier, has joined a yard that does well with her type and she was the only one capable of mixing it with the winner, although in the end was well held. She'll find easier opportunities. (op 13-2)
Groove Master had finished unplaced in six starts up to 2m on the Flat. His yard has traditionally enjoyed plenty of success with its juvenile hurdlers, but he's clearly going to be one for the lesser tracks. (op 10-1)
Highland Cadett, rated just 46 on turf, never really recovered from a blunder at the first. (tchd 33-1)
Whiepa Snappa(IRE) could have been expected to show more considering he had some fair placed form to his name on the Flat.

Naseby(USA) Official explanation: jockey said that the gelding had a breathing problem

1773 FOLLOW NICHOLLS ON TWITTER & FACEBOOK NOVICES' HURDLE (7 hdls 1 omitted) 2m 110y

2:50 (2:50) (Class 4) 4-Y-0+ **£3,252** (£955; £477; £238)

Form RPR

120- **1** **William Hogarth**[175] 5222 5-11-5 127 RhysFlint 125+
(Keith Goldsworthy) *mde virtually all: clr w runner-up at 4th: rdn and jnd next: mstke 2 out: edgd lft bef last: bttr jump and gained advantage last: kpt on wl u.p on flat* **7/2**[2]

22-1 **2** *1* **Karasenir (IRE)**[14] 1613 4-11-5 0 RichardJohnson 125+
(Philip Hobbs) *chsd wnr: nt fluent 3rd: jnd wnr gng best whn hit 3 out: rdn and stl upsides whn blnd next: stl ev ch whn nt fluent and outj. last: kpt on same pce u.p after* **4/7**[1]

F0F- **3** *8* **Pennellis (FR)**[247] 3848 6-10-12 0 RWalsh 108+
(Paul Nicholls) *hld up off the pce towards rr: hdwy and jst in tch in midfield after 4th: chsd ldng pair bef 2 out: rdn and styd on same pce between last 2* **15/2**[3]

/32- **4** *13* **Beside The Fire**[186] 5078 5-10-12 0 JoeTizzard 96
(Colin Tizzard) *chsd ldrs: rdn and btn appr 4th: nt fluent and no ch w ldrs fr next: plugged on u.p flat to go 4th last strides* **12/1**

0- **5** *hd* **Salybia Bay**[173] 5278 4-10-5 0 NickScholfield 89
(Andy Turnell) *t.k.h: chsd ldng pair: mstke 3rd: rdn and outpcd by ldng pair 4th: wl btn 4th bef 2 out* **66/1**

30- **6** *4 1/2* **Park Lane**[227] 4231 4-10-12 0 JamesDavies 92
(Miss J R Tooth) *in tch: rdn and struggling appr 4th: wkng and wl btn whn mstke and wnt lft 3 out* **28/1**

036/ **7** *3 3/4* **Puerto Azul (IRE)**[706] 1970 6-10-12 0 SamJones 89
(Oliver Sherwood) *t.k.h: hld up in rr: struggling wl bef 4th: sn wl btn* **40/1**

5 **8** *17* **Don Jose (USA)**[39] 1445 7-10-5 0 JakeGreenall(7) 73
(Richard Lee) *racd in midfield: in tch tl rdn and wknd qckly wl bef 4th: t.o fr 3 out* **50/1**

9 *64* **Bemused (IRE)**[181] 5-10-12 0 DarylJacob 16
(Simon Earle) *hld up wl off the pce towards rr: lost tch qckly after 3rd: wl t.o on long run bef next* **33/1**

00- **10** *24* **Contentwithmyluck (IRE)**[173] 5284 4-10-12 0 NoelFehily —
(Tom Gretton) *t.k.h: hld up wl off the pce towards rr: lost tch qckly after 3rd: wl t.o on long run bef next* **100/1**

00/ **P** **Comanche Kriek**[660] 2856 7-10-12 0 MattieBatchelor —
(George Yardley) *rel to r and v.s.a: a bhd: rdn and lost tch qckly after 3rd: t.o whn p.u next* **125/1**

3m 58.7s (-11.90) **Going Correction** -0.625s/f (Firm) **11** Ran SP% **119.4**
Speed ratings (Par 105): **103,102,98,92,92 90,88,80,50,39** —
toteswingers:1&2:£1.10, 1&3:£9.00, 2&3:£2.40 CSF £6.03 TOTE £3.30: £1.30, £1.02, £2.70; EX 6.00.

Owner ROL Plant Hire Ltd **Bred** Pinnacle Bloodstock **Trained** Yerbeston, Pembrokes

FOCUS

Jumping under pressure was the difference between the front pair here, with Karasenir making notable blunders at both the third-last and second from home. The winner is rated 6lb off last season's best.

NOTEBOOK

William Hogarth was allowed another shot when the favourite blundered, which he duly took. Rated 127 and by far the more experienced of the pair, he was well held in the Scottish Champion Hurdle when last seen, but he's clearly returned in good shape and overcame the lack of a recent outing to register his second victory over hurdles. Still a novice until the end of the October, he'll now head to either Ascot or Kempton later this month. (op 3-1 tchd 4-1)

Karasenir(IRE), who won in a canter on his hurdles debut at Market Rasen, was understandably made a red-hot favourite, and he looked the winner coming into three out, but made a mess of it, and just as he was beginning to re-find his stride, he messed up the next as well. He did rally gamely, despite again being outjumped at the last, and would surely have won with a bit in hand but for the errors. This was a setback, but he remains capable of winning more races. (op 8-11 tchd 4-5 in places)

Pennellis(FR), who fell on two of his three starts last year, had has a breathing operation over the summer and he travelled well under Ruby Walsh, who was at pains not to give him a hard race. And although unable to match the front pair, there was plenty of promise in the run and he'll be one to look for in handicaps. (op 7-1 tchd 8-1)

Beside The Fire, as had been the case in bumpers, showed promise in defeat and he'll be one to watch out for over further.

Salybia Bay, beaten a long way on her hurdles debut back in May, showed considerably more on this second start and she'll find easier opportunities against her own sex. (tchd 80-1)

Puerto Azul(IRE) tried to make some late headway on this first start in 706 days and could be of interest further down the line.

1774 DAYBREAK DAIRIES NOVICES' CHASE (18 fncs) 3m

3:25 (3:25) (Class 3) 5-Y-0+ **£5,204** (£1,528; £764; £381)

Form RPR

06-1 **1** **Balthazar King (IRE)**[15] 1602 6-11-4 0 RichardJohnson 135+
(Philip Hobbs) *j.w: mde all: qcknd gallop and gd jump 14th: rdn after 2 out: hld on wl u.p flat* **3/1**[2]

110- **2** *1/2* **Watamu Bay (IRE)**[204] 4712 7-10-12 0 RWalsh 129+
(Paul Nicholls) *j. sltly rt at times: chsd wnr tl 4th: wnt 2nd again after 7th: j.rt and reminders 3 out: outj. and rdn next: kpt on wl u.p flat: clsng on wnr fin* **1/1**[1]

01-1 **3** *12* **Aberdale (IRE)**[153] 225 6-10-9 0 RichieMcLernon(3) 119
(Jonjo O'Neill) *chsd ldrs: pushed along after 13th: rdn and outpcd by ldng pair 15th: styd on same pce fr next* **11/2**[3]

305- **4** *1 1/2* **Clyffe Hanger (IRE)**[285] 3120 10-10-12 0 AndrewGlassonbury 116
(Bob Buckler) *chsd wnr 4th tl after 7th: chsd ldrs after: hit 13th: rdn and outpcd 15th: one pce and wl hld fr next* **16/1**

0-12 **5** *21* **The Shoe (NZ)**[45] 1365 8-11-4 0 AndrewTinkler 115+
(Nicky Henderson) *t.k.h: hld up wl in tch: effrt 14th: rdn and btn 3 out: last whn mstke last: heavily eased flat* **6/1**

6m 5.10s (-16.90) **Going Correction** -0.75s/f (Firm) **5** Ran SP% **110.6**
Speed ratings: **98,97,93,93,86**
CSF £6.83 TOTE £4.30: £1.70, £1.30; EX 8.60.

Owner The Brushmakers **Bred** Sunnyhill Stud **Trained** Withycombe, Somerset

FOCUS

An interesting novice chase which should produce winners. The form could have been rated up to 6lb higher using the hurdles marks of the first four.

NOTEBOOK

Balthazar King(IRE) put his experience over the favourite to good use and won the race with slick jumping in the straight. He's clearly set to make a very useful staying handicap chaser and now heads to Cheltenham next week for a 3m novice chase. (tchd 10-3)

Watamu Bay(IRE), a dual hurdles winner for Charlie Mann, has joined a top yard and he jumped perfectly well, if a little to his right, on this first start over fences, but the winner was too quick for him in the straight and that was ultimately the difference between the two. He'll have no trouble going one better. (op 11-8 after 13-8 in places, tchd 6-4 in places)

Aberdale(IRE) ◆ finally got it together over hurdles late last year and he very much has the scope to be a nice staying chaser. Although unable to match the front pair, he wasn't given an overly hard time and, like the runner-up, it surely won't be long before he's off the mark as a chaser. He already appeals as a likely type for a race such as the Kim Muir or National Hunt Chase at the Cheltenham Festival. (op 4-1)

Clyffe Hanger(IRE) hadn't run over fences since early 2008, and for all that he was well held, it's much more likely he'll make an impact in handicaps. (tchd 14-1 and 20-1)

The Shoe(NZ), who had already won a race over fences, proved disappointing. He was already last when hitting the final fence and clearly isn't up to this level. (op 5-1 tchd 13-2)

1775 40% BETTER OFF ON BETFAIR SP HURDLE LIMITED H'CAP (7 hdls 1 omitted) 2m 110y

4:00 (4:00) (Class 2) 4-Y-0 **£16,262** (£4,775; £2,387; £1,192)

Form RPR

F16- **1** **Escort'men (FR)**[183] 5108 4-11-10 **146** RWalsh 149+
(Paul Nicholls) *hld up in last: hdwy gng wl appr 4th: wnt 2nd 2 out: led between last 2: rdn and hit last: sn hrd pressed: hld on wl towards fin* **5/1**[3]

104- **2** *nse* **Olofi (FR)**[184] 5094 4-10-8 **130** PaddyBrennan 132+
(Tom George) *hld up in tch: hdwy to trck ldrs after 3rd: wnt 2nd after 3 out tl mstke next: rallied and chal between horses sn after last: kpt on u.p: jst hld* **2/1**[1]

120- **3** *1 1/2* **Westlin' Winds (IRE)**[204] 4710 4-10-7 **136** JakeGreenall(7) 137+
(Charles Egerton) *t.k.h: chsd ldr bef 2nd: led 4th: rdn bef 2 out: hdd between last 2: stl ev ch but keeping on same pce whn squeezed out and swtchd lft after last: nt rcvr* **14/1**

126- **4** *6* **Rougham**[174] 5245 4-10-8 **130** RichardJohnson 125
(Philip Hobbs) *led: hit 1st: hdd 4th: hit 3 out: rdn and btn between last 2* **5/1**[3]

225- **5** *8* **Barwell Bridge**[204] 4710 4-10-11 **133** NoelFehily 119
(Warren Greatrex) *t.k.h: hld up wl in tch: rdn and struggling whn hit 3 out: wl btn fr next* **7/1**

105- **6** *8* **Troubletimestwo (FR)**[16] 5245 4-9-13 **126** oh3 LeeEdwards(5) 105
(Tony Carroll) *chsd ldr tl after 1st: pushed along 3rd: lost pl and rdn appr 4th: wl btn fr next* **25/1**

240- **7** *37* **George Nympton (IRE)**[206] 4675 4-10-4 **126** oh4 DarylJacob 72
(Nick Williams) *chsd ldrs tl lost pl qckly appr 4th: t.o fr 3 out* **4/1**[2]

33P- **8** *3 3/4* **Prince Pippin (IRE)**[206] 4675 4-9-11 **126** oh6 (t) AnthonyFreeman(7) 69
(Sean Curran) *chsd ldrs tl rdn and dropped to rr wl bef 4th: sn lost tch: t.o fr 3 out* **50/1**

3m 56.0s (-14.60) **Going Correction** -0.625s/f (Firm) **8** Ran SP% **111.6**
Speed ratings: **109,108,108,105,101 97,80,78**
toteswingers:1&2:£3.60, 1&3:£3.20, 2&3:£6.20 CSF £15.13 CT £125.56 TOTE £4.70: £2.10, £1.40, £3.00; EX 11.90.

Owner Donlon, Doyle & MacDonald **Bred** Michel Larobe & Haras De St Voir **Trained** Ditcheat, Somerset

■ Stewards' Enquiry : R Walsh one-day ban: careless riding (Oct 23)

FOCUS

A really good handicap hurdle that's gone to the likes of Mahogany Blaze, Gwanako and Crack Away Jack in recent times. Arguably slight improvement from the first two, with Escort'men a potential 155+ hurdler.

NOTEBOOK

Escort'men(FR), in defying a mark of 146, marked himself down as a smart prospect for the season ahead. Conceding at least 10lb to all his rivals which his trainer had worried would be too much, the winner travelled extremely well, as was often the case last term, and looked set for a cosy victory having hit the front before the last, but he made a mess of it, losing valuable momentum, and looked sure to be claimed by Olofi, despite squeezing that one up on the rail. Ruby Walsh was in no mood to be denied, though, and the pair held on, having to survive a stewards' enquiry also. A horse who put up one of the best juvenile performances of last season when running away with the Grade 2 Dovecote Novices' Hurdle against his elders last February, chasing had been the plan, but this victory is likely to bring about a change of thinking and he'll go up in grade now. It would be nice to see him put two good runs together, though, as he's yet to convince he's the most consistent in a short career. (op 9-2 tchd 11-2)

Olofi(FR), well held in the juvenile Grade 1s at Cheltenham and Aintree last spring, was well fancied to defy a mark of 130 on this handicap debut, and he conjured a strong challenge on the run-in but couldn't quite get past the winner. It's possible he'd have won had Paddy Brennan been able to properly get stuck in to him after the last, but he'd have only been second anyway had the winner jumped the final flight cleanly. (tchd 15-8 and 9-4)

Westlin' Winds(IRE) would have been beaten no more than half a length had he not been squeezed out against the rail on the run-in. Well beaten in last season's Triumph, behind Olofi, his rider was claiming a valuable 7lb and will need to continue to do so if he's to continue to make his mark in handicaps. (op 11-1)

Rougham has plenty of pace and this track wouldn't be ideal for him. He will be better off back on a less testing course. (op 7-1)

Barwell Bridge, fifth in the Triumph, should have run better and it's possible he needs a stiffer test now. (op 5-1)

George Nympton(IRE), representing last year's winning connections, had to race from 4lb 'wrong' and was beaten quickly in the straight on this first start in 206 days. (op 5-1 tchd 7-2)

1776 WYVERN ICES H'CAP HURDLE (10 hdls 1 omitted) 2m 4f

4:35 (4:35) (Class 3) (0-130,130) 4-Y-0+ **£5,204** (£1,528; £764; £381)

Form RPR

643- **1** **For Non Stop (IRE)**[213] 4517 5-10-8 **112** DarylJacob 128+
(Nick Williams) *a travelling strly: chsd ldrs tl wnt 2nd and mstke 6th: led after next: sn clr and in command: v easily* **9/2**[2]

/11- **2** *6* **Pavillon Bleu (FR)**[296] 2927 7-11-0 **118** RichardJohnson 121
(Philip Hobbs) *hld up in tch in midfield: nt fluent 1st: hdwy after 6th: rdn to chse clr wnr 3 out: no imp but kpt on for clr 2nd* **6/1**

3412 **3** *6* **Santera (IRE)**[14] 1608 6-11-2 **120** (p) RhysFlint 118
(John Flint) *chsd ldrs: rdn and outpcd by ldrs appr 7th: no ch w wnr after: plugged on to go 3rd after last* **7/1**

3031 **4** *2* **Winsley Hill**[16] 1590 8-11-3 **121** RodiGreene 118
(Neil Mulholland) *chsd ldr tl led 4th: hdd and rdn after 7th: sn outpcd by wnr: 3rd and wl hld fr next: hit last: lost 3rd flat* **20/1**

-131 **5** *hd* **Earth Dream (IRE)**[48] 1345 7-11-6 **124** RWalsh 121
(Paul Nicholls) *hld up in tch in midfield: pushed along and effrt to chse ldrs wl bef 7th: rdn and btn appr 7th: no ch whn hit 3 out* **10/3**[1]

100- **6** *6* **Blazing Buck**[10] 5245 4-10-13 **122** LeeEdwards(5) 113
(Tony Carroll) *led tl mstke and hdd 4th: chsd ldr tl 6th: rdn and wknd appr 7th: wl btn whn hit 3 out* **16/1**

0-34 **7** *12* **Apache Chant (USA)**[123] 678 6-10-0 **104** oh1 WayneHutchinson 84
(Tony Carroll) *in tch tl rdn and wknd bef 7th: sn bhd* **22/1**

05-1 **8** *1 1/4* **Tin Pot Man (IRE)**[116] 754 4-10-5 **109** (t) PaulMoloney 88
(Evan Williams) *hld up in last trio: pushed along and effrt on long run after 6th: rdn and wknd bef next: wl btn fr 3 out* **10/1**

010- **9** *2 1/4* **Majaales (USA)**[184] 5099 7-11-12 **130** PaddyBrennan 107
(Tom George) *hld up in last trio: sme prog into midfield after 6th: rdn and wknd appr next: wl btn whn hit 3 out* **5/1**[3]

U5-5 **10** *1/2* **Magic Sky (FR)**[162] 78 10-10-11 **122** JakeGreenall(7) 98
(Milton Harris) *t.k.h: hld up in last trio: in tch tl rdn and wknd bef 7th: sn wl bhd* **12/1**

1150 **11** *54* **Tarvini (IRE)**[31] 1508 5-11-7 **128** (p) RichieMcLernon(3) 56
(Jonjo O'Neill) *in tch: pushed along and dropped to last sn after 6th: lost tch wl bef next: t.o fr 7th* **33/1**

4m 46.6s (-15.20) **Going Correction** -0.625s/f (Firm)
WFA 4 from 5yo+ 10lb **11** Ran SP% **119.4**
Speed ratings (Par 107): **105,102,100,99,99 96,92,91,90,90 68**
toteswingers:1&2:£3.00, 1&3:£2.60, 2&3:£7.40 CSF £31.76 TOTE £5.70: £2.10, £2.40, £2.10; EX 35.90.
Owner Jared Sullivan **Bred** Raymond O'Rourke **Trained** George Nympton, Devon

FOCUS
A decent handicap hurdle and a big step forward from the easy winner.

NOTEBOOK
For Non Stop(IRE) ◆ moved comfortably through the race and cruised clear to make light of a mark of 112 on this handicap debut. A former point winner, the five-year-old didn't run without promise for Charlie Mann in novice hurdles last term, but he looks to have progressed over the summer and rates a very useful chasing prospect. First, though, there are surely more races to be won with him over hurdles, despite an inevitable rise for this. (op 7-2)
Pavillon Bleu(FR) had made the track only three times since February 2008 prior to today, but he had won all those starts, which were over fences at Exeter, and he was off his latest successful mark for this return to hurdles. He stayed on to take a clear second and should improve on this first outing of the year. (op 5-1)
Santera(IRE) has elevated her form again since joining current connections, and she ran well in third off what was a career-high mark. (op 15-2)
Winsley Hill found this more difficult off 8lb higher, but she was far from disgraced.
Earth Dream(IRE), handily weighted on his improved chase form, didn't find for pressure and was disappointing. (op 9-2)
Blazing Buck could do with a hand from the handicapper. (op 14-1)
Tin Pot Man(IRE) foudn this a bit too competitive. (op 12-1)
Majaales(USA) made no impact on this first start in 184 days and was another to disappoint. (op 15-2)

1777 RHYS HOWELLS MEMORIAL H'CAP CHASE (18 fncs) 3m
5:10 (5:10) (Class 2) (0-150,144) 4-Y-0+ **£11,383** (£3,342; £1,671; £834)

Form RPR
2051 **1** **Ballycarney (IRE)**[35] 1469 6-10-10 **128** JackDoyle 141+
(Emma Lavelle) *led tl 3rd: chsd ldrs after tl led again bef 14th: mde rest: clr w runner-up and rdn whn mstke 3 out: mstke last: kpt on wl and outbattled rival u.p flat* **8/1**

2552 **2** *1 1/4* **Templer (IRE)**[18] 1570 9-10-9 **127** RichardJohnson 137
(Philip Hobbs) *in tch: chsd wnr 14th: clr w wnr fr 3 out: rdn bef 2 out: finding little and looking hld tl lft w ch last: nt qckn u.p flat* **6/1**[3]

3P3- **3** *12* **Mount Oscar (IRE)**[187] 5032 11-11-3 **135** (t) JoeTizzard 134
(Colin Tizzard) *w ldr tl led 3rd: hdd after 14th: outpcd by ldng pair and rdn after 15th: wl btn fr next* **20/1**

P22- **4** *2 3/4* **Gullible Gordon (IRE)**[199] 4827 7-11-4 **136** RWalsh 136+
(Paul Nicholls) *in tch in midfield: reminders after 9th: sme hdwy to chse ldrs after 13th: blnd bdly next: no imp and wl btn after* **5/2**[1]

PPP- **5** *14* **Beat The Boys (IRE)**[182] 5127 9-11-12 **144** PaddyBrennan 131
(Nigel Twiston-Davies) *in tch in rr of main gp: hdwy 8th: chsd wnr after 13th: mstke and lost 2nd next: sn wknd: wl btn bef 3 out: eased after last* **6/1**[3]

1325 **6** *10* **Cullahill (IRE)**[15] 1606 8-9-12 **123** NathanSweeney(7) 98
(Bob Buckler) *chsd ldrs: j. slowly 1st: mstke 10th: lost pl 11th: rallied briefly u.p bef 14th: sn wknd and wl btn fr 15th: t.o* **9/1**

13P- **7** *1/2* **Le Beau Bai (FR)**[203] 4740 7-11-4 **143** JakeGreenall(7) 118
(Richard Lee) *w ldrs tl lost pl and rdn 11th: rallied u.p bef 14th: wknd bef 15th: wl btn next: t.o* **10/1**

UU-0 **8** *5* **Ellerslie George (IRE)**[14] 1611 10-10-12 **137** MrRGHenderson(7) 107
(Nick Mitchell) *in tch in midfield: mstke 2nd: wkng whn mstke 15th: sn lost tch: t.o* **22/1**

225- **9** *32* **Dom D'Orgeval (FR)**[175] 5223 10-10-9 **127** DarylJacob 68
(Nick Williams) *in tch in rr tl pushed along and detached in last pair after 7th: lost tch 12th: wl t.o fr 14th* **11/2**[2]

1-15 **P** **Tempsford (USA)**[84] 1020 10-10-9 **130** (t) RichieMcLernon(3) —
(Jonjo O'Neill) *in tch: mstke 7th: losing pl qckly whn p.u 12th* **33/1**

4402 **P** **Postmaster**[34] 1486 8-11-2 **134** PaulMoloney —
(Evan Williams) *hld up in last: lost tch 10th: wl t.o fr 12th tl p.u 14th* **33/1**

5m 58.1s (-23.90) **Going Correction** -0.75s/f (Firm) **11** Ran SP% **117.7**
Speed ratings (Par 109): **109,108,104,103,99 95,95,93,83,— —**
toteswingers:1&2:£7.10, 1&3:£10.00, 2&3:£25.00 CSF £53.32 CT £926.88 TOTE £5.30: £1.60, £2.40, £5.70; EX 66.80.
Owner Elite Racing Club **Bred** Aaron Metcalfe **Trained** Wildhern, Hants

FOCUS
A good, competitive handicap chase. The front two pulled clear and the progressive winner is rated up another 10lb+ with the second rated to his best.

NOTEBOOK
Ballycarney(IRE) held on well despite having made a mess of the last. A winner off 6lb lower at Stratford last month, he was on the pace throughout and really kicked on at the top of the straight, pinging four out and leaving all bar the runner-up trailing. He had to really dig in, but was more than up to it and he's well worth his place in a more valuable handicap now, with the United House Gold Cup at Ascot later this month looking a possible target. (op 10-1)
Templer(IRE) stays well and runs his race more often than not. He was the only one capable of matching the winner, but despite being let in by a mistake from him at the last, he couldn't capitalise. (op 7-1)
Mount Oscar(IRE) isn't on a bad mark, but he was comfortably held back in third. He should come on for this. (op 18-1)
Gullible Gordon(IRE), winner of the 3m novices' chase on the card a year ago, proved frustrating afterwards, but he clearly goes well fresh and was expected to feature off 136, but hopes he had of getting involved went when he was squeezed out on landing at the first in the straight. (op 9-4 tchd 11-4)
Beat The Boys(IRE), 17lb higher than when winning this a year ago, was held up on this occasion and, having made a promising forward move to go prominent down the back, he got tired in the straight. This broke his sequence of either winning or pulling up, but he's sure to pop up again at some stage this season, as he will soon be back on a good mark. (op 5-1 tchd 9-2)
Cullahill(IRE) started to stay on again having lost his position, but made mistakes in the straight and ended up well held. He'll find easier opportunities. (tchd 10-1)
Le Beau Bai(FR) is a slow horse and this was never going to be enough of a test for him. He needs the ground barely raceable. (op 11-1)
Dom D'Orgeval(FR) wasn't on one of his going days and never left the rear. (op 6-1 tchd 13-2)

1778 BETFAIR IPHONE & ANDROID APP STANDARD OPEN NATIONAL HUNT FLAT RACE 2m 110y
5:45 (5:45) (Class 6) 4-6-Y-0 **£1,463** (£429; £214; £107)

Form RPR
1 **1** **Kartanian (IRE)**[15] 1607 4-11-7 0 RichardJohnson 117+
(Philip Hobbs) *chsd ldrs: wnt 2nd over 3f out: rdn to chal over 2f out: led ent fnl f: edgd rt but styd on wl fnl f: rdn out* **11/4**[2]

034- **2** *2 1/2* **Golden Chieftain (IRE)**[224] 4309 5-11-0 0 JoeTizzard 108
(Colin Tizzard) *t.k.h early: chsd ldrs tl rdn to ld over 3f out: clr w wnr fr 3f out: hdd ent fnl f: no ex and btn ins fnl f: eased towards fin* **12/1**

2- **3** *17* **Merehead (FR)**[196] 4893 4-11-0 0 RWalsh 93
(Paul Nicholls) *t.k.h early: hld up in tch: effrt 5f out: rdn and outpcd by ldrs wl over 3f out: wnt modest 3rd over 2f out: no imp and n.d after* **11/10**[1]

1/ **4** *3/4* **Royal Scoundrel (IRE)**[769] 1322 6-11-7 0 PaddyBrennan 99
(Peter Bowen) *led tl hdd and rdn over 3f out: sn outpcd by ldng pair: wl btn and lost 3rd over 2f out* **14/1**

5 *8* **Mocambo (GER)** 4-10-8 0 ow1 SClements(7) 86
(Colin Tizzard) *t.k.h early: hld up towards rr: clsd and in tch 1/2-way: outpcd and poor 9th ent fnl 5f: kpt on steadily fnl 2f: nvr trbld ldrs* **66/1**

6 *3* **Hawkaller** 5-10-7 0 RachaelGreen(7) 82
(Anthony Honeyball) *hld up in midfield: hdwy 7f out: in tch and rdn ent fnl 4f: sn outpcd by ldng pair: wl btn fnl 3f* **16/1**

2 **7** *2* **Don Pooleoni (IRE)**[45] 1374 5-11-0 0 DarylJacob 80
(David Arbuthnot) *t.k.h: chsd ldr after 2f tl ent fnl 4f: sn dropped out: wl btn fnl 3f* **16/1**

8 *16* **Blues And Twos**[216] 4-11-0 0 JackDoyle 66
(Emma Lavelle) *hld up off the pce in midfield: hdwy 7f out: rdn and wknd 5f out: sn wl bhd: t.o* **11/1**[3]

9 *12* **Double Fun** 4-10-0 0 MrJBarnes(7) 48
(Martin Hill) *wl in tch tl rdn: rn green and wknd qckly 5f out: t.o fnl 3f* **100/1**

10 *13* **Smart Catch (IRE)** 4-10-9 0 LeeEdwards(5) 43
(Tony Carroll) *racd in midfield: hdwy 1/2-way: rdn and wknd qckly over 5f out: t.o* **50/1**

11 *2 1/2* **El Pescadero (IRE)** 4-10-7 0 RodiGreene 34
(Nick Ayliffe) *a towards rr and rn green: rdn along after 4f: lost tch over 5f out: t.o fnl 4f* **100/1**

12 *4 1/2* **A Splash Of Green (IRE)** 5-11-0 0 JamieMoore 37
(Jonathan Portman) *t.k.h: chsd ldrs tl wknd rapidly over 4f out: t.o fnl 2f* **66/1**

5 **13** *24* **Logan Rock**[18] 1572 6-11-0 0 AidanColeman 16
(Susan Gardner) *a in rr: detached and struggling bdly after 6f: t.o fnl 6f* **100/1**

14 *44* **Pentopyn Harry** 4-11-0 0 AndrewTinkler —
(Tony Newcombe) *hld up in rr of main gp: lost tch rapidly over 5f out: sn t.o: virtually p.u fnl f* **80/1**

15 *72* **Silver Peninsula** 5-10-7 0 HaddenFrost —
(Martin Hill) *a bhd: lost tch after 4f out: wl t.o fr 1/2-way* **100/1**

3m 55.5s (-9.50) **Going Correction** -0.625s/f (Firm) **15** Ran SP% **118.9**
Speed ratings: **97,95,87,87,83 82,81,73,68,62 60,58,47,26,—**
toteswingers:1&2:£6.60, 1&3:£1.10, 2&3:£5.40 CSF £34.86 TOTE £3.90: £1.30, £2.80, £1.20; EX 36.50 Place 6 £19.74, Place 5 £18.96.
Owner Louisville Syndicate III **Bred** His Highness The Aga Khan's Studs S C **Trained** Withycombe, Somerset

FOCUS
They went a decent gallop and the front two pulled a long way clear. The winner looks a decent prospect.

NOTEBOOK
Kartanian(IRE) ◆, who created a very favourable impression when making a winning debut at Worcester two weeks earlier, was up to defying the penalty. Whereas he outclassed the opposition on debut, he was made to work for it here, and considering his relative inexperience, it was taking to see him stay on so strongly for pressure and seal the deal inside the final furlong. He's evidently very useful and it looks likely that he'll now go hurdling, with 2m4f expected to suit. (op 3-1 tchd 7-2 in a place)
Golden Chieftain(IRE) travelled strongly throughout and readily moved clear with the winner, but the lack of a recent run possibly started to tell late on. This was a big step up on last season's effort and he too is a nice jumping prospect. (op 16-1)
Merehead(FR), who is well thought of, ended up well held back in third. A good second to a promising sort in a juvenile bumper over 1m4f at Newbury in March, he was under pressure early in the straight and never picked up. Ruby Walsh wasn't hard on him, and he seems sure to come on for the run, so is probably worth another chance. (tchd Evens and 5-4 in a place)
Royal Scoundrel(IRE), returning from a 769-day absence, having won on his debut at Newton Abbot, ensured it was truly run, but he was always likely to pay for it in the straight. He did well to take fourth and looks to have a future over hurdles. (op 12-1 tchd 10-1)
Mocambo(GER), a stablemate to the runner-up, cost only £2,000 but kept on late and should improve. (op 80-1)
Hawkaller, from a yard that does well in this sphere, showed some promise and will find easier opportunities. (op 10-1)
Blues And Twos, runner-up in a point, never got into it having been held up. (op 10-1 tchd 9-1)
Pentopyn Harry Official explanation: jockey said that the gelding had a breathing problem
Silver Peninsula Official explanation: jockey said that the mare was never travelling
T/Plt: £23.30 to a £1 stake. Pool of £59,069.26. 1,845.28 winning tickets. T/Qpdt: £21.40 to a £1 stake. Pool of £3,811.10. 131.60 winning tickets. SP

1660 HEXHAM (L-H)
Saturday, October 9

OFFICIAL GOING: Soft (good to soft in places on hurdle course; chase 6.6, hurdle 7.0)
Wind: Light, half behind Weather: Dull

1779 METROCENTRE ALWAYS A WINNER BEGINNERS' CHASE (12 fncs) 2m 110y
2:00 (2:00) (Class 4) 4-Y-0+ **£2,998** (£931; £501)

Form RPR
21-6 **1** **Saveiro (FR)**[148] 315 6-11-3 0 BrianHughes 123+
(Alan Swinbank) *j.rt on occasions: mde most to 3 out: rallied to ld bef last: styd on wl* **11/4**[2]

-211 **2** *5* **Twentyninenblack (FR)**[129] 576 6-11-3 0 BrianHarding 119+
(Donald McCain) *in tch: hdwy whn lft cl 3rd 6th: gd jump to ld 3 out: hdd bef last: rallied: one pce run-in* **10/3**[3]

522- **3** *18* **Kellystown Lad (IRE)**[168] 5386 7-11-3 0 GrahamLee 103+
(Ferdy Murphy) *t.k.h: cl up: chal 6th to after 4 out: wknd fr 2 out* **7/1**

62B- **U** **Indian Groom (IRE)**[168] 5393 5-11-3 0 TimmyMurphy —
(Howard Johnson) *trckd ldr: j.rt 5th: j.rt and uns rdr next* **5/4**[1]

0-P **P** **Alaskan Prince (IRE)**[104] 847 5-11-3 0 TomMessenger —
(Peter Salmon) *hld up: outpcd 7th: rallied and in tch 3 out: sn wknd: t.o whn p.u bef last* **66/1**

4m 14.8s (5.00) **Going Correction** +0.475s/f (Soft) **5** Ran SP% **108.2**
Speed ratings (Par 105): **107,104,96,—,—**
CSF £11.75 TOTE £4.40: £1.90, £2.20; EX 10.20.
Owner Solway Stayers **Bred** Satwa Farm **Trained** Melsonby, N Yorks

FOCUS
All of these had no chasing experience under rules and were having their first run in more than 104 days. The first two look fair prospects, with the winner rated in line with his hurdles best, while the third will no doubt be better in time.

NOTEBOOK
Saveiro(FR), off the track since a disappointing effort at Aintree in May, is a half-brother to the decent chaser Sa Suffit and shows a lot of bravery, as he lost the lead a couple of times before fighting back to get in front after the final fence. (op 7-2)
Twentynineblack(FR) ◆ won his last two starts over hurdles, a maiden and novice hurdle, and looks the one to take from the race. He was much too free under restraint and will win something similar, especially if tried on a flatter track next time. (op 5-2)
Kellystown Lad(IRE), whose only win over hurdles came over 2m4f last Dececmber, shaped with promise but was readily left behind by the front two after being alongside them down the back straight. (op 5-1)
Indian Groom(IRE), representing a trainer in form, was much the best of these over hurdles and the stable sent out Striking Article to win this in 2008 on his chasing debut. He jumped okay to start with but stuttered into the fifth before jumping out to his right over the next, causing Timmy Murphy to unseat. (tchd 50-1)
Alaskan Prince(IRE), having his first start for this trainer, took a really good grip early and never really got involved after losing his place. (tchd 50-1)

1780 CHEVY CHASE MARES' NOVICES' HURDLE (8 hdls) 2m 110y
2:35 (2:35) (Class 4) 4-Y-O+ **£2,992** (£878; £439; £219)

Form RPR

0-24 **1** **Diamond MM (IRE)**[61] 686 4-10-10 0 BrianHughes 93
(Alan Swinbank) *cl up: led 2 out: qcknd appr last: rdn and hld on wl run-in* **85/40**[2]

2 *1/2* **Sophonie (FR)**[176] 4-10-10 0 GrahamLee 93
(Ferdy Murphy) *t.k.h: cl up: ev ch 2 out: rdn appr last: styd on wl run-in* **7/4**[1]

3 *1/2* **Louisa (GER)**[20] 6-10-10 0 WilsonRenwick 92
(P Monteith) *prom: effrt after 2 out: rdn bef last: kpt on u.p run-in* **12/1**

0-56 **4** *16* **Knockaveen (IRE)**[142] 421 5-10-7 79 FearghalDavis(3) 76
(Andrew Crook) *hld up: rdn and outpcd bef 2 out: plugged on fr last: no imp* **16/1**

P3 **5** *2 1/4* **Le Petit Vigier**[19] 1003 4-10-10 0 (tp) PaddyAspell 74
(Patrick Holmes) *led tl hdd 2 out: sn rdn and wknd* **18/1**

0 **6** *nk* **Are Olive**[14] 1613 7-10-10 0 RobertWalford 74
(Tim Walford) *hld up: rdn and outpcd bef 2 out: sn btn* **10/1**

3-0 **7** *26* **Sara's Smile**[153] 230 4-10-10 0 BrianHarding 48
(Donald McCain) *nt fluent: in tch tl rdn and wknd 2 out* **11/2**[3]

4m 21.6s (4.20) **Going Correction** +0.175s/f (Yiel)
WFA 4 from 5yo+ 9lb **7** Ran SP% **111.7**
Speed ratings (Par 105): **97,96,96,89,87 87,75**
toteswingers:1&2:£1.02, 1&3:£4.70, 2&3:£30.00 CSF £6.15 TOTE £3.00: £1.90, £1.90; EX 5.90.
Owner R Haggas **Bred** Newlands House Stud **Trained** Melsonby, N Yorks

FOCUS
A very moderate mares' contest in which the early gallop was far from strong. The winner is rated in line with her best bumper run.

NOTEBOOK
Diamond MM(IRE) has taken a keen hold in the past in bumpers, and did so again on her hurdling debut, but she jumped quickly and fluently in the main and just had enough in hand to hold off two rallying rivals. Evidently well regarded, she is due to head to the Doncaster sales. (op 3-1)
Sophonie(FR), winner and second over fences in her previous two outings when last seen back in the spring, went away from the rest of the field at one point with Diamond MM but could not quicken. It was slightly disappointing that she was so readily beaten off initially, although she took a strong hold for a long time, and it might be that all her stable's runners will be straighter for the outing. (op 13-8 tchd 2-1 and 6-4 in a place)
Louisa(GER) was unable to win on the Flat after moving across from Germany in July 2009 (she did manage a success in that country), but gave her connections optimism for the future over hurdles if she can at least maintain this form. (op 11-1)
Knockaveen(IRE) officially rated just 79, plugged on but never threatened. (op 12-1)
Le Petit Vigier was given a positive ride early but got easily outpaced when joined. (tchd 16-1 and 20-1)
Sara's Smile needs a stronger gallop to chase, as she took a strong hold again early on, which may have caused her to jump poorly on occasions. (op 5-1 tchd 9-2)

1781 METROCENTRE HOT FAVOURITE H'CAP CHASE (15 fncs) 2m 4f 110y
3:10 (3:10) (Class 4) (0-115,115) 4-Y-O+ **£3,252** (£955; £477; £238)

Form RPR

00-U **1** **Quinder Spring (FR)**[149] 310 6-10-8 97 PeterBuchanan 103
(Lucinda Russell) *hld up in tch: hdwy and cl up 11th: rdn and outpcd bef 2 out: rallied bef last: styd on wl run-in: led cl home* **7/2**[2]

6P04 **2** *nk* **Tifoso (FR)**[13] 1628 5-10-6 95 (v) BrianHughes 103+
(Richard Guest) *hld up: hdwy and prom 4 out: effrt and led whn hit last: kpt on run-in: hdd cl home* **8/1**

3565 **3** *2* **Stagecoach Amber (USA)**[40] 1424 8-11-6 114 ShaneByrne(5) 118
(Sue Smith) *cl up: pushed along fr 1/2-way: rallied: led 3 out to bef last: kpt on u.p run-in* **10/1**

01-P **4** *8* **Oscar Honey (IRE)**[149] 308 9-11-12 115 WilsonRenwick 111
(Rose Dobbin) *hld up in tch: lost pl 1/2-way: rallied appr 3 out: rdn and outpcd bef last* **16/1**

04F- **5** *3/4* **Primrose Time**[181] 5141 7-10-5 101 AlexanderVoy(7) 96
(Lucy Normile) *cl up: led 2nd: clr bef 5th to 9th: hdd 3 out: no ex between last 2* **8/1**

04-U **6** *15* **Seek The Truth (IRE)**[6] 1701 7-10-0 89 oh5 TomMessenger 69
(Sue Bradburne) *prom: blnd 3rd: lost pl 9th: shortlived effrt bef 3 out: sn btn* **10/1**

2/65 **7** *2 1/4* **Rare Society (IRE)**[55] 1255 12-11-2 105 TjadeCollier 83
(Sue Smith) *prom: nt fluent 4th: pushed along 1/2-way: struggling fr 11th* **14/1**

44-5 **8** *73* **Just For Men (IRE)**[154] 213 10-11-4 107 GrahamLee 12
(Martin Todhunter) *hld up: niggled along 1/2-way: blnd 11th: effrt after next: wknd fnl 3* **3/1**[1]

P-00 **P** **Norminster**[150] 290 9-9-11 89 oh7 (p) RyanMania(3) —
(Rayson Nixon) *hld up towards rr: struggling fr 10th: t.o whn p.u bef 2 out* **40/1**

F213 **P** **Emotive**[42] 1403 7-10-7 99 CampbellGillies(3) —
(Barry Murtagh) *led to 2nd: cl up: rdn 3 out: wknd after next: p.u bef last: sn dismntd* **6/1**[3]

5m 24.4s (10.90) **Going Correction** +0.475s/f (Soft) **10** Ran SP% **116.9**
Speed ratings (Par 105): **98,97,97,94,93 88,87,59,—,—**
toteswingers:1&2:£13.70, 1&3:£3.10, 2&3:£27.40 CSF £32.00 CT £257.68 TOTE £5.50: £2.20, £2.20, £2.90; EX 40.00.
Owner Peter J S Russell **Bred** Pascal Sachot Et Al **Trained** Arlary, Perth & Kinross
■ Stewards' Enquiry : Brian Hughes one-day ban: used whip with excessive frequency (23 Oct)

FOCUS
Unlike the earlier contests, this appeared to be run at a respectable pace, even though a few still held a chance in the final stages. Ordinary handicap form.

NOTEBOOK
Quinder Spring(FR) ◆, a multiple winning pointer, unseated his rider when odds-on for a hunter chase in May and hardly looked likely to take this rounding the home bend, but stamina seems his strong suit, as he battled on strongly and mugged the runner-up on the line. A step up to 3m (the distance he collected his six straight wins over between flags) will surely benefit him, and the handicapper cannot be too hard on him for this, so a follow up success looks to be on the cards.
Official explanation: trainer said regarding the apparent improvement of form, the gelding had won five point to points and unseated its rider on its last run (op 5-1)
Tifoso(FR) ran a cracker for a horse having only his second start over fences. He travelled noticeably well at the rear in the early stages before bounding to the front coming to the last. He possibly idled once in front and did hit the final fence, but this was certainly a step in the right direction for him and he may be able to add to his two wins in France over hurdles if running the same sort of way next time. (op 10-1)
Stagecoach Amber(USA) has been steadily coming down the weights after a couple of wins in the spring of 2009, and looks the sort of ride any jockey would love if they needed to get fit, as the horse needed pushing along for some way. However, he responded to Shane Byrne every time; indeed, the pair hit the front for a while, and ran with credit. (op 8-1)
Oscar Honey(IRE), dropped 5lb since his last start in May, lost his place early but made some good late headway after getting behind.
Primrose Time, absent since falling when going well at Kelso in April, got to a clear lead and held a good advantage until the pack closed up to her. To be fair, she didn't drop away and plugged on.
Just For Men(IRE) hasn't won for a long time but is down to a decent-looking mark now. He was making some ground when hitting the eleventh quite hard. That was probably enough to end his chances of getting seriously involved. It was reported afterwards that he jumped moderately.
Official explanation: jockey said the gelding jumped poorly throughout (op 11-4 tchd 7-2)
Emotive Official explanation: jockey said the gelding lost action

1782 NEW MAN AT SQUARE H'CAP HURDLE (12 hdls) 3m
3:45 (3:45) (Class 4) (0-100,100) 4-Y-O+ **£3,151** (£918; £459)

Form RPR

40-5 **1** **Whatdoidowiththat**[31] 1507 7-10-12 91 ShaneByrne(5) 99
(Sue Smith) *prom: effrt 2 out: led bef last: gd jump last: styd on strly run-in* **9/2**[2]

2F-P **2** *3/4* **Delightfully (FR)**[154] 212 6-11-9 97 (p) PeterBuchanan 105+
(Lucinda Russell) *hld up in tch: smooth hdwy to chse wnr whn nt fluent last: drvn and kpt on towards fin* **11/1**

-0F0 **3** *9* **Solway Bee**[8] 1666 10-10-11 88 HarryHaynes(3) 86
(Lisa Harrison) *mde most to after 3 out: rallied and ev ch next: one pce bef last* **16/1**

4-F2 **4** *1/2* **Political Pendant**[137] 458 9-10-3 80 RyanMania(3) 78
(Rayson Nixon) *prom: drvn after 2 out: outpcd bef last* **11/1**

4-52 **5** *1/2* **Bled (FR)**[115] 766 5-11-5 100 (b) MrJHamer(7) 97
(Donald McCain) *trckd ldrs: outpcd bef 2 out: rallied last: no imp* **13/2**[3]

0-02 **6** *1/2* **Manoubi**[8] 1666 11-10-7 86 JamesHalliday(5) 83
(Martin Todhunter) *hld up: stdy hdwy 2 out: rdn and outpcd bef last* **4/1**[1]

3315 **7** *5* **Maolisa (IRE)**[49] 1339 8-11-6 97 CampbellGillies(3) 90
(S R B Crawford, Ire) *disp ld tl after 2 out: sn rdn and wknd* **11/1**

P0OU **8** *2 1/2* **Oniz Tiptoes (IRE)**[6] 1694 9-11-2 90 (v) PaddyAspell 79
(John Wainwright) *trckd ldrs tl rdn and wknd bef last* **16/1**

056/ **9** *4 1/2* **Dee Cee Bolter (IRE)**[146] 8-10-12 93 MrGJCockburn(7) 78
(Lucinda Russell) *hld up towards rr: rdn whn nt fluent 2 out: sn btn* **25/1**

-565 **10** *20* **Catleen (IRE)**[129] 577 6-10-13 94 MrBGCrawford(7) 59
(S R B Crawford, Ire) *hld up: rdn 2 out: sn btn* **8/1**

4U2 **P** **Sparkling Zola**[90] 946 8-11-6 97 EwanWhillans(3) —
(Alistair Whillans) *hld up in tch: outpcd 4 out: p.u after next* **8/1**

6m 14.2s (1.00) **Going Correction** +0.175s/f (Yiel) **11** Ran SP% **114.3**
Speed ratings (Par 105): **105,104,101,101,101 101,99,98,97,90 —**
toteswingers:1&2:£25.90, 1&3:£6.00, 2&3:£4.90 CSF £51.41 CT £722.65 TOTE £4.80: £1.70, £3.40, £4.00; EX 51.70.
Owner M F Spence **Bred** Mrs S L Dent **Trained** High Eldwick, W Yorks

FOCUS
It appeared that a decent pace had been set by these modest types, so it was surprising that there was a bunch of horses all going fairly well with around 3f to go. The first two were both very well in on their best old form.

NOTEBOOK
Whatdoidowiththat didn't show a lot on his return from a 459-day layoff last time under a 10lb claimer, but that effort had clearly done him good as he pressed off the final bend and did enough to hold on. He obviously loves this C&D, and took this race back in 2008. (op 6-1 tchd 4-1)
Delightfully(FR) has been tried in different variations of headgear, and today it was cheekpieces that were tried again for her reappearance. The winner got first run on her and she was never quite able to reel him in.
Solway Bee, a winner over this sort of trip at Ayr last season off a 3lb lower mark, went to post early and then helped to set what looked a good gallop, so the fact she was able to keep on again to claim a place suggests she isn't far away from winning again. (tchd 14-1)
Political Pendant, back over hurdles on her return to action and without headgear, was never far away but got outpaced before keeping on. She will be straighter for the run. (op 10-1)
Manoubi caught the eye last time at this course over just over 2m4f but failed to build on that run. (tchd 7-2)

1783 METROCENTRE BRITAIN'S BEST SHOPPING CENTRE MAIDEN HURDLE (10 hdls) 2m 4f 110y
4:20 (4:20) (Class 4) 4-Y-O+ **£2,602** (£764; £382; £190)

Form RPR

12-0 **1** **Monogram**[16] 1593 6-11-0 0 TimmyMurphy 118+
(Howard Johnson) *t.k.h: a cl up: led briefly 3 out: styd w ldr: led bef last: styd on wl* **11/8**[1]

0 **2** *1 1/4* **Blenheim Brook (IRE)**[148] 319 5-11-0 0 PeterBuchanan 116
(Lucinda Russell) *t.k.h: hld up in midfield: hdwy to ld after 3 out: sn hrd pressed: hdd bef last: hung lft run-in: styd on* **7/2**[2]

4 **3** *13* **Twentypoundluck (IRE)**[123] 679 5-10-11 0............. JamesO'Farrell(3) 103
(Patrick Griffin, Ire) *trckd ldrs: rdn and outpcd bef 2 out: rallied bef last: no ch w first two* **20/1**

24- **4** *11* **Oil Burner**[212] 4530 5-10-11 105.................................. CampbellGillies(3) 92
(William Amos) *hld up: hdwy to chse clr ldng pair whn nt fluent last: wknd bef last* **4/1**[3]

5 *14* **Melua Maid (IRE)**[916] 8-10-7 0.. TjadeCollier 71
(Sue Smith) *in tch tl lost pl 1/2-way: n.d after* **28/1**

40- **6** *1* **Goffa Crag**[181] 5144 6-10-11 0..................................... FearghalDavis(3) 77
(Nicky Richards) *hld up: stdy hdwy bef 3 out: wknd bef next* **33/1**

40/ **7** *2 ¼* **Errington**[552] 4864 5-11-0 0.. BrianHughes 75
(Howard Johnson) *led to 3 out: wkng whn nt fluent next* **18/1**

8 *10* **Domoly (FR)** 7-10-7 0.. MrAPKelly(7) 65
(Ferdy Murphy) *bhd: struggling bef 4 out: nvr on terms* **33/1**

305- **9** *13* **Glingermill (IRE)**[203] 4730 7-11-0 0.................................. BrianHarding 52
(Nicky Richards) *in tch: rdn after 3 out: wkng whn hit next* **7/1**

00-0 **10** *11* **Its Bobkat (IRE)**[8] 1660 4-11-0 0.. PaddyAspell 41
(Robert Smith) *bhd: struggling bef 4 out: nvr on terms* **100/1**

0-00 **11** *nk* **Solway Silver**[8] 1664 4-10-11 0.................................... HarryHaynes(3) 40
(Lisa Harrison) *cl up tl wknd fr 1/2-way* **33/1**

06- **P** **Barr Head (IRE)**[195] 4910 6-10-7 0................................ AlexanderVoy(7) —
(Lucy Normile) *prom tl rdn and wknd bef 2 out: t.o whn p.u bef last* **80/1**

5m 16.4s (3.90) **Going Correction** +0.175s/f (Yiel) **12** Ran SP% **121.3**
Speed ratings (Par 105): **99,98,93,89,84 83,82,79,74,69 69,—**
toteswingers:1&2:£2.30, 1&3:£21.10, 2&3:£21.10 CSF £6.05 TOTE £2.20: £1.60, £1.20, £3.50; EX 9.50.
Owner Andrea & Graham Wylie **Bred** Mrs J K M Oliver **Trained** Billy Row, Co Durham

FOCUS
Hardly any of these could be fancied on anything they had done on a racecourse, but this was probably a fair race for the track and time of year and the first two are above average. They pulled miles clear, which doesn't say a lot for the rest as both took fierce holds for a lot of the contest.

NOTEBOOK
Monogram, back on a left-handed track after running out at Perth's paddock bend, was always going well and kept on the stronger of the pair that move away to record his first win over hurdles. There were a couple of small hints that he may not be completely straightforward again, but he is obviously talented and a exciting prospect. (op 6-4 tchd 7-4 and 15-8 in a place)
Blenheim Brook(IRE) ◆ has apparently always been held in high regard by those who had ridden him, and he proved their faith was not misplaced on his first outing over hurdles. He seems sure to win any ordinary contest. (op 5-1)
Twentypoundluck(IRE) appeared to improve on his opening try over hurdles at Bangor in June, but one would suspect that this former winning pointer will be one for handicaps rather than maiden or novice hurdles. (op 22-1 tchd 18-1)
Oil Burner showed some ability on two starts last season and ran well for a long time here before not getting home. (op 5-1)
Errington Official explanation: jockey said the gelding hung right handed throughout

1784 ELDON SQUARE SIMPLY BEST IN SHOPPING H'CAP CHASE (19 fncs) 3m 1f
4:55 (4:55) (Class 5) (0-95,95) 4-Y-0+ **£2,797** (£821; £410; £205)

Form RPR

PP-2 **1** **Sierra Victor (IRE)**[126] 625 7-11-9 92........................... WilsonRenwick 100+
(P Monteith) *prom: hdwy and ev ch 3 out: led next: drvn clr fr last* **5/1**[3]

P-33 **2** *11* **Murphys Beau (IRE)**[8] 1663 8-10-0 69 oh2......................... GrahamLee 68+
(Kate Walton) *led: mstke 3 out: hdd next: rallied bef last: no ex run-in* **3/1**[2]

P-10 **3** *8* **Benbeoch**[143] 398 11-11-9 95..(p) RyanMania(3) 84
(Sandy Thomson) *in tch: rdn and outpcd 14th: rallied to chse clr ldrs after 2 out: no imp* **10/1**

5PU5 **4** *dist* **Dougall (IRE)**[8] 1661 7-10-6 80..................................(p) JamesHalliday(5) 19
(Joanne Foster) *cl up: wnt 2nd 13th: outpcd whn blnd 3 out: t.o* **8/1**

2-32 **P** **Reckless Venture (IRE)**[8] 1663 9-11-3 89..............(t) CampbellGillies(3) —
(Lucinda Russell) *cl up: hit 7th: outpcd whn mstke 14th: rallied bef 3 out: sn chsng clr ldrs: wknd after next: p.u bef last* **7/4**[1]

343 **P** **Adrianeo (IRE)**[49] 1341 7-11-5 95...............................(p) MrBGCrawford(7) —
(S R B Crawford, Ire) *hld up in tch: struggling 13th: t.o whn p.u bef 4 out* **11/2**

6m 39.5s (7.30) **Going Correction** +0.475s/f (Soft) **6** Ran SP% **113.6**
Speed ratings (Par 103): **107,103,100,84,— —**
toteswingers:1&2:£2.00, 1&3:£11.90, 2&3:£3.00 CSF £21.04 TOTE £5.00: £2.30, £2.10; EX 31.70.
Owner Hamilton House Limited **Bred** Mrs Brenda Cunningham **Trained** Rosewell, Midlothian
■ Stewards' Enquiry : Wilson Renwick caution: careless riding

FOCUS
A weak contest, rated through ther winner to his best.

NOTEBOOK
Sierra Victor(IRE) was still searching for his first win under rules coming into this race, but he travelled smoothly for most of the race before going on at the right time. He wasn't hard pressed to maintain his advantage and won cosily. (op 4-1)
Murphys Beau(IRE), running from out of the handicap, was allowed an easy lead and plugged on quite well once joined and passed. (op 9-2)
Benbeoch won a novice hunter chase in May before being beaten in an open contest over the same C&D a couple of weeks later. Off since, he got outpaced early and never got back into the race with a winning chance. (op 8-1)
Dougall(IRE) attracted some market support and got close up going well before going backwards quickly. (op 11-1 tchd 15-2)
Reckless Venture(IRE) is a consistent sort but had not got his head in front since a couple of successes in March 2008. He looked unhappy for some reason quite a way out, possibly due to mistakes, and was most disappointing. Official explanation: jockey said the gelding was never travelling and hung left handed throughout (op 5-2)
Adrianeo(IRE) showed his most solid piece of form last time when tried in a handicap (also cheekpieces fitted for the first time) but was beaten early in this. (op 5-2)

1785 METROCENTRE ALWAYS A SAFE BET INTERMEDIATE NATIONAL HUNT FLAT RACE (CONDITIONALS/AMATEURS) 2m 110y
5:30 (5:30) (Class 5) 4-6-Y-O **£1,644** (£479; £239)

Form RPR

1 **Cool Vic (IRE)**[160] 6-10-11 0.. MrJARichardson(7) 103
(David Carr) *in tch: hdwy 3f out: styd on to ld wl ins fnl f: r.o* **10/1**

2 *nk* **Dunowen Point (IRE)**[195] 4-11-1 0................................ JohnKington(3) 102+
(Donald McCain) *t.k.h: trckd ldrs: rdn to ld over 1f out: hdd wl ins fnl f: r.o* **4/5**[1]

22-5 **3** *2 ¼* **River Dragon (IRE)**[13] 1629 5-10-13 0......................... JamesHalliday(5) 100
(Malcolm Jefferson) *led: rdn and hdd over 1f out: kpt on same pce last 100yds* **5/1**[3]

3- **4** *14* **Lady Counsellor**[241] 3980 4-10-8 0............................ RichardKilloran(3) 79
(Alan Swinbank) *in tch: rdn and outpcd 4f out: no imp over 2f out* **4/1**[2]

5 *9* **Gun And More** 5-10-13 0... ShaneByrne(5) 77
(Sue Smith) *w ldr tl rdn and outpcd over 3f out: sn n.d* **22/1**

6 *13* **Katie's Prince (IRE)**[209] 6-10-13 0................................. MissLHorner(5) 64
(Chris Grant) *trckd ldrs: drvn and outpcd 5f out: sn btn* **16/1**

7 *5* **Highland Cathedral**[146] 6-10-11 0................................ MissCWalton(7) 59
(James Walton) *bhd: struggling over 5f out: sn btn* **100/1**

8 *4* **Adin Abroad (IRE)** 5-10-8 0... HarryHaynes(3) 48
(John Wainwright) *towards rr: struggling over 4f out: sn btn* **66/1**

9 *99* **Phar Beyond** 5-10-4 0.......................................(t) MissAngelaBarnes(7) —
(Maurice Barnes) *t.k.h: hld up: rdn over 6f out: sn struggling: virtually p.u last 2f* **66/1**

4m 22.3s (9.60) **Going Correction** +0.175s/f (Yiel) **9** Ran SP% **115.5**
Speed ratings: **84,83,82,76,71 65,63,61,15**
toteswingers:1&2:£2.40, 1&3:£4.80, 2&3:£1.40 CSF £18.42 TOTE £10.00: £3.10, £1.10, £1.80; EX 24.50 Place 6 £62.94, Place 5 £33.08.
Owner David Carr **Bred** J J Fisher **Trained** Hexham, Northumberland
■ Stewards' Enquiry : Mr J A Richardson one-day ban: use of whip (TBA)

FOCUS
Probably only a fair bumper, but the first three pulled nicely clear. The form is rated through the third and fourth.

NOTEBOOK
Cool Vic(IRE), a half-brother to a couple of winners, most notably Were In Touch, was runner-up in a point at Mosshouses in May and proved just the stronger in a tight finish. It was a good ride by his 7lb claiming rider, and stamina is clearly not a problem for the horse. (op 14-1)
Dunowen Point(IRE) didn't complete in his only outing in a point but was still thereabouts when unseating at penultimate fence. New connections paid 75,000gns to secure his services two weeks later and he possibly lost out here after taking a strong hold for almost the whole race. It might be that he heads for a flatter track next time. (op 5-6 tchd 8-11)
River Dragon(IRE), having his first start away from Market Rasen, helped to lead and kept on after being challenged. (op 6-1 tchd 9-2)
Lady Counsellor, a sister to Turbo Linn, a very smart bumper winner who went on to land the Lancashire Oaks, seemed to be disappointing on her first start when beaten at 8/11 in a Fibresand bumper, although the horse that finished in front of her there has gone on to win two of her three subsequent races. She lost ground quite easily here but made some late headway. (op 7-2 tchd 9-2)
Gun And More, whose stable won this the previous year, was prominent for a long way before weakening. (op 20-1)
T/Plt: £349.00 to a £1 stake. Pool of £41,001.37 - 85.76 winning tickets T/Qpdt: £75.70 to a £1 stake. Pool of £3,450.90 - 33.70 winning tickets RY

1786 - 1792a (Foreign Racing) - See Raceform Interactive

1389 FFOS LAS (L-H)
Sunday, October 10

OFFICIAL GOING: Good (good to firm in places) changing to good to firm (good in places) after race 2 (2:45)
Wind: modest, across Weather: bright and sunny

1793 CRABBIES ALCOHOLIC GINGER BEER MARES' "NATIONAL HUNT" MAIDEN HURDLE (8 hdls) 2m
2:10 (2:10) (Class 4) 4-Y-0+ **£2,927** (£859; £429; £214)

Form RPR

1 **Ixora (IRE)**[64] 1210 4-10-12 0.. TomO'Brien 101+
(Jamie Snowden) *wandering at sme hurdles: chsd ldrs: lft 3rd 2nd: pressed ldr next: led 4th: mde rest: clr bef 3 out: styd on wl flat: rdn out* **9/4**[2]

3 **2** *4 ½* **Clarach (IRE)**[12] 1643 5-10-12 108............................. RichardJohnson 98+
(Tim Vaughan) *t.k.h: hld up in rr: hdwy to chse ldng pair 3 out: rdn to chse wnr next: stmbld last: kpt on same pce and no imp flat* **2/1**[1]

3 *5* **Cailin Ceol (IRE)**[24] 1536 5-10-12 0...............................(t) DenisO'Regan 92
(Michael C Griffin, Ire) *hld up in last pair: hmpd 2nd: hdwy on inner after 5th: rdn and outpcd 3 out: styd on same pce after: wnt 3rd after last* **33/1**

56-1 **4** *3 ½* **Dipity Doo Dah**[14] 1629 6-10-5 0................................ MichaelByrne(7) 88
(Peter Bowen) *j. novicey: in tch: rdn wl bef 3 out: outpcd and no threat to ldrs fr 3 out* **4/1**[3]

010- **5** *6* **Reinriver**[184] 5114 4-10-12 0.. AidanColeman 83
(Brendan Powell) *t.k.h: chsd ldrs: lft 2nd at 2nd tl next: chsd wnr 3 out tl next: sn wknd* **16/1**

3235 **6** *5* **Salford Rose (IRE)**[16] 1603 4-10-9 0.......................... LeeStephens(3) 80
(David Evans) *plld hrd: wandering at hurdles: lft in ld and hmpd 2nd: hdd 4th: chsd wnr after tl lost 2nd and hit 3 out: sn wknd* **7/1**

6-40 **F** **My Viking Bay (IRE)**[80] 1069 6-10-5 0......................... CharlieWallis(7) —
(John O'Shea) *led tl j.lft and fell 2nd* **33/1**

3m 47.1s (-1.90) **Going Correction** -0.725s/f (Firm) **7** Ran SP% **108.4**
Speed ratings (Par 105): **88,85,83,81,78 76,—**
toteswingers:1&2:£1.10, 1&3:£13.80, 2&3:£7.80 CSF £6.63 TOTE £4.20: £2.90, £1.10; EX 5.80.
Owner J E Snowden **Bred** John Harvey **Trained** Ebbesbourne Wake, Wilts
■ Bachley Gale was withdrawn on vet's advice at start (14/1, deduct 5p in the £ under R4).

FOCUS
This looked a competitive race for its type in the morning, but after a couple of fancied horses were declared non-runners and another was withdrawn at the start, it may not have taken a lot of winning.

NOTEBOOK
Ixora(IRE), making her debut for Jamie Snowden after running five times in Ireland, had plenty of fair form over hurdles and took this under an intelligent ride by Tom O'Brien, who kicked on at the right time and gained a healthy advantage. She was still a little green at some stages, so should have more to come. Her dam certainly knew where the winning post was, as she collected ten wins, mainly for Martin Pipe. (op 5-2)
Clarach(IRE), dropping in distance after seemingly running below market expectations on her first outing for Tim Vaughan after leaving Ireland, settled in behind from the start and was making steady ground on Ixora when jumping untidily at the final flight. It probably didn't cost her a win but it certainly came at the wrong time. (tchd 15-8 and 9-4)
Cailin Ceol(IRE) continues to be well held and never had a chance of making a big impact in the outcome.
Dipity Doo Dah, who won on her first start for Peter Bowen after a 400-day layoff in a Market Rasen bumper, looked interesting on her hurdling debut but probably wasn't helped by a lack of pace, as she needed pushing along leaving the back straight while her rivals were travelling fairly well. (op 7-2)
Reinriver, absent since April, made a promising move at the top of the home straight but got tired. (op 14-1)

Salford Rose(IRE) takes a strong hold and will have trouble winning something until she races more kindly. (op 10-1)

1794 E.P.S. LTD NOVICES' CHASE (17 fncs) 2m 5f
2:45 (2:45) (Class 4) 4-Y-0+ **£3,252** (£955; £477; £238)

Form RPR
-U11 **1** **Cappagh (IRE)**[18] 1575 5-11-4 115 RichardJohnson 124+
(Philip Hobbs) *hld up in last pair: mstke 10th: hdwy and blnd 13th: rdn to join ldr and lft in ld 2 out: clr last: r.o wl flat* **15/8**[1]
453- **2** *3 1/4* **Sonny Mullen (IRE)**[190] 4991 6-11-1 115 SeanQuinlan(3) 119+
(Kim Bailey) *chsd ldrs: mstke 7th: lft 2nd bef 9th: led 10th: j.rt 3 out: jnd whn pckd and hdd next: no ex and btn last* **5/2**[2]
22P- **3** *4* **Prince Du Beury (FR)**[228] 4233 7-11-4 114 AndrewTinkler 114
(Nicky Henderson) *chsd ldrs: lft 3rd bef 9th: chsd ldr 10th: ev ch and rdn bef 3 out: wknd between last 2* **13/2**
450F **4** *12* **Agente Romano (USA)**[41] 1432 5-11-4 115 PaulMoloney 107+
(Evan Williams) *t.k.h: hld up in tch in midfield: hdwy to chse ldrs after 13th: mstke and pckd next: sn btn and wknd fr next* **6/1**[3]
32P1 **5** *10* **Chevy To The Levy (IRE)**[39] 1452 8-10-11 109 (p) CharlieWallis(7) 92
(John O'Shea) *chsd ldr tl lft in ld bef 9th: hdd 10th: rdn and wknd bef 14th* **12/1**
1060 **6** *35* **Vintage Fabric (USA)**[49] 1347 8-11-4 94 (t) DavidDennis 57
(Nigel Hawke) *nt fluent: mstke 1st: in rr fr 3rd: lost tch 14th: t.o and eased flat* **50/1**
5P20 **P** **Michigan Assassin (IRE)**[35] 1486 8-10-11 115 AodhaganConlon(7) —
(Debra Hamer) *led: blnd 6th: mstke 8th: eased: hdd and p.u bef 9th: b.b.v* **7/1**

5m 18.6s (-11.40) **Going Correction** -0.60s/f (Firm) 7 Ran SP% **113.1**
Speed ratings (Par 105): **105,103,102,97,93 80,—**
toteswingers:1&2:£2.10, 1&3:£2.90, 2&3:£2.80 CSF £7.05 TOTE £2.60: £1.10, £3.10; EX 7.30.
Owner John P McManus **Bred** Legends Stud **Trained** Withycombe, Somerset

FOCUS
A fair-looking contest that should produce a few winners.

NOTEBOOK
Cappagh(IRE) ◆, back up in trip on his attempt to land a hat-trick, has looked a tricky ride in the past but has found a knack of getting the job done. The biggest worry for his supporters this time came as he hit five out hard, but he battled his way back into contention and got to the front at the right time to win with a bit in hand, albeit in workmanlike style. (tchd 2-1)
Sonny Mullen(IRE) ◆ looked an interesting recruit to fences. Lightly raced, he hardly put a foot wrong and looks a sure-fire winner of a similar event. (op 11-4)
Prince Du Beury(FR), a modest but capable sort over hurdles, seemed to enjoy his first taste of fences but was a little one-paced in the final stages. (op 11-2 tchd 7-1)
Agente Romano(USA) had shown plenty of aptitude for chasing before falling on his chasing debut at Huntingdon, and his trainer reported before the off that the horse's schooling since that mishap had not been particularly good at home. He travelled nicely in behind and was still thereabouts when hitting four out really hard. That mistake was enough to end any chance he may have had of winning, and his jumping was awkward over the next three fences.
Chevy To The Levy(IRE) has plenty of chasing experience and finally got off the mark over fences on his previous outing with cheekpieces on for the first time. Down in distance for this, he was beaten off at a relatively early stage after racing prominently. (op 11-1)
Michigan Assassin(IRE) was in front when pulled up heading out on the final circuit. It turned out he burst a blood vessel. Official explanation: vet said that the gelding had bled from the nose (op 9-1)

1795 DRIVESHAFT SERVICES "NATIONAL HUNT" MAIDEN HURDLE (10 hdls) 2m 4f
3:20 (3:20) (Class 4) 4-Y-0+ **£2,998** (£931; £501)

Form RPR
24- **1** **Silver Token**[217] 4461 5-10-7 118 MattGriffiths(7) 108+
(David Brace) *nt a fluent: t.k.h: chsd ldrs: mstke and reminders after 6th: led gng best after next: rdn clr bef 3 out: wl clr and mstke 2 out: stdd into last: drvn and kpt on flat* **2/1**[1]
3212 **2** *3 3/4* **Jump Up**[49] 1344 4-11-0 0 RhysFlint 100
(Keith Goldsworthy) *led: nt fluent 2nd: rdn and hdd after 7th: sn outpcd by wnr: wl btn after next: rallied u.p last: no imp fnl 100yds* **2/1**[1]
210P **3** *38* **Call Me Bill (IRE)**[7] 1703 4-10-11 0 DonalDevereux(3) 74
(Peter Bowen) *t.k.h: chsd ldr: ev ch and rdn after 7th: sn struggling: 3rd and wl btn next: t.o bef last* **7/1**[3]
2413 **F** **Whereveryougoigo (IRE)**[36] 1472 4-11-0 0 TomO'Brien —
(Peter Bowen) *hld up in tch tl j. awkwardly and fell 3rd* **9/4**[2]

4m 46.6s (-2.40) **Going Correction** -0.725s/f (Firm) 4 Ran SP% **109.9**
Speed ratings (Par 105): **81,79,64,—**
CSF £6.49 TOTE £3.80; EX 7.70.
Owner David Brace **Bred** David Brace **Trained** Pyle, Bridgend

FOCUS
With the ground getting quicker and the official going changed after the previous contest to good to firm, good in places, this decent-looking maiden cut up when promising Bens Moor, expensive purchase Mediolanum and Rash Call were all taken out. Littledean Jimmy also didn't line up, so it was disappointing field of four that faced the starter. The gallop was predictably slow.

NOTEBOOK
Silver Token, off since March, needed to be pushed along first, but once he got to the lead, there was little danger of him losing. His jumping wasn't always perfect and can get better. (op 9-4 tchd 5-2 and 15-8)
Jump Up was allowed to lead but came under strong pressure rounding the home bend. He looked like being well held at one stage, but rallied to some extent and made some late ground on the winner. (tchd 9-4)
Call Me Bill(IRE), disappointing on both his previous tries over hurdles, once again made no meaningful impression. (op 9-2)
Whereveryougoigo(IRE), beaten in a Stratford bumper when last seen at odds of 8-11, departed at the third after appearing to twist slightly in the air and crumple on landing. (op 2-1tchd 5-2 in a place)

1796 TRUSTMARK STATIONERY STORES NOVICES' CHASE (13 fncs) 2m
3:55 (3:56) (Class 4) 4-Y-0+ **£3,998** (£1,241; £668)

Form RPR
P-12 **1** **Mam Ratagan**[19] 1568 9-11-7 120 PeterToole(3) 129+
(Heather Main) *mde all: blnd 1st: drew clr 10th: wl in command whn blnd 2 out: eased after last* **3/1**[2]
3233 **2** *10* **Quedillac (FR)**[17] 1587 6-10-10 103 MrTomDavid(7) 108
(Tim Vaughan) *racd in last pair: mstke 1st and 2nd: clsd and lft 3rd 5th: mstke 7th: rdn and btn after 9th: wnt 2nd but no ch w wnr 3 out* **13/2**
61-0 **3** *25* **National Trust**[117] 756 8-11-3 0 PaddyBrennan 97+
(Nigel Twiston-Davies) *racd in last pair: blnd 2nd: clsd and lft 2nd 5th: mstke 7th: rdn and btn 10th: no ch whn mstke and dropped to last 3 out: j.lft last 2: eased after last* **11/10**[1]
1522 **F** **Blacktoft (USA)**[35] 1485 7-11-10 128 PaulMoloney —
(Evan Williams) *t.k.h: chsd ldr tl fell 5th* **10/3**[3]

3m 56.0s (-9.00) **Going Correction** -0.60s/f (Firm) 4 Ran SP% **109.0**
Speed ratings (Par 105): **98,93,80,—**
CSF £17.61 TOTE £4.10; EX 16.20.
Owner Highnote Thoroughbreds **Bred** Cyril Humphris **Trained** Kingston Lisle, Oxon

FOCUS
The form of this contest is unlikely to be that informative because it was riddled with some bad jumping.

NOTEBOOK
Mam Ratagan, down in trip, hit the first quite hard after getting the lead but stayed upright That error seemed to settle him down, as he still enjoyed himself in front and fought off any rival that got close to him. (op 4-1)
Quedillac(FR), out the back early and 17lb inferior to the winner on official ratings, never promised to make the winner work for success once getting into a challenging position. (op 6-1 tchd 9-2)
National Trust a mainly useful hurdler for a few different trainers since being purchased from top connections on the Flat, hardly took off at the second fence and forfeited a lot of ground. He got back into contention but then hit another fence hard in the back straight and had no chance of making a big impact when considering those errors. (op 6-4 tchd 13-8)
Blacktoft(USA) raced keenly behind Mam Ratagan, the pair clear of the other two early, but dived at the first down the back straight and came down. (op 2-1 tchd 15-8)

1797 SAXTON DRILLING H'CAP HURDLE (8 hdls) 2m
4:30 (4:30) (Class 2) (0-145,137) 4-Y-0+ **£7,604** (£2,246; £1,123; £561; £280)

Form RPR
2F-P **1** **Black Jack Blues (IRE)**[155] 207 7-11-5 137 (t) AodhaganConlon(7) 151+
(Rebecca Curtis) *mde virtually all: j.w: rdn clr bef 3 out: in n.d fr 3 out: eased flat: easily* **11/2**[3]
4652 **2** *9* **Exulto (IRE)**[19] 1569 5-10-4 115 RichardJohnson 115
(Philip Hobbs) *in tch: hdwy to chse clr ldr bef 3 out: rdn and no imp after next: drvn and kpt on same pce between last 2* **7/2**[2]
6122 **3** *1 3/4* **Rio Gael (IRE)**[41] 1426 4-10-6 117 TomO'Brien 117
(Peter Bowen) *chsd ldrs: wnt 2nd bef 5th tl rdn and outpcd by wnr bef 3 out: 3rd and no ch w wnr whn j.lft 2 out: kpt on same pce u.p flat* **6/1**
0205 **4** *1/2* **Gloucester**[51] 1311 7-11-6 131 TomScudamore 129
(Michael Scudamore) *hld up in tch in last trio: hdwy bef 3 out: rdn and no imp on wnr bef 2 out: styd on same pce after* **11/2**[3]
2360 **5** *shd* **Dishdasha (IRE)**[15] 1609 8-10-11 129 (t) OliverDayman(7) 126
(Alison Thorpe) *in tch in midfield: rdn after 5th: no prog u.p fr next* **16/1**
56P1 **6** *2 1/2* **Bolton Hall (IRE)**[46] 1370 8-10-6 117 (bt) RhysFlint 112
(Keith Goldsworthy) *chsd wnr: reminders after 4th: lost 2nd bef next: bhd and wl btn fr 3 out* **16/1**
1116 **7** *5* **Points Of View**[15] 1609 5-11-3 131 (t) SeanQuinlan(3) 124
(Kim Bailey) *t.k.h: hld up in tch in last trio: rdn and effrt bef 3 out: no prog and wl btn whn j.lft and hit last* **11/4**[1]
4-50 **8** *13* **Enlightenment (IRE)**[15] 1611 10-10-8 119 PaulMoloney 96
(Evan Williams) *t.k.h: hld up in tch in last trio: rdn and dropped to last whn mstke 5th: lost tch next: j.lft last 2* **9/1**

3m 38.8s (-10.20) **Going Correction** -0.725s/f (Firm)
WFA 4 from 5yo+ 9lb 8 Ran SP% **115.7**
Speed ratings (Par 109): **109,104,103,103,103 102,99,93**
toteswingers:1&2:£4.50, 1&3:£7.00, 2&3:£3.80 CSF £25.89 CT £119.78 TOTE £6.80: £3.00, £1.10, £2.60; EX 40.10.
Owner Peter Neary **Bred** B J Griffiths **Trained** Newport, Dyfed

FOCUS
A decent handicap hurdle and a well- executed ride by the winning jockey.

NOTEBOOK
Black Jack Blues(IRE)' rider quickened things up heading into the home bend and went so far clear that the pair were never going to get caught. It would be amazing if he was allowed to get away with those sort of tactics again on Black Jack Blues, and the Greatwood Hurdle is being considered as a future target. Official explanation: trainer said, regarding the apparent improvement of form, his best races when fresh and had benefited from today's drop in class (tchd 6-1)
Exulto(IRE) didn't always have much room in the pack but proved to be one-paced under pressure. (op 4-1)
Rio Gael(IRE) jumped exuberantly at some hurdles while racing prominently in the chasing pack, but made little impression down the home straight. (op 15-2)
Gloucester ran his usual sort of race, travelling strongly before not producing as much as looked likely. (op 5-1)
Points Of View, who looked to be sweating, was keen in the rear and failed to get competitive. It looks as though the handicapper might have his measure. (op 7-2 tchd 5-2)

1798 LINDLEY CATERING CONDITIONAL JOCKEYS' H'CAP HURDLE (12 hdls) 3m
5:05 (5:05) (Class 5) (0-90,90) 4-Y-0+ **£2,276** (£668; £334; £166)

Form RPR
0452 **1** **Scotsbrook Cloud**[36] 1468 5-11-5 82 TomMolloy 106+
(David Evans) *hld up wl in tch: mstke 6th: trckd ldrs gng wl after 9th: led next: sn clr: comf* **3/1**[1]
6062 **2** *12* **Calypso Bay (IRE)**[21] 1559 4-11-8 89 RichieMcLernon(3) 99+
(Jonjo O'Neill) *in tch in midfield: hmpd 2nd: lft chsng ldrs 9th: outpcd by wnr next: rdn and chsd clr wnr whn nt fluent 2 out: no imp and wl hld after* **4/1**[2]
62-2 **3** *10* **Brave Bugsy (IRE)**[41] 1434 7-11-6 83 GemmaGracey-Davison 82
(Graham Smith) *led tl 3rd: chsd clr ldr after: rdn along after 6th: clsng on ldr whn lft in ld 9th: hdd next: sn no ch w wnr: 3rd and wl btn fr 2 out* **5/1**[3]
-030 **4** *25* **Flag Flier**[95] 930 7-10-8 79 NathanSweeney(8) 58
(Bob Buckler) *in tch: mstke 1st: rdn 8th: lft handy next: wknd u.p next: t.o* **12/1**
6633 **5** *16* **Saddlewood (IRE)**[7] 1694 7-11-8 85 (tp) DavidBass 43
(Jamie Snowden) *chsd ldrs: lft 3rd 9th: sn fdd u.p: t.o bef 2 out* **11/2**
U00 **6** *nse* **Abulharith**[17] 1451 4-11-5 83 (p) JohnKington 40
(Michael Scudamore) *hld up in tch: hdwy to chse ldrs 8th: lft handy next: rdn and wknd bef next: fin tired: t.o* **33/1**
7 *75* **Paradise Ally (IRE)**[379] 1544 8-11-7 89 (t) PeterCarberry(5) —
(P Budds, Ire) *in tch tl dropped to rr and rdn 8th: sn lost tch: wl t.o bef 3 out* **25/1**
-2P0 **P** **Treasury Counsel (IRE)**[21] 1551 8-11-6 86 (p) DPFahy(3) —
(Evan Williams) *in tch in rr: hmpd 2nd: mstke and reminders 4th: rdn and struggling after 6th: wl t.o after 9th tl p.u 2 out* **10/1**
310- **P** **Lucky Pearl**[343] 2020 9-11-1 84 MrTomDavid(6) —
(Tim Vaughan) *chsd ldrs tl eased and p.u 2nd: dismntd* **7/1**

501P R Stafford Charlie[21] 1559 4-11-6 90............................(b[1]) CharlieWallis(6) —
(John O'Shea) *t.k.h: hld up in tch in rr tl hdwy to ld 3rd: clr next: mstke 7th: nt fluent next: reduced ld whn rn out 9th* **16/1**

5m 51.1s (4.10) **Going Correction** -0.725s/f (Firm)
WFA 4 from 5yo+ 11lb **10** Ran SP% **119.0**
Speed ratings (Par 103): **100,96,92,84,79 78,53,—,—,—**
toteswingers:1&2:£4.30, 1&3:£6.70, 2&3:£2.30 CSF £16.22 CT £58.94 TOTE £3.80: £1.70, £1.50, £2.20; EX 19.80.
Owner Walters Plant Hire Ltd **Bred** A E And P E Price **Trained** Pandy, Monmouths

FOCUS
A modest conditional jockeys' hurdle.

NOTEBOOK
Scotsbrook Cloud was well supported on his debut for David Evans, and those who supported him rarely had a moment's worry once he surged to the front, although on occasions he needed a bit of rousting along. A half-brother to the promising Lamb's Cross, this was a shrewd bit of business by his trainer after buying him out of a seller last time having not won a race. (op 11-4)
Calypso Bay(IRE), whose best effort for these connections came last time when stepped up to 3m, bumped into a horse a mile in front of the handicapper and had no chance of beating him. (tchd 3-1)
Brave Bugsy(IRE), making his debut for this trainer, inherited the lead when Stafford Charlie ran out, but he never really threatened to prove successful. (op 6-1)
Flag Flier shaped with some promise on her return to action and can find a small handicap. (op 14-1)
Lucky Pearl Official explanation: jockey said mare had been struck into (op 20-1)
Stafford Charlie, who had beaten Scotsbrook Cloud by nine lengths in the seller David Evans purchased him from, was in front and still going reasonably well when running out at the ninth. (op 20-1)

1799 DIGIBET.COM MAIDEN OPEN NATIONAL HUNT FLAT RACE 2m
5:40 (5:40) (Class 5) 4-6-Y-O **£1,712** (£499; £249)

Form RPR
22 **1** **Youralltalk (IRE)**[3] 1748 6-10-7 0.............................. PeterCarberry(7) 107+
(Keith Goldsworthy) *mde all: rdn along over 4f out: wandered u.p 2f out: hrd pressed 1f out: kpt on wl fnl 100yds* **5/4**[1]
2 1 ½ **Charles** 4-10-9 0.............................. JimmyDerham(5) 105
(Seamus Mullins) *hld up in tch in last pair: hdwy 4f out: rdn to chse wnr over 1f out: ev ch 1f out: no ex and btn fnl 100yds* **5/1**[3]
4-4 **3** 11 **Sothisisit (FR)**[144] 412 4-10-11 0..........................(t) RichieMcLernon(3) 94
(Jonjo O'Neill) *t.k.h: chsd ldrs: wnt 2nd 6f out: rdn and fnd little over 2f out: 3rd and wl btn over 1f out* **7/1**
0-42 **4** 5 **Pontyates**[14] 1629 5-10-11 0.............................. DonalDevereux(3) 89
(Peter Bowen) *chsd wnr: racing awkwardly and rdn 6f out: wknd 3f out* **3/1**[2]
5 4 ½ **Redbridge Flyer (IRE)**[210] 6-11-0 0.............................. HarrySkelton 85
(Nick Mitchell) *t.k.h: hld up in tch in last: rdn and btn 3f out* **8/1**

3m 37.2s (-6.20) **Going Correction** -0.725s/f (Firm) **5** Ran SP% **109.7**
Speed ratings: **99,98,92,90,88**
toteswingers:1&2:£10.50, 1&3:£8.20, 2&3:£5.30. totesuper7: Win: Not won. Place: £268.30. CSF £7.79 TOTE £2.10: £1.10, £2.70; EX 9.40 Place 6 £59.28; Place 5 £43.46.
Owner M Duthie **Bred** Mrs Tessa Gunn **Trained** Yerbeston, Pembrokes

FOCUS
An ordinary bumper.

NOTEBOOK
Youralltalk(IRE) was made to work hard by the runner-up for success, but a combination of experience and getting a bit of weight possibly told late on. Peter Carberry once again looked great value for his 7lb claim. (op 6-4 tchd 6-5)
Charles had no runs behind him at all, so one would expect him to reverse form with the winner if they met again. He moved well early on and looked sure to win before Youralltalk rallied. If he can build on this, he should be competitive in similar events. (op 7-1 tchd 15-2)
Sothisisit(FR) impressed when he was chasing the winner but found disappointingly little when asked to quicken. (op 9-2)
Pontyates was in trouble down the back straight and regressed to the sort of form he showed in his two starts. (op 11-4)
Redbridge Flyer(IRE), who changed hands for £8,000 after two starts in Irish points, was keen in rear and may have needed this after a long break. (op 15-2)
T/Plt: £442.00 to a £1 stake. Pool of £64,923.70 - 107.21 winning tickets T/Qpdt: £69.30 to a £1 stake. Pool of £5,090.66 - 54.30 winning tickets SP

1800 - (Foreign Racing) - See Raceform Interactive

1072 LIMERICK (R-H)
Sunday, October 10

OFFICIAL GOING: Good

1801a PRICEWATERHOUSECOOPERS CHASE (GRADE 3) (11 fncs) 2m 1f
3:00 (3:00) 4-Y-0+ **£18,119** (£5,296; £2,508; £836)

RPR
1 **Cornas (NZ)**[173] 5302 8-11-5.............................. DarylJacob 144+
(Nick Williams) *trckd ldr: 3rd 1/2-way: impr to ld appr 2 out: rdn to assert bef last: kpt on wl* **11/8**[2]
2 3 **Cruising Katie (IRE)**[43] 1408 8-10-9 123.............................. PFMangan 131
(R A Cotter, Ire) *chsd ldr: 2nd 1/2-way: impr to ld bef st: rdn and hdd appr 2 out: no ex in 2nd bef last: kpt on same pce* **8/1**[3]
3 1 ¼ **Salesin**[13] 1637 7-10-10..............................(p) NPMadden 131
(Niall Madden, Ire) *hld up in rr: slt mstke 5th: rdn in rr 3 out: styd on into 3rd and slt peck 2 out: no ex bef last: kpt on same pce* **16/1**
4 9 **Nicanor (FR)**[15] 1619 9-11-1 134.............................. DJCondon 127
(Noel Meade, Ire) *hld up in 4th: mstke 4th: slow 5 out: rdn 3 out: no imp in 4th 2 out: kpt on one pce* **10/1**
5 dist **Let Yourself Go (IRE)**[171] 5350 8-11-8 150.............................. PCarberry —
(Adrian Maguire, Ire) *led: mstke 6th: rdn and hdd bef st: no ex and wknd appr 2 out: t.o* **5/4**[1]

4m 4.80s (244.80) **5** Ran SP% **112.6**
CSF £11.89 TOTE £2.20: £1.40, £2.10; DF 10.10.
Owner The Gascoigne Brookes Partnership Iii **Bred** D P And Mrs K C Fleming **Trained** George Nympton, Devon

FOCUS
The winner did not need to repeat his best chase form.

NOTEBOOK
Cornas(NZ), a faller five out when favourite for this race a year ago, made amends on his first start since finishing fifth in a Grade 1 event at the Punchestown festival in April. Best in at the weights on official figures, this was his third win over fences and after being close up throughout, he went to the front before two out and kept on well. (op 5/4 tchd 11/10)
Cruising Katie(IRE), both of whose chase wins were recorded over 2m4f at this track, was close up all the way and landed disputing the lead at the sixth fence. Ridden in second after three out, she kept on without being able to trouble the winner from the final fence. (op 10/1)
Salesin, a dual winner on the Flat and over hurdles, had won a beginners' chase over this trip at Wexford. Held up in rear, he was slow over the fifth fence and remained out the back until going third before two out. He nodded slightly on landing over that fence and kept on without finding a lot. (op 12/1)
Nicanor(FR), a first-fence faller at Navan on his previous start, was back in distance here over a trip short of his best. He fluffed the fourth fence and was slow five out before making some headway under pressure after three out. However, he was unable to make any impression from two out. (op 8/1)
Let Yourself Go(IRE), whose four wins over fences included this event a year ago when he made all the running, was making his first appearance since running second to Captain Cee Bee in a Grade 1 novice at the Punchestown festival in April. A confirmed front-runner, he was soon clear but he took a chance with the sixth fence and that seemed to unsettle him. He dropped away tamely when headed well before two out. Official explanation: jockey said gelding made a bad mistake in the back straight in this race and never travelled thereafter (op 6/4 tchd 13/8)

PARDUBICE (L-H)
Sunday, October 10

OFFICIAL GOING: Turf: good

1811a VELKA PARDUBICKA CESKE POJISTOVNY (CROSS-COUNTRY CHASE) (6YO+) (TURF) 4m 2f 110y
2:25 (12:00) 6-Y-0+
£60,463 (£33,254; £21,162; £15,115; £10,581; £6,046)

RPR
1 **Tiumen (POL)**[364] 1732 9-10-10 0.............................. JVanaJr 143
(Josef Vana II, Czech Republic) **5/2**[1]
2 nse **Amant Gris (FR)**[728] 1695 11-10-10 0.............................. MStromsky 143
(R Holcak, Czech Republic) **5/1**[3]
3 3 ¼ **Sixteen (FR)**[364] 1732 10-10-6 0.............................. JosefBartos 136
(Josef Vana II, Czech Republic) **13/4**[2]
4 2 ¼ **Mandarino (CZE)**[364] 1732 9-10-10 0.............................. JMyska 137
(S Popelka Jr, Czech Republic) **31/4**
5 3 ¾ **Teviot (CZE)** 7-10-10 0.............................. LUrbanek 134
(Jiri Janda, Czech Republic) **44/1**
6 ¾ **Lirain (CZE)**[331] 2256 9-10-10 0.............................. JVanaIII 133
(Josef Vana II, Czech Republic) **10/1**
7 dist **Aspirant (POL)** 7-10-10 0.............................. JanFaltejsek —
(F Holcak, Czech Republic) **11/1**
8 4 ¼ **Kobuz (POL)** 8-10-10 0.............................. LSimunek —
(Josef Vana II, Czech Republic) **77/1**
9 nk **Lakreg (CZE)**[364] 1732 10-10-10 0.............................. MLiska —
(Jana Minarikova, Czech Republic) **100/1**
10 3 ¼ **Juventus (POL)**[695] 2192 11-10-10 0.............................. JKorpas —
(Josef Vana II, Czech Republic) **20/1**
11 17 **Bejrut (POL)**[1975] 9-10-10 0.............................. PKasny —
(Jiri Janda, Czech Republic) **50/1**
12 16 **Mr Big (IRE)**[19] 1570 9-10-10 0.............................. NoelFehily —
(Charlie Mann) *trckd ldrs (disputing 7th) early: sn settled in midfield jumping wl: towards rr 13th (of 32): slt mstke 15th: mstke 19th (water): last fr 21st: t.o: fin w only two shoes* **16/1**
P **Il En Reve (FR)**[21] 12-10-12 0 ow2.............................. PavelSlozil —
(Milan Theimer, Czech Republic) **150/1**
P **Jung (POL)**[364] 1732 10-10-10 0.............................. BMatl —
(Pavlina Bastova, Czech Republic) **77/1**
F **Ligreta (CZE)** 10-10-6 0.............................. LucieBaluchova —
(V Hrbacek, Czech Republic) **120/1**
U **Valldemoso (CZE)** 6-10-10 0.............................. DusanAndres —
(J Uhl, Czech Republic) **14/1**
U **Bremen Plan (POL)**[393] 7-10-10 0.............................. JKousek —
(R Holcak, Czech Republic) **6/1**
U **Teresina (GER)** 8-10-6 0.............................. MNovak —
(F Zobal, Czech Republic) **100/1**
U **Rubin (CZE)** 8-10-10 0.............................. MartinaRuzickova —
(Martina Ruzickova, Czech Republic) **77/1**

9m 3.73s (543.73) **19** Ran SP% **140.7**
.
Owner Koi Dent **Bred** Moszna Stud **Trained** Czech Republic

NOTEBOOK
Tiumen(POL), last year's winner, survived an enquiry to give the legendary Josef Vana his seventh Pardubicka as a jockey and eighth as a trainer.
Amant Gris(FR), an unlucky runner-up, had been disqualified when first past the post two years ago.
Mr Big(IRE), who dropped his hind legs in the water jump, found things happening too quickly for him and was never really in the race.

1688 HUNTINGDON (R-H)
Tuesday, October 12

OFFICIAL GOING: Good (8.2)
Wind: Virtually nil Weather: bright and sunny

1812 TURFTV NOVICES' HURDLE (10 hdls) 2m 4f 110y
2:20 (2:25) (Class 4) 4-Y-0+ **£2,602** (£764; £382; £190)

Form RPR
53- **1** **Iceman George**[6] 5045 6-10-5 0..............................(p) MrJMQuinlan(7) 113+
(Giles Bravery) *hld up in tch in midfield: hdwy bef 3 out: rdn to chse ldr 2 out: swtchd rt between last 2: mstke last: qcknd u.p to ld flat: r.o wl* **5/1**[3]
0-54 **2** 1 ½ **Keep Talking (IRE)**[9] 1689 6-10-9 0.............................. AlexMerriam(3) 110
(Neil King) *hld up in tch in rr: hdwy into midfield 7th: led jst bef 2 out: clr w wnr last: rdn flat: hdd and one pce fnl 150yds* **20/1**
13 **3** 7 **Sircozy (IRE)**[9] 1689 4-11-5 0..............................(p) JamieMoore 112
(Gary Moore) *hld up in tch in rr: hdwy bef 3 out: nt clr run on inner bnd bef 2 out: sn swtchd lft and rdn to chse ldng pair 2 out: hung rt and no imp between last 2* **5/1**[3]
4 8 **See You Jack**[199] 5-10-12 0.............................. AndrewThornton 97
(Caroline Bailey) *t.k.h: chsd ldr tl 2nd: styd handy tl rdn and wknd 2 out* **40/1**
04U6 **5** 3 ½ **Martin Scruff (IRE)**[9] 1688 4-10-12 0.............................. MattieBatchelor 94
(Michael Quinlan) *hld up in tch in rr: hdwy bef 7th: sltly outpcd 3 out: kpt on steadily fr next* **40/1**

PU1- **6** 1 ½ **Polmar (FR)**174 5324 7-10-12 0 DarylJacob 92
(Jamie Snowden) *led tl rdn and hdd 2 out: sn wknd* **9/2**2

022- **7** 1 ¼ **Teenage Kicks (IRE)**170 8 5-10-5 106 MissGAndrews(7) 91
(Pam Sly) *chsd ldrs: wnt 2nd bef 6th: pressed ldr 3 out: rdn and wknd next* **7/4**1

25-1 **8** 1 ½ **Ben Cee Pee M (IRE)**155 254 5-10-12 0 LeightonAspell 92+
(Oliver Sherwood) *t.k.h: chsd ldrs: blnd bdly 2nd: rdn and wknd qckly bef 2 out* **8/1**

0/ **9** 31 **Peintre Du Roi (USA)**655 2937 6-10-12 0 JamesDavies 62
(Natalie Lloyd-Beavis) *hld up in tch: wknd qckly bef 2 out: t.o fr 2 out* **100/1**

10 nk **Body Gold (ARG)**333 7-10-12 0 PaddyBrennan 62
(Nigel Twiston-Davies) *t.k.h: j.rt: chsd ldr 2nd tl after 6th: wkng whn j. bdly rt and blnd 3 out: t.o bef last* **20/1**

00- **11** 22 **Hot Chipotle**239 4083 4-9-12 0 MrTJCannon(7) 35
(Paul Henderson) *nt a fluent: in tch towards rr tl wknd qckly 7th: t.o after next* **250/1**

0- **12** 46 **Lureyno**184 5158 4-10-12 0 JimmyMcCarthy —
(Renee Robeson) *hld up in tch in midfield: mstke 2nd: wknd qckly bef 3 out: t.o bef 2 out* **50/1**

0 **13** 9 **Fen Farm**149 362 5-10-9 0 TomMolloy(3) —
(Emma Baker) *in tch towards rr: lost tch qckly bef 7th: t.o fr next* **150/1**

0-0 **P** **The Dark Witch**156 238 6-10-0 0 MarcGoldstein(5) —
(Alan Blackmore) *in tch in rr: j. slowly 5th: sn rdn: lost tch next: wl t.o and p.u 3 out* **200/1**

P **Stawell Gift (AUS)**667 6-10-12 0 PaulMoloney —
(Nick Littmoden) *t.k.h: chsd ldrs early: dropped to rr and j.v.slowly 6th: t.o fr next: p.u 2 out* **50/1**

4m 45.7s (-13.30) **Going Correction** -0.40s/f (Good) **15 Ran SP% 119.9**
Speed ratings (Par 105): **109,108,105,102,101 100,100,99,87,87 79,61,58,—,—**
Tote Swingers:1&2:£16.30, 2&3:£20.50, 1&3:£6.00 CSF £94.81 TOTE £5.20: £2.00, £4.90, £2.60; EX 93.20.

Owner John Mangan **Bred** T J And J Wells **Trained** Cowlinge, Suffolk

FOCUS

A wide-open novices' hurdle, rated around the penalised third. Not form to get carried away with.

NOTEBOOK

Iceman George, in really good form on the Flat this year, improved markedly on his two previous efforts over hurdles, coming to hold every chance on the run to two out and eventually doing the runner-up for speed on the run-in. Whether or not he can defy a penalty, he is the type to do well in handicaps, with this new trip clearly to his liking.

Keep Talking(IRE), twice a runner-up in bumpers, was another to improve notably on his previous runs over hurdles, travelling really well before just getting done for pace on the run-in. He remains capable of better. (op 18-1)

Sircozy(IRE) came up short under a penalty at the course earlier in the month and that was the case once more, the first-time cheekpieces and a step up in trip not having enough of an effect. He didn't get the best of runs, though, so may have been a bit closer. (op 13-2 tchd 7-1)

See You Jack had won his only completed start in points. He should improve for the experience and be seen to better effect over 3m.

Martin Scruff(IRE) ran his best race to date, keeping on down the straight, and he will do better handicapping, especially over 3m.

Polmar(FR) had won a valuable handicap chase for Willie Mullins at Punchestown when last seen, yet was sold for only £10,000. He looks a resolute galloper and should improve markedly for this first run in 174 days. Races such as the Badger Ales and Beecher Chase will now come under consideration for his next outing. (tchd 5-1)

Teenage Kicks(IRE) had been running well when last seen and another good effort seemed assured, but his trainer did warn beforehand that the run would be needed and he stopped very quickly. Therefore, he should step forward considerably next time. (op 9-4)

Ben Cee Pee M(IRE) deserves another chance as he blundered badly at the second and could never really recover.

Body Gold(ARG), a Group 2 winner on the Flat when trained in Argetina, hadn't run in 333 days and was too keen. He showed enough to suggest he has a future and deserves another chance. Official explanation: jockey said gelding hung badly left (op 16-1)

Stawell Gift(AUS) Official explanation: vet said gelding finished distressed

1813 HUNTINGDON FOR ALL YOUR OUTSIDE EVENTS NOVICES' H'CAP CHASE (16 fncs) 2m 4f 110y

2:50 (2:56) (Class 4) (0-105,105) 4-Y-0+ **£3,252** (£955; £477; £238)

Form RPR

3-22 **1** **Fidelis (IRE)**152 299 6-11-9 102 NoelFehily 118+
(Ben De Haan) *hld up in rr: hmpd by loose horse after 5th: mstke next: clsd to chse ldrs 10th: wnt 2nd 13th: hit next: led and j.lft 2 out: clr last: comf: dismntd after fin* **7/1**

5405 **2** 6 **Ovthenight (IRE)**23 1556 5-11-5 105 MissGAndrews(7) 112
(Pam Sly) *hmpd and dropped to last 1st: nt fluent and wl bhd after: hmpd by loose horse after 5th and next: rdn 9th: hdwy 11th: wnt 3rd and pckd 2 out: pckd again last: chsd wnr flat: nvr able to chal* **9/1**

00-0 **3** 9 **Corredor Sun (USA)**16 1628 4-10-8 101 (p) SamTwiston-Davies(3) 89
(Nigel Twiston-Davies) *w ldrs: led 11th: rdn after 3 out: hdd: hmpd and mstke next: sn btn: wknd and lost 2nd after last* **16/1**

4-P4 **4** 5 **Vasodilator (IRE)**37 1476 7-11-10 103 LeightonAspell 97
(Pat Murphy) *t.k.h: lft 3rd 1st: sn clr in ldng trio: struggling 13th: 3rd btn after next: wknd bef 2 out* **10/1**

40-3 **5** 46 **Persian Gates (IRE)**17 1612 6-11-2 95 TomMessenger 78+
(Chris Bealby) *chsd clr ldng trio: clsd and wl in tch whn blnd bdly 10th: trying to rcvr whn mstke 12th: btn next: t.o after 3 out* **7/2**2

3P-0 **F** **Notmorebrandy (IRE)**135 530 6-10-13 95 AlexMerriam(3) —
(Diana Grissell) *w ldrs whn fell 1st* **40/1**

33-P **P** **Laneguy (FR)**159 171 5-11-2 95 PaddyBrennan —
(Tom George) *mstkes: led tl 11th: wkng whn mstke 12th: p.u next* **6/1**3

1005 **U** **Pool Of Knowledge (FR)**9 1709 4-10-13 103 AidanColeman —
(Venetia Williams) *towards rr whn bdly hmpd and uns rdr 1st* **15/2**

4322 **F** **Rebel Hunter (IRE)**14 1645 5-11-12 105 APMcCoy —
(Steve Gollings) *midfield whn fell 1st* **5/2**1

(-5.30) **Going Correction** -0.30s/f (Good)
WFA 4 from 5yo+ 10lb **9 Ran SP% 116.8**
Speed ratings (Par 105): **98,95,92,90,72 —,—,—,—**
Tote Swingers:1&2:£3.90, 2&3:£13.70, 1&3:£10.70 CSF £67.24 CT £976.14 TOTE £9.20: £1.70, £2.70, £5.00; EX 41.70.

Owner Mr & Mrs Nicholas Tatman **Bred** Nicholas Purcell **Trained** Lambourn, Berks

FOCUS

A highly eventful handicap and the already moderate form is suspect. A step up from the winner with the second rated to the level of his hurdles form.

NOTEBOOK

Fidelis(IRE) got an ideal tow into things and staying on strongly having jumped to the front two out. Well held on his one previous try over fences, he did finish second off 3lb higher on his latest outing over hurdles in May and this new, longer trip was clearly a help to the 6-y-o. Unfortunately, though, he was dismounted after the line and it emerged had suffered quite a bad tendon injury to his hind leg. (op 8-1 tchd 6-1)

Ovthenight(IRE) was soon last having been hampered at the first and his jumping lacked conviction. He did stay on past tiring rivals for second and should improve for the experience, but would like to see him show a bit more before he can be considered a betting proposition. (op 12-1)

Corredor Sun(USA) showed considerably more than he had done on his chasing debut at Market Rasen, the cheekpieces having some sort of effect, but he stopped very quickly as stamina began to ebb away in the straight and ended up well held. Official explanation: vet said gelding returned lame (op 14-1 tchd 20-1 in a place)

Vasodilator(IRE) didn't get home having helped disputed the early lead. (op 11-1 tchd 16-1)

Persian Gates(IRE), well held on his chase debut at Market Rasen, was in the process of running an improved race when blundering and losing his back legs on landing at the first in the back straight. He completed in his own time and can be given another chance. (tchd 4-1)

Laneguy(FR) Official explanation: jockey said gelding lost its action (op 11-4 tchd 3-1 in places)

Rebel Hunter(IRE) came down at the first and caused some carnage. He reportedly suffered a career-threatening injury. (op 11-4 tchd 3-1 in places)

1814 JOHN O'CONNER BIRTHDAY H'CAP HURDLE (12 hdls) 3m 2f

3:20 (3:27) (Class 4) (0-110,110) 4-Y-0+ **£2,602** (£764; £382; £190)

Form RPR

430- **1** **Go Amwell**26 3653 7-11-9 107 (v) TimmyMurphy 114+
(J R Jenkins) *hld up in last pair: hdwy to trck ldrs bef 2 out: pushed into ld on inner bef 2 out: looking like wnr whn lft wl clr after 2 out: pushed out* **15/2**

P-63 **2** 9 **Inghwung**48 1368 8-11-11 109 LeightonAspell 107+
(Oliver Sherwood) *in tch: hdwy 8th: rdn next: struggling bef 2 out: lft 3rd and hmpd 2 out: sn lft chsng wnr: no imp: dismntd qckly after fin* **4/1**2

3553 **3** 5 **Manadam (FR)**23 1555 7-10-8 99 MattGriffiths(7) 91
(Anthony Middleton) *chsd ldr tl 9th: sn rdn and struggling: wknd next: hmpd 2 out: lft modest 3rd between last 2* **6/1**3

2-P1 **4** 1 ¾ **Thai Vango (IRE)**17 1612 9-11-7 105 PaddyBrennan 96
(Nigel Twiston-Davies) *chsd ldrs: rdn and unable qck bef 3 out: wknd sn after next: hmpd 2 out: lft modest 4th between last 2* **10/3**1

0620 **5** 19 **Englishtown (FR)**23 1556 10-11-2 110 (p) GeraldQuinn(10) 85
(Jonjo O'Neill) *j.lft: chsd ldrs tl j. bdly lft and lost pl 8th: hdwy to chse ldrs again next: wknd qckly 3 out* **18/1**

/250 **6** 54 **Herne Bay (IRE)**48 1364 10-11-11 109 TomScudamore 32
(Ian Williams) *hld up in tch: wknd qckly after 9th: wl t.o after next* **22/1**

P6-F **P** **Ordelia**23 1559 6-10-6 90 TomMessenger —
(Chris Bealby) *hld up in last: rdn and struggling after 7th: lost tch next: t.o whn p.u 3 out* **14/1**

4154 **F** **Pairc Na Gcapall (IRE)**21 1570 8-11-12 110 (b) AidanColeman 107
(Neil King) *led: hdd and mstke 3 out: sn drvn: 3rd and btn whn fell next* **6/1**3

6U1P **P** **Pinerock (IRE)**9 1709 6-11-12 110 APMcCoy 110
(Jonjo O'Neill) *chsd ldrs: wnt 2nd 9th: led next: hdd bnd bef 2 out: stl pressing wnr whn mstke 2 out: sn lost action and p.u: fatally injured* **7/1**

6m 9.00s (-13.90) **Going Correction** -0.40s/f (Good) **9 Ran SP% 112.2**
Speed ratings (Par 105): **105,102,100,100,94 77,—,—,—**
Tote Swingers:1&2:£6.60, 2&3:£7.20, 1&3:£8.00 CSF £36.84 CT £190.78 TOTE £9.40: £3.60, £1.20, £2.90; EX 40.00.

Owner Robin Stevens **Bred** Michael Ng **Trained** Royston, Herts

FOCUS

A modest handicap hurdle and an eventful race. The cosy winner is rated back to the best of his 2008 form.

NOTEBOOK

Go Amwell, who's notoriously difficult to win with, got a peach of a rider from Timmy Murphy. Held up under restraint, he always looked to be travelling powerfully and, having nipped round the inside to lead on straightening, he had Pinerock held when that was broke down with fatal consequence after the second-last. This was his first victory over jumps since March 2008 and connections will no doubt be keen to get him out under a penalty, as he holds upcoming entries at Cheltenham and Plumpton. (op 7-1 tchd 13-2)

Inghwung finished a fortunate second, but she was dismounted after the last having appeared to go lame. Official explanation: vet said mare was lame (tchd 7-2)

Manadam(FR) kept on again despite having been hampered. (op 9-1 tchd 10-1)

Thai Vango(IRE) was off the same mark as when winning over fences at Market Rasen latest and should have done better. He was already beaten when hampered. (op 3-1)

Pairc Na Gcapall(IRE), better known as a chaser, had run well but was beaten in third when coming down two out. (tchd 7-1)

Pinerock(IRE) sadly broke down with tragic consequences. (tchd 7-1)

1815 HUNTINGDON NOVICES' CHASE (19 fncs) 3m

3:50 (3:56) (Class 3) 4-Y-0+ **£5,529** (£1,623; £811; £405)

Form RPR

01-1 **1** **Swincombe Rock**19 1598 5-11-8 135 PaddyBrennan 138+
(Nigel Twiston-Davies) *chsd ldrs: blnd 12th: outpcd and rdn after next: hdwy and reminders bef 3 out: chsd ldr after next: led and j.rt 2 out: clr whn j.rt last: eased towards fin* **4/11**1

1355 **2** 19 **Pheidias (IRE)**93 957 6-11-5 118 (p) MissGAndrews(7) 126+
(Pam Sly) *led: nt fluent 2nd and 3rd: sn hdd: chsd ldr after: mstke 11th: led 14th: rdn: hdd and hmpd 2 out: sn btn* **20/1**

3 17 **Canticle**199 5-11-2 0 TomMessenger 98+
(Chris Bealby) *chsd ldrs after 12th: wknd sn after 3 out* **7/1**2

22-5 **4** ½ **Silver Bay**156 234 9-11-2 110 LeightonAspell 103+
(Oliver Sherwood) *chsd ldrs tl led after 3rd: hdd and blnd 14th: rdn and wknd bef 3 out* **18/1**

12-P **P** **Ravenclaw (IRE)**21 1568 7-11-2 0 JackDoyle —
(Emma Lavelle) *hld up in last: pckd 2nd: losing tch whn p.u 15th* **8/1**3

5m 58.8s (-11.50) **Going Correction** -0.30s/f (Good) **5 Ran SP% 106.9**
Speed ratings (Par 107): **107,100,95,94,—**
CSF £7.28 TOTE £1.30: £1.10, £5.30; EX 7.60.

Owner Mills & Mason Partnership **Bred** M C And Mrs Yeo **Trained** Naunton, Gloucs

FOCUS

An uncompetitive novice chase, rated around the runner-up. The easy winner was below the level of his Perth run.

NOTEBOOK

Swincombe Rock spent most of the race trailing due to some careful jumping, but eventually his class saw him go clear. Having made a successful debut for the yard off 120 in a handicap at Perth, this was expected to prove straightforward, but he failed to travel as well on this quicker ground/speedier track. There should be better to come back on a slower surface and he'll be more at home on a stiffer course, so don't expect this to be the last of his wins. (op 2-5 tchd 4-9 in a place)

Pheidias(IRE), shouldering a double penalty, was aided by his capable rider's 7lb claim and he made the winner work, despite a blunder, but in the end was left trailing. He's been struggling in handicaps and isn't that easy to place at present. (op 18-1)
Canticle, unbeaten in three point-to-points, showed up well for a long way until he got tired. It's also possible this was enough of a test of stamina at this stage. (op 13-2)
Ravenclaw(IRE), who burst a blood vessel when pulled up on his chasing debut at Stratford, was never really travelling and again pulled up, suggesting something was amiss once more. Official explanation: vet said gelding bled from the nose

1816 RACING UK H'CAP HURDLE (8 hdls) 2m 110y
4:20 (4:26) (Class 4) (0-115,115) 4-Y-O+ **£2,927** (£859; £429; £214)

Form				RPR
-U56	1		**Cruchain (IRE)**[9] [1692] 7-11-12 **115** APMcCoy (Jonjo O'Neill) *chsd clr ldr: mstke 1st: hdwy to join ldrs and rdn along 5th: drvn and clr w rival next: led 2 out: kpt on reluctantly u.p flat* **11/2**[2]	118+
3545	2	2	**Phoenix Eye**[6] [1732] 9-10-5 **94** LeightonAspell (Michael Mullineaux) *stdd s: hld up wl off the pce in rr: hdwy but stl plenty to do 3 out: wnt 4th next: rdn between last 2: kpt on u.p flat: wnt 2nd nr fin* **9/2**[1]	93
10-0	3	*nk*	**Superius (IRE)**[38] [1470] 5-11-5 **108** JackDoyle (Emma Lavelle) *chsd ldr and clr of remainder: blnd 3rd: swtchd lft sn after 5th: led bef next and sn clr w wnr: hdd 2 out: styd on same pce flat: lost 2nd nr fin* **13/2**[3]	108+
-345	4	*3/4*	**Sonic Anthem (USA)**[21] [1569] 8-10-6 **95** RhysFlint (John Mackie) *led: sn clr w rival: j.lft 5th: hdd bef next: kpt on same pce u.p fr bef 2 out* **9/2**[1]	94
6360	5	*8*	**Alfloramoor**[14] [1646] 8-10-11 **103** (p) AdamPogson(3) (Charles Pogson) *t.k.h: hld up wl off the pce in midfield: nt fluent 3rd: rdn and no real prog bef 3 out:* **14/1**	96
-1FF	6	*7*	**Forget It**[138] [494] 5-11-8 **111** JamieMoore (Gary Moore) *hld up wl off the pce in rr: mstke 4th: n.d* **11/2**[2]	99
106-	7	*12*	**Sam Whiskey (GER)**[438] [1108] 7-10-6 **102** MissHGrissell(7) (Diana Grissell) *chsd ldng trio: clsd and in tch 5th: rdn and wknd after next* **33/1**	76
F/	P		**Outaouais (FR)**[955] [4205] 8-11-12 **115** (t) AndrewTinkler (George Baker) *t.k.h: hld up wl off the pce in rr: mstke 4th and immediately p.u* **20/1**	—
133-	P		**King Brex (DEN)**[177] [5259] 7-11-10 **113** (tp) NoelFehily (Charlie Mann) *hld up in midfield: hdwy to chse ldrs 5th: mstke next: no prog bef 2 out: wl hld whn p.u last* **7/1**	101
-P	P		**Baltrap (FR)**[72] [1147] 5-10-11 **100** AndrewThornton (Clarissa Caroe) *hld up wl off the pce towards rr: lost tch rapidly bef 4th: t.o and p.u 5th* **80/1**	—
/00-	P		**Nothing's Easy (IRE)**[211] [4648] 6-11-0 **110** JosephAkehurst(7) (Philip Middleton) *t.k.h: hld up wl off the pce in rr: sme prog after 4th: rdn and lost tch after next: t.o and p.u after 3 out* **16/1**	—

3m 49.2s (-5.70) **Going Correction** -0.40s/f (Good) 11 Ran SP% **114.5**
Speed ratings (Par 105): **97,96,95,95,91 88,82,—,—,— —**
Tote Swingers:1&2:£4.20, 2&3:£9.80, 1&3:£9.20 CSF £29.60 CT £163.93 TOTE £5.60: £1.20, £2.50, £3.60; EX 26.30.
Owner P McCarthy **Bred** Dunmanway Breeding Club **Trained** Cheltenham, Gloucs

FOCUS
A moderate handicap, run at a fair gallop. The second is rated to the best of his recent form.

NOTEBOOK
Cruchain(IRE) eventually wore down Superius and then did the bare minimum once in front. Clearly not straightforward, this was his first win since the summer of last year but you wouldn't want to be relying on him to follow it up. (op 13-2 tchd 5-1)
Phoenix Eye stayed on again having got a bit behind, but never looked like winning. His losing run continues. (op 4-1)
Superius(IRE), a winner at Wincanton earlier in the year, had failed to run to anything like that form in two subsequent attempts, including on his handicap debut, but he's clearly come on appreciably for that run and this was a much-improved display. He did have quite a hard race, but looks up to winning off this sort of mark. (op 6-1 tchd 7-1)
Sonic Anthem(USA) hasn't won in well over two years and he slowly faded having made the early running. (op 15-2)
Outaouais(FR) Official explanation: jockey said gelding lost its action (op 11-2 tchd 5-1)
King Brex(DEN) seemed to tire on this first start in 177 days, so should improve. It also emerged he had lost a shoe. Official explanation: jockey said gelding lost a front shoe (op 11-2 tchd 5-1)

1817 BRAMPTON STANDARD OPEN NATIONAL HUNT FLAT RACE 2m 110y
4:50 (4:58) (Class 6) 4-6-Y-O **£1,370** (£399; £199)

Form				RPR
221-	1		**Mawsem (IRE)**[167] [53] 4-11-0 0 PeterCarberry(7) (George Baker) *hld up in tch: hdwy to chse ldrs 4f out: rdn to ld over 1f out: kpt on wl fnl f* **4/1**[2]	112+
	2	*1/2*	**Midies Prince (IRE)** 4-10-7 0 MrJMQuinlan(7) (Terry Clement) *hld up in tch in rr: gd hdwy on outer over 2f out: ev ch over 1f out: kpt on wl fnl f but a jst hld* **16/1**	105+
-	3	*8*	**Bach To Back (IRE)** 5-11-0 0 PaddyBrennan (Nigel Twiston-Davies) *hld up in tch towards rr: hdwy to chse ldrs 4f out: rdn ent fnl 2f: nt pce of ldng pair and btn 1f out: kpt on* **6/1**	97+
	4	*4 1/2*	**Yesyoucan (IRE)** 5-11-0 0 TimmyMurphy (Alan Fleming) *hld up wl in tch: chsd ldrs and rdn ent fnl 2f: rn green and btn over 1f out* **3/1**[1]	92+
	5	*1 1/2*	**Ebony Diamond (IRE)**[71] [1171] 6-11-7 0 NoelFehily (Charlie Mann) *t.k.h: hld up wl in tch: hdwy to chse ldrs and stl pulling over 4f out: led ent fnl 2f: rdn and hdd over 1f out: sn wknd* **4/1**[2]	98+
0/	6	*13*	**Knowsall**[164] 5-11-0 0 LeightonAspell (Ms A E Embiricos) *led: hdd 9f out: styd upsides ldr: rdn to ld again over 2f out: sn hdd & wknd qckly* **80/1**	78
5	7	*3/4*	**Sound Judgment (IRE)**[34] [1510] 4-11-0 0 TomScudamore (Mark Rimell) *chsd ldrs: rdn 4f out: wknd over 3f out:* **50/1**	77
	8	*2*	**Wonmorenomore (IRE)** 4-10-7 0 MattGriffiths(7) (Anthony Middleton) *t.k.h: hld up in midfield tl hdwy to chse ldrs 12f out: wknd over 3f out* **50/1**	75
	9	*15*	**Hijack The Duke (IRE)** 4-11-0 0 PaulMoloney (John Ferguson) *t.k.h: chsd ldr after 2f: led 9f out tl hdd over 2f out: sn wknd* **22/1**	60
	10	*13*	**Sleep In First (FR)** 4-11-0 0 AndrewTinkler (Anna Bramall) *t.k.h: hld up in tch in rr: carried wd bnd 10f out: struggling fr 1/2-way: t.o* **25/1**	47
	11	*10*	**Miss Lala (IRE)** 5-10-4 0 DPFahy(3) (Nicholas Pomfret) *hld up in tch towards rr: wknd 5f out: t.o* **125/1**	30
	12	*25*	**Billy Teal** 5-11-0 0 DaveCrosse (G P Kelly) *rn green in rr: lost tch over 5f out: t.o* **100/1**	12
	P		**Lying Eyes** 4-11-0 0 DarylJacob (Paul Henderson) *bolted to post: t.k.h: hld up in rr tl lost action and p.u 10f out: fatally injured* **5/1**[3]	—

3m 48.9s (-0.20) **Going Correction** -0.40s/f (Good)
WFA 4 from 5yo+ 9lb 13 Ran SP% **117.0**
Speed ratings: **84,83,80,77,77 71,70,69,62,56 51,40,—**
Tote Swingers:1&2:£12.30, 2&3:£22.00, 1&3:£6.10 CSF £61.00 TOTE £5.20: £1.70, £4.60, £3.50; EX 76.90 Place 6 £237.46, Place 5 £94.16..
Owner George Baker & Partners **Bred** 6c Racing **Trained** Whitsbury, Hants

FOCUS
An ordinary bumper that developed into something of a sprint and two came clear. Probably a fair race of its type.

NOTEBOOK
Mawsem(IRE), off since winning a bumper at Southwell in April, had the assistance of Peter Carberry, who is really catching the eye, and he was brought with a perfectly timed challenge in the straight, his experience in the end telling over debutant Midies Prince. It will presumably be hurdles next for the son of Monsun, who should stay further. (op 5-1)
Midies Prince(IRE) made little appeal on breeding and his yard is 0-8 in bumpers in recent years, but he made swift headway to challenge and draw clear with the winner. He couldn't quite match him, but this was a very pleasing start. (op 18-1)
Bach To Back(IRE), who cost just 8,500euros, is from a yard that does well in this sphere and he stayed on nicely into third. He should improve for this initial experience. (op 8-1)
Yesyoucan(IRE), a half-brother to two bumpers winners whose dam is related to Harbour Pilot, travelled well on this racecourse debut before getting outpaced in the straight. He could be the one to take from the race. (op 7-2 tchd 4-1)
Ebony Diamond(IRE), making his debut for the yard, was last seen wining a Cork bumper in impressive fashion in August, but he proved too keen for his own good and was readily swept aside in the end. He's better than this, but needs to settle. (op 3-1)
Knowsall, poor in points, had the run of things and was probably flattered. (op 100-1)
Sound Judgment(IRE)
Sleep In First(FR) Official explanation: jockey said gelding ran too free
Lying Eyes, bought for only £460 at Ascot sales earlier in the year, was surprisingly popular in the market, but having bolted to post, he lost his action in the race and was pulled up with a fatal injury. (op 9-2 tchd 7-2)
T/Jkpt: £87,059.00 to a £1 stake. Pool of £183,927.48. 1.50 winning tickets. T/Plt: £311.90 to a £1 stake. Pool of £87,398.99. 204.55 winning tickets. T/Qpdt: £19.40 to a £1 stake. Pool of £7,544.84. 286.70 winning tickets. SP

1703 UTTOXETER (L-H)
Wednesday, October 13

OFFICIAL GOING: Chase course - good to soft; hurdle course - good (good to soft in places: chase 5.9, hurdle 6.6)
First flight in the back straight omitted in all hurdle races; Last fence in the home straight omitted in all chases; damaged ground.
Wind: Nil Weather: Warm and sunny

1818 RED SQUARE JUVENILE HURDLE (9 hdls 1 omitted) 2m
2:10 (2:10) (Class 4) 3-Y-O **£2,211** (£649; £324; £162)

Form				RPR
F63	1		**Frameit (IRE)**[4] [1545] 3-10-12 108 (vt) RichardJohnson (Tim Vaughan) *wnt 2nd after 6th: led 3 out: sn clr: mstke last: rdn out* **11/4**[2]	95+
0	2	*13*	**Royal Torbo (ISR)**[24] [1545] 3-10-12 0 AndrewTinkler (George Baker) *mstke first: sn getting reminders: hdwy after 6th: wnt mod 2nd and hit last* **25/1**	82
	3	*2 1/2*	**Miss Miracle**[112] 3-10-2 0 RichieMcLernon(3) (Jonjo O'Neill) *chsd ldr u.p after 6th: outpcd three out: lost 2nd flat* **3/1**[3]	72
	4	*22*	**Admiral Breese**[13] 3-10-12 0 PaulMoloney (Evan Williams) *led: nt fluent 4th: j.rt 5th: hdd and blnd 7th: 4th and fading whn blnd next* **5/2**[1]	66+
	5	*17*	**Astrovenus**[22] 3-10-5 0 ColinBolger (Mark H Tompkins) *hit 4th and rdn: blnd 5th and nrly uns rdr: last whn mstke sixth: sn t.o* **6/1**	37
	6	*10*	**Daisy Dolittle**[91] 3-10-5 0 JamieGoldstein (John Holt) *bhd: t.o after 6th* **66/1**	28
3	P		**Bojangles Andrews**[36] [1498] 3-10-5 0 (p) BrianToomey(7) (Tim Pitt) *j. modly: chsd ldrs tl blnd 5th: sn t.o: p.u three out* **10/1**	—

3m 55.2s **Going Correction** -0.15s/f (Good) 7 Ran SP% **109.0**
Speed ratings (Par 103): **94,87,86,75,66 61,—**
toteswingers:1&2 £10.40, 2&3 £11.60, 1&3 £1.50 CSF £49.33 TOTE £4.60: £2.30, £12.80; EX 38.80.
Owner M Khan X2 **Bred** Liam Butler **Trained** Aberthin, Vale of Glamorgan

FOCUS
Ground conditions on the hurdle course were officially advertised as being good all over, but the way they came home in this weak juvenile event would suggest it was pretty tacky.

NOTEBOOK
Frameit(IRE) emphatically opened his account in this sphere at the fourth attempt. The winner had paid for not settling when eighth at Wolverhampton on the Flat four days earlier, but had scored at Lingfield the time before and does stay well. That stood him in good stead in this line up and, while he is flattered by the wide-winning margin, he is a likeable horse in this sort of class. His confidence should be sky high now. (op 5-2 tchd 9-4 and 3-1 in a place)
Royal Torbo(ISR) got somewhat closer to the winner than was the case when well beaten on his hurdling debut last month, but still has a long way to go before becoming a betting proposition. (op 28-1)
Miss Miracle, a half-sister to Katchit, was last seen belatedly getting off the mark on the level in June and ended up with a mark of 75 in that sphere. Even if that mark may have slightly flattered her, she was no doubt the best of these on the Flat and has joined a top yard for her new career, but proved easy to back. She didn't settle that well and looked very novicey, ending up well beaten off. She isn't the biggest for this game, but will surely fare better as she becomes more streetwise. (op 11-4 tchd 7-2)
Admiral Breese, a 57-rated maiden on the Flat, was bought by his new connections after finishing second in a soft-ground seller over 1m6f 13 days earlier. He set out to make all, but was a sitting duck for the winner before his jumping went to pot in the home straight and needs more practice. A stiffer test will also be what he wants down the line. (op 3-1)

1819 EUROPEAN BREEDERS' FUND LAMBRINI "NATIONAL HUNT" NOVICES' HURDLE (QUALIFIER) (9 hdls 1 omitted) 2m
2:40 (2:40) (Class 4) 4-6-Y-O **£2,341** (£687; £343; £171)

Form				RPR
	1		**Nicene Creed**[172] [5402] 5-10-12 0 TomO'Brien (Philip Hobbs) *2nd untl led bef 2 out: sn rdn clr: hit last: easily* **30/100**[1]	106+

2 *10* **Rash Call (IRE)**[191] 6-10-12 0 PaulMoloney 89
(Evan Williams) *led at mod pce: hit 4th: rdn and hdd bef 2 out: sn no ch w wnr: all out to hold 2nd* **8/1**[3]

3 *1 3/4* **Taketimeout (IRE)** 5-10-12 0 APMcCoy 89+
(Jonjo O'Neill) *green and mstkes in midfield: effrt in 4th 2 out: nt rch ldrs after: snatched 3rd: do bttr* **7/1**[2]

660- 4 *shd* **Midnight Opera**[177] 5283 4-10-5 0 MarkQuinlan(7) 89
(Neil Mulholland) *chsd ldrs: stmbld bdly 3 out: outpcd whn hit next: lost 3rd nr fin* **20/1**

PP0- 5 *15* **Totally Beat**[231] 4229 5-10-12 0 NoelFehily 72
(Ian Williams) *mstke 1st: rdn and lost bef 3 out: mstke next* **25/1**

200- 6 *1 1/2* **Finger Spin**[251] 3846 4-10-5 0 ColinBolger 67+
(Mark H Tompkins) *3rd tl wknd bef 3 out: blnd next* **25/1**

6 7 *dist* **Secret Palm (IRE)**[53] 1325 5-10-12 0 AndrewThornton —
(Caroline Bailey) *bhd: lost tch 6th: sn t.o* **80/1**

8 *dist* **Action Hawk (GER)**[242] 6-10-9 0 RichieMcLernon(3) —
(Ben Pollock) *nt jump wl in last: t.o 5th: fin 2f bhd* **50/1**

3m 53.8s (-1.40) **Going Correction** -0.15s/f (Good)
WFA 4 from 5yo+ 9lb **8** Ran SP% **116.2**
Speed ratings: **97,92,91,91,83 82,—,—**
toteswingers:1&2 £1.40, 2&3 £2.70, 1&3 £1.10 CSF £3.21 TOTE £1.20: £1.02, £1.60, £1.60; EX 3.10.
Owner Mrs Diana L Whateley **Bred** Aylesfield Farms Stud Ltd **Trained** Withycombe, Somerset

FOCUS
The riders after the opener generally confirmed that the ground was tacky and hard work, despite riding like good to soft.

NOTEBOOK
Nicene Creed arrived for this British debut with a tall reputation and went a fair way to justifying that with a clear-cut success on this introduction to hurdling. This 5-y-o son of Hernando was purchased for £175,000 after finishing second in a bumper at the Punchestown Fesitval - so often a breeding ground for future jumping stars - behind the ready winner that day Backspin (subsequently joined Jonjo O'Neill). The race wasn't really run to suit him there as it was something of a dawdle and, looking at the way he had to be niggled to pick up the runner-up before three out here, a longer trip is going to be what he wants as a hurdler. He likes a sound surface and left the impression he would come on nicely for the experience, so he could well be a big player in this division as the season develops. His next assignment is eagerly anticipated. (op 2-5)
Rash Call(IRE), whose pointing form figures read P1F, is bred to make his mark in this sphere and ran a nice race from the front. He was no match when the winner found his full stride, but ought to improve a good deal for the outing and is another that should enjoy racing over further. (op 7-1)
Taketimeout(IRE) is from a family his yard knows well, but it's a little surprising he bypassed a bumper for his debut and the market suggested this would be needed. Indeed he looked inexperienced and made errors, but was keeping on under an educational ride late in the day. His yard did win this race with the high-class pair Albertas Run and Refinement in the past decade, and he should leave this form behind as he gains more practice. (tchd 6-1)
Midnight Opera failed to really build on an encouraging debut in his bumper season last term. He shaped with some promise on this seasonal/hurdling debut and, the sort his trainer does well with, he too should come into his own over a stiffer test in due course. (op 25-1)
Finger Spin deserves a mention as she was still in with a chance of placing off the home turn, but her jumping was messy over the last three flights and ultimately this seasonal debut was needed. She ought to learn for this initial experience of hurdles and will find her level when going handicapping. (op 28-1)

1820 RICHARD BRADFORD AT CRAIG TARA HAVEN H'CAP CHASE (16 fncs 2 omitted) 3m
3:15 (3:15) (Class 5) (0-90,90) 4-Y-O+ **£1,951** (£573; £286; £143)

Form RPR
2442 1 **Heezagrey (IRE)**[10] 1694 7-9-11 **68** MarkQuinlan(7) 79+
(James Evans) *bhd: pckd 2nd: mstke 3rd: hdwy and stmbld 12th: sn u.p: led 2 out: in command last: drvn out* **7/2**[1]

121- 2 *5* **Portrait Royale (IRE)**[191] 5056 8-11-11 **89** FelixDeGiles 94
(Anna Newton-Smith) *bhd: effrt bef 3 out: wnt 2nd last: drvn and nt rch wnr* **11/2**[3]

000- 3 *3 3/4* **Dromore Hill (IRE)**[204] 4798 6-11-9 **87** JimmyMcCarthy 90+
(Charlie Morlock) *bhd: reminders after 5th: hmpd 9th: sn drvn: effrt to press ldrs 3 out: one pce after* **16/1**

146F 4 *14* **Bynack Mhor (IRE)**[7] 1733 9-10-13 **77** (tp) AidanColeman 67
(Lawney Hill) *drvn 7th: nt gng wl in rr next: effrt to go 2nd 12th tl bef 2 out: 4th and wkng whn mstke last* **9/2**[2]

31P- 5 *22* **Ukrainian Star (IRE)**[203] 4824 7-11-7 **85** WarrenMarston 61+
(Martin Keighley) *nt fluent 3rd and 4th: lft 3rd at 9th: led 11th: hdd and blnd 2 out: fdd bdly* **6/1**

4P4U 6 *15* **Little Girl**[6] 1747 12-10-2 **66** oh6 ow2 (p) ColinBolger 20
(Ray Peacock) *chsd ldr tl bdly hmpd 9th: sn lost pl: t.o: b.b.v* **28/1**

P00/ U **Quintus (FR)**[601] 4019 6-11-9 **90** SeanQuinlan(3) —
(Chris Bealby) *hit 2nd: led and abt 5 l clr tl nrly fell 9th and eventually uns rdr* **14/1**

-1P0 P **Glacial Call (IRE)**[7] 1730 7-11-8 **86** (b) HaddenFrost —
(James Frost) *chsd ldrs: mstke 7th: wknd 9th: lost tch 11th: t.o and p.u last* **11/1**

50P5 P **Delgany Gunner**[7] 1733 6-10-7 **71** (vt) AndrewThornton —
(Ben Pollock) *handy: lft in ld and hmpd 9th: rdn and hdd 10th: stopped to nil after next: t.o and p.u 2 out* **9/1**

000- P **Lots Of Fun (IRE)**[231] 4229 6-10-13 **77** APMcCoy —
(Jonjo O'Neill) *reminders 7th: last whn mstke 10th: t.o and p.u 12th* **8/1**

6m 20.3s (5.20) **Going Correction** +0.275s/f (Yiel) **10** Ran SP% **115.5**
Speed ratings (Par 103): **102,100,99,94,87 82,—,—,—,—**
toteswingers:1&2 £2.30, 2&3 £28.00, 1&3 £17.30 CSF £23.48 CT £270.59 TOTE £4.10: £1.60, £2.00, £5.50; EX 17.60.
Owner Miss S Troughton **Bred** Anne Sexton **Trained** Broadwas, Worcs

FOCUS
A wide-open staying handicap. It was a race of changing fortunes, but overall the form looks fair for the class.

NOTEBOOK
Heezagrey(IRE) finally lost his maiden status and came right away after the last fence, but any of his backers would've almost thrown away their tickets before the final circuit. He seemed to lose interest early on out the back on this return to chasing as he put in some slow jumps and came under pressure. The longer the race went on the better he became, however, and he arrived on the scene going strongly turning into the home straight. He was always doing enough after hitting the front and this really should do his confidence the power of good, so perhaps turning out under a penalty would be wise. (op 4-1)
Portrait Royale(IRE), who looked fit enough, travelled nicely for most of the race and she too moved into contention powerfully. She just looked to blow up nearing the home turn, but kept on gamely and it was a pleasing return from this very consistent mare. Watch out for her back at Plumpton in due course. (tchd 9-2)
Dromore Hill(IRE) was beaten out of sight in one bumper and four hurdle races last term. He is bred to make a better chaser, though, and this was much more encouraging on his seasonal return. He clearly stays very well and should find a race, probably when getting back on softer ground. (op 25-1)
Bynack Mhor(IRE) was turning out after an unlucky fall at Towcester a week earlier. He needs very strong handling in his races and things didn't look good for him as he began to go backwards passing the stands for the first time. Not that surprisingly, he rallied on the final circuit but again didn't help his rider after another sloppy jump at the first in the home straight. Now may be the time to try another form of headgear, as he still looks weighted to go in when in the mood. (op 4-1)
Ukrainian Star(IRE), making his debut for a new yard, went well towards the front end prior to an error three out that saw him soon treading water. He should be sharper for the run. (op 5-1 tchd 9-2)
Little Girl Official explanation: vet said mare bled from the nose
Quintus(FR) was still looking to be enjoying himself out in a clear lead prior to getting the ninth all wrong and eventually unseating. It was his first outing since February last year and he may well have emptied had he stood up, but on this showing he will make up into a better chaser. (op 12-1 tchd 16-1)

1821 BRIAN RUTHVEN AT SETON SANDS HAVEN NOVICES' HURDLE (10 hdls 2 omitted) 2m 6f 110y
3:45 (3:46) (Class 4) 4-Y-O+ **£2,211** (£649; £324; £162)

Form RPR
22-1 1 **Ackertac (IRE)**[24] 1553 5-11-5 118 PaddyBrennan 126+
(Nigel Twiston-Davies) *2nd tl led 6th: clr fr 2 out: r.o stoutly* **5/6**[1]

560- 2 *4 1/2* **Hear My Song (IRE)**[289] 3123 5-10-12 0 APMcCoy 114+
(Jonjo O'Neill) *handy on outside: effrt and hit 3 out: chsd wnr next: v one pce* **25/1**

13-2 3 *6* **Like A Hurricane (IRE)**[133] 583 7-11-5 115 WayneHutchinson 117+
(Alan King) *nt fluent 3rd: hdwy 6th: v one pce and no imp between last 2* **5/1**[2]

203- 4 *1 1/2* **Super Villan**[174] 5344 5-10-12 0 MattieBatchelor 107
(Mark Bradstock) *cl up: mstke 6th: 3rd and drvn bef 3 out: wknd next: mstke last* **7/1**[3]

52-P 5 *2* **Bobbisox (IRE)**[156] 249 5-10-5 98 TomO'Brien 97
(Alex Hales) *hdwy after 6th: rdn and no imp fr 3 out* **25/1**

4024 6 *2* **Leitra House (IRE)**[54] 1308 7-10-12 106 NickScholfield 103
(Jeremy Scott) *led at v stdy pce tl 6th: wknd u.p bef 3 out* **20/1**

6/60 7 *1/2* **Little Dibber**[24] 1555 7-10-12 0 JackDoyle 102
(Peter Pritchard) *chsd ldrs tl wknd 3 out* **100/1**

110- 8 *7* **Carrickmines (IRE)**[200] 4890 8-10-12 0 JamieMoore 95
(Dr Richard Newland) *effrt 7th: lost tch tamely next* **9/1**

9 *4 1/2* **Glens Boy (IRE)**[220] 6-10-12 0 HaddenFrost 90
(Henrietta Knight) *t.k.h in midfield: lost tch bef 3 out* **16/1**

5 10 *1* **Lagan Katie**[42] 1455 4-9-11 0 MarkQuinlan(7) 81
(Neil Mulholland) *bhd: rdn 4th: lost tch bef 3 out* **100/1**

/0P- 11 *17* **Dash Of Salt**[217] 4516 5-10-12 0 FelixDeGiles 72
(Charlie Longsdon) *bhd: mstke 6th: sn t.o* **100/1**

12 *30* **Bohemian Rock**[269] 6-10-12 0 AndrewThornton 42
(Caroline Bailey) *t.k.h: chsd ldrs to 7th: t.o bef 2 out* **40/1**

00- 13 *18* **Duffy Moon**[183] 5178 6-10-12 0 JimmyMcCarthy 24
(Charlie Morlock) *bhd: mstkes 2nd and 5th: hopelessly t.o 3 out* **100/1**

P **Real Dandy**[29] 4-10-11 0 JamieGoldstein —
(Lucinda Featherstone) *bhd: rdn 5th: t.o 7th: p.u 3 out* **150/1**

0-00 P **Knottage Hill (IRE)**[19] 1600 5-10-12 0 JohnnyFarrelly —
(Reg Hollinshead) *t.k.h: chsd ldrs to 7th: t.o and p.u 3 out* **150/1**

P **Hot Candy** 6-10-5 0 PaulMoloney —
(Reg Hollinshead) *j. poorly in last: t.o after 6th: p.u 3 out* **100/1**

5m 24.02s (-6.88) **Going Correction** -0.15s/f (Good)
WFA 4 from 5yo+ 10lb **16** Ran SP% **120.8**
Speed ratings (Par 105): **105,103,101,100,100 99,99,96,95,94 89,78,72,—,— —**
toteswingers:1&2 £9.50, 2&3 £12.10, 1&3 £2.90 CSF £31.01 TOTE £1.90: £1.20, £3.90, £1.70; EX 38.00.
Owner Mark Aspey & Steve Catton **Bred** Jerry Capliss **Trained** Naunton, Gloucs

FOCUS
Despite the large field this wasn't the most competitive novice hurdle.

NOTEBOOK
Ackertac(IRE) had more on his plate than when winning on his return at this venue 24 days earlier, but he followed up with a ready effort under his penalty. Stepping up in trip suited and his trainer's belief that he had strengthened up during his off-season is evidently spot on. Things will be plenty harder under a double penalty in this division, so connections will probably have to raise his sights now. His official mark of 118 will now go up, but he remains open to more improvement over this sort of distance while his yard continues in such grand form. (op Evens tchd 4-5 and 11-10 in places)
Hear My Song(IRE) proved backward last season, but has obviously done well for his time off the track and posted a promising effort in defeat. He got the longer trip well, indeed he looks a horse that will relish racing over 3m and this is a performance he should build on.
Like A Hurricane(IRE), having his first outing for 133 days, ran a sound enough race under his penalty. He probably needs better ground over this far, but should come on for the run and may now appreciate a switch to handicaps. One imagines he will also go chasing before all that long. (tchd 6-1)
Super Villan is well regarded and took in the Cheltenham Bumper on his penultimate outing last season. He took a bit of a hold when beaten on his final start, though, and that was again his undoing on this hurdling/seasonal debut over the longer trip. The experience will not be lost on him, however, and dropping back to 2m4f looks a wise move in the short term. (op 8-1 tchd 13-2)
Bobbisox(IRE), last seen pulling up in May, wasn't done many favours three out and shaped a little better than the bare form. She has the option of reverting to races against her own sex and should pick up a race before too long.
Carrickmines(IRE) wasn't fluent on this seasonal debut back over hurdles. His yard has yet to hit form and the run should bring him on plenty. (op 15-2 tchd 10-1)
Glens Boy(IRE) won two of his five outings between the flags in Ireland and was expected to need this outing on debut for new connections. He moved nicely through the race before fitness became an issue and is one to keep an eye on. (op 14-1)
Hot Candy Official explanation: jockey said mare made a noise

1822 NICKY PROCTOR AT ALLHALLOWS HAVEN H'CAP HURDLE (10 hdls 2 omitted) 2m 4f 110y
4:20 (4:20) (Class 5) (0-95,92) 4-Y-O+ **£1,561** (£458; £229; £114)

Form RPR
0PP- 1 **Prince Massini (IRE)**[219] 4487 9-10-13 **79** PaulMoloney 104+
(Evan Williams) *chsd ldrs fr 4th: led after 5th: clr w one rival 3 out: level whn mstke last: drvn to assert flat* **8/1**[3]

044- 2 *1 1/2* **Babilu**[4] 4677 5-11-1 **81** TomO'Brien 103+
(Dai Burchell) *taken down early: effrt to press wnr fr 6th: upsides fr 3 out tl blnd last: outbattled flat* **17/2**

0P-1 **3** *19* **Quam Celerrime**[10] 1707 5-10-1 **67** 7ex.............................. HaddenFrost 73
(Roger Curtis) *bhd: clsd on suffernce after 7th: 5th whn mstke 3 out: chsd ldng trio vainly after: wnt poor 3rd flat: lost front shoe* **7/2**[1]

03-5 **4** *3 ¼* **Present Your Case (IRE)**[151] 336 5-11-7 **87**..................(t) DarylJacob 88
(Ben Case) *hdwy to go 3rd 7th: outpcd fr next: hit 2 out: lost poor 3rd flat* **18/1**

005- **5** *3 ½* **Blazing Sun (IRE)**[213] 4618 7-11-7 **90**..........................(t) SeanQuinlan(3) 89
(Kim Bailey) *rdn and hdwy 7th: 4th and bmpd along bef 3 out where mstke struggling after* **12/1**

0013 **6** *15* **Simone Martini (IRE)**[6] 1741 5-10-3 **74** 7ex...........(tp) JimmyDerham(5) 59
(Milton Harris) *effrt and n.m.r 7th: wnt poor 5th and mstke 2 out: fdd after* **9/2**[2]

3F50 **7** *21* **Wisteria Lane (IRE)**[7] 1735 7-10-12 **78**.......................(p) GerardTumelty 44
(Anabel L M King) *led: j.rt 5th: sn hdd: drvn and nt keen and wknd after 7th: bdly t.o* **9/1**

005- **8** *1 ¼* **Salpierre (IRE)**[221] 4439 5-11-12 **92**.. APMcCoy 56
(Jonjo O'Neill) *in rr whn mstke 1st: struggling after 7th: bdly t.o* **8/1**[3]

P0-0 **9** *¾* **Little Roxy (IRE)**[166] 84 5-10-12 **78**.................................. FelixDeGiles 42
(Anna Newton-Smith) *bhd early: bdly t.o fr 3 out* **40/1**

10 *¾* **Kilbready Star (IRE)**[955] 4252 10-11-5 **85**............................ JackDoyle 48
(Peter Pritchard) *struggling fr 6th: bdly t.o* **28/1**

P6-6 **11** *26* **Utern**[39] 737 6-10-12 **78**... AidanColeman 18
(Venetia Williams) *struggling 6th: bdly t.o: b.b.v* **25/1**

/00- **12** *½* **Carys's Lad**[488] 689 7-11-10 **90**....................................... LeightonAspell 29
(Michael Mullineaux) *w ldr tl bmpd 5th: lost tch after next: hopelessly t.o* **25/1**

13 *dist* **Blackwater Sparkle (IRE)**[72] 1170 6-11-2 **89**.............. MichaelByrne(7) —
(A J Kennedy, Ire) *t.k.h: chsd ldrs tl after 5th: bdly t.o 3 out* **66/1**

PP-0 **14** *1* **Oscar Trial (IRE)**[12] 1666 8-10-4 **70**..............................(p) NickScholfield —
(Sharon Watt) *chsd ldrs to 5th: hopelessly t.o* **25/1**

P5P5 **P** **Winter Holly**[17] 1623 4-11-8 **88**.. RobertWalford —
(Tim Walford) *t.k.h in last: struggling 5th: t.o and p.u last* **25/1**

4m 59.1s (-4.90) **Going Correction** -0.15s/f (Good)
WFA 4 from 5yo+ 10lb **15** Ran SP% **118.9**
Speed ratings (Par 103): **103,102,95,93,92 86,78,78,78,77 67,67,—,—,—**
toteswingers:1&2 £16.00, 2&3 £7.60, 1&3 £10.50 CSF £67.41 CT £285.00 TOTE £10.20: £3.80, £3.30, £1.40; EX 94.90.
Owner R E R Williams **Bred** Robert McCarthy **Trained** Llancarfan, Vale Of Glamorgan

FOCUS
A very weak handicap, run at an ordinary gallop and the first pair dominated off the home turn.

NOTEBOOK
Prince Massini(IRE), who is better known as a chaser, ran out a very game winner on this return from a 219-day break and belatedly ended his losing run. He came into this with a poor completion rate last season next to his name, but his best previous effort for current connections came on his debut for them and he is probably the sort of horse best caught when fresh. It's anyone's guess whether he will build on this, but his trainer later declared his wind was operated on about a month previously and it has obviously done him good. (op 13-2)
Babilu was beaten a long way on her latest outing on the Flat four days earlier, but the cheekpieces were dispensed with for this return to hurdling and she was the only one to give Prince Massini a serious race. She looked to be going better than the winner from three out, but was starting to feel the pinch before the last when she met it all wrong and couldn't get by him thereafter. Her official mark will now go up, but she remains open to some improvement as a hurdler. (op 12-1)
Quam Celerrime was a bloodless winner at this venue on his seasonal and handicap return ten days earlier. He was the one to beat on that form under his penalty, but was facing much different ground over a different trip here and it was clear from two he was labouring. The run probably came soon enough for him and he wants softer ground, but things will be tougher off his future mark. He was later reported to have lost a shoe. Official explanation: jockey said gelding lost a front shoe (op 4-1 tchd 9-2)
Present Your Case(IRE) looked a player when making smooth headway in the back straight, but eventually tired out of things on this first run since May. (tchd 16-1 and 20-1)
Blazing Sun(IRE), equipped with a first-time tongue tie, wasn't given too hard a time on this seasonal debut and ought to come on for it. (op 14-1)
Simone Martini(IRE) failed to get home over this longer trip and has now had three runs in quick succession. (op 4-1 tchd 7-2)
Utern Official explanation: jockey said mare bled from the nose

1823 CRABBIES ALCOHOLIC GINGER BEER H'CAP CHASE (10 fncs 2 omitted) 2m
4:55 (4:55) (Class 4) (0-110,110) 4-Y-0+ **£3,065** (£951; £512)

Form RPR

32-3 **1** **Kilkenny All Star (IRE)**[127] 676 9-11-7 **110**.................. ShaneByrne(5) 119+
(Sue Smith) *led fr 4th: rdn and kpt on gamely flat: all out* **2/1**[1]

53-0 **2** *2 ½* **Wingull (IRE)**[156] 252 6-10-9 **93**..................................... AndrewTinkler 101+
(George Baker) *wnt 3rd at 4th: tk 2nd 3 out: look tired and hld whn blnd last: no imp after* **11/4**[2]

PU04 **3** *dist* **Benefit Game (IRE)**[10] 1708 6-10-12 **96**................................. APMcCoy 75
(Jonjo O'Neill) *chsd ldr fr 4th tl rdn and no rspnse 3 out: t.o next: eased after* **7/2**[3]

3P-6 **P** **Colliers Court**[24] 1552 13-10-10 **94**.................................. LeightonAspell —
(Lisa Williamson) *led to 4th: t.o 6th: p.u 7th* **11/2**

-41P **P** **Arcadia Boy (IRE)**[35] 1505 7-11-4 **105**............................. AdrianLane(3) —
(Donald McCain) *sn pushed along and nt looking keen: t.o bef 7th: p.u 2 out* **6/1**

3m 57.9s (2.30) **Going Correction** +0.275s/f (Yiel) **5** Ran SP% **111.9**
Speed ratings (Par 105): **105,103,—,—,—**
CSF £8.23 TOTE £2.30: £1.10, £2.00; EX 8.10.
Owner The McGoldrick Partnership **Bred** Mrs Brenda Cunningham **Trained** High Eldwick, W Yorks

FOCUS
This moderate handicap was run at a fair gallop.

NOTEBOOK
Kilkenny All Star(IRE) looked to have been found a decent opportunity and it was surprising to see him drift in the betting. He did things well throughout, but tired near the finish and had to kept right up to his work after the last. He is capable of holding his form, but this was just his second win to date and he's probably one to be taking on from a higher mark next time. (op 7-4 tchd 9-4)
Wingull(IRE) was heavily backed on this first outing for 156 days and was the chief danger to the winner from three out. He was held by that rival prior to hitting the final fence, though, and may just prefer stepping up in trip. He is yet to win a race, but this was better on his chasing debut and there ought to be something for him before all that long. (op 9-2)
Benefit Game(IRE) was ridden to dispute the lead with the winner four out, but came under heavy pressure rounding the home turn and was done with soon after. He seems happiest on quicker ground. (tchd 3-1)
Colliers Court was reported to have suffered from a fibrillating heart. Official explanation: vet said gelding had a fibrillating heart (op 11-2 tchd 7-1)
Arcadia Boy(IRE) was left behind in the back straight and has now pulled up the last twice. (op 11-2 tchd 7-1)

1824 HAVEN HOLIDAYS LITTLE STAR FOUNDATION STANDARD OPEN NATIONAL HUNT FLAT RACE 2m
5:25 (5:25) (Class 6) 4-6-Y-O **£1,301** (£382; £191; £95)

Form RPR

1 **Bear's Affair (IRE)** 4-11-0 0... AndrewTinkler 109+
(Nicky Henderson) *effrt on outside bef st: led over 3f out: rdn 1f out: rn green and drvn: hld on gamely* **3/1**[1]

2 *hd* **Champion Court (IRE)**[165] 106 5-11-7 0.................... WarrenMarston 116+
(Martin Keighley) *bhd: effrt to chse ldrs 4f out: wnt 2nd 2f out: styd on strly cl home: jst failed* **7/2**[2]

3 *10* **Heliopsis (IRE)** 5-11-0 0.. AidanColeman 100
(Venetia Williams) *effrt on outside appr st: wnt 3rd over 1f out: no imp on ldrs after* **28/1**

0-3 **4** *1 ¼* **Father Probus**[19] 1607 4-11-0 0.................................... PaddyBrennan 99
(Nigel Twiston-Davies) *bhd: rdn after 5f: rn in snatches: struggling 3f out: sme late prog* **7/1**

5 *¾* **Just Dave (IRE)** 4-11-0 0.. PaulMoloney 98
(Evan Williams) *t.k.h: pressing ldrs: tk 2nd over 3f out tl 2f out: sn wknd* **9/2**[3]

6 *6* **Pompan (IRE)** 4-11-0 0... WayneHutchinson 93
(Peter Niven) *t.k.h: chsd ldrs tl wknd wl over 2f out* **66/1**

0/ **7** *1 ¼* **Tanners Emperor**[576] 4536 6-11-0 0................................ LiamTreadwell 91
(Claire Dyson) *led: rdn and hdd over 3f out: lost pl qckly* **100/1**

0- **8** *½* **Deputy Dog (IRE)**[177] 5283 4-11-0 0.................................... APMcCoy 91
(Jonjo O'Neill) *handy: chal briefly 5f out: fdd 2f out* **6/1**

9 *12* **High Kite (IRE)** 4-11-0 0.. HaddenFrost 80
(Henrietta Knight) *a bhd: struggling bef st: t.o* **50/1**

10 *12* **Moorlands Jack** 5-11-0 0.. RichardJohnson 69
(Tim Vaughan) *last and rdn 5f out: sn t.o* **5/1**

06 **11** *dist* **The Ridge**[130] 637 6-11-0 0... SamJones —
(Michael Scudamore) *pressed ldr tl wknd u.p over 5f out: hopelessly t.o* **125/1**

3m 43.2s (-6.40) **Going Correction** -0.15s/f (Good)
WFA 4 from 5yo+ 9lb **11** Ran SP% **117.5**
Speed ratings: **110,109,104,104,103 100,100,100,94,88 —**
toteswingers:1&2:£3.20, 1&3:£15.10, 2&3:£6.60 CSF £13.42 TOTE £5.50: £2.80, £1.10, £4.90; EX 10.70 Place 6 £13.57; Place 5 £3.29.
Owner G B Barlow **Bred** T J Whitley **Trained** Upper Lambourn, Berks

FOCUS
There is every chance that this will turn out to be a good heat and the race is a clear indication the bumper division is now starting to hot up.

NOTEBOOK
Bear's Affair(IRE) did enough to make a winning debut for his powerful stable. This 67,000euros purchase is bred to enjoy racing over further when sent jumping and has his share of scope. Being by Presenting, it wasn't surprising this goodish ground suited and he rates value for better than the bare margin, as he proved distinctly green when asked to win the race. It wouldn't be surprising to see him defy a penalty, but he has reportedly schooled well at home so could well go hurdling. (op 11-4 tchd 7-2)
Champion Court(IRE) was snapped up by connections for £130,000 after making a winning debut at Kilbeggan in May. He came through from off the pace to have every chance and went down fighting under his penalty. This rates an improved effort in defeat and he emerges as the best horse at the weights, but wouldn't be certain to reverse the form with the winner on level terms next time. That said, he looks a lovely prospect for novice hurdles. (op 10-3)
Heliopsis(IRE) couldn't go with the first pair, but turned in a very pleasing debut effort and looks sure to enjoy a stiffer test in due course. He can win a bumper before going hurdling.
Father Probus was having his third outing and helps to set the level of the form. He will no doubt want further in due course. (op 8-1)
Just Dave(IRE), a half-brother to Black Jack Blues, was a big market mover on his racecourse debut and travelled best of all through the race. He looked sure to go close nearing the 3f marker, but lacked any sort of acceleration when asked for an effort. It may be that run was needed, but there is also every chance that he too wants a stiffer test already. (op 12-1 tchd 4-1)
Pompan(IRE) is bred to win races over jumps and posted a respectable debut display.
Deputy Dog(IRE), well backed when down the field on debut at Kempton last season, came under heavy pressure around 3f out and may have found this ground against him. (tchd 11-2)
Moorlands Jack was beaten before the home turn, however, and something may well have gone amiss. (op 7-2)
T/Plt: £14.20 to a £1 stake. Pool:£59,780.52 - 3,051.81 winning tickets T/Qpdt: £4.00 to a £1 stake. Pool:£5,337.03 - 975.44 winning tickets IM

[603]WETHERBY (L-H)
Wednesday, October 13

OFFICIAL GOING: Good (good to firm in places; watered; hurdle 8.3; chase 8.0; average 8.2)
Wind: light 1/2 behind Weather: fine and sunny

1825 RACHEL WRIGHT MEMORIAL HURDLE (JUVENILE MAIDEN HURDLE) (9 hdls) 2m 110y
2:20 (2:20) (Class 5) 3-Y-O **£1,712** (£499; £249)

Form RPR

33 **1** **Bring Sweets (IRE)**[25] 1018 3-10-9 97........................ FearghalDavis(3) 86
(Brian Ellison) *hld up in rr: nt fluent 4th: stdy hdwy next: wnt 3rd appr 3 out: lft handy 2nd next: led appr last: rdn out* **11/2**[3]

2 *3 ¾* **Makbullet**[55] 3-10-12 0.. BrianHughes 83
(Howard Johnson) *t.k.h: hdwy to trck ldrs 3rd: wnt 2nd appr 3 out: lft in ld 2 out: hdd appr last: no ex* **12/1**

6 **3** *9* **Venture Girl (IRE)**[10] 1699 3-10-5 0................................ RichieMcGrath 67
(Tim Easterby) *t.k.h in rr: hdwy 4th: tk modest 4th appr 3 out: lft 3rd 2 out* **25/1**

6 **4** *1 ½* **Always Roses**[10] 1691 3-10-5 0...................................... TomMessenger 65
(Chris Bealby) *chsd ldrs: drvn 5th: outpcd appr 3 out: kpt on between last 2* **40/1**

5 *4 ½* **Manxman (IRE)**[196] 3-10-12 0... GrahamLee 68
(Ferdy Murphy) *chsd ldrs: fdd appr 3 out* **17/2**

6 *3 ½* **Green For Luck (IRE)**[65] 3-10-12 0....................................... HenryOliver 64
(Sue Smith) *t.k.h: trckd ldrs 3rd: outpcd appr 3 out: 6th and styng on whn bdly hmpd by loose horse last* **12/1**

6 **7** *10* **Acol**[10] 1696 3-10-5 0... AlexanderVoy(7) 54
(George Foster) *t.k.h: hdwy to trck ldrs 3rd: lost pl appr 3 out* **80/1**

8 *hd* **Magic Millie (IRE)**[44] 3-10-6 0 ow1.................................. DenisO'Regan 48
(David O'Meara) *chsd ldrs: lost pl appr 3 out* **3/1**[1]

9 6 **North Shadow**[51] 3-10-7 0 JamesHalliday(5) 48
(Alan Brown) *t.k.h: sn trcking ldrs: wknd appr 3 out* **40/1**

53 10 6 **Henry Havelock**[10] 1696 3-10-12 0 PeterBuchanan 42
(Chris Grant) *chsd ldrs: lost pl 5th: bhd fr next* **8/1**

11 ¾ **Gorgeous Annie (IRE)**[56] 3-10-5 0 (t) WillKennedy 34
(John G Carr, Ire) *nt jump wl: in rr: mstke 2nd: drvn and nt fluent 5th: sn bhd* **25/1**

12 22 **Crushing (IRE)**[123] 3-10-12 0 DougieCostello 19
(Julie Camacho) *t.k.h in rr: bhd fr 6th: t.o* **80/1**

5 P **Red Barcelona (IRE)**[20] 1586 3-10-12 0 DaveCrosse —
(Mark H Tompkins) *prom: nt fluent: reminders and lost pl 5th: sn bhd: t.o whn p.u bef 3 out* **11/1**

F **Danceintothelight**[8] 3-10-12 0 BarryKeniry 93+
(Micky Hammond) *led: 7 l clr and in total command whn fell 2 out* **5/1**[2]

3m 53.6s (-2.20) **Going Correction** -0.50s/f (Good) **14** Ran SP% **117.4**
Speed ratings (Par 101): **85,83,79,78,76 74,69,69,66,64 63,53,—,—**
toteswingers:1&2:£13.90, 1&3:£29.50, 2&3:£45.60 CSF £63.18 TOTE £7.40: £2.00, £3.90, £6.00; EX 84.90.
Owner Koo's Racing Club **Bred** Kilnamoragh Stud **Trained** Norton, N Yorks

FOCUS
Just an ordinary juvenile hurdle, it was run at a modest early pace. Weak form, rated aound the third and fourth, with the faller rated a 7l winner.

NOTEBOOK
Bring Sweets(IRE) proved the chief beneficiary of the leader's fall, coming through under a patient ride to hit the front at the last. Third in a couple of hurdle races at Market Rasen in the summer and not disgraced on the Flat since, he was a fortunate winner and may prove vulnerable under a penalty. (op 6-1)
Makbullet is basically a sprinter on the Flat and there was obviously a doubt over his stamina ahead of this hurdles debut. Left in front two from home but unable to hold off the winner, he showed enough to suggest that he can win in ordinary company in this sphere. (op 11-1 tchd 10-1)
Venture Girl(IRE) was again rather keen in the first part of the race but she improved on what she had shown on her hurdles debut, staying on from the rear albeit without ever offering much of a threat.
Always Roses was another to improve on this second experience of hurdling, plugging on for fourth after coming under pressure some way from home.
Manxman(IRE), sold out of Mark Johnston's yard in the spring after winning a 1m3f maiden at Kempton, faded out of things on the home turn. He is entitled to strip fitter with the run behind him and the return of headgear would be a plus. (op 6-1)
Green For Luck(IRE) stayed on quite well from the back on this hurdles bow and debut for the Smith yard and should have learned from this. He would have been a little closer had the loose Danceintothelight not jumped into hiom at the last. (op 11-1)
Acol was not entirely disgraced on this second start and may be the type for low-grade handicaps later on. (op 50-1)
Magic Millie(IRE) paid her way at around 1m2f in the summer and came in for support ahead of this hurdles debut for her Flat-oriented yard, but after coming through to look dangerous she weakened quickly at the first flight in the home straight. She is not the biggest for hurdling. (op 6-1)
Danceintothelighthad made most of the running and was in the process of drawing clear when he stepped into the second-last and came down. A winner over 1m6f on the Flat last month, he was an unlucky loser on this hurdles debut and can make amends if none the worse, but there is room for improvement in his hurdling. (op 9-2 tchd 4-1)

1826 GET 20% DISCOUNT ONLINE @ WETHERBYRACING.CO.UK H'CAP CHASE (18 fncs) 2m 6f 110y
2:50 (2:50) (Class 5) (0-90,90) 4-Y-0+ **£2,055** (£599; £299)

Form RPR

2-34 1 **Pistol Basc (FR)**[12] 1663 6-11-3 **88** PaulGallagher(7) 100+
(Ferdy Murphy) *trckd ldrs 5th: jnd ldr 3 out: led after next: rdn clr run-in: eased towards fin* **7/1**

1F1U 2 6 **Archie's Wish**[12] 1663 6-11-3 **81** BarryKeniry 89+
(Micky Hammond) *trckd ldrs: led 4 out: jnd and mstke 2 out: sn hdd: kpt on same pce* **9/2**[1]

3P52 3 4½ **Executive's Hall (IRE)**[36] 1503 6-10-1 **65** (v) BrianHughes 65
(Andrew Crook) *w ldr: led 6th: nt fluent 10th and 12th: hdd 4 out: one pce fr next* **9/2**[1]

P534 4 3¼ **Feeling Peckish (USA)**[17] 1627 6-10-9 **73** (t) AndrewGlassonbury 69
(Michael Chapman) *prom: drvn 13th: outpcd and lost pl appr 4 out: j.rt and kpt on one pce over last 3* **11/1**

0443 5 15 **Mcqueen (IRE)**[38] 1481 10-11-9 **90** DannyCook(3) 71
(Barry Leavy) *prom: lost pl 9th: sme hdwy 11th: lost pl appr 4 out* **11/2**[3]

P6P5 6 ½ **Panthers Run**[12] 1665 10-10-4 **68** (t) DougieCostello 49
(Jonathan Haynes) *mde most: nt fluent 10th: hdd 12th: wknd appr 4 out* **20/1**

0035 7 8 **First Fought (IRE)**[15] 1642 8-9-11 **68** (vt) HenryBrooke(7) 44
(Joanne Foster) *in rr: mstke 2nd: hmpd 9th: sme hdwy 11th: lost pl 13th: sn bhd* **5/1**[2]

41-5 P **Hever Road (IRE)**[135] 549 11-11-1 **86** JoeCornwall(7) —
(David Pearson) *in rr: drvn along 7th: hmpd and lost pl 9th: bhd fr 11th: t.o whn p.u bef 4 out* **12/1**

60-5 F **Braden Brook (IRE)**[12] 1663 7-10-3 **74** (t) MrJohnDawson(7) —
(John Wade) *trckd ldrs: fell 9th* **9/1**

5m 24.9s (-12.10) **Going Correction** -0.775s/f (Firm) **9** Ran SP% **111.7**
Speed ratings (Par 103): **90,87,86,85,80 79,77,—,—**
toteswingers:1&2:£2.90, 1&3:£2.20, 2&3:£2.20 CSF £37.61 CT £154.57 TOTE £4.30: £2.20, £2.00, £1.50; EX 18.50.
Owner The DPRP Pistol Partnership **Bred** Sebastien & Alain Dufrancatel **Trained** West Witton, N Yorks

FOCUS
A low-grade handicap chase run at a fair pace. It was one for the younger brigade, with the first four home all 6-y-os, and the form looks fairly sound. The winner warrants a small personal best.

NOTEBOOK
Pistol Basc(FR) was runner-up in this race 12 months ago and his last win came off this mark over a quarter of a mile less at this track back in November. He needed his first run of this season, but is usually pretty consistent and ran out a comfortable winner back over this more suitable trip. (op 5-1)
Archie's Wish had won both his completed starts over fences, each time at Sedgefield. He generally jumped well, only to clout the second-last and hand the advantage to the winner. There may still be a little more improvement in him. (tchd 5-1)
Executive's Hall(IRE), runner-up to Archie's Wish last time, was outjumped at times by his old rival and eventually gave way after the third-last. His turn will probably come sooner rather than later. (op 5-1 tchd 4-1)
Feeling Peckish(USA) ran his race but extended his winless record over jumps to 61. (op 16-1)
Mcqueen(IRE) came in for support, but is a bit long in the tooth to be trying chasing again and he was unable to build on a reasonably encouraging run at Worcester. (op 6-1 tchd 13-2)

First Fought(IRE) was always in the last pair. (tchd 9-2)

1827 TOTESPORT.COM H'CAP HURDLE (9 hdls) 2m 110y
3:25 (3:25) (Class 3) (0-135,125) 4-Y-0+ **£4,553** (£1,337; £668; £333)

Form RPR

1311 1 **Maska Pony (IRE)**[36] 1501 6-11-5 **118** GrahamLee 129+
(George Moore) *led: hit 2 out: briefly hdd appr last: hld on gamely* **9/2**[1]

0-00 2 ½ **Amazing King (IRE)**[18] 1609 6-10-10 **116** KyleJames(7) 126+
(Philip Kirby) *hld up: hdwy 4th: 3rd whn nt fluent 3 out: chsd wnr next: narrow and brief ld appr last: no ex last 75yds* **9/2**[1]

2-20 3 10 **Dontpaytheferryman (USA)**[18] 1614 5-11-0 **116** FearghalDavis(3) 115
(Brian Ellison) *trckd ldrs: effrt 3 out: one pce fr next* **10/1**

/P2- 4 2½ **Degas Art (IRE)**[180] 5207 7-11-7 **123** JamesO'Farrell(3) 120
(Howard Johnson) *chsd ldrs: one pce fr 3 out* **8/1**[3]

1/4- 5 1¾ **Ahmedy (IRE)**[52] 4941 7-10-13 **112** DougieCostello 107
(John Quinn) *trckd ldrs: wnt 2nd 5th: hung lft appr 3 out: j.lft 2 out: stl 3rd last: sn wknd* **11/2**[2]

P0-0 6 26 **Farmers Cross (IRE)**[15] 1644 6-10-5 **104** RichieMcGrath 73
(Ferdy Murphy) *in rr: bhd fr 6th: kpt on fr 2 out: nvr on terms* **22/1**

4P-1 7 ¾ **Ashammar (FR)**[15] 1641 5-11-12 **125** DenisO'Regan 93
(Paul Webber) *trckd ldrs: effrt appr 3 out: wknd bef 2 out* **9/2**[1]

261- 8 ½ **Shadrack (IRE)**[211] 4666 6-11-1 **114** TjadeCollier 82
(Sue Smith) *chsd ldrs: drvn 6th: lost pl appr next* **11/1**

1050 9 5 **Crosby Jemma**[39] 1470 6-10-9 **108** BrianHughes 79
(Mike Sowersby) *in rr: bhd 5th: sme hdwy next: lost pl appr 3 out* **25/1**

02-U 10 3 **Teenage Idol (IRE)**[15] 1642 6-11-7 **123** RyanMania(3) 83
(Evelyn Slack) *in rr: j.rt 6th: bhd fr next: blnd 2 out* **33/1**

P633 11 ¾ **Nordwind (IRE)**[24] 1558 9-11-4 **120** DPFahy(3) 79
(Evan Williams) *in rr: reminders 6th: sn bhd: b.b.v* **14/1**

16/P 12 16 **Oakapple Express**[124] 708 10-10-10 **109** PaddyAspell 52
(Geoffrey Harker) *in rr: drvn 5th: sn bhd: t.o 3 out* **66/1**

3m 44.3s (-11.50) **Going Correction** -0.50s/f (Good) **12** Ran SP% **117.8**
Speed ratings (Par 107): **107,106,102,100,100 87,87,87,84,83 83,75**
toteswingers:1&2:£3.00, 1&3:£7.30, 2&3:£5.90 CSF £24.24 CT £194.35 TOTE £5.70: £1.90, £2.10, £2.90; EX 35.10.
Owner Mrs J M Gray **Bred** Twelve Oaks Stud Establishment **Trained** Middleham Moor, N Yorks

FOCUS
Quite a competitive handicap hurdle, and the form should stand up. It was run in a time below standard and over nine seconds quicker than the earlier juvenile event. The progressive winner produced a big step up, in a relatively fast time.

NOTEBOOK
Maska Pony(IRE) made it four wins in his last five starts with a game success from the front. Racing from 11lb higher than at Sedgefield, he had not run over this short since his bumper days but his win at Cartmel in late August was over only a furlong further than this. He is likely to have another run while the ground remains on the fast side, before being put away. (op 6-1)
Amazing King(IRE), who received a kick at the start, had every chance but the winner showed the greater battling qualities when it came down to it. He had dropped to a mark a pound lower than when gaining his last hurdles win, nearly two years ago, and this was a marked drop in grade after contesting the Galway Hurdle and a valuable handicap at Market Rasen on his last two starts. (op 11-2)
Dontpaytheferryman(USA) ran a solid race on this second run after a break, but remains 6lb higher than his most recent winning mark. He has the option of reverting to fences. (op 11-1)
Degas Art(IRE) ran a pleasing race on this first start since April, staying on again after losing his pitch, and is very well handicapped on his old form. (tchd 9-1)
Ahmedy(IRE), from a yard successful twice in this race in recent years, travelled well and looked the major threat to the winner at one stage before fading. He has run just twice over hurdles since winning in April 2007. (op 5-1 tchd 9-2)
Ashammar(FR) was found out under top weight on this handicap debut, weakening after being well enough placed turning into the straight. Official explanation: trainer had no explanation for the poor form shown (op 7-2 tchd 5-1)
Shadrack(IRE) can be expected to improve with this first run since March behind him, but he has risen 38lb in the weights since his first hurdles win back in January. (op 12-1 tchd 14-1)
Nordwind(IRE) Official explanation: trainer said gelding bled from the nose

1828 BOBBY RENTON H'CAP CHASE (16 fncs) 2m 4f 110y
3:55 (3:55) (Class 3) (0-135,133) 4-Y-0+
£5,635 (£1,665; £832; £416; £207; £104)

Form RPR

16-2 1 **Drever Route (IRE)**[159] 194 7-10-12 **119** TimmyMurphy 131+
(Howard Johnson) *hld up: wnt prom 9th: chsd ldrs 12th: led appr last: edgd rt after last: drvn out* **11/4**[1]

/223 2 1 **Film Festival (USA)**[19] 1606 7-10-3 **113** ow2 FearghalDavis(3) 122
(Brian Ellison) *t.k.h: trckd ldr: lft in ld 12th: hdd appr last: kpt on wl: a hld* **17/2**

11P2 3 8 **Kirkhammerton (IRE)**[10] 1690 8-10-5 **115** DannyCook(3) 119+
(Barry Leavy) *chsd ldrs: outpcd whn lft modest 3rd 4 out* **10/1**

31F0 4 16 **Grand Lahou (FR)**[18] 1609 7-11-5 **133** MrTomDavid(7) 124+
(Tim Vaughan) *led: j.rt: hit 11th: blnd and hdd next: sn wknd* **14/1**

21-2 5 ½ **General Hardi**[121] 746 9-10-11 **118** BrianHughes 103
(John Wade) *chsd ldrs: outpcd and lost pl 12th* **12/1**

406- 6 13 **Daldini**[169] 33 8-10-13 **120** TjadeCollier 92
(Sue Smith) *chsd ldrs: lost pl after 11th* **16/1**

0-33 P **War Party**[17] 1628 6-9-7 **107** PeterCarberry(7) —
(Dr Richard Newland) *in rr: bhd fr 8th: t.o whn blnd 4 out: p.u bef next* **6/1**[3]

32-5 F **Nikos Extra (FR)**[157] 236 6-11-5 **126** SamThomas —
(Alan King) *hld up: hdwy to trck ldrs 12th: cl 3rd whn fell next* **3/1**[2]

044- P **Fit To Drive**[178] 5246 8-11-4 **125** (t) WilsonRenwick —
(Brendan Powell) *chsd ldrs: shkn up 7th: outpcd 10th: lost pl next: bhd whn p.u bef 4 out* **10/1**

4m 47.8s (-20.00) **Going Correction** -0.775s/f (Firm) course record **9** Ran SP% **114.9**
Speed ratings (Par 107): **107,106,103,97,97 92,—,—,—**
toteswingers:1&2:£14.90, 1&3:£4.50, 2&3:£9.10 CSF £26.25 TOTE £4.20: £1.70, £2.70, £1.60; EX 25.70.
Owner Andrea & Graham Wylie **Bred** Patrick Doyle **Trained** Billy Row, Co Durham

FOCUS
A fair handicap chase in which the pace picked up on the second circuit, and the time was more than two seconds quicker than standard. The winner is on the upgrade and the third helps set the level.

NOTEBOOK
Drever Route(IRE), whose stamina for this trip was unproven, was ridden less prominently than usual on this first start since May. He got on top going to the last and stayed on well enough to give the Howard Johnson yard a third successive winner of this race. There are no immediate plans but he should have more to offer. (tchd 3-1)
Film Festival(USA)'s rider put up 2lb overweight, which meant he was effectively racing off a career-high mark. Another who usually runs over shorter, he was left in front at the last down the back and went down fighting. (op 9-1 tchd 10-1)

Kirkhammerton(IRE) lost his pitch after a mistake at the tenth and never really got back into it, although he was staying on steadily in the latter stages. (op 9-1)
Grand Lahou(FR) was 17lb above his last winning mark. He was once again let down by his jumping on this return to chasing, going out to his right and sketchy several times before he lost his lead with a shuddering error. The ability is there if he gets it together.
General Hardi, raised 6lb to a career-high mark after finishing second over this trip at Sedgefield, ran creditably on this first start for four months and will appreciate a return to further. (tchd 10-1)
Nikos Extra(FR), effectively making his seasonal return, was a close third when coming down at the first in the home straight, but for which he would surely have been in the shake-up. (op 9-1 tchd 11-1)
Fit To Drive did well last season and had conditions to suit on this reappearance, but she dropped away rather disappointingly. (op 9-1 tchd 11-1)

1829 RAMADA JARVIS WETHERBY NOVICES' HURDLE (11 hdls) 2m 4f
4:30 (4:30) (Class 4) 4-Y-0+ **£2,276** (£668; £334; £166)

Form RPR

P3-3 **1** **Icy Colt (ARG)**^{24} [1553] 4-10-5 107 (v) WillKennedy 106+
(Paul Webber) *trckd ldrs: upsides 7th: led next: styd on fr 3 out: nt fluent last: drvn rt out* **9/2**^{3}

0-10 **2** *4 1/2* **Montoya's Son (IRE)**^{20} [1594] 5-11-5 110 (t) BrianHughes 114
(Howard Johnson) *trckd ldrs: chsd wnr 3 out: rdn and no ex between last 2* **8/1**

1-55 **3** *3 3/4* **Lackamon**^{130} [632] 5-10-12 0 HenryOliver 105+
(Sue Smith) *led: hdd 6th: blnd 8th and sn wl outpcd: modest 5th: 2 out: styd on to take 3rd run-in* **22/1**

4 **4** *1* **Bavard Court (IRE)**^{28} [1526] 4-10-12 0 TomScudamore 102
(Tim Vaughan) *chsd ldrs: wnt 2nd 8th: rdn appr next: wknd run-in* **7/4**^{1}

-424 **5** *2* **Rain Stops Play (IRE)**^{15} [1641] 8-10-9 110 FearghalDavis$^{(3)}$ 102+
(Nicky Richards) *hld up in rr: stdy hdwy 7th: outpcd after next: modest 4th appr 3 out: nt fluent last: sn wknd* **14/1**

/F-6 **6** *3 3/4* **Ceasar's Return**^{15} [1643] 5-10-12 0 BarryKeniry 96
(George Moore) *in rr: sme hdwy 8th: 5th whn nt fluent next: kpt on fr 2 out: nvr nr ldrs* **33/1**

4-45 **7** *1 1/4* **Brooklyn Bay**^{15} [1643] 5-10-7 0 JamesHalliday$^{(5)}$ 95
(Malcolm Jefferson) *hld up in rr: sme hdwy 3 out: kpt on: nvr nr ldrs* **33/1**

1035 **8** *5* **Knar Mardy**^{17} [1625] 5-11-2 110 AdamPogson$^{(3)}$ 97
(Charles Pogson) *prom: outpcd 5th: lost pl 8th* **16/1**

6/0- **9** *2* **Dance Sauvage**^{400} [1410] 7-10-9 0 CampbellGillies$^{(3)}$ 88
(Mike Sowersby) *chsd ldrs: wknd after 8th* **150/1**

1-1F **10** *15* **Eliza Doalott (IRE)**^{147} [398] 8-10-5 0 DougieCostello 66
(Mrs M Stirk) *chsd ldrs: wl outpcd 8th: bhd whn heavily eased run-in* **7/2**^{2}

05- **11** *18* **Mannered**^{302} [2896] 5-10-5 0 MrJohnDawson$^{(7)}$ 55
(John Wade) *t.k.h: j lft 1st: sn w ldrs: led 6th: hdd 8th: sn wknd: t.o next* **33/1**

12 *51* **Astroleo**^{69} 4-10-12 0 DaveCrosse 4
(Mark H Tompkins) *hmpd 1st: in rr: hdwy and prom 5th: reminders 7th: sn wknd: t.o 3 out* **40/1**

4m 53.2s (-6.30) **Going Correction** -0.50s/f (Good)
WFA 4 from 5yo+ 10lb **12** Ran SP% **116.7**
Speed ratings (Par 105): **92,90,88,88,87 86,85,83,82,76 69,49**
toteswingers:1&2:£6.30, 1&3:£15.30, 2&3:£18.10 CSF £36.62 TOTE £5.40: £2.00, £1.50, £5.30; EX 34.20.
Owner Robert Kirkland **Bred** Alfredo Gorostiza **Trained** Mollington, Oxon

FOCUS
Ordinary novice hurdle form but not easy to pin a rating on with the first two on the upgrade.

NOTEBOOK
Icy Colt(ARG) has looked an improved performer since being fitted with headgear and he built on a promising reappearance at Uttoxeter, idling in front but still winning decisively. Bred in the southern hemisphere, he is six months behind the rest of his age group and has understandably taken time to mature, but is getting his act together now. His trainer thinks he'll make a chaser in time. (op 7-1)
Montoya's Son(IRE), who may still have some strengthening to do, was tried in a tongue tie. He ran a decent race but this longer trip just seemed to stretch him late on. (op 7-1 tchd 17-2)
Lackamon lost ground with a mistake at the last down the back, but was staying on stoutly again late on. Easier ground will help his cause. (op 20-1 tchd 25-1)
Bavard Court(IRE) showed a respectable level of form in Ireland for Michael Hourigan, but he was found wanting on this British debut after holding every chance. (op 15-8 tchd 13-8)
Rain Stops Play(IRE) looked to be travelling well when improving down the far side only to allow the leaders to get away from him on the approach to the home straight. He did plug on from there, but the return to this longer trip did not look to suit. (op 10-1)
Ceasar's Return stayed on from the back and overturned Sedgefield running with Brooklyn Bay.
Brooklyn Bay made modest late gains. (op 28-1)
Eliza Doalott(IRE), a prolific pointer/hunter chaser, was well beaten on this return to hurdles after a five-month absence. Her rider eased her after the last. Official explanation: jockey said, regarding running and riding, that his orders were to jump off handy, giving the mare plenty of room, not to get crowded and do his best, adding that having jumped off wide it became very keen as it was the first run of the season and there was no pace, as the race quickened down the back straight, it became outpaced, at which point it blew up, staying on one paced to the line. (op 9-2)

1830 INVESTEC BEGINNERS' CHASE (18 fncs) 3m 1f
5:00 (5:01) (Class 5) 4-Y-0+ **£1,951** (£573; £286; £143)

Form RPR

U **1** **Sweden (IRE)**^{161} [152] 6-11-5 0 GrahamLee 102+
(Evan Williams) *chsd ldrs: led 4 out: sn hdd: styd on and upsides last: led narrowly run-in: all out* **5/2**^{2}

46-P **2** *nk* **New Shuil (IRE)**^{15} [1645] 6-10-12 0 MrJohnDawson$^{(7)}$ 103+
(John Wade) *stdd s: hld up in rr: smooth hdwy 11th: led on bit after 4 out: jnd last: sn narrowly hdd: no ex towards fin* **8/1**

P2-6 **3** *12* **Greenbelt**^{15} [1642] 9-11-5 114 (p) BarryKeniry 90
(George Moore) *w ldrs: led briefly appr 4 out: 3rd and one pce whn pckd 2 out* **6/1**^{3}

4 *9* **Ramborob (IRE)**^{150} 5-11-5 0 PeterBuchanan 81
(Mike Sowersby) *wnt prom 8th: hit 12th: drvn 14th: wknd appr 2 out* **12/1**

FP **5** *42* **Wapiti Creek (IRE)**^{44} [1426] 6-10-12 0 (t) WillKennedy 31
(John G Carr, Ire) *led: j.rt 7th: hdd appr 4 out: sn wknd: t.o 3 out* **28/1**

0/P- **P** **The Client (IRE)**^{150} 9-10-12 0 JoeCornwall$^{(7)}$ —
(David Pearson) *chsd ldrs: reminders 7th: wknd 9th: t.o next: p.u bef 4 out* **66/1**

U **Macs Lad (IRE)**^{128} 7-11-0 0 MissLHorner$^{(5)}$ —
(Liam Corcoran) *prom: mstke and rdr briefly lost iron 2nd: sddle slipped and uns rdr bef next* **13/2**

0/0- **U** **Long Strand (IRE)**^{8} [1721] 6-11-2 110 DGHogan$^{(3)}$ —
(C F Swan, Ire) *t.k.h: trckd ldrs: stdd 5th: blnd and uns rdr next* **9/4**^{1}

6m 1.00s (-8.40) **Going Correction** -0.775s/f (Firm) course record **8** Ran SP% **110.7**
Speed ratings (Par 103): **92,91,88,85,71 —,—,—**
toteswingers:1&2:£6.50, 1&3:£2.50, 2&3:£3.80 CSF £21.12 TOTE £3.40: £1.20, £2.00, £1.40; EX 23.80.
Owner Mr & Mrs William Rucker **Bred** Patrick Condon **Trained** Llancarfan, Vale Of Glamorgan

FOCUS
A very weak beginners' chase and not form to treat too seriously. The first two may go on to rate higher.

NOTEBOOK
Sweden(IRE), one of several point-to-pointers in this line-up, has joined Evan Williams from the Sheila Crow yard, the same route taken by Foxhunters' winner Cappa Bleu. An unseater in a Cheltenham hunter chase when last seen in May, he jumped soundly bar getting in too close three out and rallied well to snatch the race close home. While he might struggle under a penalty, there is improvement in him and he will not mind easier ground. (op 11-4)
New Shuil(IRE)'s saddle slipped early on his recent chase debut. He looked set to win when taking it up travelling easily, but might have been in front soon enough and was run out of it late on. (op 10-1)
Greenbelt, the pick on official figures, had the cheekpieces on for the first time over jumps and was fitter for his recent return. He ran his race without any obvious excuses, and continues below par. (op 5-1)
Ramborob(IRE) won a maiden point when last seen in May and he performed respectably on this debut under rules, if looking rather one-paced. (op 10-1)
Wapiti Creek(IRE) jumped well out in front, but was swallowed up turning into the home straight. She has won a 3m point, but the trip looked to stretch her here. (op 22-1 tchd 33-1)
Macs Lad(IRE) Official explanation: jockey said saddle slipped (op 5-2)
Long Strand(IRE) was out of the race at an early stage. (op 5-2)

1831 BET365 CHARLIE HALL - 29/30 OCTOBER MAIDEN HURDLE (DIV I) (9 hdls) 2m 110y
5:30 (5:32) (Class 5) 4-Y-0+ **£1,370** (£399; £199)

Form RPR

320- **1** **Warrior One**^{215} [4552] 4-10-11 101 RyanMania$^{(3)}$ 114+
(Howard Johnson) *trckd ldrs: wnt 2nd appr 3 out: led on bit after 2 out: sn qcknd clr: v readily* **6/4**^{1}

03 **2** *13* **Red Skipper (IRE)**^{44} [1426] 5-11-0 0 WilsonRenwick 96
(Noel Wilson) *hld up: trckd ldrs 4th: hit next: sn outpcd: styd on fr 2 out: tk 2nd run-in* **5/1**^{3}

3 **3** *2 1/2* **Global**^{12} [1278] 4-10-11 0 FearghalDavis$^{(3)}$ 95
(Brian Ellison) *w ldr: led after 3rd: hit next: hdd after 2 out: one pce and lost 2nd run-in* **7/2**^{2}

4 *3 1/4* **Morocchius (USA)**^{14} 5-11-0 0 LiamHeard 92
(Julie Camacho) *stdd s: hld up towards rr: stdy hdwy 6th: chsng ldrs next: one pce* **10/1**

234- **5** *10* **Otto Quercus (FR)**^{217} [4511] 5-11-0 0 BrianHughes 80
(John Wade) *led to 4th: wknd appr 2 out* **8/1**

00-6 **6** *1/2* **Railway Park (IRE)**^{17} [1624] 6-11-0 95 (v) PaddyAspell 80
(John Wainwright) *chsd ldrs: upsides 4th: lost pl after 3 out* **12/1**

0 **7** *16* **Furius**^{17} [1629] 4-11-0 0 HenryOliver 64
(Sue Smith) *t.k.h towards rr: drvn 5th: lost pl after next sn bhd* **66/1**

-F60 **8** *1* **Simplified**^{60} [1249] 7-10-7 65 (t) AndrewGlassonbury 56
(Michael Chapman) *towards rr: bhd and drvn 6th* **100/1**

5 **P** **Rowaad**^{56} [1280] 5-10-7 0 MrJFlook$^{(7)}$ —
(Andrew Price) *prom to 3rd: drvn and lost pl 5th: sn bhd: t.o whn p.u bef 3 out* **100/1**

0-0P **U** **Still Royal**^{139} [494] 4-11-0 84 (t) GrahamLee —
(John Davies) *trckd ldrs: stmbld landing and uns rdr 3rd* **66/1**

3m 51.4s (-4.40) **Going Correction** -0.50s/f (Good) **10** Ran SP% **111.7**
Speed ratings (Par 103): **90,83,82,81,76 76,68,68,—,—**
toteswingers:1&2:£2.50, 1&3:£2.80, 2&3:£4.90 CSF £8.93 TOTE £2.50: £1.20, £1.70, £2.20; EX 11.30.
Owner Mrs B Halman & J H Johnson **Bred** Ermyn Lodge Stud Limited **Trained** Billy Row, Co Durham

FOCUS
A very modest maiden hurdle. A big step up from the easy winner with the next two close to their marks.

NOTEBOOK
Warrior One was placed on his first three starts last term, but had not been seen since dropping away tamely on his handicap debut back in March. He ran out an easy winner and, while the opposition was distinctly limited, he gave the impression that he can win again if not overfaced. (op 7-4)
Red Skipper(IRE) was third to Maska Pony, an earlier winner on this card, on his latest start at Cartmel. He was never close enough to mount a challenge, but stayed on well past toiling rivals from the second-last. (op 9-2)
Global again keen on this second try over hurdles, was allowed to go on with a circuit to run. He had no chance when the winner eased past and lost second on the run-in, appearing to confirm that he lacks stamina. (op 3-1 tchd 11-4)
Morocchius(USA) was without the regular tongue strap on this hurdles debut. A 56-rated handicapper on the Flat, he made good progress from the rear to get into contention before his effort flattened out. (op 12-1)
Otto Quercus(FR), formerly with Charlie Longsdon, was the clear top-rated on BHA ratings. Reverting to hurdles, he shaped as if this first run since March was needed. (op 6-1)
Rowaad Official explanation: trainer said gelding had a breathing problem

1832 BET365 CHARLIE HALL - 29/30 OCTOBER MAIDEN HURDLE (DIV II) (9 hdls) 2m 110y
6:00 (6:00) (Class 5) 4-Y-0+ **£1,370** (£399; £199)

Form RPR

1 **Delphi Mountain (IRE)**^{16} [1639] 5-10-11 110 DGHogan$^{(3)}$ 114+
(C F Swan, Ire) *chsd ldrs: shkn up after 6th: upsides 2 out: led last: rdn out* **6/4**^{1}

2 *1 1/4* **Buddy Holly**^{11} 5-11-0 0 WillKennedy 111+
(F Jordan) *trckd ldrs: led 2 out: hdd last: no ex* **10/1**

60-2 **3** *9* **Altan Khan**^{18} [1613] 5-10-9 0 JamesHalliday$^{(5)}$ 105+
(Malcolm Jefferson) *hld up: hdwy to trck ldrs 4th: ev ch tl wknd between last 2* **5/1**^{3}

4 **4** *6* **Hustle (IRE)**^{5} [1433] 5-11-0 0 GrahamLee 98
(Gay Kelleway) *trckd ldr: led after 5th: hdd 2 out: 4th and wl btn whn mstke last* **8/1**

5 *1/2* **Bagutta Sun**^{11} 4-10-4 0 DannyCook$^{(3)}$ 90
(Barry Leavy) *in rr: styd on fr 3 out: nvr nr ldrs* **33/1**

P/5- **6** *15* **Bergonzi (IRE)**^{38} [1499] 6-11-0 0 TimmyMurphy 80
(Howard Johnson) *hld up: nt fluent: hdwy 6th: chsng ldrs appr next: sn rdn and btn* **11/4**^{2}

7 *1 3/4* **Kimberley Downs (USA)**^{48} 4-10-11 0 HarryHaynes$^{(3)}$ 79
(Noel Wilson) *chsd ldrs: lost pl appr 3 out* **18/1**

PP **P** **That's All Right (IRE)**^{15} [1643] 7-10-7 0 (v^{1}) BrianToomey$^{(7)}$ —
(Kevin M Prendergast) *led and sn clr: blnd 3rd: wknd 5th: sn hdd: t.o next: p.u bef 3 out* **100/1**

P **Willent**^{251} 4-11-0 0 DougieCostello —
(Julie Camacho) *nt jump wl in rr: bhd fr 3rd: t.o 6th: p.u bef next* **80/1**

PPPF F **Modestine**[53] 1337 8-10-4 0 RyanMania(3) —
(Jane Walton) *in rr: nt fluent 1st: fell heavily 2nd* **150/1**

3m 51.6s (-4.20) **Going Correction** -0.50s/f (Good) **10** Ran SP% **114.6**
Speed ratings (Par 103): **89,88,84,81,81 74,73,—,—,—**
totesuper7: Win: Not won. Place: £30.70. CSF £17.67 TOTE £2.60: £1.30, £2.50, £2.40; EX 17.30 Place 6 £185.06; Place 5 £44.38.
Owner Mrs T P Hyde/Mrs T Hyde/Mrs P Shanahan **Bred** Tim Hegarty **Trained** Cloughjordan, Co Tipperary

FOCUS
This looked the weaker division, although the time was only slightly slower. The time reads sound enough.

NOTEBOOK
Delphi Mountain(IRE), an Irish raider, had run creditably behind three previous winners at Roscommon last time and this was an easier assignment. He won reasonably comfortably, but defying a penalty may be beyond him. (op 15-8 tchd 2-1)
Buddy Holly, third on the Flat on his recent debut for the yard, ran creditably on this hurdles debut, finishing clear of the third, but it should be emphasised that this was a very moderate event. (op 15-2)
Altan Khan, an eye-catching second to Karasenir last time, was unable to build on that under a more prominent ride but was not given a hard time when held. (op 6-1)
Hustle(IRE) failed to settle and was still keen when finding himself in front. His exertions told from the second-last. (op 7-1)
Bagutta Sun stayed on quite well from the back and would have been fourth but for a last-flight mistake. She might be up to winning a seller somewhere. (tchd 40-1)
Bergonzi(IRE) seemed to confirm that hurdling is not for him. Official explanation: jockey said gelding did not jump with any fluency (op 10-3)
T/Jkpt: Not won. T/Plt: £221.20 to a £1 stake. Pool:£61,365.59 - 202.48 winning tickets T/Qpdt: £63.20 to a £1 stake. Pool:£4,330.72 - 50.70 winning tickets WG

1833 - 1839a (Foreign Racing) - See Raceform Interactive

180 WINCANTON (R-H)

Thursday, October 14

OFFICIAL GOING: Good to firm (good in places)
Wind: Moderate across Weather: Overcast

1840 HIGOS INSURANCE SERVICES 20TH ANNIVERSARY H'CAP HURDLE (11 hdls) 2m 6f
2:20 (2:20) (Class 5) (0-95,95) 4-Y-O+ **£1,951** (£573; £286; £143)

Form RPR
4060 1 **Heir To Be**[7] 1745 11-11-12 **95** (b) NickScholfield 115+
(Michael Blake) *mde all: jnd wl bef 2 out: c readily clr sn after and in n.d: easily* **12/1**
4221 2 12 **Northern Lad (IRE)**[7] 1741 8-11-12 **95** APMcCoy 105+
(Jim Best) *stdd and plld hrd in rr: stl keen after 6th: stdy hdwy to go 2nd after 3 out: jnd wnr wl bef next: sn rdn and continually hung rt: fnd no ex and sn btn* **1/1**[1]
1-65 3 10 **Bollywood (IRE)**[8] 1735 7-10-11 **80** (t) AndrewThornton 76
(Alison Batchelor) *in rr: sme hdwy 7th: hrd rdn fr 2 out to take n.d 3rd last* **8/1**[3]
5545 4 ½ **Vacario (GER)**[7] 1745 6-11-8 **94** (t) TommyPhelan(3) 90
(Mark Gillard) *chsd ldrs: drvn along fr 7th: hit 3 out: wnt one pce 3rd 3 out: nvr rchd ldng duo and dropped to 4th last: styd on to press fr that position run-in* **12/1**
44 5 14 **Himitas (FR)**[25] 1559 5-11-0 **90** MattGriffiths(7) 72
(Graeme McPherson) *in tch: nt fluent 3rd: j. slowly 7th: chsd ldrs 3 out: wknd sn after* **7/2**[2]
2212 6 4½ **Rash Moment (FR)**[12] 1678 11-11-5 **88** (p) TomScudamore 65
(Michael Scudamore) *chsd wnr tl after 3 out: wknd sn after* **10/1**
P-PP 7 19 **Rapid Return (IRE)**[130] 650 7-11-7 **90** RichardJohnson 48
(Richard Phillips) *chsd ldrs: rdn 3 out: wknd wl bef next* **25/1**
6464 8 3¾ **Singapore Harbour (IRE)**[56] 1289 4-11-7 **90** LeightonAspell 44
(Oliver Sherwood) *nt fluent: bhd fr 4th* **33/1**
P P **Laureus (GER)**[25] 1552 7-10-9 **78** (v[1]) AidanColeman —
(Rachel Hobbs) *in rr: hit 3rd: stl bhd whn hit 3 out: sn wknd: t.o whn p.u bef 2 out* **66/1**

4m 57.77s (-28.73) **Going Correction** -1.40s/f (Hard) course record
WFA 4 from 5yo+ 10lb **9** Ran SP% **116.1**
Speed ratings (Par 103): **96,91,88,87,82 81,74,72,—**
toteswingers:1&2: £4.70, 2&3: £2.90, 1&3: £10.70 CSF £25.34 CT £109.88 TOTE £11.30: £2.90, £1.30, £1.70; EX 42.30.
Owner Staverton Owners Group **Bred** I Stewart-Brown And M Meacock **Trained** Trowbridge, Wilts

FOCUS
The ground, which was officially good, good to firm in places, must have been quick as this opening handicap hurdle was run in a course record time. This was a weak race but the winner was very well in on his best 2009 form.

NOTEBOOK
Heir To Be, well beaten in a selling handicap hurdle just last week, returned to form in no uncertain terms, making every yard, and he even had the luxury of being eased having galloped on relentlessly to go clear. It's possible he will be retired now, if so it was a fine way to go out. (op 14-1 tchd 16-1)
Northern Lad(IRE) was expected to follow up last week's Exeter win, as he's due to go up 13lb from Saturday, but he refused to settle and then hung under strong pressure down the straight, in the end proving no match for the back-to-form winner. Things are only going to get tougher. (tchd 11-10 in places)
Bollywood(IRE) kept on late for third, but was never a threat.
Vacario(GER) was again comfortably held and remains winless in handicaps. (op 16-1)
Himitas(FR) was the disappointment of the race, failing to build on what was a promising run at Uttoxeter latest. (op 9-2)

1841 HIGOS INSURANCE SERVICES H'CAP CHASE (17 fncs) 2m 5f
2:50 (2:50) (Class 4) (0-110,110) 4-Y-O+ **£3,252** (£955; £477; £238)

Form RPR
4403 1 **Intac (IRE)**[21] 1589 8-11-12 **110** JoeTizzard 123+
(Colin Tizzard) *trckd ldr: hit 8th: led appr 3 out: styd on strly fr next and in command whn nt fluent last: drvn out* **5/1**[3]
3512 2 6 **Morestead (IRE)**[21] 1589 5-11-8 **106** (b) LeightonAspell 112
(Brendan Powell) *led tl hdd appr 3 out: styd on same pce fr next* **13/2**
46P4 3 8 **Hereweareagain (IRE)**[21] 1589 7-11-3 **101** (bt) TomO'Brien 101
(Philip Hobbs) *towards rr but in tch: hdwy 13th: nt fluent 3 out: styd on to take one pce 3rd next* **4/1**[2]
U3F0 4 4½ **Nawow**[21] 1589 10-11-1 **102** (tp) PeterToole(3) 96
(Matt Hazell) *chsd ldrs: rdn 13th: no ch w ldrs fr 3 out: styd on for mod 4th run-in* **25/1**
0-01 5 3½ **The Darling Boy**[7] 1744 5-10-5 **89** (t) PaddyBrennan 88+
(Tom George) *chsd ldrs: nt fluent 6th and 7th: hit 10th: styng on strly in 3rd whn blnd 3 out: rcvrd and stl ch whn blnd bdly next and nt rcvr: mstke last* **7/4**[1]
-23P 6 ¾ **Chilbury Hill (IRE)**[109] 848 7-11-0 **98** LiamHeard 89
(Kevin Bishop) *hit 1st: in tch: hdwy 9th: chsd ldrs 4 out: wknd: next* **14/1**
6036 P **Some Craic (IRE)**[21] 1589 10-11-10 **108** RichardJohnson —
(Paul Henderson) *chsd ldrs: blnd 7th: in rr fr 9th: t.o whn p.u bef 3 out* **7/1**

5m 5.70s (-19.50) **Going Correction** -0.80s/f (Firm) **7** Ran SP% **109.4**
Speed ratings (Par 105): **105,102,99,97,96 96,—**
toteswingers:1&2: £3.50, 2&3: £3.80, 1&3: £3.50 CSF £33.02 CT £128.85 TOTE £7.00: £2.80, £3.80; EX 28.30.
Owner Stranger, Mogridge, Romans **Bred** Patrick A Keogh **Trained** Milborne Port, Dorset

FOCUS
Just a modest handicap chase. The winner's Newton Abbot second to Classic Swain could be rated to this sort of level but he produced a big turnaround on his latest run compared with the second.

NOTEBOOK
Intac(IRE)ran better when third off this mark at Fontwell and he built on that with a workmanlike victory, leading three out and staying on well. This was his first win in a handicap over fences, but he's not the most consistent. (op 6-1)
Morestead(IRE) was up another 6lb and seemed to run his race, finishing clear of the third. (op 5-1)
Hereweareagain(IRE), swapping cheekpieces for blinkers, plodded on in third but never looked like winning. (op 5-1)
Nawow still doesn't look to have recovered from a fall he took at Stratford on his penultimate start. Official explanation: vet said gelding lost a near-fore shoe (op 16-1)
The Darling Boy blundered his chance away. Despite a catalogue of mistakes, he still came to hold every chance in the straight, but he hit the third-last, and a more serious error two out ended his hopes. This was a disconcerting performance and some extensive schooling is clearly required. (tchd 6-4)

1842 HIGOS IS SOMERSET BUSINESS OF THE YEAR NOVICES' H'CAP HURDLE (10 hdls) 2m 4f
3:20 (3:20) (Class 4) (0-115,114) 3-Y-O+ **£2,602** (£764; £382; £190)

Form RPR
00-0 1 **Uffa Fox (IRE)**[106] 864 7-10-4 **92** ow2 (t) DarylJacob 96+
(Ben De Haan) *in rr but in tch: nt fluent 4 out: hdwy 3 out: pressed ldrs fr 2 out: edgd lft and rt last: r.o strly run-in to ld last stride: dismntd* **6/1**[3]
4P63 2 nse **Unleashed (IRE)**[23] 1571 5-11-3 **105** NoelFehily 107
(Charlie Mann) *in rr but in tch: hdwy and hit 4 out: chsd ldrs next: led after 2 out: styd on wl run-in: ct last stride* **5/1**[1]
1453 3 ¾ **Folie A Deux (IRE)**[20] 1604 8-11-1 **103** (t) JoeTizzard 104
(Colin Tizzard) *led after 1st: rdn and hdd after 2 out: wl there whn n.m.r and swtchd lft last: rallied and kpt on run-in: nt quite gng pce of ldng duo fnl 50yds* **11/2**[2]
0/32 4 2 **Prince Tom**[114] 820 6-11-7 **114** IanPopham(5) 114
(Paul Nicholls) *chsd ldrs: ev ch 2 out tl rt there whn nt fluent last: styd on same pce* **5/1**[1]
1235 5 4 **Forest Rhythm (IRE)**[101] 914 6-11-5 **110** WayneKavanagh(3) 107
(Seamus Mullins) *chsd ldrs: t.k.h: wnt 2nd after 3 out: ev ch 2 out tl mstke last and sn btn* **11/2**[2]
513U 6 28 **Grand Bay (USA)**[25] 1546 9-11-3 **105** (vt[1]) APMcCoy 84+
(Jonjo O'Neill) *in rr: hit 6th: hdwy to get in tch w main gp after 3 out: wknd bef next* **7/1**
3440 7 24 **Parazar (FR)**[21] 1592 5-10-3 **91** LeightonAspell 34
(Oliver Sherwood) *prom early: mstke 6th and sn bhd* **5/1**[1]
6-53 8 10 **Sir Bere (FR)**[20] 1600 4-11-8 **110** (p) TomScudamore 43
(Rebecca Curtis) *led tl after 1st: rdn 6th: chsd ldr tl after 3 out: sn btn* **20/1**

4m 29.46s (-27.34) **Going Correction** -1.40s/f (Hard) **8** Ran SP% **112.3**
Speed ratings (Par 105): **105,104,104,103,102 91,81,77**
toteswingers:1&2: £4.60, 2&3: £7.10, 1&3 £9.70 CSF £34.87 CT £172.51 TOTE £7.80: £3.20, £3.00, £1.10; EX 37.80.
Owner Lady V Aitken Mrs F Walwyn D Heath **Bred** Mrs Margaret O'Donnell **Trained** Lambourn, Berks

FOCUS
They went 5-1 the field for this novices' handicap hurdle, despite there being just the eight runners, and it was no surprise to see more than half of them in with a chance two out. Ordinary handicap form with the winner 4lb off his best and the next three close to their marks.

NOTEBOOK
Uffa Fox(IRE), off since finishing well beaten on his chase debut at Worcester in June, had the blinkers removed and travelled like a much-improved horse. Having moved through to challenge, he made a mistake two out that could easily have cost him the race, but he rallied well and just managed to get back up on the line. Considering his rider was putting up 2lb overweight, he'll be thankful he got the horse back up, but it was unfortunate to see him dismounted after the line, reportedly returning lame behind. (op 5-1 tchd 13-2)
Unleashed(IRE) was always likely to improve for the switch to handicaps and he came through to lead after two out, but got in a bit close to the last and was nailed by the winner in the final stride. The ground seemed to suit him well and he should go one better before long. (op 11-2)
Folie A Deux(IRE), rated 8lb lower over hurdles compared to fences, was soon in front and tried to rally once headed, but became a bit squeezed for room and was always being held late on. (op 5-1 tchd 6-1)
Prince Tom, dropping 2f in trip for this handicap debut, had his chance but couldn't quicken late on and will be suited by a step up to 3m. (tchd 9-2)
Forest Rhythm(IRE), 13lb higher than when winning here back in May, was held when hitting the last and again looked to find this trip beyond him. (op 6-1 tchd 13-2)
Parazar(FR) dropped right out of contention and has a bit to prove following this. (op 7-1)

1843 HIGOS INSURANCE SERVICES SOMERTON H'CAP CHASE (21 fncs) 3m 1f 110y
3:50 (3:51) (Class 4) (0-100,97) 4-Y-O+ **£3,252** (£955; £477; £238)

Form RPR
0-00 1 **Outside Investor (IRE)**[88] 1027 10-9-12 **74** (p) KeiranBurke(5) 89
(Patrick Rodford) *trckd ldr: upsides fr 10th tl led 14th: narrowly hdd 16th: sn led again: rdn and styd on appr 3 out: hit 2 out: kpt on wl* **12/1**
4426 2 5 **Lord Lescribaa (FR)**[54] 1331 7-10-9 **80** (tp) RhysFlint 89
(Philip Hobbs) *prom: wnt 2nd 4 out: rdn and styd on: no imp on wnr fr next* **4/1**[2]
4154 3 5 **Keltic Lord**[25] 1550 14-11-10 **95** NickScholfield 99
(Peter Hiatt) *led: jnd fr 10th: hdd14th: styd challnging and led again 16th: sn hdd: dropped to 3rd appr 4 out and styd on same pce fr 3 out* **9/1**
63-1 4 10 **Orion Star (IRE)**[163] 132 8-10-2 **78** (p) JimmyDerham(5) 75+
(Seamus Mullins) *chsd ldrs: hit 2nd: rdn and bhd 17th: styd on to take wl hld 4th 3 out* **11/4**[1]

0023 **5** *2 ¼* **Classic Clover**[25] 1550 10-11-12 **97**..............................(t) AidanColeman 91
(Colin Tizzard) *in tch: rdn 12th and lost position: rallied to chse ldrs after next: wknd and blnd 17th* **5/1**[3]
4434 **6** *18* **Converti**[11] 1710 6-11-5 **90**..............................(p) RodiGreene 64
(Simon Burrough) *in rr: rdn 10th: wknd and hit 16th* **8/1**
143- **P** **Wizard Of Edge**[216] 4571 10-11-10 **95**.............................. TimmyMurphy —
(Ron Hodges) *sn bhd: t.o whn p.u bef 9th* **5/1**[3]
PP6P **P** **Hazelbury**[12] 1678 9-10-0 **71** oh13.............................. TomMessenger —
(Nigel Hawke) *rdn and bhd fr 12th: t.o whn p.u bef 16th* **40/1**
6m 20.0s (-19.50) **Going Correction** -0.80s/f (Firm) **8** Ran SP% **111.2**
Speed ratings (Par 105): **98,96,94,91,91 85,—,—**
CSF £57.35 CT £444.54 TOTE £20.00: £5.90, £2.10, £1.60; EX 78.60.
Owner E T Wey **Bred** Moyglare Stud Farm Ltd **Trained** Ash, Somerset

FOCUS
A low-grade handicap chase. The surprise winner was 5lb off his best 2009 form, with the second rated to his mark.

NOTEBOOK
Outside Investor(IRE) had run dreadfully on each of his six starts since winning 14 months ago. Swapping blinkers for cheekpieces, he was never far from the pace and, having taken over quite a way out, he galloped on relentlessly for a hard-fought success. It remains to be seen whether he can back this up. (tchd 14-1)
Lord Lescribaa(FR) bounced back from a below-par effort at Newton Abbot and clearly benefited from a short break.
Keltic Lord couldn't match the front pair in the end but continues to give a good account. (op 17-2 tchd 8-1)
Orion Star(IRE) made mistakes and in the end wasn't up to it off 10lb higher. (op 7-2)
Classic Clover was a bit below his best. (op 9-2)
Wizard Of Edge probably needed this first start in 216 days. Official explanation: jockey said gelding was unsuited by the good to firm (good in places) ground (op 9-2)

1844 ELITE RACING CLUB H'CAP HURDLE (8 hdls) 2m
4:20 (4:24) (Class 4) (0-110,110) 4-Y-0+ **£2,602** (£764; £382; £190)

Form RPR
4143 **1** **Nothing Is Forever (IRE)**[38] 1492 6-10-11 **95**..............(p) DarylJacob 100+
(Liam Corcoran) *chsd ldr: led appr 2 out: rdn and jnd last: kpt on u.p run-in: edgd rt cl home* **9/1**
P450 **2** *¾* **Raise Again (IRE)**[21] 1592 7-9-10 **85** oh5 ow1............(b) KeiranBurke(5) 88
(Nerys Dutfield) *chsd ldrs: wnt 2nd after 2 out: n.m.r on ins appr last: sn chalng: kpt on: a jst hld* **20/1**
00 0 **3** *3 ½* **Slam**[161] 185 6 10 8 **92**.............................. PaddyBrennan 92
(Tom George) *hld up in rr: stdy hdwy fr 4 out: trckd ldrs after next: rdn and kpt on same pce after 2 out* **7/2**[1]
26 **4** *1 ½* **Society Venue**[39] 1487 5-11-12 **110**.............................. TomScudamore 109
(Michael Scudamore) *in rr: hdwy fr 3f out: hdwy on ins appr 2 out: then nt fluent: styd on again run-in* **16/1**
31-5 **5** *¾* **Mayberry**[137] 534 5-11-10 **108**.............................. JackDoyle 109+
(Emma Lavelle) *mstkes 1st: 2nd and 3rd: sn towards rr: hdwy 2 out: sn rdn: styd on same pce appr last* **7/1**
6-32 **6** *shd* **Halling Gal**[57] 1280 4-11-6 **104**.............................. PaulMoloney 102
(Evan Williams) *led tl hdd appr 2 out: styd on same pce appr last* **8/1**
100/ **7** *¾* **Master Mahogany**[43] 4533 9-11-4 **109**.............................. MattGriffiths(7) 106
(Ron Hodges) *in rr hdwy 3 out and chsd ldrs appr next: kpt on same pce appr last* **28/1**
2544 **8** *shd* **Foreign King (USA)**[14] 1548 6-10-12 **101**.............................. JimmyDerham(5) 99+
(Seamus Mullins) *in rr: rdn 4 out: styd on fr 2 out: keeping on whn blnd last* **6/1**[3]
P-10 **9** *hd* **Tiermore (IRE)**[25] 1553 6-11-5 **110**.............................. MrPJTolman(7) 107
(Sirrell Griffiths) *chsd ldrs: blnd 2nd: rdn 2 out: styd on one pce* **20/1**
P463 **10** *2 ¼* **Timoca (IRE)**[43] 1453 5-10-6 **93**.............................. DPFahy(3) 87
(Evan Williams) *in tch 4th: pushed along fr 3 out: no imp on ldrs fr 2 out* **9/2**[2]
P0 **11** *4 ½* **Rolanta (FR)**[20] 1601 5-10-6 **90**.............................. HaddenFrost 80
(James Frost) *nvr beyond mid-div* **100/1**
U-P5 **12** *52* **Holden Caulfield (IRE)**[38] 1488 5-10-11 **95**..............(t) RodiGreene 33
(Nick Ayliffe) *in rr: sme hdwy 4th: sn wknd: t.o* **50/1**
6-23 **P** **Windpfeil (IRE)**[152] 338 4-10-11 **95**..............(tp) ColinBolger —
(Simon Burrough) *in rr hdwy 4th: chsd ldrs 3 out: wknd 2 out p.u after last: lame* **16/1**
3m 26.8s (-22.10) **Going Correction** -1.40s/f (Hard) course record
WFA 4 from 5yo+ 9lb **13** Ran SP% **116.0**
Speed ratings (Par 105): **99,98,96,96,95 95,95,95,95,94 91,65,—**
toteswingers:1&2: £23.50, 2&3: £19.70, 1&3: £9.60 CSF £172.36 CT £751.39 TOTE £11.80: £3.60, £6.80, £1.30; EX 196.10.
Owner The Globe Partnership **Bred** Reg Griffin And Jim McGrath **Trained** Charlton Adam, Somerset

FOCUS
An ordinary handicap hurdle where they finished in a heap despite the apparent fast time. The first two were well in on 2009 form with the next pair posting small personal bests.

NOTEBOOK
Nothing Is Forever(IRE) battled on gamely when joined to win his second race of the season. This was the highest mark he has won off, and it remains to be seen whether he's up to defying much of a rise. (op 8-1 tchd 10-1)
Raise Again(IRE) ran a blinder considering he was 5lb out of the handicap. This was easily his best effort in 18 months, but it remains to be seen whether he can repeat the form. (tchd 18-1)
Slam was expected to return an improved performer having been given a breathing operation. He travelled well, but didn't have the speed to win the race and looks in need of a stiffer test. There are races to be won with him. Official explanation: vet said gelding had been struck into left-hind (op 9-2)
Society Venue bounced back from a poor effort at Worcester, appreciating the move into handicaps.
Mayberry looks to slowly be working her way back to form, so watch out for her in the coming weeks. (op 9-2)
Halling Gal was readily swept aside having made the running, but did keep on. (op 17-2 tchd 10-1)
Master Mahogany made a satisfactory return. (op 25-1 tchd 33-1)
Foreign King(USA), a winner on the Flat last month, was trying to stay on when meeting the last wrong. (op 11-2 tchd 5-1)
Timoca(IRE) failed to reproduce the form of her Hereford third off this 3lb higher mark. (op 6-1)
Windpfeil(IRE) Official explanation: vet said gelding pulled up lame but was subsequently found to be sound

1845 HIGOS INSURANCE SERVICES WELLS JUVENILE MAIDEN HURDLE (8 hdls) 2m
4:50 (4:51) (Class 4) 3-Y-O **£2,665** (£827; £445)

Form RPR
4 **1** **Until The Man (IRE)**[8] 1728 3-10-12 0.............................. APMcCoy 82+
(Jim Best) *chsd ldr: led appr 2 out: nt fluent last: strly chal fnl 100yds: edgd lft: drvn out* **5/4**[1]
0 **2** *¾* **Lady Willa (IRE)**[21] 1586 3-10-2 0.............................. TommyPhelan(3) 71
(Mark Gillard) *in rr: hdwy appr 2 out: styd on to chse wnr last and kpt on to chal fnl 100yds: no ex nr fin* **12/1**
5 **3** *6* **Royal Etiquette (IRE)**[56] 1298 3-10-12 0.............................. AidanColeman 73
(Lawney Hill) *led: j. slowly 2nd: hdd appr 2 out: styd pressing wnr tl wknd after last* **7/2**[3]
P **Revelator (IRE)**[352] 3-10-12 0..............................(t) HarrySkelton —
(Paul Nicholls) *blnd bdly 2nd: chsd ldrs tl wknd 3 out: t.o whn p.u bef next* **5/2**[2]
P **Guppy's Girl (IRE)**[10] 3-10-5 0.............................. JamesDavies —
(Sam Davison) *plld hrd: blnd and rdr lost iron 2nd: nt rcvr: sddle slipped and p.u sn after* **18/1**
3m 35.18s (-13.72) **Going Correction** -1.40s/f (Hard) **5** Ran SP% **108.2**
Speed ratings (Par 103): **78,77,74,—,—**
Place 6: £207.63 Place 5: £152.43 CSF £14.36 TOTE £1.70: £1.10, £7.70; EX 13.60.
Owner S. G. M. **Bred** Tally-Ho Stud **Trained** Lewes, E Sussex

FOCUS
A weak juvenile hurdle rated around the winner and third.

NOTEBOOK
Until The Man(IRE), well held when fourth at Ludlow on debut, capitalised on this weaker opportunity, overcoming a slight mistake at the last and staying on well. He'll do well to defy a penalty, though. (op 6-4 tchd 6-5)
Lady Willa(IRE), 50-1 when beaten a long way on her hurdles debut, was nibbled in the market and this much-improved display clearly wasn't a surprise to everyone. She can probably win a small race. (op 25-1)
Royal Etiquette(IRE) was another to improve markedly on his debut effort, though was still well held in the end. (op 11-4 tchd 5-2)
Revelator(IRE), a 6f maiden winner just under a year ago, never really recovered from a bad blunder at the second where his rider did almost came off. The way he stopped suggests there is a major stamina doubt with the son of One Cool Cat and has plenty to prove. (op 9-4 tchd 11-4)
Guppy's Girl(IRE) was never able to recover from an early blunder, with the saddle slipping. Official explanation: jockey said saddle slipped (op 9-4 tchd 11-4)
T/Plt: £222.30 to a £1 stake. Pool of £59,158.22 - 194.24 winning tickets. T/Qpdt: £25.90 to a £1 stake. Pool of £4,005.16 - 114.00 winning tickets. ST

1846 - (Foreign Racing) - See Raceform Interactive

1833 PUNCHESTOWN (R-H)
Thursday, October 14

OFFICIAL GOING: Good

1847a RYAN'S CLEANING EVENTS SPECIALISTS HURDLE (GRADE 3) (9 hdls) 2m
3:15 (3:15) 5-Y-0+ **£17,544** (£5,128; £2,429; £809)

RPR
1 **Luska Lad (IRE)**[174] 5381 6-11-10 150.............................. AndrewJMcNamara 141+
(John Joseph Hanlon, Ire) *trckd ldr in 2nd: led appr 2 out: sn drew clr: eased fr last: nt extended: v easily* **4/6**[1]
2 *2 ½* **Der Spieler (GER)**[264] 3620 5-11-1 118..............................(t) BarryGeraghty 124+
(J G Coogan, Ire) *settled 4th: slt mstke 1st: 3rd 4 out: rdn fr 2 out: 2nd and kpt on fr last wout troubling wnr* **8/1**[3]
3 *3 ½* **Imperial Shabra (IRE)**[11] 1713 6-11-1 116.............................. MWBowes 121
(Patrick O Brady, Ire) *led: hdd appr 2 out: sn rdn and outpcd: 3rd and no ex fr last* **16/1**
4 *3* **Baron De'L (IRE)**[33] 5299 7-11-5 120..............................(b) RWalsh 122
(Edward P Harty, Ire) *chsd ldrs in 3rd: reminders 1/2-way: 4th u.p 4 out: last 2 out: kpt on same pce* **9/4**[2]
5 *3* **Winner Takes Itall**[60] 1262 6-10-11 .... MPWalsh 111?
(T J Taaffe, Ire) *lost grnd s: hld up in rr: tk clsr orde 3 out: 4th and rdn 2 out: no imp: no ex appr last* **66/1**
3m 46.8s (-23.20) **Going Correction** -1.15s/f (Hard) **5** Ran SP% **109.2**
Speed ratings: **112,110,109,107,106**
CSF £6.68 TOTE £1.50: £1.02, £2.30; DF 5.30.
Owner Magestic Syndicate **Bred** D Phelan **Trained** Bagenalstown, Co Carlow

FOCUS
A messy race where all five runners finished fairly close-up. The fifth limits the form, which could easily be rated 5lb higher.

NOTEBOOK
Luska Lad(IRE) did the job that was expected of him but connections probably learned one or two things from this performance. The main thing was that sitting in behind a lead didn't really seem to suit him. It didn't help his jumping and he certainly seemed happier when McNamara sent him on after the third last and allowed him to use his stride as he settled the issue quite quickly. It will be interesting as the season goes on to see where he rates among the best hurdlers. He's a horse capable of causing an upset in a good race. (op 1/3)
Der Spieler(GER) was having his first run since his very tame effort in the MCR Hurdle back in January. He ran on well in pursuit of the winner, who beat him easily, but it was a decent effort. (op 10/1 tchd 12/1)
Imperial Shabra(IRE) made the pace and kept going at the same pace once headed after the third last. (op 20/1)
Baron De'L(IRE) was the one horse in the race that could be said to have run disappointingly. He really seemed to be done for pace after the winner went on and dropped back to last place. He ended up keeping on at one pace without threatening and gives the impression that he could be a hard enough horse to place this season. (op 4/1)
Winner Takes Itall, beaten out of sight in a Tramore maiden hurdle on his previous start, was travelling so well behind the leaders three out that it looked as though his rider would have to take a pull. In the end, he was found wanting when the pace quickened but his proximity again does give a fair idea of how messy a race it mostly was. (op 40/1)

1849a BUCK HOUSE NOVICE CHASE (GRADE 3) (13 fncs) 2m 2f
4:15 (4:18) 4-Y-0+ **£16,393** (£4,792; £2,269)

RPR
1 **Loosen My Load (IRE)**[27] 1537 6-11-5 .... AELynch 143+
(Henry De Bromhead, Ire) *racd in 2nd tl lft in ld fr 3rd: jnd briefly 5 out: drvn along whn pressed after 2 out: rdn to assert after last: comf* **1/4**[1]

2 2 1/2 **Darceys Dancer (IRE)**[12] 1685 7-11-1 ....(b) PCarberry 134
(Noel Meade, Ire) *trckd ldrs in 3rd: lft 2nd fr 3rd: disp ld briefly 5 out: drvn along to keep in tch after 3 out: rdn fr next: no imp fr last: styd on wout threatening clsng stages* **6/1**[2]

3 19 **Norther Bay (FR)**[1] 1837 7-11-1 121................................ BarryGeraghty 115
(Eoin Griffin, Ire) *hld up in rr: wknd bef 3 out: eased fr next* **11/1**[3]

U **Strongpoint (IRE)**[11] 1698 6-11-5 124...........................(t) AndrewTinkler —
(Patrick Griffin, Ire) *led tl blnd and uns rdr 3rd* **20/1**

4m 34.4s (-6.90) **Going Correction** -0.275s/f (Good) **4** Ran SP% **107.4**
Speed ratings: **104,102,94,—**
CSF £2.34 TOTE £1.20; DF 1.70.
Owner Alan & Ann Potts Partnership **Bred** John Roche **Trained** Knockeen, Co Waterford

FOCUS
The runner-up is rated back to his hurdles best and the winner built on his promising debut.

NOTEBOOK
Loosen My Load(IRE) had to work a little bit but he was never in danger. What he really seems to need is a step up in trip and his rider probably would have preferred not to have to make his own running, something he was forced into when leader Strongpoint capsized early. As usual, he jumped superbly and used that as well as his ability to pull out a bit extra when he needed to in order to beat off a rival who may well prove to be a good horse. He's likely, it seems, to have a scouting mission to Cheltenham next month to see how he gets on over 2m there and that would seem to be a sensible move. It's likely to determine what his March target is likely to be. (op 3/10)
Darceys Dancer(IRE) ◆ made the winner work a little bit and left a very slight impression of what might have been had his jumping stood up better in the closing stages. Awkward at the third last when the winner began to up the tempo, he came back at him but his measure was probably just being taken when another less than fluent jump at the last settled it. It's becoming apparent that this horse is a bit better than may have been thought and he belongs in graded company. (op 5/1 tchd 9/2)
Norther Bay(FR) is well enough exposed, although is a reasonable yardstick in his own right, and the fact that he was beaten before the third last augurs well for the runner-up in particular. (op 11/1 tchd 10/1)

1850a STAR 'BEST FOR RACING COVERAGE' CHASE (GRADE 3) 2m 7f
4:45 (4:48) 5-Y-0+ **£18,119** (£5,296; £2,508)

RPR

1 **China Rock (IRE)**[12] 1684 7-11-8 142.. RWalsh 156
(M F Morris, Ire) *mde all: mstke 4th: edgd clr 4 out: rdn fr 2 out: styd on wl u.p fr last: comf* **6/4**[2]

2 7 **Sizing Europe (IRE)**[177] 5302 8-11-10 160.............................. AELynch 151+
(Henry De Bromhead, Ire) *settled 3rd: nt fluent early: 2nd fr 6 out: outpcd after 4 out: drvn along next: sme prog appr 2 out: no imp fr bef last* **5/4**[1]

3 5 **Siegemaster (IRE)**[176] 5322 9-11-8 148................................ RLoughran 144+
(D T Hughes, Ire) *racd in 2nd: slt mstke 3rd: dropped to 3rd after mstke 6 out: lost tch fr 4 out: kpt on same pce fr next* **11/2**[3]

F **Jadanli (IRE)**[177] 5303 8-11-10 145.. DJCondon —
(Paul John Gilligan, Ire) *hld up in rr: bad mstke 6th: fell 6 out* **14/1**

5m 47.6s (-9.90) **Going Correction** -0.275s/f (Good) **4** Ran SP% **106.5**
Speed ratings: **106,103,101,—**
CSF £3.80 TOTE £2.50; DF 3.40.
Owner Michael O'Flynn **Bred** Brian Griffin **Trained** Fethard, Co Tipperary

FOCUS
Sizing Europe, last season's Arkle Trophy winner, was entering new distance territory and while he came up short, Henry de Bromhead's eight year old is likely to be given another chance over this sort of trip before any decisions are made about long-term targets. The winner had a fitness edge over the next two but rates a slight personal best, with the next two well off.

NOTEBOOK
China Rock(IRE), a winner over 2m6f at Galway a year ago and of a Grade 2 event over 2m4f at Gowran Park on his reappearance early this month, made all the running and, although lucky to survive a bad blunder at the fourth fence, he jumped well the rest of the way and took control of the race when ridden clear before three out. He kept on well and afterwards trainer Mouse Morris said: "He's finished in handicaps after that and we'll look at maybe the Charlie Hall Chase or the JNwine.com Champion Chase for him next." (op 2/1)
Sizing Europe(IRE) jumped adequately, if a little sluggishly at times, and was close enough to trouble the winner leaving the back straight. However, the picture changed four out where he was a bit slow, allowing the winner to increase his advantage. Struggling to make much impression on China Rock, he kept on and deserves another shot at around this distance with the benefit of this race behind him. According to de Bromhead, Andrew Lynch reported that the horse gave "a big blow" after four out. (op 4/5)
Siegemaster(IRE), who hit the third fence, was making his reappearance and was close up until outpaced after four out. He stayed on but is a a horse who appreciates further and also slower ground. (op 7/1 tchd 5/1)
Jadanli(IRE), a surprise winner of the Grade 1 Powers Gold Cup last season when he showed his ability to handle heavy ground, survived a bad mistake at the sixth fence only to fall at the tenth fence when trailing his three rivals. (op 12/1)

1851 - 1852a (Foreign Racing) - See Raceform Interactive

[148] CHELTENHAM (L-H)
Friday, October 15

OFFICIAL GOING: Good (good to firm in places; watered; 7.9)
Wind: Virtually nil Weather: Overcast

1853 NEPTUNE INVESTMENT MANAGEMENT NOVICES' HURDLE (10 hdls) 2m 5f
2:10 (2:11) (Class 2) 4-Y-0+
£12,524 (£3,700; £1,850; £926; £462; £232)

Form RPR

11- 1 **Final Day (IRE)**[79] 1120 6-11-6 133...(t) PCarberry 134+
(Gordon Elliott, Ire) *hld up in rr but in tch: stdy hdwy fr 3 out: trckd ldr last: drvn and qcknd to ld fnl 120yds: kpt on wl* **11/8**[1]

/F-0 2 1/2 **Queiros Bleu (FR)**[30] 1526 6-11-6 134.................................... AELynch 134
(Henry De Bromhead, Ire) *hld up in rr in tch: hdwy on ins after 2 out to ld appr last: sn rdn: hdd and one pce fnl 120yds* **5/1**[3]

211 3 6 **There's No Panic (IRE)**[66] 1228 5-11-6 123............................... RWalsh 129
(Paul Nicholls) *trckd ldrs in 4th tl qcknd to go 2nd 4 out: chal fr next tl slt ld 2 out: hdd appr last and sn one pce* **5/2**[2]

001- 4 20 **Flaming Gorge (IRE)**[193] 5030 5-11-3 0................................. DarylJacob 108
(Nick Williams) *led: jnd 3 out narrowly hdd 2 out: wknd sn after* **12/1**

01-1 5 2 1/4 **Total Submission**[167] 93 5-11-3 0.......................... WarrenMarston 106
(Martin Keighley) *chsd ldr to 4 out: wknd fr 3 out* **14/1**

042- 6 47 **Ceepeegee (IRE)**[203] 4867 5-10-12 122.................................. JoeTizzard 58
(Colin Tizzard) *racd in cl 3rd tl wknd after 4 out: t.o* **14/1**

5m 11.1s (-2.30) **Going Correction** -0.30s/f (Good) **6** Ran SP% **108.4**
Speed ratings (Par 109): **92,91,89,81,81 63**
toteswingers:1&2:£2.50, 1&3:£1.10, 2&3:£2.90 CSF £8.11 TOTE £2.30: £1.50, £3.50; EX 8.50.
Owner B Kane **Bred** Pat Kinsella **Trained** Trim, Co Meath

FOCUS
The ground appeared to be riding on the fast side of good for the opening meeting of the season (officially described as good, good to firm), although the time recorded in the first race suggested it was riding slower than that. The two Irish runners ultimately drew clear in this novices' hurdle. Easy form to rate with the first three to their marks.

NOTEBOOK
Final Day(IRE) made it win number three over hurdles with a likeable performance over a new trip. Off since finishing second at Galway in the summer, he was clearly straight enough to make a winning return, but gave the impression he would improve for it and, although no star, he's the type to make an impact in good handicaps later in the season. He'll either head for a race at Navan in two weeks time, or return here next month for the Open meeting, with wherever he can get decent ground being favoured. (op 13-8 tchd 7-4 in places)
Queiros Bleu(FR), below par last time, had looked a bit flattered by his British rating, but he showed it to be about right with this battling effort in defeat, just getting run out of it late on. (op 7-1)
There's No Panic(IRE) did his winning at the lesser tracks earlier in the year and, although ultimately no match for the front pair, he showed enough to suggest he'll make his mark in decent handicaps, with 3m likely to suit. (op 2-1 tchd 15-8)
Flaming Gorge(IRE) made a winning hurdles debut in heavy ground back in April and he ran as though he would come on for this first start since. A return to slower conditions will also suit and he can show himself better than this in time. (op 10-1)
Total Submission, off since making a winning hurdles debut at Uttoxeter in May, could have been expected to last a bit longer, with the extra distance expected to suit, but he's likely to come on for it and will find easier opportunities. (op 10-1)
Ceepeegee(IRE) stopped quickly and, for all that he's entitled to benefit from this first outing in 203 days, it would have been nice to see more. (op 12-1)

1854 CHELTENHAM WORLD OF JUMP RACING NOVICES' CHASE (16 fncs) 2m 4f 110y
2:45 (2:45) (Class 3) 4-Y-0+ **£7,514** (£2,220; £1,110; £555)

Form RPR

021- 1 **Rebel Du Maquis (FR)**[180] 5256 5-11-4 0.................................. RWalsh 132+
(Paul Nicholls) *mde all: jnd 3 out: sn clr: pushed out run-in* **9/4**[2]

5-61 2 20 **Frontier Dancer (IRE)**[22] 1595 6-11-11 0........................ PaddyBrennan 123+
(Nigel Twiston-Davies) *chsd wnr most of way: chal 3 out and no fluent: sn no ch and wl hld whn mstke 2 out: wknd run-in and jst hld on for 2nd* **7/4**[1]

1P0- 3 hd **Wolf Moon (IRE)**[190] 5093 7-11-4 0.............................. WarrenMarston 113
(Martin Keighley) *racd off pce in 4th: tk modest 3rd after 11th: rdn after next: styd on fr 2 out to almost rch 2nd last strides but nvr any ch w wnr* **11/4**[3]

-122 4 82 **Gee Dee Nen**[54] 1345 7-11-11 130.. JamieMoore 46
(Gary Moore) *racd in 3rd tl chal for 2nd fr 7th to 9th: stl cl up whn mstke 11th and sn no ch: t.o* **7/1**

5m 5.17s (-5.83) **Going Correction** -0.20s/f (Good) **4** Ran SP% **106.3**
Speed ratings (Par 107): **103,95,95,64**
CSF £6.48 TOTE £2.60; EX 5.40.
Owner Mrs Kathy Stuart **Bred** Daniel & Mme Jeannine Laupretre **Trained** Ditcheat, Somerset

FOCUS
This was the steeplechase since the repositioning of the controversial second-last fence. The race didn't prove to be as tight as the market suggested it may be. The easy winner was up 6lb on his hurdles best and should rate higher, with the second to his Perth mark.

NOTEBOOK
Rebel Du Maquis(FR) led throughout, jumping well, and scooting clear for an easy success on this return to fences. Twice a runner-up when chasing in France, he created a good impression with two wins over hurdles last season and good-ground conditions again looked to suit him well. He'll stick to this sort of trip, with races back here and at Newbury next month likely to come under consideration. (op 2-1 tchd 15-8)
Frontier Dancer(IRE) ran out a good winner on his chasing debut at Perth, but faster conditions and a 7lb penalty made things tougher this time and, having been left trailing by the winner, he was nearly claimed late on for second by the fast-finishing Wolf Moon. He'll probably defy the penalty at some stage, but handicaps may be more his bag. (tchd 15-8 and 2-1 in places)
Wolf Moon(IRE) always looks the type to make a better chaser and this was a thoroughly likeable first effort. He raced adrift of the front two, looking a bit rusty on this first start in 190 days, but his jumping improved as the contest progressed and there'll be considerable improvement to come with this under his belt upped to 3m. (op 7-2)
Gee Dee Nen ended up well held, stopping quickly following a mistake and clearly failing to give his true running. (op 6-1)

1855 PERTEMPS H'CAP HURDLE (QUALIFIER) (12 hdls) 3m
3:20 (3:21) (Class 2) 4-Y-0+
£9,393 (£2,775; £1,387; £694; £346; £174)

Form RPR

4F-3 1 **Amber Brook (IRE)**[160] 206 9-10-13 **140**........................ PaddyBrennan 144+
(Nigel Twiston-Davies) *chsd ldrs: led after 2 out: rdn last: hung lft then rt run-in: hld on all out* **8/1**[3]

1-F4 2 hd **King Ar Aghaidh (IRE)**[114] 830 9-9-7 **127** oh6........(p) PeterCarberry(7) 131+
(Charlie Longsdon) *towards rr but in tch: hdwy 3 out: styng on whn hmpd next: styd on strly run-in and edgd rt fnl 100yds: fin wl: jst failed* **7/1**[2]

0012 3 2 3/4 **Raslan**[19] 1626 7-10-12 **142**...(vt) DannyCook(3) 142
(David Pipe) *pressed ldr tl def ld 8th: rdn and hdd 2 out: styd chsng wnr and rallied fnl 100yds: one pce whn swtchd lft cl home* **9/1**

2123 4 2 1/4 **Battle Group**[30] 1526 5-10-8 **135**.. APMcCoy 134
(David Pipe) *blnd 1st: in rr but in tch: hdwy fr 2 out: chsd ldrs next: styd on same pce run-in* **6/1**[1]

1140 5 2 **Barnhill Brownie (IRE)**[19] 1626 7-9-12 **130**................(t) GilesHawkins(5) 128+
(Philip Hobbs) *j. slowly 1st: in rr: hit 6th: stl plenty to do 2 out whn pushed rt: styd on strly appr last: gng on cl home* **25/1**

12-P 6 3/4 **Viking Blond (FR)**[160] 206 5-9-13 **129**...........(b) SamTwiston-Davies(3) 126
(Nigel Twiston-Davies) *chsd ldrs: drvn to ld and mstke 2 out: hdd sn after and squeezed out: kpt on same pce* **9/1**

014- 7 17 **Buena Vista (IRE)**[189] 5113 9-10-13 **140**........................... HaddenFrost 120
(David Pipe) *in rr: no ch whn slighlty hmpd 2 out: mod prog run-in* **10/1**

04-0 8 2 **King's Forest (IRE)**[19] 1626 6-10-2 **129**........................... JackDoyle 109
(Emma Lavelle) *in rr: hit 2nd: blnd 4 out: nvr in contention after* **8/1**[3]

U11- 9 50 **Chester Lad**[179] 5273 5-10-3 **130**.. JanFaltejsek 63
(George Charlton) *chsd ldrs but j. poorly thrght: wknd 3 out: t.o* **16/1**

P066 10 6 **Jug Of Punch (IRE)**[9] 1735 11-9-7 **127** oh63.................. MissCBoxall(7) 55
(Simon Lewis) *sn bhd: t.o fr 1/2-way* **125/1**

055- 11 10 **Lough Derg (FR)**[229] 4328 10-11-12 **153**......................(v) TomScudamore 72
(David Pipe) *disp ld to 8th: wknd qckly: t.o* **22/1**

/11- 12 42 **Hills Of Aran**[488] 716 8-11-9 **150**...................................... RhysFlint 31
(Keith Goldsworthy) *chsd ldrs tl wknd 8th: t.o* **20/1**

3-21 P **Markington**[18] 708 7-10-4 **131**..(b) TomO'Brien —
(Peter Bowen) *p.u after 1st: dismntd* **12/1**

33-5 **F** **Sangfroid**[160] 206 6-10-2 **128** ow1 .... DarylJacob 128+
(Nick Williams) *trckd ldrs: disputing cl 3rd and travelling wl whn fell 2 out*
6/1[1]

5m 50.77s (-12.63) **Going Correction** -0.30s/f (Good) **14** Ran SP% **119.7**
Speed ratings (Par 109): **109,108,108,107,106 106,100,100,83,81 78,64,—,—**
toteswingers:1&2:£10.20, 1&3:£15.60, 2&3:£50.10 CSF £60.73 CT £523.16 TOTE £9.30: £3.10, £2.50, £3.70; EX 78.90 Trifecta £780.50 Pool: £1,308.01 - 1.24 winning units.
Owner The Yes No Wait Sorries **Bred** Larry Mealiffe **Trained** Naunton, Gloucs
■ Stewards' Enquiry : Peter Carberry three-day ban: careless riding (Oct 29-31)

FOCUS
A competitive staying handicap hurdle and solid form with the third and fourth setting the level. A surprise personal best from the winner but the stable are in great form.

NOTEBOOK
Amber Brook(IRE), third off this mark in a good race at Haydock back in May, hasn't got the best of records fresh, but she's returned at a time when many of her trainer's horses are going well and, having travelled strongly under Paddy Brennan, she just found enough to hold on, having hung both ways on the run-in. This was the highest mark she's ever won off and, not being the most consistent of mares, there has to be some doubt as to whether she can follow it up next time, despite looking likely to head back to Wincanton. (op 17-2)
King Ar Aghaidh(IRE), 6lb out of the handicap but ridden by very promising conditional Peter Carberry, who was claiming 7lb, always looked to be travelling well and he made steady headway into a challenging position prior to being hampered by the fall of Sangfroid two out. To his credit, though, he rallied strongly and very nearly caught the idling winner, just needing another stride or two. He's lightly raced for is age and has had only two runs over fences, so may yet have more to offer. (op 8-1 tchd 13-2)
Raslan's been in good form and he again displayed his toughness, trying to rally once headed, but in the end he couldn't quite match the front pair. This mark may continue to just prove beyond him. (op 12-1)
Battle Group was 8lb higher than when second to Raslan on his penultimate start, but ran right up to form, keeping on as though a more forceful ride will suit in future. (tchd 11-2)
Barnhill Brownie(IRE) bounced back from a couple of shocking efforts, staying on from an impossible position, and he'll no doubt appeal to many next time off what still looks a reasonable mark.
Viking Blond(FR), off since pulling up at Haydock in May, was never far away and took it up two out, but he was untidy there and then got squeezed for room having just been headed. He ultimately weakened out of it, but should improve and remains capable of better, being just a 5-y-o. (op 12-1)
Buena Vista(IRE), winner of the Final of this series last season, was beginning to make a little late headway when hampered. (op 12-1)
King's Forest(IRE) was just beginning to make a forward move when hitting the fourth-last, and he could make no headway thereafter.
Chester Lad jumped poorly on this handicap debut, but is sure to improve and will find easier opportunities. (op 20-1)
Lough Derg(FR) offered little, dropping away very quickly. (op 20-1)
Markington Official explanation: jockey said gelding was lame (tchd 11-2)
Sangfroid ran well without winning in many good handicaps last season and this may have been his day had he not come down two out. He still appeared to be full of running and, although he's often found a way to get beaten in the past, he would surely have gone close. (tchd 11-2)

1856 SPORTINGBET.COM H'CAP CHASE (19 fncs) 3m 110y
3:55 (3:55) (Class 2) (0-150,149) 4-Y-0+
£14,089 (£4,162; £2,081; £1,041; £519; £261)

Form RPR

1-41 **1** **Midnight Chase**[143] 458 8-11-0 **137** .... DougieCostello 150+
(Neil Mulholland) *mde most: jnd fr 8th and briefly hdd 13th but sn narrow ld: jnd again 3 out: forged clr appr 2 out: styd on gamely: eased cl home*
6/1[3]

033- **2** *10* **Lacdoudal (FR)**[174] 5395 11-10-13 **136** .... RichardJohnson 139
(Philip Hobbs) *chsd ldrs: rdn 11th: styd on again to press ldrs 3 out: dropped bk to 4th after next: rallied to retake 2nd appr last but no ch w wnr*
8/1

1-01 **3** *1 3/4* **Ouzbeck (FR)**[110] 844 8-11-12 **149** .... JackDoyle 150
(Emma Lavelle) *in rr: hit 5th: lost tch 13th: blnd 3 out: plenty to do whn styd on fr 2 out: fin strly run-in to cl on 2nd: nvr any ch w wnr*
12/1

P1P- **4** *6* **Meanus Dandy (IRE)**[181] 5223 7-10-5 **128** .... RWalsh 124
(Paul Nicholls) *in tch: hit 14th: chsd ldrs fr next: wl there 3 out and rdn to go 2nd appr 2 out: no ch w wnr and wknd last*
11/4[1]

164- **5** *2* **Calgary Bay (IRE)**[190] 5095 7-11-12 **149** .... HaddenFrost 142+
(Henrietta Knight) *hit 3rd: in rr: gd hdwy 4 out: drvn to chal next: wknd 2 out*
6/1[3]

44-5 **6** *5* **Lead On (IRE)**[167] 98 9-11-0 **137** .... TomO'Brien 126
(Philip Hobbs) *hit 1st: in rr: no ch whn blnd 12th*
16/1

20F- **7** *8* **Double Dizzy**[193] 5067 9-10-1 **131** .... NathanSweeney(7) 113
(Bob Buckler) *chsd ldrs: rdn 15th and sn wknd*
14/1

2-53 **8** *10* **Qulinton (FR)**[20] 1611 6-10-5 **128** ....(p) TomScudamore 105
(David Pipe) *w wnr fr 11th: led briefly 13th: wknd 4 out*
5/1[2]

-1P4 **F** **Victor Daly (IRE)**[59] 1275 9-10-2 **125** .... WayneHutchinson —
(Martin Keighley) *in rr tl fell 3rd*
14/1

1-53 **P** **Diablo (IRE)**[51] 1365 8-10-7 **130** .... PaddyBrennan —
(Nigel Twiston-Davies) *chsd ldrs: rdn 12th: wknd quickly appr 4 out: t.o whn p.u bef 3 out*
14/1

6m 7.38s (-10.92) **Going Correction** -0.20s/f (Good) **10** Ran SP% **116.6**
Speed ratings (Par 109): **109,105,105,103,102 101,98,95,—,—**
toteswingers:1&2:£9.70, 1&3:£6.10, 2&3:£12.60 CSF £53.21 CT £560.79 TOTE £5.70: £1.90, £2.30, £3.20; EX 68.40 Trifecta £763.40 Pool: £1,031.67 - 1.00 winning units.
Owner Lady Clarke **Bred** Conkwell Grange Stud Ltd **Trained** Burlescombe, Devon

FOCUS
A good handicap chase, run at a decent pace. There were reasons to oppose just about all of these and it is unlikely the second and third were at their best after breaks, otherwise the form could be rated higher.

NOTEBOOK
Midnight Chase kept the gallop up remarkably well and raced to win number four over fences (now 2-2 over this track). Clearly ready to roll on this first start since May, he proved unrelenting, despite looking vulnerable on occasions, and powered up the hill to ultimately win eased down. He can expect some harsh treatment from the handicapper, but remains on the up and will return for next month's Open meeting. (op 5-1)
Lacdoudal(FR), off the same mark as when third in the Bet365 Gold Cup on his latest outing, shows no signs of deteriorating, despite his age, being bang there turning in but not staying on as well as the younger, more progressive winner. He's sure to feature in some decent staying handicaps again this term. (op 12-1)
Ouzbeck(FR), 7lb higher than when winning the Summer National over 3m4f at Uttoxeter, got well behind following a couple of sloppy jumps, but he stayed on really well down the straight, as one would expected for a strong stayer, and is another who looks set to have a say in some decent races this season. (op 9-1 tchd 17-2)
Meanus Dandy(IRE) looked good when winning at Sandown last season, but he was pulled up off this new 9lb higher mark in the Scottish National and ended up well held on this first start since, fading late on in a manner to suggest the run was needed. (op 4-1)
Calgary Bay(IRE), only 7lb higher than when last winning a handicap, having struggled to make an impact in either the Gold Cup or Totesport Bowl last backend, moved well on this seasonal reappearance and looked a threat at the top of the hill, but he ultimately appeared to blow up and will have other days. (op 11-2)
Lead On(IRE) made a few mistakes and never really threatened. (op 14-1)
Diablo(IRE) Official explanation: vet said gelding finished lame right-fore

1857 LEMINGTON MAIDEN HURDLE (8 hdls) 2m 110y
4:30 (4:31) (Class 3) 4-Y-0+
£6,262 (£1,850; £925; £463; £231; £116)

Form RPR

121- **1** **King Of The Night (GER)**[175] 5368 6-11-0 0 .... RWalsh 126+
(Paul Nicholls) *hld up in rr and wl bhd clr ldr: stdy hdwy appr 3 out: trckd ldr next: chal on bit last: sn c clr: v easily*
5/2[2]

00- **2** *9* **Fiulin**[163] 4657 5-11-0 0 .... PaulMoloney 114+
(Evan Williams) *led after 1st: sn 15 l clr: hit 4 out: 4 l clr whn hit 2 out: jnd by wnr last: sn no ch but kpt on u.p for 2nd*
11/8[1]

10-2 **3** *3* **Caught By Witness (IRE)**[162] 168 5-11-0 0 .... WarrenMarston 110+
(Milton Harris) *in rr and wl bhd clr ldr tl hdwy after 4 out: styd on to go 3rd after 2 out: edgd rt and kpt on u.p run-in but no imp*
4/1[3]

4 *10* **Mannlichen**[41] 4-11-0 0 .... AidanColeman 100
(Venetia Williams) *in tch w main gp: wl bhd clr ldr: drvn and styd on fr 3 out: nvr rchd ldrs fr next and wknd bef last*
12/1

346- **5** *1 1/2* **Prince Of Denial (IRE)**[193] 5035 6-11-0 0 .... PaddyBrennan 101
(Nigel Twiston-Davies) *chsd 15 l ldr fr 3rd whn nt fluent: lost 2nd and nt fluent 3 out: no imp and one pce whn blnd next*
20/1

20P0 **6** *20* **Hi Wycombe (IRE)**[13] 1679 6-11-0 90 .... RodiGreene 81
(David Bridgwater) *led tl after 1st: nt fluent 3rd: bhd fr next*
100/1

7 *3* **Eddie Boy**[423] 4-11-0 0 .... APMcCoy 78
(Rebecca Curtis) *hit 3rd: a towards rr*
20/1

8 *12* **Gallego**[16] 8-11-0 0 .... GerardTumelty 67
(Richard Price) *wl bhd tl brief effrt fr rr 3 out: sn dropped away*
50/1

9 *62* **Iwakuni (NZ)**[468] 6-10-11 0 .... SamTwiston-Davies(3) 11
(Nigel Twiston-Davies) *hit 1st: lost tch fr 4th: t.o*
22/1

3m 58.56s (-3.44) **Going Correction** -0.30s/f (Good)
WFA 4 from 5yo+ 9lb **9** Ran SP% **115.2**
Speed ratings (Par 107): **96,91,90,85,84 75,74,68,39**
toteswingers:1&2:£1.70, 1&3:£2.60, 2&3:£1.70 CSF £6.14 TOTE £3.60: £1.10, £1.30, £1.70; EX 7.90 TRIFECTA Pool: £1,172.30 - 41.84 winning units.
Owner Mr & Mrs G Calder **Bred** Gestut Norina **Trained** Ditcheat, Somerset

FOCUS
An interesting maiden hurdle. There is a case for rating the race a lot higher through the second, he time was relatively slow and that horse is rated 20lb+ off his Festival mark. The easy winner is sure to rate higher.

NOTEBOOK
King Of The Night(GER) had closed the gap to the favourite Fiulin considerably running down the hill and, having taken over still cantering jumping the last, he was nudged clear for a very ready success. Although a dual scorer in bumpers, his best effort probably came in defeat, when just failing to give the highly regarded Sprinter Sacre 13lb at Ascot in February, and this effort seems to confirm he's going to make a smart hurdler. He'll now return here for the 2m Grade 2 novices' hurdle at the Open meeting. (tchd 11-4 in a place)
Fiulin, seventh in last season's Supreme Novices' but still a maiden, ensured there was no hanging around, but it was clear from the second-last he was a mere sitting duck for the winner. He'll have no trouble winning, probably back up in trip, but it's in handicaps where he'll ply his trade. (op 2-1 tchd 9-4)
Caught By Witness(IRE), well beaten on his hurdles debut at Newton Abbot, having run respectably in the Grade 1 bumper at Punchestown last season, fared better here, considering it was a stronger heat, and he'll be seen to better effect over a longer trip. (op 9-2 tchd 7-2)
Mannlichen, rated 72 on the Flat, ended up well held, but did at least pull clear with the front trio racing down the hill, and he'll find easier opportunities than this. (tchd 10-1)
Prince Of Denial(IRE), making his debut for the yard, shaped well and will be of interest once handicapping over further. (op 16-1)
Eddie Boy, a regressive maiden on the Flat, offered little on this debut for connections. (op 14-1)
Gallego has embarked on a hurdles career rather late in life. (op 66-1)

1858 CHELTENHAM BUSINESS CLUB AMATEUR RIDERS' H'CAP CHASE (19 fncs) 3m 110y
5:05 (5:05) (Class 3) (0-125,125) 4-Y-0+
£6,002 (£1,875; £937; £469; £234; £118)

Form RPR

0-40 **1** **Quattrocento (FR)**[51] 1373 6-11-0 **113** ....(v[1]) MrMPFogarty 126+
(Peter Bowen) *in tch: hdwy 11th: drvn to chal 3 out and sn led: rdn clr appr last*
14/1

-144 **2** *6* **Swing Bill (FR)**[20] 1611 9-11-9 **125** .... MrTWeston(3) 133
(David Pipe) *chsd ldrs: led 4 out: jnd next and hdd sn after: styd chsng wnr but no imp fr 2 out*
7/1[1]

1F-4 **3** *6* **Oscar Glory (IRE)**[42] 1463 10-10-11 **110** ....(tp) MissNCarberry 113
(Edward Cawley, Ire) *in rr: hdwy 13th: blnd next: hdwy fr 3 out: styd on fr 2 out to take 3rd run-in but nvr any ch*
12/1

1201 **4** *1/2* **Presentandcorrect (IRE)**[59] 1274 9-11-11 **124** ....(p) MrRMahon 129+
(Nigel Twiston-Davies) *chsd ldrs: chal 10th: led 12th: hit 4 out and hdd: stl pressing ldrs 3 out: wknd bef next and lost 3rd run-in*
16/1

6-14 **5** *1* **Lucky Luk (FR)**[134] 599 11-10-7 **113** ....(p) MrCGreene(7) 115
(Kim Bailey) *nt fluent in rr: hdwy and wl there 10th: lost position appr 4 out: styd on again fr 2 out: gng on nr fin*
20/1

3214 **6** *14* **I Need A Hero (IRE)**[59] 1274 5-11-0 **120** ....(t) MrMEnnis(7) 108
(Sarah Humphrey) *in rr tl hdwy appr 3 out: styd on fr next but nvr in contention*
25/1

0-0P **7** *8* **Au Courant (IRE)**[26] 1557 10-11-12 **125** .... MrJETudor 106
(Sophie Leech) *hit 8th: in rr tl sme hdwy fr 3 out*
66/1

350- **8** *1 1/4* **Gaora Lane (IRE)**[189] 5111 9-11-10 **123** .... MrSWaley-Cohen 108+
(Charlie Mann) *led to 2nd: styd chsng ldrs tl blnd 15th and sn btn* **12/1**

23-1 **9** *nk* **Mont Present (FR)**[159] 234 6-11-2 **122** .... MrTCheesman(7) 102
(Philip Hobbs) *chsd ldrs to 4 out*
10/1

-415 **10** *hd* **Dusty Dane (IRE)**[54] 1348 8-10-9 **113** ....(t) MrDGPrichard(5) 92
(Bill Turner) *bhd fr 6th*
33/1

21P- **11** *4* **Scots Dragoon**[181] 5223 8-11-3 **123** .... MrNdeBoinville(7) 101
(Nicky Henderson) *chsd ldrs to 13th: wknd next*
8/1[3]

3221 **12** *hd* **Royal Kicks (FR)**[6] 1769 9-10-9 **113** 7ex .... MrTJCannon(5) 89
(Suzy Smith) *chsd ldrs: hit 3rd and 5th: wknd 13th*
8/1[3]

1303 **13** *12* **Marblehead (IRE)**[19] 1625 8-11-5 **123** ....(b) MrMWall(5) 88
(Nigel Twiston-Davies) *led 2nd tl hdd 12th: wknd 13th*
14/1

0- **14** *16* **Larry Luso (IRE)**[13] 1686 8-11-5 **121** ....(t) MrMJO'Hare(3) 71
(Daniel William O'Sullivan, Ire) *hit 8th: blnd 12th: a in rr*
11/1

0116 **U** **Cold Mountain (IRE)**[24] 1570 8-11-4 **124**.................... MrKevinJones(7) —
(Seamus Mullins) *mstke and uns rdr 2nd* **40/1**
06-P **P** **The Walnut Tree (IRE)**[8] 1745 9-9-7 **99** oh33.............(b) MissCBoxall(7) —
(Simon Lewis) *j. slowly in rr: t.o whn p.u bef 3 out* **100/1**
U221 **P** **King Roonah**[9] 1725 6-11-9 **122** 7ex....................................(t) MrJJCodd —
(Gordon Elliott, Ire) *in rr: hdwy 13th: wknd after 4 out: t.o whn p.u bef 2 out* **15/2**[2]
1211 **P** **Mad Jack Duncan (IRE)**[40] 1486 8-10-10 **112**.......... MissGAndrews(3) —
(Lawney Hill) *chsd ldrs tl p.u qckly bef 14th* **7/1**[1]
6m 13.7s (-4.60) **Going Correction** -0.20s/f (Good) **18** Ran SP% **127.5**
Speed ratings (Par 107): **99,97,95,95,94 90,87,87,87,87 85,85,81,76,— —,—,—**
toteswingers:1&2:£48.00, 1&3:£48.10, 2&3:£21.40 CSF £108.37 CT £1248.25 TOTE £17.10: £4.30, £2.40, £3.50, £4.20; EX 214.20 Trifecta £526.20 Pool: £711.11 - 1.00 winning units.
Owner Roddy Owen & Paul Fullagar **Bred** Guy Cherel **Trained** Little Newcastle, Pembrokes
■ Stewards' Enquiry : Mr D G Prichard caution: used whip when out of contention.
Mr S Waley-Cohen caution: used whip when out of contention.

FOCUS
This is often a competitive handicap chase and this year's was no different, with the bookmakers betting 7-1 the field. Ordinary but sound form. The winner had slipped to a good mark.

NOTEBOOK
Quattrocento(FR), with conditions to suit, was nibbled at earlier in the day and he sprung back to life in the first-time visor, receiving a good ride from his promising jockey, who produced a fine leap out of him at the last to seal the deal. He had slipped to a very good mark and will presumably return next month for the Open meeting, but it remains to be seen whether the headgear works again. (op 16-1)
Swing Bill(FR) had twice run respectably off this mark since making a winning return from an almighty absence in the summer, and this was possibly his best effort yet, going on four out and trying his best to rally having been headed by the winner. It's hoped he can remain sound. (op 8-1)
Oscar Glory(IRE) kept on for a never-nearer third, leaving behind a miserable effort at Kilbeggan in the process. (op 14-1)
Presentandcorrect(IRE), back on track when winning a novices' chase at Worcester in the first-time cheekpieces, took it up a fair way out but was always likely to prove vulnerable late on off his career-high mark.
Lucky Luk(FR) stayed on again having lost his position, but never got close enough to challenge and remains 9lb above his last winning mark. (op 16-1)
I Need A Hero(IRE), well behind Presentandcorrect at Worcester, had earlier scored off 8lb lower and this was certainly a more encouraging display, keeping on late having been well behind. (op 20-1)
Gaora Lane(IRE), runner-up off 4lb lower a year ago, was still in with a chance when making a race-ending blunder at the 15th. (op 11-1 tchd 10-1)
Mont Present(FR), winner of a beginners' chase at Worcester in May, was well held on this return to handicaps/first start since.
Scots Dragoon ended up well held on this first start in 181 days.
Royal Kicks(FR) never looked like defying the penalty. (op 9-1)
King Roonah, a winner at Ludlow recently, stopped quickly in the end having briefly made a forward move running down hill. (op 10-1)
Mad Jack Duncan(IRE) was pulled up quickly with something amiss, and sadly had to be put down. (op 10-1)

1859 SPORTINGBET.COM SPONSORS THE CONDITIONAL JOCKEYS' CHAMPIONSHIP H'CAP HURDLE (CONDITIONAL JOCKEYS) (8 hdls) 2m 110y

5:40 (5:41) (Class 3) (0-135,131) 4-Y-0+

£6,262 (£1,850; £925; £463; £231; £116)

Form RPR
-113 **1** **Astracad (FR)**[20] 1609 4-11-6 **128**........................ SamTwiston-Davies(3) 143+
(Nigel Twiston-Davies) *in tch: chsd ldrs 3 out: chal and mstke next: sn led: drvn and edgd lft run-in: styd on strly* **9/4**[1]
11- **2** *4* **Organisateur (IRE)**[190] 5102 5-11-6 **128**........................ IanPopham(3) 136+
(Paul Nicholls) *in tch: hdwy to chse ldrs 3 out: drvn and styd on to dispute 2nd last: sn chsng wnr and edgd lft: no imp* **7/1**[3]
2-11 **3** *3 3/4* **Lucaindubai (IRE)**[49] 1392 4-11-0 **122**........................ DPFahy(3) 128+
(Evan Williams) *chsd ldr tl lft in ld after 2nd: rdn and jnd 2 out: hdd sn after: lost 2nd after last: one pce* **6/1**[2]
1113 **4** *8* **Beidh Tine Anseo (IRE)**[15] 870 4-11-0 **122**........... CampbellGillies(3) 121
(Lucinda Russell) *chsd ldrs: hit 3rd: rdn 3 out: wknd appr last* **9/1**
222 **5** *4* **Scene Two**[54] 1343 4-10-1 **114**.. ChrisDavies(8) 110+
(Philip Hobbs) *in rr: nt fluent 4th: hdwy 4 out: styd on fr 2 out but nvr a threat* **7/1**[3]
40-0 **6** *3/4* **Oceana Gold**[20] 1609 6-11-4 **131**........................ StephenO'Donovan(8) 125
(Emma Lavelle) *chsd ldrs: hit 2 out: sn wknd* **20/1**
0123 **7** *2 1/4* **Boogie Dancer**[26] 1548 6-10-1 **111**........................ PeterCarberry(5) 103
(Stuart Howe) *in rr: sme hdwy 2 out but nvr a threat* **10/1**
62 **8** *shd* **Makhaaleb (IRE)**[9] 1594 4-10-7 **115**........................ KMDonoghue(3) 106
(Gordon Elliott, Ire) *hit 2nd: in rr: sme hdwy appr 2 out: sn wknd* **20/1**
0-10 **9** *26* **Shalamiyr (FR)**[151] 372 5-10-6 **114**........................ GilesHawkins(3) 82
(Philip Hobbs) *chsd ldrs: chal and nt fluent 4th: wknd after 3 out* **20/1**
01/0 **10** *3 3/4* **Higgy's Boy (IRE)**[20] 1609 5-11-7 **129**........................(b) DavidBass(3) 94
(Nicky Henderson) *chsd ldrs tl hit 3 out and sn wknd* **9/1**
4112 **R** **Dereks (IRE)**[61] 1260 8-11-1 **120**........................ RichieMcLernon —
(Sophie Leech) *led tl slipped bdly and rn out at crse bnd after 2nd* **25/1**
3m 53.4s (-8.60) **Going Correction** -0.30s/f (Good) course record
WFA 4 from 5yo+ 9lb **11** Ran SP% **117.3**
Speed ratings (Par 107): **108,106,104,100,98 98,97,97,85,83 —**
toteswingers:1&2:£3.70, 1&3:£3.50, 2&3:£8.10 CSF £17.26 CT £84.70 TOTE £2.80: £1.30, £3.00, £2.20; EX 17.20 Trifecta £144.90 Pool: £380.09 - 1.94 winning units. Place 6 £204.71; Place 5 £123.54.
Owner H R Mould **Bred** Charlotte Thoreau **Trained** Naunton, Gloucs

FOCUS
An open conditional jockeys' handicap hurdle, run in a good time for the grade. The winner produced another big step forward and the second is on the upgrade too.

NOTEBOOK
Astracad(FR), held off 3lb lower on his reappearance at Market Rasen, had been most progressive in the spring and he resumed that here with a thoroughly professional performance, really knuckling down for pressure and staying on strongly. Successful here from a mark of 128, he'll find himself in the mid-to-high 130s next time, but this was only his eighth start, so it would be foolish to assume there's not more to come. (op 11-4 tchd 2-1, 3-1 in a place)
Organisateur(IRE), left clear at the last in both previous starts over hurdles (looked booked for second latest), was weak in the market on this seasonal/handicap debut, but actually ran a race full of promise, staying on in pursuit of the winner without ever looking likely to match him. He should improve and remains one to keep on-side. (tchd 10-1)
Lucaindubai(IRE) held a contested lead for much of the way, but he was headed soon after two out and couldn't stay on as well as either of the front two. This was still another decent effort from this improving sort, and he'll find easier opportunities. (op 7-1)
Beidh Tine Anseo(IRE), who had a recent pipe-opener on the Flat, was 16lb higher than when last winning a handicap and he ran about as well as could have been expected. (op 17-2 tchd 11-1)
Scene Two made mistakes, but did stay on late and he's another who will find easier opportunities. (op 6-1)
Oceana Gold ran with promise and should come on again.
Boogie Dancer never got into it from the rear. (op 8-1)
Makhaaleb(IRE), who was weak in the market, briefly made a forward move, but ended up well held on this handicap debut. (op 25-1)
Higgy's Boy(IRE) hasn't shown much in two starts since returning. (tchd 7-1)
Dereks(IRE) ran out having slipped on the bend. Official explanation: jockey said gelding slipped on first bend (op 33-1)
T/Plt: £259.00 to a £1 stake. Pool:£101,160.76 - 285.12 winning tickets T/Qpdt: £33.20 to a £1 stake. Pool:£9,573.72 - 212.90 winning tickets ST

[1853] CHELTENHAM (L-H)
Saturday, October 16

OFFICIAL GOING: Good (good to firm in places; 7.9)
Wind: Moderate behind Weather: Sunny Intervals

1860 RUBY WALSH - THE AUTOBIOGRAPHY NOVICES' HURDLE (13 hdls) 3m 1f 110y

2:05 (2:05) (Class 3) 4-Y-0+

£6,262 (£1,850; £925; £463; £231; £116)

Form RPR
322- **1** **Aiteen Thirtythree (IRE)**[224] 4450 6-10-12 130........................ RWalsh 137+
(Paul Nicholls) *led but jnd fr 3rd tl def advantage 4 out: drvn appr last: hdd fnl 120yds: rallied gamely to ld again fnl 30yds* **1/1**[1]
1201 **2** *1* **Supercede (IRE)**[23] 1593 8-11-6 122..................................(bt) PCarberry 145+
(Gordon Elliott, Ire) *hld up in rr: blnd 8th: j. slowly 9th: stdy hdwy to trck ldrs 3 out: chsd wnr after next: rdn and tk slt ld fnl 120yds: hdd and no ex fnl 30yds* **9/1**[3]
00-2 **3** *32* **Smooth Classic (IRE)**[169] 82 6-10-12 115........................ NoelFehily 108
(Warren Greatrex) *t.k.h: hit 1st: in rr but in tch: hit 2nd: blnd 8th and sn chsng ldrs: rdn and lft one pce 3rd 2 out: sn no ch w ldng duo* **20/1**
2-11 **4** *4 1/2* **Pure Anticipation (IRE)**[136] 583 5-10-10 0............... RichardJohnson 103+
(Tim Vaughan) *w wnr tl blnd 4 out and sn lost pl: styd on again u.p run-in for poor 4th* **12/1**
6333 **5** *nk* **Doubletoilntrouble (IRE)**[52] 1369 4-10-11 105........................ RhysFlint 101
(Keith Goldsworthy) *chsd ldrs: j. slowly 8th: wnt 3rd 9th: wknd 3 out: no ch whn hit 2 out* **66/1**
555- **6** *24* **No Woman No Cry**[181] 5256 5-10-12 0................................ JoeTizzard 80
(Colin Tizzard) *t.k.h: in tch tl wknd after 4 out* **50/1**
4P40 **7** *30* **Smiling Applause**[27] 1559 11-10-9 66........................(p) TommyPhelan(3) 53
(Harry Chisman) *t.o fr 7th* **200/1**
1024 **B** **Majestic Mayhem (IRE)**[15] 1662 7-11-6 123........................ TomO'Brien 112
(George Moore) *chsd ldrs: j. slowly 5th: rdn and one pce bhd ldrs whn b.d 2 out* **25/1**
F **Acey (IRE)**[216] 4627 5-10-12 0... PaddyBrennan 115+
(Nigel Twiston-Davies) *j. slowly 6th: hit 9th: in rr tl gd hdwy 4 out: drvn to chse ldrs and hit 3 out: disputing cl 2nd under pressre whn fell 2 out: fatally injured* **2/1**[2]
6m 22.83s (-3.27) **Going Correction** -0.30s/f (Good)
WFA 4 from 5yo+ 11lb **9** Ran SP% **113.6**
Speed ratings (Par 107): **93,92,82,81,81 73,64,—,—**
Tote Swingers: 1&2 £1.90, 1&3 £5.90, 2&3 £10.30 CSF £10.32 TOTE £1.90: £1.10, £1.90, £3.30; EX 8.90 Trifecta £53.60 Pool: £1,538.83 - 21.24 winning units..
Owner Paul K Barber & The Stewart Family **Bred** Mrs Rosemary Ross **Trained** Ditcheat, Somerset

FOCUS
This opening novice hurdle wasn't the strongest of contests for the grade. The first pair came a long way clear in a battling finish off the home turn. The winner was just about the form pick but looks on the upgrade.

NOTEBOOK
Aiteen Thirtythree(IRE) was massively hyped last year but he proved a big disappointment in his three outings as a novice last term. Making his seasonal debut in new ownership, he once more proved a very popular choice for his leading trainer/jockey combination, who have both hit the ground running this autumn. He looked very slow last season so it wasn't surprising to see him try to make this a test and he finally got his head in front over hurdles, but was made to work very hard to land his prize by the penalised runner-up. To his credit he kept finding after the last having come over to the near rail with his effort, and it looks a case of the stiffer test the better for him. Being a 6-y-o with few miles on the clock who has won a point-to-point, it is probable that a switch to chasing will figure in his plans before long. Indeed he often jumped these hurdles like a chaser, certainly possesses the size for that game and so there is every chance he will rate higher when taking in fences. A sound surface also suits him well and it will be interesting to see where he turns up next, as a current mark of 130 in this sphere flatters him at this stage. (op 5-4 tchd 11-8 in a place)
Supercede(IRE), a dual winner over hurdles and fences, ran a big race in defeat conceding 8lb to the winner. He was officially raised 7lb despite being greatly flattered by his clear-cut success over hurdles at Perth last month, and this proved the handicapper to have been spot on with his assessment. He would have very likely won this had he not made a mess of the ninth as he lost vital momentum, and no doubt his shrewd trainer will be eyeing a return to this track with him later in the season. (tchd 10-1)
Smooth Classic(IRE) proved keen on this return from a 169-day break and that wouldn't have helped him over this longer trip. He still needs more practice and his optimum distance is uncertain, but he should come on for the outing. (tchd 18-1)
Pure Anticipation(IRE), seeking a hat-trick, was last seen scoring on her hurdling debut in June and proved easy to back. She put it up to the winner on the front end, but lost any chance with a mistake four out that saw her go backwards. The best of her has likely still to be seen. (op 11-1)
Doubletoilntrouble(IRE), returning from a 52-day break, hadn't shown enough in two previous outings to think he could be figuring at the finish in this company. He left the impression the trip stretched him at this stage of his career and will be better off in a handicap off his current mark of 105. (op 50-1)
Majestic Mayhem(IRE) faced his stiffest task at the weights and, while making heavy weather of things, was in the process of running a more encouraging race again prior to departing. (op 7-4 tchd 9-4)
Acey(IRE), a useful bumper performer in Ireland, sadly fell at the second-last with tragic consequences on this debut for new connections. (op 7-4 tchd 9-4)

1861 ZETURF.COM H'CAP CHASE (16 fncs) 2m 4f 110y

2:40 (2:40) (Class 2) (0-150,150) 4-Y-0+

£31,310 (£9,250; £4,625; £2,315; £1,155; £580)

Form RPR
310- **1** **Edgbriar (FR)**[189] 5126 8-10-13 **137**........................(p) DominicElsworth 142
(Paul Webber) *chsd ldrs: wnt 2nd 4 out: chal 2 out: rdn to take narrow ld last: rdn out* **14/1**

14P- **2** ½ **Chaninbar (FR)**[175] 5394 7-11-8 **149**............................(v) SeanQuinlan(3) 155
(Milton Harris) *chsd ldrs: hit 5th: blnd 6th: slt ld fr 3 out: sn rdn: narrowly hdd last: kpt on wl run-in but a jst hld* **40/1**

1F2- **3** 6 **Free World (IRE)**[181] 5246 8-10-0 **124** oh4......................... JamieMoore 124
(Warren Greatrex) *in rr: hdwy 4 out: styng on one pce in 3rd whn hit 2 out: kpt on run-in but no ch w ldng duo* **14/1**

1PP- **4** ½ **You're The Top (FR)**[175] 5398 6-11-1 **139**....................... BarryGeraghty 139
(Nicky Henderson) *in rr: j. slowily 3rd: hit 5th: hdwy after 4 out: styd on to chse ldrs 3 out: no imp on ldng duo fr next* **9/1**[3]

50-0 **5** 3½ **Private Be**[169] 78 11-10-8 **132**.................................... RichardJohnson 130+
(Philip Hobbs) *in tch: rdn 3 out: styng on same pce and no imp on ldrs whn bdly hmpd 2 out: kpt on again run-in* **9/1**[3]

402- **6** ½ **Rory Boy (USA)**[176] 5371 5-10-10 **134**............................ PaddyBrennan 131
(Nigel Twiston-Davies) *in rr and hit 5th: hdwy 12th: chsd ldrs u.p 3 out: one pce and hld whn hmpd 2 out* **8/1**[2]

1111 **7** 17 **Passato (GER)**[56] 1332 6-11-4 **142**......................................(t) APMcCoy 129+
(Joanna Davis) *in tch: hit 9th: rdn and no imp on ldrs after 4 out: no ch whn bdly hmpd 2 out* **15/2**[1]

0/0- **8** hd **Il Duce (IRE)**[336] 2269 10-10-13 **137**........................... WayneHutchinson 124+
(Alan King) *in tch early: in rr and hit 10th: mstke 4 out and no ch whn bdly hmpd 2 out* **8/1**[2]

2112 **9** 2¼ **Classic Swain (USA)**[56] 1332 5-11-5 **143**............................(bt) RWalsh 123
(Paul Nicholls) *blnd 4th and bhd: stl in rr and nvr travelling whn hit 12th* **15/2**[1]

P3-P **10** 13 **Pocket Aces (IRE)**[168] 98 8-10-9 **133**.......................... LeightonAspell 114+
(Richard Rowe) *in rr: hit 2nd and 5th: hit 11th: no ch whn blnd 3 out: hmpd last* **33/1**

04P- **11** 13 **Moon Over Miami (GER)**[211] 4716 9-10-13 **137**................(t) NoelFehily 97
(Charlie Mann) *a in rr: wl bhd whn hmpd last* **20/1**

00-P **12** 6 **Star Of Germany (IRE)**[56] 1332 10-10-10 **134**............. TomScudamore 90
(Ian Williams) *chsd ldrs to 11th: no ch whn hmpd 2 out* **33/1**

-464 **P** **Cossack Dancer (IRE)**[41] 1486 12-10-0 **124** oh7.......(p) MattieBatchelor —
(Mark Bradstock) *chsd ldr to 10th: asn wknd: t.o whn p.u bef 3 out* **33/1**

056- **F** **Gwanako (FR)**[185] 5183 7-11-7 **150**.................................... MrRMahon(5) —
(Paul Nicholls) *chsd ldrs: styng on one pce u.p for 4 l 3rd whn fell 2 out* **8/1**[2]

1122 **F** **Yellow Flag**[50] 1390 7-10-0 **127**.................................. RichieMcLernon(3) —
(Jonjo O'Neill) *in rr tl fell 4th* **14/1**

P32- **U** **Oiseau De Nuit (FR)**[176] 5394 8-11-8 **146**..........................(t) JoeTizzard 140
(Colin Tizzard) *in rr tl gd hdwy fr 11th: hit 12th: wkng and no ch whn bdly hmpd: swvd and uns rdr 2 out* **16/1**

2115 **F** **Frosted Grape (IRE)**[22] 1604 4-9-9 **134**...........................(b) CO'Farrell(5) 121
(David Pipe) *led: sn clr but j.rt fr 8th: narrowly hdd 3 out: wkng and no ch whn fell 2 out* **22/1**

5m 1.91s (-9.09) **Going Correction** -0.20s/f (Good)
WFA 4 from 5yo+ 10lb **17** Ran SP% **123.1**
Speed ratings (Par 109): **109,108,106,106,105 104,98,98,97,92 87,85,—,—,— —,—**
Tote Swingers: 1&2 £84.80, 1&3 £67.60, 2&3 £193.50 CSF £497.39 CT £7744.29 TOTE £18.30: £3.80, £12.50, £5.10, £2.80; EX 856.80 TRIFECTA Not won..

Owner D Allen **Bred** Jean-Michel Duperret **Trained** Mollington, Oxon

■ A winner for Dominic Elsworth on his first ride since suffering serious head injuries in August 2009.

FOCUS

A very competitive handicap run at a solid gallop and they were strung out early on. The first two dominated from three out and, although there was carnage at the newly aligned second-last fence, the pair were clear at that stage. The first four are only rated in line with their previous best.

NOTEBOOK

Edgbriar(FR) made light of a 189-day break and ran out a very gutsy winner, giving Dominic Elsworth a dream return on his comeback from a lengthy injury layoff. He was always handy and that proved to be an advantage as the race panned out, but there was an awful lot to like about his attitude up the climbing finish. The winner was 3l higher than when last winning at Bangor in March two runs back and so this does rate a personal-best effort. A stiff 2m4f also now looks to be his optimum distance and this display fully entitles him to come back and try his luck in the Paddy Power over C&D at the Open meeting next month. However, not since 2001 when Shooting Light succeeded has the winner of this event gone on to follow up. (op 16-1)

Chaninbar(FR) has to be considered very unfortunate to have bumped into the winner as he was a clear second-best and he went down fighting on his seasonal return. Better known as a two-miler last term, he just got outstayed by Edgbriar up the run-in but clearly stays the trip. It should also be remembered he was conceding the best part of a stone to that rival, so he too fully deserves to come back for the Paddy Power. (op 50-1)

Free World(IRE) came in for support on his return to action, despite being 4lb out of the handicap. He was gifted third following the melee two out, but ideally wants a stiffer test, and perhaps a more positive ride would have seen him finish closer to the first pair. With that in mind it was a pleasing comeback effort and he is one to bear in mind next time out despite the likelihood of a rise. (op 22-1)

You're The Top(FR) looked like making up into a decent novice chaser last season, but he was disappointingly pulled up when tried in better company on his final two outings. He was ridden to get the trip on this seasonal debut and began his move around four out but was never a serious threat. He is also a touch flattered by his finishing position due to the fallers in the home straight and may not be the easiest to place this season. However, he is entitled to improve and could be happier again when going right handed again. (op 15-2)

Private Be knows his way around here very well, but he was laboured on his return from a summer break and was beaten before getting badly hampered. He should improve for this, but probably wants his sights lowered. (op 12-1)

Rory Boy(USA) won first time up as a novice last term and was representing an in-form yard. He too posted a laboured effort, but is still only a 5-y-o and there will be better to come from him this season.

Passato(GER) proved a revelation during the summer and arrived for this return from a 56-day break unbeaten in his last four outings. He was 9lb higher in this much tougher company, though, and was beaten well before he got hampered two out. (tchd 8-1)

Il Duce(IRE) (op 10-1)

Classic Swain(USA), still just a 5-y-o, did not take to this much more competitive assignment on his return from a break and is not going to prove simple to place off his current sort of mark. (op 13-2 tchd 8-1 in a place)

Gwanako(FR) came down at the newly sited second-last as he was battling away for third place. (tchd 25-1)

Oiseau De Nuit(FR) unseated after jumping two out as he got badly hampered. A drop back in trip now looks firmly on the cards for that one. (tchd 25-1)

Frosted Grape(IRE), still just a filly, came down two out when held. (tchd 25-1)

1862 SPORTINGBET.COM HURDLE (8 hdls) 2m 110y

3:15 (3:15) (Class 2) 4-Y-O

£31,310 (£9,250; £4,625; £2,315; £1,155; £580)

Form RPR

1-11 **1** **Clerk's Choice (IRE)**[153] 356 4-10-12 131......................... TomMolloy 157+
(Michael Banks) *hld up off a str pce: hdwy after 5th: disp 2nd travelling wl gng to 2 out: led wl bef last: r.o strly: impressive* **14/1**

1- **2** 21 **Royal Mix (FR)**[323] 2550 4-10-12 141.. RWalsh 137
(Paul Nicholls) *wnt lft 1st: hld up in mid-div: stdy prog fr after 4th: disp 2nd after next: rdn after 2 out: styd on same pce: wnt 2nd sn after last: no ch w wnr* **13/8**[2]

221- **3** 4½ **Barizan (IRE)**[175] 5399 4-11-6 146......................................(v) APMcCoy 142
(Evan Williams) *w ldr: led after 2nd: hit 4th: rdn after 2 out: sn hdd: kpt on same pce: lost 2nd sn after last* **6/4**[1]

166- **4** 11 **Gilded Age**[175] 5399 4-10-12 132................................ WayneHutchinson 123
(Alan King) *hld up in last trio: styd on fr after 2 out: wnt 4th towards fin: nvr able to get on terms w ldrs* **12/1**

233- **5** ½ **Ultimate**[28] 4643 4-10-12 134... DannyCook 124
(Brian Ellison) *chsd clr ldrs: wnt 2nd after 4th tl after next: outpcd after 2 out: lost 4th towards fin* **10/1**[3]

314- **6** 17 **Orsippus (USA)**[175] 5399 4-11-6 142....................................... DJCondon 115
(Michael Smith) *hld up in mid-div: mstke 5th: sn struggling: wknd bef 2 out: t.o* **12/1**

1 **7** 6 **Dark Ranger**[13] 1689 4-10-12 0... BrianToomey 102
(Tim Pitt) *hld up wl off str pce: nvr able to get on terms: t.o* **33/1**

0-16 **8** dist **My Brother Sylvest**[7] 1768 4-10-12 0...................................... RhysFlint —
(David Brace) *j.lft: led at str pce tl after 2nd: chsd ldr tl after 4th: sn wknd: t.o* **66/1**

3m 49.25s (-12.75) **Going Correction** -0.30s/f (Good) course record **8** Ran SP% **113.7**
Speed ratings: **118,108,106,100,100 92,89,—**
Tote Swingers: 1&2 £5.60, 1&3 £5.50, 2&3 £1.02 CSF £38.03 TOTE £18.30: £2.60, £1.20, £1.30; EX 63.70 Trifecta £151.20 Pool: £1,574.72 - 7.70 winning units..

Owner M C Banks **Bred** N Coman **Trained** Waresley, Cambs

FOCUS

This was a decent event for 4-y-os and as expected there was a frantic early gallop on. Most were found out around the third-last. Seemingly a massive step up from the facile winner although this might have him a few pounds too high.

NOTEBOOK

Clerk's Choice(IRE) was a useful handicapper when trained on the Flat and proved very progressive when landing a hat-trick over hurdles back in the spring. He had never raced against anything of this calibre, however, and his pre-race odds of 14-1 seemed a fair enough reflection of his chance at these weights. There was no fluke about the manner in which he went about his business in winning easily, though, and he must be treated as a big improver. The strong early gallop played right into this strong-traveller's hands and this proves his effectiveness away from a flat track. A hike in the ratings is now a certainty and it is never straightforward for a horse of this age when finally going up against the big boys in the 2m hurdle division. However, last year's winner of this event Starluck went on to be a Champion Hurdle contender and a likely rise should see him a get a run in next month's Greatwood Hurdle back over C&D. He is certainly worth aiming at that classy handicap after this bloodless win, but it may also be that connections follow the same path that Starluck took after this last year and take in the valuable 4-y-o hurdle at Haydock next month instead. Whatever the case he will not be running on proper soft ground and it will be fascinating to see how far up the ladder he can climb this season. (op 12-1)

Royal Mix(FR) was having his first outing since beating subsequent Grade 1 winner Me Voici on his hurdling debut for connections in November last year. There seemed to be deal of confidence about him on this belated return, but ultimately he left the impression the run was needed as he proved somewhat ring rusty. Softer ground may also suit this former French Flat winner better, and also a step up in trip could be what he wants this season, so he certainly remains a horse of potential. (tchd 15-8 in a place and 7-4 in places)

Barizan(IRE) was just about the toughest juvenile hurdler around last term and, while his Grade 1 success at Punchestown on his final outing wasn't a strong event for the class, his second in the Triumph Hurdle made him the clear pick at these weights. He wasn't helped by getting into a duel for the early lead on this return, however, as he did an awful lot through the first half. He unsurprisingly came under pressure around three out and, while he responded in typically game fashion, he was a sitting duck for the winner. He was a bit unlucky to lose second place late on and should come on a deal for the run, but will need to up his game if he is to win against his elders this season. (op 7-4 tchd 15-8 in places)

Gilded Age was well held by Barizan on the form of his two outings at the top level last season, and found things happening all too quickly on this first run back. His mark of 132 is probably a workable one, though, and he too should come on for the run. (tchd 14-1)

Ultimate, who had a spin on the level last month, liked getting out in front last season so the fact he couldn't get near the lead early on this time is a decent indication of how quickly the pace-setters went. He is another entitled to come on for the run and should enjoy getting back on a flatter track, but won't find things easy off his current perch. (op 12-1 tchd 9-1)

Orsippus(USA) caused a surprise when beating Barizan in the Grade 1 Anniversary Hurdle at Aintree at last season's Grand National meeting, but was put in his place by him again when signing off at the Punchestown festival. He wasn't on a going day on his seasonal debut here, tending to make mistakes, but it's a fair bet he'll improve plenty for the outing. Whether he will prove up to his mark of 142 this term remains to be seen, though. (op 17-2 tchd 8-1)

Dark Ranger won well on debut at Huntingdon 13 days earlier, but was taken off his feet from the offset in this vastly better race and never figured. (op 25-1)

1863 ROYAL GLOUCESTERSHIRE HUSSARS NOVICES' CHASE (19 fncs) 3m 110y

3:50 (3:51) (Class 2) 5-Y-O+

£9,393 (£2,775; £1,387; £694; £346; £174)

Form RPR

05-3 **1** **Chicago Grey (IRE)**[21] 1619 7-11-8 138..............................(t) PCarberry 150+
(Gordon Elliott, Ire) *hld up in rr: hit 5th and 6th: rdn appr 3 out: gd hdwy sn after and styd on to ld appr 2 out: rdn out* **13/2**

61-1 **2** 6 **Picture This (IRE)**[161] 206 7-11-0 0... RWalsh 137+
(Paul Nicholls) *trckd ldrs tl blnd 7th: in tch again whn nt fluent 12th: chsng ldrs whn hit 3 out and lost position: pushed along and stl 5th 2 out: styd on run-in and fin wl to take 2nd last strides but no ch w wnr* **6/5**[1]

1111 **3** nk **Billie Magern**[20] 1627 6-11-8 0.. PaddyBrennan 143
(Nigel Twiston-Davies) *led: hit 3rd: rdn 3 out: hdd appr next: no imprssion on wnr run-in: ct for 2nd last strides* **9/2**[2]

6-11 **4** shd **Balthazar King (IRE)**[7] 1774 6-11-8 132...................... RichardJohnson 142
(Philip Hobbs) *chsd ldr: hit 12th: lost 2nd 4 out but styd pressing ldrs: one pce 2 out: styd on again run-in: gng on cl home* **11/2**[3]

-601 **5** 22 **Hell's Bay (FR)**[46] 1444 8-11-5 0.. JoeTizzard 124+
(Colin Tizzard) *in tch: chsng ldrs whn mstkes 14th and next: wnt 2nd 4 out: chal 3 out: wkng whn nt fluent 2 out* **14/1**

0156 **6** 2 **Pilgrims Lane (IRE)**[20] 1626 6-11-8 130......................(p) JimmyDerham 120
(Milton Harris) *in tch: hit 8th: bhd fr 12th* **40/1**

120- 7 3¼ **Babysitter (IRE)**185 5182 7-11-0 0 SamTwiston-Davies 109
(Nigel Twiston-Davies) *chsd ldrs: j. slowly 8th: rdn 13th: wknd after 3 out* **10/1**

6m 12.45s (-5.85) **Going Correction** -0.20s/f (Good) **7** Ran SP% **110.6**
Speed ratings: **101,99,98,98,91 91,90**
Tote Swingers: 1&2 £2.90, 1&3 £4.00, 2&3 £1.10 CSF £14.55 TOTE £7.10: £3.20, £1.30; EX 17.50 Trifecta £40.10 Pool: £948.97 - 17.51 winning units..
Owner John Earls **Bred** Mrs R H Lalor **Trained** Trim, Co Meath

FOCUS
A good novice chase that should prove the benchmark for the staying division until the Open meeting back here next month. It was run at something of an uneven gallop, but the form still looks sound enough. The winner is a 149 hurdler and dhould match that over fences.

NOTEBOOK
Chicago Grey(IRE) landed his third success from six outings since embarking on his chase career and completed the task in decent fashion. The step up in trip was of some concern and things didn't look good for him on the final circuit as his sluggish jumping looked to be taking a toll. However, he really picked up strongly from the fourth-last and arrived on the scene going easily after a decent leap over the next. He took control coming to the penultimate fence and, although he wasn't too clever again over that fence, he was always doing enough thereafter. Now connections can be confident he fully gets the trip it opens up more opportunities for him. Indeed he may well be aimed towards the RSA Chase now and it must be remembered he was a very useful hurdler (carried top weight in last season's Coral Cup). An outing in Graded company will reveal more as to his credentials for that. (op 15-2 tchd 6-1)
Picture This(IRE), last seen readily winning a competitive handicap hurdle at Haydock in May, attracted plenty of money on this chasing debut. He had also prevailed on both his outings in that sphere at this track and he looked a natural over the first six fences here. However, he made a bad mistake at the seventh and went backwards. Despite getting back into a rhythm shortly after, he failed to really convince from that point on and looked in trouble as the pace increased on the final circuit. Indeed he seemed well beaten turning into the home straight, but he motored up the run-in to grab second near the finish. A sound surface is a must for him and providing he can brush up his jumping, which he is fully entitled to do, he will no doubt be winning races as a chaser. (op 6-4 tchd 13-8 in places)
Billie Magern had slammed the winner at Perth when they met back in July and was bidding to emulate his half-brother Ollie Magern, who won this event in 2004. His grinding style has drawn comparison with his sibling and, unsurprisingly, he set out to make all. He was no match for the winner when that rival asserted for home, but did things well enough through the race and may well have been better off making this more of a test. It could be that he still has a bit more to offer. (op 10-3)
Balthazar King(IRE) came into this unbeaten in two previous outings over fences. He was never far away, but hit something of a flat spot before rallying after the last. He wasn't at all disgraced considering he endured a hard race at Chepstow a week earlier. (op 6-1 tchd 13-2)
Hell's Bay(FR) was going strongly around three out and looked a likely winner, but his stamina blatantly gave way before the second-last. He has been rejuvenated since joining the yard and is one to side with when reverting to a sharper test. (op 12-1)

1864 RACING WITH STYLE H'CAP HURDLE (10 hdls) 2m 5f
4:25 (4:25) (Class 2) (0-140,137) 4-Y-0+
£9,393 (£2,775; £1,387; £694; £346; £174)

Form RPR

-101 **1** **Russian War (IRE)**18 1643 7-10-11 **122** (t) PCarberry 127+
(Gordon Elliott, Ire) *hld up in rr tl stdy hdwy and mstke 2 out: stl on bit whn chal last: led sn after: rdn fnl 75yds: jst hld on* **8/1**3

3442 **2** *hd* **Is It Me (USA)**23 1590 7-9-12 **112** (t) RichieMcLernon(3) 116
(Sophie Leech) *led 2nd: narrowly hdd whn hit 2 out: rallied to press ldrs last: rallied u.p fnl 50yds: fin wl: jst failed* **33/1**

1025 **3** *1* **Son Of Flicka**21 1609 6-11-5 **137** HenryBrooke(7) 139
(Donald McCain) *chsd ldrs: blnd 6th: rallied u.p fr 2 out to take slt ld last: hdd sn after: kpt on same pce fnl 100yds* **20/1**

2352 **4** *3* **Aohna (FR)**13 1692 5-10-4 **115** WayneHutchinson 115
(Alan King) *hld up towards rr: hit 3 out: hdwy 2 out: kpt on wl to take 4th fnl 100yds but no imp on ldng trio* **12/1**

0-52 **5** *1* **Mickmacmagoole (IRE)**21 1614 8-9-13 **120** JSMcGarvey(10) 120
(Evan Williams) *hit 2nd: in rr: stl wl bhd 2 out tl drvn and styd on appr last: fin strly* **28/1**

664- **6** *hd* **Dingat (IRE)**207 4801 5-10-0 **111** oh1 AidanColeman 111
(Tim Vaughan) *hit 2nd: in tch: rdn after 3 out: styd on appr last and kpt on run-in but nvr a threat* **16/1**

-220 **7** *¾* **Dantari (IRE)**79 1133 5-11-2 **130** DPFahy(3) 128
(Evan Williams) *in tch: rdn after 3 out: styd on fr 2 out but nvr rchd ldrs* **16/1**

0-P3 **8** *4½* **Secret Tune**55 1346 6-11-5 **130** (b) PaddyBrennan 128+
(Tom George) *mid-div: hit 6th: hdwy 4 out: chal 3 out: slt ld and hit next: upsides and narrowly hdd last: wknd run-in* **14/1**

-255 **9** *6* **Rajeh (IRE)**19 1198 7-11-7 **132** (p) TomO'Brien 121
(John Spearing) *in rr: hit 3 out: hdwy 2 out: kpt on same pce run-in* **33/1**

-611 **10** *nse* **Great Mates (IRE)**71 1196 6-10-7 **118** RWalsh 108
(Paul Nicholls) *in rr: stl bhd whn hit 4 out: rdn after next: sme prog appr last* **7/2**1

313- **11** *½* **Scampi Boy (IRE)**183 5209 6-10-9 **120** WillKennedy 108
(Paul Webber) *chsd ldrs: rdn to chal 3 out: wknd after next* **8/1**3

041- **12** *1* **General Ting (IRE)**194 5045 5-10-5 **116** LeightonAspell 103
(Lucy Wadham) *in rr: sme hdwy 4 out: btn whn hmpd 2 out* **20/1**

34-0 **13** *16* **Fin Vin De Leu (GER)**161 206 4-11-2 **127** NoelFehily 100
(Charlie Mann) *chsd ldrs: wnt 2nd 4 out: chal 3 out to next: wknd sn after* **25/1**

2121 **14** *62* **Benedict Spirit (IRE)**46 1443 5-10-7 **118** (p) RhysFlint 35
(John Flint) *led tl after 1st: wknd after 4 out* **12/1**

120- **P** **Benartic (IRE)**190 5119 6-10-8 **119** BarryGeraghty —
(Nicky Henderson) *chsd ldrs tl wknd qckly 4 out: p.u sn after* **12/1**

U-11 **P** **Comehomequietly (IRE)**52 1372 6-10-13 **124** PaulMoloney —
(David Rees) *t.o fr 6th: p.u bef 3 out* **14/1**

46-1 **U** **Pro Pell (IRE)**157 282 5-10-1 **112** JamieMoore 112+
(Gary Moore) *in tch: rdn and styng on to dispute cl 4th whn blnd and uns rdr 2 out* **15/2**2

5m 9.70s (-3.70) **Going Correction** -0.30s/f (Good)
WFA 4 from 5yo+ 10lb **17** Ran SP% **127.1**
Speed ratings (Par 109): **95,94,94,93,93 92,92,90,88,88 88,88,81,58,— —,—**
Tote Swingers: 1&2 £91.40, 1&3 £78.40, 2&3 £79.90 CSF £264.77 CT £5050.57 TOTE £11.10: £2.80, £6.90, £5.40, £3.10; EX 333.70 TRIFECTA Not won..
Owner T D Howley Jnr **Bred** Tommy Howley **Trained** Trim, Co Meath

FOCUS
This wasn't the strongest of contests for the class, but it was certainly competitive. There was an average gallop on and the first three came clear after the last. The winner is rated in line with his best Irish form.

NOTEBOOK
Russian War(IRE) received another fine winning ride from Paul Carberry to follow up his Sedgefield success last month and gave his yard a quick-fire double. He isn't that straightforward and benefited from a superb ride from Tony McCoy on his previous outing. Once again assistance from the saddle was top-class as he scythed his way through the pack from off the pace on the inside nearing two out and it was apparent he had plenty in the tank for the climb up the home straight. He could have been better at the last and that forced Carberry to play his hand. Not for the first time he then idled out in front and that allowed the runner-up another crack at him, but he was always doing enough. This was the winner's handicap debut, despite it being his tenth outing over hurdles and he is evidently still on an upwards curve. It wouldn't be at all surprising to see him back here for the festival in March. (op 12-1)
Is It Me(USA) made a really bold bid from the front and, despite again finding one too good, he richly deserves to add to his tally. There should be plenty of easier assignments in the coming weeks.
Son Of Flicka turned in a solid effort in defeat from the top of the handicap back over a suitably stiffer test. He helps to set the standard as he does look handicapped to his best. (op 25-1 tchd 28-1)
Aohna(FR) got going late in the day and posted another sterling effort in defeat. She is a model of consistency and is another that can find less competitive assignments again in the near future, but she doesn't find it easy to get her head in front. (op 14-1)
Mickmacmagoole(IRE), who made an early mistake, once again did his best work towards the finish and turned in a sound effort. Official explanation: jockey said gelding bled from the nose (op 25-1)
Dingat(IRE) ♦, a dual bumper winner, was a disappointment in three novice hurdles last term, but he came in for support on this seasonal/handicap debut and ran a lot more encouragingly. He was 1lb out of the handicap and should be able to find an opening before long. (op 10-1)
Dantari(IRE) left the impression he would come on for this first outing since finishing eighth in the Galway Hurdle, and is worth another try over this trip on a less demanding circuit.
Secret Tune, returning from a 55-day break, took it up two out but wasn't clever there and also could have been better at the last when under heavy pressure. He probably made his move that bit too soon, but still just looks held by the handicapper. (op 16-1)
Great Mates(IRE), seeking a hat-trick, was disappointing on his handicap debut and now has something to prove. Official explanation: trainer said, regarding running, that the gelding suffered interference early and was never able to get into a challenging position. (tchd 10-3 and 4-1)
Scampi Boy(IRE) looked a big player when making his move nearing the second-last, but he wasn't helped when Secret Tune went out to his right there and soon came under pressure. He is better than the bare form and has evidently begun life in handicap company on a fair mark. (tchd 15-2, 9-1 in a place)
General Ting(IRE), up in trip, deserves a mention as he moved nicely until feeling the pinch three out. He is not exposed as a hurdler and should improve a deal for the run, so is well worth keeping an eye on. (op 18-1)
Comehomequietly(IRE) Official explanation: jockey said gelding lost its action

1865 KLEINWORT BENSON NOVICES' CHASE (13 fncs) 2m
5:00 (5:00) (Class 2) 4-Y-0+ **£9,427** (£2,809; £1,422; £729; £381)

Form RPR

1 **Kilmurry (IRE)**49 1408 5-11-10 0 JoeTizzard 152+
(Colin Tizzard) *trckd ldrs: chal 9th: led 4 out: pushed along and qcknd whn pressed 2 out: drvn clr run-in: readily* **5/1**3

100- **2** *11* **Ghizao (GER)**189 5128 6-11-2 0 RWalsh 136+
(Paul Nicholls) *trckd ldrs: j. slowly 5th: trckd wnr 3 out: pushed along and 1 l down 2 out: sn rdn and outpcd but clr 2nd best* **13/8**1

510- **3** *19* **Pigeon Island**191 5097 7-11-10 137 PaddyBrennan 127
(Nigel Twiston-Davies) *in rr: j. slowly 5th: rdn and strugggling 4 out: hit 3 out: styd on to take wl hld 3rd last* **6/1**

01-0 **4** *3½* **Captive Audience (IRE)**161 206 7-11-2 0 APMcCoy 115+
(Rebecca Curtis) *trckd ldr: slt ld 9th: hdd 4 out: hit next and lost 2nd: sn wknd: lost mod 3rd last* **4/1**2

F-0 **5** *10* **Kotkidy (FR)**33 1519 4-10-12 126 AELynch 104
(Henry De Bromhead, Ire) *led: blnd 6th: mstke and hdd 9th: wl btn whn blnd 2 out* **6/1**

11F1 **F** **Shopfrontspecialst (IRE)**18 1642 7-11-7 122 (t) PCarberry —
(Gordon Elliott, Ire) *blnd 3rd: in rr tl fell 8th* **16/1**

3m 51.58s (-6.42) **Going Correction** -0.20s/f (Good)
WFA 4 from 5yo+ 9lb **6** Ran SP% **109.2**
Speed ratings (Par 109): **108,102,93,91,86** —
Tote Swingers: 1&2 £1.80, 1&3 £3.30, 2&3 £1.90 CSF £13.44 TOTE £5.20: £2.40, £1.30; EX 12.80.
Owner J P Romans **Bred** Dan O'Connor **Trained** Milborne Port, Dorset

FOCUS
An interesting novice chase over the minimum trip. It was run at a decent pace and the impressive winner is rated up a stone+ and within 10lb of a typical Arkle winner.

NOTEBOOK
Kilmurry(IRE) made a successful British debut for new connections. The 5-y-o had only a maiden hurdle to his name prior to going chasing in the summer when with Henry de Bromhead in Ireland, but improved markedly to score on his last two outings at Galway for his previous trainer. He proved easy enough to back here, but travelled with real enthusiasm through the race and went to the front after the fourth-last. He looked a little vulnerable as Ghizao loomed up nearing the second-last, but he pinged that fence and another fine leap at the last saw him hit the ground running. He came right away thereafter and still looked to have a fair bit left in the tank at the business end. Considering the runner-up was rated 135 over hurdles and he gave that rival 8lb here it has to rate a decent effort. This display fully entitles him to try his hand in something more valuable now and the Grade 2 Independent Newspapers Novices' Chase back here at next month's Open meeting looks just the right race for him. That is a well-known trial for the Arkle and he would be facing much stiffer opposition, but with his liking for the track now well advertised he would still have plenty of backers there. (op 9-2 tchd 11-2 in a place)
Ghizao(GER) attracted good support for this chasing and seasonal debut. He took a little time to warm to the task, but was the only threat to the winner after three out. He wasn't nearly so good as that rival over the final two fences, however, and ultimately this experience just looked needed. It shouldn't be long before he's winning and stepping up in trip may well suit, but he is probably more a handicap prospect for this discipline. (op 2-1 tchd 5-2 in places and 9-4 in places)
Pigeon Island's sole win as a novice last term came when he ran out a ready winner of the Grand Annual at the festival over C&D. He should have enjoyed the way the race was run, but went in snatches from an early stage and was never a serious player. He has developed into an enigmatic character and will shortly lose his novice status, but it wouldn't be surprising if he pops up in something valuable again later on. (op 9-2 tchd 13-2)
Captive Audience(IRE) bombed out on his handicap debut when last seen in May, but he was a progressive novice hurdler prior to that. He was backed for this switch to chasing, but not that surprisingly found this drop back from 3m too sharp. He is one to be with back over further now he has some experience of fences under his belt. (op 11-2 tchd 6-1)
Kotkidy(FR) was representing the Irish yard that used to train the winner. He had fallen six out when still a long way in front at the Listowel fesitval last month and looked open to improvement. He is a headstrong character, though, and, while this probably wasn't his track, he must learn to settle better. (op 9-2)

Shopfrontspecialst(IRE), a recent Sedgefield winner, was behind and hadn't convinced prior to crashing out at the eighth. He was soon back up on his feet. (op 11-1)

1866 CHAMPAGNE LANSON STANDARD OPEN NATIONAL HUNT FLAT RACE 2m 110y

5:35 (5:36) (Class 4) 4-6-Y-O **£3,903** (£1,146; £573; £286)

Form RPR

1 **Lets Get Serious (IRE)** 4-11-0 0 BarryGeraghty 121+
(Nicky Henderson) *hld up in rr: stdy hdwy on outside 4f out: shkn up and qcknd wl over 1f out: led jst ins fnl f: sn clr: comf* **4/1**[2]

2- 2 2 ½ **Dark Lover (GER)**[189] 5137 5-11-0 0 RWalsh 115
(Paul Nicholls) *in tch hdwy fr 4f out: trckd ldrs over 2f out: drvn to take slt ld appr fnl f: sn hdd: one pce* **2/1**[1]

1 3 7 **Sybarite (FR)**[38] 1510 4-11-7 0 PaddyBrennan 115
(Nigel Twiston-Davies) *trckd ldr: upsides fr 7f out: drvn to take slt advantage over 2f out: stl hrd pressed whn hdd appr fnl f: sn wknd* **2/1**[1]

4 1 **Teaforthree (IRE)**[194] 5061 6-11-0 0 APMcCoy 107
(Rebecca Curtis) *led: jnd 7f out: drvn and kpt slt advantage tl narrowly hdd over 2f out: wknd ins fnl f* **6/1**[3]

5 2 ½ **Vico Road (IRE)** 5-10-11 0 RichieMcLernon(3) 105
(Jonjo O'Neill) *chsd ldrs: rdn 4f out: styd wl there tl wknd fr 2f out* **33/1**

5- 6 3 ½ **Accordintolawrence (IRE)**[235] 4213 4-10-7 0 PeterCarberry(7) 101
(Charlie Longsdon) *chsd ldrs tl wknd over 3f out* **12/1**

53 7 10 **Robello**[108] 869 6-10-7 0 CharlieWallis(7) 91
(John O'Shea) *chsd ldrs 10f* **40/1**

00- 8 6 **Koralsdarling (IRE)**[176] 5368 6-10-11 0 RichardKilloran(3) 85
(Alan Jones) *bhd most of way* **66/1**

3m 58.7s (2.30) **Going Correction** -0.30s/f (Good) **8** Ran SP% **115.5**
Speed ratings: **82,80,77,77,75 74,69,66**
Tote Swingers: 1&2 £1.40, 1&3 £4.00, 2&3 £1.10 CSF £12.50 TOTE £5.00: £1.90, £1.10, £1.40; EX 15.70 Trifecta £20.30 Pool: £1,146.62 - 41.59 winning units. Place 6: £97.88 Place 5: £60.26..
Owner Michael Buckley **Bred** Stuart Weld **Trained** Upper Lambourn, Berks

FOCUS
This bumper has thrown up some decent winners in the past, indeed Imperial Commander made a winning debut here in 2006, and this year's running looked a small, but select field. The first pair came clear of the penalised third late on and both look potentially very useful. The form is solid enough despite the slow time.

NOTEBOOK
Lets Get Serious(IRE) ◆ overcame greenness and ran out a very ready debut winner. A half-brother to a point winner, he hails from a yard that has always boasted a serious bunch of bumper horses, but he proved fairly easy to back. Perhaps the experience was expected to be needed and he looked clueless at times, but the further he went the better he was. He displayed a neat turn of foot to master the runner-up inside the final furlong and, with plenty of improvement assured for the outing, ought to defy a penalty if kept to this division. He could turn up at next month's Open Meeting for the decent bumper. (op 9-2 tchd 5-1)
Dark Lover(GER) ◆, second on debut at Chepstow in April, also hails from a leading stable with plenty of talent among its bumper performers. He got a patient ride before being asked for his effort off the home bend and lost nothing in defeat. He really ought to pick up one of these before he goes hurdling. (op 11-4 tchd 3-1)
Sybarite(FR) was an impressive debut winner at Uttoxeter last month and he gives this form a solid look. He raced more positively than the first two home and his rider looked fairly confident rounding the final turn. However, having mastered Teaforthree shortly afterwards he still looked green when asked for maximum effort and was comfortably swallowed up with around a furlong to go. He was the only penalised runner here and time should tell he faced a very difficult task, so he remains a nice prospect for novice hurdling. (op 13-8)
Teaforthree(IRE) was making his British debut for new connections having finished third at Cork in April. A former winning pointer, he unsurprisingly got a positive ride and proved game but was a sitting duck off the home turn. He essentially looks a stayer and, while he may well be able to win one of these, will enjoy stepping up in trip once sent hurdling. (op 7-1)
Vico Road(IRE), a £21,000 purchase, wasn't given too hard a time of things on this racecourse debut and should come on a good deal foe the run. He too ought to prove suited by further once sent hurdling. (op 22-1)
T/Plt: £347.60 to a £1 stake. Pool:£145,834 - 306.25 winning tickets T/Qpdt: £25.00 to a £1 stake. Pool:£7,168 - 211.90 winning tickets ST

1695 KELSO (L-H)

Saturday, October 16

OFFICIAL GOING: Good to firm (good in places; 7.0)
Wind: Almost nil Weather: Overcast

1867 CLIFFORD FIRTH MEMORIAL "NATIONAL HUNT" MAIDEN HURDLE (8 hdls) 2m 110y

2:30 (2:30) (Class 4) 4-Y-0+ **£2,341** (£687; £343; £171)

Form RPR

-315 1 **Mr Jay Dee (IRE)**[53] 1357 5-11-0 0 BrianHughes 119+
(Alan Swinbank) *trckd ldrs: hdwy to ld last: rdn out* **3/1**[2]

F4-2 2 6 **Maggio (FR)**[15] 1664 5-11-0 112 (p) AndrewTinkler 112
(Patrick Griffin, Ire) *led tl hdd last: kpt on same pce u.p run-in* **6/1**[3]

26F2 3 hd **Flichity (IRE)**[25] 1567 5-10-11 108 AdrianLane(3) 112
(Donald McCain) *t.k.h: hld up: hdwy and prom 3 out: effrt 2 out: kpt on u.p run-in* **8/1**

220- 4 6 **Si Bien (FR)**[188] 5142 5-11-0 111 GrahamLee 108+
(James Ewart) *t.k.h: cl up: hit 3rd: ev ch tl outpcd after last* **3/1**[2]

04-2 5 3 ½ **County Colours (IRE)**[8] 1757 5-11-0 107 TimmyMurphy 104
(Howard Johnson) *t.k.h: in tch: effrt bef 2 out: wknd last* **11/4**[1]

0- 6 9 **Scarvagh Rose**[180] 5277 5-10-7 0 WilsonRenwick 89
(Rose Dobbin) *hld up: stdy hdwy and in tch bef 3 out: wknd next* **66/1**

44-6 7 8 **Accordingtotheboss (IRE)**[144] 457 5-10-11 0 FearghalDavis(3) 86
(Nicky Richards) *hld up: outpcd 4 out: n.d after* **40/1**

3-43 8 4 ½ **Wicked Streak (IRE)**[113] 841 5-11-0 0 BarryKeniry 82
(Micky Hammond) *trckd ldrs tl rdn and wknd 2 out* **25/1**

50- 9 10 **Smithy The Horse (IRE)**[182] 5235 4-11-0 0 BrianHarding 71
(Donald McCain) *hld up: outpcd whn hit 4 out: sn btn* **33/1**

10 18 **Fred Grass** 4-10-11 0 JamesO'Farrell(3) 53
(Jonathan Haynes) *midfield: blnd 1st: nt fluent 4 out: wknd next* **200/1**

00-6 11 18 **Bunacurry**[15] 1664 5-10-11 0 CampbellGillies(3) 35
(Barry Murtagh) *bhd: struggling 4 out: sn btn* **100/1**

P56- 12 6 **Return Perk (IRE)**[205] 4833 7-11-0 0 RichieMcGrath 29
(Jim Goldie) *in tch to 1/2-way: sn lost pl and struggling* **66/1**

3m 50.0s (-11.80) **Going Correction** -0.725s/f (Firm) **12** Ran SP% **115.8**
Speed ratings (Par 105): **98,95,95,92,90 86,82,80,75,67 58,56**
CSF £20.26 TOTE £3.90: £1.30, £2.40, £2.50; EX 22.30.
Owner R Dooly **Bred** Noel Dooly **Trained** Melsonby, N Yorks

FOCUS
Racing took place in dry, cool, windless conditions, and Brian Hughes described the mostly good to firm going as perfect ground after taking this opener. A fair novice for the track, with the easy winner rated up a stone.

NOTEBOOK
Mr Jay Dee(IRE) was well placed throughout, and wasn't too hard pressed to pick off Maggio from the last and stay on well. Early over-keenness and mid-race mistakes might have fudged the issue over whether he didn't truly stay 2m4f at Sedgefield last time, but either way he looks perfectly capable back at 2m on this evidence, and can be placed to find a northern novice contest in the short term. (op 4-1)
Maggio(FR), retaining the cheekpieces which inspired a revival at Hexham last time, got his preferred uncontested lead once more but couldn't offer sufficient fight once joined. A current handicap mark of 120 looks a bit high on balance, yet at the same time he's not blessed with enough late tactical speed to repel any halfway-decent novice. (op 9-2)
Flichity(IRE) found more and jumped better than has often been the case and nearly demoted the runner-up close home. A step up in trip and switch to handicaps may not go amiss. (op 10-1)
Si Bien(FR), a first runner since May for James Ewart, was right there until his challenge flattened out from the last, and it's not hard to conclude that a lack of match-fitness played a greater role in his defeat than the effect of an early mistake. He remains capable of better in the coming weeks. (op 10-3 tchd 7-2)
County Colours(IRE), sent wide for most of the race to get a good sight of the hurdles, failed to pick up. He was a little keen early, but then he had been when still managing a second at Carlisle eight days earlier, so maybe this just came too soon after. (tchd 3-1)
Scarvagh Rose shaped with a little promise before being left behind up the straight, and could be one for ordinary mares' handicaps in due course.

1868 EDINBURGH CITY F.C. NOVICES' H'CAP CHASE (17 fncs) 2m 6f 110y

3:05 (3:06) (Class 4) (0-115,115) 4-Y-0+ **£2,927** (£859; £429; £214)

Form RPR

F005 1 **Lindseyfield Lodge (IRE)**[13] 1701 9-10-3 92 (p) KennyJohnson 98+
(Robert Johnson) *mde all: hmpd by loose horse bef 3 out: sn rcvrd: qcknd after next: kpt on wl run-in* **25/1**

363 2 1 ½ **More Equity**[23] 1598 8-10-10 102 RyanMania(3) 106+
(P Monteith) *blnd 1st: prom: hdwy whn lft 2nd 12th to 2 out: sn rdn: kpt on u.p run-in: regained 2nd nr fin* **5/1**[2]

6443 3 ½ **Storm Prospect**[49] 1405 7-10-4 93 (b) PeterBuchanan 97+
(Lucinda Russell) *hld up: hdwy and prom 3 out: chsd wnr run-in: one pce and lost 2nd nr fin* **9/2**[1]

0P3- 4 1 ½ **Border Reiver**[171] 43 6-10-11 100 (t) RichieMcGrath 102
(Tim Easterby) *trckd wnr to 10th: effrt and wnt 2nd 2 out to run-in: kpt on same pce towards fin* **5/1**[2]

-02P 5 5 **Kyber**[8] 1598 9-10-13 102 GrahamLee 99
(Jim Goldie) *hld up: hdwy and prom 2 out: outpcd run in* **11/1**

-F54 6 36 **Poseidon (GER)**[18] 1645 8-10-10 99 DenisO'Regan 69
(John Wade) *hld up: stdy hdwy after 4 out: wknd after next* **7/1**

3P4- 7 11 **Sirkeel (FR)**[183] 5203 8-10-7 106 NathanMoscrop(10) 71
(James Ewart) *nt fluent: bhd: hmpd 5th: blnd 10th: struggling fr next* **7/1**

0-21 F **Amalfi Coast**[18] 1645 11-11-12 115 BrianHughes —
(Karen Tutty) *trckd ldrs tl fell 5th* **7/1**

P-62 U **Dukeofchesterwood**[93] 1002 8-10-10 102 FearghalDavis(3) —
(Sandy Forster) *cl up: chsd wnr 11th: blnd and uns rdr next* **11/2**[3]

5m 39.7s (-4.80) **Going Correction** -0.475s/f (Good) **9** Ran SP% **116.6**
Speed ratings (Par 105): **89,88,88,87,86 73,69,—,—**
CSF £148.27 CT £681.89 TOTE £38.10: £6.20, £2.00, £1.80; EX 295.20.
Owner Toon Racing **Bred** Mrs M Brophy **Trained** Newburn, Tyne & Wear

FOCUS
An ordinary contest that lost much of its lustre with Amalfi Coast and Duke Of Chesterwood's departures. Sound form, the winner rated back to his best.

NOTEBOOK
Lindseyfield Lodge(IRE)'s jumping held together fine today and apart from nearly being carried out with three to jump, nothing managed to head him or find enough up the run-in. A follow-up is hard to predict confidently, given the litter of non-completions that followed a May course and distance selling chase win (off 7lb lower) before today. (op 22-1)
More Equity was also checked briefly by a loose horse before the turn in and had to wind up her effort once more up the straight, but it would be pushing it to call her unlucky as the winner was always finding plenty. She has at least dropped 8lb since sent handicap chasing and is getting a little closer to a first win in the discipline. (op 11-2)
Storm Prospect, still available at 8-1 in some places mid-morning, wasn't as inconvenienced as some by the fall of Amalfi Coast, and just couldn't get there in time up the run-in. Another small step up in trip might assist. (tchd 5-1)
Border Reiver could never recover sufficiently from getting a touch outpaced early in the straight. Second over 3f further than this at Catterick a year earlier, he's another with slightly better prospects back over 3m plus. (op 7-1)
Sirkeel(FR)'s tardy jumping display on this chasing debut did for him long before fitness after his sixth-month break became an issue. (op 13-2 tchd 8-1)
Dukeofchesterwood had mostly jumped reasonably (bar a small error at the second) before departing at two-thirds distance. (op 5-1)

1869 DOC HARVEY NOVICES' HURDLE (11 hdls) 2m 6f 110y

3:35 (3:37) (Class 4) 4-Y-0+ **£2,602** (£764; £382; £190)

Form RPR

3P-1 1 **Jurisdiction**[164] 163 6-11-5 115 GrahamLee 118+
(Rose Dobbin) *cl up: reminders and drvn 1/2-way: rallied to ld 7th: hrd pressed fr next: edgd rt and styd on gamely u.p run-in* **10/11**[1]

/ 2 4 **Dove Hill (IRE)**[636] 7-10-12 0 BrianHughes 110+
(Howard Johnson) *prom: rdn and outpcd after 4 out: rallied 2 out: styd on to chse wnr towards fin: no imp* **3/1**[2]

1U2P 3 1 ¾ **Bow School (IRE)**[97] 947 9-10-12 102 DenisO'Regan 105+
(Mrs A C Hamilton) *trckd ldrs: chal gng wl bef 3 out: rdn after last: one pce run-in: lost 2nd towards fin* **8/1**[3]

4 63 **Sam Hall (FR)**[237] 5-10-9 0 (t) JamesO'Farrell(3) 48
(Patrick Griffin, Ire) *bhd: lost tch fr 1/2-way: t.o* **33/1**

-UP4 5 6 **Glaced Over**[13] 1698 5-9-12 106 GaryRutherford(7) 36
(Raymond Shiels) *plld hrd: nt fluent: led to 7th: rdn and wknd fr 3 out* **9/1**

00P/ 6 49 **Craicneasy (IRE)**[558] 4891 7-10-9 0 RyanMania(3) —
(Bruce Mactaggart) *chsd ldng gp: struggling after 7th: lost tch fr next* **100/1**

-226 P **Elevenses**[8] 1757 6-11-5 114 PaddyAspell —
(James Moffatt) *hld up: p.u after 3rd* **16/1**

5m 26.3s (-14.70) **Going Correction** -0.725s/f (Firm) **7** Ran SP% **108.3**
Speed ratings (Par 105): **96,94,94,72,70 52,—**
CSF £3.45 TOTE £1.70: £1.50, £2.20; EX 3.80.
Owner River Tweed Syndicate **Bred** Mrs J Cadzow **Trained** South Hazelrigg, Northumbria

FOCUS
Few to consider in a novice hurdle lacking strength in depth. Ordinary form but the winner may have more to offer.

NOTEBOOK
Jurisdiction, acquired after landing a bumper for Graham Hollis in spring 2009, now has a career return of three wins from four on going good or faster. This second consecutive C&D score looked far harder work than the first in May, though, with Graham Lee already riding the gelding with over a circuit to go and the issue not really settled in the partnership's favour until the elbow. Regarded by connections as a big, lazy animal that will stay further, maybe he would take more kindly to a switch to a galloping 3m on this preferred surface hereafter. (op 11-8 tchd 6-4 in places)
Dove Hill(IRE), easy to back before this first run for 636 days, recovered from being outpaced midway through the final circuit to gain second place late on. An Irish point winner on heavy going when last seen and already rising eight, a switch to novice chasing can't be far off after this pleasing pipe-opener. (op 11-4 tchd 7-2)
Bow School(IRE) was having only his second try over this far under rules and didn't see it out despite being asked for his effort as late as possible. He is still eligible for point-to-points and hunter chases this winter so long as he doesn't run again after October 31, and it wouldn't surprise to see him being aimed at the same northern 2m4f hunter chases in 2011 as he was this year (winning one at Wetherby in May). (op 7-1)
Glaced Over proved keen early, and spent a bit too long in the air at some of her obstacles. The ability to take a small hurdle is there, though getting her to channel all her energies in the right direction is proving a little tough. Official explanation: vet said mare finished distressed (op 15-2 tchd 10-1)

1870 PETER DOYLE H'CAP HURDLE (8 hdls) 2m 110y
4:05 (4:07) (Class 4) (0-115,114) 4-Y-0+ **£2,602** (£764; £382; £190)

Form RPR
-232 **1** **Grand Diamond (IRE)**[7] [1766] 6-10-10 **105** PaulNorton(7) 112+
(Jim Goldie) *hld up: hdwy bef 2 out: rdn to ld last 200yds: kpt on wl* **9/2**[2]
3351 **2** 2 ½ **Midnite Blews (IRE)**[13] [1695] 5-10-5 **96** (t) RyanMania(3) 102+
(Maurice Barnes) *trckd ldrs: hdwy to chal after 4 out: led bef 2 out: sn rdn: hdd last 200yds: kpt on same pce* **12/1**
-005 **3** 2 ½ **Long Distance (FR)**[13] [1695] 5-10-4 **95** (p) CampbellGillies(3) 98
(Lucinda Russell) *hld up: rdn and hdwy bef 2 out: chsd wnr briefly run-in: kpt on same pce towards fin* **8/1**[3]
6 **4** 6 **Benmadigan (IRE)**[80] [1118] 8-11-9 **114** FearghalDavis(3) 111
(Nicky Richards) *hld up: stdy hdwy after 4 out: rdn bef 2 out: no imp run-in* **22/1**
P0-0 **5** 6 **Knock Three Times (IRE)**[13] [1695] 4-10-7 **102** (t) MissLAlexander(7) 94
(Wilf Storey) *hld up in midfield: outpcd 4 out: rallied bef 2 out: sn no imp* **80/1**
004- **6** nk **Pillar Of Hercules (IRE)**[240] [4126] 6-10-12 **100** GrahamLee 93+
(Ferdy Murphy) *t.k.h: led 1st: hdd bef 2 out: rallied: hit last: wknd run-in* **13/8**[1]
1-32 **7** 2 ¾ **Pyracantha**[143] [468] 5-11-11 **113** BrianHughes 102
(Alan Swinbank) *trckd ldrs: effrt bef 2 out: wknd run-in* **10/1**
/0-3 **8** shd **Quai Du Roi (IRE)**[6] [1802] 8-11-10 **112** DenisO'Regan 101
(T G McCourt, Ire) *bhd: pushed along after 4 out: sme late hdwy: nvr on terms* **22/1**
-035 **9** nk **Morning Time (IRE)**[18] [1641] 4-10-11 **99** PeterBuchanan 88
(Lucinda Russell) *trckd ldrs tl rdn and wknd bef 2 out* **14/1**
3-45 **10** 5 **Border Tale**[133] [472] 10-10-12 **100** (v) PaddyAspell 85
(James Moffatt) *led to 1st: trckd ldrs tl rdn and wknd 2 out* **12/1**
/00- **11** 3 ½ **Just Posh**[344] [2102] 8-9-7 **88** oh3 PaulGallagher(7) 69
(Rayson Nixon) *bhd: drvn and outpcd 4 out: nvr on terms* **100/1**
201- **12** 9 **Waterloo Corner**[194] [4665] 8-10-13 **101** WilsonRenwick 74
(Ray Craggs) *towards rr: struggling 4 out: sn btn* **40/1**
242 **13** ½ **Heart Of Dubai (USA)**[18] [1644] 5-10-11 **99** (p) BarryKeniry 72
(Micky Hammond) *trckd ldrs tl wknd after 3 out* **8/1**[3]
31P- **14** 23 **Gwyre (IRE)**[200] [4940] 4-11-3 **105** RichieMcGrath 57
(Tim Easterby) *bhd: struggling fnl circ: t.o* **33/1**

3m 47.0s (-14.80) **Going Correction** -0.725s/f (Firm)
WFA 4 from 5yo+ 9lb **14** Ran SP% **125.9**
Speed ratings (Par 105): **105,103,102,99,97 96,95,95,95,93 91,87,86,76**
TOTE £4.50: £1.30, £3.20, £3.60; EX 36.40.
Owner Jim Goldie Racing Club **Bred** Newberry Stud Company **Trained** Uplawmoor, E Renfrews

FOCUS
A competitive handicap hurdle run at a solid gallop and those played later started to swamp the pacesetters from the last. the time was good for the grade and the form is solid.

NOTEBOOK
Grand Diamond(IRE) got more of a test at the trip than he had over this C&D two starts earlier, and was far less keen in rear as a result. This well-judged and strong-finishing effort rates just reward for some consistent hurdling efforts this autumn, though an Ayr entry this coming week suggest attentions may yet turn back to the Flat now. (op 13-2)
Midnite Blews(IRE), 8lb worse (including riders' claims) than when beating the winner three and a half lengths in a recent course and distance race, was found out by a combination of a stronger pace and a 7lb higher mark out close home. Successful twice in 20 hurdles outings, this former sprinter still sometimes gives the impression of barely seeing out this trip. (op 16-1)
Long Distance(FR) ◆, like the winner, had trailed Midnite Blews here last time and was another to appreciate the stronger gallop, though a bit of cut would have helped yet further. Already 15lb lower than when starting in handicaps, he could rate a very tempting proposition in one of these once underfoot conditions change enough. (op 17-2 tchd 9-1)
Benmadigan(IRE) had his ground but is more effective around 2m2f-2m4f nowadays, and this still didn't constitute enough of a test for him. (op 18-1 tchd 25-1)
Pillar Of Hercules(IRE) was still available at 5-1 in the morning, but having refused to settle under a switch to front-running tactics was unable to produce anything once taken on between the last two. It's unlikely a mistake at the last proved crucial, and he continues to frustrate, despite now being 23lb below his initial hurdles mark in this country. Official explanation: jockey said gelding ran too free (op 7-4 tchd 11-8)
Pyracantha's fading effort bore out his trainer's assertion beforehand that he was less far forward than some in his yard. A little more give would have been appreciated in any event. (op 17-2)
Morning Time(IRE) Official explanation: jockey said, regarding running and riding, that his orders were to make the running but was unable to do so because of the strong pace. adding that with a circuit to go he was outpaced and gave the gelding a chance to fill its lungs going down the hill, staying on through tired horses.
Heart Of Dubai(USA)'s untimely mistake emptied him out completely and this effort is safest ignored. (op 11-1)

1871 ELLIOT LANDELLS ROADSWEEPER H'CAP CHASE (FOR THE MARSHALL TROPHY) (19 fncs) 3m 1f
4:40 (4:40) (Class 3) (0-135,129) 4-Y-0+ **£5,204** (£1,528; £764; £381)

Form RPR
P-3U **1** **Or De Grugy (FR)**[23] [1598] 8-10-10 **120** AlexanderVoy(7) 131+
(Sue Bradburne) *led to 5th: cl up: lft in ld 12th: mde rest: hld on gamely u.p run-in* **11/1**
0/1- **2** 2 ¾ **Always Right (IRE)**[224] [4437] 8-11-1 **118** BrianHughes 130+
(John Wade) *t.k.h early: trckd ldrs: effrt and ev ch last: kpt on u.p run-in* **7/2**[1]
44-4 **3** shd **Cast Iron Casey (IRE)**[13] [1695] 8-11-1 **118** WilsonRenwick 126
(P Monteith) *hld up in tch: effrt after 2 out: rdn and styd on run-in* **5/1**[3]
5F-2 **4** 6 **Casadei (IRE)**[13] [1697] 11-10-0 **103** oh2 (tp) BarryKeniry 105
(T G McCourt, Ire) *trckd ldrs: drvn and outpcd after 2 out: no imp fr last* **9/2**[2]
2P3- **5** 5 **Youngstown (IRE)**[196] [4982] 7-11-8 **125** GrahamLee 125+
(Donald McCain) *t.k.h: cl up: led 5th tl blnd and hdd 12th: rallied: wknd fr last* **7/1**
3P5- **6** 17 **Zitenka (IRE)**[180] [5274] 8-11-12 **129** (p) RichieMcGrath 110
(Tim Easterby) *hld up: outpcd 14th: n.d after* **12/1**
3441 **7** 15 **Soubriquet (IRE)**[24] [1577] 7-11-5 **125** (t) RyanMania(3) 93
(Maurice Barnes) *in tch on outside tl rdn and wknd fr 2 out* **8/1**
10 **8** 43 **Native Coral (IRE)**[71] [1198] 12-11-5 **122** BrianHarding 51
(Nicky Richards) *hit 2nd and sn towards rr: struggling 14th: sn btn* **18/1**
1-45 **9** 59 **Top Dressing (IRE)**[23] [1598] 9-11-1 **118** TimmyMurphy —
(Howard Johnson) *in tch tl dropped to rr 5th: lost tch fnl circ* **9/1**
/23- **U** **Blaze Trailer (IRE)**[6] [1805] 7-11-3 **120** DenisO'Regan —
(T G McCourt, Ire) *hld up: stdy hdwy and in tch whn blnd 13th: 4 l down and stl gng wl whn uns rdr 2 out* **18/1**

6m 15.1s (-16.40) **Going Correction** -0.475s/f (Good) **10** Ran SP% **117.2**
Speed ratings (Par 107): **107,106,106,104,102 97,92,78,59,—**
CSF £51.29 CT £222.35 TOTE £11.60: £2.80, £2.00, £2.00; EX 38.90.
Owner Lord Cochrane And Partners **Bred** Earl La Grugerie **Trained** Cunnoquhie, Fife

FOCUS
A fair handicap for the track with the winner rated back to his best. Just a steady pace for most of the way round, such that the field was still well bunched approaching three out.

NOTEBOOK
Or De Grugy(FR) was always in the firing line, and what pace there was proved enough for him to get into a nice jumping rhythm quickly. Clearly none the worse physically or mentally for a bizarre incident at Perth last time, when bundled over by a loose horse up the run-in, he is 4-7 around this course now, though marks in excess of today's 120 have proved beyond him even here before. (op 10-1)
Always Right(IRE) ◆ is the one to take out of the race, having held on for second despite early keenness and a less fluent round of jumping than the winner. Far more assured granted soft going here last March, and also a winner over as far as 3m5f in points since a midfield finish in the 2009 Cheltenham Foxhunter, a more thorough test than today's is likely to see him raise his game. (op 4-1 tchd 9-2)
Cast Iron Casey(IRE) didn't see out this trip on his only previous try at Hexham in the spring, but did better up to a point around this less exacting course. Still to win a handicap chase, a few pounds' respite would help. (op 7-2)
Casadei(IRE) performed below the form of his recent C&D second with no obvious excuses, and his monster losing run over fences endures. (op 8-1 tchd 4-1)
Youngstown(IRE) doesn't need to have his own way out in front to win races, but a combination of the attentions of the winner and going faster than ideal seemed to play on his mind this time and the errors started to creep in. He's better than this. (op 11-2)

1872 HUTCHINSON SEWAGE TREATMENT NOVICES' H'CAP CHASE (12 fncs) 2m 1f
5:15 (5:16) (Class 4) (0-110,107) 4-Y-0+ **£2,927** (£859; £429; £214)

Form RPR
F-10 **1** **Kosta Brava (FR)**[24] [1575] 6-11-8 **103** WilsonRenwick 112+
(Howard Johnson) *cl up: rdn to ld last: styd on strly run-in* **5/1**[3]
6311 **2** 3 **Morning Sunshine (IRE)**[7] [1767] 7-11-9 **107** AdrianLane(3) 114+
(Donald McCain) *hmpd 1st: hld up in tch: stdy hdwy 1/2-way: effrt 2 out: styd on to chse wnr towards fin* **7/4**[1]
340- **3** 1 **Saddlers Deal (IRE)**[188] [5142] 5-11-9 **104** DenisO'Regan 108+
(Chris Grant) *j.rt: led: blnd 3 out: hdd last: kpt on same pce run-in: bttr for r* **15/2**
-P23 **4** 3 ½ **Tranos (USA)**[18] [1646] 7-10-13 **94** (p) BarryKeniry 98
(Micky Hammond) *cl up: rdn 3 out: outpcd next: no imp fr last* **9/2**[2]
6-63 **5** nk **Best Horse (FR)**[24] [1575] 8-10-9 **90** GrahamLee 90
(Ferdy Murphy) *hld up and bhd: stdy hdwy and prom 3 out: rdn next: one pce run-in* **17/2**
34P0 **6** ¾ **Tiger King (GER)**[13] [1695] 9-9-12 **82** CampbellGillies(3) 82
(P Monteith) *hld up in tch: effrt and prom 3 out: outpcd after next* **8/1**
PP/P **7** 99 **Steel Man (IRE)**[8] [1759] 8-9-8 **81** oh21 ow1 PaulGallagher(7) —
(Bruce Mactaggart) *nt jump wl: in rr: lost tch fnl circ* **40/1**
P523 **U** **More Shennanigans**[15] [1665] 9-10-0 **80** oh8 PaddyAspell —
(Jean McGregor) *in tch: blnd and uns rdr 1st* **12/1**

4m 10.9s (-7.10) **Going Correction** -0.475s/f (Good) **8** Ran SP% **114.7**
Speed ratings (Par 105): **97,95,95,93,93 92,46,—**
CSF £14.96 CT £64.47 TOTE £4.90: £1.70, £1.40, £2.80; EX 12.70.
Owner Andrea & Graham Wylie **Bred** Guy Blasco **Trained** Billy Row, Co Durham

FOCUS
A good gallop to this handicap chase from the outset, and 12l split first and last after just two fences. The second, fourth and fifth set the level.

NOTEBOOK
Kosta Brava(FR)'s chasing career trajectory so far hasn't been the smoothest, with a close second at Catterick followed by an early fall and a run out last time. He was entirely tractable and pretty accomplished at his fences on this occasion, however, and found plenty up the run-in to produce a pleasing, if workmanlike first win over fences. An extra furlong or two should be within compass. (op 9-2 tchd 11-2)
Morning Sunshine(IRE) lost ground and momentum when hampered by the first-fence departure of More Shennanigans and took some time to recover from it, and although close enough by two out was ultimately outgunned by a decent rival with that bit better luck on the day. He remains in decent heart, and granted a clear run next time may tell us whether he's up to defying this 9lb higher mark. (tchd 11-8 and 15-8 in places)
Saddlers Deal(IRE) ◆ ensured a proper test on his chasing debut. It was race-fitness rather than pitching out to the right on a few occasions that did for his finishing effort, and he can be placed to advantage in a similar contest with this first outing for 188 days entitled to do this lightly raced gelding the world of good. (op 8-1 tchd 9-1)
Tranos(USA) put in a slow one just when it wasn't needed at the final ditch and had too much to claw back after that. Frequently outpaced at a pivotal moment over 2m, he's surely due a longer try over 2m4f than the two attempts he's had so far (both rendered inconclusive after early errors). (tchd 4-1 and 5-1and 11-2 in places)
Best Horse(FR) made some gains approaching the last, but produced another tepid finishing effort. (op 8-1 tchd 9-1)

1873 BETFAIR TRAINING SERIES CONDITIONAL JOCKEYS' H'CAP HURDLE (RACING EXCELLENCE INITIATIVE) (11 hdls) 2m 6f 110y
5:50 (5:50) (Class 4) (0-100,99) 4-Y-0+ **£2,341** (£687; £343; £171)

Form RPR
40-6 **1** **Buckstruther (IRE)**[168] [90] 8-10-6 **84** NathanMoscrop(5) 88+
(Andrew Parker) *set stdy pce: mde all: qcknd after 3 out: rdn and hld on wl run-in* **5/2**[2]

-153 **2** *1* **Planetarium**[53] 1362 5-11-7 **99**......................(p) JakeGreenall(5) 102
(P Monteith) *trckd ldrs: rdn and outpcd after 3 out: rallied after 2 out: chsd wnr run-in: kpt on* **15/8**[1]

-F24 **3** *3 ¾* **Political Pendant**[7] 1782 9-10-3 **79**...................... PaulGallagher(3) 78
(Rayson Nixon) *prom: hdwy to chse wnr bef 7th: rdn and outpcd after 3 out: rallied next: one pce and lost 2nd run-in* **9/2**[3]

46P4 **4** *56* **Solway Blue**[81] 1102 8-9-10 **74**...................... CallumWhillans(5) 31
(Lisa Harrison) *hld up: hmpd by faller 7th: sn pushed along: rallied and prom 3 out: struggling bef next* **7/1**

5341 **F** **Desert Soul**[18] 1647 6-11-5 **92**......................(t) AlexanderVoy —
(Maurice Barnes) *t.k.h: cl up: fell heavily 7th* **9/2**[3]

5m 31.2s (-9.80) **Going Correction** -0.725s/f (Firm) **5** Ran SP% **112.2**
Speed ratings (Par 105): **88,87,86,66,—**
CSF £8.00 TOTE £4.00: £3.10, £1.70; EX 10.40 Place 6: £48.25 Place 5: £14.33..
Owner Alastair and Rachel Bell **Bred** Mrs Rita Doocey **Trained** Ecclefechan, D'fries & G'way
■ Stewards' Enquiry : Paul Gallagher caution: used whip in the forehand.

FOCUS
Just the five runners in this poor finale, and a very steady pace saw a couple of them racing keenly early on. The second and third are rated to their marks.

NOTEBOOK
Buckstruther(IRE) had a most productive time in points when owner-trained last winter, and finally landed a rules contest at the 22nd attempt having set the fractions from flagfall. He looked to be a little more in hand over the second up the run-in than the distance between them implied, with Nathan Moscrop not having to resort to the whip until the final 25 yards or so just to make sure. This win excludes Buckstruther from points and hunter chases this winter, but there might be a poor novice handicap or two in him over hurdles or fences if building on this. (op 11-4)
Planetarium, winner of a quickly run 2m4f seller in the summer, shaped as if in need of this far now when third at Sedgefield last time. The slow fractions were little help in that regard, and he could never quite get recover from the winner's injection of pace turning in. He remains winless over hurdles outside of the lowest grade. (op 9-4)
Political Pendant's rider was hard at work some way out and she may still have needed this. She is slipping to a quietly dangerous mark, though it would require a bad contest for her to double her tally of one win from 26. (op 11-2)
Desert Soul, a winner when receiving a lead at Sedgefield last time, was proving less amenable to the same strategy when crashing out. (op 4-1)
T/Plt: £40.30 to a £1 stake. Pool:£58,649 - 1,062.30 winning tickets T/Qpdt: £9.00 to a £1 stake. Pool:£4,459 - 363.42 winning tickets RY

1874 - 1881a (Foreign Racing) - See Raceform Interactive

KEMPTON (R-H)
Sunday, October 17

OFFICIAL GOING: Good (good to firm in places) (chs 8.1, hdl 8.1)
Wind: Virtually nil Weather: Bright, light cloud

1882 WILLIAMHILL.COM/MOBILE JUVENILE HURDLE (8 hdls) 2m
2:20 (2:20) (Class 3) 3-Y-O **£4,033** (£1,184; £592; £295)

Form RPR

3 **1** **Jubail (IRE)**[22] 1610 3-10-12 0...................... WayneHutchinson 110+
(Alan King) *hld up in tch: trckd ldrs after 3 out: rdn to chal between last 2: led last: r.o wl and a jst holding runner-up flat* **1/1**[1]

2 *nk* **Plan A (IRE)**[13] 3-10-12 0...................... APMcCoy 109+
(Michael Quinlan) *t.k.h: chsd ldrs: pressed ldr sn after 3 out: led bef next: rdn between last 2: hdd last: r.o wl u.p flat: a jst hld* **11/4**[2]

2 **3** *7* **Denton Ryal**[28] 1545 3-10-5 0...................... JamieGoldstein 95
(Sheena West) *t.k.h: hld up wl in tch in last pair: hdwy to trck ldrs 3 out: rdn to press ldrs and hung rt whn rdn between last 2: no ex and btn whn mstke last* **13/2**[3]

4 *9* **Il Portico**[37] 3-10-12 0...................... JamieMoore 95+
(Gary Moore) *chsd ldrs: mstke 2nd: chsd ldr next: jnd ldr 5th: led sn after next: rdn and hdd bef 2 out: wknd between last 2: wl btn whn mstke last* **16/1**

1410 **5** *1 ¾* **Gulf Punch**[22] 1610 3-10-10 109......................(p) JimmyDerham(5) 94
(Milton Harris) *mde most tl hdd after 3 out: rdn and wknd bef next* **20/1**

6 *23* **Professeur Emery (FR)** 3-10-12 0...................... NoelFehily 71
(Warren Greatrex) *plld hrd: hld up in tch in last: blnd 1st: rdn and wknd qckly bef 2 out: t.o* **10/1**

3 **7** *52* **Big Talk**[15] 1674 3-10-12 0......................(b) RodiGreene 16
(David Bridgwater) *j.rt: chsd ldr: j.rt and mstke 1st: j. slowly and lost pl 3rd: j. bdly rt 5th: sn lost tch: t.o fr next* **50/1**

8 *20* **Magic Spirit**[229] 3-10-5 0...................... ColinBolger —
(Suzy Smith) *chsd ldrs tl blnd and dropped to rr 4th: lost tch qckly next: wl t.o fr 3 out* **66/1**

3m 50.1s (-9.90) **Going Correction** -0.70s/f (Firm) **8** Ran SP% **113.2**
Speed ratings (Par 105): **96,95,92,87,86 75,49,39**
toteswingers: 1&2 £1.40, 1&3 £5.10, 2&3 £3.30 CSF £3.85 TOTE £2.30: £1.40, £1.60, £1.60; EX 4.30.
Owner David Mason **Bred** A F O'Callaghan **Trained** Barbury Castle, Wilts

FOCUS
Dual bends configuration utilised and distances as advertised. It was described as "nice, fast ground with a good covering of grass" by one of the riders in the first. They went a steady pace before picking up and the time was nearly a second inside the standard. There was not much depth to this, and the form is a little suspect, but the first two drew clear and are decent juveniles for this stage of the season.

NOTEBOOK
Jubail(IRE), who made a promising hurdles debut at Market Rasen, settled better here and jumped nicely. Quickening up between the last two flights, he took a slim lead which he maintained to the line. The yard won this event two years ago with a useful sort in Saticon and, while this one may not reach the same level, he should certainly win again over hurdles. He is likely to be kept to flat, sharp tracks for now and would not want the ground too soft. (op 5-4 tchd 11-8 in a place)
Plan A(IRE) ◆, in contrast to the winner, would prefer some cut. He has the same BHA rating, 71, as the winner on the Flat and came here having won two of his last three starts in that sphere, each time in soft conditions. He had every chance and went down fighting on this hurdles debut and should soon go one better, with a stiffer track likely to help his cause. (tchd 5-2)
Denton Ryal, whose trainer won this a year ago with Mohanad, ran a promising race, just outpaced by the first two from the approach to the final flight. This was an improvement on what she had shown in weaker company at Plumpton and a race should come her way. (tchd 7-1)
Il Portico, a tough performer at trips of around 1m4f on the Flat, is currently rated 54. He was only put in his place between the final two flights and hopefully can jump a bit better with the experience behind him. (tchd 14-1 and 18-1)
Gulf Punch was well behind Jubail at Market Rasen and faced a very stiff task under a 10lb penalty, but appeared to run her race. (tchd 25-1)
Professeur Emery(FR) was well beaten in the end but there was a glimmer of promise. Unraced on the Flat, this brother to a winning hurdler in France was very keen early on and blundered at the first, but travelled well until the leaders got away from him turning out of the back straight. He was not knocked about when held and should improve on this in time. His rider reported that the gelding had run too free. Official explanation: jockey said gelding ran too freely (op 7-1)
Big Talk jumped out to his right, alarmingly so at the fourth from home. (tchd 66-1)

1883 WILLIAMHILL.COM - POKER BEGINNERS' CHASE (12 fncs) 2m
2:50 (2:51) (Class 4) 4-Y-O+ **£3,252** (£955; £477; £238)

Form RPR

100- **1** **Chain Of Command (IRE)**[215] 4657 7-11-2 0...................... NoelFehily 118+
(Warren Greatrex) *nt a fluent: hld up wl off the pce in last pair: clsd 7th: lft cl 3rd 9th: led 2 out: pushed clr and in command whn wnt lft and mstke last: pushed out and r.o wl flat* **11/4**[2]

4-35 **2** *3* **Sonning Star (IRE)**[144] 479 6-11-2 114...................... LiamTreadwell 112
(Nick Gifford) *chsd ldrs: lft cl 4th 9th: rdn bef next: chsd clr wnr between last 2: styd on wl u.p flat but nt pce to threaten wnr* **12/1**

42-0 **3** *9* **Ray Diamond**[158] 282 5-10-11 0...................... MarcGoldstein(5) 104
(Michael Madgwick) *j.lft: chsd ldr tl after 3rd: lft in ld 9th: sn rdn: mstke and hdd 2 out: wknd bef last* **25/1**

63P- **4** *4* **Benfleet Boy**[23] 5099 6-11-2 0...................... APMcCoy 102+
(Brendan Powell) *led: mstke 3rd: hdd bef next: styd pressing ldr tl lft 2nd 9th: rdn bef next: wknd 2 out* **11/8**[1]

F00- **5** *18* **Vino Griego (FR)**[190] 5123 5-11-2 0...................... JamieMoore 87+
(Gary Moore) *in tch in midfield: mstke 4th and next: struggling whn mstke 7th: lft modest 5th 9th: wl btn bef next* **3/1**[3]

-0F4 **6** *34* **Hi Tide (IRE)**[14] 1693 6-11-2 0...................... TimmyMurphy 47
(J R Jenkins) *t.k.h: hld up in last pair: lost tch 6th: t.o fr 9th* **14/1**

0265 **U** **Bold Pioneer (USA)**[24] 1587 7-10-11 71....... GemmaGracey-Davison(5) —
(Zoe Davison) *t.k.h: chsd ldrs: mstke 2nd: led after next: hrd pressed whn blnd and uns rdr 9th* **100/1**

3m 56.4s (-1.60) **Going Correction** -0.475s/f (Good) **7** Ran SP% **113.0**
Speed ratings (Par 105): **85,83,79,77,68 51,—**
toteswingers: 1&2 £8.40, 1&3 £15.80, 2&3 £10.20 CSF £31.25 TOTE £4.30: £2.80, £6.30; EX 49.50.
Owner Malcolm C Denmark **Bred** Miss Catherine McCaghey **Trained** Upper Lambourn, Berks

FOCUS
This novice chase has gone to some decent performers in recent years, most notably I'msingingtheblues and Mahogany Blaze. They went just a fair pace and the winner clocked a time over six seconds outside the standard. The bare form is ordinary but the winner can rate higher.

NOTEBOOK
Chain Of Command(IRE) was a useful hurdler, thought good enough to contest the Supreme Novices' on his final start. He showed a distinct tendency to pull last season but settled well enough under restraint here and he jumped fluently on this chasing debut. Picking up ground nicely and coming clear after touching down ahead two out, he looks a horse with a future. The return to softer ground will suit. (op 9-2 tchd 5-1 in a place)
Sonning Star(IRE) made a pleasing chase debut on this first run since May, jumping soundly. He needed niggling along at times and came off the bridle on the home turn before running on determinedly from the last. This trip and a sound surface are ideal. (op 9-1 tchd 14-1)
Ray Diamond had a fair bit to find with most of these on his hurdles form and produced a thoroughly satisfactory chasing debut. He is well at home on soft ground and should pay his way round the minor tracks during the winter. (op 16-1)
Benfleet Boy was a very useful handicapper over hurdles with an official rating of 138. Taken on for the lead by no-hoper Bold Pioneer on this chase debut, his jumping suffered as a result and he had been seen off before the second-last. This was somehat disappointing, but the ground may have been quicker than he would have preferred and he is worth another chance. (op 5-4 tchd 6-4)
Vino Griego(FR) was a very useful hurdler, finishing eighth (eight places ahead of Chain Of Command) in the Supreme Novices' last season. He was weak in the market ahead of this chase debut, after reports that his schooling had not entirely gone to plan, and in the race his lack of fluency was evident and he could never reach a dangerous position. He possesses the size and scope to do better but has something to prove. (op 7-2 tchd 4-1)
Hi Tide(IRE) has been well beaten in his two starts since taking a nasty fall at Worcester. (op 9-1)

1884 WILLIAMHILL.COM - CASINO NOVICES' HURDLE (LISTED RACE) (8 hdls) 2m
3:25 (3:26) (Class 1) 4-Y-O+
£8,551 (£3,208; £1,606; £801; £402; £201)

Form RPR

2-12 **1** **Karasenir (IRE)**[8] 1773 4-11-6 127...................... RichardJohnson 132+
(Philip Hobbs) *nt a fluent: chsd ldrs: nt fluent 2nd: led and blnd 3 out: mstke next: clr and in command between last 2* **10/11**[1]

1120 **2** *10* **Dereks (IRE)**[2] 1859 8-11-8 120...................... PaulMoloney 120+
(Sophie Leech) *racd in midfield: clsd and chsng ldrs bef 3 out: rdn to chse wnr and mstke 2 out: no ch w wnr after: plugged on* **25/1**

364- **3** *6* **Marleno (GER)**[215] 4669 4-11-0 0...................... WarrenMarston 104
(Milton Harris) *stdd s: plld hrd and hld up wl bhd: hdwy 5th: chsd ldrs after next: wknd 2 out* **40/1**

20-1 **4** *nk* **William Hogarth**[8] 1773 5-11-6 127...................... RhysFlint 110
(Keith Goldsworthy) *led tl bef 5th: chsd ldrs after: drvn after 3 out: wkng whn mstke next* **10/3**[2]

35- **5** *3 ¼* **Rajamand (FR)**[253] 3890 4-11-0 0...................... NoelFehily 102+
(Warren Greatrex) *t.k.h: hld up wl off pce towards rr: clsd and in tch bef 3 out: wknd bef 2 out: wl hld whn mstke 2 out and last* **40/1**

6 *¾* **Hatton Flight**[36] 6-11-0 0...................... FelixDeGiles 100
(Andrew Balding) *hld up off the pce in midfield: mstke 4th: clsd and in tch bef 3 out: rdn and wknd bef 2 out* **7/1**[3]

- **7** *19* **Mister New York (USA)**[31] 5-11-0 0...................... WillKennedy 81
(Noel Chance) *hld up wl off the pce in rr: j. awkwardly 2nd: reminder after next: hdwy 5th: drvn and wknd qckly after next: t.o* **66/1**

8 *¾* **Goodwood Starlight (IRE)**[19] 5-11-0 0...................... JamieGoldstein 80
(Sheena West) *plld hrd: hld up wl in rr: hdwy to chse ldrs 3rd: mstke next: hanging bdly lft after: led 5th: hdd and mstke next: stl hanging and lost pl qckly bnd bef next: t.o* **14/1**

9 *14* **Rajnagan (IRE)**[448] 6-11-0 0...................... DenisO'Regan 66
(Paul Webber) *hld up wl off the pce: clsd and in tch bef 3 out: wknd qckly bef 2 out: t.o* **66/1**

2341 **P** **Marc Aurele (IRE)**[28] 1547 5-11-6 116......................(bt[1]) NickScholfield —
(Paul Nicholls) *w ldrs: rdn and struggling whn j. slowly 5th: sn dropped out: t.o next tl p.u 2 out* **17/2**

3m 45.8s (-14.20) **Going Correction** -0.70s/f (Firm)
WFA 4 from 5yo+ 9lb **10** Ran SP% **116.9**
Speed ratings (Par 111): **107,102,99,98,97 96,87,86,79,—**
toteswingers: 1&2 £40.40, 1&3 £21.20, 2&3 £7.70 CSF £30.36 TOTE £1.90: £1.02, £4.30, £7.90; EX 26.90.
Owner Louisville Syndicate **Bred** His Highness The Aga Khan's Studs S C **Trained** Withycombe, Somerset

FOCUS
Some good novices feature on this Listed event's roll of honour, among them Marcel, Deep Purple and last year's winner Cootehill. The latest edition did not appear especially strong for the grade, with the second favourite below par, but the pace was sound and the time was five seconds inside the standard. The winner is on the upgrade and the second sets the level.

NOTEBOOK
Karasenir(IRE) ought to be unbeaten in three starts over hurdles, but his jumping let him down against William Hogarth at Chepstow last weekend. He again hurdled moderately, showing a rather scruffy technique, but came right away from the home turn to record a very comfortable victory. Things will be tougher under his double penalty and he is set to go handicapping now. He is clearly a useful novice who has shown that he acts on soft ground too. (op 6-5 tchd 11-8 and 5-4 in places)
Dereks(IRE), who was conceding 2lb to the winner, was making a quick reappearance after an early departure at Cheltenham on Friday. He has done well since joining this yard, who snapped him up after he won a seller for Jim Best, and ran well again in the face of a pretty stiff task without seriously threatening the winner. He may not prove easy to place. (op 16-1)
Marleno(GER) pulled hard in each of his bumpers last term and he did so again through the early stages of this hurdles debut. After making promising progress to reach the leaders' heels his effort flattened out again from the second-last. There is plenty of ability there but he is not yet getting home. Official explanation: jockey said, regarding running and riding, that the gelding pulled hard early stages and hit a flat spot turning into home straight. (op 28-1 tchd 50-1)
William Hogarth was fortunate to beat Karasenir at Chepstow and the pair were evenly matched here on BHA ratings. He encountered opposition for the lead and had run his race by the home turn, failing to perform to his best. The ground was on the fast side for him. (op 7-2 tchd 4-1)
Rajamand(FR) showed ability on his two starts last winter and again here. He should strip fitter with the outing behind him and a little race should come his way, with handicaps an option now. (op 25-1)
Hatton Flight was a smart middle-distance performer on the Flat, rated 99 at his peak, but he proved hard to place this year. Making his hurdling debut, he worked his way into contention before fading in the straight. He is capable of building on this but it would be no surprise if some headgear was back on next time. (op 15-2 tchd 8-1)
Marc Aurele(IRE) had 11lb to find with the winner and fourth on this rise in grade, but even so should have run better than he did. He was unable to get to the front, and after shadowing William Hogarth he dropped away tamely down the far side, looking less than enthusiastic in the first-time blinkers. (op 9-1 tchd 10-1)

1885 WILLIAMHILL.COM - VEGAS H'CAP CHASE (18 fncs) 3m
4:00 (4:00) (Class 4) (0-115,112) 4-Y-0+ **£3,577** (£1,050; £525; £262)

Form RPR
51-P **1** **Basoda**^{161} 229 7-11-5 **108**............(t) SeanQuinlan(3) 123+
(Kim Bailey) *hld up in rr of main gp: hmpd 1st and 5th: bmpd 8th: hdwy to trck ldrs 14th: swtchd rt and led 2 out: rdn clr and in command last: comf* **4/1**^{1}
204- **2** *7* **Runshan (IRE)**^{207} 4813 10-10-12 **98**............ TomScudamore 101
(David Bridgwater) *j.lft: led: rdn and hrd pressed bef 3 out: hdd 2 out: outpcd by wnr and btn whn j.lft last: kpt on* **9/2**^{2}
122- **3** *3/4* **Sea Cadet**^{181} 5281 8-11-11 **111**............ RhysFlint 115+
(Laura Mongan) *lft 2nd 1st: chsd ldr after: rdn to chal bef 3 out: outpcd by wnr and btn after 2 out: plugged on* **4/1**^{1}
06-0 **4** *21* **Qianshan Leader (IRE)**^{23} 1604 6-11-12 **112**............ JackDoyle 96+
(Emma Lavelle) *t.k.h: hld up in rr of main gp: hmpd 1st: rdn and wknd 14th: wl btn whn mstke 2 out* **14/1**
063- **5** *10* **Nagam (FR)**^{234} 4261 9-11-11 **111**............ TimmyMurphy 82
(Alan Fleming) *j.rt: nvr travelling wl in midfield and pushed along at times: in tch: rdn along after 11th: wknd 14th: wl btn after next* **4/1**^{1}
2465 **6** *140* **Indian Pipe Dream (IRE)**^{14} 1706 8-10-11 **100**...(p) EamonDehdashti(3) —
(Aytach Sadik) *hmpd 1st: mstke next: detached and mstkes in last after: t.o fr 11th* **25/1**
1-P5 **P** **Alfie's Sun**^{11} 1725 11-11-10 **110**............ NoelFehily —
(Don Cantillon) *chsd ldrs tl wknd qckly after 13th: t.o after 15th tl p.u last* **13/2**^{3}
430- **P** **Phar Again (IRE)**^{191} 5120 7-10-4 **90**............(t) LiamTreadwell —
(Claire Dyson) *in tch in rr of main gp: mstke 1st: mstke 10th: sn lost tch: t.o after next tl p.u 14th* **10/1**
2P5P **F** **Tampa Boy (IRE)**^{26} 1570 8-11-7 **112**............(vt^{1}) JimmyDerham(5) —
(Milton Harris) *chsd ldr tl hmpd and fell 1st* **20/1**

6m 0.10s (-14.90) **Going Correction** -0.475s/f (Good) **9** Ran SP% **115.9**
Speed ratings (Par 105): **105,102,102,95,92** —,—,—,—
toteswingers: 1&2 £7.30, 1&3 £2.50, 2&3 £4.30 CSF £23.06 CT £76.27 TOTE £6.00: £1.20, £1.90, £1.50; EX 41.90.
Owner Angie & Michael Storey **Bred** S V Parry **Trained** Andoversford, Gloucs

FOCUS
This is not the race it was in its former guise of the Charisma Gold Cup and is just an ordinary 0-115 handicap these days. It had an open look to it and the first three pulled clear, suggesting the form is sound. The winner is on the upgrade.

NOTEBOOK
Basoda had not run since pulling up off this mark in May, when he suffered from sore shins, but came in for support after his summer break. His jumping was not blemish-free, but he closed up stylishly from the rear and came away for a ready success. This was only his fourth completed outing over fences and it is reasonable to expect further improvement. He may run under a penalty. (op 11-2 tchd 6-1)
Runshan(IRE) had conditions to suit on this first start since March. He jumped well, if slightly out to his left, and battled on for second after the winner had taken his measure. Hard to win with, he has made the frame nine times since his most recent victory. (op 6-1)
Sea Cadet, in common with the pair who beat him, was seeing action for the first time since the spring. He ran well for a long way before appearing to blow up and, while he has been beaten three times from this mark now, he is probably capable of winning from it when things go his way. (op 9-2 tchd 7-2)
Qianshan Leader(IRE) jumped better than he had on his chasing debut and was staying on at the end over this extra half mile. He was well beaten though and needs to show more. (op 12-1)
Nagam(FR) won this event 12 months ago from the same mark and everything appeared in place for another big run, but he was disappointing. He has been retired. (op 10-3)
Alfie's Sun, dropped 2lb since his second run back from a long absence, was close enough for a long way but a mistake at the last ditch soon had him on the retreat. (op 11-2)

1886 WILLIAMHILL.COM HURDLE (8 hdls) 2m
4:35 (4:35) (Class 2) 4-Y-0+
£9,393 (£2,775; £1,387; £694; £346; £174)

Form RPR
1F-1 **1** **Australia Day (IRE)**^{57} 1017 7-11-8 157............ DenisO'Regan 146+
(Paul Webber) *mde all at gd gallop: sn clr: unchal* **1/2**^{1}
230- **2** *10* **Katchit (IRE)**^{213} 4701 7-11-8 155............ WayneHutchinson 134
(Alan King) *chsd wnr tl after 2nd: 4th and rdn after 3 out: no ch w wnr but kpt on gamely fr next: j.rt last: wnt 2nd towards fin* **11/4**^{2}
116- **3** *1* **Noble Alan (GER)**^{190} 5124 7-11-8 0............ BrianHarding 133
(Nicky Richards) *t.k.h: hld up in midfield: nt fluent 2nd: chsd clr wnr bef 2 out: no imp: j.lft last: lost 2nd towards fin* **7/1**^{3}
10- **4** *23* **Farleigh House (USA)**^{295} 3028 6-11-0 120............ MarkBradburne 104
(Neil King) *chsd wnr 2nd: nvr on terms: rdn and wknd bef 2 out: 4th and wl btn whn mstke 2 out* **40/1**
4124 **5** *18* **Rock Me (IRE)**^{28} 1551 5-11-0 103............(tp) DavidBass 84
(Lawney Hill) *sn outpcd in last: reminders after 1st: t.o fr 3rd* **80/1**
-P53 **6** *4* **Spider Boy**^{129} 692 13-11-5 79............(b) GemmaGracey-Davison 85
(Zoe Davison) *sn outpcd in last pair: mstke 2nd: t.o fr 3rd* **150/1**

3m 40.4s (-19.60) **Going Correction** -0.70s/f (Firm) **6** Ran SP% **110.2**
Speed ratings (Par 109): **121,116,115,104,95 93**
toteswingers: 1&2 £1.10, 1&3 £1.30, 2&3 £1.70 CSF £2.17 TOTE £1.50: £1.10, £1.80; EX 2.60.
Owner Skippy & The Partners **Bred** Kenilworth House Stud **Trained** Mollington, Oxon

FOCUS
A good conditions hurdle. Australia Day set a brisk pace and recorded a new record time over ten seconds inside the standard, underlining that conditions were pretty quick. He is rated a few pounds off his Market Rasen win with Katchit a stone the best of his form last season.

NOTEBOOK
Australia Day(IRE), a faller at the first in the novice hurdle on this card 12 months ago, bolted up in a valuable Listed handicap at Market Rasen in July on his only run over hurdles since and was put up no less than 22lb as a result. Again going out in front, he jumped slickly and had his race won turning for home. He will go for the Elite Hurdle at Wincanton next month provided the ground remains suitable and is then likely to be put away until the Champion Hurdle. He would need to show further improvement to figure there and the left-handed track would be a bit of a worry, although he did win going that way round at Worcester as a novice. (op 8-13 tchd 4-6 in places)
Katchit(IRE) fractured a hind pastern in the World Hurdle in March and needed three months' box rest. He found 2m here much too sharp at this stage of his career and looked set to finish well held in third at one stage, but came home strongly after the last to grab second close home. Also runner-up in this race two years ago, behind Snap Tie, he last won in the Champion Hurdle of 2008 and he will not be easy to place successfully, but this effort shows that the fire remains and he should prove competitive in good races at 2m4f-3m again. Next month's Ascot Hurdle should be his next port of call. (op 10-3 tchd 7-2)
Noble Alan(GER), a very useful novice chaser last term, last ran over hurdles when landing the Scottish Champion at Ayr in April 2009. Held up, he moved into second place off the home turn but the favourite was away and clear by that stage and he never really threatened to bridge the gap. He was cut down for second place close home, but this was still a satisfactory reappearance. The Haldon Gold Cup at Exeter could be next for him provided the ground is decent. (op 9-2)
Farleigh House(USA) had not run since finishing well behind in a warm novice event won by Menorah here on Boxing Day. Running for only the third time over hurdles, he had no chance on these terms but did as well as could be expected. Mark Bradburne was having his first ride for six months after injuring his back. (op 33-1)

1887 WILLIAMHILL.COM - BINGO "NATIONAL HUNT" NOVICES' HURDLE (10 hdls) 2m 5f
5:10 (5:10) (Class 4) 4-Y-0+ **£2,602** (£764; £382; £190)

Form RPR
603- **1** **Heez A Cracker (FR)**^{208} 4801 4-10-12 0............ NoelFehily 112+
(Emma Lavelle) *t.k.h: hld up in midfield: clsd to chse ldrs bef 3 out: led on bit sn after 2 out: pushed out flat: comf* **2/1**^{1}
06-5 **2** *1 1/2* **Jay J**^{10} 1743 6-10-9 0............ TomMolloy(3) 110+
(Andrew Price) *t.k.h: wandering at hurdles: w ldrs tl 5th: hdwy to jnd ldr again whn blnd 7th: led bef 2 out: j.rt 2 out: sn hdd: kpt on same pce flat* **9/1**^{3}
666- **3** *1/2* **Wyck Hill (IRE)**^{214} 4683 6-10-12 0............ RodiGreene 107
(David Bridgwater) *t.k.h: j.rt and nt a fluent: hld up in rr: hdwy 7th: chsd ldrs bef 2 out: hanging rt fr 2 out: sltly hmpd last: kpt on flat: swtchd rt nr fin* **16/1**
4- **4** *29* **Benarchat (FR)**^{273} 3490 5-10-12 0............ NickScholfield 83+
(Paul Nicholls) *t.k.h: mstkes: chsd ldr tl led 5th: hdd bef 2 out: sn btn: lft poor 4th and mstke last: hmpd by loose horse flat* **7/2**^{2}
P4-0 **5** *19* **Canyouseeme**^{10} 1736 7-10-12 0............ LiamTreadwell 59
(Claire Dyson) *a towards rr: struggling after 6th: t.o after 3 out* **50/1**
-14P **P** **Prescelli (IRE)**^{11} 1724 6-11-5 115............(p) TomO'Brien —
(Keith Goldsworthy) *led tl 5th: sn rdn along: chsd ldrs after tl wknd sn after 3 out: t.o and p.u 2 out* **2/1**^{1}
0- **F** **Sussex Sunset**^{248} 3995 4-10-5 0............ DenisO'Regan 99
(Paul Webber) *t.k.h: hld up in rr: hdwy 7th: chsd ldrs bef 2 out: rdn between last 2: 3rd and keeping on same pce whn fell last* **25/1**

5m 6.30s (-17.70) **Going Correction** -0.70s/f (Firm)
WFA 4 from 5yo+ 10lb **7** Ran SP% **110.6**
Speed ratings (Par 105): **105,104,104,93,85** —,—
toteswingers: 1&2 £4.40, 1&3 £6.00, 2&3 £22.20 CSF £19.52 TOTE £3.40: £2.10, £2.70; EX 21.10.
Owner Gdm Partnership **Bred** Henrietta Charlet & Daniel Charlesworth **Trained** Wildhern, Hants

FOCUS
A very modest event and a weak race for the track. The leaders went off quite quick before coming back and the race rather fell apart. The cosy winner is open to more improvement.

NOTEBOOK
Heez A Cracker(FR) is closely related to stable star Crack Away Jack and has matured since last season, when he showed minor promise in three starts. He won this nicely enough under a patient ride and has more to offer, but it should be emphasised that the bare form is very limited. (tchd 7-4 and 5-2)
Jay J came in for support and he ran better on this step up in trip, leading off the home turn but no match for the winner in the end. His hurdling has room for improvement and he did not look entirely straightforward. (op 18-1 tchd 8-1)
Wyck Hill(IRE) was staying on all the while on this hurdling debut and looks likely to appreciate 3m in time. A sound surface seems important to him. (tchd 14-1)
Benarchat(FR) pulled his way to the front on this hurdles debut and his exertions told as he dropped away very tamely on the home turn. A big, chasing type, already a winner of a point-to-point, he looks some way from the finished article physically. (op 11-4 tchd 5-2)
Canyouseeme (op 33-1)
Prescelli(IRE) had run poorly on her reappearance, where she lost a shoe, and put up another poor showing under her double penalty. Her rider reported that she was never travelling. Official explanation: jockey said mare never travelled (op 3-1 tchd 7-2 in places)
Sussex Sunset, tailed off in her one bumper start, looked set to finish well adrift for much of this hurdles debut, but she stayed on well and was a close third when coming dwon at the last. Her dam was a decent jumper and she should win a little race. (op 3-1 tchd 7-2 in places)

1888 WILLIAMHILL.COM - SPORTS BETTING H'CAP CHASE (12 fncs) 2m
5:40 (5:41) (Class 4) (0-115,110) 4-Y-0+ **£3,577** (£1,050; £525; £262)

Form RPR
3442 **1** **Woodlark Island (IRE)**^{8} 1767 4-11-3 **110**............(bt) TomScudamore 111+
(David Pipe) *chsd ldr: lft disputing ld 2nd: led 7th: mde rest: rdn bef 3 out: kpt on wl u.p flat* **11/8**^{1}
4033 **2** *3/4* **Cortinas (GER)**^{43} 1471 8-11-12 **110**............(t) NoelFehily 118
(Charlie Mann) *t.k.h: hld up in last trio: hdwy to chse ldng trio 9th: mstke 2 out: chal last: rdn flat: fnd little u.p and a hld by wnr* **15/2**
120 **3** *8* **January**^{26} 1569 7-11-7 **105**............(t) TimmyMurphy 108+
(Liam Corcoran) *t.k.h: chsd ldrs: wnt 2nd bef 3 out: rdn and fnd little between last 2: wknd flat* **12/1**

210 **4** *19* **Red Birr (IRE)**[8] 1767 9-11-3 **101**..(t) SamThomas 82
(Paul Webber) *bhd: mstke 4th: lost tch next: rallied briefly 7th: sn toiling again: t.o after 9th: plugged on to go modest 4th flat* **10/1**

1PF2 **5** *2 3/4* **Bushwacker (IRE)**[43] 1471 6-11-7 **108**...........................(t) TomMolloy(3) 88
(Seamus Mullins) *led: blnd bdly and jnd 2nd: mstke 6th: hdd next: wknd qckly after 9th wl btn whn mstke 3 out* **8/1**

2365 **6** *29* **Indiana Gold (FR)**[24] 1589 6-11-6 **104**.................................(p) APMcCoy 53
(Alison Thorpe) *chsd ldrs tl after 5th: struggling whn j.lft 7th: t.o bef 3 out* **11/2[2]**

3032 **7** *nk* **Shinnecock Bay**[59] 1290 6-11-7 **105**...........................(b) LeightonAspell 54
(Oliver Sherwood) *mstkes: a towards rr: lost tch after 7th: t.o bef 3 out* **13/2[3]**

3m 56.8s (-1.20) **Going Correction** -0.475s/f (Good)
WFA 4 from 6yo+ 9lb **7** Ran SP% **110.5**
Speed ratings (Par 105): **84,83,79,70,68 54,54**
toteswingers: 1&2 £3.70, 1&3 £3.70, 2&3 £9.40 CSF £11.38 TOTE £2.30: £1.70, £5.90; EX 13.50 Place 6 £13.70, Place 5 £12.30.
Owner Eminence Grise Partnership **Bred** Stone Ridge Farm **Trained** Nicholashayne, Devon

FOCUS
A moderate handicap chase, and not form to treat too seriously, but the winner stepped up on his recent chase debut.

NOTEBOOK
Woodlark Island(IRE) was always towards the fore on this second run over fences and he found extra when challenged after the last. His trainer has done well in handicap chases this autumn with another four-year-old, Frosted Grape, and this one might have more improvement in him. He gets further. (op 13-8 tchd 7-4 and 2-1 in a place and 15-8 in places)
Cortinas(GER), eased 3lb to his last winning mark, was ridden with kid gloves. He loomed up to look a threat, but when let down on the flat he did not find as much as he had promised. (op 8-1 tchd 13-2)
January is less than straightforward, and after closing to have his chance he once again failed to produce much. He is 8lb higher than when winning for a different yard at Hereford in August. (op 9-1)
Red Birr(IRE) was soon in trouble but stayed on late past beaten rivals. (tchd 8-1 and 11-1)
Bushwacker(IRE)'s jumping let him down again, although he did well to find a leg at the second. Weakening quickly on the home turn, he is a very dicey proposition. (op 13-2)
T/Plt: £64.50 to a £1 stake. Pool: £64,433.56. 728.13 winning tickets. T/Qpdt: £9.00 to a £1 stake. Pool: £5,337.80. 434.85 winning tickets. SP

1889 - 1898a (Foreign Racing) - See Raceform Interactive

1545 PLUMPTON (L-H)

Monday, October 18

OFFICIAL GOING: Good to firm (good in places; watered; 8.9)
Single bends for all races.
Wind: virtually nil Weather: light cloud, bright spells

1899 TOTESPORT.COM MAIDEN HURDLE (DIV I) (9 hdls) 2m
2:20 (2:20) (Class 5) 4-Y-0+ **£1,712** (£499; £249)

Form RPR

P-3 **1** **Beaubrav**[29] 1547 4-10-9 0..(t) MarcGoldstein(5) 110+
(Michael Madgwick) *led 1st tl after next: chsd ldr after: mstke 4th: led again and mstke 6th: mde rest: clr after 3 out: kpt on: rdn out* **7/2[2]**

0-4 **2** *2 1/2* **Addwaitya**[27] 1466 5-11-0 0.. RichardJohnson 106
(Laura Mongan) *j. modly: led tl wandered bdly and hdd 1st: chsd ldrs after: ev ch whn outj. 3 out: rdn and styd on same pce fr bef 2 out* **10/11[1]**

3 *12* **Mut'Ab (USA)**[40] 5-11-0 0.. JamieMoore 99+
(Gary Moore) *hld up in midfield: j.rt 2nd: clsd to chse ldrs and hmpd 5th: mstke next: rdn and wknd after 3 out* **12/1**

500- **4** *9* **Top Smart**[205] 4893 4-10-9 0.. JimmyDerham(5) 84
(Seamus Mullins) *hld up wl in rr: hmpd 1st: lost tch after 5th: rdn and kpt on steadily after 3 out: nvr trbld ldrs* **25/1**

6P- **5** *10* **Empire Seeker (USA)**[250] 3978 5-10-11 0........................ PeterToole(3) 79
(Heather Main) *t.k.h: hld up in last pair: hdwy 4th: hmpd next: clr in ldng quintet 6th: wnt 3rd bef next: rdn and wknd qckly bef 2 out: 4th and tired whn pckd bdly 2 out* **66/1**

6 *2* **Gtaab**[24] 4-11-0 0.. DominicElsworth 75
(Paul Webber) *mistrake 1st: chsd ldrs tl 2nd: hld up in midfield after: j.rt 3rd: hmpd 5th: sn lost tch: t.o whn j.rt last* **4/1[3]**

0-50 **7** *22* **Tocatchaprince (IRE)**[15] 1705 4-11-0 0........................ DaveCrosse 50
(Milton Harris) *hld up off the pce towards rr: nt fluent 4th: lost tch after next: t.o whn mstke 3 out* **25/1**

P **Musical Script (USA)**[20] 7-10-11 0........................ RichardKilloran(3) —
(Mouse Hamilton-Fairley) *plld hrd: chsd ldrs after 1st: led after next: mstke 3rd: hdd 6th: wknd rapidly next: t.o whn p.u 2 out* **50/1**

P **Swirl Tango**[79] 4-10-7 0.. WillKennedy —
(F Jordan) *hld up wl off the pce towards rr: blnd 1st: hmpd 5th: sn lost tch: wl t.o whn mstke 3 out: sn p.u* **250/1**

0-0 **F** **Quahadi (IRE)**[16] 1680 4-10-11 0.. CharlieStudd(3) —
(Chris Gordon) *t.k.h: hld up in midfield: hdwy 4th: 4th and wl in tch whn fell next* **100/1**

3m 43.5s (-17.30) **Going Correction** -0.95s/f (Hard) **10** Ran SP% **114.8**
Speed ratings (Par 103): **105,103,97,93,88 87,76,—,—,—**
toteswingers:1&2:£1.50, 1&3:£2.90, 2&3:£1.80 CSF £7.05 TOTE £3.70: £1.20, £1.10, £2.20; EX 6.90.
Owner The B B Partnership **Bred** Star Pointe Ltd,Brosnan And Williamson **Trained** Denmead, Hants

FOCUS
The first division of what looked a very ordinary maiden hurdle. The winner produced a step up but the fourth, fifth and the time limit the rating.

NOTEBOOK
Beaubrav, third to a decent sort over C&D latest, only had to repeat that form to go close in this lesser event and he stayed on strongly down the straight to win with a bit in hand. He's the type to do well in handicaps down the line. (tchd 3-1)
Addwaitya, not beaten far on the Flat last month, had run creditably on his most recent outing over hurdles and he again showed enough to suggest he'll be winning races at a modest level. (op Evens, tchd 5-4 in a place and 6-5 in places)
Mut'Ab(USA), going the wrong way on the Flat, showed a little ability without proving his stamina for the trip. (op 11-1 tchd 10-1)
Top Smart didn't build on a promising start in bumpers, but he kept on late on this first try over hurdles and will be suited by a stiffer test.
Empire Seeker(USA) again failed to see his race out, but may do better once handicapping.
Gtaab, solid in the market, was already looking in trouble when impeded and he ended up well beaten. (op 6-1)
Quahadi(IRE) caused some trouble when coming down at the fifth. (op 66-1)

1900 TOTESPORT.COM MAIDEN HURDLE (DIV II) (9 hdls) 2m
2:50 (2:52) (Class 5) 4-Y-0+ **£1,712** (£499; £249)

Form RPR

1 **Clu Agus Cail (IRE)**[35] 1521 5-10-7 106........................ TimmyMurphy 104+
(Alison Batchelor) *chsd ldr tl led after 5th: mde rest: rdn after 3 out: j.rt and collided w rival 2 out: hung rt after: mstke last: kpt on u.p flat* **2/1[2]**

2 **2** *2 1/4* **Betabob (IRE)**[15] 1688 7-11-0 106........................ RichardJohnson 107
(Tim Vaughan) *hld up wl in tch: chsd ldng pair bef 3 out: rdn and effrt between last 2: chsd wnr and drvn flat: styd on same pce and no imp* **7/4[1]**

3 *3/4* **Sinbad The Sailor**[188] 5-11-0 0.. AndrewTinkler 108+
(George Baker) *t.k.h: chsd ldrs: wnt 2nd after 5th: ev ch and rdn after 3 out: j.lft and collided w wnr next: carried rt and mstke last: kpt on same pce u.p flat* **4/1[3]**

/F-5 **4** *12* **Sail And Return**[15] 1689 6-10-7 0........................ JosephAkehurst(7) 96
(Philip Middleton) *racd freely: led: blnd 5th: sn hdd: chsd ldrs after: wkng whn hmpd and stmbld 3 out: lft modest 4th bef next* **14/1**

50-6 **5** *6* **Magusta (GER)**[165] 168 6-11-0 0..(t) DarylJacob 87
(Jamie Snowden) *hld up off the pce in last trio: mstke 4th: hdwy 5th: mstke next: no hdwy after and wl btn next: mstke last* **66/1**

6 **6** *14* **Bold Warning**[22] 1629 6-11-0 0.. WillKennedy 73
(Alex Hales) *racd in midfield: struggling after 5th: losing tch whn mstke next: t.o after 3 out* **20/1**

0-0P **7** *6* **Out To Impress (IRE)**[141] 528 5-11-0 0..................(t) AndrewThornton 67
(Murty McGrath) *hld up in last trio: lost tch 6th: t.o fr next* **250/1**

-556 **8** *28* **Pursuit Of Purpose**[99] 953 4-10-4 83........................ CharlieStudd(3) 32
(Philip Sharp) *racd in last trio: mstke 1st: lost tch qckly after 5th: t.o bef 3 out* **200/1**

0 **9** *53* **Me Fein**[15] 1688 6-11-0 0.. PaulMoloney —
(Barney Curley) *t.k.h early: hld up towards rr: hung rt and lost tch qckly 5th: wl t.o fr next* **33/1**

P **Prohibition (IRE)**[21] 4-11-0 0.. JamieMoore —
(Gary Moore) *t.k.h: hld up in midfield: hdwy to chse ldrs 5th: mstke 3 out: 5th and wkng whn p.u bef next: dismntd* **12/1**

3m 41.9s (-18.90) **Going Correction** -0.95s/f (Hard)
WFA 4 from 5yo+ 9lb **10** Ran SP% **114.1**
Speed ratings (Par 103): **109,107,107,101,98 91,88,74,48,—**
toteswingers:1&2:£2.00, 1&3:£2.50, 2&3:£1.90 CSF £5.80 TOTE £3.20: £1.10, £1.10, £1.80; EX 6.30.
Owner Mrs Alison Batchelor **Bred** March Thoroughbreds **Trained** Petworth, W Sussex

FOCUS
This was fought out by the market leaders. A similar standard to division I. The winner was the form pick but 5lb off her best Irish efforts.

NOTEBOOK
Clu Agus Cail(IRE) stayed on best despite having banged into the third taking the first in the straight and then hung right. She had shown more than enough back home to win a race such as this, and it would be no surprise were she to go in again, with her having the obvious option of mares-only events. (op 5-2, tchd 11-4 in places)
Betabob(IRE), an 8l second at Huntingdon on his debut for the yard, appeared to run his race once more and a race will surely fall his way at some stage. (op 9-4 tchd 13-8)
Sinbad The Sailor, a four-timer winner at up to 2m on the Flat, came off worst when colliding with the winner two out and a mistake at the last, when intimidated by that same rival, didn't help matters either. This was a reasonable first effort and he should have no trouble finding something similar. (op 7-2, tchd 9-2 in a place)
Sail And Return was already beaten when hampered and then stumbling at the third-last. (op 12-1)
Prohibition(IRE) proved disappointing on this first start over hurdles, although he was dismounted having been pulled up. Official explanation: jockey said gelding lost its action (op 9-1)

1901 BETFAIR SUPPORTS MOORCROFT RETRAINING OF RACEHORSES NOVICES' H'CAP CHASE (14 fncs) 2m 4f
3:20 (3:21) (Class 5) (0-95,95) 4-Y-0+ **£2,729** (£832; £435; £236)

Form RPR

3-0P **1** **Chord**[12] 1735 6-11-3 **86**.. AndrewThornton 98+
(Simon Earle) *in tch in midfield: chsd ldrs 9th: j.rt 3 out: sn rdn: kpt on u.p to chal last: led flat: all out* **22/1**

4P-P **2** *nk* **Normandy Landings**[167] 132 7-10-12 **81**........................ DougieCostello 91
(Neil Mulholland) *chsd ldng pair: wnt 2nd 8th: pressed ldr and travelling wl 11th: mstke 2 out: rdn hands and heels between last 2: mstke last: ev ch flat: nt qckn* **5/1[2]**

2 **3** *nk* **Mister Micheau (IRE)**[29] 1546 7-11-10 **93**........................(t) JamieMoore 103
(Joanna Davis) *j.rt: led: mstke 3rd: rdn and forged ahd after 3 out: hrd pressed last: hdd and no ex flat* **5/2[1]**

P-F4 **4** *63* **Drombeg Pride (IRE)**[29] 1546 6-9-12 **72**........................ MarcGoldstein(5) 18
(Gerry Enright) *a in rr: mstke 4th and 6th: hmpd next: struggling and rdn after 8th: t.o fr 11th: lft poor 4th 2 out: t.o* **16/1**

-101 **P** **Mycenean Prince (USA)**[47] 1450 7-11-1 **84**........................ APMcCoy —
(Jim Best) *chsd ldr: hmpd 3rd: rdn and nt travelling after 6th: drvn bef 9th: struggling whn lft 5th and bdly hmpd 10th: t.o whn p.u next* **5/2[1]**

0PP5 **F** **Poacher's Dream (IRE)**[43] 1474 8-10-0 **69** oh2................(t) FelixDeGiles —
(Jonathen de Giles) *chsd ldrs: mstke 3rd and 4th: fell 7th* **25/1**

0102 **F** **Tegan Lee**[25] 1592 7-11-9 **95**.. DPFahy(3) 99
(Liam Corcoran) *hld up in last pair: mstke 1st: hdwy to trck ldrs 10th: bmpd 3 out: cl 4th and shkn up whn fell 2 out* **11/2[3]**

43 **F** **Royial (FR)**[42] 1494 5-11-5 **93**.. JimmyDerham(5) —
(Seamus Mullins) *hld up in last pair: mstke 6th: hdwy and j.rt 8th: chsng ldrs whn fell next* **10/1**

5m 1.80s (-5.50) **Going Correction** -0.275s/f (Good) **8** Ran SP% **112.4**
Speed ratings (Par 103): **100,99,99,74,— —,—,—**
toteswingers:1&2:£17.10, 1&3:£9.10, 2&3:£3.90 CSF £123.99 CT £377.03 TOTE £23.20: £4.00, £2.10, £1.20; EX 101.20.
Owner The Plum Merchants **Bred** Cheveley Park Stud Ltd **Trained** Tytherington, Wilts

FOCUS
This had the look of a tricky little handicap beforehand and the front three were separated by two necks. Ordinary form but solid enough, with the winner capable of rating higher.

NOTEBOOK
Chord, placed off 8lb higher at Towcester last October, ran a shocker back there on his reappearance but the blinkers were dispensed with on this occasion and he got up close home under an all-out drive from Andrew Thornton. (op 20-1)
Normandy Landings had been struggling when last seen, but he's clearly benefited from a break and may well have won had he jumped better in the straight. His rider could have been harder, but it surely won't be long before he gets off the mark. (op 11-2 tchd 13-2)
Mister Micheau(IRE), runner-up off 3lb lower over C&D latest, tended to jump to his right, but still gave it a good go and very nearly held on. He's another who will surely be winning before long. (op 9-4 tchd 2-1 and 11-4)

Tegan Lee was by no means out of it when coming down two out, in fact she almost certainly would have made it a four-way finish. (tchd 8-1 and 11-1)
Royial(FR) was still going okay when coming down on this first start over fences. (tchd 8-1 and 11-1)

1902 ISIRIS SUPPORTS MOORCROFT CHARITY RACEDAY NOVICES' H'CAP HURDLE (9 hdls) 2m
3:50 (3:50) (Class 4) (0-100,100) 3-Y-0+ **£2,740** (£798; £399)

Form RPR
33 **1** **Rimini (FR)**124 766 5-11-12 **100**........ PaulMoloney 104+
(David Rees) *chsd ldr tl led 3 out: rdn bef next: styd on gamely fr last* **8/1**
006P **2** 1 1/4 **Motor Home**47 1451 4-10-11 **85**........(t) JimmyMcCarthy 86+
(Charlie Morlock) *in tch in midfield: rdn and outpcd 3 out: rallied u.p between last 2: styd on strly flat: wnt 2nd towards fin: nt rch wnr* **40/1**
200- **3** 1/2 **Luthien (IRE)**262 3724 4-11-7 **95**........ WillKennedy 96+
(Alex Hales) *led tl outj. and hdd 3 out: sn rdn: chsd wnr after tl last: kpt on same pce u.p flat* **33/1**
364- **4** hd **Uncle Bunge (IRE)**174 36 4-11-7 **95**........ TimmyMurphy 96
(Liam Corcoran) *in tch in midfield: switching rt bef 3 out: hdwy u.p to chse ldrs 2 out: wnt 2nd and blnd last: styd on same pce flat* **6/1**3
042 **5** 1 3/4 **Red Current**42 1488 6-11-12 **100**........ TomScudamore 98
(Michael Scudamore) *hld up in rr: gd hdwy bef 6th: rdn to chse ldng pair after: no ex u.p between last 2: btn after last* **11/2**2
20-4 **6** 1 1/2 **San Silvestro (IRE)**70 470 5-11-7 **95**........(p) RichardJohnson 92
(Tim Vaughan) *chsd ldrs: rdn bef 3 out: one pce u.p bef 2 out: btn between last 2* **13/8**1
2-00 **7** 2 1/4 **Mid Wicket (USA)**27 865 4-11-5 **96**........(p) RichardKilloran(3) 92+
(Mouse Hamilton-Fairley) *chsd ldrs: rdn and outpcd bef 3 out: rallied u.p bef 2 out: wknd between last 2* **25/1**
3605 **8** 2 3/4 **Mulaazem**15 1704 7-10-6 **85**........ DavidBass(5) 77
(Derek Frankland) *chsd ldrs: drvn after 3rd: lost pl and dropped to rr after: no threat to ldrs after: styd on same pce fr 3 out* **16/1**
000- **9** 2 1/4 **Kaycee (IRE)**188 5172 5-11-4 **92**........ MarkGrant 83
(Roger Curtis) *hld up in last trio: blnd 6th: no real prog bef next: rdn after 3 out: btn whn blnd last* **25/1**
254 **10** 1 1/4 **Django Reinhardt**12 1734 4-11-4 **99**........ MrDavidTurner(7) 87
(Sam Davison) *t.k.h: in tch: rdn and struggling bef 3 out: wl btn bef 2 out: no ch whn hmpd last* **7/1**
44P- **11** 1/2 **Raspbary**174 41 4-11-7 **100**........ JimmyDerham(5) 90
(Seamus Mullins) *hld up in rr: rdn and sme hdwy into midfield bef 2 out: no hdwy fr 2 out and wl hld whn j.lft and pckd last* **33/1**
6000 **12** 29 **Jim Job Jones**16 1675 6-9-11 **78**........ MarkQuinlan(7) 37
(Neil Mulholland) *hld up in tch in last trio: rdn and struggling after 6th: lost tch next* **50/1**

3m 43.4s (-17.40) **Going Correction** -0.95s/f (Hard)
WFA 4 from 5yo+ 9lb **12** Ran SP% **115.2**
Speed ratings (Par 105): **105,104,104,104,103 102,101,99,98,98 97,83**
toteswingers:1&2:£57.80, 1&3:£18.30, 2&3:£92.90 CSF £280.86 CT £9532.48 TOTE £7.70: £2.40, £11.50, £7.30; EX 351.50.
Owner D Rees **Bred** Haras D'Ecouves & Uplifting B'Stock Ltd **Trained** Clarbeston, Pembrokes

FOCUS
A low-grade handicap hurdle, but it was certainly open. They finished in a heap but the time was fair for the grade. The winner produced a big step up but can rate higher, with the second another improver.

NOTEBOOK
Rimini(FR), a promising third on his hurdles debut at Fontwell prior to being disqualified at Worcester in June, had a bit to prove under top weight dropped to 2m, but he was backed beforehand and always looked in control having taken over at the third-last. This was a likeable effort from the 5-y-o, who should have more to offer upped in trip. (op 14-1)
Motor Home, dropped 4lb having pulled up on his handicap debut at Hereford, shaped considerably better with a first-time tongue-tie on, keeping on well for second, and he'll be able to pick up a small race if the breathing aid continues to work. (op 33-1)
Luthien(IRE) put up an improved display switched to a handicap, making the running and keeping on admirably once headed. (op 25-1)
Uncle Bunge(IRE), as expected, found the drop in trip against him, but he did well to get himself into a challenging position and he'll find better opportunities back up in trip. (op 11-2 tchd 5-1)
Red Current didn't see it out having reached a challenging position. (op 6-1)
San Silvestro(IRE), twice a beaten favourite at selling level on the Flat in the summer, was well fancied on this debut for the yard, but he couldn't quicken for pressure and was again well held. (op 11-8 tchd 7-4)

1903 SIMON GIBSON H'CAP CHASE (18 fncs) 3m 2f
4:20 (4:21) (Class 4) (0-110,110) 4-Y-0+ **£3,809** (£1,162; £607; £329)

Form RPR
U **1** **Macs Lad (IRE)**5 1830 7-10-7 **91**........ TimmyMurphy 109+
(Liam Corcoran) *a gng wl: hld up in last pair: hdwy 8th: led after 11th: cruised clr after 13th: in n.d after: comf* **11/2**
5004 **2** 6 **Mzuri Bay**27 1568 5-11-5 **103**........(bt) NoelFehily 108
(Brendan Duke) *in tch: rdn after 12th: rallied briefly next: 4th and wl btn after 14th: lft disputing modest 2nd 3 out: kpt on u.p: chsd wnr between last 2: nvr a threat to wnr* **12/1**
4651 **3** 2 3/4 **Sarahs Gift (IRE)**29 1550 7-11-7 **110**........(t) DavidBass(5) 113
(Lawney Hill) *hld up in last: mstke 11th: rdn and hdwy on inner after 13th: no hdwy and wl btn after next: lft disputing modest 2nd and hmpd 3 out: plugged on same pce u.p but no ch w wnr* **13/8**1
511P **4** 65 **What A Scientist (IRE)**22 1626 10-11-9 **110**........ SamTwiston-Davies(3) 67+
(Nigel Twiston-Davies) *chsd ldrs: nt fluent 1st: rdn and struggling after 12th: 3rd and wl btn 15th: lft 2nd: bdly hmpd and rdr lost iron 3 out: 4th and t.o bef next* **11/4**2
4F-0 **U** **September Moon**49 1434 12-10-11 **95**........ RodiGreene —
(Graham Smith) *led tl after 11th: rdn and dropped to last after 13th: lost tch next: wl bhd whn blnd and uns rdr 15th* **25/1**
133P **F** **Strong Coffee**29 1550 8-11-10 **108**........(b) LeightonAspell —
(Oliver Sherwood) *chsd ldr 3rd tl 11th: rdn to chse wnr 13th: no imp and wl hld whn fell 3 out* **5/1**3

6m 39.8s (-10.90) **Going Correction** -0.275s/f (Good) **6** Ran SP% **108.4**
Speed ratings (Par 105): **105,103,102,82,—** —
toteswingers:1&2:£5.00, 1&3:£2.40, 2&3:£3.30 CSF £52.55 TOTE £6.80: £2.10, £1.80; EX 39.90.
Owner Balios Racing **Bred** Kieran Hanlon **Trained** Charlton Adam, Somerset
■ Stewards' Enquiry : Noel Fehily one-day ban: careless riding (Nov 1)

FOCUS
Just a modest handicap chase. The winner posted a big step up on his old hurdles form and can rate higher.

NOTEBOOK
Macs Lad(IRE) had been running well in points prior to unseating returned to rules at Wetherby five days earlier (saddle slipped), and he put in a good effort under Timmy Murphy, who always seemed confident and just had to nudge him out for a cosy success. There's more to come from the 7-y-o and he may well follow up. (op 17-2)
Mzuri Bay improved markedly on his initial outing over fences, staying on well for second without proving a match for the winner. (op 10-1)
Sarahs Gift(IRE), 9lb higher, failed to reproduce the form and was left looking laboured in third. (op 6-4 tchd 7-4 and 15-8 in a place)
What A Scientist(IRE), 8lb lower for this return to fences, was badly hampered by the fall of Strong Coffee and was allowed to come home in his own time. (op 10-3 tchd 5-2)
Strong Coffee was beaten when coming down. (op 4-1)

1904 FITZDARES H'CAP HURDLE (14 hdls) 3m 1f 110y
4:50 (4:51) (Class 3) (0-120,120) 4-Y-0+ **£4,553** (£1,337; £668; £333)

Form RPR
30-1 **1** **Firm Order (IRE)**158 303 5-11-7 **115**........ WillKennedy 118+
(Paul Webber) *mostly chsng ldr: mstke 1st: rdn after 3 out: ev ch last: kpt on wl to ld fnl 100yds: drvn out* **6/1**3
0314 **2** 3/4 **Winsley Hill**9 1776 8-11-12 **120**........ RodiGreene 123
(Neil Mulholland) *led: mstke 1st and 9th: qcknd 11th: rdn bef 2 out: kpt on gamely u.p: hit last: edgd lft u.p flat: hdd and no ex fnl 100yds* **13/2**
40P- **3** 3/4 **Lupanar (IRE)**183 5248 6-11-2 **110**........(p) JamieMoore 113+
(Gary Moore) *hld up in tch in rr: hdwy to chse ldrs 11th: rdn after 3 out: mstke next: kpt on same pced u.p between last 2* **8/1**
6410 **4** nse **Cubism**12 1726 4-10-2 **102**........(t) JimmyDerham(5) 102
(Milton Harris) *in tch in midfield: rdn 3 out: kpt on same pce u.p between last 2* **13/2**
F-P **5** nk **Clifton Debut**59 1317 7-10-11 **108**........ SeanQuinlan(3) 110+
(Kim Bailey) *chsd ldrs: drvn after 3 out: j.lft next: styd on same pce between last 2* **4/1**2
2105 **6** 11 **Makena (FR)**11 1746 8-10-9 **108**........(p) DavidBass(5) 98
(David Rees) *in tch: rdn after 11th: wknd u.p bef 2 out* **8/1**
345 **7** 4 **Whenever**54 1364 6-11-10 **118**........(t) RichardJohnson 104
(Richard Phillips) *in tch: mstke 4th: rdn wl bef 3 out: wknd u.p bef 2 out: eased after last* **7/2**1
100- **8** 34 **Global Flyer**241 4150 6-11-7 **115**........ AndrewThornton 67
(Caroline Bailey) *hld up in tch: hdwy to chse ldrs after 10th: rdn after next: wknd qckly 3 out: t.o 2 out* **20/1**
-266 **9** 19 **Canni Thinkaar (IRE)**25 1590 9-10-9 **108**.(p) GemmaGracey-Davison(5) 41
(Zoe Davison) *in tch in last pair: rdn and struggling 10th: t.o fr 3 out* **22/1**

5m 59.1s (-29.70) **Going Correction** -0.95s/f (Hard) course record
WFA 4 from 5yo+ 11lb **9** Ran SP% **114.5**
Speed ratings (Par 107): **107,106,106,106,106 103,101,91,85**
toteswingers:1&2:£4.80, 1&3:£4.90, 2&3:£9.40 CSF £44.33 CT £313.43 TOTE £9.50: £2.70, £3.60, £2.20; EX 33.90.
Owner The Syndicators **Bred** Edmund Arthur **Trained** Mollington, Oxon

FOCUS
A competitive handicap hurdle and solid form. The winner is rated up 5lb and the next two were well in on their best old form.

NOTEBOOK
Firm Order(IRE) responded to strong pressure from Will Kennedy to get up close home. Having travelled well for much of the way on this step up in trip, he quickly became outpaced towards the end of the back straight, but showed himself to be a strong stayer with this performance. He should make a chaser in time, but can win more races over hurdles first. (op 7-1 tchd 15-2)
Winsley Hill kept finding off the front under top weight and only gave in close home. She continues in good form. (op 5-1 tchd 9-2 and 15-2)
Lupanar(IRE) looked potentially interesting upped in trip with the cheekpieces on, returning from a six-month break, but he couldn't quite stay on as well as the front pair. It's hoped he goes the right way from this. (op 9-1)
Cubism ran a solid race and remains capable of winning off this mark. (op 8-1)
Clifton Debut proved rather one-paced in the end. (tchd 9-2)
Whenever again proved disappointing in the first-time tongue-tie, finding little and ending up well held. (op 4-1 tchd 9-2)

1905 D & D CONSTRUCTION H'CAP CHASE (12 fncs) 2m 1f
5:20 (5:22) (Class 5) (0-90,87) 4-Y-0+ **£2,759** (£861; £464)

Form RPR
2-33 **1** **Sean Og (IRE)**120 794 8-9-11 **61** oh1........(t) RichardKilloran(3) 70+
(Tim Vaughan) *a gng wl: j.rt: chsd clr ldr tl lft in ld 7th: mde rest: clr fr 3 out: easily* **8/11**1
3P06 **2** 12 **Space Cowboy (IRE)**25 1591 10-10-5 **66**........ JamieMoore 65
(Gary Moore) *chsd clr ldr: lft cl 2nd 7th: mstke next: struggling and rdn 3 out: keeping on but hld whn slipped bnd bef 2 out: wl btn after* **11/4**2
624 **3** 52 **Temple Place (IRE)**15 1707 9-11-12 **87**........ WillKennedy 32
(Alan Jones) *hld up in last: lft 3rd and in tch 7th: sn pushed along: btn 9th: lost tch next: t.o whn mstke 2 out* **6/1**3
06P/ **U** **Shouldntbethere (IRE)**143 591 6-10-10 **76**........(t) JimmyDerham(5) —
(Joanna Davis) *racd freely: led: wl clr tl blnd and uns rdr 7th* **9/1**

4m 22.2s (-3.70) **Going Correction** -0.275s/f (Good) **4** Ran SP% **108.9**
Speed ratings (Par 103): **97,91,66,—**
CSF £3.24 TOTE £1.70; EX 2.70.
Owner Dave Prince, Jim Reuter & Jeff Wadley **Bred** Camogue Stud Ltd **Trained** Aberthin, Vale of Glamorgan

FOCUS
A very weak handicap chase. The winner could be rated a few pounds higher but the second is regressive.

NOTEBOOK
Sean Og(IRE), although 1lb 'wrong' on this debut for the yard, looked to hold very strong claims and never had a moment's worry, readily coming clear from the third-last and winning easily. Winning from a mark of 61, it would be most surprising were he not to go in again before the handicapper has his say. (tchd 5-6 and 10-11 in a place)
Space Cowboy(IRE), making a rare trip away from Fontwell, is on a good mark again and, but he proved no match for the winner, a slight slip on the bend turning in making no difference. His usual blinkers were left off. (tchd 9-4)
Temple Place(IRE) never threatened to make an impact. (op 11-2 tchd 13-2)
Shouldntbethere(IRE) still held a commanding lead when blundering and unseating his rider at the seventh. (op 14-1)

1906 ANDY STEWART CHARITABLE FOUNDATION SUPPORTS MOORCROFT MAIDEN OPEN NATIONAL HUNT FLAT RACE 2m 2f
5:50 (5:50) (Class 6) 4-6-Y-0 **£1,370** (£399; £199)

Form RPR
06- **1** **Bad Sir Brian (IRE)**222 4522 5-11-0 0........ LiamTreadwell 104+
(Nick Gifford) *w ldr tl led 8f out: mde rest: rdn over 2f out: in command 1f out: styd on wl* **7/2**2

2 4 1/2 **Border Station (IRE)**[60] 1307 4-11-0 0 TimmyMurphy 99+
(Alison Batchelor) *hld up in tch in last pair: hdwy 5f out: chsd wnr over 3f out: rdn and tried to chal ent fnl 2f: no ex and btn ent fnl f* **5/6**[1]

3 11 **Oscar Mac (IRE)** 4-11-0 0 RichardJohnson 88
(Tim Vaughan) *in tch: chsd ldrs 7f out tl over 3f out: sn drvn and wl btn over 2f out* **7/2**[2]

6- 4 9 **Salut Honore (FR)**[177] 5391 4-11-0 0 SamJones 79
(Alex Hales) *t.k.h: chsd ldrs: rdn over 3f out: wknd over 2f out* **12/1**[3]

0 5 24 **Hard To Tell (IRE)**[12] 1729 4-10-9 0 TomO'Connor(5) 55
(Bill Turner) *plld hrd early: in tch: hanging fr 9f out: lost tch qckly over 4f out: t.o fnl 2f* **66/1**

0-00 6 17 **Poesmulligan (IRE)**[16] 1680 4-11-0 0 JamieMoore 38
(Linda Jewell) *plld hrd: hld up in tch in last pair: rdn and lost tch qckly over 4f out: t.o fnl 3f* **66/1**

00/0 7 11 **My Only Boy**[16] 1680 5-10-9 0 MarcGoldstein(5) 27
(Michael Madgwick) *led at stdy gallop tl hdd and pushed along 8f out: dropped to rr and rdn 7f out: sn lost tch: t.o fnl 4f* **40/1**

4m 11.5s (-15.50) **Going Correction** -0.95s/f (Hard) 7 Ran SP% **112.1**
Speed ratings: **96,94,89,85,74 66,62**
toteswingers:1&2:£1.60, 1&3:£2.00, 2&3:£1.70. totesuper7: Win: Not won. Place: Not won. CSF £6.54 TOTE £4.50: £1.80, £1.10; EX 9.00 Place 6 £872.12; Place 5 £690.48..
Owner Core Strength **Bred** Killian Lynch **Trained** Findon, W Sussex

FOCUS
Probably a fair little bumper for the course. The winner produced a big step forward.

NOTEBOOK
Bad Sir Brian(IRE) put in an improved effort on this third attempt. Outright leader before halfway, it was clear from over 4f out that he was still going well in front and he galloped on relentlessly for what ultimately proved a comfy success. He'll have no trouble staying further over hurdles. (tchd 10-3)
Border Station(IRE) was brought through to challenge the winner turning in, but he couldn't stay on as strongly and ended up well held. This former pointer will no doubt fare better over hurdles. (op 11-8)
Oscar Mac(IRE), whose dam won in bumpers and over hurdles, travelled well until getting outpaced and should improve. (op 11-4 tchd 4-1)
Salut Honore(FR) stepped up on his sole previous effort and is bred to do better over jumps. (op 9-1)
T/Plt: £879.30 to a £1 stake. Pool:£74,996.73 - 62.26 winning tickets T/Qpdt: £379.40 to a £1 stake. Pool:£4,922.18 - 9.60 winning tickets SP

1736 EXETER (R-H)
Tuesday, October 19

OFFICIAL GOING: Good (chs 6.9, hdl 6.5)
Wind: mild against Weather: sunny periods with light showers

1907 EXETER RACECOURSE CHRISTMAS RACEDAY HOSPITALITY AMATEUR RIDERS' NOVICES' HURDLE (12 hdls) 2m 7f 110y
2:10 (2:11) (Class 4) 4-Y-0+ **£2,498** (£774; £387; £193)

Form RPR

1 **Garton King**[157] 6-11-4 0 MrWBiddick 117+
(Paul Nicholls) *mid-div: hdwy 7th: led appr 2 out: styd on: rdn out* **7/2**[3]

356- 2 4 **Royal Collonges (FR)**[238] 4218 5-10-11 120 MrHDerham(7) 114+
(Paul Nicholls) *t.k.h: trckd ldrs: led appr 3 out: hdd whn mstke 2 out: sn rdn: styd on same pce* **3/1**[2]

650- 3 3/4 **Kauto The Roc (FR)**[183] 5282 6-10-11 105 MrRJarrett(7) 113+
(Alan King) *trckd ldrs: jnd ldrs appr 3 out: ev ch 2 out: sn rdn: hld whn awkward last: lost 2nd nr fin* **7/1**

5 4 11 **Mtpockets (IRE)**[17] 1675 5-10-4 0 MrDLavery(7) 94
(Neil Mulholland) *in tch: hit 2nd: lost pl 9th: styd on again fr 3 out but nvr gng to rch ldrs* **40/1**

35/2 5 15 **Easement**[30] 1555 7-10-11 0 (v) MrTGarner(7) 88
(Charlie Morlock) *in tch: led 8th: rdn and hdd appr 3 out: wknd bef next: t.o* **10/1**

603- 6 15 **Doctor Foxtrot (IRE)**[183] 5282 5-10-11 114 MrTCheesman(7) 74
(Philip Hobbs) *mid-div: rdn after 9th: sn wknd: t.o* **2/1**[1]

0 7 43 **Inishrush (IRE)**[12] 1742 9-10-13 0 ow2 MrWPotter(7) 37
(Adrian Chamberlain) *a bhd: t.o fr 6th* **200/1**

P 8 27 **Battle Bridge (IRE)**[12] 1739 5-10-13 0 MrRGHenderson(5) 11
(Nick Mitchell) *wnt lft 1st 2: led tl hdd 8th: wknd after next: t.o* **100/1**

P/3- P **Matako (FR)**[157] 7-10-11 0 MissSJBerry(7) —
(Caroline Keevil) *mstke 4th: a in rr: t.o whn p.u bef 3 out* **20/1**

0 P **Sarah's Boy**[142] 538 5-10-11 0 (t) MrKEdgar(7) —
(David Pipe) *a towards rr: lost tch 7th: p.u bef 3 out* **33/1**

0P-4 P **Emmaslegend**[13] 1724 5-10-6 0 MrTJCannon(5) —
(Suzy Smith) *trckd ldr tl wknd 7th: t.o whn p.u bef 3 out* **16/1**

5m 39.8s (-19.20) **Going Correction** -0.775s/f (Firm) 11 Ran SP% **119.7**
Speed ratings (Par 105): **101,99,99,95,90 85,71,62,—,— —**
Tote Swingers: 1&2 £1.40, 1&3 £40.80, 2&3 £5.60 CSF £14.66 TOTE £7.20: £3.40, £1.70, £2.50; EX 14.00.
Owner Trailer Resources Ltd **Bred** D & C Clapham & Tweenhills Farm & Stud **Trained** Ditcheat, Somerset
■ Will Biddick's first winner since reverting to amateur status.

FOCUS
This was an interesting staying novice hurdle to kick off proceedings, confined to amateur riders. There was just an average gallop on and the principals dominated from the home turn. Ordinary novice form but the winner should go on to rate higher.

NOTEBOOK
Garton King joined Paul Nicholls after winning three times from as many outings between the flags earlier this year. The stable ran two here, but despite being the morning line favourite the market eventually suggested he was the second string. That didn't stop him from running out a ready winner, though, and he clearly has a little bit of class about him. Whether he is up to contesting Graded races in this division is doubtful and no doubt chasing will be on his agenda before long, but it's a fair bet he has more to offer over hurdles. He clearly stays very well and it will be interesting to see where he goes next. (op 10-3 tchd 9-2)
Royal Collonges(FR), the winner's stablemate, failed to live up to expectations in three outings for the yard last term and looked flattered by a mark of 120. He was well backed for this seasonal return and, despite running freely, shaped with plenty more encouragement for the step back up in trip. Indeed he probably needs an even stiffer test looking at the way he finished off his race here. He also lacked fluency late on and it wouldn't be surprising to see him sent over fences in the near future, where he should fare better. (tchd 11-4)
Kauto The Roc(FR) ◆ failed to really convince in six outings as a novice last term, but appeared in need of a stiffer test and this comeback over the longer trip brought about a personal-best effort. He travelled nicely through the race and was the chief danger to the winner coming to the last flight, but he wasn't fluent over it. His stamina just looked to be giving way at that stage, however, and he lost second near the finish. There really should be a race for him over this sort of trip on a sharper circuit and he could well be set for a better season. (op 11-1 tchd 13-2)
Mtpockets(IRE) plugged on late in the day without ever threatening over this stiffer test. This former winning pointer will be more interesting when switching to low-grade handicaps.
Easement was second in a seller on his return last month and found this too hot, but goes some way to helping set the level of this form. (op 12-1)
Doctor Foxtrot(IRE) failed to score in six runs in this sphere last term, but signed off with his best effort when third at Kempton and has looked in need of this stiffer test of stamina. He was very well backed, but his fate was sealed shortly after halfway as he came under pressure and he proved a big disappointment. (op 5-2 tchd 11-4)
Emmaslegend Official explanation: jockey said mare was unsuited by the good ground

1908 CHRISTMAS PARTIES HERE AT EXETER RACECOURSE BEGINNERS' CHASE (18 fncs) 3m
2:40 (2:40) (Class 3) 4-Y-0+ **£5,854** (£1,719; £859; £429)

Form RPR

510- 1 **Quinz (FR)**[193] 5113 6-11-4 130 RichardJohnson 129+
(Philip Hobbs) *led 3rd: j. fluently in the main: in command whn rchd for 3 out: easily* **11/10**[1]

P-01 2 23 **Cashel Blue (USA)**[43] 1490 8-10-13 0 (p) KeiranBurke(5) 110+
(Patrick Rodford) *led tl 3rd: w wnr: nudged along 11th: rdn after 14th: sn no ch w wnr* **8/1**

2-05 3 16 **Persian Run (IRE)**[12] 1739 6-11-4 0 JoeTizzard 87
(Colin Tizzard) *chsd ldrs: hit 5th: rdn after 11th: wnt 3rd 13th but no ch w ldng pair sn after* **11/4**[2]

40-6 4 61 **Landenstown Star (IRE)**[12] 1742 5-11-4 0 AndrewThornton 32
(Seamus Mullins) *prom: hit 5th: stmbld 10th: blnd 13th: sn wknd* **25/1**

31-0 F **Estates Recovery (IRE)**[13] 1725 5-11-4 117 TomO'Brien —
(Philip Hobbs) *trckd ldrs: hit 1st: fell 3rd* **4/1**[3]

5m 51.3s (-18.00) **Going Correction** -0.775s/f (Firm) 5 Ran SP% **109.2**
Speed ratings (Par 107): **99,91,86,65,—**
CSF £9.58 TOTE £1.40: £1.30, £3.70; EX 8.60.
Owner Andrew L Cohen **Bred** Michael Blond **Trained** Withycombe, Somerset

FOCUS
This beginners' chase has been contested by some decent novices in the past, but it was a disappointing turnout this year. There should be more to come from Quinz over fences, and the second is rated in line with his hurdles form.

NOTEBOOK
Quinz(FR) didn't convince in three outings when initially tried over fences last term, but showed his class when reverting to hurdles and was the clear form pick in this line-up. He raced enthusiastically through the early parts and, jumping nicely, was soon in the firing line as a result. He had matters in control turning for home, but seemed to get confused when Richard Johnson asked him to go big at the third-last fence and does still have something to learn in the jumping department as a chaser. He is entitled to learn from this confidence-boosting comeback success, however, and providing he does that, there could be a fair staying handicap in him over fences this season. (op 4-5)
Cashel Blue(USA) was last seen making all over 3m3f on testing ground off a mark of 95 over hurdles 43 days previously and was another that arrived here with something to prove back over fences. He faced a near impossible task with the winner at the weights, but made a good fist of it and he too is entitled to learn for the experience, but will need his sights lowering again before coming good as a chaser. (op 9-1)
Persian Run(IRE) was the biggest danger to the winner on hurdles form, but was well beaten on his chasing debut 12 days earlier over C&D. He ultimately left the impression the run would again bring him on and he needs more practice over fences, but he ought to show his true colours as the season develops. (op 10-3)
Landenstown Star(IRE) was out the back in three novice hurdles last term and faced a very difficult assignment on this switch to fences. He was in trouble before clouting seven out, but should improve for the experience and will find his feet as he gains more experience. (tchd 28-1)
Estates Recovery(IRE), the winner's stablemate, didn't jump well when beaten a long way on his chase debut 13 days earlier and failed to convince prior to falling at the third this time. He can only be watched at present. (op 6-1)

1909 BEST MATE BEGINNERS' CHASE (12 fncs) 2m 1f 110y
3:10 (3:10) (Class 3) 4-Y-0+ **£5,997** (£1,862; £1,002)

Form RPR

102- 1 **Diamond Brook (IRE)**[199] 4991 5-11-2 0 DarylJacob 112
(Nick Williams) *hld up 4th: outpcd after 8th: lft prom 4 out: led next: rdn whn hrd pressed after 3 out: edgd rt run-in: hld on: all out* **9/1**[3]

-0UU 2 hd **Jocheski (IRE)**[58] 1345 6-11-2 0 AndrewThornton 112
(Tony Newcombe) *hld up bhd ldng quartet: outpcd after 8th: lft prom 4 out: rdn and ev ch fr next: kpt on run-in: nudged whn carried sltly rt: jst hld* **50/1**

6630 3 8 **The Brimmer (IRE)**[12] 1737 6-10-11 0 JimmyDerham(5) 107
(Seamus Mullins) *trckd ldr tl 6th: outpcd after 8th: lft in ld whn hmpd next: sn hdd: one pce fr 3 out* **40/1**

44F- F **Celestial Halo (IRE)**[192] 5125 6-11-2 0 (t) RWalsh —
(Paul Nicholls) *trckd ldrs: disp fr 6th: 2 l clr and travelling wl whn fell 4 out* **1/4**[1]

26-4 F **Rougham**[10] 1775 4-10-7 0 RichardJohnson —
(Philip Hobbs) *led: nt fluent 1st: disp fr 6th: hdd and 2 l down whn fell 4 out* **6/1**[2]

4m 10.6s (-8.40) **Going Correction** -0.775s/f (Firm)
WFA 4 from 5yo+ 9lb 5 Ran SP% **108.7**
Speed ratings (Par 107): **87,86,83,—,—**
CSF £128.10 TOTE £6.80: £2.50, £9.20; EX 107.90.
Owner Paul Duffy Diamond Partnership **Bred** Ms Barbara Johnston **Trained** George Nympton, Devon
■ Stewards' Enquiry : Daryl Jacob two-day ban: careless riding (Nov 2-3)

FOCUS
The general consensus of the riders after the first two races was that the ground was riding pretty much as officially advertised. This is traditionally an exciting beginners' chase but the falls of the two market leaders four out blew the race wide open. The form is rated through the second and third to the level of their hurdles form.

NOTEBOOK
Diamond Brook(IRE) and Jocheski were left to to fight it out when two came down four out, and just edged the verdict. Nick Williams's 5-y-o won his novice hurdle at this track back in February and has always been thought of as more of a chaser in the making, though he wasn't expected to take this. Obviously he was a very fortunate winner, and hadn't been given a hard time from off the pace prior to the two market leaders falling, but he responded well when asked to win the race from that stage. There should be some more to come from him.
Jocheski(IRE) had unseated on his two previous outings since going chasing and was in the process of being given an educational ride prior to being left in with every chance. He dug deep to make the winner pull out the stops, and wasn't done too many favours by that rival after the last, which resulted in a stewards' enquiry. This should do his confidence plenty of good and he deserves to go one better, but will remain vulnerable in novice company now the division is hotting up.
The Brimmer(IRE), on his chasing debut, was left in the lead when a couple fell in front of him four out, but he was hampered too and quickly headed. (op 33-1)

Celestial Halo(IRE), champion class over hurdles and officially rated 165 in that sphere, was making an eagerly anticipated chasing debut. He was unsurprisingly towards the top of the betting for the Arkle next March despite not having jumped a fence in public, and things were going well enough for him through the race until everything dramatically changed complexion as he fell at the first in the home straight. He didn't look a complete natural prior to guessing at that fence and coming down, perhaps befitting of a horse that started his career on the Flat, and it was not a forgone conclusion that he would've beaten Rougham, who also came down independently at the same fence. He was soon up on his feet, but this was anything but a good introduction to chasing and it remains to be seen how badly his confidence is affected. He is still only a 6-y-o, however, and should things not go to plan for him in this division he always has the option of going back over hurdles. (tchd 2-7 in places)
Rougham was a dual winner over hurdles as a juvenile last season and signed off with a mark of 130. He likes to race from the front and was given a positive ride on this seasonal/chasing debut. He had jumped satisfactorily prior to coming down, perhaps as a result of being put off by Celestial Halo, and wasn't totally done with at the time, though his rider was later of the opinion he was beat. It's hoped he emerges okay from this experience as there are clearly races to be won with him in this sphere if he does. (tchd 2-7 in places)

1910 BATHWICK TYRES TAUNTON NOVICES' HURDLE (8 hdls) 2m 1f
3:40 (3:41) (Class 4) 4-Y-0+ **£2,602** (£764; £382; £190)

Form				RPR
162-	**1**		**Dare Me (IRE)**[192] 5129 6-10-12 0 RichardJohnson (Philip Hobbs) *trckd ldr: sltly hmpd 3rd: led next: hit 3 out: a in command: easily* **4/9**[1]	130+
4-1	**2**	*12*	**Kasbadali (FR)**[156] 355 5-10-12 0 LeightonAspell (Oliver Sherwood) *mid-div: hdwy after 4th: hit next: rdn bef 3 out: chsd wnr fr 2 out but nvr any ch* **14/1**	111+
36/0	**3**	*13*	**Puerto Azul (IRE)**[10] 1773 6-10-12 0 DominicElsworth (Oliver Sherwood) *t.k.h: hld up in rr: j. sltly lft: hdwy after 5th: wnt bdly lft last: styd on: snatched 3rd fnl stride: nvr trbld ldng pair* **50/1**	99+
3-	**4**	*shd*	**Sunwise (USA)**[247] 4055 4-10-12 0 RWalsh (Paul Nicholls) *in tch: pushed along and hdwy after 5th: rdn bef next: wnt 3rd after 2 out: styd on same pce: lost 3rd fnl stride* **7/2**[2]	97
1-02	**5**	*16*	**Dean's Grange**[12] 1736 5-11-5 112 JoeTizzard (Colin Tizzard) *trckd ldrs: rdn to chse wnr appr 3 out tl 2 out: wknd* **7/1**[3]	92
P55-	**6**	*2*	**Reefer Beefer (IRE)**[189] 5178 5-10-12 0 AndrewThornton (Tony Newcombe) *a towards rr* **100/1**	81
46U0	**7**	*10*	**Cruise In Style (IRE)**[12] 1736 4-10-0 0 GilesHawkins(5) (Kevin Bishop) *mid-div tl wknd after 5th: t.o* **100/1**	65
	8	*1 3/4*	**Magic Show**[1127] 6-10-12 0 TomO'Brien (Peter Bowen) *mid-div tl wknd after 5th: t.o* **40/1**	70
06	**9**	*1/2*	**Le Roi Max (FR)**[26] 1594 6-10-12 0 PaddyBrennan (Nigel Twiston-Davies) *led: wnt lft 3rd: hdd whn hit next: rdn after 5th: wknd bef next: t.o* **25/1**	70
00/	**P**		**Lindengrove**[582] 4536 5-10-12 0 LiamTreadwell (Claire Dyson) *mid-div tl 3rd: sn wl bhd: p.u bef 3 out* **100/1**	—

3m 57.4s (-18.10) **Going Correction** -0.775s/f (Firm)
WFA 4 from 5yo+ 9lb **10** Ran SP% **121.9**
Speed ratings (Par 105): **111,105,99,99,91 90,86,85,84,—**
Tote Swingers: 1&2 £15.30, 1&3 £21.80 CSF £9.15 TOTE £1.50: £1.10, £3.50, £12.40; EX 12.90.
Owner Trevor Hemmings **Bred** Aaron Metcalfe **Trained** Withycombe, Somerset

FOCUS
Not much strength in depth but the winner is a smart recruit. He transferred his bumper form to hurdling and was value for further.

NOTEBOOK
Dare Me(IRE) ◆ was a dual bumper winner and posted a career-best when second to Megastar in Grade 2 company at Aintree's Grand National meeting on his final outing last season. Held in very high regard by his powerful stable, he proved all the rage for this hurdling debut and didn't disappoint, running out a most decisive winner to enhance the yard's already excellent record in the race. He was given a no-nonsense ride and could've been called the winner three out, where he wasn't that clever. Indeed he has something to work on with his jumping, but is certainly entitled to improve on that score and it's probable that he will want a stiffer test in this division to be seen at his very best. A sound surface looks important to his cause and he should be well up to defying a penalty should connections wish to get more experience into him before tackling something more valuable. (op 8-15 after 8-13 in places)
Kasbadali(FR) ◆ was last seen narrowly winning a bumper at the second time of asking at Market Rasen in May. He was allowed time to find his feet on this switch to hurdling and eventually finished a clear second-best. This rates a pleasing introduction and, with improvement assured for the outing, he should get off the mark before all that long.
Puerto Azul(IRE), the runner-up's stablemate, is a headstrong 6-y-o and proved very unruly beforehand, produced an interesting run. He unsurprisingly took time to settle under restraint, but caught the eye running on at the finish and, despite going markedly out left at the last, sneaked a place at the finish. He clearly has some temperament issues, but also has ability and it will be interesting to see what mark he gets for handicaps.
Sunwise(USA) cost his owners 130,000gns after showing useful form on the level in Ireland, but took time to acclimatise and was somewhat of a disappointment on his hurdling debut over C&D in February. Better was expected of him on this seasonal return back on a sounder surface, but he found little after travelling into the home straight and lost third near the line. It may be that he wants a longer trip in this sphere as he stayed 1m4f well on the Flat, but he also sported headgear in that sphere and it may be that some form of aid would help his cause. (op 10-3)
Dean's Grange, who was penalised, was easily shaken off from three out and ran well below his recent level. (op 13-2)

1911 BATHWICK TYRES BARNSTAPLE H'CAP HURDLE (10 hdls) 2m 3f
4:10 (4:10) (Class 4) (0-115,110) 4-Y-0+ **£3,252** (£955; £477; £238)

Form				RPR
332-	**1**		**Lemon Silk (IRE)**[209] 4831 6-10-10 **94** TomO'Brien (Alex Hales) *mid-div: hdwy 7th: led appr 3 out: rdn after 2 out: all out: jst hld on* **14/1**	97+
1600	**2**	*hd*	**Captain Becket**[12] 1740 7-10-6 **95** TomO'Connor(5) (James Frost) *mid-div: hdwy 7th: rdn 3 out: styd on to chse wnr after 2 out: str chal run-in: jst failed* **14/1**	98
052-	**3**	*3 1/4*	**John's Gift**[194] 5103 6-11-2 **100** HarrySkelton (Bob Buckler) *prom: hit 6th: rdn and ev ch appr 3 out: lost 2nd bef last: styd on same pce* **13/2**[3]	100
21-2	**4**	*nk*	**Maurisca (FR)**[166] 169 5-10-12 **103** PeterCarberry(7) (Charlie Longsdon) *t.k.h: hld up towards rr: hdwy on ins bnd after 7th: swtchd lft appr 3 out: sn rdn: styng on same pce whn awkward last* **10/3**[1]	106+
2F0	**5**	*1 1/2*	**Dark Energy**[13] 1726 6-11-12 **110** (t) TomScudamore (Michael Scudamore) *hld up towards rr: hdwy after 7th: rdn after 3 out: styd on same pce* **33/1**	108
032/	**6**	*4*	**Russian Epic**[533] 4959 6-11-12 **110** RichardJohnson (Philip Hobbs) *hld up twards rr: sme prog after 7th: sn rdn: styd on same pce fr next* **7/1**	106
0554	**7**	*2 1/4*	**Royal Max (IRE)**[24] 1614 4-11-8 **106** (t) PaddyBrennan (Ian Williams) *mid-div: hdwy 6th: rdn after 3 out: one pce fr next* **4/1**[2]	99
0-34	**8**	*1/2*	**Miller's Dawn**[162] 249 6-11-0 **98** (b[1]) HaddenFrost (Henrietta Knight) *towards rr: hit 4th: sn rdn along: nvr any imp on ldrs* **16/1**	90
535	**9**	*nse*	**Party Palace**[12] 1740 6-11-3 **101** RodiGreene (Stuart Howe) *chsd eaders: rdn after 7th: one pce fr next* **14/1**	93
0-P2	**10**	*18*	**Princess Flame (GER)**[17] 1677 8-10-13 **97** JimmyMcCarthy (Brendan Powell) *in tch: led 6th tl appr 3 out: sn wknd* **11/1**	73
U20/	**11**	*1 3/4*	**Mud Monkey**[581] 4546 6-11-7 **105** (t) LiamTreadwell (Claire Dyson) *led tl blnd 2nd: trckd ldrs: blnd 5th: wknd 7th: t.o* **40/1**	82
-4F0	**12**	*3 1/2*	**Predateur (FR)**[16] 1692 7-11-12 **110** (t) DavidEngland (Giles Smyly) *led after 2nd tl mstke and hdd 6th: rdn after next: wknd bef 3 out: t.o* **28/1**	81
4451	**13**	*23*	**The Wee Midget**[13] 1735 5-10-11 **95** NickScholfield (Arthur Whiting) *chsd ldrs early: midfield 4th: wknd 7th: t.o* **8/1**	46

4m 27.8s (-14.90) **Going Correction** -0.775s/f (Firm)
WFA 4 from 5yo+ 9lb **13** Ran SP% **123.1**
Speed ratings (Par 105): **100,99,98,98,97 96,95,94,94,87 86,85,75**
Tote Swingers: 1&2 £36.60, 1&3 £33.20, 2&3 £22.40 CSF £195.13 CT £1413.46 TOTE £18.50: £4.20, £4.20, £2.90; EX 345.40.
Owner A S Helaissi **Bred** Duncan Grimley **Trained** Wardington, Oxon

FOCUS
This moderate handicap was a competitive affair for the grade and there was a fair gallop on. The first pair drew clear nearing the last. Both were very well in on the best of their old form.

NOTEBOOK
Lemon Silk(IRE) just did enough to repel the runner-up at the business end. This 6-y-o only had four outings last season and, having fallen in the first of them, was placed each time he completed. This comeback task looked warm enough for him, but he was the bottom weight and the return to a sounder surface evidently helped. It was a deserved win from a horse that was a Grade 2 winning juvenile back in 2007. This was his first win since then and he has tumbled down the handicap, so it wouldn't be surprising to see him build on this now his confidence should be high. (op 16-1)
Captain Becket bounced right back to form and went down narrowly. He wouldn't be sure to improve on this next time, but looking at the manner in which he finished his race it could be that returning to a stiffer test would suit ideally. (op 16-1)
John's Gift attracted support on this return from his summer break and had his chance, but didn't help his cause by refusing to settle early on. He has the scope to improve this term and has begun life in handicaps on a workable mark. (op 15-2 tchd 6-1)
Maurisca(FR) was 3lb lower than when finishing second over fences on his previous outing 166 days earlier and also came in for support with his yard among the winners. He travelled smoothly into contention, but proved one-paced when it mattered and was well held prior to a messy jump at the last. He is better as chaser, but may appreciate stepping up in trip over hurdles. (op 7-2 tchd 4-1)
Dark Energy was given a very patient ride and crept into things rounding the home turn, but could only muster the same pace when push came to shove. (tchd 28-1)
Russian Epic was making his handicap debut and having his first run for Philip Hobbs after a 533-day layoff. He too got a patient ride, but wasn't always fluent and ultimately shaped as though the run would do him good. Returning to a sharper track is also likely to suit better. (op 13-2 tchd 10-1)
Royal Max(IRE) was another that began to get involved nearing the final bend, but found little when asked for maximum effort and his losing run continues. (op 5-1 tchd 11-2)

1912 BATHWICK TYRES PLYMOUTH H'CAP CHASE (15 fncs) 2m 3f 110y
4:40 (4:40) (Class 4) (0-110,117) 4-Y-0+ **£3,903** (£1,146; £573; £286)

Form				RPR
-P46	**1**		**I'm A Legend**[23] 1628 8-11-5 **103** (p) DougieCostello (Neil Mulholland) *mid-div: hdwy after 11th: chal 2 out: sn led: kpt on wl: rdn out* **8/1**	111
4421	**2**	*4*	**Woodlark Island (IRE)**[2] 1888 4-11-9 **117** 7ex (bt) TomScudamore (David Pipe) *prom: led 9th: rdn clr 4 out: hdd sn after 2 out: kpt on but no imp on wnr fr last* **3/1**[1]	112+
0U0-	**3**	*3/4*	**Inside Dealer (IRE)**[188] 5184 6-11-4 **102** JoeTizzard (Colin Tizzard) *mid-div: hit 7th: hdwy next: trckd ldr 10th: hit next: sn rdn: styng on u.str.p whn mstke last: no ch after* **15/2**	111+
11P-	**4**	*nk*	**Ere Alfie (IRE)**[271] 3572 6-10-7 **91** (p) DarylJacob (Nick Williams) *trckd ldrs: hit 7th: wnt 2nd after 11th tl rdn after 4 out: styd on same pce* **11/2**[2]	95+
00-1	**5**	*6*	**De Bansha Man (IRE)**[26] 1596 5-11-9 **110** SamTwiston-Davies(3) (Nigel Twiston-Davies) *trckd ldrs: rdn after 8th: lost pl after 11th: styd on same pce fr 4 out* **7/1**[3]	109
5440	**6**	*10*	**Foreign King (USA)**[5] 1844 6-11-5 **108** JimmyDerham(5) (Seamus Mullins) *hld up towards rr: rdn and hdwy after 11th: j. bdly lft fr 4 out: no further imp on ldrs: wknd after 2 out* **14/1**	100
3-44	**7**	*12*	**Swainson (USA)**[131] 687 9-11-4 **102** OwynNelmes (Helen Nelmes) *a towards rr* **66/1**	80
546-	**8**	*2 1/4*	**Honourable Arthur (IRE)**[220] 4583 7-11-6 **104** TomO'Brien (Victor Dartnall) *trckd ldrs: nt fluent 8th and 9th: rdn and wknd after 11th* **15/2**	80
4120	**9**	*14*	**Beauchamp Viking**[126] 755 6-10-1 **85** (t) RodiGreene (Simon Burrough) *mstke last: a towards rr* **20/1**	49
/05-	**10**	*5*	**Charming Oscar (IRE)**[364] 1844 8-9-13 **90** NathanSweeney(7) (Bob Buckler) *mid-div tl wknd after 11th: t.o* **16/1**	49
030-	**11**	*29*	**Manmoon (FR)**[193] 5120 7-11-5 **103** (p) DavidDennis (Nigel Hawke) *led tl 9th: wknd 11th: t.o* **16/1**	36
005U	**P**		**Pool Of Knowledge (FR)**[7] 1813 4-10-9 **103** SamThomas (Venetia Williams) *nvr particularly fluent: a bhd: t.o whn p.u bef 4 out* **12/1**	—

4m 39.2s (-18.10) **Going Correction** -0.775s/f (Firm)
WFA 4 from 5yo+ 9lb **12** Ran SP% **119.9**
Speed ratings (Par 105): **105,103,103,102,100 96,91,90,85,83 71,—**
Tote Swingers: 1&2 £6.40, 1&3 £51.60, 2&3 £14.30 CSF £33.74 CT £193.89 TOTE £10.70: £2.80, £2.20, £2.40; EX 33.74.
Owner Wincanton Race Club **Bred** Conkwell Grange Stud Ltd **Trained** Burlescombe, Devon

FOCUS
An ordinary handicap, run at a fair enough gallop. The form looks solid with the winner rated to his C/D mark.

NOTEBOOK
I'm A Legend was second off the same mark in this race last term and, well backed, went one better with a determined display. He dug deep to get on top in the home straight and showed a decent attitude when pressed nearing the last. While he doesn't really appeal as one to back this up, he will no doubt continue to pay his way. (op 12-1 tchd 7-1)
Woodlark Island(IRE) was penalised for winning at Kempton just two days earlier and, given an aggressive ride, made a bold bid to follow up. This longer trip on a stiffer track just found him out. (op 10-3 tchd 7-2)
Inside Dealer(IRE), who often travels well in his races, was making his seasonal and chasing debut. He was in with every chance prior to making a mess of the final fence and would've no doubt gone very close with a better leap there. This was just about his best effort to date and he shouldn't be too long in making amends providing he brushes up his fencing. (op 7-1)

Ere Alfie(IRE) was last seen pulling up at Taunton in January when bidding for a hat-trick. He shaped encouragingly on this first run back and should come on nicely for the outing. (op 9-2)
De Bansha Man(IRE) belatedly got his head in front when easily winning over hurdles off a 13lb lower mark at Perth last month. He didn't live up to expectations over fences on his debut in this sphere the time before, and made heavy weather of things here, but it was still a more accomplished jumping display from him. He could still be weighted to win when stepping up in trip as a chaser. (op 8-1)

1913 BATHWICK TYRES "JUNIOR" STANDARD OPEN NATIONAL HUNT FLAT RACE — 1m 5f
5:10 (5:12) (Class 6) 3-Y-O — **£1,301** (£382; £191; £95)

Form	Pos	Dist	Horse	Jockey	RPR
	1		**Cousin Khee** 3-10-12 0	TomScudamore	105+
			(Hughie Morrison) *trckd ldrs: nt clr run 3f out: led 2f out: qcknd clr: readily*	**1/1**[1]	
	2	10	**Bathcounty (IRE)** 3-10-5 0	CDTimmons(7)	89
			(Barry Brennan) *led: rdn 3f out: hdd 2f out: kpt on but nt pce of wnr: jst hld on for 2nd*	**50/1**	
	3	shd	**Shinko Moon** 3-10-12 0	DarylJacob	89
			(Jo Crowley) *trckd ldrs: rdn and ev ch 3f out tl 2f out: kpt on but nt pce of wnr*	**28/1**	
	4	1	**Watledge (FR)** 3-10-12 0	PaddyBrennan	88
			(Tom George) *mid-div: hdwy over 4f out: rdn 3f out: styd on same pce*	**11/4**[2]	
	5	9	**Mollycarrs Dream** 3-9-12 0	MarkQuinlan(7)	69
			(Bill Turner) *mid-div: pushed along 1/2-way: one pce fnl 2f*	**40/1**	
	6	½	**Firescent** 3-10-9 0	PeterToole(3)	75
			(Dominic Ffrench Davis) *hld up towards rr: styd on fnl 3f: nvr trbld ldrs*	**66/1**	
	7	¾	**Direct Flo (IRE)** 3-9-12 0	PeterCarberry(7)	67
			(Keith Goldsworthy) *trckd ldrs: rdn 3f out: one pce fr over 2f out*	**7/1**[3]	
	8	3 ¾	**Generous Bob** 3-10-9 0	WayneKavanagh(3)	69
			(Seamus Mullins) *pushed along fr 1/2-way: nvr bttr than mid-div*	**25/1**	
	9	4 ½	**Ondeafears (IRE)** 3-10-5 0	TimmyMurphy	57
			(Stuart Howe) *a towards rr*	**14/1**	
	10	¾	**Knight Blaze** 3-10-5 0	TomO'Brien	56
			(David Brace) *mid-div: hdwy over 4f out: rdn 3f out: sn wknd*	**28/1**	
	11	2 ¾	**Upton Mead (IRE)** 3-10-5 0	MissJBuck(7)	59
			(Chris Down) *trckd ldrs: rdn over 3f out: sn wknd*	**40/1**	
	12	9	**Present Accepted** 3-10-7 0	KeiranBurke(5)	47
			(Nerys Dutfield) *a towards rr*	**66/1**	
	13	4	**Burning Light (IRE)** 3-10-12 0	JamesDavies	42
			(Andrew Haynes) *mid-div tl wknd 3f out*	**28/1**	
	14	27	**Zateen Star** 3-10-5 0	JackDoyle	—
			(Susan Gardner) *mid-div tl wknd 4f out*	**22/1**	

3m 3.30s (-13.40) — **14** Ran SP% **124.2**
Tote Swingers: 1&2 £20.50, 1&3 £15.60, 2&3 £59.10 CSF £89.32 TOTE £1.90: £1.02, £23.00, £12.20; EX 54.40 Place 6: £635.18 Place 5: £333.60..
Owner Rory Sweet **Bred** Miss B Swire **Trained** East Ilsley, Berks

FOCUS
Junior bumpers are most often races to tread carefully with and there was no previous form on offer here, but it still proved a lively betting heat. There was an ordinary gallop on and the first four came nicely clear from around 2f out. Cousin Khee promises to be well above average.

NOTEBOOK
Cousin Khee ◆ ran out a taking debut winner and gave his yard a third win in the race from the last four seasons. This well-bred son of Sakhee is a half-brother to There And Then amongst others, who won also bumper on debut earlier this year, and proved very strong in the betting ring. He moved strongly just off the leaders and, after having to momentarily wait for his effort in the home straight, powered clear once the gap came. It's not at all hard to envisage him going in again and there is a Listed event at Cheltenham on New Year's Day, which his stable took with the smart Cill Rialaig (who also made a winning debut in this event) last year that is likely to be his big target. His trainer later revealed that this colt's future is most likely to be over jumps, rather than on the level. (op 10-11 tchd 11-10)
Bathcounty(IRE), the first foal of a 7f-1m winner, posted a solid effort from the front on debut. He clearly stays well and has a future. (op 28-1)
Shinko Moon is a half-brother to the AW winners Champagne Fizz and Sorbiesharry, who both ran in the same ownership. He failed to settle early on, so this rates a pleasing introduction and there could be one of these for him before the year is out. (tchd 25-1)
Watledge(FR), half-brother to a 1m2f Flat winner in France, was a big market mover. He travelled nicely and held every chance, but lacked the toe to stay with the principals from the furlong marker. He too clearly has a future and should improve for the experience. (op 7-1)
T/Plt: £603.60 to a £1 stake. Pool:£76,361 - 92.34 winning tickets T/Qpdt: £249.20 to a £1 stake. Pool:£5,288 - 15.70 winning tickets TM

1674 FONTWELL (L-H)
Wednesday, October 20

OFFICIAL GOING: Good (7.0)
Rail realignment added 15yds per circuit to advertised distances.
Wind: Fresh becoming light races 6 and 7, half against Weather: Sunny and cool

1914 HENNINGS WINE MERCHANTS NOVICES' HURDLE (7 hdls 2 omitted) — 2m 2f 110y
2:20 (2:21) (Class 4) 4-Y-O+ — **£2,341** (£687; £343; £171)

Form	Pos	Dist	Horse	Jockey	RPR
24-4	1		**Present To You (IRE)**[28] [1573] 5-10-12 124	TomO'Brien	103+
			(Philip Hobbs) *chsd ldr: hmpd and lft in ld 2nd: jnd by runner-up by-passing omitted last: edgd rt: drvn clr fnl 75yds*	**1/1**[1]	
6-	2	1 ½	**Penchesco (IRE)**[35] [3659] 5-10-12	LiamTreadwell	103+
			(Amanda Perrett) *hld up towards rr: mstk and rdr lost whip 4th: hdwy 3 out: jnd wnr by-passing omitted last: n.m.r on rail: no ex fnl 75yds*	**13/2**[3]	
433/	3	4	**The Bishops Baby (IRE)**[580] [4591] 7-10-5	LeightonAspell	91
			(Richard Rowe) *mid-div: hdwy 6th: chsd wnr 3 out tl next: one pce*	**28/1**	
51	4	1	**Moonwolf (NZ)**[18] [1675] 6-11-5	JamieGoldstein	104+
			(Sheena West) *hld up and bhd: r.o promisingly fr 3 out: nvr nrr*	**7/1**	
04-4	5	5	**Balustrade (IRE)**[18] [1675] 4-10-12	ColinBolger	93
			(Chris Gordon) *in tch: pressed ldrs 6th: outpcd fr 3 out*	**25/1**	
	6	2 ¼	**Galant Star (FR)**[181] 4-10-5	JamieMoore	85
			(Gary Moore) *mid-div: hdwy to chse ldrs 3 out: hrd rdn appr 2 out: sn wknd*	**14/1**	
20	7	6	**Kasban**[13] [1742] 6-10-12	MattieBatchelor	85
			(Luke Dace) *bhd: sme hdwy 3 out: nvr trbld ldrs*	**33/1**	
3-0	8	3 ½	**Zuwaar**[31] [1547] 5-10-12	(tp) AndrewGlassonbury	82
			(Paddy Butler) *in tch: effrt and mstk 3 out: sn wknd*	**66/1**	
462-	9	8	**Dalrymple (IRE)**[16] [2754] 4-10-7	(t) MarcGoldstein(5)	75
			(Michael Madgwick) *t.k.h in tch: wknd 6th*	**66/1**	
0/	10	48	**Red Law (IRE)**[198] 6-10-9	TommyPhelan(3)	32
			(Mark Gillard) *towards rr: nt fluent 4th: n.d fr 6th*	**100/1**	
0-P	11	28	**Idol Deputy (FR)**[17] [1705] 4-10-12	(t) MarkGrant	6
			(James Bennett) *mid-div tl wknd 6th*	**150/1**	
0	12	15	**Aragall (GER)**[31] [1547] 5-10-12	DavidEngland	—
			(George Baker) *prom: hmpd 2nd: mstk 4th: wknd 6th*	**25/1**	
00-	13	4	**King Richard (IRE)**[290] [3275] 6-10-12	AndrewThornton	—
			(Richard Rowe) *led tl blnd bdly and nrly fell 2nd: mstke and wknd 5th: wl bhd fr next*	**100/1**	
30-4	P		**Lady Karinga**[13] [1742] 5-10-2	LeeStephens(3)	—
			(David Evans) *prom: mstk 1st: hanging bdly rt and losing pl whn p.u after next*	**5/1**[2]	

4m 29.0s (-5.30) **Going Correction** -0.10s/f (Good)
WFA 4 from 5yo+ 9lb — **14** Ran SP% **118.9**
Speed ratings (Par 105): **107,106,104,104,102 101,98,97,93,73 61,55,53,—**
Tote Swingers: 1&2 £3.00, 1&3 £13.70, 2&3 £45.60 CSF £7.19 TOTE £2.00: £1.10, £2.20, £6.40; EX 12.10.
Owner R A Green **Bred** A W Young **Trained** Withycombe, Somerset

FOCUS
A moderate novice hurdle. The first pair drew clear after the omitted last flight. The sixth flight was also bypassed.

NOTEBOOK
Present To You(IRE) was left in the lead a lot sooner than ideal, finally got off the mark over hurdles. The ground certainly suited better than it had done when disappointing at Perth last time and he can still develop into a useful staying handicapper, with the best of him going to be seen over fences. (op 10-11 tchd 11-10)
Penchesco(IRE), tailed off in heavy ground on his one previous run over hurdles, was in fair form on the Flat earlier in the year and, like the winner, he proved well suited by the good ground. He looked to be going best of the pair bypassing the last, but his rider lost his whip soon after and he couldn't stay on as strongly as the winner. It may have made a difference, but the likelihood is he'd have just come off second best anyway. (op 7-1 tchd 6-1)
The Bishops Baby(IRE), making her hurdles debut following a 580-day absence, was clearly straight enough to run well and it's hoped she can built on it. (op 25-1 tchd 33-1)
Moonwolf(NZ) appeared not to be asked for an effort until after the last, and only then was he given a token slap. Considering he had won over further, surely a more positive ride should have been given to the 6-y-o and it can't really be argued that he should have finished a good bit closer. The Stewards did look into it, but according to his trainer Sheena West, he was scoped after the race and there were signs of blood, so no action was taken. Official explanation: trainer said gelding scoped post-race showed signs of bleeding (op 13-2 tchd 5-1)
Balustrade(IRE), 12l behind Moonwolf at the course last time, wasn't necessarily helped by the drop in trip, but he again ran well and should find an opening once handicapping. (op 20-1)
Galant Star(FR), who won and placed on the Flat in France, failed to see it out having reached a challenging position, but can probably be given another chance against her own sex over 2m. (op 16-1 tchd 12-1)
Lady Karinga, expected to be suited by the drop in trip, quickly lost her position and was eventually pulled up. This clearly wasn't her form and her rider reported she was hanging badly. Official explanation: jockey said mare hung badly right and had been virtually unsteerable (op 10-1)

1915 PARITUA VINEYARDS CONDITIONAL JOCKEYS' NOVICES' H'CAP HURDLE (10 hdls) — 2m 4f
2:50 (2:52) (Class 5) (0-90,85) 3-Y-O+ — **£1,561** (£458; £229; £114)

Form	Pos	Dist	Horse	Jockey	RPR
0	1		**Curragh Dancer (FR)**[14] [1735] 7-11-2 77	NathanSweeney(5)	80+
			(Paddy Butler) *in tch on outer: pressed ldrs and rdn 3 out: cl 2nd whn lft in ld next: blnd last: drvn out*	**33/1**	
350	2	1 ½	**O'Callaghan Strand (AUS)**[31] [1547] 4-11-6 85	RichieMcLernon(3)	79
			(Jonjo O'Neill) *hld up in rr of midfield: hdwy 3 out: hmpd and lft 3 l 2nd 2 out: pressed wnr after last: kpt on*	**17/2**	
60-0	3	2	**Dancing Daffodil**[14] [1735] 5-10-4 68	ChristopherWard(8)	66
			(Robin Dickin) *rn in snatches: chsd ldrs: rdn and lost pl 6th: rallied 2 out: styd on*	**15/2**[3]	
/P-P	4	30	**Roughing It (IRE)**[44] [1494] 7-11-12 82	JohnKington	52
			(Michael Scudamore) *bhd: rdn and sme hdwy fr 3 out: nt trble ldrs*	**16/1**	
5046	5	shd	**Atabaas Allure (FR)**[18] [1679] 4-10-12 73	PeterCarberry(5)	43
			(Chris Gordon) *bhd: rdn 7th: modest late hdwy*	**5/1**[2]	
0-45	6	3 ¼	**Hawk Gold (IRE)**[27] [1592] 6-11-2 72	(b) IanPopham	39
			(Michelle Bryant) *disp ld tl wknd 3 out*	**12/1**	
-60P	7	4 ½	**Knockvicar (IRE)**[139] [593] 8-11-1 71	GilesHawkins	34
			(Richard Mitchell) *disp ld tl wknd after 3 out*	**16/1**	
500-	8	13	**She Is A Cracker (FR)**[226] [4493] 5-11-2 80	JosephAkehurst(8)	31
			(Gary Moore) *in tch: rdn appr 7th: wknd 3 out*	**5/1**[2]	
5F3	9	9	**Yes Minister (IRE)**[27] [1592] 6-10-13 69	(p) CO'Farrell	12
			(Sophie Leech) *pushed along towards rr: dropped to last and drvn along 4th: n.d after*	**15/2**[3]	
-2P1	F		**Winning Show**[27] [1592] 6-11-9 82	(tp) CharlieWallis(3)	87
			(Chris Gordon) *chsd ldrs: led after 3 out: slt ld whn fell next*	**10/3**[1]	

4m 58.5s (-0.90) **Going Correction** -0.10s/f (Good)
WFA 4 from 5yo+ 10lb — **10** Ran SP% **112.9**
Speed ratings (Par 103): **97,96,95,83,83 82,80,75,71,—**
Tote Swingers: 1&2 £42.80, 1&3 £30.10, 2&3 £16.60 CSF £280.36 CT £2330.83 TOTE £86.10: £16.00, £2.70, £3.10; EX 309.70.
Owner Alistair M J Elliott **Bred** Haras De Bois Carrouges & Coolmore Stud **Trained** East Chiltington, E Sussex

FOCUS
A very weak handicap, confined to conditional riders.

NOTEBOOK
Curragh Dancer(FR), who beat only two home on his return from a 22-month absence/debut for the yard, had clearly come on a lot in a short space of time and he was all set to battle it out with Winning Show when that one came down two out, leaving him with a lead which he would maintain, despite a mistake at the last. This was his first success at the 23rd attempt and he may add to it at the right level, with a switch to fences not out of the question. (op 28-1)
O'Callaghan Strand(AUS) ◆ qualified for a mark of 85 with three down-the-field runs in novice only events and it was no surprise to see him produce something better on this first start in a handicap. He's going to stay further and should have little trouble finding a small race or two. (op 15-2)
Dancing Daffodil was never travelling that well and lost her position having lost an iron, but did keep on again for pressure and promises to stay 3m. (op 6-1)
Roughing It(IRE) was never in the hunt, but at least managed to complete this time. (tchd 14-1)
Atabaas Allure(FR) posted a very laboured effort from off the pace. (op 6-1)
She Is A Cracker(FR) was particularly disappointing on this first start for Gary Moore. (op 9-2 tchd 4-1)

Winning Show, 8lb higher than when winning over C&D latest, was putting in a good effort and still held the lead, albeit a narrow one, when coming down two out. It was too early to say whether he'd have won or not for sure. (tchd 7-2)

1916 CHAMPAGNE JOSEPH PERRIER H'CAP CHASE (16 fncs) 2m 6f

3:25 (3:26) (Class 4) (0-115,106) 4-Y-0+ **£2,862** (£840; £420; £209)

Form RPR

F46- **1** **High Oscar**[312] 2843 9-10-13 **93** LeightonAspell 102
(Richard Rowe) *hld up in rr: mstke 2nd: hdwy 4 out: drvn to ld fnl 100yds* **11/4**[2]

4S43 **2** *1 1/4* **Take A Mile (IRE)**[31] 1546 8-11-5 **104** JimmyDerham[(5)] 112
(Seamus Mullins) *chsd ldrs: wnt 2nd 4 out: slt ld jst after last: hdd and nt qckn fnl 100yds* **11/2**

6P43 **3** *nk* **Hereweareagain (IRE)**[6] 1841 7-11-7 **101** (bt) TomO'Brien 109
(Philip Hobbs) *trckd ldr 4th: led 12th: hit last and sn hdd: one pce fnl 100yds* **10/3**[3]

5122 **4** *32* **Morestead (IRE)**[6] 1841 5-11-12 **106** (b) NoelFehily 90
(Brendan Powell) *led at gd pce: rdn along fr 10th: hdd 12th: wknd 4 out* **7/4**[1]

0/3 **5** *35* **Mister Virginian (IRE)**[18] 1676 11-11-1 **102** MrTJCannon[(7)] 49
(Chris Gordon) *chsd ldr early: mainly 4th tl wknd 12th* **12/1**

5m 39.5s (-3.50) **Going Correction** -0.175s/f (Good) **5** Ran SP% **109.2**
Speed ratings (Par 105): **99,98,98,86,74**
CSF £16.44 TOTE £3.30: £2.00, £1.50; EX 16.90.

Owner Richard Rowe Racing Partnership **Bred** R T Crellin **Trained** Sullington, W Sussex

FOCUS
A moderate handicap chase run at a decent clip.

NOTEBOOK
High Oscar, returning from a 312-day absence and without a win in almost two years, has won on his return in the past and was running well when falling first time back last year, so this was probably the time to catch him, and he came through late in a race run to suit, getting on top as they climbed to the line. Richard Rowe had concerns over the suitability of the track, but he coped better than he had done on a previous occasion and may return next time. (op 9-4)
Take A Mile(IRE) is still 6lb above his last winning mark, but he travelled well for much of the way before taking over at the last, only to be claimed in the final half furlong. (op 5-1 tchd 9-2)
Hereweareagain(IRE) took over at the 12th travelling well, but he's proved a tough horse to win with and was eventually outstayed having been headed at the last. (op 3-1 tchd 11-4 and 7-2)
Morestead(IRE), 8l ahead of Hereweareagain when third at Worcester just six days earlier, took them along at a good clip but ultimately paid the price, dropping right away. (op 5-2)

1917 REDBANK LONG PADDOCK WINES BEGINNERS' CHASE (15 fncs) 2m 4f

4:00 (4:00) (Class 4) 4-Y-0+ **£2,862** (£840; £420; £209)

Form RPR

154- **1** **Fruity O'Rooney**[188] 5197 7-11-3 JamieMoore 120
(Gary Moore) *j. soundly: mde all: hld on wl whn pressed fr 2 out: drvn out* **5/6**[1]

155- **2** *1 1/4* **Double Dash**[200] 4991 6-11-3 MarkBradburne 119
(George Baker) *hld up in tch: trckd wnr 9th: hit 4 out: drvn to chal last: kpt on* **13/2**[3]

122- **3** *7* **Plunkett (IRE)**[192] 5156 7-11-3 PaulMoloney 120+
(Evan Williams) *t.k.h in rr: wnt 3rd at 9th: cl up and ch whn mstke and nrly uns rdr last: nt rcvr* **5/2**[2]

4 **4** *2 3/4* **Kylenoe Fairy (IRE)**[18] 1677 6-10-3 (t) MattGriffiths[(7)] 103
(Paul Henderson) *in tch in last pair tl outpcd 3 out* **20/1**

5 *29* **Forever Emo (IRE)**[253] 3963 7-11-0 RichieMcLernon[(3)] 84
(Jonjo O'Neill) *chsd wnr tl 9th: lost pl and last at 11th: lost tch after 4 out* **12/1**

5m 1.80s (-5.50) **Going Correction** -0.175s/f (Good) **5** Ran SP% **108.9**
Speed ratings (Par 105): **105,104,101,100,89**
CSF £6.54 TOTE £1.80: £1.20, £2.00; EX 6.50.

Owner Heart Of The South Racing **Bred** R W Russell **Trained** Lower Beeding, W Sussex

FOCUS
Not a bad little beginners' chase.

NOTEBOOK
Fruity O'Rooney jumped with enthusiasm and found plenty to make a winning debut over fences, although whether he'd have won had Plunkett not nearly unseated his rider at the last is doubtful. Rated 132 over hurdles, he's a strong stayer at the trip and his jumping should enable him to win again at some stage. (op 5-4 tchd 11-8 in a place)
Double Dash, who seemed well at home in heavy ground last season, jumped well in the main on this first start over fences, but always looked to be held by the winner. He'll appreciate a stiffer test. (op 15-2 tchd 8-1 and 6-1)
Plunkett(IRE) ◆, rated 123 over hurdles, was a bit keen under restraint, but he crept through the field to hold every chance from two out and was ridden to just about join the winner when blundering and nearly unseating Paul Moloney, who did well to recover, at the last. He'd probably have won had he jumped it cleanly and can gain compensation before long. (op 15-8 tchd 11-4)
Kylenoe Fairy(IRE) ran better than expected on this first run over fences since joining her current yard. (op 14-1)
Forever Emo(IRE), ex-Irish, ended up well held and may find better opportunities once handicapping. Official explanation: jockey said gelding hung right-handed (tchd 11-1 and 14-1)

1918 HILDON H'CAP HURDLE (11 hdls) 2m 6f 110y

4:30 (4:30) (Class 4) (0-105,105) 4-Y-0+ **£2,341** (£687; £343; £171)

Form RPR

4521 **1** **Scotsbrook Cloud**[10] 1798 5-10-0 **82** LeeStephens[(3)] 101+
(David Evans) *hld up in 5th: a gng wl: smooth hdwy 8th: led after 3 out: clr fr next: easily* **4/7**[1]

FP0- **2** *12* **Friends Of Tina (IRE)**[248] 4058 7-10-9 **88** NoelFehily 89
(Alex Hales) *hld up in rr: hdwy to chse ldng pair 3 out: wnt 2nd run-in: no ch w wnr* **8/1**[3]

3-03 **3** *1 1/2* **Romney Marsh**[14] 1732 9-10-6 **92** DannyBurton[(7)] 92
(Roger Curtis) *towards rr: hrd rdn 8th: styd on fr 3 out: wnt 3rd run-in: nt trble wnr* **11/1**

6-32 **4** *5* **Bon Spiel**[41] 1291 6-11-3 **103** (vt) MrTJCannon[(7)] 100
(Chris Gordon) *prom: led 7th tl after 3 out: 2nd and btn whn mstke next: wknd run-in* **5/1**[2]

U040 **5** *54* **Keckerrockernixes (IRE)**[27] 1592 4-10-7 **87** LeightonAspell 33
(Richard Rowe) *t.k.h: prom: hit 5th: nt fluent 6th: wknd 3 out* **50/1**

-420 **6** *14* **Casual Garcia**[71] 1230 5-11-9 **105** (bt) TommyPhelan[(3)] 39
(Mark Gillard) *led: reminders bnd after 3rd: hdd and rdn after 7th: wknd next* **14/1**

460/ **P** **Idris (GER)**[607] 4042 9-11-2 **98** CharlieStudd[(3)] —
(Philip Sharp) *in tch: rdn and wknd 8th: sn wl bhd: p.u bef 2 out* **40/1**

5m 37.0s (-5.50) **Going Correction** -0.10s/f (Good)
WFA 4 from 5yo+ 10lb **7** Ran SP% **110.8**
Speed ratings (Par 105): **105,100,100,98,79 74,—**
Tote Swingers: 1&2 £2.40, 1&3 £2.80, 2&3 £3.70 CSF £5.69 TOTE £1.50: £1.30, £2.90; EX 6.40.

Owner Walters Plant Hire Ltd **Bred** A E And P E Price **Trained** Pandy, Monmouths

FOCUS
A bloodless win for the well-handicapped winner.

NOTEBOOK
Scotsbrook Cloud ◆ escaped a penalty for his Ffos Las win and hacked up here. Always travelling strongly, he drew right away having taken the second-last and, for all that things will be tougher in future, he'll surely complete a hat-trick in this mood. (op 8-13 tchd 8-15 and 4-6 in places)

Friends Of Tina(IRE), still 9lb above her last winning mark, shaped well on this first start since February, keeping on again for second. (op 15-2)

Romney Marsh seems to be finding her form again, but remains high enough in the weights. (op 8-1)

Bon Spiel could have been expected to run a little better, and remains winless over hurdles. (op 13-2)

1919 LOUIS LATOUR H'CAP CHASE (13 fncs) 2m 2f

5:05 (5:10) (Class 4) (0-105,104) 4-Y-0+ **£2,862** (£840; £420; £209)

Form RPR

32-5 **1** **Sumdancer (NZ)**[164] 221 8-11-0 **97** MarcGoldstein[(5)] 104
(Michael Madgwick) *led: hdd and mstke 3rd: led 4 out: hung rt and hrd rdn 2 out: drvn out* **12/1**

55-6 **2** *1 1/4* **Nautical Approach (IRE)**[115] 843 7-11-3 **95** NoelFehily 102+
(Alex Hales) *hld up: hdwy to ld 9th: j. slowly and hdd next: pressed wnr after: kpt on run-in: a hld* **11/4**[2]

13P4 **3** *4 1/2* **Good Old Days (IRE)**[14] 1732 11-11-12 **104** TomSiddall 105
(Kim Bailey) *chsd ldrs: mstke and lost pl 7th: rallied 3 out: no imp run-in* **11/2**

06-1 **4** *2 1/2* **Randjo (FR)**[167] 183 5-11-3 **95** TomO'Brien 94
(Victor Dartnall) *chsd ldrs: mstke 4 out: rdn and outpcd fr 2 out* **9/4**[1]

4-43 **5** *21* **Space Star**[13] 1744 10-11-3 **95** DominicElsworth 75
(Paul Webber) *last at 4th: reminders 7th: sn wl bhd* **9/2**[3]

42U- **6** *10* **Littleton Aldor (IRE)**[184] 5289 10-10-0 **81** TommyPhelan[(3)] 57
(Mark Gillard) *reluctant to line up: s.s: j.rt: t.k.h and hdwy to ld 3rd: hdd 9th: sn wknd* **6/1**

4m 32.4s (-2.30) **Going Correction** -0.175s/f (Good) **6** Ran SP% **113.0**
Speed ratings (Par 105): **98,97,95,94,85 80**
Tote Swingers: 1&2 £4.60, 1&3 £4.00, 2&3 £3.80 CSF £46.16 TOTE £18.60: £10.00, £1.70; EX 54.00.

Owner Los Leader **Bred** Miss H M Thompson **Trained** Denmead, Hants

FOCUS
A competitive little handicap chase for the class.

NOTEBOOK
Sumdancer(NZ), just 3lb above his last successful mark, has done his winning in the past with cut in the ground, but having gone on again after four out, he kept finding under strong pressure and was always doing enough on the run-in. (op 17-2)

Nautical Approach(IRE) came tanking through to take it up before four out, but a slow jump there handed the momentum to Sumdancer and he was unable to stay on as well as that rival after the last. (op 5-1)

Good Old Days(IRE) ran better returned to fences, albeit he never looked like winning. (op 5-1 tchd 6-1)

Randjo(FR), making his debut for the yard, was 6lb higher than when winning on his final start for the Alners in May and he ran as though the race was needed. He's only five and we've still to see the best of him. (tchd 2-1 and 5-2)

1920 888SPORT AFFILIATES MARES' INTERMEDIATE OPEN NATIONAL HUNT FLAT RACE 1m 6f

5:40 (5:40) (Class 6) 4-6-Y-0 **£1,370** (£399; £199)

Form RPR

20- **1** **Violin Davis (FR)**[194] 5114 4-10-12 0 RWalsh 95+
(Paul Nicholls) *mde all: rdn clr 2f out: readily* **8/15**[1]

2 *3 3/4* **Lady Everywhere** 5-10-12 0 DarylJacob 91
(Nick Williams) *trckd wnr: stl gng wl 3f out: rdn and outpcd fnl 2f* **8/1**[3]

3 *2 1/2* **Tech Zinne** 4-10-12 0 DavidEngland 88
(George Baker) *chsd ldrs: rdn over 2f out: one pce* **7/2**[2]

4 *17* **Blue Lovell (FR)** 4-10-7 0 IanPopham[(5)] 67
(Caroline Keevil) *chsd ldrs: outpcd and lost pl 5f out: n.d after* **25/1**

5 *5* **Round About**[192] 5-10-5 0 MrJBarber[(7)] 63
(Paul Nicholls) *t.k.h in rr: sme hdwy after 4f: disp 2nd 4f out: wknd over 2f out* **8/1**[3]

6 *36* **Schmetterling (IRE)** 6-10-12 0 PaulMoloney 18
(Sophie Leech) *hld up in 6th: outpcd 5f out: sn bhd* **33/1**

7 *4* **Brandy N' Lovage** 5-10-5 0 MrJBanks[(7)] 13
(Richard Mitchell) *a bhd: rdn and no ch fnl 6f* **33/1**

8 *38* **So Jo Beach** 4-10-9 0 CharlieStudd[(3)] —
(Philip Sharp) *in tch: wknd over 6f out: sn bhd* **50/1**

3m 24.5s (-6.60) **8** Ran SP% **121.4**
Tote Swingers: 1&2 £1.80, 1&3 £1.50, 2&3 £2.00 CSF £6.28 TOTE £1.70: £1.02, £1.20, £1.90; EX 6.00.

Owner Andrew Polson **Bred** Claude Quellier **Trained** Ditcheat, Somerset

FOCUS
An uncompetitive mares' bumper.

NOTEBOOK
Violin Davis(FR), the only ride on the card for Ruby Walsh, she was soon in front and gradually drew clear down the straight. Seventh in last season's Listed mares' bumper at Aintree, she will be suited by a return to 2m and could be the type to win a few once sent hurdling. (tchd 4-7 and 8-13 in places)

Lady Everywhere, whose dam won on the Flat and over hurdles, made a satisfactory debut in second and will prove well suited further once hurdling. (op 9-1 tchd 10-1)

Tech Zinne, related to some useful Flat winners, shaped encouragingly back in third and looks capable of winning something similar for her in-form yard. (op 9-2)

Blue Lovell(FR), a half-sister to winning jumpers in France and Britain, made some late ground and should improve over further.

Round About, the Nicholls second string, had shown little in points prior to placing in April, but she was too keen on this first start in a bumper and dropped right away late on. Official explanation: jockey said mare ran too freely (tchd 9-1)

T/Plt: £272.70 to a £1 stake. Pool:£57,846 - 154.83 winning tickets T/Qpdt: £62.90 to a £1 stake. Pool:£5,178 - 60.90 winning tickets LM

[1742]WORCESTER (L-H)

Wednesday, October 20

OFFICIAL GOING: Good (good to firm in places on run-in and cathedral bend)

Cathedral bend Inside, run-in bends out 9yds adding 27yds to a 2m race.

Wind: Light half-against Weather: Fine and sunny

1921 BOOK CHRISTMAS PARTIES AT WORCESTER RACECOURSE MARES' NOVICES' HURDLE (8 hdls) 2m

2:10 (2:10) (Class 4) 4-Y-0+ **£2,397** (£698; £349)

Form RPR

043- **1** **Sparky May**[188] [5200] 5-10-5 0 KeiranBurke(5) 111+
(Patrick Rodford) *hld up: hdwy and hmpd appr 3 out: rdn to ld flat: hung lft: r.o* **6/1**[3]

3-2 **2** *2* **Boragh Princess (IRE)**[14] [1724] 6-11-3 112 APMcCoy 117
(Gordon Elliott, Ire) *a.p: chsd ldr 4th: led 3 out: rdn and hdd flat: styd on same pce* **13/8**[1]

5U5- **3** *14* **Sally's Idea**[206] [4907] 4-10-7 0 AdrianLane(3) 99+
(Donald McCain) *chsd ldrs: rdn appr 3 out: wkng whn blnd last* **66/1**

2 **4** *1* **Lucy's Perfect**[17] [1689] 4-10-10 0 (b) TomScudamore 96
(David Pipe) *chsd ldrs tl led after 2nd: rdn and hdd 3 out: wknd bef last* **7/1**

5 *6* **Aine's Delight (IRE)**[20] 4-10-10 0 NickScholfield 90
(Andy Turnell) *hld up: hdwy 4th: rdn appr 3 out: sn wknd* **28/1**

20 **6** *1 1/2* **Try Cat**[14] [1724] 4-10-10 0 (t) RichardJohnson 88
(Philip Hobbs) *led to 2nd: chsd ldrs tl rdn and wknd appr 3 out: mstke next* **14/1**

7 *9* **Sworn Tigress (GER)**[165] 5-10-10 0 AndrewTinkler 80
(George Baker) *hld up: wknd after 4th* **3/1**[2]

-220 **8** *1/2* **Stir On The Sea (IRE)**[13] [1746] 4-10-10 100 HaddenFrost 80
(James Frost) *hld up: bhd fr 5th* **16/1**

9 *2 1/2* **Primera Rossa**[21] 4-10-10 0 JamesDavies 77
(J S Moore) *hld up: a in rr: bhd fr 5th* **100/1**

4-5 **10** *1/2* **Genny Wren**[26] [1607] 4-10-10 0 SamJones 77
(Renee Robeson) *mid-div: wknd 5th* **40/1**

11 *25* **Illysantachristina**[192] 7-10-10 0 ChristianWilliams 55
(Bernard Llewellyn) *led 2nd: sn hdd: mstke 4th: wknd next* **50/1**

F- **P** **Abby Belle (IRE)**[507] [539] 4-10-10 0 WayneHutchinson —
(Mrs H Parrott) *hld up: a in rr: t.o whn p.u bef 3 out* **66/1**

6- **P** **Fraam Lea**[131] [3980] 4-10-3 0 MrJFlook(7) —
(Andrew Price) *hld up: a in rr: t.o whn p.u bef 3 out* **150/1**

00FP **P** **La Chemme**[17] [1688] 4-10-10 0 GerardTumelty —
(Reg Hollinshead) *bhd whn blnd 2nd: t.o whn p.u bef 3 out* **100/1**

3m 43.5s (-3.80) **Going Correction** +0.075s/f (Yiel)
WFA 4 from 5yo+ 9lb **14** Ran SP% **115.9**
Speed ratings (Par 105): **112,111,104,103,100 99,95,95,93,93 81,—,—,—**
Tote Swingers: 1&2 £2.30, 1&3 £47.50, 2&3 £28.20 CSF £15.60 TOTE £6.70: £2.20, £1.30, £10.70; EX 17.30.
Owner Bill Muddyman **Bred** Ruxley Holdings Ltd **Trained** Ash, Somerset

FOCUS

The ground was good to firm in the view of one of the senior riders in the first. A modest mares' event lacking strength in depth. The pace was sound enough.

NOTEBOOK

Sparky May showed ability in bumpers last term without winning and made a successful hurdles bow following her summer break. She had work to do entering the straight, having been slightly hampered on the home turn when attempting to improve, but stayed on strongly to claim the favourite on the lengthy run-in. There is likely to be a bit more to come from her over further. (op 15-2 tchd 11-2)

Boragh Princess(IRE) was the only previous winner in the line-up and the pick on previous form. Dropped in trip, she looked set to win when going clear, only to be worn down on the run-in. She did not do a whole lot wrong other than perhaps getting to the front a shade early. (tchd 6-4)

Sally's Idea, appearing for the first time since March, was one-paced from the home turn but did stay on again after a last-flight mistake. This was an advance on what she had shown last season and a step up in trip might pay off. She does not look straightforward though. (op 50-1)

Lucy's Perfect ran respectably without building on what she showed at Huntingdon on her hurdles debut. (op 11-2 tchd 15-2 in a place)

Aine's Delight(IRE) won a 1m2f handicap a year ago but did not show much in a light Flat campaign this year. A half-sister to her trainer's smart hurdler Blue Bajan, she travelled quite well but did not appear to get home. (op 25-1)

Try Cat, equipped with a tongue tie for the first time on this drop in trip, was on the retreat turning in and does not seem to be progressing. (op 20-1)

Sworn Tigress(GER) had a successful AW campaign in the spring and is currently rated 76 on the Flat, but showed little on this first try over hurdles. (op 10-3 tchd 7-2)

Stir On The Sea(IRE) Official explanation: jockey said filly hung right-handed

1922 WS-PROMOTIONS.CO.UK TRIBUTE BANDS MAIDEN HURDLE (10 hdls) 2m 4f

2:40 (2:40) (Class 4) 4-Y-0+ **£2,329** (£678; £339)

Form RPR

06- **1** **Spock (FR)**[190] [5178] 5-11-0 0 HarrySkelton 101+
(Paul Nicholls) *hld up: racd keenly: hdwy 6th: led 2 out: hung rt flat: drvn out* **15/2**

0 **2** *1 1/4* **Alnwick**[14] [1734] 6-11-0 0 WillKennedy 95
(Peter Cundell) *hld up: pushed along after 5th: hdwy next: chsd wnr 2 out: rdn and ev ch flat: r.o* **4/1**[2]

5P-U **3** *18* **Spiritonthemount (USA)**[23] [797] 5-10-11 0 (b) WayneKavanagh(3) 80
(Peter Hiatt) *chsd ldrs: led 4th: hdd 2 out: wknd last* **25/1**

034- **4** *8* **Royal Role**[185] [5250] 6-11-0 85 JackDoyle 69
(Peter Pritchard) *hld up: hdwy after 4th: wknd 3 out* **33/1**

413F **5** *shd* **Whereveryougoigo (IRE)**[10] [1795] 4-10-11 0 DonalDevereux(3) 69
(Peter Bowen) *hld up: hdwy 5th: rdn and ev ch 3 out: wknd bef last* **5/1**[3]

65 **6** *14* **Casper's Shadow (IRE)**[18] [1680] 4-11-0 0 RhysFlint 55
(Keith Goldsworthy) *prom: chsd ldr 5th: rdn 7th: wknd appr 2 out* **25/1**

43 **7** *1 1/4* **Twentypoundluck (IRE)**[11] [1783] 5-11-0 0 AndrewTinkler 54
(Patrick Griffin, Ire) *chsd ldrs tl wknd appr 3 out* **7/2**[1]

00P- **8** *32* **Tiffany Jones**[192] [5154] 7-10-7 0 AidanColeman 15
(John Spearing) *hld up: hdwy 4th: wknd 7th: t.o* **25/1**

0P **P** **Mr Johnson (IRE)**[46] [1467] 7-10-7 0 MrJEngland(7) —
(Michael Gates) *led to 4th: wknd after next: t.o whn p.u bef 3 out* **80/1**

0-0P **P** **Middleton Red (IRE)**[17] [1703] 6-11-0 0 JodieMogford —
(Graham Smith) *a in rr: mstke 1st: t.o whn p.u bef 3 out* **100/1**

P **Rebel High (IRE)**[136] 6-10-9 0 DavidBass(5) —
(Derek Frankland) *hld up: bhd fr 5th: t.o whn p.u bef 3 out* **16/1**

43-4 **P** **Big Knickers**[24] [1629] 5-10-7 0 DougieCostello —
(Neil Mulholland) *mid-div: lost pl and rdn after 4th: t.o whn p.u bef next* **7/2**[1]

P **Sourchamp (FR)**[402] 4-11-0 0 NickScholfield —
(Arthur Whiting) *hld up in tch: lost pl 4th: t.o whn p.u bef 6th* **40/1**

4m 46.3s (-1.10) **Going Correction** +0.075s/f (Yiel) **13** Ran SP% **117.9**
Speed ratings (Par 105): **105,104,97,94,94 88,87,75,—,— —,—,—**
Tote Swingers: 1&2 £11.00, 1&3 £27.40, 2&3 £25.60 CSF £35.63 TOTE £10.40: £3.80, £1.10, £5.90; EX 42.30.
Owner Jeffrey Hordle **Bred** Jaques Cypres Et Al **Trained** Ditcheat, Somerset

FOCUS

A weak maiden hurdle in which the first two finished clear.

NOTEBOOK

Spock(FR) shaped with limited promise in a couple of bumpers in the spring but represents a top stable and was good enough to go in first time over hurdles. Noticeably green, he raced keenly and tended to wander going into his obstacles, then once in front hung over to the stands' rail like quite a few horses do at this track. He won comfortably enough when straightened up and ought to improve on the bare form, although he won't reach his full potential until he switches to chasing. (op 11-2)

Alnwickdid not have things go his way on his hurdling debut, but he ran a much better race here. He was perhaps flattered by the eventual margin of defeat, but this decent handicapper at 2m on the Flat looks well capable of winning in modest company over hurdles. However, he was reported to have finished distressed. Official explanation: jockey said gelding finished distressed (tchd 7-2 and 9-2)

Spiritonthemount(USA), another stayer on the Flat, had not shown much in previous hurdles ventures and unseated on his chase debut in the summer. He tried to kick away on the home turn but was reeled in two out and soon on the retreat.

Royal Role was well held in fourth on this seasonal reappearance and may be worth stepping back up in trip. (op 25-1)

Whereveryougoigo(IRE), an early casualty on his hurdles debut at Ffos Las, has the scope to make a go of it at this game but weakened rather tamely after holding every chance. (tchd 4-1 and 11-2)

Twentypoundluck(IRE), an Irish challenger, probably needs further. (op 9-2 tchd 5-1)

Middleton Red(IRE) Official explanation: jockey said gelding made a noise (op 5-1)

Big Knickers made the frame in each of her bumpers but was in trouble and pulled up by halfway on this hurdles bow. She was reported by her trainer to have a breathing problem. Official explanation: trainer said mare had a breathing problem (op 5-1)

1923 FRED RIMELL MEMORIAL NOVICES' CHASE (18 fncs) 2m 7f

3:15 (3:15) (Class 3) 5-Y-0+ **£4,860** (£1,467; £755; £400)

Form RPR

365- **1** **The Giant Bolster**[194] [5112] 5-11-0 0 RodiGreene 141+
(David Bridgwater) *chsd ldrs: nt fluent 3rd and 5th: wnt 2nd after 12th: led 3 out: j.rt last 2: rdn clr flat* **5/2**[2]

523- **2** *11* **Bob 'N' You (IRE)**[194] [5113] 7-11-0 0 DougieCostello 132+
(Ian Williams) *a.p: mstke 8th: chal 3 out: hmpd last 2 fences: no ex flat* **13/8**[1]

3F-6 **3** *15* **Ballydub (IRE)**[11] [1769] 7-11-0 125 (b) RichardJohnson 123+
(Philip Hobbs) *chsd ldr: mstke 9th: led next: mstke and hdd 11th: led again 12th: hit 13th: hdd 3 out: wknd last* **7/2**[3]

0/P- **4** *111* **Slash And Burn (IRE)**[83] [1130] 8-11-0 130 (t) APMcCoy —
(Gordon Elliott, Ire) *led to 10th: led again next: hdd & wknd 12th: t.o* **5/1**

4656 **P** **Indian Pipe Dream (IRE)**[3] [1885] 8-11-0 100 TomMessenger —
(Aytach Sadik) *j.rt and mstkes: a bhd: t.o whn p.u bef 13th* **66/1**

5m 45.3s (2.70) **Going Correction** +0.075s/f (Yiel) **5** Ran SP% **107.0**
Speed ratings: **98,94,88,—,—**
CSF £6.85 TOTE £2.70: £1.40, £1.80; EX 7.20.
Owner Simon Hunt **Bred** Gestut Fahrhof **Trained** Icomb, Gloucs

FOCUS

A race with some smart performers on its winners' roll, including Pride Of Dulcote and Heltornic in recent years, and Call Equiname and Barton Bank when it was run over 3f shorter in the 90s. None of this year's field is likely to reach the same heights.

NOTEBOOK

The Giant Bolster was quite impressive on this chasing debut and can progress to better things. Rated 140 over hurdles following good efforts in Grade 1s at Cheltenham and Aintree in the spring, he moved smoothly into the lead before clearing away. His jumping was solid, although he did go out to his right over each of the last two fences, and he handles softer ground too. (tchd 11-4)

Bob 'N' You(IRE) was another useful novice hurdler and he made a pleasing chase debut, coming through to hold every chance three out. He could not go with the winner from the last but is entitled to strip fitter for this. There is room for a bit of improvement in his jumping. (op 15-8 tchd 2-1 in a place)

Ballydub(IRE) has been let down byy his jumping in his previous chases and that was the case again. He has more than enough ability to win races over fences but looks a risky proposition, and the reapplied blinkers did not have a positive effect here as he appeared a shade reluctant once he had forfeited the lead. (op 10-3 tchd 4-1)

Slash And Burn(IRE), who has left Charlie Swan's care since his last run in July, is officially rated 130 over fences. He made the running, jumping soundly in the main, but dropped out very quickly down the back and completed in his own time. (op 9-2 tchd 4-1)

1924 CLEANEVENT H'CAP CHASE (12 fncs) 2m

3:50 (3:50) (Class 5) (0-85,85) 4-Y-0+ **£1,712** (£499; £249)

Form RPR

6F4P **1** **Buds Dilemma**[18] [1678] 6-10-5 **67** DonalDevereux(3) 79+
(Peter Bowen) *chsd ldrs: lost pl appr 4th: rallied 3 out: led flat: rdn out* **8/1**

F **2** *8* **Turn Up (IRE)**[17] [1710] 7-11-4 **84** (t) MrJMRidley(7) 90+
(Matt Sheppard) *led: clr 4 out: mstke 2 out: rdn and hdd flat: no ex* **20/1**

5640 **3** *3 1/4* **Fongoli**[13] [1745] 4-10-6 **79** (b) MrMMO'Connor(5) 73
(Brendan Powell) *chsd ldr: rdn appr 4 out: wknd flat* **5/1**[1]

U-66 **4** *11* **Secret Cavern (USA)**[158] [339] 8-10-13 **72** JackDoyle 66
(Peter Pritchard) *hld up: hmpd 5th: hdwy 8th: wkng whn mstke last* **14/1**

523U **5** *5* **More Shennanigans**[4] [1872] 9-10-10 **72** RyanMania(3) 61
(Jean McGregor) *hld up: mstke 5th: hmpd 3 out: nvr on terms* **7/1**[3]

4/1- **6** *5* **Guns Of Love (IRE)**[531] [199] 8-11-2 **75** CharliePoste 58
(Robin Dickin) *chsd ldrs: rdn appr 4 out: wknd 2 out* **9/1**

322- **7** *1/2* **Lerida**[208] [4864] 8-11-4 **80** (p) FearghalDavis(3) 63
(Sharon Watt) *mid-div: j.lft 1st: hdwy 4th: wknd appr 4 out* **8/1**

3041 **8** *1* **Janal (IRE)**[19] [1665] 7-10-5 **71** GaryRutherford(7) 53
(Stuart Coltherd) *hld up: mstke 5th: bhd fr 7th* **6/1**[2]

-U00 **9** *10* **Commanche Dream**[13] [1742] 7-10-11 **77** PaulGallagher(7) 50
(Simon Lewis) *hld up: bhd fr 6th: t.o* **9/1**

0F/P **10** *15* **Hollandia (IRE)**[44] [1494] 9-10-3 **69** MrRHawkins(7) 28
(Kathleen Sanderson) *hmpd 1st: hld up: hdwy after 3rd: rdn and wknd appr 4 out: t.o* **16/1**

-406 **F** **Shadow Wood (IRE)**[17] 1700 6-11-12 **85**....................(p) AndrewTinkler —
(Patrick Griffin, Ire) *bhd: hdwy 6th: wkng whn mstke and fell 3 out: fatally injured* **7/1**[3]

3m 56.3s (4.70) **Going Correction** +0.075s/f (Yiel)
WFA 4 from 6yo+ 9lb 11 Ran SP% **115.5**
Speed ratings (Par 103): **91,87,85,79,77 74,74,74,69,61** —
Tote Swingers: 1&2 £41.80, 1&3 £5.70, 2&3 £27.60 CSF £142.49 CT £880.80 TOTE £9.30: £2.70, £10.30, £2.00; EX 266.70.

Owner Monty Belton **Bred** M P B Bloodstock Ltd **Trained** Little Newcastle, Pembrokes

FOCUS
A low-grade handicap chase and not form to treat too positively. Runner-up Turn Up set a sound pace and few got into it.

NOTEBOOK
Buds Dilemma, rated just 67 and carrying bottomweight, was suited in the end by the brisk pace of this race. Down in trip, she had lost a prominent early pitch and had only a couple behind her turning out of the back straight, but she began to pick up ground once in line for home and won going away after leading on the flat. This was her first career win but her confidence ought to have been boosted and there might be more to come from her now. (op 9-1)

Turn Up(IRE), an ex-Irish gelding, was a faller on his debut for this yard earlier this month. The drop in trip and better ground seemed to suit and he ran a bold race from the front, only giving best late on to a mare who was receiving 17lb. (op 16-1)

Fongolicame in for a support and she ran better than she had been doing. She was never far from the pace and the drop back to 2m was a positive. (op 9-1 tchd 9-2)

Secret Cavern(USA) was appearing for the first time since May and he ran respectably. (op 12-1)

More Shennanigans didn't get far at Kelso four days earlier but had been in fair form prior to that. He was never seen with a chance but did reverse Hexham running with Janal. (op 13-2 tchd 11-2)

Guns Of Love(IRE) ran creditably on this first start since winning at Wincanton in May 2009. (op 7-1 tchd 13-2)

Janal(IRE) was 7lb higher than when wining at Hexham and racing on a much faster surface. She was soon struggling after a mistake down the back. (op 9-2 tchd 7-1)

1925 MYSON RADIATORS H'CAP HURDLE (10 hdls) 2m 4f
4:20 (4:21) (Class 4) (0-105,105) 4-Y-0+ **£3,425** (£998; £499)

Form RPR

454- **1** **Jeanry (FR)**[207] 4897 7-9-11 **83**.. CDTimmons(7) 82
(Arthur Whitehead) *chsd ldrs: rdn appr 3 out: styd on u.p to ld nr fin* **12/1**

3-42 **2** *shd* **Lord Landen (IRE)**[154] 407 5-11-12 **105**........................ AidanColeman 105+
(Rachel Hobbs) *led: rdn and hung rt flat: hdd nr fin* **5/1**[2]

0F/0 **3** *2* **Sumner (IRE)**[4] 1723 6-10-11 **90**....................................(v) RichardJohnson 88+
(David Evans) *hld up: hdwy 6th: chsd wnr after next: j.rt 2 out: no ex nr fin* **5/1**[2]

-042 **4** *1 1/4* **Santamina (IRE)**[94] 1028 4-11-2 **98**..........................(p) DonalDevereux(3) 95
(Peter Bowen) *a.p: chsd ldr 4th: tl pushed along after 7th: rdn and hung rt flat: styd on* **20/1**

41F3 **5** *4 1/2* **Kilmore West (IRE)**[17] 1709 5-11-0 **100**........................ MrPJTolman(7) 92
(Tim Vaughan) *hld up: hdwy 4th: outpcd after 7th: styd on flat* **7/1**

5F6- **6** *9* **Spot The Ball (IRE)**[226] 4490 5-10-11 **90**............................. APMcCoy 75
(Jonjo O'Neill) *hld up: hdwy 7th: rdn bef next: wknd appr last* **7/1**

2405 **7** *23* **Art Man**[26] 1601 7-11-0 **93**..(b) HaddenFrost 56
(James Frost) *hld up: hdwy 4th: wknd appr 3 out: t.o* **11/1**

-642 **8** *1* **Kilvergan Boy (IRE)**[132] 698 6-11-4 **97**........................ PaddyBrennan 59
(Nigel Twiston-Davies) *prom: nt fluent: drvn along 4th: sn wknd: t.o* **9/2**[1]

000- **9** *3 3/4* **Stage Right**[413] 1376 9-9-7 **79** oh15.................................... MissCBoxall(7) 38
(Simon Lewis) *hld up: bhd fr 4th: t.o* **100/1**

/FP- **P** **All Things Equal (IRE)**[256] 11-10-11 **90**............................ DaveCrosse —
(Claire Dyson) *chsd ldr to 4th: sn lost pl: t.o whn p.u bef next* **40/1**

-344 **P** **Pocket Too**[17] 1709 7-11-7 **100**...................................(p) AndrewTinkler —
(Matthew Salaman) *mid-div: rdn and wknd after 4th: t.o whn p.u bef 7th* **11/2**[3]

4m 51.8s (4.40) **Going Correction** +0.075s/f (Yiel)
WFA 4 from 5yo+ 10lb 11 Ran SP% **116.1**
Speed ratings (Par 105): **94,93,93,92,90 87,78,77,76,— —**
Tote Swingers: 1&2 £16.50, 1&3 £22.30, 2&3 £6.10 CSF £70.12 CT £344.88 TOTE £10.40: £2.60, £2.70, £1.90; EX 90.60.

Owner A J Whitehead **Bred** Jean Biraben And Henri Soler **Trained** Aston on Clun, Shropshire

FOCUS
A moderate handicap run in a time more than five seconds slower than the earlier maiden hurdle.

NOTEBOOK
Jeanry(FR) ran some fair races last term and stepped up on those on this seasonal bow, staying on relentlessly to lead on the flat. He has reportedly strengthened up, and judging by his action he may not mind a return to softer conditions. (op 14-1 tchd 16-1)

Lord Landen(IRE) settled better and tried to make all, but after seeing off the third he succumbed on the run-in. This was a solid effort under top weight and he should get off the mark before long. (op 8-1)

Sumner(IRE) came in for support and loomed up going well, but did not find as much as he had promised and was just held after jumping out to his right two out. He is well treated on his old Flat form and this was a step forward on his recent return to hurdling. (op 11-1)

Santamina(IRE) was never far from the action on this handicap debut and gave the impression that he won't mind a return to further. (op 16-1)

Kilmore West(IRE) had track and ground to suit, but the trip was on the sharp side and he was coming home well after the leaders had pulled away from him. He was reported to have hung left-handed throughout. Official explanation: jockey said gelding hung left-handed throughout (op 9-2 tchd 8-1 and 17-2 in a place)

Spot The Ball(IRE) could never reach a threatening position on this handicap bow but may improve for his first run since March. (op 11-2)

Kilvergan Boy(IRE) was racing from a 7lb higher mark but should still have shown more than he did. Paddy Brennan reported that the gelding was never travelling, and the vet added that the horse had sustained a wound on its foreleg. Official explanation: jockey said gelding never travelled; vet said gelding sustained a wound on its foreleg

Pocket Too was unbeaten in two previous starts at Worcester and has become very well handicapped, but he was in trouble at an early stage and eventually pulled up. Official explanation: trainer said gelding finished distressed (tchd 13-2)

1926 RICHARD DAVIS MEMORIAL H'CAP CHASE (15 fncs) 2m 4f 110y
4:55 (4:55) (Class 3) (0-130,123) 4-Y-0 **£5,703** (£1,684; £842; £421; £210)

Form RPR

3F-1 **1** **Sir Ian (IRE)**[26] 1604 7-11-7 **118**.................................... TomScudamore 134+
(Charlie Longsdon) *mde all: clr fr 3 out: rdn out* **9/4**[1]

3-31 **2** *6* **Alesandro Mantegna (IRE)**[18] 1676 5-11-10 **121**..............(p) RhysFlint 129
(Keith Goldsworthy) *chsd wnr to 8th: remained handy: rdn appr 3 out: wnt 2nd again last: styd on same pce* **9/2**[2]

3601 **3** *13* **Another Trump (NZ)**[45] 1481 6-11-6 **117**................................ APMcCoy 115
(Jonjo O'Neill) *hld up: hdwy 11th: rdn and hung lft after 2 out: wkng whn j.rt and lost 2nd last* **9/2**[2]

213- **4** *5* **Holmwood Legend**[194] 5118 9-11-3 **119**.......................... KieranBurke(5) 111
(Patrick Rodford) *prom: chsd ldr 8th: mstke next: rdn and wknd after 2 out* **7/1**

-552 **5** *nk* **Storm Of Applause (IRE)**[26] 1604 9-11-8 **119**............ RichardJohnson 110
(Philip Hobbs) *chsd ldrs: mstke 9th: wknd 4 out* **5/1**[3]

3335 **6** *10* **Nudge And Nurdle (IRE)**[28] 1577 9-11-11 **122**............... PaddyBrennan 104
(Nigel Twiston-Davies) *hld up: wknd appr 4 out: t.o* **9/1**

22-B **U** **Haar**[164] 234 6-11-12 **123**..(t) NickScholfield —
(Andy Turnell) *chsd ldrs: nt fluent 4th and next: wknd appr 4 out: t.o whn mstke and uns rdr last* **20/1**

5m 4.30s (-2.40) **Going Correction** +0.075s/f (Yiel) 7 Ran SP% **111.1**
Speed ratings (Par 107): **107,104,99,97,97 93,—**
Tote Swingers: 1&2 £2.30, 1&3 £3.10, 2&3 £5.90 CSF £12.31 TOTE £2.10: £1.10, £4.60; EX 14.70.

Owner Mrs Phillip Stevenson **Bred** Mrs Valerie Hore **Trained** Over Norton, Oxon

FOCUS
A competitive event contested by several progressive types, and the form appears solid.

NOTEBOOK
Sir Ian(IRE) shrugged off a 10lb rise for his win over C&D, making all and staying on well, and is clearly still on the upgrade. He needs decent ground and around a month between races, so it could be that he won't be seen out again until the spring. (op 5-2 after 11-4 early in a place, tchd 15-8)

Alesandro Mantegna(IRE) ran well off this 7lb higher mark, keeping on for second in a manner which suggests he will appreciate a return to further. (op 5-1 tchd 6-1)

Another Trump(NZ)'s course-and-distance win has been advertised by runner-up Frosted Grape, but he went up no less than 16lb for that. The rise appeared to tell, as he flattened out after improving to look a threat. (tchd 4-1 and 5-1)

Holmwood Legend ◆ put in a couple of scruffy jumps on this seasonal return but gave strong indications that he is capable of winning more races from this sort of mark, only fading two from home. (op 13-2 tchd 8-1)

Storm Of Applause(IRE), one of the more exposed in the field, was 10lb better off with Sir Ian on their meeting here but was beaten a lot further this time. He was plugging on at the end. (tchd 9-2)

Nudge And Nurdle(IRE) had no excuses on acount of trip and ground and had been eased 2lb, but this was more competitive and he had been seen off by the home turn. (op 8-1 tchd 10-1)

Haar is yet to win over fences and his record includes four seconds and five non-completions now. Equipped with a tongue-tie on this first start in six months, he dropped away turning in and was well adrift when unshipping his rider at the last. (op 16-1 tchd 22-1)

1927 P BROWN FENCING "NEWCOMERS" STANDARD OPEN NATIONAL HUNT FLAT RACE 2m
5:30 (5:30) (Class 6) 3-5-Y-0 **£1,370** (£399; £199)

Form RPR

1 **Twirling Magnet (IRE)** 4-11-10 0.. APMcCoy 104+
(Jonjo O'Neill) *hld up: hdwy over 5f out: led 2f out: drvn out* **11/10**[1]

2 *1 1/2* **I Know The Code (IRE)** 5-11-10 0............................. RichardJohnson 100+
(Noel Chance) *trckd ldrs: hung lft over 3f out: rdn and ev ch 2f out: styd on same pce ins fnl f* **9/2**[3]

3 *2 3/4* **Divine Folly (IRE)** 5-11-5 0.. DavidBass(5) 97
(Lawney Hill) *chsd ldr: rdn over 3f out: outpcd over 2f out: hung rt and styd on ins fnl f* **10/1**

4 *6* **Vinomore** 4-11-0 0.. SamTwiston-Davies(3) 84
(Shaun Lycett) *prom: rdn over 2f out: wknd over 1f out* **20/1**

5 *3/4* **Midnight Molly** 3-10-0 0... TimmyMurphy 67
(John Spearing) *hld up: pushed along over 3f out: nvr on terms* **4/1**[2]

6 *1 1/4* **Onetokeep (IRE)** 5-11-10 0.. TomScudamore 89
(Anabel L M King) *set stdy pce tl qcknd 6f out: rdn and hdd 2f out: sn hung rt and wknd* **12/1**

7 *12* **Megan May** 4-11-3 0.. DougieCostello 70
(Ian Williams) *hld up in tch: racd keenly: pushed along 7f out: wknd over 3f out* **33/1**

8 *2 3/4* **Haydens Mount** 5-11-10 0.. HaddenFrost 75
(James Frost) *chsd ldrs: rdn over 3f out: wknd over 2f out* **40/1**

9 *2* **Kayf Paradis** 5-11-3 0... WillKennedy 66
(John Spearing) *hld up: hdwy 10f out: wknd over 3f out* **25/1**

10 *6* **Cladding** 4-11-7 0.. DannyCook(3) 67
(John Panvert) *hld up: wknd 4f out: t.o* **50/1**

11 *28* **Sleeping Policeman (FR)** 4-11-10 0................................ AndrewTinkler 39
(Anna Bramall) *hld up: wknd 4f out: t.o* **40/1**

4m 2.80s (21.10) **Going Correction** +0.075s/f (Yiel)
WFA 3 from 4yo 17lb 4 from 5yo 9lb 11 Ran SP% **121.0**
Speed ratings (Par 101): **50,49,47,44,44 43,37,36,35,32 18**
Tote Swingers: 1&2 £2.30, 1&3 £4.40, 2&3 £5.40. totesuper7: Win: Not won. Place: Not won. CSF £5.86 TOTE £2.50: £1.70, £2.50, £3.10; EX 7.70.

Owner Mrs Gay Smith **Bred** G Quirk **Trained** Cheltenham, Gloucs

FOCUS
No previous form to go on in this bumper, which was slowly run until the pace picked up towards the end of the back straight.

NOTEBOOK
Twirling Magnet(IRE), well supported ahead of this debut, is closely related to smart jumper Massini's Maguire (by Dr Massini) and he cost 150,000euros as a 3-y-o. He had to work a bit to hold the runner-up but looks a decent prospect and may take in another bumper before switching to hurdles. (tchd 10-11, after early 6-4 in places)

I Know The Code(IRE), a half-brother to the stable's bumper winner Gentle Drifter, has more scope than a lot of these and he shaped with plenty of promise, holding every chance and rallying close home. He should win a race or two when switched to hurdles. (op 5-1 tchd 11-2)

Divine Folly(IRE), from the family of smart Irish jumper Colnel Rayburn, was renewing his effort late on after becoming slightly outpaced. (op 13-2)

Vinomore, a half-sister to fair hurdler/chaser More Equity but a cheap buy, ran creditably but would have more chance in races confined to her own sex. (op 16-1 tchd 25-1)

Midnight Molly, a 3-y-o filly getting all the allowances, came in for a deal of support. Held up, she was outpaced when the tempo lifted and could never get back into it, but was running on at the end to suggest that she has ability. (op 12-1 tchd 7-2)

Onetokeep(IRE), the long-time leader, ran green but finished well clear of the others.

T/Plt: £1,188.30 to a £1 stake. Pool:£59,989 - 36.85 winning tickets T/Qpdt: £245 to a £1 stake. Pool:£5,596 - 16.90 winning tickets CR

[1757]CARLISLE (R-H)

Thursday, October 21

OFFICIAL GOING: Good (good to firm in places on hurdle course; 7.4)

Wind: Fairly strong, half against Weather: Fresh, half against

1928 MOLSON COORS MAIDEN HURDLE (12 hdls) 3m 1f

2:20 (2:20) (Class 4) 4-Y-0+ **£2,740** (£798; £399)

Form RPR

56- **1** **Rupin (FR)**[226] 4502 5-10-11 0 .... RyanMania(3) 115+
(Howard Johnson) *sn trcking ldr: led gng wl 3 out: drew clr fr next: easily* **4/1**[3]

4-P **2** *36* **Imperial Breeze (IRE)**[12] 1787 5-10-9 97 .... EJO'Connell(5) 83
(J J Lambe, Ire) *hld up: stdy hdwy 8th: rdn 3 out: sn outpcd: wnt mod 2nd after last: no ch w wnr* **11/10**[1]

6-3U **3** *20* **Keoghs Bar (IRE)**[20] 1663 6-11-0 95 .... JPByrne 72+
(Irene J Monaghan, Ire) *j.lft: led to 3 out: wknd next: btn whn j. bdly lft last: sn lost 2nd pl: t.o* **5/2**[2]

U6 **4** *1 1/4* **Tenth Avenue (IRE)**[54] 1401 5-10-11 0 .... AdrianLane(3) 60
(Donald McCain) *t.k.h: trckd ldrs: nt fluent and rdn 4 out: wknd fr next* **11/1**

0-65 **P** **Glen Vale**[44] 1499 7-11-0 0 .... BrianHughes —
(John Wade) *prom: outpcd whn nt fluent 7th: sn wknd: t.o whn p.u bef 3 out* **16/1**

6m 15.4s (-22.80) **Going Correction** -1.05s/f (Hard) 5 Ran SP% **110.4**
Speed ratings (Par 105): **94,82,76,75,—**
CSF £9.25 TOTE £4.40: £2.30, £1.30; EX 7.30.
Owner J Howard Johnson **Bred** Fernand Sellier **Trained** Billy Row, Co Durham

FOCUS
A poor race but the easy winner may turn out to be decent. The second was well below the form he has shown over shorter.

NOTEBOOK
Rupin(FR), well beaten in a bumper and a novice hurdle, was having his first start since March. Keen early, he was soon on the heels of the leader. Jumping ahead three out, he was out on his own between the last two flights but what he actually achieved is open to doubt. One thing is certain, though, he just stays. (op 11-4)
Imperial Breeze(IRE), dropped right out in last, was in contention when he made a mistake five out. Under pressure three out, he took a remote second spot on the run-in. He looks more of a chaser and this trip might be beyond him. (op 15-8)
Keoghs Bar(IRE), his rider's first mount here for three years after serving a ban, raced without the tongue strap. He took them along but jumped left-handed. He was still in second spot when heavily eased between the last two and in the end just held on to third. Official explanation: jockey said, regarding running and riding, that the gelding was hanging badly left and had no more to give from the second last. (op 9-4 tchd 2-1)
Tenth Avenue(IRE), struggling with a full circuit to go, dropped right away going to three out and looks limited in the extreme. (op 14-1)

1929 SOL H'CAP HURDLE (11 hdls) 2m 4f

2:55 (2:55) (Class 4) (0-110,107) 4-Y-0+ **£2,740** (£798; £399)

Form RPR

4P-0 **1** **What's Occurrin**[168] 176 6-10-11 **92** .... RobertWalford 99+
(Tim Walford) *mde all: hit 6th: rdn and hrd pressed last: hld on gamely towards fin* **8/1**

12P- **2** *hd* **Of Course (FR)**[209] 4862 8-11-1 **103** .... (p) MrSFMagee(7) 109
(Simon West) *hld up in midfield: hdwy after 4 out: str chal last: kpt on: jst hld* **11/1**

0-00 **3** *11* **Appeal Denied (IRE)**[13] 1762 8-9-9 **83** .... PaulGallagher(7) 79
(Sandy Forster) *hld up in midfield: effrt and drvn after 4 out: styd on fr 2 out: nt rch first two* **22/1**

0043 **4** *1 1/2* **Inner Voice (USA)**[20] 1660 7-11-0 **100** .... (p) EJO'Connell(5) 96
(J J Lambe, Ire) *hld up in midfield: hdwy and cl up 1/2-way: effrt whn nt fluent 2 out: sn one pce* **12/1**

02P- **5** *3/4* **Sonara (IRE)**[38] 4556 6-10-5 **86** .... BrianHughes 82
(Howard Johnson) *trckd ldrs: effrt whn hit 3 out: outpcd after next* **4/1**[1]

5510 **6** *1/2* **Fly Tipper**[18] 1700 10-10-10 **91** .... (t) GrahamLee 85
(Wilf Storey) *towards rr: effrt u.p after 4 out: styd on fr last: no imp* **33/1**

5121 **7** *3/4* **Rebel Swing**[32] 1559 4-11-3 **98** .... HenryOliver 91
(Sue Smith) *bhd: pushed along bef 4 out: styd on fr last: nvr rchd ldrs* **9/2**[2]

0-54 **8** *12* **Sambelucky (IRE)**[149] 457 5-10-5 **86** .... JamesReveley 71
(Keith Reveley) *nt fluent: bhd: hdwy after 4 out: hit next: sn no ex* **16/1**

P5-2 **9** *5* **King Penda (IRE)**[149] 459 7-10-12 **96** .... FearghalDavis(3) 74
(Nicky Richards) *hld up in midfield: hdwy and prom 7th: rdn bef 3 out: wknd next* **6/1**[3]

U00- **10** *7* **Waltham Abbey**[258] 3867 9-11-1 **103** .... MrRUtley(7) 74
(Lynsey Kendall) *trckd ldrs to 4 out: sn wknd* **80/1**

1PU/ **11** *8* **Balamory Dan (IRE)**[684] 2639 9-11-12 **107** .... PaddyAspell 71
(Geoffrey Harker) *prom: lost pl 6th: struggling fr next* **33/1**

005P **12** *9* **Osolomio (IRE)**[11] 1644 7-11-12 **107** .... (b) AlanO'Keeffe 63
(Jennie Candlish) *cl up tl rdn and wknd bef 3 out* **18/1**

6620 **13** *11* **Lady Wright (IRE)**[23] 1644 7-10-2 **90** .... JakeGreenall(7) 36
(Michael Easterby) *bhd: struggling 7th: nvr on terms* **14/1**

504- **14** *23* **Faith And Reason (USA)**[258] 3872 7-11-9 **107** .... CampbellGillies(3) 32
(Chris Grant) *midfield: lost pl 1/2-way: sn struggling* **33/1**

-1F0 **15** *2 1/4* **Eliza Doalott (IRE)**[8] 1829 8-11-9 **104** .... DougieCostello 27
(Mrs M Stirk) *midfield on outside: lost pl 6th: struggling fr next* **16/1**

4m 59.0s (-23.80) **Going Correction** -1.05s/f (Hard)
WFA 4 from 5yo+ 10lb 15 Ran SP% **117.7**
Speed ratings (Par 105): **105,104,100,99,99 99,99,94,92,89 86,82,78,69,68**
toteswingers: 1&2 £17.70, 1&3 £37.60, 2&3 £43.20. CSF £85.64 CT £1861.49 TOTE £9.70: £3.00, £3.20, £9.50; EX 86.30.
Owner Miss Jill Gittus **Bred** Miss Jill Gittus **Trained** Sheriff Hutton, N Yorks

FOCUS
A modest handicap hurdle with plenty of the runners having something to prove at present. Ordinary form rated through the second, and potentially more to come from the winner.

NOTEBOOK
What's Occurrin, who started life in handicaps from an 8lb higher mark, was having his first outing since May. Reckoned to have strengthened and matured during his absence, he jumped well apart from one mistake a mile out. Brought wide in the straight, he showed real battling qualities to edge ahead near the line. A potential chaser, he should stay 3m. (op 12-1)
Of Course(FR), absent since March, won from a 6lb lower mark here in November. He showed clear second two out and in the end, racing towards the running rail, was just edged out. This was a good effort as he is best with much more give in the ground. (op 16-1)
Appeal Denied(IRE), a winner in Ireland a year ago, has plummeted down the weights since arriving here and this was his best effort for some time. (op 33-1)
Inner Voice(USA) had finished third in selling company at Hexham, but seemed to appreciate the step up to 2m4f. (op 14-1 tchd 16-1)
Sonara(IRE), rated 70 on the Flat, does not look a natural jumper. (op 9-2)
Fly Tipper, off the mark at the 27th attempt at Perth in August, was raised 6lb to a career high mark and is likely to continue to struggle. (op 28-1)
Rebel Swing, raised 9lb for his win over 3m in testing ground at Uttoxeter, was struggling to keep up with a full circuit to go. (op 11-2)
Sambelucky(IRE), absent since May, shaped nicely on his handicap bow, coming from way off the pace to chase the leaders three out. By no means knocked about, there is surely better to come.
King Penda(IRE), very weak in the market on his first start since May, was another given a patient ride. He looked a possible threat at the bottom of the hill and in the end was given a sympathetic ride when his chance had gone. He looks every inch a potential chaser and is unlikely to waste time over hurdles. (op 7-2 tchd 10-3)

1930 MOLSON COORS NOVICES' CHASE (12 fncs) 2m

3:25 (3:25) (Class 3) 4-Y-0+ **£5,854** (£1,719; £859; £429)

Form RPR

2-03 **1** **Divers (FR)**[15] 1731 6-11-2 0 .... GrahamLee 129+
(Ferdy Murphy) *hld up: hdwy and prom 5 out: nt fluent and rdn 3 out: rallied after next: led run-in: drvn out* **4/1**[2]

0-1U **2** *2* **Tara Royal**[12] 1770 5-11-8 0 .... TimmyMurphy 134+
(Donald McCain) *t.k.h: sn prom: hdwy to ld bef 4 out: rdn after next: hdd run-in: kpt on: hld towards fin* **11/4**[1]

320- **3** *9* **Premier Sagas (FR)**[193] 5142 6-11-2 0 .... BrianHarding 122+
(Nicky Richards) *prom: reminders 7th: outpcd after next: rallied 2 out: kpt on fr last to take 3rd cl home: no ch w first two* **10/1**

1P1- **4** *nse* **Hold Fast (IRE)**[213] 4779 6-11-2 0 .... WilsonRenwick 121+
(Howard Johnson) *t.k.h: cl up: led 4th to bef 4 out: rdn whn hit 2 out: edgd rt and outpcd last* **11/4**[1]

0240 **5** *19* **Terenzium (IRE)**[13] 1759 8-11-2 113 .... (p) BarryKeniry 102
(Micky Hammond) *hld up in tch: rdn and outpcd 1/2-way: n.d after* **100/1**

213- **6** *2 3/4* **Benny Be Good**[188] 5201 7-11-2 0 .... JamesReveley 104+
(Keith Reveley) *prom: lost pl whn blnd 5th: sn struggling: n.d after* **7/1**

0 **7** *3/4* **Seigneur Des Bois (FR)**[13] 1759 4-10-7 0 .... RichieMcGrath 90
(Ferdy Murphy) *hld up: struggling 1/2-way: nvr on terms* **50/1**

1-61 **F** **Saveiro (FR)**[12] 1779 6-11-8 121 .... BrianHughes —
(Alan Swinbank) *led to 4th: cl up: 3 l 3rd whn fell heavily 5 out* **11/2**[3]

4m 7.20s (-8.90) **Going Correction** -0.85s/f (Firm)
WFA 4 from 5yo+ 9lb 8 Ran SP% **113.3**
Speed ratings (Par 107): **88,87,82,82,72 71,71,—**
toteswingers: 1&2 £1.70, 1&3 £6.40, 2&3 £10.00. CSF £15.74 TOTE £6.80: £1.80, £1.40, £1.40; EX 17.00.
Owner The DPRP Divers Partnership **Bred** Alec Head And Mme Ghislaine Head **Trained** West Witton, N Yorks

FOCUS
A very interesting novices' chase and decent form. The race seems sure to throw up future winners.

NOTEBOOK
Divers(FR), third on his chasing debut at Towcester, is a 125-rated hurdler. He stuck to his guns and after being unsighted at the last and stayed on to gain the upper hand on the run-in. He is better suited by 2m4f and he should progress further. (tchd 9-2)
Tara Royal, who unseated his rider at Bangor on his first start since winning at Haydock in May, is a free-going sort. Landing in front four out, in the end the penalty proved too much. He is better suited by 2m4f and his trainer believes his will stay 3m in time. (op 2-1)
Premier Sagas(FR), 118 over hurdles, was very keen early on. He struggled to keep up at the halfway mark but stayed on from the last to snatch third place on the line and looks sure to make a better chaser than hurdler. (op 12-1)
Hold Fast(IRE), a 128-rated hurdler, was another to race with the choke out. Jumping ahead at the fourth, two errors took their toll and he tired badly on the run-in. He will improve for the outing and should make his mark in ordinary novice chases. (op 5-1)
Terenzium(IRE), a 113-rated hurdler, was having his second start over fences and his longer-term future lies in modest handicaps. (op 66-1)
Benny Be Good, rated 127 over hurdles, found himself out of contention after two serious jumping errors in the first half of the race. Staying on in his own time up the final hill he looks capable of much better. Official explanation: jockey said gelding jumped poorly (op 15-2 tchd 8-1)
Saveiro(FR), expected to be suited by going right-handed, lost the advantage with a clumsy jump at the fourth and he looked to be struggling when crashing out five from home. (op 5-1)

1931 GROLSCH INTERMEDIATE H'CAP HURDLE (9 hdls) 2m 1f

3:55 (3:55) (Class 3) (0-125,125) 4-Y-0+ **£6,505** (£1,910; £955; £477)

Form RPR

502- **1** **Amir Pasha (UAE)**[28] 4601 5-9-10 **100** .... (v) JamesHalliday(5) 104+
(Micky Hammond) *hld up in tch: hdwy 3 out: led appr last: kpt on wl run-in* **15/2**

3206 **2** *1* **High Bird Humphrey**[13] 1761 11-10-3 **107** .... PaulCallaghan(5) 109
(Simon West) *racd wd: prom: j.lft 5th and next: ev ch bef 2 out to last: pushed along and kpt on run-in* **8/1**

340- **3** *3 1/2* **Papa Caruso**[201] 4990 6-10-13 **112** .... TjadeCollier 112
(Sue Smith) *trckd ldrs: drvn and outpcd after 4 out: rallied 2 out: kpt on wl run-in: nt rch first two* **12/1**

664- **4** *8* **Ascendant**[187] 5220 4-11-6 **119** .... BrianHughes 111
(Howard Johnson) *t.k.h: hld up: hdwy and cl up after 3rd: rdn and wknd after 4 out* **7/1**[3]

4011 **5** *hd* **Zahara Joy**[18] 1700 7-9-11 **99** .... (t) RyanMania(3) 91
(Maurice Barnes) *t.k.h: led 1st to 5th: led bef 2 out to appr last: wknd run-in* **9/2**[1]

-212 **6** *1* **Worth A King'S**[135] 679 4-11-4 **120** .... AdrianLane(3) 111
(Donald McCain) *hld up in tch: drvn and outpcd bef 3 out: rallied after next: grad wknd run-in* **12/1**

0FP- **7** *5* **Cranky Corner**[273] 3574 6-10-13 **117** .... ShaneByrne(5) 104+
(Sue Smith) *hld up: hdwy on outside and prom bef 3 out: wknd after next* **9/1**

111- **8** *3 1/2* **Skylancer**[12] 1788 6-11-6 **124** .... EJO'Connell(5) 109
(J J Lambe, Ire) *led to 1st: cl up: led 5th to bef 2 out: wknd after 2 out* **28/1**

404- **9** *15* **Bocamix (FR)**[198] 5076 4-11-1 **117** .... FearghalDavis(3) 87
(Andrew Crook) *trckd ldrs tl rdn and wknd bef 3 out: t.o* **9/1**

263- **10** *35* **Monsieur Jourdain (IRE)**[187] 5220 4-11-12 **125** .... (p) RichieMcGrath 63
(Tim Easterby) *nt fluent on occasions: prom: lost pl bef 4th: sn struggling: t.o* **14/1**

F244 **P** **Trumpstoo (USA)**[28] 1597 4-11-4 **117** GrahamLee —
(Richard Fahey) *hld up: struggling 1/2-way: sn btn: t.o whn p.u bef 2 out* **6/1**[2]

4m 14.8s (-15.00) **Going Correction** -1.05s/f (Hard) **11** Ran SP% **113.3**
Speed ratings (Par 107): **93,92,90,87,87 86,84,82,75,59** —
toteswingers: 1&2 £20.70, 1&3 £14.70, 2&3 £27.40. CSF £63.99 CT £709.30 TOTE £7.00: £1.90, £2.90, £3.40; EX 61.70.

Owner J McAllister **Bred** Darley **Trained** Middleham Moor, N Yorks

FOCUS

An interesting intermediate handicap hurdle run at a sound pace, and all but two were still in contention three out. A hurdles personal best from the winner.

NOTEBOOK

Amir Pasha(UAE), in good form and a winner twice on the level this summer, wore a visor rather than the usual cheekpieces. He proved more willing than the runner-up on the run-in and gave his rider a welcome winner. He may turn out under a penalty at Wetherby next Friday. (op 8-1 tchd 7-1)

High Bird Humphrey, better treated over hurdles than fences, had been placed five times in six previous visits here, including when edged out of this prize a year ago. Tending to jump left-handed, he went round in cruise control but in the end the winner proved too strong. His overall strike-rate (1-32) tells all. (tchd 17-2)

Papa Caruso, having just his second start in handicap company on his first outing since April, stayed on in good style after jumping right-handed at the final flight. He will improve for the outing.

Ascendant, impressive on his first try over hurdles, is rated 93 on the level and resumed here from a possible lenient mark. He came again when it was all over and will be suited by an extra half-mile. (op 6-1)

Zahara Joy, a stone higher than her Kelso success, helped force the pace but came up well short. (op 5-1 tchd 11-2)

Worth A King'S was only sticking on in his own time when knocked into at the final flight. He needs a stiffer test but does not look well treated. (op 11-1 tchd 14-1)

Cranky Corner, a smart bumper horse, travelled very strongly and looked a big threat when he landed in a heap three out. This was his first outing for his third trainer and his first start since January. The ability is definitely there if only the key to him can be found. (op 8-1)

Bocamix(FR), who has been gelded and had a wind operation, could not keep up from three out. He will come on for the outing but is at his best in the mud. (op 8-1 tchd 10-1)

Trumpstoo(USA) Official explanation: jockey said gelding hung badly left throughout

1932 ENNERDALE H'CAP CHASE (18 fncs) 3m 110y

4:30 (4:30) (Class 3) (0-130,127) 4-Y-0+ **£5,854** (£1,719; £859; £429)

Form				RPR
202-	**1**		**Presenting Forever (IRE)**[193] 5148 6-11-5 **120** BrianHughes (Howard Johnson) *mostly j.lft: mde all: rdn 2 out: styd on strly fr last* **6/5**[1]	131+
2153	**2**	*4*	**Rifleman (IRE)**[46] 1482 10-10-5 **111** (t) GilesHawkins(5) (Richard Lee) *cl up: chsd wnr fr 1/2-way: effrt 3 out: 2 l down last: one pce run-in* **7/1**[3]	114
5653	**3**	*20*	**Stagecoach Amber (USA)**[12] 1781 8-10-13 **114** TjadeCollier (Sue Smith) *cl up tl drvn and wknd fr 2 out* **12/1**	98
2042	**4**	*hd*	**Flying Doctor**[13] 1759 7-11-5 **127** StevenGagan(7) (Elliott Cooper) *hld up in tch: hdwy and prom 12th: outpcd 5 out: rallied next: wknd after 3 out* **10/1**	112
5P-5	**P**		**Not Left Yet (IRE)**[18] 1697 9-10-9 **110** TimmyMurphy (P Monteith) *hld up in last: j. slowly 2nd and v slowly next 2: tailing off whn p.u bef 5th* **10/3**[2]	—
2240	**P**		**Chorizo (IRE)**[30] 1570 9-11-2 **117** PaddyAspell (Richard Guest) *cl up tl dropped to rr and outpcd bef 10th: sn lost tch: t.o whn p.u bef 3 out* **17/2**	—

6m 16.6s (-26.00) **Going Correction** -0.85s/f (Firm) **6** Ran SP% **108.3**
Speed ratings (Par 107): **107,105,99,99**,— —
toteswingers: 1&2 £2.30, 1&3 £2.70, 2&3 £4.20. CSF £9.23 TOTE £2.00: £1.10, £4.20; EX 8.90.

Owner Andrea & Graham Wylie **Bred** John P Cahill **Trained** Billy Row, Co Durham

FOCUS

A modest handicap chase. The easy winner has the potential to rate higher.

NOTEBOOK

Presenting Forever(IRE), who changed hands for 370,000gns after his Irish point win, looked potentially well treated on just 120 on his effort when runner-up to Wogan at Doncaster in January. Tending to jump left and hanging badly that way on the paddock bend, he sealed it with a fine leap three from home. He is relatively unexposed and, much happier going right-handed, he should be able to pick up a good prize. (op 11-8 tchd 11-10, tchd 13-8 in a place)

Rifleman(IRE), having his 24th start over fences and 8lb higher than his last success, went down fighting. His last three wins have been at Worcester, but that track is out of action now for the winter. (op 11-2)

Stagecoach Amber(USA) is another strong traveller but he has yet to show he stays beyond 2m4f. (op 8-1)

Flying Doctor, who joined this stable rated 75 over hurdles, ran from a mark of 127. Averaging a race a week since May, he shaped as if his busy time has at last caught up with him. Seeing as he needs decent ground, now may be the time to give him a winter's rest. (op 7-1)

Not Left Yet(IRE), now rated 110 but once as high as 130, was never going and, jumping without any fluency in a detached last, was soon pulled up. Official explanation: jockey said gelding never travelled or jumped fluently (op 9-2 tchd 5-1 in a place)

1933 MOLSON COORS CLUB OF YEAR H'CAP CHASE (18 fncs) 3m 110y

5:00 (5:00) (Class 5) (0-95,95) 4-Y-0+ **£1,756** (£515; £257; £128)

Form				RPR
56-5	**1**		**Isla Pearl Fisher**[161] 306 7-10-13 **82** PaddyAspell (N W Alexander) *hld up and bhd: smooth hdwy and in tch 5 out: effrt 3 out: led bef last: rdn and styd on strly run-in* **8/1**	97+
0550	**2**	*5*	**Rossini's Dancer**[13] 1759 5-11-10 **93** MarkBradburne (Sue Bradburne) *prom: hdwy to ld 3 out: hdd bef last: rallied: kpt on same pce run-in* **16/1**	102
0-5F	**3**	*24*	**Braden Brook (IRE)**[8] 1826 7-10-5 **74** (t) BrianHughes (John Wade) *cl up: led 4 out to next: sn drvn and outpcd: mod 3rd whn blnd last* **11/2**	63
-332	**4**	*5*	**Murphys Beau (IRE)**[12] 1784 8-10-0 **69** oh2 (p) RichieMcGrath (Kate Walton) *led to 1st: cl up: drvn and outpcd bef 3 out: sn n.d* **10/3**[1]	51
01/3	**5**	*4 ½*	**Springaway**[13] 1760 11-10-2 **78** MrSFMagee(7) (Simon West) *t.k.h: led 1st and sn clr: hdd 4 out: wknd next* **7/2**[2]	60
P-00	**6**	*1 ¼*	**Nelliedonethat (IRE)**[18] 1697 10-11-12 **95** PeterBuchanan (Lucinda Russell) *bhd: nt fluent 8th: outpcd and detached next: sme late hdwy: nvr on terms* **12/1**	72
00-0	**7**	*½*	**Yes Mate**[13] 1757 6-9-11 **69** oh2 RyanMania(3) (Dianne Sayer) *mstkes: in tch: effrt 5 out: ev ch 3 out: hit and wknd 2 out* **28/1**	48
4152	**8**	*11*	**Red Dynamite**[18] 1701 9-11-12 **95** (p) GrahamLee (Geoffrey Harker) *hld up: effrt u.p after 5 out: struggling fr next* **9/2**[3]	62
614-	**9**	*6*	**Matmata De Tendron (FR)**[198] 5077 10-11-7 **93** (p) FearghalDavis(3) (Andrew Crook) *cl up tl lost pl 12th: n.d after* **11/1**	54

6m 32.6s (-10.00) **Going Correction** -0.85s/f (Firm) **9** Ran SP% **115.3**
Speed ratings (Par 103): **82,80,72,71,69 69,69,65,63**
toteswingers: 1&2 £15.60, 1&3 £9.20, 2&3 £16.00. CSF £115.57 CT £763.85 TOTE £7.80: £1.60, £3.80, £1.10; EX 143.60.

Owner Mrs J E B Gammell **Bred** Mrs D Marshall **Trained** Kinneston, Perth & Kinross

FOCUS

A very moderate handicap chase. The pace was steady and there were four in line three out. The winner is rated to his previous best.

NOTEBOOK

Isla Pearl Fisher, having his first start since May and only his second try over 3m, has needed to learn to settle. Relaxed in last, he edged forward in the final mile and, upsides two out, he put his stamp firmly on the race on the run-in, scoring with something to spare. His rating will shoot up but there is better to come, though his trainer may be in no hurry to pull him out again. (op 15-2 tchd 9-1)

Rossini's Dancer, having just his second start over fences, finished clear second best and connections must be hoping his rating does not go up by too much. He finished a long way clear of the third.

Braden Brook(IRE) travelled strongly but was a tired and well-beaten third when jumping left at the final fence. A drop back in distance might be in his favour for the time being. (op 8-1)

Murphys Beau(IRE), 0-8 over fences and a long-standing maiden, wore cheekpieces for the first time. He was hard at work four out and was soon left flagging. (op 4-1)

Springaway, having his second start in two weeks after two and a half years on the sidelines, raced keenly in front but, headed four out, he was allowed to complete in his own time. He may need a short break before he returns to action. (op 9-2)

Red Dynamite, 6lb higher than his Wetherby success in May over 2m6f, was in trouble before stamina became an issue. He was reported to have hung and jumped left and is much happier going the other way round. Official explanation: jockey said gelding jumped and hung left (tchd 4-1)

1934 MOLSON COORS MARES' STANDARD NATIONAL HUNT FLAT RACE (CONDITIONALS/AMATEURS) 2m 1f

5:30 (5:31) (Class 6) 4-6-Y-0 **£1,370** (£399; £199)

Form				RPR
	1		**Sparkling Hand** 4-10-7 0 PaulGallagher(7) (Peter Atkinson) *hld up: hdwy over 6f out: effrt 3f out: led ins fnl f: hld on wl* **40/1**	95
43-	**2**	*nk*	**Hannah Jacques (IRE)**[225] 4515 5-10-11 0 FearghalDavis(3) (Nicky Richards) *t.k.h early: in tch: hdwy to ld over 2f out: rdn over 1f out: hdd ins fnl f: r.o: hld cl home* **9/2**[2]	95
0	**3**	*3 ½*	**Alexander Road (IRE)**[165] 230 5-10-11 0 JohnKington(3) (Donald McCain) *hld up in tch: drvn and outpcd over 4f out: rallied to chse ldrs over 1f out: one pce fnl f* **8/1**	92
5	**4**	*8*	**Mrs Eff**[158] 355 4-10-7 0 HenryBrooke(7) (Kate Walton) *bhd: drvn along 1/2-way: rallied 3f out: kpt on: nvr able to chal* **7/1**	85
	5	*2 ¼*	**Baileys Ruffit (IRE)**[26] 5-10-9 0 EJO'Connell(5) (Neil McKnight, Ire) *t.k.h early: w ldrs: led 1/2-way to over 2f out: wknd over 1f out* **13/2**[3]	83
5	**6**	*11*	**Floraclock**[13] 1764 5-10-9 0 ShaneByrne(5) (Sue Smith) *cl up tl rdn and wknd fr 2f out* **9/1**	73
	7	*19*	**Bartleny Native (IRE)** 5-10-7 0 MrMatthewBarber(7) (Tom Gretton) *bhd: outpcd 1/2-way: nvr on terms* **25/1**	56
6-	**8**	*1 ¾*	**Corston Star (IRE)**[193] 5150 5-10-9 0 JamesHalliday(5) (Malcolm Jefferson) *led 5f: cl up tl rdn and wknd over 2f out* **11/1**	54
	9	*17*	**Mollyash (IRE)**[193] 5-10-11 0 CampbellGillies(3) (S R B Crawford, Ire) *t.k.h: in tch: rdn over 3f out: wknd over 2f out* **5/2**[1]	39
0	**10**	*14*	**Overpriced**[43] 1510 4-10-7 0 (t) MissAngelaBarnes(7) (Maurice Barnes) *bhd: hdwy and in tch over 6f out: outpcd whn rn v wd bnd ent st: t.o* **100/1**	26
0-	**11**	*20*	**Onetwobeat**[336] 2381 5-10-8 0 ow1 MrTPark(7) (Lisa Williamson) *cl up: led after 5f to 1/2-way: sn lost pl: t.o* **100/1**	9
	12	*33*	**Princess Cherry (IRE)**[167] 205 5-10-7 0 GaryRutherford(7) (Harriet Graham) *hld up ins: drvn 1/2-way: sn struggling: t.o* **66/1**	—
0	**13**	*71*	**Phar Beyond**[12] 1785 5-10-11 0 (t) RyanMania(3) (Maurice Barnes) *t.k.h: cl up: lost pl bef 1/2-way: sn t.o and eased* **100/1**	—
	14	*shd*	**Last Chorus** 4-10-7 0 MissStephanieBowey(7) (Tracy Waggott) *bhd: lost tch 1/2-way: eased whn no ch* **66/1**	—

4m 14.5s (-9.70) **Going Correction** -1.05s/f (Hard) **14** Ran SP% **114.3**
Speed ratings: **80,79,78,74,73 68,59,58,50,43 34,18**,—,—
toteswingers: 1&2 £30.20, 1&3 £36.90, 2&3 £6.80. totesuper7: WIN: Not won. PLACE: Not won. CSF £201.93 TOTE £83.40: £20.10, £1.30, £5.60; EX 350.70 Place 6: £407.11, Place 5: £260.49..

Owner P G Atkinson **Bred** Victor G And Mrs Izabel Palmer **Trained** Yafforth, N Yorks

■ Stewards' Enquiry : Fearghal Davis two-day ban: used whip with excessive frequency (Nov 4-5)
John Kington nine-day ban: used whip with excessive frequency (Nov 4-12)

FOCUS

A modest mares' only bumper run at a sensible pace. Plenty of deadwood and they came home well strung out.

NOTEBOOK

Sparkling Hand, a half-sister to a 3m hurdle winner, stayed on in determined fashion to force her head in front near the line. She looks a weak type and will struggle under a penalty.

Hannah Jacques(IRE), in the frame on her two previous starts, is a mare with quite a bit of size and scope. Absent since March, she worked hard to get her head in front only to miss out near the line. She will need stiff tracks over hurdles. (op 3-1)

Alexander Road(IRE), who did not run up to expectations on her previous outing in May, stuck on under a forceful ride. She looks a real stayer. (tchd 9-1 in a place)

Mrs Eff, off the pace and under pressure at halfway, did well to finish so close but she looks a tricky customer. (op 15-2)

Baileys Ruffit(IRE), a heavy-ground Irish mares' only maiden point winner, took it up at the foot of the hill but proved too slow to retain the advantage. (op 9-1)

Floraclock, fifth on her debut here two weeks ago, did not improve on that effort. (tchd 10-1)

Mollyash(IRE), another Irish mares' only maiden point winner, is from a stable with a 33% record in bumpers here. She raced quite keenly and dropped right away before the home turn. Official explanation: jockey said mare ran too free (op 3-1 tchd 9-4)

T/Plt: £1,581.60 to a £1 stake. Pool:£53,624.50 - 24.75 winning tickets T/Qpdt: £63.90 to a £1 stake. Pool:£4,866.70 - 56.30 winning tickets RY

[1723]LUDLOW (R-H)

Thursday, October 21

OFFICIAL GOING: Good

All bends moved to provide fresh ground but impact on distances not quantified.
Wind: Almost nil Weather: Clear but chilly

1935 STOURPORT HIGH SCHOOL "RACING TO SCHOOL" JUVENILE HURDLE (9 hdls) 2m

2:10 (2:10) (Class 4) 3-Y-O **£3,252** (£955; £477; £238)

Form RPR

1 **1** **Al Dafa (USA)**[13] 1576 3-11-5 0 APMcCoy 96+
(Gordon Elliott, Ire) *kpt hanging and jumping lft: prom: wnt bdly lft 4th: drvn to chal 3 out: led and j.lft and rdr lost iron 2 out: hdd and hit last: forced ahd again fnl 100yds* **11/8**[1]

U **2** *3/4* **Tom Wade (IRE)**[15] 1728 3-10-12 0 CharliePoste 87
(John Harris) *settled in 6th pl: mstke 6th: chal 3 out: led last: rdn and hdd 100yds out: kpt on* **11/1**

F631 **3** *4* **Frameit (IRE)**[8] 1818 3-11-5 104 (vt) RichardJohnson 91
(Tim Vaughan) *chsd ldr tl drvn bef 3 out: no great rspnse: one pce and btn 2 out* **11/4**[2]

4 *3/4* **Free As A Lark**[29] 3-10-5 0 PaulMoloney 77+
(Evan Williams) *plld hrd: hld up in tch: effrt 3 out: hanging rt next and sn btn: mstke last* **6/1**[3]

4 **5** *1/2* **Highland Cadett**[12] 1772 3-10-12 0 (v) TomScudamore 83+
(Rod Millman) *trckd ldrs: blnd 5th: rdn to ld 3 out: hdd next: no ex between last two* **40/1**

2523 **6** *3* **Sansili**[72] 1226 3-10-9 99 DonalDevereux(3) 80
(Peter Bowen) *led: drvn and hdd 3 out: sn wknd* **13/2**

0200 **7** *23* **A P Ling**[18] 1691 3-10-5 82 DarylJacob 52
(Christopher Kellett) *t.k.h early: last whn mstke 4th: drvn and lost tch after 6th: t.o whn mstke next* **100/1**

3m 53.6s (4.10) **Going Correction** -0.175s/f (Good) 7 Ran SP% **108.2**
Speed ratings (Par 103): **82,81,79,79,79 77,66**
toteswingers: 1&2 £6.00, 1&3 £1.10, 2&3 £5.50. CSF £15.49 TOTE £2.30: £1.60, £3.40; EX 13.50.

Owner Sean F Gallagher **Bred** Darley **Trained** Trim, Co Meath

■ Tony McCoy's 100th winner of the season.

FOCUS

A moderate juvenile event run at just an average gallop and there was something of a sprint finish off the home turn. The first pair eventually forged clear. This is modest form and the winner is entitled to rate higher on his Flat efforts.

NOTEBOOK

Al Dafa(USA), despite tending to hang to his left pretty much throughout, ran out a game enough winner on this return to hurdling and has now won his last two in this sphere. He still showed some signs of inexperience, but once Tony McCoy got serious with him after the last he was always going to master the runner-up. He is versatile regards ground and is in the right hands to progress a little further over hurdles, but things will be much tougher under a double penalty in this division. (tchd 11-10)

Tom Wade(IRE) unseated on his hurdling debut over C&D 15 days earlier when far from done with, and he confirmed he has a future in this sphere with a solid effort in defeat. This maiden would have likely enjoyed more of a test and can be found a small opening before that long. (op 8-1)

Frameit(IRE) was faced with different ground than he raced on when winning easily at Uttoxeter eight days earlier and, as a horse who gets 1m4f well on the level, basically found this too sharp. It wasn't a bad run under his penalty and he could still win another one of these when reverting to a stiffer test. (op 3-1 tchd 7-2 and 4-1 in a place)

Free As A Lark was snapped up by her new connections after finishing second in a 1m2f claimer at Redcar last month. She needed this initial experience over hurdles and showed enough to think she can be found a race or two in due course. (tchd 7-1)

Highland Cadett spoilt his chance with a first-flight mistake on his hurdling debut 12 days earlier, but this was more like it. It's not hard to see why he sports headgear, and it will be a weak race he wins, but it looks as though he will be more effective as a hurdler than he was on the level. (op 33-1)

Sansili, rated 99, came into this return from a 72-day break having been placed in three of his four previous outings in this sphere. It wasn't surprising to see him attempt to make all and, looking at his action, softer ground should suit. He probably needs further too, and he could win at some point before the year is out. (op 8-1 tchd 9-1 in a place)

1936 PLYMOUTH CARVERY BEGINNERS' CHASE (13 fncs) 2m

2:40 (2:40) (Class 4) 4-Y-O+

£3,757 (£1,110; £555; £277; £138; £69)

Form RPR

11-0 **1** **William's Wishes (IRE)**[166] 207 5-11-2 0 PaulMoloney 133+
(Evan Williams) *trckd ldrs gng wl: wnt 3rd at 7th: led 3 out: readily drew clr: hit last: r.o strly: impressive* **5/4**[1]

30-1 **2** *8* **Wikaala (USA)**[16] 1720 5-11-2 118 (b) APMcCoy 119
(Gordon Elliott, Ire) *chsd ldr: led bef 6th tl 9th: ev ch 3 out: rdn and wl hld fr next* **11/2**[3]

00-6 **3** *5* **Potemkin (USA)**[14] 1737 5-10-13 0 (t) LeeStephens(3) 115
(David Evans) *t.k.h: led 4th tl bef 6th: led again 9th tl rdn and hdd 3 out: btn next* **66/1**

2112 **4** *3 1/4* **Twentynineblack (FR)**[12] 1779 6-11-2 0 NoelFehily 113+
(Donald McCain) *hld up: pushed along bef 10th: little rspnse: 7 l 4th and btn whn blnd 2 out* **9/4**[2]

F3-3 **5** *14* **Laureate Des Loges (FR)**[160] 313 6-10-9 0 RichardJohnson 97+
(Henry Daly) *blnd 2nd: j. modly in last: 5th and struggling fr 8th* **9/1**

6P16 **6** *47* **Bolton Hall (IRE)**[11] 1797 8-11-2 114 (bt) RhysFlint 56
(Keith Goldsworthy) *allowed soft 12 l ld tl j. wildly lft 1st and 2nd: hdd 4th: continued to hang and jump lft: last fr 8th: fence bhd 10th: b.b.v* **18/1**

4m 0.70s (2.20) **Going Correction** +0.275s/f (Yiel) 6 Ran SP% **107.4**
Speed ratings (Par 105): **105,101,98,96,89 66**
toteswingers: 1&2 £1.60, 1&3 £30.50, 2&3 £22.10. CSF £7.89 TOTE £2.20: £1.50, £1.70; EX 7.50.

Owner Mrs D E Cheshire **Bred** Mrs M O'Driscoll **Trained** Llancarfan, Vale Of Glamorgan

FOCUS

A modest beginners' chase, but an impressive debut winner who can do better. The second and fourth were below their best.

NOTEBOOK

William's Wishes(IRE) is rated 133 over hurdles and his last outing saw him finish seventh in the Swinton Hurdle back in May. As such it wasn't surprising to see the money come for him, particularly as his yard do well at this venue. He bided his time before getting involved around the seventh fence and a fine leap at the fourth-last saw him get to the front. He soon had matters in control and was in no danger when getting in low at the last. This should do his confidence a lot of good, he will not mind returning to further over fences and could well rate a fair bit higher as a novice chaser. A sound surface seems important to him and he may just be the sort that needs space between his races, so it would not surprise to see him miss out the winter months. (op 15-8 tchd 6-5)

Wikaala(USA), friendless in the betting ring, was nonetheless expected to step up on the form he showed on his return to chasing at Tipperary 16 days earlier and did just that. However, he was made to look slow by the winner and probably needs more of a test over fences. (op 7-2)

Potemkin(USA), still a maiden, was awash with sweat. He showed much more on this switch to chasing, though, and there is surely a small race for him provided he comes on for the experience. (op 33-1)

Twentynineblack(FR) had finished second on his chasing debut at Hexham 12 days earlier. He pulled hard that day and so it wasn't surprising to see him settled well off the pace here. He emerged with his chance turning for home, but his jumping let him down thereafter and he found nothing when put under pressure. It may be that this run came soon enough for him and reverting to a left-handed track may see him back in a better light, but this does leave him with something to prove. (op 2-1 tchd 15-8)

Bolton Hall(IRE) Official explanation: trainer said gelding bled from the nose

1937 RACING WELFARE WEEK (S) HURDLE (11 hdls) 2m 5f

3:15 (3:15) (Class 5) 4-Y-O+ **£1,951** (£573; £286; £143)

Form RPR

1-03 **1** **National Trust**[11] 1796 8-11-4 130 PaddyBrennan 116+
(Nigel Twiston-Davies) *nt fluent 1st and 2nd: bhd: 8th at 6th: stdy prog 8th: sustained effrt fr 3 out: drvn to ld last: forged clr* **3/1**[2]

4022 **2** *6* **Armenian Boy (FR)**[15] 1726 7-11-4 114 (bt) TomScudamore 113+
(David Pipe) *prom: led 8th: rdn bef 3 out: nt fluent next: hdd last: outbattled flat* **5/4**[1]

-4P0 **3** *1 1/2* **Tighe Caster**[15] 1726 11-10-12 104 JodieMogford 105
(Graeme McPherson) *hld up: hdwy 8th: wnt 2nd gng wl bef 3 out: 3rd and wkng whn blnd next: plugged on* **8/1**[3]

0-50 **4** *23* **Petrosian**[15] 1731 6-11-1 105 MissIsabelTompsett(7) 96
(Dai Burchell) *carried hd v high: pressed ldrs: 3rd and rdn bef 3 out: racd wd and dropping out qckly in 12 l 4th whn blnd 2 out* **22/1**

P **5** *10* **Tibetan Dragon (IRE)**[26] 1608 6-10-12 109 (v[1]) PaulMoloney 73
(Evan Williams) *bhd: effrt after 6th: rdn and outpcd 8th: btn whn wnt rt 2 out* **11/1**

0204 **6** *77* **Bachley Gale**[63] 1296 5-10-5 0 (p) RhysFlint —
(Keith Goldsworthy) *prom: hit 4th: 4th and rdn bef 3 out: fdd rapidly: bdly t.o* **20/1**

-PFP **7** *6* **Prestbury Knight**[15] 1725 10-10-9 0 (t) RichieMcLernon(3) —
(Sophie Leech) *kpt away fr others in preliminaries and mounted on crse: j. slowly 1st and pushed along: midfield tl hit 5th: rdn and lost tch next: sn tailed himself off: probably retired* **25/1**

P-PP **P** **Tayman (IRE)**[113] 868 8-11-1 104 (b) TomMolloy(3) —
(Nigel Twiston-Davies) *pressed ldr tl rdn and downed tools and j.v.slowly 7th: sn t.o: p.u after next* **12/1**

00/U **P** **Penny King**[18] 1705 9-10-5 0 MrRGHenderson(7) —
(Ken Wingrove) *bhd: drvn 5th: t.o next: continued forlornly tl eventually p.u 2 out* **150/1**

00-P **P** **Nothing's Easy (IRE)**[9] 1816 6-11-4 110 NoelFehily —
(Liam Corcoran) *t.k.h: led tl 8th: rapidly lost pl: t.o and p.u 3 out* **20/1**

60 **P** **John Sixteen (IRE)**[15] 1729 5-10-9 0 DonalDevereux(3) —
(Peter Bowen) *last pair and nvr gng wl: rdn 5th: t.o next: p.u after 8th* **66/1**

5m 5.90s (-8.90) **Going Correction** -0.175s/f (Good) 11 Ran SP% **116.5**
Speed ratings (Par 103): **109,106,106,97,93 64,61,—,—,— —**
toteswingers: 1&2 £1.60, 1&3 £6.00, 2&3 £2.80. CSF £6.68 TOTE £4.00: £1.90, £1.10, £2.80; EX 7.20.The winner was sold to Christian Leech for £6,250.

Owner Walters Plant Hire Ltd **Bred** Cheveley Park Stud Ltd **Trained** Naunton, Gloucs

FOCUS

An uncompetitive seller, rated around the placed horses. The winner is tough to beat in this grade.

NOTEBOOK

National Trust didn't take to fences when thrashed on his chasing debut 11 days earlier and, having just his second outing for the stable, was quickly dropped in class on this return to hurdling. An official mark of 130 greatly flatters him, but he was still the one to beat on previous form and he got the job done under a strong ride. His confidence should be boosted by this and he has now evidently found his sort of level. (op 11-4 tchd 9-4)

Armenian Boy(FR) finished second off a mark of 110 in a handicap over C&D 15 days earlier and was well backed to give his yard success in the race for the second year running. He took it up at the eighth and was the only one to give the winner a serious race after three out, but was a sitting duck for that rival prior to meeting the last two flights wrong. He needs a strong ride, but is well up to winning in this grade. (op 7-4 tchd 6-5)

Tighe Caster, well beaten by the runner-up over C&D last time, looked a big player going into the final turn. He was feeling the pinch before whacking the penultimate flight, but this was much more encouraging from this veteran and he is worth persevering with in such company. (op 15-2 tchd 9-1)

Petrosian had his chance on this return to hurdling back down in grade, but faced a stiff task on these terms and cried enough after three out. (tchd 25-1)

1938 LUDLOW RACECOURSE SUPPORTS RACING WELFARE H'CAP HURDLE (9 hdls) 2m

3:45 (3:45) (Class 4) (0-115,115) 4-Y-O+ **£3,903** (£1,146; £573; £286)

Form RPR

1101 **1** **Skye But N Ben**[15] 1723 6-11-12 **115** (b) APMcCoy 121+
(Michael Chapman) *w ldr tl lft in ld 6th: urged to qckn clr bef 3 out: 5 l ahd last: idled bdly and jst scraped home: fine ride* **11/2**

1455 **2** *nk* **Lodgician (IRE)**[28] 1597 8-10-8 **100** SamTwiston-Davies(3) 105+
(Nigel Twiston-Davies) *plld hrd and cl up: rdn and outpcd by wnr 3 out: 6 l 3rd whn blnd last: styd on as wnr idled: nrly got up but jst too much to do* **11/4**[1]

35-0 **3** *1/2* **Tom O'Tara**[164] 252 6-10-6 **98** WayneKavanagh(3) 102
(Robin Dickin) *t.k.h: pressed ldrs: wnt 2nd bef 3 out: sn outpcd by wnr and hanging in both directions and racing most awkwardly up st: styng on after last: gave himself too much to do* **11/1**

-P14 **4** *6* **Liberty Seeker (FR)**[61] 1328 11-11-0 **110** MattCrawley(7) 109
(John Harris) *last and pushed along 4th: outpcd wl bef 3 out: kpt on steadily but nvr looked like chalng* **9/1**

05U6 **5** *19* **Coach And Four (USA)**[27] 1600 5-10-4 **100** MrJEngland(7) 82
(Michael Gates) *cl up: rdn after 6th: dropped out qckly bef next* **25/1**

5452 **6** *5* **Phoenix Eye**[9] 1816 9-10-4 **93** LeightonAspell 80+
(Michael Mullineaux) *hld up in rr: wl in tch whn v bdly hmpd 6th: lost all ch* **3/1**[2]

-326 **F** **Halling Gal**[7] 1844 4-11-1 **104** PaulMoloney —
(Evan Williams) *nt fluent 4th: slt ld tl fell 6th* **7/2**[3]

3m 47.7s (-1.80) **Going Correction** -0.175s/f (Good)
WFA 4 from 5yo+ 9lb **7** Ran SP% **111.5**
Speed ratings (Par 105): **97,96,96,93,84 81,—**
toteswingers: 1&2 £6.80, 1&3 £7.50, 2&3 £13.00. CSF £20.36 CT £154.64 TOTE £4.00: £3.70, £1.80; EX 16.10.
Owner Mrs M Chapman **Bred** Charles And David Hodge **Trained** Market Rasen, Lincs

FOCUS
A very ordinary handicap, run at an uneven gallop. Another step forward from the winner.

NOTEBOOK
Skye But N Ben was purchased by his new connections after winning a C&D seller 15 days earlier and, raised 7lb for that, he proved easy to back under top weight on this return to better company. His last success was a personal best, though, and he made it four wins from his last five outings under a typically strong ride from Tony McCoy, who is now 2-2 aboard him. He was idling late on and ought to remain competitive after another weight rise. (op 4-1)
Lodgician(IRE) took time to settle, but responded to strong pressure from three out and was coming back at the winner at the business end. He enjoyed this return to quicker ground, but ideally needs a stiffer 2m. (tchd 3-1 and 10-3 in a place)
Tom O'Tara ◆ looked the biggest danger to the winner off the home turn, but didn't look to fully let himself down on ground that would've been plenty lively enough for him. It was a pleasing comeback effort from him and he is one to be interested in next time if reverting to a stiffer test on an easier surface. (op 10-1)
Liberty Seeker(FR) proved one-paced when it mattered on this sharper track. This veteran could still find another race down in plating company. (op 8-1)
Phoenix Eye was all but stopped when the well-backed Halling Gal crashed out with four to jump. (op 7-2)

1939 AMATEUR JOCKEYS ASSOCIATION AMATEUR RIDERS' H'CAP CHASE (FOR THE COURT OF HILL CHALLENGE CUP) (19 fncs) 3m
4:15 (4:15) (Class 4) (0-100,100) 4-Y-O+
£3,301 (£1,031; £515; £257; £128; £64)

Form RPR

5344 **1** **Feeling Peckish (USA)**[8] 1826 6-9-7 **74** oh1 (t) MrTGarner[(7)] 85+
(Michael Chapman) *nt fluent 3rd: trckd ldrs: pushed along bef 12th: led appr 16th: drew rt away next: easily* **9/1**

4421 **2** *15* **Heezagrey (IRE)**[8] 1820 7-9-12 **75** 7ex RobertKirk[(3)] 71
(James Evans) *lost gd pl 6th: in rr and rdn 10th: 15 l 4th and styng on 3 out: wnt 2nd flat but nvr nr wnr* **9/2**[2]

-324 **3** *¾* **Havenstone (IRE)**[14] 1741 9-10-8 **89** MrJEngland[(7)] 85
(Evan Williams) *led: j.lft at times: drvn and hdd bef 16th: sn lost tch w wnr: 17 l 2nd and fading last* **13/2**

/432 **4** *8* **Autumn Red (IRE)**[14] 1747 10-11-1 **96** (bt) MrJonathanBailey[(7)] 85
(Paul Webber) *cl up but nvr looked to be gng wl: reminders 5th and 8th: mstke 13th and rdn: struggling after 15th: tk poor 4th flat* **5/1**[3]

2P3- **5** *4½* **One More Dinar**[193] 5152 7-10-3 **84** MrJamieJenkinson[(7)] 71
(John Bryan Groucott) *chsd ldrs: wnt 2nd on wd outside and looked to be gng wl 14th tl next: outpcd by wnr 16th: tiring fr 2 out* **11/1**

0235 **6** *2¾* **Classic Clover**[7] 1843 10-11-2 **97** (t) MrMLegg[(7)] 79
(Colin Tizzard) *dropped to rr 6th: rdn and sulking in last at 8th: t.o 13th* **16/1**

U1 **7** *24* **Macs Lad (IRE)**[3] 1903 7-11-10 **98** 7ex MissLHorner 58
(Liam Corcoran) *last whn j.v.slowly 2nd (water): slow again 3rd: virtually t.o 4th: in tch in last pair 6th tl 12th: sn floundering: t.o bef 16th* **7/4**[1]

0/50 **P** **Cilrhiwviv**[15] 1730 7-11-7 **100** MrMWall[(5)] —
(Sue Wilson) *bhd: hdwy 10th: wknd 15th: remote 6th whn blnd 3 out: p.u next* **33/1**

6m 11.7s (3.40) **Going Correction** +0.275s/f (Yiel) **8** Ran SP% **111.7**
Speed ratings (Par 105): **105,100,99,97,95 94,86,—**
toteswingers: 1&2 £5.60, 1&3 £4.30, 2&3 £4.10. CSF £47.51 CT £278.31 TOTE £6.60: £1.90, £1.80, £3.10; EX 38.50.
Owner J E Reed **Bred** Juddmonte Farms Inc **Trained** Market Rasen, Lincs

FOCUS
A weak handicap for amateur riders, run at a sound gallop. The winner is rated to the level of his previous best.

NOTEBOOK
Feeling Peckish(USA) finally shed his maiden tag at the 79th time of asking. It has taken him 62 outings over jumps to come good and he was obviously very hard to fancy, but the track clearly suited as he took it up going strongly nearing the third-last. It's anyone's guess whether he will build on this after a likely rise and this is suspect form, but his confidence should be sky high. (op 10-1)
Heezagrey(IRE) went in snatches when belatedly getting off the mark at Uttoxeter eight days earlier and was easy enough to back under his penalty. Having set off in a handy position, he once again went backwards from halfway before rallying all too late in the day to grab second. This sharper track and quicker ground wouldn't have been ideal given the way his running style has developed, plus he really needs stronger handling to be seen at his best. (op 11-2)
Havenstone(IRE) set out to make all and proved game once headed by the winner, but a 6lb rise for finishing in front of the runner-up on his previous outing in this sphere looks a bit harsh. (op 7-1)
Autumn Red(IRE) went close to getting off the mark at Worcester last time and was closely matched with the placed horses on the form of his penultimate outing at that venue. Another 3lb higher here, went in snatches from an early stage and it's no coincidence he has yet to win. (tchd 11-2)
One More Dinar looked a big player when moving up easily on the final circuit, but he faded from the home turn and this return to action was needed. (op 9-1 tchd 12-1)
Macs Lad(IRE) ran out an easy winner at Plumpton on Monday as he was well ahead of the handicapper under a penalty. He was behind from the start on this different circuit, however, and presumably found the run coming too soon. Official explanation: jockey said gelding never travelled and lost its action (tchd 6-4 and 15-8)

1940 CHRISTMAS FAIR ON 16 NOVEMBER H'CAP CHASE (13 fncs) 2m
4:50 (4:50) (Class 4) (0-105,102) 4-Y-O+
£3,757 (£1,110; £555; £277; £138; £69)

Form RPR

3F-P **1** **Pistolet Dove (IRE)**[153] 427 8-11-9 **102** RichieMcLernon[(3)] 107+
(Sophie Leech) *settled in rr: 9 l 4th and prog 9th: wnt rt and mstke next: drvn and styd on steadily after: led after last: all out* **10/1**

1653 **2** *nk* **Papradon**[18] 1710 6-11-0 **93** SamTwiston-Davies[(3)] 98+
(Nigel Twiston-Davies) *settled pressing ldng pair: rdn 8th: sltly outpcd 10th: drvn into 2nd 3 out: trying to chal whn mstke last: styng on cl home* **4/1**[3]

5225 **3** *4½* **Peak Seasons (IRE)**[25] 1628 7-9-7 **76** oh2 GaryDerwin[(7)] 76
(Michael Chapman) *j. sltly lft at times: sn 2nd: led 7th: 5 l clr and looked wnr 10th: wknd bef last: bmpd along and hdd and no ex flat* **7/2**[2]

540 **4** *1* **Blue Express (IRE)**[46] 1474 11-11-0 **90** (t) PaulMoloney 89
(Evan Williams) *reminder 3rd: chsd ldrs: outpcd 9th: cajoled along 3 out: kpt on flat but nvr unable to chal* **8/1**

P-6P **5** *9* **Colliers Court**[8] 1823 13-10-11 **94** HarryChalloner[(7)] 85
(Lisa Williamson) *set a brisk pce: hd str: led tl mstke 7th: lost 2nd 3 out: no ex* **14/1**

05U- **6** *½* **Thievery**[176] 48 9-10-9 **85** RichardJohnson 76
(Henry Daly) *blnd 3rd: bhd: n.d fr 8th: plugging on fr 2 out* **5/2**[1]

/P0P **P** **Sternenzelt (GER)**[46] 1481 7-11-2 **92** DavidEngland —
(Michael Gates) *in rr and str reminders after 5th: no rspnse: t.o and p.u 10th* **11/1**

P-P **P** **Your Night Out (FR)**[64] 1283 5-11-2 **92** (t) AidanColeman —
(Matt Sheppard) *bhd: j. slowly 6th: rdn and struggling 8th: t.o and p.u 10th* **14/1**

4m 4.70s (6.20) **Going Correction** +0.275s/f (Yiel) **8** Ran SP% **112.7**
Speed ratings (Par 105): **95,94,92,92,87 87,—,—**
toteswingers: 1&2 £3.00, 1&3 £5.50, 2&3 £2.10. CSF £49.20 CT £168.69 TOTE £12.20: £4.20, £3.20, £1.10; EX 43.70.
Owner C J Leech **Bred** W And Mrs S May **Trained** Kingsbridge, Devon

FOCUS
Another weak handicap, run at a fair gallop. The first two are rated pretty much to their marks.

NOTEBOOK
Pistolet Dove(IRE) developed into a tricky customer when with Phillip Hobbs and was having his first outing since pulling up on his final outing for him back in May. He proved easy to back on this return to the track, but got up under a finely judged ride and rates value for a little further than the bare margin. His rider tends to excel on such characters and this 8-y-o wouldn't be sure to build on this. However, he is entitled to come on for the run and the change of scenery has obviously done him good. (op 6-1 tchd 12-1)
Papradon, with the blinkers abandoned, came under heavy pressure on the back straight, but to his credit he rallied and was only just denied by the winner. He prefers a slightly stiffer test and this was better again, but he does look to be handicapped about right. (op 7-2 tchd 3-1)
Peak Seasons(IRE) came into this on the back of a long losing run, but it looked for a long way as though he was going to end it and hand his yard a treble on the card. He just tired nearing the final fence and would've probably scored had his rider held onto him for a little longer. (op 9-2 tchd 5-1)
Blue Express(IRE) shaped more encouragingly on this second outing as a chaser, but remains winless since 2008 and is one to carefully with. (op 17-2 tchd 9-1)
Thievery, returning from a 178-day break, was second in this race last term on his comeback and was back down to his last winning mark. He was always playing catch up after getting behind when guessing at the third fence. (op 3-1 tchd 10-3)

1941 HAVE YOUR CHRISTMAS PARTY AT LUDLOW NOVICES' HURDLE (11 hdls) 2m 5f
5:20 (5:20) (Class 4) 4-Y-O+ **£3,252** (£955; £477; £238)

Form RPR

1 **1** **Natureofthebeast (IRE)**[15] 1729 5-10-12 0 PaulMoloney 119+
(Evan Williams) *dropped out last: clsd bef 3 out: sn led: racd lazily up st but a doing enough: rdn clr fr last* **4/6**[1]

3-32 **2** *2¼* **Zakatal**[157] 370 4-10-12 120 (t) RichardJohnson 115
(Philip Hobbs) *lacked fluency: hld up: effrt w wnr bef 3 out: chsd him after: rdn and ev ch last: wl hld flat* **5/4**[2]

3 *36* **Eternal City** 5-10-12 0 SamJones 87
(Paul Webber) *j. slowly 2nd: pressed ldr tl rdn to ld after 8th: hdd bef next: dropped out rapidly* **12/1**[3]

604P **4** *49* **Youandme (IRE)**[15] 1730 8-10-12 75 (p) ColinBolger 39
(Ray Peacock) *led tl after 8th: last bef next: sn bdly t.o* **80/1**

5m 13.9s (-0.90) **Going Correction** -0.175s/f (Good)
WFA 4 from 5yo+ 10lb **4** Ran SP% **113.4**
Speed ratings (Par 105): **94,93,79,60**
CSF £2.05 TOTE £2.10; EX 1.90 Place 6: £39.70, Place 5: £19.82..
Owner Mrs Janet Davies **Bred** Mr And Mrs R A St George **Trained** Llancarfan, Vale Of Glamorgan

FOCUS
This predictably developed into a match off the home turn and the winner can rate higher. The time was slow and this is not form to be confident about, though.

NOTEBOOK
Natureofthebeast(IRE) ◆ added to his two point wins when readily winning a bumper on debut for connections at this venue 15 days earlier, and he maintained his unbeaten record on this switch to hurdling. The extra distance suited and he again showed a likeable attitude when sent about his business. It's hard to know how good he may be at this stage, but connections obviously have a decent prospect on their hands and he looks up to defying a penalty if found another race on this sort of ground. (op 4-5)
Zakatal, placed on his three previous outings, was bumped up to a mark of 120 after finishing a clear second in what has proved to be a fair event at Newton Abbot on his previous outing in May. Given a breathing operation during his time off the track, he proved easy to back on this return and, not for the first time, tended to run with the choke out. He failed to match the winner in the jumping department from three out and that cost him. No doubt he is capable of winning races if consenting to settle better and time may tell he faced a difficult task here. (tchd 6-4)
Eternal City has more of a Flat pedigree but is a brother to hurdles winning Hereditary. He was given a positive ride, but proved novicey at his hurdles and was easily beaten off from the third-last. There ought to be more to come from him after this experience and he should get 3m. (op 16-1 tchd 18-1)
T/Plt: £39.50 to a £1 stake. Pool:£49,175.33 - 907.02 winning tickets T/Qpdt: £8.70 to a £1 stake. Pool:£3,972.09 - 337.10 winning tickets IM

1942 - 1948a (Foreign Racing) - See Raceform Interactive

436 FAKENHAM (L-H)
Friday, October 22

OFFICIAL GOING: Good (7.2)
Wind: moderate against Weather: sunny and chilly

1949 PRINCE OF WALES STAND CONDITIONAL JOCKEYS' (S) H'CAP HURDLE (9 hdls) 2m
2:00 (2:01) (Class 5) (0-85,85) 4-Y-O+ **£2,397** (£698; £349)

Form RPR

35/P **1** **Brilliant (GER)**[15] 1745 7-10-7 **69** (p) AodhaganConlon[(3)] 76
(Debra Hamer) *pressed ldng pair: rdn bef 6th: outpcd 2 out: rallied for driving to ld jst after last: sn clr* **8/1**

6-53 **2** *3* **Mister Fizzbomb (IRE)**[17] 745 7-11-12 **85** (v) HarryHaynes 89
(John Wainwright) *pressed ldr: led 2 out: 2 l clr and rdn between last two: hdd jst after last: fnd nthing* **13/2**[3]

55P5 **3** *2* **Bari Bay**[46] 1489 4-11-1 **74** PeterToole 77
(Michael Blake) *j. slowly 2nd: chsd ldrs: effrt 3 out: wnt 2nd but hrd rdn next: wknd bef last* **13/2**[3]

3-34 **4** *1 3/4* **Stravita**19 1704 6-11-3 **79**............(p) MarcGoldstein(3) 80
(Jim Best) *bhd: sme prog whn stmbld bef 3 out: rdn and plugged on wout threatening fr next: tk 4th bef last* **7/2**1

500 **5** *6* **Granakey (IRE)**27 1613 7-10-7 **74**............ MichaelByrne(8) 73+
(Peter Bowen) *hit 1st: led: mstke 3 out: hdd next: 6 l 5th and wkng last: eased flat* **15/2**

-P44 **6** *1 3/4* **Daraybad (FR)**62 1340 8-10-12 **76**............(v) PaulGallagher(5) 71
(Andrew Crook) *j. poorly in rr: last after 5th: rdn 3 out: toiled on: mstke last* **8/1**

/0P6 **7** *9* **Ful Of Grace (IRE)**19 1707 6-10-13 **72**............(b) CO'Farrell 58
(James Frost) *towards rr: rdn 3 out: struggling to rch ldrs whn blnd next* **14/1**

F600 **8** *1* **Simplified**9 1831 7-10-6 **65**............(t) SamTwiston-Davies 50
(Michael Chapman) *t.k.h chsng ldrs: nt fluent 3rd: rdn and btn after mstke 3 out* **16/1**

0362 **9** *hd* **We'Re Delighted**33 1549 5-11-12 **85**............(t) RyanMania 70
(Michael Blake) *hld up in midfield: rdn after 3 out: btn bef next* **9/2**2

4m 12.5s (7.10) **Going Correction** -0.125s/f (Good)
WFA 4 from 5yo+ 9lb **9** Ran SP% **113.6**
Speed ratings (Par 103): **77,75,74,73,70 69,65,64,64**
toteswingers:1&2:£17.90, 1&3:£6.40, 2&3:£22.90 CSF £58.07 CT £357.98 TOTE £8.60: £3.20, £1.50, £2.70; EX 68.80.There was no bid for the winner.
Owner John Cole **Bred** Horst-D Beyer **Trained** Nantycaws, Carmarthens

FOCUS
The going was decribed as good, beautiful jumping ground for this tricky but modest conditional jockeys' seller which was run at just an ordinary pace. The winner is rated to his 2009 best.

NOTEBOOK
Brilliant(GER), a winner at this lowly level back in 2007, had been pulled up on reappearance earlier this month but had clearly benefited from the outing. His form is rather hit-and-miss at this level so, whether he can go on can only be taken on trust. There was no bid for him at the subsequent auction.
Mister Fizzbomb(IRE) looked as though he had the upper hand turning in but was eventually run out of it from the last. Soundly beaten on the Flat recently, this was respectable effort back over hurdles under top weight even at this level. (op 11-2)
Bari Bay produced a better effort than that of late but would have found this sharp enough. (op 8-1)
Stravita had been performing respectably in sellers and a claimer and was sent off favourite, but lost her pitch when stumbling going to three out and, although she was staying on turning in, she was always fighting a losing battle. Official explanation: jockey said gelding stumbled approaching final 3f (op 5-2)
Granakey(IRE) tried to make this a test on handicap debut in this lowly grade but needs to brush up on her jumping and was soundly beaten after being headed going to two out. (op 11-1 tchd 12-1)

1950 ROA GOLD STANDARD AWARD FOR FAKENHAM H'CAP CHASE (18 fncs) 3m 110y
2:35 (2:35) (Class 3) (0-135,130) 4-Y-0+ **£8,261** (£2,425; £1,212; £605)

Form RPR

/523 **1** **Sporting Rebel (IRE)**33 1557 10-10-7 **111**............ HaddenFrost 127+
(James Frost) *enthusiatic and tended to jump really wl: 2nd tl led 6th: 4 l clr whn hit 15th: ballooned 2 out and rdn: a in command* **8/1**

3552 **2** *9* **Pheidias (IRE)**10 1815 6-10-7 **118**............(p) MissGAndrews(7) 126+
(Pam Sly) *hld up early: wnt 2nd at 8th: bmpd along fr bef 15th: nvr win 4 l of wnr: fnd nthing 2 out: eased flat* **3/1**2

141P **3** *21* **No Panic (IRE)**27 1611 7-11-12 **130**............(v1) TomO'Brien 117
(Peter Bowen) *pressed ldrs tl outpcd and j. slowly 10th: 3rd and rdn and struggling fr next: 17 l 3rd 3 out: laboured on* **7/2**3

103- **4** *nk* **Emperor Concerto**197 5101 7-11-12 **130**............ LeightonAspell 120+
(Lucy Wadham) *led tl hdd and blnd 6th: plentiful slow jumps after: struggling 11th: 22 l 4th 3 out: plodding on after last* **11/4**1

3PP- **P** **Antonius Caesar (FR)**191 5181 7-10-8 **112**............ PaulMoloney —
(Alex Hales) *j. deliberately and nvr gng wl: last after mstke 7th: t.o 11th tl p.u 2 out* **3/1**2

6m 27.7s (-8.00) **Going Correction** -0.125s/f (Good) **5** Ran SP% **110.0**
Speed ratings (Par 107): **107,104,97,97,—**
CSF £31.33 TOTE £8.50: £2.80, £2.50; EX 24.70.
Owner Peter Farthing **Bred** John F Gibbons **Trained** Scorriton, Devon

FOCUS
A decent prize on offer for this staying handicap chase but a disappointing turnout, with jumping errors ultimately taking the favourite out of the race. The winner was back to the sort of form he showed for a different yard in 2008.

NOTEBOOK
Sporting Rebel(IRE) ran out a comfortable winner returning to 3m. Taking over with two circuits to go, he never looked as though he was in any real trouble and only had to be pushed out. Jimmy Frost continues to do particularly well with his runners here and this horse had shaped as though he was steadily coming to hand, but in all fairness this race was up for the taking off his light weight with most of the runners below par. (op 7-1 tchd 9-1)
Pheidias(IRE) performs well around this tight track since fitted with cheekpieces and made a pleasing return to action here earlier this month. He tried to make a race of it going down the back straight but was always being held. Another good effort, he's always one to take into consideration around here. (op 7-2 tchd 4-1)
No Panic(IRE) was running in a first-time visor after pulling up in a valuable contest at Market Rasen last time. This was another disappointing effort as after flattering briefly with a circuit to go he dropped away very tamely after five out. (op 3-1 tchd 5-2)
Emperor Concerto was a progressive novice last year ad was well supported to make a winning return on handicap debut. He landed very awkwardly whilst leading the field with two circuits to go, though, and his jumping was far from fluent from then on. Whether he injured himself, time will only tell but, he is worth giving another chance as he is better than this. (tchd 9-4)
Antonius Caesar(FR), making his seasonal debut, made a mistake with two circuits to go and soon found himself detached, eventually being pulled up. (op 4-1 tchd 9-2)

1951 JOHN WARD LIFETIME IN RACING NOVICES' HURDLE (11 hdls) 2m 4f
3:10 (3:10) (Class 3) 4-Y-0+ **£4,553** (£1,337; £668; £333)

Form RPR

1- **1** **Carribs Leap (IRE)**232 4405 5-10-12 0............ APMcCoy 114+
(Charles Egerton) *trckd ldrs: wnt 3rd at 5th: hit 7th: hrd drvn bef 3 out: led last: forced along to hold on* **11/10**1

22-1 **2** *1* **Frontier Spirit (IRE)**30 1573 6-11-4 0............ PaddyBrennan 119+
(Nigel Twiston-Davies) *nt a fluent: pressed ldr: led after 3 out: hit next: drvn and hdd last: kpt on but carrying hd high* **2/1**2

1261 **3** *2 1/2* **Occasionally Yours (IRE)**19 1688 6-11-3 119............ MarcGoldstein(5) 120
(Alan Blackmore) *towards rr: effrt in 4th at 8th: wnt 3rd 2 out: rdn and kpt on gamely but a 3rd best* **7/1**3

0226 **4** *30* **Astrolibra**16 1724 6-10-11 110............ ColinBolger 82
(Mark H Tompkins) *midfield: mstke 2nd: rdn 6th: outpcd 8th: poor 7th 3 out* **16/1**

125- **5** *3/4* **L'Eldorado (FR)**230 4427 5-10-12 0............ TomMessenger 84+
(Chris Bealby) *led: 6 l clr early: hit 6th: rdn and hdd after 3 out: stopped to nil next: t.o* **20/1**

04- **6** *3 1/2* **Morcambe**192 5179 5-10-12 0............ BarryGeraghty 81
(Nicky Henderson) *chsd ldrs: blnd 7th: struggling after next: t.o* **9/1**

6 **7** *1 3/4* **Panama Canal (IRE)**26 1623 5-10-9 0............ AdamPogson(3) 78
(Charles Pogson) *t.k.h in rr: drvn and lost tch in 5th at 8th: t.o* **66/1**

400- **8** *19* **Erin Dancer (IRE)**256 3931 5-10-5 0............ PaulGallagher(7) 61
(Ferdy Murphy) *bhd: mstke 4th: struggling after 7th: drvn and t.o bef 3 out* **50/1**

5m 6.00s (-6.60) **Going Correction** -0.125s/f (Good) **8** Ran SP% **117.5**
Speed ratings (Par 107): **108,107,106,94,94 92,92,84**
toteswingers:1&2:£1.10, 1&3:£2.40, 2&3:£2.90 CSF £3.69 TOTE £2.40: £1.10, £1.30, £2.10; EX 4.80.
Owner Charles Egerton **Bred** Pat Grogan **Trained** Chaddleworth, Berks

FOCUS
A couple of interesting contenders for this novices' hurdle which was run at just an ordinary pace, with the front three pulling well clear of the remainder.

NOTEBOOK
Carribs Leap(IRE), an Irish point winner and with an easy victory in a Ludlow bumper already to his name, was made to work very hard to come out on top on hurdling debut. He clearly has bags of potential, but was never really travelling on this tight track, although jumping fluently enough. Highly regarded with a likeable attitude, he has plenty of ticks in the right boxes and considerable improvement can be expected when on a more galloping track. (op 5-4 tchd 11-8)
Frontier Spirit(IRE) has confirmed promise of bumpers when scoring on hurdling debut last time and again posted a decent effort. She handled the track better than the winner, but was ultimately out-gunned from the last. She remains open to further improvement and handled the faster surface. (op 9-4)
Occasionally Yours(IRE) set the standard under a double penalty and ran a blinder in defeat. He remains in great heart since joining present connections. He stuck to his task gamely after coming under pressure from a fair way out, but could not quite reel in the front pair. (op 8-1)
Astrolibra had won a maiden hurdle in May and likes this ground, but was coming here off the back of a disappointing effort last time and again performed below par. (tchd 14-1 and 20-1)
L'Eldorado(FR) took them along at an ordinary pace but did himself no favours jumping to his right and probably needs a softer surface to be seen to better effect.

1952 NORTHERN NORFOLK NOVICES' CHASE (16 fncs) 2m 5f 110y
3:45 (3:45) (Class 3) 4-Y-0+ **£6,960** (£2,043; £1,021; £510)

Form RPR

10-2 **1** **Robo (FR)**169 170 5-11-2 114............ SamJones 137+
(Renee Robeson) *bhd: hit 2nd: blnd 5th: mstke 6th: plentiful reminders fr 8th: clsd 11th: wnt 4th and mstke 12th: chal 2 out: sn led: forged clr bef last and j. it wl* **9/1**

25-2 **2** *5* **Anquetta (IRE)**162 303 6-11-2 0............ BarryGeraghty 129+
(Nicky Henderson) *wnt 2nd at 5th: led 13th: gng wl after 3 out: pressed next: sn hdd and drvn: swished tail bef last and gave up v tamely* **11/4**1

56-3 **3** *10* **Bugsy's Boy**12 401 6-11-2 0............ AndrewTinkler 119
(George Baker) *chsd ldrs: j. slowly 7th: rdn 12th: 7 l 4th and btn 3 out* **11/4**1

4052 **4** *11* **Ovthenight (IRE)**10 1813 5-10-9 105............ MissGAndrews(7) 112+
(Pam Sly) *mstkes 3rd and 5th: lost tch 8th: nvr gng or jumping w any zest: wl bhd 11th* **12/1**

23-1 **5** *9* **Circus Of Dreams**170 155 7-11-12 125............(b1) DominicElsworth 111
(Oliver Sherwood) *led: pckd 1st: hdd 13th: drvn and j. slowly next: dropped out rapidly* **5/1**3

-3PP **P** **Grenoli (FR)**48 1469 9-11-1 94............(bt) JoeCornwall(7) —
(John Cornwall) *j. slowly 1st: chsd ldr tl 5th: rdn 8th: sn lost tch: t.o and p.u 3 out* **66/1**

211- **P** **Hoback Junction (IRE)**201 5013 6-11-2 0............ LeightonAspell —
(Lucy Wadham) *j.rt: chsd ldrs tl wknd 12th: t.o next: p.u 2 out* **3/1**2

5m 34.9s (-6.90) **Going Correction** -0.125s/f (Good) **7** Ran SP% **114.2**
Speed ratings (Par 107): **107,105,101,97,94 —,—**
toteswingers:1&2:£7.50, 1&3:£5.10, 2&3:£2.90 CSF £34.84 TOTE £12.80: £4.40, £2.20; EX 46.50.
Owner The Ravenstone Partnership **Bred** Yvon Madiot **Trained** Tyringham, Bucks

FOCUS
An ordinary novice but the winner can rate higher if his jumping improves.

NOTEBOOK
Robo(FR)'s progression over hurdles flattened out somewhat when with Philip Hobbs, but he was always considered to be a better proposition when his attention was switched to fences and that duly proved to be the case. Apart from finding the track on the tight side and producing some novicey mistakes, he ran out a convincing winner. Rated 113 over hurdles, he looks capable of being better than that over fences and shaped as though stepping up in distance would also be to be his advantage. (tchd 10-1)
Anquetta(IRE) had been pleasing in his schooling at home and fenced well here and after looking as though he was travelling better than the winner from two out, but found little when push came to shove. He is no doubt capable and with his top connections he should find a similar opportunity before long. (op 15-8 tchd 3-1)
Bugsy's Boy, the highest-rated of these over hurdles, had run well over fences on chasing debut in the spring and came here in good heart after winning on the Flat earlier this month. He moved up to press the leaders with a circuit to run, but clouted five out and soon came under pressure. Ultimately, he could only stay on at the same pace. (op 4-1)
Hoback Junction(IRE) had shown some fairly useful form over hurdles, but threw away any chance he had by jumping continually to his right. (op 11-4)

1953 FAKENHAM SUPPORTS RACING WELFARE H'CAP HURDLE (9 hdls) 2m
4:20 (4:20) (Class 4) (0-110,106) 4-Y-0+ **£4,228** (£1,241; £620; £310)

Form RPR

6/4- **1** **Motarjm (USA)**29 4721 6-11-8 **102**............(t) GerardTumelty 107+
(Jeff Pearce) *towards rr on ins: hdwy 3 out: led gng wl bef next: 3 l clr last: stamina ebbed away flat: all out cl home* **13/2**2

1353 **2** *3/4* **Galley Slave (IRE)**26 1624 5-9-13 **86**............ GaryDerwin(7) 89
(Michael Chapman) *a 2nd or 3rd: chsd wnr fr 2 out: outpcd between last two: rallied under unorthodox handling flat: catching wnr cl home* **7/2**1

00-2 **3** *6* **Blackstone Vegas**33 1552 4-10-9 **92**............ SeanQuinlan(3) 92+
(Derek Shaw) *bhd: rdn 5th: mstke 3 out: kpt on after: wnt 8 l 3rd at last: nvr looked like rching ldrs* **7/1**3

364- **4** *5* **Tricky Tree (IRE)**179 25 4-11-5 **106**............ MissGAndrews(7) 99
(Pam Sly) *towards rr on outside: rdn and effrt 3 out: 8 l 4th next: no further prog* **17/2**

662- **5** *2* **Kinsya**44 4722 7-11-6 **100**............ ColinBolger 92+
(Mark H Tompkins) *t.k.h pressing ldrs: led after 3 out: hdd next: fdd tamely: mstke last* **13/2**2

14-P **6** *15* **Bromhead (USA)**[26] 1624 4-10-12 **92** .... LeightonAspell 70
(Kevin Morgan) *taken gingerly to s: plld hrd in rr: mstke 6th: rdn and struggling after 3 out: eased after next* **14/1**

P-P0 **7** *12* **Orpen Wide (IRE)**[7] 1569 8-11-4 **98** ....(bt) AndrewGlassonbury 65
(Michael Chapman) *wnt 3rd at 5th and 2nd at next: ev ch 3 out: dropped out rapidly: eased and t.o* **20/1**

42-4 **8** *27* **Tae Kwon Do (USA)**[63] 1313 4-11-6 **100** .... DougieCostello 43
(Julie Camacho) *midfield: rdn and wknd bef 3 out: eased and hopelessly t.o* **8/1**

-030 **9** *6* **Renege The Joker**[54] 760 7-10-3 **90** .... MissCBoxall(7) 27
(Sean Regan) *tubed: bhd: struggling whn hmpd 6th: sn lost tch: eased and hopelessly t.o* **50/1**

144- **10** *14* **Calaficial (IRE)**[358] 1975 7-11-7 **104** ....(t) AdamPogson(3) 29
(Charles Pogson) *led at brisk pce: j.rt: hdd after 3 out and stopped to nthing: eased and hopelessly t.o* **16/1**

50-0 **11** *3 1/2* **Zepnove (IRE)**[161] 313 4-11-6 **100** .... RichardJohnson 21
(Neil King) *chsd ldr tl rdn 5th: last after next: eased and hopelessly t.o* **13/2**[2]

4m 6.10s (0.70) **Going Correction** -0.125s/f (Good)
WFA 4 from 5yo+ 9lb **11** Ran SP% **115.6**
Speed ratings (Par 105): **93,92,89,87,86 78,72,59,56,49 47**
toteswingers:1&2:£5.10, 1&3:£9.70, 2&3:£4.60 CSF £29.58 CT £165.32 TOTE £9.10: £3.00, £2.40, £2.40; EX 31.30.
Owner P D Band **Bred** Darley **Trained** Newmarket, Suffolk

FOCUS
A competitive handicap hurdle run at a fair pace. The winner is rated in line with his recent Flat form with the next three close to their marks.

NOTEBOOK
Motarjm(USA), rarely seen over hurdles (only fifth run), has been coming back to hand on the Flat recently and wasn't beaten far off this mark over C&D in March. He travelled well for most of the trip and had the race put to bed turning in, although the runner-up was closing at the finish. Probably likes a sharp track like this and does not find much off the bridle, but fairly unexposed in this sphere so possible improvement could not easily be ruled out. (op 9-2)
Galley Slave(IRE) is not easy to predict but has been running at a consistent level of late and again ran respectably. He held every chance from two out until the winner just edged ahead going to the last, but stayed on again on the run to the line. (op 11-2)
Blackstone Vegas's form of his second has not held up after the winner was soundly beaten next time and he was 5lb higher here. He stayed on from after two out after being readily outpaced in the back straight. (op 15-2)
Tricky Tree(IRE) was progressive in bumpers but improvement seemed to have flattened out since switched to hurdles. He looked to be on a high enough mark for handicap debut and that remains to the case as he could not get involved here. (op 10-1 tchd 8-1)
Kinsya improved on previous hurdling form when chasing home easy winner over C&D in May and looked to be on a reasonable mark for handicap debut, but he was soon brushed aside after holding every chance going to two out. (op 6-1 tchd 5-1)
Calaficial(IRE) jumped to the right at a lot of hurdles and found little once joined. (op 17-2)
Zepnove(IRE), down to a decent mark, came in for some market support but showed nothing the moment she came under pressure. Official explanation: jockey said filly stopped quickly (op 8-1 tchd 6-1)

1954 1824 H'CAP CHASE (16 fncs) 2m 5f 110y
4:55 (4:55) (Class 5) (0-85,82) 4-Y-0+ **£2,797** (£821; £410; £205)

Form RPR

600- **1** **Reelwill (FR)**[213] 4811 5-11-0 **70** .... TomMessenger 76+
(Chris Bealby) *led tl 4th: nrly a 2nd after: upsides 3 out: led and nt fluent last: asserted flat: all out* **10/1**

P523 **2** *1 1/4* **Executive's Hall (IRE)**[9] 1826 6-10-9 **65** ....(v) BrianHughes 71+
(Andrew Crook) *mde nrly all fr 4th: mstke 10th: j. slowly 11th: hit 3 out and jnd: hit next: hdd last: fnd nthing* **2/1**[2]

34P1 **3** *2 3/4* **Great Ocean Road (IRE)**[20] 1678 7-11-12 **82** .... WillKennedy 84
(David Thompson) *trckd ldng trio: mstke 13th: wnt 3rd next: sn drvn and effrt: woefully one pce between last two* **11/1**

-331 **4** *35* **Sean Og (IRE)**[4] 1905 8-10-11 **67** 7ex ....(t) RichardJohnson 49+
(Tim Vaughan) *trckd ldrs: 2nd briefly at 11th: blnd 13th and rdn: struggling after next: eased flat* **5/4**[1]

6364 **5** *16* **Mad Professor (IRE)**[15] 1744 7-10-10 **73** ....(p) JoeCornwall(7) 29
(John Cornwall) *nt a fluent: bhd: hit 5th and rdn: drvn after 11th: t.o 3 out* **16/1**

030P **P** **Devilfishpoker Com**[21] 1660 6-11-2 **75** ....(p) AdamPogson(3) —
(Shaun Harris) *2nd tl blnd 3rd: sddle slipped and p.u* **40/1**

5454 **P** **Safe Investment (USA)**[16] 1733 6-11-5 **75** ....(p) AndrewThornton —
(Ben Pollock) *a last: j. slowly 7th: struggling 10th: t.o and blnd 12th: p.u 3 out* **17/2**[3]

5m 44.4s (2.60) **Going Correction** -0.125s/f (Good) **7** Ran SP% **114.0**
Speed ratings (Par 103): **90,89,88,75,70** —,—
toteswingers:1&2:£3.70, 1&3:£30.50, 2&3:£2.00 CSF £31.51 CT £228.71 TOTE £9.30: £5.10, £1.90; EX 32.80.
Owner Michael Hill **Bred** Jean-Andre Quesny **Trained** Barrowby, Lincs

FOCUS
A sound pace for this open looking, if somewhat ordinary, handicap chase. The form is rated through the second.

NOTEBOOK
Reelwill(FR) had shown glimmers of ability over hurdles but never built on a fair second back in April 2009 and got in here off a mark of 70 as a result. She had reportedly taken to fences almost immediately and jumped well to get the better of a prolonged duel with the runner-up throughout the final circuit. Whether she can go on from this will remain to be seen, but any substantial rise in her mark will make life difficult to do so. Nonetheless, it was a welcome return to the winner's enclosure for Tom Messenger after injury. (op 9-1 tchd 8-1)
Executive's Hall(IRE) has been running consistently well off this mark and can continue to do so. This was a game effort from the front and after rallying gamely after being headed twice, only gave best on the run to the line. (op 5-2)
Great Ocean Road(IRE) outstayed rivals at Fontwell three weeks ago, but faced an 8lb rise and that seemed enough to anchor him after moving through to threaten briefly two out. (op 10-1 tchd 9-1)
Sean Og(IRE) was all the rage in the market to make it 2-2 since joining Tim Vaughan but the writing was on the wall before clattering four out and this might have come too quickly after winning an uncompetitive affair at Plumpton on Monday. (tchd 7-4)
Devilfishpoker Com Official explanation: jockey said saddle slipped (op 8-1 tchd 15-2)
Safe Investment(USA) is likely to be retired now. (op 8-1 tchd 15-2)

1955 FAKENHAM INTERMEDIATE OPEN NATIONAL HUNT FLAT RACE 2m
5:25 (5:26) (Class 5) 4-5-Y-0 **£2,055** (£599; £299)

Form RPR

3- **1** **Catspan (FR)**[216] 4744 4-11-2 0 .... APMcCoy 99+
(Charles Egerton) *midfield: pushed along and effrt 5f out: led 2f out: in command after* **7/4**[1]

3 **2** *4* **Dontupsettherhythm (IRE)**[26] 1629 5-10-13 0 .... AdamPogson(3) 96
(Charles Pogson) *led: rdn over 3f out: hdd 2f out: one pce and wl hld by wnr after* **9/2**[2]

3 *1 1/4* **Stanley's Choice** 4-11-2 0 .... PaulMoloney 94
(John Ferguson) *last trio tl 5f out: styd on fr over 2f out: 5th st: wnt 3rd ins fnl f: unable to chal but kpt on* **20/1**

0- **4** *6* **Ceilidh Royal**[316] 2793 5-10-9 0 .... BarryGeraghty 81
(Nicky Henderson) *midfield: rdn over 4f out: sn flat footed: n.d fnl 2f* **7/4**[1]

5 *1 1/2* **Iznt Getting Court (IRE)** 4-10-13 0 .... HarryHaynes(3) 87
(John Wainwright) *prom tl rdn 3f out: wknd steadily* **50/1**

6 *1 1/2* **Hanahoe** 5-11-2 0 .... TomO'Brien 86
(Alex Hales) *prom tl lost pl 5f out: plodded on* **8/1**[3]

0 **7** *33* **Hijack The Duke (IRE)**[10] 1817 4-11-2 0 .... LeightonAspell 60
(John Ferguson) *in last trio: struggling 5f out: t.o and eased* **50/1**

0 **8** *3 1/4* **Amazingreyce**[77] 1201 5-10-6 0 .... PeterToole(3) 46
(Owen Brennan) *in last pair: struggling 6f out: t.o fnl 3f: eased* **50/1**

4m 4.80s (5.00) **Going Correction** -0.125s/f (Good)
WFA 4 from 5yo 9lb **8** Ran SP% **112.7**
Speed ratings: **82,80,79,76,75 74,58,56**
toteswingers:1&2:£1.10, 1&3:£13.20, 2&3:£8.10 CSF £9.83 TOTE £2.90: £1.30, £1.10, £5.40; EX 9.00 Place 6: £107.85, Place 5: £39.92..
Owner Bailey-Carvill Equine **Bred** Eric Puerari And Marc De Chambre **Trained** Chaddleworth, Berks

FOCUS
An ordinary bumper, with the first two rated in line with their previous efforts.

NOTEBOOK
Catspan(FR) landed a double for Charlie Egerton and Tony McCoy. The Turgeon-bred 5-y-o had run with promise when a staying on third in similar affair on soft ground at Uttoxeter in March but handled this faster surface just as well. Nice individual who can only go on from this and will probably be sent over hurdles in the near future. (tchd 11-8)
Dontupsettherhythm(IRE) won an Irish point in May and was subsequently bought for £12,000 at Doncaster in August. He showed promise here after trying to make all and kept on well enough when headed. (op 7-1)
Stanley's Choice ran green and got going all to late. He will have benefited from the experience. (op 28-1)
Ceilidh Royal is well related but had to put behind her a disappointing debut on soft ground in December when well beaten at odds on. She handled this quicker surface well enough, but once again, failed to get home and has plenty of questions to answer now. (op 5-4 tchd 6-5 and 2-1)
T/Plt: £202.80 to a £1 stake. Pool:£64,171.38 - 230.97 winning tickets T/Qpdt: £15.00 to a £1 stake. Pool:£7,906.93 - 390.02 winning tickets IM

706 AINTREE (L-H)
Saturday, October 23

OFFICIAL GOING: Good to soft (soft in places; chs 7.6, hdl 7.9)
Wind: Light, across Weather: Cloudy with showers

1956 TOTEPLACEPOT H'CAP HURDLE (9 hdls) 2m 110y
2:10 (2:10) (Class 2) (0-140,136) 4-Y-0+ **£8,871** (£2,620; £1,310; £655; £327)

Form RPR

2-01 **1** **Nearby**[14] 1766 6-11-4 **135** .... ChrisDavies(7) 145+
(Philip Hobbs) *midfield: hdwy appr 3 out: led last: drvn out and r.o wl run-in: wl in command fnl 100yds* **8/1**[3]

0246 **2** *3* **Heron Bay**[27] 1625 6-10-3 **116** .... DonalDevereux(3) 122
(Peter Bowen) *a.p: led appr 3 out: rdn and hdd last: one pce and wl hld by wnr fnl 100yds* **12/1**

3 *9* **Kauto Relko (FR)**[172] 142 6-10-12 **125** .... SeanQuinlan(3) 124
(Rachel Hobbs) *hld up: hdwy appr 3 out: effrt to chal 2 out: nt fluent last: sn hung lft and btn: no ch w front pair after* **28/1**

6F-6 **4** *nk* **Charingworth (IRE)**[169] 194 7-10-5 **115** .... GrahamLee 113
(Ferdy Murphy) *hld up: shkn up appr 2 out: styd on steadily after: nt trble ldrs* **28/1**

B11- **5** *5* **Mille Chief (FR)**[269] 3681 4-11-12 **136** .... WayneHutchinson 130
(Alan King) *midfield: managed to avoid fallers 6th: effrt and hdwy 3 out: sn chsd ldrs: one pce bef last* **10/3**[1]

50-P **6** *2 1/2* **Cheshire Prince**[162] 316 6-10-10 **120** .... MarkBradburne 112
(Neil King) *midfield: effrt and hdwy 2 out: rdn bef last: no further imp* **14/1**

20-3 **7** *3 1/4* **Westlin' Winds (IRE)**[14] 1775 4-11-5 **136** .... JakeGreenall(7) 125
(Charles Egerton) *led: hdd appr 3 out: rdn bef 2 out: wknd bef last* **4/1**[2]

0/0- **8** *3/4* **Culcabock (IRE)**[342] 2295 10-11-3 **130** .... CampbellGillies(3) 117
(Lucinda Russell) *prom: stl chalng 3 out: rdn and wknd appr 2 out* **16/1**

0-31 **9** *3/4* **Regent's Secret (USA)**[30] 1597 10-9-9 **112** ....(v) PaulNorton(7) 98
(Jim Goldie) *in rr: nt fluent 2nd: strrugling appr 3 out: nvr on terms* **20/1**

1-25 **10** *1 1/2* **Master Fong (IRE)**[145] 548 4-10-6 **119** ....(b) AdrianLane(3) 104
(Donald McCain) *trckd ldrs: nt fluent 3 out: btn whn nt fluent 2 out: sn dropped away* **28/1**

/4V- **11** *29* **Hector's Choice (FR)**[315] 2840 6-11-0 **124** .... TomScudamore 83
(Richard Lee) *in tch: rdn to chse ldrs 2 out: abt 5 l 4th and u.p whn slipped bdly last: nt rcvr and dropped away* **33/1**

2-U0 **12** *28* **Teenage Idol (IRE)**[10] 1827 6-10-10 **120** .... TjadeCollier 54
(Evelyn Slack) *a bhd: j.rt 6th: lost tch after* **80/1**

10P- **B** **Caravel (IRE)**[196] 5128 6-11-4 **131** .... RyanMania(3) —
(Howard Johnson) *midfield tl b.d 6th* **12/1**

243- **B** **Gifted Leader (USA)**[213] 4818 5-10-5 **122** .... TrevorWhelan(7) —
(Ian Williams) *hld up: b.d 6th* **17/2**

213- **F** **Hector's House**[306] 3001 4-9-10 **113** ....(b[1]) PeterCarberry(7) 108
(David Brace) *midfield: trcking ldrs whn fell 6th* **33/1**

613- **P** **Drumshambo (USA)**[185] 5308 4-10-9 **119** .... AidanColeman —
(Venetia Williams) *in tch: reminders after 5th: wknd after 6th: t.o whn p.u bef 3 out* **12/1**

4m 8.90s (2.70) **Going Correction** +0.40s/f (Soft) **16** Ran SP% **122.6**
Speed ratings (Par 109): **109,107,103,103,100 99,98,97,97,96 83,69,**—,—,— —
toteswingers:1&2:£31.30, 2&3:£61.20, 1&3:£61.20 CSF £92.95 CT £2578.27 TOTE £8.70: £2.30, £2.50, £5.30, £7.50; EX 116.10 TRIFECTA Not won..
Owner Andy Ash **Bred** Juddmonte Farms Ltd **Trained** Withycombe, Somerset

FOCUS
This was a competitive handicap. The pace did not look strong early and there was a nasty incident four out, when Hector's House fell when in midfield, bringing down both Gifted Leader and Caravel. The cosy winner is on the upgrade and should be competitive in top two-mile handicaps.

NOTEBOOK
Nearby ◆ had been put up 10lb for a clear victory at Bangor on his previous start. The stable took this race last season with a horse ridden by a claimer, and Chris Davies looks to have a bright future in front of him judged on this well-timed effort. Nearby has looked an improved performer this season and like Nampour last season, it would be no surprise to see him take in the Gerry Feilden next time at Newbury. (op 17-2 tchd 10-1 in places)

Heron Bay, taking a sharp drop in trip and without any headgear, hasn't been the most reliable of types since going hurdling, but this was by far his best effort. The one thing that does stand out in his jumps form is his liking for this course, so one would imagine connections will look for opportunities at Aintree whenever they arise. (op 14-1)
Kauto Relko(FR) ◆, making his debut for Rachel Hobbs after changing hands for £27,000, travelled really well for the majority of the race and was an eyecatcher. If he progresses for this effort, he seems sure to win races this season. (op 33-1)
Charingworth(IRE), back over hurdles on his first outing since May, was another to run on well after being held up at the back of the field.
Mille Chief(FR), having his first outing since January due to a small fracture at the top of a cannon bone, appeared to take a strong hold in the early stages while being covered up and didn't offer a great deal when given the chance to get involved after three out. That said, one would imagine connections were delighted with the performance after his layoff and injury, and his next start will give us a better idea of what he is capable of. (op 3-1 tchd 4-1)
Westlin' Winds(IRE) looked slightly unlucky last time, as he was undoubtedly short of room at a crucial time at Chepstow, but had no excuses here. Allowed to lead, he couldn't raise his game as the field turned in and weakened steadily. (op 9-2 tchd 5-1)
Hector's Choice(FR) went nicely for a long way but was beaten when sprawling after the last.
Hector's House (op 25-1)

1957 BET TOTEPOOL ON ALL UK RACING H'CAP CHASE (16 fncs) 2m 4f
2:45 (2:45) (Class 3) (0-135,129) 4-Y-0+ **£6,505** (£1,910; £955; £477)

Form				RPR
1P-4	1		**Just Smudge**[176] 78 8-11-4 **121** AidanColeman (Venetia Williams) *chsd ldrs: lft 2nd 9th: effrt 2 out: led between last 2: styng on wl whn j.rt last: drew clr run-in* **8/1**	130+
215-	2	7	**Its Crucial (IRE)**[190] 5208 10-11-0 **117** PaddyBrennan (Nigel Twiston-Davies) *j.rt: led to 2nd: chsd ldr tl regained ld appr 8th: blnd 10th: nt fluent 4 out: rdn and hdd between last 2: no ex and n.d to wnr run-in* **9/2**[2]	120
P6-5	3	1 ½	**Russian Flag (FR)**[20] 1690 7-11-12 **129** MarkBradburne (Neil King) *hld up: hmpd 9th: hdwy appr 3 out: wnt 3rd bef last: styd on run-in: nvr able to rch front 2* **7/1**	132+
214-	4	6	**Fortysecond Street (IRE)**[189] 5221 6-11-7 **124** WilsonRenwick (Howard Johnson) *hld up in midfield: hmpd 9th: hdwy 10th: trckd ldrs gng ok bef 3 out: rdn and failed to pick up after 2 out: n.d after* **10/3**[1]	122+
PUP-	5	41	**Lorum Leader (IRE)**[189] 5223 9-11-4 **121** AndrewThornton (Dr Richard Newland) *chsd ldrs: mstke and j.rt 3rd: hmpd 9th: wknd 10th: toiling whn mstke 4 out* **16/1**	78
3234	6	8	**Baaher (USA)**[14] 1767 6-10-7 **110** BarryKeniry (Jim Goldie) *hld up in rr: forced wd 9th: wnt remote 4th after 12th: wknd 3 out* **12/1**	60
31	7	3 ¼	**Adajal (IRE)**[21] 1676 7-11-11 **128** (t) APMcCoy (Jonjo O'Neill) *a bhd: toiling fr 12th: nvr on terms* **10/1**	75
5-31	F		**Safari Adventures (IRE)**[134] 707 8-11-11 **128** PeterBuchanan (Lucinda Russell) *led 2nd: clr fr 4th to 7th: hdd appr 8th: 2 l 2nd whn fell 9th* **5/1**[3]	—
U0-1	U		**Big Burrows (IRE)**[157] 401 8-11-10 **127** GrahamLee (Ferdy Murphy) *blnd and uns rdr 1st* **11/1**	—

5m 17.4s (9.20) **Going Correction** +0.40s/f (Soft) **9** Ran SP% **112.5**
Speed ratings (Par 107): **97,94,93,91,74 71,70,—,—**
toteswingers:1&2 £13.90, 2&3 £55.70, 1&3 £16.60 CSF £43.47 CT £263.75 TOTE £11.50: £2.40, £1.70, £2.70; EX 31.00 Trifecta £232.90 Pool: £355.65 - 1.13 winning units..
Owner Sastastic Partnership **Bred** A E Price **Trained** Kings Caple, H'fords

FOCUS
A fair handicap chase with a small personal best from the winner.

NOTEBOOK
Just Smudge, 4lb above his highest winning chase mark, slowly worked his way into contention before finding enough once in front to claim the prize. This was a great start to his season and he will undoubtedly improve again when stepped back up to 3m again.
Its Crucial(IRE), stepping back up in trip on his first run since April, came from a stable with a good record in this contest and got to the lead early when Safari Adventures started to ease up a touch. His jumping was mostly fairly good, albeit out to his right, but he was unable to hang on to his lead coming to the final fence. (op 11-2)
Russian Flag(FR) hasn't been in great form on his last three starts after showing plenty of consistency earlier, and his jockey did well to stay on here after the horse side-stepped Safari Adventures on the floor. Given time to get back into the race, the combination did well to claim third after losing valuable momentum. (tchd 8-1)
Fortysecond Street(IRE) closed up on the leaders going strongly and it looked a matter of time before he got to the front. However, he couldn't quicken after two out and failed to make any impression thereafter. (op 9-2)
Adajal(IRE) was in fine form for Charlie Swan in May but didn't show a great deal on his first start for this trainer at Fontwell in early October. Trying this trip for the first time, this was little better (op 9-1)
Safari Adventures(IRE) set a good early gallop, but he started to slow into a few fences down the home straight first time, and then lost the lead. The jockey managed to get him nicely settled as they started off on their final circuit but the pair took a horrible-looking fall at the ninth. (op 4-1)

1958 TOTETENTOFOLLOW OLD ROAN CHASE (LIMITED H'CAP) (GRADE 2) (16 fncs) 2m 4f
3:25 (3:25) (Class 1) 4-Y-0+ **£34,366** (£12,994; £6,586; £3,364; £1,768)

Form				RPR
613-	1		**Monet's Garden (IRE)**[197] 5110 12-11-7 **165** DougieCostello (Nicky Richards) *mde all: rchd for 8th: shkn up 2 out: rdn and kicked on between last 2: jnd by runner-up last: gamely plld out more run-in: a doing enough towards fin* **4/1**[3]	165
12U-	2	½	**Poquelin (FR)**[197] 5110 7-11-6 **164** BarryGeraghty (Paul Nicholls) *chsd wnr: chalng fr 3 out: swtchd rt between last 2: moved upsides wnr last: nt qckn sn after: kpt on towards fin: a looked hld* **7/2**[2]	165
554-	3	28	**Tartak (FR)**[197] 5110 7-10-9 **153** PaddyBrennan (Tom George) *hld up: nt fluent 9th: wnt 3rd appr 3 out: outpcd by front pair between last 2: wl btn after* **15/8**[1]	130
211-	4	16	**Albertas Run (IRE)**[197] 5110 9-11-10 **168** APMcCoy (Jonjo O'Neill) *in tch: nt fluent 5th: clsd 8th: pushed along appr 4 out: wknd bef 2 out* **11/2**	128
10U-	5	12	**Watch My Back**[198] 5097 9-10-4 **148** oh6 GrahamLee (Ferdy Murphy) *a bhd and nvr able to get on terms: lost tch bef 3 out: t.o* **18/1**	97
302-	F		**I'msingingtheblues (IRE)**[245] 4157 8-10-10 **154** TomScudamore (David Pipe) *racd keenly: chsd ldrs: 3rd abt 2 l off the pce whn fell 4 out* **8/1**	—

5m 6.60s (-1.60) **Going Correction** +0.40s/f (Soft) **6** Ran SP% **108.8**
Speed ratings (Par 115): **119,118,107,101,96** —
toteswingers:1&2 £1.70, 2&3 £1.70, 1&3 £2.70 CSF £17.31 TOTE £4.50: £2.70, £2.70; EX 17.50.
Owner David Wesley Yates **Bred** William Delahunty **Trained** Greystoke, Cumbria

FOCUS
Quite a few of these have met on plenty of occasions in the past, so what the value of this form will prove to be is debatable. The pace looked good and the first two pulled well clear of the remainder down the home straight. Monet's Garden ran to the level of last year's win in this race, with Poqelin 3lb off last season's best. Tartak and Albertas Run were well below their best, the latter to the tune of 3st.

NOTEBOOK
Monet's Garden(IRE), chasing his third victory in this race, seemed to have plenty going for him despite his advancing years and he produced a wonderful display of jumping from the front to take this again. He seemed certain to be gathered in by the runner-up, but he showed all his usual determination and enthusiasm to gain another victory. Connections reported afterwards that he would be aimed at the Peterborough Chase. (tchd 9-2)
Poquelin(FR) made a bright start to last season but saw the rear end of Albertas Run twice, albeit he didn't complete on one of those occasions. He settled beautifully in behind and looked guaranteed to get past the winner from two out on a couple of occasions. However, Monet's Garden was in no mood to surrender and he couldn't get his nose in front. He would have wanted better ground ideally and this performance suggested he can have another good season. (op 11-4)
Tartak(FR), well beaten by Monet's Garden in this last season, was much better off with Albertas Run on their meeting in the Melling Chase but compromised his chance with some modest jumping at times. He should have been a lot closer under his low weight, so this has to be considered a disappointing effort. (op 5-2 tchd 7-4, 11-4 in a place)
Albertas Run(IRE) appeared resurgent last season, winning three times, including the Grade 1 Ryanair Chase and Melling Chase, the latter coming over this C&D in April. He has a good record fresh but looked to be not enjoying things some way out here, possibly because of the ground. (op 9-2)
Watch My Back, running from out of the handicap, set off at the back of the pack and never threatened to get involved. (op 16-1 tchd 20-1)
I'msingingtheblues(IRE), sold out of Paul Nicholls' yard for £48,000 at Doncaster in May, was trying a trip he wasn't too familiar with but still looked a big player when falling four from home. It was too far out to know what would have happened to him, but he would have done well to win given his possible stamina doubts. Connections will hope he comes out unscathed from this, as they look to have a decent horse to have some fun with. (op 9-1)

1959 TOTESWINGER FLEXI BETTING NOVICES' H'CAP HURDLE (13 hdls) 3m 110y
4:00 (4:01) (Class 3) (0-120,119) 4-Y-0+ **£5,204** (£1,528; £764; £381)

Form				RPR
/212	1		**Corso Palladio (IRE)**[58] 1380 8-11-0 **107** (p) TomScudamore (Peter Bowen) *trckd ldrs: led after 3 out: sn rdn: r.o wl and in command run-in* **6/1**[2]	117+
-541	2	4	**Court Red Handed (IRE)**[17] 1726 5-11-3 **110** (tp) BarryGeraghty (Rebecca Curtis) *midfield: mstke 8th: hdwy appr 3 out: effrt to chse wnr between last 2: nt fluent last: no imp run-in* **6/1**[2]	117+
04-1	3	9	**Rey Nacarado (IRE)**[20] 1694 5-10-5 **105** PeterCarberry[(7)] (Charlie Longsdon) *trckd ldrs: chal 3 out: rdn bef 2 out: one pce after last* **4/1**[1]	104+
22F-	4	7	**Daring Origyn (FR)**[246] 4150 5-11-3 **117** JakeGreenall[(7)] (Richard Lee) *hld up in rr: hdwy 4 out: rdn to chse ldrs appr 3 out: 4th and styng on abt 8 l off pce whn blnd last: unable to get on terms after* **16/1**	110
20-P	5	nk	**Top It All**[15] 1762 7-10-2 **95** WilsonRenwick (Rose Dobbin) *prom: lost pl after 4th: hdwy 9th: chalng u.p 3 out: wknd bef last* **28/1**	85
5-01	6	8	**Bescot Springs (IRE)**[31] 1578 5-11-12 **119** PeterBuchanan (Lucinda Russell) *led: hdd after 4th: remained w ldr: led again after 4th: rdn and hdd after 3 out: wknd 2 out* **16/1**	103
3-03	7	5	**Lost Glory (NZ)**[17] 1726 5-11-1 **108** APMcCoy (Jonjo O'Neill) *hld up: pushed along after 4 out: outpcd after: nvr able to get on terms* **11/1**	87
23	8	25	**You Know Yourself (IRE)**[15] 1758 7-10-8 **101** TjadeCollier (Sue Smith) *in tch: lost pl bef 8th: rdn after 4 out: no imp after* **9/1**[3]	57
2-32	9	hd	**Phare Isle (IRE)**[167] 231 5-10-11 **109** JamesHalliday[(5)] (Ben Case) *hld up: hdwy 4 out: chsd ldrs 3 out but no real imp on ldrs: wknd bef last* **16/1**	65
1125	10	8	**Caheerloch (IRE)**[29] 1605 8-10-3 **96** PaddyBrennan (Nigel Twiston-Davies) *midfield: pushed along 9th: wknd after 4 out* **10/1**	45
40-1	11	3 ¼	**Musical Wedge**[177] 59 6-10-3 **99** TommyPhelan[(3)] (Claire Dyson) *midfield: hdwy appr 8th: rdn to chse ldrs bef 3 out: wknd bef 2 out* **50/1**	45
3F6-	12	26	**Aspolan (GER)**[348] 2197 7-9-12 **94** SeanQuinlan[(3)] (Rachel Hobbs) *a bhd* **33/1**	17
PP-3	P		**Inchloch**[177] 59 8-9-10 **94** (t) IanPopham[(5)] (Claire Dyson) *prom tl wknd 9th: t.o whn p.u bef 3 out* **33/1**	—
1-1P	P		**Liz's Dream**[31] 1578 10-10-10 **103** (tp) BrianHarding (Lisa Harrison) *hld up: struggling 4 out: t.o whn p.u bef 3 out* **22/1**	—
212	P		**Cailin Na Ri (IRE)**[25] 1643 7-11-7 **114** GrahamLee (Martin Todhunter) *w ldr: led after 4th: hdd appr 8th: remained prom tl wknd after 4 out: t.o whn p.u bef 3 out* **10/1**	—
0P-0	P		**Sam Patch**[20] 1700 7-9-4 **93** oh5 CallumWhillans[(10)] (Donald Whillans) *midfield: wknd 4 out: t.o whn p.u bef 3 out* **66/1**	—
2-11	P		**Identity Parade (IRE)**[147] 514 6-11-2 **116** MrJHamer[(7)] (Donald McCain) *midfield: hdwy after 7th: rdn and wknd after 4 out: t.o whn p.u bef 3 out* **16/1**	—

6m 25.2s (8.90) **Going Correction** +0.40s/f (Soft) **17** Ran SP% **125.7**
Speed ratings (Par 107): **101,99,96,94,94 91,90,82,82,79 78,70,—,—,— —,—**
toteswingers:1&2 £7.90, 2&3 £8.80, 1&3 £12.30 CSF £40.86 CT £167.72 TOTE £7.20: £1.90, £1.80, £1.70, £4.70; EX 40.60 Trifecta £117.40 Pool: £555.67 - 3.50 winning units..
Owner F Lloyd **Bred** Des De Vere Hunt **Trained** Little Newcastle, Pembrokes
■ Stewards' Enquiry : Tom Scudamore two-day ban: used whip with excessive frequency (Nov 6-7)

FOCUS
Even though the early gallop was far from strong, the runners came home very tired in stamina-sapping ground. There should be more to come from the winner.

NOTEBOOK
Corso Palladio(IRE) has definitely improved since joining the Peter Bowen stable and being raised in trip. He showed that he has lots of stamina with a solid effort after tracking the leaders. His trainer had taken two of the previous five renewals of this contest, so it remains to be seen whether this one can prove to be as good as both Souffleur and Blue Splash. (op 15-2)
Court Red Handed(IRE), who won when cheekpieces were fitted for the first time on his previous outing, didn't look like he'd have a problem with these conditions judged on his pointing form, and made the winner work for victory after also going well for much of the contest. He had looked held when making a mistake at the last. (op 7-1)
Rey Nacarado(IRE) probably stayed on the bridle the longest but didn't seem to get home in these conditions. The 15lb rise for his win last time undoubtedly didn't help, but it is possible that the going was a contributing factor to his not lasting for longer. (op 5-1 tchd 11-2)
Daring Origyn(FR), absent since February, was trying this trip for the first time and plugged on throughout the final half a mile. (op 12-1)

Top It All got behind but stayed on. (op 33-1)

Bescot Springs(IRE), raised 7lb for possibly mugging a victory at Perth in late September, was always thereabouts but couldn't quicken once the field closed up on him again. (op 14-1)

Lost Glory(NZ), not beaten far by Court Red Handed last time, came under pressure quite a way out and failed to build on the promise of that Ludlow start. (op 8-1)

1960 TOTETENTOFOLLOW.CO.UK VETERANS' H'CAP CHASE (19 fncs) 3m 1f

4:35 (4:36) (Class 2) (0-145,140)
10-Y-0+

£15,655 (£4,625; £2,312; £1,157; £577; £290)

Form RPR

05P- **1** **Alderburn**[182] 5395 11-11-3 **131** .... TomScudamore 139
(Henry Daly) *prom: led appr 3rd: hdd 5th: remained prom: led again 2 out: rdn and hdd last: rallied to reagin ld towards fin: kpt up to work fnl strides* **17/2**

5-50 **2** *3/4* **Magic Sky (FR)**[14] 1776 10-10-9 **130** .... JakeGreenall(7) 136
(Milton Harris) *hld up: nt fluent 1st: hdwy 11th: chsd ldrs 4 out: tried to chal bef last: r.o and clsd towards fin* **25/1**

000- **3** *1* **Character Building (IRE)**[196] 5127 10-11-11 **139** .... MissNCarberry 144
(John Quinn) *hld up bhd: hdwy after 15th: gd prog and styd on to ld last: all out and hdd towards fin: no ex* **6/1**[1]

P5U- **4** *1* **Royal Rosa (FR)**[196] 5127 11-10-8 **122** .... WilsonRenwick 127
(Howard Johnson) *midfield: outpcd 12th: hdwy appr 2 out: r.o after last: gng on at fin* **7/1**[3]

00U5 **5** *10* **Valley Ride (IRE)**[28] 1611 10-10-12 **129** .... (p) DonalDevereux(3) 127+
(Peter Bowen) *midfield: j. slowly 4th: mstke 7th: reminders after 10th: hdwy 14th: chsd ldrs 3 out: cl up briefly bef last: sn btn* **9/1**

5F0- **6** *2 1/4* **Irish Raptor (IRE)**[182] 5395 11-11-5 **133** .... PaddyBrennan 130
(Nigel Twiston-Davies) *prom: led and nt fluent 5th: mstke 6th: mstke 14th: rdn appr 3 out: hdd 2 out: wknd bef last* **13/2**[2]

C00- **7** *22* **Cornish Sett (IRE)**[221] 4661 11-10-10 **129** .... IanPopham(5) 103
(Caroline Keevil) *midfield: hmpd by loose horse 6th: outpcd by hmpd 4 out: no impresion fr 2 out* **25/1**

F35- **P** **Laskari (FR)**[190] 5204 11-11-12 **140** .... DominicElsworth —
(Paul Webber) *nt jump wl: a bhd: t.o whn p.u bef 2 out* **20/1**

0223 **P** **Midnight Gold**[14] 1769 10-10-10 **124** .... (p) WayneHutchinson —
(Peter Bowen) *trckd ldrs: hit 13th: sn rdn and wknd: t.o whn p.u bef last* **8/1**

P1-0 **P** **Fine By Me (IRE)**[14] 1769 11-10-0 **114** .... (p) GerardTumelty —
(Julian Smith) *trckd ldrs: niggled along and lost pl appr 9th: struggling after: t.o whn p.u bef 3 out* **14/1**

/0-2 **U** **Our Jasper**[17] 1725 10-10-9 **123** .... (b) APMcCoy —
(Donald McCain) *led tl appr 3rd: remained prom: niggled along 4th and abt 5 l off pce whn bludnered bdly and uns rdr 4 out* **7/1**[3]

6/51 **U** **Retrievethelegend (IRE)**[77] 1212 11-11-2 **130** .... GrahamLee —
(J T R Dreaper, Ire) *racd keenlu in midfield: blnd bdly and uns rdr 3rd* **33/1**

2P- **P** **Rock Diplomat (IRE)**[183] 5378 10-10-8 **122** .... (p) BarryGeraghty —
(Dr Richard Newland) *a bhd: blnd 7th: t.o whn p.u bef 8th* **8/1**

6m 40.0s (10.00) **Going Correction** +0.40s/f (Soft) **13** Ran SP% **117.4**
Speed ratings: **100,99,99,99,95 95,88,—,—,— —,—,—**
toteswingers:1&2 £37.90, 2&3 £28.70, 1&3 £9.10 CSF £198.68 CT £1372.95 TOTE £12.10: £3.60, £7.90, £2.40; EX 197.20 TRIFECTA Not won..

Owner Mrs D P G Flory **Bred** Mrs D P G Flory **Trained** Stanton Lacy, Shropshire

FOCUS
Plenty of well-known horses took their chance in this contest designed for those of advancing years. It produced a thrilling finish, in which the lead changed hands a few times in the latter stages. The winner is rated to the best of last season's form.

NOTEBOOK
Alderburn doesn't have a particularly strong record fresh, although he did run well first time out last season, but he certainly appeared to want victory than the third here under pressure. He was winning for the first time since 2007, but in fairness to the horse, it had taken him a long time to get down to a winning mark. He is booked in to have a breathing operation on Tuesday (he reportedly made a noise in this) and is heading to another veterans chase at Huntingdon next over 2m4f. (op 10-1 tchd 11-1)

Magic Sky(FR) needed pushing along from some way out and never threatened to win off a mark 4lb above his highest winning one. (op 20-1)

Character Building(IRE) was out the back popping away over the fences, albeit to his right a lot, before making his way through the field. Produced at what looked the right time, the pair got about two lengths up well after the final fence before the horse showed little inclination to stay there, and was even being closed down by the fourth after surrendering the lead. He clearly has an abundance of talent but will need riding with nerves of steel in future to get him to the front even later than was the case here. (op 13-2 tchd 15-2)

Royal Rosa(FR) was going nowhere quickly at one point but plugged on while others were stopping. (op 10-1)

Valley Ride(IRE) has no problems staying extended distances but isn't the quickest, and never looked like winning. (op 17-2 tchd 8-1 in a place)

Irish Raptor(IRE) took it up from the winner, who had led early, and proceeded to enjoy himself out in front. He looked to be holding every chance of placing at least jumping three out, but tired quickly and lost quite a few places. (op 9-2)

1961 TOTEEXACTA FLEXI BETTING NOVICES' CHASE (11 fncs 1 omitted) 2m

5:10 (5:10) (Class 3) 4-Y-0+ **£6,982** (£2,387)

Form RPR

104- **1** **Medermit (FR)**[183] 5380 6-11-2 0 .... WayneHutchinson 150+
(Alan King) *chsd ldr: hit 1st: led narrowly 4 out: blnd and lft wl clr 3 out: unchal after* **1/5**[1]

0-PP **2** *88* **Alaskan Prince (IRE)**[14] 1779 5-11-2 0 .... DavidEngland 71
(Peter Salmon) *racd in last pl thrght: lost tch after 4 out: lft poor 2nd 3 out: nvr on terms* **25/1**[3]

1-33 **U** **Wessex King (IRE)**[14] 1770 6-11-8 122 .... TomScudamore —
(Henry Daly) *led: hdd narrowly 4 out: stl cl 2nd whn blnd bdly and uns rdr 3 out* **4/1**[2]

4m 4.20s (4.20) **Going Correction** +0.40s/f (Soft) **3** Ran SP% **107.2**
Speed ratings (Par 107): **105,61,—**
CSF £3.96 TOTE £1.30; EX 5.80.

Owner The Dunkley & Reilly Partnership **Bred** Philippe Gasdoue **Trained** Barbury Castle, Wilts

FOCUS
This looked as though it could be an informative race despite the small field, but the late defection of Rock Noir removed a lot of the interest. This was not an easy race to put a fugure on but Medermit was a 160 hurdler at his peak and looks sure to rate higher than this.

NOTEBOOK
Medermit(FR) looked to get his chasing career off to a flying start, but those who had taken short odds about him doing so would have had their hearts in their mouths when he made a mistake at the first fence. He understandably put in some awkward leaps at some fences given his lack of racecourse experience over them, but did jump others nicely, although he appeared to take off a little early at three out and hit it quite hard just before main market rival Wessex King hit it even harder and came down when starting to look held. One would imagine that the winner will have learned plenty from this and can improve his jumping. (op 1-4 tchd 2-7 in a place)

Alaskan Prince(IRE) was a lucky runner-up after the fall of the second favourite, as he was in another parish at the time. (op 20-1)

Wessex King(IRE) was just in behind Medermit when coming down at the third-last fence. He probably wouldn't have beaten the winner when considering their best form, but would have been a clear second. (op 3-1)

1962 TOTEPOOL A BETTER WAY TO BET MAIDEN HURDLE (9 hdls) 2m 110y

5:40 (5:41) (Class 3) 4-Y-0+ **£4,553** (£1,337; £668; £333)

Form RPR

315- **1** **Ballybriggan (IRE)**[196] 5128 6-11-0 124 .... DougieCostello 110+
(John Quinn) *racd keenly: trckd ldrs: led appr 3 out: rdn bef last: styd on wl and plld out more fnl 100yds* **11/8**[1]

2 *3 1/4* **Mediolanum (IRE)**[166] 262 5-11-0 0 .... PaddyBrennan 105+
(Nigel Twiston-Davies) *in tch: chsd wnr 3 out: rdn to cl win 1 1/2 l of wnr 200yds out: one pce fnl 100yds* **3/1**[2]

4-1 **3** *2 1/4* **Scoter Fontaine (FR)**[177] 60 4-11-0 0 .... APMcCoy 104+
(Rebecca Curtis) *midfield: hdwy appr 6th: chsd ldrs bef 2 out: str effrt whn cl 3rd 200yds out: no ex fnl 100yds* **4/1**[3]

4 *6* **Kaolak (USA)**[113] 4-11-0 0 .... ColinBolger 97
(John Ryan) *plld hrd: trckd ldrs: led 4th: hdd appr 3 out: wknd after 2 out* **40/1**

5 *1* **Art Broker (IRE)**[154] 4-10-7 0 .... JakeGreenall(7) 96
(Henry Daly) *midfield: j. slowly 4th: hdwy 3 out: rdn bef next: no imp on ldrs sn after* **28/1**

5 **6** *2* **Cygnet**[20] 1705 4-10-11 0 .... AdrianLane(3) 94
(Donald McCain) *racd keenly: hld up: hdwy after 6th: chsd ldrs bef 2 out: no imp after* **50/1**

7 *8* **Well Hello There (IRE)** 4-11-0 0 .... DominicElsworth 87
(Jonjo O'Neill) *hld up: struggling 6th: kpt on fr 3 out: nvr trbld ldrs* **40/1**

U46 **8** *8* **Echo Dancer**[20] 1705 4-10-4 0 .... JoshWall(10) 80
(Trevor Wall) *in rr: impr into midfield appr 2 out: nvr on terms w ldrs* **80/1**

533- **9** *6* **Steel Edge (IRE)**[179] 35 5-11-0 0 .... GrahamLee 77
(Ferdy Murphy) *midfield: hmpd 4th: sme hdwy appr 3 out: no further prog fr 2 out* **66/1**

10 *21* **Ben Chorley**[170] 6-11-0 0 .... (t) BarryGeraghty 60
(Tim Vaughan) *midfield: blnd 4th: sme hdwy 3 out: eased whn no imp bef 2 out* **11/1**

0 **11** *nk* **Barrie Burn (IRE)**[14] 1768 4-11-0 0 .... RichieMcGrath 55
(Jonjo O'Neill) *plld hrd: trckd ldrs: wknd appr 3 out* **80/1**

20- **12** *7* **Pamoja**[232] 4418 4-11-0 0 .... BrianHarding 49
(Martin Todhunter) *a bhd: nvr on terms* **100/1**

160- **13** *4* **Jaques Vert (FR)**[189] 5227 4-11-0 0 .... PaddyAspell 45
(Robert Wylie) *racd keenly: trckd ldrs tl wknd appr 3 out* **28/1**

2- **14** *3 1/4* **Dhaular Dhar (IRE)**[15] 2835 8-11-0 0 .... JamesReveley 42
(Jim Goldie) *led: hdd 2nd: led again after 3rd: hdd 4th: remained cl up tl wknd 2 out* **12/1**

003- **15** *16* **Solway Flight**[184] 5340 7-10-11 0 .... HarryHaynes(3) 28
(Lisa Harrison) *a bhd* **100/1**

0-00 **16** *21* **Why So Serious**[105] 732 4-11-0 0 .... DavidEngland 9
(Peter Salmon) *led 2nd: hdd after 3rd: nt fluent 5th: wknd after 6th* **150/1**

4m 13.5s (7.30) **Going Correction** +0.40s/f (Soft) **16** Ran SP% **123.5**
Speed ratings (Par 107): **98,96,95,92,92 91,87,83,80,70 70,67,65,64,56 46**
toteswingers:1&2 £2.00, 2&3 £4.40, 1&3 £2.40 CSF £5.29 TOTE £2.50: £1.30, £1.90, £1.40; EX 7.40 Trifecta £20.70 Place 6: £229.69, Place 5: £49.60. Pool: £783.63 - 27.89 winning units..

Owner Stewart Andrew & Jim Shaw **Bred** C Kenneally **Trained** Settrington, N Yorks

FOCUS
An open looking contest, with any amount of runners seeming to have a chance for various reasons. The form is just ordinary with the winner rated 10lb below his best.

NOTEBOOK
Ballybriggan(IRE), officially rated 124 after some good form already over hurdles, did set a good standard and won with a bit in hand after racing close to the leaders throughout. This was his second 'win' over hurdles despite this being a maiden contest, as he was disqualified after landing a race at Doncaster in March for a banned substance being found in his urine. (op 7-4 tchd 15-8, 2-1 in a place)

Mediolanum(IRE) ◆ was never far away on his first outing for Nigel Twiston-Davies after being purchased for £100,000 out of the Charlie Swan stable. His jumping wasn't always slick but he looks a promising sort and will surely become more fluent with experience. (op 11-2)

Scoter Fontaine(FR) ◆, making his hurdling debut, looks destined to collect a few wins this season. Covered up early, McCoy made his way through the field and came with a good run that just petered out late on. He looks a nice prospect. (op 3-1)

Kaolak(USA) ◆, rated 95 at his peak on the Flat, hadn't run since early July in a hot Sandown handicap but showed plenty of aptitude for hurdling on ground that would not have played to his strengths. (tchd 50-1)

Art Broker(IRE) ◆ was a capable sort on the Flat and had decent form for Dermot Weld prior to joining this stable. He made pleasing late progress and can find an opportunity to win. (op 25-1 tchd 20-1)

Cygnet wasn't completely disgraced after making a positive move late on.

Well Hello There(IRE), whose dam was unraced but from the family of Native Upmanship, looks capable of winning something in time. (tchd 33-1)

Ben Chorley ◆, a four-time winner on the Flat for a couple of different trainers, was knocked sideways at one point on his first outing for Tim Vaughan and ran better than his final position suggests. (op 8-1)

Dhaular Dhar(IRE), runner-up on his only previous start over hurdles, raced prominently but weakened quickly approaching two out. This wasn't a bad effort, despite his finishing position, on ground he would not have liked. He can win a small race. (op 9-1)

T/Plt: £454.50 to a £1 stake. Pool:£84,332.74 - 135.45 winning tickets. T/Qpdt: £15.60 to a £1 stake. Pool:£6,123.72 - 289.40 winning tickets. DO

[1772]CHEPSTOW (L-H)

Saturday, October 23

OFFICIAL GOING: Good to soft changing to soft after race 1 (2.00)
Last flight in back straight omitted on all circuits of all hurdle races. Hurdles in back straight sited on Flat course.
Wind: mild across Weather: overcast

1963 BEST ODDS GUARANTEED AT TOTESPORT.COM MAIDEN HURDLE (10 hdls 2 omitted) 3m

2:00 (2:00) (Class 5) 4-Y-O+ **£2,276** (£668; £334; £166)

Form RPR

133- **1** **Alverstone**[311] [2912] 7-10-2 0 .... DavidBass(5) 125+
(Lawney Hill) *travelled wl: trckd ldrs: led sn after 4 out: hit next: styd on strly: readily* **7/2**[2]

2 *14* **Carlicue (IRE)**[297] 5-11-0 0 .... DarylJacob 121+
(Paul Nicholls) *t.k.h early: trckd ldrs: hit 4 out: chsd wnr fr next: sn rdn: styd on: a being comf hld* **11/4**[1]

53-2 **3** *11* **Bobbie Magern**[27] [1625] 5-10-11 0 .... SamTwiston-Davies(3) 108
(Nigel Twiston-Davies) *mid-div: rdn on long run after 6th: wnt 4th 4 out: mstke 3 out: awkward 2 out: lft 3rd whn hit last: styaed on same pce: nvr trbld ldrs* **11/4**[1]

4-0 **4** *31* **Dashing John**[17] [1734] 8-10-7 0 .... MrSParish(7) 80
(Audrey Manners) *hld up towards rr: hdwy 6th: wknd bef 4 out: lft modest 4th last* **80/1**

1- **5** *26* **Bens Moor (IRE)**[234] [4391] 5-11-0 0 .... RichardJohnson 56
(Tim Vaughan) *mid-div: rdn on long run after 6th: wknd bef 4 out: t.o* **4/1**[3]

6 *18* **Sir Mattie (IRE)**[196] 5-11-0 0 .... RhysFlint 40
(David Rees) *trckd ldr: hit 1st and 6th: wknd on long run after 6th: t.o* **14/1**

/00- **P** **Rebus (IRE)**[452] [1076] 6-10-7 0 .... HenryBrooke(7) —
(Tom Gretton) *t.o fr 4th: p.u after 6th* **150/1**

0F- **P** **No Tears (IRE)**[213] [4823] 7-11-0 0 .... SamThomas —
(Alan King) *trckd ldrs tl wknd 6th: sn t.o: p.u bef 4 out* **16/1**

0P2- **F** **Double Chocolate**[196] [5134] 7-10-9 0 .... MrWBiddick(5) 108
(Matt Sheppard) *led: hit 4 out: sn rdn and hdd: lost 2nd next: styng on same pce in 3rd whn fell last* **22/1**

0-0 **P** **It's Molly**[16] [1742] 8-10-7 0 .... DavidDennis —
(Simon Earle) *mid-div tl wknd after 4th: t.o whn p.u on long run after 6th* **200/1**

45- **P** **Spring Moon (IRE)**[257] [3944] 5-11-0 0 .... WarrenMarston —
(Martin Keighley) *hld up towards rr: wknd after 6th: t.o whn p.u bef 4 out* **40/1**

P **Bank The Bucks (IRE)**[31] [1579] 4-10-13 97 ....(tp) NoelFehily —
(Aidan Anthony Howard, Ire) *t.k.h: hld up towards rr: hdwy 5th: wknd on long run after 6th: t.o whn p.u bef 4 out* **66/1**

6m 6.40s (-13.40) **Going Correction** -0.125s/f (Good)
WFA 4 from 5yo+ 11lb **12** Ran SP% **118.8**
Speed ratings (Par 103): **117,112,108,98,89 83,—,—,—,— —,—**
toteswingers:1&2 £2.50, 2&3 £1.90, 1&3 £1.30 CSF £13.69 TOTE £4.70: £1.30, £1.80, £1.40; EX 15.60.
Owner The Freudians **Bred** Mrs M L Luck **Trained** Aston Rowant, Oxon

FOCUS
A fair staying maiden in which ground conditions took a toll. The easy winner is up a stone on her best hurdles form and looks a decent staying prospect.

NOTEBOOK
Alverstone moved up stylishly to the leader ready for the turn for home and she stayed on well to put some distance back to her nearest pursuers. She fluffed the second-last, but her jumping was assured in the main and she travelled well, no doubt helped by her mares' and conditionals' allowances. She looks a lovely, big chasing type and should fare well in better contests. (op 4-1 tchd 10-3)
Carlicue(IRE) was a bit keen early on and, although he was poised to pounce as they turned in, he was unable to deliver. This was his first outing since his wide-margin success in an Irish point last December, so he can be forgiven some freshness and should pay his way in due course (tchd 3-1 and 10-3 in places)
Bobbie Magern was under pressure for much of the final circuit and could only plod on. His brothers Ollie Magern and Billie Magern took a while to register their first hurdling successes and it looks to be the same pattern with him. He might also require faster going. On this ground, however, he looked devoid of pace. (op 7-2)
Dashing John plugged on but was never a factor and will need to improve to win over hurdles. (op 100-1)
Bens Moor(IRE) made some good progress in the back straight but did not last home and finished tired. He won a soft-ground bumper in March and as an Irish point winner was expected to stay, so this run was a little disappointing Official explanation: jockey said gelding finished distressed (op 10-3 tchd 9-2 in places)
Sir Mattie(IRE), another Irish point winner, held a prominent position until midway down the back straight but, with his head on one side, he weakened badly from there to suggest he did not like the ground. (op 16-1)
Rebus(IRE) Official explanation: jockey said gelding never travelled (op 20-1 tchd 25-1)
Double Chocolate led until the home straight and mostly jumped well, but he got tired and fell when looking booked for third. He deserves another chance. (op 20-1 tchd 25-1)

1964 FREE RACING POST FORM AT TOTESPORT.COM BEGINNERS' CHASE (18 fncs) 3m

2:30 (2:30) (Class 4) 4-Y-O+ **£4,553** (£1,337; £668; £333)

Form RPR

5/4 **1** **Keel Road (IRE)**[16] [1739] 8-10-8 0 .... TomMolloy(3) 107
(Giles Smyly) *a.p: led 6th tl next: led 9th tl next: styd pressing ldrs: rdn after 2 out: styd on wl to ld fnl 100yds: rdn out* **16/1**

200- **2** *1* **Earth Planet (IRE)**[191] [5197] 8-11-4 0 ....(t) HarrySkelton 114+
(Paul Nicholls) *disp cl 5th/6th: trckd ldng pair travelling wl after 4 out: led whn nt fluent last: sn rdn: edgd rt and hdd fnl 100yds: no ex* **11/4**[2]

1/4- **3** *nse* **Theophrastus (IRE)**[337] [2396] 8-11-4 0 .... LiamTreadwell 113
(Nick Gifford) *trckd ldrs: led 4 out: rdn after 2 out: hdd bef last: styd on: no ex run-in* **6/1**

310- **4** *16* **City Theatre (IRE)**[220] [4674] 6-11-1 0 .... RichieMcLernon(3) 99
(Jonjo O'Neill) *disp cl 5th/6th: rdn after 5 out: styd on same pce tl wknd appr last* **9/2**[3]

45P- **5** *11* **Lord Generous**[197] [5112] 6-11-1 0 .... SamTwiston-Davies(3) 91
(Nigel Twiston-Davies) *led: hdd 6th tl next: reminders after 8th: hdd 9th tl next: rdn appr 5 out: hdd 4 out: wknd after 2 out* **15/8**[1]

11P- **6** *19* **Winterwood (IRE)**[231] [4442] 7-11-4 0 ....(p) SamThomas 67
(Tim Vaughan) *trckd ldrs: rdn after 5 out: wknd 3 out: t.o* **10/1**

6m 32.6s (10.60) **Going Correction** +0.225s/f (Yiel) **6** Ran SP% **108.9**
Speed ratings (Par 105): **91,90,90,85,81 75**
toteswingers:1&2 £7.10, 2&3 £3.50, 1&3 £7.10 CSF £57.03 TOTE £18.10: £4.20, £2.10; EX 76.10.
Owner N Sutton **Bred** Mrs S Neville **Trained** Wormington, Worcs
■ Stewards' Enquiry : Tom Molloy five-day ban: used whip in incorrect place (Nov 6-10)

FOCUS
An ordinary beginners' chase in which the winner and third are rated in line with their previous best.

NOTEBOOK
Keel Road(IRE) was keen to challenge for the lead until giving way in the back straight and that may have proved decisive, as she was able to be galvanised for a renewed effort to grab victory in game fashion. She has been pointing with some success since leaving Donald McCain's yard after just one appearance and that experience helped her build on the promise she had showed at Exeter on her previous start. However, against race-fit rivals she would not have been allowed to come back into it. (op 12-1)
Earth Planet(IRE) looked the likeliest winner turning in, but he veered right on the run-in and allowed the winner to get back on terms. He did not clear the early fences with much athleticism and, although it did not hinder his momentum, it might be an issue further down the road. He will also need to demonstrate a little more resolve in a finish. (op 3-1)
Theophrastus(IRE) jumped more competently than on his previous chasing start last November and rallied on the flat, suggesting this lightly raced 8yo might improve on this if he stays sound. (op 5-1)
City Theatre(IRE) jumped ponderously and did not seem to act on the track. (op 4-1)
Lord Generous has done the rounds of the stables and was making his debut for yet another yard here. He got the better of an early battle for the lead with the winner, but after that effort and some rather big early jumps, he was readily outpaced in the straight. He might prefer faster ground. (op 11-4)
Winterwood(IRE), whose winning form is on slightly better ground, was the first to crack in the home straight. (op 15-2)

1965 MORE LIVE FOOTBALL BETTING AT TOTESPORT.COM NOVICES' H'CAP CHASE (16 fncs) 2m 3f 110y

3:05 (3:06) (Class 4) (0-115,116) 4-Y-O+ **£3,903** (£1,146; £573; £286)

Form RPR

P0P- **1** **Digger Gets Lucky (IRE)**[227] [4520] 8-10-11 **100** .... LiamTreadwell 110
(Nick Gifford) *t.k.h: in tch: hdwy to chse ldr 5 out: chal 2 out: led last: styd on wl: rdn out* **10/1**

2P-2 **2** *2* **Mister Wiseman**[20] [1710] 8-10-5 **94** ....(p) DavidDennis 104+
(Nigel Hawke) *led: 6 l clr 5 out: blnd 3 out: sn rdn: hdd last: kpt on: no ex* **6/1**

26P- **3** *27* **Quintessentially (IRE)**[106] [5130] 8-11-11 **114** .... NoelFehily 95
(Warren Greatrex) *trckd ldrs: rdn after 4 out: wnt 3rd next but no ch w ldng pair: sn wknd* **7/2**[2]

60-1 **4** *2 ¾* **Quipe Me Posted (FR)**[146] [541] 6-11-6 **109** .... SamThomas 87
(Jonjo O'Neill) *patiently rdn in rr: little prog whn mstke 4 out: sn rdn: wknd after 3 out: wnt modest 4th bef last* **7/1**

10-P **5** *14* **Power Shared (IRE)**[170] [169] 6-10-9 **103** .... MichaelMurphy(5) 73
(Pat Murphy) *hld up in tch: hit 2nd: rdn after 5 out: lft 4th whn blnd 3 out: wknd* **8/1**

4031 **6** *14* **Intac (IRE)**[9] [1841] 8-11-6 **116** .... MrRGHenderson(7) 66
(Colin Tizzard) *disp tl 9th: chsd ldr: rdn whn slow jump 4 out: wknd next* **5/1**[3]

0-01 **U** **Russellstown Boy (IRE)**[20] [1710] 10-10-1 **93** .... DPFahy(3) —
(Evan Williams) *hld up: rdn after 5 out: 4th but no ch w ldrs whn stmbld bdly and uns rdr eventually 3 out* **10/3**[1]

P0- **P** **Lucciolina**[275] [3574] 7-11-1 **107** .... WayneKavanagh(3) —
(Robin Dickin) *trckd ldrs tl wknd qckly after 11th: t.o whn p.u bef last* **25/1**

5m 12.8s (1.50) **Going Correction** +0.225s/f (Yiel) **8** Ran SP% **112.8**
Speed ratings (Par 105): **106,105,94,93,87 82,—,—**
toteswingers:1&2 £23.60, 2&3 £9.20, 1&3 £9.70 CSF £66.18 CT £252.34 TOTE £13.90: £2.70, £2.00, £1.50; EX 83.70.
Owner The Chanctonbury Ring **Bred** Donal Barnwell **Trained** Findon, W Sussex

FOCUS
A moderate handicap which only began to develop from halfway. The winner produced a massive step up on his previous chase best.

NOTEBOOK
Digger Gets Lucky(IRE) was keen initially on his first start since March, but he settled once he had got into a rhythm over the fences. He began to make achingly slow progress in the back straight and still had seven lengths to make up turning for home, but the result became somewhat inevitable, although he had to battle. His first three attempts over fences were plagued by mishaps, but he looks a better chaser than hurdler and hopefully he can build on this. (tchd 9-1)
Mister Wiseman ought off the challenge of Intac and valiantly tried to maintain his lead, but the writing was on the wall from three out and he did really well to battle as gamely as he did. On this effort he looks capable of gaining a deserved first win over fences, but might need a bit of time to get over this. (op 11-2 tchd 5-1 and 13-2)
Quintessentially(IRE) never threatened under his big weight on his first start since April. (op 10-3 tchd 9-4)
Quipe Me Posted(FR) did not jump that fluently on his chasing debut and made no impact from the rear of the field on this step up in trip on softer ground than ideal. (op 13-2 tchd 15-2)
Intac(IRE) duelled for the lead and, although he was seen off in the back straight, he maintained his position until his stamina emptied in the home straight. (tchd 13-2)
Russellstown Boy(IRE) was well supported to follow up his Uttoxeter win despite a 14lb rise but, although he has been competitive from his current mark in the past, he was never going well this time and was making only modest late headway when parting company with his jockey three out. (op 9-2)

1966 TOTESPORT.COM PERSIAN WAR NOVICES' HURDLE (GRADE 2) (10 hdls 1 omitted) 2m 4f

3:35 (3:36) (Class 1) 4-Y-O+
£14,252 (£5,347; £2,677; £1,335; £670; £335)

Form RPR

1 **1** **Silviniaco Conti (FR)**[14] [1768] 4-11-7 135 .... NoelFehily 158+
(Paul Nicholls) *trckd clr ldrs: clsd on ldrs after 6th: led appr 3 out: styd on strly: impressive* **7/2**[3]

111- **2** *10* **Captain Chris (IRE)**[191] [5194] 6-11-7 146 .... RichardJohnson 149+
(Philip Hobbs) *trckd clr ldrs: clsd on ldrs after 6th: rdn after 4 out: wnt 2nd after 3 out: styd on: a being hld by wnr* **7/4**[1]

322- **3** *13* **Frascati Park (IRE)**[200] [5081] 6-11-0 132 .... SamTwiston-Davies 131+
(Nigel Twiston-Davies) *led: j.lft at times: rdn on long run after 6th: narrowly hdd whn blnd 3 out: wknd next: mstke last* **5/2**[2]

0-14 **4** *6* **William Hogarth**[6] [1884] 5-11-4 127 .... RhysFlint 125
(Keith Goldsworthy) *chsd ldr in clr 2nd: rdn on long run after 6th: no ch fr next* **28/1**

2 **5** *11* **Shalimar Fromentro (FR)**[23] 1659 4-11-0 0 DarylJacob 109
(Nick Williams) *hld up: nvr any imp* **16/1**
10- **6** *1 1/2* **Cavite Beta (IRE)**[184] 5351 4-11-0 0 AndrewTinkler 108
(Nicky Henderson) *hld up: lost tch after 6th* **8/1**
41-3 **P** **Lidar (FR)**[162] 315 5-11-4 122 SamThomas —
(Alan King) *hld up: wknd after 6th: t.o whn p.u bef next* **20/1**
-210 **P** **Quo Video (FR)**[122] 830 6-11-4 130 MrTomDavid —
(Tim Vaughan) *hld up: rdn appr 6th: sn wknd: t.o whn p.u bef 4 out* **40/1**

4m 53.6s (-8.20) **Going Correction** -0.125s/f (Good) **8** Ran SP% **114.8**
Speed ratings (Par 115): **111,107,101,99,95 94,—,—**
toteswingers:1&2 £1.60, 2&3 £1.10, 1&3 £2.20 CSF £10.23 TOTE £5.30: £1.80, £1.30, £1.50; EX 10.00.
Owner Potensis Limited **Bred** Patrick Joubert **Trained** Ditcheat, Somerset

FOCUS
Another quality line-up for what is usually an informative and high-class event. The easy winner produced a top-class performance with the second rated in line with their previous best.

NOTEBOOK
Silviniaco Conti(FR) ◆ travelled supremely well, allowed the leader to run out of steam and was produced to pounce in the home straight, from where he came home comfortably. This was a stiffer test than his British debut at Bangor a fortnight earlier, but he handled it with aplomb to dispense with some smart rivals. He seems versatile regarding ground conditions, possesses tactical pace and looks a high-class hurdler already. The Ascot Hurdle next month could be his next appearance. (op 5-1 tchd 11-2 and 6-1 in places)
Captain Chris(IRE), a triple hurdle winner last spring and attempting to make the most of his novice status before it expires at the end of the month, led the chasing pack but could not pick up when needed and was unable to offer a serious challenge to the winner. He may not have fully appreciated the ground, but this was still a reasonable performance and he was just beaten by a smarter rival. He is set to switch to fences now. Official explanation: jockey said gelding had a breathing problem (op 6-4 tchd 15-8)
Frascati Park(IRE) showed he retains his headstrong tendencies by setting off at a good-ground pace, not helped by being hassled for the lead, and he set the field a stern test, before running on empty from the third-last. Second in this race last year, he is a useful benchmark, but the three-time bumper winner remains vulnerable over hurdles until he settles better. (op 3-1 tchd 9-4and 7-2 in places)
William Hogarth briefly challenged for the early lead and held his position once seen off to run a decent race considering he was outclassed. (op 16-1)
Shalimar Fromentro(FR), whose yard won this last term with Reve De Sivola, had run reasonably at Auteuil last month, but he had a bit to find. (op 12-1)
Cavite Beta(IRE), winner of a bumper and point-to-point, had a stiff introduction to hurdling but made a little progress before fading. (op 10-1)

1967 TOTESPORT 0800 221 221 SILVER TROPHY H'CAP HURDLE (LISTED RACE) (10 hdls 1 omitted) 2m 4f
4:10 (4:10) (Class 1) 4-Y-O+
£17,103 (£6,417; £3,213; £1,602; £804; £402)

Form RPR
00-2 **1** **Any Given Day (IRE)**[20] 1698 5-10-8 137 HenryBrooke(7) 152+
(Donald McCain) *travelled strly: mid-div: hdwy after 5th to join ldrs: led 4 out: sn qcknd clr: blnd 2 out: mstke last: pushed out: comf* **7/1**
2200 **2** *10* **Dantari (IRE)**[7] 1864 5-10-5 130 DPFahy(3) 130
(Evan Williams) *trckd ldrs: mstke 3rd: rdn after 4 out: wnt 2nd next: styd on: no ch w wnr* **11/1**
1F1- **3** *1 1/2* **Restless Harry**[190] 5209 6-11-9 145 HenryOliver 144+
(Robin Dickin) *lft 12 l at s: bhd: hdwy after 5th to join ldrs after next: rdn after 4 out: styd on same pce* **6/1**[3]
11-0 **4** *3 1/4* **Hills Of Aran**[8] 1855 8-11-12 148 RhysFlint 143
(Keith Goldsworthy) *prom tl lost pl u.p on long run after 6th: kpt on gamely fr after next: nvr gng to threaten ldrs: wnt 4th bef last* **50/1**
51F2 **5** *9* **Mad Moose (IRE)**[31] 1578 6-9-11 122 oh5 SamTwiston-Davies(3) 108
(Nigel Twiston-Davies) *trckd ldrs: ev ch 4 out: sn rdn: lost 2nd and hld fr next: wknd after 2 out* **16/1**
00-0 **6** *1 1/4* **Chief Yeoman**[175] 94 10-10-8 130 SamThomas 115
(Venetia Williams) *mid-div: hdwy after 6th: rdn after 4 out: one pce fr next* **33/1**
/31- **7** *10* **Benbane Head (USA)**[371] 1783 6-10-6 128 WarrenMarston 103
(Martin Keighley) *trckd ldrs tl rdn after 6th: sn btn* **9/1**
411- **8** *21* **Pickamus (FR)**[188] 5252 7-10-4 126 AndrewTinkler 80
(Henry Daly) *led: rdn and hdd appr 4 out: wknd bef 3 out* **16/1**
502- **9** *8* **Tullamore Dew (IRE)**[220] 4674 8-11-3 139 LiamTreadwell 90+
(Nick Gifford) *hld up towards rr: rdn whn hmpd 4 out: sn wknd* **15/2**
123- **10** *2 3/4* **Duke Of Lucca (IRE)**[183] 5381 5-11-12 148 RichardJohnson 91
(Philip Hobbs) *mid-div tl blnd bdly and dropped in rr 5th: rdn appr 4 out: sn btn* **5/1**[1]
203- **11** *20* **Pistolet Noir (FR)**[198] 5099 4-11-3 139 HarrySkelton 62
(Paul Nicholls) *a towards rr: wknd 4 out* **11/2**[2]
4352 **12** *11* **Mohanad (IRE)**[13] 1150 4-10-7 129 JamieGoldstein 41
(Sheena West) *mid-div tl after 6th: sn bhd* **20/1**
01-0 **F** **Sir Harry Ormesher**[175] 94 7-11-9 145 ChristianWilliams —
(Alan King) *hld up towards rr: hdwy after 6th: nudged along in cl 5th whn fell 4 out* **14/1**

4m 53.6s (-8.20) **Going Correction** -0.125s/f (Good)
WFA 4 from 5yo+ 10lb **13** Ran SP% **117.0**
Speed ratings (Par 111): **111,107,106,105,101 101,97,88,85,84 76,71,—**
toteswingers:1&2 £22.50, 2&3 £24.50, 1&3 £23.60 CSF £78.18 CT £492.38 TOTE £10.00: £3.50, £4.40, £2.40; EX 76.70 TRIFECTA Not won..
Owner T G Leslie **Bred** Ralph And Helen O'Brien **Trained** Cholmondeley, Cheshire

FOCUS
A competitive event turned into a romp as the winner powered clear in the straight, producing a high-class performance. The second is rated to his best.

NOTEBOOK
Any Given Day(IRE) travelled well and and when asked he readily stretched clear for a wide-margin success on this softer ground. He competed in some hot contests last season but was perhaps overmatched and so could not make much impression. However, he had run consistently to his mark and evidently had improved for his reappearance run when narrowly beaten at Kelso. Life will be much tougher in handicaps after this. (op 8-1)
Dantari(IRE) raced prominently and held every chance but was readily outpaced by a more progressive rival. He is a solid handicapper and C&D winner and should be up to picking up a race at a lower level. (op 16-1)
Restless Harry ◆ gave the field around a ten-length start but soon fought his way into contention, although those earlier efforts must have told at the finish. He is on a fair mark and there must be more races to be won with him. (tchd 7-1)
Hills Of Aran was beaten out of sight at Cheltenham last week on his return from a lengthy absence, but he put up a better display here. Helping to set the early pace, he lost position around the final turn but rallied a bit near the finish. He is still on the comeback trail but looks to be gradually coming into form. (op 40-1)
Mad Moose(IRE) led on the final turn but faded badly from the second-last and did not last home on this galloping track. (op 20-1)
Chief Yeoman has been given a chance by the handicapper but has only one win to his name in over three years. It does not look likely that his winning tally will be increasing any time soon. (op 28-1)
Duke Of Lucca(IRE) was placed in top-class novice hurdles at the Aintree and Punchestown festivals in the spring, but he has winning form on soft ground. He was on a potentially lenient mark but he did not jump with any fluency and was never travelling. Official explanation: jockey said gelding was unsuited by the soft ground (op 9-2 tchd 4-1)
Pistolet Noir(FR) was never in the hunt and could not find a change of gear. The 4-y-o has reportedly matured over the summer and presumably will come on for this lacklustre run. (tchd 5-1 and 6-1)

1968 GET LIVE FOOTBALL STATS AT TOTESPORT.COM H'CAP CHASE (18 fncs) 3m
4:45 (4:45) (Class 3) (0-135,134) 4-Y-O+ **£6,505** (£1,910; £955; £477)

Form RPR
10-5 **1** **Incentivise (IRE)**[144] 567 7-9-11 110 MichaelMurphy(5) 119+
(C Roberts) *hld up last but wl in tch: hdwy 5 out: chal fr next: led appr last: styd on: rdn out* **11/4**[2]
FP1- **2** *1 3/4* **Den Of Iniquity**[211] 4870 9-11-12 134 NoelFehily 142+
(Warren Greatrex) *trckd ldrs: led 4 out: rdn after next: wnt rt and pckd 2 out: hdd whn wnt rt last: styd on* **5/2**[1]
23P- **3** *12* **Le Burf (FR)**[210] 4890 9-11-11 133 LiamTreadwell 131
(Giles Smyly) *j.rt: led: mstke 7th: rdn after 5 out: hdd next: hld whn pckd bdly 3 out: wknd* **6/1**[3]
300- **4** *6* **Made In Japan (JPN)**[210] 4884 10-11-3 128 SamTwiston-Davies(3) 118
(Nigel Twiston-Davies) *trckd ldrs: nudged along after 11th: ev ch 5 out: sn rdn: hld fr next: wknd after 3 out* **11/4**[2]
-111 **P** **Baily Storm (IRE)**[122] 828 8-11-7 129 (p) DarylJacob —
(Tim Vaughan) *trckd ldr: rchd for 3rd: hit 5th: rdn after 13th: wknd bef 5 out: p.u bef 4 out* **13/2**

6m 23.2s (1.20) **Going Correction** +0.225s/f (Yiel) **5** Ran SP% **109.5**
Speed ratings (Par 107): **107,106,102,100,—**
CSF £10.10 TOTE £4.20: £2.00, £2.10; EX 11.20.
Owner Ron Bartlett, F J Ayres & Jeff Hulston **Bred** Thomas Maher **Trained** Coedkernew, Newport

FOCUS
A fair handicap and a tight two-way finish. The winner is rated in line with last season's best.

NOTEBOOK
Incentivise(IRE) saved energy with low efficient jumping and that gave him enough to fight off a strong challenge from the last. He is a better horse at Chepstow and has now gained all three of his wins here, so even a 10lb higher mark than his last win was no problem. This was a step up on his previous victories, but he was getting lumps of weight from all his rivals, which was a distinct advantage in this ground. (op 7-2 tchd 4-1 in places)
Den Of Iniquity goes particularly well on soft ground, but in the end the topweight found the weight concession too much. This was a good performance and should set him up for a winter campaign. (op 9-4 tchd 11-4)
Le Burf(FR) led the field but started jumping out to the right as he began to tire. He habitually needs his first run of the season and that again looked the case. (tchd 13-2)
Made In Japan(JPN) was given plenty of time to recover after pulling up lame on his sole previous visit to this track in April 2007, and that patience paid off when he landed a competitive hurdle at Cheltenham in April 2009. However, an 8lb higher mark did not seem that favourable for the resumption of his chasing career and he looked less than sharp as he began to labour in the back straight. Official explanation: jockey said gelding was unsuited by the soft ground (op 3-1 tchd 5-2)
Baily Storm(IRE) made too many errors and was toiling before the home turn. (op 11-2)

1969 40 LIVE FOOTBALL MARKETS AT TOTESPORT.COM CONDITIONAL JOCKEYS' H'CAP CHASE (18 fncs) 3m
5:20 (5:20) (Class 5) (0-95,90) 4-Y-O+ **£2,276** (£668; £334; £166)

Form RPR
555P **1** **Canal Bank (IRE)**[20] 1710 6-11-9 90 (p) RichieMcLernon(3) 99+
(Jonjo O'Neill) *hld up: hdwy after 5 out: sn rdn: styd on to draw upsides last: sn led: drvn out* **14/1**
32-P **2** *2* **Hobb's Dream (IRE)**[21] 1678 6-10-6 73 (p) MrMMO'Connor(3) 79
(Neil Mulholland) *in tch: hdwy after 13th: rdn after 5 out: chsd ldr after next: led whn nt fluent last: sn hdd: styd on: no ex* **9/2**[1]
243- **3** *2* **Kiltimoney (IRE)**[201] 5056 10-10-6 70 GilesHawkins 76
(Richard Mitchell) *in tch: cl 4th whn v awkward 5 out: sn rdn: styd on same pce: wnt 3rd towards fin* **9/2**[1]
323P **4** *3/4* **Gift Of The Gods (IRE)**[22] 1663 7-11-1 85 (v) MrTomDavid(6) 88
(Tim Vaughan) *trckd ldrs: led after 7th: rdn after 4 out: hdd appr last: no ex* **7/1**
3P5P **5** *28* **Thyne Spirit (IRE)**[17] 1733 11-10-0 64 oh12 (p) JohnKington 39
(Simon Lewis) *towards rr: rdn after 10th: wknd 5 out: t.o* **28/1**
2P-1 **6** *3/4* **Gerrard (IRE)**[166] 251 12-11-10 88 (b) SamTwiston-Davies 63
(Althea Barclay) *trckd ldrs: rdn and ev ch 5 out: wknd next: t.o* **6/1**[3]
-400 **P** **Arceye**[17] 1733 13-11-0 78 (p) RichardKilloran —
(William Davies) *a detached: t.o whn p.u after 13th* **12/1**
FP-6 **P** **Maidstone Mixture (FR)**[46] 1500 5-11-12 90 (bt[1]) CO'Farrell —
(David Pipe) *led: hit 2nd: mstke 6th: hdd next: wkng whn blnd 11th: t.o whn p.u bef 5 out* **5/1**[2]
PP1- **P** **Wide Receiver (IRE)**[229] 4487 7-11-7 85 (v) DavidBass —
(Charlie Morlock) *trckd ldr: rdn along fr 8th: blnd 12th: sn wknd: t.o whn p.u bef 5 out* **5/1**[2]

6m 30.6s (8.60) **Going Correction** +0.225s/f (Yiel) **9** Ran SP% **114.3**
Speed ratings (Par 103): **94,93,92,92,83 82,—,—,—**
toteswingers:1&2 £13.90, 2&3 £2.20, 1&3 £13.90 CSF £76.53 CT £333.99 TOTE £13.30: £4.00, £2.10, £1.50; EX 130.30 Place 6: £51.81, Place 5: £41.23..
Owner John P McManus **Bred** Glenn Turley **Trained** Cheltenham, Gloucs

FOCUS
A weak staying handicap.

NOTEBOOK
Canal Bank(IRE) was held up at the rear and was able to gain ground steadily without coming under any serious pressure to deliver a late and decisive challenge. This was a marked improvement on his previous chases and his jumping was not always convincing, but he has enough of an engine to offset that in this grade. Official explanation: trainer said, regarding apparent improvement in form, that on its previous run the gelding made a bad mistake, lost its confidence, and pulled up. (tchd 16-1)
Hobb's Dream(IRE) never travelled on her reappearance at Fontwell three weeks earlier, but she responded to cheekpieces to put in a much-improved effort. She stayed on under pressure but had been in the vanguard for the length of the straight, so was somewhat vulnerable to a late finisher. (op 15-2)
Kiltimoney(IRE) had made his seasonal debut in the equivalent race in the previous two seasons, finishing second each time, but this year it has been reduced by 2.5f and that just counted against him. He will need a weak race to go on from this. (op 7-2)
Gift Of The Gods(IRE) finished best of those ridden near the pace, but she eventually paid the price by weakening to lose third place. She does not look close to breaking her maiden. (op 15-2 tchd 8-1)
Thyne Spirit(IRE) Official explanation: jockey said gelding finished lame

Gerrard(IRE) held a challenging position turning for home but weakened tamely. As a veteran he is not improving and is handicapped to the hilt, but he prefers faster ground and is a bit better than this. (op 5-1)
Arceye Official explanation: jockey said gelding never travelled (op 9-2 tchd 4-1)
Maidstone Mixture(FR) was too free in newly fitted headgear and tongue tie, and did not jump with any fluency on his debut for David Pipe. (op 9-2 tchd 4-1)
Wide Receiver(IRE) lost interest after a mistake in the back straight and was eventually pulled up. (op 9-2 tchd 4-1)
T/Plt: £115.00 to a £1 stake. Pool:£57,790.31 - 366.70 winning tickets. T/Qpdt: £12.40 to a £1 stake. Pool:£4,326.56 - 258.00 winning tickets. TM

1567 STRATFORD (L-H)

Saturday, October 23

OFFICIAL GOING: Good (good to firm in places on hurdle course)
Hurdle rails out 3m from inner line incr races by about 50m a circuit and chase track out 2m increasing races by about 33m a circuit.
Wind: Fresh half-against Weather: Showers

1970 100% NEW PLAYER BONUS AT TOTESPORTCASINO.COM NOVICES' CHASE (14 fncs) 2m 4f

2:20 (2:20) (Class 3) 5-Y-O+ **£5,069** (£1,497; £748; £374; £187)

Form				RPR
210-	1		**On Borrowed Wings (IRE)**[218] 4715 7-10-12 0 .... TimmyMurphy (Alan Fleming) *hld up: hdwy 2 out: rdn and r.o to ld towards fin* **6/4**[1]	133+
52-U	2	1 1/4	**Ikorodu Road**[134] 714 7-10-12 124 .... JohnnyFarrelly (Martin Keighley) *chsd ldr to 3 out: wnt 2nd again after next: rdn to ld last: hdd towards fin* **3/1**[2]	130
240/	3	16	**Mexican Pete**[570] 3404 10-10-12 0 .... DaveCrosse (Ian Williams) *hld up: hdwy 10th: rdn and mstke 2 out: wkng whn lft 3rd and hmpd last* **25/1**	120+
33-5	4	9	**Marley Roca (IRE)**[14] 1770 6-10-12 0 .... SamJones (Paul Webber) *hld up: hdwy 11th: wknd after 2 out* **11/1**	108
3UP4	5	hd	**Smack That (IRE)**[48] 1485 8-11-1 127 ....(vt[1]) PeterToole[(3)] (Milton Harris) *prom: chsd ldr 3 out tl rdn after next: wknd bef last* **12/1**	113
-121	6	4 1/2	**Alldunnandusted (IRE)**[147] 522 6-10-7 0 .... JimmyDerham[(5)] (Seamus Mullins) *hld up: wknd after 3 out* **6/1**	103
-1F4	F		**Otage De Brion (FR)**[14] 1770 8-11-3 134 .... MrSWaley-Cohen[(5)] (Nigel Twiston-Davies) *led: j lft 2nd and 8th: hdd and fell last* **11/2**[3]	138

4m 56.0s (1.80) **Going Correction** +0.35s/f (Yiel) **7 Ran SP% 114.5**
Speed ratings: **110,109,103,99,99 97,—**
toteswingers:1&2 £1.40, 2&3 £7.00, 1&3 £15.30 CSF £6.63 TOTE £2.40: £1.50, £2.00; EX 6.00.
Owner A T A Wates **Bred** Peter Mooney **Trained** Beare Green, Surrey

FOCUS
A blustery wind was blowing into the runners' faces in the home straight. This opener looked an interesting novices' chase, despite the smallish field. The winner is rated in line with his hurdles form with the second to his mark.

NOTEBOOK
On Borrowed Wings(IRE), a 133-rated hurdler making his debut over fences, notched a workmanlike victory. Held up in rear for the first circuit, he began to make progress approaching the 12th and had moved into third by the last. He did not get away from that fence as quickly as his jockey might have hoped, but showed a useful change of gear to edge ahead close to the finish. This was an encouraging start to his chasing career and, while nobody should get too carried away with the bare form, he ought to improve for the experience. A Grade 2 chase at Newbury's Hennessy fixture is now seemingly under consideration. (op 7-4)
Ikorodu Road, raised 5lb since finishing second in a novice handicap chase at Newbury last November, looks a feasible guide to the standard achieved by the winner. He was always close up, chasing the pace-setting Otage de Brion from the outset, and jumped adequately throughout. He lacked his conqueror's zip on the run-in, but went down fighting. (op 7-2)
Mexican Pete, a chasing debutant having his first outing for 570 days, ran reasonably well considering that layoff. He raced in fourth for much of the journey and lost touch with the leaders only in the home straight. (op 16-1)
Marley Roca(IRE), still a maiden over hurdles, never promised to finish closer than he did and seems to lack pace. (op 14-1)
Otage De Brion(FR), twice success at Bangor for previous connections but disappointing on his last two starts, would undoubtedly have made the significant placings had he not come down when still in contention at the last. He had taken the field along from the start and was galloping on resolutely before his fall. (op 5-1 tchd 9-2 and 13-2)

1971 OVER 60 INSTANT GAMES AT TOTESPORTGAMES.COM (S) HURDLE (9 hdls) 2m 110y

2:50 (2:50) (Class 5) 4-6-Y-O **£1,951** (£573; £286; £143)

Form				RPR
0-05	1		**Hibiki (IRE)**[135] 687 6-10-12 127 ....(p) TomO'Brien (Philip Hobbs) *chsd ldrs: wnt 2nd 6th: led 2 out: clr last: comf* **4/7**[1]	117+
56	2	8	**Lindsay's Dream**[20] 1689 4-10-5 0 .... JamesDavies (Andrew Haynes) *hld up: hdwy 3 out: sn rdn: styd on same pce fr next* **33/1**	99
010-	3	1/2	**Tayarat (IRE)**[61] 1840 5-11-7 0 ....(vt) PaulMoloney (Evan Williams) *led and sn clr: rdn and hdd 2 out: no ex last* **14/1**	115
-33P	4	23	**War Party**[10] 1828 6-10-10 107 .... MrTWeston[(7)] (Dr Richard Newland) *hld up: rdn 5th: nvr on terms* **15/2**[3]	91
3300	5	2 1/2	**Ladies Best**[16] 1741 6-10-5 93 ....(v) MattGriffiths[(7)] (Gordon Edwards) *chsd ldrs: rdn after 4th: wknd bef 6th* **25/1**	83
15-3	6	1 1/2	**Feeling (IRE)**[32] 1569 6-10-10 99 .... MissIsabelTompsett[(7)] (Dai Burchell) *chsd ldr to 6th: wknd after 3 out* **15/2**[3]	88
05-1	7	52	**Musashi (IRE)**[17] 1549 5-11-3 98 .... LeightonAspell (Laura Mongan) *hld up: rdn after 5th: a bhd: t.o* **5/1**[2]	40
0-	F		**Optimaxer (IRE)**[229] 4495 5-10-12 0 .... DaveCrosse (Jamie Snowden) *bhd whn fell 4th* **66/1**	—

3m 56.2s (0.20) **Going Correction** -0.025s/f (Good)
WFA 4 from 5yo+ 9lb **8 Ran SP% 118.8**
Speed ratings: **98,94,94,83,82 81,56,—**
toteswingers:1&2 £13.80, 2&3 £6.90, 1&3 £7.40 CSF £27.60 TOTE £1.50: £1.10, £4.20, £2.70; EX 30.10.The winner was bought in for 8,700gns.
Owner R A Green **Bred** Albert Conneally **Trained** Withycombe, Somerset

FOCUS
There was not a lot of depth to this ordinary selling hurdle. The winner stood out and was a stone+ off his previous best.

NOTEBOOK
Hibiki(IRE), placed from a mark of 128 at Market Rasen in September 2009, was not hard-pressed to take this weak event. Patiently ridden early on, he went second three out and jumped into the lead at the next. The race was quickly in the bag. (op 8-11 tchd 4-5 and 8-15)
Lindsay's Dream, a modest sixth in novice grade on her previous outing, appeared to improve on that effort. In mid-field for much of he race, she went third three out and grabbed second on the run-in. (op 28-1)
Tayarat(IRE) was dropped in grade for this seasonal bow and his rider apparently set out with the intention of making all the running. He was perhaps ten lengths clear at one stage, but came under pressure three out and had no response when the winner swept past. Official explanation: jockey said gelding had a breathing problem (op 10-1)
War Party was reverting to hurdles after a modest effort over fences at Wetherby and fared a little better. He never promised to make the first three, however, after disputing fifth for most of the race. (op 7-1 tchd 8-1)
Ladies Best, a fair Flat performer at one stage, has been disappointing over hurdles and ran modestly again. (op 20-1)
Feeling(IRE), third from a mark of 99 here a month earlier, was well below that level in this contest. He chased the pace early on, but faded out of contention from the third-last. (tchd 7-1 and 8-1)
Musashi(IRE) Official explanation: jockey said gelding hung right-handed

1972 £10 FREE PLAY AT TOTESPORTBINGO.COM H'CAP HURDLE (FOR THE KEOGH AND HOWS CHALLENGE TROPHY) (10 hdls) 2m 3f

3:20 (3:20) (Class 3) (0-130,124) 4-Y-0+
£6,262 (£1,850; £925; £463; £231; £116)

Form				RPR
413-	1		**Hidden Keel**[182] 5386 5-11-6 118 .... FelixDeGiles (Charlie Longsdon) *mde all: mstke 3 out: sn clr: blnd last: comf* **9/2**[2]	133+
4104	2	7	**Cubism**[5] 1904 4-9-13 102 ....(t) JimmyDerham[(5)] (Milton Harris) *a.p: rdn to chse wnr appr 2 out: no imp* **9/2**[2]	106
2163	3	5	**Topenhall (IRE)**[28] 1614 9-11-1 113 ....(t) CharliePoste (Ben Case) *prom: chsd wnr appr 6th tl rdn bef 2 out: styd on same pce* **10/1**	113
26-P	4	3/4	**The Rainbow Hunter**[20] 1692 6-10-10 115 .... EdCookson[(7)] (Andy Turnell) *hld up: hdwy 5th: styd on same pce appr 2 out* **8/1**	115
3-21	5	1 1/2	**Cantabilly (IRE)**[16] 1740 7-11-0 119 .... MattGriffiths[(7)] (Ron Hodges) *hld up: sme hdwy after 3 out: nvr on terms* **6/1**[3]	116
025	6	16	**Consulate (IRE)**[59] 1372 6-11-5 117 .... NickScholfield (Gordon Edwards) *chsd ldrs tl wknd appr 7th: t.o* **12/1**	100
1102	7	14	**Pure Faith (IRE)**[69] 1257 6-11-12 124 .... TomO'Brien (Peter Bowen) *chsd wnr to appr 6th: wknd after next: t.o* **7/2**[1]	94
0-16	8	3	**Le Corvee (IRE)**[17] 1731 8-11-1 118 .... LeeEdwards[(5)] (Tony Carroll) *mid-div: drvn along after 5th: wknd bef 7th: t.o* **16/1**	86
3-40	F		**Dot's Delight**[16] 1746 6-10-4 105 .... PeterToole[(3)] (Mark Rimell) *hld up: in rr whn fell 7th* **14/1**	—

4m 31.3s (-0.20) **Going Correction** -0.025s/f (Good)
WFA 4 from 5yo+ 9lb **9 Ran SP% 113.3**
Speed ratings (Par 107): **107,104,101,101,101 94,88,87,—**
toteswingers:1&2 £3.00, 2&3 £9.10, 1&3 £11.90 CSF £24.97 CT £189.59 TOTE £6.40: £2.00, £1.90, £3.80; EX 26.00.
Owner Mrs Peter Matthey & John F Horn **Bred** Mrs M J Matthey **Trained** Over Norton, Oxon

FOCUS
Just a mid-range handicap hurdle, but apparently competitive on paper. The easy winner produced a massive step up.

NOTEBOOK
Hidden Keel, making his handicap debut and returning from a six-month break, galloped his rivals into submission. Sent into the lead from the start, he had established a clear advantage by the home turn and never looked likely to be caught. He was not pretty at the final flight, getting over it bunny-style and landing awkwardly, but that did not stop him and he scored with something in hand. The plan now is to send him over fences and connections feel a stiffer track will be in his favour. (tchd 4-1 and 11-2)
Cubism was making a quick reappearance after finishing fourth at Plumpton five days earlier and looks a decent yardstick for the form. He raced in fourth for much of the journey and hurdled respectably. Third two out, he picked up another place in the closing stages. (tchd 4-1)
Topenhall(IRE) was 5lb higher than when scoring at Market Rasen in August and seems to be struggling a little off his current rating. He was always in the leading trio, but could not quicken at the business end. (op 11-1 tchd 9-1)
The Rainbow Hunter, who landed a handicap from a 3lb lower mark in January, is another seemingly over-rated now. He did make some late progress, after racing in rear early on, but it was nothing like enough to put him in with a leading chance. (op 15-2)
Cantabilly(IRE) had been raised 7lb for his success at Exeter 16 earlier and comprehensively failed to handle that rise. He was held up in the early stages and never closer than at the finish. (op 11-2 tchd 7-1)
Pure Faith(IRE) had racked up a hat-trick in novice events in the summer, but disappointed here. He chased the winner for more than a circuit, but folded tamely before the home turn. Official explanation: jockey said gelding ran too free (op 4-1)

1973 PLAY BLACKJACK AT TOTESPORT.COM H'CAP CHASE (FOR THE JOHN H. KENNY MEMORIAL CUP) (15 fncs) 2m 5f 110y

3:50 (3:50) (Class 3) (0-135,125) 4-Y-0+ **£7,935** (£2,420; £1,264; £687)

Form				RPR
PPP-	1		**Minella Theatre (IRE)**[191] 5195 7-11-12 125 .... HaddenFrost (Henrietta Knight) *a.p: lft 2nd and hmpd 3 out: rdn to ld last: styd on wl* **13/2**	141+
1266	2	7	**Sunday City (JPN)**[28] 1611 9-11-6 119 .... JamieMoore (Peter Bowen) *w ldr: mstke 8th (water): lft in ld 3 out: rdn and hdd last: no ex flat* **9/2**[2]	128
16-	3	19	**Emergency Exit (IRE)**[185] 5309 7-11-12 125 .... TomO'Brien (Philip Hobbs) *hld up: mstke 7th: hdwy 11th: rdn after 2 out: wkng whn hit last* **7/2**[1]	122+
44-P	4	hd	**Fit To Drive**[10] 1828 8-11-10 123 ....(t) LeightonAspell (Brendan Powell) *prom tl wknd after 10th* **14/1**	115
0-P0	P		**Gaelic Flight (IRE)**[132] 735 12-11-10 123 .... NickScholfield (Jeremy Scott) *chsd ldrs tl wknd 8th: j. slowly next: t.o whn p.u bef 12th* **14/1**	—
5P0-	P		**Ordre De Bataille (FR)**[223] 4610 8-11-9 122 .... TimmyMurphy (Henry Daly) *a bhd: t.o whn p.u bef 3 out* **9/1**	—
4533	F		**Folie A Deux (IRE)**[9] 1842 8-10-12 111 ....(t) JoeTizzard (Colin Tizzard) *led tl fell 3 out* **7/2**[1]	—
P5PF	U		**Tampa Boy (IRE)**[6] 1885 8-10-8 112 ....(vt) JimmyDerham[(5)] (Milton Harris) *prom: pushed along 9th: wknd after 12th: blnd and uns rdr 2 out* **6/1**[3]	91

5m 18.7s (3.70) **Going Correction** +0.35s/f (Yiel) **8 Ran SP% 113.6**
Speed ratings (Par 107): **107,104,97,97,— —,—,—**
toteswingers:1&2 £2.30, 2&3 £3.60, 1&3 £12.80 CSF £35.81 CT £118.33 TOTE £7.30: £1.90, £2.10, £1.90; EX 49.30.
Owner Trevor Hemmings **Bred** Gerard Mullins **Trained** West Lockinge, Oxon

FOCUS
An interesting handicap chase, though several had something to prove judged on recent form. The winner is rated to the level of last season's first-time out win.

NOTEBOOK
Minella Theatre(IRE) had failed to complete in decent company on his last three outings of last season, but took advantage of this drop in grade to win decisively. Always well placed, he disputed third for much of the race before going second approaching two out. He hit the front jumping the last and showed a much better finishing kick than the runner-up. There was no sign here of the burst blood vessels that have occasionally blighted his career and, while he may not be suited to testing underfoot conditions, he can win again this winter if his wellbeing can be maintained. (op 6-1 tchd 5-1 and 7-1)
Sunday City(JPN) had run creditably from out of the weights in a Listed chase at Market Rasen last time and posted another highly commendable effort here. Second early on, he took the lead three out, when Folie A Deux came down, and was still in front approaching the last. He had no answer to the winner's run-in kick, but was still far too good for the rest. (tchd 4-1)
Emergency Exit(IRE) had disappointed off this mark on his final outing of last season, but fared better in this. His jumping was not entirely fault-free, but he plugged in gamely towards the finish.
Fit To Drive, three times successful last term but disappointing on her reappearance, was always in mid-field. She has not yet regained the form she showed when scoring three times last term, but this was an improvement on her modest reappearance. (op 11-1)
Folie A Deux(IRE) was in front when falling three out. (op 9-2)

1974 PLAY ROULETTE AT TOTESPORT.COM MAIDEN HURDLE (9 hdls) 2m 110y
4:25 (4:25) (Class 3) 4-Y-0+ **£4,119** (£1,216; £608; £304; £152)

Form					RPR
533-	1		**Paint The Clouds**[192] 5182 5-11-0 **120**	LeightonAspell	111+
			(Warren Greatrex) *chsd ldr tl led after 3 out: shkn up flat: comf* **4/6**[1]		
32-4	2	1	**Beside The Fire**[14] 1773 5-11-0 0	JoeTizzard	107
			(Colin Tizzard) *a.p: chsd wnr after 3 out: rdn flat: r.o* **10/3**[2]		
	3	3 1/4	**Pilgreen (FR)** 5-11-0 0	PaulMoloney	106+
			(Evan Williams) *hld up: hdwy to go 3rd appr 2 out: nvr nr to chal* **8/1**[3]		
	4	26	**Mister Fantastic**[10] 4-10-11 0	CharlieHuxley(3)	80
			(Nicky Vaughan) *nt fluent in rr: mod late prog: t.o* **40/1**		
0/0-	5	11	**Sir Mark (IRE)**[23] 2546 6-11-0 0	JodieMogford	70
			(Anna Bramall) *led: mstke 67th: sn hdd & wknd: t.o* **33/1**		
-500	6	16	**Tocatchaprince (IRE)**[5] 1899 4-11-0 0	DaveCrosse	56
			(Milton Harris) *hld up: wknd appr 6th: t.o* **40/1**		
	7	hd	**Irish Joe (USA)**[813] 4-10-11 0	PeterToole(3)	56
			(Ray Peacock) *hld up: drvn along 6th: sn wknd: t.o* **66/1**		
6	8	36	**Sablazo (FR)**[16] 1743 4-11-0 0	NickScholfield	23
			(Andy Turnell) *hld up: hdwy 6th: wknd after 3 out: t.o* **40/1**		
0-0	9	50	**Citrus Mark**[20] 1689 5-11-0 0	WillKennedy	—
			(Paul Webber) *chsd ldrs tl rdn and wknd after 3 out: t.o* **14/1**		
0-5	P		**Bahr Nothing (IRE)**[177] 60 4-11-0 0	TimmyMurphy	—
			(Henry Daly) *hld up in tch: rdn and wknd after 3 out: p.u and dismntd bef next* **20/1**		

4m 0.30s (4.30) **Going Correction** -0.025s/f (Good) **10** Ran SP% **117.4**
Speed ratings (Par 107): **88,87,86,73,68 61,60,44,20,—**
toteswingers:1&2 £1.02, 2&3 £2.20, 1&3 £1.50 CSF £2.90 TOTE £1.60: £1.10, £1.20, £1.90; EX 3.60.
Owner Peter Deal & Jill & Robin Eynon **Bred** Guy Reed And Mrs A H Daniels **Trained** Upper Lambourn, Berks

FOCUS
There looked little depth to this weak maiden hurdle and the winner stood out. The time was relatively slow and the winner is rated a stone off.

NOTEBOOK
Paint The Clouds had finished third from a mark of 117 at Cheltenham on his final outing of last season and, although he did not need to reach anything like that standard to take this, won cosily enough. He raced in second in the early stages, took the lead four from home, and was clear approaching the last. The second closed him down on the run-in, but he was probably only idling and is worth more than the winning margin might suggest. That said, he may find life tougher from now on, either carrying a penalty or going back into handicaps. (op 5-6 tchd 10-11)
Beside The Fire, fourth at Chepstow on his hurdling debut two weeks previously, almost certainly improved on that performance. He too was prominent from the start and, by the second-last, was in a clear second place. He tried hard from the final flight, cutting the winner's lead with every stride, but never quite looked likely to get his head in front before the post. (op 11-4 tchd 5-2)
Pilgreen(FR), a half-brother to a hurdles winner in France, made an eye-catching debut. In rear early on, he had worked his way into fourth before three out. Although he made a mistake there, he eventually stayed on well to take third. Even better can be expected next time. (op 9-1)
Mister Fantastic, a maiden after ten starts on the Flat, was another who made late progress. He had been a long way adrift in the middle of the race - and ultimately well beaten overall - but passed several rivals after the home turn. (tchd 50-1)
Sir Mark(IRE), rated 60 on the Flat and well beaten on his only previous outing over hurdles, did a decent job of pace-setting before getting tired in the closing stages and dropping rather tamely out of contention.
Bahr Nothing(IRE) Official explanation: jockey said gelding lost its action

1975 PLAY SLOTS AT TOTESPORT.COM H'CAP CHASE (11 fncs 1 omitted) 2m 1f 110y
5:00 (5:00) (Class 3) (0-125,125) 4-Y-0 **£6,337** (£1,872; £936; £468; £234)

Form					RPR
1322	1		**Quito Du Tresor (FR)**[30] 1597 6-11-9 **125**	CampbellGillies(3)	141+
			(Lucinda Russell) *hld up: hdwy to chse ldr 7th: led next: shkn up flat: r.o strly* **13/8**[1]		
5664	2	19	**Mibleu (FR)**[29] 1606 10-11-6 **119**	(t) JoeTizzard	118
			(Colin Tizzard) *hld up: hdwy 8th: chsd wnr after 3 out: rdn appr last: wknd flat* **8/1**		
2464	3	16	**Kikos (FR)**[20] 1690 8-11-3 **116**	SamJones	101
			(Renee Robeson) *hld up: hdwy appr 2 out: rdn and wknd bef last* **13/2**[3]		
P105	4	3 3/4	**Blast The Past**[14] 1767 8-10-0 **106**	MrJohnDawson(7)	87
			(Dai Burchell) *hld up: hdwy appr 2 out: sn rdn and wknd: t.o* **10/1**		
5532	5	12	**Marodima (FR)**[21] 1676 7-11-10 **123**	(p) TomO'Brien	93
			(Jamie Snowden) *led and sn clr: hdd 8th: wknd appr 2 out: t.o* **4/1**[2]		
-121	6	2 1/4	**Mam Ratagan**[13] 1796 9-11-7 **123**	PeterToole(3)	91
			(Heather Main) *blnd 1st: chsd clr ldr to 7th: ev ch 3 out: rdn and wknd after next: t.o* **4/1**[2]		

4m 19.7s (12.60) **Going Correction** +0.35s/f (Yiel) **6** Ran SP% **111.6**
Speed ratings (Par 107): **86,77,70,68,63 62**
toteswingers:1&2 £4.50, 2&3 £12.40, 1&3 £2.50 CSF £14.16 TOTE £2.60: £2.00, £2.70; EX 20.70.
Owner Mrs Jo Tracey **Bred** Mme Claude Menard & Jacques Cherel **Trained** Arlary, Perth & Kinross

FOCUS
On paper, this looked a competitive handicap chase, but it was won decisively. The open ditch going away from the stands was omitted due to a broken frame. There is a case for rating the form up to 8lb higher.

NOTEBOOK
Quito Du Tresor(FR) had been raised 3lb since finishing second over fences at Perth in July, but overcame that increase in style. Held up just off the pace in the early stages, he went third on the second circuit and jumped into the lead four out. Nothing got near him after that and he might have collected by a greater margin had his rider not been relatively easy on him up the straight. (op 2-1)
Mibleu(FR), 9lb higher than when winning at Worcester in June, was tried in a tongue-tie. Just how much difference it made is hard to judge, but he was no match for the winner and does not seem obviously well-treated from his current mark. (op 9-1)
Kikos(FR) has not been at his best since collecting from a 4lb higher mark at Uttoxeter in April and never threatened to win this. He raced in mid-field throughout and could not muster a significant change of pace in the closing stages. (tchd 6-1)
Blast The Past, twice disappointing since collecting from 2lb lower here in September, was another held up off the pace for much of the journey. She made a little progress on the second circuit, but weakened approaching the last. (tchd 11-1)
Marodima(FR), a habitual front-runner who finished a clear second at Fontwell on his latest outing, set off in front as usual. He was headed at the fourth-last, however, and dropped away tamely thereafter. (op 9-2)
Mam Ratagan, switched back to handicap company after scoring on two of his last three runs in novice grade, was disappointing. He weakened quite quickly after hitting the third-last. Official explanation: jockey said gelding was unsuited by the good ground (op 10-3)

1976 PLAY BINGO AT TOTESPORT.COM LADY RIDERS' H'CAP HURDLE (9 hdls) 2m 110y
5:30 (5:30) (Class 4) (0-100,100) 4-Y-0+ **£2,740** (£798; £399)

Form					RPR
0030	1		**Lean Burn (USA)**[82] 1164 4-9-9 **74** oh4	RachaelGreen(5)	82+
			(Barry Leavy) *hld up: hdwy appr 6th: led 2 out: rdn out* **7/1**[3]		
0003	2	2 3/4	**Henry Hook (IRE)**[16] 1737 6-11-5 **100**	(p) MissAPearn(7)	105
			(Victor Dartnall) *hld up in tch: plld hrd: led 6th: hdd 2 out: styd on same pce flat* **7/1**[3]		
3P52	3	11	**Ruby Valentine (FR)**[65] 1300 7-9-7 **74** oh2	MissBAndrews(7)	69
			(Jim Wilson) *hld up: hdwy 3 out: styd on same pce fr next* **7/1**[3]		
-000	4	8	**Monfils Monfils (USA)**[8] 1468 8-9-10 **77** oh5 ow3	MissLucyBell(7)	65
			(Philip Kirby) *chsd ldrs tl wknd after 3 out* **17/2**		
P-05	5	3	**Kyoto (GER)**[20] 1707 6-9-9 **76**	MsLisaO'Neill(7)	61
			(Nigel Hawke) *chsd ldr tl after 5th: wknd appr 2 out* **8/1**		
P-50	6	2 1/2	**Art Value**[17] 1723 5-9-11 **78**	MissJBuck(7)	61
			(Carroll Gray) *hld up: hdwy appr 5th: wknd bef 2 out* **17/2**		
20-U	7	3/4	**Chalice Welcome**[12] 439 7-10-6 **85**	GemmaGracey-Davison(5)	67
			(Neil King) *led to 6th: wknd 2 out* **11/2**[2]		
P-34	8	17	**Leulahleulahlay**[34] 1549 4-10-12 **93**	MissIsabelTompsett(7)	60
			(Evan Williams) *prom: pushed along 5th: wknd 3 out: t.o* **9/2**[1]		
530	9	31	**Monsieur (FR)**[67] 1272 10-10-1 **82**	MissJennyCarr(7)	21
			(Carroll Gray) *hld up: rdn and wknd after 3 out: t.o* **8/1**		

4m 1.90s (5.90) **Going Correction** -0.025s/f (Good)
WFA 4 from 5yo+ 9lb **9** Ran SP% **114.3**
Speed ratings (Par 105): **85,83,78,74,73 72,71,63,49**
toteswingers:1&2 £3.80, 2&3 £3.30, 1&3 £13.30 CSF £54.44 CT £355.83 TOTE £13.10: £3.90, £2.40, £2.00; EX 57.00 Place 6: £10.79, Place 5: £8.03..
Owner N Heath **Bred** George Ruggiero Jr **Trained** Forsbrook, Staffs

FOCUS
A weak finale, with the top weight rated just 100. The form is rated through the runner-up.

NOTEBOOK
Lean Burn(USA), running without any sort of headgear after being tried in blinkers, cheekpieces and a tongue-tie, notched his first-ever success over hurdles. He was racing from 4lb out of the handicap, but quickly asserted after taking the lead at the second-last and was not hard-pressed to collect. He obviously deserves credit for winning, but his victory, from a mark of just 74, hardly reflects well on the opposition. (op 8-1)
Henry Hook(IRE), apparently improved for the addition of cheekpieces last time out, again ran commendably in those aids. Always close up, he stayed on gamely in the closing stages, without promising to trouble the winner. (op 4-1)
Ruby Valentine(FR), racing from 2lb out of the handicap, did most of her best work in the home straight. She finished second over 2m3f here in August and may well benefit from stepping back up in distance. (tchd 15-2)
Monfils Monfils(USA), 5lb out of the handicap and further disadvantaged by his rider putting up overweight, ran as well as could be expected. He was beaten comprehensively in sellers on three starts leading up to this, so his fourth place puts the form firmly into perspective. (op 11-1)
T/Plt: £21.50 to a £1 stake. Pool:£45,080.26 - 1,529.71 winning tickets. T/Qpdt: £10.90 to a £1 stake. Pool:£3,512.26 - 237.70 winning tickets. CR

1977 - 1983a (Foreign Racing) - See Raceform Interactive

1956 AINTREE (L-H)
Sunday, October 24

OFFICIAL GOING: Good to soft (chs 6.3; hdl 6.6)
All hurdles and bends moved out from Saturday's position.
Wind: Moderate, across Weather: Fine

1984 HALLOWEEN AT MATALAN INTRODUCTORY JUVENILE HURDLE (9 hdls) 2m 1f
2:10 (2:12) (Class 3) 3-Y-O **£5,204** (£1,528; £764; £381)

Form					RPR
	1		**Mason Hindmarsh**[20] 3-11-0 0	BrianHarding	109+
			(Karen McLintock) *w ldr to 1st: sn dropped to midfield: hdwy 3 out: chalng 2 out: led jst bef last: styd on for press run-in: a jst doing enough towards fin* **50/1**		
1	2	1/2	**Pena Dorada (IRE)**[21] 1699 3-11-5 0	BarryKeniry	114+
			(Mrs K Burke) *led: dived at 5th: hdd 6th: regained ld 3 out: rdn and hdd jst bef last: continued to chal run-in: styd on but jst hld* **15/8**[2]		
	3	17	**Franklino (FR)**[195] 3-11-0 0	WayneHutchinson	94+
			(Alan King) *plld hrd early: hld up: hdwy 6th: effrt to chal appr 2 out: btn jst after last and lost tch w front pair* **10/11**[1]		
2	4	3 1/4	**Almutaham (USA)**[21] 1696 3-11-0 0	PaddyAspell	90
			(James Moffatt) *racd keenly: trckd ldrs: w ldr 3rd: led 6th: hdd 3 out: fading whn mstke 2 out: n.d after* **25/1**		
	5	9	**Ibn Hiyyan (USA)**[201] 3-11-0 0	GrahamLee	82
			(Ferdy Murphy) *trckd ldrs: pushed along whn j.big 3 out: wknd appr 2 out* **11/1**[3]		
	6	1 3/4	**Antoella (IRE)**[30] 3-10-7 0	JamesReveley	73
			(Philip Kirby) *hld up bhd: j. slowly 4th: struggling 6th: mod hdwy appr 2 out: no imp on ldrs and sn no further prog* **100/1**		
3	7	2 1/4	**Stags Leap (IRE)**[21] 1699 3-11-0 0	(v) WilsonRenwick	88+
			(P Monteith) *hld up: hdwy to go handy 5th: cl up abt 1 l off the pce whn blnd 3 out: 5th abt 7 l down whn mstke 2 out: wknd bef last* **14/1**		
	8	37	**Escape Artist**[19] 3-11-0 0	RichieMcGrath	45
			(Tim Easterby) *racd keenly: trckd ldrs tl pushed along and wknd after 6th: t.o* **20/1**		
	P		**Prince Of Vasa (IRE)**[55] 3-11-0 0	DougieCostello	—
			(Michael Smith) *plld hrd early: hld up: mstke 1st: nt fluent 5th: bhd whn p.u bef 3 out* **100/1**		

4 **P** **Master Performer (USA)**[32] 1576 3-11-0 0........................ BrianHughes —
(Barry Murtagh) *in tch: j. slowly and lost pl 6th: sn bhd: p.u bef 3 out* **66/1**
4m 22.0s (8.30) **Going Correction** +0.40s/f (Soft) **10** Ran SP% **116.2**
Speed ratings (Par 105): **96,95,87,86,82 81,80,62,—,—**
toteswingers: 1&2 £1.80, 1&3 £6.70, 2&3 £6.20. CSF £144.78 TOTE £82.00: £10.10, £1.10, £1.30; EX 210.90 TRIFECTA Not won..
Owner I R Clements **Bred** Newsells Park Stud **Trained** Ingoe, Northumberland

FOCUS
This had the look of a really interesting juvenile hurdle and all the attention was on Alan King's highly regarded newcomer Franklino, a dual winner on the Flat in France, but he failed to meet with expectations.

NOTEBOOK
Mason Hindmarsh, a 68-rated Flat performer, stayed on too strongly for the penalised Pena Dorada after the last, the pair some 17l clear. He stayed 1m2f on the level and responded well to pressure to edge ahead before the last. It would be unwise to assume this was a fluke, although he will find life tougher under a penalty.
Pena Dorada(IRE)'s impressive Kelso win on debut received a boost when the runner-up went in next time, and he ran a good, solid race under the penalty in a stronger contest, pulling clear of the third. He can probably defy it in a lesser contest. (op 3-1 tchd 10-3 in places)
Franklino(FR), who pulled early, was on edge beforehand and also got a little warm, but he travelled well into contention and held every chance from the first in the straight. However, it was clear from after two out that he wasn't going to be winning, and he was soon left trailing by the front pair, looking quite tired. He'll no doubt improve for the run, but this wasn't the performance of a future Triumph winner. (op 8-11 tchd evens in places)
Almutaham(USA), runner-up at Kelso on debut, disputed it for much of the way until slowly fading in the straight. He looks capable of winning races, but at a lower level than this. (op 28-1)
Ibn Hiyyan(USA), rated 68 on the Flat and winner of a 1m4f handicap at Southwell for Mark Johnston back in April, offered plenty of promise on this hurdles debut and, although well beaten, he's sure to improve for the run. (op 9-1)
Antoella(IRE), a 47-rated maiden on the Flat, made modest late headway and may make a better hurdler. Official explanation: jockey said, regarding running and riding, that his orders were to get the filly settled as it is inclinded to be a little buzzy, adding that having jumped big over the first couple of flights it lost ground but was able to make it up up round bend staying on in straight past beaten horses.
Stags Leap(IRE), third and some 22l behind Pena Dorada on debut, closed up well and was in the process of running an improved race when making a race-ending blunder three out. (op 16-1)
Escape Artist, rated 51 on the Flat, was a bit keen early and ultimately dropped right out. (op 28-1 tchd 33-1)

1985 MATALAN AND NSPCC NOVICES' CHASE (16 fncs) 2m 4f
2:45 (2:45) (Class 3) 4-Y-O+ **£7,039** (£2,574)

Form RPR
2-2 **1** **Cool Friend (IRE)**[169] 200 7-10-9 100................................ TomO'Brien 120+
(Jeremy Scott) *lft in 2nd pl 1st: chsd ldr: j. awkwardly 7th: moved upsides ldr 2 out: sn led and wnt clr: unchal after* **6/1**[3]
142- **2** *12* **Adams Island (IRE)**[218] 4724 6-11-2 0.......................... TomScudamore 125+
(Rebecca Curtis) *j.rt a few times: led: mstke 11th: rdn and jnd 2 out: sn hdd: wl btn appr last* **5/1**[2]
1F0- **F** **Wishfull Thinking**[199] 5099 7-11-2 0.............................. RichardJohnson —
(Philip Hobbs) *racd in 2nd pl whn fell 1st* **4/7**[1]
225- **F** **Galaxy Rock (IRE)**[192] 5197 6-11-2 0.................................... APMcCoy —
(Jonjo O'Neill) *racd in last pl: nt fluent 3rd: fell 5th* **7/1**
5m 20.8s (12.60) **Going Correction** +0.40s/f (Soft) **4** Ran SP% **107.1**
Speed ratings (Par 107): **90,85,—,—**
CSF £28.54 TOTE £5.30; EX 13.90.
Owner Mrs Messer-Bennetts Mrs Clarke-Hall **Bred** James Barry **Trained** Brompton Regis, Somerset

FOCUS
A race with an impressive roll of honour - Star De Mohaison, Turko, Tidal Bay and Kicks For Free all winning it in recent years. This year's edition had looked an interesting one.

NOTEBOOK
Cool Friend(IRE), the only one with previous experience of fences, having finished second on all five starts over them last season, jumped better than her one remaining rival and, having been level taking three out, she asserted soon after the next and stayed on strongly for a ready success. A most consistent sort, she should win her share this season, with her having the option of reverting to mares' only company, and the final at Newbury next year must already be to the forefront of connections' minds. (op 9-2 tchd 4-1)
Adams Island(IRE) quickly developed into a useful novice hurdler last season and, being a former point winner, he's expected to prove even better over fences. He made a satisfactory debut, throwing in the odd sketchy jump, notably when just getting to the other side of six out, but the experience won't be lost on him and he'll appreciate a return to 3m and softer conditions. (op 7-2)
Wishfull Thinking had reportedly schooled really well at home, but he clipped the top of the first fence and landed too steeply to stay upright. This was an unfortunate start for him and it's hoped his confidence isn't dented. (op 8-1 tchd 10-1)
Galaxy Rock(IRE) was hampered at the first and seemed to lose all confidence before crashing out at the fifth. (op 8-1 tchd 10-1)

1986 HELICENTRE LIVERPOOL H'CAP HURDLE (13 hdls) 3m 110y
3:20 (3:20) (Class 3) (0-135,133) 4-Y-O **£6,337** (£1,872; £936; £468; £234)

Form RPR
1PP- **1** **The Shy Man (IRE)**[196] 5141 7-10-11 **118**............................ BarryKeniry 123+
(George Moore) *hld up: hdwy 8th: nt fluent 4 out: chalng fr 3 out: lft appr last where big jump: r.o wl to draw clr fnl 175yds* **25/1**
040- **2** *11* **Racing Demon (IRE)**[221] 4674 10-11-12 **133**...................... HaddenFrost 127
(Henrietta Knight) *a.p: w ldr after 4 out: led 3 out: rdn and hdd appr last: one pce and n.d to wnr fnl 175yds* **7/1**[2]
212- **3** *2* **Sound Stage**[192] 5195 7-10-11 **123**.................................... IanPopham[(5)] 117+
(Caroline Keevil) *in tch: chsd ldrs 3 out: cl up 2 out: rdn appr last: styd on same pce and no imp run-in* **10/1**
4-00 **4** *½* **Parlesotho (FR)**[60] 1364 7-10-11 **118**.......................... WayneHutchinson 113+
(Ben Case) *trckd ldrs: blnd 9th: nt fluent 4 out: sn rdn: outpcd appr last: styd on for late gains but no ch towards fin* **20/1**
130- **5** *9* **Predictive (FR)**[198] 5113 7-11-3 **131**................................ HenryBrooke[(7)] 115
(Donald McCain) *prom: led appr 2nd: hdd 3 out: stl chalng 2 out: u.p between last 2: wknd after last* **9/2**[1]
146- **6** *6* **Cross Kennon (IRE)**[198] 5113 6-11-11 **132**....................... AlanO'Keeffe 111
(Jennie Candlish) *nt fluent: towards rr: hdwy 9th: rdn and outpcd appr 3 out: no imp after* **9/2**[1]
1-11 **7** *¾* **Solway Sam**[135] 710 7-11-12 **133**.................................... RichieMcGrath 111+
(Lisa Harrison) *bhd: nt fluent 6th: niggled along after 7th: sme hdwy after 4 out: nvr able to get to ldrs* **8/1**[3]
132- **8** *13* **Dance Island (IRE)**[198] 5109 7-11-8 **129**............................ CharliePoste 102+
(Ben Case) *midfield: hdwy after 4 out: chsd ldrs but no real imp 3 out: wknd appr last* **16/1**
-33P **9** *3¾* **Risk Runner (IRE)**[23] 1661 7-10-7 **114**.............................(b) PaddyAspell 77
(James Moffatt) *towards rr: struggling appr 9th: nvr on terms* **14/1**
1500 **10** *25* **Tarvini (IRE)**[15] 1776 5-11-4 **125**...(p) APMcCoy 65
(Jonjo O'Neill) *bhd: pushed along after 7th: toiling 4 out: nvr on terms* **14/1**
-21P **11** *3½* **Markington**[9] 1855 7-11-10 **131**..(b) TomO'Brien 68
(Peter Bowen) *led: hdd appr 2nd: remained prom: pushed along and lost pl appr 8th: rdn and bhd 4 out* **10/1**
513- **12** *28* **Moorlands Teri**[222] 4663 7-10-13 **120**............................ RichardJohnson 32
(Tim Vaughan) *prom: lost pl 7th: struggling whn mstke 8th: bhd after: t.o* **7/1**[2]
3-00 **13** *20* **Baccalaureate (FR)**[29] 1609 4-10-9 **120**............(t) SamTwiston-Davies[(3)] 13
(Nigel Twiston-Davies) *midfield: hdwy to trck ldrs after 7th: lost pl 8th: rdn appr 4 out: wknd bef 3 out: t.o* **20/1**
6m 21.0s (4.70) **Going Correction** +0.40s/f (Soft)
WFA 4 from 5yo+ 11lb **13** Ran SP% **123.2**
Speed ratings (Par 107): **108,104,103,103,100 98,98,94,93,85 84,75,68**
toteswingers: 1&2 £50.20, 1&3 £46.00, 2&3 £27.60. CSF £194.21 CT £1904.69 TOTE £36.10: £8.80, £3.00, £4.10; EX 329.90 TRIFECTA Not won..
Owner Sean P Graham **Bred** Peadar Byrne **Trained** Middleham Moor, N Yorks

FOCUS
A decent staying handicap hurdle.

NOTEBOOK
The Shy Man(IRE), very hit-and-miss over fences last season, winning twice but failing to complete on five other occasions, has gone well fresh in the past and he didn't look on too badly treated off a mark 6lb above his last winning one. Racing without the usual cheekpeices, he travelled sweetly and, having closed right up two out, he was clear by the last and ran powered clear to win with ease. This was a really encouraging display from the 7-y-o, and it's hoped he can prove more consistent this year, with a return to fences likely sooner rather than later.

Racing Demon(IRE) clearly still has some juice in the tank and his chase rating looks quite attractive now, so there will be opportunities for him this season. (op 8-1)

Sound Stage ◆, a consistent and progressive chaser last term, is rated 5lb lower over hurdles and he kept on well in third. This should tee him up nicely for a return to fences and he could develop into a very useful handicapper this term over 3m. (op 11-1)

Parlesotho(FR), reportedly lame latest, had stamina to prove over this trip, but she kept on well enough. It remains to be seen whether she's up to winning off this mark, though. (op 28-1)

Predictive(FR), 4lb lower than when ninth in an ultra-competitive staying handicap at the Grand National meeting, looks likely to come on for this first start in 198 days. (op 15-2)

Cross Kennon(IRE), sixth in the same race as Predictive at the Grand National meeting, goes well fresh, has won first time up for the past two seasons, so it was surprising to see him put in such a laboured effort, jumping lazily and failing to make any ground up in the straight. He is better than this and it would be no surprise to see him sent chasing now. (op 11-2)

Solway Sam, chasing a four-timer on this handicap debut/first start since June, is already a dual course scorer, but he was very much ridden to get the trip and never got into it. He ought to improve. (op 7-1)

Dance Island(IRE), much-improved sent chasing last term, ran as though this first run in 198 days was needed.

Moorlands Teri was in trouble from quite an early stage and proved bitterly disappointing. (op 5-1 tchd 8-1 and 9-1 in places)

1987 WEATHERBYS BANK H'CAP CHASE (FOR THE JOHN PARRETT MEMORIAL TROPHY) (12 fncs) 2m
3:55 (3:59) (Class 2) (0-145,138) 4-Y-O+ **£9,427** (£2,809; £1,422; £729; £381)

Form RPR
2113 **1** **Stagecoach Pearl**[70] 1257 6-10-11 **128**............................ ShaneByrne[(5)] 150+
(Sue Smith) *mde all: rn wd on bnd after 4th: hit 4 out: drew wl clr fr 2 out: eased down run-in* **10/3**[2]
1P3- **2** *22* **Awesome George**[191] 5215 6-11-9 **138**.......................... CharlieHuxley[(3)] 141
(Alan King) *disp 2nd pl tl mstke 8th: wnt 2nd 4 out: rdn appr 2 out: sn no ch w wnr* **7/1**
P4-0 **3** *6* **Tramantano**[170] 194 11-11-1 **130**........................ SamTwiston-Davies[(3)] 128
(Nigel Twiston-Davies) *disp 2nd pl: nt fluent 6th: tk def 2nd 8th: nt fluent and lost 2nd 4 out: u.p appr 2 out: sn n.d to wnr but continued to chal for 2nd pl tl one pce run-in* **11/4**[1]
260- **4** *6* **Folk Tune (IRE)**[15] 5225 7-10-8 **120**................................. DougieCostello 109
(John Quinn) *in tch: lost gound on ldrs 5th: bhd 6th: outpcd after 4 out: n.d after* **15/2**
3F1- **5** *1¼* **Ockey De Neulliac (FR)**[261] 3872 8-10-13 **125**.................... GrahamLee 116+
(Ferdy Murphy) *bhd: rdn whn wnt wd on bnd after 4th: hdwy 6th: chsd ldrs 4 out: rdn appr 3 out: wknd bef 2 out* **13/2**
151- **P** **Bob's Dream (IRE)**[196] 5139 8-10-5 **120**..................(t) CampbellGillies[(3)] —
(William Amos) *bhd: mstke 3rd: nvr gng wl: lft wl bhd appr 3 out: t.o whn p.u bef last* **7/2**[3]
4m 3.20s (3.20) **Going Correction** +0.40s/f (Soft) **6** Ran SP% **109.6**
Speed ratings (Par 109): **108,97,94,91,90** —
toteswingers: 1&2 £3.50, 1&3 £2.80, 2&3 £4.50. CSF £23.73 TOTE £3.90: £1.80, £2.70; EX 24.90.
Owner John Conroy Jaqueline Conroy **Bred** R F Broad **Trained** High Eldwick, W Yorks

FOCUS
This was turned into a rout by Stagecoach Pearl.

NOTEBOOK
Stagecoach Pearl soon had a healthy lead and galloped on relentlessly down the straight to win as he liked. Disappointing at Southwell latest, he had been given a break and turned in a career-best on this return to handicaps, although the handicapper is sure to make life much tougher for the likeable grey in future. (op 4-1 tchd 3-1)

Awesome George, who needs more of a test than this, boxed on best of the remainder and should improve considerably. His jumping should be sharper next time also. (op 15-2 tchd 8-1)

Tramantano, winner of the race for the past two years, was 3lb lower than last season and again looked the one to beat, but he made a couple of mistakes, notably four out, and finished tired. He's usually best fresh and connections will be pinning their hopes on the reapplication of blinkers working now. (op 9-4 tchd 3-1)

Folk Tune(IRE) jumped slowly at times and was well beaten. (op 8-1)

Ockey De Neulliac(FR) made a promising mid-race move which suggests the run was simply needed. Graham Lee did well to keep him in the race after he hung badly right at the bend racing out on to the final circuit (swayed by the winner running wide), and he should give a better account next time, with a 2m4f handicap chase at Newbury's Hennessy meeting likely to be his next stop. (op 11-2)

Bob's Dream(IRE), generally progressive last season, if somewhat inconsistent, jumped slowly over the first few and received stern reminders with a circuit to race. He never threatened to get involved and was disappointing, but is just the sort of horse to bounce back next time. (op 4-1 tchd 10-3)

1988 EUROPEAN BREEDERS' FUND BESTWAY "NATIONAL HUNT" NOVICES' HURDLE (QUALIFIER) (11 hdls) 2m 4f

4:30 (4:30) (Class 3) 4-6-Y-O **£4,553** (£1,337; £668; £333)

Form RPR

11- **1** **Cue Card**[221] 4676 4-10-12 0 JoeTizzard 144+
(Colin Tizzard) *racd keenly: hld up: nt fluent 4 out: smooth hdwy sn after: upsides w big jump 3 out: sn led on bit: clr whn j.lft last: v easily* **1/2**[1]

120- **2** *13* **Dear Sam (GER)**[197] 5129 5-10-12 0 TomScudamore 117
(Steve Gollings) *handy: w ldrs appr 7th: mstke 4 out: pushed along and wnt 2nd but outpcd by wnr between last 2: j.lft last: hung lft run-in whn no ch* **10/1**[3]

2-16 **3** *1 3/4* **Mr Moonshine (IRE)**[126] 805 6-10-13 0 ShaneByrne(5) 121
(Sue Smith) *led to 2nd: remained prom: regained ld 7th: jnd 3 out: sn hdd: struggling to qckn between last 2: carried lft last: one pce run-in* **16/1**

1 **4** *4 1/2* **Nicene Creed**[11] 1819 5-11-4 0 TomO'Brien 118+
(Philip Hobbs) *in tch: effrt bhd ldrs 2 out: struggling to qckn between last 2: stmbld last: plugged on at one pce after whn n.d* **7/2**[2]

302- **5** *1* **Castlerock**[211] 4881 6-10-12 0 APMcCoy 109
(Jonjo O'Neill) *hld up: pushed along and outpcd by ldrs 2 out: nvr able to chal* **14/1**

05-F **6** *10* **Iona Days (IRE)**[22] 1675 5-10-12 0 HaddenFrost 104+
(Henrietta Knight) *prom: ev ch 3 out: pushed along and wknd appr last* **25/1**

7 *70* **Eliades Run (IRE)** 4-10-12 0 GrahamLee 29
(Ferdy Murphy) *a bhd: nvr travelling wl: lost tch after 4 out: t.o* **66/1**

8 *27* **Mind Shower (IRE)**[139] 4-10-12 0 PaddyAspell 2
(Robert Wylie) *w ldr: led 2nd: hdd 7th: rdn and wknd after 4 out: t.o* **66/1**

5m 10.5s (9.80) **Going Correction** +0.40s/f (Soft)
WFA 4 from 5yo+ 10lb **8** Ran SP% **117.4**
Speed ratings: **96,90,90,88,87 83,55,45**
toteswingers: 1&2 £1.70, 1&3 £3.10, 2&3 £5.50. CSF £7.24 TOTE £1.60: £1.10, £2.10, £3.00; EX 6.00 Trifecta £33.20 Pool: £1,093.66 - 24.34 winning units..
Owner Mrs Jean R Bishop **Bred** R T Crellin **Trained** Milborne Port, Dorset

FOCUS
No Captain Chris, but this was perhaps still the most eagerly anticipated jumps race of the weekend, with last season's deeply impressive Champion bumper winner Cue Card.

NOTEBOOK
Cue Card ◆, last season's deeply impressive Champion bumper winner, had reportedly strengthened over the summer and couldn't have made a more impressive debut over hurdles. The form of the Cheltenham contest had worked out extremely well and, having reportedly schooled like a natural, including over fences, it was no surprise to see him made a red-hot favourite, with the step up to 2m4f not expected to be a bother. Despite having taken a fierce hold for the first part of the race, he jumped well and his tank was still full as he charged ahead three out, cruising clear to win as he pleased. Colin Tizzard, who said he had him straight for this reappearance, admitted to being relieved that this first run was out of the way and will now step him up in grade, with races from 2m-2m4f under consideration. He's favourite for both the Supreme Novices' and Neptune at next year's Festival, but judging from his trainer post-race interview, the Champion Hurdle, for which he's a 33-1 shot, is by no means out of the equation. It's likely he'll be out again soon, possibly at Cheltenham's Open meeting next month. (op 8-13 tchd 4-6)
Dear Sam(GER) ◆, a dual scorer in bumpers, was nibbled at ahead of this hurdles debut and, having jumped well in the main, he stayed on best after the last for second. He'll obviously find easier opportunities and looks a winner in waiting. (op 16-1)
Mr Moonshine(IRE), one of two carrying a penalty, had been off since disappointing at Hexham in June and he showed that running to be all wrong here, keeping on and marking himself down as a useful stayer in the making. (tchd 18-1)
Nicene Creed was being niggled leaving the back and proved rather laboured for pressure in the straight. He's well thought of and deserves a chance to show this running to be wrong. (op 10-3 tchd 3-1 and 4-1 in a place)
Castlerock ◆ very much caught the eye back in fifth. Up in trip for this reappearance, he still looked to be travelling well enough turning in, but failed to get close enough to challenge and very much looks one for another day, possibly once handicapping. (op 9-1)
Iona Days(IRE), who'd probably have been second but for falling at the last at Fontwell 22 days earlier, will stand more of a chance once handicapping and may yet improve.

1989 CHAMPAGNE LANSON ROSE STANDARD OPEN NATIONAL HUNT FLAT RACE 2m 1f

5:05 (5:06) (Class 4) 4-6-Y-O **£2,602** (£764; £382; £190)

Form RPR

1 **Herdsman (IRE)** 5-11-0 0 RichardJohnson 122+
(Philip Hobbs) *midfield: hdwy 8f out: led 3f out: plld away and r.o wl fnl f* **7/2**[1]

2 *3 1/4* **Charminster (IRE)**[169] 4-10-11 0 AdrianLane(3) 119+
(Donald McCain) *midfield: hdwy 6f out: chsd ldrs 3f out: chalng and stl looked green 2f out: nt qckn jst over 1f out: no imp on wnr ins fnl f* **8/1**

3 **3** *1 1/4* **Lexicon Lad (IRE)**[163] 319 5-11-0 0 SamThomas 118
(Tom George) *a.p: rdn 3f out: chalng 2f out: nt qckn jst over 1f out: styd on same pce ins fnl f* **13/2**

4 *9* **Old Wigmore (IRE)**[189] 5-11-0 0 APMcCoy 110
(Rebecca Curtis) *led: pushed along and hdd 3f out: wknd over 1f out* **9/2**[2]

5 *18* **Eldred (IRE)** 4-11-0 0 AndrewTinkler 94
(Nicky Henderson) *chsd ldrs: pushed along after 6f: outpcd 4f out: no imp on ldrs after* **11/2**[3]

10-0 **6** *1 1/2* **Tale Of Tanganyika (FR)**[163] 319 4-11-7 0 JamesReveley 99
(John Wade) *hld up: hdwy 6f out: chsd ldng quartet 3f out: no imp: wknd fnl f* **20/1**

00/2 **7** *7* **Be My Deputy (IRE)**[134] 732 5-11-0 0 BrianHughes 86
(Richard Guest) *towards rr: pushed along 6f out: sme hdwy 4f out: nvr able to trble ldrs* **14/1**

0-4 **8** *4 1/2* **Buraimi Oasis**[105] 949 5-11-0 0 BrianHarding 85
(Karen McLintock) *trckd ldrs tl rdn and wknd 4f out* **25/1**

0-0 **9** *10* **The Tiddly Tadpole**[16] 1764 5-10-9 0 PaulCallaghan(5) 73
(Simon West) *given ld into s: racd wd early: prom: wknd 4f out* **100/1**

50- **10** *1/2* **Swallow (FR)**[227] 4536 4-10-11 0 HarryHaynes(3) 73
(James Ewart) *prom: pushed along 6f out: wknd 5f out* **25/1**

0 **11** *17* **Beau D'Argent**[16] 1764 4-10-7 0 GrahamLee 50
(Ferdy Murphy) *in rr: rdn after 6f: nvr on terms* **100/1**

0 **12** *2 3/4* **Blazing Bay (IRE)**[163] 319 5-10-7 0 PaddyAspell 48
(James Moffatt) *midfield tl wknd 4f out* **25/1**

0- **13** *20* **Mac's Haul (IRE)**[299] 3154 5-11-0 0 DougieCostello 37
(Ian Williams) *midfield: rdn after 6f: wknd 6f out* **17/2**

14 *4 1/2* **Oscar Sierra (IRE)** 4-11-0 0 WayneHutchinson 33
(Tim Vaughan) *midfield: rdn 7f out: wknd 5f out* **25/1**

0/0- **15** *44* **Inishmor (IRE)**[358] 2004 6-11-0 0 TomSiddall —
(Jeremy Scott) *midfield: pushed along 4f out: sn wknd: t.o* **100/1**

16 *17* **Solway Pete** 4-11-0 0 RichieMcGrath —
(Lisa Harrison) *nvr gng wl: a bhd: t.o* **25/1**

17 *44* **Sally O'Malley (IRE)** 4-10-7 0 AlanO'Keeffe —
(Charles Smith) *a bhd: niggled along after 4f: lost tch after 6f: t.o* **100/1**

4m 15.2s (7.80) **Going Correction** +0.40s/f (Soft) **17** Ran SP% **125.4**
Speed ratings: **97,95,94,90,82 81,78,76,71,71 63,61,52,50,29 21,—**
toteswingers: 1&2 £12.80, 1&3 £7.80, 2&3 £12.70. CSF £29.33 TOTE £4.70: £2.20, £3.70, £2.90; EX 41.00 TRIFECTA Pool: £616.88 - 2.00 winning units. Place 6: £304.71 Place 5: 259.35.

Owner Trevor Hemmings **Bred** Eddie Flavin **Trained** Withycombe, Somerset

FOCUS
The likelihood is that this was a good bumper, certainly run at a proper gallop.

NOTEBOOK
Herdsman(IRE), a son of Flemensfirth, travelled like a quality animal throughout the race. His inexperience was there for all to see when Richard Johnson asked for his effort in the straight, looking green in front and clearly not being sure of what was required, but he did keep galloping, and always looked to be holding them inside the final furlong. He had a hard enough race in the end, but is obviously open to improvement and this should toughen him up. He'll appreciate at least 2m4f over hurdles and looks a bright prospect.
Charminster(IRE), who joined these connections for £45,000, also went like a good horse, and was actually the last horse off the bridle. He too was green under pressure, though, and couldn't keep on as well as the winner. Whether he wins a bumper of not, he too is a very nice hurdling prospect. (op 11-1)
Lexicon Lad(IRE), third over C&D in May, stayed on again to bustle up the winner, but he lacked a change of gear and was made to settle for third. He's another staying prospect with a future. (op 10-1 tchd 6-1)
Old Wigmore(IRE), a winner on his third start in points, has joined a yard that does well in the bumper arena, and he ensured this was a proper test, but probably to his own detriment in the end, as he finished tired. He should win races, but lacks the potential of a few of these. (op 6-1)
Eldred(IRE), from a yard that traditionally does well in bumpers, looked in need of the experience and should be more of a betting proposition next time. (op 7-2 tchd 6-1)
Be My Deputy(IRE) was keeping on late and will be well suited by a stiffer test over hurdles. (op 12-1)
Mac's Haul(IRE) has now attracted support on both his starts, but come nowhere near to justifying it. He may come good over further once hurdling. (op 8-1 tchd 9-1)
T/Plt: £332.20 to a £1 stake. Pool:£77,461.49 - 170.20 winning tickets. T/Qpdt: £104.30 to a £1 stake. Pool:£5,935.25 - 42.10 winning tickets. DO

1730 TOWCESTER (R-H)

Sunday, October 24

OFFICIAL GOING: Good (8.6)
Wind: Fresh, across Weather: Bright and breezy

1990 HAYGAIN HAY STEAMERS NOVICES' HURDLE (11 hdls 1 omitted) 3m

1:30 (1:30) (Class 4) 4-Y-0+ **£2,927** (£859; £429; £214)

Form RPR

325- **1** **Rif (FR)**[246] 4166 5-10-12 114 [1] NoelFehily 120+
(Alex Hales) *taken down v early and led to s: hld up in rr: mstke 1st: hdwy 7th: chsd ldrs and effrt u.p bef 2 out: led and hit last: styd on wl: rdn out* **8/1**

01 **2** *1 1/2* **Tullyraine (IRE)**[17] 1742 6-11-4 0 PaddyBrennan 124
(Nigel Twiston-Davies) *in tch: hdwy to join ldrs bypassing 9th: ev ch and edgd rt next: drvn and j.lft 2 out: styd on same pce flat* **11/4**[2]

354- **3** *3 1/4* **Any Currency (IRE)**[221] 4670 7-10-12 0 WarrenMarston 116
(Martin Keighley) *led tl after 3rd: chsd ldr tl after 8th: lost pl but stl in tch bef 3 out: rallied u.p to chse ldrs 2 out: swtchd rt bef last: no ex flat* **5/2**[1]

U-3 **4** *2* **Yabora (FR)**[177] 78 5-10-12 0 TomSiddall 116+
(Charlie Longsdon) *t.k.h: chsd ldrs: wnt 2nd bypassing 9th: led bef 3 out: drvn bef 2 out: hdd and nt fluent last: fdd flat* **4/1**[3]

5- **5** *1 1/4* **Definite Dawn (IRE)**[182] 7 6-10-5 0 MrTomDavid(7) 113
(Tim Vaughan) *t.k.h: chsd ldrs: rdn and outpcd bef 2 out: plugged on same pce between last 2* **28/1**

3 **6** *18* **Jetnova (IRE)**[160] 370 5-10-12 0 ChristianWilliams 96
(Alan King) *hld up wl in tch in midfield: mstke 8th: rdn and wknd after 3 out: wl btn whn j. slowly next* **6/1**

0 **7** *7* **El Diego (IRE)**[22] 1675 6-10-7 0 DavidBass(5) 90
(Jamie Snowden) *hld up in tch in rr: hdwy after 7th: in tch bypassing 8th: rdn and wknd qckly after next* **50/1**

05 **8** *29* **Fairwood Dante (IRE)**[17] 1749 6-10-12 0 NickScholfield 63
(Simon Earle) *chsd ldrs: wnt 2nd after 8th: led bypassing next tl hdd and short of room 3 out: wknd qckly bef 2 out* **66/1**

9 *2 3/4* **Kingman Reef (IRE)**[553] 6-10-12 0 TomMessenger 61
(Chris Bealby) *hld up in tch towards rr: rdn and struggling after 8th: t.o whn blnd 3 out* **66/1**

10 *9* **Hardwick Wood**[189] 5-10-12 0 AndrewThornton 53
(Caroline Bailey) *chsd ldr tl led after 3rd: chsd ldr tl bypassing 9th: wknd rapidly 3 out: t.o* **25/1**

0/ **P** **Dareios (GER)**[759] 1480 5-10-12 0 DaveCrosse —
(John Mackie) *hld up in tch towards rr: rdn and struggling after 8th: t.o whn p.u 2 out* **100/1**

5/0- **R** **Trempari**[24] 5154 7-10-5 0 (b) MrAWilliams(7) —
(Mike Murphy) *hld up towards rr: hdwy to chse ldrs whn cocked jaw, rn out and uns rdr 3rd* **80/1**

060 **P** **The Ridge**[11] 1824 6-10-9 0 JohnKington(3) —
(Michael Scudamore) *in tch towards rr: lost tch rapidly 8th: wl t.o whn p.u 3 out* **150/1**

00 **P** **Fen Farm**[12] 1812 5-10-9 0 TomMolloy(3) —
(Emma Baker) *in tch: rdn and lost pl qckly after 7th: t.o whn p.u next* **125/1**

00 **P** **Hamalac**[18] 1734 4-10-11 0 GerardTumelty —
(Martin Keighley) *hld up in tch towards rr: rdn and struggling 8th: t.o whn mstke 3 out: p.u next* **100/1**

6m 6.60s (-8.40) **Going Correction** -0.50s/f (Good)
WFA 4 from 5yo+ 11lb **15** Ran SP% **117.5**
Speed ratings (Par 105): **94,93,92,91,91 85,83,73,72,69 —,—,—,—,—**
toteswingers: 1&2 £5.00, 1&3 £5.80, 2&3 £2.40. CSF £29.27 TOTE £9.90: £3.30, £1.40, £1.20; EX 33.20.
Owner The Patient Partnership **Bred** Francois-Marie Cottin **Trained** Wardington, Oxon

FOCUS
A few of these have already had experience of fences, and one would imagine many of these will become successful staying chasers in time. The early pace wasn't strong but it still looked a slog at the end. The fourth-last flight was bypassed on the second circuit.

NOTEBOOK
Rif(FR), wearing a hood for the first time, has given trouble in the past (he went down early here and was walked to the start) but showed that there is talent in with some possible quirks with a sound effort. Held up, he crept into contention and got to the front approaching the last hurdle. Once there, he did enough to hang on and one would imagine his future will very much depend on his mental state on the day. (op 9-1)
Tullyraine(IRE) got his hurdling career off to a perfect start last time at Worcester, also over 3m, and was the only one of these running under a penalty. Coming from a stable with a decent record in this race, he kept grinding away and ran well giving weight away. (op 7-2)
Any Currency(IRE), a very useful staying chaser last season, often hits a flat spot and did so again here a number of times, but the one thing he does do is respond, and he plugged on up the hill. (op 11-4 tchd 3-1, 10-3 in places)
Yabora(FR) ♦, whose trainer/owner took this race last season with a chaser, looked sure to go close when he took it up but weakened dramatically after two out - he took a strong hold early, which is possibly why he emptied out. Once he learns to settle or runs on a flatter course, a victory seems assured. (op 7-2 tchd 3-1 and 9-2)
Definite Dawn(IRE) shaped nicely and seems a stayer. (op 25-1)
Jetnova(IRE), absent since May, ran as though the run would bring him on. (op 11-2)
Fairwood Dante(IRE) ran well enough to suggest he has enough ability to make his mark in due course.
Hardwick Wood ran better than his eventual position would indicate. (op 20-1)

1991 COURIER COMPANY H'CAP CHASE (14 fncs) 2m 3f 110y
2:00 (2:02) (Class 4) (0-105,105) 4-Y-O+ **£2,927** (£859; £429; £214)

Form				RPR
501	**1**		**In The Zone (IRE)**[48] 1493 6-11-6 **102** RichieMcLernon(3) (Jonjo O'Neill) *hld up in last trio: stdy prog 9th: trckd ldrs on bit after 3 out: n.m.r and swtchd rt between last 2: nudged ahd flat: cleverly* **8/1**	117+
06-1	**2**	¾	**Red Rouble (IRE)**[18] 1730 5-11-12 **105** PaddyBrennan (Nigel Twiston-Davies) *in tch towards rr: mstke 1st: hdwy and hmpd 7th: chsd ldrs 11th: ev ch 2 out: rdn to ld between last 2: mstke last: hdd and unable qck flat* **3/1**[1]	114+
-560	**3**	¾	**Azulada Bay (IRE)**[30] 1601 6-11-1 **97** (t) PeterToole(3) (Mark Rimell) *in tch on outer: hmpd 7th: hdwy to chse ldr jst bef 3 out: ev ch and rdn 2 out: mstke last: styd on same pce flat* **6/1**[2]	105+
4-5P	**4**	22	**Jacarado (IRE)**[18] 1733 12-10-0 **79** (v) HenryOliver (Robin Dickin) *sn pushed up to ld: nt fluent 2nd: hdd 7th: rallied to ld 11th: drvn and hdd between last 2: sn wknd* **11/1**	66
21PP	**5**	19	**Wiesenfurst (GER)**[136] 689 6-10-5 **89** TomO'Connor(5) (John Berwick) *in tch in midfield: mstke 5th: lost pl next: hdwy 9th: rdn and btn 3 out: modest 5th and wl btn bef next* **28/1**	59
P24-	**6**	2	**Mr Ironman**[209] 4931 9-9-9 **79** oh8 MarcGoldstein(5) (Alan Jones) *in tch in midfield tl rdn and btn after 3 out: wl bhd next* **14/1**	47
2-35	**7**	nse	**Terrible Tenant**[156] 431 11-11-7 **100** AndrewThornton (Seamus Mullins) *chsd ldrs: struggling u.p bef 3 out: wl btn bef 2 out* **12/1**	68
511-	**8**	nk	**Bennynthejets (IRE)**[337] 2431 8-11-12 **105** TomMessenger (Chris Bealby) *chsd ldrs: led 7th: hit 10th: hdd next: wknd qckly u.p bef 2 out* **7/1**[3]	73
6-PP	**9**	31	**The Walnut Tree (IRE)**[9] 1858 9-10-2 **81** oh13 ow2 (b) ColinBolger (Simon Lewis) *mostly chsd ldr: j. slowly 6th: lost pl u.p 11th: t.o bef 2 out: eased flat* **80/1**	21
0504	**10**	dist	**Donovan (NZ)**[29] 1612 11-10-11 **95** JamesHalliday(5) (Richard Guest) *t.k.h: hld up in rr: blnd 6th: hdwy and in tch 8th: mstke next: wknd qckly bef 3 out: wl t.o whn blnd bdly last: virtually p.u flat* **12/1**	4
3524	**U**		**Cool Bob (IRE)**[30] 1601 7-11-3 **103** (t) MrLRPayter(7) (Matt Sheppard) *hld up in rr: j.rt 3rd and 4th: blnd and rdr trying to rcvr whn bdly hmpd and uns rdr 7th* **12/1**	—
5404	**P**		**Doheny Bar (IRE)**[18] 1727 7-10-6 **85** (p) JodieMogford (Nikki Evans) *in tch in midfield: hmpd and dropped to rr 7th: lost tch 11th: t.o whn p.u 2 out* **14/1**	—
3-5P	**F**		**Backfromthebrink (IRE)**[17] 1747 6-11-9 **102** WillKennedy (Paul Webber) *chsd ldrs tl fell 7th* **28/1**	—

5m 13.9s (-4.30) **Going Correction** -0.325s/f (Good) 13 Ran SP% **115.8**
Speed ratings (Par 105): **95,94,94,85,78 77,77,77,64,50** —,—,—
toteswingers: 1&2 £4.10, 1&3 £15.00, 2&3 £6.20. CSF £31.81 CT £156.67 TOTE £7.40: £1.80, £1.60, £2.10; EX 36.50.
Owner John P McManus **Bred** Frank Motherway **Trained** Cheltenham, Gloucs

FOCUS
There looked quite a wide range of abilities in this contest, but the winner seems to be a step ahead of the handicapper on this effort.

NOTEBOOK
In The Zone(IRE) ♦, 8lb higher than when winning at Newton Abbot in September, was given a patient ride early before coming with a cheeky effort down the home straight to win with a bit in hand. Still only six, and a horse with plenty of size, he can land the hat-trick. (op 7-1)
Red Rouble(IRE) ♦, making his chasing debut, over-jumped the first but didn't do too badly thereafter over the fences until stopped in his tracks by a faller. He looked unlucky to come up against a well handicapped horse here, and will win something similar. (op 7-2)
Azulada Bay(IRE) had been mainly well beaten over hurdles, so this appeared a much better performance, although it remains to be seen whether he can build on it. (op 7-1 tchd 15-2)
Jacarado(IRE), who has gained four of his five wins at Towcester, was hard work almost from the outset, but does respond to pressure and had his chance in the final stages. (op 16-1)
Wiesenfurst(GER), without headgear on his first start for this stable, attracted market support but was never close enough to get involved. (op 40-1 tchd 25-1)
Bennynthejets(IRE), absent since last November but chasing a hat-trick, was always close up but appeared to race a bit freely and faded on the run up the hill. (op 5-1)

1992 PP BUSINESS IMPROVEMENT H'CAP CHASE (16 fncs) 2m 6f
2:30 (2:32) (Class 4) (0-115,115) 4-Y-O+ **£3,903** (£1,146; £573; £286)

Form				RPR
46-1	**1**		**Ammunition (IRE)**[17] 1738 10-11-4 **107** (p) PaddyBrennan (Nigel Twiston-Davies) *prom in main gp: clsd on ldr 10th: bmpd 12th: trckd ldr 13th: pushed along to chal last: drvn ahd flat: kpt on* **4/1**[1]	118+
1623	**2**	¾	**Prophete De Guye (FR)**[17] 1738 7-11-1 **104** LeightonAspell (James Evans) *t.k.h: in tch in main gp: clsd on ldr 10th: led after 12th: rdn and j.rt 2 out: hdd after last: no ex* **4/1**[1]	112
2B0-	**3**	15	**Captain Smoothy**[196] 5157 10-10-0 **96** AnthonyFreeman(7) (Sean Curran) *in tch in main gp: mstke 6th: clsd on ldr 10th: j.rt 12th: rdn to chse ldng pair after 3 out: no imp fr next: btn whn j.rt and mstke last: wknd flat* **10/1**	97+
-11P	**4**	8	**House Of Bourbon (IRE)**[33] 1570 7-11-5 **115** (vt) MrTomDavid(7) (Tim Vaughan) *lft chsng clr ldr and mstke 2nd: lost 2nd 8th: mstke next: struggling u.p 12th: wl btn 3 out* **12/1**	104
/3-0	**5**	14	**Arnold Layne (IRE)**[15] 1769 11-11-6 **109** AndrewThornton (Caroline Bailey) *led: lft clr and bmpd 2nd: reduced ld 10th: hdd and rdn after 12th: wknd 3 out* **17/2**	84
63-5	**6**	27	**Machu Picchu (FR)**[124] 824 8-10-8 **102** DavidBass(5) (Jamie Snowden) *hld up in rr: mstke 5th: hdwy 9th: chsd ldrs and rdn 13th: wknd after 3 out: eased flat: t.o* **9/1**	52
0P00	**7**	32	**Keepitsecret (IRE)**[30] 1604 9-11-6 **112** RichieMcLernon(3) (Jonjo O'Neill) *hld up in last trio: hdwy 9th: wknd 12th: t.o fr 3 out* **16/1**	34
62-1	**U**		**Double The Trouble**[177] 85 9-11-7 **110** NickScholfield (Andy Turnell) *chsd ldr tl blnd bdly and uns rdr 2nd* **15/2**[3]	—
03-4	**F**		**Mister Watzisname (IRE)**[102] 986 8-11-12 **115** FelixDeGiles (Charlie Longsdon) *hld up in last trio: hdwy 9th: in tch whn fell next* **5/1**[2]	—

5m 42.6s (-10.40) **Going Correction** -0.325s/f (Good) 9 Ran SP% **111.6**
Speed ratings (Par 105): **105,104,99,96,91 81,69**,—,—
toteswingers: 1&2 £1.80, 1&3 £6.70, 2&3 £6.20. CSF £20.01 CT £143.32 TOTE £3.60: £1.70, £1.50, £3.00; EX 12.50.
Owner Miss Katharine J Holland **Bred** D Morrissey **Trained** Naunton, Gloucs

FOCUS
This was run at a good pace. The first two finished clear.

NOTEBOOK
Ammunition(IRE) again got the better of the argument despite meeting the runner-up on worse terms than at Exeter. He needed plenty of pushing to get on terms after losing his place but fought on well to get on top. (op 7-2 tchd 10-3)
Prophete De Guye(FR) travelled really well, as he can do, and looked a likely winner when he gained an advantage, but he was steadily worn down by his old rival and submitted after the last. (op 5-1)
Captain Smoothy improved greatly on his last appearance with a staying-on third. (op 17-2)
House Of Bourbon(IRE), off since pulling up over 3m4f at Stratford in September, was prominent in the chasing pack but got hard ridden after the tenth and never got involved from that point. (op 10-1)
Arnold Layne(IRE) had some useful chasing form in the distant past, but had not been showing that level for some time. He was allowed to go it alone in front and stayed there before being reeled in down the back straight. (op 10-1)
Machu Picchu(FR) made a brief effort that soon came to little. (op 10-1)
Keepitsecret(IRE) hasn't really shown anything since winning a race in May, and was once again easily disposed of. (op 12-1)
Double The Trouble, absent since April, was on the shoulder of Arnold Layne at the second fence when making a mistake that dislodged his rider. (op 15-2)
Mister Watzisname(IRE), back over fences, attracted market support and was still taking a strong grip when losing his footing at the tenth. (op 15-2)

1993 DALEPAK LTD MARES' NOVICES' HURDLE (DIV I) (8 hdls) 2m
3:05 (3:05) (Class 4) 4-Y-O+ **£2,602** (£764; £382; £190)

Form				RPR
-2P6	**1**		**Naughty Naughty**[17] 1601 5-10-10 100 NoelFehily (Brendan Powell) *hld up in tch towards rr: hdwy 4th: sltly hmpd jst bef 2 out: led 2 out: edgd rt between last 2: styd on wl: rdn out* **8/1**	114
32-2	**2**	2½	**Way Back When**[166] 263 5-10-5 0 MrSWaley-Cohen(5) (Alan King) *hld up in tch in midfield: hdwy after 3rd: chsd ldr after 5th: rdn to ld ent st: wandered u.p bef 2 out: hdd: j.rt 2 out and bmpd rival: kpt on same pce after* **4/1**[3]	113+
32	**3**	4	**Clarach (IRE)**[14] 1793 5-10-3 108 MrTomDavid(7) (Tim Vaughan) *hld up in last: prog after 5th: chalng on inner whn bdly bmpd and stmbld on landing 2 out: swtchd lft and rdn between last 2: flashed tail u.p and one pce after* **10/3**[2]	112+
40-1	**4**	2¾	**Miss Overdrive**[18] 1724 6-11-2 120 NickScholfield (Andy Turnell) *led: mstke 4th: hdd and drvn ent st: wknd 2 out* **11/10**[1]	113
4	**5**	10	**Playful Rose (IRE)**[162] 333 4-10-3 0 JakeGreenall(7) (Henry Daly) *hld up in tch: rdn and outpcd after 3 out: one pce and wl hld fr next* **14/1**	97
	6	dist	**Brunette'Sonly (IRE)**[239] 5-10-10 0 AndrewThornton (Seamus Mullins) *chsd ldr tl 2nd: styd chsng ldrs tl wknd qckly 3 out: t.o* **66/1**	65
00-0	**7**	19	**Roxane Bruere (FR)**[15] 1768 5-10-7 84 WayneKavanagh(3) (Robin Dickin) *in tch: rdn and wknd bef 3 out: t.o fr 2 out* **150/1**	48
300-	**8**	11	**Poppy Lee Brown**[202] 5042 4-10-10 0 TomMessenger (Chris Bealby) *t.k.h: hld up in tch in rr: blnd 1st: j. slowly 5th: wknd bef next: t.o bef 2 out* **66/1**	38
	9	19	**Viva Taipan (IRE)** 7-10-10 0 WillKennedy (Alex Hales) *chsd ldr 2nd tl after 5th: wknd bef 3 out: t.o bef 2 out* **33/1**	21
-PP	**10**	36	**Baltrap (FR)**[12] 1816 5-10-10 92 JamesDavies (Clarissa Caroe) *taken down early: in tch tl dropped to rr after 3rd: lost tch next: wl t.o bef 3 out: mstke last* **100/1**	—

3m 57.1s (-10.80) **Going Correction** -0.50s/f (Good)
WFA 4 from 5yo+ 9lb 10 Ran SP% **116.1**
Speed ratings (Par 105): **107,105,103,102,97 79,70,64,55,37**
toteswingers: 1&2 £4.00, 1&3 £4.70, 2&3 £2.10. CSF £39.83 TOTE £10.00: £1.70, £1.50, £1.20; EX 30.60.
Owner Mrs A Ellis **Bred** E R Hanbury **Trained** Upper Lambourn, Berks

FOCUS
Some decent mares have taken this in the past, including subsequent Grade 1 winner Refinement back in 2005, but it remains to be seen whether any of these will prove to be above average. This division was run in a time over 3 seconds faster than the second.

NOTEBOOK
Naughty Naughty, whose last start was a ninth of eleven on the Flat just over two weeks previously, finished runner-up in this contest last season but went one better here after travelling strongly for much of the race. Officially rated 100, this was her first success. (op 9-1)
Way Back When, representing a stable chasing its third consecutive success in this contest, shaped nicely behind a subsequent dual winner on her hurdling debut in May, and put in a solid performance here after chasing the pace. She should be a bit sharper next time. (tchd 5-1)
Clarach(IRE) has been very consistent but always usually takes a strong hold under restraint. She looked to have been given an excellent ride by her claiming jockey, but she was slightly impeded by the runner-up two from home, which saw her stumble. It would have been close between her and Naughty Naughty had she gained an error-free run in, but it was slightly concerning to see her flash her tail when given a smack with the whip. (op 5-2)
Miss Overdrive, dropping significantly in trip, set a good standard and was allowed an easy lead which, even allowing for the distance, should have been good enough for her to go very close to winning. However, distress signals started to show turning in and she was easily passed. (op 6-4)

Playful Rose(IRE) ◆, a half-sister to I'msingingtheblues, didn't shape too badly in a bumper (two subsequent winners in front) and again on her first outing over hurdles. She looks sure to win something if progressing. (op 16-1 tchd 12-1)

1994 DALEPAK LTD MARES' NOVICES' HURDLE (DIV II) (8 hdls) 2m
3:40 (3:40) (Class 4) 4-Y-0+ **£2,602** (£764; £382; £190)

Form RPR
12- **1** **Brixen (IRE)**[255] 3995 6-10-10 0 LeightonAspell 97+
(Lucy Wadham) *chsd ldr tl led after 3rd: mde rest: rdn bef 2 out: clr whn nt fluent last: kpt on: eased towards fin* **7/2**[2]

00-0 **2** 1 ½ **Blakeneys Pet (IRE)**[17] 1736 4-10-5 0 TomO'Connor(5) 93
(John Berwick) *hld up in tch in last trio: hdwy after 5th: chsd ldrs and n.m.r bef 2 out: drvn and styd on to go 2nd whn j.rt last: kpt on but no threat to wnr* **100/1**

12-1 **3** 1 **Cinderella Rose**[18] 1734 4-10-13 0 SeanQuinlan(3) 99+
(Kim Bailey) *chsd ldrs: mstke 4th: reminders bef next: mstke 5th: chsd ldng pair u.p bef 2 out: styd on same pce* **2/5**[1]

00-P **4** 5 **Cherokee Story**[21] 1689 4-10-10 0 (b[1]) TomMessenger 88
(Chris Bealby) *led tl after 3rd: chsd wnr after: reminders after 4th: rdn and mstke 3 out: kpt on same pce fr next: lost 2nd and hmpd last: wknd flat* **100/1**

5003 **5** shd **Reg's Ruby**[33] 1567 4-10-10 94 RodiGreene 87
(David Bridgwater) *chsd ldrs: j.big 1st: rdn after 3 out: kpt on same pce fr next* **18/1**

5-0 **6** 3 ¼ **Catch The Rascal (IRE)**[144] 589 4-10-10 0 ChristianWilliams 84
(Seamus Mullins) *in tch: rdn bef 2 out: wknd between last 2* **20/1**

000- **7** 17 **Midnight Trix**[202] 5048 4-10-10 0 WillKennedy 69
(Alex Hales) *in tch in midfield: rdn 5th: wkng whn mstke 3 out: sn lost tch* **40/1**

8 3 ½ **Mayolynn (USA)**[417] 4-10-10 0 AndrewThornton 66
(Caroline Bailey) *hld up in tch in last trio: rdn and struggling after 5th: lost tch after 3 out* **14/1**[3]

9 27 **First Spirit**[478] 4-10-7 0 WayneKavanagh(3) 41
(Robin Dickin) *plld hrd: hld up in last: nt fluent 3rd: rdn and wknd bef 3 out: t.o bef 2 out* **40/1**

4m 0.20s (-7.70) **Going Correction** -0.50s/f (Good) **9** Ran SP% **117.2**
Speed ratings (Par 105): **99,98,97,95,95 93,85,83,69**
toteswingers: 1&2 £18.70, 1&3 £1.10, 2&3 £11.30. CSF £263.21 TOTE £5.20: £1.70, £13.40, £1.02; EX 302.80.
Owner Tom Ford & Tony Regan **Bred** Neil R Tector **Trained** Newmarket, Suffolk

FOCUS
The second division of the mares' contest didn't look as strong as the first, and the proximity of the second and fourth, along with the time being the slower of the two divisions, make this look modest form at best.

NOTEBOOK
Brixen(IRE), who landed the first of her two outings in bumpers after one run in a point, raced prominently and eventually got to the front. She jumped nicely throughout and forged on at the right time to gain a lead that wasn't going to be closed down. Although she didn't beat a great deal, there should be more to come and she might be a useful sort. (op 11-4)
Blakeneys Pet(IRE) hadn't been hinting a run like this was coming, but she kept on well as the field closed up and battled on for second. Her best previous performance, indeed her only other placing, came at this course.
Cinderella Rose, who looked useful in bumpers, made a successful start to her hurdling career over C&D last time in a mixed-sex novice but came under pressure here at a fairly early stage. Well-backed, she ran a lacklustre race for some reason. (op 8-11 after early 4-5 and 5-6 in places)
Cherokee Story helped to set the pace, looking a bit keen while doing so, and still had a chance heading to the second-last hurdle. She had shown virtually nothing in her three previous starts, so maybe the blinkers made a significant difference.
Reg's Ruby kept plugging away and almost nicked fourth on the line. (op 16-1)

1995 PRINT DATA SOLUTIONS NOVICES' H'CAP CHASE (12 fncs) 2m 110y
4:15 (4:15) (Class 4) (0-100,92) 4-Y-0+ **£2,927** (£859; £429; £214)

Form RPR
500- **1** **Owner Occupier**[215] 4804 5-11-12 92 ColinBolger 101+
(Chris Gordon) *chsd ldr and sn clr of field: led 8th: rdn to forge ahd between last 2: kpt on gamely flat* **28/1**

5F43 **2** 2 ¼ **Cloonavery (IRE)**[21] 1704 8-10-3 69 (v) LiamTreadwell 75
(Tony Carroll) *racd wl off the pce in midfield: hdwy 7th: lft 3rd and hmpd 3 out: sn rdn and clsd on ldng pair: wnt 2nd bef last: pressed wnr flat: outbattled and btn fnl 100yds* **7/2**[1]

00/U **3** 11 **Quintus (FR)**[11] 1820 6-11-10 90 TomMessenger 88+
(Chris Bealby) *led and sn clr w wnr: hdd 8th but styd w wnr: rdn bef 2 out: wknd between last 2* **7/2**[1]

PP5F **4** 30 **Poacher's Dream (IRE)**[6] 1901 8-10-1 67 (t) RodiGreene 36
(Jonathen de Giles) *a wl off the pce towards rr: mstke 5th: rdn 7th: nvr trbld ldrs: t.o after 3 out* **7/1**

00U- **5** dist **Istron Bay**[199] 5104 8-11-11 91 AndrewThornton —
(Richard Lee) *chsd clr ldng pair: dived lft and blnd 4th: j.lft after: wknd 9th: lft 4th and wl btn 3 out: t.o and rdn between last 2: j.lft: stmbld and almost fell last: trotted home: btn 145 l* **8/1**

6003 **R** **National Heritage**[21] 1700 5-11-0 83 (v) FearghalDavis(3) —
(Micky Hammond) *nvr gng wl: wl off the pce in last trio: j. slowly and rdn 7th: no reponse: t.o 3 out tl distracted and ref last* **11/2**[2]

0/0- **F** **Mr Bond (IRE)**[353] 2084 7-11-7 87 NickScholfield —
(Andy Turnell) *racd wl off the pce in midfield: hdwy 7th: wnt 3rd 9th: 4 l down and clsng whn fell 3 out* **14/1**

-0P3 **F** **Wild Side Of Life (IRE)**[21] 1707 7-11-1 88 MrTomDavid(7) —
(Tim Vaughan) *t.k.h: hld up wl off the pce tl fell 5th* **6/1**[3]

U300 **P** **Humbel Lad (IRE)**[21] 1700 6-11-7 87 JamesDavies —
(Richard Guest) *wl off the pce in midfield: rdn and struggling after 4th: t.o whn p.u 8th* **20/1**

4m 17.9s (1.80) **Going Correction** -0.325s/f (Good) **9** Ran SP% **112.6**
Speed ratings (Par 105): **82,80,75,61,— —,—,—,—**
toteswingers: 1&2 £15.90, 1&3 £9.60, 2&3 £4.10. CSF £124.05 CT £438.86 TOTE £34.90: £5.60, £1.10, £2.10; EX 194.30.
Owner Mrs D M Lawes **Bred** Bearstone Stud **Trained** Morestead, Hants

FOCUS
It was difficult to make any sort of solid case for the majority of these even before they jumped off when considering their last efforts, so this is undoubtedly weak form.

NOTEBOOK
Owner Occupier ◆ collected a first win (and placing) but it was hardly a massive shock considering the calibre of rival he took on. Carrying top weight despite his best previous performance over hurdles being a 20-length fifth, he won quite nicely and could pick up another uncompetitive affair. Official explanation: trainer's rep said, regarding apparent improvement in form, that the gelding had not run since March, this being first time over fences, and appeared to benefit from racing prominently. (op 20-1)
Cloonavery(IRE) made ground from off the pace to throw down a challenge to the winner, but he wasn't good enough to get past. (tchd 4-1)
Quintus(FR), who ran over 3m when last on the track, was given a positive ride and shaped with some promise, albeit at a low grade. (tchd 3-1)
Poacher's Dream(IRE), the bottom weight, kept going but was never in with any sort of chance. (op 9-1 tchd 10-1 and 13-2)
National Heritage, with a visor back on after running in cheekpieces last time, got behind and lost interest, so much so that he refused to jump the last fence when completely tailed off. (op 11-1)
Mr Bond(IRE) was starting to make some ground when tripping over three out. He probably would have gone close had he stayed upright. (op 11-1)

1996 GG.COM AMATEUR RIDERS' H'CAP HURDLE (DIV I) (8 hdls) 2m
4:50 (4:51) (Class 4) (0-100,100) 4-Y-0+ **£1,873** (£581; £290; £145)

Form RPR
-060 **1** **Amuse Me**[18] 1734 4-10-11 85 MrAJBerry 103+
(Jonjo O'Neill) *hld up in rr: stdy hdwy 5th: led on bit bef 2 out: mstke 2 out: clr between last 2: eased flat: v easily* **5/1**[2]

P536 **2** 7 **Spider Boy**[7] 1886 13-9-12 79 (b) MrHGMiller(7) 86
(Zoe Davison) *led: rdn along and kpt finding ex fr 4th: hdd bef 2 out: no ch w wnr after: kpt on for 2nd* **6/1**[3]

/13- **3** 5 **Lightening Fire (IRE)**[203] 5007 8-10-4 85 (b) MrRJWilliams(7) 87
(Bernard Llewellyn) *t.k.h: chsd ldrs: mstke 3 out: rdn and btn bef next* **12/1**

6/5- **4** 17 **Don Pietro**[7] 1303 7-10-9 90 (p) MrTGarner(7) 78
(Barry Brennan) *t.k.h: chsd ldrs: mstke 5th: rdn next: wknd and wl btn 2 out* **16/1**

50-0 **5** ¾ **Tiger Dream**[162] 328 5-11-5 100 MrRHawkins(7) 86
(Chris Down) *in tch in midfield: outpcd after 3rd: rdn and struggling 5th: no ch but plugged on past btn horses fr 2 out* **16/1**

6 3 **Closesthingtocrazy**[32] 1582 6-11-5 100 (t) MrMEnnis(7) 84
(Sarah Humphrey) *chsd ldrs: wnt 4th: upsides ldr next tl rdn and wknd qckly after 3 out* **4/1**[1]

06P- **7** 2 ¼ **Loco Grande (IRE)**[196] 5149 5-11-2 97 MrEDavid(7) 79
(Tim Vaughan) *chsd ldrs: rdn and wknd after 3 out: wl btn next* **13/2**

0600 **8** 2 ½ **Wujood**[17] 1741 8-9-10 77 oh7 ow3 (t) MrJPark(7) 57
(Gerald Ham) *chsd ldr tl mstke 4th: wknd next: wl btn whn mstke 3 out* **28/1**

3-04 **9** ½ **Rawaaj**[146] 552 4-10-9 88 MrJHamer(5) 67
(Donald McCain) *in tch tl midfield and outpcd after 3rd: drvn and no real prog bef 3 out* **7/1**

0P06 **10** 16 **Hi Wycombe (IRE)**[9] 1857 6-10-9 90 MrSWDrinkwater(7) 54
(David Bridgwater) *a bhd: lost tch u.p 5th: t.o next* **28/1**

P-PP **11** 15 **Shara Like Magic**[16] 1760 7-9-7 74 oh12 MissECSayer(7) 25
(Dianne Sayer) *a bhd: lost tch 5th: t.o next* **50/1**

541- **U** **Carrig An Uisce (IRE)**[207] 4958 9-11-0 95 MrDHannig(7) —
(Anna Brooks) *towards rr whn j.big and uns rdr 1st* **12/1**

3P2- **P** **Aboukir Bay (IRE)**[207] 4961 6-10-9 90 MrWBlythe(7) —
(John Cornwall) *bhd fr 3rd: lost tch after 5th: wl t.o whn p.u last* **33/1**

3m 57.7s (-10.20) **Going Correction** -0.50s/f (Good)
WFA 4 from 5yo+ 9lb **13** Ran SP% **115.7**
Speed ratings (Par 105): **105,101,99,90,90 88,87,86,86,78 70,—,—**
toteswingers: 1&2 £6.50, 1&3 £10.00, 2&3 £15.50. CSF £33.15 CT £341.92 TOTE £4.60: £2.30, £2.40, £3.60; EX 51.80.
Owner John P McManus **Bred** Whatton Manor Stud **Trained** Cheltenham, Gloucs

FOCUS
The first division of this moderate contest for amateur riders.

NOTEBOOK
Amuse Me won with ridiculous ease after being given a patient ride. Making his handicap debut, it's impossible to guess why he'd run so badly in his three previous outings over hurdles, as he made his rivals here look slow. Even after being reassessed, he ought to win again, especially if found a similar race to this. Official explanation: trainer's rep said, regarding apparent improvement in form, that the gelding appeared to benefit from the fast early pace.
Spider Boy, a previous C&D winner, has been a grant servant to connections and ran his heart out again.
Lightening Fire(IRE) shaped nicely on his return to the track but ideally wants further when considering his winning form.
Don Pietro, with cheekpieces on for the first time over hurdles, pulled hard just behind the leaders but kept going to claim fourth. Official explanation: vet said gelding struck into itself
Tiger Dream got well behind at one point before staying on slowly.
Closesthingtocrazy, having his first run for this stable, and with a tongue-tie fitted for the first time, travelled into the lead going well but stopped quickly once rivals closed up on him.
Loco Grande(IRE), a market drifter, raced prominently but didn't get home on his first start for the Tim Vaughan stable.

1997 GG.COM AMATEUR RIDERS' H'CAP HURDLE (DIV II) (8 hdls) 2m
5:25 (5:25) (Class 4) (0-100,100) 4-Y-0+ **£1,873** (£581; £290; £72; £72)

Form RPR
0P00 **1** **Kensington Oval**[30] 1601 5-11-9 97 (t) MrAJBerry 98+
(Jonjo O'Neill) *hld up in tch towards rr: hdwy 4th: ev ch bef 2 out: rdn to ld between last 2: j. slowly last: hdd flat: rdn to ld again towards fin* **5/1**[2]

0430 **2** ½ **Bocciani (GER)**[21] 1700 5-10-9 90 MissECSayer(7) 90
(Dianne Sayer) *t.k.h: chsd ldr tl led after 3rd: hdd 3 out: stl pressing ldrs: chsd wnr and gd jump last: led flat tl hdd and no ex towards fin* **7/1**[3]

00-0 **3** 3 **Earl Of Thomond (IRE)**[18] 1734 5-10-6 87 MrJonathanBailey(7) 84
(Caroline Bailey) *in tch in midfield: hdwy 5th: ev ch next: led bef 2 out: rdn and hdd between last 2: styd on same pce u.p flat* **9/2**[1]

00-0 **4** 1 **Stage Right**[4] 1925 9-9-7 74 oh10 MissCBoxall(7) 71
(Simon Lewis) *chsd ldrs: led 3 out: rdn and hdd bef next: kpt on same pce fr 2 out* **28/1**

0333 **4** dht **Frosty's Gift**[68] 1272 6-9-7 74 oh2 (p) MrJBanks(7) 71+
(Jimmy Fox) *hld up in tch in last pair: hdwy bef 2 out: swtchd rt and kpt on between last 2: nvr able to chal* **9/2**[1]

0-0 **6** 3 ½ **Golden Partner**[21] 1709 5-10-9 90 (t) MrJMRidley(7) 83
(Matt Sheppard) *hld up in last pair: hdwy after 5th: chsd ldng trio and rdn bef 2 out: wknd between last 2: mstke last* **14/1**

P-00 **7** ¾ **Red Lancer**[49] 1477 9-11-5 100 MrNdeBoinville(7) 93
(Jonathen de Giles) *taken down early: in tch in midfield: rdn and effrt after 3 out: wknd after 2 out: wl hld whn hit last* **18/1**

2540 **8** 4 ½ **Django Reinhardt**[6] 1902 4-11-6 99 MrDavidTurner(5) 87
(Sam Davison) *hld up in tch towards rr: hdwy 5th: chsd ldrs bef 3 out: rdn and wknd bef 2 out* **9/1**

330- **9** 24 **Ramvaswani (IRE)**[186] 5311 7-10-13 94 (v) MrMMarris(7) 61
(Neil King) *led tl after 3rd: chsd ldr after tl jst bef 3 out: wknd wl bef 2 out* **9/1**

/F-P **10** *11* **Between Dreams**[21] 1689 7-9-13 **80**.................................. MrBJPoste(7) 37
(Andy Turnell) *hld up in tch in midfield: rdn and wknd qckly after 3 out: wl btn next: t.o* **25/1**

362- **P** **Kinkeel (IRE)**[196] 5151 11-10-8 **85**....................................... RobertKirk(3) —
(Tony Carroll) *in tch tl rdn and dropped to rr after 4th: lost tch 3 out: p.u next* **8/1**

4m 2.00s (-5.90) **Going Correction** -0.50s/f (Good)
WFA 4 from 5yo+ 9lb **11** Ran SP% **115.9**
Speed ratings (Par 105): **94,93,92,91,91 90,89,87,75,69 —**
toteswingers: 1&2 £10.10, 1&3 £6.30, 1&3 £6.70. totesuper7: WIN: Not won. PLACE: 1,738.80 - 1 winning unit. CSF £39.68 CT £169.03 TOTE £5.60: £2.00, £2.30, £2.00; EX 55.00 Place 6: £12.07 Place 5: £8.14.
Owner John P McManus **Bred** The Duke Of Devonshire And Globe Bstock **Trained** Cheltenham, Gloucs

FOCUS
The early pace set by the leaders cannot have been that strong, as virtually the whole field were in line after they jumped three out.

NOTEBOOK
Kensington Oval has been frustrating but finally got off the mark after a string of poor efforts over hurdles. He made ground from the back and battled on well to gain a narrow success. It was a good ride by his experienced jockey, as the horse needed niggling along at various stages. Official explanation: trainer's rep said, regarding apparent improvement in form, that the gelding was hampered on its previous run, has a history of wind trouble and appeared to benefit from the fitting of a tongue strap. (op 11-2)
Bocciani(GER) was always thereabouts and held a couple of positions before getting back in front after the final hurdle. He gained a slender lead before being re-passed by the winner. (op 9-1)
Earl Of Thomond(IRE) came in for market support on his handicap debut, and he rewarded punters who got on each way with a sound effort. (op 7-1)
Stage Right ran well for a horse running a long way out of the weights. (tchd 5-1)
Frosty's Gift's relatively experienced jockey appeared to leave his final effort until far too late. The mare's jumping wasn't perfect and she did seem to be hanging at times down the home straight, but one has to conclude that had she been ridden harder before two out, she would have gone close to winning, considering how strongly she came home after the final hurdle. (tchd 5-1)
Kinkeel(IRE) Official explanation: jockey had no explanation for the poor form shown
T/Jkpt: Not won. T/Plt: £13.70 to a £1 stake. Pool:£69,908.68 - 3,721.04 winning tickets. T/Qpdt: £3.80 to a £1 stake. Pool:£4,938.90 - 960.20 winning tickets. SP

1840 WINCANTON (R-H)
Sunday, October 24

OFFICIAL GOING: Good (good to firm in places; chs 9.4; hdl 10.4)
Wind: Fresh against Weather: Sunny

1998 TOTESPORT H'CAP HURDLE (8 hdls) 2m
2:20 (2:20) (Class 3) (0-120,123) 4-Y-0+ **£4,553** (£1,337; £668; £333)

Form RPR

053- **1** **Robain (FR)**[217] 4765 5-10-11 **105**.. RhysFlint 111+
(Philip Hobbs) *trckd ldrs: hit 2 out: led appr last: r.o: rdn out* **9/4**[1]

52U- **2** *6* **King's Revenge**[214] 4817 7-11-4 **119**.............................. PeterCarberry(7) 117
(Shaun Lycett) *hld up bhd ldrs: nudged along after 4th: rdn appr 2 out: styd on to go 2nd run-in: no ch w wnr* **9/2**[3]

0-03 **3** *2 ½* **Superius (IRE)**[12] 1816 5-11-1 **109**......................................(b[1]) JackDoyle 106+
(Emma Lavelle) *led: hit 2 out: rdn and hdd appr last: no ex whn lost 2nd run-in* **3/1**[2]

2612 **4** *3 ¾* **Freedom Fire (IRE)**[35] 1547 4-11-10 **118**........................... JamieMoore 109
(Gary Moore) *hld up bhd ldrs: rdn appr 2 out: styd on same pce* **9/2**[3]

13-0 **5** *1 ¾* **Bathwick Quest (IRE)**[17] 1740 6-10-13 **112**............. MrMMO'Connor(5) 102
(Brendan Powell) *hung rt most of the way: trckd ldr tl rdn appr 2 out: sn one pce* **10/1**

00/0 **6** *3 ¼* **Master Mahogany**[10] 1844 9-11-0 **108**.............................. HarrySkelton 94
(Ron Hodges) *hld up bhd ldrs: rdn appr 2 out: sn one pce* **8/1**

3m 30.4s (-18.50) **Going Correction** -1.10s/f (Hard)
WFA 4 from 5yo+ 9lb **6** Ran SP% **112.3**
Speed ratings (Par 107): **102,99,97,95,95 93**
toteswingers: 1&2 £2.90, 1&3 £1.20, 2&3 £3.20. CSF £12.81 CT £29.29 TOTE £3.60: £1.70, £2.50; EX 16.20.
Owner Mrs Joanna Peppiatt **Bred** Jean-Andre Quesny Et Al **Trained** Withycombe, Somerset
■ Stewards' Enquiry : Mr M M O'Connor Fine: £140, failed to report at scales that mare hung.

FOCUS
Not a strong handicap for the class. It was run at an average gallop and the form should work out.

NOTEBOOK
Robain(FR) scored on his seasonal and handicap debut. He took a long time to settle in mid-field, but found plenty when asked for an effort off the home turn and was well in command coming to the last. This quick ground was clearly much to his liking, and there should really be more to come from this 5-y-o. (op 3-1)
King's Revenge was outpaced from an early stage on this return to action and blatantly found this too sharp. He isn't an easy horse to win with, but should only come on for the run and prove more effective back at around 2m4f. (op 4-1 tchd 5-1)
Superius(IRE), third off 1lb lower at Huntingdon, was equipped with first-time blinkers and got himself very warm beforehand. He paid for his early exertions after two out and must learn to relax more through the early parts, but still raises a sound benchmark here. (op 10-3)
Freedom Fire(IRE) lacked the pace to land a serious blow on this switch to a handicap and he too looks worth a try over further in this sphere. The handicap likely has him where he wants him, though. (op 4-1)
Bathwick Quest(IRE) wasn't able to dictate and proved somewhat free as a result. She was very one paced, but still posted an improved effort in defeat. Official explanation: jockey said, regarding running and riding, that his orders were to bounce the mare out and if nothing else made the running to go on, adding that after jumping the first it started to hang right, continuing to do so throughout, in his opinion it was unsuited by the good, good to firm places ground; trainer confirmed, adding that the mare is better suited by softer ground. (tchd 9-1 and 11-1)

1999 F.J. CHALKE DESERT ORCHID H'CAP CHASE (FOR THE DESERT ORCHID SILVER CUP) (22 fncs) 3m 3f 110y
2:55 (2:55) (Class 2) (0-140,138) 4-Y-0+
£10,019 (£2,960; £1,480; £740; £369; £185)

Form RPR

22-4 **1** **Gullible Gordon (IRE)**[15] 1777 7-11-8 **134**......................... HarrySkelton 148+
(Paul Nicholls) *led after 1st: set str gallop: kicked clr 15th: stmbld bdly 3 out: styd on: rdn out* **6/1**

2223 **2** *7* **Ballyvesey (IRE)**[23] 1661 5-10-8 **120**...........................(v[1]) AidanColeman 125
(Peter Bowen) *chsd wnr fr 5th: rdn after 18th: styd on fr 3 out but a being hld* **11/2**

52P- **3** *2* **Present M'Lord (IRE)**[190] 5223 10-10-13 **125**....................... DarylJacob 128
(Nick Williams) *struggling to go pce early: hdwy after 13th: rdn after 18th: styd on same pce fr 4 out: wnt 3rd run-in* **9/2**[2]

5522 **4** *1 ¾* **Templer (IRE)**[15] 1777 9-11-6 **132**.. RhysFlint 134
(Philip Hobbs) *chsd wnr: rdn after 18th: styd on same pce fr 4 out* **5/1**[3]

1P-3 **5** *1 ¾* **Fairoak Lad (IRE)**[28] 1626 7-11-7 **138**........................... GilesHawkins(5) 139
(Philip Hobbs) *hld up but in tch: dropped to last and struggling fr 14th: outpcd after 18th: nvr any threat to ldrs* **4/1**[1]

116U **6** *1 ¾* **Cold Mountain (IRE)**[9] 1858 8-10-7 **124**...................... JimmyDerham(5) 122
(Seamus Mullins) *in tch: rdn after 17th: sn outpcd: styd on fr after 3 out* **14/1**

6131 **7** *14* **Simply Smashing (IRE)**[33] 1570 10-10-2 **121**................(t) KyleJames(7) 109
(Philip Kirby) *led tl after 1st: chse ldrs: sn pushed along to hold pl: rdn after 16th: outpcd after 18th: fdd fr after 4 out* **9/2**[2]

6m 37.2s (-31.00) **Going Correction** -0.875s/f (Firm) **7** Ran SP% **109.4**
Speed ratings (Par 109): **109,107,106,105,105 104,100**
toteswingers: 1&2 £4.00, 1&3 £4.40, 2&3 £4.20. CSF £34.88 CT £147.55 TOTE £7.10: £3.40, £2.40; EX 34.30.
Owner Mrs Bunty Millard **Bred** Mrs Mary Buttimer **Trained** Ditcheat, Somerset

FOCUS
A fair staying handicap, but again not the strongest of contests for the class. It proved a decent test and the winner is full value for the winning margin.

NOTEBOOK
Gullible Gordon(IRE) showed the big benefit of his seasonal return at Chepstow 15 days earlier and ran out a decisive winner from the front. He raced a lot more aggressively over this stiffer test and some fine jumping saw him open up an unassailable advantage on the final circuit. He began to feel the pinch before getting the third-last wrong and allowing the runner-up to close on him, but he was never going to get caught. This 7-y-o is clearly a proper stayer, is versatile regards going and could well come back here for the valuable Badger Ales Handicap next month. (op 7-1)
Ballyvesey(IRE), equipped with a first-time visor, began to toil nearing the turn for home but kept gamely to the task and eventually finished a clear second-best. He deserves to find another opening. (tchd 5-1)
Present M'Lord(IRE), making his debut for the yard, was given time to find his stride and began to labour going out onto the final circuit. He plugged on for pressure and this dour stayer ought to come on plenty for the run. (op 11-2)
Templer(IRE), a runner-up the last two times, had finished in front of the winner at Chepstow on his previous outing. He was in trouble around four out on this return to ground that suits, though, and looks sure to go back hunter chasing before long. (op 11-2 tchd 9-2)
Fairoak Lad(IRE) was returning to chasing defending a record of 3-3 at the course. He was on trouble a long way out as he lacked fluency and was staying on far too late in the day. He now has something to prove. Official explanation: jockey said gelding never travelled (op 3-1)
Simply Smashing(IRE) went in snatches from an early stage. (tchd 4-1)

2000 FRIENDS OF VERRINGTON HOSPITAL NOVICES' HURDLE (11 hdls) 2m 6f
3:30 (3:30) (Class 4) 4-Y-0+ **£2,793** (£955)

Form RPR

2- **1** **That'Ll Do**[162] 5-10-12 0.. HarrySkelton 130+
(Paul Nicholls) *disp ld tl outrt ldr after 3 out: drew wl clr appr 2 out: v easily* **1/5**[1]

2 *53* **Health Is Wealth (IRE)**[232] 5-10-12 0.............................. AidanColeman 77
(Colin Tizzard) *disp ld tl after 3 out: wknd bef next* **5/1**[2]

P **Seekwall** 4-10-7 0.. JimmyDerham(5) —
(Seamus Mullins) *racd green: chsd ldrs tl lost tch after 3rd: t.o whn reluctant on stable bnd and p.u bef 7th* **12/1**[3]

5m 0.50s (-26.00) **Going Correction** -1.10s/f (Hard) course record
WFA 4 from 5yo+ 10lb **3** Ran SP% **107.7**
Speed ratings (Par 105): **103,83,—**
CSF £1.72 TOTE £1.30; EX 1.60.
Owner Paul Barber & Mr & Mrs Mark Woodhouse **Bred** R G Percival And R Kent **Trained** Ditcheat, Somerset

FOCUS
A straightforward task for the promising That'll Do.

NOTEBOOK
That'Ll Do ◆ was faced with a simple task on his return from the pointing field and ran out a very easy winner on this hurdling debut. He had found only the very useful Black Jack Blues too good on his debut in a bumper last year and had impressed when winning both his outings between the flags since then. He got warm beforehand, but sauntered clear when asked to go clear and responded impressively. A sound surface clearly suits this future-chasing performer and could well be worth remembering that his leading stable won this event with Denman back in 2005. He ought to defy a penalty before going on to better things. (op 3-10, tchd 1-3 in a place)
Health Is Wealth(IRE) was last seen getting off the mark in between the flags at the fifth attempt 232 days earlier. He got a positive ride, but was left for dead when the winner asserted on the back straight. No doubt he will find easier assignments and ought to come on nicely for the run. (op 4-1 tchd 7-2)
Seekwall, whose dam won a bumper for the stable, lacked fluency and something presumably went amiss with him down the far side. (op 11-1 tchd 14-1)

2001 "NEW TRICKS" H'CAP HURDLE (11 hdls) 2m 6f
4:05 (4:05) (Class 4) (0-100,99) 4-Y-0+ **£2,602** (£764; £382; £190)

Form RPR

1310 **1** **Strumble Head (IRE)**[18] 1726 5-11-2 **92**..................(p) DonalDevereux(3) 103+
(Peter Bowen) *trckd ldrs: hit 4th: rdn appr 3 out: led 2 out: kpt on: drvn out* **9/2**[1]

-653 **2** *¾* **Bollywood (IRE)**[10] 1840 7-9-12 **78**................................(t) MrSHanson(7) 87
(Alison Batchelor) *hld up: hdwy after 3 out: ev ch next: sn rdn and hung rt: kpt on towards fin* **5/1**[2]

10-P **3** *8* **Lucky Pearl**[14] 1798 9-10-8 **84**....................................... RichardKilloran(3) 86
(Tim Vaughan) *trckd ldrs: rdn after 3 out: kpt on same pce fr next: wnt 3rd towards fin* **5/1**[2]

5552 **4** *1* **Mangonel**[17] 1741 6-10-3 **76**..(v) HarrySkelton 77
(Stuart Howe) *led: j.lft: rdn and hdd appr 2 out: kpt on same pce: hung lft run-in: lost 3rd towards fin* **9/2**[1]

5454 **5** *4 ½* **Vacario (GER)**[10] 1840 6-11-0 **90**................................(t) TommyPhelan(3) 86
(Mark Gillard) *trckd ldrs: pushed along appr 6th: rdn after next: one pce fr after 3 out* **13/2**

0606 **6** *1 ½* **Vintage Fabric (USA)**[14] 1794 8-11-5 **99**.....................(t) MsLisaO'Neill(7) 93
(Nigel Hawke) *chsd ldrs: rdn appr 3 out: sn one pce* **16/1**

0544 **7** *2 ¼* **Sir Harry Cool**[95] 1062 7-11-10 **97**.. DavidEngland 89
(John Panvert) *hld up: sme prog whn nt fluent 3 out: sn rdn: one pce fr next* **6/1**[3]

4P0- **P** **Bankers Bonus (IRE)**[184] 5359 5-10-6 **82**............................ DannyCook(3) —
(Martin Hill) *trckd ldrs: rdn after 3 out: wknd bef next: p.u bef last* **8/1**

4m 59.5s (-27.00) **Going Correction** -1.10s/f (Hard) course record **8** Ran SP% **114.3**
Speed ratings (Par 105): **105,104,101,101,99 99,98,—**
toteswingers: 1&2 £8.10, 1&3 £2.80, 2&3 £5.40. CSF £27.42 CT £115.70 TOTE £5.90: £1.70, £2.40, £1.60; EX 34.30.

Owner Jonathan Martin Bred Martin J Dibbs Trained Little Newcastle, Pembrokes
■ Stewards' Enquiry : Ms Lisa O'Neill caution: used whip when out of contention.
Tommy Phelan one-day ban: used whip when out of contention (Nov 7)

FOCUS
An ordinary handicap, run at an average gallop until they went out onto the final circuit.

NOTEBOOK
Strumble Head(IRE) was asked for everything after making up ground towards the home turn and was in no serious danger from the penultimate flight. He idled after the last and that saw the runner-up come back at him, but he was always doing enough. He stays well and this was a career-best effort, but consistency has not been his strong suit thus far. (op 5-1)
Bollywood(IRE) was given a very patient ride and made his move approaching the turn for home. He couldn't match the winner from two out and is a touch flattered by his proximity to the winner, but did finish a clear second-best. He rates a solid enough benchmark.
Lucky Pearl, pulled up at Ffos Las when reportedly struck into last time, had won this race off a 5lb lower mark last season and had raced just twice since then. She proved laboured from the fourth-last, but still ran more encouragingly on this return to suitably quicker ground. (op 4-1 tchd 11-2)
Mangonel, 4lb higher, again set out to make all but proved a sitting duck for the first pair and this maiden probably needs dropping back in distance. (op 11-2)

2002 JOYCE JOYCE 50TH BIRTHDAY NOVICES' H'CAP CHASE (21 fncs) 3m 1f 110y
4:40 (4:40) (Class 4) (0-100,100) 4-Y-O+ £3,332 (£1,034; £557)

Form				RPR
022-	1		**Might As Well**[189] 5257 7-11-7 **100**................................ JimmyDerham(5)	105+
			(Seamus Mullins) *hld up bhd ldrs: wnt 2nd after 16th: rdn to chal whn mstke 3 out: slt ld whn mstke 2 out: blnd and narrowly hdd last: rdr lost iron: kpt on: led nr fin* **11/4**[2]	
54P1	2	hd	**Von Galen (IRE)**[18] 1733 9-11-2 **90**................................(p) SamJones	95+
			(Michael Scudamore) *trckd/pressed ldr most of way: led 16th: rdn whn pckd 3 out: pckd whn narrowly hdd 2 out: regained narrow advantage last: kpt on: hdd nr fin* **4/1**[3]	
4262	3	20	**Lord Lescribaa (FR)**[10] 1843 7-10-6 **80**................................(tp) RhysFlint	64
			(Philip Hobbs) *j.lft: trckd ldrs: rdn after 16th: wknd appr 3 out* **85/40**[1]	
00P/	P		**Morgan The Mighty (IRE)**[857] 741 8-10-0 **74** oh10....... DavidEngland	—
			(Nigel Twiston-Davies) *led tl mstke 16th: sn rdn: wknd qckly after next: p.u bef 4 out* **8/1**	
00-U	U		**Rossmill Lad (IRE)**[21] 1710 6-10-2 **79**......................(t) RichardKilloran(3)	—
			(Tim Vaughan) *hld up in cl 5th: mstke 3rd: slow 4th (water): hit 10th and 14th: rdn after 16th: 4th and btn whn wnt lft and uns rdr 3 out* **4/1**[3]	

6m 25.8s (-13.70) **Going Correction** -0.875s/f (Firm) 5 Ran SP% **109.8**
Speed ratings (Par 105): **86,85,79,—,—**
CSF £13.58 TOTE £3.90: £1.40, £2.20; EX 8.00.
Owner Dr & Mrs John Millar **Bred** Shade Oak Stud **Trained** Wilsford-Cum-Lake, Wilts

FOCUS
A weak staying handicap for novices, run at a fair enough gallop.

NOTEBOOK
Might As Well, who has changed stables, rallied most gamely off the home turn and looked the most likely winner coming to the last. He got in too close at it, however, and had to work very hard to get up on the run-in. He pipped the runner-up nearing the line and won despite his rider losing his irons towards the business end, so rates value for a bit further. He was back up another 3lb on this seasonal return, but that still left on the same mark as when winning over hurdles last year. There should be some improvement in him for the run, but he doesn't appeal as one for a follow up. (tchd 3-1)
Von Galen(IRE) was raised 9lb for winning at Towcester on his previous outing and that ultimately only just found him out. This was another decent effort on this sharper track, though, and he remains in decent form. (op 7-2 tchd 3-1)
Lord Lescribaa(FR), second off this mark over C&D last time, came under heavy pressure a fair way out and there is no coincidence he had yet to score under rules. (op 9-4 tchd 2-1)
Morgan The Mighty(IRE) was 10lb out of the weights on his return from a long layoff and, after setting out to make this a fair test, was pulled up soon after capitulating on the final circuit. (op 17-2)
Rossmill Lad(IRE) unseated on his debut for the yard 21 days earlier and again lacked fluency, but at least completed. He needs more practice in this sphere. (op 17-2)

2003 PAUL NICHOLLS RACING "NATIONAL HUNT" NOVICES' HURDLE (7 hdls 1 omitted) 2m
5:15 (5:19) (Class 4) 4-Y-O+ £2,602 (£764; £382; £190)

Form				RPR
40-0	1		**Great Esteem (IRE)**[148] 519 5-10-12 0....................(p) JimmyMcCarthy	91+
			(Charles Egerton) *trckd ldrs: chal 2 out: led appr last: awkward hd-carriage but kpt on: pushed out* **8/1**[3]	
2-4	2	nk	**Royale's Charter**[17] 1743 4-10-12 0.................................. DarylJacob	91+
			(Nick Williams) *tk str hold: trckd ldrs: rdn to chal 2 out: ev ch thereafter: kpt on but a being narrowly hld* **15/8**[2]	
1-	3	7	**Bottman (IRE)**[197] 5137 5-10-9 0.......................... RichardKilloran(3)	86+
			(Tim Vaughan) *led: rn green at hurdles: rdn and hdd after mstke 2 out: kpt on same pce* **10/11**[1]	
00P-	4	nk	**Born To Be Wilde (IRE)**[207] 4963 5-10-12 0.................... PaulMoloney	83
			(Evan Williams) *prom: hit 3 out: short of room on bnd turning in: rdn and ev ch 2 out: swtchd rt appr last: kpt on same pce* **10/1**	

3m 40.7s (-8.20) **Going Correction** -1.10s/f (Hard) 4 Ran SP% **107.4**
Speed ratings (Par 105): **76,75,72,72**
CSF £22.62 TOTE £8.60; EX 18.80 Place 6: £719.13 Place 5: £367.24.
Owner Bailey-Carvill Equine **Bred** Beech Hill Stud **Trained** Chaddleworth, Berks

FOCUS
A modest novice hurdle, run at a steady gallop.

NOTEBOOK
Great Esteem(IRE) just did enough to prevail. He is clearly a headstrong sort as he got warm beforehand, racing very enthusiastically through the race, proved a tricky ride. He was best suited by the run of the race, though, and always just held the runner-up near the finish. His yard is having a good time of it at present, but first-time cheekpieces have to go down as having held the desired effect here and he will look vulnerable under a penalty in this division. (op 7-1 tchd 13-2)
Royale's Charter got involved off the home turn and held every chance, but the winner always just had his measure. The quicker ground here suited and he remains open to some improvement for this added experience, but his future looks to lie with the handicapper. (op 7-4 tchd 6-4)
Bottman(IRE), a debut bumper winner in April, looked something of a reluctant early leader and would've likely been seen in a better light going off quicker on this hurdling debut. He is not one to judge too harshly on the back of this effort and should learn for the experience. (op Evens tchd 6-5)
Born To Be Wilde(IRE) showed more on this return from his summer break and is another that would've appreciated more of a test. (op 14-1 tchd 16-1)
T/Plt: £338.70 to a £1 stake. Pool:£55,667.84 - 119.98 winning tickets. T/Qpdt: £20.20 to a £1 stake. Pool:£4,206.10 - 154.00 winning tickets. TM

2004 - 2007a (Foreign Racing) - See Raceform Interactive

1415 GALWAY (R-H)
Sunday, October 24

OFFICIAL GOING: Good (good to yielding in places on chase course)

2008a BARNA WASTE BALLYBRIT NOVICE CHASE (GRADE 3) (12 fncs) 2m 1f
4:45 (4:45) 4-Y-O+ £18,119 (£5,296; £2,508; £836)

			RPR
1		**Head Of The Posse (IRE)**[34] 1564 7-11-1 .... DJCasey	140+
		(John E Kiely, Ire) *trckd ldrs in 3rd: lft 2nd 4 out: impr to chal 2 out: led last: rdn and pressed early st: kpt on wl ins fnl f* **6/4**[2]	
2	1 3/4	**Son Of Oscar (IRE)**[19] 1720 9-11-1 .... BTO'Connell	137
		(Philip Fenton, Ire) *hld up towards rr: lft mod 4th 4 out: clsr 2 out: 3rd last: impr in 2nd ent st: rdn to press ldr early st: no ex ins fnl f: kpt on same pce* **9/1**	
3	27	**Salesin**[14] 1801 7-11-1 ....(p) NPMadden	113
		(Niall Madden, Ire) *hld up towards rr: lft mod 3rd 4 out: clsr 2 out: rdn in 4th and no ex last: wknd ent st* **8/1**[3]	
4	dist	**Blindspin**[112] 902 5-11-0 ....(t) RCColgan	—
		(Andrew Lee, Ire) *led: disp briefly bef 4 out: chal 2 out: slt mstke and hdd last: rdn and wknd: t.o* **40/1**	
F		**Realt Dubh (IRE)**[29] 1620 6-11-1 .... PCarberry	—
		(Noel Meade, Ire) *trckd ldr in 2nd: impr to dispute bef 4 out where fell* **11/10**[1]	

4m 44.8s (9.30) 5 Ran SP% **111.2**
CSF £13.56 TOTE £2.10: £1.30, £1.90; DF 12.90.
Owner John P McManus **Bred** Miss Catherine O'Donovan **Trained** Dungarvan, Co Waterford

FOCUS
An interesting novice chase rated though the runner-up. The time was slow.

NOTEBOOK
Head Of The Posse(IRE) had to work hard enough, but isn't a horse to ever win spectacularly and one got the idea that he would dearly have liked a fence in the straight. He got a lead for as long as he could and swept to the front before the straight, but as soon as he got there he started to idle and almost opened the door for the runner-up. However he was always in control and the runner-up was flattered by his proximity to him. This horse only has one run really and needs something to run at, something which he will have when stepping up to better company. (op 11/8)
Son Of Oscar(IRE) ran a big race on his return from an absence of almost two years earlier in the month, and continued his progression here. He was ridden to be doing his best work at the finish, having sat off the pace, and did move up to track the winner into the straight but was always being held. He does have the tendency to make the odd mistake, but shouldn't have much difficulty in picking up a beginners chase. (op 12/1)
Salesin was ridden similarly to the runner-up, but while jumping well enough he was never close enough to make an impression. (op 7/1)
Blindspin jumped really well in front, but folded completely once the winner went past him after the final fence.
Realt Dubh(IRE) was still going nicely prior coming down, his rider later reasoning a shadow after the fence had put him off. (op 11/10 tchd 1/1)

2009 - 2019a (Foreign Racing) - See Raceform Interactive

TAUNTON (R-H)
Tuesday, October 26

OFFICIAL GOING: Good to firm (firm in places)
Rail moved out on bends adding 50m per circuit to distances.
Wind: mild across Weather: rain

2020 SUPPORT RACING WELFARE RAFFLE JUVENILE HURDLE (9 hdls) 2m 1f
2:10 (2:10) (Class 4) 3-Y-O £4,000 (£1,174; £587; £293)

Form				RPR
5	1		**Pullyourfingerout (IRE)**[20] 1728 3-10-12 0........................(t) APMcCoy	116+
			(Brendan Powell) *racd keenly: prom: led 4th: drew wl clr after 3 out: v easily* **7/2**[3]	
246	2	22	**Royal And Ancient (IRE)**[17] 1610 3-10-12 113............. WarrenMarston	93
			(Milton Harris) *trckd ldrs: rdn in 2nd appr 6th: no ch w wnr fr 3 out* **9/4**[1]	
02	3	7	**Lady Willa (IRE)**[12] 1845 3-10-2 0................................ TommyPhelan(3)	79
			(Mark Gillard) *trckd ldrs: effrt after 6th: wknd after 3 out* **8/1**	
	4	6	**Call To Arms (IRE)**[87] 3-10-12 0................................ RichardJohnson	83
			(Peter Bowen) *nt fluent: wnt rt 1st: hld up: hdwy 6th: rdn after 3 out: sn wknd* **7/2**[3]	
0	5	93	**Kingspark Boy (IRE)**[17] 1772 3-10-12 0............................ RodiGreene	—
			(David Rees) *a last: t.o fr after 5th* **80/1**	
4	F		**Free As A Lark**[5] 1935 3-10-5 0.. PaulMoloney	—
			(Evan Williams) *led tl 4th: w wnr: losing pl whn fell 6th* **3/1**[2]	

4m 3.10s (-4.90) **Going Correction** -0.475s/f (Good) 6 Ran SP% **112.6**
Speed ratings (Par 103): **92,81,78,75,31 —**
toteswingers:1&2 £4.70, 2&3 £3.90, 1&3 £9.60 CSF £12.19 TOTE £5.10: £4.00, £1.10; EX 17.60.
Owner K Rhatigan **Bred** T Quayle **Trained** Upper Lambourn, Berks

FOCUS
The course endured rain in the morning before racing commenced and the ground was expected to ride a bit easier than the official description of good to firm, firm in places, but A P McCoy said it still rode fast. The easy winner improved towards the level of his Flat form. The time was slow compared with the later novice hurdle.

NOTEBOOK
Pullyourfingerout(IRE), equipped with a first-time tongue tie, proved far too good for his rivals in this weak juvenile event and, jumping nicely, opened his account at the second attempt over hurdles with a much-improved effort. He was given a positive ride and took up a clear lead nearing the fourth-last. The race was his to lose soon after as he powered clear off the home turn and this should boost his confidence no end. A quick surface was important to him on the level and he should get further down the line judged on his form in that sphere, so could well prove better as a hurdler. (tchd 3-1)
Royal And Ancient(IRE) came under pressure down the back straight on this return to hurdling and, despite responding, was no match for the winner. His official mark of 113 needs looking at, but he still helps to set the standard. (op 10-3 tchd 7-2)
Lady Willa(IRE) improved when a close second on her latest outing, but that did come in a dire event and she was well beaten off here. She remains winless. (op 15-2 tchd 7-1)
Call To Arms(IRE) was just about the best of these on the Flat and arrived for this hurdling debut for new connections having been placed on his last three outings in that arena. Stamina was a worry for this new discipline, though, and he never seriously figured after being ridden to get the trip. (tchd 10-3 and 4-1)

Free As A Lark, who ran freely when fourth on her hurdling debut five days earlier, was well backed and settled a little better as a result of being sent to the front here. However, she was going backwards prior to falling and most probably found the run coming too soon. (tchd 7-2)

2021 SOMERSET COUNTY GAZETTE NOVICES' HURDLE (9 hdls) 2m 1f
2:40 (2:40) (Class 4) 4-Y-0+ **£4,000** (£1,174; £587; £293)

Form				RPR
11-2	**1**		**Organisateur (IRE)**[11] 1859 5-11-7 133 IanPopham(5) (Paul Nicholls) *mid-div: tk clsr order 6th: led sn after 2 out: hit last: pushed out: comf* **1/4**[1]	128+
0-	**2**	*11*	**Ballinteni**[34] 2382 8-10-12 0 JoeTizzard (Colin Tizzard) *trckd ldrs: rdn to ld 2 out: sn hdd: kpt on same pce: no ch w wnr* **16/1**	97
1263	**3**	*1 1/4*	**Tignello (IRE)**[20] 1723 5-11-2 111 (t) TomMolloy(3) (Emma Baker) *prom: led after 2nd: rdn and hdd 2 out: kpt on same pce* **10/1**[3]	103
0P-0	**4**	*9*	**Jumpjack Flint**[19] 1743 4-10-12 0 RichardJohnson (Charlie Longsdon) *hld up bhd: stdy prog past btn horses fr after 3 out: nvr nrr* **28/1**	88+
	5	*shd*	**Magroom**[57] 6-10-5 0 MattGriffiths(7) (Ron Hodges) *hld up towards rr: rdn and hdwy after 3 out: one pce fr next* **20/1**	88
5-	**6**	*14*	**Classically (IRE)**[27] 3992 4-10-12 0 TomScudamore (Hughie Morrison) *racd keenly: prom: rdn after 3 out: wkng whn hit 2 out* **6/1**[2]	75
	7	*6*	**Spinning Waters**[35] 4-10-12 0 JimmyMcCarthy (Eve Johnson Houghton) *mid-div tl wknd after 3 out* **28/1**	70
200/	**8**	*14*	**Aureate**[162] 4109 6-10-9 0 WayneKavanagh(3) (Brian Forsey) *mid-div: hdwy after 5th: rdn after 3 out: sn wknd* **25/1**	57
4-00	**9**	*21*	**Operachy**[50] 1488 5-10-12 84 HaddenFrost (James Frost) *trckd ldrs: rdn after 6th: sn wknd: t.o* **66/1**	38
0P-P	**10**	*5*	**Lethal Gun (IRE)**[174] 148 8-10-5 0 (t) MrJBanks(7) (Richard Mitchell) *led tl after 2nd: trckd ldrs tl wknd after 5th: t.o* **100/1**	34
	11	*dist*	**General Sam (USA)**[634] 4-10-12 0 JohnnyFarrelly (Richard Mitchell) *a towards rr: rdn after 4th: t.o fr next* **100/1**	—

3m 59.7s (-8.30) **Going Correction** -0.475s/f (Good)
WFA 4 from 5yo+ 9lb **11** Ran SP% **128.2**
Speed ratings (Par 105): **100,94,94,90,89 83,80,73,64,61** —
toteswingers:1&2 £4.60, 2&3 £14.40, 1&3 £2.10 CSF £7.29 TOTE £1.20: £1.02, £4.70, £2.10; EX 10.60.
Owner Mrs Angela Tincknell & W Tincknell **Bred** Wertheimer Et Frere **Trained** Ditcheat, Somerset

FOCUS
The easy winner stood out in this very ordinary novice hurdle. There is a case for rating the form a few pounds higher through the third.

NOTEBOOK
Organisateur(IRE) met his first defeat at Cheltenham on his seasonal/handicap debut 11 days earlier, but that effort still represented a clear personal-best and, despite carrying a double penalty, he proved all the rage on this return to a novice event. He was asked for his effort after travelling nicely into the home straight and, despite taking a little time to hit top gear, he motored clear from the second-last. He wasn't great at the final flight, but looked to be going at his quickest near the finish and is clearly a very useful performer in the making. His mark of 133 shouldn't really be affected by this display, but he could well stick to novice company and, providing he comes out of the race okay, have his third run in quick succession at Ascot on Saturday. That would be a lot tougher again, but he will still be the one to beat on previous form if heading there. (op 2-5 tchd 4-9 in a place)
Ballinteni, a one-time very useful horse on the Flat, had flopped on his hurdling debut last November but was returning to jumping for a new yard and he ran a lot better. He only found the progressive winner too strong from the penultimate flight and this gives his current yard something to work on. (op 14-1)
Tignello(IRE) is a former stablemate of the winner and was having his first outing for new connections after finishing third in a seller 20 days earlier. He raced with enthusiasm out in front and ultimately paid the price, but this was still a step back in the right direction. (op 9-1)
Jumpjack Flint proved a horribly tricky ride for Richard Johnson out the back as he took a fierce hold and lacked fluency. He stayed on stoutly towards the finish, though, and clearly has some sort of an engine. This was his best effort yet, but he remains one to tread carefully with until showing more sign of relaxing through his races. (op 25-1)
Magroom is a seven-times winner on the level and is officially rated 66 in that sphere. He had stamina to prove on this belated switch to hurdling, but as keeping on late after briefly looking in trouble on the back straight, and will find his level as he gains more practice.
Classically(IRE) had pulled hard when beaten miles on his hurdling debut last term, but he was returning to jumping having been in decent form on the AW and a better effort was expected. He once again spoilt his cause by proving keen on the front end, but there was a little more encouragement to be taken from this display. (tchd 11-2)

2022 READ PAUL NICHOLLS EXCLUSIVELY ON BETFAIR H'CAP CHASE (12 fncs) 2m 110y
3:10 (3:10) (Class 3) (0-125,120) 4-Y-0+ **£8,781** (£2,578; £1,289; £643)

Form				RPR
6-04	**1**		**Qianshan Leader (IRE)**[9] 1885 6-11-4 112 JackDoyle (Emma Lavelle) *trckd ldrs: rdn whn outpcd appr 3 out: styd on to ld run-in: rdn out* **13/2**	119+
4126	**2**	*1*	**Rockiteer (IRE)**[32] 1604 7-11-7 115 (p) RichardJohnson (Henry Daly) *trckd ldrs: jnd ldr 7th: tk narrow advantage after 4 out: rdn after next: kpt on but no ex whn hdd run-in* **5/1**[2]	122+
4212	**3**	*4 1/2*	**Woodlark Island (IRE)**[7] 1912 4-11-1 118 7ex (bt) TomScudamore (David Pipe) *led: rdn and hdd after 4 out: remained w ev ch tl mstke last: no ex* **11/4**[1]	112
6642	**4**	*6*	**Mibleu (FR)**[3] 1975 10-11-11 119 (t) JoeTizzard (Colin Tizzard) *hld up: tk clsr order 7th: wnt lft next: sn rdn: one pce fr after 4 out: lft 4th last* **5/1**[2]	116
3255	**5**	*3/4*	**Red Jester**[37] 1557 9-10-6 100 AndrewGlassonbury (Gerald Ham) *in tch: drvn along fr 6th: one pce fr after 4 out* **16/1**	95
1203	**F**		**January**[9] 1888 7-10-11 105 (t) TimmyMurphy (Liam Corcoran) *hld up: hdwy after 8th: rdn in 4th gng to 3 out: styng on same pce whn stmbld and fell last* **7/1**	106
33-P	**P**		**King Brex (DEN)**[14] 1816 7-11-10 118 (tp) NoelFehily (Charlie Mann) *nvr fluent: trckd ldrs: hit 2nd: dropped to last after 5th: t.o whn p.u after 4 out* **12/1**	—
50F4	**P**		**Agente Romano (USA)**[16] 1794 5-11-3 111 PaulMoloney (Evan Williams) *nt particularly fluent: hld up: wknd after 8th: t.o whn p.u after 4 out* **11/2**[3]	—

4m 4.30s (-5.70) **Going Correction** -0.40s/f (Good)
WFA 4 from 5yo+ 9lb **8** Ran SP% **114.8**
Speed ratings (Par 107): **97,96,94,91,91** —,—,—
toteswingers:1&2 £10.30, 2&3 £2.30, 1&3 £4.50 CSF £39.37 CT £110.14 TOTE £5.10: £2.20, £1.10, £2.00; EX 47.10.
Owner The Pick 'N' Mix Partnership **Bred** Robin Harold-Barry **Trained** Wildhern, Hants

FOCUS
This wasn't a strong event for the class. They went a fair gallop and there were changing fortunes in the home straight. The winner produced a big step up on his previous chase best and the form seems solid enough.

NOTEBOOK
Qianshan Leader(IRE) ◆ unsurprisingly got going late in the day on this big drop back in trip and won under a decent ride from Jack Doyle. He didn't settle well over 3m last time, but the tempo over the minimum trip helped on that front. He got outpaced nearing the home turn as the placed horses kicked on, but his rider didn't panic and a good jump at the last saw him land running. Such tactics looked ideal for him, a bit further should prove his optimum distance in this sphere and his confidence will be nicely boosted after this first win over fences. There ought to be more to come. (op 9-1)
Rockiteer(IRE) really enjoys a sound surface and he returned to form on this drop back to 2m, just giving way to the winner near the line. He likes this track and could well add to his tally back over a slightly stiffer test, if found a suitable race on this sort of ground next time. (op 6-1)
Woodlark Island(IRE) was beaten under this penalty at Exeter a week previously, but this drop back in trip seemed a good move. He turned in a brave effort from the front, only going down after a slight error at the last, and is a consistent sort. (op 9-4 tchd 3-1)
Mibleu(FR) attracted support, but his jumping let him down after being asked to make up his ground on the back straight. (op 7-1 tchd 17-2 in a place)
January was given a typical waiting ride by Timmy Murphy, but his effort proved short-lived off the home turn and he was held in fourth prior to falling at the last. He was quickly up on his feet. (op 15-2)
Agente Romano(USA) Official explanation: jockey said gelding never travelled (op 15-2)

2023 BEST OF TAUNTON H'CAP HURDLE (12 hdls) 3m 110y
3:40 (3:40) (Class 4) (0-115,113) 4-Y-0+ **£4,000** (£1,174; £587; £293)

Form				RPR
S665	**1**		**Kristoffersen**[50] 1490 10-10-13 100 OwynNelmes (Helen Nelmes) *hld up towards rr: blnd 8th: sn struggling: plenty to do 3 out: hdwy next: lft 2nd last: swtchd lft: str run fnl 100yds to ld towards fin* **9/1**	107
0601	**2**	*2 3/4*	**Heir To Be**[12] 1840 11-11-9 110 (b) NickScholfield (Michael Blake) *led: sn clr: rdn after 3 out: hdd next: 2 l 2nd and looked hld whn lft in ld last: tiring whn hdd towards fin* **11/2**	115
6002	**3**	*12*	**Captain Becket**[7] 1911 7-10-8 95 HaddenFrost (James Frost) *trckd ldrs: rdn after 9th: sn one pce: lft 3rd last* **2/1**[1]	89
2F14	**4**	*3 1/2*	**North Island (IRE)**[51] 1482 8-11-12 113 TomScudamore (Peter Bowen) *chsd clr ldr: rdn and ev ch sn after 3 out: grad fdd: lft 4th last* **9/2**[3]	107+
-566	**5**	*38*	**Mauricetheathlete (IRE)**[20] 1730 7-10-7 101 MrNSlatter(7) (Martin Keighley) *trckd ldrs tl lost pl after 5th: rdn whn mstke 9th: sn lost tch* **7/1**	57
2145	**U**		**Admiral Dundas (IRE)**[20] 1726 5-11-2 106 (t) SeanQuinlan(3) (Kim Bailey) *trckd ldrs: chal 3 out: sn rdn: led next: 2 l up whn wnt lft and uns rdr bef last* **10/3**[2]	116+

5m 51.8s (-15.30) **Going Correction** -0.475s/f (Good) **6** Ran SP% **112.5**
Speed ratings (Par 105): **105,104,100,99,87** —
toteswingers:1&2 £4.40, 2&3 £4.00, 1&3 £5.70 CSF £54.69 TOTE £6.20: £2.50, £2.90; EX 43.00.
Owner T M W Partnership **Bred** Five Horses Ltd **Trained** Warmwell, Dorset

FOCUS
This weak staying handicap was run at a sound gallop and the race changed complexion twice in the home straight. Suspect form. The winner is rated to his mark and the unseater was heading for a big personal best.

NOTEBOOK
Kristoffersen looked a hopeless cause on the final circuit, but his rider kept at him and he consented to hit top gear from two out. He motored past the second after the last to win with plenty in hand in the end. It was his first win since 2008 and he often performs this way, so is a very unlikely sort for a follow up. (tchd 7-1)
Heir To Be was 15lb higher than when ending his losing run at Wincanton 12 days earlier and set out to make this a decent test. Booked for second prior to being left in the lead at the last, he looked sure to collect only to be mown down on the flat. The handicapper looks to have his measure again. (op 6-1)
Captain Becket, a close second off this mark at Exeter a week previously, was well backed to go one better back up in trip. He hit a flat spot at a crucial stage on the final circuit before plugging on again late in the day, and is not an easy horse to predict. (op 5-2)
North Island(IRE) was left behind nearing the home turn and has run well below his mark the last twice. (tchd 5-1)
Admiral Dundas(IRE)had got on top coming to the last, but he jinked when eased into it and unseated was in the process of running a personal-best on this further step up in trip prior to his exit. It may be a case that he wants delivering as late as possible in his races, and he is worth another chance. (tchd 3-1 and 7-2)

2024 CRINKLE BIRR H'CAP CHASE (17 fncs) 2m 7f 110y
4:10 (4:10) (Class 4) (0-115,113) 4-Y-0+ **£4,943** (£1,451; £725; £362)

Form				RPR
154F	**1**		**Pairc Na Gcapall (IRE)**[14] 1814 8-11-12 113 (b) MarkBradburne (Neil King) *disp ld: hmpd 2nd: outrt ldr 11th tl next: rdn after 4 out: led after 3 out: styd on: rdn out* **7/2**[2]	122
43-5	**2**	*3 1/2*	**Topless (IRE)**[179] 85 9-11-0 101 DougieCostello (Neil Mulholland) *hld up: hmpd 1st: stdy prog fr 11th: rdn after next: styd on same pce fr 4 out: wnt 2nd last* **7/2**[2]	107
036P	**3**	*3*	**Some Craic (IRE)**[12] 1841 10-11-4 105 RichardJohnson (Paul Henderson) *trckd ldrs: led appr 12th: rdn and hdd after 3 out: hit next: styd on same pce: lost 2nd last* **5/1**[3]	109
2356	**4**	*6*	**Classic Clover**[5] 1939 10-10-9 96 (t) AidanColeman (Colin Tizzard) *in tch: rdn after 12th: plugged on: nvr any real imp on ldrs* **8/1**	94
3243	**5**	*18*	**Havenstone (IRE)**[5] 1939 9-9-9 89 MrJEngland(7) (Evan Williams) *disp ld: wnt bdly lft 2nd: reminder after 7th: rdn and hdd 11th: sn hld: wknd 2 out* **3/1**[1]	73
-001	**6**	*7*	**Outside Investor (IRE)**[12] 1843 10-9-10 88 oh6 ow1 (p) KeiranBurke(5) (Patrick Rodford) *in tch: struggling fr after 10th: wknd after 13th: mstke 2 out* **13/2**	63

6m 1.80s (-12.80) **Going Correction** -0.40s/f (Good) **6** Ran SP% **110.6**
Speed ratings (Par 105): **105,103,102,100,94** **92**
CSF £15.77 TOTE £5.00: £2.80, £1.50; EX 19.50.
Owner So What Is Your Role In Life Partnership **Bred** Hugh Douglas **Trained** Newmarket, Suffolk
■ Mark Bradburne's first winner after a lengthy injury lay-off.

FOCUS
A very ordinary handicap that was made up of exposed chasers. It was run at a strong gallop as the two early leaders rather took each other on and the form is straightforward. Sound form with the winner posting his best effort since this time last year.

NOTEBOOK

Pairc Na Gcapall(IRE), who fell over hurdles last time, produced a really game effort to regain winning ways considering he was unable to dictate and did so much through the first half of the race. He took it up six out, but was readily passed at the next and it looked a case of him feeling the pinch. However, he was back on the bridle round the home turn and it was clear three out he was the one to be on. This likeable performer was having his first outing at the track and obviously enjoyed himself. (op 4-1)

Topless(IRE) got going too late in the day and is a very hard horse to win with. That said, this was her first outing since April and she does want softer ground.\n (op 11-4)

Some Craic(IRE) was backed to show his true colours on this return to quick ground and it looked nearing the final turn as though he was going to get his head back in front. He wilted soon after the renewed challenge of the winner materialised, though, and he was running on empty coming to the last. (op 7-1)

Classic Clover again ran in snatches and was never in the hunt. (op 13-2)

Havenstone(IRE) not surprisingly weakened on the final circuit on this quick reappearance. Official explanation: vet said gelding lost a right fore shoe and had been struck into (op 7-2 tchd 4-1 and 11-4)

Outside Investor(IRE) was 7lb higher for his recent Wincanton success, but that still left him 6lb out of the handicap. He was in trouble before the final lap and this was in keeping with his inconsistent profile. (op 6-1 tchd 7-1)

2025 TOTAL STAR RADIO SOMERSET 102.4 STANDARD OPEN NATIONAL HUNT FLAT RACE — 2m 1f

4:40 (4:40) (Class 5) 4-6-Y-O **£1,541** (£449; £224)

Form				RPR
	1		**Buck Magic (IRE)**[191] 4-10-9 0 KeiranBurke(5) — (Patrick Rodford) *t.k.h: trckd ldrs: led over 5f out: rdn over 2f out: styd on: drvn out* **11/10**[1]	88+
4	2	2 3/4	**Lucky Sun**[166] [304] 4-11-0 0 RichardJohnson — (Brian Eckley) *cl up: rdn to chal briefly over 2f out: styd on same pce* **6/1**[3]	86
-0	3	6	**Wychwoods Kaddy**[20] [1729] 4-11-0 0 (t) JodieMogford — (Graeme McPherson) *hld up last: tk clsr order 6f out: rdn over 2f out: styd on same pce* **40/1**	81
	4	6	**Prince Of King** 5-11-0 0 OwynNelmes — (Helen Nelmes) *in tch: hdwy over 4f out: rdn to chse wnr briefly over 2f out: sn one pce* **10/1**	75
0	5	2 1/4	**Double Fun**[17] [1778] 4-10-0 0 MrJBarnes(7) — (Martin Hill) *trckd ldrs: rdn over 3f out: one pce fnl 2f* **20/1**	66
5	6	3 3/4	**Mocambo (GER)**[17] [1778] 4-11-0 0 JoeTizzard — (Colin Tizzard) *led tl over 5f out: sn rdn: one pce fnl 3f* **2/1**[2]	70
0	7	44	**Cladding**[6] [1927] 4-10-11 0 DannyCook(3) — (John Panvert) *trckd ldrs tl 6f out: sn wknd* **33/1**	30

4m 4.60s (2.20) **Going Correction** -0.475s/f (Good) 7 Ran SP% **114.5**
Speed ratings: **75,73,70,68,67 65,44**
toteswingers:1&2 £1.80, 2&3 £6.00, 1&3 £8.00 CSF £8.41 TOTE £1.90: £1.10, £2.80; EX 8.40 Place 6: £80.94 Place 5: £47.39.
Owner Brian Derrick **Bred** Sean Culleton **Trained** Ash, Somerset

FOCUS

Probably a very moderate bumper, run at an uneven gallop and in a slow time. The form is given a token rating through the second.

NOTEBOOK

Buck Magic(IRE) was snapped up by connections having opened his account at the fourth attempt in Irish points in April and proved a popular choice here. He got the job done with a ready enough effort considering he took a keen hold towards the front and looks well suited by a sound surface. This was just his yard's second win in a bumper and this 4-y-o should prove well suited by stepping up to around 2m4f over hurdles. (op 7-4)

Lucky Sun, fourth on debut in May, travelled smoothly on the inside turning into the home straight but was ultimately outstayed by the winner. Now looks the time to go hurdling with him, and he too should enjoy a step up in distance in that sphere. (op 7-2 tchd 3-1)

Wychwoods Kaddy, who played up in the preliminaries, was given a very patient ride and crept into contention coming out of the back straight. He proved one-paced when it mattered, but this was still an improvement on his debut at Ludlow 20 days earlier.

Prince Of King couldn't go with them from 3f out, but still posted a respectable enough debut for a yard not associated with bumper winners. (op 12-1)

Mocambo(GER) had got going late when well beaten on debut at Chepstow 17 days previously, but was ridden from the front this time. He began to labour around 5f out, though, and looks to need more time. (op 9-4 tchd 11-4)

T/Plt: £74.20 to a £1 stake. Pool of £70,610.09 - 693.93 winning tickets. T/Qpdt: £31.00 to a £1 stake. Pool of £5,536.73 - 131.80 winning tickets. TM

2026 - 2032a (Foreign Racing) - See Raceform Interactive

206 HAYDOCK (L-H)

Wednesday, October 27

OFFICIAL GOING: Good (good to soft in places on chase course; good to firm in places on hurdle course; chs 5.7, hdl 7.9)

Chases on same course as last season but hurdles run on new inner course.
Wind: Half, across Weather: Fine

2033 COSTCO HAYDOCK JUVENILE HURDLE (9 hdls) — 2m

2:20 (2:20) (Class 4) 3-Y-O **£3,903** (£1,146; £573; £286)

Form				RPR
	1		**Palawi (IRE)**[23] 3-10-12 0 DougieCostello — (John Quinn) *hmpd 1st: sn chsd ldr: hit 2nd and 3rd: led sn after: effrtlessly wnt clr fr 3 out: v easily* **5/4**[1]	106+
4105	2	11	**Gulf Punch**[10] [1882] 3-11-7 109 (p) JimmyDerham(5) — (Milton Harris) *chsd ldrs: rdn after 5th: wnt 2nd u.p 3 out but nvr any danger to wnr* **10/1**	103
3	3	26	**Miss Miracle**[14] [1818] 3-10-2 0 RichieMcLernon(3) — (Jonjo O'Neill) *midfield: outpcd after 6th: kpt on steadily fr2 out: wnt mod 3rd run-in: nvr nr to chal* **7/1**[3]	59
3	4	4	**Groove Master**[18] [1772] 3-10-12 0 (b[1]) WayneHutchinson — (Alan King) *mstkes: chsd ldrs: wnt 2nd biefly bef 3 out where blnd: sn rdn and wknd* **16/1**	64
0	5	1 3/4	**Capricornus (USA)**[24] [1696] 3-10-12 0 GrahamLee — (Ferdy Murphy) *hld up: racd in midfield after 6th: hit 2 out: nvr nr to chal* **16/1**	60
4	6	11	**Plus Ultra (IRE)**[34] [1586] 3-10-5 0 KyleJames(7) — (Philip Kirby) *hld up bhd: pushed along after 6th: nvr on terms* **13/2**[2]	51
0	7	8	**North Shadow**[14] [1825] 3-10-7 0 JamesHalliday(5) — (Alan Brown) *led: hdd after 3rd: chsd ldr tl appr 3 out: sn wknd* **100/1**	43
U	8	17	**Dazeen**[47] [1498] 3-10-12 0 AndrewThornton — (Paul Midgley) *racd keenly: hld up: bhd after 6th: eased whn n.d run-in* **33/1**	28
0	9	hd	**Vittachi**[24] [1699] 3-10-9 0 EwanWhillans(3) — (Alistair Whillans) *nt fluent: a bhd* **14/1**	28
63	10	14	**Venture Girl (IRE)**[14] [1825] 3-10-5 0 RichieMcGrath — (Tim Easterby) *a bhd* **10/1**	8
	11	2 1/2	**Nephele (IRE)**[44] 3-10-5 0 BrianHughes — (Tim Easterby) *mstkes: midfield: rdn and wknd after 6th: t.o* **25/1**	6

3m 48.9s (-15.30) 11 Ran SP% **114.7**
toteswingers:1&2:£3.00, 1&3:£2.30, 2&3:£18.50 CSF £14.04 TOTE £2.20: £1.30, £2.70, £2.00; EX 15.90.
Owner Bob McMillan **Bred** Jim McCormack **Trained** Settrington, N Yorks

FOCUS

A moderate juvenile event and an impressive debut winner. He was value for further but has the potential to rate a lot higher.

NOTEBOOK

Palawi(IRE) ◆ ran out an impressive debut winner. This scopey son of Dubawi had failed to win in eight attempts prior to this switch in codes, but he had shown useful form in defeat on his last two outings in that sphere. He proved all the rage here and won easily despite looking to do far too much through the early parts as he was lit up after being hampered at the first. His jumping therefore also wasn't fluent over the next couple, but the further he went the better he was and he flew the third-last to go clear. Value for a good bit further, he rates one of the better prospects to be seen out so far in this division and ought to be well up to defying a penalty, considering he should improve for the experience. (op 11-8, tchd 6-4 in places)

Gulf Punch, who like the winner is by Dubawi, returned to something like her best form in defeat yet was never a threat to the winner. This triple winner was giving that rival a stone, however, and was a clear second-best. She is a solid benchmark and will probably find life easier again when switching to handicaps.

Miss Miracle, well beaten on debut a fortnight earlier, was back on some better ground here yet still posted a laboured effort. She is looking more one for low-grade handicaps. (op 15-2 tchd 8-1)

Groove Master, a distant third on debut 18 days earlier, was equipped with first-time blinkers. He wasn't that fluent in the back straight, but made his worst mistake when meeting the third-last all wrong. It made little difference to the overall result and he is clearly one of his stable's lesser lights. (op 14-1)

Capricornus(USA) stepped up on his hurdling debut 24 days earlier and is another that will be more interesting when going handicapping, but he still has stamina to prove for this discipline. (op 10-1)

2034 GERARD O'SULLIVAN 70TH BIRTHDAY H'CAP CHASE (15 fncs) — 2m 4f

2:50 (2:50) (Class 4) (0-115,115) 4-Y-0+ **£3,903** (£1,146; £573; £286)

Form				RPR
236-	1		**Deuteronomy (IRE)**[275] [3666] 9-10-4 **93** BrianHughes — (John Wade) *a.p: led 3 out: rdn whn mstke last: jnd by runner-up run-in: r.o willingly and on top towards fin* **9/1**	105+
2-62	2	1/2	**Restezen D'Armor (FR)**[20] [1737] 5-11-0 **103** FelixDeGiles — (Charlie Longsdon) *hld up: hdwy appr 4 out: chsd ldng pair bef 3 out: travelling wl 2 out: sn wnt cl 2nd: shkn up bef last: moved upsides wnr to chal run-in: no ex towards fin* **3/1**[1]	114+
136P	3	15	**Badger Foot (IRE)**[49] [1509] 5-11-7 **110** APMcCoy — (Jonjo O'Neill) *prom: led 11th: hdd 3 out: rdn but stl chalng 2 out: nt qckn appr last: no ex run-in* **14/1**	108
0244	4	4 1/2	**The Duke's Speech (IRE)**[20] [1738] 9-11-10 **113** PaulMoloney — (Sophie Leech) *bhd: u.p 11th: kpt on fr 3 out: nvr able to rch ldrs* **8/1**	106
0310	5	6	**Magnetic Pole**[33] [1604] 9-11-0 **108** (v) GilesHawkins(5) — (Richard Lee) *trckd ldrs: effrt in 4th abt 3 l off the pce whn blnd 4 out: wknd 3 out* **22/1**	99
05-3	6	13	**Ballabrook (IRE)**[29] [1645] 8-10-12 **104** AdrianLane(3) — (Donald McCain) *midfield: rdn appr 10th: wknd 11th* **6/1**[3]	80
2/0-	7	3 1/2	**Guns And Butter (IRE)**[382] [1702] 8-11-2 **105** WilsonRenwick — (Rose Dobbin) *in tch: effrt 4 out: outpcd next: wknd bef last* **28/1**	78
42-F	8	nk	**Master Somerville**[180] [78] 8-11-12 **115** (b) RichardJohnson — (Henry Daly) *led: blnd 1st: rdn and hdd 11th: wknd 3 out* **7/1**	90
461P	9	30	**Ragador**[38] [1557] 9-10-13 **102** TjadeCollier — (Sue Smith) *in tch: blnd 1st: lost pl 4th: in rr and nt travelling wl after* **25/1**	47
13-1	P		**Desperate Dex (IRE)**[24] [1701] 10-10-8 **97** GrahamLee — (Ferdy Murphy) *midfield: pushed along appr 9th: bhd after 11th: t.o whn p.u bef 2 out* **5/1**[2]	—
2234	U		**Ormello (FR)**[34] [1598] 8-11-12 **115** PeterBuchanan — (Lucinda Russell) *midfield: blnd bdly and uns rdr 9th* **14/1**	—
65-0	F		**Pelo Du Bief (FR)**[18] [1767] 7-9-11 **93** JoeCornwall(7) — (John Cornwall) *towards rr: fell 9th* **40/1**	—

5m 3.80s (-6.20) **Going Correction** -0.225s/f (Good) 12 Ran SP% **117.0**
Speed ratings (Par 105): **103,102,96,95,92 87,86,85,73,— —,—**
toteswingers:1&2:£3.90, 2&3:£18.00, 1&3:£16.30 CSF £35.50 CT £383.98 TOTE £8.20: £2.70, £1.30, £3.90; EX 47.00.
Owner John Wade **Bred** Mrs R Coghlan **Trained** Mordon, Co Durham

FOCUS

A moderate handicap that looked competitive for the class and it was run at a fair gallop. The first pair came clear on the run-in. The winner is rated back to the level of his best 2009 form.

NOTEBOOK

Deuteronomy(IRE) made light of a 275-day absence and ran out a very game winner, ending a two-year losing run in the process. He was never far away and made his effort from three out. Having mastered the third, he then looked a sitting duck for the runner-up coming to the last and got in very close to that fence. It cost him no momentum, though, and he proved the most resolute on the run-in. He has gone well fresh in the past and his profile would suggest he is one to be taking on next time, but this should do his confidence a lot of good. (op 8-1)

Restezen D'Armor(FR) was making his chasing debut off a 4lb higher mark than when second at Exeter 20 days earlier and, not for the first time, came in for decent support. He raced enthusiastically off the pace, but jumped soundly and arrived on the scene going sweetly around three out. He met the final fence better than the winner, but didn't help his rider when asked to get on top and his attitude will now rightly come under scrutiny. There must surely be a race for him, however, and perhaps dropping back in trip in this sphere will do the trick. (op 9-2)

Badger Foot(IRE) showed up a lot more encouragingly on this return from a 49-day break with Tony McCoy back aboard and only tired out of it after the second-last. (op 11-1)

The Duke's Speech(IRE) got going all too late on this drop back from 3m having been ridden out the back and has a moderate strike-rate, but goes some way to setting the level. (op 15-2 tchd 17-2)

Magnetic Pole was in the process of running an improved race prior to whacking the fourth-last, but for which he would have been closer. (op 25-1)

Ballabrook(IRE) looked to have solid claims back on this easier surface despite being 4lb higher, but his jumping let him down as the pace began to lift in the back straight and he was disappointing. (op 8-1)

Desperate Dex(IRE) was up 2lb for winning on his return in a classified chase 24 days earlier. He may have been better off racing more handily on this drop back in trip, but he was another whose jumping lacked fluency on the far side and he was eventually pulled up. Perhaps something went amiss. Official explanation: jockey said gelding ran flat and was unsuited by the good (good to soft in places) ground (op 6-1 tchd 9-2)

2035 PARAMOUNT LEGAL COSTS H'CAP HURDLE (10 hdls) 2m 4f
3:25 (3:25) (Class 3) (0-135,132) 4-Y-O+ **£5,529** (£1,623; £811; £405)

Form RPR
012- **1** **Riptide**[193] 5224 4-11-5 **128**...(b) AdrianLane(3) 132+
(Donald McCain) *trckd ldr: led 4 out: rdn appr 3 out: styd on wl towards fin* **11/1**

25-5 **2** *2* **Barwell Bridge**[18] 1775 4-11-12 **132**...(t) NoelFehily 133
(Warren Greatrex) *hld up: hdwy 3 out: rdn appr last: styd on run-in: tk 2nd fnl stride but no imp on wnr* **17/2**

51-3 **3** *hd* **Accordingtoemandem (IRE)**[180] 76 6-10-13 **119**... DougieCostello 120
(Ian Williams) *hld up: hdwy appr 3 out: wnt 2nd 2 out: hung lft run-in: no imp on wnr towards fin: lost 2nd fnl stride* **14/1**

3-63 **4** *5* **Soft Spoken Guy (IRE)**[18] 1766 7-11-9 **129**...(t) MichaelMcAlister 127+
(Maurice Barnes) *in tch: pushed along after 4 out: effrt to chse ldrs 3 out: styd on same pce fr bef last* **5/1**[2]

11F5 **5** *3* **Three Ships**[18] 1766 9-10-8 **119**... GilesHawkins(5) 113
(Richard Lee) *hld up: hdwy fr 6th: chsng ldrs whn hit 3 out: one pce run-in* **18/1**

136- **6** *nse* **Pipe Banner**[218] 4802 6-11-0 **120**... APMcCoy 114
(Nicky Henderson) *in tch: effrt to chse ldrs 3 out: rdn appr last: wknd run-in* **6/1**[3]

-411 **7** *1 ¾* **Summer Soul (IRE)**[40] 581 8-11-2 **125**...(p) CampbellGillies(3) 117
(Lucinda Russell) *in tch: lost pl after 4th: rdn along after 5th: kpt on again run-in but nvr able to get on terms w ldrs* **14/1**

21-1 **8** *3 ¾* **Mostly Bob (IRE)**[173] 191 7-11-8 **128**... RichardJohnson 117
(Philip Hobbs) *hld up: hdwy 6th: effrt 3 out: rdn whn chsng ldrs appr 2 out: wknd last* **5/2**[1]

04-0 **9** *4* **Flake**[171] 236 10-10-4 **110**... TjadeCollier 95
(Sue Smith) *trckd ldrs tl rdn and wknd 4 out* **33/1**

11U- **10** *18* **Raysrock (IRE)**[194] 5204 8-10-11 **117**... WilsonRenwick 96+
(P Monteith) *led: nt fluent 5th: hdd 4 out: wkng whn blnd 3 out: eased whn wl btn bef last* **18/1**

45-0 **11** *25* **Cassius (IRE)**[173] 196 8-10-10 **116**... GrahamLee 62
(Bruce Mactaggart) *nt fluent 4th: a bhd: t.o* **11/1**

4m 36.3s (-37.20) **11** Ran SP% **113.5**
toteswingers:1&2:£15.10, 1&3:£12.80, 2&3:£35.10 CSF £97.65 CT £1313.59 TOTE £8.60: £2.30, £2.10, £6.80; EX 60.20.
Owner Gone To The Bar Racing **Bred** D Robb **Trained** Cholmondeley, Cheshire

FOCUS
A wide-open looking handicap and an interesting race. There was a fair enough gallop on, but there was still something of a dash finish off the home turn. Fair form, with the first three all on the upgrade.

NOTEBOOK
Riptide made most to resume winning ways on this return from his seasonal break. He takes plenty of stoking up, but his positive response at the top of the home straight proved the difference between winning and a place. He kept responding when strongly challenged from two out and it's a fair bet this 4-y-o had more left in the tank at the finish. This rates a career-best effort, he goes on most surfaces and there is very probably more to come from him this term. (op 12-1)
Barwell Bridge arrived with every chance on the outside from the second-last, but this was his first outing over the longer trip and he was just outstayed by the winner. This quicker ground suited and it was a much-improved effort under top weight in a tongue strap, so there could be a nice pot in him at some stage this season. (op 7-1 tchd 13-2)
Accordingtoemandem(IRE) ◆ posted a very encouraging return from his summer break. Ridden to get the longer trip, he made smooth headway in the home straight and looked a big threat nearing the last. The winner outstayed him when it mattered, but he looks well up to adding to his tally in the coming weeks if out again on a similarly sound surface. (op 18-1)
Soft Spoken Guy(IRE) ◆ had run a nice race in defeat on his return behind a subsequent winner 18 days earlier. He would've likely been better off under more positive handling on this step back up in trip, but this was another sound effort and he is one to side when reverting to easier ground. (tchd 11-2)
Three Ships ran close enough to his last-time-out form with the fourth over this suitably stiffer test, and helps to give the form a fair look. (tchd 20-1)
Pipe Banner wasn't disgraced on this seasonal debut and should appreciate getting back on some softer ground. (op 11-2 tchd 5-1)
Mostly Bob(IRE) was last seen making it three wins from four career outings when scoring at Aintree in May. Well supported for this handicap debut, he looked to find it too sharp and probably wants easier ground to be seen at his best. It would be unwise to write him off on the back of this effort. (op 10-3)

2036 HAGER SOLLYSTA H'CAP CHASE (18 fncs) 3m
4:00 (4:00) (Class 3) (0-120,117) 4-Y-O+ **£6,505** (£1,910; £955; £477)

Form RPR
41-6 **1** **Le Platino (GER)**[168] 287 8-10-11 **102**...(p) BrianHughes 115+
(John Wade) *in tch: led after 14th: clr bef last: styd on wl* **8/1**

130- **2** *6* **Double Mead**[226] 4646 8-11-5 **117**... MrsAlexDunn(7) 125
(Kim Bailey) *midfield: hdwy after 14th: chsd wnr 4 out: one pce and no imp bef last* **12/1**

3F-6 **3** *9* **Garleton (IRE)**[19] 1763 9-10-8 **106**...(t) AlexanderVoy(7) 106
(Maurice Barnes) *trckd ldrs: rdn and outpcd after 4 out: chsd front 2 appr last: no imp and one pce* **6/1**[3]

P604 **4** *4* **Catch The Perk (IRE)**[35] 1577 13-11-8 **113**... PeterBuchanan 109
(Lucinda Russell) *prom: rdn and outpcd appr 4 out: kpt on u.p run-in but no imp* **14/1**

54-3 **5** *16* **Marleybow (IRE)**[21] 1725 7-11-7 **112**... RichardJohnson 98
(Richard Lee) *in tch: cl up appr 4 out: mstke 2 out: sn wknd* **9/2**[1]

516- **6** *21* **Fine Parchment (IRE)**[204] 5077 7-11-6 **111**... NoelFehily 74
(Charlie Mann) *midfield: hdwy 10th: mstke 11th: chsd ldrs 4 out: rdn appr 2 out: sn wknd* **5/1**[2]

/120 **7** *23* **Twelve Paces**[19] 1763 9-10-12 **103**...(v[1]) WilsonRenwick 45
(P Monteith) *hld up: struggling bef 13th: nvr on terms* **16/1**

P-30 **8** *4* **Island Flyer (IRE)**[21] 1725 8-11-5 **110**...(p) PaddyBrennan 48
(Tom George) *led: hdd after 14th: wknd appr 3 out* **14/1**

0/24 **P** **Cebonne (FR)**[21] 1725 9-11-4 **109**... PaulMoloney —
(Sophie Leech) *hld up: blnd 5th: struggling after 14th: bhd whn p.u bef 4 out* **6/1**[3]

6/0- **P** **Stagecoach Opal**[525] 402 9-11-2 **112**... ShaneByrne(5) —
(Sue Smith) *trckd ldrs: lost pl bef 5th: j. slowly 6th: hmpd 9th: toiling 10th: t.o 12th: p.u bef 14th* **22/1**

1-P4 **P** **Oscar Honey (IRE)**[18] 1781 9-11-6 **111**... GrahamLee —
(Rose Dobbin) *blnd 1st: sn bhd: rdn appr 5th: p.u after 9th* **14/1**

31-5 **F** **Dawn Ride (IRE)**[160] 425 9-11-7 **112**...(p) BarryKeniry —
(Micky Hammond) *hld up: fell 9th* **25/1**

6m 3.80s (-10.20) **Going Correction** -0.225s/f (Good) **12** Ran SP% **116.3**
Speed ratings (Par 107): **108,106,103,101,96 89,81,80,—,— —,—**
toteswingers:1&2:£11.70, 1&3:£24.30, 2&3:£15.20 CSF £96.95 CT £619.39 TOTE £10.10: £3.60, £6.00, £3.10; EX 161.80.
Owner John Wade **Bred** Carlton Consultants Ltd **Trained** Mordon, Co Durham

FOCUS
A moderate handicap for the class. The winner produced a step up and the second is rated to form.

NOTEBOOK
Le Platino(GER) ran out a ready winner on his return from a 168-day break and handed his stable a double on the card, which had previously been winless since May. This is his second season as a chaser and, although he wasn't proven over this far, he obviously stays very well now. His jumping was decent, bar a slight error at the last, and a sound surface does look important to his cause. He doesn't have many miles on the clock for an 8-y-o and should continue to pay his way at least after a likely rise. (op 12-1)
Double Mead was giving over a stone to the winner without taking her rider's claim into account and turned in a very pleasing seasonal return. She stayed on to finish nicely clear of the rest, fully proving she gets the trip, and also enjoyed the ground. Another relatively lightly raced 8-y-o, this is a performance she is more than entitled to build on, but it should be noted she has a good record when fresh.
Garleton(IRE) ◆ came under heavy pressure turning for home, but kept on gamely without threatening the first two and this was a step back in the right direction. He has not long been with the stable, is now back on his last winning mark and should improve again when reverting to a stiffer track. (op 13-2)
Catch The Perk(IRE), who won this race last year, rallied bravely from three out and was coming back towards the finish. This 14-time winner now heads off for an honourable retirement. (op 12-1)
Marleybow(IRE) ran below the level of his Ludlow debut for his new connections 21 days earlier. He ought to pop up at some stage this term, though. (op 5-1)
Fine Parchment(IRE) was easy to back on this seasonal debut despite having won on his return last term. He looked a player off the home turn but ultimately paid for running too freely and dropping back in trip looks a wise move. (tchd 6-1)
Cebonne(FR) was another that was proved easy to back. He never looked like getting involved from out the back and was pulled up with something presumably going amiss at the top of the home straight. (op 11-2)
Oscar Honey(IRE) Official explanation: jockey said gelding made an early mistake and never travelled thereafter (op 11-2)

2037 HAYDOCK PARK PONY CLUB NOVICES' H'CAP CHASE (13 fncs) 2m
4:35 (4:35) (Class 4) (0-115,115) 4-Y-O+ **£3,903** (£1,146; £573; £286)

Form RPR
-055 **1** **Kack Handed**[21] 1734 7-11-3 **106**... RichardJohnson 114+
(Henry Daly) *led: mstke and hdd 3rd: chsd ldr after: nt fluent 6th: rdn appr last: styd on to ld towards fin* **4/1**[1]

2240 **2** *½* **Prioryjo**[19] 1761 7-11-4 **107**... BrianHarding 112
(Martin Todhunter) *hld up: hdwy fr 4 out: wnt 2nd 2 out: led appr last: u.p and hdd towards fin* **18/1**

0-P6 **3** *3 ¾* **That's The Deal (IRE)**[18] 1770 6-9-9 **91**... JoeCornwall(7) 94
(John Cornwall) *chsd ldr: led 3rd: rdn and hdd appr last: kpt on same pce after* **12/1**

2P-3 **4** *23* **Prince Du Beury (FR)**[17] 1794 7-11-11 **114**... AndrewTinkler 95
(Nicky Henderson) *chsd ldrs: rdn and outpcd 9th: rallied briefly appr 4 out: wknd bef 3 out* **9/2**[2]

2353 **B** **Blossom King (FR)**[18] 1767 6-11-5 **108**...(t) PaddyBrennan —
(Tom George) *hld up: 5th and in tch whn b.d 9th* **5/1**[3]

2-53 **P** **Quatro Pierji (FR)**[147] 576 6-11-9 **112**... PaddyAspell —
(James Moffatt) *bhd: struggling whn j.rt 8th: p.u bef 9th* **10/1**

026- **F** **Catch Bob (IRE)**[186] 5393 6-11-12 **115**... GrahamLee —
(Ferdy Murphy) *hld up: fell 5th* **11/2**

61-0 **F** **Shadrack (IRE)**[14] 1827 6-11-5 **113**... ShaneByrne(5) —
(Sue Smith) *chsd ldrs: 3rd abt 4 l off the pce whn fell 9th* **9/2**[2]

4m 12.9s (1.90) **Going Correction** -0.225s/f (Good) **8** Ran SP% **110.5**
Speed ratings (Par 105): **86,85,83,72,— —,—,—**
toteswingers:1&2:£8.70, 1&3:£7.10, 2&3:£13.00 CSF £59.07 CT £746.18 TOTE £4.60: £1.50, £5.20, £3.40; EX 62.80.
Owner A J Haden **Bred** Patrick And Roslyn Burling **Trained** Stanton Lacy, Shropshire

FOCUS
An ordinary novice handicap in which none of the runners had previously won over fences. It was run at a solid gallop and the form is worth treating with a degree of caution. The winner is rated 5lb off his best chase figure.

NOTEBOOK
Kack Handed finally shed his maiden tag on this return to fences. Too keen on his return over hurdles last time, he again did plenty through the early parts up front and wasn't foot perfect. He briefly looked held coming to the penultimate fence, but to his credit he rallied and got on top of the idling runner-up near the finish. He is talented enough to defy a rise after going back up in the weights and his confidence should be boosted, but he isn't certain to build on this. (tchd 7-2)
Prioryjo was still going strongly two out, but after being asked to win the race on the run-in she looked to markedly idle in front and was mugged at the business end. This was a much more encouraging display on her second outing as a chaser and, despite her two hurdle successes coming in selling company, there is evidently a handicap to be won with her over fences. She clearly needs producing as late as possible in this sphere, though, and the problem is she will be going up in the weights for this. (op 16-1)
That's The Deal(IRE)had previously shown very little under rules, including in two outings over fences since joining the yard. It was this former point winner's handicap debut, however, and, well backed, he posted a vastly improved display. Stepping back up in trip should help and he has obviously now found his level, so his turn isn't looking far off. (op 22-1 tchd 25-1)
Prince Du Beury(FR) found the drop back to the minimum trip too sharp and continues to frustrate. (tchd 5-1)
Blossom King(FR) was travelling nicely and creeping into the race prior to being brought down when Shadrack crashed out with five to jump. (tchd 5-1)
Catch Bob(IRE), making his chasing debut, had been taken off his feet but was starting to make some inroads before coming down on the back straight. (tchd 5-1)
Shadrack(IRE) was not done with before he fell. He was shortly back up on his feet. (tchd 5-1)

2038 RACING UK HOME OF JUMP RACING NOVICES' HURDLE (9 hdls) 2m
5:10 (5:10) (Class 4) 4-Y-O+ **£3,252** (£955; £477; £238)

Form RPR
12 **1** **Drill Sergeant**[18] 1765 5-11-5 0... APMcCoy 127+
(Donald McCain) *led: sn clr: abt 15 l ahd whn plld himself up and hdd on paddock bnd after 3rd: continued in rr but sn gd hdwy and prom 5th: led appr 3 out: rdn whn pressed run-in: kpt on wl towards fin* **11/10**[1]

00-3 **2** *1* **Brother Bob (IRE)**[24] 1688 4-10-12 0... RichardJohnson 105+
(Charlie Longsdon) *hld up: hdwy appr 3 out: wnt 2nd and chalng whn nt fluent last: ev ch on run-in: r.o u.p: hld cl home* **6/1**[3]

2/0- **3** 3 1/4 **Morning Farewell**[544] 89 6-10-12 0............(p) LeightonAspell 101
(William Clay) *midfield: hmpd 1st: hdwy to chse ldrs 3 out: chalng appr last: ev ch run-in: no ex fnl 75yds* **66/1**
5 **4** 4 **Bagutta Sun**[14] 1832 4-10-2 0............ DannyCook(3) 90
(Barry Leavy) *in rr: hdwy appr last: styd on wl run-in: nrst fin* **33/1**
0/4 **5** 1/2 **Wild Desert (FR)**[32] 1613 5-10-12 0............ ChristianWilliams 96
(Alan King) *hld up in midfield: hdwy 3 out: chsd ldrs 2 out: styd on same pce run-in* **20/1**
230- **6** 5 **Mister Wall Street (FR)**[225] 4657 5-10-12 110............ GrahamLee 91
(Ferdy Murphy) *in tch: chalng appr 3 out: stl ch 2 out: rdn bef last: wknd run-in* **9/2**[2]
53-4 **7** 7 **Attaglance**[172] 209 4-10-7 0............ JamesHalliday(5) 84
(Malcolm Jefferson) *hld up: pushed along appr last: nvr on terms w ldrsa fa* **20/1**
8 1 3/4 **Stevie Thunder**[147] 5-10-12 0............ DougieCostello 84
(Ian Williams) *in tch: effrt to chse ldrs appr 2 out: wknd bef lastroe* **9/2**[2]
05- **9** 7 **Robertewenutter**[204] 5078 6-10-12 0............ HenryOliver 76
(Sue Smith) *pckd 1st: chsd ldr fr 2nd: led 6th: hdd appr 3 out where mstke: wknd bef 2 out:* **80/1**
0P-P **10** nk **Vallani (IRE)**[174] 176 5-10-2 73............ CampbellGillies(3) 68
(P Monteith) *mstke 1st: chsd ldrs: lft in ld on paddock bnd after 3rd: hdd 6th: sn wknd* **150/1**
11 1 3/4 **Daggerman**[609] 5-10-5 0............ HarryChalloner(7) 75
(Barry Leavy) *in tch: blnd 4th: wknd 3 out* **100/1**
44- **12** nk **Hallstatt (IRE)**[26] 1368 4-10-12 0............ DaveCrosse 75
(John Mackie) *midfield: pushed along whn j. slowly 3 out: sn wknd* **50/1**
13 16 **Real Desire**[5] 4-10-12 0............ WilsonRenwick 57
(P Monteith) *midfield: lost pl bef 4th: bhd after* **200/1**

3m 50.7s (-13.50)
WFA 4 from 5yo+ 9lb **13** Ran SP% **117.6**
toteswingers:1&2:£2.90, 1&3:£18.60, 2&3:£29.20 CSF £7.62 TOTE £1.90: £1.10, £2.50, £11.30; EX 7.00 Place 6: £321.93, Place 5 £233.72..
Owner T G Leslie **Bred** D G Hardisty Bloodstock **Trained** Cholmondeley, Cheshire
■ Stewards' Enquiry : Danny Cook three-day ban: weighed-in 2lb heavy (Nov 10-12)

FOCUS
A modest novice event. The wayward winner, given an unbelievable ride by the champion, was value for further and can probably rate a lot higher.

NOTEBOOK
Drill Sergeant was given a simply incredible ride by the champion. Having set out to make all and attained a clear early advantage, the winner all but refused as he went around the paddock bend, which saw him quickly drop from first to last place. McCoy got him back interested, however, and, due to there not being much of a gallop on the pair made their way back into a handy position on the back straight. He was in front again off the home turn, but looked vulnerable as he came under pressure two out. His rider kept making his mind up for him, though, and he was always just doing enough the run-in. Few jockeys would've been able to get this 5-y-o to resume winning ways here, but this formerly smart Flat performer obviously rates better than the bare form. Things will be tougher under a double penalty now, so perhaps connections will switch him to a handicap as a likely mark in the 120s would look tempting. (op Evens tchd 5-4)
Brother Bob(IRE) was an eye-catcher on his hurdling debut 24 days earlier and stepped up on that form as expected, only going down narrowly. A stiffer test will probably be what he wants in due course, but there could well be one of these in him before he goes handicapping. (op 15-2 tchd 11-2)
Morning Farewell was having his first outing since running poorly on his debut for connections 544 days previously and he ran a big race in defeat. This was in keeping with his previous best effort, he is another that will likely peak over further and he should come on a lot for the run. One will have to be somewhat mindful of the bounce factor next time, though.
Bagutta Sun ◆ really caught the eye doing her best work towards the finish under a fairly considerate ride. This was a nice improvement on her hurdling debut a fortnight earlier and she can be found an opening when switching to a handicap.
Wild Desert(FR) stayed on well in the home straight and this was much more encouraging than his hurdling debut last month. He may prefer further judged on his Flat form and is one to note when going handicapping.
Mister Wall Street(FR) has long been well thought of by connections and, while never a threat, had taken in the Supreme Novice on his final outing last term. He had his chance on this return, but didn't help his cause by running freely and weakened from the second-last.
Stevie Thunder is a useful performer on the level, but has gone two years without success and had stamina to prove on this switch to hurdling. It ultimately looked to be a case of him not lasting home. (op 6-1)
T/Plt: £544.20 to a £1 stake. Pool:£70,643.78 - 94.75 winning tickets T/Qpdt: £199.70 to a £1 stake. Pool:£5,911.32 - 21.90 winning tickets DO

2039 - 2045a (Foreign Racing) - See Raceform Interactive

[1914]FONTWELL (L-H)
Thursday, October 28

OFFICIAL GOING: Good to soft (6.5)
Rail realignment increased distances by about 65m per circuit on both courses.
Wind: Fresh, across Weather: Cloudy

2046 EUROPEAN OFFICE PRODUCTS NOVICES' CHASE (15 fncs) 2m 4f
2:00 (2:01) (Class 4) 4-Y-0+ **£2,992** (£878; £439; £219)

Form RPR
01P- **1** **Bai Zhu (IRE)**[197] 5184 6-11-3 0............ FelixDeGiles 129+
(Nicky Henderson) *mde all: jinked rt after 9th: hrd rdn appr last: hld on wl whn jnd run-in* **2/1**[2]
100- **2** nk **Balzaccio (FR)**[195] 5213 5-11-3 0............ WayneHutchinson 129+
(Alan King) *chsd ldrs: wnt 2nd at 7th: drvn to join wnr run-in: nt qckn nr fin* **11/8**[1]
206- **3** 20 **Psi (USA)**[336] 2518 5-11-3 0............ JamieMoore 114
(Gary Moore) *hld up in 5th: hdwy whn mstke 8th: disp 2nd fr 4 out tl rdn and wknd 2 out* **15/2**
303 **4** 10 **Not So Sure Dick (IRE)**[22] 1727 5-11-3 0............ MarkBradburne 102
(George Baker) *trckd ldrs gng wl tl rdn and wknd 4 out* **12/1**
0P/3 **5** 51 **Kitley Hassle**[25] 1706 8-10-10 0............(b) MrTJCannon(7) 56
(James Frost) *in tch: rdn 7th: wknd 9th: sn bhd* **7/1**[3]
/0P- **6** 23 **Daring Approach (IRE)**[221] 4762 9-11-3 0............ WillKennedy 35
(Helen Nelmes) *chsd wnr tl 7th: wknd 9th: sn bhd* **33/1**
-FP4 **P** **Open Range (IRE)**[140] 692 10-11-3 56............(t) LeightonAspell —
(George Wareham) *reluctant to s and lost 20 l: j. bdly: a wl bhd: blnd and p.u 9th* **100/1**
P-0F **P** **Notmorebrandy (IRE)**[16] 1813 6-10-12 95............ MarcGoldstein(5) —
(Diana Grissell) *towards rr: mstke and struggling 8th: wl bhd whn p.u bef 10th* **40/1**

5m 12.9s (5.60) **Going Correction** +0.525s/f (Soft) **8** Ran SP% **113.8**
Speed ratings (Par 105): **109,108,100,96,76 67**,—,—
Tote Swingers: 1&2 £2.30, 1&3 £4.30, 2&3 £3.00 CSF £5.35 TOTE £3.00: £1.10, £1.30, £1.90; EX 5.90.
Owner The Perfect Day Partnership **Bred** Coisdeel Syndicate **Trained** Upper Lambourn, Berks

FOCUS
The going remained good to soft and the bends were dolled out, meaning the course was at minimum width. This didn't look the most competitive novices' chase but it was a fair race for the track. The winner stepped up on his best hurdles form and is the type to rate higher.

NOTEBOOK
Bai Zhu(IRE), a 118-rated hurdler, narrowly came out on top. Soon in front on this chase debut, he jumped well, as is often the case with novices from this yard, and found plenty for pressure. He'll find it tougher under a penalty, but still looked a bit green and should make his mark in handicaps later in the season. (tchd 15-8, 85-40 in a place)
Balzaccio(FR), rated 127 over hurdles, was never far from the winner and threw down a strong challenge in the straight, but always just looked to be coming off second best. This was a satisfactory start and he should go one better at some stage. (op 15-8 tchd 2-1)
Psi(USA), without a win over hurdles but rated 110, travelled well on this chase debut, but he couldn't match the classier front pair at the business end. He's in good hands to win races at an ordinary level. (op 13-2 tchd 6-1 and 8-1)
Not So Sure Dick(IRE) showed enough to suggest he'll be of interest once handicapping. (op 10-1)

2047 CROWN RACING BEST FOR SERVICE JUVENILE HURDLE (9 hdls) 2m 2f 110y
2:30 (2:30) (Class 4) 3-Y-O **£2,341** (£687; £343; £171)

Form RPR
1 **1** **Zakeeta (IRE)**[26] 1674 3-10-12 0............ LeightonAspell 105+
(Oliver Sherwood) *prom: led 4th: pushed clr 2 out: readily* **11/4**[2]
P4 **2** 4 1/2 **Freckle Face**[26] 1674 3-10-7 0............ TomO'Connor(5) 99
(Bill Turner) *plld hrd: sn prom: jnd wnr and mstke 3 out: outpcd next* **14/1**
3 3 1/2 **Ultravox (USA)**[75] 3-10-12 0............ NickScholfield 96
(Jeremy Scott) *hld up in rr of midfield: hdwy whn mstke 6th: one pce 2 out: 3rd and btn whn mstke last* **16/1**
4 **4** 12 **Il Portico**[11] 1882 3-10-12 0............(p) JamieMoore 86
(Gary Moore) *hld up in midfield: hdwy after 5th: rdn and wknd 2 out* **2/1**[1]
5 4 1/2 **Rahaala (IRE)**[173] 3-10-5 0............ DougieCostello 74
(Lucy Wadham) *hld up towards rr: hdwy 5th: wknd appr 2 out* **7/1**[3]
1U00 **6** 34 **Joe Rua (USA)**[25] 1691 3-11-5 100............(b[1]) ColinBolger 57
(John Ryan) *led tl hit 4th: wknd 6th* **33/1**
5 **7** 3 1/4 **On The Right Path**[59] 1422 3-10-5 0............ MrSHanson(7) 47
(Alison Batchelor) *a in mid-div: outpcd after 5th: n.d fr 3 out* **80/1**
8 3 **Brave Enough (USA)**[140] 3-10-12 0............ DaveCrosse 44
(Roger Curtis) *bhd: blnd 2nd: rdn 3rd: blnd bdly 6th: no ch after* **50/1**
02 **9** 3 **Royal Torbo (ISR)**[15] 1818 3-10-12 0............ GerardTumelty 41
(George Baker) *chsd ldrs tl rdn and wknd 6th* **16/1**
10 4 1/2 **Pursestrings**[43] 3-10-5 0............ RhysFlint 30
(Laura Mongan) *plld hrd: prom: hmpd by loose horse appr 6th: sn wknd* **40/1**
U **Claimant (IRE)**[106] 3-10-12 0............ JamesDavies —
(Miss J R Tooth) *bhd: mstke 5th: blnd and uns rdr next* **50/1**
F **Juwireya**[47] 3-10-2 0............ WayneKavanagh(3) —
(Peter Hiatt) *bhd tl fell 2nd* **8/1**
0 **P** **Magic Spirit**[11] 1882 3-10-5 0............(b) RodiGreene —
(Suzy Smith) *t.k.h: prom: j. slowly 2nd: lost pl after next: hrd rdn and lost tch 5th: wl bhd whn p.u bef next* **50/1**
P **You Mug**[37] 3-10-5 0............ AnthonyFreeman(7) —
(Sean Curran) *sn wl bhd: hmpd 2nd: t.o whn p.u after 5th* **100/1**

4m 48.8s (14.50) **Going Correction** +0.525s/f (Soft) **14** Ran SP% **115.5**
Speed ratings (Par 103): **90,88,86,81,79 65,64,62,61,59** —,—,—,—
Tote Swingers: 1&2 £8.80, 1&3 £10.80, 2&3 £25.40 CSF £37.17 TOTE £2.60: £1.20, £3.10, £3.90; EX 33.50.
Owner B G Fillery **Bred** Sean Collins **Trained** Upper Lambourn, Berks

FOCUS
An ordinary juvenile novices' hurdle. Zakeeta produced a step up and looks a fair juvenile.

NOTEBOOK
Zakeeta(IRE) defy the penalty, having won well over C&D earlier in the month. In front with a circuit to go, her quick, fluent jumping was a massive help and she gradually pulled clear from the second-last. She's clearly taken very well to hurdles and may well be up to defying a double penalty, with her expected to keep improving. (op 3-1 tchd 9-4)
Freckle Face, some 14lb behind the winner latest, narrowed the gap significantly and showed much improved form. He's going the right way.
Ultravox(USA) didn't live up to expectations on the Flat, but he shaped promisingly on this first start over hurdles and looks to have a future at the right level. (op 20-1 tchd 12-1)
Il Portico, a well-beaten fourth at Kempton on debut, was expected to improve in the first-time cheekpieces, but he didn't see it out and this has to go down as disappointing. (tchd 9-4)
Rahaala(IRE), unplaced in two starts for Sir Michael Stoute on the Flat and sold for just 6,000gns, didn't seem to get home, but may fare better on a flatter, more speed-reliant track. (op 11-2)
Joe Rua(USA) continues to struggle under his penalty, the first-time blinkers making no difference. (op 28-1)

2048 EXPRESS PRINTING H'CAP CHASE (15 fncs) 2m 4f
3:00 (3:01) (Class 5) (0-90,90) 4-Y-0+ **£1,821** (£534; £267; £133)

Form RPR
P6-5 **1** **Qualypso D'Allier (FR)**[21] 1747 6-11-8 86............ NickScholfield 106+
(Andy Turnell) *pressed ldr: led 4th: clr fr 3 out: kpt up to work run-in* **4/1**[2]
11-P **2** 27 **Kappelhoff (IRE)**[169] 280 13-10-11 75............(b) MattieBatchelor 70
(Lydia Richards) *outpcd and sn wl bhd: styd on fr 11th: wnt mod 2nd after last* **10/1**
P-P2 **3** 2 3/4 **Normandy Landings**[10] 1901 7-11-3 81............ DougieCostello 74
(Neil Mulholland) *led tl 4th: pressed wnr after tl wknd appr 3 out* **3/1**[1]
3P-U **4** 12 **Killfinnan Castle (IRE)**[26] 1678 7-10-10 74............ WillKennedy 59
(F Jordan) *chsd ldrs: hrd rdn 8th: wknd 11th* **9/2**[3]
P062 **P** **Space Cowboy (IRE)**[10] 1905 10-10-2 66............(b) JamieMoore —
(Gary Moore) *hld up in 5th: hdwy 7th: mstke next: wknd 9th: bhd whn p.u bef 2 out* **6/1**
-F44 **P** **Drombeg Pride (IRE)**[10] 1901 6-10-3 72............(v[1]) MarcGoldstein(5) —
(Gerry Enright) *mstke 1st: trckd ldng pair tl 8th: wknd after next: t.o whn p.u after 11th* **20/1**
/11- **P** **Brushford (IRE)**[263] 3913 6-11-12 90............ LeightonAspell —
(Chris Gordon) *sn bhd: t.o 10th: p.u after 4 out* **4/1**[2]

5m 23.9s (16.60) **Going Correction** +0.525s/f (Soft) **7** Ran SP% **111.3**
Speed ratings (Par 103): **87,76,75,70**,— —,—
Tote Swingers: 1&2 £6.30, 1&3 £4.30, 2&3 £5.00 CSF £37.67 TOTE £7.10: £3.40, £3.80; EX 45.60.
Owner M Tedham **Bred** Yves Maupoil **Trained** Broad Hinton, Wilts

FOCUS
A very moderate handicap chase. The winner is rated back to the level of last season's Towcester unseat.

NOTEBOOK

Qualypso D'Allier(FR) finally put it all together to get off the mark at the tenth attempt over fences, being ridden positively, jumping well, and staying on dourly to win with plenty in hand. He had become very well weighted and will have had his confidence boosted by this success, so may now progress, with there being plenty of scope for improvement. He's expected to be a better horse next year. (tchd 10-3, 9-2 in places)

Kappelhoff(IRE), making his reappearance, got behind before staying on late and is entitled to come on for it, but whether he's up to winning off this mark remains to be seen. (op 9-1 tchd 8-1)

Normandy Landings, off the same mark as when second at Plumpton latest, was soon up with the pace and still looked in with a chance rounding for home, but he got tired from after the third-last and eventually lost second. (op 5-2 tchd 10-3)

Killfinnan Castle(IRE) received an early reminder and never really looked like winning. (op 11-2 tchd 4-1)

Brushford(IRE), bidding for a hat-trick, having won twice at the course early in the year, was 9lb higher for this return and found himself in trouble from an early stage. Official explanation: jockey said gelding never travelled and pulled up (op 9-2 tchd 5-1)

2049 HEART OF THE SOUTH RACING H'CAP HURDLE (10 hdls) 2m 4f

3:30 (3:31) (Class 4) (0-110,110) 4-Y-0+ **£2,341** (£687; £343; £171)

Form RPR

-2 **1** **Silver Accord (IRE)**[166] 328 7-11-7 **105**.......................... LeightonAspell 114
(Oliver Sherwood) *hld up in tch: effrt 7th: led and gng wl after 3 out: hld on wl whn chal last: drvn out* **11/2**[2]

5-05 **2** *1 ¾* **Lepido (ITY)**[26] 1677 6-11-2 **100**.......................... JamieMoore 107
(Gary Moore) *towards rr: hdwy 6th: wnt 2nd 2 out: jnd wnr last: hrd rdn: nt qckn fnl 100yds* **7/1**

P-65 **3** *19* **Porters War (IRE)**[93] 1108 8-11-10 **108**.......................... NickScholfield 98
(Peter Hiatt) *led tl 3rd: w ldrs tl wknd 2 out* **12/1**

3-02 **4** *1 ½* **Crystal Prince**[22] 1735 6-10-7 **91**..........................(tp) FelixDeGiles 82
(Charlie Longsdon) *towards rr: effrt and mstke 3 out: fair 4th and styng on whn blnd 2 out: no imp* **6/1**[3]

PP6- **5** *18* **Ballinderry Park (FR)**[200] 5147 7-11-12 **110**..........................(t) NoelFehily 82
(Charlie Mann) *bhd: blnd 5th: sme hdwy on wd outside appr 3 out: sn wknd* **8/1**

453- **6** *3 ½* **Ready Or Not (IRE)**[203] 5105 7-10-11 **102**.......................... NathanSweeney(7) 71
(Bob Buckler) *in tch: jnd ldr 5th: led appr 7th tl after 3 out: sn wknd* **15/2**

140- **7** *13* **Home**[45] 2518 5-10-9 **100**.......................... MissCLWills(7) 58
(Brendan Powell) *w ldrs: led 3rd: mstke 6th: hdd appr next: hrd rdn and wknd 3 out* **17/2**

42-P **8** *6* **Oncle Kid (FR)**[164] 371 8-10-9 **98**.......................... JimmyDerham(5) 50
(Paul Henderson) *prom tl wknd 6th* **16/1**

-6P3 **9** *8* **Galantos (GER)**[26] 1679 9-10-0 **84**.......................... WillKennedy 29
(Helen Nelmes) *in rr of midfield tl rdn and wknd after 6th* **9/2**[1]

06-0 **10** *117* **Sam Whiskey (GER)**[16] 1816 7-10-8 **99**.......................... MissHGrissell(7) —
(Diana Grissell) *towards rr: nt fluent and dropped to last at 3rd: n.d after: wl bhd fr 7th* **40/1**

4U-0 **P** **Princely Hero (IRE)**[26] 1677 6-11-3 **108**.......................... MrTJCannon(7) —
(Chris Gordon) *prom: drvn along and lost pl 6th: bhd whn p.u bef next* **20/1**

5m 7.10s (7.70) **Going Correction** +0.525s/f (Soft) **11** Ran SP% **114.5**

Speed ratings (Par 105): **105,104,96,96,88 87,82,79,76,— —**

Tote Swingers: 1&2 £7.10, 1&3 £6.90, 2&3 £9.90 CSF £42.95 CT £441.94 TOTE £5.20: £1.80, £2.40, £2.80; EX 21.80.

Owner Mrs Sue Griffiths **Bred** Cyril O'Hara **Trained** Upper Lambourn, Berks

■ Stewards' Enquiry : Jamie Moore one-day ban: used whip with excessive frequency (Nov 11)

FOCUS

The front two drew clear in what was a modest handicap hurdle. The winner produced a step up and the second is rated to last season's best form.

NOTEBOOK

Silver Accord(IRE), off since finishing runner-up off 3lb lower 166 days earlier, came there travelling well and, although having to fight hard for it in the end, always looked to be coming out best on the run-in. This was his first win and there may be more to come from this future chaser upped to 3m. (op 5-1 tchd 6-1)

Lepido(ITY) has slipped back to a good mark and he emerged as a major threat in the straight, but having joined the winner, he was unable to stay on as well on the rise to the line. (op 15-2 tchd 8-1)

Porters War(IRE), formerly with Alan King, showed up well for a long way until tiring in the straight. He should come on for this first outing in three months. (op 8-1)

Crystal Prince kept on again for fourth, but was never close enough to challenge. (op 11-2 tchd 7-1)

Ballinderry Park(FR), wearing a first-time tongue-tie, could make no impression in the straight, having made some ground down the back, but may have needed it and deserves another chance. (op 9-1)

Ready Or Not(IRE) got tired on this first run in 203 days. (op 8-1)

Galantos(GER) never made a move and failed to build on his recent course third. Official explanation: jockey said gelding moved poorly (op 6-1)

Princely Hero(IRE) Official explanation: jockey said gelding lost its action

2050 ESPORTA HEALTH CLUB RUSTINGTON 01903 859777 H'CAP CHASE (19 fncs) 3m 2f 110y

4:00 (4:00) (Class 5) (0-95,95) 4-Y-0+ **£1,865** (£579; £311)

Form RPR

/531 **1** **Panzer (GER)**[21] 1745 9-11-2 **92**.......................... HenryBrooke(7) 105+
(Donald McCain) *bhd early: hdwy 8th: chsd ldr 3 out: drvn to ld last: styd on wl* **5/2**[2]

P622 **2** *12* **You Can Of Course (IRE)**[26] 1679 7-10-7 **76**.......................... DougieCostello 75
(Neil Mulholland) *chsd tearaway ldr: led 13th: sn rdn: hdd and no ex last* **9/4**[1]

451- **3** *30* **Quartz Du Montceau (FR)**[207] 5010 6-11-12 **95**.......................... FelixDeGiles 81+
(Anna Newton-Smith) *hld up in 3rd and 4th: wnt 2nd and gng wl at 14th: wknd 3 out* **9/2**[3]

4236 **P** **Monsieur Georges (FR)**[22] 1733 10-10-0 **69** oh3.......................... WillKennedy —
(F Jordan) *sn outpcd and bhd: 4th and no ch whn blnd and p.u 15th* **13/2**

P6PP **P** **Hazelbury**[14] 1843 9-9-10 **70** oh20 ow1..........................(p) KeiranBurke(5) —
(Nigel Hawke) *led at str early pce: hdd & wknd 13th: bhd whn p.u bef next* **16/1**

P/P- **P** **Giggles O'Shea (IRE)**[221] 4759 8-9-9 **69**.......................... JayPemberton(5) —
(Richard Rowe) *sn wl bhd: p.u bef 5th* **17/2**

7m 23.7s (22.60) **Going Correction** +0.525s/f (Soft) **6** Ran SP% **107.3**

Speed ratings (Par 103): **87,83,74,—,— —**

Tote Swingers: 1&2 £1.10, 1&3 £2.70, 2&3 £1.90 CSF £8.06 TOTE £2.70: £1.20, £1.40; EX 7.70.

Owner D McCain Jnr **Bred** Baron N C J Rothschild **Trained** Cholmondeley, Cheshire

FOCUS

A low-grade staying handicap chase. Complete outsider Hazelbury soon had them strung out. A personal best from the winner and the form could be rated 7lb higher through the second.

NOTEBOOK

Panzer(GER), winner of a Worcester selling hurdle latest, had finished well held in one previous try over fences, but he jumped well in the main and, having taken a narrow lead at the last, he powered clear for a ready success. (op 9-4)

You Can Of Course(IRE) pressed on at a fair way out and kept finding until headed at the last, at which point he suddenly became very tired. (op 2-1 tchd 15-8)

Quartz Du Montceau(FR) travelled well for a long way on this seasonal return, but he ultimately became quite tired and was comfortably held. He'll come on for it, though, and remains capable of better at this sort of level. (op 4-1)

Monsieur Georges(FR) was struggling a long way out and was eventually pulled up. (op 12-1)

Giggles O'Shea(IRE), backed beforehand, never went a yard. (op 12-1)

2051 888SPORT MOBILE BETTING NOVICES' HURDLE (13 hdls) 3m 3f

4:30 (4:30) (Class 4) 4-Y-0+ **£2,602** (£764; £382; £190)

Form RPR

54 **1** **Mtpockets (IRE)**[9] 1907 5-10-5 0.......................... DougieCostello 109+
(Neil Mulholland) *trckd ldrs: led 8th to 10th: led after 3 out: rdn clr next: styd on wl* **7/2**[2]

U1P- **2** *18* **Mic Aubin (FR)**[188] 5369 7-10-12 104.......................... WarrenMarston 100
(Giles Smyly) *led tl after 1st: led 2nd tl 8th: outpcd 3 out: wnt wl-btn 2nd run-in* **13/2**

2/23 **3** *1 ½* **Rith Bob (IRE)**[134] 763 7-10-5 109.......................... RhysFlint 93
(David Rees) *trckd ldrs on inner: led 10th tl after 3 out: btn whn hit next: wknd and lost 2nd run-in* **4/5**[1]

4 *dist* **Charming Lad (IRE)**[228] 5-10-12 0..........................(t) NoelFehily 82+
(Charlie Mann) *in tch on outer: jnd ldrs and hit 6th: gng wl tl rdn and wknd 3 out* **11/2**[3]

00-0 **5** *dist* **Hot Chipotle**[16] 1812 4-9-11 0.......................... MrTJCannon(7) 28
(Paul Henderson) *in tch: rdn along fr 7th: wknd appr 3 out* **100/1**

0/35 **6** *3* **Mister Virginian (IRE)**[8] 1916 11-10-9 0..........................(p) CharlieStudd(3) 33
(Chris Gordon) *nt fluent: led after 1st tl stmbld on landing next: rdn 4th: sn bhd: t.o fr 8th* **33/1**

5P5- **7** *46* **Island News**[189] 5326 6-10-7 0.......................... MarcGoldstein(5) —
(Michael Madgwick) *t.k.h: w ldrs tl wknd 9th: bhd whn mstke 3 out* **22/1**

00 **8** *88* **Seaview Lad (IRE)**[164] 370 7-10-5 0.......................... NathanSweeney(7) —
(Bob Buckler) *a bhd: reminder after 5th: sn struggling: t.o fr 8th* **66/1**

7m 9.60s (16.80) **Going Correction** +0.525s/f (Soft)

WFA 4 from 5yo+ 11lb **8** Ran SP% **116.3**

Speed ratings (Par 105): **96,90,90,79,69 68,54,28**

Tote Swingers: 1&2 £3.90, 1&3 £1.90, 2&3 £2.10 CSF £25.02 TOTE £4.50: £1.10, £2.20, £1.10; EX 23.50.

Owner Neil Mulholland Racing Club **Bred** Joseph Smiddy **Trained** Burlescombe, Devon

FOCUS

A modest novices' hurdle. The winner produced a big step forward over this longer trip.

NOTEBOOK

Mtpockets(IRE) asserted turning in and stayed on well to go clear. A former point winner, she's improving with each start over hurdles and looks capable of winning again. (tchd 10-3)

Mic Aubin(FR) was a hunter chase winner last season. He plugged on again for second, although it proved very hard work. (op 6-1)

Rith Bob(IRE) had shown enough to suggest she would take the beating, but she started to look in trouble leaving the back and finished very tired, having been left behind by the winner. (op 10-11 tchd Evens, 11-10 in places)

Charming Lad(IRE) travelled well before tiring and should improve. His yard has yet to hit top form. (tchd 6-1)

Mister Virginian(IRE) Official explanation: jockey said gelding never travelled

2052 DIGIBET.COM "JUNIOR" STANDARD OPEN NATIONAL HUNT FLAT RACE 1m 6f

5:00 (5:01) (Class 6) 3-Y-O **£1,370** (£399; £199) **Stalls** Far side

Form RPR

1 **Cinders And Ashes** 3-10-9 0.......................... AdrianLane(3) 99
(Donald McCain) *hld up in tch: led 2f out: hrd rdn over 1f out: hld on wl* **5/1**[3]

2 *½* **Zahirah Moon** 3-10-5 0.......................... MattieBatchelor 91
(Lady Herries) *t.k.h: in tch on outer: wnt prom 9f out: led 5f out tl 2f out: kpt on wl to regain 2nd fnl 50yds* **7/2**[2]

3 *½* **Go Set Go** 3-10-12 0.......................... MarkBradburne 98
(James Eustace) *towards rr: hdwy 3f out: chsd wnr over 1f out tl fnl 50yds: kpt on* **15/2**

4 *4 ½* **Hightown (IRE)** 3-10-5 0.......................... MrJMQuinlan(7) 92
(Don Cantillon) *hld up towards rr: last at 1/2-way: hdwy 4f out: one pce appr fnl f* **11/4**[1]

5 *2* **Painted Tail (IRE)** 3-10-5 0.......................... TomO'Brien 83
(James Frost) *mid-div: effrt on outer 3f out: wnt 2nd 2f out tl wknd over 1f out* **13/2**

6 *2 ¾* **Super Ken (IRE)** 3-10-12 0.......................... ColinBolger 87
(Chris Gordon) *led tl 5f out: wknd over 2f out* **20/1**

7 *20* **Brambley** 3-10-0 0.......................... JimmyDerham(5) 56
(Seamus Mullins) *t.k.h: chsd ldrs tl rdn and wknd 5f out* **9/1**

8 *1 ¼* **Dance Til Midnight** 3-10-5 0.......................... LeightonAspell 54
(Richard Rowe) *chsd ldrs tl wknd 3f out* **20/1**

9 *18* **Champagne Mary** 3-10-0 0.......................... JayPemberton(5) 33
(Raymond York) *chsd ldr: rdn and wknd over 5f out: sn bhd* **66/1**

10 *28* **Mr Grumpalot** 3-10-7 0.......................... TomO'Connor(5) —
(Bill Turner) *in rr: hdwy to chse ldrs on inner 9f out: wknd 4f out* **33/1**

3m 42.2s (11.10) **10** Ran SP% **114.6**

Tote Swingers: 1&2 £4.20, 1&3 £8.30, 2&3 £8.90 CSF £21.43 TOTE £3.30: £1.10, £2.40, £3.10; EX 15.00 Place 6: £54.14 Place 5: £45.17..

Owner D McCain **Bred** Juddmonte Farms Ltd **Trained** Cholmondeley, Cheshire

■ Stewards' Enquiry : Jay Pemberton one-day ban: used whip when out of contention (Nov 11)
Tom O'Connor one-day ban: used whip when out of contention (Nov 11)

FOCUS

A competitive junior bumper. There was no previous form to go on.

NOTEBOOK

Cinders And Ashes, whose dam is related to the likes of Brian Boru and Kitty O'Shea, cost only £4,500 as a 2-y-o, but looks to have a definite future on this evidence, with further likely to suit. (tchd 6-1)

Zahirah Moon, a half-sister to several winners, including a few decent ones, stayed on well for second and should improve. (tchd 4-1)

Go Set Go, half-brother to a claiming winner, stayed on from the rear to just miss second and will stay further over hurdles. (op 7-1 tchd 13-2)

Hightown(IRE) was solid enough in the market, but he was given a fair bit to do and never really got close enough to challenge seriously. (tchd 5-2)

T/Plt: £68.80 to a £1 stake. Pool:£61,674.65 - 654.17 winning tickets T/Qpdt: £18.50 to a £1 stake. Pool:£4,563.75 - 182.50 winning tickets LM

[1970]STRATFORD (L-H)

Thursday, October 28

OFFICIAL GOING: Good to soft (good in places on hurdle course, soft in places on chase course; hdl 8.6, chs 8.2)

Chase rail moved out increasing distances by about 50m per circuit.

Wind: fresh against Weather: overcast

2053 MORETON-IN-MARSH H'CAP CHASE (12 fncs) 2m 1f 110y

2:20 (2:20) (Class 4) (0-105,105) 4-Y-0+ **£4,553** (£1,337; £668; £333)

Form RPR

33P4 **1** **War Party**[5] 1971 6-10-13 **99**....(b) MrTWeston(7) 114+
(Dr Richard Newland) *led to 3rd: led again 5th: clr fr 3 out: rdn out* **13/2**[3]

3-02 **2** *5* **Wingull (IRE)**[15] 1823 6-11-0 **93**.... AndrewTinkler 101
(George Baker) *a.p: chsd wnr 9th: styd on same pce appr last* **3/1**[1]

F2 **3** *6* **Turn Up (IRE)**[8] 1924 7-9-12 **84**....(t) MrJMRidley(7) 91+
(Matt Sheppard) *chsd ldr tl led 3rd: hdd 5th: blnd and lost pl 8th: wnt 3rd again flat* **4/1**[2]

331 **4** *2* **Rimini (FR)**[10] 1902 5-11-7 **100**.... PaulMoloney 102
(David Rees) *chsd ldrs: slipped bnd after 6th: rdn 3 out: styd on same pce fr next* **3/1**[1]

6303 **5** *7* **The Brimmer (IRE)**[9] 1909 6-11-12 **105**.... AndrewThornton 102
(Seamus Mullins) *hld up: hdwy 7th: hit 9th: sn wknd* **8/1**

3-PP **6** *9* **Laneguy (FR)**[16] 1813 5-11-2 **95**.... PaddyBrennan 81
(Tom George) *hld up: sme hdwy 9th: sn wknd* **11/1**

13P0 **7** *2* **Kristallo (GER)**[25] 1692 5-11-11 **104**....(v) SamJones 89
(Paul Webber) *prom tl wknd 7th* **14/1**

4m 22.8s (15.70) **Going Correction** +0.55s/f (Soft) **7** Ran SP% **109.4**

Speed ratings (Par 105): **87,84,82,81,78 74,73**

Tote Swingers: 1&2 £9.80, 1&3 £5.30, 2&3 £2.80 CSF £24.71 TOTE £10.90: £4.30, £3.50; EX 30.20.

Owner J A Provan,C E Stedman,Prof D E Newland **Bred** Dayton Investments Ltd **Trained** Claines, Worcs

FOCUS

This was a very ordinary handicap, run at a fair enough gallop and most were found out around the third-last. The form makes sense.

NOTEBOOK

War Party bounced back to form under a positive ride and landed his first success as a chaser. He arrived for this return to fences with a good bit to prove, but the switch to front-running tactics over this trip worked the oracle and his attitude was a lot better as a result. The handicapper's decision to drop him 8lb also proved a big help and he's entitled to improve a little in this sphere, but doesn't appeal as one for a follow-up. (op 7-1 tchd 6-1)

Wingull(IRE), who got warm beforehand, had finished second off this mark on his chasing debut 15 days earlier and again found one too good. He once again left the impression more of a test would suit better over fences. (op 9-2 tchd 11-4)

Turn Up(IRE) was a runner-up off his current mark when attempting to make all eight days earlier. He couldn't dictate here, but was putting it up to the winner prior to going backwards after he hit the eighth fence. Looking at the way he rallied from two out he would've likely been second at least but for that and is worth another chance. (tchd 9-2)

Rimini(FR) came good off this mark over hurdles ten days previously and this triple winning pointer was expected to enjoy the switch to regulation fences. He jumped well enough, but the easier ground looked to blunt him when push came to shove and he finished tired. Perhaps the run came too soon. (op 11-4 tchd 5-2)

The Brimmer(IRE) failed to raise his game as might have been expected on this return to a handicap as he lacked fluency. A stiffer test suits ideally and he should win over fences as he gains more experience. (op 5-1)

2054 STRATFORD-ON-AVON RACECOURSE RACING EXCELLENCE "HANDS AND HEELS" (S) HURDLE (CONDITIONALS') (10 hdls) 2m 3f

2:50 (2:50) (Class 5) 4-7-Y-0 **£1,951** (£573; £286; £143)

Form RPR

1 **Baynes Cross (IRE)**[7] 1948 7-10-12 100....(b) PeterCarberry 100
(Ms Joanna Morgan, Ire) *prom: chsd ldr 3 out: styd on same pce: 15 l down whn lft clr last* **7/2**[3]

006 **2** *8* **Nouailhas**[50] 1506 4-10-9 90.... PeterHatton(3) 92
(Reg Hollinshead) *hld up and bhd: hdwy 6th: wknd appr 2 out: lft 2nd last* **33/1**

F05 **3** *15* **Dark Energy**[9] 1911 6-11-7 110....(t) JakeGreenall(3) 91+
(Michael Scudamore) *hld up and bhd: lft 3rd last: nvr nr to challnge* **9/4**[1]

P060 **4** *39* **Hi Wycombe (IRE)**[4] 1996 6-10-9 90....(v[1]) MrSWDrinkwater(3) 43
(David Bridgwater) *led and sn clr: hdd 7th: wknd after next* **11/1**

2521 **5** *hd* **Tri Nations (UAE)**[50] 1506 5-11-12 113.... EdCookson 57
(Milton Harris) *prom tl wknd after 3 out* **7/1**

P0 **6** *2 ½* **Battle Bridge (IRE)**[9] 1907 5-10-9 0....(p) MrRGHenderson(3) 41
(Nick Mitchell) *chsd ldrs: lost pl 5th: bhd fr next* **100/1**

U043 **7** *1* **Benefit Game (IRE)**[15] 1823 6-11-0 0.... MrRobertHawker(5) 47
(Richard Hawker) *hld up: bhd fr 6th* **22/1**

46-P **8** *5* **Kirkum (IRE)**[80] 847 5-10-12 0....(p) MattCrawley 36
(Diana Weeden) *sn pushed along in rr: bhd fr 6th* **66/1**

/4P- **9** *4 ½* **Highly Elaborate (IRE)**[515] 540 5-10-0 64....(p) MrMTStanley(5) 25
(James Bennett) *hld up: effrt 6th: sn wknd* **150/1**

-0P3 **10** *13* **Nicky Nutjob (GER)**[150] 555 4-11-5 95.... AodhaganConlon 27
(John O'Shea) *hld up: bhd fr 6th* **12/1**

P **Captain Jack Black**[739] 5-10-9 0.... MrJFlook(3) —
(Edward Bevan) *hld up: drvn along 6th: sn wknd: t.o whn p.u bef 2 out* **125/1**

631/ **F** **No To Trident**[24] 2454 5-10-7 101.... ThomasFlint(5) 113+
(John Flint) *chsd ldr 2nd tl led 7th: clr fr 2 out: 15 l ahd whn hung rt and fell last* **3/1**[2]

4m 31.5s **Going Correction** +0.075s/f (Yiel)

WFA 4 from 5yo+ 9lb **12** Ran SP% **117.7**

Speed ratings: **103,99,93,76,76 75,75,73,71,65 —,—**

Tote Swingers: 1&2 £0.00, 1&3 £3.60, 2&3 £31.10 CSF £110.17 TOTE £5.90: £2.00, £6.20, £1.50; EX 181.30.No bid for the winner.

Owner Boher Richdale Syndicate **Bred** Rathbarry Stud **Trained** Ballivor, Co Meath

■ Stewards' Enquiry : Jake Greenall ten-day ban: failed to take all reasonable and permissable measures (Nov 11-20)

FOCUS

A dire affair. The lucky winner is rated in line with his best Irish form and the form was heading for a big hurdles best.

NOTEBOOK

Baynes Cross(IRE), an Irish-trained gelding, came into this 0-14 over hurdles, but he used to be a useful performer on the Flat and had been found a very winnable race for his British debut. He was under heavy pressure and booked for the runner-up spot prior to being left in front at the last, so obviously rates a very lucky winner. (op 3-1 tchd 5-2)

Nouailhas showed much-improved form on this return from a 50-day absence, but certainly doesn't look an imminent winner. (op 40-1)

Dark Energy, who ran up to his mark in a handicap on his previous outing and had gone without success since winning back-to-back races last year, came in for a lot of support. However, his rider gave him far too much to do out the back and, this being a hands and heels race, he was always going to struggle to make up ground sufficiently. He should have finished closer. Official explanation: jockey said, regarding running and riding, that his orders were to settle the gelding in rear, see how the race progressed and creep into the contest, the front runners appeared to get away a little in the back straight when he was making his effort and stayed on past tiring horses; trainer confirmed the waiting tactics were usual for the gelding which is headstrong and doesn't find much off the bridle, however, he felt the rider would have been closer to the main body in the back straight. (op 11-4)

Tri Nations(UAE) posted a tame effort on this easier ground, but was later reported to have had a breathing problem. Official explanation: trainer said gelding had a breathing problem (op 9-2)

No To Trident looked to have the race in the bag when clear coming to the last, but he wandered badly coming to it, jumped it awkwardly, clipped the top and came down. Given a spin on the level 24 days earlier, he was having his first outing over hurdles since winning a novice race of this class for another yard in 2008. He obviously threw it away, but with more patient handling should be well up to making amends so long as he comes out of this okay. (op 5-1 tchd 11-2)

2055 RIVER AVON H'CAP CHASE (FOR THE J. H. ROWE CHALLENGE TROPHY) (20 fncs) 3m 4f

3:20 (3:20) (Class 3) (0-120,116) 4-Y-0+

£6,262 (£1,850; £925; £463; £231; £116)

Form RPR

04-2 **1** **Runshan (IRE)**[11] 1885 10-10-8 **98**.... TomScudamore 113+
(David Bridgwater) *chsd ldr tl led 4th: clr 2 out: easily* **10/3**[1]

-205 **2** *11* **Balladeer (IRE)**[53] 1477 12-11-2 **106**.... AidanColeman 110
(Lawney Hill) *chsd ldrs: mstke 12th: rdn 17th: wnt 2nd bef last: no imp* **16/1**

4424 **3** *5* **Petite Margot**[19] 1769 11-11-8 **115**.... SamTwiston-Davies(3) 113
(Nigel Twiston-Davies) *led to 4th: chsd wnr to 12th: sn drvn along: outpcd fr 3 out* **13/2**

33U- **4** *2 ¼* **Helm (IRE)**[213] 4927 9-10-6 **96**.... RichardJohnson 93
(Richard Rowe) *hld up: hit 12th: hdwy 15th: wknd 2 out* **9/2**[2]

4F2- **5** *7* **Peut Etre Sivola (FR)**[214] 4915 7-11-9 **113**....(tp) JohnnyFarrelly 102
(David Pipe) *prom: chsd wnr 12th tl wknd appr last* **9/1**

-113 **6** *4 ½* **Volcanic Rock (IRE)**[61] 1404 10-11-12 **116**.... MrDerekO'Connor 105
(John Anthony Staunton, Ire) *hld up: bdly hmpd 13th: hdwy 17th: wknd next* **6/1**

2-P5 **P** **Michigan D'Isop (FR)**[19] 1769 10-10-8 **103**.... IanPopham(5) —
(John Ryall) *hld up: hdwy 15th: wknd next: t.o whn p.u bef last* **11/2**[3]

3F46 **F** **Whataboutya (IRE)**[22] 1725 9-11-9 **113**....(p) APMcCoy —
(Jonjo O'Neill) *hld up: fell 13th* **8/1**

7m 13.5s (10.50) **Going Correction** +0.55s/f (Soft) **8** Ran SP% **111.3**

Speed ratings (Par 107): **107,103,102,101,99 98,—,—**

Tote Swingers: 1&2 £10.20, 1&3 £1.20, 2&3 £11.80 CSF £46.65 CT £317.15 TOTE £5.70: £1.50, £3.90, £2.00; EX 63.40.

Owner Terry & Sarah Amos **Bred** White Barn Stud **Trained** Icomb, Gloucs

FOCUS

The general consensus of the riders after the first two races was that the ground was riding more like soft. This marathon event was not a strong race for the grade, but it was full of well-known handicappers and the form should work out. The winner is rated back to his best.

NOTEBOOK

Runshan(IRE) was well backed and went one better than his comeback second at Kempton 11 days earlier with a taking display, putting in some fine leaps along the way. He wasn't certain to see out this longer trip, but loves it out in front and the extra 4f clearly suited. He was able to ease down after the last and, although the handicapper will now make things tougher, his confidence should be high after this first win since 2008. (op 9-2 tchd 5-1 in places)

Balladeer(IRE), returning from a 53-day break, was 4lb lower for this first outing in a handicap chase since 2006. He stayed on to finish a clear second-best, getting the longer trip well enough, and this likeable veteran deserves a change of fortune. (op 18-1 tchd 14-1)

Petite Margot once more went in snatches, but stays all day long and she rates the benchmark here. She remains one to swerve for win-only purposes. (op 6-1)

Helm(IRE) attracted some support on this seasonal return and did his best to get involved on the final circuit, but ultimately his lack of fitness told. He should be spot on next time and ought to be up to winning over fences this term. (op 5-1 tchd 4-1)

Peut Etre Sivola(FR), equipped with first-time cheekpieces, had won on his comeback last season but proved easy to back on this first run since March and it was significant that Tom Scudamore (stable jockey) was aboard the winner. He ought to come on for the run, but currently has to prove he is not held by the handicapper. (op 15-2 tchd 10-1)

Volcanic Rock(IRE), a dour stayer, was a market drifter on this slower surface and hadn't convinced with his fencing out the back prior to being very badly hampered at the 13th. He was pretty much allowed to complete in his own time thereafter. (op 5-1)

Michigan D'Isop(FR) Official explanation: jockey said gelding never travelled

2056 EUROPEAN BREEDERS' FUND "NATIONAL HUNT" NOVICES' HURDLE (QUALIFIER) (8 hdls 1 omitted) 2m 110y

3:50 (3:50) (Class 3) 4-6-Y-0 **£5,069** (£1,497; £748; £374; £187)

Form RPR

13-1 **1** **Owen Glendower (IRE)**[21] 1743 5-11-4 0.... BarryGeraghty 122+
(Nicky Henderson) *chsd ldrs: mstke 2nd: led 2 out: r.o wl* **4/6**[1]

003- **2** *2 ½* **Mister Hyde (IRE)**[218] 4822 5-10-12 0.... APMcCoy 110+
(Jonjo O'Neill) *mid-div: stdy hdwy 6th: r.o wl flat: nt rch wnr* **25/1**

2- **3** *1* **Timesawastin (IRE)**[278] 3622 4-10-12 0.... PaulMoloney 109
(Evan Williams) *led after 2nd: hit 4th: hdd 6th: ev ch whn hit 2 out: one pce flat* **20/1**

4 *1 ½* **San Remo Bello (FR)**[168] 4-11-3 0.... IanPopham(5) 119+
(Paul Nicholls) *led tl after 2nd: led again 6th: hdd and hit 2 out: no ex last* **6/1**[2]

5 *5* **Renard D'Irlande (FR)**[242] 5-10-12 0.... AidanColeman 103+
(Venetia Williams) *prom: rdn appr 2 out: wknd flat* **7/1**[3]

0-53 **6** *8* **What An Oscar (IRE)**[19] 1765 5-10-12 0.... PaddyBrennan 96
(Nigel Twiston-Davies) *prom: j. slowly 1st: wknd after 6th* **10/1**

6-2F **7** *3 ¼* **Cityar (FR)**[147] 591 6-10-5 0.... CharlieWallis(7) 91
(John O'Shea) *hld up: n.d* **100/1**

0 **8** *4 ½* **Smoking (FR)**[137] 739 4-10-12 0.... SamJones 86
(Sean Curran) *hld up: racd keenly: nvr on terms* **125/1**

041- **9** *6* **Madame Jasmine**[189] 5332 5-10-5 0.... DarylJacob 73
(Suzy Smith) *hld up: sme hdwy after 6th: sn wknd* **40/1**

06-0 **10** *9* **Kayfton Pete**[19] 1768 4-10-5 0 PeterHatton(7) 71
(Reg Hollinshead) *hld up: hdwy 5th: wknd appr 2 out* **150/1**

6- **11** *1 1/4* **Beau Colonel (FR)**[202] 5122 4-10-12 0 HaddenFrost 70
(Henrietta Knight) *trckd ldrs tl wknd appr 2 out* **50/1**

06- **12** *25* **Sebennytos**[239] 4391 5-10-5 0 MrTGarner(7) 45
(Warren Greatrex) *hld up: a in rr* **66/1**

4-4 **13** *2* **Benarchat (FR)**[11] 1887 5-10-12 0 HarrySkelton 43
(Paul Nicholls) *hld up: a in rr* **16/1**

0 **14** *1 1/2* **Bemused (IRE)**[19] 1773 5-10-12 0 AndrewThornton 42
(Simon Earle) *hld up: drvn along 5th: bhd fr next* **200/1**

00-0 **15** *31* **Contentwithmyluck (IRE)**[19] 1773 4-10-7 0 LeeEdwards(5) 11
(Tom Gretton) *hld up: a in rr: bhd fr 6th* **200/1**

3m 58.2s (2.20) **Going Correction** +0.075s/f (Yiel)
WFA 4 from 5yo+ 9lb **15** Ran SP% **119.7**
Speed ratings: **97,95,95,94,92 88,87,84,82,77 77,65,64,63,49**
Tote Swingers: 1&2 £4.00, 1&3 £7.20, 2&3 £18.40 CSF £25.77 TOTE £1.40: £1.10, £4.40, £3.00; EX 25.50.

Owner The Ten From Seven **Bred** Kenilworth House Stud **Trained** Upper Lambourn, Berks

FOCUS
An interesting novice hurdle for the track, which should produce winners. It was run at an average gallop and the first five all look capable of rating higher as the season develops. The cosy winner is rated in line with his recent win.

NOTEBOOK
Owen Glendower(IRE) proved all the rage under his penalty and duly followed up his Worcester success 21 days earlier with a ready effort. He was asked to win the race off the home turn and was just about on top prior to his two main rivals at the time hitting the penultimate flight. This likeable 5-y-o is now 2-2 since going hurdling and again shaped as though he will relish a stiffer test as he matures. A step up in class now beckons, but he is fully entitled to take his chance in something more valuable. (op 4-5)

Mister Hyde(IRE) ◆ didn't show that much in three outings over hurdles last term and there wasn't any obvious confidence behind him on this seasonal debut despite Tony McCoy taking over the reins. He got badly outpaced three out, but motored once straightening for home and this was a promising display. He needs a stiffer test and should soon be winning. Official explanation: jockey said, regarding running and riding, that his orders were to get the gelding to run as well as possible and most of all to get it to the finish, he made an effort at the end of the back straight but felt that the front runners were not coming back, having picked it up at the second last, it responded and finished well past tiring horses; trainer confirmed, adding that it has been very disappointing in its previous runs and is very flighty at home. (op 20-1)

Timesawastin(IRE) ◆ found only subsequent Grade 1 winner Hidden Universe too good on his debut in a Leopardstown bumper on heavy ground in January. He proved easy to back on this British/hurdling debut for new connections, but turned in a pleasing display from the front and is another that should really enjoy racing on a stiffer track. (op 12-1)

San Remo Bello(FR), another 4-y-o, was snapped up by his leading connections after winning on his hurdling debut over 2m2f in France in May. He was another that was easy to back conceding weight all round, but he only tired out of the places late on and can build on this when reverting to more of a test. (op 13-2 tchd 15-2)

Renard D'Irlande(FR) is out of a dam who is distantly related to My Way De Solzen and has already produced the fair mare O'Hana, who won a bumper and two hurdles in Ireland for Willie Mullins. This 5-y-o won both his bumpers in France prior to joining his new connections and there was a plenty of promise in this initial outing as a hurdler. He is yet another that will be better off over further in due course and can soon find an opening. (op 13-2 tchd 6-1 and 8-1)

2057 SHOTTERY BEGINNERS' CHASE (17 fncs) 2m 7f
4:20 (4:20) (Class 4) 4-Y-O+ **£3,903** (£1,146; £573; £286)

Form				RPR
11P-	**1**		**Tell Massini (IRE)**[223] 4712 6-11-4 0 PaddyBrennan (Tom George) *chsd ldr tl led 5th: shkn up flat: comf* **8/11**[1]	135+
1PF-	**2**	*3 1/4*	**Fredo (IRE)**[196] 5197 6-11-4 0 TomScudamore (Ian Williams) *hld up: hdwy after 11th: styd on to go 2nd nr fin: no ch w wnr* **8/1**	130+
0-22	**3**	*1/2*	**Triggerman**[21] 1739 8-11-4 0 RichardJohnson (Philip Hobbs) *hld up: hdwy 6th: chsd wnr next to 3 out: rdn to go 2nd again bef last: lost 2nd nr fin* **11/2**[3]	127
1-04	**4**	*14*	**Captive Audience (IRE)**[12] 1865 7-11-4 0 APMcCoy (Rebecca Curtis) *led to 5th: remained handy: chsd wnr 3 out tl rdn and wknd appr last* **7/2**[2]	119+
P40	**5**	*dist*	**No Reception (IRE)**[22] 1725 9-10-11 104 MissLBrooke(7) (Lady Susan Brooke) *chsd ldrs tl wknd after 13th* **100/1**	73
42-2	**6**	*8*	**Picture In The Sky (IRE)**[172] 234 9-11-1 119 SamTwiston-Davies(3) (Susan Nock) *chsd ldrs: lost pl 5th: hdwy 8th: wknd 12th* **33/1**	65
P-U0	**7**	*1 1/2*	**Factotum**[137] 738 6-11-1 0 RichieMcLernon(3) (Jonjo O'Neill) *hld up: a in rr: bhd fr 13th* **66/1**	64

5m 51.4s (9.80) **Going Correction** +0.55s/f (Soft) **7** Ran SP% **112.0**
Speed ratings (Par 105): **104,102,102,97,83 81,80**
Tote Swingers: 1&2 £4.40, 1&3 £1.70, 2&3 £5.40 CSF £7.08 TOTE £2.10: £2.20, £4.60; EX 6.30.

Owner Mr & Mrs R Cornock **Bred** Colm Griffin **Trained** Slad, Gloucs

FOCUS
There were some useful performers in this beginners' chase, but all eyes were on Tell Massini. He is rated 151 over hurdles and should match that over fences.

NOTEBOOK
Tell Massini(IRE), a smart staying novice hurdler last season, made a winning chase debut. This was his first outing since losing his unbeaten record when pulling up in the Albert Bartlett at the Cheltenham Festival in March, and this former point winner has always been regarded as more of a chasing prospect by connections. He was accompanied by a pony in the preliminaries, something his trainer intends to stick with this term, and did prove somewhat reluctant to go out onto the course, which suggests he has a few quirks. Having set out to make all he was deliberate at the first and took time to get into a clear lead. His jumping got better as the race progressed, though, and it was clear turning for home he had his rivals in trouble. He didn't extend as might have been expected thereafter and was only workmanlike in the end, but this course wouldn't have been ideal for him. He is probably the sort to show more in a better races, should learn plenty for the experience and could now head for the Grade 2 novice Chase over 3m at Newbury's Hennessy meeting late next month. This display was enough for most bookmakers to cut him for the RSA Chase next March, with 10/1 being the general price on offer. (op 4-6 tchd 4-5)

Fredo(IRE), rated 130 over hurdles, had failed to complete on his final two outings last term and he turned in an encouraging display on this seasonal/chasing debut. He found this track too sharp and was doing his best work at the finish so should be up to going one better when reverting to a stiffer test. (op 12-1 tchd 7-1)

Triggerman finished runner-up on both his previous outings over fences and he rates the benchmark here. He isn't the biggest for this game, but should gain a deserved success before long. (op 6-1 tchd 9-2)

Captive Audience(IRE) was well backed on his chasing debut at Cheltenham 12 days earlier over a trip short of his best and in good company, and was expected to be happier back over this longer trip. He refused to settle, though, and still looked in need of the experience. He was later reported to have hung throughout. Official explanation: jockey said gelding hung badly (op 4-1 tchd 9-2 in places)

2058 STRATFORD ANNUAL MEMBERS' MAIDEN HURDLE (DIV I) (12 hdls) 2m 6f 110y
4:50 (4:50) (Class 4) 4-Y-O+ **£2,927** (£859; £429; £214)

Form				RPR
06-U	**1**		**Educated Evans (IRE)**[35] 1594 5-10-11 0 SamTwiston-Davies(3) (Nigel Twiston-Davies) *hld up: hdwy 8th: led 3 out: rdn out* **66/1**	110+
20-	**2**	*6*	**Murrell (IRE)**[230] 4575 5-11-0 0 HarrySkelton (Paul Nicholls) *hld up in tch: rdn appr 2 out: no ex flat* **12/1**	103
/3-P	**3**	*4*	**Matako (FR)**[9] 1907 7-10-9 0 IanPopham(5) (Caroline Keevil) *hld up: hdwy 9th: mstke last: wknd flat* **50/1**	101+
	4	*11*	**If I Had Him (IRE)**[12] 3833 6-11-0 114 AndrewTinkler (George Baker) *chsd ldrs: led 8th to 3 out: wknd next* **3/1**[2]	91
360-	**5**	*1/2*	**Island Jim (IRE)**[278] 3603 6-11-0 0 TomScudamore (Charlie Longsdon) *chsd ldrs: led 4th to 8th: wknd after 3 out* **10/1**	89
	6	*1/2*	**Rockabilly (FR)**[172] 5-11-0 0 PaddyBrennan (Nigel Twiston-Davies) *prom: drvn along 7th: wknd 9th* **9/2**[3]	88
00-P	**7**	*8*	**Our Little Dreamer (IRE)**[172] 223 6-11-0 0 DominicElsworth (Jeremy Scott) *led to 3rd: remainded handy tl wknd after 3 out* **10/1**	81
/P-3	**8**	*7*	**Ballyoliver**[172] 225 6-11-0 0 AidanColeman (Venetia Williams) *prom tl wknd 3 out* **9/2**[3]	75
	9	*25*	**Whispering Jack**[193] 5-10-11 0 PeterToole(3) (Charlie Mann) *hld up: hdwy 8th: wknd after 3 out* **25/1**	52
500-	**10**	*2*	**Everdon Brook (IRE)**[192] 5283 5-11-0 0 DarylJacob (Ben Case) *hld up: hdwy 9th: wknd after 3 out* **100/1**	50
00	**P**		**Inishrush (IRE)**[9] 1907 9-10-7 0 MrRHawkins(7) (Adrian Chamberlain) *chsd ldrs: wknd bef 8th: t.o whn p.u bef next* **250/1**	—
2	**P**		**Blue Signal (IRE)**[22] 1729 5-11-0 0 APMcCoy (Tom George) *chsd ldr: led 3rd to 4th: mstke and lost pl 7th: t.o whn p.u bef 9th* **5/2**[1]	—
04-	**P**		**Fidelor (FR)**[207] 5019 4-10-13 0 RichardJohnson (Henry Daly) *a in rr: t.o whn p.u bef last* **33/1**	—

5m 29.4s (1.30) **Going Correction** +0.075s/f (Yiel)
WFA 4 from 5yo+ 10lb **13** Ran SP% **119.3**
Speed ratings (Par 105): **100,97,96,92,92 92,89,87,78,77 —,—,—**
Tote Swingers: 1&2 £29.20, 1&3 £36.80 CSF £701.20 TOTE £88.40: £13.20, £4.90, £14.90; EX 831.50.

Owner Mrs Caroline Beresford-Wylie **Bred** Donie O'Brien **Trained** Naunton, Gloucs

FOCUS
This novice event was a moderate heat, but the faster of the two divisions. Not an easy race to put a figure on, but the winner showed considerable improvement on his bumper form.

NOTEBOOK
Educated Evans(IRE), Nigel Twiston-Davies's second-string, had shown little in four previous outings and unseated on his hurdling debut last month, but is clearly an improver. The longer trip made all the difference to him and his next outing, likely to be under a penalty in this division, should tell us more as to his true potential. (op 40-1)

Murrell(IRE) was a beaten favourite in his two bumpers last season, but was very easy to back on this hurdling debut and return to action. He came under pressure around three out and wants an even stiffer test in this sphere, but will need to improve a deal to win one of these. (op 9-1)

Matako(FR), better known as a hunter chaser, was done with from the home turn and looked slow. It was good to see him complete this time, though, and he will look more interesting in a handicap.

If I Had Him(IRE), a dual AW winner back in May, was popular on this first run over hurdles for the yard. He got a positive ride, but was well beat prior to hitting the last and looks to want dropping back in trip. (op 10-3 tchd 11-4)

Rockabilly(FR), the winner's stablemate, failed to score in three attempts between the flags, but was unlucky not to collect in the last of them and got well backed for this hurdling debut for his new yard. He was laboured, however, and may need a sounder surface. (op 7-2)

Ballyoliver attracted support on this first run for Venetia Williams, but he was beaten before his jumping got sloppy and the outing looked much needed. (op 8-1)

Inishrush(IRE) Official explanation: jockey said gelding lost its action (op 3-1 tchd 10-3)

Blue Signal(IRE) looked to have been found a good opening for his hurdling debut, but he was never going prior to being pulled up. Official explanation: jockey said gelding never travelled (op 3-1 tchd 10-3)

2059 STRATFORD ANNUAL MEMBERS' MAIDEN HURDLE (DIV II) (12 hdls) 2m 6f 110y
5:25 (5:25) (Class 4) 4-Y-O+ **£2,927** (£859; £429; £214)

Form				RPR
120-	**1**		**Made In Time (IRE)**[225] 4676 5-11-0 0 (t) APMcCoy (Rebecca Curtis) *a.p: chsd ldr 8th: led on bit appr 2 out: sn clr: easily* **4/6**[1]	131+
	2	*13*	**Time For Spring (IRE)**[243] 6-11-0 0 TomScudamore (Charlie Longsdon) *led tl after 2nd: led again after 7th: hdd appr 2 out: sn btn* **14/1**	109+
	3	*15*	**Ratify** 6-10-9 0 MrMMO'Connor(5) (Brendan Powell) *hld up: hdwy 8th: nt fluent next: wknd after 3 out* **80/1**	94
1/4-	**4**	*8*	**Shacklesborough (IRE)**[368] 1922 6-11-0 0 HarrySkelton (Paul Nicholls) *hld up: drvn along 9th: nvr on terms* **6/1**[2]	87
564-	**5**	*8*	**Grey Missile**[201] 5137 5-11-0 0 TomSiddall (Jeremy Scott) *hld up in tch: plld hrd: hit 3 out: sn wknd* **16/1**	79
	6	*6*	**Shoudhavenownbettr (IRE)**[187] 6-11-0 0 (t) DavidDennis (Matt Sheppard) *hld up: hdwy after 5th: wknd 9th* **100/1**	74
0	**7**	*37*	**Body Gold (ARG)**[16] 1812 7-11-0 0 PaddyBrennan (Nigel Twiston-Davies) *racd keenly: led after 2nd: j.rt next: mstke 7th: sn hdd: wknd bef 9th* **25/1**	41
	8	*18*	**Brockton Scrumpy** 5-10-11 0 CharlieHuxley(3) (Lisa Williamson) *a in rr: bhd fr 7th* **100/1**	25
1-	**9**	*2 1/2*	**Sizing Santiago (IRE)**[232] 4522 4-10-13 0 RichardJohnson (Philip Hobbs) *chsd ldrs: hit 7th: wknd after next* **7/1**[3]	21
60/	**P**		**Miss Nut Nut**[934] 4923 7-10-4 0 DannyCook(3) (Sophie Leech) *a in rr: bhd whn hit 7th: t.o whn p.u bef last* **100/1**	—

5m 37.1s (9.00) **Going Correction** +0.075s/f (Yiel)
WFA 4 from 5yo+ 10lb **10** Ran SP% **107.4**
Speed ratings (Par 105): **87,82,77,74,71 69,56,50,49,—**
Tote Swingers: 1&2 £3.00, 1&3 £18.70, 2&3 £37.20. Totesuper7: Win: Not won. Place: £148.70. CSF £9.50 TOTE £2.00: £1.10, £3.00, £15.40; EX 9.90 Place 6: £374.29 Place 5: £153.39..

Owner John P McManus **Bred** J And J Lawler **Trained** Newport, Dyfed

■ Glens Boy (12/1) was withdrawn after spreading a plate at the start. Deduct 5p in the £ under R4.

FOCUS
This second division of the staying novice hurdle was much more interesting than the first, but the first pair dominated from four out. The easy winner was value for a lot further and is sure to rate higher.

NOTEBOOK
Made In Time(IRE) was a decent bumper horse last term and he proved far too classy for his rivals on this hurdling debut. It was slightly surprising to see him upped so markedly in distance for his initial outing, but he obviously stays very well and could hardly have won this any easier. Easy ground is what he wants, dropping back in trip should not bother him and he ought to be well up to defying a penalty should connections wish to get more experience into him before going up in class. (op 4-5)
Time For Spring(IRE) cost 25,000gns after a game win in an Irish point, came from an in-form yard and showed up well under a positive ride, but he was firmly put in his place when the winner asserted for home. The market suggested this would be needed and he should come on nicely for the outing.
Ratify, out of a point winner, was never a threat to the first pair yet still posted an encouraging enough debut. He too stays well and ought to improve a bundle for the experience. (op 100-1)
Shacklesborough(IRE) was a very disappointing favourite on his hurdling debut at Wincanton last year and had not been seen since. This comeback didn't offer a great deal of encouragement, but he will look more interesting in a staying handicap, for which he is now eligible. As a former pointer it is also fair to expect him to go chasing before long. (op 5-1 tchd 13-2)
Grey Missile ran very freely on this return over hurdles, but will probably improve a lot for the run and find his level as he gains more experience. (op 20-1)
Sizing Santiago(IRE), a debut bumper winner at Fontwell in March, was given a positive ride on this switch to hurdling but was in trouble a long way out. This softer ground was probably to blame. Official explanation: trainer said gelding lost a shoe (op 9-2)
T/Plt: £277.60 to a £1 stake. Pool:£65,687.09 - 172.70 winning tickets T/Qpdt: £50.20 to a £1 stake. Pool:£5,313.96 - 78.30 winning tickets CR

2060 - 2066a (Foreign Racing) - See Raceform Interactive

1818 UTTOXETER (L-H)

Friday, October 29

OFFICIAL GOING: Heavy (soft in places; chs 5.4 hdl 6.0)
Final flight in back straight omitted in all hurdle races due to ground under repair.
Divided bends with hurdlers on inside.
Wind: Strong, behind Weather: Cloudy

2067 TOTEL SOLUTIONS "NATIONAL HUNT" NOVICES' HURDLE (DIV I) (10 hdls 2 omitted) 2m 4f 110y

1:30 (1:36) (Class 4) 4-Y-0+ **£1,886** (£553; £276; £138)

Form				RPR
1	**1**		**Kilcrea Kim (IRE)**[20] 1765 5-11-5 0 RichardJohnson (Philip Hobbs) *a.p: w ldr 5th: led 6th: nt fluent 7th: pressed by runner-up fr 3 out: styd on wl and plld out more run-in* **5/2**[2]	127+
	2	*1 ½*	**My Boy Paddy (IRE)**[207] 5061 6-10-12 0 PaddyBrennan (Nigel Twiston-Davies) *in tch: w ldr after 7th: str chal after: jinked sltly rt after last: nt qckn and hld towards fin* **1/1**[1]	119+
	3	*7*	**Cornish Ice**[207] 6-10-12 0 HenryOliver (Robin Dickin) *nt fluent: chsd ldrs: outpcd after 3 out: kpt on u.p after but no ch w front pair* **50/1**	112+
120-	**4**	*shd*	**Mic's Delight (IRE)**[202] 5129 6-10-12 0 TomO'Brien (Victor Dartnall) *in tch: outpcd by ldrs after 3 out: kpt on u.p whn chalng for 3rd after: no ch w front pair* **6/1**[3]	111
40-2	**5**	*17*	**Grafite**[20] 1768 5-10-12 0 WarrenMarston (Milton Harris) *hld up in rr: hdwy after 7th: chsd ldng bunch 3 out but no imp: wknd 2 out* **14/1**	96
	6	*27*	**Valley View (IRE)**[236] 4-10-12 0 APMcCoy (Jonjo O'Neill) *hld up: outpcd after 3 out: nvr a danger* **12/1**	67
40	**7**	*27*	**Up And Away (IRE)**[124] 843 5-10-12 0 AndrewThornton (Caroline Bailey) *prom: led 3rd: hdd 6th: rdn and wknd appr 3 out: eased 2 out* **100/1**	40
5	**8**	*15*	**Melua Maid (IRE)**[20] 1783 8-10-5 0 TjadeCollier (Sue Smith) *led: hdd 3rd: reminder appr 4th: bhd bef 6th: t.o fr 7th* **66/1**	18
	P		**Stadium Arcadium (IRE)**[1265] 7-10-2 0 StephenO'Donovan[(10)] (Emma Lavelle) *hld up in rr: nt a fluent: struggling after 5th: lost tch after 7th: p.u bef last* **20/1**	—
450-	**P**		**Roi De Garde (FR)**[188] 5391 4-10-12 0 TomMessenger (Chris Bealby) *midfield: mstke 2nd: struggling whn nt fluent 7th: bhd after: t.o whn p.u bef last* **100/1**	—

5m 7.00s (3.00) **Going Correction** +0.50s/f (Soft)
WFA 4 from 5yo+ 10lb **10** Ran SP% **117.4**
Speed ratings (Par 105): **114,113,110,110,104 93,83,77,—,—**
Tote Swingers: 1&2 £1.10, 1&3 £17.00, 2&3 £14.00 CSF £5.49 TOTE £3.80: £1.60, £1.10, £5.90; EX 4.20.
Owner James and Jean Potter **Bred** Francis O'Brien **Trained** Withycombe, Somerset

FOCUS
This event has been won by useful types in Oscar Park, Here's Johnny and Great Endeavour, and the first two home this year look decent recruits. The pace was only moderate, unsurprising in ground that was described as "very tacky" and "hard work", and the time was over 20 seconds outside the standard, but it was much the faster division. The form is rated through the fifth.

NOTEBOOK
Kilcrea Kim(IRE) won well on his hurdling debut on good ground at Bangor and produced a nice effort to follow up under a penalty. He and the runner-up were locked together over the last three flights, and it was only after the last that he was able to get on top. Things will be harder under a double penalty but he has the right attitude. He will stick to this sort of trip for now but will get 3m when required. (op 13-8 tchd 11-4)
My Boy Paddy(IRE) was successful in a Cork bumper in heavy ground in April on his last start for Denis Ahern and there was plenty of confidence behind him. This winning Irish pointer held every chance over the last three flights, but did not jump the last as well as the winner then jinked to his right shortly afterwards, handing the initiative to his rival. He had been rather keen too and may not be wholly straightforward, but he is not short on ability and should soon get off the mark for his new connections. (op 6-4)
Cornish Ice, bought for £10,000 after winning a maiden point in April, ran a very pleasing race on this rules debut. His jumping lacked fluency, but that should improve in time and he does not lack for stamina. (op 66-1 tchd 40-1)
Mic's Delight(IRE), a bumper winner, could not go with the front pair from the third-last and was just edged out of minor honours. The tongue-tie he wore on his last start in bumpers was missing. (op 8-1)
Grafite was a remote second to subsequent Grade 2 winner Silviniaco Conti on his hurdles debut and was unable to build on that over this longer trip. (op 16-1 tchd 20-1)
Valley View(IRE) was successful in his only start in an Irish point back in March. A chasing type, he was never able to get competitive on this rules debut but should leave this running behind in time. (op 8-1)

2068 MIKE JONES MEMORIAL MARES' MAIDEN HURDLE (9 hdls 1 omitted) 2m

2:00 (2:04) (Class 5) 3-Y-0+ **£1,561** (£458; £229; £114)

Form				RPR
1-	**1**		**L'Accordioniste (IRE)**[223] 4742 5-11-4 0 PaddyBrennan (Nigel Twiston-Davies) *midfield: stdy hdwy fr after 6th: chsd ldr after 3 out: upsides whn hit 2 out: nosed ahd appr last: styd on gamely in duel w runner-up run-in: a doing enough* **9/4**[1]	126+
1-	**2**	*nk*	**Silver Gypsy (IRE)**[207] 5042 5-11-1 0 (t) SeanQuinlan[(3)] (Kim Bailey) *led: hrd pressed fr 2 out: hdd narrowly appr last: styd on and continued to chal strly run-in: jst hld* **9/1**	125
403-	**3**	*19*	**Seren Cwmtudu (IRE)**[186] 20 6-11-4 0 PaulMoloney (Evan Williams) *t.k.h: trckd ldrs: chalng whn nt fluent 3 out: outpcd by front pair whn j.lft 2 out: n.d after* **25/1**	108
	4	*8*	**Lastroseofsummer (IRE)**[48] 4-10-11 0 MattCrawley[(7)] (Rae Guest) *hld up: stdy hdwy after 3 out: hmpd 2 out: kpt on wout troubling ldrs* **16/1**	99
5-5	**5**	*14*	**Bianco Fuji**[167] 332 5-11-4 0 LeightonAspell (Oliver Sherwood) *midfield: pushed along and outpcd after 3 out: no imp whn blnd and hmpd 2 out: n.d after* **11/1**	88+
64	**6**	*7*	**Always Roses**[16] 1825 3-10-1 0 TomMessenger (Chris Bealby) *prom tl pushed along and wknd after 6th* **18/1**	60
	7	*1 ½*	**Pepite Rose (FR)**[136] 3-10-1 0 AidanColeman (Venetia Williams) *trckd ldrs tl wknd after 3 out* **7/2**[3]	59
	8	*2*	**Rumballina**[151] 3-10-1 0 DaveCrosse (Amy Weaver) *hld up: struggling after 6th: sn btn* **150/1**	57
5	**9**	*5*	**Electric City (IRE)**[27] 1674 3-9-8 0 MrJMQuinlan[(7)] (Michael Quinlan) *hld up: n.m.r after 4th: j. slowly 6th: struggling after* **50/1**	52
0	**10**	*4 ½*	**Illysantachristina**[9] 1921 7-11-4 0 ChristianWilliams (Bernard Llewellyn) *hld up: lost pl after 6th: struggling after* **100/1**	64
	11	*4*	**Attainable**[98] 4-11-4 0 RhysFlint (Jim Old) *prom tl rdn and wknd appr 3 out* **100/1**	60
	12	*9*	**Sun Des Mottes (FR)**[354] 4-11-4 0 TimmyMurphy (David Pipe) *racd keenly in midfield: hdwy gng wl after 6th: wknd qckly 3 out* **3/1**[2]	51
0-4R	**P**		**Orpen Bid (IRE)**[72] 858 5-11-4 0 MarkBradburne (Michael Mullineaux) *bhd: u.p after 6th: t.o whn p.u bef 3 out* **150/1**	—
	P		**Catawollow**[53] 3-10-1 0 TjadeCollier (Richard Guest) *hld up: struggling after 6th: t.o whn p.u bef 2 out* **66/1**	—
50-	**U**		**Lady Karabaya**[207] 5042 5-11-4 0 HaddenFrost (Henrietta Knight) *cl up: hit 3 out: outpcd and looking hld in 4th whn blnd and uns rdr 2 out* **33/1**	99

4m 1.60s (6.40) **Going Correction** +0.50s/f (Soft)
WFA 3 from 4yo 17lb 4 from 5yo+ 9lb **15** Ran SP% **121.0**
Speed ratings (Par 103): **104,103,94,90,83 79,79,78,75,73 71,66,—,—,—**
Tote Swingers: 1&2 £4.90, 1&3 £16.90, 2&3 £51.60 CSF £23.34 TOTE £3.10: £1.30, £3.50, £7.60; EX 26.00.
Owner David Maxwell **Bred** J F C Maxwell **Trained** Naunton, Gloucs

FOCUS
A reasonable mares' hurdle, but only the first two, who fought out a good finish, really saw it out in the conditions. The first two are rated up around 5lb on their bumper wins.

NOTEBOOK
L'Accordioniste(IRE) won a bumper here in March from Mic's Delight, who was fourth in the opener on this card. On her hurdles debut, she did well to close the gap to the winner after the third-last flight but made an error at the next. It cost her little momentum and she knuckled down well to get on top. Likely to stick to mares' races, she looks well capable of winning again. (tchd 5-2)
Silver Gypsy(IRE) was trained in Ireland when landing a good-ground Fakenham bumper in April. Given a forcing ride on this hurdles debut, she tried to kick clear at the first in the home straight but the winner was alert to the move. She went down fighting, a long way clear of the rest, and should soon go one better. (op 15-2 tchd 10-1)
Seren Cwmtudu(IRE) was beaten in a fair way into third, but this was still a respectable hurdling debut after six months off. It was the first time she has encountered ground softer than good.
Lastroseofsummer(IRE) came in for a bit of support and showed ability for all that she was beaten a long way in fourth. Better ground should help this modest winning stayer on the Flat. (op 33-1 tchd 14-1)
Bianco Fuji, also fifth in both her bumpers, was well beaten when blundering two out on this hurdles debut but the ground was no good to her. (op 12-1 tchd 14-1)
Always Roses did not improve on her Wetherby effort but did best of the juveniles and is now eligible for handicaps. (op 50-1 tchd 14-1)
Pepite Rose(FR) made the frame in each of her four starts for Guillaume Macaire, but she stopped quickly on this British debut. She had plenty of experience in testing ground in France. (op 9-2)
Sun Des Mottes(FR) was placed in all seven of her 'bumpers' in France. Having raced keenly on this hurdles debut, she moved up stylishly, only to stop very quickly and finish tailed off. She might well be worth another chance on better ground, but still has her stamina to prove. (op 9-4 tchd 2-1 and 7-2)
Lady Karabaya, well behind today's runner-up in a bumper, was running a pleasing race and holding a modest fourth when she blundered away her rider two out.

2069 TOTEL SOLUTIONS "NATIONAL HUNT" NOVICES' HURDLE (DIV II) (10 hdls 2 omitted) 2m 4f 110y

2:35 (2:35) (Class 4) 4-Y-0+ **£1,886** (£553; £276; £138)

Form				RPR
	1		**Stolen Thunder** 5-10-12 0 JackDoyle (Emma Lavelle) *hld up bhd: j.lft 5th: hdwy after 7th: chsd ldrs 3 out: wnt 2nd appr 2 out: sn chalng: led bef last: styd on wl to draw clr run-in* **12/1**	110+
	2	*12*	**Back Bob Back (IRE)**[258] 5-10-12 0 PaddyBrennan (Tom George) *hld up: hdwy whn nt fluent 6th: led appr 3 out: pressed 2 out: hdd bef last: no ex run-in* **3/1**[2]	101+
2	**3**	*22*	**Foynes Island (IRE)**[35] 1603 4-10-12 0 RichardJohnson (Philip Hobbs) *hld up: hdwy 6th: wnt 2nd appr 7th: chalng 3 out: wknd bef 2 out* **13/8**[1]	76
12U/	**4**	*13*	**Paquet Cadeau (FR)**[672] 2974 7-10-12 0 ChristianWilliams (Henry Daly) *led hurdling wl: hdd appr 3 out: sn wknd* **13/2**	63
	5	*19*	**Corrigans Road (IRE)**[202] 5-10-12 0 APMcCoy (Donald McCain) *chsd ldrs: j. slowly 2nd: wknd after 7th: eased whn wl btn bef 2 out* **4/1**[3]	44
0-50	**6**	*2*	**Chaser's War (IRE)**[73] 1275 6-10-5 0 JodieMogford (Nikki Evans) *chsd ldrs: nt fluent 7th: wknd appr 3 out* **125/1**	35
0/	**P**		**Hendaway**[580] 6-10-12 0 TomMessenger (Chris Bealby) *chsd ldr tl appr 7th: sn wknd: t.o whn p.u bef 3 out* **66/1**	—

000- **P** **Master Paddy (IRE)**[274] 3696 6-10-12 0 .... NickScholfield —
(Andy Turnell) *midfield: struggling after 5th: sn bhd: t.o whn p.u bef 7th* **66/1**

0- **P** **Sunday Sharpner (IRE)**[248] 4213 4-10-12 0 .... JimmyMcCarthy —
(Renee Robeson) *midfield: nt fluent 6th: wknd 7th: t.o whn p.u bef 2 out* **33/1**

00 **P** **Orlittlebylittle**[21] 1758 4-10-9 0 .... AdrianLane(3) —
(Donald McCain) *midfield: reminder after 5th: wknd appr 7th: t.o whn p.u bef 3 out* **33/1**

P **P** **Hot Candy**[16] 1821 6-10-5 0 ....(t) PaulMoloney —
(Reg Hollinshead) *hld up in rr: blnd 5th: struggling after: t.o whn p.u bef 7th* **100/1**

5m 13.9s (9.90) **Going Correction** +0.50s/f (Soft) **11** Ran SP% **114.8**
Speed ratings (Par 105): **101,96,88,83,75 75,—,—,—,— —**
Tote Swingers: 1&2 £6.50, 1&3 £4.10, 2&3 £1.90 CSF £47.04 TOTE £14.20: £2.60, £1.70, £1.10; EX 71.50.

Owner Colin Bothway & Roger Hetherington **Bred** Colin Bothway **Trained** Wildhern, Hants

FOCUS
In all likelihood the weaker of the two divisions, and the time was nearly seven seconds slower. The form could be rated higher through the third and fourth.

NOTEBOOK
Stolen Thunder is out of a dam who won a bumper and a hurdle from just three starts and is from the family of Stayers' Hurdle winner Rose Ravine. After looking set to finish out the back for the first half of the race, he began to pick up down the far side. Going after the runner-up down the outside in the straight, he was well on top at the end although the eventual margin of victory perhaps flattered him. This win surprised his trainer, who reported him difficult to get fit, and there should be improvement to come. (op 16-1)

Back Bob Back(IRE) dead-heated for an Irish point with Blue Signal, who was runner-up in a bumper on his British debut. He ran well on this first start under rules, leading early in the straight and coming down the outer for the better ground before giving best from the final flight. He looks a chasing type. (op 4-1)

Foynes Island(IRE) had his chance but, after remaining on the inside in the straight, where the ground was more poached, he had run his race with two to jump. The testing conditions are an obvious excuse. (op 11-8 tchd 15-8)

Paquet Cadeau(FR) won a handicap chase here in November 2008 but had not been seen since unseating his rider on Boxing Day that year. After setting the pace as usual, he was headed before the first in the home straight and immediately beaten. He is just 2lb above his winning chase mark and is entitled to come on considerably for this run. (op 6-1 tchd 5-1)

Corrigans Road(IRE), a former Irish pointer, is a half-brother to Will Be Done and Fiendish Flame, both useful performers for these connections. Although well beaten on this debut under rules he should improve on this in time. (op 7-2)

2070 SEVERN VALLEY CATERING H'CAP HURDLE (10 hdls) 2m

3:10 (3:11) (Class 5) (0-95,94) 4-Y-0+ **£1,561** (£458; £229; £114)

Form RPR

44-2 **1** **Babilu**[16] 1822 5-11-8 **90** ....(p) TomO'Brien 109+
(Dai Burchell) *hld up: tk clsr order after 4th: prom 6th: chalng 3 out: led appr 2 out and looked in command: asserted bef last: styd on wl* **7/2**[1]

0301 **2** *2 1/4* **Lean Burn (USA)**[6] 1976 4-10-6 **77** 7ex .... DannyCook(3) 93
(Barry Leavy) *sn chsd ldrs: led after 6th: hdd appr 2 out: kpt on u.p but hld after* **5/1**[2]

P53 **3** *20* **Bari Bay**[7] 1949 4-10-6 **74** ....(b) TimmyMurphy 70
(Michael Blake) *midfield early: bhd after 4th: hdwy fr 3 out: pluugged on at one pce but no imp on front 2 fr 2 out* **10/1**

P-13 **4** *3/4* **Quam Celerrime**[16] 1822 5-10-8 **76** .... HaddenFrost 71
(Roger Curtis) *chsd ldrs: effrt 3 out: wknd appr 2 out* **7/2**[1]

0-60 **5** *7* **Not A Bob (IRE)**[104] 1021 5-11-6 **91** .... RichieMcLernon(3) 79+
(Jonjo O'Neill) *hld up: sme hdwy after 6th: no imp on ldrs: wknd 3 out* **20/1**

-321 **6** *2 3/4* **Royal Flynn**[40] 1554 8-11-3 **92** ....(tp) HenryBrooke(7) 78
(Kate Walton) *midfield: hdwy 6th: cl up tl rdn and wknd 3 out* **11/2**[3]

5005 **7** *36* **Granakey (IRE)**[7] 1949 7-10-6 **74** .... RichardJohnson 23
(Peter Bowen) *midfield: u.p and bhd after 6th: n.d whn mstke last: t.o* **12/1**

03/0 **8** *10* **She's Little Don**[107] 992 10-10-8 **83** .... MattGriffiths(7) 22
(Stephen Hughes) *in rr: struggling after 5th: nvr on terms: t.o* **50/1**

000- **P** **Kingscourt Lad (IRE)**[346] 2342 12-11-0 **85** ....(t) AdamPogson(3) —
(Charles Pogson) *chsd ldr: led appr 6th: hdd after 6th: sn wknd: t.o whn p.u bef 3 out* **40/1**

30PP **P** **Devilfishpoker Com**[7] 1954 6-10-0 **75** ....(p) BrianToomey(7) —
(Shaun Harris) *led: hdd appr 6th: rdn and wknd after 6th: t.o whn p.u bef 2 out* **33/1**

P **Desert Mirage (IRE)**[29] 1653 6-11-4 **89** ....(t) DonalDevereux(3) —
(P J Goodwin, Ire) *chsd ldrs: wknd 6th: t.o whn p.u bef 2 out* **28/1**

312- **P** **My Les**[256] 4078 4-11-12 **94** .... APMcCoy —
(Jim Best) *midfield: reminders after 5th: in tch after 6th: wknd appr 3 out: t.o whn p.u bef 2 out* **11/2**[3]

4m 1.70s (6.50) **Going Correction** +0.50s/f (Soft) **12** Ran SP% **124.2**
Speed ratings (Par 103): **103,101,91,91,88 86,68,63,—,— —,—**
Tote Swingers: 1&2 £2.90, 1&3 £10.60, 2&3 £18.00 CSF £21.65 CT £167.41 TOTE £5.50: £2.10, £2.70, £3.60; EX 31.60.

Owner Mr & Mrs A J Mutch **Bred** Paul Wyatt Ranby Hall **Trained** Briery Hill, Blaenau Gwent

FOCUS
This moderate handicap was run in a slightly slower time than the earlier maiden hurdle, which was confined to mares. The first two finished a long way ahead of the rest and showed reasonable form for the grade. Both lok progressive.

NOTEBOOK
Babilu was second to the well-handicapped Prince Massini here last month and a 9lb rise was insufficient to stop her going one better. Showing ahead early in the straight, she was switched about in front as her rider looked to keep her on the better ground and won pretty comfortably in the end. Taken to post early again, she found the drop in trip no problem in the stamina-sapping conditions and the cheekpieces were back in place. She is set to go for a mares' race at Hereford next. (op 5-1)

Lean Burn(USA) was effectively only 3lb higher under the penalty he picked up when landing a lady riders' race at Stratford, and was officially 6lb ahead of the handiapper. After taking up the running going well, he was soon headed and unable to cope with the winer, but kept on to finish well clear of the third home. (op 7-1)

Bari Bay, fitted with blinkers again, stayed on from the rear for a well-beaten third. Still a maiden, she was due for a 2lb ease in her rating before this. (op 12-1)

Quam Celerrime won over C&D in heavy ground two starts back and there were excuses next time. He ran creditably here, but was 12lb higher than when winning, which anchored him. (op 4-1)

Not A Bob(IRE) was well held on this handicap debut and first start since July, but not without showing a glimmer of promise. The stewards looked into his running, and noted the vet's explanation that the gelding was sore in the back. Official explanation: jockey said, regarding running and riding, that his orders were to drop the gelding in, do his best and try to get it home as it had run prominent previously and faded closing stages, adding that having run keenly early off a slow pace, it settled at the end of the straight and was happy with the way it travelled until coming down the hill when it came off the bit, jumped deliberately in home straight and plugged on to the finish; vet said gelding was sore in its back. (op 16-1)

Royal Flynn's victory here last month has been boosted by the runner-up and he has winning form on the Flat in heavy ground, but he was well beaten in the end off a 7lb higher mark. (op 6-1)

My Les jumped better than when last in action back in February but was on the retreat before the home turn and eventually pulled up. Tony McCoy reported that she was never travelling. Official explanation: jockey said filly never travelled (op 9-2 tchd 7-1)

2071 PARWICH LEES HOLIDAY COTTAGES BEGINNERS' CHASE (12 fncs) 2m

3:45 (3:45) (Class 4) 4-Y-0+ **£2,856** (£892; £480)

Form RPR

003- **1** **Abey M'Boy**[212] 4963 7-11-2 107 .... LeightonAspell 110+
(Oliver Sherwood) *chsd ldr fr 2nd: led 7th: clr 2 out: eased towards fin* **5/1**[3]

60 **2** *11* **Panama Canal (IRE)**[7] 1951 5-10-13 0 ....(p) AdamPogson(3) 101
(Charles Pogson) *led: hdd 7th: w ldr after 8th: rdn and btn appr 2 out: eased whn n.d fnl 75yds* **14/1**

F0- **3** *28* **Sway (FR)**[227] 4662 4-9-11 0 .... RichieMcLernon(3) 65
(Jonjo O'Neill) *hld up in last pl: nt fluent 4 out: pushed along and nt pick-up whn j.rt 3 out: j.rt whn lost tch 2 out* **8/11**[1]

20-0 **P** **Border Castle**[153] 521 9-11-2 0 .... TimmyMurphy —
(Michael Blake) *chsd ldr to 2nd: j. slowly and dopped to last pl 5th: looked reluctant whn qckly lost tch and p.u bef next* **3/1**[2]

4m 9.70s (14.10) **Going Correction** +0.80s/f (Soft)
WFA 4 from 5yo+ 9lb **4** Ran SP% **106.2**
Speed ratings (Par 105): **96,90,76,—**
CSF £37.89 TOTE £4.90; EX 18.80.

Owner Furrows Ltd **Bred** Furrows Limited **Trained** Upper Lambourn, Berks

FOCUS
An interesting beginners' chase, but the best two of these over hurdles failed to give their running and the form is of dubious value. The winner was a 114 hurdler at best. The time was over 24 seconds outside the standard.

NOTEBOOK
Abey M'Boy won a bumper but failed to score over hurdles despite some decent efforts. He jumped safely enough on this chase debut and came clear of the outsider for a fairly comfortable victory. Things will be tougher for him under a penalty for this rather bloodless success, but he gets further which increases the options open to him. (op 11-2 tchd 9-2)

Panama Canal(IRE) was placed in Irish points but raced too keenly in a couple of hurdles runs for this yard. Fitted with first-time cheekpieces for this chase debut, he jumped soundly in front and stuck to his task once headed down the back. (op 16-1)

Sway(FR) was a very useful hurdler and as a 4-y-o filly was in receipt of a lot of weight on this chase debut. Held up in last place, she jumped adequately, but found nothing from the home turn and finished well beaten. She had shown an aptitude for testing ground in France and this was disappointing. (op 4-6 tchd 8-13 and 5-6 in places)

Border Castle suddenly decided he didn't fancy continuing and pulled himself up in the back straight. He was a one-time smart hurdler but has something to prove now after this first taste of chasing. Timmy Murphy confirmed that his mount had refused to race. Official explanation: jockey said gelding refused to race (tchd 7-2)

2072 LADIES AT THE RACES MARES' H'CAP HURDLE (12 hdls) 2m 6f 110y

4:20 (4:20) (Class 4) (0-115,114) 4-Y-0+ **£2,211** (£649; £324; £162)

Form RPR

03-3 **1** **Malindi Bay**[20] 1768 5-10-8 **99** .... SeanQuinlan(3) 115+
(Kim Bailey) *hld up: hdwy appr 3 out: led bef 2 out: styd on wl to draw clr run-in: eased towards fin* **4/1**[2]

2333 **2** *11* **Saintly Lady (IRE)**[35] 1605 5-10-7 **98** ....(p) DonalDevereux(3) 103+
(Peter Bowen) *hld up: hdwy 7th: led after 3 out: hdd appr 2 out: one pce and no ch w wnr after last* **3/1**[1]

31-5 **3** *12* **Bringewood Belle**[173] 223 7-10-9 **100** .... TommyPhelan(3) 89
(John Needham) *chsd ldrs tl rdn and wknd appr 2 out* **11/2**[3]

5-35 **4** *7* **Be My Light (IRE)**[23] 1724 4-10-2 **94** ....(p) RichieMcLernon(3) 75
(Charlie Longsdon) *chsd ldrs: effrt whn hit 3 out: sn wknd* **4/1**[2]

0362 **5** *10* **Himayna**[26] 1703 6-10-11 **99** .... RichardJohnson 71
(Tim Vaughan) *j.rt most of way: led: hdd after 3 out: sn wknd* **15/2**

P14- **6** *28* **Noun De La Thinte (FR)**[209] 4987 9-11-12 **114** .... AidanColeman 58
(Venetia Williams) *in tch: pushed along after 6th: bhd and toiling bef next: t.o* **8/1**

1F00 **P** **Eliza Doalott (IRE)**[8] 1929 8-11-2 **104** .... LiamTreadwell —
(Mrs M Stirk) *hld up: struggling after 7th: t.o whn p.u bef 2 out* **20/1**

2-0F **P** **Playing With Fire (IRE)**[20] 1766 6-11-5 **107** .... CharliePoste —
(Robin Dickin) *chsd ldr tl rdn appr 3 out: sn wknd: t.o whn p.u bef 2 out* **11/1**

5m 41.0s (10.10) **Going Correction** +0.50s/f (Soft)
WFA 4 from 5yo+ 10lb **8** Ran SP% **116.4**
Speed ratings (Par 105): **102,98,94,91,88 78,—,—**
Tote Swingers: 1&2 £2.00, 1&3 £5.30, 2&3 £3.40 CSF £17.19 CT £66.01 TOTE £5.40: £1.70, £1.30, £2.10; EX 14.10.

Owner Lucky Bin Racing **Bred** R Chugg **Trained** Andoversford, Gloucs

FOCUS
An ordinary handicap hurdle, confined to mares. The runner-up looks a fair guide to the form and the winner produced a big step up.

NOTEBOOK
Malindi Bay was a remote third to the smart Silviniaco Conti first time out and the runner-up, Grafite, was well beaten in the opening race here. Making her handicap debut, she took up the running going well before staying on strongly for pressure over this longer trip. Her bumper win had also come in heavy ground and she is clearly well at home when the mud's flying. (op 7-2)

Saintly Lady(IRE) ran another solid race and has now been placed on her last six starts, but still awaits her first win over hurdles. She stays further and acts on bertter ground, too. (op 9-2)

Bringewood Belle ◆ was well beaten on this return to action but showed enough to suggest she will pay her way in handicaps this term. She will get this trip in better ground. (op 7-1)

Be My Light(IRE), fitted with cheekpieces for the first time, showed up for a long way on this handicap bow before the conditions began to tell. Her stamina for this sort of trip remains unproven. (op 7-2)

Himayna, runner-up in a C&D maiden hurdle in similar ground latest, weakened rapidly on the lengthy run from the third-last to the next. Another handicap debutante, she had jumped out to her right in front. (op 7-1 tchd 8-1)

Noun De La Thinte(FR) was adeptly placed to pick up six races last season, five of them over fences. It was asking a lot of her to shoulder top weight in bad ground on this seasonal return and this run can be written off. (op 7-1 tchd 9-1)

Eliza Doalott(IRE) Official explanation: jockey said mare had a breathing problem (op 14-1)

Playing With Fire(IRE) is a winner in heavy ground but did not get home over this trip. (op 14-1)

2073 ALEC ROBINSON 60TH BIRTHDAY H'CAP CHASE (15 fncs) 2m 4f

4:55 (4:55) (Class 4) (0-110,110) 4-Y-0+ **£2,788** (£823; £411; £205; £102)

Form RPR

P5-3 **1** **Mohi Rahrere (IRE)**[167] 328 7-11-3 **104** DannyCook(3) 117+
(Barry Leavy) *midfield: hmpd 3rd: hdwy to chse ldr 9th: rdn appr 4 out: led 2 out: drvn out after last: hld on wl cl home* **14/1**

5011 **2** ½ **In The Zone (IRE)**[5] 1991 6-11-8 **109** 7ex RichieMcLernon(3) 120+
(Jonjo O'Neill) *hld up: hdwy appr 11th: trckd ldrs 3 out: rdn 2 out: r.o after last: clsng towards fin* **5/2**[1]

-442 **3** 1 ½ **Supreme Plan (IRE)**[145] 651 7-11-9 **110** (t) SeanQuinlan(3) 119
(Kim Bailey) *hld up: hdwy 11th: chsd ldrs 4 out: rdn bef 2 out: styd on same pce fnl 50yds* **9/2**[3]

P-31 **4** 6 **Festival Dreams**[26] 1708 5-10-4 **95** (p) DannyBurton(7) 100
(Joanna Davis) *prom: lft in ld 3rd: rdn and hdd 2 out: mstke last: wknd run-in* **4/1**[2]

P4P- **5** 9 **Cold Harbour**[433] 1286 6-10-6 **90** PaulMoloney 84
(Evan Williams) *prom: outpcd fr 11th: wl btn after 2 out* **8/1**

F06- **6** 13 **Pacco (FR)**[207] 5034 7-11-3 **101** DominicElsworth 84
(Oliver Sherwood) *hld up: hmpd 3rd: pushed along appr 4 out: no imp bef next* **7/1**

4F00 **7** 10 **Predateur (FR)**[10] 1911 7-11-9 **110** (t) TomMolloy(3) 81
(Giles Smyly) *hld up: j. slowly 8th: sme hdwy appr 4 out: btn bef 3 out* **22/1**

604- **U** **Mylord Collonges (FR)**[216] 4896 10-10-13 **100**(p) SamTwiston-Davies(3) —
(Susan Nock) *cl up tl hmpd and uns rdr 3rd* **14/1**

P0-P **P** **Lucciolina**[6] 1965 7-11-9 **107** CharliePoste —
(Robin Dickin) *handy tl lost pl appr 11th: wl bhd bef 4 out: t.o whn p.u bef 2 out* **50/1**

1-31 **F** **High Jack (IRE)**[161] 427 8-11-12 **110** NickScholfield —
(Andy Turnell) *led tl fell 3rd* **10/1**

5m 18.7s (13.20) **Going Correction** +0.80s/f (Soft) **10** Ran SP% **119.1**
Speed ratings (Par 105): **105,104,104,101,98 93,89,—,—,—**
Tote Swingers: 1&2 £17.50, 1&3 £13.00, 2&3 £2.90 CSF £52.21 CT £191.81 TOTE £19.70: £5.00, £2.50, £1.90; EX 82.40.
Owner Mrs S D Ashford **Bred** Thomas Lennon **Trained** Forsbrook, Staffs

FOCUS
An ordinary handicap chase. The form seems sound enough with the winner up 10lb on his hurdles best.

NOTEBOOK
Mohi Rahrere(IRE), off the track since finishing third off this mark over hurdles in May, made a successful chasing debut. Hampered in a third-fence melee which saw two exit the race, his jockey doing well to stay aboard, he came under pressure turning out of the back. He stayed on willingly once striking the front and promises to get a bit further than this. (op 16-1 tchd 20-1)
In The Zone(IRE), bidding for a hat-trick, was 15lb higher than when scoring at Newton Abbot last month. After reaching the leaders' heels he was outpaced three out and appeared safely held, but began to stay on from there and was closing down the winner at the end. A forthcoming rise for his Towcester win will not aid his cause, but he is on the upgrade. (op 11-4 tchd 3-1)
Supreme Plan(IRE) was another staying on to good effect late in the day. This was a pleasing chase debut and he will be suited by a return to further. It would not be a surprise to see the cheekpieces deployed again on him. (op 11-2 tchd 4-1)
Festival Dreams was an easy winner of a weak race over 3m here last month. Now 5lb higher, he ran a bold race from the front but was beginning to fade when he clouted the last. (op 5-1)
Cold Harbour remains a maiden but he is fully entitled to improve for this first run since August 2009. (op 14-1 tchd 16-1)
Pacco(FR) was minus the cheekpieces on this first run since April. (op 11-2)
Predateur(FR) ran a bit better than the bare facts on ground that was no use to him. (op 20-1 tchd 25-1)

2074 DIGIBET.COM STANDARD OPEN NATIONAL HUNT FLAT RACE 2m

5:30 (5:30) (Class 6) 4-6-Y-0 **£1,301** (£382; £191; £95)

Form RPR

2- **1** **Rose Of The Moon (IRE)**[242] 4358 5-11-4 0 WarrenMarston 109
(Milton Harris) *hld up: hdwy 1/2-way: effrt to chal strly fr 2f out: styd on for press ins fnl f: led towards fin: edgd lft fnl stride* **4/1**[2]

2 nk **Koup De Kanon (FR)** 4-11-4 0 JackDoyle 109
(Emma Lavelle) *hld up: hdwy and gng wl 5f out: led over 2f out: sn pressed: rdn whn strly chal ins fnl f: hdd towards fin and sn bmpd* **7/2**[1]

33- **3** 9 **Aviador (GER)**[262] 3951 4-10-11 0 MattCrawley(7) 100
(Lucy Wadham) *trckd ldrs: effrt 3f out: outpcd over 1f out: no ch w front pair and kpt on same pce fnl f* **9/1**

32 **4** ½ **Music In The Air**[55] 1472 6-10-11 0 CharliePoste 92
(Robin Dickin) *led: rdn over 3f out: hdd over 2f out: plugged on at one pce fnl f* **16/1**

5 shd **Elton Fox** 5-11-1 0 (t) TommyPhelan(3) 99
(John Needham) *hld up: pushed along 3f out: styd on fnl 2f: nt rch ldrs* **16/1**

6 9 **Letmespeak (IRE)** 5-10-11 0 MrJHamer(7) 90
(Donald McCain) *prom tl rdn and wknd 3f out* **9/1**

7 ½ **Otter Mist** 5-11-4 0 TomO'Brien 89
(Victor Dartnall) *midfield: rdn and outpcd over 2f out: no imp after* **13/2**[3]

8 4 ½ **A Patchy Dancer (IRE)** 5-11-4 0 HenryOliver 85
(Sue Smith) *trckd ldrs: chalng 3f out: wknd wl over 1f out* **22/1**

9 2 ¾ **Furrows** 5-11-4 0 LeightonAspell 82
(Oliver Sherwood) *hld up in midfield: outpcd fr over 2f out* **8/1**

10 ½ **A M Xpress** 5-11-4 0 TjadeCollier 82
(Sue Smith) *prom tl rdn and wknd 3f out* **10/1**

11 2 ½ **Radmores Oscar** 4-10-11 0 CharlieWallis(7) 79
(John O'Shea) *midfield: lost pl and dropped to rr bef 1/2-way: struggling after* **25/1**

12 18 **Go To The Edge** 4-10-11 0 HarryChalloner(7) 61
(John Bryan Groucott) *hld up: struggling fnl 5f* **40/1**

13 ¾ **North Stack** 4-11-4 0 SamJones 60
(Michael Scudamore) *midfield: struggling 4f out: sn btn* **40/1**

14 4 ½ **Dapple Prince (IRE)** 5-10-13 0 LeeEdwards(5) 56
(Tom Gretton) *hld up: struggling fnl 5f: nvr on terms w ldrs* **50/1**

40 **15** 51 **Teals Star**[33] 1629 6-11-4 0 (t) DaveCrosse 5
(C I Ratcliffe) *midfield: bhd 6f out: t.o fnl 4f* **40/1**

3m 57.6s (8.00) **Going Correction** +0.50s/f (Soft)
WFA 4 from 5yo+ 9lb **15** Ran SP% **125.0**
Speed ratings: **100,99,95,95,95 90,90,88,86,86 85,76,75,73,48**
Tote Swingers: 1&2 £4.50, 1&3 £5.00, 2&3 £6.90. Totesuper7: Win: Not won. Place: Not won. CSF £17.75 TOTE £4.50: £2.30, £1.30, £3.60; EX 21.70 Place 6: £60.26 Place 5: £46.12..
Owner D Shorey **Bred** Mrs Teresa Mulcahy **Trained** Herridge, Wiltshire

■ Stewards' Enquiry : Warren Marston two-day ban: careless riding (Nov 12-13); caution: used whip with excessive frequency.

FOCUS
A reasonable bumper run at a fair pace given the conditions. The first two came clear to fight out a stirring finish and the winner and fourth are rated up to their marks.

NOTEBOOK
Rose Of The Moon(IRE) had been runner-up on his Hereford debut in March, and winner Fishoutofwater gave the form a boost when fourth in the big Aintree bumper. The grey has left John Spearing since, but remains in the same ownership. He stuck his neck out gamely to get the better of a prolonged tussle with the runner-up, and his battling qualities will stand him in good stead when he switches to hurdles. (op 9-2 tchd 7-2)
Koup De Kanon(FR) has a modest pedigree but his dam was placed on the Flat in France. Carrying his head low, he improved to lead going well, but despite battling on he could not fight off an opponent who had the benefit of previous experience.He was held when getting a bumper from the winner in the dying strides. (op 5-1)
Aviador(GER) also filled third place in his two runs last term. He ran well for a long way on this seasonal return but could not race on with the first two and was tying up at the end. (tchd 10-1)
Music In The Air was placed on both her first two starts, and she ran creditably from the front on this markedly different ground. (op 12-1)
Elton Fox was staying on steadily on this debut. He represents a small but capable yard, who won two races with this one's half-brother Native Fox. (op 25-1)
Letmespeak(IRE)'s dam won a bumper and is a half-sister to the McCain yard's smart performer Regal Heights. The gelding was under pressure a good way out to hold his pitch but looks to possess ability. (op 10-1)
Otter Mist's trainer has a good record with his bumper runners at Uttoxeter and won this race with Broomhill Flyer in 2007. Out of a winning selling hurdler, the grey was a cheap buy as a 2-y-o but he showed enough to suggest that he will pay his way in time. (op 5-1)
A Patchy Dancer(IRE), who has reportedly been working well, shaped with promise but may need more time. (op 20-1)
T/Plt: £64.40 to a £1 stake. Pool:£68,820.60 - 779.65 winning tickets T/Qpdt: £31.20 to a £1 stake. Pool:£5,069.28 - 119.74 winning tickets DO

1825 WETHERBY (L-H)

Friday, October 29

OFFICIAL GOING: Good (7.6)
Wind: fresh 1/2 against Weather: overcast and breezy

2075 WETHERBY RACECOURSE & CONFERENCE CENTRE "NATIONAL HUNT" NOVICES' HURDLE (11 hdls) 2m 4f

2:10 (2:10) (Class 4) 4-Y-0+ **£2,397** (£698; £349)

Form RPR

314- **1** **Habbie Simpson**[195] 5227 5-10-12 0 WayneHutchinson 109+
(Alan King) *trckd ldrs: t.k.h: wnt 2nd appr 3 out: led appr last: lft clr: pushed out* **4/1**[2]

0-1P **2** 11 **Front Of House (IRE)**[26] 1703 8-11-5 119 BarryKeniry 108+
(Ben Haslam) *hld up: trckd ldrs 5th: hmpd bnd appr 3 out: kpt on same pce: lft 10 l 2nd last* **4/1**[2]

0 **3** 8 **Howizee**[21] 1764 4-10-12 0 (t) MichaelMcAlister 92
(Maurice Barnes) *in rr: hdwy to chse ldrs 8th: outpcd next: kpt on to take modest 3rd towards fin* **150/1**

120- **4** ¾ **Eagle Owl (IRE)**[202] 5129 4-10-12 0 RichieMcGrath 92
(Tim Easterby) *trckd ldrs: nt fluent 5th: effrt 3 out: 3rd and one pce whn j.rt last* **3/1**[1]

306/ **5** 5 **Pikasso (FR)**[986] 3944 7-10-12 0 DavidEngland 88
(Pam Sly) *trckd ldrs: 4th and btn whn mstke 2 out* **33/1**

03- **6** 28 **Rushing Nature (IRE)**[206] 5076 6-10-12 0 GrahamLee 62
(David O'Meara) *towards rr: sme hdwy 6th: rdn and lost pl 8th: wl bhd whn hmpd 3 out* **20/1**

06 **7** 2 ¾ **Are Olive**[20] 1780 7-10-5 0 RobertWalford 52
(Tim Walford) *towards rr: sme hdwy appr 3 out: sn wknd* **100/1**

P- **8** 106 **Rockstown**[194] 5243 6-10-12 0 WillKennedy —
(Paul Webber) *trckd ldr: lost pl after 8th: sn bhd: wl t.o whn hmpd last: virtually p.u* **12/1**

40/0 **F** **Errington**[20] 1783 5-10-9 0 JamesO'Farrell(3) —
(Howard Johnson) *led tl after 8th: wknd rapidly: wl bhd whn fell next* **22/1**

30- **F** **Jago River (IRE)**[193] 5277 4-10-12 0 BrianHughes 104+
(Howard Johnson) *j.rt: trckd ldrs: led after 8th: hit 2 out: hdd appr last: 3 l down whn fell last* **5/1**[3]

P **Cloudy Too (IRE)**[180] 4-10-7 0 ShaneByrne(5) —
(Sue Smith) *prom: lost pl after 5th: sn bhd: t.o whn p.u bef 7th* **10/1**

4m 58.1s (-1.40) **Going Correction** +0.025s/f (Yiel)
WFA 4 from 5yo+ 10lb **11** Ran SP% **112.2**
Speed ratings (Par 105): **103,98,95,95,93 81,80,—,—,— —**
Tote Swingers: 1&2 £4.30, 1&3 £17.20, 2&3 £22.40 CSF £18.73 TOTE £3.90: £1.70, £1.40, £11.90; EX 13.60.
Owner Sandy Love **Bred** Moniabrock Farming **Trained** Barbury Castle, Wilts

FOCUS
An ordinary novices' hurdle. The form could be rated a stone higher but the winner is assessed as having improved by 5lb on his best bumper form.

NOTEBOOK
Habbie Simpson, winner of a Southwell bumper last season, was always likely to improve for a stiffer test now hurdling and he'd started to assert when left clear by the fall of Jago River at the last. He'll find it tougher going under a penalty, but can probably win again at some stage, with him likely to end up in handicaps. (op 7-2 tchd 9-2)
Front Of House(IRE), moved from Nicky Henderson after flopping in heavy ground at Uttoxeter latest, shaped better on this going and would have been closer but for getting hampered. He'll make more appeal in handicaps. (tchd 7-2)
Howizee, well beaten in a bumper on debut, took a step forward switched to hurdles in a first-time tongue-tie, keeping on in the manner of a horse likely to want further.
Eagle Owl(IRE), a fair bumper performer last season, proved one-paced under pressure on this hurdles debut and a more testing surface should suit. (op 7-2)
Pikasso(FR) travelled well before tiring on this return from a 986-day absence. (op 28-1)
Jago River(IRE), off since disappointing in a Hexham bumper in April, showed considerably more on this first start over hurdles and was booked for second when coming down at the last. It's hoped this doesn't affect his confidence too badly. (op 6-1)

2076 BET365.COM H'CAP HURDLE (9 hdls) 2m 110y

2:45 (2:45) (Class 3) (0-125,125) 4-Y-0+ **£4,228** (£1,241; £620; £310)

Form RPR

5540 **1** **Royal Max (IRE)**[10] 1911 4-10-7 **106** (t) TomScudamore 111+
(Ian Williams) *mde all: hrd pressed fr 3 out: nt fluent last: styd on gamely* **13/2**[3]

02-1 **2** 1 ¼ **Amir Pasha (UAE)**[8] 1931 5-10-1 **107** 7ex....(v) AlexanderVoy(7) 110+
(Micky Hammond) *hld up in mid-div: hdwy to chse ldrs 5th: chal appr last: rdr dropped whip sn after last: styd on same pce* **11/2**[2]

3512 **3** 4 **Midnite Blews (IRE)**[13] 1870 5-9-12 **100** ow1....(t) RyanMania(3) 100
(Maurice Barnes) *chsd ldrs: kpt on same pce appr last* **4/1**[1]

6-U5 **4** 3 ¼ **Calatagan (IRE)**[148] 606 11-10-11 **115**.... JamesHalliday(5) 111
(Malcolm Jefferson) *chsd ldrs: outpcd 3 out: hung rt and styd on appr last* **20/1**

0126 **5** 1 ¾ **Dream Risk (FR)**[13] 1695 4-10-9 **108**....(t) RichieMcGrath 103
(Kate Walton) *trckd ldrs: wnt cl 2nd after 3 out: wknd appr last* **14/1**

33 **6** 9 **Global**[16] 1831 4-10-3 **102**.... GrahamLee 90
(Brian Ellison) *hld up in rr: t.k.h: hdwy 6th: sn chsng ldrs: 5th and hld whn mstke 2 out* **10/1**

10-4 **7** 3 ¾ **Farleigh House (USA)**[12] 1886 6-11-4 **120**.... AlexMerriam(3) 103
(Neil King) *in rr: hdwy to chse ldrs 5th: lost pl appr 3 out* **10/1**

13-1 **8** hd **Hi Dancer**[67] 179 7-11-2 **115**.... BarryKeniry 97
(Ben Haslam) *prom: outpcd and lost pl 5th* **15/2**

63-0 **9** 11 **Monsieur Jourdain (IRE)**[8] 1931 4-11-7 **125**....(p) ShaneByrne(5) 98
(Tim Easterby) *chsd ldrs: rdn 6th: sn lost pl and bhd: t.o last* **25/1**

604/ **P** **Bywell Beau (IRE)**[615] 4067 11-11-11 **124**....(t) JanFaltejsek —
(George Charlton) *chsd wnr: t.k.h: lost pl 6th: bhd whn p.u bef next* **14/1**

11-4 **P** **Knight In Purple**[167] 331 6-10-13 **112**....(v) AndrewTinkler —
(John Mackie) *in rr: bhd and drvn 5th: t.o whn p.u bef next* **13/2**[3]

3m 54.6s (-1.20) **Going Correction** +0.025s/f (Yiel)
WFA 4 from 5yo+ 9lb **11** Ran SP% **113.9**
Speed ratings (Par 107): **103,102,100,99,98 93,92,92,86,— —**
Tote Swingers: 1&2 £5.50, 1&3 £6.70, 2&3 £4.50 CSF £41.33 CT £160.89 TOTE £6.80: £2.40, £1.60, £2.40; EX 42.70.
Owner R S Brookhouse **Bred** Mrs Jacqueline Donnelly **Trained** Portway, Worcs

FOCUS
A fair handicap hurdle and pretty solid form. The winner is rated in line with his juvenile best.

NOTEBOOK
Royal Max(IRE), racing off a career-low mark over hurdles, set off in front and kept pulling out more when strongly pressed for a well-earned victory. (op 15-2 tchd 6-1)
Amir Pasha(UAE), who made a winning return to hurdles at Carlisle last week, again had the visor on and emerged as the big threat to the winner in the straight, but his rider lost his whip after the last and he was unable to make any further impression. (op 6-1)
Midnite Blews(IRE), whose rider was 1lb overweight, could only keep on at the one pace under pressure, but remains capable of winning a lesser race off this sort of mark. (op 5-1 tchd 11-2)
Calatagan(IRE) kept on at the one pace and it's been almost three years since he won a race now. (op 18-1)
Dream Risk(FR) had her chance before weakening and remains a bit below her best. (op 12-1)
Global, switching to handicaps having had just the two runs in novice events, slowly faded down the straight and doesn't yet look up to winning off this mark. (op 9-1 tchd 11-1)
Knight In Purple, comfortably held off this new career-high mark latest, was never travelling and his rider eventually accepted the situation. (tchd 7-1)

2077 BET365 H'CAP CHASE (LISTED RACE) (16 fncs) 2m 4f 110y

3:20 (3:20) (Class 1) (0-150,139) 4-Y-O+

£11,402 (£4,278; £2,142; £1,068; £536; £268)

Form RPR

2-11 **1** **Neptune Equester**[43] 605 7-10-4 **120**.... FearghalDavis(3) 136+
(Brian Ellison) *hld up in rr: hdwy 12th: chsng ldr next: led 3 out: styd on strly: eased towards fin* **5/1**[2]

-530 **2** 5 **Qulinton (FR)**[14] 1856 6-11-1 **128**....(p) TomScudamore 137
(David Pipe) *chsd ldrs: wnt 2nd 12th: led appr next and hit fence: j.lft after: hdd 3 out: kpt on same pce* **7/2**[1]

430- **3** 6 **Mister McGoldrick**[196] 5204 13-11-7 **139**.... ShaneByrne(5) 141
(Sue Smith) *w ldrs: led after 7th: wnt 7 l clr sn after 12th: hdd appr next: kpt on same pce fr 2 out* **7/1**

050- **4** 12 **According To Pete**[203] 5113 9-11-7 **134**.... GrahamLee 129
(Malcolm Jefferson) *in rr: sme hdwy whn blnd 7th: sme hdwy 12th: tk modest 4th sn after 2 out* **11/2**[3]

21-6 **5** 11 **Soulard (USA)**[174] 214 7-11-6 **133**.... SamThomas 119
(Tom George) *trckd ldrs: wknd 4 out: 4th and wl btn whn blnd 2 out* **10/1**

54-5 **6** 6 **My Moment (IRE)**[175] 194 7-11-3 **130**.... AndrewTinkler 106
(Henry Daly) *chsd ldrs: 3rd and wkng whn hit 12th: sn lost pl* **14/1**

0-P0 **7** 11 **Star Of Germany (IRE)**[13] 1861 10-11-2 **129**.... DougieCostello 95
(Ian Williams) *led to 3rd: lost pl after 12th* **16/1**

116- **8** 20 **Lease Lend**[209] 4988 7-11-8 **135**....(tp) RichieMcGrath 83
(Tim Easterby) *towards rr and nt fluent: pushed along 7th: sme hdwy 9th: sn lost pl: wl bhd whn blnd 4 out* **9/1**

F3U- **P** **Frankie Figg (IRE)**[203] 5111 8-11-5 **132**.... WilsonRenwick —
(Howard Johnson) *led 3rd: hdd after 7th: lost pl 12th: wl bhd whn p.u bef next* **11/2**[3]

4m 54.9s (-12.90) **Going Correction** -0.325s/f (Good) **9** Ran SP% **113.8**
Speed ratings (Par 111): **111,109,106,102,98 95,91,83,—**
Tote Swingers: 1&2 £3.70, 1&3 £6.30, 2&3 £7.30 CSF £23.26 CT £121.31 TOTE £6.30: £1.70, £1.80, £2.40; EX 22.30.
Owner Koo's Racing CLub II **Bred** Mrs Joanna Daniell **Trained** Norton, N Yorks

FOCUS
A good, competitive handicap chase. A big step forward from the progressive winner with the second rated to his best.

NOTEBOOK
Neptune Equester ◆ got a decent pace to run at on this first start over fences in 148 days, and showed himself fully effective at this shorter trip, having won his last two over 3m1f (both at this course). Having already finished second over 3m4f, it's clear stamina is his forte, and as a 7-y-o, connections must be hopeful he can develop into a National horse one day. As for this season, he'll presumably be aimed at some of the top staying handicap chases, with the Grade 3 Rowland Meyrick back here over Christmas presumably to the forefront of connections minds. As for later in the season, the Eider Chase was mentioned as his main long-term aim. (tchd 6-1 in a place)
Quintonn(FR) bounced back from a below-par run at Cheltenham earlier in the month, looking suited by this shorter trip. (op 5-1)
Mister McGoldrick, a winner on eight of his previous 12 visits here, hasn't won since springing a 66-1 shock at the 2008 Cheltenham Festival, but he's nicely treated again and shot into a clear lead after five out. He couldn't sustain the gallop, however, and was ultimately left trailing by the front pair. (op 13-2 tchd 6-1)
According To Pete made a satisfactory reappearance, not being knocked about, and he'll benefit from a return to further. (op 13-2 tchd 7-1)
Soulard(USA) was weak in the market and ran as though this first run in 174 days was needed. He showed enough to suggest he'll be up to winning off this sort of mark, though. (op 11-1 tchd 12-1)
My Moment(IRE) was keen on this reappearance and didn't get home. (op 11-1)
Lease Lend made mistakes and ended up well beaten. (op 8-1)
Frankie Figg(IRE) stopped quickly and something was presumably amiss. Official explanation: jockey said gelding stopped quickly (tchd 5-1)

2078 WEATHERBYS BANK WENSLEYDALE JUVENILE HURDLE (LISTED RACE) (9 hdls) 2m 110y

3:55 (3:55) (Class 1) 3-Y-O

£8,551 (£3,208; £1,606; £801; £402; £201)

Form RPR

1 **Maoi Chinn Tire (IRE)**[44] 3-10-12 0.... AlanO'Keeffe 120+
(Jennie Candlish) *stdd s: t.k.h in rr: stdy hdwy 5th: chsd ldrs appr 3 out: led appr 2 out: clr whn nt fluent last* **200/1**

110 **2** 9 **Meetings Man (IRE)**[34] 1610 3-11-4 115.... GrahamLee 115
(Micky Hammond) *t.k.h in midfield: hdwy appr 3 out: sn 3rd: styd on to go modest 2nd between last 2* **50/1**

2112 **3** ¾ **Two Kisses (IRE)**[34] 1610 3-10-11 125.... SamThomas 108
(Brendan Powell) *w ldrs: t.k.h: tk modest 3rd 3 out: kpt on same pce between last 2* **9/1**

31 **4** 2 ¼ **Jubail (IRE)**[12] 1882 3-11-6 121.... WayneHutchinson 114
(Alan King) *mid-div: wnt prom 4th: kpt on one pce and tk modest 4th 2 out* **12/1**

3- **5** 2 ½ **Grandouet (FR)**[189] 3-11-6 0.... BarryGeraghty 114+
(Nicky Henderson) *trckd ldrs: qcknd to ld and hit 5th: wnt clr after 3 out: hdd appr 2 out: wknd qckly between last 2* **3/1**[2]

6 4 ½ **Bonfire Knight**[49] 3-10-12 0.... DougieCostello 101
(John Quinn) *trckd ldrs: wknd appr 3 out* **5/1**[3]

30 **7** 16 **Dr Finley (IRE)**[18] 1610 3-10-12 0....(p) GerardTumelty 87
(Jeff Pearce) *chsd ldrs: lost pl 5th* **50/1**

1 **8** 3 **Domtaline (FR)**[20] 1772 3-11-4 0.... RWalsh 89
(Paul Nicholls) *led to 2nd: led 4th to next: wknd 3 out* **6/4**[1]

12 **9** 2 **Kahfre**[26] 1691 3-11-4 114.... JamieMoore 87
(Gary Moore) *t.k.h: led 2nd tl after next: hit 4th: lost pl next* **40/1**

11 **10** 23 **Turf Trivia**[26] 1696 3-11-4 109.... BarryKeniry 66
(George Moore) *chsd ldrs: hmpd and lost pl after 3rd: bhd fr 5th: t.o* **28/1**

4 **11** 24 **Maison Brillet (IRE)**[26] 1696 3-10-12 0.... BrianHughes 38
(Howard Johnson) *chsd ldrs to 5th: sn lost pl: t.o 3 out* **100/1**

1 **F** **Whipperway (IRE)**[36] 1586 3-10-11 0.... MarcGoldstein —
(Sheena West) *w ldrs: led after 3rd: hdd next: wknd appr 3 out: 8th and bhd whn fell 2 out* **33/1**

0 **P** **Magic Millie (IRE)**[16] 1825 3-10-5 0.... RichieMcGrath —
(David O'Meara) *stdd s: nt fluent in rr: bhd fr 5th: t.o whn p.u bef 3 out* **100/1**

3m 58.0s (2.20) **Going Correction** +0.025s/f (Yiel) **13** Ran SP% **114.6**
Speed ratings (Par 109): **95,90,90,89,88 86,78,77,76,65 54,—,—**
Tote Swingers: 1&2 £75.60, 1&3 £88.40, 2&3 £46.50 CSF £3451.47 TOTE £224.40: £21.10, £8.00, £2.50; EX 3616.20.
Owner Alan Baxter **Bred** Mrs E Thompson **Trained** Basford Green, Staffs

FOCUS
This had looked a quality juvenile hurdle, certainly up on last year's field, but the shock victory of 200-1 shot Maoi Chinn Tire (the biggest-priced winner in over five years/also 999-1 SP on Betfair), somewhat changes the overall impression of the race, especially when considering there was a 50-1 shot in second, and neither of the 'big' two in market ran up to expectations. The winner is rated in line with his Flat form and the second is on the upgrade.

NOTEBOOK
Maoi Chinn Tire(IRE) caused a massive shock at 200-1. A three-time scorer at up to 7f when trained on the Flat by Stan Moore, including twice in claiming company, didn't look an obvious one with promise to make a good hurdler, but the way he tanked into contention before breezing past Grandouet was quite impressive. He certainly wasn't stopping at the line and it will be fascinating to see where he goes next. (tchd 300-1 in places)
Meetings Man(IRE), already twice a winner over hurdles, jumped poorly when disappointing behind a couple of these at Market Rasen latest, but he was sharper going back left-handed and stayed on well to take a distant second. He's the type with more to offer and will stay further than 2m in time. (tchd 66-1)
Two Kisses(IRE), unable to complete the hat-trick when bumping into Architrave at Market Rasen, but still ahead of both Jubail and Meetings Man, was outpaced down the back before plugging on again, but she was always comfortably being held. (op 12-1)
Jubail(IRE), narrowly off the mark at Kempton, needed to pull out considerably more with a 6lb penalty and he just wasn't up to it. (op 14-1)
Grandouet(FR) has joined top connections, won by 26l at Enghien in April and was certainly the best looking horse in the race. However, he refused to settle, and despite Geraghty giving him his head and allowing him to go into a clear lead leaving the back, he was never going to last, especially with a 6lb penalty to shoulder. He was quickly swept aside and finished pretty tired, but this would have taken the fizz out of him and he deserves another chance. (op 15-8)
Bonfire Knight, a useful Flat performer who was backed beforehand, didn't appear to get home, but probably deserves another chance on a more speed-favouring track. (op 13-2)
Domtaline(FR) isn't the biggest and he started to look in trouble once his main market rival went on, finding very little and coming home in his own time. This was bitterly disappointing and he's left with plenty to prove. Official explanation: trainer's rep said gelding finished distressed (op 7-4 tchd 15-8)
Turf Trivia was quickly in trouble having been hampered. (op 40-1 tchd 25-1)
Whipperway(IRE) had run her race and was tired when coming down. (tchd 28-1)

2079 BOOK ON-LINE @ WETHERBYRACING.CO.UK H'CAP CHASE (18 fncs) 3m 1f

4:30 (4:30) (Class 4) (0-110,110) 4-Y-O+ **£2,927** (£859; £429; £214)

Form RPR

311- **1** **Palos Conti (FR)**[207] 5039 7-11-0 **98**.... DougieCostello 118+
(Tim Pitt) *stdd s: hld up in rr: stdy hdwy 10th: wnt handy 3rd appr 4 out: led 2 out: sn wnt clr: heavily eased last 75yds* **13/2**[3]

-036 **2** 22 **Timpo (FR)**[23] 1726 7-11-0 **98**.... AndrewTinkler 97
(Henry Daly) *trckd ldrs: reminders after 9th: wnt 2nd 12th: upsides 3 out: sn wknd: lft 10 l 2nd last* **6/1**[2]

345P **3** 21 **Sycho Fred (IRE)**[89] 1152 9-9-11 **84** oh8....(t) CampbellGillies(3) 62
(Mike Sowersby) *in rr: hit 7th: kpt on fr 4 out: lft poor 3rd last* **10/1**

01P- **4** 3 ¾ **Star Beat**[196] 5202 7-11-8 **106**....(p) RichieMcGrath 81
(Kate Walton) *mde most to 8th: hit 12th: wknd appr 4 out* **16/1**

1 **5** 2 **Ihaventabob (IRE)**[45] 1524 6-10-13 **97**.... JohnnyFarrelly 70
(Aidan Anthony Howard, Ire) *chsd ldrs: wknd appr 4 out* **10/3**[1]

P-36 **6** 30 **Shrewd Investor (IRE)**[140] 716 10-11-8 **106**....(p) RobertWalford 52
(Henry Hogarth) *t.k.h: w ldr: wknd after 14th: sn bhd: t.o* **16/1**

/1-1 **U** **La Pantera Rosa (IRE)**[26] 1697 7-11-4 **102**....(p) BarryKeniry 108
(Micky Hammond) *hdwy to trck ldrs 5th: led 8th: mistke 4 out: hdd 2 out: 6 l 2nd whn blnd and uns rdr last* **6/1**[2]

P-5P **P** **Not Left Yet (IRE)**[8] 1932 9-11-12 **110**....(v) BrianHughes —
(P Monteith) *nt jump wl: prom: lost pl 10th: sn bhd: t.o whn p.u bef 14th* **25/1**

3634 **P** **Western Gale (IRE)**[21] 1763 7-11-10 **108**............................ GrahamLee —
(Martin Todhunter) *chsd ldrs: reminders and lost pl 9th: sn bhd: t.o whn p.u bef 14th* **13/2**[3]

P-21 **P** **Sierra Victor (IRE)**[20] 1784 7-11-3 **101**........................... WilsonRenwick —
(P Monteith) *in tch: blnd 3rd: lost pl 10th: sn t.o: p.u bef 13th* **17/2**

6m 2.20s (-7.20) **Going Correction** -0.325s/f (Good) course record **10** Ran SP% **113.5**
Speed ratings (Par 105): **98,90,84,83,82 72**,—,—,—,—
Tote Swingers: 1&2 £9.60, 1&3 £22.60, 2&3 £13.60 CSF £44.66 CT £385.13 TOTE £8.80: £2.60, £2.20, £2.80; EX 53.10.

Owner C N Barnes **Bred** Patrick Joubery & Jean-Andre Quesny **Trained** Norton, N Yorks

FOCUS
A modest staying handicap chase. The winner was well in on his hurdles form but this was another step forward.

NOTEBOOK
Palos Conti(FR) was in fine form over hurdles earlier in the year, winning his last two starts, and he actually got to return to fences off 6lb lower (having done little in three previous tries over them). Jumping wasn't a problem for the 7-y-o, who quickly asserted after two out before being left well clear at the last. He remains capable of better and looks the sort to win again. (op 7-1 tchd 15-2)

Timpo(FR), having only his third start over fences, inherited second at the last and remains off little interest off this sort of mark. (op 11-2 tchd 5-1)

Sycho Fred(IRE) ended up well held from 8lb out of the handicap (op 14-1)

Star Beat failed to get home on this first start for a new yard, but should improve. (tchd 14-1)

La Pantera Rosa(IRE), up another 8lb, had run a fine race, but was held, when making a mess of the last and losing his rider. (op 4-1)

2080 WETHERBY RACECOURSE FOR WEDDING RECEPTIONS CONDITIONAL JOCKEYS' NOVICES' H'CAP HURDLE (12 hdls) 2m 6f

5:05 (5:05) (Class 4) (0-105,102) 3-Y-0+ **£2,397** (£698; £349)

Form RPR

40-5 **1** **Wheyaye**[31] 1644 8-11-0 **90**.. JamesO'Farrell 96+
(Valerie Jackson) *hdwy to trck ldrs 5th: wnt handy 2nd appr 3 out: led appr last: hld on wl* **14/1**

F022 **2** *1 ¼* **Nobby Kivambo (IRE)**[23] 1730 5-11-9 **99**..................... MrMMO'Connor 103+
(Brendan Powell) *trckd ldr: led appr 3 out: narrowly hdd appr last: no ex last 100yds* **17/2**

2123 **3** *2* **Auberge (IRE)**[40] 1559 6-11-1 **91**................................ FearghalDavis 92
(Dianne Sayer) *mid-div: hdwy to chse ldrs 7th: styd on wl to take 3rd run-in* **4/1**[1]

40-4 **4** *4* **Ouest Eclair (FR)**[21] 1758 5-10-11 **93**.......................... PaulGallagher(6) 91
(Ferdy Murphy) *mid-div: hdwy 9th: wnt 3rd 2 out: kpt on one pce* **16/1**

436- **5** *3 ½* **Lady De La Vega (FR)**[226] 4680 6-11-1 **97**...............(v[1]) MrTomDavid(6) 91
(Tim Vaughan) *in tch: effrt appr 3 out: one pce* **9/1**

-030 **6** *3 ½* **The Magic Bishop**[40] 1556 5-11-7 **100**........................ JamesHalliday(3) 91
(Malcolm Jefferson) *hld up in rr: sme hdwy 9th: kpt on: nvr nr ldrs* **33/1**

54- **7** *3 ¼* **Aghill (IRE)**[20] 6-11-9 **99**.. EwanWhillans 87
(Rose Dobbin) *prom: hit 8th: lost pl completely next: t.o 3 out: styd on steadily fr next* **22/1**

32F- **8** *3* **Iris's Flyer**[354] 2191 8-10-10 **89**.. KyleJames(3) 74
(Brian Rothwell) *led tl appr 3 out: wknd between last 2* **25/1**

/0-0 **9** *10* **Dance Sauvage**[16] 1829 7-10-0 **76** oh6.......................... CampbellGillies 52
(Mike Sowersby) *chsd ldrs: lost pl appr 3 out* **28/1**

420 **10** *6* **Heart Of Dubai (USA)**[13] 1870 5-10-13 **99**.................(p) JoeColliver(10) 70
(Micky Hammond) *chsd ldrs: drvn 8th: sn lost pl* **28/1**

455- **11** *3 ¼* **Echoes Of Dawn (IRE)**[232] 4531 6-11-1 **94**..................... RyanMania(3) 62
(Howard Johnson) *chsd ldrs: lost pl appr 3 out* **13/2**[2]

5-45 **12** *37* **Pollen Jock (IRE)**[23] 1730 6-11-5 **95**................................... PeterToole 30
(Chris Bealby) *in rr: bhd fr 8th: t.o 3 out* **12/1**

U2P3 **13** *nk* **Bow School (IRE)**[13] 1869 9-11-7 **102**.......................... JakeGreenall(5) 37
(Mrs A C Hamilton) *chsd ldrs: lost pl 8th: t.o 3 out* **15/2**[3]

P **14** *31* **Bank The Bucks (IRE)**[6] 1963 4-11-7 **97**............................(tp) RTDunne 4
(Aidan Anthony Howard, Ire) *in rr: sme hdwy 7th: lost pl after 9th: sn bhd: wl t.o* **50/1**

0/0- **P** **Jazrawy**[227] 4665 8-11-2 **95**... ShaneByrne(3) —
(Sue Smith) *in rr: bhd fr 8th: t.o whn p.u bef 3 out* **28/1**

-435 **P** **Major Miller**[36] 1590 9-11-5 **98**.. DavidBass(3) —
(Nicky Henderson) *in rr: last and drvn 6th: t.o whn p.u bef 3 out* **13/2**[2]

5106 **P** **Fly Tipper**[8] 1929 10-10-12 **91**............................(t) AlexanderVoy(3) —
(Wilf Storey) *in rr: bhd whn p.u bef 3 out* **33/1**

5m 24.5s (-2.30) **Going Correction** +0.025s/f (Yiel)
WFA 4 from 5yo+ 10lb **17** Ran SP% **125.6**
Speed ratings (Par 105): **105,104,103,102,101 99,98,97,93,91 90,77,76,65**,—,—,—
Tote Swingers: 1&2 £44.70, 1&3 £29.80, 2&3 £10.30 CSF £119.97 CT £580.81 TOTE £18.30: £3.30, £1.70, £2.10, £4.40; EX 145.20 Place 6: £519.86 Place 5: £223.42..

Owner Mrs V Jackson **Bred** Mrs Valerie Jackson **Trained** Belsay, Northumberland

■ Stewards' Enquiry : James O'Farrell caution: careless riding.

FOCUS
A wide-open conditional jockeys' handicap hurdle. The third and fourth set the level.

NOTEBOOK
Wheyaye, without a win in seven previous attempts over hurdles, had been dropped a further 2lb and she found improvement for the extra 2f, battling on well having taken it up before the last. (op 22-1)

Nobby Kivambo(IRE) has now finished runner-up on each of his last three starts. Up 4lb for finishing second at Towcester latest, he gave it another good go, but things aren't going to get any easier. (op 10-1 tchd 8-1)

Auberge(IRE) again ran her race and will be suited by a return to 3m. (op 5-1)

Ouest Eclair(FR)'s sure to come good at some stage, possibly over 3m. (op 14-1)

Lady De La Vega(FR) had her chance on this return from a 226-day absence, but is likely to continue to fall short off this mark. (op 13-2)

The Magic Bishop made some late ground and we've still to see the best of him. He'll be of interest over 3m switched to fences.

Major Miller has still to win a race over hurdles and he never looked like getting into this, eventually pulling up. (op 15-2)

T/Jkpt: Not won. T/Plt: £819.60 to a £1 stake. Pool:£76,294.03 - 67.95 winning tickets T/Qpdt: £301.60 to a £1 stake. Pool:£6,114.99 - 15 winning tickets WG

ASCOT (R-H)

Saturday, October 30

OFFICIAL GOING: Good (chase 7.7, hurdle 8.0)
Wind: Almost nil Weather: Fine, mild

2081 WINDSOR + MAIDENHEAD TOWN PARTNERSHIPS NOVICES' H'CAP HURDLE (11 hdls) 2m 3f 110y

1:50 (1:50) (Class 3) (0-120,120) 3-Y-0+

£6,888 (£2,035; £1,017; £509; £254; £127)

Form RPR

3-23 **1** **Like A Hurricane (IRE)**[17] 1821 7-11-7 **115**.............. WayneHutchinson 124+
(Alan King) *a w ldrs: rdn in 3rd after 3 out: chsd ldr sn after next: led bef last: drvn out* **13/2**[1]

4FP- **2** *½* **Ballybach (IRE)**[231] 4589 6-11-12 **120**............................ LiamTreadwell 127
(Nick Gifford) *w ldr: blnd 5th: led 7th: drvn and pressed bef 2 out: hdd bef last: styd on flat: a hld* **14/1**

53-1 **3** *2 ¼* **Iceman George**[18] 1812 6-10-11 **112**.........................(p) MrJMQuinlan(7) 117
(Giles Bravery) *towards rr: mstke 4th: rdn in rr of gp 8th: stl there after 3 out: styd on stoutly fr 2 out: tk 3rd flat and fin strly* **9/1**[3]

F-24 **4** *3* **Phoenix Flight (IRE)**[19] 1111 5-11-5 **113**...................... DougieCostello 116
(James Evans) *hld up in last trio: stdy prog fr 8th: gng bttr than most after 3 out in 5th: shkn up and nt qckn 2 out: hanging but wnt 3rd briefly last: one pce* **12/1**

P632 **5** *7* **Unleashed (IRE)**[16] 1842 5-11-0 **108**.................................... NoelFehily 104
(Charlie Mann) *hld up in midfield: prog 8th: rdn to chse ldng trio after 3 out: no imp next: fdd last* **7/1**[2]

1345 **6** *2 ¼* **Wilbury Star (IRE)**[59] 1453 4-11-0 **108**............................ AndrewTinkler 102
(Nicky Henderson) *hld up in midfield: rdn in 7th after 3 out: no imp on ldrs next: fdd* **16/1**

410- **7** *4* **Manele Bay**[195] 5253 7-11-2 **110**...................................... LeightonAspell 100
(Richard Rowe) *hld up wl in rr: pushed along 8th: hit 3 out: poor 12th 2 out: stl only 11th whn hit last: r.o strly flat: nrst fin: eyecatcher* **20/1**

-324 **8** *shd* **Bon Spiel**[10] 1918 6-10-8 **102**..(vt) ColinBolger 93
(Chris Gordon) *pressed ldrs: blnd 5th: stl wl there 8th: wl btn in 6th after 3 out* **20/1**

-542 **9** *nk* **Keep Talking (IRE)**[18] 1812 6-10-13 **110**.......................... AlexMerriam(3) 102+
(Neil King) *hld up wl in rr: stdy prog on outer fr 6th: trckd ldr after 8th: rdn to chal after 3 out: lost 2nd sn after 2 out: wkng rapidly whn mstke last* **16/1**

432- **10** *1 ¾* **Lively Fling (USA)**[217] 4887 4-10-13 **107**........................ AidanColeman 95
(Venetia Williams) *hld up in midfield: shkn up and no prog 3 out: struggling next* **9/1**[3]

-234 **11** *11* **Woodmore (IRE)**[27] 1692 6-11-2 **110**................................ FelixDeGiles 98+
(Charlie Longsdon) *trckd ldrs: hmpd 5th and dropped to last pair: tried to rcvr fr 8th: wknd after 3 out* **7/1**[2]

6/03 **12** *shd* **Puerto Azul (IRE)**[11] 1910 6-11-2 **110**........................ DominicElsworth 88
(Oliver Sherwood) *t.k.h: hld up in midfield: stl keen 1/2-way: shkn up after 3 out: wkng whn hit 2 out* **9/1**[3]

42/0 **13** *21* **Bob Casey (IRE)**[23] 1742 8-10-11 **105**................................ TomO'Brien 64
(Keith Goldsworthy) *mstke 1st: led to 7th: wknd v rapidly after next: t.o* **14/1**

0323 **14** *22* **Minneapolis**[69] 1343 5-10-11 **105**...................................... TimmyMurphy 44
(Alison Batchelor) *hld up last: sltly hmpd 5th: no prog at any stage: t.o* **10/1**

0-3F **U** **Al Amaan**[130] 823 5-11-1 **109**... JamieMoore —
(Gary Moore) *t.k.h: hld up wl in rr: bdly hmpd and uns rdr 5th* **33/1**

25P- **F** **Divy (FR)**[249] 4212 5-11-7 **115**................................(v[1]) MarkBradburne —
(George Baker) *prom: cl 5th whn hmpd by rival and fell 5th* **20/1**

4m 38.3s (-9.70) **Going Correction** -0.30s/f (Good)
WFA 4 from 5yo+ 9lb **16** Ran SP% **127.4**
Speed ratings (Par 107): **107,106,105,104,101 101,99,99,99,98 94,94,85,76**,—,—
toteswingers:1&2:£33.90, 1&3:£10.80, 2&3:£94.10 CSF £93.43 CT £845.72 TOTE £7.00: £1.70, £4.00, £2.10, £3.70; EX 117.50 Trifecta £367.90 Part won. Pool £497.16 - 0.30 winning units..

Owner Mel Fordham **Bred** Miss Miriam S Regan **Trained** Barbury Castle, Wilts

FOCUS
The going was good, following 4.5mm of overnight rain, for the opening jumping fixture of the season at the course. A competitive novices' handicap hurdle, and fair form. The first three are all on the upgrade.

NOTEBOOK
Like A Hurricane(IRE), who returned with a satisfactory effort at Uttoxeter, was always likely to fare better once handicapping and he showed the benefit of that initial outing, leading before the last and holding on despite appearing to do very little in front. The 3f drop in trip was clearly not a problem, and perhaps he's best kept to this sort of distance for the time being, with a switch to fences now on the agenda. (op 15-2 tchd 6-1)

Ballybach(IRE), pulled up in the EBF Final on his final outing last season, had earlier taken a heavy fall when still in with every chance at Plumpton, but he's had more than seven months to rebuild some confidence and this was a fine effort under top weight. He rallied having been headed and shapes like a horse who will stay 3m in time.

Iceman George ◆, a Huntingdon novice winner, was down slightly in trip for this handicap debut, and really finished his race off strongly, having got behind, and he'd probably have won in another furlong. This was only his fourth start and he's one to watch out for back up in distance. (op 8-1)

Phoenix Flight(IRE), who had a recent spin on the Flat, travelled strongly on this handicap debut but, not for the first time, he didn't find a great deal and started to hang after the last. (tchd 11-1)

Unleashed(IRE) slowly faded from the second-last and remains a maiden. (op 8-1)

Wilbury Star(IRE), down 3lb, ran a little better on this return from a break, although he remains 7lb above his last winning mark.

Manele Bay ◆, 3lb lower than when disappointing on her handicap debut back in April (raced keenly), was dropped right out on this occasion and found herself with plenty of running to do. In fact she still had more than half the field ahead of her approaching the last, but she fairly rattled home and looks sure to be of interest next time. (op 18-1)

Keep Talking(IRE) travelled well until emptying as they straightened for home, ending up well held. This was only his fourth start over hurdles and he can be found an opening at some stage. (op 20-1)

Lively Fling(USA), from a yard yet to hit top form, ended up well held, but he's run well off this mark before and should come good at some stage. He was later reported to have lost a shoe. Official explanation: vet said gelding lost a shoe (op 13-2)

Woodmore(IRE) was hampered, which caused him to lose his place, and was never able to recover. (op 15-2 tchd 8-1)

Puerto Azul(IRE) failed to run his race, having been very keen. (tchd 10-1)

2082 ASCOT UNDERWRITING BEGINNERS' CHASE (16 fncs) 2m 3f
2:25 (2:25) (Class 3) 4-Y-0+

£6,888 (£2,035; £1,017; £509; £254; £127)

Form RPR

320- **1** **Radium (FR)**^{189} 5401 5-11-3 0 APMcCoy 145+
(Nicky Henderson) *nt a fluent: hld up in tch: prog 8th: mstke 10th: pushed along in 3rd after 3 out: effrt to ld next where mstke: clr last: r.o wl* **2/1**^{1}

224- **2** *3 ½* **Othermix (FR)**^{205} 5098 6-11-3 142 NoelFehily 138
(Ian Williams) *prom: pressed ldr 9th: chal fr 12th: upsides 2 out: nt qckn and vain chse of wnr after* **10/3**^{3}

222- **3** *14* **Cois Farraig**^{204} 5115 5-11-3 0 DominicElsworth 127
(Paul Webber) *mde most: looked to be gng bttr than 2 chalrs after 3 out: hdd & wknd 2 out* **8/1**

U1-2 **4** *4 ½* **Pause And Clause (IRE)**^{34} 1627 6-11-3 0 JackDoyle 125+
(Emma Lavelle) *trckd ldng pair: blnd 6th: nt convincing after: nt fluent 7th and reminder: lft bhd fr 12th: styd on wl flat* **3/1**^{2}

0/1- **5** *12* **County Zen (FR)**^{218} 4873 7-11-3 0 RichardJohnson 113+
(Philip Hobbs) *in tch: awkward jump 8th: mstke 10th: struggling after: lft bhd fr 12th* **9/1**

POP- **6** *¾* **Quartano (GER)**^{218} 4873 7-11-3 0 WayneHutchinson 111
(Warren Greatrex) *in tch in rr: grad outpcd fr 11th: no ch 3 out* **16/1**

5/3- **7** *66* **Fiftyonefiftyone (IRE)**^{260} 4018 6-11-3 122 LeightonAspell 96+
(Oliver Sherwood) *j. sltly lft: pressed ldr to 9th: wknd rapidly 13th: virtually p.u between last 2 fences* **33/1**

4m 40.2s (-6.80) **Going Correction** -0.30s/f (Good) **7** Ran SP% **111.3**
Speed ratings (Par 107): **102,100,94,92,87 87,59**
toteswingers:1&2:£2.80, 1&3:£5.20, 2&3:£3.30 CSF £8.82 TOTE £3.10: £1.80, £2.30; EX 9.70.
Owner Simon Munir **Bred** Mme Michele Juhen Cypres **Trained** Upper Lambourn, Berks

FOCUS
An interesting beginners' chase, featuring a winner and two runners-up from last season's Cheltenham Festival. Radium stepped up on his hurdles form and is a smart chase prospect. The runner-up is rated 4lb below his best.

NOTEBOOK
Radium(FR) ◆, although beaten in receipt of 6lb from Pause And Clause in the Martin Pipe, is a year younger and looked the one with the greater scope for fences. Favourite in the hands of Tony McCoy, he made a couple of novicey mistakes, including when screwing at the second-last, but his class enabled him to assert before the final fence, where a stunning leap well and truly sealed the deal. This was a very likeable first effort from the 5-y-o, who should improve a good deal for the experience, and he's expected to prove best at this sort of trip, making the new 2m4f Jewson Novices' Chase at Cheltenham in March an obvious target at this early stage. (tchd 15-8)
Othermix(FR), runner-up in the race formerly known as the Jewson last season, had been off since disappointing at Aintree the following month and didn't have the blinkers on for this reappearance, but still seemed to run his race and simply got beaten by a better horse. He seems sure to break his duck over fences at some stage and will no doubt end up contesting some decent handicaps once again this season. (op 7-2)
Cois Farraig ◆, a three-time runner-up over hurdles last season, including behind the smart Oscar Whisky at Sandown, is a fine chasing type and ran really well, jumping soundly before getting a little tired late on. He's a useful prospect for the season ahead and could end up in something like the Centenary Novices' Handicap Chase at Cheltenham (formerly known as the Jewson). (op 13-2 tchd 6-1)
Pause And Clause(IRE), hesitant at his fences when second to the useful Billie Magern on debut at Market Rasen, seemed to lose his confidence completely after a mistake at the sixth, staying on late only having been given time to find some rhythm again. He's better than this and should come good at some stage. He looks another obvious type for the Centenary. (op 7-2, tchd 5-1 in places)
County Zen(FR), a winner on his only start last season, has long looked the type for fences, but his jumping wasn't the best and he ended up well held. The experience should do him good, though. (op 8-1 tchd 10-1)
Quartano(GER), useful but inconsistent over hurdles, was one of the first beaten and offered little immediate promise, although this was a stiff introduction. (op 33-1 tchd 14-1)
Fiftyonefiftyone(IRE) stopped quickly and something was presumably amiss. (op 25-1)

2083 CUSHMAN & WAKEFIELD NOVICES' HURDLE (FOR THE JOHN TRAVERS' MEMORIAL TROPHY) (9 hdls) 2m
3:00 (3:00) (Class 2) 4-Y-0+

£6,888 (£2,035; £1,017; £509; £254; £127)

Form RPR

01-1 **1** **Dunraven Storm (IRE)**^{23} 1736 5-11-3 0 RichardJohnson 140+
(Philip Hobbs) *led 2nd: maintained stdy pce tl upped tempo fr 6th: nt fluent 2 out and rdn: hrd pressed last: styd on strly flat* **11/8**^{1}

1 **2** *4* **Recession Proof (FR)**^{22} 1757 4-11-3 0 DougieCostello 134
(John Quinn) *trckd ldng pair: rdn to chse wnr after 2 out: 1 l down last and styng on: outpcd fnl 100yds* **8/1**

00-2 **3** *6* **Fiulin**^{15} 1857 5-10-12 135 APMcCoy 124
(Evan Williams) *led at stdy pce to 2nd: trckd wnr: rdn to chal 2 out: nt qckn and sn lost 2nd: fdd tamely* **11/4**^{2}

1-21 **4** *7* **Organisateur (IRE)**^{4} 2021 5-11-6 133 IanPopham 126
(Paul Nicholls) *trckd ldrs: pushed along sn after 3 out: lost tch u.p bef 2 out* **3/1**^{3}

0-42 **5** *12* **Addwaitya**^{12} 1899 5-10-12 108 (b^{1}) LeightonAspell 108
(Laura Mongan) *hld up last: nt fluent 4th: easily outpcd fr 6th: no ch fr next (3 out)* **28/1**

044/ **6** *2 ¼* **Excape (IRE)**^{593} 4531 5-10-12 0 AndrewTinkler 104
(Nicky Henderson) *t.k.h: hld up in tch: nt fluent 6th and sn easily outpcd: no ch fr 3 out: mstke last* **20/1**

3m 52.3s (3.30) **Going Correction** -0.30s/f (Good) **6** Ran SP% **113.1**
Speed ratings (Par 109): **79,77,74,70,64 63**
toteswingers:1&2:£3.00, 1&3:£1.60, 2&3:£2.70 CSF £13.29 TOTE £2.60: £1.50, £2.00; EX 12.30.
Owner Mrs Karola Vann **Bred** Miss Violet Sweeney **Trained** Withycombe, Somerset

FOCUS
A good-looking novices' hurdle, although it was run at quite a steady pace and in a slow time. Form to be positive about though, and the winner has the potential to develop into one of the better British novices.

NOTEBOOK
Dunraven Storm(IRE), who won a course bumper, had the run of things when making a winning hurdles debut at Exeter, and he took it up at quite an early stage here, Johnson eager to see the race wasn't run at a complete dawdle. It became apparent he had everything in trouble as he upped the tempo, and despite a clumsy jump at the second-last, things always seemed under control. There's little doubt his future lies over further, but Johnson is keen to keep him to this trip for the time being, and he's now likely to head for the Grade 2 2m novices' hurdle at Cheltenham's Open meeting, where Cue Card will be lying in wait. (op 7-4)
Recession Proof(FR), a useful Flat-racer who made a tidy debut over hurdles at Carlisle, stayed on to challenge the winner, having briefly been outpaced, but always looked held. He's clearly up to defying the penalty in a lesser race and could be the type to develop into a decent handicapper. (op 7-1 tchd 13-2)
Fiulin, well beaten by a smart prospect at Cheltenham on his reappearace, having raced in a clear lead for much of the way, was content to take a lead this time, but he was never going to have the pace to win off a steady gallop and became outpaced before fading late on. He'll break his duck at some point. Tony McCoy later reported that the gelding lost a front shoe. Official explanation: jockey said gelding lost a front shoe (op 3-1 tchd 10-3 and 7-2 in a place)
Organisateur(IRE), an easy winner at Taunton just four days earlier, didn't travel as sweetly as he has done and was quickly beaten when the tempo lifted. This was a rather flat performance and the race evidently came too soon. (op 11-4)
Addwaitya failed improve for the addition of blinkers. (op 25-1)
Excape(IRE) seemed very rusty on this return from a 593-day absence and should improve. (tchd 22-1)

2084 UNITED HOUSE GOLD CUP H'CAP CHASE (LISTED RACE) (20 fncs) 3m
3:40 (3:40) (Class 1) 4-Y-0+

£56,330 (£21,220; £10,620; £5,310; £2,660; £1,330)

Form RPR

5/3- **1** **Massini's Maguire (IRE)**^{305} 3149 9-11-3 **146** TomScudamore 158+
(David Pipe) *mstke 2nd: prom: wnt 2nd 15th: led 3 out: drvn and jnd last: styd on wl flat* **8/1**

103- **2** *1 ½* **Take The Breeze (FR)**^{204} 5109 7-11-2 **145** HarrySkelton 156
(Paul Nicholls) *hld up in midfield: prog to go prom 15th: short of room briefly after 3 out in 4th: chsd wnr 2 out: upsides last: nt qckn flat* **11/2**^{2}

313- **3** *9* **From Dawn To Dusk**^{199} 5183 11-11-4 **147** (t) RichardJohnson 150
(Philip Hobbs) *settled in midfield: prog fr 14th: rdn to chse wnr after 3 out tl mstke next: fdd last* **17/2**

2B4- **4** *1 ¼* **Exmoor Ranger (IRE)**^{199} 5183 8-11-2 **145** TomO'Brien 147+
(Victor Dartnall) *nt fluent and wl in rr: mstke 3rd: gd prog fr 15th to rch 5th after 3 out: kpt on: nvr able to rch ldrs* **14/1**

F0-1 **5** *½* **Dover's Hill**^{23} 1739 8-10-0 **132** (t) SamTwiston-Davies$^{(3)}$ 134+
(Mary Hambro) *mstke 1st: w ldr: led 5th: blnd 13th: hdd 3 out: sn lost pl u.p: plugged on flat* **5/1**^{1}

242- **6** *11* **Carruthers**^{205} 5095 7-11-12 **155** MattieBatchelor 149+
(Mark Bradstock) *trckd ldrs: cl 3rd fr 12th: lost pl and rdn 17th: wl btn in 6th after 3 out: j. bdly lft last* **7/1**^{3}

F2-3 **7** *¾* **Free World (IRE)**^{14} 1861 8-10-0 **129** oh5 WayneHutchinson 118
(Warren Greatrex) *hld up in last trio: sme prog fr 15th: rchd 8th after 3 out but nt on terms: kpt on: nrst fin* **8/1**

16F- **8** *25* **Can't Buy Time (IRE)**^{203} 5127 8-11-4 **147** APMcCoy 133+
(Jonjo O'Neill) *hld up wl in rr: sltly hmpd 4th: sme prog into midfield 15th: 7th and nt on terms after 3 out: wknd and eased next* **12/1**

532- **9** *27* **Possol (FR)**^{192} 5306 7-11-4 **147** AndrewTinkler 109+
(Henry Daly) *tended to jump lft: chsd ldrs: reminders 9th: struggling fr 15th: wl btn in 9th after 3 out: j.lft last: t.o* **10/1**

1F-S **10** *hd* **Eric's Charm (FR)**^{182} 98 12-11-6 **149** DominicElsworth 91
(Oliver Sherwood) *led to 5th: dropped out rapidly fr 11th: last fr 13th: mstke 15th: t.o* **33/1**

P1-0 **11** *7* **Always Waining (IRE)**^{35} 1611 9-10-11 **140** (p) JamieMoore 76
(Peter Bowen) *prom: pressed ldr 11th tl wknd rapidly 15th: t.o* **33/1**

2311 **12** *27* **Silmi**^{35} 1611 6-9-13 **131** RichieMcLernon$^{(3)}$ 42
(Sophie Leech) *hld up in last trio: nt fluent 4th: mstke 9th and reminder next: no prog 14th: t.o* **9/1**

12-U **P** **Burren Legend (IRE)**^{182} 98 9-10-3 **132** LeightonAspell —
(Richard Rowe) *nt a fluent: a towards rr: struggling fr 15th: t.o 3 out: p.u bef last* **20/1**

5m 54.3s (-14.70) **Going Correction** -0.30s/f (Good) **13** Ran SP% **121.4**
Speed ratings (Par 111): **112,111,108,108,107 104,104,95,86,86 84,75,—**
toteswingers:1&2:£25.00, 1&3:£20.00, 2&3:£13.40 CSF £52.55 CT £390.35 TOTE £10.10: £2.70, £2.60, £2.70; EX 65.90 Trifecta £533.70 Pool: £41,017.50 - 56.86 winning units..
Owner Alan Peterson **Bred** G Quirk **Trained** Nicholashayne, Devon

FOCUS
This is often a highly competitive handicap chase, underlined by a shock 33-1 winner a year ago, and this season's edition produced a cracking finish. Solid handicap form with high-class efforts from the first two.

NOTEBOOK
Massini's Maguire(IRE), on his debut for David Pipe, rallied bravely on the run-in to deny Take The Breeze, the pair clear. The pace was a good one, and that suited the ex-Philip Hobbs inmate down to the ground, the 9-y-o having been placed in the 2009 RSA Chase. Running in his first handicap over fences, off a reasonable mark of 146, he travelled like a class horse through the race and a change of yard has clearly freshened him up. Apparently not the easiest to get fit, he's expected to improve a bit by his trainer, and both the Paddy Power Gold Cup and the Hennessy will come under consideration now. (op 11-2)
Take The Breeze(FR) had a good first year over fences, winning four times and finishing third to Burton Port in a Grade 2 at Aintree when last seen in April. He travelled strongly into contention down the back but, having picked up well to draw alongside and narrowly head the winner at the last, he was reclaimed on the flat. This was a promising start to his season and he could be one for the Badger Ales at Wincanton in a couple of weeks' time. (op 6-1 tchd 5-1)
From Dawn To Dusk, third in last season's Byrne Group Plate, stays this trip well, as highlighted by his win at Aintree the following month, but a mistake at the second-last did for his chance. Racing from a career-high mark, this near 12-y-o still seems on an upward curve and he, too, would be one to consider for something like the Badger Ales. (op 8-1 tchd 9-1)
Exmoor Ranger(IRE) ◆ did well to finish fourth considering his jumping was sticky to say the least, a notable blunder at the third taking a bit out of him, but he did stay on well and he'll be contending for plenty of decent handicap chases once again if his jumping improves. (op 12-1)
Dover's Hill, a good winner at Exeter on his previous start and now returning to handicaps, stuck on surprising well considering he made a lot of the running at a good gallop and suffered a notably bad blunder down the back. (op 7-1)
Carruthers, runner-up to What A Friend in last season's Totesport Bowl, didn't contest the lead like he normally does and connections clearly didn't want him to have too hard a race first time back. He should come on plenty and will be suited by a return to slower ground, with the Hennessy presumably the target. (op 15-2)
Free World(IRE) plugged on late from the rear and isn't yet up to this level. (op 10-1 tchd 7-1)
Can't Buy Time(IRE), an early faller in the National, travelled well until getting tired and McCoy was at pains not to be hard on him once his chance had gone. His campaign will presumably be geared towards Aintree once again. (tchd 14-1)
Possol(FR), another likely to have Aintree at the top of his agenda this season, kept jumping out to his left and gave himself little chance. His rider reported the gelding to have both hung and jumped left-handed. Official explanation: jockey said gelding hung and jumped left throughout (tchd 12-1)
Eric's Charm(FR), as good as ever last year, showed disappointingly little on this first start since May, dropping out quickly at rather an early stage. One hates to say it, but perhaps age has finally caught up with him. We'll no doubt learn more next time.
Always Waining(IRE) paid for sitting so close to the pace.

Silmi, seeking a hat-trick, found this calibre of race all a bit too competitive. (op 12-1)

2085 WILLIAMHILL.COM H'CAP HURDLE (LISTED RACE) (9 hdls) 2m

4:15 (4:15) (Class 1) 4-Y-O+

£12,392 (£4,668; £2,336; £1,168; £585; £292)

Form				RPR
140-	1		**Tocca Ferro (FR)**[231] 4591 5-10-2 **126** JackDoyle (Emma Lavelle) *bmpd 1st: trckd ldrs: wnt 3rd after 3 out: clsd on bit to ld last: drvn flat: jst hld on* **5/2**[1]	132+
-051	2	*hd*	**Hibiki (IRE)**[7] 1971 6-10-0 **124** (p) TomScudamore (Philip Hobbs) *bmpd 1st: trckd ldrs: lost pl and dropped to last pair 3 out: rallied strly fr 2 out: drvn to go 2nd after last: clsd on wnr flat: jst failed* **14/1**	129
P-15	3	*2*	**Pascha Bere (FR)**[147] 633 7-10-10 **134** (p) LiamTreadwell (Nick Gifford) *pressed ldr: drvn ahd bef 2 out: hdd last: styd on same pce* **8/1**[3]	137
P2-0	4	*4 ½*	**Aather (IRE)**[175] 207 5-10-1 **125** TimmyMurphy (Alan Fleming) *hld up in tch: nt fluent 5th: lost pl 3 out and in rr: prog on inner after: chsd ldng pair bef last: fdd flat* **5/1**[2]	124
520-	5	*2 ½*	**Oldrik (GER)**[13] 4711 7-11-0 **138** (p) RichardJohnson (Philip Hobbs) *hld up in last pair: sme prog 3 out: nt qckn and no imp on ldrs 2 out: kpt on: nvr able to chal* **8/1**[3]	136
/0F-	6	*6*	**Alsadaa (USA)**[189] 5392 7-11-2 **140** LeightonAspell (Laura Mongan) *led at decent pce: drvn and hdd bef 2 out: steadily lost pl* **25/1**	132
112-	7	*¾*	**Get Me Out Of Here (IRE)**[228] 4657 6-11-12 **150** APMcCoy (Jonjo O'Neill) *t.k.h: hld up in 9th: effrt 3 out and in tch: nudged along and no hdwy 2 out: fdd* **5/2**[1]	141
66-4	8	*nk*	**Gilded Age**[14] 1862 4-10-8 **132** WayneHutchinson (Alan King) *j.rt 1st: trckd ldng pair tl after 3 out: wkng whn blnd 2 out* **16/1**	123
121/	9	*6*	**Levera**[29] 1892 7-10-5 **132** CharlieHuxley(3) (Alan King) *t.k.h: hld up in 7th: no prog 3 out and sn dropped to rr: n.d after* **25/1**	117
11-0	10	*51*	**Ciceron (IRE)**[175] 207 4-10-11 **135** AidanColeman (Venetia Williams) *hld up in 8th: smooth prog fr 6th to trck ldrs 3 out: sn wknd rapidly: t.o* **25/1**	74
2403	F		**Forty Thirty (IRE)**[16] 1127 4-10-4 **128** JamieGoldstein (Sheena West) *hld up: last but in tch whn fell 4th* **40/1**	—

3m 42.5s (-6.50) **Going Correction** -0.30s/f (Good)
WFA 4 from 5yo+ 9lb **11 Ran SP% 122.6**
Speed ratings (Par 111): **104,103,102,100,99 96,96,95,92,67** —
toteswingers:1&2:£2.00, 1&3:£24.60, 2&3:£42.20 CSF £36.84 CT £257.91 TOTE £3.20: £1.40, £4.30, £2.90; EX 61.30 Trifecta £270.60 Pool: £1,850.76 - 5.06 winning units..
Owner Prior Syder **Bred** Ian Kellitt Et Al **Trained** Wildhern, Hants

FOCUS
Perhaps not the strongest field overall for a Listed handicap hurdle. It was left to two horses at the bottom of the weights to fight out the finish.

NOTEBOOK
Tocca Ferro(FR) ◆, who had just the four starts over hurdles in his novice season, ran better than his finishing position suggested in the Imperial Cup off this mark back in March and, now a stronger-looking horse, he was able to see his race out better, having again travelled like a dream. He was made to sweat as the runner-up clawed him back with every stride on the run-in, appearing to idle, but it's likely he'll come on for this and connections looks to have a horse capable of contesting all the big 2m handicap hurdles. The Gerry Feilden could be next. (op 9-2)
Hibiki(IRE) has still to win a handicap over hurdles but, to the surprise of many, he nearly got up to take this, just seven days after winning a selling hurdle at Stratford. He's on a decent mark again and last week's easy win has clearly given his confidence a boost. (op 16-1)
Pascha Bere(FR), an honest sort who was 9lb higher than when winning at Worcester in May, was always likely to find something too good, but he kept on dourly for pressure. (op 11-1)
Aather(IRE), well beaten in the Swinton when last seen, tried to get back into it, having lost his place, and showed enough to suggest he'll be winning again at some stage. (op 9-2)
Oldrik(GER), fit from the Flat, was running for the first time off his new rating of 138 and could never get into it. He won't find it easy to defy this mark.
Alsadaa(USA), seventh off 2lb higher a year ago, ran a similar race this time round. (op 20-1)
Get Me Out Of Here(IRE), touted as a possible Champion Hurdle contender by many, was 15lb higher than when winning last season's Totesport Trophy and should have been perfectly capable of winning off this mark, but he never got close to the leaders, McCoy very much looking after the 6-y-o with an eye to the future. He'll no doubt leave this form behind, although obviously he needs to, with the Greatwood the next possible stop. (tchd 9-4 and 11-4)

2086 BYRNE GROUP H'CAP CHASE (LISTED RACE) (13 fncs) 2m 1f

4:50 (4:50) (Class 1) (0-150,148) 4-Y-O+

£17,103 (£6,417; £3,213; £1,602; £804; £402)

Form				RPR
603-	1		**Safari Journey (USA)**[36] 5210 6-10-8 **130** (b[1]) RichardJohnson (Philip Hobbs) *hld up in tch: prog 7th: led 4 out gng v easily: sn clr and in n.d: eased fnl 75yds* **10/1**	150+
63-0	2	*12*	**Fiendish Flame (IRE)**[21] 1766 6-11-4 **140** BrianHarding (Donald McCain) *led at str pce: hdd and mstke 4 out: no ch w wnr after but kpt on wl to hold on to 2nd* **8/1**	144
313-	3	*1 ½*	**I Have Dreamed (IRE)**[195] 5244 8-11-1 **137** JamieMoore (Gary Moore) *hld up in rr: latched on to ldng gp 7th: prog fr 3 out to go 3rd after next: one pce after* **25/1**	139
121-	4	*½*	**King Edmund**[195] 5244 7-11-6 **142** (t) RodiGreene (Chris Gordon) *pressed ldr: hit 8th: upsides next: outpcd fr 4 out: kpt on* **10/1**	143
PP-4	5	*4 ½*	**You're The Top (FR)**[14] 1861 6-11-3 **139** APMcCoy (Nicky Henderson) *trckd ldrs: nt fluent fr 8th whn trying to cl: no imp fr 3 out: one pce* **11/4**[1]	138
32-U	6	*4 ½*	**Oiseau De Nuit (FR)**[14] 1861 8-11-8 **144** (t) JoeTizzard (Colin Tizzard) *in tch: rdn 9th: no prog next: n.d bef 2 out* **6/1**[3]	138
002/	7	*13*	**Sizing Africa (IRE)**[29] 1671 8-11-0 **136** AELynch (Henry De Bromhead, Ire) *prom: mstke 6th: blnd next and lost pl: struggling fr 9th* **4/1**[2]	121
14F-	8	*28*	**Panjo Bere (FR)**[204] 5111 7-11-5 **148** JoshuaMoore(7) (Gary Moore) *j. sluggishly and nvr gng wl: a in last trio: lost tch fr 6th: t.o* **16/1**	104
4-02	9	*3 ¼*	**Nikola (FR)**[36] 1606 9-10-5 **130** SamTwiston-Davies(3) (Nigel Twiston-Davies) *sn in rr: nt fluent and lost tch fr 5th: t.o* **7/1**	83
612-	P		**Danehill Willy (IRE)**[236] 4485 8-10-11 **136** (t) DPFahy(3) (Evan Williams) *prom to 4th: sn dropped to rr and struggling: t.o whn p.u bef 9th* **20/1**	—

4m 4.60s (-10.40) **Going Correction** -0.30s/f (Good) **10 Ran SP% 117.2**
Speed ratings (Par 111): **112,106,105,105,103 101,95,81,80,**—
toteswingers:1&2:£4.70, 1&3:£9.30, 2&3:£7.00 CSF £87.41 CT £1947.41 TOTE £12.80: £2.80, £2.30, £4.90; EX 82.40 Trifecta £1123.70 Part won. Pool: £1,518.58 - 0.10 winning units..
Owner Hill, Trembath, Bryan & Outhart **Bred** Juddmonte Farms Inc **Trained** Withycombe, Somerset

FOCUS
This good handicap was turned into a rout by Safari Journey, who produced a big step up in the first-time blinkers. The next three are all rated to their marks.

NOTEBOOK
Safari Journey(USA) travelled strongly in the first-time blinkers and, having powered to the front at the end of the back straight, continued to gallop on relentlessly for a bloodless victory. He's long looked capable of becoming a really good 2m handicap chaser, although whether the headgear works as well in future remains to be seen. It'll probably be a 2m handicap chase at next month's Cheltenham Open meeting for the 6-y-o.

Fiendish Flame(IRE), last season's Jewson sixth but well held over hurdles on his reappearance at Bangor, ensured there was no hanging around and picked up again having made a blunder at the fourth-last, but he was made to look pedestrian by the winner.

I Have Dreamed(IRE), consistent in his first season over fences, closed up well from the rear to take a place. He was going without the usual cheekpieces and remains capable of better this season.

King Edmund ◆, another to do well in his first season over fences, couldn't get an easy lead but still travelled strongly until becoming outpaced. He'll come on for this and could be a horse to keep on-side this season, as he's still got plenty of scope. (op 7-1)

You're The Top(FR), fourth at Cheltenham on his reappearance, couldn't cope with the drop in trip, plugging on late. (op 3-1)

Oiseau De Nuit(FR) isn't going to find it easy winning off this mark. (op 9-2)

Sizing Africa(IRE), an Irish raider, was disappointing, although he was another who may have found everything happening a bit quickly. (op 9-2)

2087 CHYPS CHILDRENS HOSPICE STANDARD OPEN NATIONAL HUNT FLAT RACE 2m

5:25 (5:25) (Class 4) 4-6-Y-O

£3,131 (£925; £462; £231; £115; £58)

Form				RPR
	1		**Persian Snow (IRE)**[195] 4-11-0 0 RichardJohnson (Philip Hobbs) *hld up wl in tch: jnd ldrs 4f out: rdn to ld 2f out: forged clr fnl f* **3/1**[2]	122+
	2	*6*	**Balding Banker (IRE)** 4-11-0 0 NoelFehily (Paul Nicholls) *trckd ldrs: cl up 5f out gng strly: rdn to chal and upsides 2f out: sn lft bhd by wnr* **11/4**[1]	114
	3	*2 ¼*	**No Secrets (IRE)** 6-11-0 0 WayneHutchinson (Warren Greatrex) *prom: jnd ldr 4f out: rdn to ld 3f out to 2f out: outpcd after* **3/1**[2]	112
26-3	4	*3 ¼*	**Natural Spring**[168] 332 5-10-7 0 ColinBolger (Suzy Smith) *disp ld at gd pce to 3f out: steadily fdd* **6/1**[3]	102
	5	*15*	**Jimmy The Hat (IRE)** 4-10-11 0 TomMolloy(3) (Giles Smyly) *hld up in last pair: prog on outer 6f out: nvr on terms w ldrs: wl btn 5th over 1f out: nt disgracd* **16/1**	96
20	6	*1 ¾*	**Don Pooleoni (IRE)**[21] 1778 5-11-0 0 TimmyMurphy (David Arbuthnot) *hld up in last pair: prog to go 5th 4f out but nt on terms w ldrs: hanging and fdd 2f out* **20/1**	94
	7	*11*	**Turf Legends (IRE)** 4-11-0 0 TomO'Brien (Philip Hobbs) *sn pushed along and rn green: struggling fr 1/2-way: sme late prog: nvr a factor* **12/1**	84
	8	*9*	**Rathconrath (FR)**[207] 5-10-11 0 SamTwiston-Davies(3) (Althea Barclay) *pressed ldrs: pushed along after 6f: u.p 6f out: wknd 4f out* **20/1**	76
	9	*20*	**Radmores Sam Evans** 5-10-7 0 CharlieWallis(7) (John O'Shea) *in tch: rdn 7f out: sn struggling: wl bhd fnl 3f: t.o* **66/1**	58
	10	*1 ¼*	**Candlefort Lady (IRE)** 5-10-7 0 JamieMoore (Linda Jewell) *trckd ldrs: rdn over 6f out: sn wknd: t.o* **40/1**	50
	11	*9*	**Topthorn** 4-10-7 0 (v[1]) AnthonyFreeman(7) (Martin Bosley) *t.k.h: disp ld aftr 3f tl wknd rapidly 5f out: t.o* **66/1**	49
	12	*4*	**Spell Shot**[224] 6-11-0 0 MarkBradburne (Jimmy Fox) *a in rr: rdn sn after 1/2-way: struggling after: wl bhd fnl 3f: t.o* **40/1**	45

3m 35.9s (-7.10) **Going Correction** -0.30s/f (Good)
WFA 4 from 5yo+ 9lb **12 Ran SP% 121.9**
Speed ratings: **105,102,100,99,91 90,85,80,70,70 65,63**
toteswingers:1&2:£3.00, 1&3:£3.90, 2&3:£3.90 CSF £11.28 TOTE £3.50: £1.60, £2.00, £1.60; EX 10.10 Trifecta £25.80 Pool: £642.93 - 18.43 winning units. Place 6 £382.83, Place 5 £128.64.

Owner D R Peppiatt **Bred** Garryhankard House Stud **Trained** Withycombe, Somerset

FOCUS
No Heather Royal, the morning favourite, but this still looked a decent bumper, with the big yards dominatiing.

NOTEBOOK
Persian Snow(IRE) ◆, a faller when in contention on his sole point-to-point start, created a favourable impression on debut for the red-hot Philip Hobbs stable. Reportedly going well at home, he was always travelling kindly under Johnson, and the pair gradually drew clear in the straight. His future ultimately lies over fences, but that a long way off for the 4-y-o, who can first make his mark over hurdles. He'll be suited by further and looks one to keep on-side. (op 5-2, tchd 10-3 in a place and 9-4 in places)

Balding Banker(IRE), out of an unraced half-sister to Celestial Gold and Fiveforthree, closed up readily to challenge in the straight, but the winner proved a little too classy late on. This was a promising start and he'll be well suited by further once he goes hurdling. (op 5-2 tchd 3-1)

No Secrets(IRE), from a yard that traditionally does well in this sphere, couldn't match the front pair in the straight but was a few lengths ahead of the remainder and should be good enough to win a bumper before being sent hurdling. (op 15-2)

Natural Spring, having her fourth start, disputed it at a decent clip before fading late on. She'll find opportunities against her own sex over hurdles. (op 5-1 tchd 9-2)

Jimmy The Hat(IRE), whose dam is a half-sister to Cornish Sett, was a bit adrift of the front four but showed more than enough, considering his breeding points to 3m and fences being needed.

Turf Legends(IRE), half-brother to a couple of bumper winners, was quite badly in need of the experience and looks almost certain to improve. He'll require further over hurdles. (tchd 14-1)

T/Jkpt: Not won. T/Plt: £541.30 to a £1 stake. Pool: £159,741.72. 215.41 winning tickets. T/Qpdt: £120.10 to a £1 stake. Pool: £8,112.39. 49.95 winning tickets. JN

2075 WETHERBY (L-H)

Saturday, October 30

OFFICIAL GOING: Good (watered; chase 7.8, hurdle 8.1, average 8.0)

Wind: fresh 1/2 behind Weather: fine and sunny but very breezy

2088 BET365.COM NOVICES' CHASE (13 fncs) 2m

1:40 (1:41) (Class 3) 4-Y-0+ **£5,041** (£1,480; £740; £369)

Form				RPR
521-	**1**		**Gilbarry (IRE)**[189] 5386 5-11-2 0 GrahamLee (Malcolm Jefferson) *t.k.h: trckd ldrs: blnd 4th: nt fluent 9th: led 3 out: drvn out* **4/1**[3]	137+
3-11	**2**	*5*	**Osric (IRE)**[149] 591 7-11-2 0 BarryGeraghty (Nicky Henderson) *j.lft: led 1st: hit next: hdd sn after 4th: j.lft and bmpd 7th: led appr 4 out: hdd 3 out: kpt on same pce* **6/5**[1]	130+
231-	**3**	*30*	**Knockavilla (IRE)**[186] 32 7-11-9 125 BrianHughes (Howard Johnson) *led to 1st: bmpd 7th: led sn after 9th: hdd appr next: wknd 3 out* **15/8**[2]	110
-PP2	**4**	*16*	**Alaskan Prince (IRE)**[7] 1961 5-11-2 0 DavidEngland (Peter Salmon) *trckd ldrs: led sn after 4th: hdd sn after 9th: wknd next* **100/1**	86
P-14	**5**	*21*	**Quell The Storm (FR)**[41] 1558 6-11-4 0 (t) JimmyDerham(5) (Milton Harris) *t.k.h: j.lft: trckd ldrs: outpcd and lost pl 5th: sn bhd: t.o 9th* **12/1**	70

3m 47.4s (-8.40) **Going Correction** -0.30s/f (Good) **5** Ran SP% **108.9**

Speed ratings (Par 107): **109,106,91,83,73**

CSF £9.51 TOTE £4.90: £2.10, £1.30; EX 10.80.

Owner Highbank Stud **Bred** Colin Kennedy **Trained** Norton, N Yorks

FOCUS

The ground was described as "lovely" by the winning jockey in the first. A fair novice chase, it was run at what looked an ordinary pace, but the time was more than four seconds inside the standard. Gilbarry is rated up a stone on his hurdles form and looks a decent prospect.

NOTEBOOK

Gilbarry(IRE), a big gelding, progressed over hurdles last season and looks likely to make an even better chaser on the evidence of this debut win. Held up, and keen once again, he covered the runner-up's move turning for home and jumped ahead three out. Staying on well, he will not mind a step back up in trip, but there is room for improvement in his jumping. This sort of ground is ideal. (op 6-1)

Osric(IRE) won his last two races over hurdles in the early summer and has the highest BHA rating of this line-up in that sphere. His rider soon had him settled and he moved smoothly to the front facing up to the last line of fences, but he was quickly headed by the winner and was unable to get back at him. He probably just needed this seasonal bow, as a number of his stablemates have been doing. (op Evens tchd 5-4)

Knockavilla(IRE), the most experienced chaser in the field, got off the mark at Sedgefield in April after several solid placed efforts. Outpaced by the principals from the third-last, he will probably be suited by a return to further. He goes on soft ground too and there should be opportunities for him in handicaps. (op 2-1)

Alaskan Prince(IRE) achieved little when a distant second to Medermit last week. He was out of his depth again, but wasn't disgraced and picked up a welcome fourth prize on his home track. (op 66-1)

Quell The Storm(FR) has left Paul Nicholls since his last start. The soft ground was a legitimate excuse at Uttoxeter, but this performance was harder to explain as, after being restrained in rear, he was left trailing from the first down the back. He might be one to be wary of on this evidence.

Official explanation: jockey said gelding ran too free (op 11-1 tchd 10-1)

2089 BET365 MARES' HURDLE (LISTED RACE) (9 hdls) 2m 110y

2:15 (2:15) (Class 1) 4-Y-0+

£17,103 (£6,417; £3,213; £1,602; £804; £402)

Form				RPR
25U-	**1**		**Alegralil**[189] 5397 5-10-12 127 GrahamLee (Donald McCain) *trckd ldrs: hit 5th: upsides 3 out: led sn after last: hld on* **7/2**[3]	128+
12-3	**2**	*nk*	**Issaquah (IRE)**[175] 207 8-10-12 145 JamesHalliday (Malcolm Jefferson) *led to 2nd: w ldr: led 3 out: hung lft and hdd sn after last: no ex clsng stages* **11/4**[2]	128+
F-31	**3**	*12*	**Amber Brook (IRE)**[15] 1855 9-10-12 146 PaddyBrennan (Nigel Twiston-Davies) *chsd ldrs: blnd and lost pl 6th: kpt on to take modest 3rd appr last* **9/4**[1]	120+
51-2	**4**	*½*	**Je Ne Sais Plus (FR)**[23] 1746 6-10-12 113 PaulMoloney (Tom George) *hit 3rd: hdwy 5th: chsng ldrs whn bdly hmpd 3 out: wnt modest 4th appr last* **12/1**	119+
0500	**5**	*8*	**Crosby Jemma**[17] 1827 6-10-12 106 BrianHughes (Mike Sowersby) *hld up: hdwy 6th: modest 3rd 2 out: wknd appr last* **66/1**	106
2023	**6**	*shd*	**Edgefour (IRE)**[23] 1746 6-10-12 107 (v) DarylJacob (Ben Case) *chsd ldrs: modest 4th 2 out: wknd between last 2* **28/1**	106
3524	**7**	*9*	**Aohna (FR)**[14] 1864 5-10-12 115 SamThomas (Alan King) *t.k.h: trckd ldrs: lost pl 3 out: sn bhd* **11/1**	97
221-	**F**		**Bogside Theatre (IRE)**[141] 4512 6-10-12 126 BarryKeniry (George Moore) *led 2nd: hdd and fell 3 out* **8/1**	—
50-0	**P**		**Politelysed**[27] 1702 4-10-12 0 KennyJohnson (Robert Johnson) *detached in last: sn bhd: j. slowly: t.o 3rd: p.u bef 3 out* **150/1**	—

3m 52.1s (-3.70) **Going Correction** +0.125s/f (Yiel) **9** Ran SP% **112.4**

Speed ratings (Par 111): **113,112,107,106,103 103,98,—,—**

toteswingers:1&2:£2.20, 1&3:£2.00, 2&3:£1.60 CSF £13.41 TOTE £4.60: £1.30, £1.40, £1.50; EX 11.90 Trifecta £45.70 Pool: £646.98 - 10.45 winning units..

Owner Tony Meehan **Bred** R D Chugg And C M A Aston **Trained** Cholmondeley, Cheshire

FOCUS

There was not a great deal of depth to this mares' Listed event, which is now in its fourth year. The pace seemed sound but the time was over six seconds outside the standard, suggesting that the hurdles course was riding slower than the chase track. The winner is rated to her mark with the next pair below their best.

NOTEBOOK

Alegralil goes well fresh, so her lack of a recent run was not expected to prove a problem, and has had a minor wind operation over the summer. Closing three from home, she took a narrow lead at the last and fended off the runner-up in brave style. She had no less than 18lb to find with the runner-up, so this was a smart performance from a mare who has more improvement in her. She gets further and the logical target would be the David Nicholson Hurdle at the Cheltenham festival, a race the McCain stable won with Whiteoak in 2008. (tchd 4-1)

Issaquah(IRE), whose regular jockey was unable to claim his 5lb allowance, had been third in the hotly contested Swinton Hurdle when last seen in early May. Always up with the pace, she was left in the lead three from home and looked set to rise in front at the last, only to falter going into the flight and lose momentum. She battled on from there but was always just being held. Softer ground will aid her cause but she is on a career-high mark, which will not make life easy for her. (op 2-1)

Amber Brook(IRE) put up a career-best effort in a Cheltenham handicap last time and was best in at the weights in this company, a pound ahead of Issaquah and 19lb and more clear of the rest. She does most of her racing over further, which was a concern, but was moving well enough when she dived at the last flight down the back and lost her hind legs. That knocked her to the back of the field, the rank outsider apart, and while she could never get back into the race she was staying on steadily at the end. Perhaps an unlucky loser, this was an opportunity missed and she has now been found wanting in each of her eight tries in Listed races. (op 7-2)

Je Ne Sais Plus(FR) was nearly brought down at the third-last and it is to her credit that she stayed on to claim fourth. She won't mind a return to further but her jumping remains a concern. (op 11-1 tchd 9-1)

Crosby Jemma had an awful lot on at the weights and ran well in the circumstances, even finding herself briefly in third place between the last two flights.

Edgefour(IRE), a 107-rated handicapper, ran creditably but could not overturn recent Worcester form with Je Ne Sais Plus. (op 33-1)

Aohna(FR) was another facing a thankless task at the weights, and she probably prefers a longer trip. (tchd 10-1 and 12-1)

Bogside Theatre(IRE) soon reached the front where she likes to be, but she was being tackled on both sides when she stepped into the third-last and took a heavy fall. She was up quickly and it is to be hoped that this useful mare is none the worse. (tchd 15-2)

Politelysed Official explanation: jockey said, regarding running and riding, that his orders were to jump off with the others, give the filly some daylight at first, creep away and try to win, adding that it jumped the first three very slowly and became detached. (tchd 15-2)

2090 JOHN SMITH'S HURDLE (REGISTERED AS THE WEST YORKSHIRE HURDLE RACE GRADE 2) (13 hdls) 3m 1f

2:50 (2:50) (Class 1) 4-Y-0+

£18,528 (£6,951; £3,480; £1,735; £871; £435)

Form				RPR
500-	**1**		**Fair Along (GER)**[226] 4701 8-11-8 158 (p) RhysFlint (Philip Hobbs) *w ldr: led appr 2nd: hdd appr 8th: led appr 3 out: hit 2 out: edgd lft: hld on wl* **6/1**	159+
550-	**2**	*1 ¼*	**Kayf Aramis**[14] 5348 8-11-0 148 PaddyBrennan (Nigel Twiston-Davies) *chsd ldrs: hrd drvn and wnt 2nd appr 3 out: swtchd rt between last 2: styd on run-in: nvr quite able to chal* **11/2**[3]	148
104-	**3**	*8*	**Tidal Bay (IRE)**[205] 5093 9-11-8 160 BrianHughes (Howard Johnson) *chsd ldrs: pushed along and lost pl after 7th: hdwy 10th: nt fluent next: kpt on to take modest 3rd last* **5/2**[2]	149
211-	**4**	*4*	**Duc De Regniere (FR)**[199] 5183 8-11-0 154 BarryGeraghty (Nicky Henderson) *trckd ldrs: effrt appr 3 out: 3rd and btn whn hit 2 out* **9/4**[1]	138
0123	**5**	*17*	**Raslan**[15] 1855 7-11-0 145 (vt) DannyCook (David Pipe) *led tl appr 2nd: chsd ldr: led and qcknd appr 8th: hdd & wknd appr 3 out* **10/1**	122
313-	**6**	*6*	**Blazing Bailey**[233] 4540 8-11-0 147 ChristianWilliams (Alan King) *chsd ldrs: drvn 7th: lost pl after next: t.o 3 out* **12/1**	113
024B	**7**	*68*	**Majestic Mayhem (IRE)**[14] 1860 7-11-0 123 SamThomas (George Moore) *nt fluent in rr: bhd fr 8th: t.o 3 out* **66/1**	45
1-20	**P**		**Coastley (IRE)**[147] 627 8-11-0 129 GrahamLee (David Carr) *t.k.h towards rr: hdwy and prom 8th: blnd next: sn lost pl: t.o whn p.u bef 3 out* **28/1**	—

6m 10.1s (-6.40) **Going Correction** +0.125s/f (Yiel) **8** Ran SP% **110.7**

Speed ratings (Par 115): **115,114,112,110,105 103,81,—**

toteswingers:1&2:£7.10, 1&3:£4.80, 2&3:£3.60 CSF £36.42 TOTE £6.50: £1.90, £1.50, £1.30; EX 38.40 Trifecta £124.60 Pool: £657.01 - 3.90 winning units..

Owner Alan Peterson **Bred** Gestut Harzburg **Trained** Withycombe, Somerset

FOCUS

A decent edition of this Grade 2 hurdle. The pace seemed reasonable but the time was around 11 seconds outside the standard. The principals are all smart performers but the position of Big Buck's at the top of the stayers' ranks remains untroubled on this evidence. Fair Along is rated 3lb off last year's winning mark with the second to his best and the next pair a stone off.

NOTEBOOK

Fair Along(GER) won this race by 18l last season and he was saddled with an 8lb penalty this time round. He did not have things his own way in front, having to share the lead with Raslan, but was back in front early in the home straight and battled on in his usual gritty fashion to repel the runner-up. He failed to add to his win in a light campaign last season and although there were no immediate plans, his trainer has been reported as saying that he may switch back to fences now, the reasoning being that he is unexposed in chases over 3m. There are more races to be won with this thoroughly admirable individual. (op 13-2 tchd 11-2)

Kayf Aramis had a couple of recent runs on the Flat and lacked nothing in fitness. From a yard successful in this event in recent years with Pettifour and Redemption, he was never far away and was staying on resolutely all the way to the line. His last win over hurdles came in the 2009 Pertemps Final, when trained by Venetia Williams, but this tough sort should continue to run with credit. (op 6-1 tchd 13-2)

Tidal Bay(IRE), whose connections won this with Inglis Drever five years ago, was penalised for his win in the Cleeve Hurdle in January. This famously quirky character was never going that sweetly and was held turning out of the back for the final time, but did stay on late for third. He had an alternative entry in the Charlie Hall and could revert to fences if required. (op 11-4)

Duc De Regniere(FR), another who appeared among the Charlie Hall entries, had some smart hurdling form a couple of seasons back and was top rated on official figures. After briefly looking a threat turning out the back, he appeared to blow up, but he should be spot-on next time. Unbeaten in three chases last season, he is now rated 156 over fences and finding winning opportunities for him won't be easy. (op 15-8)

Raslan has hit a rich vein of form recently and he ran well for a long way on this rise in grade. His rider tried to quicken things up on the final circuit, but the gelding could never shake off Fair Along and and was a spent force with three to jump. (op 12-1)

Blazing Bailey is not the force of old and was one of the first in trouble, but he did stay on a bit in the latter stages. He is another who may switch back to fences, although he didn't look a natural as a novice. (op 11-1 tchd 10-1)

Coastley(IRE) faced a big ask on this first run since June, but he was close enough when a blunder in the back straight cost him any chance he may have had. Official explanation: jockey said gelding made a mistake 5th last (op 25-1)

2091 BET365 CHARLIE HALL CHASE (GRADE 2) (18 fncs) 3m 1f

3:25 (3:25) (Class 1) 5-Y-0+

£57,010 (£21,390; £10,710; £5,340; £2,680; £1,340)

Form				RPR
423-	**1**		**Nacarat (FR)**[205] 5095 9-11-0 158 SamThomas (Tom George) *trckd ldr: upsides 10th: led appr 4 out: 3 l ahd whn blnd 3 out: styd on wl: drvn out* **6/1**[3]	164+
205-	**2**	*4*	**The Tother One (IRE)**[228] 4659 9-11-0 155 RWalsh (Paul Nicholls) *chsd ldrs: 3rd whn hit 12th: hrd drvn and outpcd 4 out: kpt on to chse wnr appr last: no imp* **9/4**[1]	160
P46-	**3**	*2 ½*	**Deep Purple**[204] 5110 9-11-10 160 PaulMoloney (Evan Williams) *chsd ldrs: drvn and lost pl 14th: sn bhd: styd on fr 3 out: hung rt and tk 3rd run-in: gng on at fin* **15/2**	166

P2-1 **4** 5 **Ollie Magern**[160] 446 12-11-4 147 .... PaddyBrennan 156
(Nigel Twiston-Davies) *led: qcknd appr 10th: hdd appr 4 out: wknd run-in* **11/1**

3010 **5** 2¾ **That's Rhythm (FR)**[35] 1611 10-11-0 142 ....(v) GrahamLee 150
(Martin Todhunter) *in rr: blnd 9th: sme hdwy 14th: kpt on fr 2 out* **33/1**

64-5 **6** 4½ **Calgary Bay (IRE)**[15] 1856 7-11-4 146 .... HaddenFrost 148
(Henrietta Knight) *trckd ldrs: pushed along 14th: outpcd fr 4 out* **7/1**

30P- **7** 65 **Barbers Shop**[192] 5322 8-11-0 156 ....(p) BarryGeraghty 108
(Nicky Henderson) *hld up: nt fluent 11th: sn drvn and hung lft: lost pl 14th: hit next: sn bhd: t.o* **4/1[2]**

245- **P** **Knockara Beau (IRE)**[204] 5109 7-11-6 149 .... JanFaltejsek —
(George Charlton) *sn pushed along: bhd fr 5th: t.o whn p.u bef 9th* **8/1**

5m 52.1s (-17.30) **Going Correction** -0.30s/f (Good) course record **8** Ran SP% **111.7**
Speed ratings: **115,113,112,111,110 109,88,—**
toteswingers:1&2:£3.80, 1&3:£11.20, 2&3:£4.70 CSF £19.81 TOTE £6.30: £2.40, £1.40, £2.10; EX 19.30 Trifecta £77.20 Pool: £1,686.30 - 16.16 winning units..
Owner Simon W Clarke **Bred** Francis Maze **Trained** Slad, Gloucs

FOCUS

An up-to-scratch renewal of the season's first big chase. The pace was brisk and the time was nearly two seconds inside the standard. Nacarat is rated 6lb off last season's Racing Post Chase mark but will come on for this and produced his best figure to date on a left-handed track. The Tother One ran to the level of last season's reappearance with Deep Purple 4lb off his best.

NOTEBOOK

Nacarat(FR) conceded the early lead to fellow front-runner Ollie Magern before easing back to the front at the entrance to the home straight. He walked through the third-last but kept galloping to score in decisive style. Reportedly treated for a shoulder problem during the summer, he was clearly fit enough here but his trainer had left a bit to work on, so there could be more to come from him. He will be targeted at the King George again, a race in which he faded into fourth behind Kauto Star last season, and the return to a right-handed track where he goes so well will suit him. Another bold run looks assured, but he cannot keep affording the blunders. sdf sdf sdf sdf sdfsdf sd sdf conceded the early lead to fellow front-runner Ollie Magern before easing back to the front at the entrance to the home straight. He walked through the third-last but kept galloping to score in decisive style. Reportedly treated for a shoulder problem during the summer, he was clearly fit enough here but his trainer had left a bit to work on, so there could be more to come from him. He will be targeted at the King George again, a race in which he faded into fourth behind Kauto Star last season, and the return to a right-handed track where he goes so well will suit him. Another bold run looks assured, but he cannot keep affording the blunders. King George again, a race in which he faded into fourth behind Kauto Star last season, and the return to a right-handed track where he goes so well will suit him. Another bold run looks assured, but he cannot keep affording the blunders. (op 11-2)

The Tother One(IRE) rather ran in snatches and his jumping lacked a bit of fluency, but he was staying on stoutly at the end. This was a pleasing reappearance and a stiffer test of stamina will suit him, but he remains a difficult horse to catch right. The option is there to try him in blinkers again. (op 3-1)

Deep Purple, last year's winner, faced a stiff task attempting to concede a 10lb penalty to the likes of the first two. After losing his pitch he was running on again late, and this was a brave performance from a horse who broke blood vessels on a couple of occasions last season. He will bid for a repeat win in the Peterborough Chase at Huntingdon and the Betfair Ascot Chase looks an obvious target in the new year. (op 6-1)

Ollie Magern is a regular in this race and won it in 2005 and 2007. Now well into the veteran stage of his career, he ran another enthusiastic race from the front and although he could not go with Nacarat up the straight, he only weakened out of second spot late on. He goes well fresh and it is asking a lot for him to build on this. (tchd 10-1 and 12-1)

That's Rhythm(FR)'s Bangor win in August was smart form and he was worth a crack at this sort of company. He was not quite up to the task and was never seen with a realistic chance, but did come home well from the rear.

Calgary Bay(IRE) had ground conditions to suit and had made a pleasing return at Cheltenham. He needed to find improvement at these weights and it was not forthcoming, but he seemed to run his race. (op 17-2)

Barbers Shop was rated just 2lb off Nacarat on these terms and this was a disappointing effort. Running here rather than shoulder top weight at Ascot, he had the cheekpieces back for this seasonal return but was in trouble down the far side and ended up well beaten. He usually goes well fresh and, while his fitness may improve, he has something to prove after a couple of lacklustre efforts in the latter part of last season. Official explanation: jockey said gelding hung left throughout (op 10-3)

Knockara Beau(IRE) was a smart novice last term but he did not want to know on this return, dropping himself out before being pulled up with a circuit to run Official explanation: vet said gelding finished distressed (op 9-1)

2092 CAROLINE BAILEY WINS WITH YORKSHIRE POST NOVICES' HURDLE (9 hdls) 2m 110y

4:00 (4:00) (Class 3) 4-Y-O+ **£4,228** (£1,241; £620; £310)

Form RPR

24 **1** **Andhaar**[141] 712 4-11-0 110 .... BarryGeraghty 120+
(Steve Gollings) *chsd ldrs: wnt 2nd 3 out: upsides last: sn led: styd on wl* **11/1[3]**

-121 **2** 1¾ **Karasenir (IRE)**[13] 1884 4-11-8 131 .... RhysFlint 127+
(Philip Hobbs) *trckd ldr: led appr 3 out: nt fluent 2 out: jnd last: sn hdd and no ex* **8/13[1]**

65- **3** 11 **Highland Love**[14] 2837 5-10-11 0 .... DannyCook(3) 107
(Jedd O'Keeffe) *hld up in mid-div: racd wd: hdwy to chse ldrs 4th: kpt on same pce fr 3 out: tk modest 3rd next* **40/1**

52- **4** 4½ **Solis**[154] 4730 4-11-0 0 .... ChristianWilliams 103+
(John Quinn) *chsd ldrs: one pce fr 3 out: hit last* **12/1**

43-F **5** ¾ **Luso's Lad (IRE)**[29] 1661 6-10-11 117 .... JamesO'Farrell(3) 103+
(Howard Johnson) *hld up in mid-div: hdwy to chse ldrs 6th: 6th and one pce whn mstke 2 out* **25/1**

046- **6** 3½ **Along Came Rosie**[239] 4416 6-10-4 92 .... FearghalDavis(3) 91
(Andrew Crook) *mid-div: hdwy 6th: chsng ldrs whn stmbld on landing next: one pce after* **66/1**

10- **7** 3½ **Rupert Lamb**[203] 5129 4-11-0 0 .... BrianHughes 97+
(Howard Johnson) *nt fluent: trckd ldrs: wnt 2nd appr 3 out: 5th and wkng whn mstke last* **11/2[2]**

8 6 **Zefooha (FR)**[14] 6-10-7 0 .... RobertWalford 83
(Tim Walford) *j.lft 1st: nt fluent: sn towards rr: sme hdwy 3 out: nvr nr ldrs* **50/1**

23/ **9** 3½ **Motafarred (IRE)**[22] 1951 8-11-0 0 ....(t) RichieMcGrath 85
(Tina Jackson) *hld up in midfield: sme hdwy 6th: wknd fr next: j.lft last* **40/1**

-430 **10** 1¾ **Wicked Streak (IRE)**[14] 1867 5-10-9 0 .... JamesHalliday(5) 82
(Micky Hammond) *towards rr: nvr on terms* **100/1**

56 **11** 12 **Media Stars**[29] 1660 5-11-0 0 .... KennyJohnson 70
(Robert Johnson) *t.k.h in midfield: sme hdwy 5th: wknd next* **100/1**

/43- **12** 1¼ **Lap Of Honour (IRE)**[345] 2382 6-11-0 0 .... GrahamLee 69
(Ferdy Murphy) *in rr-div: reminders appr 3 out: nvr a factor* **12/1**

13 ½ **Lindoro**[8] 5-10-7 0 .... BrianToomey(7) 69
(Kevin M Prendergast) *stdd s: t.k.h in rr: sme hdwy 6th: sn wknd* **66/1**

0 **14** ¾ **Wicked Times**[34] 1629 5-11-0 0 .... HenryOliver 68
(Sue Smith) *chsd ldrs: lost pl appr 3 out* **100/1**

000 **15** 11 **Tuckers Treasure**[29] 1664 4-10-9 0 .... ShaneByrne(5) 57
(Sue Smith) *led tl appr 3 out: sn lost pl* **100/1**

36-0 **16** 14 **Jersey Boys**[29] 1664 4-11-0 0 .... WilsonRenwick 43
(Howard Johnson) *stdd s: hld up in rr: a bhd* **50/1**

-000 **17** 1 **Why So Serious**[7] 1962 4-11-0 0 .... DavidEngland 42
(Peter Salmon) *in rr: bhd and rdn 6th* **100/1**

0P **18** 71 **Balwyllo (IRE)**[107] 1003 5-11-0 0 .... AndrewThornton —
(Ben Haslam) *in rr: mstke 1st: bhd fr 6th: t.o next: eventually completed* **100/1**

3m 56.0s (0.20) **Going Correction** +0.125s/f (Yiel) **18** Ran SP% **122.6**
Speed ratings (Par 107): **104,103,98,95,95 93,92,89,87,86 81,80,80,80,74 68,67,34**
toteswingers:1&2:£2.00, 1&3:£24.60, 2&3:£42.20 CSF £17.99 TOTE £15.30: £3.40, £1.10, £10.50; EX 25.10.
Owner P J Martin **Bred** Shadwell Estate Company Limited **Trained** Scamblesby, Lincs

FOCUS

A fair novice hurdle which was run at a fairly steady pace considering the size of the field, and they finished in a bit of a heap. A big step up from the winner but the runner-up was 5lb off his best.

NOTEBOOK

Andhaar had made the frame in both his previous runs over hurdles back in the early summer, making mistakes each time. Jumping better here, he gunned down the odds-on favourite at the last and ran on well. Things will be tougher under a penalty, but he is well regarded. (op 16-1)

Karasenir(IRE) had won two of his three races this term and was well supported to successfully concede a double penalty. Slipshod jumping had been a feature of his previous outings and it was once again here, as he landed flat-footed over the third-last and the next as he attempted to race clear. He met the final flight better but could not repel the winner. (op 10-11 tchd 4-7)

Highland Love scored twice on the Flat at about 1m2f this year. He ran a nice race on this return to hurdles, if holding no chance with the first two late on, and is now qualified for a handicap mark. A sharp 2m looks required. (op 33-1)

Solis ◆, another having his third run over hurdles, ran a pleasing race, keeping on after the leaders had got away from him. A winning opportunity should be found. (op 10-1)

Luso's Lad(IRE), back over hurdles after a fall on his chasing debut, settled better under restraint and plugged on for fifth. (op 22-1)

Along Came Rosie ran creditably, but is rated 92 and puts the form into some sort of perspective.

Rupert Lamb, a bumper winner, showed up for a long way on this hurdles debut but will need to jump better. (op 10-3 tchd 6-1 in a place)

Zefooha(FR) shaped with a bit of promise on this hurdles debut but may need further and has to jump better.

Motafarred(IRE), third in this race two years ago on his last hurdles start, faded out of things from the third-last. (op 50-1)

2093 WETHERBYRACING.CO.UK NOVICES' H'CAP CHASE (16 fncs) 2m 4f 110y

4:35 (4:36) (Class 3) (0-120,118) 4-Y-O+ **£5,041** (£1,480; £740; £369)

Form RPR

2232 **1** **Film Festival (USA)**[17] 1828 7-11-9 118 .... FearghalDavis(3) 131+
(Brian Ellison) *mde all: styd on wl fr 4 out: hit 2 out: 9 l ahd last: eased last 75yds* **3/1[1]**

-015 **2** 8 **The Darling Boy**[16] 1841 5-10-10 102 ....(t) PaddyBrennan 104
(Tom George) *nt fluent in rr: hdwy to chse ldrs 12th: hit next: kpt on to take modest 2nd last* **13/2**

P3-4 **3** 4½ **Border Reiver**[14] 1868 6-10-7 99 ....(t) RichieMcGrath 99
(Tim Easterby) *trckd wnr: j.rt and hit 2 out: j.rt and wknd run-in* **4/1[3]**

1P23 **4** 2¾ **Kirkhammerton (IRE)**[17] 1828 8-11-6 115 .... DannyCook(3) 110
(Barry Leavy) *chsd ldrs: outpcd and lost pl 12th: kpt on fr 2 out* **7/1**

3112 **5** 13 **Morning Sunshine (IRE)**[14] 1872 7-10-13 108 .... AdrianLane(3) 92
(Donald McCain) *hld up in rr: hdwy 11th: rdn after next: wknd appr 4 out* **7/2[2]**

P234 **6** 4 **Tranos (USA)**[14] 1872 7-10-1 93 ....(p) BrianHughes 72
(Micky Hammond) *prom: wknd appr 4 out: sn bhd: last whn mstke 2 out* **8/1**

2-63 **P** **Greenbelt**[17] 1830 9-10-6 98 ....(p) GrahamLee —
(George Moore) *in tch: reminders 7th: outpcd and lost pl 9th: sn bhd: t.o whn hit 12th: sn p.u* **10/1**

4m 57.6s (-10.20) **Going Correction** -0.30s/f (Good) **7** Ran SP% **113.3**
Speed ratings (Par 107): **107,103,102,101,96 94,—**
toteswingers:1&2:£5.60, 1&3:£3.70, 2&3:£3.20 CSF £21.91 TOTE £3.70: £2.30, £2.80; EX 29.10.
Owner Koo's Racing Club **Bred** Jim Ryan And Geraldine Ryan **Trained** Norton, N Yorks

FOCUS

An ordinary novice handicap. A chase personal best from the winner with the second 6lb off his best.

NOTEBOOK

Film Festival(USA) made all the running, and although he got in too close to the second-last his nearest pursuer did likewise. He deserved this after being placed on each of his four previous starts this term, and readily defied a 5lb rise for his latest C/D second. (op 10-3 tchd 11-4)

The Darling Boy is 13lb higher now than when winning over 2m at Worcester two starts back. His jumping was again not the best, but he stayed on for second after the last. (op 8-1)

Border Reiver chased the winner for much of the way but a mistake two out ended any lingering hopes. He won't mind a return to further and is well handicapped at the moment. (op 9-2 tchd 5-1)

Kirkhammerton(IRE) was 1lb better off with Film Festival but finished further behind him than he had here last time. (op 13-2)

Morning Sunshine(IRE), who was 16lb higher than when scoring at Cartmel in August, did not stay this longer trip. Official explanation: jockey said gelding ran flat (op 4-1)

Tranos(USA) did not find the anticipated improvement for the extra half mile. (op 7-1)

2094 WETHERBY RACECOURSE & CONFERENCE CENTRE H'CAP HURDLE (11 hdls) 2m 4f

5:10 (5:10) (Class 3) (0-120,120) 4-Y-O+ **£4,228** (£1,241; £620; £310)

Form RPR

-P00 **1** **Viva Colonia (IRE)**[72] 1292 5-10-8 102 .... GrahamLee 116+
(David O'Meara) *hld up towards rr: hdwy to chse ldrs 8th: styd on wl to ld last: drvn clr* **10/1**

/13- **2** 4 **First Stream (GER)**[255] 4104 6-11-12 120 .... BrianHughes 129+
(Howard Johnson) *hld up in mid-div: hdwy to trck ldrs 6th: led appr last: hit last and hdd: no ex* **7/2[1]**

30P- **3** 5 **Peter Grimes (IRE)**[33] 4737 4-11-5 113 .... SamThomas 116
(Alan King) *trckd ldrs: hit 3 out: led next: hdd appr last: kpt on same pce* **10/1**

-203 **4** 3¼ **Dontpaytheferryman (USA)**[17] 1827 5-11-5 116 .... FearghalDavis(3) 115
(Brian Ellison) *trckd ldrs: one pce fr 2 out* **4/1[2]**

431- **5** 4½ **Munlochy Bay**[199] 5184 6-10-5 106 .... MrLRPayter(7) 102
(Matt Sheppard) *in rr: mstke 6th: hdwy 8th: hit next: kpt on one pce* **14/1**

U 6 nse **San Deng**[67] 1358 8-10-4 **98** RichieMcGrath 93
(Micky Hammond) *chsd ldrs: lost pl 5th: kpt on fr 2 out* **22/1**
54F- 7 2 3/4 **Political Paddy**[216] 4908 8-11-7 **118** RyanMania(3) 109
(Rayson Nixon) *in rr: hdwy 8th: outpcd next: kpt on one pce fr 2 out* **33/1**
52/1 8 1 3/4 **Dakota Boy (IRE)**[136] 765 8-11-2 **110** (t) RhysFlint 105+
(Alex Hales) *chsd ldrs: upsides 3 out: 4th and hld whn stmbld bdly landing last: eased* **9/1**
0-05 9 nk **Knock Three Times (IRE)**[14] 1870 4-9-13 **100** (t) MissLAlexander(7) 89
(Wilf Storey) *in rr: hdwy to chse ldrs 8th: outpcd and hit next: kpt on between last 2* **40/1**
-450 10 1 **Border Tale**[14] 1870 10-10-0 **94** PaddyAspell 82
(James Moffatt) *in rr: drvn 5th: chsng ldrs after 8th: one pce fr next* **22/1**
60-6 11 ½ **Blazing Desert**[21] 1766 6-10-11 **105** (t) ChristianWilliams 93
(John Quinn) *chsd ldrs: wknd 2 out* **17/2**
43-3 12 ½ **Wot Way Chief**[141] 715 9-11-2 **115** JamesHalliday(5) 102
(Malcolm Jefferson) *w ldrs: led 4th tl 2 out: sn wknd* **8/1**[3]
253- 13 3/4 **Yeoman Spirit (IRE)**[190] 5356 7-11-2 **110** (p) PaulMoloney 97
(John Mackie) *led to 2nd: chsd ldrs: wknd 2 out* **20/1**
04-0 14 24 **Faith And Reason (USA)**[9] 1929 7-10-6 **105** (p) MissLHorner(5) 68
(Chris Grant) *in rr: hdwy 5th: lost pl after 8th: sn bhd: t.o* **40/1**
41/ P **Banquet (IRE)**[69] 2444 5-11-10 **118** (p) RobertWalford —
(Tim Walford) *w ldrs: led 2nd to 4th: reminders after 7th: wknd rapidly after next: t.o whn p.u bef 3 out* **33/1**

4m 58.2s (-1.30) **Going Correction** +0.125s/f (Yiel)
WFA 4 from 5yo+ 10lb **15** Ran SP% **122.9**
Speed ratings (Par 107): **107,105,103,102,100 100,99,98,98,97 97,97,97,87,—**
toteswingers:1&2:£34.90, 1&3:£27.10, 2&3:£9.20 CSF £42.88 CT £372.03 TOTE £10.70: £3.30, £1.90, £3.40; EX 67.30 Trifecta £399.50 Part won. Pool: £539.89 - 0.20 winning units. Place 6 £10.58, Place 5 £6.37.
Owner Mrs Elizabeth Offord **Bred** Schwindibode Ag **Trained** Nawton, N Yorks

FOCUS
A competitive handicap hurdle and there were a lot in with a chance turning for home. The winner was nicely in but produced a step up, and the second can rate higher on his Flat form.

NOTEBOOK
Viva Colonia(IRE) ◆, who was buried in the pack, made up ground in eyecatching fashion. Sent out after the runner-up going to the last, he produced the better jump there and quickened right away for a most impressive win. He had become disappointing for Charlie Mann, but has been edging down the weights and was without the tongue-tie and cheekpieces he had been wearing. His new stable has revitalised him since his break and in this mood he can win again. (tchd 9-1)
First Stream(GER) ran a fine race under top weight on this seasonal return and looked set to win when striking the front after the second-last, but he jinked going to the final flight and a mistake there sealed his fate. He would not have beaten the winner in any case but is well capable of scoring off this sort of mark, although his hurdling remains a concern. (op 9-2 tchd 3-1)
Peter Grimes(IRE) lost his way last season after a winning debut, but he showed the benefit of a recent pipe-opener on the Flat and ran well, showing ahead briefly before the front two asserted. He is on a decent mark at present. (op 8-1)
Dontpaytheferryman(USA) ran a solid race over this longer trip and looks a decent marker for the form. (op 11-2)
Munlochy Bay was 10lb higher than when winning at Cheltenham in April. Surviving a bad mistake down the far side, she was staying on at the end as she tends to do. It would be no surprise to see the cheekpieces back on next time, with a return to further sure to suit. (op 11-1 tchd 16-1)
San Deng was making late headway on this return to hurdles without posing a threat. (op 18-1 tchd 25-1)
Dakota Boy(IRE) showed up for a long way off this 8lb higher mark and was still in fourth when stumbling badly just after the last. (op 14-1)
Wot Way Chief ran better than his final position suggests. (tchd 13-2)
Yeoman Spirit(IRE), back over hurdles, only faded out of it two from home. (op 12-1)
T/Plt: £19.80 to a £1 stake. Pool: £95,410.68. 3,506.18 winning tickets. T/Qpdt: £10.90 to a £1 stake. Pool: £5,461.82. 370.80 winning tickets. WG

2095 - (Foreign Racing) - See Raceform Interactive

[1896]NAAS (L-H)
Saturday, October 30

OFFICIAL GOING: Soft

2096a POPLAR SQUARE CHASE (GRADE 3) (10 fncs) 2m
2:35 (2:35) 5-Y-0+ **£16,393** (£4,792; £2,269; £756)

RPR
1 **Captain Cee Bee (IRE)**[191] 5350 9-11-12 158 MPWalsh 162+
(Edward P Harty, Ire) *chsd ldr: cl up 4 out: travelling best st: gained narrow ld bef last: pushed out to assert run-in* **9/10**[1]
2 4 **Archie Boy (IRE)**[13] 1892 8-11-8 145 (p) DNRussell 148+
(Paul W Flynn, Ire) *led: reduced ld bef 5 out: strly pressed st: narrowly hdd bef last: no imp and kpt on same pce run-in* **12/1**
3 4 **Catch Me (GER)**[306] 3133 8-11-1 143 AndrewJMcNamara 137+
(E J O'Grady, Ire) *racd in 3rd: struggling fr bef st: sn no imp and kpt on same pce* **11/4**[2]
4 2 **Psycho (IRE)**[191] 5350 9-11-5 145 RMPower 139+
(A J Martin, Ire) *racd in rr: t.k.h early: no ex and kpt on same pce fr bef st* **7/2**[3]

4m 21.1s (-2.20) **4** Ran SP% **109.2**
CSF £9.25 TOTE £1.30; DF 7.60.
Owner John P McManus **Bred** Maurice Stack **Trained** The Curragh, Co Kildare

FOCUS
The time was poor and the front-running runner-up possibly limits the form somewhat.

NOTEBOOK
Captain Cee Bee(IRE) ◆ got a nice lead into the race and his jumping really improved as the race developed. The way he quickened between the final two fences to take control of the race was probably the most pleasing aspect. Not much more could be asked of a seasonal debut and every indication points to him having potentially improved since last year. (op 9/10 tchd 1/1)
Archie Boy(IRE) had the fitness edge and came back to form after a very disappointing effort at Cork a couple of weeks previously. He enjoyed himself dictating a gradually increasing pace and jumped well, although he was ultimately outclassed.
Catch Me(GER) jumped pretty well in the main and kept on again after seeming to blow up entering the straight. (op 3/1 tchd 5/2)
Psycho(IRE) didn't look sharp and didn't really jump with the fluency he showed last year. He also seemed to have a good blow around the turn into the straight and kept on again at the finish. There will be much better to come from him. (op 10/3)

[1928]CARLISLE (R-H)
Sunday, October 31

OFFICIAL GOING: Soft (good to soft in places in the home straight on hurdle course; 6.3)
Rail on entire hurdles track moved out 2yds.
Wind: Almost nil Weather: Fine

2102 NORTHERN RACING CLUB 30TH ANNIVERSARY NOVICES' HURDLE (11 hdls) 2m 4f
1:00 (1:00) (Class 4) 4-Y-0+ **£2,740** (£798; £399)

Form RPR
4- 1 **Yurok (IRE)**[224] 4757 6-10-7 0 ShaneByrne(5) 121+
(Sue Smith) *hld up and bhd: smooth hdwy and in tch whn blnd 3 out: sn rcvrd: lft after last: kpt on wl* **10/1**
-5 2 2 **Rival D'Estruval (FR)**[170] 319 5-10-12 0 TimmyMurphy 118+
(Pauline Robson) *hld up midfield on outside: hdwy and in tch after 5th: effrt and led 2 out: hdd after last: kpt on same pce: improve* **11/2**
310- 3 13 **Seren Rouge**[197] 5227 5-10-12 0 JamesReveley 105
(Keith Reveley) *hld up: hdwy and prom 1/2-way: outpcd after 3 out: kpt on fr last: nt rch first two* **16/1**
3-11 4 shd **Noble Scholar (IRE)**[141] 731 5-10-12 0 BrianHughes 105
(Alan Swinbank) *chsd ldr to 3rd: cl up: effrt and ev ch 3 out to next: wknd bef last* **10/1**
02 5 3 3/4 **Blenheim Brook (IRE)**[22] 1783 5-10-12 0 PeterBuchanan 102
(Lucinda Russell) *t.k.h: cl up: chsd ldr 3rd tl led after 4 out: hdd 2 out: wknd bef last* **10/3**[1]
22-1 6 5 **Sunnyside**[30] 1662 5-10-12 0 AlexanderVoy(7) 104
(Lucy Normile) *j.lft: led to after 4 out: rdn and wknd bef 2 out* **7/2**[2]
4-P4 7 16 **Lady Jinks**[33] 1643 5-10-12 111 (t) MichaelMcAlister 80
(Maurice Barnes) *midfield: effrt bef 4 out: wknd bef next* **25/1**
60- 8 6 **Frontier Boy (IRE)**[224] 4757 6-10-9 0 HarryHaynes(3) 74
(James Ewart) *in tch tl rdn and wknd bef 3 out* **100/1**
9 2 3/4 **Forty Something (IRE)** 5-10-9 0 CampbellGillies(3) 71
(William Amos) *towards rr: stdy hdwy 1/2-way: wknd bef 3 out* **100/1**
1- 10 4 ½ **Tiptoeaway (IRE)**[195] 5277 5-10-12 0 GrahamLee 67
(Tim Easterby) *t.k.h: trckd ldrs tl rdn and wknd fr 3 out* **5/1**[3]
55- 11 8 **Emperor Charlie**[186] 53 6-10-12 0 RichieMcGrath 59
(Ferdy Murphy) *bhd: nt fluent 2nd: rdn 1/2-way: sn struggling* **80/1**
12 14 **Taras Joy (IRE)**[169] 5-10-12 0 BrianHarding 45
(John Wade) *midfield: struggling 1/2-way: n.d after* **50/1**
2PP/ 13 16 **Sacred Mountain**[674] 2951 9-10-5 0 MissCWalton(7) 29
(James Walton) *midfield: struggling fr 6th: sn btn* **80/1**
00/ 14 8 **Transparency**[550] 60 5-10-12 0 HenryOliver 21
(Sue Smith) *t.k.h in rr: struggling 7th: sn btn* **125/1**
15 7 **Blue Bertie** 4-10-12 0 AidanColeman 14
(Chris Grant) *a bhd: no ch fr 7th* **100/1**
0/ 16 4 **Euro One**[225] 6-10-2 0 RyanMania(3) 3
(Dianne Sayer) *a bhd: no ch fr 1/2-way* **200/1**
3 17 5 **Louisa (GER)**[22] 1780 6-10-5 0 WilsonRenwick —
(P Monteith) *hld up on ins: struggling bef 4 out: sn btn* **33/1**

5m 10.8s (-12.00) **Going Correction** -0.475s/f (Good) **17** Ran SP% **116.9**
Speed ratings (Par 105): **105,104,99,98,97 95,89,86,85,83 80,74,68,65,62 60,58**
toteswingers: 1&2 £10.70, 1&3 £27.20, 2&3 £14.00 CSF £60.51 TOTE £14.40: £4.50, £1.90, £5.50; EX 82.60.
Owner Trevor Hemmings **Bred** D W Macauley **Trained** High Eldwick, W Yorks

FOCUS
Rail on entire hurdles track moved out 2yds. Ground described as "a bit dead but a lovely cover of grass" for Carlisle's richest jumps card. Quite an interesting novice hurdle with plenty of deadwood and just seven still in contention three out. The first two look decent prospects.

NOTEBOOK
Yurok(IRE), a half-brother to Brave Inca, is a big horse who has had his problems. On the back of one run in bumper company in March he was settled towards the rear. Making his move four out, his inexperience showed in a head-to-head on the run-in but in the end he came out on top. He looks to have plenty of improvement in him and his long term target is the EBF Final. (tchd 11-1)
Rival D'Estruval(FR) came into this on the back of one promising run in a bumper in May. Well backed, he looked to be travelling best when taking charge but in the end had to accept defeat. He still looks very raw and is sure to improve and win races for his good yard. (op 15-2 tchd 5-1)
Seren Rouge, who took a soft ground bumper here in March, is out of Bayrouge, a smart NH mare who did so well for this yard. After getting tapped for toe at the foot of the hill he stayed on from the last to snatch third spot on the line. He looks a real stayer and will come on for the outing. (op 25-1 tchd 28-1)
Noble Scholar(IRE), a dual bumper winner, was making his hurdling debut on his first start since June. In the thick of things from the off, he became leg weary on the run-in and will improve for the outing. (op 9-1)
Blenheim Brook(IRE), who looks every inch a potential chaser, showed ahead going to three out but rather surprisingly did not seem to get home. He is better than he showed on the day. (op 11-4 tchd 7-2)
Sunnyside, penalised for his Hexham 3m win, took them along but continually jumped left-handed. He just stays and will be better suited by going the other way round. Official explanation: jockey said gelding hung and jumped left (tchd 4-1)
Tiptoeaway(IRE), who had Noble Scholar seven lengths back when scoring on his only previous outing in a bumper at Hexham in April, was weak in the market. He ran with the choke out and, running out of petrol three out, he was given a very easy time of it. He can do considerably better with this prep outing under his belt.
Emperor Charlie Official explanation: jockey said gelding hung left in straight

2103 LLOYD MINI COUNTRYMAN AMATEUR RIDERS' NOVICES' H'CAP HURDLE (12 hdls) 3m 1f
1:30 (1:30) (Class 5) (0-90,90) 3-Y-0+ **£1,977** (£608; £304)

Form RPR
5F-0 1 **Bardolet (IRE)**[183] 88 7-11-4 **87** MrColmMcCormack(5) 97+
(Keith Reveley) *mstkes: hld up and bhd: stdy hdwy bef 3 out: led whn hit last: styd on strly to go clr run-in* **12/1**
60P- 2 7 **Flaming Breeze (IRE)**[193] 5315 5-11-4 **85** MrMSeston(3) 87
(Henry Hogarth) *led to 4th: cl up: led 7th to 4 out: rdn and outpcd appr 2 out: rallied to chse wnr run-in: styd on: no imp* **16/1**
06-6 3 1 1/4 **Stormion (IRE)**[23] 1758 5-10-8 **79** MrDOckenden(7) 79
(Lucinda Russell) *bhd: rdn and outpcd 1/2-way: plenty to do 4 out: styd on wl fr 2 out: nt rch first two* **9/2**[2]
0653 4 shd **Make It Blossom (IRE)**[33] 1647 8-10-3 **72** MrJMQuinlan(5) 72
(John G Carr, Ire) *cl up: ev ch 4 out: hit next: led briefly 2 out: no ex and lost two pls run-in* **15/2**

05-4 **5** *2 3/4* **The Rustlin Rhino**[23] 1760 5-11-4 **87** MrJHamer(5) 87+
(Donald McCain) *mstkes: cl up: led 4 out to 2 out: rallied: cl 3rd whn mstke last: sn btn* **11/4**[1]
524- **6** *16* **Native Coll**[211] 4984 10-9-13 **70** MissLAlexander(7) 51
(N W Alexander) *nt fluent and rdr lost iron briefly 1st: prom tl rdn and wknd bef 3 out* **7/1**[3]
6-50 **7** *12* **Soldiers Tree (IRE)**[23] 1760 5-11-1 **84** MrGCrow(5) 53
(Sue Bradburne) *bhd: drvn along fr 8th: no ch after next* **16/1**
6P65 **8** *36* **Samizdat (FR)**[23] 1762 7-11-4 **89** MissECSayer(7) 22
(Dianne Sayer) *cl up: led 4th to 7th: cl up tl wknd fr 4 out* **10/1**
56/0 **9** *12* **Dee Cee Bolter (IRE)**[22] 1782 8-11-5 **90** (p) MrGJCockburn(7) 11
(Lucinda Russell) *towards rr: drvn after 5th: struggling fnl circ* **14/1**
FP/0 **10** *1 1/4* **King's Envoy (USA)**[28] 1700 11-9-7 **64** oh2 MissAMcGregor(7) —
(Jean McGregor) *bhd: struggling fr 7th: nvr on terms* **100/1**
0-00 **P** **Whatevertheweather**[23] 1760 6-9-7 **64** oh6 MrAdamNicol(7) —
(Sandy Forster) *in tch tl rdn and wknd after 4 out: t.o whn p.u bef 2 out* **14/1**
00-0 **P** **Samaret**[153] 547 5-9-9 **64** oh6 MissPernillaHermansson(5) —
(Harriet Graham) *midfield: hit 5th: lost tch fr 7th: t.o whn p.u bef 2 out* **50/1**

6m 32.5s (-5.70) **Going Correction** -0.15s/f (Good) 12 Ran SP% **113.9**
Speed ratings (Par 103): **103,100,100,100,99 94,90,78,75,74** —,—
toteswingers: 1&2 £67.30, 1&3 £12.40, 2&3 £42.00 CSF £178.46 CT £994.33 TOTE £9.70: £3.60, £5.60, £2.60; EX 285.20.
Owner Mrs Stephanie Smith **Bred** George Durrheim & Mrs Maria Mulcahy Durr **Trained** Lingdale, Redcar & Cleveland
■ Colm McCormack's first winner in Britain.

FOCUS
A low-grade amateur riders' novice handicap hurdle run at a sensible pace and just five still in serious contention at the third last flight. Straightforward, sound form.

NOTEBOOK
Bardolet(IRE), a disappointing favourite over fences when last seen out at Hexham in May, was making his hurdling handicap bow. Ridden from well off the pace, he moved up going to three out and in the end came clear on the run-in. He is relatively unexposed and is clearly a real stayer. (op 15-2)
Flaming Breeze(IRE), who doesn't have many miles on the clock, had been dropped a stone after two poor runs in handicaps in the spring. In the thick of things throughout, he was left for dead by the winner on the run-in. He looks very one-paced. (op 22-1)
Stormion(IRE), making his handicap debut, was last and struggling setting out on to the final circuit. Only seventh at the second-last flight, despite a clumsy jump at the last he finished with a real flourish. No distance looks like being too far for him. (op 6-1)
Make It Blossom(IRE), a maiden after 17 previous starts, looked a big danger at the foot of the final hill but didn't seem to see it out. (op 17-2 tchd 7-1)
The Rustlin Rhino, a half-brother to Grand National winner Silver Birch, is a clumsy jumper. He was in the mix from the off but after blundering at the final two flights he was very leg weary on the run-in. (op 7-2)
Native Coll, racing from a mark a stone lower than his chase mark on his return, survived an early scare but he doesn't look to stay beyond two and a half miles. (op 5-1 tchd 15-2)
Samizdat(FR) was too keen and is another who finds three miles beyond him. (tchd 8-1 and 11-1)

2104 GEOFFREY AND GRAHAM MCLEAN H'CAP HURDLE (9 hdls) 2m 1f
2:05 (2:05) (Class 4) (0-115,115) 4-Y-0+ **£2,602** (£764; £382; £190)

Form RPR
45-0 **1** **Cocoa Key (IRE)**[168] 350 6-10-9 **98** PaddyAspell 102
(Richard Guest) *t.k.h: hld up midfield: hdwy to ld bef 2 out: hrd pressed run-in: hld on wl* **14/1**
-320 **2** *1/2* **Pyracantha**[15] 1870 5-11-9 **112** BrianHughes 116
(Alan Swinbank) *midfield: hdwy bef 3 out: chsd wnr bef last: kpt on run-in: hld nr fin* **6/1**[2]
3000 **3** *2 1/4* **Daytime Dreamer (IRE)**[33] 1644 6-10-11 **100** GrahamLee 101
(Martin Todhunter) *hld up: hdwy to chse ldrs bef 2 out: sn rdn: one pce run-in* **20/1**
0/5- **4** *9* **Simonside**[15] 2187 7-10-5 **97** FearghalDavis(3) 90+
(Brian Ellison) *cl up: led bef 5th: hit 3 out: hdd bef next: wknd bef last* **2/1**[1]
035- **5** *1/2* **Cool Operator**[187] 34 7-11-12 **115** WilsonRenwick 107
(Howard Johnson) *hld up: stdy hdwy 3 out: drifted rt run in: nvr nr to chal* **10/1**
0115 **6** *10* **Zahara Joy**[10] 1931 7-10-9 **98** (t) MichaelMcAlister 80
(Maurice Barnes) *midfield: hdwy bef 5th: rdn bef 3 out: wknd bef next* **14/1**
440- **7** *nk* **Euro American (GER)**[208] 5074 10-10-9 **105** AlexanderVoy(7) 86
(Rose Dobbin) *in tch tl rdn and wknd fr 3 out* **14/1**
0-B1 **8** *8* **No Supper (IRE)**[23] 1762 6-10-10 **102** HarryHaynes(3) 75
(George Bewley) *hld up: hdwy and prom 4th: rdn and wknd bef 2 out* **7/1**[3]
001/ **9** *2 3/4* **Kings Guard (IRE)**[598] 4440 7-9-11 **89** EwanWhillans(3) 60
(Alistair Whillans) *t.k.h: in tch: hdwy 1/2-way: wknd fr 3 out* **10/1**
050- **10** *4* **Heart O' The West (IRE)**[239] 4433 6-10-13 **102** JamesReveley 69
(Andrew Parker) *hld up: outpcd 1/2-way: n.d after* **22/1**
5P-0 **11** *8* **Kempski**[171] 309 10-10-7 **99** (b) RyanMania(3) 58
(Rayson Nixon) *led to bef 5th: wknd fr next* **33/1**
F **12** *43* **Knockbaun Prince (IRE)**[39] 1574 6-10-9 **98** CharliePoste 14
(John G Carr, Ire) *trckd ldrs: lost pl 4th: sn struggling: t.o* **40/1**
5/P- **F** **Palm Reader (IRE)**[330] 2715 7-11-7 **110** AdrianLane —
(Donald McCain) *trckd ldrs: 4th and outpcd whn fell 3 out* **20/1**

4m 25.0s (-4.80) **Going Correction** -0.15s/f (Good) 13 Ran SP% **117.6**
Speed ratings (Par 105): **105,104,103,99,99 94,94,90,89,87 83,63**,—
toteswingers: 1&2 £34.10, 1&3 £47.60, 2&3 £19.80 CSF £88.46 CT £1695.91 TOTE £16.40: £3.60, £1.70, £5.30; EX 197.40.
Owner Richard Collins **Bred** M M Woods **Trained** Stainforth, S Yorks

FOCUS
A competitive 89-115 handicap and again the pace was sound. The winner ran to his mark, with a step up from the second.

NOTEBOOK
Cocoa Key(IRE), having his first start since May for this in form yard, is a big type. He carries his head high but in the end did just enough. His new handler will not waste any time before he sends him over fences. (op 12-1)
Pyracantha, having his second start in two weeks after his summer break, likes to get his toe in and went down fighting on just his second start in handicap company. He deserves to go one better. (op 8-1)
Daytime Dreamer(IRE), who scored for this yard on the Flat in the summer, put two below-par efforts over hurdles behind him without seriously threatening the first two. (tchd 25-1)
Simonside, twelfth in the Cesarewitch, looked potentially well treated just 23lb higher than his Flat mark. He was in the firing line from the off but was beaten two out. He prefers much more lively ground. (op 9-4)
Cool Operator, out of sorts since his last win over fences two years ago, caught the eye staying on up the hill from the rear. He looked fourth best on merit and all his best form has been on quicker ground. (op 11-1 tchd 9-1)
Zahara Joy will continue to struggle off a stone higher than her most recent success. (tchd 18-1)
No Supper(IRE), raised 9lb after his win here on his second start for this yard, travelled strongly but stopped to nothing up the final hill. Consistency has never been his strong point. (tchd 15-2)
Palm Reader(IRE), who has clearly had his problems, was having his first run since pulling up at Wetherby in December. He shaped nicely but was at the end of his tether when departing three out. (op 14-1)

2105 COLIN PARKER MEMORIAL INTERMEDIATE CHASE (16 fncs) 2m 4f
2:40 (2:40) (Class 2) 5-Y-0+ **£8,415** (£8,415; £1,910; £954)

Form RPR
F16- **1** **Little Josh (IRE)**[228] 4672 8-11-4 140 SamTwiston-Davies 153
(Nigel Twiston-Davies) *led: gd jump to go 3 l clr 4 out: 4 l up last: styd on u.p run-in: jnd on line* **7/2**[3]
111- **1** *dht* **Weird Al (IRE)**[267] 3898 7-11-10 152 NoelFehily 159
(Ian Williams) *prom: hdwy to go 2nd 9th: ev ch 4 out: outpcd bef next: rallied and 4 l down last: styd on wl to dead-heat on line* **5/2**[2]
3F6- **3** *18* **Door Boy (IRE)**[205] 5109 7-11-4 137 BrianHughes 135
(Howard Johnson) *t.k.h: trckd ldrs: effrt and ev ch 4 out: wknd after next* **13/2**
21P- **4** *62* **The Hollinwell**[227] 4698 7-11-4 138 GrahamLee 73
(Ferdy Murphy) *j.lft on occasions: cl up tl wknd bef 4 out: t.o whn j. bdly lft next* **10/1**
40-1 **P** **Cape Tribulation**[30] 1661 6-10-12 0 TimmyMurphy —
(Malcolm Jefferson) *j.lft: hld up in last: hit 8th: lost tch after 10th: t.o whn p.u bef 5 out* **7/4**[1]

5m 12.6s (-14.80) **Going Correction** -0.40s/f (Good) 5 Ran SP% **109.6**
Speed ratings: **113,113,105,81**,—
WIN: WA £1.60, LJ £3.00; PL: WA £1.30, £2.50; EX: WA-LJ £4.90, LJ-WA £4.40; CSF: WA-LJ £5.70, LJ-WA £6.34.
Owner Brannon Dennis Dick Holden **Bred** C Ronaldson **Trained** Portway, Worcs
Owner Tony Bloom **Bred** Michael Kearns **Trained** Naunton, Gloucs

FOCUS
Quite a valuable 2m4f intermediate chase whose roll of honour includes Monet's Garden and Tidal Bay. A thrilling finish and the best possible verdict, neither deserved to lose. Little Josh is rated to his best with Weird Al 3lb off.

NOTEBOOK
Little Josh(IRE), very useful but a bit hit and miss in his first season over fences, was in receipt of 6lb. He jumped as straight as a die in front and looked to have it in the bag when setting out up the run in with a three-length advantage. He was joined right on the line and is just the type of progressive second-season chaser his top yard excels with. His next target is reported to be the Paddy Power Gold Cup. (op 7-4 tchd 11-4 and 7-2 in a place)
Weird Al(IRE) proved himself one of last season's leading novices, winning his three starts over fences before a small fracture ruled him out of the RSA Chase. He had to carry a 6lb penalty and looked booked for second spot until staging a tremendous rally in the last 100 yards to divide the spoils on the line. This return over a trip that will be his bare minimum will have put him spot on, though if Denman turns out he will be a couple of pounds out of the weights in the Hennessy at Newbury. The one doubt and one cloud over his performance is that he looked in some distress afterwards in the unsaddling enclosure, but he was later reported to be fine. (op 7-4 tchd 11-4 and 7-2 in a place)
Door Boy(IRE), who had won first time out in each of the last two seasons, looked very fit. He had 9lb to find with Weird Al and 3lb with Little Josh and had no more to give three out. (op 17-2 tchd 9-1)
The Hollinwell, pulled up after bleeding in the Jewson, showed a tendency to hang and jump left. He stopped to nothing at the foot of the hill and after this has something to prove. (op 8-1)
Cape Tribulation, rated 154 over hurdles, was in receipt of 12lb from the 152-rated chaser Weird Al. Winner in much lower grade at Hexham on his only previous try over fences he was very warm at the gate, jumped badly left and never looked happy. He stopped to nothing at the first fence on the final circuit and it was only a question of time before he was pulled up. This was simply too bad to be true and it transpired that he had pulled some muscles in his hind quarters. Official explanation: jockey said gelding hung and jumped left throughout (op 9-4 tchd 13-8)

2106 CUMBERLAND H'CAP CHASE (19 fncs) 3m 2f
3:10 (3:10) (Class 3) (0-135,134) 4-Y-0+ **£26,020** (£7,640; £3,820; £1,908)

Form RPR
PU4- **1** **Etxalar (FR)**[260] 4026 7-10-10 **121** CampbellGillies(3) 132+
(Lucinda Russell) *hld up: plenty to do 5 out: hdwy next: lft 4th 3 out: styd on to ld run-in: drifted lft: styd on wl* **9/1**
42P- **2** *2* **Minster Shadow**[191] 5373 11-10-9 **120** (v) RyanMania(3) 128
(Chris Grant) *trckd ldrs: ev ch fr 5 out and sn clr of rest: rdn 4 out: nt fluent 2 out: mstke last: swtchd rt run-in: kpt on same pce towards fin* **16/1**
112- **3** *2 1/2* **Vodka Brook (IRE)**[211] 4987 7-11-6 **128** (p) RobertWalford 135+
(Tim Walford) *cl up: led 12th and clr w one other after 5 out: rdn 3 out: hdd run-in: no ex* **14/1**
UPF- **4** *9* **Jaunty Journey**[247] 4283 7-11-3 **125** (b) PaddyBrennan 123
(Nigel Twiston-Davies) *mstkes: trckd ldrs: drvn and outpcd after 4 out: no imp fr next* **9/1**
36-0 **5** *4* **Camden George (IRE)**[23] 1761 9-10-7 **115** HenryOliver 108
(Sue Smith) *mstkes: racd wd in midfield: outpcd bef 14th: plugged on fr 2 out: nvr rchd ldrs* **22/1**
06-6 **6** *14* **Daldini**[18] 1828 8-10-3 **118** AlexanderVoy(7) 96
(Sue Smith) *trckd ldrs tl rdn and wknd after 4 out* **22/1**
P34/ **7** *12* **See You There (IRE)**[631] 3779 11-10-12 **120** (t) PeterBuchanan 92
(Lucinda Russell) *towards rr: rdn along bef 4 out: nvr able to chal* **16/1**
3P-P **P** **Echo Point (IRE)**[39] 1577 10-11-5 **127** BrianHarding —
(Nicky Richards) *bhd: and sn rdn: t.o whn p.u after 10th* **50/1**
/00- **P** **Officier De Reserve (FR)**[209] 5067 8-11-10 **132** AidanColeman —
(Venetia Williams) *bhd: struggling fr 11th: p.u bef 14th* **12/1**
2P-U **F** **Mr Woods**[165] 394 8-11-2 **124** JamesReveley —
(Harriet Graham) *hld up: hdwy 5 out: 7 l 4th and no imp whn fell 3 out* **40/1**
5F1- **P** **Gentle Ranger (IRE)**[198] 5212 8-11-12 **134** (p) TomScudamore —
(David Pipe) *led to 12th: wknd after 5 out: t.o whn p.u bef 2 out* **10/3**[1]
P32- **R** **Bay Cherry (IRE)**[195] 5274 8-11-3 **125** BrianHughes —
(Howard Johnson) *in tch tl wknd after 5 out: wl btn whn ref 2 out* **11/2**[2]
F0-P **U** **Heathcliff (IRE)**[176] 206 8-11-3 **130** (b) GilesHawkins(5) —
(Richard Lee) *midfield: outpcd whn blnd and uns rdr 13th* **22/1**
331- **P** **Nicto De Beauchene (FR)**[261] 4022 9-11-3 **125** DarylJacob —
(Victor Dartnall) *midfield: struggling 11th: t.o whn p.u bef 4 out* **8/1**[3]

0/1- **P** **Palace Merano (FR)**[191] 5378 7-11-4 **126**............................ GrahamLee —
(Donald McCain) *nt fluent: a bhd: t.o whn p.u after 10th* **16/1**

7m 6.40s (-0.80) **Going Correction** +0.15s/f (Yiel) **15** Ran SP% **119.0**
Speed ratings (Par 107): **107,106,105,102,101 97,93,—,—,— —,—,—,—,—**
toteswingers: 1&2 £54.30, 1&3 £40.50, 2&3 £54.30 CSF £129.02 CT £2004.50 TOTE £9.90: £3.40, £6.60, £3.40; EX 227.40.
Owner Mrs Elizabeth Ferguson **Bred** Elie Lellouche And Bertrand Clin **Trained** Arlary, Perth & Kinross
■ Stewards' Enquiry : Campbell Gillies three-day ban: careless riding (Nov 14-16)

FOCUS
A highly competitive and valuable 115-134 stayers' handicap chase and the gallop was unremitting. Solid form and the winner is well handicapped at present.

NOTEBOOK
Etxalar(FR), whose trainer was taking this £26,000 prize for the third consecutive time, was an impressive winner from an 11lb lower mark on his first outing last season. He had problems with his jumping afterwards but clearly returned here in peak form. Patiently ridden, he crept forward in the final mile but still had plenty of work to do when landing third two out. Staying on in really gutsy fashion, despite a tendency to hang left under an untidy ride on the run-in he was on top at the line. It remains to be seen if he is capable of building on this this time. (op 8-1)
Minster Shadow, now a pensioner, has a good record round here. Having his first outing since April, he showed clear second four out. After an untidy jump at the final fence he pushed the winner hard all the way to the line despite being forced to switch late on. (op 25-1)
Vodka Brook(IRE), who has changed stables in the summer, took on the pacesetter. After gaining the advantage, he looked in command until flagging setting out up the run-in. He deserves to find consolation. (op 16-1)
Jaunty Journey, who failed to complete on his final three outings last term, did well to finish so close considering he made numerous jumping errors.
Camden George(IRE) is on a long losing run. (op 28-1)
Mr Woods improved from the rear but looked tired in fourth when hitting the deck three out. (op 11-4 tchd 7-2 in places)
Gentle Ranger(IRE), a big danger to all when falling at the fourth last in the four-miler at the Cheltenham Festival and from a stable with a temendous recent record here, set out to make all but he was overtaken by Viodka Brook then stopped to nothing at the foot of the hill. He will no doubt bounce back. Official explanation: trainer had no explanation for the poor form shown (op 11-4 tchd 7-2 in places)
Nicto De Beauchene(FR) Official explanation: jockey said gelding never travelled (op 11-4 tchd 7-2 in places)

2107 EDINBURGH WOOLLEN MILL NOVICES' H'CAP CHASE (12 fncs) 2m
3:45 (3:45) (Class 4) (0-105,105) 4-Y-O+ **£2,927** (£859; £429; £214)

Form RPR
4F-5 **1** **Primrose Time**[22] 1781 7-10-10 **96**................................ AlexanderVoy(7) 115+
(Lucy Normile) *trckd ldrs: wnt handy 2nd 4 out: led 2 out: drvn clr: eased fnl 75yds* **8/1**
-P53 **2** *6* **Dallas Bell**[108] 1002 8-11-0 **96**................................ EwanWhillans(3) 105
(Alistair Whillans) *trckd ldrs: led 7th: hdd 2 out: styd on same pce* **12/1**
-163 **3** *6* **Ormus**[119] 891 7-11-0 **93**.. PaddyAspell 96
(Christopher Wilson) *racd wd in rr: hdwy 6th: chsng ldrs 8th: wnt modest 3rd 3 out: one pce* **12/1**
305/ **4** *13* **Mighty Magnus (IRE)**[556] 5168 7-10-3 **85**.................. FearghalDavis(3) 75
(Martin Todhunter) *in rr: hdwy 8th: modest 4th 3 out: wknd next* **22/1**
312 **5** *10* **Stolen Light (IRE)**[33] 1646 9-10-10 **89**............................(b) BrianHughes 69
(Andrew Crook) *chsd ldrs: drvn 8th: wknd next* **14/1**
626- **6** *2 ¼* **Locked Inthepocket (IRE)**[224] 4756 6-11-10 **103**........... TimmyMurphy 81
(Pauline Robson) *hld up in midfield: hdwy 8th: outpcd: 7th and short of room on ins whn blnd and lost pl 4 out* **9/2**[2]
40-3 **7** *½* **Saddlers Deal (IRE)**[15] 1872 5-11-11 **104**.................... PaddyBrennan 83
(Chris Grant) *led to 7th: blnd 4 out: sn wknd* **8/1**
53-6 **8** *½* **Devil Water**[171] 306 7-11-5 **105**................................ NathanMoscrop(7) 82
(James Ewart) *in rr-div: hit 3rd: sme hdwy 6th: wknd 8th* **40/1**
300- **9** *2 ½* **Tchikita (FR)**[227] 4704 7-11-3 **99**.................................. HarryHaynes(3) 73
(James Ewart) *in rr: blnd 5th: bhd fr 4 out* **40/1**
142- **10** *25* **Pete**[518] 534 7-11-2 **95**..(t) BrianHarding 44
(Barry Murtagh) *hld up in rr: blnd 1st: sme hdwy 8th: sn wknd: blnd 3 out: sn eased: t.o* **6/1**[3]
44-4 **11** *46* **Prince Tam**[161] 444 6-10-7 **86**..................................(p) PeterBuchanan —
(Lucinda Russell) *prom: lost pl and blnd 6th: bhd 8th: sn t.o* **20/1**
03P- **P** **Arc Warrior (FR)**[191] 5374 6-11-12 **105**..........................(t) JamesReveley —
(Andrew Parker) *in rr: bhd fr 6th: t.o whn p.u bef 4 out* **50/1**
4- **P** **Roudoudou Ville (FR)**[237] 4492 5-11-11 **104**..................... TomO'Brien —
(Victor Dartnall) *trckd ldrs to 5th: wknd 8th: bhd whn p.u bef 2 out* **4/1**[1]
005- **U** **Sundown Trail (IRE)**[220] 4835 5-10-10 **89**.................... DominicElsworth —
(Nicky Richards) *hld up towards rr: blnd and uns rdr 4th* **10/1**

4m 14.8s (-1.30) **Going Correction** +0.15s/f (Yiel) **14** Ran SP% **121.8**
Speed ratings (Par 105): **109,106,103,96,91 90,90,89,88,76 53,—,—,—**
toteswingers: 1&2 £21.10, 1&3 £17.80, 2&3 £20.60 CSF £94.04 CT £1162.33 TOTE £10.30: £3.40, £2.50, £5.00; EX 85.40.
Owner The Explorers **Bred** Mrs D A Whitaker **Trained** Duncrievie, Perth & Kinross

FOCUS
A modest 85-105 handicap chase and only two in it from three out. The easy winner was value for further and there may be more to come.

NOTEBOOK
Primrose Time, going well when falling from a 5lb higher mark at Kelso in April, had run well for a long way before tiring late on on her return over 2m4f at Hexham. She went clear on the run-in and, heavily eased in the end, was value at least 10 lengths. This was just her seventh start over fences and there should be even better to come. Her jumping is excellent value for his claim. (op 15-2)
Dallas Bell, a close third over 3m2f when last seen at Cartmel in July, kicked for home but in the end was readily outspeeded by the winner. He deserves credit for this. (op 16-1)
Ormus, who took the scenic route, showed a return to form after two below-par efforts on ground much more in his favour. (op 10-1)
Mighty Magnus(IRE), making his chase debut for his new yard, was having his first outing since April 2009. (op 33-1)
Locked Inthepocket(IRE), well beaten on his chasing debut over an extra half mile here in March, was outpaced when left short of room bang on the inner at the final ditch, four out. He gave the impression that he may be capable of a fair bit better over a fair bit further. (op 5-1)
Saddlers Deal(IRE) Official explanation: vet said gelding finished distressed
Arc Warrior(FR) Official explanation: jockey said gelding lost action after mistake 6th (op 9-2)
Roudoudou Ville(FR), winner of two bumpers in France, made his debut over fences from a possibly lenient mark of 104. He looked very fit but dropped away in a matter of strides before being pulled up. He has a lot to prove now. (op 9-2)

2108 E B F "JUNIOR" STANDARD OPEN NATIONAL HUNT FLAT RACE 1m 6f
4:15 (4:15) (Class 5) 3-Y-O **£2,055** (£599; £299)

Form RPR
1 **Opera North** 3-10-12 0.. JamesReveley 95+
(Tom Tate) *trckd ldrs: led 3f out: pushed out fnl f* **9/2**[2]
2 *2* **Thackeray** 3-10-12 0.. BrianHarding 91
(Chris Fairhurst) *hld up: smooth hdwy over 3f out: pressed wnr over 1f out: rdn and kpt on same pce fnl f* **25/1**
3 *6* **Serenader** 3-10-12 0.. RichieMcGrath 83
(David O'Meara) *hld up on outside: hdwy and prom after 6f: effrt and cl up 3f out: one pce over 1f out* **6/1**[3]
4 *4* **Lure of The Night (IRE)** 3-10-12 0.................................. TomO'Brien 79
(Brian Rothwell) *trckd ldrs tl rdn and outpcd fnl 2f* **9/2**[2]
5 *3* **Tasman Tiger** 3-9-12 0...................................... HenryBrooke(7) 68
(Kate Walton) *hld up in tch: effrt over 3f out: outpcd fnl 2f* **12/1**
6 *3 ½* **Jersey Joe (IRE)** 3-10-9 0.............................. FearghalDavis(3) 71
(Brian Ellison) *t.k.h: hld up: rdn over 3f out: sn no imp* **13/2**
7 *¾* **Jack's Rocket** 3-10-12 0.. PaddyAspell 70
(Richard Guest) *t.k.h: hld up: sme hdwy over 3f out: nvr rchd ldrs* **18/1**
8 *1* **Josie's Set** 3-9-12 0... AlistairFindlay(7) 62
(George Charlton) *set slow pce: qcknd after 6f: hdd 3f out: wknd fr 2f out* **8/1**
9 *shd* **Playing Truant (IRE)** 3-10-9 0.............................. HarryHaynes(3) 69
(James Ewart) *midfield: rdn and outpcd over 3f out: sn n.d* **22/1**
10 *3 ½* **Touch Of Spring** 3-10-12 0.. BrianHughes 64
(Alan Swinbank) *trckd ldrs tl edgd rt and wknd fr over 2f out* **4/1**[1]
11 *9* **Escapee** 3-10-5 0.. DavidEngland 47
(Terry Caldwell) *in tch tl wknd fr 4f out* **50/1**
12 *65* **Shaw Cross** 3-10-5 0.. MrAdamNicol(7) —
(Robert Johnson) *t.k.h: hld up on outside: struggling over 5f out: eased whn no ch* **50/1**

3m 54.7s (234.70) **12** Ran SP% **120.2**
toteswingers: 1&2 £14.70, 1&3 £3.90, 2&3 £22.50 CSF £119.22 TOTE £5.70: £2.10, £6.50, £1.90; EX 144.40 Place 6 £4,750.51, Place 5 £931.22.
Owner T P Tate **Bred** Ermyn Lodge Stud Limited **Trained** Tadcaster, N Yorks

FOCUS
A mile six 'Junior' bumper contested entirely by unraced three-year-olds. No one wanted to jump off in front and the pace was farcical for the first mile, but nonetheless a decisive winner of some potential.

NOTEBOOK
Opera North, quite a big, commanding looking individual, cost 48,000gns as a yearling. He knew his job and, taking charge with over two furlongs left to run, had only to be kept up to his work to score with something in hand in the end. Two miles and more testing conditions will not bother him and he looks destined to go on to better things.
Thackeray, bred more for speed than stamina, emerged as a serious threat but was very much second best at the line. He can be found an opportunity to go one better.
Serenader, picked up for £6,200, ran a respectable first race and this will have taught him something.
Lure of The Night(IRE) did not go un-backed but was beaten some way in the end.
Tasman Tiger, unable to find a buyer when offered for sale this summer, stayed on in her own time in the closing stages.
Touch Of Spring was a handful in the paddock and was led riderless to post. He was far too keen and stopped to nothing with over two furlongs left to run. He will no doubt be next seen out over shorter on the all-weather this winter.
T/Jkpt: Not won. T/Plt: £7,044.10 to a £1 stake. Pool: £71,406.49. 7.40 winning tickets. T/Qpdt: £185.70 to a £1 stake. Pool £7,965.48. 31.74 winning tickets. RY

1812 HUNTINGDON (R-H)
Sunday, October 31

OFFICIAL GOING: Good changing to good to soft after race 4 (3.00)
Wind: Almost nil Weather: Overcast with heavy rain mid afternoon

2109 BRAMPTON "NATIONAL HUNT" MAIDEN HURDLE (8 hdls) 2m 110y
1:20 (1:21) (Class 5) 4-Y-O+ **£2,397** (£698; £349)

Form RPR
1- **1** **Muldoon's Picnic (IRE)**[192] 5344 4-10-11 0.................. SeanQuinlan(3) 115+
(Kim Bailey) *chsd ldrs: wnt 2nd after 3 out: led 2 out: r.o wl to draw clr run-in* **4/1**[2]
5 **2** *5* **Roper (IRE)**[22] 1768 5-10-11 0.................................. RichieMcLernon(3) 110+
(Jonjo O'Neill) *hld up: hdwy after 5th: hdwy 3 out: sn shkn up to trck ldrs: nt fluent at last: styd on to take 2nd towards fin: nvr gng pce to trble wnr: one to nte* **28/1**
10-2 **3** *nk* **Milgen Bay**[167] 375 4-11-0 0.. LeightonAspell 111+
(Oliver Sherwood) *midfield: mstke 4th: hdwy next: effrt to chse ldrs appr 2 out: wnt 2nd last: outpcd by wnr run-in: lost 2nd towards fin* **9/4**[1]
030- **4** *8* **Up To The Mark**[196] 5255 5-11-0 103.............................. RichardJohnson 103
(Henry Daly) *led: hdd 2 out: pushed along appr last: wknd run-in* **15/2**
3 **5** *9* **Taketimeout (IRE)**[18] 1819 5-11-0 0.. APMcCoy 92
(Jonjo O'Neill) *in tch: chsd ldrs 5th: nt fluent 2 out: no imp bef last: eased whn n.d after* **9/2**[3]
6 *hd* **All For Free (IRE)**[91] 1157 4-11-0 0.............................. WarrenMarston 92
(Milton Harris) *midfield: hdwy 5th: nt fluent 3 out: effrt to chse ldrs 2 out: no imp bef last: wknd sn after* **12/1**
4- **7** *7* **Richmond (FR)**[275] 3732 5-11-0 0.. DougieCostello 85
(Ian Williams) *racd keenly: chsd ldr: nt fluent 5th: rdn and lost 2nd after 3 out: wknd 2 out* **6/1**
00- **8** *17* **South Stack**[250] 4213 5-11-0 0.. SamJones 68
(Michael Scudamore) *hld up: outpcd after 3 out: sn wl btn* **100/1**
50/0 **9** *26* **Patrick Dee**[179] 154 5-10-7 0.. MattCrawley(7) 42
(Christine Dunnett) *hld up: nt fluent 4th: struggling after: nvr on terms: t.o* **200/1**
10 *½* **Topalena (IRE)** 7-10-11 0.. TomMolloy(3) 41
(Michael Banks) *hld up: hdwy to chse ldrs appr 4th: wknd bef 3 out: t.o: lame* **25/1**
6P-0 **11** *1 ¾* **Beat In Time**[169] 327 4-10-7 0.. DaveCrosse 33
(John Mackie) *in tch: nt fluent 5th: sn wknd: wl btn whn mstke 3 out: t.o* **200/1**
065- **F** **Salto Angel (FR)**[291] 3422 4-11-0 0.. JamieMoore —
(Gary Moore) *bhd: struggling whn fell 5th* **28/1**

3m 42.9s (-12.00) **Going Correction** -0.75s/f (Firm)
WFA 4 from 5yo+ 9lb **12** Ran SP% **115.4**
Speed ratings (Par 103): **98,95,95,91,87 87,84,76,63,63 62,—**
toteswingers: 1&2 £21.10, 1&3 £3.30, 2&3 £15.20 CSF £106.97 TOTE £5.90: £1.90, £4.70, £1.50; EX 90.30.
Owner Clive Washbourn **Bred** Peter McCrea **Trained** Andoversford, Gloucs

FOCUS
A reasonable maiden hurdle contested by some promising types. The first and third improved on their bumper figures with a big step up from the second. The ground was riding as advertised at this stage and the time was a respectable 2.90 seconds outside the standard.

NOTEBOOK

Muldoon's Picnic(IRE) won a Uttoxeter bumper in April on his one previous start. Hurdling well, he was always well placed and came away in nice style to score with something to spare, pricking his ears and running a little green in front. A big, strong individual, he is a useful prospect and can win again. (tchd 7-2)

Roper(IRE) ◆ showed a glimpse of potential on his debut behind the useful Silviniaco Conti at Bangor and stepped up on that with a taking effort. A tall gelding who became warm beforehand, he lacked the pace of the winner from the turn in but kept on nicely to secure second without his rider being overly hard on him. A step up in trip will suit him and he should be winning before long. (tchd 25-1)

Milgen Bay, a bumper winner at this course, made a pleasing return to action. He made a couple of slight mistakes and was under pressure leaving the far side, but stayed on to dispute second on the run-in. His dam was a prolific winning jumper and he looks capable of making his mark, perhaps on a stiffer track. (op 7-2, tchd 4-1 in places)

Up To The Mark made the running as he often does but could not prevent the winner easing by. He stuck on for fourth and, seemingly exposed and with a BHA mark of 103, looks a decent pointer to the form's worth. (op 7-1 tchd 13-2)

Taketimeout(IRE), the runner-up's stablemate, showed promise first time at Uttoxeter and confirmed that he has ability, although he could not race on with the principals from the second-last. A step up to 2m4f may suit him. (tchd 11-2)

All For Free(IRE) won a fast-ground bumper at Kilbeggan in the summer and joined his current connections for £33,000. He was outpaced by the leaders in the latter stages and may be the type for handicaps further down the line. (tchd 10-1)

Richmond(FR) should strip fitter for this hurdles debut and first run since January. Dougie Costello reported that the gelding ran too keenly and was tired turning for home. Official explanation: jockey said gelding ran too keenly and tired turning for home

Topalena(IRE) Official explanation: vet said gelding returned lame

2110 JEREMY REYNOLDS 50TH BIRTHDAY NOVICES' CHASE (19 fncs) 3m
1:55 (1:56) (Class 3) 4-Y-0+ **£5,529** (£1,623; £811; £405)

Form RPR

121- **1** **Wayward Prince**[205] [5112] 6-11-2 0 DougieCostello 143+
(Ian Williams) *in tch: wnt 2nd 14th (water): sn pressed ldr: led appr 2 out: clr and in command whn j.lft and mstke last: pushed out* **10/11**[1]

1-13 **2** *9* **Aberdale (IRE)**[22] [1774] 6-11-2 0 APMcCoy 133+
(Jonjo O'Neill) *prom: led 3rd: hdd appr 2 out: already looking hld whn hit 2 out: no ch w wnr after* **11/2**[3]

160- **3** *10* **Quentin Collonges (FR)**[205] [5113] 6-11-2 0 RichardJohnson 125+
(Henry Daly) *hld up in tch: hit 8th: chsd clr front pair fr 15th: no imp whn j. and mstke 2 out: plugged on at one pce but no threat* **3/1**[2]

5522 **4** *8* **Pheidias (IRE)**[9] [1950] 6-11-5 118 (p) MissGAndrews(7) 126
(Pam Sly) *led to 3rd: remained w ldr tl blnd and nrly uns rdr 13th: struggling and dropped away fr 16th* **28/1**

3P0- **5** *18* **Outlaw Tom (IRE)**[219] [4869] 6-11-2 0 SamJones 96
(Alex Hales) *hld up: struggling to keep up fr 12th: wl outpcd whn mstke 16th: n.d after* **40/1**

23-0 **6** *11* **Arkose (IRE)**[183] [94] 6-11-2 0 LeightonAspell 96+
(Oliver Sherwood) *trckd ldrs: j. slowly 2nd: blnd 8th: nt fluent 11th: wknd 16th* **10/1**

4 **P** **Ramborob (IRE)**[18] [1830] 5-11-2 0 AndrewThornton —
(Mike Sowersby) *j.lft thrght: bhd: wnt eratically lft 9th and off the crse: p.u bef next* **100/1**

6m 2.50s (-7.80) **Going Correction** -0.225s/f (Good) **7** Ran SP% **108.7**
Speed ratings (Par 107): **104,101,97,95,89 85,—**
toteswingers: 1&2 £1.10, 1&3 £1.10, 2&3 £2.90 CSF £5.82 TOTE £2.00: £1.60, £2.10; EX 4.80.
Owner T J & Mrs H Parrott **Bred** M G Kilroe **Trained** Portway, Worcs

FOCUS

The chase course rails were out a couple of yards, adding six yards to race distances. A fascinating novice chase, this was run at a solid gallop and saw an impressive chasing debut from Wayward Prince, who should better his hurdles mark of 147 over fences. Good novice form.

NOTEBOOK

Wayward Prince ran out an impressive winner on this chasing debut. A former winning Irish pointer, he progressed well last term, never out of the first two in five starts and successful in the Grade 1 Sefton Novices' Hurdle at Aintree on his final appearance. Closing into second place early on the last circuit, he soon locked horns with the runner-up and the pair matched strides before he asserted off the home turn. He was clear with his race won when he got in too close to the last, probably due to his idling, but that was the only real error in an otherwise fine round of jumping. It takes a real stayer to land the Sefton and he is a gutsy individual with plenty of class too. He looks a very smart recruit to the 3m chasing division and the RSA Chase is firmly the target. (op 4-5 tchd 8-11)

Aberdale(IRE) ◆ had the benefit of a recent run over fences, when third to Balthazar King at Chepstow. He tried to serve it up to the field on the second circuit but, while he soon had most of them in trouble, he could not shake off the winner. Just getting the worse of the argument when he slipped slightly on the home turn, he hit the second-last and McCoy quickly accepted defeat. He had jumped very well before that tired mistake and lost nothing in defeat against a smart opponent. It should not be long before he gets off the mark over fences. (op 5-1)

Quentin Collonges(FR) was a useful hurdler, with a BHA rating of 134 at that game. Not the biggest for fences, he made more than one minor error and was left trailing by the big two down the back straight, but he should certainly be winning soon in lesser company. A stiffer test of stamina than this sharp 3m will benefit him. (op 4-1)

Pheidias(IRE) faced a very difficult task giving away 10lb to the rest of the field. He raced more enthusiastically than is sometimes the case but was left behind after an error seven from home, where his rider did well to stay aboard. (op 25-1 tchd 33-1)

Outlaw Tom(IRE) was not up to tackling this company but will face easier tasks over fences. (tchd 50-1)

Arkose(IRE) won over hurdles on this card a year ago. Returning from a six-month break, he made one or two jumping errors on this chase debut and was another who was put in his place when the big two kicked away down the far side. (op 11-1 tchd 12-1)

Ramborob(IRE) Official explanation: jockey said gelding jumped badly left before being pulled up

2111 HUNTINGDON NOVICES' HURDLE (10 hdls) 2m 4f 110y
2:30 (2:30) (Class 4) 4-Y-0+ **£2,740** (£798; £399)

Form RPR

1 **1** **Mossley (IRE)**[148] [637] 4-10-12 0 APMcCoy 121+
(Nicky Henderson) *hld up: nt fluent 1st: wnt into midfield 4th: clsd 7th: led appr 2 out where nt fluent: j.rt last: pushed clr run-in: comf* **8/13**[1]

4 **2** *5* **See You Jack**[19] [1812] 5-10-12 0 AndrewThornton 107
(Caroline Bailey) *led 2nd: rdn and hdd appr 2 out: continued to chse wnr: outpcd fnl 75yds* **6/1**[3]

11-P **3** *3 1/4* **Hoback Junction (IRE)**[9] [1952] 6-11-12 127 LeightonAspell 119
(Lucy Wadham) *sn trckd ldrs: chalng appr 2 out: hung rt and nt qckn bef last: kpt on same pce run-in* **7/2**[2]

00-1 **4** *15* **Harvest Song (IRE)**[172] [279] 4-11-5 120 WillKennedy 98
(Henrietta Knight) *in tch: effrt 3 out: rdn and outpcd fr 2 out: no imp after* **7/1**

0 **5** *8* **Kilbready Star (IRE)**[18] [1822] 10-10-12 85 JackDoyle 85
(Peter Pritchard) *hld up: hdwy 7th: in tch whn nt fluent 3 out: outpcd appr 2 out: no imp after* **50/1**

00/P **6** *3 3/4* **Lindengrove**[12] [1910] 5-10-9 0 TommyPhelan(3) 80
(Claire Dyson) *led to 2nd: remained prom: rdn appr 3 out: wknd bef 2 out* **100/1**

0/P **7** *3* **Dareios (GER)**[7] [1990] 5-10-12 0 DaveCrosse 77
(John Mackie) *in tch tl pushed along and wknd 3 out* **100/1**

00P- **8** *14* **Northwold**[210] [5017] 6-10-12 0 RodiGreene 64
(Christopher Kellett) *prom tl lost pl 7th: struggling after* **100/1**

0- **9** *2* **Frankie Falco**[15] [2238] 4-10-12 0 JodieMogford 63
(Giuseppe Fierro) *hld up: nt fluent 2nd: struggling and detached 7th: nvr on terms* **100/1**

10 *50* **Colonel Alf** 5-10-12 0 SamJones 18
(Alex Hales) *hld up: nt fluent 2nd: j. slowly 6th: struggling and detached next: t.o* **33/1**

11 *42* **Be Back In Time (IRE)**[154] 8-10-7 0 DavidBass(5) —
(Derek Frankland) *hld up: struggling and detached 7th: t.o* **100/1**

4m 48.2s (-10.80) **Going Correction** -0.25s/f (Good)
WFA 4 from 5yo+ 10lb **11** Ran SP% **120.8**
Speed ratings (Par 105): **110,108,106,101,98 96,95,90,89,70 54**
toteswingers: 1&2 £1.60, 1&3 £1.10, 2&3 £2.50 CSF £5.49 TOTE £1.90: £1.10, £2.10, £1.10; EX 5.10.
Owner Michael Buckley **Bred** Pipe View Stud **Trained** Upper Lambourn, Berks

FOCUS

It started to rain heavily during this contest, in which there was plenty of dead wood and where they bet 33-1 bar four. The time was reasonable, just over ten seconds above the standard. The easy winner was value for further and is potentially a smart novice.

NOTEBOOK

Mossley(IRE) easily won a Worcester bumper in June and he did not have to work hard to land the odds on this hurdling debut. His jumping was not as slick as it might have been, but he came away readily from the final flight and will have learned considerably from the outing. He did not have a great deal to beat but looks sure to progress to better things. (op 4-6 tchd 8-11)

See You Jack showed ability on his hurdling debut over C/D and he stepped up on that here. After making the running he could only stick on at the one pace when the winner went by, and he may be ready to move back up to 3m. (op 9-1)

Hoback Junction(IRE) won two novice hurdles in the spring and the double penalty meant he was conceding a stone to the bulk of this field. Back hurdling after an inauspicious chasing debut, he ran respectably, but will no longer be eligible for this type of race now and may not be the easiest to place. (op 9-2)

Harvest Song(IRE), a surprise winner when last seen at Fontwell in May, was under pressure three from home and safely held under his penalty. His BHA mark looks harsh. (op 11-2)

Kilbready Star(IRE), an ex-Irish veteran rated 85, did best of the no-hopers. (op 40-1)

Colonel Alf is out of a unraced half-sister to Party Politics who has produced several winners, but is going to need more time.

2112 MACER GIFFORD H'CAP CHASE (12 fncs) 2m 110y
3:00 (3:03) (Class 3) (0-130,130) 4-Y-0+ **£6,635** (£1,948; £974; £486)

Form RPR

2662 **1** **Sunday City (JPN)**[8] [1973] 9-11-1 **119** JamieMoore 139+
(Peter Bowen) *led: hdd 4th: regained ld after 5th: mde rest: clr fr 3 out: nt fluent 2 out: unchal after* **9/2**[2]

1F04 **2** *28* **Grand Lahou (FR)**[18] [1828] 7-11-4 **129** MrTomDavid(7) 124
(Tim Vaughan) *w ldr: led 4th: mstke 5th: sn hdd: outpcd by wnr appr 3 out: kpt on u.p after: jst hld on for 2nd cl home* **8/1**

4424 **3** *nk* **Knight Legend (IRE)**[65] [1390] 11-11-7 **125** (t) RhysFlint 123+
(Philip Hobbs) *mstkes: trckd ldrs: outpcd after 5th and fnl circ tl styd on fr 2 out: clsng on 2nd cl home* **5/1**[3]

4410 **4** *12* **Viable**[28] [1690] 8-10-11 **122** MissGAndrews(7) 105
(Pam Sly) *racd keenly: prom: lost pl 3rd: outpcd fr 6th: n.d after* **12/1**

10-5 **5** *10* **Award Winner**[29] [1676] 7-11-2 **120** APMcCoy 94
(Brendan Powell) *in rr: hit 1st: struggling fr 6th: nvr on terms* **10/1**

-21P **6** *1/2* **Marc Of Brilliance (USA)**[29] [1676] 7-10-7 **118** (b) JoshuaMoore(7) 91
(Gary Moore) *in tch: pckd 1st: outpcd after 3 out: wknd and wl btn bef last* **14/1**

434- **7** *2 1/4* **Arctic Ben (IRE)**[193] [5316] 6-10-9 **113** RichardJohnson 84
(Henry Daly) *a bhd: toiling after 5th: nvr on terms* **3/1**[1]

2062 **P** **High Bird Humphrey**[10] [1931] 11-10-8 **117** PaulCallaghan(5) —
(Simon West) *a bhd: t.o 5th: p.u bef 9th* **8/1**

11P- **P** **Fighting Chance (IRE)**[226] [4716] 10-11-12 **130** AndrewThornton —
(Richard Lee) *trckd ldrs: nt fluent whn outpcd 3 out: wkng in 5th whn jinked lft and p.u appr 2 out* **8/1**

4m 11.6s (1.40) **Going Correction** +0.275s/f (Yiel) **9** Ran SP% **116.6**
Speed ratings (Par 107): **107,93,93,88,83 83,82,—,—**
toteswingers: 1&2 £3.70, 1&3 £2.80, 2&3 £10.00 CSF £40.34 CT £187.61 TOTE £5.90: £2.10, £2.30, £1.50; EX 50.80.
Owner R Greenway **Bred** Shiraoi Farm **Trained** Little Newcastle, Pembrokes

FOCUS

The continuing rain looked to be getting into the ground by this stage. There were several regular front-runners in this fair handicap chase. There is a case for rating the form higher and it will be interesting to see how the winner is reassessed.

NOTEBOOK

Sunday City(JPN) won the right to play the front-running role. Drawing steadily clear from the home turn, he put some toiling rivals to the sword for a wide-margin victory. Arriving here in good heart, he had been running over further but had plenty of form over this sort of trip in his younger days. He will be hit by the handicapper for this. (tchd 11-2)

Grand Lahou(FR) could not get to the front, but although he was ultimately left well behind by the winner he stuck on for a commendable second, with the right-handed track seeming to suit. He just needs to get his jumping together.

Knight Legend(IRE) put in a scruffy round of jumping too and was beaten a good way out, but he did plug on to dispute second on the flat. He is hard to win with these days. (tchd 6-1)

Viable has not matched his Market Rasen effort in two runs here since, and was beaten a long way into fourth.

Award Winner found this too sharp and was always trailing. He made a string of jumping errors. (op 8-1)

Marc Of Brilliance(USA) ran a bit more sweetly in the reapplied blinkers and was still in third place entering the home straight before weakening.

Arctic Ben(IRE) would have been suited by the ease in the ground on this chasing debut, but he was taken off his feet and always towards the rear. He will have learned from this, though, and better can be expected. Richard Johnson reported that the gelding was never travelling. Official explanation: jockey said gelding never travelled (op 4-1)

High Bird Humphrey Official explanation: trainer said gelding was unsuited by the good to soft ground (op 9-1, tchd 12-1 in a place)

Fighting Chance(IRE), another who likes to make the running, made a reasonable return to action but was well adrift in fifth when pulling up before the second-last. Andrew Thornton reported that his mount had tired quickly. Official explanation: jockey said gelding tired quickly and pulled up (op 9-1, tchd 12-1 in a place)

2113 TURFTV BETTING SHOP SERVICE H'CAP CHASE (16 fncs) 2m 4f 110y
3:35 (3:35) (Class 5) (0-90,90) 4-Y-O+ £2,797 (£821; £410; £205)

Form RPR
4435 1 **Mcqueen (IRE)**[18] 1826 10-11-1 82 .... DannyCook[(3)] 98+
(Barry Leavy) *led fr 2nd: mde rest: drawing clr and in command whn pckd 2 out: unchal after* 7/2[1]
005- 2 10 **Handtheprizeover**[193] 5315 5-11-9 90 .... PeterToole[(3)] 96+
(Ben Case) *hld up: hdwy whn rdr lost whip 4 out: chsd wnr 3 out: outpcd fr 2 out: no ch bef last* 9/2[3]
30-P 3 12 **Phar Again (IRE)**[14] 1885 7-11-4 82 ....(tp) LiamTreadwell 79
(Claire Dyson) *led to 2nd: remained prom: effrt to chal whn mstke 3 out: wknd bef 2 out* 11/2
-000 4 2 **That Man Fox**[25] 1730 9-10-6 75 ....(b) LeeEdwards[(5)] 67
(Tony Carroll) *j.lft several times: in tch: mstke 6th: wnt prom whn racing keenly 8th: outpcd appr 3 out: n.d after* 4/1[2]
3645 5 16 **Mad Professor (IRE)**[9] 1954 7-9-12 69 ....(p) JoeCornwall[(7)] 48
(John Cornwall) *bhd: nvr looked happy: plugged on to pass btn horses fr bef 2 out: nvr on terms* 10/1
F4P1 6 6 **Buds Dilemma**[11] 1924 6-10-9 76 .... DonalDevereux[(3)] 48
(Peter Bowen) *prom to 10th: struggling 12th: sn wknd* 7/2[1]
7 4 1/2 **Killiney Ranger (IRE)**[31] 1657 12-10-5 69 .... RodiGreene 37
(P J Goodwin, Ire) *hld up: hdwy appr 10th: lost pl 11th (water): wknd appr 3 out* 14/1

5m 19.4s (14.10) **Going Correction** +0.775s/f (Soft) 7 Ran SP% 113.8
Speed ratings (Par 103): **104,100,95,94,88 86,84**
toteswingers: 1&2 £3.50, 1&3 £4.00, 2&3 £4.10 CSF £19.58 CT £83.46 TOTE £4.70: £2.30, £3.10; EX 25.10.
Owner Moorland Racing & Mrs Laura Leavy **Bred** Philip Newton **Trained** Forsbrook, Staffs

FOCUS
The official going was amended to good to soft before this race, a very moderate handicap chase. The winner is rated in line with his Worcester run.

NOTEBOOK
Mcqueen(IRE), who was well handicapped on his third at Worcester two starts back, appreciated being allowed to bowl along in front and burnt off the runner-up for a bloodless success. This was his first chase victory and he may win again if he jumps as well as he did here. (op 3-1 tchd 4-1)
Handtheprizeover did not show much over hurdles and he was saddled with topweight on this chase debut. He ran respectably, if put in his place by the winner from the turn in, and looks like he should pay his way in time over fences. (op 11-2 tchd 6-1)
Phar Again(IRE), tried in first-time cheekpieces, made jumping errors and was being shoved along with a circuit to run, but remained in contention until the third-last. (op 9-2)
That Man Fox came in for a bit of support on this switch to fences, but he was well beaten off and remains a maiden. (op 15-2)
Mad Professor(IRE) Official explanation: trainer said gelding was unsuited by the good to soft ground
Buds Dilemma was 9lb higher for winning a weak race which rather fell in her lap at Worcester. Back up in trip, which shouldn't have posed a problem, she lost her pitch early on the final circuit and was left well behind following a mistake at the middle fence down the back. The ground was a possible excuse. (tchd 4-1)
Killiney Ranger(IRE) Official explanation: trainer said gelding finished distressed

2114 HUNTINGDON FOR ALL YOUR OUTSIDE EVENTS H'CAP HURDLE (8 hdls) 2m 110y
4:05 (4:07) (Class 5) (0-95,97) 4-Y-O+ £2,397 (£698; £349)

Form RPR
0601 1 **Amuse Me**[7] 1996 4-11-9 92 7ex .... APMcCoy 106+
(Jonjo O'Neill) *midfield: hdwy 5th: mstke 3 out: travelling wl and led 2 out: a in full control on bit: effrtlessly wnt clr fnl 75yds: easily* 2/5[1]
41-U 2 3 1/2 **Carrig An Uisce (IRE)**[7] 1996 9-11-12 95 .... AndrewTinkler 96
(Anna Brooks) *in tch: led 5th: hdd 2 out: stl upsides but u.p last: a fighting losing battle w wnr whn ev ch run-in: outpcd fnl 75yds* 12/1
0-U0 3 6 **Chalice Welcome**[8] 1976 7-10-13 82 .... MarkBradburne 80+
(Neil King) *hld up: hdwy 5th: chsd ldrs appr 2 out: rdn and hung rt whn nt qckn bef last: kpt on u.p run-in but no dnager to front pair* 8/1[2]
320 4 1/2 **Wicklewood**[143] 697 4-11-3 93 ....(p) MattCrawley[(7)] 89
(Christine Dunnett) *racd keenly in midfield: hdwy after 5th: chsd ldrs 3 out: wnt 2nd briefly bef 2 out: nt qckn and outpcd by ldrs appr last: kpt on u.p run-in* 40/1
6050 5 8 **Mulaazem**[13] 1902 7-10-9 83 .... DavidBass[(5)] 71
(Derek Frankland) *trckd ldrs: hit 5th: rdn and wknd after 3 out* 20/1
4-P6 6 1 1/4 **Bromhead (USA)**[9] 1953 4-11-7 90 .... LeightonAspell 78
(Kevin Morgan) *hld up: hdwy 3 out: no imp on ldrs whn nt fluent last: fdd* 28/1
0-00 7 2 1/2 **Madman (FR)**[28] 1689 6-11-2 85 .... RodiGreene 69
(Christopher Kellett) *led: hdd 5th: pushed along appr 3 out: wknd bef 2 out* 50/1
P 8 13 **Desert Mirage (IRE)**[2] 2070 6-11-3 89 ....(tp) DonalDevereux[(3)] 62
(P J Goodwin, Ire) *hld up: bhd and niggled along appr 5th: nvr a threat* 14/1
500 9 3/4 **Chadwell Spring (IRE)**[36] 1613 4-11-2 85 .... AndrewThornton 57
(Mike Sowersby) *hld up: shkn up after 3 out: nvr nr ldrs: sn eased* 33/1
5-P4 10 1 **Three Boars**[25] 1735 8-10-11 80 ....(tp) LiamTreadwell 51
(Claire Dyson) *chsd ldr tl niggled along after 5th: wknd appr 2 out* 9/1[3]

3m 57.8s (2.90) **Going Correction** +0.25s/f (Yiel)
WFA 4 from 5yo+ 9lb 10 Ran SP% 122.4
Speed ratings (Par 103): **103,101,98,98,94 93,92,86,86,85**
toteswingers: 1&2 £3.40, 1&3 £2.10, 2&3 £5.50 CSF £6.64 CT £24.15 TOTE £1.50: £1.10, £1.80, £2.60; EX 5.10 Place 6 £9.27, Place 5 £5.47.
Owner John P McManus **Bred** Whatton Manor Stud **Trained** Cheltenham, Gloucs

FOCUS
There were five non-runners in this low-grade handicap hurdle, including three of the more plausible dangers to the odds-on Amuse Me. He was value for further and confirmed the merit of his Towcester win.

NOTEBOOK
Amuse Me, well treated under just a 7lb penalty for last weekend's effortless Towcester victory, was unsurprisingly sent off a warm odds-on shot to dispose of some very limited opposition. Always going well, his only anxious moment came when he was clumsy at the third-last. The runner-up was still alongside him over the final flight, but he pulled away from there to win very easily. He will be facing a rise in the weights but is really getting his act together now. (op 4-7)
Carrig An Uisce(IRE) was effectively having his first race of the season and ran well for a long way, although the favourite was only toying with him in the latter stages. He is 10lb higher than when scoring at Hereford in March but may be up to winning another minor handicap, probably in easy ground. (tchd 11-1 and 14-1)
Chalice Welcome had been dropped 3lb and had a squeak on his best form, but he was comfortably beaten off and remains a maiden over hurdles. (op 9-1)
Wicklewood ran respectably in a change of headgear on this first start since June, but may have stamina limitations. (op 33-1)
Mulaazem was under a shove from a long way out. (op 25-1)
T/Plt: £12.20 to a £1 stake Pool: £61,200.39. 3,644.20 winning tickets. T/Qpdt: £5.70 to a £1 stake. Pool £5,236.92. 674.72 winning tickets. DO

2115 - (Foreign Racing) - See Raceform Interactive

1889 CORK (R-H)
Sunday, October 31

OFFICIAL GOING: Heavy

2116a DIAL-A-BET 1800 721 821 EUROPEAN BREEDERS FUND NOVICE HURDLE (GRADE 3) (13 hdls) 3m
1:45 (1:45) 4-Y-O+ £24,446 (£7,146; £3,384; £1,128)

RPR
1 **Mount Helicon**[25] 1188 5-11-0 109 ....(t) JLCullen 126+
(T Hogan, Ire) *trckd ldrs in 3rd: impr to chal whn bmpd 3 out: rdn to ld bef next: kpt on wl fr last* 9/10[1]
2 1 3/4 **Original Option (IRE)**[26] 1717 5-11-0 .... PCarberry 124
(Noel Meade, Ire) *led tl hdd after jumping bdly lft at 3rd: hung lft and j.lft most of way: rdn fr 3 out: kpt on fr next* 11/4[2]
3 2 1/2 **Tango Knight (IRE)**[21] 1800 6-11-0 106 .... RMPower 122
(Mrs John Harrington, Ire) *hld up in last: 4th fr 4th: rdn in 4th fr 3 out: 3rd next: kpt on same pce* 9/2[3]
4 14 **King Maker (IRE)**[26] 1718 6-11-0 94 .... EFPower 108
(John Joseph Murphy, Ire) *racd 2nd: led after 3rd: rdn and hdd after 3 out: sn wknd* 33/1
5 10 **Moon Over Moscow (IRE)**[22] 1786 6-10-9 .... RWalsh 93
(T Hogan, Ire) *racd 4th: last fr 4th: rdn fr 4 out: no imp* 10/1

6m 29.5s (-2.60) 5 Ran SP% 109.5
CSF £3.72 TOTE £1.80: £1.10, £1.60; DF 6.40.
Owner Miss M A Masterson **Bred** Highclere Stud & Hmh Management **Trained** Nenagh, Co Tipperary
■ Stewards' Enquiry : J L Cullen advice: careless riding

FOCUS
An uncompetitive Grade 3, won in game fashion by the outstanding pick pre-race. The third and fourth help set the level.

NOTEBOOK
Mount Helicon stayed the trip well and coped reasonably with the ground, which jockeys reported was not as deep as it looked. He jumped fluently in the main, and his rider reported that he picked up instantly when given a squeeze around the third-last. He is a bit lazy in his races, which is no harm, and he looks one of the best-handicapped horses in Ireland, though he might get a few pounds for this. He will go for a novices' hurdle here in December over 3m. (op 4/5 tchd 1/1)
Original Option(IRE) ran a strange race. He had a soft lead initially but hung for much of the race thereafter. To his credit, he was slightly hemmed in by the winner before the last, after which he ran on well. He was beaten fair and square. (op 11/4 tchd 5/2)
Tango Knight(IRE) might have found 3m on this ground a bit difficult but travelled as well as he usually does. He looks quite well handicapped. (op 11/2 tchd 6/1)
King Maker(IRE) was out of his depthbut did not run badly all the same. (op 25/1)
Moon Over Moscow(IRE) probably struggled over the trip but was outclassed in any case. (op 7/1)

2119a DIAL-A-BET 1800 721 821 EUROPEAN BREEDERS FUND NOVICE CHASE (GRADE 3) (14 fncs) 2m 4f
3:25 (3:25) 5-Y-O+ £20,420 (£5,969; £2,827; £942)

RPR
1 **Back Of The Pack (IRE)**[14] 1893 8-10-12 .... MDarcy 135
(Colin Kidd, Ire) *trckd ldr in 2nd: led fr 6 out and mde rest: rdn clr fr 2 out: kpt on wl* 12/1
2 4 1/2 **Beau Michael**[28] 1712 6-11-6 ....(tp) BarryGeraghty 138
(Adrian McGuinness, Ire) *trckd ldrs in mod 3rd: rdn in 4th 3 out: 2nd 2 out: kpt on same pce wout threatening wnr* 7/1
3 1 3/4 **Farringdon**[41] 1565 7-11-0 .... AndrewJMcNamara 130+
(Mrs Prunella Dobbs, Ire) *hld up: last 4 out: sn rdn: mod 5th 2 out: kpt on into 3rd fr last* 10/3[2]
4 shd **Sam Adams (IRE)**[259] 4065 7-11-0 134 ....(t) DNRussell 130
(Paul Nolan, Ire) *trckd ldrs: mod 4th 6 out: rdn in 5th 3 out: no ex* 9/2
5 7 **Muirhead (IRE)**[18] 1839 7-11-0 .... PCarberry 123
(Noel Meade, Ire) *hld up: mstke 5 out: rdn fr next: 6th 3 out: no imp* 7/2[3]
6 hd **Pay The Bounty**[30] 1672 7-11-0 ....(t) PTEnright 129
(Robert Tyner, Ire) *hld up: clsr in 4th 4 out: rdn in 3rd 3 out: sn no imp: 5th whn bad mstke at last* 11/4[1]
7 12 **Turtle Gale (IRE)**[80] 1244 7-11-3 104 .... DJCondon 114
(P C O'Connor, Ire) *led: hdd 6 out: wknd st* 33/1

5m 21.4s (321.40) 7 Ran SP% 113.3
CSF £86.16 TOTE £17.20: £4.50, £2.70; DF 46.40.
Owner Raheenwood Syndicate **Bred** Michael Fennessy **Trained** Bagenalastown, Co Carlow

FOCUS
This looked a hottish Grade 3 but there were a few disappointments. The fourth, sixth and seventh have been rated close to their recent bests.

NOTEBOOK
Back Of The Pack(IRE) has been transformed since tackling fences, even though she is not the biggest. She simply loves jumping them and took it up a long way out here from off the strong pace. She kept galloping thereafter and had everything beaten by the second-last. An ordinary enough hurdler, she has really been transformed over fences, and one would be wary of opposing her around this trip or closer to 3m. She is comparitavely well treated back over hurdles, but her trainer is concerned as to how she would jump if reverting to that sphere.
Beau Michael has been a credit to connections and ran another solid race, despite being friendless in the ring. He is unlikely to tackle ground worse than this over the winter and will likely get a break now. (op 6/1)
Farringdon had every chance. He was ridden along quite a bit from home but kept on. He may be better on better ground. (op 10/3 tchd 3/1)
Sam Adams(IRE) will probably be better for the race. (op 11/2)
Muirhead(IRE) was very disappointing. His jumping was pretty good on his debut, but he made a bad mistake five out and never got into it thereafter. He does not appeal as a horse who will excel over fences, though in his defence a testing 2m4f would hardly have been ideal. (op 11/4)
Pay The Bounty flattered to deceive, as he often did over hurdles. His jumping was hit-and-miss and he cut out from the second-last. (op 7/2)
Turtle Gale(IRE) wants better ground and was outclassed. (op 25/1)

2120 - 2121a (Foreign Racing) - See Raceform Interactive

1882 KEMPTON (R-H)

Monday, November 1

OFFICIAL GOING: Good (watered; chs 7.6; hdl 7.5)

Wind: Moderate, across Weather: Fair

2122 LONDON IRISH BIGGEST TACKLE NOVICES' HURDLE (8 hdls) 2m

1:00 (1:02) (Class 4) 4-Y-0+ **£2,602** (£764; £382; £190)

Form				RPR
60-	1		**Iolith (GER)**[268] 3881 5-10-12 0 WayneHutchinson (Alan King) *hld up in midfield: hdwy 2 out: led and mstke last: rdn out* **7/1**	114+
0-2	2	2 3/4	**Ballinteni**[6] 2021 8-10-12 0 JoeTizzard (Colin Tizzard) *w ldr: led 2 out tl last: kpt on same pce* **8/1**	107
6-2	3	3/4	**Penchesco (IRE)**[12] 1914 5-10-12 0 LeightonAspell (Amanda Perrett) *trckd ldrs: shkn up after 2 out: 3rd and hld whn mstke last* **3/1**[2]	105
6-	4	5	**According**[156] 3890 4-10-12 0 BarryGeraghty (Nicky Henderson) *plld hrd: chsd ldrs: ev ch whn slt mstke 2 out: sn outpcd* **11/4**[1]	101
6	5	nse	**Gtaab**[14] 1899 4-10-12 0 DominicElsworth (Paul Webber) *led tl 2 out: no ex* **66/1**	102
	6	1 3/4	**Smokey Oakey (IRE)**[30] 6-10-12 0 ColinBolger (Mark H Tompkins) *hld up towards rr: sme hdwy and nt fluent 2 out: sn rdn and styd on same pce* **10/1**	98
6	7	7	**Remember Now (IRE)**[25] 1736 4-10-12 0 APMcCoy (Nicky Henderson) *plld hrd in rr: hdwy on outside 5th: wknd appr 2 out* **9/1**	95+
-0	8	3	**Mister New York (USA)**[15] 1884 5-10-12 0 WillKennedy (Noel Chance) *hld up in tch: rdn appr 2 out: sn wknd* **50/1**	88
/26-	9	2 1/2	**King Olav (UAE)**[30] 3028 5-10-12 0 TomScudamore (Tony Carroll) *t.k.h: prom: mstke 1st: wknd appr 2 out* **9/2**[3]	86
36	10	9	**Kilcommon Pride (IRE)**[38] 1607 5-10-12 0 HaddenFrost (Roger Curtis) *chsd ldrs tl lost pl 5th: bhd fr 3 out* **100/1**	77
0	11	6	**The Snatcher (IRE)**[169] 360 7-10-9 0 SeanQuinlan(3) (Richard Phillips) *bhd: mstke 1st: j.lft 4th: n.d after* **66/1**	71
P	12	32	**Prohibition (IRE)**[14] 1900 4-10-12 0 AndrewGlassonbury (Gary Moore) *plld hrd in rr: hdwy and in tch 3 out: rdn and wknd appr next* **66/1**	39
	P		**Saints Bay (IRE)**[554] 4-9-12 0 RobertKirk(7) (Steven Dixon) *a in rr: stmbld 2nd: nt fluent next: struggling fr 5th: wl bhd whn p.u bef 2 out* **100/1**	—

3m 57.2s (-2.80) **Going Correction** -0.55s/f (Firm)
WFA 4 from 5yo+ 7lb **13 Ran SP% 121.0**
Speed ratings (Par 105): **85,83,83,80,80 79,76,74,73,69 66,50,—**
toteswingers:1&2:£11.10, 1&3:£5.90, 2&3:£4.00 CSF £61.63 TOTE £7.00: £3.10, £1.50, £1.30; EX 102.70.
Owner Favourites Racing XI **Bred** Gestut Schlenderhan **Trained** Barbury Castle, Wilts

FOCUS
A fairly ordinary novices' hurdle. The pace was slow and this is not form to be too confident about. A step up from the winner but he is entitled to rate much higher on his Flat form.

NOTEBOOK
Iolith(GER) ran out a good winner, defying a significant market drift in the process. Placed at Group level on the Flat in Germany, he didn't live up to expectations in two starts last season, although there were excuses, and he had since been gelded. Reportedly working well with some 'proper' horses at home, he made good headway to challenge under Wayne Hutchinson and readily asserted, a mistake at the last not enough to slow him down. He looks capable of winning again and could make his mark in decent handicaps later in the season. (op 7-2)
Ballinteni, runner-up to a useful sort at Taunton just six days earlier (debut for yard), was never far away and probably improved a little. He looks capable of winning something similar. (tchd 12-1)
Penchesco(IRE), not beaten far at Fontwell latest (rider dropped whip/squeezed up run-in), held his chance and just lacked a bit of pace dropped back to a bare 2m on good ground. (op 7-2 tchd 4-1)
According, fancied by some to make a Triumph Hurdle candidate last season, met with a disappointing defeat on his sole start and was also a beaten favourite on the Flat in the spring. Again made market leader, he refused to settle and was readily outpaced in the straight. He isn't the biggest and looks limited, with ordinary handicap hurdles likely to be his thing. (op 9-2)
Gtaab didn't get home having made the running, but he won't be seen at his best until sent handicapping. (op 40-1)
Smokey Oakey(IRE), rated 111 at his peak on the Flat following victory in the 2008 Group 3 Brigadier Gerard, never got into it, but was keeping on at the finish and he'll probably benefit from a more positive ride next time. (tchd 9-1)
Remember Now(IRE), well beaten on his debut at Exeter, made a brief forward move, but he had pulled hard early and didn't get home. He looks one for handicaps. (op 12-1)
King Olav(UAE), a three-time Flat winner this year, was another who failed to settle adequately on this return to hurdles, although to see him drop away so tamely was worrying. (op 5-1 tchd 4-1)

2123 LONDON IRISH FAMILY ZONE "NATIONAL HUNT" NOVICES' HURDLE (10 hdls) 2m 5f

1:30 (1:30) (Class 4) 4-Y-0+ **£2,602** (£764; £382; £190)

Form				RPR
6-52	1		**Jay J**[15] 1887 6-10-9 109 TomMolloy(3) (Andrew Price) *t.k.h: w ldr: nt fluent 4th: led 7th: rdn appr 2 out: styd on wl whn chal* **13/2**	117+
03/2	2	3 1/2	**Representingceltic (IRE)**[38] 1607 5-10-12 0 ColinBolger (Pat Phelan) *trckd ldrs: wnt 2nd 3 out: chal and gng wl next: rdn and mstke last: no ex* **17/2**	115+
35-3	3	8	**Molanna View (IRE)**[25] 1736 5-10-12 0 JackDoyle (Emma Lavelle) *trckd ldrs: slt mstke 7th: rdn and outpcd fr 2 out* **5/2**[1]	107
0/0-	4	4	**Half Cocked**[243] 4385 8-10-12 0 LeightonAspell (Richard Rowe) *towards rr: sme hdwy 3 out: rdn and no imp appr next* **33/1**	103
100-	5	18	**The Laodicean**[229] 4683 4-10-12 0 WayneHutchinson (Alan King) *in tch tl hrd rdn and wknd appr 2 out* **9/2**[2]	90
P60-	6	23	**Pak Jack (FR)**[206] 5111 10-10-9 0 SeanQuinlan(3) (Richard Phillips) *led tl 7th: wknd 3 out* **5/1**[3]	66
24-2	7	1	**Inner Steel (IRE)**[184] 92 5-10-12 0 MarkBradburne (Lydia Richards) *sn bhd: struggling fr 6th* **8/1**	65
41-	8	23	**Dusky Bob (IRE)**[259] 4083 5-10-12 0 SamThomas (Nick Gifford) *a bhd: struggling 5th: no ch fr 7th* **11/2**	45
0-0	9	18	**Monty's Revenge (IRE)**[26] 1734 5-10-12 0 WarrenMarston (Martin Keighley) *t.k.h: chsd ldrs tl wknd 6th* **66/1**	28

5m 10.9s (-13.10) **Going Correction** -0.55s/f (Firm)
WFA 4 from 5yo+ 8lb **9 Ran SP% 118.2**
Speed ratings (Par 105): **102,100,97,96,89 80,80,71,64**
toteswingers:1&2:£8.30, 1&3:£4.00, 2&3:£7.40 CSF £61.04 TOTE £9.70: £3.50, £3.50, £1.10; EX 53.10.
Owner The Silverlining Partnership **Bred** Silver Lining Partnership **Trained** Leominster, H'fords

FOCUS
Just a modest novices' hurdle, although it should produce winners in the handicap sphere. The winner produced a big step up on his recent course run.

NOTEBOOK
Jay J, who improved to finish second over C&D last time, was soon up disputing it and stayed on best down the straight, ultimately winning with a bit in hand. He's the type to make his mark in handicap hurdles. (op 11-2 tchd 5-1)
Representingceltic(IRE), runner-up to a decent type on his third and final start in bumpers, was up in trip for this hurdles debut and couldn't see it out quite as well as the winner. It was a promising start, though, and he should have no trouble going one better. (op 10-1 tchd 11-1)
Molanna View(IRE) failed to improve as expected for the step back up in trip, but it's unlikely he'll be seen at his best until handicapping anyway. (op 9-4 tchd 11-4)
Half Cocked, well beaten on his hurdles debut in March when returning from a lengthy absence, made a little late headway on this first starts since and, despite his age, he remains capable of better.
The Laodicean, who had reportedly done well over the summer, failed to offer much encouragement on this first start over hurdles, but will presumably improve for the run. (op 5-1 tchd 6-1)
Pak Jack(FR), best known as a staying chaser, recorded his only win way back in January 2005 and, for all that this will have blown the cobwebs away for a return to fences, he didn't shown an awful lot. (op 8-1)
Inner Steel(IRE) soon got behind and doesn't look the quickest, but it's still early days for him. (tchd 7-1)
Dusky Bob(IRE) was never going on this first start over hurdles and it would come as no surprise to learn something was amiss. (op 6-1)

2124 LONDON IRISH BIG 5 NOVICES' H'CAP CHASE (16 fncs) 2m 4f 110y

2:05 (2:05) (Class 4) (0-110,110) 4-Y-0+ **£3,903** (£1,146; £573; £286)

Form				RPR
1FF6	1		**Forget It**[20] 1816 5-11-12 **110** AndrewGlassonbury (Gary Moore) *hld up in rr: hdwy 10th: chsd ldr 12th: mstke and hrd rdn 2 out: styd on to ld run-in* **13/2**	119+
33-0	2	1	**Solitary Palm (IRE)**[176] 231 7-10-12 **96** CharliePoste (Brian Forsey) *pressed ldr: led 10th: 3 l clr whn mstke last: no ex and hdd run-in* **9/2**[2]	104+
0-00	3	7	**Lordsbridge (USA)**[25] 1740 8-11-12 **110** NickScholfield (Andy Turnell) *plld hrd: hld up in 5th: mstke 9th: hdwy into 3rd at 11th: one pce fr 4 out* **9/2**[2]	111
52P-	4	17	**Alteranthela (IRE)**[217] 4930 6-11-11 **109** LeightonAspell (Richard Rowe) *mde most tl 10th: wknd 4 out* **5/1**[3]	94
PF25	5	18	**Bushwacker (IRE)**[15] 1888 6-11-7 **105** AndrewThornton (Seamus Mullins) *bhd: mstke 4th: blnd 10th: sme hdwy and fair 5th whn pckd 4 out: n.d after* **7/2**[1]	80
62-6	6	17	**Cockatoo (USA)**[185] 85 7-11-7 **108** (b) EamonDehdashti(3) (Gary Moore) *in tch: mstke 7th: drvn along fr 9th: finding little and lost pl steadily fr next* **12/1**	61
P2-P	7	2 1/2	**Itea Du Fau (FR)**[169] 353 5-11-4 **102** WayneHutchinson (Alan King) *t.k.h: sn chsng ldrs: blnd and wknd 11th* **11/2**	53

5m 18.2s (-1.30) **Going Correction** -0.125s/f (Good) **7 Ran SP% 111.7**
Speed ratings (Par 105): **97,96,93,87,80 74,73**
toteswingers:1&2:£8.40, 1&3:£6.90, 2&3:£6.00 CSF £34.03 CT £142.04 TOTE £10.00: £6.00, £1.30; EX 33.40.
Owner The Cockpit Crew **Bred** Mrs J Chandris **Trained** Lower Beeding, W Sussex

FOCUS
Only the seven runners, but this still looked a competitive handicap chase. The winner is rated up 4lb but the form is not that strong.

NOTEBOOK
Forget It probably needed his reappearance run for a confidence boost, having fallen on his two previous starts, but he jumped well in the main on this first start over fences and capitalised on a mistake from the runner-up at the last, staying on strongly to get up close home. This was a promising start and the 5-y-o remains capable of better. (op 15-2 tchd 6-1)
Solitary Palm(IRE) managed just one win from 23 over hurdles, but on this evidence he's going to make a much better chaser. He jumped well and looked all over the winner coming to the last, but got in too close and made a mistake, which cost him the race. He should go one better at some stage. (op 13-2 tchd 4-1)
Lordsbridge(USA) looked well treated on the pick of his efforts and considering he jumped well, or at least by his standards, it was disappointing to see him dropped by the front pair in the straight. (op 4-1 tchd 5-1)
Alteranthela(IRE) ended up well held but should improve for both the outing and experience of fences.
Bushwacker(IRE) made mistakes and, having bit the turf four out, his race was done with. (op 5-1)
Cockatoo(USA) Official explanation: vet said gelding lost its left fore shoe
Itea Du Fau(FR) found little having raced keenly, but she's said to want softer ground. (op 4-1)

2125 PERTEMPS H'CAP HURDLE (SERIES QUALIFIER) (10 hdls) 2m 5f

2:40 (2:40) (Class 2) 4-Y-0+
£9,393 (£2,775; £1,387; £694; £346; £174)

Form				RPR
0-61	1		**Working Title (IRE)**[54] 1508 8-11-3 **142** BarryGeraghty (Nicky Henderson) *hld up in tch: wnt 2nd 3 out: chal and lft 6 l clr 2 out: eased run-in* **10/3**[2]	148+
240P	2	3	**Backbord (GER)**[23] 1769 8-10-1 **126** (t) DougieCostello (Lucy Wadham) *bhd: sn on and off the bridle: hdwy 3 out: lft 6 l 2nd next: no ch w wnr* **10/1**	123
P20-	3	29	**Tasheba**[254] 4154 5-11-7 **151** DavidBass(5) (Nicky Henderson) *bhd: hdwy to chse ldrs 7th: rdn and wknd 2 out* **9/1**	127
110-	4	8	**Maraafeq (USA)**[207] 5099 6-10-3 **128** AidanColeman (Venetia Williams) *in tch: mstke 3rd: rdn and lost pl appr 7th: n.d after* **12/1**	92
2335	5	7	**Always Bold (IRE)**[26] 1727 5-9-7 **125** oh3 (b[1]) HenryBrooke(7) (Donald McCain) *chsd ldrs tl rdn and wknd 7th* **11/2**	83
1P0-	6	23	**Rodrigo Gonzales (IRE)**[310] 3033 8-10-5 **130** TomSiddall (Martin Keighley) *trckd ldrs: rdn 7th: sn wknd* **33/1**	67
55-0	7	12	**Lough Derg (FR)**[17] 1855 10-11-11 **150** (v) TomScudamore (David Pipe) *hit 4th: mde most tl after 7th: sn lost pl: bhd and eased after 3 out* **16/1**	76
10-P	F		**Alderluck (IRE)**[177] 206 7-10-10 **135** LeightonAspell (Nick Gifford) *pressed ldr: led after 7th: slt ld whn fell 2 out* **6/1**	135
4-00	F		**King's Forest (IRE)**[17] 1855 6-10-2 **127** JackDoyle (Emma Lavelle) *nt jump wl in rr: hdwy and in tch 7th: wknd appr 2 out: 4th and no ch whn fell heavily last* **11/4**[1]	92

5m 7.50s (-16.50) **Going Correction** -0.55s/f (Firm) **9 Ran SP% 115.0**
Speed ratings (Par 109): **109,107,96,93,91 82,77,—,—**
toteswingers:1&2:£8.90, 1&3:£5.20, 2&3:£11.80 CSF £35.89 CT £274.19 TOTE £4.20: £2.30, £3.30, £2.90; EX 49.20.

Owner Auld Hayes & Murphy **Bred** Mrs Caroline O'Driscoll **Trained** Upper Lambourn, Berks

FOCUS

A decent handicap hurdle. The winner would probably won despite Alderluck's fall and is rated up 6lb on his previous best.

NOTEBOOK

Working Title(IRE) would have been made to work considerably harder had Alderluck, who still held a slight advantage, not come down two out. Raised 12lb for scoring at Uttoxeter in early September, he seems to like this track, but he'll now be forced up in grade, although Nicky Henderson hasn't ruled out sending him back chasing. (tchd 3-1 and 7-2)

Backbord(GER), reverting to hurdles, having been struggling over fences, didn't seem to want to know early without the usual blinkers, but he eventually decided to put it all in and stayed on well to end up a clear second. (op 9-1)

Tasheba would probably have needed this under top weight and ended up well held. (op 15-2)

Maraafeq(USA), from a yard yet to hit form, should improve. (tchd 11-1)

Always Bold(IRE), 3lb out of the handicap, didn't fire in the first-time blinkers. (op 6-1 tchd 5-1)

Alderluck(IRE), runner-up off 8lb lower in the race a year ago and since a C&D scorer, looked ready for this seasonal debut and he had everything beaten bar the winner turning for home. He was in the process of being joined, though, and would probably have been second anyway, when crashing out two from home. (op 11-2 tchd 13-2)

King's Forest(IRE) made numerous jumping errors and was beaten off in fourth when taking a heavy fall at the last. (op 11-2 tchd 13-2)

2126 WEATHERBYS BLOODSTOCK INSURANCE GRADUATION CHASE (16 fncs) 2m 4f 110y

3:10 (3:12) (Class 2) 4-Y-0+

£15,655 (£4,625; £2,312; £1,157; £577; £290)

Form				RPR
15F-	**1**		**Riverside Theatre**[193] 5350 6-11-9 154 BarryGeraghty *(Nicky Henderson) trckd ldrs: led 3 out: sn clr: easily* **6/4**[1]	166+
230-	**2**	*9*	**Free World (FR)**[227] 4716 6-11-6 152 (t) RWalsh *(Paul Nicholls) hld up in 5th: blnd 2nd: effrt 4 out: disputing 2nd whn hit 3 out: one pce* **3/1**[2]	151
0UP-	**3**	*1 1/4*	**Tatenen (FR)**[205] 5126 6-11-9 143 LeightonAspell *(Richard Rowe) chsd ldr: led 11th tl 3 out: nt pce of wnr: mstke and lost 2nd at last* **20/1**	154
P4-1	**4**	*1 1/2*	**Golan Way**[26] 1727 6-11-2 0 JamieGoldstein *(Sheena West) led at gd pce: hdd 11th: wknd 3 out* **6/4**[1]	145
1U1-	**5**	*31*	**Bakbenscher**[266] 3934 7-11-9 141 ChristianWilliams *(Alan King) in tch: mstke 4th: wknd 10th: 5th and no ch whn mstke 4 out* **16/1**[3]	129
405/	**6**	*18*	**Altilhar (USA)**[555] 5225 7-11-2 0 AndrewGlassonbury *(Gary Moore) a last: rdn appr 10th: sn wl bhd* **66/1**	100

5m 7.40s (-12.10) **Going Correction** -0.125s/f (Good) **6** Ran SP% **117.1**

Speed ratings (Par 109): **118,114,114,113,101 94**

toteswingers:1&2:£1.70, 1&3:£5.40, 2&3:£7.80 CSF £7.18 TOTE £2.70: £1.20, £2.00; EX 6.20.

Owner Jimmy Nesbitt Partnership **Bred** Goldford Stud **Trained** Upper Lambourn, Berks

FOCUS

A really interesting graduation chase, run at a good gallop, and a thoroughly likeable performance from Riverside Theatre. He stepped up over this longer trip, but Free World was below his best 2m form.

NOTEBOOK

Riverside Theatre ◆ came really strong in the straight, having looked a bit rusty for the first 2m of the race, and pulled clear following a cracking jump three out. Last year's Arkle fifth, off since falling at Punchestown, but with an excellent record fresh and at this course (now 4-4), could take high rank this season, with races such as the Peterborough Chase, Ascot Chase, Ryanair and Melling Chase all likely to come under consideration for the 6-y-o, who is reportedly a stronger, more mature horse this season. Expected to come on for this, he may even get 3m, and considering his excellent course record one wouldn't be in a rush to dismiss him in a King George, but with Henderson already having Long Run, and maybe even Punchestowns, in mind for that race, he probably won't run (op 5-4 tchd 7-4,15-8 in a place)

Free World(FR) would often spoil his chance by refusing to settle last season, which was a worry considering he was now going up in trip, but he settled well under restraint and came out best of the remainder. He won't be easy to place off this mark and it would be no surprise were he to end up contesting some good handicap hurdles, given he's rated only 140, which it 12lb lower than he is over fences. (op 7-2)

Tatenen(FR), making his debut with Richard Rowe, travelled and jumped like a good horse before tiring and he's become well handicapped, so it would be no surprise were he to win a good handicap this season. The Byrne Group Plate looks an obvious long-term aim. (tchd 25-1)

Golan Way made quite an impressive debut over fences at Ludlow, but this was a considerably tougher ask against more experienced rivals and he couldn't maintain the gallop. This won't stop him winning more races back in novice company, though. (op 9-4 tchd 5-2 in places)

Bakbenscher made mistakes, but wasn't given a hard time and he'll be a big player in plenty of decent handicaps this season, especially back on softer ground and upped to 3m. (op 14-1)

Altilhar(USA), returning from a 555-day absence on this debut over fences, duly struggled.

2127 WEATHERBYS PRINTING H'CAP CHASE (18 fncs) 3m

3:45 (3:45) (Class 4) (0-115,120) 4-Y-0+ **£3,903** (£1,146; £573; £286)

Form				RPR
-2P1	**1**		**Victory Surge (IRE)**[68] 1366 6-11-1 102 (p) APMcCoy *(Jonjo O'Neill) sn chsng ldrs: blnd 10th: led after next: hit 13th: rdn clr 2 out: styd on wl* **4/1**[3]	118+
431-	**2**	*7*	**Coup Royale (FR)**[224] 4786 6-11-11 112 JoeTizzard *(Colin Tizzard) t.k.h in rr: hdwy 11th: mstke 4 out: rdn to chse wnr after 3 out: no ex* **7/2**[2]	121+
22-3	**3**	*7*	**Sea Cadet**[15] 1885 8-11-10 111 RhysFlint *(Laura Mongan) chsd ldrs: pressed wnr after 11th: chal 3 out: sn hrd rdn and btn* **11/4**[1]	112
54F1	**4**	*33*	**Pairc Na Gcapall (IRE)**[6] 2024 8-12-2 120 7ex (b) AlexMerriam(3) *(Neil King) chsd ldr tl lost pl 9th: sn bhd* **8/1**	91
1224	**5**	*1*	**Morestead (IRE)**[12] 1916 5-11-5 106 (b) LeightonAspell *(Brendan Powell) led: mstke 11th: sn hdd: wknd 4 out* **8/1**	76
-315	**6**	*72*	**Petroupetrov (FR)**[124] 868 7-11-6 107 TomSiddall *(Richard Phillips) nt fluent in rr: wl bhd fr 7th* **7/1**	13
3656	**P**		**Indiana Gold (FR)**[15] 1888 6-10-7 101 (p) OliverDayman(7) *(Alison Thorpe) a towards rr: lost tch and rdn after 10th: wl bhd whn p.u after 3 out* **12/1**	—

6m 8.80s (-6.20) **Going Correction** -0.125s/f (Good) **7** Ran SP% **111.3**

Speed ratings (Par 105): **105,102,100,89,89 65,—**

toteswingers:1&2:£3.00, 1&3:£2.80, 2&3:£2.40 CSF £17.79 TOTE £3.70: £3.30, £2.20; EX 14.70.

Owner Mrs Gay Smith **Bred** Mary Fanning McCormack **Trained** Cheltenham, Gloucs

FOCUS

Just a fair handicap chase, but the front two both put up performances that mark them down as horses to keep on-side. The form is rated through the third.

NOTEBOOK

Victory Surge(IRE), raised 5lb for winning at Bangor in August when he wore first-time cheekpieces, took another marked step forward and the headgear has clearly been the making of him. He stayed on too strongly for the runner-up and looks as though there may be more improvement to come as he goes beyond 3m. (tchd 9-2)

Coup Royale(FR) ◆, who didn't hang around long over hurdles, having only the four runs, winning his last, is a magnificent-looking beast who is expected to develop into a very useful chaser. The only surprise was that he was making his debut over fences at 3m, considering he hadn't run beyond 2m1f over hurdles, and that ultimately proved his undoing, as having travelled like much the best horse in the race, he couldn't match the winner in the final 2f. With this run under his belt and dropped to 2m4f, he'll make immense appeal in something similar. (op 10-3 tchd 3-1)

Sea Cadet had his chance and, although on the face of it disappointing, it's probable he was beaten by two progressive and unexposed sorts. (op 5-2)

Pairc Na Gcapall(IRE), penalised for winning at Taunton, struggled in this better race under a penalty. Consistency isn't his strong point. (tchd 9-1)

2128 LONDON IRISH TOP TRY SCORER CONDITIONAL JOCKEYS' H'CAP HURDLE (8 hdls) 2m

4:20 (4:20) (Class 4) (0-115,114) 4-Y-0+ **£2,602** (£764; £382; £190)

Form				RPR
256/	**1**		**Mark Of Love (IRE)**[981] 4096 6-10-9 97 SamTwiston-Davies *(Martin Keighley) plld hrd: in tch: led appr 2 out: drvn to hold on run-in* **5/1**[2]	105+
4313	**2**	*1 1/4*	**Crystal Rock (IRE)**[30] 1677 5-11-9 114 DavidBass(3) *(Nicky Henderson) t.k.h: prom: hrd rdn appr 2 out: kpt on to take 2nd fnl 50yds: a hld* **10/3**[1]	119
002-	**3**	*hd*	**Quetzal (IRE)**[192] 5363 5-10-9 100 CharlieHuxley(3) *(Alan King) in tch: drvn to chse ldrs appr 2 out: 3rd and hld whn mstke last: styd on same pce* **8/1**	105
-025	**4**	*1 1/4*	**Dean's Grange**[13] 1910 5-11-2 112 SClements(8) *(Colin Tizzard) hld up towards rr: smooth hdwy and looked dangerous 2 out: hrd rdn appr last: one pce* **15/2**[3]	115
14-5	**5**	*7*	**Sun Quest**[176] 235 6-11-0 105 RobertKirk(3) *(Steven Dixon) led tl 3 out: mstke and wknd next* **14/1**	102
1-55	**6**	*7*	**Mayberry**[18] 1844 5-10-12 108 StephenO'Donovan(8) *(Emma Lavelle) hld up in rr: hdwy and in tch whn stmbld on landing 3 out: wkng whn wandered and hit next* **5/1**[2]	100+
60/-	**7**	*5*	**The Cayterers**[12] 3279 8-10-9 100 LeeEdwards(3) *(Tony Carroll) t.k.h: chsd ldr: led 3 out: sn hdd: 6th and btn whn mstke next* **8/1**	85
64	**8**	*17*	**Society Venue**[18] 1844 5-11-8 110 JohnKington *(Michael Scudamore) towards rr: effrt on inner after 3 out: sn wknd* **16/1**	80
2633	**9**	*1*	**Tignello (IRE)**[6] 2021 5-11-9 111 (t) TomMolloy *(Emma Baker) plld hrd in rr: hdwy 3rd: blnd and dropped to last next: wl bhd fr 5th* **11/1**	80
2/5-	**10**	*5*	**Trump Call (IRE)**[222] 4822 6-10-10 104 HarryChalloner(6) *(Venetia Williams) towards rr: j. slowly 2nd: lost tch 3 out* **25/1**	69
1-00	**11**	*26*	**King Of The Titans (IRE)**[11] 1292 7-11-5 107 (b[1]) MichaelMurphy *(Patrick Gilligan) prom tl wknd rapidly 3 out* **33/1**	48

3m 54.9s (-5.10) **Going Correction** -0.55s/f (Firm) **11** Ran SP% **118.1**

Speed ratings (Par 105): **90,89,89,88,85 81,79,70,70,67 54**

toteswingers:1&2:£3.30, 1&3:£4.00, 2&3:£5.70 CSF £22.62 CT £133.26 TOTE £5.70: £2.30, £1.10, £4.30; EX 18.10.

Owner 7 Day Catering Limited **Bred** G Swift **Trained** Condicote, Gloucs

FOCUS

Four drew clear in what had looked a fairly modest handicap hurdle. The winner is rated a bit better than the bare result and to the level of his old form.

NOTEBOOK

Mark Of Love(IRE), returning from a 981-day absence, had already placed twice over C&D in novice events and found himself returning off a mark 13lb lower. Often a strong-traveller, he refused to settle early, but was clearly so well handicapped that is didn't make a difference, leading before two out and staying on well. It's hoped he goes on from this, although there's never a guarantee. (op 11-2 tchd 6-1)

Crystal Rock(IRE) kept finding for pressure and battled on well close home to take second, but was always being held by the winner. He looks ready for 2m4f now. (op 7-2 tchd 3-1)

Quetzal(IRE), always likely to do better once handicapping, has a bit of size and scope and he should be more than capable of winning off this mark. (tchd 9-1)

Dean's Grange, returning to the scene of his sole previous victory, travelled well and left behind a disappointing run at Exeter last time, but couldn't quicken sufficiently from before the last. He'll be at his best once sent chasing. (op 8-1)

Sun Quest ended up well held, having made the running. Official explanation: vet said gelding lost his off hind shoe (tchd 12-1)

Mayberry can be rated better than her finishing position, as she had closed to a challenging position when stumbling on landing at the third-last. (op 9-2 tchd 11-2)

Tignello(IRE) Official explanation: jockey said gelding ran too free

T/Jkpt: Part won. £56,394.50 to a £1 stake. Pool: £79,428.98 - 0.50 winning tickets. T/Plt: £147.30 to a £1 stake. Pool:£75,550.66 - 374.21 winning tickets T/Qpdt: £17.20 to a £1 stake. Pool:£5,290.09 - 226.80 winning tickets LM

1899 PLUMPTON (L-H)

Monday, November 1

OFFICIAL GOING: Good (chs 7.5, hdl 7.3)

Wind: virtually nil Weather: dry, bright

2129 BREEDERS' CUP LIVE ONLY ON ATR MAIDEN HURDLE (9 hdls) 2m

12:50 (12:50) (Class 4) 4-Y-0+ **£2,397** (£698; £349)

Form				RPR
311-	**1**		**Brackloon High (IRE)**[292] 3423 5-11-0 0 RichardJohnson *(Noel Chance) chsd ldrs: j.rt 2nd: hdwy to chse ldr bef 3 out: drvn 2 out: styd on strly u.p flat to ld fnl 75yds* **2/1**[1]	117+
60-4	**2**	*3/4*	**Midnight Opera**[19] 1819 4-10-7 0 MarkQuinlan(7) *(Neil Mulholland) travelled wl: chsd ldrs: wnt 2nd after 5th: bttr jump to ld next: mstke 2 out: sn rdn: hdd and no ex fnl 75yds* **16/1**	117+
4	**3**	*4 1/2*	**Mannlichen**[17] 1857 4-11-0 0 AidanColeman *(Venetia Williams) in tch: mstke 5th: hdwy to chse ldrs after next: rdn and chsd ldng pair after 2 out: one pce and hld whn j.rt last* **11/4**[2]	113+
00-4	**4**	*9*	**Top Smart**[14] 1899 4-10-9 0 JimmyDerham(5) *(Seamus Mullins) hld up in rr: sme hdwy into modest 7th bef 3 out: styd on steadily after: wnt 4th after last: nvr trbld ldrs* **33/1**	104
5	*4 1/2*	**Uncle Keef (IRE)**[64] 4-11-0 0 AndrewTinkler *(Nicky Henderson) chsd ldrs: mstke 1st: reminder after 4th: chsd ldng pair bef 3 out: rdn and wknd sn after 2 out* **17/2**	100

3 **6** *21* **Mut'Ab (USA)**[14] 1899 5-11-0 0 JamieMoore 81
(Gary Moore) *t.k.h early: in tch in midfield: rdn and mstke 3 out: sn wknd u.p: wl btn whn mstke last* **14/1**

7 *1* **Josr's Magic (IRE)**[7] 6-11-0 0 MattieBatchelor 80
(Peter Hedger) *t.k.h early: hld up in last: sme hdwy after 5th: no hdwy and struggling next: wl btn 3 out: t.o* **16/1**

/P-4 **8** *15* **Kathleen Kennet**[29] 1705 10-10-0 0 MrJBanks(7) 60
(Martin Bosley) *led: hung lft appr 3rd: j.big next: hdd bef 5th: wknd qckly 3 out: t.o* **100/1**

3- **9** *21* **Stormy Morning**[12] 2754 4-11-0 0 ChristianWilliams 48
(Lawney Hill) *a towards rr: mstke 2nd and 5th: sn struggling and j. slowly 6th: sn lost tch: t.o after 3 out* **8/1**[3]

10 *3 ¼* **Twilight Star (IRE)**[79] 6-10-7 0 MrTJCannon(7) 45
(Roger Teal) *t.k.h early: hld up in midfield: blnd and lost pl 3rd: rallied briefly 5th: sn lost pl again: t.o fr 3 out* **66/1**

0-P0 **11** *36* **Idol Deputy (FR)**[12] 1914 4-11-0 0 (t) MarkGrant 13
(James Bennett) *a in rr: rdn and struggling after 4th: wl t.o bef 3 out: j.lft and mstke last* **250/1**

P **Double Banded (IRE)**[408] 6-10-9 0 MarcGoldstein(5) —
(Jim Best) *chsd ldr: led after 5th: dived and hdd next: 4th and stl wl in tch whn lost action and p.u qckly 3 out: dismntd* **8/1**[3]

3m 46.7s (-14.10) **Going Correction** -0.575s/f (Firm) **12** Ran SP% **117.0**
Speed ratings (Par 105): **112,111,109,104,102 92,91,84,73,72 54,—**
toteswingers:1&2:£10.50, 1&3:£2.30, 2&3:£19.50 CSF £35.51 TOTE £3.10: £1.20, £3.50, £1.70; EX 43.70.
Owner T Conway,Mrs Conway,T G Warren **Bred** Barry O'Connor **Trained** Upper Lambourn, Berks

FOCUS
Not a bad maiden. It was run at a sound gallop and the form is probably worth being postitive about.

NOTEBOOK
Brackloon High(IRE) is well regarded by Noel Chance and won two of his three outings in the bumper division last term, which included success at this track. His one defeat came on a quick surface so there was a slight doubt about this ground on his hurdling debut, but he just got away with it and showed a decent attitude when asked to get on top up the run-in. Returning to softer ground is really what he wants and a stiffer test is also very likely to suit ideally, so he could well be up to defying a penalty if kept to this sort of grade next time out. His trainer later said he has one eye on the Grade 1 Challow Hurdle (2m5f) at Newbury in December for him. (tchd 9-4)
Midnight Opera showed the clear benefit of his return at Uttoxeter (when well behind the promising Nicene Creed) and only gave way to the winner near the finish. He shaped as though a stiffer test was required on his previous outing, and so it wasn't surprising that he was more effective under positive tactics here. He is a nice prospect and can land one of these over a bit further. (op 20-1)
Mannlichen finished fourth on debut at Cheltenham last month in better company and attracted support this time. He still looked a bit novicey at times and would've probably been better suited by a more positive ride, but this was still another fair effort. (op 7-2)
Top Smart ◆ caught the eye staying on steadily from off the pace and this was a definite step in the right direction. He should be winning when switched to handicap company over a longer trip.
Uncle Keef(IRE) has joined a top yard that very often improve horses sent there from the Flat, but he didn't look a typical recruit being rated just 56 and having scored just once from 11 outings in that sphere. He had his chance, but dropped out tamely off the home turn and is likely to struggle to win in novice company. His win on the level came over this trip, though, so it's a fair bet he will appreciate further over hurdles (op 8-1 tchd 9-1)
Mut'Ab(USA) was in front of the fourth when placed over C&D a fortnight previously, but taking a keen hold on this slower surface didn't help his stamina. (op 12-1)
Double Banded(IRE) was a very useful stayer at best on the level yet was a cheap purchase for his new connections and this was his first outing for 408 days. He was just feeling the pinch before pulling up after he clipped the fourth-last, and was later found to have come back lame. Official explanation: vet said gelding was lame when he was pulled up (tchd 9-1)

2130 ATTHERACES.COM/BREEDERSCUP MARES' NOVICES' HURDLE (12 hdls) 2m 5f
1:20 (1:20) (Class 4) 4-Y-0+ **£2,740** (£798; £399)

Form RPR

0-5 **1** **Kaituna (IRE)**[170] 333 4-10-10 0 SamJones 104+
(Oliver Sherwood) *hld up in tch: hmpd 3rd and 4th: hdwy to join ldr gng wl and mstke 3 out: hit next: rdn to ld between last 2: in command last: r.o wl* **12/1**

340- **2** *6* **The Hon Tara**[232] 4620 6-10-10 0 FelixDeGiles 96
(Charlie Longsdon) *in tch: hmpd 3rd: rdn to chse ldng pair after 3 out: j.lft last: chsd wnr flat: no imp: kpt on* **6/1**[3]

45P- **3** *1 ½* **Twin Bud**[231] 4636 5-10-5 0 (p) JimmyDerham(5) 94+
(Anna Newton-Smith) *hld up in tch: hmpd 1st: hdwy 9th: rdn after 3 out: kpt on same pce fr 2 out: wnt 3rd after last* **33/1**

53-2 **4** *2 ½* **Hill Forts Gloria (IRE)**[30] 1675 5-10-7 0 WayneKavanagh(3) 92
(Seamus Mullins) *led: jnd 3 out: rdn wl bef next: hit 2 out: sn hdd and nt pce of wnr: lost 2 pls flat* **13/8**[2]

115F **5** *2 ¼* **Frosted Grape (IRE)**[16] 1861 4-11-3 123 (b) JohnnyFarrelly 96
(David Pipe) *chsd ldrs: hmpd 1st: lft 2nd 3rd tl bef 3 out: sn rdn and fnd little: wl btn between last 2* **11/8**[1]

/00- **6** *19* **Bella Medici**[342] 2485 5-10-5 0 MichaelMurphy(5) 72
(Pat Murphy) *hld up in tch in rr: hmpd 3rd: j. slowly 5th: rdn and struggling whn mstke 3 out: sn wknd* **80/1**

60- **7** *33* **Noir Noir**[266] 3931 5-10-10 0 (t) MattieBatchelor 42
(Anna Newton-Smith) *j.lft and many mstkes: chsd ldrs: tl dropped to rr 8th: lost tch next: t.o* **40/1**

F **Sonus Weld (IRE)**[197] 5265 5-10-3 0 (b[1]) NathanSweeney(7) —
(Paddy Butler) *in tch tl bdly hmpd and fell 3rd* **33/1**

5m 9.40s (-12.90) **Going Correction** -0.575s/f (Firm) **8** Ran SP% **111.7**
Speed ratings (Par 105): **101,98,98,97,96 89,76,—**
toteswingers:1&2:£3.70, 1&3:£22.90, 2&3:£22.30 CSF £73.47 TOTE £6.50: £2.10, £2.00, £9.80; EX 41.10.
Owner P Deal & N Chamberlain **Bred** Miss Jane Mangan **Trained** Upper Lambourn, Berks

FOCUS
An ordinary mares' novice event. There was an average gallop on. The winner produced a big step up on her bumper form.

NOTEBOOK
Kaituna(IRE) ◆, who relished the step up in trip, should go on to better things. Oliver Sherwood's 4-y-o showed ability in two bumpers earlier this year and had obviously done well for her summer break. Despite her stable being in good form the market strongly suggested this hurdling debut would be needed, so there should be more to come and one can see her defying a penalty in this division before tackling something a little better. (op 9-1)
The Hon Tara made the frame in her first two bumper starts last season, but was well beaten on her final outing. She met support for this seasonal/hurdling debut, with the longer trip likely to suit on pedigree, and she showed there is a race to be won with her in this division. The way she tended to go in snatches would suggest the run will bring her on a fair deal and a stiffer track ought to help. (op 7-1 tchd 11-2)
Twin Bud, whose dam was a five-time winner at this venue for her stable, started to get involved from the third-last and kept on to post a career-best on this return from a 231-day absence. (op 40-1)
Hill Forts Gloria(IRE) was very well backed to go one better than her debut second in this sphere last month, with the extra distance expected to suit. She set out to make all, but was a sitting duck after an error two out and probably wants softer ground. Official explanation: jockey said mare had a breathing problem (op 5-2)
Frosted Grape(IRE), who fell over fences last time, came under heavy pressure nearing three out and was well held. This course may not have been ideal and her confidence should be restored somewhat, but she is probably in need of a break all the same. (op 11-10 tchd 13-8)

2131 AT THE RACES SKY 415 H'CAP HURDLE (9 hdls) 2m
1:55 (1:55) (Class 4) (0-105,102) 3-Y-0+ **£2,740** (£798; £399)

Form RPR

-466 **1** **Just Beware**[30] 1677 8-10-5 **86** (p) GemmaGracey-Davison(5) 96+
(Zoe Davison) *in tch: hdwy to chse ldr after 4th: led after next: mde rest: rdn clr between last 2: in command last: pushed out flat* **16/1**

05-6 **2** *10* **Switched Off**[38] 472 5-11-3 **98** MichaelMurphy(5) 99
(Ian Williams) *t.k.h early: hld up in tch in midfield: hdwy 6th: chsd ldrs 3 out: lft 2nd 2 out: sn rdn: hld hd awkwardly and fnd nil bef last* **11/8**[1]

5012 **3** *3* **Dormouse**[26] 1732 5-11-5 **102** (p) MrOJMurphy(7) 101
(Anabel L M King) *chsd ldr tl nt fluent 4th: in tch after: cl 4th and rdn bef 2 out: nt pce of wnr between last 2: wnt 3rd but wl hld whn mstke last* **5/1**[2]

3300 **4** *½* **Ghaill Force**[43] 1551 8-9-8 **77** NathanSweeney(7) 79+
(Paddy Butler) *chsd ldrs: wnt 2nd 6th: ev ch next tl blnd bdly 2 out: no ch w wnr after: lost 3rd last* **15/2**[3]

0425 **5** *9* **Red Current**[14] 1902 6-11-10 **100** SamJones 89
(Michael Scudamore) *t.k.h early: hld up in last trio: nt fluent 4th: pushed along and effrt after 6th: rdn and no prog after next: wl btn 2 out* **10/1**

006/ **6** *3 ¼* **Baby Car (FR)**[606] 4311 6-10-12 **88** RichardJohnson 78
(Noel Chance) *in tch in midfield: mstke 5th: rdn and wknd sn after 3 out* **8/1**

6P-5 **7** *2 ½* **Empire Seeker (USA)**[14] 1899 5-10-9 **88** PeterToole(3) 72
(Heather Main) *t.k.h: hld up in rr: short-lived effrt 3 out: rdn and wl btn bef 2 out* **20/1**

P-1 **8** *24* **Killowenabbey (IRE)**[185] 75 6-11-2 **99** (p) AodhaganConlon(7) 62
(Debra Hamer) *hld up in tch in last trio: rdn after 5th: struggling whn mstke 3 out: sn wl bhd: t.o* **14/1**

-000 **9** *38* **Mid Wicket (USA)**[14] 1902 4-11-2 **95** (p) RichardKilloran(3) 23
(Mouse Hamilton-Fairley) *led: clr tl after 4th: hdd after 5th: wkng qckly whn j.lft 3 out: t.o 2 out: eased flat* **33/1**

0-34 **P** **Tuppenny Piece**[119] 908 4-11-7 **97** GerardTumelty —
(Alan King) *nt fluent: chsd ldrs: j. slowly 2nd and 3rd: dropped to rr 6th: t.o whn p.u last* **12/1**

3m 49.4s (-11.40) **Going Correction** -0.575s/f (Firm)
WFA 4 from 5yo+ 7lb **10** Ran SP% **118.7**
Speed ratings (Par 105): **105,100,98,98,93 92,90,78,59,—**
toteswingers:1&2:£15.50, 1&3:£23.10, 2&3:£4.30 CSF £40.37 CT £137.10 TOTE £19.70: £5.00, £1.70, £1.70; EX 64.00.
Owner The Secret Circle **Bred** A Walder **Trained** Hammerwood, E Sussex
■ Stewards' Enquiry : Michael Murphy two-day ban: used whip with excessive force (15-16 Nov)

FOCUS
This was a moderate handicap, run at a sound tempo. The winner was very well in on the bset of last season's form and is rated to that level.

NOTEBOOK
Just Beware had been out the back in two previous outings since resuming, but had been placed on her last two visits to this course and she showed vastly improved form to score. This was her first success since September 2008 and, while she did the business readily here, her profile dictates she is one to oppose again next time after a rise. Official explanation: trainer was unable to offer any explanation for the apparent improvement of form (op 14-1)
Switched Off had improved a bundle since joining current connections and appeared nicely handicapped on this return to hurdles. He moved well through the race, but couldn't go with the winner when it mattered and raced most awkwardly when put under maximum pressure. Looking at this Flat wins this year he wants further as a hurdler and he is well up to winning off this mark, but it's not at all hard to see why his previous yard tried him in blinkers. (op 6-4 tchd 13-8)
Dormouse, another 5lb higher, found this sharp enough yet posted another creditable effort in defeat. He is consistent and rates the benchmark. (op 6-1)
Ghaill Force, the subject of a gamble and third in this last year, is still winless and was returning from a 43-day break with something to prove. He was in the process of running a much-improved race prior to clouting the penultimate flight and would've been closer but for that. He wouldn't have beaten the winner, though. (op 16-1)

2132 BREEDERS' CUP LIVE ONLY ON ATR NOVICES' H'CAP CHASE (18 fncs) 3m 2f
2:30 (2:30) (Class 5) (0-90,85) 4-Y-0+ **£2,602** (£764; £382; £190)

Form RPR

3-14 **1** **Orion Star (IRE)**[18] 1843 8-10-12 **76** (p) JimmyDerham(5) 84+
(Seamus Mullins) *chsd ldr: mstke 3rd and reminder: led 5th: j.rt next: j.rt 13th but sn pushed clr: rdn after 3 out: pckd and hdd next: kpt on gamely u.p to ld again flat: all out* **10/3**[2]

234- **2** *nk* **Sailor's Sovereign**[211] 5010 9-10-5 **64** GerardTumelty 70
(Julian Smith) *hld up in tch: chsd ldng pair 14th: rdn to chal and lft in ld 2 out: drvn and hdd after last: one pce after* **3/1**[1]

-PP0 **3** *3 ¼* **Rapid Return (IRE)**[18] 1840 7-11-0 **73** RichardJohnson 77
(Richard Phillips) *in tch: chsd ldr: wnt 2nd gng wl after 13th: shkn up 2 out: rdn and fnd nil between last 2: styd on same pce flat* **10/1**

423- **4** *9* **Mister Pink**[196] 5288 10-11-4 **77** PaddyBrennan 72
(Richard Rowe) *in tch in last pair: cajoled along fr 8th: sme hdwy to go 4th after 3 out: swtchd lft: drvn and no imp between last 2* **9/2**[3]

6000 **5** *½* **Wujood**[8] 1996 8-10-8 **67** LiamHeard 62
(Gerald Ham) *hld up in last: hdwy 13th: 4th and rdn 3 out: sn struggling: wl btn next* **16/1**

46F4 **6** *23* **Bynack Mhor (IRE)**[19] 1820 9-11-2 **75** (p) TomMessenger 54
(Lawney Hill) *led tl 5th: chsd ldr after: mstke and reminder 12th: lost pl and mstke 14th: wl bhd fr 3 out: t.o whn j.rt last* **11/2**

4P-6 **P** **Wild Bay**[30] 1675 7-11-12 **85** (p) LiamTreadwell —
(Nick Gifford) *t.k.h early: chsd ldrs: mstke and reminder 7th: more reminders after 10th: dropped to rr 13th: blnd next: t.o whn p.u 3 out* **9/2**[3]

6m 46.3s (-4.40) **Going Correction** -0.075s/f (Good) **7** Ran SP% **114.8**
Speed ratings (Par 103): **103,102,101,99,98 91,—**
toteswingers:1&2:£2.70, 1&3:£6.60, 2&3:£7.30 CSF £14.36 TOTE £4.10: £2.70, £1.30; EX 12.40.
Owner C A Green **Bred** Dr J O'Keeffe **Trained** Wilsford-Cum-Lake, Wilts

FOCUS
A weak staying handicap with an open look about it. The winner should still be competitive when reassessed and the next two ran to their marks.

NOTEBOOK
Orion Star(IRE) just did enough to resume winning ways. He was a beaten favourite on his previous outing, but that was on his return to action and he did win at Exeter on his penultimate outing in May. He is best from the front, this ground was easy enough for his liking and he deserves a lot of credit for rallying after meeting the penultimate fence wrong. (op 7-2 tchd 3-1)
Sailor's Sovereign ◆, well backed, was given a patient ride and made his move nearing three out. He was soon under pressure thereafter, but kept responding and only just lost out near the business end. This rates a very pleasing return to action and there is surely a race for him this year. (op 4-1)
Rapid Return(IRE) got a nice ride through the race and had every chance, but ultimately failed to see it out like the first two. This was a lot more like it again from him and dropping back to 3m in this sphere should help. (op 12-1 tchd 14-1)
Mister Pink was never seriously in the hunt on this seasonal return and, again showing an awkward head carriage, remains one to have reservations about. (tchd 4-1)
Wujood, racing without any aids, went in snatches through the first half but began to creep closer on the final circuit and looked a player. He failed to get home in the end, but this was one of his more encouraging efforts. (tchd 20-1)
Bynack Mhor(IRE) is a lazy performer so it wasn't too worrying when he came under pressure around the 12th fence. He was in trouble shortly afterwards, though, and could now benefit from a break. (op 9-2)

2133 ATTHERACES.COM/BREEDERSCUP JUVENILE CLAIMING HURDLE (9 hdls) 2m
3:00 (3:00) (Class 5) 3-Y-O **£1,541** (£449; £224)

Form				RPR
0515	1		**Pobs Trophy**29 1700 3-11-0 90 (p) PaddyBrennan	91+
			(David Bourton) *racd in midfield: clsd and pushed along to chse ldrs after 3 out: bmpd and blnd next: chsd ldr last: rdn to ld fnl 100yds: drvn out* **9/2**3	
P6	2	½	**Moonbalej**23 1772 3-10-5 0 (v1) JimmyDerham(5)	83
			(Milton Harris) *led: sn clr: hung lft after 6th: hrd pressed and rdn bef 2 out: drvn and hld hd awkwardly after last: hdd fnl 100yds: no ex* **50/1**	
6313	3	1¼	**Frameit (IRE)**11 1935 3-11-0 107 (vt) RichardJohnson	87
			(Tim Vaughan) *in tch in main gp: wnt 2nd after 6th: clsd on ldr next: rdn 2 out: nt fluent and lost 2nd last: hung rt u.p and styd on same pce flat* **3/1**2	
3	4	nk	**Jazz Age (IRE)**26 1728 3-10-13 0 (b) COFarrell(5)	90
			(David Pipe) *prom in main gp: wnt 2nd and clsd on ldr bef 3 out: pressing ldr whn j.lft 2 out: styd on same pce between last* **17/2**	
	5	3¼	**State Visit**13 3-10-8 0 SamJones	77
			(Amy Weaver) *prom in main gp: lost pl 6th: 8th and looked wl hld 3 out: rallied u.p next: styd on flat* **9/1**	
364	6	2¼	**Massachusetts**42 1473 3-10-8 77 (p) JohnnyFarrelly	75
			(Brendan Powell) *racd off the pce in midfield: mstke 1st: clsd and in tch 6th: rdn and unable qck after 3 out: kpt on same pce fr next* **50/1**	
	7	1	**Best Catch (USA)**39 3-11-0 0 JamieMoore	81
			(Gary Moore) *t.k.h early: hld up in last trio: hdwy after 5th: chsd ldrs 3 out: rdn next: wknd between last 2* **33/1**	
45	8	hd	**Highland Cadett**11 1935 3-10-10 0 (v) PaulMoloney	77
			(Rod Millman) *chsd clr ldr tl after 6th: wknd u.p bef 2 out: wl hld whn j. slowly last* **14/1**	
101	9	5	**Joan D'Arc (IRE)**29 1691 3-10-8 109 MrJMQuinlan(7)	76
			(Michael Quinlan) *racd in last trio: stl rr but jst in tch and rdn after 5th: no prog: 9th and wl hld fr 3 out* **9/4**1	
0	10	2¼	**Baggsy (IRE)**13 1691 3-10-1 0 MattieBatchelor	60
			(Julia Feilden) *hld up in last trio: rdn and no hdwy bef 3 out: n.d* **66/1**	
2P5	11	nk	**Glen Lass**83 1226 3-10-11 95 (b) DarylJacob	70
			(Jamie Snowden) *racd in midfield: blnd 1st: mstke 3rd: rdn after next: dropped to rr and u.p after 5th: no ch fr 3 out* **18/1**	

3m 53.3s (-7.50) **Going Correction** -0.575s/f (Firm) 11 Ran SP% **114.8**
Speed ratings (Par 102): **95,94,94,93,92 91,90,90,88,87 86**
toteswingers:1&2:£37.30, 1&3:£3.70, 2&3:£28.10 CSF £192.56 TOTE £5.10: £1.80, £12.70, £1.20; EX 420.30.Frameit was claimed by J. G. Given for £8,000.
Owner Stan Wright **Bred** Mrs S Joint **Trained** Abberley, Worcs
■ Pobs Trophy was Dave Bourton's first runner over jumps.

FOCUS
A typically moderate juvenile claimer. It was run at a solid enough gallop and the first four dominated. The winner is better than the bare result but the form is very limited.

NOTEBOOK
Pobs Trophy, who has changed stables, attracted solid support on this drop back down in class and regained the winning thread, but needed all of his rider's strength to prevail. He came under heavy pressure around three out and, after rallying to hold every chance at the second-last, a mistake as things got tight there looked to have cost him. However, his rider picked him back up and he eventually found most up the run-in. This is clearly his sort of level, but a stiffer test should suit ideally as he matures. (op 7-1 tchd 15-2)
Moonbalej had been a bitter disappointment in his career to date and struggled in two previous runs as a hurdler. He was sent to the front with a first-time visor replacing cheekpieces and looked sure to fold as the challengers mounted on the back straight, having done so much early on. However, despite looking awkward, he kept responding and only got reeled in near the finish. His current stable could find him a race of this class, but whether he will build on this is anyone's guess.
Frameit(IRE) had every chance on this drop in class and appeared to give his all. He sets the standard. (op 11-4 tchd 5-2)
Jazz Age(IRE), a well-held third on debut last month, had blinkers on for the first time in this sphere. He proved easy to back conceding weight all round, but was given every chance and his stamina only gave way after the last. He clearly appreciated the easier grade. (op 6-1)
State Visit had won two of her three previous outings in this sphere and unsurprisingly proved popular on this drop in class. She was taken wide throughout, presumably to find the better ground, and it was clear on the back straight that she was in trouble. (op 12-1)
Joan D'Arc(IRE) Official explanation: jockey said that the filly was never traveling

2134 AT THE RACES VIRGIN 534 H'CAP CHASE (14 fncs) 2m 4f
3:35 (3:35) (Class 4) (0-105,99) 4-Y-O+ **£3,252** (£955; £477; £238)

Form				RPR
2452	1		**Glengarra (IRE)**25 1744 13-11-11 98 (tp) TimmyMurphy	109+
			(Liam Corcoran) *led: hdd 11th: drvn and ev ch after 3 out: blnd and pckd next: looked btn between last 2: gd jump to ld again last: sn clr: rdn out* **4/1**2	
412-	2	4½	**The Hardy Boy**211 5011 10-11-4 91 MattieBatchelor	97
			(Anna Newton-Smith) *chsd ldr: hit 1st: led 11th: rdn after 3 out: looked wnr between last 2: hit last and hdd: wknd flat* **5/1**3	
46-1	3	2	**High Oscar**12 1916 9-11-9 96 RichardJohnson	100
			(Richard Rowe) *hld up in rr: blnd 4th: mstke 9th: hdwy next: chsd ldng pair 11th: rdn and no prog fr 2 out* **6/4**1	
422-	4	2	**Massini Sunset (IRE)**210 5031 10-11-7 99 GilesHawkins(5)	99
			(Richard Mitchell) *chsd clr ldrs: clsd after 9th: rdn and outpcd after 3 out: kpt on again u.p flat* **8/1**	
43F	5	hd	**Royial (FR)**14 1901 5-11-1 93 JimmyDerham(5)	94
			(Seamus Mullins) *hld up in rr: mstke 7th: clsd after 9th: rdn and outpcd 3 out: styd on again u.p flat: dismntd after fin* **6/1**	
0-46	6	36	**Maximix**152 586 7-11-11 98 JamieMoore	86
			(Gary Moore) *racd in midfield: rdn along after 9th: struggling bef 11th: mstke and lost tch 3 out: virtually p.u flat: t.o* **10/1**	

5m 3.20s (-4.10) **Going Correction** -0.075s/f (Good) **6** Ran SP% **111.2**
Speed ratings (Par 105): **105,103,102,101,101 87**
toteswingers:1&2:£3.10, 1&3:£2.00, 2&3:£1.80 CSF £23.02 TOTE £4.30: £1.80, £1.90; EX 19.80.
Owner Starlight Racing **Bred** T J Whitley **Trained** Charlton Adam, Somerset

FOCUS
Not a strong event for the class with the top weight being rated 6lb below the race ceiling. The winner is rated close to the best of his recent form.

NOTEBOOK
Glengarra(IRE) deservedly got back to winning ways and he got a fine ride from his bang in-form jockey. He cut out a lot of the running, but was hassled for a lot of the way for that position by the runner-up and wasn't going as well as that rival turning for home. He also wasn't that clever two out, but Timmy Murphy gave him a smack as he took off at the last and he flew it, which ultimately won him the race. He was 7lb lower than when last winning in 2009, but doesn't appeal as one to follow up. (tchd 9-2)
The Hardy Boy, a course specialist, turned in a brave effort on his seasonal debut and only gave way up the run-in. He is currently 6lb higher than his last win at the track, but often comes on for his first run back and so this was a very pleasing comeback. (op 11-2)
High Oscar was up 3lb for winning on his return over 2m6f last month, but had landed this race in 2008 off a 9lb higher mark and was in with every chance when departing two out last season. His rider still looked fairly confident turning for home in third place, but he found just the one pace when it mattered and the run probably came that bit too soon. It may well be that he wants further these days, however (tchd 5-4 and 13-8)
Massini Sunset(IRE) often needs a few races before coming good each season and wasn't disgraced on this return from his seasonal break. (tchd 10-1)
Royial(FR) wasn't done with prior to falling on his chasing debut over C&D last time. He was given time to get into things and looked a player four out, but lacked the pace to get seriously involved. That would suggest he wants a longer trip, but he was found to be lame shortly after the finish and could be set for some time off. Official explanation: vet said gelding finished lame (op 13-2 tchd 7-1)
Maximix was the first beaten and was later reported to have lost a shoe. Official explanation: vet said gelding had lost a right fore shoe (tchd 12-1)

2135 ATTHERACES.COM/BREEDERSCUP CONDITIONAL JOCKEYS' H'CAP HURDLE (12 hdls) 2m 5f
4:10 (4:10) (Class 5) (0-90,90) 4-Y-O+ **£1,712** (£499; £249)

Form				RPR
-P00	1		**Just The Job (IRE)**25 1741 6-11-4 85 MrMMO'Connor(3)	103+
			(Neil Mulholland) *a gng wl: hld up in midfield: mstke 1st: hdwy to trck ldrs 7th: led on bit and nt fluent 2 out: clr last: r.o strly: easily* **20/1**	
5362	2	12	**Spider Boy**8 1996 13-10-12 79 (b) GemmaGracey-Davison(3)	78
			(Zoe Davison) *w ldr tl led 4th: rdn after 3 out: hdd nt pce of wnr between last 2: plugged on to hold 2nd* **9/2**2	
2P1F	3	½	**Winning Show**12 1915 6-11-5 86 (tp) CharlieWallis(3)	87+
			(Chris Gordon) *chsd ldrs: mstke 7th: rdn to press ldr and hit next: stl ev ch 2 out: nt pce of wnr between last 2: wl hld whn nt fluent last* **5/1**3	
01	4	5	**Curragh Dancer (FR)**12 1915 7-10-12 81 (p) NathanSweeney(5)	77
			(Paddy Butler) *in tch in midfield: mstke 4th and 8th: hdwy after 8th: rdn and outpcd by ldng trio after 3 out: one pce and wl hld after: mstke 2 out* **17/2**	
0-00	5	2½	**Little Roxy (IRE)**19 1822 5-10-7 71 MarcGoldstein	63
			(Anna Newton-Smith) *in tch: mstke 4th: rdn and outpcd by ldng trio after 3 out: styd on same pce u.p and wl hld after* **33/1**	
3P-0	6	4	**Midnight Diamond (IRE)**151 597 7-10-5 75 (p) MrTomDavid(6)	63
			(Tim Vaughan) *midfield: sn niggled along and nvr travelling: dropped towards rr and rdn 5th: toiling u.p bef 9th: 8th and no ch 3 out: plugged on past btn horses between last 2* **4/1**1	
2-34	7	4	**Pete The Feat (IRE)**30 1679 6-11-7 85 PeterToole	70
			(Anna Newton-Smith) *chsd ldrs: drvn and wknd after 3 out: wl btn next* **13/2**	
/0-0	8	4½	**Monash Lad (IRE)**176 220 8-11-2 80 RichardKilloran	61
			(Michelle Bryant) *hld up in last trio: hdwy after 8th: chsd ldrs and rdn after 3 out: sn wknd* **33/1**	
5/P1	9	10	**Brilliant (GER)**10 1949 7-10-6 73 (p) AodhaganConlon(3)	45
			(Debra Hamer) *led tl 4th: pushed along after: chsd ldr tl bef 3 out: wknd qckly u.p wl bef 2 out: t.o* **4/1**1	
45-5	10	26	**Brigadore (USA)**174 264 7-11-7 90 ChrisDavies(5)	38
			(Gerald Ham) *hld up in rr: rdn and lost tch after 8th: t.o after 3 out* **22/1**	
60P0	P		**Knockvicar (IRE)**12 1915 8-10-4 68 GilesHawkins	—
			(Richard Mitchell) *a bhd: pushed along after 4th: lost tch bef 9th: t.o whn p.u 2 out* **25/1**	

5m 9.80s (-12.50) **Going Correction** -0.575s/f (Firm) 11 Ran SP% **117.5**
Speed ratings (Par 103): **100,95,95,93,92 90,89,87,83,73** —
toteswingers:1&2:£19.40, 1&3:£25.60, 2&3:£5.30 CSF £103.58 CT £530.18 TOTE £41.50: £8.80, £2.90, £2.30; EX 237.80.
Owner Brian Mulholland **Bred** Mrs A R Mulholland **Trained** Burlescombe, Devon

FOCUS
This moderate handicap for conditional riders was run at a decent gallop and the form looks sound enough for the class. The easy winner was up 20lb+ on his previous best and looks sure to win again.

NOTEBOOK
Just The Job(IRE) ◆, from an in-form yard, was partnered by a talented conditional rider and he ran out a fairly effortless winner. He went easily through the race and it was clear nearing the second-last he was the one to be on. He didn't have to be extended to go clear from that point, and this was a hugely improved effort on just his second run in a handicap. Surely connections will look to get him out before his new mark kicks in as he would escape a penalty, and he ought to prove hard to stop from going in again should that be the case. He holds an entry at Hereford on Sunday. Official explanation: trainer said, regarding the running and riding, that the race was run to suit him and he benefitted from a change of training regime (op 25-1)
Spider Boy, second at Towcester eight days earlier, again ran a solid race in defeat but was no match for the winner. He helps to set the standard and, fairly handicapped at present, deserves to go one better again. (tchd 5-1)
Winning Show was 4lb higher than when departing two out at Fontwell 12 days earlier and gave his all here. This ground was as easy as he wants it, but the handicapper probably just has his measure now. (op 7-1 tchd 9-2)
Curragh Dancer(FR) was the one to benefit from Winning Show's fall at Fontwell last month and he was 4lb higher for that initial success. He tended to go in snatches here, but kept on and ran close enough to his previous form. (tchd 8-1 and 10-1)
Little Roxy(IRE) was under pressure a fair way out, but did keep on and turned in her most encouraging effort to date. (op 25-1)

Midnight Diamond(IRE) was well treated on his previous best efforts and met support on this debut for Tim Vaughan. Returning from a 151-day break, he raced lazily and is likely to prove a challenge for his new trainer. (op 9-2)
Brilliant(GER), winner of a seller at Fakenham ten days earlier, didn't seem to enjoy being taken on for the lead and downed tools on the final lap. (op 9-2)
T/Plt: £541.60 to a £1 stake. Pool:£55,456.37 - 74.74 winning tickets T/Qpdt: £13.40 to a £1 stake. Pool:£8,035.08 - 443.04 winning tickets SP

1907 EXETER (R-H)

Tuesday, November 2

OFFICIAL GOING: Chase course - good to soft (soft in places; 6.1); hurdle course - soft (good to soft in places; 5.9)

Wind: Moderate, across Weather: Overcast but dry

2136 TOTEPLACEPOT "NATIONAL HUNT" NOVICES' HURDLE (DIV I) (11 hdls) 2m 5f 110y

1:35 (1:36) (Class 3) 4-Y-0+ £4,228 (£1,241; £620; £310)

Form				RPR
1	1		**Mr Hudson (IRE)**[169] [375] 5-10-12 0 RWalsh (Paul Nicholls) *trckd ldr: shkn up to ld last: edgd rt: styd on wl: rdn out* 2/1[2]	124+
44F-	2	1 ¾	**Madison Du Berlais (FR)**[206] [5127] 9-10-12 0 (p) TomScudamore (David Pipe) *led: rdn appr 3 out: hdd last: swtchd lft run-in: styd on but no ex* 13/8[1]	120
5-	3	7	**Ace High**[363] [2058] 6-10-12 0 TomO'Brien (Victor Dartnall) *mid-div: hdwy after 8th: rdn in cl 3rd after 3 out: styd on same pce fr next* 17/2	114+
06-	4	11	**Grey Wulff (IRE)**[207] [5121] 5-10-12 0 JackDoyle (Emma Lavelle) *mid-div: hdwy 8th: rdn in cl 3rd appr 3 out tl wknd 2 out* 33/1	102
3	5	14	**The Clyda Rover (IRE)**[31] [1675] 6-10-12 0 OwynNelmes (Helen Nelmes) *mid-div: rdn after 8th: no imp on ldrs: wknd 2 out* 50/1	88
00-	6	12	**Graduation Night**[241] [4429] 4-10-12 0 SamThomas (Jamie Snowden) *chsd ldrs tl dropped to rr 6th: nvr any danger after* 100/1	76
5	7	2	**Driving Onwards (IRE)**[26] [1748] 6-10-5 0 MattGriffiths(7) (Ron Hodges) *mid-div: hit 6th: rdn after 8th: wknd 3 out* 100/1	74
0-	8	2	**Ballyegan (IRE)**[242] [4420] 5-10-12 0 HarrySkelton (Bob Buckler) *trckd ldrs: rdn after 8th: wknd bef next: hit 2 out* 66/1	72
40-0	9	8	**George Nympton (IRE)**[24] [1775] 4-10-12 120 BarryGeraghty (Nick Williams) *hld up towards rr: sme prog into midfield 7th: rdn after next: sn wknd* 7/2[3]	64
	10	24	**Quiet Alice** 5-10-5 0 RodiGreene (Neil Mulholland) *hit 1st: a towards rr: t.o* 33/1	33
/4-4	P		**The Grifter**[185] [93] 8-10-12 109 AndrewGlassonbury (John Ryall) *t.k.h: hit 1st: a towards rr: struggling 7th: bhd whn p.u bef 2 out* 20/1	—

5m 25.5s (-7.50) **Going Correction** -0.15s/f (Good)
WFA 4 from 5yo+ 8lb 11 Ran SP% 118.3
Speed ratings (Par 107): **107,106,103,99,94 90,89,88,86,77** —
Tote Swingers:1&2:£1.50, 2&3:£5.90, 1&3:£5.10 CSF £5.71 TOTE £2.80: £1.10, £1.50, £2.00; EX 7.50.
Owner Mrs Angela Tincknell & W Tincknell **Bred** Margo & Julie Harty **Trained** Ditcheat, Somerset

FOCUS
A fair novices' hurdle and the winner should go on to rate higher.

NOTEBOOK
Mr Hudson(IRE) made it 2-2 under rules, having won a Newton Abbot bumper back in May. Up 5f in trip now sent hurdling, he was always travelling kindly under Ruby Walsh and did what he had to once taking over from the front-running favourite. He'll stay 3m and looks capable of defying a penalty. (tchd 9-4)
Madison Du Berlais(FR), last seen falling in the Grand National and looking a bit burly beforehand, hadn't run over hurdles since his juvenile days back in 2004, but he was strong in the market regardless, and made it a good test under a positive ride. He couldn't match the winner late on, but this will have set him up nicely for a return to fences, with either the Betfair Chase or Hennessy likely to be his aim. (op 9-4)
Ace High, a promising fifth on his sole bumper start at Chepstow almost a year ago, is a fine, big sort and his rider was keen not to give him a hard time of it once he was held. The way he travelled suggest he's got a definite future, though, and he should have no trouble winning something similar. (op 9-1)
Grey Wulff(IRE), unplaced in a couple of bumpers, shaped nicely despite ending up well held, but he's likely to improve and is another with a future.
George Nympton(IRE), disappointing in a good 4-y-o handicap hurdle on his reappearance at Chepstow, showed very little again and is now left with plenty to prove. (op 3-1)

2137 TOTETENTOFOLLOW NOVICES' HURDLE (8 hdls) 2m 1f

2:05 (2:06) (Class 3) 4-Y-0+ £4,553 (£1,337; £668; £333)

Form				RPR
62-1	1		**Dare Me (IRE)**[14] [1910] 6-11-4 0 RichardJohnson (Philip Hobbs) *mde virtually all: mstke 4th: wl in command fr 3 out: unextended* 1/6[1]	130+
	2	4 ½	**Alla Svelta (IRE)**[177] 4-10-12 0 PaulMoloney (Evan Williams) *in tch: pckd 5th: rdn in 4th appr 3 out: styd on fr 2 out: snatched 2nd fnl strides: no ch w v easy wnr* 25/1	105
	3	shd	**Sorcillera**[368] 4-10-5 0 RhysFlint (John Flint) *chsd wnr virtually thrght: rdn appr 3 out: nvr able to chal and sn comf hld by wnr: lost 2nd fnl strides* 20/1[3]	97
0P0-	4	4	**Forty Knights**[206] [5130] 5-9-12 0 MrRHawkins(7) (Chris Down) *in tch: rdn appr 3 out: styd on but nt pce to mount chal* 100/1	93
0	5	7	**Silver Roque (FR)**[181] [154] 4-10-12 0 HaddenFrost (Henrietta Knight) *trckd ldrs: effrt appr 3 out: wkng whn hit 2 out* 12/1[2]	95
	6	3 ¾	**Ladies Dancing**[163] 4-10-12 0 LiamHeard (Chris Down) *mid-div: hdwy after 4th: rdn appr 3 out: sn one pce* 66/1	90
40/	7	3 ¾	**Arrayan**[656] [3376] 5-10-12 0 TomScudamore (David Pipe) *hld up towards rr: j.lft: rdn whn sme prog into midfield after 5th: nvr trbld ldrs* 33/1	86
0U3-	8	4 ½	**Baraquet**[208] [5103] 4-10-5 0 JamesDavies (Chris Down) *towards rr: sme late prog: nvr a factor* 80/1	74
0P	9	10	**Sarah's Boy**[14] [1907] 5-10-7 0 (t) CO'Farrell(5) (David Pipe) *nvr bttr than mid-div* 66/1	71
	10	3 ½	**Cridda Boy**[511] 4-10-12 0 AndrewThornton (Simon Burrough) *nvr fluent: mstke 3rd: a towards rr* 100/1	68
0-0	11	1	**Gallimaufry**[26] [1736] 4-10-5 0 RodiGreene (Neil Mulholland) *mid-div tl wknd 5th* 100/1	60
0	12	1 ¾	**Eddie Boy**[18] [1857] 4-10-12 0 APMcCoy (Rebecca Curtis) *t.k.h early: led tl 1st: trckd wnr tl after 4th: wknd bef 3 out* 12/1[2]	65
	13	18	**Trouble Digger** 5-10-12 0 SeanQuinlan (Kim Bailey) *nvr fluent: a in rr: t.o 5th* 28/1	47
0	14	shd	**Tooney Maloney**[171] [333] 5-9-12 0 MarkQuinlan(7) (Neil Mulholland) *a in rr: t.o fr 3rd* 80/1	40
0	15	8	**Haydens Mount**[13] [1927] 5-10-9 0 WayneKavanagh(3) (James Frost) *mid-div: rdn appr 5th: sn wknd: t.o* 100/1	39
	P		**Tiger Breeze (USA)**[465] 4-10-5 0 NathanSweeney(7) (Bob Buckler) *mid-div tl sddle slipped 2nd: sn p.u* 100/1	—
0	P		**Chase Gate**[26] [1736] 5-10-12 0 SamThomas (James Frost) *mid-div: pushed along 3rd: wknd 5th: t.o whn p.u bef 3 out* 100/1	—
0-	P		**Midnight Paradise**[193] [5368] 4-10-5 0 JohnnyFarrelly (Neil Mulholland) *a in rr: t.o whn p.u after 5th* 66/1	—

4m 11.7s (-3.80) **Going Correction** -0.15s/f (Good)
WFA 4 from 5yo+ 7lb 18 Ran SP% 129.0
Speed ratings (Par 107): **102,99,99,97,94 92,91,89,84,82 82,81,72,72,69** —,—,—
Tote Swingers:1&2:£5.10, 2&3:£48.50, 1&3:£4.80 CSF £12.73 TOTE £1.10: £1.02, £5.20, £4.20; EX 9.80.
Owner Trevor Hemmings **Bred** Aaron Metcalfe **Trained** Withycombe, Somerset

FOCUS
A seriously uncompetitive novices' hurdle, despite the large field, and 1-6 shot Dare Me always had things under control off the front end. The fifth and eighth are the best guides to the level of the form.

NOTEBOOK
Dare Me(IRE), an easy C&D winner on debut over hurdles, did what was expected. We learned nothing new about this formerly smart bumper performer, but he's almost certainly going to improve for a longer trip down the line and remains a horse of some potential. As for where he goes next, his trainer's not sure, but it will almost certainly be up in grade. (op 1-5, tchd 2-9 in places)
Alla Svelta(IRE) had run out on his only start in points. He never got close enough to challenge the favourite, but did travel nicely into contention for second and looks likely to be suited by further.
Sorcillera, a 1m2f Flat winner in Germany last year, went well for a long way and didn't give up second without a fight. She'll have no trouble finding opportunities, with her having the option of racing in mares' only events.
Forty Knights stayed on late to record a much-improved effort. We'll learn more next time, but she too will find it easier against her own sex.
Silver Roque(FR) improved on his initial effort and will be of more interest once handicapping.
Arrayan, returning from a 656-day absence on this debut for David Pipe, kept on late without being given a hard time and he too will be of some interest sent handicapping. (op 40-1)
Eddie Boy looked a peculiar purchase by his owner, considering his lowly achievements on the Flat, and for a second straight race he looked a non-stayer.
Tiger Breeze(USA) Official explanation: jockey said saddle slipped

2138 TOTESPORT.COM HALDON GOLD CUP CHASE (LIMITED H'CAP) GRADE 2 (12 fncs) 2m 1f 110y

2:35 (2:35) (Class 1) 4-Y-0+

£39,907 (£14,973; £7,497; £3,738; £1,876; £938)

Form				RPR
212-	1		**Tchico Polos (FR)**[199] [5221] 6-10-4 153 oh5 (t) RWalsh (Paul Nicholls) *chsd ldrs: mstke 1st: lft disputing 2nd 8th: outpcd appr 4 out: rallied 3 out: led 2 out: hit last: drifted rt run-in: hld on: all out* 3/1[2]	153
PR3-	2	½	**Twist Magic (FR)**[192] [5394] 8-11-10 173 NoelFehily (Paul Nicholls) *reluctant to line up and led in: in tch: tk clsr order after 6th: lft disputing 2nd 8th tl mstke 4 out: sn rdn: rallied after 2 out: kpt on gamely but drifted sltly rt run-in: hld nr fin* 16/1	174+
122-	3	3	**Somersby (IRE)**[208] [5098] 6-10-7 156 HaddenFrost (Henrietta Knight) *travelled wl for most of way in tch: lft disputing 2nd 8th: nt fluent 4 out: sn rdn: ev ch 2 out: kpt on same pce* 9/4[1]	154+
02-F	4	5	**I'msingingtheblues (IRE)**[10] [1958] 8-10-5 154 TomScudamore (David Pipe) *chsd ldrs: wnt 2nd 5th: lft in ld 8th: rdn after 4 out: hdd 2 out: no ex* 11/1	145
300-	5	5	**The Sawyer (BEL)**[195] [5324] 10-9-11 153 oh7 NathanSweeney(7) (Bob Buckler) *disp tl 3rd: chsd ldrs: outpcd after 6th: styd on same pce fr 4 out* 66/1	140
45-1	6	hd	**Cornas (NZ)**[23] [1801] 8-10-4 153 oh3 BarryGeraghty (Nick Williams) *hld up but in tch: hit 5th: outpcd after 7th: rdn after next: styd on same pce fr 4 out: nvr a threat: fin lame* 7/2[3]	140
F5F-	U		**Mahogany Blaze (FR)**[192] [5394] 8-10-4 153 oh3 (b) PaddyBrennan (Nigel Twiston-Davies) *hld up: blnd and uns rdr 4th* 10/1	—
4P-2	P		**Chaninbar (FR)**[17] [1861] 7-10-6 155 (v) SeanQuinlan (Milton Harris) *reluctant at s: dwlt: a last: losing tch whn p.u bef 8th* 11/1	—
U53-	R		**Herecomesthetruth (IRE)**[247] [4327] 8-10-6 155 ColinBolger (Chris Gordon) *disp ld tl clr ldr 3rd: rn out 8th* 33/1	—

4m 14.8s (-4.20) **Going Correction** +0.025s/f (Yiel) 9 Ran SP% 114.1
Speed ratings (Par 115): **110,109,108,106,104 103**,—,—,—
Tote Swingers:1&2:£8.20, 2&3:£9.50, 1&3:£1.80 CSF £46.01 CT £125.80 TOTE £5.20: £1.50, £3.00, £1.10; EX 26.00.
Owner Chris Giles **Bred** Claude Leroy & Mrs Colette Leroy **Trained** Ditcheat, Somerset

FOCUS
A race that's traditionally one of the first real highlights of the season, with it often attracting one or two with ambitions of Champion Chase, Ryanair, or even Gold Cup glory. The pace was a good one, courtesy of Herecomesthetruth and The Sawyer, and it turned into a proper test at the distance. This was a decent renewal Tchico Polos is rated to the best of his novice form, with Twist Magic right up to his mark.

NOTEBOOK
Tchico Polos(FR), a previous C&D winner who had been tried at up to 3m last season, was solid in the market despite racing from 5lb out of the handicap. He had long been targeted at this race by his trainer and Ruby Walsh was content to sit back and chase the pace aboard this often front-runner. It was a good job he did, as it enabled him to keep a bit in reserve for the slog up the home straight, rallying well to take over two out and overcoming a mistake at the last to hold on well from his stablemate, the pair drifting right. Placed at Grade 1 level last season, he isn't going to be the easiest to place, but he is at least fairly versatile with regards to trip. (tchd 10-3)
Twist Magic(FR), a regular in this race who was conceding 17lb or more to all his rivals, ran a cracking race. Dismissed in the market, he had to be led into the start (refused to race at Punchestown last May), but did jump off and travelled powerfully through the contest. He looked beaten when coming under pressure and making a mistake four out, but rallied strongly to press his stablemate on the run-in and there was no disgrace in just losing out to a considerably lower-weighted rival. Third to Planet Of Sound off 6lb lower a year ago, before registering back-to-back Grade 1 wins in the Tingle Creek and Victor Chandler, he will presumably contest those races again and be a major player, with this effort confirming him at least as good as ever.

Somersby(IRE), last year's Arkle runner-up who was being touted as a Gold Cup contender by many last spring until his trainer confirmed he'll be aimed at the Champion Chase, was solid in the market and expected to take the beating off a mark of 156, carrying just 10-7. He travelled strongly and arguably looked the winner turning in, but was untidy at the fourth-last and started to look tired from the next. He was disappointing on the face of it, but knowing his trainer there'll be plenty left to work on and we'll get more of an idea of which route he should go down when he contests the Tingle Creek, his next intended target. (op 5-2)

I'msingingtheblues(IRE), still travelling when falling four out in the Old Roan Chase (debut for David Pipe), ran really well considering he chased the early gallop and was left in front quite a way out. Considering he's yet to win over this sort of trip it was no surprise to see him fade late on, but he's clearly capable of winning a good races. (op 10-1)

The Sawyer(BEL), 7lb out of the handicap but with a very capable rider of that claim aboard, was an improved horse last year, toughing it out best in two valuable handicaps before finishing third to Monet's Garden in the Grade 1 Ascot Chase. Considering the gallop which he helped force, he did well to keep on again, and he may even develop into a Grand National horse this year.

Cornas(NZ), a Grade 3 winner at Limerick on his return, was 3lb 'wrong', but he's a course winner who had the form to go close in this, so to see him run such a laboured race was disappointing. It later transpired he had finished lame. Official explanation: vet said gelding returned lame (op 9-2)

Mahogany Blaze(FR), second and fourth for the last two years, got no further than the fourth. (op 17-2 tchd 8-1)

Chaninbar(FR) lost ground at the start after proving reluctant to race and was eventually pulled up. (op 17-2 tchd 8-1)

Herecomesthetruth(IRE), a classy sort on his day, ideally wants further than this, so it was no surprise to see him help force the pace. However, he ran out at the eighth when still appearing to be going well enough and this wasn't the first time, having done the same at Cheltenham as a novice. His new connections have a talented horse on their hands, but keeping him on the straight and narrow may prove a challenge. (op 17-2 tchd 8-1)

2139 TOTESPORT 0800 221 221 NOVICES' CHASE (12 fncs) 2m 1f 110y

3:05 (3:05) (Class 2) 4-Y-O+ **£9,505** (£2,808; £1,404; £702)

Form RPR

0-2 **1** **Rock Noir (FR)**[30] 1693 5-11-1 0 APMcCoy 141+
(Jonjo O'Neill) *trckd ldng trio: wnt 3rd 8th: chal 2 out: slt ld last: rdn clr nr fin: readily* **9/2**[3]

110- **2** *1* **Phidippides (IRE)**[207] 5112 6-11-1 0 PaulMoloney 138+
(Evan Williams) *j.rt at times: trckd ldrs: slt ld whn pckd 8th: rdn and hrd pressed fr 4 out: narrowly hdd whn edgd lft last: kpt on* **2/1**[2]

16U- **3** *19* **Qozak (FR)**[247] 4328 6-11-1 0 RWalsh 122+
(Paul Nicholls) *trckd ldr: wnt rt 1st: led after 4th: narrowly hdd 8th: remained w ev ch tl rdn 3 out: wknd last* **4/5**[1]

3-05 **4** *4 ½* **Bathwick Quest (IRE)**[9] 1998 6-10-8 0 MrMMO'Connor 110
(Brendan Powell) *hung rt thrght: led tl after 4th: chsd ldrs fr after next tl outpcd after 8th* **28/1**

4m 18.4s (-0.60) **Going Correction** +0.025s/f (Yiel) **4** Ran SP% **110.5**
Speed ratings (Par 109): **102,101,93,91**
CSF £13.86 TOTE £4.20; EX 6.80.
Owner John P McManus **Bred** Scea Terres Noires **Trained** Cheltenham, Gloucs

FOCUS
A good novices' chase, despite the small field, and two potentially smart types pulled clear of the slightly disappointing favourite. The winning time was 3.6secs slower than the Haldon Gold Cup, which was understandable given the way the races were run. Rock Noir can go on to rate higher on his hurdles form, and the second was up 6lb on his hurdles figure.

NOTEBOOK
Rock Noir(FR), a Grade 1 winner in France who made no impact off 152 in the County Hurdle on his debut for connections last spring, failed to settle and made mistakes when beaten at short odds on his chase debut at Huntingdon, but he had been schooled intensively and a considerably more fluent round back on this sort of ground enabled him to get off the mark. This will have done his confidence no harm at all and, given his hurdles rating, it's not unreasonable to expect him to take pretty high rank as a chaser, although there's little doubt he needs a good cut in the ground to be at his best. The Henry VIII at Sandown in early December could be a viable target. (op 4-1 tchd 5-1)
Phidippides(IRE), winner of a decent novices' hurdle at Kempton last season prior to finishing well held in a Grade 1 at Aintree (reportedly came home sore), is held in the highest regard by his trainer and it's not hard to see why following this effort. Considering he was racing over a trip short of his best on ground softer than ideal, it was a cracking run to go down by just 1l, looking green at his fences, but showing a likeable attitude under pressure. With this run out the way, he can really kick on and should have little trouble going one better before being upped in grade. It would be no surprise to see him contest something like the Grade 1 Feltham at Kempton on Boxing Day and end up going down the RSA route. (tchd 85-40 in places)
Qozak(FR) was disappointing on the face of it, but it's possible he was just beaten by two good horses. He should improve and can land an ordinary novices' chase before no doubt ending up in handicaps later in the season. (op Evens)
Bathwick Quest(IRE) got round safely for some fourth-place prize money and will find easier opportunities. Official explanation: jockey said mare hung right-handed (op 25-1 tchd 22-1)

2140 TOTEPOOL H'CAP CHASE (18 fncs) 3m

3:35 (3:35) (Class 3) (0-125,125) 4-Y-O+ **£7,806** (£2,292; £1,146; £572)

Form RPR

1P3- **1** **Iconoclast (IRE)**[213] 4987 9-11-8 121 PaddyBrennan 133+
(Alex Hales) *hld up: hdwy 11th: chal 4 out: led 2 out: sn hrd rdn: styd on: all out* **10/1**

1F-2 **2** *¾* **Vamizi (IRE)**[26] 1738 7-11-4 117 MattieBatchelor 129+
(Mark Bradstock) *disp ld most of way: mstke 9th: rdn after 4 out: narrowly hdd 2 out: kpt battling: ev ch whn pckd last: styd on: hld nr fin* **7/2**[1]

41-5 **3** *8* **Son Histoire (FR)**[26] 1738 6-10-13 112 (b) RichardJohnson 115
(Philip Hobbs) *in tch: hit 7th and 12th: rdn after 14th: wnt 3rd 2 out: styd on but nvr gng pce to get on terms* **11/2**[3]

05-4 **4** *13* **Clyffe Hanger (IRE)**[24] 1774 10-10-13 112 AndrewGlassonbury 104
(Bob Buckler) *trckd ldrs: rdn after 14th: nvr quite able to chal: lost 3rd whn wkng 2 out: dismntd after line: fin lame* **6/1**

1442 **5** *12* **Swing Bill (FR)**[18] 1858 9-11-12 125 TimmyMurphy 105
(David Pipe) *disp ld most of way tl wknd after 4 out* **9/2**[2]

P34- **6** *30* **Moleskin (IRE)**[242] 4420 7-11-9 122 TomO'Brien 75
(Victor Dartnall) *in tch: nt fluent 8th (water): pushed along 11th: wknd bef 4 out: t.o* **8/1**

/PP- **7** *6* **Deep Quest**[277] 3719 11-11-1 114 (t) RodiGreene 61
(Simon Burrough) *trckd ldrs early: in rr fr 7th: lost tch fr 14th: t.o* **33/1**

11P4 **P** **What A Scientist (IRE)**[15] 1903 10-10-3 105 SamTwiston-Davies(3) —
(Nigel Twiston-Davies) *in last pair: struggling fr 7th: t.o whn p.u after 14th* **14/1**

343- **P** **Victory Parade (IRE)**[321] 2913 7-11-5 118 APMcCoy —
(Rebecca Curtis) *prom whn stirrup leather broke after 10th: sn p.u* **11/2**[3]

6m 5.20s (-4.10) **Going Correction** +0.025s/f (Yiel) **9** Ran SP% **115.3**
Speed ratings (Par 107): **107,106,104,99,95 85,83,—,—**
Tote Swingers:1&2:£9.70, 2&3:£4.60, 1&3:£12.90 CSF £46.27 CT £215.70 TOTE £15.80: £4.80, £1.50, £1.90; EX 59.70.
Owner John & Lorraine Barlow **Bred** Andrew Kavanagh And Mary Cunnion **Trained** Wardington, Oxon

FOCUS
A competitive handicap chase run at a decent gallop. The form looks solid.

NOTEBOOK
Iconoclast(IRE), still 7lb higher than when winning at Kempton last season, is lightly raced for his age and there was every chance he'd have improved. Held up under Paddy Brennan, he crept through the field, travelling strongly, and having jumped ahead two out, he kept finding when pressed by the rallying runner-up after the last. He'll go up for this, but could have more to offer. (op 8-1)
Vamizi(IRE), narrowly beaten by a subsequent winner off 5lb lower on his reappearance at the course, seemed assured to run well again and he duly did, fending them all off bar the winner. A good, honest type, he stays really well and certainly deserves to get his head in front again, although will be nudged up again for losing. (tchd 9-2)
Son Histoire(FR) bounced back from a disappointing effort on his return and will be of interest for the win once the tongue-tie is reapplied. (op 7-1)
Clyffe Hanger(IRE), having only his fourth start over fences at the age of ten, was dismounted after the line and it transpired he had gone lame. Official explanation: jockey said gelding was lame (op 8-1)
Swing Bill(FR), in good form since returning from a three-year absence, looked vulnerable under top weight, especially back on softer ground, and he slowly faded having disputed it for much of the race. (op 5-1 tchd 11-2 and 4-1)
Moleskin(IRE) made a couple of mistakes on this first start over fences, but his yard has yet to hit form and he's almost certain to improve. (op 6-1)
Victory Parade(IRE), making his chasing debut, was still very much in contention when McCoy's stirrup leather broke, leaving him with the only option to pull up. Official explanation: jockey said stirrup leather broke (op 8-1)

2141 TOTESUPER7 H'CAP HURDLE (12 hdls) 2m 7f 110y

4:05 (4:05) (Class 4) (0-115,114) 4-Y-O+ **£3,252** (£955; £477; £238)

Form RPR

030- **1** **Victors Serenade (IRE)**[261] 4055 5-11-2 104 AidanColeman 110+
(Anthony Honeyball) *hld up towards rr: stdy hdwy fr 8th: rdn appr 3 out: swtchd lft 2 out: styd on wl to ld fnl 100yds: rdn out* **10/1**

51-5 **2** *1 ½* **Five Star Wilsham (IRE)**[169] 370 6-11-10 112 NickScholfield 117+
(Jeremy Scott) *mid-div: hdwy fr 7th: rdn to ld appr 2 out: hung lft run-in: hdd fnl 100yds: no ex* **16/1**

52-3 **3** *5* **John's Gift**[14] 1911 6-10-13 101 HarrySkelton 101
(Bob Buckler) *hld up towards rr: hdwy fr after 7th: rdn to chal whn mstke 3 out: ev ch fr next tl awkward last: no ex* **5/1**[2]

/324 **4** *½* **Prince Tom**[19] 1842 6-11-12 114 RWalsh 112
(Paul Nicholls) *in tch: outpcd appr 3 out: styd on again fr after 2 out* **7/2**[1]

64-6 **5** *7* **Dingat (IRE)**[17] 1864 5-11-8 110 RichardJohnson 102
(Tim Vaughan) *prom: led 4th: hit next: rdn and hdd after 3 out: fdd fr next* **7/1**

22-P **6** *9* **Monsieur Cadou (FR)**[178] 212 5-10-9 97 PaddyBrennan 82
(Tom George) *hld up towards rr: rdn and sme prog after 9th: no further imp fr 3 out* **13/2**[3]

151- **7** *14* **Days Of Pleasure (IRE)**[194] 5330 5-11-1 110 MrTJCannon(7) 78
(Chris Gordon) *mid-div: hdwy 7th: effrt bef 3 out: sn wknd* **25/1**

3 **8** *¾* **Oscar Close (IRE)**[174] 279 5-11-12 114 AndrewTinkler 81
(George Baker) *hld up and a towards rr* **20/1**

311- **9** *17* **Omix D'Or (FR)**[193] 5373 8-11-5 107 DavidDennis 57
(James Evans) *mid-div: rdn after 8th: wknd after next: t.o* **8/1**

1-43 **10** *7* **Boomtown Kat**[26] 1740 6-11-9 111 AndrewThornton 54
(Karen George) *trckd ldrs: ev ch after 9th: sn rdn: wknd bef 3 out: t.o* **14/1**

60P- **11** *1 ¾* **Bally Conn (IRE)**[208] 5107 8-11-3 105 SamThomas 47
(Martin Hill) *chsd ldrs tl wknd appr 3 out: t.o* **16/1**

F/PP **12** *13* **Krackatara**[26] 1740 8-11-3 112 MissLGardner(7) 41
(Susan Gardner) *racd keenly: trckd ldrs: ev ch after 9th: wknd bef 3 out: t.o* **16/1**

6P-6 **13** *3 ¼* **Dawn At Sea**[26] 1746 8-11-3 105 (p) RhysFlint 30
(John Flint) *led tl 4th: wknd after 7th: t.o* **14/1**

5m 52.1s (-6.90) **Going Correction** -0.15s/f (Good) **13** Ran SP% **124.5**
Speed ratings (Par 105): **105,104,102,102,100 97,92,92,86,84 83,79,78**
Tote Swingers:1&2:£54.60, 2&3:£23.90, 1&3:£16.10 CSF £163.30 CT £911.13 TOTE £12.30: £3.40, £5.70, £1.90; EX 243.50.
Owner Michael & Angela Bone **Bred** Thomas Horgan **Trained** Seaborough, Dorset

FOCUS
An open-looking handicap hurdle. Ordinary form, but the first two are on the upgrade.

NOTEBOOK
Victors Serenade(IRE), fairly treated for this handicap debut based on his Taunton third last February, looked a likely improve for the longer trip and he really came strong inside the final 2f, getting well on top close home. Soft ground is reportedly very important to him and he remains open to further improvement. (tchd 11-1)
Five Star Wilsham(IRE), making his handicap debut after only two starts over hurdles, gave it a bold go, but couldn't fend off the winner late on. This was his first start in 169 days and he should improve. (tchd 18-1)
John's Gift, third off 1lb lower at the course on his reappearance, came to hold every chance, but didn't see out this longer trip as well as expected. He won't be at his best until chasing. (op 11-2 tchd 9-2)
Prince Tom kept on again and looks in need of this longer trip. He's still a maiden, but is in the right hands to be found a small race. (op 6-1)
Dingat(IRE) didn't appear to get home on this step up in trip. (op 11-2)
Monsieur Cadou(FR) took a step back in the right direction on this return from 178 days off. (op 8-1)

2142 TOTEPLACEPOT "NATIONAL HUNT" NOVICES' HURDLE (DIV II) (11 hdls) 2m 5f 110y

4:35 (4:35) (Class 3) 4-Y-O+ **£4,228** (£1,241; £620; £310)

Form RPR

3F2- **1** **Court In Motion (IRE)**[249] 4279 5-10-12 0 JackDoyle 127+
(Emma Lavelle) *in tch: trckd ldrs 8th: led appr 2 out: shkn up run-in: comf* **4/6**[1]

21- **2** *1 ¼* **Oscar Papa**[211] 5057 5-10-12 0 LiamTreadwell 123+
(Nick Gifford) *hld up towards rr: hdwy fr 6th: rdn after 3 out: cl 2nd whn hit last: styd on but a being hld* **8/1**[3]

3 *1 ¾* **Join Together (IRE)**[216] 5-10-12 0 RWalsh 119
(Paul Nicholls) *trckd ldr: led 3 out: sn rdn and hdd: lost 2nd at the last: styd on same pce* **10/3**[2]

6- **4** *20* **The Boss (IRE)**[206] 5137 5-10-12 0 NickScholfield 102
(Jeremy Scott) *trckd ldrs: rdn after 8th: styd chsng ldrs tl wknd 2 out* **66/1**

0 **5** *9* **Glens Boy (IRE)**[20] 1821 6-10-12 0 HaddenFrost 90
(Henrietta Knight) *mid-div: rdn after 8th: wknd after next* **40/1**

60P/ **6** *21* **Jayjay Valentine**[205] 7-10-12 0 TomO'Brien 75
(Victor Dartnall) *j.lft: led tl rdn 3 out: sn hung bdly lft: wknd 2 out* **16/1**

50 **7** *11* **Lagan Katie**[20] 1821 4-9-12 0 MarkQuinlan(7) 51
(Neil Mulholland) *mid-div: rdn after 8th: blnd 3 out: wknd* **100/1**

0 **8** *19* **Glenfly (IRE)**[172] 319 5-10-12 0.................................... RichardJohnson 39
(Philip Hobbs) *hld up towards rr: lost tch after 8th: t.o* **25/1**
00- **9** *10* **Mi Money**[194] 5332 5-10-5 0.. TomScudamore 22
(David Pipe) *a towards rr: t.o* **40/1**
502- **10** *4* **De Forgotten Man (IRE)**[190] 25 5-10-12 0................ WarrenMarston 25
(Martin Keighley) *trckd ldrs: rdn after 8th: sn wknd: t.o* **12/1**
5m 30.1s (-2.90) **Going Correction** -0.15s/f (Good)
WFA 4 from 5yo+ 8lb **10** Ran SP% **119.0**
Speed ratings (Par 107): **99,98,97,90,87 79,75,68,65,63**
Tote Swingers:1&2:£2.50, 2&3:£3.20, 1&3:£1.60. Totesuper7: Win: Not won. Place: £66.20. CSF £7.11 TOTE £1.50: £1.02, £2.00, £2.50; EX 7.60.
Owner N Mustoe **Bred** Peter O'Reilly **Trained** Wildhern, Hants

FOCUS
Undoubtedly the stronger of the two divisions, the slower time down to there being considerably lesser pace on than in the opener. The front three drew clear and the race should produce its share of winners. The cosy winner is rated 12lb off his best.

NOTEBOOK
Court In Motion(IRE), who had placed form behind the likes of Oscar Whiskey and Peveril to his name last season, travelled strongly on this reappearance and never had to come out of second gear according to his rider. Emma Lavelle believes he will benefit from a stronger pace in future and he rates a very useful prospect. He'll be aimed at something a bit better now. (tchd 5-6)
Oscar Papa, easy winner of a Plumpton bumper in April, is a fine-looking individual and he made good headway to reach a challenging position, but just lacked the pace of the winner late on. He's probably going to want 3m and fences one day, but can win over hurdles first.
Join Together(IRE), a point winner at the third attempt, was soon tracking the pace and Walsh took him to the front at the first in the straight, but he was soon pressed and could find no extra from before the last. This was still a pleasing first effort, considering the lack of pace, and he should have no trouble getting off the mark in the coming weeks. (op 4-1 tchd 11-4)
The Boss(IRE) improved on the form shown in his bumper at Chepstow and looks a promising type for staying events. (op 50-1)
Glens Boy(IRE), reportedly quite a robust sort who takes a bit of getting fit, again travelled well, as he had done at Uttoxeter, but he tired in the straight and it's unlikely he'll be winning until sent handicapping, possibly over fences.
Jayjay Valentine looked a bit wayward in front at times and ended up well held, but his yard are struggling for winners at present and he should do better down the line. Official explanation: jockey said gelding hung left-handed
Glenfly(IRE) has shown little in both starts now, but it's hard to believe this is as good as he is given breeding and connections. More of a long term project, perhaps.
Mi Money should do better in handicaps.
De Forgotten Man(IRE) had finished a promising second to Lidar on his debut over hurdles, but was quickly beaten here after a mistake.
T/Plt: £44.70 to a £1 stake. Pool:£95,374.30. 1,556.53 winning tickets. T/Qpdt: £42.80 to a £1 stake. Pool:£5,441.34. 93.98 winning tickets. TM

1963 CHEPSTOW (L-H)
Wednesday, November 3

OFFICIAL GOING: Good to soft (soft in places) changing to soft (good to soft in places) after race 3 (2.10)
Wind: breezy Weather: steady rain from 1.30

2143 SPIFFING CRABBIE'S ALCOHOLIC GINGER BEER MAIDEN HURDLE (10 hdls 1 omitted) 2m 4f
1:05 (1:06) (Class 5) 4-Y-0+ **£1,561** (£458; £229; £114)

Form RPR
1 **Sonofvic (IRE)**[241] 5-11-0 0.. RWalsh 131+
(Paul Nicholls) *trckd ldrs: led after bypassed 4 out: shkn up run-in: easily* **10/3**[1]
4 **2** *5* **Teaforthree (IRE)**[18] 1866 6-11-0 0... APMcCoy 119
(Rebecca Curtis) *chsd ldr fr 5th: chal by bypassed 4th last: chsd wnr fr next: styd on same pce fr 2 out* **7/2**[2]
14- **3** *1 1/4* **Ohio Gold (IRE)**[242] 4429 4-11-0 0.. JoeTizzard 119+
(Colin Tizzard) *in tch: chsd ldrs 6th: wnt 3rd 3 out: rdn whn blnd 2 out: styd on same pce run-in* **7/2**[2]
516- **4** *9* **Awesome Freddie**[249] 4309 5-10-11 0........................... CharlieHuxley(3) 110
(Alan King) *t.k.h: chsd ldrs: rdn appr bypassed 4th last: wknd next* **15/2**[3]
5 *27* **Lobby Ludd**[234] 5-11-0 0.. RichardJohnson 89+
(Philip Hobbs) *w ldr tl ld after 4th: hdd after bypassed 4th last: wknd qckly* **10/1**
00-5 **6** *12* **Double Or Quitz**[64] 1448 5-10-7 0............................ NathanSweeney(7) 75
(Bob Buckler) *in tch: rdn 6th: wknd bypassed 4th last: no ch whn mstke next* **100/1**
P- **7** *2 3/4* **Robin Will (FR)**[312] 3064 5-11-0 0.. HarrySkelton 72
(Paul Nicholls) *blnd 3 out: a bhd* **16/1**
5/25 **8** *7* **Easement**[15] 1907 7-11-0 0...(v) JimmyMcCarthy 66
(Charlie Morlock) *chsd ldrs 5th: wknd after next* **14/1**
014 **9** *2 3/4* **Littledean Jimmy (IRE)**[43] 1567 5-10-7 0........................ CharlieWallis(7) 64
(John O'Shea) *chsd ldrs tl 7th* **50/1**
10 *11* **Saint Denis (FR)**[206] 5164 4-11-0 0.. NoelFehily 54
(Alex Hales) *hit 4th a bhd* **14/1**
11 *dist* **The Beat Is On**[379] 4-10-7 0... LiamTreadwell —
(Tony Carroll) *hit 2nd: sn t.o* **200/1**
0/0 **P** **Tanners Emperor**[21] 1824 6-10-11 0........................... TommyPhelan(3) —
(Claire Dyson) *mde most tl hdd after 4th: wknd rapidly: t.o whn p.u after 6th* **100/1**
00- **P** **Rahotep (FR)**[212] 5050 5-10-7 0.. JakeGreenall(7) —
(Henry Daly) *chsd ldrs tl 6th: t.o whn p.u bef 3 out* **100/1**
3- **F** **Seymour Eric**[228] 4742 5-11-0 0.. SamJones —
(Michael Scudamore) *fell 1st* **25/1**
U **Goodtimetoby (IRE)** 7-11-0 0.. CharliePoste —
(Richard Lee) *bdly hmpd and uns rdr 1st* **100/1**
4m 55.02s (-6.78) **Going Correction** -0.10s/f (Good)
WFA 4 from 5yo+ 8lb **15** Ran SP% **117.9**
Speed ratings (Par 103): **109,107,106,102,92 87,86,83,82,77 —,—,—,—,—**
toteswingers:1&2 £2.30, 2&3 £2.80, 1&3 £4.10 CSF £14.68 TOTE £5.30: £2.20, £2.60, £1.10; EX 14.70.
Owner Mrs Angela Hart **Bred** Mrs Rosemary Ross **Trained** Ditcheat, Somerset

FOCUS
An interesting maiden. There was an average gallop on and the first four came clear from the third-last so the form ought to work out. The winner looks a decent novice and can rate higher The fourth-last was bypassed following two horses departing at the first flight.

NOTEBOOK
Sonofvic(IRE) ◆ was having his first outing since comfortably getting off the mark at the second attempt between the flags in March and he ran out a taking winner on this debut for Paul Nicholls, who has now taken this race three times in the past four seasons. He was allowed time to get into a rhythm before making his move coming out of the back straight and ran on strongly when asked to win the race from three out. He was well on top prior to an exuberant leap at the last that saw him go further clear and he is clearly a promising stayer, being related to stable companions Aiteenthirtythree and the very useful Forest Pennant. Chasing will ultimately be his game, but he could rate a good bit higher over hurdles before making that switch. Nicholls later said the horse wants time between his races and is likely to be out again around Christmas. (op 7-2 tchd 3-1)
Teaforthree(IRE) ran respectably on his debut for connections in a bumper at Cheltenham 18 days earlier and appreciated stepping back up in trip on this switch to hurdling. He wasn't able to live with the winner, but should be capable winning one of these and may even prefer 3m already. (op 4-1 tchd 3-1)
Ohio Gold(IRE) won a heavy-ground bumper on debut last term before signing off with a solid effort in defeat in a valuable contest at Doncaster. He made smooth headway from off the pace on the back straight and had his chance, but ultimately ran as though this comeback would do him good. This was an encouraging introduction to hurdling and he might just be better suited by dropping back in trip in the short term. (op 4-1)
Awesome Freddie, a soft-ground bumper winner last season, was another who got involved nearing the home turn and was asked for everything around three out. He proved one-paced, but should come on appreciably for this return and get closer on his next assignment. (op 8-1)
Lobby Ludd had unseated on his pointing debut in Ireland back in March where he sustained a knee injury. He pulled his way to the front and paid the price when the first four went for home, but is another who should be capable of better with the experience under his belt.
Tanners Emperor Official explanation: jockey said gelding was distressed

2144 LINDLEY CATERING H'CAP HURDLE (11 hdls) 2m 4f
1:35 (1:39) (Class 5) (0-95,95) 4-Y-0+ **£1,561** (£458; £229; £114)

Form RPR
PP-1 **1** **Prince Massini (IRE)**[21] 1822 9-11-7 90.............................. PaulMoloney 105+
(Evan Williams) *chsd ldrs: wnt 3rd appr 4 out: chal 2 out: sn led: rdn whn jnd and hit last: styd on strly* **3/1**[1]
060- **2** *2* **Radmores Revenge**[206] 5157 7-11-5 95........................ CharlieWallis(7) 108+
(John O'Shea) *in rr tl stdy hdwy fr 5th: trckd ldrs 4 out: led appr 3 out: narrowly hdd after next: chalng whn mstke last: kpt on same pce* **16/1**
00-4 **3** *15* **Cockney Prince (IRE)**[186] 100 5-11-7 90.................................. APMcCoy 90+
(Jonjo O'Neill) *towards rr but in tch: hdwy whn j. slowly 7th: chsd ldrs appr 4 out: rdn next: sn no ch but kpt on for wl hld 3rd* **9/2**[2]
4-05 **4** *1* **Canyouseeme**[17] 1887 7-10-9 78.. NoelFehily 77
(Claire Dyson) *trckd ldrs: chal 5th: blnd next: led appr 4 out: hdd appr 3 out: sn no ch* **16/1**
00/0 **5** *3/4* **Giollacca (IRE)**[32] 1675 6-10-8 77................................. JodieMogford 73
(Graeme McPherson) *bhd: pushed along 4 out: drvn and styd on fr 2 out: kpt on run-in: nvr a threat* **12/1**
3005 **6** *2 3/4* **Ladies Best**[11] 1971 6-11-3 93.. MattGriffiths(7) 90
(Gordon Edwards) *chsd ldrs: blnd 5th: hit 7th: wknd 4 out: wl bhd whn blnd last* **22/1**
0F-5 **7** *16* **All The Fashion (IRE)**[32] 1679 6-10-3 72............................ WillKennedy 51
(F Jordan) *bhd: slow jump 2nd: rdn 5th: hit 7th: no ch after* **18/1**
010- **8** *nk* **French Leave (IRE)**[204] 5172 8-11-7 95............(t) MrJoshuaGuerriero(5) 74
(Victor Dartnall) *led: hit 7th: hdd appr 4 out: wknd sn after* **8/1**
0063 **9** *3 3/4* **Satindra (IRE)**[28] 1735 6-10-7 76................................(tp) TomMessenger 52
(Carole Ikin) *a towards rr* **9/1**
015- **10** *7* **Delcombe**[321] 2924 9-10-9 83... GilesHawkins(5) 53
(Richard Mitchell) *chsd ldrs tl wknd appr 4 out* **20/1**
01P- **11** *2* **Walls Way**[191] 16 6-11-7 90... LiamTreadwell 58
(Tony Carroll) *chsd ldrs tl 6th* **40/1**
63-4 **12** *dist* **A Fistful Of Euros**[178] 225 6-11-5 95............................ DannyBurton(7) —
(Chris Down) *sn bhd* **22/1**
03P- **13** *30* **Chilla Cilla**[517] 595 7-10-7 76... NickScholfield —
(Anthony Honeyball) *chsd ldrs tl wknd qckly after 7th* **7/1**[3]
3/00 **P** **She's Little Don**[5] 2070 10-10-9 83............................(p) MrBMoorcroft(5) —
(Stephen Hughes) *lost tch 6th: t.o whn p.u after 3 out* **100/1**
5m 3.22s (1.42) **Going Correction** -0.10s/f (Good) **14** Ran SP% **118.4**
Speed ratings (Par 103): **93,92,86,85,85 84,78,77,76,73 72,—,—,—**
toteswingers:1&2 £5.50, 2&3 £10.80, 1&3 £2.80 CSF £46.21 CT £217.91 TOTE £3.70: £1.40, £6.50, £2.20; EX 70.90.
Owner R E R Williams **Bred** Robert McCarthy **Trained** Llancarfan, Vale Of Glamorgan

FOCUS
An ordinary handicap run at a fair enough gallop, and the first pair fought it out from the third-last. The winner was well in and the second is rated back to his best.

NOTEBOOK
Prince Massini(IRE) benefited from a wind operation prior to making a winning return at Uttoxeter last month, where he beat a subsequent scorer, and he followed up with another gutsy effort off this 11lb higher mark. He cut through the pack to get competitive on the far side and was moving strongly four out. He kept finding for pressure against the stands' rail when pressed by the runner-up and, despite a less than fluent leap at the last which that rival also hit, he went clear on the run-in. This 9-y-o has clearly resumed in top form this term and, despite already being due to run off an 8lb higher mark from this weekend, one wouldn't rule out him landing a hat-trick while in such form. (op 10-3 tchd 7-2 and 4-1 in places)
Radmores Revenge ◆, off the mark at this venue last year, ran a big race on his seasonal debut. He was probably just held prior to hitting the final flight, but as a clear second-best and should enjoy returning to a stiffer test. (op 14-1)
Cockney Prince(IRE) looked a threat when making up his ground from off the pace, but he could not find an extra gear down the home straight and was well held from two out. This was his best effort yet on his first outing since May. (tchd 4-1 and 5-1)
Canyouseeme was always front rank on this handicap debut, but tired from three out. He won his bumper on good ground at Towcester and it would be little surprise to see him appreciate going back there this year. (op 20-1 tchd 14-1)
Giollacca(IRE) took an age to pick up, but caught the eye keeping on late in the day and this was more encouraging on her handicap debut. She can build on this. (tchd 14-1)
Chilla Cilla was making her debut for the yard and must have been doing something right in her home work, as the money came for her. She didn't settle on this first outing for 517 days, though, and then went backwards after hitting a flat spot coming out of the back straight. (tchd 6-1 and 15-2)

2145 LINDLEY CATERING MAIDEN HURDLE (8 hdls) 2m 110y
2:10 (2:11) (Class 5) 4-Y-0+ **£1,561** (£458; £229; £114)

Form RPR
3- **1** **Arthurian Legend**[207] 5137 5-11-0 0............................. RichardJohnson 127+
(Philip Hobbs) *chsd ldrs: shkn up 3 out: led after 2 out: edgd lft last: styd on strly* **7/2**[2]
6/2 **2** *11* **Gurtacrue (IRE)**[27] 1743 5-11-0 0.. PaulMoloney 116+
(Evan Williams) *chsd ldrs: led sn after 4 out: hdd sn after 2 out: sn no ch w wnr: kpt on wl for 2nd* **5/2**[1]

5 **3** *5* **Redbridge Flyer (IRE)**24 1799 6-10-11 0........................ DannyCook(3) 110
(Nick Mitchell) *led tl after 4 out: sn no ch w wnr: styd on same pce* **100/1**

234- **4** *9* **Pride In Battle (IRE)**198 5283 5-11-0 0.............................. SamThomas 101
(Alan King) *in tch: drvn to chse ldrs 4 out: wknd after 3 out* **16/1**

150- **5** *1 1/2* **Another Kate (IRE)**265 3995 6-10-7 0............................. AidanColeman 93
(David Richards) *towards rr: hdwy 4th: outpcd 3 out: styd on again run-in* **22/1**

6 *4* **Teshali (IRE)**364 4-11-0 0... RWalsh 98+
(Paul Nicholls) *chsd ldrs: wnt 2nd after 4 out: rdn next: wknd fr 2 out* **5/2**1

23-4 **7** *3 1/2* **Bally Legend**27 1736 5-10-9 0.............................. IanPopham(5) 95
(Caroline Keevil) *chsd ldrs: rdn appr 4 out: wknd sn after: no ch whn blnd last* **33/1**

0-20 **8** *1/2* **Great Hero**77 1284 5-11-0 0.. SeanQuinlan 93
(Richard Phillips) *in rr: drvn and sme late prog fr 3 out: nvr a threat* **100/1**

3- **9** *14* **Mr Chow (IRE)**198 5284 6-11-0 0.. NoelFehily 80
(Warren Greatrex) *chsd ldrs: hit 3rd: wknd 4 out* **8/1**3

46 **10** *30* **Jigsaw Financial (IRE)**28 1729 4-10-7 0........................ DannyBurton(7) 53
(Roger Curtis) *mid-div: rdn and wknd appr 4 out: t.o* **125/1**

0102 **11** *1 1/2* **Thomas Bell (IRE)**43 1572 6-10-7 0.............................. CharlieWallis(7) 52
(John O'Shea) *a bhd: t.o* **100/1**

6- **12** *4* **Belvidera**21 4945 4-10-0 0... RobertKirk(7) 41
(Tony Carroll) *hit 3rd: a bhd: t.o* **200/1**

13 *10* **In The Sand (IRE)** 4-11-0 0.. APMcCoy 39
(Jonjo O'Neill) *a bhd: t.o* **25/1**

5 **14** *14* **Ask The Oracle**27 1736 4-10-7 0......................... MissIsabelTompsett(7) 26
(John Price) *chsd ldrs: hit 3rd: wknd next: t.o* **40/1**

P5- **15** *6* **Valid Point (IRE)**221 4891 4-11-0 0...................................... TimmyMurphy 21
(Jim Old) *a bhd: t.o* **33/1**

4m 7.29s (-3.31) **Going Correction** -0.10s/f (Good) **15** Ran SP% **117.1**
Speed ratings (Par 103): **103,97,95,91,90 88,87,86,80,66 65,63,58,52,49**
toteswingers:1&2 £3.70, 2&3 £34.90, 1&3 £50.60 CSF £11.76 TOTE £4.40: £1.50, £1.40, £24.50; EX 10.10.
Owner R T Kanter & A J Scrimgeour **Bred** Mrs L M Northover **Trained** Withycombe, Somerset

FOCUS
Another interesting maiden hurdle. The winner fulfilled the promise of a good bumper run.

NOTEBOOK
Arthurian Legend ◆, whose stable won this with Planet Of Sound in 2007, came home a ready winner on this seasonal and hurdling debut. He didn't look too comfortable on quicker ground when third on debut in a bumper here last term, but this easier surface proved much more up his street. He completed the task in the style of a horse who has a good deal more to offer. (op 6-1)
Gurtacrue(IRE) ◆, beaten by a subsequent winner on his British debut 27 days earlier, made a bold bid to give his in-form yard a double but lacked the gear change displayed by the winner nearing the last. He was nicely clear in second and deserves to go one better in this sphere, but does shape as though a slightly stiffer test would be ideal. (tchd 9-4)
Redbridge Flyer(IRE) was sent to the front on this switch to hurdling and posted a promising effort. He was swamped around three out, but rallied for pressure after the penultimate flight and surely wants a longer trip.
Pride In Battle(IRE) showed ability in his three bumpers last term and was representing the yard that took this with Manyriverstocross last year. He proved friendless in the betting, however, and clearly needed the run. There should be improvement in him when stepping up in trip. (op 10-1)
Another Kate(IRE) showed her best form on good ground in four bumpers last season. She wasn't disgraced on her hurdling debut and first outing since February, leaving the impression she too will enjoy a little further now. (op 16-1 tchd 25-1)
Teshali(IRE) was purchased by his leading connections for 100,000euros after winning three of his six outings on the level in France for Alain De Royer-Dupre. He had reportedly taken time to get over being gelded, but proved solid in the betting for this hurdling debut and things looked good for his supporters turning for home. He dropped out tamely after three out, however, and presumably the outing was needed.

2146 LINDLEY CATERING NOVICES' H'CAP CHASE (18 fncs) 3m
2:45 (2:45) (Class 4) (0-110,110) 4-Y-0+ **£2,927** (£859; £429; £214)

Form RPR

UFO/ **1** **Major Malarkey (IRE)**573 4920 7-11-11 **109**..................... PaddyBrennan 130+
(Nigel Twiston-Davies) *trckd ldrs: chal 13th: led whn nt fluent next: sn clr: eased down run-in* **9/1**

0P-F **2** *3 1/2* **Bobby Gee**39 1612 9-11-12 **110**.. NoelFehily 120
(Renee Robeson) *led tl hdd 14th: sn outpcd but styd 2nd: clsd on eased down wnr run-in* **12/1**

231 **3** *14* **Dunkelly Castle (IRE)**27 1747 6-11-12 **110**.................... LeightonAspell 109
(Roger Curtis) *in tch: hit 10th: styd on for wl hld 3rd fr 3 out* **6/1**2

46-0 **4** *9* **Honourable Arthur (IRE)**15 1912 7-10-12 **96**.................. HarrySkelton 85
(Victor Dartnall) *blnd 2nd: a towards rr: mod late prog* **6/1**2

040- **5** *7* **Glebehall Bay (IRE)**203 5184 7-11-5 **103**....................... AidanColeman 86
(Venetia Williams) *a towards rr* **8/1**3

P2-F **6** *10* **Double Chocolate**11 1963 7-11-6 **109**........................... MrWBiddick(5) 83
(Matt Sheppard) *chsd ldrs 7th: slow jump 11th: chal 13th: wknd after next* **10/1**

5126 **7** *8* **Justabout**27 1738 7-10-11 **95**...(t) JoeTizzard 62
(Colin Tizzard) *chsd ldrs: blnd 6th and 11th: j. slowly 12th: sn wknd* **9/2**1

P-22 **8** *dist* **Mister Wiseman**11 1965 8-10-12 **96**.................................. DavidDennis —
(Nigel Hawke) *in rr: hdwy 7th: rdn and wknd appr 14th: t.o* **9/2**1

2P15 **P** **Chevy To The Levy (IRE)**24 1794 8-11-4 **109**..........(v1) CharlieWallis(7) —
(John O'Shea) *hit 1st: bhd: blnd 7th: sme hdwy 12th: sn rdn and wknd: t.o whn p.u bef 4 out* **28/1**

P/U- **B** **Miss Fleur**233 4641 7-10-0 **84** oh1.................................... LiamTreadwell —
(Nick Mitchell) *in tch whn b.d 4th* **20/1**

0-50 **F** **No More Whispers (IRE)**27 1747 5-10-6 **90**...................... PaulMoloney —
(Evan Williams) *chsng ldrs whn fell 4th* **22/1**

6m 29.0s (7.00) **Going Correction** +0.15s/f (Yiel) **11** Ran SP% **115.4**
Speed ratings (Par 105): **94,92,88,85,82 79,76,—,—,— —**
toteswingers:1&2 £26.10, 2&3 £26.70, 1&3 £23.30 CSF £103.18 CT £701.64 TOTE £8.10: £4.30, £3.40, £1.90; EX 103.60.
Owner Baker Dodd & Cooke **Bred** Bill Ronayne **Trained** Naunton, Gloucs

FOCUS
A wide-open looking novice handicap, run at an average gallop and most were in trouble before the home straight. A step up from the winner who was value for further.

NOTEBOOK
Major Malarkey(IRE) comes from a yard well known for readying one after a layoff and he made light of a 573-day absence to score pretty much as he pleased. He had failed to complete in two previous runs as a chaser, but jumped like an old hand and was given a very confident ride. He was eased off as he began to tire near the finish, so rates value for further and there was plenty to like about this display. It's hoped he comes out of this sound and one will have to be mindful of the bounce factor next time, but on this evidence he should be rating higher over fences this term. (op 6-1 tchd 11-2)
Bobby Gee was always up there and was the runner only still with the winner at the top of the home straight. He was made to look slow when that rival asserted, but rallied under maximum pressure and was coming back after the last. This should do his confidence a lot of good. (op 9-1)
Dunkelly Castle(IRE), 5lb higher, hit a flat spot on the back straight and was never a serious player thereafter. This course may not have been that much to his liking. (op 15-2 tchd 8-1)
Honourable Arthur(IRE), 8lb lower, was dropped out in last place over this longer trip and proved free under restraint. He moved up a little nearing the home turn, but was soon under the pump and looks to need a bit more experience. (op 8-1)
Glebehall Bay(IRE) was making his seasonal/chasing debut. Ridden to get the trip, he was in trouble around seven out but did plug onto to suggest he will come on for the run. (op 9-1)
Justabout came under heavy pressure on the back straight and, having made errors, was miles below his best. This deeper ground may have been partly to blame. (op 5-1)
Mister Wiseman turned in a laboured effort. (op 6-1)

2147 REAL RADIO LISTENERS CHOICE H'CAP HURDLE (12 hdls) 3m
3:20 (3:20) (Class 3) (0-125,123) 4-Y-0+ **£4,553** (£1,337; £668; £333)

Form RPR

2F40 **1** **Thelobstercatcher**57 1501 6-10-12 **112**...................(p) DonalDevereux(3) 129+
(Peter Bowen) *chsd ldrs 5th: led on bit appr 3 out: c clr: easily* **16/1**

11-2 **2** *5* **Pavillon Bleu (FR)**25 1776 7-11-9 **120**......................... RichardJohnson 121
(Philip Hobbs) *in tch: pushed along fr 6th: styd on to chse ldrs 4 out: chsng wnr whn nt fluent 3 out: sn no ch w wnr: hld on for 2nd* **3/1**1

6-41 **3** *1/2* **Young Albert (IRE)**31 1709 9-11-4 **115**.............................. FelixDeGiles 115
(Charlie Longsdon) *t.k.h in tch: j. slowly 3rd: chsd ldrs after 4 out: styd on to press 2nd run-in: nvr any ch w wnr* **9/1**

1PP- **4** *2 1/2* **Saphire Night**333 2704 9-11-0 **121**.............................. CiaranMckee(10) 118
(Tom George) *chsd ldrs: hit 6th: led after 8th: hdd appr 3 out: sn outpcd* **25/1**

40-1 **5** *shd* **Rhum (FR)**31 1705 5-11-6 **117**... PaddyBrennan 114
(Nigel Twiston-Davies) *in tch: hdwy to chse ldrs 8th: rdn 4 out: one pce fr next* **8/1**

151/ **6** *5* **Nodforms Paula (IRE)**977 4191 7-11-8 **119**.............................. RWalsh 112
(Paul Nicholls) *in rr: pushed along appr 4 out: drvn 3 out: kpt on fr next: nvr any ch* **7/1**3

-215 **7** *15* **Cantabilly (IRE)**11 1972 7-11-0 **118**................................. MattGriffiths(7) 97
(Ron Hodges) *bhd tl sme hdwy 8th: nvr rchd ldrs: wknd 3 out* **16/1**

133- **8** *2 1/2* **Timetoring**223 4844 8-10-1 **105**.......................(p) MissIsabelTompsett(7) 86
(Bernard Llewellyn) *led tl after 1st: styd chsng ldrs: rdn appr 3 out: wknd bef next* **5/1**2

46-P **9** *7* **Stow**180 193 5-11-4 **115**... AidanColeman 86
(Venetia Williams) *chsd ldrs: rdn after 8th: wknd 4 out* **11/1**

210- **10** *16* **Deep Pockets (IRE)**219 4930 11-10-9 **111**....................... IanPopham(5) 67
(Caroline Keevil) *led after 1st tl 4th: rdn and wknd after 8th* **14/1**

2PP/ **11** *6* **Only Vintage (USA)**1026 10-11-5 **123**............................ MrTJCannon(7) 74
(Paul Henderson) *a towards rr* **66/1**

/1-3 **12** *6* **Native Taipan (IRE)**168 409 8-11-4 **115**............................ APMcCoy 60
(Rebecca Curtis) *pressed ldr: led 4th tl after 8th: sn wknd* **12/1**

00P1 **13** *5* **Two Miles West (IRE)**67 1405 9-10-12 **119**................... GeraldQuinn(10) 60
(Jonjo O'Neill) *a struggling in rr* **33/1**

6m 26.85s (7.05) **Going Correction** +0.475s/f (Soft) **13** Ran SP% **118.0**
Speed ratings (Par 107): **107,105,105,104,104 102,97,96,94,89 87,85,83**
CSF £63.47 CT £476.16 TOTE £21.30: £4.10, £1.80, £2.50; EX 91.80.
Owner G A Moore **Bred** J H Ray, M Mulholland & A M Varmen **Trained** Little Newcastle, Pembrokes

FOCUS
This looked to be a competitive handicap and there were a host of chances turning for home, but the impressive winner did it easily. This was a big step forward from him.

NOTEBOOK
Thelobstercatcher could hardly have won any easier in the end. The winner had disappointed in five previous outings for the stable, but he was a fair novice hurdler when trained in Ireland. He had something to prove on such ground, but he went through it easily and could've been called the winner approaching the third-last. Connections would do very well to find him something under a penalty now. (tchd 18-1)
Pavillon Bleu(FR), well backed, was 2lb higher for this step up in trip and, despite hitting three out, had no chance with the easy winner. It was his first run over this far and he saw it out well enough. (tchd 11-4)
Young Albert(IRE) was 5lb higher than when scoring at Uttoxeter a month previously and made heavy weather of it here. He was staying on dourly towards the finish and helps to set the level. (op 10-1)
Saphire Night showed up a lot more encouragingly again on this return from a 333-day absence. She won first time out last year, but did enough this time to suggest she will improve for the outing. (tchd 33-1)
Rhum(FR) showed his true colours when winning nicely over 2m on heavy ground when resuming a month earlier and another improved effort looked likely on this handicap debut. However, he was laboured from three out and a drop back in trip is probably what he wants. (op 7-1)
Nodforms Paula(IRE) was last seen winning his novice hurdle at Doncaster back in 2008 and proved easy to back on this return and debut over the longer distance. Patiently ridden, he appeared to blow up off the home turn and should be much sharper with the run now behind him. (op 11-2)
Timetoring came in for decent support throughout the day and had his chance on ground that suits, but was another who ultimately looked in need of this seasonal return. (op 9-1)

2148 LINDLEY CATERING H'CAP CHASE (12 fncs) 2m 110y
3:55 (3:55) (Class 4) (0-115,114) 4-Y-0+ **£3,577** (£1,050; £525; £262)

Form RPR

23-0 **1** **Cadoudalas (FR)**178 234 7-11-8 **110**........................... RichardJohnson 122+
(Richard Lee) *chsd ldrs: outpcd 8th: rallied 4 out: chal next: sn led: styd on u.p run-in: all out* **7/1**3

00-4 **2** *1 1/4* **Forty Five (IRE)**26 1761 8-11-10 **112**.. APMcCoy 124+
(Jonjo O'Neill) *chsd ldrs: wnt 2nd after 7th: led after 4 out: jnd next: sn hdd: pckd last: rallied run-in: a being jst hld* **11/10**1

/13- **3** *23* **Oscar Gogo (IRE)**217 4959 8-11-10 **112**.................... ChristianWilliams 102
(Evan Williams) *bhd: styd on fr 8th: kpt on fr 2 out to take wl hld 3rd cl home* **8/1**

4/2- **4** *3/4* **Riddleofthesands (IRE)**406 1501 6-11-6 **108**................ PaddyBrennan 100
(Nigel Twiston-Davies) *led: mstke whn jnd 4 out: sn hdd: wknd bef 2 out: lost wl hld 3rd cl home* **4/1**2

2U-6 **5** *36* **Littleton Aldor (IRE)**14 1919 10-9-11 **88** oh7............. TommyPhelan(3) 45
(Mark Gillard) *hit 2nd: blnd 6th: a bhd: t.o* **28/1**

4FP- **P** **Rouge Et Blanc (FR)**247 4360 5-11-5 **107**..................... LeightonAspell —
(Oliver Sherwood) *bhd fr 5th: t.o whn p.u bef 4 out* **16/1**

3PP- **P** **El Distintivo (ARG)**208 5117 6-11-10 **112**....................... AidanColeman —
(Venetia Williams) *blnd 3rd: a bhd: t.o whn p.u bef 8th* **25/1**

F5F- **P** **Henry King (IRE)**[242] 4446 6-11-12 **114**.............................. HarrySkelton —
(Victor Dartnall) *t.k.h: sn chsng ldrs: blnd 3rd: lost 2nd after 7th: sn wknd: t.o whn p.u bef 4 out* **9/1**

4m 17.3s (0.20) **Going Correction** +0.15s/f (Yiel) **8** Ran SP% **114.4**
Speed ratings (Par 105): **105,104,93,93,76** —,—,—
toteswingers:1&2 £2.60, 2&3 £3.70, 1&3 £6.00 CSF £16.02 CT £63.90 TOTE £7.20: £1.70, £2.50, £1.80; EX 19.10.
Owner Six To Five Against G D Thorp, R L Baker **Bred** Mme Evelyne Van Haaren **Trained** Byton, H'fords

FOCUS
This moderate handicap was run at a brisk gallop considering the ground and the two horses for money dominated from the fourth-last. The winner is rated back to his best and the second posted a chase best.

NOTEBOOK
Cadoudalas(FR) met support and finally ended his losing run, under a strong ride from Richard Johnson. He momentarily looked held at the top of the home straight, but began to rally after the fourth-last and a decent leap over the last saw him fend off the runner-up. This was his first success over fences and his first win since winning a novice hurdle for Malcolm Jefferson in 2008. The ground was much to his liking on this first outing for 178 days and he could well have more to offer now he's got his head back in front. (op 9-1 tchd 13-2)
Forty Five(IRE) was heavily backed to open his account as a chaser. He moved up going well turning for home, but having mastered the long-time leader he lacked an extra gear when challenged by the winner. He looked like getting back into it, but wasn't too clever at the last and was always being held thereafter. There is surely a race for him in this sphere, perhaps over a stiffer test, but his mark will go up again after this. (op 7-4)
Oscar Gogo(IRE), who showed a preference for such ground in two outings last season, was making his chasing debut after a 217-day break. He kept on encouragingly after lacking the pace to land a serious blow and wasn't given too hard a time, so ought to improve on this. (op 6-1)
Riddleofthesands(IRE) was having his first outing since finishing runner-up on his chase debut in September last year. He got warm beforehand and did plenty from the front, ensuring this was a decent test. Unsurprisingly he folded when pressed in the home straight, but should really come on a deal for the run and prove more effective when reverting to a sounder surface. (tchd 9-2)

2149 DIGIBET.COM H'CAP HURDLE (8 hdls) 2m 110y
4:25 (4:25) (Class 5) (0-90,90) 4-Y-0+ **£1,561** (£458; £229; £114)

Form				RPR
P00-	**1**		**Black Phantom (IRE)**[221] 4891 4-11-7 **85**........ NickScholfield (Andy Turnell) *trckd ldrs: slt ld 4 out: drew clr after next: easily* **22/1**	100+
300	**2**	*7*	**Monsieur (FR)**[11] 1976 10-11-1 **79**........ HarrySkelton (Carroll Gray) *in rr tl hdwy to chse ldrs appr 4 out: wnt 2nd 2 out: kpt on: no ch w wnr* **33/1**	85
-043	**3**	*10*	**Catholic Hill (USA)**[58] 1489 5-11-4 **85**........ TommyPhelan(3) (Mark Gillard) *chsd ldrs: drvn to chal 4 out: chsd wnr next: no imp: wknd into 3rd next* **12/1**	84
00P0	**4**	*1 ½*	**Lady Of Ashcott**[106] 1049 4-10-0 **64** oh6........(p) DougieCostello (Neil Mulholland) *chsd ldrs: drvn to chal 4 out: wknd after next* **20/1**	60
30-6	**5**	*4 ½*	**Keyneema**[28] 1732 8-11-4 **85**........(p) DannyCook(3) (Cathy Hamilton) *chsd ldrs: drvn to chal 4 out: wknd fr next* **7/1**[2]	77
4P0/	**6**	*¾*	**Dansilver**[21] 2267 6-10-11 **82**........ RobertKirk(7) (Tony Carroll) *chsd ldrs: hit 2nd: drvn to chse ldr 4 out: wknd after next* **4/1**[1]	73
6-34	**7**	*1 ¾*	**River Rhapsody (IRE)**[45] 1554 4-11-4 **82**........ ChristianWilliams (Evan Williams) *bhd: pushed along and styd on fr 3 out: nvr rchd ldrs* **9/1**[3]	71
00-6	**8**	*½*	**Queenstown Lad**[33] 1666 5-9-7 **64** oh36........(v[1]) BrianToomey(7) (Gary Brown) *t.k.h: sn led: blnd 4th: hdd 4 out: wknd next* **20/1**	53
-030	**9**	*5*	**Galant Eye (IRE)**[153] 593 11-10-4 **75**........ DannyBurton(7) (Chris Down) *mid-div: hit 4th: rdn and sme prog appr 4 out: n.d after* **25/1**	59
F6-6	**10**	*nk*	**Spot The Ball (IRE)**[14] 1925 5-11-12 **90**........ APMcCoy (Jonjo O'Neill) *bhd: sme hdwy 4 out: sn wknd* **4/1**[1]	74
462-	**11**	*10*	**Tiger Line**[223] 4840 6-11-11 **89**........ TomSiddall (Richard Phillips) *bhd most of way* **10/1**	64
60-0	**12**	*11*	**Smokey George**[31] 1705 5-11-5 **83**........ SeanQuinlan (Kim Bailey) *bhd most of way* **16/1**	48
U460	**13**	*2*	**Echo Dancer**[11] 1962 4-11-2 **90**........ JoshWall(10) (Trevor Wall) *blnd 2nd: hdwy to chse ldrs 4th: wl there 4 out: wknd qckly* **33/1**	53
566/	**14**	*15*	**Trotters Bottom**[906] 232 9-10-12 **76**........ RichardJohnson (Edward Bevan) *j. slow 1st: in rr whn bdly hmpd 3rd: no ch after* **22/1**	26
056	**15**	*15*	**Roc De Guye (FR)**[59] 1485 5-11-10 **88**........ DavidDennis (James Evans) *bhd most of way* **50/1**	24
01PO	**U**		**Stafford Charlie**[24] 1798 4-11-5 **90**........(b) CharlieWallis(7) (John O'Shea) *in rr whn blnd bdly and uns rdr 3rd* **20/1**	—
-04P	**P**		**Strictly Business**[63] 1453 5-11-12 **90**........ PaddyBrennan (Tom George) *hit 2nd: bhd whn bdly hmpd next: no ch after: t.o whn p.u bef 3 out* **16/1**	—

4m 17.85s (7.25) **Going Correction** +0.475s/f (Soft)
WFA 4 from 5yo+ 7lb **17** Ran SP% **125.7**
Speed ratings (Par 103): **101,97,93,92,90 89,89,88,86,86 81,76,75,68,61** —,—
toteswingers:1&2 £123.30, 2&3 £79.40, 1&3 £63.60 totesuper7: Win: Not won. Place: Not won. CSF £580.54 CT £8795.16 TOTE £36.60: £6.90, £7.60, £4.40, £5.70; EX 469.20.
Owner T L Morshead **Bred** R Frisby **Trained** Broad Hinton, Wilts

FOCUS
A very weak handicap, run at a fair gallop and they came home pretty strung out on the deep surface. A massive step up from the easy winner with the second to his mark.

NOTEBOOK
Black Phantom(IRE) had not shown much in four outings last term, but has obviously done very well for his time off the track as he ran out a most convincing winner on this handicap debut. He shot clear when asked to win the race and was able to coast home near the finish. This 4-y-o proved right at home on the ground and it will be very interesting to see how he fares after a likely hike in the weights as he is completely unexposed. Official explanation: trainer said, regarding tha apparent improvement in form shown, gelding had strengthened up from last season (op 25-1)
Monsieur(FR) is a tricky customer and had to be kidded into the start. He then took a keen hold, but easily made up his ground nearing the home turn and eventually finished nicely clear of the rest in second. He used to be capable of a lot better, but has gone four years without a win and is far from certain to build on this.
Catholic Hill(USA), 4lb lower, was produced with every chance towards the stands' side four out, but was feeling the pinch prior to hitting the penultimate flight. He may not be one to have too much faith in, but may be happier further in this sphere. (op 10-1)
Lady Of Ashcott, 6lb out of the weights, kept on to register her best effort yet on this return from a 106-day break in first-time cheekpieces. Her yard is in decent form at present and she may just be coming to herself, but probably has some temperament issues all the same. (op 16-1)
Keyneema ran her race under a positive ride and helps to set the standard. (op 8-1)
Dansilver, fit from the Flat, was held from three out and probably wants further these days as a hurdler. (op 5-1 tchd 6-1)
Spot The Ball(IRE) was well supported, but was done with before the fourth-last and continues to frustrate. (op 11-2)

T/Jkpt: Not won. T/Plt: £14.40 to a £1 stake. Pool of £60,988.03 - 3,073.02 winning tickets. T/Qpdt: £8.70 to a £1 stake. Pool of £5,037.98 - 431.90 winning tickets. ST

WARWICK (L-H)
Wednesday, November 3

OFFICIAL GOING: Good (hdl 6.0, chs 6.2)
Wind: Nil Weather: showers

2150 TURFTV H'CAP HURDLE (8 hdls) 2m
12:55 (12:57) (Class 4) (0-110,110) 4-Y-0+ **£3,425** (£998; £499)

Form				RPR
30-6	**1**		**Park Lane**[25] 1773 4-11-10 **108**........ JamieMoore (Miss J R Tooth) *chsd ldr: led appr 3 out: rdn and hdd narrowly bef 2 out: regained ld bef last: drvn out and r.o wl run-in: rdr dropped rein towards fin* **20/1**	117+
-322	**2**	*3*	**Goat Castle (IRE)**[31] 1704 6-10-3 **90**........(t) SamTwiston-Davies(3) (Nigel Twiston-Davies) *in tch: led 4th: hdd appr 3 out: stl chalng: led narrowly bef 2 out: hdd bef last: nt qckn run-in* **9/4**[1]	97
5-03	**3**	*7*	**Tom O'Tara**[13] 1938 6-10-12 **99**........ WayneKavanagh(3) (Robin Dickin) *in tch: prom 4th: carried hd high: rdn whn chsng ldng pair after 3 out: styd on same pce and no imp fr 2 out* **6/1**[3]	100
24	**4**	*7*	**Lucy's Perfect**[14] 1921 4-11-6 **104**........(b) TomScudamore (David Pipe) *racd keenly: in tch: rdn and wknd 3 out* **10/1**	99
13-4	**5**	*shd*	**Bosamcliff (IRE)**[27] 1746 5-11-4 **105**........ LeeStephens(3) (David Evans) *hld up: struggling 4 out: styd on u.p fr 2 out: nvr able to chal* **5/1**[2]	99
400-	**6**	*4*	**Mr Tingle**[310] 3123 6-11-1 **99**........ WarrenMarston (Richard Phillips) *hld up: struggling 4th: nvr able to get on terms* **33/1**	89
-100	**7**	*8*	**Shalamiyr (FR)**[19] 1859 5-11-12 **110**........ RhysFlint (Philip Hobbs) *led: hdd 4th: lost pl and outpcd 4 out: wl btn whn hit 2 out* **10/1**	96
4P0/	**8**	*4*	**Wise Hawk**[681] 2920 5-11-0 **98**........ JamesDavies (Chris Down) *midfield: hdwy 4 out: chsd ldrs 3 out: sn rdn and wknd* **50/1**	77
40-1	**9**	*5*	**Mauritino (GER)**[136] 793 6-10-12 **99**........ RichieMcLernon(3) (Jonjo O'Neill) *midfield: rdn 4th: wknd appr 3 out* **7/1**	74
26-1	**10**	*43*	**Crazy Bold (GER)**[171] 350 7-11-2 **105**........ LeeEdwards(5) (Tony Carroll) *racd keenly: in tch: lost pl 4th: struggling after: t.o* **16/1**	41
1P0-	**P**		**Petroglyph**[212] 5043 6-11-3 **108**........ MrJMQuinlan(7) (Michael Quinlan) *a bhd: struggling appr 4th: t.o fr 4 out: p.u bef 2 out* **16/1**	—

3m 42.8s (-13.70) **Going Correction** -0.725s/f (Firm)
WFA 4 from 5yo+ 7lb **11** Ran SP% **113.8**
Speed ratings (Par 105): **105,103,100,96,96 94,90,88,85,64** —
toteswingers:1&2 £10.30, 2&3 £3.90, 1&3 £11.90 CSF £63.69 CT £314.56 TOTE £27.70: £6.40, £1.80, £2.40; EX 77.20.
Owner Raymond Tooth **Bred** D J And Mrs Deer **Trained** Upper Lambourn, Berks

FOCUS
An ordinary handicap hurdle in which the first three were always handy. A big hurdles best from the winner.

NOTEBOOK
Park Lane, making his handicap debut having been twice well beaten since a promising hurdling debut for Nicky Henderson back in February, is a fast-ground winner on the Flat so these conditions were in his favour. Always close up, he took over in front at halfway but looked beaten when the favourite headed him on the home turn. However, to his credit he never gave up and a fast jump at the last took him back to the front and sealed the victory. He still has a bit of scope for this game, but is viewed as a potential chaser in the longer term. (op 25-1)
Goat Castle(IRE) has improved plenty since being fitted with a tongue-tie and this return to a sound surface was expected to suit him. He looked to have the race in his grasp when leading coming to two out, but could never stamp his authority and a hesitant jump at the last handed the initiative back to the winner. He is beginning to look a bit of a bridesmaid. (op 3-1)
Tom O'Tara, a dual winner over C&D in February and still 9lb higher than for the second of those, ran well on his return to action at Ludlow last month, but although he had every chance here, he had pulled hard early and possesses an awkward head carriage. He also needs softer ground than this. (op 5-1)
Lucy's Perfect, making her handicap debut after showing ability in a couple of novice hurdles, was never too far off the pace but didn't improve on previous efforts. (op 9-1 tchd 17-2)
Bosamcliff(IRE), who seemed to find 2m4f beyond her on her return to hurdles at Worcester last month, got going too late over this shorter trip and still looks to be on a stiff-enough mark. (op 11-2 tchd 9-2)
Mr Tingle, a former Irish point winner making his handicap debut having not been seen since finishing well beaten in three novice hurdles at the end of last year, should come on for the run but needs a stiffer test. (tchd 28-1)

2151 WEATHERBYS BANK JUVENILE HURDLE (8 hdls) 2m
1:25 (1:28) (Class 4) 3-Y-0 **£2,602** (£764; £382; £190)

Form				RPR
	1		**Pantxoa (FR)**[124] 3-11-5 0........ WayneHutchinson (Alan King) *mde all: shkn up whn nt fluent last: pushed out run-in: a in full control* **4/9**[1]	105+
0	**2**	*1 ¼*	**Omaruru (IRE)**[31] 1691 3-10-12 0........ MarkBradburne (Renee Robeson) *hld up: hdwy appr 3 out: rdn to chse wnr between last 2: nt fluent last: r.o run-in: clsd on wnr cl home: nvr gng to get there* **25/1**	94+
	3	*5*	**Jolly Roger (IRE)**[32] 3-10-12 0........ RhysFlint (John Flint) *chsd ldrs: j. slowly 4th: wnt 2nd appr 2 out where nt fluent: rdn and nt qckn whn lost 2nd bef last: styd on same pce run-in* **4/1**[2]	88
U	**4**	*5*	**Claimant (IRE)**[6] 2047 3-10-12 0........ JamieMoore (Miss J R Tooth) *hld up: hdwy appr 4th: chsd ldrs bef 2 out: no imp and btn bef last* **33/1**	84
	5	*½*	**Dragon's Den (IRE)**[127] 3-10-12 0........ JamesDavies (Chris Down) *racd keenly: sn chsd ldr: rdn and lost 2nd appr 2 out: wknd bef last* **9/1**[3]	83
30	**6**	*6*	**Big Talk**[17] 1882 3-10-12 0........ RodiGreene (David Bridgwater) *chsd ldrs: nt fluent 1st: rdn along briefly after 3rd: rdn and wknd after 3 out* **20/1**	78
	7	*4 ½*	**Rigid**[21] 3-10-7 0........ LeeEdwards(5) (Tony Carroll) *hld up: hdwy appr 4th: nt fluent 3 out: rdn and wknd bef 2 out* **25/1**	74
	8	*24*	**If I Were A Boy (IRE)**[17] 3-10-5 0........ GerardTumelty (Dominic Ffrench Davis) *racd keenly: in tch: racd wd and clsd bef 4th: wknd appr 4 out* **10/1**	45
	9	*15*	**Steely Bird**[53] 3-10-9 0........ PeterToole(3) (Richard Hawker) *j. slowly 2nd: a bhd* **66/1**	39

10 23 **Penshurst Lad (IRE)**[18] 3-10-12 0 WarrenMarston 18
(Richard Phillips) *midfield: rdn whn j. slowly and wknd 4 out: t.o* **66/1**

P 11 5 **Guppy's Girl (IRE)**[20] 1845 3-10-5 0 AndrewGlassonbury 7
(Sam Davison) *a bhd: j. slowly 1st and 3rd: nvr on terms: t.o* **66/1**

3m 47.7s (-8.80) **Going Correction** -0.725s/f (Firm) **11** Ran SP% **128.2**
Speed ratings (Par 104): **93,92,89,87,87 84,81,69,62,50 48**
toteswingers:1&2 £7.90, 2&3 £12.00, 1&3 £1.10 CSF £22.33 TOTE £2.00: £1.10, £6.90, £1.40; EX 14.40.
Owner The Dunkley & Reilly Partnership **Bred** Pierre De Maleissye Melun **Trained** Barbury Castle, Wilts

FOCUS
An uncompetitive juvenile hurdle and the early pace was pedestrian. The winning time was almost five seconds slower than the opener. Not much to go on but the first two can rate higher.

NOTEBOOK
Pantxoa(FR), making his debut for the yard (which had won this race twice in the previous five years) and carrying a 7lb penalty for a convincing success over 15 rivals at Clairefontaine in July, managed to land the odds but wasn't that impressive. To be fair to him, the moderate early tempo caused him to pull his way to the front before the first flight and he had to make all the running from that point. He eventually travelled well and, apart from an untidy jump at the last, didn't look like being beaten even though he had to be ridden out on the run-in. He will need to settle better and is likely to be kept to ordinary company for the time being. (tchd 1-2 in early places)
Omaruru(IRE) ◆, a 65-rated maiden on the Flat for Mark Johnston, finished tailed off on his hurdling debut at Huntingdon last month but this was much better. Having settled well at the back of the field early, he made his move racing down the back straight and made sure the favourite wasn't allowed to ease off. He should be winning over hurdles before too long. (op 33-1)
Jolly Roger(IRE), rated 75 on the Flat after just two outings and bought for £8,000 by current connections after winning a 1m2f Redcar seller last month for Neville Bycroft, was sent off well backed and, having been handy from the start, kept on right to the line. He can win races at this game. (op 11-2)
Claimant(IRE), a 65-rated maiden on the Flat, was behind when unseating on his hurdling debut at Fontwell six days earlier but improved on that here. After moving into contention at halfway, he was bang there with every chance under pressure turning in but couldn't then find any more.
Dragon's Den(IRE), a 73-rated maiden on the Flat in Ireland, was picked up for £20,000 by current connections and showed enough on this hurdles debut to suggest that the money wasn't wasted. (op 10-1)
If I Were A Boy(IRE), 2-20 on the Flat and rated 75 in that sphere, was a springer in the market but she took a strong hold on the outside of the field and looked almost unrideable at times. (op 20-1)

2152 WEATHERBYS BLOODSTOCK INSURANCE H'CAP CHASE (12 fncs) 2m
2:00 (2:00) (Class 4) (0-105,100) 4-Y-0+ **£3,252** (£955; £477; £238)

Form RPR

-P63 1 **That's The Deal (IRE)**[7] 2037 6-10-10 **91** JoeCornwall(7) 103+
(John Cornwall) *hld up in tch: dropped to rr bef 6th: hdwy 7th: upsides 3 out: led 2 out: drew clr after last: comf* **5/1**[2]

0-03 2 12 **Corredor Sun (USA)**[22] 1813 4-10-12 **97** (p) SamTwiston-Davies(3) 89
(Nigel Twiston-Davies) *w ldr: nt fluent 4th: led appr 6th: hdd 2 out: 3rd and hld whn blnd last: styd on to take 2nd cl home: no ch w wnr* **3/1**[1]

2555 3 nk **Red Jester**[8] 2022 9-11-12 **100** AndrewGlassonbury 98
(Gerald Ham) *towards rr after 2nd: hdwy appr 6th: led 3 out: hdd 2 out: wl btn and no ch w wnr after last: lost 2nd cl home* **8/1**

045P 4 4 ½ **Rince Donn (IRE)**[31] 1710 8-10-3 **84** (t) MrTGarner(7) 78
(Roger Curtis) *in tch: rdn and outpcd bef 4 out: tried to get bk on terms: no real imp bef 2 out: wl hld bef last* **12/1**

351- 5 23 **Devils River (IRE)**[191] 26 8-11-9 **97** (p) AndrewTinkler 70
(Anna Brooks) *led: hdd appr 6th: wknd 8th* **17/2**

-P44 6 2 ½ **Vasodilator (IRE)**[22] 1813 7-11-4 **97** MichaelMurphy(5) 68
(Pat Murphy) *bhd: nt fluent 3rd: j. carefully 4th: effrt 7th: wknd 8th* **11/2**[3]

-664 F **Secret Cavern (USA)**[14] 1924 8-10-2 **76** oh7 ow2 JackDoyle —
(Peter Pritchard) *hld up in rr: fell 2nd* **6/1**

50P- F **Bobby Donald (IRE)**[207] 5133 8-10-12 **86** WarrenMarston —
(Richard Phillips) *hld up: fell 2nd* **6/1**

3m 58.7s (-6.90) **Going Correction** -0.725s/f (Firm)
WFA 4 from 6yo+ 7lb **8** Ran SP% **115.0**
Speed ratings (Par 105): **88,82,81,79,68 66,—,—**
toteswingers:1&2 £4.20, 2&3 £3.40, 1&3 £10.60 CSF £21.25 CT £117.70 TOTE £8.70: £3.50, £2.10, £2.00; EX 20.80.
Owner J R Cornwall **Bred** P Magill **Trained** Long Clawson, Leics

FOCUS
A moderate handicap chase, especially following the early departures of Bobby Donald and Secret Cavern, and not form to get too carried way with. That said the winner is on the upgrade. They went a decent early pace nonetheless with a disputed lead.

NOTEBOOK
That's The Deal(IRE), a former Irish point winner, improved plenty on previous efforts under rules when third off this mark on his handicap debut at Haydock seven days earlier, whilst this victory was mainly down to a well-judged waiting ride by Joe Cornwall, who was content to sit off the pace whilst the leaders got on with it. However, it was clear from some way out that he was running all over his opponents and he fairly bolted up. Unfortunately this form amounts to little and a significant rise in his mark could leave him vulnerable. (op 11-2)
Corredor Sun(USA), whose only win came over hurdles here last December, was having only his third start over fences and didn't stay the extended 2m4f at Huntingdon last month. This trip seemed to suit him better and he did well to regain second on the run-in as he was involved in a protracted duel for the lead with Devils River in the first half of the contest. (op 10-3 tchd 7-2)
Red Jester, whose most recent success came in this race last year off 4lb lower, moved through to take it up jumping three out but faded after losing the advantage before the next. (op 6-1)
Rince Donn(IRE), 6lb lower than when winning at Folkestone in January, raced prominently early but dropped away from the final bend. He is 1-27 over fences and prefers softer ground. (op 16-1)
Devils River(IRE), not seen since winning off 6lb lower at Towcester in April, has no great record fresh and has shown all his best form going right handed. (op 15-2)

2153 COMMSCOPE AND ANIXTER BUSINESS PARTNERS NOVICES' CHASE (12 fncs) 2m
2:35 (2:35) (Class 3) 4-Y-0+ **£5,854** (£1,719; £859; £429)

Form RPR

5/ 1 **Darby's Turn (IRE)**[195] 5346 8-11-1 125 WarrenMarston 129+
(Richard Phillips) *chsd ldrs: blnd 2nd: wnt 2nd at 6th: chalng 2 out: led last: drvn out and styd on wl* **10/1**

05-0 2 2 ½ **Dan Breen (IRE)**[179] 207 5-11-1 0 TomScudamore 128+
(David Pipe) *led: nt fluent and hdd 4th: led 5th: rchd for 7th: rdn and hdd last: no ex fnl 75yds* **4/5**[1]

252- 3 2 ¾ **Shakalakaboomboom (IRE)**[217] 4959 6-11-1 0 AndrewTinkler 125+
(Nicky Henderson) *chsd ldrs: nt fluent 3 out: rdn and nt qckn bef last: kpt on same pce run-in and no imp on ldrs* **7/1**[3]

P-10 4 8 **Ashammar (FR)**[21] 1827 5-11-1 0 (p) DominicElsworth 120+
(Paul Webber) *hld up: clsd to chse ldrs 8th: nt fluent 2 out: no imp whn blnd last: n.d after* **11/1**

341P 5 1 ¾ **Marc Aurele (IRE)**[17] 1884 5-10-10 0 (t) JimmyDerham(5) 115
(Milton Harris) *w ldr: led 4th: hdd 5th: lost pl 8th: outpcd and wl btn bef 2 out* **25/1**

U-02 6 1 ¾ **Shadow Dancer (IRE)**[31] 1706 5-11-12 0 RichieMcLernon(3) 113
(Jonjo O'Neill) *hld up: rdn and outpcd after 3 out: nvr a danger* **5/1**[2]

1-06 7 40 **I'm In The Pink (FR)**[145] 500 6-10-12 0 LeeStephens(3) 92
(David Evans) *j. poorly: a bhd: nvr on terms: t.o* **33/1**

3m 55.5s (-10.10) **Going Correction** -0.45s/f (Good) **7** Ran SP% **108.9**
Speed ratings (Par 107): **107,105,104,100,99 98,78**
toteswingers:1&2 £3.10, 2&3 £2.80, 1&3 £8.80 CSF £17.85 TOTE £13.60: £4.90, £1.30; EX 26.60.
Owner John Nicholls (Trading) Ltd **Bred** Miss Emma Jane Gallagher **Trained** Adlestrop, Gloucs

FOCUS
The favourite had taken four of the previous five runnings and it has been won by some high-class novices, including Afsoun and Somersby in the last two years. Whether this year's winner reaches their heights seems unlikely, even though the winning time was 3.2 seconds faster than the preceding handicap. The winner is rated in line with his best Irish form with the second a stone below his hurdles best.

NOTEBOOK
Darby's Turn(IRE) was making his debut for the yard and already has a chase mark of 125 after showing ability in seven starts over fences in Ireland last season. Despite racing keenly enough early, he travelled powerfully into the race and maintained his momentum to lead at the last and battle on well up the run-in. His best efforts in Ireland had come on much softer ground, so this effort shows that he is versatile in terms of going and, although he is a more exposed type, he may well have improved. He is likely to stick to the novice route and will be tried at one of the bigger tracks. (op 11-1 tchd 12-1)
Dan Breen(IRE), a 135-rated hurdler, was tried in some red-hot company during the spring. The market expected him to make a winning chasing debut and it's hard to work out why he was beaten, as he didn't seem to do a lot wrong. Admittedly he was involved in a battle for the early lead with Marc Aurele and was racing for the first time since May, but fitness isn't normally an issue with horses from the yard and he probably ran into one that was just more streetwise on the day. He can still make his mark at this game. (op 5-6)
Shakalakaboomboom(IRE), not seen since a promising hurdling debut at Hereford in March, proved weak in the market but he never stopped trying and was still staying on at the line. He remains unexposed. (op 9-2)
Ashammar(FR), a 124-rated hurdler, had cheekpieces on for this chasing debut and had a chance turning in before fading. (tchd 10-1 and 12-1)
Shadow Dancer(IRE), a 125-rated hurdler, showed some ability when second of five on his chase debut at Uttoxeter last month, but his jumping here was often less than fluent and he could never get into the race. This trip would have been sharp enough. (op 10-2)

2154 PAUL AND PAULA DALY WEDDING DAY NOVICES' HURDLE (12 hdls) 3m 1f
3:10 (3:10) (Class 4) 4-Y-0+ **£2,602** (£764; £382; £190)

Form RPR

66-1 1 **Cotswold Charmer (IRE)**[31] 1703 5-10-9 0 SamTwiston-Davies(3) 117+
(Nigel Twiston-Davies) *hld up: hdwy whn mstke 4 out: chsd ldrs 3 out: upsides 2 out: sn led: drvn out and r.o wl fnl 75yds: edgd lft cl home whn wl on top* **9/4**[2]

60-2 2 2 **Hear My Song (IRE)**[21] 1821 5-10-9 0 RichieMcLernon(3) 114+
(Jonjo O'Neill) *hld up: nt fluent 5th: hdwy appr 8th: wnt 2nd after 3 out: led narrowly 2 out: sn hdd: rdn whn nt fluent last: outpcd by wnr fnl 75yds* **7/4**[1]

22-0 3 4 **Teenage Kicks (IRE)**[22] 1812 5-10-12 106 WarrenMarston 111
(Pam Sly) *led: nt fluent 3 out: hdd 2 out: sn rdn: styd on same pce run-in* **9/2**[3]

66-3 4 ½ **Wyck Hill (IRE)**[17] 1887 6-10-12 0 RodiGreene 109
(David Bridgwater) *racd keenly: in tch: chsd ldr bef 2nd tl rdn after 3 out: kpt on same pce fr 2 out* **11/2**

34-4 5 20 **Royal Role**[14] 1922 6-10-12 85 JackDoyle 89
(Peter Pritchard) *chsd ldr tl appr 2nd: remained prom: rdn and wknd after 3 out* **50/1**

0/ 6 18 **Front Street (IRE)**[184] 6-10-7 0 MichaelMurphy(5) 71
(Pat Murphy) *chsd ldrs tl wknd 3 out* **25/1**

55-6 7 37 **No Woman No Cry**[18] 1860 5-10-12 0 DaveCrosse 34
(Colin Tizzard) *in tch: rdn and wknd after 3 out: eased whn wl btn bef 2 out* **33/1**

8 16 **Duke Of Ormond (IRE)**[207] 7-10-12 0 CharliePoste 18
(Anna Brooks) *hld up in rr: struggling after 8th: sn lft bhd* **33/1**

P 9 9 **Harry Oscar (IRE)**[27] 1742 9-10-5 0 MrBJPoste(7) —
(Ken Wingrove) *hld up: struggling appr 8th: lost tch after* **66/1**

6m 19.8s (-7.70) **Going Correction** -0.45s/f (Good) **9** Ran SP% **113.9**
Speed ratings (Par 105): **94,93,92,91,85 79,67,62,59**
toteswingers:1&2 £1.90, 2&3 £2.00, 1&3 £4.40 CSF £6.43 TOTE £3.90: £1.70, £1.20, £1.10; EX 8.30.
Owner The Double Octagon Partnership **Bred** Raymond McDonnell **Trained** Naunton, Gloucs

FOCUS
The rain started to come down before this race. The early pace was very moderate and as a result this wasn't the test of stamina it might have been. The winner is on the upgrade but this form is not too solid.

NOTEBOOK
Cotswold Charmer(IRE) was unpenalised for his easy win in a heavy-ground conditional jockeys' novice hurdle at Uttoxeter last month. Given a waiting ride, he moved into contention halfway down the back straight on the final circuit, but seemed to be going worse than his most of his main rivals turning in. However, stamina seems to be the key to him and he forged his way to the front in between the last two flights. There should be more to come from him given a decent test and connections believe he is a chaser in the making. (op 11-4)
Hear My Song(IRE), 6l ahead of a subsequent winner when runner-up on his return from a break at Uttoxeter last month, moved into the race travelling better than anything racing inside the final mile and had every chance turning in, but he couldn't match the winner's turn of foot after jumping two out. Here probably needs a race run at a proper pace, but his breeding suggests that he will truly come into his own over fences. (op 6-4 tchd 15-8 in places)
Teenage Kicks(IRE), rated 106 over hurdles, needed the run over an inadequate 2m4f at Huntingdon last month and made a bold bid to make all until headed two out. This was a good effort, but he did enjoy the run of the race. (op 13-2)
Wyck Hill(IRE) seemed likely to be suited by this extra half-mile judged on his promising hurdling debut at Kempton last month and he ran well having been handy throughout. He still has the scope for further improvement. (op 4-1)

Royal Role ended up well beaten and is only rated 85 over hurdles.

2155 MRS B IS ALWAYS RIGHT CONDITIONAL JOCKEYS' H'CAP CHASE (20 fncs) 3m 2f
3:40 (3:40) (Class 4) (0-100,99) 4-Y-0+ **£2,927** (£859; £429; £214)

Form RPR
-P02 **1** **Chico Time (IRE)**[74] 1336 9-10-7 **85**....................(p) StephenO'Donovan(5) 100+
(Jonathan Geake) *j.rt several times: hld up: mstke 10th: hdwy 11th: wnt cl 2nd bef 14th: led 4 out: drew clr appr 2 out: kpt up to work run-in* **7/2**[2]
40PP **2** 3 ¾ **Overton Lad**[28] 1733 9-10-1 **74**....................(b) RichieMcLernon 81
(Peter Pritchard) *chsd along in rr early: chsd ldrs fr 4th: wnt 2nd appr 10th: lost 2nd bef 14th: rdn after 3 out: sn wl outpcd: hit last: kpt on to take 2nd run-in: unable to threaten wnr* **15/2**
F-0U **3** 6 **September Moon**[16] 1903 12-10-11 **87**.................... KyleJames(3) 89
(Graham Smith) *led: hdd 4 out: u.p and outpcd by wnr appr 2 out: lost 2nd whn wl hld run-in* **16/1**
14-P **4** 7 **Fourpointone**[187] 83 9-10-12 **85**....................(p) DavidBass 79
(Michael Scudamore) *in tch: rdn and outpcd appr 14th: kpt on modly bef 2 out: no imp* **11/2**
1-5P **5** hd **Hever Road (IRE)**[21] 1826 11-10-9 **85**.................... JoeCornwall(3) 79
(David Pearson) *bhd bef 4th: struggling appr 14th: kpt on modly bef 2 out: no imp on ldrs* **10/1**
P15/ **P** **Randolph O'Brien (IRE)**[720] 2170 10-11-9 **99**.... SamTwiston-Davies(3) —
(Nigel Twiston-Davies) *chsd ldr: mstke 7th: lost 2nd appr 10th: wknd 14th: t.o whn p.u bef 2 out* **5/1**[3]
4324 **P** **Autumn Red (IRE)**[13] 1939 10-11-1 **93**....................(bt) JakeGreenall(5) —
(Paul Webber) *nt fluent 2nd: a bhd and nvr travelling: t.o whn p.u bef 2 out* **5/2**[1]

6m 44.3s (-8.40) **Going Correction** -0.45s/f (Good) **7** Ran SP% **109.6**
Speed ratings (Par 105): **94,92,91,88,88** —,—
toteswingers:1&2 £6.30, 2&3 £8.90, 1&3 £6.30 CSF £26.23 TOTE £4.80: £2.90, £5.60; EX 25.60.
Owner Antell & Twomey **Bred** Maurice Barry **Trained** Marlborough, Wilts

FOCUS
A modest conditional jockeys' handicap chase, but at least the pace was sound. A chase best from the winner.

NOTEBOOK
Chico Time(IRE), making her debut for the yard, was able to race off a 19lb lower mark than over hurdles. Held up early, she took over in front halfway down the back straight on the final circuit and soon held a clear advantage. She tended to run down the last two fences as she lost concentration, but never looked like being caught. She can avoid a penalty for this. (tchd 10-3)
Overton Lad, 4lb higher than when grinding out success in this race last year, didn't come into this year's renewal in any sort of form and seemed reluctant to race in the early stages, but he had every chance in the final mile and kept plugging on. A mistake at the last made little difference to the result. (op 8-1)
September Moon, lightly raced in the last couple of seasons, had a record of 2-27 over fences coming into this and hadn't been at her best in two starts since returning from a layoff. Given her usual positive ride, she lasted much longer this time and seems to be on the way back, though she will soon be a teenager. (op 10-1)
Fourpointone is well handicapped on his best form, but he hadn't been seen since losing his action and pulling up at Fontwell in April. He was being shoved along with a circuit still to run here, but the outing should have brought him on. (op 5-1 tchd 6-1)
Hever Road(IRE), back down to his last winning mark, was pulled up on his return at Wetherby last month and was inclined to run in snatches here. (op 17-2 tchd 15-2)
Randolph O'Brien(IRE) is well handicapped these days and has a fine record fresh, so the two-year absence shouldn't have been a worry, but his previous form at 3m-plus is poor and he looked a non-stayer again. (op 9-2 tchd 6-1)
Autumn Red(IRE) usually makes the frame, but is now 0-18 over jumps and didn't want to know at all this time. Official explanation: jockey said gelding never travelled (op 9-2 tchd 6-1)

2156 WARWICK MARES' STANDARD OPEN NATIONAL HUNT FLAT RACE 2m
4:15 (4:15) (Class 5) 4-6-Y-0 **£2,055** (£599; £299)

Form RPR
1 **Wassailing Queen** 4-10-9 0.................... SamTwiston-Davies(3) 109+
(Colin Tizzard) *in tch: led over 5f out: j. path whn asserting 1f out: green: readily drew clr ins fnl f* **6/1**[3]
1- **2** 6 **Whoops A Daisy**[200] 5235 4-11-2 0.................... RichardKilloran(3) 109
(Nicky Henderson) *in tch: effrt 4f out: chsd wnr u.p over 1f out: one pce and no imp ins fnl f* **5/2**[2]
3 2 **Dream Function (IRE)** 5-10-12 0.................... RhysFlint 100
(Philip Hobbs) *midfield: hdwy 5f out: wnt 2nd 4f out: rdn over 2f out: lost 2nd over 1f out: styd on same pce* **9/4**[1]
4 7 **Golden Gael** 4-10-12 0.................... WillKennedy 94
(Jeremy Scott) *trckd ldrs: pushed along 4f out: styd on same pce fnl 2f* **14/1**
5 nk **Bounds And Leaps**[211] 5-10-12 0.................... TomScudamore 93
(Michael Scudamore) *led: hdd over 5f out: outpcd 3f out: n.d after* **25/1**
6 ½ **Farewellatmidnight** 4-10-12 0.................... JimmyMcCarthy 93
(Alex Hales) *midfield: hdwy 1/2-way: chsd ldrs 3f out: no further imp and btn wl over 1f out* **33/1**
0 **7** 8 **Withy Mills**[27] 1748 5-10-7 0.................... GilesHawkins(5) 87
(Kevin Bishop) *hld up: pushed along 5f out: kpt on fnl 2f: nvr on terms w ldrs* **66/1**
2- **8** 7 **Blazing Empress**[539] 284 5-10-12 0.................... JackDoyle 79
(Sarah Humphrey) *midfield: pushed along 6f out: plugged on at one pce fnl 2f: no imp on ldrs* **20/1**
3 **9** 3 ¼ **Living Proof (IRE)**[77] 1284 5-10-5 0.................... StephenO'Donovan(7) 76
(Jonathan Geake) *prom tl rdn and wknd 4f out* **8/1**
10 19 **Menepresents (IRE)** 5-10-12 0.................... HaddenFrost 59
(Henrietta Knight) *in tch: rdn over 4f out: wknd 3f out* **20/1**
11 6 **Icansayno (IRE)** 4-10-7 0.................... DavidBass(5) 54
(Lawney Hill) *hld up: pushed along after 5f: nvr on terms* **33/1**
06- **12** ¾ **Lilac Belle**[253] 4213 4-10-9 0.................... ChrisHonour(3) 53
(Alex Hales) *midfield: hdwy to chse ldrs 7f out: wknd 3f out* **66/1**
6-0 **13** 11 **Corston Star (IRE)**[13] 1934 5-10-7 0.................... JamesHalliday(5) 43
(Malcolm Jefferson) *chsd ldrs tl over 6f out: struggling and n.d after* **40/1**
14 2 ¾ **Dani (IRE)** 4-10-9 0.................... PeterToole(3) 41
(Mark Rimell) *a bhd* **25/1**
15 34 **Sussex Lass** 5-10-7 0.................... GemmaGracey-Davison(5) 10
(Zoe Davison) *a bhd: pushed along 1/2-way: nvr on terms: t.o* **40/1**
0 **16** 33 **Spring A Suprise**[27] 1748 6-10-5 0.................... MrBJPoste(7) —
(Ken Wingrove) *a bhd: t.o* **200/1**

3m 41.7s (-9.20) **Going Correction** -0.45s/f (Good) **16** Ran SP% **122.9**
Speed ratings: **105,102,101,97,97 97,93,89,87,78 75,75,69,68,51 34**
toteswingers:1&2 £4.30, 2&3 £3.00, 1&3 £3.10 CSF £19.07 TOTE £6.80: £1.90, £1.10, £2.90; EX 28.10.
Owner Robert And Sarah Tizzard **Bred** Jethro Bloodstock **Trained** Milborne Port, Dorset

FOCUS
A more truly run race than many bumpers, though it still paid to race handily, and a most taking winner. The winning time was quicker than both hurdle races run over the same trip earlier on the card. The first two look above-avergae mares.

NOTEBOOK
Wassailing Queen ◆, a £25,000 half-sister to four winners including her smart stable companion Bob Bob Bobbin, was always handy but looked as green as grass at various stages, especially when in a clear lead racing up the home straight, but she still won with any amount in hand and looks a very nice prospect indeed. (op 15-2)
Whoops A Daisy ◆, whose stable had won two of the previous four runnings of this race, was an impressive winner of a Bangor bumper on debut in April. She kept staying on having been handy all the way and time may show that this was a decent effort against a nice prospect under her 7lb penalty. (tchd 9-4 and 11-4)
Dream Function(IRE) ◆, a sister to the smart Captain Chris, moved powerfully into the race down the back straight and looked a threat, but she couldn't match the winner for speed down the home straight. She has a future. (op 5-2 tchd 2-1)
Golden Gael ◆ showed up for a long way on this racecourse debut and this half-sister to the hurdles/bumper winner Magellan Straits is one to note. (op 25-1)
Bounds And Leaps, last seen winning a mares' point in April, made much of the early running and ran on again after looking likely to drop away rounding the home bend. She will appreciate a greater test of stamina in due course and should come on for the run.
Farewellatmidnight, out of a half-sister to Beantown and Dun An Doras, showed her inexperience by hanging wide off the final bend but still showed enough to suggest she will make her mark. (op 50-1)
T/Plt: £16.40 to a £1 stake. Pool of £41,269.24 - 1,831.36 winning tickets. T/Qpdt: £7.00 to a £1 stkae. Pool of £3,106.21 - 324.28 winning tickets. DO

2157 - 2160a (Foreign Racing) - See Raceform Interactive

2033 HAYDOCK (L-H)
Thursday, November 4

OFFICIAL GOING: Chase course - good to soft (good in places; 5.9); hurdle course - good (good to firm in places; 7.0)
Wind: Moderate - strong, half-against Weather: Overcast, turning wet

2161 TAYLORMADE BETTING CONDITIONAL JOCKEYS' H'CAP HURDLE (12 hdls) 3m
12:55 (12:55) (Class 4) (0-115,109) 4-Y-0+ **£3,252** (£955; £477; £238)

Form RPR
5211 **1** **Scotsbrook Cloud**[15] 1918 5-11-3 **100**.................... TomMolloy 107+
(David Evans) *midfield: hdwy gng wl appr 3 out: upsides 2 out: sn led: drvn out and r.o wl after last: kpt on but in control cl home* **4/1**[1]
5-01 **2** 1 ¼ **Rare Coincidence**[30] 1004 9-11-5 **105**....................(p) AlexanderVoy(3) 108
(Roger Fisher) *set stdy pce: pressed 2 out: sn rdn and hdd: nt qckn w wnr after last: styd on towards fin but a hld* **16/1**
145U **3** 8 **Admiral Dundas (IRE)**[9] 2023 5-11-1 **106**....................(t) EdCookson(8) 102+
(Kim Bailey) *chsd ldrs: rdn and nt qckn appr last: hung lft run-in: styd on fnl 100yds but no imp on front 2* **9/2**[2]
6624 **4** ¾ **Kings Riches (IRE)**[68] 1401 5-11-2 **102**.................... DonalDevereux(3) 98
(Peter Bowen) *chsd ldr: mstke 7th: lost 2nd appr 2 out but stl ev ch: nt fluent last: wknd run-in* **7/1**[3]
111- **5** 3 ½ **Willandrich (IRE)**[227] 4790 8-11-4 **109**.................... TrevorWhelan(8) 101
(Ian Williams) *midfield: hdwy appr 3 out: sn chsd ldrs: rdn bef last: sn one pce and btn* **7/1**[3]
034- **6** 8 **Watercolours (IRE)**[195] 5372 5-10-11 **102**.................... PaulNorton(8) 87
(Jim Goldie) *hld up: struggling appr 3 out: nvr a threat* **8/1**
2F4- **7** 2 ¼ **Young Buddy**[194] 5389 5-10-11 **97**.................... JamesHalliday(3) 81
(Malcolm Jefferson) *hld up: pushed along after 2 out: no imp* **7/1**[3]
2-6U **8** 4 ½ **Phoenix Des Mottes (FR)**[28] 1747 7-10-6 **95**.................... JoeCornwall(6) 74
(John Cornwall) *in tch: pushed along and wknd appr last* **22/1**
6205 **9** 1 ¾ **Englishtown (FR)**[23] 1814 10-11-7 **107**....................(p) RichieMcLernon(3) 84
(Jonjo O'Neill) *midfield: rdn and dropped to rr 3 out: no imp after* **14/1**
-PPP **10** 36 **Tayman (IRE)**[14] 1937 8-11-0 **100**.................... SamTwiston-Davies(3) 45
(Nigel Twiston-Davies) *hld up: toiling whn hit 3 out: nvr on terms: t.o* **20/1**

5m 53.3s (-6.70) **10** Ran SP% **108.5**
toteswingers:1&2:£9.80, 1&3:£2.60, 2&3:£40.40 CSF £57.44 CT £263.33 TOTE £4.20: £1.80, £3.80, £1.60; EX 39.40.
Owner Walters Plant Hire Ltd **Bred** A E And P E Price **Trained** Pandy, Monmouths
■ Stewards' Enquiry : Tom Molloy two-day ban: careless riding (Nov 18-19)

FOCUS
Despite the course enduring 25mm of rain in the 48 hours leading up to racing the ground on the hurdles course was still on the quick side. This handicap for conditional riders was run at an ordinary gallop despite there being a clear early leader. It looked competitive for the class despite the top weight being rated 6lb below the race ceiling. There is probably more to come from the winner, and the second is rated to his mark.

NOTEBOOK
Scotsbrook Cloud landed the hat-trick with an authoritative display. He had won his first two outings for current connections, but was fully 18lb higher in this better grade. He shrugged that off in great style, going to the front easily nearing the last, and it was probably a case of him idling as the runner-up rallied late on. He is obviously fast improving and another rise may not be enough to stop him, seeing as he has now proven himself on easier ground. (tchd 7-2 and 9-2 in a place)
Rare Coincidence ran well when second on the level last time out and had won off a 5lb lower mark on his previous outing over hurdles at Cartmel in July. He got very much the run of the race from the front, but there was plenty to like about his attitude when headed and he finished clear of the rest. (op 12-1)
Admiral Dundas(IRE) threw his race away when unseating before the last at Taunton off this mark nine days earlier. He had his chance in this better event, but proved one-paced when it mattered and is now due to race off a 6lb higher mark. (op 4-1 tchd 5-1)
Kings Riches(IRE) came in for support on this return from a 68-day absence and ran a respectable race in defeat. This was a step back in the right direction, but his stamina did appear to just give way over this stiffer test. (op 11-1)
Willandrich(IRE) won three of his four outings last season, which made it six from his last seven, and was 6lb higher for this return. It was just his second outing over this far and he wasn't disgraced, but was another that left the impression the trip just stretched him. It could be he will see it out better now he has a run under his belt, though. (op 13-2 tchd 6-1)

Watercolours(IRE) was doing all of her best work towards the finish and should be much sharper for this seasonal debut. (op 7-1)

2162 BEGBIES TRAYNOR NOVICES' HURDLE (9 hdls) 2m
1:30 (1:30) (Class 4) 4-Y-0+ **£3,252** (£955; £477; £238)

Form					RPR
2-31	1		**Al Qeddaaf (IRE)**34 1664 4-11-5 117 ... JasonMaguire (Donald McCain) *chsd ldrs: led 2 out: rdn abt 3 l clr whn nt fluent last: drvn out and r.o* **4/6**1		114+
4F6-	2	4 ½	**Tahiti Pearl (IRE)**227 4779 6-10-12 0 ... HenryOliver (Sue Smith) *led: j. slowly 1st: hdd 2 out: kpt on same pce and no imp on wnr run-in* **16/1**		98
2-	3	5	**Quiet Whisper (IRE)**295 3419 4-10-5 0 ... (t) MrCGreene(7) (Kim Bailey) *hld up: mstke 5th: hdwy after 3 out: chsd ldrs next: chal for 2nd briefly last: no ex fnl 120yds* **14/1**3		95
3-40	4	1 ¾	**Attaglance**8 2038 4-10-7 0 ... JamesHalliday(5) (Malcolm Jefferson) *hld up in rr: niggled along after 6th: styd on fr last: tk 4th towards fin: nt trble ldrs* **14/1**3		92+
	5	2	**King Fingal (IRE)**29 5-10-12 0 ... DougieCostello (John Quinn) *racd keenly: prom: chalng whn stmbld 2 out: sn lost pl and no imp on ldrs after: wknd fnl 150yds* **6/1**2		92
	6	11	**Mill Beattie**597 5-10-5 0 ... DaveCrosse (John Mackie) *prom tl rdn and wknd 2 out* **100/1**		73
	7	11	**Lyrical Intent**29 4-10-12 0 ... (t) MichaelMcAlister (Maurice Barnes) *in tch: pushed along appr 3 out: wknd bef 2 out* **50/1**		70
5	8	29	**Vico Road (IRE)**19 1866 5-10-12 0 ... NoelFehily (Jonjo O'Neill) *hld up in rr: lft wl bhd after 6th* **6/1**2		44
0/-	9	115	**Bob Jackson (IRE)**1070 2518 8-10-12 0 ... JohnnyFarrelly (Elliott Cooper) *in tch: rdn and wknd 6th: t.o* **40/1**		—
00-	P		**Sacco D'Oro**78 2716 4-10-2 0 ... CharlieStudd(3) (Michael Mullineaux) *hld up in midfield: sddle sn slipped: lost pl and p.u bef 4th* **150/1**		—

4m 3.00s (-1.20) **10** Ran SP% **113.8**
toteswingers:1&2:£4.80, 1&3:£2.50, 2&3:£35.70 CSF £13.08 TOTE £1.60: £1.10, £3.30, £2.70; EX 16.30.

Owner T G Leslie **Bred** Gerrardstown House Stud **Trained** Cholmondeley, Cheshire

■ Stewards' Enquiry : James Halliday ten-day ban: breach of Rule (B)59.4 (Nov 18-27)

FOCUS
The opinion of some riders after the opener was that the ground on the inner course was quite tacky in places and softer round the bends. This ordinary novice event was steadily run and most took a keen hold early on. Easy form to rate, and the winner is 10lb off his best.

NOTEBOOK
Al Qeddaaf(IRE) defied his penalty with a determined display. This 4-y-o had shown his true colours when belatedly off the mark at Hexham last month and was all the rage to follow up. He could've done with a bit more of a test as he took time to settle, and he didn't extend as might have been expected after the last, but despite hitting the last he was never going to get caught after hitting the front. His attitude is now much more convincing and a return to softer ground could see him improve again. Indeed he may get further this term, but things will be tougher under a double penalty in this sphere, so handicaps may now be his best option. (op 8-11 tchd 4-5 in places)

Tahiti Pearl(IRE) showed up a lot more encouragingly on his return from a 227-day break and looks to have benefited for his time away from the track. He may be a little flattered as he dictated here, but this late-maturing 6-y-o should be treated as a potential improver and now qualifies for a mark. (op 18-1 tchd 20-1)

Quiet Whisper(IRE), narrowly denied on his debut in a Southwell bumper last season, was making his hurdling debut for a new yard that has been among the winners and was equipped with a first-time tongue tie. He left the impression he wants more of a test and should learn a good deal for the experience. (op 10-1)

Attaglance was another that would've no doubt enjoyed a stronger overall gallop as he was keeping on with some purpose all too late in the day having been ridden with great restraint. Stepping up in trip in a low-grade handicap should really see him in a better light. This display caught the attention of the stewards, who looked into the running and riding, and later banned the rider James Halliday for ten days for failing to take all reasonable and permissible measures to ensure the best possible placing. Halliday stated his instructions were to drop his mount in and get him switched off, and that he became outpaced on the home turn. The stewards' verdict did seem somewhat harsh. Official explanation: jockey said, regarding running and riding, that his orders were to drop the gelding in, get it settled and switched off, but he got caught flat footed on the final bend. (op 12-1)

King Fingal(IRE), rated 76 on the Flat, hails from a decent dual-purpose yard and got 1m2f on the level. He too took time to settle off the sedate early gallop, but was going as well as the winner prior to hitting the second-last and would've surely been placed at least but for that. He has a future in this game and deserves another chance. (op 11-2 tchd 13-2)

Bob Jackson(IRE) Official explanation: trainer said gelding finished distressed

Sacco D'Oro Official explanation: jockey said saddle slipped

2163 SNG COMMERCIAL LAW H'CAP CHASE (18 fncs) 3m
2:05 (2:05) (Class 3) (0-135,132) 4-Y-0+ **£6,505** (£1,910; £955; £477)

Form					RPR
211-	1		**King Fontaine (IRE)**194 5388 7-11-2 122 ... GrahamLee (Malcolm Jefferson) *hld up: hdwy 4 out: mstke 13th: effrt 2 out whn chsng ldrs: led last: styd on gamely to prevail in duel on run-in* **11/2**3		138+
211-	2	hd	**Maktu**215 4987 8-11-7 132 ... MichaelMurphy(5) (Pat Murphy) *hld up: hdwy 7th: hit 11th: wnt 2nd 4 out: led 2 out: rdn and hdd last: continued to chal strly run-in: styd on gamely in duel: jst hld* **13/2**		146+
11P-	3	3 ¼	**Categorical**9 4980 7-11-1 121 ... JamesReveley (Keith Reveley) *hld up: hdwy 14th: rdn to chal appr last: no ex fnl 75yds* **9/1**		130
2P2-	4	19	**Dark Ben (FR)**225 4813 10-10-1 112 ... PaulCallaghan(5) (Simon West) *led to 2nd: remained prom tl rdn and wknd appr last* **9/2**2		107
4-00	5	25	**Flake**8 2035 10-10-9 115 ... TjadeCollier (Sue Smith) *in tch: pushed along appr 13th: lft bhd after 14th* **18/1**		84
532F	6	28	**Mizen Raven (IRE)**40 1611 7-11-9 129 ... (tp) TomScudamore (Peter Bowen) *chsd ldrs tl rdn and wknd appr 3 out* **8/1**		73
41F-	F		**The Jazz Musician (IRE)**210 5098 8-11-6 126 ... (t) JoeTizzard (Colin Tizzard) *racd keenly: chsd ldr: led 2nd: hit 12th: hdd 2 out: 4th and hld whn fell last* **11/2**3		130+
F21-	R		**Ernst Blofeld (IRE)**228 4754 6-11-11 131 ... JasonMaguire (Donald McCain) *in tch: nt fluent 2nd: rdn after 5th: rdn in 6th and wl hld whn ref 3 out* **7/2**1		—

6m 15.7s (1.70) **Going Correction** +0.25s/f (Yiel) **8** Ran SP% **110.9**
Speed ratings (Par 107): **107,106,105,99,91 81,—,—**
toteswingers:1&2:£2.60, 1&3:£14.40, 2&3:£13.10 CSF £38.14 CT £301.55 TOTE £5.90: £2.00, £2.40, £3.20; EX 24.20.

Owner Trevor Hemmings **Bred** Peter McCarthy **Trained** Norton, N Yorks

FOCUS
The ground was officially described as good to soft, good in places on the chase course. An interesting handicap with four second-season chasers in attendance that all looked capable of further progression. It was run at a fair gallop. The winner can rate higher still and the second was close to form.

NOTEBOOK
King Fontaine(IRE) came good over fences towards the end of last season, winning his last two races, and picked up where he left off with a game effort on this seasonal debut. He was 5lb higher than when winning despite a blunder at the last on his previous outing in April and again lacked fluency at times off the pace here. Despite those errors, he crept into things going strongly in the home straight and really dug deep for his rider's urgings when it mattered on the run-in. He has now won five of his eight outings since joining the stable and this was his first outing over 3m as a chaser, so it opens up more options for him now. (op 5-1)

Maktu ◆ had also scored on his final two outings last term and was popular in the betting for this first run back, despite racing off a career-high mark back in handicap company. He too made a few errors on the final circuit, but still threw down a strong challenge from three out and was only narrowly denied. This was a very pleasing comeback from a horse who seems sure to improve for the outing, and it wouldn't be surprising to see him aimed the Welsh National next month. (op 11-2 tchd 5-1)

Categorical, fit from the Flat, was having his first outing over fences since pulling up in April but was a back-to-back winner prior to that. He got his usual patient ride and moved sweetly into contention turning for home but eventually gave way to the first pair after the last. This was still a sterling effort in defeat and he helps to set the level. (op 12-1 tchd 14-1)

Dark Ben(FR)'s one win last term was first time out and he showed up well enough under a positive ride but was outclassed when things got really serious in the home straight. (op 13-2)

The Jazz Musician(IRE) was making his seasonal debut and having his first outing in a handicap over fences. He pulled his way to the front and took an age to settle. He was not surprisingly done with after two out back over this longer trip, but took a heavy fall at the last and has now come down on his last two starts. It later transpired he had injured a hock and sadly he had to be put down. (op 3-1 tchd 4-1 and 9-2 in a place)

Ernst Blofeld(IRE), a dual winner as a novice last term, looked the most interesting of these with the future in mind. He proved easy to back for his handicap debut, though, went in snatches from an early stage and was done with prior to attempting to refuse at the third-last, where he ended up unseating and landing pretty much on top of that fence. He is capable of rating higher as the season develops, but this comeback effort leaves him with something to prove. (op 3-1 tchd 4-1 and 9-2 in a place)

2164 BETDAQ THE BETTING EXCHANGE H'CAP HURDLE (9 hdls) 2m
2:40 (2:40) (Class 3) (0-135,125) 4-Y-0+ **£5,204** (£1,528; £764; £381)

Form					RPR
1223	1		**Rio Gael (IRE)**15 1797 4-11-4 117 ... (p) TomScudamore (Peter Bowen) *mde all: rdn steadily clr fr bef last: r.o wl* **7/1**		125+
43-B	2	4	**Gifted Leader (USA)**12 1956 5-11-9 122 ... DougieCostello (Ian Williams) *in tch: effrt to chse wnr appr 3 out: styd on u.p whn pressed for 2nd on run-in: no imp on wnr* **5/1**2		124
3P4-	3	shd	**Dr Livingstone (IRE)**33 4779 5-11-9 125 ... SamTwiston-Davies(3) (Charles Egerton) *hld up: pushed along after 6th: hdwy 3 out: chsd ldrs 2 out: styd on run-in to chal for 2nd: no imp on wnr* **15/2**		127
-112	4	16	**Rubipresent (IRE)**39 1623 6-11-6 124 ... JamesHalliday(5) (Malcolm Jefferson) *in tch: rdn and outpcd appr 3 out: no imp whn nt fluent last* **12/1**		112
3	5	1	**Kauto Relko (FR)**12 1956 6-11-12 125 ... HarrySkelton (Rachel Hobbs) *hld up: hdwy to chse ldrs after 6th: pushed along appr 2 out: wknd bef last* **8/1**		112
-250	6	1 ½	**Master Fong (IRE)**12 1956 4-11-2 115 ... AdrianLane (Donald McCain) *midfield: pushed along appr 5th: wknd bef 3 out* **16/1**		100
2321	7	1 ½	**Grand Diamond (IRE)**19 1870 6-10-13 112 ... GrahamLee (Jim Goldie) *hld up: rdn appr 3 out: nvr on terms* **4/1**1		96
2346	8	1 ¾	**Baaher (USA)**12 1957 6-10-10 116 ... PaulNorton(7) (Jim Goldie) *hld up: j. slowly 3rd: pushed along and outpcd whn nt fluent 3 out: nvr on terms* **20/1**		98
3/6-	9	6	**Laredo Sound (IRE)**544 226 8-11-7 120 ... NoelFehily (Alex Hales) *chsd ldrs: wnt 2nd after 6th: effrt whn hung lft and mstke 3 out: wknd 2 out* **11/2**3		97
030-	P		**Singapore Reef (FR)**193 3 4-10-13 112 ... DarylJacob (Nick Williams) *chsd wnr tl after 6th: j. slowly 3 out: wknd qckly: bhd whn p.u bef 3 out* **11/1**		—

3m 53.2s (-11.00)
WFA 4 from 5yo+ 7lb **10** Ran SP% **114.1**
toteswingers:1&2:£7.60, 1&3:£5.80, 2&3:£5.70 CSF £41.56 CT £270.16 TOTE £7.40: £3.50, £1.10, £3.40; EX 47.70.

Owner Mrs Karen Bowen **Bred** Glending Bloodstock **Trained** Little Newcastle, Pembrokes

FOCUS
With the top weight being rated 10lb below the race ceiling this wasn't a strong race for the class, but the form is still fair. There was a sound enough gallop on and the first three came clear. The winner produced a step up.

NOTEBOOK
Rio Gael(IRE) ran out a gutsy winner from the front on this return to hurdling and posted a career-best effort. He ran close to his mark over 1m6f on the level last time out and his stamina was a big asset here. There was a lot to like about his attitude when not fluent three out and this proves he doesn't have to have genuinely quick ground to shine. Still only a 4-y-o, he is just the sort his trainer tends to do well with and further improvement cannot not ruled out, especially as he should get further. It remains to be seen whether connections now put him away for a spring campaign. (op 8-1)

Gifted Leader(USA), brought down at Aintree on his return 12 days earlier, didn't settle that well and that wouldn't have helped him when pressing the winner from three out. This was still an effort he should build on, though, and he rates a fair enough benchmark. (op 6-1 tchd 9-2)

Dr Livingstone(IRE) shaped a lot better again on the level at Newmarket last month and was making his handicap debut back over hurdles. He got going late in the day, looks in need of a stiffer test now in this sphere and should enjoy returning to softer ground. (op 9-1)

Rubipresent(IRE) was a progressive novice hurdler during the summer. He lacked the speed to land a serious blow and probably wants further in this sort of company, but does look high enough in the weights. (op 11-1 tchd 14-1)

Kauto Relko(FR) travelled like a player into the home bend, but was another that ran somewhat freely and failed to build on his encouraging third at Aintree 12 days earlier. Perhaps the run came soon enough for him. (op 7-1)

Grand Diamond(IRE) was up 7lb for winning at Kelso 19 days earlier, but proved laboured from off the pace and probably needs quicker ground. He was later reported to have never been travelling. Official explanation: jockey said gelding never travelled (op 5-1 tchd 11-2)

2165 MICHAEL "OSCAR" WILD RETIREMENT NOVICES' CHASE (15 fncs) 2m 4f

3:15 (3:15) (Class 4) 4-Y-0+ **£3,998** (£1,241; £668)

Form				RPR
20-5	1		**Born Again (IRE)**[27] 1759 5-10-13 0 .... RichieMcLernon(3) (Jonjo O'Neill) *chsd ldr tl after 11th: lft in 2nd pl 4 out: chalng fr 2 out: upsides after last: led and pushed out towards fin* **10/3**[3]	129+
4-14	2	½	**Alderley Rover (IRE)**[27] 1759 6-11-2 0 .... NoelFehily (Donald McCain) *hld up: effrt to go cl 2nd after 11th: blnd and lost 2nd 4 out: lost grnd on front 2: rallied and lugged lft between last 2: lft in ld jst after last: pressed strly after: hdd and no ex towards fin* **6/4**[1]	129+
4/4-	3	17	**Our Bob (IRE)**[336] 2677 8-11-2 0 .... RhysFlint (Philip Hobbs) *led: rdn appr 2 out: strly pressed whn blnd last: sn hdd: wknd qckly* **5/2**[2]	116
116/	F		**Gray Mountain (USA)**[740] 1837 7-11-2 0 .... PeterBuchanan (Lucinda Russell) *j.rt several times: hld up: losing grnd on ldrs whn fell 8th* **6/1**	—

5m 12.9s (2.90) **Going Correction** +0.25s/f (Yiel) **4** Ran SP% **105.9**
Speed ratings (Par 105): **104,103,97,—**
CSF £8.59 TOTE £3.80; EX 9.80.

Owner John P McManus **Bred** S And S Hubbard Rodwell **Trained** Cheltenham, Gloucs

FOCUS
This was a competitive little novice chase. The race was run at a fair gallop and there were changing fortunes in the home straight. The first two are rated in line with their hurdles form.

NOTEBOOK
Born Again(IRE), who does like soft ground, just did enough to get off the mark at the second attempt over fences and this was another advertisement of his jockey Richie McClernon's skills in the saddle. He went nicely through the race and looked by far the most likely winner when moving up to the tiring Our Bob after three out. He didn't find any extra when asked to get on top, though, and it looked a case of him tiring. However, once the runner-up headed him on the run-in he picked up again and was cajoled to lead near the line under hands-and-heels riding. He evidently has some temperament issues, but rates value for further than the bare margin and there is every chance he will make up into a better chaser this season as he has relatively few miles on the clock. (op 4-1 tchd 3-1)

Alderley Rover(IRE) jumped neatly on his chasing debut when one place ahead of the winner at Carlisle last month and was well backed to open his account. He made mistakes here, though, and looked sure to finish third when he clouted the fourth-last. However, as the pair in front of him began to wane, he rallied for pressure and was only just held in the end. He must brush up his jumping again, but he too should rate higher as a chaser and should be most effective over a longer trip in this sphere. (op 7-4)

Our Bob(IRE), thought good enough to run in Graded company as a novice hurdler when with Willie Mullins, was having his first outing since tiring out of things on his chasing debut for this yard last year. He posted a similar display here, jumping enthusiastically out in front before fading. It is hoped he comes out of this soundly as he surely still has a future if that's the case. (op 2-1)

Gray Mountain(USA) was making his first appearance on the track since 2008, a season in which his only defeat in four outings as a novice hurdler came in Graded company on his final outing. He wasn't clever at the first and hadn't really convinced prior to departing in the back straight. He was quick to his feet, though, and should learn from this. (tchd 11-2 and 13-2 in places)

2166 BET365 "FIXED BRUSH" NOVICES' HURDLE (10 hdls) 2m 4f

3:50 (3:50) (Class 4) 4-7-Y-0 **£3,252** (£955; £477; £238)

Form				RPR
01	1		**Lively Baron (IRE)**[27] 1764 5-10-12 0 .... JasonMaguire (Donald McCain) *led: hdd 3rd: remained prom: regained ld appr 3 out: pressed run-in: styd on and plld out more towards fin* **2/7**[1]	111+
4-	2	¾	**Palace Jester**[196] 5344 5-10-9 0 .... RichieMcLernon(3) (Jonjo O'Neill) *trckd ldrs: smoothly wnt 2nd 3 out: chalng run-in: nt qckn towards fin* **8/1**[2]	108+
/5-P	3	13	**The Portonion (IRE)**[27] 1758 6-10-12 0 .... DougieCostello (Malcolm Jefferson) *hld up in rr: hdwy after 7th: nt fluent 3 out: chsd ldrs 2 out: pushed along appr last: lost tch w front pair run-in* **14/1**[3]	96
04-0	4	6	**Original Prankster (IRE)**[179] 238 5-10-9 0 .... SamTwiston-Davies(3) (Nigel Twiston-Davies) *hld up in tch: effrt to chsd ldrs 2 out: wknd last* **16/1**	89
05-0	5	7	**Robertewenutter**[8] 2038 6-10-12 0 .... HenryOliver (Sue Smith) *racd keenly: chsd ldr: led 3rd: hdd appr 3 out: wknd 2 out* **20/1**	82
060-	6	20	**Rester Vrai (FR)**[242] 4461 5-10-5 0 .... JoeCornwall(7) (John Cornwall) *in tch: pushed along and wknd appr 3 out* **50/1**	62
	7	11	**Jam Tomorrow (FR)** 5-10-12 0 .... NoelFehily (Ian Williams) *hld up: niggled along after 7th: nvr on terms* **8/1**[2]	51
0/	8	17	**Dr Light (IRE)**[112] 4256 6-10-12 0 .... JodieMogford (Anna Bramall) *racd keenly: prom 2nd: blnd 6th: sn wknd: t.o* **80/1**	34

4m 53.5s (-20.00) **8** Ran SP% **120.5**
toteswingers:1&2:£1.40, 2&3:£6.90, 1&3:£3.60 CSF £3.99 TOTE £1.40: £1.02, £2.30, £3.30; EX 4.30.

Owner Trevor Hemmings **Bred** Michael Gowen **Trained** Cholmondeley, Cheshire

FOCUS
This was run at a very steady pace. The first two can rate higher.

NOTEBOOK
Lively Baron(IRE) looked a horse of real potential when hacking up in a Carlisle bumper last month on his second start and unsurprisingly proved all the rage for this hurdling debut over the longer trip. He duly followed up, but was made to pull out all the stops to hold off the runner-up, who also runs in the same ownership. That was very likely down to this being run at a dawdling gallop, however, as the race developed into something of a sprint nearing the third-last, which he over jumped. He wasn't fluent at the last and appeared in trouble, but he displayed a very willing attitude under pressure and was always just holding his rival near the finish. These brush hurdles may not have been all that much to his liking and there is a strong chance time will tell he beat a useful rival here, so his next outing ought to reveal some more regarding his real potential. (op 2-5 tchd 40-85 in a place and 4-9 in places)

Palace Jester ◆ had undergone a wind operation since finishing fourth on quick ground in a bumper at Uttoxeter in April. He travelled with real purpose through the race and loomed up strongly nearing the last flight. He was just outpaced near the finish, but this rates a very promising introduction to hurdling and he looks a sure-fire winner in the coming weeks. (op 13-2)

The Portonion(IRE), who has evidently had his problems, made up his ground turning for home and had his chance. This was a lot more encouraging again and he should find his feet when going handicapping, but his optimum trip remains unknown. (op 12-1)

Original Prankster(IRE) showed up more promisingly on this switch to hurdling, but looks much more of one for handicaps in due course. (op 14-1)

2167 HAYDOCK MARES' STANDARD OPEN NATIONAL HUNT FLAT RACE 2m

4:20 (4:20) (Class 6) 4-6-Y-0 **£1,301** (£382; £191; £95)

Form				RPR
	1		**Elegant Touch (IRE)**[236] 4-10-12 0 .... NoelFehily (Don Cantillon) *midfield: hdwy to trck ldrs 6f out: led over 1f out: r.o wl to draw clr fnl 100yds* **8/1**	101+
3-	2	5	**Aneyeforaneye (IRE)**[179] 245 4-10-12 0 .... GrahamLee (Malcolm Jefferson) *led: rdn and hdd over 1f out: no ex fnl 75yds* **9/2**[3]	96
2	3	1½	**Lady Everywhere**[15] 1920 5-10-12 0 .... DarylJacob (Nick Williams) *chsd ldr tl rdn 2f out: nt qckn over 1f out: styd on same pce ins fnl f* **14/1**	95
	4	½	**Lady Hight (FR)** 4-10-12 0 .... FelixDeGiles (Nicky Henderson) *in tch: rdn over 3f out: outpcd 2f out: styd on ins fnl f: one pce fnl strides* **11/4**[1]	94
	5	5	**Cue To Cue** 4-10-12 0 .... JamesReveley (Keith Reveley) *trckd ldrs tl rdn and wknd over 1f out* **3/1**[2]	91+
0-	6	10	**Lady Ida**[196] 5344 5-10-12 0 .... AlanO'Keeffe (Jennie Candlish) *hld up in rr: rdn over 2f out: kpt on fnl f: nvr able to chal* **66/1**	81
	7	3½	**Heather Glen (IRE)** 4-10-12 0 .... TjadeCollier (Sue Smith) *trckd ldrs tl rdn and wknd 4f out* **25/1**	78
	8	hd	**Congella** 5-10-12 0 .... RobertWalford (Tim Walford) *hld up: niggled along 5f out: wl outpcd 3f out: nvr a threat* **50/1**	77
6	9	1½	**Erin Vogue**[26] 1771 4-10-12 0 .... BrianHarding (Nicky Richards) *midfield: hdwy to trck ldrs 6f out: rdn and wknd 3f out* **33/1**	76
00	10	14	**Overpriced**[14] 1934 4-10-5 0 .... (t) MissAngelaBarnes(7) (Maurice Barnes) *hld up: outpcd 3f out: nvr a threat* **125/1**	63
4-	11	¾	**Landenstown Rose (IRE)**[239] 4515 4-10-12 0 .... JasonMaguire (Donald McCain) *in tch: rdn and wknd 3f out* **16/1**	63
	12	shd	**Luccombe Chine** 5-10-12 0 .... DougieCostello (John Quinn) *midfield: pushed along and lost pl 6f out: no imp after* **25/1**	63
	13	29	**Royal Daffodil** 4-10-12 0 .... AdrianLane (Donald McCain) *hld up: rdn along 5f out: nvr on terms* **33/1**	37
	14	13	**Tobayornottobay** 4-10-12 0 .... (b[1]) BrianHughes (Bruce Hellier) *hld up: hdwy into midfield 7f out: rdn and wknd 4f out* **150/1**	25
	15	140	**Lemon Queen (IRE)** 4-10-5 0 .... StevenGagan(7) (Elliott Cooper) *hld up: struggling 6th: lost tch over 4f out: t.o* **14/1**	—

3m 57.8s (-0.80) **Going Correction** +0.25s/f (Yiel) **15** Ran SP% **118.7**
Speed ratings: **100,97,96,96,94 89,87,87,86,79 79,78,64,57,—**
toteswingers:1&2:£6.80, 1&3:£10.00, 2&3:£4.40. totesuper7: Win: Not won. Place: 431.50. CSF £40.63 TOTE £11.00: £2.80, £1.90, £3.40; EX 51.00.

Owner Don Cantillon **Bred** D E Cantillon **Trained** Newmarket, Suffolk

FOCUS
This mares' bumper wasn't easy to assess beforehand, but the first five came well clear when the race got serious at the top of the home straight and the form looks sound rated around the placed horses. The winner should go on to rate higher.

NOTEBOOK
Elegant Touch(IRE) ◆ hails from a stable that really know the time of day in this division and she ran out a taking debut winner. She fell two out when in with every chance in her sole outing between the flags in March, but went off at odds-on that day and didn't go unbacked here. She was settled in midfield towards the outside to find the better ground and also kept wide for her challenge from 3f out. She found plenty after travelling well into the race and this half-sister to her yard's former fair hurdler/chaser Be Fair looks an above-average prospect for novice hurdling, where a longer trip ought to suit ideally. (tchd 9-1 in a place)

Aneyeforaneye(IRE) had finished placed on her two previous outings in fair company and was making her debut for new connections. She was never far away and had every chance, so rates a decent benchmark. There should be one of these for her before she goes hurdling and a sound surface is probably what she wants. (op 5-1 tchd 11-2 in a place)

Lady Everywhere finished second at Fontwell on debut and this represents an improved effort over the longer trip. She is another that ought to enjoy an even stiffer test when switching to hurdles. (tchd 12-1)

Lady Hight(FR) ◆, representing a very powerful yard in this division, is related to two winners on the level at up to 1m4f, one of whom scored over hurdles. She got tapped for toe when it mattered in the home straight and looks to need a stiffer test. She should come on nicely for the run and prove hard to beat next time out. (op 3-1 tchd 5-2)

Cue To Cue is from a family her stable knows all about and there was money for her She had her chance, but couldn't stay with the first four late on and she too looks to need more of a test already. There should be a deal of improvement in her. (op 4-1)

T/Plt: £68.50 to a £1 stake. Pool:£46,273.53 - 492.56 winning tickets T/Qpdt: £24.10 to a £1 stake. Pool:£3,438.29 - 105.15 winning tickets DO

1990 TOWCESTER (R-H)

Thursday, November 4

OFFICIAL GOING: Good to soft (good in places up the hill; 7.7)
Wind: Very strong ahead Weather: Light cloud

2168 LADBROKES.COM MARES' "NATIONAL HUNT" NOVICES' HURDLE (8 hdls) 2m

1:10 (1:12) (Class 4) 4-Y-0+ **£2,927** (£859; £429; £214)

Form				RPR
/P2-	1		**Line Freedom (FR)**[203] 5199 5-10-10 0 .... AndrewTinkler (Nicky Henderson) *trckd ldrs: pushed along after 4 out: chal next: rdn again to chal last: styd on to ld fnl 20yds* **11/2**[3]	106+
320-	2	1¾	**Risaala**[209] 5114 4-10-3 0 .... MissGAndrews(7) (Pam Sly) *trckd ldrs: led after 3 out: gng wl whn blnd 2 out: jnd next: kpt on tl hdd and no ex fnl 20yds* **13/2**	106+
	3	6	**Bunglasha Lady (IRE)**[193] 5-10-10 0 .... WayneHutchinson (Warren Greatrex) *sn chsng ldrs: rdn to chal 3 out: no imp 2 out and sn one pce* **22/1**	99
0-60	4	¾	**Definitley Lovely**[26] 1771 5-10-10 0 .... PaddyBrennan (Nigel Twiston-Davies) *led tl hdd after 3 out: outpcd fr 2 out* **16/1**	98
2	5	2¾	**Fiddledee (IRE)**[26] 1771 5-10-10 0 .... APMcCoy (Jonjo O'Neill) *t.k.h: chsd ldrs: rdn and hit 3 out: wknd fr 2 out* **5/2**[1]	96
-40F	6	½	**My Viking Bay (IRE)**[25] 1793 6-10-3 0 .... CharlieWallis(7) (John O'Shea) *in rr: j. slowly 2nd: in rr stl wl bhd 3 out: kpt on fr next and styng on whn blnd last: one pce* **100/1**	96

0/4- **7** *15* **Peveril Pandora**[224] 4840 7-10-10 0............................(t) MarkBradburne 81
(Jimmy Fox) *in rr tl mod prog fr 3 out* **50/1**

3- **8** *1 1/4* **Karinga Dream**[222] 4899 4-10-10 0.................................. AidanColeman 80
(Venetia Williams) *in rr: sme hdwy 4 out: no imp on ldrs fr next* **16/1**

340- **9** *1 3/4* **Francesa**[203] 5200 5-10-3 0.. JakeGreenall(7) 78
(Henry Daly) *chsd ldrs tl blnd 4 out and sn wknd* **40/1**

1 **10** *20* **Ixora (IRE)**[25] 1793 4-10-11 114.. DavidBass(5) 66
(Jamie Snowden) *chsd ldrs to 4 out* **15/2**

6 **11** *20* **Brunette'Sonly (IRE)**[11] 1993 5-10-10 0...................... AndrewThornton 42
(Seamus Mullins) *chsd ldrs to 4 out* **125/1**

030 **12** *9* **Restless Harriet**[41] 1607 4-10-10 0..................................... CharliePoste 34
(Robin Dickin) *j. slowly 3rd: in tch and hit 4th: sn wknd* **150/1**

50- **13** *2* **Atared**[202] 5218 4-10-10 0... WarrenMarston 33
(Pam Sly) *a bhd: blnd last* **100/1**

02-0 **14** *3 3/4* **Dark Sensation**[173] 332 5-10-10 0...................................... SeanQuinlan 29
(Stuart Kittow) *t.k.h: chsd ldrs tl wknd 4 out* **50/1**

1- **F** **Instabella**[203] 5200 4-10-10 0.. RichardJohnson —
(Philip Hobbs) *t.k.h: in rr: blnd 4th: stl in rr whn fell 3 out* **4/1**[2]

4m 1.66s (-6.24) **Going Correction** 0.0s/f (Good) **15** Ran SP% **115.0**
Speed ratings (Par 105): **115,114,111,110,109 109,101,101,100,90 80,75,74,72,—**
toteswingers:1&2:£10.30, 1&3:£62.60, 2&3:£5.80 CSF £37.95 TOTE £6.00: £2.60, £2.80, £9.40; EX 51.60.

Owner Mr & Mrs R Kelvin Hughes **Bred** Mme Georges Vuillard **Trained** Upper Lambourn, Berks

FOCUS
The front two ended up a little way clear in what was a fair mares' hurdle. The race has been given a compromise sort of rating and should throw up a few winners.

NOTEBOOK
Line Freedom(FR), useful in bumpers, looked a likely type to do well hurdling and she stayed on best on the climb to the line. She is from a yard that traditionally does well with this type and can probably defy the penalty at some stage. (op 4-1)

Risaala ◆, runner-up in a Listed bumper at Sandown last season, having made a winning debut in the bumper on this card a year ago, wasn't helped by a mistake at the second-last, when travelling strongly, and the winner eventually outstayed her. This was still a promising start and she should have no trouble going one better. (op 8-1)

Bunglasha Lady(IRE) made a very encouraging debut back in third and will prove suited by a stiffer test. She's got a future and can win one of these. (tchd 20-1)

Definitley Lovely was unable to race on with the front pair in the end, but this was a promising first effort and she too will be suited by further.

Fiddlededee(IRE), runner-up at Bangor on her debut for the yard (beaten favourite), again failed to live up to expectations switched to hurdles, racing keenly and dropping out late on. She's presumably better than this, but is left with a bit to prove. (tchd 11-4)

My Viking Bay(IRE) caught the eye staying on late and this will have helped to restore some confidence.

Ixora(IRE), the only previous hurdles winner, proved very disappointing and it can't solely be put down to the penalty. Official explanation: jockey said filly lost an off-fore shoe (op 17-2)

Atared Official explanation: jockey said filly lost an off-fore shoe

Instabella, ready winner of a Cheltenham bumper in April, was in the rear throughout and stood no chance when taking a heavy fall at the third from home. (op 7-2)

2169 LADBROKES SHOP MANAGERS CLUB (S) HURDLE (8 hdls) 2m

1:45 (1:45) (Class 5) 4-Y-0+ **£1,626** (£477; £238; £119)

Form RPR

P144 **1** **Liberty Seeker (FR)**[14] 1938 11-10-11 108...................... MattCrawley(7) 109+
(John Harris) *in rr tl stdy hdwy 4 out: led after 3 out: styd on run-in: all out* **3/1**[1]

5F-0 **2** *4* **Vivarini**[32] 1692 6-11-3 110... MrJonathanBailey(7) 114+
(Caroline Bailey) *trckd ldrs: wnt lft and led 3 out: hdd sn after: rallied to chal 2 out: u.p and fading whn blnd last: hung lft and sn btn* **9/1**

053 **3** *17* **Dark Energy**[7] 2054 6-11-8 110.. PaddyBrennan 93
(Michael Scudamore) *in rr: styd on fr 3 out to take mod 3rd appr last* **4/1**[2]

3334 **4** *2 3/4* **Frosty's Gift**[11] 1997 6-9-12 72..(p) MrJBanks(7) 74
(Jimmy Fox) *in rr: j. slowly 3rd: hdwy to cl on ldrs appr 3 out: wknd wl bef next and btn whn j. slowly: lost 3rd appr last* **16/1**

6-51 **5** *3 1/4* **Holiday Cocktail**[34] 1660 8-11-4 109...................................(p) APMcCoy 84
(John Quinn) *in rr but in tch whn hmpd 2nd: in tch after 3rd: rdn after 4 out: wknd next* **4/1**[2]

113- **6** *10* **Perfect Reward**[195] 5367 6-11-8 113.................................. JamieMoore 81
(Gary Moore) *led tl hdd 3 out: wknd qckly* **8/1**

-0P0 **7** *18* **Out To Impress (IRE)**[17] 1900 5-10-12 0...................(t) AndrewThornton 53
(Murty McGrath) *bhd fr 3rd: no ch whn blnd 2 out* **100/1**

UP50 **P** **Simiola**[106] 1064 11-9-12 53.. MissCBoxall(7) —
(Simon Lewis) *chsd ldrs tl j. slowly 4 out and sn wknd: t.o: p.u 2 out* **200/1**

13P/ **P** **Wyeth**[615] 4185 6-10-5 0.. JoshuaMoore(7) —
(Gary Moore) *j. slowly 1st: chsd ldrs: hmpd 2nd: wknd 4 out: t.o whn p.u after next* **5/1**[3]

006- **F** **Arthurian (IRE)**[367] 2039 5-10-12 0...............................(tp) CharliePoste —
(Anthony Middleton) *in tch whn fell 2nd* **33/1**

4m 5.44s (-2.46) **Going Correction** 0.0s/f (Good) **10** Ran SP% **113.1**
Speed ratings (Par 103): **106,104,95,94,92 87,78,—,—,—**
toteswingers:1&2:£22.30, 1&3:£5.70, 2&3:£12.10 CSF £29.86 TOTE £2.80: £1.10, £3.40, £2.50; EX 41.70.There was no bid for the winner. Vivarini was claimed by J. G. M. O'Shea for £6,000.

Owner Mrs A E Harris **Bred** Aylesfield Farms Stud Ltd **Trained** Eastwell, Leics

FOCUS
The front pair were clear and are decent in this grade. They are rated to their marks but the third was again well below his best.

NOTEBOOK
Liberty Seeker(FR) came through the field to lead before the straight and stayed on well under pressure. This is his level these days, and he can probably win again. (op 7-2 tchd 4-1)

Vivarini, who got upset and failed to run his race latest, looked a big player dropping in grade and he made the winner work for it, but he started to hang left and could make no further impression from the last. (op 12-1)

Dark Energy stayed on all too late and remains without a win for a year. Official explanation: vet said gelding lost a shoe (op 9-2)

Frosty's Gift didn't get home having briefly made a promising move.

Holiday Cocktail was beaten very quickly under McCoy, but did get hampered early. (op 7-2 tchd 9-2)

Simiola Official explanation: vet said mare returned lame off-fore (tchd 9-2)

Wyeth, returning from a 615-day absence, stopped quickly, but was another who got hampered. (tchd 9-2)

2170 ICANCOPY.COM H'CAP CHASE (16 fncs) 2m 6f

2:20 (2:20) (Class 4) (0-100,99) 4-Y-0+ **£3,252** (£955; £477; £238)

Form RPR

5P-2 **1** **Aztec Treasure (NZ)**[32] 1708 6-11-5 92................................. APMcCoy 111+
(Jonjo O'Neill) *in tch: j. slowly 3rd: stdy hdwy to trck ldrs 4 out: led 2 out: drvn out run-in* **9/2**[1]

033 **2** *3* **Romney Marsh**[15] 1918 9-10-2 75................................. MattieBatchelor 88
(Roger Curtis) *blnd 1st: in tch fr 6th: chsd ldrs 4 out: rdn after next: chsd wnr after 2 out and rallied u.p last but a readily hld* **6/1**[2]

145- **3** *19* **Ballymorn (IRE)**[246] 4387 6-10-13 86................................. HaddenFrost 82
(Henrietta Knight) *slt ld but hrd pressed tl narrowly hdd 10th: styd upsides and led again 4 out: hdd 2 out: wknd rapidly* **9/1**

35-P **4** *2 1/2* **Me Julie**[29] 1730 7-11-1 93... JimmyDerham(5) 88
(Arthur Whiting) *chsd ldrs: bmpd 2nd: chal 9th: slt ld next: hdd 4 out: wknd after 3 out* **8/1**

3F04 **5** *4* **Nawow**[21] 1841 10-11-9 99..(tp) PeterToole(3) 89
(Matt Hazell) *in rr: tl mod hdwy fr 3 out* **25/1**

443- **6** *3/4* **Sir Peter (IRE)**[224] 4842 8-11-8 95................................ RichardJohnson 84
(Henry Daly) *rdn 6th: nvr travelling and a in rr* **9/2**[1]

P1-P **7** *5* **Wide Receiver (IRE)**[12] 1969 7-10-10 83.................(p) JimmyMcCarthy 68
(Charlie Morlock) *disp ld: hit 11th: wknd 3 out* **9/1**

400P **P** **Arceye**[12] 1969 13-10-4 77..(p) RodiGreene —
(William Davies) *rdn after 4th: sn bhd and nvr really travelling: t.o whn p.u bef 3 out* **40/1**

24-6 **P** **Mr Ironman**[11] 1991 9-10-0 73 oh2.................................. TomMessenger —
(Alan Jones) *in tch: j. slowly 9th: hdwy to chse ldrs 10th: wknd and blnd 3 out: t.o whn p.u after 2 out* **7/1**[3]

PP0 **P** **The Walnut Tree (IRE)**[11] 1991 9-10-1 73 oh7 ow1.........(p) ColinBolger —
(Simon Lewis) *bmpd 2nd: chsd ldrs: chal 7th: j. slowly and rdn 9th: wknd after 4 out: t.o whn p.u bef 2 out* **50/1**

604/ **P** **Walk Tall (IRE)**[637] 3755 7-11-10 97................................ AidanColeman —
(Venetia Williams) *chsd ldrs fr 6th: wknd qckly 3 out: t.o whn p.u bef next* **10/1**

P-50 **P** **Foxesbow (IRE)**[27] 1763 6-11-10 97............................ DominicElsworth —
(Jonjo O'Neill) *blnd 8th and 10th: a in rr: t.o whn p.u bef 3 out* **20/1**

5m 50.88s (-2.12) **Going Correction** +0.05s/f (Yiel) **12** Ran SP% **116.4**
Speed ratings (Par 105): **105,103,97,96,94 94,92,—,—,— —,—**
toteswingers:1&2:£4.50, 1&3:£5.60, 2&3:£8.10 CSF £30.35 CT £234.00 TOTE £4.80: £1.40, £1.90, £3.70; EX 25.40.

Owner John P McManus **Bred** W L Spring **Trained** Cheltenham, Gloucs

FOCUS
This was just a modest handicap chase. The easy winner is on the upgrade and the second is well handicapped.

NOTEBOOK
Aztec Treasure(NZ), up 2lb having finished second at Uttoxeter on his chase debut, put in a competent round of jumping and stayed on well having hit the front two out. Only six, he hasn't had much racing and can continue to climb the ladder further. (tchd 5-1)

Romney Marsh, who hadn't run over fences since refusing in the summer of 2008, has generally been running well over hurdles and is rated 17lb lower in this sphere, so it was no surprise to see her put in a good show. She was clear of the third and can go one better at some stage. (tchd 9-2)

Ballymorn(IRE), 4lb higher than when winning at the course in January, lost his form afterwards and, although well held on this return, he very much ran like a horse in need of the run, getting very tired late on.

Me Julie, pulled up over hurdles on her return, ran better back over fences and is only 3lb higher than when last winning.

Sir Peter(IRE) didn't look fully tuned up, racing lazily and never threatening to get involved. He should be sharper next time. (op 5-1 tchd 11-2)

Walk Tall(IRE), off for 637 days, is bred to do better chasing and should improve markedly for this outing, as he stopped sharply late on when looking tired.

2171 AGETUR UK 25TH ANNIVERSARY H'CAP HURDLE (11 hdls) 2m 5f

2:55 (2:56) (Class 3) (0-125,120) 4-Y-0+ **£4,878** (£1,432; £716; £357)

Form RPR

03-2 **1** **Mister Hyde (IRE)**[7] 2056 5-11-1 109................................... APMcCoy 124+
(Jonjo O'Neill) *hld up in rr: hit 4th: stdy hdwy 7th: led and jnd appr 2 out: drvn and styd on strly run-in: readily* **11/8**[1]

-40P **2** *1 1/2* **Earcomesthedream (IRE)**[154] 601 7-10-1 95.................(b) TomSiddall 102
(Peter Pritchard) *mid-div: hdwy to trck ldrs 7th: styd on to chal 2 out: stl rt there u.p last: kpt on but readily outpcd by wnr* **16/1**

00-0 **3** *23* **Global Flyer**[17] 1904 6-11-4 115..................................... AdamPogson(3) 103
(Caroline Bailey) *chsd ldrs: drvn to chal 3 out: led sn after: hdd appr 2 out: sn wknd* **28/1**

00/3 **4** *12* **Bellflower Boy (IRE)**[32] 1708 7-10-11 105................(p) RichardJohnson 81
(Dr Richard Newland) *trckd ldr: led appr 6th: jnd 3 out: sn hdd & wknd* **16/1**

5533 **5** *1 3/4* **Manadam (FR)**[23] 1814 7-9-11 98 ow1........................... MattGriffiths(7) 72
(Anthony Middleton) *hit 4th and bhd: sme hdwy 7th: wknd after 4 out* **12/1**

51P/ **6** *1 3/4* **Sexy Rexy (IRE)**[698] 2625 9-10-12 106............................ PaddyBrennan 78
(Nigel Twiston-Davies) *hit 1st: j. slowly 2nd: bhd most of way* **11/2**[2]

2P4- **7** *2 1/2* **Dashing George (IRE)**[187] 104 8-11-11 119..................(p) JamieMoore 89
(Dr Richard Newland) *in rr: hdwy 7th: chsd ldrs fr 4 out tl wknd rapidly fr 3 out* **16/1**

14P- **8** *6* **Merry Music (IRE)**[195] 5365 11-10-3 97........................ GerardTumelty 62
(Julian Smith) *chsd ldrs to 4 out* **100/1**

105- **9** *16* **Dan Buoy (FR)**[17] 4426 7-11-2 110..................................(b) PaddyAspell 60
(Richard Guest) *nvr really travelling: a in rr* **10/1**

-112 **10** *12* **American World (FR)**[100] 1108 6-11-8 116................... JimmyMcCarthy 56
(Brendan Powell) *in rr: sme hdwy 7th: wknd 4 out: wl bhd whn blnd last* **20/1**

F2P- **P** **Arctic Echo**[229] 4738 11-11-7 115.................................... LiamTreadwell —
(Rob Summers) *in rr: sme hdwy 7th: in tch 4 out: sn wknd: t.o whn p.u bef 2 out* **66/1**

515- **P** **Chaim (IRE)**[210] 5107 8-11-7 115.................................... LeightonAspell —
(Lucy Wadham) *sn bhd: t.o whn p.u bef 4 out* **8/1**[3]

621- **P** **Flanagan (IRE)**[218] 4963 6-11-9 117.............................. AidanColeman —
(Venetia Williams) *chsd ldrs tl wknd 7th: t.o whn p.u after 3 out* **16/1**

F10- **P** **Evella (IRE)**[222] 4889 6-11-9 120................................... AlexMerriam(3) —
(Neil King) *led tl hdd appr 6th: sn wknd: t.o whn p.u bef 4 out* **16/1**

5- **P** **True Grit (NZ)**[267] 3984 6-11-9 117............................... CampbellGillies —
(Lucinda Russell) *blnd 6th: a in rr: t.o whn p.u bef 4 out* **33/1**

5m 23.44s (-3.76) **Going Correction** 0.0s/f (Good) **15** Ran SP% **128.4**
Speed ratings (Par 107): **107,106,97,93,92 91,90,88,82,77 —,—,—,—,—**
toteswingers:1&2:£9.40, 1&3:£27.70, 2&3:£82.50 CSF £26.10 CT £492.01 TOTE £2.80: £1.40, £5.90, £11.70; EX 49.40.

Owner Bensaranat Club & Ocean Trailers Ltd **Bred** Mrs Catherine Kenneally **Trained** Cheltenham, Gloucs

FOCUS
The front pair drew some 23l clear in this handicap hurdle. A big step foward from the winner over this longer trip with the second rated to form.

NOTEBOOK
Mister Hyde(IRE) showed much-improved form when second to a fair type at Stratford last week, but his new mark hadn't kicked in yet, so he was officially 10lb well in for this handicap debut. Strong at the head of the market, he was given a waiting ride by McCoy, who always looked confident of victory, and the pair did what was required without wanting to win by too far. There should be more to come and, although things will be tougher next time, it would be a surprise were he not to go in again. (op 13-8)
Earcomesthedream(IRE), back down to a decent mark, had clearly been refreshed by a break and he was the only one capable of giving the winner a race, but couldn't quite match him on the run-in. (op 25-1)
Global Flyer improved on his reappearance effort and will soon be on a winnable mark again. (op 33-1)
Bellflower Boy(IRE), well weighted on his old Irish form, had the cheekpieces back on and he ran only a little better, although still ended up well beaten. (op 18-1)
Sexy Rexy(IRE) looked rusty on this return from a 698-day absence and never threatened to challenge. Official explanation: jockey said gelding hung (op 15-2 tchd 8-1)
Chaim(IRE) Official explanation: jockey said gelding made a noise

2172 AGETUR UK 25TH ANNIVERSARY NOVICES' H'CAP CHASE (14 fncs) 2m 3f 110y
3:30 (3:30) (Class 4) (0-100,97) 4-Y-0+ **£3,252** (£955; £477; £238)

Form				RPR
P6F-	1		**Bobby Bullock (IRE)**[192] 24 8-10-11 **82**........ PaddyBrennan (Nigel Twiston-Davies) *mde all: c clr fr 3 out: eased run-in: unchal* **5/2**[1]	107+
5603	2	*17*	**Azulada Bay (IRE)**[11] 1991 6-11-9 **97**........(t) PeterToole(3) (Mark Rimell) *in tch: hdwy to take 3rd 7th: hit 9th: styd on u.p to take wl hld 2nd 2 out* **5/2**[1]	105
20P-	3	*16*	**Doctor Disny**[226] 4798 7-11-11 **96**........(p) SeanQuinlan (Kim Bailey) *chsd wnr: rdn 8th: no ch w wnr fr 4 out: wl hld 3rd fr 2 out* **5/1**[2]	96+
531-	4	*76*	**Sawpit Supreme**[214] 5015 8-11-12 **97**........ AidanColeman (Venetia Williams) *in rr: hdwy 5th: nvr in contention and wknd 4 out t.o* **15/2**[3]	21
S0-0	P		**Nearly A Breeze**[176] 273 10-10-2 **73**........(p) JamesDavies (Chris Down) *sn bhd: t.o whn p.u bef 3 out* **15/2**[3]	—
0	P		**Bohemian Rock**[22] 1821 6-11-10 **95**........(t) AndrewThornton (Caroline Bailey) *in rr: j. slowly 7th: hit 10th: t.o whn p.u bef 3 out* **10/1**	—
66-0	P		**Peter Sent**[158] 538 8-11-12 **97**........ SamThomas (Tom George) *chsd ldr to 4th: wknd next: t.o whn j.v.slowly and p.u 3 out* **14/1**	—

5m 19.2s (1.00) **Going Correction** +0.05s/f (Yiel) **7** Ran SP% **113.1**
Speed ratings (Par 105): **100,93,86,56,—,—,—**
toteswingers:1&2:£2.10, 1&3:£3.70, 2&3:£2.70 CSF £9.39 TOTE £2.90: £1.10, £2.70; EX 10.50.
Owner The Yes No Wait Sorries **Bred** George Durrheim & Mrs Maria Mulcahy Durr **Trained** Naunton, Gloucs

FOCUS
A moderate handicap chase. The winner improved to the level of his best hurdles form.

NOTEBOOK
Bobby Bullock(IRE), a fine, big sort who had always looked capable of better than he'd shown, was solid in the market on this first start for Nigel Twiston-Davies and turned it into a rout, leading from the off and gradually coming clear from before the third-last. Now he's got this first win out the way, from a mark of just 82, it would be no surprise to see him go on and add another, with him being lightly raced for his age. (op 10-3)
Azulada Bay(IRE), up 4lb having finished third at the course latest, probably ran his race and just bumped into a well handicapped horse. (op 11-4)
Doctor Disny, expected to fare better now switched to fences/tried in cheekpieces, dropped away in the end and didn't exactly shape with much promise. (tchd 6-1)
Sawpit Supreme, a course winner over hurdles on her final start in April, was 9lb higher switched to fences and she ran as though the run was needed. Her yard has yet to hit form. (op 7-1)

2173 E B F "JUNIOR" FILLIES' STANDARD OPEN NATIONAL HUNT FLAT RACE 1m 5f 110y
4:00 (4:00) (Class 5) 3-Y-O **£1,951** (£573; £286; £143)

Form				RPR
	1		**Doynosaur** 3-11-0 0........ BarryKeniry (Mrs K Burke) *hld up towards rr: rdn and stl plenty to do ins fnl 2f: stl only 5th ins fnl f but styng on: kpt on strly fnl 50yds to ld cl home* **13/2**[3]	85+
	2	*nk*	**Pearl Mountain (IRE)** 3-11-0 0........ GerardTumelty (Jeff Pearce) *hld up in rr: hdwy over 2f out: green but styng on appr fnl f: kpt on to ld fnl 30yds: ct cl home* **5/1**[1]	85
	3	*1 ½*	**Reveal The Light** 3-11-0 0........ PaddyAspell (Garry Woodward) *hld up in rr: hdwy 3f out to ld ins fnl 2f: edgd rt ins fnl f: hdd and no ex fnl 30yds* **12/1**	83
	4	*1*	**Ophelia's Kiss** 3-11-0 0........ JimmyMcCarthy (Brendan Powell) *hld up in rr: hdwy 3f out: rdn: green and hung rt ins fnl 2f: one pce* **13/2**[3]	81
0	5	*2 ½*	**Brambley**[7] 2052 3-10-9 0........ JimmyDerham(5) (Seamus Mullins) *chsd ldrs: rdn and outpcd 3f out: styd on again fnl f* **16/1**	78
	6	*hd*	**Tild'Or Du Granit (FR)** 3-10-7 0........ RobertKirk(7) (James Evans) *chsd ldrs: led ins fnl 3f: hdd ins fnl 2f: kpt on same pce fnl f* **16/1**	78
	7	*13*	**Bathwick Tigger (IRE)** 3-11-0 0........ PaddyBrennan (John Flint) *chsd ldrs: rdn over 2f out: no imp on ldrs: sn wknd* **5/1**[1]	61
	8	*7*	**Dusty Showbiz** 3-10-7 0........ MattGriffiths(7) (Anthony Middleton) *chsd ldrs: rdn 3f out: wknd 2f out* **18/1**	52
5	9	*15*	**Mollycarrs Dream**[16] 1913 3-10-9 0........ TomO'Connor(5) (Bill Turner) *led tl hdd ins fnl 3f: sn wknd* **12/1**	32
5	10	*6*	**Tasman Tiger**[4] 2108 3-10-7 0........ HenryBrooke(7) (Kate Walton) *chsd ldrs 9f: wknd 3f out* **6/1**[2]	25
	11	*13*	**Go Flo Go** 3-11-0 0........ ColinBolger (Mark Hoad) *a in rr* **33/1**	8
	12	*67*	**Good Golly (IRE)** 3-11-0 0........ AndrewThornton (Tony Newcombe) *in tch: hdwy to get wl in tch over 4f out: wknd qckly sn after* **10/1**	—

3m 40.57s (-0.03) **12** Ran SP% **118.7**
toteswingers:1&2:£7.50, 1&3:£23.00, 2&3:£12.70 CSF £39.04 TOTE £6.00: £2.40, £2.50, £4.70; EX 48.10.
Owner J Wilson & Mrs E Burke **Bred** J C S Wilson Bloodstock & Mrs E M Burke **Trained** Middleham Moor, North Yorks

FOCUS
Probably nothing more than a modest mares' bumper, although it should produce winners. The principals finished in a heap.

NOTEBOOK
Doynosaur, half-sister to a couple of Flat winners (dam won an Ayr Gold Cup), produced a late burst up the hill to make a successful debut. She was only fifth with 1f to run, but really rocketed once given a couple of slaps and should improve for the experience, although it is hard to defy a penalty in this sphere. (op 8-1)
Pearl Mountain(IRE), who has an interesting Flat pedigree, stayed on well for pressure to briefly hit the front inside the final 100 yards, but no sooner had she got there, the winner took over. This was a promising start. (op 6-1)
Reveal The Light ♦, whose dam was placed at up to 1m6f in France, travelled like the best horse in the race and looked all over the winner sent to the front inside the final 2f, but she started to run green and get a little tired, and the final climb to the line proved too much. She'd almost certainly have won had her rider delayed his challenge a tough longer, although she should have no trouble gaining compensation.
Ophelia's Kiss, unlike the front three, has more a jumpers pedigree, and she'll improve once given the chance to race over 2m and hurdles. (op 11-2)
Brambley tayed on again and took a step forward from her first effort (tchd 20-1)
Tasman Tiger Official explanation: jockey said filly stopped quickly
T/Jkpt: Not won. T/Plt: £554.50 to a £1 stake. Pool:£60,928.90 - 80.20 winning tickets T/Qpdt: £32.40 to a £1 stake. Pool:£6,169.16 - 140.60 winning tickets ST

2174 - 2180a (Foreign Racing) - See Raceform Interactive

2046 FONTWELL (L-H)
Friday, November 5

OFFICIAL GOING: Good to soft (6.8)
Wind: quite strong across Weather: overcast with light rain

2181 BET IN-PLAY AT LADBROKES.COM CONDITIONAL JOCKEYS' NOVICES' HURDLE (10 hdls) 2m 4f
1:20 (1:20) (Class 4) 4-Y-0+ **£2,602** (£764; £382; £190)

Form				RPR
50-3	1		**Kauto The Roc (FR)**[17] 1907 6-10-4 112........ PeterHatton(8) (Alan King) *mid-div: hdwy after 3 out: rdn whn blnd next: kpt on run-in u.p: swtchd rt fnl 100yds: led towards fin: all out* **11/4**[1]	107+
4-41	2	*nk*	**Present To You (IRE)**[16] 1914 5-10-13 124........ MattGriffiths(6) (Philip Hobbs) *in tch: smooth hdwy after 3 out: led next: idled quite bdly and sn drvn: wandered after last: hdd ins fnl 100yds: rallying nr fin* **7/2**[2]	112+
21-	3	*1 ¼*	**Inga Bird**[247] 4384 5-10-4 0........ JakeGreenall(8) (Henry Daly) *trckd ldrs: pckd 3rd: jnd ldrs 7th: led after 3 out: hdd whn mstke next: ev ch fnl 150yds: no ex nring fin* **9/2**[3]	104+
	4	*26*	**Admirable Duque (IRE)**[67] 4-10-12 0........ DavidBass (Dominic Ffrench Davis) *hld up towards rr: hdwy after 6th: effrt after 3 out: wknd next* **7/1**	79
0-P0	5	*½*	**Bright Decision**[33] 1705 4-10-9 0........ DannyBurton(3) (Joanna Davis) *led tl 3rd: prom: led 7th: rdn and hdd after 3 out: wknd next* **80/1**	79
0	6	*3 ¼*	**Jack The Soldier (IRE)**[34] 1675 6-10-12 0........ RichardKilloran (Chris Gordon) *a towards rr* **33/1**	76
43-P	7	*4*	**Like Ice**[171] 379 5-10-7 0........ JosephAkehurst(5) (Philip Middleton) *a towards rr* **40/1**	72
06	8	*7*	**Downe Payment (IRE)**[34] 1680 5-10-5 0........ GemmaGracey-Davison (Diana Grissell) *mid-div: rdn after 7th: wknd next* **100/1**	59
665-	9	*23*	**Aerospace**[200] 5287 6-10-12 0........ GilesHawkins (Nick Mitchell) *mid-div tl 6th: sn struggling: t.o* **66/1**	45
	10	*4 ½*	**Maringo Bay (IRE)**[243] 5-10-9 0........ PeterToole(3) (Charlie Mann) *trckd ldr: prom whn hit 6th: wknd next: t.o* **8/1**	41
F-	11	*33*	**Richardlionheart (USA)**[5] 2335 4-10-12 0........ MarcGoldstein (Michael Madgwick) *t.k.h: hld up towards rr: midfield whn hit 7th: sn wknd: t.o* **100/1**	12
06-1	P		**Bad Sir Brian (IRE)**[18] 1906 5-10-3 0 ow1........ FinianO'Toole(10) (Nick Gifford) *t.k.h: sn prom: led 3rd tl appr 7th: sn wknd: t.o whn p.u bef last* **6/1**	—

5m 11.7s (12.30) **Going Correction** +0.725s/f (Soft)
WFA 4 from 5yo+ 8lb **12** Ran SP% **115.1**
Speed ratings (Par 105): **104,103,103,92,92 91,89,87,77,76 62,—**
toteswingers:1&2 £2.40, 2&3 £3.40, 1&3 £3.90 CSF £11.97 TOTE £3.60: £1.30, £1.60, £1.80; EX 12.00.
Owner Mrs Rachel King **Bred** Mme Marie-Louise Aubert **Trained** Barbury Castle, Wilts
■ Stewards' Enquiry : Matt Griffiths one-day ban: used whip with excessive frequency (Nov 19)

FOCUS
The front three drew clear in what was a modest novices' hurdle. The winner was a few pounds of his Exeter mark with the second posting a small personal best.

NOTEBOOK
Kauto The Roc(FR) reappeared with an improved effort at Exeter and he built on that here under a well-timed ride, coming through to lead late on despite making a complete mess of the second-last. He's going the right way, stays further, and should make his mark in handicaps. (op 3-1 tchd 10-3)
Present To You(IRE) comes out the best horse at the weights, having shouldered a penalty he picked up for winning at the course last time. He looked all over the winner turning in, but not for the first time looked clueless in the lead, and despite rallying again near the line having been headed, he couldn't get back up in time. (tchd 3-1and 4-1 in places)
Inga Bird didn't help his cause with a mistake two out, but he still held a chance until fading on the final climb to the line. Clear of the fourth, this was a promising start and he should win something similar. (tchd 5-1)
Admirable Duque(IRE), a fair sort at up to 1m6f on the Flat, never really got into it and ended up well held, but he's likely to improve for the experience and can make his mark at a modest level. (op 13-2)
Maringo Bay(IRE), a dual runner-up in Irish points, was beaten a worryingly long way on this debut under rules. (tchd 13-2)
Bad Sir Brian(IRE), a recent bumper winner at Plumpton, took a good grip through the early stages of the race and the way he dropped up before being pulled up suggests something was amiss. Official explanation: trainer said gelding was unsuited by the good to soft ground (op 13-2 tchd 15-2)

2182 LADBROKES SUPPORTING GREAT ORMOND STREET HOSPITAL MARES' BEGINNERS' CHASE (15 fncs) 2m 4f
1:50 (1:50) (Class 4) 4-Y-0+ **£3,252** (£955; £477; £238)

Form				RPR
250-	1		**Easter Legend**[204] 5196 6-11-0 0........ JackDoyle (Emma Lavelle) *mde all: nt fluent 4 out: hit next: sn wl in command: comf* **4/6**[1]	130+

130- **2** *14* **Cobbler's Queen (IRE)**223 4889 6-11-0 0 RichardJohnson 111+
(Henry Daly) *trckd wnr: hit 4 out: sn rdn: kpt on but a being hld fr next: hit last* **15/2**

50 **3** *12* **Sieglinde (FR)**78 1291 4-10-5 0 LeightonAspell 87
(Alison Batchelor) *trckd wnr: rdn after 4 out: one pce fr next* **66/1**

0/P0 **4** *20* **Dora Explora**21 1549 6-11-0 0 AndrewThornton 78
(Linda Jewell) *a in last pair: nt fluent 6th: hmpd 8th: struggling 10th: no ch fr 4 out* **100/1**

240- **5** *18* **Raise You Five (IRE)**223 4889 6-11-0 0 APMcCoy 62
(Jonjo O'Neill) *hld up in last pair: awkward 4th: struggling 10th: no ch fr 4 out* **11/2**3

200- **F** **Dansimar**204 5196 6-11-0 0 AidanColeman —
(Venetia Williams) *trcking ldrs whn fell 8th* **4/1**2

5m 16.8s (9.50) **Going Correction** +0.60s/f (Soft)
WFA 4 from 6yo 8lb **6** Ran SP% **109.6**
Speed ratings (Par 105): **105,99,94,86,79** —
toteswingers:1&2 £1.50, 2&3 £5.90, 1&3 £4.10 CSF £6.16 TOTE £1.90: £1.50, £3.20; EX 6.40.
Owner Simon Willes **Bred** Simon Willes **Trained** Wildhern, Hants

FOCUS
Probably a fair mares' beginners' chase. The winner was a 138-rated hurdler and should better that over fences.

NOTEBOOK
Easter Legend, a useful hurdler, made all the running and came clear for a smooth success on this debut over fences. Fifth behind Quevega in the David Nicholson at last season's Cheltenham Festival, she should take very high rank in the mares' division as a chaser, and this is surely the first of many victories. (op 4-7 tchd 8-11)
Cobbler's Queen(IRE), rated 118 over hurdles, made a couple of novicey mistakes, but she jumped soundly in the main on this first start over fences and should find easier opportunities. (tchd 13-2)
Sieglinde(FR), rated just 90 as a hurdler and having only her third start in this country, wasn't beaten as far as many would have expected on this debut over fences and she should have a future in handicaps with the allowances.
Raise You Five(IRE), rated 113 over hurdles, never threatened to get into this and was allowed to coast home in the end under McCoy. This initial experience of fences won't be lost on her and she should do better next time. (op 13-2 tchd 7-1 and 5-1)
Dansimar, rated just 6lb below the winner over hurdles, would probably have been the one to give the winner most to do had she not come down at the eighth. It's hoped this spill doesn't affect her confidence too badly. (op 6-1)

2183 GOT THE FEELING? GET TO LADBROKES H'CAP HURDLE (13 hdls) 3m 3f
2:20 (2:20) (Class 5) (0-95,95) 4-Y-O+ **£1,951** (£573; £286; £143)

Form RPR

0622 **1** **Calypso Bay (IRE)**26 1798 4-11-6 **89** APMcCoy 113+
(Jonjo O'Neill) *racd wd: hld up towards rr: hdwy after 9th to trck ldrs next: led 2 out: clr last: easily* **5/2**3

5311 **2** *9* **Panzer (GER)**8 2050 9-11-5 **95** HenryBrooke(7) 102+
(Donald McCain) *hld up towards rr: hdwy to trck ldrs after 7th: pushed along 10th: led u.p after 3 out: hdd next: kpt on but sn no ch w wnr* **13/8**1

6335 **3** *11* **Saddlewood (IRE)**26 1798 7-11-0 **83** (tp) DarylJacob 79
(Jamie Snowden) *trckd ldrs tl lost pl after 8th: hdwy 10th: rdn in cl 3rd appr 2 out: styd on same pce* **9/1**3

/0P- **4** *14* **My Rosie Ribbons (IRE)**197 5330 11-10-6 **80**(p) GemmaGracey-Davison(5) 64
(Zoe Davison) *racd wd in tch: led appr 9th: rdn and hdd after 3 out: hld fr next: fdd* **20/1**

4545 **5** *17* **Vacario (GER)**12 2001 6-11-4 **90** (t) TommyPhelan(3) 58
(Mark Gillard) *in tch: nt fluent 2nd: hmpd on bnd after 7th: sn rdn: wknd after 10th* **11/1**

4P0- **6** *1 3/4* **Acosta**240 4521 6-10-8 **80** (b) EamonDehdashti(3) 47
(Dr Jeremy Naylor) *trckd ldr: led briefly after 8th: rdn after 9th: wknd appr 3 out* **12/1**

5P0- **7** *3 1/4* **Whitcombe Spirit**29 4916 5-11-10 **93** MattieBatchelor 57
(Jamie Poulton) *a towards rr: no ch fr 10th* **33/1**

FF-0 **8** *11* **Toomuchinformation**34 1679 6-11-0 **88** JimmyDerham(5) 42
(Anna Newton-Smith) *reminders after 5th: a towards rr* **16/1**

P-U3 **9** *8* **Spiritonthemount (USA)**16 1922 5-11-6 **92** (b) WayneKavanagh(3) 39
(Peter Hiatt) *led tl mstke 8th: sn rdn: wknd after 9th* **25/1**

30-0 **10** *3 3/4* **Ramvaswani (IRE)**12 1997 7-11-8 **94** (p) AlexMerriam(3) 37
(Neil King) *in tch tl wknd appr 10th* **25/1**

56P/ **F** **Commanche Dawn**638 3756 8-9-9 **69** oh5 MarcGoldstein(5) —
(Gerry Enright) *hld up towards rr: fell 7th* **33/1**

7m 10.1s (17.30) **Going Correction** +0.725s/f (Soft)
WFA 4 from 5yo+ 9lb **11** Ran SP% **116.9**
Speed ratings (Par 103): **103,100,97,92,87 87,86,83,80,79** —
toteswingers:1&2 £1.10, 2&3 £3.10, 1&3 £2.80 CSF £6.56 CT £28.57 TOTE £3.30: £1.30, £1.90, £1.40; EX 6.50.
Owner John P McManus **Bred** T Hirschfeld **Trained** Cheltenham, Gloucs

FOCUS
A moderate handicap hurdle. The winner took a big step forward and was value for further, and the second is rated in line with his recent chase win.

NOTEBOOK
Calypso Bay(IRE) has shown improved form since switched to handicaps the last twice, and this step up to a marathon trip enabled him to show improved form, travelling strongly under McCoy and drawing right away having taken over at the first in the straight. Successful off a mark of 89, he's sure to be nudging 100 following this, so connections will probably want him out under a penalty. He's only four and remains a horse to keep onside. (op 9-4)
Panzer(GER), a cosy winner over fences at the course last week, was well-in returned to hurdles, his new mark having not kicked in yet, and he was understandably made favourite. However, he proved no match for the younger, less exposed winner in the end. (op 2-1)
Saddlewood(IRE) travelled well to a point and there was no disgrace in being unable to race on with the front pair. She's still a maiden, but should put that right at some point. (op 10-1 tchd 17-2)

2184 PLAY CASINO AT LADBROKES.COM H'CAP CHASE (16 fncs) 2m 6f
2:50 (2:50) (Class 4) (0-115,114) 4-Y-O+ **£3,252** (£955; £477; £238)

Form RPR

1P-4 **1** **Ere Alfie (IRE)**17 1912 6-10-3 **91** (p) DarylJacob 102
(Nick Williams) *mde all: hrd rdn after 3 out whn pressed: styd on wl to assert run-in* **2/1**1

S432 **2** *3* **Take A Mile (IRE)**16 1916 8-10-11 **104** (p) JimmyDerham(5) 112
(Seamus Mullins) *trckd wnr: pressed wnr fr 4 out: rdn after 3 out: ev ch 2 out tl sn after last: no ex* **15/2**

105- **3** *6* **Stoney's Treasure**237 4589 6-11-11 **113** WayneHutchinson 120+
(Alan King) *travelled wl in tch: trckd wnr fr 11th tl stmbld bdly 4 out: bk on terms next: ev ch whn pckd 2 out: sn rdn: kpt on same pce* **11/4**2

-440 **4** *28* **Swainson (USA)**17 1912 9-10-7 **95** OwynNelmes 72
(Helen Nelmes) *in last: reminders fr 1st: wnt modest 4th after 12th: nvr threatened ldrs* **25/1**

2-1U **5** *12* **Double The Trouble**12 1992 9-11-8 **110** NickScholfield 77
(Andy Turnell) *trckd wnr tl appr 11th: rdn after 12th: wknd bef 3 out: t.o* **12/1**

6013 **6** *2 3/4* **Another Trump (NZ)**16 1926 6-11-12 **114** APMcCoy 78
(Jonjo O'Neill) *trcking wnr whn mstke 10th: nt travelling fr next: wknd bef 4 out: t.o* **5/1**3

-450 **7** *10* **Lidjo De Rouge (FR)**102 1093 11-10-4 **99** MrTJCannon(7) 54
(Paul Henderson) *in tch: pushed along 7th: wknd bef 4 out: t.o* **8/1**

5m 53.2s (10.20) **Going Correction** +0.60s/f (Soft) **7** Ran SP% **111.1**
Speed ratings (Par 105): **105,103,101,91,87 86,82**
toteswingers:1&2 £2.50, 2&3 £4.30, 1&3 £1.70 CSF £16.11 TOTE £2.80: £2.50, £3.20; EX 16.60.
Owner Mrs Sally & Miss Isobel Noott **Bred** R S Bennett **Trained** George Nympton, Devon

FOCUS
This was quite an interesting race for the grade. A small step up from the winenr with the second rated to form.

NOTEBOOK
Ere Alfie(IRE) returned with a promising effort at Exeter last month and he proved suited by the return to a longer trip, finding plenty for strong pressure and drawing away again on the climb to the line. He's improved since joining his current yard and may well have more to offer back up to 3m. (op 9-4 tchd 5-2)
Take A Mile(IRE), runner-up off this mark over C&D latest, again looked a player and he ran his race, but found the lightly-weighted winner too strong from the last. He's holding his form and deserves a win. (op 8-1 tchd 7-1)
Stoney's Treasure, a promising type over hurdles who had reportedly schooled like a 'natural chaser' at home, looked very well weighted off a mark of 113 for this debut over fences and travelled like the best horse throughout. However, he became very tired in the straight and ended up well held back in third. Assuming the run was needed, he should go close next time. (op 5-2 tchd 9-4)
Swainson(USA) kept on again for a distant fourth, but achieved little.
Another Trump(NZ) was never going after a blunder at the tenth and is in danger of going the wrong way. Official explanation: jockey said gelding lost left-fore shoe (op 6-1)

2185 LADBROKES.COM H'CAP HURDLE (10 hdls) 2m 4f
3:20 (3:20) (Class 4) (0-115,109) 4-Y-O+ **£2,602** (£764; £382; £190)

Form RPR

6011 **1** **Amuse Me**5 2114 4-11-2 **99** 14ex APMcCoy 117+
(Jonjo O'Neill) *in tch: hdwy after 3 out: chalng whn squeezed up and hit 2 out: sn led: pushed clr fr last: comf* **11/10**1

-052 **2** *5* **Lepido (ITY)**8 2049 6-11-3 **100** (v1) JamieMoore 107
(Gary Moore) *hld up towards rr: hdwy after 3 out: chsd ldrs next: sn rdn and ev ch: kpt on but a hld fr jst bef last* **10/3**2

130- **3** *6* **Posh Emily**211 5105 7-10-12 **102** MattGriffiths(7) 104
(Ron Hodges) *trckd ldrs: short of room but ev ch 2 out: sn rdn: kpt on same pce fr last* **16/1**

F-54 **4** *1/2* **Sail And Return**18 1900 6-10-10 **93** (t) AndrewGlassonbury 94
(Philip Middleton) *led: mstke 4 out: rdn and hdd sn after 2 out: cl up whn mstke last: no ex* **16/1**

P4-F **5** *13* **Near The Water (IRE)**177 281 6-11-11 **108** LeightonAspell 96
(Richard Rowe) *a towards rr: nvr threatened* **16/1**

00-2 **6** *35* **Cardinal James (IRE)**29 1740 6-11-4 **104** SamTwiston-Davies(3) 61
(Tor Sturgis) *chsd ldrs tl rdn and wknd after 3 out: t.o* **10/1**3

00-P **7** *4* **Celtic Ballad (IRE)**29 1737 4-10-7 **90** (t) JoeTizzard 43
(Colin Tizzard) *trckd ldr: mstke 7th: sn rdn: wknd next: t.o* **18/1**

62-0 **8** *13* **Dalrymple (IRE)**16 1914 4-10-7 **95** (tp) MarcGoldstein(5) 37
(Michael Madgwick) *a towards rr: t.o* **66/1**

64-4 **9** *69* **Uncle Bunge (IRE)**18 1902 4-11-0 **97** TimmyMurphy —
(Liam Corcoran) *in tch: rdn after 3 out: sn wknd: t.o* **16/1**

2355 **U** **Forest Rhythm (IRE)**22 1842 6-11-9 **109** WayneKavanagh(3) —
(Seamus Mullins) *stmbld/clipped heels and uns rdr sn after 1st* **16/1**

5m 13.7s (14.30) **Going Correction** +0.725s/f (Soft)
WFA 4 from 6yo+ 8lb **10** Ran SP% **116.0**
Speed ratings (Par 105): **100,98,95,95,90 76,74,69,41,**—
toteswingers:1&2 £2.00, 2&3 £11.70, 1&3 £7.60 CSF £5.42 CT £35.58 TOTE £2.30: £1.10, £1.10, £4.50; EX 4.90.
Owner John P McManus **Bred** Whatton Manor Stud **Trained** Cheltenham, Gloucs

FOCUS
A low-grade handicap hurdle. Another step forward from the easy winner and the second ran to his mark.

NOTEBOOK
Amuse Me defied the double penalty to complete a hat-trick with a bit in hand, overcoming a mistake two out when short of room near the rail and getting well on top from the last. This new, longer trip was clearly not a problem for the son of Daylami and, although the 4-y-o will be asked a tougher question in future, there's nothing to say he's done improving. (op 10-11 tchd 6-5 and 5-4 in places)
Lepido(ITY), back to form when second at the course last week, was off the same mark here and probably improved a little for the first-time visor, looking unfortunate to bump into the well-handicapped winner. (op 9-2 tchd 3-1and 5-1 in places)
Posh Emily, returning from a 211-day absence, travelled well into contention, but was another a bit squeezed for room coming to two out, and her lack of an outing told late on. (op 20-1)
Sail And Return, wearing a tongue tie for this handicap debut, has been keen and struggled to get home over shorter in the past, so it was perhaps no surprise to see him outstayed upped to this trip. There are definitely races to be won with him, though, as he may yet improve. (op 20-1)
Near The Water(IRE), a faller last time over fences, never posed a threat but kept on for fifth and this should have restored some confidence. (op 18-1)

2186 BE FREE WITH LADBROKES MOBILE STANDARD OPEN NATIONAL HUNT FLAT RACE 2m 2f 110y
3:50 (3:52) (Class 6) 4-6-Y-O **£1,370** (£399; £199)

Form RPR

1 **Camden (IRE)**223 4-11-4 0 LeightonAspell 108+
(Oliver Sherwood) *t.k.h early: prom: led over 8f out: rdn whn pressed over 2f out: styd on wl: rdn out* **11/2**2

2 *1* **Water Garden (FR)** 4-11-4 0 TimmyMurphy 107+
(Paul Nicholls) *in tch on outer: trck wnr fr over 7f out: rdn and ev ch over 2f out: kpt on: a jst being hld: drew wl clr of remainder* **2/1**1

3 *17* **Be Extraordinary (IRE)** 4-11-4 0 JackDoyle 92
(Sarah Humphrey) *in tch: rdn over 4f out: styd on same pce to go 3rd wl ins fnl f: no ch w ldng pair* **33/1**

4 *3/4* **Charlotte's Ball (IRE)** 4-10-6 0 JayPemberton(5) 84
(Raymond York) *trckd ldrs: rdn to chse ldng pair over 3f out: sn no ch: styd on same pce: lost 3rd ins fnl f* **66/1**

4 **5** *2 1/4* **Brannoc (IRE)**[29] 1749 5-11-4 0 AndrewThornton 89
(Tony Newcombe) *hld up towards rr: hdwy into midfield 1/2-way: styd on same pce fnl 3f* **40/1**

30- **6** *2 3/4* **Venetian Lad**[258] 4158 5-11-4 0 MarkBradburne 87
(Lydia Richards) *hld up towards rr: sme late prog: nvr a danger* **8/1**[3]

7 *4 1/2* **Thewellmeadow (IRE)**[279] 5-10-11 0 MrTJCannon(7) 82
(Paul Henderson) *mid-div: rdn over 4f out: nvr any imp: wknd 3f out* **66/1**

1- **8** *10* **Custer Of The West (IRE)**[199] 5296 5-11-11 0 WayneHutchinson 80
(Alan King) *mid-div: rdn over 4f out: wknd 3f out* **9/1**

6- **9** *15* **Society Shares (IRE)**[179] 262 5-11-4 0 JodieMogford 60
(Graeme McPherson) *chsd ldrs tl over 5f out: t.o* **9/1**

10 *2 1/2* **Bestwood Lodge** 4-10-11 0 OwynNelmes 51
(Helen Nelmes) *a bhd: t.o* **33/1**

11 *18* **Blantyre** 4-11-4 0 HaddenFrost 42
(Henrietta Knight) *hld up towards rr: hdwy into midfield over 6f out: wknd 4f out* **12/1**

2 **12** *14* **Midies Prince (IRE)**[24] 1817 4-10-11 0 MrJMQuinlan(7) 29
(Terry Clement) *mid-div tl wknd over 6f out: t.o* **11/2**[2]

0-4 **13** *15* **All But Beat**[110] 1029 5-11-4 0 AidanColeman 15
(Ron Hodges) *t.o fnl 6f* **33/1**

3- **14** *127* **Rebelious (IRE)**[214] 5057 5-10-13 0 JimmyDerham(5) —
(Seamus Mullins) *sn led: hdd over 8f out: wknd over 5f out: t.o* **14/1**

4m 41.0s (12.30) **Going Correction** +0.725s/f (Soft)
WFA 4 from 5yo 7lb **14 Ran SP% 123.8**
Speed ratings: **103,102,95,95,94 93,91,86,80,79 71,66,59,—**
toteswingers:1&2 £5.00, 2&3 £20.30, 1&3 £47.70 CSF £16.62 TOTE £7.20: £2.40, £1.60, £6.40; EX 20.60.
Owner T D J Syder **Bred** Fran Kavanagh **Trained** Upper Lambourn, Berks

FOCUS
The front pair drew some 17l clear and look above average in what looked an ordinary bumper all told.

NOTEBOOK
Camden(IRE), from a yard that can get them ready to win a bumper, was clearly straight enough to make a winning debut as he had to work hard to maintain his advantage over the runner-up in the straight. He's going to stay further over hurdles and rates a promising sort, whether or not he manages to defy a penalty. (tchd 5-1)
Water Garden(FR), whose dam was a half-sister to a couple of winning jumpers, is from a top yard and he looked the likely winner at one stage, but Camden kept pulling out more and he was always being held in the final half furlong. Clear of the remainder, this was a promising start and he should go one better before long. (op 5-2 tchd 11-4)
Be Extraordinary(IRE), whose dam was a distant relation of Jodami, is from a yard that had a well-backed bumper winner last season and, for all that he was well held back in third, he did stay on in the manner of a horse with a future.
Charlotte's Ball(IRE) has some smart performers in her family and, considering she's more of a staying chase prospect, this wasn't a bad start.
Brannoc(IRE) again kept on late and will be of interest once upped in grade over hurdles. (op 50-1)
Venetian Lad again kept on in the manner of a horse in need of a stiffer test. He'll get it once sent hurdling. (op 11-1)
Custer Of The West(IRE), the only penalised runner in the race having won at Towcester on his sole outing last season, was weak in the market and never posed a serious threat. (op 7-1 tchd 6-1 and 10-1)
Midies Prince(IRE), runner-up at Huntingdon on debut, failed to confirm that promise with a rather tame effort. (op 5-1 tchd 9-2)
Rebelious(IRE) Official explanation: jockey said gelding made a noise

2187 BEST ODDS GUARANTEED AT LADBROKES.COM H'CAP CHASE (13 fncs) 2m 2f
4:20 (4:20) (Class 5) (0-95,95) 4-Y-0+ **£1,951** (£573; £286; £143)

Form RPR

653/ **1** **Golden Duck (IRE)**[596] 4588 10-11-12 **95** DarylJacob 118+
(Nick Williams) *trckd ldrs: clsd on clr ldr 4 out: led next: sn clr: v easily* **9/2**[3]

6403 **2** *8* **Fongoli**[16] 1924 4-10-1 **78** (b) MattieBatchelor 73
(Brendan Powell) *led tl 2nd: chsd ldr: reminders afer 7th: lost 2nd gng to 4 out: lft 3rd 3 out: regained 2nd run-in: no ch w wnr* **11/4**[2]

434- **3** *9* **Rileyev (FR)**[196] 5353 5-11-12 **95** AidanColeman 93+
(Venetia Williams) *chsd ldrs: clsd on clr ldr 4 out: ev ch sn after: hld whn stmbld next: wknd and lost 2nd run-in* **11/2**

U4-P **4** *1* **Wishes Or Watches (IRE)**[185] 136 10-9-11 **69** oh3 SamTwiston-Davies(3) 64
(John Upson) *hld up in tch: hit 9th: rdn after 4 out: nvr threatened: lft 4th 3 out* **12/1**

0-65 **5** *42* **Magusta (GER)**[18] 1900 6-11-2 **90** DavidBass(5) 46
(Jamie Snowden) *hld up but in tch: nvr able to get on terms: wknd bef 4 out: t.o* **16/1**

6P/U **F** **Shouldntbethere (IRE)**[18] 1905 6-10-2 **76** (t) JimmyDerham(5) —
(Joanna Davis) *led 2nd: sn clr: rdn whn hdd and fell 3 out* **12/1**

102F **P** **Tegan Lee**[18] 1901 7-11-8 **91** TimmyMurphy —
(Liam Corcoran) *hld up: j.lft progively worse: p.u after 6th* **5/2**[1]

4m 56.9s (22.20) **Going Correction** +0.60s/f (Soft)
WFA 4 from 5yo+ 7lb **7 Ran SP% 110.1**
Speed ratings (Par 103): **74,70,66,66,47 —,—**
toteswingers:1&2 £4.00, 2&3 £2.90, 1&3 £2.00 CSF £16.51 TOTE £4.80: £3.00, £1.20; EX 20.60.
Owner Mrs Sally & Miss Isobel Noott **Bred** Miss C Hayes **Trained** George Nympton, Devon

FOCUS
The runners came home well strung out in what was a modest handicap chase. The facile winner recorded a personal best.

NOTEBOOK
Golden Duck(IRE), making his debut for Nick Williams on the back of a 596-day absence (formerly with Nigel Twiston-Davies), was clearly straight enough and it all proved rather easy, travelling strongly and drawing clear with ease. He was only 2lb higher than when last winning and, assuming he goes the right way from this, he could win again. (op 10-3)
Fongoli appeared to run his race, but was quickly left trailing by the winner. (op 10-3 tchd 5-2)
Rileyev(FR) made a reasonable comeback under top weight, especially as most of his yard's runners are needing a run. (tchd 5-1 and 6-1)
Wishes Or Watches(IRE), off since pulling up at Fakenham in May, never threatened from 3lb out of the handicap but should be straighter next time. (op 11-1 tchd 10-1)
Shouldntbethere(IRE), clear from an early stage, had been headed and looked a tired horse when taking a heavy fall three out. (op 10-1)
Tegan Lee, still in with every chance when falling on her chase debut at Plumpton recently, had clearly been jolted by that incident as she was never jumping and her rider eventually accepted the situation. Official explanation: jockey said mare jumped badly left throughout and pulled up (op 10-1)

T/Jkpt: £999.50. Pool of £12,669.74 - 9.00 winning tickets. T/Plt: £6.60 to a £1 stake. Pool of £64,791.80 - 7,128.18 winning tickets. T/Qpdt: £3.90 to a £1 stake. Pool of £4,532.96 - 848.30 winning tickets. TM

1779 HEXHAM (L-H)
Friday, November 5

OFFICIAL GOING: Heavy (5.9)
The third fence in the back straight was omitted on all circuits of all chases due to unsafe ground.
Wind: Fresh, half against Weather: Overcast

2188 TOTEPLACEPOT (S) HURDLE (10 hdls) 2m 4f 110y
1:10 (1:10) (Class 4) 4-Y-0+ **£2,397** (£698; £349)

Form RPR

0-F4 **1** **Earth Magic (IRE)**[181] 208 10-10-12 129 PaulMoloney 117+
(Evan Williams) *led: hdd briefly bef 2 out: drew clr after 2 out: v easily* **4/11**[1]

FP-6 **2** *33* **Bubses Boy**[82] 1258 4-10-12 0 KennyJohnson 79
(Robert Johnson) *chsd ldng pair: outpcd bef 2 out: rallied to chse (clr) wnr bef last: no imp* **16/1**

3230 **3** *3/4* **Treason Trial**[20] 1573 9-10-12 103 BrianHughes 79
(Andrew Crook) *nt fluent: cl up: wnt 2nd 4th: led briefly bef 2 out: outpcd after 2 out: lost 2nd bef last: kpt on same pce* **9/2**[2]

0-0 **P** **Maree Prince (IRE)**[35] 1660 9-10-5 93 MrJosephPalmowski(7) —
(Ferdy Murphy) *trckd wnr to 4th: sn broke down and p.u after 4th* **9/1**[3]

5m 41.6s (29.10) **Going Correction** +1.025s/f (Soft)
WFA 4 from 6yo+ 8lb **4 Ran SP% 107.4**
Speed ratings (Par 105): **85,72,72,—**
CSF £6.10 TOTE £1.30; EX 5.30.There was no bid for the winner.
Owner R E R Williams **Bred** James Bowe **Trained** Llancarfan, Vale Of Glamorgan
■ Stewards' Enquiry : Mr Joseph Palmowski seven-day ban: Rule (D) 45, failed to pull up gelding when lame (tbn)

FOCUS
The track had to pass an inspection and the riders in the first confirmed that conditions were pretty testing. The opener was run more than 50 seconds outside the standard. This selling hurdle was rendered even less competitive by three non-runners and the form will have little relevance for the future. Earth Magic is rated below his best.

NOTEBOOK
Earth Magic(IRE) made virtually all for an easy win, his first victory since the Grade 3 Galmoy Hurdle at Gowran early in 2008. Trained then by Michael Bowe, he did not show much in three starts for the Evan Williams yard in the spring, two of them over fences, but this represented a huge drop in class. He was more than two stone clear on the figures and it is impossible to gauge from this win just how much of his old ability remains, but this experience cannot have done his confidence any harm. (op 2-5)
Bubses Boy showed nothing for Alison Thorpe and he achieved little in struggling into a remote second on his debut for this yard. (op 12-1)
Treason Trial was placed over hurdles on better ground in the summer for Joss Saville, who is now training in the USA. He momentarily put it up to the favourite in the dip before the second-last, but was beaten in a matter of strides. Not for the first time he jumped sketchily. (op 5-1)

2189 HEXHAM RACECOURSE BOOKMAKERS CONDITIONAL JOCKEYS' H'CAP CHASE (13 fncs 2 omitted) 2m 4f 110y
1:40 (1:40) (Class 4) (0-105,101) 4-Y-0+ **£3,577** (£1,050; £525; £262)

Form RPR

F6-1 **1** **Ocarina (FR)**[181] 213 8-11-9 **101** (p) HarryHaynes(3) 114+
(James Ewart) *trckd ldrs: hdwy to ld 3 out: drew clr after next: rdn out run-in* **5/1**[3]

-026 **2** *15* **Manoubi**[27] 1782 11-10-11 **86** JamesHalliday 87
(Martin Todhunter) *hld up in tch: effrt 3 out: chsd (clr) wnr bef last: no imp* **7/2**[2]

/13- **3** *15* **Do It For Dalkey**[269] 3955 8-10-8 **86** CampbellGillies(3) 69
(Lucinda Russell) *led to 3 out: rdn and outpcd after next: wknd and lost 2nd bef last* **13/8**[1]

350- **4** *6* **Cybora (FR)**[312] 3128 8-10-9 **90** PaulGallagher(6) 67
(Ferdy Murphy) *hld up last: shortlived effrt appr 3 out: sn btn* **12/1**

22P- **5** *17* **Paddys Unyoke (IRE)**[208] 5139 9-10-10 **90** GaryRutherford(5) 50
(Stuart Coltherd) *chsd ldrs: lost pl 8th: lost tch fr 4 out* **17/2**

P/P- **P** **Cloudmor (IRE)**[244] 4432 9-11-5 **97** EwanWhillans(3) —
(Alistair Whillans) *pressed ldr: wkng whn j. slowly 3 out: p.u bef next* **7/1**

5m 45.9s (32.40) **Going Correction** +1.375s/f (Heavy) **6 Ran SP% 107.7**
Speed ratings (Par 105): **93,87,81,79,72 —**
CSF £21.01 TOTE £4.20: £2.50, £1.50; EX 15.10.
Owner Mrs Ray Calder **Bred** Bernard Cypres **Trained** Langholm, Dumfries & G'way

FOCUS
A moderate handicap chase, run in a time 45.90 seconds above the standard. The winner is rated back to his 2008 best.

NOTEBOOK
Ocarina(FR) won over C&D last time out, but that was six months ago and on good ground. Resuming off a 5lb higher mark, he made rapid progress to lead going to three out and the race was as good as over soon afterwards. He avoids a penalty for this win and connections may look to turn him out before he can be reassessed. (tchd 9-2)
Manoubi was back down in trip on this return to fences. He has a good record at Hexham, but although he moved into second place on the home turn he never really looked like adding to his three course wins. (op 10-3 tchd 11-4)
Do It For Dalkey was up with the pace for a long way, but was never allowed his own way in front and his efforts told on this first run since February. He jumped soundly on this chasing debut and can win races in this sphere, but is not going to be as good as his dam, who won ten races over fences for the same owner and was runner-up in a Scottish National. The gelding was reported to have hung badly right. Official explanation: jockey said gelding hung right-handed (op 7-4 tchd 2-1)
Cybora(FR) was always in rear and probably needed this first start in more than ten months. (op 10-1 tchd 14-1)
Cloudmor(IRE) disputed the lead before dropping away very quickly. He has now been pulled up in all three starts since winning at Carlisle in November 2007. (op 8-1 tchd 13-2)

2190 ROWLANDS CHARTERED ACCOUNTANTS H'CAP HURDLE (8 hdls) 2m 110y
2:10 (2:10) (Class 5) (0-95,90) 4-Y-0+ **£2,397** (£698; £349)

Form RPR

2-P0 **1** **Rolecarr (IRE)**[113] 1005 7-11-4 **82** AdrianLane 100+
(Ann Hamilton) *hld up in tch: reminders after 3 out: hdwy to ld after next: rdn clr: unchal* **7/1**

4303 **2** *23* **Knight Valliant**[28] 1762 7-11-3 **84** JamesO'Farrell(3) 79
(Barbara Butterworth) *cl up: wnt 2nd after 2nd: ev ch 2 out: no ch w wnr bef last* **3/1**[1]

0051 **3** *11* **Lindseyfield Lodge (IRE)**[20] 1868 9-11-6 **84** (p) KennyJohnson 66
(Robert Johnson) *racd wd: led to after 2 out: wknd bef last* **4/1**[2]

-254 **4** *5* **Devils Delight (IRE)**[28] 1762 8-10-13 **77** PaddyAspell 54
(James Moffatt) *prom tl rdn and wknd after 2 out* **3/1**[1]

00-0 **5** *49* **Lisdonagh House (IRE)**[181] 209 8-11-4 **82** TomSiddall 10
(Lynn Siddall) *bhd: struggling after 4th: lost tch fr next* **13/2**[3]

64-0 **P** **Dollar Express (USA)**[35] 1664 4-11-12 **90** BrianHarding —
(Edwin Tuer) *hld up: rdn and struggling bef 2 out: t.o whn p.u bef last* **14/1**

P35 **P** **Le Petit Vigier**[27] 1780 4-11-7 **85** (t) DougieCostello —
(Patrick Holmes) *hld up: effrt after 3 out: wknd appr next: t.o whn p.u bef last* **14/1**

0PP- **P** **Bombie Boy**[213] 5072 5-10-3 **67** BrianHughes —
(Brian Storey) *chsd ldr to 2nd: lost pl bef 4 out: struggling fr next: t.o whn p.u bef last* **18/1**

4m 33.2s (15.80) **Going Correction** +1.025s/f (Soft) 8 Ran SP% **114.4**
Speed ratings (Par 103): **103,92,87,84,61** —,—,—
toteswingers:1&2 £4.70, 2&3 £4.00, 1&3 £10.30 CSF £28.98 CT £95.79 TOTE £12.40: £3.90, £1.20, £1.10; EX 31.90.
Owner Ian Hamilton **Bred** A W Buller **Trained** Great Bavington, Northumbland

FOCUS
A selling-class handicap hurdle in which they finished well strung out. A step up from the winner but nothing else seemed to handle the ground and all are rated upwards of 8lb off.

NOTEBOOK
Rolecarr(IRE) looked in a spot of trouble down the far side, but he responded to lead at the foot of the hill and stayed on stoutly for a wide-margin win. A horse who has had a lot of training problems, he was well treated on his second in a novice hurdle at Sedgefield in May last year, but this was only his third run since. (op 9-1)
Knight Valliant travelled quite well in the context of this race, but was left trailing once the winner asserted. This was a reasonable effort in the ground. (op 4-1)
Lindseyfield Lodge(IRE), who landed a Kelso chase on fast ground last time, was not best suited by the underfoot conditions. Racing off an 8lb lower hurdles mark and down in trip, he made the running but was quickly beaten once headed by the winner. (op 10-3)
Devils Delight(IRE) recorded her one win to date in heavy ground and was able to race off her correct mark here, but was instantly beaten two from home. (tchd 10-3)

2191 JANE BENNETT 30TH BIRTHDAY NOVICES' CHASE (17 fncs 2 omitted) 3m 1f
2:40 (2:40) (Class 3) 5-Y-0+ **£5,703** (£1,684; £842; £421; £210)

Form RPR

264- **1** **Club Class**[222] 4910 7-10-5 0 MrJohnDawson(7) 112
(John Wade) *led to after 2 out: rallied to regain ld last: edgd lft u.p run-in: hld on wl* **22/1**

-016 **2** *hd* **Bescot Springs (IRE)**[13] 1959 5-10-12 0 PeterBuchanan 115+
(Lucinda Russell) *pressed wnr: led after 2 out to last: rallied run-in: crowded nr fin: styd on* **5/1**[3]

112- **3** *10* **Milans Man (IRE)**[222] 4910 5-10-12 0 BrianHughes 103
(Howard Johnson) *trckd ldrs: effrt 2 out: outpcd after last* **7/4**[1]

041- **4** *7* **Only The Best**[222] 4910 7-10-12 0 GrahamLee 97
(Ferdy Murphy) *hld up: hdwy and in tch whn hmpd 3 out: nt fluent next: sn outpcd: no imp fr last* **11/4**[2]

U1 **5** *hd* **Sweden (IRE)**[23] 1830 6-11-4 0 PaulMoloney 102
(Evan Williams) *hld up in tch: lost pl whn nt fluent 13th: rallied bef 3 out: no imp fr next* **11/2**

6 *9* **Golfer's Crossing (IRE)**[909] 7-10-12 0 CampbellGillies 86
(Lucinda Russell) *hld up in tch: rdn bef 3 out: wknd fr next* **28/1**

24-4 **U** **Oil Burner**[27] 1783 5-10-9 0 HarryHaynes(3) —
(William Amos) *hld up: blnd and uns rdr 2nd* **16/1**

0U- **P** **Columbus Secret (IRE)**[208] 5140 5-10-12 0 JamesReveley —
(Keith Reveley) *hld up in tch: outpcd whn mstke 4 out: sn lost tch: t.o whn p.u after 2 out* **80/1**

7m 2.10s (29.90) **Going Correction** +1.375s/f (Heavy) 8 Ran SP% **110.0**
Speed ratings: **107,106,103,101,101 98**,—,—
toteswingers:1&2 £16.70, 2&3 £3.80, 1&3 £7.90 CSF £119.14 TOTE £38.60: £10.50, £1.10, £2.80; EX 135.90.
Owner John Wade **Bred** D G L Llewellin **Trained** Mordon, Co Durham
■ Stewards' Enquiry : Mr John Dawson one-day ban: careless riding (tbn)

FOCUS
A fair novice chase where it proved difficult to make up ground from the rear. The winner is rated up 10ln on his best hurdles form but the second is rated below his hurdles best.

NOTEBOOK
Club Class failed to win over hurdles, but he is out of a half-sister to Gold Cup second Go Ballistic and he jumped soundly on this debut over fences. Making the vast majority of the running, he was headed by the runner-up on the home turn before rallying tenaciously to lead at the last. This was a pleasing start to his chasing career, but things will be tougher under a penalty. (op 33-1)
Bescot Springs(IRE) was a fair hurdler and he looks like reaching a similar level over fences, but he is not straightforward. Racing in second place, he lost ground on the winner with slow jumps at quite a number of obstacles and it is to his credit that he managed to show in front on the home turn. He was quickly headed again and was just held when the winner edged into him near the line. (op 8-1)
Milans Man(IRE), twice a winner over hurdles last winter, jumped well enough on this chasing bow as he tracked the leading pair, but he lacked anything like a change of gear to deliver a telling challenge. Conditions were fine for him. (tchd 13-8 and 2-1)
Only The Best, a winning Irish pointer, looked a useful prospect when slamming Milans Man and Club Class over hurdles here in March. On his first run since, he was being niggled along with a circuit to run and a mistake at the second-last ended his hopes of reaching the leaders. This was a little disappointing, but he is entitled to strip fitter and he should win races over fences if he can get his jumping together. (tchd 9-4)
Sweden(IRE) shouldn't have been troubled by the different ground, but his Wetherby win came in a weak race and he was well beaten under the penalty. Official explanation: jockey said gelding was unsuited by heavy going (op 4-1 tchd 7-2)
Golfer's Crossing(IRE), the runner-up's stablemate, won an Irish point in May 2008 on his one previous racecourse outing. He was well beaten in the end, but not without showing a glimpse of promise. (op 22-1 tchd 33-1)

2192 WEATHERBYS BLOODSTOCK INSURANCE NOVICES' HURDLE (10 hdls) 2m 4f 110y
3:10 (3:10) (Class 4) 4-Y-0+ **£3,252** (£955; £477; £238)

Form RPR

5 **1** **Code Blue**[33] 1703 7-10-12 0 JasonMaguire 90+
(Donald McCain) *trckd ldrs: wnt 2nd bef 2 out: effrt and led last: drvn out* **3/1**[1]

-3 **2** *1 1/4* **Bear Dancing (IRE)**[35] 1662 6-10-12 0 PeterBuchanan 87
(Lucinda Russell) *cl up: led 5th: rdn after 2 out: hdd last: rallied: hld towards fin* **4/1**[2]

50- **3** *16* **Papamoa**[208] 5144 5-10-12 0 PaddyAspell 71
(N W Alexander) *prom: outpcd 4 out: rallied 2 out: kpt on run-in: no ch w first two* **25/1**

4 *5* **Mansonien L'As (FR)**[129] 4-10-12 0 GrahamLee 67
(Ferdy Murphy) *hld up: hdwy bef 2 out: sn rdn and no imp* **5/1**[3]

5 *14* **King Sandor (IRE)** 5-10-12 0 DougieCostello 52
(Nicky Richards) *hld up: stdy hdwy and in tch after 3 out: wknd fr next* **4/1**[2]

-442 **6** *1/2* **Corky Dancer**[40] 876 5-10-12 0 WilsonRenwick 51
(P Monteith) *hld up in midfield: outpcd after 3 out: btn next* **5/1**[3]

0 **7** *2* **Domoly (FR)**[27] 1783 7-10-5 0 MrAPKelly(7) 49
(Ferdy Murphy) *bhd: pushed along bef 3 out: struggling bef next* **50/1**

000/ **P** **Riskier**[223] 5-10-12 0 BrianHughes —
(John Wade) *led to 5th: styd w ldr tl wknd qckly bef 2 out: t.o whn p.u bef last* **16/1**

0/0 **P** **Euro One**[5] 2102 6-10-2 0 RyanMania(3) —
(Dianne Sayer) *in tch tl lost pl 4 out: struggling fr next: t.o whn p.u bef 2 out* **100/1**

60- **P** **Paul Revere (IRE)**[196] 5370 6-10-12 0 BrianHarding —
(Nicky Richards) *hld up: struggling 4 out: t.o whn p.u bef 2 out* **20/1**

5m 38.5s (26.00) **Going Correction** +1.025s/f (Soft)
WFA 4 from 5yo+ 8lb 10 Ran SP% **115.8**
Speed ratings (Par 105): **91,90,84,82,77 77,76**,—,—,—
toteswingers:1&2 £2.40, 2&3 £12.50, 1&3 £7.80 CSF £14.76 TOTE £4.70: £2.60, £2.20, £8.70; EX 16.10.
Owner D McCain **Bred** J Singleton **Trained** Cholmondeley, Cheshire

FOCUS
A very moderate novice hurdle run in worsening conditions. The time was around three seconds faster than the opening seller. The first two came clear and this is probably weak form.

NOTEBOOK
Code Blue, who shaped with promise on his debut at Uttoxeter, is out of a dam who won a novice hurdle for the McCain yard as well as a heavy-ground bumper at this track. Going after the runner-up two from home, he led at the last for a gritty win. He is entitled to improve for the experience and looks a tough sort who should pay his way in handicaps down the line. (op 7-2)
Bear Dancing(IRE) made a lot of the running and went down fighting. It could be worth running him over further again, as although he was a well-beaten third over 3m on his reappearance here last month, he is a dual winner over that trip in points. (op 5-1)
Papamoa was never a serious threat back in third, but it was a step up on what he showed in a couple of bumpers back in the spring and he looks a stayer. (op 20-1)
Mansonien L'As(FR), the subject of a favourable report from his trainer, is a big, chasing type, and he has already had a run over fences in France. He was outpcd on the second circuit, but plugged on for a remote fourth. (op 7-2)
King Sandor(IRE) is a half-brother to a couple of minor winners out of a mare who was second in a bumper. He made a promising mid-race move before fading and looks to have a bit of ability. (op 5-1 tchd 7-2)
Riskier, winner of a 2m4f point-to-point in the spring, weakened rapidly after disputing the lead with the runner-up. (op 11-1)

2193 SIS H'CAP CHASE (17 fncs 2 omitted) 3m 1f
3:40 (3:40) (Class 5) (0-95,95) 5-Y-0+ **£2,740** (£798; £399)

Form RPR

14-0 **1** **Matmata De Tendron (FR)**[15] 1933 10-11-1 **91** (p) NathanMoscrop(7) 94
(Andrew Crook) *prom: chsd clr ldr 4th: led gng wl bef 3 out: jnd appr last: hld on wl run-in* **9/2**

12P- **2** *hd* **Seeking Power (IRE)**[216] 4983 9-11-5 **95** MissLAlexander(7) 98
(N W Alexander) *hld up in tch: stdy hdwy to chse wnr 3 out: effrt and disp ld appr last: kpt on: hld cl home* **11/4**[2]

P44P **3** *dist* **The Green Hat (IRE)**[138] 804 10-10-4 **80** MrMEnnis(7) —
(Theresa Gibson) *led and wl clr to 13th: hdd bef 3 out: wknd next: t.o whn tried to refuse last: continued* **3/1**[3]

-32P **P** **Reckless Venture (IRE)**[27] 1784 9-11-6 **89** (t) PeterBuchanan —
(Lucinda Russell) *chsd clr ldr to 4th: outpcd 6th: sn struggling: p.u bef 8th* **7/4**[1]

7m 11.2s (39.00) **Going Correction** +1.375s/f (Heavy) 4 Ran SP% **106.2**
Speed ratings: **92,91**,—,—
CSF £15.66 TOTE £3.70; EX 13.00.
Owner Lucky Catch Partnership **Bred** Gerard Mercier **Trained** Middleham Moor, N Yorks
■ Stewards' Enquiry : Mr M Ennis six-day ban: failed to pull up exhausted gelding (tbn); one-day ban: used whip when gelding showed no response (tbn)

FOCUS
Just the four runners in this low-grade handicap chase, but it still produced a rousing finish. The first two are rated to their marks.

NOTEBOOK
Matmata De Tendron(FR) may not be the biggest, but he is certainly tough and he stuck his neck out bravely to land the spoils. He has a respectable strike rate and should continue to pay his way in marathon chases in testing ground. Surprisingly this was only his second trip to Hexham, a course that seems tailor-made for him. (op 7-2 tchd 10-3)
Seeking Power(IRE), a much bigger individual than the runner-up, did nothing wrong but was just held. Lack of a recent run probably told on this lightly raced gelding, who is capable of winning again when the emphasis is on stamina. (op 9-4)
The Green Hat(IRE) was a long way clear beginning the final circuit but was soon reeled in by the other two, and was pretty tired by the time he virtually stopped at the final fence. He is a very moderate maiden. (op 9-2)
Reckless Venture(IRE) was pulled up at an early stage and has now run two successive poor races at a track he usually goes well at. Official explanation: trainer said gelding had a breathing problem (op 15-8 tchd 2-1)

2194 TOTESWINGER H'CAP CHASE (11 fncs 1 omitted) 2m 110y
4:10 (4:10) (Class 5) (0-95,95) 4-Y-0+ **£2,602** (£764; £382; £190)

Form RPR

0410 **1** **Janal (IRE)**[16] 1924 7-9-9 **71** GaryRutherford(7) 83
(Stuart Coltherd) *chsd ldrs: hdwy to join ldr 1/2-way: led after 2 out: hrd pressed last: hld on gamely* **7/1**

3P-2 **2** *nk* **Against The Wind**[35] 1665 7-11-7 **90** PeterBuchanan 102
(Lucinda Russell) *trckd ldrs: effrt and chal last: kpt on run-in: jst hld* **4/1**[1]

304- **3** *13* **Soul Angel**[224] 4861 6-11-0 **83** PaddyAspell 82
(Sandy Forster) *hld up: outpcd 4 out: rallied after 2 out: lft 12 l 3rd last: no imp* **14/1**

P0P- **4** *13* **Nifty Roy**[194] 9 10-11-11 **94** RichieMcGrath 80
(Brian Storey) *led tl hdd after 2 out: rdn and sn wknd* **50/1**

06-0 **5** *7* **Dark Gentleman**[38] 1644 7-10-8 **77** TjadeCollier 56
(Evelyn Slack) *hld up: struggling after 4 out: nvr on terms* **9/1**

-00P **6** *1/2* **Norminster**[27] 1781 9-10-7 **79** (p) RyanMania(3) 57
(Rayson Nixon) *bhd: struggling fr 7th: nvr on terms* **16/1**

22-0 **P** **Lerida**[16] 1924 8-10-8 **77** (p) BrianHarding —
(Sharon Watt) *cl up tl wknd qckly appr 3 out: t.o whn p.u bef last* **13/2**[3]

4P06 **P** **Tiger King (GER)**[20] 1872 9-10-11 **80** GrahamLee —
(P Monteith) *sn bhd: struggling fr 3rd: t.o whn p.u bef 3 out* **17/2**

-026 **P** **Duke Of Malfi**[27] 1767 7-11-12 **95**.................................(p) CampbellGillies —
(Lucinda Russell) *in tch: mstke 2nd: nt fluent next: lost pl after 6th: sn struggling: t.o whn p.u bef last* **9/2**[2]

U03- **F** **Gavroche Gaugain (FR)**[269] 3952 6-10-4 **80**............... PaulGallagher(7) 89
(Ferdy Murphy) *hld up: stdy hdwy in tch 1/2-way: effrt and disputing ld whn fell last* **7/1**

4m 31.8s (22.00) **Going Correction** +1.375s/f (Heav) **10** Ran SP% **111.6**
Speed ratings (Par 103): **103,102,96,90,87 87,—,—,—,—**
CSF £34.56 CT £372.52 TOTE £8.10: £3.50, £1.10, £2.60; EX 31.70.
Owner S Coltherd **Bred** Niall McGrady **Trained** Selkirk, Borders
■ Stewards' Enquiry : Ryan Mania two-day ban: careless riding (Nov 19,21)

FOCUS
They were soon stretched out in this very ordinary handicap chase, which was quite a test at the trip in this bad ground. The time was reasonable for the grade and the first two are rated in line with their recent C/D efforts.

NOTEBOOK
Janal(IRE) beat Against The Wind over C&D last month and she repeated the trick despite being 7lb worse off, just getting the better of a good tussle from the last. In between her two wins here she was never a threat at Worcester, but the good ground there was an obvious excuse. (op 8-1 tchd 6-1)
Against The Wind could not turn the tables on Janal despite his 7lb pull, but got considerably closer and this was another solid effort. He won't mind a return to further when conditions are not quite so testing. (tchd 7-2)
Soul Angel, a winner in heavy ground over hurdles, stayed on from off the pace for a modest third on only his second run over fences.
Nifty Roy showed his first form for a long while but was well beaten off in the end after making the running. (op 33-1)
Duke Of Malfi was bidding for a third successive win in this event, and while a recent 5lb ease in his rating enabled him to qualify, he was still 11lb higher than for those two victories. His regular rider partnered the runner-up instead and he was struggling after successive early errors. (op 6-1 tchd 15-2)
Gavroche Gaugain(FR) was arguably an unlucky loser on his chase debut, as he was upsides the first two and staying on when he tipped up at the last. He looks likely to make a better chaser than hurdler and should find compensation at some point if none the worse. (op 6-1 tchd 15-2)
T/Plt: £47.30 to a £1 stake. Pool of £53,723.02 - 828.01 winning tickets. T/Qpdt: £17.50 to a £1 stake. Pool of £3,688.17 - 155.50 winning tickets. RY

2195 - (Foreign Racing) - See Raceform Interactive

1393 DOWN ROYAL (R-H)
Friday, November 5

OFFICIAL GOING: Hurdle course - soft (yielding in places); chase course - yielding to soft (soft in places)

2196a EUROPEAN BREEDERS FUND LOUGH CONSTRUCTION LTD MARES NOVICE HURDLE (GRADE 3) (9 hdls) 2m
1:35 (1:35) 4-Y-0+ **£20,995** (£6,137; £2,907; £969)

RPR

1 **Macville (IRE)**[26] 1800 6-11-3 123... PTownend 138
(Patrick Neville, Ire) *chsd ldr in mod 2nd: clr of field: clsd appr 4 out: led 4 out: rdn and chal bef 2 out: asserted bef last: kpt on strly* **8/1**[3]

2 *8* **Oilily (IRE)**[33] 1713 7-11-3 .... MrSPByrne 130
(Sean Byrne, Ire) *settled mid-div early: hdwy into 5th 1/2-way: impr in 3rd bef 3 out: travelled wl to chal bef 2 out: rdn and no imp on ldr appr 2 out: kpt on same pce* **3/1**[2]

3 *12* **Araucaria (IRE)**[13] 1979 6-11-0 .... RWalsh 115+
(John E Kiely, Ire) *chsd ldrs in mod 3rd: clsd 4 out: 2nd bef 3 out: rdn in 3rd ent st: no ex in 4th bef 2 out: kpt on one pce to 3rd run-in* **8/11**[1]

4 *1 3/4* **Shop Dj (IRE)**[41] 1616 5-10-10 ....(t) ADLeigh 109
(P Fahey, Ire) *chsd ldrs: mod 4th 1/2-way: clsr 4 out: rdn bef 3 out: no imp in mod 3rd bef 2 out: kpt on one pce: lost 3rd run-in* **8/1**[3]

5 *11* **Firm Foundations (IRE)**[6] 2097 4-10-7 104........................... PCarberry 95
(Michael Mulvany, Ire) *hld up towards rr: hdwy into 6th bef 3 out: sn rdn and no imp: kpt on one pce* **40/1**

6 *shd* **Benefit Scheme (IRE)**[13] 1979 6-10-10 .... JLCullen 98
(Miss Bernadette A K Murphy, Ire) *chsd ldrs: mod 6th 1/2-way: mstke 5th: clsr 4 out: rdn in 5th and no ex bef 3 out: kpt on one pce* **25/1**

7 *5* **Lizzie Bennett (IRE)**[13] 1979 5-10-10 .... AELynch 93
(W McCreery, Ire) *mid-div: rdn in 8th and no imp bef 3 out* **25/1**

8 *10* **Flying Bella**[26] 1803 4-10-7 .... EJO'Connell 80
(J J Lambe, Ire) *a towards rr* **33/1**

9 *nk* **Diyla (IRE)**[11] 2016 7-11-0 109...(p) BMCash 87
(M Flannery, Ire) *led and clr: reduced advantage bef 4 out where hdd: sn rdn and wknd* **33/1**

10 *18* **Tovaria**[19] 1786 6-10-10 .... AndrewJMcNamara 65
(Edward P Harty, Ire) *chsd ldrs early: dropped towards rr 1/2-way: no imp after* **50/1**

4m 6.60s (3.30)
WFA 4 from 5yo+ 7lb **10** Ran SP% **123.1**
CSF £32.49 TOTE £5.30: £1.60, £1.50, £1.02; DF 46.10.
Owner Carrig Syndicate **Bred** Patrick Neville **Trained** Askeaton, Co Limerick

NOTEBOOK
Macville(IRE) continued her rate of progression over a trip that may have been thought too short and ran out an emphatic winner. They went a very good clip which obviously helped, as did Paul Townend making plenty of use of her. She sat a clear second until taking the lead off the front-running Diyla before three out and from there she just poured it on and burned the finish out of the possibly speedier runner-up. It was a very good performance from an improving mare who may not be seen again until Cheltenham. (op 7/1)
Oilily(IRE) was held up off the pace and improved on the bridle to chase the winner three out but was unable to make any impression on her from the top of the hill. It was a reasonable performance but she just ran into a mare that was far too good on the day. (op 5/2)
Araucaria(IRE) was concerned about the drop back in trip but that would hardly explain what was a below par effort. She travelled well at the head of the pack chasing the two early leaders and improved smoothly into a competitive position after the third last, but she went from travelling to struggling in a few strides and was beaten before two out. She did stay on a bit close home but that does little to mask a performance that was well short of her best. (op 11/10)
Shop Dj(IRE) seemed to run out of stamina a bit. She was certainly close enough if good enough at the third last, but was under pressure and making no impression from the second last. In the end she emptied further after the final flight. 2m on good ground seems to be what she requires. (op 7/1)
Firm Foundations(IRE) effort flattening out after she did make some headway after the fourth last.

2197a WKD CORE HURDLE (GRADE 2) (9 hdls) 2m
2:05 (2:05) 4-Y-0+ **£28,761** (£8,407; £3,982; £1,327)

RPR

1 **Gimli's Rock (IRE)**[19] 1803 4-11-2 133.................................(b) TPTreacy 142
(Mrs John Harrington, Ire) *chsd ldrs: 3rd 1/2-way: lft 2nd 5 out: impr to chal ent st: led travelling wl bef 2 out: rdn and kpt on strly after last: comf* **10/1**

2 *4* **Der Spieler (GER)**[22] 1847 5-11-2 123...........................(t) BarryGeraghty 138?
(J G Coogan, Ire) *hld up in last: 4th bef 3 out: rdn into 3rd bef 2 out: styd on to 2nd bef last: no imp on wnr: kpt on same pce* **25/1**

3 *1 3/4* **Summit Meeting**[233] 4671 5-11-2 143.. RMPower 137
(Mrs John Harrington, Ire) *settled bhd ldrs: 5th 1/2-way: lft 4th 5 out: 3rd bef 4 out: rdn in 4th bef 2 out: styd on to 3rd last: no imp run-in: kpt on same pce* **2/1**[2]

4 *3 1/2* **Luska Lad (IRE)**[22] 1847 6-11-8 150.. DNRussell 141
(John Joseph Hanlon, Ire) *chsd ldr in cl 2nd: led appr 5 out: pushed along after 3 out: rdn and hdd bef 2 out: wknd bef last (scoped bdly post r)* **5/4**[1]

5 *22* **Blackstairmountain (IRE)**[199] 5299 5-11-10 146...................... RWalsh 119
(W P Mullins, Ire) *settled bhd ldrs: 4th 1/2-way: lft 3rd 5 out: sn 4th again: dropped to last bef 3 out: pushed along and no imp ent st: wknd (blowing hrd post r)* **4/1**[3]

U **Magnum Force (IRE)**[71] 1384 6-11-5 122.......................(b[1]) EJO'Connell —
(C A McBratney, Ire) *led: hdd appr 5 out where slt mstke and uns rdr* **50/1**

4m 10.0s (6.70)
WFA 4 from 5yo+ 7lb **6** Ran SP% **112.7**
CSF £152.67 TOTE £12.50: £3.50, £4.40; DF 60.50.
Owner Geoffrey Ruddock **Bred** Mrs Ann Marie O'Brien **Trained** Moone, Co Kildare

NOTEBOOK
Gimli's Rock(IRE) put these to the sword in the manner of a very good horse. His improvement is hard to quantify and his ability to handle this ground in company such as this would have been questionable, but he travelled really strongly throughout and when he came to challenge on the steel at the second last he proceeded to go and win his race very quickly. It was a very classy effort from this individual who looks likely to have a break and be seen out around February. (op 10/1 tchd 12/1)
Der Spieler(GER) ran up to his mark and if the handicapper doesn't have an averse reaction there is probably a very good handicap to be won with this horse. Held up out the back he just stayed on from the second last without looking a danger to the favourite but it was a very decent effort. (op 20/1)
Summit Meeting ◆ ran very well over a trip short of his best. He was given time to get into the race and closed up behind the leaders two out before his effort just flattened out from the last. He looks likely to go to the Hatton's Grace at Fairyhouse but there's no reason why he shouldn't be able to step up to 3m in due course. (op 9/4)
Luska Lad(IRE) was a disappointing favourite. His jumping was patchy early on but he did gradually get into a rhythm, but the way he capitulated when challenged at the second last was untypical of him. There is a sense of back to the drawing board after this performance. Official explanation: trainer's rep said gelding scoped badly post-race (op 11/10)
Blackstairmountain(IRE) was labouring from the top of the straight. He seemed to blow up quite badly and the fact that he was found to be blowing hard post race would back that up. Official explanation: vet said gelding was found to be blowing hard post-race (op 7/2)

1867 KELSO (L-H)
Saturday, November 6

OFFICIAL GOING: Good (good to soft in places; 6.0)
Wind: Almost nil Weather: Sunny

2202 BORDER SKIP HIRE "NATIONAL HUNT" NOVICES' HURDLE (11 hdls) 2m 6f 110y
12:30 (12:31) (Class 4) 4-Y-0+ **£2,602** (£764; £382; £190)

Form RPR

P-11 **1** **Jurisdiction**[21] 1869 6-11-12 116..(p) GrahamLee 123+
(Rose Dobbin) *mde all: rdn bef 2 out: hrd pressed fr last: hld on gamely u.p* **4/1**[3]

000- **2** *nk* **Arctic Court (IRE)**[238] 4576 6-10-12 0.............................. RichieMcGrath 109+
(Jim Goldie) *hld up: stdy hdwy 4 out: rdn fr next: no imp tl rallied 2 out: styd on wl u.p run-in: wnt 2nd nr fin: a hld* **3/1**[1]

32- **3** *nk* **Senor Alco (FR)**[235] 4669 4-10-12 0....................................... BrianHughes 110+
(Howard Johnson) *trckd ldrs: effrt and wnt 2nd between last 2: kpt on run-in: hld and lost 2nd nr fin* **10/3**[2]

00- **4** *11* **What A Dream**[339] 2639 4-10-9 0..................................... HarryHaynes(3) 98
(William Amos) *midfield: effrt and chsng ldrs 2 out: edgd rt and outpcd run-in* **66/1**

40-6 **5** *5* **Goffa Crag**[28] 1783 6-10-9 0.. FearghalDavis(3) 94
(Nicky Richards) *hld up: hdwy and in tch 3 out: rdn and outpcd fr next* **28/1**

66 **6** *8* **Bertie Milan (IRE)**[34] 1698 5-10-12 0.............................. MarkBradburne 87
(Sue Bradburne) *trckd ldrs: ev ch 3 out: lost 2nd and wknd bef last* **9/1**

/15- **7** *2 1/2* **Willie Hall**[325] 2915 6-10-12 0... CampbellGillies 84
(William Amos) *hld up: hdwy and in tch bef 3 out: wknd fr next* **13/2**

5- **8** *36* **Night In Milan (IRE)**[197] 5376 4-10-12 0............................ JamesReveley 51
(Keith Reveley) *nt fluent in rr: rdn 3 out: nvr on terms* **11/1**

P5-P **9** *1 3/4* **I Witness (IRE)**[185] 163 8-10-5 89................................... AlistairFindlay(7) 50
(Jane Walton) *in tch: lost pl bef 7th: n.d after* **100/1**

43-6 **10** *nse* **Fightstar (FR)**[45] 1573 6-10-12 0....................................... PeterBuchanan 50
(Lucinda Russell) *in tch to 4 out: sn rdn and wknd* **33/1**

5/0- **11** *18* **Froggy Lane**[358] 2259 7-10-7 0....................................... PaulCallaghan(5) 34
(Simon West) *trckd wnr tl wknd fr 3 out* **80/1**

06P/ **12** *3 3/4* **Flighty Mist**[857] 815 8-9-12 0....................................... PaulGallagher(7) 23
(Sandy Forster) *bhd: drvn along 7th: nvr on terms* **125/1**

P **The Skanky Farmer**[931] 10-10-9 0.. RyanMania(3) —
(Sandy Thomson) *in tch tl wknd and p.u bef 7th: b.b.v* **66/1**

4/0 **U** **Belmore Baron**[48] 1553 8-10-7 0.. ShaneByrne(5) —
(Sue Smith) *cl up whn tried to refuse and uns rdr 1st* **28/1**

50-4 **P** **Tomzatackman (IRE)**[44] 1599 5-10-12 0............................. WilsonRenwick —
(Raymond Shiels) *bhd: blnd and struggling 7th: t.o whn p.u bef 3 out* **80/1**

4- **P** **Northern Flame (IRE)**[197] 5376 5-10-12 0.......................... PaddyAspell —
(N W Alexander) *bhd: struggling 7th: sn btn: t.o whn p.u bef 2 out* **50/1**

5m 41.4s (0.40) **Going Correction** -0.10s/f (Good)
WFA 4 from 5yo+ 8lb **16** Ran SP% **118.8**
Speed ratings (Par 105): **95,94,94,90,89 86,85,73,72,72 66,64,—,—,— —**
toteswingers:1&2 £3.00, 2&3 £2.90, 1&3 £1.70 CSF £15.52 TOTE £3.20: £1.40, £1.90, £1.50; EX 14.50.
Owner River Tweed Syndicate **Bred** Mrs J Cadzow **Trained** South Hazelrigg, Northumbria

FOCUS

The ground had eased slightly overnight and was riding on the slow side of good. The opening time was more than 23 seconds outside the standard. Winners should emerge from this novices' hurdle, which saw a group of seven pull a long way clear prior to the home turn. The winner was the form pick and is rated up another 5lb with a big step up from the second.

NOTEBOOK

Jurisdiction completed a C/D hat-trick with a bold front-running performance, fighting off his challengers well after getting to the stands' rail on the long run-in. A lazy type who hates being covered up, he was helped by the cheekpieces and, while the plan had been to switch to fences, he may stay over hurdles while he is in this sort of form, with the Grade 2 Winter Novices' Hurdle at Sandown next month making some appeal as a suitable target. He was conceding a stone all round and this was a decent effort. (op 10-3 tchd 3-1)

Arctic Court(IRE), whose run at Ayr in March attracted the attention of the stewards and who has still not been allotted a BHA mark, was well supported. He gradually worked his way through the field from off the pace and, still with ground to make up taking the last, stayed on all the way to the line. His turn should come. (op 5-2)

Senor Alco(FR) was placed in both his bumpers last term, on the second occasion behind subsequent dual winner Lovey Dovey. He was always well placed on this hurdles debut and stuck on willingly after a last-flight error, losing second only close home. (op 4-1)

What A Dream did not show much in a couple of bumpers last winter but is a half-brother to the Amos yard's stable star Lie Forrit. He was apparently the second string here but shaped with a good deal of promise, the stiffer test clearly helping. There are races to be won with him.

Goffa Crag could not race on with the leaders from two out but this effort confirms he has ability and he should come into his own as he gains experience. (op 40-1)

Bertie Milan(IRE) was well beaten on his recent hurdling debut over C/D but showed a lot more here. The form of his Irish pointing win in February has worked out particularly well. (op 12-1)

Willie Hall, a bumper winner, ran a pleasing race on this hurdles debut but was the first of the leading seven to drop away as lack of a recent outing started to tell. (op 8-1)

Night In Milan(IRE) was beaten a long way on this hurdling debut and first start for this yard but is not a lost cause. (tchd 10-1)

The Skanky Farmer Official explanation: jockey said gelding bled from the nose (op 100-1)

Tomzatackman(IRE) was eventually pulled up but he had just started a forward move when his progress was halted by a bad blunder at the seventh. He was reported to have a breathing problem. Official explanation: jockey said gelding had a breathing problem (op 100 1)

2203 SHIP INN, DALKEITH NOVICES' H'CAP CHASE (19 fncs) 3m 1f

1:00 (1:00) (Class 4) (0-110,105) 4-Y-0+ **£2,927** (£859; £429; £214)

Form RPR

6-51 **1** **Isla Pearl Fisher**[16] 1933 7-10-12 **91**.............................. PaddyAspell 102+
(N W Alexander) *hld up: hdwy and in tch whn nt fluent 14th: effrt after 2 out: led last 200yds: drvn out* **7/2**[1]

3632 **2** ¾ **More Equity**[21] 1868 8-11-6 **102**.............................. RyanMania(3) 110
(P Monteith) *prom: rdn to ld 2 out: hdd last 200yds: kpt on u.p* **9/2**[2]

0-P5 **3** 8 **Top It All**[14] 1959 7-11-2 **95**.............................. WilsonRenwick 96
(Rose Dobbin) *cl up: led after 4 out to 2 out: rdn and one pce fr last* **9/1**

21/3 **4** 2¾ **Lockstown**[70] 1402 7-11-12 **105**.............................. GrahamLee 103
(Ann Hamilton) *trckd ldrs: rdn fr 14th: rallied: outpcd between last 2: plugged on run-in* **9/2**[2]

4433 **5** ½ **Storm Prospect**[21] 1868 7-11-0 **93**..............................(b) PeterBuchanan 91
(Lucinda Russell) *hld up in tch: outpcd after 4 out: rallied between last 2: sn no imp* **7/1**[3]

5502 **6** nk **Rossini's Dancer**[16] 1933 5-11-2 **95**.............................. MarkBradburne 95
(Sue Bradburne) *nt fluent on occasions: hld up in tch: lost pl 12th: rallied bef 3 out: no ex after next* **10/1**

-62U **7** 24 **Dukeofchesterwood**[21] 1868 8-11-6 **102**.............................. FearghalDavis(3) 82
(Sandy Forster) *led to after 4 out: rdn and wknd fr next* **12/1**

060- **8** 6 **Flaming Thistle (IRE)**[226] 4833 6-11-3 **96**.............................. BrianHarding 67
(Nicky Richards) *hld up: nt fluent 4th: stdy hdwy and in tch after 4 out: wknd fr next* **10/1**

02P5 **9** 25 **Kyber**[21] 1868 9-11-7 **100**.............................. JamesReveley 48
(Jim Goldie) *cl up: blnd and lost pl 12th: lost tch fr 14th* **25/1**

6m 38.1s (6.60) **Going Correction** +0.40s/f (Soft) **9** Ran SP% **110.8**
Speed ratings (Par 105): **105,104,102,101,101 101,93,91,83**
toteswingers:1&2 £3.80, 2&3 £15.30, 1&3 £21.50 CSF £18.93 CT £121.69 TOTE £4.30: £2.20, £1.70, £2.60; EX 19.60.
Owner Mrs J E B Gammell **Bred** Mrs D Marshall **Trained** Kinneston, Perth & Kinross

FOCUS

An ordinary novices' handicap run in a time 35 seconds outside the standard and suggesting that the ground was softer than advertised. The pace was fairly steady and most of the field were still in contention at the third from home. Isla Pearl Fisher produced a big step up on his previous win.

NOTEBOOK

Isla Pearl Fisher won nicely after settling better at Carlisle last month and followed up under a similar ride, a rise of 9lb proving insufficient to stop him. He seems to be improving belatedly, but things will be tougher after he is reassessed. Genuine good ground is ideal for him and there is a chance he will be put away until the spring now. (op 5-1)

More Equity made her bid for glory two out and gave best only on the run-in. The longer trip was not a problem and she has now been placed in seven of her nine starts over fences, but that first win eludes her. There doesn't seem a lot wrong with her application. (op 5-1 tchd 4-1)

Top It All generally jumped well on this chasing debut and was up with the pace until fading going to the last. This half-brother to a couple of chase winners looks up to picking up a race or two in this sphere, perhaps at 2m4f. (op 12-1)

Lockstown lacked the pace of the principals from the second-last but kept plugging away for a respectable fourth. (op 11-2)

Storm Prospect ran his race over this longer trip but is without a win since the summer of 2008 and has yet to hit the target in a dozen tries over fences now.

Rossini's Dancer was 7lb better off with Isla Pearl Fisher on their Carlisle meeting but finished further behind this time. Some untidy jumping didn't help. (op 9-1)

Flaming Thistle(IRE), who was unplaced in three tries over hurdles last season, was well beaten off in the end, but there was a hint of promise in this chase debut. (op 6-1)

Kyber Official explanation: jockey said gelding had a breathing problem

2204 PREMIER TRAFFIC MANAGEMENT H'CAP CHASE (17 fncs) 2m 6f 110y

1:30 (1:30) (Class 3) (0-130,129) 4-Y-0+ **£5,204** (£1,528; £764; £381)

Form RPR

-126 **1** **Sheriff Hutton (IRE)**[129] 859 7-11-12 **129**.............................. RobertWalford 139+
(Tim Walford) *led 2nd: mde rest: rdn bef 2 out: styd on gamely run-in* **7/1**

4-43 **2** 1¼ **Cast Iron Casey (IRE)**[21] 1871 8-11-1 **118**.............................. WilsonRenwick 126
(P Monteith) *in tch: hit 13th: hdwy and wnt 2nd 3 out: effrt 2 out: kpt on u.p run-in* **7/2**[1]

-3U1 **3** 1¼ **Or De Grugy (FR)**[21] 1871 8-11-1 **125**.............................. AlexanderVoy(7) 131
(Sue Bradburne) *trckd ldrs: ev ch after 4 out: rdn and outpcd after 2 out: rallied run-in: kpt on same pce* **9/2**[2]

6533 **4** 38 **Stagecoach Amber (USA)**[16] 1932 8-10-6 **114**.............................. ShaneByrne(5) 86
(Sue Smith) *cl up: chal 10th tl after 4 out: mstke next: wknd fr 2 out* **6/1**[3]

P5-6 **5** 5 **Zitenka (IRE)**[21] 1871 8-11-10 **127**..............................(p) RichieMcGrath 94
(Tim Easterby) *in tch tl rdn and wknd fr 4 out: t.o* **9/1**

-31F **6** 23 **Safari Adventures (IRE)**[14] 1957 8-11-11 **128**.............................. CampbellGillies 75
(Lucinda Russell) *led to 2nd: stdd in tch: nt fluent next: struggling bef 4 out: sn btn* **8/1**

/2-P **U** **Jack The Blaster**[167] 446 10-11-8 **125**.............................. BrianHughes —
(Howard Johnson) *hld up last: blnd and uns rdr 9th* **8/1**

21P- **P** **Middleton Dene (IRE)**[203] 5226 8-11-10 **127**.............................. GrahamLee —
(Rose Dobbin) *j. bdly: sn wl bhd: p.u bef 5th* **10/1**

5m 51.2s (6.70) **Going Correction** +0.40s/f (Soft) **8** Ran SP% **108.5**
Speed ratings (Par 107): **104,103,103,89,88 80,—,—**
toteswingers:1&2 £2.00, 2&3 £1.10, 1&3 £7.90 CSF £29.29 CT £108.28 TOTE £8.50: £2.10, £1.70, £1.80; EX 29.70.
Owner Richard Adcock Joe Grindal Nigel Skinner **Bred** Joe Slattery **Trained** Sheriff Hutton, N Yorks

FOCUS

A fair handicap chase which numbers Hello Bud and King Harald among recent winners. The first three finished well clear and the form looks solid.

NOTEBOOK

Sheriff Hutton(IRE) was third in this a year ago and was 6lb higher now, but looked well treated on his winning form at Perth in May. Off the track since a lacklustre effort at the same track the following month, he made most of the running and saw it out bravely up the run-in. He was a little low at some of his fences but jumped safely enough and could have further progress in him as this was only his seventh run in chases. An easy 3m is his optimum trip. (op 10-1)

Cast Iron Casey(IRE) ran a solid race, sticking on willingly and turning around recent course form with the third home on these 5lb better terms. A step back up to 3m won't bother him. (tchd 10-3)

Or De Grugy(FR) likes it at Kelso and ran well off a 5lb higher mark than when winning here last time, rallying at the last after looking held. That latest win was over 3m1f and he won't mind a return to that sort of trip. (op 4-1)

Stagecoach Amber(USA) was always at the sharp end, but a couple of mistakes did for him. He still has to prove that he gets as far as this. (op 15-2 tchd 8-1)

Zitenka(IRE), well held in Or De Grugy's race here on his seasonal return, dropped away tamely and is not one for maximum faith. (op 8-1)

Safari Adventures(IRE) was the early leader until his rider opted to steady him at the back of the field. He was left behind over the final four fences but this should have restored some confidence after a heavy fall at Aintree. (op 7-1 tchd 13-2)

Middleton Dene(IRE) Official explanation: jockey said gelding never travelled after two early mistakes

2205 GRAEME TODD HAULAGE AND FRIENDS H'CAP HURDLE (13 hdls) 3m 3f

2:05 (2:05) (Class 3) (0-125,125) 4-Y-0+ **£4,228** (£1,241; £620; £310)

Form RPR

006- **1** **Captain Americo (IRE)**[204] 5203 8-11-4 **120**.............................. HarryHaynes(3) 131+
(James Ewart) *midfield: smooth hdwy to ld bef 2 out: drew clr run-in: readily* **11/2**[2]

052- **2** 9 **Rambling Minster**[209] 5141 12-11-12 **125**.............................. JamesReveley 123
(Keith Reveley) *hld up: drvn along 8th: hdwy after 4 out: chsd ldrs bef 2 out: styd on run-in to take 2nd last stride: no ch w wnr* **20/1**

462- **3** shd **Silent Cliche (IRE)**[225] 4874 6-11-9 **122**.............................. BrianHughes 122+
(Howard Johnson) *cl up: hit 9th: ev ch whn nt fluent 3 out: chsd wnr 2 out: one pce last: lost 2nd last stride* **15/2**

1210 **4** 1¼ **Rebel Swing**[16] 1929 4-10-0 **99** oh1.............................. HenryOliver 97
(Sue Smith) *midfield: hit 8th: effrt and cl up bef 3 out: outpcd fr next* **4/1**[1]

4110 **5** 27 **Summer Soul (IRE)**[10] 2035 8-11-10 **123**..............................(p) CampbellGillies 95
(Lucinda Russell) *towards rr: drvn along fr 6th: struggling fr 4 out: nvr on terms* **14/1**

3P5- **6** 3½ **Wild Cane Ridge (IRE)**[197] 5372 11-11-7 **120**..............................(b) WilsonRenwick 89
(Rose Dobbin) *led to bef 2 out: one pce whn hit last: sn wknd* **33/1**

00-0 **7** 6 **Elzahann (IRE)**[182] 206 8-11-3 **123**.............................. PaulGallagher(7) 87
(Ferdy Murphy) *hld up: stdy hdwy and in tch after 4 out: rdn next: wknd fr 2 out* **20/1**

261- **8** 2 **Merigo (FR)**[203] 5223 9-11-4 **117**.............................. RichieMcGrath 79
(Andrew Parker) *in tch: outpcd 9th: struggling fr next* **13/2**

312- **9** 47 **Fiftyfive Degrees (IRE)**[239] 4553 9-10-8 **107**..............................(p) BrianHarding 27
(Pauline Robson) *midfield on outside: outpcd after 8th: wknd next: t.o* **12/1**

1532 **10** 2 **Planetarium**[21] 1873 5-9-7 **99**..............................(p) HenryBrooke(7) 17
(P Monteith) *hld up: hdwy and in tch 8th: wknd fr 4 out: t.o* **7/1**

010- **P** **Tillietudlem (FR)**[19] 5338 4-11-12 **125**.............................. GrahamLee —
(Jim Goldie) *trckd ldrs: rdn 9th: wknd next: t.o whn p.u bef 2 out* **6/1**[3]

6m 40.4s (-7.80) **Going Correction** -0.10s/f (Good) **11** Ran SP% **114.1**
Speed ratings (Par 107): **107,104,104,103,95 94,93,92,78,78 —**
toteswingers:1&2 £27.40, 2&3 not won, 1&3 £11.80 CSF £104.90 CT £823.75 TOTE £5.60: £2.30, £4.80, £2.20; EX 113.90.
Owner M Tedham **Bred** Paddy Molloy **Trained** Langholm, Dumfries & G'way

FOCUS

A marathon handicap hurdle contested by an interesting mix of runners. The winner was very well in on his best 2009 form and was value for further, and the form has a solid look.

NOTEBOOK

Captain Americo(IRE) had become well handicapped on his best form and made it pay on this first start since leaving Andy Turnell, running out a smooth winner. He will take a hike in the weights for this, but that is not an immediate problem as the plan now is to switch him back to fences, and he has reportedly schooled well. (op 5-1 tchd 6-1)

Rambling Minster ran a remarkable race on this rare venture over hurdles, looking set to lose touch at one stage but staying on well from the third-last and snatching second on the post. He was generally well held over fences last season but finished second in blinkers (left off here) at Perth on his final outing and still has life in him yet. The Borders National over 4m here next month looks ideal. (op 16-1)

Silent Cliche(IRE), an Irish point winner with a good deal of scope, ran a big race but could not live with the easy winner from the last and was pipped for second on the line. This was only his fourth run over hurdles and he is still eligible for novice races and, alternatively, he looks the type to make a nice chaser. (op 9-1)

Rebel Swing, a pound out of the weights, ran with credit against some experienced handicappers and clearly possesses plenty of stamina. (tchd 7-2)

Summer Soul(IRE) was in trouble from an early stage but plugged on over this longer trip for a remote fifth. (op 18-1)

Wild Cane Ridge(IRE) is an infrequent runner over hurdles but enjoyed himself out in front and was relegated out of the places only approaching the final flight.

Elzahann(IRE) did not shape badly on this first run for six months and, although she is attractively handicapped again over hurdles, the plan is to switch her to mares' novices' chases. She should do well in that sphere. (op 22-1 tchd 25-1 and 18-1)

Merigo(FR), currently rated 20lb lower over hurdles, ran a satisfactory race on this first start since winning the Scottish National and it should have put him right for the Becher Chase at Aintree later this month. That event will tell us more about his Grand National credentials. (op 8-1)

Fiftyfive Degrees(IRE), representing the same connections as Merigo, was one of the first beaten but should come on for the outing. (op 10-1)

Planetarium did not see out the trip. (op 10-1)

Tillietudlem(FR), five times a winner on the Flat since his last hurdles outing, was reported to have been struck into. Official explanation: jockey said gelding was struck into (op 5-1 tchd 9-2)

2206 MAYFIELD RESTAURANT CHASE (LIMITED H'CAP) (12 fncs) 2m 1f

2:40 (2:41) (Class 2) 5-Y-0+ **£8,781** (£2,578; £1,289; £643)

Form				RPR
16-3	1		**Noble Alan (GER)**[20] 1886 7-10-4 **145** oh2 BrianHarding (Nicky Richards) *chsd ldr: 1 l down and gng wl whn lft 3 l clr last: kpt on wl* **11/10**[1]	136+
011-	2	5	**Gringo**[197] 5371 8-10-4 **145** oh13 BrianHughes (Howard Johnson) *prom: effrt and rdn after 2 out: lft 3 l 2nd last: kpt on same pce* **7/1**	130
3F4-	3	7	**Kalahari King (FR)**[200] 5302 9-11-10 **165** GrahamLee (Ferdy Murphy) *hld up in tch: rdn and outpcd after 2 out: lft 7 l 3rd last: no imp* **5/2**[2]	144
/P-2	4	2 1/4	**Cantgeton (IRE)**[29] 1761 10-10-4 **145** oh26 WilsonRenwick (P Monteith) *hld up last: outpcd 3 out: no imp fr next* **16/1**	122
206-	F		**I'm Delilah**[203] 5225 8-10-4 **145** oh7 RichieMcGrath (Ferdy Murphy) *led: qcknd after 4 out: 1 l in front and rdn whn fell last* **11/2**[3]	133

4m 23.0s (5.00) **Going Correction** +0.40s/f (Soft) **5** Ran SP% **110.0**

Speed ratings: **104,101,98,97,—**

CSF £8.79 TOTE £2.60: £1.60, £1.90; EX 9.30.

Owner Craig Bennett **Bred** Gestut Kussaburg **Trained** Greystoke, Cumbria

FOCUS

The second edition of this limited handicap, it was run in a time 17 seconds outside the standard. The presence of Kalahari King meant the other four were all out of the weights to varying degrees. The fourth liomits the rating and Noble Alan is rated 6lb off, I'm Delilah heading for something similar and Kalhari King 20lb+off.

NOTEBOOK

Noble Alan(GER) was just 2lb 'wrong' and had run a pleasing race on his return to action over hurdles at Kempton. A smart novice chaser last season, he jumped nicely back over fences and was closing right in on the long-time leader I'm Delilah, going well, when the mare came down at the last. There is little doubt that he would have won in any case. Provided the ground is decent he could go for the Paddy Power Gold Cup at Cheltenham next weekend, for which he picks up a 5lb penalty, but the extended 2m4f there might be something of a worry. (op 6-4)

Gringo won both his races over fences last spring but was nearly a stone out of the weights on this reappearance. He could not race on with the leaders from the second-last but inherited second spot at the final fence and this rates a highly satisfactory comeback. (tchd 8-1)

Kalahari King(FR) had this race designed specifically for him a year ago but he had to miss it following a setback. In the frame in the Queen Mother Champion Chase and the equivalent race at Punchestown in the spring, he was returning to handicaps off 8lb higher than when winning at Doncaster in February. Class act though he is, he had a job on his hands attempting to concede the weight to Noble Alan, who had the benefit of a previous run, and while he ran creditably, this effort seemed to confirm that this trip is on the short side for him now, especially given the modest pace here. He will go for the Peterborough Chase at Huntingdon next and a big run should be expected, especially on better ground. (op 15-8 tchd 11-4)

Cantgeton(IRE) had had no realistic chance from 26lb out of the weights and always brought up the rear. (op 22-1)

I'm Delilah, a stablemate of Kalahari King, went out in front and quickened it up from the third-last. That move had most of her opponents in trouble, but not Noble Alan, and she was only just in front of him when she took quite a heavy fall at the last. Racing from 7lb out of the weights, she is a useful and likeable mare but may not be too easy to place successfully in this second season over fences. (op 6-1 tchd 5-1)

2207 HAZELRIGG RACING H'CAP CHASE (12 fncs) 2m 1f

3:15 (3:15) (Class 4) (0-115,115) 4-Y-0+ **£2,927** (£859; £429; £214)

Form				RPR
1633	1		**Ormus**[6] 2107 7-10-4 **93** PaddyAspell (Christopher Wilson) *hld up in tch: stdy hdwy bef 3 out: shkn up to ld run-in: hld on wl nr fin* **15/8**[1]	104+
-101	2	shd	**Kosta Brava (FR)**[21] 1872 6-11-7 **110** WilsonRenwick (Howard Johnson) *cl up: blnd 8th: led 2 out: hdd run-in: edgd lft u.p: kpt on: jst hld* **5/2**[2]	118+
030-	3	14	**Super Baby (FR)**[199] 5309 8-11-1 **107** (p) HarryHaynes[(3)] (James Ewart) *led to 2 out: rallied: rdn and wknd after last* **9/2**[3]	101
4-40	4	10	**Prince Tam**[6] 2107 6-10-0 **89** oh3 CampbellGillies (Lucinda Russell) *cl up tl rdn and wknd after 2 out* **9/1**	76
5	5	7	**The Cockney Squire (IRE)**[44] 1594 5-11-12 **115** PeterBuchanan (Lucinda Russell) *hld up in tch: stdy hdwy 3 out: blnd and outpcd next: btn whn hit last* **5/1**	96

4m 25.4s (7.40) **Going Correction** +0.40s/f (Soft) **5** Ran SP% **108.2**

Speed ratings (Par 105): **98,97,91,86,83**

CSF £6.90 TOTE £2.90: £1.10, £1.80; EX 6.60.

Owner David Bartlett **Bred** Mrs Andrea Bartlett **Trained** Manfield, N Yorks

FOCUS

An ordinary handicap chase run in a time just 2.4 seconds slower than the preceding limited handicap. The first two pulled well clear and both could pay to follow in the near future, with the winner still likely to be competitive after being reassessed.

NOTEBOOK

Ormus, given a patient ride, quickened up to take a narrow lead on the run-in and just held the runner-up's sustained challenge. He had run a promising race on his return from a break at Carlisle last weekend and was quite well handicapped on his best form. (op 5-2 tchd 7-4)

Kosta Brava(FR), 7lb higher than when winning on fast ground over C/D last month, travelled well but had to survive one particularly bad blunder. After taking it up on the home turn, he was headed halfway up the run-in but stuck to his guns and was just inched out. There is room for improvement in his jumping but he is still on an upward curve. (op 2-1)

Super Baby(FR) made a lot of the running and this rates a pleasing reappearance. He is without a win since scoring here in March last year but is currently operating off 5lb lower than he was that day. (op 4-1 tchd 7-2)

Prince Tam, without the cheekpieces, was 3lb out of the weights and this ground was easier than ideal. Official explanation: jockey said gelding hung left (op 12-1)

The Cockney Squire(IRE), making his chasing debut, was let down by his jumping at the business end of the race. (op 11-2 tchd 13-2)

2208 MERRY FARRIERS STAG H'CAP HURDLE (10 hdls) 2m 2f

3:45 (3:45) (Class 4) (0-110,109) 4-Y-0+ **£2,602** (£764; £382; £190)

Form				RPR
6PP-	1		**Sunarri (IRE)**[192] 44 6-11-0 **104** AlistairFindlay[(7)] (Jane Walton) *mde all: clr bef 2 out: hld on wl fr last* **14/1**	115+
F45-	2	1	**Texas Holdem (IRE)**[209] 5141 11-11-4 **104** JamesO'Farrell[(3)] (Michael Smith) *t.k.h: hld up: pushed along after 4 out: hdwy bef 2 out: chsd wnr run-in: rdn and r.o* **25/1**	112
-060	3	10	**Itstooearly**[157] 582 7-10-7 **90** PaddyAspell (James Moffatt) *hld up: pushed along bef 3 out: hdwy after next: styd on run-in: nrst fin* **40/1**	89
00-0	4	nk	**Winter Alchemy (IRE)**[183] 191 5-9-10 **89** StephenMulqueen[(10)] (Nicky Richards) *hld up in midfield: outpcd after 4 out: rallied bef 2 out: kpt on run-in: no imp* **18/1**	88
00-0	5	5	**Just Posh**[21] 1870 8-9-11 **83** oh1 RyanMania[(3)] (Rayson Nixon) *disp ld to 2nd: cl up: rdn after 3 out: no imp whn hit last* **20/1**	77
0053	6	1/2	**Long Distance (FR)**[21] 1870 5-10-12 **95** (p) CampbellGillies (Lucinda Russell) *in tch: lost pl after 3rd: hdwy bef 2 out: nvr rchd ldrs* **5/1**[2]	89
265	7	1/2	**Mountskip**[39] 1645 6-10-12 **102** MrAdamNicol[(7)] (Rose Dobbin) *cl up: wnt 2nd 3 out to run-in: sn wknd* **8/1**	95
4-60	8	11	**Accordingtotheboss (IRE)**[21] 1867 5-10-4 **90** FearghalDavis[(3)] (Nicky Richards) *t.k.h: hld up: hit 5th: rdn bef 3 out: wknd bef next* **9/2**[1]	77
-445	9	3 1/2	**Heavenly Chorus**[147] 728 8-11-9 **106** JamesReveley (Keith Reveley) *hld up: stdy hdwy after 4 out: wknd bef 2 out* **14/1**	86
3-F	10	2 1/2	**St Killian's Run (IRE)**[189] 88 6-11-8 **105** WilsonRenwick (P Monteith) *hld up: rdn after 4 out: nvr on terms* **12/1**	83
114-	11	2 1/4	**Bene Lad (IRE)**[204] 5202 8-10-7 **90** RichieMcGrath (Jim Goldie) *plld hrd: prom tl rdn and wknd fr 3 out* **11/2**[3]	66
2100	12	11	**Front Rank (IRE)**[34] 1695 10-11-5 **109** MissECSayer[(7)] (Dianne Sayer) *prom: lost pl after 6th: struggling fr next* **22/1**	75
01-0	13	3 1/2	**Waterloo Corner**[21] 1870 8-11-3 **100** KennyJohnson (Ray Craggs) *hld up: hdwy and prom 1/2-way: rdn and wknd appr 2 out* **28/1**	63
-B10	14	12	**No Supper (IRE)**[6] 2104 6-10-12 **102** BrianToomey[(7)] (George Bewley) *hld up: hdwy and in tch after 4 out: wknd bef 2 out* **16/1**	54
0-31	15	15	**Weetfromthechaff**[139] 800 5-11-3 **100** (t) MichaelMcAlister (Maurice Barnes) *mstkes: in tch tl rdn and wknd bef 2 out* **12/1**	39

4m 42.1s (15.10) **Going Correction** -0.10s/f (Good) **15** Ran SP% **120.1**

Speed ratings (Par 105): **62,61,57,56,54 54,54,49,47,46 45,40,39,33,27**

toteswingers:1&2 £41.60, 2&3 £18.30, 1&3 £39.30 CSF £327.47 CT £12832.65 TOTE £22.50: £4.40, £12.00, £13.50; EX 542.80.

Owner Fresh Start Partnership **Bred** Mrs Moira O'Byrne **Trained** Otterburn, Northumberland

FOCUS

Not many became seriously involved in this modest handicap hurdle. The winner is rated back to the level of last season's good run first time out.

NOTEBOOK

Sunarri(IRE) lost his way last term and was sold out of George Charlton's yard for £10,000 after his last run in the spring. Making much of the running, he skipped clear on the home turn and was always holding the second up the lengthy run-in. He was not always fluent and blundered at the last flight with a circuit to run.

Texas Holdem(IRE) stayed on from the rear division to emerge as the only threat to the winner after the last. Without a win for the best part of five years, but lightly raced in that period, he was limited to just three chase runs last season, and this was his first outing since April.

Itstooearly was another staying on from the back, but while this was a satisfactory seasonal return she was never a factor and is now winless in 24 career starts.

Winter Alchemy(IRE) didn't show much in a bumper and three novice hurdles last season, and this was a step in the right direction on his handicap debut. He is a half-brother to winning hurdler Johnny Mullen.

Just Posh, again without the regular cheekpieces, shaped as if the return to further will suit.

Long Distance(FR) was keeping on at the end on this step back up in trip but is a difficult horse to catch right.

Mountskip, back over hurdles, ran well for a long way and was still in second over the last. The ground was softer than he would have liked.

Accordingtotheboss(IRE), who came here with a similar profile to his stablemate Winter Alchemy, was keen and had been seen off with two to jump.

No Supper(IRE) ran better than his final position indicates.

T/Plt: £20.40 to a £1 stake. Pool of £57,238.91 - 2,040.64 winning tickets. T/Qpdt: £9.60 to a £1 stake. Pool of £3,343.98 - 256.60 winning tickets. RY

SANDOWN (R-H)

Saturday, November 6

OFFICIAL GOING: Chase course - good (good to soft in places); hurdle course - good to soft (good in places)

Wind: Light, half against Weather: Fine, pleasant

2209 BET @ BLUESQ.COM CONDITIONAL JOCKEYS' H'CAP HURDLE (9 hdls) 2m 4f

12:45 (12:45) (Class 3) (0-120,120) 4-Y-0+ **£4,000** (£1,174; £587; £293)

Form				RPR
44P-	1		**Gold Reef**[221] 4940 7-10-13 **115** PeterHatton[(8)] (Alan King) *hld up in last pair: stl there after 3 out: gd prog but stl only 9th bef 2 out: wnt 4th last: urged along and styd on strly to ld fnl strides* **11/1**	119
32-1	2	1/2	**Lemon Silk (IRE)**[18] 1911 6-10-5 **99** DavidBass (Alex Hales) *hld up towards rr: gd prog after 3 out: led bef last: rdn 2 l clr flat: kpt on: collared fnl strides* **15/2**[2]	103
03-6	3	2	**Doctor Foxtrot (IRE)**[18] 1907 5-11-3 **114** (b[1]) GilesHawkins[(3)] (Philip Hobbs) *trckd ldrs: prog after 3 out to ld bef next: hdd bef last: kpt on same pce* **12/1**	116
1-24	4	nse	**Maurisca (FR)**[18] 1911 5-10-2 **104** (p) PeterCarberry[(8)] (Charlie Longsdon) *t.k.h: cl up: chal and w ldr bef 2 out: nt qckn bef last: kpt on* **4/1**[1]	106
/P4-	5	10	**Slew Charm (FR)**[24] 4233 8-11-7 **115** (t) PeterToole (Noel Chance) *hld up in midfield: smooth prog to join ldrs bef 2 out: sn rdn: wknd bef last* **10/1**[3]	108
2212	6	5	**Northern Lad (IRE)**[23] 1840 8-10-10 **107** MarcGoldstein[(3)] (Jim Best) *hld up in last pair: gd prog 3 out to press ldrs bef next: sn rdn and wknd* **12/1**	95

4304 **7** *4 1/2* **Dream Catcher (SWE)**[30] 1740 7-11-0 **111**.............. RichieMcLernon(3) 95
(Jonjo O'Neill) *hld up in midfield: prog 3 out: pressed ldrs bef next and n.m.r: wknd after 2 out* **14/1**

410- **8** *1 3/4* **Preuty Boy (FR)**[211] 5119 5-11-9 **117**.............................. RichardKilloran 100
(Alan Fleming) *trckd ldr: pushed along after 6th: chal and upsides bef 2 out: sn wknd* **16/1**

-525 **9** *1 3/4* **Mickmacmagoole (IRE)**[21] 1864 8-11-2 **120**............(p) JSMcGarvey(10) 101
(Evan Williams) *hld up towards rr: rdn and struggling in last pair after 6th: decided to keep on fr 2 out: n.d* **14/1**

3P-0 **10** *3/4* **Prince Pippin (IRE)**[28] 1775 4-11-3 **117**.................(t) AnthonyFreeman(6) 101
(Sean Curran) *trckd ldng pair: lost pl fr 6th but stl gng wl: midfield after next: rallying u.p whn mstke 2 out: wknd* **50/1**

-340 **11** *13* **Apache Chant (USA)**[28] 1776 6-10-4 **101**....................(p) LeeEdwards(3) 70
(Tony Carroll) *rdn in rr after 3rd: a struggling after: lost tch sn after 3 out* **25/1**

0424 **12** *3 1/2* **Santamina (IRE)**[17] 1925 4-10-1 **98**..........................(p) DonalDevereux(3) 64
(Peter Bowen) *prom: j. slowly 4th: u.p and wknd after 3 out* **14/1**

223- **13** *1 3/4* **Latin America (IRE)**[198] 5326 5-11-2 **120**.................... FinianO'Toole(10) 84
(Nick Gifford) *t.k.h: hld up in rr: lost tch w ldrs after 3 out in last quartet: jst pushed along after* **14/1**

150/ **14** *15* **Cathedral Rock (IRE)**[252] 8-11-7 **118**.........................(b) CharlieWallis(3) 69
(Ms A E Embiricos) *led: hdd & wknd rapidly bef 2 out: t.o* **33/1**

-305 **15** *76* **Wade Farm Billy (IRE)**[34] 1693 6-11-4 **120**.............. JosephAkehurst(8) 2
(Gary Moore) *hld up in rr: effrt after 3 out: in tch u.p bef 2 out: sn wknd: virtually p.u flat* **25/1**

3-4 **P** **Sunwise (USA)**[18] 1910 4-10-13 **110**..............................(b) IanPopham(3) —
(Paul Nicholls) *t.k.h: trckd ldrs: j. slowly 4th: sn rdn: dropped away fr 6th: t.o in last whn p.u bef 2 out* **15/2**[2]

5m 11.8s (6.10) **Going Correction** +0.275s/f (Yiel)
WFA 4 from 5yo+ 8lb **16** Ran SP% **121.5**
Speed ratings (Par 107): **98,97,97,96,92 90,89,88,87,87 82,80,80,74,43** —
toteswingers:1&2 £39.50, 2&3 £24.80, 1&3 £53.40 CSF £88.45 CT £1025.76 TOTE £15.80: £3.60, £2.10, £3.30, £1.60; EX 132.10.

Owner Ms Caroline Rowland **Bred** Mrs S C Welch **Trained** Barbury Castle, Wilts

■ Stewards' Enquiry : Peter Carberry ten-day ban: failed to ride out for third (Nov 20-29)

FOCUS
After 7.2mm of rain fell in the previous 24 hours, clerk of the course Andrew Cooper was forced to change the going from an overnight report of no worse than good, to good, good to soft in places' on the chase course and good to soft, good in places' on the hurdles course. The first two stepped up but the runner-up was a lot better than this at one time.

NOTEBOOK
Gold Reef was almost last leaving the back straight. However, she responded to pressure while others faltered, and got in front at just the right time. Absent since pulling up after breaking a blood vessel in March, this was good start to her season. (op 12-1)

Lemon Silk(IRE) was another to come from off the pace, but it was heartbreak for his supporters when the winner mugged him late on. He did, at least, confirm the form with the fourth. (op 8-1)

Doctor Foxtrot(IRE) almost certainly improved for the fitting of the blinkers, but, although he was close up at the end, his rider had to work hard on him almost as soon as the pair got to the front. (op 16-1)

Maurisca(FR), in first-time cheekpieces, can often move powerfully under restraint and did so again here, but he couldn't lengthen when Peter Carberry wanted him to, although he stayed on well enough at the one pace. The jockey, however, was banned for 10 days for failed to ride his mount out to the line - he reportedly rode to the wrong finishing line. (op 5-1)

Slew Charm(FR) represented a stable with a two-from-two record in this contest, so had to be respected for that fact alone. He moved up going well at what looked the right time but failed to get home as strongly as the four in front of him. (op 7-1)

Northern Lad(IRE), running off a 12lb higher mark than last time, cruised through runners after sitting at the rear, which he can often do, but didn't find another gear once the battle up front started. (op 14-1)

Wade Farm Billy(IRE) Official explanation: trainer said gelding was unsuited by the good to soft (good in places) ground

Sunwise(USA), with blinkers on for the first time over hurdles, jumped slowly at the fourth and appeared to lose interest from that point. His jockey did his best to get him going again but they never made any meaningful impact. Official explanation: jockey said gelding stopped quickly (op 11-2, tchd 5-1 in places)

2210 JOS RODOSTHENOUS BEGINNERS' CHASE (13 fncs) 2m
1:15 (1:17) (Class 3) 4-Y-0+ **£5,204** (£1,528; £764; £381)

Form RPR

33-P **1** **Pepe Simo (IRE)**[44] 1587 6-11-1 0...................................... SamThomas 138+
(Paul Nicholls) *hld up: mstke 3rd: wnt 2nd and mstke 8th: waited bhd ldr tl cruised into ld last: easily* **10/11**[1]

146- **2** *4 1/2* **Lord Singer (FR)**[216] 5009 5-11-1 0.................................... JamieMoore 124+
(Gary Moore) *t.k.h: led and sn clr: several bold leaps but also j.lft: mstke 9th: hdd last: no match for wnr* **13/2**[3]

41P5 **3** *25* **Marc Aurele (IRE)**[3] 2153 5-10-10 0..........................(t) JimmyDerham(5) 104
(Milton Harris) *a abt same pl: outpcd and wl btn 3rd fr 4 out: wknd 2 out* **8/1**

012- **4** *29* **Fahrisee (IRE)**[237] 4606 7-10-12 0.. DPFahy(3) 87
(Evan Williams) *pckd 1st: chsd ldr: mstkes 3rd and 6th: lost 2nd pl 8th: mstke next: sn wknd: t.o* **5/2**[2]

4m 1.30s (-0.50) **Going Correction** +0.15s/f (Yiel) **4** Ran SP% **105.4**
Speed ratings (Par 107): **107,104,92,77**
CSF £6.20 TOTE £1.70; EX 3.80.

Owner Highclere Thoroughbred Racing-Pepe Simo **Bred** Grange Stud **Trained** Ditcheat, Somerset

FOCUS
A race won by some decent sorts in the past, like Crack Away Jack and Jack The Giant, but this looked fairly uncompetitive. The easy winner ran to the level expected from the best of his hurdles form.

NOTEBOOK
Pepe Simo(IRE)'s jumping wasn't fluent early while held up, but he warmed to his task the further he went and was given a beautiful ride by Sam Thomas to win nicely, and with a bit in hand. There is plenty of room for improvement with his jumping, although some of his leaps down the back straight were good, and one would slightly worry for him in a fast-run contest. (op 8-11)

Lord Singer(FR) got to the front early enough after taking a strong hold but jumped out to his left at virtually every fence, some times worse than others. However, despite being no match for the winner after the last, he had the third a long way behind and will surely be going left-handed next time. (op 8-1)

Marc Aurele(IRE) wasn't able to dominate and got round in his own time. (op 11-1)

Fahrisee(IRE) was disappointing. A bad peck at the second of the railway fences didn't help, but most of his rivals met one of those three awkwardly, so that isn't really an excuse. Official explanation: trainer said gelding bled from the nose (op 9-4)

2211 BLUE SQUARE EXCLUSIVE LIVE SHOWS JUVENILE HURDLE (8 hdls) 2m 110y
1:45 (1:47) (Class 4) 3-Y-O **£3,252** (£955; £477; £238)

Form RPR

1 **Dolatulo (FR)**[242] 3-11-5 0.. APMcCoy 129+
(Paul Nicholls) *mde all: stdy pce tl stretched field fr 5th: drew rt away bef 2 out: easily* **10/11**[1]

20 **2** *23* **Optimistic Duke (IRE)**[23] 1674 3-10-12 0.................... JimmyMcCarthy 94
(William Muir) *settled in 6th: outpcd after 3 out: 5th and rdn whn mstke 2 out: styd on to take 2nd flat* **50/1**

3 *1 3/4* **Kitty Koo (IRE)**[23] 3-10-0 0... LeeEdwards(5) 89+
(Tony Carroll) *chsd ldng pair: stmbld bdly on landing 3 out and rdr lost iron: rallied to press for 2nd 2 out: plugged on* **66/1**

4 *3* **Meglio Ancora**[33] 3-10-12 0.. SamThomas 90
(Jonathan Portman) *settled in 7th: outpcd after 5th: no ch after: rdn and kpt on fr 2 out* **16/1**

5 *5* **Balerina (FR)**[231] 3-10-5 0... ChristianWilliams 77
(Alan King) *chsd ldrs in 6th: outpcd after 3 out: n.d after: one pce fr 2 out* **15/2**

6 *3/4* **Bun Oir (USA)**[24] 1833 3-10-12 0..................................... FelixDeGiles 88+
(Charlie Longsdon) *chsd wnr: only one on terms after 3 out: rdn and tired whn mstkes 2 out and last: wknd and lost pls flat* **5/1**[2]

5 **7** *1 1/2* **Jinksy Minx**[34] 1691 3-10-5 0... ColinBolger 75
(Suzy Smith) *hld up in rr: mstke 3rd: wl bhd after 3 out: jst pushed along fr 2 out: clsd on tiring rivals flat* **40/1**

8 *15* **L'Eminence Grise (IRE)** 3-10-12 0.................................... DarylJacob 69
(Nick Williams) *nt jump wl: mostly last: t.o after 3 out* **6/1**[3]

9 *43* **Deux Etoiles (IRE)**[195] 3-10-12 0..................................... JamieMoore 30
(Gary Moore) *chsd ldrs in 5th: wknd 3 out: t.o after 2 out: virtually p.u flat* **10/1**

4m 12.2s (5.00) **Going Correction** +0.275s/f (Yiel) **9** Ran SP% **116.0**
Speed ratings (Par 104): **99,88,87,85,83 83,82,75,55**
toteswingers:1&2 £8.70, 2&3 £26.10, 1&3 £17.50 CSF £55.71 TOTE £2.00: £1.10, £7.10, £7.50; EX 54.00.

Owner Simon Munir **Bred** Claude Michel **Trained** Ditcheat, Somerset

FOCUS
No more than a fair event, which generally hasn't produced too many stars in previous years. That said, you could not fail to be seriously impressed by the wide-margin winner, who rates the best juvenile of the season so far.

NOTEBOOK
Dolatulo(FR) ◆ won his sole start over hurdles in France, and thanks to a new rule introduced this season, he is allowed to take his place in juvenile events, despite winning in March - the rule means that any horse winning in France this year as a 3-y-o in February, March or April can run in juvenile contests until the end of this season. Soon afforded a lengthy lead, he was never in any danger and sauntered home to an easy success. He beat very little judged on their previous form but will surely be stepped up in grade next time. (tchd Evens, 11-10 in places and 6-5 in a place)

Optimistic Duke(IRE), modest on the Flat, shaped with a little bit of promise on the first of his two previous outings over hurdles, but was never involved in this until passing some tired horses.

Kitty Koo(IRE), whose stable won this last season, hadn't really shown much on the Flat to suggest she was going to shine here, but this was a lot better, as even though she clouted three out really hard, which saw her jockey lose his stirrup for some time, she galloped on strongly and stayed on in pleasing style. This effort suggests she'll want a test of stamina.

Meglio Ancora, a fair sort on the Flat with mixed form, made only a satisfactory debut, but no more than that.

Balerina(FR), a Listed winner at Marseille last November, was having her first outing for this stable and didn't make a big impact once she started up the hill despite the weight allowance. (op 13-2 tchd 6-1)

Bun Oir(USA) showed promise for Jessica Harrington on his sole start over hurdles almost a month previously, but he fell to pieces in the latter stages after racing prominently in the chasing pack. (tchd 9-2 and 11-2)

L'Eminence Grise(IRE) was nicely supported for a stable that can ready an unraced horse for a juvenile hurdle, but he seemed green and in need of the experience. (op 10-1)

2212 BLUE SQUARE H'CAP CHASE (17 fncs) 2m 4f 110y
2:20 (2:20) (Class 3) (0-135,135) 4-Y-0+
£8,766 (£2,590; £1,295; £648; £323; £162)

Form RPR

-U21 **1** **Songe (FR)**[34] 1690 6-11-12 **135**... NoelFehily 145+
(Charlie Longsdon) *hld up in tch gng wl: prog on inner whn mstke 12th: stl only 5th 3 out: hdwy to chse clr ldr 2 out: clsd to chal last: led flat: drvn and jst hld on* **11/4**[1]

-312 **2** *hd* **Alesandro Mantegna (IRE)**[17] 1926 5-10-12 **121**..........(p) JamieMoore 130+
(Keith Goldsworthy) *tended to jump lft: mde most: drew clr 3 out: 5 l up whn j. markedly lft 2 out: hdd flat: rallied: jst failed* **7/2**[3]

02P- **3** *12* **Or Bleu (FR)**[224] 4883 8-11-7 **130**..................................... TomO'Brien 126
(Philip Hobbs) *trckd ldng pair: nt fluent 7th: rdn bef 3 out: disp 2nd briefly 2 out: sn btn* **11/2**

0F-0 **4** *8* **Double Dizzy**[22] 1856 9-11-3 **126**... APMcCoy 115
(Bob Buckler) *w ldr: bmpd 6th: reminder bnd bef next: led briefly 10th: drvn and lost 2nd 2 out: wknd* **3/1**[2]

00-4 **5** *1 1/2* **Commemoration Day (IRE)**[167] 438 9-10-4 **120**........ JoshuaMoore(7) 107
(Gary Moore) *hld up last: pair: pushed along and prog 10th: disp 3rd after 4 out: wknd 2 out* **16/1**

P0P- **6** *8* **Bible Lord (IRE)**[204] 5204 9-11-12 **135**.................................. MarkGrant 115
(Andy Turnell) *trckd ldrs: nt fluent 8th: pushed along 10th: rdn whn mstke 4 out: sn wknd* **7/1**

U1-6 **P** **Polmar (FR)**[25] 1812 7-11-6 **129**... DarylJacob —
(Jamie Snowden) *chsd ldrs: nt fluent 3rd: wknd 12th: t.o whn p.u bef 3 out* **14/1**

5m 17.6s (-0.80) **Going Correction** +0.15s/f (Yiel) **7** Ran SP% **114.3**
Speed ratings (Par 107): **107,106,102,99,98 95,—**
toteswingers:1&2 £1.60, 2&3 £5.50, 1&3 £5.90 CSF £13.21 CT £48.13 TOTE £2.90: £2.00, £2.30; EX 10.00.

Owner Alan Halsall **Bred** Alec Head And Mme Ghislaine Head **Trained** Over Norton, Oxon

FOCUS
This will probably be good and reliable form, as a few of these looked nicely weighted and a couple have the potential to hold their own at a slightly higher level. The first two are rated a bit better than the bare result.

NOTEBOOK

Songe(FR) finally gained a first win over fences last time after showing plenty of promise over them, but had been put up 13lb for that easy success. Held up towards the rear, he could be seen going well throughout, but a mistake at the first of the Railway Fences stopped his progress for a few strides. Soon gathered together, he looked dangerous again but only got the verdict on the line after finding a little less than appeared likely at one stage. There is a race at Kempton over the Christmas period for him to be aimed towards. (op 10-3, tchd 7-2 in places)

Alesandro Mantegna(IRE) ◆ was possibly unlucky in some ways, as he managed to get to the lead, but gave away lengths during the last circuit jumping out to his left, something he has done in the past. Considering the winning margin, he may have won had he been able to keep straighter at the fences. (op 9-2)

Or Bleu(FR), absent since a disappointing favourite at Bangor in March, looks fairly treated but needed niggling early and was one paced when in a position to challenge. (tchd 13-2)

Double Dizzy has finally dropped down to a mark he is capable of winning off, but he never looked entirely happy, and dispite the best efforts of the champion jockey, the pair were readily left behind once in the home straight. (op 7-2 tchd 4-1)

Commemoration Day(IRE), without blinkers on his reappearance, came through to look dangerous rounding the final bend but was unable to sustain that effort.

Bible Lord(IRE) didn't have a great time of things last season after winning on his seasonal reappearance, albeit in some quality races, and was back down to a 1lb lower mark that that victory. He was still in with a chance when making a bad error at the last of the railway fences, which was enough to end his bid. (op 6-1 tchd 11-2)

Polmar(FR), well beaten on his first start for this stable over hurdles after leaving the Willie Mullins stable, got behind and pulled up. (op 10-1 tchd 9-1)

2213 BLUE SQUARE SUPPORTING CLAYGATE CLUBHOUSE H'CAP HURDLE (8 hdls) — 2m 110y

2:55 (2:55) (Class 3) (0-125,125) 4-Y-0+

£7,514 (£2,220; £1,110; £555; £277; £139)

Form — RPR

0-P6 **1** **Cheshire Prince**[14] 1956 6-11-4 **120** .... AlexMerriam(3) 127+
(Neil King) *hld up in rr: prog to trck ldrs after 3 out: nt fluent 2 out and rdn: wnt 3rd last: styd on wl to ld flat* **8/1**

133 **2** *2* **Sircozy (IRE)**[25] 1812 4-11-5 **118** .... JamieMoore 123+
(Gary Moore) *hld up last: prog on outer after 5th: chal bef 2 out: pressed ldr after but hanging: upsides after last: wnr sn wnt by* **7/1**

1/00 **3** *1 1/4* **Higgy's Boy (IRE)**[22] 1859 5-11-7 **125** ....(b) DavidBass(5) 128
(Nicky Henderson) *hld up towards rr: lost pl 5th: rdn in last after 3 out and struggling: rallied bef 2 out: kpt on u.p to take 3rd flat* **10/1**

41-0 **4** *1 1/2* **General Ting (IRE)**[21] 1864 5-11-2 **115** .... LeightonAspell 118+
(Lucy Wadham) *t.k.h: hld up in midfield: prog after 3 out: led 2 out but hrd pressed: blnd last: hdd & wknd flat* **11/2[3]**

2102 **5** *9* **Alph**[48] 1548 13-11-1 **121** .... MrTJCannon(7) 115
(Roger Teal) *hld up in rr: effrt after 3 out: nt pce to threaten ldrs bef 2 out: plugged on* **9/1**

6522 **6** *3* **Exulto (IRE)**[27] 1797 5-10-11 **115** .... GilesHawkins(5) 106
(Philip Hobbs) *cl up: wnt 3rd 5th: chal and upsides bef 2 out: nt qckn bef last: wknd* **5/1[2]**

U561 **7** *3/4* **Cruchain (IRE)**[25] 1816 7-11-6 **119** .... APMcCoy 109
(Jonjo O'Neill) *trckd ldrs: led briefly bef 2 out gng wl: wknd tamely sn after 2 out* **9/2[1]**

014- **8** *31* **Outside The Box**[201] 5278 6-11-8 **121** .... TomSiddall 83
(Noel Chance) *trckd ldng pair to 5th: lost pl: dropped to last pair and struggling after 3 out: t.o* **16/1**

062P **9** *nse* **High Bird Humphrey**[6] 2112 11-10-5 **111** .... MrSFMagee(7) 73
(Simon West) *led to 5th: w ldr after 3 out: wkng rapidly whn sltly hmpd 2 out: t.o* **16/1**

410- **10** *8* **Drussell (IRE)**[180] 258 4-11-12 **125** .... SeanQuinlan 80
(Richard Phillips) *hld up in rr: rdn and struggling for room bnd after 3 out: wknd bef next: t.o* **25/1**

01-4 **11** *20* **Flaming Gorge (IRE)**[22] 1853 5-11-7 **120** .... DarylJacob 57
(Nick Williams) *racd freely: w ldr: led 5th: hdd & wknd rapidly bef 2 out: t.o* **11/1**

05-6 **F** **Troubletimestwo (FR)**[28] 1775 4-11-5 **123** .... LeeEdwards(5) 114
(Tony Carroll) *trckd ldrs: lost pl 3 out: tight for room and u.p bnd sn after: 7th and getting outpcd whn fell 2 out* **25/1**

4m 8.60s (1.40) **Going Correction** +0.275s/f (Yiel) **12** Ran SP% **120.7**
Speed ratings (Par 107): **107,106,105,104,100 99,98,84,84,80 70,—**
toteswingers:1&2 £44.30, 2&3 £11.30, 1&3 £9.90 CSF £64.79 CT £570.55 TOTE £10.90: £2.90, £2.70, £3.70; EX 100.10 Trifecta £323.00.
Owner Across The Pond Partnership **Bred** The National Stud **Trained** Newmarket, Suffolk

FOCUS

A fair handicap run at what seemed a solid pace. The winner is a potential 140+ horse on his Flat form, and the runner-up improved to the level expected of his best Flat form.

NOTEBOOK

Cheshire Prince has taken well to hurdling and saw his Aintree form behind Nearby boosted earlier in the day when that horse took the Elite Hurdle at Wincanton. Towards the rear early, he stayed on really well after the final hurdle to gain another success. Ascot in a couple of weeks is on the agenda next. (op 6-1)

Sircozy(IRE), making his handicap debut without the cheekpieces he wore last time, certainly knows how to win both over hurdles and on the Flat and came from a stable that had won this race three times since 2001. Held up, he came through to have every chance but was unable to hold off the winner, especially as he was hanging under pressure. (op 8-1)

Higgy's Boy(IRE), whose trainer won this with Caracciola back in 2003, looked on a good mark after two poor efforts since a long absence, and bounced back to something close to his best in this. (op 12-1)

General Ting(IRE) ◆, back down in distance after being well beaten on his handicap debut last time, looked to pull much too hard in behind, and unsurprisingly didn't have a lot left at the end. Better ground or a flatter track will help him. (op 13-2)

Alph is a talented veteran and got some market support, but couldn't get involved when it mattered. (op 14-1)

Exulto(IRE) chased the leaders but had nothing left for the charge up the hill, and steadily weakened. (tchd 9-2 and 11-2)

Cruchain(IRE) hasn't always looked the easiest to win with but he got his head back in front on his previous outing at Huntingdon. Now 4lb higher, he made his way into the lead, seemingly going well, but was soon held. (op 5-1, tchd 11-2 in places)

2214 MARLBOROUGH SURFACING H'CAP CHASE (22 fncs) — 3m 110y

3:30 (3:30) (Class 3) (0-125,122) 4-Y-0+

£7,514 (£2,220; £1,110; £555; £277; £139)

Form — RPR

4-P4 **1** **Fit To Drive**[14] 1973 8-11-9 **119** ....(t) NoelFehily 132+
(Brendan Powell) *trckd ldng pair: let them get on w it fr 12th: dropped to 5th at 18th: renewed effrt to go 3rd 3 out: clsd to ld bef last: bounded clr* **14/1**

6513 **2** *10* **Sarahs Gift (IRE)**[19] 1903 7-10-12 **108** ....(t) AidanColeman 112
(Lawney Hill) *settled towards rr: mstke 10th: effrt 17th: no imp after 4 out and struggling in 5th 3 out: rallied fr next: styd on to take 2nd flat* **8/1**

PP-P **3** *2 1/4* **Antonius Caesar (FR)**[15] 1950 7-10-8 **107** .... PeterToole(3) 109
(Alex Hales) *mstke 1st: pressed ldr: narrow ld fr 11th and clr of rest: bef off chalr 2 out: nthing lft whn hdd bef last: wknd and lost 2nd flat* **15/2**

42P- **4** *9* **Appleaday (IRE)**[217] 4980 9-11-12 **122** .... APMcCoy 117
(Paul Webber) *nt a fluent: narrow ld to 11th: duelled w ldr after and clr of rest: btn off 2 out: wknd last: fin tired* **6/1[3]**

3212 **5** *5* **Magical Legend**[36] 1661 9-11-4 **117** ....(t) RichieMcLernon(3) 106
(Sophie Leech) *wl in tch: chsd clr ldng pair 17th: no imp after 4 out: lost 3rd next: fdd* **10/1**

53-2 **6** *4 1/2* **Sonny Mullen (IRE)**[27] 1794 6-11-6 **116** .... SeanQuinlan 103
(Kim Bailey) *hld up in detached last pair: mstke 6th: blnd 15th whn in 7th: no prog after* **11/4[1]**

2-54 **7** *11* **Silver Bay**[25] 1815 9-10-13 **109** .... LeightonAspell 88
(Oliver Sherwood) *wl in tch: wnt 4th at 18th: no prog next: wknd 3 out* **12/1**

3-4F **8** *17* **Mister Watzisname (IRE)**[13] 1992 8-11-5 **115** .... FelixDeGiles 75
(Charlie Longsdon) *hld up in detached last pair: hmpd 1st: no real prog whn mstke 17th: nvr a factor* **12/1**

P/0- **9** *41* **Verasi**[358] 2253 9-10-13 **112** ....(b) EamonDehdashti(3) 35
(Gary Moore) *sloppy rnd of jumping: dropped to last after mstkes 12th and 13th: t.o whn v slow 18th* **25/1**

1P-0 **F** **Scots Dragoon**[22] 1858 8-11-6 **121** .... DavidBass(5) —
(Nicky Henderson) *fell 1st* **9/2[2]**

6m 28.2s (0.40) **Going Correction** +0.15s/f (Yiel) **10** Ran SP% **117.0**
Speed ratings (Par 107): **105,101,101,98,96 95,91,86,73,—**
Swingers:1&2:£102.00, 2&3:£8.60, 1&3:£102.00 CSF £120.73 CT £914.02 TOTE £17.60: £4.90, £2.30, £2.90; EX 165.50 Trifecta £265.10.
Owner The Meon Golfing Partnership **Bred** W Smith **Trained** Upper Lambourn, Berks

FOCUS

Not an easy race to assess because both Antonius Caesar and Appleaday went off at a decent pace, and leaving the back straight they looked to be the only two that mattered. However, both had seemingly gone off at least a stride too quickly, and the pair tired from three out, and allowed closers to get past. The winner is rated back to her best 2009 form.

NOTEBOOK

Fit To Drive was back down to a fair mark but the trip looked an unknown considering her winning form. However, she showed no shortage of stamina when those in front of her weakened, and won by a wide margin. (op 16-1)

Sarahs Gift(IRE) was another to get well behind before keeping on in relentless style. This was a better effort after a disappointing performance last time, but he is a little high in the weights on his winning form, and all of his wins have come going left-handed. (tchd 9-1 in places)

Antonius Caesar(FR) hadn't finished on his last three starts, so this was a return to something better. He seemed to enjoy himself out in front but probably went too fast early. (op 9-1 tchd 7-1)

Appleaday(IRE) helped to set the decent pace but didn't get home under his big weight. (tchd 9-2)

Sonny Mullen(IRE), a good second on his chase debut at Ffos Las, raced in the rear and lost his position with a bad mistake at the fifteenth. (op 7-2 tchd 4-1 and 9-2 in places)

Mister Watzisname(IRE) took a strong hold in rear and made no impression. (op 16-1)

Verasi didn't look like he was enjoying himself for much of the contest and didn't jump very well. (op 22-1)

2215 PRINCE OF WALES PUB ESHER STANDARD OPEN NATIONAL HUNT FLAT RACE — 2m 110y

4:05 (4:08) (Class 5) 4-6-Y-0 **£1,951** (£573; £286; £143)

Form — RPR

1 **Knight Pass (IRE)** 4-11-0 0 .... NoelFehily 120+
(Warren Greatrex) *hld up bhd ldrs: smooth prog to ld jst over 2f out: r.o wl and drew clr over 1f out* **4/1[2]**

2 *8* **Sire De Grugy (FR)** 4-11-0 0 .... JamieMoore 107
(Gary Moore) *t.k.h: hld up in last trio: prog over 2f out: rdn and styd on to take 2nd jst ins fnl f: no ch w wnr* **6/1**

3 *1 1/2* **Loch Ba (IRE)** 4-11-0 0 .... HaddenFrost 106
(Henrietta Knight) *cl up: led 3f out gng wl: hdd and outpcd jst over 2f out: lost 2nd jst ins fnl f* **12/1**

4 *1/2* **El Padrino (IRE)** 5-11-0 0 .... LeightonAspell 105
(Nick Gifford) *cl up: effrt on inner 3f out: shkn up and kpt on: nt pce to threaten* **12/1**

5 *6* **Master Milan (IRE)**[182] 4-11-0 0 .... APMcCoy 101
(Jonjo O'Neill) *hld up in last trio: prog over 2f out: nudged along and one pce fr over 1f out* **11/2[3]**

0- **6** *1* **Carabinier (FR)**[201] 5283 4-10-9 0 .... DavidBass(5) 98
(Nicky Henderson) *w ldr: nt qckn once pce lifted 3f out: sn lost pl: one pce after* **10/3[1]**

7 *3/4* **Practice Round (IRE)** 4-10-11 0 .... MrAJBerry(3) 97
(Jonjo O'Neill) *hld up in last trio: pushed along 5f out: sme prog fnl 2f: nvr a factor* **28/1**

8 *1 1/4* **Sulpius (GER)** 5-11-0 0 .... SamThomas 96
(Paul Nicholls) *led: set slow gallop tl past 1/2-way: hdd 3f out: sn btn* **14/1**

9 *3 3/4* **Tenby Jewel (IRE)** 5-10-7 0 .... PeterCarberry(7) 92
(Keith Goldsworthy) *in tch: pushed along and outpcd fr 3f out* **25/1**

1/4 **10** *nk* **Royal Scoundrel (IRE)**[28] 1778 6-11-7 0 .... TomO'Brien 99
(Peter Bowen) *hld up in tch: outpcd and dropped to last over 3f out: no ch after* **10/1**

1 **11** *1* **Vicpol (ITY)**[146] 739 4-11-2 0 .... LeeEdwards(5) 98
(Tom Gretton) *trckd ldng pair to 4f out: wknd 3f out* **7/1**

4m 22.4s (16.30) **Going Correction** +0.275s/f (Yiel)
WFA 4 from 5yo+ 7lb **11** Ran SP% **123.7**
Speed ratings: **72,68,67,67,64 64,63,63,61,61 60**
toteswingers:1&2 £46.70, 2&3 £24.30, 1&3 £46.70 CSF £30.06 TOTE £7.00: £2.10, £2.80, £3.60; EX 34.90.
Owner Malcolm C Denmark **Bred** D J Fitzpatrick **Trained** Upper Lambourn, Berks

FOCUS

Good horses have won this race down the years. The last three renewals had been won by Megastar, Bensalem and Big Eared Fran. The early pace here was really slow and this is not form to be confident about, but the winner looks a decent prospect.

NOTEBOOK

Knight Pass(IRE) ◆ looks capable of being a force in top bumpers for the rest of the season. Solid in the betting, he was held up behind but stormed clear once asked to quicken in the manner of an above-average performer. (op 5-1)

Sire De Grugy(FR) finished second, but one can't be sure what he achieved given the lack of any early pace. Described as big and strong in a Stable Tour, he should have more to come. (op 9-2)

Loch Ba(IRE) looked to have plenty of size about him and kept on well after racing prominently, albeit a bit keen. He seems sure to improve for the experience. (op 11-1)

El Padrino(IRE), a half-brother to I'msingingtheblues, confirmed he had a future with a pleasing debut effort. (op 14-1)

Master Milan(IRE), who fell and won in two Irish points, was the stable's first choice on jockey bookings, and kept on well after being towards the rear. His dam is a half-sister to Go Ballistic, so one would imagine he'll appreciate a stiffer test in time. (op 7-1)
Carabinier(FR) was a disappointment on his sole start last season, and dropped away tamely here once under pressure. (tchd 3-1 and 7-2)
Practice Round(IRE), the second of the two McManus-owned runners, looked green and in need of the experience, and should be straighter mentally next time for this outing. (op 33-1 tchd 25-1)
Vicpol(ITY), who won a Stratford bumper at 80-1 for Bill Turner, had experience on his side but was disappointing once off the bridle. (op 10-1 tchd 11-1)
T/Plt: £318.60 to a £1 stake. Pool £65,239.78 - 149.46 winning tickets. T/Qpdt: £80.20 to a £1 stake. Pool of £4,659.90 - 42.95 winning tickets. JN

1998 WINCANTON (R-H)
Saturday, November 6

OFFICIAL GOING: Good (chs 8.0, hdl 9.0)
Wind: mild breeze Weather: sunny

2216 TOTEPLACEPOT E B F "NATIONAL HUNT" NOVICES' HURDLE (QUALIFIER) (8 hdls) 2m
12:35 (12:37) (Class 3) 4-6-Y-O **£4,553** (£1,337; £668; £333)

Form RPR
1- **1** **Skint**[224] 4899 4-10-12 0 .... AndrewTinkler 118+
(Nicky Henderson) *mid-div: trckd ldrs 3rd: nt clr run briefly appr 2 out: rdn sn after: led last: r.o wl* **11/4**[2]
2- **2** *1 1/4* **The Reformer (IRE)**[201] 5283 5-10-12 0 .... HarrySkelton 114+
(Paul Nicholls) *mid-div: trckd ldrs 3rd: rdn to ld sn after 2 out: hdd last: kpt on: nt gng pce of wnr* **11/8**[1]
03-2 **3** *2 1/2* **Sweet Irony (FR)**[174] 355 4-10-12 0 .... WayneHutchinson 113+
(Alan King) *hld up towards rr: hdwy fr 4th: led appr 2 out: rdn and hdd wl bef last: kpt on* **5/1**[3]
5 **4** *7* **Just Dave (IRE)**[24] 1824 4-10-12 0 .... PaulMoloney 104+
(Evan Williams) *t.k.h: nt a fluent: trckd ldrs: slow 1st: lost pl 4th: hdwy after 3 out: shkn up after 2 out: no further imp* **16/1**
04- **5** *9* **Rayon Vert (FR)**[240] 4541 5-10-12 0 .... (t) RichardJohnson 95
(Philip Hobbs) *hld up towards rr: prog to chse ldrs after 3 out: sn rdn and one pce* **8/1**
0/0 **6** *10* **Red Law (IRE)**[17] 1914 6-10-9 0 .... TommyPhelan(3) 85
(Mark Gillard) *trckd ldrs: rdn after 3 out: sn btn* **200/1**
0- **7** *3/4* **Medicine Man (IRE)**[345] 2522 6-10-12 0 .... JackDoyle 85
(Ben De Haan) *led tl after 3 out: rdn appr 2 out: wknd sn after* **80/1**
060 **8** *3 1/4* **Le Roi Max (FR)**[18] 1910 6-10-12 0 .... PaddyBrennan 82
(Nigel Twiston-Davies) *nt a fluent: struggling 4th: a towards rr* **33/1**
60 **9** *58* **Sablazo (FR)**[14] 1974 4-10-12 0 .... NickScholfield 23
(Andy Turnell) *mid-div: hit 4th: struggling in rr whn mstke 6th: wknd after next* **100/1**
0 **10** *14* **Sun Des Mottes (FR)**[8] 2068 4-10-5 0 .... TimmyMurphy —
(David Pipe) *trckd ldr: led after 3 out: rdn and hdd bef next: wknd qckly* **25/1**

3m 32.9s (-16.00) **Going Correction** -1.10s/f (Hard) **10** Ran SP% **111.9**
Speed ratings: **96,95,94,90,86 81,80,79,50,43**
toteswingers:1&2:£1.60, 2&3:£1.30, 1&3:£3.00 CSF £6.69 TOTE £3.10: £1.50, £1.40, £1.40; EX 8.00.
Owner Paul Murphy **Bred** David Jenks **Trained** Upper Lambourn, Berks

FOCUS
The front three drew clear in what was probably a decent novice hurdle. It was steadily run.

NOTEBOOK
Skint ◆, ready winner of a Stratford bumper in March, is reportedly quite a sharp sort and was expected to prove suited by 2m on a speed-favouring track like this. Although done no favours coming to two out, he picked up really well on the run to the last, where he led, and then stayed on well to win with a bit in hand. This was a likeable performance from a horse who can probably defy a penalty before going up in grade. (tchd 3-1)
The Reformer(IRE), runner-up in a Kempton bumper on debut (may have won but for looking very inexperienced), is from a yard that had won three of the last four runnings of this race, and he looked the likely winner coming to lead after the second-last. Skint soon had him in his sights, though, and he was done for speed late on. He should improve again and will have no trouble going one better at some stage. (op 6-4 tchd 5-4)
Sweet Irony(FR) ◆, twice placed in bumpers and held in quite high regard by connections, being described as a 'classy individual' by Alan King, made good headway to and, although unable to match the front pair late on, he's almost certain to improve and looks another ready-made winner. (op 9-2 tchd 11-2)
Just Dave(IRE) ◆, too keen when fifth on his bumper debut at Uttoxeter, again refused to settle, but did show enough, without being given anything like a hard time by Paul Moloney, to suggest he'll be winning races. He gave the impression he could have got involved with the principals under a more vigorous ride and was the obvious eyecatcher of the race. The stewards later looked into his running and riding, but were happy that no wrong doing took place. (tchd 14-1)
Rayon Vert(FR), who has had a breathing operation since last seen, needed this to qualify for a handicap mark. He should fare better in that sphere. (op 11-1)
Medicine Man(IRE) ended up well held, but is a good-looker and has a future. (op 66-1)
Sun Des Mottes(FR) has now stopped quickly on both starts since joining David Pipe and has plenty to prove for now. Official explanation: jockey said filly hung badly left-handed (op 20-1)

2217 TOTEEXACTA H'CAP CHASE (17 fncs) 2m 5f
1:10 (1:10) (Class 4) (0-115,113) 4-Y-0+ **£5,204** (£1,528; £764; £381)

Form RPR
P461 **1** **I'm A Legend**[18] 1912 8-11-9 **110** .... (p) DougieCostello 118+
(Neil Mulholland) *hld up: hdwy 10th: nudged along after 12th: chalng whn awkward 3 out: narrow advantage next: pckd last: styd on: rdn out* **7/2**[3]
44 **2** *2 3/4* **Kylenoe Fairy (IRE)**[17] 1917 6-10-13 **100** .... (t) RichardJohnson 106+
(Paul Henderson) *trcking ldrs whn pckd bdly 1st: sn in last pair: shkn up and hdwy appr 4 out: slt advantage 3 out: rdn and narrowly hdd 2 out: ev ch last: no ex* **8/1**
5440 **3** *9* **Sir Harry Cool**[13] 2001 7-10-2 **89** .... DavidEngland 84
(John Panvert) *chsd ldng trio: nt fluent 9th (water): sn pushed along: rdn after 4 out: styd on same pce fr next: wnt 3rd last* **3/1**[2]
533F **4** *2 3/4* **Folie A Deux (IRE)**[14] 1973 8-11-10 **111** .... (t) JoeTizzard 106
(Colin Tizzard) *j.lft thrght: led: guessed at 7th: rdn and hdd appr 3 out: no ex whn lost 3rd bef last* **11/4**[1]
260- **5** *20* **Pacha D'Oudairies (FR)**[247] 4402 7-11-12 **113** .... TimmyMurphy 96
(Michael Blake) *trckd ldr: mstke 3rd: rdn after 13th: outpcd whn bdly hmpd 4 out: no ch after: wknd after next* **9/2**
0-P5 **6** *2* **Power Shared (IRE)**[14] 1965 6-10-7 **99** .... MichaelMurphy(5) 79
(Pat Murphy) *trckd ldrs: pckd 6th: mstke 10th: u.p whne hit 4 out and slithered on landing: no ch after: wknd after next* **9/1**

5m 10.6s (-14.60) **Going Correction** -0.775s/f (Firm) **6** Ran SP% **113.2**
Speed ratings (Par 105): **96,94,91,90,82 82**
toteswingers:1&2 £9.10, 2&3 £5.00, 1&3 £5.30 CSF £28.89 TOTE £3.20: £1.30, £3.30; EX 25.90.
Owner Wincanton Race Club **Bred** Conkwell Grange Stud Ltd **Trained** Burlescombe, Devon

FOCUS
This was just a modest handicap chase. The form is solid enough.

NOTEBOOK
I'm A Legend, 7lb higher than when winning at Exeter last month, is ideally served by small fields and, despite a brief scare at the last, he stayed on to win with a bit in hand. He's clearly in the form of his life, but it remains to be seen whether he's up to completing a hat-trick. (op 3-1 tchd 11-4)
Kylenoe Fairy(IRE), switched to handicaps on her third start over fences, hasn't had many chances for connections and this represented much-improved form. She remains a maiden in 13 attempts, but should put that right before long. (op 6-1 tchd 11-2)
Sir Harry Cool, rated 5lb lower over fences compared with hurdles, came in for good support but was readily left behind by the front pair. (op 9-2)
Folie A Deux(IRE), an early faller at Stratford, didn't help his cause by jumping left at his fences and, having been headed, he was quickly beaten. This was disappointing, but he at least got round and could do better next time. (tchd 3-1)
Pacha D'Oudairies(FR), a disappointing sort for Paul Nicholls, was already beaten when badly hampered four out, but probably deserves another chance now this run is out of the way. (op 6-1)
Power Shared(IRE) had made mistakes and was beaten when slithering badly on landing at the fourth-last. He was allowed to come home in his own time after. (op 11-1)

2218 TOTESWINGER MARES' H'CAP HURDLE (11 hdls) 2m 6f
1:40 (1:40) (Class 2) 4-Y-0+
£15,655 (£4,625; £2,312; £1,157; £577; £290)

Form RPR
4123 **1** **Santera (IRE)**[28] 1776 6-10-0 **122** oh2 .... (p) WillKennedy 130+
(John Flint) *chsd ldrs: wnt 2nd after 3 out: chalng whn pckd bdly 2 out: led last: r.o wl: rdn out* **12/1**
121- **2** *3* **Banjaxed Girl**[205] 5196 6-11-9 **148** .... SamTwiston-Davies(3) 152+
(Nigel Twiston-Davies) *led: rdn whn pressed appr 2 out: hdd whn sltly awkward last: kpt on: no ex* **3/1**[2]
3142 **3** *11* **Winsley Hill**[19] 1904 8-10-0 **122** .... RodiGreene 115
(Neil Mulholland) *w ldr: hit 5th: rdn after 3 out: styd on same pce* **9/1**
13F- **4** *2 3/4* **Kerada (FR)**[205] 5196 6-10-5 **127** .... AndrewTinkler 117
(Nicky Henderson) *hld up: hdwy 7th: effrt after 3 out: one pce fr next: lft 4th at the last* **7/4**[1]
302- **5** *5* **Alasi**[205] 5196 6-10-8 **130** .... DominicElsworth 117
(Paul Webber) *t.k.h: hld up: hdwy 3 out: rdn appr 2 out: sn one pce: lft 5th last* **9/2**[3]
01-0 **6** *30* **Love Of Tara**[182] 206 8-10-7 **129** .... WarrenMarston 87
(Martin Keighley) *chsd ldrs: nt fluent 2nd: nudged along after 6th: rdn after 3 out: sn one pce: wknd after 2 out* **16/1**
0-14 **U** **Miss Overdrive**[13] 1993 6-9-7 **122** oh2 .... MrBJPoste(7) 118
(Andy Turnell) *hld up: hit 1st: nudged along after 5th: rdn after 7th: prog whn rdr dropped whip between last 2 hurdles: 4th and styng on whn awkward and uns rdr last* **12/1**
4B-5 **P** **Thedeboftheyear**[186] 131 6-10-0 **122** oh7 .... JamesDavies —
(Chris Down) *chsd ldrs tl 5th: lost tch fr 7th: t.o whn p.u bef last* **40/1**

4m 57.0s (-29.50) **Going Correction** -1.10s/f (Hard) course record **8** Ran SP% **113.3**
Speed ratings (Par 109): **109,107,103,102,101 90,—,—**
toteswingers:1&2 £4.60, 2&3 £3.10, 1&3 £14.30 CSF £48.11 CT £344.35 TOTE £14.10: £3.10, £1.30, £2.40; EX 50.70 Trifecta £256.20 Part won. Pool: £346.33 -0.03 winning units..
Owner Jason Tucker **Bred** Pedro Rosas **Trained** Kenfig Hill, Bridgend

FOCUS
Often a competitive mares' hurdle and this year's running was no different. They went a decent pace. A step up from the winenr with another personal best from the runner-up.

NOTEBOOK
Santera(IRE), 2lb 'wrong' and beaten in selling hurdles towards the end of the summer, emerged victorious. In fairness to her, she has done nothing but improve since joining this yard and the step back up in trip on decent ground really suited, staying on strongly having hit to the front at the last (overcoming a bad peck on landing two out). On this evidence she'll stay 3m, although further progress will be required if she's to defy another rise. (op 16-1)
Banjaxed Girl, whose yard has taken this with Amber Brook for the past two years, won four of her last five starts over hurdles last season, often in gritty fashion, and she signed off with victory in a Listed handicap hurdle at Cheltenham in April - narrowly denying Alasi. Returning off a mark of 148 and conceding at least 18lb to all her rivals, she ran mightily well considering she was there to be picked off the whole time, only giving way at the last. She was clear of the remainder and, for all that winning handicaps won't be easy this season, she should add to her tally in mares' conditions/pattern races, with the David Nicholson at the Cheltenham Festival presumably the aim. Chasing is the other option. (op 10-3)
Winsley Hill was left trailing in the end, but should be able to win off this sort of mark down in grade. (op 10-1)
Kerada(FR), a faller in the Cheltenham race won by Banjaxed Girl last April, was 12lb better off at the weights and made favourite to reverse the form, but never really looked like delivering. She's now set to go chasing. (tchd 13-8 and 2-1)
Alasi, weighted to reverse Cheltenham form with the runner-up, was keen and didn't see it out. She's likely to come on for this and it will probably be in her interests to go chasing now. (op 4-1)
Miss Overdrive, 2lb out of the handicap, was beginning to stay on again when her rider lost his whip and then the pair split ways at the last. A try at 3m now looks in order. (op 16-1 tchd 11-1)

2219 TOTESCOOP6 ELITE HURDLE (LIMITED H'CAP) (GRADE 2) (8 hdls) 2m
2:10 (2:10) (Class 1) 4-Y-0+
£34,206 (£12,834; £6,426; £3,204; £1,608; £804)

Form RPR
-011 **1** **Nearby**[14] 1956 6-10-5 **145** .... ChrisDavies(7) 151+
(Philip Hobbs) *in tch: trckd ldrs 3 out: slt advantage 2 out: 3 l clr whn hit last: r.o strly: rdn out* **11/2**[2]
300- **2** *6* **Tito Bustillo (FR)**[203] 5222 5-10-4 **137** .... NickScholfield 135
(Paul Nicholls) *in tch: trckd ldrs 3 out: ev ch 2 out: sn rdn: nt gng pce of wnr gng to last: kpt on for 2nd* **13/2**
31-0 **3** *1 1/4* **Dee Ee Williams (IRE)**[182] 207 7-11-2 **149** .... (b) LiamTreadwell 147
(Nick Gifford) *outpcd towards rr early: hdwy after 3 out: chalng whn hit 2 out: styd on same pce fr last* **12/1**
011- **4** *1 1/4* **Ashkazar (FR)**[196] 5392 6-11-8 **155** .... TimmyMurphy 151
(David Pipe) *outpcd in detached last: hdwy after 3 out: 5th whn sltly hmpd 2 out: styd on same pce fr last* **9/1**

33-5 **5** 3¾ **Ultimate**[21] 1862 4-10-1 **137** oh5 .... DannyCook[(3)] 129
(Brian Ellison) *led at str pce tl 2nd: chsd ldr: led appr 2 out: sn rdn and hdd: kpt on same pce* **20/1**

403- **6** 4½ **Leslingtaylor (IRE)**[28] 5128 8-10-4 **137** oh3 .... DougieCostello 125
(John Quinn) *outpcd towards rr: hdwy after 3 out but nvr able to get on terms w ldrs* **8/1**

21-3 **7** 15 **Barizan (IRE)**[21] 1862 4-10-13 **146** ....(v) PaulMoloney 119
(Evan Williams) *nvr able to get prom off str pce: in tch: pushed along 4th: rdn bef 3 out: wknd sn after* **8/1**

F-P1 **8** 3 **Black Jack Blues (IRE)**[27] 1797 7-10-10 **150** ....(t) AodhaganConlon[(7)] 120
(Rebecca Curtis) *led 2nd: continued to set v str pce: rdn and hdd appr 2 out: sn wknd* **6/1**[3]

F-11 **9** 14 **Australia Day (IRE)**[20] 1886 7-11-10 **157** .... DominicElsworth 113
(Paul Webber) *chsd ldrs: vying for ld whn blnd 2nd: chsd ldrs: mstke 3 out: sn rdn: wknd bef next:* **4/1**[1]

123/ **F** **American Trilogy (IRE)**[560] 5224 6-11-1 **148** ....(b) HarrySkelton 133
(Paul Nicholls) *hld up: hdwy after 3 out: rdn in 3 l 6th whn fell heavily 2 out* **14/1**

3m 25.8s (-23.10) **Going Correction** -1.10s/f (Hard) course record
WFA 4 from 5yo+ 7lb **10** Ran SP% **114.3**
Speed ratings (Par 115): **113,110,109,108,106 104,97,95,88,—**
CSF £40.59 CT £410.08 TOTE £8.00: £2.50, £2.60, £3.20; EX 55.80 Trifecta £487.20 Pool: £724.35 - 1.10 winning units..
Owner Andy Ash **Bred** Juddmonte Farms Ltd **Trained** Withycombe, Somerset

FOCUS
A handicap hurdle that has gone to some classy performers over the years. There was always likely to be plenty of pace on, with numerous front-runners in opposition (run in course record time), and we saw a very smart performance from the rapidly progressive Nearby. The time was good and the form looks solid.

NOTEBOOK
Nearby, rapidly progressive, tanked through the race under regular rider now Chris Davies, and readily drew clear when asked, making it three wins in less than a month. Successful off 125 at Bangor in early Ocotber, he was defying a mark of 145 here, and can now expect to be rated in the low-to-mid 150s, so isn't that far off progressive out of handicaps. The Greatwood will come too soon, but he has to be considered a possible for the Gerry Feilden and there's no telling how far he might go. (op 13-2)
Tito Bustillo(FR), favourite and still in contention when all but brought down in the County Hurdle, has had a breathing operation since last season and only the winner was travelling better turning for home. However, he was readily outpaced by him from before the final hurdle and had to settle for second. This still represented improved form and he's capable of winning a decent prize or two this season, with it being possible a longer trip may suit at some stage. (op 15-2 tchd 6-1)
Dee Ee Williams(IRE) is now on a high mark, 149, but he got himself into the mix, having initially looked a bit rusty, and this has to go down as a decent effort. He remains capable of running well in big handicaps. (op 11-1)
Ashkazar(FR) finally took advantage of his declining mark last April, winning twice, but his handicap rating went up 20lb in total as a result and it was no surprise to see him come up short here, for all that he ran very promisingly. (op 8-1)
Ultimate, racing from 5lb out of the handicap, did remarkably well considering he chased a strong pace, going on again in the straight and not being beaten far at all. Rated just 132, he's capable of landing a decent handicap hurdle this season. (op 28-1)
Leslingtaylor(IRE), racing from 3lb 'wrong', has had a couple of spins on the Flat recently and he plugged on late having been unable to go the gallop for much of the race. (op 10-1)
Barizan(IRE)'s well beaten reappearance run at Cheltenham suggested he was going to struggle this season, and an example of how quickly they went early was that this often trail-blazing front-runner couldn't get anywhere near the lead. He was in trouble from an early stage and needs assistance from the handicapper. (op 9-1)
Black Jack Blues(IRE), 13lb higher in a considerably stronger race, gave himself no chance of winning by setting such a strong gallop. (op 13-2)
Australia Day(IRE) returned with a comfy win, albeit he beat little, at Kempton on his reappearance, but he was 22lb higher than when winning his last handicap, and this front-runner was never going to get an easy lead. He stopped quickly and isn't going to be the easiest to place. (op 7-2)
American Trilogy(IRE) took a heavy fall two out, which was a shame, as he had travelled well throughout the race and been set to go chasing after this. Connections will presumably want to give him another spin over hurdles now, as his confidence is sure to be dented, but if he takes to it, he's the type to win a Grand Annual. (op 11-1)

2220 TOTETENTOFOLLOW RISING STARS NOVICES' CHASE (GRADE 2) (17 fncs) 2m 5f

2:45 (2:45) (Class 1) 4-Y-0+ **£18,457** (£7,059; £3,641; £1,923)

Form RPR

F0-F **1** **Wishfull Thinking**[13] 1985 7-11-2 0 .... RichardJohnson 140+
(Philip Hobbs) *j.lft most of way: trckd ldrs: led 4th: nodded on landing whn jnd 4 out: 1/2 l down and pushed along whn lft in ld 3 out: drew clr fr next: easily* **5/4**[1]

-1U2 **2** 12 **Tara Royal**[16] 1930 5-11-8 133 .... JasonMaguire 136+
(Donald McCain) *nt particularly fluent early: hld up last but in tch: hdwy after 13th to trck ldng pair: outpcd whn lft 2nd 3 out: no ch w wnr* **5/1**[3]

0316 **3** 9 **Intac (IRE)**[14] 1965 8-11-6 116 .... JoeTizzard 123
(Colin Tizzard) *trckd ldrs: outpcd 12th: no ch after: kpt on to regain 3rd at the last* **40/1**

-113 **4** 6 **Cootehill (IRE)**[34] 1693 6-11-6 0 .... PaddyBrennan 119
(Nigel Twiston-Davies) *led tl 4th: slow jump next: chsd wnr tl 10th: rdn after 13th: one pce fr next: lft 3rd 3 out: fading whn lost 3rd at the last* **8/1**

4-1 **F** **Robinson Collonges (FR)**[28] 1770 5-11-8 0 .... NickScholfield 146+
(Paul Nicholls) *trckd ldrs: jnd wnr 4 out: 1/2 l up and appeared to be travelling the bttr whn knuckled on landing and fell 3 out* **2/1**[2]

5m 8.60s (-16.60) **Going Correction** -0.775s/f (Firm) **5** Ran SP% **108.0**
Speed ratings (Par 115): **100,95,92,89,—**
CSF £7.52 TOTE £2.50: £1.70, £2.60; EX 8.30.
Owner Mrs Diana L Whateley **Bred** Cobhall Court Stud **Trained** Withycombe, Somerset

FOCUS
This is often an interesting novice chase, won by the likes of Comply Or Die and Turko in recent years, and two potentially smart sorts were drawing clear when Robinson Collonges, who had just taken it up looking the winner, knuckled on landing three out, leaving it to Wishfull Thinking. The winner is rated to the level of his hurdles form with the second pretty much to his mark, but the third limits the race's rating. The faller looks a smart novice.

NOTEBOOK
Wishfull Thinking was fortunate to get off the mark over fences at the second attempt. Useful over hurdles, the winner had taken an unfortunate first-fence fall on his debut at Aintree 13 days earlier, but showed no signs of that having affected him here, albeit he jumped as though he'd appreciate going the other way round. He had them all on the stretch as they left the back, barring his market rival, but had been headed and even by his rider's own admission was travelling second best when the race took a dramatic twist. Although fortunate, he rates a bright prospect, with 3m likely to suit at some stage. He remains a general 25-1 shot for the RSA. (op 13-8 tchd 6-5)
Tara Royal, who fell when favourite for the race won by Robinson Collonges at Bangor, again made mistakes and had been left trailing by the 'big' two when inheriting second at the first in the straight. He's likely to be sent handicapping once his jumping improves. (op 11-2)
Intac(IRE) stayed on again to claim third-place money. He isn't up to this level. (op 25-1)
Cootehill(IRE) finished well beaten at Huntingdon last time, but for all that he was an unlikely winner, it was surprising he couldn't beat 40-1 outsider Intac. Handicaps are surely the route for him. (tchd 15-2 and 17-2)
Robinson Collonges(FR) was deeply impressive on his chasing debut at Bangor last month, winning by a hard-held 20l despite racing keenly for much of the contest, and despite having to concede 6lb to Wishfull Thinking, it was surprising to see him deposed as favourite. Again racing freely throughout, his jumping had been sure-footed for a novice, and Nick Scholfield had just allowed him to edge on when falling at the first in the straight. It was a shame because he had jumped the fence well, but just couldn't get his front legs down in time. One can be fairly confident in saying he'd have won, and it's just hoped this doesn't affect him, as he looks a top-notch prospect. (op 13-8)

2221 BADGER ALES TROPHY (HANDICAP CHASE) (LISTED RACE) (21 fncs) 3m 1f 110y

3:20 (3:21) (Class 1) (0-150,150) 4-Y-0+
£39,907 (£14,973; £7,497; £3,738; £1,876; £938)

Form RPR

1P-4 **1** **Meanus Dandy (IRE)**[22] 1856 7-9-11 **126** ....(b[1]) IanPopham[(5)] 141+
(Paul Nicholls) *chsd clr ldr: str chal fr 4 out: sn rdn: led appr last: styd on stoutly: rdn out* **5/1**[2]

14-0 **2** 3½ **Buena Vista (IRE)**[22] 1855 9-10-5 **132** ....(p) DannyCook[(3)] 145+
(David Pipe) *chsd ldrs: led whn j.rt 4 out: sn rdn and hrd pressed: hdd last: styd on: sn hld* **17/2**

U-00 **3** 19 **Ellerslie George (IRE)**[28] 1777 10-10-2 **133** ....(b[1]) MrRGHenderson[(7)] 127
(Nick Mitchell) *j. occassionally rt: led: sn clr: hdd 4 out: sn rdn: rallied briefly appr next: no ch w ldng pair fr bef 2 out: jst hld on for 3rd* **16/1**

P0-2 **4** hd **I'moncloudnine (IRE)**[28] 1769 7-10-9 **133** .... DougieCostello 127
(Neil Mulholland) *mid-div: hdwy fr 15th: rdn to chse ldrs after 4 out: styd on same pce but sn no ch w ldng pair* **6/1**[3]

2U5- **5** 6 **The Package**[196] 5395 7-11-9 **147** .... TimmyMurphy 138
(David Pipe) *hld up towards rr of midfield: hmpd 12th: hdwy fr 14th: rdn to chse ldrs after 4 out: wl hld fr next* **6/1**[3]

F0-6 **6** 3½ **Irish Raptor (IRE)**[14] 1960 11-10-6 **130** .... PaddyBrennan 116
(Nigel Twiston-Davies) *mid-div: chsd ldr fr 8th: rdn whn hit 17th: no ch fr next* **14/1**

3256 **7** 3¾ **Cullahill (IRE)**[28] 1777 8-9-7 **124** oh4 .... NathanSweeney[(7)] 109
(Bob Buckler) *mid-div: nt fluent 5th: rdn after 15th: nvr any imp* **25/1**

10-0 **8** 6 **Carrickmines (IRE)**[24] 1821 8-10-0 **124** oh3 .... AndrewGlassonbury 100
(Dr Richard Newland) *towards rr: hdwy to get in tch 16th: sn rdn: wknd 4 out* **28/1**

-013 **9** hd **Ouzbeck (FR)**[22] 1856 8-11-11 **149** .... JackDoyle 125
(Emma Lavelle) *mid-div: rdn after 15th: wknd after 17th* **12/1**

232- **10** 12 **Forest Pennant (IRE)**[230] 4768 8-11-1 **139** .... NickScholfield 104
(Paul Nicholls) *hld up towards rr of midfield: awkward 4th (water): hmpd 12th: struggling fr 14th: sn in rr* **16/1**

-223 **11** 14 **Triggerman**[9] 2057 8-10-8 **132** .... RichardJohnson 85
(Philip Hobbs) *a towards rr* **9/1**

000- **12** 63 **Comply Or Die (IRE)**[210] 5127 11-11-12 **150** ....(p) JohnnyFarrelly 46
(David Pipe) *chsd ldrs tl hmpd 12th: sn in rr: t.o* **40/1**

20P- **F** **Niche Market (IRE)**[210] 5127 9-11-7 **148** ....(t) SamTwiston-Davies[(3)] —
(Paul Nicholls) *in tch whn fell 12th* **9/2**[1]

2-UP **P** **Burren Legend (IRE)**[7] 2084 9-10-8 **132** .... AndrewThornton —
(Richard Rowe) *hmpd 12th: a in rr: t.o whn p.u bef 4 out* **40/1**

6m 10.3s (-29.20) **Going Correction** -0.775s/f (Firm) **14** Ran SP% **122.2**
Speed ratings (Par 111): **113,111,106,106,104 103,101,100,100,96 92,72,—,—**
toteswingers:1&2 £14.60, 2&3 £37.10, 1&3 £22.40 CSF £46.79 CT £643.05 TOTE £6.80: £2.40, £3.50, £4.00; EX 67.80 Trifecta £746.00 Pool: £1119.05 - 1.11 winning units..
Owner Mr & Mrs Mark Woodhouse & Paul Barber **Bred** Gerard Murphy **Trained** Ditcheat, Somerset

FOCUS
A race that is always well contested, this year's edition was no different, and the pace set by last season's winner Ellerslie George was a good one, ensuring it was a proper test. Two handled it considerably better the rest and drew 19l clear. Meanus Dandy produced a big step up, with Buena Vista rated to his old chase form.

NOTEBOOK
Meanus Dandy(IRE), wearing first-time blinkers, stayed on too strongly for Buena Vista. He had disappointed on both starts since winning off 7lb lower at Sandown last March, but is reportedly ideally suited by 3m on a flat track, which he got here, and the headgear enabled him to travel much better than he had done in the past. It was clear from some way out that he was going to play a pleading role in the outcome of the race, and his rider kept at him in the straight before the pair began to assert from the last, a good jump helping. He's the type to develop into a Grand National horse one day, but for now at least it is more likely to be the Topham come April. He has no specific short-term plans, although a race like the Eider at Newcastle later in the season could suit. (op 8-1)
Buena Vista(IRE), last season's Pertemps winner off just 1lb higher, had only had two runs over fences since finishing sixth in the Arkle as a novice way back in 2007, his last being in the summer of 2008, but he jumped well with the cheekpieces back on and was the only one capable of giving the winner a race. He couldn't stay on as strongly in the end, but is clearly up to mixing it in good handicap chases as well as hurdles. (tchd 9-1)
Ellerslie George(IRE) , just 1lb higher than when successful a year ago, sprung back into life with the first-time blinkers on, racing in a clear lead, and it was surprising to see him rally, having been headed at the fourth from home. To his credit he managed to keep on down the straight to hold on for a place.
I'moncloudnine(IRE), runner-up at Bangor off 4lb lower on his reappearance, was solid in the market and ran well in this stronger heat, just missing third. (op 13-2)
The Package, 6lb higher than when narrowly denied in last season's William Hill at Cheltenham, is still only seven and expected to take another step forward in top staying handicap chases this season. He didn't shape badly, assuming the run would have been needed, and will presumably head to Cheltenham's December meeting now, as he did last year. (tchd 5-1)
Irish Raptor(IRE) is back on a very good mark now and he'll presumably head for the Becher next, a race he often contends without success. (op 16-1 tchd 18-1)
Cullahill(IRE) was racing from 4lb 'wrong' and will find easier opportunities than this (op 33-1)
Carrickmines(IRE) will find easier opportunities.
Ouzbeck(FR) never got into it. (op 9-1)
Forest Pennant(IRE) was let down by his jumping.
Triggerman found it too competitive. (op 17-2)
Comply Or Die(IRE) very much ran as though the race was needed. (op 33-1)

Niche Market(IRE), making his debut for Paul Nicholls off a very reasonable mark, was going nicely enough when coming down at the 12th, but it was too early to determine how he would have fared. (op 5-1)

2222 BET TOTEPOOL ON ALL UK RACING INTERMEDIATE OPEN NATIONAL HUNT FLAT RACE 2m

3:55 (3:57) (Class 6) 4-6-Y-O **£1,301** (£382; £191; £95)

Form				RPR
	1		**Peckhamecho (IRE)** 4-11-4 0 JasonMaguire (Rebecca Curtis) *mde all: kpt on wl: rdn out* 6/1	113+
	2	3/4	**Harry Le Fise Lake (IRE)** 4-11-4 0 RhysFlint (Philip Hobbs) *trckd ldrs: rdn over 2f out: chsd wnr fr wl over 1f out: swtchd rt ins fnl f: kpt on* 14/1	112+
	3	3 1/2	**Bowntobebad (IRE)**266 5-11-0 0 ow1 MrNHarris(5) (Jeremy Scott) *mid-div: making hdwy whn hmpd 4f out: swtchd lft ent st: sn rdn: styd on fnl 2f* 9/1	110
	4	1	**Five Rivers (IRE)** 4-11-4 0 PaddyBrennan (Warren Greatrex) *in tch: rdn over 2f out: styd on same pce* 14/1	108
	5	3 1/4	**Two Bob (IRE)** 5-11-4 0 RichardJohnson (Philip Hobbs) *unsettled prelimaries: prom: rdn wl over 2f out: styd on same pce* 3/1²	105
130-	6	1/2	**Lifestyle**211 5114 4-11-4 0 AndrewTinkler (Nicky Henderson) *hld up bhd: hdwy 3f out: sn rdn: kpt on: nvr gng pce to threaten* 9/2³	104
23-	7	1/2	**Romulus D'Artaix (FR)**250 4358 4-11-4 0 WayneHutchinson (Alan King) *mid-div: hdwy 4f out: rdn over 2f out: styd on same pce* 9/4¹	104
	8	21	**Filimoss** 5-10-11 0 GerardTumelty (Charlie Morlock) *trckd ldrs tl over 5f out: sn rdn: wknd 4f out* 66/1	76
	9	21	**Twentyten (IRE)**167 5-10-11 0 MrMEnnis(7) (Paul Henderson) *a towards rr* 66/1	62
4	10	53	**Long Row**173 375 4-10-11 0 TimmyMurphy (Stuart Howe) *a towards rr: virtually p.u fnl 3f* 33/1	2

3m 49.1s (5.80) **Going Correction** -1.10s/f (Hard) **10** Ran SP% **117.5**

Speed ratings: **41,40,38,38,36 36,36,25,15,—**

toteswingers:1&2 £31.20, 2&3 £35.60, 1&3 £14.50 CSF £85.24 TOTE £7.60: £3.30, £5.30, £2.20; EX 100.10.

Owner C R Trembath & G Costelloe **Bred** D Nolan **Trained** Newport, Dyfed

FOCUS

This had looked a decent bumper beforehand and, despite none of the front three in the market being able to get into the race, it should still prove a source of winners. It was slowly run and is not form to be too confident about.

NOTEBOOK

Peckhamecho(IRE), from a yard that often get them ready to win on debut, knew his job well and galloped on relentlessly for a workmanlike success. He'll stay further over hurdles, but will presumably try and defy a penalty first. (op 5-1 tchd 7-1)

Harry Le Fise Lake(IRE), the supposed stable second string, looked green under pressure, but stayed on well enough to hassle the winner late on. This was a promising start and he too looks likely to benefit from a greater test over hurdles. (op 10-1)

Bowntobebad(IRE), easy winner of a point in February, stayed on well down the straight and took third inside the final furlong. There was plenty to like about this performance and he can probably win a bumper before going hurdling. (op 13-2)

Five Rivers(IRE), whose dam was a half-sister to useful chaser Bother Na, is from a yard that does well in this sphere and he made a pleasing start. It won't be until he's faced with a staying test over fences, though, that he's at his best. (op 18-1)

Two Bob(IRE), the shorter of the two Hobbs runners in the betting, was on edge beforehand and that may have affected his performance in the race. He did keep on, but never looked like winning, and probably deserves another chance. (op 7-2 tchd 5-2)

Lifestyle, the only previous winner under rules in the field, ended last season on a low note in the Aintree mares' bumper and she never threatened to get into this. She'll go hurdling now and should do well, with her trainer often excelling with his mares. (op 4-1 tchd 5-1)

Romulus D'Artaix(FR), twice placed last season and expected to have improved, was very well backed beforehand, but yet another who failed to get into it. He should leave this form behind sent hurdling. (op 9-2)

T/Plt: £202.70 to a £1 stake. Pool of £74,222.50 - 267.21 winning tickets. T/Qpdt: £77.70 to a £1 stake. Pool of £5,125.93 - 48.80 winning tickets. TM

2223 - 2225a (Foreign Racing) - See Raceform Interactive

2195 DOWN ROYAL (R-H)

Saturday, November 6

OFFICIAL GOING: Soft (yielding to soft in places)

2226a JNWINE.COM CHAMPION CHASE (GRADE 1) (15 fncs) 3m

2:25 (2:27) 5-Y-O+

£74,336 (£23,539; £11,150; £3,716; £1,858; £619)

			RPR
1		**Kauto Star (FR)**232 4713 10-11-10 (t) RWalsh (Paul Nicholls) *trckd ldr in 2nd: cl up 5 out: pushed along in 2nd appr 3 out: led 3 out: rdn bef next: kpt on strly fr last* 4/7¹	164+
2	4	**Sizing Europe (IRE)**23 1850 8-11-10 160 AELynch (Henry De Bromhead, Ire) *slow 1st and 2nd: trckd ldrs: 4th 1/2-way: hdwy in 3rd travelling wl 4 out: rdn 3 out: no imp on ldr in 2nd appr 2 out: kpt on same pce: jst hld 2nd run-in* 5/1²	160
3	nk	**China Rock (IRE)**23 1850 7-11-10 152 BarryGeraghty (M F Morris, Ire) *chsd ldrs: 3rd 1/2-way: impr to dispute 9th: led bef 4 out: rdn and hdd 3 out: u.p in 3rd bef 2 out: kpt on same pce: jst hld for 2nd* 5/1²	160
4	dist	**Coolcashin (IRE)**35 1684 9-11-10 138 DJCondon (Michael J Bowe, Ire) *hld up towards rr: rdn in 6th and no imp 5 out: kpt on one pce st* 20/1	—
5	9	**Killyglen (IRE)**16 1945 8-11-10 PCarberry (S R B Crawford, Ire) *led: disp fr 9th: rdn and hdd bef 4 out: sn wknd* 16/1³	—
6	14	**Mossbank (IRE)**927 5165 10-11-10 153 DNRussell (Michael Hourigan, Ire) *hld up towards rr: 5th 6 out: rdn and no imp bef 4 out where bad mstke: wknd* 33/1	—
P		**Trafford Lad**371 2013 8-11-10 TJDoyle (Laurence James Butler, Ire) *settled bhd ldrs in 5th early: mstke 7th: sn dropped towards rr: p.u bef 3 out* 20/1	—

6m 22.2s (4.00) **7** Ran SP% **115.3**

CSF £4.11 TOTE £1.40: £1.50, £2.80; DF 3.60.

Owner Clive D Smith **Bred** Mme Henri Aubert **Trained** Ditcheat, Somerset

FOCUS

The form is rated around the third. Kauto Star can improve on this satisfactory return, and it was a better run from Sizing Europe.

NOTEBOOK

Kauto Star(FR) needed to be more fully wound up to win this year's renewal of this particular race than when beating Light On The Broom two years ago. He obviously beat better horses this year but what value this was as a Gold Cup trial is very much open to question. They went no pace on the soft ground for the first half of the race until Barry Geraghty on China Rock attempted to inject a bit of pace into it. From there it wasn't until the fourth last or so that they went close to Gold Cup or King George pace. It looked as if it might be a race as they descended but the winner pulled out enough to keep his two main rivals comfortably at bay. He'll obviously improve for this and it was a classy performance, but at this stage it would be hard to see either of the two immediately behind him being competitive in a Gold Cup for varying reasons. In short, Kauto's real opposition still awaits him. He could line up in the Hennessy next. Ruby Walsh broke his leg in a fall later on the card which will rule him out for around three months.

Sizing Europe(IRE) seemed to see out this 3m at a mostly slow gallop but on the evidence seen so far whether he would see it out at King George pace is very much a horse of a different colour. The slow pace didn't do anything for his jumping early on, although he did get it together very soon after and he stuck it out well from the final fence to see off his Punchestown conqueror China Rock. Better ground would suit, he'll get that at Kempton. A faster pace would suit, he'll also get that at Kempton. What he'll also get at Kempton is the acid test of whether he's a 3m horse, that question wasn't really answered here. (op 9/2)

China Rock(IRE) would need much better ground to be seen at his best and he did try to inject some pace into it at about halfway. He truly ran a cracker to be still close enough to make a race of it with the winner at the second last, and while he would want better ground the two horses in front of him wouldn't object to it either. This run is just about as good as he is and it's likely to be as close as he will manage to get to either Kauto Star or Sizing Europe. (op 6/1)

Mossbank(IRE) had a huge task for him to be competitive after an absence of over two years but he travelled well until he began to feel the pinch before the fourth last and a bad mistake at that fence was the end of his flailing challenge.It will take another run or two before he can be truly assessed. (op 25/1)

Trafford Lad was struggling soon after making a bad mistake at the seventh fence. (op 20/1 tchd 22/1)

2227a LADBROKES.COM CHASE (GRADE 2) (13 fncs) 2m 4f

3:00 (3:04) 5-Y-O+ **£28,761** (£8,407; £3,982; £1,327)

			RPR
1		**The Nightingale (FR)**212 5098 7-11-10 RWalsh (Paul Nicholls) *trckd ldrs: travelled wl to chal 3 out: led bef next: rdn and kpt on strly fr bef last* 3/1¹	160+
2	11	**Roberto Goldback (IRE)**198 5350 8-11-10 145 BarryGeraghty (Mrs John Harrington, Ire) *chsd ldrs: 4th 1/2-way: hdwy to chal in 2nd and mstke 3 out: rdn in 3rd and no ex bef 2 out: 2nd after 2 out: no ch w wnr: kpt on same pce* 7/1³	149
3	8	**Osana (FR)**198 5350 8-11-5 150 (p) AndrewJMcNamara (E J O'Grady, Ire) *chsd ldr in 2nd: led 4 out: rdn and chal 3 out: hdd bef next where mstke: no ex* 9/2²	136
4	3	**Lucky At Last (IRE)**14 1981 8-11-1 131 (t) DJCondon (Patrick Martin, Ire) *hld up towards rr: hdwy into 5th bef 4 out: rdn in 6th and no imp 4 out: kpt on one pce st* 14/1	129
5	1 1/2	**Apt Approach (IRE)**287 3618 7-11-5 (t) PTownend (W P Mullins, Ire) *led: rdn and hdd 4 out: no ex in 4th 3 out: kpt on one pce* 12/1	132
6	dist	**Jadanli (IRE)**23 1850 8-11-12 145 AELynch (Paul John Gilligan, Ire) *chsd ldrs early: 5th 1/2-way: rdn and wknd bef 4 out* 16/1	—
F		**See U Bob (IRE)**164 481 7-11-5 144 MPWalsh (Paul Nolan, Ire) *hld up towards rr: mstke 8th: slt mstke 5 out: rdn in 5th and no imp 4 out: fell next* 12/1	130

5m 18.8s (318.80) **7** Ran SP% **83.6**

CSF £11.65 TOTE £2.30: £1.30, £3.10; DF 10.40.

Owner C G Roach **Bred** Frederique Brisac **Trained** Ditcheat, Somerset

■ Pandorama was withdrawn on vet's advice at the start (6/4F, deduct 40p in the £ under R4).

FOCUS

A third successive win in this race for Paul Nicholls. The first two home are rated to their best form of last season.

NOTEBOOK

The Nightingale(FR) seemed to stay on better than any of his rivals in a race ruined really by the withdrawal at the start of Pandorama. He jumped and travelled well and while it took a little time for him to really warm to his task, he picked up better than anything from the second last and drew clear nicely. It was his seasonal debut and he was entitled to need it, but this probably topped anything he had done previously and one would see him as a leading Ryanair Chase contender on this evidence. He certainly didn't beat any mugs here. (op 7/2)

Roberto Goldback(IRE) should be well able to win a good chase this season. He travelled and jumped while tracking the leaders and despite a mistake at the third last he was still close enough at the second last before the winner drew away. He's one that looks sure to appreciate further and may get his chance this season to see if he can make the transition to 3m. (op 11/2)

Osana(FR) raced towards the front rank, raced with plenty of enthusiasm and jumped well, but just seemed to blow up after the second last and perhaps empty over this trip. He was just starting to feel the pinch when he pecked on landing jumping the second last and had nothing left from there. He'll improve for the run but it will be interesting to see how they place him this season. (op 9/2 tchd 4/1)

Lucky At Last(IRE) ran very well. Held up at the back of the field, he began to get a bit closer well inside the final mile and while he could never really land a blow he kept on reasonably well. It might be interesting to see if the handicapper reacts any to this performance. (op 14/1)

Apt Approach(IRE) made the running but made a mistake five out and was probably just beginning to send out some distress signals at that point. He kept on to a degree but was a tired horse in the straight and should improve hugely for the run. (op 10/1)

Jadanli(IRE) was quite well behind and struggling for much of the way. (op 14/1)

See U Bob(IRE) was in rear for most of the way and was beaten when making a mistake three out. (op 10/1)

2228 - 2229a (Foreign Racing) - See Raceform Interactive

1881 AUTEUIL (L-H)

Saturday, November 6

OFFICIAL GOING: Turf: heavy

2230a GRAND PRIX D'AUTOMNE (HURDLE) (GRADE 1) (5YO+) (TURF) 3m

2:45 (12:00) 5-Y-O+

£147,345 (£72,035; £42,566; £29,469; £16,371; £11,460)

		RPR
1	**Questarabad (FR)**27 1809 6-10-8 0 RegisSchmidlin (M Rolland, France) *settled in midfield: taken on wd outside of bkst and tk clsr order: wnt 4th bef 5 out and 2nd bef 3 out: disp ld gng wl 2 out: led appr last: r.o wl* 2/5¹	—

2 2 1/2 **Coralhasi (FR)**14 8-10-8 0 SylvainDehez —
(J-P Gallorini, France) *trckd ldng gp (racing in 4th for much of r): hdwy fr 4 out: j. 2 out disputing 2nd: chal wnr run-in: unable qck fnl 100yds* **42/1**
3 15 **Good Bye Simon (FR)**7 7-10-8 0 BenoitDelo —
(T Doumen, France) *hld up towards rr: hdwy 4 out: running on and cl 8th 2 out: tk 3rd w a gd jump at the last: one pce run-in and no ch w first two* **17/1**
4 8 **Avenue Marceau (FR)**14 5-9-13 0 JeremyDaSilva —
(Y Fouin, France) *hld up: r.o fr 4 out: tk 4th appr last: nvr nr to chal* **23/1**
5 1 1/2 **Oeil Du Maitre (FR)**7 8-10-8 0 (p) StevenColas —
(J-P Gallorini, France) *w ldrs (2nd or 3rd much of the way): led 4 out: hdd 2 out and no ex* **34/1**
6 nk **Tyko (FR)**27 1809 5-10-3 0 (p) DavidBerra —
(P Peltier, France) *a.p: rdn and wknd fr 2 out* **7/1**2
7 hd **Royal Penny (FR)**7 6-10-8 0 ChristophePieux —
(B Barbier, France) *chsd ldrs: qcknd to ld appr 2 out: jnd 2 out: sn hdd: fdd appr last* **18/1**
8 8 **Palmier (FR)**27 1809 7-10-8 0 DavidCottin —
(F-M Cottin, France) *midfield: rdn and btn after 3 out* **37/1**
9 dist **Really Hurley (FR)**21 5-10-3 0 Jean-LucBeaunez —
(Mme P Alexanian, France) *a bhd* **32/1**
P **Zhukov (IRE)**168 8-10-8 0 RaymondO'Brien —
(Kevin Tork) *bhd fr 1/2-way: p.u 3 out* **83/1**
P **Sucess River (FR)**52 1532 5-10-3 0 CyrilleGombeau —
(G Cherel, France) *led tl hdd 4 out: wknd qckly and p.u after 3 out* **12/1**3

5m 59.47s (359.47) **11 Ran SP% 118.6**
PARI-MUTUEL (all including 1 euro stakes): WIN 1.40; PLACE 1.20, 5.00, 2.50; DF 21.50; SF 25.30.
Owner Mme Roger Polani **Bred** Scea Terres Noires **Trained** France

NOTEBOOK
Questarabad(FR) repeated his win in this race last year and is now apparently to be aimed at the World Hurdle. He'll first get a taster of Cheltenham in the Relkeel Hurdle.

1793 FFOS LAS (L-H)

Sunday, November 7

OFFICIAL GOING: Good to soft (good in places; 7.5)
Wind: Virtually nil Weather: Bright and sunny

2231 LINDLEY GROUP "NATIONAL HUNT" NOVICES' HURDLE (8 hdls) 2m
1:10 (1:11) (Class 4) 4-Y-0+ **£2,927** (£859; £429; £214)

Form RPR
2 1 **Mediolanum (IRE)**15 1962 5-10-12 0 PaddyBrennan 102+
(Nigel Twiston-Davies) *chsd ldng pair: wnt 2nd after 5th: mstke next: rdn to ld after 2 out: hdd last: sn lft in ld again: heavily eased flat* **1/4**1
13F5 2 2 1/2 **Whereveryougoigo (IRE)**18 1922 4-10-12 0 TomO'Brien 91
(Peter Bowen) *led: mstke 5th: rdn after 3 out: hdd between last 2: sn wknd: lft 2nd sn after last: clsd on eased wnr but wl hld after* **10/1**3
5- 3 5 **Oddjob (IRE)**262 4123 6-10-12 0 NoelFehily 86
(Warren Greatrex) *t.k.h: hld up in midfield: nt fluent 3rd: clsd on ldrs after 5th: rdn and wknd bef 2 out: lft 3rd last* **6/1**2
0-01 4 1 **Great Esteem (IRE)**14 2003 5-11-5 0 (p) JimmyMcCarthy 92
(Charles Egerton) *plld hrd: hld up in last trio: clsd on ldrs bef 3 out: 4th whn j.lft and wknd after 2 out: sn wknd* **16/1**
00 5 5 **Illysantachristina**9 2068 7-10-5 0 ChristianWilliams 73
(Bernard Llewellyn) *reluctant to line up: hld up in last pair: struggling bef 3 out: n.d after: lft modest 5th and hmpd last* **100/1**
2046 6 17 **Bachley Gale**17 1937 5-10-5 0 (p) JamieMoore 56
(Keith Goldsworthy) *mstke 1st: chsd ldr tl after 5th: sn struggling u.p: wl btn bef 2 out* **50/1**
36 7 49 **Naughtyatiz (IRE)**67 1455 4-10-12 0 FelixDeGiles 14
(Debra Hamer) *hld up in rr: rdn and lost tch 5th: t.o fr next* **66/1**
2540 F **Grand Award**130 862 5-10-12 100 JasonMaguire 106
(Donald McCain) *t.k.h: hld up in midfield: hdwy bef 3 out: rdn to ld and hit last: slipped and fell 2 strides later* **11/1**

3m 53.6s (4.60) **Going Correction** 0.0s/f (Good)
WFA 4 from 5yo+ 7lb **8 Ran SP% 122.0**
Speed ratings (Par 105): **101,99,97,96,94 85,61,—**
toteswingers: 1&2 £1.90, 1&3 £1.30, 2&3 £3.70 CSF £4.94 TOTE £1.30: £1.02, £1.60, £1.70; EX 4.10.
Owner Walters Plant Hire Ltd **Bred** David Carey **Trained** Naunton, Gloucs

FOCUS
Grand Award looked the winner when falling, leaving Mediolanum clear. A modest novice hurdle. The winner is rated close to his mark with the second rated to the level of his best bumper form.

NOTEBOOK
Mediolanum(IRE) had a real fight on his hands from Grand Award and had been headed when that one slipped on landing after the last, leaving him clear. He had finished runner-up at Aintree on his hurdles debut, was undoubtedly fortunate and clearly needs to improve to defy a penalty, but he'll benefit from a step up in trip and a longer distance wouldn't hurt either. (op 4-11 tchd 2-5 in places)
Whereveryougoigo(IRE) improved on his Worcester effort, although he was flattered by his close proximity to the winner and did have the run of the race. He'll do better in handicaps down the line. (op 12-1)
Oddjob(IRE), fifth behind the smart Dare Me in a course bumper last season, was disappointing on the face of it, although he did race keenly on this return from a 262-day absence, so probably deserves another chance. (op 9-2)
Great Esteem(IRE), another who failed to settle, looked vulnerable under the penalty in this stronger contest and was beaten from before the second-last.
Grand Award, disappointing on his handicap debut when last seen in June, was worth considering on the pick of his efforts and had just taken over when getting the last wrong and falling awkwardly having landed. He looked unlucky, but probably isn't one to get sucked into backing next time. (op 10-1)

2232 PEARN'S PHARMACIES LTD NOVICES' HURDLE (12 hdls) 3m
1:40 (1:40) (Class 4) 4-Y-0+ **£2,927** (£859; £429; £214)

Form RPR
0-31 1 **Alpine Breeze (IRE)**152 684 4-10-12 111 TimmyMurphy 123+
(Don Cantillon) *t.k.h: hld up in tch in last trio: hdwy to trck ldrs gng wl after 3 out: led last: rdn clr flat: comf* **4/1**2
221 2 3 1/4 **Youralltalk (IRE)**28 1799 6-10-12 0 JamieMoore 115
(Keith Goldsworthy) *led: rdn wl bef 2 out: hdd last: styd on same pce flat* **9/2**3
0- 3 2 3/4 **Round Tom (FR)**216 5-10-12 0 PaddyBrennan 112
(Paul Nicholls) *t.k.h: hld up in tch: wnt 2nd and j.lft 3 out: hung lft after: swtchd rt and lost 2nd 2 out: styd on same pce after* **11/2**
5-5 4 3 1/2 **Definite Dawn (IRE)**14 1990 6-10-12 0 ChristianWilliams 111+
(Tim Vaughan) *in tch: chsd ldrs and mstke 8th: rdn 3 out: wknd next: wl hld whn mstke last* **5/1**
2423 5 6 **Stormyisland Ahead**31 1742 5-11-2 112 (t) DPFahy(3) 111
(Evan Williams) *t.k.h: hld up in tch in last trio: hdwy to chse ldrs 9th: rdn and wknd after 3 out* **7/2**1
F144 6 23 **North Island (IRE)**12 2023 8-11-2 111 (p) DonalDevereux(3) 90
(Peter Bowen) *chsd ldrs: wnt 2nd after 8th: rdn after next: lost 2nd 3 out: sn wknd* **13/2**
10P3 7 39 **Call Me Bill (IRE)**28 1795 4-10-12 0 TomO'Brien 48
(Peter Bowen) *chsd ldr tl after 8th: rdn and lost tch after next: t.o fr 2 out* **16/1**
0P-0 P **Dash Of Salt**25 1821 5-10-12 0 (p) FelixDeGiles —
(Charlie Longsdon) *hld up in tch in last: mstke 6th: sn eased and p.u* **100/1**

6m 7.80s (20.80) **Going Correction** 0.0s/f (Good)
WFA 4 from 5yo+ 9lb **8 Ran SP% 112.7**
Speed ratings (Par 105): **102,100,100,98,96 89,76,—**
toteswingers: 1&2 £2.30, 1&3 £4.40, 2&3 £7.60 CSF £21.94 TOTE £4.60: £2.40, £1.40, £4.80; EX 16.10.
Owner Don Cantillon **Bred** D E Cantillon **Trained** Newmarket, Suffolk

FOCUS
A competitive-looking novices' hurdle and all bar one still looked in with a chance leaving the back. Decent form for the track with the easy winner up a stone+.

NOTEBOOK
Alpine Breeze(IRE), off since winning at Southwell in June, is bred to be suited by this sort of distance and, having travelled strongly throughout under Timmy Murphy, asserted on the run-in for a ready success. She'll be asked to carry a double penalty next time but is clearly on the up and may well complete a hat-trick, with her having the option of mares-only events. (op 7-2)
Youralltalk(IRE), successful in a course bumper latest, was soon in front and stole a couple of lengths on the field turning in, but having fought off the challenge of Round Tom, he couldn't repel the winner from the last. This was a pleasing first effort, though, and he should go one better before long. (op 5-1)
Round Tom(FR), twice a runner-up in points since being a beaten favourite on his bumper debut in May of last year, is reportedly a big, strong sort who's expected to improve this season. He travelled smoothly and briefly looked the winner coming to three out but still looked inexperienced under pressure and ended up well held in third. He should improve and can win one of these without much hassle. (op 9-2)
Definite Dawn(IRE) again showed promise but may not be winning until he's sent handicapping. (op 4-1)
Stormyisland Ahead continues to fall short under the penalty and will stand more of a chance in handicaps. (op 11-2)
North Island(IRE) failed to run his race and perhaps didn't take to the cheekpieces. (op 6-1 tchd 7-1)
Dash Of Salt Official explanation: jockey said gelding was lame

2233 LINDLEY CATERING NOVICES' CHASE (13 fncs) 2m
2:15 (2:15) (Class 3) 4-Y-0+ **£5,204** (£1,528; £764; £381)

Form RPR
0-63 1 **Potemkin (USA)**17 1936 5-11-1 115 (t) JamieMoore 118
(David Evans) *in tch: in tch: lft 3rd 6th: rdn to chal and hit 10th: led next: clr and j.rt last: styd on: rdn out* **16/1**
00-1 2 2 1/4 **Chain Of Command (IRE)**21 1883 7-11-7 127 NoelFehily 124+
(Warren Greatrex) *j.rt: hld up in last: mstke 2nd: hdwy 9th: chsd wnr 2 out: styd on same pce and no imp after* **10/11**1
522F 3 7 **Blacktoft (USA)**28 1796 7-11-0 128 AdamWedge(7) 119
(Evan Williams) *w ldr: j. v awkwardly 2nd: led 4th: jnd and blnd 10th: hdd next: wknd 2 out* **11/1**
3P-4 4 8 **Benfleet Boy**21 1883 6-11-1 0 JimmyMcCarthy 108+
(Brendan Powell) *led: mstke 2nd: outj. and hdd 4th: j. slowly and lost 2nd next: in tch after: rdn and rallying whn hit 3 out: btn whn j.rt 2 out: wknd* **5/1**3
5 3 **More Claret (IRE)**15 1982 4-10-6 113 TimmyMurphy 94
(Kevin F O'Donnell, Ire) *chsd ldng pair: lft 2nd 6th tl 10th: rdn and wknd bef 2 out: hung lft after 2 out* **11/4**2

4m 2.20s (-2.80) **Going Correction** -0.05s/f (Good)
WFA 4 from 5yo+ 7lb **5 Ran SP% 109.9**
Speed ratings (Par 107): **105,103,100,96,94**
CSF £33.07 TOTE £23.00: £5.10, £1.10; EX 50.30.
Owner Mr & Mrs David Thornhill **Bred** Epona, Llc **Trained** Pandy, Monmouths

FOCUS
A fairly weak novices' chase. Not an easy race to assess and the ratings could be 5lb+ out either way.

NOTEBOOK
Potemkin(USA) failed to win on the Flat or over hurdles but shaped quite encouragingly on his chase debut at Ludlow and found enough improvement to deny the favourite, receiving a fine ride and quickening best over the last couple of fences. He's clearly on the up, but the form isn't worth much and it would be a surprise were he good enough to defy a penalty. (op 18-1 tchd 20-1)
Chain Of Command(IRE) won with a bit in hand on his chasing debut at Kempton, so it was disappointing he couldn't follow up under a penalty in this lowly event. Noel Fehily perhaps got caught out a little on him, not banking on the winner picking up in the manner he did, but on this evidence he's going to remain vulnerable until going handicapping. He may also benefit from going back right-handed. (op Evens tchd 11-10 in places)
Blacktoft(USA) has generally been running well under his penalty but fell at the course last time and never looked like winning here. (op 8-1)
Benfleet Boy, well behind the favourite on debut, fared no better this time, jumping poorly, and is likely to continue to struggle until he goes handicapping. (tchd 13-2)
More Claret(IRE), a ready winner at Wexford last month, was again getting all the allowances, so it was disappointing to see her run so poorly. (tchd 10-3 in places)

2234 PROFESSIONAL SECURITY MANAGEMENT H'CAP CHASE (13 fncs) 2m
2:45 (2:46) (Class 3) (0-135,133) 4-Y-0+ **£5,854** (£1,719; £859; £429)

Form RPR
4P-0 1 **Moon Over Miami (GER)**22 1861 9-11-12 133 (t) NoelFehily 141
(Charlie Mann) *hld up in midfield: effrt to chse ldng pair 10th: rdn 3 out: no imp tl lft 4 l 2nd last: kpt on flat to ld towards fin* **13/2**3
6621 2 1 **Sunday City (JPN)**7 2112 9-11-5 126 7ex JamieMoore 133
(Peter Bowen) *led: hdd 3 out: sn rdn: 6 l down and wl hld whn lft in 4 l ld last: drvn flat: hdd towards fin* **6/4**1
0F4P 3 19 **Agente Romano (USA)**12 2022 5-9-10 110 AdamWedge(7) 100
(Evan Williams) *hld up in last pair: mstke 4th: effrt to go modest 4th 10th: no prog after and wl hld fr 3 out: lft 3rd last* **7/1**

5525 **4** 2 3/4 **Storm Of Applause (IRE)**[18] 1926 9-10-12 **119**................. TomO'Brien 107
(Philip Hobbs) *disp 2nd: j. awkwardly 2nd: rdn and wknd bef 10th: wl btn 3 out: lft modest 4th and hmpd last* **10/3**[2]

316- **5** 12 **The Snail**[220] 4969 7-10-7 **124**.................................. JSMcGarvey(10) 101
(Evan Williams) *j.rt: a in last: lost tch 9th* **7/1**

-500 **F** **Enlightenment (IRE)**[28] 1797 10-11-3 **127**...........................(p) DPFahy(3) 140+
(Evan Williams) *chsd ldr: led 3 out: j.lft next: 6 l clr and in command whn j.lft and fell heavily last* **10/1**

3m 59.6s (-5.40) **Going Correction** -0.05s/f (Good) **6** Ran SP% **110.5**
Speed ratings (Par 107): **111,110,101,99,93** —
toteswingers: 1&2 £2.70, 1&3 £6.60, 2&3 £3.90 CSF £16.99 TOTE £8.60: £4.50, £1.70; EX 14.40.
Owner Safest Syndicate 3 **Bred** R Kuhne U A **Trained** Upper Lambourn, Berks

FOCUS
There was a dramatic conclusion to this handicap chase, with Enlightenment, clear and with the race at his mercy, falling heavily at the last, and Sunday City, who looked to have inherited the victory, being run down close home by Moon Over Miami. The winner is rated 4lb off last season's best and the faller is assessed as a 5l winner.

NOTEBOOK
Moon Over Miami(GER), although clearly fortunate, is well weighted on his old form and his extra stamina for this trip won him the day. This was his first win since December 2007 and consistency is a worry, so don't be banking on a follow up. (op 11-2 tchd 7-1)
Sunday City(JPN), expected to take the beating under a 7lb penalty, again set about making all but had been swept aside by Enlightenment and couldn't even hang on having been gifted the race at the last. (op 5-4)
Agente Romano(USA) is still learning as a chaser. (op 10-1)
Storm Of Applause(IRE), last year's winner, was beaten before the home turn. (op 5-1)
The Snail jumped badly right and slowly lost touch. He'll come on for this, though, and should be sharper next time. (op 15-2)
Enlightenment(IRE), very well treated on the pick of his efforts, looked transformed by the cheekpieces, travelling strongly and readily asserting, but he guessed at the last and got it badly wrong, falling heavily. He would have won but it remains to be seen how this affects his confidence. (op 8-1)

2235 FFOS LAS AWARD WINNING CATERING H'CAP HURDLE (12 hdls) 3m
3:20 (3:20) (Class 3) (0-135,134) 4-Y-O+ **£4,553** (£1,337; £668; £333)

Form RPR

436- **1** **Harouet (FR)**[226] 4869 5-10-6 **114**..................................... PaddyBrennan 119+
(Paul Nicholls) *hld up in tch in last trio: mstke 9th: hdwy bef next: led and j.lft 2 out: sn rdn: kpt on wl to assert after last* **11/4**[1]

5-10 **2** 1 1/2 **Tin Pot Man (IRE)**[29] 1776 4-9-7 **108** oh3.......................(t) MrJEngland(7) 109
(Evan Williams) *hld up in tch in midfield: hdwy to chse ldrs bef 3 out: ev ch fr bef 2 out: rdn between last 2: no ex and btn after last* **18/1**

1042 **3** 1 1/2 **Cubism**[15] 1972 4-9-9 **108** oh3......................................(t) JimmyDerham(5) 108
(Milton Harris) *t.k.h early: in tch in midfield: rdn bef 3 out: chsd ldng pair and drvn between last 2: styd on same pce after last* **8/1**

21P0 **4** 2 1/2 **Markington**[14] 1986 7-11-7 **129**...(b) TomO'Brien 126
(Peter Bowen) *chsd ldng pair: rdn and j. slowly 3 out: outpcd u.p bef next: kpt on same pce between last 2* **14/1**

3335 **5** 9 **Doubletoilntrouble (IRE)**[22] 1860 4-10-0 **108** oh3............ JamieMoore 97
(Keith Goldsworthy) *chsd ldr: rdn bef 3 out: wknd u.p 2 out* **16/1**

12-1 **6** 1 3/4 **Cool Mission (IRE)**[178] 305 6-11-12 **134**........................ JasonMaguire 123
(Donald McCain) *led: hdd and hmpd 2 out: sn wknd: wl btn last* **6/1**[3]

123- **7** 34 **Money Order (IRE)**[225] 4884 8-11-6 **131**..................... MrAJBerry(3) 88
(Brendan Powell) *hld up in tch in last trio: rdn and btn bef 3 out: t.o last* **6/1**[3]

16P- **8** 9 **Crazy Eyes (IRE)**[207] 5184 5-10-5 **113**..........................(t) TimmyMurphy 62
(Charlie Mann) *t.k.h: hld up in tch in last trio: mstke 6th: rdn and wknd 3 out: t.o last: eased flat* **13/2**

41-4 **9** 9 **Al Co (FR)**[183] 206 5-11-10 **132**.. NoelFehily 73
(Jonjo O'Neill) *chsd ldrs: rdn and lost pl after 9th: wl bhd bef 2 out: t.o and eased after last* **9/2**[2]

6m 9.50s (22.50) **Going Correction** 0.0s/f (Good)
WFA 4 from 5yo+ 9lb **9** Ran SP% **115.7**
Speed ratings (Par 107): **99,98,98,97,94 93,82,79,76**
toteswingers: 1&2 £11.50, 1&3 £4.80, 2&3 £23.10 CSF £48.25 CT £356.76 TOTE £4.10: £1.50, £6.20, £2.60; EX 56.40.
Owner Walters Plant Hire Ltd Egan Waste Ltd **Bred** Jean Pierre Roussel **Trained** Ditcheat, Somerset

FOCUS
A decent handicap hurdle that proved a bit of a slog in the end. The winner is rated to his mark.

NOTEBOOK
Harouet(FR), who ended last year with a keeping-on sixth over this trip at Newbury, looked a likely improver this term and received a fine ride from Paddy Brennan to score, asserting on the run-in and keeping on well. He remains capable of better at this sort of distance. (op 3-1 tchd 10-3)
Tin Pot Man(IRE), 3lb out of the handicap, was disappointing on his handicap debut at Chepstow, but this was more like it, clearly appreciating the step up to 3m. He remains capable of better. (tchd 16-1)
Cubism, another who was 3lb 'wrong', rallied well and stayed on for third, but was always being held by the front pair (op 15-2)
Markington became outpaced leaving the back straight but stays well and plugged on again for fourth.
Doubletoilntrouble(IRE), also 3lb out of the handicap, made a lot of the running before gradually fading on this handicap debut. (op 20-1)
Cool Mission(IRE), off since winning at Perth in May, hadn't finished out the first three in eight previous attempts but looked to be making his handicap debut off a high enough mark and, having been on the pace for much of the way, he slowly faded once headed. He's entitled to come on, but is left with a bit to prove.
Crazy Eyes(IRE) travelled well until appearing to get tired on this first start in 207 days. (op 9-1)
Al Co(FR), fourth off this mark at Haydock in May, was disappointing considering he'd looked a promising type for the season ahead. He's likely to come on for it, though, so probably deserves another chance. (op 4-1)

2236 HEATHCOTES OUTSIDE CATERING NOVICES' H'CAP CHASE (17 fncs) 2m 5f
3:55 (3:55) (Class 4) (0-115,115) 4-Y-O+ **£3,252** (£955; £477; £238)

Form RPR

6-P4 **1** **The Rainbow Hunter**[15] 1972 6-11-4 **114**.......................... EdCookson(7) 130+
(Andy Turnell) *t.k.h: hld up in tch: lft 3rd 6th: wnt 2nd and j.rt fr 11th: led 14th: clr and mstke next: in command whn wnt rt last 2: easily* **13/2**[3]

333- **2** 6 **Regal Approach (IRE)**[207] 5184 7-11-12 **115**.................. JasonMaguire 122+
(Kim Bailey) *in tch: hmpd 6th: wnt 2nd 12th: led next: j.rt and hdd 14th: kpt on same pce and no threat to wnr fr next* **11/10**[1]

2/00 **3** 17 **Bob Casey (IRE)**[8] 2081 8-10-11 **100**.............................. TimmyMurphy 94
(Keith Goldsworthy) *j.rt: led tl 13th: cl 3rd and mstke next: wknd 3 out* **11/1**

4 7 **Trooper Clarence**[386] 6-10-9 **105**.................................. AdamWedge(7) 88
(Evan Williams) *t.k.h: chsd ldrs tl wnt 2nd 4th: mstke 7th: lost 2nd 11th: styd in tch tl wknd 14th: burst blood vessel* **5/1**[2]

U210 **F** **Builteoir (IRE)**[45] 1591 8-10-4 **96**................................... DPFahy(3) —
(Evan Williams) *hld up in last: hmpd 6th: in tch whn fell 9th* **13/2**[3]

2-P0 **U** **Oncle Kid (FR)**[10] 2049 8-10-4 **98**................................. JimmyDerham(5) —
(Paul Henderson) *chsd ldr tl 4th: 3rd whn mstke and uns rdr 6th* **8/1**

5m 38.4s (8.40) **Going Correction** -0.05s/f (Good) **6** Ran SP% **110.4**
Speed ratings (Par 105): **89,86,80,77**,— —
toteswingers: 1&2 £2.30, 1&3 £4.60, 2&3 £3.00 CSF £14.46 TOTE £8.20: £3.60, £1.30; EX 16.90.
Owner The Hon Mrs Cookson **Bred** M Massarella **Trained** Broad Hinton, Wilts

FOCUS
Just a modest novices' handicap chase. the form is rated around the front two.

NOTEBOOK
The Rainbow Hunterlooked potentially interesting on this first start over fences and, despite continually jumping out to his right down the straight, always had things under control once taking over three out. This was a promising start and he may well win again. (op 7-1 tchd 6-1)
Regal Approach(IRE), another open to improvement switched to fences, failed to win over hurdles but made a promising start here and should go one better at some stage. (op 11-8 tchd 6-4 and Evens)
Bob Casey(IRE) ran well in this first start over fences, despite jumping out to his right, and looks capable of finding a small race at some stage. (op 9-1 tchd 8-1)
Trooper Clarence could make no impression in the straight on this first start in over a year, but he's joined a yard that does well with this type and is likely to come good at some stage. Official explanation: jockey said gelding bled from the nose (op 11-2)
Builteoir(IRE) fell before the race had got going. (op 11-2)

2237 GREEN'S OF ST JAMES "JUNIOR" STANDARD OPEN NATIONAL HUNT FLAT RACE 1m 6f
4:25 (4:25) (Class 5) 3-Y-O **£1,626** (£477; £238; £119)

Form RPR

1 **Keys (IRE)** 3-10-12 0.. PaddyBrennan 105+
(Roger Charlton) *t.k.h: hld up in last pair: hdwy 5f out: trckd ldrs gng wl over 2f out: pushed into ld ins fnl f: sn in command: comf* **7/4**[1]

2 1 1/2 **Kuilsriver (IRE)** 3-10-12 0.......................................(t) ChristianWilliams 100
(Alison Thorpe) *chsd ldr tl 6f out: styd chsng ldrs: rdn and ev ch jst over 2f out: led over 1f out tl hdd and nt pce of wnr ins fnl f* **20/1**

3 4 **Awaywiththegreys (IRE)** 3-10-12 0.................................. TomO'Brien 95
(Peter Bowen) *chsd ldrs: wnt 2nd 6f out: upsides ldr gng wl over 3f out: rdn to ld jst over 2f out: hdd over 1f out: wknd ins fnl f* **7/1**

4 3/4 **It's A Gimme (IRE)** 3-10-9 0.. MrAJBerry(3) 95
(Jonjo O'Neill) *hld up in rr: hdwy 6f out: chsd ldrs 4f out: rdn over 2f out: styd on same pce fr over 1f out* **4/1**[2]

5 3 1/2 **Fairy Trader (IRE)** 3-10-5 0.. TimmyMurphy 83
(Keith Goldsworthy) *led: rdn over 2f out: hdd jst over 2f out: wknd over 1f out* **5/1**[3]

6 5 **Conigre** 3-10-12 0.. DominicElsworth 84
(Tor Sturgis) *in tch in midfield: stl travelling wl ent fnl 4f: rdn and wknd qckly over 2f out* **25/1**

7 1 1/4 **Magical Man** 3-10-5 0.. AodhaganConlon(7) 83
(Debra Hamer) *chsd ldrs tl rdn and wknd 3f out* **20/1**

6 **8** 16 **Firescent**[19] 1913 3-10-12 0.. JasonMaguire 64
(Dominic Ffrench Davis) *in tch: rdn and wknd over 3f out: wl btn fnl 2f* **25/1**

9 3 1/2 **Silver Commander** 3-10-12 0... NoelFehily 59
(Alison Thorpe) *chsd ldrs tl lost pl 6f out: wl bhd fnl 4f* **18/1**

10 12 **Jay Jays Lady** 3-9-12 0.. MissIsabelTompsett(7) 38
(Bernard Llewellyn) *in tch in midfield: rdn and lost pl qckly over 5f out: sn lost tch: t.o* **33/1**

5 **11** nk **Midnight Molly**[18] 1927 3-10-5 0....................................... JamieMoore 38
(John Spearing) *t.k.h: in tch: rdn and wknd qckly over 3f out: t.o* **16/1**

12 36 **The Pundit** 3-10-7 0... TomO'Connor(5) 1
(Bill Turner) *in tch in midfield: puhed along and dropped to rr over 7f out: lost tch 5f out: t.o* **50/1**

3m 19.7s (199.70) **12** Ran SP% **118.8**
toteswingers: 1&2 £11.50, 1&3 £3.70, 2&3 £19.70. totesuper7: Win: Not won; Place £16.00. CSF £47.26 TOTE £2.70: £1.20, £5.20, £3.00; EX 42.50.
Owner Seasons Holidays **Bred** B Hurley **Trained** Beckhampton, Wilts

FOCUS
Little to go on but this was pobably an above-average junior bumper.

NOTEBOOK
Keys(IRE), a rare National Hunt runner for Roger Charlton, put up a likeable performance. A half-brother to the yard's Oaks fourth Clowance, he made good headway down the straight under Paddy Brennan and, despite looking green once in front, was always doing enough. This was a promising first start and he can probably defy a penalty. (tchd 6-4 and 15-8)
Kuilsriver(IRE), a son of Cape Cross whose dam won up to 1m4f, wore a tongue-tie and travelled well into the straight but, despite sticking on well, couldn't quite match the winner. He looks capable of winning something similar, with good ground likely to suit better. (op 25-1 tchd 18-1)
Awaywiththegreys(IRE), whose dam is a half-sister to useful staying hurdler Souffleur, travelled strongly but failed to see it out as well as the front pair. He should improve. (op 6-1)
It's A Gimme(IRE), whose dam is a half-sister to top staying chaser Commanche Court, stayed on in pleasing fashion and looks almost certain to improve for a stiffer test over hurdles. (op 5-1 tchd 7-2)
Fairy Trader(IRE), a half-sister to numerous winners, including Flipando, went well for a long way up on the pace but was green under pressure and should improve. (op 6-1)
T/Plt: £18.60 to a £1 stake. Pool: £57,928.09. 2,272.86 winning tickets. T/Qpdt: £6.20 to a £1 stake. Pool: £4,204.61. 497.00 winning tickets. SP

[1449] HEREFORD (R-H)
Sunday, November 7

OFFICIAL GOING: Good to soft (good in places; chs 6.5; hdl 6.4)
Wind: Nil Weather: Fine becoming cloudy

2238 LINDLEY CATERING MAIDEN HURDLE (11 hdls) 2m 6f 110y
1:00 (1:00) (Class 5) 4-Y-O+ **£1,691** (£496; £248; £124)

Form RPR

4 **1** **Old Wigmore (IRE)**[14] 1989 5-10-7 0....................... AodhaganConlon(7) 120+
(Rebecca Curtis) *trckd ldrs: wnt 2nd after 3 out: rdn whn chalng appr 2 out: led between last 2: clr and in command fr last: pushed out and r.o wl* **13/2**

03-4 **2** 5 **Super Villan**[25] 1821 5-11-0 0.. MattieBatchelor 113
(Mark Bradstock) *led: hdd 3 out: pushed along and outpcd appr 2 out: kpt on to take 2nd bef last: no ch w wnr* **4/1**[3]

	3	3	**Iron Chancellor (IRE)**[238] 5-11-0 0 WayneHutchinson (Alan King) *trckd ldrs: pushed along and outpcd 2 out: kpt on but no imp fr last* **10/1**	110
2	4	5	**Causing Chaos (IRE)**[32] 1734 4-10-11 0 SamTwiston-Davies(3) (Nigel Twiston-Davies) *in tch: rdn bhd ldrs whn mstke 3 out: wl outpcd bef 2 out: styd on fr bef last but unable to chal ldrs* **3/1**2	107
030-	5	nk	**Vin De Roy (FR)**[204] 5228 5-11-0 0 SeanQuinlan (Rachel Hobbs) *hld up: struggling to keep up after 3 out: kpt on modly fr bef last: nvr able to chal* **100/1**	106
	6	10	**Forlovenormoney (IRE)**[552] 6-11-0 0 SamThomas (Paul Nicholls) *j.w but a bit big: w ldr: led 3 out: rdn and hdd between last 2: sn wknd and dropped away qckly* **7/4**1	101+
6-	7	28	**Saffron Lord**[268] 4016 5-11-0 0 TomSiddall (Martin Keighley) *j.rt at times: a bhd: lost tch 8th: nvr on terms* **66/1**	71
5-	8	22	**Ben The Horse (IRE)**[244] 4488 4-11-0 0 RichardJohnson (Henry Daly) *a towards rr: rdn and lost tch 8th: t.o* **25/1**	52
	9	61	**Tom Bach (IRE)**[196] 6-11-0 0 GerardTumelty (Richard Price) *trckd ldrs to 4th: sn lost pl: bhd and struggling 7th: lost tch next: t.o* **100/1**	—
	P		**Rageon (IRE)** 7-10-9 0 MrMMO'Connor(5) (Milton Harris) *bhd: struggling 7th: lost tch next: t.o whn p.u bef 2 out* **50/1**	—

5m 31.8s (-6.20)
WFA 4 from 5yo+ 8lb **10** Ran SP% **113.1**
toteswingers: 1&2 £4.50, 1&3 £8.20, 2&3 £6.90 CSF £31.36 TOTE £9.50: £3.30, £1.10, £1.30; EX 32.30.
Owner Sea Partnership **Bred** Noel O'Brien **Trained** Newport, Dyfed

FOCUS
The ground had eased slightly overnight from the advertised good, and riders in the first described it as 'perfect'. The time was over 28 seconds outside the standard, suggesting that the ground was indeed slightly on the easy side. This was an interesting maiden hurdle, contested by several winning point-to-pointers. The winner confirmed his bumper promise with the second and fourth close to their marks, but the fifth was a bit of a worry.

NOTEBOOK
Old Wigmore(IRE) was successful in a point-to-point in Ireland in the spring. He was fourth on his British debut in a bumper at Aintree, where he went off quickly over 2m1f, but was ridden a little less forcefully upped in trip on this hurdles debut. Getting past the favourite on the home turn, he was never in any danger of being caught. His trainer described him as still weak, and regards him as a chasing type. (op 8-1)
Super Villan set a fair standard on his fourth over this trip at Uttoxeter last month. After making the running, the game was soon up when he was collared by the favourite but he stuck on for second. (op 9-2 tchd 5-1)
Iron Chancellor(IRE) won a brace of Irish points in good style earlier in the year and he ran a pleasing race on this debut under rules, just lacking a change of pace from the turn out of the back straight. He is a 3m chaser in the making. (tchd 17-2)
Causing Chaos(IRE) was runner-up at Towcester over 2m1f on his debut. He was being shoved along a good away out here and stayed on to suggest that this sort of trip is well within his compass. (op 10-3 tchd 7-2 and 4-1 in places)
Vin De Roy(FR) showed nothing on his hurdling debut in the spring and this was an improved effort, but his proximity perhaps holds down the form slightly. (tchd 125-1)
Forlovenormoney(IRE), bought by his leading connections for £85,000 after winning an Irish point in May 2009 and given time since to recover from a minor fracture, proved a disappointment. A warm order to make a winning hurdles debut, things looked to be going to plan when he struck the front three from home. He was still going best at the next, but was soon headed and dropped away rapidly, being relegated to sixth and appearing to finish tired. A chasing type, he gave his flights plenty of air and the best is unlikely to be seen of him until he switches to fences, but he is surely capable of better than he showed here. Official explanation: trainer said gelding had a breathing problem (op 6-4 tchd 11-8)

2239 LINDLEY CATERING H'CAP HURDLE (13 hdls) 3m 2f

1:30 (1:31) (Class 5) (0-85,84) 4-Y-0+ **£1,691** (£496; £248; £124)

Form				RPR
-0P0	1		**Bernard**[31] 1741 10-10-13 **76** (p) GilesHawkins(5) (Kevin Bishop) *midfield: hdwy 8th: chsd ldrs bef 2 out: styd on after last: r.o to ld towards fin* **11/1**	82
-3P4	2	nk	**Elegant Olive**[69] 1434 7-11-8 **80** HaddenFrost (Roger Curtis) *midfield: hdwy 10th: chsd ldrs bef 2 out: led between last 2: over 2 l clr whn pckd last: hrd pressed after: hdd narrowly towards fin and jst hld* **11/2**1	87+
0304	3	8	**Flag Flier**[28] 1798 7-10-11 **76** NathanSweeney(7) (Bob Buckler) *chsd ldr to 10th: stl cl up 2 out: outpcd bef last: kpt on run-in but n.d to front pair* **17/2**	75
6222	4	1	**You Can Of Course (IRE)**[10] 2050 7-11-8 **80** DougieCostello (Neil Mulholland) *led: rdn and hdd between last 2: kpt on same pce after* **6/1**2	77
4212	5	¾	**Heezagrey (IRE)**[17] 1939 7-10-12 **77** MarkQuinlan(7) (James Evans) *midield: rdn and outpcdd fr bef 8th: styd on appr last: nvr able to get competitve* **11/2**1	73
0660	6	1½	**Jug Of Punch (IRE)**[23] 1855 11-9-13 **64** MissCBoxall(7) (Simon Lewis) *bhd: struggling fr 6th: styd on for press fr bef last: nvr able to rch ldrs* **17/2**	59
P0-0	7	¾	**Woodlands Gem (IRE)**[157] 601 8-11-3 **75** (b) JackDoyle (Peter Pritchard) *chsd ldrs: pushed along appr 8th: outpcd 9th: no imp after* **25/1**	69
0-P3	8	hd	**Lucky Pearl**[14] 2001 9-11-5 **84** MrTomDavid(7) (Tim Vaughan) *in tch: wnt 2nd 10th: rdn whn chalng 2 out: fdd appr last* **7/1**3	78
42-P	9	1¾	**Lonesome Boatman (IRE)**[173] 383 10-10-9 **74** JoshWall(7) (Arthur Whitehead) *hld up: struggling 8th: nvr on terms* **16/1**	66
3P3-	10	12	**Rojabaa**[346] 2528 11-10-6 **71** MattGriffiths(7) (Simon Burrough) *led into strart: hld up: pushed along bef 3 out: nvr on terms* **20/1**	52
/604	11	12	**Stowford Press (IRE)**[31] 1745 7-10-11 **76** KyleJames(7) (Nikki Evans) *reluctant to line-up: wl bhd to 2nd: stl in rr but in tch w others after: struggling 4 out: wl btn after* **11/1**	47
60-0	12	½	**Lupita (IRE)**[187] 134 6-10-12 **70** (t) DarylJacob (Derrick Scott) *in tch tl rdn and wknd bef 2 out* **16/1**	40

6m 35.7s (4.00) **Going Correction** +0.225s/f (Yiel) **12** Ran SP% **115.6**
Speed ratings (Par 103): **102,101,99,99,98 98,98,98,97,93 90,90**
toteswingers: 1&2 £16.10, 1&3 £19.90, 2&3 £13.90 CSF £69.63 CT £545.37 TOTE £19.20: £4.20, £4.20, £3.10; EX 115.50.
Owner K Bishop **Bred** Mountgrange Stud Ltd **Trained** Spaxton, Somerset
■ Stewards' Enquiry : Giles Hawkins three-day ban: used whip with excessive frequency (Nov 21-23)

FOCUS
A very modest handicap with the emphasis firmly on stamina, and the form is pretty weak. The winner was well handicapped on his old form, and there was a personal best from the second.

NOTEBOOK
Bernard was under pressure a fair way from home, but his rider's persistence was eventually rewarded. Equipped with first-time cheekpieces, the gelding was down to his last winning hurdles mark and was a stone lower than when scoring over fences in May last year. This was a big improvement on his recent efforts, and the trainer reported that the cheekpieces and the longer trip had rekindled the horse's enthusiasm. Official explanation: trainer said, regarding apparent improvement in form, that the gelding had rekindled its enthusiasm by wearing first-time cheekpieces and possibly the longer trip. (op 10-1)
Elegant Olive looked an unlucky loser. She was going much the best when easing to the front on the inside turning for home, but she stumbled on landing at the last and the lost momentum proved decisive. She was not beaten for lack of stamina but 3m might prove to be her optimum. (op 8-1 tchd 17-2)
Flag Flier ran one of her best races since finishing second in this event 12 months ago when 3lb higher. (op 9-1)
You Can Of Course(IRE) made a lot of the running but was unable to hold on from the turn. He is running consistently and has the option of reverting to fences, over which he is currently rated 6lb lower. (op 13-2 tchd 7-1)
Heezagrey(IRE) raced closer to the pace than he does usually, but was under pressure for most of the final circuit and only began to run on when it was too late. (op 5-1 tchd 6-1)
Lucky Pearl ran well for a long way but was found out by this longer trip in the end. (op 6-1)
Lonesome Boatman(IRE)
Stowford Press(IRE) lost a lot of ground at the start, something she has done before, and could never get into it prior to being pulled up. She does not look one for maximum faith. (op 17-2)

2240 LINDLEY CATERING H'CAP CHASE (19 fncs) 3m 1f 110y

2:00 (2:00) (Class 4) (0-100,97) 4-Y-0+ **£2,862** (£840; £420; £209)

Form				RPR
6F-1	1		**Bobby Bullock (IRE)**[3] 2172 8-11-1 **89** 7ex SamTwiston-Davies(3) (Nigel Twiston-Davies) *chsd ldrs: wnt 2nd bef 12th: led appr 16th: sn clr: unchal after* **1/1**1	113+
422-	2	14	**Sir Winston (IRE)**[229] 4796 8-11-10 **95** DarylJacob (Victor Dartnall) *hit 1st: towards rr: reminders appr 5th: hdwy 12th: wnt 2nd bef 16th but a chsng wnr in vain: kpt on whn hrd pressed for 2nd run-in* **9/2**2	99
-340	3	nk	**Miller's Dawn**[19] 1911 6-11-12 **97** HaddenFrost (Henrietta Knight) *towards rr and nvr gng wl: rdn to go mod 3rd 3 out: styd on to chal for 2nd run-in: no ch w wnr* **12/1**	100
1-1P	4	33	**Gunship (IRE)**[166] 463 9-11-9 **97** (b) DannyCook(3) (Cathy Hamilton) *led to 1st: remained prom: regained ld 11th: hdd appr 16th: wknd bef 3 out: t.o* **11/1**3	83
-031	F		**Marked Man (IRE)**[109] 1061 14-11-11 **96** CharliePoste (Richard Lee) *in tch: 3rd but niggled along whn fell 13th* **16/1**	—
433-	B		**Heart Springs**[198] 5361 10-10-10 **84** EamonDehdashti(3) (Dr Jeremy Naylor) *in rr: struggling to keep up whn b.d 13th: injured fatally* **14/1**	—
501B	P		**Lansdowne Princess**[32] 1733 8-10-1 **77** DavidBass(5) (Gerald Ham) *bhd: rdn appr 12th: p.u bef 13th* **11/1**3	—
PP0P	P		**The Walnut Tree (IRE)**[3] 2170 9-10-1 **72** oh5 ow1 (b) ColinBolger (Simon Lewis) *led 1st: rdn appr 9th: hdd 11th: wknd 12th: t.o whn p.u bef 3 out* **25/1**	—
/FP-	P		**Raki Rose**[246] 4441 8-11-6 **91** (p) JohnnyFarrelly (Michael Scudamore) *chsd ldrs: rdn and lost pl 9th: bhd after 10th: t.o whn p.u bef 12th* **28/1**	—

6m 26.5s (-5.30) **Going Correction** -0.125s/f (Good) **9** Ran SP% **112.4**
Speed ratings (Par 105): **103,98,98,88,—, —,—,—,—**
toteswingers: 1&2 £2.50, 1&3 £6.40, 2&3 £6.20 CSF £6.15 CT £31.22 TOTE £2.40: £1.30, £1.80, £2.20; EX 6.10.
Owner The Yes No Wait Sorries **Bred** George Durrheim & Mrs Maria Mulcahy Durr **Trained** Naunton, Gloucs

FOCUS
Only four completed in this ordinary handicap chase. The time was over 25 seconds outside the standard. The easy winner was thrown in on his recent win but this was another step up.

NOTEBOOK
Bobby Bullock(IRE) took up the running going to the fourth-last and the contest was as good as over as he quickly pulled well clear. He looked well treated under a 7lb penalty for his easy win at Towcester three days earlier and this longer trip did obviously didn't pose him a problem. That's two out of two for his new yard, and he is likely to be given a break now. (op 11-10 tchd 6-5 and 10-11)
Sir Winston(IRE) was steadily left behind by the winner and it looked like he might be caught for second as he tired. This was a satisfactory first run since March and his jumping was sound enough after an early mistake, but he remains vulnerable from this mark. (tchd 11-2)
Miller's Dawn was without the usual headgear for this chasing debut. A good way adrift of the leaders starting the final circuit, he plugged on doggedly to challenge for second going to the last but remains essentially a disappointing type. (tchd 11-1)
Gunship(IRE) weakened quickly once headed and this first run since May will have done him good. (op 8-1)
Marked Man(IRE) took a crashing fall when in third place. (tchd 28-1)
The Walnut Tree(IRE)was a shock winner of this event last year but was well beaten from 5lb out of the weights this time round. (tchd 28-1)

2241 HAPPY BIRTHDAY MRS OTTESEN NOVICES' HURDLE (10 hdls) 2m 4f

2:35 (2:36) (Class 4) 4-Y-0+ **£2,341** (£687; £343; £171)

Form				RPR
	1		**Court By Surprise (IRE)**[588] 5-10-12 0 JackDoyle (Emma Lavelle) *a.p: led between last 2: nt fluent last: drvn clr run-in: comf* **12/1**	112+
0-34	2	7	**Father Probus**[25] 1824 4-10-9 0 SamTwiston-Davies(3) (Nigel Twiston-Davies) *hld up in tch: pushed along to chse ldrs 2 out: styd on to take 2nd towards fin: no ch w wnr* **9/1**	105+
14-1	3	½	**Fountains Flypast**[36] 1680 6-10-7 0 (t) RachaelGreen(5) (Anthony Honeyball) *hld up: nt fluent 6th: hdwy appr 2 out: chsd wnr between last 2: no imp whn mstke last: styd on same pce: lost 2nd towards fin* **7/2**1	104+
	4	3	**Kingsmere**[182] 5-10-12 0 RichardJohnson (Henry Daly) *led 2nd: hdd between last 2: sn u.p and btn* **13/2**	101
523-	5	4	**Mister Chancer (IRE)**[240] 4575 5-10-9 0 CharlieHuxley(3) (Alan King) *midfield: rdn after 7th: hdwy to chse ldrs 3 out: mstke whn one pce last* **5/1**3	97
453/	6	11	**King Of Dubai**[636] 3823 5-10-12 0 RhysFlint (John Flint) *racd keenly in midfield: lost pl 5th: styd on fr after 2 out: unable to rch ldrs* **40/1**	86
2135	7	1	**Hadron Collider (FR)**[31] 1742 5-11-2 112 DannyCook(3) (Christopher Nenadich) *trckd ldrs: rdn after 4 out: wknd 2 out* **8/1**	92
06-0	8	1¼	**Boosha**[31] 1749 5-10-5 0 SeanQuinlan (Rachel Hobbs) *in tch: lost pl after 4th: n.d after* **100/1**	77

The Form Book, Raceform Ltd, Compton, RG20 6NL

000 **9** ½ **Sheezatreasure (IRE)**[31] 1743 5-9-12 0 MarkQuinlan(7) 77
(James Evans) *a bhd: nvr on terms* **100/1**

-100 **10** 11 **Tiermore (IRE)**[24] 1844 6-10-12 109 MrPJTolman(7) 84
(Sirrell Griffiths) *led to 2nd: remained prom: nt fluent 6th: mstke 7th: wknd appr 2 out* **16/1**

10-2 **11** *shd* **Life Long (IRE)**[182] 224 6-10-12 0 GerardTumelty 74
(Anabel L M King) *trckd ldrs: pushed along after 5th: bhd and toiling 7th* **20/1**

U **12** 7 **Goodtimetoby (IRE)**[4] 2143 7-10-12 0 CharliePoste 67
(Richard Lee) *hld up in midfield: hdwy 6th: no imp on ldrs bef 2 out: wknd* **100/1**

0-0 **13** 9 **Benny The Swinger (IRE)**[31] 1736 5-10-12 0 HaddenFrost 59
(Henrietta Knight) *hld up: u.p 4 out: nvr on terms* **50/1**

00P/ **U** **Bristol Delauriere (FR)**[174] 629 6-10-5 0 MrJamieJenkinson(7) —
(Natalie Lloyd-Beavis) *hld up: mstke: slipped and almost fell whn uns rdr 4th* **150/1**

02- **P** **Ballagio (IRE)**[204] 5235 5-10-12 0 SamThomas —
(Paul Nicholls) *in tch: lost pl bef 7th: dropped away qckly 3 out: t.o whn p.u bef last* **4/1**[2]

5m 0.50s (5.00) **Going Correction** +0.225s/f (Yiel)
WFA 4 from 5yo+ 8lb **15** Ran SP% **119.7**
Speed ratings (Par 105): **99,96,96,94,93 88,88,87,87,83 83,80,76,—,—**
toteswingers: 1&2 £24.40, 1&3 £9.40, 2&3 £10.50 CSF £111.58 TOTE £12.60: £3.60, £2.50, £2.20; EX 175.80.
Owner N Mustoe **Bred** Noel McLoughlin **Trained** Wildhern, Hants

FOCUS
An interesting novices' hurdle likely to prove a source of future winners at an ordinary level. The pace was fairly steady. The winner looks a decent recruit.

NOTEBOOK
Court By Surprise(IRE) has been off with a leg problem since falling in an Irish point in March 2009. Never far from the pace, he led off the home turn, where he ran a little wide, and was in command when overjumping slightly at the last. A chasing type, he is still green and it bodes well for his future that he was able to win this.
Father Probus shaped in his bumpers as if this sort of trip was what he needed and, after finding himself outpaced by the leaders, he stayed on for pressure to snatch second near the line. A step up to 3m may well suit him. (tchd 10-1)
Fountains Flypast, a dual bumper winner, was a first ride for his jockey since she turned professional. Improving steadily on the second circuit, he looked a threat on the home turn but could make no further inroads from there, and lost second after a last-flight mistake. He can win races over hurdles. (tchd 9-2)
Kingsmere is out of a half-sister to his connections' high-class staying hurdler Mighty Man. Winner of a maiden point over this trip in May, he made much of the running until weakening in between the last two flights. Faster ground might be what he wants. (op 6-1 tchd 11-2)
Mister Chancer(IRE) showed ability in bumpers and he ran a pleasing race on this first try over hurdles. A slightly longer trip may suit. (tchd 6-1)
King Of Dubai ◆ made the frame in bumpers for two different Welsh yards two seasons ago and he shaped with definite promise on this hurdles debut after a long absence. He looks one to keep an eye on.
Hadron Collider(FR), 112-rated by the BHA, was well held under his penalty on this second run for the yard. (op 9-1 tchd 10-1)
Goodtimetoby(IRE) did not get far on his debut earlier in the week but showed a glimmer of promise here despite only beating one home.
Ballagio(IRE) was runner-up in a bumper in the spring and looked a leading contender on his hurdles debut, but dropped away in disappointing fashion and was eventually pulled up. (op 11-2 tchd 3-1)

2242 LINDLEY CATERING MARES' H'CAP HURDLE (8 hdls) 2m 1f
3:05 (3:05) (Class 3) (0-125,120) 3-Y-0+ **£4,163** (£1,222; £611; £305)

Form RPR

1-53 **1** **Princess Rainbow (FR)**[161] 541 5-10-11 105 AlanO'Keeffe 117+
(Jennie Candlish) *j.lft: mde all: qcknd up appr last: clr and in command run-in: eased towards fin* **11/1**

4-21 **2** 6 **Babilu**[9] 2070 5-10-4 98 (p) RichardJohnson 104
(Dai Burchell) *hld up: hdwy 5th: chsd wnr after 3 out: chalng 2 out: no imp fr last* **2/1**[1]

3P2- **3** 9 **Asturienne**[201] 5294 6-11-12 120 GerardTumelty 117
(Alan King) *chsd ldr to 3rd: remained handy: rdn and outpcd after 2 out: kpt on to take 3rd after last: n.d to front 2* **6/1**[3]

5223 **4** 1¼ **Josephine Malines**[18] 1511 6-10-7 101 (p) RhysFlint 97
(John Flint) *midfield: effrt and hdwy to chse ldrs 2 out: kpt on same pce and btn bef last* **9/2**[2]

225- **5** *hd* **Covert Mission**[270] 3974 7-11-2 113 LeeStephens(3) 111
(David Evans) *hld up: hdwy to chse ldrs appr 2 out: no imp and one pce bef last* **9/1**

126- **6** 27 **Cloudy Spirit**[206] 5196 5-11-8 116 SamThomas 87
(Reg Hollinshead) *hld up: struggling appr 3 out: nvr on terms* **8/1**

03-0 **7** 8 **Diktalina**[12] 1609 4-11-7 115 (bt[1]) DarylJacob 79
(Alison Thorpe) *chsd ldrs tl after 4 out: struggling and wl btn bef 2 out* **14/1**

05/5 **P** **Ruthenoise (FR)**[43] 1614 5-11-7 115 AndrewTinkler —
(Nicky Henderson) *plld hrd in midfield: hdwy to chse ldr 3rd: lost 2nd after 3 out: wknd qckly bef 2 out: t.o whn p.u bef last* **6/1**[3]

4m 1.70s (2.30) **Going Correction** +0.225s/f (Yiel)
WFA 4 from 5yo+ 7lb **8** Ran SP% **112.1**
Speed ratings (Par 107): **103,100,95,95,95 82,78,—**
toteswingers: 1&2 £3.80, 1&3 £10.00, 2&3 £3.30 CSF £33.05 CT £146.49 TOTE £17.30: £3.10, £1.20, £2.40; EX 41.30.
Owner P and Mrs G A Clarke **Bred** Societe Sogir **Trained** Basford Green, Staffs

FOCUS
A fair handicap hurdle for mares. A big step forward from the winner to beat the well handicapped second.

NOTEBOOK
Princess Rainbow(FR) was performing creditably when last seen back in the spring and she made all the running here, winning quite cosily after brushing off the runner-up in between the last two flights. A quirky mare who carried her head a shade high and jinked left going into some of her hurdles, she would ideally be suited by softer conditions than these. (op 12-1)
Babilu came here in fine heart but was raised 8lb for her win at Uttoxeter recently. She looked to be going better than the winner after the second-last, but was soon outpaced by her. This might have proved too sharp a test for her on this ground. (op 9-4)
Asturienne is well regarded, but although she won twice in her novice season, she was also a beaten favourite three times. This trip was too short for her and better can be expected when she reverts to further. (op 9-2)
Josephine Malines having her first run over hurdles for this yard, showed enough to suggest she can pay her way at a slightly lower level. (op 5-1 tchd 11-2)
Covert Mission was without the cheekpieces for this reappearance. She ran respectably but probably needs further, although her optimum trip remains something of a mystery. (op 12-1)
Cloudy Spirit ran well in Listed company on her final start last term but she was untidy at the first on this reappearance and could never get involved. (op 10-1)
Diktalina's first-time blinkers failed to bring out any improvement. (op 12-1 tchd 11-1)
Ruthenoise(FR) dropped away rather tamely before pulling up and still needs to settle better.
Official explanation: jockey said mare pulled up quickly (tchd 15-2)

2243 HOMESTART HEREFORDSHIRE H'CAP CHASE (14 fncs) 2m 3f
3:40 (3:40) (Class 4) (0-105,105) 4-Y-0+ **£2,862** (£840; £420; £209)

Form RPR

U0-3 **1** **Inside Dealer (IRE)**[19] 1912 6-11-9 102 JoeTizzard 122+
(Colin Tizzard) *led to 3rd: remained prom: regained ld 8th: asserted fr last: styd on wl* **11/4**[1]

20/0 **2** 2½ **Mud Monkey**[19] 1911 6-11-2 100 (t) IanPopham(5) 117
(Claire Dyson) *a.p: led 3rd to 8th: stl chalng 3 out and 2 out: sn rdn: one pce and no imp on wnr fr last* **16/1**

3P43 **3** 18 **Good Old Days (IRE)**[18] 1919 11-11-9 102 SeanQuinlan 108+
(Kim Bailey) *trckd ldrs: hit 8th: rdn and outpcd by ldrs fr after 4 out: wl hld in 3rd whn hit last: no daner to front 2* **9/1**

2P-2 **4** 7 **Reland (FR)**[46] 1575 5-11-6 102 SamTwiston-Davies(3) 100
(Nigel Twiston-Davies) *prom: nt fluent 4 out: sn rdn: wknd 2 out* **7/2**[2]

243 **5** 32 **Temple Place (IRE)**[20] 1905 9-10-0 79 WillKennedy 44
(Alan Jones) *hld up: struggling 4 out: nvr able to trble ldrs* **28/1**

05-0 **6** 7 **Charming Oscar (IRE)**[19] 1912 8-10-6 85 DarylJacob 44
(Bob Buckler) *in tch tl rdn and wknd 4 out* **12/1**

601- **7** ¾ **Monn Royal (FR)**[518] 635 6-11-12 105 AidanColeman 63
(Venetia Williams) *in tch: lost pl struggling and wl btn 3 out* **11/1**

404P **8** ¾ **Doheny Bar (IRE)**[14] 1991 7-9-8 80 (p) PeterHatton(7) 38
(Nikki Evans) *hld up: rdn 4 out: sn outpcd: n.d after* **16/1**

2104 **9** *shd* **Red Birr (IRE)**[21] 1888 9-11-5 98 (t) SamThomas 56
(Paul Webber) *bhd: niggled along 4th: nvr on terms* **18/1**

PP00 **10** 4½ **I'm The Decider (IRE)**[45] 1589 8-11-7 103 (p) RichieMcLernon(3) 57
(Jonjo O'Neill) *hld up: toiling fr 11th: nvr on terms* **22/1**

05 **F** **Kilbready Star (IRE)**[7] 2111 10-10-9 88 JackDoyle —
(Peter Pritchard) *midfield tl fell 6th* **8/1**[3]

23P6 **P** **Chilbury Hill (IRE)**[24] 1841 7-11-3 96 LiamHeard —
(Kevin Bishop) *a bhd: lost tch 10th: t.o whn p.u bef last* **11/1**

4m 44.7s (-2.00) **Going Correction** -0.125s/f (Good) **12** Ran SP% **119.2**
Speed ratings (Par 105): **99,97,90,87,73 71,70,70,70,68 —,—**
toteswingers: 1&2 £14.10, 1&3 £8.20, 2&3 £30.20 CSF £46.09 CT £359.22 TOTE £4.00: £1.70, £6.00, £2.70; EX 81.60 Trifecta £240.90 Pool: £361.46 - 1.11 winning units..
Owner J M Dare, T Hamlin, J W Snook **Bred** B D Darrer **Trained** Milborne Port, Dorset

FOCUS
Not many got into this modest handicap chase and the first four were always in the front rank. The winner and second came clear over the final three fences and the winner should have more to offer.

NOTEBOOK
Inside Dealer(IRE) was undone by late errors on his chasing debut at Exeter but he jumped better this time. Racing from the same mark, he fought off the runner-up from the home turn. A lightly raced six-year-old, he looks to have further improvement in him. He stays further and and remains eligible for novice races. (op 3-1 tchd 10-3)
Mud Monkey showed more than he had on his recent return to action over hurdles and renewed his challenge two out before giving best. Like the winner he was having only his second run over fences. (op 25-1)
Good Old Days(IRE) was well held back in third but probably gave his running. He remains 7lb above his last winning mark, though. (op 17-2 tchd 8-1)
Reland(FR) could not hold on to third after a mistake two out and was beaten a fair way in the end, but may be worth persevering with over this sort of trip. (op 4-1)
Monn Royal(FR) is entitled to improve on this, his first outing since winning a handicap hurdle at Worcester in the summer of 2009. This was his first run over fences since a couple of tries as a 3yo in France and he jumped soundly enough. (op 8-1)

2244 DIGIBET.COM CONDITIONAL JOCKEYS' H'CAP HURDLE (10 hdls) 2m 4f
4:15 (4:15) (Class 5) (0-95,95) 4-Y-0+ **£1,951** (£573; £286; £143)

Form RPR

P523 **1** **Ruby Valentine (FR)**[15] 1976 7-10-3 72 MichaelMurphy 88+
(Jim Wilson) *midfield: hdwy to trck ldrs bef 4th: led 2 out: pushed along whn pressed appr last: plld out more run-in: styd on* **13/2**[2]

P001 **2** 1 **Just The Job (IRE)**[6] 2135 6-11-6 92 7ex MrMMO'Connor(3) 108+
(Neil Mulholland) *midfield: hdwy appr 7th: chal gng wl fr 2 out: upsides whn hit last: sn rdn and failed to pick up: hld towards fin* **13/8**[1]

0062 **3** 18 **Nouailhas**[10] 2054 4-11-2 90 PeterHatton(5) 91
(Reg Hollinshead) *led: nt fluent 6th: rdn and hdd 2 out: wknd appr last* **20/1**

2053 **4** 8 **Can't Remember**[45] 1590 5-11-4 90 OliverDayman(3) 82
(Alison Thorpe) *midfield: rdn and outpcd after 3 out: styd on fr bef last: nvr able to chal ldrs* **10/1**

F/03 **5** 1 **Sumner (IRE)**[3] 1925 6-11-5 91 (v) KyleJames(3) 82
(David Evans) *hld up: rdn and hdwy appr 2 out: outpcd by ldrs between last 2: [nvr able to chal* **11/1**

60-P **6** 15 **Honourable Dreamer (IRE)**[31] 1741 5-10-13 85 RichieMcLernon(3) 62
(Jonjo O'Neill) *trckd ldrs: rdn after 3 out: wknd bef 2 out* **20/1**

0-00 **7** 35 **Roxane Bruere (FR)**[14] 1993 5-10-1 78 ChristopherWard(8) 24
(Robin Dickin) *w ldr: rdn 3 out and sn wknd* **40/1**

/0P- **8** 1¼ **Aymard Des Fieffes (FR)**[228] 4820 8-9-11 69 RobertKirk(3) 14
(Nikki Evans) *trckd ldrs tl rdn and wknd 4 out* **66/1**

0-06 **9** 8 **Golden Partner**[14] 1997 5-11-4 87 (t) LeeEdwards 25
(Matt Sheppard) *hld up: struggling 3 out: n.d whn blnd 2 out* **33/1**

00-0 **10** 6 **Over The Hill**[47] 1567 6-11-3 89 SamTwiston-Davies(3) 21
(Nigel Twiston-Davies) *midfield: hdwy 3 out: pushed along to chse clr ldrs 2 out: nt pce to chal: wknd last* **10/1**

0-04 **P** **Stage Right**[14] 1997 9-10-4 73 DavidBass —
(Simon Lewis) *prom: blnd 1st and rdr lost iron briefly: niggled along and lost pl after 3rd: bhd after 4th: t.o whn p.u bef 5th* **25/1**

33-0 **P** **Everyman**[178] 299 6-11-9 95 HarryChalloner(3) —
(John Bryan Groucott) *bhd: struggling 5th: p.u bef last* **50/1**

4P- **P** **Speedy Directa (GER)**[531] 465 7-10-13 85 BrianToomey(3) —
(Patrick Morris) *a bhd: struggling 5th: t.o whn p.u bef 2 out* **28/1**

464U **P** **Karzelle**[44] 1605 6-11-6 89 CharlieHuxley —
(Milton Harris) *towards rr: pushed along after 3rd: toiling fr 6th: t.o whn p.u bef 2 out* **16/1**

445 **P** **Himitas (FR)**[24] [1840] 5-10-13 **85**.. MattGriffiths(3) —
(Graeme McPherson) *hld up: hdwy to go handy 3rd: wknd 3 out: p.u after 2 out* **15/2**[3]

5m 0.50s (5.00) **Going Correction** +0.225s/f (Yiel)
WFA 4 from 5yo+ 8lb **15** Ran SP% **121.2**
Speed ratings (Par 103): **99,91,84,81,81 75,61,60,57,54 —,—,—,—,—**
toteswingers: 1&2 £3.40, 1&3 £11.00, 2&3 £11.00 CSF £16.21 CT £211.74 TOTE £6.40: £2.30, £1.60, £6.10; EX 27.10.
Owner The Winbledon Partnership **Bred** Earl Elevage De La Source **Trained** Ham, Gloucs

FOCUS
A moderate handicap which only involved three from the third-last. The winner was well handicapped on her best old form, and the second, who was very well in, probably stepped up on his Plumpton form.

NOTEBOOK
Ruby Valentine(FR) had been running well and this step back up in trip looked sure to suit. She was there to be shot at from the home turn, but battled on well, something she has not always done in the past. She was 12lb lower than when last getting her head in front in the summer of 2009 and avoids a penalty for this win. (tchd 6-1)
Just The Job(IRE) looked to have a gilt-edged opportunity to supplement his recent Plumpton gains and he was travelling better than the mare when upsides going to the last, but hit the flight and found little from there. He finished well clear of the rest but things are likely to be tougher when his new mark comes into effect. The ground might have been easier than he would have liked. (op 11-8 tchd 7-4)
Nouailhas, a well beaten second in a seller latest, ran creditably from the front on this handicap bow without fully seeing out the trip. (op 22-1 tchd 16-1)
Can't Remember remains vulnerable from this sort of mark but did make modest late gains. (tchd 9-1)
Sumner(IRE) ran a lacklustre race on the AW the other day and this was slightly better. (op 12-1 tchd 14-1 and 10-1)
T/Jkpt: Not won. T/Plt: £167.90 to a £1 stake. Pool: £73,582.51. 319.74 winning tickets. T/Qpdt: £8.80 to a £1 stake. Pool: £5,190.03. 435.35 winning tickets. DO

1623 MARKET RASEN (R-H)
Sunday, November 7

OFFICIAL GOING: Soft (chs 5.4, hdl 5.2)
Wind: Light, half behind Weather: Fine and sunny

2245 MARKET RASEN RACECOURSE JUVENILE HURDLE (8 hdls) 2m 1f
1:20 (1:21) (Class 4) 3-Y-O **£2,602** (£764; £382; £190)

Form RPR
51 **1** **Pullyourfingerout (IRE)**[12] [2020] 3-11-5 0...........................(t) APMcCoy 111+
(Brendan Powell) *mde all: j.lft: 6 l ahd whn hit last: pushed rt out* **6/4**[1]
5 **2** 3 **Manxman (IRE)**[25] [1825] 3-10-12 0............................ GrahamLee 97
(Ferdy Murphy) *chsd ldrs: reminders 3rd: rdn and outpcd 3 out: styd on same pce fr next: snatched 2nd line* **10/1**
3 nse **Marsh Warbler**[33] 3-10-9 0.............................. FearghalDavis(3) 98+
(Brian Ellison) *chsd ldrs: j.lft and nt fluent: outpcd 3 out: kpt on same pce fr next: edgd lft run-in* **3/1**[2]
5 **4** ½ **Rahaala (IRE)**[10] [2047] 3-10-5 0.............................. LeightonAspell 89
(Lucy Wadham) *mid-div: hdwy 3 out: styd on same pce fr next* **12/1**
5 7 **Rare Malt (IRE)**[44] 3-10-5 0.................................... WarrenMarston 86+
(Milton Harris) *t.k.h in mid-div: hdwy 5th: wnt 2nd next: wknd last* **8/1**[3]
0 **6** 30 **Escape Artist**[14] [1984] 3-10-12 0..........................(t) RichieMcGrath 59
(Tim Easterby) *chsd ldrs: wknd 3 out: bhd fr next* **22/1**
F **7** 3½ **Juwireya**[10] [2047] 3-10-2 0.............................. WayneKavanagh(3) 49
(Peter Hiatt) *mid-div: j. bdly rt 1st: bhd fr 4th* **33/1**
8 30 **Layla's Boy**[23] 3-10-12 0.. BrianHughes 26
(John Mackie) *chsd ldrs: rdn 5th: sn lost pl: bhd 2 out: t.o* **50/1**
P **9** 10 **Catawollow**[9] [2068] 3-10-5 0.. PaddyAspell 9
(Richard Guest) *stdd s: plld hrd in rr: sme hdwy 4th: sn wknd: t.o 2 out* **66/1**
6 **10** 9 **Green For Luck (IRE)**[25] [1825] 3-10-12 0.......................... HenryOliver 7
(Sue Smith) *mid-div: drvn 3rd: lost pl next: bhd whn mstke 3 out: t.o* **16/1**
11 ½ **Storming Redd**[34] 3-10-12 0.. MarkBradburne 6
(James Eustace) *in rr-div: lost pl 4th: t.o 3 out* **14/1**
P **Frequency**[19] 3-10-9 0.. AlexMerriam(3) —
(Amy Weaver) *in rr: j. slowly and rdr lost irons 2nd: immediately p.u* **50/1**
P **Polebrook**[53] 3-10-12 0.. DavidEngland —
(J R Jenkins) *mid-div: bdly hmpd: sddle slipped and rdr lost irons 1st: sn p.u* **100/1**

4m 13.0s (6.30) **Going Correction** +0.425s/f (Soft) **13** Ran SP% **119.1**
Speed ratings (Par 104): **102,100,100,100,97 82,81,67,62,58 57,—,—**
toteswingers: 1&2 £3.10, 1&3 £1.60, 2&3 £5.30 CSF £17.14 TOTE £2.40: £1.10, £3.10, £1.50; EX 14.40.
Owner K Rhatigan **Bred** T Quayle **Trained** Upper Lambourn, Berks

FOCUS
The ground had eased to soft, which was the overall opinion of the jockeys. The hurdles were situated at their innermost position. An ordinary juvenile contest that was run at a sound pace with the front five finishing well clear of the remainder. The winner stood out on his previous form and is value for further.

NOTEBOOK
Pullyourfingerout(IRE) had shaped a lot better than on debut when easily accounting for a modest bunch at Taunton last time and this looked to be a good opportunity to build upon that giving weight all round. It was a decent front-running display by the winner, which had his nearest pursuers in trouble going to the second-last. Apart from a mistake at the last and a tendency to jump to his left he has taken well to this game, but he would not want the ground any easier than this. A double penalty will make life difficult so he will have to step up in grade. (op 11-8 tchd 5-4)
Manxman(IRE) showed enough on hurdling debut that he should be ready to make an impact in this sphere before long. He could not quite get on terms with Pullyourfingerout turning in and just stayed on at the same pace to get the better of a fair four-way tussle for second. Going in the right direction and should be going one better before long. (op 17-2)
Marsh Warbler was making his hurdling debut on his first run for Brian Ellison off the back of scoring in a seller on the Flat. He jumped well enough and this was a respectable effort, and he should be capable of getting off the mark in a similar affair. (op 4-1)
Rahaala(IRE) had shown a degree of promise in maidens on the Flat but, shaped a little better on her hurdling debut at Fontwell and this was another step forward. Although, never threatening to lay down a serious challenge, she kept on well enough in the straight. (tchd 14-1)
Rare Malt(IRE) has proved she has the ability on the Flat, but came here after being sold cheaply since being well backed when refusing to start at Haydock in September so, clearly has issues. This was a fair debut, as she looked as though she was capable of giving the winner a race turning in, but her effort eventually flattened out going to the last. (op 11-1)
Frequency Official explanation: jockey said he lost his irons
Polebrook Official explanation: jockey said saddle slipped

2246 DIGIBET.COM NOVICES' HURDLE (10 hdls) 2m 3f
1:50 (1:50) (Class 4) 4-Y-O+ **£2,602** (£764; £382; £190)

Form RPR
21 **1** **Get It On (IRE)**[42] [1623] 5-11-5 122.......................... PaulMoloney 127+
(Evan Williams) *hld up in rr: hdwy 7th: chsng ldrs next: chalng whn mstke 2 out: led appr last: drvn out* **5/2**[2]
243- **2** 2 **Mac Aeda**[222] [4942] 6-10-12 0.................................... GrahamLee 114
(Malcolm Jefferson) *trckd ldrs: led 6th: hdd appr last: styd on same pce* **5/1**[3]
0/20 **3** 4 **Be My Deputy (IRE)**[14] [1989] 5-10-12 0.......................... PaddyAspell 110
(Richard Guest) *led tl appr 4th: chsd ldrs: outpcd appr 2 out: kpt on same pce* **25/1**
2-53 **4** 7 **River Dragon (IRE)**[29] [1785] 5-10-12 0............................ BarryKeniry 103
(Neville Bycroft) *chsd ldrs: outpcd 6th: one pce fr 3 out* **28/1**
0-23 **5** 4½ **Caught By Witness (IRE)**[23] [1857] 5-10-12 122............ WarrenMarston 104+
(Milton Harris) *t.k.h towards rr: hdwy to chse ldrs 3 out: hung lft: wknd and mstke next: 5th whn mstke last* **11/8**[1]
33 **6** 1¾ **Moufatango (FR)**[157] [609] 4-10-9 0............................ FearghalDavis(3) 97
(Nicky Richards) *trckd ldrs: hit 3 out: sn rdn: wknd appr next: 6th whn mstke last* **28/1**
7 nk **And The Man** 4-10-12 0.. BrianHarding 96
(Nicky Richards) *in rr: hdwy 7th: rdn after next: lost pl bef 2 out* **50/1**
6-14 **8** 7 **Dipity Doo Dah**[28] [1793] 6-9-13 0 ow1.......................... MichaelByrne(7) 83
(Peter Bowen) *t.k.h: trckd ldrs: rdn 3 out: sn lost pl appr next* **14/1**
- **9** 51 **Alonso De Guzman (IRE)**[724] 6-10-12 0............................ APMcCoy 38
(Tim Vaughan) *racd wd: w ldr: led appr 4th: hdd 6th: wknd rapidly after 7th: t.o after next* **11/1**

4m 45.4s (6.00) **Going Correction** +0.425s/f (Soft)
WFA 4 from 5yo+ 7lb **9** Ran SP% **115.0**
Speed ratings (Par 105): **104,103,101,98,96 95,95,92,71**
toteswingers: 1&2 £1.40, 1&3 £9.00, 2&3 £25.40 CSF £14.88 TOTE £2.40: £1.02, £2.80, £5.90; EX 16.10.
Owner John Lee Jones **Bred** G Martin **Trained** Llancarfan, Vale Of Glamorgan

FOCUS
A fair novice hurdle for the track. The easy winner is on the upgrade and should rate higher.

NOTEBOOK
Get It On(IRE) defied a penalty for a recent C/D success. A blunder two out was the only scare for his supporters as he eventually stayed on strongly to draw clear from the last. He handled the softer conditions well and has been progressing well since joining Evan Williams from Ireland earlier this season, but a double penalty could force a switch to handicapping for which a current mark of 122 looks reasonable. (op 3-1)
Mac Aeda is a lovely stamp of a horse and has run respectably on two previous efforts over hurdles, although not jumping that fluently last time. He just got outstayed by the winner from the last and his turn cannot be far away, and he looks a chaser for the future. (op 11-2)
Be My Deputy(IRE) set just an ordinary gallop before getting outpaced by the front pair when headed. He was staying on again at the finish and posted a respectable effort on his hurdling debut. (op 18-1)
River Dragon(IRE) had some solid efforts in bumpers to his name and ran with credit on his hurdling debut for new connections before tiring going to the last. (op 33-1)
Caught By Witness(IRE) had been progressing steadily over hurdles, but this was a disappointing effort as he was never that fluent and looked unsuited by going right-handed. He's clearly better than this. Official explanation: jockey said gelding hung badly left (tchd 6-4 and 7-4 in a place)
Moufatango(FR) will come on for the race as a blunder three out did not aid his cause before getting outpaced turning in. (op 33-1 tchd 25-1)
And The Man, out of a fairly useful mare, shaped with some promise on his racecourse debut and should come on for the experience.
Alonso De Guzman(IRE), a fairly useful Flat performer, dropped out of contention rather quickly three out suggesting something was amiss. (op 9-1)

2247 RACING EXCELLENCE "HANDS AND HEELS" H'CAP HURDLE (FOR CONDITIONAL JOCKEYS AND AMATEUR RIDERS) (10 hdls) 2m 3f
2:25 (2:25) (Class 4) (0-115,115) 4-Y-O+ **£2,927** (£859; £429; £214)

Form RPR
463- **1** **Viscount Rossini**[197] [5388] 8-11-2 **105**..........................(b) PeterCarberry 107+
(Steve Gollings) *chsd ldrs: led 6th: styd on to go 5 l ahd last: drvn rt out: hld on towards fin* **7/1**[3]
-550 **2** 1 **Hippodrome (IRE)**[32] [1726] 8-10-2 **96**........................(p) MrRyanClark(5) 96
(John Harris) *in rr: drvn along 5th: hdwy 3 out: chsng ldrs next: wnt 2nd between last 2: styd on: nt quite rch wnr* **12/1**
3 **3** 9 **Quel Ballistic**[40] [1644] 6-10-8 **100**.............................. MrJohnDawson(3) 91
(John Wade) *in rr: hdwy 7th: wl outpcd appr 2 out: styd on to take modest 3rd nr fin* **7/2**[2]
0-66 **4** nk **Railway Park (IRE)**[25] [1831] 6-9-11 **89**.......................... MrOGarner(3) 80
(John Wainwright) *chsd ldrs: wnt 2nd appr 2 out: 3rd and btn whn mstke last* **17/2**
P001 **5** 17 **Kensington Oval**[14] [1997] 5-10-10 **102**........................(t) GeraldQuinn(3) 79
(Jonjo O'Neill) *trckd ldrs: chsd wnr 3 out: sn hrd drvn: 4th: wkng and nt fluent next* **9/4**[1]
2-P0 **6** 6 **Muntami (IRE)**[126] [888] 9-10-9 **103**............................(p) JoeCollivier(5) 71
(John Harris) *chsd ldrs: drvn 5th: lost pl after 7th: sn bhd* **16/1**
25-5 **7** 19 **L'Eldorado (FR)**[16] [1951] 5-11-9 **115**.......................... MrOJMurphy(3) 64
(Chris Bealby) *mde most to 6th: lost pl 3 out: sn bhd* **7/2**[2]
P2-0 **P** **Art Exhibition (IRE)**[179] [282] 5-11-1 **109**..............(bt) MrKieranWatson(5) —
(Charlie Mann) *w ldr: lost pl 6th: sn wl bhd: t.o whn p.u after next* **16/1**

4m 49.8s (10.40) **Going Correction** +0.425s/f (Soft) **8** Ran SP% **117.7**
Speed ratings (Par 105): **95,94,90,90,83 80,72,—**
toteswingers: 1&2 £25.30, 1&3 £4.30, 2&3 £9.60 CSF £83.67 CT £346.08 TOTE £5.10: £2.00, £3.70, £2.00; EX 103.30.
Owner Richard Atterby & Christine Atterby **Bred** M R M Bloodstock **Trained** Scamblesby, Lincs

FOCUS
A low-grade "hands and heels" handicap hurdle run at just an ordinary pace. The first two werre well in and are rated around 5lb below their best.

NOTEBOOK
Viscount Rossini was returning to action after 197 days off, and he was well up to the task. He had to be driven out by the up-and-coming Peterjon Carberry, but had enough in hand to repel the late thrust of the runner-up. Although the winner wears blinkers, he usually gives his best and he should find a little opportunity when his attention is switched back to fences. (op 5-1)
Hippodrome(IRE) had won off 95 back in April 2009, but had failed to add to that success. He ran with credit here and was staying on well in the latter stages, but the winner always had enough in hand. (tchd 16-1)
Quel Ballistic was only having his second start in this country after a enforced spell on the sidelines since crossing the channel and shaped as though he would appreciate a step up in trip after getting outpaced in the straight. (op 4-1)
Railway Park(IRE) had been given a chance by the handicapper, but failed to seize upon that had been given a chance by the handicapper, but failed to seize upon that. (op 16-1)

Kensington Oval, a winner last time and with the yard in such good form at present, ran disappointingly and dropped away very tamely. (tchd 2-1 after early 11-4 in places)

2248 VICTOR LUCAS MEMORIAL NOVICES' CHASE (14 fncs) 2m 6f 110y

2:55 (2:55) (Class 3) 4-Y-0+ **£5,529** (£1,623; £811; £405)

Form				RPR
264-	**1**		**Ashfield's Dream**[216] 5045 6-11-3 120 PaulMoloney (Evan Williams) *hld up: hdwy to chse ldr appr 3 out: led last: hung lft and qcknd clr* **9/1**	127+
-163	**2**	4 ½	**Mr Moonshine (IRE)**[14] 1988 6-10-12 120 ShaneByrne(5) (Sue Smith) *t.k.h: trckd ldr: led 4 out: jnd 2 out: hdd last and sn outpcd* **11/4**[1]	121
30-3	**3**	1 ¾	**C'Monthehammers (IRE)**[30] 1759 7-11-3 117 DavidEngland (Nigel Twiston-Davies) *led: nt fluent: hrd drvn 9th: hdd 4 out: kpt on same pce fr 2 out* **6/1**	119
20-3	**4**	1 ¼	**Premier Sagas (FR)**[17] 1930 6-11-3 118 BrianHarding (Nicky Richards) *hld up wl in tch: hit 7th and reminders: drvn 10th: chsng ldrs next: kpt on one pce fr 3 out* **9/2**	118
2232	**5**	1 ¾	**Ballyvesey (IRE)**[14] 1999 5-11-3 120 (v) BrianHughes (Peter Bowen) *trckd ldrs: one pce fr 3 out* **7/2**[2]	115
3621	**U**		**Diaco (IRE)**[42] 1628 6-11-3 119 APMcCoy (Jonjo O'Neill) *trckd ldrs: broke leg: stmbld and uns rdr jst bef 9th: fatally injured* **4/1**[3]	—

5m 55.0s (9.00) **Going Correction** +0.425s/f (Soft) **6** Ran SP% **111.4**
Speed ratings (Par 107): **101,99,98,98,97** —
toteswingers: 1&2 £6.50, 1&3 £20.10, 2&3 £3.90 CSF £33.91 TOTE £12.60: £3.40, £3.10; EX 49.50.

Owner Mr & Mrs William Rucker **Bred** A C R Stubbs **Trained** Llancarfan, Vale Of Glamorgan

FOCUS
A tight contest for this novice chase and they finished in a bit of a heap, so this is probably not form to get carried away with. The winner should go on to rate higher.

NOTEBOOK
Ashfield's Dream ran out a ready winner. Held up off the pace, jumping economically, he moved through to take a narrow advantage two out and only had to be shaken up to draw clear from the last. The winner rather lost his way after finishing second at Newbury at the back end of last year, but he had been freshened up after a good summer break, and if going on from this there should no reason why he can't defy a penalty. (op 7-1)

Mr Moonshine(IRE), a winning Irish pointer who had finished a well-held third over hurdles behind Cue Card at Aintree, recently looked every inch a natural back over fences and will be opening his account sooner rather than later. He simply lacked the pace of Ashfield's Dream from the last. (op 7-2 tchd 5-2)

C'Monthehammers(IRE) cut out just an ordinary pace and looked as though he would be swallowed up when headed in the straight but, to his credit, kept battling away. Step up to 3m should see him off the mark. (op 13-2 tchd 8-1)

Premier Sagas(FR) ran respectably on his second start over fences, but he could only stay on at the same pace. (op 4-1 tchd 7-2)

Ballyvesey(IRE) has the most experience of these over fences and has been performing consistently since winning here in July. He again ran respectably, but could only find the one pace in the straight. (op 9-2 tchd 5-1)

Diaco(IRE) was travelling very comfortably behind the leaders when stumbling and unseating his rider going to five out. Sadly he was fatally injured. (tchd 7-2)

2249 MARGARET TUNBRIDGE 50 GLORIOUS YEARS RACING H'CAP CHASE (17 fncs) 3m 1f

3:30 (3:30) (Class 3) (0-120,119) 4-Y-0+ **£5,529** (£1,623; £811; £405)

Form				RPR
43-1	**1**		**Roseneath (IRE)**[186] 158 6-11-3 **110** (p) PaulMoloney (Alex Hales) *hld up wl in tch: t.k.h: stdy hdwy 4 out: chsd ldr appr next: nt fluent last: edgd lft and styd on to ld last 100yds: all out* **3/1**[1]	120+
0P5-	**2**	½	**Rebel Melody (IRE)**[224] 4915 9-10-10 **106** (bt) PeterToole(3) (Charlie Mann) *led: hdd run-in: no ex clsng stages* **6/1**	115
F46F	**3**	¾	**Whataboutya (IRE)**[10] 2055 9-11-6 **113** (p) APMcCoy (Jonjo O'Neill) *nt fluent: trckd ldrs: hit 10th and 12th: hdwy to chse 2 ldrs appr 3 out: swtchd rt and nt qckn last 150yds* **6/1**	121
UP-5	**4**	10	**Lorum Leader (IRE)**[15] 1957 9-11-3 **117** MrTWeston(7) (Dr Richard Newland) *prom: chsng ldrs 12th: lost pl appr 3 out* **4/1**[2]	117
-P14	**5**	11	**Thai Vango (IRE)**[26] 1814 9-11-5 **112** DavidEngland (Nigel Twiston-Davies) *chsd ldrs: nt fluent 11th: sn hrd drvn: lost pl appr 3 out* **9/2**[3]	101
PP0-	**6**	118	**Tot O'Whiskey**[225] 4884 9-11-7 **119** JamesHalliday(5) (Malcolm Jefferson) *last but wl in tch: pushed along 10th: sn lft bhd: t.o 12th: eventually completed* **6/1**	—
1/6-	**F**		**Wenger (FR)**[374] 1974 10-10-10 **106** RichardKilloran(3) (Shaun Lycett) *chsd ldrs: 4th and outpcd whn hit 3 out: 5th and btn whn fell last: fatally injured* **16/1**	96

6m 36.4s (5.10) **Going Correction** +0.425s/f (Soft) **7** Ran SP% **111.9**
Speed ratings (Par 107): **108,107,107,104,100** —,—
toteswingers: 1&2 £4.80, 1&3 £2.10, 2&3 £8.50 CSF £20.17 TOTE £3.60: £2.20, £2.60; EX 20.20.

Owner The Strathclyders **Bred** N J Connors **Trained** Wardington, Oxon

FOCUS
A modest handicap chase but a step up from the winner.

NOTEBOOK
Roseneath(IRE) has been a much better proposition since switching to fences, and he added a third success to his name in that sphere. He came into the race after the fourth-last but, although, he has to be produced as late as possible, he had to dig deep to get on top of the long-time leader nearing the finish to land this ordinary staying handicap chase. Returning here after a six-month break and, only being a six-year-old, the winner is entitled to further improvement, but a bigger field and a stronger pace will also see him in a better light. (op 10-3 tchd 7-2)

Rebel Melody(IRE) cut out just an ordinary pace until increasing the tempo going to three out only to get collared close home. He stays on dourly in his races but, failed to shine after taking a fall on his seasonal reappearance last year, and this was a welcome return to form. (op 11-2 tchd 13-2)

Whataboutya(IRE) had questions marks regarding ground but seemed to handle it well enough, and he was coming here off the back of a fall. He had his chance going to the last and was staying on well enough in the closing stages. He remains on a reasonable mark. (op 5-1)

Lorum Leader(IRE) was the winner of this race last season off a 3lb higher mark, but he was a spent force after three out and does not possess the most convincing profile. (tchd 7-2)

Thai Vango(IRE), a winner here over 2m6f in September, had been soundly beaten back over hurdles recently, and he did not quite see out the step back up to 3m here.

2250 WEDDING RECEPTIONS AT MARKET RASEN RACECOURSE H'CAP CHASE (14 fncs) 2m 4f

4:05 (4:05) (Class 5) (0-95,95) 4-Y-0+ **£2,055** (£599; £299)

Form				RPR
0-35	**1**		**Persian Gates (IRE)**[26] 1813 6-11-12 **95** TomMessenger (Chris Bealby) *w ldr: led 4th to 8th: led appr 3 out: hung rt and hit last 2: styd on run-in* **11/4**[1]	100+
3125	**2**	1 ¼	**Stolen Light (IRE)**[7] 2107 9-11-6 **89** (b) BrianHughes (Andrew Crook) *trckd ldrs: led 8th: hdd appr 3 out: styd on same pce run-in* **7/1**	91
5040	**3**	6	**Donovan (NZ)**[14] 1991 11-11-5 **88** (p) GrahamLee (Richard Guest) *in tch: hdwy to chse ldrs 4 out: one pce fr next* **9/1**	84
05-U	**4**	11	**Sundown Trail (IRE)**[7] 2107 5-11-6 **89** BrianHarding (Nicky Richards) *nt jump wl in rr: mstke 10th: hdwy next: 4th and outpcd whn hit 3 out: sn wknd* **5/1**[3]	76
/50P	**5**	8	**Cilrhiwviv**[17] 1939 7-11-7 **93** (t) WayneKavanagh(3) (Sue Wilson) *trckd ldrs: j.rt: wknd appr 3 out* **11/1**	70
-5P1	**6**	15	**Mischief Man**[69] 1423 8-11-3 **91** ShaneByrne(5) (Sue Smith) *chsd ldrs: lost pl appr 3 out: sn bhd* **3/1**[2]	53
2-0P	**7**	4 ½	**Kercabellec (FR)**[63] 1483 12-9-7 **69** oh1 JoeCornwall(7) (John Cornwall) *led to 4th: drvn and outpcd 9th: sn bhd: t.o 3 out* **7/1**	27

5m 16.9s (11.20) **Going Correction** +0.425s/f (Soft) **7** Ran SP% **111.7**
Speed ratings (Par 103): **94,93,91,86,83 77,75**
toteswingers: 1&2 £3.40, 1&3 £6.20, 2&3 £5.00 CSF £20.72 TOTE £3.50: £1.40, £4.50; EX 23.30.

Owner Mrs Robert Bingley & Mrs Bryan Spooner **Bred** Thistletown Stud **Trained** Barrowby, Lincs

FOCUS
A good duel between the first two for this 0-95 handicap chase. The winner is on the upgrade.

NOTEBOOK
Persian Gates(IRE) eventually outstayed the runner-up on the run from the last. He was disappointing last time out when he made a costly mistake, and he still has a bit to learn in the jumping department as he clouted two out here. The winner has been a weak finisher in the past, but he did nothing to suggest that here as he was drawing away at the finish. He has time on his side and can only improve with experience. (op 3-1 tchd 5-2)

Stolen Light(IRE) came here off the back of a poor run at Carlisle last time (ground) and remained 10lb higher than his Sedgefield success. He ran a solid race here and lost nothing in defeat now dropping back to this more suitable trip. (op 13-2 tchd 6-1)

Donovan(NZ) has been slipping down the ratings, but that has been due to some lacklustre performances. This was a step back in the right direction for he does possess ability but he will have to build on this. (op 8-1)

Sundown Trail(IRE) unshipped his rider at an early stage on his chasing debut, and again his jumping was unconvincing here. He looked as though he was travelling well enough turning in, but found little when asked to get involved. Official explanation: jockey said gelding jumped poorly (op 11-2)

Cilrhiwviv could never get involved and clearly needs to come down the weights if he is to get competitive. (op 16-1)

Mischief Man got off the mark at Cartmel in August and looked to have a good chance here, but the ease in the ground counted against him and this run can be ignored. (op 11-4)

T/Plt: £88.80 to a £1 stake. Pool: £54,805.94. 450.05 winning tickets. T/Qpdt: £23.00 to a £1 stake. Pool: £3,349.22. 107.50 winning tickets. WG

2251 - 2258a (Foreign Racing) - See Raceform Interactive

1615 NAVAN (L-H)

Sunday, November 7

OFFICIAL GOING: Soft (soft to heavy in places)

2259a LISMULLEN HURDLE (GRADE 2) (11 hdls) 2m 4f

1:25 (1:27) 4-Y-0+ **£23,008** (£6,725; £3,185; £1,061)

			RPR
1		**Oscar Dan Dan (IRE)**[199] 5348 8-11-12 148 PTownend (Thomas Mullins, Ire) *chsd ldr in 2nd: rdn after 2 out: pressed ldr whn lft in ld last: kpt on wl u.p run-in* **11/4**[2]	156
2	4	**Jumbo Rio (IRE)**[141] 791 5-11-12 152 AndrewJMcNamara (E J O'Grady, Ire) *chsd ldrs in 3rd: lft 2nd last: rdn and no imp on ldr run-in: kpt on same pce* **11/4**[2]	152+
3	2 ½	**Moskova (IRE)**[168] 5067 7-11-0 136 RMPower (Paul Nolan, Ire) *hld up in tch: rdn in 4th bef 2 out: no ex whn lft 3rd last and sltly hmpd: kpt on same pce* **9/2**[3]	138
4	10	**Baron De Feypo (IRE)**[693] 2798 12-11-5 MWBowes (Patrick O Brady, Ire) *hld up in 4th: rdn 3 out: sn no ex in last: lft mod 4th last* **33/1**	133
F		**Aitmatov (GER)**[12] 2027 9-11-10 148 (bt) DJCondon (Noel Meade, Ire) *led: rdn after 2 out: 1 l advantage whn fell last* **7/4**[1]	155

5m 10.0s (8.20) **5** Ran SP% **110.8**
CSF £10.85 TOTE £3.90: £2.40, £2.00; DF 10.80.

Owner Mrs Paul Duffin **Bred** Mary F Fogarty **Trained** Goresbridge, Co Kilkenny

FOCUS
The winner is rated to his best but may have been lucky with Aitmatov a falle. the fourth limits the form.

NOTEBOOK
Oscar Dan Dan(IRE) fell at the second-last when Aitmatov was just about to challenge him last year and there was a remarkable role reversal here. Paul Townend felt that he had things under control and it could perhaps be said that Oscar Dan Dan was travelling that bit better coming to the last, but he was still a length or so down. Regardless, this was an excellent effort from a horse who tends to run well fresh. He is without question best at this trip and will now go for the Hatton's Grace, which he won last year. He will face better rivals there, but is nearly sure to run well. (op 11/4 tchd 5/2)

Jumbo Rio(IRE)'s trainer says his horses are coming on for their seasonal returns and the evidence supports that. He ran a very solid race here over a stiff 2m4f that perhaps stretches his stamina a shade, but he will be a big player if he goes for the Hatton's Grace. For a few second he seemed to be travelling best going to the last, before he probably got tired. (op 3/1)

Moskova(IRE) is an enigmatic performer who was always likely to struggle over this trip in this company. She ran about as well as could be expected. (op 5/1)

Baron De Feypo(IRE) was not disgraced on his first run in over two years. (op 20/1)

Aitmatov(GER) jumped really well up until his fall at the last - which was one of those things and no more. He was under pressure but he was still very much in it when falling. (op 7/4 tchd 15/8)

2260a "FOR AUCTION" NOVICE HURDLE (GRADE 3) (10 hdls) 2m
1:55 (1:56) 4-Y-0+ £16,393 (£4,792; £2,269; £756)

RPR
1 **Hidden Cyclone (IRE)**[33] 1717 5-11-1 AndrewJMcNamara 136+
(John Joseph Hanlon, Ire) *trckd ldrs: 4th 1/2-way: impr to chal 3 out: led travelling wl bef 2 out: slt mstke 2 out: rdn bef last: kpt on strly: comf* **13/8**[1]
2 6 **Hazeymm (IRE)**[12] 2028 7-11-5 126 (p) PTownend 132
(E J O'Grady, Ire) *hld up: 7th 1/2-way: hdwy into 4th 3 out: rdn into 3rd 2 out: 2nd last: no imp on ldr: kpt on same pce: jst hld 2nd* **7/1**[3]
3 shd **Maggio (FR)**[22] 1867 5-11-1 (p) JamesO'Farrell 128
(Patrick Griffin, Ire) *chsd ldrs: 3rd 1/2-way: hdwy in 2nd 4 out: sn impr to ld: rdn and chal 3 out: hdd bef 2 out: 3rd last: kpt on: jst hld for 2nd* **20/1**
4 5 1/2 **Save My Blushes**[41] 1637 4-11-2 115 (t) APCrowe 123
(Paul W Flynn, Ire) *chsd ldr in 2nd: rdn in 3rd 3 out: no ex in 4th next: kpt on same pce* **10/1**
5 11 **Imperial Shabra (IRE)**[8] 2095 6-11-5 115 MWBowes 115
(Patrick O Brady, Ire) *settled bhd ldrs: 5th 1/2-way: rdn 3 out: sn no imp: kpt on one pce* **10/1**
6 dist **Steel Park (IRE)**[15] 1977 6-11-1 107 (tp) MrSPByrne —
(Sean Byrne, Ire) *led: rdn and hdd after 4 out: wknd and t.o* **7/1**[3]
F **Prima Vista**[13] 2014 5-11-1 DJCondon —
(Noel Meade, Ire) *hld up: fell 3rd* **9/4**[2]
U **Meitheamh (IRE)**[25] 1838 5-10-10 BarryGeraghty —
(Mrs John Harrington, Ire) *hld up towards rr: last 1/2-way: hdwy in 5th 4 out: stmbld and uns rdr after 4 out* **14/1**

4m 9.10s (1.10)
WFA 4 from 5yo+ 7lb **8** Ran SP% **123.5**
CSF £15.47 TOTE £3.00: £1.30, £2.30, £8.30; DF 16.20.
Owner Mrs A F Mee **Bred** Ronald O'Neill **Trained** Bagenalstown, Co Carlow

FOCUS
The form is rated around the winner, second and fourth, but the third could limit it.
NOTEBOOK
Hidden Cyclone(IRE) was always tanking and the testing ground seemed to suit him well, though he handles better. His trainer says he will be better over another half-mile, but a strongly run 2m on soft ground should not be a problem. He will come back here for the race formerly known as the Barry & Sandra Kelly Memorial. (op 6/4)
Hazeymm(IRE), rated 126, had to give weight to the winner and has had a fairly busy time of it. He was outclassed but ran a solid race. (op 11/2)
Maggio(FR) ran above expectations on his Irish debut. He is still eligible for maiden hurdles and this display implies he should win one, at least.
Save My Blushes was very much up against it and this is as good as he is.
Prima Vista remains a decent prospect. (op 3/1)
Meitheamh(IRE) was not going badly at the point of departure. Official explanation: jockey said mare clipped heels, stumbled and slipped up after 4 out (op 3/1)

2262a FRIENDS OF NAVAN FORTRIA CHASE (GRADE 2) (11 fncs) 2m
3:00 (3:01) 5-Y-0+ £24,159 (£7,061; £3,345; £1,115)

RPR
1 **Big Zeb (IRE)**[235] 4673 9-11-12 174 BarryGeraghty 160+
(C A Murphy, Ire) *settled 3rd: 2nd 5 out: chal bef 3 out: niggled along in 2nd 2 out: styd on to ld after last: kpt on wl run-in: cosily* **8/15**[1]
2 1 1/4 **Golden Silver (FR)**[201] 5302 8-11-12 166 PTownend 157+
(W P Mullins, Ire) *chsd ldr in 2nd: 3rd 5 out: rdn 2 out: no imp on ldrs bef last: kpt on wl run-in to take 2nd cl home* **11/4**[2]
3 1 3/4 **Carthalawn (IRE)**[252] 4351 9-11-10 146 DJCondon 153
(Gordon Elliott, Ire) *led: chal bef 3 out: rdn after 2 out: hdd after last: no ex and kpt on same pce: lost 2nd cl home* **25/1**
4 18 **Joncol (IRE)**[273] 3928 7-11-12 161 APCawley 137
(Paul Nolan, Ire) *a in rr: j.rt: rdn and no imp 3 out* **6/1**[3]

4m 25.0s (14.50) **4** Ran SP% **110.0**
CSF £2.57 TOTE £1.50; DF 2.70.
Owner Patrick Joseph Redmond **Bred** Lyle Buttimer **Trained** Gorey, Co Wexford

FOCUS
The third, who set a steady pace, limits the form, but Big Zeb won with a bit to spare.
NOTEBOOK
Big Zeb(IRE) did everything that was asked of him and with each passing race, less doubt remains about his jumping. It was virtually flawless here on ground he would not have loved and the relationship between jockey and horse at this stage is key. He has no problems running well fresh and this will tee him up perfectly for the rest of the season. He is unquestionably the horse to beat in the 2m chasing division. (op 4/6)
Golden Silver(FR) never looked like winning and he can probably jump better, but there was still enough for his trainer to be pleased about. He ran exactly as his trainer's horses are at present - in need of a run generally - and it was encouraging how he ran on from the last. He remains a very big force in deep-ground 2m chases.
Carthalawn(IRE), on his debut for the yard, made it a good clip and loves being out in front. For a moment before the last he nearly seemed to be travelling best, but probably just got a bit tired. The MCR Hurdle is his seasonal target, but he is definitely a better chaser. (op 20/1)
Joncol(IRE) was very disappointing, particularly as his trainer's horses are generally in good form. He jumped badly right and never had any chance to get near horses with more toe than him. He is a massive horse who will be better for the race but this was a worrying display of jumping. (op 11/2)

2261a, 2264a, 2266a-2268a (Foreign Racing) - See Raceform Interactive

2230 AUTEUIL (L-H)
Sunday, November 7

OFFICIAL GOING: Turf: heavy

2265a PRIX ALFRED DE DREUX (PRIX ALADDIN) (CONDITIONS) (4-5YO FILLIES & MARES) (TURF) 2m 2f
11:55 (12:00) 4-5-Y-0 £21,238 (£10,619; £6,194; £4,203; £1,991)

RPR
1 **Sister Palma (FR)**[25] 4-10-6 0 ChristophePieux —
(J Bertran De Balanda, France) **41/10**[3]
2 8 **Net Lovely (FR)**[16] 4-10-8 0 JonathanPlouganou —
(E Clayeux, France) **7/1**
3 3 **Sissi De Teille (FR)**[131] 4-10-6 0 ow3 DavidCottin —
(E Leray, France) **10/1**
4 snk **Font Froide (FR)**[43] 5-11-0 0 SylvainDupuis —
(F Belmont, France) **14/5**[2]
5 10 **My Destination (FR)**[16] 5-10-10 0 DavidBerra —
(P Journiac, France) **9/2**
6 15 **Full Atraction (FR)**[16] 4-10-10 0 MrChristopheCorduan —
(M Nicolau, France) **5/2**[1]
7 20 **Mojo Moon (IRE)**[15] 4-10-6 0 (b) LaurentGerard —
(D Darlix, France) **41/1**
P **Karingabay Queen**[63] 1480 5-10-6 0 GaelBarbedette —
(Kevin Tork) *settled towards rr: bhd at 1/2-way: p.u bef 5 out* **57/1**

4m 49.24s (289.24)
WFA 4 from 5yo 7lb **8** Ran SP% **118.4**
PARI-MUTUEL (all including 1 euro stakes): WIN 5.10; PLACE 2.40, 2.40, 3.10; DF 14.40; SF 34.10.
Owner Francois Hoffet **Bred** A Baudouin, J Bertran De Balanda & F Hoffet **Trained** France

2102 CARLISLE (R-H)
Monday, November 8

OFFICIAL GOING: Heavy (5.2)
Wind: Strong, half against Weather: Overcast

2269 EXPLOSIVEPRODUCTIONSLTD.CO.UK NOVICES' HURDLE (10 hdls 2 omitted) 3m 1f
12:50 (12:50) (Class 4) 4-Y-0+ £2,740 (£798; £399)

Form RPR
/2 1 **Dove Hill (IRE)**[23] 1869 7-10-12 0 BrianHughes 117+
(Howard Johnson) *trckd ldrs: rdn and outpcd bef 3 out: rallied bef last: styd on wl to ld towards fin* **15/8**[1]
1-5 2 3/4 **Bally Wall (IRE)**[16] 1981 7-10-12 113 JohnnyFarrelly 114
(I R Ferguson, Ire) *trckd ldrs: wnt 2nd 1/2-way: rdn and led 3 out: edgd lft after last: kpt on: hdd towards fin* **13/2**
42- 3 3 1/4 **Bring On The Judge (IRE)**[254] 4295 7-10-9 0 SamTwiston-Davies(3) 114+
(Nigel Twiston-Davies) *nt fluent: led: hung lft after 4 out: hdd and hit next: hit last two: kpt on same pce run-in* **2/1**[2]
4 dist **Russinrudi (IRE)**[246] 7-10-12 0 JasonMaguire —
(Donald McCain) *in tch: outpcd and struggling 4 out: lost tch fr next: virtually p.u* **11/4**[3]

6m 41.7s (3.50) **Going Correction** +0.275s/f (Yiel) **4** Ran SP% **108.1**
Speed ratings (Par 105): **105,104,103,—**
CSF £11.91 TOTE £2.90; EX 11.10.
Owner Andrea & Graham Wylie **Bred** Michael Byrne **Trained** Billy Row, Co Durham

FOCUS
The runners finished out on their feet in this opening contest, as they did in more or less every race. The runner-up sets the standard.
NOTEBOOK
Dove Hill(IRE), only third taking the last, stayed on best. A former point winner in heavy ground, who had finished second to a subsequent winner on his rules debut at Kelso (good to firm), clearly had no problem with the going, but he will need to improve to defy a penalty. The best of him won't be until he's sent chasing next season. (tchd 2-1)
Bally Wall(IRE), a winner over fences at Ayr last season, stays well and acts in these conditions, but he couldn't hold off the winner, finishing tired. (op 7-1 tchd 15-2)
Bring On The Judge(IRE), runner-up over 2m4f at Chepstow in similar conditions on his hurdles debut, made mistakes that ultimately took their toll late on. (tchd 9-4)
Russinrudi(IRE) proved most disappointing, quickly being beaten and possibly failing to handle the ground. (tchd 5-2 and 3-1)

2270 BAINES WILSON LLP NOVICES' CHASE (11 fncs 1 omitted) 2m
1:20 (1:21) (Class 4) 4-Y-0+ £3,577 (£1,050; £525; £262)

Form RPR
0P-0 1 **Sonowyouno (IRE)**[33] 1731 6-11-2 0 DominicElsworth 120+
(Jonjo O'Neill) *t.k.h: mde all: rdn whn nt fluent last: styd on strly* **9/2**[3]
22-3 2 1 **Kellystown Lad (IRE)**[30] 1779 7-11-2 0 GrahamLee 118+
(Ferdy Murphy) *hld up: hdwy 3 out: effrt and styd on wl fr last: nt rch wnr* **8/1**
20-4 3 1 1/4 **Si Bien (FR)**[23] 1867 5-10-13 0 HarryHaynes(3) 116
(James Ewart) *hld up: hdwy and prom 4th: effrt bef 2 out: ev ch last: kpt on same pce towards fin* **7/2**[2]
15-3 4 2 **Mohayer (IRE)**[192] 80 8-10-13 0 RichieMcLernon(3) 114
(Jonjo O'Neill) *hld up: hdwy on ins and prom last: rdn and kpt on same pce run-in* **9/2**[3]
40-3 5 3 1/2 **Papa Caruso**[18] 1931 6-11-2 0 TjadeCollier 112+
(Sue Smith) *cl up: effrt and ev ch 3 out: edgd rt and outpcd run-in* **9/1**
1124 6 26 **Twentynineblack (FR)**[18] 1936 6-11-2 112 JasonMaguire 85
(Donald McCain) *hld up: hdwy and prom after 4 out: wkng whn j.lft 2 out* **11/4**[1]
00 7 4 1/2 **Seigneur Des Bois (FR)**[18] 1930 4-10-8 107 RichieMcGrath 73
(Ferdy Murphy) *trckd ldrs tl rdn and wknd fr 3 out* **33/1**
-53P U **Quatro Pierji (FR)**[12] 2037 6-11-2 110 (p) PaddyAspell 81
(James Moffatt) *w ldr: bdly blkd and uns rdr 7th* **20/1**
0PP- F **Hard To Name**[199] 5374 7-11-2 80 BrianHarding —
(Alan Mactaggart) *in tch: hit 4 out: wknd bef next: 9 l down and btn whn fell 2 out* **100/1**

4m 26.8s (10.70) **Going Correction** +0.70s/f (Soft)
WFA 4 from 5yo+ 7lb **9** Ran SP% **115.1**
Speed ratings (Par 105): **101,100,99,98,97 84,81,—,—**
toteswingers:1&2 £16.00, 2&3 £6.30, 1&3 £8.00 CSF £38.48 TOTE £7.70: £2.40, £2.10, £1.30; EX 48.50.
Owner John P McManus **Bred** T F Duggan **Trained** Cheltenham, Gloucs

FOCUS
Just a modest novices' chase rated around the placed horses.
NOTEBOOK
Sonowyouno(IRE), never involved on his chase debut at Towcester, liked plenty of cut in the ground over hurdles and he seemed more comfortable in these conditions, jumping well in the main under a positive ride and staying on well. His future lies in handicaps and he remains capable of better. (op 8-1)
Kellystown Lad(IRE), a well-beaten third at Hexham on his chase debut, had clearly come on appreciably for that and stayed on well without ever looking like getting to the winner. He stays further than this and is another likely to do better once handicapping. (tchd 13-2)
Si Bien(FR), twice a runner-up over hurdles, made a satisfactory start to his chasing career and should be winning at a similarly modest level. (op 4-1)
Mohayer(IRE), a faller on both previous starts over fences in late 2008 (would probably have won on second occasion), jumped soundly enough but couldn't quicken out of the ground. (op 3-1)
Papa Caruso has plenty of size and scope and, although ultimately well held on this first starts over fences, he really needs further. He'll be one to look for next time. (op 15-2)
Twentynineblack(FR), well ahead of the runner-up at Hexham, disappointed last time at Ludlow when finding little, and he again emptied quickly, looking uncomfortable on the ground. (op 7-2)

Hard To Name had run his race and was comfortably held when coming down two out.

2271 ASTSIGNS NOVICES' H'CAP HURDLE (10 hdls 1 omitted) 2m 4f
1:55 (1:55) (Class 4) (0-100,95) 3-Y-0+ **£2,740** (£798; £399)

Form RPR
-P21 **1** **Douglas Julian**[38] 1666 8-10-13 82 .... HenryOliver 90+
(Sue Smith) *w ldr: led 3rd to 5th: led again bef 3 out: asserting whn mstke last: styd on strly* **11/10**[1]
46F- **2** *8* **Border Flora**[335] 2762 5-11-10 93 .... CampbellGillies 91
(William Amos) *in tch: effrt 3 out: outpcd next: rallied run-in: tk 2nd cl home: no ch w wnr* **8/1**
5-43 **3** *hd* **Lukey Luke**[161] 552 7-10-11 80 .... PaddyAspell 78
(James Turner) *prom: hdwy to press wnr appr 2 out: one pce fr last: lost 2nd cl home* **9/2**[2]
5P-0 **4** *10* **Play The Rock (FR)**[187] 156 7-10-12 81 .... JamesReveley 70
(Philip Kirby) *led to 3rd: led 5th to bef 3 out: wknd fr next* **12/1**
/2P- **5** *7* **Paddys Honour (IRE)**[494] 851 7-11-11 94 .... PeterBuchanan 75
(Lucinda Russell) *hld up in tch: outpcd after 5th: n.d after* **12/1**
6-0P **6** *22* **Transact (IRE)**[41] 1647 5-10-2 76 .... JamesHalliday(5) 35
(Martin Todhunter) *hld up: shortlived effrt after 4 out: sn btn: t.o* **50/1**
030- **P** **Allanard (IRE)**[265] 4096 6-11-2 85 .... GrahamLee —
(Martin Todhunter) *trckd ldrs: hit 6th: wknd next: t.o whn p.u bef 3 out* **7/1**[3]
00-0 **P** **Lochore (IRE)**[46] 1594 4-10-11 87 .... AlexanderVoy(7) —
(Lucy Normile) *t.k.h: hld up: hdwy and prom 1/2-way: wknd 4 out: t.o whn p.u bef next* **40/1**
020P **P** **Overyou**[150] 706 5-11-8 91 .... JohnnyFarrelly —
(Elliott Cooper) *hld up in tch: rdn after 4 out: wknd and p.u bef next* **20/1**

5m 33.4s (10.60) **Going Correction** +0.575s/f (Soft)
WFA 4 from 5yo+ 8lb **9** Ran SP% **114.0**
Speed ratings (Par 105): **101,97,97,93,90 82,—,—,—**
CSF £10.39 CT £29.33 TOTE £2.60: £1.10, £2.50, £1.60; EX 12.00.
Owner Mrs S Smith **Bred** A M Armitage **Trained** High Eldwick, W Yorks
■ Stewards' Enquiry : Campbell Gillies three-day ban: used whip with excessive frequency (22-24 Nov)

FOCUS
A moderate handicap hurdle, but it was another decent effort from last month's Hexham winner. The placed horses are the best guides to the level.

NOTEBOOK
Douglas Julian defied the 7lb rise with a fair bit in hand. Although he was tired at the finish, he did stay on strongly to draw clear from the last, despite a slight mistake, and he's likely to head over fences at some stage, a division he should do well in. (op 6-5 tchd Evens)
Border Flora, a faller last time, looked a possible improver switched to handicaps and she kept on well to just snatch second, suggesting she'll improve for a step up to 3m. (op 13-2)
Lukey Luke is still a maiden, but his last two efforts here have been better and he'll probably go forward again switched to fences. (op 8-1)
Play The Rock(FR) was made plenty of use of on this return to hurdles, but didn't get home in the conditions. (op 8-1)

2272 DAVID-ALLEN.CO.UK H'CAP CHASE (14 fncs 2 omitted) 2m 4f
2:25 (2:25) (Class 3) (0-125,125) 4-Y-0+ **£6,505** (£1,910; £955; £477)

Form RPR
P3-U **1** **Sibenek (IRE)**[31] 1759 6-11-5 118 .... JamesReveley 125+
(Martin Todhunter) *hld up in tch: smooth hdwy to ld after 3 out: j.lft next: rdn and kpt on wl run-in* **15/2**
31-0 **2** *2* **Et Maintenant (FR)**[31] 1761 8-11-7 120 .... PeterBuchanan 124
(Lucinda Russell) *prom: hdwy and ev ch 3 out: kpt on same pce fr last* **8/1**
02-0 **3** *2* **Le Roi Rouge (FR)**[31] 1761 8-11-10 123 .... GrahamLee 125
(Ferdy Murphy) *hld up: mstke 10th: hdwy 3 out: kpt on fr last: no imp* **5/1**[3]
411- **4** *22* **Diamond Frontier (IRE)**[219] 4979 7-11-11 124 .... BrianHughes 108+
(Howard Johnson) *cl up: led briefly appr 3 out: rdn and wknd fr next* **7/2**[1]
/2U- **5** *41* **Hockenheim (FR)**[219] 4980 9-11-3 119 .... RyanMania(3) 58
(George Bewley) *led tl hdd appr 3 out: sn wknd* **7/2**[1]
130- **P** **Jimmy Bond**[216] 5075 11-11-1 114 ....(p) RichieMcGrath —
(Kate Walton) *bhd: lost tch bef 7th: p.u bef 10th* **12/1**
3-11 **P** **Sotovik (IRE)**[31] 1761 9-10-11 113 .... EwanWhillans(3) —
(Alistair Whillans) *hit 1st: cl up: rdn and ev ch after 4 out: wknd fr next: p.u bef last* **9/2**[2]
340 **P** **Adajal (IRE)**[16] 1957 7-11-9 125 ....(t) RichieMcLernon(3) —
(Jonjo O'Neill) *hld up: outpcd 8th: nvr on terms: t.o whn p.u bef last* **25/1**

5m 39.8s (12.40) **Going Correction** +0.70s/f (Soft) **8** Ran SP% **113.7**
Speed ratings (Par 107): **103,102,101,92,76 —,—,—**
toteswingers:1&2 £15.00, 2&3 £3.40, 1&3 £16.10 CSF £62.92 CT £328.32 TOTE £8.90: £3.00, £1.30, £2.50; EX 75.80.
Owner Leeds Plywood And Doors Ltd **Bred** Tom Hughes **Trained** Orton, Cumbria

FOCUS
A fair handicap chase with the winner having more to offer, and the second and third setting the level.

NOTEBOOK
Sibenek(IRE), who unseated early on his recent chase debut at the course, looked potentially interesting switched to handicaps and he relished the heavy ground, winning with a tad more in hand than it may have looked. Only six, he's entitled to improve further and can win again when conditions are in his favour. (op 10-1 tchd 11-1)
Et Maintenant(FR), held off this mark on his reappearance, went on coming to three out, but was soon overtaken by the winner. He had clearly improved and can probably win again once eased a little in the weights. (tchd 6-1)
Le Roi Rouge(FR) showed the benefit of his reappearance run, keeping on for a clear third, but he remains 6lb above his last winning mark. (op 13-2)
Diamond Frontier(IRE) ended last year on a higher, but he couldn't pick up where he left off on this handicap debut, dropping right out late on. (op 5-2)
Hockenheim(FR) has gone well fresh in the past and handled these conditions well, so it was disappointing to see him put up such a poor display. (op 5-1)
Sotovik(IRE) showed his versatility when dropped back to 2m at the course latest, but he didn't put up much of a fight and was beaten too far for the 6lb rise to be put forward as an excuse. Official explanation: trainer was unable to offer any explanation for the poor performance shown (op 7-2 tchd 11-2)

2273 WEATHERBYS BANK GRADUATION CHASE (16 fncs 2 omitted) 3m 110y
3:00 (3:00) (Class 2) 4-Y-0+ **£15,799** (£4,769; £2,456; £1,301)

Form RPR
1UF- **1** **Hey Big Spender (IRE)**[214] 5098 7-11-10 146 .... JoeTizzard 153+
(Colin Tizzard) *t.k.h: cl up: led appr 3 out: hit and hdd next: 3 l down last: rallied to pass idling ldr run-in: drvn out* **5/2**[1]
U14- **2** *1* **Big Fella Thanks**[212] 5127 8-11-10 151 .... GrahamLee 152+
(Ferdy Murphy) *hld up last but in tch: stdy hdwy to ld 2 out: 3 l clr last: rdn: idled and hdd run-in: kpt on fin* **5/1**[3]
130- **3** *7* **Massasoit (IRE)**[236] 4670 8-11-3 140 ....(b) NickScholfield 140+
(Paul Nicholls) *prom: hit and pushed along 4 out: rallied next: no imp whn lft 8 l 3rd last* **5/2**[1]
0/1- **4** *28* **Hunters Ploy (IRE)**[384] 1843 8-11-7 0 .... PaddyBrennan 122
(Nigel Twiston-Davies) *mstkes: led tl hdd appr 3 out: sn rdn and wknd* **8/1**
201- **U** **Prince De Beauchene (FR)**[219] 4988 7-11-10 140 .... BrianHughes 143
(Howard Johnson) *trckd ldrs: effrt and ev ch 3 out: rdn next: 6 l 3rd and one pce whn blnd and uns rdr last* **3/1**[2]

7m 1.20s (18.60) **Going Correction** +0.70s/f (Soft) **5** Ran SP% **109.9**
Speed ratings (Par 109): **98,97,95,86,—**
CSF £14.43 TOTE £2.80: £1.70, £2.40; EX 12.70.
Owner Brocade Racing **Bred** Oliver Brennan **Trained** Milborne Port, Dorset

FOCUS
The front pair drew clear in what looked a decent graduation chase, although the picture changed somewhat on the run-in as Big Fella Thanks, who travelled like the best horse and looked all over the winner when going on, suddenly began to tire and was worn down by second-season chaser Hey Big Spender. The form looks suspect with the first three all rated below their best.

NOTEBOOK
Hey Big Spender(IRE) had his trouble jumping last season, and again made mistakes on this return, but clearly stays the trip well and he was probably fitter than the runner-up, which would obviously have been a help on the final climb to the line. He looks just the type for the Hennessy, although can expect to find himself racing from out of the handicap there in what promises to be another vintage edition. (op 9-4)
Big Fella Thanks, making his debut for Ferby Murphy, showed himself to be a classy sort at shorter when winning a 2m4f Grade 3 handicap at Newbury last year, and in the end it was the heavy ground over this trip that found him out. Given the way he travelled, though, it's reasonable to expect him to do well again this season. He'll also head for the Hennessy. (tchd 11-2)
Massasoit(IRE), receiving 7lb from the front two, had some good form against Burton Port to his name last season, including in these conditions, but he was a bit sketchy at a few of his fences and never really looked like winning. Rated 140, he should make his mark in handicap chases this season. (tchd 11-4)
Hunters Ploy(IRE), who started off with this yard before joining Ian Williams and winning his only start over fences last term, isn't going to be easy to place given his lack of experience, and it was there for all to see here, making numerous mistakes before dropping out. (op 9-1)
Prince De Beauchene(FR), a winner off 132 on his final outing last term, was in the process of running a sound race when parting company with Brian Hughes at the last, and he should make his mark in northern handicaps this term. (op 7-2 tchd 11-4)

2274 CUBBY CONSTRUCTION H'CAP CHASE (17 fncs 2 omitted) 3m 2f
3:30 (3:30) (Class 4) (0-105,104) 4-Y-0+ **£2,927** (£859; £429; £214)

Form RPR
3412 **1** **Overquest**[31] 1763 8-11-5 97 .... JohnnyFarrelly 112+
(Elliott Cooper) *hld up in tch: smooth hdwy bef 3 out: led between last 2: styd on strly to go clr run-in* **10/3**[1]
-103 **2** *7* **Benbeoch**[30] 1784 11-10-11 92 ....(p) RyanMania(3) 99
(Sandy Thomson) *cl up: led 3rd: rdn 3 out: hdd between last 2: kpt on same pce run-in* **10/1**
PP-3 **3** *4 1/2* **Star Player (IRE)**[31] 1763 8-11-12 104 ....(t) PaddyBrennan 109+
(Chris Grant) *cl up: effrt and ev ch whn hit 3 out: sn rdn: one pce fr next* **7/2**[2]
55P1 **4** *15* **Canal Bank (IRE)**[16] 1969 6-11-1 96 ....(p) RichieMcLernon(3) 86
(Jonjo O'Neill) *hld up: smooth hdwy to trck ldrs bef 3 out: wknd bef next* **13/2**
P-35 **5** *37* **Master Sebastian**[31] 1763 11-11-10 102 .... PeterBuchanan 53
(Lucinda Russell) *prom: outpcd 13th: lost tch bef 3 out* **11/2**[3]
1216 **6** *2 1/4* **Finbin (IRE)**[161] 549 8-11-10 102 ....(t) RobertWalford 62
(Henry Hogarth) *led to 3rd: cl up tl rdn and wknd fr 3 out* **17/2**
24P- **7** *42* **Sammy Spiderman**[199] 5373 7-11-10 102 .... BrianHarding 8
(Alistair Whillans) *hld up in tch: reminders 1/2-way: outpcd 12th: btn bef 3 out: virtually p.u run-in* **8/1**
243- **P** **Smart Mistress**[263] 4125 8-11-9 101 .... GrahamLee —
(Ferdy Murphy) *bhd: struggling 10th: t.o whn p.u bef 3 out* **14/1**

7m 37.0s (29.80) **Going Correction** +0.70s/f (Soft) **8** Ran SP% **111.4**
Speed ratings (Par 105): **82,79,78,73,62 61,48,—**
toteswingers:1&2 £5.80, 2&3 £8.50, 1&3 £3.00 CSF £33.14 CT £119.03 TOTE £3.90: £1.10, £3.20, £1.10; EX 34.60.
Owner Derrick Mossop **Bred** Mrs Joy Maund-Powell **Trained** Brigham, Cumbria
■ Stewards' Enquiry : Johnny Farrelly caution: use of whip

FOCUS
Just an ordinary handicap chase rated around the placed horses.

NOTEBOOK
Overquest, beaten off 4lb lower at the course latest, had earlier romped home at Hexham and the return to more testing conditions were clearly in his favour, leading before the last and staying on strongly. A progressive staying chaser, this was only his sixth start under rules and this is unlikely to have been the last of his wins. (op 3-1)
Benbeoch made a lot of the running and stayed on again after the last, but was always being held. (tchd 9-1)
Star Player(IRE) has returned in considerably better form than he was last season and looks very well weighted on old form, so he may soon be winning. (tchd 4-1)
Canal Bank(IRE) again had the cheekpieces on, but produced a disappointing finishing effort. (tchd 15-2 and 6-1 in places)

2275 J&S WILKINSON CONDITIONAL JOCKEYS' H'CAP HURDLE (8 hdls 1 omitted) 2m 1f
4:05 (4:05) (Class 4) (0-110,105) 4-Y-0+ **£2,740** (£798; £399)

Form RPR
0-11 **1** **Fair Spin**[21] 729 10-11-0 93 ....(v) JamesHalliday 96+
(Micky Hammond) *prom: hdwy whn nt fluent and rdn 2 out: led run-in: styd on strly* **2/1**[1]
0-5F **2** *2 1/4* **Leith Walk (IRE)**[149] 729 7-10-8 95 .... CallumWhillans(8) 96
(Donald Whillans) *t.k.h: cl up: chal on bit bef last: rdn run-in: edgd rt and kpt on towards fin* **7/2**[3]
02P- **3** *5* **Also Jo**[242] 4534 7-11-6 99 .... CampbellGillies 94
(William Amos) *t.k.h: led tl hdd and no ex run-in* **5/1**
P-5P **4** *12* **Black Apache (IRE)**[163] 522 6-11-4 105 ....(t) HenryBrooke(8) 88
(Donald McCain) *trckd ldrs tl rdn and wknd bef 2 out* **5/2**[2]
-564 **5** *10* **Knockaveen (IRE)**[30] 1780 5-10-6 85 .... FearghalDavis 58
(Andrew Crook) *cl up tl rdn and wknd fr 3 out* **7/1**

4m 43.3s (13.50) **Going Correction** +0.575s/f (Soft) **5** Ran SP% **113.3**
Speed ratings (Par 105): **91,89,87,81,77**
CSF £9.69 TOTE £1.80: £1.10, £2.20; EX 11.40.
Owner Bendery Properties Holdings Ltd **Bred** A S Reid **Trained** Middleham Moor, N Yorks

FOCUS
A low-grade conditional jockeys' handicap hurdle in which the runner-up sets the level.

NOTEBOOK

Fair Spin, who's been running just okay on the Flat, had won his last two starts over hurdles, the latest off 9lb lower, and he showed himself to still be on the up with a hard-fought victory. He's doing well considering he's rising 11, and is likely to bid for a four-timer at Hexham next week. (op 5-2)

Leith Walk(IRE), under pressure and looking held behind the winner last time on her latest start in June, was entitled to go well with the swing at the weights and she duly did, but just couldn't stay on as strongly as the winner in the ground. (op 4-1 tchd 5-1)

Also Jo did his best to hang in there under pressure, but in the end could find no extra from the last. This was a satisfactory reappearance. (op 6-1 tchd 9-2)

Black Apache(IRE) failed to improve for the fitting of a tongue-tie. (op 11-4 tchd 9-4)

Knockaveen(IRE) did no better for the switch to fences. (op 5-1)

T/Plt: £192.90 to a £1 stake. Pool £54,890.30 - 207.63 winning tickets. T/Qpdt: £22.80 to a £1 stake. Pool of £5,262.10 - 170.45 winning tickets. RY

1255 SOUTHWELL (L-H)

Monday, November 8

OFFICIAL GOING: Good (good to firm in places) changing to good after race 1 (12.40) changing to good (good to soft in places) after race 2 (1.10)

Fences were situated 16metres off inside rail and both bends in the centre.

Wind: fresh 1/2 against Weather: wet and windy

2276 CE PROPERTY SERVICES GROUP H'CAP CHASE (13 fncs) 2m

12:40 (12:40) (Class 4) (0-115,122) 4-Y-O+ **£3,577** (£1,050; £525; £262)

Form				RPR
2-31	1		**Kilkenny All Star (IRE)**[26] 1823 9-11-7 **115**.................... ShaneByrne(5) (Sue Smith) *trckd ldng pair: mstke 4th: wnt prom 7th: led appr 3 out: clr 2 out: easily* **2/1**[1]	123+
2253	2	11	**Peak Seasons (IRE)**[18] 1940 7-9-7 **89** oh15.................... GaryDerwin(7) (Michael Chapman) *chsd ldr: led appr 4th: hdd appr 3 out: kpt on: no ch w wnr* **12/1**	84
353B	3	8	**Blossom King (FR)**[12] 2037 6-11-5 **108**..........................(t) SamThomas (Tom George) *hld up: hdwy and 3rd whn pckd landing 9th: chsng ldrs after next: one pce fr 3 out* **5/1**	98
0332	4	12	**Cortinas (GER)**[22] 1888 8-11-12 **115**..................................(t) NoelFehily (Charlie Mann) *hld up in rr: blnd 3rd: hdwy to chse ldrs 4 out: wknd appr next: modest 4th whn blnd last* **11/4**[2]	101
2P-P	5	21	**Majy D'Auteuil (FR)**[192] 81 8-11-0 **103**.................... RichardJohnson (Alan Jessop) *nt j.w in rr: bhd fr 7th: t.o 3 out* **4/1**[3]	65
P2-P	P		**Aboukir Bay (IRE)**[15] 1996 6-9-8 **90**..............................(b) JoeCornwall(7) (John Cornwall) *led tl appr 4th: hit 8th: wknd next: t.o whn p.u bef 3 out* **12/1**	—

4m 16.5s (6.50) **Going Correction** +0.50s/f (Soft) **6** Ran SP% **112.1**

Speed ratings (Par 105): **103,97,93,87,77** —

toteswingers:1&2 £3.50, 2&3 £5.70, 1&3 £2.20 CSF £22.50 TOTE £4.00: £2.70, £7.80; EX 21.40.

Owner The McGoldrick Partnership **Bred** Mrs Brenda Cunningham **Trained** High Eldwick, W Yorks

FOCUS

A moderate handicap, run at a solid gallop and the form is a little suspect, but the winner still impressed. The form is limited by the proximity of the runner-up from well out of the weights.

NOTEBOOK

Kilkenny All Star(IRE) ran out an easy winner. Sue Smith's 9-y-o was up 5lb for registering just his second career success at Uttoxeter last month, but he shrugged that off without bother and could have been called the winner soon after straightening for home. His main rivals ran well below par, but he is clearly at the very top of his game at present. The handicapper will now have his say, but would surely take all the beating again if found another race under a penalty. (tchd 13-8)

Peak Seasons(IRE) was a sitting duck for the winner after four out, but gave his all and ran another game race from the front. However, he was just over a stone out of the handicap so his finishing position dictates this form should be treated with some caution. (op 16-1 tchd 18-1)

Blossom King(FR), not done with when brought down on his previous outing, was allowed to bide his time and made a move around five out. He was brilliant at that fence, but still had his chance turning for home and proved laboured when asked for maximum effort. He is a tricky character. (tchd 11-2)

Cortinas(GER) was 5lb higher than when finishing second at Kempton last time out and thus 5lb higher than when last winning in this race last year. He crept into contention coming out of the back straight, but didn't appear too willing when push came to shove and was soon beaten. He is best on quick ground and so perhaps the rain was not to his liking, but this was still disappointing. (op 9-4)

Majy D'Auteuil(FR) had been pulled up on his last two outings and is another that enjoys a sound surface. He was outpaced from halfway and never threatened. Official explanation: jockey said that the gelding jumped poorly in the back straight and got tired (op 11-2 tchd 6-1)

2277 CLEANEVENT H'CAP CHASE (19 fncs) 3m 110y

1:10 (1:10) (Class 4) (0-100,94) 4-Y-O+ **£3,252** (£955; £477; £238)

Form				RPR
P-16	1		**Gerrard (IRE)**[16] 1969 12-11-1 **86**..............................(b) CharlieHuxley(3) (Althea Barclay) *in rr: wnt prom 10th: reminders 12th: led appr 2 out: j. slowly last: drvn out* **12/1**	95
P3-5	2	10	**One More Dinar**[18] 1939 7-10-7 **82**.......................... HarryChalloner(7) (John Bryan Groucott) *trckd ldrs: led 14th: blnd 4 out: sn hdd: one pce fr 3 out: tk 2nd between last 2* **9/2**[1]	85
3441	3	1 ½	**Feeling Peckish (USA)**[18] 1939 6-10-7 **82**......................(t) MrTGarner(7) (Michael Chapman) *chsd ldrs: outpcd 13th: one pce fr 4 out* **9/2**[1]	82
00-1	4	hd	**Reelwill (FR)**[17] 1954 5-10-8 **76**.. TomMessenger (Chris Bealby) *trckd ldrs: rdn 4 out: sn outpcd: nt jump wl last 3* **5/1**[2]	76
2126	5	31	**Rash Moment (FR)**[25] 1840 11-11-12 **94**..................(p) TomScudamore (Michael Scudamore) *trckd ldrs: led 10th: hdd 14th: led after 4 out: blnd next: hdd appr 2 out: 4th and wl btn whn blnd last: heavily eased: fin tired* **8/1**	88+
3-50	6	2 ¾	**Donald Will Do (IRE)**[174] 383 10-10-12 **80**................ AndrewThornton (Caroline Bailey) *j.rt: led 2nd: hdd 10th: drvn next: lost pl 14th: sn bhd: t.o 3 out* **11/2**[3]	52
404-	P		**Ortega (FR)**[356] 2343 8-10-1 **76**.....................................(p) JoeCornwall(7) (John Cornwall) *t.k.h: led to 2nd: drvn and hit 12th: lost pl 14th: t.o whn p.u bef 3 out* **17/2**	—
340/	P		**Mickwell Bay**[592] 4731 9-10-7 **75**.................................... DougieCostello (Tim Pitt) *in tch: wnt prom 11th: drvn 13th: lost pl next: t.o whn p.u bef 3 out* **6/1**	—

6m 57.8s (31.80) **Going Correction** +1.35s/f (Heav) **8** Ran SP% **112.0**

Speed ratings (Par 105): **103,99,99,99,89 88,—,—**

toteswingers:1&2 £9.20, 2&3 £4.30, 1&3 £6.30 CSF £63.26 CT £281.39 TOTE £14.50: £3.50, £1.10, £2.40; EX 86.50.

Owner Mrs Althea Barclay **Bred** Niall Delany **Trained** Oddington, Gloucs

FOCUS

A weak staying handicap that looked wide open. There was just an ordinary gallop on, but the majority finished leg-weary. The fourth rated to her fakenham form is the best guide.

NOTEBOOK

Gerrard(IRE), who needed his comeback last month, got back to winning ways and was well on top after the penultimate fence. He isn't always the easiest to predict and tends to need plenty of driving in his races, which was again the case here. He kept responding for his rider's urgings, though, and has now won two of his last three outings. This better ground was much more up his street and it was his joint-highest winning mark to date. (op 14-1)

One More Dinar was expected to step up on his comeback effort at Ludlow last month, and it looked as he went to the front on the back straight as though he was a likely winner. However, he hit the fourth-last and soon came under the pump. It was still a more encouraging effort and a slight drop back in trip may suit ideally. (tchd 4-1)

Feeling Peckish(USA) was a long way ahead of the runner-up when finally shedding his maiden tag at Ludlow off an 8lb lower mark 18 days earlier. He tended to go in snatches and got behind when the pace became serious, before plugging on stoutly in the home straight. He helps to set the level. (tchd 5-1)

Reelwill(FR) was raised 6lb for getting off the mark on her chasing debut at Fakenham 17 days earlier. She had her chance, but ultimately failed to really see out the longer trip as her fencing was messy from three out. Although it could also be this second outing came that bit too soon for her. (op 9-2)

Rash Moment(FR) enjoyed this return to chasing and made his move off the home turn. He was going that bit better than the winner prior to clouting the third-last and that cost him. He has yet to score beyond 2m7f, though, and the winner would have probably outstayed him in any case. (op 15-2)

2278 CLEAN CONCIERGE BEGINNERS' CHASE (19 fncs) 3m 110y

1:45 (1:45) (Class 4) 4-Y-O+ **£2,927** (£859; £429; £214)

Form				RPR
56-F	1		**Sheshali (IRE)**[43] 1627 6-11-3 0.. PaulMoloney (Evan Williams) *j.rt: t.k.h: trckd ldrs: nt fluent 14th: upsides 3 out: led on bit after 2 out: styd on u.p run-in* **2/1**[2]	125+
5-33	2	1	**Night Orbit**[35] 1602 6-11-3 0.. MattieBatchelor (Julia Feilden) *led: hdd 9th: upsides 15th: rdn next: hit 3 out: no ex last 75yds* **11/2**	121
64	3	12	**The Wifes Pet (IRE)**[33] 1731 6-10-10 0.......................... AidanColeman (Lawney Hill) *t.k.h: trckd ldr: led 9th: jnd 3 out: hdd after next: wknd appr last* **6/4**[1]	106+
1P-6	4	48	**Winterwood (IRE)**[16] 1964 7-11-3 0................................(p) SamThomas (Tim Vaughan) *chsd ldrs: nt fluent 3rd: outpcd 7th: drvn 10th: lost pl 12th: sn bhd: t.o 15th* **10/3**[3]	72

6m 57.4s (31.40) **Going Correction** +1.35s/f (Heav) **4** Ran SP% **111.8**

Speed ratings (Par 105): **103,102,98,83**

CSF £11.62 TOTE £2.20; EX 13.50.

Owner Edwards, Swinnerton, Babb, Howell **Bred** His Highness The Aga Khan's Studs S C **Trained** Llancarfan, Vale Of Glamorgan

FOCUS

The ground was officially eased to good, good to soft in places prior to this modest little beginners' chase. The second sets the level.

NOTEBOOK

Sheshali(IRE) got off the mark as a chaser at the second time of asking with a fairly ready effort. He had fallen on his debut over fences in September, but was patiently ridden here and allowed time to find his feet. It was apparent he was still full of running coming to three out and it looked as though he would win nicely when hitting the front near the last, but ultimately he had to dig deep to fend off the runner-up. He didn't always do a lot when in front over hurdles, though, and there's every chance he had more in hand than the bare margin. There is still room for improvement with his jumping, but he is fully entitled to improve on that and this will have done his confidence a lot of good. (tchd 9-4)

Night Orbit was returning from the Flat and had finished third on his previous two outings in this sphere, so he rates the best guide for the overall form. He was the first of the principals to come under pressure and wasn't helped by a mistake three out, but there was no faulting his attitude under pressure. He deserves to get his head back in front. (op 9-2)

The Wifes Pet(IRE), having her third run for current connections, had returned to something like the pick of her hurdling form when fourth at Towcester in a decent heat over 2m on her chasing debut last month. She took time to settle here and was in front from the ninth fence. She still appeared to be going well nearing three out, but found little when pressed thereafter and probably paid for running freely over this much longer trip. This added experience will not be lost on her. (op 2-1)

Winterwood(IRE), beaten a long way on his chasing debut 16 days earlier, seemed to lose interest after four fences or so and failed to raise his game for this return to better ground. He now has a bit to prove. (op 3-1)

2279 SOUTHWELL-RACECOURSE.CO.UK CLAIMING HURDLE (13 hdls) 3m 110y

2:15 (2:16) (Class 4) 4-Y-O+ **£2,740** (£798; £399)

Form				RPR
-031	1		**National Trust**[18] 1937 8-11-0 130.. PaulMoloney (Sophie Leech) *trckd ldr: led 6th: wnt clr appr 2 out: 15 l ahd last: heavily eased* **8/13**[1]	114+
1250	2	13	**Caheerloch (IRE)**[16] 1959 8-11-2 95.................................. DavidEngland (Nigel Twiston-Davies) *led: j.lft 2nd: hdd 6th: drvn along 8th: wnt 2nd 2 out: no ch w wnr* **7/1**	97
243F	3	25	**Kilshannig (IRE)**[32] 1747 5-11-6 99..................................(bt[1]) APMcCoy (Jonjo O'Neill) *t.k.h: trckd ldrs: hit 8th: chsd wnr next: drvn 10th: wknd 2 out: sn eased* **5/1**[2]	87
/600	4	24	**Little Dibber**[26] 1821 7-10-8 103.. AidanColeman (Peter Pritchard) *nt fluent in last: mstke 1st: outpcd 9th: sn bhd: t.o 3 out* **11/2**[3]	45

6m 44.8s (37.30) **Going Correction** +1.15s/f (Heav) **4** Ran SP% **106.5**

Speed ratings (Par 105): **86,81,73,66**

.National Trust was claimed by E. J. Creighton for £7000\n\x\x

Owner C J Leech **Bred** Cheveley Park Stud Ltd **Trained** Kingsbridge, Devon

FOCUS

An uncompetitive claimer. The winner did not have to improve and is value for further, with the runner-up rated to his mark.

NOTEBOOK

National Trust resumed winning ways in selling company at Ludlow last month and was having his first outing for new connections. It was very surprising his official mark of 130 was not lowered after that win, but he was still the clear form pick in this line up and he duly scored as he pleased. It was his first success over 3m, but this is a sharp track and he had previously scored over 2m6f at Ascot so stamina wasn't a worry. There should be more of these to be won with him, as he will be high on confidence now. (op 4-9)

Caheerloch(IRE), faced with a tough task at the weights, set out to make all but had to be content to let the winner go by when that rival put some pace into the race. He was easily shaken off from the home turn, but kept to his task and it was a more encouraging effort again from this dour stayer. (op 8-1)

Kilshannig(IRE), who fell over fences last time, was equipped with first-time blinkers on this drop in grade. He faced a very stiff task conceding 6lb to the winner, but didn't convince with his jumping of these smaller obstacles and was in trouble off the home turn. He looks one to swerve. (op 6-1 tchd 9-2)
Little Dibber is lightly raced and was back down in grade here, but was beaten a long way out. His mark needs looking at. (op 7-1)

2280 BOOK CHRISTMAS PARTIES AT SOUTHWELL RACES H'CAP HURDLE (11 hdls) 2m 4f 110y
2:45 (2:46) (Class 4) (0-100,99) 4-Y-O+ **£2,341** (£687; £343; £171)

Form RPR
05-0 **1** **Salpierre (IRE)**[26] 1822 5-11-3 **90** APMcCoy 109+
(Jonjo O'Neill) *nt fluent: hld up in rr: hdwy 6th: sn trcking ldrs: led 3 out: shkn up between last 2: pushed clr run-in: v readily* **7/2**[1]
00 **2** *3 ¾* **Spice Bar**[13] 1199 6-10-0 **73** BarryKeniry 82
(Declan Carroll) *trckd ldrs: jnd wnr after 3 out: styd on same pce between last 2* **8/1**
0-00 **3** *6* **Dance Sauvage**[10] 2080 7-9-7 **73** oh3 (b[1]) PaulGallagher[(7)] 76
(Mike Sowersby) *hld up in rr: hdwy 6th: sn chsng ldrs: mstke next: one pce fr 2 out* **12/1**
-005 **4** *¾* **Hot Tottie (IRE)**[32] 1737 6-10-12 **90** (p) IanPopham[(5)] 92
(Jeremy Scott) *chsd ldrs: pushed along 7th: led next: hdd 3 out: one pce* **4/1**[2]
5PP- **5** *12* **Najca De Thaix (FR)**[23] 4377 9-11-10 **97** JamieMoore 88
(John Spearing) *prom: mstke 3rd: outpcd and nt fluent 8th: lost pl after next* **25/1**
0-P3 **6** *30* **Phar Again (IRE)**[8] 2113 7-10-9 **82** (tp) NoelFehily 46
(Claire Dyson) *trckd ldrs: led after 6th: hdd 8th: wknd next: eased between last 2* **9/1**
P-3P **7** *27* **Inchloch**[16] 1959 8-11-2 **92** (t) TommyPhelan[(3)] 32
(Claire Dyson) *prom: lost pl 8th: sn bhd: t.o 2 out* **10/1**
3532 **P** **Galley Slave (IRE)**[17] 1953 5-10-11 **91** GaryDerwin[(7)] —
(Michael Chapman) *led: hdd after 6th: lost pl after next: sn bhd: t.o whn p.u bef 3 out* **8/1**
6 **P** **Closesthingtocrazy**[15] 1996 6-11-4 **98** (t) MrMEnnis[(7)] —
(Sarah Humphrey) *trckd ldrs: t.k.h: wknd appr 3 out: sn bhd: t.o whn p.u bef 2 out* **15/2**[3]
06-0 **P** **Keep Guessing**[188] 129 7-11-5 **99** MrTGarner[(7)] —
(Warren Greatrex) *hld up towards rr: lost pl 8th: sn bhd: t.o whn p.u bef 2 out* **8/1**

5m 32.2s (21.50) **Going Correction** +1.15s/f (Heav) **10** Ran SP% **117.9**
Speed ratings (Par 105): **105,103,101,101,96 85,74,—,—,—**
toteswingers:1&2 £12.80, 2&3 £24.00, 1&3 £13.50 CSF £32.29 CT £306.18 TOTE £7.60: £4.40, £5.80, £1.60; EX 48.80.
Owner F Gillespie **Bred** Mrs Mary Furlong **Trained** Cheltenham, Gloucs

FOCUS
Winning form was thin on the ground in this weak handicap. There was a fair gallop on and the form ought to work out with the first pair coming clear and the second rated to his mark.

NOTEBOOK
Salpierre(IRE) ◆, well backed, showed much-improved form to open his account at the seventh time of asking and completed the task with a fair bit left in the tank. He was confidently ridden by McCoy and only had the runner-up to worry about in the home straight. He asserted his authority over that rival coming to the last and was comfortably on top at the finish. This 5-y-o looked promising when second in both his bumpers, but had disappointed over hurdles coming into this. It was just his second outing in a handicap though, and the sort his yard does well with, so there should be more to come now. Official explanation: trainer's representative said regarding the apparent improvement of form, that the gelding has benefited from its first run of the season and considered today's race to be a weak race (op 9-2)
Spice Bar ran freely for most of the contest. He travelled into contention going strongly though, and, although put in his place by the winner from the last, he did finish well clear of the remainder. This was probably his best effort to date on his second outing for the stable. (op 15-2 tchd 10-1)
Dance Sauvage, 3lb out of the weights, made up ground easily to get involved coming out of the back straight. He was laboured from the third-last, but this was more encouraging from him in first-time blinkers. (op 10-1)
Hot Tottie(IRE), equipped with first-time cheekpieces, had her chance but couldn't raise her game from the home turn and probably paid for running freely. (op 5-1)
Galley Slave(IRE) Official explanation: trainer said the gelding was unsuited by the good, good to soft in places, going.

2281 SOUTHWELL GOLF CLUB LADY MEMBERS NOVICES' HURDLE (11 hdls) 2m 4f 110y
3:20 (3:20) (Class 4) 4-Y-O+ **£2,602** (£764; £382; £190)

Form RPR
-1P2 **1** **Front Of House (IRE)**[10] 2075 8-11-5 118 APMcCoy 122+
(Ben Haslam) *trckd ldrs: led on bit 2 out: clr last: easily* **5/2**[2]
4-12 **2** *5* **Kasbadali (FR)**[20] 1910 5-10-12 0 LeightonAspell 106
(Oliver Sherwood) *trckd ldrs: upsides 2 out: styd on same pce between last 2: no ch w wnr* **11/8**[1]
3 *5* **Awareiness (IRE)**[212] 4-10-12 0 TomMessenger 100
(Chris Bealby) *trckd ldrs: outpcd whn nt fluent 8th: kpt on one pce fr 2 out* **16/1**
4 *4* **Native Gallery (IRE)**[212] 5-10-12 0 DarylJacob 100+
(Ben De Haan) *trckd ldr: led 8th: hdd whn mstke 2 out: wknd last* **9/1**[3]
32 **5** *10* **Dontupsettherhythm (IRE)**[17] 1955 5-10-9 0 AdamPogson[(3)] 86
(Charles Pogson) *t.k.h: trckd ldrs: wknd appr 2 out* **9/1**[3]
0 **6** *22* **Hardwick Wood**[15] 1990 5-10-12 0 AndrewThornton 64
(Caroline Bailey) *set modest pce: hdd 8th: rdn and wknd next: sn bhd* **40/1**
00-0 **7** *6* **Midnight Trix**[15] 1994 4-10-5 0 FelixDeGiles 51
(Alex Hales) *chsd ldrs: outpcd 7th: lost pl next* **80/1**
00 **8** *31* **Body Gold (ARG)**[11] 2059 7-10-12 0 DavidEngland 27
(Nigel Twiston-Davies) *nt jump wl in rr: blnd 1st: mstke 7th: sn bhd: t.o 3 out* **40/1**
20- **9** *4* **Royal Mile (IRE)**[269] 4023 6-10-12 0 NoelFehily 23
(Warren Greatrex) *hld up in rr: bhd fr 7th: t.o 2 out* **10/1**
5 **10** *36* **Gun And More**[30] 1785 5-10-7 0 ShaneByrne[(5)] —
(Sue Smith) *prom: lost pl 6-7th: t.o 3 out: blnd next: eventually completed* **66/1**

5m 38.5s (27.80) **Going Correction** +1.15s/f (Heav)
WFA 4 from 5yo+ 8lb **10** Ran SP% **113.3**
Speed ratings (Par 105): **93,91,89,87,83 75,73,61,59,46**
toteswingers:1&2 £1.70, 2&3 £5.80, 1&3 £7.70 CSF £6.21 TOTE £3.30: £1.10, £1.10, £6.20; EX 5.70.
Owner John P McManus **Bred** Newtownbarry House Stud **Trained** Middleham Moor, N Yorks

FOCUS
A modest novice event run at an ordinary gallop, and the two market leaders eventually pulled clear. The winner is rated to his mark.

NOTEBOOK
Front Of House(IRE) bounced back to winning ways under his penalty and got off the mark for his current yard at the second attempt. The easing ground was of a little concern for him considering his best form had been on a quicker surface, but his proven stamina was a big advantage as the race panned out. Things will be much tougher for him under a double penalty in this division, but he should be full of confidence after this and the very best of him may well have yet to be seen. (op 3-1 tchd 7-2)
Kasbadali(FR) was a popular pick to go one better than his encouraging comeback effort at Exeter behind Dare Me last month. He was given every chance, but didn't travel as fluently as the winner and failed to see out the longer trip like that rival, perhaps on account of the deteriorating ground. This was just his second outing over hurdles and he was still nicely clear of the remainder, so success shouldn't be too far off in this sphere. (op 6-4 tchd 5-4)
Awareiness(IRE) was last seen winning at the second attempt between the flags in Ireland and was debuting for a yard that won this event last season. He shaped with definite ability, but lacked the pace to land a serious blow and this 40,000gns purchase very likely needs a stiffer test. (op 12-1)
Native Gallery(IRE) ◆ cost his new connections £46,000 having landed two of his three outings in Irish points. He got a positive ride, did things nicely in the race and was still upsides the first pair prior to getting the second-last all wrong. That saw him go backwards, but this was a very encouraging debut display and he won't mind racing on softer ground. (tchd 8-1)
Dontupsettherhythm(IRE) had been placed in both his bumpers and didn't go unbacked for this switch to hurdling. He raced too enthusiastically and was done with at the top of the home straight, but left the impression he will have little problem winning races down the line. (op 8-1 tchd 13-2)

2282 CLEAN WASTE SOLUTIONS NOVICES' HURDLE (9 hdls) 2m
3:55 (3:56) (Class 4) 4-Y-O+ **£2,602** (£764; £382; £190)

Form RPR
1 **Break The Chain** 4-10-12 0 AndrewThornton 107+
(Caroline Bailey) *trckd ldrs: led appr 2 out: 3 l ahd last: drvn rt out* **16/1**
0 **2** *1 ½* **Well Hello There (IRE)**[16] 1962 4-10-12 0 APMcCoy 104+
(Jonjo O'Neill) *in rr: hdwy 3 out: sn hrd drvn: wnt 2nd between last 2: styd on: no imp* **11/4**[2]
54 **3** *10* **Bagutta Sun**[12] 2038 4-10-2 0 DannyCook[(3)] 88
(Barry Leavy) *chsd ldrs: drvn 3 out: one pce fr next* **5/2**[1]
4 **4** *3 ¾* **Morocchius (USA)**[26] 1831 5-10-12 0 LiamHeard 92
(Julie Camacho) *stdd s: t.k.h in rr: hdwy 6th: kpt on one pce fr 2 out* **9/1**
0 **5** *1 ¼* **First Spirit**[15] 1994 4-10-2 0 WayneKavanagh[(3)] 84
(Robin Dickin) *mid-div: hdwy to chse ldrs 3 out: one pce fr next* **66/1**
1-12 **6** *hd* **Tharaya**[149] 726 5-11-5 108 RichardJohnson 99+
(James Turner) *chsd ldr: blnd 6th: wknd between last 2* **7/2**[3]
/0-5 **7** *8* **Sir Mark (IRE)**[16] 1974 6-10-12 0 AndrewTinkler 85
(Anna Bramall) *led: j.rt: hdd appr 2 out: wknd between last 2* **14/1**
00 **8** *¾* **Furius**[26] 1831 4-10-7 0 ShaneByrne[(5)] 82
(Sue Smith) *prom: outpcd and lost pl 3 out* **40/1**
50-P **9** *4 ½* **Roi De Garde (FR)**[10] 2067 4-10-12 0 TomMessenger 78
(Chris Bealby) *chsd ldrs: nt fluent 5th: drvn 3 out: wknd appr next* **25/1**
P- **10** *10* **Breadstick**[197] 4 4-10-5 0 (t) WillKennedy 62
(Jeremy Scott) *prom: lost pl after 3 out: sn bhd* **16/1**
P **Admirals Way**[121] 5-10-12 0 JimmyMcCarthy —
(Christopher Kellett) *t.k.h detached in last: bhd fr 5th: t.o whn p.u bef 2 out* **50/1**

4m 21.2s (24.10) **Going Correction** +1.15s/f (Heav)
WFA 4 from 5yo+ 7lb **11** Ran SP% **115.6**
Speed ratings (Par 105): **85,84,79,77,76 76,72,72,70,65 —**
toteswingers:1&2 £8.20, 2&3 £2.50, 1&3 £11.60 CSF £59.31 TOTE £20.10: £4.20, £1.50, £2.20; EX 85.60.
Owner Mr & Mrs R Scott **Bred** Whitley Stud **Trained** Brixworth, Northants

FOCUS
An ordinary novice hurdle in which the third and fourth set the level.

NOTEBOOK
Break The Chain ran out a ready debut winner. He moved sweetly through the race and found plenty when asked for an effort in between the final two flights. He was probably idling somewhat as the runner-up closed after the last and, considering his yard had been previously going through a lean spell, he could be above average. His dam won a Grade 1 in France over a bit further and he should enjoy stepping up in trip in due course. It will be interesting to see how he fares under a penalty.
Well Hello There(IRE) ◆ was never in the hunt on debut when sent off at 40-1 at Aintree 16 days earlier, but this was easier and he came in for support. He was patiently ridden, but couldn't quicken sufficiently when asked for his effort at the top of the home straight and needed strong driving. He responded positively and was closing on the winner after the last though, so is clearly going the right way. A longer trip should also prove more in his favour, and he ought to be off the mark before long. (op 2-1 tchd 3-1)
Bagutta Sun caught the eye finishing well at Haydock 12 days earlier and was well backed here. She had her chance, but proved somewhat laboured on the easier ground and probably found the sharper track against her. She is not one to abandon just yet. (op 3-1 tchd 7-2)
Morocchius(USA) was again ridden to get the trip and, having made up his ground from four out, hit something of a flat spot in the home straight before running on towards the finish. He may need better ground over hurdles.
First Spirit, last of nine on her hurdling debut, showed improved form in defeat. She got 1m4f on the level and would've probably enjoyed a better early gallop, so could build on this again. (tchd 50-1)
Tharaya was in good form when last seen earlier in the year and set the standard with an official mark of 108. He didn't help his cause by refusing to settle on this return from a 149-day break and was beaten after the penultimate flight, but should be sharper for the outing. (op 11-4 tchd 5-2)
T/Plt: £84.00 to a £1 stake. Pool of £58,997.75 - 512.26 winning tickets. T/Qpdt: £23.00 to a £1 stake. Pool of £5,176.54 - 166.50 winning tickets. WG

2136 EXETER (R-H)
Tuesday, November 9

OFFICIAL GOING: Chase course - good to soft (soft in places; 6.0); hurdle course - soft (heavy in places on the home turn bend)
Wind: strong partly across Weather: Raining at times, easing from 2.15.

2283 CHRISTMAS PARTIES HERE AT EXETER RACECOURSE NOVICES' HURDLE (11 hdls) 2m 5f 110y
1:20 (1:22) (Class 4) 4-Y-O+ **£2,602** (£764; £382; £190)

Form RPR
1- **1** **Highland Valley (IRE)**[278] 3853 5-10-12 0 SamThomas 132+
(Emma Lavelle) *trckd ldrs: wnt into narrow advantage travelling wl gng to 3 out: easily drew clr fr after gng lft last: impressive* **5/1**[3]
2F-4 **2** *10* **Daring Origyn (FR)**[17] 1959 5-10-5 117 (t) JakeGreenall[(7)] 112+
(Richard Lee) *j.lft at times: in tch: hdwy to ld 6th: rdn whn narrowly hdd 3 out: remained w wnr u.str.p: readily hld whn carried lft last* **9/4**[1]

424- **3** *8* **Simply Wings (IRE)**[229] 4844 6-10-12 112 .... RichardJohnson 107+
(Richard Lee) *hld up towards rr: hit 6th: hdwy whn pckd next: rdn to chse ldng pair 3 out: stmbld whn hit 2 out: styd on same pce* **6/1**

352- **4** *4 1/2* **Shrewd Investment**[210] 5178 4-10-9 0 .... CharlieHuxley(3) 100
(Alan King) *mid-div: rdn aftert 8th: styd on same pce: lft 4th appr 2 out* **9/1**

00 **5** *2 3/4* **El Diego (IRE)**[16] 1990 6-10-7 0 .... DavidBass(5) 97
(Jamie Snowden) *hld up towards rr: sme hdwy u.p after 8th: no further imp whn lft 5th appr 2 out* **66/1**

400/ **6** *14* **One And All (IRE)**[599] 4607 7-10-12 0 .... DavidDennis 83
(Nigel Hawke) *mid-div: hdwy to trck ldrs 6th: rdn and wknd appr 3 out* **80/1**

7 *22* **That'lldoboy (FR)**[233] 4-10-12 0 .... NoelFehily 61
(Paul Nicholls) *plld hrd off stdy pce: trckd ldr: led 2nd tl 6th: wknd bef 3 out: t.o* **7/2**[2]

6 **8** *1* **Sir Mattie (IRE)**[17] 1963 5-10-12 0 ....(p) PaulMoloney 60
(David Rees) *led at stdy pce tl 2nd: trckd ldrs tl wknd after 8th: t.o* **28/1**

5P0- **U** **History Lesson**[246] 4482 4-10-12 0 .... ChristianWilliams —
(Alan Jones) *jinked lft appr 1st and uns rdr* **28/1**

/0F- **P** **Master Alfredo**[270] 4019 6-10-9 0 .... SamTwiston-Davies(3) —
(Susan Nock) *t.k.h in mid-div: wknd bef 8th: t.o whn p.u bef 3 out* **66/1**

P **Waldsee (GER)**[14] 5-10-5 0 .... AnthonyFreeman(7) —
(Sean Curran) *mid-div tl wknd appr 8th: t.o whn p.u bef 3 out* **100/1**

31-4 **U** **Skipper Robin (FR)**[44] 1623 4-10-12 0 .... PaddyBrennan —
(Nigel Twiston-Davies) *trckd ldrs: rdn appr 3 out: fading in 4th whn wnt rt and uns rdr appr 2 out* **8/1**

0-0 **P** **Rabbitkettle Lake (IRE)**[176] 375 6-10-12 0 .... GerardTumelty —
(Michael Blanshard) *lost tch 6th: t.o whn p.u after 8th* **150/1**

6m 2.90s (29.90) **Going Correction** +0.60s/f (Soft)
WFA 4 from 5yo+ 8lb 13 Ran SP% **117.8**
Speed ratings (Par 105): **69,65,62,60,59 54,46,46,—,— —,—,—**
Tote Swingers: 1&2 £3.40, 1&3 £6.20, 2&3 £3.10 CSF £16.48 TOTE £8.40: £2.30, £1.50, £2.10; EX 20.00.

Owner M E Thompson **Bred** Patrick Myers **Trained** Wildhern, Hants

FOCUS

A modest novice event in which most were found out by the testing surface. The runners stood still for around ten seconds at the tape went up, with nothing wanting to go on, and there was a very steady gallop when they eventually got going, which saw most take a keen hold. The winner looks a decent prospect with the runner-up below his best and the third setting the standard.

NOTEBOOK

Highland Valley(IRE) ◆ ran out a taking winner and followed up his debut bumper success at Wincanton back in February. That win also came on testing ground and he is another of his sire's progeny that obviously loves it when the mud is flying. He was travelling all over the runner-up in the home straight and, although he didn't help that rival when going out to his left over the last two flights, he was still able to coast home on the run-in. This 5-y-o is yet another promising novice from his stable and the longer trip proved much to his liking, so it will be interesting to see where he turns up next. His trainer later added he is very much a chaser in the making, so he may not be tried too highly this season. (op 10-3 tchd 11-2)

Daring Origyn(FR) was having his fifth outing as a hurdler and with an official mark of 117 set the standard in this field. He had every chance back down in trip and, although firmly put in his place by the winner, finished a clear second-best. His bumper win came on good ground and returning to a sounder surface is probably what he ideally wants. (op 3-1)

Simply Wings(IRE), a stablemate of the runner-up, was having his fourth outing over hurdles and also came in for support on this seasonal return. He kept on under maximum pressure without threatening and should improve nicely for the run, but his best chance of success probably lies in a handicap. (op 10-1 tchd 5-1)

Shrewd Investment was a well-beaten third behind the winner on debut last term, but improved on his final two outings without winning. He proved easy to back for this seasonal/hurdling debut and found it hard to quicken on this testing surface. He too should come on plenty for the outing.

El Diego(IRE) was never seriously in the hunt, but was noted keeping on towards the finish and this was his most encouraging effort in this sphere. He is now eligible for handicaps.

That'lldoboy(FR) joined Paul Nicholls having won a point on debut in March. He has scope, but refused to settle off the sedate early gallop and was running on empty from three out. He may appreciate racing on better ground and dropping back in trip could also benefit in the short term.

Sir Mattie(IRE) Official explanation: jockey said gelding hung left-handed

2284 BATHWICK TYRES PLYMOUTH H'CAP HURDLE (12 hdls) 2m 7f 110y

1:50 (1:52) (Class 4) (0-115,112) 4-Y-O+ **£3,252** (£955; £477; £238)

Form RPR

/P1- **1** **Kathleens Pride (IRE)**[231] 4798 10-11-2 **102** .... FelixDeGiles 111
(Robin Dickin) *mde all: mstke 8th: styd on v gamely whn hrd pressed 2 out: rdn out* **8/1**

1-52 **2** *1 3/4* **Five Star Wilsham (IRE)**[7] 2141 6-11-7 **112** .... IanPopham(5) 119
(Jeremy Scott) *trckd wnr thrght: ev ch 2 out: sn rdn: edgd lft: styd on same pce* **7/4**[1]

30-1 **3** *5* **Victors Serenade (IRE)**[7] 2141 5-11-11 **111** 7ex .... AidanColeman 114
(Anthony Honeyball) *j.lft at times: hld up in last pair: hdwy into 3rd at the 5th: rdn appr 3 out: styd on same pce* **5/2**[2]

4206 **4** *22* **Casual Garcia**[20] 1918 5-11-0 **103** ....(t) TommyPhelan(3) 83
(Mark Gillard) *trckd ldrs: rdn after 9th: wknd 3 out: t.o* **50/1**

0023 **5** *32* **Captain Becket**[14] 2023 7-10-13 **99** .... HaddenFrost 47
(James Frost) *hld up last but in tch: rdn after 9th: nvr any imp on ldrs: wknd 3 out: t.o* **14/1**

2111 **6** *3 1/2* **Scotsbrook Cloud**[5] 2161 5-10-11 **100** .... LeeStephens(3) 70+
(David Evans) *trckd ldrs: rdn appr 3 out: wknd sn after: t.o whn eased run-in* **10/3**[3]

6m 10.3s (11.30) **Going Correction** +0.60s/f (Soft) 6 Ran SP% **107.8**
Speed ratings (Par 105): **105,104,102,95,84 83**
Tote Swingers: 1&2 £3.90, 1&3 £2.00, 2&3 £1.60 CSF £21.30 TOTE £8.20: £3.40, £1.10; EX 30.90.

Owner Solihull Syndicate **Bred** Rory Collins **Trained** Atherstone on Stour, Warwicks

FOCUS

An moderate staying handicap, run at an average sort of gallop and the first pair were always to the fore. The placed horses were rated to their marks.

NOTEBOOK

Kathleens Pride(IRE) was last seen winning off an 8lb lower mark on soft ground over C&D in March and, making his debut for a new yard, followed up in game fashion. He was given a positive ride and his jockey emerges with top marks for keeping wide to find the best ground in the straight, as that no doubt helped him from three out. This 10-y-o hasn't stood much racing in the past two seasons, but has evidently resumed at the top of his game, and it won't be surprising to see him back over fences this season. He was a winner on his previous start in that sphere back in 2007 and is currently rated 5lb lower as a chaser. (op 15-2)

Five Star Wilsham(IRE) was a game second off this mark over C&D on his handicap debut after a break a week earlier and was well backed to go one better. He was never far away, keeping more to the inside, and looked to be going best nearing two out. He came under pressure after that flight, though, and ended up more towards the outside as he struggled to master the winner. It must be noted he was conceding 5lb to the winner, taking into account his rider's claim, and this was another fine effort in defeat considering the run came plenty soon enough. He richly deserves to win one of these, but life will be tougher off his higher future mark. (op 5-2)

Victors Serenade(IRE) showed his true colours when just getting the better of Five Star Wilsham here last week, but was 7lb worse off with that rival under his penalty on this quick reappearance. He had his chance, but proved once paced under maximum pressure and just left the impression the run came that bit too soon, even though he ran close to his winning form on the revised terms. (op 11-4 tchd 3-1)

Casual Garcia, whose last win came on heavy ground, proved laboured from four out with the blinkers left off, yet reversed his last-time-out form with Scotsbrook Cloud. He needs to show more again before becoming of betting interest. (op 28-1)

Captain Becket was the first beaten and can't operate on such ground.

Scotsbrook Cloud came into this in great form having won his last three and was unpenalised for winning another conditional riders' handicap at Haydock five days earlier. This ground was an unknown for him, though, and it was a combination of that and the run coming too soon that appeared to find him out. He was later reported to have been unsuited by the ground. Official explanation: trainer's rep said, regarding running, that the gelding was unsuited by the soft (heavy on home turn bend) ground. (op 5-2 tchd 9-4 and 7-2 in places)

2285 BATHWICK TYRES TAUNTON NOVICES' CHASE (18 fncs) 3m

2:20 (2:20) (Class 3) 5-Y-O+ **£9,199** (£2,948; £1,638)

Form RPR

10-2 **1** **Watamu Bay (IRE)**[31] 1774 7-10-12 0 .... NoelFehily 140+
(Paul Nicholls) *j.w: disp ld tl lft outrt ldr 13th: jnd after next tl appr 4 out: in command after: comf* **8/11**[1]

11P- **2** *18* **Voramar Two**[214] 5112 7-10-12 0 ....(t) RichardJohnson 127+
(Philip Hobbs) *trckd ldrs: jnd wnr sn after 14th tl rdn appr next: kpt on for clr 2nd but sn hld* **10/3**[2]

22-3 **3** *45* **Plunkett (IRE)**[20] 1917 7-10-12 123 .... PaulMoloney 98
(Evan Williams) *hld up bhd ldrs: keen early: pckd 9th: lft 3rd 13th: hit next: wkng whn mstke 3 out: eased sn after* **16/1**

43-P **U** **Victory Parade (IRE)**[7] 2140 7-10-12 118 .... APMcCoy —
(Rebecca Curtis) *disp ld tl mstke and uns rdr 13th* **5/1**[3]

/4-3 **F** **Theophrastus (IRE)**[17] 1964 8-10-12 122 .... LiamTreadwell —
(Nick Gifford) *slithered on landing and fell 1st* **14/1**

6m 27.5s (18.20) **Going Correction** +0.60s/f (Soft) 5 Ran SP% **110.2**
Speed ratings: **93,87,72,—,—**
CSF £3.73 TOTE £1.90: £1.10, £3.00; EX 3.40.

Owner Jared Sullivan **Bred** Gerry McIntyre And R J Whitford **Trained** Ditcheat, Somerset

FOCUS

A novice chase that is often won by a promising stayer and Watamu Bay kept up that tradition. The ground on the chase course was not quite as testing as the hurdle track, and they went a fair enough gallop.

NOTEBOOK

Watamu Bay(IRE) was just held on his chasing debut when having his first outing for Paul Nicholls at Chepstow last month, and was the all the rage to give his new yard a fourth consecutive win in the race. He made just about all and completed the task readily. His jumping was slicker on this right-handed track, and there was plenty to like about the professional attitude he showed when asked to go clear from the third-last. There should really be more to come from him as he has few miles on the clock, but whether he is quite up to RSA Chase standard remains open to some debate, though his next outing should reveal more on that front. It may well prove to be that he is more of one for the 4m National Hunt Chase at next year's Cheltenham Festival, though it should be noted soft ground is thought to be important to his cause. (op 4-5 tchd 5-6)

Voramar Two ◆ created a decent impression when winning back-to-back novice hurdles last season and has always looked to crying out for a switch to fences. This was his first run back after pulling up in Grade 1 company at Aintree, since which he has undergone a breathing operation, and the market suggested this chase debut may be needed. He duly tired from the third-last, but jumped like a natural through the race and is sure to open his account before long. (op 7-2 tchd 3-1)

Plunkett(IRE), who would've probably won on his chasing debut last time but for an error at the last, didn't look too happy on this easier ground. This was a stiffer task, though, and he too is very likely to find an opening before the year is out. (op 10-1)

Victory Parade(IRE) was not done with prior to being pulled up on his chasing debut over C&D a week earlier after his stirrup broke. He got a positive ride on this switch to novice company and had jumped well enough prior to getting the 13th wrong and unseating. He again wasn't done with prior to departing, but it would be over doing things to think he would've beaten the winner. (op 8-1)

2286 DESERT ORCHID RESTAURANT BEGINNERS' CHASE (12 fncs) 2m 1f 110y

2:50 (2:50) (Class 4) 4-Y-O+ **£5,204** (£1,528; £764; £381)

Form RPR

113- **1** **Royal Charm (FR)**[283] 3737 5-11-1 0 .... NoelFehily 142+
(Paul Nicholls) *j.w: led 3rd: mde rest: drew wl clr fr after 4 out: unextended: impressive* **8/13**[1]

004/ **2** *22* **Carrickboy (IRE)**[586] 4830 6-11-1 0 .... AidanColeman 123+
(Venetia Williams) *trckd wnr fr 3rd: rdn appr 4 out: kpt on for clr 2nd but nvr any ch w wnr* **16/1**

3-02 **3** *17* **Solitary Palm (IRE)**[8] 2124 7-10-10 96 .... IanPopham(5) 104
(Brian Forsey) *led tl 3rd: chsd ldrs: rdn after 8th: wknd 4 out* **50/1**

200- **4** *4* **South O'The Border**[215] 5099 8-10-12 135 .... SamTwiston-Davies(3) 97
(Nigel Twiston-Davies) *hld up: awkward 4th: pushed along fr 6th: no ch fr 8th* **4/1**[2]

P/35 **5** *4 1/2* **Kitley Hassle**[12] 2046 8-11-1 0 ....(b) HaddenFrost 93
(James Frost) *in tch tl outpcd 6th and dropped in rr: no ch after* **80/1**

120/ **6** *1/2* **Belcantista (FR)**[633] 3906 8-11-1 0 .... APMcCoy 93
(Philip Hobbs) *hld up: wnt 3rd briefly after 8th: rdn bef 4 out: sn wknd: dismntd after line: fin lame* **5/1**[3]

PP4/ **7** *16* **Quicolai (FR)**[604] 4504 6-11-1 0 ....(t) PaddyBrennan 79
(Tom George) *hld up: wknd after 8th: t.o* **80/1**

4m 29.3s (10.30) **Going Correction** +0.60s/f (Soft) 7 Ran SP% **108.9**
Speed ratings (Par 105): **101,91,83,81,79 79,72**
Tote Swingers: 1&2 £3.10, 1&3 £9.10, 2&3 £11.70 CSF £9.87 TOTE £1.50: £1.10, £4.90; EX 9.00.

Owner Mrs Angela Tincknell & W Tincknell **Bred** Jean-Philippe Dubois **Trained** Ditcheat, Somerset

FOCUS

A fair novice chase and a very impressive winner although the third limits things slightly.

NOTEBOOK

Royal Charm(FR) ◆ won his two novice hurdles at this venue last season before finding 2m5f at Cheltenham too stiff when upped to Grade 2 company on his final outing in January. He ended up with an official mark of 145 over hurdles, which entitled him to win in such company on this chasing debut, but it was hard not to be very impressed with the way he went about his business. He was always near the front and took the race by the scruff of the neck at the sixth fence. It was clear turning out of the back straight he was going to win barring accidents, and he put in some very neat jumps along the way. This 5-y-o still has relatively few miles on the clock, and so could turn out to be one of the big players in the 2m novice chase division this term, as it's hard to know how good he may be at this stage. He will be full of confidence after this, and should have little trouble defying a penalty should connections wish to get further experience into him before returning to a graded event. He was generally cut to odds of 16/1 for the Arkle next March after this, but his trainer was not sure that race will be for him on the likely quicker ground there. He could come back here next month for a race over 2m3f, which his stablemate Take The Breeze followed up in after winning this last year, or the Grade 2 Henry VIII Novices' Chase at Sandown could also figure in his plans. One could see him relishing the proper jumping test in that. (tchd 4-6)

Carrickboy(IRE), a dual novice hurdle winner, was having his first outing since finishing fourth off a mark of 128 at Aintree's Grand National meeting last year. He did things nicely enough on this chasing debut, and wasn't given too hard a time when it became apparent the classy winner was not for catching. His yard has yet to hit top gear this season and there was more than enough in this effort to think he will be winning races as a novice chaser, but one will have to be mindful of the bounce factor next time. (tchd 14-1)

Solitary Palm(IRE) ran his race on ground soft enough for his liking and will look more interesting when switching to a handicap in this sphere. (op 40-1)

South O'The Border, a stablemate of the runner-up, proved ring rusty on this seasonal debut and was in trouble before the fifth-last. He should prove sharper for the run, but with an official rating of 136 is not simple to place. (tchd 9-2)

Kitley Hassle got badly outpaced in the back straight, but plugged on from four out and will surely prove more effective when returned to further in handicaps, for which he is now eligible. (op 66-1)

Belcantista(FR), a 134-rated hurdler, was returning from a 633-day layoff on this chasing debut having been off with a leg problem. He proved friendless in the betting and looked much in need of the outing. Unfortunately, he was dismounted after the finish as he finished lame and looks set for another spell on the sidelines. Official explanation: jockey said gelding finished lame (op 11-2 tchd 9-2)

2287 BOOK EARLY FOR NEW YEAR'S DAY H'CAP CHASE (15 fncs) 2m 3f 110y

3:20 (3:20) (Class 4) (0-100,97) 4-Y-O+ **£3,252** (£955; £477; £238)

Form RPR

600- **1** **Robbers Bridge (IRE)**^{250} 4411 6-11-8 **93**............ AndrewGlassonbury 103+
(Victor Dartnall) *trckd ldrs: untidy 1st: rdn to chse ldr 4 out: drvn and styd on wl to take narrow advantage last: drvn clr* **7/2**^{3}

000- **2** *4* **Quapriland (FR)**^{256} 1270 6-11-1 **80**.................... SamTwiston-Davies$^{(3)}$ 98
(Althea Barclay) *led: blnd 9th: mstke 2 out: sn rdn: hdd whn wnt rt and hit last: no ex* **11/4**^{2}

-42P **3** *21* **Whatcanisay**^{37} 1710 11-10-2 **73**..(t) HaddenFrost 63
(James Frost) *trckd ldrs: blnd 4th: outpcd after 11th: regained modest 3rd at the last* **9/4**^{1}

30-0 **4** *2* **Manmoon (FR)**^{21} 1912 7-11-12 **97**...................................... DavidDennis 82
(Nigel Hawke) *trckd ldr: rdn appr 3 out: sn hld: wknd 2 out: lost 3rd at the last* **9/2**

06-0 **5** *39* **Xtravaganza (IRE)**^{178} 340 5-11-1 **91**............................(t) DavidBass$^{(5)}$ 41
(Jamie Snowden) *nvr that fluent: hld up last but in tch: struggling 8th: mstke 10th: wknd 4 out: t.o* **8/1**

5m 7.20s (9.90) **Going Correction** +0.60s/f (Soft) **5** Ran SP% **109.0**
Speed ratings (Par 105): **104,102,94,93,77**
CSF £13.26 TOTE £4.90: £1.40, £2.20; EX 12.90.
Owner G D Hake **Bred** Michael Kennedy **Trained** Brayford, Devon

FOCUS

A weak handicap but the first two can do better over fences.

NOTEBOOK

Robbers Bridge(IRE) ◆ showed little in three outings in novice hurdles last season, but his debut third on soft ground in a bumper at Chepstow was encouraging and he has always looked more of a chaser in the making. He took time to warm to the fences, but eventually got on top after the last to open his account at the fifth time of asking on this handicap debut. He displayed a decent attitude when it mattered and his jumping was at its best towards the end of the race, so there is every chance he will improve enough to defy a higher mark. A stiffer test should also suit ideally as he matures and this was a welcome winner for the stable. Official explanation: trainer said, regarding apparent improvement in form, that the gelding was backward and prefers fences to hurdles. (op 11-4)

Quapriland(FR) ◆, another lightly raced horse making her handicap debut, was given a very positive ride. She survived a blunder on the back straight and was still going best three out. However, she got in low at the penultimate fence and then wasn't clever at the last, which handed the momentum to the winner. It was her first outing for 256 days and her first taste of fences, so improvement ought to be forthcoming after this career-best effort. (op 3-1 tchd 10-3)

Whatcanisay, pulled up on her return last month, got badly outpaced on the back straight before running on late and may come on again for the run. However, her losing run continues. (op 3-1)

Manmoon(FR) was still going nicely around the home turn, but he found very little for pressure nearing the fourth-last and most probably found the ground against him. He has slipped in the handicap and there is a chance he may still have needed this outing, so shouldn't be discounted when reverting to a suitably sounder surface. (op 5-1)

2288 EXETER RACECOURSE CONFERENCE CENTRE MARES' NOVICES' HURDLE (10 hdls) 2m 3f

3:50 (3:50) (Class 4) 4-Y-O+ **£2,602** (£764; £382; £190)

Form RPR

105- **1** **Animation (IRE)**^{214} 5114 6-10-5 0............................... JimmyDerham$^{(5)}$ 112
(Seamus Mullins) *led tl 5th: trckd ldrs: stmbld 3 out: rdn after next: led sn after last: kpt on gamely: all out* **15/2**

2P61 **2** *½* **Naughty Naughty**^{16} 1993 5-11-2 111.. APMcCoy 118+
(Brendan Powell) *hld up towards rr: stdy prog fr after 4th to trck ldrs 7th: led 3 out: hit 2 out: rdn and hdd sn after last: kpt on but no ex* **7/1**^{3}

3 *13* **Dun See Dee (IRE)**^{218} 5063 6-10-10 0.................................. NoelFehily 99
(Charlie Mann) *cl up: wnt 2nd 5th: rdn and ev ch fr 3 out tl sn after 2 out: 3rd and hld whn hit last* **13/2**^{2}

2-22 **4** *5* **Way Back When**^{16} 1993 5-10-5 108........................ MrSWaley-Cohen$^{(5)}$ 93
(Alan King) *chsd ldrs: rdn after 7th: one pce fr 3 out* **11/4**^{1}

5 *2 ¼* **Overnight Fame (IRE)**^{261} 6-10-10 0.............................. PaddyBrennan 91
(Tom George) *mid-div: hdwy after 7th: rdn bef 3 out: sn one pce and no further imp* **9/1**

5- **6** *10* **Calico Rose**^{253} 4358 6-10-10 0................................. AndrewGlassonbury 84+
(Victor Dartnall) *chsd ldrs: led 5th tl drvn appr 3 out: fading in 4th whn nt fluent last 2 hurdles* **40/1**

563- **7** *24* **Inkberrow Rose (IRE)**^{219} 5019 6-10-10 0........................ MarkBradburne 57
(Tom Gretton) *chsd ldrs: rdn after 7th: wknd bef 3 out: t.o* **66/1**

5- **8** *¾* **Victoria Rose (IRE)**^{315} 3154 5-10-10 0.................................. RodiGreene 56
(Simon Burrough) *mid-div tl drvn after 4th: sn in rr: t.o* **33/1**

05/0 **P** **Tracy Road (FR)**^{33} 1736 6-10-3 0..................................... MattGriffiths$^{(7)}$ —
(Carroll Gray) *a towards rr: t.o whn p.u bef 3 out* **100/1**

/233 **P** **Rith Bob (IRE)**^{12} 2051 7-10-10 109....................................... PaulMoloney —
(David Rees) *hung lft thrght: chsd ldr tl appr 5th: wknd 7th: bhd whn p.u bef 3 out* **11/4**^{1}

2- **P** **Ballestra (IRE)**^{294} 3528 6-10-10 0.................................... AidanColeman —
(Venetia Williams) *mid-div: effrt after 7th: wknd qckly and p.u bef 3 out* **16/1**

20-4 **P** **Some Secret**^{184} 230 5-10-10 0.. JamesDavies —
(Chris Down) *mid-div: stmbld 2nd: bhd fr after 6th: p.u bef 2 out* **40/1**

00-0 **P** **Shared Secret**^{33} 1742 6-10-5 0................................. RachaelGreen$^{(5)}$ —
(Anthony Honeyball) *a in rr: t.o whn p.u bef 3 out* **66/1**

60 **P** **Rolline (IRE)**^{161} 568 5-10-10 0.................................. ChristianWilliams —
(Stuart Kittow) *mstke 1st: bhd fr 5th: t.o whn p.u bef 3 out* **100/1**

P **Flameproof (IRE)** 5-10-5 0... IanPopham$^{(5)}$ —
(Caroline Keevil) *a towards rr: t.o whn p.u bef 3 out* **80/1**

4m 48.9s (6.20) **Going Correction** +0.60s/f (Soft) **15** Ran SP% **120.8**
Speed ratings (Par 105): **110,109,104,102,101 97,86,86,—,— —,—,—,—,—**
Tote Swingers: 1&2 £9.00, 1&3 £13.40, 2&3 £7.50 CSF £57.72 TOTE £6.10: £1.50, £2.60, £2.60; EX 53.10.
Owner Dr R Jowett **Bred** Desmond Loy **Trained** Wilsford-Cum-Lake, Wilts

FOCUS

A modest mares' novice hurdle. It was run at an ordinary gallop and the first pair, who look above average, drew clear from two out.

NOTEBOOK

Animation(IRE) dug deep to master the runner-up near the finish and make a winning debut over hurdles on her seasonal return. A heavy-ground bumper winner last season, this ground obviously held no fears for her and she responded gamely to strong handling in the home straight. She ought to get even further this term and is entitled to improve for the run, but things will be tougher under a penalty in this division. (op 12-1)

Naughty Naughty, belatedly off the mark at Towcester 16 days earlier, crept into the race nearing the home turn and was going best of all after coming wide into the home straight. She got in low at the second-last, but only gave way to the winner near the business end and finished well clear of the rest. She emerges the best horse at the weights and will probably be happiest back on some better ground, so another success in this division cannot be ruled out. (op 8-1)

Dun See Dee(IRE) followed up her Irish point win when decisively taking a bumper at Cork in April, both on heavy ground. Easy to back on this British and hurdling debut for new connections, she had her chance before tiring from the second-last. She ought to last longer on her next assignment. (op 4-1)

Way Back When had been placed on each of her five previous outings coming into this, but she came unstuck on this more demanding surface. (op 3-1 tchd 7-2)

Overnight Fame(IRE) was last seen comfortably winning an Irish point at the third attempt in February and is now racing for the same connections as the smart Tell Massini. She travelled well enough into contention, but began to toil at the top of the home straight and may well be more effective when faced with a stiffer test. (op 8-1 tchd 10-1)

Calico Rose went well for a long way on this hurdling/seasonal debut and should prove a deal sharper with the run under her belt. (op 33-1)

Rith Bob(IRE), well backed, was in trouble a long way out on this big drop back in trip and was later reported to have hung left. Official explanation: jockey said mare hung left-handed throughout. (op 7-2 tchd 5-2)

T/Plt: £41.70 to a £1 stake. Pool of £66,060.21 - 1,154.26 winning tickets. T/Qpdt: £13.10 to a £1 stake. Pool of £4,916.06 - 277.16 winning tickets TM

LINGFIELD (L-H)

Tuesday, November 9

OFFICIAL GOING: Chase course - soft (good to soft in places; 6.8); hurdle course - soft (heavy in places; 6.3); all-weather - standard

Wind: light, across Weather: raining

2289 MARSH GREEN MARES' NOVICES' HURDLE (8 hdls) 2m 110y

1:10 (1:10) (Class 4) 4-Y-O+ **£2,740** (£798; £399)

Form RPR

43-1 **1** **Sparky May**^{20} 1921 5-10-12 0... KeiranBurke$^{(5)}$ 122+
(Patrick Rodford) *hld up in midfield: hdwy to trck ldrs and nt clr run bnd bef 2 out: effrt to ld and stmbld 2 out: rdn clr and mstke last: styd on wl: rdn out* **9/2**^{2}

2 *5* **American Ladie**^{543} 4-10-10 0.................................... WayneHutchinson 108+
(Alan King) *t.k.h: trckd ldrs: effrt and ev ch 2 out: kpt on same pce between last 2* **7/1**^{3}

12-1 **3** *13* **Brixen (IRE)**^{16} 1994 6-11-3 0... LeightonAspell 103+
(Lucy Wadham) *j.rt: led tl 2 out: sn rdn and btn: wl hld whn j.rt last* **3/1**^{1}

33/3 **4** *¾* **The Bishops Baby (IRE)**^{20} 1914 7-10-3 0.................... MrTJCannon$^{(7)}$ 94
(Richard Rowe) *t.k.h: hld up in midfield: hdwy to chse ldrs after 3 out: mstke next: sn rdn and btn* **9/1**

0-5 **5** *½* **Salybia Bay**^{31} 1773 4-10-10 0... NickScholfield 93
(Andy Turnell) *chsd ldng pair: mstke 3rd: rdn and wknd 2 out: 5th and wl hld whn sltly hmpd last* **20/1**

6 **6** *12* **Galant Star (FR)**^{20} 1914 4-10-10 0..................................... JamieMoore 83
(Gary Moore) *hld up in midfield: hdwy bef 3 out: rdn and wknd bef 2 out* **8/1**

7 *1 ¾* **Free Falling**^{49} 4-10-10 0... WillKennedy 82
(Alastair Lidderdale) *chsd ldrs: j. slowly 3 out: sn rdn and struggling: wknd bef 2 out* **66/1**

0-02 **8** *5* **Blakeneys Pet (IRE)**^{16} 1994 4-10-5 100........................ TomO'Connor$^{(5)}$ 74
(John Berwick) *a towards rr: pushed along 4th: toiling 3 out: wl btn whn j.rt 2 out: t.o* **20/1**

323 **9** *7* **Clarach (IRE)**^{16} 1993 5-10-3 108..................................... MrTomDavid$^{(7)}$ 67
(Tim Vaughan) *hld up in rr: hdwy and wl in tch 3 out: wknd bef 2 out: t.o* **9/2**^{2}

0 **10** *¾* **Sworn Tigress (GER)**^{20} 1921 5-10-10 0....................(v[1]) AndrewTinkler 72
(George Baker) *w ldr: j.rt and mstke 2nd: ev ch bef 2 out: wknd qckly 2 out: wl btn whn mstke last: t.o* **16/1**

11 *28* **Old Dungarvan Oak (IRE)** 4-10-7 0........................ EamonDehdashti$^{(3)}$ 39
(Gary Moore) *racd in midfield: lost pl and dropped to rr 5th: rdn and lost tch next: wl t.o bef 2 out* **66/1**

006- **12** *nk* **Polly's Star**^{310} 3281 5-10-10 0.. AndrewThornton 38
(Gerry Enright) *a bhd: lost tch 5th: wl t.o after next* **250/1**

305/ **13** *39* **Golbelini**[598] 4639 5-10-10 0 WarrenMarston —
(Martin Keighley) *t.k.h: hld up in midfield: rdn and struggling bef 3 out: wl t.o bef 2 out* **25/1**

4m 13.5s (-0.60) **Going Correction** +0.10s/f (Yiel)
WFA 4 from 5yo+ 7lb **13** Ran SP% **117.6**
Speed ratings (Par 105): **105,102,96,96,95 90,89,87,83,83 70,70,51**
Tote Swingers: 1&2 £4.80, 1&3 £4.10, 2&3 £4.00 CSF £33.22 TOTE £9.90: £2.70, £1.30, £1.40; EX 25.70.
Owner Bill Muddyman **Bred** Ruxley Holdings Ltd **Trained** Ash, Somerset

FOCUS
18mm of rain fell in the 24 hours on the run up to the meeting but the planned early morning inspection was cancelled as the forecast overnight deluge failed to materialise. The first race was run in driving rain, though, and the jockeys reported the ground on the hurdle track to be heavy. Not much strength-in-depth in an ordinary mares' novice event and one in which the gallop was not surprisingly an ordinary one. The first two pulled clear and the level is set by the fourth and fifth.

NOTEBOOK
Sparky May had shown improved form to win on her hurdling debut, and she bettered that effort in these much more testing conditions under her penalty. She should prove equally at home over further and, given the manner of this victory, she looks the type to hold her own in slightly stronger company. (op 10-3 tchd 3-1)
American Ladie ◆, placed on the Flat in the French provinces last year, missed last season through injury, but this apparently well-regarded sort shaped with a good deal of promise on this racecourse debut. She jumped soundly, travelled strongly and, although held late on, showed more than enough to suggest a similar event at least can be found. (op 4-1)
Brixen(IRE) had more on her plate under her penalty, and she failed to build on that win in these much more testing conditions. A sounder surface and a right-handed track may suit better, and she is worth another chance in ordinary company. (op 4-1)
The Bishops Baby(IRE) was nibbled at in the market and again showed ability on this second fairly quick run after a lengthy absence. She may improve for longer distances once switched to run-of-the-mill handicaps and she should improve. (op 10-1 tchd 8-1)
Salybia Bay was far from disgraced but again underlined her vulnerability in this type of event. She may do better over hurdles, although it's worth bearing in mind she failed to win in 19 Flat starts for Richard Hannon. (op 22-1)
Galant Star(FR), who was placed on the Flat in France last year, was backed at big odds on this second hurdle start but she didn't look totally at home in these conditions and was well beaten. She will be worth another chance in due course. (op 40-1)

2290 BET PREMIER LEAGUE FOOTBALL - BETDAQ NOVICES' H'CAP CHASE (18 fncs) 3m
1:40 (1:40) (Class 5) (0-90,85) 4-Y-0+ **£2,797** (£821; £410; £205)

Form RPR
/U-B **1** **Miss Fleur**[6] 2146 7-11-7 **83** DannyCook(3) 92+
(Nick Mitchell) *a gng wl: led 1st tl 3rd: styd prom tl led again 13th: c clr after 3 out: rdn flat: kpt on* **11/2**
P-06 **2** *5* **Midnight Diamond (IRE)**[8] 2135 7-10-6 **72** (v1) MrTomDavid(7) 78
(Tim Vaughan) *led: j. slowly and hdd 1st: reminders bef next: chsd ldrs after: rdn along fr 7th: u.p and clr w wnr bef 15th: btn after 3 out: plugged on* **4/1**[1]
00-3 **3** *7* **Dromore Hill (IRE)**[27] 1820 6-11-12 **85** (p) JimmyMcCarthy 82
(Charlie Morlock) *w ldrs tl 4th and struggling 14th: chsd ldng pair bef 3 out: no imp and wl btn after* **9/2**[2]
0P5P **4** *18* **Delgany Gunner**[27] 1820 6-9-7 **59** oh1 (vt) NathanSweeney(7) 38
(Ben Pollock) *w ldrs tl led 3rd: hdd 13th: wknd wl bef 3 out* **4/1**[1]
6532 **5** *54* **Bollywood (IRE)**[16] 2001 7-11-9 **82** (t) LeightonAspell 7
(Alison Batchelor) *in tch in last pair: rdn and losing tch whn blnd bdly 10th: t.o fr 13th* **4/1**[1]
00-P **P** **Lots Of Fun (IRE)**[27] 1820 6-10-10 **72** (t) RichieMcLernon(3) —
(Jonjo O'Neill) *in tch in last pair: struggling whn blnd 12th: t.o after 14th tl p.u 3 out* **5/1**[3]

6m 33.1s (9.40) **Going Correction** +0.475s/f (Soft) **6** Ran SP% **110.2**
Speed ratings (Par 103): **103,101,99,93,75** —
Tote Swingers: 1&2 £5.60, 1&3 £5.60, 2&3 £1.70 CSF £26.36 TOTE £6.30: £3.20, £3.00; EX 29.20.
Owner Milcombe Racing **Bred** Mrs K J And D M Holmes **Trained** Piddletrenthide, Dorset

FOCUS
A very moderate handicap chase run at a fair gallop on ground the riders described as "pretty soft". The form is weak with the winner back to her 2009 form and the second to his mark.

NOTEBOOK
Miss Fleur had failed to get round on her last three starts, but she was proven over the trip, and in the conditions, and did enough (attracted support) after a fluent round of jumping to notch her first victory. This was a weak race, but she did the job in pleasing style and she may be capable of a little better. (op 8-1)
Midnight Diamond(IRE) wasn't always fluent and didn't look an easy ride with the first-time visor replacing cheekpieces back over fences, but he kept responding to pressure and, although he may not be one for skinny odds, showed enough to suggest a similarly weak event can be found for current connections. Official explanation: three-day ban: used whip with excessive frequency (Nov 23-25) (op 7-2)
Dromore Hill(IRE), who proved easy in the market, looks slow but he wasn't totally disgraced in the first-time cheekpieces. He'll be suited by an even stiffer test of stamina and is lightly raced enough to be open to a little improvement. (op 3-1 tchd 5-1)
Delgany Gunner's profile has a very shaky look to it and he was again well beaten after attracting a fair bit of market support. He'll have to fare a good deal better before he's of any short-term interest. (op 7-1)
Bollywood(IRE) came here on the back of a solid run on a sound surface, but he floundered in these softer conditions returned to fences. He'll be worth another chance back on quicker ground. (tchd 10-3 and 9-2)

2291 E B F "NATIONAL HUNT" NOVICES' HURDLE (QUALIFIER) (10 hdls) 2m 3f 110y
2:10 (2:12) (Class 4) 4-6-Y-0 **£2,740** (£798; £399)

Form RPR
1 **On Trend (IRE)**[219] 4-10-12 0 WarrenMarston 123+
(Nick Gifford) *w ldr tl led 3rd: rdn and hit 2 out: clr whn mstke last: eased towards fin* **14/1**
342- **2** *4 ½* **Raduis Bleu (FR)**[224] 4943 5-10-12 114 WayneHutchinson 116+
(Alan King) *hld up in tch: hdwy after 7th: chsd ldr bef 2 out: hit 2 out: styd on same pce between last 2* **13/8**[1]
2- **3** *15* **Filbert (IRE)**[214] 5121 4-10-12 0 TomO'Brien 100
(Philip Hobbs) *in tch: chsd ldrs 3 out: 3rd and btn 2 out: sn wknd* **3/1**[2]
55- **4** *8* **Current Climate (IRE)**[218] 5057 6-10-12 0 JamieMoore 92
(Richard Rowe) *in tch in midfield: rdn and wknd bef 2 out: wl btn between last 2* **50/1**
020- **5** *1* **Beau Lake (IRE)**[218] 5055 6-10-5 106 MrTJCannon(7) 91
(Suzy Smith) *in tch on outer: j. slowly 1st: chsd ldrs 3 out: rdn and wknd bef next* **14/1**
6 *4 ½* **Croan Rock (IRE)**[219] 5-10-12 0 TomScudamore 88
(Ian Williams) *w ldrs tl wknd qckly bef 2 out* **6/1**[3]
34- **7** *39* **Point West (IRE)**[243] 4531 6-10-9 0 DannyCook(3) 48
(Nick Mitchell) *led tl 3rd: stl cl up whn slipped on landing 3 out: sn rdn and dropped out: t.o bef next* **12/1**
00 **8** *38* **Bemused (IRE)**[12] 2056 5-10-12 0 AndrewThornton 10
(Simon Earle) *a bhd: in tch: rdn and lost tch 7th: wl t.o fr next* **100/1**
P **Norwich Well (IRE)**[198] 5-10-12 0 LeightonAspell —
(Oliver Sherwood) *chsd ldrs: mstke 6th and 7th: rdn and lost tch qckly bef 3 out: wl t.o whn p.u 2 out* **16/1**
2 **P** **Border Station (IRE)**[22] 1906 4-10-12 0 TimmyMurphy —
(Alison Batchelor) *in tch: mstke 5th and 6th: lost tch qckly next: t.o and p.u 3 out* **12/1**

5m 17.4s (10.70) **Going Correction** +0.45s/f (Soft)
WFA 4 from 5yo+ 7lb **10** Ran SP% **114.9**
Speed ratings: **96,94,88,85,84 82,67,52,—,—**
Tote Swingers: 1&2 £5.60, 1&3 £8.60, 2&3 £2.30 CSF £37.70 TOTE £11.80: £4.20, £1.40, £1.30; EX 59.70.
Owner Ham Manor Farms Ltd **Bred** Jonathan Murphy **Trained** Findon, W Sussex

FOCUS
A handful of interesting newcomers to the hurdling ranks and, although the pace was steady, the first two pulled clear in the straight. The third is rated close to his bumper mark.

NOTEBOOK
On Trend(IRE) ◆, an Irish point winner, was allowed an easy time of it in front, but he handled the testing ground well and created a favourable impression on this hurdles debut, despite fluffing the last two flights on this first run for new connections. He will stay further and, although his future lies over fences, he's the type to progress and win again over hurdles. (op 12-1)
Raduis Bleu(FR) was well supported and ran another solid race on this return to hurdles and first run since March. He looks the best guide to the worth of this form, and he's more than capable of picking up a race away from the more progressive types around this trip over hurdles or fences. (tchd 15-8)
Filbert(IRE) had shown ability at an ordinary level in a good-ground bumper on his debut in April, and he ran well for a long way before getting tired in these much more testing conditions on this hurdle debut. He should be better for this experience and remains capable of picking up a similar event back on better ground. (tchd 11-4 and 10-3 in a place)
Current Climate(IRE) wasn't totally disgraced on this hurdles debut, and left the impression that he may be capable of a little better once qualified for a handicap mark granted a sufficient test of stamina. (tchd 66-1)
Beau Lake(IRE)'s form has a patchy look to it, and he had his limitations firmly exposed back in this grade in the softest ground he's encountered to date. Ordinary handicaps should be the way forward with him but his previous run in that grade confirms he's not one to be taking too short a price about. (tchd 16-1)
Croan Rock(IRE), a £32,000 first foal of a mare from the family of very useful staying chaser Nil Desperandum, was nibbled at in the market on this hurdles debut and first run since April, but after showing up well to a point, seemed to get very tired in the conditions. He should be able to better this bare form in due course. (op 8-1)

2292 BETDAQ THE BETTING EXCHANGE H'CAP CHASE (13 fncs 1 omitted) 2m 4f 110y
2:40 (2:41) (Class 5) (0-90,90) 4-Y-0+ **£2,797** (£821; £410; £205)

Form RPR
4150 **1** **Ponchatrain (IRE)**[34] 1735 10-11-12 **90** (v1) WarrenMarston 101
(Martin Keighley) *chsd ldr tl 9th: clr 3 out: reduced ld and j.rt last 3: hung rt u.p flat: kpt on towards fin* **5/1**[3]
/0-F **2** *1* **Mr Bond (IRE)**[16] 1995 7-11-9 **87** NickScholfield 97
(Andy Turnell) *hld up towards rr: mstke 5th: hdwy bef next: chsd clr ldr sn after 3 out: clsd bef next: no imp 2 out tl kpt on u.p flat: pressed wnr fnl 150yds: hld towards fin* **5/1**[3]
00U/ **3** *30* **Oponce (FR)**[854] 865 8-11-8 **86** WillKennedy 71
(Noel Chance) *in tch towards rr: lost tch w ldrs 10th: wnt modest 3rd 3 out: no imp* **11/1**
1PP5 **4** *15* **Wiesenfurst (GER)**[16] 1991 6-11-4 **87** TomO'Connor(5) 52
(John Berwick) *chsd ldrs: pushed along 8th: rdn 10th 3rd and wl btn after 3 out: t.o fr 3 out* **6/1**
265U **5** *9* **Bold Pioneer (USA)**[23] 1883 7-10-2 **71** GemmaGracey-Davison(5) 27
(Zoe Davison) *led: hdd 9th: rdn after 10th: lost 2nd and wknd sn after 3 out: 5th and wl btn bef 2 out: t.o* **9/2**[2]
0P-F **6** *10* **Bobby Donald (IRE)**[6] 2152 8-11-8 **86** SeanQuinlan 32
(Richard Phillips) *a in rr: mstke and struggling 9th: wl t.o wl bef 3 out* **4/1**[1]
11-P **7** *7* **Brushford (IRE)**[12] 2048 6-11-10 **88** LeightonAspell 27
(Chris Gordon) *chsd ldrs tl rdn and losing pl 9th: t.o wl bef 3 out* **4/1**[1]

5m 30.1s (11.90) **Going Correction** +0.675s/f (Soft) **7** Ran SP% **114.1**
Speed ratings (Par 103): **104,103,92,86,83 79,76**
Tote Swingers: 1&2 £2.70, 1&3 £5.30, 2&3 £5.00 CSF £29.78 CT £260.93 TOTE £5.20: £2.70, £3.40; EX 32.90.
Owner The League Of Gentlemen **Bred** Lady Melissa Brooke **Trained** Condicote, Gloucs

FOCUS
A moderate handicap chase, but one run at a fair gallop in the worsening conditions. The first two pulled clear from some way out, with the winner rated to his best in a weak handicap.

NOTEBOOK
Ponchatrain(IRE) hadn't been at his best in cheekpieces on good ground on his last two starts, but returned to something like his best - travelling strongly and jumping soundly - back in testing ground in the first-time visor. He has now passed the post in front in four of his last eight starts over fences and, given he appeared to idle late on, he may be capable of a little better. (op 9-2)
Mr Bond(IRE) turned in easily his best effort back up in trip and in these much more testing conditions. There is room for plenty of improvement in the fencing department, but he pulled clear of the remainder and looks sure to pick up a similarly moderate event when his jumping holds up. (op 4-1 tchd 11-2)
Oponce(FR) was soundly beaten, but he is entitled to be all the better for this first run in over two years. The step up to 3m could suit, he is in good hands and wouldn't be one to write off just yet. (op 6-1)
Wiesenfurst(GER) attracted a bit of market support, but turned in a laboured effort back in testing ground and was again a long way below the level he showed when scoring at Fontwell in May in first-time cheekpieces (no headgear again). He has plenty to prove at present. (op 8-1)
Bold Pioneer(USA), an inconsistent performer whose sole win came over hurdles three years ago, wasn't suited by the return to this trip in these testing conditions, but his overall profile means he remains one to tread carefully with. (op 7-1)
Bobby Donald(IRE), who was proven in testing ground, completed this time but was soundly beaten and remains best watched at present. (op 5-1)

Brushford(IRE), who was reportedly never travelling when well beaten on his reappearance last month, attracted support but fared no better this time. He is best watched at present. (tchd 7-2)

2293 T FROST (BAWTRY) RACING SADDLERS H'CAP CHASE (11 fncs 1 omitted) 2m

3:10 (3:10) (Class 3) (0-125,123) 4-Y-0+ £5,854 (£1,719; £859; £429)

Form RPR

650- 1 **Noble Crusader (USA)**[218] 5046 7-11-9 120.............(p) TomScudamore 129
(Richard Lee) *in tch tl dropped to last and rdn 6th: drvn after next: rallied to chse ldng pair bef 3 out: chsd ldr bef 2 out: kpt on u.p to ld towards fin* 11/2

140 2 ½ **King Ozzy (IRE)**[31] 1766 6-11-4 115.............................(t) WarrenMarston 125+
(Martin Keighley) *chsd ldr: wnt 2nd and clsd bypassing 4th: led 9th: clr bef next: rdn bef last: hrd drvn flat: hdd and no ex towards fin* 11/2

3-15 3 6 **Circus Of Dreams**[18] 1952 7-11-11 122........................(v) LeightonAspell 126
(Oliver Sherwood) *chsd ldr tl bypassing 4th: ev ch and mstke 10th: rdn and outpcd bef next: lost 2nd after 3 out: plugged on same pce after* 11/4[1]

-253 4 19 **Prince Des Marais (FR)**[157] 636 7-11-12 123........... AndrewThornton 106
(Caroline Bailey) *hld up in tch: mstke 2nd and 7th: struggling wl bef 3 out: wl btn whn j.lft 2 out: wnt modest 4th flat* 4/1[2]

5325 5 2¾ **Marodima (FR)**[17] 1975 7-11-12 123..................................(p) DarylJacob 103
(Jamie Snowden) *taken down early: led: clr tl bypassing 4th: hdd 9th: wknd wl bef next* 4/1[2]

U1F- 6 8 **Captain Tidds (IRE)**[228] 4870 9-11-12 123......................... SeanQuinlan 99
(Richard Phillips) *hld up in rr: j.big 1st: hdwy to trck ldrs 7th: rdn and wknd bef 3 out: wl btn whn j.lft 2 out* 5/1[3]

4m 19.0s (11.20) **Going Correction** +0.875s/f (Soft) 6 Ran SP% 114.1
Speed ratings (Par 107): **107,106,103,94,92 88**
Tote Swingers: 1&2 £6.40, 1&3 £3.80, 2&3 £4.20 CSF £34.54 TOTE £5.60: £4.30, £4.50; EX 36.30.
Owner Nicola Shields Peter Phillips Will Roseff **Bred** Moyglare Stud Farm Ltd **Trained** Byton, H'fords

FOCUS
A fair handicap in which the gallop was a reasonable one. The third is the best guide to the level.

NOTEBOOK
Noble Crusader(USA) had been disappointing over further since winning over this trip at Ludlow in December but he ran as well as he ever has done, despite losing his place around halfway, and showed a good attitude with the cheekpieces refitted to score on this first run since April. He goes well in soft ground and is worth another try over a bit further, but it remains to be seen whether this will be built on next time. (op 6-1 tchd 13-2)
King Ozzy(IRE), returned to fences and with the tongue-tie refitted, put a couple of disappointing runs behind him and he may be a bit better than the bare result suggests as he was up with the decent gallop throughout. His best recent form has been with give in the ground, and he should be able to pick up a similar event if this can be reproduced. (op 5-1 tchd 6-1)
Circus Of Dreams hadn't been at his best in the first-time blinkers at Fakenham after a break on his previous start, but fared much better with his usual visor refitted on this return to 2m. He may be best when able to dominate, but he has little margin for error from his current mark. (op 7-2)
Prince Des Marais(FR), a dual winner on a sound surface in April, wasn't foot-perfect and was a fair way below that level in this much softer ground after this five-month break. He'll be of more interest returned to a sound surface, but he too looks high enough in the weights at present. (tchd 9-2)
Marodima(FR), with the cheekpieces again fitted, has form in testing conditions, but he was again a fair way below his best after setting a decent gallop. He figures on a reasonable mark but will have to show a fair bit more before he's a solid betting proposition. (op 5-1)
Captain Tidds(IRE), a 3m heavy ground winner early this year, had conditions to suit but didn't jump with much fluency and was well beaten on this first run since falling in March. He'll be suited by the return to further and will be worth another chance with this run behind him. (op 4-1)

2294 TRY BETDAQ FOR AN EXCHANGE COPTHORNE H'CAP HURDLE (8 hdls) 2m 110y

3:40 (3:40) (Class 4) (0-110,109) 3-Y-0+ £2,602 (£764; £382; £190)

Form RPR

1-U2 1 **Carrig An Uisce (IRE)**[9] 2114 9-10-12 95....................(p) AndrewTinkler 99+
(Anna Brooks) *in tch: hdwy to chse ldrs 3 out: clr in ldng trio bef next: led 2 out: drvn between last 2: hrd pressed fnl 100yds: all out* 9/2[2]

4661 2 hd **Just Beware**[8] 2131 8-10-5 93 7ex..............(p) GemmaGracey-Davison[(5)] 97+
(Zoe Davison) *in tch: hdwy and gd jump to ld 3 out: c towards centre st: hdd 2 out: hung lft u.p between last 2: pressing wnr whn mstke last: ev ch fnl 100yds: no ex last strides* 9/2[2]

0U-3 3 11 **Just One Thing (IRE)**[194] 58 5-11-3 107.................... AdamWedge[(7)] 102+
(Evan Williams) *t.k.h: chsd ldrs tl led after 2nd: hdd 3 out: clr in ldng trio bef next: struggling whn blnd 2 out: wknd bef last* 16/1

62-5 4 2¾ **Kinsya**[18] 1953 7-11-2 99.. ColinBolger 87
(Mark H Tompkins) *hld up in tch in last trio: rdn and btn after 3 out: 6th and wl btn whn j.rt 2 out: wnt modest 4th after last* 8/1[3]

23 5 9 **Denton Ryal**[23] 1882 3-10-4 103.. JamieGoldstein 68
(Sheena West) *t.k.h: hld up in rr: short-lived effrt after 3 out: no hdwy and wl btn next* 9/2[2]

23-2 6 14 **Sagredo (USA)**[37] 1705 6-11-9 109..........................(t) RichieMcLernon[(3)] 74
(Jonjo O'Neill) *in tch in midfield: chsd ldng trio and rdn after 3 out: wknd bef next: eased after last* 7/2[1]

23- 7 34 **Mister Matt (IRE)**[367] 2123 7-11-7 104................................ WillKennedy 35
(Bob Buckler) *t.k.h: chsd ldr tl after 2nd: styd chsng ldrs tl wknd qckly 3 out: t.o next* 12/1

3FU 8 20 **Al Amaan**[10] 2081 5-11-12 109.. JamieMoore 20
(Gary Moore) *a in rr: mstke 2nd: lost tch qckly sn after 3 out: t.o next* 20/1

3-60 P **Watergate (IRE)**[127] 914 4-11-0 97................................... LeightonAspell —
(Richard Rowe) *led tl after 2nd: pressed ldr after tl lost pl rapidly sn after 3 out: t.o whn p.u next* 11/1

4m 25.3s (11.20) **Going Correction** +0.80s/f (Soft)
WFA 3 from 4yo 15lb 4 from 5yo+ 7lb 9 Ran SP% 114.5
Speed ratings (Par 105): **105,104,99,98,94 87,71,62,—**
Tote Swingers: 1&2 £4.20, 1&3 £18.20, 2&3 £17.00 CSF £25.27 CT £294.97 TOTE £4.80: £1.10, £2.60, £3.50; EX 27.60.
Owner Robinsons Blick & Brooks **Bred** Miss Margaret Flynn **Trained** Alderton, Northants

FOCUS
A modest handicap run at an ordinary gallop and one in which the two that had something in hand of their current marks pulled clear in the closing stages. The form is easy to rate around the first three.

NOTEBOOK
Carrig An Uisce(IRE), who chased home an in-form sort at Huntingdon last time and who will be 5lb higher in future, showed a good attitude in first-time cheekpieces to confirm himself fully effective in testing ground. He had a hard race and life will obviously be tougher in future, but he seems to be getting his act together and it may be unwise to rule out further progress. (op 5-1)
Just Beware came here on the back of an improved effort to break a losing run on good ground at Plumpton and was narrowly denied after showing battling qualities under her penalty. She'll be 4lb higher in future handicaps and, while capable of winning again if this can be reproduced, she may not forget this race in a hurry. (op 11-2)
Just One Thing(IRE) got tired in the closing stages after fluffing the penultimate flight, but had run creditably for a long way on this handicap debut after a break against a couple of rivals that were in front of their current handicap marks. Less testing ground may suit better and he's capable of picking up an ordinary race. (op 12-1 tchd 18-1)
Kinsya is unexposed over hurdles but despie shaping as though a step up in distance would suit, he has flattered to deceive in the past and it's worth remembering he hasn't won since scoring on the Flat just over three years ago. He remains one to tread carefully with. (tchd 9-1)
Denton Ryal had shaped well on both previous starts on a sound surface over hurdles, but floundered on this handicap debut in these much more testing conditions. She'll be worth another chance back on better ground. (op 11-2)
Sagredo(USA) had run creditably in heavy ground over hurdles early last month, but failed by a long chalk to reproduce that effort returned to handicap company in the first-time tongue-tie. His yard has been in good form but he may not be entirely straightforward. (tchd 3-1)

2295 BURSTOW INTERMEDIATE OPEN NATIONAL HUNT FLAT RACE 2m

4:10 (4:10) (Class 5) 4-6-Y-O £1,712 (£499; £249)

Form RPR

1 **Daymar Bay (IRE)** 4-10-8 0................................ StephenO'Donovan[(10)] 107+
(Emma Lavelle) *hld up in tch in midfield: hdwy to trck ldr gng wl over 4f out: led jst over 2f out: pushed clr wl over 1f out: pushed out fnl f: easily* 5/1[3]

30- 2 7 **Management (IRE)**[248] 4429 4-11-4 0....................... WayneHutchinson 96+
(Alan King) *chsd ldrs: rdn over 4f out: drvn to ld over 2f out: sn hdd: nt pce of wnr wl over 1f out: styd on same pce after* 15/8[1]

00- 3 5 **Joker Choker (IRE)**[204] 5283 5-11-4 0........................ AndrewTinkler 91
(Nicky Henderson) *t.k.h: hld up in tch in rr: hdwy 5f out: chsd ldrs over 2f out: outpcd and rn green bnd ent fnl 2f: 3rd and wl hld fr over 1f out* 11/2

3 4 nk **Tech Zinne**[20] 1920 4-10-11 0...................................... DavidEngland 83
(George Baker) *w ldr tl led 5f out: rdn and hdd over 2f out: wknd wl over 1f out* 10/3[2]

0 5 3½ **Ellie Wiggins**[184] 237 4-10-4 0................................ NathanSweeney[(7)] 79
(Bob Buckler) *t.k.h: chsd ldrs: rdn and outpcd over 3f out: plugged on same pce and no threat to ldrs fnl 3f* 66/1

0 6 1¼ **Oscar Sierra (IRE)**[16] 1989 4-10-11 0........................ MrTomDavid[(7)] 85
(Tim Vaughan) *in tch: chsd ldrs and rdn ent fnl 3f: wknd over 2f out* 25/1

00- 7 nk **Polarity**[212] 5158 4-10-11 0.. JamieMoore 78
(James Bethell) *in tch tl rdn and wknd over 3f out* 33/1

6 8 3½ **Subtle Approach (IRE)**[33] 1749 5-11-4 0........................ NickScholfield 81
(Emma Baker) *in tch: pushed along 1/2-way: wknd u.p 4f out* 33/1

0-0 9 10 **Late Red**[181] 222 5-11-4 0.. MattieBatchelor 71
(Jamie Poulton) *t.k.h: led tl 5f out: rdn and wknd 4f out: sn bhd* 66/1

10 ¾ **Bit Of A Clown (IRE)** 4-11-4 0.. AndrewThornton 70
(Caroline Bailey) *a bhd: lost tch over 4f out* 22/1

P **Lord Arion (IRE)** 5-11-4 0.. WillKennedy —
(Jeremy Scott) *in tch in last trio tl lost action and p.u over 5f out: dismntd: fatally injured* 17/2

3m 30.6s (-7.40) **Going Correction** -0.425s/f (Stan) 11 Ran SP% 117.5
Speed ratings: **101,97,95,94,93 92,92,90,85,85 —**
Tote Swingers: 1&2 £3.00, 2&3 £4.70. Totesuper7: Win: Not won. Place: Not won. CSF £13.92 TOTE £5.90: £1.40, £1.20, £1.90; EX 26.50.
Owner The Second Fox Inn Syndicate **Bred** Barry Noonan **Trained** Wildhern, Hants

FOCUS
A steadily run bumper. Those with previous experience were nothing out of the ordinary but the winner looks a useful prospect.

NOTEBOOK
Daymar Bay(IRE) ◆, who cost 20,000 euros last year and who is a half-brother to a 2m hurdle winner, created a very favourable impression despite his apparent greenness, on this racecourse debut when scoring with plenty in hand. He has physical scope, is open to stacks of improvement and can win again in this grade before switching to hurdles. (op 11-2 tchd 6-1)
Management(IRE) failed to reproduce the bit of debut promise when last seen in February, but was well supported and ran creditably against one that could hold hold his own in stronger company on this reappearance and Polytrack debut. He should be able to pick up an uncompetitive race in due course. (op 9-4 tchd 7-4)
Joker Choker(IRE) had been soundly beaten in ordinary company in spring but shaped better on this reappearance, and first run for a yard that has a tremendous record in this type of event. He travelled strongly for a long way and he should be able to pick up an ordinary event over hurdles. (op 9-2)
Tech Zinne was well supported but, although enjoying the run of the race, failed to build on the form she showed at Fontwell on her debut. She's likely to remain vulnerable in this type of event. (tchd 11-4 and 7-2)
Ellie Wiggins wasn't totally disgraced on this first run since May, but she is going to have to raise her game by some way to make her of any short-term interest in bumper company. (op 100-1)
Oscar Sierra(IRE) bettered the form of his racecourse debut run but will have to show a fair bit more before he's worth a bet. (tchd 28-1)
T/Plt: £378.10 to a £1 stake. Pool of £60,705.38 - 117.20 winning tickets. T/Qpdt: £65.70 to a £1 stake. Pool of £5,423.88 - 61.00 winning tickets. SP

1641 SEDGEFIELD (L-H)

Tuesday, November 9

OFFICIAL GOING: Good to soft (good in places on straight, soft in places in back straight) changing to soft after race 4 (2.30)

Wind: Light into Weather: cold, intermittent heavy showers

2296 EUROPEAN BREEDERS' FUND "NATIONAL HUNT" NOVICES' HURDLE (QUALIFIER) (8 hdls) 2m 1f

1:00 (1:00) (Class 4) 4-6-Y-O £2,471 (£725; £362; £181)

Form RPR

1020 1 **Pure Faith (IRE)**[17] 1972 6-11-8 122.................................... BrianHughes 126+
(Peter Bowen) *mde all: clr whn nt fluent last: kpt on wl* 9/2[3]

435- 2 8 **Bridlingtonbygones (IRE)**[196] 35 5-10-12 0.................. GrahamLee 108
(Karen McLintock) *trckd ldrs in 3rd: racd keenly: chsd wnr bef 2 out: kpt on same pce: regained 2nd nr fin* 8/1

3-4 3 nk **Ebony River (IRE)**[32] 1757 4-10-12 0............................... JasonMaguire 108
(Donald McCain) *midfield: rdn and outpcd bef 3 out: hdwy bef 2 out: chsd wnr after 2 out: no imp run-in: lost 2nd nr fin* 9/1

5F2/ 4 hd **Carndonagh (IRE)**[619] 4192 6-10-12 0............................ DougieCostello 107
(Malcolm Jefferson) *trckd wnr: rdn after 3 out: kpt on one pce* 16/1

3-1 5 2 **Catspan (FR)**[18] 1955 4-10-12 0................................... DominicElsworth 108+
(Charles Egerton) *trckd ldrs: rdn and outpcd 3 out: keeping on to dispute 3rd whn mstke 2 out: one pce after* 4/1[2]

1-23 **6** *23* **Dr Flynn (IRE)**[32] 1764 5-10-12 0 WilsonRenwick 88+
(Howard Johnson) *trckd ldrs: wnt lft 2nd: rdn and lost pl after 4 out* **15/2**

7 *5* **Artic Night (FR)** 4-10-9 0 FearghalDavis(3) 80
(Nicky Richards) *hld up: rdn 4 out: sn wknd* **33/1**

/4-1 **8** *2 1/2* **Seam Of Diamonds**[159] 602 5-10-5 0 BrianHarding 71
(Martin Todhunter) *hld up: brief hdwy after 4th: n.d* **33/1**

045- **9** *63* **Hidden In Time**[229] 4839 5-10-12 0 JamesReveley 21
(Keith Reveley) *hld up: rdn after 4th: sn t.o* **50/1**

20-4 **P** **Eagle Owl (IRE)**[11] 2075 4-10-12 0 RichieMcGrath —
(Tim Easterby) *in tch: nt fluent 4 out and sn lost pl: wl bhd whn p.u bef last* **3/1**[1]

00- **P** **Tommy Gun**[204] 5277 4-10-12 0 (t) MichaelMcAlister —
(Maurice Barnes) *hld up: rdn 4th: sn t.o: p.u bef 2 out* **250/1**

4-04 **U** **Shooting Times**[39] 1664 5-10-7 0 JamesHalliday(5) —
(Andrew Parker) *midfield: uns rdr 1st* **33/1**

4m 14.9s (8.00) **Going Correction** +0.425s/f (Soft)
WFA 4 from 5yo+ 7lb **12 Ran SP% 113.1**
Speed ratings: **98,94,94,94,93 82,79,78,49,— —,—**
Tote Swingers: 1&2 £6.30, 1&3 £5.50, 2&3 £10.60 CSF £36.91 TOTE £3.90: £1.40, £3.00, £2.60; EX 38.60.
Owner P Bowling,S Scott,R Harvey & K Bowen **Bred** P J Carmody **Trained** Little Newcastle, Pembrokes

FOCUS
A bright, breezy day and the ground, after 6mm of overnight rain, rode on the soft side of good. Quite an interesting novices' hurdle run at a sound pace and the first two are rated around previous form.

NOTEBOOK
Pure Faith(IRE), a winner three times over hurdles in the summer, had finished runner-up on his chasing debut at Southwell in August. He was found to have scoped badly after finishing well beaten in a handicap hurdle at Stratford two weeks earlier. Rated 122, he made every yard and stayed on in very willing fashion. The plan is to go back over fences next May. (op 5-1 tchd 11-2)
Bridlingtonbygones(IRE), who took a bumper at Musselburgh on his debut a year ago, was making his hurdling debut on his first start since April. He stuck on to claim second spot near the line and looks sure to be found an opening. (op 7-1 tchd 9-1)
Ebony River(IRE), too keen when well beaten on his first try over hurdles at Carlisle last month, settled better and stayed on from off the pace to chase the leaders two out. He can progress further. (op 7-1 tchd 13-2)
Carndonagh(IRE), absent since finishing runner-up at Doncaster in February 2009, made a highly satisfactory return and will be suited by a return to 2m4f. (op 14-1 tchd 12-1)
Catspan(FR), who took an ordinary bumper at Fakenham, was starting to struggle when he made a mess of the second-last. (op 5-1 tchd 11-2)
Dr Flynn(IRE), who showed fair form in three bumpers, jumped erratically and was beaten off three out. (op 9-1 tchd 7-1)
Artic Night(FR), who cost £40,000, never really figured but is quite well regarded and he ought to be capable of better. (tchd 28-1)
Eagle Owl(IRE), fourth on his hurdling debut at Wetherby, didn't jump well and was struggling to get into contention at the halfway mark. He stopped to nothing three out was was eventually pulled up. This was simply too bad to be true. Official explanation: jockey said gelding never travelled (op 10-3 tchd 4-1)

2297 JOHN WADE RECYCLING NOVICES' HURDLE (QUALIFIER) (10 hdls) 2m 4f
1:30 (1:30) (Class 4) 4-Y-O+ **£2,471** (£725; £362; £181)

Form RPR

130- **1** **Carpincho (FR)**[237] 4676 6-10-12 0 JasonMaguire 125+
(Sarah Humphrey) *mde all: racd keenly: clr after 3 out: easily* **2/9**[1]

0 **2** *46* **Kalulushi (IRE)**[139] 832 5-10-12 0 AdrianLane 76
(Donald McCain) *trckd ldrs: outpcd after 4 out: kpt on to take distant 2nd after 2 out* **18/1**

0 **3** *1 1/4* **Eliades Run (IRE)**[16] 1988 4-10-12 0 GrahamLee 74
(Ferdy Murphy) *nt fluent in rr: bhd tl hdwy after 3 out: wnt 3rd after last: n.d* **33/1**

60-4 **4** *9* **Ballet D'Anges (FR)**[37] 1702 4-10-5 0 AlexanderVoy(7) 66
(Lucy Normile) *midfield: rdn after 4 out and lost tch: tk distant 4th after 2 out* **16/1**[3]

5 *2 3/4* **Seminal Moment**[339] 4-10-5 0 CampbellGillies 57
(William Amos) *hld up: outpcd after 4 out: nvr a factor* **40/1**

6 *1* **Bravello (IRE)** 5-10-12 0 BrianHughes 63+
(Howard Johnson) *trckd wnr in 2nd: outpcd 3 out: stl remote 2nd 2 out: wknd qckly bef last* **10/1**[2]

00- **7** *2* **Steadys Breeze**[244] 4515 6-10-2 0 HarryHaynes(3) 54
(R MacDonald) *midfield: rdn and wknd after 4 out* **66/1**

8 *47* **Farmer Henry** 6-10-12 0 TomMessenger 19
(Sandy Forster) *hld up: a bhd* **66/1**

0- **F** **Twice Lucky**[233] 4757 6-10-7 0 ShaneByrne(5) —
(Sue Smith) *trckd ldrs: wknd after 4 out: bhd whn fell 2 out* **40/1**

U **Rock Relief (IRE)**[133] 4-10-7 0 MissLHorner(5) —
(Chris Grant) *midfield: mstke and uns rdr 1st* **20/1**

0/0- **P** **Forrest Lemons**[538] 385 6-10-12 0 JamesReveley —
(Andrew Parker) *hld up: nt fluent 5th: sn lost pl: t.o whn p.u after 4 out* **80/1**

0 **P** **Last Chorus**[19] 1934 4-10-5 0 PaddyAspell —
(Tracy Waggott) *hld up: t.o after 3rd: p.u after 5th* **150/1**

5m 13.6s (20.90) **Going Correction** +0.425s/f (Soft)
WFA 4 from 5yo+ 8lb **12 Ran SP% 119.5**
Speed ratings (Par 105): **75,56,56,52,51 51,50,31,—,— —,—**
Tote Swingers: 1&2 £3.10, 1&3 £3.90, 2&3 £11.50 CSF £5.57 TOTE £1.20: £1.02, £3.50, £3.90; EX 7.30.
Owner W D Glover & P Chapman **Bred** Patrice Perraud **Trained** West Wratting, Cambs

FOCUS
A one-sided novices' hurdle, with plenty of dead wood, run at a very steady pace and the winner's only problem was the loose horse. He is rated in line with his bumper form for now.

NOTEBOOK
Carpincho(FR), who won on his only start in Irish points, was a very useful bumper horse and took his chance in the Cheltenham Festival bumper. He looked in really good trim on his first start since and, making every yard, was out on his own from three out. He is a naturally keen sort and will need careful handling, but looks potentially a very useful recruit who will come into his own over fences next season. (op 4-9)
Kalulushi(IRE), another Irish point winner, had finished last on his sole start in bumper company on his first start for this stable at Worcester in June. He tried to keep tabs on the two leaders and in the end did enough to secure a remote second spot. He looks to just stay. (op 11-1 tchd 25-1)
Eliades Run(IRE), tailed off behind Cue Card at Aintree on his debut, still looks very inexperienced. Struggling with a circuit to go, he stayed on to capture third spot and should improve again. He looks to have been blessed with a lot more stamina than speed.
Ballet D'Anges(FR), a well-beaten fourth at Kelso on his first try over hurdles, was another struggling setting out on to the final circuit.

Bravello(IRE) kept tabs on the winner and was clear second until stopping to nothing between the last two flights. (op 8-1)

2298 COLLINS SEAFOODS H'CAP CHASE (16 fncs) 2m 4f
2:00 (2:00) (Class 4) (0-110,110) 4-Y-O+ **£3,041** (£898; £449; £224; £112)

Form RPR

56-6 **1** **Tyrone House (IRE)**[32] 1759 6-11-7 **105** BrianHughes 115+
(John Wade) *in tch: rdn and outpcd bef 3 out: hdwy to chse ldrs 2 out: lft 2nd last: kpt on wl to ld fnl 75yds* **3/1**[1]

6-10 **2** *2 1/4* **Baltic Pathfinder (IRE)**[159] 608 6-11-3 **106** ShaneByrne(5) 113
(Sue Smith) *prom: led 11th: rdn whn hdd 3 out: regained ld bef last: hdd fnl 75yds: no ex* **11/2**[3]

3-54 **3** *14* **Marley Roca (IRE)**[17] 1970 6-11-12 **110** DominicElsworth 108+
(Paul Webber) *hld up: hdwy to trck ldrs 12th: rdn 3 out: hld in 4th whn lft 3rd and sltly hmpd last* **6/1**

3UF- **4** *36* **Lahib The Fifth (IRE)**[275] 3921 10-11-0 **101** FearghalDavis(3) 63
(Nicky Richards) *midfield: rdn and outpcd 12th: lft distant 4th last* **18/1**

0600 **5** *27* **Toulouse Express (IRE)**[37] 1697 11-11-3 **101** (v) KennyJohnson 39
(Robert Johnson) *led: hdd 10th: sn wknd* **16/1**

42/P **P** **Julius Caesar**[32] 1763 10-11-9 **107** RichieMcGrath —
(Ferdy Murphy) *midfield: wknd after 4 out: bhd whn p.u and dismntd run-in* **16/1**

34P- **U** **Le Vert Galant (FR)**[329] 2893 7-11-6 **104** GrahamLee —
(Ferdy Murphy) *hld up: j.rt: blnd and uns rdr 10th* **8/1**

16/6 **P** **Banoge (IRE)**[32] 1762 8-11-9 **107** WilsonRenwick —
(Rose Dobbin) *midfield: rdn 4 out: hld in 5th whn p.u bef last* **5/1**[2]

F **Arctic Mick (IRE)**[276] 3907 9-10-5 **89** AELynch 90
(Michael O'Hare, Ire) *trckd ldrs: wnt 2nd after 10th: led 3 out: rdn and hdd appr last: 1 l down and hld whn fell last* **11/2**[3]

5m 8.90s (5.90) **Going Correction** +0.425s/f (Soft) **9 Ran SP% 114.9**
Speed ratings (Par 105): **105,104,98,84,73 —,—,—,—**
Tote Swingers: 1&2 £4.30, 1&3 £2.60, 2&3 £6.60 CSF £20.26 CT £92.30 TOTE £5.30: £1.60, £2.20, £2.10; EX 25.70.
Owner John Wade **Bred** Michael Martin Sheehan **Trained** Mordon, Co Durham

FOCUS
A modest handicap chase run at a sound pace and plenty of incidents. The runner-up is rated to his mark although the race could rate a little higher.

NOTEBOOK
Tyrone House(IRE), from a stable enjoying a purple patch with their chasers, was a dual Irish point winner in the past. He showed little over hurdles and, well beaten on his first try over fences at Carlisle, made his handicap debut from his hurdle race mark of 105. Well backed, he kept tabs on the two leaders and, left 3l second at the last, stayed on much the better up the final hill. He will be even better suited by 3m and should make further progress. (op 4-1)
Baltic Pathfinder(IRE), 7lb higher than when opening his account over fences at Hexham in May, ran badly next time and was back after a five-month break. He regained the lead going to the last, but was worn down up the final hill. (tchd 5-1 and 6-1)
Marley Roca(IRE), 9lb below his hurdles mark, was ridden from off the pace on just his third chase start. He was only keeping on at the one pace when after a mistake at the last he was then hampered by the faller. His stamina looks strictly limited.
Lahib The Fifth(IRE), absent since falling in February, was a distant sixth going to the final fence. (op 14-1)
Toulouse Express(IRE), seeking his fourth course win, was soon taking them along, but his jumping was erratic and a blunder a mile out finished him completely. (op 14-1)
Julius Caesar Official explanation: trainer said gelding pulled up lame (op 7-1 tchd 5-1)
Le Vert Galant(FR) was struggling to take a hand when blundering his rider out of the saddle early on the final circuit. (op 7-1 tchd 5-1)
Banoge(IRE) Official explanation: jockey said gelding lost its action but returned sound (op 7-1 tchd 5-1)
Arctic Mick(IRE), an Irish raider, making his handicap debut on his fourth start over fences and his first outing since February, went on three out but looked cooked in second when falling at the last. (op 7-1 tchd 5-1)

2299 COLLINS SEAFOODS NOVICES' CHASE (QUALIFIER) (PART OF COLLINS SEAFOODS YOUNG CHASERS SERIES) (16 fncs) 2m 4f
2:30 (2:30) (Class 4) 4-Y-O+ **£3,168** (£936; £468; £234; £117)

Form RPR

13-6 **1** **Benny Be Good**[19] 1930 7-11-2 0 JamesReveley 127+
(Keith Reveley) *prom: led 4th: hdd narrowly 2 out: nt fluent but led again last: kpt on wl* **11/4**[1]

26-F **2** *3 3/4* **Catch Bob (IRE)**[13] 2037 6-10-9 115 PaulGallagher(7) 123+
(Ferdy Murphy) *midfield: hdwy 8th: jnd ldrs 4 out: led narrowly 2 out: rdn and hdd last: no ex run-in* **14/1**

-040 **3** *9* **Pokanoket (IRE)**[44] 1626 7-10-4 0 JamesHalliday(5) 109+
(Malcolm Jefferson) *led: hdd 4th: remained w ldrs tl rdn and wknd 2 out* **7/2**[3]

3-00 **4** *13* **Monsieur Jourdain (IRE)**[11] 2076 4-10-7 0 RichieMcGrath 92
(Tim Easterby) *trckd ldrs: rdn and wknd 4 out* **12/1**

5-5 **5** *3/4* **Willie Martin (IRE)**[17] 5-11-2 0 AELynch 101
(Michael O'Hare, Ire) *midfield: j.rt 4th: rdn 5 out: wknd after 3 out* **12/1**

0/0 **6** *24* **Cockleshell Road (IRE)**[32] 1759 7-11-2 0 BrianHarding 79
(Martin Todhunter) *nt fluent: hld up: a towards* **20/1**

2405 **P** **Terenzium (IRE)**[19] 1930 8-11-2 110 (p) BarryKeniry —
(Micky Hammond) *hld up: rdn and lost pl 9th: t.o whn p.u 3 out* **33/1**

140- **U** **Hollo Ladies (IRE)**[237] 4671 5-11-2 0 GrahamLee —
(Ferdy Murphy) *midfield: uns rdr 2nd* **3/1**[2]

003- **F** **Don't Tell Nina (IRE)**[228] 4867 6-11-2 0 DominicElsworth —
(Paul Webber) *hld up: bhd whn fell 3 out* **9/1**

5m 10.8s (7.80) **Going Correction** +0.425s/f (Soft)
WFA 4 from 5yo+ 8lb **9 Ran SP% 113.6**
Speed ratings (Par 105): **101,99,95,90,90 80,—,—,—**
Tote Swingers: 1&2 £8.10, 1&3 £4.30, 2&3 £10.00 CSF £38.96 TOTE £4.70: £1.10, £4.20, £1.80; EX 23.60.
Owner John Wade **Bred** Maurice Ramshaw **Trained** Lingdale, Redcar & Cleveland

FOCUS
A fair novice chase run in a mixture of heavy rain and hail stones. The winner should rate higher.

NOTEBOOK
Benny Be Good ◆, a 127-rated hurdler, had been let down by his jumping on his chasing bow at Carlisle. He was much better this time and after seeing off the third, he dug deep to get the better of the runner-up on the run-in. Highly progressive, he will build on this. (op 2-1)
Catch Bob(IRE), winner of his only start in Irish points, won twice over hurdles earning a mark of 115. A faller on his chasing debut, he was the stable's second string behind Hollo Ladies. He took a narrow advantage at the second-last and in the end went down fighting. He deserves to go one better. (op 12-1)
Pokanoket(IRE), rated 123 over hurdles, took on the winner on her first try over fences but she started to flag soon after two out. She looks nailed on for a mares-only novices' chase. (op 6-1)
Monsieur Jourdain(IRE), rated 118 over hurdles, is a bit hit-and-miss and he was struggling to keep up some way out on his chasing bow. (op 20-1)

Hollo Ladies(IRE), winner of a Grade 1 novices' hurdle for Noel Meade at Leopardstown's Christmas meeting, did not get far on this chase debut. (op 11-4, tchd 10-3 in a place)

2300 DIGIBET.COM H'CAP HURDLE (10 hdls) 2m 4f
3:00 (3:00) (Class 3) (0-130,125) 4-Y-O+ £3,928 (£1,160; £580; £290; £145)

Form				RPR
212-	1		**King O'The Gypsies (IRE)**[226] 4907 5-11-4 **120** RyanMania(3)	125+
			(Howard Johnson) *trckd ldr: rdn after 2 out: chal last: kpt on wl to ld line* 5/1[2]	
5-26	2	*nse*	**Mini Beck**[181] 291 11-10-4 **110** AlexanderVoy(7)	116+
			(Sandy Thomson) *led: rdn after 2 out: half l up whn hit last: kpt on: hdd line* 9/1	
54-1	3	*18*	**Bale O'Shea (IRE)**[10] 2100 6-11-3 **116** (p) AELynch	104
			(Michael O'Hare, Ire) *trckd ldr: rdn appr 2 out: wknd bef last* 5/2[1]	
200	4	*3/4*	**Heart Of Dubai (USA)**[11] 2080 5-10-0 **99** oh3 (p) BarryKeniry	86
			(Micky Hammond) *prom: hit 3 out: rdn and wknd appr 2 out* 9/1	
-U00	5	*4*	**Teenage Idol (IRE)**[17] 1956 6-11-1 **114** TjadeCollier	97
			(Evelyn Slack) *in tch on outer: rdn 3 out: wknd bef 2 out* 40/1	
FP-0	6	*1 1/2*	**Cranky Corner**[19] 1931 6-10-11 **115** ShaneByrne(5)	96
			(Sue Smith) *racd keenly: hld up in tch: hdwy to trck ldrs 3 out: rdn appr 2 out: sn wknd* 6/1[3]	
42-6	7	*12*	**Last Of The Bunch**[179] 313 5-10-10 **109** BrianHughes	78
			(Alan Swinbank) *hld up: rdn 4 out: wknd after 3 out* 8/1	
534-	8	*42*	**Premier Dane (IRE)**[195] 44 8-11-12 **125** DougieCostello	52
			(Nicky Richards) *hld up: rdn 4 out: sn wknd* 9/1	
51-P	P		**Bob's Dream (IRE)**[16] 1987 8-10-13 **112** (t) CampbellGillies	—
			(William Amos) *hld up: hit 3 out and sn wknd: bhd whn p.u bef 2 out* 12/1	
2410	P		**Bucephalus (IRE)**[42] 1641 6-11-10 **123** (t) MichaelMcAlister	—
			(Maurice Barnes) *trckd ldrs: rdn 5th and qckly lost pl: t.o whn p.u bef 2 out* 40/1	

5m 12.6s (19.90) **Going Correction** +1.075s/f (Soft) 10 Ran SP% **113.2**
Speed ratings (Par 107): **103,102,95,95,93 93,88,71,—,—**
Tote Swingers: 1&2 £8.00, 1&3 £2.90, 2&3 £6.30 CSF £47.70 CT £136.14 TOTE £3.90: £1.20, £4.00, £1.30; EX 63.30 Trifecta £222.10 Pool: £522.29 - 1.74 winning units..
Owner Andrea & Graham Wylie **Bred** Premier Bloodstock **Trained** Billy Row, Co Durham

FOCUS
The going was changed to soft before this competitive handicap hurdle which was run in heavy rain. There was a sound gallop and just half a dozen were still in serious contention three out. The winner stepped up for the longer trip and the second is rated to his Kelso form.

NOTEBOOK
King O'The Gypsies(IRE), rated 90 on the Flat, returned to action on his handicap bow from a possibly lenient mark of 120 - though his trainer thought otherwise. He went in pursuit of the leader two out and came out on top by a whisker. He had a tough race on his first outing since March (tchd 9-2 and 11-2)
Mini Beck, a winning pointer, has now finished runner-up five times. Having his first start since May, he enjoyed himself out in front, but had been joined when he made a mess of the final flight. He battled hard, but came off a luckless second best at the line. He deserves to go one better. (op 12-1)
Bale O'Shea(IRE), a narrow winner over 2m at Naas, was upsides at the second-last flight, but did not see out the trip anywhere near as well as the first two and in the end struggled to hang on to third. (op 9-4 tchd 11-4)
Heart Of Dubai(USA), well supported despite running from out of the handicap, was readily left behind on the run round to two out and continues to under-perform. (op 18-1)
Cranky Corner, who shaped in encouraging fashion at Carlisle on his first start for this stable, tends to race with the choke out and might be better suited by a drop back to 2m. (op 11-2)

2301 NEWCASTLE FLOORING H'CAP CHASE (13 fncs) 2m 110y
3:30 (3:30) (Class 5) (0-95,93) 4-Y-O+ £2,341 (£687; £343; £171)

Form				RPR
0523	1		**Schinken Otto (IRE)**[63] 1502 9-11-5 **91** JamesHalliday(5)	105+
			(Malcolm Jefferson) *led: hdd 4th: regained ld 9th: stl on bridle between last 2: pushed clr after last: comf* 9/1	
-635	2	*8*	**Best Horse (FR)**[24] 1872 8-11-1 **89** PaulGallagher(7)	91
			(Ferdy Murphy) *hld up on outer: hdwy 8th: trckd ldrs 9th: wnt 2nd appr 2 out: rdn to chse wnr bef last: no ex run-in* 8/1	
6P56	3	*1 1/4*	**Panthers Run**[27] 1826 10-10-0 **67** oh4 (t) DougieCostello	67
			(Jonathan Haynes) *trckd ldrs: wnt 2nd 4 out: rdn whn lost 2nd appr 2 out: kpt on same pce* 10/1	
406-	4	*9*	**Go On Be A Lady**[233] 4753 7-11-7 **88** BrianHughes	81
			(Alan Swinbank) *midfield: rdn 4 out: sn no imp* 17/2	
4406	5	*21*	**Well Oiled (IRE)**[42] 1646 9-10-9 **76** (tp) TomMessenger	46
			(Sandy Forster) *hld up: rdn 4 out: wknd 3 out* 5/1[1]	
2U6/	6	*18*	**Kit Carson (IRE)**[745] 1849 10-11-0 **88** GaryRutherford(7)	40
			(R MacDonald) *hld up: rdn 9th: wknd bef next* 14/1	
1P/	P		**Clearly Now (IRE)**[976] 4347 12-11-3 **84** AELynch	—
			(Michael O'Hare, Ire) *midfield: mstke and dropped to rr 6th: hit 8th and sn t.o: p.u bef 3 out* 11/2[2]	
F615	P		**Troodos Jet**[42] 1646 9-10-11 **81** (p) RyanMania(3)	—
			(Dianne Sayer) *midfield: rdn 4 out: sn wknd: bhd whn p.u bef 2 out* 11/2[2]	
0-50	P		**Apache Brave (IRE)**[121] 955 7-10-0 **67** oh8 (p) RobertWalford	—
			(Henry Hogarth) *midfield: blnd 5th: sn lost pl and bhd: p.u bef 2 out* 7/1[3]	
0F	P		**Follow The Sun (IRE)**[40] 1062 6-11-12 **93** WilsonRenwick	—
			(Peter Niven) *prom: led 4th: clr 6th: nt so far clr 8th: hdd 9th: wknd qckly 3 out: p.u bef 2 out* 20/1	

4m 25.6s (17.00) **Going Correction** +1.075s/f (Soft) 10 Ran SP% **112.1**
Speed ratings (Par 103): **103,99,98,94,84 76,—,—,—,—**
Tote Swingers: 1&2 £5.00, 1&3 £18.80, 2&3 £15.90 CSF £75.67 CT £729.67 TOTE £5.60: £1.60, £4.10, £3.60; EX 25.80.
Owner John Donald **Bred** T Burns And Mrs P F N Fanning **Trained** Norton, N Yorks

FOCUS
A modest but wide-open handicap chase run at a sound pace in the deteriorating underfoot conditions and only the first three home were still in serious contention at the third last fence. The winner is value for further.

NOTEBOOK
Schinken Otto(IRE) was making his fourth appearance in this race, having won it in 2007 from an 11lb higher mark. He seemed to thoroughly enjoy himself and came clear on the run-in. His rider is excellent value for his claim. (op 7-1)
Best Horse(FR), given a patient ride, went in pursuit of the winner at the top of the hill and had closed the gap down to 3l jumping the last. He gives the impression that a much easier track will suit him better. (op 13-2)
Panthers Run, whose last success over a year ago at Hexham came from an 8lb higher mark, ran his best race for some time. He came up the run-in in spirited fashion and prefers a much stiffer test. (op 12-1)
Go On Be A Lady, tailed off on her chasing debut when last seen in March, will come on for the outing, but she still looks to need more experience over fences yet. (op 9-1 tchd 8-1)
Well Oiled(IRE), without a win for over three years, has tumbled down the ratings, but he could never take a hand. (op 6-1)

Troodos Jet Official explanation: jockey said gelding never travelled

2302 SPORTPOOL.CO.UK H'CAP HURDLE (8 hdls) 2m 1f
4:00 (4:00) (Class 5) (0-95,95) 4-Y-O+ £1,561 (£458; £229; £114)

Form				RPR
000-	1		**Emirate Isle**[14] 42 6-10-13 **82** (p) BrianHughes	94+
			(Brian Storey) *prom: led 5th: rdn clr after 2 out: comf* 13/2[2]	
050-	2	*13*	**Scrum V**[233] 4752 6-11-9 **92** PaddyAspell	89+
			(John Davies) *trckd ldrs: rdn bef 2 out: kpt on to take 2nd fnl 100yds: no match for wnr* 8/1[3]	
-660	3	*hd*	**Barbarian**[90] 697 4-10-11 **85** JamesHalliday(5)	82
			(Alan Brown) *led: hdd 5th: chsd wnr tl appr 2 out: kpt on* 14/1	
6F-3	4	*2 1/4*	**Secret Desert**[187] 174 4-11-2 **92** PaulGallagher(7)	88
			(Ferdy Murphy) *hld up: gd hdwy after 3 out: rdn to go 2nd 2 out: hit last: wknd fnl 100yds* 16/1	
5	5	*5*	**Accordion To Paddy (IRE)**[32] 1757 6-11-7 **90** AELynch	80
			(Michael O'Hare, Ire) *hld up: hdwy to trck ldrs after 3 out: rdn bef 2 out: wknd appr last* 9/2[1]	
3502	6	*6*	**Authentic Act (IRE)**[37] 1700 6-10-11 **80** CampbellGillies	64
			(Martin Todhunter) *midfield: rdn after 3 out: sn no imp* 9/2[1]	
P0-5	7	*1*	**Papa Drew (IRE)**[185] 212 6-10-12 **81** RichieMcGrath	64
			(Andrew Parker) *midfield: rdn after 3 out: sn no imp* 17/2	
P06P	P		**Tiger King (GER)**[4] 2194 9-11-0 **83** (b[1]) WilsonRenwick	—
			(P Monteith) *midfield: wknd quckly after 3 out: p.u bef last* 11/1	
/60-	P		**Nonotreally**[233] 4755 9-11-5 **95** (p) MrRUtley(7)	—
			(Lynsey Kendall) *trckd ldrs tl wknd qckly after 3 out: bhd whn p.u bef last* 50/1	
-555	P		**Harcas (IRE)**[35] 1361 8-10-9 **78** BrianHarding	—
			(Martin Todhunter) *hld up: reminders bef 4th: sn bhd: t.o whn p.u bef 2 out* 10/1	
062-	U		**Cosmetic**[198] 12 5-10-5 **77** RyanMania(3)	—
			(Howard Johnson) *midfield: blnd and uns rdr 3rd* 8/1[3]	

4m 27.6s (20.70) **Going Correction** +1.075s/f (Soft)
WFA 4 from 5yo+ 7lb 11 Ran SP% **114.4**
Speed ratings (Par 103): **94,87,87,86,84 81,81,—,—,— —**
Tote Swingers: 1&2 £12.40, 1&3 £17.40, 2&3 £31.70 CSF £56.23 CT £701.26 TOTE £8.80: £3.70, £2.60, £3.30; EX 77.70.
Owner John Wade **Bred** J Wade **Trained** Boltonfellend, Cumbria

FOCUS
A modest but competitive handicap hurdle. Only five were in with a shout at the top of the hill going to two out. The winner can rate higher and the third and fifth are rated to their marks and set the level.

NOTEBOOK
Emirate Isle, on the back of a Flat success at Catterick last month, went on three out and came clear to score with something in hand, local owner John Wade's third success of the day at a track where he is a director. Official explanation: trainer said, regarding apparent improvement in form, that the gelding had been better suited by the softer ground. (op 11-2)
Scrum V, runner-up three times in bumpers, has struggled to make an impact over hurdles and was making his handicap bow here from a mark of just 92. (op 11-1)
Barbarian, who has yet to taste success, survived a blunder at the first hurdle to take them along. He kept on surprisingly well in the closing stages. (op 12-1 tchd 16-1)
Secret Desert, having his first outing for Ferdy Murphy and another making his handicap bow, stayed on from off the pace and will be suited by an extra half mile. (tchd 14-1)
Accordion To Paddy(IRE) continued a wretched day for his Irish stable and seemed to find things happening too quickly over a trip short of his best. (op 4-1 tchd 11-2)
Cosmetic, who refused to settle, lost his rider at the third flight, the last with a circuit to go. (op 6-1)

T/Jkpt: £1,566.50 to a £1 stake. Pool of £35,303.10 - 16 winning tickets. T/Plt: £34.50 to a £1 stake. Pool of £66,919.17 - 1,411.90 winning tickets. T/Qpdt: £7.30 to a £1 stake. Pool of £5,374.52 - 539.12 winning tickets. AS

1765 BANGOR-ON-DEE (L-H)
Wednesday, November 10

OFFICIAL GOING: Soft (6.0)
Wind: Light, across Weather: part cloudy

2303 MAXILEAD METALS BEGINNERS' CHASE (15 fncs) 2m 4f 110y
1:10 (1:10) (Class 4) 4-Y-O+ £3,903 (£1,146; £573; £286)

Form				RPR
121-	1		**Wymott (IRE)**[263] 4161 6-11-2 0 JasonMaguire	144+
			(Donald McCain) *mde all: rdn appr last: styd on wl to draw clr run-in: comf: useful prospect* 5/2[2]	
124-	2	*4*	**Pearlysteps**[221] 4990 7-10-9 0 JakeGreenall(7)	137
			(Henry Daly) *chsd wnr to 3 out: pushed along and outpcd after: rallied to regain 2nd run-in: no ch w wnr* 18/1	
211/	3	*1 1/4*	**Tarablaze**[634] 3915 7-11-2 0 RichardJohnson	138+
			(Philip Hobbs) *hld up: hdwy 7th: chsd wnr 3 out: jst over 1 l down 2 out: one pce fr last: lost 2nd run-in: no ex* 2/1[1]	
310-	4	*11*	**Alfie Sherrin**[237] 4699 7-11-2 0 APMcCoy	126+
			(Jonjo O'Neill) *in tch: pushed along and outpcd after 3 out: kpt on wout troubling ldrs fr between last 2* 7/2[3]	
310-	5	*9*	**Silver Kate (IRE)**[236] 4712 7-10-9 0 SamThomas	112+
			(David Richards) *j. carefully in rr: sme way bhd fr 9th to 10th: in tch w field tl u.p and wknd after 3 out* 9/2	
0P-3	6	*8*	**Alexander Beetle**[195] 62 5-11-2 102 HaddenFrost	108
			(Henrietta Knight) *hld up: outpcd after 3 out: nvr able to chal* 100/1	
5	7	*39*	**Forever Emo (IRE)**[21] 1917 7-11-2 0 NoelFehily	69
			(Jonjo O'Neill) *prom: lost pl 10th: mstke 11th: struggling 4 out: lost tch after 3 out: t.o* 100/1	

5m 17.2s (8.10) **Going Correction** +0.25s/f (Yiel) 7 Ran SP% **109.6**
Speed ratings (Par 105): **94,92,92,87,84 81,66**
toteswingers:1&2 £8.20, 2&3 £3.90, 1&3 £1.70 CSF £35.59 TOTE £3.40: £1.70, £4.90; EX 47.90.
Owner Trevor Hemmings **Bred** Mrs Mary Fennell **Trained** Cholmondeley, Cheshire

FOCUS
A cracking beginners' chase, which was won last year by Burton Port. The gallop was a steady one, but the form should be followed. Wymott should at least match his hurdles best and Pearlysteps stepped up on his hurdles form.

NOTEBOOK
Wymott(IRE) was an impressive winner. He developed into a smart novice hurdler last season, beating subsequent Grade 1 winner Wayward Prince when taking the Albert Bartlett (Prestige) Novices' Hurdle at Haydock on his final start. Soon showing in front on this chase debut, he gradually wound up the pace in the final mile and had seen off his pursuers from the second-last. He put in a fine round of jumping and looks sure to make up into a smart novice, with the RSA Chase the long-term target if things go to plan. (tchd 9-4, 11-4 in a place)

Pearlysteps ◆ could not counter when the winner began to wind it up but stayed on to grab second on the run-in. He was a dual winning hurdler last season but considerably inferior to several of these in that discipline, and this rates a very pleasing chase debut. He made his share of mistakes as a hurdler but there was not much wrong with his jumping here. (tchd 20-1)
Tarablaze's last racecourse appearance was back in February 2009, when he won same Grade 2 novices' hurdle that Wymott won last season, the Prestige at Haydock. Sidelined since, he raced keenly on this chasing debut until moving closer to the pace with a circuit to run. In a close second going to the penultimate fence, he made a slight error there and then seemed to blow up, losing second on the run-in. Another who will not mind a step back up in trip, he should soon be winning over fences. He has had a tendency to break blood-vessels in the past but hopefully that is now behind him. (op 15-8 tchd 85-40 in a place)
Alfie Sherrin was sold out of Paul Nicholls' yard at the Harry Findlay dispersal for £110,000. Off the track since finishing sore when a beaten favourite in the Pertemps Final at Cheltenham, he jumped solidly enough on this chasing debut but got in a bit too close to a couple as the pace was lifting in the final mile, and was outpaced by the principals from the fourth-last. A return to 3m will suit this winning pointer, who looked fit enough but ought to come on for the outing. (op 9-2)
Silver Kate(IRE) developed into a smart mare last season but she was a shade disappointing on this chase debut, albeit in a warm race. She jumped most of the first few fences slowly and, although she did make a little progress from the rear as she started to warm to her task, she was never really a factor. A mares' race may be the way forward with her.
Alexander Beetle was not disgraced on his chasing debut. (op 80-1)

2304 SPORTECH PLC SIR JOHN HANMER GRADUATION CHASE (12 fncs) 2m 1f 110y

1:40 (1:41) (Class 2) 4-Y-0+ **£16,040** (£5,010; £2,698)

Form				RPR
3-02	**1**		**Fiendish Flame (IRE)**[11] 2086 6-11-8 140 ... JasonMaguire (Donald McCain) *mde all: clr tl after 6th: clr again appr 2 out: rdn after last: styd on wl: unchal* **5/2**[3]	152+
4-56	**2**	*8*	**Calgary Bay (IRE)**[11] 2091 7-11-8 145 ... HaddenFrost (Henrietta Knight) *chsd wnr: pushed along after 4 out: outpcd by wnr after 3 out: plugged on u.p after: no imp* **9/4**[2]	144
0-21	**3**	*39*	**Rock Noir (FR)**[8] 2139 5-11-8 0 ... APMcCoy (Jonjo O'Neill) *racd in last pl: nt fluent 3 out: sn u.p and wl btn: nt fluent last 2: t.o* **7/4**[1]	119+
0PP-	**F**		**Atouchbetweenacara (IRE)**[237] 4702 9-11-8 137 ... AidanColeman (Venetia Williams) *racd in 3rd pl tl fell 4th* **9/1**	—

4m 25.1s (3.00) **Going Correction** +0.25s/f (Yiel) **4 Ran SP% 105.7**
Speed ratings (Par 109): **103,99,82,—**
CSF £8.06 TOTE £3.30; EX 6.90.
Owner Mr & Mrs R N C Hall **Bred** Richard Hall **Trained** Cholmondeley, Cheshire

FOCUS
An interesting race and a personal-best from the winner, but the form is not strong.

NOTEBOOK
Fiendish Flame(IRE) made all the running and handed his trainer/jockey a quick-fire double. Given a breather at halfway, he allowed the others to close before coming clear again before the home turn. He jumped well and showed no signs of going out to his right, as he had done on his two most recents runs on a left-handed circuit. This was a pleasing performance, but it won't help his handicap mark and he may not be too easy to find winning opportunities for now. (op 9-4)
Calgary Bay(IRE) had not tackled a trip this short since the 2009 Arkle, and he duly ran as if this was much too sharp. He is a smart chaser, but the fact that he is still contesting graduation chases underlines that he is not a simple horse to place. (op 11-4)
Rock Noir(FR), comfortably off the mark in novice company at Exeter eight days earlier, lacked the chasing experience of his rivals. Settled in last place, he made a slight error at the third-last, just as the winner was increasing the pace, and produced a minimal response thereafter under pressure. This was disappointing. McCoy reported that his mount stopped quickly. Official explanation: jockey said gelding stopped quickly (tchd 15-8)
Atouchbetweenacara(IRE) came down too early to tell how he would have fared. He had been let down by his jumping in a light campaign last season, but remains relatively unexposed. (op 8-1 tchd 15-2)

2305 ANNE DUCHESS OF WESTMINSTER MEMORIAL H'CAP CHASE (18 fncs) 3m 110y

2:10 (2:12) (Class 3) (0-135,129) 4-Y-0+ **£8,871** (£2,620; £1,310; £655; £327)

Form				RPR
/1P-	**1**		**Summery Justice (IRE)**[235] 4738 6-11-9 126 ... AidanColeman (Venetia Williams) *hld up: pushed along and hdwy bef 13th: rdn appr 2 out: styd on to ld last: drew clr run-in* **16/1**	144+
225-	**2**	*8*	**Buffalo Bob (IRE)**[221] 4980 7-11-8 125 ... SeanQuinlan (Kim Bailey) *led: rdn and hdd last: wknd run-in: jst hld on for 2nd cl home* **7/2**[2]	134+
F0/1	**3**	*nk*	**Major Malarkey (IRE)**[7] 2146 7-10-13 116 7ex ... PaddyBrennan (Nigel Twiston-Davies) *midfield: pushed along appr 14th: effrt 4 out whn chsng ldrs: outpcd bef 2 out: styd on run-in: clsng on runner-up cl home* **3/1**[1]	127+
32P-	**4**	*½*	**Minella Boys (IRE)**[252] 4389 8-11-2 119 ...(t) FelixDeGiles (Charlie Longsdon) *hld up: hdwy 6th: prom 8th: chsd ldr 13th: chalng whn nt fluent 2 out: lost 2nd bef last: no ex fr last* **13/2**[3]	128+
5142	**5**	*24*	**Jimbatai (IRE)**[52] 1557 7-10-13 119 ... PeterToole(3) (Barry Leavy) *towards rr: pckd 3rd: hdwy 6th: chsd ldrs 14th: wknd appr 2 out* **9/1**	102
504-	**6**	*15*	**Rate Of Knots (IRE)**[247] 4491 7-11-0 117 ... APMcCoy (Jonjo O'Neill) *hld up: lost tch 13th: t.o* **10/1**	85
3PP-	**P**		**Kilbeggan Blade**[277] 3887 11-11-9 129 ... WayneKavanagh(3) (Robin Dickin) *prom: losing pl whn nt fluent 5th: bhd 6th: struggling after 9th: t.o whn p.u bef 2 out* **33/1**	—
2F1-	**P**		**Costa Courta (FR)**[228] 4882 8-11-8 125 ... JimmyMcCarthy (Charlie Morlock) *prom: lost pl 10th: bhd 11th: t.o whn p.u after 12th* **25/1**	—
406-	**P**		**The Vicar (IRE)**[231] 4816 7-11-8 125 ... HaddenFrost (Henrietta Knight) *prom fr 2nd: rchd for 9th: lost pl 13th: wknd 4 out: t.o whn p.u bef 2 out* **16/1**	—
31-P	**P**		**Sagalyrique (FR)**[180] 314 6-11-8 125 ... JasonMaguire (Donald McCain) *prom tl wknd 4 out: t.o whn p.u bef 2 out* **9/1**	—
41P3	**P**		**No Panic (IRE)**[19] 1950 7-11-12 129 ...(p) RichardJohnson (Peter Bowen) *in tch: nt fluent 3rd: lost pl 6th: struggling after 10th: j. slowly 12th: t.o whn p.u bef 2 out* **16/1**	—

6m 21.6s (1.80) **Going Correction** +0.25s/f (Yiel) **11 Ran SP% 114.1**
Speed ratings (Par 107): **107,104,104,104,96 91,—,—,—,— —**
toteswingers:1&2 £15.40, 2&3 £3.80, 1&3 £17.30 CSF £71.62 CT £218.58 TOTE £26.10: £5.40, £2.00, £2.20; EX 135.00.
Owner Mrs H Brown **Bred** Michael Long **Trained** Kings Caple, H'fords

FOCUS
A competitive handicap chase run at a good pace, and the form should work out. The winner can rate higher.

NOTEBOOK
Summery Justice(IRE) had run just twice before over fences so lacked the experience of most of his rivals. His trainer had been concerned about the 3m trip first time out, the gelding having pulled up on his one previous try over this far, but he stayed on well to wear down the winner at the last and was not stopping at the end. There is more to come from him when the emphasis is on stamina and hopefully this was a sign of a return to form for his stable, which has not been firing.
Buffalo Bob(IRE) had his ground on this seasonal return. He produced a bold display from the front and was only caught at the final fence, but he was tired up the run-in and would have been only fourth with a little further to run. This was a very solid effort and he is capable of winning off his current mark. (op 9-2 tchd 5-1)
Major Malarkey(IRE) was officially 6lb ahead of the handicapper under his penalty. He never really looked like following up, a couple of untidy jumps not helping, but stayed on stoutly from the home turn and nearly snatched second. Things will obviously be tougher from his new mark. (op 4-1 tchd 11-4, 9-2 in places)
Minella Boys(IRE) won over hurdles here last winter and is currently rated 9lb lower over fences. Equipped with a first-time tongue tie, he ran well for a long way but weakened out of second spot between the last two fences. (op 9-2 tchd 4-1)
Rate Of Knots(IRE) was well beaten on this seasonal return and although she has become well handicapped, she continues to operate below her best. (op 9-1)
Costa Courta(FR) Official explanation: jockey said gelding never travelled (op 10-1)
Sagalyrique(FR), formerly with Alan King and having his first run since May, dropped away after pecking six from home and was eventually pulled up. (op 10-1)

2306 CORAL JUVENILE MAIDEN HURDLE (9 hdls) 2m 1f

2:40 (2:41) (Class 4) 3-Y-0 **£2,927** (£859; £429; £214)

Form				RPR
3	**1**		**Marsh Warbler**[3] 2245 3-10-9 0 ... FearghalDavis(3) (Brian Ellison) *led: hdd 2nd: regained ld 3rd: mde rest: drew clr appr 2 out: wl in command whn nt fluent last: v easily* **85/40**[2]	132+
4	**2**	*23*	**Call To Arms (IRE)**[15] 2020 3-10-9 0 ... DonalDevereux(3) (Peter Bowen) *j.rt 1st: racd keenly: trckd ldrs: nt fluent 4th: wnt 2nd 3 out: sn outpcd by wnr and no ch* **18/1**	103+
2462	**3**	*2¾*	**Royal And Ancient (IRE)**[15] 2020 3-10-12 113 ... WarrenMarston (Milton Harris) *trckd ldrs: carried rt 1st: outpcd after 3 out: kpt on to chal for pls run-in* **15/2**	100
6	**4**	*1¼*	**Bonfire Knight**[12] 2078 3-10-12 0 ... DougieCostello (John Quinn) *prom: led 2nd to 3rd: remained w ldr: mstke 5th: lost 2nd 3 out: sn btn: kpt on whn chalng for pls run-in* **13/8**[1]	100+
	5	*2¼*	**Dhaafer**[20] 3-10-12 0 ... SamThomas (Alan King) *in tch: rdn and wkng whn mstke 3 out* **7/1**[3]	96
	6	*10*	**Beneath**[32] 3-10-12 0 ... PaddyAspell (Kevin Ryan) *hld up: hdwy 5th: wknd appr 3 out* **18/1**	86
6	**7**	*6*	**Celtic Intrigue (IRE)**[71] 1442 3-10-12 0 ... PaddyBrennan (Tom George) *hld up: hdwy after 4th: lost pl 5th: struggling whn nt fluent 4 out: wl bhd after* **40/1**	81
	8	*½*	**Lamps**[132] 3-10-12 0 ... NickScholfield (Michael Blake) *a bhd: struggling appr 5th: nvr on terms* **22/1**	79

4m 20.3s (9.40) **Going Correction** +0.625s/f (Soft) **8 Ran SP% 111.7**
Speed ratings (Par 104): **102,91,89,89,88 83,80,80**
toteswingers:1&2 £9.00, 2&3 £9.80, 1&3 £2.20 CSF £34.99 TOTE £3.50: £1.90, £3.60, £2.30; EX 48.20.
Owner Dan Gilbert & Kristian Strangeway **Bred** Darley **Trained** Norton, N Yorks

FOCUS
Not much strength in depth to this juvenile hurdle and there was an easy winner, who produced a massive step up on his recent debut form.

NOTEBOOK
Marsh Warbler slammed the opposition. Third on his hurdles debut at Market Rasen on Sunday, he was untroubled by this quick reappearance and made most of the running before pulling right away from the third-last. He wandered going into the second-last and wasn't fluent at the final flight, but was well in command by then. The opposition was limited and we will learn more about his prospects when he has run under a penalty, but this was a good effort. Soft ground suits him very well. (op 11-4 tchd 3-1 in a place)
Call To Arms(IRE) tried to run out at the first and pulled his rider's arms out for much of the trip, so it's to his credit that he stuck on for second. He was beaten a long way though and his stamina is still not fully proven. (op 14-1)
Royal And Ancient(IRE) has not really progressed but he made the frame for the fourth time in five outings over hurdles. He has a BHA rating of 113 and helps set the level of this form. (tchd 7-1 and 8-1)
Bonfire Knight was down in grade after making his hurdling debut in a Listed race. A little keen, if nowhere near as much as the runner-up, he was no match for the winner and faded in the latter stages. He is another who has yet to convince he gets this far. (op 7-4 tchd 6-4, 15-8 in a place)
Dhaafer, who had a run on the AW recently on his debut for his powerful yard, had reportedly schooled pleasingly ahead of this hurdling bow. He was outpaced by the principals from the third-last, but was staying on at the end and may prove more effective over a little further. (op 5-1 tchd 15-2)
Beneath, a fair middle-distance performer on the Flat who lost his way in the second half of the season, weakened from the third-last. (op 25-1 tchd 16-1)

2307 RACING WELFARE 24/7 NOVICES' HURDLE (9 hdls) 2m 1f

3:10 (3:11) (Class 4) 4-Y-0+ **£3,252** (£955; £477; £238)

Form				RPR
11-	**1**		**Safran De Cotte (FR)**[221] 4992 4-10-12 0 ... RichardJohnson (Henry Daly) *mde all: pressed fr 2 out: rdn bef last: styd on and plld out more towards fin: nice prospect* **7/1**[3]	114+
4-13	**2**	*1¾*	**Scoter Fontaine (FR)**[18] 1962 4-10-12 0 ... APMcCoy (Rebecca Curtis) *in tch: chalng 2 out: ev ch whn hit last: nt qckn towards fin* **4/6**[1]	111
2462	**3**	*½*	**Heron Bay**[18] 1956 6-11-2 123 ...(p) DonalDevereux(3) (Peter Bowen) *chsd wnr: lost 2nd appr 2 out: rdn bef last: kpt on: hld run-in* **7/2**[2]	118
6-00	**4**	*2¾*	**Kayfton Pete**[13] 2056 4-10-5 0 ... PeterHatton(7) (Reg Hollinshead) *chsd ldrs: wnt 2nd and chalng appr 2 out: lost 2nd but stl ch u.p last: no ex run-in* **100/1**	108
0-25	**5**	*4*	**Grafite**[12] 2067 5-10-12 0 ... WarrenMarston (Milton Harris) *hld up: hdwy to chse ldrs after 3 out: hit 2 out: one pce after* **25/1**	103
46-5	**6**	*5*	**Prince Of Denial (IRE)**[26] 1857 6-10-12 0 ... PaddyBrennan (Nigel Twiston-Davies) *hld up: nt fluent 3 out: pushed along appr 2 out: styd on for press bef last: nvr able to rch ldrs* **20/1**	98
03-4	**7**	*12*	**Pie At Midnight**[32] 1768 4-10-12 106 ... JasonMaguire (Donald McCain) *midfield: hdwy appr 4th: rdn bef 2 out: sn wknd* **16/1**	86
50	**8**	*4*	**Don Jose (USA)**[32] 1773 7-10-12 0 ... CharliePoste (Richard Lee) *midfield: hit 2nd: u.p and btn appr 2 out* **150/1**	83
35-	**9**	*½*	**Dune Shine**[251] 4405 5-10-9 0 ... CharlieHuxley(3) (Oliver Sherwood) *racd keenly: hld up: rdn 4 out: nvr able to get on terms* **66/1**	81

The Form Book, Raceform Ltd, Compton, RG20 6NL

3/ **10** *2 ¼* **Russian Music (USA)**[42] [4632] 5-10-12 0 NoelFehily 79
(Ian Williams) *midfield: wkng whn nt fluent 2 out* **33/1**
00 **11** *shd* **Barrie Burn (IRE)**[18] [1962] 4-10-12 0 SamThomas 79
(Jonjo O'Neill) *a bhd: niggled along appr 4 out: nvr on terms* **100/1**
0 **12** *6* **Daggerman**[14] [2038] 5-10-12 0 LiamHeard 73
(Barry Leavy) *hld up: mstke 4 out: struggling 3 out: nvr a threat* **100/1**
4m 23.8s (12.90) **Going Correction** +0.625s/f (Soft)
WFA 4 from 5yo+ 7lb **12** Ran SP% **117.3**
Speed ratings (Par 105): **94,93,92,91,89 87,81,79,79,78 78,75**
toteswingers:1&2 £1.90, 2&3 £1.70, 1&3 £4.00 CSF £12.06 TOTE £6.70: £1.90, £1.10, £1.60; EX 12.40.
Owner Mrs A Timpson **Bred** Mme Pierre Richardot & Georges Richardot **Trained** Stanton Lacy, Shropshire

FOCUS
Straightforward enough novice form and the winner can rate a lot higher. The second and fourth ran to their marks. The time was slower than the previous juvenile hurdle.

NOTEBOOK
Safran De Cotte(FR) ◆ made all the running and he stuck his neck out gamely on the run-in to fend off his challengers. Stretching his unbeaten record to three, having won a pair of bumpers earlier in the year, he is tough and talented but perhaps a little quirky too, as he momentarily looked like running off the course near the stables, having done something similar at Haydock in April. He will get 2m4f in time and is one to keep on the right side. (op 15-2)
Scoter Fontaine(FR) was never far away and was delivered to challenge at the last, but he did not meet the flight as well as the winner did and was unable to quicken up. He is getting closer to his first win over hurdles. (op 5-6)
Heron Bay was runner-up to Saturday's Elite Hurdle winner Nearby off 116 in an Aintree handicap last time. Reverting to novice company under a penalty, and with the headgear back on, he ran a solid race and was staying on without quite being able to deliver a challenge. (op 3-1 tchd 4-1)
Kayfton Pete was close to the pace all the way and only gave best from the final flight. This was a big step up on what he had shown previously and he clearly possesses ability, but his proximity perhaps lends doubts to the form. (op 200-1)
Grafite stayed on from the rear in a race which favoured those who raced prominently. He may be worth another try over further.
Prince Of Denial(IRE) ◆ found this too sharp but was staying on when it was all over. He is one to look out for over further. (op 16-1)
Pie At Midnight was again rather keen.

2308 CASTLE CONSTRUCTION BUILDING CONDITIONAL JOCKEYS' H'CAP HURDLE (9 hdls) 2m 1f
3:40 (3:41) (Class 4) (0-100,99) 3-Y-O+ **£3,252** (£955; £477; £238)

Form RPR
002 **1** **Monsieur (FR)**[7] [2149] 10-10-3 **79** MattGriffiths(3) 84+
(Carroll Gray) *racd keenly: hld up: hdwy whn mstke 5th: wnt 2nd after 4 out: sn rdn: no imp whn hit 2 out: abt 6 l down and wl hld whn ldr eased down 110yds out: styd on for press to ld cl home: lucky wnr* **5/1**[3]
54-1 **2** *¾* **Jeanry (FR)**[21] [1925] 7-10-11 **87** CDTimmons(3) 97+
(Arthur Whitehead) *led: rdn clr appr last: abt 6l ahd and wl in command whn rdr sed to ease down 110yds out: rdn along too late whn hdd by wnr cl home: should have won* **4/1**[2]
510/ **3** *14* **Fujin Dancer (FR)**[10] [5141] 5-11-9 **99** BrianToomey(3) 87
(Kevin Ryan) *hld up: hdwy 3 out: rdn whn chsng ldrs appr 2 out: sn no imp: wl btn bef last* **12/1**
0136 **4** *2 ¾* **Simone Martini (IRE)**[28] [1822] 5-10-4 **77** (tp) SamTwiston-Davies 63
(Milton Harris) *hld up in tch: hit 2nd: j. slowly 4th: outpcd 3 out: n.d after* **9/4**[1]
5236 **5** *17* **Sansili**[20] [1935] 3-10-7 **99** DonalDevereux(3) 52
(Peter Bowen) *chsd ldr to 5th: rdn appr 4 out: wknd 3 out: eased bef 2 out 34* **6/1**
42-0 **6** *17* **Pete**[10] [2107] 7-11-8 **95** (t) EwanWhillans 47
(Barry Murtagh) *hld up: hdwy 4 out: nt fluent 3 out: sn btn: eased bef 2 out* **11/1**
004- **7** *14* **Royal Chatelier (FR)**[224] [4963] 5-11-10 **97** PeterToole 35
(Michael Blake) *trckd ldrs tl wknd 5th: lost tch 4 out: t.o* **7/1**
50P- **P** **Cybergenic (FR)**[263] [4168] 12-11-5 **95** KyleJames(3) —
(Tracey Watkins) *trckd ldrs: wnt 2nd 5th: lost 2nd after 4 out: wkng whn blnd 3 out: sn eased: p.u bef 2 out* **50/1**
4m 25.3s (14.40) **Going Correction** +0.625s/f (Soft)
WFA 3 from 5yo+ 15lb **8** Ran SP% **112.2**
Speed ratings (Par 105): **91,90,84,82,74 66,60,—**
toteswingers:1&2 £3.80, 2&3 £6.50, 1&3 £9.60 CSF £24.70 CT £223.39 TOTE £5.50: £1.90, £1.50, £2.30; EX 26.80.
Owner Miss Jacqueline Howard **Bred** Francois Cottin **Trained** Moorland, Somerset
■ Stewards' Enquiry : C D Timmons 28-day ban: failed to ride out gelding that would have won (tbn)

FOCUS
An ordinary handicap hurdle, but one with a dramatic outcome as the runner-up was eased when clear inside the final furlong and got caught by the winner near the line. Jockey Chris Timmons got a 28-day ban. Monsieur is rated to his mark, with Jeanry heading for a personal best.

NOTEBOOK
Monsieur(FR) rates as one of the season's luckiest winners, but credit goes to his rider for taking his opportunity. The gelding was ending a losing sequence of four years, but had run well at Chepstow last time and was 4lb ahead of the handicapper here. He does not pick up a penalty for this win. (op 13-2 tchd 7-1)
Jeanry(FR) was well in command with the race apparently in the bag when Timmons, having had a quick look over both shoulders, began easing him right up with half a furlong left. The jockey checked over his right shoulder again but inexplicably did not see Monsieur bearing down on him, and the pair were caught close home. It is no consolation to those who backed him, but the gelding is clearly in fine heart at present. (tchd 9-2)
Fujin Dancer(FR) had not run over hurdles since the spring of 2009. Held up as usual, he closed into third place before his effort petered out. He is the type who needs things to fall just right. (op 10-1)
Simone Martini(IRE) was back down in trip after a couple of runs over further and the ground seemed more suitable. He was well supported, but could not race on with the leaders from the third-last and ended up well held. (op 3-1)

2309 HORSEYHOTTIES.COM "NEWCOMERS" STANDARD OPEN NATIONAL HUNT FLAT RACE 2m 1f
4:10 (4:10) (Class 5) 3-5-Y-O **£1,712** (£499; £249)

Form RPR
1 **King's Grace** 4-11-9 0 JasonMaguire 111+
(Donald McCain) *mde all: rdn over 1f out: r.o to draw clr fnl 110yds: won gng away* **9/4**[2]
2 *5* **Tarn Hows (IRE)** 4-11-9 0 AlanO'Keeffe 103
(Jennie Candlish) *hld up in rr: hdwy over 3f out: rdn to stay on to take 2nd over 1f out: no imp on wnr fnl 110yds* **12/1**
3 *1 ½* **Flemi Two Toes (IRE)** 4-11-9 0 APMcCoy 102
(Rebecca Curtis) *w ldr: rdn to chal 2f out: nt qckn over 1f out: styd on same pce ins fnl f* **13/8**[1]
4 *2 ¼* **Coolbeg (IRE)** 4-11-9 0 PaddyBrennan 100
(Tom George) *hld up: hdwy 5f out: chsd ldrs 3f out: kpt on u.p fnl f: nt gng pce to trble front 3* **9/2**[3]
5 *6* **Qualitee** 5-11-2 0 DaveCrosse 86
(Claire Dyson) *in tch: rdn to chse ldrs over 2f out: wknd over 1f out* **66/1**
6 *7* **Carlos Gardel** 5-11-6 0 PeterToole(3) 86
(Mark Rimell) *trckd ldrs: rdn 4f out: wknd 2f out* **50/1**
7 *6* **Absolution (IRE)** 4-11-9 0 HaddenFrost 80
(Henrietta Knight) *hld up: pushed along over 4f out: wl btn over 2f out* **25/1**
8 *13* **The De Thaix (FR)** 3-10-7 0 CharliePoste 51
(Robin Dickin) *trckd ldrs: pushed along 6f out: wknd over 4f out* **20/1**
9 *3 ¼* **Ben Brierley** 3-10-7 0 BarryKeniry 48
(Bruce Hellier) *hld up: pushed along 1/2-way: nvr on terms* **80/1**
10 *1 ¾* **Bennys Mist (IRE)** 4-11-9 0 AidanColeman 62
(Venetia Williams) *racd keenly: cl up: w ldrs 1/2-way: niggled along whn lugged rt and lost pl 6f out: toling after* **14/1**
4m 31.2s (25.90) **Going Correction** +0.625s/f (Soft)
WFA 3 from 4yo+ 15lb **10** Ran SP% **114.7**
Speed ratings (Par 103): **64,61,60,59,57 53,50,44,43,42**
toteswingers:1&2 £3.40, 2&3 £5.10, 1&3 £2.20. totesuper7: Win: Not won. Place: £87.80. CSF £26.64 TOTE £3.30: £1.10, £2.10, £1.80; EX 24.10.
Owner T G Leslie **Bred** R T Crellin **Trained** Cholmondeley, Cheshire

FOCUS
No previous form to go on in this bumper, which was very steadily run until past halfway.

NOTEBOOK
King's Grace ◆ was always up with the pace and he ran on well when asked to stretch in the final furlong. Out of a useful hurdler, and a half-brother to, amongst others, progressive chaser Bradford Boris, he looks a decent prospect but his next run will tell us more. (op 15-8)
Tarn Hows(IRE) is a half-brother to several winners, notably staying chaser Kings Orchard. He improved from the back of the field to have his chance before the winner cleared away from him. (op 14-1 tchd 16-1)
Flemi Two Toes(IRE) lacked a change of pace late on, but had travelled well and would appear to have ability. The most expensive member of this field, he is out of a sister to high-class staying hurdler Mysilv and he should win races further down the line. (op 7-4 tchd 6-4)
Coolbeg(IRE), whose half-brother Dingat won a couple of bumpers, shaped with a bit of promise and a more strongly run race will suit him. (op 7-1)
Qualitee, out of a winning stayer on the Flat who went well in the mud, was a cheap buy and ran respectably.
T/Jkpt: Not won. T/Plt: £71.70 to a £1 stake. Pool of £59,830.35 - 609.04 winning tickets. T/Qpdt: £6.40 to a £1 stake. Pool of £4,073.03 - 469.00 winning tickets. DO

[2109] HUNTINGDON (R-H)
Wednesday, November 10
OFFICIAL GOING: Good to soft (good in places)
Wind: Light half-behind Weather: Cloudy with sunny spells

2310 EQUIMARK HORSEBOXES NOVICES' HURDLE (8 hdls) 2m 110y
1:20 (1:22) (Class 4) 4-Y-O+ **£2,602** (£764; £382; £190)

Form RPR
1 **Gibb River (IRE)**[446] 4-10-12 0 BarryGeraghty 115+
(Nicky Henderson) *a.p: led 2 out: shkn up flat: r.o wl* **1/1**[1]
65P- **2** *6* **Strongbows Legend**[201] [5354] 5-10-12 0 AndrewTinkler 105+
(Charlie Longsdon) *chsd ldrs: rdn whn nt fluent last: styd on to go 2nd nr fin: no ch w wnr* **33/1**
622- **3** *½* **Featherbed Lane (IRE)**[200] [5391] 5-10-12 0 TomScudamore 103
(Anabel L M King) *chsd ldrs: led 5th: rdn and hdd 2 out: styd on same pce last: lost 2nd nr fin* **5/1**[3]
06- **4** *1 ¼* **Soleil D'Avril (FR)**[202] [5344] 4-10-12 0 WayneHutchinson 102
(Alan King) *hld up: hdwy appr 3 out: styd on: nt rch ldrs* **18/1**
040- **5** *3 ¾* **Robin De Creuse (FR)**[228] [4893] 4-10-12 0 TomO'Brien 99
(Philip Hobbs) *hld up: hdwy after 5th: rdn whn mstke 2 out: sn wknd* **18/1**
0 **6** *7* **Mayolynn (USA)**[17] [1994] 4-10-5 0 AndrewThornton 85
(Caroline Bailey) *chsd ldrs: rdn after 3 out: wknd appr last* **100/1**
00 **7** *4 ½* **Me Fein**[23] [1900] 6-10-12 0 LeightonAspell 88
(Barney Curley) *hld up: hdwy appr 3 out: shkn up and wknd bef next* **66/1**
320- **8** *3* **Eastern Supreme (IRE)**[214] [5129] 5-10-12 0 (t) TomSiddall 86
(Kim Bailey) *led: hdd after 3rd: led again bef next: hdd 5th: wknd appr 2 out* **7/2**[2]
0- **9** *38* **Agapanthus (GER)**[29] [3505] 5-10-12 0 PaulMoloney 51
(Barney Curley) *hld up in tch: rdn and wknd appr 3 out: t.o* **25/1**
10 *1 ¾* **Mick's Dancer**[401] 5-10-9 0 RichieMcLernon(3) 50
(Richard Phillips) *hld up: hdwy 5th: wknd bef next: t.o* **33/1**
00- **11** *9* **Betty Browneyes**[196] [50] 5-10-5 0 RhysFlint 35
(Tom George) *prom tl wknd appr 3 out* **80/1**
0- **12** *3 ¾* **Mandalay Prince**[236] [4460] 6-10-12 0 TimmyMurphy 38
(Willie Musson) *a bhd: t.o* **150/1**
13 *nk* **Cluain Alainn (IRE)**[152] 4-10-7 0 MichaelMurphy(5) 38
(Ian Williams) *hld up: mstke 4th: a in rr: t.o* **50/1**
006- **14** *3 ¾* **Uncle Ant (IRE)**[240] [4636] 5-10-12 0 DominicElsworth 35
(Paul Webber) *hld up: plld hrd: a bhd: t.o* **100/1**
0-00 **P** **Driving Seat**[101] [1148] 6-10-12 0 MarkBradburne —
(Michael Mullineaux) *hld up: plld hrd: a bhd: t.o whn p.u bef 3 out* **200/1**
460 **P** **Jigsaw Financial (IRE)**[7] [2145] 4-10-5 0 DannyBurton(7) —
(Roger Curtis) *hld up: plld hrd: hdwy to ld after 3rd: hung lft and hdd bef next: sn wknd: t.o whn p.u bef 5th* **150/1**
3m 53.9s (-1.00) **Going Correction** 0.0s/f (Good) **16** Ran SP% **117.6**
Speed ratings (Par 105): **102,99,98,98,96 93,91,89,71,71 66,65,64,63,— —**
toteswingers:1&2 £8.20, 2&3 £3.90, 1&3 £1.70 CSF £46.09 TOTE £2.00: £1.20, £5.90, £1.80; EX 39.50.
Owner Corbett Stud **Bred** Scuderia Pieffegi Sas **Trained** Upper Lambourn, Berks

FOCUS
A routine novice event, but the winner is in good hands and should go on from here. The pace was ordinary, and probably favoured those who raced handily, but that should not seriously detract from the winner's highly promising performance. It is probably worth being positive about the form.

NOTEBOOK
Gibb River(IRE), a useful maiden rated around 80 at 1m4f-plus on the Flat, has the stamina for hurdling and this successful debut suggests that jumping will be his game. A big horse with plenty of scope, he looked the part in the paddock and is likely to win again. (tchd 5-6 and 11-10 in places)

Strongbows Legend ran by far his best race to date and on this evidence is improving with age. He shaped well without being subjected to a harder race than necessary, and should stay a bit further too. (tchd 28-1)
Featherbed Lane(IRE) failed to win in his four bumpers but he should have no trouble getting off the mark now he is jumping. A brother to two hurdlers, he has good credentials and this was an encouraging first effort. (op 13-2)
Soleil D'Avril(FR) ◆ disappointed Alan King in two bumpers, but the trainer has not lost faith in him and will have been heartened by this first run over hurdles. He is likely to do even better when he finally begins to strengthen. (op 12-1)
Robin De Creuse(FR), beaten a long way in four bumpers, has improved significantly for a breathing operation during the summer, and a switch to hurdling. A big, strong individual, he has a fine physique that suggests there is plenty more to come, with chasing an obvious long-term probability. (op 14-1)
Eastern Supreme(IRE) is not the most natural jumper, according to trainer Kim Bailey, but this decent bumper winner showed enough in front to suggest he is nonetheless getting the hang of it. (op 11-2 tchd 10-3)
Mick's Dancer Official explanation: jockey said gelding hung

2311 INGREBOURNE VALLEY H'CAP CHASE (19 fncs) 3m
1:50 (1:53) (Class 4) (0-115,115) 4-Y-0+ **£3,252** (£955; £477; £238)

Form RPR
0524 **1** **Ovthenight (IRE)**[19] 1952 5-10-9 **105** MissGAndrews(7) 115+
(Pam Sly) *chsd ldr tl led after 3rd: hdd 9th: led again 12th: styd on wl* **6/1**
443- **2** *12* **Reblis (FR)**[246] 4499 5-11-10 **113** JamieMoore 115
(Gary Moore) *prom: ev ch appr 2 out: wknd flat* **9/2**[2]
P-2 **3** *12* **Darn Hot**[189] 158 6-11-2 **108** ChrisHonour(3) 100
(Alex Hales) *hld up: hdwy 13th: ev ch appr 2 out: wkng whn blnd last* **5/1**[3]
P0P- **4** *3* **Pancake (FR)**[275] 3937 7-11-12 **115** (p) TomO'Brien 104
(Philip Hobbs) *led: j. slowly 3rd: sn hdd: chsd wnr tl led again 9th: hdd 12th: mstke 14th: sn wknd* **9/2**[2]
2P11 **5** *5* **Victory Surge (IRE)**[9] 2127 6-11-3 **109** 7ex (p) RichieMcLernon(3) 90
(Jonjo O'Neill) *chsd ldrs: mstkes: drvn along 13th: wknd 15th* **5/4**[1]
6m 14.1s (3.80) **Going Correction** +0.325s/f (Yiel) **5** Ran SP% **111.8**
Speed ratings (Par 105): **106,102,98,97,95**
CSF £30.86 TOTE £8.10: £2.90, £2.30; EX 31.20.
Owner D Bayliss, T Davies, G Libson & P Sly **Bred** Derek Veitch And Mark Tong **Trained** Thorney, Cambs

FOCUS
With two of the runners, including the favourite, running poorly, this was easier to win than might have been. The form is rated through the second.

NOTEBOOK
Ovthenight(IRE), rated lazy by his trainer, responded well to a positive ride. The longer trip suited him well, so he looks capable of maintaining a better level of form around 3m, though his jumping does not always inspire confidence. (op 8-1)
Reblis(FR) ran his usual solid race but it is now 11 races without success since arriving from France. He is probably a few pounds too high, but his consistency continues to keep his weight up. (op 5-1 tchd 11-2)
Darn Hot, off since May, made a creditable comeback but was fading when blundering at the last. She came on a lot for her seasonal debut this time last year, so she should last longer next time. (op 4-1)
Pancake(FR), out of form last season, did little to suggest that he is on the way back yet.
Victory Surge(IRE) failed to have a cut at several fences and was beaten over a mile from home. He threw in a bad run in July just before winning twice in succession, so it is too early to write him off. (op 11-8 tchd 6-4 and 13-8 in places)

2312 EQUIMARK ADVANTAGE RACING RANGE H'CAP HURDLE (8 hdls) 2m 110y
2:20 (2:21) (Class 4) (0-115,115) 4-Y-0+ **£2,927** (£859; £429; £214)

Form RPR
206- **1** **Dona**[254] 4356 6-11-7 **110** WayneHutchinson 127+
(Alan King) *a.p: led appr 2 out: r.o wl* **9/2**[2]
3P-0 **2** *11* **Olympian Boy (IRE)**[150] 736 6-10-11 **100** TomScudamore 102
(Anabel L M King) *led: hdd appr 3 out: rdn and hung rt appr last: no ex flat* **20/1**
0/21 **3** *3 ¼* **Manshoor (IRE)**[35] 1732 5-10-6 **102** MattCrawley(7) 101
(Lucy Wadham) *hld up: hdwy 4th: rdn appr 3 out: wknd flat* **11/4**[1]
-653 **4** *5* **Porters War (IRE)**[13] 2049 8-11-2 **105** TomO'Brien 100
(Peter Hiatt) *chsd ldrs tl rdn and wknd appr 2 out* **8/1**
14P- **5** *1 ½* **I'Ve Been Framed (IRE)**[210] 5184 6-11-9 **115** (b[1]) AlexMerriam(3) 109
(Neil King) *chsd ldr tl led appr 3 out: hdd bef next: sn wknd* **12/1**
2335 **6** *3* **Decision**[100] 1160 4-10-7 **101** (t) DavidBass(5) 92
(Lawney Hill) *hld up: hdwy 5th: sn rdn: wknd appr 2 out* **15/2**[3]
4526 **7** *21* **Phoenix Eye**[20] 1938 9-10-6 **95** LeightonAspell 67
(Michael Mullineaux) *hld up: rdn and wknd after 5th: t.o* **12/1**
44-0 **8** *½* **Calaficial (IRE)**[19] 1953 7-10-8 **100** (t) AdamPogson(3) 71
(Charles Pogson) *hld up: plld hrd: hdwy appr 3 out: wknd bef next: t.o* **25/1**
-130 **9** *17* **Barrel Of Fun (IRE)**[143] 798 4-11-12 **115** (t) BarryGeraghty 71
(Jim Best) *chsd ldrs: reminders after 3rd: wknd 3 out: t.o* **8/1**
-460 **10** *46* **Sommersturm (GER)**[35] 1732 6-10-6 **95** PaulMoloney 9
(Barney Curley) *hld up: bhd and hung lft fr 4th: t.o* **8/1**
3m 54.3s (-0.60) **Going Correction** 0.0s/f (Good) **10** Ran SP% **113.9**
Speed ratings (Par 105): **101,95,94,91,91 89,79,79,71,50**
toteswingers:1&2 £11.80, 2&3 £33.10, 1&3 £3.30 CSF £82.82 CT £290.44 TOTE £4.40: £1.70, £7.40, £1.40; EX 67.00.
Owner The Hallowed Turf Partnership **Bred** A Lestorte & D Lamarque **Trained** Barbury Castle, Wilts

FOCUS
A decent pace set this up for a relatively unexposed horse who looks likely to have a good winter. He produced a massive step up on last season's form.

NOTEBOOK
Dona did not set the world alight in four runs last season after arriving from France, but he appears to have thrived during a break since March. This was a big step up on previous form, and he is likely to operate at a higher level now he has hit the groove, though the handicapper will have the final say. (op 5-1, tchd 11-2 in places)
Olympian Boy(IRE) had lost his form badly in recent outings, but he has been lightly raced in the last year and he seemed to have been freshened up. Though no match for the winner, he ran an honest race and is capable of winning off this mark if he can build on it. (op 16-1)
Manshoor(IRE) was 12lb higher than when winning last time at Towcester, a track where the demands on stamina can flatter. He remains in good shape but has plenty of weight now. (op 3-1 tchd 10-3)
Porters War(IRE) is too inconsistent to be of great appeal, but he did run as if likely to appreciate a return to trips around 2m4f. (tchd 17-2)
I'Ve Been Framed(IRE), blinkered for the first time, ran better than when last seen in the spring but needs to find more to suggest he is getting back to his best. He goes particularly well round this track and is capable of winning from 2m to 3m2f. (op 14-1)
Decision has had trouble winning for a while now, and this was not one of his better efforts. (op 17-2)

2313 TOM JONES MEMORIAL HTJ CENTRE LTD NOVICES' CHASE (12 fncs) 2m 110y
2:50 (2:50) (Class 3) 4-Y-0+ **£5,664** (£1,758; £946)

Form RPR
2F-1 **1** *¾* **Harry Tricker**[48] 1587 6-11-7 0 (p) JamieMoore 133+
(Gary Moore) *chsd ldr tl lft in ld 6th: hdd next: led again 3 out: pckd next: rdn and hdd flat: carried rt and hmpd: styd on: fin 2nd: plcd 1st* **7/1**[2]
03P- **2** **Sergeant Pink (IRE)**[221] 4990 4-10-7 0 TomScudamore 118+
(Steve Gollings) *hld up: lft 3rd 6th: chsd wnr after 3 out: and hung rt bef next: blnd last: led flat: rdr dropped reins and continued to hang rt: all out: fin 1st: plcd 2nd* **12/1**[3]
0F46 **3** *84* **Hi Tide (IRE)**[24] 1883 6-11-1 109 TimmyMurphy 94
(J R Jenkins) *hld up: lft 2nd 6th: led next: hdd 3 out: sn wknd and eased: t.o* **66/1**
04-1 **R** **Medermit (FR)**[18] 1961 6-11-7 0 WayneHutchinson —
(Alan King) *led: hung lft and ref 6th* **1/5**[1]
4m 16.1s (5.90) **Going Correction** +0.325s/f (Yiel)
WFA 4 from 6yo 7lb **4** Ran SP% **105.0**
Speed ratings (Par 107): **98,99,59,—**
CSF £47.62 TOTE £5.30; EX 23.70.
Owner R A Green **Bred** Lawn Stud **Trained** Lower Beeding, W Sussex

FOCUS
A dramatic but unsatisfactory race all round, with the highly touted favourite disgracing himself and the stewards reversing the placings of the first two. They are rated pretty much in line with their hurdles marks.

NOTEBOOK
Harry Tricker was awarded the race after being prevented from changing course, as he and Sergeant Pink ran straight towards the dolled-off open ditch in front of the stands on the run-in. It was his second slice of luck, since the long odds-on favourite had refused earlier in the race. (tchd 13-2 and 8-1)
Sergeant Pink(IRE), hanging as his saddle slipped, prevented Harry Tricker from changing course as the pair of them headed towards the dolled-off open ditch after the final fence. The stewards' decision to demote him suggests that they believed he would not have won had the incident not taken place. (tchd 11-1 and 14-1)
Hi Tide(IRE) was beaten a long way for the third time running, and has yet to recover the form he was in the process of showing when falling at Worcester in September. (op 33-1)
Medermit(FR)'s refusal was as sudden as it was unexpected, with jockey Wayne Hutchinson suggesting, without being entirely convinced, that he may have been distracted by a member of the groundstaff. It may be that this was just a freak "blip" in an otherwise excellent career, but he did make two jumping mistakes in his bloodless win at Aintree, so he still has to prove that he is as reliable over fences as he was over hurdles. Connections, who say the incident was quite out of character, do not intend to repeat these front-running tactics and hope that he will find something to lead him next time. (op 2-9)

2314 EQUIMARKHORSEBOXES.COM H'CAP HURDLE (10 hdls) 2m 5f 110y
3:20 (3:20) (Class 5) (0-95,94) 4-Y-0+ **£2,055** (£599; £299)

Form RPR
0012 **1** **Just The Job (IRE)**[3] 2244 6-10-10 **85** MarkQuinlan(7) 106+
(Neil Mulholland) *mid-div: hdwy 4th: led after 7th: mstke 3 out: clr next: hit last: easily* **10/11**[1]
0-03 **2** *16* **Earl Of Thomond (IRE)**[17] 1997 5-11-5 **87** AndrewThornton 89+
(Caroline Bailey) *mid-div: outpcd 5th: hdwy 7th: wknd appr 2 out: wnt 2nd flat* **16/1**
0-00 **3** *5* **Ramvaswani (IRE)**[5] 2183 7-11-5 **94** (v) MrMMarris(7) 90
(Neil King) *led to 5th: sn drvn along: wknd appr 2 out* **66/1**
6P-0 **4** *½* **Loco Grande (IRE)**[17] 1996 5-11-5 **94** MrTomDavid(7) 90
(Tim Vaughan) *hld up: hdwy 7th: chsd wnr 3 out: wknd next* **14/1**
6/2- **5** *½* **Massini Moon (IRE)**[559] 80 6-11-8 **90** JamieMoore 85
(Gary Moore) *hld up: rdn after 6th: nvr trbld ldrs* **11/1**
P0-2 **6** *16* **Friends Of Tina (IRE)**[21] 1918 7-11-0 **89** PeterCarberry(7) 70
(Alex Hales) *hld up: hdwy 7th: wknd after 3 out: t.o* **7/1**[2]
060- **7** *4* **Zero Six Zoo (IRE)**[278] 3871 7-11-8 **90** BrianHarding 67
(Karen McLintock) *prom: mstke 5th: drvn along 7th: wknd 3 out: t.o* **16/1**
00-0 **8** *2 ½* **Carys's Lad**[28] 1822 7-11-8 **90** LeightonAspell 65
(Michael Mullineaux) *hld up: mstke 6th: wknd 3 out: t.o* **40/1**
00-0 **9** *43* **Kaycee (IRE)**[23] 1902 5-11-8 **90** MarkGrant 26
(Roger Curtis) *chsd ldrs: drvn along 6th: wknd after next: t.o* **33/1**
234- **10** *12* **Bearneen Boy (IRE)**[519] 659 7-9-12 **71** (p) GilesHawkins(5) —
(Neil King) *chsd ldrs: led 5th: hdd after 7th: sn wknd: t.o* **9/1**[3]
-U03 **11** *hd* **Chalice Welcome**[10] 2114 7-11-0 **82** MarkBradburne 7
(Neil King) *hld up: rdn appr 7th: sn wknd: t.o* **14/1**
P0-5 **P** **Totally Beat**[28] 1819 5-11-12 **94** TomScudamore —
(Ian Williams) *hld up: bhd fr 3rd: t.o whn p.u after 5th* **20/1**
5m 17.4s (6.80) **Going Correction** 0.0s/f (Good) **12** Ran SP% **119.9**
Speed ratings (Par 103): **87,81,79,79,79 73,71,70,55,50 50,—**
toteswingers:1&2 £6.20, 2&3 £46.40, 1&3 £19.90 CSF £16.66 CT £628.71 TOTE £1.80: £1.10, £4.70, £12.80; EX 16.90.
Owner Brian Mulholland **Bred** Mrs A R Mulholland **Trained** Burlescombe, Devon

FOCUS
A good pace sorted out the best from the rest. The easy winner was value for further.

NOTEBOOK
Just The Job(IRE), an impressive winner, is due to go up 15lb. However, on this evidence he would be capable of winning even off that new mark, so the handicapper will be tempted to top him up a bit more. (op 5-4)
Earl Of Thomond(IRE), no match for the winenr but clearly best of the rest, has run much better in his last two races and now looks capable of winning. (op 14-1)
Ramvaswani(IRE) ran his best race for a while, and showed dogged determination in slogging on after helping to set the pace, but his record of one win in 53 over jumps does not inspire confidence. (op 50-1)
Loco Grande(IRE) had shown nothing since winning in February 2009 and, while this was a little better, he needs to do more to attract major support. (op 16-1)
Massini Moon(IRE) ran a respectable first race for 18 months and can win off this mark if going the right way. (op 12-1)
Friends Of Tina(IRE) went backwards after threatening to return to form last time. (op 6-1)

2315 E B F EQUIMARK HORSEBOXES "JUNIOR" STANDARD OPEN NATIONAL HUNT FLAT 1m 6f
3:50 (3:52) (Class 5) 3-Y-O **£2,055** (£599; £299)

Form RPR
1 **Broughtons Star** 3-10-12 0 TimmyMurphy 102
(Willie Musson) *hld up: hdwy over 2f out: rdn to ld ins fnl f: jst hld on* **6/1**[3]

2 nse **Close House** 3-10-12 0 BrianHarding 102
(Karen McLintock) *chsd ldrs: led over 1f out: rdn and hdd ins fnl f: styd on* **20/1**

2 **3** 5 **Bathcounty (IRE)**[22] 1913 3-10-12 0 TomO'Brien 96
(Barry Brennan) *led: rdn and hdd over 1f out: styd on same pce* **16/1**

4 3 1/4 **Polurrian (IRE)** 3-10-12 0 MarkGrant 92
(Charles Egerton) *chsd ldr: rdn over 2f out: styd on same pce fnl 2f* **16/1**

5 3 1/4 **Trade On** 3-10-12 0 WayneHutchinson 88
(Alan King) *prom: rdn over 2f out: wknd over 1f out* **9/2**[2]

4 **6** hd **Watledge (FR)**[22] 1913 3-10-12 0 BarryGeraghty 88
(Tom George) *hld up: hdwy over 5f out: wknd over 1f out* **10/1**

7 3 **Megagrace** 3-10-5 0 JamieMoore 77
(Gary Moore) *hld up: hdwy over 5f out: wknd over 1f out* **9/4**[1]

8 7 **Tango Master** 3-10-5 0 JeremiahMcGrath(7) 76
(Mouse Hamilton-Fairley) *hld up: hdwy over 4f out: rdn and wknd 2f out* **50/1**

4 **9** 1 1/2 **Hightown (IRE)**[13] 2052 3-10-12 0 LeightonAspell 74
(Don Cantillon) *hld up: rdn over 3f out: sn wknd* **9/2**[2]

10 3/4 **Powder King** 3-10-12 0 TomMessenger 73
(Chris Bealby) *hld up in tch: plld hrd: lost pl over 4f out: sn bhd* **28/1**

11 10 **Peintre Ster (IRE)** 3-10-9 0 AlexMerriam(3) 61
(Neil King) *hld up: effrt over 4f out: sn wknd* **50/1**

12 1 3/4 **Cheeky Boy** 3-10-12 0 TomScudamore 59
(Steve Gollings) *hld up: a in rr: bhd fnl 5f* **20/1**

13 3 3/4 **Eastern Chariot** 3-9-12 0 MrRichardCollinson(7) 48
(Tobias B P Coles) *hld up: a in rr: wknd over 4f out* **66/1**

14 8 **Lyford Lad** 3-10-2 0 SamuelWelton(10) 45
(George Moore) *hld up: a in rr* **33/1**

15 1 3/4 **Divine Eric** 3-10-12 0 BrianHughes 43
(Peter Niven) *hld up: effrt over 5f out: wknd over 3f out* **40/1**

16 hd **Roe Valley (IRE)** 3-10-12 0 AndrewThornton 43
(Linda Jewell) *chsd ldrs tl wknd over 3f out* **125/1**

3m 13.9s (-6.10) **Going Correction** -0.425s/f (Good) **16** Ran SP% **126.8**
Speed ratings (Par 102): **100,99,97,95,93 93,91,87,86,86 80,79,77,72,71 71**
toteswingers:1&2 £21.20, 2&3 £33.70, 1&3 £15.80 CSF £129.73 TOTE £9.00: £2.80, £7.90, £3.10; EX 212.70.
Owner Broughton Thermal Insulation **Bred** Michael E Broughton **Trained** Newmarket, Suffolk

FOCUS
The pace, though not flat-out, was pretty good for a bumper, but the race was largely dominated by handily ridden runners. The first two look above-average 3yo bumper horses.

NOTEBOOK
Broughtons Star, patiently ridden in contrast to the other placed horses, just got the verdict. His dam won on the Flat and over hurdles, and he is also likely to have a future. (op 12-1)
Close House, a 41,000euros foal but sold for £6,000 earlier this year, rewarded his new connections with a fine debut. He and the winner finished clear of the rest, and he can win a similar race if repeating this performance. (op 18-1 tchd 16-1)
Bathcounty(IRE) has run well in two bumpers but needs to improve a little to win one. However, both performances bode well when he switches to hurdles. (op 12-1)
Polurrian(IRE), at 65,000gns the most expensive in the field, is a brother to a 1m Listed winner. Making a satisfactory debut, he can do better as he matures.
Trade On, half-brother to the winning hurdler Mystic Forest, made a satisfactory debut and can be expected to improve. (op 6-1)
Watledge(FR) had shown promise on his debut, and ran another fair race here, but he is falling short in bumpers so the switch to hurdling will show what he is made of. (op 15-2 tchd 7-1)
Megagrace, a half-sister to the smart bumper winner Megastar, did not live up to the market support. However, she showed enough to suggest there may be something better to come in the longer term. (tchd 11-4)
Hightown(IRE) started joint second-favourite but did not repeat the promise of his debut. (op 5-1 tchd 11-2)
T/Plt: £768.00 to a £1 stake. Pool of £54,974.21 - 52.25 winning tickets. T/Qpdt: £69.60 to a £1 stake. Pool of £2,968.27 - 31.52 winning tickets. CR

2316 - 2321a (Foreign Racing) - See Raceform Interactive

1935 LUDLOW (R-H)

Thursday, November 11

OFFICIAL GOING: Good to soft (good in places; 7.4)
Bends moved out to provide fresh ground.
Wind: Light across Weather: Sunny intervals

2322 JOY PRICE BIRTHDAY MAIDEN HURDLE (9 hdls) 2m
1:00 (1:00) (Class 4) 4-Y-0+ **£3,252** (£955; £477; £238)

Form RPR

4/ **1** **Colleoni (IRE)**[205] 5300 5-11-0 123 (t) PaulMoloney 124+
(Evan Williams) *in tch: led appr 3 out where j.rt: edgd lft after last: drvn out* **4/1**[2]

3-2 **2** 2 **Silverlord (FR)**[121] 973 6-11-0 110 (t) JasonMaguire 120
(Gordon Elliott, Ire) *hld up: hdwy after 6th: rdn to chse wnr appr 2 out: ch after last: no ex fnl 50yds* **6/1**[3]

21-1 **3** 9 **Mawsem (IRE)**[30] 1817 4-11-0 0 APMcCoy 114+
(George Baker) *a.p: ev ch whn bmpd 3 out: rdn whn mstke next: kpt on same pce* **10/3**[1]

4 7 **Piroulet (FR)**[522] 4-11-0 0 RichardJohnson 106
(Philip Hobbs) *in tch: pushed along appr 3 out: kpt on same pce* **9/1**

5-F6 **5** 4 1/2 **Iona Days (IRE)**[18] 1988 5-11-0 109 HaddenFrost 104
(Henrietta Knight) *led: hdd briefly after 3rd: hdd appr 3 out: nt fluent next: wl btn after* **17/2**

6 **6** 11 **Hatton Flight**[25] 1884 6-11-0 0 (v) FelixDeGiles 95+
(Andrew Balding) *plld hrd: prom: led briefly after 3rd: rdn and wknd appr 3 out* **4/1**[2]

7 2 1/2 **Cruise Control**[17] 4-11-0 0 GerardTumelty 90
(Richard Price) *hmpd 1st: hld up: kpt on fr 3 out: nvr on terms w ldrs* **125/1**

0- **8** 5 **Chapter (IRE)**[336] 2787 8-10-7 0 MrJSherwood(7) 85
(Simon Sherwood) *in tch: j. slowly 5th: lost pl 4 out: n.d after* **125/1**

0 **9** 12 **Rajnagan (IRE)**[25] 1884 6-11-0 0 DominicElsworth 80
(Paul Webber) *midfield: hdwy appr 6th: wknd bef 3 out* **66/1**

0-5P **10** 26 **Bahr Nothing (IRE)**[19] 1974 4-11-0 0 ChristianWilliams 51
(Henry Daly) *midfield: pushed along after 4 out: wkng whn wnt rt to avoid faller 3 out* **100/1**

0-20 **11** 1 **Carbon Print (USA)**[107] 1111 5-11-0 100 (t) WillKennedy 50
(Paul Webber) *prom: mstkes 1st and 3rd: rdn and wknd after 4 out: no ch whn wnt rt to avoid faller next* **40/1**

0 **12** 22 **Irish Joe (USA)**[19] 1974 4-10-11 0 DPFahy(3) 30
(Ray Peacock) *sn bhd* **100/1**

-2F0 **F** **Cityar (FR)**[14] 2056 6-10-7 0 CharlieWallis(7) —
(John O'Shea) *hld up: j.rt 1st: sme hdwy 4 out: eighth and u.p whn fell next* **66/1**

632- **F** **Highway Code (USA)**[258] 4280 4-10-9 110 GilesHawkins(5) —
(Richard Lee) *hld up: j.lft and fell 1st* **18/1**

P-04 **U** **Jumpjack Flint**[16] 2021 4-11-0 0 TomO'Brien —
(Charlie Longsdon) *plld hrd: hld up: mstke and uns rdr 3rd* **22/1**

3m 55.5s (6.00) **Going Correction** +0.55s/f (Soft) **15** Ran SP% **116.5**
Speed ratings (Par 105): **107,106,101,98,95 90,89,86,80,67 67,56,—,—,—**
toteswingers:1&2:£12.30, 1&3:£2.80, 2&3:£14.70 CSF £26.63 TOTE £4.30: £2.10, £2.50, £1.90; EX 24.10.
Owner John Lee Jones & P Conway **Bred** Swettenham Stud And Ben Sangster **Trained** Llancarfan, Vale Of Glamorgan

FOCUS
A fair novices' hurdle. The winner stood out on his Irish form and is rated a few pounds off his best.

NOTEBOOK
Colleoni(IRE), winless in nine attempts over hurdles in Ireland, was going without the regular cheekpieces on this debut for Evan Williams and he turned in a much-improved display, taking over at the first in the straight and staying on well. He'll be vulnerable under a penalty, but could win again switched to handicaps. (op 3-1 tchd 11-4)
Silverlord(FR), twice a runner-up in the summer, had been below par on his final start in July, but this was a return to something like his best. He's capable of going one better. (op 13-2 tchd 17-2)
Mawsem(IRE) was keen on this switch to hurdles and, having been impeded three out, he made a mess of the next and was ultimately left trailing. He's better than the bare form and deserves another chance. (op 7-2 tchd 4-1)
Piroulet(FR), winless in five attempts on the Flat in France, has joined a good yard and should improve, with a stiffer test likely to suit. (op 11-1)
Iona Days(IRE) ended up well held, but he again showed some promise and will be of interest once sent handicapping. (op 10-1 tchd 8-1)
Hatton Flight, with the visor back on, was unable to improve on his initial effort, but couldn't get any cover and one of the loose horses did him few favours on the stable bend. He'll be another to watch for once sent handicapping. (tchd 7-2)

2323 TEME (S) HURDLE (9 hdls) 2m
1:30 (1:30) (Class 5) 4-7-Y-0 **£1,951** (£573; £286; £143)

Form RPR

10-3 **1** **Tayarat (IRE)**[19] 1971 5-11-8 (bt1) PaulMoloney 118+
(Evan Williams) *mde all: drew clr appr 3 out: unchal* **5/4**[1]

0533 **2** 19 **Dark Energy**[7] 2169 6-11-8 (t) PaddyBrennan 99+
(Michael Scudamore) *midfield: hdwy to take 2nd after 4 out: no ch w wnr* **7/4**[2]

0P30 **3** 41 **Nicky Nutjob (GER)**[14] 2054 4-10-11 (p) CharlieWallis(7) 55
(John O'Shea) *chsd wnr tl after 4 out: sn wknd* **16/1**

50 **4** 2 **Ask The Oracle**[8] 2145 4-10-12 (t) TomMessenger 47
(John Price) *chsd ldrs tl wknd after 4 out* **10/1**[3]

0P **5** 49 **Kheskianto (IRE)**[36] 1723 4-9-12 (t) GaryDerwin(7) —
(Michael Chapman) *hld up: struggling after 4 out: sn lost tch: t.o* **50/1**

000/ **P** **Murfreesboro**[592] 4784 7-10-12 (p) WillKennedy —
(Alan Jones) *in rr: pushed along appr 4th: t.o whn p.u bef 5th* **10/1**[3]

P **Edge End**[17] 6-10-5 HarryChalloner(7) —
(Lisa Williamson) *racd keenly: hld up bhd: lost tch after 4 out: tailled off whn p.u bef 3 out* **80/1**

3m 56.3s (6.80) **Going Correction** +0.55s/f (Soft)
WFA 4 from 5yo+ 7lb **7** Ran SP% **108.1**
Speed ratings: **105,95,75,74,49 —,—**
toteswingers:1&2:£1.10, 1&3:£5.10, 2&3:£1.70 CSF £3.29 TOTE £2.80: £1.90, £1.10; EX 3.10.There was no bid for the winner.
Owner D J Burchell **Bred** Golden Garden Stud **Trained** Llancarfan, Vale Of Glamorgan

FOCUS
An uncompetitive selling hurdle.The winner ran to a similar level to Stratford, and the second was again well below his best.

NOTEBOOK
Tayarat(IRE) took well to the first-time blinkers and made every yard for an easy victory. It would be a surprise were he not to win again at this level. (op 11-8 tchd 6-4)
Dark Energy, rated 4lb inferior to the winner, has been struggling to make an impact in similar events and the return of a tongue-tie made little difference. (op 2-1 tchd 9-4)
Nicky Nutjob(GER) ran better than he had done at Stratford latest, although that's not saying much. (op 14-1 tchd 12-1)
Ask The Oracle, dropped into this grade for the first time, was again beaten a long way, with the first-time tongue-tie having no effect. (op 17-2)
Murfreesboro Official explanation: jockey said gelding was never travelling

2324 WEATHERBYS 2011 POINT-TO-POINT ANNUAL H'CAP CHASE (19 fncs) 3m
2:00 (2:00) (Class 3) (0-120,120) 4-Y-0+ **£6,285** (£1,873; £948; £486; £254)

Form RPR

121- **1** **Midnight Haze**[280] 3851 8-11-12 120 JasonMaguire 132+
(Kim Bailey) *mde all: j.rt fnl 3 fences: clr 2 out: styd on wl* **9/4**[1]

20-2 **2** 5 **Key Cutter (FR)**[36] 1727 6-11-10 118 (t) WillKennedy 125+
(Paul Webber) *in tch: nt fluent 6th: pushed along 14th: chsd wnr appr 4 out: no imp fr 2 out* **12/1**

6232 **3** 2 **Prophete De Guye (FR)**[18] 1992 7-10-13 107 LeightonAspell 112
(James Evans) *hld up: hdwy to chse ldrs appr 15th: kpt on same pce fr 2 out* **5/1**[2]

1532 **4** 16 **Rifleman (IRE)**[21] 1932 10-11-0 113 (t) GilesHawkins(5) 105
(Richard Lee) *hld up: struggling 15th: nvr on terms* **10/1**

13-4 **5** 60 **Holmwood Legend**[22] 1926 9-11-5 118 KeiranBurke(5) 54
(Patrick Rodford) *hld up: rdn and lost tch after 15th: t.o* **5/1**[2]

1500 **P** **Tyup Pompey (IRE)**[36] 1725 9-10-9 110 MrBJPoste(7) —
(Ann Price) *sn prom: wknd 12th: t.o whn p.u bef 3 out* **25/1**

4/3 **P** **Chrysander**[73] 1429 8-11-12 120 (t) PaulMoloney —
(Evan Williams) *midfield early: bhd fr 5th: t.o 13th: p.u bef next* **10/1**

3-1P **P** **Tisfreetdream (IRE)**[151] 738 9-11-9 120 (p) RichieMcLernon(3) —
(Peter Pritchard) *prom: wknd 4 out: blnd next: t.o whn p.u bef 2 out* **14/1**

P0-P **P** **Ordre De Bataille (FR)**[19] 1973 8-11-5 113 RichardJohnson —
(Henry Daly) *in tch: nt fluent 12th: sn rdn and wknd: t.o whn p.u bef 15th* **8/1**[3]

6m 25.0s (16.70) **Going Correction** +0.875s/f (Soft) **9** Ran SP% **111.6**
Speed ratings (Par 107): **107,105,104,99,79 —,—,—,—**
toteswingers:1&2:£5.70, 1&3:£3.20, 2&3:£7.30 CSF £27.35 CT £119.01 TOTE £4.00: £1.10, £5.90, £1.80; EX 30.00.
Owner Kim Bailey Racing Partnership **Bred** Phillip C And Mrs Kathryn M Dando **Trained** Andoversford, Gloucs

FOCUS
A fair handicap chase. The solid third sets the level and the progressive winner produced another step up.

NOTEBOOK
Midnight Haze jumped well and led throughout on this first start since February. Now successful in three of his last four starts, the 8-y-o is going to be forced into a better class of race soon, but it's probable he'll improve for this, like many from the yard often do, so don't be surprised if there's more to come. Interestingly, all his wins have come right-handed. (op 11-4 tchd 85-40)
Key Cutter(FR), a well-beaten second to the useful Golan Way at the course on his debut over fences, was surprisingly weak in the market switched to handicaps, but that didn't stop him running a good race on this return to 3m. He should get off the mark at some stage and looks a decent handicapper in the making.
Prophete De Guye(FR), raised 3lb having finished second at Towcester latest, leaving him on a career-high mark, again seemed to run his race, pulling clear of the remainder. (op 9-2)
Rifleman(IRE) was unable to back up his recent Carlisle second. (op 17-2 tchd 8-1)
Holmwood Legend has now disappointed on both starts this term. (op 6-1)
Chrysander Official explanation: jockey said gelding had a breathing problem
Ordre De Bataille(FR) Official explanation: jockey said gelding stopped quickly

2325 WEATHERBYS BLOODSTOCK INSURANCE INTRODUCTORY HURDLE (11 hdls) 2m 5f
2:30 (2:31) (Class 3) 4-Y-O+ **£4,553** (£1,337; £668; £333)

Form RPR
10-6 **1** **Cavite Beta (IRE)**[19] 1966 4-11-0 0 BarryGeraghty 121+
(Nicky Henderson) *led after field was stationary for several 2nds: hdd after 1st: cl up: led 4 out: clr fr last: easily* **4/9**[1]
2 *11* **Ultimate Quest (IRE)**[45] 5-10-7 0 GaryDerwin(7) 100
(Michael Chapman) *hld up: hdwy appr 3 out: rdn to take 2nd 2 out: no ch w wnr* **14/1**[3]
3 *5* **Kilvoydansouth (IRE)**[559] 107 6-11-0 0 TomO'Brien 95
(N F Glynn, Ire) *hld up: hit 3rd: nt fluent 3 out: effrt and chsd ldrs next: one pce run-in* **28/1**
2- **4** *6* **Gortenbuie (IRE)**[362] 2278 5-11-0 0 HaddenFrost 89
(Henrietta Knight) *chsd ldrs: effrt 3 out: wknd fr next* **20/1**
5 *12* **Mashdood (USA)**[20] 4-11-0 0 LiamTreadwell 77
(Peter Hiatt) *led after 1st: hit next: hdd 4 out: rdn and wknd appr 2 out* **80/1**
06-1 **6** *½* **Spock (FR)**[22] 1922 5-11-0 0 IanPopham(5) 82
(Paul Nicholls) *hld up: hdwy to chse ldrs appr 3 out: wknd next* **7/2**[2]
5m 43.1s (28.30) **Going Correction** +0.875s/f (Soft) **6** Ran SP% **107.6**
Speed ratings (Par 107): **81,76,74,72,68 67**
toteswingers:1&2:£2.40, 1&3:£4.20, 2&3:£3.80 CSF £6.62 TOTE £1.50: £1.10, £3.20; EX 6.10.
Owner Ann & Alan Potts **Bred** Christopher Maye **Trained** Upper Lambourn, Berks

FOCUS
What had looked an interesting novices' hurdle was turned into a rout by Cavite Beta, who is rated to a similar level to last season's bumper form. The pace was slow.

NOTEBOOK
Cavite Beta(IRE) found this considerably easier than the Grade 2 event he had contested at Chepstow on his reappearance. Although behind some potentially high-class sorts, it's fairly safe to assume he wasn't at his best that day, and he ran out an easy winner despite failing to settle. Stiffer tests await this former point winner, but he'll benefit from more of a pace to chase in better races. The best of him won't be seen until he's faced with 3m and fences. (op 8-13)
Ultimate Quest(IRE), just the type to do well over hurdles, was staying on dourly in the final furlong and he'll appreciate 3m before long. There are races to be won with him. (op 10-1 tchd 16-1)
Kilvoydansouth(IRE), a former point winner who failed to shine in to bumpers, shaped quite well on this first starts over hurdles and is another who'll appreciate a stiffer test. (op 25-1)
Gortenbuie(IRE), a promising second in a Uttoxeter bumper a year ago, has plenty of physical scope and, judging by the way he dropped out, this run was badly needed, as can sometimes be the case with runners from this yard. (op 18-1 tchd 16-1)
Mashdood(USA), possibly flattered by his Flat rating of 68, didn't run too badly and should have a future as a lowly level. (op 66-1 tchd 100-1)
Spock(FR), conceding weight all round, dropped out quickly, having closed up to challenge leaving the back, and something was presumably amiss. (op 11-4)

2326 ROSEMARY WRIGHT THREE SCORE YEARS AND TEN BEGINNERS' CHASE (13 fncs) 2m
3:00 (3:00) (Class 4) 4-Y-O+ **£3,771** (£1,123; £568; £291; £152)

Form RPR
F0-3 **1** **Sway (FR)**[13] 2071 4-9-11 0 RichieMcLernon(3) 113+
(Jonjo O'Neill) *a.p: led between last 2: swtchd lft to avoid water jump fnl 75yds: kpt on wl* **8/1**[3]
6-4F **2** *½* **Rougham**[23] 1909 4-10-7 0 RichardJohnson 120+
(Philip Hobbs) *j.lft several times: led to 3 out: rallying whn bmpd fnl 75yds: hld cl home* **10/11**[1]
2P-4 **3** *8* **Sambulando (FR)**[33] 1766 7-11-1 0 PaddyBrennan 123+
(Tom George) *trckd ldrs: chal 9th: led 3 out: hdd between last 2: rdn whn blnd last: sn btn* **2/1**[2]
-504 **4** *34* **Petrosian**[21] 1937 6-10-8 0 (p) HarryChalloner(7) 89
(Lisa Williamson) *chsd ldr tl after 9th: wknd appr 4 out: t.o* **20/1**
0313 **5** *29* **Mujamead**[104] 1137 6-10-10 0 (p) LeeEdwards(5) 63
(Sally-Anne Wheelwright) *hld up: nt fluent 8th: lost tch next: t.o* **40/1**
0-0P **R** **Border Castle**[13] 2071 9-11-1 0 (b) DominicElsworth —
(Michael Blake) *racd reluctantly: j. slowly 1st: wnt prom briefly 5th: bhd whn ref 7th* **25/1**
4m 14.9s (16.40) **Going Correction** +0.875s/f (Soft)
WFA 4 from 6yo+ 7lb **6** Ran SP% **107.9**
Speed ratings (Par 105): **94,93,89,72,58** —
toteswingers:1&2:£2.80, 1&3:£2.30, 2&3:£1.10 CSF £15.48 TOTE £6.20: £3.50, £1.10; EX 12.70.
Owner John P McManus **Bred** Guy Cherel **Trained** Cheltenham, Gloucs

FOCUS
Probably a fair beginners' chase. Sway was again well below her best hurdling level, with the form limited by the second and third.

NOTEBOOK
Sway(FR), useful over hurdles in France, got tired and began to jump right when disappointing on her chasing debut at Uttoxeter, but she had clearly come on appreciably and was again receiving plenty of weight all round, being a 4-y-o filly. Hunted round by Richie McClernon, she jumped well in the main and, having come to challenge three out, she was level at the next and just managed to hold on from a rallying Rougham. The stewards took a look, as she did edge across and bump Rougham on the run-in, which would have intimidated him, but she was the best horse in the race on the day and deserved to keep the race. There should be more to come from her, looking at much she improved in such a short space of time from runs one to two, and it would be a surprise were she not to defy a penalty before possibly going up in grade. Official explanation: trainer had no explanation for the apparent improvement in form (op 5-1 tchd 9-2)
Rougham, not out of it when coming down on his debut at Exeter, was hesitant at a few of his early fences, but got better as the race went on and he stayed on again having been headed and looked beaten three out, but couldn't quite get back up. The winner did him few favours close home, but it probably made no difference, and he looks ready for a step up in trip now. (op Evens tchd 5-6)
Sambulando(FR) edged ahead at the first in the straight on this return to fences, but the winner had him covered from two out, and he was beaten when taking a tired lunge at the last. (op 11-4)

2327 LUDLOW TRI NATIONS CHALLENGE AMATEUR RIDERS' H'CAP HURDLE (FOR GENTLEMAN AMATEUR RIDERS) (11 hdls) 2m 5f
3:30 (3:30) (Class 5) (0-95,95) 4-Y-O+ **£2,186** (£677; £338; £169)

Form RPR
0121 **1** **Just The Job (IRE)**[1] 2314 6-11-9 **92** 7ex MrJean-PhilippeBoisgontier 108+
(Neil Mulholland) *hld up: hdwy appr 7th: wnt 2nd 4 out: blnd and led 2 out: drew clr run-in* **1/2**[1]
524U **2** *16* **Cool Bob (IRE)**[18] 1991 7-11-11 **94** (t) MrMSeston 95+
(Matt Sheppard) *cl up: nt fluent 4th: led 7th: hdd 2 out: no ch w wnr fr last* **7/1**[2]
-003 **3** *39* **Ramvaswani (IRE)**[1] 2314 7-11-11 **94** (v) MrROHarding 60
(Neil King) *rel to r: bhd: tk poor 3rd appr 3 out: nvr on terms* **14/1**
-50F **4** *26* **No More Whispers (IRE)**[8] 2146 5-11-7 **90** MrFlorentGuy 32
(Evan Williams) *chsd ldr tl appr 7th: wknd after 4 out* **9/1**
3000 **5** *7* **Mayor Of Kilcock**[36] 1726 7-11-12 **95** MrJTCarroll 31
(James Danahar) *led: sn clr: blnd 5th: hdd 7th: wknd after 4 out* **8/1**[3]
5m 31.3s (16.50) **Going Correction** +0.875s/f (Soft) **5** Ran SP% **106.9**
Speed ratings (Par 103): **103,96,82,72,69**
CSF £4.29 TOTE £1.60: £1.10, £3.00; EX 3.70.
Owner Brian Mulholland **Bred** Mrs A R Mulholland **Trained** Burlescombe, Devon

FOCUS
Not much of a race, it was won easily by the consistent and hardy Just The Job.

NOTEBOOK
Just The Job(IRE), an easy winner at Huntingdon 24 hours earlier (his second victory of the month), defied the 7lb penalty with ease. He is clearly a fast-improving 6-y-o, though the handicapper is sure to catch up eventually. (tchd 4-9)
Cool Bob(IRE), back over hurdles, is now 0-36, but he was the only one capable of getting anywhere near the winner and certainly deserves to win a race. (op 11-2)
Ramvaswani(IRE) , behind Just The Job the previous day, was again beaten out of sight. (op 12-1)
No More Whispers(IRE), back over hurdles following a failed experiment chasing, was quickly brushed aside. (op 11-1 tchd 12-1)
Mayor Of Kilcock did too much too soon and paid for it late on. (op 11-1 tchd 12-1)

2328 VYRNWY INTERMEDIATE OPEN NATIONAL HUNT FLAT RACE 2m
4:00 (4:00) (Class 5) 4-6-Y-O **£1,951** (£573; £286; £143)

Form RPR
1 **Chasing Aces**[186] 245 4-11-2 0 APMcCoy 99+
(Rebecca Curtis) *prom: led 4f out: rdn 2f out: edgd lft whn pressed ent fnl f: hung rt fnl 110yds: kpt on wl* **11/4**[1]
4- **2** *¾* **Forever Waining (IRE)**[236] 4744 4-11-2 0 TomO'Brien 98+
(Peter Bowen) *hld up: hdwy 5f out: chsd wnr over 2f out: edgd lft whn ev ch ent fnl f: carried rt fnl 110yds: nt qckn cl home* **5/1**[2]
3 *6* **Deciding Moment (IRE)** 4-11-2 0 JasonMaguire 92
(Ben De Haan) *hld up: hdwy over 4f out: rdn and edgd lft whn ev ch over 2f out: styd on same pce fr over 1f out* **12/1**
0- **4** *¾* **Drumlang (IRE)**[236] 4742 4-11-2 0 HaddenFrost 91
(Henrietta Knight) *hld up: hdwy 1/2-way: rdn to chse ldrs over 2f out: styd on same pce fr over 1f out* **15/2**[3]
5 *3 ¼* **Automaticman (IRE)**[220] 4-11-2 0 RichardJohnson 88
(Henry Daly) *in tch: effrt to chse ldrs over 2f out: one pce fr over 1f out* **10/1**
0 **6** *3 ¼* **Lieutenant Miller**[178] 375 4-11-2 0 BarryGeraghty 85
(Nicky Henderson) *midfield: hdwy 5f out: rdn and outpcd over 2f out* **11/4**[1]
3 **7** *2 ¾* **Egypt Mill Spirit (IRE)**[36] 1729 4-10-11 0 IanPopham(5) 82
(Paul Nicholls) *in tch: ev ch 3f out: rdn and wknd 2f out* **5/1**[2]
0 **8** *7* **Hidden Springs**[36] 1729 5-11-2 0 JodieMogford 75
(Brian Baugh) *prom: rdn 5f out: wknd 4f out* **100/1**
530 **9** *1 ¼* **Robello**[26] 1866 6-10-9 0 CharlieWallis(7) 74
(John O'Shea) *midfield: pushed along 5f out: sn wknd* **40/1**
0 **10** *7* **Go To The Edge**[13] 2074 4-10-9 0 MrJamieJenkinson(7) 67
(John Bryan Groucott) *led: hdd 4f out: sn rdn and wknd* **200/1**
11 *5* **Midnight Charmer** 4-10-13 0 TomMolloy(3) 62
(Emma Baker) *hld up: struggling 5f out: nvr on terms* **66/1**
12 *4* **Summer De Baune (FR)** 5-10-9 0 HarryChalloner(7) 58
(John Bryan Groucott) *trckd ldrs tl rdn and wknd 5f out* **100/1**
13 *shd* **Midnight Dove** 5-10-9 0 MrJFlook(7) 57
(Andrew Price) *hld up: struggling 5f out: nvr on terms* **50/1**
0 **14** *65* **Harry Masters**[185] 254 6-11-2 0 LiamTreadwell —
(Edward Bevan) *midfield: hdwy 1/2-way: rdn and wknd over 4f out: t.o* **150/1**
4m 1.70s (17.80) **Going Correction** +0.875s/f (Soft)
WFA 4 from 5yo+ 7lb **14** Ran SP% **124.2**
Speed ratings: **90,89,86,86,84 83,81,78,77,74 71,69,69,36**
toteswingers:1&2:£4.90, 1&3:£9.00, 2&3:£16.30 CSF £17.24 TOTE £5.60: £2.70, £2.20, £5.00; EX 17.80.
Owner Miss Rebecca Curtis **Bred** Goldford Stud **Trained** Newport, Dyfed
■ Stewards' Enquiry : Tom O'Brien caution: careless riding.

FOCUS
A modest bumper and perhaps not form to get too carried away with, but it should still produce winners.

NOTEBOOK
Chasing Aces, hampered when held on his bumper debut for Tom Taaffe, has joined a yard that does well in this division and, despite showing signs of inexperience late on, he was always just doing enough under McCoy inside the final furlong. He should stay further over hurdles and can win more races. (op 9-2)
Forever Waining(IRE), fourth at Uttoxeter on debut last season, showed improved form and, although unable to stay on as strongly as the winner, he should have no trouble winning races. (op 9-2 tchd 4-1)
Deciding Moment(IRE), who's from a family of good staying chasers, shaped promisingly. He appeared to get tired, but the way he travelled suggests he has a bright future and he will be of particular interest faced with a stiffer test over hurdles. (op 11-1)
Drumlang(IRE), well held at Uttoxeter on debut last term, kept on in encouraging fashion and appeared to take a step forward, although it's unlikely he'll be winning until sent hurdling. (op 8-1)
Automaticman(IRE), who shaped with promise despite failing to win in two points, made an encouraging debut and will benefit from a stiffer test over hurdles. (op 14-1)
Lieutenant Miller was disappointing on this first start since May, shaping like a horse who lacks the pace to win a bumper. (op 5-2 tchd 10-3)
Egypt Mill Spirit(IRE), fifth in an ordinary bumper on debut, didn't get home having held his chance and was disappointing. (op 13-2 tchd 9-2)
T/Plt: £5.30 to a £1 stake. Pool:£42,401.95 - 5,799.34 winning tickets T/Qpdt: £3.40 to a £1 stake. Pool:£2,684.88 - 570.26 winning tickets DO

[2020]TAUNTON (R-H)

Thursday, November 11

OFFICIAL GOING: Good (good to firm in places; 8.1)

Rail on bends moved out to provide fresh ground and distances increased by 63metres each circuit.

Wind: very strong across Weather: cloudy with sunny periods

2329 BATHWICK TYRES TAUNTON MARES' H'CAP HURDLE (10 hdls) 2m 3f 110y

1:10 (1:10) (Class 4) (0-110,108) 4-Y-0+ **£4,110** (£1,198; £599)

Form RPR

-431 **1** **Detroit Red**[129] 910 4-11-8 **104**.......................... SamThomas 112+
(Martin Hill) *in tch: rdn to cl on ldrs appr 2 out: chalng whn mstke last: pushed in to ld run-in: kpt on to assert towards fin* **25/1**

0011 **2** ¾ **Am I Blue**[66] 1494 4-11-2 **105**.......................... MrTomDavid(7) 107
(Mrs D Thomas) *chsd ldrs: rdn appr 3 out: led 2 out: hdd run-in: kpt on but no ex towards fin* **7/1**[2]

-2UP **3** 2¾ **Topflight Wildbird**[144] 796 7-11-6 **102**.......................... WayneHutchinson 102
(Alan King) *mid-div: rdn after 3 out to chse ldrs: styd on wout chalng: wnt 3rd sn after last* **8/1**[3]

5524 **4** *nk* **Mangonel**[18] 2001 6-10-0 **82** oh6..........................(v) RodiGreene 81
(Stuart Howe) *chsd ldrs: rdn appr 3 out: ev ch last: kpt on but no ex* **10/1**

-0FP **5** 1½ **Playing With Fire (IRE)**[13] 2072 6-11-4 **103**.......... WayneKavanagh(3) 102
(Robin Dickin) *hld up towards rr: hit 5th: rdn and stdy prog fr after 6th: styd on same pce fr 2 out* **14/1**

000- **6** *1* **Time To Think**[202] 5364 5-10-7 **89**.......................... AndrewThornton 86
(Seamus Mullins) *in tch: rdn to chse ldrs appr 2 out: one pce fr last* **6/1**[1]

3-45 **7** 1½ **Bosamcliff (IRE)**[8] 2150 5-11-6 **105**.......................... LeeStephens(3) 102
(David Evans) *mid-div: rdn after 3 out: one pce fr next: mstke last* **9/1**

-556 **8** ½ **Mayberry**[10] 2128 5-11-2 **108**.......................... StephenO'Donovan(10) 105
(Emma Lavelle) *hld up bhd: sme hdwy into midfield whn nt clr run on home bnd: one pce fr next* **7/1**[2]

P00 **9** *11* **Rolanta (FR)**[28] 1844 5-10-3 **85**.......................... JamesDavies 70
(James Frost) *hld up towards rr: hdwy after 6th: rdn in midfield after 3 out: wknd next* **50/1**

206 **10** 2¾ **Try Cat**[22] 1921 4-11-8 **104**..........................(t) RhysFlint 99+
(Philip Hobbs) *led: hdd whn mstke 2 out: sn wknd* **25/1**

305 **11** 1¼ **Daliarose (FR)**[91] 1233 4-11-9 **105**..........................(t) TomScudamore 87
(David Pipe) *hld up towards rr: short lived effrt after 3 out: wknd bef next* **10/1**

244 **12** 2¾ **Lucy's Perfect**[8] 2150 4-11-8 **104**..........................(b) JohnnyFarrelly 83
(David Pipe) *mid-div: rdn after 3 out: wknd bef next* **18/1**

P-4P **13** *13* **Emmaslegend**[23] 1907 5-10-10 **92**.......................... ColinBolger 60
(Suzy Smith) *in tch tl wknd 7th: t.o whn mstke last* **28/1**

21-3 **14** 3¼ **Tarabela**[186] 220 7-10-13 **100**.......................... DavidBass(5) 65
(Gerald Ham) *mid-div tl after 5th: sn drvn in rr: t.o* **14/1**

1 **15** 3½ **Clu Agus Cail (IRE)**[24] 1900 5-11-10 **106**.......................... TimmyMurphy 67
(Alison Batchelor) *prom tl 3 out: sn wknd: t.o* **9/1**

4m 55.2s (9.20) **Going Correction** +0.325s/f (Yiel)
WFA 4 from 5yo+ 7lb **15** Ran SP% **116.4**
Speed ratings (Par 105): **94,93,92,92,91 91,90,90,86,85 84,83,78,77,75**
toteswingers:1&2:£11.70, 1&3:£33.90, 2&3:£6.30 CSF £181.45 CT £1545.37 TOTE £19.80: £6.70, £2.70, £3.10; EX 91.30.
Owner Martin Hill **Bred** Martin Hill **Trained** Littlehempston, Devon

FOCUS
Things don't come much more open than this modest mares' handicap. The cosy winner was value for further with the next three all fairly close to their marks.

NOTEBOOK
Detroit Red picked up where she left off at Newton Abbot in July and readily followed up on this switch to a handicap. This drop in distance was partially negated by the easier ground and there should be more improvement in her, considering she ought to come on for the run. The EBF Mares' Final at Newbury next year is reportedly her big target.
Am I Blue was 15lb higher on this return from a 66-day break and posted brave effort in defeat. As a 4-y-o she remains open a little more improvement and may enjoy getting back over further.
Topflight Wildbird had been pulled up on her previous outing 144 days earlier so this was a welcome return to form. She hasn't won since 2003, but hasn't been with her current trainer all that long and she too is entitled to benefit from the outing.
Mangonel wasn't disgraced from 6lb out of the handicap and probably could've done without the rain. She remains a maiden, though.
Time To Think, making her debut for the stable, came in for some support on this seasonal debut for a new yard but shaped as though it was needed.
Mayberry Official explanation: vet said mare lost fore shoe

2330 BATHWICK TYRES BRIDGWATER NOVICES' CHASE (14 fncs) 2m 3f

1:40 (1:40) (Class 4) 4-Y-0+ **£5,204** (£1,528; £764; £381)

Form RPR

21-1 **1** **Rebel Du Maquis (FR)**[27] 1854 5-11-9 0.......................... NoelFehily 146+
(Paul Nicholls) *mde all: drawing clr whn mstke 3 out: wl in command whn blnd 2 out: easily* **10/11**[1]

55-2 **2** *9* **Double Dash**[22] 1917 6-11-2 117.......................... MarkBradburne 120+
(George Baker) *chsd wnr: disputing 2nd whn hit 4 out: rdn sn after: comf hld by wnr fr 3 out: wnt clr 2nd appr last* **14/1**

110- **3** *10* **Lake Legend**[239] 4674 6-11-2 0.......................... WayneHutchinson 114+
(Alan King) *in tch: disp 2nd appr 4 out: sn rdn: comf hld by wnr fr 3 out: blnd 2 out: fdd last* **2/1**[2]

5-22 **4** *16* **Anquetta (IRE)**[20] 1952 6-11-2 0.......................... AndrewTinkler 96
(Nicky Henderson) *in tch: 4th whn mstke 4 out: sn rdn and btn* **6/1**[3]

0UU2 **5** *19* **Jocheski (IRE)**[23] 1909 6-11-2 113.......................... AndrewThornton 79
(Tony Newcombe) *a in last pair: no ch fr bef 4 out: t.o* **33/1**

-060 **6** *33* **I'm In The Pink (FR)**[8] 2153 6-10-13 0.......................... LeeStephens(3) 49
(David Evans) *nt fluent 1st: trckd wnr tl mstke 8th: wkng whn mstke 10th: t.o* **100/1**

1P5/ **P** **Abstract Art (USA)**[616] 4311 7-11-2 0.......................... AidanColeman —
(Rachel Hobbs) *a last: lost tch after 7th: p.u bef next* **66/1**

4m 53.6s (-2.90) **Going Correction** +0.025s/f (Yiel) **7** Ran SP% **112.1**
Speed ratings (Par 105): **107,103,99,92,84 70,—**
toteswingers:1&2:£6.30, 1&3:£4.30, 2&3:£5.20 CSF £13.08 TOTE £2.30: £1.10, £4.50; EX 12.60.
Owner Mrs Kathy Stuart **Bred** Daniel & Mme Jeannine Laupretre **Trained** Ditcheat, Somerset

FOCUS
Not a bad novice chase and an impressive winner, who was value for further and who can rate higher.

NOTEBOOK
Rebel Du Maquis(FR) jumped neatly for a debutant when winning first time up over fences at Cheltenham on his comeback last month and followed up with another clear-cut success under his penalty. He set off at a decent gallop in front and had the race in safe keeping coming to the third-last, having again jumped accurately to that point. However, he hit that fence and, clearly affected, also got the penultimate fence wrong. He was okay at the last again, though, and would've won even further with a cleaner round in the home straight. It was his third consecutive success, having landed his second win as a novice hurdler when signing off last term, and this 5-y-o is quickly making up into a very useful chaser. He does seem happiest on a sound surface and his trainer later confirmed that he is more of a spring horse. With that in mind he is likely to have one more outing in such company before being put away through the winter. (tchd Evens)
Double Dash made a respectable start over fences when second at Fontwell 22 days earlier, but he was completely outclassed by the penalised winner here. The added experience will not be lost on him, though, and stepping up in trip is likely to suit ideally in this sphere. (op 16-1 tchd 18-1)
Lake Legend was a four-time winner over hurdles and is officially rated 145 in that sphere, which made him of obvious interest for this chasing debut. He made his move on the back straight, but was never going to get near the winner. He would have probably finished runner-up but for hitting the second-last and this is an effort he ought to build on next time. (op 9-4)
Anquetta(IRE) was somewhat disappointing on his chasing debut at Fakenham last month, despite finishing second, and this was a definite step backwards. It could be that reverting to a left-handed circuit would help again, though. (op 15-2 tchd 5-1)
I'm In The Pink(FR) Official explanation: jockey said gelding finished lame

2331 BATHWICK TYRES NOVICES' HURDLE (9 hdls) 2m 1f

2:10 (2:10) (Class 3) 4-Y-0+ **£5,480** (£1,597; £799)

Form RPR

2-2 **1** **Dark Lover (GER)**[26] 1866 5-10-12 0.......................... NoelFehily 115+
(Paul Nicholls) *trckd ldrs: led after 4th: drew clr fr after 3 out: v easily* **1/2**[1]

41-0 **2** *13* **Madame Jasmine**[14] 2056 5-10-5 0.......................... ColinBolger 86
(Suzy Smith) *mid-div: trckd ldrs after 4th: rdn after 3 out: wnt 2nd at the last: no ch w wnr* **14/1**

0 **3** *6* **Attainable**[13] 2068 4-10-5 0..........................(t) RhysFlint 81
(Jim Old) *mid-div: hdwy 6th: rdn to chse wnr but no ch after 3 out: lost 2nd at the last: kpt on same pce* **50/1**

000- **4** *11* **Fun Guy**[264] 4158 5-10-12 0.......................... AndrewGlassonbury 78
(Bob Buckler) *in tch: chsd wnr fr 6th tl after 3 out: wknd after next* **66/1**

-506 **5** *22* **Art Value**[19] 1976 5-10-9 78.......................... SamTwiston-Davies(3) 58
(Carroll Gray) *hld up: sme prog 6th: rdn after 3 out: sn wknd: t.o* **28/1**

55-6 **6** *6* **Reefer Beefer (IRE)**[23] 1910 5-10-12 0.......................... AndrewThornton 53
(Tony Newcombe) *a towards rr: t.o fr after 3 out* **28/1**

5 **7** *21* **Aine's Delight (IRE)**[22] 1921 4-10-5 0.......................... NickScholfield 27
(Andy Turnell) *plld hrd: trckd ldrs: lft in ld after 3rd: hdd bef 5th: wknd qckly after 3 out: t.o* **15/2**[3]

8 2½ **Kilshanna (IRE)**[15] 2039 5-10-12 0.......................... AlanO'Keeffe 32
(Daniel William O'Sullivan, Ire) *prom tl 4th: wknd after next: t.o* **50/1**

0 **P** **Ben Chorley**[19] 1962 6-10-12 0..........................(t) TomScudamore —
(Tim Vaughan) *led tl p.u after 3rd: fatally injured* **4/1**[2]

4m 15.0s (7.00) **Going Correction** +0.325s/f (Yiel)
WFA 4 from 5yo+ 7lb **9** Ran SP% **117.4**
Speed ratings (Par 107): **96,89,87,81,71 68,58,57,—**
toteswingers:1&2:£2.30, 1&3:£11.50, 2&3:Not won CSF £8.94 TOTE £1.60: £1.02, £3.20, £8.60; EX 6.20.
Owner Des Nichols & Peter Hart **Bred** W Lohmann Jr **Trained** Ditcheat, Somerset

FOCUS
A weak and uncompetitive novice hurdle. The winner stood out and was value for further

NOTEBOOK
Dark Lover(GER) ◆ had finished second on both his previous outings in bumpers and proved all the rage to go one better on this switch to hurdling. He duly scored, making all for an easy success, and rates yet another decent prospect for his leading stable. He should get further as he matures and is sure to come into his own when sent chasing, but it will be interesting to see how high up the ladder he can climb in this sphere beforehand. He is likely to return here for a more valuable novice event next time. (op 4-9)
Madame Jasmine, a Fontwell bumper winner last term, kept on to prevail in the battle for second place and stepped up on her hurdling debut at Stratford last month. She likes a sound surface and should really appreciate a stiffer test. (op 20-1)
Attainable shaped much more encouragingly for the application of a first-time tongue-tie and she will be more interesting when switching to a handicap.
Fun Guy failed to build on an encouraging debut effort in bumpers last season, but this was a satisfactory introduction to hurdling and he should come on a deal for the experience.

2332 BATHWICK TYRES YEOVIL H'CAP CHASE (17 fncs) 2m 7f 110y

2:40 (2:40) (Class 5) (0-95,95) 4-Y-0+ **£2,740** (£798; £399)

Form RPR

1260 **1** **Justabout**[8] 2146 7-11-12 **95**..........................(tp) JoeTizzard 102+
(Colin Tizzard) *led: jinked lft 2nd: hdd after 4th: led 10th: hrd rdn after 3 out: styd on: all out* **3/1**[2]

5325 **2** ¾ **Bollywood (IRE)**[2] 2290 7-10-13 **82**..........................(t) TimmyMurphy 86
(Alison Batchelor) *hld up bhd ldrs: nt fluent 1st: disp 2nd 4 out: rdn next: sn chsng wnr: flattered sn after: styd on* **7/1**

36-5 **3** *8* **Lady De La Vega (FR)**[13] 2080 6-11-12 **95**..........................(v) SamThomas 84
(Tim Vaughan) *prom most of way: hit 6th: blnd 12th: rdn and ch whn pckd 3 out: styd on same pce fr next* **9/2**[3]

F6-0 **4** *55* **Aspolan (GER)**[19] 1959 7-11-9 **92**.......................... SeanQuinlan 40
(Rachel Hobbs) *nt fluent 1st: hld up: wnt 4th after 12th: rdn after next: sn wknd: t.o* **7/1**

P3-0 **P** **Rojabaa**[4] 2239 11-10-2 **71**.......................... RodiGreene —
(Simon Burrough) *plld hrd: led after 4th: clr 7th tl heavily restrained bef next: hdd 10th: wknd after next: t.o whn p.u after 4 out* **6/1**

PP03 **P** **Rapid Return (IRE)**[10] 2132 7-10-4 **73**.......................... WayneHutchinson —
(Richard Phillips) *trckd ldrs: rdn after 13th: sn wknd: t.o whn p.u bef 3 out* **11/4**[1]

6m 26.8s (12.20) **Going Correction** +0.025s/f (Yiel) **6** Ran SP% **109.1**
Speed ratings (Par 103): **80,79,77,58,—,—**
toteswingers:1&2:£8.70, 1&3:£3.70, 2&3:£3.30 CSF £21.36 TOTE £2.40: £1.02, £5.30; EX 20.00.
Owner Brocade Racing **Bred** H T Cole **Trained** Milborne Port, Dorset
■ Stewards' Enquiry : Joe Tizzard five-day ban: used whip with excessive force (Nov 25-29)

FOCUS
A weak handicap. The winner is rated to his mark.

NOTEBOOK
Justabout got back to winning ways under a strong ride from Joe Tizzard. His jumping had let him down the last twice and he wasn't that clever over the first two here. The application of first-time cheekpieces helped his cause as the race got serious off the home turn, however, and he was always just doing enough from two out. This was his third win of the year and it has to rate a career-best effort, but this is his level and he will now be forced back up in class. Official explanation: vet said gelding had been wealed as a result of the whip (tchd 10-3)

Bollywood(IRE) appreciated this sounder surface and ran an awful lot better than had been the case when returned to chasing at Lingfield two days earlier. He met the last running and went down fighting, so deserves a change of fortune. (op 11-2)
Lady De La Vega(FR) had her chance, but came under pressure from three out and was well held by the first pair. Her stable continues its quiet spell. (tchd 5-1)
Aspolan(GER) lacked fluency and was never seriously in the hunt. (tchd 6-1)
Rojabaa had her chance, but came under pressure from three out and was well held by the first pair. He stable continues its quiet spell. (op 3-1)
Rapid Return(IRE) came back to form at Plumpton ten days earlier, but the writing was on the wall a long way out for him here and he is one to tread carefully with. (op 3-1)

2333 BATHWICK TYRES PLYMOUTH H'CAP HURDLE (9 hdls) 2m 1f
3:10 (3:12) (Class 4) (0-115,115) 4-Y-O+ **£4,110** (£1,198; £599)

Form				RPR
0F-3	1		**Pennellis (FR)**[33] 1773 6-11-7 **110** ... NoelFehily (Paul Nicholls) *travelled wl in chsng gp: trckd ldrs after 3 out: jnd ldrs 2 out: led last: pushed clr* **5/4**[1]	126+
4-55	2	5	**Sun Quest**[10] 2128 6-10-9 **105** ... RobertKirk(7) (Steven Dixon) *chsd ldr: rdn after 3 out: led next: hdd last: nt pce of wnr* **6/1**[2]	104
256	3	8	**Consulate (IRE)**[19] 1972 6-11-5 **115** ...(p) MrDEdwards(7) (Gordon Edwards) *chsd ldr: jnd ldr 3 out: sn hung rt: rdn to ld briefly bef 2 out: sn one pce* **14/1**	107
-230	4	1 ½	**Sweet World**[42] 1548 6-11-2 **112** ... MissIsabelTompsett(7) (Bernard Llewellyn) *hld up: hdwy after 5th: rdn to chse ldrs appr 2 out: sn one pce* **11/1**	102
1431	5	12	**Nothing Is Forever (IRE)**[28] 1844 6-10-13 **102** ...(p) SeanQuinlan (Liam Corcoran) *led tl rdn after 3 out: fading whn mstke next* **15/2**[3]	85+
542	6	12	**Shipboard Romance (IRE)**[127] 933 5-10-6 **98** ...(t) PeterToole(3) (Mark Rimell) *hld up and a towards rr: wknd after 3 out: t.o* **14/1**	67
4502	7	14	**Raise Again (IRE)**[28] 1844 7-9-12 **90** ...(b) SamTwiston-Davies(3) (Nerys Dutfield) *hld up: mstke 3 out: sn wknd: t.o* **8/1**	46
-500	P		**Freddy's Star (IRE)**[178] 372 8-11-5 **115** ... DannyBurton(7) (Gerald Ham) *chsd ldng trio tl wknd after 5th: t.o whn p.u after 3 out* **20/1**	—
30-P	P		**Singapore Reef (FR)**[7] 2164 4-11-9 **112** ...(t) DarylJacob (Nick Williams) *hld up: nt fluent 5th: sn struggling: wknd bef 3 out: t.o whn p.u bef 2 out* **8/1**	—

4m 11.4s (3.40) **Going Correction** +0.325s/f (Yiel) **9** Ran SP% **119.1**
Speed ratings (Par 105): **105,102,98,98,92 86,80,—,—**
toteswingers:1&2:£2.00, 1&3:£8.20, 2&3:Not won CSF £10.21 CT £75.09 TOTE £2.70: £1.30, £1.80, £4.30; EX 12.90.
Owner Ken Ellis **Bred** Kenneth Bourke **Trained** Ditcheat, Somerset

FOCUS
This moderate handicap was run at a sound gallop and the form should work out. The winner was value for a lot further.

NOTEBOOK
Pennellis(FR) showed the benefit of his seasonal return at Chepstow last month and opened his account with plenty left in the tank on this handicap debut, making it three winners from as many runners for his trainer/jockey on the card. The breathing operation he had during his summer break has evidently worked the oracle and he has clearly begun life in handicaps on a decent mark. He should go on from this now. (op 6-4)
Sun Quest raced handily and responded most gamely to pressure around the home turn. In front at the second-last, he was a sitting duck for the winner but this was an improved effort. (op 7-1 tchd 11-2)
Consulate(IRE), dropping back in trip, took time to settle just off the early leader in first-time cheekpieces. He had his chance, but couldn't go with the first pair off the home turn and probably is happiest on quicker ground. He helps to set the level. (op 16-1 tchd 20-1)
Sweet World improved in the back straight but was done with from the penultimate flight. He looks held by the handicapper. (op 12-1)
Nothing Is Forever(IRE) was 7lb higher than when winning at Wincanton last month and set out to make all. He paid for his exertions off the home bend and wasn't given too hard a time when beat. (op 8-1)

2334 BATHWICK TYRES BATH H'CAP CHASE (12 fncs) 2m 110y
3:40 (3:40) (Class 5) (0-95,93) 4-Y-O+ **£2,602** (£764; £382; £190)

Form				RPR
/1-6	1		**Guns Of Love (IRE)**[22] 1924 8-10-5 **72** ... CharliePoste (Robin Dickin) *chsd ldng pair: wnt 2nd 6th: led next: hit 8th: rdn appr 3 out: kpt on gamely: drvn out* **13/2**[3]	83+
1200	2	2 ½	**Beauchamp Viking**[23] 1912 6-11-0 **81** ...(t) RodiGreene (Simon Burrough) *hld up: hdwy after 4 out: lft 3rd but sn 2nd after 3 out: rdn and styd on but a being hld* **13/2**[3]	88
-6P5	3	21	**Colliers Court**[21] 1940 13-11-9 **90** ... AidanColeman (Lisa Williamson) *j.lft 1st: led at str pce: hdd 7th: styd pressing wnr tl 4 out: hld whn lft 2nd briefly 3 out: wknd* **14/1**	78
4050	4	½	**Art Man**[22] 1925 7-11-6 **90** ...(t) ChrisHonour(3) (James Frost) *hld up: 33 l last 4 out: pluged on fr 3 out: wnt modest 4th bef last* **20/1**	78
0-65	5	8	**Keyneema**[8] 2149 8-11-4 **90** ... JimmyDerham(5) (Cathy Hamilton) *chsd clr trio tl wknd appr 4 out: t.o* **17/2**	72
3314	6	12	**Sean Og (IRE)**[20] 1954 8-9-11 **71** ...(t) MrTomDavid(7) (Tim Vaughan) *led chsng gp but a wl adrift of front three: wkng whn lft modest 4th 3 out* **6/1**[2]	45
5U-6	U		**Thievery**[21] 1940 9-10-11 **78** ... AndrewTinkler (Henry Daly) *a in rr: no ch whn mstke and uns rdr 4 out* **7/1**	—
3P-0	F		**Chilla Cilla**[8] 2144 7-10-9 **76** ...(t) NickScholfield (Anthony Honeyball) *hld up in chsng gp: prog fr 7th: pushed along in 4 l 2nd but clsng whn fell 3 out* **9/1**	83
-055	P		**Kyoto (GER)**[19] 1976 6-10-7 **74** ... DavidDennis (Nigel Hawke) *stmbld bdly 2nd: blnd 6th: sn wl bhd: p.u bef 4 out* **12/1**	—
6-14	P		**Randjo (FR)**[22] 1919 5-11-7 **93** ...(v¹) MrJoshuaGuerriero(5) (Victor Dartnall) *prom: hit 2nd and 7th: wknd after next: t.o whn p.u bef 3 out* **10/3**[1]	—

4m 22.8s (12.80) **Going Correction** +0.025s/f (Yiel) **10** Ran SP% **116.2**
Speed ratings (Par 103): **70,68,58,58,54 49,—,—,—,—**
toteswingers:1&2:£14.70, 1&3:£8.10, 2&3:£7.30 CSF £48.66 CT £574.10 TOTE £7.00: £2.60, £2.00, £3.50; EX 59.10.
Owner Whoops 72! **Bred** Pat O'Rourke **Trained** Atherstone on Stour, Warwicks
■ Stewards' Enquiry : Charlie Poste one-day ban: used whip in incorrect place (Nov 25)

FOCUS
There was always likely to be a decent gallop on in this weak handicap and so it played out as the two early leaders went off too quickly for their own good. The first two are rated to their marks.

NOTEBOOK
Guns Of Love(IRE) ran out a game winner. He needed his return at Worcester last month and had dropped back to his last winning mark for this. His rider's decision to just sit off the two pacemakers paid off and this 8-y-o showed a decent attitude under pressure in the home straight. (op 7-1 tchd 11-2)
Beauchamp Viking ◆, 4lb lower, showed the clear benefit of his comeback at Exeter 23 days previously and was the only one to make a significant impact under a waiting ride. A return to more positive handling over this trip is probably a wise move and his turn isn't looking that far off again. (op 11-1 tchd 6-1)
Colliers Court predictably made his way to the front, but the presence of Randjo ensured he had to go off quicker than he really wanted to. He was cooked from four out, but did keep on in the home straight and this was more encouraging again.
Art Man, with the blinkers left off for this chasing debut, kept on past beaten rivals in the home straight yet is entitled to come on a bit for the experience. (op 22-1)
Chilla Cilla was keeping on nicely and was still in with every chance prior to tipping up at the third-last. On this evidence she will make into a better chaser, but it was anything but an ideal introduction to fences. (op 3-1 tchd 7-2 in places)
Randjo(FR) looked to have been found a decent opportunity, but he was lit up by the first-time visor and stopped quickly on the back straight. (op 3-1 tchd 7-2 in places)

2335 BATHWICK TYRES BRISTOL MAIDEN OPEN NATIONAL HUNT FLAT RACE 2m 1f
4:10 (4:10) (Class 5) 4-6-Y-O **£2,055** (£599; £299)

Form				RPR
3	1		**Hes Our Lad (IRE)**[35] 1748 4-10-11 0 ... RachaelGreen(5) (Anthony Honeyball) *hld up: hdwy fr over 6f out: jnd ldr travelling wl over 2f out: edgd narrowly ahd ins fnl f: hung bdly lft: hld on* **2/1**[2]	107+
2	2	hd	**Billy Merriott (IRE)**[162] 589 4-11-2 0 ... NoelFehily (Paul Nicholls) *trckd ldrs: led 4f out: hrd pressed fr over 2f out: narrowly hdd ins fnl f: rallied nr fin* **5/4**[1]	105+
	3	6	**Dineur (FR)** 4-10-9 0 ... CDTimmons(7) (Alan King) *trckd ldrs: rdn over 2f out: styd on same pce tl no ex ins fnl f* **9/2**[3]	99+
006-	4	24	**Taylors Secret**[200] 7 4-10-9 0 ... PeterCarberry(7) (Shaun Lycett) *trckd ldrs tl outpcd over 7f out: plugged on to regain modest 4th over 1f out* **33/1**	75
0-	5	1 ½	**Pirans Car**[215] 5137 4-11-2 0 ... DavidDennis (Nigel Hawke) *led tl 4f out: sn rdn: wknd 2f out* **40/1**	74
	6	5	**Wosayu** 4-11-2 0 ... JoeTizzard (Colin Tizzard) *rn green: in tch: rdn over 6f out: sn btn* **7/1**	69
	7	47	**Mister Gold** 5-10-13 0 ... LeeStephens(3) (David Evans) *lost tch 1/2-way* **14/1**	22

4m 9.70s (7.30) **Going Correction** +0.325s/f (Yiel) **7** Ran SP% **120.5**
Speed ratings: **95,94,92,80,80 77,55**
toteswingers:1&2:£1.02, 1&3:£2.10, 2&3:£1.30 CSF £5.29 TOTE £2.70: £1.60, £1.10; EX 4.40.
Owner A J Honeyball S E Wall A J Forde **Bred** Alistair Corrigan **Trained** Seaborough, Dorset

FOCUS
There was a satisfactory gallop on in this maiden bumper and the first three had it to themselves off the home turn. The first two are fair bumper horses.

NOTEBOOK
Hes Our Lad(IRE), third on debut at Worcester last month, opened his account at the second time of asking and won with a fair bit more in hand than the narrow margin indicates. He made smooth headway coming out of the back straight and was travelling all over the runner-up 2f out. His rider was very confident, but he proved green when asked to win the race and ended up hanging right over to the stands' rail. He was always just holding sway, though, and edged the verdict without need for the whip. This added experience should teach him a good deal and he rates a fair prospect for novice hurdling. (tchd 9-4)
Billy Merriott(IRE), second on debut at Fontwell in June, was a popular choice to give his trainer/jockey a four-timer and nearly went one better. He travelled well off the home turn and, coming under heavy pressure from 2f out, proved game in defeat. He could come on for the run and deserves a change of fortune. (op 13-8)
Dineur(FR) is a good-looking 4-y-o and met support for this racecourse debut. He didn't help his cause by refusing to settle, though, and paid the price from 3f out. There should be a nice bit of improvement in him. (op 13-2 tchd 7-1)
Wosayu looked well for his debut, but ran green on the back straight and was eventually well beaten off. (op 11-2 tchd 5-1)
T/Plt: £124.40 to a £1 stake. Pool:£64,554.23 - 378.69 winning tickets T/Qpdt: £23.90 to a £1 stake. Pool:£4,422.83 - 136.71 winning tickets TM

2336 - 2338a (Foreign Racing) - See Raceform Interactive

2060 CLONMEL (R-H)
Thursday, November 11

OFFICIAL GOING: Soft to heavy (heavy in places) changing to heavy after race 3 (1:55)

2339a CLONMEL OIL CHASE (GRADE 2) (14 fncs) 2m 4f
2:25 (2:25) 5-Y-O+ **£25,884** (£7,566; £3,584; £1,194)

			RPR
1		**Tranquil Sea (IRE)**[204] 5322 8-11-10 157 ... AndrewJMcNamara (E J O'Grady, Ire) *racd in 4th: 3rd 7 out: 2nd 5 out: led bef 2 out: clr last: pushed out run-in* **10/11**[1]	163
2	2	**Let Yourself Go (IRE)**[32] 1801 8-11-4 150 ... SJHassett (Adrian Maguire, Ire) *led: nt fluent 7 out: strly pressed and hdd bef 2 out: no imp last: kpt on again run-in* **5/1**[3]	155
3	1 ¾	**Scotsirish (IRE)**[205] 5302 9-11-10 154 ... PTownend (W P Mullins, Ire) *hld up: clsr in 4th 6 out: 3rd fr 3 out: no imp u.p and kpt on same pce fr 2 out* **9/2**[2]	159
4	18	**Oscar Looby (IRE)**[32] 1804 7-11-6 137 ...(t) DJCondon (Noel Meade, Ire) *towards rr: reminder 4th: pushed along and prog fr 3 out: 4th appr st: sn no imp and kpt on same pce* **11/2**	137
5	17	**One Cool Cookie (IRE)**[17] 2016 9-11-8 137 ...(bt) DNRussell (C F Swan, Ire) *prom: wknd fr 3 out* **20/1**	122
P		**Mansony (FR)**[219] 5082 11-11-10 147 ... PWFlood (A L T Moore, Ire) *trckd ldrs: wknd and p.u bef 5 out* **16/1**	—

5m 31.3s (13.70) **6** Ran SP% **113.3**
CSF £6.30 TOTE £2.40: £1.40, £2.70; DF 7.20.
Owner D Cox **Bred** Edward Curtin **Trained** Ballynonty, Co Tipperary

FOCUS
This wasn't run much quicker than the following mares' race and only the winner was seemingly on his game.

NOTEBOOK
Tranquil Sea(IRE) eased to the front coming to the second-last and while he didn't open up and leave them for dead, he did more than enough without having any really serious questions asked of him. All being well, this could be the season where he shows himself to be a genuine Grade 1 quality chaser. (op 1/1)
Let Yourself Go(IRE) ran a cracker. After leading and jumping well, the winner had too much class for him, but to his credit he really kept on well. (op 4/1)

Scotsirish(IRE) ◆ ran a real cracker. Hitting the front two coming down the hill, he didn't have the pace to challenge the winner but was running on well enough to chase him home before he probably got a bit tired from the last. It was a very good effort and while it's hard to predict where he'll go next, he could have a good season. (op 9/2 tchd 5/1)
Oscar Looby(IRE) ended up well beaten. His jumping lacked fluency on occasions and after he seemed to be staying on for pressure early in the straight, he eventually got a bit tired from the second-last. (op 9/1)
One Cool Cookie(IRE) was never able to get into it. (op 16/1 tchd 25/1)
Mansony(FR) weakened quickly on the final circuit before pulling up. (op 14/1)

2340 - 2342a (Foreign Racing) - See Raceform Interactive

1860 CHELTENHAM (L-H)

Friday, November 12

OFFICIAL GOING: Chase & hurdle courses - good (good to soft in places) changing to good to soft (good in places) after race 3 (2.25); cross-country course - good
Moderate aheadOvercast

2343 IRISH TIMES AMATEUR RIDERS' H'CAP CHASE (19 fncs) 3m 110y
1:15 (1:15) (Class 2) (0-140,140) 4-Y-0+
£8,402 (£2,625; £1,311; £656; £327; £165)

Form RPR
46U- **1** **Rustarix (FR)**^{245} 4565 9-9-13 **120** .... MrJBanks$^{(7)}$ 128
(Alan King) *in rr: hdwy 14th: chsd ldrs 4 out: chal 3 out: rdn to take narrow ld next: styd on u.p run-in: hld on wl* **14/1**
4425 **2** *1* **Swing Bill (FR)**^{10} 2140 9-10-11 **125** .... MrSWaley-Cohen 132
(David Pipe) *trckd ldrs: qcknd to take slt ld 3 out: narrowly hdd but upsides next and last: kpt on run-in but a jst hld by wnr* **7/1**
F3-P **3** *1 1/2* **Knowhere (IRE)**^{138} 844 12-11-9 **137** .... MrDerekO'Connor 145
(Nigel Twiston-Davies) *led after 1st: kpt narrow advantage tl hdd 3 out: rdn and hit 2 out: rallied run-in and kpt on again cl home* **7/1**
14-6 **4** *1 1/2* **Noun De La Thinte (FR)**^{14} 2072 9-10-1 **122** .... MrJSherwood$^{(7)}$ 126
(Venetia Williams) *chsd ldrs: wnt 2nd 8th: chal fr 10th to 3 out: sn rdn: kpt on run-in but no imp* **16/1**
140- **5** *1/2* **Qhilimar (FR)**^{217} 5111 6-10-12 **126** .... (b) MrWBiddick 130
(Alan Jones) *hit 8th: in tch: rdn and rr 4 out: styd on wl fr 2 out: r.o wl cl home but nt rch ldrs* **6/1^{2}**
-401 **6** *2 1/4* **Quattrocento (FR)**^{28} 1858 6-10-8 **122** .... (v) MrMPFogarty 126
(Peter Bowen) *in rr: j. slowly 13th: hdwy and hit 3 out: nvr quite rchd ldrs and one pce fr 2 out* **11/2^{1}**
120- **7** *8* **Notabotheronme (IRE)**^{230} 4890 8-9-8 **115** .... (p) MrTCheesman$^{(7)}$ 111
(Philip Hobbs) *chsd ldrs tl dropped to rr 12th: apparently losing tch after 4 out but styd on again after 2 out wout ever looking a threat* **12/1**
00-2 **8** *shd* **Earth Planet (IRE)**^{20} 1964 8-10-9 **128** .... (t) MrDGPrichard$^{(5)}$ 124
(Paul Nicholls) *in tch fr 7th: hdwy 14th: rdn and lost tch 3 out: kpt on again run-in* **13/2^{3}**
143- **9** *1 1/4* **Richard's Sundance (IRE)**^{236} 4768 8-11-12 **140**... MrJoshuaGuerriero 136
(Victor Dartnall) *led tl after 1st: hit 9th: wknd: bhd fr 14th* **20/1**
5P0- **10** *6* **Martys Mission (IRE)**^{202} 5395 8-10-8 **127** .... MrTJCannon$^{(5)}$ 118
(Richard Rowe) *in rr: hdwy 14th: in tch whn rdn 3 out: btn whn mstke 2 out* **14/1**
16P- **11** *28* **Theatrical Moment (USA)**^{209} 5223 7-11-11 **139** .... MrAJBerry 102
(Jonjo O'Neill) *in rr: j. slowly 4th: hit 6th: sme hdwy 11th: rdn and wknd 4 out* **8/1**
00-0 **U** **Cornish Sett (IRE)**^{20} 1960 11-10-2 **123** .... MrRHawkins$^{(7)}$ —
(Caroline Keevil) *trckd ldrs tl mstke and uns rdr 3rd* **20/1**

6m 26.88s (8.58) **Going Correction** +0.05s/f (Yiel) **12 Ran SP% 115.5**
Speed ratings (Par 109): **88,87,87,86,86 85,83,83,82,80 71,—**
Tote Swingers: 1&2 £49.90, 1&3 £12.90, 2&3 £5.70 CSF £107.40 CT £746.11 TOTE £17.30: £5.20, £2.10, £2.60; EX 119.70 Trifecta £1327.80 Pool: £1,794.42 - 1 winning unit..
Owner Mrs R J Skan **Bred** Gheorghe Codre **Trained** Barbury Castle, Wilts
■ Stewards' Enquiry : Mr D G Prichard one-day ban: used whip when out of contention (tbn)
Mr T Cheesman two-day ban: used whip when out of contention (tbn)

FOCUS
The ground for the first day of the Open meeting was officially described as good, good to soft in places on both the hurdle and chase tracks. It certainly looked to be riding nearer good in this opening handicap for amateur riders, but the jockeys afterwards were of the opinion it was dead in places and would still take some getting. They went something of an uneven gallop in the race, but it still provided a decent test and the first two dominated off the home turn. Solid handicap form, the winner back to form and the next two pretty much on their marks.

NOTEBOOK
Rustarix(FR), who failed to score in four outings last term, attracted support on this seasonal return and ran out a gutsy winner. He got seriously involved on the back straight and it was clear that he and Swing Bill were travelling by far the best nearing the final bend. The pair locked horns from the second-last and he saw the trip out really well up the run-in, in receipt of 12lb from the runner-up taking into account his rider's 7lb claim. He was resuming off a career-low mark and he clearly likes this venue, having finished second as a novice hurdler on his only previous visit here. He seems happiest on a sounder surface, but has scored on soft ground and now he has won over the trip it opens up more options for him. (op 16-1 tchd 12-1)
Swing Bill(FR) was having his sixth outing back since returning from an injury layoff in July. He flopped on soft ground at Exeter ten days earlier, but this return to better ground brought about a vast improvement again, and he was a little unfortunate to have bumped into the winner as he finished a clear second-best. He got outstayed by that rival as a result of racing enthusiastically, but was giving a fair bit of weight away and this rates a personal-best display. (op 8-1)
Knowhere(IRE) has fallen in the handicap over the past year and was last seen pulling up in the Summer National 138 days earlier. He got an aggressive ride by his senior Irish amateur and he posted a brave effort in defeat, despite an indifferent round of jumping. This is an outing he could build upon, although it must be noted he has a decent record first time up. (op 15-2)
Noun De La Thinte(FR) was beaten a long way on her return over hurdles a fortnight previously, but her trainer is in better form now and has a decent record in this event. With that in mind it wasn't surprising to see her turn in a much-improved effort, but this trip stretches her and she does look weighted around her best.
Qhilimar(FR) ◆ had fallen at the old second-last in this race last season on just his second outing for connections and is now officially rated a stone higher despite having won just once since. He hit a flat spot at a crucial stage on this seasonal debut, but caught the eye staying on stoutly from the last and looks sure to improve for the outing. (op 7-1)
Quattrocento(FR) was hiked up 9lb for resuming winning ways at Exeter 28 days earlier, when a long way in front of Swing Bill. He was battling away prior to an error at the third-last which didn't help his cause, and was unable to find an extra gear up the home straight. He helps to set the standard. (tchd 6-1 in places)
Notabotheronme(IRE) is a dour stayer and, faced with a stiff enough task on this return to action, wasn't disgraced on ground plenty quick enough for him. His rider was overly hard on him after the last, though, so he did have a tough race. (op 16-1 tchd 18-1)
Earth Planet(IRE), whose best effort over hurdles came in a very competitive 3m handicap at this meeting last year, rather threw it away when second on his comeback at Chepstow last month. He was another that hit a flat spot on this handicap debut over fences, and probably found the ground quicker than he cares for, but he isn't one for maximum faith. (op 6-1 tchd 7-1)
Richard's Sundance(IRE) recovered from a blunder at the ninth and had his chance, but ultimately left the impression this return was needed - in keeping with the majority from his yard so far this term. He also should appreciate reverting to an easier surface. (op 16-1)
Martys Mission(IRE) looked a player when responding to pressure coming out of the back straight, but had begun to feel the pinch prior to an error at the second-last and was treading water up the run-in. He has the talent to defy this mark when things click for him and is yet another entitled to improve for the outing. (op 16-1 tchd 25-1 in a place)
Theatrical Moment(USA) was pulled up in the Scottish National on his final outing last term, but his sixth off a 3lb higher perch in the William Hill Handicap at last year's Festival entitled him to respect. He tried to get involved going out onto the final lap, but jumping errors mounted up and he ran well below his best. It's a good bet he will improve as the season develops and may well prove happier back on a right-handed track. (op 13-2)

2344 CHELTENHAM COLLECTION SHARP NOVICES' HURDLE GRADE 2 (8 hdls) 2m 110y
1:50 (1:51) (Class 1) 4-Y-0+
£14,252 (£5,347; £2,677; £1,335; £670; £335)

Form RPR
11-1 **1** **Cue Card**^{19} 1988 4-11-7 0 .... JoeTizzard 154+
(Colin Tizzard) *trckd ldrs: hit 3rd: trckd ldr after 3 out: chal on bit 2 out: led wl bef last: pushed clr run-in: comf* **8/13^{1}**
1-11 **2** *8* **Dunraven Storm (IRE)**^{13} 2083 5-11-7 138 .... RichardJohnson 145+
(Philip Hobbs) *trckd ldr: led appr 3 out: jnd and hit 2 out: sn rdn: hdd bef last and sn no ch w wnr but styd on wl for clr 2nd* **5/1^{2}**
2 **3** *10* **Ballyadam Brook (IRE)**^{40} 1713 6-11-7 140 .... PTownend 137
(Terence O'Brien, Ire) *led: hit 1st: sn clr: stdd 3rd: hdd appr 3 out: sn outpcd by ldng duo and hit 2 out: wl hld whn mstke last* **11/1**
3-11 **4** *6* **Owen Glendower (IRE)**^{15} 2056 5-11-7 135 .... BarryGeraghty 130
(Nicky Henderson) *in tch: trckd ldrs fr 3rd: rdn 3 out: no ch fr next: mstke last* **16/1**
21-1 **5** *15* **King Of The Night (GER)**^{28} 1857 6-11-7 0 .... NoelFehily 115
(Paul Nicholls) *a towards rr: lost tch appr 3 out* **15/2^{3}**
3111 **6** *nk* **Maska Pony (IRE)**^{30} 1827 6-11-7 127 .... GrahamLee 117
(George Moore) *in rr: pushed along and effrt after 4 out: sn wknd and no ch fr 3 out* **40/1**
50- **7** *28* **Far Away So Close (IRE)**^{17} 2028 5-11-7 134 .... DNRussell 106
(Paul Nolan, Ire) *a in rr: j. slowly 1st: and 4 out: wl bhd whn j. slowly again next* **18/1**

3m 56.4s (-5.60) **Going Correction** +0.05s/f (Yiel) **7 Ran SP% 112.3**
Speed ratings (Par 115): **115,111,106,103,96 96,83**
Tote Swingers: 1&2 £1.40, 1&3 £3.50, 2&3 £5.60 CSF £4.02 TOTE £1.60: £1.40, £2.30; EX 4.40 Trifecta £14.90 Pool: £1,808.97 - 89.66 winning units..
Owner Mrs Jean R Bishop **Bred** R T Crellin **Trained** Milborne Port, Dorset

FOCUS
The strongest running of this race for a while, all bar one of the runners having scored last time out, with the one who hadn't winning his previous four. A top-class performance from Cue Card who is already operating at a level good enough to win a typical Supreme Novices'. The second is a smart novice and the third is the best guide to the form.

NOTEBOOK
Cue Card ◆ was returning to the scene of his devastating Champion Bumper victory, and the good pace set by Irish raider Ballyadam Brook enabled him to settle considerably better than he had done on his hurdles debut at Aintree, when still managing to run out an easy winner. Keen not to allow main market rival Dunraven Storm too much of a start, Tizzard kept him within a few lengths throughout, and a quick jump two out, when the runner-up blundered, handed him the advantage. He just had to be squeezed to assert coming to the last and, as one would have expected, he stormed clear up the hill. Although he clearly possesses a lot of speed, there's little doubt his future lies over further, and the Neptune would seem the more sensible long-term target, being a race that goes to the best horse a high percentage of the time, whereas that isn't the case in the Supreme Novices', where there's always the danger he'll be done for speed by an ex-Flat racer. However, as was the case after Aintree, Colin Tizzard hinted the Champion Hurdle is very much an option, and we'll no doubt learn more again after his next appearance around Christmas time. (op 8-11 tchd 4-5 in places)
Dunraven Storm(IRE), some 27l behind Cue Card in the Festival bumper, had won all three starts since, including his two starts over hurdles this term, and he looked the one most capable of testing the favourite. He still held a narrow lead until hitting two out, but looking at how readily he was left trailing from the last, it's clear he was beaten by a far superior horse. He will surely go up in distance now, which should suit on breeding and run-style, and he has every chance of developing into a leading Neptune contender, with the Challow Hurdle over Christmas a possible target. (tchd 11-2)
Ballyadam Brook(IRE), who notched a four-timer between May and September, came up short tried in Grade 3 company last time, but the return to better ground seemed to suit and he stayed on valiantly back in third, having been dropped by the front two. (op 12-1 tchd 14-1)
Owen Glendower(IRE), 2-2 over hurdles, having won at Worcester and Stratford, looked a bit out of his depth on this rise in grade and was quickly dropped by the classy front pair, but there's every chance he improve for a stiffer test and there could be a decent handicap in him later in the season. His future lies over fences, though, being a half-brother to the following winner Dave's Dream. (op 14-1)
King Of The Night(GER), who had created such a good impression when winning a maiden hurdle over C&D on last month's seasonal reappearance. Usually a strong-travelling type, he was in trouble a long way out, beaten too soon for the rise in grade to be blamed, and perhaps the ground had become a bit tacky for him. He's not a winter horse, so it would be no surprise to see him kept back for the spring. (op 7-1)
Maska Pony(IRE), who has gone up 37lb in the handicap, winning four times since May, had a massive class gap to bridge and he simply wasn't up to it. (op 33-1 tchd 50-1)
Far Away So Close(IRE), ninth in last season's Supreme Novices' as a maiden, came into this having won his last two, but made numerous mistakes and never threatened to get involved. (op 20-1 tchd 16-1)

2345 PADDYPOWER.COM H'CAP CHASE (13 fncs) 2m
2:25 (2:26) (Class 2) (0-145,144) 4-Y-0+
£25,048 (£7,400; £3,700; £1,852; £924; £464)

Form RPR
340- **1** **Dave's Dream (IRE)**^{239} 4698 7-11-5 **137** .... BarryGeraghty 154+
(Nicky Henderson) *trckd ldrs: pushed along fr 4 out: chal 3 out: led wl bef 2 out: c clr sn after: readily* **10/3^{1}**
F042 **2** *8* **Grand Lahou (FR)**^{12} 2112 7-10-4 **129** .... MrTomDavid$^{(7)}$ 138
(Tim Vaughan) *t.k.h: led: jnd 3 out: hdd wl bef 2 out and sn no ch w wnr but hld on wl for 2nd* **25/1**
120- **3** *2 3/4* **Rivaliste (FR)**^{239} 4698 5-11-5 **137** .... NoelFehily 143
(Paul Nicholls) *chsd ldrs: rt there whn hit 3 out and sn outpcd: rdn and styd on fr 2 out and kpt on to cl on 2nd run-in but nvr any ch w wnr* **7/2^{2}**

03-1 **4** *2 ¾* **Safari Journey (USA)**[13] 2086 6-11-12 **144**...............(b) RichardJohnson 148
(Philip Hobbs) *in tch: chsd ldrs fr 8th: drvn to chal 3 out: no ch w wnr next and styd on same pce* **6/1**

3-P0 **5** *7* **Pocket Aces (IRE)**[27] 1861 8-10-12 **130**.......................... LeightonAspell 127
(Richard Rowe) *mid-div: dropped to rr 4 out: hit next and plenty to do but styd on again appr last wout ever looking a threat* **25/1**

2/6- **6** *5* **Keelaghan (IRE)**[26] 1892 10-10-13 **131**.................................. APMcCoy 123
(A J Martin, Ire) *in tch: rdn appr 3 out: wknd sn after* **5/1³**

3221 **7** *6* **Quito Du Tresor (FR)**[20] 1975 6-11-3 **135**...................... CampbellGillies 125
(Lucinda Russell) *chsd ldrs: rdn and wknd 3 out* **15/2**

/30- **8** *23* **Rookery Rebel (IRE)**[26] 1892 8-9-11 **118** oh1..................... DGHogan⁽³⁾ 84
(C W J Farrell, Ire) *j. slowly 1st: blnd 3rd: a in rr and no ch fr 4 out* **25/1**

-P00 **9** *5* **Star Of Germany (IRE)**[14] 2077 10-10-5 **123**.............. TomScudamore 85
(Ian Williams) *in tch tl wknd 4 out* **25/1**

113- **10** *11* **De Boitron (FR)**[204] 5337 6-11-2 **134**.............................. GrahamLee 86
(Ferdy Murphy) *in tch 7th: hit 9th and sn wknd* **12/1**

/PP- **11** *6* **Perce Rock**[204] 5346 8-11-3 **138**.................................. RichieMcLernon⁽³⁾ 84
(Jonjo O'Neill) *nvr jumping w any real fluency: a bhd* **25/1**

4m 1.27s (3.27) **Going Correction** +0.45s/f (Soft) **11** Ran SP% **114.9**
Speed ratings (Par 109): **109,105,103,102,98 96,93,81,79,73 70**
Tote Swingers: 1&2 £18.50, 1&3 £2.80, 2&3 £21.70 CSF £83.71 CT £305.48 TOTE £4.00: £1.90, £7.60, £1.60; EX 98.70 Trifecta £822.10 Pool: £2,466.30 - 2.22 winning units..

Owner David Murdoch & Jenny Murdoch **Bred** Kenilworth House Stud **Trained** Upper Lambourn, Berks

FOCUS
A good-quality handicap chase, featuring a couple of interesting second-season chasers. They didn't go overly fast early on and it paid to race handily. Solid handicap form. A big step up from the impressive winner, and the second was back to the form of his Stratford win.

NOTEBOOK
Dave's Dream(IRE) didn't go on as expected having made a winning start over fences last season, disappointing in the Jewson on his final start, but a wind operation over the summer has clearly done the trick, and he ran out a most convincing winner, pinging the two fences in the straight in the manner of a horse with plenty left in the tank. He'll return next month for the December Gold Cup (formerly the Boylesports), where the longer trip promises to suit. (op 7-2 tchd 3-1)

Grand Lahou(FR), who made a lot of the running, is still 12lb higher than when last winning, but he returned to something like his best in second, staying on again in a manner to suggest he'll appreciate a return to further.

Rivaliste(FR) made a promising start last season, having formerly been trained in France, but he could only manage seventh when favourite for the Jewson and the drop in trip, which was expected to suit, didn't appear to work in his favour judging by the way he kept on up the hill having been outpaced. Perhaps he'll strip fitter next time and, being just a 5-y-o, he remains capable of better. Official explanation: vet said gelding lost left-fore shoe (op 4-1 tchd 9-2)

Safari Journey(USA) went up 14lb for routing his rivals in first-time blinkers at Ascot and there's every reason to believe he ran his race in defeat in what looked a much stronger contest. (op 11-2)

Pocket Aces(IRE) ◆ was the eyecatcher as, having been badly outpaced and got well behind, he stayed on taking in the final 2f and is clearly crying out for a return to further. Rated 130 here, he looks more than capable of winning a decent prize off that mark.

Keelaghan(IRE) had to be respected, following his win at Cork last month, but he produced a rather tame finishing effort. Official explanation: vet said gelding was lame left-hind (tchd 9-2 and 11-2 in places)

Quito Du Tresor(FR), the easy Stratford winner, never got involved in this better race off a 10lb higher mark. (op 8-1)

De Boitron(FR), a progressive sort last season, is from a yard whose runners have been needing a run and he can be expected to leave this form behind in due course.

2346 GLENFARCLAS CROSS COUNTRY CHASE (32 fncs) 3m 7f
3:00 (3:01) (Class 2) 5-Y-0+

£15,655 (£4,625; £2,312; £1,157; £577; £290)

Form RPR

33-2 **1** **Lacdoudal (FR)**[28] 1856 11-10-10 135.......................... RichardJohnson 140+
(Philip Hobbs) *in tch: hdwy 15th: led 22nd: jnd fr 27th: strly chal last and run-in: styd on gamely to assert fnl 25yds* **9/2²**

115- **2** *nk* **Garde Champetre (FR)**[19] 2007 11-11-8 161............ MissNCarberry 152+
(E Bolger, Ire) *in tch: j. slowly and in rr 25th: styd on fr 3 out: drvn to chal last: stl upsides run-in: kpt on gamely but no ex fnl 25yds* **6/5¹**

204- **3** *4 ½* **Sizing Australia (IRE)**[22] 1943 8-11-5 137.............................. AELynch 143
(Henry De Bromhead, Ire) *chsd ldrs: chal 12th: led 13th: hdd 17th: led 19th to 22nd: mstke 27th: ev ch 4 out to 2 out: one pce appr last* **6/1³**

62-0 **4** *18* **Freneys Well**[58] 1526 10-11-5 137.. MrAJBerry 125
(E Bolger, Ire) *chsd ldrs: rdn 4 out: wknd next* **16/1**

6-50 **5** *1* **Mr Big (IRE)**[33] 1811 9-11-5 132.. NoelFehily 123
(Charlie Mann) *chsd ldrs: led 14th to 17th: wknd after 4 out* **50/1**

300- **6** *1 ¾* **Joe Lively (IRE)**[216] 5127 11-11-8 145............................. JoeTizzard 126
(Colin Tizzard) *in tch tl dropped towards rr 18th: stl bhd whn blnd and no ch 27th* **9/2²**

-145 **7** *16* **Lucky Luk (FR)**[28] 1858 11-11-2 111.............................. SeanQuinlan 106
(Kim Bailey) *j. slowly 4th: a towards rr* **50/1**

0P- **8** *18* **Changing Course (IRE)**[15] 2063 8-10-10 127...................... MrPPower 78
(Henry De Bromhead, Ire) *in rr: hdwy 21st: mstke and wknd 28th* **66/1**

600- **9** *dist* **Heads Onthe Ground (IRE)**[26] 13-10-12 133 ow2..... MrJTMcNamara 30
(E Bolger, Ire) *led to 13th: led again 17th to 22nd: wknd 28th: t.o* **16/1**

/PP- **P** **Flintoff (USA)**[216] 5127 9-10-10 136................................. AidanColeman —
(Venetia Williams) *nvr travelling or jumping: in rr tl t.o and p.u bef 15th* **18/1**

8m 13.17s (-24.83) **Going Correction** -0.575s/f (Firm) course record **10** Ran SP% **118.5**
Speed ratings: **109,108,107,103,102 102,98,93,80,—**
Tote Swingers: 1&2 £1.10, 1&3 £3.30, 2&3 £2.80 CSF £10.99 TOTE £4.60: £1.60, £1.20, £1.80; EX 11.80 Trifecta £31.70 Pool: £3,350.30 - 78.04 winning units..

Owner Mrs R J Skan **Bred** Scea Terres Noires **Trained** Withycombe, Somerset

FOCUS
The opening of the three cross-county events at this track is the only non-handicap event. The course didn't water this unique circuit and the ground was officially advertised at good to firm, good in places. The rain did arrive again just before the race, though, and it did appear to have got into the ground somewhat. As usual they went an ordinary gallop until things began to wind up nearing the Aintree fence, and the first three had it to themselves turning for home. Lacdoudal is probably capable of rating higher over this track. Garde Champetre was a stone off his best but rates higher than when winning this last year.

NOTEBOOK
Lacdoudal(FR) just did enough to hold off Garde Champetre and finally strike a blow for the domestic challenge in this sphere. The winner finished third at the Festival over C&D last season and had returned here last month with a solid second in a handicap over 3m. That must have put him spot on for a return to these fences and, taking the race by the scruff of the neck a fair way out, he displayed a really game attitude to end a losing run that dated back to the Betfred Gold Cup (as it was formerly known) in 2006. He was 13lb worse off with the runner-up on their previous meeting here in March, but was getting 12lb off him this time and used to rate a good bit higher himself in his heyday. No doubt a return to this course next month will be on his agenda, but it will be back in handicap company on even less favourable terms with his old rival, and so he will need to step up again to follow up there. (op 5-1)

Garde Champetre(FR) took this event last season and his record of 5-7 over C&D was there for all to see. At the Festival he didn't get a great passage in what was a very messy race and he again endured a troubled run this time. He also tended to fiddle a few of his fences which meant he had to come from a fair way back to get to the front pair nearing the home turn. His response when asked to quicken was immediate and he still looked a likely winner at the last, but ultimately a 12lb concession to the winner proved beyond him. Next month's race here back in a handicap will see him go off top weight again, but the likely softer ground there should only play to his strengths and he will be better off again with Lacdoudal, so he will still be the one to beat again. (op 11-8 tchd 11-10)

Sizing Australia(IRE) showed a real liking for this track last season and, surprisingly, his comeback win at Thurles last month was his first as a chaser so he should've been high on confidence. He got a positive ride and held every chance, but couldn't go with the first pair from the final fence. He rates a solid benchmark along with the runner-up and, while he should again run well, it would be surprising to see him reverse form in the handicap here next month.

Freneys Well, one of three from the Enda Bolger yard, is himself a well-known performer in this discipline. He lacked the tactical pace to land a serious blow, but has yet to strike here and there is probably no coincidence that his two wins under rules have come at the Punchestown festival. (op 20-1)

Mr Big(IRE), fourth in this race last term, was well beaten again in the Pardubicka last time out but showed his true colours here. (op 33-1)

Joe Lively(IRE) was in decline last season, but there was always a chance switching to these fences would rekindle some enthusiasm. Patiently ridden, he looked a possible player nearing the Aintree fence but was left behind as the pace lifted from that stage. He was plugging on towards the end and should come on for the run. (op 6-1)

2347 ARKLE BOOKSHOP CONDITIONAL JOCKEYS' H'CAP HURDLE (10 hdls) 2m 5f
3:35 (3:37) (Class 3) (0-125,123) 4-Y-0+

£6,262 (£1,850; £925; £463; £231; £116)

Form RPR

1/1- **1** **Aegean Dawn**[360] 2349 5-11-0 **114**...................................... DavidBass⁽³⁾ 146+
(Nicky Henderson) *in tch: hmpd 4 out: smooth hdwy fr 3 out to trck ldr after next: chal on bit last: sn clr and styd on bridle: v easily* **6/4¹**

3 **2** *3 ½* **Dynaste (FR)**[36] 1743 4-11-5 **119**.. CO'Farrell⁽³⁾ 137+
(David Pipe) *trckd ldr: led 4th: drvn clr after 2 out: jnd by smooth-travelling wnr last: sn no ch but kpt on wl for easy 2nd* **20/1**

2131 **3** *17* **Entertain Me**[154] 706 6-10-10 **115**........................... ChristopherWard⁽⁸⁾ 117
(Robin Dickin) *in rr: impr 6th: chsd ldrs fr 3 out and styd on wl fr next but nvr any ch w ldng duo* **33/1**

12-3 **4** *2 ½* **Sound Stage**[19] 1986 7-11-12 **123**.. IanPopham 122
(Caroline Keevil) *chsd ldrs fr 4th: rdn and readily outpcd fr 2 out* **11/1³**

1/1- **5** *2 ¾* **Max Bygraves**[411] 1555 7-10-7 **112**.................................. EdCookson⁽⁸⁾ 110
(Kim Bailey) *in rr tl rdn and styd on appr 2 out: kpt on run-in but nvr any ch* **14/1**

-320 **6** *hd* **Phare Isle (IRE)**[20] 1959 5-10-12 **109**.................................... PeterToole 108
(Ben Case) *in rr styng on whn hmpd 4 out: styd on fr next but nvr a thrr* **66/1**

411- **7** *2 ¾* **Chance Du Roy (FR)**[225] 4969 6-11-7 **121**.................. GilesHawkins⁽³⁾ 115
(Philip Hobbs) *hit 3rd: towards rr: hdwy 3 out: nvr rchd ldrs* **12/1**

562- **8** *¾* **Amore Mio (GER)**[236] 4759 5-11-6 **122**................. StephenO'Donovan⁽⁵⁾ 116
(Richard Phillips) *in rr: hdwy fr 3 out: nvr rchd ldrs* **25/1**

1230 **9** *10* **Boogie Dancer**[28] 1859 6-10-13 **110**.............................. DonalDevereux 95
(Stuart Howe) *in rr: styd on fr 2 out: nvr rchd ldrs* **50/1**

334- **10** *1 ¾* **Sandofthecolosseum (IRE)**[222] 5017 5-11-2 **113**....... RichieMcLernon 96
(Alex Hales) *mid-div: sme hdwy fr 2 out* **33/1**

5250 **11** *3 ½* **Mickmacmagoole (IRE)**[6] 2209 8-10-13 **120**............... JSMcGarvey⁽¹⁰⁾ 100
(Evan Williams) *j. slowly 4th: in rr tl sme hdwy fr 2 out* **33/1**

5000 **12** *2* **Tarvini (IRE)**[19] 1986 5-11-3 **122**..................................(p) GeraldQuinn⁽⁸⁾ 100
(Jonjo O'Neill) *chse ldrs to 3 out* **80/1**

2U-2 **13** *4 ½* **King's Revenge**[19] 1998 7-11-4 **120**..........................(b) NathanSweeney⁽⁵⁾ 94
(Shaun Lycett) *hdwy to trck ldrs fr 4th: chal 3 out: wknd sn after* **50/1**

13-0 **14** *1* **Scampi Boy (IRE)**[27] 1864 6-11-4 **120**.......................... PeterCarberry⁽⁵⁾ 95
(Paul Webber) *chsd ldrs tl hmpd 4 out: tried to rally next: sn wknd* **10/1²**

0-15 **15** *14* **Rhum (FR)**[9] 2147 5-11-3 **117**............................ SamTwiston-Davies⁽³⁾ 78
(Nigel Twiston-Davies) *chsd ldrs to tl wknd 5th* **14/1**

03S- **16** *2 ½* **Stripe Me Blue**[202] 5393 8-11-1 **115**................................ DannyBurton⁽³⁾ 76
(Peter Jones) *chsd ldrs tl hmpd and wknd 4 out* **16/1**

0-03 **17** *3* **Global Flyer**[8] 2171 6-11-1 **115**.. KyleJames⁽³⁾ 71
(Caroline Bailey) *a in rr* **66/1**

36-0 **18** *1 ¼* **Ponmeoath (IRE)**[18] 2016 10-11-6 **123**..................................(p) RJJones⁽⁶⁾ 78
(E McNamara, Ire) *chsd ldrs: hit 5th: in tch whn hmpd 4 out: sn wknd* **50/1**

6-1U **19** *½* **Pro Pell (IRE)**[27] 1864 5-10-9 **112**..................................... JoshuaMoore⁽⁶⁾ 66
(Gary Moore) *hit 5th: sn in rr* **14/1**

0-F5 **20** *2 ½* **Bally Sands (IRE)**[149] 763 6-11-2 **113**..(p) DPFahy 65
(Robin Mathew) *chsd ldrs untl wknd 5th* **100/1**

00-6 **21** *1 ½* **Blazing Buck**[34] 1776 4-11-6 **120**...................................... LeeEdwards⁽³⁾ 73
(Tony Carroll) *led to 4th: stl wl there whn hmpd 4 out: sn wknd* **66/1**

40-4 **F** **Turner Brown (IRE)**[17] 2029 6-11-6 **120**................................... LMcNiff⁽³⁾ —
(Michael O'Hare, Ire) *chsd ldrs tl fell 4 out* **16/1**

3 **F** **Traffic Article (IRE)**[27] 1875 6-11-7 **118**.................................(t) EJO'Connell —
(Gordon Elliott, Ire) *chsd ldrs: stl travelling ok whn fell 4 out* **16/1**

5m 18.87s (5.47) **Going Correction** +0.45s/f (Soft)
WFA 4 from 5yo+ 8lb **23** Ran SP% **132.8**
Speed ratings (Par 107): **107,105,99,98,97 97,96,95,91,91 89,89,87,87,81 80,79,79,79,78 77,—,—**
Tote Swingers: 1&2 £5.80, 1&3 £96.10 CSF £39.20 CT £823.90 TOTE £2.70: £1.10, £3.50, £9.20, £2.70; EX 45.60 Trifecta £1981.80 Part won. Pool: £2,678.17 - 0.70 winning units..
Owner Paul Murphy **Bred** P Murphy **Trained** Upper Lambourn, Berks
■ Stewards' Enquiry : J S McGarvey caution: used whip when out of contention.

FOCUS
This was nowhere near as competitive as one would expect for a such a big field, two evidently well handicapped horses drawing well clear. Facile winner Aegean Dawn was very impressive and the second a big step up. The next four were all within a few pounds of their marks.

NOTEBOOK

Aegean Dawn ◆, who was held in the highest regard when with the Alners, cruising clear on the run-in to win with any amount in hand; impressive considering this was his first run in 360 days and he was hampered by the fall of Traffic Article at the top of the hill. David Bass didn't panic, allowing him to re-establish his stride and readily going in pursuit of the runner-up rounding the final bend. He was receiving 5lb, but being such a big horse, it's hard to believe there isn't plenty left to work on and, although he can be expected to get hit hard by the handicapper, it would be a surprise were he not to win again. Whatever he does over hurdles, he'll surely improve on it over fences, his dam being an unraced half-sister to Gold Cup winner Cool Dawn. (op 2-1)

Dynaste(FR) ◆, readily outpaced over 2m on his British debut, was expected to improve for this longer trip and he duly did, opening up a clear advantage running down the hill and leaving all bar the winner trailing. Time may show he faced an impossible task trying to give 5lb to the winner and, although he can expect a rise for finishing 17l clear of the third, he's still a novice, so shouldn't have any trouble winning races. (op 25-1)

Entertain Me, up 10lb in a better race, stayed on best of the remainder without ever looking a threat. She remains capable of better and is likely to get 3m.

Sound Stage reappeared with a promising effort at Aintree, but there was a doubt as to whether he'd have the speed to cope with this trip over hurdles, given he's best known as a chaser, and he simply couldn't quicken on. He will surely return to fences now and looks capable of further success in what division, with him currently rated 128. (tchd 10-1 and 12-1)

Max Bygraves hadn't run since winning over fences 411 days earlier, and was only 4lb higher for this return to hurdles. It was a very promising run, staying on nicely from the rear, and he looks capable of winning something similar before going back chasing.

Phare Isle(IRE) bounced back from a disappointing run at Aintree, staying on from well back having been hampered at the fourth-last.

Chance Du Roy(FR), a dual winner over fences in the spring, the latest off this mark, never got into it, but was going on at the finish and should improve. (tchd 14-1 in places)

Amore Mio(GER), back over hurdles having been sold from the Emma Lavelle stable, isn't badly weighted on his old form.

Sandofthecolosseum(IRE) never got involved on this switch to handicaps, but should come good once chasing.

Scampi Boy(IRE) was one of those most affected by the fall of Traffic Article four out and can safely be given another chance. (op 11-1 tchd 9-1)

Stripe Me Blue, a seasonal debutant, was another affected by a melee four out.

Pro Pell(IRE) was a notable disappointment and needs to bounce back. (op 12-1)

Bally Sands(IRE) Official explanation: trainer said gelding got bumped during race and finished injured

Turner Brown(IRE), 16lb higher than when winning at Punchestown last month, was still in the mix when falling four out.

2348 STEEL PLATE AND SECTIONS NOVICES' CHASE (16 fncs) 2m 4f 110y

4:05 (4:05) (Class 2) 4-Y-O+

£9,393 (£2,775; £1,387; £694; £346; £174)

Form			Horse	Jockey	RPR
122-	**1**		**Time For Rupert (IRE)**[239] 4701 6-11-2 0 (Paul Webber) *trckd ldrs: pushed along to cl up after 4 out: chsd ldr after 3 out: drvn and upsides whn lft w 1 l advantage 2 out: rdn and styd on strly run-in* **7/2**[3]	WillKennedy	153+
6015	**2**	*8*	**Hell's Bay (FR)**[27] 1863 8-11-7 125 (Colin Tizzard) *hld up in rr tl hdwy after 4 out: styng on 3rd whn lft 1 l 2nd 2 out: sn hrd drvn: no ex and one pce run-in* **33/1**	JoeTizzard	152+
24-2	**3**	*9*	**Othermix (FR)**[13] 2082 6-11-2 142 (Ian Williams) *chsd ldr: chal 3rd to 6th: styd chsng ldr tl appr 3 out: no ch whn hmpd and lft 3rd 2 out* **11/2**	NoelFehily	138
121-	**4**	*14*	**Reve De Sivola (FR)**[203] 5381 5-11-2 0 (Nick Williams) *chsd ldrs: blnd 4 out: wknd bef next* **3/1**[1]	DarylJacob	131+
-031	**5**	*10*	**Divers (FR)**[22] 1930 6-11-7 131 (Ferdy Murphy) *hmpd 12th: a in rr* **40/1**	GrahamLee	122+
00-5	**6**	*36*	**Vino Griego (FR)**[26] 1883 5-11-2 0 (Gary Moore) *in rr: sme hdwy 11th: wknd next: t.o* **66/1**	JamieMoore	83
250-	**7**	*14*	**Quantitativeeasing (IRE)**[203] 5381 5-11-2 0 (Nicky Henderson) *chsd ldrs: wkng whn hit 4 out: t.o* **7/1**	APMcCoy	70
100-	**8**	*14*	**Copper Sound**[418] 1478 6-11-2 0 (Michael Scudamore) *sn bhd* **150/1**	JamesDavies	58
65-1	**F**		**The Giant Bolster**[23] 1923 5-11-7 0 (David Bridgwater) *chsd ldrs: blnd 8th: hit 11th: stl wl there whn fell next* **14/1**	RodiGreene	—
300-	**F**		**Mr Thriller (FR)**[239] 4699 5-11-2 0 (David Pipe) *led: hit 5th: jnd but stl gng ok whn fell 2 out* **10/3**[2]	TomScudamore	147

5m 18.07s (7.07) **Going Correction** +0.45s/f (Soft) **10** Ran SP% **112.4**

Speed ratings (Par 109): **104,100,97,92,88 74,69,64,—,—**

Tote Swingers: 1&2 £8.90, 1&3 £3.90, 2&3 £22.70. Totesuper7: Win: Not won. Place: £186.80. CSF £91.18 TOTE £4.20: £1.50, £5.10, £2.00; EX 134.50 Trifecta £927.70 Pool: £2,682.85 - 2.14 winning units..

Owner Littlecote Racing Partnership **Bred** Robert O'Callaghan **Trained** Mollington, Oxon

FOCUS

A novice chase that has been won by subsequent Gold Cup heroes Denman and Imperial Commander in the past decade and always proves informative for the staying division. One will do well to see a higher-quality contest for the level than this year's line-up and the race will look stronger than many graded novice chases run through the season. It included three horses that finished second at last season's Festival here in Othermix (Jewson Novices' Handicap), Reve De Sivola (Neptune Novice Hurdle) and Time For Rupert (World Hurdle). There were also a host of other decent prospects in attendance and they went a fair enough gallop through the race. The pace got really serious from four out. Strong form, with the winner up a stone+ on his hurdles best and a massive step up from the second, and there is a case for rating the form up to 8lb higher through the third.

NOTEBOOK

Time For Rupert(IRE) ◆ was the only one to give Big Buck's any sort of a race in the World Hurdle in March and has always had the size to make up into a chaser, so this chase debut was eagerly anticipated. He proved easy enough to back and there was a niggling worry that he badly needed his first run back over hurdles last term. His trainer Paul Webber said beforehand he had done his share of work and had schooled nicely at home, though. This trip was also on the sharp side for him, but he jumped like a professional pretty much throughout (bar reaching at the tenth) under a positive ride and was in the right place jumping four out. He got outpaced when the leaders kicked for home, but kept finding for pressure and it was no surprise that he stayed on best up the rising finish. He looked to have mastered Mr Thriller prior to that one departing at the penultimate fence, and it was hard not to be impressed by the way he came away near the finish. He has all the credentials to go right to the top of the chasing tree and, while the RSA is his big target this season, connections may do well to take a look at the Gold Cup division, as that seems to be at its most open for years. The last novice to win that race was Midnight Court back in 1978, but this 6-y-o should only improve for the experience and stepping up in trip is what he really wants, so a tilt at the big one next March would not be beyond him if building on his hurdling form. The safe option would be to stick to the novice route, though, and returning here for a similar event next month is likely to be next up for him. He was cut to as low as 6/1 with Paddy Power for the RSA straight after the race, but was more generally available at 7/1. (tchd 10-3 and 4-1 in places)

Hell's Bay(FR) should not be used to hold this form down. This strong-travelling 8-y-o has returned to his best since joining current connections and travelled like a winner before stamina became an issue over 3m1f here last month. He again travelled really sweetly and momentarily looked like getting on top, but eventually his 5lb concession to the winner told. He clearly likes the track and will probably be aimed at something at next year's Festival, with the new Grade 2 Novice Chase over 2m4f looking a viable target.

Othermix(FR)'s finest hour last season saw him finish runner-up in the Jewson Handicap at the Festival, and he had posted a sound effort on his debut for this stable at Ascot last month. He was never far away and did things nicely in the race, but was made to look one paced off the home turn. This somewhat enigmatic character should really have no trouble getting off the mark on one of the smaller tracks, and it wouldn't be that surprising to see blinkers back on at some stage. Dropping back in trip also looks well worth a go with him. (op 6-1)

Reve De Sivola(FR) finished second to Peddlers Cross in the Neptune last term and went one better with a very game effort to gain his Grade 1 success at the Punchestown Festival. He didn't always jump hurdles that convincingly and it was his jumping on this chase debut that caught him out. It may be deemed as somewhat disappointing from him, but he couldn't have found a hotter race for his introduction and he should be able to step up now he has some experience under his belt. Most bookmakers eased him to 20/1 for the RSA. (tchd 10-3 and 7-2 in places)

Divers(FR), off the mark at Carlisle 22 days earlier, was up in trip for this third outing over fences. He got behind early and was always playing catch-up. It would be folly to judge him on this effort, however, and keeping in mind his yard's record at the Festival, the Centenary Novices' Handicap (formerly known as a Jewson) here next March is likely to be his big target. (op 33-1 tchd 50-1 in a place)

Vino Griego(FR) is a talented horse, but he jumped horribly on his chase debut at Kempton last month and again failed to convince over his fences in this better company. (op 50-1)

Quantitativeeasing(IRE) came unstuck when well-fancied for the Coral Cup last season and looked over the top when well beaten by Reve De Sivola on his final outing at Punchestown. He has the scope to make his mark over fences, but did not look great in his coat and, from the 11th fence on his comeback, was found out. This experience will not be lost on him and he can obviously find easier assignments in the coming weeks. (op 8-1)

The Giant Bolster, sixth in last season's Supreme Novice, won really well on his chasing debut when returning last month. He hit the eighth, but was still going okay prior to crashing out at the 12th. (op 3-1 tchd 11-4 and 7-2 in places)

Mr Thriller(FR) won his first two over hurdles last year and looked really progressive, but the last of them at Haydock on demanding ground seemed to bottom him, as he struggled thereafter. Well backed for this seasonal/chase debut, he set out to make all and was not totally done with prior to coming down on landing after the second-last. He had jumped well to that point and it is hoped this doesn't overly dent his confidence as, on this evidence, he looks like rating higher over fences. (op 3-1 tchd 11-4 and 7-2 in places)

T/Jkpt: Part won. £12,830.40 to a £1 stake. Pool:£18,701.03 - 0.50 winning tickets. T/Plt: £43.40 to a £1 stake. Pool:£213,401.76 - 3,582.53 winning tickets T/Qpdt: £11.40 to a £1 stake. Pool:£13,261.43 - 855.14 winning tickets ST

NEWCASTLE (L-H)

Friday, November 12

OFFICIAL GOING: Good to soft (soft in places; 5.8)

The final flight of hurdles and the cross hurdle after the winning post, and the two cross fences after the winning post, were omitted due to high winds.

Wind: Strong, half against Weather: Bright

2349 WSR NOVICES' HURDLE (6 hdls 3 omitted) 2m

12:35 (12:35) (Class 4) 4-Y-O+ **£2,788** (£823; £411; £205; £102)

Form			Horse	Jockey	RPR
/31-	**1**		**Storm Brig**[215] 5144 5-10-12 0 (Alistair Whillans) *hld up in midfield: hdwy and cl up 3 out: led next: sn rdn: r.o strly to go clr run-in* **11/2**[3]	BrianHarding	120+
3-3	**2**	*8*	**Flinty Bay (IRE)**[35] 1757 5-10-12 0 (Nicky Richards) *hld up in tch: smooth hdwy to chal 2 out: sn rdn: one pce run-in* **15/8**[1]	DougieCostello	112
	3	*4 ½*	**Crackentorp**[20] 5-10-12 0 (Tim Easterby) *hld up in tch: rdn and outpcd appr 2 out: styd on run-in: no ch w first two* **7/2**[2]	RichieMcGrath	108
20-1	**4**	*½*	**Warrior One**[30] 1831 4-11-2 117 (Howard Johnson) *prom: drvn and outpcd 2 out: no imp fr last* **13/2**	RyanMania(3)	115
10-	**5**	*nk*	**Kings Grey (IRE)**[248] 4508 6-10-12 0 (Keith Reveley) *chsd ldr: led 2nd to 2 out: edgd lft and sn outpcd* **14/1**	JamesReveley	107
0	**6**	*5*	**Tippering (IRE)**[180] 355 5-10-12 0 (Sue Smith) *in tch tl rdn and outpcd bef 2 out: n.d after* **40/1**	TjadeCollier	103
15U-	**7**	*7*	**Fairynuff**[203] 5376 6-10-12 0 (Kate Walton) *midfield: nt fluent 3rd: outpcd after 3 out: no imp fr next* **10/1**	BrianHughes	98
0/F-	**8**	*12*	**Canal Cottage (IRE)**[383] 1914 6-10-12 0 (Lucinda Russell) *t.k.h: hld up in midfield: outpcd 3 out: n.d after* **66/1**	PeterBuchanan	86
	9	*20*	**Alsahil (USA)**[21] 4-10-12 0 (Micky Hammond) *trckd ldrs: nt fluent 3rd or next: sn wknd* **12/1**	JasonMaguire	68
0-60	**10**	*2 ½*	**Bunacurry**[27] 1867 5-10-5 0 (Barry Murtagh) *bhd: struggling bef 3 out: nvr on terms* **200/1**	AlexanderVoy(7)	65
4300	**11**	*3*	**Wicked Streak (IRE)**[13] 2092 5-10-12 0 (Micky Hammond) *midfield: drvn and outpcd bef 3 out: btn bef next* **100/1**	BarryKeniry	63
600-	**12**	*32*	**Benluna (IRE)**[203] 5370 6-10-9 0 (Alistair Whillans) *t.k.h: hld up: struggling bef 3 out: sn btn: t.o* **100/1**	EwanWhillans(3)	34
0	**13**	*20*	**Real Desire**[16] 2038 4-10-12 0 (P Monteith) *bhd: struggling bef 3 out: t.o* **200/1**	WilsonRenwick	16
	P		**Cigalas**[55] 5-10-12 0 (Jean McGregor) *led to 2nd: wknd 3 out: t.o whn p.u bef next* **200/1**	RobertWalford	—
	P		**Moon Lightning (IRE)**[41] 4-10-9 0 (Tina Jackson) *in tch on outside: mstke 2nd: sn lost pl: t.o whn p.u after 3 out* **100/1**	HarryHaynes(3)	—
0	**P**		**Fred Grass**[27] 1867 4-10-7 0 (Jonathan Haynes) *bhd: struggling 1/2-way: t.o whn p.u after 3 out* **200/1**	JamesHalliday(5)	—

4m 4.20s (-5.80) **Going Correction** -0.05s/f (Good) **16** Ran SP% **118.1**

Speed ratings (Par 105): **112,108,105,105,105 102,99,93,83,82 80,64,54,—,— —**

Tote Swingers: 1&2 £2.70, 1&3 £5.20, 2&3 £1.60 CSF £16.23 TOTE £7.50: £2.30, £1.40, £1.50; EX 18.90.

Owner W J E Scott & Mrs M A Scott **Bred** Mrs D H Mathias **Trained** Newmill-On-Slitrig, Borders

■ Stewards' Enquiry : Dougie Costello caution: careless riding.

FOCUS

The hurdle after the winning post was omitted, and so too was the final flight in the home straight, resulting in a much longer run-in than usual. The pace was modest, which was understandable considering the wind. This looked a good novice hurdle for the track and it should produce winners. The winner is rated in line with his decent bumper form.

NOTEBOOK
Storm Brig ◆ created a good impression, scoring tidily on his debut over obstacles after an absence of 215 days. He was a fair type in bumpers, winning two of his three starts, and is a useful recruit to hurdling. Last off the bridle, he had the benefit of the stands' rail in the straight and drew nicely clear when asked. Stiffer tasks no doubt await, but he's obviously decent and could pick up a nice prize this winter. (op 9-2 tchd 6-1)
Flinty Bay(IRE), third on his hurdling debut at Carlisle in October, had the benefit of race-fitness over the winner, but was ultimately no match at all for that rival. It's fair to say he bumped into quite a nice type, but clearly he has his limitations. (op 5-2 tchd 11-4)
Crackentorp, a useful dual 1m2f Polytrack winner on the Flat, was race-fit for his hurdling debut and did enough to suggest he has a future at this game, staying on for third without threatening the winner. (op 9-2 tchd 5-1)
Warrior One had no easy task under the penalty picked up for winning a similar event at Wetherby on his reappearance. (op 5-1 tchd 7-1)
Kings Grey(IRE) travelled well in a prominent position for much of the way and looks a bit better than his finishing position indicates. This bumper winner, who was having his first start since March, simply got tired in the straight and raced more towards the far side than the principals. (tchd 16-1)

2350 ITPS BEGINNERS' CHASE (14 fncs 2 omitted) 2m 4f
1:05 (1:06) (Class 4) 4-Y-0+ **£3,022** (£968; £538)

Form / RPR
2-22 **1** **Lord Larsson**[45] 1642 7-11-2 0........(t) DougieCostello 127+
(Malcolm Jefferson) *mde all: drew clr fr 5 out: easily* **3/1**[2]
222- **2** *11* **Mr Syntax (IRE)**[199] 30 6-11-2 0........ RichieMcGrath 110+
(Tim Fitzgerald) *t.k.h: chsd wnr thrght: blnd 2nd: outpcd whn blnd 4 out: sn btn* **7/1**[3]
P- **3** *81* **Chester Ridge**[235] 4784 6-11-2 0........ JamesReveley 34
(William Amos) *hld up in tch: outpcd 8th: lost tch fr 5 out* **50/1**
-63P **F** **Greenbelt**[13] 2093 9-11-2 93........(p) BrianHarding —
(George Moore) *hld up: outpcd 7th: 4th and no imp whn fell 5 out* **28/1**
105- **F** **The Knoxs (IRE)**[205] 5306 7-11-2 0........ BrianHughes —
(Howard Johnson) *trckd ldrs: overj. and fell 5th* **8/15**[1]

5m 33.1s (5.90) **Going Correction** +0.175s/f (Yiel) **5** Ran SP% **108.1**
Speed ratings (Par 105): **95,90,58,—,—**
CSF £20.28 TOTE £3.60: £1.50, £2.50; EX 11.20.
Owner Mrs K S Gaffney & Mrs Alix Stevenson **Bred** Mrs K S Gaffney & Mrs Alix Stevenson **Trained** Norton, N Yorks

FOCUS
The two fences heading away from the stands' were omitted owing to the strong wind. Market leader The Knox fell early, and as a consequence this was an uncompetitive event. Modest novice form.

NOTEBOOK
Lord Larsson, equipped with a tongue tie for the first time since his bumper debut, was never seriously challenged. He fell in this race 12 months ago, and followed that by unseating twice, but he had run some solid races in defeat on his last three outings and finally got off the mark. His jumping was fine this time, though this wasn't much of a race. (tchd 11-4 and 10-3)
Mr Syntax(IRE), over fences for the first time after 199 days off, didn't settle early, pecked on landing at the fourth fence, and then made a serious mistake at the fourth last. He still ran on in the closing stages, but could get nowhere near the easy winner. (op 5-1)
Chester Ridge is a point-to-point winner but was pulled up on his sole start under Rules in March, after which his then trainer said that on returning home the gelding coughed and subsequently scoped dirty. Making his debut for a new yard after 235 days off, he offered very little, almost walking over the line for third-place prizemoney. (op 40-1 tchd 66-1)
Greenbelt, pulled up over fences two weeks earlier, travelled with no enthusiasm before falling. This won't have helped his outlook on the game. (op 8-11 tchd 4-5 in a place)
The Knoxs(IRE), an Irish point winner making his chasing debut after an absence of 205 days, fell too early to know how he might have fared. (op 8-11 tchd 4-5 in a place)

2351 OLIVER AND GREGS H'CAP HURDLE (10 hdls 3 omitted) 3m
1:40 (1:40) (Class 5) (0-90,89) 4-Y-0+ **£2,081** (£611; £305; £152)

Form / RPR
03-0 **1** **Not Talking (IRE)**[42] 1666 7-10-1 **64**........ DougieCostello 71
(John Quinn) *in tch: effrt after 2 out: led last: rdn and edgd rt run-in: styd on wl* **5/1**[2]
6-63 **2** *3 ½* **Stormion (IRE)**[12] 2103 5-11-2 **79**........ PeterBuchanan 83
(Lucinda Russell) *led: reminders 1/2-way: hdd 6th: led bef 3 out to last: kpt on u.p* **10/3**[1]
0U4/ **3** *3* **Talesofriverbank**[890] 606 7-9-13 **65**........ EwanWhillans(3) 67
(Alistair Whillans) *hld up: hdwy and prom 3 out: effrt and ev ch between last 2: edgd lft and one pce u.p run-in* **50/1**
510- **4** *24* **Quay Meadow (IRE)**[228] 4930 8-11-5 **89**........ AlexanderVoy(7) 69
(John Norton) *hld up: reminders 1/2-way: outpcd 4 out: rallied after 2 out: kpt on run-in: no ch w first three* **16/1**
35P5 **5** *1 ¾* **Cute N You Know It**[40] 1694 7-10-1 **64**........(p) BrianHughes 42
(Andrew Crook) *hld up: hdwy and prom 3 out: outpcd fr next* **8/1**
63-0 **6** *½* **Bob Will (IRE)**[35] 1757 5-11-11 **88**........ RichieMcGrath 68
(Chris Grant) *cl up: led 6th to bef 3 out: rdn whn hit next: btn whn nt fluent last* **12/1**
-003 **7** *2 ¼* **Appeal Denied (IRE)**[22] 1929 8-10-13 **83**........ PaulGallagher(7) 59
(Sandy Forster) *hld up: rdn bef 3 out: sn outpcd* **12/1**
-540 **8** *7* **Sambelucky (IRE)**[22] 1929 5-11-7 **84**........ JamesReveley 53
(Keith Reveley) *hld up: pushed along and outpcd after 4 out: nvr rchd ldrs* **13/2**[3]
0-61 **9** *6* **Buckstruther (IRE)**[27] 1873 8-11-3 **87**........ NathanMoscrop(7) 51
(Andrew Parker) *trckd ldrs: lost pl 4 out: struggling fr next* **8/1**
32 **10** *½* **Soul Magic (IRE)**[35] 1760 8-11-1 **85**........ GaryRutherford(7) 49
(Harriet Graham) *hld up: hdwy to chse ldrs 1/2-way: effrt bef 2 out: wknd qckly bef last* **9/1**
P-0P **11** *63* **Sam Patch**[20] 1959 7-11-1 **88**........ CallumWhillans(10) —
(Donald Whillans) *trckd ldrs tl nt fluent and outpcd 3 out: sn lost tch* **40/1**
/40- **P** **Ravensbill (IRE)**[205] 5310 8-11-5 **85**........ HarryHaynes(3) —
(William Amos) *hld up: struggling 6th: tailing off whn p.u next* **33/1**

6m 16.7s (2.70) **Going Correction** -0.05s/f (Good) **12** Ran SP% **113.9**
Speed ratings (Par 103): **93,91,90,82,82 82,81,79,77,76 55,—**
Tote Swingers: 1&2 £5.20, 2&3 £27.70 CSF £21.26 CT £735.06 TOTE £5.10: £2.00, £1.40, £12.40; EX 15.80.
Owner J N Blackburn **Bred** Mrs Mary Smyth **Trained** Settrington, N Yorks

FOCUS
A moderate handicap. The first two are rated to their best.

NOTEBOOK
Not Talking(IRE) ◆ travelled well for much of the way and found enough for pressure. He was well beaten over an extended 2m4f on his reappearance, but proved suited by the step up in trip, as his breeding suggested (two of his brothers won over this distance). Unexposed at around 3m, it wouldn't surprise to see him defy a rise. (op 11-2)
Stormion(IRE) plugged on dourly under a forward ride, responding every time he came under pressure and seeing off a few challengers, but ultimately he had to give best to the winner. He's all stamina. (op 6-1 tchd 3-1)
Talesofriverbank, off the track since finishing fourth in a selling hurdle in June 2008, ran with real credit on her return. There might me more to come provided she continues to stand training.
Quay Meadow(IRE) was under pressure a fair way out, but this was a respectable return from a 228-day absence and he's obviously entitled to strip fitter next time. (op 20-1)
Cute N You Know It had cheekpieces back on in place of a visor, but she was well held. (tchd 9-1)
Ravensbill(IRE) Official explanation: trainer said gelding pulled up lame off-fore

2352 CELLULAR SOLUTIONS H'CAP CHASE (11 fncs 2 omitted) 2m 110y
2:15 (2:15) (Class 4) (0-115,115) 4-Y-0+ **£3,022** (£968; £538)

Form / RPR
F-51 **1** **Primrose Time**[12] 2107 7-10-7 **103** 7ex........ AlexanderVoy(7) 115+
(Lucy Normile) *cl up: effrt and ev ch 3 out: rdn next: styd on wl fr last: led nr fin* **7/4**[1]
FU-P **2** *¾* **Polar Gunner**[35] 1761 13-11-7 **115**........ JamesHalliday(5) 121
(Malcolm Jefferson) *led to 3rd: led next: rdn bef last: kpt on run-in: hdd nr fin* **25/1**
31P- **3** *53* **Something Silver**[198] 46 9-10-4 **93**........(v) RichieMcGrath 64
(Jim Goldie) *cl up: led 3rd to next: outpcd whn hmpd and lft 3rd 5 out: sn btn and eased* **9/2**[3]
2346 **U** **Tranos (USA)**[13] 2093 7-10-1 **90**........(p) BarryKeniry —
(Micky Hammond) *hld up in tch: mstke and uns rdr 1st* **7/1**
2P-6 **U** **Pamak D'Airy (FR)**[181] 330 7-11-7 **110**........ RobertWalford —
(Henry Hogarth) *cl up whn mstke and uns rdr 2nd* **7/2**[2]
2402 **F** **Prioryjo**[16] 2037 7-11-8 **111**........ BrianHarding —
(Martin Todhunter) *hld up in tch: rdn along and 4 l down whn fell 6th: fatally injured* **10/1**
0P-0 **F** **Peachey Moment (USA)**[35] 1758 5-10-6 **98**........ FearghalDavis(3) —
(Nicky Richards) *hld up in tch: stdy hdwy and 3 l down in 3rd whn fell 5 out* **11/1**

4m 22.3s (1.20) **Going Correction** +0.175s/f (Yiel) **7** Ran SP% **110.5**
Speed ratings (Par 105): **104,103,78,—,— —,—**
Tote Swingers: 1&2 £7.90, 1&3 £1.40, 2&3 £6.70 CSF £32.88 TOTE £2.30: £1.50, £11.20; EX 55.20.
Owner The Explorers **Bred** Mrs D A Whitaker **Trained** Duncrievie, Perth & Kinross

FOCUS
Over half the field failed to complete, and only two of the seven runners mattered. The winner is rated better than the bare result and the second to last season's best.

NOTEBOOK
Primrose Time was slower over the fences in the straight than the runner-up, but clearly had that bit much more to offer on the level. She was 3lb well-in under the penalty picked up for her recent Carlisle success, but made work hard of winning what was effectively a match race and won't appeal as worth backing when going for the hat-trick. (op 13-8 tchd 15-8 in a place)
Polar Gunner, pulled up when reported to have lost his action last time, returned to form with a gallant effort in defeat, proving he can still be competitive. (op 20-1)
Something Silver offered nothing after an absence of 198 days. He emptied quickly before the bend into the straight and was beaten when slightly hampered by a faller five out. (op 6-1 tchd 4-1)
Pamak D'Airy(FR) got rid of his rider too early to know how he might have fared. (op 12-1 tchd 14-1)
Prioryjo sadly took a fatal fall six out. (op 12-1 tchd 14-1)
Peachey Moment(USA), pulled up on his only previous chasing start, was still in with a shout when coming down five from the finish. (op 12-1 tchd 14-1)

2353 DIGIBET.COM MARES' MAIDEN HURDLE (8 hdls 3 omitted) 2m 4f
2:50 (2:53) (Class 5) 4-Y-0+ **£2,211** (£649; £324; £162)

Form / RPR
46-6 **1** **Along Came Rosie**[13] 2092 6-10-7 97........ FearghalDavis(3) 106+
(Andrew Crook) *hld up: hdwy after 4 out: wnt 2nd bef 2 out: 6 l down last: styd on to ld run-in: kpt on wl* **5/1**[3]
/23- **2** *3* **Empress Orchid**[521] 662 5-10-10 0........ JasonMaguire 105+
(Donald McCain) *t.k.h: led 2nd: blnd 4th: rdn bef 2 out: 6 l clr last: hdd and no ex run-in* **7/4**[1]
5650 **3** *8* **Catleen (IRE)**[7] 2198 6-10-5 94........ MrStevenCrawford(5) 97
(S R B Crawford, Ire) *trckd ldrs: wnt 2nd bef 3 out to bef next: sn outpcd: no imp whn blnd last* **9/2**[2]
3P-P **4** *4* **Roll Over Rose (IRE)**[42] 1662 5-10-7 0........ EwanWhillans(3) 92
(William Amos) *hld up: hdwy bef 3 out: rdn and no imp fr next* **20/1**
P-P0 **5** *11* **Vallani (IRE)**[16] 2038 5-10-10 79........ WilsonRenwick 82
(P Monteith) *trckd ldrs: drvn and outpcd after 3 out: n.d after* **100/1**
00-0 **6** *31* **Tchikita (FR)**[12] 2107 7-10-7 99........ HarryHaynes(3) 55
(James Ewart) *prom tl rdn and wknd after 2 out* **8/1**
7 *6* **Sported And Played (IRE)** 7-10-3 0........ AlexanderVoy(7) 48
(Lucy Normile) *hld up: shortlived effrt and prom bef 4th: wknd bef next* **80/1**
55-0 **8** *9* **Bach Street Girl (IRE)**[188] 214 6-10-10 86........ TomSiddall 40
(Lynn Siddall) *hld up: struggling bef 4 out: sn btn* **66/1**
50- **9** *5* **Hole In One (IRE)**[209] 5227 4-10-10 0........ PeterBuchanan 36
(Lucinda Russell) *hld up: rdn and outpcd 4 out: nvr on terms* **12/1**
5 **10** *11* **Baileys Ruffit (IRE)**[22] 1934 5-10-10 0........ AdrianLane 26
(Neil McKnight, Ire) *hld up in midfield: rdn and outpcd whn j.rt and mstke 3 out: sn wknd* **33/1**
6-44 **P** **Almond Court (IRE)**[171] 461 7-10-10 74........ KennyJohnson —
(Robert Johnson) *in tch: lost pl bef 4th: sn struggling: t.o whn p.u bef 2 out* **33/1**
PPP- **P** **Basford Lady (IRE)**[232] 4851 6-10-10 0........(t) AlanO'Keeffe —
(Jennie Candlish) *led to 2nd: cl up tl wknd qckly appr 3 out: p.u bef next* **10/1**
P **Airey Scarey**[180] 7-10-5 0 ow2........ NathanMoscrop(7) —
(James Ewart) *bhd: struggling bef 4 out: t.o whn p.u bef 2 out* **100/1**

5m 24.9s (3.80) **Going Correction** -0.05s/f (Good)
WFA 4 from 5yo+ 8lb **13** Ran SP% **114.5**
Speed ratings (Par 103): **90,88,85,84,79 67,64,61,59,54 —,—,—**
Tote Swingers: 1&2 £3.40, 1&3 £4.70, 2&3 £3.70 CSF £13.33 TOTE £5.20: £2.20, £1.50, £1.90; EX 15.50.
Owner Friends of Rosie & Select Racing Club **Bred** Longdon Stud Ltd **Trained** Middleham Moor, N Yorks

FOCUS
A fairly standard mares' maiden.

NOTEBOOK
Along Came Rosie appreciated the switch to mares-only company and benefited from the runner-up tiring late on. Things are set to get tougher now. (op 11-2 tchd 4-1)

Empress Orchid touched 1.06 in-running, but she got tired on the unusually long run-in. She had flattened the fourth and briefly lost her footing on landing, which can't have helped, for all that she soon recovered. However, she hadn't been seen since June 2009 and seemingly just needed this fitness-wise. A similar race should be hers for the taking provided she gets over this okay. (op 11-8 tchd 15-8 in a place)
Catleen(IRE) ran respectably but wasn't quite good enough. (op 5-1 tchd 4-1)
Roll Over Rose(IRE) showed ability on debut before pulling up twice. This was a step back in the right direction. (op 16-1 tchd 22-1)

2354 THOMPSONS SOLICITORS H'CAP CHASE (16 fncs 2 omitted) 3m
3:25 (3:25) (Class 4) (0-110,107) 4-Y-O+ **£2,915** (£861; £430; £215; £107)

Form | | | | RPR
514- **1** **Eyre Square (IRE)**[209] [5226] 7-11-11 **106** .... JamesReveley 118+
(Keith Reveley) *trckd ldrs: rdn and outpcd 3 out: rallied and lft jst over 4 l 3rd last: led fnl 50yds: styd on* **7/1**
P532 **2** *3/4* **Dallas Bell**[12] [2107] 8-10-12 **96** .... EwanWhillans(3) 108+
(Alistair Whillans) *hld up: stdy hdwy bef 5 out: effrt 3 out: rallying and lft 4 l 2nd whn mstke last: chsd wnr fnl 50yds: r.o* **5/1**[3]
6-11 **3** *1 1/4* **Ocarina (FR)**[7] [2189] 8-11-3 **101** .... (p) HarryHaynes(3) 111
(James Ewart) *cl up: led bef 9th: hrd pressed 4 out: sn rdn: hdd and no ex fnl 50yds* **4/1**[2]
4-U6 **4** *21* **Seek The Truth (IRE)**[34] [1781] 7-10-2 **83** .... TomMessenger 74
(Sue Bradburne) *led to bef 9th: cl up tl outpcd 4 out: n.d after* **10/1**
3F-0 **5** *6* **Blazing Diva (IRE)**[35] [1763] 7-11-9 **107** .... RyanMania(3) 94
(Sandy Thomson) *hld up in tch: rdn and outpcd bef 5 out: no imp fr next* **16/1**
3-43 **6** *12* **Border Reiver**[13] [2093] 6-11-3 **98** .... (t) RichieMcGrath 75
(Tim Easterby) *prom: mstke 5 out: rdn and wknd fr next* **9/1**
-21P **7** *4* **Sierra Victor (IRE)**[14] [2079] 7-11-5 **100** .... WilsonRenwick 71
(P Monteith) *hld up: rdn and outpcd 1/2-way: no ch fnl circ* **18/1**
3PP- **8** *15* **Royal Mackintosh**[203] [5373] 9-11-11 **106** .... BrianHarding 64
(Alan Mactaggart) *in tch: outpcd 9th: struggling fr next: t.o* **25/1**
/650 **9** *39* **Rare Society (IRE)**[34] [1781] 12-11-2 **97** .... TjadeCollier 20
(Sue Smith) *prom: lost pl 6th: rdn after 8th: wknd fr next: t.o* **40/1**
4121 **F** **Overquest**[4] [2274] 8-11-9 **104** 7ex .... JohnnyFarrelly 114
(Elliott Cooper) *hld up: hdwy and prom 6th: chal after 4 out: sn rdn: 2 l down and jst outpcd whn fell last* **7/2**[1]
43P- **P** **Waterski**[215] [5141] 9-11-1 **96** .... RobertWalford —
(Jean McGregor) *towards rr: lost tch 9th: t.o whn p.u bef 4 out* **28/1**

6m 23.5s (1.00) **Going Correction** +0.175s/f (Yiel) **11** Ran SP% **111.4**
Speed ratings (Par 105): **105,104,104,97,95 91,90,85,72,— —**
Tote Swingers: 1&2 £4.10, 1&3 £4.60, 2&3 £3.50 CSF £39.72 CT £154.50 TOTE £6.20: £1.10, £2.90, £1.20; EX 10.00.
Owner John Wade **Bred** William Neville **Trained** Lingdale, Redcar & Cleveland

FOCUS
This is quite good form for the grade - Ocarina and Overquest, both last-time-out winners, looked likely to fight out the finish when heading to the last, while the eventual runner-up was 3lb well in. The winner has the potential to rate a bit higher.

NOTEBOOK
Eyre Square(IRE) had been given a chance by the handicapper and showed himself on a good mark on his return from 209 days off. This was only his fifth start over fences and he can rate higher. (tchd 13-2)
Dallas Bell was second over 2m on his return from a break, but he has won over 3m1f and, back up in trip, he ran really well, just failing to get up after making a mistake at the last. He is due to go up 3lb. (op 11-2 tchd 9-2)
Ocarina(FR) had won his last two starts under this rider over an extended 2m4f at Hexham, the latest on his return from six months off, and he avoided a penalty for that, making him 9lb well-in. He looked likely to take advantage for much of the closing stages, but he had been plenty keen enough and his exertions told on the run-in as he emptied quite quickly and lost two places. This longer trip stretched him. (tchd 7-2)
Seek The Truth(IRE) couldn't take advantage of a mark 2lb lower than when winning over C&D last October. (op 12-1)
Overquest, the winner of two of his last three, the latest four days earlier, wasn't far away in second behind Ocarina and still in with a shout when falling at the last. His stride shortened noticeably going into that fence and he met it all wrong, but he was in the process of running a big race under his penalty. (op 3-1 tchd 4-1)

2355 STP CONSTRUCTION MAIDEN OPEN NATIONAL HUNT FLAT RACE 2m
3:55 (3:58) (Class 6) 4-6-Y-O **£1,431** (£420; £210; £104)

Form | | | | RPR
2- **1** **Master Murphy (IRE)**[207] [5277] 5-10-9 0 .... AlistairFindlay(7) 98+
(Jane Walton) *mde all: pushed along over 2f out: styd on strly* **14/1**
2 *2* **Kent Street (IRE)** 5-10-6 0 .... BenjaminStephens(10) 96
(Sue Smith) *a cl up: effrt over 2f out: kpt on ins fnl f* **40/1**
2 **3** *7* **High Hoylander**[131] [892] 4-11-2 0 .... HenryOliver 90
(Sue Smith) *t.k.h: hld up: hdwy and prom over 5f out: pushed along and one pce fr 2f out* **9/1**[3]
0-5 **4** *9* **Farm Pixie (IRE)**[50] [1599] 4-11-2 0 .... AdrianLane 82
(Ann Hamilton) *prom: pushed along 1/2-way: plugged on fnl 2f: no imp* **50/1**
5 *3/4* **Brave Spartacus (IRE)** 4-11-2 0 .... JasonMaguire 81
(Chris Grant) *hld up in midfield: outpcd 1/2-way: styd on fnl 2f: nvr rchd ldrs* **14/1**
0-4 **6** *8* **Harris Hawk**[35] [1764] 5-11-2 0 .... BrianHarding 74
(John Wade) *midfield: rdn and outpcd over 6f out: sme late hdwy: nvr rchd ldrs* **6/1**[2]
3- **7** *1 1/2* **Allbarkanobite**[280] [3873] 5-10-9 0 .... RichieMcGrath 66
(Kate Walton) *midfield: hdwy and prom 6f out: rdn and edgd lft over 2f out: sn outpcd* **16/1**
0-5 **8** *5* **Darkan Road**[162] [609] 5-11-2 0 .... JanFaltejsek 68
(George Charlton) *hld up: stdy hdwy and in tch 1/2-way: wknd over 2f out* **33/1**
0 **9** *3 1/2* **Knockando**[183] [311] 5-11-2 0 .... PeterBuchanan 65
(Lucinda Russell) *midfield: outpcd 1/2-way: sn struggling: sme late hdwy: nvr on terms* **9/1**[3]
0- **10** *6* **Saddlers' Secret (IRE)**[251] [4429] 5-10-4 0 .... JamesHalliday(5) 53
(Mark Campion) *trckd ldrs tl rdn and wknd over 4f out* **66/1**
2 **11** *5* **Middlebrook (IRE)**[35] [1764] 5-11-2 0 .... BrianHughes 55
(Peter Niven) *hld up: rdn over 5f out: sn struggling* **9/2**[1]
0 **12** *11* **Sleep In First (FR)**[31] [1817] 4-11-2 0 .... BarryKeniry 45
(Anna Bramall) *in tch: struggling over 6f out: sn btn* **100/1**
4 **13** *2* **Thurnham**[177] [399] 4-11-2 0 .... JamesReveley 43
(Keith Reveley) *hld up: rdn over 6f out: btn and eased fnl 2f* **9/2**[1]
0 **14** *3 1/2* **Velvet Vic (IRE)**[182] [319] 4-11-2 0 .... PaddyAspell 40
(Richard Guest) *hld up: struggling over 6f out: sn btn* **25/1**
0- **15** *28* **Mister Daniel Dee**[411] [1556] 5-11-2 0 .... TomMessenger 15
(Richard Whitaker) *sn cl up: rdn and wknd over 4f out* **80/1**

4m 8.30s (3.90) **Going Correction** -0.05s/f (Good) **15** Ran SP% **104.8**
Speed ratings: **88,87,83,79,78 74,73,71,69,66 64,58,57,55,41**
Tote Swingers: 1&2 £0.00, 1&3 £11.80, 2&3 £36.50 CSF £374.44 TOTE £15.90: £4.30, £10.70, £2.50; EX 448.90.
Owner Mrs J M Walton **Bred** R Ryan **Trained** Otterburn, Northumberland

FOCUS
Ordinary bumper form, with the winner, third and fourth rated in line with their pre-race marks. The time was slow.

NOTEBOOK
Master Murphy(IRE) confirmed the promise he showed when runner-up at Hexham on his only previous start in April. A strong-galloping type who seems sure to stay further, he's a nice prospect for jumping. (op 16-1)
Kent Street(IRE), an 8,500euros half-brother to four point winners, including 2m4f-2m5f hunter chase winner Craiglands, made a pleasing debut. He lacked the winner's experience and should come on plenty for this.
High Hoylander, runner-up for a different stable on debut in July, was sold for £25,000 in August. He's a Flat-bred, so may have lacked the stamina of the front two, especially after being keen, but he clearly has ability. (op 7-1)
Farm Pixie(IRE) showed ability and could do okay over obstacles. (tchd 40-1)
Brave Spartacus(IRE) ◆, a half-brother to 2m4f hurdle winner Hamelsmead Lady, caught the eye keeping on steadily. He seems sure to do better. (op 11-1)
Middlebrook(IRE) was below the form he showed when second on debut at Carlisle. (tchd 4-1)
Thurnham was another to underperform, not confirming the promise he showed on his only previous start 177 days earlier, but he was soon heavily eased in the straight and can be given another chance. (op 4-1 tchd 5-1)
T/Plt: £24.80 to a £1 stake. Pool:£55,294.96 - 1,626.57 winning tickets T/Qpdt: £10.30 to a £1 stake. Pool:£3,814.93 - 272.92 winning tickets RY

2343 CHELTENHAM (L-H)
Saturday, November 13

OFFICIAL GOING: Good to soft (good in places; 7.6)
Wind: Virtually nil Weather: Overcast

2356 JCB TRIUMPH HURDLE TRIAL (REGISTERED AS THE PRESTBURY JUVENILE HURDLE RACE) (GRADE 2) (8 hdls) 2m 110y
12:50 (12:50) (Class 1) 3-Y-O
£14,252 (£5,347; £2,677; £1,335; £670; £335)

Form | | | | RPR
1 **Sam Winner (FR)**[197] 3-10-12 0 .... NoelFehily 141+
(Paul Nicholls) *hld up towards rr early: hdwy to trck ldrs after 3rd: led 2 out: c stands' side and pushed clr after last: easily* **4/1**[2]
3-5 **2** *15* **Grandouet (FR)**[15] [2078] 3-11-6 0 .... APMcCoy 132
(Nicky Henderson) *hld up in rr: hdwy 3 out: chsd wnr after 2 out: styd far side and kpt on appr last but nvr any ch: kpt on for clr 2nd* **8/1**
2 **3** *9* **Plan A (IRE)**[27] [1882] 3-10-12 0 .... JamieMoore 116
(Michael Quinlan) *in tch: hdwy and hit 4 out: chsd ldrs next and wnt 3rd after 2 out: nvr any ch w ldng trio and keeping on same pce whn hit last* **12/1**
0 **4** *hd* **Horatio Caine (FR)**[44] [1658] 3-10-12 0 .... DarylJacob 115+
(Nick Williams) *in rr: stl plenty to do and pushed along 3 out: styd on after 2 out and kpt on wl run-in to take 4th run-in and clsng on 3rd nr fin but no ch w ldng duo* **33/1**
5 *8* **Titan De Sarti (FR)**[146] 3-10-12 0 .... BarryGeraghty 109
(Nicky Henderson) *in tch: chsd ldrs after 3rd: rt there whn j. slowly and lost position 4 out: rallied to chse ldrs 2 out: sn rdn and wknd* **11/4**[1]
2 **6** *2 1/2* **Kalamill (IRE)**[42] [1674] 3-10-12 0 .... (t) SamTwiston-Davies 106
(Shaun Lycett) *in rr: pushed along after 4 out: rdn 3 out: styd on appr last: kpt on run-in* **40/1**
1123 **7** *hd* **Two Kisses (IRE)**[15] [2078] 3-10-9 125 .... AidanColeman 105
(Brendan Powell) *chsd ldrs: nt fluent 2nd: led after 4 out: hdd 2 out and sn wknd* **16/1**
11 **8** *12* **Zakeeta (IRE)**[16] [2047] 3-10-9 117 .... LeightonAspell 95
(Oliver Sherwood) *chsd ldrs: led appr 4th: hdd after 4 out: stl upsides whn hit 3 out: wknd next* **14/1**
12 **9** *1/2* **Pena Dorada (IRE)**[20] [1984] 3-11-2 120 .... BrianHughes 98
(Mrs K Burke) *led tl after 1st: styd prom to 3 out* **20/1**
1 **10** *3/4* **Palawi (IRE)**[17] [2033] 3-11-2 0 .... DougieCostello 101
(John Quinn) *chsd ldrs: t.k.h: stl wl there 3 out: wknd next: no ch whn blnd last* **8/1**
1052 **11** *7* **Gulf Punch**[17] [2033] 3-10-9 109 .... (p) WayneHutchinson 84
(Milton Harris) *hit 1st: a towards rr* **100/1**
12 *9* **Tatispout (FR)**[173] 3-10-5 0 .... FelixDeGiles 72
(Charlie Longsdon) *in rr: sme hdwy fr 3 out: nvr on terms and wknd bef last* **100/1**
111 **13** *17* **Architrave**[49] [1610] 3-11-6 138 .... RichardJohnson 72
(Tim Vaughan) *chsd ldrs to 3 out: sn wknd* **5/1**[3]
1 **14** *3/4* **Mason Hindmarsh**[20] [1984] 3-11-6 0 .... BrianHarding 71
(Karen McLintock) *chsd ldrs: rdn and wknd 4 out* **33/1**
15 *64* **Green Art (IRE)**[72] 3-10-12 0 .... MrGBarfoot-Saunt 6
(Tracey Barfoot-Saunt) *led after 1st: hdd & wknd appr 4th: t.o* **200/1**

4m 2.00s **Going Correction** +0.40s/f (Soft) **15** Ran SP% **121.4**
Speed ratings (Par 114): **116,108,104,104,100 99,99,93,93,93 90,85,77,77,47**
toteswingers: 1&2 £8.60, 1&3 £11.70, 2&3 £74.40. CSF £34.90 TOTE £5.10: £2.10, £2.50, £3.90; EX 38.30 Trifecta £255.80 Pool: £1,735.49 - 5.02 winning units..
Owner Mrs Angela Yeoman **Bred** Ecurie Winning **Trained** Ditcheat, Somerset

FOCUS
After a dry night the going was given as good to soft, good in places (GoingStick 7.6) on both the chase and hurdles tracks. Jockeys returning after the first reported that the ground was soft/dead/sticky/hard work, and the winning time, ten seconds slower than standard, confirmed that view. A race that has in recent years done its job in identifying a leading candidate for the Triumph, with winners including Fair Along, Franchoek and Katchit, while last year's runner-up Barizan also filled the same position in the main event. As the betting suggested, those with winning form in this country didn't appear to set too high a standard, and looked vulnerable to one of the French imports representing the big two stables. Sam Winner was just about the form pick on his French efforts but this still rates a big step up and he will be a player in the Triumph Hurdle on this evidence. This was by some way best juvenile hurdle of the season to date.

NOTEBOOK

Sam Winner(FR) announced himself as the early favourite for the Triumph with an impressive, wide-margin success. Three times a runner-up at Auteuil in the spring, he travelled strongly on his British debut, was kept wide for most of the race, brought stands' side in the straight, and powered up the hill. He was getting 8lb from the runner-up but would have beaten him at levels and this was a taking performance, one which prompted bookmakers to introduce him as a top-priced 8-1 favourite for the Triumph. While one could question the depth in this race, he very much sets the standard for others to aim at. (tchd 9-2)

Grandouet(FR) was much too keen at Wetherby on his British debut but was given a more patient ride this time and settled better. Saving ground towards the inside throughout, he couldn't go with the winner from the turn in, but it was still a good effort in defeat considering he was giving 8lb to him. He was well clear of the third and won't be long in going one better.

Plan A(IRE), another who took the inside route, promised to be better suited to this stiffer track than Kempton last time, and he did run well, albeit while outclassed by the first two. He looks one for handicaps in due course.

Horatio Caine(FR), given a waiting ride out the back, had plenty to do running down the hill, but stamina is clearly his thing and he got going once in line for home. He looks the type who will improve for proper winter ground. (op 40-1)

Titan De Sarti(FR), winner of both his starts in the French provinces, was the subject of good support, but he was slow at the fourth-last, began to come under pressure heading down to the second-last and soon beat a retreat. Perhaps he needs better ground than this - his wins in France came on good and good to soft. (tchd 10-3 and 5-2 in places)

Kalamill(IRE) was under the pump from some way out but he did respond and kept on. He got 1m6f on the Flat and a greater test of stamina is going to suit him in time. (op 50-1 tchd 33-1)

Two Kisses(IRE) hit the second-last and dropped away quite quickly from there. (tchd 14-1)

Zakeeta(IRE) hit the third-last and was soon beating a retreat.

Palawi(IRE), who was a bit keen and wasn't given a hard time once his chance had gone, remains capable of better at a lower level. (tchd 17-2 in a place)

Architrave came here seeking a four-timer, but the competition was hotter than he has been up against over the summer/autumn. He has an official mark of 138 but has yet to record an RPR above 118, so perhaps this is one the handicapper got wrong. (op 7-1)

2357 ULTIMA FRONTRUNNER IN IT SOLUTIONS NOVICES' CHASE (19 fncs) 3m 110y

1:20 (1:21) (Class 2) 5-Y-0+

£9,393 (£2,775; £1,387; £694; £346; £174)

Form			Horse	RPR
21-1	1		**Wayward Prince**[13] 2110 6-11-4 0 ... DougieCostello (Ian Williams) *trckd ldrs: hit 3rd: chal fr 3 out: slt ld sn after: hdd and nk 2nd whn lft in ld 2 out: hrd rdn last: edgd lft u.p run-in: all out* **9/4**[1]	147+
-114	2	4 ½	**Balthazar King (IRE)**[28] 1863 6-11-7 137 ... RichardJohnson (Philip Hobbs) *trckd ldr: led 8th to 12th: styd chalng and led again 15th: jnd 3 out: hdd sn after and one-pced 4th whn lft 2 l 2nd u.p 2 out: rallied last: no imp run-in and hld whn swtchd rt run-in* **16/1**	144
213-	3	4	**Cannington Brook (IRE)**[218] 5112 6-10-13 0 ... JoeTizzard (Colin Tizzard) *in tch: hit 3rd: blnd 9th: hdwy to cl on ldrs 3 out: sn rdn and one pce: btn in 5th whn lft 3rd 2 out: styd on same pce* **13/2**	133+
341-	4	22	**Berties Dream (IRE)**[19] 2017 7-10-13 150 ... AELynch (Paul John Gilligan, Ire) *chsd ldrs: hit 5th and 7th: mstke 11th and 4 out: no ch whn blnd 3 out: lft mod 4th 2 out* **7/2**[2]	117
1113	5	4 ½	**Billie Magern**[28] 1863 6-11-7 137 ... PaddyBrennan (Nigel Twiston-Davies) *led to 8th: styd perssing ldr: led and pckd 12th: hit 14th: hdd next: wknd after 4 out* **14/1**	122
P0-3	6	¾	**Wolf Moon (IRE)**[29] 1854 7-10-13 0 ... WayneHutchinson (Martin Keighley) *chsd ldrs: reminders 11th: wknd bef 4 out* **10/1**	110
411-	B		**Beshabar (IRE)**[266] 4154 8-10-13 0 ... ChristianWilliams (Tim Vaughan) *pckd 1st: in rr: hit 3rd and 5th: mstke 10th: hdwy and mstke 4 out: drvn and gd prog after 3 out and styng on 2 l 3rd whn b.d 2 out* **10/1**	136+
5-31	F		**Chicago Grey (IRE)**[28] 1863 7-11-7 145 ... (t) DJCondon (Gordon Elliott, Ire) *hld up in rr: hdwy 3 out: drvn to chal sn after: nk ldr and styng on wl whn fell 2 out* **5/1**[3]	150+

6m 28.27s (9.97) **Going Correction** +0.40s/f (Soft) **8** Ran SP% **113.7**

Speed ratings: **100,98,97,90,88 88,—,—**

toteswingers: 1&2 £12.60, 1&3 £3.10, 2&3 £22.40. CSF £35.55 TOTE £3.30: £1.60, £3.50, £1.90; EX 50.80 Trifecta £345.30 Pool: £2,239.79 - 4.80 winning units..

Owner T J & Mrs H Parrott **Bred** M G Kilroe **Trained** Portway, Worcs

FOCUS

This decent novice chase has been won by some high-class performers in recent seasons, most notably subsequent Grand National winner Comply Or Die and dual Festival winner Albertas Run. This is good novice form and the winner is rated in line with his hurdles best. Chicago Grey rates a dead-heater and to the level of his recent course win.

NOTEBOOK

Wayward Prince, a Grade 1-winning hurdler and impressive winner of his only previous start over fences, was favourite and duly obliged. However, that does not tell the whole story, as he looked likely to come off second-best at least when headed by Chicago Grey going to the second last, only for that one to fall and bring down the running-on Beshabar. Nevertheless, he galloped on resolutely from that point and is a reliable sort that always gives his running. He appeared to jump adequately, although his trainer thought he could have been better and was inclined to blame the ground. He is likely to be campaigned in a similar way to how his stable companion Weird Al was last season, with the RSA Chase the ultimate aim. (tchd 5-2)

Balthazar King(IRE) finished behind Chicago Grey here last time and had 6 1/2l to find on the same terms. That run might have come too soon though and he ran pretty well, having been up with the pace throughout. He would probably have been third at best had his old rival stood up, but he looks a fair guide to the level of the form. (tchd 20-1 in a place)

Cannington Brook(IRE), a dual point winner, finished runner-up on his debut over fences under rules but was pulled up next time and switched to hurdles, winning over 3m on soft and finishing placed behind today's winner in a Grade 1 at Aintree. He ran pretty well on this turn to fences, recovering from losing his place on the second circuit to get into contention on the downhill run before having nothing more to offer from two out. He should be winning races before too long. (op 15-2)

Berties Dream(IRE) won the Grade 1 Albert Bartlett at the Festival in March (his only previous try at 3m). He had run well before blowing up on his chasing debut, and ran reasonably here, but compromised his chance with a couple of mistakes, most notably at the first ditch. (op 4-1)

Billie Magern, whose trainer had been responsible for three of the previous ten winners, made the running but a couple of errors on the second circuit saw him lose his place, and he was beaten running down the hill. The ground was reportedly sticky and dead and it might not have suited him. (tchd 12-1)

Wolf Moon(IRE), a winner three times over hurdles, including twice here (both times with today's runner-up behind), had made a promising debut over shorter here behind a subsequent winner. However, he was getting reminders with a circuit to go and was beaten a long way from home. In all probability the tacky ground did not suit him. (tchd 11-1)

Beshabar(IRE) ◆ was well beaten on his only previous try over fences last December (3m heavy) but had won his two hurdles starts subsequently, both valuable handicaps. Having his first start for a new trainer, he looked interesting back over fences but a mistake at the first ditch resulted in him being at the back and not appearing to be going that well for much of the way. However, he came back on the bridle running down the hill and was staying on when the leader fell right in front of him two out, giving his rider no chance of staying aboard. He appeared to prove his stamina for the trip and is one to bear in mind for similar races. (tchd 12-1)

Chicago Grey(IRE) ◆ had won three of his six starts over fences, including over C&D last time with today's second and fourth behind. Held up early, he looked set to improve his record when striking the front off the home turn, but he clipped the top of the fence and took a heavy fall. Hopefully, he is none the worse for this, as he looks sure to make his mark in good races this winter. (tchd 12-1)

2358 MORSON GROUP H'CAP CHASE (GRADE 3) (22 fncs) 3m 3f 110y

1:55 (1:58) (Class 1) 4-Y-0+

£28,505 (£10,695; £5,355; £2,670; £1,340; £670)

Form			Horse	RPR
-411	1		**Midnight Chase**[29] 1856 8-11-9 146 ... DougieCostello (Neil Mulholland) *mde virtually all: outrt ldr 6th: hit 3 out: galloped on relentlessly: mstke last: v game: rdn out* **8/1**[3]	165+
54-3	2	8	**Any Currency (IRE)**[20] 1990 7-10-9 132 ... (p) NoelFehily (Martin Keighley) *hld up towards rr: hdwy fr 14th: chsd ldrs 17th: rdn after 3 out: wnt 3rd bef next: chal for 2nd last: hung bdly rt: wnt 2nd fnl 100yds: no ch w wnr* **6/1**[1]	143
131-	3	1	**Junior**[108] 5101 7-10-11 134 ... (b) TomScudamore (David Pipe) *disp tl 6th: chsd wnr: rdn after 3 out: hld by wnr next: styd on but no ex whn lost 2nd run-in* **12/1**	143
1/1-	4	20	**Bluesea Cracker (IRE)**[14] 2099 8-11-4 141 ... AndrewJMcNamara (J Motherway, Ire) *hld up towards rr of midfield: gd hdwy appr 4 out: disputing 2nd whn nodded on landing 3 out: sn rdn: wknd bef 2 out* **20/1**	132
13-3	5	10	**From Dawn To Dusk**[14] 2084 11-11-10 147 ... (t) RichardJohnson (Philip Hobbs) *mid-div: reminders after 14th: nvr able to get on terms: plugged on fr 3 out* **14/1**	129
4-56	6	5	**Lead On (IRE)**[29] 1856 9-10-10 133 ... (b[1]) TomO'Brien (Philip Hobbs) *mid-div: plugged on fr 3 out but nvr able to get on terms* **20/1**	111
130-	7	10	**Ogee**[218] 5109 7-11-5 142 ... JimmyMcCarthy (Renee Robeson) *hld up in mid-div: hdwy fr 14th: chsng ldrs whn stmbld bdly 4 out: sn rdn: 5th and btn whn hit 3 out: blnd 2 out* **11/1**	116+
40F-	8	8	**Ballyfitz**[217] 5127 10-10-12 138 ... SamTwiston-Davies[(3)] (Nigel Twiston-Davies) *mid-div: hit 8th: rdn after 14th: nvr any imp: wknd after 4 out* **15/2**[2]	99
F-S0	9	7	**Eric's Charm (FR)**[14] 2084 12-11-9 146 ... LeightonAspell (Oliver Sherwood) *a towards rr: lost tch fr 16th: t.o* **66/1**	101
153-	10	1	**Wind Instrument (IRE)**[213] 5181 9-10-3 126 ... (b) WayneHutchinson (Alan King) *hld up towards rr of midfield: nvr any imp: wknd 4 out: t.o* **14/1**	80
1P4-	11	5	**Razor Royale (IRE)**[210] 5223 8-11-9 146 ... PaddyBrennan (Nigel Twiston-Davies) *mid-div: hdwy fr 17th: rdn to chse ldrs after 4 out: wknd bef next* **10/1**	96
00-3	12	31	**Character Building (IRE)**[21] 1960 10-11-3 140 ... (t) APMcCoy (John Quinn) *a in rr: t.o fr 18th* **8/1**[3]	62
5/0-	P		**New Alco (FR)**[242] 4659 9-11-2 139 ... GrahamLee (Ferdy Murphy) *hld up towards rr: sme hdwy but no ch whn blnd 4 out: p.u bef next* **33/1**	—
503-	P		**Zacharova (IRE)**[211] 5212 7-10-3 126 ... AidanColeman (Venetia Williams) *chsd ldrs: losing pl whn hit 9th: grad fdd: t.o whn p.u bef 4 out* **25/1**	—
F1-P	P		**Gentle Ranger (IRE)**[13] 2106 8-10-11 134 ... (tp) JohnnyFarrelly (David Pipe) *disp ld tl 6th: chsd ldrs tl 16th: sn wknd: t.o whn p.u bef 2 out* **20/1**	—
123-	P		**Giles Cross (IRE)**[238] 4740 8-10-11 134 ... TimmyMurphy (Victor Dartnall) *in tch tl wkng whn slow jump 18th: bhd whn p.u bef 3 out* **20/1**	—
100-	P		**Tricky Trickster (IRE)**[217] 5127 7-11-12 149 ... SamThomas (Paul Nicholls) *struggling fr 12th: a in rr: t.o fr 16th: p.u bef 4 out* **10/1**	—

7m 11.9s (2.50) **Going Correction** +0.40s/f (Soft) **17** Ran SP% **123.1**

Speed ratings (Par 113): **112,109,109,103,100 99,96,94,92,92 90,81,—,—,— —,—**

Tote Swingers: 1&2 £4.40, 1&3 £12.20, 2&3 £6.90 CSF £51.19 CT £589.86 TOTE £7.10: £2.30, £2.00, £2.70, £3.20; EX 31.10 Trifecta £198.80 Pool: £3,598.77 - 13.39 winning units..

Owner Lady Clarke **Bred** Conkwell Grange Stud Ltd **Trained** Burlescombe, Devon

FOCUS

On paper there looked to be plenty of pace in this race, and sure enough the early gallop was pretty strong. It was somewhat surprising that two of the three forcing it early were able to maintain the gallop well enough to finish third and first, but the tacky ground appeared to play into the hands of those up front as those held up struggled to make an impression. The winner has improved into a top-class handicapper and the second ran to his best, with the third getting towards the best of his hurdles form.

NOTEBOOK

Midnight Chase is a progressive staying chaser and has a good record round here. The even greater test of stamina he faced this time suited him well and he successfully kept up a relentless gallop to see off his rivals. He was given 33-1 quotes for the Grand National by Paddy Power and Stan James, but his trainer thinks it's unlikely he'll show up for the race as he considers the gelding too young and inexperienced at the moment. Given his liking for this track, though, it won't be a surprise to see him back here again quite soon. (tchd 15-2)

Any Currency(IRE), who was fourth in the four-miler at the Festival, is not short of stamina, but he tends to get outpaced in his races before running on again late. Fitted with first-time cheekpieces, he ran to type, staying on well up the hill, albeit while hanging badly right under pressure. (op 7-1, tchd 8-1 in places)

Junior, last seen finishing second at the Glorious Goodwood meeting, ran a blinder back over fences, especially as he's best suited by good ground. Still lightly raced in this sphere, there's room for more improvement. (op 9-1)

Bluesea Cracker(IRE), the Irish Grand National winner, came there going well running down the hill but there was nothing in the locker from three out and she could only keep on one-paced. She has never won on anything quicker than yielding/soft. (op 16-1)

From Dawn To Dusk showed he was as good as ever at Ascot last time, but he's very much a good-ground horse and this tacky surface may not have been entirely to his liking.

Lead On(IRE), beaten 25l by Midnight Chase here last time out, had blinkers for the first time. They didn't have a dramatically positive effect, as he simply kept on without ever troubling the principals. (op 33-1)

Ogee was in the leading group when making a mistake at the fourth last which knocked him back, and he was tired when making another blunder at the second-last. He's another who wouldn't have been at home on this tacky surface. (op 17-2, tchd 12-1 in places)

Ballyfitz still jumps fences poorly. (op 9-1)

Razor Royale(IRE), who was in fourth heading down the hill, didn't get home on his seasonal reappearance. (op 11-1)

Character Building(IRE) ran well at Aintree on his reappearance, albeit he threw the race away on the run-in, but he never threatened to get involved from off the pace here, with McCoy taking over in the saddle from Nina Carberry. (op 9-1 tchd 10-1)
Tricky Trickster(IRE), who faced a stiff task off top weight, was never going at any point, but he needs better ground and his long-term target is the National. (op 14-1)

2359 PADDY POWER GOLD CUP CHASE (H'CAP) GRADE 3 (16 fncs) 2m 4f 110y
2:35 (2:37) (Class 1) 4-Y-0+

£85,515 (£32,085; £16,065; £8,010; £4,020; £2,010)

Form RPR
16-1 **1** **Little Josh (IRE)**[13] 2105 8-10-5 **146**.................... SamTwiston-Davies(3) 160+
(Nigel Twiston-Davies) *mde all: drvn 5 l clr after 3 out: hrd drvn fr 2 out: hld on wl u.p run-in* **20/1**
4R-2 **2** 2 ¾ **Dancing Tornado (IRE)**[14] 2099 9-9-13 **142**....................... APHeskin(5) 154+
(Michael Hourigan, Ire) *in rr tl rdn and styd on appr 3 out: kpt on to take 3rd after 2 out: kpt on u.p run-in to chse wnr fnl 50yds but no imp* **20/1**
113- **3** 2 **Long Run (FR)**[241] 4672 5-11-1 **158**......................... MrSWaley-Cohen(5) 170+
(Nicky Henderson) *trckd ldrs: nt fluent 6th: mstke 7th: hit 12th: hdwy 4 out: chsd wnr 3 out but no imp: one pce whn blnd 2 out: kpt on same pce run-in and lost 2nd fnl 50yds* **2/1**[1]
341- **4** 12 **Mad Max (IRE)**[219] 5098 8-11-5 **157**................................. BarryGeraghty 156
(Nicky Henderson) *chsd ldrs: hit 5th: chsd wnr 4 out: disputing 2nd 3 out but no imp: wknd bef next* **15/2**[3]
2U-2 **5** 6 **Poquelin (FR)**[21] 1958 7-11-7 **164**...................................... IanPopham(5) 159
(Paul Nicholls) *hld up in mid-div: hdwy after 4 out: nvr gng pce to rch ldrs and one pce whn hit 2 out* **14/1**
441- **6** 2 ¼ **Great Endeavour (IRE)**[240] 4702 6-10-4 **142**................. TimmyMurphy 134
(David Pipe) *chsd ldrs tl wknd sn after 3 out* **5/1**[2]
312- **7** 3 ¾ **Sunnyhillboy (IRE)**[240] 4702 7-9-12 **139**.................. RichieMcLernon(3) 129
(Jonjo O'Neill) *in rr tl hdwy fr 4 out: styd on fr 3 out but no imp whn mstke last* **12/1**
10-1 **8** 4 ½ **Edgbriar (FR)**[28] 1861 8-10-7 **145**..............................(p) DominicElsworth 133
(Paul Webber) *chsd ldrs to 10th: dropped to rr sn after: sme prog again run-in* **33/1**
10-3 **9** 1 ½ **Pigeon Island**[28] 1865 7-10-0 **138** oh3..........................(b) PaddyBrennan 120
(Nigel Twiston-Davies) *in rr: blnd 9th: mod prog fr 3 out* **25/1**
43-3 **10** 1 ½ **Catch Me (GER)**[14] 2096 8-10-5 **143**....................... AndrewJMcNamara 130
(E J O'Grady, Ire) *in tch whn blnd 9th: hdwy appr 4 out: nvr rchd ldrs and no ch whn bdly hmpd 2 out* **10/1**
1110 **11** 14 **Passato (GER)**[28] 1861 6-10-1 **139**....................................(t) JamieMoore 107
(Joanna Davis) *nvr beyond mid-div: no ch whn hmpd 4 out* **66/1**
U-13 **12** 5 **Finger Onthe Pulse (IRE)**[59] 1527 9-10-11 **149**.................(t) APMcCoy 113
(T J Taaffe, Ire) *trckd ldrs: hit 4th: chsd wnr 7th to 4 out: wknd and hit next* **18/1**
00-5 **13** 6 **The Sawyer (BEL)**[11] 2138 10-10-1 **146**.................... NathanSweeney(7) 104
(Bob Buckler) *hit 2nd: chsd ldrs tl wknd after 9th* **25/1**
56-F **F** **Gwanako (FR)**[28] 1861 7-10-10 **148**............................ NickScholfield 139
(Paul Nicholls) *in rr tl hdwy after 4 out: no imp and wl hld whn fell 2 out* **33/1**
6F-0 **P** **Can't Buy Time (IRE)**[14] 2084 8-10-7 **145**...................... DougieCostello —
(Jonjo O'Neill) *in rr: hit 4th blnd 6th: t.o whn p.u bef 3 out* **50/1**
F6-3 **P** **Door Boy (IRE)**[13] 2105 7-10-0 **138** oh1.............................. BrianHughes —
(Howard Johnson) *towards rr: no ch whn bdly hmpd 4 out: t.o whn p.u bef 2 out* **40/1**
P3-2 **P** **Awesome George**[20] 1987 6-9-11 **138**.......................... CharlieHuxley(3) —
(Alan King) *blnd 5th: in rr 7th: t.o whn p.u bef 11th* **33/1**
12-1 **F** **Tchico Polos (FR)**[11] 2138 6-11-1 **153** 5ex..........................(t) NoelFehily —
(Paul Nicholls) *mid-div: hit 9th: sme hdwy whn fell 4 out* **20/1**

5m 12.26s (1.26) **Going Correction** +0.40s/f (Soft) **18** Ran SP% **127.2**
Speed ratings (Par 113): **113,111,111,106,104 103,102,100,99,99 93,91,89,—,— —,—,—**
Tote Swingers: 1&2 £174.90, 1&3 £18.90, 2&3 £33.10 CSF £341.61 CT £1172.27 TOTE £22.90: £3.60, £4.60, £1.40, £2.00; EX 732.90 Trifecta £4925.50 Pool: £42,066.87 - 6.32 winning units..
Owner Tony Bloom **Bred** Michael Kearns **Trained** Naunton, Gloucs
■ Gonebeyondrecall was withdrawn at the start (66/1, not wearing declared visor).

FOCUS
The highlight of the open meeting, this ultra-competitive handicap chase is the first really big race of the jumps season proper. Plenty of good horses have taken this recently, although perhaps the best have been subsequent Gold Cup winner Imperial Commander and the talented but ill-fated Exotic Dancer. This is rock-solid handicap form. Little Josh produced another step forward with Dancing Tornado rated in line with his recent hurdles effort and a cracking effort at the weights from Long Run.

NOTEBOOK
Little Josh(IRE), a consistent performer at up to 2m4f, dead-heated with Weird Al on his reappearance and was put up 6lb for that. His best form had been on softer but he made the running and jumped pretty well, going clear before the home turn and running on gamely up the hill. This was a terrific effort despite the fact that things might have fallen right on a day when, over fences at least, it paid to be up with the pace. Presumably, the former Boylesports Gold Cup at the December meeting here will be next. (op 25-1)
Dancing Tornado(IRE), a winner at up to 2m3f including a Grade 2, was something of a market springer. Held up early, he made progress in the last mile and chased the winner up the hill without looking likely to catch him. He might renew rivalry back here next month. (op 33-1)
Long Run(FR), the winner of the Grade 1 Feltham over 3m on his British debut and subsequently winner of a Grade 2 over 2m, looked likely to find this trip ideal. Making his handicap debut off 158, he was always in the leading half-dozen but made a couple of mistakes, the worst at the last on the first circuit. He kept galloping on but gives the impression that this track does not suit his racing style ideally, and that we may see a more potent effort at Kempton in the King George (for which his priced eased only slightly with the bookmakers), and later at Aintree. (op 5-2, tchd 11-4 in places)
Mad Max(IRE), the winner of two of four starts over fences at 2m-2m4f (including Grade 2), both on flat tracks, performed well in the Arkle around here before mistake two out and ran a similar race on this handicap debut. He looks to have more to offer and his record at Newbury suggests there could be good races to be won with him back there. (op 8-1)
Poquelin(FR), a consistent performer since switching to fences, finished runner-up in this last season (off 150) before winning the Boylesports in December and finishing second in Grade 1 Ryanair Chase. He made a good return when second to Monet's Garden at Aintree but had a stiff task off 164 and, although he ran really creditably, it looks as though he will have to contest graded races in future. (op 16-1, tchd 18-1 in a place)
Great Endeavour(IRE) is lightly raced over fences but had won 2-4 including the Byrne Group Plate over 2m5f around here. He showed up in the leading group from the start but got tired after three out and was well beaten when making a mistake at the final fence. (tchd 11-2 in places)
Sunnyhillboy(IRE) had mixed form over fences last season but his best effort was when second to Great Endeavour in the Byrne Group Plate here at the Festival. He didn't look great in his coat and, held up, he made an early mistake before running on down the hill, only to tire once hitting the rising ground. He was well held when having a coming together with his old rival on landing at the final fence. (op 11-1)
Edgbriar(FR) is finding his feet over fences and won a decent handicap over C&D at the October meeting. However, despite running well he was not up to making his mark in this tougher race.
Pigeon Island's only win over fences came when taking Grand Annual at Festival in March but he had also been placed several times around here, including at this sort of trip. He was right out the back early on and only stayed on past beaten rivals up the hill.
Catch Me(GER), a Grade 1 hurdles winner, a winner at this trip over fences and placed in graded company, was making his handicap debut off 143. He tracked the pace from the start but made several minor jumping errors and was fading when hampered at the penultimate fence. (op 8-1)
Passato(GER) won four in a row on a sound surface during the spring and summer, but was well held behind Edgbriar at the last meeting here and was only 3lb lower. He did his best but was another who found this too tough a contest. (op 80-1, tchd 100-1 in places)
Finger Onthe Pulse(IRE), the Galway Plate winner, ran well for a long way before fading. (op 20-1)
The Sawyer(BEL) showed up early before dropping away in the second half of the race.
Gwanako(FR) ran reasonably well but was held when falling two out. (tchd 22-1)
Door Boy(IRE) was in the rear when seriously hampered at the last ditch. (tchd 22-1)
Tchico Polos(FR) was chasing the leading group when taking a heavy fall at the last ditch, four out. (tchd 22-1)

2360 JARDINE LLOYD THOMPSON H'CAP HURDLE (LISTED RACE) (13 hdls) 3m 1f 110y
3:10 (3:11) (Class 1) 4-Y-0+

£14,252 (£5,347; £2,677; £1,335; £670; £335)

Form RPR
46-6 **1** **Cross Kennon (IRE)**[20] 1986 6-10-11 **130**.......................... AlanO'Keeffe 137
(Jennie Candlish) *hld up towards rr: hdwy after 3 out: rdn after 2 out: led sn after last: hung rt: styd on: rdn out* **9/2**[1]
2-P6 **2** 3 **Viking Blond (FR)**[29] 1855 5-10-10 **129**........................(b) PaddyBrennan 132
(Nigel Twiston-Davies) *racd wd: cl up: led after 9th: sn jnd: rdn after 3 out: 2 l clr after 2 out: hdd sn after last: swtchd lft: styd on but no ex* **13/2**[2]
40P2 **3** 1 **Backbord (GER)**[12] 2125 8-10-7 **126**............................(t) DougieCostello 128
(Lucy Wadham) *racd wd: prom tl 5th: sn pushed along in rr: stdy prog u.str.p fr 3 out: chsd ldng pair jst bef last: no further imp run-in* **14/1**
1235 **4** 6 **Raslan**[14] 2090 7-11-9 **145**..(vt) DannyCook(3) 142
(David Pipe) *disp ld tl rdn after 3 out: kpt chsng ldrs: styd on same pce* **25/1**
2-11 **5** 1 ¼ **Ackertac (IRE)**[31] 1821 5-10-6 **128**........................ SamTwiston-Davies(3) 125
(Nigel Twiston-Davies) *mid-div: hdwy to trck ldrs after 6th: jnd ldrs appr 3 out: rdn and ev ch bef 2 out: fdd last* **9/2**[1]
1-0F **6** 13 **Sir Harry Ormesher**[21] 1967 7-11-9 **145**....................... CharlieHuxley(3) 129
(Alan King) *hld up in mid-div: hdwy 9th: rdn in 4th appr 3 out: fdd appr last* **10/1**
2012 **7** 1 **Supercede (IRE)**[28] 1860 8-11-4 **137**............................(bt) TimmyMurphy 120
(Gordon Elliott, Ire) *hld up towards rr: nvr any imp on ldrs* **13/2**[2]
2/4- **8** 4 **Our Bomber Harris**[213] 5182 6-10-13 **132**............................. NoelFehily 116+
(Paul Nicholls) *hld up towards rr: hdwy 10th: rdn whn hit 3 out: sn wknd* **8/1**[3]
322- **9** 37 **Quickbeam (IRE)**[212] 5197 8-10-11 **130**.......................... AidanColeman 76
(Venetia Williams) *trckd ldrs: hit 5th: rdn and wknd after 10th: t.o* **16/1**
400- **F** **Maucaillou (GER)**[155] 724 7-10-11 **130**........................ WayneHutchinson —
(Martin Keighley) *a towards rr: wknd 3 out: wl bhd whn fell last* **20/1**
4422 **P** **Is It Me (USA)**[28] 1864 7-9-11 **119** oh3....................(t) RichieMcLernon(3) —
(Sophie Leech) *led tl after 9th: mstke 3 out: sn wknd: t.o whn p.u bef last* **20/1**
0UP- **P** **Nozic (FR)**[203] 5395 9-11-7 **140**..(t) LiamTreadwell —
(Nick Gifford) *trckd ldrs: hit 4th: struggling 7th: sn in rr: t.o whn p.u bef last* **33/1**
03-0 **F** **Pistolet Noir (FR)**[21] 1967 4-11-1 **139**..........................(b[1]) IanPopham(5) 122
(Paul Nicholls) *mid-div: hit 6th: in tch 8th: rdn and wkng whn fell 2 out* **14/1**

6m 36.3s (10.20) **Going Correction** +0.40s/f (Soft)
WFA 4 from 5yo+ 9lb **13** Ran SP% **118.8**
Speed ratings (Par 111): **100,99,98,96,96 92,92,91,79,— —,—,—**
Tote Swingers: 1&2 £7.50, 1&3 £20.20, 2&3 £46.60 CSF £31.91 CT £384.36 TOTE £5.00: £2.10, £2.60, £4.80; EX 34.20 Trifecta £260.10 Pool: £3,114.68 - 8.86 winning units..
Owner P and Mrs G A Clarke **Bred** Mrs Cora Cronin **Trained** Basford Green, Staffs

FOCUS
A competitive handicap and solid form, rated around the fourth and fifth.

NOTEBOOK
Cross Kennon(IRE), fourth in last season's Pertemps Handicap, tends to get outpaced in his races, but does stay on well in the closing stages, and the extra bit of distance he had to cover this time helped him get home in front. He began to struggle at the top of the hill, but got rolling down it and responded to pressure to hit the front after jumping the last. The obvious target will again be the Pertemps final, and he'll apparently be given a break over Christmas beforehand. (op 5-1)
Viking Blond(FR), all the better for his reappearance run here last month, has stamina in abundance and ran a fine race in defeat. He's the type who'll be hoping it's a wet winter and conditions become borderline unraceable, as he's an honest sort who just keeps going. (op 17-2)
Backbord(GER) is a monkey and doesn't want the ground any worse than this. He looked thoroughly uncooperative for most of this race, but his rider knew the score, kept at him, and in the end his perseverance paid off as the gelding stayed on for an unlikely third place. He is not a ride for the unfit.
Raslan ran a solid race from towards the front but he's handicapped up to the hilt and was always going to be vulnerable off top weight. (tchd 28-1)
Ackertac(IRE), winner of both his starts in lesser company this term, had been put up 10lb for the latest of those successes, and that, combined with the increased test of stamina just found him out. He's only a 5-y-o though, lightly raced and sure to have further improvement in him. (op 5-1, tchd 11-2 in places and 6-1 in a place)
Sir Harry Ormesher couldn't quite go with the principals running down the hill and failed the stamina test over this much longer trip. A strongly run race over shorter should suit him better. (op 8-1)
Supercede(IRE), who had a successful summer/autumn and is now on a pretty stiff mark, was unable to land a blow from off the pace. (op 7-1 tchd 6-1)
Our Bomber Harris, who was restricted to just one start last season, was expected to need this outing, and is to have his attention switched to fences next.
Pistolet Noir(FR), who is still only a 4-y-o, was stepping up massively in distance. He was dropping back in the field, his stamina running out, when taking a crunching fall at the second-last. (op 12-1 tchd 11-1)

2361 ULTIMA BUSINESS SOLUTIONS NOVICES' H'CAP HURDLE (8 hdls) 2m 110y
3:40 (3:43) (Class 3) (0-125,124) 3-Y-0+

£6,262 (£1,850; £925; £463; £231; £116)

Form RPR
432- **1** **Devil To Pay**[178] 4380 4-10-6 **107**.............................. CharlieHuxley(3) 111+
(Alan King) *in tch: chsd ldrs 4 out: chal next: rdn after 2 out: str run to chse ldr run-in: styd on gamely u.p to ld last strides* **7/1**[2]

3132 **2** *shd* **Crystal Rock (IRE)**[12] 2128 5-11-5 **117**........................ BarryGeraghty 119
(Nicky Henderson) *trckd ldrs: chal 3 out tl slt ld next: travelling wl appr last: rdn run-in: ct last strides* **10/1**

15-1 **3** *2 3/4* **Ballybriggan (IRE)**[21] 1962 6-11-12 **124**........................ DougieCostello 124
(John Quinn) *in rr: hdwy 3 out: chsd ldrs fr 2 out: styd on u.p run-in but nt pce of ldng duo* **8/1**[3]

122- **4** *nk* **Bold Addition (FR)**[335] 2856 5-11-5 **117**........................ NoelFehily 116
(Paul Nicholls) *towards rr: hdwy fr 4th: chsd ldrs and hit 3 out: styd on fr next and chal last: one pce run-in* **5/1**[1]

5 *5* **Khayar (IRE)**[18] 2029 4-10-3 **108**........................(t) RJJones(7) 103
(E McNamara, Ire) *in rr tl gd hdwy 3 out: chsd ldrs last: wknd run-in* **16/1**

3-33 **6** *2* **Nodforms Violet (IRE)**[11] 943 6-11-7 **119**........................ GrahamLee 112
(Karen McLintock) *chsd ldrs: rt there u.p fr 2 out: stl in tch whn hmpd last: kpt on again nr fin* **50/1**

-235 **7** *1/2* **Caught By Witness (IRE)**[6] 2246 5-11-7 **122**........ RichieMcLernon(3) 115
(Milton Harris) *in tch 4th: drvn to chal fr 3 out: stl ev ch next: wknd last* **25/1**

0/45 **8** *hd* **Wild Desert (FR)**[17] 2038 5-10-9 **107**........................ WayneHutchinson 99
(Alan King) *chsd ldrs: chal 4 out: slt ld next: hdd and hit 2 out: wknd after last* **25/1**

-113 **9** *4 1/2* **Lucaindubai (IRE)**[29] 1859 4-11-11 **123**........................ PaulMoloney 112
(Evan Williams) *in tch: dropped to rr 4th: sme hdwy 3 out: nvr rchd ldrs and one pce fr next* **11/1**

2-42 **10** *2 1/2* **Beside The Fire**[21] 1974 5-10-10 **108**........................ AidanColeman 94
(Colin Tizzard) *chsd ldrs: stl wl there 3 out: hit 2 out and sn wknd* **25/1**

0-22 **11** *6* **Ballinteni**[12] 2122 8-10-13 **111**........................ JoeTizzard 92
(Colin Tizzard) *chsd ldrs: chal 4 out to next: wknd 2 out* **25/1**

53-1 **12** *14* **Robain (FR)**[20] 1998 5-11-2 **114**........................ TomO'Brien 82
(Philip Hobbs) *mid-div: hdwy to chse ldrs 4 out to next: sn wknd* **7/1**[2]

1134 **13** *3/4* **Beidh Tine Anseo (IRE)**[29] 1859 4-11-8 **120**..........(p) CampbellGillies 87
(Lucinda Russell) *t.k.h: led after 1st: narrowly hdd 3 out: wknd 2 out* **22/1**

42-1 **14** *5* **Vertueux (FR)**[17] 299 5-10-8 **111**........................ LeeEdwards(5) 74
(Tony Carroll) *chsd ldrs to 3 out: wknd next* **25/1**

1120 **15** *2 3/4* **American World (FR)**[9] 2171 6-11-4 **116**........................ APMcCoy 76
(Brendan Powell) *led tl after 1st: wknd 4 out* **25/1**

65-3 **16** *11* **Highland Love**[14] 2092 5-11-0 **112**........................ BrianHarding 62
(Jedd O'Keeffe) *nvr bttr than mid-div: bhd fr 4 out* **66/1**

56/1 **P** **Mark Of Love (IRE)**[12] 2128 6-10-3 **104**.......... SamTwiston-Davies(3) —
(Martin Keighley) *in tch: chsd ldrs fr 4 out and stl wl there 2 out: wknd qckly and p.u bef last* **10/1**

P **Captain Sully (IRE)**[72] 1456 5-10-8 **106**........................ DominicElsworth —
(Jim Wilson) *prom to 4th: t.o whn p.u bef 3 out* **40/1**

35-5 **F** **Rajamand (FR)**[27] 1884 4-11-0 **112**........................ PaddyBrennan 112+
(Warren Greatrex) *in rr tl gd hdwy appr 3 out: trcking ldrs: styng on: looking for a run and n.m.r whn fell last* **10/1**

4m 6.30s (4.30) **Going Correction** +0.40s/f (Soft)
WFA 4 from 5yo+ 7lb **19** Ran SP% **127.6**
Speed ratings (Par 107): **105,104,103,103,101 100,99,99,97,96 93,87,86,84,83 78,—,—,—**
Tote Swingers: 1&2 £10.30, 1&3 £14.80, 2&3 £17.50 CSF £68.52 CT £591.84 TOTE £9.40: £2.60, £2.10, £2.80, £1.80; EX 80.60 Trifecta £2539.20.
Owner Horace 5 **Bred** G Russell **Trained** Barbury Castle, Wilts

FOCUS
Another race that was dominated by Martin Pipe in the first half of the last decade. This year's big field included plenty of unexposed sorts and the gallop could not have been that strong, as there were plenty in with a chance turning towards the last flight and the time was 4.30 secs slower than the opening juvenile contest. The form makes sense but this is probably not a race to get carried away with.

NOTEBOOK
Devil To Pay, a fair stayer on the Flat, was making his handicap debut over hurdles having been in the frame in all three previous hurdles starts last season. He was held up until after the last and only just did enough once getting his head in front. He could be the type to keep ahead of the handicapper. (op 11-2)
Crystal Rock(IRE) had more experience than most in this and got to the front three out travelling well. He held off a number of challenges from that point, but the winner just got the better of him. (op 14-1)
Ballybriggan(IRE), a winner at up to 2m3f on good and easy ground (disqualified once) had not been put up for a win on his return in October but still shouldered top weight. He had to squeeze his way through around the outside going to the third last but had his chance afterwards, and was only found out up the hill. This was another creditable performance.
Bold Addition(FR) ◆, a French-bred bumper winner, had only two previous starts over hurdles and this was his first run since December after striking into himself on his latest start. He race a creditable race after being produced late and this should sharpen him up for future targets. (tchd 11-2)
Khayar(IRE) might have been unlucky at Punchestown last time but came to have his chance only to have nothing more to offer up the hill. (op 14-1)
Nodforms Violet(IRE), fit from a couple of recent runs on the Flat, was another making her handicap debut but, after looking held, ran on again despite being hampered at the final flight.
Caught By Witness(IRE) finished behind Lucaindubai in the summer but was placed around here at the October meeting. He came to have his chance on the home turn but faded up the hill.
Wild Desert(FR) ◆, the stable companion of the winner, was right in the firing line when hitting two out but kept battling and only tired from the last. This lightly raced individual looks capable of winning races on sharper tracks.
Lucaindubai(IRE) showed up for a long way but was quite keen early and paid for it in the latter stages. (op 16-1)
Beside The Fire was anorher who showed up well for a long way.
Ballinteni, a well-established Flat performer but runner-up in two starts over hurdles this autumn, was making his handicap debut and ran well until tiring going to two out. He probably needs better ground. (op 33-1)
Robain(FR), a winner on his handicap debut last time, was up 9lb and this looked tougher. After creeping onto the heels of the leaders, he dropped away quickly before the second last. (op 10-1)
Mark Of Love(IRE), who beat today's runner-up on his return from a 981-day absence, was reappearing after just 12 days. He was bang there going to two out but stopped quickly soon after and was pulled up before the last flight. It is to be hoped he has not suffered a recurrence of previous problems and that he just bounced. (tchd 9-1 and 11-1 in a place)
Rajamand(FR) ◆ was the unlucky horse of the race. Making his handicap debut, he had shown signs of ability on varying ground in three starts and was noted travelling well from some way out. He had moved on to the heels of the leaders, apparently full of running, when short of room going to the last. He had to be switched to avoid clipping heels and lost his stride pattern, causing him to guess at the final flight and came down. Providing he is none the worse, he should be able to gain compensation before too long. (tchd 9-1 and 11-1 in a place)
T/Jkpt: Not won. T/Plt: £118.90 to a £1 stake. Pool:£273,848.57 - 1,680.94 winning tickets. T/Qpdt: £19.10 to a £1 stake. Pool:£19,213.53 - 743.34 winning tickets. ST

2067 UTTOXETER (L-H)
Saturday, November 13

OFFICIAL GOING: Heavy (soft in places; chs 5.5; hdl 6.2)
Bends divided and hurdles track moved out 6-8metre to provide fresh ground.
Final flight of hurdles in the back straight was omitted in all hurdle races.
Wind: Moderate 1/2 against Weather: Fine and sunny

2362 MARSTON'S BEER COMPANY NOVICES' HURDLE (9 hdls 1 omitted) 2m
12:40 (12:42) (Class 4) 4-Y-O+ £2,602 (£764; £382; £190)

Form RPR
130- **1** **Pret A Thou (FR)**[219] 5097 7-10-5 0........................ HarryChalloner(7) 116+
(John Bryan Groucott) *mde all: j.rt: drvn clr 2 out: rdn rt out* **5/2**[1]

32-F **2** *2 1/2* **Highway Code (USA)**[2] 2322 4-10-12 110........................ CharliePoste 112
(Richard Lee) *hld up: hdwy to chse ldrs 6th: kpt on to chse wnr between last 2: styd on same pce* **11/2**[3]

64-3 **3** *9* **Marleno (GER)**[27] 1884 4-10-7 0........................ JimmyDerham(5) 102
(Milton Harris) *chsd ldr: wknd 2 out: 3rd whn hit last* **5/2**[1]

134- **4** *hd* **Lucky Sunny (IRE)**[223] 5012 7-10-12 0........................ SeanQuinlan 102
(Richard Phillips) *stdd s: hld up in rr: hdwy 6th: wknd 2 out* **15/2**

244 **5** *1/2* **Yeomanry**[129] 932 5-10-7 103........................(p) MichaelMurphy(5) 101
(Ian Williams) *chsd ldrs: drvn and lost pl 5th: rallied to chse ldrs after 6th: wknd 2 out* **4/1**[2]

00-P **6** *18* **Sacco D'Oro**[9] 2162 4-10-2 0........................ CharlieStudd(3) 76
(Michael Mullineaux) *in rr: bhd fr 6th: t.o 2 out* **100/1**

6 **U** **All For Free (IRE)**[13] 2109 4-10-7 0........................ MrMMO'Connor(5) —
(Milton Harris) *chsd ldng pair to 6th: wkng whn blnd and uns rdr next* **14/1**

4m 5.10s (9.90) **Going Correction** +0.55s/f (Soft)
WFA 4 from 5yo+ 7lb **7** Ran SP% **111.9**
Speed ratings (Par 105): **97,95,91,91,90 81,—**
toteswingers: 1&2 £3.40, 1&3 £1.10, 2&3 £3.50. CSF £16.17 TOTE £3.80: £2.50, £4.20; EX 22.80.
Owner C J Tipton **Bred** Mme Robert Jeannin **Trained** Bourton, Shropshire

FOCUS
All bends were divided, and the hurdles course had been pushed out 6-8 metres in search of better ground. The winner can probably improve this hurdles mark and the form is rated around the second and third.

NOTEBOOK
Pret A Thou(FR) was given a good ride, Challoner briefly stacking the field to within 6l leaving the back straight before kicking on again, and then securing the inner rail to help get his mount home as he started to tire late on. A much-improved performer over fences last term, rising from 110 to 137 after a deep-ground 2m hat-trick, the gelding has further hurdles races in him granted optimum conditions and an uncontested lead, though will need to avoid the better novices as they continue to emerge to defy the penalty. (op 9-4 tchd 3-1)
Highway Code(USA) showed no ill effects from a first-flight fall on his seasonal reappearance two days earlier, and ultimately saw out the trip more convincingly than on any of his juvenile hurdle starts last term. On this evidence a previously stiff-looking mark of 110 may be within compass after all if switched to handicaps now. (op 6-1 tchd 7-1 and 5-1)
Marleno(GER), third in an ordinary Listed contest at Kempton last time, wasn't as destructively keen as has frequently been the case, but still failed to see it out after trying to go with the winner for much of the race. The basic ability to win a moderate 2m novice hurdle is there, albeit one placing less of an emphasis on stamina. (tchd 9-4)
Lucky Sunny(IRE)'s C&D bumper win came on soft last year, but that was in a typically very steadily run example of the type, and he too may need a less stamina-sapping assignment to show up better over hurdles. (op 7-1)
Yeomanry, with cheekpieces replacing blinkers, was the first under pressure and his effort turning in proved very short-lived. He doesn't appear one to place maximum faith in. (op 5-1 tchd 7-2)

2363 WYCHWOOD HOBGOBLIN BEGINNERS' CHASE (18 fncs) 3m
1:10 (1:10) (Class 4) 4-Y-O+ £3,642 (£1,069; £534; £267)

Form RPR
42-2 **1** **Adams Island (IRE)**[20] 1985 6-10-10 0................(p) AodhaganConlon(7) 128+
(Rebecca Curtis) *chsd ldr: lft in ld 8th: blnd 10th: drvn clr after 3 out: 8 l ahd last: eased towards fin* **15/8**[2]

1-54 **2** *6* **Federstar (GER)**[41] 1706 8-10-12 0........................ JimmyDerham(5) 117
(Milton Harris) *towards rr: hdwy to chse ldrs 14th: chsd wnr 2 out: kpt on same pce* **15/2**

213- **3** *1 1/4* **Double Pride**[244] 4615 6-11-3 0........................ AndrewThornton 116
(Alan King) *chsd ldrs: lft 2nd 8th: drvn 14th: lft 2nd 3 out: one pce* **9/2**[3]

6/0- **4** *27* **Mortimers Cross**[357] 2425 9-11-0 0........................ TommyPhelan(3) 96+
(John Needham) *mstkes: in rr: chsd ldrs 10th: wnt 2nd 4 out: 4 l down whn blnd next: sn wknd: t.o last* **10/1**

30-5 **U** **Predictive (FR)**[20] 1986 7-11-3 130........................ JasonMaguire —
(Donald McCain) *led: blnd and uns rdr 8th* **7/4**[1]

0 **P** **Brockton Scrumpy**[16] 2059 5-10-10 0........................ HarryChalloner(7) —
(Lisa Williamson) *in rr: drvn 9th: sn lost tch: t.o 11th: p.u bef 13th* **66/1**

6m 36.5s (21.40) **Going Correction** +1.025s/f (Soft) **6** Ran SP% **111.7**
Speed ratings (Par 105): **105,103,102,93,— —**
toteswingers: 1&2 £2.70, 1&3 £2.30, 2&3 £5.30. CSF £15.36 TOTE £2.50: £1.30, £3.50; EX 16.90.
Owner Naughty Boys Partnership **Bred** Robert Finnegan **Trained** Newport, Dyfed

FOCUS
Not a bad contest, albeit one that took a bit less winning than it might after Predictive's unseat at halfway, with Adams Island, who shared the lead with that rival up to that point, able to come home in isolation. The winner was value for further but is only rated in line with his Aintree run.

NOTEBOOK
Adams Island(IRE), left in the lead when Predictive unseated, was able to come home in isolation. Connections rightly asserted after that this trip suited him better than the 2m4f of his Aintree chasing debut last time, and his jumping improved as the race went on barring one shuddering error at the last fence first time round. It was noticeable that Predictive was consistently outjumping him until he departed, though, and he may prove to prefer an uncontested lead and/or a more galloping track to give himself enough time to organise himself at his fences. (op 2-1)
Federstar(GER) ◆ jumped better than on his chasing debut over 4f shorter here last time, and here too the extra distance looked the key to that. He can be placed to advantage this winter, with more galloping courses and better going than today's no impediment (as reiterated by last April's Ayr hurdles win on good). (op 9-1 tchd 10-1)
Double Pride ◆, twice a winner on heavy ground at Warwick at up to 3m1f, jumped pleasingly on this chasing debut but lacked the extra gears to run the winner closer. He could prove one for chases over extreme distances in the not too distant future. (tchd 4-1)

Mortimers Cross made mistakes on the way round (in particular at the final ditch) and that proved costlier than a lack of recent match practice. Out of a half-sister to Red Marauder and Red Striker, it's probably too early to be writing him off over fences, though the jumping will clearly need to improve. (op 12-1 tchd 14-1)
Predictive(FR) had put in the best display of jumping on this chasing debut until his departure, and is likely to be given plenty of chances to make amends around a course he handles well in the coming months. (op 6-4)

2364 BANK'S PARK BREWERY H'CAP HURDLE (10 hdls 2 omitted) 2m 4f 110y
1:40 (1:40) (Class 4) (0-115,113) 4-Y-0+ **£2,602** (£764; £382; £190)

Form				RPR
-525	1		**Bled (FR)**[35] 1782 5-10-11 **98**......(b) JasonMaguire (Donald McCain) *led tl after 1st: led 5th to next: led 7th tl appr next: led 2 out: styd on strly to go 6 l clr last: eased towards fin* **3/1**[2]	108+
F-02	2	17	**Vivarini**[9] 2169 6-11-2 **110**...... CharlieWallis(7) (John O'Shea) *trckd ldrs: chal 7th: led appr next: hdd 2 out: sn btn* **10/3**[3]	105+
01F-	3	13	**Laborec (IRE)**[343] 2718 7-11-12 **113**......(p) MarkBradburne (Neil King) *chsd ldrs: drvn 6th: wknd after next: tk modest 3rd last* **14/1**	90
030-	4	2	**Playing The Field (IRE)**[205] 5334 5-11-6 **112**...... GilesHawkins(5) (David O'Meara) *chsd ldrs: drvn and outpcd 7th: one pce: lost 3rd last* **11/4**[1]	87
P6-5	5	46	**Ballinderry Park (FR)**[16] 2049 7-11-1 **105**......(tp) PeterToole(3) (Charlie Mann) *trckd ldrs: led after 1st: hdd 5th: led next: hdd 7th: sn wknd: t.o 2 out* **6/1**	34
P0-P	P		**Petroglyph**[10] 2150 6-10-11 **105**...... MrJMQuinlan(7) (Michael Quinlan) *in rr: reminders 5th: bhd fr next: t.o 7th: p.u bef 2 out* **16/1**	—
U16/	P		**Troys Run (IRE)**[1260] 538 7-10-8 **95**...... RodiGreene (Bill Moore) *chsd ldrs: drvn 5th: lost pl next: sn bhd: t.o 7th: p.u bef next* **40/1**	—
32P-	P		**No Wonga**[262] 4237 5-10-13 **103**...... LeeStephens(3) (Katie Stephens) *in rr: bhd fr 6th: t.o next: p.u bef 3 out* **10/1**	—

5m 12.5s (8.50) **Going Correction** +0.55s/f (Soft) 8 Ran SP% **113.1**
Speed ratings (Par 105): **105,98,93,92,75** —,—,—
Tote Swingers: 1&2 £1.20, 1&3 £44.30, 2&3 £12.30 CSF £13.48 CT £116.41 TOTE £3.70: £1.10, £1.60, £4.40; EX 12.90.
Owner Essential Racing 1 **Bred** Francois-Marie Cottin **Trained** Cholmondeley, Cheshire

FOCUS
Few were meaningfully involved at any stage of this contest. The winner produced a big step up and the time was creditable.

NOTEBOOK
Bled(FR) ultimately coasted to a first win at the 11th attempt after his sole pursuer folded tamely up the straight. It wasn't quite as straightforward as that implies, however, with the winner's mind seemingly on other things on a few occasions (needed a reminder passing the paddock) and Jason Maguire was hard at work before the turn in. Donald McCain thought the assessor had hit the gelding hard after his second in a Worcester maiden previously, and fears another punitive rise for having beaten very little here may prevent a follow-up. (op 9-2)
Vivarini, claimed from Caroline Bailey after finishing second in a Towcester seller last time, produced a limited response after appearing to be travelling all over the winner turning in. He had won on both his previous breaks of 10 days or fewer (each time on soft) so this quick reappearance was nothing alien him, and having faded from a similarly promising position in that Towcester contest may just be becoming a little untrustworthy. (op 4-1)
Laborec(IRE), weak in the market beforehand, has never won a handicap of any description and didn't look like putting that right at any stage today. The ground would have suited and he has shaped well on most of his previous seasonal reappearances, though, so he may have been expected to fare a little better. (op 10-1)
Playing The Field(IRE) displayed none of the wayward tendencies of his final outing for Malcolm Jefferson, but did seem to be finding it all happening a bit too quickly halfway down the final back straight. A return to somewhere like Wetherby or Carlisle, scenes of his place finishes for previous connections, may see him in a better light. (tchd 10-3)
Ballinderry Park(FR) still didn't see out the trip, albeit under a more prominent ride than in recent starts. (tchd 11-2)

2365 BANK'S BITTER NOVICES' HURDLE (10 hdls 2 omitted) 2m 4f 110y
2:10 (2:10) (Class 4) 4-Y-0+ **£2,602** (£764; £382; £190)

Form				RPR
/32-	1		**Silver Footnote**[234] 4826 5-10-12 0...... JamesDavies (Emma Lavelle) *t.k.h: mde all: wnt clr after 3 out: drvn out* **4/6**[1]	96+
P-	2	3	**Our Columbus (IRE)**[226] 4968 6-10-9 0...... TomMolloy(3) (Nigel Twiston-Davies) *nt fluent: chsd ldrs: 2nd whn hit 5th: outpcd after 7th: styd on to go 2nd 2 out: kpt on same pce* **10/1**	90
000-	3	15	**Glamorous Gg**[249] 4496 5-10-0 0...... MichaelMurphy(5) (Ian Williams) *reminders after 2nd: drvn 5th: sn bhd: kpt on fr 3 out: tk modest 3rd after 2 out* **20/1**	68
60	4	11	**Just Unique**[37] 1749 6-10-9 0...... PeterToole(3) (Mark Rimell) *prom: outpcd 5th: wknd after 7th* **20/1**	66
	5	47	**Gentle Bob (IRE)**[222] 5-10-12 0...... AndrewThornton (Tom George) *wnt prom 6th: wknd after next: sn bhd: t.o 2 out* **7/1**[3]	17
6/	P		**Wheretheres A Will**[1269] 425 8-10-12 0...... MarkBradburne (Michael Mullineaux) *t.k.h: trckd ldrs: lost pl 5th: sn bhd: t.o 7th: p.u bef next* **25/1**	—
3-F	P		**Seymour Eric**[10] 2143 5-10-9 0...... JohnKington(3) (Michael Scudamore) *trckd ldrs: clr 2nd 6th: 4 l down and wkng whn mstke 3 out: sn lost pl: poor 5th whn p.u bef last* **4/1**[2]	—

5m 19.9s (15.90) **Going Correction** +0.55s/f (Soft) 7 Ran SP% **114.9**
Speed ratings (Par 105): **91,89,84,79,62** —,—
Tote Swingers: 1&2 £2.10, 1&3 £5.10, 2&3 £19.50 CSF £8.25 TOTE £1.60: £1.20, £4.50; EX 8.40.
Owner James Thorburn-Muirhead&john Kevin Lomax **Bred** J Thorburn-Muirhead And K Lomax **Trained** Wildhern, Hants

FOCUS
The defection of Realmont left this thinly contested novice hurdle at the mercy of Silver Footnote. He is only rated in line with his previous form.

NOTEBOOK
Silver Footnote made all, and apart from one sticky leap down the back straight there was rarely a moment's alarm for favourite backers. A sound second, albeit short of late gears, over about this far on hurdling debut at Warwick last March, he rates a cosier winner than the final margin implies having proven over-keen early on. Doubtless more will be required to defy a penalty, but he can step up on this effort again if racing calmer and stepped up in trip next time. (op 8-11 tchd 10-11)
Our Columbus(IRE) had failed to finish in two Irish points and a novice hurdle last season, so he is entitled to derive confidence from this first completion despite not convincing overly over some hurdles. The proximity to the winner does flatter him a touch, but at the same time he was certainly staying on to a degree having been outpaced at a pivotal stage of the race, and a return to 3m ought not be far off. (op 11-1)
Glamorous Gg's third place owes plenty to the perseverance of Michael Murphy and the floundering of several better fancied rivals up the straight. She hadn't always looked entirely enthusiastic in her two previous hurdles starts last season, either, and an experiment with some form of headgear might be worth a try. (op 18-1 tchd 16-1)
Gentle Bob(IRE), well held when departing through a wing late on in a 2m4f maiden point eight months earlier, again didn't convince as up to staying this trip yet. (op 8-1 tchd 6-1)
Seymour Eric, a good third to the promising L'Accordioniste in a bumper here last March, got no further than the first on his recent hurdling debut and an untimely error late on here emptied him out completely. Already just starting to feel the pinch at the time, a drop back to 2m may be prudent, but even then the jumping still needs to improve. (tchd 7-2)

2366 MARSTON'S PEDIGREE H'CAP CHASE (14 fncs 1 omitted) 2m 4f
2:45 (2:45) (Class 4) (0-115,112) 4-Y-0+ **£3,512** (£1,031; £515; £257)

Form				RPR
16-6	1		**Fine Parchment (IRE)**[17] 2036 7-11-4 **107**......(t) PeterToole(3) (Charlie Mann) *j.w: travelled strly: trckd ldrs: wnt 2nd 9th: led 11th: wnt clr omitted 3 out: pushed out* **3/1**[2]	130+
36-1	2	23	**Deuteronomy (IRE)**[17] 2034 9-11-2 **102**...... MarkBradburne (John Wade) *led: hdd 11th: one pce fr next* **5/2**[1]	105+
04U-	3	22	**Corlande (IRE)**[228] 4943 10-11-8 **108**......(b) JasonMaguire (Donald McCain) *chsd ldr: outpcd 9th: bhd 11th: tk distant 3rd 2 out* **9/2**[3]	86
11U-	4	35	**Ayemdee (IRE)**[283] 3816 7-11-9 **112**...... MrAJBerry(3) (Jonjo O'Neill) *in rr: mstke 2nd and rdr briefly lost iron: nvr gng after: reminders 4th: hmpd next: bhd and drvn 8th: wnt poor 3rd after 11th: wknd 2 out: virtually p.u run-in* **9/2**[3]	55
445-	F		**Western Whisky (FR)**[222] 5034 8-11-6 **106**......(b) AndrewThornton (Richard Lee) *mstke 1st: reminders 2nd: 4th and prom whn fell 5th* **11/2**	—
60-5	U		**Pacha D'Oudairies (FR)**[7] 2217 7-11-5 **110**...... JimmyDerham(5) (Michael Blake) *hld up in tch: 5th whn bdly hmpd and uns rdr 5th* **8/1**	—

5m 23.5s (18.00) **Going Correction** +1.025s/f (Soft) 6 Ran SP% **116.4**
Speed ratings (Par 105): **105,95,87,73**,— —
Tote Swingers: 1&2 £2.70, 1&3 £4.10, 2&3 £1.30 CSF £11.87 TOTE £5.40: £2.40, £1.90; EX 16.50.
Owner N W A Bannister **Bred** Timothy Considine **Trained** Upper Lambourn, Berks

FOCUS
A fairly tight-looking contest on paper proved to be anything but, with two casualties smashing the open ditch to matchwood on the first circuit and two others running no sort of race. The easy winner may go on to rate higher and the second is rated in line with his previous heavy-ground form.

NOTEBOOK
Fine Parchment(IRE), tried in a tongue tie, was having his second run back after a wind operation, but the first of those, at Haydock last month, was reckoned to have been needed by Charlie Mann, and the yard has just started to creep back into better form since then in any event. There could be more to come from this grand chasing type either kept at this trip or stepped back up to 3m, although connections hope to escape a "silly" rise off what is already a career-high mark for having beaten little here. (op 4-1)
Deuteronomy(IRE), representing a yard in decent nick in recent weeks, has won at this trip on bad ground as well as the good of Haydock victory last time, so it was likeliest the 9lb rise to a highest handicap mark that found him out. It's two and a half years since he last tried a longer trip, and he did manage a neck second over 3m3f back then, so there may be no harm in seeing whether he can regain the winning thread stepped back up to further. (op 3-1)
Corlande(IRE) struggled for consistency during a light 2009-10 campaign, and while an uninspiring reappearance here is nothing new (very mixed record fresh), he still enters this campaign with a deal to prove despite now rating 8lb below his last winning mark. (op 7-2)
Ayemdee(IRE)'s hat-trick last term included a 3m score on soft here, but he lost interest completely after an early mistake last time out (eventually unseated) and did exactly the same after hitting the second here. Whether a mark 14lb above his highest winning one is beyond him consequently remains unclear, but either way he has to be trodden carefully with until proving less moody when things don't go his way. (op 4-1)

2367 MARSTON'S EPA H'CAP HURDLE (9 hdls 1 omitted) 2m
3:20 (3:20) (Class 5) (0-95,95) 4-Y-0+ **£1,626** (£477; £238; £119)

Form				RPR
1364	1		**Simone Martini (IRE)**[3] 2308 5-10-3 **77**......(vt[1]) JimmyDerham(5) (Milton Harris) *chsd ldrs: hmpd after 3 out: styd on to ld appr last: hld on wl* **5/2**[1]	84
-134	2	3/4	**Quam Celerrime**[15] 2070 5-10-5 **74**...... HaddenFrost (Roger Curtis) *hld up in tch: effrt appr 3 out: swtchd rt between last 2: hrd rdn and chsd wnr run-in: no ex clsng stages* **3/1**[2]	79
533	3	3 1/4	**Bari Bay**[15] 2070 4-10-0 **72**......(b) PeterToole(3) (Michael Blake) *hld up: hdwy to trck ldrs 4th: swvd lft after 3 out: led next: wnt lft and hdd appr last: wknd fnl 100yds* **8/1**	75
2544	4	2 1/2	**Devils Delight (IRE)**[8] 2190 8-9-10 **75**...... JamesSmith(10) (James Moffatt) *t.k.h: trckd ldrs: led 4th: hdd appr 2 out: wknd appr last* **5/1**[3]	76
0056	5	18	**Ladies Best**[10] 2144 6-11-0 **90**...... MattGriffiths(7) (Gordon Edwards) *chsd ldrs: reminders 4th: drvn 6th: sn lost pl* **9/1**	72
003-	6	4	**Diddley Dee**[287] 3749 6-9-11 **76** ow3...... DerekSmith(10) (Bill Moore) *t.k.h: mstke 1st and rdr temporalily lost an iron: sn chsng ldrs: drvn 6th: sn lost pl* **20/1**	54
-000	P		**Madman (FR)**[13] 2114 6-10-13 **82**...... RodiGreene (Christopher Kellett) *led to 4th: chsd ldrs: wknd 6th: bhd fr next: t.o and p.u bef 3 out* **25/1**	—

4m 7.90s (12.70) **Going Correction** +0.55s/f (Soft)
WFA 4 from 5yo+ 7lb 7 Ran SP% **100.0**
Speed ratings (Par 103): **90,89,88,86,77 75**,—
Tote Swingers: 1&2 £2.00, 1&3 £8.10, 2&3 £4.10 CSF £8.07 CT £30.24 TOTE £3.30: £1.60, £2.40; EX 6.50.
Owner Paul Frank Barry **Bred** Epona Bloodstock Ltd **Trained** Herridge, Wiltshire
■ Nous Voila (13/2) was withdrawn after the rider was injured at the start. Deduct 10p in the £ under R4.
■ Stewards' Enquiry : Hadden Frost one-day ban: used whip with excessive frequency (Nov 28)

FOCUS
A poor affair thinned further by Nous Voila's withdrawal at the start. The winner is rated back to his C/D mark.

NOTEBOOK
Simone Martini(IRE) took a step back in the right direction after two lesser recent efforts. Defeat would have been tough on the five-year-old, who had lost some momentum after being broadsided by the third several strides after three out. Changes of headgear seem to be key with him, as a course-and-distance win in a near-identical contest last month had been gained in first-time cheekpieces and his best ever Flat effort with blinkers debuted. As such, it may not pay to place too much store in the visor tried out today working as well next time. (op 3-1 tchd 9-4)
Quam Celerrime, who took the other division of Simone Martini's handicap hurdle here last month, had similarly posted lesser efforts in defeat since then, but like the winner reappeared here still 10lb above his winning mark of that day. He never quite looked like getting up at any stage, but slightly more patient tactics this time saw him meaningfully involved for longer again and there may still be another comparably weak heat in him.

Bari Bay, under a length behind the runner-up on identical terms over course and distance last time, was the first to play her hand after the leader capitulated, but her finishing effort has not always been the strongest and she was overcome at the last pretty easily. She remains winless after 25 starts and will need plenty to fall right to correct that. (tchd 9-1)
Devils Delight(IRE) remains 5lb above her sole winning mark (gained under this 10lb claimer last February), though her refusal to settle any better early on was at least as instrumental in her fading effort this time. (op 9-2 tchd 11-2)
Ladies Best wasn't enjoying it from some way out, and although a Flat winner on good to soft in the past probably doesn't need it quite as deep as this. (tchd 8-1)

2368 NUMARK STANDARD OPEN NATIONAL HUNT FLAT RACE 2m
3:50 (3:50) (Class 6) 4-6-Y-0 **£1,301** (£382; £191; £95)

Form RPR
1 **Lucky Landing (IRE)**^{244} 4-11-0 0 JasonMaguire 109
(Donald McCain) *trckd ldrs: reminders and outpcd over 4f out: wnt 4th 3f out: edgd rt 2f out: styd on wl fnl f: led post* **5/1**^{3}
0- 2 *shd* **Poole Master**^{374} [2058] 5-10-11 0 ChrisHonour$^{(3)}$ 109
(David Pipe) *trckd ldrs: led over 3f out: hdd last stride* **12/1**
3 *3¾* **Black Noddy (IRE)** 4-11-0 0 SamThomas 105
(Emma Lavelle) *hld up towards rr: hdwy 6f out: chsd ldr 3f out: styd on same pce over 1f out* **9/4**^{1}
4 *9* **Bunclody**^{230} 5-10-4 0 SamuelWelton$^{(10)}$ 96
(George Moore) *mid-div: hdwy to chse ldrs 6f out: wnt 3rd 3f out: sltly hmpd 2f out: sn wknd* **33/1**
5 *6* **Gallant Oscar (IRE)** 4-11-0 0 TomScudamore 90
(Rebecca Curtis) *led: hdd over 3f out: sn wknd* **4/1**^{2}
6 *1* **Two Cloudy (IRE)**^{196} 4-10-9 0 MichaelMurphy$^{(5)}$ 89
(Pat Murphy) *trckd ldrs: n.m.r bnd after 5f: lost pl over 4f out* **25/1**
7 *nk* **Rojo Vivo** 4-11-0 0 TomSiddall 89
(Karen McLintock) *trckd ldrs: wknd over 3f out* **40/1**
8 *5* **Be True (IRE)** 6-10-11 0 JohnKington$^{(3)}$ 84
(Donald McCain) *hld up in rr: hdwy 7f out: outpcd and lost pl over 5f out* **33/1**
23- 9 *10* **Shammick Boy (IRE)**^{218} [5122] 5-11-0 0 AndrewGlassonbury 74
(Victor Dartnall) *hld up: hdwy to trck ldrs after 5f: drvn over 4f out: sn lost pl* **5/1**^{3}
5 10 *½* **Elton Fox**^{15} [2074] 5-10-11 0 (t) TommyPhelan$^{(3)}$ 73
(John Needham) *hld up towards rr: drvn 7f out: sn bhd* **25/1**
11 *32* **Black Cache (IRE)** 4-10-11 0 TomMolloy$^{(3)}$ 41
(Nigel Twiston-Davies) *t.k.h: trckd ldrs: wknd over 5f out: sn bhd: t.o* **7/1**
12 *2½* **Little Frano (IRE)** 6-10-7 0 MichaelByrne$^{(7)}$ 39
(Peter Bowen) *chsd ldrs: drvn 6f out: sn lost pl and bhd: t.o* **25/1**
13 *30* **Bollistick** 4-11-0 0 AndrewThornton 9
(Michael Mullineaux) *in rr: reminders 8f out: sn bhd: t.o 4f out: virtually p.u* **100/1**

3m 59.3s (9.70) **Going Correction** +0.55s/f (Soft) **13** Ran SP% **125.1**
Speed ratings: **97,96,95,90,87 87,86,84,79,79 63,61,46**
Tote Swingers: 1&2 £14.40, 1&3 £1.50, 2&3 £4.30 CSF £61.87 TOTE £5.10: £2.20, £3.90, £1.50; EX 157.00.
Owner Twenty Four Seven Recruitment **Bred** James McGrath **Trained** Cholmondeley, Cheshire

FOCUS
In all probability this was quite a decent bumper, with a number of contenders attracting support during the day and both Sam Thomas and Tom Scudamore travelling from Cheltenham for their respective sole rides on the card. It is likely to produce a few winners.

NOTEBOOK
Lucky Landing(IRE) has been described by his trainer as a fine big horse whom he loved at the sales despite not having the strongest pedigree (dam out of a half-sister to Grand National winner Papillon, though). He had been outpaced late on in both starts in four-year-old 2m4f Irish points last winter, and again found the field getting away from him before the turn for home here, but a fulsome, withering late response just wrested the spoils. This was a splendid start, while at the same time probably something of a bonus, as a longer trip and obstacles will be the making of him under rules. (op 9-2 tchd 7-2)
Poole Master had shown nothing in one bumper for another stable 12 months earlier, and was weak in the market here, but very nearly pinched it after getting first run once the pacemakers subsided at the 3f marker. Two half-sisters have proven to be modest winning hurdlers from 2m3f to 3m, but he looks more blessed with tactical speed than either on this showing and could yet oblige in a bumper. (op 8-1)
Black Noddy(IRE) ◆ looked a huge threat appearing on the leaders' coat-tails 3f from home but raced a little greenly from that point, drifting further into the middle of the course. He pulled a fair way clear of the fourth, though, and definitely looks to have a future once working out more what's required. (op 3-1)
Bunclody, who had useful-looking recent course hurdles winner Kilcrea Kim behind him when falling late on his sole Irish pointing start, posted a fair effort, albeit off a flyweight. A routine northern bumper may be within his grasp, though time, a trip and obstacles are what he'll require eventually.
Gallant Oscar(IRE)'s connections were bullish beforehand and their debutant duly faded up the straight, though his racing a shade freely may well have been as much a cause as the going. Related to a stack of quality staying chasers as well as banks legend Risk Of Thunder, all his best days are ahead of him. (op 9-2 tchd 5-1 in places)
Shammick Boy(IRE), placed under a 10lb claimer on his two previous starts, never threatened to add to his trainer's tally of 4-9 in course bumpers in the last five seasons. (tchd 9-2 and 11-2)
Black Cache(IRE) needs to learn to settle far better than he did here. (op 6-1 tchd 15-2)
T/Plt: £39.30 to a £1 stake. Pool:£54,354.96 - 1,008.45 winning tickets. T/Qpdt: £3.70 to a £1 stake. Pool:£906.86 - 4,601.29 winning tickets. WG

2088 WETHERBY (L-H)
Saturday, November 13
OFFICIAL GOING: Good to soft (soft in places; chs 7.2; hdl 6.9)
Wind: Moderate Weather: Bright and sunny

2369 FOLLOW WETHERBY RACECOURSE ON FACEBOOK JUVENILE (S) HURDLE (9 hdls) 2m 110y
12:45 (12:45) (Class 5) 3-Y-0 **£1,951** (£573; £286; £143)

Form RPR
20 1 **Lady Pacha**^{119} [1018] 3-9-12 0 BrianToomey$^{(7)}$ 83
(Tim Pitt) *trckd ldrs: rdn 3 out: edgd lft fr 2 out: styd on wl after last: led post* **11/1**
630 2 *shd* **Venture Girl (IRE)**^{17} [2033] 3-10-5 82 RichieMcGrath 84
(Tim Easterby) *trckd ldrs: pushed along to ld 3 out: wandered and jnd appr last: kpt on: ct post* **8/1**^{3}
6 3 *¾* **Antoella (IRE)**^{8} [1984] 3-10-5 0 JamesReveley 85+
(Philip Kirby) *midfield: hdwy after 6th: ev ch fr 3 out: upsides whn blnd last: kpt on run-in* **7/1**^{2}
P62 4 *13* **Moonbalej**^{12} [2133] 3-10-12 95 (v) DaveCrosse 78
(Milton Harris) *led: rdn whn hdd 3 out: wknd after 2 out* **7/1**^{2}
35 5 *8* **Valantino Oyster (IRE)**^{67} [1498] 3-10-12 0 BarryKeniry 70
(Ben Haslam) *hld up: nt fluent 4th: rdn appr 3 out: sn no imp* **8/1**^{3}
6 *1½* **Eeny Mac (IRE)**^{59} 3-10-9 0 FearghalDavis$^{(3)}$ 70
(Neville Bycroft) *hld up: hdwy appr 3 out: sn no further imp* **50/1**
34 7 *35* **Jazz Age (IRE)**^{12} [2133] 3-10-7 102 (b) CO'Farrell$^{(5)}$ 57
(David Pipe) *w ldr: rdn and wknd appr 3 out: wl btn whn blundering 2 out* **15/8**^{1}
60 P **Green For Luck (IRE)**^{6} [2245] 3-10-12 0 HenryOliver —
(Sue Smith) *trckd ldrs: mstke 3rd: wknd after 6th: t.o whn p.u bef 3 out* **14/1**
3P P **Bojangles Andrews**^{31} [1818] 3-10-5 0 KyleJames$^{(7)}$ —
(Tim Pitt) *midfield: wknd qckly after 6th: p.u bef 3 out* **22/1**
00P4 P **Teela**^{67} [1498] 3-9-9 80 SeveBrumpton$^{(10)}$ —
(Ben Haslam) *slowly away: in rr: t.o fr 1/2-way: p.u bef 3 out* **16/1**
P0 U **Catawollow**^{6} [2245] 3-10-5 0 PaddyAspell —
(Richard Guest) *hld up: mstke and uns rdr 5th* **28/1**
P **Amylyn**^{30} 3-10-5 0 TomMessenger —
(John Holt) *midfield: wknd qckly after 6th: t.o whn p.u bef 3 out* **80/1**

4m 6.60s (10.80) **Going Correction** +0.625s/f (Soft) **12** Ran SP% **113.9**
Speed ratings (Par 102): **99,98,98,92,88 88,71,—,—,— —,—**
toteswingers: 1&2 £13.30, 1&3 £18.10, 2&3 £13.00. CSF £89.52 TOTE £14.40: £3.90, £2.80, £2.80; EX 131.00.There was no bid for the winner.
Owner Pacha Bloodstock **Bred** Hascombe And Valiant Studs **Trained** Norton, N Yorks

FOCUS
A very ordinary juvenile seller which was run at an even pace and the first three pulled well clear. It proved difficult to come from off the pace and the first three home were all fillies. The fourth and fifth help set the level.

NOTEBOOK
Lady Pacha having her third start, was running without the cheeckpieces that she wore when disappointing last time out. Not looking the most likely winner approaching the final hurdle, she is very tough and should continue to pay her way at this level. (op 16-1 tchd 10-1)
Venture Girl(IRE)third at this track on her penultimate start, looked the most likely winner until getting caught close home. She appeared to do little wrong and can lose her maiden tag at some point this season.\n (op 14-1)
Antoella(IRE)having her second start, held every chance of winning when making a bad mistake at the final hurdle. Although limited on the Flat, this was a solid effort and she can also make her mark in due course (op 8-1)
Moonbalejwas bang there turning for home, but in the end was well held and can only be watched on this evidence. (op 13-2)
Jazz Age(IRE) weakened quickly and is clearly one of the yard's lesser lights. (op 6-4)

2370 HARRATTS VOLVO LEEDS AND WAKEFIELD MARES' NOVICES' HURDLE (9 hdls) 2m 110y
1:15 (1:15) (Class 4) 4-Y-0+ **£2,276** (£668; £334; £166)

Form RPR
-21P 1 **Dorabelle (IRE)**^{125} [956] 5-11-3 0 AdrianLane 115+
(Donald McCain) *midfield: trckd ldrs 5th: led 3 out: pushed clr after next: comf* **9/2**^{2}
2 *10* **Glorybe (GER)**^{270} 4-10-10 0 TomMessenger 94
(Chris Bealby) *midfield: hdwy to trck ldrs appr 3 out: wnt 2nd after 2 out: kpt on but no match wnr* **33/1**
100- 3 *3* **Chicklemix**^{218} [5114] 4-10-10 0 DavidEngland 94+
(Pam Sly) *trckd ldrs: hdwy to ld after 6th: hdd 3 out: stl ev ch whn hit 2 out: one pce after* **13/2**^{3}
00 4 *14* **Beau D'Argent**^{20} [1989] 4-10-3 0 PaulGallagher$^{(7)}$ 79
(Ferdy Murphy) *hld up: hdwy after 6th: no further imp after 3 out* **100/1**
5 *4* **Dispol Diva**^{39} 4-10-10 0 PaddyAspell 75
(Paul Midgley) *hld up: rdn and sme hdwy after 6th: no further imp after 3 out* **33/1**
042- 6 *15* **Flora's Pride**^{18} [4512] 6-10-10 104 JamesReveley 62
(Keith Reveley) *led: hdd after 6th: wknd qckly appr 3 out* **13/8**^{1}
7 *5* **Drop The Hammer**^{18} 4-10-7 0 FearghalDavis$^{(3)}$ 57
(David O'Meara) *trckd ldrs: wknd after 6th: sn wknd* **9/2**^{2}
0 8 *4½* **Zefooha (FR)**^{14} [2092] 6-10-10 0 RobertWalford 53
(Tim Walford) *nt fluent: hld up: a towards rr* **13/2**^{3}
9 *3½* **Lady Norlela**^{18} 4-10-3 0 KyleJames$^{(7)}$ 50
(Brian Rothwell) *hld up: nt fluent 1st: mstke 3rd: a towards rr* **28/1**
0-0P 10 *20* **Politelysed**^{14} [2089] 4-10-10 0 KennyJohnson 32
(Robert Johnson) *trckd ldrs: lost pl 5th: wknd after next* **66/1**
P-P P **Mujada**^{19} [92] 5-10-10 0 MichaelMcAlister —
(David O'Meara) *w ldr: wknd qckly after 6th: t.o whn p.u bef last* **100/1**

4m 4.10s (8.30) **Going Correction** +0.625s/f (Soft)
WFA 4 from 5yo+ 7lb **11** Ran SP% **113.9**
Speed ratings (Par 105): **105,100,98,92,90 83,81,78,77,67 —**
toteswingers: 1&2 £11.80, 1&3 £1.60, 2&3 £60.40. CSF £129.24 TOTE £4.80: £1.40, £5.40, £2.30; EX 238.20.
Owner Brendan Richardson **Bred** Tommy James **Trained** Cholmondeley, Cheshire

FOCUS
An even pace for this mares' novice hurdle, which provided a runaway winner in Dorabelle who was value for further. The first three pulled well clear.

NOTEBOOK
Dorabelle(IRE), who was coming back from a break, was easy to back beforehand but travelled well throughout. Already a winner of a bumper and a novice hurdle before this fine effort, she could well carry a double penalty in similar company with her stable going so well. (op 11-4 tchd 5-1)
Glorybe(GER), rated 63 on the Flat, showed up well on her hurdling debut. Coming from a stable that does well with these types, she can go one better in similar company next time out. (op 20-1)
Chicklemix, also winner of a bumper, travelled well throughout and can make her mark over timber as well. Another mares-only novice hurdle should be well within her grasp. (op 6-1 tchd 5-1)
Beau D'Argent, who has shown little in two starts in bumpers, stayed on from a long way back. She looks the type her trainer well does well with later in the season – most likely in modest handicaps.
Flora's Pride appeared to get the run of the race in front and this was disappointing. Official explanation: trainer's rep had no explanation for the poor form shown (op 9-4)
Drop The Hammer, prominent in the betting, was well held on her debut over hurdles and can only be watched next time. (op 5-1)
Zefooha(FR) Official explanation: trainer's rep said mare was unsuited by the good to soft (soft in places) ground

2371 PROAM IMAGING H'CAP CHASE (16 fncs) 2m 4f 110y
1:45 (1:45) (Class 4) (0-105,103) 4-Y-0+ **£2,927** (£859; £429; £214)

Form RPR
230 1 **You Know Yourself (IRE)**^{21} [1959] 7-11-5 101 ShaneByrne$^{(5)}$ 112+
(Sue Smith) *trckd ldr: led 8th: rdn 3 out: mstke last: kpt on wl* **7/2**^{3}

-341 **2** 3 1/2 **Pistol Basc (FR)**[31] 1826 6-11-0 **98** PaulGallagher(7) 103
(Ferdy Murphy) *hld up: hdwy 8th: chsd wnr after 4 out: kpt on: a hld run-in* **3/1**[2]
F1U2 **3** 7 **Archie's Wish**[31] 1826 6-10-7 **84** BarryKeniry 85
(Micky Hammond) *trckd ldrs: chsd wnr fr 10th tl 4 out: wknd after 3 out* **5/2**[1]
/0-0 **4** 16 **Guns And Butter (IRE)**[17] 2034 8-11-12 **103** WilsonRenwick 87
(Rose Dobbin) *trckd ldrs: rdn appr 4 out: wknd after 2 out* **10/1**
/4P- **P** **Jeringa**[221] 5077 11-11-3 **94** (b) JamesReveley —
(John Wade) *led: hdd 8th: sn rdn and lost pl: mstke 10th: p.u bef next* **9/2**
514- **P** **Northern Quest (IRE)**[395] 1744 9-11-11 **102** RobertWalford —
(Henry Hogarth) *hld up: racd keenly: rdn and wknd after 11th: t.o whn p.u bef 4 out* **9/1**

5m 14.6s (6.80) **Going Correction** +0.45s/f (Soft) 6 Ran SP% **113.1**
Speed ratings (Par 105): **105,103,101,94,— —**
toteswingers: 1&2 £3.30, 1&3 £2.50, 2&3 £1.02. CSF £14.92 TOTE £5.00: £2.50, £2.10; EX 19.80.
Owner Mrs S Smith **Bred** Patrick O'Connell **Trained** High Eldwick, W Yorks

FOCUS
An even pace for this 0-105 handicap. The cosy winner will make a better chaser than he was a hurdler.

NOTEBOOK
You Know Yourself(IRE), a comfortable winner, was making his chasing debut after a few starts over hurdles for a yard that does particularly well with these types. Not lacking for size or scope, he can go one from this and win again. (op 11-2)
Pistol Basc(FR), who has a fine record at this track including a win in this race last year, travelled well throughout. His jumping appears to be getting better and time might prove he ran into a well-handicapped winner. (op 11-4)
Archie's Wish, who was ridden along four from home, was well held at the finish. There is still room for improvement in the jumping department with him.
Guns And Butter(IRE), who hasn't won in well over two years, could do with some help from the handicapper. (op 12-1)
Jeringa, from a yard going well, stopped quickly and was pulled up. Official explanation: jockey said gelding never travelled (op 8-1 tchd 10-1)
Northern Quest(IRE), coming back from a break, looked badly in need of the run. (op 8-1 tchd 10-1)

2372 DRANSFIELDS CIU CHARITY RACEDAY H'CAP HURDLE (13 hdls) 3m 1f
2:20 (2:20) (Class 4) (0-115,111) 4-Y-0+ **£2,276** (£668; £334; £166)

Form RPR
3332 **1** **Saintly Lady (IRE)**[15] 2072 5-10-10 **98** (p) DonalDevereux(3) 106+
(Peter Bowen) *trckd ldrs: led after 10th: nt fluent whn hdd 3 out: regained ld after 2 out: on olr* **7/2**[1]
00U0 **2** 5 **Oniz Tiptoes (IRE)**[35] 1782 9-10-0 **85** (v) PaddyAspell 85
(John Wainwright) *hld up: hdwy appr 3 out: wnt 2nd sn after last: kpt on: nrst fin* **16/1**
2104 **3** 3 1/4 **Rebel Swing**[7] 2205 4-10-13 **98** HenryOliver 95
(Sue Smith) *trckd ldrs: rdn and outpcd 8th: kpt on again fr appr 3 out* **7/2**[1]
2-03 **4** 1 1/4 **Teenage Kicks (IRE)**[10] 2154 5-11-3 **109** MissGAndrews(7) 105
(Pam Sly) *trckd ldrs: hdwy to ld 3 out: hdd after 2 out: wknd qckly appr last* **4/1**[2]
4500 **5** 15 **Border Tale**[14] 2094 10-10-2 **90** RyanMania(3) 76
(James Moffatt) *hld up: hdwy after 10th: no further imp after 3 out* **20/1**
3P30 **6** 27 **Miss Tarantella**[152] 749 7-10-3 **88** (t) MichaelMcAlister 46
(Maurice Barnes) *midfield: prom fr 8th: led briefly after 10th: wknd appr 3 out* **12/1**
U6 **7** 3/4 **San Deng**[14] 2094 8-10-10 **95** BarryKeniry 52
(Micky Hammond) *hld up: pushed along 8th: a towards rr* **16/1**
53-0 **8** 1/2 **Yeoman Spirit (IRE)**[14] 2094 7-11-9 **108** (p) AndrewTinkler 65
(John Mackie) *prom: led 8th: hdd 10th: sn wknd* **18/1**
-012 **9** 10 **Rare Coincidence**[9] 2161 9-11-4 **110** (p) AlexanderVoy(7) 58
(Roger Fisher) *led: hdd 8th: sn rdn: wknd after 9th* **12/1**
400- **10** 2 1/2 **Roko Dancer (FR)**[262] 4228 5-11-8 **107** GerardTumelty 52
(Alan King) *hld up: reminders bef 1/2-way: a bhd* **8/1**[3]
2P-P **11** 5 **Arctic Echo**[9] 2171 11-11-9 **111** (p) AlexMerriam(3) 52
(Rob Summers) *midfield: rdn after 8th: wknd after next* **25/1**

6m 34.1s (17.60) **Going Correction** +0.625s/f (Soft)
WFA 4 from 5yo+ 9lb 11 Ran SP% **116.6**
Speed ratings (Par 105): **96,94,93,92,88 79,79,79,75,75 73**
Tote Swingers: 1&2 £9.30, 1&3 £3.20, 2&3 £16.90 CSF £56.86 CT £211.31 TOTE £4.90: £2.20, £4.20, £1.50; EX 70.30.
Owner The Hedonists **Bred** Chris Glynn **Trained** Little Newcastle, Pembrokes

FOCUS
A 0-115 handicap which was full of exposed horses. The early pace was even and most of the runners were ridden along four from home. The winner has progressed in the cheekpieces and the second was very well in on the best of last season's form.

NOTEBOOK
Saintly Lady(IRE), who has been very consistent in her seven starts so far, deserved to lose her maiden tag. Travelling well throughout, it will take a career best once the handicapper has had his say. (op 9-2)
Oniz Tiptoes(IRE), who has been a great servant to connections in recent years, stayed on strongly to snatch second place close home. He is 10lb below his last winning mark, so could well go one better shortly. (op 14-1)
Rebel Swing stayed on over the last couple of hurdles, but the handicapper would appear to be in charge since his win three starts ago. (tchd 3-1)
Teenage Kicks(IRE) looked like taking a major say in things turning for home until he weakened at the final flight, and he is definitely worth a try back in trip. (op 5-1)
Roko Dancer(FR), coming back from a break, never travelled and can only be watched for the time being. (op 7-1 tchd 13-2)

2373 TOTESCOOP6 H'CAP HURDLE (9 hdls) 2m 110y
2:55 (2:55) (Class 3) (0-130,126) 4-Y-0+ **£6,505** (£1,910; £955; £477)

Form RPR
6/3- **1** **Nine Stories (IRE)**[199] 44 5-11-8 **125** RyanMania(3) 129+
(Howard Johnson) *midfield: hdwy to trck ldr appr 3 out: led after 2 out: narrow ld whn nt fluent last: hld on wl towards fin* **7/1**
P001 **2** nk **Viva Colonia (IRE)**[14] 2094 5-10-10 **113** FearghalDavis(3) 119+
(David O'Meara) *midfield: smooth hdwy on inner to trck ldr appr 3 out: chal after 2 out: upsides whn nt fluent last: kpt on but a jst hld towards fin* **10/3**[1]
2231 **3** 8 **Rio Gael (IRE)**[9] 2164 4-11-9 **126** (p) DonalDevereux(3) 123
(Peter Bowen) *led: rdn whn hdd after 2 out: wknd run-in* **6/1**[3]
2-12 **4** nk **Amir Pasha (UAE)**[15] 2076 5-10-6 **111** (v) JamesHalliday(5) 107
(Micky Hammond) *hld up: hdwy to trck ldrs after 6th: rdn and kpt on same pce after 3 out* **15/2**
00P- **5** 6 **European Dream (IRE)**[58] 5128 7-11-11 **125** (p) AndrewTinkler 115
(Richard Fahey) *hld up: brief hdwy appr 3 out: sn rdn: no further imp* **7/2**[2]
4P6- **6** 19 **Melange (USA)**[11] 4781 4-10-7 **107** (t) JanFaltejsek 80
(George Charlton) *trckd ldrs: rdn after 6th: wknd appr 3 out* **20/1**
532/ **7** 2 1/4 **Burnt Oak (UAE)**[609] 4459 8-11-3 **117** BarryKeniry 88
(Chris Fairhurst) *hld up: rdn appr 3 out: sn no imp* **14/1**
12-2 **8** 1 1/4 **Fred Bojangals (IRE)**[46] 1641 8-11-3 **117** (p) AdrianLane 87
(Ann Hamilton) *trckd ldrs: rdn and wknd appr 3 out* **12/1**
02-S **9** hd **Nomadic Warrior**[181] 351 5-10-0 **100** oh1 TomMessenger 70
(John Holt) *midfield: rdn and wknd after 6th* **12/1**
23/0 **10** 3 1/2 **Motafarred (IRE)**[14] 2092 8-10-5 **105** (t) RichieMcGrath 72
(Tina Jackson) *trckd ldr: wknd after 6th* **40/1**

4m 3.10s (7.30) **Going Correction** +0.625s/f (Soft)
WFA 4 from 5yo+ 7lb 10 Ran SP% **113.1**
Speed ratings (Par 107): **107,106,103,102,100 91,90,89,89,87**
Tote Swingers: 1&2 £4.80, 1&3 £9.10, 2&3 £5.90 CSF £30.28 CT £147.88 TOTE £9.80: £2.50, £1.80, £2.10; EX 31.40 Trifecta £618.30 Part won. Pool: £835.56 - 0.92 winning units..
Owner Andrea & Graham Wylie **Bred** Stefano Stivali **Trained** Billy Row, Co Durham
■ Stewards' Enquiry : Fearghal Davis caution: used whip without giving gelding time to respond.

FOCUS
A competitive 0-130 handicap hurdle run at a sound pace and the form should prove reliable. The winner improved to the level of his best Flat form and the second confirmed the merit of his good recent win.

NOTEBOOK
Nine Stories(IRE), having his first start since last April, had conditions to suit here and showed a determined attitude to hold on close home. Only a 5yo, this was only his seventh start and can go on from this. (op 6-1 tchd 15-2)
Viva Colonia(IRE) had made a winning start with current connections over 2m4f last time at this track, and went up 11lb for that. He didn't help his chance with a mistake at the final flight, but this was still a solid run and he can win again shortly. (op 4-1 tchd 3-1)
Rio Gael(IRE), 9lb higher than his recent Haydock success, ran up to form. Largely consistent, he can continue to pay his way.
Amir Pasha(UAE) has also been very consistent of late. He ran well here but leaves the impression that the handicapper is in charge now. (op 11-2)
European Dream(IRE), having his first start over hurdles for his respected trainer, is still on the same mark that his last win came off and could do with some help from the handicapper. (op 9-2 tchd 5-1)
Burnt Oak(UAE) showed up well on his first start after a long lay-off. If remaining sound there are races to be won with him. (op 18-1)

2374 BET ON LIVE FOOTBALL AT TOTESPORT.COM H'CAP CHASE (18 fncs) 3m 1f
3:26 (3:26) (Class 3) (0-130,130) 4-Y-0+ **£6,505** (£1,910; £955; £477)

Form RPR
P1-1 **1** **Gilsland (IRE)**[192] 162 7-10-9 **113** (v1) AdrianLane 120
(Donald McCain) *chsd ldr: outpcd and dropped to 4th appr 4 out: styd on again to ld narrowly 2 out: hld on wl: drvn out* **9/2**[2]
1-5F **2** hd **Dawn Ride (IRE)**[17] 2036 9-10-8 **112** (p) BarryKeniry 121+
(Micky Hammond) *hld up: nt fluent 8th: mstke 10th: outpcd 11th: wl bhd 5 out: styd on after 4 out: chsd ldr last: styd on to go 2nd towards fin* **12/1**
1P-4 **3** 1 3/4 **Star Beat**[15] 2079 7-9-7 **104** oh2 (p) HenryBrooke(7) 109
(Kate Walton) *hld up: mstke 7th: outpcd after 12th: hdwy after 5 out: wnt 2nd appr 4 out: chal fr 2 out: no ex nr fin* **8/1**
1-25 **4** 2 **General Hardi**[31] 1828 9-10-5 **116** MrJohnDawson(7) 118
(John Wade) *trckd ldrs: outpcd after 5 out: styd on again after 3 out: ev ch last: no ex run-in* **8/1**
F/6- **5** 8 **Patman Du Charmil (FR)**[392] 1784 8-11-3 **121** (b) DavidEngland 119+
(Nigel Twiston-Davies) *cl up: led 2nd: clr 4 out: only 5 l up whn hit 3 out: rdn and hdd 2 out: wknd after last* **13/2**
5-65 **6** 1 **Zitenka (IRE)**[7] 2204 8-11-6 **124** (b1) RichieMcGrath 121
(Tim Easterby) *hld up: nt fluent: reminders and outpcd after 10th: hdwy after 4 out: ev ch last: wknd run-in* **6/1**[3]
6-66 **P** **Daldini**[13] 2106 8-10-4 **115** AlexanderVoy(7) —
(Sue Smith) *led to 2nd: lost pl 5th: wknd after 10th: bhd whn p.u bef 5 out* **15/2**
12-3 **P** **Vodka Brook (IRE)**[13] 2106 7-11-12 **130** (p) RobertWalford —
(Tim Walford) *midfield: wknd 6 out: p.u bef next* **3/1**[1]

6m 15.8s (6.40) **Going Correction** +0.45s/f (Soft) 8 Ran SP% **112.5**
Speed ratings (Par 107): **107,106,106,105,103 102,—,—**
Tote Swingers: 1&2 £8.40, 1&3 £7.20, 2&3 £8.00 CSF £51.13 CT £414.73 TOTE £4.40: £1.70, £2.50, £2.90; EX 55.80 Trifecta £207.50 Pool: £692.75 - 2.47 winning units..
Owner Brendan Richardson and Jon Glews **Bred** The Well Dunne Racing Syndicate **Trained** Cholmondeley, Cheshire
■ Stewards' Enquiry : Adrian Lane seven-day ban: used whip with excessive frequency without giving gelding time to respond (Nov 27-30,Dec 1-3)

FOCUS
With plenty of front-runners in the line-up this 0-130 handicap chase was always going to be run at a sound pace. A race the handicapper will enjoy watching as six of the eight runners touched down over the final fence within a length of each other. The winner is rated to form.

NOTEBOOK
Gilsland(IRE), having his first start after a break, landed his third straight win for his in-form stable. This was only his eighth start over fences, so there might be more to come and his sound jumping will always be an advantage. (tchd 5-1)
Dawn Ride(IRE), a four times course winner, stayed on well up the home straight but never helps himself on the way round with some sloppy jumping. (op 11-1)
Star Beat, having his second start for current connections, also ran on after hitting a flat spot down the back straight. On this evidence there are races to be won with him. (op 12-1)
General Hardi normally runs his race, as he did here, but holds no secrets from the handicapper. (op 15-2)
Patman Du Charmil(FR), who hasn't won in over three years, looked the most likely winner three from home, however he stopped very quick and his overall profile doesn't convince. That said he might be worth bringing back in trip. (op 9-2)
Zitenka(IRE), who won this race last year off a 3lb lower mark, ran a moody race in first-time blinkers. Whether he didn't fancy the headgear, only time will tell. (op 8-1)
Daldini Official explanation: jockey said gelding never travelled (tchd 5-2)
Vodka Brook(IRE), having his second start for current connections, might have found this race coming to soon from his last outing. Official explanation: trainer said, regarding running, that the race came too soon (tchd 5-2)

2375 BOOK ONLINE @ WETHERBYRACING.CO.UK NOVICES' HURDLE (11 hdls) 2m 4f
3:55 (3:55) (Class 4) 4-Y-0+ **£2,397** (£698; £349)

Form RPR
2 **1** **Moon Indigo**[43] 1662 4-10-12 0 WilsonRenwick 116+
(Howard Johnson) *trckd ldrs: hit 3rd: hdwy to ld appr 3 out: rdn whn nt fluent 2 out: hld on towards fin: drvn out* **11/8**[1]

644- **2** *nk* **Bless The Wings (IRE)**[252] 4452 5-10-12 0 GerardTumelty 115+
(Alan King) *midfield: hdwy after 7th: wnt 3rd appr 3 out: chsd wnr after 2 out: styd on strly run-in* **7/1**

64-4 **3** *8* **Tricky Tree (IRE)**[22] 1953 4-10-5 105 MissGAndrews(7) 106
(Pam Sly) *trckd ldrs: rdn 3 out: kpt on same pce* **14/1**

4/0U **4** *9* **Belmore Baron**[7] 2202 8-10-7 0 ShaneByrne(5) 98
(Sue Smith) *midfield: racd keenly: rdn and outpcd appr 3 out: kpt on after 2 out* **100/1**

10 **5** *7* **Dark Ranger**[28] 1862 4-10-12 0 BrianToomey(7) 101
(Tim Pitt) *hld up: sme hdwy appr 3 out: rdn whn blnd 2 out: n.d* **22/1**

6 *8* **Under The Stars (IRE)**[160] 5-10-9 0 FearghalDavis(3) 84
(Nicky Richards) *led: hdd appr 3 out: sn wknd* **28/1**

3-31 **7** *½* **Icy Colt (ARG)**[31] 1829 4-11-0 107 (v) WillKennedy 86
(Paul Webber) *trckd ldrs: rdn and wknd appr 3 out* **9/2**[2]

52-3 **8** *1* **Pegasus Prince (USA)**[11] 289 6-10-12 110 JamesReveley 83
(Keith Reveley) *trckd ldrs: lost pl 7th: wknd appr 3 out* **6/1**[3]

54-0 **9** *23* **Exotic Man (FR)**[41] 1702 5-10-5 0 MrJohnDawson(7) 62
(John Wade) *hld up: racd keenly: rdn appr 3 out: n.d* **40/1**

0 **10** *15* **Kingman Reef (IRE)**[20] 1990 6-10-12 0 TomMessenger 49
(Chris Bealby) *prom: wknd after 7th* **125/1**

0 **11** *2¼* **Mind Shower (IRE)**[20] 1988 4-10-12 0 PaddyAspell 47
(Robert Wylie) *hld up: mstke 6th: a towards rr* **125/1**

2-33 **P** **Classic Contours (USA)**[18] 1148 4-10-12 110 AndrewTinkler —
(John Quinn) *midfield: wknd 7th: bhd whn hit 8th: p.u bef 3 out* **18/1**

5P-6 **P** **Rationing (IRE)**[132] 892 4-10-12 0 (t) RichieMcGrath —
(Tim Easterby) *hld up: wl bhd whn blnd 8th: p.u bef 3 out* **66/1**

0 **P** **Smart Command (IRE)**[183] 319 6-10-5 0 PaulGallagher(7) —
(Ferdy Murphy) *hld up: a bhd: p.u bef 3 out* **100/1**

5m 11.5s (12.00) **Going Correction** +0.625s/f (Soft) **14 Ran SP% 114.3**
Speed ratings (Par 105): **101,100,97,94,91 88,87,87,78,72 71,—,—,—**
Tote Swingers: 1&2 £3.00, 1&3 £4.80, 2&3 £16.00 CSF £10.21 TOTE £2.20: £1.30, £3.10, £3.90; EX 13.40.
Owner Andrea & Graham Wylie **Bred** Britton House Stud Ltd **Trained** Billy Row, Co Durham

FOCUS
A decent gallop for this novice hurdle which should throw up future winners. Ordinary form with the winner rated pretty much to his mark.

NOTEBOOK
Moon Indigo, useful on the Flat, probably didn't stay the 3m first time out over hurdles but made amends here. Never far away, he looks the type to improve with racing and can win again for a stable going well. (tchd Evens)
Bless The Wings(IRE), having his first start over hurdles after showing ability in bumpers, stayed on strongly and didn't help his chance with a couple of slow jumps at an important stage. This experience will not have been lost on him and he can go one better shortly. (op 8-1)
Tricky Tree(IRE), rated 105 after four starts, ran well and puts the form in some context. He will be seen in a better light in novice handicaps. (tchd 16-1)
Belmore Baron stayed on late in the day and is now qualified for a handicap mark. It would be very surprising if he didn't make his mark at some point.
Dark Ranger was easy to back beforehand. The handicap route might see him in a better light. (op 16-1 tchd 25-1)
Under The Stars(IRE), winner of a point-to-point, cut out the early running before getting tired. He showed enough here to keep on the right side of later in the season. (op 18-1)
Icy Colt(ARG), a winner over C&D last time out, looks the type for handicaps. (op 5-1)
T/Plt: £566.10 to a £1 stake. Pool:£56,108.82 - 72.35 winning tickets. T/Qpdt: £12.70 to a £1 stake. Pool:£5,382.46 - 311.65 winning tickets. AS

2376 - 2383a (Foreign Racing) - See Raceform Interactive

2356 CHELTENHAM (L-H)
Sunday, November 14

OFFICIAL GOING: Good to soft (soft in places)
Rail realignment increased hurdles races by 15yds each circuit.
Wind: Virtually nil Weather: Overcast

2384 INDEPENDENT NEWSPAPER NOVICES' CHASE (REGISTERED AS THE NOVEMBER NOVICES' STEEPLE CHASE) (GRADE 2) (13 fncs) 2m
1:10 (1:10) (Class 1) 4-Y-0+ **£17,103** (£6,417; £3,213; £1,602; £804)

Form RPR

00-2 **1** **Ghizao (GER)**[29] 1865 6-11-2 0 TimmyMurphy 156+
(Paul Nicholls) *trckd ldr: led 5th: kpt narrow advantage tl qcknd clr appr 2 out: easily* **13/2**

11-2 **2** *10* **Captain Chris (IRE)**[22] 1966 6-11-2 0 (t) RichardJohnson 148+
(Philip Hobbs) *in tch: chsd ldrs fr 6th tl rdn and outpcd after 4 out: styd on again appr 2 out to take 2nd fnl 30yds but nvr any ch w wnr* **5/2**[1]

45-1 **3** *nk* **Loosen My Load (IRE)**[31] 1849 6-11-8 146 AELynch 153
(Henry De Bromhead, Ire) *led to 5th: styd pressing wnr and stl upsides after 3 out: rdn and outpcd bef next: wknd run-in and lost 2nd fnl 30yds* **7/2**[3]

1 **4** *12* **Kilmurry (IRE)**[29] 1865 5-11-8 143 JoeTizzard 143
(Colin Tizzard) *pressed ldrs to 6th: rdn 8th: lost tch fr 4 out: styd on again to take mod 4th run-in* **10/3**[2]

20-1 **5** *1* **Radium (FR)**[15] 2082 5-11-6 147 BarryGeraghty 142+
(Nicky Henderson) *in tch: hit 1st and 3rd: nt fluent 5th: 6th and 7th: j. slowly 8th: wknd after 4 out and hung rt fr next* **4/1**

4m 2.38s (4.38) **Going Correction** +0.35s/f (Yiel) **5 Ran SP% 107.2**
Speed ratings (Par 115): **103,98,97,91,91**
CSF £21.91 TOTE £7.90: £2.50, £1.30; EX 20.70.
Owner The Johnson & Stewart Families **Bred** Baron G Von Ullman **Trained** Ditcheat, Somerset
■ Stewards' Enquiry : A E Lynch one-day ban: used whip with excessive frequency (Nov 28)

FOCUS
Despite a dry night the going was changed to good to soft, good in places before racing. The rails were moved out on the hurdles track to provide fresh ground, adding 15yds per circuit to race distances. This Grade 2 chase has been the jumping-off point for a series of good horses in recent years, the best of them being Best Mate and Azertyuiop. Despite the small field this year's contest held plenty of interest but there was something of a surprise and, although the winner was impressive, the form might be suspect with the next three all possibly unsuited by the ground. Ghizao would need to improve upwards of 7lb to win a typical Arkle, and the second is rated in line with his hurdles form.

NOTEBOOK
Ghizao(GER), the winner of a bumper round here and runner-up to General Miller in a hurdle, had been well beaten by Killmurry on his chasing debut here and was worse off at the weights. However, his trainer believed he needed that run after having a breathing operation in the summer and that was borne out by his performance. Always up with the pace, his jumping was fluent and, when he and the third quickened down the hill, they soon had the others in trouble. He got the better of that rival on the home turn and came away to win in emphatic fashion. He looks a good chasing prospect and will be aimed at the Arkle, for which he is best priced 12-1, with the Henry VIII Chase at Sandown possibly the next port of call. (op 6-1 tchd 15-2)
Captain Chris(IRE) was a progressive hurdler last season, completing his hat-trick on this track in April (all wins on good). He was beaten by a useful import on his return on soft and was equipped with a first-time tongue-tie for this chasing debut. He jumped pretty well, if a little to the right under a positive ride, and came up well when asked for a long one. However, he was left behind on the run down to three out and, although he stayed on, could never land a serious blow at the winner. This was a creditable debut though on ground which is probably softer than ideal, and he looks to have a future over fences. He reportedly gurgled in the race though and will have a second wind operation, which will only keep him out for about a month. (op 11-4 tchd 3-1 in a place)
Loosen My Load(IRE) has a good strike-rate and had won all three starts over fences at 2m2f-2m4f. He was dropping in trip but had won a Grade 2 hurdle over this distance at this meeting last season and was ridden positively. He looked to be going as well as the winner on the run down to the third-last but was in trouble soon after that fence and lost second on the run-in. He is ideally suited by a sound surface and was probably found out by this ground. (tchd 4-1)
Kilmurry(IRE), a winner twice over fences in Ireland before making a successful debut for current connections over course and distance in October, beating today's winner, is another well suited by a sound surface although he won on heavy over hurdles. A former stablemate of Loosen My Load, he was struggling after losing his pitch nearing the top of the hill and is another who was probably unsuited by the ground. (op 3-1)
Radium(FR) was useful over hurdles last season, winning here and being placed in a Grade 2, and won on his chasing debut over 2m3f from the useful Othermix. However, he was not that fluent at his fences and, after making a brief forward move four out, was left behind down the hill. (tchd 7-2 and 3-1 in places)

2385 SINBAD TESTIMONIAL 2010/2011 CHASE (13 fncs) 2m
1:45 (1:46) (Class 2) 5-Y-0+
£31,310 (£9,250; £4,625; £2,315; £1,155; £580)

Form RPR

P11/ **1** **Gauvain (GER)**[576] 5066 8-11-0 142 DarylJacob 166+
(Nick Williams) *hld up in rr: stdy hdwy fr 4 out to trck ldrs fr 3 out: upsides appr 2 out: chal last: sn led: drvn and styd on strly* **16/1**

222- **2** *4* **Forpadydeplasterer (IRE)**[208] 5302 8-11-0 167 BarryGeraghty 164+
(Thomas Cooper, Ire) *in rr: hdwy 6th: chsd ldrs 4 out: chal and hit 3 out: drvn to take slt ld 2 out: jnd by wnr last and hdd sn after: no ex fnl 50yds* **11/8**[1]

121- **3** *6* **Tataniano (FR)**[218] 5124 6-11-5 160 NoelFehily 162
(Paul Nicholls) *led: j.rt 4 out: hit 3 out: rdn sn after: narrowly hdd and hit 2 out: wknd last* **7/4**[2]

2-U6 **4** *6* **Oiseau De Nuit (FR)**[15] 2086 8-11-4 142 JoeTizzard 155
(Colin Tizzard) *in rr: rdn along 6th: lost tch after 4 out: styd on again fr 2 out: nvr any threat* **33/1**

5F-U **5** *12* **Mahogany Blaze (FR)**[12] 2138 8-11-0 150 (b) SamTwiston-Davies 141
(Nigel Twiston-Davies) *hit 1st: chsd ldrs: wnt 2nd 7th: hit 8th: wknd and hit 3 out* **14/1**

504- **6** *14* **Oh Crick (FR)**[204] 5394 7-11-0 152 WayneHutchinson 127
(Alan King) *in rr: sme hdwy 4 out: sn wknd* **7/1**[3]

P-2P **7** *5* **Chaninbar (FR)**[12] 2138 7-11-6 155 (v) SeanQuinlan 130
(Milton Harris) *reluctant to post: led in s: chsd ldr to 6th: wknd 8th* **40/1**

4m 0.26s (2.26) **Going Correction** +0.35s/f (Yiel) **7 Ran SP% 108.9**
Speed ratings: **108,106,103,100,94 87,84**
Tote Swingers: 1&2 £3.90, 1&3 £3.20, 2&3 £1.10 CSF £36.86 TOTE £17.20: £4.40, £1.70; EX 37.80.
Owner Jared Sullivan & Simon Brown **Bred** Stall Epona **Trained** George Nympton, Devon

FOCUS
The winning time was 2.12sec quicker than the novices recorded in the previous race. The market had this down as a two-horse race, but it proved anything but. Gauvain is rated up a stone on his smart novice form and looks a realistic Champion Chase contender. The next two were below their best but the form does look solid.

NOTEBOOK
Gauvain(GER), who looked fit for his return and was debuting for his new stable, created an upset. There was no fluke about the result either, as the winner travelled well in behind the pace, was going best turning in and, after jumping the last alongside Forpadydeplasterer, stayed on well to see off the Champion Chase runner-up. Last seen on the track back in April of last year, when trained by Charlie Mann, he was returning from a tendon injury and went without the headgear he wore back in those days. Clearly an improved horse for switching to the Nick Williams stable, it's difficult to believe there won't be improvement to come on the back of this given how long he'd been off the track, and Hills might regret going biggest post-race for the Champion Chase, quoting 25-1. That looks a big price considering the doubts over some of those in front of him in the betting.
Forpadydeplasterer(IRE) was heavily favoured by the weights, as he was getting 6lb from the likes of Tataniano, and he'd won first time out in two of his previous three seasons. This looked an ideal opportunity for him to finally put an end to his run of second places, but he came up short once again. He didn't have the defence of there being insufficient pace in the race, and perhaps it's simply time to stop making excuses for him - he did carry his head slightly to one side running down the hill and up the straight. The plan is for him to be stepped up to 3m now, with the King George his next target, providing the ground is good. He'll also be given an entry in the Lexus Chase. (op 6-4 tchd 13-8 in places and 7-4 in places)
Tataniano(FR) didn't face a simple task at the weights but this was his chance to prove himself a serious Champion Chase candidate. Soon out in front, where he likes to be, he set a strong gallop but got tired running down the hill and was left behind by the first two after the second-last. The ground was probably not quick enough for him to be seen at his best, and he might well be seen in a better light in the spring, but his style of running - he seems to need to dominate - will always leave him vulnerable. The Tingle Creek is next for him providing the ground isn't too soft, otherwise he might wait for the Desert Orchid at Kempton. (op 6-4)
Oiseau De Nuit(FR), without the tongue-tie this time, stayed on for fourth without ever threatening the main players. His performance anchors the form somewhat. (tchd 28-1)
Mahogany Blaze(FR), who finished second in this race last year, continues to be let down by his jumping. He's still to win over fences out of novice company. (tchd 16-1)
Oh Crick(FR) would have been suited by better ground, but he proved a difficult horse to place last season and this reappearance effort suggests he's likely to remain in that boat for a while. (op 8-1)
Chaninbar(FR), who has proved reluctant to race on more than one occasion in the past, was led in away from the rest and got away on terms. He raced near the pace early but dropped out of contention before the top of the hill. (op 33-1)

2386 GREATWOOD H'CAP HURDLE GRADE 3 (8 hdls) 2m 110y
2:20 (2:20) (Class 1) 4-Y-0+
£57,010 (£21,390; £10,710; £5,340; £2,680; £1,340)

Form RPR

212- **1** **Menorah (IRE)**[219] 5108 5-11-12 151 RichardJohnson 165+
(Philip Hobbs) *nt fluent 1st: in rr early: hdwy to trck ldrs after 3rd: mstke 3 out: chal 2 out: slt ld and pckd last: strly chal fnl 75yds: fnd ex and r.o gamely* **6/1**[2]

110- **2** *nk* **Bothy**[22] 4675 4-9-13 127 DannyCook(3) 140
(Brian Ellison) *pressed ldrs tl slt advantage fr 4th: rdn 2 out: narrowly hdd last: rallied gamely to chal fnl 75yds: no ex cl home* **16/1**

030- **3** *5* **Manyriverstocross (IRE)**[242] 4671 5-10-13 **138**....... WayneHutchinson 145
(Alan King) *in rr tl hdwy 4th: chsd ldrs fr 3 out: rdn next: styd on appr last but no imp on ldng duo run-in* **11/2**[1]

0-21 **4** *3/4* **Any Given Day (IRE)**[22] 1967 5-11-1 **147**...................... HenryBrooke(7) 153
(Donald McCain) *chsd ldrs: rdn after 3 out: styd on same pce appr last* **11/1**

04-2 **5** *1 3/4* **Olofi (FR)**[36] 1775 4-10-7 **132**.. PaddyBrennan 137
(Tom George) *in rr: hdwy appr 3 out: rdn next: styd on same pce appr last* **12/1**

12-0 **6** *15* **Get Me Out Of Here (IRE)**[15] 2085 6-11-11 **150**.................... APMcCoy 143
(Jonjo O'Neill) *chsd ldrs: chalng whn hit 3 out: wl there next: wknd sn after* **7/1**[3]

14-6 **7** *2 1/2* **Orsippus (USA)**[29] 1862 4-11-0 **139**.................................... SamThomas 128
(Michael Smith) *in rr: stl plenty to do 2 out: styd on appr last and kpt on run-in but nvr a threat* **50/1**

1131 **8** *1* **Astracad (FR)**[30] 1859 4-10-12 **140**...................... SamTwiston-Davies(3) 128
(Nigel Twiston-Davies) *blnd 1st: in rr: sme hdwy 3 out: one pce and no imp whn hit 2 out* **12/1**

101- **9** *1 1/4* **Sure Josie Sure (FR)**[207] 5308 5-10-2 **127**.................. TomScudamore 117
(David Pipe) *pressed ldrs: chal fr 4 out to 2 out: wknd sn after* **9/1**

U14- **10** *17* **General Miller**[208] 5299 5-11-7 **146**............................. BarryGeraghty 118
(Nicky Henderson) *chsd ldrs tl wknd qckly 4 out* **8/1**

03-6 **11** *2 1/4* **Leslingtaylor (IRE)**[8] 2219 8-10-9 **134**............................ DougieCostello 104
(John Quinn) *chsd ldrs to 4th: bhd whn hmpd after 4 out* **33/1**

001- **12** *1 3/4* **Puzzlemaster**[196] 5180 4-10-2 **127**...............................(t) AndrewTinkler 95
(Hughie Morrison) *prom early: in rr fr 1/2-way* **66/1**

/0-0 **13** *1 1/4* **Culcabock (IRE)**[22] 1956 10-9-9 **127**.............................. PeterCarberry(7) 94
(Lucinda Russell) *prom tl wknd 4th* **40/1**

/36- **14** *1* **St Devote (FR)**[59] 1534 5-10-3 **133**.................................... EJO'Connell(5) 99
(Eoin Griffin, Ire) *in tch to 4th: sn wknd* **33/1**

2-32 **15** *3/4* **Issaquah (IRE)**[15] 2089 8-11-1 **145**............................... JamesHalliday(5) 110
(Malcolm Jefferson) *led to 4th: sn wknd: no ch whn hmpd 3 out* **50/1**

0-2 **F** **Tarkari (IRE)**[50] 1609 5-10-7 **132**... PaulMoloney —
(Evan Williams) *in rr: sme hdwy whn fell 3 out* **20/1**

113- **F** **Sanctuaire (FR)**[220] 5094 4-11-7 **146**...................................... NoelFehily 131+
(Paul Nicholls) *in rr tl hdwy 3 out: styng on and gng ok whn fell next* **8/1**

4m 2.34s (0.34) **Going Correction** +0.35s/f (Yiel)
WFA 4 from 5yo+ 7lb **17 Ran SP% 122.5**
Speed ratings (Par 113): **113,112,110,110,109 102,101,100,100,92 90,90,89,89,00 —,—**
Tote Swingers: 1&2 £4.80, 1&3 £20.00, 2&3 £20.90 CSF £91.42 CT £569.37 TOTE £6.50: £1.80, £5.10, £1.80, £2.90; EX 142.50 Trifecta £568.50 Pool: £4,225.48 - 5.50 winning units..

Owner Mrs Diana L Whateley **Bred** Mrs E Grant And Miss Anna Brislane **Trained** Withycombe, Somerset

FOCUS

One of the very best of the pre-Christmas handicap hurdles, having been won this century by such as Rooster Booster, Detroit City, Sizing Europe and last year's subsequent Champion Hurdle runner-up Khyber Kim. This year's line-up featured several of the top novices of 2009-2010, all with ambitions to join the roll of honour and propel themselves into the reckoning for the Champion Hurdle, including the first two from the Supreme Novices'. Menorah is rated up 10lb on his best novice form and looks a realistic Champion Hurdle contender, with the second up over a stone and the third and fourth pretty much to their marks.

NOTEBOOK

Menorah(IRE) ◆ won the Supreme Novices' last season and put himself in the Champion Hurdle picture with a terrific performance under top weight. He was worse off with both Get Me Out Of Here and General Miller compared with close battles last season, but has clearly progressed and looks set to be tested in one of the trials, either the Stan James International (formerly Boylesports and Bula) Hurdle at the next meeting, or the Christmas Hurdle at Kempton. He is consistent and is now 2-2 here, so 12-1 with the sponsors for the Champion Hurdle looks fair at this stage. (op 11-2)

Bothy ◆ won his first three starts over hurdles on soft ground last season before finishing well behind Sanctuaire in the Fred Winter. He was 19lb better off with that rival and put up a game performance, having been in the leading group throughout. He kept battling away up the hill and looks set to win good races this year, especially on soft ground. (op 33-1)

Manyriverstocross(IRE), a useful novice last season (Grade 2 winner), stays 2m4f and had gained both wins on testing ground. He travelled really well into contention but his rider felt he would have appreciated a stronger gallop, and he could not find and extra gear from the home turn. He could be campaigned over a bit further in future, with the Coral Cup a possible long-term target, but in the shorter term he's likely to be aimed at The Ladbroke, over 2m at Ascot. (op 5-1)

Any Given Day(IRE), a progressive sort last season, built on his return this term with an impressive success over 2m4f at Chepstow. Raised 10lb for that and dropped in trip, he ran a creditable race but did not have the pace to go with the first two from the second-last. He is another for whom the Coral Cup might be a suitable aim. (op 14-1)

Olofi(FR) finished third in a Grade 2 at this meeting last year then won at the December meeting before being well held at the spring festivals. He ran well when touched off by Escort'Men on his return at Chepstow and built on that here, moving into contention down the hill before being unable to find extra once in line for home. He was well clear of the rest though. (op 16-1)

Get Me Out Of Here(IRE), a useful novice who was still unbeaten when taking the Totesport Trophy last season, was touched off by today's winner in the Supreme Novices' next time and was 1lb better off today. He had been too keen on his return at Ascot but was again a little free here and faded having been right in the mix three out. He has something to prove now and really needs to learn to settle better. (tchd 13-2)

Orsippus(USA), a surprise winner of the Grade 1 novices' hurdle at Aintree but third in the Fred Winter before that, was 5lb better off with Sanctuaire on that running. Well beaten on his return at the October meeting here, he showed a bit more, staying on from the rear past beaten horses up the hill.

Astracad(FR), a useful novice at up to 2m4f on a sound surface last spring, had beaten a subsequent winner on his return over C&D in October. Raised 12lb for that, he did not run badly considering he made a bad mistake at the first flight. (op 16-1)

Sure Josie Sure(FR) beat subsequent hat-trick scorer Nearby at Perth in April and was just 7lb higher but had not run since. She showed up for a long way, only tiring up the hill, so the run should bring her on. She may be best suited by a flatter track. (op 10-1 tchd 8-1)

General Miller won here on his hurdling debut before unseating at the first in the Supreme Novices'. He showed how well he would have gone had he stood up there by beating Menorah narrowly at Aintree, and was 5lb better off with that rival today. He was right there going to four out but was ridden and dropped away soon after that flight. He might have needed the run but better could have been expected on last year's efforts. (op 13-2)

Tarkari(IRE), a three-time winner over 2m on soft ground, had run well behind Palomar on his debut for the yard. He was chasing the leaders when taking a heavy fall three out. (op 7-1)

Sanctuaire(FR) won the Fred Winter here in impressive style before being beaten by Orsippus at Aintree, when he was too keen. Making his seasonal debut, he was settled in the rear before making progress onto the heels of the leaders three out, but was just beginning to be nudged along when departing at the penultimate flight. Hopefully he is none the worse. (op 7-1)

2387 PADDY POWER INTERMEDIATE H'CAP HURDLE (10 hdls) 2m 5f

2:55 (2:56) (Class 2) (0-140,139) 4-Y-0+

£12,524 (£3,700; £1,850; £926; £462; £232)

Form RPR

212- **1** **Grands Crus (FR)**[264] 4216 5-10-13 **126**.....................(t) TomScudamore 149+
(David Pipe) *trckd ldrs: chal 3 out and sn led: drvn and styd on strly appr last: readily* **5/1**[2]

43-1 **2** *6* **For Non Stop (IRE)**[36] 1776 5-10-12 **125**............................. DarylJacob 140+
(Nick Williams) *trckd ldrs: led appr 6th: jnd 3 out: sn hdd: continued to chse wnr but no imp after 2 out: styd on wl for clr 2nd* **9/2**[1]

/1U- **3** *11* **King's Legacy (IRE)**[220] 5102 6-11-4 **131**.............................. NoelFehily 135+
(Paul Nicholls) *in rr tl hdwy fr 4 out: styd on for 3rd 2 out: kpt on but nvr any ch w ldng duo* **18/1**

13-1 **4** *1 1/2* **Hidden Keel**[22] 1972 5-11-3 **130**.. PaddyBrennan 132
(Charlie Longsdon) *a wl there: rdn after 3 out: styd on fr 2 out and kpt on run-in but nvr any ch w ldng duo* **14/1**

U111 **5** *nk* **Cappagh (IRE)**[35] 1794 5-10-4 **117**................................ RichardJohnson 120+
(Philip Hobbs) *in tch: rdn and hit 4 out: sn one pce: styd on again after 2 out and kpt on run-in* **11/1**

3-21 **6** *3* **Mister Hyde (IRE)**[10] 2171 5-10-12 **125**.................................. APMcCoy 124
(Jonjo O'Neill) *in tch: chsd ldrs fr 6th tl wknd 2 out* **9/1**

7 *8* **Rock County (IRE)**[21] 2007 6-10-9 **122**.. MDarcy 114
(Sabrina J Harty, Ire) *in tch: hdwy fr 4 out: chsd ldrs 2 out: wknd sn after* **16/1**

03-1 **8** *2 3/4* **Heez A Cracker (FR)**[28] 1887 4-10-7 **120**.......................... SamThomas 109
(Emma Lavelle) *in rr: sme hdwy after 3 out: nvr rchd ldrs* **12/1**

311- **9** *9* **Lush Life (IRE)**[247] 4568 5-11-12 **139**............................... BarryGeraghty 123
(Nicky Henderson) *chsd ldrs tl wknd qckly 2 out* **15/2**[3]

1011 **10** *4* **Russian War (IRE)**[29] 1864 7-11-1 **128**..........................(t) TimmyMurphy 106
(Gordon Elliott, Ire) *in rr: hit 3rd: nvr beyond mid-div and no ch after 4 out* **12/1**

002- **11** *10* **Rigadin De Beauchene (FR)**[293] 3661 5-10-0 **113** oh4. AidanColeman 82
(Venetia Williams) *chsd ldrs tl wknd after 4 out* **40/1**

0/U- **12** *6* **Baracas (FR)**[19] 2028 5-10-11 **129**.................................... EJO'Connell(5) 92
(Eoin Griffin, Ire) *j. slowly 1st: bhd most of way* **33/1**

12-1 **13** *12* **Riptide**[18] 2035 4-11-6 **133**..(b) JasonMaguire 85
(Donald McCain) *led to 4th: wknd 6th* **14/1**

1-P3 **14** *25* **Hoback Junction (IRE)**[14] 2111 6-10-12 **125**..................... WillKennedy 55
(Lucy Wadham) *chsd ldrs: led 4th tl appr 6th: sn wknd* **66/1**

11P- **15** *45* **Sophies Trophy (IRE)**[45] 5393 5-11-1 **128**......................... PaulMoloney 17
(Pat Phelan) *bhd fr 1/2-way* **33/1**

1-33 **P** **Accordingtoemandem (IRE)**[18] 2035 6-10-9 **122**......... DougieCostello —
(Ian Williams) *a in rr: t.o whn p.u bef 2 out* **25/1**

460- **P** **Politeo (FR)**[28] 1897 4-10-10 **123**.. APCawley —
(Paul Nolan, Ire) *prom tl hit 6th: sn wknd: t.o whn p.u bef 2 out* **20/1**

5m 18.47s (5.07) **Going Correction** +0.35s/f (Yiel)
WFA 4 from 5yo+ 8lb **17 Ran SP% 123.2**
Speed ratings (Par 109): **104,101,97,96,96 95,92,91,88,86 82,80,75,66,49 —,—**
Tote Swingers: 1&2 £5.80, 1&3 £29.60, 2&3 £22.10 CSF £26.23 CT £388.25 TOTE £6.20: £2.70, £1.90, £5.20, £2.70; EX 23.50 Trifecta £1091.20 Pool: £2,500.47 - 1.69 winning units..

Owner Roger Stanley & Yvonne Reynolds III **Bred** Jean-Marie Prost Alamartine **Trained** Nicholashayne, Devon

FOCUS

A really competitive handicap but a couple of unexposed horses came clear heading towards the straight. The winner produced a massive step up and the second is improving fast, and overall this is form to be positive about.

NOTEBOOK

Grands Crus(FR) stayed on strongest to make a winning reappearance. There had been a fair amount of support for him in the morning, and it's easy to see why, considering his form with the likes of Wishfull Thinking and Sanctuaire last season, and he proved himself a well-handicapped animal off a mark of 126. He'll be due a hefty rise now, but that won't bother his connections, as he's due to make a quick reappearance at Haydock next Saturday and will only have to carry a 6lb penalty in a valuable handicap over the brush hurdles there. That race is over 3m, and the step up in trip promises to suit him well so he should take a bit of beating. According to his trainer he could well go chasing after that. (op 9-2 tchd 6-1 in places)

For Non Stop(IRE), an impressive winner at Chepstow on his first start for his new stable, had been put up 13lb for that success and ran a blinder in his bid to follow up. He finished well clear of the rest and was simply unlucky to bump into a handicap blot. He'll no doubt go up again for this, but is firmly on an upward curve. (tchd 5-1 in places)

King's Legacy(IRE), whose trainer had suggested he would need this reappearance outing, ran a promising race. He was travelling as well as anything coming down the hill and, while the first two got away from him, he stayed on nicely for third, despite flattening the final hurdle. The plan had been to go chasing after this pipe-opener and he has the potential to do well in that sphere. (op 16-1)

Hidden Keel, raised 12lb for winning at Stratford, stayed on again after getting a little outpaced and posted a solid effort. He clearly doesn't have to lead to show his best. (op 16-1)

Cappagh(IRE), who didn't look great in his coat, was back over hurdles following a couple of chase wins and had to race off a 27lb higher mark than when last successful in this sphere, but he is rated 5lb higher than this over fences. A winner over as far as 3m, he kept on after getting outpaced running down the hill. (op 14-1)

Mister Hyde(IRE), put up 16lb for winning at Towcester, was found out off his higher mark. He was still in the battle for the places turning in but weakened in the straight. (op 11-1 tchd 12-1 in places)

Rock County(IRE), an Irish challenger chasing a four-timer, has been doing his winning on quicker ground and presumably conditions were just that bit softer than ideal here. (op 20-1)

Heez A Cracker(FR), cosy winner from a subsequent scorer at Kempton last time, was unable to land a blow from off the pace, but perhaps he's another who needs better ground to be seen at his best - his close relative Crack Away Jack is at his best on a sound surface. (tchd 14-1 in places)

Lush Life(IRE) didn't face an easy task off top weight, especially over this longer trip. It's possible he wants dropping back to 2m. (op 11-2 tchd 8-1)

Russian War(IRE) has been on the go through the summer and autumn and this tougher competition and softer ground seemed to find him out. (op 16-1)

Riptide, more exposed than many in the field, was up there early but struggling from the top of the hill. (op 16-1)

2388 NEPTUNE INVESTMENT MANAGEMENT NOVICES' HURDLE (REGISTERED AS THE HYDE NOVICES' HURDLE) (GRADE 2) (10 hdls) 2m 5f

3:30 (3:31) (Class 1) 4-Y-0+

£14,252 (£5,347; £2,677; £1,335; £670; £335)

Form				RPR
2	1		**Champion Court (IRE)**32 [1824] 5-11-0 0 WarrenMarston (Martin Keighley) *hld up in rr: hdwy and nt fluent 3 out: styng on whn nt fluent again next: drvn and qckned to ld bef last: rdn and styd on strly run-in* **5/1**2	135+
13	2	7	**Sybarite (FR)**29 [1866] 4-11-0 0 PaddyBrennan (Nigel Twiston-Davies) *chsd ldrs: hit 2 out: led sn after: hdd bef last: styd on same pce run-in* **8/1**3	125+
30-1	3	nk	**Mount Helicon**14 [2116] 5-11-7 127 (t) JLCullen (T Hogan, Ire) *chsd ldrs: chal 2 out and upsides sn after: nt fluent last and sn one pce* **5/1**2	132
1-15	4	6	**Total Submission**30 [1853] 5-11-0 0 WayneHutchinson (Martin Keighley) *chsd ldr: blnd 5th: lost 2nd after 3 out: styd on same pce and no ch whn hit last* **33/1**	121+
11-1	5	nk	**Final Day (IRE)**30 [1853] 6-11-7 136 (t) JasonMaguire (Gordon Elliott, Ire) *in rr: hdwy 3 out: chsng ldrs whn nt fluent 2 out: wknd bef last* **3/1**1	125
U-34	6	4	**Yabora (FR)**21 [1990] 5-11-0 122 RichardJohnson (Charlie Longsdon) *led tl hdd after 2 out: sn wknd* **11/1**	116
	7	26	**Drumfire (IRE)**35 [1800] 6-11-0 125 BarryGeraghty (Eoin Griffin, Ire) *j. slowly 2nd: in rr: in tch whn blnd 4th: nt fluent 4 out: hdwy to chse ldrs next: wknd sn after* **3/1**1	101
-210	P		**One Cool Tornado (IRE)**42 [1713] 5-11-7 138 (p) AELynch (Paul John Gilligan, Ire) *chsd ldrs tl in rr and hit 6th: t.o whn p.u bef 2 out* **10/1**	—

5m 33.74s (20.34) **Going Correction** +0.35s/f (Yiel)
WFA 4 from 5yo+ 8lb **8** Ran SP% **114.8**
Speed ratings (Par 115): **75,72,72,69,69 68,58,—**
Tote Swingers: 1&2 £7.60, 1&3 £5.30, 2&3 £8.00 CSF £43.70 TOTE £6.40: £2.20, £2.10, £2.40; EX 31.50 Trifecta £632.60 Pool: £1,213.99 - 1.42 winning units..
Owner Sureinvestment Partnership **Bred** Larry O'Connor **Trained** Condicote, Gloucs

FOCUS
Another race that has had some high-class winners in recent seasons, the last two being Tell Massini and Diamond Harry, while they were preceded by subsequent Festival winners Massini's Maguire and Black Jack Ketchum. This year's line-up was equally split between runners from Ireland and the home contingent. The pace was steady and the time was much slower than the preceding handicap, suggesting this was not the strongest renewal of this contest. The first two look decent recruits though.

NOTEBOOK
Champion Court(IRE) ◆, the winner of an easy-ground bumper in Ireland, was bought for £130,000 afterwards and was narrowly beaten under a penalty on his first start for new connections. Making his hurdling debut, he was settled in the rear and showed signs of inexperience. He was ridden along after landing rather flat-footed three out, but soon came back on the bridle and swept past his rivals turning into the straight, before coming away for a quite taking success. He looks sure to progress with time and distance, and his trainer intends to aim him for the Albert Bartlett at the Festival.
Sybarite(FR) ◆ won on his bumper debut in September before finishing third under a penalty here at the October meeting. Stepping up in grade for this hurdling debut, he was a little keen but was upsides the leader when making quite a bad error two out. He recovered to lead briefly on the home turn but could not respond when the winner came past, although he ran on to get the better of a more-experienced rival for second. He looks a nice type and should have little difficulty winning races over hurdles. (op 15-2)
Mount Helicon, a dual winner over hurdles - 2m on good and 3m on heavy ground - was ridden patiently before moving into contention down the hill. He had every chance on the home turn but could not quicken and represents the best guide to the level of this form. (op 4-1)
Total Submission, a stablemate of the winner and successful in a bumper on good and on his hurdles debut on easy ground, had been beaten a long way by Final Day on his return over course and distance at the October meeting. He ran pretty well under a positive ride, especially as he made a bad mistake at the first flight going away from the stands, and would have preferred a sounder surface.
Final Day(IRE) had won three of his six starts over hurdles on a sound surface at 2m-2m5f, including here at the October meeting. He was held up in rear before making ground travelling well, but once under pressure the response was limited. He was probably unsuited by this softer surface. (op 4-1)
Yabora(FR), ex-French, had run well in both chase starts in this country, despite unseating on one occasion, then was keen and got tired over 3m at Towcester over hurdles on his reappearance. Dropping in trip but up in grade, he made the running but could not respond when the challenges arrived and tired up the hill. A flatter track might suit best. (op 12-1 tchd 14-1 in places)
Drumfire(IRE), placed in all three starts over hurdles, at 2m-2m5f on good and soft ground, made more than one jumping error and had nothing in reserve from the penultimate flight. (op 7-2)
One Cool Tornado(IRE), a three-time winner on fast and easy ground in late summer, all at 2m4f, was in trouble a long way out and is another who was unsuited by the going. (op 8-1)

2389 CLEANEVENT STANDARD OPEN NATIONAL HUNT FLAT RACE (LISTED RACE) 2m 110y

4:00 (4:02) (Class 1) 4-6-Y-0

£6,841 (£2,566; £1,285; £640; £321; £160)

Form				RPR
411-	1		**Rock On Ruby (IRE)**253 [4452] 5-11-4 0 (t) NoelFehily (Paul Nicholls) *hld up in rr: stdy hdwy fr 4f out: led appr fnl 2f: pushed clr fnl f: comf* **11/4**1	125+
46-1	2	5	**Laveroque (FR)**38 [1748] 4-11-4 0 TomScudamore (Charlie Longsdon) *chsd ldrs: disp 2nd fr 2f out and kpt on to chse wnr fnl 50yds but nvr any ch* **16/1**	121
11	3	½	**Kartanian (IRE)**36 [1778] 4-11-4 0 TomO'Brien (Philip Hobbs) *chsd ldrs: led after 5f: hdd 1/2-way: led again 3f out: hdd appr fnl 2f: sn no chanve w wnr but styd disputing 2nd tl no ex fnl 50yds* **11/4**1	120
2-1	4	½	**Rose Of The Moon (IRE)**16 [2074] 5-11-4 0 WarrenMarston (Milton Harris) *in rr tl drvn and hdwy over 4f out: styd on wl fnl f and clsng for 3rd nr fin but nvr any ch w wnr* **22/1**	120
221-	5	1 ½	**Cucumber Run (IRE)**219 [5122] 5-11-4 0 BarryGeraghty (Nicky Henderson) *chsd ldrs: rdn 3f out: wknd ins fnl 2f* **9/2**2	119
	6	8	**Theatrical Star** 4-11-0 0 JoeTizzard (Colin Tizzard) *in rr: hdwy 7f out: rdn over 3f out and no imp on ldrs* **15/2**3	108+
	7	4	**Go On Arch (IRE)** 4-11-0 0 PaddyBrennan (Nigel Twiston-Davies) *in rr: rdn along and styd on fr over 3f out: nvr a threat* **14/1**	104
0-	8	9	**Rogue Dancer (FR)**267 [4158] 5-11-0 0 TimmyMurphy (Michael Banks) *prom early: dropped to rr 1/2-way: mod late prog* **50/1**	96
1	9	¾	**Panache**54 [1572] 5-10-11 0 MrPJTolman(7) (Debra Hamer) *chsd ldrs: led 1/2-way: hdd 3f out: sn wknd* **33/1**	99
4	10	8	**Vinomore**25 [1927] 4-10-0 0 PeterCarberry(7) (Shaun Lycett) *rdn 1/2-way: a in rr* **66/1**	81
	11	16	**Graiguecullen (IRE)**59 [1536] 6-11-0 0 APMcCoy (Eoin Griffin, Ire) *chsd ldrs over 10f* **16/1**	73
-3	12	1	**Bach To Back (IRE)**33 [1817] 5-10-11 0 SamTwiston-Davies(3) (Nigel Twiston-Davies) *a in rr* **25/1**	73
	13	2 ¼	**For Valour**36 [1792] 6-11-0 0 (t) MDarcy (Sabrina J Harty, Ire) *a in rr* **50/1**	70
0-0	14	80	**Castle Legend**199 [60] 5-10-7 0 MissCBoxall(7) (Simon Lewis) *t.k.h: led 5f: sn wknd: t.o* **200/1**	—
0	R		**Radmores Sam Evans**15 [2087] 5-10-7 0 CharlieWallis(7) (John O'Shea) *w ldrs whn rein broke: carried st on and tk wrong crse after 3f* **200/1**	—

4m 1.62s (5.22) **Going Correction** +0.35s/f (Yiel) **15** Ran SP% **119.3**
Speed ratings: **101,98,98,98,97 93,91,87,87,83 75,75,74,36,—**
Tote Swingers: 1&2 £6.90, 1&3 £2.50, 2&3 £13.80. Totesuper7: Win: Not won. Place: Not won. CSF £48.94 TOTE £3.40: £1.60, £3.80, £1.70; EX 53.20 Trifecta £209.10 Pool: £1,741.14 - 6.16 winning units..
Owner The Festival Goers **Bred** John O'Dwyer **Trained** Ditcheat, Somerset

FOCUS
This is quite often a decent bumper - winners include Best Mate, Back In Front and Rhinestone Cowboy - and with the form horses coming to the fore, this looked a solid enough renewal, albeit nothing to frighten the Irish, with the Champion Bumper in mind. The form horses dominated and the principals are all likely to switch to hurdles before long.

NOTEBOOK
Rock On Ruby(IRE), who sported a tongue-tie for the first time, arguably set the standard and, having turned into the straight in front, ran on strongly up the hill for a comfortable success. This was his fourth start in this sphere and his attentions will now be switched to hurdling, where he's expected to appreciate 2m4f. He has plenty of potential. (tchd 5-2 and 3-1 in places)
Laveroque(FR) won at Worcester on his reappearance and that form has worked out nicely. He ran well on this step up in class and is another who should make it pay over hurdles. (op 14-1)
Kartanian(IRE), successful in his previous two bumper starts, was up with the pace throughout and was just outstayed by the winner up the hill. It was a good effort and he has a future over hurdles. (op 4-1)
Rose Of The Moon(IRE), a narrow winner in heavy ground at Uttoxeter last time, lacked the speed of the principals but kept plugging away and his stamina kicked in up the hill. He's likely to stay well over hurdles. (op 16-1)
Cucumber Run(IRE) might do better back on a more speed-favouring track. (tchd 5-1)
Theatrical Star, a brother to Alegralil, who won her first two starts in bumpers, didn't shape badly on his debut despite running green. (op 8-1)
Go On Arch(IRE) also ran green but showed more than enough to suggest he'll go close in ordinary bumper company next time. (op 10-1 tchd 9-1)
Rogue Dancer(FR) Official explanation: jockey said gelding did not come down the hill
Radmores Sam Evans Official explanation: jockey said rein broke and pulled up
T/Jkpt: Not won. T/Plt: £90.70 to a £1 stake. Pool:£205,485.45 - 1,652.48 winning tickets T/Qpdt: £18.70 to a £1 stake. Pool:£14,914.11 - 587.84 winning tickets ST

2181 FONTWELL (L-H)

Sunday, November 14

OFFICIAL GOING: Heavy
All races were on inner course.
Wind: mild behind Weather: overcast with showers after heavy rain before racing

2390 HAPPY 7TH BIRTHDAY OLIVER ELNER-GIBBS NOVICES' H'CAP HURDLE (11 hdls) 2m 6f 110y

12:20 (12:20) (Class 5) (0-95,94) 3-Y-0+ **£2,016** (£592; £296; £147)

Form				RPR
-340	1		**Pete The Feat (IRE)**13 [2135] 6-11-1 83 FelixDeGiles (Anna Newton-Smith) *trckd ldr: led 2 out: styd on but idled run-in: rdn out* **11/2**	92+
-544	2	7	**Sail And Return**9 [2185] 6-11-11 93 (t) JamieMoore (Philip Middleton) *led: rdn whn edgd lft and hdd appr 2 out: hung rt run-in: styd on same pce* **7/1**	94
014	3	¾	**Curragh Dancer (FR)**13 [2135] 7-10-6 81 NathanSweeney(7) (Paddy Butler) *trckd ldrs: rdn appr 8th: one pce whn lft 3rd 2 out* **11/1**	81
0-03	4	nk	**Dancing Daffodil**25 [1915] 5-10-0 68 CharliePoste (Robin Dickin) *in tch: slow jump 2nd: trckd ldrs 5th: rdn after 3 out: styng on same pce whn lft 5th 2 out: wnt 4th run-in* **9/2**3	69
0405	5	4	**Keckerrockernixes (IRE)**25 [1918] 4-11-1 83 (p) LeightonAspell (Richard Rowe) *trckd ldrs: disputing ld whn hit 3rd: nt fluent 6th: hdd bef 3 out: sn rdn: hld whn lft 4th 2 out: fdd run-in* **50/1**	79
P0-0	6	38	**Whitcombe Spirit**9 [2183] 5-11-8 90 MattieBatchelor (Jamie Poulton) *in tch: hit 6th: nudged along 7th: wknd after 8th: t.o fr after 3 out* **14/1**	48
3502	7	½	**O'Callaghan Strand (AUS)**25 [1915] 4-10-10 87 RichieMcLernon(3) (Jonjo O'Neill) *in tch: trckd ldrs 5th: effrt after 3 out: sn wknd: t.o* **4/1**2	38
0-P0	8	24	**Our Little Dreamer (IRE)**17 [2058] 6-11-8 90 NickScholfield (Jeremy Scott) *trckd ldrs tl 5th: rdn after 7th: wkng whn mstke next: t.o* **33/1**	23
0-UU	P		**Rossmill Lad (IRE)**21 [2002] 6-10-4 79 JoshuaMoore(7) (Luke Dace) *a last: lost tch 8th: t.o whn p.u after 3 out* **33/1**	—
4U65	U		**Martin Scruff (IRE)**33 [1812] 4-11-5 94 MrJMQuinlan(7) (Michael Quinlan) *hld up towards rr: hdwy after 8th: rdn to dispute cl 2nd whn stmbld/slipped bdly on landing and uns rdr 2 out* **11/4**1	95+

5m 58.9s (16.40) **Going Correction** +0.85s/f (Soft)
WFA 4 from 5yo+ 8lb **10** Ran SP% **115.6**
Speed ratings (Par 103): **105,102,102,102,100 87,87,79,—,—**
Tote Swingers: 1&2 £4.40, 1&3 £23.10, 2&3 £6.80 CSF £42.70 TOTE £5.30: £1.80, £2.40, £2.70; EX 54.80.
Owner G J Larby & P J Smith **Bred** Michael O'Keeffe **Trained** Jevington, E Sussex

FOCUS
A weak handicap in which the winner was left clear at the second-last. He is rated back to last winter's best.

NOTEBOOK

Pete The Feat(IRE) saw it out best, although whether that would have been the case had Martin Scruff not crashed out at the second-last when challenging is debatable. Third in this race 12 months ago, he was left clear to land his first success at the 20th time of asking. He doesn't have the profile of a horse capable of following up and will probably be vulnerable off a slightly higher mark in future. (op 7-1)

Sail And Return, who got warm beforehand and was keen early on in the race, kept on well in the circumstances and posted an encouraging effort. (op 8-1)

Curragh Dancer(FR)'s improved recent showings have come on much better ground than this and he couldn't run to the same level, although he didn't fare badly. (op 12-1)

Dancing Daffodil rallied in the closing stages and arguably finished her race better than anything. This was her first time on ground this testing but her light weight would have helped. She is at the right end of the handicap and could do better again over even further. (op 5-1)

Martin Scruff(IRE), who looked uneasy around the bends, began to make good headway in the straight and was throwing down a big challenge when unseating his rider. He may well have won despite this track clearly not suiting and the cat is out of the bag to some extent now as this opening handicap mark looks like one one he can exploit. (op 5-2 tchd 3-1)

2391 TOTEEXACTA FLEXI BETTING H'CAP HURDLE (13 hdls) 3m 3f

12:50 (12:50) (Class 5) (0-95,90) 4-Y-O+ **£2,016** (£592; £296; £147)

Form RPR

0-60 **1** **Queenstown Lad**[11] 2149 5-10-0 **64** oh14 JamesDavies 76+
(Gary Brown) *hld up last but in tch: wnt 3rd after 3 out: sn rdn: sprawled on landing next: led last: styd on wl* **14/1**

2-P2 **2** *5* **Hobb's Dream (IRE)**[22] 1969 6-10-4 **75** (p) MarkQuinlan(7) 81
(Neil Mulholland) *j.lft at times: trckd ldrs: rdn to ld appr 2 out: hdd last: styd on same pce* **13/8**[1]

6P/F **3** *18* **Commanche Dawn**[9] 2183 8-10-0 **64** JamieMoore 55
(Gerry Enright) *trckd ldr: chalng whn hmpd 10th: led briefly after 3 out: sn rdn: lost 2nd next: wknd run-in* **6/1**

-401 **4** *29* **Isintshelovely (IRE)**[43] 1679 7-11-5 **83** LeightonAspell 42
(Chris Gordon) *trckd ldrs: hmpd 1st: rdn appr 10th: wknd after 3 out: t.o* **11/4**[2]

0P-4 **P** **My Rosie Ribbons (IRE)**[9] 2183 11-10-6 **75**(p) GemmaGracey-Davison(5) —
(Zoe Davison) *led tl rdn appr 3 out: sn wknd: p.u bef 2 out* **10/3**[3]

7m 19.1s (26.30) **Going Correction** +0.85s/f (Soft) **5** Ran SP% **108.8**
Speed ratings (Par 103): **95,93,88,79,—**
CSF £37.16 TOTE £18.70: £5.40, £1.80; EX 67.20.
Owner T Bramble **Bred** R W Huggins **Trained** East Garston, Berks

FOCUS

A real war of attrition and a shock result in this low-greade handicap. A big step up from the winner.

NOTEBOOK

Queenstown Lad was racing from a stone out of the handicap, but stayed on best to land a first career success. Although the winner appeared to have a mountain to climb on these terms, he is very lightly raced and clearly improved markedly for the step up in trip. Stamina is his strong suit and, given how unexposed he is, he ought to remain interesting after being reassessed. Official explanation: trainer said, regarding apparent improvement in form, that the gelding was better suited by the step up in trip. (tchd 16-1)

Hobb's Dream(IRE) stays well and, racing off a similar mark to her hurdles one, looks to have run her race. She has just been foiled by a much less exposed rival. (tchd 6-4)

Commanche Dawn's effort petered out in the final couple of furlongs but at least she managed to stay on her feet this time. (op 7-1 tchd 15-2)

Isintshelovely(IRE) proved disappointing and it surely can't just have been the 9lb higher mark that proved her undoing. (op 5-2 tchd 9-4 and 3-1)

My Rosie Ribbons(IRE) is slipping down the handicap but she didn't last long enough to be of interest next time. (op 4-1)

2392 JOHN ROGERSON MEMORIAL BEGINNERS' CHASE (13 fncs) 2m 2f

1:25 (1:25) (Class 4) 4-Y-O+ **£2,992** (£878; £439; £219)

Form RPR

02-0 **1** **Tullamore Dew (IRE)**[22] 1967 8-11-1 0 LiamTreadwell 130+
(Nick Gifford) *j.w: mde all: wl in command fr 4 out: v easily* **1/5**[1]

41/P **2** *23* **Zhukov (IRE)**[8] 2230 8-10-10 0 JayPemberton(5) 100
(Kevin Tork) *trckd wnr fr 4th: blnd 4 out: sn rdn but no ch w v easy wnr: j.lft last 2* **8/1**[2]

0P-6 **3** *17* **Daring Approach (IRE)**[17] 2046 9-11-1 0 OwynNelmes 80
(Helen Nelmes) *trckd wnr tl after 4th: dropped to 4th after 7th but in tch: outpcd after 9th: plugged on to regain modest 3rd sn after last* **12/1**[3]

65U5 **4** *19* **Bold Pioneer (USA)**[5] 2292 7-10-10 71 GemmaGracey-Davison(5) 65
(Zoe Davison) *racd in cl 4th: disp 2nd 8th tl after 4 out: sn rdn: wknd after next: mstke last: sn lost modest 3rd* **20/1**

4m 56.6s (21.90) **Going Correction** +1.10s/f (Heav)
WFA 4 from 5yo+ 7lb **4** Ran SP% **106.9**
Speed ratings (Par 105): **95,84,77,68**
CSF £2.44 TOTE £1.10; EX 2.40.
Owner Give Every Man His Due **Bred** Michael Daly **Trained** Findon, W Sussex

FOCUS

A straightforward task on paper for 139-rated hurdler Tullamore Dew. The form could be rated up to 10lb higher.

NOTEBOOK

Tullamore Dew(IRE) was a league apart from these rivals if translating his hurdles ability to fences and his supporters never had a moment's worry as this scopey individual jumped like an old hand en route to dotting up. Although this was an easy task, these were tricky conditions and he'd ideally prefer better ground, so he deserves credit for this exemplary performance and he looks a really nice prospect for the novice chase division this year. (op 1-4)

Zhukov(IRE) was rated 24lb inferior to the winner over hurdles and he was no match for that rival on this first try over fences. Still, connections will be encouraged by the way he jumped, and he'll not always be bumping into such classy rivals. (tchd 9-1)

Daring Approach(IRE) isn't showing anywhere near enough to be of interest at the moment. (op 11-1)

2393 TIKRAM H'CAP HURDLE (FOR THE SALMON SPRAY CHALLENGE TROPHY) (9 hdls) 2m 2f 110y

2:00 (2:00) (Class 3) (0-130,127) 4-Y-O+ **£6,337** (£1,872; £936; £468; £234)

Form RPR

34P- **1** **Warne's Way (IRE)**[18] 5231 7-11-0 **115** (b) LiamTreadwell 123
(Brendan Powell) *racd wd: disp ld: outrt ldr 3 out: rdn and hdd last: rallied gamely: led towards fin: drvn out* **7/2**[1]

/05- **2** *nk* **Ned Ludd (IRE)**[38] 4423 7-10-11 **115** (p) RichieMcLernon(3) 124
(Jonathan Portman) *racd wd: trckd ldrs: wnt 2nd appr 3 out: chal 2 out: rdn to ld whn mstke last: kpt on but no ex whn hdd towards fin* **17/2**

2613 **3** *17* **Occasionally Yours (IRE)**[23] 1951 6-10-13 **119** DavidBass(5) 110
(Alan Blackmore) *racd wd: trckd ldrs: rdn after 3 out: styd chsng front pair tl fdd last* **15/2**

45-U **4** *½* **Sparrow Hills (IRE)**[194] 138 6-10-4 **112** RobertKirk(7) 103
(Steven Dixon) *disp ld tl rdn appr 3 out: styd chsng ldrs: mstke next: fdd last* **20/1**

366- **5** *23* **Johnny Mullen (IRE)**[233] 4873 7-10-10 **118** MattGriffiths(7) 85
(Paul Henderson) *hld up towards rr: nt fluent 1st: rdn after 5th: nvr on terms: t.o fr 2 out* **7/1**

10-4 **6** *13* **Maraafeq (USA)**[13] 2125 6-11-5 **127** HarryChalloner(7) 81
(Venetia Williams) *in tch: rdn appr 6th: wknd 3 out: t.o* **11/2**[2]

/11- **P** **Oenologue (FR)**[272] 4074 8-11-8 **123** JohnnyFarrelly —
(Alison Thorpe) *racd wd: hld up towards rr: nt fluent 4th: hdwy 3 out: sn rdn: wknd next: p.u bef last* **17/2**

10-0 **P** **Olympian (FR)**[184] 316 8-11-5 **120** AndrewGlassonbury —
(Philip Middleton) *mid-div: rdn after 6th: wknd sn after next: bhd whn p.u bef 2 out* **17/2**

163/ **P** **Special Day (FR)**[926] 78 6-10-9 **110** (t) LeightonAspell —
(Lucy Wadham) *mid-div: rdn after 6th: sn wknd: t.o whn p.u bef 2 out* **6/1**[3]

4m 47.1s (12.80) **Going Correction** +0.85s/f (Soft) **9** Ran SP% **112.5**
Speed ratings (Par 107): **107,106,99,99,89 84,—,—,—**
Tote Swingers: 1&2 £3.80, 1&3 £4.10, 2&3 £5.90 CSF £32.04 CT £206.57 TOTE £4.40: £1.50, £2.50, £2.90; EX 32.30.
Owner Nigel Stafford **Bred** Mrs Ann Kennedy **Trained** Upper Lambourn, Berks

FOCUS

A modest handicap where the first pair came well clear. There is a case for rating the race a fair bit higher through the beaten horses.

NOTEBOOK

Warne's Way(IRE) got back up in the final 50 yards to snatch the prize. The winner, who won on his only previous visit to this track, was potentially well handicapped on the pick of some of his old hurdle form, and he confirmed the promise of two good runs on the Flat this autumn by carrying that form back to this sphere. He clearly stays well and handles conditions but his overall profile of three wins from 30 starts doesn't suggest he's a good thing to follow up. (tchd 3-1)

Ned Ludd(IRE), also fit from the Flat, travelled and jumped with eyecatching ease but began to idle and failed to put the race to bed when hitting the front before the last flight of hurdles. He is another with a poor strike rate (2-47). (op 9-1 tchd 10-1)

Occasionally Yours(IRE) deserves some credit as he would prefer a much sounder surface, so he was far from disgraced. (op 8-1 tchd 17-2)

Johnny Mullen(IRE) shaped with some encouragement on his first start since March and his record suggests he'll be able to build on this. (op 17-2)

Maraafeq(USA) has to rate disappointing. (op 5-1)

Oenologue(FR) Official explanation: jockey said gelding stopped quickly

2394 TOTEPOOL CONDITIONAL JOCKEYS' H'CAP CHASE (16 fncs) 2m 6f

2:35 (2:35) (Class 5) (0-95,95) 4-Y-O+ **£2,065** (£641; £345)

Form RPR

1-P2 **1** **Kappelhoff (IRE)**[17] 2048 13-10-6 **75** (b) DavidBass 80
(Lydia Richards) *chsd ldrs: rdn along fr 10th: pressed ldr fr 4 out: led 2 out: all out: hld on* **4/1**

43-3 **2** *½* **Kiltimoney (IRE)**[22] 1969 10-10-1 **70** IanPopham 76
(Richard Mitchell) *trckd ldrs: pckd 1st: jnd ldrs 9th: hit 12th: rdn to chse ldng pair after 4 out: styd on fr last: swtchd rt and clsng at fin* **2/1**[1]

12-2 **3** *71* **The Hardy Boy**[13] 2134 10-11-3 **91** NathanSweeney(5) 76
(Anna Newton-Smith) *w ldr most of way tl outrt ldr 11th: pressed by wnr fr 4 out: rdn after 3 out: hdd 2 out: 3rd and hld whn knuckled bdly on landing last: walked home* **3/1**[3]

F1U- **P** **Prince Louis (FR)**[205] 5353 7-11-9 **95** (t) PeterToole(3) —
(Charlie Mann) *j.lft progively worse: led: hit 7th: hdd whn blunderd 11th: sn btn: t.o whn p.u bef 3 out* **5/2**[2]

6m 14.7s (31.70) **Going Correction** +1.10s/f (Heav) **4** Ran SP% **106.9**
Speed ratings (Par 103): **86,85,60,—**
CSF £12.01 TOTE £4.30; EX 7.60.
Owner Mrs Lydia Richards **Bred** Tom Curran **Trained** Funtington, W Sussex

FOCUS

A weak handicap which saw a slow-motion finish. The first two are rated close to their marks.

NOTEBOOK

Kappelhoff(IRE) just did enough to hold off the Kiltimoney. He was the first to come off the bridle, so all credit to David Bass, who was rewarded for his perseverence as his mount responded gamely to jump to the front two out and just have enough left to see his race out. He looks vulnerable off this mark nowadays but at least the handicapper can't do much with his rating after this narrow success and he does have a terrific record at this venue. (op 10-3)

Kiltimoney(IRE) has a poor strike rate (1-32) but this is another solid effort in defeat and he deserves to find another race. (op 5-2)

The Hardy Boy ran out of steam in the straight and almost stopped to a walk going over the last. Plumpton is his track though. (tchd 11-4)

Prince Louis(FR) eventually paid the price for some far from fluent jumping. (op 9-4 tchd 11-4)

2395 TOTESUPER7 SOUTHERN NATIONAL H'CAP CHASE (21 fncs) 3m 4f

3:10 (3:10) (Class 3) (0-135,132) 4-Y-O+ **£12,697** (£3,873; £2,023; £1,099)

Form RPR

F2-5 **1** **Peut Etre Sivola (FR)**[17] 2055 7-10-4 **110** (vt) JohnnyFarrelly 122+
(David Pipe) *in tch: nudged along fr 16th: rdn to ld 3 out: styd on dourly: rdn out* **3/1**[1]

315- **2** *6* **Kawagino (IRE)**[239] 4738 10-11-5 **125** AndrewThornton 130+
(Seamus Mullins) *trckd ldrs: nt fluent 12th and 4 out: sn rdn: chsd wnr 2 out: styd on same pce:* **16/1**

FP/F **3** *2* **Pass Me By**[185] 312 11-10-8 **114** DavidEngland 115
(Suzy Smith) *j.rt: led tl after 9th: styd chsng ldrs: sn drvn along: styd on same pce fr 3 out* **20/1**

4-21 **4** *17* **Runshan (IRE)**[17] 2055 10-10-2 **108** JamieMoore 96
(David Bridgwater) *chsd ldr: led after 9th: rdn and hdd 4 out: styd on same pce tl wknd appr last* **9/2**[3]

541 **P** **Mtpockets (IRE)**[17] 2051 5-9-11 **110** MarkQuinlan(7) —
(Neil Mulholland) *hld up: reminder after 5th: blnd 15th: wknd after next: t.o whn p.u bef 3 out* **7/2**[2]

4243 **P** **Petite Margot**[17] 2055 11-10-4 **113** TomMolloy(3) 101
(Nigel Twiston-Davies) *mid-div: reminders after 14th: in rr u.p 16th: styd on fr 3 out: wnt 4th briefly whn p.u bef last: dismntd* **15/2**

16U6 **P** **Cold Mountain (IRE)**[21] 1999 8-10-10 **121** JimmyDerham(5) —
(Seamus Mullins) *hld up towards rr: p.u bef 9th* **25/1**

03-4 **P** **Emperor Concerto**[23] 1950 7-11-5 **125** LeightonAspell —
(Lucy Wadham) *in tch: trckd ldrs 12th: wknd qckly 15th: p.u bef next* **17/2**

2560 **P** **Cullahill (IRE)**[8] 2221 8-10-7 **120** NathanSweeney(7) —
(Bob Buckler) *hld up: rdn after 16th: sme prog after 4 out: disputing 10 l 7th whn blnd 2 out: wknd and p.u bef last* **12/1**

232- **F** **Bench Warrent (IRE)**[257] 4375 7-11-9 **132**......................(p) PeterToole(3) —
(Charlie Mann) *in tch: jnd ldr 15th: mstke 17th: led after 4 out tl next: disputing 7th but fading whn fell heavily 2 out* **12/1**
7m 53.0s (25.70) **Going Correction** +1.10s/f (Heavy) **10** Ran SP% **117.6**
Speed ratings (Par 107): **107,105,104,99,**— —,—,—,—,—
Tote Swingers: 1&2 £25.90, 2&3 £77.80 CSF £48.35 CT £826.21 TOTE £3.50: £2.00, £4.50, £4.60; EX 75.90.
Owner Third Time Lucky **Bred** Gilles Trapenard **Trained** Nicholashayne, Devon

FOCUS
Only four finishers, such was the gruelling nature of this contest, and they were virtually walking after the last. The winner is rated back to the form he showed in this race last year.

NOTEBOOK
Peut Etre Sivola(FR), winner of the race last year off a 1lb lower mark, repeated the feat in emphatic style having travelled and jumped well. He jumped to the front three out and soon had the race in safe keeping. His overall profile is patchy but he had clearly benefited from his reappearance at Stratford and connections had him at his peak for this. (tchd 5-2, tchd 7-2 in a place)
Kawagino(IRE) travelled well in the main but didn't jump with a great deal of fluency and that wouldn't have helped his momentum, especially in these conditions. In the circumstances he ran really well on his first start of the season.
Pass Me By, who was front rank early, came under striong driving a long way out but, to his creit, he rallied and briefly looked likely to take a hand in the finish again until tiring in the straight. He is potentially well handicapped on old form and this was encouraging, so he's one to keep an eye on.
Runshan(IRE) has been in fine form of late, indeed he was a long way in front of Peut Etre Sivola when scoring at Stratford last time. However, the combination of that busy spell and a 10lb rise meant he was unable to run to a similar level this time, despite getting weight from all of his rivals. He wasn't disgraced though. (op 5-1 tchd 11-2)
Mtpockets(IRE) was in trouble from a fairly early stage. Official explanation: jockey said mare never travelled (op 9-2 tchd 5-1)
Petite Margot Official explanation: jockey said mare stopped quickly (op 9-2 tchd 5-1)
Cold Mountain(IRE) Official explanation: jockey said gelding was unsuited by the heavy ground (op 9-2 tchd 5-1)

2396 TOTEPOOL A BETTER WAY TO BET MAIDEN HURDLE (10 hdls) 2m 4f
3:40 (3:40) (Class 4) 4-Y-0+ **£2,471** (£725; £362; £181)

Form RPR
22- **1** **Amirico (IRE)**[230] 4932 5-10-9 0.. MrWBiddick(5) 115+
(Venetia Williams) *trckd ldrs: chal 2 out: sn led: wandered but kpt on wl run-in: rdn out* **9/2**[2]
0-0 **2** *8* **Ballyegan (IRE)**[12] 2136 5-10-7 0.............................. NathanSweeney(7) 103
(Bob Buckler) *hld up towards rr: rdn after 7th: styd on wl fr 2 out: wnt 2nd run-in: nvr gng to rch wnr* **33/1**
05- **3** *12* **Bubbly Bruce (IRE)**[207] 5323 6-10-11 0............................ PeterToole(3) 95+
(Charlie Mann) *trckd ldrs: jnd ldr 7th: led 3 out: rdn whn jnd and blnd 2 out: sn hdd: wknd run-in* **1/2**[1]
4 *10* **Double Whammy**[35] 4-11-0 0... MattieBatchelor 81
(Jamie Poulton) *disp ld tl 4th: chsd ldr: hit 5th: rdn after 7th: wknd after 3 out: wnt modest 4th run-in* **8/1**[3]
3/ **5** *4 1/2* **Bentley Brook (IRE)**[320] 1131 8-11-0 0................................. MarkGrant 76
(Barry Brennan) *trckd ldrs: led 4th tl 3 out: sn rdn: styd chsng ldng pair tl wknd bef last* **40/1**
06 **6** *3 1/4* **Jack The Soldier (IRE)**[9] 2181 6-10-11 0...................... CharlieStudd(3) 73
(Chris Gordon) *in tch: rdn after 6th: no ch fr 3 out* **28/1**
4-45 **7** *1/2* **Balustrade (IRE)**[25] 1914 4-11-0 0.. ColinBolger 72
(Chris Gordon) *disp ld tl 4th: chsd ldrs: rdn after 6th: wknd after 3 out* **14/1**
5m 21.1s (21.70) **Going Correction** +0.85s/f (Soft)
WFA 4 from 5yo+ 8lb **7** Ran SP% **111.5**
Speed ratings (Par 105): **90,86,82,78,76 74,74**
Tote Swingers: 1&2 £1.10, 1&3 £3.90, 2&3 £13.30 CSF £98.84 TOTE £4.70: £1.80, £10.60; EX 41.60 TRIFECTA Not won..
Owner Alan Didlick **Bred** Michael D Hickey **Trained** Kings Caple, H'fords

FOCUS
Conditions played a big part in this moderate novice hurdle and the winner relished the ground. The fifth and sixth help set the level.

NOTEBOOK
Amirico(IRE) benefited from a cool ride and eventually came home clear. He shaped with plenty of promise in two bumpers last season and built on that with an impressive performance given the conditions. He wandered around when clear in the straight but was always doing enough to come home clear and he looks the type who can build on this. He certainly travelled and jumped like a horse with future. (op 7-2)
Ballyegan(IRE) took a marked step forward having been thrashed on both previous starts over hurdles. Maybe testing conditions are the key to him, as he stayed on steadily without looking likely to get to the winner. He could be a force over staying trips. (op 25-1)
Bubbly Bruce(IRE) got very tired and probably shouldn't be judged too harshly for this defeat. He definitely showed promise and probably just found conditions too testing on return. (op 4-7)
Double Whammy showed enough to suggest he might have a future at this game, although there is room for improvement in his jumping. (op 17-2)
T/Plt: £309.80 to a £1 stake. Pool:£54,980.05 - 129.55 winning tickets T/Qpdt: £59.70 to a £1 stake. Pool:£14,914.11 - 587.84 winning tickets TM

2245 MARKET RASEN (R-H)
Sunday, November 14

OFFICIAL GOING: Soft (chs 5.9 hdl 5.3)
Rails on both courses moved out 3yds to give fresh ground.
Wind: almost nil Weather: fine

2397 TURFTV NOVICES' HURDLE (8 hdls) 2m 1f
12:30 (12:30) (Class 4) 4-Y-0+ **£2,602** (£764; £382; £190)

Form RPR
241 **1** **Andhaar**[15] 2092 4-11-5 **126**.. RhysFlint 122+
(Steve Gollings) *trckd ldrs: wnt 2nd after 3rd: clsd up 3 out: led sn after 2 out: nt fluent last: drvn out* **10/11**[1]
35 **2** *5* **Taketimeout (IRE)**[14] 2109 5-10-12 0........................... DominicElsworth 110+
(Jonjo O'Neill) *hld up: wnt 3rd after 3rd: handy whn mstke 2 out: wnt 4 l 2nd appr last: hit last: kpt on same pce* **6/1**[3]
24-1 **3** *8* **Bow Badger**[37] 1758 4-11-5 0... BrianHughes 112+
(Howard Johnson) *t.k.h: reluctant ldr: qcknd 2nd: nt fluent: stmbld landing 2 out: sn hdd: wknd appr last* **15/8**[2]
00-2 **4** *22* **Meridiem**[188] 254 6-10-9 0.. ChrisHonour(3) 78
(Sean Regan) *in tch: t.k.h: lost pl 4th: no ch after* **66/1**
5 *13* **Short Supply (USA)**[18] 4-10-5 0... RobertWalford 58
(Tim Walford) *nt fluent 1st: lost pl 4th: sn bhd* **40/1**
0 **P** **In The Sand (IRE)**[11] 2145 4-10-12 0.................................. RichieMcGrath —
(Jonjo O'Neill) *t.k.h: trckd ldr to 3rd: lost pl and bhd next: sn t.o: p.u after 5th* **66/1**
4m 29.1s (22.40) **Going Correction** +0.625s/f (Soft) **6** Ran SP% **106.9**
Speed ratings (Par 105): **72,69,65,55,49** —
Tote Swingers: 1&2 £1.10, 1&3 £1.20, 2&3 £1.40 CSF £6.22 TOTE £1.70: £1.20, £2.70; EX 5.30.
Owner P J Martin **Bred** Shadwell Estate Company Limited **Trained** Scamblesby, Lincs

FOCUS
A reasonable novice hurdle with the betting centring around two previous winners and with nothing keen to go on it was run at a sedate early pace. The form is suspect and the winner is rated below his best.

NOTEBOOK
Andhaar had the leader in his sights and moved up well to assert in the home straight. He got in close to the final two and will need to improve his jumping, but he possesses a decent engine. He had won on faster ground at Wetherby in a good time in a race that has already thrown up a subsequent winner, and with a rating rising to 126 in light of that effort he was well placed to defy a penalty here. Connections were encouraged that he handled this softer ground and have entered him for the valuable 4yo hurdle at Haydock next weekend. (tchd 11-10)
Taketimeout(IRE) was not pushed once his chance had gone at Huntingdon last time and he looked a likely improver. He kept tabs on the winner but just lacked that rival's pace, but it was an improved effort and he looks up to winning races, and appears suited to longer trips in time. (op 13-2 tchd 11-2)
Bow Badger eventually took up the running and held the initiative, but he stumbled at the second-last and that cost him vital momentum. This was still a good performance and he should be up to adding to his Carlisle win, especially on better ground. (tchd 13-8 and 2-1)
Meridiem did not settle on his first run since May and was never going to be involved, but he made some progress from off the pace around the final turn and should come on for this hurdling debut. (op 50-1)
Short Supply(USA), a dual winner on the Flat this year and rated 53, struggled on her hurdling debut. (tchd 50-1)
In The Sand(IRE) never looked happy and showed little promise. Official explanation: vet said gelding pulled up distressed

2398 BOOK YOUR TICKETS FOR BOXING DAY H'CAP HURDLE (8 hdls) 2m 1f
1:00 (1:01) (Class 5) (0-90,89) 4-Y-0+ **£1,951** (£573; £286; £143)

Form RPR
002 **1** **Spice Bar**[6] 2280 6-10-10 **73**.. BarryKeniry 95+
(Declan Carroll) *t.k.h in midfield: hit 5th: smooth hdwy next: shkn up to chse ldr appr 2 out: led on bit appr last: rdn clr: eased towards fin* **3/1**[2]
6F5 **2** *5* **Marino Prince (FR)**[97] 678 5-11-7 **89**......................... MarcGoldstein(5) 103+
(Jim Best) *hld up in tch: smooth hdwy to join ldrs 3 out: led gng wl appr next: hdd appr last: styd on same pce* **7/4**[1]
3-05 **3** *15* **Pinewood Legend (IRE)**[40] 1001 8-11-3 **80**.....................(p) GrahamLee 79
(Peter Niven) *trckd ldrs: drvn 3 out: outpcd appr next: kpt on run-in to take modest 3rd towards fin* **15/2**
/PP- **4** *3/4* **Trans Sonic**[12] 489 7-11-12 **89**.. BrianHughes 88
(David O'Meara) *t.k.h: trckd ldr: led briefly bef 2 out: sn wknd: 10 l 3rd whn mstke last* **11/2**[3]
5000 **5** *18* **Chadwell Spring (IRE)**[14] 2114 4-11-3 **80**..................... PeterBuchanan 60
(Mike Sowersby) *mid-div: mstke and lost pl 3 out* **25/1**
0000 **6** *nk* **Tuckers Treasure**[15] 2092 4-10-6 **69**..................................... TjadeCollier 49
(Sue Smith) *chsd ldrs: reminders 5th: lost pl bef 2 out* **18/1**
204/ **7** *3 3/4* **Miss Champagne (IRE)**[719] 2422 7-10-2 **65**........................ PaddyAspell 41
(Andrew Wilson) *towards rr: sme hdwy 4th: lost pl 3 out* **16/1**
0000 **8** *10* **Vogarth**[39] 1723 6-10-6 **76**.. GaryDerwin(7) 42
(Michael Chapman) *chsd ldrs: drvn 3rd: reminders 5th: lost pl next* **40/1**
00-P **9** *1/2* **Kingscourt Lad (IRE)**[16] 2070 12-11-2 **82**...................(t) AdamPogson(3) 48
(Charles Pogson) *led: hdd & wknd bef 2 out* **25/1**
-0PU **10** *nk* **Still Royal**[32] 1831 4-11-4 **84**... RyanMania(3) 49
(John Davies) *in rr: mstke 3rd: bhd 3 out* **40/1**
-PP0 **P** **Baltrap (FR)**[21] 1993 5-10-12 **80**...................................... GilesHawkins(5) —
(Clarissa Caroe) *gave problems leaving paddock: in rr: nt fluent 2nd: bhd fr 5th: last whn p.u bef 2 out* **100/1**
4m 20.2s (13.50) **Going Correction** +0.625s/f (Soft)
WFA 4 from 5yo+ 7lb **11** Ran SP% **113.2**
Speed ratings (Par 103): **93,90,83,83,74 74,72,68,67,67** —
Tote Swingers: 1&2 £1.90, 1&3 £3.30, 2&3 £3.70 CSF £8.12 CT £33.37 TOTE £2.50: £1.10, £1.80, £4.30; EX 9.20.
Owner Kevin McConnell **Bred** Littleton Stud **Trained** Sledmere, E Yorks

FOCUS
A weak contest ripe for the taking by a well-backed improver, but in this case the gamble went astray. The winner produced a step up and the second matched his best old form, but the rest were all upwards of 8lb off.

NOTEBOOK
Spice Bar was the form pick on the basis of his second at Southwell last week despite pulling too hard, and off the same mark he was fancied to go one better. Driven up to improve in the back straight, he was a bit outpaced around the home turn but was soon back into stride and came home smoothly. He will reportedly have a bit of a break now but should soon be resuming his improvement. (tchd 7-2)
Marino Prince(FR) came into this as a longstanding maiden over hurdles but he had been inching down the weights and was strongly fancied on his first start for Jim Best. He travelled up smoothly to take up the running as they entered the straight and looked set to coast home, but could find no extra once challenged. He is a smallish, nippy type which goes some way to explaining his vulnerability in fending off lighter-weighted rivals. (op 7-2)
Pinewood Legend(IRE) got outpaced but plugged on to claim third, but will need to improve to make the most of a handy mark. (op 13-2 tchd 8-1)
Trans Sonic has been in good form on the Flat this year with five wins at distances up to a mile and was in good enough form to improve on his previous dismal efforts over hurdles, but he did not fully see out the trip. (op 3-1)
Chadwell Spring(IRE) has been unable to transfer his Flat racing ability to hurdles thus far. (tchd 28-1)
Tuckers Treasure ran well for a way but again weakened disappointingly. (op 22-1)

2399 DIGIBET.COM H'CAP HURDLE (10 hdls) 2m 3f
1:35 (1:35) (Class 3) (0-135,135) 4-Y-0+ **£5,703** (£1,684; £842; £421; £210)

Form RPR
505- **1** **Keki Buku (FR)**[214] 5182 7-11-2 **130**................................... GilesHawkins(5) 139+
(Philip Hobbs) *hld up in rr: hdwy to trck ldrs 7th: led appr 2 out: clr last: pushed out* **11/4**[2]
P2-4 **2** *11* **Degas Art (IRE)**[32] 1827 7-10-11 **123**................................. RyanMania(3) 120
(Howard Johnson) *trckd ldrs: drvn 7th: outpcd after next: kpt on to take 3rd 2 out: styd on to take modest 2nd towards fin* **9/2**[3]
2034 **3** *3/4* **Dontpaytheferryman (USA)**[15] 2094 5-10-3 **115**........ FearghalDavis(3) 111
(Brian Ellison) *trckd ldr: drvn to ld after 3 out: hdd appr next: kpt on same pce* **9/4**[1]

4-00 **4** *3* **Fin Vin De Leu (GER)**29 1864 4-11-2 **125** GrahamLee 118
(Charlie Mann) *set str pce: pushed along 7th: hdd after 3 out: one pce appr next: fdd last 100yds* **10/1**
F-1P **5** *12* **Auroras Encore (IRE)**140 844 8-11-7 **135** ShaneByrne(5) 116
(Sue Smith) *chsd ldrs: drvn 7th: outpcd and lost pl sn after next* **7/1**
010- **6** *72* **Sir Tantallus Hawk**220 5099 6-11-12 **135** BrianHughes 44
(Alan Swinbank) *hld up: wl in tch tl drvn and lost pl 6th: sn bhd: eased 2 out: t.o last: virtually p.u* **9/1**

4m 47.7s (8.30) **Going Correction** +0.625s/f (Soft)
WFA 4 from 5yo+ 7lb **6** Ran SP% **107.2**
Speed ratings (Par 107): **107,102,102,100,95 65**
Tote Swingers: 1&2 £2.30, 1&3 £1.90, 2&3 £1.80 CSF £13.95 TOTE £2.90: £1.10, £2.00; EX 15.30.
Owner Mrs Diana L Whateley **Bred** Ecurie Passing **Trained** Withycombe, Somerset

FOCUS
This was run at a reasonable pace with three pulling clear on the home turn, although only the winner could sustain it to the line. He produced improved form, with the next three setting the level.

NOTEBOOK
Keki Buku(FR) was ridden with confidence, gradually improving his position on the final circuit, held together before delivering his challenge, and stretching clear in effortless fashion to stay on well to the line. He goes well on soft ground that is not too testing, so conditions were ideal today, and he was on a reasonable mark to do himself justice on his seasonal bow. He ran respectably in some hot handicaps last season and, with a wind operation evidently having done its job in the interim, he should be able to pick up more races this term. (op 2-1 tchd 3-1)
Degas Art(IRE) could not go with the increase in pace leaving the back straight but stayed on late to grab second on the line. He has been relatively light raced since his last win in February 2007 but is now on a reasonable enough mark and looks to be gradually coming into form. (op 11-2)
Dontpaytheferryman(USA) held every chance as he was driven up to challenge on the home turn but tired markedly. He tends to go well in his first few runs after a break but has had three outings already so was probably not fresh enough to make use of ideal conditions and a light weight. (op 11-4 tchd 2-1)
Fin Vin De Leu(GER) set a good pace but could find no extra once swamped by the two market leaders. He is capable enough and has run creditably in better contests, but seems to be struggling to cope with a stiff mark imposed after winning a weak juvenile event at Warwick in February. (op 9-1 tchd 8-1)
Auroras Encore(IRE) usually goes better with a recent run so should come on for this first start since June. (op 13-2)
Sir Tantallus Hawk is suited by soft ground but may have needed this run and will need to improve on this. (op 17-2 tchd 8-1)

2400 1STSECURITYSOLUTIONS.COM H'CAP CHASE (14 fncs) 2m 4f
2:10 (2:10) (Class 3) (0-135,135) 4-Y-0+ **£6,395** (£1,930; £994; £526)

Form RPR
0636 **1** **Ursis (FR)**42 1690 9-10-6 **115** RhysFlint 122+
(Steve Gollings) *led to 1st: nt fluent 2nd: trckd ldrs: led gng best appr 3 out: drvn clr 2 out: eased towards fin* **5/1**
1P-P **2** *9* **Victorias Groom (GER)**197 98 8-11-7 **130** PaddyAspell 126
(Lucy Wadham) *led 1st: hdd after 4th: led 7th to 4 out: kpt on one pce fr next: 6 l 2nd whn mstke last* **5/1**
133- **3** *3/4* **Riguez Dancer**205 5371 6-11-2 **125** GrahamLee 120
(Ferdy Murphy) *hld up in rr: j.big: hdwy to trck ldrs 9th: styd on same pce fr 3 out* **8/1**
425- **4** *57* **Four Strong Winds (IRE)**263 4228 6-10-8 **117** DominicElsworth 87+
(Jonjo O'Neill) *mstke 1st: nt fluent in rr: hdwy to chse ldrs 4 out: lost pl appr next: sn bhd and eased: wl t.o* **7/2**2
F/1- **P** **Bleak House (IRE)**289 3725 8-11-5 **128** BrianHughes —
(Howard Johnson) *trckd ldrs: blnd 10th: wknd next: t.o whn p.u bef 3 out* **4/1**3
U10- **F** **Gansey (IRE)**241 4698 8-11-7 **135** ShaneByrne(5) 123+
(Sue Smith) *t.k.h: trckd ldr 2nd: led after 4th to 7th: led 4 out: hdd appr next: 4th and wl hld whn fell 3 out* **3/1**1

5m 9.10s (3.40) **Going Correction** +0.35s/f (Yiel) **6** Ran SP% **111.7**
Speed ratings (Par 107): **107,103,103,80,— —**
Tote Swingers: 1&2 £5.40, 1&3 £5.80, 2&3 £7.40 CSF £28.67 TOTE £6.30: £4.50, £3.50; EX 30.10.
Owner P J Martin **Bred** Serge Bernereau Sarl **Trained** Scamblesby, Lincs

FOCUS
A small field but it looked competitive on paper, although most would improve for this outing. The winner's best run since 2008.

NOTEBOOK
Ursis(FR) was well backed to continue his stable's excellent recent form, despite having not won for two years and arguably being better over hurdles than fences. He lost position at the first two jumps but that turned out to be to his advantage as he was then racing off the pace, and he came through powerfully for a convincing victory. Credit should go to his jockey who made his mind up after those early fences and that gave him confidence to attack the subsequent obstacles. He goes well here and was well handicapped for this, and there are no definite plans as this race was his target. (op 15-2 tchd 9-2)
Victorias Groom(GER) ran a sound race at the head of the pace throughout, but had no answer as the winner swept by. He seems back on track after pulling up in his last two races in the spring and may also come on for the run. (tchd 4-1)
Riguez Dancer made some progress in the back straight but was eventually outpaced. He is on a fair mark and should come on for the run and can pay his way in soft-ground handicaps this season. (op 11-2)
Four Strong Winds(IRE) faced a stiff enough test for his chasing debut and may have needed the run, but was never in the race. (op 9-2 tchd 11-2)
Bleak House(IRE) has previously been at his best on flat, galloping tracks when fresh, so this might have been a wasted opportunity on his first run of the season, but he weakened too early to suggest that he was at his peak this time round. (op 7-2)
Gansey(IRE) was still up there when falling at the first in the home straight, although he was coming to the end of his tether at the time. He might need to come down a bit in the ratings but should make the transition to handicaps. (op 7-2)

2401 1STSECURITYSOLUTIONS.CO.UK NOVICES' H'CAP CHASE (17 fncs) 3m 1f
2:45 (2:45) (Class 3) (0-130,128) 4-Y-0+ **£6,505** (£1,910; £955; £477)

Form RPR
0-U1 **1** **Quinder Spring (FR)**36 1781 6-10-0 **102** oh1 PeterBuchanan 114+
(Lucinda Russell) *trckd ldrs: t.k.h: hit 7th: led after 4 out: styd on wl between last 2: drvn out* **9/4**2
5-36 **2** *5* **Ballabrook (IRE)**18 2034 8-9-9 **104** MrJHamer(7) 109
(Donald McCain) *t.k.h: trckd ldrs: reminders 12th: disp 2nd 3 out: styd on same pce appr last* **11/2**
320- **3** *9* **Pennek (FR)**242 4670 7-11-6 **122** JamesReveley 121+
(Philip Kirby) *led: qcknd 10th: hdd after 4 out: outpcd appr next: 5 l 4th whn hmpd last* **4/1**3
11P- **4** *17* **Herald Angel (FR)**223 5039 7-10-1 **110** (t) CDTimmons(7) 93
(Barry Brennan) *w ldrs: upsides 11th: lost pl appr 3 out: sn bhd* **12/1**
-111 **F** **Neptune Equester**16 2077 7-11-9 **128** FearghalDavis(3) 134+
(Brian Ellison) *nt fluent and j.rt-handed in rr: hdwy to chse ldrs12th: drvn 4 out: disputing 3 l 2nd whn fell last* **15/8**1

6m 44.0s (12.70) **Going Correction** +0.35s/f (Yiel) **5** Ran SP% **108.6**
Speed ratings (Par 107): **93,91,88,83,—**
CSF £13.57 TOTE £2.90: £3.20, £2.50; EX 12.10.
Owner Peter J S Russell **Bred** Pascal Sachot Et Al **Trained** Arlary, Perth & Kinross

FOCUS
A competitive novice handicap that should throw up some future winners. Quinder Spring is on the upgrade and the second ran to form. The faller was heading for a figure close to his best.

NOTEBOOK
Quinder Spring(FR) jumped ponderously at a couple of early fences, but got into his stride and responded to pressure to maintain his advantage from the home turn. He was only a moderate hurdler but showed much more promise when winning six point-to-points in the spring, and converted that ability into a first chasing success at Hexham last month. Putting his light weight to full use, there is still some leeway for this fast-improving chaser, handicapper permitting. (tchd 5-2)
Ballabrook(IRE) took a while to get into a rhythm but could never really pose a threat to the winner. He is consistent and again ran up to form but looks a bit limited in stronger contests. (op 6-1 tchd 15-2)
Pennek(FR) jumped at full stretch over several fences but in the main jumped well at the head of affairs, but after fighting off the attentions of Herald Angel in the back straight he could find no extra and set the race up for the closers. He went well on plenty of occasions without managing to convert that to a win when with Alan King, so still has something to prove for his new stable if he is to make anything of a handy-looking mark. (op 6-1 tchd 7-2)
Herald Angel(FR) moved up to challenge in the back straight but was beaten off by the home turn. He won twice on soft ground on his return from a lengthy layoff last season so unless he improves for this run he might not be able to recapture that peak. (tchd 16-1)
Neptune Equester has won three times on fast ground at Wetherby since May but took a long time to get to grips with the softer ground here. His jumping was never that fluent but he still moved up to get on terms with the winner in the home straight, but clipped the last when jumping at speed and came down. He will be of interest again on faster ground if dropping down a few pounds. (op 6-4 tchd 11-8)

2402 HOST YOUR WORK CHRISTMAS PARTY HERE H'CAP CHASE (19 fncs) 3m 5f
3:20 (3:20) (Class 5) (0-95,93) 4-Y-0+ **£2,602** (£764; £382; £190)

Form RPR
P021 **1** **Chico Time (IRE)**11 2155 9-11-5 **93** (p) StephenO'Donovan(7) 102
(Jonathan Geake) *in rr: effrt 13th: chsd ldr 5 out: 4 l down last: styd on to ld last 150yds: drvn out* **7/2**1
6351 **2** *2* **Rudinero (IRE)**85 1331 8-10-11 **83** (t) MichaelMurphy(5) 90
(Barry Brennan) *chsd ldr: led 14th: hdd and no ex run-in* **4/1**2
4-01 **3** *1 1/2* **Matmata De Tendron (FR)**9 2193 10-11-4 **92** (p) NathanMoscrop(7) 98
(Andrew Crook) *chsd ldrs: wnt 2nd 14th: outpcd appr 3 out: 7 l 3rd last: kpt on* **4/1**2
45P3 **4** *2 1/4* **Sycho Fred (IRE)**16 2079 9-10-9 **76** (t) GrahamLee 79
(Mike Sowersby) *hld up in rr: hdwy 5 out: drvn and wl outpcd next: wnt modest 4th 3 out: 3 l down in 4th last: kpt on* **9/2**3
-0P0 **5** *34* **Kercabellec (FR)**7 2250 12-9-8 **68** JoeCornwall(7) 51
(John Cornwall) *led: clr 6th: hdd 14th: wknd 4 out: bhd whn mstke next: sn t.o* **11/1**
4-P4 **P** **Fourpointone**11 2155 9-11-2 **83** (p) RhysFlint —
(Michael Scudamore) *chsd ldrs: pckd 2nd: lost pl 14th: sn bhd: t.o whn p.u bef 2 out* **4/1**2

7m 59.5s (479.50) **6** Ran SP% **108.7**
Tote Swingers: 1&2 £2.10, 1&3 £2.30, 2&3 £3.40 CSF £16.68 TOTE £3.50: £1.90, £1.70; EX 14.80.
Owner Antell & Twomey **Bred** Maurice Barry **Trained** Marlborough, Wilts

FOCUS
A reasonable contest for the grade with three last-time-out winners filling the first three places. The three are rated to their marks.

NOTEBOOK
Chico Time(IRE) gradually wore down the leader and dug deep against the rail to overhaul a four-length deficit from the last in a gruelling finish. She continued the resurgence for her new stable to notch up her second win in a fortnight and jumped much straighter on this right-handed track. Despite the 8lb rise there is still some room for manoeuvre before she reaches her hurdling mark so there could be another win in her. (tchd 10-3)
Rudinero(IRE) was the first to make his move on the final circuit and still held the advantage coming to the last, but just got tired on the flat. Both his wins have come in the summer months, but he showed he could cope with softer ground, which increases his options, and should be up to winning again. (op 10-3)
Matmata De Tendron(FR) won a slow-motion contest in heavy ground at Hexham last week and kept going at his own pace. He is consistent and game but is a bit slow. (op 9-2 tchd 7-2)
Sycho Fred(IRE) was a bit ponderous in rear and was never able to get competitive. (op 13-2)
Kercabellec(FR) opened up a clear lead but was too keen and was never likely to sustain it. (op 10-1 tchd 9-1)
Fourpointone was soon struggling once the race began to develop on the final circuit and this was a disappointing effort. (op 9-2)

2403 WATCH RACING UK IN YOUR PUB 0870 351 8834 STANDARD OPEN NATIONAL HUNT FLAT RACE 2m 1f
3:50 (3:51) (Class 6) 4-6-Y-O **£1,370** (£399; £199)

Form RPR
4 **1** **Jukebox Melody (IRE)**182 355 4-11-2 0 GrahamLee 105
(Malcolm Jefferson) *t.k.h in midfield: effrt over 5f out: chsng ldrs over 3f out: wnt 2nd 2f out: edgd lft and styd on strly to ld last 50yds* **17/2**
1- **2** *1 1/2* **Our Mick**204 5391 4-11-6 0 JohnKington(3) 110
(Donald McCain) *led: rdn 4 l clr over 2f out: hdd towards fin* **7/2**3
- **3** *5* **Victor Lynch (IRE)** 4-11-2 0 RichieMcGrath 98
(Kate Walton) *chsd ldrs: pushed along 7f out: outpcd over 2f out: rallied to take 3rd last 150yds* **16/1**
4 *2 1/2* **Brunswick Gold (IRE)**199 74 5-11-2 0 RhysFlint 96
(Steve Gollings) *trckd ldr: effrt over 3f out: wknd 2f out* **85/40**1
1- **5** *12* **Rocks Rule (IRE)**250 4508 5-11-9 0 BrianHughes 91
(Alan Swinbank) *trckd ldrs: drvn over 3f out: wknd over 2f out* **5/2**2
01- **6** *7* **Comeragh King**234 4839 6-11-2 0 AlexanderVoy(7) 84
(Tim Fitzgerald) *hld up in rr: drvn over 5f out: wknd 3f out* **10/1**
7 *38* **Don't Call Harry** 5-11-2 0 RobertWalford 39
(Tim Walford) *hld up in rr: drvn 6f out: bhd fnl 4f: t.o* **40/1**
8 *2 1/4* **Remmyniss** 6-10-9 0 TomMessenger 29
(Derek Shaw) *t.k.h in rr: drvn and lost tch over 6f out: t.o 5f out* **80/1**
9 *nk* **Mill Run** 4-10-2 0 MrTGarner(7) 29
(Sean Regan) *mid-div: drvn 9f out: sn lost pl: t.o 6f out* **66/1**

10 *130* **Ash Holt** 4-11-2 0 .... TomSiddall —
(Charles Smith) *in rr: drvn after 4f: sn wl bhd: t.o 9f out: eventually completed* **100/1**

4m 18.3s (17.20) **Going Correction** +0.625s/f (Soft)
WFA 4 from 5yo+ 7lb **10** Ran SP% **114.4**
Speed ratings: **84,83,80,79,74 70,52,51,51,—**
Tote Swingers: 1&2 £5.70, 1&3 £6.10, 2&3 £6.30 CSF £37.51 TOTE £8.60: £1.80, £2.20, £3.50; EX 27.90.
Owner Richard Collins **Bred** Finbar Leahy **Trained** Norton, N Yorks

FOCUS
This was a fair bumper with three previous winners and a former point winner in the line-up. The form is rated around the second and fourth and the fifth was over a stone off.

NOTEBOOK
Jukebox Melody(IRE) was on his toes in the paddock, carried his head high, looked an awkward ride and got outpaced on the home turn, but once he got into his stride he stayed on powerfully to cut down the leader as the post loomed. He was wayward on the turn in his previous bumper at this track but looks green and keyed up rather than unruly. As he gains experience he should be quite useful when able to utilise his stamina. (op 8-1)
Our Mick dictated the pace and got first run on the field, but he was eventually run out of it near the line. This was a solid performance from the C&D winner who made a valiant effort to defy his winner's penalty. (op 9-4 tchd 4-1)
Victor Lynch(IRE) needed to be kept interested down the back and he got a bit tapped for toe racing on the inside rail, but he stayed on as well as the winner in the closing stages, albeit having already forfeited too much ground. (op 22-1)
Brunswick Gold(IRE), who had previously finished second in a bumper at Tipperary before changing hands for £75,000, was well backed to give his trainer a treble at the meeting. He tracked the leader but could only stay on at one pace once the tempo lifted. He has already won a point and might not be seen to best effect until tackling fences once more. (op 7-2)
Rocks Rule(IRE), representing the stable that won this last year, was with the leading bunch when going a bit wide round the home turn, but he faded rather tamely from there on his first run since making a winning debut in March. (op 9-4 tchd 2-1)
T/Plt: £178.20 to a £1 stake. Pool:£41,512.54 - 169.98 winning tickets T/Qpdt: £96.30 to a £1 stake. Pool:£2,696.16 - 20.70 winning tickets WG

2404 - 2411a (Foreign Racing) - See Raceform Interactive

2376 PUNCHESTOWN (R-H)
Sunday, November 14

OFFICIAL GOING: Soft to heavy (heavy in places)

2412a CRADDOCKSTOWN NOVICE CHASE (GRADE 2) (11 fncs) 2m
1:05 (1:05) 4-Y-0+ **£23,008** (£6,725; £3,185; £1,061)

RPR
1 **Realt Dubh (IRE)**[21] 2008 6-11-4 .... DJCondon 144+
(Noel Meade, Ire) *trckd ldrs in 4th: j.w: prog 4 out: led fr 3 out: rdn and styd on wl fr after 2 out: comf* **4/7**[1]
2 *6* **Gates Of Rome (IRE)**[18] 2042 6-11-4 .... DNRussell 138
(C A Murphy, Ire) *trckd ldrs in 3rd: 4th 4 out: impr into 2nd after 3 out: rdn and no imp fr next: kpt on u.p* **6/1**[3]
3 *11* **Jigalo (IRE)**[9] 2200 9-11-4 125 .... (p) AndrewJMcNamara 127
(Ms Joanna Morgan, Ire) *hld up in rr: mod 4th 3 out: no imp fr bef next: one pce* **8/1**
4 *4* **Save My Blushes**[7] 2260 4-10-9 .... (t) RMPower 114
(Paul W Flynn, Ire) *led: j.lft 2nd and 3rd: hdd bef 4th: regained ld 6th: hit 4 out and hdd: cl up u.p whn blnd 3 out: no ex* **12/1**
5 *10* **Darceys Dancer (IRE)**[31] 1849 7-11-4 .... (b) PWFlood 113
(Noel Meade, Ire) *cl up: led bef 4th: hdd 6th: led again 4 out: hdd 3 out: sn rdn and wknd* **11/2**[2]

4m 20.7s (6.80) **Going Correction** +0.80s/f (Soft)
WFA 4 from 6yo+ 7lb **5** Ran SP% **112.1**
Speed ratings: **115,112,106,104,99**
CSF £4.83 TOTE £1.60: £1.20, £2.50; DF 5.50.
Owner D J Sharkey **Bred** R Hartigan **Trained** Castletown, Co Meath

FOCUS
A small field for this Grade 2. The first two came clear and both are rated close to their hurdles bests.

NOTEBOOK
Realt Dubh(IRE) ◆ headed the market and he ran out a decisive winner to make it 2-3 over fences having fallen at Galway after his chasing debut win over 2m4f at Navan. He jumped well and was always close up before going to the front approaching three out. He ran about a bit after taking up the running, but asserted in good style from the final fence. He is heading for the Grade 1 Drinmore Novice Chase at Fairyhouse on November 28 where reverting to 2m4f should suit. (op 4/6)
Gates Of Rome(IRE), a winning pointer and twice successful over hurdles, had been unplaced behind Thegreatjohnbrowne on his chasing debut over 2m4f here last month. Down in trip here, he produced a better effort and put it up to the winner after going second away from three out. Racing well apart from the winner, he had every chance two out but was unable to make much impression from before the final fence. (op 8/1)
Jigalo(IRE), a four-time winner over hurdles, has plenty of expereince over fences and won a handicap over a slightly longer trip at Gowran Park last month. Rated 125, he was held up in rear but could make no impression after going third between the last two fences.
Save My Blushes, winner of a Grade 3 event over this trip at Roscommon in September on his second start over fences, led and disputed until approaching three out. He had been headed when he blundered at that fence and was quickly done with. (op 10/1 tchd 14/1)
Darceys Dancer(IRE), once successful from four previous attempts over fences, had run second to Loosen My Load over 2m2f here last month. He raced in second place and disputed the lead for much of the way before weakening three out. (op 9/2)

2413a FLORIDA PEARL NOVICE CHASE (GRADE 3) (15 fncs) 2m 6f
1:40 (1:40) 5-Y-0+ **£16,393** (£4,792; £2,269; £756)

RPR
1 **Thegreatjohnbrowne (IRE)**[18] 2042 6-11-0 .... DJCondon 148+
(Noel Meade, Ire) *mde all: j.w: drew clr 3 out: styd on wl: v easily* **11/8**[1]
2 *7* **Tharawaat (IRE)**[399] 1723 5-10-13 .... (t) RMPower 136+
(Gordon Elliott, Ire) *mostly 4th: nt fluent 8th: slt mstke 5 out: prog after 3 out: mod 2nd into st: no imp whn blnd 2 out: kpt on same pce* **12/1**
3 *dist* **Sam Adams (IRE)**[14] 2119 7-11-0 134 .... (t) DNRussell —
(Paul Nolan, Ire) *trckd ldr in 2nd: rdn and outpcd 3 out: 4th and no ex 2 out: lft remote 3rd fr last: t.o* **4/1**[3]
4 *dist* **Healys Bar (IRE)**[18] 2041 6-11-0 .... RCColgan —
(Oliver McKiernan, Ire) *veered lft s and v.s.a: in tch in rr fr 2nd: rdn and wknd fr 5 out: mstke 3 out: completely t.o* **10/3**[2]
U **Erritt Lake (IRE)**[24] 1942 7-11-0 .... PWFlood 117
(D T Hughes, Ire) *trckd ldrs: mostly 3rd: rdn and outpcd 3 out: no imp fr next: blnd and uns rdr last* **5/1**

5m 59.6s (17.60) **Going Correction** +0.80s/f (Soft) **5** Ran SP% **109.5**
Speed ratings: **100,97,—,—,—**
CSF £15.02 TOTE £2.00: £1.40, £2.20; DF 19.80.
Owner Martin Doran **Bred** Noel Guiry **Trained** Castletown, Co Meath

FOCUS
The easy winner has more to offer and the runner-up ran to his hurdles mark.

NOTEBOOK
Thegreatjohnbrowne(IRE) ◆ created a big impression when making all and jumping superbly on his chasing debut over 2m4f here last month and he produced a similar performance on this occasion to win this Grade 3 event impressively. He again gave an exhibition of jumping and, after kicking clear of his pursuers approaching three out, he won very much as he liked. He will facer stiffer tests in future but, on what he has shown so far, he is an exciting prospect for the better staying novice chases. Trainer Noel Meade said of the winner: "He's been brilliant since the first day he schooled over fences. He was good here the last time and he was very good today. He'll probably go for the Grade 1 Drinmore Novice Chase at Fairyhouse in two weeks' time and if, for any reason, he doesn't go there, then we'll look at the Grade 1 3m novice at Leopardstown's Christmas meeting." (op 11/8 tchd 6/4)
Tharawaat(IRE), twice a winner over hurdles as a juvenile two seasons back, was making his chasing debut on his first appearance since October 2009. He was driven up between horses to go second on the bend after three out, but made a very bad mistake at the second last, which he was lucky to survive. He could make no impression on the winner who was given an easy time of it in the closing stages. (op 10/1)
Sam Adams(IRE), a dual winner over hurdles, had been placed once from four previous attempts over fences and after racing in second place throughout, he was unable to raise his game when the winner stretched clear before three out and was soon struggling. (op 5/1)
Healys Bar(IRE) lost a lot of ground at the start before closing to track his rivals before the third fence. He was a spent force after five out and was out of contention when making a mistake three out. Official explanation: jockey said gelding ducked left at the start and lost considerable ground (op 5/2)
Erritt Lake(IRE), winner of a 2m2f novice event at Thurles last month, raced close up but could make no impression from three out and was quite a remote third when he blundered badly and ditched his rider at the final fence. (op 5/1 tchd 11/2)

2414a DOBBINS & MADIGANS AT PUNCHESTOWN HURDLE (GRADE 1) (9 hdls) 2m
2:15 (2:17) 4-Y-0+ **£48,893** (£14,292; £6,769; £2,256)

RPR
1 **Solwhit (FR)**[205] 5380 6-11-10 165 .... DNRussell 161+
(C Byrnes, Ire) *cl up in 2nd: chal after 2 out: led early st: rdn clr last: kpt on wl: comf* **11/10**[1]
2 *2 ½* **Voler La Vedette (IRE)**[32] 1835 6-11-5 149 .... PTownend 153+
(C A Murphy, Ire) *in tch in rr: cl up whn pushed along 3 out: 3rd after 2 out: 2nd and styd on after last wout threatening wnr* **5/2**[2]
3 *1 ½* **Donnas Palm (IRE)**[20] 1711 6-11-10 155 .... DJCondon 157
(Noel Meade, Ire) *led: rdn and strly pressed fr 2 out: hdd early st: 3rd and no ex after last* **3/1**[3]
4 *23* **Sublimity (FR)**[294] 3638 10-11-10 158 .... (t) AndrewJMcNamara 138
(Robert Alan Hennessy, Ire) *cl up in 3rd: rdn and dropped to rr after 2 out: no ex early st: eased fr last* **10/1**

4m 4.40s (-5.60) **Going Correction** +0.075s/f (Yiel) **4** Ran SP% **110.3**
Speed ratings: **117,115,115,103**
CSF £4.33 TOTE £1.90; DF 4.80.
Owner Top Of The Hill Syndicate **Bred** Haras De Preaux **Trained** Ballingarry, Co Limerick

FOCUS
Only the four runners but for this time of year a good-quality Grade 1 that went the way most expected it would. The time was nearly six seconds faster than last year (when the going was heavy), but it was by not a strongly run race. Solwhit did not need to be at his best.

NOTEBOOK
Solwhit(FR) is extremely hard to beat and he did the job in a typically professional style. Though his trainer said he would be better for the race, he does not take much work to get fit and the chances are he was more than forward enough for his seasonal bow. Davy Russell was keen not to be far off the speed and the race went to plan. He took it up on the turn in, having jumped well, and was in control thereafter. He goes next to the Hatton's Grace, when the trip of 2m4f will hold no fears at all, but it is unlikely that he will be good enough to win a Cheltenham Champion Hurdle on the likely ground. He should be very hard to beat in the Hatton's Grace. (op 5/4 tchd 11/8)
Voler La Vedette(IRE)'s run was always going to tell us more about where she stands relative to the top hurdlers and it has to be said she came up short. She had a run under her belt but was outclassed by Solwhit. Against that, she ran on well to beat two decent horses and very few would have lived with the winner on the day. She would have little chance of reversing the form in the Hatton's Grace, and will probably fall a bit short when pitched against the males, but she is a very classy sort all the same.
Donnas Palm(IRE) is not a top-class hurdler and he had the run of the race. Davy Condon slowed it down after the second before gradually winding it up. He was left behind from the turn-in but was in no way disgraced and would probably be better over a shade further. (op 11/4)
Sublimity(FR), who has had a wind operation, ran no sort of race. He will be worth another chance but will find it hard to win at this level, even on his favoured better ground, as he gets on in years.

2415 - 2418a (Foreign Racing) - See Raceform Interactive

LEICESTER (R-H)
Monday, November 15

OFFICIAL GOING: Hurdle course - soft; chase course - good (good to firm in places and soft on the flat crossings; hurdle 6.5; chase 8.1)
Wind: nil Weather: bright and sunny, chilly

2419 BURTON OVERY NOVICES' HURDLE (8 hdls) 2m
12:50 (12:50) (Class 4) 4-Y-0+ **£3,252** (£955; £477; £238)

Form RPR
6P/ 1 **Alarazi (IRE)**[464] 4402 6-10-12 0 .... DominicElsworth 104+
(Lucy Wadham) *plld hrd: hld up in rr: j.rt 1st: hdwy to trck ldng pair 5th: wnt 2nd bef next: led gng wl jst bef 2 out: nt fluent last: rdn and kpt on wl flat* **7/2**[3]
040- 2 *1 ½* **Call It On (IRE)**[187] 5243 4-10-12 108 .... JamesReveley 100
(Philip Kirby) *chsd ldr tl bef 3 out: styd chsng ldrs: rdn 2 out: chsd wnr last: kpt on u.p flat but a hld* **4/1**
05 3 *4 ½* **Silver Roque (FR)**[13] 2137 4-10-12 0 .... HaddenFrost 96
(Henrietta Knight) *t.k.h: hld up in tch: clsd to chse ldrs 5th: rdn and hanging rt bef 2 out: styd on same pce between last 2* **11/4**[2]
-160 4 *hd* **My Brother Sylvest**[30] 1862 4-11-5 124 .... RhysFlint 103
(David Brace) *led: rdn and hdd jst bef 2 out: 3rd and btn whn mstke last: wknd flat* **9/4**[1]

00 **5** *16* **The Snatcher (IRE)**[14] 2122 7-10-12 0................................ SeanQuinlan 82+
(Richard Phillips) *hld up in tch in midfield: clsd and chsd ldrs after 5th: wknd jst bef 2 out* **50/1**

0-0 **6** *4* **Frankie Falco**[15] 2111 4-10-12 0.. JodieMogford 75
(Giuseppe Fierro) *hld up in rr: j.rt 1st: hdwy 5th: j.rt next: sn wknd* **150/1**

50 **7** *7* **Vico Road (IRE)**[11] 2162 5-10-12 0....................................... NoelFehily 68
(Jonjo O'Neill) *t.k.h: hld up in midfield: lost pl and dropped towards rr 5th: wknd next* **25/1**

0-0 **8** *3/4* **Deputy Dog (IRE)**[33] 1824 4-10-9 0........................... RichieMcLernon(3) 68
(Jonjo O'Neill) *nt fluent: hld up in last trio: struggling after 5th: wknd next* **16/1**

0 **9** *28* **Action Hawk (GER)**[33] 1819 6-10-12 0......................... AndrewThornton 40
(Ben Pollock) *chsd ldrs: mstke 5th: sn pushed along and struggling: bhd next: t.o fr 2 out* **100/1**

3m 53.1s (-7.90) **Going Correction** -0.475s/f (Good) **9** Ran SP% **113.0**
Speed ratings (Par 105): **100,99,97,96,88 86,83,83,69**
toteswingers:1&2:£3.90, 1&3:£1.70, 2&3:£3.40 CSF £17.49 TOTE £2.50: £1.10, £1.60, £1.50; EX 22.90.
Owner Johnny Eddis **Bred** His Highness The Aga Khan's Studs S C **Trained** Newmarket, Suffolk

FOCUS
Not a race that took much winning. Alarazi should be capable of a lot better but the form is rated around the second and third.

NOTEBOOK
Alarazi(IRE) proved good enough on this first start in 464 days. He hadn't run over jumps since pulling up in the Supreme Novices' in 2009, only his second start over hurdles, and despite refusing to settle, he saw it out well. There should be significant improvement to come with this run out the way, and he may well be good enough to defy a penalty before going handicapping. (op 7-4)
Call It On(IRE) stepped up on what he showed last season and will be of interest sent handicapping off this sort of mark. (op 11-2)
Silver Roque(FR) stayed on well after the last to grab third. He had finished behind smart types on both previous starts over hurdles and, for all that his future lies over fences, there are races to be won as a hurdler first, with a longer trip/switch to handicaps likely to help. (op 7-2)
My Brother Sylvest, the only penalised runner, having won on fast ground at Stratford in September, has run poorly in two starts since, admittedly behind smart sorts, and this was more like his true form. He wasn't good enough, but the ground was as soft as he would want. (op 4-1)
The Snatcher(IRE) should do better once sent handicapping.
Vico Road(IRE) will be of more interest sent handicapping. (op 20-1 tchd 16-1)

2420 JOHN MCKINNON (BIG RED) MEMORIAL H'CAP CHASE (18 fncs) 2m 7f 110y
1:20 (1:20) (Class 4) (0-105,105) 4-Y-O+ **£3,903** (£1,146; £573; £286)

Form RPR
1-P6 **1** **Backfromthecongo (IRE)**[39] 1747 0 11 0 **102**........(bt) RichardJohnson 100
(Richard Lee) *prom: led 6th: mde most after: kpt on wl fr 2 out: drvn out* **13/2**

3-05 **2** *2 1/2* **Arnold Layne (IRE)**[22] 1992 11-11-9 **102**..................... AndrewThornton 107
(Caroline Bailey) *chsd ldr tl led 2nd: hdd 5th: styd prom and w wnr fr 8th: rdn bef 2 out: swtchd lft between last 2: lost 2nd and mstke last: chsd wnr again fnl 150yds: styd on same pce* **9/2[2]**

5P5 **3** *nk* **Hever Road (IRE)**[12] 2155 11-9-11 **83**............................ JoeCornwall(7) 88
(David Pearson) *in tch in rr: hmpd and rdr unbalanced 2nd: bdly bmpd next: outpcd 8th: hdwy 13th: chsd ldrs and rdn bef 15th: chsd wnr last: styd on same pce and lost 2nd fnl 150yds* **11/2[3]**

-366 **4** *42* **Shrewd Investor (IRE)**[17] 2079 10-11-9 **102**...............(p) RobertWalford 69
(Henry Hogarth) *chsd ldrs: led 5th tl 6th: chsd ldrs after: rdn 13th: stl cl up whn slipped bnd after 14th: mstke and wknd next: t.o between last 2* **7/1**

/320 **5** *51* **Gothic Charm (IRE)**[143] 840 8-11-4 **104**........................... MrJMahot(7) 13
(Rachel Hobbs) *chsd ldrs: mstke 9th and reminders: rdn 13th: stl in tch but struggling whn slipped bnd after 14th: sn wl bhd: t.o fr 3 out* **8/1**

B0-3 **P** **Captain Smoothy**[22] 1992 10-10-7 **93**........................ AnthonyFreeman(7) —
(Sean Curran) *in tch: in last pair: stmbld bnd after 4th: reminders after next: outpcd 8th: lost tch 13th: p.u after next* **85/40[1]**

3156 **P** **Petroupetrov (FR)**[14] 2127 7-11-12 **105**............................... TomSiddall —
(Richard Phillips) *led: j. bdly rt and hdd 2nd: j. bdly rt again next: sn eased and p.u* **12/1**

5m 50.5s (-13.50) **Going Correction** -0.625s/f (Firm) course record **7** Ran SP% **110.2**
Speed ratings (Par 105): **97,96,96,82,65 —,—**
toteswingers:1&2:£6.90, 1&3:£3.40, 2&3:£5.80 CSF £33.16 TOTE £3.00: £1.60, £2.10; EX 29.40.
Owner D Cound, J Jackson & A Compton **Bred** Stan Doyle **Trained** Byton, H'fords

FOCUS
As is often the case here, the ground on the chase course was significantly faster than on the hurdles track, being good, good to firm in places. This was just a modest handicap chase. The winner stepped up on his previous form.

NOTEBOOK
Backfromthecongo(IRE), still 5lb above his last winning mark, had been freshened up by a short break and, ridden positively, he stayed on strongly from the last, always looking the winner. This was the highest mark he has ever won off, so it remains to be seen whether he's able to follow up after a rise. (op 7-1 tchd 6-1)
Arnold Layne(IRE) is very well handicapped on old form, and this was easily his best effort in a couple of years. He already looked held when less than fluent at the last, but something similar should come his way if he can build on it. (op 7-2 tchd 5-1)
Hever Road(IRE) is another who's on a decent mark and, although run out of second late on, he was interfered with badly early in the race. He too can pick up a small race. (op 8-1)
Shrewd Investor(IRE) was going okay until he slipped, and having made a mistake soon after, he was quickly beaten. (op 13-2 tchd 6-1)
Gothic Charm(IRE) was another who slipped. (tchd 15-2 and 10-1)
Captain Smoothy was never going after stumbling on the bend, soon receiving remainders and pulling up, with something possibly amiss. Official explanation: jockey said gelding never travelled (op 5-2 tchd 2-1)

2421 EASTWELL (S) HURDLE (8 hdls) 2m
1:50 (1:50) (Class 5) 3-5-Y-O **£1,951** (£573; £286; £143)

Form RPR
306 **1** **Big Talk**[12] 2151 3-10-6 104...................................(v1) RodiGreene 84+
(David Bridgwater) *in tch: j.rt 1st: hdwy to chse ldrs 5th: pressed ldr bef 3 out: led gng wl bef 2 out: clr 2 out: drvn between last 2: kpt on and in command whn hit rail after last: drvn out* **9/2[3]**

0 **2** *5* **Primera Rossa**[26] 1921 4-11-1 0.. WillKennedy 88
(J S Moore) *hld up in tch: hdwy 4th: chsd ldrs and rdn 5th: chsd wnr 2 out: styd on same pce and no imp after* **22/1**

3-35 **3** *nse* **Helieorbea**[50] 1624 4-11-12 103... RichieMcGrath 99
(Tim Easterby) *chsd ldrs: rdn and outpcd bef 3 out: 6th and wl hld whn j.rt 2 out: rallied between last 2: j.rt last: styd on wl u.p flat: no ch w wnr* **9/4[2]**

P303 **4** *1 3/4* **Nicky Nutjob (GER)**[4] 2323 4-11-5 91..........................(p) CharlieWallis(7) 97
(John O'Shea) *taken down early: hld up in tch in rr: hdwy 5th: chsd ldrs next: sn rdn and outpcd bef 2 out: plugged on u.p flat: no ch w wnr* **25/1**

12-3 **5** *4 1/2* **Dr Valentine (FR)**[13] 210 4-11-12 104................................ PaddyAspell 95
(Ann Duffield) *led tl after 3 out: sn rdn and nt pce of wnr: blnd and lost 2nd 2 out: wknd last* **85/40[1]**

6 *23* **Good Buy Dubai (USA)**[11] 4-11-8 0.................................. JamesReveley 71
(Edward Creighton) *hld up in tch in rr: rdn and effrt after 5th: chsd ldrs next: wknd qckly bef 2 out: wl btn bef last* **66/1**

6 **7** *36* **Mill Beattie**[11] 2162 5-11-1 0.. DaveCrosse 23
(John Mackie) *w ldr tl bef 3 out: wknd rapidly 3 out: t.o fr 2 out* **14/1**

P **Apurna**[95] 5-10-8 0.. MattCrawley(7) —
(John Harris) *in tch towards rr: hmpd and mstke 2nd: nt travelling wl after: pushed along and struggling 4th: lost tch next: t.o whn p.u 3 out:* **50/1**

020 **P** **Royal Torbo (ISR)**[18] 2047 3-10-6 92..........................(p) AndrewTinkler —
(George Baker) *in tch: pushed along 4th: dropped towards rr and mstke next: sn lost tch: t.o whn p.u 3 out* **7/1**

3m 55.0s (-6.00) **Going Correction** -0.475s/f (Good)
WFA 3 from 4yo+ 15lb **9** Ran SP% **111.8**
Speed ratings (Par 103): **96,93,93,92,90 78,60,—,—**
toteswingers:1&2:£19.60, 1&3:£2.90, 2&3:£13.20 CSF £84.52 TOTE £4.50: £1.90, £4.30, £1.40; EX 128.70.There was no bid for the winner.
Owner Deauville Daze Partnership **Bred** Miss K Rausing **Trained** Icomb, Gloucs

FOCUS
Not the most competitive selling hurdle, and ordinary form for the grade rated around the second and third.

NOTEBOOK
Big Talk, down in grade and fitted with a first-time visor, made good headway to challenge, travelling strongly, and he readily asserted to win with a fair bit in hand, despite knocking into the rail after the last. He looks capable of winning again. (op 15-2 tchd 8-1)
Primera Rossa stepped up on her initial effort, clearly appreciating the drop in grade. (op 20-1 tchd 25-1)
Helieorbea stayed on again to take third, but never looked like winning. (tchd 2-1)
Nicky Nutjob(GER), a well-beaten third at Ludlow four days earlier, ran better but continues to fall short. (op 16-1)
Dr Valentine(FR), already a winner at this level in similar conditions, had a recent spin on the Flat and was expected to take the beating, but he was readily brushed aside and a mistake two out ended any chance he had of rallying. (op 15-8)

2422 JOHN O'GAUNT NOVICES' CHASE (12 fncs) 2m
2:20 (2:20) (Class 3) 4-Y-O+ **£4,816** (£1,422; £711; £355; £177)

Form RPR
1 01 **1** **William's Wishes (IRE)**[25] 1036 5-11-7 136....................... PaulMoloney 138+
(Evan Williams) *t.k.h: hld up in 3rd: wnt 2nd 9th: upsides ldr 2 out: rdn to ld last: asserted flat and in command fnl 150yds: eased towards fin* **2/9[1]**

-352 **2** *11* **Sonning Star (IRE)**[29] 1883 6-11-1 121........................... LiamTreadwell 120+
(Nick Gifford) *chsd clr ldr: led bef 9th: hit next: rdn and jnd next: hdd last: outpcd after last: eased whn btn fnl 100yds* **13/2[2]**

-145 **3** *19* **Quell The Storm (FR)**[16] 2088 6-11-7 0............................(t) DaveCrosse 103
(Milton Harris) *led: sn clr: hdd and pushed along bef 9th: wknd bef 3 out* **28/1**

1P53 **4** *5* **Marc Aurele (IRE)**[9] 2210 5-11-1 0................................(t) WarrenMarston 92
(Milton Harris) *a in last pair: rdn after 8th: lost tch next* **14/1[3]**

-P06 **5** *24* **Muntami (IRE)**[8] 2247 9-10-8 0.. MattCrawley(7) 68
(John Harris) *a in rr: pushed along 6th: lost tch after 8th: t.o* **100/1**

3m 54.5s (-13.70) **Going Correction** -0.625s/f (Firm) course record **5** Ran SP% **106.3**
Speed ratings (Par 107): **109,103,94,91,79**
CSF £2.10 TOTE £1.10: £1.02, £2.10; EX 2.20.
Owner Mrs D E Cheshire **Bred** Mrs M O'Driscoll **Trained** Llancarfan, Vale Of Glamorgan

FOCUS
An easy win in the end for William's Wishes, who is a smart novice. There is a cae for rating the race a few pounds higher.

NOTEBOOK
William's Wishes(IRE) did take time to assert, although ultimately won with ease. An impressive winner at Ludlow on his recent chase debut, he again saw his race out strongly and can be expected to improve as he goes up to 2m4f. He's likely to be placed to pick up another minor event before going up in grade. (op 2-7)
Sonning Star(IRE), runner-up on his chasing debut at Kempton (winner since beaten under a penalty), tried to get the favourite at it, but in the end proved no match. (op 11-2)
Quell The Storm(FR) hasn't gone on from August's Newton Abbot victory (trained by Paul Nicholls), and he was never going to last home having gone into a clear early lead. (op 18-1)
Marc Aurele(IRE) liked to make the running for Paul Nicholls, and he never looked happy under restraint. (op 12-1 tchd 11-1)

2423 WEATHERBYS PRINTING H'CAP HURDLE (8 hdls) 2m
2:50 (2:50) (Class 3) (0-125,123) 4-Y-O+ **£4,553** (£1,337; £668; £333)

Form RPR
60P- **1** **Spear Thistle**[20] 5009 8-11-12 **123**.......................................(p) NoelFehily 129+
(Charlie Mann) *mde all: dived 5th: rdn and clr 2 out: styd on wl* **9/1**

03-3 **2** *3 3/4* **Numide (FR)**[15] 96 7-11-10 **121**................................... TomScudamore 124+
(Rod Millman) *t.k.h: hld up in tch in rr: taken wd in bk st: hdwy to trck ldrs after 5th: chsd wnr after 3 out: rdn next: hung rt and no imp whn mstke last* **5/1**

FU35 **3** *2 1/4* **Ajman (IRE)**[57] 1548 5-10-9 **106**...(t) PaulMoloney 105
(Evan Williams) *hld up in rr: stmbld 2nd: hdwy 3 out: rdn to chse ldng pair after 2 out: no imp after* **10/3[2]**

-U54 **4** *2 1/2* **Calatagan (IRE)**[17] 2076 11-10-13 **115**....................... JamesHalliday(5) 112
(Malcolm Jefferson) *chsd wnr tl after 5th: rdn: racd awkwardly and outpcd bef 2 out: plugged on same pce u.p between last 2* **13/2**

10-0 **5** *3 1/4* **Drussell (IRE)**[9] 2213 4-11-9 **120**... SeanQuinlan 113
(Richard Phillips) *hld up in tch in midfield: pushed along after 5th: hit next and sn outpcd: styd on at same pce and no threat to ldrs after* **25/1**

44-0 **6** *3* **Karky Schultz (GER)**[36] 80 5-11-9 **120**............................. FelixDeGiles 111
(James Eustace) *chsd ldrs: wnt 2nd 5th tl after 3 out: wknd next: btn and eased after last* **9/2[3]**

52-4 **7** *12* **Solis**[16] 2092 4-11-0 **111**.. DougieCostello 92
(John Quinn) *t.k.h: hld up in tch in midfield: rdn and hit 3 out: sn struggling and wl btn next: eased flat* **3/1[1]**

3m 50.4s (-10.60) **Going Correction** -0.475s/f (Good)
WFA 4 from 5yo+ 7lb **7** Ran SP% **110.1**
Speed ratings (Par 107): **107,105,104,102,101 99,93**
toteswingers:1&2:£3.80, 1&3:£14.30, 2&3:£4.40 CSF £48.86 TOTE £11.70: £6.00, £1.40; EX 25.50.
Owner Tony Hayward & Sue Head **Bred** Side Hill Stud **Trained** Upper Lambourn, Berks

FOCUS
A fair handicap hurdle and the first two are rated pretty much to their marks.

NOTEBOOK

Spear Thistle kept grinding away off the front and stayed on too strongly for his rivals. He had been struggling for form when last seen, but he found himself back on his last winning mark and clearly relished the conditions. He'll go back up in the weights now, though, so will be doing well to follow up. (op 15-2)

Numide(FR) came there travelling, but couldn't race on with the winner, having not found as much as had looked likely once coming under pressure. He did box on to hold second, though. (op 10-3 tchd 3-1)

Ajman(IRE), although not beaten far, was always being held and remains 7lb above his last winning mark. (op 13-2 tchd 3-1)

Calatagan(IRE) again ran creditably, but doesn't look up to winning off this mark. (op 11-2 tchd 7-1)

Drussell(IRE) was noted staying on in encouraging fashion and he's soon going to be of interest, having shown fair form when trained in Ireland last season. (op 18-1)

Karky Schultz(GER) was disappointing on this return to hurdles. (op 4-1)

Solis failed to improve for the switch to handicaps, a mistake three out sealing his fate. Official explanation: jockey said gelding never travelled (op 4-1 tchd 11-4)

2424 CASTLE CONDITIONAL JOCKEYS' H'CAP CHASE (15 fncs) 2m 4f 110y

3:20 (3:20) (Class 5) (0-95,90) 4-Y-O+ **£2,443** (£835)

Form — RPR

P00- **1** **Irish Guard**[203] 24 9-11-9 **90**.................................. AnthonyFreeman(3) 101+
(John O'Neill) *trckd ldr and a gng best: wnt upsides 10th: led 12th: clr and rdn whn j.lft 2 out: kpt on wl* **10/3**[3]

-506 **2** *9* **Donald Will Do (IRE)**[7] 2277 10-10-13 **80**........................ KyleJames(3) 83
(Caroline Bailey) *led: jnd 10th: rdn after next: hdd 12th: sn btn* **6/4**[2]

360- **F** **Here's The Key (FR)**[224] 5043 6-11-7 **90**..................(t) PeterCarberry(5) —
(Paul Webber) *j.rt and fell 1st* **11/8**[1]

5m 14.4s (-4.50) **Going Correction** -0.625s/f (Firm) **3** Ran SP% **105.2**
Speed ratings (Par 103): **83,79,**—
CSF £7.98 TOTE £3.60; EX 6.80.

Owner J G O'Neill **Bred** J G O'Neill **Trained** Stratton Audley, Oxon

FOCUS

With Here's The Key coming down at the first, it was left to just two. It is difficult to know what Irish Guard acheived but he was rated 110+ at his peak.

NOTEBOOK

Irish Guard, 21lb lower than when he started out in handicaps, was always travelling strongly and could be called the winner once going on before the straight. He's capable of going in again. (op 5-2 tchd 9-4)

Donald Will Do(IRE), whose only previous win came here back in February 2009, towed the winner along until readily being left behind in the straight. This still represented a step back in the right direction. (tchd 11-8 and 13-8)

2425 STONESBY MARES' NOVICES' H'CAP HURDLE (10 hdls) 2m 4f 110y

3:50 (3:50) (Class 4) (0-105,100) 3-Y-O+ **£2,602** (£764; £382; £190)

Form — RPR

0-34 **1** **Little Carmela**[166] 577 6-11-12 **100**................................ DougieCostello 103
(Neil King) *chsd ldrs: rdn bef 3 out: led wl bef 2 out: drvn and hdd last: battled on gamely u.p to ld again fnl 100yds: kpt on wl* **11/2**[3]

3-54 **2** *1 ¼* **Present Your Case (IRE)**[33] 1822 5-10-11 **85**..................(t) DarylJacob 87
(Ben Case) *t.k.h: hld up in tch: hdwy to trck ldrs 5th: jnd ldr on bit bef 2 out: led last: sn rdn and fnd little: hdd and outbattled fnl 100yds* **9/4**[2]

5P5P **3** *24* **Winter Holly**[33] 1822 4-10-13 **87**.. RobertWalford 65
(Tim Walford) *hld up in last pair: pushed along 6th: hdwy to chse ldrs next: struggling bef next: 6th and wl btn after 3 out: plugged on to go poor 3rd after last* **14/1**

00-P **4** *7* **Autumn Spirit**[39] 1737 6-10-8 **85**.............................. WayneKavanagh(3) 56
(Robin Dickin) *t.k.h: chsd ldr 2nd: jnd ldr next: rdn to ld after 3 out: sn hdd: wknd 2 out: lost poor 3rd after last* **20/1**

30-0 **5** *nse* **Jaunty Dove**[39] 1746 8-10-2 **83**.. MrJFlook(7) 54
(Andrew Price) *in tch: mstke 7th: sn rdn and struggling: wl btn next* **16/1**

0035 **6** *2 ¼* **Reg's Ruby**[22] 1994 4-11-6 **94**.. RodiGreene 63
(David Bridgwater) *led: jnd 3rd: rdn and hdd sn after 3 out: wknd and mstke next* **18/1**

2-P5 **7** *4 ½* **Bobbisox (IRE)**[33] 1821 5-11-10 **98**...................................... TomO'Brien 62
(Alex Hales) *in tch in midfield: rdn and outpcd bef 3 out: 5th and wl btn bef 2 out: t.o* **2/1**[1]

000- **8** *42* **Kielder Rise**[416] 1529 6-10-12 **86**...................................... PaulMoloney 8
(Evan Williams) *chsd ldr tl 2nd: lost pl and dropped to rr 6th: lost tch next: sn wl t.o* **9/1**

5m 17.1s (-7.60) **Going Correction** -0.475s/f (Good)
WFA 4 from 5yo+ 8lb **8** Ran SP% **112.1**
Speed ratings (Par 105): **95,94,85,82,82 81,80,64**
toteswingers:1&2:£3.40, 1&3:£9.50, 2&3:£5.20 CSF £18.05 CT £160.70 TOTE £3.50: £1.30, £1.10, £3.80; EX 18.20.

Owner A Whyte J Custerson & R Swinfen **Bred** O Pointing **Trained** Newmarket, Suffolk

■ Stewards' Enquiry : Daryl Jacob two-day ban: careless riding (Nov 29-30)

FOCUS

Two drew clear in what was a moderate mares' handicap. A step up from the winner with the second to her best.

NOTEBOOK

Little Carmela, making her handicap debut on this return from a 166-day absence, seemed to improve for the softer ground and found plenty when challenged by Present Your Case, getting back up in plenty of time. Her stamina got her through, and she may well be suited by a return to 3m. (op 3-1)

Present Your Case(IRE) is still a maiden, but the way she travelled before getting outstayed by the winner late on suggests she'll find a race at some stage. (op 7-2)

Winter Holly, pulled up on three of her five previous starts over hurdles, plugged on late and may be suited by a stiffer test. (op 16-1 tchd 18-1)

Bobbisox(IRE) was the disappointment of the race, failing to improve as expected for the switch to handicaps. It would come as no surprise to learn something was amiss. (op 3-1)

T/Plt: £103.40 to a £1 stake. Pool:£50,804.77 - 358.67 winning tickets T/Qpdt: £35.60 to a £1 stake. Pool:£4,001.83 - 83.00 winning tickets SP

2129 PLUMPTON (L-H)

Monday, November 15

OFFICIAL GOING: Soft (heavy in places on chase course; 6.7)

Wind: Almost nil Weather: Overcast

2426 STARSPORTSBET.CO.UK NOVICES' HURDLE (9 hdls) 2m

1:00 (1:00) (Class 3) 4-Y-O+ **£5,204** (£1,528; £764; £381)

Form — RPR

3 **1** **Union Island (IRE)**[51] 1613 4-10-12 0........................ WayneHutchinson 102+
(Alan King) *hld up in tch: trckd ldng pair 3 out: rdn next: wnt 2nd last: r.o wl flat to ld fnl stride* **11/4**[2]

33P- **2** *shd* **Beau Fighter**[23] 3659 5-10-12 123....................................(p) JamieMoore 104+
(Gary Moore) *t.k.h: pressed ldr fr 2nd: nt fluent 3rd and 3 out: led and hit 2 out: flattened last: hdd u.p fnl stride* **5/6**[1]

33-3 **3** *3* **Aviador (GER)**[17] 2074 4-10-12 0.................................... LeightonAspell 100
(Lucy Wadham) *led: set stdy pce to 1/2-way: nt fluent 6th: hdd 2 out: one pce u.p* **5/1**[3]

4 *7* **Golden Prospect**[32] 6-10-12 0.. JamesDavies 92
(Miss J R Tooth) *hld up: wnt prom 6th: lost pl next: cl enough in 4th bef 2 out: pushed along and grad outpcd: nt disgracd* **33/1**

4 **5** *1 ¼* **Mister Fantastic**[23] 1974 4-10-12 0.................................. AidanColeman 91
(Sarah Humphrey) *nt a fluent: wl in tch tl outpcd fr 3 out* **12/1**

6 *2 ¾* **Drummers Drumming (USA)**[164] 4-10-12 0.............. JimmyMcCarthy 88
(Charlie Morlock) *trckd ldr to 2nd: styd wl in tch tl outpcd fr 3 out* **100/1**

6/0- **7** *9* **Street Devil (USA)**[212] 2275 5-10-12 0.............................. MarkGrant 79
(Barry Brennan) *hld up in last pair: wl in tch 3 out: pushed along and steadily wknd* **33/1**

3m 57.8s (-3.00) **Going Correction** -0.20s/f (Good) **7** Ran SP% **112.5**
Speed ratings (Par 107): **99,98,97,93,93 91,87**
toteswingers:1&2:£1.10, 1&3:£2.50, 2&3:£1.20 CSF £5.44 TOTE £3.20: £1.80, £1.20; EX 5.30.

Owner Clipper Logistics **Bred** Barouche Stud Ireland Ltd **Trained** Barbury Castle, Wilts

FOCUS

An ordinary juvenile event. They finished in a bit of a heap and this is not form to be confident about, with the winner entitled to rate a lot higher on his Flat form.

NOTEBOOK

Union Island(IRE) stuck his head down on the line and just edged the verdict. This was a lot better than his third on debut at Market Rasen in September, probably down to his yard being in much better form now, and he should be capable of rating higher as he gains further experience. A stiffer test is also likely to ideally suit in due course. (op 4-1)

Beau Fighter showed more on the Flat on his previous outing and, fitted with cheekpieces, was well backed to open his account on this return to hurdling. He was produced with that appeared to be a winning challenge at the second-last, but wasn't clever at it and then ran through the final flight. He only lost out by the smallest margin at the line, but would've surely held on with better jumping in the home straight. A mark of 123 probably flatters him, but he should be capable of gaining compensation in something similar before that long. (op 5-4)

Aviador(GER) has now finished third on his four career starts. He set out to make all, but was held after the last and probably needs more of a test. (op 3-1)

Golden Prospect, a six-time winner on the Flat, often ran freely on the level and could've settled better on this switch to hurdling. He found the rising finish too much, but showed he has a future for this discipline. (op 22-1)

2427 HEPWORTH CONQUEROR STOUT NOVICES' CHASE (14 fncs) 2m 4f

1:30 (1:30) (Class 3) 4-Y-O+ **£6,262** (£1,850; £925; £463; £231)

Form — RPR

436- **1** **Bouggler**[221] 5093 5-11-2 0.. SamThomas 136+
(Emma Lavelle) *trckd ldng pair fr 5th: nt fluent next: ct flat-footed after 4 out: rdn to chse clr ldr next: clsd fr 2 out: styd on wl to ld flat* **1/2**[1]

UP-1 **2** *1* **Have You Seen Me (IRE)**[40] 1731 7-11-5 0.................... TomMolloy(3) 137
(Nigel Twiston-Davies) *t.k.h: pressed ldr: led 10th: kicked on 4 out: 7 l clr after next: styd on: hdd flat* **3/1**[2]

1224 **3** *37* **Gee Dee Nen**[31] 1854 7-11-8 126....................................(v) JamieMoore 112
(Gary Moore) *led to 10th: sn drvn: lost 2nd 3 out: wknd and lft wl bhd* **12/1**[3]

3- **4** *32* **Gandalfe (FR)**[220] 5117 5-11-2 0.. TimmyMurphy 62
(Alan Fleming) *hld up in detached last: wnt modest 4th at 8th: sn no ch: t.o* **12/1**[3]

2-03 **5** *3* **Ray Diamond**[29] 1883 5-10-11 0.................................. MarcGoldstein(5) 59
(Michael Madgwick) *mstke 2nd: chsd ldng pair tl blnd 5th: last and struggling fr 8th: t.o* **40/1**

5m 2.40s (-4.90) **Going Correction** -0.20s/f (Good) **5** Ran SP% **109.5**
Speed ratings (Par 107): **101,100,85,73,71**
CSF £2.50 TOTE £1.50: £1.30, £1.10; EX 2.60.

Owner Axom (XXI) **Bred** David Brown, Slatch Farm Stud & G B Turnbull Ltd **Trained** Wildhern, Hants

FOCUS

The ground was more testing on the chase course. The first pair came well clear here and the second sets a decent standard. The winner can match his hurdles best over fences.

NOTEBOOK

Bouggler was a Grade 2 winner as a novice hurdler and is currently rated 148 in that sphere, so it wasn't surprising he proved all the rage for this seasonal/chase debut. He duly scored, but anyone who took the odds would have all but torn up their tickets turning into the home straight as he hit a marked flat spot. To his credit, though, he motored up the home straight and was doing his best work just as the penalised runner-up was feeling the pinch. There was a fair bit to like about his jumping and there is every chance he will want 3m to really shine as a chaser. His yard remains in decent form and it will be interesting to see whether he is now kept to this sort of company or tried in a higher grade. (op 4-7)

Have You Seen Me(IRE) was a gutsy winner on his chasing debut in a good event at Towcester 40 days earlier and he made a bold bid to follow up. He looked to have the winner well held two out, but he again ran with the choke out through the early parts and that probably cost him at the business end. He rates a solid benchmark and there will still be other days for him. (tchd 7-2)

Gee Dee Nen was having his fifth outing over fences and racing in visor for the first time in this sphere. He ensured it was a decent test, but again made the odd error and was done with soon after getting in tight at the tenth. The ground was more demanding than he cares for, though, and it wouldn't be that surprising to see him win a handicap at some stage this term. (op 11-1)

Gandalfe(FR) didn't jump that well on his debut for connections last term and was allowed to find his feet on this switch to fences. He was never in the hunt, but should come on for the outing and experience. (op 14-1)

2428 STAR SPORTS "LAY A BET" "NATIONAL HUNT" NOVICES' HURDLE (12 hdls) 2m 5f

2:00 (2:00) (Class 4) 4-Y-0+ **£2,740** (£798; £399)

Form RPR

36 **1** **Jetnova (IRE)**[22] 1990 5-10-12 0 WayneHutchinson 117+
(Alan King) *wl plcd: chsd ldng pair fr 6th: wnt 2nd sn after 3 out: clsd next: rdn to ld last: styd on wl* **7/2**[3]

4 **2** *1* **Native Gallery (IRE)**[7] 2281 5-10-12 0 JasonMaguire 114
(Ben De Haan) *led and allowed easy advantage: pressed 2 out: hdd last: styd on but hld last 100yds* **4/1**

2-12 **3** *1 ½* **Frontier Spirit (IRE)**[24] 1951 6-11-5 117 PaddyBrennan 119
(Nigel Twiston-Davies) *trckd ldng trio fr 6th: effrt 3 out: wnt 3rd bef next: kpt on but nvr looked willing enough to chal* **15/8**[1]

33-1 **4** *16* **Paint The Clouds**[23] 1974 5-11-5 120 LeightonAspell 103
(Warren Greatrex) *t.k.h: prom: chsd ldr 5th tl sn after 3 out: sn wknd: hung rt after last* **11/4**[2]

30-6 **5** *nse* **Venetian Lad**[10] 2186 5-10-12 0 MattieBatchelor 97+
(Lydia Richards) *nt jump wl in last trio: struggling 1/2-way: lost no more grnd fr 9th: plugged on flat* **20/1**

5P-3 **6** *1 ¼* **Twin Bud**[14] 2130 5-10-0 0 (p) JimmyDerham(5) 89
(Anna Newton-Smith) *hld up in last trio: outpcd whn mstke 9th: mstke next: plugged on* **22/1**

2 **7** *3* **Health Is Wealth (IRE)**[22] 2000 5-10-12 0 JoeTizzard 92
(Colin Tizzard) *t.k.h: hld up in midfield: pushed along to chse ldng quartet after 9th: no imp next: lost pl last* **25/1**

060 **8** *38* **Downe Payment (IRE)**[10] 2181 5-10-2 0 AlexMerriam(3) 47
(Diana Grissell) *chsd ldr to 5th: lost pl qckly: t.o 3 out* **100/1**

60-0 **F** **Noir Noir**[14] 2130 5-10-0 0 (t) MarcGoldstein(5) —
(Anna Newton-Smith) *in tch in last trio tl fell 6th* **150/1**

5m 17.0s (-5.30) **Going Correction** -0.20s/f (Good) **9** Ran SP% **118.3**
Speed ratings (Par 105): **102,101,101,94,94 94,93,78,—**
toteswingers:1&2:£3.40, 1&3:£2.00, 2&3:£3.00 CSF £17.50 TOTE £5.10: £1.90, £1.30, £1.30; EX 18.00.
Owner David Sewell **Bred** Paddy Kennedy **Trained** Barbury Castle, Wilts

FOCUS
This fair novice hurdle for the track was run at a reasonable gallop and the first three dominated from three out. The winner showed improved form.

NOTEBOOK
Jetnova(IRE) was well backed and handed his yard two winners from as many runners on the card. He showed the clear benefit of his seasonal return over 3m last month and looks a real stayer in the making, getting on top late in the day here. It was probably a case of him idling somewhat when in front, but while he remains open to improvement he would look somewhat vulnerable under a penalty in this division. (op 9-2 tchd 10-3 and 5-1 in a place)
Native Gallery(IRE) ran better than the bare form on his hurdling debut a week previously and showed his true colours here with a brave effort in defeat. This dual point winner will get further without much fuss, clearly likes this sort of ground and deserves to go one better. (op 5-1 tchd 11-2)
Frontier Spirit(IRE) hit a flat spot off the home turn and looked held from the second-last, but was coming back at them on the run-in. He remains in fair form and rates a solid benchmark for the race, but his attitude under pressure still leaves a little to be desired. (op 2-1 tchd 7-4)
Paint The Clouds, whose yard won the race last season with Quartano, got off the mark as a hurdler when reappearing last month. He was a player here till emptying out off the home turn, but his best form had all come on much better ground and he failed to see out this longer trip as a result of the deep surface. (tchd 5-2 and 3-1 and 10-3 in places)
Venetian Lad, making his hurdling debut, took time to settle and lacked fluency early on. He came under pressure passing the stands for the first time and was seventh turning for home, but picked up to nearly grab fourth at the finish. He may not be the most straightforward, but his Newbury third on debut last season showed he has ability and he is one to note when going handicapping. (tchd 18-1)

2429 STRAIGHT FORWARD RACING H'CAP CHASE (12 fncs) 2m 1f

2:30 (2:30) (Class 3) (0-120,118) 4-Y-0+
£6,262 (£1,850; £925; £463; £231; £116)

Form RPR

213- **1** **Mister Stickler (IRE)**[208] 5316 6-11-12 118 WayneHutchinson 128+
(Alan King) *a gng wl: hld up in last pair: stdy prog fr 7th: pressed ldr after 3 out: led after 2 out: rdn out* **4/1**[2]

6-13 **2** *3 ½* **High Oscar**[14] 2134 9-9-11 96 MrTJCannon(7) 100
(Richard Rowe) *trckd ldrs: prog on inner to ld sn after 3 out: drvn and hdd sn after 2 out: one pce* **15/2**[3]

03-1 **3** *1 ¾* **Abey M'Boy**[17] 2071 7-11-1 107 LeightonAspell 114+
(Oliver Sherwood) *hld up in last: stdy prog after 7th: effrt and cl up on outer whn blnd 3 out: chsd ldng pair next: kpt on: nvr able to chal* **5/2**[1]

2-51 **4** *7* **Sumdancer (NZ)**[26] 1919 8-10-4 101 MarcGoldstein(5) 97
(Michael Madgwick) *pressed ldr fr 3rd: led 4 out: drvn and hdd sn after 3 out: wknd fr next* **8/1**

31F- **5** *2 ¾* **Inthejungle (IRE)**[245] 4637 7-10-11 103 AndrewGlassonbury 96
(Daniel O'Brien) *pressed ldr tl blnd 3rd: styd prom tl fdd fr 3 out* **16/1**

423- **6** *9* **She's Humble (IRE)**[210] 5289 8-10-2 94 JamieMoore 78
(Linda Jewell) *hld up: in tch tl outpcd fr 8th: nvr nr ldrs after* **18/1**

0-55 **7** *11* **Award Winner**[15] 2112 7-11-12 118 APMcCoy 91
(Brendan Powell) *racd wd: prom: nt fluent 2nd: pushed along and struggling fr 7th: wl bhd after next: sltly hmpd 4 out* **9/1**

6P-P **8** *2* **Amble Forge (IRE)**[190] 236 8-11-8 114 JoeTizzard 85
(Colin Tizzard) *in tch: rdn and struggling after 7th: wl adrift of ldrs after next* **15/2**[3]

00-1 **F** **Owner Occupier**[22] 1995 5-10-8 100 ColinBolger —
(Chris Gordon) *led at decent pce but pressed thrght: jst hdd whn fell 4 out* **12/1**

4m 19.3s (-6.60) **Going Correction** -0.20s/f (Good) **9** Ran SP% **112.0**
Speed ratings (Par 107): **107,105,104,101,99 95,90,89,—**
toteswingers:1&2:£9.00, 1&3:£4.10, 2&3:£6.40 CSF £32.64 CT £87.54 TOTE £4.30: £1.80, £1.40, £2.10; EX 33.90.
Owner Trevor Hemmings **Bred** Thomas Meagher **Trained** Barbury Castle, Wilts

FOCUS
A pretty competitive race for the class. It was run at a solid early gallop and the form should work out. The winner produced a decent level for a chase debutant.

NOTEBOOK
Mister Stickler(IRE) ◆ ran out a ready winner to give his yard a hat-trick. This 6-y-o did win a novice hurdle, but had looked pretty ordinary in that sphere last season. However, he has always had the size to make a better chaser and, judging by the way he went about his business on this debut over fences, that will be the case this term. It was the softest ground he had run on so far and he could well follow up off a likely higher mark. (op 7-2 tchd 9-2)
High Oscar won on his return in October and posted a sound enough effort back at this venue last month. The drop back in trip was far from sure to suit, but he actually enjoyed it and only gave way to the winner after the last, improving on his fourth in this event last season. He helps to set the standard. (op 8-1 tchd 7-1)
Abey M'Boy ◆ somewhat belatedly showed his true colours on his chase debut 17 days earlier and proved popular for this switch to a handicap with the ground in his favour. He was ridden patiently and crept into things going strongly on the final lap. He lost vital momentum when hitting the tenth, though, and was always being held by the first pair in the home straight. Considering this was just his second outing over fences he wasn't disgraced and is worth another chance. (op 3-1 tchd 10-3 in a place)
Sumdancer(NZ) resumed winning ways off a 4lb lower mark at Fontwell last time out and is a dual winner over this C&D. He ran his race, but was done with from two out and now looks to be in the handicapper's grip.
Inthejungle(IRE), having his fourth consecutive outing here, got a positive ride on this return from a 245-day absence and his rider did well to stay aboard after he blundered at the third fence. He was still in with a chance prior to hitting the tenth and should come on nicely for the run.
She's Humble(IRE) should prove sharper for this seasonal debut. (op 14-1 tchd 20-1)
Owner Occupier wasn't done with prior to departing at the ninth and it's hoped this doesn't dent his confidence. (tchd 11-1)

2430 CALL STAR SPORTS ON 08000 521 321 H'CAP HURDLE (10 hdls) 2m 2f

3:00 (3:02) (Class 4) (0-100,100) 4-Y-0+ **£2,397** (£698; £349)

Form RPR

413- **1** **Ban Uisce (IRE)**[246] 4601 5-11-5 100 MarkQuinlan(7) 107+
(Neil Mulholland) *led 2nd: mde rest: drew clr 2 out: pushed out flat* **4/9**[1]

356- **2** *2 ½* **Wheres Johnny**[259] 4361 9-11-9 97 MattieBatchelor 98
(Jamie Poulton) *led to 2nd: chsd wnr to 3 out: sn rdn: regained 2nd 2 out: kpt on: nvr able to chal* **20/1**

66F- **3** *5* **Doctored**[257] 4388 9-10-1 80 DavidBass(5) 76
(Daniel O'Brien) *cl up: rdn after 6th: steadily outpcd after 3 out: kpt on fr next* **12/1**[3]

600- **4** *6* **Across The Straits (FR)**[232] 4913 6-11-5 98 JimmyDerham(5) 91
(Jonathan Geake) *hld up last: nt fluent 7th: prog to trck wnr 3 out gng strly: wknd and mstke 2 out* **22/1**

0-00 **5** *8* **Monash Lad (IRE)**[14] 2135 8-9-7 74 oh2 MrTGarner(7) 56
(Michelle Bryant) *cl up: rdn and outpcd after 7th: n.d after* **14/1**

3004 **6** *4* **Ghaill Force**[14] 2131 8-10-3 77 AndrewGlassonbury 55
(Paddy Butler) *in tch: mstke 4th: disp 2nd pl after 6th: sn dropped to rr u.p and btn* **9/2**[2]

4m 32.2s (272.20) **6** Ran SP% **110.9**
toteswingers:1&2:£2.20, 1&3:£2.90, 2&3:£10.70 CSF £9.75 TOTE £1.80: £1.10, £2.70; EX 9.70.
Owner The Don't Tell Daddy Racing Partnership **Bred** Cecil Ashe **Trained** Burlescombe, Devon

FOCUS
A weak handicap, run at a fair gallop. The winner produced a small step up and the second is rated in line with his best chase form last year.

NOTEBOOK
Ban Uisce(IRE) hails from a bang in-form stable and was heavily backed for this seasonal debut. He took the race by the scruff of the neck early on and, despite looking to feel the pinch somewhat from two out, was in no real danger from the home turn. This ground is right up his street and he has now won three of his five races since going handicapping, so further improvement cannot be ruled out. (op 4-6, tchd 8-11 in places)
Wheres Johnny stayed on dourly to finish a clear second-best and, entitled to improve a deal for the outing, ought to relish getting back over a longer trip. (op 12-1)
Doctored, whose sole success over hurdles came on heavy ground in 2008, was last seen falling on his previous outing in March. He came under pressure a fair way out and the run looked needed. (op 16-1 tchd 22-1)
Across The Straits(FR) travelled sweetly into contention on the back straight and looked the chief threat to the winner. He felt the pinch turning for home and dropped out thereafter, but this was much more encouraging on his first run back for his original yard. He ought to last longer next time. (op 12-1)

2431 DON MURCH 90TH NOVICES' H'CAP CHASE (18 fncs) 3m 2f

3:30 (3:30) (Class 4) (0-100,98) 4-Y-0+ **£2,887** (£901; £485)

Form RPR

F34- **1** **Beware Chalk Pit (IRE)**[221] 5101 6-11-3 94 JimmyDerham(5) 97+
(Jonathan Geake) *hld up last: trckd ldr 4 out: led after 3 out: hrd pressed and gd jump last: rdn out* **9/2**

34-2 **2** *2 ¾* **Sailor's Sovereign**[14] 2132 9-10-0 72 oh3 (p) GerardTumelty 73
(Julian Smith) *hld up in 3rd: wnt 2nd briefly after 14th: rdn to chse wnr 2 out: cl enough whn outj. last: nt qckn* **7/4**[1]

23-4 **3** *47* **Mister Pink**[14] 2132 10-10-5 77 LeightonAspell 48
(Richard Rowe) *w ldr: outj. 13th and next: sn dropped away: t.o whn lft remote 3rd last: fin lame* **2/1**[2]

1044 **U** **Ethiopia**[75] 1452 7-11-5 98 NathanSweeney(7) 97
(Bob Buckler) *led at v stdy pce: hdd after 3 out: lost 2nd next: 5 l down whn blnd and uns rdr last* **7/2**[3]

7m 6.70s (16.00) **Going Correction** -0.20s/f (Good) **4** Ran SP% **110.1**
Speed ratings (Par 105): **67,66,51,—**
CSF £12.92 TOTE £6.80; EX 11.90.
Owner Dr & Mrs Peter Leftley **Bred** Miss Helena Gaskin **Trained** Marlborough, Wilts

FOCUS
An ordinary novice handicap run at a steady gallop. The second sets the level.

NOTEBOOK
Beware Chalk Pit(IRE) ◆ readily shed his maiden tag on this return to action and looks an improver this season. He hadn't shown much previously, but kept decent company in novice races last term and was making his handicap debut over a longer trip. He proved free under restraint, but there was plenty in the tank when his rider asked him for his effort after three out and he was always just doing enough when in front. There should be more to come. (op 7-2)
Sailor's Sovereign was hiked up 5lb for his near miss over C&D on his seasonal return on better ground a fortnight previously, but was still 3lb out of the handicap this time. The cheekpieces were back on and he looked to have been brought with a well-timed challenge two out. However, he didn't find what might have been expected under maximum pressure and ultimately lost out when getting in tight at the last. He rates the best guide for this form and is up to getting off the mark, but looks as though he needs delivering as late as possible in his races. (op 2-1)
Mister Pink didn't have that much to find with the runner-up on their last time out form here, but as soon as the tempo increased going out onto the final circuit he was in trouble. He was found to be lame afterwards. Official explanation: vet said gelding was lame post race (op 5-2)

Ethiopia, a dual winner at this course, showed more under a positive ride on this return from a 75-day absence but was done with prior to meeting the last wrong and unseating. (tchd 4-1)

2432 STAR SPORTS LEADER IN US SPORTS STANDARD OPEN NATIONAL HUNT FLAT RACE 2m 2f

4:00 (4:00) (Class 6) 4-6-Y-O **£1,370** (£399; £199)

Form				RPR
	1		**Global Power (IRE)**[254] 4-11-2 0 LeightonAspell (Oliver Sherwood) *hld up: last to 1/2-way: gd prog over 5f out to chse ldng pair 3f out: rdn to ld over 1f out: styd on wl* 9/2[2]	108+
3	2	3	**Divine Folly (IRE)**[26] 1927 5-10-11 0 DavidBass(5) (Lawney Hill) *cl up: jnd ldr over 3f out: stl upsides wl over 1f out: nt qckn after* 9/2[2]	105
	3	1	**Ballabrace (IRE)** 5-11-2 0 AidanColeman (Venetia Williams) *hld up: prog 1/2-way: led 4f out: sn jnd: hdd and one pce over 1f out* 11/10[1]	104
2	4	14	**Willy Be Lucky (IRE)**[190] 222 4-10-11 0 JimmyDerham(5) (Seamus Mullins) *in tch: pushed along fr 6f out: outpcd over 3f out: wnt modest 4th 2f out* 5/1[3]	90
	5	1 3/4	**Ben Eva (IRE)** 4-10-9 0 MarkGrant (Barry Brennan) *led 2f: chsd ldr to 4f out: steadily wknd* 25/1	81
	6	13	**Grey Cruzene (USA)** 4-11-2 0 ColinBolger (Chris Gordon) *hld up in midfield: dropped to rr 1/2-way: sn lost tch: passed 3 toiling rivals fnl 3f* 25/1	75
	7	8	**Carbis Bay** 4-10-11 0 (p) GemmaGracey-Davison(5) (Zoe Davison) *plld way up to ld after 2f: hanging bnd over 6f out: hdd & wknd 4f out* 40/1	67
	8	7	**Albert Saxe** 4-11-2 0 JamesDavies (Miss J R Tooth) *cl up: rdn 5f out: wknd rapidly over 3f out* 66/1	60
0	9	12	**Kidajo**[39] 1749 4-11-2 0 MattieBatchelor (Roger Curtis) *t.k.h: in tch to 1/2-way: sn t.o* 100/1	48

4m 25.5s (-1.50) **Going Correction** -0.20s/f (Good) 9 Ran SP% **113.3**
Speed ratings: **95,93,93,87,86 80,76,73,68**
toteswingers:1&2:£4.10, 1&3:£2.90, 2&3:£2.90 CSF £23.23 TOTE £9.40: £1.80, £2.10, £1.60; EX 22.20.
Owner It Wasn't Us **Bred** R J Whitford **Trained** Upper Lambourn, Berks

FOCUS
A steadily run bumper in which the principals dominated off the home bend and the form looks fair for the track.

NOTEBOOK
Global Power(IRE) won his sole start between the flags in Ireland in March and subsequently joined his new connections for £14,000. He got a patient ride and became slightly outpaced as the tempo increased on the back straight. His response under pressure from the bottom of the home straight was pleasing, though, and he ultimately came home well on top despite running green when in front. His point success came on a sounder surface so he seems versatile on that front and he looks a nice recruit for novice hurdling, where a longer trip will suit. (op 7-2)
Divine Folly(IRE) was doing his best work late on when third on his debut at Worcester last month. He too got a little tapped for toe on the back straight, but responded gamely and held every chance over this stiffer test. He should relish racing over further once sent hurdling and is another fair prospect.
Ballabrace(IRE) is a half-brother to the useful Irish hurdler Silver Friend (debut bumper winner) and proved popular for this racecourse debut. He travelled nicely into contention and went to the front leaving the back straight. It was clear soon after that he was feeling the pinch, however, and he was eventually outstayed by the first pair. Dropping back to 2m on better ground in this sphere could see him off the mark. (op 13-8 tchd 7-4)
Willy Be Lucky(IRE), who was last seen finishing second on his debut over C&D in May. That came on quick ground, though, and he wasn't able to raise his game when it mattered on this testing surface. (op 4-1)
Ben Eva(IRE), bred to make her mark over jumps, was always to the fore and shaped with some ability. She looks more of one for handicap hurdles over further down the line, though. (tchd 28-1)
T/Plt: £26.00 to a £1 stake. Pool:£62,871.15 - 1,759.15 winning tickets T/Qpdt: £17.40 to a £1 stake. Pool:£3,944.41 - 167.70 winning tickets JN

1949 FAKENHAM (L-H)

Tuesday, November 16

OFFICIAL GOING: Good to soft (good in places) changing to good to soft after race 2 (1.30)
Wind: nil Weather: bright, chilly

2433 WENSUM VALLEY (S) H'CAP HURDLE (11 hdls) 2m 4f

1:00 (1:00) (Class 5) (0-95,89) 4-Y-O+ **£2,397** (£698; £349)

Form				RPR
5006	1		**Tocatchaprince (IRE)**[24] 1974 4-10-6 69 (v[1]) DaveCrosse (Milton Harris) *hld up wl in tch: hdwy after 7th: jnd ldr gng wl 3 out: led next: rdn clr between last 2: kpt on* 8/1	73+
P0/6	2	5	**Dansilver**[13] 2149 6-11-3 80 PaulMoloney (Tony Carroll) *t.k.h: hld up in tch in rr: nt fluent 2nd: hdwy after 8th: rdn to chse ldng pair after 3 out: drvn and chsd clr wnr between last 2: no imp* 11/4[1]	80
0465	3	4	**Atabaas Allure (FR)**[27] 1915 4-10-6 69 ColinBolger (Chris Gordon) *t.k.h: chsd ldrs: mstke 6th: 4th and outpcd u.p after 3 out: plugged on same pce fr next* 9/1	66
06P5	4	8	**Standing Order**[39] 1760 7-10-13 76 BrianHughes (Richard Ford) *t.k.h: chsd ldrs: mstke 5th: led 7th: qcknd after next: rdn and hdd whn hit 2 out: wknd between last 2* 14/1	67
-664	5	9	**Railway Park (IRE)**[9] 2247 6-11-12 89 PaddyAspell (John Wainwright) *t.k.h: hld up wl in tch in last pair: hdwy to chse ldrs after 7th: rdn and wknd sn after 3 out* 7/1	70
0630	6	1 1/2	**Satindra (IRE)**[13] 2144 6-10-11 74 (tp) TomMessenger (Carole Ikin) *in tch in midfield: hdwy to join ldrs 7th: rdn and lost pl next: wl btn after 3 out* 6/1[3]	53
3-05	7	2 1/2	**Just Dan**[180] 420 4-10-7 77 MrTomDavid(7) (David Thompson) *chsd ldr tl after 8th: wknd qckly sn after next* 20/1	54
-3	8	45	**Adage**[58] 1549 7-11-8 85 (bt) TomScudamore (Jim Best) *led at stdy gallop tl hdd 7th: sn rdn: downed tools and dropped to rr: t.o fr 3 out* 3/1[2]	22

5m 28.6s (16.00) **Going Correction** +0.875s/f (Soft)
WFA 4 from 6yo+ 8lb 8 Ran SP% **111.0**
Speed ratings (Par 103): **103,101,99,96,92 92,91,73**
toteswingers:1&2:£8.20, 1&3:£11.00, 2&3:£5.50 CSF £29.22 CT £194.86 TOTE £12.90: £3.40, £1.10, £3.10; EX 38.30.There was no bid for the winner.
Owner Mrs D Dewbery **Bred** Laurence & Martin Curran **Trained** Herridge, Wiltshire
■ Dave Crosse's first winner in Britain following 11 months out with a badly broken leg.

FOCUS
This poor selling handicap hurdle was won with ease by Tocatchaprince, who stepped up on his previous hurdles form.

NOTEBOOK
Tocatchaprince(IRE) scooted clear in the straight and seemed helped by the drop in grade/switch to handicaps. Clearly improving for a first-time visor, it's possible he'll win again if the headgear continues to have this effect. Official explanation: trainer said, regarding apparent improvement in form, that the gelding benefited from wearing the first-time visor, a fair handicap mark and the first run in a seller. (tchd 15-2)
Dansilver ran better on this drop in grade without proving a match for the winner, to whom he was conceding 11lb. (tchd 5-2 and 3-1)
Atabaas Allure(FR) is still a maiden over hurdles and, not for the first time, she ran as though a step up to 3m may suit. (op 8-1)
Standing Order was quickly swept aside in the straight. (op 11-1 tchd 16-1)
Adage seemed to decide she wasn't up for it and her rider allowed her to coast home in her own time. Official explanation: jockey said mare blundered and never travelled thereafter (op 4-1)

2434 HD CLINICAL CONDITIONAL JOCKEYS' H'CAP CHASE (11 fncs 1 omitted) 2m 110y

1:30 (1:30) (Class 5) (0-85,85) 4-Y-O+ **£2,865** (£889; £479)

Form				RPR
0560	1		**Roc De Guye (FR)**[13] 2149 5-11-7 83 RobertKirk(3) (James Evans) *t.k.h: hld up in tch and a travelling wl: trckd ldrs 6th: led and j. awkwardly 3 out: readily drew clr and in command bef next: rdn out flat* 20/1	97+
4032	2	9	**Fongoli**[11] 2187 4-10-12 78 (b) MrMMO'Connor (Brendan Powell) *led tl 4th: dropped to last and rdn 6th: nvr gng wl after: drvn and wl btn after 3 out: lft 2nd and mstke last: no ch w wnr* 11/4[1]	78
P/UF	3	9	**Shouldntbethere (IRE)**[11] 2187 6-10-12 74 (t) DannyBurton(3) (Joanna Davis) *t.k.h: nt a fluent: chsd ldrs tl led 4th: mstke 9th: hdd and j. awkwardly 3 out: sn wknd u.p: lft 3rd and hmpd last* 15/2[3]	73
4-P4	F		**Wishes Or Watches (IRE)**[11] 2187 10-10-7 66 SamTwiston-Davies (John Upson) *hld up in tch tl fell 2nd* 8/1	—
2532	U		**Peak Seasons (IRE)**[8] 2276 7-10-10 74 GaryDerwin(5) (Michael Chapman) *chsd ldr tl 3rd: wnt 2nd again 6th tl after 9th: chsd clr wnr and drvn after 3 out: no imp and wl hld whn uns rdr last* 11/4[1]	81
40-P	F		**Art Gallery**[42] 1428 6-11-5 81 MrTomDavid(3) (David Thompson) *chsd ldrs: dived 1st: fell next* 20/1	—
03-F	F		**Gavroche Gaugain (FR)**[11] 2194 6-11-6 85 PaulGallagher(6) (Ferdy Murphy) *hld up wl in tch tl fell 6th* 3/1[2]	—

4m 28.8s (12.20) **Going Correction** +0.225s/f (Yiel)
WFA 4 from 5yo+ 7lb 7 Ran SP% **110.7**
Speed ratings (Par 103): **80,75,71,—,—,— —,—**
toteswingers:1&2:£7.30, 1&3:£17.40, 2&3:£3.60 CSF £71.84 TOTE £35.00: £12.40, £1.20; EX 105.80.
Owner S Crawley, T Crawley, N Goodger **Bred** G A E C Delorme Gerard & Vincent **Trained** Broadwas, Worcs
■ Robert Kirk's first winner since turning professional.

FOCUS
The fifth-last fence was bypassed. A weak handicap chase in which three of the runners departed early, and another, Peak Seasons, unseated when in second at the last. A big step up from the easy winner.

NOTEBOOK
Roc De Guye(FR), well beaten in a novices' chase at Worcester in September, hardly looked an obvious winner switched to handicaps, but he found the necessary improvement from somewhere and was clear before the last. This was only his sixth start and it's reasonable to expect further improvement from the 5-y-o. Official explanation: trainer said, regarding apparent improvement in form, this was the gelding's second run over fences, which it preferred, and also appreciated the good to soft (good in places) ground, not pulling so hard and only three runners completed. (op 33-1 tchd 40-1)
Fongoli was one of the first in trouble, losing his position before plugging on again to inherit second. (op 4-1)
Shouldntbethere(IRE), still ahead of Fongoli when falling latest, at least managed to complete this time, but was comfortably held. (op 13-2)
Peak Seasons(IRE) kept finding for pressure and looked to have second in the bag when parting company with his rider at the last. (op 5-2 tchd 3-1)
Gavroche Gaugain(FR), in with every chance when falling at the last at Hexham earlier this month, was expected to go close if none the worse, despite being 5lb higher, and he may well have done had he not come down again. His confidence may need restoring after this. (op 5-2 tchd 3-1)

2435 SIS FILLIES' JUVENILE HURDLE (9 hdls) 2m

2:00 (2:00) (Class 3) 3-Y-O **£4,553** (£1,337; £668; £333)

Form				RPR
1010	1		**Joan D'Arc (IRE)**[15] 2133 3-11-1 109 MrJMQuinlan(7) (Michael Quinlan) *racd in last pair: hdwy after 5th: chsd ldr next: mstke 3 out: rdn bef next: looked hld tl rallied and fast jump to chal last: led fnl 75yds: kpt on: sddle slipped* 11/1	92
353	2	1/2	**Doyenne Dream**[44] 1691 3-10-12 100 MarkBradburne (James Eustace) *chsd clr ldr: clsd to ld after 5th: clr w wnr fr 3 out: rdn and mstke next: idling between last 2: outj. and hrd pressed last: kpt on u.p tl hdd and no ex fnl 75yds* 8/1[3]	82
201	3	9	**Lady Pacha**[3] 2369 3-10-11 0 BrianToomey(7) (Tim Pitt) *in tch in main gp: clsd after 5th: rdn and outpcd wl bef 3 out: 3rd and wl btn bef 2 out: plugged on u.p between last 2* 8/1[3]	80
	4	34	**Fantastic Sam (IRE)**[141] 3-10-12 0 BrianHughes (Kate Walton) *t.k.h: hld up in rr: hdwy after 5th: chsd ldng pair after 6th: sn rdn and wkng whn hit 3 out: wl btn next: t.o* 33/1	43
5	5	10	**Rare Malt (IRE)**[9] 2245 3-10-9 0 SamTwiston-Davies(3) (Milton Harris) *racd in midfield: mstke 4th: rdn and dropped to last after next: lost tch 6th: t.o after 3 out* 5/4[1]	34
2	P		**Fine Lace (IRE)**[38] 1772 3-10-12 0 PaulMoloney (Evan Williams) *led and sn clr: rdn and stopping after 5th: hdd bef next: mstke 6th: sn t.o and p.u bef next: b.b.v.* 2/1[2]	—

4m 21.3s (15.90) **Going Correction** +0.875s/f (Soft) 6 Ran SP% **111.3**
Speed ratings (Par 103): **95,94,90,73,68** —
toteswingers:1&2:£3.00, 1&3:£5.00, 2&3:£4.90 CSF £83.73 TOTE £12.20: £4.90, £4.50; EX 39.30.
Owner Newtown Anner Stud Farm Ltd **Bred** Lynn Lodge Stud **Trained** Newmarket, Suffolk

FOCUS
A moderate juvenile hurdle that turned into a good test at the distance. The principals disappointed and the first three are rated pretty much to form.

NOTEBOOK
Joan D'Arc(IRE), already a dual winner over hurdles, disappointed in a claiming hurdle latest, but her stable took this race a year ago and she came right back to form, eventually wearing down the idle runner-up whom she had also beaten at Huntingdon last month. Given her limited ability, she's been well placed to pick up three races. If she's to add a fourth, it will have to be at a lower level or switched to handicaps. (op 15-2 tchd 7-1)

Doyenne Dream looked the winner when taking it up, but she was idling with ears pricked from the turn in and was eventually run down. She's got the ability to win a minor contest. (op 9-1 tchd 15-2)

Lady Pacha never got involved in this slightly better contest, and probably found it coming too soon. (op 5-1)

Rare Malt(IRE) had run promisingly on her debut nine days earlier. She was never going a yard, being the first one beaten, and is left with plenty to prove now. (op 9-4)

Fine Lace(IRE), a distant second at Cheltenham on debut (winner disappointing next time), was weak in the market and never gave herself much chance of lasting home by tearing into a clear early lead. That said, it was surprising to see her stop as soon as she did and it came as no surprise to learn that she had broken a blood vessel. Official explanation: trainer's rep said filly bled from the nose (op 15-8 tchd 9-4)

2436 AT THE RACES NOVICES' CHASE (12 fncs 6 omitted) 3m 110y

2:30 (2:30) (Class 3) 4-Y-0+ **£6,505** (£1,910; £955; £477)

Form / RPR

0-21 **1** **Robo (FR)**[25] 1952 5-11-9 125 .... TomO'Brien 140+
(Renee Robeson) *chsd ldr 3rd: n.m.r on inner bef 15th (actual 3 out): led next: sn wl clr: nudged out: v easily* **13/8**[1]

2-33 **2** *33* **Plunkett (IRE)**[7] 2285 7-11-2 123 .... PaulMoloney 98
(Evan Williams) *hld up towards rr: hdwy to chse ldng pair 6th: rdn and btn bef 3 out (actual 2 out) wnt poor 2nd on long run-in* **7/2**[3]

6/ **3** *4* **Bentota (IRE)**[719] 2464 9-11-2 0 .... TomScudamore 95
(Michael Scudamore) *a in rr: lost tch 7th: mstke 10th: no ch 15th (actual 3 out): styd on bypassing last to go poor 3rd towards fin* **11/1**

2321 **4** *2* **Film Festival (USA)**[17] 2093 7-11-6 127 .... FearghalDavis(3) 100
(Brian Ellison) *led tl 3 out (actual 2 out) sn no ch w wnr: tired and lost 2 pls on long run-in* **7/4**[2]

60-6 **5** *22* **Rester Vrai (FR)**[12] 2166 5-10-9 0 .... JoeCornwall(7) 73
(John Cornwall) *chsd ldr tl 3rd: lost pl 5th: toiling fr 1/2-way: t.o fr 15th (actual 3 out)* **50/1**

6m 29.8s (-5.90) **Going Correction** +0.225s/f (Yiel) **5** Ran SP% **107.0**
Speed ratings (Par 107): **118,107,106,105,98**
CSF £7.31 TOTE £2.40: £1.40, £1.40; EX 6.90.
Owner The Ravenstone Partnership **Bred** Yvon Madiot **Trained** Tyringham, Bucks

FOCUS
The last fence was omitted on all circuits in this novices' chase due to low sun, and the fifth-last was omitted too as it was damaged. A big step up from the winner and there is a caase for rating the race much higher.

NOTEBOOK
Robo(FR) took over jumping what turned out to be the second last and quickly drew clear. Formerly with Philip Hobbs over hurdles, he ran out a good winner over 2f shorter at the course on debut and it would be no surprise were this relation to Royal Auclair to win a decent prize as a chaser, his relatively low-key trainer having done well with Ogee over the past two seasons. (op 15-8 tchd 6-4 and 2-1 in places)

Plunkett(IRE), beaten a long way at Exeter last week, did a little better here but he was still under pressure with a circuit to run. He could do better once handicapping. Official explanation: jockey said gelding hung left throughout (op 3-1)

Bentota(IRE), a dual point winner who had finished well beaten in a chase nearly two years earlier for a different yard, was soon tailed off but he wasn't given an overly hard time and should learn from the experience. (op 12-1 tchd 8-1)

Film Festival(USA), a winner off 118 at Wetherby, didn't see out this longer trip, quickly being swept aside by the winner and looking tired late on. (tchd 15-8)

Rester Vrai(FR) was never involved on this debut over fences, but should have a long-term future in low-grade handicap chases.

2437 RACING AT FAKENHAM ON NEW YEAR'S DAY H'CAP CHASE (11 fncs 5 omitted) 2m 5f 110y

3:00 (3:00) (Class 4) (0-105,96) 4-Y-0+ **£5,204** (£1,528; £764; £381)

Form / RPR

5-62 **1** **Nautical Approach (IRE)**[27] 1919 7-11-12 96 ....(t) PaddyBrennan 113+
(Alex Hales) *t.k.h: a travelling wl: trckd ldrs: mstke 5th: led bef 3 out (actual 2 out): clr bef next: in total command on long run-in: eased towards fin* **11/8**[1]

4P13 **2** *9* **Great Ocean Road (IRE)**[25] 1954 7-10-12 82 .... WillKennedy 85
(David Thompson) *hld up in tch: hdwy to chal wnt bmpd and mstke 9th (actual 3 out): chsd wnr after next: kpt on after last but no threat to wnr* **11/4**[2]

4413 **3** *9* **Feeling Peckish (USA)**[8] 2277 6-10-5 82 ....(t) GaryDerwin(7) 76
(Michael Chapman) *led: reminders after 1st: hdd after 5th: styd w ldr: pushed along fr 7th: lj.rt and bmpd rival 9th (actual 3 out): wknd 2 out (actual last)* **5/1**[3]

-6U0 **4** *32* **Phoenix Des Mottes (FR)**[12] 2161 7-11-4 95 .... JoeCornwall(7) 59
(John Cornwall) *t.k.h: chsd ldr tl led after 5th: hdd bef 3 out: (actual 2 out): wknd qckly after next: t.o* **7/1**

62-P **P** **Kinkeel (IRE)**[23] 1997 11-10-12 85 ....(p) EamonDehdashti(3) —
(Tony Carroll) *a in rr: in tch: rdn and struggling after 8th: lost tch and j. slowly 9th (actual 3 out): p.u after next* **12/1**

5m 51.0s (9.20) **Going Correction** +0.225s/f (Yiel) **5** Ran SP% **105.6**
Speed ratings (Par 105): **92,88,85,73,—**
CSF £5.21 TOTE £1.70: £1.10, £3.20; EX 4.20.
Owner A M Hales **Bred** N J Connors **Trained** Wardington, Oxon

FOCUS
The last fence was omitted on all circuits due to low sun, and the fifth-last was omitted too as it was damaged.A low-grade handicap chase in which the easy winner took a step forward off.

NOTEBOOK
Nautical Approach(IRE), fitted with a tongue strap for the first time, took over at the last down the back and quickly drew clear. Just 1lb higher than when runner-up at Fontwell latest, he easily took care of this lesser opposition and, now he's got this first win out the way, it would be no surprise were he to go in again. (tchd 5-4 and 6-4)

Great Ocean Road(IRE) has been in good form and had run well off this mark over C&D latest, but he proved no match for the runaway winner and is clearly vulnerable off this mark. (tchd 3-1)

Feeling Peckish(USA), held off this mark at Southwell last week, was readily dropped by the winner. (op 11-2 tchd 6-1 and 9-2)

Phoenix Des Mottes(FR) remains too high in the weights. (op 13-2)

Kinkeel(IRE) wasn't going from an early stage. (op 8-1)

2438 PRINCE OF WALES STAND NOVICES' H'CAP HURDLE (9 hdls) 2m

3:30 (3:30) (Class 4) (0-105,104) 3-Y-0+ **£4,163** (£1,222; £611; £305)

Form / RPR

1 **Venetian Dove (IRE)**[51] 1631 4-11-7 97 .... PaulMoloney 100+
(Evan Williams) *t.k.h: a travelling: hld up prom in main gp: clsd on ldr 5th: wnt 2nd bef 3 out: led bef 2 out: rdn and in command last: eased fnl 75yds: comf* **10/1**

0-44 **2** *1 3/4* **Ouest Eclair (FR)**[18] 2080 5-10-9 92 .... PaulGallagher(7) 91
(Ferdy Murphy) *t.k.h: hld up off the pce in midfield: clsd on ldr 5th: rdn bef 3 out: rdn to press wnr and nt fluent 2 out: nt qckn u.p and styd on same pce bef last* **7/2**[2]

300 **3** *nse* **Dr Finley (IRE)**[18] 2078 3-10-13 104 ....(p) GerardTumelty 90+
(Jeff Pearce) *bhd: clsd on ldr and rdn along after 5th: chsd ldrs and drvn 2 out: kpt on u.p flat: no threat to wnr* **3/1**[1]

U030 **4** *8* **Chalice Welcome**[6] 2314 7-10-6 82 .... MarkBradburne 73
(Neil King) *racd off the pce in last trio: clsd on ldr 5th: chsd ldrs and rdn bef 2 out: wknd between last 2* **9/2**[3]

532P **5** *5* **Galley Slave (IRE)**[8] 2280 5-10-8 91 .... GaryDerwin(7) 77
(Michael Chapman) *led: lft wl clr 2nd: c bk to field 5th: rdn after next: hdd bef 2 out: wknd qckly between last 2* **11/1**

032 **6** *19* **Red Skipper (IRE)**[34] 1831 5-11-12 102 .... WilsonRenwick 71
(Noel Wilson) *t.k.h: hld up chsng clr ldng pair: lft 2nd at 2nd: clsd on ldr 5th: lost 2nd bef 3 out: wknd u.p bef 2 out* **7/1**

3204 **P** **Wicklewood**[16] 2114 4-10-10 93 ....(p) MattCrawley(7) —
(Christine Dunnett) *hld up off the pce in rr: clsd and in tch 5th: rdn and struggling whn mstke next: wl btn whn rdr lost iron 3 out: t.o and p.u last* **11/1**

00-3 **F** **Luthien (IRE)**[29] 1902 4-11-6 96 .... WillKennedy —
(Alex Hales) *chsd ldr and clr of field tl fell 2nd* **8/1**

4m 18.4s (13.00) **Going Correction** +0.875s/f (Soft)
WFA 3 from 4yo 15lb 4 from 5yo+ 7lb **8** Ran SP% **114.8**
Speed ratings (Par 105): **102,101,101,97,94 85,—,—**
toteswingers:1&2:£10.40, 1&3:£1.30, 2&3:£3.90 CSF £45.91 CT £132.52 TOTE £12.40: £2.40, £1.70, £2.00; EX 42.60.
Owner R E R Williams **Bred** Martin Doran **Trained** Llancarfan, Vale Of Glamorgan

FOCUS
Not much of a race, but there were a few potential improvers. A big step up from surprise winner, but in line with her Flat form.

NOTEBOOK
Venetian Dove(IRE) had been unplaced in four maiden hurdles, made a successful debut for Evan Williams. The switch to handicaps was clearly a help and, having travelled best, she found enough in front to hold on, although there's little doubt the third should have given her more of a race. Considering the market drift, it's possible she'll improve and it will be interesting to see whether she's up to defying a rise. Official explanation: trainer's rep said, regarding apparent improvement in form, that the filly, previously trained in Ireland, had not been in the yard long and he could not offer a comment on its previous form. (op 7-1)

Ouest Eclair(FR) showed improved form upped to 2m6f latest, so it was surprising to see him dropped to 2m. He came in for support, though, and ran well without having the pace to win. (op 5-1)

Dr Finley(IRE), seventh in a Listed event at Wetherby latest, looked potentially interesting on this switch to handicaps, but he was given enough to do and the way he kept on close home to just miss out on second suggests there'll be improvement to come once he's upped in trip. (op 4-1)

Chalice Welcome, runner-up off 3lb higher in the race a year ago, never looked like winning. (op 5-1 tchd 4-1)

Red Skipper(IRE) was under strong pressure a long way from he finish and ended up well held. (op 13-2)

T/Plt: £289.90 to a £1 stake. Pool:£65,527.30 - 164.95 winning tickets T/Qpdt: £26.60 to a £1 stake. Pool:£6,366.23 - 176.60 winning tickets SP

292 FOLKESTONE (R-H)

Tuesday, November 16

OFFICIAL GOING: Hurdle course - heavy (soft in places); chase course - soft (hurdle: 6.5 chase: 6.8)

Wind: Almost nil Weather: Fine

2439 DAILY MAIL JUVENILE HURDLE (8 hdls) 2m 1f 110y

12:40 (12:40) (Class 4) 3-Y-0 **£2,602** (£764; £382; £190)

Form / RPR

0 **1** **Pepite Rose (FR)**[18] 2068 3-10-5 0 .... AidanColeman 93+
(Venetia Williams) *trckd ldrs: led sn after 2 out gng easily: pushed clr bef last: v comf* **5/2**[2]

120 **2** *5* **Kahfre**[18] 2078 3-10-12 114 .... JoshuaMoore(7) 98
(Gary Moore) *trckd ldrs: rdn 3 out: led briefly 2 out: brushed aside by wnr on long run towards last* **11/4**[3]

1F **3** *13* **Whipperway (IRE)**[18] 2078 3-10-7 0 .... MarcGoldstein(5) 79
(Sheena West) *hld up in tch: hit 2nd: effrt 3 out: drvn to chse ldng pair after 2 out: no imp: wknd flat* **15/8**[1]

33 **4** *9* **Miss Miracle**[20] 2033 3-10-2 0 .... RichieMcLernon(3) 62
(Jonjo O'Neill) *t.k.h: pressed ldr: led 3 out to 2 out: sn btn* **5/1**

0 **5** *3 1/4* **Rumballina**[18] 2068 3-10-2 0 .... AlexMerriam(3) 60
(Amy Weaver) *mde most to 3 out: sn wknd and bhd* **33/1**

50 **6** *30* **On The Right Path**[19] 2047 3-10-12 0 .... LeightonAspell 36
(Alison Batchelor) *in tch tl wknd rapidly 3 out: sn t.o* **66/1**

4m 32.9s (-2.70) **Going Correction** +0.05s/f (Yiel) **6** Ran SP% **111.1**
Speed ratings (Par 104): **97,94,89,85,83 70**
CSF £9.82 TOTE £4.50: £2.10, £2.10; EX 8.20.
Owner Potensis Limited **Bred** Pegasus Breeding Ltd **Trained** Kings Caple, H'fords

FOCUS
Testing ground on the hurdles course saw the ground officially advertised as heavy, soft in places and that played a massive part in this opening juvenile hurdle. The runners went steadily until they went out onto the back straight. The easy winner stood out in a weak race on his French form but is rated below that level here.

NOTEBOOK
Pepite Rose(FR) was clearly going to take all the beating from the penultimate flight. She showed promise on such ground in four outings in France prior to joining connections and it was her ability to act on it here that saw her come home an easy winner. She had clearly come on a bundle for her debut for connections at Uttoxeter last month and was very well backed earlier in the day, but proved friendless near the off. Venetia Williams' yard is now hitting top gear and, looking at the way she went about her business here, this scopey filly would be up to defying a penalty in such company before having a crack at something more valuable. (op 7-4 tchd 13-8 and 11-4)

Kahfre, who had yet to run on this sort of ground, came under heavy pressure around three out and was a sitting duck for the winner turning for home. He kept on gamely to finish a clear second-best and was giving a stone to that rival. Returning to a sounder surface is what he wants. (tchd 3-1)

Whipperway(IRE), well held when falling two out in Listed company last time, was heavily supported late on. She lacked fluency early on and made heavy weather of it when asked to close up from three out. She was another unproven on the contrasting surface, though, and it was most likely to blame for this laboured effort. (op 7-2)

Miss Miracle had disappointed in two runs since switching to this sphere and was yet another not to have run on such a surface, but her illustrious half-brothers Katchit and Prince Erik have both won on heavy ground. She proved free due to the steady gallop on and was in trouble before the third-last. A firm-ground winner on the level, this surface evidently wasn't for her and she will surely be capable of upping her game in this sphere down the line. (tchd 9-2, 11-2 in a place)

2440 E B F DAILY MAIL "NATIONAL HUNT" NOVICES' HURDLE QUALIFIER (8 hdls) 2m 1f 110y

1:10 (1:10) (Class 4) 4-6-Y-O **£2,602** (£764; £382; £190)

Form RPR

440- **1** **Oscar Prairie (IRE)**[216] 5184 5-10-12 108 NoelFehily 115+
(Warren Greatrex) *trckd ldr: led 3rd: drew clr 5th: in command after: shkn up flat: unchal* **8/13**[1]

0-44 **2** *5* **Top Smart**[15] 2129 4-10-7 101 JimmyDerham(5) 107
(Seamus Mullins) *hld up: hit 2nd: chsd clr wnr 5th: rdn and kpt on fr 2 out: nvr able to chal* **10/3**[2]

60- **3** *27* **Chervonet (IRE)**[225] 5050 4-10-12 0 (t) LiamTreadwell 80
(Nick Gifford) *mstke 1st: hld up: prog to chse wnr after 3rd to 5th: sn struggling: wknd bef last* **14/1**

0P-1 **4** *3* **Lomitaar**[121] 1028 5-11-5 0 AndrewTinkler 84
(Tony Newcombe) *hld up: outpcd fr 5th: disp modest 3rd u.p 2 out: wknd bef last* **5/1**[3]

0 **5** *dist* **Candlefort Lady (IRE)**[17] 2087 5-10-5 0 JamieMoore —
(Linda Jewell) *in tch to 5th: sn wknd: wl t.o after 2 out* **100/1**

00-0 **6** *dist* **King Richard (IRE)**[27] 1914 6-10-12 0 AndrewThornton —
(Richard Rowe) *racd freely: j.lft: led to 3rd: wknd and mstke 5th: sn t.o* **66/1**

4m 27.1s (-8.50) **Going Correction** +0.05s/f (Yiel)
WFA 4 from 5yo+ 7lb **6** Ran SP% **110.8**
Speed ratings: **110,107,95,94,—,—**
toteswingers:1&2:£1.02, 1&3:£7.80, 2&3:£8.60 CSF £3.03 TOTE £2.10: £1.10, £1.60; EX 3.20.
Owner The Weathercocks **Bred** Noel O'Connor **Trained** Upper Lambourn, Berks

FOCUS

A moderate novice hurdle but the fastest race over the trip. The winner was the form pick but this looks a step up.

NOTEBOOK

Oscar Prairie(IRE) had been found a decent opportunity to get off the mark and enhance his yard's excellent record at the course. He duly obliged with a decisive effort on this seasonal debut and is probably value for better than the winning margin as he got tired from the last. He stays further and his rider's decision to kick on down the back straight proved to be a winning move. He will look a bit vulnerable under a penalty in novice company, but looks to have done well for his time off the track and could have more to offer back in handicap company over a stiffer test. He also has the size to make up into a better chaser in due course. (op 5-4 tchd 11-8 in a place)

Top Smart posted an encouraging effort in defeat at Plumpton on his previous outing, but looked to want around 2m4f there and had yet to prove himself on soft ground. He was never going to get to the winner, but stuck to his task well in defeat and finished miles clear in second. There are definitely races to be won with him this season and now looks the time to switch to a handicap. (op 3-1 tchd 11-4)

Chervonet(IRE) had shown some ability on his debut in a bumper at Plumpton last term, but was well beaten next time. Equipped with a first-time tongue tie for this introduction to hurdling, he looked uneasy on the ground and in need of the experience. (op 9-1 tchd 16-1)

Lomitaar was last seen winning over 2m6f on good ground in July. He was in trouble from the third-last over this sharper test and wants further, but will struggle to defy his penalty in novice company. (op 3-1 tchd 11-2)

2441 DAILY MAIL NOVICES' CHASE (15 fncs) 2m 5f

1:40 (1:40) (Class 3) 4-Y-0+ **£6,505** (£1,910; £955; £477)

Form RPR

514- **1** **Ravethebrave (IRE)**[214] 5201 6-11-1 122 WayneHutchinson 118+
(Alan King) *hld up: prog 11th: blnd 4 out: effrt to ld 2 out: rdn out* **6/4**[1]

2660 **2** *1* **Canni Thinkaar (IRE)**[29] 1904 9-10-10 107(b) GemmaGracey-Davison(5) 115
(Zoe Davison) *trckd ldrs: led 8th: rdn 3 out: hdd next: kpt on wl but hld after last* **80/1**

643- **3** *5* **Rear Gunner (IRE)**[221] 5116 8-11-1 117 AndrewThornton 110
(Diana Grissell) *trckd ldr: led 6th tl nt fluent and hdd 8th: chsd ldr tl one pce and nt fluent 2 out* **4/1**[3]

1216 **4** *hd* **Alldunnandusted (IRE)**[24] 1970 6-10-10 118 JimmyDerham(5) 111
(Seamus Mullins) *in tch: nt fluent 9th: rdn to chse ldng trio 3 out: no imp fr next* **12/1**

241- **5** *12* **General Kutuzov (IRE)**[295] 3659 6-11-1 125 LiamTreadwell 99
(Nick Gifford) *inclined to hang lft: t.k.h: sn prom: lost pl 10th: outpcd fr next: wl btn after* **5/2**[2]

3-06 **6** *12* **Arkose (IRE)**[16] 2110 6-11-1 125 (v1) LeightonAspell 95+
(Oliver Sherwood) *nt fluent: led to 6th: lost pl 11th: bhd fr 3 out: no ch whn blnd 2 out* **11/2**

5m 22.8s (0.60) **Going Correction** +0.15s/f (Yiel) **6** Ran SP% **112.9**
Speed ratings (Par 107): **104,103,101,101,97 92**
toteswingers:1&2:£10.90, 1&3:£4.50, 2&3:£3.80 CSF £46.71 TOTE £2.30: £1.10, £8.20; EX 61.90.
Owner David Mason **Bred** Andrew Pierce **Trained** Barbury Castle, Wilts

FOCUS

A modest novice chase, run at an ordinary gallop. The winner is rated in line with his best hurdles form, with a surprise step up from the second.

NOTEBOOK

Ravethebrave(IRE) kept up the very good recent work of his stable and just did enough to get his account on this seasonal/chase debut. This former point winner looked to be waiting to go chasing in his novice hurdling campaign last term and was starting off over the trip that saw him winning at Kempton in March. He acted on the ground without much fuss, but wasn't foot perfect and had to work hard to fend off the 107-rated second after the last. He is entitled to improve on this, though, and may even prefer returning to further over fences. (op 13-8 tchd 11-8, 7-4 in places)

Canni Thinkaar(IRE), a dual winner over hurdles at this venue, had a tough task at the weights yet ran a solid race under his usual positive ride and evidently enjoyed this switch to chasing. His mark could suffer should the handicapper take this form too literally and so it wouldn't be that surprising to see him turned out quickly in a handicap over fences. (op 50-1)

Rear Gunner(IRE), returning from a 221-day break, was having his fifth outing as a chaser and his previous form was the best on offer here. He had also won his maiden hurdle at the course last year and he came in for support. He was given his chance under a prominent ride, but again made the odd error and ultimately left the impression the outing was needed. He is probably the best guide for this form. (op 5-1)

Alldunnandusted(IRE) tried to get involved from two out and, although he proved one paced under maximum pressure, this was a little more encouraging on his second outing as a chaser. (tchd 9-1)

General Kutuzov(IRE) produced a disappointing effort on this chasing debut considering he had the ground to suit for this seasonal return. This imposing sort took a keen grip over hurdles last term and again refused to settle here. He was undone by a mistake at the tenth, but his response thereafter was unconvincing and he now has a little bit to prove. It may be that reverting to a left-handed track will suit, though. Official explanation: jockey said gelding ran too free (op 2-1 tchd 3-1)

Arkose(IRE) again lacked fluency and the application of a first-time visor failed to work out. (op 7-1 tchd 5-1)

2442 DAILY MAIL HBLB MARES' H'CAP HURDLE (8 hdls) 2m 1f 110y

2:10 (2:11) (Class 3) (0-120,112) 4-Y-0+ **£5,204** (£1,528; £764; £381)

Form RPR

442 **1** **Kylenoe Fairy (IRE)**[10] 2217 6-11-1 99 (t) RichardJohnson 106+
(Paul Henderson) *trckd ldr to 3rd: styd prom: wnt 2nd again 3 out: rdn to ld bef last: drvn and styd on wl flat* **4/1**[3]

12-6 **2** *2* **Ocean Transit (IRE)**[13] 80 5-11-12 110 APMcCoy 114+
(Richard Price) *cl up: lost pl 4th: rdn 3 out: rallied u.p after 2 out: wnt 2nd last and ch: nt qckn flat* **11/8**[1]

-40F **3** *3* **Dot's Delight**[24] 1972 6-11-4 105 PeterToole(3) 105
(Mark Rimell) *hld up in tch: effrt 3 out: rdn to chse ldng pair after 2 out: one pce and nvr able to chal* **14/1**

-531 **4** *3* **Princess Rainbow (FR)**[9] 2242 5-12-0 112 7ex AlanO'Keeffe 109
(Jennie Candlish) *led at decent pce: hung lft bnd after 3rd: hdd and carried hd high bef last: wknd* **15/8**[2]

6612 **5** *21* **Just Beware**[7] 2294 8-10-8 97 (p) GemmaGracey-Davison(5) 76
(Zoe Davison) *hld up: prog 4th: chsd ldr 5th to next: wknd 2 out: t.o* **8/1**

2200 **6** *dist* **Stir On The Sea (IRE)**[27] 1921 4-11-2 100 HaddenFrost —
(James Frost) *chsd ldr 3rd to 5th: wknd rapidly next: sn t.o* **33/1**

4m 29.8s (-5.80) **Going Correction** +0.05s/f (Yiel)
WFA 4 from 5yo+ 7lb **6** Ran SP% **117.6**
Speed ratings (Par 107): **104,103,101,100,91 —**
toteswingers:1&2:£1.10, 1&3:£24.20, 2&3:£8.80 CSF £10.95 TOTE £4.00: £1.30, £1.90; EX 11.30.
Owner The Rockbourne Partnership **Bred** Eamon Hanrahan **Trained** Rockbourne, Hants

FOCUS

A fair mares' handicap with the top weight being rated 8lb below the race ceiling. There was a fair gallop on and the first four were closely covered at the last, but the first two came clear from that point. The winner ran to the level of her best form in Ireland.

NOTEBOOK

Kylenoe Fairy(IRE) was nicely handicapped on this return to hurdles if her much-improved effort over fences at Wincanton ten days earlier was to be believed. She confirmed she is an improving performer with a gutsy success, her career first at the 14th attempt under rules, and the drop in trip on more demanding ground worked the oracle. There could be some more to come back over fences from this ex-Irish mare.

Ocean Transit(IRE) arrived for this return to hurdling at the top of her game having signed off on the Flat with back-to-back wins. Well backed, she came under pressure a fair way out and it was only really due to her rider's strength that she managed to get so close in the end. Perhaps this ground was just that bit too demanding for her. (op 13-8 tchd 7-4 in a place)

Dot's Delight, who fell on her previous outing, stayed on dourly after coming under pressure round the final bend yet was done with from the final flight. This was more encouraging again. (op 16-1)

Princess Rainbow(FR) was penalised for her win at Hereford nine days earlier and again set out to make all. She showed her customary high head carriage at times, but still had her chance. It just looked a case of this more demanding ground on her quick reappearance taking its toll in the end. (op 5-2)

2443 DAILY MAIL RACEDAY H'CAP CHASE (IN MEMORY OF LADY HARMSWORTH BLUNT) (15 fncs) 2m 5f

2:40 (2:40) (Class 3) (0-125,121) 4-Y-0+
£9,393 (£2,775; £1,387; £694; £346; £174)

Form RPR

545- **1** **Zarrafakt (IRE)**[236] 4844 6-11-8 117 SamThomas 137+
(Emma Lavelle) *hld up in last: j. deliberately 2nd and 3rd: prog 11th: wnt 2nd after 3 out gng easily: chal and outj. 2 out: led after last: cruised clr* **2/1**[1]

111- **2** *3 3/4* **Ray Mond**[211] 5286 9-10-13 115 AnthonyFreeman(7) 119
(Sean Curran) *led: rdn and hrd pressed 2 out: styd on wl but hdd and easily outpcd after last* **6/1**

5231 **3** *14* **Sporting Rebel (IRE)**[25] 1950 10-11-11 120 HaddenFrost 110
(James Frost) *prom: chsd ldr 8th: rdn 11th: lost 2nd next: sn wl outpcd: plugged on to take modest 3rd last stride* **9/1**

0P0- **4** *shd* **Stradbrook (IRE)**[214] 5213 8-11-4 113 APMcCoy 105+
(Jonjo O'Neill) *hld up in tch: prog to trck ldr 4 out gng wl: lost 2nd after next: sn drvn and outpcd: lost modest 3rd last stride* **9/2**[2]

016- **5** *3/4* **Plein Pouvoir (FR)**[290] 3734 7-11-11 120 AidanColeman 110
(Venetia Williams) *chsd ldr 4th to 8th: mstke next: rdn in 4th after 3 out: sn lft bhd* **11/2**[3]

-P0U **6** *3 1/4* **Oncle Kid (FR)**[9] 2236 8-10-3 98 JamieMoore 84
(Paul Henderson) *in tch: jnd ldrs 10th: lost pl 12th: wl btn after next* **10/1**

50-0 **7** *shd* **Gaora Lane (IRE)**[32] 1858 9-11-12 121 NoelFehily 107
(Charlie Mann) *chsd ldr to 4th: steadily lost pl: last fr 10th: lost tch 12th: no ch after* **6/1**

5m 21.5s (-0.70) **Going Correction** +0.15s/f (Yiel) **7** Ran SP% **114.6**
Speed ratings (Par 107): **107,105,100,100,99 98,98**
toteswingers:1&2:£9.80, 1&3:£7.70, 2&3:£11.60 CSF £14.62 TOTE £3.70: £2.10, £2.10; EX 20.10.
Owner G P MacIntosh **Bred** Gerry Carroll **Trained** Wildhern, Hants

FOCUS

This looked to be an average handicap for the class, but the first pair came nicely clear and the form should work out. The easy winner was value for further and is rated up a stone on his best hurdles form.

NOTEBOOK

Zarrafakt(IRE), who won his bumper on this card in 2008, was well supported for this chase debut and came home an effortless winner under an ultra-confident ride by Sam Thomas. He bided his time out the back and jumped nicely considering it was his first taste of fences, though he improved on that front as the race went on. He scythed through the pack on the final lap and was cantering all over the runner-up at the top of the straight. That rival kept most gamely to his task and the winner made his only semblance of an error two out, but it made no difference as he coasted clear when asked to win after the last. He loves soft ground and, on this evidence, looks like making up into a better chaser. Indeed he would be all the rage if turned out under penalty before the handicapper can strike as he will be going up plenty for this. However, it must be noted he has now scored first time up in each of his three seasons of racing and this could well be the time to catch him. (op 5-2)

Ray Mond had a brilliant time of it last term, scoring on his return and going unbeaten in his last five outings, and was returning off a 12lb higher mark. He had his own way out in front and, although a sitting duck for the easy winner, he still looks on an upwards curve as he finished a clear second-best. (tchd 15-2)

Sporting Rebel(IRE) just got up for third. He had more on his plate than when winning off a 9lb higher mark last month and appeared to get found out by this drop back in trip. (op 7-1)
Stradbrook(IRE) lost the plot last season, but was resuming here off a very good mark if fully tuned up back over fences. He ran better than the bare form as he made a positive move in the back straight, but ultimately tired out of things and found the trip too far. A drop back in trip could well see him off the mark over fences, now he has a run under his belt. (tchd 4-1)
Plein Pouvoir(FR) had won well off an 8lb lower mark on his penultimate outing, but flopped off this mark at Cheltenham on his final start. The fact he wasn't seen afterwards last term would suggest something went amiss there and he ran a fair race on this comeback, shaping as though he would improve for it. (op 6-1 tchd 7-1)
Gaora Lane(IRE) Official explanation: jockey said, regarding running and riding after final fence, that he had continued to push with hands and heels and had achieved the best possible placing.

2444 DAILY MAIL H'CAP CHASE (16 fncs 2 omitted) 3m 1f
3:10 (3:11) (Class 5) (0-90,90) 4-Y-0+ **£2,797** (£821; £410; £205)

Form RPR
21-2 **1** **Portrait Royale (IRE)**[34] 1820 8-11-12 **90**.......................... FelixDeGiles 103+
(Anna Newton-Smith) *j. proficiently: led 2nd: mde most after at stdy pce: kicked on fr 3 out: styd on gamely u.p fr next* **2/1**[2]
2224 **2** *3¾* **You Can Of Course (IRE)**[9] 2239 7-10-10 **74**............... DougieCostello 80
(Neil Mulholland) *hld up: trckd wnr fr 4 out: rdn 2 out: nt qckn and no imp after* **7/4**[1]
-141 **3** *21* **Orion Star (IRE)**[15] 2132 8-10-13 **82**......................(p) JimmyDerham[(5)] 70
(Seamus Mullins) *led to 2nd: w wnr: reminder 11th: lost pl 4 out and sn bhd: tk remote 3rd again flat* **7/2**[3]
0332 **4** *4* **Romney Marsh**[12] 2170 9-11-2 **80**....................................... HaddenFrost 63
(Roger Curtis) *cl up: pushed along 12th: sn lft bhd by ldng pair: lost remote 3rd flat* **9/2**

6m 36.3s (0.50) **Going Correction** +0.15s/f (Yiel) **4** Ran SP% **110.1**
Speed ratings (Par 103): **105,103,97,95**
CSF £6.11 TOTE £1.70; EX 5.30.
Owner Pps Racing **Bred** Patrick Nagle **Trained** Jevington, E Sussex

FOCUS
The second fence after the winning post was omitted due to a low sun. This low-grade handicap saw a repeat of last year's 1-2 as Portrait Royale followed up her win last season over You Can Of Course. A personal best from the winner.

NOTEBOOK
Portrait Royale(IRE) had turned in a pleasing comeback effort at Uttoxeter last month and a 1lb rise for that meant she was 16lb higher than when taking this event in 2009. She jumped boldly for most of the way, but began to feel the pinch around four out and the runner-up appeared to still have plenty in the tank in behind her. She kept responding for her rider's urgings, however, and it was apparent throughout the home straight her old rival was going to struggle to get to the front. She has ultra-consistent form figures and this has to rate a career best display. (op 13 8)
You Can Of Course(IRE) gave 6lb to the winner in this last term and was in receipt of 16lb from her this time, so it wasn't surprising to see him well backed to reverse the form with his yard in such good form. He jumped well enough on this return to fences and looked to be going much better than his old rival nearing the home straight. The distress signals were being sent out soon after, though, and while he did his best to close from two out he was always being held. He does deserve to go one better again and is probably happier on better ground. (tchd 6-4)
Orion Star(IRE) was easily shaken off from the third-last. Runner-up in this race in 2008, he was up 6lb for making all at Plumpton 15 days earlier, but wasn't left alone in the lead here. He lacked fluency at times and it was clear after embarking on the final lap he was in trouble. The softer ground probably did for him. (op 5-1 tchd 11-2)
Romney Marsh was found out when the first two asserted on the final circuit and ran well below her recent level. (op 5-1 tchd 11-2)

2445 DAILY MAIL STANDARD OPEN NATIONAL HUNT FLAT RACE 2m 1f 110y
3:40 (3:40) (Class 5) 4-6-Y-0 **£1,712** (£499; £249)

Form RPR
1 **Penny Max (IRE)**[275] 4-11-2 0.. SamThomas 94+
(Emma Lavelle) *hld up last: prog 5f out: led 2f out: shkn up and clr 1f out: pushed out* **1/4**[1]
2 *4½* **Armedanddangerous (IRE)** 5-11-2 0......................... DougieCostello 85
(Tom Gretton) *t.k.h: prom: chsd ldr 10f out to over 2f out: kpt on to take 2nd ins fnl f* **14/1**
0 **3** *2½* **Thewellmeadow (IRE)**[11] 2186 5-11-2 0.................... RichardJohnson 82
(Paul Henderson) *led at stdy pce: kicked on 5f out: hdd and one pce 2f out: lost 2nd ins fnl f* **12/1**[3]
4 *3½* **Ice 'N' Easy (IRE)** 4-11-2 0.. AndrewThornton 79
(Richard Rowe) *trckd ldr to 10f out: styd cl up: rdn 4f out: outpcd fr over 2f out* **16/1**
0 **5** *5* **Smart Catch (IRE)**[38] 1778 4-10-11 0............................ LeeEdwards[(5)] 74
(Tony Carroll) *hld up in last pair: rdn and prog 4f out: disp 3rd 2f out: fdd* **20/1**
- **6** *10* **Sterling Chief** 6-11-2 0.. LeightonAspell 64
(Oliver Sherwood) *hld up: rdn and dropped to last pair 4f out: struggling after* **9/2**[2]
7 *10* **Luna Lightning** 6-10-9 0.. JamieMoore 47
(Linda Jewell) *trckd ldrs: lost pl and dropped to last pair 5f out: sn struggling* **50/1**
0/6 **8** *13* **Knowsall**[35] 1817 5-10-13 0.. AlexMerriam[(3)] 41
(Ms A E Embiricos) *prom on outer: disp 2nd 1/2-way: rdn and wknd 4f out* **33/1**

4m 38.4s (13.20) **Going Correction** +0.05s/f (Yiel) **8** Ran SP% **128.1**
Speed ratings: **72,70,68,67,65 60,56,50**
toteswingers:1&2:£3.70, 1&3:£2.70, 2&3:£11.50 CSF £7.65 TOTE £1.50: £1.02, £3.60, £2.90; EX 9.30.
Owner Highclere Thoroughbred Racing-Penny Max **Bred** Micheal Woodlock **Trained** Wildhern, Hants

FOCUS
A moderate bumper, but Penny Trix won well and has a future. The form has been given a token rating through the third.

NOTEBOOK
Penny Max(IRE), whose trainer won this with Zarrafakt in 2008, was snapped up by connections for £45,000 after finishing a close second on his sole outing in an Irish point in February, a race working out nicely. He was backed to the exclusion of his rivals on this bumper debut and ran out a convincing winner, handing his trainer/rider a double on the card. He was settled in last early and took a bit of time to settle off the ordinary gallop. He made smooth headway to get involved out of the back straight and looked all over the most likely winner, but just ran somewhat green when initially asked to seal the race. It was clear when he was in front 2f out he was going to collect, though, and the experience should be to his benefit. His dam is closely related to Cousin Vinny and Scottish National winner Four Trix, and a longer trip will be to his liking once sent hurdling. (op 3-10)
Armedanddangerous(IRE) is related to both hurdle and Flat winners. He travelled nicely and, while firmly put in his place when the winner kicked for home, there was a fair bit to like about his finishing effort. He should come on a bundle for the experience and has a future. (op 18-1)

Thewellmeadow(IRE) had the run of things out in front, but refused to go down lightly when headed and this was a marked improvement on his debut effort earlier this month. (tchd 10-1)
Ice 'N' Easy(IRE) is out of a dam that is half-sister to winners of bumpers, points and to the dam of Tranquil Sea. He looks in need of a stiffer test already and should improve for this debut outing. (op 25-1)
Sterling Chief, whose yard sent out a debut bumper winner at Plumpton the previous day, is bred to enjoy further over jumps and got badly outpaced as the tempo lifted on this racecourse debut. (tchd 4-1)
T/Plt: £33.40 to a £1 stake. Pool:£58,908.82 - 1,283.91 winning tickets T/Qpdt: £13.00 to a £1 stake. Pool:£4,037.25 - 229.60 winning tickets JN

2188 HEXHAM (L-H)
Wednesday, November 17

OFFICIAL GOING: Heavy (5.0)
Last fence in back straight omitted all chases. First and last hurdles in the back straight omitted all hurdle races. Rails moved in back straight and top bend.
Wind: Fresh, half behind Weather: Overcast, dull

2446 EBF D SQUADRON THE ROYAL DRAGOON GUARDS "NATIONAL HUNT" NOVICES' HURDLE (QUALIFIER) (5 hdls 3 omitted) 2m 110y
1:10 (1:10) (Class 4) 4-6-Y-0 **£2,797** (£821; £410; £205)

Form RPR
025 **1** **Blenheim Brook (IRE)**[17] 2102 5-10-12 0...................... PeterBuchanan 111+
(Lucinda Russell) *cl up: led 1st: mde rest: rdn and r.o strly bef last* **13/8**[1]
F-66 **2** *1* **Ceasar's Return**[35] 1829 5-10-12 0....................................... BarryKeniry 109
(George Moore) *midfield: outpcd after 2 out (usual 3 out): sn rallied: effrt and chsd wnr run-in: kpt on fin* **11/1**[3]
-114 **3** *4½* **Noble Scholar (IRE)**[17] 2102 5-10-12 0............................. BrianHughes 105
(Alan Swinbank) *sn chsng wnr: effrt passing omitted 2 out: one pce last: no ex and lost 2nd run-in* **3/1**[2]
-553 **4** *9* **Lackamon**[35] 1829 5-10-12 0.. TjadeCollier 95
(Sue Smith) *cl up: rdn and outpcd passing omitted 2 out: no imp whn lft 4th last* **3/1**[2]
-04U **5** *7* **Shooting Times**[8] 2296 5-10-7 0.................................. JamesHalliday[(5)] 88
(Andrew Parker) *hld up: short lived effrt after 2 out (usual 3 out); outpcd passing omitted 2 out* **25/1**
0PP/ **6** *20* **Borderhopper**[592] 4844 6-10-5 0... MrAPKelly[(7)] 68
(Ferdy Murphy) *hld up: rdn bef omitted 2 out: sn struggling* **33/1**
5 **7** *15* **Pagan Lightning (USA)**[79] 1426 5-10-9 0.......................... JamesO'Farrell[(3)] 53
(Dianne Sayer) *prom tl rdn and wknd bef omitted 2 out* **50/1**
/00- **8** *3* **Monsoon Music (IRE)**[208] 5370 6-10-12 0.................... CampbellGillies 50
(Lucinda Russell) *hld up in midfield: effrt after 2 out (usual 3 out): wknd fr omitted 2 out* **100/1**
9 *4* **Some Catch (IRE)**[228] 4999 4-10-2 0.............................. HarryHaynes[(3)] 39
(Elliott Cooper) *sn rdn in midfield: wknd bef omitted 2 out* **100/1**
0- **10** *54* **King Puc**[384] 1970 5-10-9 0.. RyanMania[(3)] —
(Barry Murtagh) *bhd: struggling after 2 out (usual 3 out): nvr on terms* **200/1**
2-0 **F** **Kvarner Riviera (IRE)**[40] 1764 4-10-12 0............................ GrahamLee 95
(Malcolm Jefferson) *t.k.h: in tch: effrt passing omitted 2 out: outpcd bef last: 9 l 4th and hld whn fell last* **16/1**

4m 56.5s (39.10) **Going Correction** +1.025s/f (Soft) **11** Ran SP% **113.5**
Speed ratings: **49,48,46,42,38 29,22,21,19,—,—**
toteswingers:1&2 £4.60, 2&3 £6.50, 1&3 £1.10 CSF £19.58 TOTE £3.50: £1.10, £4.70, £1.10; EX 17.50.
Owner The County Set Three **Bred** Richard Frisby **Trained** Arlary, Perth & Kinross

FOCUS
The rail was moved in the back straight and at the top bend to provide as much fresh ground as possible. This ordinary novice hurdle was run at a steady pace in the conditions, riders confirming that the ground was testing and hard work, and the time was over a minute outside the standard. They jumped only five flights instead of the usual eight. The winner was the form pick but is rated 5lb off his best.

NOTEBOOK
Blenheim Brook(IRE) is quite a keen sort and he was allowed to take over in front with a full circuit left to run. As a winning pointer his stamina was not in much doubt and he stayed on well to hold off his pursuers, turning around Carlisle form with the third home over this shorter trip. He is likely to remain over hurdles this term and a return to further will not trouble him when conditions are less extreme. (op 9-4)
Ceasar's Return lost his pitch heading away past the stands but began to stay on from the home turn, and things would have been interesting had the run-in been a little longer. A return to 2m4f should suit him. (op 18-1)
Noble Scholar(IRE) was the best part of four lengths in front of Blenheim Brook on the same terms at Carlisle, but that was over half a mile further. He was never far from the pace and gave his running, but was held in second when rapping the final flight. (op 5-2)
Lackamon was outpaced by the principals from the home turn and is another who will benefit from returning to a longer trip. (tchd 11-4)
Shooting Times was never a factor but again showed a glimmer of promise. (op 28-1 tchd 33-1)
Kvarner Riviera(IRE) was runner-up in a bumper in the spring but was down the field on his return last month. He went well for a long way on this hurdles debut, looking sure to reach a place, but dropped away quickly as they began the final incline and was a tired fourth when coming down at the last. He may well have further strengthening to do. (op 12-1 tchd 11-1)

2447 DURHAM COUNTY CRICKET CLUB NOVICES' CHASE (10 fncs 2 omitted) 2m 110y
1:40 (1:41) (Class 3) 4-Y-0+ **£5,464** (£1,696; £913)

Form RPR
321/ **1** **Best Lover (FR)**[591] 4859 8-10-11 0............................... HarryHaynes[(3)] 130
(James Ewart) *prom: rdn and outpcd 2 out: rallied to ld bef last: drvn out run-in* **22/1**
312- **2** *2¾* **Glenwood Knight (IRE)**[228] 4990 7-11-0 0...................... JasonMaguire 127
(Donald McCain) *cl up: led 1st: rdn and hdd bef last: kpt on u.p run-in: hld towards fin* **2/1**[2]
511- **3** *10* **Lord Villez (FR)**[236] 4876 6-10-7 116.............................. PaulGallagher[(7)] 119
(Ferdy Murphy) *trckd ldrs: effrt after 2 out: no imp on first two whn nt fluent last: one pce* **14/1**[3]
53PU **P** **Quatro Pierji (FR)**[9] 2270 6-11-0 110................................(p) PaddyAspell —
(James Moffatt) *nt fluent: led to 1st: chsd ldrs: outpcd after 5th: lost tch next: t.o whn p.u bef 2 out* **66/1**
214- **P** **Bygones Of Brid (IRE)**[221] 5123 7-11-0 0........................... GrahamLee —
(Karen McLintock) *t.k.h: sn w ldr tl wknd qckly and p.u bef last* **4/7**[1]

4m 21.2s (11.40) **Going Correction** +0.85s/f (Soft) **5** Ran SP% **109.5**
Speed ratings (Par 107): **107,105,101,—,—**
CSF £66.02 TOTE £14.50: £7.30, £2.00; EX 37.80.
Owner The Best Lovers **Bred** Mlle Lara Kovenko **Trained** Langholm, Dumfries & G'way

FOCUS
An interesting novice chase, run in a time 21 seconds outside the standard.
NOTEBOOK
Best Lover(FR) picked up a minor leg injury when winning a novice hurdle over C&D in April 2009 and this was his first appearance since. A tall gelding, he jumped soundly on this chasing debut but the three in front of him looked to be going better after the second-last. He stayed on for pressure though and, having led before the final fence, was pulling away at the line. Racing here without the regular tongue tie he wore before his lay-off, he will stay further and is already proven on better ground. (op 12-1 tchd 25-1)
Glenwood Knight(IRE) ◆, making his chase debut after more than seven months off the course, showed up well for a long way on the sharp end but could not hold off the winner from the home turn. He jumped solidly and has the look of a chaser, so should not be long in getting off the mark in this sphere. He is proven over further. (op 5-2)
Lord Villez(FR) won a brace of novice hurdles at the end of last season and was making his chasing debut in this country, but he had run no fewer than 16 times over fences for his previous connections in France. He ran well enough but lacked the pace of the principals from the second-last. (op 17-2)
Quatro Pierji(FR) soon made it clear that he didn't fancy this, putting the brakes on at the first, and was eventually pulled up after jumping slowly again more than once. He has yet to complete over fences. (op 8-11 tchd 4-5 in a place)
Bygones Of Brid(IRE), a Grade 2-winning novice last season and rated 20lb or more superior to his opponents over hurdles, was the disappointment. An athletic gelding, if not the biggest, he jumped well on this chase debut, matching strides with Glenwood Knight for much of the way, but was brought under pressure after the second-last and stopped very quickly, to the extent that he was pulled up before the final fence. His trainer had expressed concern beforehand that he may need the race, as he did first time out last season, and he should not be written off. Official explanation: trainer had no explanation for the poor form shown (op 8-11 tchd 4-5 in a place)

2448 NORTHUMBRIA H'CAP HURDLE (6 hdls 4 omitted) 2m 4f 110y
2:10 (2:10) (Class 4) (0-110,110) 4-Y-0+ **£1,893** (£1,893; £429; £214)

Form				RPR
-111	1		**Fair Spin**[9] 2275 10-10-4 **93**.....(v) JamesHalliday(5)	98
			(Micky Hammond) *cl up: hdwy to ld last: hdd cl home: rallied to dead-heat on post* **5/2**[1]	
P-00	1	*dht*	**Kempski**[12] 2104 10-10-8 **95**..... RyanMania(3)	100
			(Rayson Nixon) *led tl hdd passing omitted 2 out: rallied to chal last: led nr fin: jnd post* **40/1**	
6-00	3	*1 1/4*	**Mister Pete (IRE)**[40] 1762 7-10-7 **96**.....(p) AlexanderVoy(5)	100
			(Chris Grant) *trckd ldrs: led passing omitted 2 out: hdd last: rallied: hld towards fin* **10/1**	
01/0	4	*2*	**Kings Guard (IRE)**[17] 2104 7-9-13 **86**..... EwanWhillans(3)	90+
			(Alistair Whillans) *hld up: hdwy passing omitted 2 out: rdn and ev ch whn nt fluent last: one pce* **8/1**[3]	
45-2	5	*8*	**Texas Holdem (IRE)**[11] 2208 11-11-9 **110**..... JamesO'Farrell(3)	105
			(Michael Smith) *midfield: hdwy 1/2-way: ev ch passing omitted 2 out: wknd after last* **12/1**	
F-P2	6	*3*	**Delightfully (FR)**[39] 1782 6-11-5 **103**.....(p) PeterBuchanan	94
			(Lucinda Russell) *hld up: rdn after 3 out (usual 2 out): effrt passing omitted 2 out: no imp bef last* **8/1**[3]	
4-4U	7	*7*	**Oil Burner**[12] 2191 5-11-5 **103**..... CampbellGillies	87
			(William Amos) *t.k.h: in tch tl rdn and wknd bef last* **18/1**	
01-P	8	*14*	**Bollin Fiona**[194] 193 6-10-11 **105**..... CallumWhillans(10)	75
			(Donald Whillans) *in tch: lost pl bef 2 out (usual 3 out): n.d after* **33/1**	
40-0	9	*3 3/4*	**Euro American (GER)**[17] 2104 10-11-4 **102**..... WilsonRenwick	76
			(Rose Dobbin) *midfield: hdwy to trck ldrs bef omitted 2 out: wknd bef last* **16/1**	
0262	10	*hd*	**Manoubi**[12] 2189 11-10-2 **86**..... JamesReveley	52
			(Martin Todhunter) *hld up: rdn bef omitted 2 out: sn btn* **13/2**[2]	
/34-	P		**Nodform William**[252] 4509 8-11-2 **107**..... NathanMoscrop(7)	—
			(Karen McLintock) *in tch tl wknd passing omitted 2 out: t.o whn p.u bef last* **22/1**	
133/	P		**Spirit Calling (IRE)**[867] 833 9-10-2 **93**..... MrGJCockburn(7)	—
			(Lucinda Russell) *in tch: rdn after 2 out (usual 3 out): wknd at omitted 2 out: t.o whn p.u bef last* **14/1**	
644-	P		**Perfectus (IRE)**[214] 5229 6-10-11 **95**..... GrahamLee	—
			(Malcolm Jefferson) *hld up: rdn bef omitted 2 out: sn btn: t.o whn p.u bef last* **20/1**	
2P-3	P		**Also Jo**[9] 2275 7-10-12 **99**..... HarryHaynes(3)	—
			(William Amos) *w ldr tl wknd after omitted 2 out: t.o whn p.u bef last* **33/1**	

5m 31.4s (18.90) **Going Correction** +1.025s/f (Soft) **14** Ran SP% **116.2**
Speed ratings (Par 105): **105,105,104,103,100 99,96,91,90,90** —,—,—,—WIN: Kempski £22.20, Fair Spin £1.70 PL: K £13.50, FS £1.60 MP £4.30. EX: K/FS £77.00 FS/K £147.90 CSF: K/FS £65.85, FS/K £58.09 TRI K/FS/Mister Pete £563.96 FS/K/MP £434.79 toteswingers: Kempski & Fair Spin £39.80, K&3 £17.10, FS&3 £14.10: £27, £Owner, £Bendery Properties Holdings Ltd, £BredA S Reid Trained Trifecta £Middleham Moor, N Yorks.
Owner Rayson & Susan Nixon **Bred** W T Kemp **Trained** Ettrickbridge, Borders

FOCUS
Quite a competitive handicap hurdle, and the form has a solid look to it. The whole field was still in with a shout on the extended run between the final two flights, and there were still five in contention over the last. In the end the first two home could not be separated. The dead-heaters have been rated to their marks.
NOTEBOOK
Fair Spin took a narrow lead at the last and boxed on for a share of the spoils. Completing a four-timer over hurdles, stretching back to the summer, he escaped a penalty for his latest win and was officially 7lb ahead of the handicapper, so things will obviously be tougher off his revised mark. He is in fine heart and acts on all types of ground. (tchd 11-4)
Kempski made the running as usual but looked set to be swallowed up on the home turn. He refused to give in and rallied well, seeming to have snatched the race outright in the last strides but having to settle for a dead-heat. Heavy ground and 2m4f are his conditions, and he was almost a stone lower than when last winning in March last year. This was his first success away from Ayr. (tchd 11-4)
Mister Pete(IRE), a previous winner in heavy ground, was sharper for his recent return to action. He could not adopt his favoured front-running role, but was never far from the pace and only gave best on the run-in. This was a sound effort. (op 11-1)
Kings Guard(IRE) ◆ was back up in trip for this second run back following an absence of over 19 months. The only one to get involved from the rear, he was staying on when appearing to jump into the back of Fair Spin at the last, costing him valuable momentum. He is capable of winning off this mark. (op 9-1 tchd 13-2)
Texas Holdem(IRE) won this race all of five years ago, but has presumably had his problems and has appeared only a dozen times since. Raised 6lb for his Kelso second, he looked to be going as well as anything turning into the home straight but his big weight then began to tell. (op 14-1)
Delightfully(FR), 6lb higher than when second over 3m here but still a pound well-in, will be suited by a return to a longer trip. (op 15-2)
Oil Burner, a second-fence casualty on his recent chasing debut here, travelled nicely to the home turn on this handicap debut and it will be interesting to see which way connections go with him. (op 20-1)
Manoubi was ultimately well held on this return to hurdling, and connections could offer no explanation. Official explanation: trainer had no explanation for the poor form shown (op 8-1)
Spirit Calling(IRE), usually a chaser and not seen since July 2008, ran better than the bare facts. (tchd 12-1)

2449 SOLAR SIGNS NORTHUMBERLAND NATIONAL (HANDICAP CHASE) (22 fncs 3 omitted) 4m
2:40 (2:41) (Class 3) (0-135,132) 4-Y-0+ **£7,185** (£2,332; £1,284)

Form				RPR
/22-	1		**Belon Gale (IRE)**[346] 2728 7-11-12 **132**..... WilsonRenwick	143+
			(Howard Johnson) *set stdy pce: mde all: drew clr fr 2 out* **7/2**[3]	
6-05	2	*8*	**Camden George (IRE)**[17] 2106 9-10-7 **113**..... HenryOliver	110
			(Sue Smith) *pressed wnr thrght: rdn and outpcd 2 out: no imp after* **11/4**[1]	
34/0	3	*63*	**See You There (IRE)**[17] 2106 11-10-12 **118**.....(t) PeterBuchanan	52
			(Lucinda Russell) *in tch: blnd 16th: outpcd whn lft 6 l 3rd 3 out: wknd fr next* **4/1**	
/4F-	P		**Carry Duff**[349] 2669 9-9-7 **106** oh10..... PaulGallagher(7)	—
			(Ferdy Murphy) *hld up last: hit 7th and 11th: outpcd bef 17th: sn struggling: t.o whn p.u bef next* **7/1**	
44P3	P		**The Green Hat (IRE)**[12] 2193 10-9-7 **106** oh28..... HenryBrooke(7)	—
			(Theresa Gibson) *prom: struggling after 17th: t.o whn p.u bef last* **25/1**	
U13-	F		**Classic Cut**[241] 4754 6-11-2 **125**.....(p) HarryHaynes(3)	—
			(James Ewart) *trckd ldrs: 3 l down and gng wl whn fell 3 out* **3/1**[2]	

9m 46.0s (50.60) **Going Correction** +1.675s/f (Heav) **6** Ran SP% **110.2**
Speed ratings (Par 107): **103,101,85,**—,—,—
CSF £13.38 TOTE £3.70: £1.40, £1.80; EX 15.90.
Owner Andrea & Graham Wylie **Bred** Roland Rothwell **Trained** Billy Row, Co Durham

FOCUS
This marathon proved a dour test of stamina as expected, and only three completed despite a very steady pace. Not form to be overly confident about but the winner looks decent.
NOTEBOOK
Belon Gale(IRE) was runner-up in both his starts last season, the second of them behind the smart Money Trix at Kelso back in December, and was able to resume on the same mark as when running from 11lb out of the handicap in that race. Out in front all the way, jumping soundly, he had seen off the runner-up two from home and is obviously blessed with abundant stamina. This was a fine effort under topweight and this promising young stayer could be the type for the Eider Chase at Newcastle. (op 4-1)
Camden George(IRE) tracked the winner for most of the way but was beaten with two to jump. He saw out the trip better than most but has still never won a handicap. (op 4-1)
See You There(IRE), who was fifth in this event when it was last held in 2007, made an error early on the final circuit and could never get back into the race from that point. This Carlisle specialist is currently 4lb below his last winning mark. (op 7-2 tchd 3-1)
Carry Duff took a bad fall at Market Rasen on his most recent start in December last year, and reportedly lost his confidence. Racing from 10lb out of the weights on this return, he made more than one mistake in rear and was pulled up on the final circuit. (tchd 6-1)
Classic Cut was going well enough in third when crashing out three from home, but was about to enter uncharted territory as far as his stamina was concerned. He is only six and there are more races to be won with him over fences provided he is none the worse. (tchd 6-1)

2450 AT THE RACES VIRGIN 534 NOVICES' H'CAP CHASE (11 fncs 4 omitted) 2m 4f 110y
3:10 (3:11) (Class 4) (0-115,110) 4-Y-0+ **£2,927** (£859; £429; £214)

Form				RPR
P211	1		**Douglas Julian**[9] 2271 8-10-0 **84** oh2..... HenryOliver	106+
			(Sue Smith) *pressed ldr: rdn to ld after 2 out: asserting whn lft 21 l clr last: eased run-in* **13/8**[1]	
PU3/	2	*12*	**Innominate (IRE)**[636] 4015 8-10-12 **96**..... CampbellGillies	92
			(Lucinda Russell) *hld up: struggling 1/2-way: hdwy 2 out: lft mod 4th last: styd on to chse wnr run-in: no imp* **20/1**	
P042	3	*8*	**Tifoso (FR)**[39] 1781 5-10-13 **97**.....(v) BrianHughes	84
			(Richard Guest) *hld up: hdwy and in tch 1/2-way: rdn and outpcd in 3rd whn lft 21 l 2nd last: no ex* **9/2**[2]	
26-6	4	*12*	**Locked Inthepocket (IRE)**[17] 2107 6-11-3 **101**..... RichieMcGrath	76
			(Pauline Robson) *prom: effrt 2 out: sn struggling: no imp whn lft mod 3rd last* **8/1**	
/22-	5	*9*	**Time Out (IRE)**[277] 4028 7-11-5 **110**..... NathanMoscrop(7)	78
			(James Ewart) *cl up: rdn and outpcd whn mstke 2 out: sn wknd* **11/1**	
F4-0	6	*30*	**Young Buddy**[13] 2161 5-10-6 **95**..... JamesHalliday(5)	31
			(Malcolm Jefferson) *in tch: lost pl 1/2-way: lost tch fr 3 out: t.o* **17/2**	
PF0-	F		**Tartan Snow**[220] 5139 10-11-2 **107**..... GaryRutherford(7)	—
			(Stuart Coltherd) *in tch: rdn 4 out: 8 l sixth and outpcd whn fell 2 out* **33/1**	
50P-	P		**Golden Globe (IRE)**[225] 5074 8-11-2 **100**..... GrahamLee	—
			(Ferdy Murphy) *hld up: blnd 2nd: struggling fr 1/2-way: t.o whn p.u bef 2 out* **28/1**	
P-22	F		**Against The Wind**[12] 2194 7-10-11 **95**..... PeterBuchanan	102
			(Lucinda Russell) *led tl hdd after 2 out: 7 l 2nd and hld whn fell last* **6/1**[3]	

5m 46.0s (32.50) **Going Correction** +1.675s/f (Heav) **9** Ran SP% **111.7**
Speed ratings (Par 105): **105,100,97,92,89 77,**—,—,—
toteswingers:1&2 £1.90, 2&3 £15.20, 1&3 £2.20 CSF £32.50 CT £122.04 TOTE £2.00: £1.02, £8.00, £1.20; EX 39.20.
Owner Mrs S Smith **Bred** A M Armitage **Trained** High Eldwick, W Yorks

FOCUS
Few got involved in this modest novice handicap chase, in which most of them came home tired. The easy winner was value for a lot further with faller Against The Wind rated to his course form.
NOTEBOOK
Douglas Julian was always in the first two and had seen off long-time leader Against The Wind prior to being left a mile clear when that one fell at the last. This successful chasing debut followed two recent wins over hurdles, and the overweight meant he was effectively only 2lb higher here. That left him 6lb well-in, and receiving lumps of weight from his rivals, and he took full advantage. Apart from jumping rather low at the last there were none of the jumping errors he made over hurdles, and he should win more races. (op 9-4)
Innominate(IRE), who went without any headgear, had not run since February 2009 but had been dropped 9lb in his absence. He was struggling a long way out and was still a remote eighth taking the second-last, but stayed on past some tired horses for an unlikely runner-up spot. He is yet to win under rules but has finished second six times now. (op 22-1 tchd 25-1)
Tifoso(FR)'s narrow C&D second has been well advertised since by the winner Quinder Spring. He did not see this out in the ground and was a tired horse when left briefly in second place at the last. (op 4-1)
Locked Inthepocket(IRE) seemingly had trip and ground to suit but had been seen off with two to jump. (tchd 7-1)
Time Out(IRE) ◆ made smooth progress to tack on to the leaders, but was under pressure when stumbling two out and quickly beaten. He showed enough to suggest that he will pay his way over fences with this run under his belt. (op 12-1 tchd 14-1 and 10-1)
Tartan Snow was just starting to retreat on this seasonal bow when he fell two from home. (op 28-1)

Against The Wind had been runner-up in a pair of handicaps over the extended 2m here on his last two starts but was 5lb higher now. He tried to make all, but his legs turned to jelly after the second-last and he was held in second when coming down at the last. (op 28-1)

2451 AT THE RACES SKY 415 JUVENILE MAIDEN HURDLE (5 hdls 3 omitted) 2m 110y
3:40 (3:42) (Class 4) 3-Y-O £2,397 (£698; £349)

Form				RPR
F	1		**Danceintothelight**[22] 1825 3-10-12 0 BarryKeniry (Micky Hammond) *led: blnd 2 out (usual 3 out): hdd passing omitted 2 out: rallied bef last: led run-in: hld on wl u.p* **9/4**[2]	103+
	2	3/4	**Molon Labe (IRE)**[53] 3-10-12 0 JamesReveley (Tom Tate) *hld up in tch: stdy hdwy 1/2-way: led after omitted 2 out: rdn and hdd run-in: kpt on* **8/1**	100
52	3	3	**Manxman (IRE)**[10] 2245 3-10-12 0 GrahamLee (Ferdy Murphy) *chsd ldrs: pushed along fr 2nd: led briefly passing omitted 2 out: rdn and kpt on same pce last* **5/4**[1]	97
	4	3	**Vosges (FR)**[183] 3-10-9 0 HarryHaynes(3) (James Ewart) *prom: outpcd briefly bef omitted 2 out: effrt bef last: outpcd run-in* **7/2**[3]	94
	P		**Kai Broon (IRE)**[447] 3-10-12 0 CampbellGillies (Lucinda Russell) *hld up in tch: hdwy and ev ch passing omitted 2 out: wknd and p.u bef last* **25/1**	—
	P		**Brootommitty (IRE)**[181] 3-10-5 0 WilsonRenwick (P Monteith) *prom: struggling after 3rd: t.o whn p.u bef last* **80/1**	—
0	P		**Jack's Rocket**[17] 2108 3-10-12 0 PaddyAspell (Richard Guest) *t.k.h: hld up: struggling 2 out (usual 3 out): t.o whn p.u bef last* **66/1**	—
0	P		**Shaw Cross**[17] 2108 3-10-12 0 KennyJohnson (Robert Johnson) *bhd: lost tch 2nd: t.o whn p.u bef 2 out (usual 3 out)* **200/1**	—

4m 46.5s (29.10) **Going Correction** +1.85s/f (Heav) **8** Ran SP% **115.6**
Speed ratings (Par 104): **105,104,103,101,—,—,—,—**
toteswingers:1&2 £3.60, 2&3 £3.10, 1&3 £2.10 CSF £19.45 TOTE £2.40: £1.10, £2.10, £1.40; EX 23.10.
Owner Roland Roper **Bred** Mrs David Low **Trained** Middleham Moor, N Yorks

FOCUS
An ordinary juvenile hurdle. The time was ten seconds quicker than the opening novice event. The winner is entitled to rate higher on his Flat form.

NOTEBOOK
Danceintothelight was an unlucky loser on his hurdling debut at Wetherby last month, crashing out when clear two from home, but obviously suffered no ill-effects and has finished second on the Flat since. Making the running, he had to be picked up off the ground two out, still a good way from home, and seemed set to drop away when coming under pressure heading into the home straight. To his credit he rallied well and stayed on to show in front again near the line. He had a tough race and his jumping remains a concern, but he has the ability to rate higher than the bare form. (op 15-8 tchd 5-2)
Molon Labe(IRE) posted modest placed form on the Flat and stayed at least 1m4f. He looked set for a winning hurdles debut when striking the front going best, but idled a little in front and could not hold off the winner. His turn should come. (op 9-1 tchd 11-1 and 7-1)
Manxman(IRE) would have finished well behind Danceintothelight at Wetherby had it not been for the latter's fall but he ran better at Market Rasen, finishing just ahead of subsequent winner Marsh Warbler. He had his chance here but looked a hard ride, and the option of headgear remains open to connections. (op 15-8)
Vosges(FR) was runner-up in a pair of hurdles for Guillaume Macaire in France in the spring and the ground should not have been a problem on this British debut. He was not discredited, but if anything he possibly needs further. (tchd 10-3)
Kai Broon(IRE), who ran three times as a 2yo for this yard but had not been seen since, joined the leading group at the foot of the hill but his stamina soon failed him. (op 14-1)
T/Plt: £28.30 to a £1 stake. Pool of £68,015.84 - 1,750.12 winning tickets. T/Qpdt: £5.60 to a £1 stake. Pool of £5,189.88 - 676.64 winning tickets. RY

2150 WARWICK (L-H)
Wednesday, November 17

OFFICIAL GOING: Good to soft (good in places) changing to good to soft after race 1 (1.00)
Wind: Virtually nil Weather: Dull, overcast

2452 RACING UK H'CAP HURDLE (9 hdls) 2m 3f
1:00 (1:00) (Class 4) (0-100,100) 4-Y-0+ £2,602 (£764; £382; £190)

Form				RPR
5-01	1		**Salpierre (IRE)**[9] 2280 5-11-9 97 7ex APMcCoy (Jonjo O'Neill) *hld up towards rr: hdwy 5th: trcking ldrs whn nt fluent 3 out: wnt cl 2nd sn after: drvn to take slt advantage last: sn pushed clr: comf* **9/4**[1]	114+
-033	2	3	**Tom O'Tara**[14] 2150 6-11-8 99 WayneKavanagh(3) (Robin Dickin) *chsd ldr: wnt 2nd after 4th: slt ld 4 out: rdn appr 2 out: narrowly hdd last: sn no ch w wnr: styd on wl for 2nd* **12/1**	110
4-12	3	4 1/2	**Jeanry (FR)**[7] 2308 7-10-6 87 CDTimmons(7) (Arthur Whitehead) *led tl after 1st: chsd ldr to 5th: styd wl there and rdn 3 out: one pce fr 2 out* **7/2**[3]	94
06/6	4	24	**Baby Car (FR)**[16] 2131 6-10-12 86 RichardJohnson (Noel Chance) *in rr tl hdwy 5th: styd on to tae mod 4th appr 2 out* **20/1**	71
030-	5	10	**It's A Date**[19] 2664 5-11-7 95 WayneHutchinson (Alan King) *hit 1st and led sn after: hdd 4 out: wknd next* **11/4**[2]	71
0-05	6	4	**Lisdonagh House (IRE)**[12] 2190 8-10-5 79 TomSiddall (Lynn Siddall) *in rr: mod progress after 3 out* **80/1**	52
066-	7	2	**Royaume Bleu (FR)**[220] 5154 5-11-0 88 PaulMoloney (Alex Hales) *in rr: hung rt appr 5th: nvr any ch* **33/1**	59
/00-	8	hd	**Perkin Warbeck**[282] 3943 8-11-9 100 PeterToole(3) (Mark Rimell) *in rr: sme hdwy 5th: sn wknd* **40/1**	71
20P-	9	1/2	**French Ties (IRE)**[242] 4736 8-11-5 93 (p) AlanO'Keeffe (Jennie Candlish) *chsd ldrs to 4 out* **33/1**	63
0/15	10	2 3/4	**Washango (IRE)**[114] 1090 8-11-8 99 SamTwiston-Davies(3) (Shaun Lycett) *in tch to 5th* **40/1**	67
0-05	11	11	**Tiger Dream**[24] 1996 5-11-3 98 DannyBurton(7) (Chris Down) *chsd ldrs to 4th* **66/1**	56
1	12	14	**Baynes Cross (IRE)**[20] 2054 7-11-5 100 (b) PeterCarberry(7) (David Bourton) *j. slowly 5th: a in rr* **22/1**	45
/60-	P		**Red Perfection**[361] 2416 7-11-3 91 AidanColeman (Tony Carroll) *chsd ldrs: hit 4th: sn wknd: t.o whn p.u bef 2 out* **25/1**	—
06/5	P		**Pikasso (FR)**[19] 2075 7-11-4 92 WarrenMarston (Pam Sly) *mstke 1st: in tch: tl wknd and hit 4 out: t.o whn p.u bef 2 out* **20/1**	—

4m 29.38s (-13.32) **Going Correction** -0.575s/f (Firm) **14** Ran SP% **118.6**
Speed ratings (Par 105): **105,103,101,91,87 85,85,84,84,83 78,73,—,—**
toteswingers:1&2 £6.40, 2&3 £5.50, 1&3 £2.00 CSF £24.76 CT £95.08 TOTE £4.50: £1.90, £2.50, £1.30; EX 29.70.
Owner F Gillespie **Bred** Mrs Mary Furlong **Trained** Cheltenham, Gloucs

FOCUS
A good contest for the grade and three came nicely clear of the remainder. Steps up from the first two.

NOTEBOOK
Salpierre(IRE), whose win last time had already been boosted by the runner-up, took his time to get into contention but grinded out a tough victory from the second last. Due to go up 6lb, things will be tougher from now on but he promises to stay further, and he will no doubt be a chaser in the making if taking after his brother Ballyagran, a Grade 3 chase winner in Ireland. (op 5-2 tchd 11-4)
Tom O'Tara, a dual winner over 2m at this course last season, didn't reveal any stamina issues at this distance and merely bumped into an improving sort. No doubt his connections will find opportunities for him during the winter at this course. (op 14-1)
Jeanry(FR) settled just behind the leader, appeared to travel the best of those who came clear for the longest but couldn't pick up. Up 12lb from the coming weekend, he will possibly have a break now. (op 4-1)
Baby Car(FR) kept on from the rear. The step up in distance looked to suit but even further may be needed in time. (op 25-1)
It's A Date, up in trip, was prominent in the market, but not for any obvious reason on what he has shown over hurdles. He adopted front-running tactics shortly after the start, something he has done successfully on the Flat, but was beaten heading towards the end of the back straight. (op 5-2)
Royaume Bleu(FR) looked a tricky ride towards the rear, pulling hard and seeming to hang under pressure.
Perkin Warbeck Official explanation: jockey said gelding hung right
Red Perfection Official explanation: jockey said mare had a breathing problem

2453 DENNIS JORDAN HAPPY 80TH BIRTHDAY H'CAP CHASE (17 fncs) 2m 4f 110y
1:30 (1:30) (Class 4) (0-110,110) 4-Y-0+ £3,577 (£1,050; £525; £262)

Form				RPR
45-3	1		**Flemish Invader (IRE)**[41] 1747 7-11-9 107 PaddyBrennan (Nigel Twiston-Davies) *trckd ldrs: wnt 2nd after 10th: led 11th: hdd after 3 out: drvn to chal next and sn led: c clr run-in: readily* **5/2**[1]	124+
04-U	2	8	**Mylord Collonges (FR)**[19] 2073 10-10-13 100(p) SamTwiston-Davies(3) (Susan Nock) *j. slowly 3rd: hdwy 7th: chsd ldrs fr 10th: one pce whn mstke 2 out: kpt o to take wl hld 2nd fnl 100yds* **17/2**	107
0-14	3	4	**Quipe Me Posted (FR)**[25] 1965 6-11-7 105 APMcCoy (Jonjo O'Neill) *nt fluent 2nd: 3rd and 4th: in tch: hdwy to chse ldrs 11th: wnt 2nd 13th: chal 3 out: led sn ater: hit next and narrowly hdd: 1 l down and u.p whn blnd last: no ch after and lost wl hld 2nd fnl 100yds* **9/2**[2]	113+
-31F	4	16	**High Jack (IRE)**[19] 2073 8-11-12 110 NickScholfield (Andy Turnell) *in rr: hit 11th: mod prog after 3 out: no ch whn hit last* **8/1**	96
3-14	5	9	**Brimham Boy**[182] 409 8-11-7 105 (t) WarrenMarston (Martin Keighley) *led 3rd: hdd 9th: led after 10th: hdd 11th: wknd 4 out* **5/1**[3]	82
F-P1	6	1 1/4	**Pistolet Dove (IRE)**[27] 1940 8-11-6 107 RichieMcLernon(3) (Sophie Leech) *in rr: brief effrt 12th: sn bhd* **16/1**	83
21-3	7	28	**Karasakal (IRE)**[168] 584 7-11-4 102 JamieMoore (Gary Moore) *in tch 7th: hit 12th and sn wknd* **9/1**	50
4521	P		**Glengarra (IRE)**[16] 2134 13-11-6 104 (tp) TimmyMurphy (Liam Corcoran) *led to 3rd: led 9th tl after next: wknd bef 11th: t.o whn p.u bef 3 out* **10/1**	—

5m 17.12s (-3.88) **Going Correction** -0.15s/f (Good) **8** Ran SP% **110.0**
Speed ratings (Par 105): **101,97,96,90,86 86,75,—**
toteswingers:1&2 £12.10, 2&3 £13.80, 1&3 £3.20 CSF £21.84 CT £82.74 TOTE £4.10: £1.60, £4.20, £1.10; EX 27.30.
Owner Mrs E M Bathurst **Bred** Robert McCarthy **Trained** Naunton, Gloucs

FOCUS
The going changed from good to soft, good in places after the first race, which was on the hurdles course, to good to soft all round. An ordinary handicap chase with a small personal best from the winner.

NOTEBOOK
Flemish Invader(IRE) ◆ pressed on when getting to the front for the first time, but the horse almost immediately jumped right at the fences and lost the lead, but rather than panic, the rider did the right thing and got his mount interested again just in behind, and the pair got back into the race. A mistake at the last fence by the third no doubt helped, but it is also obvious that the winner has plenty of ability when in the mood, and was idling once in front, pricking his ears constantly. It should be onwards and upwards for him now. (op 11-4)
Mylord Collonges(FR) was given a never-say-die ride by Sam Twiston-Davies and kept on to claim second place. He might not be easy to win with, as he hasn't won since taking four races in 2008, but this was a fair effort. (op 11-1)
Quipe Me Posted(FR) ◆, having only his second try at chasing, ran much better than he had done on his chasing debut and was almost handed the race when the winner started to jump erratically. A mistake two out wasn't helpful but he met the final fence badly and sprawled on landing, almost certainly costing him second place. A drop in trip certainly wouldn't be an issue on this showing. (op 5-1)
Brimham Boy made the running until folding quite a way out on his first start since May. (op 9-2)

2454 BANBURY NOVICES' HURDLE (11 hdls) 2m 5f
2:00 (2:01) (Class 4) 4-Y-0+ £2,602 (£764; £382; £190)

Form				RPR
14-1	1		**Habbie Simpson**[19] 2075 5-11-5 0 WayneHutchinson (Alan King) *hld up towards rr: hdwy 7th: led 2 out: pushed out run-in: in n.d whn edgd rt fnl 75yds* **10/3**[2]	130+
2212	2	6	**Youralltalk (IRE)**[10] 2232 6-10-12 0 APMcCoy (Keith Goldsworthy) *led tl hdd 2 out: one pce sn after but styd on wl for clr 2nd* **7/2**[3]	115+
6-4	3	7	**The Boss (IRE)**[15] 2142 5-10-12 0 NickScholfield (Jeremy Scott) *chsd ldrs: wnt 2nd briefly 3 out: rdn appr 2 out: sn no ex and styd on same pce* **25/1**	109
/0-	4	1	**Don't Turn Bach (IRE)**[221] 5129 6-10-12 0 SamThomas (Paul Nicholls) *hld up in rr: hdwy appr 7th: chsd ldrs after 3 out: one pce whn mstke 2 out: sn no ch* **7/2**[3]	110+
220/	5	5	**The Old Pretender (IRE)**[580] 5053 7-10-12 0 PaddyBrennan (Nigel Twiston-Davies) *chsd ldrs: rdn and outpcd 3 out: kpt on same pce after next* **2/1**[1]	103
0-20	6	6	**Life Long (IRE)**[10] 2241 6-10-12 0 TomScudamore (Anabel L M King) *chsd ldrs: chal 5th to 4 out: wknd after 3 out* **80/1**	97

6-00 **7** *7* **Boosha**^{10} 2241 5-10-5 0 SeanQuinlan 84
(Rachel Hobbs) *in rr 5th: mod prog fr 2 out* **125/1**

04-6 **8** *3 ½* **Morcambe**^{26} 1951 5-10-12 0 FelixDeGiles 88
(Nicky Henderson) *chsd ldrs tl wknd 7th: no ch whn mstke 2 out* **28/1**

30-5 **9** *nse* **Vin De Roy (FR)**^{10} 2238 5-10-12 0 AidanColeman 88
(Rachel Hobbs) *in rr: hdwy and wl in tch 7th: wknd 3 out* **50/1**

04-P **10** *½* **Fidelor (FR)**^{20} 2058 4-10-12 0 RichardJohnson 87
(Henry Daly) *pressed ldrs tl wknd qckly appr 3 out* **66/1**

11 *20* **Coral Point (IRE)**^{228} 4-10-12 0 JoeTizzard 69
(Alan Jessop) *chsd ldrs to 4 out* **100/1**

/4- **12** *10* **Artic Pride (IRE)**^{564} 120 6-10-12 0 LeightonAspell 60
(Oliver Sherwood) *a in rr* **33/1**

0 **13** *42* **Colonel Alf**^{17} 2111 5-10-12 0 WillKennedy 23
(Alex Hales) *in tch tl wknd 7th* **125/1**

00/- **P** **Racing With Angels**^{695} 2921 8-10-12 0 JamesDavies —
(Pam Ford) *blnd 5th: a in rr: t.o whn p.u bef 4 out* **200/1**

004- **P** **Direct Approach (IRE)**^{242} 4741 6-10-12 83 TomSiddall —
(Lynn Siddall) *j. slowly 2nd: a in rr: t.o whn p.u bef 2 out* **150/1**

P **P** **Real Dandy**^{35} 1821 4-10-12 0 JamieGoldstein —
(Lucinda Featherstone) *hit 1st: in rr: mstke 6th: t.o whn p.u after 3 out* **200/1**

505- **P** **Flying Flagship**^{223} 5102 5-10-12 0 LiamHeard —
(Chris Down) *in rr tl hdwy 7th: sn wknd: t.o whn p.u bef 2 out* **150/1**

5m 9.00s (-6.00) **Going Correction** -0.15s/f (Good)
WFA 4 from 5yo+ 8lb **17** Ran SP% **120.7**
Speed ratings (Par 105): **105,102,100,99,97 95,92,91,91,91 83,79,63,—,— —,—**
toteswingers:1&2 £2.70, 2&3 £12.70, 1&3 £18.00 CSF £14.99 TOTE £4.60: £2.10, £1.10, £4.70; EX 14.40.
Owner Sandy Love **Bred** Moniabrock Farming **Trained** Barbury Castle, Wilts

FOCUS
A decent contest judged on previous form, and won by classy chaser Weird Al in 2008. The winner is on the upgrade and should rate higher.

NOTEBOOK
Habbie Simpson ◆, the only runner carrying a penalty, travelled really strongly throughout, so it was pleasing that he found so much once asked to quicken, in the manner of a smart sort. The runner-up from his Wetherby victory had already come out and won, and Alan King's horse looks certain to hold his own in much better company next time. The long-term aim is to get him qualified for the E.B.F Final at Sandown. (op 11-4 tchd 7-2)
Youralltalk(IRE), down in trip, got to the lead easily and made it a fair test before battling on bravely to collect second. He should win any ordinary novice, especially when stamina is required. (op 9-2)
The Boss(IRE) hinted at ability under rules last time at Exeter and proved that effort was no fluke with a sound performance behind a potentially classy type. (op 28-1)
Don't Turn Bach(IRE) was given a quiet ride in rear before making progress, but hit a flat spot on the final bend and could never make any meaningful impression thereafter A horse with a bit of size about him, he should be given another chance. (op 11-4 tchd 4-1 in places)
The Old Pretender(IRE) attracted solid market support but raced keenly and didn't get home. He was fully entitled to be rusty after his long absence, and will be better judged after his next outing. (op 10-3)
Life Long(IRE) was always prominent and showed some ability. (tchd 66-1)
Boosha didn't shape too badly in a slowly-run affair. (op 150-1)
Vin De Roy(FR) showed up well for a lot of the race and is probably not devoid of ability. (op 40-1)
Flying Flagship Official explanation: vet said gelding finished lame

2455 HIGHFLYER BLOODSTOCK FOUR YEARS OLD NOVICES' CHASE (12 fncs) 2m
2:30 (2:32) (Class 3) 4-Y-O **£5,854** (£1,719; £859; £429)

Form RPR

1 **Nadiya De La Vega (FR)**^{269} 4-10-3 0 AndrewTinkler 140+
(Nicky Henderson) *mde all: c clr fr 3 out: easily: unchal* **11/10**^{1}

2 *13* **Sir Du Bearn (FR)**^{319} 4-10-10 0 NoelFehily 134+
(Paul Nicholls) *hit 1st: in tch: chsd wnr fr 7th: no imp whn hit 4 out: styd on same pce appr 2 out* **11/4**^{2}

6-40 **3** *17* **Gilded Age**^{18} 2085 4-10-10 0 WayneHutchinson 115
(Alan King) *chsd wnr to 7th: no ch fr 4 out* **13/2**

25 **4** *4 ½* **Shalimar Fromentro (FR)**^{25} 1966 4-10-10 0 DarylJacob 115+
(Nick Williams) *in tch whn blnd 6th: no ch fr 8th: mstke 3 out* **6/1**^{3}

3P-1 **5** *3 ¾* **Sergeant Pink (IRE)**^{7} 2313 4-10-10 0 TomScudamore 112
(Steve Gollings) *disp 2nd: j. slowly 6th: rdn bef next: wknd 4 out: mstke next: blnd last* **9/1**

3m 56.1s (-9.50) **Going Correction** -0.15s/f (Good) **5** Ran SP% **111.9**
Speed ratings: **117,110,102,99,97**
CSF £4.79 TOTE £2.50: £1.70, £1.20; EX 5.30.
Owner Million In Mind Partnership **Bred** Haras de la Vega **Trained** Upper Lambourn, Berks

FOCUS
Traditionally a good race, which has produced a future Arkle winner in Voy Por Ustedes. There was not much form to go on but the first two are probably well above average.

NOTEBOOK
Nadiya De La Vega(FR), who had two handlers in the paddock, was nicely on her toes for her British debut and soon got into the lead. She jumped nicely on her first outing over fences, making only a few minor mistakes, and bounded on to a clear-cut success. Visually this was a pleasing start, and she certainly isn't short of size, so one would imagine that connections should be keen to use both her weight-for-age and sex allowance where possible over fences, which would make her difficult to beat off low weights. (op 6-5 tchd Evens and 5-4 in places)
Sir Du Bearn(FR), a winner over hurdles at Pau in January, was the only one to make the winner do any work in the latter stages but was readily held once the filly lengthened. (op 5-2 tchd 7-2)
Gilded Age took quite a keen hold in the early stages, which probably caused him to weaken quite early. (op 8-1 tchd 11-2)
Shalimar Fromentro(FR), keen in rear under restraint, made a blunder about halfway round and was unable to make any impact. (op 9-1)
Sergeant Pink(IRE), disqualified after winning on his chasing debut at Huntingdon, was never involved and appeared to run well below the level of his previous effort, and may not have recovered from a hard race there. (op 17-2 tchd 11-1)

2456 ANABEL KING RACING "NATIONAL HUNT" NOVICES' HURDLE (8 hdls) 2m
3:00 (3:00) (Class 4) 4-Y-O+ **£2,602** (£764; £382; £190)

Form RPR

13- **1** **High Benefit (IRE)**^{208} 5383 5-10-5 0 SamThomas 99+
(Alan King) *trckd ldrs: led 3 out: idled appr 2 out: jnd last and hdd sn after: rallied and qcknd to ld again fnl 30yds: readily* **2/5**^{1}

6-56 **2** *1* **Prince Of Denial (IRE)**^{7} 2307 6-10-12 0 PaddyBrennan 101
(Nigel Twiston-Davies) *hld up in tch: hdwy appr 3 out: chsd wnr sn after: drvn to chal last and led sn after: hdd and outpcd fnl 30yds* **6/1**^{2}

3 *8* **Bishophill Jack (IRE)**^{263} 4-10-12 0 SeanQuinlan 94
(Kim Bailey) *trckd ldrs: hit 3rd: led 4th: hdd 3 out: outpcd by ldng duo fr next but kpt on* **18/1**

4-0 **4** *2* **Richmond (FR)**^{17} 2109 5-10-12 0 DougieCostello 91
(Ian Williams) *in rr: t.k.h: hdwy 4th: chsd ldrs 3 out: outpcd fr next* **16/1**

6-4 **5** *1 ½* **Thoresby (IRE)**^{192} 237 4-10-12 0 DarylJacob 90
(Ben Case) *chsd ldrs to 3 out: sn outpcd* **40/1**

50-0 **6** *2 ½* **Atared**^{13} 2168 4-10-5 0 DavidEngland 80
(Pam Sly) *in rr: hdwy 4th: chsd ldrs 3 out: styd on same pce* **66/1**

7 *2* **Light Dragoon** 5-10-12 0 PaulMoloney 85
(Evan Williams) *hdwy 4th: tracing ldrs: keen and green appr 3 out and lost position: styd on wl appr last: kpt on run-in* **20/1**

-200 **8** *3 ½* **Great Hero**^{14} 2145 5-10-12 0 TomSiddall 82
(Richard Phillips) *in rr: hdwy and hit 3 out: wknd sn after* **50/1**

0- **9** *11* **Crackerjac Boy (USA)**^{221} 5137 5-10-12 0 WarrenMarston 71
(Richard Phillips) *in rr: hit 4 out: mod prog fr 2 out* **125/1**

00/ **10** *4 ½* **Niceboy (IRE)**^{623} 4287 6-10-12 0 LeightonAspell 66
(Nick Gifford) *bhd: mod late prog* **100/1**

11 *2 ¾* **Tanwood Boy (FR)** 6-10-12 0 AidanColeman 63
(Venetia Williams) *chsd ldrs to 3 out* **33/1**

545 **12** *4 ½* **Superior Knight**^{84} 1374 6-10-12 0 DavidDennis 59
(James Evans) *chsd ldrs to 4th* **66/1**

P **13** *11* **Sourchamp (FR)**^{28} 1922 4-10-9 0 JimmyDerham$^{(3)}$ 48
(Arthur Whiting) *led tl after 2nd: wknd 4th* **100/1**

-04U **14** *27* **Jumpjack Flint**^{6} 2322 4-10-12 0 (e^{1}) RichardJohnson 21
(Charlie Longsdon) *plld hrd: chsd ldrs after 2nd: wknd qckly appr 3 out* **12/1**^{3}

00-P **15** *6* **Master Paddy (IRE)**^{19} 2069 6-10-12 0 NickScholfield 15
(Andy Turnell) *chsd ldrs to 4 out* **100/1**

0/P- **P** **Dark Haven**^{231} 4959 7-10-5 0 LiamTreadwell —
(James Evans) *plld hrd: led after 2nd: hdd 4th: p.u sn after* **200/1**

4m 1.47s (4.97) **Going Correction** -0.15s/f (Good)
WFA 4 from 5yo+ 7lb **16** Ran SP% **123.9**
Speed ratings (Par 105): **81,80,76,75,74 73,72,70,65,63 61,59,53,40,37** —
toteswingers:1&2 £2.60, 2&3 £4.40, 1&3 £6.30 CSF £3.04 TOTE £1.40: £1.10, £1.50, £2.80; EX 4.10.
Owner J Hales **Bred** Kenneth Parkhill **Trained** Barbury Castle, Wilts

FOCUS
Some good horses have taken this contest in the past, but obviously last year's Supreme Novices' Hurdle winner Menorah stands out as being the best of them. This renewal was run at a slow early pace, which saw many of these fighting for their heads. Not form to get carried away with.

NOTEBOOK
High Benefit(IRE) was punted as though defeat was out of the question, but those who had taken short odds about her must have had a few heart palpitations when the runner-up got past her after the final hurdle - she seemed to idle after establishing a comfortable advantage. However, she showed good resilience under pressure and got to the front again where it mattered. She is better that the performance suggests and it will be interesting to see in what direction connections go with her now, as she can, of course, head to mares-only events. (op 4-7 tchd 8-13 in places)
Prince Of Denial(IRE) had taken a fierce hold early, and his stopping rapidly (plus High Benefit picking up again after idling) shouldn't have been a surprise. In fact, it was a good performance by both jockey and horse to have the chance of victory, considering that the horse was still fighting for his head jumping three out. (op 5-1)
Bishophill Jack(IRE) would have wanted a strong pace considering he'd won a 2m4f point on his only previous start, so this was a fair start under rules. (op 14-1 tchd 20-1)
Richmond(FR) was another to take a strong hold. He appeals as the sort to make his mark when handicapping. (op 22-1)
Light Dragoon, making his racecourse debut, was an eyecatcher but it remains to be seen whether he can build on the run, as he looked very green. Official explanation: jockey said gelding had a breathing problem (op 16-1 tchd 22-1)
Dark Haven Official explanation: jockey said mare hung badly right

2457 NICK DAVENPORT 60TH BIRTHDAY H'CAP CHASE (20 fncs) 3m 2f
3:30 (3:30) (Class 5) (0-95,93) 4-Y-O+ **£2,055** (£599; £299)

Form RPR

1P-5 **1** **Ukrainian Star (IRE)**^{35} 1820 7-11-0 81 WarrenMarston 98+
(Martin Keighley) *led 3rd: jnd 10th: hdd sn after: styd pressing ldrs: led again 14th: hit 3 out: rdn sn after: u.p whn blnd last: sn rcvrd and styd on wl u.p* **7/4**^{1}

0P0/ **2** *1 ¼* **Atherstone Hill (IRE)**^{610} 4540 8-10-8 78 (v^{1}) WayneKavanagh$^{(3)}$ 91
(Robin Dickin) *chsd ldrs: wnt 2nd 8th: chal 10th: led sn after hdd 14th: chal after next: styd on u.p fr 2 out: rallied run-in: a hld* **11/2**

U-B1 **3** *19* **Miss Fleur**^{8} 2290 7-11-6 90 7ex DannyCook$^{(3)}$ 92+
(Nick Mitchell) *pressed ldrs: chal 14th to 16th: pckd 3 out: styd chsng ldrs tl wknd last* **5/2**^{2}

0PP2 **4** *74* **Overton Lad**^{14} 2155 9-10-6 76 (b) RichieMcLernon$^{(3)}$ —
(Peter Pritchard) *led to 3rd: blnd 6th and rdn: blnd 10th: wknd and blnd 14th: t.o* **10/3**^{3}

010/ **5** *37* **Bringewood Fox**^{583} 4988 8-11-9 93 (t) TommyPhelan$^{(3)}$ —
(John Needham) *chsd ldrs: rdn 13th: sn wknd: hit 14th: blnd next and t.o* **12/1**

6m 51.0s (-1.70) **Going Correction** -0.15s/f (Good) **5** Ran SP% **111.1**
Speed ratings (Par 103): **96,95,89,67,55**
CSF £11.29 TOTE £3.60: £2.20, £3.60; EX 13.10.
Owner The Class Act Partnership **Bred** Mrs G O'Connell **Trained** Condicote, Gloucs

FOCUS
This race was steadily thinned out the further they went. Weak form, the winner rated to the level of last season's Huntingdon win.

NOTEBOOK
Ukrainian Star(IRE) always looked to be going the best, although appearing to hang a bit under pressure. He hit the last quite hard, which gave the runner-up another chance, but he pulled out more and can obviously get the job done at a low level. (op 2-1)
Atherstone Hill(IRE) hadn't been on a racecourse since March 2009, and was fitted with a visor for the first time. He plugged on in relentless style after always being prominent, but there is no telling whether he'll run as well next time after having such a hard race here. (op 13-2)
Miss Fleur, raised 7lb for winning at Lingfield, kept on after getting outpaced as the tempo increased but wasn't able to get back on terms. That said, it was a good run and she can be given every chance next time in a similar contest. (op 11-4 tchd 3-1 in places)

Overton Lad soon lost his place due to some moderate jumping and never got involved. (op 4-1 tchd 3-1)

2458 E B F DAVID NICHOLSON MEMORIAL "JUNIOR" STANDARD OPEN NATIONAL HUNT FLAT RACE 1m 6f

4:00 (4:00) (Class 5) 3-Y-O **£2,055** (£599; £299)

Form RPR
1 **Zama Zama** 3-10-7 0 BrianToomey(5) 100+
(Kevin Ryan) *mde virtually all: travelling wl fr 4f out: shkn up over 1f out: styd on strly* **5/1**3

2 *8* **Cardinal Rose** 3-10-12 0 APMcCoy 87
(Jonjo O'Neill) *in rr early: hdwy 1/2-way: chsd ldrs 6f out: rdn and styd on fr 3 out: wnt 2nd over 1f out: styd on u.p ins fnl f: no imp on wnr* **7/2**2

3 *2* **Revani** 3-10-9 0 DannyCook(3) 85
(Nick Mitchell) *chsd ldrs: wnt 2nd 6f out: rdn and no imp fr 3f out: one pce and lost 2nd over 1f out* **16/1**

4 *14* **Unnecessary Xpense** 3-10-12 0 TomScudamore 68
(Michael Scudamore) *chsd ldrs tl lost position 1/2-way: styd on again fr over 2f out: kpt on ins fnl f* **33/1**

0 5 *5* **Cheeky Boy**7 [2315] 3-10-12 0 (p) AidanColeman 62
(Steve Gollings) *rdn in mid-div 1/2-way: sn in rr: drvn and mod prog fnl 2f* **33/1**

6 *1 3/4* **Money Bridge** 3-10-12 0 RhysFlint 60
(Steve Gollings) *in rr: hdwy 7f out: chsd ldrs 5f out: wknd fr 3f out* **9/1**

7 *nk* **Kala Patthar** 3-10-12 0 JoeTizzard 60
(Colin Tizzard) *chsd ldrs: rdn 4f out: wknd 3f out* **7/4**1

8 *2 1/2* **The Languid One** 3-10-5 0 MrJMQuinlan(7) 57
(Michael Quinlan) *in rr tl styd on fnl 2f* **20/1**

9 *7* **Ellis** 3-10-5 0 MissSusannahWileman(7) 48
(Christopher Kellett) *wl bhd untl styd on fnl 2f* **200/1**

5 10 *3 1/4* **Fairy Trader (IRE)**10 [2237] 3-10-5 0 RichardJohnson 37
(Keith Goldsworthy) *chsd ldrs: rdn 5f out: wknd fr 3f out* **10/1**

4 11 *21* **Ophelia's Kiss**13 [2173] 3-10-5 0 JimmyMcCarthy 12
(Brendan Powell) *in tch 1/2-way: sn bhd* **16/1**

12 *2* **Racey Lacey** 3-10-5 0 LiamHeard 10
(Chris Down) *chsd ldrs tl rdn and wknd 5f out: v green and hung bdly rt bnd 2f out* **28/1**

13 *52* **John The Glass** 3-10-12 0 LiamTreadwell —
(Mark Wellings) *chsd ldrs to 1/2-way: t.o* **200/1**

3m 21.14s (2.04) **13** Ran SP% **121.2**
toteswingers:1&2 £5.30, 2&3 £19.70, 1&3 £37.00. totesuper7: Win: Not won. Place: £74.60. CSF £22.08 TOTE £10.50: £2.80, £1.60, £8.40; EX 40.90.
Owner S C B Limited **Bred** Cheveley Park Stud Ltd **Trained** Hambleton, N Yorks

FOCUS
A glorified Flat maiden given some of the pedigrees of show. Little to go on but the easy winner is the type to rate higher.

NOTEBOOK
Zama Zama raced prominently and galloped on in good style down the home straight. He should have a decent future but this race has had a history of winners that don't race a lot afterwards. (op 8-1)
Cardinal Rose, who does have a jumping pedigree, was dwarfed by those around him, but responded to pressure after sitting in rear early, and kept on for second. His half-sister landed a bumper, and he should win something if keeping up the family tradition. (op 9-2 tchd 5-1)
Revani is nicely bred and attracted some support at long odds, which didn't looked misplaced with this sound effort. (op 33-1)
Unnecessary Xpense, who was stood away from his rivals at the start for some time, kept on and passed some rivals in the latter stages.
Kala Patthar evidentially came to the track with a good reputation but didn't show anything to suggest he is out of the ordinary. Obviously, he should be allowed another chance but he will need to make some serious improvement between now and his next run to be winning. (op 10-11)
Racey Lacey Official explanation: jockey said filly hung right
T/Jkpt: £507.10 to a £1 stake. Pool of £10,000.00 - 14.00 winning tickets. T/Plt: £21.60 to a £1 stake. Pool of £53,738.60 - 1,811.90 winning tickets. T/Qpdt: £5.30 to a £1 stake. Pool of £3,744.83 516.71 winning tickets ST

2459 - 2465a (Foreign Racing) - See Raceform Interactive

2238 HEREFORD (R-H)

Thursday, November 18

OFFICIAL GOING: Good to soft (soft in places) changing to soft after race 4 (2.30)
Wind: Brisk across Weather: Cloudy

2466 LINDLEY CATERING JUVENILE HURDLE (8 hdls) 2m 1f

1:00 (1:00) (Class 4) 3-Y-O **£2,276** (£668; £334; £166)

Form RPR
1 **Tiptronic (FR)** 3-10-9 0 DPFahy(3) 107+
(Reginald Brown) *t.k.h: trckd ldrs: pushed along 2 out: sn upsides: slt ld last: hdd sn after: rallied and styd on chalng: led again last strides* **100/1**

2 *nse* **Harry Hunt**15 [1681] 3-10-12 0 JodieMogford 106
(Graeme McPherson) *led to 5th: rdn and one pce 3 out: rallied fr next and chal last: led sn after: a hrd pressed: hdd last strides* **28/1**

3 *7* **Rock Of Deauville (IRE)**173 3-10-12 0 NoelFehily 102+
(Paul Nicholls) *trckd ldr: led 5th: rdn after 2 out: hdd & wknd last* **11/8**1

3 4 *5* **Ultravox (USA)**21 [2047] 3-10-12 0 NickScholfield 95
(Jeremy Scott) *chsd ldrs to 3 out: wknd after 2 out* **20/1**

P42 5 *1 3/4* **Freckle Face**21 [2047] 3-10-7 110 TomO'Connor(5) 96
(Bill Turner) *sn in tch: chsd ldrs 4th: wknd 2 out: no ch whn blnd last* **16/1**

6 *2 1/2* **Matrow's Lady (IRE)** 3-9-12 0 MarkQuinlan(7) 84
(Neil Mulholland) *in rr: brief effrt 3 out: sn wknd* **66/1**

3 7 *nse* **Franklino (FR)**25 [1984] 3-10-12 0 WayneHutchinson 91
(Alan King) *in tch: rdn 3 out: no imp on ldrs and wknd bef next* **11/8**2

60 8 *18* **Celtic Intrigue (IRE)**8 [2306] 3-10-12 0 PaddyBrennan 75
(Tom George) *blnd 1st: chsd ldrs: rdn 5th: wknd 3 out* **80/1**

9 *18* **Zambuka (FR)**45 3-10-5 0 MarkGrant 52
(Barry Brennan) *bhd fr 1/2-way* **80/1**

10 *45* **Royal Box**10 3-10-12 0 WillKennedy 18
(Dai Burchell) *uns rdr bef s: blnd 1st: rdn after 3rd: a wl bhd: t.o* **66/1**

11 *4* **Admission**26 3-10-12 0 PaulMoloney 15
(Sophie Leech) *chsd ldrs 3rd: wknd bef 3 out: t.o* **7/1**3

4m 9.86s (10.46) **Going Correction** +0.75s/f (Soft) 11 Ran SP% **117.2**
Speed ratings (Par 104): **105,104,101,99,98 97,97,88,80,59 57**
toteswingers:1&2 £33.90, 2&3 £26.90, 1&3 £8.80 CSF £1564.12 TOTE £113.30: £38.50, £8.20, £1.70; EX 1123.90.
Owner R L Brown **Bred** Julien Merienne & Michel Cahu **Trained** Cross Ash, Monmouths

FOCUS
This looked a potentially interesting juvenile contest but there was a turn up, as two outsiders fought out the finish. The form is best rated around the fourth and fifth to downgraded Fontwell form.

NOTEBOOK
Tiptronic(FR) was said to be in good order for his racecourse debut and stuck on well to win by a narrow margin. It would be dangerous to write this off as a fluke, but he will obviously find things tougher under a penalty.
Harry Hunt came under pressure a long way from home, but he responded well and kept going to almost steal an unlikely victory. His previous form over hurdles seems to suggest this wasn't much of a race.
Rock Of Deauville(IRE), making his debut for these connections, got to the front going nicely but did not get home. The winner of two of his three races on the Flat in France at 1m5f, he should be given another chance. (op 6-4 tchd 5-4)
Ultravox(USA) probably ran to the same sort of level as on his hurdling debut, and at least doesn't seem to be regressing.
Franklino(FR) was a disappointing favourite at Aintree on his previous run and again failed to live up to expectations. It's a bit too early to judge him harshly, but he may appreciate further in time. (op 5-4 tchd 13-8)
Admission Official explanation: jockey said the gelding had a breathing problem

2467 LINDLEY CATERING H'CAP HURDLE (8 hdls) 2m 1f

1:30 (1:30) (Class 5) (0-95,95) 4-Y-O+ **£1,626** (£477; £238; £119)

Form RPR
F52 1 **Marino Prince (FR)**4 [2398] 5-11-1 89 MarcGoldstein(5) 109+
(Jim Best) *hld up in rr: in tch: stdy hdwy to trck ldrs 3 out: led sn after: gng clr whn mstke 2 out: eased run-in* **11/8**1

/312 2 *6* **Maizy Missile (IRE)**73 [1489] 8-11-2 85 PaulMoloney 88
(Mary Evans) *led: jnd 4th: hdd 5th: rdn and lost position after 3 out: rallied after 2 out and styd on to go 2nd after last: nvr any ch w eased down wnr* **7/2**2

021 3 *1 3/4* **Monsieur (FR)**8 [2308] 10-10-9 83 GilesHawkins(5) 84
(Carroll Gray) *in tch fr 3rd: trckd ldrs 4th: wnt 2nd 2 out: nvr any ch w eased down wnr: wknd into 3rd after last* **11/2**3

0300 4 *2 3/4* **Galant Eye (IRE)**15 [2149] 11-9-11 73 DannyBurton(7) 73
(Chris Down) *trckd ldr: chal and mstke 4th: led next: hdd after 3 out: nvr any ch w eased down wnr and wknd into 4th run-in* **12/1**

66/0 5 *13* **Trotters Bottom**15 [2149] 9-10-4 73 WillKennedy 60
(Edward Bevan) *in tch whn hit 3rd: chsd ldrs 5th: wknd fr 2 out* **25/1**

4600 6 *3 1/2* **Echo Dancer**15 [2149] 4-10-11 90 JoshWall(10) 74
(Trevor Wall) *in tch: effrt 5th: wknd after 3 out* **33/1**

016 7 *1 1/4* **Aughcarra (IRE)**46 [1704] 5-10-11 83 TommyPhelan(3) 66
(Harry Chisman) *chsd ldrs: nt fluent 4th: wknd 3 out* **14/1**

0P-P 8 *4* **Cybergenic (FR)**8 [2308] 12-11-5 95 KyleJames(7) 74
(Tracey Watkins) *t.k.h early: nt fluent: a bhd: blnd last* **66/1**

-060 9 *1 1/2* **Golden Partner**11 [2244] 5-11-4 87 (bt1) DavidDennis 65
(Matt Sheppard) *in rr: brief effrt 3 out: sn wknd* **25/1**

5400 10 *16* **Django Reinhardt**25 [1997] 4-11-5 95 MrDavidTurner(7) 58
(Sam Davison) *hit 3rd: blnd 2 out: a in rr* **14/1**

50-0 11 *14* **The Boss Rock (IRE)**193 [232] 7-11-2 85 (t) RhysFlint 36
(Jim Old) *chsd ldrs: blnd 4th: wknd qckly appr 3 out* **25/1**

4m 10.87s (11.47) **Going Correction** +0.75s/f (Soft) 11 Ran SP% **116.7**
Speed ratings (Par 103): **103,100,99,98,91 90,89,87,87,79 73**
toteswingers:1&2 £1.10, 2&3 £1.50, 1&3 £1.90 CSF £6.23 CT £19.93 TOTE £3.40: £1.40, £2.20, £1.10; EX 7.00.
Owner Miss J S Dollan **Bred** Newsells Park Stud Ltd **Trained** Lewes, E Sussex

FOCUS
A moderate handicap but the time was reasonable and the placed horses are rated to their marks.

NOTEBOOK
Marino Prince(FR), on his second outing for the yard, was an emphatic winner. Plenty was clearly expected at Market Rasen last time, but he found one too strong. This result didn't look in any danger as soon as he took up the running, but the handicapper is certain to push him up the weights, and it remains to be seen whether he can defy a higher mark. (op 6-4 tchd 13-8)
Maizy Missile(IRE) ran a strange race, as she helped to set the pace before losing her place quite a way out. It seemed certain she'd drop away but she started to run on again when it was all too late, and was keeping on strongly. A step up in trip will suit her. (tchd 4-1)
Monsieur(FR) was driven up to hold every chance off the slow early tempo, but could only manage the one pace off the bridle. He has still to win going right-handed. (op 6-1 tchd 5-1)
Galant Eye(IRE) helped to force the pace with Maizy Missile and battled on to claim fourth. (op 14-1)
The Boss Rock(IRE) Official explanation: vet said the gelding lost a shoe and finished lame

2468 LINDLEY CATERING NOVICES' H'CAP CHASE (12 fncs) 2m

2:00 (2:00) (Class 5) (0-95,95) 4-Y-O+ **£2,081** (£611; £305; £152)

Form RPR
-440 1 **Bedarra Boy**54 [1429] 4-11-9 95 DarylJacob 97+
(David Arbuthnot) *hit 1st: trckd ldrs 4th: wnt 2nd 4 out: led 2 out: hdd sn after: rallied: rdn and hd in front whn lft in clr ld last: drvn out* **9/1**

0-00 2 *2 3/4* **Mamba (GER)**190 [272] 8-10-1 66 JamesDavies 70
(Chris Down) *in tch: chsd ldrs 4 out: rdn and one pce next: no imp on ldng duo whn lft 2nd last: kpt on* **20/1**

3135 3 *6* **Mujamead**7 [2326] 6-11-7 91 (p) LeeEdwards(5) 92
(Sally-Anne Wheelwright) *chsd ldr: chal and blnd 5th: lost 2nd 4 out: wknd next: lft wl hld 3rd last* **14/1**

2-60 4 *10* **Form And Beauty (IRE)**114 [1106] 8-10-2 72 MrBMoorcroft(5) 65
(Bernard Llewellyn) *in rr mstkes 5th: 6th and 7th: sme hdwy appr 3 out: nvr nr ldrs and lft poor 4th last* **6/1**3

P-0F 5 *6* **Chilla Cilla**7 [2334] 7-10-11 76 (t) NickScholfield 61
(Anthony Honeyball) *in rr: sme hdwy after 4 out: sn wknd* **3/1**2

P50P 6 *14* **Simiola**14 [2169] 11-10-1 66 oh12 ow1 ColinBolger 38
(Simon Lewis) *chsd ldrs tl wknd 4 out* **50/1**

/035 7 *2 1/4* **Sumner (IRE)**11 [2244] 6-11-9 91 (v) LeeStephens(3) 61
(David Evans) *in tch: rdn and wkng whn mstke 4 out* **13/2**

F23 F **Turn Up (IRE)**21 [2053] 7-10-12 84 (t) MrJMRidley(7) 91
(Matt Sheppard) *led: hdd 2 out: led again sn after: hdd and rdn and a hd down but styng on whn fell last* **2/1**1

-655 P **Magusta (GER)**13 [2187] 6-11-8 87 (p) FelixDeGiles —
(Jamie Snowden) *blnd 3rd and 5th: a in rr: t.o whn p.u bef 3 out* **22/1**

4m 7.30s (3.70) **Going Correction** +0.325s/f (Yiel) 9 Ran SP% **113.7**
Speed ratings (Par 103): **103,101,98,93,90 83,82,—,—**
toteswingers:1&2 not won, 2&3 £8.90, 1&3 £6.60 CSF £146.03 CT £2471.40 TOTE £10.40: £4.00, £7.90, £3.70; EX 247.30.
Owner P M Claydon **Bred** Mickley Stud & E Kent **Trained** Compton, Berks

FOCUS
This only concerned two from quite a way out and the winner is rated to his hurdles mark, although the form is ordinary.

NOTEBOOK

Bedarra Boy's main threat departed at the last, but the impression was he would have done enough to win whatever the case, indeed his jockey felt he would have won. The only 4-y-o in the contest, it was a good performance on his chasing debut and he could win something similar while in the mood. Connections suggested afterwards that he may be put away until next summer if the ground continues to soften. (op 12-1)
Mamba(GER), making her chasing debut, took a while to get going but stayed on respectably from the home bend. (op 16-1)
Mujamead chased the pace but made a blunder at the fifth. That was more than enough to knock him out of having a chance of winning. (op 12-1 tchd 16-1)
Chilla Cilla was a little disappointing after showing promise on her chasing debut last time before departing three out. Held up, she was another to make no impact. (op 11-4)
Turn Up(IRE) soon took up the running and responded well to pressure. However, he looked to be held when sprawling after the last. (op 5-2)

2469 DIGIBET.COM NOVICES' H'CAP HURDLE (10 hdls) 2m 4f
2:30 (2:30) (Class 4) (0-100,100) 3-Y-0+ £2,276 (£668; £334; £166)

Form				RPR
2-P6	1		**Monsieur Cadou (FR)**[16] 2141 5-11-7 95 PaddyBrennan (Tom George) *in rr: in tch: hdwy 4 out: styd on fr 3 out to press ldrs 2 out: upsides sn after and led bef last: drvn out* 11/4[1]	102+
0/	2	3 ¾	**The Gripper (IRE)**[44] 1721 6-10-12 93 MrJMahot(7) (Rachel Hobbs) *sn chsng ldrs: rdn 4 out: chal fr next tl slt ld after 2 out: hdd appr last: styd on same pce* 80/1	95
003-	3	3 ¼	**Constant Cupid (IRE)**[215] 5234 6-10-10 84 (v) JodieMogford (Graeme McPherson) *chsd ldrs: chal fr 4 out tl slt ld after 3 out: hdd next: sn one pce* 16/1	83
0-10	4	1	**Musical Wedge**[26] 1959 6-11-8 99 TommyPhelan(3) (Claire Dyson) *slt ld to 6th: styd upsides and slt ld again 2 out: hdd sn after: kpt on same pce* 16/1	97
4023	5	6	**Coeur Brule (FR)**[60] 1551 4-11-5 100 MrDavidTurner(7) (Sam Davison) *pressed ldrs: led 6th: hdd after 3 out: wknd fr next* 14/1	93
503-	6	32	**Diamond Eclipse (IRE)**[205] 41 4-11-3 91 DarylJacob (Nick Williams) *in rr: hdwy fr 4 out: rdn next nvr rchd ldrs: sn wknd: t.o* 3/1[2]	55
3-0P	7	8	**Everyman**[11] 2244 6-11-0 95 HarryChalloner(7) (John Bryan Groucott) *chsd ldrs tl after 4 out: t.o* 50/1	52
000-	8	2 ¾	**Midnight Appeal**[209] 5359 5-11-12 100 WayneHutchinson (Alan King) *chsd ldrs to 3 out: sn wknd t.o* 6/1[3]	54
006-	9	60	**Witch's Hat (IRE)**[240] 4798 7-11-4 92 RhysFlint (Jim Old) *chsd ldrs tl wknd qckly 4 out: t.o* 40/1	—
11P-	P		**Dusk**[359] 2488 5-11-1 89 PaulMoloney (Evan Williams) *sn bhd: t.o whn p.u bef 5th* 9/1	—
434	P		**Royal Entourage**[46] 1700 5-10-11 92 KyleJames(7) (Philip Kirby) *prom to 4th: t.o whn p.u bef 2 out* 17/2	—
	P		**Back The Rock (IRE)**[160] 721 7-11-7 98 WayneKavanagh(3) (Roy Brotherton) *bhd fr 4th: t.o whn p.u bef 2 out* 33/1	—
-506	P		**Chaser's War (IRE)**[20] 2069 6-9-7 74 oh5 RobertKirk(7) (Nikki Evans) *pressed ldrs tl wknd 4 out: t.o whn p.u bef 2 out* 80/1	—
0P-0	P		**Tiffany Jones**[29] 1922 7-10-11 85 WillKennedy (John Spearing) *sn bhd: t.o whn p.u bef 2 out* 33/1	—

5m 10.27s (14.77) **Going Correction** +0.75s/f (Soft)
WFA 4 from 5yo+ 8lb **14** Ran SP% **117.7**
Speed ratings (Par 105): **100,98,97,96,94 81,78,77,53,— —,—,—,—**
CSF £231.47 CT £2989.60 TOTE £3.10: £1.30, £20.00, £6.90; EX 311.20 TRIFECTA Not won..
Owner The 'Ye Of Little Faith' Partnership **Bred** Jerome Brion & Frederique Brion **Trained** Slad, Gloucs

FOCUS

This turned into a war of attrition and, once again, few got involved. The winner was rated to the best of last season's form with the third and fourth close to their marks.

NOTEBOOK

Monsieur Cadou(FR) could have been given a chance on some of his form last season, but his previous two performances hardly suggested he was a solid betting proposition, even allowing for the weakeness of the event. However, he was still nicely backed and gamely justified support. He stays further, which probably helped in these conditions. (op 4-1)
The Gripper(IRE), back over hurdles on his first start for this trainer, hadn't shown a lot for a while so this looked a better effort. He would be interesting in a weak race next time if reproducing this sort of form.
Constant Cupid(IRE), having his first run since April, once again showed enough to suggest he can find a little contest. (op 18-1)
Musical Wedge bounced back to the sort of form he showed when winning at this course in April, and has something to build on again.
Coeur Brule(FR) has been running to a modest level recently and is one to rate the race through, as he appeared to run to somewhere near his best. (tchd 12-1)
Diamond Eclipse(IRE), returning from a layoff and making his handicap debut, took a strong hold in rear and couldn't make the ground up from the back to get involved. Official explanation: jockey said that the gelding was unsuited by the trip (op 9-4)
Dusk Official explanation: jockey said gelding had a breathing problem

2470 LINDLEY CATERING MARES' H'CAP CHASE (16 fncs) 2m 5f 110y
3:00 (3:00) (Class 4) (0-115,115) 4-Y-0+ £2,732 (£802; £401; £200)

Form				RPR
362-	1		**Take It There**[233] 4936 8-11-5 108 (t) FelixDeGiles (Alastair Lidderdale) *trckd ldrs fr 6th: chal 11th: led 12th: pushed along and styd on wl fr 2 out: readily* 10/1	119+
31F4	2	3 ¾	**Moulin De La Croix**[55] 1604 6-11-9 115 (t) SamTwiston-Davies(3) (Nigel Twiston-Davies) *mstke 1st: in rr: hit 7th: hdwy and hit 12th: rdn 4 out: styd on fr 3 out: drvn to chse wnr after last: no imp* 4/1[2]	120
5-P4	3	1	**Me Julie**[14] 2170 7-10-3 92 NickScholfield (Arthur Whiting) *chsd ldr to 4 out: rdn and outpcd sn after: rallied u.p fr 2 out and kpt on wl ro take 3rd cl home: no ch w wnr* 5/1	96
31F-	4	1 ¼	**Fleur De Vassy**[233] 4939 6-9-8 90 HarryChalloner(7) (Venetia Williams) *t.k.h early: trckd ldrs: chsd wnr 3 out: sn rdn and no imp: one pce last: lost two pls run-in* 15/8[1]	92
40-5	5	40	**Raise You Five (IRE)**[13] 2182 6-11-7 113 RichieMcLernon(3) (Jonjo O'Neill) *chsd ldrs: hit 8th: in rr 9th: mstke and wknd next: no ch whn hit 11th: t.o* 14/1	85
10-P	P		**Evella (IRE)**[14] 2171 6-11-9 115 AlexMerriam(3) (Neil King) *led tl hdd12th: wknd qckly appr 4 out and p.u sn after* 9/2[3]	—
2-P0	P		**Itea Du Fau (FR)**[17] 2124 5-10-7 99 CharlieHuxley(3) (Alan King) *chsd ldrs to 7th: in rr 8th: rdn 10th: t.o whn p.u bef 4 out* 14/1	—

5m 36.62s (16.62) **Going Correction** +0.75s/f (Soft) **7** Ran SP% **112.1**
Speed ratings (Par 105): **99,97,97,96,82 —,—**
toteswingers:1&2 £3.20, 2&3 £7.60, 1&3 £4.60 CSF £47.92 CT £224.34 TOTE £9.00: £3.00, £4.00; EX 48.00.
Owner Entertainments Committee **Bred** The Queen **Trained** Eastbury, Berks

FOCUS

The going was changed to soft all round before this race. Most of these were tightly bunched on the back straight on the final circuit. The cosy winner is rated back to her best with the next three home close to form in a easy to rate handicap.

NOTEBOOK

Take It There could be spotted going strongly as others started to come under pressure. She moved easily to the front and never showed any signs of stopping once in a commanding position. This victory came off a career-high mark, so she'll have work to do when bidding to follow up.
Moulin De La Croix plugged on under a strong ride and this was a respectable effort, but she's high enough in the weights. (op 10-3 tchd 3-1)
Me Julie had shown mixed form since winning last season, so this was better, although she was under strong pressure a long way out. (tchd 9-2 and 11-2)
Fleur De Vassy sat just behind the pacesetters, taking a bit of a grip, and looked a real threat when making ground, but it soon became apparent she had no change of gear, and was made to look woefully one paced. (op 11-4)
Evella(IRE), pulled-up on her reappearance, looked interesting on her chasing debut but was a disappointment. (op 5-1 tchd 4-1)

2471 HEREFORD UNITED NOVICES' CHASE (16 fncs) 2m 5f 110y
3:30 (3:30) (Class 3) 4-Y-0+ £4,943 (£1,451; £725)

Form				RPR
4-1F	1		**Robinson Collonges (FR)**[12] 2220 5-11-7 0 NoelFehily (Paul Nicholls) *trckd ldr fr 6th: led 8th: sn clr in own time: fin on bridle* 1/10[1]	138+
P-30	2	46	**Brimley**[43] 1726 7-10-12 0 LeeStephens(3) (Ann Price) *trckd ldr tl blnd 6th: j.big 9th: chsd wnr fr 12th: nvr the remotest ch* 18/1[3]	86
P5/P	3	30	**Abstract Art (USA)**[7] 2330 7-11-1 0 AndrewThornton (Rachel Hobbs) *led: hit 2nd: hit 7th: mstke and hdd next: lost poor 2nd and hit 12th: sn t.o: blnd 3 out* 12/1[2]	56

5m 31.83s (11.83) **Going Correction** +0.75s/f (Soft) **3** Ran SP% **103.9**
Speed ratings (Par 107): **108,91,80**
CSF £2.27 TOTE £1.10; EX 2.60.
Owner Mr & Mrs G Calder **Bred** Gaec Delorme Freres **Trained** Ditcheat, Somerset

FOCUS

A seriously uncompetitive novice chase wth the winner rated in line with his recent mark when falling here.

NOTEBOOK

Robinson Collonges(FR) won in the manner you'd expect from a long odds-on shot. He only needed to negotiate the fences fluently to collect, which he did without any fuss. This will have boosted his confidence after his fall at Wincanton, and he is a horse to follow at a higher level. (op 1-9)
Brimley got behind after making a blunder and was no match at all for the winner. (op 16-1)
Abstract Art(USA) jumped poorly and was beaten a long way.

2472 LINDLEY CATERING MARES' MAIDEN OPEN NATIONAL HUNT FLAT RACE 2m 1f
4:00 (4:00) (Class 6) 4-6-Y-0 £1,301 (£382; £191; £95)

Form				RPR
4-	1		**Semi Colon (FR)**[217] 5200 4-11-0 0 AndrewTinkler (Nicky Henderson) *trckd ldrs: led over 4f out: clr whn rdn over 1f out: styd on strly* 5/6[1]	104+
	2	7	**Varkala (IRE)** 4-11-0 0 JimmyMcCarthy (Charles Egerton) *in rr tl hdwy fr 6f out: chsd ldrs 3f out: wnt 2nd ins fnl 2f: styd on ins fnl f: no ch w wnr* 16/1	96
	3	2 ½	**Hazy Dawn** 5-11-0 0 RhysFlint (Michael Scudamore) *in rr early: hdwy 1/2-way: chsd ldrs fr 4f out: rdn and chsd wnr fr 3f out: no imp: lost 2nd ins fnl 2f: kpt on to hold 3rd ins fnl f* 50/1	94
	4	½	**Addiction** 5-11-0 0 LeightonAspell (Oliver Sherwood) *in rr: rdn 6f out hdwy over 3f out: styd on wl fnl 2f to cl for 3rd nr fin: nvr any ch w wnr* 12/1	93
23	5	6	**Lady Everywhere**[14] 2167 5-11-0 0 DarylJacob (Nick Williams) *mde most tl hdd over 4f out: lost 2nd 3f out: sn btn* 5/1[2]	88
	6	9	**Lights Of Broadway (IRE)** 4-11-0 0 MarkGrant (Barry Brennan) *chsd ldrs to 4f out* 40/1	78
	7	24	**Countess Susy** 5-10-7 0 MrDGPrichard(7) (Phillip Dando) *chsd ldrs: chal 7f out to 6f out: wknd 3f out* 33/1	54
0-	8	3 ¼	**Top Bob (IRE)**[217] 5200 5-11-0 0 TimmyMurphy (David Arbuthnot) *rdn 1/2-way: a bhd* 13/2[3]	51
3-0	9	12	**Sheila's Rose (IRE)**[158] 739 5-10-7 0 CDTimmons(7) (Barry Brennan) *chsd ldrs tl wknd fr 4f out* 25/1	39
0	10	4	**Kayf Paradis**[29] 1927 5-11-0 0 WillKennedy (John Spearing) *chsd ldrs 10f* 66/1	35
	11	nk	**Quand Je Reve De Toi (FR)**[235] 6-11-0 0 CharliePoste (Mrs Pauline Harkin) *chsd ldrs tl wknd over 4f out* 25/1	34
0B0-	12	76	**Silver Monet**[249] 4620 6-10-11 0 DPFahy(3) (Matt Sheppard) *bhd fr 1/2-way: t.o* 50/1	—
0-	13	5	**Lady Exe**[243] 4744 5-11-0 0 (t) JamesDavies (Chris Down) *bhd fr 1/2-way: t.o* 66/1	—

4m 10.63s (16.83) **Going Correction** +0.75s/f (Soft)
WFA 4 from 5yo+ 7lb **13** Ran SP% **118.1**
Speed ratings: **90,86,85,85,82 78,66,65,59,57 57,21,19**
toteswingers:1&2 £7.10, 2&3 £39.90, 1&3 £15.80 CSF £15.29 TOTE £2.20: £1.10, £3.50, £6.30; EX 16.10.
Owner Mrs Caroline Mould **Bred** Michel Bourgneuf **Trained** Upper Lambourn, Berks

FOCUS

An uncompetitive mares' bumper that could be rated higher.

NOTEBOOK

Semi Colon(FR) set what looked a good standard judged on her sole start last season at Cheltenham (two of those in front of her that day have subsequently won) and took this with plenty in hand after leading about 4f out. She certainly has the scope to make a jumper. (op Evens)
Varkala(IRE), out of a well-related bumper winner, travelled like a decent sort and kept on nicely to make an eyecatching debut. She appeared to flounder in the ground and might want a better surface. (op 20-1)
Hazy Dawn, a half-sister to three winning hurdlers and a winning pointer, looks to have plenty of stamina. She will be interesting on a more demanding course.
Addiction, out of a prolific winning hurdler, is related to winners and showed more than enough ability to suggest she'll be winning something in due course. (op 11-1)
Lady Everywhere travelled strongly at the head of affairs but weakened tamely when the race got interesting. She looked tired and may not have handled the going. (op 4-1)
Top Bob(IRE) was behind the winner at Cheltenham on her only start last season and doesn't seem to have made progress from that run. (op 7-1 tchd 6-1)
T/Plt: £474.50 to a £1 stake. Pool of £54,479.36 - 83.80 winning tickets. T/Qpdt: £113.60 to a £1 stake. Pool of £5,405.85 - 35.20 winning tickets. ST

2397 MARKET RASEN (R-H)

Thursday, November 18

OFFICIAL GOING: Good to soft (good in places)

Hurdle rail in home straight and bends moved out 3yds, chase rail moved in 3yds.
Wind: moderate 1/2 behind Weather: fine, becoming overcast, light rain last 2

2473 PHS WASHROOMS CONSUMABLES "NATIONAL HUNT" NOVICES' HURDLE (10 hdls) 2m 3f

12:40 (12:40) (Class 4) 4-Y-O+ £2,740 (£798; £399)

Form				RPR
-404	1		**Attaglance**14 2162 4-10-9 0 ... RyanMania(3) (Malcolm Jefferson) *trckd ldrs: blnd 2 out: 4th last: hung rt and styd on to ld last 100yds* 12/1	117+
20-2	2	2	**Dear Sam (GER)**25 1988 5-10-12 0 ... APMcCoy (Steve Gollings) *led 2nd: 4 l ahd whn mstke last: hdd and no ex clsng stages* 1/2[1]	115+
1-0	3	3 3/4	**Tiptoeaway (IRE)**18 2102 5-10-12 0 ... GrahamLee (Tim Easterby) *trckd ldrs: t.k.h: styd on same pce run-in* 9/1[3]	109
120-	4	2 1/2	**Basford Bob (IRE)**246 4676 5-10-12 0 ... AlanO'Keeffe (Jennie Candlish) *t.k.h in midfield: hit 4th: chsd ldr 2 out: wknd fnl 150yds* 9/2[2]	107
3-40	5	18	**Pie At Midnight**8 2307 4-10-12 106 ... JasonMaguire (Donald McCain) *in rr: hdwy and wl in tch whn blnd 3 out: sn wknd* 20/1	94+
0-P0	6	6	**Roi De Garde (FR)**10 2282 4-10-12 0 ... TomMessenger (Chris Bealby) *led to 2nd: chsd ldr: lost pl appr 2 out* 100/1	85
	7	4	**Our Matti**973 4606 9-10-12 0 ... BrianHarding (Chris Grant) *chsd ldrs: nt fluent 5th: lost pl 3 out* 16/1	82
6	8	2 1/4	**Upper Deck (IRE)**156 759 5-10-12 0 ... SeanQuinlan (Richard Phillips) *nt fluent in rr: bhd fr 7th* 150/1	80
	9	92	**Another Mystery** 5-10-5 0 ... TjadeCollier (Evelyn Slack) *nt jump wl in last: reminders 2nd: bhd fr 7th: t.o 2 out* 200/1	—

4m 56.4s (17.00) **Going Correction** +1.05s/f (Soft)
WFA 4 from 5yo+ 7lb 9 Ran SP% 115.3
Speed ratings (Par 105): **106,105,103,102,94 92,90,89,51**
toteswingers:1&2 £2.10, 2&3 £2.60, 1&3 £12.50 CSF £19.38 TOTE £17.60: £3.60, £1.02, £2.10; EX 27.40.
Owner H Young, G Eifert, R Snyder **Bred** H Young **Trained** Norton, N Yorks

FOCUS
This average novice event was run at something of an uneven gallop, but the form still looks sound with the first four coming nicely clear. The form is rated around those in the frame behind the winner.

NOTEBOOK
Attaglance had caught the attention of the stewards after his fourth at Haydock a fortnight earlier, after which his jockey James Halliday received a ten-day ban for failing to ensure his mount attained the best possible position. He attracted a little support under a different pilot here and ultimately ran out a cosy winner, rating value for a deal further than the bare margin. The longer trip no doubt helped his cause, and it wouldn't be that surprising to see him defy a penalty in this division now he has shown his true colours. (op 14-1)
Dear Sam(GER) beat all bar Cue Card on his hurdling debut at Aintree last month and was all the rage to go one better over this slightly shorter trip. He didn't help his cause by getting warm beforehand, though, and after hitting the last, was running on empty near the finish having done plenty from the front. There ought to be a race in him before too long, but he must learn to relax more through the early parts. (tchd 8-15 and 4-7 in places)
Tiptoeaway(IRE) was bitterly disappointing on his hurdling debut at Carlisle 18 days earlier, but this was more like it and he left the impression he would have been seen in a better light off a stronger early gallop. He has the scope to rate higher as the season develops. (op 10-1 tchd 12-1)
Basford Bob(IRE) showed promise last season and was having his first outing since nearly being carried out in the Cheltenham Bumper in March. He did show errant traits in his first few bumper outings, however and, after being produced with every chance two out here, he again proved tricky when put under pressure. The experience will not be lost on him and he has the talent to win a novice hurdle, but he isn't one for maximum faith. (op 4-1)
Our Matti was a useful sort when previously trained by Willie Mullins and was making his debut for a new yard after a whopping 973-day layoff. He unsurprisingly began to feel the pinch three out, but should come on plenty for the run.

2474 PHS PAPER PRODUCTS CLAIMING HURDLE (10 hdls) 2m 3f

1:10 (1:10) (Class 5) 4-Y-O+ £2,055 (£599; £299)

Form				RPR
532/	1		**Hernando's Boy**16 4995 9-11-0 0 ... JamesReveley (Keith Reveley) *led: qcknd appr 2 out: jnd last: sn narrowly hdd: styd on to regain narrow ld clsng stages* 8/1[3]	111
43F3	2	nk	**Kilshannig (IRE)**10 2279 5-11-6 99 ... (bt) APMcCoy (Jonjo O'Neill) *hld up: hdwy to chse ldr 2 out: hung lft: led narrowly sn after last: hdd and no ex last 100yds* 14/1	117
1441	3	11	**Liberty Seeker (FR)**14 2169 11-10-3 109 ... MattCrawley(7) (John Harris) *trckd ldrs: wnt cl 2nd 3 out: drvn appr next: sn wl outpcd: wknd between last 2* 13/2[2]	98
P3-1	P		**Rathcor**46 1692 8-10-9 128 ... TrevorWhelan(7) (Ian Williams) *trckd ldr to 3 out: sn drvn: wknd and p.u bef 2 out: lame* 1/3[1]	—

4m 57.5s (18.10) **Going Correction** +1.05s/f (Soft) 4 Ran SP% 106.1
Speed ratings (Par 103): **103,102,98,—**
CSF £59.54 TOTE £8.40; EX 30.00.
Owner Crack of Dawn Partnership **Bred** T E Pocock **Trained** Lingdale, Redcar & Cleveland

FOCUS
This was an uncompetitive claimer at it turned out, but there was still a cracking finish and the second sets the level. The winner is rated in line with last year's Flat form with the third 11lb off his best.

NOTEBOOK
Hernando's Boy arrived here fit from the Flat and ensured it was a fair test when going into a clear early lead. He was headed after the last, but refused go give way and battled back under strong handling at the business end. This was his first outing over jumps since April and his first over hurdles since 2008, and he could now head for another one of these at Wetherby next week. (tchd 10-1)
Kilshannig(IRE) is a tricky sort and, after being produced with what looked a winning run by McCoy, he couldn't cope with the winner's renewed challenge when it mattered most. This was still a lot better from him again back down in trip. (tchd 12-1)
Liberty Seeker(FR), back to winning ways at Towcester a fortnight earlier, cried enough before the second-last. (op 4-1)
Rathcor would've won this with if running near to his official mark, but he was the first beaten and unfortunately pulled up lame. Official explanation: vet said gelding was lame (op 4-9)

2475 PHS SMARTDRI HAND DRYER BEGINNERS' CHASE (14 fncs) 2m 6f 110y

1:40 (1:40) (Class 4) 4-Y-O+ £3,903 (£1,146; £573; £286)

Form				RPR
/1-1	1		**Smuglin**190 285 7-10-9 0 ... JasonMaguire (Donald McCain) *trckd clr ldr: led 3 out: hit next: edgd lft and styd on run-in: rdn rt out* 85/40[1]	120+
40-U	2	1 1/2	**Hollo Ladies (IRE)**9 2299 5-11-2 0 ... GrahamLee (Ferdy Murphy) *hld up in rr: wnt prom 7th: dropped bk next: hdwy to trck ldrs 4 out: chsd wnr next: swtchd rt between last 2: kpt on same pce run-in: no imp* 3/1[2]	126+
40/3	3	13	**Mexican Pete**26 1970 10-11-2 123 ... DaveCrosse (Ian Williams) *chsd ldrs: one pce appr 3 out: tk modest 3rd appr last* 8/1	115
602	4	10	**Panama Canal (IRE)**20 2071 5-10-13 0 ... (p) AdamPogson(3) (Charles Pogson) *led: sn clr: nt fluent 10th and next: hdd 3 out: 4th and wkng whn blnd last* 10/1	108
3	5	32	**Canticle**37 1815 5-11-2 0 ... TomMessenger (Chris Bealby) *chsd ldrs: 5th and wkng whn mstke 4 out: t.o next* 9/2[3]	76
-U00	6	25	**Factotum**21 2057 6-11-2 0 ... APMcCoy (Jonjo O'Neill) *chsd ldrs: drvn 7th: sn lost pl: bhd fr 10th: t.o 3 out* 8/1	54
1P0	7	13	**Deep Reflection**104 1195 10-11-2 0 ... GerardTumelty (Martin Keighley) *in rr: reminders 7th: bhd fr 8th: t.o 4 out* 28/1	42

5m 49.3s (3.30) **Going Correction** +0.375s/f (Yiel) 7 Ran SP% 109.9
Speed ratings (Par 105): **109,108,103,100,89 80,76**
toteswingers:1&2 £2.10, 2&3 £6.60, 1&3 £2.80 CSF £8.39 TOTE £2.20: £1.10, £4.00; EX 8.40.
Owner Broadband Partnership **Bred** R F Broad **Trained** Cholmondeley, Cheshire

FOCUS
This modest novice chase was run at a decent gallop and the first pair came clear from the penultimate flight. The fourth helps set the level.

NOTEBOOK
Smuglin, who has had niggling back problems, picked up where she left off last season and got her chase career off to a perfect start. She kept finding for pressure in the home straight, despite having proved keen through the race, and has now won on each of her three outings for connections. She probably doesn't want the ground too soft and it was a little better here on the chase course. This experience should see her go forward, she will likely be given time to recover sufficiently and her trainer is eyeing the EBF Mares' Final at Newbury in the spring for her. (op 15-8 tchd 9-4)
Hollo Ladies(IRE) had got no further than the first on his chasing debut for connections at Sedgefield nine days earlier. He proved free out the back here and his jumping got better as the race went on. He emerged with every chance from three out, but couldn't get past the more resolute winner. He was clear in second and this former Grade 1 winning hurdler clearly gets this trip. His yard is going through a lean spell at present, and it's a good chance he will only really come into his own over fences later in the season. (op 11-4 tchd 5-2 and 10-3 in places)
Mexican Pete had his chance and stepped up a little on the level of his chase debut at Stratford last month. He ideally wants quicker ground. (op 9-1)
Panama Canal(IRE), up in trip, did plenty in a clear early lead and paid the price from the third-last fence. He should find his feet when going handicapping. (op 14-1)
Canticle was in trouble from the ninth fence and ran below the level of his debut under rules last month. (op 5-1 tchd 11-2)
Factotum wants quicker ground, but still again ran disappointingly. (op 9-1 tchd 15-2)

2476 PHS WATER SAVING H'CAP CHASE (14 fncs) 2m 6f 110y

2:10 (2:11) (Class 3) (0-125,122) 4-Y-O+ £5,529 (£1,623; £811; £405)

Form				RPR
414-	1		**Sarde (FR)**226 5073 6-11-7 117 ... (t) SeanQuinlan (Kim Bailey) *trckd ldrs: shkn up 10th: n.m.r after next: led appr 3 out: styd on strly* 7/2[3]	130+
P3-5	2	5	**Youngstown (IRE)**33 1871 7-11-12 122 ... JasonMaguire (Donald McCain) *trckd ldr: upsides 7th: led 10th: hdd after next: sn rdn: kpt on same pce fr 2 out* 11/8[1]	131
142-	3	11	**Work Boy**216 5202 9-10-9 110 ... ShaneByrne(5) (Sue Smith) *led to 10th: edgd rt and led after 4 out: hdd appr next: stmbld landing: wknd appr 2 out* 5/2[2]	110
422-	4	25	**Rebeccas Choice (IRE)**237 4869 7-11-6 116 ... GrahamLee (Mark Rimell) *settled in last: outpcd 9th: bhd fr 4 out* 5/1	92

6m 2.50s (16.50) **Going Correction** +0.375s/f (Yiel) 4 Ran SP% 109.6
Speed ratings (Par 107): **86,84,80,71**
CSF £9.04 TOTE £5.70; EX 8.50.
Owner Bill Ives **Bred** E A R L Haras De Nonant Le Pin **Trained** Andoversford, Gloucs

FOCUS
This tight little handicap was run at an ordinary gallop. It saw the first three in with every chance. The winner is rated to his best with the runner-up close to his mark.

NOTEBOOK
Sarde(FR) came under pressure as the pace lifted nearing four out, but responded kindly and was in front at the next. He came away in between the final two fences and has evidently resumed at the top of his game. He wore cheekpieces last term, but clearly doesn't need them to shine and he could well be set for a better time of things this season. (op 9-4)
Youngstown(IRE), back on more suitably easier ground, raced enthusiastically and looked the one to be on four out. He began to feel the pinch nearing the next fence, though, and couldn't go with the winner try as he might thereafter. He is probably in need of some respite from the handicapper, but may just come on a touch again for the run. (tchd 5-4 and 6-4)
Work Boy, whose connections won this race last year, got a positive ride on his return to action. He cried enough after three out, but should come on nicely for the outing. (op 4-1)
Rebeccas Choice(IRE) was consistent over hurdles last season and was pitched straight into handicap company for this chase debut. She was the first beaten and really the run looked much needed. (op 11-2 tchd 6-1)

2477 PHS TREADSMART ENTRANCE MATTING H'CAP HURDLE (10 hdls) 2m 5f

2:40 (2:41) (Class 3) (0-120,114) 4-Y-O+ £5,204 (£1,528; £764; £381)

Form				RPR
400-	1		**No Principles**222 5132 7-11-9 111 ... JasonMaguire (Julian Smith) *hld up in rr: stdy hdwy 3 out: upsides last: rdn to ld last 200yds: styd on wl* 22/1	123+
360-	2	5	**Full Of Joy (IRE)**257 4446 5-11-3 105 ... APMcCoy (Jonjo O'Neill) *trckd ldrs: led 2 out: hdd and no ex run-in* 3/1[1]	109
35-6	3	3 1/2	**Stick Together**46 1709 7-11-2 109 ... (b) BrianToomey(5) (Malcolm Jefferson) *trckd ldrs: mstke 2nd: led appr 2 out: sn hdd and mstke: kpt on same pce appr last* 8/1[3]	111
5502	4	6	**Hippodrome (IRE)**11 2247 8-10-1 96 ... (p) MattCrawley(7) (John Harris) *in rr: drvn 5th: hdwy to chse ldrs after 7th: outpcd next: kpt on and n.d 4th whn mstke last* 10/1	93

405P **5** *1* **Terenzium (IRE)**[9] 2299 8-11-1 **113**...(p) JoeColliver(10) 108
(Micky Hammond) *hld up in rr: hdwy 7th: chsng ldrs next: wknd appr 2 out* **66/1**
2P- **6** *6* **Descaro (USA)**[27] 3724 4-11-5 **107**... GrahamLee 98
(David O'Meara) *trckd ldrs: t.k.h: led briefly after 3 out: 4th and btn whn hit 2 out* **3/1**[1]
203- **7** *25* **King Mak**[241] 4783 8-11-2 **104**... RobertWalford 71
(Marjorie Fife) *w ldr: led 5th: hdd after 3 out: lost pl appr next: t.o last* **10/1**
/0-P **8** *30* **Stagecoach Opal**[22] 2036 9-10-12 **105**... ShaneByrne(5) 45
(Sue Smith) *mde most: reminders 4th: hdd next: wknd 7th: t.o next* **33/1**
3P0/ **9** *36* **Hoh Viss**[592] 10-11-9 **114**... AdamPogson(3) 21
(Caroline Bailey) *chsd ldrs: drvn and lost pl 5th: bhd next: t.o fr 7th* **50/1**
0P-3 **P** **Peter Grimes (IRE)**[19] 2094 4-11-11 **113**... GerardTumelty —
(Alan King) *chsd ldrs: blnd 7th: sn p.u: fatally injured* **5/1**[2]
435 **F** **Hypnotic Gaze (IRE)**[75] 983 4-11-1 **106**... JimmyDerham(3) —
(Martin Keighley) *in rr: sme hdwy whn fell 7th* **14/1**

5m 28.2s (19.40) **Going Correction** +1.05s/f (Soft) **11** Ran SP% **113.4**
Speed ratings (Par 107): **105,103,101,99,99 96,87,75,62,—** —
CSF £84.71 CT £588.85 TOTE £23.20: £6.10, £1.20, £2.70; EX 89.10.
Owner Exors Of The Late Donald Smith **Bred** D E S Smith **Trained** Tirley, Gloucs

FOCUS
A moderate handicap for the grade with the top weight being rated 6lb below the race ceiling. It was run at a solid gallop and the form looks fair, rated through the third.

NOTEBOOK
No Principles raced enthusiastically on this return from his 222-day break and came through late on to run out a ready winner. The decent gallop was right up his street and he has evidently done well for his time off the track, as this was his first success over hurdles at the fifth attempt. This former bumper winner doesn't have many miles on the clock and it will be interesting to see what he can do off a likely higher mark. (op 25-1 tchd 20-1)
Full Of Joy(IRE) ◆, another bumper winner, was tailed off on his handicap debut when last seen in March. He proved a popular choice for this comeback over the longer trip, however, and did things nicely in the race. He was given every chance, but ultimately got outstayed by the winner from the last. He ought to prove hard to beat next time out, even though he faces a rise in the handicap. (tchd 11-4, 10-3 and 4-1 in a place)
Stick Together, who registered her sole success over C&D last season, was ridden more patiently and stepped up on the level of her comeback at Uttoxeter last month. She helps to set the standard. (op 9-1)
Hippodrome(IRE) was ridden to get the longer trip and probably performed close to his recent level. He will be better off back down in grade. (tchd 9-1 and 11-1)
Terenzium(IRE) ran one of his more encouraging races.
Descaro(USA) dropped out tamely after looking a big player entering the home straight. This was his first outing over hurdles for a trainer who improved him plenty on the Flat during the summer, and it may be that he wants dropping back in trip, despite staying well on the level. Official explanation: jockey said that the gelding failed to stay the two miles and five furlongs (op 5-2 tchd 9-4)
Peter Grimes(IRE) sadly broke down on the final lap. (tchd 9-2 and 11-2)

2478 PHS WORKPLACE SERVICES LADY AMATEUR RIDERS' H'CAP HURDLE (8 hdls) 2m 1f
3:10 (3:10) (Class 5) (0-95,95) 4-Y-0+ **£1,977** (£608; £304)

Form RPR
3012 **1** **Lean Burn (USA)**[20] 2070 4-10-11 **83**... MissIsabelTompsett(3) 101+
(Barry Leavy) *trckd ldrs: led 3 out: drew clr appr next: 10 l ahd last: eased towards fin* **1/1**[1]
-354 **2** *11* **Be My Light (IRE)**[20] 2072 4-11-1 **91**...(p) MissJennyCarr(7) 96
(Charlie Longsdon) *trckd ldrs: chsd wnr 5th: styd on same pce appr 2 out* **3/1**[2]
0260 **3** *10* **The Fox's Decree**[43] 1730 6-11-5 **95**...(t) MissSLBrett(7) 95+
(Martin Keighley) *racd wd: trckd ldrs: outpcd 5th: hit next: modest 3rd whn rdr almost c off 2 out: kpt on* **16/1**
0004 **4** *2½* **Monfils Monfils (USA)**[13] 1976 8-9-7 **69**...(p) MissLucyBell(7) 62
(Philip Kirby) *led: hdd 3 out: lost pl bef next* **4/1**[3]
F-34 **5** *19* **Secret Desert**[9] 2302 4-11-2 **92**... MissCWalton(7) 68
(Ferdy Murphy) *in last: hit 5th: bhd fr next* **10/1**

4m 26.2s (19.50) **Going Correction** +1.05s/f (Soft)
WFA 4 from 6yo+ 7lb **5** Ran SP% **110.0**
Speed ratings (Par 103): **96,90,86,84,76**
CSF £4.56 TOTE £1.60: £1.02, £2.00; EX 4.00.
Owner N Heath **Bred** George Ruggiero Jr **Trained** Forsbrook, Staffs

FOCUS
A weak handicap, confined to lady amateur riders, that was run at a fair tempo. The runner-up sets the level.

NOTEBOOK
Lean Burn(USA), well backed, arrived here in the best form and he easily resumed winning ways. He was up 5lb for finishing second Uttoxeter last time, but this return to better ground was right up his street and he could have been called the winner rounding the home bend. The handicapper will again have his say, so this progressive horse would probably be best turned out quickly as he didn't have a much of a race. (tchd 10-11 and 11-10)
Be My Light(IRE) was the only one to give the winner any sort of a challenge, but she lacked the pace to stay with that rival from the home turn and found this that bit too sharp. She is struggling to find her optimum trip, but there was enough in this effort to think she can find a race back over a slightly stiffer test. (op 11-4)
The Fox's Decree, who often runs over further, hit a flat spot before keeping on under considerate handling and nearly came down two out. He remains winless. (op 11-1)
Monfils Monfils(USA) paid for his early exertions from three out. (op 13-2 tchd 7-1)
Secret Desert was never in the hunt from off the pace. (op 17-2)

2479 PHS GROUP H'CAP CHASE (14 fncs) 2m 4f
3:40 (3:40) (Class 4) (0-100,100) 4-Y-0+ **£2,927** (£859; £429; £214)

Form RPR
-50P **1** **Foxesbow (IRE)**[14] 2170 6-11-6 **94**... APMcCoy 103
(Jonjo O'Neill) *trckd ldrs: wnt 2nd 9th: led after 4 out: styd on u.p run-in: hld on wl* **3/1**[2]
6-05 **2** *1¼* **Dark Gentleman**[13] 2194 7-10-0 **74** oh2... TjadeCollier 82
(Evelyn Slack) *led: hit 8th: hdd appr 3 out: upsides last: kpt on same pce* **6/1**[3]
540F **3** *5* **Grand Award**[11] 2231 5-11-12 **100**... JasonMaguire 106+
(Donald McCain) *hld up in rr: hdwy 4 out: sn trcking ldrs: cl 3rd whn blnd last: nt rcvr* **9/4**[1]
04-P **4** *20* **Ortega (FR)**[10] 2277 8-9-9 **76**...(p) JoeCornwall(7) 61
(John Cornwall) *nt fluent: chsd ldr: outpcd whn hit 11th: sn wknd* **9/1**
0403 **5** *17* **Donovan (NZ)**[11] 2250 11-11-0 **88**...(p) GrahamLee 65
(Richard Guest) *in rr: nt fluent 7th: drvn and outpcd whn sltly hmpd appr 3 out: sn lost pl* **3/1**[2]
103/ **6** *¾* **Jubilee George**[584] 4986 10-11-2 **90**... TomMessenger 64
(Christopher Kellett) *trckd ldrs: hit 8th: outpcd 4 out: bhd whn mstke 3 out and next* **12/1**

5m 18.0s (12.30) **Going Correction** +0.375s/f (Yiel) **6** Ran SP% **112.7**
Speed ratings (Par 105): **90,89,87,79,72 72**
toteswingers:1&2 £2.90, 2&3 £3.00, 1&3 £2.50 CSF £20.52 TOTE £3.20: £1.10, £2.70; EX 18.80.
Owner John P McManus **Bred** Mrs Eleanor Hadden **Trained** Cheltenham, Gloucs

FOCUS
An ordinary handicap, weakened by the non-runner. The third is rated to his hurdles mark.

NOTEBOOK
Foxesbow(IRE) bounced back to winning ways and justified good support in the process. He had shown little of late and was pulled up on his latest outing, but was well treated on his previous best efforts. His jumping was much more assured on this sounder surface and the experience ought to boost his confidence nicely, but his profile dictates he is one to take on again next time. Official explanation: trainer's representative said, regarding the apparent improvement of form, that the gelding made several mistakes last time, but jumped much better in this race (op 9-2 tchd 11-4)
Dark Gentleman, 2lb out of the weights, ran a game race under a positive ride and finished a clear second-best. He too enjoyed this sounder surface and it was by far his best run to date over fences, so his turn may well be nearing. (op 7-1)
Grand Award, whose in-form yard won this in 2008, fell at the last when just in front on his previous outing and was making his chasing debut here. He crept into things off the home turn and had every chance in the straight, but blundered at the last. That cost him, but the experience should be to his benefit and he ought to be placed to strike before that long. (op 15-8)
Ortega(FR) could have jumped better, but this was still more encouraging and he will enjoy stepping back up in trip. (op 10-1 tchd 12-1)
Donovan(NZ) posted one of his better efforts when third off this mark over C&D 11 days earlier. He didn't get a clear run on the final bend, but was well held at the time and remains hard to predict. (tchd 10-3)
T/Plt: £504.80 to a £1 stake. Pool of £36,412.87 - 52.65 winning tickets. T/Qpdt: £25.10 to a £1 stake. Pool of £3,586.14 - 105.40 winning tickets. WG

2216 WINCANTON (R-H)
Thursday, November 18

OFFICIAL GOING: Chase course - good to soft; hurdle course - good (good to soft in places)
Wind: mild breeze against Weather: overcast with sunny periods and showers.

2480 BATHWICK TYRES H'CAP HURDLE (10 hdls) 2m 4f
1:20 (1:20) (Class 4) (0-105,104) 4-Y-0+ **£2,602** (£764; £382; £190)

Form RPR
3-P3 **1** **Matako (FR)**[21] 2058 7-11-4 **101**... IanPopham(5) 104+
(Caroline Keevil) *cl up: led 2 out: sn rdn and hdd: kpt on to ld sn after last: all out* **8/1**
046- **2** *hd* **Perception (IRE)**[76] 5328 4-10-12 **100**... PeterHatton(10) 104+
(Alan King) *cl up: chal 2 out: led sn after and rdn: nt fluent last: sn hdd: kpt on towards fin: jst hld* **7/2**[2]
P-30 **3** *7* **Ballyoliver**[21] 2058 6-11-10 **102**... AidanColeman 99
(Venetia Williams) *trckd ldrs: rdn after 3 out: styd on same pce fr next: no ch w ldng pair* **11/2**
566- **4** *8* **Stagehand (IRE)**[221] 5157 6-11-8 **100**... LiamHeard 91
(Chris Down) *led tl rdn 2 out: fdd last* **10/1**
5244 **5** *5* **Mangonel**[7] 2329 6-10-0 **78** oh2...(v) RodiGreene 63
(Stuart Howe) *trckd ldr: chal fr 6th tl appr 2 out: sn wknd* **9/2**[3]
5231 **F** **Ruby Valentine (FR)**[11] 2244 7-9-9 **78** oh6... MichaelMurphy(5) —
(Jim Wilson) *cl up whn fell heavily 7th* **2/1**[1]

4m 46.5s (-10.30) **Going Correction** -0.55s/f (Firm)
WFA 4 from 6yo+ 8lb **6** Ran SP% **109.3**
Speed ratings (Par 105): **105,104,102,98,96** —
toteswingers:1&2 £1.90, 2&3 £5.60, 1&3 £2.10 CSF £33.98 TOTE £12.10: £3.70, £1.60.
Owner P M Bryant **Bred** Carol Garmond & Mme Carol Garmond **Trained** Blagdon, Somerset

FOCUS
Two drew clear in this opening handicap. The first two are on the upgrde and the third is rated to his mark.

NOTEBOOK
Matako(FR) proved too resolute for the runner-up after the last. A multiple point winner, he improved markedly on his previous efforts switched to handicaps, and a return to 3m is likely to suit at some stage. (op 17-2)
Perception(IRE), in good form on the Flat, was another to raise her game switched to handicaps but, having travelled best, she was headed at the last and couldn't get back up. (op 11-4)
Ballyoliver improved on his initial effort for the yard and will be of interest once returned to 3m. (op 5-1 tchd 6-1)
Stagehand(IRE) slowly faded and was disappointing. (op 12-1)
Ruby Valentine(FR), officially 12lb well in, having won at Hereford the previous week, looked the one to beat, despite racing from out of the handicap, but her race came to an abrupt end when taking a crashing fall at the seventh. It's hoped her confidence isn't affected too badly by this. (tchd 9-4 in places)

2481 EUROPEAN BREEDERS' FUND/THOROUGHBRED BREEDERS' ASSOCIATION MARES' NOVICES' CHASE (15 fncs 2 omitted) 2m 5f
1:50 (1:50) (Class 4) 4-Y-0+ **£3,998** (£1,241; £668)

Form RPR
50-1 **1** **Easter Legend**[13] 2182 6-11-6 0... SamThomas 126+
(Emma Lavelle) *j.w: lft in ld 4th: mde rest: in command fr 2 out: easily* **1/3**[1]
-450 **2** *8* **Bosamcliff (IRE)**[7] 2329 5-11-0 0... JohnnyFarrelly 111+
(David Evans) *trckd ldrs: mstke 2nd: lft trcking wnr 4th: rdn after 3 out: hld fr next: wnt rt last* **20/1**
14PP **3** *53* **Prescelli (IRE)**[32] 1887 6-11-0 112...(p) TomO'Brien 58
(Keith Goldsworthy) *led tl rchd for 4th: trckd ldrs: rdn after 4 out: wknd bef next: t.o* **12/1**[3]
00-F **U** **Dansimar**[13] 2182 6-11-0 0... AidanColeman —
(Venetia Williams) *trcking ldrs: nt fluent 2nd: blnd bdly and uns rdr 4th* **9/2**[2]

5m 29.2s (4.00) **Going Correction** -0.425s/f (Good) **4** Ran SP% **105.7**
Speed ratings (Par 105): **75,71,51,—**
CSF £5.94 TOTE £1.20; EX 4.30.
Owner Simon Willes **Bred** Simon Willes **Trained** Wildhern, Hants

FOCUS
The last fence in the straight was omitted in all chase races. A fair mares' chase with the winner value for further.

NOTEBOOK
Easter Legend made it 2-2 over fences. She was much more polished in the jumping department than she had been at Fontwell on her reappearance, and will reportedly be kept to mares' company for now. The final of this series at Newbury next spring is the long-term target. (op 3-10)
Bosamcliff(IRE) won only once as a hurdler, where she was rated inferior to these three rivals, but she jumped well enough on this first start over fences and should pick up a small race at some stage. (op 25-1)
Prescelli(IRE) had lost her form over hurdles and the switch to fences did little to help matters. (op 14-1)
Dansimar departed early and has now failed to complete in both starts over fences. (tchd 5-1)

2482 SOUTH WEST RACING CLUB NOVICES' HURDLE (11 hdls) 2m 6f
2:20 (2:20) (Class 4) 4-Y-O+ **£2,602** (£764; £382; £190)

Form				RPR
1	**1**		**Buck Magic (IRE)**[23] 2025 4-10-7 0 .... KeiranBurke(5) (Patrick Rodford) *t.k.h: mid-div: hdwy to trck ldrs 5th: led appr 2 out: styd on strly to assert run-in: pushed out* **25/1**	119+
2-	**2**	½	**Vico (IRE)**[364] 2389 6-10-7 0 .... MrRMahon(5) (Paul Nicholls) *a.p: led 6th tl appr 2 out: styd pressing ldr u.p: hung rt: ev ch last: no ex* **8/15**[1]	118
	3	23	**Roalco De Farges (FR)**[207] 5-10-12 0 .... RichardJohnson (Philip Hobbs) *racd keenly towards rr: hdwy to trck ldrs 4th: wnt prom 6th tl rdn after 3 out: no ch w ldng pair whn hit 2 out* **13/2**[2]	97+
10P-	**4**	1	**Fortification (USA)**[243] 4740 7-10-12 125 ....(p) DominicElsworth (Michael Blake) *chsd ldrs: drvn along fr 7th: one pce fr 3 out* **13/2**[2]	96
45-	**5**	nk	**Takamaru (FR)**[264] 4301 4-10-12 0 .... JohnnyFarrelly (David Pipe) *hld up towards rr: pushed along after 6th: hdwy appr 3 out: one pce fr 2 out* **25/1**	96+
	6	shd	**Gunna Be A Devil (IRE)**[227] 6-10-7 0 .... IanPopham(5) (Jeremy Scott) *chsd ldrs: rdn after 3 out: sn one pce* **66/1**	96
0/	**7**	3½	**Noddies Way**[33] 4649 7-10-12 0 .... DavidEngland (John Panvert) *prom tl pckd 4th: chsd ldrs: rdn after 8th: wknd 2 out* **66/1**	93
05	**8**	1	**Glens Boy (IRE)**[16] 2142 6-10-12 0 .... HaddenFrost (Henrietta Knight) *a towards rr* **40/1**	92
4-4P	**9**	4	**The Grifter**[16] 2136 8-10-12 109 .... AndrewGlassonbury (John Ryall) *hit 1st: mid-div: rdn after 8th: nvr any imp: wknd 2 out* **33/1**	88
4-20	**10**	½	**Inner Steel (IRE)**[17] 2123 5-10-12 0 .... MarkBradburne (Lydia Richards) *mid-div: mstke 4th: wknd bef 3 out* **25/1**	88
0/06	**11**	3¼	**Red Law (IRE)**[12] 2216 6-10-5 0 .... MrPJTolman(7) (Mark Gillard) *prom tl rdn appr 8th: wknd* **100/1**	85
42-6	**12**	32	**Ceepeegee (IRE)**[34] 1853 5-10-12 118 .... JoeTizzard (Colin Tizzard) *led tl appr 6th: hit 7th: wknd after next: t.o* **20/1**[3]	56
05	**13**	2½	**The Clyda Rover (IRE)**[16] 2136 6-10-12 0 .... JamieMoore (Helen Nelmes) *a towards rr: t.o* **66/1**	54
0	**14**	3½	**Quiet Alice**[16] 2136 5-10-5 0 .... RodiGreene (Neil Mulholland) *a bhd: t.o* **100/1**	44
00-4	**15**	6	**Silver Twilight**[78] 1455 5-10-0 0 .... MichaelMurphy(5) (John Allen) *a bhd: t.o* **125/1**	38
P	**P**		**Stadium Arcadium (IRE)**[20] 2067 7-10-12 0 .... SamThomas (Emma Lavelle) *in tch tl wknd 8th: t.o whn p.u bef 2 out* **25/1**	—

5m 8.10s (-18.40) **Going Correction** -0.55s/f (Firm)
WFA 4 from 5yo+ 8lb **16** Ran SP% **124.7**
Speed ratings (Par 105): **111,110,102,102,101 101,100,100,98,98 97,85,84,83,81** —
toteswingers:1&2 £9.50, 2&3 £2.60, 1&3 £15.20 CSF £38.97 TOTE £42.50: £7.20, £1.02, £2.80; EX 87.60.
Owner Brian Derrick **Bred** Sean Culleton **Trained** Ash, Somerset

FOCUS
An ordinary novice hurdle. The front pair drew clear.

NOTEBOOK
Buck Magic(IRE), winner of a Taunton bumper on his recent rules debut, came out on top, upsetting red-hot favourite Vico. The winner, who also scored in the pointing field, travelled well throughout and, having engaged in a tussle with the favourite, it was he who stayed on the stronger. This was a likeable performance and he can probably defy a penalty, with 3m likely to suit. (tchd 22-1)
Vico(IRE), runner-up in this race on his hurdles debut a year ago, had failed to make the track since, but the market suggested he was ready to go. However, he could not stay on as well as the winner and was hanging late on. Clear of the third, he's clearly got a race in him, but is no star. He'll probably do better over fences. (op 4-5 tchd 5-6 in places)
Roalco De Farges(FR), placed on both completed starts in Irish points, ran well enough, but he had failed to settle early on and that ultimately took its toll. This run should have taken any fizz out of him and he's likely to post an improvement on this next time. (tchd 11-2)
Fortification(USA), who progressed into a useful handicap chaser last term, was making his debut for yet another yard and ran with some encouragement. This should set him up for a return to fences. (op 7-1)
Takamaru(FR) never got into it on this debut over hurdles, but he wasn't exactly given a hard time of it and should improve. (op 22-1)

2483 BATHWICK TYRES H'CAP CHASE (17 fncs 5 omitted) 3m 3f 110y
2:50 (2:51) (Class 4) (0-115,113) 4-Y-O+ **£5,331** (£1,655; £891)

Form				RPR
P5-2	**1**		**Rebel Melody (IRE)**[11] 2249 9-11-2 106 ....(bt) PeterToole(3) (Charlie Mann) *chsd ldrs: jnd ldr 12th: rdn after 3 out: slipped on landing 2 out: narrow advantage whn lft wl clr last* **9/4**[1]	119
11P4	**2**	61	**House Of Bourbon (IRE)**[25] 1992 7-11-11 112 ....(vt) RichardJohnson (Tim Vaughan) *chsd ldrs: wnt 3rd appr 12th: sn rdn: no ch fr 14th: lft remote 2nd last* **13/2**	70
0016	**3**	45	**Outside Investor (IRE)**[23] 2024 10-9-11 89 oh6 ow2..(b) KeiranBurke(5) (Patrick Rodford) *disp ld tl wnt rt 10th: rdn after next: lost tch fr 12th: lft v remote 3rd last* **12/1**	7
1-0P	**P**		**Fine By Me (IRE)**[26] 1960 11-11-5 113 ....(p) AnthonyFreeman(7) (Julian Smith) *virtuall brought to a stand stl 1st: nvr rcvrd wl adrift: p.u bef 7th* **9/1**	—
63-2	**F**		**Newbay Bob**[196] 181 10-11-0 108 ....(p) MrRGHenderson(7) (Nick Mitchell) *fell 1st: fatally injured* **7/2**[3]	—
102-	**F**		**Shaking Hands (IRE)**[234] 4929 6-11-5 106 ....(bt) TomScudamore (David Pipe) *mde most: pckd 9th: bmpd next: jnd by wnr 12th: rdn whn slipped on bnd appr 2 out: narrowly hdd whn fell last* **11/4**[2]	116

6m 52.3s (-15.90) **Going Correction** -0.425s/f (Good) **6** Ran SP% **110.7**
Speed ratings (Par 105): **105,87,74,—,— —**
toteswingers:1&2 £5.70, 2&3 £4.80, 1&3 £7.50 CSF £16.06 TOTE £4.10: £3.60, £2.80; EX 17.60.
Owner Mrs Judy Maynard **Bred** Donal Keane **Trained** Upper Lambourn, Berks

FOCUS
An eventful handicap chase, with Newbay Bob's first-fence fall sadly having fatal consequences, and Shaking Hands, who was still in with a chance, falling heavily at the last and leaving Rebel Melody to collect. The winner and faller are rated to form in an ordinary race.

NOTEBOOK
Rebel Melody(IRE), who would probably have come home in front anyway, was just 1lb higher than when second on his reappearance and can continue to give a good account, assuming the handicapper doesn't put him up too much. (tchd 2-1 and 5-2)
House Of Bourbon(IRE) inherited second, but he hasn't shown much since returning to fences. (op 10-1)
Fine By Me(IRE) Official explanation: jockey said gelding was badly hampered by a faller at the first fence (op 5-2 tchd 3-1)
Newbay Bob took a fatal fall at the first fence. (op 5-2 tchd 3-1)
Shaking Hands(IRE) looked capable of going well off this mark and, although headed, he was by no means beaten when falling. He did get up after laying winded for a while, but it remains to be seen how this affects his confidence. (op 5-2 tchd 3-1)

2484 JOCKEY CLUB CATERING H'CAP CHASE (11 fncs 2 omitted) 2m
3:20 (3:21) (Class 4) (0-115,122) 4-Y-O+ **£3,903** (£1,146; £573; £286)

Form				RPR
4611	**1**		**I'm A Legend**[12] 2217 8-11-12 115 ....(p) DougieCostello (Neil Mulholland) *chsd ldng pair: clsd on ldrs fr 8th: narrow advantage last: sn hrd rdn: kpt on gamely run-in: won on nod* **7/2**[2]	125+
0-31	**2**	shd	**Inside Dealer (IRE)**[11] 2243 6-11-6 109 7ex .... JoeTizzard (Colin Tizzard) *disp ld: rdn appr 2 out: ramianed w narrow advantage tl last: kpt on gamely all the way to line: lost on nod* **10/11**[1]	119+
2245	**3**	3½	**Morestead (IRE)**[17] 2127 5-11-3 106 ....(b) LiamTreadwell (Brendan Powell) *disp ld: rdn after 3 out: ev ch last: kpt on but no ex* **14/1**	112
203F	**4**	20	**January**[23] 2022 7-11-0 103 ....(t) TomScudamore (Liam Corcoran) *hld up 4th: clsng on ldrs whn nt fluent 3 out: sn rdn: wknd next* **10/1**	91
2444	**5**	9	**The Duke's Speech (IRE)**[22] 2034 9-11-9 112 .... JohnnyFarrelly (Sophie Leech) *hld up in last pair: nvr any imp: t.o* **10/1**	92
2002	**F**		**Beauchamp Viking**[7] 2334 6-10-0 89 oh8 ....(t) RodiGreene (Simon Burrough) *hld up in last pair: nvr any imp: t.o whn fell 2 out* **9/1**[3]	—

3m 53.4s (-6.50) **Going Correction** -0.425s/f (Good) **6** Ran SP% **109.5**
Speed ratings (Par 105): **99,98,97,87,82** —
toteswingers:1&2 £1.60, 2&3 £4.20, 1&3 £4.30 CSF £7.13 CT £30.52 TOTE £4.80: £2.30, £1.10; EX 5.90.
Owner Wincanton Race Club **Bred** Conkwell Grange Stud Ltd **Trained** Burlescombe, Devon
■ Stewards' Enquiry : Dougie Costello three-day ban: used whip without giving time to respond (2-5 Dec)

FOCUS
A fair handicap chase in which the first two are on the upgrade and the third sets the level.

NOTEBOOK
I'm A Legend came out on top in a bobbing finish. On a hat-trick following wins at Exeter and at this course earlier in the month, he was up another 5lb, but it wasn't quite enough to stop him. He'll find it more difficult extending his winning sequence to four, but he's clearly in the form of his life. (op 11-4)
Inside Dealer(IRE), shouldering a penalty for last week's Hereford win, leaving him 5lb well-in, looked the one to beat and he certainly showed a good attitude, but his head was down at the wrong time as they flashed past the post. This defeat shouldn't be held against him and he'll probably appreciate a return to further. (op 6-5)
Morestead(IRE) bounced back from a couple of lesser efforts. (op 16-1)
January may have been feeling the effects of his last time out fall. (op 8-1 tchd 11-1)

2485 WINCANTON RACECOURSE RACING EXCELLENCE "HANDS AND HEELS" NOVICES' H'CAP HURDLE (CONDITIONAL/AMAT) (8 hdls) 2m
3:50 (3:50) (Class 4) (0-100,100) 3-Y-O+ **£2,602** (£764; £382; £190)

Form				RPR
5-62	**1**		**Switched Off**[17] 2131 5-11-8 99 ....(p) MrJHodson(3) (Ian Williams) *trckd ldrs: hmpd 2nd: jnd ldrs 5th: led after 2 out: pushed ahd flat* **9/4**[1]	108+
2150	**2**	2	**J'Adhere (FR)**[146] 837 5-11-5 98 .... MrEDavid(5) (Tim Vaughan) *restrained in rr: hdwy after 4th: jnd ldrs 5th: led appr 2 out: hdd but ev ch flat: kpt on: no ex* **15/2**	104
023	**3**	4	**Lady Willa (IRE)**[23] 2020 3-10-2 91 .... AodhaganConlon (Mark Gillard) *racd wd: prom tl lost pl on bnd appr 3rd: chsd ldrs 5th: rdn after 3 out: kpt on same pce* **10/1**	77
254-	**4**	9	**Taste The Wine (IRE)**[40] 4828 4-11-5 96 .... MrRJWilliams(3) (Bernard Llewellyn) *hld up: barged way through to ld 5th: hdd appr 2 out: wknd last* **9/2**[2]	89
P0/0	**5**	4½	**Wise Hawk**[15] 2150 5-11-7 95 .... PeterCarberry (Chris Down) *chsd ldrs: rdn after 3 out: wknd after next* **7/1**[3]	84
450	**6**	12	**Highland Cadett**[17] 2133 3-10-6 95 ....(v) NathanSweeney (Rod Millman) *in rr after 3rd: nvr a threat* **8/1**	58
/5-0	**7**	9	**Trump Call (IRE)**[17] 2128 6-11-9 100 .... MrJSherwood(3) (Venetia Williams) *chsd ldrs tl wknd after 3 out* **7/1**[3]	70
3620	**8**	30	**We'Re Delighted**[27] 1949 5-10-9 83 ....(t) MrPJTolman (Michael Blake) *led at gd pce: hmpd and hdd 5th: wknd after 3 out: t.o* **16/1**	26

3m 39.1s (-9.80) **Going Correction** -0.55s/f (Firm)
WFA 3 from 4yo 15lb 4 from 5yo+ 7lb **8** Ran SP% **111.8**
Speed ratings (Par 105): **102,101,99,94,92 86,81,66**
toteswingers:1&2 £5.10, 2&3 £5.40, 1&3 £6.60. totesuper7: Win: Not won. Place: £105.40. CSF £18.63 CT £135.67 TOTE £2.10: £1.10, £3.10, £1.90; EX 17.70.
Owner P Nicholls **Bred** Mrs Byron Paterson **Trained** Portway, Worcs

FOCUS
A low-grade handicap hurdle rated around the placed horses.

NOTEBOOK
Switched Off posted a career-best when finishing second at Plumpton on his recent return to hurdles, and the addition of cheekpieces enabled him to improve again. He travelled like a horse with more to offer, but is by no means going to be getting carried away with. (tchd 5-2 in places)
J'Adhere(FR), returning from a 146-day absence, travelled well into the straight and had his chance, but the winner always looked to have him covered. (op 7-1 tchd 8-1)
Lady Willa(IRE) showed improved form switched to handicaps, although was still comfortably held and it may require a drop in grade for her to be successful. (op 11-1 tchd 12-1)
Taste The Wine(IRE) contested some fair contests as a novice, so it was disappointing he couldn't make more of an impact switched to handicaps, having been fit from the Flat. (op 7-1)
T/Plt: £11.10 to a £1 stake. Pool of £44,564.96 - 2,928.57 winning tickets. T/Qpdt: £2.70 to a £1 stake. Pool of £4,567.28 - 1,214.30 winning tickets. TM

2486 - 2492a (Foreign Racing) - See Raceform Interactive

2081 ASCOT (R-H)

Friday, November 19

OFFICIAL GOING: Good to soft (good in places; chs 7.0 hdl 6.9)

Wind: Almost nil Weather: Fine

2493 REDSTONE "NATIONAL HUNT" NOVICES' HURDLE (11 hdls) 2m 3f 110y

1:00 (1:00) (Class 3) 4-Y-0+

£5,009 (£1,480; £740; £370; £184; £92)

Form				RPR
22-3	1		**Frascati Park (IRE)**[27] 1966 6-10-12 132 PaddyBrennan (Nigel Twiston-Davies) *mde all: clr to 5th: rdn and maintained gallop after 3 out: hld 3 l ld flat tl eased fnl strides* **10/3**[3]	136+
11-	2	1 ¾	**Sprinter Sacre (FR)**[216] 5227 4-10-12 0 BarryGeraghty (Nicky Henderson) *t.k.h early: prom: chsd wnr 7th: rdn bef 2 out: cl enough last: no imp flat* **6/5**[1]	134+
1	3	8	**Poungach (FR)**[187] 362 4-10-7 0 MrRMahon(5) (Paul Nicholls) *settled midfield: pushed along 4th: rdn in 7th pl after 7th: struggling next: styd on stoutly fr 2 out to take 3rd flat* **25/1**	124
3-	4	1 ½	**Easter Meteor**[237] 4893 4-10-12 0 SamThomas (Emma Lavelle) *hld up last: stdy prog fr 8th: shkn up after 3 out: wnt 3rd after 2 out tl flat: shaped wl* **25/1**	123
20-1	5	3 ¾	**Made In Time (IRE)**[22] 2059 5-11-4 0 (t) APMcCoy (Rebecca Curtis) *t.k.h: prom: chsd wnr 5th to 7th: jst pushed along and steadily lost pl after 3 out* **11/4**[2]	127+
	6	5	**Imperial Circus (IRE)**[167] 4-10-12 0 RichardJohnson (Philip Hobbs) *settled in midfield: outpcd fr 8th: sme hdwy 3 out but nvr a threat: nt disgracd* **40/1**	116+
1-3P	7	12	**Lidar (FR)**[27] 1966 5-11-4 122 WayneHutchinson (Alan King) *prom: 4th and wl in tch after 7th: rdn and wknd sn after 3 out* **16/1**	108
6	8	24	**Hawkaller**[41] 1778 5-10-7 0 RachaelGreen(5) (Anthony Honeyball) *hld up in last trio: lost tch 7th: wl bhd next: t.o* **100/1**	78
0	9	14	**Whispering Jack**[22] 2058 5-10-9 0 PeterToole(3) (Charlie Mann) *in tch in rr tl after 7th: wl bhd next: t.o* **125/1**	64
	P		**Buffalo Creek (FR)**[564] 6-10-12 0 LiamTreadwell (Giles Smyly) *mstke 2nd: chsd wnr to 5th: wknd rapidly 7th: t.o whn p.u bef next* **100/1**	—
	B		**Humbel Times (IRE)**[239] 4857 6-10-5 0 MrRichardCollinson(7) (Neil King) *mstkes: hld up in last trio: jst in tch whn b.d 7th* **200/1**	—
	F		**Beefeater (IRE)** 5-10-12 0 RhysFlint (Philip Hobbs) *hld up in rr: in tch whn fell 7th: fatally injured* **100/1**	—

4m 38.6s (-9.40) **Going Correction** -0.025s/f (Good)
WFA 4 from 5yo+ 7lb **12 Ran SP% 115.5**
Speed ratings (Par 107): **117,116,113,112,111 109,104,94,89,— —,—**
Tote Swingers: 1&2 £1.90, 1&3 £12.00, 2&3 £6.20 CSF £7.55 TOTE £3.50: £1.50, £1.20, £4.30; EX 8.90 Trifecta £80.90 Pool: £1,088.22 - 9.95 winning units..
Owner Barry Connell **Bred** J Mangan **Trained** Naunton, Gloucs

FOCUS

The front pair drew clear in what looked a good novice hurdle. The winner ensured a decent pace and the time was good. There were a few performances of note and the race should produce its share of winners, with the winner rated to his best.

NOTEBOOK

Frascati Park(IRE) brought placed form behind the likes of Reve De Sivola, Escort'men and Silviniaco Conti into this, setting a high standard, and he was always likely to prove tough to pass. Despite the favourite travelling well in his slipstream, he found plenty under strong pressure in the straight, and the fact he had already had a run this season made the difference. This was his first win as a hurdler and he's good enough to defy a penalty before going handicapping. (op 7-2 tchd 4-1)

Sprinter Sacre(FR) ◆ was unbeaten in bumpers last yehere and at Ayr last season. He was understandably made favourite on this first start over hurdles and he travelled like a class horse. However, he had been plenty keen enough early on, and it became apparent off the final bend that Geraghty wasn't holding on to much. He did stay on though, and had a really good blow afterwards, which suggests he'll improve plenty for it. Undoubtedly the one to take from the race, he should have no trouble going one better before possibly going up in grade. He'll make a fine chaser. (op Evens tchd 5-4)

Poungach(FR) ◆, off since winning a Stratford bumper in May, is a big, scopey, chasing type, and little was expected on this debut over hurdles judging by his SP of 25-1. Therefore, it was pleasing to see him shape so well in third, staying on nicely without being given an overly hard time. He couldn't match the front pair, but that's understandable and he too looks a winner in waiting once he's granted a stiffer test of stamina. (op 22-1 tchd 20-1)

Easter Meteor ◆, described as a 'big, gangly, unfurnished type' by his trainer, hadn't run since finishing third to Kid Cassidy in a junior bumper in the spring and, although unable to make any impression on the principals, he travelled nicely until becoming outpaced and was another who wasn't given a hard time. He'll improve for this and can win once upped in trip. (op 20-1)

Made In Time(IRE), who had finished ninth in last season's Champion bumper and won with ease on his hurdles debut at Stratford, proved disappointing. Whilst he looked vulnerable to his market rivals under a penalty on this drop in trip, he was unable to put up much of a fight under pressure, backing out of it from the final bend. From a yard that gets its horses fit first time, it remains to be seen how much improvement he's got in him. (op 7-2)

Imperial Circus(IRE), a point winner, made some late headway and should relish a stiffer test. (op 50-1)

Lidar(FR) hasn't lived up to expectations and may be best off down the handicap route now. (op 18-1 tchd 20-1)

Beefeater(IRE)

2494 NOT FORGOTTEN ASSOCIATION BEGINNERS' CHASE (17 fncs) 2m 5f 110y

1:35 (1:35) (Class 3) 4-Y-0+

£7,514 (£2,220; £1,110; £555; £277; £139)

Form				RPR
113-	1		**Master Of The Hall (IRE)**[267] 4260 6-11-1 0 BarryGeraghty (Nicky Henderson) *racd wd: hld up: wnt 3rd 10th: pressed ldr 12th: led 4 out: drew clr 2 out: 7 l up whn blnd bdly last: drvn and looked vulnerable briefly flat: sn in command again* **10/11**[1]	142+
PF-2	2	3 ½	**Fredo (IRE)**[22] 2057 6-11-1 133 TomScudamore (Ian Williams) *cl up: led 10th: pressed 12th: hdd and mstke 4 out: wl hld tl lft w slim ch after last: one pce* **9/2**[3]	133
/1-5	3	7	**County Zen (FR)**[20] 2082 7-11-1 0 RichardJohnson (Philip Hobbs) *in tch: blnd 7th: sn struggling in last: plugged on fr 12th to take 3rd 2 out: no further hdwy* **14/1**	127
1-24	4	2 ¼	**Pause And Clause (IRE)**[20] 2082 6-11-1 0 SamThomas (Emma Lavelle) *j. stickily early: pressed ldr: led 7th to 10th: mstke 12th and lost tch w ldng pair: lost 3rd 2 out* **10/3**[2]	127+
-044	5	33	**Captive Audience (IRE)**[22] 2057 7-10-8 0 AodhaganConlon(7) (Rebecca Curtis) *led to 7th: blnd 9th and lost pl: t.o whn mstke 12th* **10/1**	97
1/P2	6	1 ¼	**Zhukov (IRE)**[5] 2392 8-10-8 0 MrBJPoste(7) (Kevin Tork) *in tch: drvn 11th: sn wknd: t.o fr 13th* **100/1**	93

5m 22.4s (-3.60) **Going Correction** -0.025s/f (Good) **6 Ran SP% 110.4**
Speed ratings (Par 107): **105,103,101,100,88 87**
Tote Swingers: 1&2 £2.10, 1&3 £3.20, 2&3 £4.50 CSF £5.47 TOTE £1.80: £1.30, £2.00; EX 5.20.
Owner Martin Landau & Jonathan Duffy **Bred** Sweetmans Bloodstock **Trained** Upper Lambourn, Berks

FOCUS

A really interesting beginners' chase with the winner looking a smart prospect and the placed horses to last season's hurdle marks.

NOTEBOOK

Master Of The Hall(IRE) ◆, barring a scare at the last, where he blundered and did well to stand up, made a smooth transition to fences. That mistake cost him all momentum, and he briefly looked vulnerable to Fredo, but did pick up again and can be rated value for much more than the official winning margin. His jumping down the side of the course was good, and he still looks a bit green, understandable with this being only the former point winner's fifth start under rules. His form over hurdles came in testing ground, but he is just as effective on this better surface and he looks in for a fruitful novice campaign, with him having the option of going either up or down in distance. He should have no trouble defying a penalty before going up in grade, with the new Jewson-sponsored event at Cheltenham the possible long-term aim. (tchd Evens)

Fredo(IRE), runner-up to Tell Massini on his chase debut at Stratford, jumped well in the main, but was swiftly overtaken by the winner coming to three out and, despite being allowed back in with a chance at the last, he didn't have enough left to run the winner close. A strong stayer over hurdles, he's going to relish the step up to 3m and could be one to make an impact in some decent handicaps later in the season. (op 4-1 tchd 5-1)

County Zen(FR) looked low on confidence at his fences when a well-beaten fifth here on debut, and he again looked set to struggle when dropping to last with a circuit to run. However, he warmed to it, staying on inside the final 4f, and will be of interest switched to handicaps down the line. (tchd 20-1)

Pause And Clause(IRE), disappointing when fourth at the course latest (ahead of County Zen), had been schooled intensively since then, but he still looked far from confident at his fences and again ended up well held. This was his third run, so he's now qualified for a mark, and it would be no surprise to see him improve once handicapping. He'll no doubt be aimed towards the Centenary Novices' Handicap at the Festival (formerly the Jewson). (op 4-1 tchd 3-1)

Captive Audience(IRE) should come to life once faced with 3m in handicaps. (tchd 9-1)

2495 ROBERT GILES AGENCIES INTRODUCTORY HURDLE (9 hdls) 2m

2:10 (2:10) (Class 2) 4-Y-0+

£6,888 (£2,035; £1,017; £509; £254; £127)

Form				RPR
251-	1		**Megastar**[223] 5129 5-11-0 0 JamieMoore (Gary Moore) *nt entirely fluent: hld up: t.k.h downhill fr 3rd: prog to trck ldng pair 6th: led 2 out: sn clr: easily* **1/2**[1]	130+
6	2	16	**Smokey Oakey (IRE)**[18] 2122 6-11-0 0 ColinBolger (Mark H Tompkins) *pressed ldr: led 5th: qcknd pce fr next: hit 3 out: hdd 2 out and sn easily outpcd* **8/1**[3]	104
4/	3	4 ½	**Highly Regal (IRE)**[25] 2378 5-11-0 0 (b) TomScudamore (Roger Teal) *t.k.h: hld up bhd ldrs: wnt 2nd 6th tl bef 2 out: sn outpcd* **25/1**	100
5	4	1 ¼	**Ebony Diamond (IRE)**[38] 1817 6-11-0 0 PaulMoloney (Charlie Mann) *t.k.h: hld up bhd ldrs: mstke 6th: effrt and cl enough in 4th after 3 out: sn outpcd* **12/1**	99
2	5	15	**Koup De Kanon (FR)**[21] 2074 4-11-0 0 SamThomas (Emma Lavelle) *nt fluent 1st: hld up last: t.k.h downhill fr 3rd: nvr on terms w ldrs: wnt modest 5th 3 out* **4/1**[2]	87+
	6	11	**By Command**[16] 5-11-0 0 LiamHeard (Gerald Ham) *hld up in tch: struggling once pce lifted 6th: wl bhd fr 3 out: t.o* **66/1**	72
4P	7	nk	**Karingabay Queen**[12] 2265 5-10-7 0 (b[1]) MrBJPoste (Kevin Tork) *led at stdy pce to 5th: wknd and mstke next: t.o* **66/1**	65
	8	7	**Marvo**[49] 6-11-0 0 MattieBatchelor (Mark H Tompkins) *hld up: t.k.h downhill fr 3rd: mstke 6th: sn btn: t.o* **16/1**	67

3m 55.8s (6.80) **Going Correction** -0.025s/f (Good) **8 Ran SP% 118.2**
Speed ratings (Par 109): **82,74,71,71,63 58,57,54**
Tote Swingers: 1&2 £2.60, 1&3 £5.90, 2&3 £8.20 CSF £5.92 TOTE £1.60: £1.10, £1.50, £3.90; EX 5.00 Trifecta £41.40 Pool: £854.98 - 15.27 winning units..
Owner Hinds, Waddingham, Arthur, Herbert, Day **Bred** Pleasure Palace Racing **Trained** Lower Beeding, W Sussex

FOCUS

There wasn't much pace on, but the time was still 7.8secs slower than the later handicap won by Aegean Dawn. This wasn't competitive but the winner can rate higher.

NOTEBOOK

Megastar ◆ was one of last season's leading bumper horses, having finished fifth behind Cue Card at Cheltenham before taking the Aintree championship event. A big, imposing sort with the looks to match, connections were cagey over his chance beforehand, saying he would come on for it and had schooled just 'okay', and he refused to settle early having found no cover. His jumping improved as the race progressed, albeit he doesn't look a natural, typical of many big horses who would probably find it easier to jump a fence, and it became clear as they rounded the final bend that he had the race in the bag, galloping on strongly and looking better the further he went. He's certainly got an action on him, but was beaten on his only previous try on soft ground, and this sort of surface seems to suit him best. Despite initial thoughts that he would require further than this, which is backed up by his breeding, being by dual Ascot Gold Cup winner Kayf Tara, his trainer sees him very much as a speed horse, and he'll be kept to this distance, with him likely to remain low-key for time being. Having been well and truly thrashed by Cue Card last year, he won't be taking him on in a rematch, so may even bypass this season's Festival in favour of a return trip to Aintree. Wherever he goes, there are few brighter jumps prospect around than this fellow. He's a 16-1 shot for the Supreme Novices' with Paddy Power and William Hill. (op 4-7 tchd 8-13 in places)

Smokey Oakey(IRE), a keeping-on sixth at Kempton on debut, appeared to take a step forward despite proving no match for the easy winner. He'll find an opening at some stage. (op 7-1)

Highly Regal(IRE), a Kempton AW specialist, had finished tailed off on his sole previous outing over hurdles in November 2008, but he's much improved on the level since then and did enough here to suggest he can win races as a hurdler.

Ebony Diamond(IRE), a former bumper winner in Ireland who was held at Huntingdon on his debut for Charlie Mann, travelled well to a point on this first start over hurdles and should benefit from a longer distance. (op 14-1)

Koup De Kanon(FR), runner-up in a Uttoxeter bumper three weeks earlier, was slow at a few of his hurdles and never threatened to get involved. He should improve for the experience, but may not come good until he's handicapping. Official explanation: jockey said gelding stopped quickly. (tchd 7-2)

2496 INTRINSIC FINANCIAL SERVICES H'CAP CHASE (16 fncs) 2m 3f
2:45 (2:45) (Class 3) (0-135,135) 4-Y-0+ £6,262 (£1,850; £925; £463)

Form				RPR
33F-	1		**Matuhi**[232] 4967 7-11-2 125 ....(t) TomScudamore (David Pipe) *led: jnd 11th: drew clr after 3 out: shkn up after 2 out: eased flat but maintained advantage* 15/8[1]	142+
2-62	2	9	**Five Dream (FR)**[55] 1611 6-11-7 135 ....(b) MrRMahon(5) (Paul Nicholls) *trckd wnr 5th: chal and upsides fr 11th tl drvn and btn off after 3 out* 2/1[2]	142
500F	3	11	**Enlightenment (IRE)**[12] 2234 10-11-4 127 ....(p) PaulMoloney (Evan Williams) *trckd wnr to 5th: dropped to last by 7th: lft wl bhd 11th: wnt remote 3rd 3 out: rdn and kpt on after next* 9/2	124
6-53	4	58	**Russian Flag (FR)**[27] 1957 7-11-3 129 .... AlexMerriam(3) (Neil King) *mstke 1st: in tch in last pair to 10th: sn lft bhd: lost remote 3rd 3 out: mstke last: virtually p.u* 4/1[3]	88

4m 47.2s (0.20) **Going Correction** -0.025s/f (Good) **4** Ran SP% **106.3**
Speed ratings (Par 107): **98,94,89,65**
CSF £5.89 TOTE £2.90; EX 6.30.
Owner Willsford Racing Incorporated **Bred** Mrs A Yearley **Trained** Nicholashayne, Devon

FOCUS
This had looked an open contest, despite there being just the four runners, but Matuhi, on his debut for David Pipe, showed improved form to run out a ready winner. The winner sets the level.

NOTEBOOK
Matuhi, on his debut for David Pipe, showed improved form to run out a ready winner, jumping well and drawing clear in the straight. He isn't the biggest, but certainly jumps his fences with relish, and could win again before the handicapper gets a hold of him. (tchd 2-1)
Five Dream(FR) was the only one capable of giving him a race, although in the end was comfortably left trailing. He doesn't find it easy to win. (tchd 95-40 in places)
Enlightenment(IRE), who fell heavily at the last with the race secure at Ffos Las latest, had gone up 7lb and failed to run to the same level, possibly finding it coming too soon. (tchd 4-1)
Russian Flag(FR) was disappointing considering he's now just 1lb higher than when last winning. (tchd 9-2 in places)

2497 ATLANTIC ENTERPRISES H'CAP CHASE (20 fncs) 3m
3:20 (3:20) (Class 3) (0-135,134) 4-Y-0+ £7,618 (£2,324; £1,214; £659)

Form				RPR
10-1	1		**Quinz (FR)**[31] 1908 6-11-8 130 .... RichardJohnson (Philip Hobbs) *j.w: racd wd: led 3rd: mde rest: drew clr fr 3 out: quite impressive* 15/8[1]	150+
120-	2	14	**Far More Serious (IRE)**[247] 4670 10-11-10 132 .... TomScudamore (Charlie Longsdon) *led to 3rd: settled bhd ldng pair: pressed wnr after 14th: rdn to chal 4 out: brushed aside after 3 out* 5/2[2]	135
3P-3	3	23	**Le Burf (FR)**[27] 1968 9-11-9 131 .... LiamTreadwell (Giles Smyly) *pressed ldr fr 4th tl mstke 14th: wl btn in 3rd fr next: wknd* 13/2	112
/0-0	4	59	**Verasi**[13] 2214 9-10-0 108 oh1 ....(b) JamieMoore (Gary Moore) *in tch: nt fluent 3rd: rdn and struggling fr 11th: t.o 15th: j. last fence as wnr fin* 20/1	36
-1PP	P		**Tisfreetdream (IRE)**[8] 2324 9-10-12 120 ....(p) TomSiddall (Peter Pritchard) *j. ponderously: lost tch 4th: wl t.o fr 11th: p.u bef 15th* 16/1	—
P1-2	P		**Den Of Iniquity**[27] 1968 9-11-12 134 .... WayneHutchinson (Warren Greatrex) *in tch: blnd 8th: wknd 12th: j. slowly 14th: t.o whn p.u bef next* 7/2[3]	—

6m 4.10s (-4.90) **Going Correction** -0.025s/f (Good) **6** Ran SP% **109.6**
Speed ratings (Par 107): **107,102,94,75,—,—**
Tote Swingers: 1&2 £2.00, 1&3 £2.80, 2&3 £2.90 CSF £6.91 TOTE £2.70: £1.40, £1.80; EX 7.00.
Owner Andrew L Cohen **Bred** Michael Blond **Trained** Withycombe, Somerset

FOCUS
The two market leaders stood out beforehand and they had it between themselves a long way from the finish. The winner looks a smart novice and the form could be rated higher.

NOTEBOOK
Quinz(FR) ◆ emerged clear best, asserting from three out and staying on strongly. Not a lot went his way in three runs over fences last season, falling when still travelling well in a race won by the runner-up at Newbury, but he looked transformed in the jumping department when winning with ease on his reappearance at Exeter, and made light work of his 130 rating returned to handicaps. A fine looking sort, his jumping is sure to face sterner tests in the future, but he won't be aimed too high too soon, so for that reason should be able to complete a hat-trick. Richard Johnson was complimentary afterwards. (tchd 7-4 and 2-1)
Far More Serious(IRE), progressive last term, had been aimed at this race and he came to join the winner quite a way out, but started to look vulnerable from four out, and was a beaten horse by the next. Time may shown he faced a tough task conceding 2lb to the much-improved winner, so this defeat shouldn't be held against him. (op 11-4 tchd 10-3 in places)
Le Burf(FR) is exposed as a chaser and will remain vulnerable to unexposed, more progressive sorts. (op 5-1)
Verasi was struggling a long way out. (op 25-1)
Tisfreetdream(IRE) jumped poorly. (tchd 20-1)
Den Of Iniquity was unable to build on a promising reappearance effort at Chepstow, never really going after a blunder at the eighth and eventually pulling up. (tchd 20-1)

2498 CANACCORD GENUITY H'CAP HURDLE (9 hdls) 2m
3:55 (3:56) (Class 2) (0-145,145) 4-Y-0+
£7,514 (£2,220; £1,110; £555; £277; £139)

Form				RPR
/1-1	1		**Aegean Dawn**[7] 2347 5-9-9 119 oh5 .... DavidBass(5) (Nicky Henderson) *trckd ldrs: chal 3 out: led next: pressed last: pushed along and qcknd away flat* 4/11[1]	140+
11-5	2	4 ½	**Mille Chief (FR)**[27] 1956 4-11-3 136 .... WayneHutchinson (Alan King) *hld up in midfield: cl up 3 out: trckd wnr gng strly last and tried to chal: r.o flat but no match* 6/1[2]	149+
202/	3	11	**Tuanku (IRE)**[27] 2617 5-9-11 119 .... CharlieHuxley(3) (Alan King) *prom: pressed ldr after 5th: led 3 out: hdd 2 out: easily outpcd fr last* 20/1	119
0512	4	1 ¼	**Hibiki (IRE)**[20] 2085 6-10-11 130 ....(p) AidanColeman (Sarah Humphrey) *trckd ldrs: cl up 3 out: drvn bef next: readily outpcd fr last* 20/1	129
P4-3	5	1 ¾	**Dr Livingstone (IRE)**[15] 2164 5-10-10 129 ....(b¹) APMcCoy (Charles Egerton) *hld up in last: prog fr 6th: pushed along in 7th after 3 out: no imp on ldrs next: r.o flat* 16/1	128
0/1-	6	3 ¾	**Simply Blue**[390] 1924 6-10-6 125 .... AndrewGlassonbury (Simon Burrough) *chsd ldr to 5th: styd prom tl wknd u.p bef 2 out* 50/1	119
P-44	7	1 ¾	**Benfleet Boy**[12] 2233 6-11-5 138 .... LeightonAspell (Brendan Powell) *led and clr: blnd 3rd and c bk to field: hdd 5th: rallied and w ldr 3 out: wknd 2 out* 66/1	130
2/0-	8	3	**Wingman (IRE)**[559] 225 8-9-12 127 .... JosephAkehurst(10) (Gary Moore) *hld up in midfield: getting outpcd whn mstke 3 out and dropped to last pair: no ch after: modest late prog* 50/1	116
564-	9	½	**Spring Jim**[28] 5194 9-11-4 137 .... PaulMoloney (James Fanshawe) *hld up in last quartet: effrt 3 out and rchd 8th sn after: pushed along and no hdwy 2 out: fdd* 20/1	125
30-3	10	2	**Afsoun (FR)**[21] 94 8-11-9 145 .... AlexMerriam(3) (Neil King) *hld up in rr: rdn bef 3 out: sn outpcd and wl btn* 25/1	131
350-	11	½	**Secret Dancer (IRE)**[245] 4711 5-11-0 133 .... SamThomas (Alan Jones) *hld up in last quartet: dropped to last 6th: nudged along and no prog after next* 12/1[3]	119
1-4	12	¾	**Alhaque (USA)**[165] 662 4-10-0 119 .... JamieMoore (Gary Moore) *trckd ldrs: lost pl 5th: rdn and no prog after 3 out: wl btn after* 40/1	104
150-	13	5	**Dani's Girl (IRE)**[92] 4591 7-9-10 122 .... NathanSweeney(7) (Pat Phelan) *t.k.h: hld up in midfield: prog to ld 5th: hdd & wknd 3 out* 25/1	102

3m 48.0s (-1.00) **Going Correction** -0.025s/f (Good)
WFA 4 from 5yo+ 7lb **13** Ran SP% **131.0**
Speed ratings (Par 109): **101,98,93,92,91 89,89,87,87,86 86,85,83**
Tote Swingers: 1&2 £2.30, 1&3 £6.00, 2&3 £9.30 CSF £3.25 CT £29.24 TOTE £1.40: £1.10, £1.70, £4.20; EX 4.10 Trifecta £51.20 Pool: £2,383.01 - 34.43 winning units..
Owner Paul Murphy **Bred** P Murphy **Trained** Upper Lambourn, Berks

FOCUS
Interesting the winning time was 7.8secs quicker than that recorded by impressive novice winner Megastar earlier on the card. An intriguing end to a cracking meeting with the winner value for further with the third and fourth to their marks.

NOTEBOOK
Aegean Dawn ◆, officially 16lb well-in (due to race off 21lb higher in future but 5lb out of the handicap here), taking the drop in trip on this quick reappearance after last week's Cheltenham victory in his stride. Defending an unbeaten record, this giant son of Alflora was ridden handily by David Bass, and it was clear from a long way out that he was absolutely hacking. Still, as he turned into the straight, it looked for all the world as though the apparently speedier Mille Chief, who was also apparently full of running, would do him for speed on touching down after the last, but it was actually he who found the greater acceleration, quickening on again close home. A fine effort considering his three previous runs had come with lengthy gaps in between, things are obviously going to be tougher off his new mark, but there's no telling how much this strapping 5-y-o has left in the locker, and it says something that a horse viewed as being a future 3m chaser (dam half-sister to Gold Cup winner Cool Dawn), can win a 2m handicap hurdle by showing such speed. Indeed, his rider David Bass was gushing about him afterwards, describing him as 'special', and for all that he's clearly capable of winning good races a hurdler, there can be few better chasing prospects around. He won't be over-faced, being such a young horse, and we probably won't see him too often season, but when we do it's clearly an occasion to relish. (op 4-9 tchd 1-2 in places)
Mille Chief(FR), in need of the run on his Aintree reappearance, had clearly sharpened up and he menacingly tracked the winner through into the straight, but proved no match for him having taken the last. Time will probably show he faced an impossible task at the weights, but in finishing a clear second, he may have ruled himself out of winning a top handicap, as the handicapper's sure to react. (tchd 15-2 in a place)
Tuanku(IRE), rated just 119, took over at the third last, but soon had the big guns on his tail and was ultimately left trailing. This was an improved effort and he'll no doubt be bumped up a few pounds, but should still be capable of winning something similar.
Hibiki(IRE), narrowly denied in a Listed handicap hurdle at the course last time, was up 6lb on this debut for a new yard and probably ran up to form.
Dr Livingstone(IRE) kept on late, having been restrained early in the first-time blinkers, but isn't one to put maximum faith in. (op 20-1)
Simply Blue, off since winning at Wincanton 390 days earlier, was up 7lb for this return and ran well, just getting a little tired and weakening in the straight. He should improve and will be of interest next time.
Benfleet Boy was readily reeled in and eventually weakened in the straight.
Wingman(IRE) shaped encouragingly on this first start in 559 days, making some late headway, and he's nicely treated now, so looks for him to be winning something in the coming months.
Secret Dancer(IRE) never featured on this reappearance, but should come on for it and will have other days. (op 11-1 tchd 10-1)
Alhaque(USA), although 40-1, was expected to show more by connections and may be dropped right out in future. (op 50-1 tchd 33-1)
Dani's Girl(IRE), another previous course winner, dropped right out in the end to finish last. (op 20-1)
T/Plt: £9.90 to a £1 stake. Pool of £83,577.10 - 9.95 winning tickets. T/Qpdt: £7.00 to a £1 stake. Pool of £5,290.54 - 553.13 winning tickets. JN

2283 EXETER (R-H)
Friday, November 19

OFFICIAL GOING: Chase course - soft (6.1); hurdle course - heavy (5.7)
All hurdle races run on chase bend entering home straight increasing each circuit by about 40yds. Hurdle on bend after stands omitted.
Wind: mild across Weather: overcast with showers and sunny periods

2499 JACK FLETCHER NOVICES' HURDLE (7 hdls 1 omitted) 2m 1f
12:45 (12:45) (Class 4) 4-Y-0+ £2,602 (£764; £382; £190)

Form				RPR
5-6	1		**Accordintolawrence (IRE)**[34] 1866 4-10-12 0 .... FelixDeGiles (Charlie Longsdon) *trckd ldrs: bmpd whn chalng 3 out: sn rdn: nt fluent 2 out: narrow advantage sn after last: kpt on wl: drvn out* 16/1	119+
00-4	2	nk	**The Chazer (IRE)**[188] 327 5-10-12 104 .... CharliePoste (Richard Lee) *mid-div: hdwy after 3rd: led jst bef 3 out: sn rdn: edgd lft appr last: hdd sn after: kpt on* 12/1	117+
	3	18	**Pateese (FR)**[515] 5-10-12 0 .... TomO'Brien (Philip Hobbs) *mid-div: hdwy after 3rd: chalng whn edgd lft 3 out: sn rdn: hld fr next: wkng whn blnd last* 9/2[2]	101+
5	4	2 ¼	**Renard D'Irlande (FR)**[22] 2056 5-10-12 0 .... AidanColeman (Venetia Williams) *trckd ldrs: led after 4th: hdd jst bef 3 out: sn rdn: hld fr next: wknd last* 11/10[1]	99
/4-0	5	1 ¾	**Peveril Pandora**[15] 2168 7-10-5 0 ....(t) MarkBradburne (Jimmy Fox) *hld up towards rr: hdwy after 4th: pushed along after 3 out: styd on same pce* 33/1	88
64-5	6	hd	**Grey Missile**[22] 2059 5-10-12 0 .... NickScholfield (Jeremy Scott) *in tch tl lost pl after 3rd: sme prog after 4th: rdn and styd on same pce fr 3 out* 13/2[3]	95

0/ **7** *15* **Molly Round (IRE)**565 131 6-10-2 0 DonalDevereux(3) 73
(Grant Cann) *mid-div: rdn afer 4th: wknd bef next: t.o* **150/1**

0P/6 **8** *½* **Jayjay Valentine**17 2142 7-10-7 0 GilesHawkins(5) 80
(Victor Dartnall) *led: sn clr: rdn and hdd appr 3 out: hung lft and sn wknd: t.o* **18/1**

0P0 **9** *4 ½* **Sarah's Boy**17 2137 5-10-7 0 (t) CO'Farrell(5) 75
(David Pipe) *a towards rr: t.o* **66/1**

0 **10** *9* **Mr Bachster (IRE)**186 375 5-10-12 0 AndrewGlassonbury 66
(Victor Dartnall) *mid-div: drvn along fr after 3rd: wknd 3 out: t.o* **33/1**

0-00 **11** *20* **Gallimaufry**17 2137 4-10-5 0 RodiGreene 39
(Neil Mulholland) *a in rr: t.o fr 3rd* **100/1**

0- **12** *1 ¾* **Mac Beattie**376 2152 4-10-9 0 DPFahy(3) 44
(Evan Williams) *mid-div tl wknd after 4th: t.o* **50/1**

P-0 **13** *38* **Breadstick**11 2282 4-10-5 0 (t) JamesDavies —
(Jeremy Scott) *struggling in rr fr 2nd: sn t.o* **125/1**

P **14** *2* **Tiger Breeze (USA)**17 2137 4-10-12 0 WillKennedy 4
(Bob Buckler) *trckd clr ldr tl after 3rd: rdn and wknd after next: t.o* **100/1**

00 **15** *6* **Haydens Mount**17 2137 5-10-12 0 HaddenFrost —
(James Frost) *mid-div tl wknd after 4th: t.o* **150/1**

34- **U** **Setter's Princess**15 4620 4-10-0 0 IanPopham(5) —
(Ron Hodges) *stmbld bdly whn uns rdr 1st* **11/1**

4m 13.1s (-2.40) **Going Correction** 0.0s/f (Good)
WFA 4 from 5yo+ 7lb **16** Ran SP% **119.7**
Speed ratings (Par 105): **105,104,96,95,94 94,87,87,85,80 71,70,52,51,48** —
Tote Swingers: 1&2 £20.20, 1&3 £5.80, 2&3 £11.40 CSF £183.95 TOTE £22.80: £4.20, £3.40, £2.00; EX 130.00.
Owner Johnnie Lightfoot **Bred** James Lacy **Trained** Over Norton, Oxon

FOCUS
This has been won by some smart types in recent years, namely St Pirran, Ashley Brook, Racing Demon and The Tother One. However, this latest running looked an ordinary contest, with the runner-up rated just 104, albeit that one's entitled to be improving. That said, the pace was reasonable and the time was 7.30 seconds quicker than the later 0-105 handicap. The first two are worth being positive about, the third can rate higher and the fourth is rated to his recent mark.

NOTEBOOK
Accordintolawrence(IRE) had shown ability in two starts in bumpers, notably at Cheltenham on his reappearance in October, and he improved for the switch to hurdling. He was a bit green on the approach to the first two hurdles in the straight, wandering around on the run to three out, but his actual jumping was fine, and he then battled on well on the run-in. He can do better. (op 18-1 tchd 20-1)
The Chazer(IRE), returning from a 188-day break, was just about last off the bridle, but once under pressure after the third last it was soon clear he wasn't fully applying himself, with him initially edging left and also pricking his ears. Despite that, he kept on well enough to draw clear of all bar the winner, who just too determined, and this was his best effort to date over hurdles. (tchd 10-1)
Pateese(FR) won twice over staying trips on the Flat in France, but had been off for 515 days. He received a slight bump going to three out, but was beginning to struggle at the time and gradually got tired, walking through the last. It seems this run was needed. (tchd 4-1)
Renard D'Irlande(FR), a well-related dual bumper winner at around 1m4f in France, had shaped okay before fading on his hurdling debut at Stratford, but he failed to build on that and was disappointing. He travelled strongly, looking a horse with plenty of ability, but once more offered little off the bridle. It remains to be seen whether he has sufficient stamina. (tchd 5-4)
Peveril Pandora was ridden patiently and never really seen with a chance, but she hardly made any progress when asked in the straight. Official explanation: jockey said mare had a breathing problem. (op 20-1)
Grey Missile wasn't given a hard time and looked as though he'll be capable of better, but he did have a sheepskin noseband fitted and carried his head a little high in the straight. (op 9-1)
Jayjay Valentine raced in a clear lead before fading. Official explanation: jockey said gelding hung left. (tchd 22-1)

2500 PERTEMPS H'CAP HURDLE SERIES (QUALIFIER) (11 hdls 1 omitted) 2m 7f 110y
1:15 (1:15) (Class 2) 4-Y-0+

£9,393 (£2,775; £1,387; £694; £346; £174)

Form RPR

2F-0 **1** **Superior Wisdom (IRE)**195 206 10-10-8 **125** WillKennedy 135
(Alex Hales) *hld up but in tch: hdwy after 5th to trck ldrs: pckd next: rdn to chal 3 out: led 2 out: hld on gamely: all out* **15/2**

3P-0 **2** *nk* **Le Beau Bai (FR)**41 1777 7-11-1 **137** GilesHawkins(5) 147
(Richard Lee) *disp ld tl outrt ldr after 8th: rdn whn pressed after 3 out: hdd next: rallied gamely: ev ch fr last: styd on* **6/1**3

21-R **3** *25* **Ernst Blofeld (IRE)**15 2163 6-11-0 **131** (t) JasonMaguire 116
(Donald McCain) *trckd ldrs tl lost pl after 5th: nudged along fr next: rdn after 7th: regained 3rd 3 out: wknd next* **6/1**3

3-5F **4** *8* **Sangfroid**35 1855 6-10-11 **128** DarylJacob 105
(Nick Williams) *trckd ldrs tl blnd 7th and lost pl: rdn after 8th: regain 4th after 3 out: wknd next* **4/1**2

131- **5** *2 ½* **Synchronised (IRE)**244 4740 7-11-9 **143** RichieMcLernon(3) 117
(Jonjo O'Neill) *trckd ldrs: pckd 1st: lost pl on long run bef 6th: hmpd 7th: rdn after 3 out: nvr bk on terms* **9/1**

240- **6** *22* **Sullumo (GER)**237 4884 7-11-4 **135** NoelFehily 87
(Charlie Mann) *hld up but in tch: reminders after 6th: rdn and no imp whn hit wing and mstke 3 out: sn wknd* **12/1**

/2-6 **P** **Karanja**199 131 11-10-13 **130** AndrewThornton —
(Simon Burrough) *trckd ldrs: rdn after 8th: wknd after 3 out: p.u bef last* **25/1**

1-22 **P** **Pavillon Bleu (FR)**16 2147 7-10-4 **121** TomO'Brien —
(Philip Hobbs) *disp ld tl rdn after 8th: wkng whn hmpd and blnd 3 out: p.u bef next* **5/2**1

6m 3.90s (4.90) **Going Correction** +0.45s/f (Soft) **8** Ran SP% **110.4**
Speed ratings (Par 109): **109,108,100,97,97 89**,—,—
Tote Swingers: 1&2 £12.40, 1&3 £13.70, 2&3 £8.50 CSF £48.06 CT £272.43 TOTE £8.80: £2.50, £2.30, £3.00; EX 44.70.
Owner Andrew L Cohen **Bred** James Farnan **Trained** Wardington, Oxon

FOCUS
An ordinary handicap hurdle for the class with the winner rated back to his 2008 form.

NOTEBOOK
Superior Wisdom(IRE) is a strong stayer who acts well on testing ground, so clearly plenty was in his favour for his first run in 195 days and he was a game winner. He was successful over fences last season, but has also fallen twice from just four starts over the larger obstacles, so it would not surprise to see him kept to hurdling, and he should remain competitive. (op 8-1 tchd 9-1)
Le Beau Bai(FR), back over hurdles after being well held over fences on his reappearance, had conditions to suit and only just failed. He was well clear of the remainder and is one to have on-side over hurdles or back over fences when the ground is like this. (op 13-2)
Ernst Blofeld(IRE) went without his usual tongue-tie over fences on his reappearance, when he ran in snatches before getting tired and unseating three from the finish. Back over hurdles, he had the breathing aid re-fitted, but was again on and off the bridle and couldn't go with the front two when it mattered. He's best watched for the time being. (op 7-1)
Sangfroid, in with every chance until falling two out at Cheltenham in October, had just started to come under pressure prior to completely losing his chance with a momentum-halting mistake at the seventh. He recovered as well as could have been expected, but it's quite possibly a lack of concentration that's costing him these days, and it's no surprise headgear has been tried in the past. (tchd 7-2)
Synchronised(IRE), the Midlands Grand National winner when last seen in March, had yet to be asked for an effort when badly hampered at the seventh, an incident that cost him his chance. He wasn't given a particularly hard time thereafter and this was the sort of reappearance that he really ought to improve from, presumably back over fences. Well suited by testing ground and already a winner of a chase at Chepstow, the Welsh National is a logical target. The stewards enquired into his running, but accepted the explanations provided by connections and took no further action. Official explanation: jockey said his instructions were to jump off in the middle of the field and get his mount jumping and travelling and get as close as he could adding gelding was badly hampered. trainers representative was unable to confirm instuctions. (tchd 10-1)
Karanja, racing on heavy ground for the first time on his return from a 199-day break, travelled well for a long way and, although eventually pulled up, there was encouragement in this performance. There might be more to come back on a better surface. (op 3-1)
Pavillon Bleu(FR), a three-time winner here over fences, was beaten when hampered and making a mistake three out, after which he was soon pulled up. This was disappointing seeing as he came into the race in good form. Official explanation: jockey said gelding was badly hampered. Vet said gelding had an irregular heartbeat. (op 3-1)

2501 DEVON COUNTY SHOW EXETER NOVICES' CHASE (18 fncs) 3m
1:50 (1:50) (Class 3) 5-Y-0+ **£6,505** (£1,910; £955)

Form RPR

0-21 **1** **Watamu Bay (IRE)**10 2285 7-11-4 0 NoelFehily 144+
(Paul Nicholls) *led tl 8th: w ldr: led 11th: clr 13th: in command whn mstke 4 out: comf* **1/5**1

020- **2** *5* **Tarateeno**239 4844 7-10-7 0 MichaelMurphy(5) 123
(Pat Murphy) *j.lft thrght: patiently rdn bhd ldng pair: nodded on landing 10th: wnt 2nd 14th: clsd on wnr appr 4 out: rdn after 3 out: styd on but a being comf hld:* **7/1**2

222- **3** *106* **Penn Da Benn (FR)**245 4718 7-10-12 **127** (p) JasonMaguire —
(Bernard Llewellyn) *racd keenly trcking wnr: led 8th tl 11th: wknd qckly after next: sn t.o* **9/1**3

6m 20.1s (10.80) **Going Correction** +0.525s/f (Soft) **3** Ran SP% **105.8**
Speed ratings: **103,101**,—
CSF £2.02 TOTE £1.10; EX 2.10.
Owner Jared Sullivan **Bred** Gerry McIntyre And R J Whitford **Trained** Ditcheat, Somerset

FOCUS
An uncompetitive novice chase with the winner value for further and the second in line with his hurdles form.

NOTEBOOK
Watamu Bay(IRE) was never seriously challenged, despite losing his concentration when clear in the straight. He wasn't that quick over the fourth last, having started to idle, and he soon received a reminder, but he did enough. It's possible he'll be given a break now, and the 4m National Hunt Chase is a possible Cheltenham target. (op 1-4 tchd 2-7)
Tarateeno, a 124-rated hurdler returning from a 239-day break, is flattered to get so close to the winner, but this was still a pleasing effort. He pecked on landing at the tenth, but recovered okay and, despite being inclined to go to his left over his obstacles, he stuck on for pressure. There should be more to come. (op 6-1 tchd 11-2)
Penn Da Benn(FR), debuting for a new yard after 245 days off, had cheekpieces on for the first time but ran no sort of race. This leaves him with plenty to prove. (op 8-1 tchd 15-2)

2502 BATHWICK TYRES PLYMOUTH NOVICES' H'CAP CHASE (15 fncs) 2m 3f 110y
2:25 (2:25) (Class 3) (0-130,119) 4-Y-0+ **£6,505** (£1,910; £955; £477)

Form RPR

02-1 **1** **Diamond Brook (IRE)**31 1909 5-11-12 **119** DarylJacob 121+
(Nick Williams) *disp ld tl 6th: trckd ldr: rdn to chal 4 out: led next: enough in hand and a gng to hold on run-in: drvn out* **85/40**2

0-45 **2** *nk* **Russian Song (IRE)**175 503 6-11-0 **107** JoeTizzard 111+
(Colin Tizzard) *trckd ldrs: led appr 4 out: hdd 3 out: rdn whn mstke 2 out: swtchd rt and rallied fnl 75yds: fin wl* **7/2**3

2150 **3** *9* **Cantabilly (IRE)**16 2147 7-11-3 **117** SClements(7) 112
(Ron Hodges) *trckd ldrs: nt fluent 9th: rdn appr 4 out: styd on same pce lft 3rd 3 out* **8/1**

2-F6 **4** *10* **Double Chocolate**16 2146 7-11-2 **109** TomO'Brien 92
(Matt Sheppard) *disp ld tl outrt ldr 6th: rdn and hdd appr 4 out: grad fdd: lft 4th 3 out* **10/1**

-622 **F** **Restezen D'Armor (FR)**23 2034 5-11-3 **110** (b1) FelixDeGiles 114+
(Charlie Longsdon) *hld up: hit 11th: travelling wl in cl 3rd whn fell 3 out* **15/8**1

5m 3.90s (6.60) **Going Correction** +0.525s/f (Soft) **5** Ran SP% **109.2**
Speed ratings (Par 107): **107,106,103,99**,—
CSF £9.75 TOTE £3.10: £1.70, £1.70; EX 9.10.
Owner Paul Duffy Diamond Partnership **Bred** Ms Barbara Johnston **Trained** George Nympton, Devon

FOCUS
An ordinary novices' handicap chase with the winner rated in line with his hurdles mark and the second to his bumper rating.

NOTEBOOK
Diamond Brook(IRE)'s chance was clearly made that bit easier by the fall of Restezen D'Armor, and this not the first time he has had things fall kindly for him. When making a successful chasing debut around here on his reappearance, he had looked held until Celestial Halo and Rougham fell four out, and his sole hurdles success, also at Exeter, was gained after the leader fell at the last, earning him the close-up comment 'lucky'. He was all out to hold on this time and, all things considered, won't appeal as one to back to follow up. (op 7-4 tchd 9-4)
Russian Song(IRE), making his chasing debut after a 175-day break, didn't help himself with a mistake two out, but he still only just failed to get up. He should build on this. (op 4-1)
Cantabilly(IRE) was comfortably held on his chasing debut but is entitled to improve for this (op 10-1)
Double Chocolate, well held on his chasing debut over 3m at Chepstow, again made no real impression. (op 11-1 tchd 14-1)
Restezen D'Armor(FR), blinkered for the first-time after finishing runner-up on his chasing debut at Haydock in October, was in with every chance and apparently full of running when taking a heavy fall three out. It's impossible to know how much he would have found. (op 2-1 tchd 7-4)

2503 BATHWICK TYRES TAUNTON H'CAP CHASE (12 fncs) 2m 1f 110y
3:00 (3:00) (Class 3) (0-125,121) 4-Y-0+ **£5,464** (£1,696; £913)

Form RPR

0P0- **1** **Baseball Ted (IRE)**348 2739 8-10-8 **103** TomO'Brien 114+
(Charlie Longsdon) *trckd ldr: led 6th: mstke 4 out: 8 l clr 3 out: rdn after next: kpt on: drvn out* **7/4**1

1-40 **2** *¾* **Flaming Gorge (IRE)**13 2213 5-11-6 **115** DarylJacob 124+
(Nick Williams) *on his toes befhand: led untl 6th: chsd wnr: rdn appr 4 out: kpt on fr last but a being hld* **2/1**2

144- 3 23 **Wheels Up (IRE)**[218] 5195 9-11-9 **121**......(t) RichieMcLernon(3) 111
(Jonjo O'Neill) *trckd ldrs: nt fluent 5th: rdn appr 4 out: j.rt fr 4 out: wknd 3 out* **7/2**[3]
PP-0 F **Deep Quest**[17] 2140 11-11-1 **110**......(t) RodiGreene —
(Simon Burrough) *fell 1st* **5/1**
4m 29.4s (10.40) **Going Correction** +0.525s/f (Soft) **4 Ran SP% 108.6**
Speed ratings (Par 107): **97,96,86,—**
CSF £5.72 TOTE £7.80: £4.10, £1.10; EX 13.70.
Owner Alan Peterson **Bred** Donal Fennessy **Trained** Over Norton, Oxon

FOCUS
Not form to get carried away with with the winner rated to his heavy ground form and the second to his hurdles mark.

NOTEBOOK
Baseball Ted(IRE), 10lb higher than when gaining his only previous win in a novices' handicap chase in December 2008, made a successful debut for his new trainer after an absence of 348 days. However, he only clambered home, having got noticeably tired in the straight, being slow over the fourth last, as well as the final fence. Connections will no doubt hope he comes on a good deal for this. (op 9-4 tchd 13-8 and 11-4 in places)
Flaming Gorge(IRE), making his chasing debut, only just failed to take advantage of the winner getting tired in the straight. (op 13-8)
Wheels Up(IRE) ran as though this first run in 218 days was needed. (op 3-1)
Deep Quest, whose last win came over 4m, departed at the first. (op 15-2)

2504 GREAT VALUE RACEDAY HOSPITALITY CONDITIONAL JOCKEYS' H'CAP HURDLE (7 hdls 1 omitted) 2m 1f
3:35 (3:35) (Class 4) (0-105,105) 4-Y-0+ **£2,602** (£764; £382; £190)

Form RPR
44P- 1 **Minnie Hill (IRE)**[215] 5258 6-11-8 **101**...... GilesHawkins 115+
(Victor Dartnall) *trckd ldrs: led 2nd: styd on wl fr 2 out: rdn out* **8/1**
40/0 2 10 **Arrayan**[17] 2137 5-10-10 **92**...... CO'Farrell(3) 98+
(David Pipe) *hld up: hdwy after 4th: trcking wnr whn mstke 3 out: sn rdn: kpt on same pce* **9/4**[1]
0123 3 9 **Dormouse**[18] 2131 5-11-9 **102**......(p) SamTwiston-Davies 96
(Anabel L M King) *trckd ldrs: rdn appr 3 out: nt pce to chal: wkng whn mstke last* **13/2**[3]
3622 4 2 **Spider Boy**[18] 2135 13-10-0 **82**......(b) GemmaGracey-Davison(3) 73
(Zoe Davison) *hld up: hdwy 2nd: rdn appr 4th: wl hld fr 3 out* **9/2**[2]
10-0 5 3 **French Leave (IRE)**[16] 2144 8-10-11 **95**......(t) PeterCarberry(5) 83
(Victor Dartnall) *led tl 2nd: chsd ldr tl rdn after 4th: fdd fr 3 out* **9/2**[2]
31-3 6 3/4 **Josear**[188] 330 8-11-6 **105**...... DannyBurton(6) 92
(Chris Down) *trckd ldr tl 2nd: sn struggling in last: nvr threatened after* **12/1**
0-10 7 17 **Mauritino (GER)**[16] 2150 6-11-2 **98**...... RichieMcLernon(3) 71
(Jonjo O'Neill) *chsd ldrs tl rdn after 4th: sn wknd* **25/1**
30-3 R **Posh Emily**[14] 2185 7-11-9 **102**...... IanPopham —
(Ron Hodges) *ref to r: tk no part* **9/1**
4m 20.4s (4.90) **Going Correction** +0.45s/f (Soft) **8 Ran SP% 113.1**
Speed ratings (Par 105): **106,101,97,96,94 94,86,—**
Tote Swingers: 1&2 £4.60, 1&3 £8.80, 2&3 £4.80 CSF £26.55 CT £124.54 TOTE £9.80: £2.80, £1.70, £1.60; EX 33.10.
Owner Mrs L M Northover **Bred** John Dineen **Trained** Brayford, Devon

FOCUS
A modest conditional riders' handicap hurdle and, with the pace just modest for much of the way, the time was 7.30 seconds slower than the earlier novice hurdle. The first two were improvers and the race could rate higher.

NOTEBOOK
Minnie Hill(IRE) ◆ was reported to have stopped quickly when last seen pulling up on quick ground at Wincanton in April, but she returned from her absence in top form with these vastly different conditions clearly suiting. A penalty can be avoided if she's out before being reassessed, and that could be the plan according to connections (entered in mares' event at Taunton on November 25), but whatever, she's said to be likely to go chasing sooner rather than later. (op 17-2)
Arrayan was well backed on his handicap debut, but although running respectably he was always being held by the winner, with a mistake three out not helping. It will be a surprise if he can't rate higher, maybe on better ground. (op 6-4)
Dormouse ran okay but probably wants better ground. (op 9-1)
Spider Boy doesn't win very often. (op 7-1)
French Leave(IRE) has won on heavy ground, but he wears a tongue-tie these days and probably appreciates a better surface now. (op 7-1)
T/Plt: £291.10 to a £1 stake. Pool of £48,471.12 - 121.53 winning tickets. T/Qpdt: £15.20 to a £1 stake. Pool of £4,947.70 - 239.90 winning tickets. TM

MUSSELBURGH (R-H)
Friday, November 19

OFFICIAL GOING: Good (5.9)
Rail at innermost configuration.
Wind: Almost nil Weather: Fair

2505 SCOTTISH RACING MARES' MAIDEN HURDLE (12 hdls) 2m 4f
12:25 (12:25) (Class 4) 4-Y-0+ **£2,602** (£764; £382; £190)

Form RPR
4 1 **Lastroseofsummer (IRE)**[21] 2068 4-10-5 0...... MattCrawley(7) 110+
(Rae Guest) *trckd ldr: sddle slipped and lost one iron after 8th: nrly uns rdr next: rdr continued wout irons: hdwy to ld bef last: kpt on wl: tremendous ride* **11/2**
2 2 1/4 **Madamlily (IRE)**[34] 4-10-12 0...... DougieCostello 105+
(John Quinn) *j.lft on occasions: cl up: wnt 2nd 7th: effrt and ev ch whn j.lft 2 out: kpt on run-in: nt pce of wnr* **3/1**[1]
U5-3 3 5 **Sally's Idea**[30] 1921 4-10-5 0...... HenryBrooke(7) 99
(Donald McCain) *t.k.h: led: rdn bef 2 out: hdd bef last: kpt on same pce run-in* **6/1**
103- 4 3/4 **Miss Abbey**[216] 5227 6-10-12 0...... BarryKeniry 100
(Jim Goldie) *nt fluent: hld up in tch: hdwy bef 3 out: effrt next: one pce run-in* **8/1**
5 10 **Black Rock Lake (IRE)**[34] 1874 4-10-7 102...... KMDonoghue(5) 93
(T G McCourt, Ire) *trckd ldrs: effrt bef 2 out: hung rt and wknd between last 2* **10/3**[2]
00-0 6 11 **Steadys Breeze**[10] 2297 6-10-9 0...... HarryHaynes(3) 83
(R MacDonald) *hld up: effrt after 4 out: wknd fr next* **100/1**
P **Beat The Band**[105] 1208 5-10-12 0...... PeterBuchanan —
(Lucinda Russell) *hld up in tch: p.u and dismntd after 4 out* **9/2**[3]
P **A Special Lady (IRE)**[265] 5-10-12 0...... RichieMcGrath —
(I A Duncan, Ire) *t.k.h: bhd: struggling 8th: t.o whn p.u bef 2 out* **66/1**
4m 46.3s (-5.20) **Going Correction** -0.50s/f (Good)
WFA 4 from 5yo+ 8lb **8 Ran SP% 109.5**
Speed ratings (Par 105): **90,89,87,86,82 78,—,—**
Tote Swingers: 1&2 £10.20, 1&3 £5.50, 2&3 £2.70 CSF £20.93 TOTE £9.60: £3.70, £1.90, £3.50; EX 22.30.
Owner E P Duggan **Bred** Mount Coote Stud **Trained** Newmarket, Suffolk

FOCUS
A moderate mares' hurdle run in a slow time and not form to be confident about, with the third and fourth the best guides.

NOTEBOOK
Lastroseofsummer(IRE) was given a fantastic ride to get home in front, with her rider having lost both his irons at the ninth flight, and she has to rate value for better than the bare margin. Her first error came at the eighth which saw Cawley lose an iron initially, and the saddle shot forward so he kicked both his feet out soon after. He all but came off at the next and performed miracles to get back aboard his mount, indeed one will do well to see a better recovery. That looked to be her chance gone, but the further she went the better she got and she pinged the last three hurdles. Obviously her rider emerges with top marks and, while he eventually came off after the line, it was job done by that point. This sounder surface was much more up her street and there ought to be more improvement in her over this longer trip. (op 6-1)
Madamlily(IRE), who hails from a decent dual-purpose yard, has gone two years without success on the level and is currently rated 58 in that sphere. She stays well, though, and showed more than enough on this hurdling debut to think she can win a similar event. (op 9-2)
Sally's Idea set out to make all on this fourth run over hurdles, but such tactics found out her stamina over this longer trip. She still posted a fair effort, however, and sets the standard. (op 9-2)
Miss Abbey won a bumper on her debut at this track last term and looked a likely player on this first run back over hurdles. She proved very easy to back, though, and left the impression she would come on nicely for the experience. She was later reported to have lost a shoe and suffered a cut. Official explanation: vet said mare lost a near fore shoe and sustained a cut to its fore. (op 7-1)
Black Rock Lake(IRE) travelled nicely into contention, but lacked any sort of acceleration and the longer trip looked beyond her. (op 9-2)
Beat The Band, returning from a 105-day break, had finished second on her two previous outings and was making her debut for the yard. She clipped the top of the eighth and was awkward over the next, after which she was quickly pulled up. She was later reported to have suffered an overreach. Official explanation: jockey said lost mare lost her action and suffered an over-reach. (op 3-1)

2506 DOOS AN DONTS H'CAP HURDLE (12 hdls) 2m 4f
12:55 (12:55) (Class 3) (0-130,127) 4-Y-0+ **£6,505** (£1,910; £955; £477)

Form RPR
3202 1 **Pyracantha**[19] 2104 5-11-0 **115**...... BrianHughes 120+
(Alan Swinbank) *hld up in tch: hdwy bef 3 out: led next: drvn out fr last* **9/2**[1]
35-5 2 1/2 **Cool Operator**[19] 2104 7-11-0 **115**...... WilsonRenwick 118
(Howard Johnson) *midfield on ins: n.m.r bef 3 out: hdwy after 3 out: kpt on u.p fr last: tk 2nd cl home* **5/1**[2]
12P 3 hd **Cailin Na Ri (IRE)**[27] 1959 7-10-8 **114**...... AlexanderVoy(5) 117
(Martin Todhunter) *chsd ldrs: effrt and wnt 2nd 2 out: kpt on u.p last: lost 2nd cl home* **9/1**
106- 4 7 **Grandad Bill (IRE)**[28] 5224 7-11-6 **121**...... RichieMcGrath 118+
(Jim Goldie) *trckd ldr to 1/2-way: cl up tl rdn and outpcd fr last* **10/1**
5-01 5 1/2 **Cocoa Key (IRE)**[19] 2104 6-10-2 **103**...... PaddyAspell 98
(Richard Guest) *hld up: hdwy and prom bef 2 out: edgd rt and outpcd fr last* **9/1**
0-06 6 1 1/4 **Farmers Cross (IRE)**[37] 1827 6-10-1 **102**...... GrahamLee 95+
(Ferdy Murphy) *hld up: stdy hdwy bef 3 out: shkn up next: nvr nr ldrs* **15/2**
64 7 1 **Benmadigan (IRE)**[34] 1870 8-10-10 **114**...... FearghalDavis(3) 107
(Nicky Richards) *hld up towards rr: hdwy and prom after 4 out: one pce fr 2 out: btn whn checked after last* **12/1**
1-3U 8 3/4 **Strongpoint (IRE)**[36] 1849 6-11-12 **127**......(t) JamesReveley 119
(Patrick Griffin, Ire) *led tl hdd 2 out: edgd rt and wknd fr last* **16/1**
-315 9 2 1/2 **Barron Watlass (IRE)**[170] 576 6-10-4 **105**...... BarryKeniry 94
(George Moore) *hld up towards rr: hdwy and in tch 1/2-way: lost pl 4 out: btn next* **9/1**
4- 10 7 **Almanyan (IRE)**[24] 2031 6-10-8 **114**......(b) KMDonoghue(5) 96
(Adrian McGuinness, Ire) *in tch tl rdn and wknd bef 3 out* **6/1**[3]
-310 11 14 **Regent's Secret (USA)**[27] 1956 10-10-3 **111**......(v) PaulNorton(7) 79
(Jim Goldie) *cl up: chal 7th: wknd bef 3 out* **33/1**
4m 37.8s (-13.70) **Going Correction** -0.50s/f (Good) course record **11 Ran SP% 116.5**
Speed ratings (Par 107): **107,106,106,103,103 103,102,102,101,98 93**
Tote Swingers: 1&2 £4.10, 1&3 £12.80, 2&3 £13.70 CSF £27.41 CT £195.06 TOTE £4.30: £1.80, £2.70, £2.20; EX 36.30.
Owner Ian John Clark **Bred** G Reed **Trained** Melsonby, N Yorks
■ Stewards' Enquiry : Paddy Aspell one-day ban; careless riding (3rd Dec)

FOCUS
A modest handicap, run at a fair gallop and the first three came clear. The form looks solid with the third the best guide.

NOTEBOOK
Pyracantha made his move off the home turn and, hitting top gear near the final flight, was always doing enough on the run-in. He had yet to prove himself over this far, but was ridden as though the trip wouldn't be a problem and this turning track was in his favour on that front. It was a deserved success. (op 5-1 tchd 11-2)
Cool Operator got outpaced around three out, but rallied gamely for maximum pressure and was doing his best work towards the finish. He needed all of this longer trip and evidently enjoyed this quicker surface. (op 4-1)
Cailin Na Ri(IRE) showed her previous Aintree run to be all wrong and, never far away, posted a game effort in defeat. She is weighted to near her best, but it was only her second outing in a handicap and she may well gain reward for her consistency before the year is out. (op 12-1)
Grandad Bill(IRE), fit from a recent spin on the level, was another that lacked the necessary turn of foot when asked for maximum effort, but this was a performance he could build on. (op 13-2)
Cocoa Key(IRE) narrowly beat the winner on 2lb better terms at Carlisle 19 days earlier and was ridden to get this longer trip. He emerged with a chance in the home straight, but ultimately his lack of stamina told. (op 10-1)
Farmers Cross(IRE) ◆ was never a serious factor from off the pace, but this was more encouraging and he is one to keep an eye on. (op 9-1 tchd 7-1 and 10-1 in a place)

2507 BIRDCAGE BAR & RESTAURANT ESKMILLS NOVICES' CHASE (18 fncs) 3m
1:25 (1:25) (Class 4) 4-Y-0+ **£3,252** (£955; £477; £238)

Form RPR
6-P2 1 **New Shuil (IRE)**[37] 1830 6-10-9 99...... MrJohnDawson(7) 113
(John Wade) *trckd ldr: effrt 3 out: led after last: kpt on wl u.p* **15/2**[3]

0-00 **2** ½ **Elzahann (IRE)**[13] 2205 8-10-9 0 GrahamLee 108+
(Ferdy Murphy) *set stdy pce: qcknd bef 4 out: pckd last: sn hdd: kpt on u.p* **3/1**[2]

0/5 **3** 1¾ **Ballycolin**[26] 7-11-2 107 DougieCostello 111
(I A Duncan, Ire) *trckd ldrs: lft cl 3rd 11th: effrt bef 3 out: kpt on same pce run-in* **20/1**

0-1U **4** 156 **Big Burrows (IRE)**[27] 1957 8-11-9 127 RichieMcGrath —
(Ferdy Murphy) *hld up: j. slowly 3rd: hdwy to chse ldr bef 7th: blnd and dropped to rr next: hmpd 11th: sn lost tch* **9/1**

65/ **B** **Hegrid (IRE)**[62] 1541 9-11-2 117 JohnnyFarrelly —
(A J Martin, Ire) *in tch tl b.d 11th* **18/1**

31P- **U** **Double Expresso**[224] 5112 6-11-2 0 BrianHughes —
(Howard Johnson) *cl up: hit: slipped and uns rdr 11th* **5/6**[1]

6m 14.7s (11.30) **Going Correction** +0.275s/f (Yiel) **6** Ran SP% **111.3**
Speed ratings (Par 105): **92,91,91,—,—** —
Tote Swingers: 1&2 £3.20, 1&3 £10.00, 2&3 £7.30 CSF £30.01 TOTE £9.20: £4.30, £2.10; EX 37.10.
Owner John Wade **Bred** Martin Lyons **Trained** Mordon, Co Durham

FOCUS
This modest novice chase proved an eventful race. It was run at a steady gallop and the form should be treated with some caution. The placed horses are the best guides.

NOTEBOOK
New Shuil(IRE) showed his true colours when a close second at Wetherby last month, and he deservedly went one better with a game display. He took time to settle, but was starting to really find his stride prior to the runner-up getting the last wrong, which handed him the race. He is lightly raced and this was his first success of any description at the eighth attempt. His mark of 99 will probably now shoot up, so his best option is probably to stick to novice company in the short term. (op 11-1)
Elzahann(IRE) ◆ was expected to have come on for her recent comeback over hurdles and she was soon sent to the front on this chasing debut. She travelled enthusiastically and jumped well in the main, looking the most likely winner nearing two out. She pecked on landing after the last, however, and that cost her. This was still an encouraging introduction and shouldn't be long in winning. (op 4-1)
Ballycolin, who landed his third success between the flags last month, wasn't beaten at all far and this was his best effort under rules. (op 12-1)
Big Burrows(IRE) has become frustrating. (op 8-1 tchd 10-1)
Hegrid(IRE) wasn't done with when brought down at the 11th and is one to keep an eye on. (op 11-1 tchd 20-1)
Double Expresso was a dual bumper winner who advertised his versatility for underfoot conditions when winning his novice hurdle at Sedgefield last season. Rated 129 over hurdles, he was all the rage for this seasonal/chase debut and was doing things well enough through the race prior to his departure at the 11th. (op 11-1 tchd 20-1)

2508 SALTIRE 2010 26TH-28TH NOVEMBER H'CAP HURDLE (9 hdls) 2m
2:00 (2:01) (Class 3) (0-125,112) 3-Y-0+ **£5,204** (£1,528; £764; £381)

Form RPR

0-23 **1** **Altan Khan**[37] 1832 5-11-0 **100** DougieCostello 108+
(Malcolm Jefferson) *hld up: hdwy and prom 2 out: rdn to ld run-in: styd on wl* **8/1**[3]

04-6 **2** 1½ **Pillar Of Hercules (IRE)**[34] 1870 6-11-0 **100** GrahamLee 104+
(Ferdy Murphy) *hld up: smooth hdwy bef 3 out: chal on bit next: led last: rdn and hdd run-in: kpt on: hld towards fin* **9/2**[2]

3210 **3** 2 **Grand Diamond (IRE)**[15] 2164 6-11-5 **112** PaulNorton(7) 115+
(Jim Goldie) *hld up: hdwy and in tch 2 out: rdn and kpt on run-in: nt pce of first two* **10/1**

/5-4 **4** 3 **Simonside**[19] 2104 7-10-8 **97** FearghalDavis(3) 96+
(Brian Ellison) *hld up in midfield: rdn and outpcd 1/2-way: rallied bef 2 out: kpt on run-in: nrst fin* **11/4**[1]

50-6 **5** 2¼ **Veronicas Boy**[34] 1641 4-11-3 **103** (v[1]) BarryKeniry 101
(George Moore) *trckd ldrs: hit 4 out: rdn next: one pce fr 2 out* **33/1**

650 **6** 2½ **Mountskip**[13] 2208 6-10-9 **102** MrAdamNicol(7) 97
(Rose Dobbin) *in tch: effrt bef 3 out: kpt on same pce fr next* **16/1**

5005 **7** nk **Crosby Jemma**[20] 2089 6-11-7 **107** CampbellGillies 103+
(Mike Sowersby) *hld up in midfield: hdwy whn blnd 2 out: sn no impressiopn* **28/1**

-126 **8** 2¾ **Tharaya**[11] 2282 5-11-1 **108** HenryBrooke(7) 99
(James Turner) *t.k.h: in tch: outpcd bef 3 out: no imp fr next* **25/1**

333- **9** 11 **Pokfulham (IRE)**[20] 4106 4-11-9 **109** JamesReveley 89
(Jim Goldie) *in tch tl rdn and wknd after 3 out* **10/1**

21-6 **10** shd **Spirit Of The Mist (IRE)**[83] 1406 6-11-9 **109** PaddyAspell 107
(James Moffatt) *cl up: led after 3rd: rdn 2 out: hdd last: wkng whn broke leg run-in: fatally injured* **11/1**

1-4P **11** 5 **Knight In Purple**[21] 2076 6-11-12 **112** (v) RichieMcGrath 87
(John Mackie) *led to after 3rd: styd upsides: rdn and wknd bef 2 out* **25/1**

3- **12** ½ **Five Jembs (IRE)**[9] 2319 6-10-6 **97** (t) KMDonoghue(5) 72
(Adrian McGuinness, Ire) *hld up in midfield: hdwy bef 4th: rdn and wknd bef 3 out* **14/1**

6-06 **13** 3½ **Takaatuf (IRE)**[172] 548 4-11-5 **105** BrianHughes 76
(John Hellens) *trckd ldrs tl rdn and wknd after 3 out* **50/1**

650- **14** 12 **Carters Rest**[251] 4578 7-11-0 **105** AlexanderVoy(5) 64
(Chris Grant) *racd wd: hld up: struggling bef 3 out: sn btn* **25/1**

4-00 **15** ½ **Faith And Reason (USA)**[20] 2094 7-10-9 **100** (p) MissLHorner(5) 59
(Chris Grant) *bhd: struggling after 4 out: nvr on terms* **100/1**

3m 38.4s (-10.00) **Going Correction** -0.50s/f (Good)
WFA 4 from 5yo+ 7lb **15** Ran SP% **115.9**
Speed ratings (Par 107): **105,104,103,101,100 99,99,97,92,92 89,89,87,81,81**
Tote Swingers: 1&2 £6.20, 1&3 £5.90, 2&3 £10.50 CSF £39.63 CT £367.35 TOTE £6.00: £2.30, £2.10, £3.40; EX 32.40.
Owner Mrs Jennifer E Pallister **Bred** Mrs M Barker **Trained** Norton, N Yorks

FOCUS
A weak race for the grade, though, with the top weight rated 8lb below the race ceiling. There was an average sort of gallop on and plenty were in with a chance of the home turn. The form looks solid and should work out, with the fifth and seventh setting the level.

NOTEBOOK
Altan Khan was given a lovely ride and got on top at the business end to shed his maiden tag at the sixth time of asking. He crept into things from three out and tracked the runner-up on the inside. Although he wasn't that clever at the penultimate flight, he responded kindly to a smack nearing the last and his superior stamina kicked in on the run-in. He has the scope to defy a higher mark, but his real future lies over fences in due course. (op 6-1)
Pillar Of Hercules(IRE) ◆ travelled sweetly and looked all over the winner in between the final two flights. He couldn't cope with the winner's burst after the last, but this was a much-improved effort on ground that suits, and he should be found another opening before long. (tchd 5-1)
Grand Diamond(IRE) enjoyed this return to better ground and returned to near his best in defeat, helping to set the standard. (op 12-1)
Simonside ◆ failed to really raise his game as may have been expected for this quicker ground, but he surely wants further over hurdles these days. (op 3-1 tchd 5-2)

2509 SCOTTISH RACING YOUR BETTER BET NOVICES' HURDLE (9 hdls) 2m
2:35 (2:35) (Class 4) 4-Y-0+ **£2,602** (£764; £382; £190)

Form RPR

1 **Dica (FR)** 4-10-7 0 KMDonoghue(5) 97+
(Patrick Griffin, Ire) *mde all: rdn after 2 out: hld on wl run-in* **100/1**

2-0 **2** 3¼ **Dhaular Dhar (IRE)**[27] 1962 8-10-12 0 BarryKeniry 94
(Jim Goldie) *trckd ldrs: effrt and chsd wnr after 2 out: kpt on same pce run-in* **7/1**

3 nk **Jawaab (IRE)**[39] 6-10-12 0 PaddyAspell 93
(Richard Guest) *in tch: effrt 2 out: kpt on u.p run-in* **12/1**

0-06 **4** 2¼ **Tale Of Tanganyika (FR)**[26] 1989 4-10-12 0 JamesReveley 92
(John Wade) *trckd wnr: effrt whn mstke 2 out: sn lost 2nd pl: edgd rt and outpcd run-in* **5/1**[3]

254/ **5** 6 **That'll Do Nicely (IRE)**[86] 682 7-10-12 0 BrianHarding 85
(Nicky Richards) *in tch: effrt appr 3 out: no imp fr next* **5/1**[3]

6 3 **Shy Glance (USA)**[28] 8-10-12 0 CampbellGillies 82
(P Monteith) *hld up: stdy hdwy 3 out: shkn up and no imp fr next* **100/1**

60-0 **7** 1 **Jaques Vert (FR)**[27] 1962 4-10-12 0 RichieMcGrath 81
(Robert Wylie) *bhd: nt fluent 2nd: hdwy after 2 out: kpt on: nrst fin* **20/1**

8 9 **Arabian Spirit**[20] 5-10-12 0 BrianHughes 72
(Richard Fahey) *hld up in midfield: shkn up bef 2 out: sn outpcd: no imp whn nt fluent last* **10/3**[2]

9 hd **Parc Des Princes (USA)**[142] 4-10-12 0 DougieCostello 72
(Nicky Richards) *hld up: pushed along bef 3 out: no imp bef next* **22/1**

20-0 **10** 8 **Pamoja**[27] 1962 4-10-12 0 GrahamLee 66
(Martin Todhunter) *prom tl rdn and wknd after 3 out* **40/1**

00 **11** 1½ **Velvet Vic (IRE)**[7] 2355 4-10-12 0 PeterBuchanan 63
(Richard Guest) *t.k.h: hld up: rdn bef 3 out: sn btn* **150/1**

12 1¼ **Angle Of Attack (IRE)**[25] 5-10-9 0 FearghalDavis(3) 61
(Alan Brown) *bhd: struggling 1/2-way: nvr on terms* **150/1**

13 6 **Michelle's Express (IRE)**[33] 1890 6-11-5 130 JohnnyFarrelly 62
(A J Martin, Ire) *hld up in tch: shortlived effrt on outside bef 3 out: sn wknd* **3/1**[1]

00 **14** 21 **Real Desire**[7] 2349 4-10-12 0 WilsonRenwick 34
(P Monteith) *bhd: struggling bef 3 out: nvr on terms* **150/1**

3m 40.0s (-8.40) **Going Correction** -0.50s/f (Good)
WFA 4 from 5yo+ 7lb **14** Ran SP% **117.1**
Speed ratings (Par 105): **101,99,99,98,95 93,93,88,88,84 83,83,80,69**
Tote Swingers: 1&2 £61.50, 1&3 £61.50, 2&3 £43.60 CSF £683.45 TOTE £56.90: £30.70, £2.00, £4.60; EX 1372.50.
Owner M Deren **Bred** E A R L Vernon Gil **Trained** Oldtown, Co Dublin

FOCUS
An ordinary novice hurdle. It was run at an uneven gallop and it paid to race handily. It is not a race to be confident about even though it could be rated a fair bit higher.

NOTEBOOK
Dica(FR) made all and readily got his career off to a perfect start, belying his odds of 100/1. He was gifted the early lead and his rider timed it to perfection. He has to rate a touch flattered to have had the run of things, but should only improve for the experience and his next outing will help to determine his true potential. It was his trainer's first winner for over two years.
Dhaular Dhar(IRE) was undone by the ground on his return to hurdling at Aintree last month, but this sounder surface was much more in his favour and he held every chance. He is now qualified for a mark. (op 9-1)
Jawaab(IRE) ◆ is a four-time winner on the level and is rated 75 in that sphere. He didn't go unbacked for this switch to hurdling, but wasn't suited by the stop-start gallop as he was motoring home after the last. He would've been second in another few strides and this was a very encouraging introduction. (op 16-1)
Tale Of Tanganyika(FR) looked promising when beating some fair rivals on his debut in a bumper here last season. He hadn't shown much since then, but was backed for this switch to hurdling and showed up nicely. He got very warm beforehand and may be somewhat headstrong, but ought to find one of these when faced with more of a test. (op 15-2)
That'll Do Nicely(IRE) looked interesting on this belated return to hurdling, but he was another undone by the uneven gallop and probably wants further.
Shy Glance(USA) Official explanation: jockey said gelding had a breathing problem.
Arabian Spirit, rated 86 on the Flat, tried to get involved from the third-last. He had stamina to prove, however, and on this evidence looks a short runner over hurdles. (op 7-2 tchd 3-1)
Michelle's Express(IRE) has improved of late, but he proved very easy to back on this debut for Tony Martin and stopped quickly after three out. Connections could offer no excuses afterwards. Official explanation: trainer had no explanation as to geldings poor run. (op 9-4)

2510 TURFTV H'CAP CHASE (16 fncs) 2m 4f
3:10 (3:10) (Class 3) (0-120,120) 4-Y-0+ **£5,204** (£1,528; £764; £381)

Form RPR

50-4 **1** **Cybora (FR)**[14] 2189 8-10-0 **94** oh7 GrahamLee 104+
(Ferdy Murphy) *dictated modest gallop: mde all: qcknd 4 out: kpt on wl: unchal* **6/1**

6331 **2** 5 **Ormus**[13] 2207 7-10-1 **95** PaddyAspell 104+
(Christopher Wilson) *nt fluent on occasions: hld up in tch: stdy hdwy 5 out: effrt 3 out: chsd wnr after next: no imp run-in* **11/8**[1]

60-4 **3** 4½ **Folk Tune (IRE)**[26] 1987 7-11-9 **117** DougieCostello 117
(John Quinn) *chsd wnr: rdn 3 out: lost 2nd after next: no imp* **7/2**[2]

234U **4** 11 **Ormello (FR)**[23] 2034 8-11-6 **114** PeterBuchanan 105
(Lucinda Russell) *hld up in tch: outpcd after 5 out: struggling fr next* **5/1**[3]

3460 **F** **Baaher (USA)**[15] 2164 6-10-11 **105** BarryKeniry —
(Jim Goldie) *hld up in tch: 5l 3rd and stl gng wl whn fell 11th* **7/1**

5m 2.80s (1.60) **Going Correction** +0.275s/f (Yiel) **5** Ran SP% **107.8**
Speed ratings (Par 107): **107,105,103,98,—**
CSF £14.74 TOTE £7.80: £4.10, £1.10; EX 13.70.
Owner D Clinton, S Gale, M Milns, F Murphy **Bred** Roger Treger **Trained** West Witton, N Yorks

FOCUS
A moderate handicap, run at a stop-start gallop and the winner dictated. The winner is rated back to something like her best.

NOTEBOOK
Cybora(FR), back on more suitable ground, made all from 7lb out of the handicap and handed her yard a welcome winner. She looked to be doing enough out in front early on, but her rider was allowed to dictate matters as he pleased and her neat jumping was a valuable asset as he asked her to quicken from three out. She has to rate as somewhat flattered, but positive tactics over this sharper trip worked the oracle and she ought to be high on confidence now. (op 7-1)
Ormus was 2lb higher for just getting up with something to spare at Carlisle 13 days earlier. He has won here and had his ground, but got caught out by the winner being able to dictate over this longer trip, which he has yet to score over. He still rates a sound benchmark. (op 5-4)
Folk Tune(IRE) had every chance back up in trip, but failed to see it out like the first pair and is not an easy horse to catch right. (tchd 4-1)

Ormello(FR) who unseated last time out, was left behind from the 12th fence and is another tricky horse to win with. (tchd 11-2)
Baaher(USA) had work to do, but didn't look done with prior to coming down on the back straight. (op 8-1 tchd 6-1)

2511 RACING UK "NEWCOMERS" STANDARD OPEN NATIONAL HUNT FLAT RACE 2m

3:45 (3:45) (Class 5) 3-5-Y-O **£1,951** (£573; £286; £143)

Form RPR

1 **Bygones In Brid (IRE)** 4-11-8 0 GrahamLee 105+
(Karen McLintock) *t.k.h: mde all at stdy gallop: qcknd clr over 1f out: readily* **6/1**

2 *8* **D'Gigi** 4-11-1 0 JamesReveley 87+
(Keith Reveley) *hld up: pushed along fr 1/2-way: hdwy 3f out: chsd (clr) wnr ins fnl f: styd on: no imp* **10/1**

3 *3 ¼* **Blue Blooded** 4-11-8 0 BrianHughes 91
(Alan Swinbank) *trckd ldrs: effrt and chsd wnr over 1f out: no ex appr fnl f* **11/4**[1]

4 *1* **Kasakovs Girl** 3-9-7 0 HenryBrooke(7) 68
(Simon West) *hld up in tch: rdn and outpcd over 3f out: rallied over 1f out: no imp ins fnl f* **50/1**

5 *¾* **Barello Road** 4-11-1 0 PeterBuchanan 82
(Lucinda Russell) *t.k.h: cl up tl rdn and no ex over 1f out* **20/1**

6 *6* **Way To Finish** 4-11-8 0 PaddyAspell 85
(James Moffatt) *plld hrd: hld up: hdwy and prom over 2f out: wknd fnl f* **16/1**

7 *1 ¼* **Red Rocco (IRE)** 3-9-11 0 SamuelWelton(10) 67
(George Moore) *hld up: rdn and outpcd over 4f out: n.d after* **9/1**

8 *1 ¾* **Grey Assassin** 3-10-2 0 PaulCallaghan(5) 65
(Simon West) *hld up: struggling over 4f out: nvr on terms* **40/1**

9 *1 ½* **A Beat So Far** 4-11-1 0 KennyJohnson 72
(Robert Johnson) *t.k.h: in tch tl wknd fr 3f out* **100/1**

10 *1 ¾* **Bello Regalo (IRE)** 4-11-8 0 DougieCostello 77
(Malcolm Jefferson) *trckd ldrs: rdn over 2f out: sn wknd* **7/2**[2]

11 *12* **Gin Cobbler** 4-11-8 0 WilsonRenwick 65+
(Howard Johnson) *t.k.h: trckd ldrs: hung lft fr 6f out: hung bdly lft and lost pl qckly bnd ent st: sn btn* **9/2**[3]

12 *13* **Pills Baby (IRE)** 5-10-10 0 KMDonoghue(5) 45
(Adrian McGuinness, Ire) *hld up: rdn and struggling over 3f out: sn btn* **28/1**

3m 48.8s (6.00) **Going Correction** -0.50s/f (Good)
WFA 3 from 4yo+ 15lb **12** Ran SP% **119.9**
Speed ratings (Par 103): **65,61,59,58,58 55,54,54,53,52 46,39**
Tote Swingers: 1&2 £8.00, 1&3 £5.20, 2&3 £7.30. totesuper7: Win: Not won. Place: Not won. CSF £62.17 TOTE £6.20: £1.60, £2.70, £2.30; EX 64.90.
Owner Alan Lamont **Bred** Tom Mullins **Trained** Ingoe, Northumberland

FOCUS
No previous form to go on here and so a tricky race to assess. There was a taking winner but the form is likely to prove ordinary.

NOTEBOOK
Bygones In Brid(IRE), whose dam won a bumper, is from a stable that do well in this sphere and he ran out a taking winner. He was always front rank and took an age to settle. He was in the right place when things got serious off the home turn, but he quickened smartly and was in no danger inside the final furlong. Bred to get further once sent jumping, it will be interesting to see how he fares under a penalty.
D'Gigi ran green on the back straight, but the penny dropped late on and she turned in a very pleasing effort. She has plenty of stamina in her pedigree and looks sure to improve for this initial experience. (tchd 12-1)
Blue Blooded is bred for the Flat, but is a half-brother to Supreme Novice hero Arcalis and his yard has an excellent record in the bumper division. This 80,000gns purchase had every chance, but left the impression he would come on for the run as he flattened out late on. (tchd 3-1)
Kasakovs Girl, another bred for the Flat, was ridden to get the trip and really caught the eye staying on inside the final furlong. This was an encouraging debut effort. (op 40-1)
Barello Road is bred to make her mark in this sphere and she proved suited by running on the pace. She is entitled to get closer now she has a run under her belt. (op 25-1)
Way To Finish has some scope about him and this was a fair debut run considering he ran with the choke out under heavy restraint. He has a future. (tchd 14-1 and 20-1 in a place)
Red Rocco(IRE) is another bred to come into his own over farther in due course. He got badly outpaced when the pace lifted out of the back straight, and his inexperienced rider looked to overdo the waiting tactics. (op 22-1)
Bello Regalo(IRE) was representing an in-form stable that sends out its share of bumpers winner each term and he too was well backed. The run looked much needed, though. (op 4-1 tchd 5-1 in a place)
Gin Cobbler, yet another bred to win one of these, spoilt his chance by running very wide off the home turn and disappointed. Official explanation: jockey said gelding hung left. (op 4-1 tchd 7-2)
T/Jkpt: Not won T/Plt: £724.20 to a £1 stake. Pool of £39,188.08 - 39.50 winning tickets. T/Qpdt: £109.30 to a £1 stake. Pool of £3,693.60 - 25.00 winning tickets. RY

2493 ASCOT (R-H)

Saturday, November 20

OFFICIAL GOING: Good to soft (good in places)
Wind: Virtually nil Weather: Damp, cloudy

2512 BARRETT STEEL NOVICES' HURDLE (12 hdls) 2m 6f

12:20 (12:22) (Class 2) 4-Y-0+

£6,888 (£2,035; £1,017; £509; £254; £127)

Form RPR

2 1 **Time For Spring (IRE)**[23] 2059 6-10-12 0 TomO'Brien 122+
(Charlie Longsdon) *trckd ldrs: chal 7th: led 8th: c clr fr 3 out: in n.d whn blnd last: sn rcvrd: comf* **10/1**

/F6- 2 *4 ½* **Hong Kong Harry**[344] 2814 6-10-12 0 WayneHutchinson 115
(Alan King) *in rr: rdn after 4 out: hdwy after next to chse ldr: tendency to hang rt appr 2 out: chal for 2nd last: sn chsng wnr: nvr any ch* **20/1**

3/22 3 *3 ½* **Representingceltic (IRE)**[19] 2123 5-10-12 0 TimmyMurphy 115+
(Pat Phelan) *trckd ldrs tl hmpd and lost position bnd after 8th: stdy hdwy again to trck ldrs 3 out: chsd wnr sn after: nvr any ch: lost 2nd and one pce sn after last* **11/2**[3]

6-34 4 *4 ½* **Wyck Hill (IRE)**[17] 2154 6-10-12 108 RodiGreene 110+
(David Bridgwater) *led at modest pce: mstke 6th: jnd 7th: hdd and blnd next: styd chsng wnner tl after 3 out: wknd fr 2 out* **28/1**

110- 5 *1 ¾* **Ballyfoy (IRE)**[238] 4890 9-10-12 0 MattieBatchelor 107+
(Jamie Poulton) *in rr: bmpd 1st: hit 8th: stl wl bhd 3 out: hdwy on outer appr 2 out: styd on wl u.p fr next: nvr gng pce to get into contention* **16/1**

0- 6 *11* **Troy Tempest (IRE)**[270] 4213 5-10-12 0 JamesDavies 96
(Emma Lavelle) *in rr: stl wl bhd 3 out: drvn and styd on fr 2 out: nvr in contention* **66/1**

2 7 *11* **Ultimate Quest (IRE)**[9] 2325 5-10-12 0 DaveCrosse 88
(Michael Chapman) *t.k.h in rr: hdwy 8th: hit 4 out: wknd next* **40/1**

-111 8 *3* **Jurisdiction**[14] 2202 6-11-6 129 (p) APMcCoy 96
(Rose Dobbin) *trckd ldr to 7th: stl disputing 2nd 3 out: wknd qckly* **9/2**[2]

45- 9 *3 ½* **This Masquerade**[273] 4156 7-10-12 0 JoeTizzard 81
(Warren Greatrex) *bmpd 1st: a towards rr* **33/1**

310- 10 *9* **Rebel Rebellion (IRE)**[224] 5129 5-10-12 0 NoelFehily 80+
(Paul Nicholls) *hld up in rr: hdwy 6th: trckd ldrs travelling wl 4 out: rdn after 3 out and wknd qckly* **11/10**[1]

20-0 11 *½* **Eastern Supreme (IRE)**[10] 2310 5-10-12 0 (t) SeanQuinlan 72
(Kim Bailey) *chsd ldrs: pckd 7th: stl wl there 4 out: wknd next: wl bhd whn blnd last* **40/1**

5 12 *13* **Uncle Keef (IRE)**[19] 2129 4-10-12 0 (b) BarryGeraghty 60
(Nicky Henderson) *chsd ldrs: hit 6th: wl there whn hit 4 out: wknd qckly* **20/1**

5m 19.6s (-7.40) **Going Correction** -0.25s/f (Good)
WFA 4 from 5yo+ 8lb **12** Ran SP% **118.4**
Speed ratings (Par 109): **103,101,100,98,97 93,89,88,87,84 84,79**
toteswingers: 1&2 £13.00, 1&3 £15.10, 2&3 £40.10 CSF £177.37 TOTE £11.10: £2.70, £2.90, £1.80; EX 110.30 Trifecta £490.20 Part won. Pool: £662.44 - 0.10 winning units..
Owner MacEchern, Pottinger, Badcock **Bred** John Conway **Trained** Over Norton, Oxon

FOCUS
An ordinary novice event for the track, although the first two both stepped up on previous form. The fourth and fifth set the level.

NOTEBOOK
Time For Spring(IRE) was no match for Made In Time at Stratford on his debut for connections last month but showed he had come on a bundle with a clear-cut win. He took the race by the scruff of the neck nearing four out and he had matters well in control when making an error at the last. This former point winner clearly stays well and it will be interesting to see what he can do under a penalty. (op 20-1)
Hong Kong Harry, keen to the start, had not shown a great deal coming into this, but his yard is back in much better form this season and does have a very good record in such races at this venue. He stayed on dourly to post by far his most encouraging display to date. He is now eligible for handicaps and is entitled to come on for the run. (op 22-1 tchd 25-1)
Representingceltic(IRE) was unable to land a serious blow, but kept on well enough in the home straight and has now been placed on his last four outings, so rates a fair benchmark. He too is now qualified for a mark. Official explanation: jockey said gelding stumbled a mile out. (op 5-1 tchd 6-1)
Wyck Hill(IRE) took a keen grip to post and proved free at the head affairs through the race. He got caught out by making mistakes on the far side, but was running on again late in the day and it's not hard to see why he was tried over further last time. He too helps to set the standard. (tchd 25-1)
Ballyfoy(IRE), a 138-rated chaser, was having a rare outing over hurdles on his seasonal debut. He got going late on, suggesting he will be plenty sharper for the run, and is likely to be aimed at the Welsh National next month. (op 14-1)
Troy Tempest(IRE), well beaten on his debut in a bumper last season, still looked distinctly green on this switch to hurdling. He should learn from the experience.
Jurisdiction was chasing a four-timer. His best form had been on quicker ground, but he was beaten a long way out and now has something to prove. (tchd 4-1)
Rebel Rebellion(IRE) won his bumper on Southwell's Fibresand last term and showed useful form behind the promising Megastar either side of that success. Very well backed on this hurdling debut and first outing for Paul Nicholls, things looked good for his supporters as he effortlessly made up ground near the seventh flight. However, as soon as he was asked for an effort shortly after, it was clear he was in trouble and he was later reported to have choked. Official explanation: trainer said gelding choked. (op 5-4 tchd 11-8 in places)

2513 BAM CONSTRUCT UK NOVICES' H'CAP CHASE (20 fncs) 3m

12:55 (12:55) (Class 3) (0-120,118)
4-Y-0+

£5,635 (£1,665; £832; £416; £207; £104)

Form RPR

3F2- 1 **Teddy's Reflection (IRE)**[235] 4944 7-11-9 **115** HaddenFrost 124+
(Henrietta Knight) *in rr but in tch: clsd on ldrs 14th: pushed along 16th: one pce 3 out: rallied and styd on to ld 2 out: kpt on strly* **14/1**

3-26 2 *5* **Sonny Mullen (IRE)**[14] 2214 6-11-10 **116** SeanQuinlan 122+
(Kim Bailey) *chsd ldrs: blnd 10th: styd front rnk and chalng whn blnd 3 out: rt there and rdn next: sn chsng wnr u.p: nvr any ch and styd on same pce* **6/1**[3]

534- 3 *10* **Global Warming (IRE)**[270] 4212 6-11-1 **114** StephenO'Donovan(7) 110
(Emma Lavelle) *chsd ldrs: slt ld fr 13th: jnd 15th to 16th: narrowly hdd 4 out: led after 3 out: hdd 2 out and sn wknd* **4/1**[2]

3-PU 4 *3 ¼* **Victory Parade (IRE)**[11] 2285 7-11-5 **118** AodhaganConlon(7) 114+
(Rebecca Curtis) *chsd ldrs: hit 8th: hmpd 12th: slt ld 3 out: hdd sn after: wknd and hit 2 out* **7/1**

56-2 5 *1* **Royal Collonges (FR)**[32] 1907 5-11-12 **118** NoelFehily 112+
(Paul Nicholls) *led tl narrowly hdd 13th: hit 14th chal 15th: led 4 out: mstke and hdd 3 out: sn wknd* **7/2**[1]

3163 6 *58* **Intac (IRE)**[14] 2220 8-11-10 **116** JoeTizzard 55
(Colin Tizzard) *chsd ldrs to 7th: dropped in rr next and sn wl bhd: hit 11th: t.o* **20/1**

2P-4 7 *32* **Alteranthela (IRE)**[19] 2124 6-11-3 **109** TimmyMurphy 19
(Richard Rowe) *sn bhd: no ch whn hmpd 10th: t.o* **25/1**

21P6 F **Marc Of Brilliance (USA)**[20] 2112 7-11-2 **115** (b) JoshuaMoore(7) —
(Gary Moore) *in rr: mstke 4th: in tch whn fell 10th* **40/1**

-023 F **Solitary Palm (IRE)**[11] 2286 7-10-10 **102** LiamTreadwell —
(Brian Forsey) *pressed ldrs tl fell 2nd* **11/1**

326- F **Arturo Uno (IRE)**[219] 5195 7-11-5 **111** APMcCoy —
(Nigel Twiston-Davies) *trckd ldr fr 6th: chal fr 9th tl fell 12th* **4/1**[2]

6m 6.40s (-2.60) **Going Correction** -0.25s/f (Good) **10** Ran SP% **115.1**
Speed ratings (Par 107): **94,92,89,87,87 68,57,—,—,—**
toteswingers: 1&2 £21.10, 1&3 £21.90, 2&3 £6.70 CSF £92.73 CT £403.91 TOTE £14.00: £2.60, £2.60, £2.10; EX 47.60 TRIFECTA Not won..
Owner The Bailey Family **Bred** William Brennan **Trained** West Lockinge, Oxon

FOCUS
This modest novice handicap was run at an average gallop and the form looks fairly ordinary by course standards. The second is the best guide to the level and, although the form could be rated higher, it is not a race to get carried away with.

NOTEBOOK
Teddy's Reflection(IRE) made light of a 235-day break and provided his trainer with a welcome winner. This was his fifth outing over fences and his first success since scoring on his hurdling debut in 2008. There was a lot to like about the way he rallied into the home straight and this extra distance was clearly to his liking. He was resuming off a career-low mark and should improve for the run, so will have to be respected next time despite going back up in the handicap. (op 12-1)
Sonny Mullen(IRE) proved game in defeat and finished nicely clear in second. He still has a little to learn in the jumping department, but this easier ground was more in his favour and he should find an opening over fences before long. (op 9-1)

Global Warming(IRE), who got warm beforehand, is from a yard in decent form and was having his first outing in a handicap on this chase/seasonal debut. He raced enthusiastically and did things nicely through the race. He eventually paid for his early exertions, but this was a display he should build on. (op 5-1 tchd 11-2)
Victory Parade(IRE) came under pressure a fair way out but at least completed this time. (op 8-1)
Royal Collonges(FR) had shown more on his comeback over hurdles at Exeter last month in a race that has produced winners and had been dropped 2lb for that. He has always been regarded as a chaser and was unsurprisingly sent off favourite on this switch to fences. He once again took time to settle, however, and his jumping errors eventually mounted up. He stays all day and no doubt has a race in him over fences, but needs more practice. (tchd 4-1)
Arturo Uno(IRE) came down too early to tell how he would have fared. (op 7-2 tchd 3-1)

2514 IVAN THE TERRIBLE MARES' H'CAP HURDLE (11 hdls 1 omitted) 2m 6f
1:30 (1:30) (Class 3) (0-125,122) 4-Y-O+

£5,635 (£1,665; £832; £416; £207; £104)

Form RPR
2-13 **1** **Cinderella Rose**[27] 1994 4-11-1 **111** SeanQuinlan 120+
(Kim Bailey) *trckd ldrs: hit 6th: chal 3 out: led sn after: drvn clr appr bypassed fnl flight* **8/1**[3]
25-3 **2** *3 1/4* **Devon Native (IRE)**[189] 340 7-10-6 **109** DannyBurton(7) 112
(Chris Down) *in rr: hdwy 8th: chsd ldrs fr 4 out: rdn and styd on after 3 out: kpt on fr bypassed fnl flight to take 2nd fnl 50yds* **11/1**
P2-3 **3** *2 3/4* **Asturienne**[13] 2242 6-11-9 **119** WayneHutchinson 120
(Alan King) *chsd ldrs: wnt 2nd after 3 out but no imp on wnr: styd on same pce tl wknd and lost 2nd fnl 50yds* **7/2**[1]
-0F0 **4** *3* **Giovanna**[150] 830 9-11-5 **115** (t) WarrenMarston 113+
(Richard Phillips) *in tch fr 5th: chsd ldrs next: lost pl 8th and sn in rr: hrd drvn fr and kpt on appr bypassed fnl flight: gng on cl home* **14/1**
P00- **5** *nse* **Helens Vision**[259] 4449 7-11-4 **114** LiamTreadwell 112
(James Evans) *chsd ldrs: wknd after 3 out* **20/1**
31-5 **6** *1* **Munlochy Bay**[21] 2094 6-10-3 **106** (p) MrLRPayter(7) 105+
(Matt Sheppard) *hit 2nd: in rr: mstkes 3rd and 4th: rdn and wl bhd 7th: styd on wl fr 3 out and kpt on appr bypassed fnl flight* **12/1**
0112 **7** *3 1/4* **Am I Blue**[9] 2329 4-10-7 **110** MrTomDavid(7) 105
(Mrs D Thomas) *pressed ldrs to 3 out: sn wknd* **14/1**
4311 **8** *10* **Detroit Red**[9] 2329 4-11-3 **113** HaddenFrost 102
(Martin Hill) *chsd ldrs: rdn 4 out: wknd fr next* **14/1**
113- **9** *3 3/4* **Cat Six (USA)**[22] 5196 6-11-5 **120** LeeEdwards(5) 104
(Tom Gretton) *chsd ldrs: blnd 4th: mstke 7th: sn wknd: no ch whn blnd 2 out* **25/1**
26-6 **10** *1* **Cloudy Spirit**[13] 2242 5-11-6 **116** NoelFehily 103
(Reg Hollinshead) *in tch: chsd ldrs 6th: wknd fr 3 out* **20/1**
10-0 **11** *1 3/4* **Manele Bay**[21] 2081 7-11-0 **110** TimmyMurphy 90
(Richard Rowe) *a towards rr* **5/1**[2]
0-00 **12** *2* **Zepnove (IRE)**[29] 1953 4-9-10 **97** (p) MarcGoldstein(5) 75
(Neil King) *in tch 5th: blnd and in rr 7th: no ch whn hit 3 out* **66/1**
-P50 **13** *16* **Bobbisox (IRE)**[5] 2425 5-9-9 **98** PeterHatton(7) 61
(Alex Hales) *blnd 1st: a in rr* **25/1**
1423 **P** **Winsley Hill**[14] 2218 8-11-12 **122** RodiGreene —
(Neil Mulholland) *led tl hdd after 3 out: hmpd sn after: t.o whn p.u and collapsed bypassed fnl flight* **12/1**
P612 **F** **Naughty Naughty**[11] 2288 5-11-5 **115** APMcCoy —
(Brendan Powell) *hdwy on inner and clsng whn fell 8th* **8/1**[3]

5m 22.3s (-4.70) **Going Correction** -0.25s/f (Good)
WFA 4 from 5yo+ 8lb **15** Ran SP% **123.5**
Speed ratings (Par 107): **98,96,95,94,94 94,93,89,88,87 87,86,80,—,—**
toteswingers: 1&2 £22.10, 1&3 £4.70, 2&3 £15.10 CSF £88.10 CT £372.11 TOTE £9.40: £2.60, £4.70, £1.90; EX 168.60 Trifecta £705.30 Part won. Pool: £953.10 - 0.62 winning units..
Owner Mrs Nicholas Jones **Bred** Coln Valley Stud **Trained** Andoversford, Gloucs

FOCUS
A competitive mares' handicap, which appeared to be run at a fair enough gallop. The final flight was bypassed and the form looks fair rated around the placed horses.

NOTEBOOK
Cinderella Rose bounced back and won in good style. A good winner on her hurdling/seasonal debut at Towcester last month, she may have found her next run there coming too soon. This was her first run in a handicap, and stepping up in trip proved right up her street. It rates a clear personal-best from this well-bred 4-y-o and there ought to be some more to come as she doesn't have much mileage on the clock, but she has yet to run on genuinely soft ground so may not be seen too much this winter. (op 17-2 tchd 7-1)
Devon Native(IRE) was last seen finishing third off this mark at Uttoxeter back in May. She raced lazily out the back and proved hard work for her rider. However, the further she went the better she was and this is not the first time she has run well when fresh. Along with the winner she too enjoys good ground and her proximity was an indication that the surface was sounder in the home straight. (tchd 12-1)
Asturienne travelled nicely and locked horns with the winner off the home turn. Her stamina for this longer trip appeared to give way after the penultimate flight, but this was another sound effort and she rates a decent benchmark. (op 5-1)
Giovanna, equipped with a first-time tongue tie, stayed on dourly from a long way back in the home straight and left the impression she would benefit plenty for this first outing for 150 days. She ideally needs more of a test. (op 16-1)
Helens Vision, making her debut for a new stable, was returning from her seasonal break and posted a more encouraging display. She appeared to blow up before keeping on from two out and should come on for the outing, but consistency has not been her strong suit in the past two years. (op 16-1)
Munlochy Bay was another that kept on well from a long way off the pace, and this stout stayer surely requires more positive handling.

2515 AMLIN 1965 CHASE (GRADE 2) (16 fncs) 2m 3f
2:05 (2:05) (Class 1) 4-Y-O+ **£28,639** (£10,829; £5,489; £2,804; £1,474)

Form RPR
314- **1** **Master Minded (FR)**[248] 4673 7-11-11 **173** NoelFehily 174+
(Paul Nicholls) *trckd ldrs: wnt 2nd 12th: quicknd to chal and gng wl whn lft wl clr 3 out: n.d after* **5/6**[1]
2-F4 **2** *16* **I'msingingtheblues (IRE)**[18] 2138 8-11-1 **152** (t) DannyCook 145
(David Pipe) *t.k.h: towards rr but in tch: blnd 10th: no ch w ldng duo whn lft mod 2nd 3 out: tired whn j.lft 2 out* **11/2**[3]
4F-0 **3** *5* **Panjo Bere (FR)**[21] 2086 7-11-5 **147** JoshuaMoore 142
(Gary Moore) *led 2nd: hdd 6th: rdn and dropped to rr 11th: no ch whn mstke 4 out: lft mod 4th next: styd on u.p to take mod 3rd on line* **20/1**
-2P0 **4** *nse* **Chaninbar (FR)**[6] 2385 7-11-7 **153** (vt) SeanQuinlan 142
(Milton Harris) *led in s and led to 2nd: reminders sn after: hit 4th and chsd ldrs: hit 7th: blnd 9th: chal 10th: wknd qckly 4 out: lft poor 3rd 3 out: lost that position on line* **25/1**
2-PP **5** *99* **Kinkeel (IRE)**[4] 2437 11-11-1 **85** (p) MattieBatchelor 46
(Tony Carroll) *wl bhd fr 8th: t.o* **250/1**
11-4 **F** **Albertas Run (IRE)**[28] 1958 9-11-11 **168** APMcCoy —
(Jonjo O'Neill) *trckd ldr: blnd 4th: chal 5th: led next: hrd drvn and jnd whn fell 3 out* **9/4**[2]

4m 42.74s (-4.26) **Going Correction** -0.25s/f (Good) **6** Ran SP% **109.7**
Speed ratings (Par 115): **98,91,89,89,47** —
toteswingers:1&2 £1.40, 2&3 £3.90, 1&3 £4.30 CSF £5.63 TOTE £1.70: £1.10, £2.80; EX 6.00.
Owner Clive D Smith **Bred** Marie-Christine Gabeur **Trained** Ditcheat, Somerset

FOCUS
A fascinating Grade 2 chase, run at a decent gallop. The impressive winner was left with little to beat, but was value for a lot further and rates as being back on a par with last season's Game Spirit success.

NOTEBOOK
Master Minded(FR) was left to come home as he pleased from three out and gain a confidence-boosting success on his seasonal return. This dual Champion Chase winner was last seen finishing fourth when bidding for a hat-trick in that event in March, and he had undergone a breathing operation since then. His connections had issued upbeat bulletins about him in the lead-up and their confidence proved to be spot-on, for he got the longer trip easily. His jumping was also foot-perfect, and he was electrifying at the fifth-last when asked to join Albertas Run, who was under the pump when he came down two fences later. This may tempt connections into thinking about a campaign over even further down the line, but he is still only a 7-y-o and when he shows his true colours he remains the one to side with in the 2m division. Unsurprisingly he was promoted to clear favouritism in some lists for the Champion Chase, with the Tingle Creek the next step. That will reveal more, for he really ought to be able to follow up there. (op 10-11 tchd Evens, 21-20 in a place)
I'msingingtheblues(IRE) was getting 10lb off the two Grade 1 winners, which meant he wasn't totally out of this on official figures. He spoilt his chance by refusing to settle under restraint, though, and a mistake at the tenth saw him lose vital ground as he was trying to close. The longer trip may have stretched him. (tchd 6-1)
Panjo Bere(FR) had a very stiff task at the weights and his rider was unable to claim. He set out to make it a test, but wasn't always fluent and was beaten from halfway. (tchd 16-1)
Chaninbar(FR) got worked up beforehand and needed the help of his trainer to jump off with the runners. He was out of his depth here, but went in snatches throughout and remains one to tread carefully with. (op 33-1 tchd 20-1)
Albertas Run(IRE) was expected to come on for his below-par comeback fourthat Aintree and make a bold bid to follow up last year's win on this return to better ground. He got an aggressive ride, surely attempting to expose the winner's possible stamina frailties, but just left the impression he was going quicker than he really wanted to. He was looking in trouble prior to taking a heavy tumble three out, giving his rider a third consecutive fall on the day, but it's a fair bet he would have stuck to his task had he not come down. It is hoped this does not dent his confidence, as it was the first time he has hit the deck in his career. (tchd 2-1 and 5-2)

2516 CORAL HURDLE (REGISTERED AS THE ASCOT HURDLE RACE) (GRADE 2) (11 hdls) 2m 3f 110y
2:35 (2:36) (Class 1) 4-Y-O+

£50,697 (£19,098; £9,558; £4,779; £2,394; £1,197)

Form RPR
11 **1** **Silviniaco Conti (FR)**[28] 1966 4-11-4 **153** NoelFehily 165+
(Paul Nicholls) *trckd ldrs: led 3 out: c clr appr next: easily* **10/3**[3]
240- **2** *7* **Karabak (FR)**[212] 5348 7-11-0 **163** WayneHutchinson 155
(Alan King) *towards rr: hdwy to trck ldrs 3 out: wnt 2nd sn after: rdn and no imp whn nt fluent last: hld on all out for 2nd* **3/1**[2]
F1-3 **3** *1 1/2* **Restless Harry**[28] 1967 6-11-4 **145** HenryOliver 157
(Robin Dickin) *chsd ldr to 4 out: rdn and outpcd after 3 out: rallied u.p fr 2 out to cl on 2nd nr fin: nvr any ch w wnr* **9/1**
233- **4** *1/2* **Zaynar (FR)**[224] 5125 5-11-8 **167** BarryGeraghty 162
(Nicky Henderson) *in rr: j. slowly 5th and 6th: rdn and rallied appr 4 out: hanging rt fr next and nt look keen: tk 3rd u.p wl bef 2 out: nvr any ch w wnr and styd on same pce* **13/8**[1]
040- **5** *20* **Won In The Dark (IRE)**[211] 5380 6-11-4 **154** TomO'Brien 141
(Sabrina J Harty, Ire) *in tch: chsd ldrs fr 4th: wknd appr 2 out* **25/1**
-P10 **6** *6* **Black Jack Blues (IRE)**[14] 2219 7-11-0 **149** (t) AodhaganConlon 131
(Rebecca Curtis) *chsd ldrs to 3 out: wknd qckly and no ch whn blnd 2 out* **50/1**
5-00 **7** *7* **Lough Derg (FR)**[19] 2125 10-11-0 **145** (v) HaddenFrost 131
(David Pipe) *led at gd pce tl hdd 3 out: sn wknd* **33/1**
11-4 **8** *22* **Ashkazar (FR)**[14] 2219 6-11-8 **155** TimmyMurphy 123
(David Pipe) *in rr tl hdwy 5th: rdn and wknd 3 out* **16/1**

4m 34.94s (-13.06) **Going Correction** -0.25s/f (Good)
WFA 4 from 5yo+ 7lb **8** Ran SP% **110.8**
Speed ratings (Par 115): **116,113,112,112,104 102,99,90**
toteswingers:1&2 £1.70, 2&3 £3.80, 1&3 £4.60 CSF £13.11 TOTE £3.10: £1.10, £1.50, £2.30; EX 11.60 Trifecta £75.00 Pool: £5614.06 - 55.33 winning units..
Owner Potensis Limited **Bred** Patrick Joubert **Trained** Ditcheat, Somerset

FOCUS
A strong race for the class, run at a decent gallop. It was another big step up from the impressive winner and the form is rated around the second.

NOTEBOOK
Silviniaco Conti(FR) upset the two market leaders with an impressive success on this first venture out of novice company, extending his unbeaten record. The form of his Grade 2 Persian War win at Chepstow had been boosted by Frascati Park the previous day, and while this classier event was new territory for him he answered each question asked of him with aplomb. His hurdling was particularly pleasing considering he wouldn't have raced at this sort of a pace before, and while he should get further in due course he would have little trouble dropping back to 2m. He was introduced into the Champion Hurdle market as low as 8/1, and was made as short as 7/2 for the World Hurdle, which looks ridiculous considering his stable has the reigning champion for that event. The Champion Hurdle looks the likelier route, and Paul Nicholls intends testing his credentials in the 2m StanJames.com International Hurdle (better known as the Bula) at Cheltenham. (op 4-1)
Karabak(FR) readily reversed last year's form with Zaynar on 6lb better terms. He failed to score in three outings last season after finishing second in this race, but still showed a decent engine and his trainer is in much better form this term. With Hutchinson a late substitute for the injured McCoy, he began to edge closer nearing three out and had his chance. He was firmly put in his place by the winner, though, despite getting 4lb from that one and had to settle for second once again. He is the best guide for this form and certainly deserves to find another opening, despite now having gone seven races without success. His trainer later added a return to further should bring about improvement. (op 11-4 tchd 10-3 in places)
Restless Harry, better than the bare form on his comeback at Chepstow last month, justified his trainer's decision to send him here and posted clear a personal-best. This game 6-y-o is entitled to come on a bit again for the run and he ought to relish getting back over further, but success in the division could well prove hard to come by this season. (op 11-1)

Zaynar(FR) looked tailor-made for this event, having won it readily last year. He flattened two flights on the far side and then hit what has now become his customary flat spot, but still emerged with every chance on the outside turning for home. Barry Geraghty had to work hard to get him there, however, and his response when straightening for home was worrying as he wanted to hang under maximum pressure. The cheekpieces he wore last season were abandoned for this return, but they look sure to be back on next time and, while he could leave the form behind now he has a run under his belt, he does have something to prove. He was pushed out to as big as 10/1 for the World Hurdle. (tchd 6-4 and 7-4 in places)

Won In The Dark(IRE) ideally wants quicker ground to shine and didn't help his chances here by running freely off the pace. He wasn't disgraced, but was never going to reverse his previous Aintree form with the disappointing Zaynar on 4lb better terms. (op 16-1)

2517 CAREY GROUP H'CAP CHASE (13 fncs) 2m 1f
3:10 (3:10) (Class 2) 4-Y-0+

£18,600 (£5,532; £2,772; £1,389; £702; £360)

Form RPR

101- **1** **Woolcombe Folly (IRE)**[218] [5210] 7-11-6 **142** .... NoelFehily 156+
(Paul Nicholls) *hld up in rr but in tch: smooth hdwy to chal 2 out: sn led: gng clr whn edgd lft last: comf* **7/2**[1]

00P- **2** *5* **Piraya (FR)**[210] [5395] 7-11-4 **140** .... (tp) JohnnyFarrelly 146
(David Pipe) *chsd ldrs: chal 8th: led 9th: narrowly hdd after 3 out: slt ld u.p next: sn hdd and no ch w wnr: styd on same pce to hold 2nd* **16/1**

6-31 **3** *2* **Noble Alan (GER)**[14] [2206] 7-11-7 **143** .... BrianHarding 146
(Nicky Richards) *hld up in tch: hdwy 9th: drvn and qcknd to chal 2 out: sn outpcd but styd on again to take 3rd last strides* **4/1**[2]

330- **4** *nse* **Consigliere (FR)**[226] [5097] 7-11-9 **148** .... (bt) DannyCook[(3)] 152
(David Pipe) *in tch: hdwy to chse ldrs fr 9th: drvn to press ldrs 2 out: sn outpcd: lost 3rd last strides* **11/2**

11-0 **5** *18* **Pickamus (FR)**[28] [1967] 7-11-1 **137** .... BarryGeraghty 127
(Henry Daly) *chsd ldrs: chsd ldr 6th led appr 8th: hdd next: led after 3 out: hdd next and sn wknd* **15/2**

UP-3 **6** *3 ¾* **Tatenen (FR)**[19] [2126] 6-11-7 **143** .... TimmyMurphy 128
(Richard Rowe) *led after 3rd: t.k.h: hdd after 8th: stl ev ch tl wknd qckly appr 2 out* **8/1**

21-4 **7** *73* **King Edmund**[21] [2086] 7-11-5 **141** .... (t) RodiGreene 59
(Chris Gordon) *lft in ld 2nd: hdd after 3rd: styd in tch: drvn and wl there whn blnd and sprawled 8th: nt rcvr: t.o* **8/1**

F-11 **P** **Cockney Trucker (IRE)**[48] [1693] 8-11-3 **139** .... TomO'Brien —
(Philip Hobbs) *led tl blnd 2nd: blnd 3rd and 4th: in rr whn p.u sn after* **5/1**[3]

4m 6.92s (-8.08) **Going Correction** -0.25s/f (Good) **8** Ran SP% **114.1**
Speed ratings (Par 109): **109,106,105,105,97 95,61,—**
toteswingers:1&2 £15.20, 2&3 £29.10, 1&3 £2.50 CSF £51.25 CT £232.01 TOTE £4.20: £1.80, £3.90, £1.70; EX 80.30 Trifecta £275.60 Pool: £1191.78 - 3.20 winning units..
Owner The Hon Mrs Townshend **Bred** Mrs M Doran **Trained** Ditcheat, Somerset

FOCUS
A decent handicap and a big step forward from the progressive winner. The second and fourth give the race a solid look.

NOTEBOOK
Woolcombe Folly(IRE) ◆ eventually came clear to give his trainer/rider a quick-fire treble. He has not been the easiest to train, but has an enviable strike-rate and this comeback success was his eighth win from 14 career starts. He bided his time out the back and jumped neatly in the main. His response when asked to win the race in between the final two fences was very pleasing and he sauntered clear on the run-in. A rise in the handicap is now forthcoming, but he does look the sort that can make up into a graded performer before the season is out. His trainer later added he thinks he may find more improvement for going back on a left-handed track and, with that in mind, perhaps the valuable handicap at Doncaster in February (won by Kalahari King last term) will figure in his plans. (op 3-1 tchd 11-4 and 4-1)
Piraya(FR), pulled up on his final outing last term, had cheekpieces on for this comeback run and posted a solid effort in defeat over a trip too sharp for him. He is not the easiest of rides, but will pay his way and should only improve for a return to further. (op 20-1)
Noble Alan(GER) got back to winning ways on his return to chasing a fortnight earlier and had been dropped 2lb for that. He travelled smoothly into contention and came from a similar position as the winner, but lacked anything like that one's turn of foot. This was still a sound effort in defeat and he helps to set the standard. (tchd 9-2)
Consigliere(FR), who has won over C&D, lacked the required turn of foot after the second-last and was well held under top weight. He should come on nicely for the outing, but has little room for manoeuvre off his current mark. (op 8-1 tchd 5-1)
Pickamus(FR), back over fences, took up the running turning for home but came under pressure soon after and was well beaten in the end. He needs further, though, and can find less competitive assignments so shouldn't be fully judged on this display. (op 10-1 tchd 7-1)
Tatenen(FR) proved free on the front end and ultimately paid the price. He is not going to prove easy to place successfully for his new trainer. (op 9-1)
King Edmund had come under a bit of pressure before hitting the eighth and losing any chance. He was allowed to complete in his own time thereafter. (tchd 15-2)
Cockney Trucker(IRE) arrived here on the back of two wins in novice company, but his jumping had been exposed in handicap company last season and he got the second and third fences totally wrong, which saw him go backwards. He then hit the fourth fence and was quickly pulled up. (tchd 9-2)

2518 GUY SALMON STANDARD OPEN NATIONAL HUNT FLAT RACE 2m
3:50 (3:50) (Class 4) 4-6-Y-0

£2,285 (£675; £337; £169; £84; £42)

Form RPR

1 **Twentyfourcarat (IRE)** 5-11-0 .... TimmyMurphy 109
(Ian Williams) *mde all: sn clr: pushed along as pack clsd fr over 2f out: drvn and styd on wl thrght fnl f* **11/1**

2 *¾* **Ericht (IRE)** 4-11-0 .... BarryGeraghty 108+
(Nicky Henderson) *prom in chsng gp bhd clr ldr and subsequent wnr: hdwy to go 2nd over 2f out: hrd drvn and styd on wl fr over 1f out: clsng nr fin: a hld* **13/8**[1]

3 *4 ½* **Avoca Promise (IRE)** 5-11-0 .... JoeTizzard 104
(Charles Egerton) *in tch tl stdd in rr of pursuing gp bhd clr ldr and subsequent wnr: hdwy fr 3f out: rdn to go 3rd 2f out: hung rt and green: styd on same pce* **5/1**[3]

5- **4** *¾* **Lord Liath (IRE)**[215] [5284] 4-11-0 .... WayneHutchinson 103
(Alan King) *chsd clr ldr and subsequent wnr 6f out: no imp fr 3f out: styd on same pce fnl 2f* **8/1**

5 *8* **Hard Tackle (IRE)** 4-10-11 .... MrAJBerry[(3)] 95
(Jonjo O'Neill) *in rr: rdn along 6f out: green but styd on 3f out: nvr rchd ldrs and wknd ins fnl f* **20/1**

6 *¾* **Lariat Sam (IRE)** 5-11-0 .... BrianHarding 94
(Alan King) *mid-div: rdn and sme prog over 4f out: in tch w main gp 3f out: wknd 2f out* **8/1**

0 **7** *1* **High Kite (IRE)**[38] [1824] 4-11-0 .... HaddenFrost 93
(Henrietta Knight) *chsd ldrs in main gp bhd clr ldr and subsequent wnr: wknd fr 3f out* **50/1**

0 **8** *9* **Topthorn**[21] [2087] 4-10-9 .... AnthonyFreeman[(5)] 84
(Martin Bosley) *in rr: rdn and v green 5f out: hdwy u.p but nvr any threat fr over 2f out: wknd and hung lft sn after* **100/1**

9 *18* **Mighty Monty** 5-11-0 .... TomO'Brien 66
(Victor Dartnall) *front rnk of main gp tl wknd 4f out* **14/1**

10 *¾* **Bumblebee (IRE)** 5-11-0 .... NoelFehily 66
(Warren Greatrex) *chsd ldrs in main gp tl wknd over 3f out* **4/1**[2]

11 *4 ½* **San Salito (FR)** 4-11-0 .... LiamTreadwell 61
(Giles Smyly) *in rr: sme hdwy 1/2-way: wknd 5f out* **50/1**

12 *1 ¾* **Ben Trovato (IRE)** 4-10-7 .... StephenO'Donovan[(7)] 59
(John Upson) *in tch 9f: sn wknd* **100/1**

3m 49.34s (6.34) **Going Correction** -0.25s/f (Good)
WFA 4 from 5yo 7lb **12** Ran SP% **122.6**
Speed ratings: **74,73,71,71,67 66,66,61,52,52 50,49**
toteswingers:1&2 £7.70, 2&3 £3.10, 1&3 £10.40 CSF £29.74 TOTE £12.30: £4.00, £1.20, £2.00; EX 41.60 Trifecta £448.30 Pool: £933.11 - 1.54 winning units..
Owner Jenny & Mark Pitman Gold Club No 1 **Bred** D Hickey **Trained** Portway, Worcs

FOCUS
The winner was gifted a clear early advantage here and made all, so the form is a little suspect. The third and seventh help set the level.

NOTEBOOK
Twentyfourcarat(IRE) was gifted a clear advantage and made all. This scopey 5-y-o was still well clear turning for home and did show a very willing attitude to repel the runner-up's late challenge. He should enjoy racing over further when sent hurdling and clearly has a future, but obviously has to rate as somewhat flattered by this. (op 12-1)
Ericht(IRE) ◆, whose yard is always to be feared in this division, is a half-brother to a point winner and out of a dam that won a bumper, hurdle, chase and on the Flat. He did his best to reel back the winner from 2f out and came nicely clear of the remainder, so should really prove hard to beat next time out. (op 5-4 tchd 15-8, 2-1 in places)
Avoca Promise(IRE) ◆, a brother to a point/bumper winner, proved distinctly green on this racecourse debut and looks sure to improve for the experience. He ought to take a bumper on one of the smaller tracks. (op 8-1)
Lord Liath(IRE) was one of three here that had run previously and had the best form on offer. He too gave his all in trying to close off the home bend, but tired inside the final furlong on this return from a 215-day break.
Hard Tackle(IRE) ◆ was given a patient ride and made stealthy headway turning for home. He flattened out under pressure, but the market strongly suggested the run would be needed and he is one to look out for next time.
Bumblebee(IRE), well backed, comes from a yard that know how to win bumpers and is a half-brother to a couple of winners in this sphere. He produced a limited response under pressure, though, and much better was clearly expected. (op 11-2)
T/Jkpt: Not won. T/Plt: £174.30 to a £1 stake. Pool of £125,541.40 - 525.66 winning tickets.
T/Qpdt: £17.30 to a £1 stake. Pool of £10,122.61 - 432.74 winning tickets. ST

2161 HAYDOCK (L-H)
Saturday, November 20

OFFICIAL GOING: Good to soft (good in places on hurdle course; soft in places on chase course)
All hurdle races on inner course. Bends moved out 6m for first five races inc. dist by 38m per circuit. False rail dropped last two races inc. dist by 18m.
Wind: Almost nil Weather: Fine but turned cloudy

2519 CORONATION STREET 50TH ANNIVERSARY NOVICES' HURDLE (REGISTERED THE NEWTON NOVICES' HURDLE) (LISTED) (9 hdls) 2m
12:40 (12:40) (Class 1) 4-Y-0+ **£10,412** (£3,899; £1,947; £973)

Form RPR

52-4 **1** **Toubab (FR)**[196] [207] 4-11-0 134 .... SamThomas 138+
(Paul Nicholls) *hld up in last pl: trcking front pair gng wl appr 4 out: wnt cl 2nd on bit between last 2: led last: sauntered clr run-in* **7/2**[2]

121 **2** *8* **Drill Sergeant**[24] [2038] 5-11-6 125 .... JasonMaguire 127
(Donald McCain) *led: rdn along and hdd briefly whn idled for a few strides after 3rd: rdn and hdd narrowly appr 3 out: sn regained ld but a u.p: nt fluent and hdd last: no ch w wnr after* **13/2**[3]

0201 **3** *9* **Pure Faith (IRE)**[11] [2296] 6-11-8 125 .... BrianHughes 121
(Peter Bowen) *w ldr: lft in ld briefly after 3rd: lost pl after 5th: struggling and outpcd after 4 out: kpt on to take 3rd cl home whn n.d* **20/1**

-112 **4** *shd* **Dunraven Storm (IRE)**[8] [2344] 5-11-8 150 .... RichardJohnson 122
(Philip Hobbs) *racd keenly: trckd ldrs: led narrowly appr 3 out: sn hdd: wkng whn hit last: lost 3rd cl home* **1/2**[1]

3m 53.3s (-10.90) **Going Correction** -0.475s/f (Good)
WFA 4 from 5yo+ 7lb **4** Ran SP% **107.0**
Speed ratings (Par 111): **108,104,99,99**
CSF £20.14 TOTE £4.90; EX 23.20.
Owner Hills Of Ledbury (Aga) **Bred** Bertran De Balanda & F Hoffet **Trained** Ditcheat, Somerset

FOCUS
A small field, but two potentially high-class novices on show, and while one disappointed, the other, Toubab, created a strong impression. He is value for further with the third setting the level.

NOTEBOOK
Toubab(FR), off since finishing fourth in the Swinton at this course, created a strong impression in breaking his duck. Runner-up to last season's Triumph Hurdle winner Soldatino at Kempton in February, he looked a bit on the weak side last season, often travelling strongly without being able to see his race out with menace, but he looks to have strengthened up considerably and the way he waltzed clear without being asked was impressive. Admittedly, with Dunraven Storm failing to run his race, the form doesn't amount to much, but he's highly regarded by his trainer and will almost certainly be aimed towards the Supreme Novices', for which he is quoted at around 16-1 (tchd 9-2)
Drill Sergeant, who still managed to win despite pulling himself up on the paddock bend at this course last month, did his best to give the winner a fight, but simply didn't have the class to match. He probably needs a little help with his concentration, so it would be no surprise to see him tried in some form of headgear next time. (op 6-1 tchd 5-1)
Pure Faith(IRE) was completely outclassed, but did keep on again to take third off the disappointing favourite. (op 16-1 tchd 22-1)

Dunraven Storm(IRE), already a dual winner over hurdles and runner-up to Cue Card at Cheltenham last week, had much expected of him. There was a slight concern this would come too soon, and he needed to be at his very best to give 8lb to the useful winner, but he was a long way short of it, tying up before the second last and looking very weary as he crossed the line. There will no doubt be some who use this to question the merit of Cue Card's Cheltenham effort now, but that would be unwise, as this fellow was clearly a long way below par, and must surely be given a break now. Official explanation: trainer said gelding got upset in the preliminaries. (op 4-7, tchd 8-13 in a place)

2520 FOLLOW PAUL NICHOLLS ON FACEBOOK AND TWITTER H'CAP CHASE (13 fncs) 2m

1:15 (1:15) (Class 2) (0-140,140) 4-Y-O+**£16,262** (£4,775; £2,387; £1,192)

Form				RPR
1131	**1**		**Stagecoach Pearl**[27] 1987 6-11-7 **140** ShaneByrne(5) (Sue Smith) *led: mstke 5th: mstke 4 out: sn hdd: nt fluent 3 out: rallied u.p 2 out: led between last 2: over 1l ahd whn lft over 6 l clr last: kpt up to work run-in* **7/2**[2]	155+
1U22	**2**	15	**Tara Royal**[14] 2220 5-11-5 **133** (t) JasonMaguire (Donald McCain) *hld up: hdwy to trck ldrs 8th: chalng 2 out: u.p and hld whn over 6 l down and lft 2nd last: n.d to wnr run-in* **11/4**[1]	136+
UP45	**3**	12	**Smack That (IRE)**[28] 1970 8-10-6 **123** (vt) JimmyDerham(3) (Milton Harris) *hld up: outpcd after 9th: kpt on modly fr 4 out: lft poor 3rd last: nvr a danger* **20/1**	110
30-1	**4**	18	**Pret A Thou (FR)**[7] 2362 7-11-0 **135** HarryChalloner(7) (John Bryan Groucott) *trckd ldr tl rdn after 9th: sn wknd* **12/1**	106
11-2	**5**	2 ½	**Gringo**[14] 2206 8-11-4 **132** BrianHughes (Howard Johnson) *nt fluent: hld up: struggling fr 8th: nvr on terms* **9/2**[3]	105
F1-5	**6**	19	**Ockey De Neulliac (FR)**[27] 1987 8-10-11 **125** GrahamLee (Ferdy Murphy) *in tch: nt fluent 1st: mstke 7th: nt fluent 9th: sn rdn and wknd* **7/1**	76
145-	**7**	3 ¾	**Double Vodka (IRE)**[278] 4075 9-10-9 **123** JamesReveley (Chris Grant) *in tch: lost pl 6th: bhd fr 8th* **16/1**	71
4-56	**F**		**My Moment (IRE)**[22] 2077 7-10-12 **126** RichardJohnson (Henry Daly) *trckd ldrs: wnt 2nd after 9th: led after 4 out and carried hd awkwardly: stmbld 3 out: hdd between last 2: u.p over 1 l down whn fell last* **5/1**	133

4m 12.8s (1.80) **Going Correction** +0.35s/f (Yiel) **8** Ran SP% **114.6**
Speed ratings (Par 109): **109,101,95,86,85 75,73,—**
toteswingers: 1&2 £1.70, 1&3 £17.60, 2&3 £11.30 CSF £14.18 CT £163.68 TOTE £4.60: £1.50, £1.70, £5.20; EX 15.50 Trifecta £268.80 Part won. Pool: £363.29 - 0.43 - winning units..
Owner John Conroy Jaqueline Conroy **Bred** R F Broad **Trained** High Eldwick, W Yorks

FOCUS
The runners finished well strung out in what was a decent 2m handicap chase. The winner stepped up with the second and faller pretty much to their marks.

NOTEBOOK
Stagecoach Pearl, bidding to make it four wins in his last five, is a relentless galloper and, despite successive mistakes down the far side, he ground it out doggedly, getting back to the front after two out and having My Moment held when that one came down at the last, leaving him clear. He was 12lb higher than when dominating his field at Aintree latest, and can expect to go up again for this, so he'll need to continue his progression if he's to complete a hat-trick. (tchd 4-1)
Tara Royal, a well-beaten second in a Grade 2 at Wincanton latest, was entitled to run well off a mark of 133, but he could find no extra from after two out. He's ideally suited by further. (op 10-3)
Smack That(IRE), who's on a good mark again, has really been struggling for form and again finished well held. (op 22-1)
Gringo made mistakes and was beaten a long way out. (op 4-1 tchd 7-2)
Double Vodka(IRE) failed to improve on his reappearance run. (tchd 14-1)
My Moment(IRE) was in the process of running his best race for almost a year, but was beaten when taking a crashing fall at the last. He's slipped to a very good mark, but it remains to be how this affects his confidence. (op 7-1)

2521 BETFAIR IPHONE & ANDROID APP HURDLE (9 hdls) 2m

1:50 (1:50) (Class 2) 4-Y-O **£25,048** (£7,400; £3,700; £1,852; £924)

Form				RPR
142-	**1**		**Carlito Brigante (IRE)**[8] 5399 4-11-6 140 JasonMaguire (Gordon Elliott, Ire) *chsd ldrs: wnt 2nd 5th: led 2 out: drvn out and styd on gamely run-in* **11/4**[2]	142+
04-0	**2**	2	**Bocamix (FR)**[30] 1931 4-10-12 114 FearghalDavis (Andrew Crook) *hld up: hdwy to chse ldrs 4 out: nt qckn appr last: styd on to take 2nd fnl 110yds: nt rch wnr* **66/1**	130
1-30	**3**	2 ¼	**Barizan (IRE)**[14] 2219 4-11-6 143 PaulMoloney (Evan Williams) *chsd ldr tl lost grnd 5th: rdn along whn bhd and outpcd after 4 out: styd on u.p run-in but nvr able to trble ldrs again* **5/1**[3]	137
-111	**4**	½	**Clerk's Choice (IRE)**[35] 1862 4-11-2 162 TomMolloy (Michael Banks) *hld up in rr: fiddled 4th: clsd 3 out: effrt whn chsd ldrs appr 2 out: failed to pick up bef last: kpt on run-in but n.d* **10/11**[1]	135
3-55	**5**	hd	**Ultimate**[14] 2219 4-10-12 133 DougieCostello (Brian Ellison) *led: rn wd on bnd after 3rd: hdd 2 out: stl cl 2nd whn mstke last: no ex fnl 110yds* **7/1**	130

3m 51.1s (-13.10) **Going Correction** -0.475s/f (Good) **5** Ran SP% **109.7**
Speed ratings: **113,112,110,110,110**
CSF £54.71 TOTE £3.50: £1.80, £5.20; EX 171.50.
Owner Gigginstown House Stud **Bred** Ballylinch Stud **Trained** Trim, Co Meath
■ Stewards' Enquiry : Paul Moloney three-day ban; excessive use of whip (5th-7th Dec)

FOCUS
An intriguing 4-y-o hurdle that was run at a good gallop, and the winner is rated to last season's best form.

NOTEBOOK
Carlito Brigante(IRE), one of last season's leading juveniles, emerged triumphant. Although only fourth when favourite for the Triumph, he was still a three-time winner last season, and had recently finished second at Dundalk, so was clearly fit and ready to run. A horse who likes good ground, he'd have preferred it a bit quicker, but stayed on well having taken over at the second last. Given a 50-1 quote for the Champion Hurdle by William Hill on the back of this, he isn't good enough, but may be capable of featuring in decent handicaps. (op 3-1, tchd 10-3 in a place)
Bocamix(FR) had run poorly in a handicap on his reappearance at Carlisle, and surprised many with his bold showing, staying on right the way to the line for second. Considering the small field, there's a chance he was flattered, but then again the pace was generous enough, so we'll learn more about his capabilities next time. (op 40-1)
Barizan(IRE) had disappointed on both runs this season and, although staying on again for third in the manner of a horse crying out for further, he remains well below his best juvenile form, which included a second-place finish in the Triumph and victory in a Grade 1 at Punchestown. (op 13-2)
Clerk's Choice(IRE), kept low-key last season, impressed with the way he travelled and quickened when winning on his reappearance at Cheltenham, miles clear of Barizan, but there was little response when he was asked for an effort this time, and in the end he just stayed on at the one pace. It's possible the slower ground was against him, but he has won on good to soft, so has a few questions to answer now. Official explanation: trainer said gelding was unsuited by going. (op 4-5 tchd Evens and 8-11 in a place)
Ultimate, behind a couple of these in the Cheltenham race, ran better when fifth in the Elite Hurdle last time, but he was responsible for setting the pace here, and that eventually took its toll, as he lost three places on the run-in. (op 9-1, tchd 11-1 in a place)

2522 BETFAIR.COM/PAULNICHOLLS H'CAP CHASE (18 fncs) 3m

2:20 (2:20) (Class 2) (0-145,138) 4-Y-O+

£18,786 (£5,550; £2,775; £1,389; £693; £348)

Form				RPR
11-1	**1**		**King Fontaine (IRE)**[16] 2163 7-11-1 **127** GrahamLee (Malcolm Jefferson) *mstkes: hld up in rr: blnd 8th: wnt 2nd 4 out: led appr 3 out: clr 2 out: unchal after* **7/2**[2]	146+
32-0	**2**	11	**Dance Island (IRE)**[27] 1986 7-11-11 **137** CharliePoste (Ben Case) *in tch: effrt appr 3 out: wnt 2nd bef 2 out where j.lft: nvr a threat to wnr* **14/1**	137
114-	**3**	3 ½	**Wogan**[224] 5126 10-11-10 **136** AndrewTinkler (Nicky Henderson) *prom: rdn appr 4 out: sn btn: plugged on at one pce but n.d after* **9/2**[3]	136
U4-1	**4**	14	**Etxalar (FR)**[20] 2106 7-11-2 **128** CampbellGillies (Lucinda Russell) *nt fluent: in tch early: bhd after 3rd: struggling fr 10th: dropped away after 14th* **8/1**	120
02-6	**5**	24	**Rory Boy (USA)**[35] 1861 5-11-5 **131** PaddyBrennan (Nigel Twiston-Davies) *handy: lost pl 9th: rdn bef 10th: toiling after: t.o* **9/1**	94
1P1/	**6**	½	**Nevada Royale (FR)**[739] 2130 9-11-12 **138** (t) AidanColeman (Tim Pitt) *led: rdn and hdd appr 3 out: wknd 2 out: dismntd after line* **14/1**	100
20F-	**F**		**Palypso De Creek (FR)**[224] 5127 7-11-10 **136** RichardJohnson (Charlie Longsdon) *trckd ldrs tl fell 7th* **5/2**[1]	—
0-00	**P**		**Carrickmines (IRE)**[14] 2221 8-10-8 **120** AndrewGlassonbury (Dr Richard Newland) *hld up: blnd 6th: hdwy to trck ldrs 9th: lost pl bef 12th: bhd whn p.u bef 13th* **12/1**	—

6m 23.6s (9.60) **Going Correction** +0.35s/f (Yiel) **8** Ran SP% **111.1**
Speed ratings (Par 109): **98,94,93,88,80 80,—,—**
toteswingers:1&2 £11.10, 2&3 £5.90, 1&3 £1.80 CSF £44.22 CT £214.45 TOTE £3.60: £1.10, £3.70, £2.70; EX 45.00 Trifecta £190.40 Pool: £787.67 - 3.06 winning units..
Owner Trevor Hemmings **Bred** Peter McCarthy **Trained** Norton, N Yorks
■ Stewards' Enquiry : Charlie Poste caution; excessive use of whip.

FOCUS
A good staying handicap chase won well in the end by progressive 7-y-o King Fontaine. The winner is value for further and the form is rated around the principals.

NOTEBOOK
King Fontaine(IRE) overcame numerous mistakes to have the race in the bag soon after three out. Completing a hat-trick when winning narrowly off 5lb lower at the course on his reappearance, he made notable blunders at the eighth and ninth fences, so it says a lot for him that he was able to come back on the bridle before readily drawing clear. He'll be aimed towards the Grand National one day, but it won't be this season, with perhaps the Scottish version being a sensible long-term target. (tchd 4-1 in places)
Dance Island(IRE), well held over hurdles at Aintree on his reappearance, did well as a novice chaser last term and he ran well enough to suggest he'll continue to be competitive in decent staying handicap chases. (op 12-1)
Wogan, progressive last season, was beaten after the last down the back, but did plug on and should come on appreciably for the run. (op 4-1, tchd 5-1 in a place)
Etxalar(FR), up 7lb for his Carlisle win, made mistakes and couldn't get involved. (tchd 7-1)
Nevada Royale(FR) shaped encouragingly on this first start in 739 days. He really seemed to enjoy it out in front, and briefly appeared to have his rivals in trouble, but started to get very tired from three out and he did well to jump the last, having looked legless approaching it. He was dismounted after the line, but hopefully that was because he was tired, and not injured. (op 12-1)
Palypso De Creek(FR) departed before the race got going. (op 4-1)
Carrickmines(IRE) Official explanation: jockey said gelding was never travelling or jumping. (op 4-1)

2523 40% BETTER OFF ON BETFAIR SP "FIXED BRUSH" H'CAP HURDLE (LISTED RACE) (12 hdls) 3m

2:50 (2:50) (Class 1) 4-Y-O+

£42,757 (£16,042; £8,032; £4,005; £2,010; £1,005)

Form				RPR
12-1	**1**		**Grands Crus (FR)**[6] 2387 5-10-10 **132** 6ex (t) TomScudamore (David Pipe) *hld up: hdwy 5th: led gng wl after 4 out: nt fluent 3 out: coasted clr fr 2 out: v easily* **6/4**[1]	160+
10-2	**2**	10	**Barafundle (IRE)**[196] 206 6-10-8 **130** AlanO'Keeffe (Jennie Candlish) *racd keenly: in tch: wnt 2nd 8th: rdn 3 out: no ch w wnr fr 2 out* **16/1**	143+
114-	**3**	14	**Peveril**[246] 4715 6-11-4 **140** AndrewTinkler (Nicky Henderson) *midfield: hdwy after 6th: chsd ldrs 4 out: lost tch w front pair fr 3 out* **15/2**[3]	137
0F-0	**4**	2 ¾	**Ballyfitz**[7] 2358 10-11-12 **148** DavidEngland (Nigel Twiston-Davies) *midfield: pushed along after 4th: styd on fr 2 out: nvr able to get competitive* **40/1**	142
1-04	**5**	3	**Hills Of Aran**[28] 1967 8-11-11 **147** RhysFlint (Keith Goldsworthy) *prom: lost pl 5th: sn struggling: styd on fr 2 out: nvr able to trble ldrs* **33/1**	138
PP-1	**6**	nk	**The Shy Man (IRE)**[27] 1986 7-10-7 **129** BarryKeniry (George Moore) *bhd: hdwy 4 out: plugged on wout troubling ldrs* **20/1**	120
215-	**7**	¾	**Red Harbour (IRE)**[217] 5224 6-10-3 **130** MrRMahon(5) (Paul Nicholls) *midfield: tk clsr order 5th: sn trckd ldrs: rdn and btn after 4 out* **16/1**	121
06-1	**8**	7	**Captain Americo (IRE)**[14] 2205 8-10-13 **135** NickScholfield (James Ewart) *hld up: rdn after 4 out: nvr able to get on terms* **22/1**	119
F401	**9**	7	**Thelobstercatcher**[17] 2147 6-10-0 **125** (p) DonalDevereux(3) (Peter Bowen) *hld up: struggling after 6th: nvr on terms* **18/1**	102
54-1	**10**	1	**Fruity O'Rooney**[31] 1917 7-10-10 **132** (p) AndrewGlassonbury (Gary Moore) *led to 1st: remained prom: led 8th: hdd after 4 out: rdn and wknd appr 3 out* **25/1**	108
50-4	**11**	2 ½	**According To Pete**[22] 2077 9-10-10 **132** GrahamLee (Malcolm Jefferson) *trckd ldrs: rdn after 4 out: wknd appr 3 out* **12/1**	106
0P23	**12**	1 ½	**Backbord (GER)**[7] 2360 8-10-8 **130** (t) DougieCostello (Lucy Wadham) *a bhd and nvr gng wl* **33/1**	105
423-	**13**	37	**James De Vassy (FR)**[248] 4674 5-11-8 **144** DarylJacob (Nick Williams) *in tch: effrt after 4 out: wknd appr 3 out* **7/1**[2]	83
-1P5	**14**	29	**Auroras Encore (IRE)**[6] 2399 8-10-13 **135** TjadeCollier (Sue Smith) *midfield: rdn appr 6th: struggling 8th: n.d after* **50/1**	48
15F-	**15**	34	**Khachaturian (IRE)**[225] 5109 7-10-13 **135** JasonMaguire (Donald McCain) *led 1st: hdd 8th: rdn and wknd after 4 out* **28/1**	18
11-0	**16**	12	**Chester Lad**[36] 1855 5-10-5 **127** JanFaltejsek (George Charlton) *midfield: wknd 7th: n.d whn mstke 8th* **66/1**	—

20-3 **P** **Tasheba**[19] 2125 5-11-7 148 DavidBass(5) —
(Nicky Henderson) *hld up: struggling after 7th: t.o whn p.u bef 3 out* **28/1**
5P-5 **P** **Lord Generous**[28] 1964 6-10-13 135 (b[1]) PaddyBrennan —
(Nigel Twiston-Davies) *in tch: wkng whn mstke 8th: t.o whn p.u bef 3 out* **33/1**

5m 41.7s (-18.30) **Going Correction** -0.475s/f (Good) 18 Ran SP% **123.6**
Speed ratings (Par 111): **111,107,103,102,101 100,100,98,96,95 94,94,82,72,61 57,—,—**
toteswingers:1&2 £14.30, 2&3 £40.90, 1&3 £5.10 CSF £22.29 CT £153.50 TOTE £2.20: £1.10, £4.40, £2.30, £8.50; EX 33.50 Trifecta £315.20 Pool : £23781.37 - 55.82.
Owner Roger Stanley & Yvonne Reynolds III **Bred** Jean-Marie Prost Alamartine **Trained** Nicholashayne, Devon

FOCUS
This was nowhere near as competitive as the field size suggested it was, the apparent handicap 'good thing' Grands Crus destroying his rivals. The race could rate higher and the winner is rated as having stepped up again, while the third, rated to last season's Warwick form, is the best guide.

NOTEBOOK
Grands Crus(FR) destroyed his rivals under a penalty picked up for winning with ease at Cheltenham the previous weekend. Always travelling powerfully around the inner, he came to almost dispute it taking the last down the back and quickly drew clear from the second last. The handicapper is going to ensure he find things a lot tougher in future, but the 5-y-o is clearly progressing fast and saw this new, longer trip out really well. It will be fascinating to see where he goes next. (op 15-8 tchd 11-8)
Barafundle(IRE), off since finishing second in a similarly good staying handicap over C&D in May, is still lightly raced and he appeared to take another step forward, considering he was on the pace throughout. He's a fine prospect for fences. (op 20-1)
Peveril, a useful novice last season who finished fourth in the Martin Pipe, would probably have found this ground a bit tacky, but he did stay on and is another who rates a bright chasing prospect. Interestingly connections ran Burton Port in this last year before going chasing. (op 7-1 tchd 8-1)
Ballyfitz, well held over fences at Cheltenham the previous weekend, was under pressure a long way out, but did plug on. (op 33-1)
Hills Of Aran would probably have been fourth but for losing his position earlier in the race.
The Shy Man(IRE), an easy winner off 11lb lower at Aintree on his reappearance, was probably ridden too far out of his ground, staying on when the race was all over. It would be no surprise to see him return to fences at some stage.
Red Harbour(IRE) was soon beaten once coming under pressure, and will now go chasing. (op 20-1)
Fruity O'Rooney slowly faded having been up there throughout.
James De Vassy(FR) still appeared to be going well enough towards the end of the back, so it was disappointing to see him stop the way he did. He wasn't given a hard time, though, and deserves a chance to improve. (op 6-1)

2524 BETFAIR CHASE (REGISTERED AS THE LANCASHIRE CHASE) GRADE 1 (18 fncs) 3m
3:25 (3:26) (Class 1) 5-Y-O+
£112,660 (£42,440; £21,240; £10,620; £5,320; £2,660)

Form RPR
51U- **1** **Imperial Commander (IRE)**[226] 5095 9-11-7 185 PaddyBrennan 174+
(Nigel Twiston-Davies) *a.p: wnt 2nd 8th: led 10th: styd on wl fr 4 out: over 5l clr last: kpt up to work: a looked in full control run-in* **10/11[1]**
04-3 **2** *1 1/4* **Tidal Bay (IRE)**[21] 2090 9-11-7 0 BrianHughes 172+
(Howard Johnson) *hld up in last pl: nt fluent 14th: sn rdn: clsd fr 2 out: wnt 2nd last: styd on run-in: clsd on wnr towards fin but nvr gng to get there: flattered* **16/1**
F01- **3** *8* **Planet Of Sound**[213] 5322 8-11-7 163 (t) RichardJohnson 164
(Philip Hobbs) *hld up in tch: hdwy to trck ldrs 14th: rdn and nt qckn 2 out: one pce run-in* **17/2**
23-1 **4** *2 1/4* **Nacarat (FR)**[21] 2091 9-11-7 158 PaulMoloney 162
(Tom George) *chsd ldr fr 1st: wnt 2nd 10th: rdn and no imp between last 2: lost 2nd last: sn wknd* **7/1[3]**
211- **5** *2 3/4* **What A Friend**[226] 5095 7-11-7 159 SamThomas 159
(Paul Nicholls) *hld up: hdwy 10th: nt fluent 11th: rdn whn chsng ldrs 4 out: wknd 3 out* **3/1[2]**
PP-F **6** *50* **Atouchbetweenacara (IRE)**[10] 2304 9-11-7 137 AidanColeman 113
(Venetia Williams) *led: hdd 10th: struggling 14th: wl btn bef 4 out: t.o* **80/1**
011- **7** *27* **Chief Dan George (IRE)**[249] 4659 10-11-7 148 PaddyAspell 89
(James Moffatt) *chsd ldr to 1st: remained in tch: j. slowly 3rd: struggling 12th: lost tch after 14th: t.o* **33/1**

6m 11.2s (-2.80) **Going Correction** +0.35s/f (Yiel) 7 Ran SP% **110.5**
Speed ratings: **118,117,114,114,113 96,87**
toteswingers:1&2 £5.50, 2&3 £4.90, 1&3 £2.20 CSF £14.90 TOTE £1.90: £1.60, £3.70; EX 15.00.
Owner Our Friends In The North **Bred** Laurence J Flynn **Trained** Naunton, Gloucs

FOCUS
The rail had been taken in specifically for this contest, which opened up fresh ground. No Kauto Star for the first time since 2005, Nicholls instead being represented by What A Friend, but it again featured Imperial Commander, this time as a Gold Cup winner. The race was expected to develop into a duel between the pair, but it didn't work out that way. The winner is rated below his figure in this race last season while the third is close to form.

NOTEBOOK
Imperial Commander(IRE) began to turn the screw midway down the back and had the race under control from three out, staying on well, despite appearing to idle and becoming a little weary close home, always looking to be holding on from the fast-finishing Tidal Bay. Denied by a whisker in the race a year ago, when losing out in a titanic battle with Kauto Star, his trainer admitted he may not have been as straight as he had thought, and that the ground was certainly tackier than he had expected. So it's reasonable to think there'll be a fair amount of improvement on this, which would indicate a better showing than he has was able to give in the King George a year ago, when a well-beaten fifth. His participation there was later in doubt as he suffered a cut leg in the race, which will require him to have a week's box rest. After the Christmas showpiece if he recovers in time, it will be back to Cheltenham for the defence of his crown (general 4-1 shot), and he looks sure to take the beating again at a course he adores. (tchd 5-6 and 1-1 in places)
Tidal Bay(IRE), well held in third behind Fair Along over hurdles on his reappearance, has the talent to go well in these big races if everything falls into place and he was given time to get into a rhythm by Hughes. He still had plenty of running to do coming to the second last, but really started to stay on strongly and he'd probably have won in another 100 yards, although there's a chance Imperial Commander may have appreciated the company and gone again. He's going to remain difficult to win with, but this run shows he should never be discounted and the Gold Cup is his aim. (op 22-1)
Planet Of Sound, who ended last season with a win in the Grade 1 Punchestown Gold Cup, his first try at 3m-plus, made a promising reappearance. Good ground is key to the horse, so it was no surprise to see him struggle to quicken out of this tacky surface, but he had earlier impressed with the way he travelled, and did enough to suggest his Punchestown victory wasn't a fluke. He'll also head to Kempton for the King George - a course he's likely to give the winner more of a race at - and he could easily surprise a few there. (op 8-1 tchd 9-1)
Nacarat(FR), hard-fought winner of the Charlie Hall on his reappearance (a race that can leave its mark on horses), avoided getting into an early duel for the lead, but he was readily dropped by the winner and finished quite tired. (op 15-2)
What A Friend, a dual Grade 1 winner last season who recorded a career-best when winning the Totesport Bowl on his final outing, had great things expected of him this season after a breathing operation, with many believing he would take over from Kauto Star and Denman as the leading staying chaser in the yard. He was certainly fit, but it became apparent from the mid-way down the back he wasn't travelling as well as he can, and his response to pressure was a limited once in the straight. He didn't look to be enjoying the tacky ground, something which Nicholls later confirmed, but for all that he deserves another chance, he's left with a bit to prove now. (tchd 7-2 in places)
Atouchbetweenacara(IRE) had his brief moment of glory out in front.
Chief Dan George(IRE) had plenty to find at the weights, but it was disappointing to see him run so poorly on this seasonal return.

2525 TIMEFORM BETFAIR RACING CLUB STANDARD OPEN NATIONAL HUNT FLAT RACE 2m
3:55 (3:55) (Class 3) 4-6-Y-O
£4,553 (£1,337; £668; £333)

Form RPR
2 **1** **Charminster (IRE)**[27] 1989 4-11-0 0 JasonMaguire 109+
(Donald McCain) *hld up in last pl: hdwy gng wl over 3f out: led over 1f out: rdn clr ins fnl f: r.o wl* **15/8[2]**
1 **2** *6* **Herdsman (IRE)**[27] 1989 5-11-7 0 RichardJohnson 110+
(Philip Hobbs) *in tch: pushed along and outpcd 5f out: effrt to chse ldrs 3f out: rdn whn chalng 2f out: nt qckn over 1f out: wnt 2nd ins fnl f: no ch w wnr* **8/11[1]**
5/1- **3** *4 1/2* **Flaygray**[422] 1526 6-11-2 0 AlexanderVoy(5) 104
(Chris Grant) *prom: led over 3f out: rdn and hdd over 1f out: wknd ins fnl f* **20/1**
502- **4** *2 3/4* **Forcefield**[211] 5376 4-10-7 0 MissLAlexander(7) 93
(N W Alexander) *prom: effrt to chal over 2f out: wknd jst over 1f out* **50/1**
5 *17* **Mr One Too (IRE)** 5-11-0 0 DarylJacob 76
(Keith Goldsworthy) *in tch: niggled along 5f out: wknd 3f out* **11/1[3]**
0 **6** *6* **A Patchy Dancer (IRE)**[22] 2074 5-10-9 0 ShaneByrne(5) 70
(Sue Smith) *led: rdn 4f out: hdd over 3f out: sn wknd* **25/1**

3m 51.5s (-7.10) **Going Correction** -0.475s/f (Good)
WFA 4 from 5yo+ 7lb 6 Ran SP% **111.6**
Speed ratings: **98,95,92,91,82 79**
toteswingers:1&2 £1.02, 2&3 £4.60, 1&3 £10.30 CSF £3.49 TOTE £2.90: £1.50, £1.20; EX 2.80.
Owner Tony Meehan **Bred** Raymond Cahalane **Trained** Cholmondeley, Cheshire

FOCUS
This was a straight match but the first two are rated below their Aintree form and the third and fourth set the level.

NOTEBOOK
Charminster(IRE), behind Herdsman at Aintree, had a 7lb pull at the weights and came out on top this time, quickening much the best of the steady gallop and winning in the style of a potentially smart sort. Interestingly, his yard won the race with Poddlore Cross a year ago, and while there's no suggesting he's going to be half as good, his trainer does seem excited about him as a hurdles prospect, and who could blame him. (op 7-4 tchd 13-8)
Herdsman(IRE), highly regarded by Philip Hobbs, got the job done in a professional fashion on his debut at Aintree, when the race turned into a proper test, but this time it developed into more of a sprint and he was found wanting by his old rival. That doesn't tell the whole story, as he was denied a clear run early in the straight when looking to build up momentum, but it didn't affect the result, and he'll presumably go hurdling now, with a stiffer test of stamina expected to suit. (op 10-11, tchd 1-1 in a place)
Flaygray, the only other previous winner, looked vulnerable on this return from 422 days off, but he shaped quite well and is another expected to be suited by further over hurdles. (op 16-1)
Forcefield has shown enough in bumpers to suggest he'll be winning races as a hurdler. (tchd 40-1)
T/Plt: £161.30 to a £1 stake. Pool £90,177.81 - 408.05 winning tickets. T/Qpdt: £25.30 to a £1 stake. Pool of £7,906.67 - 230.85 winning tickets. DO

2310 HUNTINGDON (R-H)
Saturday, November 20

OFFICIAL GOING: Good to soft (hdl 6.8; chs 6.2)
Wind: Nil Weather: Murky, chilly

2526 TOTEPLACEPOT E B F MARES' "NATIONAL HUNT" NOVICES' HURDLE (10 hdls) 2m 4f 110y
12:30 (12:33) (Class 3) 4-Y-O+
£5,204 (£1,528; £764; £381)

Form RPR
20-2 **1** **Risaala**[16] 2168 4-10-3 0 MissGAndrews(7) 119+
(Pam Sly) *t.k.h: hld up in rr: rapid hdwy 7th: sn chsng ldr: upsides and hit next: led gng strly bef 2 out: hit 2 out: stl hrd hld whn j.rt last: readily drew clr flat: v easily* **6/4[1]**
6-1 **2** *4 1/2* **Midnight Macarena**[171] 589 5-10-10 0 LeightonAspell 106
(Lucy Wadham) *in tch: mstke 6th: rdn to chse ldng pair after 3 out: drvn to press wnr 2 out tl last: readily brushed aside flat* **9/2[3]**
422- **3** *4* **Good Faloue (FR)**[235] 4933 5-10-7 107 AlexMerriam(3) 103+
(Neil King) *ld: clr 6th: carried rt and hmpd by loose horse next: jnd and rdn 3 out: hdd bef next: wknd between last 2* **3/1[2]**
4-50 **4** *1 1/4* **Genny Wren**[31] 1921 4-10-10 0 JimmyMcCarthy 103+
(Renee Robeson) *pressed ldr tl 6th: mstke 3rd: rdn and btn bef 2 out: mstke 2 out: wl hld whn edgd lft between last 2* **50/1**
6-34 **5** *2 1/2* **Natural Spring**[21] 2087 5-10-10 0 ColinBolger 101
(Suzy Smith) *nt fluent: in tch: chsd ldng pair 3rd: rdn and struggling bef 3 out: wknd bef 2 out: wl hld whn hung rt between last 2* **5/1**
4-4 **6** *24* **Cloudy Wager**[195] 222 5-10-10 0 AndrewThornton 76
(Diana Grissell) *chsd ldng pair tl 3rd: in tch after tl wknd qckly 3 out* **40/1**
0-P4 **7** *82* **Cherokee Story**[27] 1994 4-10-10 0 (b) TomMessenger 3
(Chris Bealby) *in tch in rr: rdn and rapidly lost tch sn after 6th: wl t.o fr 3 out* **80/1**
4-3 **U** **Lady Jannina**[195] 230 4-10-10 0 DominicElsworth —
(Henry Daly) *uns rdr 1st* **14/1**

4m 52.5s (-6.50) **Going Correction** -0.125s/f (Good)
WFA 4 from 5yo 8lb 8 Ran SP% **112.1**
Speed ratings (Par 107): **107,105,103,103,102 93,61,—**
toteswingers: 1&2 £1.10, 1&3 £1.10, 2&3 £1.10 CSF £8.46 TOTE £2.10: £1.02, £2.60, £1.30; EX 11.10.
Owner David L Bayliss **Bred** Shadwell Estate Co Ltd **Trained** Thorney, Cambs

FOCUS
This weak mares' novices' hurdle was run at a sound pace but the casualty at the first caused a few problems when running loose. The winner was improved for the longer trip, and the second and fourth to their bumper marks set the standard.

NOTEBOOK
Risaala was all the rage after her good effort when runner-up over 2m at Towcester on her first try over hurdles. Dropped in, her jumping was not error-free over the final four flights but, after taking charge, she was in total command on the run-in. (op 11-4 tchd 11-8)

Midnight Macarena, absent since taking a Fontwell bumper in June, kept on at the same pace under hard driving and will appreciate a stiffer test. (op 3-1 tchd 5-1)
Good Faloue(FR), having her fifth start over hurdles and rated 107, set the pace but was badly impeded by the loose horse four out. She just stays but lacks a finishing kick and she is the guide to the value of the overall form. (tchd 11-4 and 7-2)
Genny Wren, having her second start over hurdles, is another who looks on the slow side. (op 40-1)
Natural Spring, placed twice in four starts in bumper races, was let down by her jumping on her first try over hurdles. (tchd 11-2)

2527 BET TOTEPOOL ON ALL UK RACING NOVICES' CHASE (16 fncs) 2m 4f 110y
1:05 (1:06) (Class 3) 4-Y-O+ **£5,529** (£1,623; £811; £405)

Form				RPR
4-14	1		**Golan Way**19 2126 6-11-7 142 JamieGoldstein (Sheena West) *w ldr tl ld after 5th: mde rest: jnd 13th: kpt finding ex after: rdn and asserted after last: in command fnl 100yds* **10/11**1	146+
24-2	2	2 1/4	**Pearlysteps**10 2303 7-11-1 0 LeightonAspell (Henry Daly) *chsd ldrs: mstke 5th: hdwy to chse ldr 11th: ev ch fr 13th: rdn between last 2: no ex and btn after last* **4/1**2	136
00-2	3	1/2	**Balzaccio (FR)**23 2046 5-10-12 0 CharlieHuxley(3) (Alan King) *hld up in last pair: hdwy 8th: chsd ldng pair 11th: mstke 13th: rdn wl bef 2 out: styd on same pce fr 2 out: n.m.r towards fin* **11/2**	136
-612	4	25	**Frontier Dancer (IRE)**36 1854 6-11-4 0 SamTwiston-Davies(3) (Nigel Twiston-Davies) *in tch in rr: mstke 6th: clsd after 9th: mstke 13th and rdn: drvn after 3 out: wknd 2 out* **5/1**3	122+
0/	5	69	**Quinola Des Obeaux (FR)**350 2722 6-11-1 0 (t) DavidDennis (Frank Sheridan) *racd freely: led tl after 5th: chsd ldr tl 11th: dropped to rr after next: t.o bef 3 out* **22/1**	50
60-5	U		**Island Jim (IRE)**23 2058 6-11-1 105 FelixDeGiles (Charlie Longsdon) *blnd v bdly and eventually uns rdr 1st* **50/1**	—

5m 3.30s (-2.00) **Going Correction** +0.35s/f (Yiel) **6** Ran SP% **110.7**
Speed ratings (Par 107): **117,116,115,106,80** —
toteswingers: 1&2 £1.20, 1&3 £1.10, 2&3 £2.90 CSF £5.03 TOTE £2.30: £1.40, £2.00; EX 4.70.
Owner W R B Racing 58 **Bred** Lewis Caterers **Trained** Falmer, E Sussex

FOCUS
A good-class novices' chase run at a sound pace with the first four bang in contention rounding the home turn. The form looks solid with the winner to his best and the fourth to previous chase form.

NOTEBOOK
Golan Way ◆, a 147-rated hurdler, had won on his debut over fences at Ludlow last month before a highly creditable fourth in a better race at Kempton. Never leaving the inside, he won the battle for the lead and stepped up the gallop setting out on to the final circuit. He stuck on strongly to forge clear on the run-in and should continue to give a good account of himself, especially if faced with a stiffer test. (op 11-10 tchd 6-5)
Pearlysteps ◆, rated 127 over hurdles, had chased home smart prospect Wymott at Bangor on his first try over fences. He landed upsides two out but couldn't match the winner for foot on the run-in. He looks sure to go one better. (tchd 7-2)
Balzaccio(FR) ◆, rated 127 over hurdles, had finished second beaten a neck on his debut over fences at Fontwell. Tapped for toe two out, he stuck on in willing fashion on the run-in and looks a ready-made winner of a similar event. (op 9-2 tchd 4-1)
Frontier Dancer(IRE), a 130-rated hurdler, had won at Perth and finished runner-up at Cheltenham on his two previous tries over fences but he was in trouble going to two out, and in the end finished well beaten. This was too bad to be true. (op 6-1)
Quinola Des Obeaux(FR), absent since pulling up a year ago, was having his first start here and his first for this yard. Kept wide he raced very freely and was on the retreat at the first fence on the final circuit. A dual bumper winner and with a novice hurdle to his credit, he has a lot to prove now. (tchd 20-1)

2528 TOTESWINGER FLEXI BETTING JUVENILE HURDLE (8 hdls) 2m 110y
1:40 (1:40) (Class 4) 3-Y-O **£2,602** (£764; £382; £190)

Form				RPR
3	1		**Jolly Roger (IRE)**17 2151 3-10-12 0 WillKennedy (John Flint) *in tch: hdwy to chse ldr gng wl 3 out: led next: kpt on wl flat: rdn out* **11/4**1	103+
51	2	3/4	**Akula (IRE)**45 1728 3-11-5 0 ColinBolger (Mark H Tompkins) *led: rdn and hdd whn hit 2 out: stl ev ch last: unable qck u.p flat* **3/1**2	109+
	3	7	**Anaya**24 3-10-2 0 SamTwiston-Davies(3) (David Bourton) *t.k.h: hld up in rr: hdwy bef 5th: chsd ldng pair bef 2 out: styd on same pce after* **28/1**	88
50	4	12	**Jinksy Minx**14 2211 3-9-12 0 MrTJCannon(7) (Suzy Smith) *in rr: struggling 4th: styd on after 5th: no threat to ldrs but kpt on steadily fr 3 out to go 4th nr fin* **40/1**	77
	5	1/2	**Viviani (IRE)**34 3-10-12 0 (t) LeightonAspell (Amanda Perrett) *chsd ldrs: wnt 2nd after 5th tl blnd next: wknd u.p bef 2 out* **10/3**3	85
	6	29	**Dream Spinner**59 3-10-7 0 IanPopham(5) (Dr Richard Newland) *chsd ldrs tl wknd u.p bef 3 out: t.o bef 2 out* **9/1**	58
44	7	11	**Il Portico**23 2047 3-10-12 102 JamieMoore (Gary Moore) *hld up in rr: mstke 1st: rdn and no prog 4th: t.o fr 3 out* **8/1**	60
53	8	3 1/4	**Royal Etiquette (IRE)**37 1845 3-10-12 0 TomMessenger (Lawney Hill) *t.k.h: hld up in midfield: rdn and struggling bef 5th: wl btn whn hmpd 3 out: t.o bef 2 out* **28/1**	45
	9	8	**Flyinflyout**121 3-10-5 0 JamieGoldstein (Sheena West) *t.k.h: chsd ldrs tl wknd qckly after 5th: t.o* **16/1**	31
P	10	54	**Polebrook**13 2245 3-10-9 0 RichieMcLernon(3) (J R Jenkins) *racd in midfield: mstke 1st: mstke 4th: sn struggling and rdn: j. slowly 5th: t.o fr 3 out* **100/1**	—
	P		**Mororless**68 3-10-0 0 ow2 MrHGMiller(7) (Zoe Davison) *hld up in rr: sme hdwy after 3rd: struggling next: t.o whn blnd 3 out and immediately p.u* **100/1**	—
34	F		**Groove Master**24 2033 3-10-9 0 (b) CharlieHuxley(3) (Alan King) *chsd ldr tl after 5th: dived 2nd: 6th and fading whn fell 3 out* **16/1**	—

3m 52.4s (-2.50) **Going Correction** -0.125s/f (Good) **12** Ran SP% **118.9**
Speed ratings (Par 104): **100,99,96,90,90 76,71,70,66,40** —,—
toteswingers: 1&2 £2.10, 1&3 £18.90, 2&3 £10.90 CSF £11.10 TOTE £3.70: £1.10, £2.20, £8.50; EX 12.90.
Owner Jason Tucker **Bred** Paget Bloodstock **Trained** Kenfig Hill, Bridgend

FOCUS
An uncompetitive early season juvenile hurdle lacking any strength in depth and with just two in it over the final two flights. That pair are on the upgrade but the fourth is probably the best guide to the level of the form.

NOTEBOOK
Jolly Roger(IRE), snapped up after taking a seller on the Flat at Redcar in October and rated 75 in that sphere, had finished third on his hurdling debut at Warwick. He looked likely to score with something in hand when jumping ahead two out but in the end he had to dig deep. He will struggle to defy a penalty. (tchd 3-1)
Akula(IRE), rated just 58 on the level, is already a better hurdler. Penalised for his Ludlow success, he was keen in front yet battled back hard when headed, and in the end was only just denied. (op 5-2)
Anaya, rated just 52 on the Flat and with her third trainer, stayed on from way off the pace to capture a never dangerous third spot. Like those who followed her home, she may have to go down to claimers or sellers if she is to get off the mark. (op 25-1)
Jinksy Minx, rated only 40 on the Flat, appeared late on the scene on her third try over hurdles.
Viviani(IRE), a 63-rated maiden on the Flat, was well backed on his debut over hurdles but he back-pedalled going to two out and looked a tired horse in the end. (op 7-1)
Il Portico looked very moody and is one to have severe reservations about. (op 6-1)

2529 TOTEEXACTA FLEXI BETTING H'CAP CHASE (16 fncs) 2m 4f 110y
2:15 (2:15) (Class 4) (0-115,113) 4-Y-O+ **£3,903** (£1,146; £573; £286)

Form				RPR
0/02	1		**Mud Monkey**13 2243 6-10-13 105 (t) IanPopham(5) (Claire Dyson) *mde all and mostly j.w: clr after 3 out: styd on wl* **9/2**3	127+
06-3	2	21	**Psi (USA)**23 2046 5-11-9 110 (p) JamieMoore (Gary Moore) *hld up towards rr: mstke 5th: j.lft next: hdwy 9th: chsd ldrs and mstke 13th: drvn bef next: chsd clr wnr sn after 2 out: no imp* **11/1**	114
11-0	3	6	**Bennynthejets (IRE)**27 1991 8-11-4 105 TomMessenger (Chris Bealby) *chsd wnr: mstke 3rd: drvn and outpcd 3 out: wl hld whn hit next: lost 2nd bef last* **10/1**	106+
6534	4	3 1/4	**Porters War (IRE)**10 2312 8-11-7 108 JimmyMcCarthy (Peter Hiatt) *hld up in tch on outer: chsd ldrs 12th: rdn and no prog sn after 3 out: wl btn next: j.lft last* **14/1**	103
12U-	5	1	**Noble Bily (FR)**211 5373 9-11-3 107 AlexMerriam(3) (Neil King) *t.k.h: chsd ldrs: hmpd 7th: rdn and struggling whn mstke 13th: wl btn after next* **20/1**	101
4643	6	1/2	**Kikos (FR)**28 1975 8-11-12 113 MarkBradburne (Renee Robeson) *chsd ldrs: mstke 12th: rdn and wknd after 3 out: wl btn next* **14/1**	107
2340	7	66	**Woodmore (IRE)**21 2081 6-11-9 110 FelixDeGiles (Charlie Longsdon) *last whn blnd bdly 1st: mstkes after and a in rr: hmpd 7th: lost tch 12th: wl t.o 3 out* **7/2**2	44
22-4	8	5	**Massini Sunset (IRE)**19 2134 10-10-7 99 GilesHawkins(5) (Richard Mitchell) *in tch: hmpd 7th: dropped towards rr 9th: lost tch 12th: wl t.o after 3 out* **20/1**	29
2-66	9	44	**Cockatoo (USA)**19 2124 7-11-1 105 (b) EamonDehdashti(3) (Gary Moore) *a towards rr and nt fluent: reminders after 5th: lost tch 12th: wl t.o 3 out* **40/1**	—
32-4	P		**Quick Fix (IRE)**200 130 8-11-4 105 TomSiddall (Susan Nock) *in tch in midfield: mstke 6th: struggling after 11th: wl bhd 3 out: t.o whn p.u next* **25/1**	—
01-5	F		**Quel Bruere (FR)**195 233 6-11-5 106 (t) JodieMogford (Graeme McPherson) *hld up towards rr: hdwy 9th: in tch in midfield whn fell next* **25/1**	—
6-12	F		**Red Rouble (IRE)**27 1991 5-11-6 110 SamTwiston-Davies(3) (Nigel Twiston-Davies) *chsd ldng pair tl fell 7th* **9/4**1	—

5m 10.1s (4.80) **Going Correction** +0.35s/f (Yiel) **12** Ran SP% **121.6**
Speed ratings (Par 105): **104,96,93,92,92 91,66,64,48,—** —,—
toteswingers: 1&2 £11.60, 1&3 £5.60, 2&3 £32.50 CSF £48.78 CT £481.79 TOTE £7.80: £2.20, £3.90, £2.10; EX 64.50.
Owner B & S Vaughan & Partner **Bred** Spencer Bloodstock **Trained** Cleeve Prior, Worcs

FOCUS
A modest handicap chase with plenty of carnage and just five still in contention three from home. The winner stepped up on his previous effort with the second setting the level.

NOTEBOOK
Mud Monkey, runner-up at Hereford on just his second start over fences and his second outing after a lengthy absence, defied a 5lb rise to give his rivals a jumping lesson from the front, pulling well clear from the second last. He is still unexposed over fences and should still be competitive even from his revised mark.
Psi(USA), who survived an early mistake on just his second start over fences, kept on to take a modest second spot at the second last-fence. He has yet to win a race after 11 starts now. (op 9-1 tchd 12-1)
Bennynthejets(IRE), who took this a year ago from a 2lb lower mark, did not reappear. Having just his second start this time, he kept tabs on the winner but was left for dead in the home straight. He might still have needed it. (tchd 9-1)
Porters War(IRE), who took the bypass route, was having just his third start for this stable and a return to fences. He has defied a 5lb higher mark in the past and might be on the way back. (op 16-1)
Noble Bily(FR), having his first outing this time, stayed on in his own time from way off the pace as befits a previous winner of the near 4m Kent National. (op 16-1)
Kikos(FR), who is slipping down the ratings, has shown his best form on much quicker ground. (op 11-1)
Massini Sunset(IRE) Official explanation: jockey said gelding was hampered by a faller.
Red Rouble(IRE), unexposed and having just his second start over fences, was quite keen and departed at the final fence with a circuit to go. (op 3-1 tchd 10-3 in places)

2530 TOTETRIFECTA FLEXI BETTING H'CAP HURDLE (10 hdls) 2m 4f 110y
2:45 (2:45) (Class 3) (0-120,115) 4-Y-O+ **£4,878** (£1,432; £716; £357)

Form				RPR
4P-5	1		**I'Ve Been Framed (IRE)**10 2312 6-11-10 113 (p) MarkBradburne (Neil King) *chsd ldrs: wnt 2nd 5th: led bef next: mde rest: rdn bef 2 out: styd on wl flat: rdn out* **9/1**	119+
0PP-	2	2 1/2	**Laustra Bad (FR)**301 3612 7-11-2 110 (tp) CO'Farrell(5) (David Pipe) *chsd ldr: lft 2nd 3rd tl 5th: chsd wnr after 6th: drvn after 3 out: styd on same pce u.p flat* **5/1**1	114
05-3	3	3 3/4	**Prince Du Seuil (FR)**192 282 7-11-2 105 JimmyMcCarthy (Alan King) *t.k.h: hld up in tch in rr: hdwy after 6th: chsd ldng pair after 3 out: hit next: rdn and btn whn mstke last* **15/2**3	107+
4P03	4	6	**Tighe Caster**30 1937 11-10-11 107 MattGriffiths(7) (Graeme McPherson) *in tch towards rr on outer: hmpd 3rd: rdn and effrt after 7th: chsd ldrs after 3 out: no hdwy and wl btn whn j.rt 2 out: lft modest 4th and bdly hmpd last* **16/1**	105+
30-	5	10	**Rock 'N' Roller (FR)**203 4446 6-11-3 106 JamieMoore (Gary Moore) *in tch: chsd ldng pair 7th tl after next: wknd bef 2 out: lft modest 5th and bdly hmpd last* **40/1**	95+
6325	6	30	**Unleashed (IRE)**21 2081 5-11-2 108 (t) PeterToole(3) (Charlie Mann) *in tch in midfield on outer: rdn 3 out: sn wl btn: t.o last* **11/2**2	67
50P-	7	19	**Mr Valentino (IRE)**223 5147 5-11-0 103 TomMessenger (Lawney Hill) *chsd ldrs: hmpd 3rd: mstke next: rdn and wknd after 7th: t.o* **12/1**	45
600-	8	hd	**Yetholm (USA)**218 5213 5-11-12 115 (p) WillKennedy (John Flint) *chsd ldrs: bdly hmpd 3rd: in tch after tl wknd qckly 3 out: t.o* **10/1**	57

2050 **9** 13 **Englishtown (FR)**[16] 2161 10-10-10 **102**................(p) RichieMcLernon(3) 32
(Jonjo O'Neill) *chsd ldrs tl bdly hmpd and lost pl 3rd: bhd after 5th: lost tch after next: t.o fr 3 out* **33/1**

-324 **10** nk **Watch Out**[19] 889 6-10-6 **100**................(tp) IanPopham(5) 30
(Dai Burchell) *hld up in tch in last trio: hdwy after 5th: wknd 7th: t.o bef 2 out* **12/1**

2U/4 **11** 18 **Paquet Cadeau (FR)**[22] 2069 7-11-3 **106**................ LeightonAspell 20
(Henry Daly) *led tl after 5th: lost pl rapidly after next: t.o bef 3 out* **17/2**

3501 **F** **Petit Fleur**[91] 1335 8-10-8 **100**................ SamTwiston-Davies(3) 98
(Julian Smith) *hld up in tch in last trio: hdwy 6th: mstke 3 out: wnt 4th 2 out: no imp and hld whn fell last* **12/1**

42 **F** **See You Jack**[20] 2111 5-11-11 **114**................ AndrewThornton —
(Caroline Bailey) *chsd ldr tl fell 3rd* **8/1**

4m 52.6s (-6.40) **Going Correction** -0.125s/f (Good) **13** Ran SP% **118.9**
Speed ratings (Par 107): **107,106,104,102,98 87,79,79,74,74 67,—,—**
toteswingers: 1&2 £16.30, 1&3 £25.70, 2&3 £30.00 CSF £54.10 CT £361.80 TOTE £12.40: £3.70, £2.80, £2.20; EX 126.00 Trifecta £105.70 Part won. Pool: £142.89- 0.20 winning units..
Owner Mr & Mrs A Whyte P Edwards C Appleton **Bred** Mrs Patricia Kelly-Furey **Trained** Newmarket, Suffolk

FOCUS
A modest handicap hurdle run at a sound pace with just five still in contention starting the final turn. A slight personal best from the winner with the fourth the best guide to the form.

NOTEBOOK
I'Ve Been Framed(IRE) made the best of his way home early on the final circuit and stuck to his task in willing fashion. The cheekpieces rather than the usual blinkers seemed to do the trick and 3m should not be a problem. (op 12-1)
Laustra Bad(FR) ◆, bang out of form for a year and a half now and having been pulled up on his final two starts last season, has slipped to a very lenient mark. He made the winner dig deep and ought to be able to end his drought if reproducing this effort. (op 7-1)
Prince Du Seuil(FR), absent since May, has not tasted success since March 2008. He moved up travelling nicely and, though not the strongest of finishers, he may now be ready to have a second crack at jumping fences. (tchd 8-1)
Tighe Caster, third in a selling race last time, last tasted success over fences at Market Rasen in April.
Unleashed(IRE), kept wide, looked a big danger four out but gave way tamely at the next. (op 7-1 tchd 5-1)
Petit Fleur was another to make smooth ground three out but she was fourth and well held when coming down at the last. She had been hiked 16lb after winning by a wide margin at Newton Abbot on her previous start in August. (tchd 15-2)
See You Jack was an early casualty. (tchd 15-2)

2531 TOTEPOOL A BETTER WAY TO BET VETERANS' H'CAP CHASE (14 fncs 2 omitted) 2m 4f 110y
3:15 (3:15) (Class 2) (0-145,137) 10-Y-0+ **£19,046** (£5,810; £3,035; £1,649)

Form RPR

30-3 **1** **Mister McGoldrick**[22] 2077 13-11-12 **137**................ DominicElsworth 150+
(Sue Smith) *a travelling wl: chsd ldr tl led 11th (4 out): clr fr next: in total command 2 out: v easily* **9/2**[3]

15-2 **2** 14 **Its Crucial (IRE)**[28] 1957 10-10-3 **117**................ SamTwiston-Davies(3) 116
(Nigel Twiston-Davies) *mstkes: chsd ldrs: lft 2nd bef 3 out: drvn and no prog after next: wl btn whn mstke last* **5/2**[1]

/0-0 **3** 1 ¾ **Il Duce (IRE)**[35] 1861 10-11-7 **132**................(b) JimmyMcCarthy 130+
(Alan King) *last whn mstke 1st: nvr looked happy and nt fluent after: rdn after 8th: wl btn after 3 out: wnt 3rd and mstke last* **10/3**[2]

4243 **4** 13 **Knight Legend (IRE)**[20] 2112 11-11-0 **125**................(t) AndrewThornton 110
(Sarah Humphrey) *chsd ldrs: mstke 6th: lft 3rd bef 3 out: rdn and wknd wl bef 2 out: wl btn whn mstke last* **8/1**

5P-1 **U** **Alderburn**[28] 1960 11-11-10 **135**................ LeightonAspell —
(Henry Daly) *chsd ldrs tl blnd and uns rdr 4th* **9/2**[3]

-003 **P** **Ellerslie George (IRE)**[14] 2221 10-11-1 **133**........(b) MrRGHenderson(7) —
(Nick Mitchell) *led tl 11th: lost action and p.u qckly bef next (3 out): fatally injured* **13/2**

5m 7.50s (2.20) **Going Correction** +0.35s/f (Yiel) **6** Ran SP% **112.5**
Speed ratings: **109,103,103,98,— —**
toteswingers: 1&2 £3.70, 1&3 £3.60, 2&3 £2.50 CSF £16.68 TOTE £3.90: £2.00, £2.10; EX 15.60.
Owner Richard Longley **Bred** Mrs J Key **Trained** High Eldwick, W Yorks

FOCUS
A good class veterans' chase and a hugely popular winner. The winner is rated to the ebst of last season's form.

NOTEBOOK
Mister McGoldrick, having his 82nd start, recorded his 14th career victory from a mark of 137, having finished third from a mark of 145 a year ago. Third on his return at Wetherby, he had been dropped a further 2lb, so for once connections could have no axe to grind. Re-united with his favourite pilot, he looked to be enjoying himself and was left in total control when Ellerslie George went wrong. In the end, he scored with plenty in hand and may not be finished winning just yet. (op 4-1)
Its Crucial(IRE) was let down by his jumping, making two significant errors setting out on to the final circuit. (op 7-2)
Il Duce(IRE) owes connections nothing but, after a mistake at the first fence, he seemed to take little interest. (op 3-1)
Knight Legend(IRE), having his first outing for his third trainer, extended his losing run to 22. (op 9-1)
Alderburn, runner-up a year ago, a place ahead of Mister McGoldrick, had been raised 4lb for his comeback win at Aintree. He raced with plenty of enthusiasm but soon put himself out of the contest. (op 7-1)
Ellerslie George(IRE) suffered a serious leg injury after the fourth last fence and was pulled up. Sadly this grand servant had to be put down. (op 7-1)

2532 BET TOTEPOOL TO SUPPORT YOUR SPORT H'CAP HURDLE (12 hdls) 3m 2f
3:45 (3:46) (Class 4) (0-105,103) 4-Y-0+ **£2,602** (£764; £382; £190)

Form RPR

0/34 **1** **Bellflower Boy (IRE)**[16] 2171 7-11-4 **102**................(tp) MrTWeston(7) 128+
(Dr Richard Newland) *in tch: led bef 3 out: cruised clr bef 2 out: eased flat: v easily* **13/2**[3]

P0-6 **2** 21 **Acosta**[15] 2183 6-9-11 **77** oh2................(b) EamonDehdashti(3) 78
(Dr Jeremy Naylor) *in rr: reminders after 2nd: hdwy into midfield and mstke 4th: pressed ldrs after 7th: rdn and outpcd bef 9th: no ch w wnr but plugged on fr 2 out to go modest 2nd last* **12/1**

4-45 **3** 2 ¼ **Royal Role**[17] 2154 6-10-12 **92**................ RichieMcLernon(3) 89
(Peter Pritchard) *chsd ldrs: rdn and outpcd 9th: no ch w wnr next: plugged on u.p flat to go modest 3rd nr fin* **33/1**

30-P **4** hd **Knight Woodsman**[190] 318 6-11-5 **99**................ AlexMerriam(3) 97
(Neil King) *in tch in midfield: hdwy after 7th: led 9th: sn rdn and hdd hdd bef next: wknd 3 out* **14/1**

23-5 **5** hd **Immense (IRE)**[168] 630 6-10-7 **91**................(t) TrevorWhelan(7) 88
(Ian Williams) *t.k.h: chsd ldrs: clr w wnr 3 out: drvn and btn bef next: lost 3 pls fr last* **3/1**[1]

5335 **6** 12 **Manadam (FR)**[16] 2171 7-10-11 **95**................ MattGriffiths(7) 81
(Anthony Middleton) *w ldr tl led after 4th: hdd 9th: sn drvn and wknd bef next* **10/1**

2502 **7** 3 ¼ **Caheerloch (IRE)**[12] 2279 8-11-1 **95**................ SamTwiston-Davies(3) 78
(Nigel Twiston-Davies) *in tch in midfield: hdwy 8th: chsd ldrs after 9th: rdn and wknd next* **4/1**[2]

/250 **8** 4 **Easement**[17] 2143 7-11-7 **98**................(v) GerardTumelty 77
(Charlie Morlock) *in tch: dropped to rr and rdn after 7th: wl btn after 9th: t.o* **22/1**

11-0 **9** 23 **Omix D'Or (FR)**[18] 2141 8-11-12 **103**................ DavidDennis 62
(James Evans) *chsd ldrs: wnt 2nd after 5th: j.rt and blnd 7th: wknd bef 9th: t.o* **8/1**

-0U3 **P** **September Moon**[17] 2155 12-10-1 **85**................ KyleJames(7) —
(Graham Smith) *led tl after 4th: sn rdn along: dropped to rr and toiling after 7th: t.o 9th tl p.u 2 out* **28/1**

P-4P **P** **My Rosie Ribbons (IRE)**[6] 2391 11-9-9 **77** oh2(b[1]) GemmaGracey-Davison(5) —
(Zoe Davison) *a in rr: losing tch whn p.u bef 8th* **20/1**

355- **P** **Willow Wren**[289] 3847 5-11-7 **98**................(t) JimmyMcCarthy —
(Renee Robeson) *in tch: bdly hmpd on bnd bef 6th: wknd bef 8th: t.o whn p.u 2 out* **8/1**

6m 20.0s (-2.90) **Going Correction** -0.125s/f (Good) **12** Ran SP% **119.5**
Speed ratings (Par 105): **99,92,91,91,91 88,87,85,78,— —,—**
toteswingers: 1&2 £9.40, 1&3 £36.40, 2&3 £44.90 CSF £76.79 CT £2399.16 TOTE £8.30: £2.40, £4.20, £4.90; EX 132.30.
Owner The Five Nations Partnership **Bred** Frank Sinnott **Trained** Claines, Worcs

FOCUS
A modest stayers' handicap hurdle run in murky conditions as the fog started to descend. The gallop was sound and it was a true test but in the end it was a one-horse race. Those in the frame behind the winner help set the level of the form.

NOTEBOOK
Bellflower Boy(IRE) ◆ travelled like a dream on just his third start for this yard, having undergone a wind operation after his arrival from Ireland in the summer. Still rated 100 on the Flat, he was possibly thrown in here from a mark of just 102. He came clear without effort and despite being heavily eased on the run-in, he still scored by a wide margin. Connections will be desperate to turn him out under a penalty before his new mark kicks in. (op 7-1 tchd 9-1)
Acosta, 16lb below his last success almost two years ago, was on and off the bridle. It was a case of something had to finish second. (op 10-1)
Royal Role, making his handicap debut, stayed on when it was all over and stamina looks his forte. (op 28-1)
Knight Woodsman, absent since pulling up after breaking a blood-vessel in May, has not had that many chances and connections will be keeping his fingers crossed that he builds on this. (tchd 16-1)
Immense(IRE), rated 78 on the level, ran here from a mark of just 91. He tended to race keenly and, after showing clear second on the final turn, he stopped to nothing. (op 9-2)
T/Plt: £37.60 to a £1 stake. Pool: £42,703.53. 827.08 winning tickets. T/Qpdt: £30.40 to a £1 stake. Pool: £2,880.77. 70.10 winning tickets. SP

2533 - 2539a (Foreign Racing) - See Raceform Interactive

1984 AINTREE (L-H)
Sunday, November 21

OFFICIAL GOING: Mildmay course - good to soft (soft in places); hurdle course - soft (good to soft in places); national course - soft (mildmay 6.0, hurdle 5.7, natioAll hurdles and bends moved to outside in increasing distances by 80yds per circuit.
Light half behindFine and sunny turning overcast

2540 TOTEPLACEPOT MAIDEN HURDLE (9 hdls) 2m 110y
12:05 (12:05) (Class 3) 3-Y-0+ **£5,204** (£1,528; £764; £381)

Form RPR

0-42 **1** **Midnight Opera**[20] 2129 4-11-1 115................ MarkQuinlan(7) 121+
(Neil Mulholland) *in tch: chalng 3 out: led 2 out: drvn and styd on run-in: a doing enough towards fin* **12/1**

0-32 **2** ½ **Brother Bob (IRE)**[25] 2038 4-11-8 115................ RichardJohnson 118
(Charlie Longsdon) *racd keenly in midfield: hdwy appr 3 out: sn chsd ldrs: wnt 2nd run-in: styd on to chal fnl 100yds: a looked hld cl home* **10/1**

22- **3** ½ **Yes Tom (IRE)**[218] 5227 5-11-5 0................ SamTwiston-Davies(3) 119+
(R T J Wilson, Ire) *led: nt fluent and hdd 2 out: kpt on u.p run-in but a hld* **8/1**[3]

4 ¾ **Swinging Hawk (GER)**[36] 4-11-8 0................ DougieCostello 117
(Ian Williams) *hld up in rr: hdwy 3 out: effrt to chse ldrs 2 out: styd on u.p run-in: nt quite pce of ldrs towards fin* **33/1**

5 4 **Bollin Felix**[25] 6-11-8 0................ JamesReveley 113
(Tim Easterby) *prom early: towards rr 2nd: hdwy after 4 out: rdn whn chsng ldrs bef 2 out: one pce and edgd lft after last* **4/1**[2]

6 23 **Current Event (FR)**[196] 3-10-7 0................ NoelFehily 78+
(Paul Nicholls) *midfield: hdwy 4 out: prom appr 3 out: wknd bef last* **5/6**[1]

00 **7** 21 **Dramatic Jewel (USA)**[52] 1337 4-11-8 0................ CampbellGillies 69
(Lucinda Russell) *hld up: hdwy appr 3 out: rdn bef 2 out: sn btn* **100/1**

5 **8** 20 **Art Broker (IRE)**[29] 1962 4-11-1 0................ JakeGreenall(7) 74
(Henry Daly) *in tch: u.p whn mstke 3 out: wknd after 2 out* **12/1**

/P3- **9** 2 ¾ **Puddington Bear**[407] 1691 6-10-12 0................ DerekSmith(10) 46
(Bill Moore) *prom: mstke 4 out: sn wknd: bhd whn mstke 3 out* **150/1**

10 1 ½ **Fight Club (GER)**[414] 9-11-1 0................ MissIsabelTompsett(7) 45
(Bernard Llewellyn) *plld hrd: hld up: hdwy to go prom 2nd: chsd ldrs after 3rd tl after 4 out: sn wknd: wl bhd whn blnd 2 out* **66/1**

0 **11** 22 **Lindoro**[22] 2092 5-11-3 0................ BrianToomey(5) 23
(Kevin M Prendergast) *plld hrd: a bhd: t.o after 4 out* **150/1**

U **Jackson (BRZ)**[4] 8-11-8 0................ BarryKeniry —
(Richard Guest) *prom whn jinked rt and lft and uns rdr 1st* **100/1**

223- **P** **Vannin (IRE)**[248] 4706 4-11-8 0................ BrianHughes —
(Tim Easterby) *midfield: lost pl bef 4th: t.o 5th: p.u bef 4 out* **33/1**

4m 25.0s (18.80) **Going Correction** +1.025s/f (Soft)
WFA 3 from 4yo+ 15lb **13** Ran SP% **120.8**
Speed ratings (Par 107): **96,95,95,95,93 82,72,63,61,61 50,—,—**
toteswingers:1&2:£8.80, 1&3:£8.60, 2&3:£6.30 CSF £122.74 TOTE £17.30: £4.00, £2.30, £2.20; EX 65.50 Trifecta £362.20 Part won..
Owner D J Bridger **Bred** Avon Thoroughbreds **Trained** Burlescombe, Devon

FOCUS
An average maiden hurdle, run at a fair enough gallop. Things started to get serious nearing the home turn and it looked pretty hard work after the last as the first four were closely covered at the finish. The winner looks the best guide to the level.

NOTEBOOK
Midnight Opera went for home jumping three out and, despite hitting the last, that move proved to be a winning one as he stole a march on his rivals. He was tying up near the business end, but may have been idling a touch and was never going to be reeled in. He shapes as though he will peak over a longer trip so the more testing ground over this distance helped his cause, and his yard remains in decent form. He could now be handed a break. (op 16-1)
Brother Bob(IRE) was doing his best work towards the finish and again found one too good. He needs more positive handling over this trip as he, too, looks a horse that will come into his own over a stiffer test in due course, and he deserves to go one better. (op 12-1 tchd 9-1)
Yes Tom(IRE) ◆ showed a good engine in bumpers last season and he was unsurprisingly sent to the front on this hurdling debut. He was a sitting duck for the winner, but was coming back towards the finish and is another here that looks sure to enjoy a stiffer test. He shouldn't be long in winning.
Swinging Hawk(GER) ◆, a very useful stayer at best on the Flat, was given a very patient ride and he was another staying on dourly from the last. This was a pleasing introduction to hurdling and there should be a race for him in the coming weeks, providing he gets a more positive ride. (op 40-1)
Bollin Felix, another very useful stayer at his best on the level, had the ground in his favour on this hurdling debut and came in for support. He got behind after the first and was ultimately tapped for toe when it mattered in the home straight. He too should really prove suited by a longer trip in this sphere. (op 9-2 tchd 7-2 and 5-1 in places)
Current Event(FR) finished second on his debut in a Listed event in France in May and was well fancied for this first run for Paul Nicholls, getting over a stone from his rivals. He moved up looking a real threat around four out, but made heavy weather of it when asked for his effort and ultimately the run looked needed. (op 10-11 tchd evens in places)
Lindoro Official explanation: trainer said gelding was unsuited by the going.

2541 TOTEPOOL GRAND SEFTON H'CAP CHASE (18 fncs) 2m 5f 110y
12:35 (12:37) (Class 2) 5-Y-O+

£37,176 (£11,040; £5,520; £2,754; £1,380; £696)

Form	Pos	Dist	Horse / Details	RPR
3U-P	1		**Frankie Figg (IRE)**[23] 2077 8-11-5 **130**.................. BrianHughes (Howard Johnson) *w ldr: led 2nd: j. boldly: mde rest: styd on strly fr 2 out* **10/1**	142+
-020	2	5	**Nikola (FR)**[22] 2086 9-11-2 **127**.................. PaddyBrennan (Nigel Twiston-Davies) *mid-div: hdwy to chse ldrs 9th: wnt 2nd 2 out: styd on same pce* **20/1**	132
0-05	3	nk	**Private Be**[36] 1861 11-11-4 **129**.................. RichardJohnson (Philip Hobbs) *towards rr: mstke 12th (Canal Turn): hdwy 14th: wnt 5th 2 out: hrd rdn and styd on run-in: collapsed fatally exiting unsaddling enclosure* **13/2**[1]	135
-502	4	¾	**Magic Sky (FR)**[29] 1960 10-11-0 **132**.................. JakeGreenall(7) (Milton Harris) *hld up towards rr: mstke 8th: hdwy whn hit 12th (Canal Turn): chsng ldrs 4 out: styd on same pce fr 2 out* **14/1**	137
1-02	5	3 ¼	**Et Maintenant (FR)**[13] 2272 8-10-11 **122**.................. CampbellGillies (Lucinda Russell) *chsd ldrs: pushed along 5th: one pce appr 2 out* **14/1**	124
1-00	6	1	**Always Waining (IRE)**[22] 2084 9-11-12 **137**..................(p) TomO'Brien (Peter Bowen) *led to 2nd: chsd ldrs: mstke 14th: kpt on same pce fr 2 out* **12/1**	139
P4-0	7	2 ¼	**Dashing George (IRE)**[17] 2171 8-11-6 **131**..................(p) JamieMoore (Dr Richard Newland) *chsd ldrs: hit 5th: mstke 10th (Becher's): hit 12th (Canal Turn): 3rd last: wknd last 150yds* **12/1**	131
056/	8	18	**Lampion Du Bost (FR)**[1030] 3558 11-9-11 **111** oh2.. RichieMcLernon(3) (Jim Goldie) *mid-div: mstke 8th: sn lost pl: hdwy to chse ldrs 13th: wknd and hit 3 out* **20/1**	93
P-01	9	2 ½	**Moon Over Miami (GER)**[14] 2234 9-11-10 **135**..................(t) NoelFehily (Charlie Mann) *nt fluent in rr: hmpd 6th: bhd whn hmpd 10th (Becher's): t.o whn blnd 3 out* **16/1**	120+
0-45	10	½	**Commemoration Day (IRE)**[15] 2212 9-10-2 **120** ow3. JoshuaMoore(7) (Gary Moore) *in rr: sme hdwy 14th: mstke and lost pl 3 out* **33/1**	96
F-04	11	70	**Double Dizzy**[15] 2212 9-10-12 **123**..................(t) AndrewGlassonbury (Bob Buckler) *chsd ldrs: hit 8th: wknd 13th (Valentine's): t.o 2 out: virtually p.u run-in* **16/1**	29
P-P2	P		**Victorias Groom (GER)**[7] 2400 8-11-5 **130**.................. JasonMaguire (Lucy Wadham) *j.rt in rr: nt fluent: bhd fr 5th: t.o whn p.u bef 8th* **9/1**[3]	—
2014	F		**Presentandcorrect (IRE)**[37] 1858 9-10-8 **122**.(p) SamTwiston-Davies(3) (Nigel Twiston-Davies) *chsd ldrs: fell 6th* **12/1**	—
-	U		**Battlefront (IRE)**[8] 2376 8-11-4 **129**..................(t) MsKWalsh (T M Walsh, Ire) *hld up towards rr: stmbld landing 5th and uns rdr* **25/1**	—
66P-	R		**Craiglands (IRE)**[218] 5223 8-10-5 **116**..................(t) BarryKeniry (Jim Goldie) *towards rr: lost pl 4th: bhd whn hmpd 6th: mstke next: t.o whn ref 12th (Canal Turn)* **8/1**[2]	—
241-	F		**Stormin Exit (IRE)**[219] 5204 7-11-2 **127**.................. JamesReveley (Jim Goldie) *mid-div: hdwy to trck ldrs 5th: wnt 2nd 7th: fell 10th (Becher's)* **13/2**[1]	—

5m 41.7s (5.70) **Going Correction** +0.50s/f (Soft) 16 Ran SP% 121.4
Speed ratings: **109,107,107,106,105 105,104,97,96,96 71,—,—,—,— —**
toteswingers:1&2:£45.90, 1&3:£5.40, 2&3:£27.30 CSF £196.90 CT £1410.34 TOTE £10.60: £3.20, £4.20, £2.00, £3.40; EX 367.90 Trifecta £686.10 Part won..
Owner Andrea & Graham Wylie **Bred** Patrick Hayes **Trained** Billy Row, Co Durham
■ Stewards' Enquiry : Richard Johnson one-day ban; excessive use of whip (5th Dec)

FOCUS
With the top weight being rated 137 it wasn't the classiest running of the Grand Sefton, but it was still typically wide open. It paid to race handy but the form looks solid, rated around the runner-up, fourth and fifth.

NOTEBOOK
Frankie Figg(IRE) held off his pursuers to make most of the running. His last win came off a 6lb lower mark here last October and he had shown a real liking for these fences before, but had actually failed to complete in three previous outings over them. He had also been pulled up on his seasonal debut at Wetherby last month, but returning here enabled him to show his true colours and it was a deserved change of fortune. This ground would've been soft enough for him and he proved most game when under maximum pressure. He will always be entitled to respect here due to his exuberant jumping over these obstacles, and another crack at the Topham in April looks most likely, but he has won over 3m and it may well be that connections take a good look at the National for him. Official explanation: trainer's rep said there was no explination for previous poor run. (op 8-1 tchd 11-1 in a place)
Nikola(FR) is a tricky horse to predict, but his stable has a decent record over these fences and he moved up looking a live threat to the winner from three out. He couldn't find any extra when asked to get to that rival in between the final two fences, but kept on gamely to hold on for second and ran right up to his best.
Private Be, well backed, was fifth in the Topham on his only previous run over these fences in 2008. He was doing his best work late on and ran well. However, he sadly collapsed afterwards and died. (op 7-1)
Magic Sky(FR), who unseated in last season's Topham, was given a waiting ride and began to creep into things from three out. He could only muster the same pace when push came to shove, but this was another solid effort in defeat and he helps to set the level.
Et Maintenant(FR) jumped well over this bigger fences and posted a respectable effort in a grade that looks just beyond him.
Always Waining(IRE)saves his best for these fences nowadays. He was 9lb higher than when landing the Topham in April and showed more enthusiasm under a positive ride, but lost vital momentum when hitting the 14th. (op 11-1)
Dashing George(IRE) only dropped out of the places late in the day and this was a lot more encouraging from him. (op 14-1)
Moon Over Miami(GER) Official explanation: jockey said gelding was hampered by faller.
Craiglands(IRE) was backed but he was hampered more than once and couldn't get into the race. (op 11-1)
Stormin Exit(IRE), whose trainer Jim Goldie had won two of the past three runnings of the race, was having his first outing since winning off a 5lb lower mark at Ayr in April. He had made a positive move and was still full of running before crashing out at Becher's. (op 11-1)

2542 LIVE FOOTBALL BETTING AT TOTESPORT.COM H'CAP HURDLE (11 hdls) 2m 4f
1:10 (1:14) (Class 2) 4-Y-O+

£12,524 (£3,700; £1,850; £926; £462; £232)

Form	Pos	Dist	Horse / Details	RPR
U11-	1		**Quartz De Thaix (FR)**[213] 5338 6-11-12 **142**.................. AidanColeman (Venetia Williams) *mde all: rdn appr 2 out: styd on and drew clr towards fin* **14/1**	148+
0253	2	4 ½	**Son Of Flicka**[36] 1864 6-11-3 **140**.................. HenryBrooke(7) (Donald McCain) *in tch: effrt after 4 out: chalng 3 out: rdn 2 out: wnt 2nd fnl 120yds: no imp on wnr towards fin* **10/1**	141
4623	3	1	**Heron Bay**[11] 2307 6-10-4 **123**..................(p) DonalDevereux(3) (Peter Bowen) *prom: chalng 3 out: rdn 2 out: styd on same pce fnl 120yds* **13/2**[3]	123
/31-	4	3 ½	**Comhla Ri Coig**[357] 2593 9-11-8 **138**.................. JasonMaguire (Donald McCain) *racd keenly: hld up: blnd 7th: hdwy appr 3 out: nt fluent 2 out whn chsng ldrs: one pce run-in* **9/1**	138+
05-1	5	10	**Keki Buku (FR)**[7] 2399 7-11-7 **137** 7ex.................. RichardJohnson (Philip Hobbs) *midfield: hdwy 4 out: rdn and chsd ldrs 3 out: wknd appr last* **7/2**[1]	126
240-	6	3	**Washington Irving (IRE)**[226] 5108 5-11-2 **132**.................. BrianHughes (Howard Johnson) *midfield: hdwy 4 out: trckd ldrs gng ok 3 out: shkn up and wknd 2 out* **8/1**	118
-P30	7	37	**Secret Tune**[36] 1864 6-10-13 **129**..................(b) PaddyBrennan (Tom George) *hld up: hdwy into midfield after 4 out: no imp on ldrs: btn 3 out* **6/1**[2]	76
/11-	8	3 ¼	**Ramsden Boy (IRE)**[202] 118 9-10-0 **119**.........(t) SamTwiston-Davies(3) (R T J Wilson, Ire) *chsd ldrs tl rdn and wknd after 4 out* **7/1**	62
2126	9	1 ¾	**Worth A King'S**[31] 1931 4-10-2 **118**.................. TimmyMurphy (Donald McCain) *prom tl wknd qckly after 4 out: eased whn wl btn after 3 out* **20/1**	60
/60-	P		**Puyol (IRE)**[212] 5382 8-11-2 **139**.................. HarryChalloner(7) (Lisa Williamson) *midfield: pushed along and lost pl 7th: bhd whn p.u bef 3 out* **16/1**	—
413-	P		**Lightening Rod**[236] 4941 5-10-4 **127**.................. JakeGreenall(7) (Michael Easterby) *a bhd: nt fluent 6th: t.o whn p.u bef 3 out* **14/1**	—

5m 16.5s (15.80) **Going Correction** +1.025s/f (Soft)
WFA 4 from 5yo+ 8lb 11 Ran SP% 116.5
Speed ratings (Par 109): **109,107,106,105,101 100,85,84,83,— —**
toteswingers:1&2:£16.50, 1&3:£9.50, 2&3:£9.30 CSF £144.13 CT £1004.49 TOTE £13.30: £3.40, £3.20, £1.90; EX 95.90 Trifecta £853.50 Pool: £1,614.84 - 1.40 winning units..
Owner Roa Arkle Partnership **Bred** Michel Bourgneuf **Trained** Kings Caple, H'fords

FOCUS
A fair handicap which was run at an average gallop and it paid to race handily. Another step up from the winner with the third the best guide.

NOTEBOOK
Quartz De Thaix(FR) had scored on his final two outings last year and he picked up where he left off with a ready effort on this seasonal debut. The market suggested the run would be needed, something in keeping with his yard's runners in general this term, but fitness wasn't an issue as he made all under top weight. He was 11lb higher here and so it must rate his best effort to date, plus he once again advertised his versatility for underfoot conditions. Further improvement this season looks on the cards and it wouldn't be surprising to see him try his luck back over fences. (op 12-1)
Son Of Flicka, 3lb higher, was never far away. He came under pressure around the third-last flight, but kept finding and turned in a very game effort. The handicapper does appear to have his measure now and he rates the benchmark. (op 12-1)
Heron Bay, from a yard with a decent record in the race, also raced prominently and performed right up to his best back up in trip. He too helps to set the level and deserves to find another opening. (op 7-1)
Comhla Ri Coig ◆, making his belated handicap debut, is very lightly raced for his age and, having his first outing since winning over fences just over a year previously, was second in the Grade 1 Grand Sefton as a novice here on his last outing over hurdles. He proved keen out the back and wasn't always fluent, but stayed on steadily to get involved off the home turn. He was tiring prior to hitting the last, but this was an encouraging display and he looks to have begun life in this sphere on a very workable mark. (op 8-1)
Keki Buku(FR) didn't get a great run around the home turn, but held every chance after being brought over to the stands' side from the second-last. He flattened out from there though, and this more demanding ground probably just found him out on this quick reappearance under a penalty. (op 10-3)
Washington Irving(IRE) moved up menacingly from four out, but he was done with nearing the penultimate flight and probably needed this first outing of the campaign. (tchd 15-2)
Secret Tune lacked fluency and threw in the towel a long way out. (op 9-1)

2543 TOTESPORT.COM BECHER H'CAP CHASE (LISTED RACE) (20 fncs 1 omitted) 3m 2f
1:45 (1:45) (Class 1) 5-Y-O+

£56,378 (£21,268; £10,668; £5,357; £2,708; £1,378)

Form	Pos	Dist	Horse / Details	RPR
05P-	1		**Hello Bud (IRE)**[211] 5395 12-10-5 **133**.................. SamTwiston-Davies(3) (Nigel Twiston-Davies) *led: hdd 3 out: regained ld next: hrd rdn and styd on gamely run-in* **15/2**[1]	144+
5U-4	2	1 ¼	**Royal Rosa (FR)**[29] 1960 11-10-0 **125** oh3..................(p) BrianHughes (Howard Johnson) *in rr: hdwy 11th: hdwy and lft modest 4th 16th (Valentine's): chsng ldrs 3 out: lft 2nd 2 out: chal elbow: kpt on same pce* **14/1**	134
P0-5	3	10	**One Cool Cookie (IRE)**[10] 2339 9-10-11 **141**..................(tp) APHeskin(5) (C F Swan, Ire) *in rr: sme hdwy 8th: lost pl and bhd fr 10th: kpt on appr 2 out: 5th last: styd on to take 3rd elbow* **25/1**	142

2325 **4** *6* **Ballyvesey (IRE)**[14] 2248 5-10-0 **125** oh5....................(v) TomScudamore 118
(Peter Bowen) *chsd ldrs: chal 4 out: led next: hdd and lft 3rd 2 out: wknd and lost 3rd elbow* **25/1**

4UP- **5** *8* **Notre Pere (FR)**[17] 2175 9-11-12 **151**....................................(p) AELynch 143+
(J T R Dreaper, Ire) *trckd ldrs: hmpd 4th: blnd 8th: bdly hmpd and lost pl 13th (Becher's): poor 5th whn blnd 3 out: kpt on fr next* **8/1**[2]

0-66 **6** *3 1/4* **Irish Raptor (IRE)**[15] 2221 11-10-3 **128**............................ PaddyBrennan 119+
(Nigel Twiston-Davies) *hld up: hdwy to trck ldrs 9th: swtchd rt and chalng whn blnd bdly 2 out: 4th last: wknd run-in* **11/1**

-0P0 **7** *11* **Au Courant (IRE)**[37] 1858 10-9-11 **125** oh6.............. RichieMcLernon(3) 96
(Sophie Leech) *hld up in rr: bhd whn hmpd 13th (Becher's)* **100/1**

60-6 **F** **Pak Jack (FR)**[20] 2123 10-10-0 **125** oh3............................ LiamTreadwell —
(Richard Phillips) *in rr: sme hdwy 8th: fell 11th* **33/1**

2P-2 **F** **Minster Shadow**[21] 2106 11-10-0 **125** oh1..................(v) CampbellGillies —
(Chris Grant) *chsd ldrs: j.rt 4th: 4th and wl outpcd whn fell 16th (Valentine's)* **25/1**

223P **U** **Midnight Gold**[29] 1960 10-10-0 **125** oh1........................(p) AidanColeman —
(Peter Bowen) *prom: hmpd 4th: sn lost pl: in rr whn uns rdr 13th (Becher's)* **33/1**

53F- **F** **Maljimar (IRE)**[225] 5127 10-11-3 **142**.................................... DarylJacob —
(Nick Williams) *blnd 2nd: in rr whn fell 3rd* **8/1**[2]

06-1 **F** **Newman Des Plages (FR)**[44] 1763 9-10-2 **127** ow2...... JamesReveley —
(Martin Todhunter) *in rr: blnd 1st: fell 11th* **16/1**

61-0 **F** **Merigo (FR)**[15] 2205 9-10-12 **137**...................................... TimmyMurphy —
(Andrew Parker) *hld up towards rr: stdy hdwy whn fell 11th* **8/1**[2]

635- **F** **Whatuthink (IRE)**[24] 2063 8-10-10 **142**................................ PFMangan(7) —
(Oliver McKiernan, Ire) *chsng ldrs whn fell 1st* **12/1**

2-41 **F** **Gullible Gordon (IRE)**[28] 1999 7-10-12 **142**....................... MrRMahon(5) —
(Paul Nicholls) *hit 1st: trckd ldrs: 4th whn fell 13th (Becher's)* **12/1**

P-41 **U** **Meanus Dandy (IRE)**[15] 2221 7-10-8 **138**......................(b) IanPopham(5) —
(Paul Nicholls) *chsd ldrs: blnd 14th (Foinavon): 5th whn sddle slipped and uns rdr next (Canal Turn)* **8/1**[2]

0-24 **U** **I'moncloudnine (IRE)**[15] 2221 7-10-8 **133**...................... DougieCostello —
(Neil Mulholland) *hld up in rr: hdwy 11th: hmpd 13th (Becher's): 4th and trcking ldrs whn uns rdr 15th (Canal Turn)* **17/2**[3]

7m 5.40s (3.40) **Going Correction** +0.50s/f (Soft) **17** Ran SP% **121.4**
Speed ratings: **114,113,110,108,106 105,101,—,—,— —,—,—,—,— —,—**
toteswingers:1&2:£21.30, 1&3:£26.40, 2&3:£84.30 CSF £98.16 CT £2507.74 TOTE £7.70: £1.90, £3.50, £5.80, £5.60; EX 154.90 TRIFECTA Not won..

Owner Seamus Murphy **Bred** Peter Casey **Trained** Naunton, Gloucs

■ Stewards' Enquiry : Sam Twiston-Davies five-day ban; excessive use of whip (5th 0th Doo)

FOCUS
This year's Becher was highly eventful and it proved to be a gruelling race with only seven getting home. The first two set the level.

NOTEBOOK
Hello Bud(IRE) ran out an ultra-game winner to give Sam Twiston-Davies another big-race success. He showed a real liking for these fences in this event last season, when only tiring from the final fence, and ran a big race to finish fifth in the National in April. He was over the top before being pulled up on his final outing last term, but his yard is in cracking form and he was 7lb lower than when running in the National. His jumping was excellent once again under his usual aggressive ride, and he refused to go down when under heavy pressure from the third-last. It looked as though the runner-up might master him coming to the elbow late on, but he picked up again and was well on top at the finish. This was a much-deserved success for the veteran and, although he will be 13 next year, his campaign will be geared around another tilt at the big one in April. The likely quicker ground there will be in his favour and he ought to make another bold bid, even though it's hard to see him winning it off a higher mark. (tchd 7-1 and 8-1 in a place)

Royal Rosa(FR) was 3lb lower than when finishing in front of the winner in third in this event last year, but had to race from the same amount of the handicap. He shaped encouragingly on his return here last month and, given a patient ride here, returned to his best in defeat. He couldn't quite get on top of his old rival, but was nicely clear in second and richly deserves to go one better again. (op 16-1)

One Cool Cookie(IRE), with cheekpieces replacing blinkers, was never seriously competitive yet stayed on dourly from the last and ran a pleasing race. He stays very well and this will surely see him aimed at the National now as he is versatile regarding ground. (op 22-1)

Ballyvesey(IRE) headed the winner three from home and, while he tired from the final fence, this was a decent effort from 5lb out of the weights. (op 33-1)

Notre Pere(FR) was having his first outing in a handicap since winning the Welsh National off a 1lb higher mark, and was expected to relish this return to further after an encouraging comeback effort 17 days earlier. This big horse has always looked as though he might also take to these fences and he jumped well early on. However, he was badly hampered more than once and has to rate unlucky not to have made the places. He looks the one to take out of this event for the Grand National, but his chance in that would really be dependant on getting some cut underfoot. (op 9-1 tchd 15-2)

Merigo(FR) had warmed up for this over hurdles last month and was creeping into it the race before falling. (tchd 14-1)

Whatuthink(IRE) took a very heavy fall at the first and reportedly broke his jaw. (tchd 14-1)

Gullible Gordon(IRE), for whom the ground was soft enough, had not totally convinced with his fencing prior to falling. (tchd 14-1)

Meanus Dandy(IRE)'s rider came off at the Canal Turn in what looked a soft unseat, although it transpired the saddle had slipped. (tchd 14-1)

2544 TOTESWINGER FLEXI BETTING H'CAP CHASE (19 fncs) 3m 1f
2:20 (2:21) (Class 3) (0-125,125) 4-Y-0+ **£7,542** (£2,247; £1,137; £583; £305)

Form RPR

31/5 **1** **Cavers Glen**[44] 1761 8-10-4 **103**.. DougieCostello 117+
(Alistair Whillans) *chsd ldrs: wnt 2nd appr 8th: led after 4 out: kicked on appr last: styd on wl* **5/1**[3]

6-61 **2** *3 1/2* **Fine Parchment (IRE)**[8] 2366 7-11-2 **115**............................(t) NoelFehily 126
(Charlie Mann) *in tch: gng wl trcking ldrs 4 out: rdn and nt pick up appr last: kpt on to take 2nd run-in: no imp on wnr* **9/4**[1]

1P-3 **3** *3 3/4* **Categorical**[17] 2163 7-11-9 **122**.. JamesReveley 131
(Keith Reveley) *led: hdd after 4 out: continued to chse wnr: u.p and nt qckn appr last: lost 2nd run-in: no ex fnl 100yds* **10/3**[2]

00-4 **4** *12* **Made In Japan (JPN)**[29] 1968 10-11-9 **122**...................... PaddyBrennan 122
(Nigel Twiston-Davies) *in tch: lost pl 11th: mstke 13th: struggling 15th: rallied briefly appr 2 out wout troubling ldrs: sn wl btn* **7/1**

2-PU **5** *11* **Jack The Blaster**[15] 2204 10-11-12 **125**............................. BrianHughes 112
(Howard Johnson) *hld up: hmpd 15th: hdwy to chse ldrs appr 4 out: no real imp on ldrs: wknd 2 out* **14/1**

-542 **P** **Federstar (GER)**[8] 2363 8-11-10 **123**............................... CharliePoste —
(Milton Harris) *nt a fluent: hld up: struggling 14th: lft wl bhd bef 4 out: p.u bef 3 out* **12/1**

4016 **P** **Quattrocento (FR)**[9] 2343 6-11-8 **121**................................(v) TomO'Brien —
(Peter Bowen) *chsd ldr tl appr 8th: hit 12th: 4th whn blnd 15th: sn wknd: wl bhd whn p.u bef 3 out* **5/1**[3]

6m 46.7s (16.70) **Going Correction** +0.85s/f (Soft) **7** Ran SP% **114.0**
Speed ratings (Par 107): **107,105,104,100,97** —,—
toteswingers:1&2:£3.40, 1&3:£3.90, 2&3:£2.20 CSF £17.27 TOTE £5.60: £2.60, £1.70; EX 21.60.

Owner John & Liz Elliot, A Brunton, P Copeland **Bred** J J Elliot **Trained** Newmill-On-Slitrig, Borders

FOCUS
A modest handicap, rated around the placed horses.

NOTEBOOK
Cavers Glen showed the clear benefit of his return from a layoff last month and completed the task readily. He had yet to prove his stamina for this far, but took it up turning for home and kept finding for his rider's urgings when asked to win the race. This was his best effort to date, on ground that suits, and he is evidently improving. (op 13-2 tchd 9-2 and 15-2 in a place)

Fine Parchment(IRE) came good for the drop back to 2m4f when hosing up at Uttoxeter off an 8lb lower mark eight days earlier. He travelled sweetly and held every chance, but looked to get outstayed by the winner back over this extra distance. (op 10-3 tchd 7-2)

Categorical was only just held by subsequent clear winner King Fontaine at Haydock on his seasonal debut 17 days earlier. He was ridden differently here, sent into a clear lead, and turned in another solid display in defeat. He rates a good benchmark. (op 3-1 tchd 4-1)

Made In Japan(JPN) plugged on late after going in snatches and has become one to tread carefully with. (op 13-2)

Quattrocento(FR)'s jumping went to pot and his rider reported he was never travelling after making a bad mistake. Official explanation: jockey said gelding made a mistake and never travelled thereafter. (tchd 4-1)

2545 TOTEEXACTA FLEXI BETTING NOVICES' H'CAP HURDLE (11 hdls) 2m 4f
2:55 (2:55) (Class 3) (0-120,114) 3-Y-0+ **£5,204** (£1,528; £764; £381)

Form RPR

22-6 **1** **Eighteen Carat (IRE)**[193] 289 6-11-6 **108**....................... JasonMaguire 113+
(Donald McCain) *j.rt: trckd ldr: mstke 7th: hdwy and upsides whn hmpd 2 out: led narrowly last: kpt on to pull clr clsng stages* **10/1**

PP-1 **2** *1 3/4* **Sunarri (IRE)**[15] 2208 6-11-4 **113**.................................. AlistairFindlay(7) 115
(Jane Walton) *led: clr 3rd: jnd whn j.rt 2 out: narrowly hdd last: upsides tl no ex last 75yds* **6/1**[2]

-442 **3** *8* **Devotion To Duty (IRE)**[60] 1573 4-11-12 **114**.............. CampbellGillies 111+
(Lucinda Russell) *hld up: hdwy to trck ldrs 5th: wnt 3rd 8th: styd far side and racd alone fr 3 out: keeping on same pce whn blnd 2 out* **10/1**

4U3- **4** *2 3/4* **What A Steel (IRE)**[347] 2769 6-10-7 **95**.......................... JamesReveley 86
(Alistair Whillans) *in rr: hdwy to chse ldrs whn mstke 5th: outpcd 8th: kpt on one pce fr next* **33/1**

F-52 **5** *9* **Chapolimoss (FR)**[44] 1758 6-11-5 **107**............................... SamThomas 89
(Martin Todhunter) *hld up towards rr: drvn 8th: nvr nr ldrs* **16/1**

224- **6** *1* **Don't Rush It (IRE)**[212] 5354 8-11-2 **111**......................... MarkQuinlan(7) 92
(John Quinn) *mid-div: hmpd 3rd: sn drvn: hmpd and mstke 7th: sn wknd* **13/2**[3]

00-2 **7** *15* **Arctic Court (IRE)**[15] 2202 6-11-12 **114**........................... TimmyMurphy 80
(Jim Goldie) *in rr: drvn along 3rd: bhd fr 8th: j. violently lft last* **9/1**

3F52 **8** *17* **Whereveryougoigo (IRE)**[14] 2231 4-11-0 **102**.................. TomO'Brien 51
(Peter Bowen) *j.rt: chsd ldrs: wknd 8th: bhd whn j. violently rt 2 out* **3/1**[1]

B34- **P** **Pliny (IRE)**[242] 4826 6-11-11 **113**.. AidanColeman —
(Venetia Williams) *chsd ldrs: drvn 5th: wknd next: t.o 8th: p.u bef next* **8/1**

3101 **P** **Strumble Head (IRE)**[28] 2001 5-10-8 **99**..................(p) DonalDevereux(3) —
(Peter Bowen) *chsd ldrs: wknd 8th: t.o whn p.u bef 2 out* **6/1**[2]

5m 25.6s (24.90) **Going Correction** +1.025s/f (Soft)
WFA 4 from 5yo+ 8lb **10** Ran SP% **115.0**
Speed ratings (Par 107): **91,90,87,86,82 82,76,69,—,—**
toteswingers:1&2:£12.10, 1&3:£13.00, 2&3:£10.20 CSF £68.43 CT £619.93 TOTE £9.60: £3.00, £2.10, £3.50; EX 68.30 Trifecta £455.50 Pool: £757.16 - 1.23 winning units..

Owner D McCain **Bred** John O'Brien And Jamie O'Brien **Trained** Cholmondeley, Cheshire

FOCUS
This novice handicap wasn't a strong event for the class and it was another race where it proved hard to make up ground from off the pace. The first pair came clear, having made their challenge towards the stands' side. The form is rated around the first three.

NOTEBOOK
Eighteen Carat(IRE) just did enough to shed his maiden tag at the seventh attempt. He had shown a liking for better ground previously, but this was his first outing in a handicap and he was one of the few who here that acted on the deep surface. Entitled to come on plenty for this first outing since May, he looks an improver but did have a fairly hard race. (op 11-1)

Sunarri(IRE) made all when belatedly getting off the mark on his latest outing and set out to repeat that feat over this longer trip. He made a bold bid off his 9lb higher mark and only gave way to the winner nearing the finish as his stamina emptied out This was just his second outing for the yard and has evidently improved for a change of scenery. (op 15-2 tchd 11-2)

Devotion To Duty(IRE), second at Perth 60 days earlier, had every chance yet probably wasn't helped by sticking to the inside in the home straight. He has started off in handicaps on a fair mark. (op 17-2 tchd 12-1)

What A Steel(IRE) didn't prove he wants to go this far on his handicap debut, but should come on a bundle for the run.

Whereveryougoigo(IRE) ran poorly, with the slower ground very likely to blame. (op 7-2 tchd 4-1)

Strumble Head(IRE) was reported to have hated the ground. Official explanation: trainer said gelding was unsuited by going. (op 11-2)

2546 TOTEPOOL A BETTER WAY TO BET MARES' STANDARD OPEN NATIONAL HUNT FLAT RACE 2m 1f
3:30 (3:30) (Class 5) 4-6-Y-0 **£2,055** (£599; £299)

Form RPR

1 **Monnow Made (IRE)** 5-10-12 0.................................... JimmyMcCarthy 110+
(Charles Egerton) *hld up: hdwy 4f out: led 2f out: drew clr ins fnl f: r.o wl* **9/2**[3]

2 *11* **Inthesettlement** 5-10-12 0.. JasonMaguire 97+
(Donald McCain) *plld hrd: hld up: hdwy to trck ldrs over 4f out: upsides on bit 2f out: rdn and nt qckn over 1f out: one pce and no ch w wnr ins fnl f* **7/2**[2]

4-11 **3** *5* **With Grace**[166] 686 5-11-5 0.. DonalDevereux(3) 102
(Peter Bowen) *prom: led over 3f out: rdn and hdd 2f out: wknd ins fnl f* **9/4**[1]

5 **4** *1 3/4* **Qualitee**[11] 2309 5-10-7 0.. IanPopham(5) 89
(Claire Dyson) *led: rdn and hdd 2f out: wknd over 1f out* **25/1**

5 *47* **Panashka (IRE)** 5-10-12 0... BrianHughes 42
(Mark Campion) *hld up: struggling 1/2-way: sn lost tch: t.o* **20/1**

6 *1* **Piggy Back (IRE)** 4-10-9 0.. RichieMcLernon(3) 41
(Jonjo O'Neill) *prom: pushed along 4f out: wknd over 3f out: t.o* **5/1**

3 **7** *27* **Jaya Bella (IRE)**[43] 1771 5-10-12 0 WarrenMarston 14
(Milton Harris) *hld up rdn over 6f out: lft wl bhd over 4f out: eased over 3f out: t.o* **5/1**

4m 34.0s (26.60) **Going Correction** +1.025s/f (Soft)
WFA 4 from 5yo+ 7lb 7 Ran SP% **113.1**
Speed ratings: **78,72,70,69,47 47,34**
toteswingers:1&2:£12.00, 1&3:£9.60, 2&3:£5.90. totesuper7: Win: Not won. Place:£1,236.90. CSF £20.10 TOTE £4.70: £2.80, £2.70; EX 2.10 Trifecta £43.30 Pool: £831.77 - 14.20 winning units..
Owner R F Bailey **Bred** Ralph Bailey **Trained** Chaddleworth, Berks

FOCUS
A steadily run mares' bumper, but not form to be confident about.

NOTEBOOK
Monnow Made(IRE) came right away from her rivals when the penny dropped in the home straight, and got her career off to a perfect start. She is well bred and looks sure to learn for the initial experience, so it will be very interesting to see how she fares under a penalty. (op 6-1)
Inthesettlement ◆, out of an unraced half-sister to Iris's Gift, travelled strongly into contention and was taken to the stands' rail with her challenge. She refused to settle early on, however, and that blunted her when push came to shove. She ought to benefit for the outing and will have decent claims next time out. (tchd 10-3)
With Grace was produced with every chance under her double penalty, but could offer no more nearing the final furlong. Her two previous wins came on good ground and now looks the time to send her hurdling. (tchd 5-2 and 11-4 in places)
Qualitee ran a fair race from the front, but will likely struggle to win a bumper.
Piggy Back(IRE)'s dam won three bumpers and took the EBF Mares' Final over hurdles in 2003 for this yard. She was in trouble before the home turn and may have found the ground against her. (op 9-2 tchd 11-2)
Jaya Bella(IRE) was beaten a long way out and couldn't operate on this softer surface. She was later reported to have run flat. Official explanation: jockey said mare ran flat. (tchd 9-2)
T/Jkpt: Not won. T/Plt: £2,160.60 to a £1 stake. Pool:£143,843.27 - 48.60 winning tickets T/Qpdt: £180.00 to a £1 stake. Pool:£17,426.54 - 71.61 winning tickets WG

2202 KELSO (L-H)
Sunday, November 21

OFFICIAL GOING: Good to soft (soft in places) changing to soft (good to soft in places) after race 1 (12:15) changing to soft after race 3 (1:20)
All bends moved in 3m.
Wind: Almost nil Weather: Dull, raining

2547 2011 PUNCHESTOWN FESTIVAL MARES' MAIDEN HURDLE (8 hdls) 2m 110y
12:15 (12:15) (Class 4) 4-Y-0+ **£2,602** (£764; £382; £190)

Form RPR
P-05 **1** **Moscow Mischief**[116] 1119 6-11-0 92 PeterBuchanan 96
(Lucinda Russell) *led: hdd briefly 3rd: rdn and hdd last: regained ld last 200yds: gamely* **14/1**
3-00 **2** *½* **Sara's Smile**[43] 1780 4-11-0 0 AdrianLane 98+
(Donald McCain) *midfield: hit 4th: hdwy to chse ldrs bef 2 out: mstke last: rdn and kpt on wl run-in: wnt 2nd towards fin* **25/1**
4/2- **3** *¾* **Lady Bluesky**[22] 324 7-10-11 0 EwanWhillans(3) 96
(Alistair Whillans) *nt fluent on occasions: hld up: hdwy to chal bef 2 out: led and rdn last: hdd last 200yds: no ex towards fin* **1/2**[1]
0-6 **4** *12* **Scarvagh Rose**[36] 1867 5-11-0 0 WilsonRenwick 84
(Rose Dobbin) *hld up in tch: hdwy to trck ldrs appr 2 out: outpcd fr last* **12/1**[3]
04/F **5** *¾* **Lady Rapido (IRE)**[14] 2261 8-10-11 0 (p) JamesO'Farrell(3) 84
(J J Lambe, Ire) *cl up tl rdn and outpcd 2 out: no imp fr last* **33/1**
00-0 **6** *5* **Just Maddie**[200] 163 6-10-11 90 RyanMania(3) 81+
(Rayson Nixon) *trckd ldrs tl rdn and wknd after 2 out* **40/1**
4-10 **7** *4½* **Seam Of Diamonds**[12] 2296 5-11-0 0 BrianHarding 75
(Martin Todhunter) *hld up: hdwy and in tch 2 out: rdn and wknd last* **25/1**
060- **8** *hd* **See The Legend**[207] 42 5-11-0 0 PaddyAspell 75
(Sandy Forster) *bhd: drvn bef 3 out: nvr on terms* **40/1**
5 **9** *27* **Seminal Moment**[12] 2297 4-10-11 0 FearghalDavis(3) 51
(William Amos) *hld up: rdn bef 3 out: sn btn* **50/1**
004 **10** *11* **Beau D'Argent**[8] 2370 4-11-0 0 GrahamLee 41
(Ferdy Murphy) *nt fluent: hld up: struggling after 4 out: nvr on terms* **25/1**
6P/0 **11** *2* **Flighty Mist**[15] 2202 8-10-7 0 PaulGallagher(7) 39
(Sandy Forster) *bhd: drvn after 4 out: sn struggling* **150/1**
0/0P **12** *17* **Euro One**[16] 2192 6-10-9 0 AlexanderVoy(5) 24
(Dianne Sayer) *prom: ev ch 4 out tl after next: wknd bef 2 out* **150/1**
/00- **P** **Mrs Trellis**[212] 5354 5-11-0 0 DominicElsworth —
(Paul Webber) *in tch whn broke down and p.u after 4 out* **14/1**
UP45 **P** **Glaced Over**[36] 1869 5-10-7 106 GaryRutherford(7) —
(Raymond Shiels) *plld hrd: cl up: led briefly 3rd: wknd 4 out: t.o whn p.u bef 2 out* **10/1**[2]

4m 14.5s (12.70) **Going Correction** +0.75s/f (Soft)
WFA 4 from 5yo+ 7lb 14 Ran SP% **119.4**
Speed ratings (Par 105): **100,99,99,93,93 91,88,88,76,70 70,62,—,—**
toteswingers:1&2:£41.30, 1&3:£1.70, 2&3:£13.90 CSF £296.84 TOTE £15.70: £2.80, £4.20, £1.20; EX 89.00.
Owner A D Stewart **Bred** Mrs L V Russell **Trained** Arlary, Perth & Kinross

FOCUS
All bends moved in 3m. The ground was officially changed to soft, good to soft in places after this opening contest, and looked to be riding pretty testing. A weak race in which the seventh and eighth set the level.

NOTEBOOK
Moscow Mischief stayed on best. That wasn't surprising given she had been running over 3m, and connections will presumably return to handicaps with her now, as she won't be good enough to defy a penalty. (op 18-1 tchd 20-1)
Sara's Smile, a well-beaten last on her hurdles debut, kept on well to take second off the favourite and will be suited by a stiffer test on better ground. (op 18-1)
Lady Bluesky, fourth in the 2009 Listed mares' bumper at Aintree, showed herself to be progressive on the Flat by winning three of her last four, and she looked the clear pick on this hurdles debut. However, her jumping wasn't the slickest and she couldn't see it out as well as the front pair. Better ground will suit though, and she should find an opening at some stage. (op 4-5 tchd 5-6 and Evens in a place)
Scarvagh Rose will find better opportunities in handicaps. (op 10-1)
Mrs Trellis was quickly pulled up having gone wrong. (op 12-1 tchd 11-1)
Glaced Over Official explanation: jockey said mare bled from nose. (op 12-1 tchd 11-1)

2548 BILLY ERSKINE 80TH BIRTHDAY BEGINNERS' CHASE (12 fncs) 2m 1f
12:45 (12:45) (Class 4) 4-Y-0+ **£3,332** (£1,034; £557)

Form RPR
436/ **1** **Alfie Flits**[470] 4837 8-11-0 0 RhysFlint 120+
(Alan Swinbank) *trckd ldrs: hdwy to ld 2nd: mde most after: kpt on wl fr last* **11/8**[1]
120/ **2** *11* **Blackpool Billy (IRE)**[741] 2122 8-11-0 0 GrahamLee 110+
(Ferdy Murphy) *t.k.h: nt fluent and j.rt on occasions: led to 2nd: w wnr: rdn after 2 out: one pce last* **4/1**[3]
23U5 **3** *27* **More Shennanigans**[32] 1924 9-10-11 70 RyanMania(3) 81
(Jean McGregor) *prom tl outpcd 8th: n.d after* **40/1**
P/P0 **F** **Steel Man (IRE)**[36] 1872 8-11-0 51 AdrianLane —
(Bruce Mactaggart) *in tch: 8 l down and outpcd whn fell 8th* **100/1**
P35- **P** **Prideus (IRE)**[219] 5202 6-11-0 110 (t) RichieMcGrath —
(Brian Storey) *cl up: blnd 1st: mstke and outpcd 5th: j. slowly next: sn p.u* **12/1**
-104 **U** **Ashammar (FR)**[18] 2153 5-11-0 0 (t) DominicElsworth —
(Paul Webber) *hld up: mstke and uns rdr 4th* **15/8**[2]

4m 31.9s (13.90) **Going Correction** +1.05s/f (Soft) 6 Ran SP% **108.0**
Speed ratings (Par 105): **109,103,91,—,—,—**
toteswingers:1&2:£1.10, 1&3:£6.80, 2&3:£6.70 CSF £6.92 TOTE £2.30: £1.70, £1.90; EX 5.40.
Owner Mrs J Porter **Bred** Shadwell Estate Company Limited **Trained** Melsonby, N Yorks

FOCUS
This proved fairly straightforward for the winner, who can go on to rate higher. The third sets the level of the form.

NOTEBOOK
Alfie Flits, a formerly useful novice hurdler, made a successful debut over fences off the back of an absence. He's got the size to make a chaser and, with improvement likely, he may be able to defy a penalty. (tchd 5-4 and 13-8)
Blackpool Billy(IRE), a 116-rated hurdler who was returning from a 741-day absence, did well considering runners from the yard often come on appreciably for an outing. His jumping should be sharper next time and he has a definite future over fences. (op 7-2)
Steel Man(IRE) looked in the process of running an improved race when coming down. (op 9-4)
Ashammar(FR), the winner's main market rival, had jumped okay on his chasing debut, but was caught out early this time. (op 9-4)

2549 CLELANDS JAGUAR H'CAP HURDLE (11 hdls) 2m 6f 110y
1:20 (1:20) (Class 3) (0-125,125) 4-Y-0+ **£4,228** (£1,241; £620; £310)

Form RPR
2-60 **1** **Stopped Out**[43] 1766 5-11-5 118 RichieMcGrath 125+
(Kate Walton) *hld up: hmpd by faller 7th: hdwy after next: effrt bef last: swtchd rt and led run-in: styd on wl* **9/1**
03-6 **2** *1* **Charlie Bucket**[191] 318 7-9-4 99 oh9 CallumWhillans(10) 102
(Donald Whillans) *hld up: stdy hdwy 1/2-way: effrt 2 out: ev ch last: kpt on run-in: hld cl home* **20/1**
42-1 **3** *7* **Ballymacduff (IRE)**[193] 291 6-10-9 108 (t) JanFaltejsek 105
(George Charlton) *t.k.h: midfield: hdwy and prom bef 4th: effrt and led bef 2 out: hdd run-in: sn outpcd* **13/2**[3]
34-6 **4** *7* **Watercolours (IRE)**[17] 2161 5-10-1 100 GrahamLee 89
(Jim Goldie) *midfield: drvn and outpcd 1/2-way: rallied bef 2 out: kpt on run-in: no imp* **7/1**
U005 **5** *5* **Teenage Idol (IRE)**[12] 2300 6-10-11 110 TjadeCollier 95
(Evelyn Slack) *cl up: effrt and ev ch bef 2 out: wknd bef last* **6/1**[2]
P-UF **6** *1½* **Mr Woods**[21] 2106 8-11-5 125 GaryRutherford(7) 111+
(Harriet Graham) *j.rt: led tl hdd bef 2 out: sn wknd* **16/1**
541P **7** *19* **Mini Minster**[171] 606 8-10-12 111 PaddyAspell 75
(Peter Atkinson) *trckd ldrs: lost pl 4 out: n.d after* **18/1**
223- **8** *25* **Glingerbank (IRE)**[218] 5224 10-11-9 122 BrianHarding 61
(Nicky Richards) *hld up: stdy hdwy and prom after 3 out: rdn and wknd fr next* **9/2**[1]
00-0 **9** *½* **Waltham Abbey**[31] 1929 9-9-8 100 MrRUtley(7) 38
(Lynsey Kendall) *in tch tl rdn and wknd fr 4 out* **50/1**
/P2- **10** *1½* **Double Default (IRE)**[276] 4125 9-11-0 113 DominicElsworth 50
(Martin Todhunter) *in tch: rdn 4 out: wknd fr next* **9/1**
41P- **F** **Thatlldoforme**[238] 4909 8-10-0 99 oh1 PeterBuchanan —
(Alistair Whillans) *midfield: niggled along whn fell 7th* **8/1**
141/ **P** **Role On (IRE)**[583] 5071 8-11-0 113 WilsonRenwick —
(Rose Dobbin) *hld up: struggling 4 out: sn btn: t.o whn p.u bef 2 out* **10/1**

5m 53.7s (12.70) **Going Correction** +0.75s/f (Soft) 12 Ran SP% **116.4**
Speed ratings (Par 107): **107,106,104,101,100 99,92,84,84,83 —,—**
toteswingers:1&2:£33.30, 1&3:£8.00, 2&3:£16.20 CSF £165.85 CT £1250.10 TOTE £13.50: £3.10, £5.30, £2.60; EX 163.30.
Owner The Well Oiled Partnership **Bred** J And T Shally **Trained** Middleham Moor, N Yorks

FOCUS
An ordinary handicap hurdle with the first two improers and the third, at 4lb below his best, setting the level.

NOTEBOOK
Stopped Out, a potential improver for this step up in trip, was badly impeded by a faller at the seventh but, given time to recover, he regained his momentum and stayed on strongly up the run-in. This was his second course win, having scored here off 10lb lower in the spring, and he remains capable of better, being just a five-year-old. Official explanation: trainer said regarding apparent improvement in form gelding was better suited by soft ground (op 12-1)
Charlie Bucket ran really well from out of the weights, trying to battle back against the winner and finishing clear of the third. (op 25-1)
Ballymacduff(IRE), off since winning off 8lb lower at Perth in May, ran well considering the softer ground and shorter trip were against him. He is capable of better. (op 8-1)
Watercolours(IRE) tried to stay on again. (op 6-1 tchd 11-2)
Mr Woods gained a much-needed confidence-boosting completion.
Glingerbank(IRE) disappointed although it's possible he needed it. Official explanation: trainer said gelding failed to get the trip on soft going. (op 7-2)

2550 ASHLEYBANK INVESTMENTS REG AND BETTY TWEEDIE NOVICES' H'CAP CHASE (17 fncs) 2m 6f 110y
1:55 (1:55) (Class 3) (0-125,119) 4-Y-0+ **£6,505** (£1,910; £955; £477)

Form RPR
-P53 **1** **Top It All**[15] 2203 7-10-2 95 WilsonRenwick 102+
(Rose Dobbin) *hld up in tch: stdy hdwy to press ldr after 4 out: led 2 out: rdn last: styd on wl* **7/2**[3]
1/34 **2** *hd* **Lockstown**[15] 2203 7-10-10 103 GrahamLee 112+
(Ann Hamilton) *trckd ldrs: blnd bdly and lost pl 12th: rcvrd and hdwy bef 3 out: effrt and pressed wnr last: styd on wl: jst hld* **11/4**[2]
6322 **3** *3¾* **More Equity**[15] 2203 8-10-11 107 RyanMania(3) 110
(P Monteith) *nt fluent on occasions: hld up in tch: pushed along 11th: hdwy after 4 out: effrt 2 out: kpt on run-in: no ex last 200yds* **7/1**

-U11 **4** *26* **Quinder Spring (FR)**[7] 2401 6-11-1 **108** 7ex.................. PeterBuchanan 88
(Lucinda Russell) *prom: hdwy to ld 4 out: hdd 2 out: rdn and wknd fr last* **2/1**[1]

64-1 **5** *10* **Club Class**[16] 2191 7-11-5 **119**...................................... MrJohnDawson(7) 87
(John Wade) *cl up: chal 11th: rdn whn hit and lost pl 4 out: wknd fr 2 out* **8/1**

0513 **6** *24* **Lindseyfield Lodge (IRE)**[16] 2190 9-10-3 **96**.............(p) KennyJohnson 38
(Robert Johnson) *led to 4 out: rdn and lost tch fr next: t.o* **18/1**

6m 6.90s (22.40) **Going Correction** +1.05s/f (Soft) **6** Ran SP% **111.1**
Speed ratings (Par 107): **103,102,101,92,89 80**
toteswingers:1&2:£1.90, 1&3:£2.70, 2&3:£1.80 CSF £13.60 TOTE £6.10: £2.40, £1.30; EX 13.90.
Owner Mr & Mrs Raymond Anderson Green **Bred** R G Percival And R Kent **Trained** South Hazelrigg, Northumbria
■ Stewards' Enquiry : Wilson Renwick two-day ban; excessive use of whip

FOCUS
An interesting novices' handicap in which the first two showed improved form and the third sets the level.

NOTEBOOK
Top It All, who was having just his second start as a chaser. Third over slightly further at the course on his debut, he had clearly come on for that outing and showed a willing attitude to hold on. He should go up too much and it's likely there's more to come. (op 9-2 tchd 5-1)
Lockstown did well to get himself back into it having made a notable blunder down the far side, indeed he very nearly pulled off the win. He got closer to the winner than he had done at the course last time and looks to be going the right way. (op 6-1)
More Equity made mistakes and couldn't match the front pair, but did keep on. (op 13-2 tchd 6-1)
Quinder Spring(FR) proved rather disappointing. He looked the one to beat under a penalty for the previous week's ready Market Rasen success, but stopped pretty quickly once beaten and ended up well held. Official explanation: trainer said run came to soon after last outing. (op 11-8 tchd 5-4)
Club Class ended up well held off a mark of 119 on this switch to handicaps. (op 7-1)

2551 THREE DIAMONDS H'CAP HURDLE (8 hdls) 2m 110y
2:30 (2:31) (Class 3) (0-130,130) 3-Y-O+ **£4,553** (£1,337; £668; £333)

Form RPR

620- **1** **Doeslessthanme (IRE)**[227] 5099 6-11-6 **127**.................... RyanMania(3) 130
(Howard Johnson) *t.k.h: trckd ldrs: led bef 2 out: rdn and jnd run-in: hld on wl* **3/1**[1]

1U-0 **2** *1* **Raysrock (IRE)**[25] 2035 8-10-11 **115**................................ WilsonRenwick 117
(P Monteith) *trckd ldrs: drvn and outpcd 2 out: rallied run-in: tk 2nd cl home: nt rch wnr* **5/1**[3]

031/ **3** *1 3/4* **Best Prospect (IRE)**[22] 4067 8-11-4 **122**.....................(tp) RichieMcGrath 122
(Michael Dods) *hld up and bhd: stdy hdwy bef 2 out: rdn to chal run-in: no ex and lost 2nd towards fin* **4/1**[2]

21-F **4** *4* **Bogside Theatre (IRE)**[22] 2089 6-10-12 **126**............. SamuelWelton(10) 123
(George Moore) *led tl hdd bef 2 out: rallied: kpt on same pce run-in* **17/2**

0/2- **5** *3/4* **Beverly Hill Billy**[25] 236 6-9-7 **104** oh4......................... PaulGallagher(7) 99
(Sandy Forster) *hld up in midfield: hdwy and ev ch bef 2 out: no ex fr last* **33/1**

5-00 **6** *3 3/4* **Cassius (IRE)**[25] 2035 8-10-11 **115**.. AdrianLane 107
(Bruce Mactaggart) *cl up tl rdn and no ex fr 2 out* **15/2**

01F- **7** *1 3/4* **Toshi (USA)**[25] 1424 8-11-12 **130**... GrahamLee 120
(Jim Goldie) *hld up: effrt bef 2 out: kpt on run-in: nvr able to chal* **20/1**

10/ **8** *4 1/2* **Livvy Inn (USA)**[598] 4825 5-11-11 **129**............................. PeterBuchanan 114
(Lucinda Russell) *midfield: shkn up and outpcd bef 2 out: sn btn* **22/1**

63-P **9** *14* **Quicuyo (GER)**[197] 213 7-10-8 **112**..................................... PaddyAspell 83
(P Monteith) *hld up: effrt bef 2 out: wknd bef last* **16/1**

033/ **10** *9* **Geojimali**[30] 4032 8-9-7 **104** oh1.. PaulNorton(7) 66
(Jim Goldie) *hld up: struggling bef 3 out: nvr on terms* **14/1**

1-PP **11** *99* **Bob's Dream (IRE)**[12] 2300 8-10-3 **110**.........................(t) HarryHaynes(3) —
(William Amos) *in tch: rdn bef 2 out: sn wknd: virtually p.u run-in* **11/1**

1000 **P** **Front Rank (IRE)**[15] 2208 10-9-10 **107**............................... MissECSayer(7) —
(Dianne Sayer) *prom: lost pl after 3rd: struggling fr next: t.o whn p.u bef 2 out* **25/1**

4m 16.1s (14.30) **Going Correction** +0.75s/f (Soft)
WFA 4 from 5yo+ 7lb **12** Ran SP% **120.7**
Speed ratings (Par 107): **96,95,94,92,92 90,89,87,81,76 30,—**
toteswingers:1&2:£6.70, 1&3:£3.70, 2&3:£10.80 CSF £18.05 CT £62.30 TOTE £3.60: £1.20, £2.40, £2.40; EX 25.90.
Owner Andrea & Graham Wylie **Bred** Mrs Karin Osthus **Trained** Billy Row, Co Durham
■ Stewards' Enquiry : Wilson Renwick two-day ban; excessive use of whip (7th-8th Dec)

FOCUS
A competitive handicap hurdle and easy to rate around those in the frame behind the winner.

NOTEBOOK
Doeslessthanme(IRE) came in for support and he travelled well just in behind the leaders until taking over two out. He fought off the challenge of Best Prospect to register his third course win over hurdles. (op 9-2)
Raysrock(IRE) stayed on again having been outpaced, but couldn't get to the winner. This was a big step up on his reappearance effort. (op 6-1)
Best Prospect(IRE), just 2lb than when winning at Newcastle on his latest hurdles start (February 2009), was also a winner on the Flat latest, but he often finds little for pressure and that was again the case here, being out-battled having come to hold every chance. (tchd 7-2 and 9-2)
Bogside Theatre(IRE), a faller last time out, tried to stay on again but never threatened. (op 13-2)
Beverly Hill Billy ran a fair race considering he was 4lb 'wrong'. There's a race in him at a lower level.
Bob's Dream(IRE) Official explanation: jockey said gelding lost its action.

2552 LOUIS COPPOLA NOVICES' HURDLE (11 hdls) 2m 6f 110y
3:05 (3:06) (Class 4) 4-Y-O+ **£2,602** (£764; £382; £190)

Form RPR

0/3- **1** **Torta Nel Cielo**[400] 1791 6-10-9 0.................................... HarryHaynes(3) 103+
(James Ewart) *trckd ldrs: wnt 2nd 7th: effrt 2 out: led run-in: styd on wl* **10/1**

00-4 **2** *3/4* **What A Dream**[15] 2202 4-10-12 0.. JanFaltejsek 99
(William Amos) *prom: rdn and outpcd bef 2 out: rallied run-in: styd on wl to take 2nd cl home* **6/1**[3]

-11P **3** *nk* **Identity Parade (IRE)**[29] 1959 6-11-5 116............................. AdrianLane 107
(Donald McCain) *led: rdn bef 2 out: hdd run-in: kpt on: lost 2nd cl home* **3/1**[1]

55-0 **4** *shd* **Emperor Charlie**[21] 2102 6-10-12 0.. GrahamLee 99
(Ferdy Murphy) *hld up: stdy hdwy 4 out: rdn next: rdn and kpt on wl run-in: nrst fin* **33/1**

6- **5** *12* **Comeththehour (IRE)**[366] 2407 7-10-12 0............................... PaddyAspell 87
(James Moffatt) *bhd: outpcd bef 4 out: rallied bef 2 out: kpt on run-in: nvr able to chal* **33/1**

501- **6** *hd* **Arrow Barrow (IRE)**[229] 5078 5-10-5 0........................ MrJohnDawson(7) 87
(John Wade) *hld up: stdy hdwy and in tch bef 2 out: wknd after last* **14/1**

5- **7** *6* **Collyns Avenue**[288] 3888 7-10-12 0................................. PeterBuchanan 81
(Shelley Johnstone) *midfield: hit 3 out: rdn and wknd fr next* **7/1**

0-65 **8** *4* **Goffa Crag**[15] 2202 6-10-9 0.. FearghalDavis(3) 78
(Nicky Richards) *hld up in tch: stdy hdwy 4 out: rdn and wknd fr 2 out* **16/1**

9 *1 1/2* **Funky Munky**[10] 5-10-12 0.. WilsonRenwick 75
(Alistair Whillans) *hld up: outpcd bef 4 out: n.d after* **50/1**

15-0 **10** *3/4* **Willie Hall**[15] 2202 6-10-9 0.. EwanWhillans(3) 76
(William Amos) *t.k.h: trckd ldrs: blnd 3 out: wknd fr next* **11/2**[2]

60-P **11** *3 3/4* **Paul Revere (IRE)**[16] 2192 6-10-12 0................................. BrianHarding 71
(Nicky Richards) *hld up: hit 4th: outpcd bef 4 out: n.d after* **66/1**

0-0 **12** *nse* **Scotswell**[49] 1702 4-10-5 0.. GaryRutherford(7) 71
(Harriet Graham) *bhd: struggling bef 4 out: nvr on terms* **100/1**

0 **13** *3/4* **Davy Boy Legend (IRE)**[175] 7-10-12 0....................... DominicElsworth 70
(Josie Ross) *bhd: struggling fnl circ: nvr on terms* **16/1**

0-4P **14** *1/2* **Tomzatackman (IRE)**[15] 2202 5-10-12 0.....................(t) RichieMcGrath 69
(Raymond Shiels) *hld up: struggling 7th: sn btn* **80/1**

4 **15** *24* **Sam Hall (FR)**[36] 1869 5-10-9 0..................................(t) JamesO'Farrell(3) 45
(Patrick Griffin, Ire) *trckd ldr to 7th: rdn after next: wknd after 3 out* **40/1**

- **P** **Diamond D'Amour (IRE)** 4-10-9 0.................................. RyanMania(3) —
(Howard Johnson) *trckd ldrs: hit 5th: lost pl qckly and p.u after next* **11/2**[2]

6m 14.6s (33.60) **Going Correction** +0.75s/f (Soft)
WFA 4 from 5yo+ 8lb **16** Ran SP% **124.1**
Speed ratings (Par 105): **71,70,70,70,66 66,64,62,62,62 60,60,60,60,51 —**
toteswingers:1&2:£18.80, 1&3:£8.80, 2&3:£5.30 CSF £69.03 TOTE £15.00: £4.20, £2.70, £1.40; EX 121.70.
Owner John Macgregor **Bred** Mrs M J Matthey **Trained** Langholm, Dumfries & G'way

FOCUS
The front four drew clear in what was a modest novice hurdle. The form is rated around the placed horses.

NOTEBOOK
Torta Nel Cielo, returning from a 400-day absence on this debut for James Ewart, travelled strongly throughout and really seemed at home in the ground, mastering the favourite on the flat and staying on well. He was clearly fit, but looks a likeable type. (op 8-1)
What A Dream stayed on nicely to get up for second and looks a promising stayer in the making. He won't be seen at his best until sent chasing, but can win over hurdles first. (op 4-1)
Identity Parade(IRE), pulled up in a handicap on her reappearance when possibly in need of the run, looked vulnerable under a penalty returned to novice company, and that extra weight eventually told. She's only rated 116 though, so can win again switched back to handicaps. (op 7-2)
Emperor Charlie will be one to watch for once he's sent handicapping. This was a big step up on his initial effort over hurdles and he'll appreciate further.
Comeththehour(IRE) kept on again and improved on his first attempt as a hurdler. He probably needs 3m. (op 40-1)
Arrow Barrow(IRE) can be rated better than the bare form, having made smooth progress to challenge before tiring. (op 12-1)
Willie Hall was too keen for his own good through the early stages, and then his jumping went to pieces when it mattered. He's likely to come good once sent handicapping. (op 8-1)
Diamond D'Amour(IRE), a half-brother to Diamond Frontier, who won races for this yard, quickly lost his place and was pulled up. It's likely something went amiss. Official explanation: jockey said gelding had a breathing problem. (op 5-1)

2553 GRANNY'S BIRTHDAY TREAT FROM E.F.C. STANDARD OPEN NATIONAL HUNT FLAT RACE 2m 110y
3:40 (3:41) (Class 6) 4-6-Y-O **£1,301** (£382; £191; £95)

Form RPR

1 **Dark Glacier (IRE)** 5-11-0 0.. BrianHarding 119+
(Chris Grant) *racd wd: prom: led over 5f out: hrd pressed fr over 3f out: asserted fr over 1f out: edgd lft and styd on strly fnl f* **10/1**

2 *4* **Fourjacks** 5-11-0 0.. AdrianLane 115+
(Tim Easterby) *hld up in tch: hdwy on outside and ev ch over 3f out: rdn over 2f out: kpt on same pce fnl f* **4/1**[2]

3 *23* **Trucking Along (IRE)**[50] 4-10-9 0......................... MrStevenCrawford(5) 92
(S R B Crawford, Ire) *cl up: led after 3f: hdd over 5f out: outpcd fnl 3f* **7/2**[1]

0- **4** *11* **Four Fiddlers (IRE)**[241] 4839 5-10-7 0...................... MissLAlexander(7) 81
(N W Alexander) *trckd ldrs: effrt and ev ch 4f out: wknd wl over 2f out* **50/1**

5 *3 1/2* **Sam D'Oc (FR)** 4-10-7 0...................................... MrColmMcCormack(7) 78
(Keith Reveley) *bhd: outpcd 1/2-way: sme late hdwy: nvr on terms* **15/2**

6 *2 1/4* **Alpha One (IRE)** 4-10-9 0.. AlexanderVoy(5) 75
(Chris Grant) *hld up: pushed along over 6f out: sn no imp* **40/1**

7 *3* **Colorado Kid (IRE)** 4-10-11 0... RyanMania(3) 72
(Howard Johnson) *midfield: drvn along 1/2-way: wknd fr over 6f out* **4/1**[2]

8 *1/2* **Drum Bustible (IRE)**[16] 2201 6-11-0 0.............................. WilsonRenwick 72
(J J Lambe, Ire) *prom tl rdn and wknd over 3f out* **6/1**[3]

9 *17* **Bunratty (IRE)** 4-11-0 0.. KennyJohnson 55
(Robert Johnson) *hld up: stdy hdwy and in tch over 6f out: sn wknd* **80/1**

6/0 **10** *21* **Fairlea Bob (IRE)**[44] 1764 6-11-0 0...................................... GrahamLee 34
(Rose Dobbin) *t.k.h: trckd ldrs tl rdn and wknd over 4f out* **16/1**

0-00 **11** *15* **The Tiddly Tadpole**[28] 1989 5-10-9 0.............................. PaulCallaghan(5) 19
(Simon West) *led 3f: cl up tl rdn and struggling fr 1/2-way* **33/1**

0 **12** *6* **Over The Clyde**[182] 448 5-10-7 0.................................. MrJohnDawson(7) 13
(William Young) *cl up to 1/2-way: sn lost tch* **100/1**

13 *40* **Willowthewizard**[637] 6-11-0 0.. PeterBuchanan —
(Shelley Johnstone) *bhd: struggling after 6f: nvr on terms: eased whn no ch* **100/1**

0-0 **14** *3 1/4* **Darden Burn (IRE)**[186] 399 4-10-7 0......................... MrJARichardson(7) —
(David Carr) *a bhd: no ch fr 1/2-way: eased* **80/1**

0 **15** *166* **Mar Ocean (FR)**[46] 1729 4-10-11 0...................................... JamesO'Farrell(3) —
(Patrick Griffin, Ire) *trckd ldrs tl wknd qckly over 5f out: virtually p.u* **18/1**

4m 8.20s (12.00) **Going Correction** +0.75s/f (Soft) **15** Ran SP% **120.3**
Speed ratings: **101,99,88,83,81 80,79,78,70,60 53,51,32,30,—**
toteswingers:1&2:£12.00, 1&3:£9.60, 2&3:£5.90 CSF £48.57 TOTE £15.20: £3.30, £2.30, £1.50; EX 64.10.
Owner Trevor Hemmings **Bred** C Kenneally **Trained** Newton Bewley, Co Durham

FOCUS
The two Trevor Hemmings-owned runners drew clear in this ordinary bumper, with the supposed second-string finishing in front. The fourth looks the best guide to the level at this stage.

NOTEBOOK
Dark Glacier(IRE) is out of a half-sister to a couple of useful winners but his trainer isn't exactly renowned for his success in bumpers. The son of Flemensfirth showed a willing attitude, and drew clear from the runner-up inside the final furlong. He'll struggle to defy a penalty, but should have a decent future over jumps. (op 14-1)
Fourjacks is probably the brighter long-term prospect. A half-brother to Old Benny, he has plenty of size about him, travelled strongly, but couldn't find as much for pressure as the winner and ended up well held. He's sure to come on plenty for it, though, and can probably win a bumper before going hurdling for his Flat-associated trainer. (op 10-3)

Trucking Along(IRE), a point winner, was keen early and stayed on at the one pace back in third, looking slow. (op 4-1)
Four Fiddlers(IRE) showed more promise than he had done on debut and, being a son of Accordion, should relish a stiffer test over hurdles. (op 66-1)
Sam D'Oc(FR) shaped with promise and should improve. (op 8-1)
Colorado Kid(IRE) was a bit disappointing, but will probably want better ground. (op 6-1 tchd 7-2)
The Tiddly Tadpole Official explanation: jockey said gelding was unsuited by going.
T/Plt: £214.70 to a £1 stake. Pool:£51,499.15 - 175.05 winning tickets T/Qpdt: £78.10 to a £1 stake. Pool:£4,677.70 - 44.30 winning tickets RY

2168 TOWCESTER (R-H)

Sunday, November 21

OFFICIAL GOING: Soft (good to soft in places; 7.3)
Wind: medium, half behind Weather: cloudy

2554 GG.COM ALERTS MARES' NOVICES' HURDLE (11 hdls) 2m 5f
12:25 (12:26) (Class 4) 4-Y-0+ **£2,927** (£859; £429; £214)

Form RPR

3-31 **1** **Malindi Bay**[23] 2072 5-11-2 115 SeanQuinlan 110+
(Kim Bailey) *chsd ldrs: chsd ldr 8th: rdn to ld bef 2 out: sn clr: styd on wl: rdn out* **8/13**[1]

5 **2** *8* **Bounds And Leaps**[18] 2156 5-10-10 0 JohnnyFarrelly 96
(Michael Scudamore) *led: j.lft 2nd: clr w wnr after 3 out: hdd bef next: plugged on same pce after* **16/1**

00- **3** *18* **Aeronautica (IRE)**[271] 4210 7-10-10 0 WayneHutchinson 80
(Tor Sturgis) *hld up in tch towards rr: hmpd 5th: stdy hdwy bef next: chsd ldng pair 8th: wknd sn after next* **100/1**

40F6 **4** *2* **My Viking Bay (IRE)**[17] 2168 6-10-3 0 CharlieWallis(7) 78
(John O'Shea) *hld up in tch in rr: stdy hdwy after 5th: chsd ldrs and mstke 3 out: sn outpcd and wl btn: blnd last* **15/2**[3]

63-0 **5** *2* **Inkberrow Rose (IRE)**[12] 2288 6-10-10 0 MarkBradburne 74
(Tom Gretton) *in tch: hmpd 2nd: wknd qckly 3 out: wl btn bef next* **33/1**

5-06 **6** *3 3/4* **Catch The Rascal (IRE)**[28] 1994 4-10-7 0 JimmyDerham(3) 70
(Seamus Mullins) *in tch in midfield: wknd qckly 3 out: wl btn bef next* **33/1**

7 *22* **M'Lady Rousseur (IRE)**[25] 4-10-10 0 TomMessenger 48
(Chris Bealby) *midfield: mstke 2nd: dropped to rr and rdn along 4th: wknd u.p bef 3 out: t.o 2 out* **100/1**

0 **8** *3 3/4* **Filimoss**[15] 2222 5-10-10 0 GerardTumelty 45
(Charlie Morlock) *in tch towards rr: rdn and wknd after 8th: wl bhd whn mstke next: t.o* **200/1**

5-00 **9** *3 1/2* **Bach Street Girl (IRE)**[9] 2353 6-10-10 85 TomSiddall 41
(Lynn Siddall) *hld up in last trio: rdn and struggling 7th: t.o fr 3 out* **100/1**

/00- **10** *31* **Argentia**[252] 4620 5-10-10 0 AndrewThornton 10
(Lucy Wadham) *chsd ldrs tl wknd rapidly 3 out: t.o and bef 2 out* **100/1**

PP0P **P** **Baltrap (FR)**[7] 2398 5-10-10 80 JamesDavies —
(Clarissa Caroe) *in tch in midfield: rdn and lost pl qckly 6th: t.o whn p.u 8th* **200/1**

405- **P** **Pull The Wool (IRE)**[218] 5228 6-10-10 96 LiamHeard —
(Gerald Ham) *a towards rr: lost tch after 6th: t.o whn p.u 8th* **40/1**

0-0P **P** **The Dark Witch**[40] 1812 6-10-5 0 (b[1]) MarcGoldstein(5) —
(Alan Blackmore) *t.k.h: chsd ldr tl 8th: dropped out rapidly: t.o whn p.u 2 out* **150/1**

0-51 **F** **Kaituna (IRE)**[20] 2130 4-11-2 0 LeightonAspell —
(Oliver Sherwood) *in tch tl fell 5th* **7/2**[2]

F **Sassy Wren** 5-10-7 0 CharlieHuxley(3) —
(Sarah Humphrey) *in tch towards rr whn fell 3rd* **100/1**

5m 31.6s (4.40) **Going Correction** +0.375s/f (Yiel) **15** Ran SP% **116.7**
Speed ratings (Par 105): **106,102,96,95,94 93,84,83,82,70 —,—,—,—,—**
toteswingers:1&2:£5.20, 1&3:£27.70, 2&3:£61.70 CSF £12.58 TOTE £1.70: £1.10, £1.80, £19.30; EX 12.10.
Owner Lucky Bin Racing **Bred** R Chugg **Trained** Andoversford, Gloucs

FOCUS
After an essentially dry night the going remained soft, good to soft in places. A modest mares' hurdle with the winner rated 5lb off her Uttoxeter form.

NOTEBOOK
Malindi Bay, whose trainer reckoned she would have only Kaituna to fear if handling this very different course. In the event, the well-backed favourite was left with a simple task once that rival crashed out early on, requiring little assistance up the straight after going on turning for home. Plenty of further improvement is required for her to rate a leading player in the mares' hurdle final at Newbury next spring, for which connections will now try to qualify her, but she's clearly improved since stepped up to 2m5f+ the last twice, as befits an animal with a largely pointer and staying chase pedigree. (op 5-6 tchd 10-11 and Evens in places)
Bounds And Leaps, a daughter of a 2m6f hurdles winner, had dotted up in a mares' maiden point on holding ground around the testing, galloping Upton-on-Severn track last Easter, and was unsurprisingly not persevered with in bumpers for very long. Unable to find an extra gear once headed, she nevertheless kept on fairly pleasingly, and an even tougher test could see her step up on this effort. (op 10-1)
Aeronautica(IRE) was done few favours by Kaituna's fall, and while that was too far out to suggest it cost her a winning chance, she nevertheless probably did a shade better than the ultimate distance beaten suggests. This improved effort gives connections something to work with after two ordinary efforts previously (one in a bumper), and she could be found a small handicap in due course at least.
My Viking Bay(IRE)'s progress was checked by a sticky leap at the foot of the final hill, but it's unlikely it cost her anything more than a possible share of third place. There may be a minor handicap in her if the jumping errors evident in all three hurdles starts to date can be rubbed out. (tchd 13-2)
Baltrap(FR) Official explanation: jockey said gelding hung left. (tchd 9-2 and 5-1 in a place)
Kaituna(IRE), a winner over this trip on better ground last time, departed early on. (tchd 9-2 and 5-1 in a place)

2555 SIS H'CAP CHASE (14 fncs) 2m 3f 110y
12:55 (12:56) (Class 5) (0-95,92) 4-Y-0+ **£2,602** (£764; £382; £190)

Form RPR

311- **1** **Abbey Dore (IRE)**[235] 4964 7-10-9 78 JimmyDerham(3) 91+
(Seamus Mullins) *in tch: chsd ldng pair 5th: lft 2nd and hmpd 9th: mstke 3 out: led bef 2 out: kpt on gamely u.p between last 2* **5/2**[1]

40 **2** *1* **Flying Squad (UAE)**[57] 1608 6-11-12 92 (t) DaveCrosse 104
(Milton Harris) *nt jump wl: hld up in rr: hdwy 5th: lft 3rd 9th: clsng whn hit next: pressing ldrs and blnd 3 out: chsd wnr bef next: ev ch and nt fluent 2 out: hrd drvn between last 2: styd on same pce flat* **16/1**

-400 **3** *16* **Silver Dollars (FR)**[115] 1128 9-11-11 91 FelixDeGiles 89
(David Arbuthnot) *racd wd: sn led: rdn and hdd after 3 out: wknd next: wl hld whn mstke last* **9/2**[2]

45-3 **4** *46* **Ballymorn (IRE)**[17] 2170 6-11-6 86 HaddenFrost 34
(Henrietta Knight) *in tch in last pair: rdn along and toiling after 5th: lost tch 8th: lft poor 4th next: t.o fr 11th* **5/2**[1]

PU/P **5** *2* **Byways Boy**[45] 1747 7-11-2 82 AndrewThornton 28
(Caroline Bailey) *chsd ldrs tl dropped to rr and rdn after 5th: lost tch after 7th: t.o fr 11th* **10/1**[3]

-P36 **U** **Phar Again (IRE)**[13] 2280 7-10-11 80 (tp) TommyPhelan(3) —
(Claire Dyson) *chsd ldr: clsd and pressing ldr whn mstke 7th: ev ch whn blnd bdly and uns rdr 9th* **9/2**[2]

5m 25.1s (6.90) **Going Correction** +0.55s/f (Soft) **6** Ran SP% **108.5**
Speed ratings (Par 103): **108,107,101,82,82 —**
toteswingers:1&2:£14.60, 1&3:£1.10, 2&3:£14.60 CSF £30.74 TOTE £2.70: £1.10, £8.50; EX 38.20.
Owner Dr & Mrs Peter Leftley **Bred** Dermot Day **Trained** Wilsford-Cum-Lake, Wilts
■ Stewards' Enquiry : Dave Crosse caution; used whip without giving mount time to respond.

FOCUS
A moderate affair, but one run at a decent clip. The winner is rated to his mark with the second to the best of his hurdles form.

NOTEBOOK
Abbey Dore(IRE) has no record of going well fresh (for all that he reportedly takes little work to get fit), and had also risen another 9lb since winning at Hereford when last seen in March, which makes his game landing of the hat-trick here all the worthier of merit. Not over-big, it's noticeable that none of his victories (all on good to soft or worse) has required him to carry more than today's 10st 9lb, and it may well be that light weights in better company remain the way to go with him as he progresses. (op 2-1)
Flying Squad(UAE)'s proximity to the winner owes plenty to Dave Crosse galvanising him again after two significant errors in the back straight. He is entitled to learn from this first experience of chasing, at least, and he has started life in this discipline dropped to a feasible mark after recent maiden and handicap hurdle disappointments. (op 12-1)
Silver Dollars(FR), whose connections' fears that the ground may have gone against him were rendered irrelevant, as he ran too freely early to get home. A more sparing display of front-running, as well as a return to a speedier, easier track, could see him last longer. Notably, he's back down to just 1lb higher than when scoring over this trip on good at Musselburgh last winter. (op 11-2)
Ballymorn(IRE) looked ill at ease throughout and needs treating a little carefully now unless anything comes to light. Official explanation: vet said gelding bled from nose. (op 9-4)
Phar Again(IRE), 25lb lower than when recording his only victory two years and 20 starts earlier, crashed out too soon to say whether he would have justified the appreciable market support. He was travelling as well as anything at the time, though. (op 13-2)

2556 HAYGAIN HAY STEAMERS NOVICES' (S) HURDLE (8 hdls) 2m
1:30 (1:30) (Class 5) 3-4-Y-O **£1,712** (£499; £249)

Form RPR

00 **1** **Baggsy (IRE)**[13] 2133 3-10-0 0 MattieBatchelor 74+
(Julia Feilden) *bhd: sme hdwy and mstke 3 out: chsd ldrs between last 2: lft cl 3rd last: kpt on wl to ld nr fin* **28/1**

3061 **2** *nk* **Big Talk**[6] 2421 3-10-11 104 (v) RodiGreene 84
(David Bridgwater) *chsd ldrs: wnt 2nd 5th: rdn bef 2 out: drvn between last 2: lft in ld last: hdd nr fin* **5/2**[2]

3 *1* **Miss Wendy**[11] 3-10-0 0 ColinBolger 73
(Mark H Tompkins) *hld up in last pair: stdy hdwy after 3rd: chsd ldng pair and j.lft 2 out: n.m.r between last 2: lft 2nd last: one pce flat* **6/1**

1POU **4** *1 1/2* **Stafford Charlie**[18] 2149 4-11-1 90 (p) CharlieWallis(7) 93
(John O'Shea) *chsd ldrs: rdn and effrt bef 2 out: styd on same pce between last 2* **16/1**

63 **5** *9* **Antoella (IRE)**[8] 2369 3-10-0 0 NickScholfield 62
(Philip Kirby) *t.k.h: hld up in tch: hdwy to trck ldrs 3 out: rdn and btn bef next* **2/1**[1]

2000 **6** *9* **A P Ling**[31] 1935 3-10-0 78 TomMessenger 53
(Christopher Kellett) *t.k.h: hld up in tch towards rr: rdn and struggling 5th: wl btn after next* **33/1**

0300 **7** *hd* **Restless Harriet**[17] 2168 4-10-12 0 WayneKavanagh(3) 67
(Robin Dickin) *chsd ldr tl 5th: sn rdn: wknd 3 out* **50/1**

5 **8** *6* **Fochabers**[43] 1772 3-10-4 0 (b[1]) DPFahy(3) 53
(Bernard Llewellyn) *in tch in midfield: j.lft and rdn 3 out: sn wknd* **5/1**[3]

0 **9** *8* **The Beat Is On**[18] 2143 4-10-10 0 LeeEdwards(5) 53
(Tony Carroll) *in tch: struggling u.p after 5th: wl bhd bef 2 out* **100/1**

020P **U** **Royal Torbo (ISR)**[6] 2421 3-10-0 92 (b[1]) MrJGoss(7) 82
(George Baker) *led: rdn and hung rt bef 2 out: flashing tail u.p between last 2: plugging and maintaining ld whn mstke and uns rdr last* **20/1**

0 **P** **Dusty Showbiz**[17] 2173 3-9-7 0 RobertKirk(7) —
(Anthony Middleton) *towards rr: blnd and rdr lost iron 3rd: detached in last after: lost tch after 5th: t.o whn p.u 2 out* **66/1**

4m 10.8s (2.90) **Going Correction** +0.375s/f (Yiel)
WFA 3 from 4yo 15lb **11** Ran SP% **114.3**
Speed ratings (Par 103): **107,106,106,105,101 96,96,93,89,— —**
toteswingers:1&2:£15.30, 1&3:£18.40, 2&3:£2.50 CSF £94.56 TOTE £43.10: £5.90, £1.40, £2.10; EX 121.00.There was no bid for the winner.
Owner Miss J Feilden **Bred** Don Commins **Trained** Exning, Suffolk

FOCUS
An exciting finish to a low-grade contest, with five still holding chances at the last. The runner-up sets the level.

NOTEBOOK
Baggsy(IRE), whose rider deserves a lot of credit for redoubling his mount's effort after two out, after an error at the previous flight appeared to have dealt her forward move a sizeable blow. Little about her Flat and hurdling efforts to date anticipated this victory, although in fairness quite a different riding tactic to today's had been used on her only previous try on soft ground around Yarmouth. (op 40-1)
Big Talk didn't travel quite as kindly as when taking an identical contest in a first-time visor at Leicester six days earlier, but did reproduce the improved jumping display of that performance. It may just have been that this third start in under three weeks was a bit too much for the time being, and he can remain of interest in this grade after a little break. (tchd 11-4)
Miss Wendy ◆, a hurdling debutante who finished 6l ahead of Baggsy on the Flat at Yarmouth, recorded her sole win on the Flat up Beverley's punishing finish (1m4f), and didn't fail on stamina grounds. A return to a drier surface wouldn't inconvenience. (op 13-2 tchd 7-1 and 5-1)
Stafford Charlie did at least complete after mishaps on his last three starts, though future prospects will depend on the jumping errors staying away stepped back up to a more conducive trip. (op 10-1)
Fochabers, still available at 14-1 in places an hour before the off and sporting first-time blinkers, came under immediate pressure after a poor jump three out and dropped out very tamely. (op 14-1)

Royal Torbo(ISR), whom first-time blinkers galvanised where cheekpieces had failed to do so behind Big Talk last time, hadn't been enjoying the stronger pressure up the straight before putting down on Jamie Goss at the last. The ability to win a comparable race is there, though he doesn't look entirely straightforward. (op 16-1)

2557 TCA ENGINEERING LTD H'CAP CHASE (18 fncs) 3m 110y
2:05 (2:05) (Class 4) (0-100,99) 4-Y-O+ **£3,903** (£1,146; £573; £286)

Form RPR

06-6 **1** **Pacco (FR)**[23] 2073 7-11-12 **99**....................................(b[1]) LeightonAspell 120+
(Oliver Sherwood) *hld up in tch: hdwy and mstke 11th: led gng strly and wnt clr 14th: in command bef 2 out: kpt on wl: easily* **9/2**[3]

43-6 **2** *13* **Sir Peter (IRE)**[17] 2170 8-11-6 **93**...............................(p) AndrewTinkler 98
(Henry Daly) *pressed ldr 4th: chsd wnr fr 13th: rdn bef 14th: kpt on trying u.p: btn 2 out: plugged on* **7/2**[2]

1-P0 **3** *14* **Wide Receiver (IRE)**[17] 2170 7-10-7 **80**.......................(v) GerardTumelty 71
(Charlie Morlock) *w ldr tl led 1st: hdd bef 14th: 3rd and struggling u.p 15th: wl btn next* **9/1**

6420 **4** *1 1/4* **Kilvergan Boy (IRE)**[32] 1925 6-11-7 **97**............................ TomMolloy(3) 87
(Nigel Twiston-Davies) *hld up in tch: pckd 2nd: hdwy to chse ldrs 10th: struggling whn mstke 13th: 5th and wl btn after 15th* **7/1**

P33- **P** **Woodlands Genpower (IRE)**[231] 5016 12-11-2 **89**.........(b) TomSiddall —
(Peter Pritchard) *led tl j. slowly and hdd 1st: chsd ldr after and sn rdn along tl crawled over 4th and dropped to last: lost tch 9th: t.o whn p.u 15th* **10/1**

46-3 **P** **Caspar Of Tarsus (IRE)**[195] 251 7-11-0 **87**............... AndrewThornton —
(Gerald Ham) *in tch: mstke 11th: rdn and struggling 12th: wkng whn p.u qckly 15th* **15/2**

0P-3 **P** **Doctor Disny**[17] 2172 7-11-9 **96**.......................................(p) SeanQuinlan —
(Kim Bailey) *in tch: mstke 9th and 11th: rdn and struggling bef 14th: 4th and wl btn after next: t.o whn p.u 2 out* **11/4**[1]

6m 47.5s (10.60) **Going Correction** +0.55s/f (Soft) **7** Ran SP% **110.4**
Speed ratings (Par 105): **105,100,96,95,— —,—**
toteswingers:1&2:£3.30, 1&3:£8.00, 2&3:£8.40 CSF £19.59 TOTE £4.90: £2.00, £3.00; EX 24.70.
Owner Ray And Marian Elbro **Bred** Mme Brigitte Ricous **Trained** Upper Lambourn, Berks

FOCUS
An ordinary staying chase, albeit one contested by a number of increasingly well-handicapped rivals. The winner is rated back to his best.

NOTEBOOK
Pacco(FR), described as "in the last chance saloon" by his trainer beforehand, proved there was hope for him yet by travelling kindly in first-time blinkers and winning as he fancied. 8lb below the mark off which he won a 2m3f chase on one of two previous successful course visits (from three all told) 18 months earlier, he may be able to remain competitive despite a rise for this bloodless success, if the headgear inspires him once again. (tchd 4-1)
Sir Peter(IRE), like the winner trying out his respective headgear (cheekpieces) for the first time, was the only rival to give meaningful chase over the final half mile. Another previous course winner, he looks to be getting closer to making count over a stone's worth of clemency since sent chasing. (op 9-2)
Wide Receiver(IRE) was 3lb above his Ffos Las winning mark of last spring, but still below the 85 he defied here over 2m6f this time last year. Essentially very disappointing other than on those two occasions, the response once headed today was pretty short-lived. (tchd 10-1)
Kilvergan Boy(IRE) hadn't convinced with his jumping in any of four previous chasing starts, and similarly was never going notably well after pecking early. (op 11-2)
Woodlands Genpower(IRE)'s backers knew their fate as soon as he jumped the first cautiously and started to lose interest straight away. (op 8-1)
Doctor Disny performed better than the bare form when trying to serve it up to an improver here on his chasing debut last time, but a couple of errors at halfway cost him his chance of building on that. He can do better again, though an inconsistent hurdling profile last season does sound a small note of caution. Official explanation: jockey said never travelling. (op 8-1)

2558 BLIZZARD H'CAP HURDLE (11 hdls) 2m 5f
2:40 (2:40) (Class 4) (0-105,105) 4-Y-O+ **£3,252** (£955; £477; £238)

Form RPR

0032 **1** **Henry Hook (IRE)**[29] 1976 6-11-5 105..........................(p) MattGriffiths(7) 114
(Victor Dartnall) *chsd ldrs: wnt 2nd and mstke 7th: upsides ldr bef 3 out: rdn to ld bef 2 out: kpt on wl* **17/2**

344P **2** *2 1/2* **Pocket Too**[11] 1925 7-10-12 98...(p) MrJBanks(7) 104
(Matthew Salaman) *hld up in tch in midfield: effrt and rdn 3 out: chsd wnr between last 2: kpt on same pce and no imp flat* **25/1**

40P2 **3** *8* **Earcomesthedream (IRE)**[17] 2171 7-11-8 101.................(b) TomSiddall 99
(Peter Pritchard) *chsd ldrs: drvn and chsd ldng pair after 3 out: chsd wnr bef next tl between last 2: plugged on same pce* **9/2**[2]

-PP3 **4** *3* **Little Al**[46] 1730 7-11-4 97..(b) LeightonAspell 92
(Oliver Sherwood) *hld up towards rr: effrt and rdn 3 out: chsd ldrs and hit next: plugged on but no imp after: mstke last* **12/1**

P-01 **5** *4* **What's Occurrin**[31] 1929 6-11-6 99.................................. RobertWalford 91
(Tim Walford) *taken down early: led: sn clr: hdd and rdn after 3 out: wknd next* **12/1**

0-12 **6** *2 1/4* **Hurricane Electric (IRE)**[179] 480 5-10-12 91................. JodieMogford 80
(Graeme McPherson) *hld up in tch: hdwy 3 out: 6th and no imp whn j.lft next* **18/1**

4/P- **7** *1* **Doctor Kilbride (IRE)**[561] 230 7-10-11 90................... TomMessenger 78
(Chris Bealby) *in tch in rr: rdn along and struggling 7th: styd on past btn horses bef 2 out: nvr trbld ldrs* **33/1**

1531 **8** *18* **Miss Saffron**[45] 1737 7-11-2 102................................... MissLGardner(7) 72
(Susan Gardner) *hld up in rr: hdwy after 5th: in tch and rdn along bef 3 out: wknd wl bef 2 out* **12/1**

0-43 **9** *5* **Cockney Prince (IRE)**[18] 2144 5-10-8 90.......................... MrAJBerry(3) 55
(Jonjo O'Neill) *in tch in midfield: rdn along 4th: hdwy to chse ldrs 8th: mstke next: sn wknd* **11/4**[1]

06-F **10** *3* **Arthurian (IRE)**[17] 2169 5-9-7 79 oh1.............................(bt) MrTGarner(7) 41
(Anthony Middleton) *hld up in tch on outer: hdwy to chse ldrs 8th: rdn and hung rt sn after 3 out: sn wknd* **40/1**

2UP3 **11** *23* **Topflight Wildbird**[10] 2329 7-11-11 104..................... WayneHutchinson 43
(Alan King) *t.k.h: hld up in tch: rdn and wknd qckly 3 out: t.o next* **10/1**

3-P0 **12** *15* **Like Ice**[16] 2181 5-11-5 105.. JosephAkehurst(7) 29
(Philip Middleton) *chsd ldrs tl wknd bef 3 out: wl t.o 2 out* **66/1**

P0-4 **13** *16* **Forty Knights**[19] 2137 5-11-7 100....................................... JamesDavies 8
(Chris Down) *chsd ldrs tl after 7th: wknd next: wl t.o bef 2 out* **33/1**

0033 **R** **Ramvaswani (IRE)**[10] 2327 7-10-4 90............................(v) MrMMarris(7) —
(Neil King) *ref to r: tk no part* **40/1**

2/6- **P** **Wardington Lad**[546] 439 8-11-2 102................................ KyleJames(7) —
(Graham Smith) *chsd ldr tl bef 7th: steadily lost pl: wl bhd 3 out: t.o whn p.u next* **28/1**

/213 **P** **Manshoor (IRE)**[11] 2312 5-11-2 102................................ MattCrawley(7) —
(Lucy Wadham) *hld up in tch in midfield: rdn and btn bef 3 out: wl bhd and p.u 2 out* **8/1**[3]

1-30 **P** **Tarabela**[10] 2329 7-11-2 100.. DavidBass(5) —
(Gerald Ham) *hld up in tch in rr: rdn and struggling bef 8th: wl btn 3 out: p.u next* **40/1**

5m 32.3s (5.10) **Going Correction** +0.375s/f (Yiel) **17** Ran SP% **125.9**
Speed ratings (Par 105): **105,104,101,99,98 97,97,90,88,87 78,72,66,—,— —,—**
toteswingers:1&2:£58.20, 1&3:£11.40, 2&3:£22.20 CSF £210.30 CT £1097.16 TOTE £10.20: £2.10, £5.90, £1.30, £3.20; EX 208.20.
Owner Under The Radar **Bred** P J Hassett **Trained** Brayford, Devon

FOCUS
A pretty decent pace to this handicap hurdle from the outset. The winner is on the upgrade and the form is rated around the placed horses.

NOTEBOOK
Henry Hook(IRE) has been weak and required a lot of time, according to connections, but two recent placed handicap efforts on drier surfaces had offered hope he is finally strengthened up enough to start building significantly on his initial bumper promise of early 2009. This powerful-finishing effort at once becomes his best performance on deep going, and offers further options going forward this winter. (op 15-2 tchd 9-1)
Pocket Too's drop to a three and a half year low mark inspired a partial revival. He's not always tended to maintain his form for more than two or three races at once, so will make some appeal again next time if not much after that. (op 28-1)
Earcomesthedream(IRE)'s march back up the weights for a return to form in a 0-125 here last time has put him back 9lb above his highest winning mark, and that looked to find him out. He had not placed in any of eight previous starts off a triple-digit rating. (op 5-1)
Little Al has posted fair efforts over C&D the last twice now, but a 6lb climb for his third last time had looked a touch harsh, and that probably put paid to his bid as much as an error two out here. (op 16-1)
What's Occurrin, the trailblazer, inevitably paid for setting it cresting the final rise for home. (op 14-1)
Cockney Prince(IRE), on whom Alan Berry deputised for McCoy, looked in trouble from a long way out with the well-backed favourite never travelling from an early stage. It's disappointing he's not been able to show up better in any of his three handicap starts now, given what looks a feasible mark. Official explanation: trainer was unable to offer any explanation as to poor run. (op 7-2)
Manshoor(IRE) made no show at all stepping up nearly 4f in distance. (op 17-2 tchd 15-2)

2559 GG.COM CONDITIONAL JOCKEYS' H'CAP CHASE (12 fncs) 2m 110y
3:15 (3:15) (Class 5) (0-90,90) 4-Y-O+ **£1,951** (£573; £286; £143)

Form RPR

05-2 **1** **Handtheprizeover**[21] 2113 5-11-12 **90**.................................. PeterToole 109+
(Ben Case) *chsd ldrs: chsd ldr 6th: gng strly and led sn after 3 out: in command bef next: kpt on wl* **9/4**[1]

45P4 **2** *17* **Rince Donn (IRE)**[18] 2152 8-11-2 **80**...................................(t) DavidBass 83
(Roger Curtis) *in tch: hmpd 7th: cl 3rd 3 out: sn rdn and outpcd by wnr: plugged on u.p to go 2nd last* **9/2**

0-14 **3** *nk* **Reelwill (FR)**[13] 2277 5-10-6 **75**....................................... AdamWedge(5) 76
(Chris Bealby) *mde most tl hdd sn after 3 out: sn drvn and no ch w wnr: lost 2nd last* **11/4**[2]

POPP **4** *22* **The Walnut Tree (IRE)**[14] 2240 9-10-0 **64** oh9.................. JohnKington 47
(Simon Lewis) *chsd ldr tl 6th: hmpd next: rdn and lost tch bef 3 out: t.o* **16/1**

U-6U **F** **Thievery**[10] 2334 9-11-0 **78**.. MichaelMurphy —
(Henry Daly) *hld up in tch in last pair tl fell 6th* **9/1**

002F **F** **Beauchamp Viking**[3] 2484 6-11-4 **85**............................(t) MattGriffiths(3) —
(Simon Burrough) *in tch: 3rd whn fell 7th* **4/1**[3]

4m 25.4s (9.30) **Going Correction** +0.55s/f (Soft) **6** Ran SP% **111.5**
Speed ratings (Par 103): **100,92,91,81,— —**
toteswingers:1&2:£1.40, 1&3:£1.10, 2&3:£2.80 CSF £12.63 TOTE £3.60: £1.20, £3.50; EX 15.60.
Owner D Allen **Bred** A Buller **Trained** Edgcote, Northants

FOCUS
A weak contest that lost plenty of its interest when two of the three late players in the line-up, Thievery and Beauchamp Viking, departed at consecutive fences around halfway. The placed horses set the level.

NOTEBOOK
Handtheprizeover, a positive in the market, was left with little to beat as a consequence, though backers had one slight scare when the partnership appeared to have a difference of opinion at the second last which the gelding fiddled his way out of. Connections are hoping a punitive rise doesn't ensue for victory in a race that took little winning. (op 11-4)
Rince Donn(IRE)'s inability to deliver a telling late burst of speed in his races is well enough established to be confident that the hampering he suffered from Beauchamp Viking didn't cost him a winning chance. He remains teasingly handicapped on a 10lb lower mark than when finally nailing a chase at Folkestone last January, though will need plenty to fall his way to make that count. (tchd 4-1 and 5-1)
Reelwill(FR) was made plenty of use of early on to counter a 1m drop in trip, and also took a better cut at her fences than Southwell's portables last time, but ultimately proved too onepaced at the trip once taken on. A sharper, flatter track and trips in the region of 2m5f-2m6f have served her best up to now, and may continue to do so. (op 3-1 tchd 7-2)
Beauchamp Viking, whom it wouldn't surprise to see acquire some headgear, or alternatively take in a confidence-restoring spin over hurdles, having crashed out two races running now. (op 5-1 tchd 7-2)

2560 TIPZONE @ GG.COM INTERMEDIATE OPEN NATIONAL HUNT FLAT RACE 2m
3:50 (3:50) (Class 5) 4-6-Y-O **£1,626** (£477; £238; £119)

Form RPR

1 **Max Laurie (FR)** 5-10-11 0.. TomMolloy(3) 104+
(Michael Banks) *hld up in last pair: hdwy 5f out: chsd clr ldr ent fnl 2f: led 1f out: rn geen ins fnl f: rdn out* **33/1**

0 **2** *1* **Bardolf (IRE)**[188] 375 4-11-0 0.................................. WayneHutchinson 103+
(Alan King) *t.k.h: hld up in tch towards rr: rdn and chsd ldrs over 2f out: kpt on wl u.p fnl f: wnt 2nd towards fin* **11/2**[2]

3 *3/4* **Secret Past (IRE)** 5-11-0 0.. TomSiddall 102
(Karen McLintock) *chsd ldr: rdn and unable qck over 4f out: rallied over 2f out: chsd wnr ins fnl f: kpt on: lost 2nd towards fin* **5/2**[1]

6- **4** *3 1/4* **Newton Tonic**[207] 53 5-11-0 0... FelixDeGiles 100
(Alex Hales) *racd keenly: led: clr over 2f out: rdn ent fnl 2f: hdd 1f out: wknd fnl 150yds* **18/1**

3 **5** *1 1/2* **Stanley's Choice**[30] 1955 4-11-0 0...................................... PaulMoloney 97
(John Ferguson) *t.k.h: hld up towards rr on outer: hdwy into midfield 1/2-way: chsd ldr 4f out: hanging rt and outpcd over 2f out: sn lost 2nd: plugged on same pce fnl 2f* **8/1**

34 **6** *2* **Tech Zinne**[12] 2295 4-10-2 0 .... DavidBass(5) 88
(George Baker) *in tch: rdn and lost pl 5f out: rallied over 2f out: kpt on fnl 2f but nvr gng pce to threaten ldrs* **8/1**

7 *3 1/2* **Flying Award (IRE)**[202] 6-10-7 0 .... MissLGardner(7) 92
(Susan Gardner) *hld up in tch: hdwy 1/2-way: chsd ldrs over 4f out: rdn and wknd wl over 2f out* **16/1**

8 *1/2* **Fresher Fishing (IRE)** 6-10-7 0 .... MattGriffiths(7) 91
(Victor Dartnall) *in tch towards rr: dropped to last pair and rdn 7f out: swtchd lft over 4f out: styd on same pce and no threat to ldrs fnl 3f* **13/2**[3]

6 **9** *13* **Onetokeep (IRE)**[32] 1927 5-11-0 0 .... GerardTumelty 78
(Anabel L M King) *t.k.h: chsd ldrs tl rdn and wknd over 3f out* **25/1**

000- **10** *2* **Mister Concussion**[216] 5284 6-11-0 0 .... LeightonAspell 76
(Peter Jones) *hld up in tch in rr: sme hdwy over 4f out: wknd over 3f out* **66/1**

11 *13* **Generals Love (IRE)** 4-10-11 0 .... JohnKington(3) 63
(Donald McCain) *t.k.h: chsd ldrs tl wknd qckly over 4f out: t.o* **7/1**

12 *2* **Another Round (IRE)** 6-11-0 0 .... AndrewGlassonbury 61
(Gerald Ham) *chsd ldrs tl wknd 4f out: wl btn fnl 2f: t.o* **66/1**

3- **13** *3* **Don't Hang About**[241] 4846 5-11-0 0 .... JohnnyFarrelly 58
(Richard Mitchell) *in tch in midfield: hdwy 1/2-way: rdn and wknd 4f out: t.o* **20/1**

4m 9.50s (7.20) **Going Correction** +0.375s/f (Yiel)
WFA 4 from 5yo+ 7lb **13** Ran SP% **117.7**
Speed ratings: **97,96,96,94,93 92,91,90,84,83 76,75,74**
toteswingers:1&2:£30.60, 1&3:£24.50, 2&3:£3.10 CSF £197.31 TOTE £45.00: £10.10, £1.70, £1.70; EX 186.80.
Owner Mrs M C Banks **Bred** Alain Salmon & Regine Salmon **Trained** Waresley, Cambs

FOCUS
A stop-start pace to this concluding bumper, in which a clever ride went some way towards determining the outcome. The fifth and sixth are the best guides to the level.

NOTEBOOK
Max Laurie(FR), whose rider took the gelding widest to avoid the most poached ground, made sure he wasn't left with too much to do by continuing his forward move, even when the leader was stacking the field ahead of an attempted sprint finish. The gelding still raced green once sent on to win, offering hope of further progress as he works out all that the job entails, and he already has the look of another decent acquisition by his permit-holding handler. (tchd 40-1)
Bardolf(IRE) ◆ looked more forward and consequently shaped with far more promise than on his May debut, finishing more purposefully than anything else. A more end-to-end gallop would have been more greatly appreciated, and he has a bumper in him on this showing if finding one run to suit. (op 7-1 tchd 5-1)
Secret Past(IRE) ◆, representing a yard with a 20% strike-rate in bumpers (including a 6-1 winner and 20-1 nose second from three representatives in the preceding fortnight alone), was the clear paddock pick. Tapped for toe half a mile out, he was another for whom the race was likely not quite run to suit. Clearly in very good hands to try to emulate his dam in winning a bumper, he's not for giving up on. (op 11-4)
Newton Tonic tried to outsprint his field having briefly let the pursuers close him down at the foot of the hill, but over-keenness early on had left him with insufficient left in reserve to pull off the feat. A sharper track and less wastefulness in running can see him go closer. (op 14-1 tchd 20-1)
Stanley's Choice similarly had less to offer in the final analysis than seemed likely after a refusal to settle better at the start. The raw material required to collect an ordinary bumper seems to be there, though. (op 13-2 tchd 6-1)
Generals Love(IRE) was another not to help his cause by racing keenly, but he dropped out more tamely than others that did even so and may still be quite weak. (op 8-1)
Don't Hang About Official explanation: jockey said gelding stopped quickly.
T/Plt: £80.60 to a £1 stake. Pool:£54,986.49 - 497.65 winning tickets T/Qpdt: £20.30 to a £1 stake. Pool:£5,444.91 - 197.84 winning tickets SP

2561a, 2563a- 2569a - (Foreign Racing) - See Raceform Interactive

2258 NAVAN (L-H)

Sunday, November 21

OFFICIAL GOING: Hurdle course - soft (soft to heavy in back straight); chase course - soft to heavy

2562a FRIENDS OF NAVAN "MONKSFIELD" NOVICE HURDLE (GRADE 2) (11 hdls) 2m 4f

1:05 (1:05) 4-Y-0+ **£24,159** (£7,061; £3,345; £1,115)

RPR

1 **Fully Funded (USA)**[28] 2012 5-11-3 .... DJCondon 132+
(Noel Meade, Ire) *led: sn clr tl reduced advantage fr 4th: strly pressed and hdd bef 2 out where slt mstke: rallied u.p to ld at last: styd on wl to draw clr run-in* **6/1**

2 *4 1/2* **Gift Of Dgab (IRE)**[15] 2223 6-11-3 .... DNRussell 128+
(A J Martin, Ire) *trckd ldrs mainly 5th: clsr ent st: rdn and no imp after 2 out: 4th at last: kpt on u.p run-in to go 2nd cl home* **12/1**

3 *1* **Ballyburke (IRE)**[14] 2258 5-11-3 .... DJCasey 126
(P J Rothwell, Ire) *trckd ldrs: 3rd racing keenly 1/2-way: wnt 2nd bef 4 out: chal and led narrowly bef 2 out: hdd u.p at last: no ex run-in* **11/2**[3]

4 *2* **Aughnacurraveel (IRE)**[18] 2159 6-11-3 121 .... PTownend 124
(Garry Ducey, Ire) *trckd ldr: 2nd 1/2-way racing keenly: 3rd 4 out: rdn and dropped to 4th bef 2 out: no imp and kpt on one pce fr bef last* **11/8**[1]

5 *11* **Bacher Boy (IRE)**[94] 1302 6-11-3 122 .... BarryGeraghty 113
(Gordon Elliott, Ire) *towards rr: clsr ent st: rdn 2 out: no ex appr last* **10/1**

6 *1 1/4* **He's Our Man (IRE)**[7] 2416 5-11-3 .... (t) JLCullen 115+
(Patrick O Brady, Ire) *trckd ldrs on inner: 4th 1/2-way: 3rd and pushed along to chal whn stmbld bdly on landing 2 out: nt rcvr* **22/1**

7 *30* **Seafield (IRE)**[25] 2039 5-11-3 .... (t) APCawley 81
(Paul Nolan, Ire) *hld up on outer: in tch appr st: no ex and wknd qckly 3 out: eased* **3/1**[2]

5m 8.10s (6.30) **7** Ran SP% **117.9**
CSF £69.83 TOTE £6.20: £2.70, £4.10; DF 67.20.
Owner More The Merrier Syndicate **Bred** Juddmonte Farms Inc **Trained** Castletown, Co Meath
■ Stewards' Enquiry : D J Condon severe caution: excessive use of the whip

FOCUS
This wasn't really a vintage Grade 2 but certainly a very competitive one.

NOTEBOOK
Fully Funded(USA) nicked a good few lengths when he made the decision to go on at the start. The horse made all and the rider kept a bit in reserve for when he was challenged, and the gelding responded generously. A tactical race it may have been, but it was a good performance and he should progress. (op 11/2 tchd 7/1)
Gift Of Dgab(IRE) was left a little bit when things quickened up in the straight but then stayed on well, especially when hitting the rising ground. He probably needs further, although a truly run race over this trip should be little problem to a horse certain to win at least a maiden hurdle.
Ballyburke(IRE) ◆ was undone by the fact that he failed to settle but it was still a credit to this immensely promising horse that he ran so well. He was tanking as they turned out of the back straight and it might have been interesting to see what happened had he been sent on at that point. When he came to challenge at the second last he had every chance but the winner had that bit left and this fellow's effort was just beginning to flatten when he was awkward at the final flight. Like the runner-up, he's certain to win a maiden hurdle at least but he has to settle better in his races. (op 7/1 tchd 5/1)
Aughnacurraveel(IRE) raced quite keenly and, when asked after the third last, the response was disappointing. Despite the way the race was run it was a substandard effort and he's better than this. (op 15/8)
Bacher Boy(IRE) wasn't flattered by his rating against improving horses and, despite being close enough if good enough at the third last, could make no further impression. (op 14/1)
He's Our Man(IRE) certainly ran a lot better than his finishing position as he had closed up on the outer with a chance when making a very bad mistake at the second last. (op 25/1)
Seafield(IRE) ran no race whatsoever, dropping out completely from the top of the straight. Official explanation: jockey said gelding never travelled throughout (op 15/8 tchd 7/2)

2231 FFOS LAS (L-H)

Monday, November 22

OFFICIAL GOING: Good to soft (soft in places)
Wind: moderate against Weather: cloudy

2570 OWAIN PRICE JUVENILE HURDLE (8 hdls) 2m

12:50 (12:50) (Class 4) 3-Y-O **£2,602** (£764; £382; £190)

Form RPR

1 **First Fandango**[55] 3-10-12 0 .... (t) RichardJohnson 110+
(Tim Vaughan) *trckd ldng pair: wnt 2nd after 5th: nt fluent and sltly outpcd by ldr next: led last: sn drvn clr* **2/7**[1]

2 *3 3/4* **Killusty Fancy (IRE)**[72] 3-10-12 0 .... MarkGrant 102+
(Dominic Ffrench Davis) *disp ld tl def advantage 3rd: qcknd appr 3 out: hit next: hdd last: one pce flat* **9/1**[2]

F- **3** *23* **Katchmore (IRE)**[20] 4965 3-10-12 0 .... JimmyMcCarthy 79
(Michael Blanshard) *racd a little keenly: disp ld tl hdd 3rd: styd cl up tl rdn bef 3 out and sn lft bhd by first 2: wl hld whn hit last* **33/1**

4 *19* **Jewellery (IRE)**[28] 3-9-12 0 .... OliverDayman(7) 52
(Alison Thorpe) *chsd ldrs: wandered gng into 5th: sn drvn and lost tch* **14/1**

0 **5** *9* **Direct Flo (IRE)**[34] 1913 3-10-5 0 .... RhysFlint 52
(Keith Goldsworthy) *hld up last but in tch: mstke 1st: rdn after 5th: disputing mod 4th whn lost hind legs on landing 3 out: immediately eased* **33/1**

4F **F** **Free As A Lark**[27] 2020 3-9-12 0 .... (t) AdamWedge(7) —
(Evan Williams) *racd keenly: hld up in rr: wknd bef 3 out: poor 5th whn fell heavily next* **12/1**[3]

3m 52.2s (3.20) **Going Correction** +0.375s/f (Yiel) **6** Ran SP% **108.0**
Speed ratings (Par 104): **107,105,93,84,79** —
Tote Swingers: 1&2 £1.40, 1&3 £10.70 CSF £3.27 TOTE £1.20: £1.10, £2.40; EX 3.40.
Owner T Vaughan **Bred** Aylesfield Farms Stud Ltd **Trained** Aberthin, Vale of Glamorgan

FOCUS
Not a lot of strength in depth for this juvenile hurdle and not a lot of form to go on, but the winner looks a useful recruit.

NOTEBOOK
First Fandango was the subject of strong vibes beforehand and he duly obliged, although, having to be ridden out to assert on the run from the last. He had changed hands for £60,000 after a successful time on the Flat with John Hills and jumped fluently in the main on this hurdling debut. He was a little green when hitting the front but looked honest and responded well to his rider's urgings. The stable has been enduring a rather quiet spell of late, but feel they're turning the corner and are hopeful this promising 3-y-o can progress into a Fred Winter possible. (op 1-2 tchd 1-4)
Killusty Fancy(IRE) ran with plenty of promise and should be winning races before long. He cut out most of the running at just an ordinary pace before quickening turning in. A mistake two out didn't help his cause and he was a sitting duck for the winner, but kept on well enough to finish clear of the remainder. (op 15-2)
Katchmore(IRE), who proved free, ran with some promise although he lacked the gears to go with the principals when they upped the tempo turning in. (op 20-1 tchd 18-1)
Jewellery(IRE), on her hurdling debut, dropped away tamely entering the home straight. (op 12-1)
Direct Flo(IRE) needs to brush up on some less than convincing jumping. (op 20-1)
Free As A Lark had shown some promise on debut but needs to settle better and was a spent force before falling at the second-last. (op 15-2)

2571 INTEGRAL GEOTECHNIQUE "NATIONAL HUNT" NOVICES' HURDLE (12 hdls) 3m

1:20 (1:20) (Class 4) 4-Y-0+ **£2,602** (£764; £382; £190)

Form RPR

42 **1** **Teaforthree (IRE)**[19] 2143 6-10-12 0 .... APMcCoy 120+
(Rebecca Curtis) *trckd ldrs: wnt 2nd 7th: chal 3 out: sn led: drew clr appr last: easily* **4/5**[1]

2 *3* **Top Benefit (IRE)**[645] 8-10-12 0 .... JasonMaguire 112+
(Keith Goldsworthy) *set stdy pce: jnd 3 out: sn drvn and hdd: one pce appr last* **25/1**

3 *1 3/4* **Duneen Point (IRE)**[527] 708 6-10-12 0 .... JohnnyFarrelly 108+
(Tim Vaughan) *trckd ldr: relegated to 3rd 7th: rdn after 9th: outpcd by ldng pair fr next: styd on again flat* **10/1**[3]

011- **4** *14* **Whitewater Dash**[239] 4915 10-10-12 109 .... RhysFlint 94
(Jim Old) *in tch: pushed along after 8th: disp modest 3rd bef 3 out: sn one pce* **14/1**

-311 **5** *1 3/4* **Alpine Breeze (IRE)**[15] 2232 4-11-5 120 .... RichardJohnson 108+
(Don Cantillon) *hld up in last pl: slt mstke 5th: stdy hdwy on ins fr 8th: 3rd whn blnd bdly and dropped bk to 5th next: no imp on ldrs after* **9/4**[2]

0/6 **6** *24* **Front Street (IRE)**[19] 2154 6-10-7 0 .... MichaelMurphy(5) 73
(Pat Murphy) *hld up in 5th: last fr 6th: rdn bef 9th: sn lft wl bhd* **100/1**

6m 11.3s (24.30) **Going Correction** +0.375s/f (Yiel) **6** Ran SP% **106.9**
Speed ratings (Par 105): **74,73,72,67,67 59**
Tote Swingers: 1&2 £3.70, 1&3 £2.00, 2&3 £12.70 CSF £18.08 TOTE £2.40: £1.30, £3.20; EX 12.70.
Owner G Costelloe **Bred** M O'Sullivan **Trained** Newport, Dyfed

FOCUS
An uncompetitive staying novice hurdle run in a moderate time. The winner can rate higher and it was a good effort from the runner-up.

NOTEBOOK
Teaforthree(IRE) ran out a convincing winner having been stepped up to 3m. A former Irish point winner, he had chased home the promising Sonofvic on his hurdling debut at Chepstow earlier this month, following a promising effort in a bumper since joining connections. He should continue to pay his way this season, but looks a decent prospect for when his attention is switched to fences next season. (op 5-6 tchd 10-11 and 1-1 in places)

Top Benefit(IRE) had not been seen since racking up a hat-trick in the point-to-point field back in February in 2009 and ran with plenty of encouragement. Making the running until narrowly headed three out, he battled on gamely and only gave best going to the last. He should come on nicely for this. (op 16-1)

Duneen Point(IRE) had shown promise in a couple of maiden hurdles in Ireland and was making his debut for connections after a lengthy absence. He ran with encouragement and a race of this nature looks well within his compass before going chasing. Official explanation: jockey said gelding hung both ways (tchd 9-1)

Whitewater Dash, reverting to hurdles after landing back-to-back staying chases in the spring, ran well enough before tiring in the straight. He will be better for the run and will be of more interest when seen back over fences. (op 12-1)

Alpine Breeze(IRE) was trying to defy a double penalty, but a very bad blunder at the last in the back straight ruined any chance she had of doing so. Official explanation: jockey said filly hung left (tchd 5-2)

2572 HUGH JAMES SOLICITORS NOVICES' H'CAP CHASE (13 fncs) 2m

1:55 (1:55) (Class 3) (0-130,125) 4-Y-0+ **£5,204** (£1,528; £764; £381)

Form				RPR
22	1		**Betabob (IRE)**[35] 1900 7-10-0 **104**...(tp) MichaelMurphy(5) (Tim Vaughan) *hld up wl in tch in last pl: jnd ldrs 4 out: led 2 out: r.o strly flat* **15/2**	117+
0551	2	4 ½	**Kack Handed**[26] 2037 7-10-13 **112**... RichardJohnson (Henry Daly) *led: tended to jump rt-handed: rdn and hdd 2 out: hld in 2nd whn hit last* **11/4**[2]	117
13-3	3	6	**Oscar Gogo (IRE)**[19] 2148 8-10-6 **112**... AdamWedge(7) (Evan Williams) *trckd ldrs: hmpd 2nd: rdn and briefly dropped to last 4 out: kpt on same pce fr next* **9/2**	110
-144	4	7	**William Hogarth**[30] 1966 5-11-12 **125**... RhysFlint (Keith Goldsworthy) *trckd ldr: mstke 2nd: j. bdly rt and lost pl next: rdn along fr 7th: wnt 2nd after 9th: one pce fr 3 out: hld in 4th whn mstke last* **7/2**[3]	118+
P-43	5	1 ½	**Sambulando (FR)**[11] 2326 7-11-9 **122**...(t) JasonMaguire (Tom George) *lft trcking ldr 3rd: lost 2nd 9th: cl 3rd whn blnd bdly and relegated to last 3 out: no imp on ldrs after* **9/4**[1]	119+

4m 8.20s (3.20) **Going Correction** +0.375s/f (Yiel) **5 Ran SP% 109.6**
Speed ratings (Par 107): **107,104,101,98,97**
CSF £27.77 TOTE £7.60: £5.90, £2.70; EX 14.60.

Owner David Lovell **Bred** Miss Carmel Salley **Trained** Aberthin, Vale of Glamorgan

FOCUS
A tight novice handicap, run at just an ordinary pace, with all five runners holding a chance at some point in the straight. A step up from the winner with the second rated to his mark

NOTEBOOK
Betabob(IRE) handed his trainer another winner in ready fashion. He had plenty of placed efforts to his name but remained, until now, a maiden after 25 starts over jumps, including since joining present connections. He travelled well tracking the leaders and a fine leap four out put him bang there on the bridle, before quickening ahead just before the last. He had a fairly uninspiring profile over fences in the past but he won with plenty in hand off his light weight and, now having got his head in front, can remain competitive if being realistically reassessed. (op 13-2 tchd 6-1 and 8-1)

Kack Handed was trying to follow up, off 6lb higher, his recent Haydock success and probably stepped up on that with this performance so remains in good heart. (op 3-1)

Oscar Gogo(IRE) ran respectably on this second try over fences and had his chance in the straight before flattening out after the second-last. (tchd 5-1)

William Hogarth has raced in decent company at times over hurdles and had beaten the useful looking Karasenir at Chepstow earlier this season. This was a bit disappointing as he was off a reasonable mark for his chasing debut. He gave the first a nudge and took his time to warm to the task but got himself in with a shout in the straight, before his effort flattened out at the second-last. Official explanation: jockey said gelding lost a near-fore shoe (op 4-1 tchd 10-3)

Sambulando(FR) was equipped with a tongue-tie and would have given the winner plenty to think about as he was travelling just as strongly before clouting three out, effectively knocking himself out of the race. He should be found compensation before long in a similar affair, providing he brushes up his fencing. (tchd 5-2)

2573 INTEGRAL GEOTECHNIQUE MARES' H'CAP CHASE (17 fncs) 2m 5f

2:25 (2:25) (Class 4) (0-115,115) 4-Y-0+ **£3,252** (£955; £477; £238)

Form				RPR
4PP3	1		**Prescelli (IRE)**[4] 2481 6-11-12 **112**...(p) JasonMaguire (Keith Goldsworthy) *in tch: j. slowly and dropped to rr 2nd: reminders after 8th: hdwy to go 2nd after 4 out: led 2 out: idled and drvn out flat* **10/1**	122+
3-52	2	2 ¼	**Topless (IRE)**[27] 2024 9-11-1 **101**...(p) DougieCostello (Neil Mulholland) *mde most tl hdd 12th: led again 4 out: hdd 2 out: styd on flat* **5/2**[2]	104
62-1	3	1 ¼	**Take It There**[4] 2470 8-12-1 **115** 7ex...(t) FelixDeGiles (Alastair Lidderdale) *hld up in last pl: clsd 9th: mstke and dropped to rr again 10th: hdwy after 13th: rdn 3 out: kpt on same pce fr next* **4/1**[3]	119
-P43	4	8	**Me Julie**[4] 2470 7-9-13 **92**... NathanSweeney(7) (Arthur Whiting) *disp ld tl nt fluent 9th: dropped to rr after 4 out: kpt on one pce fr next* **15/8**[1]	88
	5	10	**Bonny Isle (IRE)**[8] 2409 7-10-4 **95**... APHeskin(5) (D McNamara, Ire) *trckd ldrs: mstke 10th: led 12th: rdn and hdd 4 out: wknd after next* **11/2**	80

5m 39.6s (9.60) **Going Correction** +0.375s/f (Yiel) **5 Ran SP% 107.8**
Speed ratings (Par 105): **96,95,94,91,87**
CSF £33.65 TOTE £6.90: £10.30, £1.40; EX 31.60.

Owner S F Barlow **Bred** Thomas Coleman **Trained** Yerbeston, Pembrokes

FOCUS
An ordinary mares' only handicap chase. The winner returned to form and the third sets the level.

NOTEBOOK
Prescelli(IRE) received a fine never-say-die ride from Jason Maguire to grind out victory. She had slipped on landing after reaching for a fence on her chasing debut at Wincanton last time and frightened herself, so it was understandable that she was not the most fluent here. It remains to be seen if she can build upon this. Official explanation: trainer said, regarding apparent improvement in form, that the mare made a bad mistake four out on its last run. (op 9-1)

Topless(IRE) was on a fair mark with her yard in fine form and ran her usual game race, but normally finds one or two too good. (op 9-4)

Take It There travelled well turning in but could never quite get on terms with the leaders and just stayed on at the same pace. This race may have come too soon after winning at Hereford last week. (op 7-2)

Me Julie won this last year and looked on good terms to reverse the placings with Take It There on their Hereford run last week. She was struggling from a fair way out, however, and the race might have come too soon for her as well. (op 2-1)

Bonny Isle(IRE) sat prominently for most of the way until leaving the back straight and was soon beaten. (op 7-1)

2574 GWYNNE PRICE H'CAP HURDLE (11 hdls) 2m 6f

3:00 (3:00) (Class 3) (0-130,125) 4-Y-0+ **£4,878** (£1,432; £716; £357)

Form				RPR
11	1		**Kilcrea Kim (IRE)**[24] 2067 5-11-12 **125**... RichardJohnson (Philip Hobbs) *trckd ldr: hit 2nd: led 8th: rdn after 3 out: jnd last: all out* **1/1**[1]	135+
-022	2	nk	**Vivarini**[9] 2364 6-10-4 **110**... CharlieWallis(7) (John O'Shea) *hld up in tch: slt mstke 4th: hdwy 4 out: wnt 2nd bef 2 out: chal and nt fluent last: r.o u.p flat: jst hld* **8/1**[3]	120+
3355	3	27	**Doubletoilntrouble (IRE)**[15] 2235 4-10-6 **105**... RhysFlint (Keith Goldsworthy) *led: rdn and jst hdd whn mstke 8th: lost 2nd bef 2 out: lft bhd by first two fr next: plugged on one pce* **9/2**[2]	88
133-	4	½	**Salontyre (GER)**[164] 4497 4-10-1 **105**...(p) MissIsabelTompsett(5) (Bernard Llewellyn) *hld up towards rr: sme hdwy 6th: mstke and dropped to rr again 7th: rdn after 8th: sn no ch w ldrs* **9/1**	89
4235	5	nk	**Stormyisland Ahead**[15] 2232 5-10-6 **112**...(t) AdamWedge(7) (Evan Williams) *in tch: chsd ldrs after 4 out: wknd fr next* **9/1**	94
6F0/	6	50	**Counting House (IRE)**[789] 4449 7-11-7 **120**... JasonMaguire (Jim Old) *hld up in rr: nvr trbld ldrs: wl bhd fr 3 out: t.o* **12/1**	52
1-30	7	43	**Native Taipan (IRE)**[19] 2147 8-10-9 **115**...(t) AodhaganConlon(7) (Rebecca Curtis) *in tch tl wknd qckly 4 out: t.o* **14/1**	4
1F5-	P		**Pearl (IRE)**[12] 4940 6-10-8 **107**...(tp) DougieCostello (Alison Thorpe) *trckd ldrs: rdn 4 out: sn wknd: wl bhd whn p.u bef 3 out* **16/1**	—

5m 30.4s (12.40) **Going Correction** +0.375s/f (Yiel)
WFA 4 from 5yo+ 8lb **8 Ran SP% 119.5**
Speed ratings (Par 107): **92,91,82,81,81 63,47,—**
Tote Swingers: 1&2 £3.50, 1&3 £3.00, 2&3 £8.90 CSF £10.76 CT £28.15 TOTE £2.50: £1.30, £2.60, £2.20; EX 10.30.

Owner James and Jean Potter **Bred** Francis O'Brien **Trained** Withycombe, Somerset

■ Stewards' Enquiry : Charlie Wallis four-day ban: used whip with excessive frequency without giving gelding time to respond (Dec 6-9)

FOCUS
A decent handicap hurdle. The first two came well clear and it's hard not to be positive about this form. The winner looks sure to rate higher.

NOTEBOOK
Kilcrea Kim(IRE) kept his unbeaten status intact, but had to dig deep to do so on his handicapping debut. A lovely, big stamp of horse who jumps his hurdles like they were fences already, he rates an exciting staying chaser in the making. He basically outstayed the runner up here and a further step up in trip should only see him in a stronger light. (op 4-5 tchd 5-4)

Vivarini ◆ won three handicaps at the beginning of the year and remained in good heart after finishing runner up at Uttoxeter last time. He laid down a serious challenge after two out and guessed at the last, but kept on in determined fashion only to be narrowly denied. In this frame of mind he should find an opening to regain the winning trend before long. (op 17-2 tchd 9-1 and 15-2)

Doubletoilntrouble(IRE), the gamble of the race, took them along at an ordinary pace but the writing was soon on the wall for his supporters after getting headed going to three out. He is off a reasonable mark at present and might appreciate a further step back in distance. (op 8-1 tchd 4-1)

Salontyre(GER), making his reappearance back over hurdles since winning on the Flat in June, could never get involved and was soundly beaten. (op 14-1)

Stormyisland Ahead had been unable to carry a penalty with any success in novice company, although running creditably, and after a brief effort going to the third-last, was soon in trouble. (op 15-2)

2575 STRADEY PARK AMATEUR RIDERS' H'CAP CHASE (15 fncs) 2m 3f 110y

3:35 (3:35) (Class 5) (0-95,94) 4-Y-0+ **£1,873** (£581; £290; £145)

Form				RPR
4P-5	1		**Cold Harbour**[24] 2073 6-10-13 **88**... MrJEngland(7) (Evan Williams) *led: gng clr whn mstke 4 out: jnd next: hdd appr last: styd on u.p to ld early flat: drvn out* **7/2**[2]	98+
-022	2	nk	**Wingull (IRE)**[25] 2053 6-11-11 **93**... MrRMahon (George Baker) *cl up: mstke and lost pl 7th: sn rdn along: styd on u.p fr 2 out: r.o flat: jst hld* **7/4**[1]	101+
1501	3	6	**Ponchatrain (IRE)**[13] 2292 10-11-5 **94**...(v) MrTBellamy(7) (Martin Keighley) *trckd ldrs: j.rt at times: w wnr 7th tl 11th: tk narrow ld appr last: hdd, edgd rt and wknd flat* **15/2**	96+
P-04	4	14	**Loco Grande (IRE)**[12] 2314 5-11-1 **90**... MrEDavid(7) (Tim Vaughan) *in tch: wnt 2nd 7th: rdn bef 4 out: 4th and one pce whn mstke 3 out: sn wknd* **7/1**[3]	78
-P23	5	5	**Normandy Landings**[25] 2048 7-10-5 **80**...(p) MrDLavery(7) (Neil Mulholland) *a towards rr: lost tch after 11th* **7/2**[2]	60
0466	U		**Bachley Gale**[15] 2231 5-10-5 **80**...(p) MissCharlotteEvans(7) (Keith Goldsworthy) *mstke 1st: in rr: bhd fr 3rd: wl bhd whn mstke and uns rdr 9th* **18/1**	—

5m 13.5s (7.50) **Going Correction** +0.375s/f (Yiel) **6 Ran SP% 110.3**
Speed ratings (Par 103): **100,99,97,91,89 —**
Tote Swingers: 1&2 £1.50, 1&3 £5.20, 2&3 £1.30 CSF £10.16 TOTE £4.10: £1.80, £1.80; EX 12.10.

Owner Fox And Hounds Racing **Bred** Crandon Park Stud **Trained** Llancarfan, Vale Of Glamorgan

■ The first winner under rules for Johnny England, younger brother of jockey David England.

■ Stewards' Enquiry : Mr J England one-day ban: used whip with excessive frequency (Dec 14)
Mr R Mahon three-day ban: used whip with excessive frequency (Dec 14,16,22)

FOCUS
A moderate amateur riders' chase. The winner is rated back to the best of his chase form.

NOTEBOOK
Cold Harbour got off the mark at the sixth time of asking over fences. He cut out a lot of the running and proved most game from two out. He had slipped to a handy mark on his old form, but doesn't possess the most encouraging of profiles so it can only be taken on trust that he will go on from this. (op 9-2)

Wingull(IRE), under the most experienced amateur in the field, made a mistake in the back straight and was soon under strong pressure. He was doing all his best work all too late but it was all to no avail as he failed to reel in the winner. The longer trip suited. (op 15-8 tchd 2-1 and 13-8)

Ponchatrain(IRE) regained the winning thread in a first-time visor at Lingfield last time and a 4lb rise looked reasonable. He gave his rider, who was having his first ride in public, an enjoyable one and laid down a strong challenge up the straight, before edging to his right and fading from the last. (op 9-2)

Loco Grande(IRE) made an encouraging reappearance and was reasonably treated on his return to fences. It was a disappointing effort, as he had his chances but was comfortably held from three out. (op 15-2)

Normandy Landings was seeking his first win in eight attempts over fences and was trying a visor for the first time. He was under pressure turning in and could never get competitive. (op 9-2)

2576 LINCWEAR STANDARD OPEN NATIONAL HUNT FLAT RACE 1m 6f

4:05 (4:05) (Class 5) 4-5-Y-O **£1,712** (£499; £249)

Form				RPR
	1		**Valley Lad (IRE)** 4-11-0 0 RichardJohnson (Tim Vaughan) *hld up bhd ldrs: wnt 2nd over 4f out: led 3f out: steadily drew clr: comf* **9/4**[2]	105+
0	**2**	8	**Tenby Jewel (IRE)**[16] 2215 5-11-0 0 JasonMaguire (Keith Goldsworthy) *led at decent pce: hdd and rdn 3f out: sn no ch w wnr but a holding 2nd* **9/2**[3]	92
	3	8	**Miss Hippy (IRE)** 5-10-4 0 JimmyDerham(3) (Milton Harris) *midfield: clsd 6f out: lft bhd by ldng pair fr 4f out: styd on same pce* **25/1**	75
0-	**4**	1 1/2	**Todareistodo**[217] 5284 4-11-0 0 RhysFlint (Jim Old) *towards rr but in tch: clsd to trck ldrs over 4f out: sn outpcd by first two: plugged on* **14/1**	81
0	**5**	1 1/4	**Radmores Oscar**[24] 2074 4-10-7 0 CharlieWallis(7) (John O'Shea) *in tch in midfield: rdn 4f out: sn one pce and no ch w ldrs* **33/1**	79
	6	13	**Grovemere (IRE)** 5-11-0 0 APMcCoy (Rebecca Curtis) *chsd ldrs: reminders 6f out: sn drvn: wknd 4f out* **6/4**[1]	63
00	**7**	39	**Mi Man Sam (IRE)**[96] 1284 5-10-11 0 (p) CharlieStudd(3) (George Jones) *chsd ldr tl over 4f out: sn wknd: t.o fnl 3f* **66/1**	17
	8	3 1/4	**Tee Shot (IRE)** 4-10-9 0 MichaelMurphy(5) (Tim Vaughan) *in rr: struggled to go the pce early: clsd and in tch 1/2-way: wknd 5f out: t.o* **7/1**	13

3m 18.8s (198.80) **8** Ran SP% **116.4**

Tote Swingers: 1&2 £3.00, 1&3 £9.70, 2&3 £14.60 CSF £12.96 TOTE £4.10: £2.20, £1.10, £4.90; EX 15.10.

Owner Walters Plant Hire Ltd **Bred** R McCarthy **Trained** Aberthin, Vale of Glamorgan

FOCUS

A good pace for this ordinary bumper, which is rated through the second and fourth. The winner could be decent.

NOTEBOOK

Valley Lad(IRE), a Flemensfirth gelding out of an Old Vic mare, made light of his rivals to turn in a very likeable performance to give Tim Vaughan's stable a treble on the day. He dropped his rider beforehand, but was very professional in the race itself and only had to be pushed clear to score. No doubt a nice prospect, but it's hard to assess what he beat here. (op 15-8 tchd 5-2)

Tenby Jewel(IRE) set out to make this a true test, but had no answer to the winner when headed. He kept on well enough to finish a clear second-best and his was a step in the right direction after a disappointing debut. (op 5-1 tchd 11-2)

Miss Hippy(IRE) ran with some credit and, although never threatening the front pair, she stayed on well enough on her racecourse debut. (op 20-1)

Todareistodo will be better for the outing as he was a little keen and was still travelling well turning in on the heels of the leaders, but his effort flattened out in the final 2f.

Radmores Oscar stepped up on debut without ever threatening.

Grovemere(IRE) came under strong pressure to keep tabs on the leaders turning in, before weakening over 3f out. He is a half-brother to Albertas Run and considered to be a stayer in the making. (op 2-1 tchd 11-8)

T/Plt: £26.40 to a £1 stake. Pool:£46,602.34 - 1,284.68 winning tickets T/Qpdt: £13.70 to a £1 stake. Pool:£5,425.14 - 292.95 winning tickets RL

2122 KEMPTON (R-H)

Monday, November 22

OFFICIAL GOING: Good (good to soft on bend adjacent to lake, chs 7.5 hdl 7.3)

Wind: Moderate, against Weather: Cloudy, raining race 3 to race 5

2577 EUROPEAN BREEDERS' FUND "NATIONAL HUNT" NOVICES' HURDLE (QUALIFIER) (8 hdls) 2m

12:30 (12:30) (Class 4) 4-6-Y-O **£2,602** (£764; £382; £190)

Form				RPR
21-	**1**		**Bobs Worth (IRE)**[227] 5121 5-10-12 0 BarryGeraghty (Nicky Henderson) *trckd ldr: led bef 2 out: briefly pressed: pushed along and drew clr bef last: promising* **4/9**[1]	136+
2	**2**	9	**Sire De Grugy (FR)**[16] 2215 4-10-12 0 JamieMoore (Gary Moore) *prom: trckd ldng pair 3 out: chal gng strly and w wnr 2 out: sn outpcd but styd on wl* **7/1**[2]	122+
0-00	**3**	5	**George Nympton (IRE)**[20] 2136 4-10-12 118 (b1) DarylJacob (Nick Williams) *led: mstke 3 out: rdn and hdd bef 2 out: sn no ch w ldng pair: hrd rdn and kpt on* **14/1**	117
65-6	**4**	10	**Smart Freddy**[187] 412 4-10-7 0 DavidBass(5) (Lawney Hill) *trckd ldrs: cl 4th 3 out: sn rdn and outpcd by ldng trio bef next* **66/1**	107
10-5	**5**	2	**Reinriver**[43] 1793 4-10-5 0 AidanColeman (Brendan Powell) *hld up wl in rr: prog fr 5th: nt on terms w ldrs after 3 out: kpt on* **100/1**	99
455-	**6**	9	**Calusa Shadow**[356] 2628 6-10-5 0 ChrisDavies(7) (Philip Hobbs) *racd wd: hld up towards rr: outpcd whn nt fluent 3 out: pushed along and kpt on fr next: n.d* **66/1**	99+
041-	**7**	3 3/4	**Pere Blanc (IRE)**[261] 4445 5-10-12 0 TimmyMurphy (David Arbuthnot) *hld up wl in rr: wnt modest 10th after 3 out: nudged along next: gng on at fin* **12/1**	94
2-3	**8**	2	**Quiet Whisper (IRE)**[18] 2162 4-10-5 0 (t) MrCGreene(7) (Kim Bailey) *pressed ldng pair tl bef 3 out: steadily fdd* **25/1**	92
20-1	**9**	2 1/2	**Violin Davis (FR)**[33] 1920 4-10-5 0 NoelFehily (Paul Nicholls) *nt fluent: trckd ldrs: mstke 5th and lost pl: 6th and struggling after 3 out: fdd* **8/1**[3]	86+
6-0	**10**	20	**Beau Colonel (FR)**[25] 2056 4-10-12 0 HaddenFrost (Henrietta Knight) *mostly in midfield: in tch after 5th: nt fluent next: sn wknd* **66/1**	72
06-0	**11**	5	**Sebennytos**[25] 2056 5-10-5 0 MrTGarner(7) (Warren Greatrex) *t.k.h: hld up towards rr: prog to chse ldrs 5th: rdn and wknd after 3 out* **100/1**	67
-30	**12**	5	**Bach To Back (IRE)**[8] 2389 5-10-12 0 PaddyBrennan (Nigel Twiston-Davies) *j.rt 2nd: a towards rr: wl bhd whn mstke 3 out: t.o* **66/1**	63
6-1P	**13**	1/2	**Bad Sir Brian (IRE)**[17] 2181 5-10-12 0 LiamTreadwell (Nick Gifford) *a wl in rr: lost tch fr 5th: wl t.o after 3 out* **66/1**	62
0/00	**14**	1	**Patrick Dee**[22] 2109 5-10-5 0 MattCrawley(7) (Christine Dunnett) *nt fluent: a in rr: wl t.o 3 out* **100/1**	61
6	**15**	10	**Calusa Catrina (IRE)**[191] 332 5-10-5 0 TomO'Brien (Philip Hobbs) *nvr bttr than midfield: rdn and wknd bef 3 out: t.o* **66/1**	45
P	**16**	88	**Captain Sully (IRE)**[9] 2361 5-10-12 102 (t) AndrewThornton (Jim Wilson) *chsd ldrs: 7th 1/2-way: wknd rapidly after 5th: mstke next: wl t.o and virtually p.u* **40/1**	—
65-F	**F**		**Salto Angel (FR)**[22] 2109 4-10-12 0 AndrewGlassonbury (Gary Moore) *nt fluent: a in rr: t.o whn mstke 3 out: poor 16th whn fell last* **100/1**	—

3m 52.9s (-7.10) **Going Correction** -0.60s/f (Firm) **17** Ran SP% **126.4**

Speed ratings: **93,88,86,81,80 75,73,72,71,61 58,56,56,55,50 6,—**

Tote Swingers: 1&2 £3.00, 1&3 £3.80, 2&3 £11.50 CSF £4.15 TOTE £1.40: £1.20, £2.00, £2.60; EX 6.50.

Owner The Not Afraid Partnership **Bred** Mrs L Eadie **Trained** Upper Lambourn, Berks

FOCUS

A race that went to Somersby two years ago. Nicky Henderson had won this four times in the last ten seasons and added another victory courtesy of Bobs Worth. The pace seemed just modest, putting those prominent at an advantage, but the time was good, being 7.50 seconds quicker than the later Class 4 handicap, and the winner looks a smart prospect. Solid novice form.

NOTEBOOK

Bobs Worth(IRE) ◆, successful in one of his two bumpers starts at this track last term, looked a smart type in the making on this hurdling debut. He was by no means a natural over his hurdles, jumping one or two of them a bit big, very much in the fashion of a future chaser. However, he was still able to draw clear after travelling strongly into the straight, and it's a sign of his potential that he still won so readily. He should learn plenty from this, but it's unlikely we'll see the very best of him until he goes over fences. According to Nicky Henderson, Bobs Worth might have another run over 2m, before maybe trying 2m4f when he goes up in class, and the trainer will consider the EBF Final at Sandown as long as he's not too badly handicapped. (op 1-2 tchd 8-13 in a place and 4-7 in places)

Sire De Grugy(FR) ◆ finished second on his debut in the same Sandown bumper his trainer won last year with Megastar, suggesting he's well regarded, and he again showed plenty of ability. He went with the winner for a long way, and although ultimately left behind, he's clearly pretty useful. (op 8-1 tchd 9-1)

George Nympton(IRE) hadn't shown much on his first two starts this season, but he took well to the fitting of blinkers for the first time and benefited from being allowed to set an ordinary pace. This was a return to something like his best form from last term. (op 16-1)

Smart Freddy was comfortably held after being well placed, but this was still a pleasing return from a 187-day break. (op 100-1)

Reinriver was never seriously involved, but she stuck on and this was an improvement on her hurdling debut at Ffos Las.

Violin Davis(FR)'s Fontwell bumper success on her reappearance is not working out, and she struggled on this hurdling debut, being pitched in against males. She'll appreciate returning to racing against her own sex. (op 7-1)

2578 TOTESPORT.COM NOVICES' CHASE (12 fncs) 2m

1:00 (1:00) (Class 3) 4-Y-O+ **£8,433**

Form				RPR
1-03	**1**		**Dee Ee Williams (IRE)**[16] 2219 7-11-0 0 (v1) LiamTreadwell (Nick Gifford) *tended to jump sltly lft: pressed ldr: led and lft alone 6th* **1/2**[1]	125+
00-2	**F**		**Oddshoes (IRE)**[79] 1470 8-11-0 0 TomO'Brien (Philip Hobbs) *led: narrowly hdd and fell 6th: fatally injured* **6/1**[3]	—
/62-	**U**		**Quasar D'Oudairies (FR)**[422] 1536 6-11-0 0 DarylJacob (Nick Williams) *hld up last: mstke 4th: swvd to avoid faller and uns rdr 6th* **3/1**[2]	—

4m 15.5s (17.50) **Going Correction** +0.10s/f (Yiel) **3** Ran SP% **106.0**

Speed ratings (Par 107): **60,—,—**

TOTE £1.40; EX 1.10.

Owner Give Every Man His Due **Bred** Michael And Fiona O'Connor **Trained** Findon, W Sussex

FOCUS

This novice chase had yet to get serious prior to the race being turned into a non-event at the sixth fence when Oddshoes took a crashing fall, forcing Quasar D'Oudairies to swerve right on landing, unseating Tom O'Brien in the process. Unrateable form.

NOTEBOOK

Dee Ee Williams(IRE), who had a visor replacing blinkers, was left without any rivals and put in a safe round of jumping to take advantage. He failed to win in three starts over fences last year, but this was a confidence boosting return to chasing for this useful performer. (op 8-15 tchd 4-9 and 4-7 in places)

Oddshoes(IRE), on his chasing debut, sadly took a fatal fall at the sixth. (op 7-2)

Quasar D'Oudairies(FR) unseated his rider when swerving to avoid the stricken Oddshoes at the sixth. (op 7-2)

2579 LADBROKES MARES' HURDLE (LISTED RACE) (12 hdls) 3m 110y

1:30 (1:30) (Class 1) 4-Y-O+

£17,103 (£6,417; £3,213; £1,602; £804; £402)

Form				RPR
221-	**1**		**Carole's Legacy**[220] 5205 6-10-12 150 BarryGeraghty (Nicky Henderson) *trckd ldr tl nt fluent 3 out: pushed along to dispute 2nd again 2 out: drvn to chal last: r.o to ld flat* **13/8**[2]	143+
21-2	**2**	1	**Banjaxed Girl**[16] 2218 6-11-2 153 SamTwiston-Davies (Nigel Twiston-Davies) *j.w: led at mod pce: kicked on fr 9th: drvn 2 out: hdd and outpcd after last* **6/4**[1]	146+
1231	**3**	1 1/2	**Santera (IRE)**[16] 2218 6-10-12 129 (p) WillKennedy (John Flint) *cl up: chsd ldr 3 out: shkn up bef next: stl disputing 2nd and ch last: one pce* **14/1**	140
-004	**4**	14	**Parlesotho (FR)**[29] 1986 7-10-12 117 WayneHutchinson (Ben Case) *hld up in 5th: blnd 8th and reminders: chsd ldng trio 3 out: no imp bef next: wknd* **66/1**	130
-313	**5**	20	**Amber Brook (IRE)**[23] 2089 9-10-12 146 PaddyBrennan (Nigel Twiston-Davies) *settled in last: nt gng that wl fr 1/2-way: stl in tch 3 out: drvn and wknd bef next* **4/1**[3]	114
1-06	**6**	57	**Love Of Tara**[16] 2218 8-10-12 125 WarrenMarston (Martin Keighley) *trckd ldng pair to 9th: sn rdn: dropped to last and mstke 3 out: wknd: t.o and eased* **33/1**	58

6m 6.90s (-20.60) **Going Correction** -0.60s/f (Firm) **6** Ran SP% **109.2**

Speed ratings (Par 111): **108,107,107,102,96 78**

Tote Swingers: 1&2 £1.20, 1&3 £2.20, 2&3 £2.10 CSF £4.33 TOTE £3.30: £1.50, £1.90; EX 4.30.

Owner Paul Murphy **Bred** Paul Murphy **Trained** Upper Lambourn, Berks

FOCUS

A quality mares' Listed event. The time, 8.80 seconds quicker than the later Class 3 handicap hurdle, was a new course record, taking 7.90 seconds off the time recorded by One Gulp in the 2008 running. It is probably worth being positive about the form and the first two are rated around 5lb off their very best.

NOTEBOOK

Carole's Legacy, marginally best off at the weights, won in game fashion on her return from a 220-day break. She briefly looked in a bit of trouble when coming off the bridle soon after making a slight mistake three out, with the runner-up getting a start on her, but she responded in most likeable fashion to pressure, ultimately getting up on the run in. She has won when fresh in the past, but it's reasonable to assume she'll come on for this. Her main aim is the David Nicholson Mares' Hurdle at the Cheltenham Festival, a race in which she was second last year, although she could go back over fences before then. (tchd 6-4 and 7-4 in a place)

Banjaxed Girl had the benefit of race-fitness over Carole's Legacy, having run second behind Santera off 148 in a mares' handicap on her reappearance, but she still found Nicky Henderson's runner too strong. This was her first run over a trip this far under rules, but she has won a point-to-point over 3m and this was hardly a severe test of stamina at the trip. (tchd 13-8)

Santera(IRE) defeated Banjaxed Girl 3l in a Wincanton handicap on her previous start, but was 22lb worse off this time. Although unable to confirm form, this was clearly a terrific effort at the revised weights and she's still improving. (op 16-1)

Parlesotho(FR) faced a tough task at the weights but ran as well as could have been expected. (op 100-1)

Amber Brook(IRE) had finished second in this race for the last two years, and came into this in decent form, but she proved bitterly disappointing. (tchd 9-2)

2580 TAKE A BREAK BEGINNERS' CHASE (18 fncs) 3m

2:05 (2:05) (Class 4) 4-Y-0+ **£3,903** (£1,146; £573; £286)

Form				RPR
0-22	**1**		**Key Cutter (FR)**[11] 2324 6-11-2 119.....(t) WillKennedy (Paul Webber) *led to 4th: nt fluent 6th: led again 8th: nt fluent13th: lft 6 l clr 4 out: in command after: pushed out flat* **7/2**[3]	128+
205-	**2**	4 ½	**Strategic Approach (IRE)**[226] 5134 8-11-2 0.....NoelFehily (Warren Greatrex) *in tch: outpcd fr 12th: lft 2nd 4 out: rdn to cl on wnr 3 out: readily hld fr next* **3/1**[2]	122
301-	**3**	66	**Andytown (IRE)**[219] 5224 7-11-2 0.....BarryGeraghty (Nicky Henderson) *j.lft and v ponderously early: settled in last tl effrt whn blnd 12th: nt jump wl after and t.o 14th: tk v remote 3rd 2 out* **1/1**[1]	79
2-35	**4**	35	**Horseshoe Reef (AUS)**[172] 594 7-11-2 0.....DarylJacob (Jamie Snowden) *tended to jump lft: pressed ldr: led 4th to 8th: rdn 12th: wknd rapidly 14th: wl t.o* **20/1**	31
2-26	**U**		**Picture In The Sky (IRE)**[25] 2057 9-10-13 115(p) SamTwiston-Davies(3) (Susan Nock) *wl in tch: chsd wnr 12th: abt 4 l down whn mstke 4 out and eventually uns rdr* **12/1**	—

6m 15.4s (0.40) **Going Correction** +0.10s/f (Yiel) **5** Ran SP% **109.7**

Speed ratings (Par 105): **103,101,79,67,—**

CSF £14.17 TOTE £6.20: £1.90, £1.90; EX 12.90.

Owner Mrs A Timpson **Bred** Kenneth Bourke **Trained** Mollington, Oxon

FOCUS

Not a particularly competitive beginners' chase, the race losing some of its depth when Picture In The Sky unseated after making a mistake four out. Ordinary form, and the winner may not have needed to improve.

NOTEBOOK

Key Cutter(FR) had shaped nicely enough on his first two starts over fences and confirmed the promise of those efforts with a straightforward success. He looks a useful staying handicap chaser in the making. According to Paul Webber, the winner may have a mid-winter break seeing as he wants good ground. (op 3-1 tchd 11-4)

Strategic Approach(IRE), a 130-rated hurdler, was no match at all for the winner, but this was a respectable chasing debut and he's entitled to improve, especially when returned to softer ground. (tchd 5-2 and 10-3)

Andytown(IRE), the winner of a handicap hurdle off 144 at Ayr when last seen in April, hadn't taken to fences on his two previous tries, despite being a point winner, and had apparently spent time with Enda Bolger to try and rectify that. However, he let his connections down with a really poor round of jumping, going out to his left more often than not and basically just losing ground at most fences. (op 11-8 tchd 7-4)

Horseshoe Reef(AUS) stopped quickly once under pressure and this performance leaves him with much to prove. (op 16-1)

Picture In The Sky(IRE), fitted with cheekpieces for the first time, was in second and had yet to be asked for his bid when unseating four out. (op 9-1 tchd 8-1)

2581 HALCYON GALLERY H'CAP HURDLE (12 hdls) 3m 110y

2:35 (2:36) (Class 3) (0-120,120) 4-Y-0+ **£4,553** (£1,337; £668; £333)

Form				RPR
0-31	**1**		**Kauto The Roc (FR)**[17] 2181 6-10-8 112.....PeterHatton(10) (Alan King) *racd wd in midfield: prog after 9th: disp 3rd after 3 out: rdn to cl on ldr 2 out: led bef last and veered lft: edgd rt flat: kpt on* **4/1**[1]	120+
0P-3	**2**	1 ½	**Lupanar (IRE)**[35] 1904 6-11-3 111.....(p) JamieMoore (Gary Moore) *nt a fluent: hld up in rr: rdn and struggling in 8th after 3 out: prog u.p 2 out: styd on to take 2nd last 50yds*	116+
200	**3**	1 ¾	**Kasban**[33] 1914 6-10-6 100.....(t) MattieBatchelor (Luke Dace) *hld up in midfield: rdn and prog after 3 out: wnt 3rd last: trying to cl whn hmpd and stmbld 100yds out: fin 4th: promoted to 3rd* **14/1**	104+
1F25	**4**	½	**Mad Moose (IRE)**[30] 1967 6-11-6 117.....SamTwiston-Davies(3) (Nigel Twiston-Davies) *trckd ldr: led sn after 3 out: drvn 2 out: hdd bef last: swtchd lft flat: lost 2nd last 50yds: fin 3rd: disqualified and plcd 4th* **8/1**	118
0-11	**5**	5	**Firm Order (IRE)**[35] 1904 5-11-10 118.....WillKennedy (Paul Webber) *led at mod pce: rdn and hdd sn after 3 out: grad wknd fr 2 out* **7/1**[3]	114
6P-0	**6**	2 ¼	**Crazy Eyes (IRE)**[15] 2235 5-11-5 113.....(t) NoelFehily (Charlie Mann) *hld up in rr: prog fr 3 out: drvn bef 2 out: no hdwy after: kpt on* **14/1**	107
2/10	**7**	1	**Dakota Boy (IRE)**[23] 2094 8-11-0 108.....(t) TomO'Brien (Alex Hales) *t.k.h: trckd ldrs: rdn to dispute 3rd after 3 out: wknd after 2 out* **20/1**	102
/06-	**8**	1	**Theatre Dance (IRE)**[361] 2520 9-11-11 119.....DarylJacob (David Arbuthnot) *trckd ldrs: lost pl 9th: stl wl in tch after 3 out: shuffled along and lost pl again bef 2 out: nvr on terms w ldrs after* **12/1**	112
45U3	**9**	30	**Admiral Dundas (IRE)**[18] 2161 5-10-11 112.....(t) EdCookson(7) (Kim Bailey) *pressed ldng pair: lost pl after 9th and sn rdn: wknd after 3 out: t.o* **16/1**	78
54-1	**10**	nk	**Moghaayer**[193] 302 5-11-7 120.....DavidBass(5) (Nicky Henderson) *mstke 2nd: mostly midfield: rdn after 9th: mstke next (3 out): sn wknd: t.o* **9/2**[2]	87
30-1	**11**	14	**Go Amwell**[41] 1814 7-11-7 115.....(v) TimmyMurphy (J R Jenkins) *hld up last: nt gng wl fr 1/2-way: jst in tch 9th: sn wknd: t.o* **16/1**	68
0423	**12**	31	**Cubism**[15] 2235 4-11-1 109.....(vt[1]) WarrenMarston (Milton Harris) *wl in tch: rdn and wknd qckly bef 3 out: t.o* **16/1**	34

6m 15.7s (-11.80) **Going Correction** -0.60s/f (Firm)

WFA 4 from 5yo+ 9lb **12** Ran SP% **116.3**

Speed ratings (Par 107): **94,93,92,93,91 90,90,89,80,80 75,65**

Tote Swingers: 1&2 £5.70, 1&3 £27.30, 2&3 £23.60 CSF £35.67 CT £408.83 TOTE £4.00: £1.50, £2.40, £6.20; EX 29.60 Trifecta £744.30 Part won. Pool: £1,005.89 - 0.10 winning units..

Owner Mrs Rachel King **Bred** Mme Marie-Louise Aubert **Trained** Barbury Castle, Wilts

■ Stewards' Enquiry : Sam Twiston-Davies three-day ban: careless riding (Dec 10-12)

FOCUS

A fair and competitive handicap. The pace wasn't particularly strong and the time was 8.80 seconds slower than the earlier mares' hurdle won by Carole's Legacy. The winner produced another step up with the next two to their marks.

NOTEBOOK

Kauto The Roc(FR), off the mark in a 2m4f novice event under this rider at Fontwell 17 days earlier, proved suited by this longer trip and coped with the return to handicap company. He idled as soon as he got to the front just before the last, pricking his ears and wandering on the approach to that flight, and soon after landing he then edged to his right. As a consequence he came under notably strong pressure, but did enough. (op 9-2 tchd 5-1 in a place)

Lupanar(IRE) reversed recent Ludlow placings with Firm Order, but couldn't get to the winner after taking an age to respond to pressure. Although he is probably not straightforward, the leaders hadn't gone that fast, and Kempton is a quick enough track when the ground is like this, so a slightly more positive ride may have helped his cause. (op 9-1 tchd 15-2)

Kasban would surely have beaten Mad Moose had that rival not badly impeded him on the run-in, forcing him to stumble in what was a potentially nasty incident, and he was rightly promoted ahead of that rival by the stewards. This handicap debutant, who had a tongue-tie on for the first time over hurdles (had it on for one of two Flat wins), was responding well to pressure prior to the trouble, and did so again in the final few yards, although it's very unlikely he would have quite got to the winner with a clear run. (op 12-1 tchd 16-1)

Mad Moose(IRE), just as at Cheltenham last time, ran okay without quite seeing his race out. (tchd 15-2)

Firm Order(IRE), going for a hat-trick, was only 3lb higher than when winning over a furlong further at Plumpton on his previous start, a race in which he had today's runner-up behind, and he had the ground to suit, but he proved slightly disappointing. (op 8-1)

Admiral Dundas(IRE) Official explanation: jockey said gelding hung left

Moghaayer has won when fresh in the past, but he proved disappointing off a 10lb higher mark than when winning at Ludlow in May. (op 4-1)

2582 PERTEMPS NETWORK H'CAP CHASE (16 fncs) 2m 4f 110y

3:10 (3:10) (Class 3) (0-135,130) 4-Y-0+ **£5,854** (£1,719; £859; £429)

Form				RPR
52-3	**1**		**Shakalakaboomboom (IRE)**[19] 2162 6-11-1 110.....BarryGeraghty (Nicky Henderson) *led 2nd: mde most after and a gng comf: shkn up to assert bef 3 out: readily* **5/2**[1]	134+
115-	**2**	7	**Calusa Caldera (IRE)**[380] 2125 8-11-1 119.....TomO'Brien (Philip Hobbs) *trckd ldrs: wnt 2nd 11th: pressed wnr next tl bef 3 out: readily hld whn mstke 2 out* **11/2**	124+
P-41	**3**	13	**Just Smudge**[30] 1957 8-11-12 130.....AidanColeman (Venetia Williams) *wl in tch: blnd 10th and dropped to last: sn struggling: rallied to go 3rd bef 3 out: no imp on ldng pair after* **11/2**	125+
2210	**4**	5	**Royal Kicks (FR)**[38] 1858 9-10-0 111.....MrTJCannon(7) (Suzy Smith) *stmbld 1st: in tch tl rdn and wl outpcd fr 11th: lft modest 3rd briefly 4 out* **4/1**[2]	100
P0-6	**5**	53	**Rodrigo Gonzales (IRE)**[21] 2125 8-11-5 123.....(b[1]) WarrenMarston (Martin Keighley) *led to 2nd: nt fluent 7th: lost 2nd and rdn 11th: wkng whn hmpd 4 out: t.o* **5/1**[3]	61
3522	**F**		**Sonning Star (IRE)**[7] 2422 6-11-3 121.....LiamTreadwell (Nick Gifford) *nt fluent: in tch: prog to go 3rd at 11th: abt 5 l down on ldng pair whn fell 4 out* **13/2**	—

5m 17.7s (-1.80) **Going Correction** +0.10s/f (Yiel) **6** Ran SP% **109.3**

Speed ratings (Par 107): **107,104,99,97,77 —**

Tote Swingers: 1&2 £3.10, 1&3 £2.30, 2&3 £3.30 CSF £15.34 TOTE £3.40: £2.00, £3.60; EX 14.30.

Owner Liam Breslin **Bred** Godfrey Moylan **Trained** Upper Lambourn, Berks

FOCUS

A fair handicap chase. The easy winner was value for further, with the second rated to his mark.

NOTEBOOK

Shakalakaboomboom(IRE), having just his second start over fences, really impressed with his jumping - he put in an almighty leap at the open ditch heading away from the stands. This was an improvement on the form he showed over 2m on his chasing debut at Warwick, and it was his first success at the sixth attempt. However, the impression was this is as far as he wants to go distance-wise, and considering this was hardly a taxing 2m4f, he may prove best back over the minimum trip. (op 9-4 tchd 11-4)

Calusa Caldera(IRE), returning from over a year off, was no match for the winner, but that one had the benefit of race fitness. This was a pleasing return, one he can be expected to improve on. (op 6-1)

Just Smudge, up 9lb for winning at Aintree on his reappearance, wasn't that quick over some of his fences but stuck on to finish closer than had looked likely at one stage. He probably wants softer ground. (op 4-1)

Royal Kicks(FR) gained his latest win over 3m and found this an insufficient test. (op 11-2)

Rodrigo Gonzales(IRE) disappointed with blinkers fitted on this return to chasing.

Sonning Star(IRE) was under pressure in third when getting rid of his rider four out. Technically speaking, the horse fell, but he didn't go over on his side and was back on his feet almost immediately. (op 7-1 tchd 6-1)

2583 WPP CONDITIONAL JOCKEYS' NOVICES' H'CAP HURDLE (8 hdls) 2m

3:45 (3:45) (Class 4) (0-100,99) 3-Y-0+ **£2,602** (£764; £382; £190)

Form				RPR
521	**1**		**Marino Prince (FR)**[4] 2467 5-11-6 96 7ex.....MarcGoldstein(3) (Jim Best) *hld up: last to 4th: prog on inner to go 2nd after next: led after 3 out: cruised clr fr next* **1/1**[1]	109+
0061	**2**	4 ½	**Tocatchaprince (IRE)**[6] 2433 4-10-3 76 7ex.....(v) MrMMO'Connor (Milton Harris) *hld up towards rr: dropped to last after 4th and pushed along: mstke 3 out: gd prog bef next: wnt 2nd and blnd last: no ch w wnr* **5/1**[2]	76
3344	**3**	2 ¾	**Frosty's Gift**[18] 2169 6-9-9 73.....(p) PeterHatton(5) (Jimmy Fox) *hld up in rr: effrt after 3 out: nt clr run bnd briefly sn after: prog 2 out: wnt 3rd last: kpt on* **10/1**	70
-60P	**4**	7	**Watergate (IRE)**[13] 2294 4-11-6 93.....DavidBass (Richard Rowe) *j. sketchily early: pressed ldr: led 4th tl after 3 out: hrd rdn and no ch w wnr bef next: wknd last* **25/1**	83
0433	**5**	5	**Catholic Hill (USA)**[19] 2149 5-10-12 85.....C'OFarrell (Mark Gillard) *hld up in tch: pushed along and effrt 3 out: no imp on ldrs bef next* **9/1**[3]	71

4P-0 **6** ½ **Raspbary**35 1902 4-11-1 **98** DarrenO'Keeffe(10) 83
(Seamus Mullins) *racd wd: hld up in tch: lost pl and pushed along in rr 5th: rallied after 3 out: fdd u.p 2 out* **20/1**

4 **7** ¾ **Holyrood**61 1574 4-11-6 **99** (tp) MrTomDavid(6) 84
(Tim Vaughan) *hld up in tch: prog to chse ldng pair after 5th: rdn and no imp after 3 out: lost 3rd and fdd 2 out* **12/1**

0600 **8** ¾ **Le Roi Max (FR)**16 2216 6-11-0 **90** SamTwiston-Davies(3) 74
(Nigel Twiston-Davies) *mstke 2nd: led to 4th: wkng whn mstke 3 out: sn bhd in last pair: plugged on* **10/1**

B5P- **9** 9 **Won More Night**357 2616 8-10-8 **86** (t) StephenO'Donovan(5) 62
(Martin Keighley) *hld up in tch: prog after 5th: chsd ldng trio 3 out: wknd bef next* **33/1**

2-00 **10** 1½ **Dalrymple (IRE)**17 2185 4-11-0 **90** (p) MattCrawley(3) 64
(Michael Madgwick) *t.k.h: trckd ldng pair to 5th: wknd* **66/1**

4m 0.40s (0.40) **Going Correction** -0.60s/f (Firm) **10** Ran SP% **115.6**
Speed ratings (Par 105): **75,72,71,67,65 65,64,64,59,59**
Tote Swingers: 1&2 £2.50, 1&3 £4.90, 2&3 £5.70 CSF £6.34 CT £31.70 TOTE £2.50: £1.10, £2.00, £2.80; EX 7.80.
Owner Miss J S Dollan **Bred** Newsells Park Stud Ltd **Trained** Lewes, E Sussex

FOCUS
The time was 7.50 seconds slower than the earlier novice hurdle won by Bobs Worth. The facile winner was value for further and is rated in line with his Hereford win. The second improved on his Fakenham form.

NOTEBOOK
Marino Prince(FR), representing last year's winning trainer, readily followed up his Hereford success from four days earlier and is a horse on the upgrade. (tchd 11-10)
Tocatchaprince(IRE) ◆, a selling winner over 2m4f in a first-time visor on his previous start, was found out by a combination of factors this time, though his penalty wasn't the issue. The drop in trip was against him, this was his first start right-handed, he didn't have the help of professional handling, and the headgear didn't work as well. He looked likely to finish out the back when struggling before the turn into the straight, but finally got going and to take an unlikely second, and he's a horse with more to offer. (tchd 9-2)
Frosty's Gift is still a maiden, but this was a reasonable effort behind a couple of in-form types. (op 11-1 tchd 8-1)
Watergate(IRE), pulled up last time, shaped with more encouragement on this occasion. (tchd 20-1)
Catholic Hill(USA) couldn't build on recent promise and probably wants softer ground. (op 12-1)
T/Plt: £744.30 to a £1 stake. Pool:£45,424.67 - 27.10 winning tickets T/Qpdt: £11.60 to a £1 stake. Pool:£3,763.87 - 240.10 winning tickets JN

2322 LUDLOW (R-H)
Monday, November 22

OFFICIAL GOING: Good to soft (7.2)
All bends moved out to provide best ground and races at maximum possible distances.
Wind: Light across Weather: Overcast

2584 PERROTT PROPERTIES / EUROPEAN BREEDERS' FUND "NATIONAL HUNT" NOVICES' HURDLE (QUALIFIER) (11 hdls) 2m 5f
12:40 (12:40) (Class 4) 4-6-Y-O **£3,903** (£1,146; £573; £286)

Form RPR
1 **Badgers Cove (IRE)**254 6-10-12 0 CharliePoste 113
(Robin Dickin) *a.p: pushed along whn hit rails appr 3 out: rdn to ld flat: styd on wl* **33/1**

6F23 **2** 1¾ **Flichity (IRE)**37 1867 5-10-12 110 AdrianLane 112+
(Donald McCain) *hld up: plld hrd: nt fluent 6th: hdwy after 8th: led bef next: rdn and hdd flat: styd on same pce* **17/2**3

0-23 **3** ¾ **Milgen Bay**22 2109 4-10-12 0 LeightonAspell 110
(Oliver Sherwood) *chsd ldr: ev ch appr 3 out: sn rdn: swtchd rt bef last: styd on same pce* **9/4**1

11 **4** 4 **Natureofthebeast (IRE)**32 1941 5-11-5 0 PaulMoloney 117
(Evan Williams) *trckd ldrs: plld hrd: shkn up after 8th: no imp fr 3 out* **9/4**1

-521 **5** 25 **Jay J**21 2123 6-11-2 117 TomMolloy(3) 106+
(Andrew Price) *led: blnd 8th: hdd whn mstke and wknd 3 out: t.o* **5/2**2

5116 **F** **Maggie Aron**140 908 4-10-2 0 RichieMcLernon(3) —
(V J Hughes) *hld up: a in rr: bhd whn fell 3 out* **18/1**

5m 30.2s (15.40) **Going Correction** +0.725s/f (Soft)
WFA 4 from 5yo+ 8lb **6** Ran SP% **108.8**
Speed ratings: **99,98,98,96,87** —
Tote Swingers: 1&2 £17.20, 1&3 £17.20, 2&3 £4.60 CSF £239.84 TOTE £28.70: £9.50, £4.00; EX 307.40.
Owner E R Clifford Beech **Bred** Miss Lillian Barry **Trained** Atherstone on Stour, Warwicks

FOCUS
The rails were moved out to their widest position making the distance of the races at their maximum. After some showers in the morning the ground looked quite testing, described as 'on the slow side' and, despite the modest early pace, they looked to finish quite tired. Ordinary novice form rated around the second and third.

NOTEBOOK
Badgers Cove(IRE), who took a maiden on the weak south-east circuit at Parham at the fifth attempt in points, was tapped for toe when the dash for home started and he was flat out when colliding with the running rail going to three out. He looked held in third at the last, but his stamina then came into play. Three miles will suit him better but he might struggle under a penalty and fences might prove a better option. (op 50-1)
Flichity(IRE), a sparsely made half-brother to Amberleigh House, is naturally keen. He looked nailed on when taking charge three out but was worried out of it near the line. A stronger gallop will help him settle better. (tchd 8-1 and 10-1)
Milgen Bay, who took his chance in the championship bumper at Aintree's Grand National meeting after a first-time out success at Huntingdon, was stepping up in trip and after having every chance looked to have no excuse. (tchd 15-8)
Natureofthebeast(IRE), unbeaten in two runs in points, a bumper and a novice hurdle here, was outpaced when fluffing his lines three out. He kept on in his own time in the home straight and looks to just stay, but better ground is probably what he needs. (op 15-8)

Jay J, the reluctant leader, did not jump well. He stepped up the pace in the final mile but had been swamped when blundering and stopping to nothing three out. The gelding was later reported to have bled from the nose. Official explanation: jockey said gelding bled from the nose (op 11-4 tchd 3-1 in places)

2585 CONCHA Y TORO NOVICES' H'CAP CHASE (19 fncs) 3m
1:10 (1:10) (Class 4) (0-110,102) 4-Y-0+
£3,757 (£1,110; £555; £277; £138; £69)

Form RPR
6032 **1** **Azulada Bay (IRE)**18 2172 6-11-8 **101** PeterToole(3) 109+
(Mark Rimell) *chsd ldrs: led 4th: hdd and hit 6th: led again 13th: drvn out* **5/1**2

0362 **2** 2 **Timpo (FR)**24 2079 7-11-6 **96** AndrewTinkler 101
(Henry Daly) *hld up in tch: racd keenly: chsd wnr after 15th: sn rdn: styd on* **11/2**3

P-24 **3** ½ **Reland (FR)**15 2243 5-11-12 **102** DavidEngland 108
(Nigel Twiston-Davies) *chsd ldr to 3rd: remained handy: drvn along 13th: styd on u.p* **7/1**

4133 **4** 11 **Feeling Peckish (USA)**6 2437 6-9-13 **80** (t) GemmaGracey-Davison(5) 76
(Michael Chapman) *led to 4th: led again 6th: pushed along after 11th: hdd 13th: sn rdn: styd on same pce fr 3 out* **14/1**

435- **5** 11 **Aconitum (GER)**245 4790 5-11-3 **100** MarkQuinlan(7) 87
(Neil Mulholland) *hld up in tch: reminders after 9th: wknd appr 4 out* **11/2**3

40-5 **6** 21 **Glebehall Bay (IRE)**19 2146 7-11-10 **100** SamThomas 76
(Venetia Williams) *prom: lost pl 3rd: hdwy 9th: drvn along 13th: wkng whn blnd 3 out: t.o* **5/1**2

-3P0 **F** **Inchloch**14 2280 8-10-9 **90** (t) IanPopham(5) —
(Claire Dyson) *hld up: fell 6th* **33/1**

3-52 **U** **One More Dinar**14 2277 7-9-12 **81** HarryChalloner(7) —
(John Bryan Groucott) *mstkes: prom: blnd 8th: rdn appr 12th: mstke and uns rdr 15th* **7/2**1

23P- **P** **Portside (IRE)**414 1635 7-11-9 **102** CharlieHuxley(3) —
(Lisa Williamson) *a in rr: bhd whn hit and hmpd 6th: t.o whn p.u bef 12th* **28/1**

6m 31.5s (23.20) **Going Correction** +1.00s/f (Soft) **9** Ran SP% **111.9**
Speed ratings (Par 105): **101,100,100,96,92 85,—,—,—**
Tote Swingers: 1&2 £6.60, 1&3 £3.50, 2&3 £5.80 CSF £31.70 CT £188.73 TOTE £8.90: £2.00, £2.40, £1.20.
Owner Rob Douglas, Mark Rimell **Bred** Louis Robinson **Trained** Leafield, Oxon

FOCUS
A moderate novice handicap and just three in serious contention over the final three fences after a sound gallop in what looked sticky ground. The form is rated around the second and third.

NOTEBOOK
Azulada Bay(IRE), a longstanding maiden, broke his duck on just his third start over fences. He jumped soundly on the whole and proved willing, in the end just doing enough. Now he has opened his account connections will be hoping he continues to progress over fences. (op 13-2)
Timpo(FR), back over fences and dropped 2lb after his second at Wetherby, emerged as the only serious threat to the winner. His sole win was four years ago. (tchd 5-1 and 6-1)
Reland(FR), another longstanding maiden, stuck on in the home straight after being tapped for toe. He looks to just stay and should appreciate a searching test of stamina. (op 8-1)
Feeling Peckish(USA), off the mark at the 79th attempt here in October, was racing from a 6lb higher mark. After being driven along to retain the lead with a circuit to go, he was simply not up to the task in the end. (op 11-1)
Aconitum(GER) had the visor left off on his first start over fences on his first outing since March. (op 13-2)
Glebehall Bay(IRE), having just his second start over fences, was never travelling and his jumping left plenty to be desired. (op 4-1)
One More Dinar was kept wide. After surviving one bad mistake he looked to be starting to struggle when departing. Another maiden, he is possibly better going left-handed. (op 4-1)

2586 WBC CLAIMING HURDLE (9 hdls) 2m
1:45 (1:45) (Class 4) 4-7-Y-O **£2,276** (£668; £334; £166)

Form RPR
0-31 **1** **Tayarat (IRE)**11 2323 5-10-10 123 (bt) PaulMoloney 120+
(Evan Williams) *trckd ldr: plld hrd: led 2nd: clr fr 3 out: hit last: eased towards fin* **11/8**1

2234 **2** 8 **Josephine Malines**15 2242 6-9-13 100 ow3 (t) MrPJTolman(7) 104
(John Flint) *chsd ldrs: wnt 2nd appr 3 out: sn rdn and no imp* **7/2**2

1166 **3** 24 **Swiss Art (IRE)**46 1740 4-10-7 102 (b) KeiranBurke(5) 91
(Patrick Rodford) *prom: racd keenly: chsd wnr after 3rd tl rdn after 6th: wkng whn hit 3 out and next: t.o* **7/1**3

1350 **4** 10 **Hadron Collider (FR)**15 2241 5-10-11 110 (p) DannyCook(3) 81
(Chris Nenadich) *hld up: a in rr: wl bhd whn blnd 3 out: t.o* **8/1**

3255 **5** nse **Marodima (FR)**13 2293 7-11-8 0 (v1) SamThomas 89
(Jamie Snowden) *led to 2nd: remained handy tl wknd after 5th: t.o* **8/1**

/4-1 **6** 9 **Motarjm (USA)**31 1953 6-11-4 110 (t) GerardTumelty 77
(Jeff Pearce) *hld up: hdwy 5th: rdn and wknd appr 3 out: t.o* **12/1**

645- **7** 71 **Twill (IRE)**428 1479 7-10-5 0 (p) MrBMoorcroft(5) 5
(Dai Burchell) *hld up: mstke 3rd: bhd fr next: t.o* **33/1**

5/0P **8** 15 **Tracy Road (FR)**13 2288 6-9-12 0 EamonDehdashti(3) —
(Carroll Gray) *a in rr: t.o fr 4th* **150/1**

3m 57.3s (7.80) **Going Correction** +0.725s/f (Soft)
WFA 4 from 5yo+ 7lb **8** Ran SP% **110.3**
Speed ratings: **109,105,93,88,87 83,47,40**
.Tayarat was claimed by M C Chapman for £6,000.\n\x\x
Owner D J Burchell **Bred** Golden Garden Stud **Trained** Llancarfan, Vale Of Glamorgan

FOCUS
An ordinary claimer. The winner stood out but arguably took another step up.

NOTEBOOK
Tayarat(IRE), who had bolted up in a C&D seller on his previous start, had 8lb and upwards in hand on official ratings and made no mistake. He had them stretched out on the run round to three out and, after crashing through the final flight, was able to ease off in the end. He is a potent force at this level and was later claimed by Michael Chapman. (tchd 5-4 and 6-4)
Josephine Malines, having her third outing for this yard, was ridden by an amateur who could not claim his full 7lb allowance. She was a clear second going to three out but never threatened. She had a stone and a half to find with the winner and should be able to find a similar event. (op 9-2)
Swiss Art(IRE), having his first start for this stable, was very keen. After joining the winner he began to tread water on the final turn and was legless when blundering two out. (op 13-2 tchd 6-1)
Hadron Collider(FR), who had run over further on his first two starts for this trainer, was never in contention and clearly needs further. (op 10-1)
Marodima(FR), with his fourth trainer, was second best on official ratings but back over hurdles and, fitted with a visor for the first time, gave up the ghost at the halfway mark. (op 13-2)

Motarjm(USA), who landed a touch in a low-grade handicap at Fakenham, had 21lb to find with the winner and stopped to nothing before the final turn. Official explanation: jockey said gelding had a breathing problem and was unsuited by the good to soft ground (tchd 9-1 and 14-1)

2587 MICKY WIGGIN RETIREMENT H'CAP CHASE (17 fncs) 2m 4f
2:15 (2:15) (Class 3) (0-125,122) 4-Y-0+ **£6,348** (£1,936; £1,011; £549)

Form RPR

3-45 **1** **Holmwood Legend**[11] 2324 9-11-3 **118** KeiranBurke[(5)] 130+
(Patrick Rodford) *hld up: hdwy 10th: chsd ldr 13th: rdn to ld 4 out: hdd next: 1 l down whn lft clr and hmpd last* **15/2**[2]

0-5U **2** *29* **Pacha D'Oudairies (FR)**[9] 2366 7-11-0 **110** NickScholfield 86
(Michael Blake) *hld up: bhd and rdn 11th: lft remote 2nd last: n.d* **17/2**

3105 **3** *16* **Magnetic Pole**[26] 2034 9-10-10 **106** (v) TomScudamore 68
(Richard Lee) *prom: chsd ldr 5th to 13th: wknd appr 4 out: lft remote 3rd last: t.o* **8/1**[3]

340P **4** *52* **Adajal (IRE)**[14] 2272 7-11-9 **122** (t) RichieMcLernon[(3)] 37
(Jonjo O'Neill) *prom: lost pl 6th: bhd fr 11th: t.o whn hmpd 3 out* **28/1**

2-F0 **P** **Master Somerville**[26] 2034 8-11-3 **113** (b) AndrewTinkler —
(Henry Daly) *chsd ldr to 5th: mstke and wknd 10th: t.o whn p.u bef 12th* **9/1**

/021 **F** **Mud Monkey**[2] 2529 6-10-11 **112** 7ex (t) IanPopham[(5)] 127+
(Claire Dyson) *led: hdd 4 out: led again next: 1l ahd whn fell last* **8/11**[1]

PP-P **F** **El Distintivo (ARG)**[19] 2148 6-10-13 **109** SamThomas —
(Venetia Williams) *chsd ldrs tl wknd appr 4 out: t.o whn fell next* **16/1**

5m 20.5s (16.10) **Going Correction** +1.00s/f (Soft) 7 Ran SP% **110.6**
Speed ratings (Par 107): **107,95,89,68,—** —,—
Tote Swingers: 1&2 £10.40, 1&3 £2.50, 2&3 £10.70 CSF £60.12 TOTE £7.90: £3.40, £3.00; EX 69.60.
Owner Brian Derrick **Bred** Mrs P M Underhill **Trained** Ash, Somerset

FOCUS
The feature event of the day, a 106-122 handicap. The eased down Holmwood Legend was value for further and is rated to his best, while Mud Monkey is rated a 3l winner.

NOTEBOOK
Holmwood Legend, a model of consistency last season, looked cherry ripe beforehand and was back over a more suitable trip. He took on the leader and gained the upper hand four out, but he seemed booked for second spot when handed it on a plate at the final fence. (op 8-1)
Pacha D'Oudairies(FR), an under-achiever for his previous yard, soon trailed the field. Left a distant third three out, he kept on to take a modest second going to the last. His record, now 1-17, tells all. (op 10-1)
Magnetic Pole, 4lb higher than his last success, prefers quicker ground and the effect of the visor is possibly wearing off.
Adajal(IRE) continues hopelessly out of form. (op 22-1)
Master Somerville, unable to dominate, quickly lost interest and was pulled up early on the final circuit. Official explanation: jockey said gelding felt wrong (op 8-1)
Mud Monkey had scored by a wide margin at Huntingdon two days earlier and was odds-on to follow up under his penalty. He was taken on by Holmwood Legend but looked to have gained the upper hand when crashing out at the final fence. His rating will have shot up after Huntingdon and he will have more on his plate when he reappears. (op 8-1)

2588 JRC BEGINNERS' CHASE (17 fncs) 2m 4f
2:50 (2:50) (Class 4) 4-Y-0+ **£3,802** (£1,123; £561; £280; £140)

Form RPR

10-2 **1** **Phidippides (IRE)**[20] 2139 6-11-1 0 PaulMoloney 120+
(Evan Williams) *mde all: nt fluent 4th: clr fr 2 out: comf* **2/7**[1]

65P- **2** *12* **Sandynow (IRE)**[235] 4968 5-11-1 0 AndrewTinkler 101+
(Henry Daly) *prom: slipped bnd after 4th: blnd 12th: chsd wnr appr 4 out: outpcd fr 2 out* **8/1**[3]

F6 **3** *8* **Gentleman Anshan (IRE)**[177] 526 6-10-8 0 MissHannahWatson[(7)] 92
(Rosemary Gasson) *prom: chsd wnr appr 10th tl rdn bef 4 out: wknd next* **66/1**

04P4 **4** *76* **Youandme (IRE)**[32] 1941 8-11-1 0 (p) ColinBolger 24
(Ray Peacock) *hld up: hdwy 7th: wknd 10th: t.o* **150/1**

6 **5** *84* **Shoudhavenownbettr (IRE)**[25] 2059 6-11-1 0 (t) DavidDennis —
(Matt Sheppard) *chsd ldrs: pushed along and lost pl appr 5th: bhd fr 10th: t.o* **50/1**

2143 **F** **Celticello (IRE)**[50] 1692 8-10-8 0 MrJMQuinlan[(7)] —
(Michael Quinlan) *chsd ldrs tl rdn and wknd appr 4 out: fell next* **6/1**[2]

P0 **P** **Harry Oscar (IRE)**[19] 2154 9-10-8 0 (tp) MrBJPoste[(7)] —
(Ken Wingrove) *a in rr: bhd and rdn 6th: t.o whn p.u bef 9th* **100/1**

5m 22.6s (18.20) **Going Correction** +1.00s/f (Soft) 7 Ran SP% **108.3**
Speed ratings (Par 105): **103,98,95,64,31** —,—
Tote Swingers: 1&2 £1.80, 1&3 £5.30, 2&3 £6.20 CSF £2.87 TOTE £1.30: £2.00, £1.40; EX 2.50.
Owner Paul Green **Bred** Mrs Sheila O'Ryan **Trained** Llancarfan, Vale Of Glamorgan

FOCUS
A long odds-on favourite for this beginners' chase in which only three could be seriously considered and on paper at least four no-hopers. The easy winner was below the level of his chase debut with the third and the time limiting the form.

NOTEBOOK
Phidippides(IRE) had taken a novice hurdles here and at Kempton before failing to do himself full justice in a Grade 1 event at Aintree. Runner-up on his chasing debut at Exeter, he jumped very safely and in the end ran out a facile wide-margin winner. His trainer thinks the world of him and will be keen to get more experience into him before bigger targets beckon in the New Year. (tchd 3-10 in places)
Sandynow(IRE), a point winner in the past, lost his way after taking a maiden hurdle at Warwick in December. Tightened up on a bend early on, he survived a blunder at the ditch six out to shake up the winner turning for home but in the end was no match. Connections will be hoping he can build on this and a stiffer track should suit. (op 9-1)
Gentleman Anshan(IRE), who looked promising when a dual point winner in the distant past, went surprisingly well for a long way. A modest novice handicap from a low mark might be feasible.
Youandme(IRE) was struggling badly with a full circuit to go, but eventually completed to claim a distant fourth spot.
Celticello(IRE), back after a seven-week break, was having just his second start over fences and, weakening five out, was a remote third when departing at the final ditch two fences later. He's potentially well treated off 10lb lower than his hurdle-race mark. (op 11-2)

2589 ERIC COLE CONDITIONAL JOCKEYS' H'CAP HURDLE (12 hdls) 3m
3:25 (3:26) (Class 5) (0-95,91) 4-Y-0+ **£2,276** (£668; £334; £166)

Form RPR

0-00 **1** **Woodlands Gem (IRE)**[15] 2239 8-10-7 **72** (bt) RichieMcLernon 82
(Peter Pritchard) *led to 4th: chsd ldr tl led again appr 3 out: rdn and edgd rt flat: styd on* **12/1**

6606 **2** *1 ¼* **Jug Of Punch (IRE)**[15] 2239 11-10-0 **65** oh1 JohnKington 73
(Simon Lewis) *chsd ldr tl led 4th: rdn and hdd appr 3 out: styd on* **7/1**

-5P4 **3** *28* **Jacarado (IRE)**[29] 1991 12-9-13 **72** (v) ChristopherWard[(8)] 55
(Robin Dickin) *chsd ldrs: rdn appr 3 out: sn wknd* **9/1**

0P30 **4** *hd* **Call Me Bill (IRE)**[15] 2232 4-11-9 **91** (t) DonalDevereux[(3)] 74
(Peter Bowen) *chsd ldrs: lost pl 8th: n.d after* **4/1**[1]

-600 **5** *2 ½* **Synonymy**[59] 1605 7-10-13 **78** (b) PeterToole 58
(Michael Blanshard) *prom: rdn after 9th: wknd bef next* **14/1**

P-04 **6** *½* **Play The Rock (FR)**[14] 2271 7-10-5 **76** KyleJames[(6)] 56
(Philip Kirby) *hld up: mstke 4th: a in rr* **6/1**[2]

0-05 **7** *shd* **Jaunty Dove**[7] 2425 8-11-4 **83** TomMolloy 63
(Andrew Price) *hld up: hdwy 8th: rdn and wknd appr 3 out* **14/1**

-P30 **8** *39* **Lucky Pearl**[15] 2239 9-11-4 **83** IanPopham 28
(Tim Vaughan) *chsd ldrs: mstke 7th: sn rdn: wknd after 9th: bhd whn blnd 2 out: t.o* **7/1**

1P-0 **9** *nk* **Walls Way**[19] 2144 6-11-7 **89** LeeEdwards[(3)] 33
(Tony Carroll) *hld up in tch: rdn and wknd bef 3 out: t.o* **11/1**

0P-0 **P** **Aymard Des Fieffes (FR)**[15] 2244 8-9-11 **65** oh1 RobertKirk[(3)] —
(Nikki Evans) *hld up: hdwy 7th: wknd after 9th: t.o whn p.u bef 3 out* **40/1**

6/P- **P** **Santo Subito (IRE)**[165] 2307 9-10-0 **65** GemmaGracey-Davison —
(Michael Chapman) *hld up: racd keenly: wknd 8th: t.o whn p.u bef 3 out* **100/1**

10-4 **P** **Quay Meadow (IRE)**[10] 2351 8-11-6 **88** AlexanderVoy[(3)] —
(John Norton) *hld up: in rr and pushed along 6th: bhd fr 8th: t.o whn p.u bef 3 out* **13/2**[3]

000- **F** **Sir John**[310] 3458 4-10-12 **85** GeraldQuinn[(8)] 78
(Jonjo O'Neill) *chsd ldrs: 8l 3rd and styng on same pce whn fell 2 out* **20/1**

6m 10.7s (18.40) **Going Correction** +0.725s/f (Soft) 13 Ran SP% **120.2**
Speed ratings (Par 103): **98,97,88,88,87 87,87,74,74,—** —,—,—
Tote Swingers: 1&2 £20.00, 1&3 £17.50, 2&3 £11.10 CSF £93.70 CT £806.92 TOTE £16.10: £4.40, £3.20, £3.50; EX 110.60.
Owner Woodlands Generators & Alison Pritchard **Bred** Cornelius O'Riordan **Trained** Whatcote, Warwicks

FOCUS
A low-grade conditional jockeys' handicap hurdle and just three still in serious contention at the third last flight. The first two came out of the same Hereford race and both were very well in on old form. This is not an easy race to pin down.

NOTEBOOK
Woodlands Gem(IRE), rated over 100 after taking a novice hurdle at Towcester two years ago, has tumbled down the ratings and here was able to race off just 72. She and the runner-up set a strong pace in the ground, and they had it to themselves up the home straight. She was clear at the last but there was precious little to spare at the line.
Jug Of Punch(IRE), whose last success at Cheltenham in April 2008 came from a mark of 108, ran off just 65 here after a long spell in the doldrums. He usually gets behind in his races these days but was ridden a lot more positively here, and to the old boy's credit he was coming back for more at the line. (op 9-1)
Jacarado(IRE), whose last four wins have been over fences at Towcester, the latest over a year ago from a 10lb higher mark, was left behind in the final straight and was handed a remote third spot two out. (op 12-1)
Call Me Bill(IRE) has an official rating of 91, but has yet to prove he is up to that. Wearing a tongue-tie on his handicap debut, he was made to look very slow. A big type, fences might see him in a more favourable light. (op 6-1)
Sir John, another making his handicap debut, is only small and lightly made. He was clinging on to a modest third spot when departing two out. (op 12-1)

2590 BORDER ENERGY MAIDEN OPEN NATIONAL HUNT FLAT RACE 2m
3:55 (3:55) (Class 5) 4-6-Y-0 **£1,951** (£573; £286; £143)

Form RPR

1 **Kawa (FR)** 4-11-2 0 CharliePoste 101+
(Robin Dickin) *chsd ldrs: led over 5f out: styd on wl* **9/2**[3]

2 *3* **A Bridge Too Far (IRE)** 4-11-2 0 DominicElsworth 98
(Paul Webber) *hld up in tch: chsd wnr over 4f out: sn rdn: styd on same pce fnl f* **9/4**[1]

0-5 **3** *14* **William Percival (IRE)**[193] 304 4-10-9 0 JakeGreenall[(7)] 85
(Henry Daly) *led: hdd over 5f out: rdn over 3f out: wknd 2f out* **15/2**

4 *3 ½* **Definite Lady (IRE)** 4-10-6 0 PeterToole[(3)] 75
(Mark Rimell) *sn prom: lost pl over 6f out: n.d after* **10/1**

0 **5** *hd* **Furrows**[24] 2074 5-11-2 0 LeightonAspell 82
(Oliver Sherwood) *hld up: hdwy over 4f out: wknd 3 out* **8/1**

6 *6* **Captain John Smith** 5-11-2 0 SamThomas 77
(Tom George) *hld up: hdwy over 6f out: wknd over 4f out* **11/4**[2]

7 *3 ¾* **Remarkable Rocket (IRE)**[555] 6-10-9 0 MrJFlook[(7)] 73
(Andrew Price) *chsd ldrs tl wknd over 3f out* **40/1**

0-0 **8** *27* **Sir Clad**[47] 1729 4-10-13 0 (t) TommyPhelan[(3)] 49
(Claire Dyson) *hld up: rdn over 5f out: sn wknd: t.o* **66/1**

9 *9* **Sam's Pride**[212] 5-10-13 0 RichieMcLernon[(3)] 41
(Peter Pritchard) *prom tl wknd over 4f out: t.o* **33/1**

3m 59.2s (15.30) **Going Correction** +0.725s/f (Soft)
WFA 4 from 5yo+ 7lb 9 Ran SP% **114.5**
Speed ratings: **90,88,81,79,79 76,74,61,56**
Tote Swingers: 1&2 £4.00, 1&3 £6.00, 2&3 £5.30. totesuper7: Win: Not won. Place: £388.80. CSF £14.76 TOTE £5.30: £1.10, £2.20, £2.20; EX 17.50.
Owner P Armour **Bred** B De La Motte Saint-Pierre Et Al **Trained** Atherstone on Stour, Warwicks

FOCUS
A modest bumper with previous form thin on the ground. The pace was very steady until passing the halfway mark.

NOTEBOOK
Kawa(FR) ◆, a good-looking newcomer, is from a stable 0-35 in bumpers in the last five seasons but one that is evidently in good form. He kept tabs on the leader and, sent to the front half a mile out, scored in convincing fashion. He will struggle under a penalty, but should make his mark over hurdles in time. (op 3-1)
A Bridge Too Far(IRE) went in pursuit of the winner with over 2f left to run, but this half-brother to two bumper winners was never going to finish any better than second best. He should learn plenty from the experience. (op 11-4 tchd 3-1 in places)
William Percival(IRE), absent since May, was having his third start. He took them along in his own time but was made to look very one-paced. No doubt he will now try his hand over hurdles. (op 8-1)
Definite Lady(IRE), described by her trainer as 'very lazy', was struggling when the pace increased. With just one behind her on the final turn she made up a fair amount of late ground and this will have taught her plenty. (op 12-1 tchd 9-1)
Furrows, who tired badly in testing conditions on his debut at Uttoxeter last month, kept on in his own time from off the pace. He looks on the slow side. (op 13-2)
Captain John Smith, the third foal of the top-class jumping mare Lady Rebecca, was the first to come under serious pressure and was made to look very one paced. Connections will be hoping he improves given a bit more time. (op 4-1)
T/Jkpt: Not won. T/Plt: £1,105.70 to a £1 stake. Pool:£47,333.86 - 31.25 winning tickets T/Qpdt: £64.60 to a £1 stake. Pool:£6,005.50 - 68.70 winning tickets CR

2289 LINGFIELD (L-H)

Tuesday, November 23

OFFICIAL GOING: Heavy (soft in places on chase course; chs 5.2, hdl 4.4); all-weather - standard

Wind: Against, moderate becoming light Weather: Mostly cloudy

2591 S M I S LTD LEADING TIPSTER MANAGEMENT H'CAP CHASE (12 fncs) 2m

12:50 (12:50) (Class 4) (0-110,105) 4-Y-O+ **£3,577** (£1,050; £525; £262)

Form RPR

4-F5 **1** **Near The Water (IRE)**[18] 2185 6-11-12 **105** LeightonAspell 114+
(Richard Rowe) *hld up: lft bhd fr 8th: wnt modest 4th after next: clsd fr 3 out: shkn up to chse ldr 2 out: rdn and r.o flat to ld nr fin* **15/2**[3]

-621 **2** 1 ½ **Nautical Approach (IRE)**[7] 2437 7-11-10 **103** 7ex (t) PaddyBrennan 111
(Alex Hales) *prog to trck ldr 4th: led 7th to 9th: led again 3 out gng wl: 3 l up last: rdn and kpt on flat: hdd nr fin* **5/4**[1]

-466 **3** 10 **Maximix**[22] 2134 7-11-4 **97** JamieMoore 95
(Gary Moore) *hld up: effrt to chse clr ldng pair after 8th: no imp: plugged on* **15/2**[3]

-514 **4** 3 ¼ **Sumdancer (NZ)**[8] 2429 8-11-5 **101** MarcGoldstein(3) 96
(Michael Madgwick) *cl up: chsd ldr 7th: led 9th tl hdd and nt fluent 3 out: lost 2nd 2 out: wknd and mstke last* **3/1**[2]

4/3- **5** 17 **Jeczmien (POL)**[562] 234 7-11-4 **97** (t) LiamTreadwell 76
(Nick Gifford) *pressed ldr: led briefly after 3rd: lost pl 5th: lft bhd after 8th: t.o* **14/1**

51-5 **P** **Devils River (IRE)**[20] 2152 8-11-4 **97** (p) AndrewTinkler —
(Anna Brooks) *mde most tl hdd and j. bdly rt 7th: sn wknd: t.o in last whn p.u bef 3 out* **10/1**

4m 14.7s (6.90) **Going Correction** +0.225s/f (Yiel) **6** Ran SP% **108.7**

Speed ratings (Par 105): **91,90,85,83,75** —

Tote Swingers:1&2:£2.90, 2&3:£2.20, 1&3:£4.70 CSF £17.18 TOTE £5.40: £2.20, £1.40; EX 19.50.

Owner Ms Jane Southall **Bred** Geoffrey Keene **Trained** Sullington, W Sussex

FOCUS

They went an average gallop in this modest handicap and the race saw changing fortunes in the home straight. The winner is rated to the level of his best hurdles form.

NOTEBOOK

Near The Water(IRE) hadn't shown much on his seasonal return over hurdles 18 days earlier and had fallen on his only previous outing over fences. He took time to warm to his task, but the further he went the better he was and he reeled in the runner-up on the run-in to score. He has mainly run over further than this in the past, but both of his wins have now been over the minimum trip and the testing surface clearly helped his cause. He should have more to offer now he has got off the mark in this sphere. (op 8-1 tchd 17-2)

Nautical Approach(IRE) was an easy winner at Fakenham the previous week and the question was whether he would be able to reproduce that level under a penalty on this more demanding surface. He had no trouble with the drop back in trip and looked to have done enough coming to the last, but he began to tire badly on the run-in. It was clear nearing the business end that he was going to get caught and he has to rate as unfortunate not to have gone in again as he was well clear of the rest. He is now due to race off a 3lb higher mark, but has improved for the recent fitting of a tongue tie. (op 6-4 tchd 13-8)

Maximix handles this ground and he plugged on without threatening to post an improved effort in defeat. (op 7-1 tchd 6-1)

Sumdancer(NZ) went clear with the winner from the eighth, but was unable to stick with that rival from the third-last and eventually paid for his earlier exertions. Some respite from the handicapper looks required before he can win again. He was later reported to have lost a front right shoe. Official explanation: vet said gelding lost a right fore shoe (tchd 5-2 and 10-3 in places)

2592 CARLHARRIS.CO.UK MARES' NOVICES' HURDLE (8 hdls) 2m 110y

1:20 (1:20) (Class 4) 4-Y-O+ £2,740 (£798; £399)

Form RPR

1-1 **1** **L'Accordioniste (IRE)**[25] 2068 5-11-3 0 PaddyBrennan 115+
(Nigel Twiston-Davies) *reluctant ldr: set slow pce to 4th: clr next: nt fluent 3 out: rdn after next: drew further away flat* **2/7**[1]

34-U **2** 12 **Setter's Princess**[4] 2499 4-10-3 0 MattGriffiths(7) 93
(Ron Hodges) *t.k.h: prom: mostly chsd wnr fr 4th: rdn and no imp after 2 out: n.d after* **8/1**[3]

6-4 **3** 10 **Sapphire Rouge (IRE)**[192] 332 4-10-7 0 JimmyDerham(3) 81
(Seamus Mullins) *trckd wnr to 4th: outpcd fr next and nudged along: no ch in v modest 4th 2 out: pushed along and styd on flat to take 3rd last strides* **14/1**

224- **4** ½ **Ragdollianna**[25] 1247 6-10-10 0 APMcCoy 81
(Murty McGrath) *trckd ldrs: nudged along in 3rd fr 3 out: lost grnd on front pair fr 2 out: lost 3rd and rdn last strides* **7/2**[2]

66 **5** 14 **Galant Star (FR)**[14] 2289 4-10-10 0 JamieMoore 67
(Gary Moore) *chsd ldrs: outpcd fr 3 out: grad fdd fr 2 out* **10/1**

60 **6** 2 **Brunette'Sonly (IRE)**[19] 2168 5-10-10 0 AndrewThornton 65
(Seamus Mullins) *in tch: reminders after 4th: struggling after next: poor 7th 3 out: no ch after* **66/1**

06-0 **7** 4 ½ **Polly's Star**[14] 2289 5-10-10 0 LeightonAspell 60
(Gerry Enright) *chsd ldrs: outpcd fr 5th: poor 6th after next* **100/1**

8 77 **Princess Janet**[588] 4-10-10 0 JimmyMcCarthy —
(Alan Coogan) *nt fluent: lost tch after 3rd: wl t.o* **66/1**

4m 22.2s (8.10) **Going Correction** +0.225s/f (Yiel)

WFA 4 from 5yo+ 7lb **8** Ran SP% **130.8**

Speed ratings (Par 105): **89,83,78,78,71 70,68,32**

Tote Swingers:1&2:£3.40, 2&3:£7.90, 1&3:£3.50 CSF £5.41 TOTE £1.40: £1.02, £2.90, £3.90; EX 5.10.

Owner David Maxwell **Bred** J F C Maxwell **Trained** Naunton, Gloucs

FOCUS

A weak mares' novice event. Not form to be confident about but the winner will rate higher.

NOTEBOOK

L'Accordioniste(IRE) appeared to face a golden opportunity to extend her unbeaten record to three and she duly completed the task by making all under her penalty. She has yet to race on anything but this sort of testing ground and is value for even further than her winning margin, as she had to cut out the donkey work. This highly regarded mare will get further without much fuss and connections will no doubt be eyeing the EBF Mares' Final at Newbury later on for her. It may be that she is now handed a break. (op 2-9)

Setter's Princess came into this with something of a disappointing profile and had unseated on her hurdling debut four days earlier. Her rider's claim meant she had very little weight on her back, however, and she posted an encouraging effort to finish a clear second-best. A step up in trip should suit ideally.

Sapphire Rouge(IRE) looked fourth best for much of the race, but she stayed on dourly from two out and nabbed a place at the finish. She will probably enjoy getting back on some better ground and ought to come on a deal for the outing.

Ragdollianna is rated 68 on the level and ran some fair races without success in that sphere during the summer. Tony McCoy (first ride for the stable) was on top for this return to hurdling and she emerged to look a player turning for home. She paid for not settling off a sedate early gallop when push came to shove, though, and was run out of third near the line. She is capable of better on a slightly sounder surface when racing off a better pace. (op 4-1)

2593 RIGHT MAN BEGINNERS' CHASE (12 fncs) 2m

1:50 (1:50) (Class 4) 4-Y-O+ £4,923

Form RPR

5-34 **1** **Mohayer (IRE)**[15] 2270 8-10-11 0 RichieMcLernon(3) 120+
(Jonjo O'Neill) *trckd ldng pair: 6 l bhd ldr whn lft alone 7th: hacked rnd* **11/4**[2]

0R-R **P** **Sacrilege**[127] 515 5-11-0 0 AndrewGlassonbury —
(Daniel O'Brien) *detached in last: j. slowly 4th: reluctant to continue and p.u bef next* **28/1**

/3-0 **B** **Fiftyonefiftyone (IRE)**[24] 2082 6-11-0 120 LeightonAspell —
(Oliver Sherwood) *t.k.h: trckd ldr: 4 l down whn b.d 7th* **8/1**[3]

46-2 **F** **Lord Singer (FR)**[17] 2210 5-11-0 0 JamieMoore —
(Gary Moore) *t.k.h: led: 4 l up whn fell 7th* **1/2**[1]

4m 40.7s (32.90) **Going Correction** +0.225s/f (Yiel) **4** Ran SP% **107.9**

Speed ratings (Par 105): **26,—,—,—**

TOTE £3.30; EX 4.10.

Owner G & P Barker Ltd/globe Engineering **Bred** Barouche Stud Ireland Ltd **Trained** Cheltenham, Gloucs

FOCUS

A beginners' chase weakened by the late defection of Pascha Bere and it turned into a non-event. Unrateable form.

NOTEBOOK

Mohayer(IRE)'s fourth at Carlisle 15 days earlier had got a boost when Kellystown Lad (runner-up that day) scored at Sedgefield earlier in the day and, rated 124 over hurdles, was entitled to go close here if stepping up a little as he does act well on the ground. He was able to hack round after the drama and his confidence should be nicely boosted. (op 5-2 tchd 9-4 and 3-1)

Sacrilege Official explanation: As this was the fifth occasion in 2010 that gelding had either refused to race or pulled itself up after covering only a short distance, the last occasion being at Windsor on 19th July 2010 where connections were notified that any future similar behaviour might result in the gelding being reported to the British Horseracing Authority, it has now been reported (op 4-6 tchd 8-11 and 4-5 in places)

Lord Singer(FR) took off far too early at the seventh and came down on top of the fence in a nasty fall. (op 4-6 tchd 8-11 and 4-5 in places)

2594 LOUISEROSE.CO.UK NOVICES' HURDLE (10 hdls) 2m 3f 110y

2:20 (2:20) (Class 4) 4-Y-O+ £2,740 (£798; £399)

Form RPR

12 **1** **Recession Proof (FR)**[24] 2083 4-11-5 134 DougieCostello 130+
(John Quinn) *hld up in tch: prog after 6th: trckd ldng pair 3 out: effrt and hit next: rdn to ld sn after last: drvn out* **9/4**[2]

11-1 **2** 1 ¼ **Brackloon High (IRE)**[22] 2129 5-11-5 0 RichardJohnson 130+
(Noel Chance) *trckd ldrs: wnt 2nd after 7th: rdn to ld and hit 2 out: hdd sn after last: kpt on* **5/4**[1]

23-0 **3** 16 **Latin America (IRE)**[17] 2209 5-10-12 118 LiamTreadwell 107+
(Nick Gifford) *prom: jnd ldr and mstke 6th: led next: rdn and hdd 2 out: wknd bef last: fin tired* **11/4**[3]

0P **4** 10 **Chase Gate**[21] 2137 5-10-12 0 HaddenFrost 95
(James Frost) *wl in tch: chsd ldng trio 3 out: cl enough bef next: sn wknd* **66/1**

5 1 ¼ **Cleaver**[396] 9-10-12 0 LeightonAspell 95+
(Lady Herries) *t.k.h: hld up in rr: blnd 5th: prog 7th: last of 5 w a ch after 3 out: wknd bef next* **12/1**

4- **6** 19 **Just Josie**[447] 1374 4-10-5 0 JamieGoldstein 68
(Sheena West) *in tch tl 6th: struggling bdly whn mstke next: wnt poor 6th bef 2 out* **33/1**

-UUP **7** 47 **Rossmill Lad (IRE)**[9] 2390 6-10-5 79 JoshuaMoore(7) 28
(Luke Dace) *in tch: mstke 6th: sn wknd: t.o* **100/1**

00-0 **8** 41 **Hammerwood**[52] 1680 4-10-7 0 GemmaGracey-Davison(5) —
(Zoe Davison) *trckd ldr: led after 4th: hdd 7th: wkng rapidly whn mstke 3 out: t.o* **100/1**

0-06 **9** 1 ½ **King Richard (IRE)**[7] 2440 6-10-12 0 AndrewThornton —
(Richard Rowe) *led tl after 4th: wknd v rapidly: hopelessly t.o after 7th* **100/1**

00 **10** 10 **Action Hawk (GER)**[8] 2419 6-10-12 0 JamesDavies —
(Ben Pollock) *in tch to 6th: wknd v rapidly: hopelessly t.o fr 3 out* **100/1**

000 **P** **Track Star (IRE)**[47] 1743 5-10-12 0 TimmyMurphy —
(Luke Dace) *sn detached in last: j.lft 6th: hopelessly t.o whn p.u bef 7th* **100/1**

5m 11.7s (5.00) **Going Correction** +0.225s/f (Yiel)

WFA 4 from 5yo+ 7lb **11** Ran SP% **119.0**

Speed ratings (Par 105): **99,98,92,88,87 80,61,44,44,40** —

Tote Swingers:1&2:£1.40, 2&3:£1.20, 1&3:£1.70 CSF £5.73 TOTE £2.30: £1.10, £1.10, £1.50; EX 6.00.

Owner Mrs Vanessa J Stone **Bred** N P Bloodstock Ltd & Morton Bloodstock **Trained** Settrington, N Yorks

FOCUS

The two penalised runners came well clear from the last in this novice hurdle.

NOTEBOOK

Recession Proof(FR) was nicely on top at the finish, despite having lost both front shoes in the race. The 4-y-o had yet to prove himself on this sort of ground but he went through it without fuss and was given a decent ride, tracking the second before taking it up at the final flight. He stayed well on the level and this extra distance was no trouble to him, indeed he ought to get even further as he matures. Now 2-3 since going hurdling, things will be tougher under a double penalty and a mark of 134 looks high enough should he go handicapping. He does remain open to improvement, though. (op 5-2)

Brackloon High(IRE) showed a decent attitude when getting up late on his hurdling debut at Plumpton and that form looked better when the runner-up went in at Aintree earlier this week. The longer trip was expected to suit, but this wasn't a severe test due to the ordinary early gallop and he was ultimately found out by the winner's superior Flat speed after getting in close to the last. He didn't help his cause by getting warm here and, granted more of a test, should be capable of winning again in this company. (op 11-10 tchd 6-4)

Latin America(IRE) is proven on such ground and got a positive ride. He was left behind when the first pair kicked for home and, while this was a step back in the right direction, he will struggle to win a novice event. (op 7-2)

Chase Gate had pulled up last time out, but he moved nicely through the race and this was much more like it. This former point winner is one to look out for when going handicapping over a stiffer test. (op 100-1)

Cleaver, returning from a 396-day layoff, enjoyed cut underfoot on the Flat and got 2m in that sphere. He took time to settle on this hurdling debut and, after making up ground to get into contention, proved very one paced under pressure. He has begun life over hurdles late in life, but should improve for the run and can win a race. (op 14-1)

2595 SECRETSAPPHIRE.COM H'CAP CHASE (18 fncs) 3m

2:50 (2:50) (Class 4) (0-115,113) 4-Y-O+ £3,577 (£1,050; £525; £262)

Form				RPR
P-F2	1		**Bobby Gee**[20] 2146 9-11-9 110 .... TomO'Brien (Renee Robeson) *mde all: in command fr 3 out: shkn up and styd on wl after last* **3/1[2]**	126+
P-21	2	5	**Aztec Treasure (NZ)**[19] 2170 6-11-1 102 .... APMcCoy (Jonjo O'Neill) *cl up: chsd ldng pair after 15th: rdn to go 2nd and mstke 2 out: no imp on wnr flat* **7/4[1]**	113+
4423	3	½	**Supreme Plan (IRE)**[25] 2073 7-11-12 113 .... (tp) SeanQuinlan (Kim Bailey) *cl up: chsd wnr 12th: rdn bef 3 out: no imp and lost 2nd next: kpt on* **3/1[2]**	122
0P-1	4	10	**Digger Gets Lucky (IRE)**[31] 1965 8-11-5 106 .... LiamTreadwell (Nick Gifford) *cl up tl drvn and struggling in 4th pl after 15th: n.d after: mstke last* **8/1**	106
P0-5	5	28	**Outlaw Tom (IRE)**[23] 2110 6-11-9 110 .... NoelFehily (Alex Hales) *chsd wnr tl nt fluent 12th: mstke next and dropped to last: struggling after: wl bhd whn mstke 2 out* **5/1[3]**	84

6m 25.5s (1.80) **Going Correction** +0.225s/f (Yiel) **5** Ran SP% **114.1**
Speed ratings (Par 105): **106,104,104,100,91**
CSF £9.38 TOTE £5.10: £2.20, £1.80; EX 9.70.

Owner The Oakley Partnership **Bred** W Ginzel And Mrs J Kehoe **Trained** Tyringham, Bucks

FOCUS

There was just an ordinary gallop on in this moderate staying handicap. The first three are rated to their marks.

NOTEBOOK

Bobby Gee ran well when second off this mark at Chepstow 20 days previously and made all for a ready success. He came into this on the back of a long-losing run, but his last success came off this mark over hurdles on similar ground back in 2007 and a reproduction of his previous run was enough here. The handicapper will now have his say and his profile suggests a follow up is likely, but he is evidently back at the top of his game. (op 4-1)

Aztec Treasure(NZ) was 10lb higher than when opening his account at Towcester. He got caught out when the pace lifted around four out and this late-maturing 6-y-o really wants more positive handling. (op 11-8 tchd 2-1)

Supreme Plan(IRE) was 3lb higher than when second on his chase debut 25 days earlier, but stepping up in trip was in his favour and the cheekpieces were back on. He looked a threat coming out of the back straight, but was under heavy pressure soon after and it may be no coincidence he has yet to win a race. (op 7-2)

Digger Gets Lucky(IRE) showed vastly improved form when getting off the mark on his comeback a month earlier and was 6lb higher. He proved very easy to back on this step up in trip, but had his chance and failed to see it out like the principals. (op 7-1)

Outlaw Tom(IRE) met support on this return to deeper ground, but he was in trouble after hitting the 12th and 13th fences. (op 7-1)

2596 HOPE'S A WINNING MACHINE FREEPHONE 0808 126 2005 H'CAP HURDLE (8 hdls) 2m 110y

3:20 (3:20) (Class 3) (0-125,121) 4-Y-O+ £5,204 (£1,528; £764; £381)

Form				RPR
1025	1		**Alph**[17] 2213 13-11-5 121 .... MrTJCannon(7) (Roger Teal) *racd wd: trckd ldng pair: led 3 out: rdn after next: kpt on gamely fr last* **20/1**	128
3-6	2	2½	**Perfect Reward**[19] 2169 6-11-1 110 .... JamieMoore (Gary Moore) *trckd ldrs: effrt 3 out: chsd wnr next: kpt on fr last but no imp* **6/1**	114
P4-5	3	3	**Slew Charm (FR)**[17] 2209 8-11-6 115 .... (t) RichardJohnson (Noel Chance) *racd on inner: trckd ldng trio: effrt to dispute 2nd 2 out: edgd rt bef last: one pce* **10/3[1]**	117
-552	4	7	**Sun Quest**[12] 2333 6-10-5 107 .... RobertKirk(7) (Steven Dixon) *disp ld tl led after 4th to 3 out: styd on inner and steadily wknd fr 2 out* **11/2[3]**	101
510-	5	20	**Don't Panic (IRE)**[360] 2563 6-11-0 109 .... TimmyMurphy (Ron Hodges) *t.k.h: hld up in last pair: prog on wd outside and wl in tch after 3 out: wknd bef next: eased* **12/1**	83
015-	6	6	**Zafranagar (IRE)**[37] 4986 5-10-12 112 .... LeeEdwards(5) (Tony Carroll) *t.k.h: hld up in tch: mstke 3 out: sn rdn and wknd* **7/1**	80
14-P	7	15	**Sebastiano (FR)**[201] 170 7-10-10 115 .... JosephAkehurst(10) (Gary Moore) *in tch tl wknd 3 out: sn t.o* **16/1**	68
1200	8	6	**American World (FR)**[10] 2361 6-11-4 113 .... APMcCoy (Brendan Powell) *disp ld tl after 5th: hit next and wknd qckly: t.o bef 2 out* **10/1**	60
-255	F		**Grafite**[13] 2307 5-11-0 109 .... WarrenMarston (Milton Harris) *hld up in last pair: prog on outer 5th: rdn and no imp 2 out: keeping on in 5 l 4th whn fell last* **7/2[2]**	109

4m 14.6s (0.50) **Going Correction** +0.225s/f (Yiel) **9** Ran SP% **114.9**
Speed ratings (Par 107): **107,105,104,101,91 88,81,79,—**
Tote Swingers:1&2:£20.70, 2&3:£5.20, 1&3:£12.00 CSF £134.50 CT £508.43 TOTE £23.20: £5.40, £2.30, £1.80; EX 106.10.

Owner Andy Chard **Bred** G A And Mrs Antill **Trained** Ashtead, Surrey

FOCUS

This open-looking handicap was run at a fair gallop, yet it proved hard to get seriously involved from off the pace. Ordinary form for the grade, but the winner's best figure since January 2009.

NOTEBOOK

Alph got back to winning ways with a fairly decisive success on this drop into an easier grade. His capable rider's 7lb claim was a big help and he looked to be idling after the last, so rates value for a bit further. It's hard to see this game veteran following up, though. (op 16-1)

Perfect Reward showed the benefit of his return to hurdles 19 days earlier and ran very close to his best, helping to set the standard. (op 13-2 tchd 11-2)

Slew Charm(FR) was well backed and had his chance, but couldn't find an extra gear when it mattered. It's not hard to see why he was tried over 2m4f last time out. (op 4-1)

Sun Quest, 2lb higher, failed to raise his game on this return to softer ground. (op 5-1 tchd 7-1)

Don't Panic(IRE), returning from a 360-day absence, made a promising move coming out of the back straight. He was very keen early on, however, and was eventually made to pay. He was later reported to have been unsuited by the ground, and could well get closer next time. Official explanation: trainer said the gelding was unsuited by the ground and ran too free (op 10-1)

Grafite got well backed, but was making heavy weather of it prior to falling at the last. He may have gained a place but for that, however, and more positive handling or a step up in trip looks in order. (op 11-2)

2597 HARLEQUIN RFU "JUNIOR" STANDARD OPEN NATIONAL HUNT FLAT RACE 1m 5f

3:50 (3:50) (Class 5) 3-Y-O £1,712 (£499; £249)

Form				RPR
1	1		**Keys (IRE)**[16] 2237 3-11-5 0 .... PaddyBrennan (Roger Charlton) *hld up towards rr: prog 3f out to trck ldr over 2f out: led over 1f out: sn clr* **1/2[1]**	109+
5	2	4½	**Painted Tail (IRE)**[26] 2052 3-10-5 0 .... HaddenFrost (James Frost) *trckd ldrs: effrt 2f out: chsd wnr fnl f: kpt on but easily outpcd* **14/1**	87
	3	nk	**Teutonic Knight (IRE)** 3-10-12 0 .... DougieCostello (Ian Williams) *hld up in rr: sme prog 3f out: gd hdwy on outer over 1f out: styd on wl to take 3rd last strides* **10/1[3]**	93+
	4	hd	**Main Beach** 3-10-12 0 .... DominicElsworth (Tobias B P Coles) *hld up in last trio: gd prog on wd outside fr 3f out: rdn to dispute 2nd 1f out: one pce* **33/1**	93
	5	1¾	**Necessity** 3-10-12 0 .... ColinBolger (Simon Dow) *hld up in midfield: cl enough on inner over 2f out: outpcd fr over 1f out: kpt on* **20/1**	91
	6	3½	**Rebel Flag (IRE)** 3-10-12 0 .... TomMessenger (Chris Bealby) *led: set v modest pce to over 4f out: hdd and easily outpcd over 1f out* **40/1**	86
	7	2	**Saint Guru** 3-10-12 0 .... TimmyMurphy (Natalie Lloyd-Beavis) *trckd ldrs on outer: cl enough over 2f out: outpcd fr over 1f out* **12/1**	84
2	8	3½	**Pearl Mountain (IRE)**[19] 2173 3-10-5 0 .... GerardTumelty (Jeff Pearce) *trckd ldrs: rdn and lost pl over 4f out: sn struggling in rr: plugged on again fnl 2f* **8/1[2]**	72
	9	¾	**The Mightie Quin** 3-10-5 0 .... MrAWilliams(7) (Terry Clement) *plld hrd: jnd ldr after 3f tl over 2f out: wknd u.str.p* **80/1**	78
	10	¾	**Lord Aldervale (IRE)** 3-10-12 0 .... LeightonAspell (Richard Rowe) *hld up last: lft bhd whn pce lifted over 4f out: passed wkng rivals fr 3f out: nvr in contention* **66/1**	77
	11	4	**Midnight Maisie** 3-10-5 0 .... AndrewTinkler (Anna Brooks) *in tch tl wknd fr 3f out* **50/1**	65
	12	3½	**Elby** 3-10-12 0 .... JimmyMcCarthy (Eve Johnson Houghton) *t.k.h: pressed ldrs tl rdn and wknd 3f out* **33/1**	67
0	13	20	**Go Flo Go**[19] 2173 3-10-5 0 .... JamesDavies (Mark Hoad) *prom tl wknd over 4f out: t.o* **150/1**	34
	14	11	**Clee Hill Wind** 3-9-12 0 .... MarkQuinlan(7) (Bill Turner) *in tch tl wknd 5f out: t.o* **33/1**	20

3m 1.50s (181.50) **14** Ran SP% **122.6**
Tote Swingers:1&2:£3.60, 2&3:£13.00, 1&3:£3.50 CSF £8.30 TOTE £1.60: £1.10, £3.60, £2.60; EX 9.50.

Owner Seasons Holidays **Bred** B Hurley **Trained** Beckhampton, Wilts

FOCUS

Quite an interesting Polytrack bumper. The easy winner was value for further but has been given only a guessy rating.

NOTEBOOK

Keys(IRE) was all the rage to follow up his debut success at Ffos Las 16 days earlier and he completed the task in taking fashion under his penalty. He was given a confident ride by Paddy Brennan, making up ground effortlessly nearing the home turn and shooting clear when asked to win the race near the furlong marker. His connections deserve credit for placing this late-maturing 3-y-o in such a way, as he can still contest an AW maiden on the Flat and would surely be up to taking one of those. However, the owner is a jumps man and is keen to aim him at the bumper at the Cheltenham Festival, taking in a Listed event on the same course in the meantime in order to test the water. Hurdling may beckon at a later date. (op 4-7 tchd 8-13 and 4-6 in places)

Painted Tail(IRE), fifth on her debut at Fontwell, was never far away and had her chance. She was made to look slow when the winner kicked for home, but this was an improved effort on the sounder surface and she goes some way to helping set the standard. (op 16-1)

Teutonic Knight(IRE) is half-brother to a Group 3 winner and also a useful sort that won twice over 1m4f at this venue. He raced upsides the winner, but lacked anything like that one's tactical pace. He stayed on very nicely when the penny dropped from 1f out, however, and is definitely one to take from the race. (op 8-1 tchd 7-1)

Main Beach, related to several Flat winners, made up his ground nicely on the outside turning for home and clearly has ability. He should prove a good deal sharper for this initial experience.

Necessity is a half-brother to Sunday's Irish Grade 2 winning novice hurdler Fully Funded, who was also very useful on the Flat. He got badly outpaced when it mattered, but kept on nicely down the home straight and he too has a future. (op 16-1)

Go Flo Go Official explanation: jockey said filly hung left

T/Plt: £51.40 to a £1 stake. Pool:£55,552.25. 788.91 winning tickets T/Qpdt: £23.90 to a £1 stake. Pool:£4,464.41. 138.10 winning tickets JN

2296 SEDGEFIELD (L-H)

Tuesday, November 23

OFFICIAL GOING: Soft (heavy in places; chs 5.8, hdl 6.2)

Wind: Fresh, behind. Weather: Cool, sunshine but odd heavy shower

2598 HARTLEPOOL CONSULTATIVE CAFFREYS CONDITIONAL JOCKEYS MARES' NOVICES' HURDLE (SERIES QUALIFER) (10 hdls) 2m 4f

1:00 (1:00) (Class 4) 4-Y-O+ £2,471 (£725; £362; £181)

Form				RPR
21P1	1		**Dorabelle (IRE)**[10] 2370 5-11-2 120 .... HenryBrooke(8) (Donald McCain) *trckd ldrs: hit 3 out: led 2 out: sn rdn: hit last: kpt on wl run-in: drvn out* **6/4[1]**	120+
3-22	2	¾	**Boragh Princess (IRE)**[34] 1921 6-11-0 114 .... KMDonoghue(3) (Gordon Elliott, Ire) *trckd ldrs: led 4 out: rdn whn hdd narrowly 2 out: kpt on but a jst hld run-in* **2/1[2]**	111
54	3	18	**Mrs Eff**[33] 1934 4-10-10 0 .... RyanMania (Kate Walton) *trckd ldrs: rdn after 4 out: wknd after 3 out: lft 3rd 2 out* **22/1**	85
56	4	29	**Floraclock**[33] 1934 5-10-7 0 .... ShaneByrne(3) (Sue Smith) *hld up: a bhd* **33/1**	56
556/	P		**Calow Green (IRE)**[998] 4177 8-10-10 0 .... BrianToomey (Ollie Pears) *hld up: a bhd: p.u bef 2 out* **80/1**	—
252-	P		**Below The Deck (IRE)**[252] 4663 7-10-10 100 .... JamesO'Farrell (Barbara Butterworth) *midfield: wknd after 4 out: t.o whn p.u bef 2 out* **11/1**	—

5645 **P** **Knockaveen (IRE)**[15] 2275 5-10-10 80 .... FearghalDavis —
(Andrew Crook) *led: hdd 4 out: wknd after next: t.o whn p.u bef last* **80/1**

2 **F** **Sophonie (FR)**[45] 1780 4-10-4 0 .... PaulGallagher(6) 102
(Ferdy Murphy) *hld up: hdwy to trck ldr after 4 out: 1 l down in 3rd whn fell 2 out* **9/2**[3]

5m 16.4s (23.70) **Going Correction** +1.25s/f (Heav)
WFA 4 from 5yo+ 8lb **8** Ran SP% **109.6**
Speed ratings (Par 105): **102,101,94,82,— —,—,—**
Tote Swingers:1&2:£1.20, 2&3:£6.70, 1&3:£5.20 CSF £4.37 TOTE £2.40: £1.10, £1.30, £3.60; EX 4.10.
Owner Brendan Richardson **Bred** Tommy James **Trained** Cholmondeley, Cheshire

FOCUS
The ground was reported to be pretty testing. This was a quite a competitive mares' novice hurdle, with three previous winners in the seven-strong field, and although the early pace was no more than ordinary, it picked up from halfway and developed into a fair test. The three previous winners drew clear from the others from the third last. The winner is rated as having stepped up on previous efforts with the second a little below her good-ground form.

NOTEBOOK
Dorabelle(IRE) put up another sound performance, despite giving weight away all round and also stepping up to this trip for the first time. She battled on well having raced prominently, and as she incurs no further penalty for this conditional riders' race success, she should continue to be competitive in this grade. (op 15-8 tchd 2-1 in a place)
Boragh Princess(IRE) is a solid yardstick to the form, and she continues in decent form even though she has yet to add to her Downpatrick success in August. She was rated 6lb inferior to the winner, who was giving her 7lb, so ran close to her best, proving that she handles this sort of ground. (op 11-4)
Mrs Eff, who showed only modest form in a couple of bumpers, was left to take third. Although she was outpointed from the third last, she wasn't entirely disgraced and should find a small race, possible when handicapped later on. (op 25-1 tchd 20-1)
Knockaveen(IRE) Official explanation: jockey said that the saddle slipped (op 11-4)
Sophonie(FR), a winner over fences on testing ground in France, settled better than on her Hexham debut despite stepping up in trip. She travelled well through the race, and was a close third with every chance when she stumbled and came down a stride after landing over the second last. On this showing she can win in similar grade. (op 11-4)

2599 BEACON MOLSON COORS BEGINNERS' CHASE (16 fncs) 2m 4f
1:30 (1:30) (Class 4) 4-Y-0+ **£3,168** (£936; £468; £234; £117)

Form RPR

2-32 **1** **Kellystown Lad (IRE)**[15] 2270 7-11-1 0 .... GrahamLee 131+
(Ferdy Murphy) *j.rt: hld up: hdwy after 9th: trckd ldrs 11th: rdn to ld bef last: kpt on wl* **11/4**[2]

0403 **2** *2 ¾* **Pokanoket (IRE)**[14] 2299 7-10-5 0 .... RyanMania(3) 120
(Malcolm Jefferson) *w ldr: led 11th: hdd 3 out: chal again next: kpt on but a hld run-in* **11/2**[3]

33P- **3** *3* **Chamirey (FR)**[228] 5112 7-11-1 0 .... JasonMaguire 123
(Donald McCain) *led: j. slowly and hdd 11th: rdn to ld again 3 out: hdd after 2 out: no ex run-in* **6/4**[1]

-004 **4** *14* **Monsieur Jourdain (IRE)**[14] 2299 4-10-7 0 ....(p) RichieMcGrath 103
(Tim Easterby) *trckd ldrs: mstke and pckd on landing 8th: sn lost pl and dropped to rr: wknd after 11th* **25/1**

0-35 **5** *1 ½* **Papa Caruso**[15] 2270 6-11-1 112 .... TjadeCollier 107
(Sue Smith) *in tch: reminders after 8th: wknd after 10th: wl hld whn hit 2 out* **16/1**

65/B **U** **Hegrid (IRE)**[4] 2507 9-11-1 117 .... BarryKeniry —
(A J Martin, Ire) *hld up in tch: trckd ldrs 9th: 3rd whn blnd and uns rdr 10th* **22/1**

-634 **P** **Soft Spoken Guy (IRE)**[27] 2035 7-11-1 0 ....(t) MichaelMcAlister —
(Maurice Barnes) *rn in snatches: in tch: nt fluent 7th: wknd after 9th: t.o whn p.u bef 3 out* **7/1**

5m 12.4s (9.40) **Going Correction** +0.60s/f (Soft)
WFA 4 from 5yo+ 8lb **7** Ran SP% **108.6**
Speed ratings (Par 105): **105,103,102,97,96 —,—**
Tote Swingers:1&2:£3.20, 2&3:£2.00, 1&3:£1.70 CSF £16.37 TOTE £4.10: £1.60, £3.40; EX 16.60.
Owner Crossed Fingers Partnership **Bred** Brendan Kehoe **Trained** West Witton, N Yorks

FOCUS
This looked an above-average beginners chase for the course, and the pace was a sound one. The winner can raten higher and the second is rated to the best of his hurdles form.

NOTEBOOK
Kellystown Lad(IRE) didn't quite fulfil his potential over hurdles, but he's always looked the sort who would do better over fences and produced a sound enough effort here, being kept wide, jumping well and coming from off the pace to lead going to the last. The step back up in trip was ideal for him, but he still looked a bit green when he hit the front, so though he's the type to improve further, he left the impression he's a horse who doesn't want to be in front for too long. (op 3-1)
Pokanoket(IRE), who had a mark of 123 over hurdles, confirmed the promise of her first run over fences, mixing it with Chamirey for a long way, but having no answer to the winner from the second last. Both her hurdle wins were at Market Rasen, and though she acts left-handed, she seems to excel at the Lincolnshire venue. (op 13-2)
Chamirey(FR) ◆, third for Alan King in the Pertemps Final last season, had run twice over fences in France in 2007. He was rated 135 over hurdles, and though he didn't run to that mark here on his first start for Donald McCain, he certainly shouldn't be written off as a chaser. He jumped well in the main, but seemed to find the trip on this track too sharp for him. Also it was his first run of the season and he left the impression he'll improve for it. He'll be winning soon. (op 7-4 tchd 15-8 in a place)
Monsieur Jourdain(IRE) made a bad mistake at halfway, and never featured after that, but will find easier opportunities than this. (op 28-1)
Soft Spoken Guy(IRE) was never going or jumping well and may struggle to be as good a chaser as hurdler. Official explanation: jockey said that the gelding finished distressed (op 5-1 tchd 8-1)

2600 DURHAM AND CLEVELAND CIU JUVENILE HURDLE (JOHN WADE HURDLE SERIES QUALIFIER) (7 hdls 1 omitted) 2m 1f
2:00 (2:00) (Class 4) 3-Y-0 **£2,471** (£725; £362; £181)

Form RPR

31 **1** **Marsh Warbler**[13] 2306 3-11-2 139 .... FearghalDavis(3) 109+
(Brian Ellison) *mde all: wnt clr on bridle appr last: easily* **2/9**[1]

11 **2** *9* **Al Dafa (USA)**[33] 1935 3-11-7 114 .... KMDonoghue(5) 96
(Gordon Elliott, Ire) *w ldr: hit 4th: rdn appr last: sn no match for wnr: j.lft last* **13/2**[2]

3 *4 ½* **Hades (IRE)**[39] 3-10-12 0 .... RichieMcGrath 76
(Tim Easterby) *racd keenly: hld up: nt fluent 4th: kpt on after 3 out: wnt 3rd last: n.d* **12/1**[3]

4 *2* **Quality Mover (USA)**[33] 3-10-5 0 .... BrianHarding 67
(Edwin Tuer) *trckd ldrs in 3rd: rdn and wknd appr last: lost 3rd last* **20/1**

5 *27* **Penny Bazaar**[94] 3-9-12 0 .... HenryBrooke(7) 40
(Dianne Sayer) *in tch: rdn after 3 out: sn wknd* **100/1**

4m 32.4s (25.50) **Going Correction** +1.25s/f (Heav) **5** Ran SP% **108.6**
Speed ratings (Par 104): **90,85,83,82,70**
CSF £2.24 TOTE £1.10: £1.10, £1.20; EX 1.80.
Owner Dan Gilbert & Kristian Strangeway **Bred** Darley **Trained** Norton, N Yorks

FOCUS
Only five runners for this juvenile event, but two were previous winners. One flight of hurdles per circuit was omitted so they jumped only six and, as the early pace wasn't strong either, the form is best treated with a degree of caution, although the easy winner is value for further.

NOTEBOOK
Marsh Warbler again won with real authority. Bought for 12,000gns after winning a Leicester seller on the Flat in October, he stepped up on his debut run over hurdles with a runaway success at Bangor on his previous start. He repeated the dose, travelling and jumping well, and drawing right away in the straight without being asked any sort of question. The handicapper put him up to 139 for his last win, a mark that might flatter him, but he once again impressed by thrashing some inferior rivals. In a season in which star juveniles are thin on the ground, he will be interesting when stepped up in grade. (op 2-7 tchd 1-5)
Al Dafa(USA) faced a particularly stiff task trying to give weight to the winner, who is rated 25lb his superior, and was no match for him from the second last. This testing ground probably wasn't ideal for him. (op 9-2 tchd 7-1)
Hades(IRE), a 62-rated Flat performer who showed his best form at 1m, took a fair grip early on, lost his place with a mistake at the third, but kept on and in the end wasn't beaten far. However, it remains to be seen whether this flatters him. (op 18-1)
Quality Mover(USA), who was keen early, travelled up well behind the first two going into the final bend, but then faded. She was a 60-rated Flat maiden, and though not disgraced, she may not be as good as the bare result suggests. Official explanation: jockey said that the filly had a breathing problem (op 25-1)

2601 MIDDLESBROUGH WORKING MEN'S CARLING H'CAP CHASE (13 fncs) 2m 110y
2:30 (2:30) (Class 4) (0-110,107) 4-Y-0+ **£3,168** (£936; £468; £234; £117)

Form RPR

3P41 **1** **War Party**[26] 2053 6-11-5 106 ....(b) MrTWeston(7) 123+
(Dr Richard Newland) *in tch: trckd ldr 5th: w ldr 8th: led 2 out: sn clr: comf* **3/1**[2]

14-P **2** *11* **Northern Quest (IRE)**[10] 2371 9-11-6 100 .... RobertWalford 102
(Henry Hogarth) *led: hdd 2 out: sn no match for wnr* **11/1**

05/4 **3** *1 ¾* **Mighty Magnus (IRE)**[23] 2107 7-10-5 85 .... JamesReveley 84
(Martin Todhunter) *hld up in rr: hdwy after 5th: trckd ldrs 8th: wnt 3rd after 4 out: rdn after 3 out: kpt on same pce* **9/4**[1]

6005 **4** *10* **Toulouse Express (IRE)**[14] 2298 11-11-4 98 ....(v) KennyJohnson 87
(Robert Johnson) *trckd ldrs on outer: rdn after 4 out: wknd after 3 out* **14/1**

5231 **5** *4* **Schinken Otto (IRE)**[14] 2301 9-11-1 100 .... BrianToomey(5) 88
(Malcolm Jefferson) *racd keenly: hld up in tch: rdn after 4 out: sn wknd* **4/1**[3]

000 **6** *10* **Seigneur Des Bois (FR)**[15] 2270 4-11-6 107 .... GrahamLee 75
(Ferdy Murphy) *hld up in rr: hit 3rd: mstkes 7th and 2 out: a bhd* **6/1**

0P-4 **7** *9* **Nifty Roy**[18] 2194 10-10-12 92 .... RichieMcGrath 58
(Brian Storey) *trckd ldrs: wknd after 7th* **16/1**

4m 21.9s (13.30) **Going Correction** +0.60s/f (Soft) **7** Ran SP% **110.9**
Speed ratings (Par 105): **92,86,86,81,79 74,70**
Tote Swingers:1&2:£7.20, 2&3:£5.30, 1&3:£1.90 CSF £30.69 CT £82.14 TOTE £3.60: £1.40, £4.00; EX 39.40.
Owner J A Provan,C E Stedman,Prof D E Newland **Bred** Dayton Investments Ltd **Trained** Claines, Worcs

FOCUS
Mainly exposed sorts in this 0-110 handicap chase which was run at a decent gallop. The race could be rated a fair amount higher.

NOTEBOOK
War Party bounced back to form when blinkers were put back on at Stratford on his previous start and, despite being put up 7lb for that win, once again scored in some style in the headgear, racing in the first two until coming right away from the second last. He's in fine form at present, and would be interesting if turning out with a penalty. (tchd 11-4 and 7-2)
Northern Quest(IRE), who was pulled up on his reappearance, shaped much better this time even though the ground wasn't ideal for him. He kept the winner company for most of the way, but though he proved no match for him from the second last, he kept on for a creditable second. (tchd 10-1)
Mighty Magnus(IRE) was the one for money, having shaped with encouragement after a break at Carlisle three weeks previously in a race whose form had worked out pretty well. Held up in the early stages, he got into contention by the fourth last but was never able to land a serious blow in a race in which the first two were in those positions throughout. (op 10-3 tchd 2-1)
Toulouse Express(IRE) hadn't been in the best of form, but though this trip is short of his best, he shaped with more encouragement. (tchd 12-1)
Schinken Otto(IRE), who won over C&D last time, never seemed happy on this occasion. Prior to that last win, all his best form had been on better ground and he perhaps found conditions too testing this time. Official explanation: jockey said gelding was unsuited by the soft, heavy in places ground (op 3-1)
Seigneur Des Bois(FR) showed a little more, but he was never in the hunt and will need to improve a fair bit more if he's to win a race. (op 7-1 tchd 15-2)

2602 BET365.COM H'CAP CHASE (21 fncs) 3m 3f
3:00 (3:00) (Class 5) (0-95,95) 4-Y-0+ **£2,602** (£764; £382; £190)

Form RPR

51- **1** **Billsgrey (IRE)**[234] 4981 8-10-8 77 .... JamesReveley 88+
(William Amos) *hld up in tch: trckd ldrs 12th: wnt 2nd after 3 out: rdn to ld 2 out: styd on wl* **3/1**[1]

4P-P **2** *10* **Jeringa**[10] 2371 11-11-9 92 ....(b) BrianHughes 89
(John Wade) *trckd ldrs: led 9th: rdn whn hdd 2 out: sn no ex* **8/1**

-006 **3** *3* **Nelliedonethat (IRE)**[33] 1933 10-11-10 93 .... PeterBuchanan 87
(Lucinda Russell) *in rr after mstke 3rd: trckd ldrs 12th: grad lost tch after 6 out: wnt modest 3rd 2 out* **15/2**

-013 **4** *23* **Matmata De Tendron (FR)**[9] 2402 10-11-6 92 ....(p) FearghalDavis(3) 70
(Andrew Crook) *prom: w ldr 11th: rdn 4 out: lost 2nd sn after slow jump 3 out: wknd 2 out* **10/3**[2]

6500 **P** **Rare Society (IRE)**[11] 2354 12-11-5 93 .... ShaneByrne(5) —
(Sue Smith) *led: hdd 9th: reminders after 12th: wknd after 14th: bhd whn p.u bef 4 out* **14/1**

1032 **P** **Benbeoch**[15] 2274 11-11-12 95 ....(p) BrianHarding —
(Sandy Thomson) *prom: hit 4th and dropped to rr: reminders 5th: mstke 12th: lost tch after 13th: p.u bef 16th* **4/1**[3]

0-00 **P** **Yes Mate**[33] 1933 6-9-7 **69** oh8 .... HenryBrooke(7) —
(Dianne Sayer) *in tch: wknd after 14th: p.u bef 4 out* **6/1**

7m 21.2s (32.20) **Going Correction** +0.60s/f (Soft) **7** Ran SP% **111.9**
Speed ratings (Par 103): **76,73,72,65,— —,—**
Tote Swingers:1&2:£4.20, 2&3:£8.00, 1&3:£5.70 CSF £24.86 TOTE £3.10: £1.50, £4.30; EX 27.30.

Owner John & Mary Stenhouse **Bred** James Keegan And Jeff Hamilton **Trained** Broadhaugh, Scottish Borders

FOCUS

This moderate staying chase was run at a fair gallop in the conditions, and is rated around the first two.

NOTEBOOK

Billsgrey(IRE), off the mark at the 25th attempt on his previous start back in April, he faced a stiffer task off a 13lb higher rating, but scored in some style, coming from off the pace to win without being asked any sort of question. He'll face another steep rise for winning what was in essence an ordinary race, but despite him being an 8-y-o with 26 runs under his belt, he gives the impression he can improve again. (op 7-2 tchd 4-1)

Jeringa had plenty to prove coming into the race as he'd failed to finish in his two previous starts, and was not certain to appreciate the longer trip. In the end he came out clear second best despite racing a touch keenly, and though it wouldn't be a performance to go overboard about, it was at least a step in the right direction. (tchd 15-2)

Nelliedonethat(IRE) was another who had been out of form coming into the race, and he also shaped a little better despite an early mistake. He's back on his last winning mark, and looks to be on the way back. (op 7-1)

Matmata De Tendron(FR) had plenty going for him, as he stays well and has a good record on the track, so it was rather disappointing the way he dropped away from the second last. (op 5-2)

Benbeoch, who'd run well on his previous start, looked a moody customer as he didn't jump or travel this time. He looks one to be wary of. Official explanation: jockey said that the gelding was never travelling (op 7-2 tchd 9-2)

Yes Mate attracted plenty of money, but faced a stiff task from out of the handicap and once again showed little. (op 7-2 tchd 9-2)

2603 MOLSON COORS WHOLESALE AT HARTLEPOOL H'CAP HURDLE (7 hdls 1 omitted) 2m 1f

3:30 (3:30) (Class 5) (0-95,95) 4-Y-0+ **£1,561** (£458; £229; £114)

Form RPR

0021 **1** **Spice Bar**[9] 2398 6-10-13 **82** 7ex .... BarryKeniry 95+
(Declan Carroll) *hld up: smooth hdwy after 4 out: led on bridle appr last: drvn sn after last: hld on towards fin* **8/13**[1]

6603 **2** *1* **Barbarian**[14] 2303 4-10-10 **86** .... FearghalDavis(5) 92
(Alan Brown) *midfield: outpcd 4 out: styd on after 3 out: wnt 2nd sn after last: kpt on wl* **20/1**

62-U **3** *6* **Cosmetic**[14] 2302 5-10-8 **77** .... WilsonRenwick 78
(Howard Johnson) *trckd ldrs: rdn after 3 out: disp 2nd last: no ex run-in* **16/1**

0-00 **4** *7* **Prize Fighter (IRE)**[164] 727 8-11-2 **85** .... TomSiddall 80
(Lynn Siddall) *hld up: hdwy after 4 out to chse ldrs next: rdn appr last: kpt on same pce* **40/1**

00-1 **5** *2* **Emirate Isle**[14] 2302 6-11-12 **95** .... (p) BrianHughes 89
(Brian Storey) *w ldr: led 3 out: rdn whn hdd appr last: sn wknd* **11/2**[2]

3216 **6** *6* **Royal Flynn**[25] 2070 8-11-2 **92** .... (tp) HenryBrooke(7) 78
(Kate Walton) *midfield: hdwy to chse ldrs 4 out: wknd appr last* **14/1**

0-50 **7** *4 ½* **Sir Mark (IRE)**[15] 2282 6-11-10 **93** .... (v[1]) JodieMogford 75
(Anna Bramall) *led: hdd 3 out: sn wknd* **80/1**

1-03 **8** *13* **Mardood**[188] 393 5-11-3 **91** .... (p) AlexanderVoy(5) 60
(Chris Grant) *midfield: rdn whn nt fluent 4 out: sn wknd* **10/1**[3]

0P0- **P** **Byron Bay**[12] 2816 8-10-8 **77** .... (p) KennyJohnson —
(Robert Johnson) *trckd ldrs on outer: nt fluent 4 out: sn wknd: t.o and p.u bef last* **80/1**

P650 **U** **Samizdat (FR)**[23] 2103 7-10-9 **85** .... MissECSayer(7) —
(Dianne Sayer) *midfield: mstke and uns rdr 1st* **16/1**

30/P **P** **Brian's Journey**[46] 1760 8-10-8 **80** .... JamesO'Farrell(3) —
(Barbara Butterworth) *mid-div: blnd 1st: bhd whn slow 4th: t.o whn p.u bef 2 out* **100/1**

4-0P **P** **Dollar Express (USA)**[18] 2190 4-11-2 **85** .... BrianHarding —
(Edwin Tuer) *hld up: a bhd: p.u bef last* **100/1**

4m 26.5s (19.60) **Going Correction** +1.25s/f (Heav)
WFA 4 from 5yo+ 7lb **12** Ran SP% **116.5**
Speed ratings (Par 103): **103,102,99,96,95 92,90,84,—,— —,—**
Tote Swingers:1&2:£4.30, 2&3:£16.00, 1&3:£5.40 CSF £19.86 CT £113.04 TOTE £1.60: £1.10, £4.60, £4.30; EX 18.60.

Owner Kevin McConnell **Bred** Littleton Stud **Trained** Sledmere, E Yorks

■ Stewards' Enquiry : Wilson Renwick five-day ban: used whip with excessive frequency

FOCUS

A 0-95 handicap hurdle run at a strong gallop, and though most of the runners appeared pretty exposed, it featured a couple of improvers. The winner is better than the bare result and rated in line with his Market Rasen form.

NOTEBOOK

Spice Bar had beaten subsequent dual winner Marino Prince in good style at Market Rasen on his previous start. Backed to odds-on under a 7lb penalty, he proved that win was no fluke. Though he travelled well into the race having been held up well in rear off the strong pace, in the end he had to be driven right out to score. These very testing conditions were perhaps not ideal for him, but he's going to face a much stiffer task at the weights in his future races over hurdles. (op 4-7 tchd 8-11 in a place and 4-6 in places)

Barbarian had finished 13l behind Emirate Isle here on his previous start, but reversed that form on 13lb better terms, staying on in good style after getting outpaced three out. A stiffer test of stamina might well suit him. (op 22-1)

Cosmetic has shown only modest form and this was one of her better efforts. (tchd 18-1)

Prize Fighter(IRE) kept plugging away without proving a real threat.

Emirate Isle, who had won his last race here in good style having previously scored on the Flat at Catterick, was 13lb higher but was a touch disappointing all the same, though he may have paid the penalty for racing up with the strong early gallop. (op 7-1 tchd 15-2)

Mardood, who was in good form earlier in the year, probably needed this race after a break of 188 days. (op 8-1)

T/Plt: £44.50 to a £1 stake. Pool:£63,387.03. 1,037.95 winning tickets T/Qpdt: £26.90 to a £1 stake. Pool:£4,252.29. 116.90 winning tickets AS

2143 CHEPSTOW (L-H)

Wednesday, November 24

OFFICIAL GOING: Soft (chs 5.7, hdl 5.6)

Wind: Moderate behind Weather: Sunny

2604 BETFAIR RACING EXCELLENCE CONDITIONAL JOCKEYS' TRAINING SERIES H'CAP CHASE (16 fncs) 2m 3f 110y

1:10 (1:12) (Class 5) (0-95,94) 4-Y-0+ **£2,276** (£668; £334; £166)

Form RPR

0-04 **1** **Manmoon (FR)**[15] 2287 7-11-11 **93** .... (t) MattGriffiths 102
(Nigel Hawke) *trckd ldr: chal fr 7th tl led 10th: drvn and hit 2 out: rdn and hld on wl run-in* **8/1**

02 **2** *½* **Flying Squad (UAE)**[3] 2555 6-11-7 **92** .... (t) EdCookson(3) 100
(Milton Harris) *hld up in rr but in tch: nt fluent 7th: hdwy appr 12th: chsd wnr 4 out: styd on u.p thrght run-in but a hld* **9/4**[1]

5004 **3** *2* **Lukie Victor (IRE)**[99] 1273 9-11-2 **87** .... AdamWedge(3) 93
(Evan Williams) *in rr but in tch: hdwy to chse wnr appr 12th and mstke lost 2nd 4 out and outpcd: rallied to take 3rd 2 out: kpt on run-in but no imp on ldng duo* **4/1**[3]

34-3 **4** *12* **Rileyev (FR)**[19] 2187 5-11-12 **94** .... HarryChalloner 91
(Venetia Williams) *in rr but in tch: j. slowly 8th: hdwy 12th: wnt 3rd 4 out: blnd and wknd 2 out* **5/2**[2]

U-65 **5** *60* **Littleton Aldor (IRE)**[21] 2148 10-10-13 **81** .... AodhaganConlon 14
(Mark Gillard) *led but j. bdly rt thrght: jnd 7th: hdd 10th: wknd appr 12th: t.o whn veered bdly rt 2 out* **5/1**

5m 11.97s (0.67) **Going Correction** -0.05s/f (Good) **5** Ran SP% **107.1**
Speed ratings (Par 103): **96,95,95,90,66**
CSF £25.16 TOTE £9.20: £4.10, £2.10; EX 20.10.

Owner D R Mead, G C Board **Bred** Olivier Delegue **Trained** Woolminstone, Somerset

FOCUS

It was dry overnight and the ground was officially described as soft. A weak conditional jockeys' handicap chase run at a decent pace. The winner was still a stone+ off his old mark.

NOTEBOOK

Manmoon(FR) had been beaten a minimum of 27l in seven completed starts on good or softer ground, but his mark had dropped 22lb in the last 12 months and he bounced back to form with a gutsy win with a tongue tie reapplied. He should not go up much for this overdue second success under rules and could have some scope to climb back up the ranks. (op 15-2 tchd 7-1)

Flying Squad(UAE) looked a strong contender on his close second to an unexposed type on chase debut at Towcester three days earlier. He travelled smoothly under a patient ride and looked the likely winner for a long way up the straight, but couldn't overhaul the leader and was held after hitting 1.14 in-running. However, he did run into a well treated and revitalised rival on this quick reappearance and the early signs over fences are encouraging. (tchd 3-1)

Lukie Victor(IRE) has been disappointing since winning three times over hurdles/fences in Ireland in 2008, but his mark has been in relentless decline and he showed signs of a revival by staying on well behind the front pair. (tchd 7-2)

Rileyev(FR) shaped like he would improve for the run when a promising third on his reappearance at Fontwell. He was strong in the market and things seemed to be going well for a long way, but he didn't pick up when asked a question and put in a tame finishing effort. (op 9-4 tchd 2-1)

Littleton Aldor(IRE) put a severe dent in his chance by jumping markedly right out in front and was in trouble a long way out before dropping away. (op 13-2 tchd 7-1)

2605 WEATHERBYS BANK NOVICES' H'CAP CHASE (12 fncs) 2m 110y

1:40 (1:40) (Class 4) (0-100,100) 4-Y-0+ **£2,927** (£859; £429; £214)

Form RPR

3314 **1** **Rimini (FR)**[27] 2053 5-11-10 **98** .... RichardJohnson 116+
(David Rees) *hit 1st: in tch: hdwy appr 8th: led after 4 out: rdn fr 2 out: 1 l up and u.p whn lft clr at last: in n.d after and eased down run-in* **10/3**[1]

0-1F **2** *8* **Owner Occupier**[9] 2429 5-11-12 **100** .... ColinBolger 107
(Chris Gordon) *trckd ldr after 1st: drvn to ld and blnd 4 out: sn hdd: wknd next: lft poor 2nd and pckd last: clsd on eased down wnr run-in* **14/1**

F23F **3** *4* **Turn Up (IRE)**[6] 2468 7-10-3 **84** .... (t) MrJMRidley(7) 86
(Matt Sheppard) *led tl hdd 4 out: sn wknd: lft poor 3rd last* **10/1**

0-F2 **4** *3 ¼* **Mr Bond (IRE)**[15] 2292 7-11-2 **90** .... NickScholfield 92+
(Andy Turnell) *in tch: hit 2nd: 3rd and 4th: blnd 6th and 7th: no ch fr 8th: mstke 4 out: lft mod 4th last* **4/1**[3]

-01U **5** *21* **Russellstown Boy (IRE)**[32] 1965 10-11-1 **89** .... PaulMoloney 72
(Evan Williams) *bdly hmpd 2nd: a in rr* **9/1**

5601 **6** *47* **Roc De Guye (FR)**[8] 2434 5-10-9 **83** .... DavidDennis 13
(James Evans) *in tch: rdn 8th and sn wknd:* **7/1**

0504 **F** **Art Man**[13] 2334 7-11-0 **88** .... (t) HaddenFrost —
(James Frost) *in rr but in tch: nt fluent 3rd and 4th: wknd and hit 8th: wl bhd whn fell 4 out* **20/1**

0U-5 **F** **Istron Bay**[31] 1995 8-11-0 **88** .... TomMessenger —
(Richard Lee) *in tch whn fell 2nd* **25/1**

423- **F** **Douryna**[233] 5055 7-10-11 **85** .... JoeTizzard 103
(Colin Tizzard) *in tch: hdwy appr 8th: outpcd appr 4 out: rallied to chse wnr next: styng on: 1 l down and gng ok whn fell last* **7/2**[2]

4m 14.11s (-2.99) **Going Correction** -0.05s/f (Good) **9** Ran SP% **112.2**
Speed ratings (Par 105): **105,101,99,97,87 65,—,—,—**
toteswingers:1&2:£12.50, 1&3:£7.60, 2&3:£18.90 CSF £44.71 CT £416.66 TOTE £3.30: £1.20, £4.60, £3.20; EX 59.50.

Owner D Rees **Bred** Haras D'Ecouves & Uplifting B'Stock Ltd **Trained** Clarbeston, Pembrokes

FOCUS

A fairly competitive minor novices' handicap. There was some drama in the closing stages and the winner was left clear at the last. He produced a big step up.

NOTEBOOK

Rimini(FR) was well backed and looked likely to run out a convincing winner after moving smoothly to the front early in the straight. He had a rallying rival to deal with approaching the last, but looked in control when that runner crashed out. This lightly raced and former fast ground hurdle winner has looked an economical jumper in his two chase starts and is open to plenty of improvement. (op 5-1)

Owner Occupier showed marked improvement on his hurdles form when winning under a prominent ride off 8lb lower on his chase debut at Towcester. He fell in his follow up bid at Plumpton and a serious mistake four out ruined his chance here. However, on the positive side he did manage to keep plugging away and gave the impression he could make a big impact off this mark if avoiding errors. (tchd 16-1)

Turn Up(IRE) ran respectably under a positive ride but this dual Irish point winner is now 0-14 over regulation fences and his jumping does not look entirely convincing. (op 8-1)

Mr Bond(IRE) was a close second in a Lingfield handicap last time, but some jumping issues resurfaced here and he was never dangerous after making several mistakes along the way. (op 9-2 tchd 5-1)

Russellstown Boy(IRE) attracted some support at biggish prices, but was never competitive and put in his second lacklustre run since destroying his opposition off 10lb lower at Uttoxeter. (op 12-1 tchd 8-1)

Roc De Guye(FR) sprang a 20-1 surprise in a conditional riders' handicap at Fakenham eight days earlier, but that race was weakened by four runners failing to complete and he put in a very disappointing effort off the same mark here. This was probably too bad to be true and may have come too soon, but he will have a bit to prove next time. (op 5-1 tchd 9-2)

Douryna took a heavy fall at the last, but she emerges with plenty of credit because she was the only one to offer some resistance to the winner and could have gone close. This was a very pleasing chase debut for a new yard after 233 days off and she could have a profitable future over fences. (tchd 3-1)

2606 WEATHERBYS BLOODSTOCK INSURANCE H'CAP HURDLE (12 hdls) 3m

2:15 (2:15) (Class 3) (0-130,127) 4-Y-0+ **£5,204** (£1,528; £764; £381)

Form RPR

6-P0 **1** **Stow**[21] 2147 5-10-11 **112** AidanColeman 115
(Venetia Williams) *chsd ldrs early: rdn and bhd 7th: stl u.p 3 out: plenty to do but styd on after next: hrd drvn and styd on wl run-in to ld last strides* **8/1**

60-2 **2** *shd* **Radmores Revenge**[21] 2144 7-9-11 **105** CharlieWallis[(7)] 108
(John O'Shea) *in rr: hit 6th: hdwy but plenty to do 3 out: chsd clr ldr 2 out: styd on wl run-in to ld cl home: hdd last strides* **6/1**[3]

3321 **3** *½* **Saintly Lady (IRE)**[11] 2372 5-10-5 **109** (p) DonalDevereux[(3)] 111
(Peter Bowen) *chsd ldrs tl rdn and outpcd after 3 out: rallied after 2 out: styd on u.p run-in and fin strly to take 3rd last strides* **11/2**[2]

-413 **4** *nk* **Young Albert (IRE)**[21] 2147 9-11-0 **115** (p) FelixDeGiles 118
(Charlie Longsdon) *t.k.h: j. slowly 1st: led after 3rd: sn 8 l clr: stl 6 l clr 2 out: sn rdn: over 2 l up whn blnd bdly last: hdd cl home and lost 2 pls last strides* **5/1**[1]

110- **5** *4* **Misstree Dancer**[223] 5196 6-11-2 **120** DannyCook[(3)] 118
(Nick Mitchell) *in tch: hdwy 4 out: rdn next: styd on fr 2 out and kpt on run-in but nvr gng pce to rch ldrs* **20/1**

0-PU **6** *nk* **Heathcliff (IRE)**[24] 2106 8-11-12 **127** (v) RichardJohnson 125
(Richard Lee) *in rr: hdwy 6th: drvn along fr 4 out: kpt on fr 2 out and styd on run-in but no imp on ldrs* **10/1**

05P0 **7** *¾* **Osolomio (IRE)**[34] 1929 7-10-3 **104** (t) LiamTreadwell 101
(Jennie Candlish) *in rr: j.big 2nd: t.k.h: rdn and wl bhd 4 out: stl plenty to do 2 out: styd on u.p run-in: fin wl* **11/1**

PP/0 **8** *¾* **Only Vintage (USA)**[21] 2147 10-10-7 **115** MrTJCannon[(7)] 112
(Paul Henderson) *chsd ldrs: wnt 2nd 8th: styd chsng wnr but no imp fr 4 out: styd on same pce fr 2 out* **50/1**

212- **9** *28* **Anak (IRE)**[291] 3890 4-11-9 **124** TomScudamore 92
(Jim Best) *chsd ldrs: wnt 2nd 6th tl rdn 8th: wknd u.p 4 out: t.o* **15/2**

PP-4 **10** *8* **Saphire Night**[21] 2147 9-10-9 **120** (t) CiaranMckee[(10)] 80
(Tom George) *chsd ldrs tl rdn 8th and sn btn: t.o* **7/1**

1P4P **11** *45* **What A Scientist (IRE)**[22] 2140 10-10-12 **116** SamTwiston-Davies[(3)] 31
(Nigel Twiston-Davies) *led tl after 3rd: rdn 7th and sn bhd: t.o* **16/1**

6m 20.35s (0.55) **Going Correction** +0.20s/f (Yiel)
WFA 4 from 5yo+ 9lb **11** Ran SP% **111.7**
Speed ratings (Par 107): **107,106,106,106,105 105,105,104,95,92 77**
toteswingers:1&2:£17.80, 1&3:£11.10, 2&3:£3.70 CSF £53.17 CT £282.72 TOTE £8.40: £2.50, £2.10, £1.80; EX 71.10.
Owner GSM Properties Ltd **Bred** Plantation Stud **Trained** Kings Caple, H'fords

FOCUS
A fair handicap. The early pace was very steady and there was a tight four-way finish. The first five are rated close to their marks but this is not a race to be confident about.

NOTEBOOK
Stow can run in snatches and make mistakes and was a remote eighth with half a mile to go before finding a power-packed finish to get up in the dying strides after being matched at 999-1 in-running. He is 25lb lower than his peak hurdle rating and may be able to build on this major revival, but there have been more bad runs than good ones in recent times and the form of this slowly run race is not certain to work out. (op 17-2)

Radmores Revenge, a close second over 2m4f on his seasonal reappearance, gave it a good try off 10lb higher stepped back up to 3m but was just mugged by a faster finisher. Very effective on testing ground, he is back near the top of his game and should be able to gain compensation for this very close call.. (op 11-2)

Saintly Lady(IRE) finished placed six times in a row before getting back in the groove with a clear cut win at Wetherby. An 11lb rise made things tougher, but she showed a good attitude to fight her way into the bunch finish and should remain dangerous in staying handicaps. (op 5-1 tchd 9-2)

Young Albert(IRE) seized the initiative a long way out and nearly collected under an enterprising ride, but he made a crucial mistake when almost tripping over at the last hurdle and was just reeled in. This 9-y-o is a reliable type who handles most ground and should be able to record a seventh career win. (op 6-1)

Misstree Dancer put in a promising return from 223 days off, particularly as she raced keenly for a long way. She is a tough battler who won back-to-back novice hurdles at around 2m5f on heavy ground last spring and could take another step forward in handicaps this season. (op 18-1 tchd 16-1)

Heathcliff(IRE) did a bit of late work switched back to hurdling with a visor replacing blinkers but he has more letters than numbers in his form figures since a beginners' chase win at Ludlow in February and may not build on this. (op 17-2 tchd 8-1)

Osolomio(IRE), backed at big prices in the morning, was very keen early on but caught the eye staying on strongly from a long way back. (op 14-1)

2607 KILSBY AND WILLIAMS NOVICES' HURDLE (11 hdls) 2m 4f

2:50 (2:51) (Class 4) 4-Y-0+ **£2,602** (£764; £382; £190)

Form RPR

34-2 **1** **Golden Chieftain (IRE)**[46] 1778 5-10-12 0 JoeTizzard 128+
(Colin Tizzard) *led 2nd: to 4th: trckd ldrs: chal 4 out: sn led: c clr fr 2 out: easily* **7/2**[2]

34-0 **2** *9* **Point West (IRE)**[15] 2291 6-10-9 0 DannyCook[(3)] 115
(Nick Mitchell) *in rr tl hdwy 7th: styng on whn blnd 4 out: styd on to go 2nd at last and kpt on but nvr any ch w easy wnr* **33/1**

20-4 **3** *3* **Mic's Delight (IRE)**[26] 2067 6-10-12 0 TomO'Brien 112
(Victor Dartnall) *trckd ldrs: slt ld 4 out: sn hdd: styd on same pce and lost 2nd last* **9/4**[1]

6-U1 **4** *7* **Educated Evans (IRE)**[27] 2058 5-11-5 0 PaddyBrennan 112
(Nigel Twiston-Davies) *in tch: chsd ldrs fr 6th: wknd fr 2 out* **10/1**

06-4 **5** *2½* **Grey Wulff (IRE)**[22] 2136 5-10-12 0 SamThomas 102
(Emma Lavelle) *in tch: hdwy and rdn 4 out: nvr rchd ldrs and styd on same pce* **17/2**

50-5 **6** *6* **Another Kate (IRE)**[21] 2145 6-10-5 0 AidanColeman 89
(David Richards) *led to 2nd: led again after 4th: wnt rt 7th: hdd 4 out: wknd next* **6/1**[3]

4 **7** *10* **Cap Elorn (FR)**[48] 1748 4-10-12 0 NoelFehily 85
(Paul Nicholls) *chsd ldrs: led 4th: sn hdd: styd in tch tl wknd 4 out* **10/1**

53/6 **8** *2½* **King Of Dubai**[17] 2241 5-10-12 0 RhysFlint 83
(John Flint) *chsd ldrs tl wknd 4 out: hit next* **8/1**

0 **9** *2* **Otter Mist**[26] 2074 5-10-12 0 AndrewGlassonbury 81
(Victor Dartnall) *in tch: hit 6th: wknd bef 4 out* **80/1**

0-24 **10** *2* **Railway Diva (IRE)**[169] 684 6-10-5 0 PaulMoloney 72
(Evan Williams) *in rr: sme hdwy appr 4 out: sn wknd* **50/1**

360 **11** *14* **Kilcommon Pride (IRE)**[23] 2122 5-10-12 0 HaddenFrost 65
(Roger Curtis) *nvr bttr than mid-div* **100/1**

20- **12** *2½* **Easton Clump**[271] 4279 7-10-12 0 MarkGrant 62
(Dominic Ffrench Davis) *in rr: sme hdwy 6th: wknd bef 4 out: no ch whn hmpd 3 out* **33/1**

-P05 **13** *2½* **Bright Decision**[19] 2181 4-10-5 0 DannyBurton[(7)] 60
(Joanna Davis) *bhd fr 1/2-way* **80/1**

0 **14** *2* **Goodwood Starlight (IRE)**[38] 1884 5-10-9 0 MarcGoldstein[(3)] 58
(Jim Best) *prom early: bhd fr 1/2-way* **50/1**

0-0 **15** *2* **Man Of Leisure**[48] 1742 6-10-7 0 KeiranBurke[(5)] 56
(Nerys Dutfield) *a towards rr* **200/1**

U0 **F** **Goodtimetoby (IRE)**[17] 2241 7-10-12 0 CharliePoste —
(Richard Lee) *in rr: sme hdwy appr 4 out: sn wknd: fell next* **150/1**

5m 4.20s (2.40) **Going Correction** +0.20s/f (Yiel)
WFA 4 from 5yo+ 8lb **16** Ran SP% **121.5**
Speed ratings (Par 105): **103,99,98,95,94 92,88,87,86,85 79,78,77,77,76** —
toteswingers:1&2:£33.20, 1&3:£4.80, 2&3:£22.90 CSF £117.47 TOTE £4.10: £1.50, £10.90, £1.50; EX 225.90.
Owner Brocade Racing **Bred** Robert Donaldson **Trained** Milborne Port, Dorset

FOCUS
An interesting novice hurdle. The winner was impressive and they finished well strung out. This looks form to be positive about.

NOTEBOOK
Golden Chieftain(IRE) was a highly promising second in a bumper here last time behind Kartanian who was third in a Listed bumper at Cheltenham next time. This half-brother to useful jumper Boychuk was always travelling easily on his hurdles debut and forged clear for an emphatic success. He looks a useful prospect who should stay 3m and the Albert Bartlett at Cheltenham is the long term plan. (op 9-2)

Point West(IRE) had quite a bit to find, but ran a big race at 33-1 on his second run back for a new trainer. He is a former point winner who shapes like a stiffer test could encourage further progress.

Mic's Delight(IRE) was a 20-1 bumper winner at Kempton in February and had decent claims on his hurdle-debut fourth at Uttoxeter. He moved well for a long way, but couldn't find a response when the winner attacked approaching the second last. (tchd 5-2)

Educated Evans(IRE) showed much improved form stepped up to 2m6f when a 66-1 winner at Stratford last time, but he was outgunned under a penalty in this stronger race. (op 11-1 tchd 9-1)

Grey Wulff(IRE) showed promise when a 33-1 fourth in a novice hurdle at Exeter on his reappearance and there was another encouraging effort in this decent race by the half-brother to bumper/2m6f-3m3f hurdle winner Rosarian. (op 11-1 tchd 8-1)

Another Kate(IRE) ran respectably under a positive ride before fading on her second hurdles run. She is a half-sister to useful bumper/2m4f-3m hurdle winner Silver Kate and should do better in time. (tchd 5-1)

Cap Elorn(FR) faded into fourth when favourite for a Worcester bumper on debut last month and was never really in contention before weakening on this hurdling debut. (op 13-2)

2608 DIGIBET.COM H'CAP CHASE (18 fncs) 3m

3:25 (3:26) (Class 5) (0-90,90) 4-Y-0+ **£2,276** (£668; £334; £166)

Form RPR

5/P- **1** **Shannons Boy (IRE)**[274] 4220 8-11-4 **82** (t) CharliePoste 99+
(Richard Lee) *led after 1st to 4th: styd pressing ldr: led 6th tl approachng 8th: led again 9th: styng on to go clr whn blnd bdly 3 out: rcvrd next: drvn out run-in* **9/2**[1]

0-33 **2** *2½* **Dromore Hill (IRE)**[15] 2290 6-11-6 **84** (v[1]) JimmyMcCarthy 93
(Charlie Morlock) *chal 3dr tl led 4th: hdd 6th: led appr 8th: hdd 9th: styd chsng wnr but no imp whn blnd 3 out: rallied and hit last: styd on same pce* **9/2**[1]

004/ **3** *16* **Billy Murphy**[579] 5186 7-11-9 **87** MarkBradburne 79
(Paul Cowley) *in rr: sme hdwy 8th: nvr rchd ldrs and no ch fr 13th: styd on fr 2 out to take wl hld 3rd run-in* **25/1**

42P3 **4** *1½* **Whatcanisay**[15] 2287 11-10-7 **71** (t) HaddenFrost 62
(James Frost) *in rr: hdwy fr 10th: wnt mod 3rd 14th: nvr any ch: no ex and lost 3rd run-in* **6/1**[2]

0-6P **5** *43* **Wasntme (IRE)**[157] 795 7-10-11 **75** (t) JoeTizzard 23
(Colin Tizzard) *in tch: j. slowly 8th: sn bhd: t.o* **6/1**[2]

0PP4 **6** *2¾* **The Walnut Tree (IRE)**[3] 2559 9-9-11 **64** oh9 JohnKington[(3)] 9
(Simon Lewis) *sn in rr: blnd 6th: wl bhd whn blnd 12th: t.o* **16/1**

0005 **P** **Wujood**[23] 2132 8-10-3 **65** ow2 LiamHeard —
(Laura Young) *t.o 8th: p.u bef 12th* **9/1**[3]

P4U6 **P** **Little Girl**[42] 1820 12-10-1 **64** oh6 ow1 (p) ColinBolger —
(Ray Peacock) *chsd ldrs early: t.o 8th: p.u bef 12th* **50/1**

FP-P **P** **Raki Rose**[17] 2240 8-11-4 **82** (p) TomScudamore —
(Michael Scudamore) *chsd ldrs: hit 7th: wknd fr 12th: t.o whn p.u bef 3 out* **9/1**[3]

1-P0 **P** **Brushford (IRE)**[15] 2292 6-11-0 **85** MrTJCannon[(7)] —
(Chris Gordon) *chsd ldrs: hit 1st and 9th: rdn 10th: sn wknd: t.o whn p.u bef 4 out* **14/1**

50F4 **P** **No More Whispers (IRE)**[13] 2327 5-11-5 **90** AdamWedge[(7)] —
(Evan Williams) *in rr: blnd 8th: t.o whn p.u bef 4 out* **18/1**

000 **P** **Seaview Lad (IRE)**[27] 2051 7-10-1 **64** ow1 AndrewGlassonbury —
(Bob Buckler) *led and blnd 1st: sn hdd: hit 7th: wknd 12th: t.o whn p.u bef 4 out* **16/1**

6m 25.06s (3.06) **Going Correction** -0.05s/f (Good) **12** Ran SP% **114.4**
Speed ratings (Par 103): **92,91,85,85,71 70,—,—,—,— —,—**
toteswingers:1&2:£4.80, 1&3:£26.20, 2&3:£15.90 CSF £24.86 CT £450.57 TOTE £5.00: £1.50, £1.20, £4.70; EX 24.80.
Owner Walters Plant Hire Ltd **Bred** Arthur England **Trained** Byton, H'fords

FOCUS
A weak handicap chase. The first two filled those positions throughout and there was a long gap back to the third. The form is rated through the second.

NOTEBOOK
Shannons Boy(IRE) put in a determined front-running effort with a tongue tie applied to justify support in decent style on return for a new trainer after 274 days off. There was a scare when he ploughed through the third last but he regained his composure and comfortably held the runner-up. He could go on from this second course win on testing ground but he has had just two runs since April 2008, and there is a question about how well he will stand up to racing. (tchd 4-1)

Dromore Hill(IRE) had less to prove than most of these after a couple of recent third-placed efforts, and ran another solid race with a first-time visor replacing cheekpieces. He can hit a flat spot in races but is on a decent mark and stays very well. (op 5-1)

Billy Murphy put in an eye-catching return from 579 days off but he is an inconsistent maiden who showed some temperament when running out on his penultimate start last spring and a step forward is not guaranteed next time.

Whatcanisay was never in a threatening position stepped back up to 3m. This veteran is very well treated on old form but it has been 22-runs and almost three years since his sole win in a novice handicap hurdle.

Wasntme(IRE) was prominent in the market but struggled back from five months off. (op 11-2)
Seaview Lad(IRE) was reported to have finished distressed after being pulled up. Official explanation: trainer said gelding finished distressed

2609 LINDLEY CATERING H'CAP HURDLE (11 hdls) 2m 4f
3:55 (3:58) (Class 5) (0-95,94) 4-Y-0+ **£1,951** (£573; £286; £143)

Form				RPR
PP-5	1		**Najca De Thaix (FR)**[16] 2280 9-11-10 **92** JamieMoore (John Spearing) *mde all: hit 3rd: c readily clr after 4 out: unchal* **8/1**	111+
62-0	2	16	**Tiger Line**[21] 2149 6-11-7 **89** WarrenMarston (Richard Phillips) *chsd ldrs: hit 3rd: styd on to take wl hld 2nd fr 2 out* **11/4**[1]	92
65-6	3	3 ¾	**The Composer**[58] 132 8-10-5 **73** JimmyMcCarthy (Michael Blanshard) *chsd ldrs: rdn appr 4 out: tk wl hld 2nd 3 out: dropped to 3rd next and one pce* **13/2**[3]	73
0-00	4	5	**Lupita (IRE)**[17] 2239 6-9-11 **68** oh1 (t) JimmyDerham(3) (Derrick Scott) *chsd wnr to 4 out but nvr any ch: wknd fr next* **13/2**[3]	62
0534	5	21	**Can't Remember**[17] 2244 5-10-12 **87** OliverDayman(7) (Alison Thorpe) *in rr: rdn and sme hdwy appr 4 out: sn wknd* **6/1**[2]	60
POU4	6	25	**Stafford Charlie**[3] 2556 4-11-1 **90** CharlieWallis(7) (John O'Shea) *in tch: hdwy 7th: wknd appr 4 out* **6/1**[2]	38
0P-4	7	5	**Born To Be Wilde (IRE)**[31] 2003 5-11-2 **94** AshleyBird(10) (Evan Williams) *chsd ldrs: hit 7th: wknd qckly 4 out* **16/1**	37
4-00	8	37	**Miss Molly Moses**[85] 1445 6-10-12 **80** LiamHeard (Laura Young) *chsd ldrs tl mstke 6th and sn wknd* **40/1**	—
P36/	P		**Queen Musa**[948] 5102 8-10-1 **72** EamonDehdashti(3) (Dr Jeremy Naylor) *in rr and hit 5th: brief effrt 7th: sn wknd: t.o whn p.u bef 3 out* **66/1**	—
5065	P		**Art Value**[13] 2331 5-10-3 **78** MattGriffiths(7) (Carroll Gray) *in rr: rdn and lost tch 7th: t.o whn p.u bef 2 out* **9/1**	—

5m 4.85s (3.05) **Going Correction** +0.20s/f (Yiel)
WFA 4 from 5yo+ 8lb **10** Ran SP% **112.8**
Speed ratings (Par 103): **101,94,93,91,82 72,70,55,—,—**
toteswingers:1&2:£6.60, 1&3:£9.30, 2&3:£3.50. totesuper7: Win: Not won. Place: £114.10. CSF £29.98 CT £151.72 TOTE £11.00: £3.10, £1.10, £2.40; EX 30.50.
Owner Peter Kelsall **Bred** Michel Bourgneuf And Danielle Paulhac **Trained** Kinnersley, Worcs

FOCUS
A weak handicap hurdle. Most of the runners had been well beaten on their latest start and more than half the field were still maidens. Arguably a hurdles best from the winner.

NOTEBOOK
Najca De Thaix(FR) has looked reluctant on occasions and arrived here on a two-year losing run, but he was supported in the morning and stormed back to form under a trailblazing ride. He will face a big rise in his mark after this runaway win, but could remain fairly treated on a couple of chase wins off marks in the 100s in 2008. (op 13-2)
Tiger Line was behind for most of the way on her seasonal reappearance, but the money arrived for her this time and she put in a much more energetic display on just her second handicap run. She is a half-sister to 2m3f-3m hurdle/chase winner Smart Man and is open to progress. (op 7-2)
The Composer finished in the frame in a number of staying Flat handicaps in the summer and it was a similar result back over hurdles, but he was ultimately well held and is now 0-18 over jumps. (op 11-2 tchd 7-1)
Lupita(IRE), well held on her last four outings, looked a big danger turning in but didn't find much and could only plug on. (op 8-1 tchd 6-1)
Can't Remember was outpaced at a crucial stage and couldn't get back into it. It is possible that the ground was softer than ideal, but she has found life tough since a hefty rise after being awarded a race at Perth in July. (op 7-1)
Stafford Charlie returned to form with a close fourth in a 2m seller at Towcester on Sunday, but was very laboured turned out quickly back in handicap company. (op 5-1 tchd 13-2)
T/Jkpt: Not won. T/Plt: £94.20 to a £1 stake. Pool:£85,585.58 - 662.83 winning tickets T/Qpdt: £10.70 to a £1 stake. Pool:£7,758.72 - 532.12 winning tickets ST

2369 WETHERBY (L-H)
Wednesday, November 24

OFFICIAL GOING: Soft (good to soft in places; 6.6)
Wind: Fresh, half-behind Weather: dry but cold and breezy

2610 HOLD YOUR CHRISTMAS PARTY HERE CONDITIONAL JOCKEYS' CLAIMING HURDLE (12 hdls) 2m 6f
12:20 (12:21) (Class 5) 4-Y-0+ **£1,712** (£499; £249)

Form				RPR
0311	1		**National Trust**[16] 2279 8-11-1 127 KyleJames(3) (Edward Creighton) *trckd ldr: upsides 7th: drvn next: led 3 out: drew clr appr 2 out* **30/100**[1]	116+
4U-3	2	14	**Corlande (IRE)**[11] 2366 10-11-0 0 (p) HenryBrooke(8) (Donald McCain) *led: hdd 3 out: sn rdn: one pce* **13/2**[2]	106
034/	3	19	**Sundae Best (IRE)**[603] 4808 6-11-5 0 JamesO'Farrell(3) (Howard Johnson) *trckd ldrs: hit 4th: drvn and outpcd 8th: lost tch and eased 3 out* **14/1**	87
055-	P		**Calfraz**[219] 4863 8-10-8 98 (p) FearghalDavis (Micky Hammond) *trckd ldrs: p.u bef 3rd: fatally injured* **17/2**[3]	—

5m 36.2s (9.40) **Going Correction** +0.425s/f (Soft) **4** Ran SP% **107.4**
Speed ratings (Par 103): **99,93,87,—**
CSF £2.76 TOTE £1.50; EX 2.20.
Owner Paul Dewey **Bred** Cheveley Park Stud Ltd **Trained** Wormshill, Kent

FOCUS
After a dry night the ground was described as soft, good to soft in places. The winner is rated to his recent best and is operating below his current mark at present.

NOTEBOOK
National Trust, for whom this looked an ideal opportunity, landed his third success in similar company but it wasn't that straightforward as the runner-up made a race out of it. Having his first start for connections since being claimed after his last win at Southwell, he should remain dangerous in this sort of grade but would appear flattered by his handicap mark of 127. (op 1-3)
Corlande(IRE), having his first start over hurdles in over four years, ran a solid race. Proven in very testing ground over fences, he is rising 11 years of age, but on the evidence of this his in-form yard can squeeze another win out of him. (op 6-1 tchd 7-1)
Sundae Best(IRE), coming back from a lay-off, comes from an in-form yard but showed very little here and can only be watched after this tame effort. (op 16-1)

Calfraz, another coming back from a break, was quickly pulled up as though something was amiss and subsequently had to be put down. (op 10-1 tchd 12-1)

2611 BOOK RACEDAY HOSPITALITY ON 01937 582035 H'CAP CHASE (18 fncs) 2m 6f 110y
12:50 (12:50) (Class 4) (0-115,114) 4-Y-0+ **£2,927** (£859; £429; £214)

Form				RPR
1-61	1		**Le Platino (GER)**[28] 2036 8-11-9 **111** (p) BrianHughes (John Wade) *led to 2nd: w ldrs: j.rt 12th: wnt 2nd after 14th: led after 3 out: rdn clr appr last* **2/1**[1]	125+
4-13	2	7	**Rey Nacarado (IRE)**[32] 1959 5-11-3 **105** AndrewTinkler (Charlie Longsdon) *w ldrs: led 11th: hdd after 3 out: kpt on same pce* **3/1**[2]	111
31-6	3	8	**Nulato (IRE)**[197] 267 7-11-12 **114** WayneHutchinson (Alan King) *hld up in tch: wnt prom 9th: bmpd 12th: drvn 4 out: one pce fr next* **9/2**[3]	112
246-	4	5	**Supreme Keano (IRE)**[235] 4980 8-11-8 **113** (p) RichieMcLernon(3) (Jonjo O'Neill) *mstke 1st: j. bdly rt 2nd: nt fluent in rr: hdwy and prom 10th: wknd 2 out: blnd last* **10/1**	110+
1-1U	5	2 ½	**La Pantera Rosa (IRE)**[26] 2079 7-11-0 **102** (p) BarryKeniry (Micky Hammond) *led 2nd: hdd 11th: wknd 4 out* **9/2**[3]	93
PP0-	P		**Borero (FR)**[243] 4869 7-11-12 **114** BrianHarding (Michael Easterby) *in rr: bhd and reminders 9th: t.o whn p.u bef 4 out* **18/1**	—

5m 43.9s (6.90) **Going Correction** +0.275s/f (Yiel) **6** Ran SP% **109.1**
Speed ratings (Par 105): **99,96,93,92,91** —
Tote Swingers:1&2:£3.00, 2&3:£2.70, 1&3:£3.20 CSF £8.18 TOTE £4.20: £2.20, £1.20; EX 7.00.
Owner John Wade **Bred** Carlton Consultants Ltd **Trained** Mordon, Co Durham

FOCUS
Probably no more than an ordinary 0-115 handicap chase. The winner is on the upgrade and the next two are rated in line with their hurdles form.

NOTEBOOK
Le Platino(GER), a winner over C&D last April (when trained by Brian Storey), was racing off a 9lb higher mark for his win at Haydock last month. This was only his sixth start over fences and his in-form trainer thinks he will improve again for better ground. (tchd 9-4)
Rey Nacarado(IRE), a half-brother to Florida Pearl, ran a sound race on his chasing debut. Never far away, he jumped soundly and his in-form trainer can place him to go one better at some point soon.
Nulato(IRE) was also making his chasing debut on his first run since last May. He also jumped well throughout and should come on for the outing. (op 11-2)
Supreme Keano(IRE) ruined his chance by jumping to the right throughout the race. (op 9-1)
La Pantera Rosa(IRE), they early pacesetter, weakened quickly approaching four from home. (op 5-1)
Borero(FR), having his first start for current connections, was running here without the cheekpieces and tongue-tie he wore when last successful. His jumping was far from fluent and he can only be watched until showing more. (op 14-1)

2612 FOLLOW WETHERBY RACECOURSE ON FACEBOOK "NATIONAL HUNT" NOVICES' HURDLE (9 hdls) 2m 110y
1:20 (1:22) (Class 4) 4-Y-0+ **£2,397** (£698; £349)

Form				RPR
4-2	1		**Palace Jester**[20] 2166 5-10-12 0 APMcCoy (Jonjo O'Neill) *trckd ldrs: led 3 out: drvn out* **11/4**[2]	111+
10-0	2	2 ¾	**Rupert Lamb**[25] 2092 4-10-12 0 BrianHughes (Howard Johnson) *trckd ldrs: styd on same pce fr 2 out* **8/1**[3]	109
3-23	3	1	**Sweet Irony (FR)**[18] 2216 4-10-12 0 WayneHutchinson (Alan King) *hld up in midfield: hdwy 6th: chsd ldrs next: kpt on same pce fr 2 out: nt fluent last* **8/11**[1]	110+
12-	4	1 ½	**Bold Sir Brian (IRE)**[247] 4785 4-10-12 0 PeterBuchanan (Lucinda Russell) *prom: chsd ldrs 3 out: kpt on one pce* **16/1**	106
5U-0	5	18	**Fairynuff**[12] 2349 6-10-12 0 RichieMcGrath (Kate Walton) *mid-div: hdwy to trck ldrs 4th: led briefly appr 3 out: sn wknd: j.rt 2 out* **16/1**	88
/40-	6	7	**Jack The Gent (IRE)**[348] 2814 6-10-12 0 BarryKeniry (George Moore) *led 2nd: hdd appr 3 out: hit 3 out: wknd next* **50/1**	84+
00	7	2 ½	**Barnack**[152] 841 4-10-12 0 DavidEngland (Pam Sly) *in rr div: sme hdwy 6th: wknd appr next* **80/1**	79
00-	8	9	**Aitch Factor**[219] 5277 4-10-9 0 FearghalDavis(3) (Henry Hogarth) *hld up in rr: sme hdwy 6th: lost pl appr next* **100/1**	70
0	9	¾	**Artic Night (FR)**[15] 2296 4-10-12 0 DougieCostello (Nicky Richards) *in rr div: sme hdwy 6th: lost pl appr next* **100/1**	69
0-4P	10	9	**Eagle Owl (IRE)**[15] 2296 4-10-12 0 (t) BrianHarding (Tim Easterby) *w ldrs: lost pl 3 out* **22/1**	60
0	11	27	**Some Catch (IRE)**[7] 2446 4-10-2 0 HarryHaynes(3) (Elliott Cooper) *in rr: hdwy on wd outside 4th: wknd 6th: sn bhd: t.o* **250/1**	26
0/0F	P		**Errington**[26] 2075 5-10-12 0 WilsonRenwick (Howard Johnson) *in rr: bhd whn j. bdly rt 5th: t.o whn p.u bef 3 out* **80/1**	—
100-	P		**Sheepclose (IRE)**[232] 5078 5-10-5 0 JakeGreenall(7) (Michael Easterby) *mid-div: sddle slipped after 3rd: p.u bef next* **66/1**	—
040-	P		**Nothing Ventured**[315] 3418 5-10-12 0 PaddyAspell (John Norton) *nt jump wl: sn bhd: j. bdly rt 2nd: t.o 5th: p.u bef 3 out* **150/1**	—
45-0	P		**Hidden In Time**[15] 2296 5-10-12 0 JamesReveley (Keith Reveley) *prom: lost pl 6th: t.o whn p.u bef next* **100/1**	—
0P	P		**Fred Grass**[12] 2349 4-10-9 0 JamesO'Farrell(3) (Jonathan Haynes) *led to 2nd: trckd ldrs: wknd 6th: t.o whn p.u bef next* **250/1**	—
0	P		**Congella**[20] 2167 5-10-5 0 RobertWalford (Tim Walford) *in rr: bhd fr 5th: t.o whn p.u bef 3 out* **100/1**	—
0	P		**Don't Call Harry**[10] 2403 5-10-9 0 AdrianLane(3) (Tim Walford) *in rr: bhd fr 6th: t.o whn p.u bef next* **80/1**	—

4m 0.80s (5.00) **Going Correction** +0.425s/f (Soft) **18** Ran SP% **124.4**
Speed ratings (Par 105): **105,103,103,102,94 90,89,85,85,80 68,—,—,—,— —,—,—**
Tote Swingers:1&2:£2.80, 2&3:£2.90, 1&3:£1.10 CSF £25.21 TOTE £4.40: £1.50, £2.20, £1.40; EX 30.30.
Owner Trevor Hemmings **Bred** Sandicroft Stud **Trained** Cheltenham, Gloucs

FOCUS
Just an ordinary gallop for this novices' hurdle in which the first four pulled well clear. The form should prove reliable and it should throw up plenty of future winners. Palace Jester can rate higher.

NOTEBOOK
Palace Jester ◆ was a very creditable second at Haydock on his hurdling debut over 2m4f earlier this month, and went one better here in decent style. Travelling well throughout, he can carry a penalty in similar company before taking a step up in grade. (op 3-1 tchd 10-3 and 7-2 in a place)
Rupert Lamb ◆ jumped better here than he did when well held over C&D last time out. A reproduction of this effort will see him go one better next time out for his in-form trainer. (op 15-2 tchd 9-1)

Sweet Irony(FR), the well-backed favourite, was held up early in the race before throwing down a challenge. This was the easiest ground he has encountered so far in his career and there are races to be won with him in due course. (op Evens tchd 5-4 in a place)

Bold Sir Brian(IRE), winner of a bumper on his debut, stayed on strongly from the final hurdle to prove he has got a bright future in this sphere. He will get further when required. (op 12-1)

Fairynuff, also a bumper winner, could have done with a stronger gallop earlier in the race. He will also stay further and there are races to be won with him. (op 14-1)

Jack The Gent(IRE), coming back from a long break, might find life easier in handicap company next time out. (op 66-1)

Eagle Owl(IRE), wearing a tongue-strap for the first time, stopped quickly. (op 20-1)

Sheepclose(IRE) Official explanation: jockey said saddle slipped

2613 BUY TICKETS FOR BOXING DAY @ WETHERBYRACING.CO.UK H'CAP CHASE (13 fncs) 2m

1:50 (1:51) (Class 3) (0-125,125) 4-Y-0+ **£5,204** (£1,528; £764; £381)

Form				RPR
33-3	1		**Riguez Dancer**[10] 2400 6-11-12 **125** GrahamLee (Ferdy Murphy) *hld up in rr: hdwy 9th: wnt cl 2nd last: styd on u.p to ld last 75yds* **4/1**[2]	131+
4104	2	1	**Viable**[24] 2112 8-11-0 **120** MissGAndrews(7) (Pam Sly) *trckd ldrs: upsides afterr 9th: styd on same pce run-in: tk 2nd nr fin* **25/1**	125
11-4	3	hd	**Diamond Frontier (IRE)**[16] 2272 7-11-11 **124** BrianHughes (Howard Johnson) *nt fluent: trckd ldrs: led after 9th: hdd and no ex clsng stages* **7/4**[1]	129
-144	4	3/4	**Elite Land**[29] 1229 7-11-5 **118** DougieCostello (Brian Ellison) *hld up in tch: hdwy to trck ldrs 9th: hit 2 out: kpt on same pce run-in: styd on towards fin* **5/1**[3]	123+
P-6U	5	9	**Pamak D'Airy (FR)**[12] 2352 7-10-8 **110** FearghalDavis(3) (Henry Hogarth) *trckd ldrs: wknd 4 out* **11/2**	106
2534	6	8	**Prince Des Marais (FR)**[15] 2293 7-11-9 **122** AndrewThornton (Caroline Bailey) *trckd ldrs: drvn and hung lft 4 out: sn wknd* **20/1**	109
P-13	7	25	**Carrietau**[47] 1761 7-11-4 **122** (bt) AlexanderVoy(5) (Barry Murtagh) *led: clr 4th: drvn 8th: hdd after next: lost pl appr 2 out: t.o whn eased run-in* **8/1**	84

3m 57.1s (1.30) **Going Correction** +0.275s/f (Yiel) **7** Ran SP% **108.1**
Speed ratings (Par 107): **107,106,106,106,101 97,85**
Tote Swingers:1&2:£14.50, 2&3:£0.00, 1&3:£3.60 CSF £64.71 TOTE £3.80: £1.50, £7.50; EX 63.90.

Owner The DPRP Second Dance Partnership **Bred** Plantation Stud **Trained** West Witton, N Yorks

FOCUS

A good gallop was always on the cards with Carrietau in the line-up for this 0-125 handicap chase. Sound form with a small chase best from the winner.

NOTEBOOK

Riguez Dancer, held up early in the race, was produced with a perfectly timed run to get up close home. Although the handicapper will have his say after this polished display, the 6-y-o is ultra consistent and should continue to pay his way. (tchd 9-2)

Viable ran bang up to form here, but holds no secrets from the handicapper after 27 career starts. All his wins have come on right-handed tracks, but he can win going left-handed on this evidence. (op 22-1 tchd 20-1)

Diamond Frontier(IRE), for whom dropping back to 2m seemed to be a positive, got outsprinted from the final fence. This was only his sixth start over fences and there could be more to come from him. (op 15-8 tchd 6-4)

Elite Land, coming from an in-form yard, also ran bang up to form but remains 7lb higher than he has ever won off. (op 11-2 tchd 6-1)

2614 SUBSCRIBE TO RACING UK JUVENILE MAIDEN HURDLE (9 hdls) 2m 110y

2:25 (2:25) (Class 5) 3-Y-0 **£1,712** (£499; £249)

Form				RPR
	1		**Local Hero (GER)**[22] 3-10-12 0 APMcCoy (Steve Gollings) *trckd ldrs: led on bit 3 out: nt fluent last: easily* **4/6**[1]	121+
5	2	6	**Dhaafer**[14] 2306 3-10-12 0 WayneHutchinson (Alan King) *trckd ldrs: upsides 3 out: 5 l down and wl hld whn mstke last* **5/1**[2]	108
0	3	20	**Tatispout (FR)**[11] 2356 3-10-5 0 AndrewTinkler (Charlie Longsdon) *led to 3 out: wknd fr next* **5/1**[2]	81
46	4	nk	**Plus Ultra (IRE)**[28] 2033 3-10-5 0 KyleJames(7) (Philip Kirby) *chsd ldrs: nt fluent 5th: one pce whn j.lft last 2* **33/1**	88
5	5	26	**Ibn Hiyyan (USA)**[31] 1984 3-10-12 0 GrahamLee (Ferdy Murphy) *hld up: in rr whn nt fluent 5th: sn bhd* **9/1**[3]	66+
	6	13	**Verluga (IRE)**[68] 3-10-12 0 RichieMcGrath (Tim Easterby) *in rr: nt fluent 3rd: bhd fr 6th* **66/1**	47
6	7	nse	**Beneath**[14] 2306 3-10-7 0 BrianToomey(5) (Kevin Ryan) *chsd ldrs: reminders 5th: wkng whn mstke next: sn bhd* **40/1**	47
	P		**Wolf Rock**[68] 3-10-12 0 BrianHughes (David Barron) *hld up towards rr: lost pl after 5th: bhd whn p.u bef last* **28/1**	—
0	P		**Penshurst Lad (IRE)**[21] 2151 3-10-12 0 SeanQuinlan (Richard Phillips) *t.k.h: trckd ldrs: wknd appr 6th: sn bhd: t.o whn p.u bef last* **150/1**	—

4m 1.30s (5.50) **Going Correction** +0.425s/f (Soft) **9** Ran SP% **114.3**
Speed ratings (Par 102): **104,101,91,91,79 73,73,—,—**
Tote Swingers:1&2:£1.10, 2&3:£2.70, 1&3:£1.10 CSF £4.26 TOTE £1.80: £1.10, £1.70, £2.10; EX 4.60.

Owner P J Martin **Bred** Gestut Evershorst **Trained** Scamblesby, Lincs

FOCUS

An ordinary gallop for this juvenile hurdle and it produced a very taking winner who was value for further and looks a decent recruit.

NOTEBOOK

Local Hero(GER) ◆ proved a class apart. Rated 84 on the Flat, he has the size and scope to go far in this sphere. He jumped well throughout and it will be interesting to see where connections decide to sent him next time out. (op 8-11 tchd 4-5 in places)

Dhaafer, rated 74 on the Flat, had the benefit of a run at Bangor two weeks previously. He certainly came on from that experience and can go one better at some point. He was unlucky to run into such a talented winner. (op 11-2 tchd 9-2)

Tatispout(FR), the winner of a 'bumper' in France, was having her third start over hurdles. She stopped quickly two from home and might prefer better ground. (op 6-1 tchd 7-1)

Plus Ultra(IRE), also having his third start over hurdles, showed a little and might find life easier in modest handicaps in due course. (op 28-1)

Ibn Hiyyan(USA) was never dangerous and can only be watched at present. Official explanation: jockey said, regarding running and riding, that his orders were to drop the gelding in and ride to obtain the best possible placing, but it had stopped on its first run at Aintree and appeared to the same here, he niggled along approaching final hurdle in the back straight and gave it several backhanders with no response, feeling he could not obtain a better position in the home straight, at which point he held it together to get home. (op 15-2)

2615 BRAMHAM HALL FOR CONFERENCES & BANQUETING BEGINNERS' CHASE (18 fncs) 3m 1f

3:00 (3:00) (Class 4) 4-Y-0+ **£2,927** (£859; £429; £214)

Form				RPR
-132	1		**Aberdale (IRE)**[24] 2110 6-11-2 128 APMcCoy (Jonjo O'Neill) *mde all: j. soundly: qcknd 10th: shkn up 4 out: styd on wl: pushed out* **8/15**[1]	132+
62-3	2	3 3/4	**Silent Cliche (IRE)**[18] 2205 6-11-2 0 BrianHughes (Howard Johnson) *chsd wnr: shkn up 10th: kpt on same pce fr 3 out: no imp* **15/8**[2]	127+
0U-P	3	55	**Columbus Secret (IRE)**[19] 2191 5-11-2 0 JamesReveley (Keith Reveley) *a 3rd: outpcd 10th: sn lost tch: t.o 4 out* **40/1**	72
4P	4	28	**Ramborob (IRE)**[24] 2110 5-11-2 0 PeterBuchanan (Mike Sowersby) *j. slowly in last: outpcd 10th: sn lost tch: t.o 4 out sn wknd* **33/1**[3]	44

6m 26.7s (17.30) **Going Correction** +0.275s/f (Yiel) **4** Ran SP% **105.4**
Speed ratings (Par 105): **83,81,64,55**
CSF £1.83 TOTE £1.60; EX 1.70.

Owner Trevor Hemmings **Bred** Simon Lambert **Trained** Cheltenham, Gloucs

FOCUS

Only two of the four runners had any sort of chance in this beginners' chase and they came home in betting order. It was run at a steady pace and the first two are decent novices who can continue on an upward curve.

NOTEBOOK

Aberdale(IRE) had finished second to a very smart sort last time out at Huntingdon. He made all the running and, wherever he ends up, his sound jumping will always stand him in good stead. A dual winner over hurdles, he looks better over fences and can win again. (op 4-9)

Silent Cliche(IRE), winner of an Irish point-to-point, tended to jump to the right at some of his fences on this chasing debut. He has only had five career starts and should have little trouble going one better shortly. (op 9-4 tchd 7-4, 11-4 and 5-2 in a place)

Columbus Secret(IRE) showed very little and modest handicaps will be the way forward if he is going to trouble the judge. (op 33-1)

2616 E.B.F./DBS MARES' STANDARD OPEN NATIONAL HUNT FLAT RACE (QUALIFIER) 2m 110y

3:35 (3:36) (Class 5) 4-6-Y-0 **£1,712** (£499; £249)

Form				RPR
	1		**Zhakiera Spirit** 4-10-12 0 BrianHughes (Howard Johnson) *sn trcking ldr: led over 2f out: pushed out* **9/4**[2]	105+
3-2	2	1 1/2	**Aneyeforaneye (IRE)**[20] 2167 4-10-12 0 GrahamLee (Malcolm Jefferson) *led: hung rt bnd after 4f: hdd over 2f out: kpt on: no real imp* **7/4**[1]	101
3-0	3	14	**Allbarkanobite**[12] 2355 5-10-12 0 RichieMcGrath (Kate Walton) *hld up in mid-div: hdwy over 4f out: styd on to take modest 3rd over 1f out* **16/1**	87
2	4	1	**Thornton Alice**[174] 609 5-10-12 0 SeanQuinlan (Richard Phillips) *chsd ldrs: wnt modest 3rd 6f out: one pce fnl 3f* **12/1**	86
	5	shd	**Lua De Itapoan** 5-10-12 0 DougieCostello (Malcolm Jefferson) *in rr: outpcd 5f out: styd on fnl 2f: gng on at fin* **12/1**	86
0-6	6	1 1/4	**Lady Ida**[20] 2167 5-10-12 0 AlanO'Keeffe (Jennie Candlish) *in rr: drvn 6f out: sn outpcd: kpt on fnl 2f* **18/1**	85
1	7	11	**Sparkling Hand**[34] 1934 4-10-12 0 PaulGallagher(7) (Peter Atkinson) *chsd ldrs: drvn over 4f out: wknd over 2f out* **11/1**	81
	8	31	**Mordetta Road** 5-10-12 0 PaddyAspell (James Turner) *chsd ldrs: drvn 6f out: lost pl 4f out: sn bhd: t.o* **50/1**	43
1-	9	7	**Silvers Spirit**[309] 3535 4-11-5 0 JamesReveley (Keith Reveley) *hld up in rr: drvn 6f out: sn lost pl: bhd fnl 4f: t.o* **9/1**[3]	43
	10	hd	**Matilda's Folly (IRE)** 5-10-2 0 SeveBrumpton(10) (Ben Haslam) *t.k.h in rr: drvn 6f out: sn lost pl and bhd: t.o 3f out* **33/1**	35

3m 56.0s (5.80) **Going Correction** +0.425s/f (Soft) **10** Ran SP% **116.9**
Speed ratings: **103,102,95,95,95 94,89,74,71,71**
Tote Swingers:1&2:£1.10, 2&3:£13.40, 1&3:£7.30 CSF £6.57 TOTE £2.90: £1.20, £1.80, £3.80; EX 7.70.

Owner Andrea & Graham Wylie **Bred** Pleasure Palace Racing **Trained** Billy Row, Co Durham

FOCUS

An interesting mares' bumper run at a sound pace and the first two home look above average. The winner should rate higher.

NOTEBOOK

Zhakiera Spirit ◆ has a very useful pedigree (sister to Megastar) and showed she clearly has ability, travelling well throughout and picking up nicely when asked. She has the size and scope to jump hurdles in time and has a bright future. (op 3-1)

Aneyeforaneye(IRE) is the benchmark to the form after showing ability on all three starts to date. She did little wrong here and time might prove she ran into a smart winner. She can make her mark over hurdles this season. (op 9-4 tchd 5-2)

Allbarkanobite plugged on and might be worth a try over further when sent over hurdles. (op 14-1)

Thornton Alice, having her first start for connections, was well held and might also need a switch to hurdles to make her mark. (tchd 10-1)

Sparkling Hand, a shock winner at Carlisle on her debut, was well held here under her penalty. (op 12-1 tchd 10-1)

Silvers Spirit, a winner on her debut at Southwell in January, ran well below par having been very edgy at the start. Official explanation: trainer had no explanation for the poor form shown (op 11-2 tchd 5-1)

T/Plt: £13.40 to a £1 stake. Pool:£42,821.48. 2,332.77 winning tickets T/Qpdt: £7.60 to a £1 stake. Pool:£2,726.83. 263.05 winning tickets WG

2617 - 2625a (Foreign Racing) - See Raceform Interactive

NEWBURY (L-H)

Thursday, November 25

OFFICIAL GOING: Good to soft (soft in places on hurdle course)

Both courses set wide increasing distances by about 40m per circuit.

Wind: Moderate across Weather: Bright intervals

2626 SPORTINGBET.COM SPONSORS CONDITIONAL JOCKEYS' CHAMPIONSHIP H'CAP HURDLE (8 hdls) 2m 110y

12:30 (12:30) (Class 3) (0-130,127)
4-Y-O+

£5,009 (£1,480; £740; £370; £184; £92)

Form				RPR
061-	**1**		**Via Galilei (IRE)**[31] 5285 5-10-1 **108** .... JoshuaMoore(6) (Gary Moore) *lw: hld up in rr: stdy hdwy 4 out: trckd ldr 3 out: slt ld sn after: jnd: mstke last: styd on strly to assert fnl 100yds* **16/1**	118+
2-24	**2**	1 1/4	**Monetary Fund (USA)**[158] 792 4-10-11 **120** .... JeremiahMcGrath(8) (Nicky Henderson) *chsd ldrs: rdn and one pce 2 out: styd on wl run-in: rallied to take 2nd last strides: nt rch wnr* **14/1**[3]	128+
10-5	**3**	1	**Super Kenny (IRE)**[193] 360 4-10-9 **113** .... DavidBass(3) (Nicky Henderson) *lw: hld up in rr: hit 4 out: stdy hdwy sn after to trck ldrs 3 out: str chal 2 out and upsides whn blnd last: kpt on to press wnr tl no ex fnl 50yds: lost 2nd last strides* **7/2**[2]	121+
F-31	**4**	9	**Pennellis (FR)**[14] 2333 6-11-9 **124** .... SamTwiston-Davies (Paul Nicholls) *chsd ldrs: led after 4 out tl after 3 out: wknd after 2 out* **7/2**[2]	122
0254	**5**	7	**Dean's Grange**[24] 2128 5-10-13 **114** .... MrMMO'Connor (Colin Tizzard) *in tch: hdwy 4 out: chsd ldrs next: wknd 2 out* **14/1**[3]	106
01-0	**6**	16	**Sure Josie Sure (FR)**[11] 2386 5-11-9 **127** .... (t) CO'Farrell(3) (David Pipe) *lw: in rr: rdn appr 4 out: sme prog u.p appr 3 out: nvr nr ldrs and sn no ch* **5/2**[1]	110+
/6-0	**7**	4 1/2	**Laredo Sound (IRE)**[21] 2164 8-11-0 **120** .... PeterHatton(5) (Alex Hales) *a towards rr* **33/1**	93
3S-0	**8**	4 1/2	**Stripe Me Blue**[13] 2347 8-10-11 **115** .... DannyBurton(3) (Peter Jones) *led tl after 1st: lft in ld 3rd: hdd after 4 out: sn wknd* **14/1**[3]	84
6-10	**9**	28	**Crazy Bold (GER)**[22] 2150 7-9-13 **103** .... LeeEdwards(3) (Tony Carroll) *rdn 4 out: a in rr* **50/1**	47
/02-	**10**	3/4	**Top Mark**[69] 835 8-11-7 **125** .... CharlieHuxley(3) (Alan King) *chsd ldrs: hit 4th: wknd appr 3 out* **28/1**	68
1000	**11**	15	**Shalamiyr (FR)**[22] 2150 6-10-4 **108** .... (t) GilesHawkins(3) (Philip Hobbs) *hit 1st: bhd fr 4th* **16/1**	30
14-0	**U**		**Outside The Box**[19] 2213 6-10-7 **118** .... RyanRaftery(10) (Noel Chance) *t.k.h: led after 1st: sn clr: uns rdr 3rd* **20/1**	—

4m 7.63s (-2.27) **Going Correction** -0.075s/f (Good)
WFA 4 from 5yo+ 7lb **12 Ran SP% 117.9**
Speed ratings (Par 107): **102,101,100,96,93 85,83,81,68,68 61,—**
toteswingers:1&2 £12.00, 2&3 £5.20, 1&3 £7.50 CSF £205.04 CT £970.27 TOTE £25.90: £4.10, £2.90, £2.00; EX 189.30 TRIFECTA Not won..
Owner C E Stedman **Bred** J S Bolger **Trained** Lower Beeding, W Sussex
■ Stewards' Enquiry : Joshua Moore one-day ban: used whip with excessive frequency (Dec 9)

FOCUS
A competitive handicap to start the meeting off, as many of the runners could be given a chance of winning. The early pace looked to be sound, and the first three were making their handicap debuts. All three made big steps up.

NOTEBOOK
Via Galilei(IRE), beaten over 80 lengths when last seen at Leicester on the Flat in October, travelled strongly throughout, and was able to go through with his effort despite those early exertions. He undoubtedly looked well handicapped on his best Flat form for another stable in Ireland, so in some ways this performance doesn't come as too much of a surprise.
Monetary Fund(USA) was having his first outing since June but kept on nicely under a tidy ride to get past his stablemate in the final half a furlong.
Super Kenny(IRE) had been off since being beaten at 1/3 at Stratford in May, so this was a lot better. He was in with every chance coming to the last, but he hit that hurdle quite hard and didn't get home as strongly as the two in front of him. (op 9-4 tchd 4-1 in places)
Pennellis(FR), 14lb higher for winning by five lengths at Taunton, was another to move nicely for a long way, but one got the impression that the rise in the weights was enough to stop him. He has the size for chasing and that may now be a wise move for him. (tchd 10-3)
Dean's Grange ran well up to a point but this competition was probably a bit too tough for him. (op 16-1 tchd 18-1)
Sure Josie Sure(FR) was highly tried in the Greatwood Hurdle on her reappearance and ran respectably without looking likely to win. Wearing a tongue tie for the first time, she was ridden with restraint but was being pushed along quite early, and was unable to get into a challenging position. (op 7-2)
Shalamiyr(FR) Official explanation: jockey said gelding never travelled

2627 E B F MARES' "NATIONAL HUNT" NOVICES' HURDLE (10 hdls) 2m 5f

1:00 (1:02) (Class 3) 4-Y-O+ **£6,505** (£1,910; £955; £477)

Form				RPR
3-11	**1**		**Sparky May**[16] 2289 5-11-3 127 .... KeiranBurke(5) (Patrick Rodford) *lw: hld up in rr: stdy hdwy fr 4th: trckd ldrs 4 out: slt ld and travelling wl appr 2 out: drvn and 1 l up whn mstke and lft clr last: stl drvn along tl eased fnl 50yds* **9/2**[3]	137+
33-1	**2**	27	**Alverstone**[33] 1963 7-11-2 0 .... APMcCoy (Lawney Hill) *racd in 3rd tl trckd ldr 6th: chal 4 out: led sn after: hdd next: wknd u.p 2 out: no ch whn hmpd and lft poor 2nd last* **5/6**[1]	115+
05-1	**3**	23	**Animation (IRE)**[16] 2288 6-10-13 0 .... JimmyDerham(3) (Seamus Mullins) *led: jnd 6th: hdd after 4 out: wknd bef next: mstke 2 out: lft poor 3rd last* **10/1**	85
3-24	**4**	12	**Hill Forts Gloria (IRE)**[24] 2130 5-10-10 0 .... NoelFehily (Seamus Mullins) *in tch tl wknd 4 out* **25/1**	68
0/P-	**5**	37	**Fillyofthevalley**[234] 5030 7-10-10 0 .... MarkGrant (Peter Jones) *lw: a in rr: wknd and mstke 4 out: t.o* **200/1**	35
0	**6**	3	**Old Dungarvan Oak (IRE)**[16] 2289 4-10-7 0 .... EamonDehdashti(3) (Gary Moore) *j. modly in rr: blnd 4 out: t.o* **100/1**	32
P2-1	**F**		**Line Freedom (FR)**[21] 2168 5-11-2 0 .... BarryGeraghty (Nicky Henderson) *lw: trckd ldr to 5th: styd rt there and led 3 out: hdd next: sn hrd drvn: 1 l down and one pce whn fell last* **3/1**[2]	124

5m 22.78s (3.78) **Going Correction** -0.075s/f (Good)
WFA 4 from 5yo+ 8lb **7 Ran SP% 112.2**
Speed ratings (Par 107): **89,78,69,65,51 50,—**
toteswingers:1&2 £1.40, 2&3 £2.80, 1&3 £2.50 CSF £8.71 TOTE £4.80: £2.30, £1.30; EX 8.90.
Owner Bill Muddyman **Bred** Ruxley Holdings Ltd **Trained** Ash, Somerset
■ Stewards' Enquiry : Keiran Burke caution: used whip when clearly winning

FOCUS
Three of these had little chance on form and were readily disposed of leaving the back straight, which left four to take control. Not form to be confident about, but seemingly big steps up from the winner and the faller.

NOTEBOOK
Sparky May, defending an unbeaten record over hurdles, was up 4.5f in trip but that made little difference, as she sprinted clear of her rivals once asked to quicken. She had the race in safe keeping when her nearest rival departed, this was a smart performance under a double penalty, and she looks well above average. (tchd 11-2)
Alverstone, a big sort, travelled strongly but had no change of gear when the tempo increased. She was a well-beaten third heading to the last hurdle. (op 11-10)
Animation(IRE) won on her hurdling debut earlier this month over 2m3f, but was readily left behind when losing the lead. (op 8-1 tchd 11-1)
Line Freedom(FR), who has looked a bit fragile in the past when considering the gaps between her races, appeared to be the first beaten of the four that went clear when her jockey started to push her along heading to the home bend. However, she responded well to pressure and came back to look dangerous. She was held when coming down at the final hurdle, but thankfully got up looking relatively unscathed. (op 11-4 tchd 5-2)

2628 ROONEY/HALL NOVICES' CHASE (13 fncs) 2m 1f

1:35 (1:36) (Class 3) 4-Y-O+ **£6,262** (£1,850; £925)

Form				RPR
315-	**1**		**Finian's Rainbow (IRE)**[253] 4671 7-11-0 0 .... BarryGeraghty (Nicky Henderson) *lw: mde all: mstkes 4th and 8th: c clr on bridle fr 3 out: v easily* **2/5**[1]	156+
0152	**2**	12	**Hell's Bay (FR)**[13] 2348 8-11-4 143 .... (t) SamTwiston-Davies(3) (Colin Tizzard) *hit 2nd: racd in 3rd: hit 6th: clsd on ldng duo 9th: wnt 2nd 3 out but nvr any ch w wnr* **7/1**[3]	147
21-	**3**	27	**Sang Bleu (FR)**[287] 3992 4-10-7 0 .... (t) NoelFehily (Paul Nicholls) *lw: trckd wnr: chal 5th: styd 2nd: rdn appr 4 out: lost 2nd 3 out and sn wknd: eased whn no ch run-in* **7/2**[2]	119+

4m 7.92s (-5.08) **Going Correction** -0.075s/f (Good)
WFA 4 from 7yo+ 7lb **3 Ran SP% 106.2**
Speed ratings (Par 107): **108,102,89**
CSF £3.12 TOTE £1.40; EX 3.20.
Owner Michael Buckley **Bred** J O'Keeffe **Trained** Upper Lambourn, Berks

FOCUS
Not many runners but a strong event. Finian's Rainbow looks a serious Arkle contender, with Hell's Bay 5lb off his mark over further.

NOTEBOOK
Finian's Rainbow(IRE) was the chosen runner for a stable that held a few entries for this contest at the five-day stage. He didn't have a lot of experience behind him but had shown plenty of ability when on the racecourse. Absent since finishing fifth in the Grade 1 Neptune Novices' Hurdle in March, his jockey took him straight into the lead and got on with the job in hand. Novicey at some of his fences, as could be expected, he travelled strongly throughout and came home a ready winner, which saw him attract plenty of interest in the ante-post market for Cheltenham next March. (tchd 1-2 in places)
Hell's Bay(FR), wearing a tongue-tie again, had plenty of chasing experience behind him and a couple of decent efforts mixed in, notably when runner-up to Time For Rupert at Cheltenham last time. Held up in rear, he made a few mistakes early but did come back into it to hold some sort of chance before being left behind. He probably didn't run up to his last performance but still sets a decent standard. (tchd 13-2)
Sang Bleu(FR), running in a first-time tongue tie, only had two starts for this stable last season, the first of which was in the Grade 1 Finale Hurdle where he finished second. Getting a handy weight allowance, this was his first outing since landing a weak contest at Huntingdon in February, and he struggled after mixing it with the winner for much of the contest. There will be other days for him but he does have something to prove now. (tchd 3-1 in places)

2629 SPORTINGBET.COM H'CAP CHASE (17 fncs) 2m 6f 110y

2:10 (2:10) (Class 3) (0-135,129) 4-Y-O+

£8,766 (£2,590; £1,295; £648; £323; £162)

Form				RPR
25-2	**1**		**Buffalo Bob (IRE)**[15] 2305 7-11-6 **126** .... SamTwiston-Davies(3) (Kim Bailey) *hit 1st: led 2nd: hdd 8th: led next: rdn fr 4 out: chal fr next: nt fluent 2 out: styd on gamely u.p run-in: all out* **7/1**	139+
2-34	**2**	2 1/4	**Sound Stage**[13] 2347 7-11-11 **128** .... BarryGeraghty (Caroline Keevil) *trckd ldrs: hit 8th: chsd wnr fr 12th: chal and blnd 4 out: stl ev ch 2 out: styd on same pce u.p run-in* **4/1**[2]	139+
F-11	**3**	10	**Sir Ian (IRE)**[36] 1926 7-11-12 **129** .... FelixDeGiles (Charlie Longsdon) *chsd ldrs: rdn 4 out: chal next: wknd bef last* **16/1**	130
400-	**4**	3 1/2	**Thetwincamdrift (IRE)**[224] 5197 8-11-4 **121** .... WayneHutchinson (Alan King) *lw: in rr: hdwy 13th: rdn 4 out: nvr rchd ldrs and wknd after 3 out* **11/1**	120
06-P	**5**	19	**The Vicar (IRE)**[15] 2305 7-11-0 **117** .... (p) HaddenFrost (Henrietta Knight) *led: hit 1st: hdd 2nd: styd pressing ldr: hit 5th: led 8th: hdd next: styd chsng ldrs: wknds 4 out* **28/1**	98
5-31	**6**	38	**Flemish Invader (IRE)**[8] 2453 7-10-11 **114** 7ex .... PaddyBrennan (Nigel Twiston-Davies) *sn chsng ldrs: wknd appr 4 out: t.o* **8/1**	61
560-	**P**		**Regal Heights (IRE)**[225] 5181 9-11-10 **127** .... NoelFehily (Tom George) *in rr and hmpd 10th: blnd 13th: t.o whn p.u bef 3 out* **14/1**	—
-004	**P**		**Nostringsattached (IRE)**[92] 1373 9-11-10 **127** .... (p) APMcCoy (Jonjo O'Neill) *lw: a in rr: t.o 8th: p.u bef 13th* **20/1**	—
2P-3	**P**		**Or Bleu (FR)**[19] 2212 8-11-11 **128** .... RichardJohnson (Philip Hobbs) *blnd 2nd: in rr: j. slowly 3rd and 4th: sn wl bhd: t.o whn p.u bef 8th* **16/1**	—
/01-	**U**		**Prince Geeno (IRE)**[329] 3194 7-10-6 **109** .... (t) TomScudamore (David Pipe) *in tch: sme hdwy whn blnd and uns rdr 10th* **6/1**[3]	—
45-1	**P**		**Zarrafakt (IRE)**[9] 2443 6-11-7 **124** 7ex .... SamThomas (Emma Lavelle) *in rr: sme hdwy whn j. slowly 12th: nvr rchd ldrs: t.o whn p.u bef 3 out* **3/1**[1]	—

5m 46.9s (-3.40) **Going Correction** -0.075s/f (Good) **11 Ran SP% 117.9**
Speed ratings (Par 107): **102,101,97,96,89 76,—,—,—,—,—**
toteswingers:1&2 £5.40, 2&3 £9.10, 1&3 £21.60 CSF £36.31 CT £439.51 TOTE £7.70: £2.20, £1.60, £4.20; EX 33.60 Trifecta £227.90 Pool: £770.25 - 2.50 winning units..
Owner The GFH Partnership **Bred** Shane A Moran **Trained** Andoversford, Gloucs

FOCUS
With a few proven front-runners taking part, this was always going to be a strongly run event, and it appeared to turn into a decent test of stamina. Improved form from the first two.

NOTEBOOK
Buffalo Bob(IRE) made a highly encouraging start to his season at Bangor after making a lot of the running, and built on it with a battling display. Always prominent, he kept finding for his in-form rider and gained a brave success. (op 17-2 tchd 9-1)
Sound Stage, back over fences after a couple of hurdles starts, moved well close to the leaders but was never able to force his head to the front, especially after making a blunder four out. (op 5-1)

Sir Ian(IRE) started his winning spree off a 21lb lower mark (his last two successes came over 2m4.5f at Worcester), so this looked a lot tougher. Unable to dominate this time, he took a good grip just in behind, which must have blunted his stamina for the end. (tchd 14-1)
Thetwincamdrift(IRE) ◆, having another try over fences, got a bit too far behind at one stage before making some eye-catching progress on the home bend. A step up in distance may help him, although he'd be competitive over this distance with a more prominent ride.
Flemish Invader(IRE), 3lb in front of the handicapper, can often travel with purpose, and did so again, but may have found this company a bit hot. (op 12-1)
Prince Geeno(IRE), a chasing debutant, was going nicely in midfield when unseating his jockey. It was too far out to know what would have happened to him, but he can be given another chance. (op 9-4 tchd 7-2 in places)
Zarrafakt(IRE), 6lb in front of the handicapper, overcame some early jumping errors to comfortably win on his chasing debut at Folkestone, but was unable to repeat that sort of effort after getting behind again early. Official explanation: jockey said gelding never travelled (op 9-4 tchd 7-2 in places)

2630 CSP NOVICES' H'CAP HURDLE (10 hdls) 2m 5f

2:45 (2:45) (Class 3) (0-120,119) 3-Y-0+ **£6,505** (£1,910; £955; £477)

Form | | | | RPR
60-2 **1** Full Of Joy (IRE)[7] 2477 5-10-12 **105** APMcCoy 120+
(Jonjo O'Neill) *in tch: hdwy 5th: styng on whn hmpd bnd appr 3 out: sn chalng and led bef 2 out: rdn appr last: hld on gamely u.p run-in: all out* **2/1**[1]
226/ **2** *hd* **Vagrant Emperor (IRE)**[632] 4262 7-11-8 **115** SamThomas 127+
(Emma Lavelle) *trckd ldrs: wnt 2nd travelling wl 2 out: chal sn after and upsides last: kpt on u.p run-in: nt quite get up* **12/1**
1P-2 **3** *16* **Mic Aubin (FR)**[28] 2051 7-10-6 **104** DavidBass(5) 104+
(Giles Smyly) *chsd ldrs: rdn and nt fluent 3 out: sn one pce: rallied appr last and tk wl hld 3rd run-in* **16/1**
24-3 **4** *2 1/4* **Simply Wings (IRE)**[16] 2283 6-11-7 **114** FelixDeGiles 110
(Richard Lee) *in tch: hdwy 5th: hit 4 out: slt ld 3 out: hdd bef next: sn wknd* **20/1**
3-23 **5** *2* **Bobbie Magern**[33] 1963 5-11-6 **113** PaddyBrennan 108
(Nigel Twiston-Davies) *j. slowly 4th ane bhd: rdn and sme hdwy 3 out: sn one pce: styd on again u.p fr 2 out* **12/1**
0222 **6** *1 3/4* **Nobby Kivambo (IRE)**[27] 2080 5-10-6 **104** MrMMO'Connor(5) 99
(Brendan Powell) *w ldr: hit 2nd: led 4 out: hdd appr 3 out and mstke: wknd next* **12/1**
0-26 **7** *2 1/4* **Cardinal James (IRE)**[20] 2185 6-10-11 **104** WayneHutchinson 95
(Tor Sturgis) *in rr: sme hdwy approachng 3 out: nvr rchd ldrs* **50/1**
20-5 **8** *22* **Beau Lake (IRE)**[16] 2291 6-10-10 **103** ColinBolger 74
(Suzy Smith) *chsd ldrs: rdn 4 out: wknd and hit 3 out* **25/1**
15F5 **9** *1/2* **Frosted Grape (IRE)**[24] 2130 4-11-12 **119** (b) TomScudamore 89
(David Pipe) *led tl hdd 4 out: wknd bef next* **33/1**
5P-F **10** *16* **Divy (FR)**[26] 2081 5-11-8 **115** (v) DavidEngland 71
(George Baker) *in rr early: hdwy 5th: chsd ldrs after 4 out: wknd next* **25/1**
-536 **11** *9* **What An Oscar (IRE)**[28] 2056 5-10-8 **104** SamTwiston-Davies(3) 52
(Nigel Twiston-Davies) *chsd ldrs: led appr 3 out: sn hdd: wknd next* **16/1**
23 **12** *28* **Foynes Island (IRE)**[27] 2069 4-11-3 **110** RichardJohnson 33
(Philip Hobbs) *hit 3rd: a bhd* **14/1**
F0-6 **P** **Commit To Memory**[203] 171 5-9-7 **93** oh1 PeterHatton(7) —
(Jimmy Fox) *a in rr: t.o whn p.u bef 3 out* **40/1**
0-14 **P** **Harvest Song (IRE)**[25] 2111 4-11-12 **119** WillKennedy —
(Henrietta Knight) *chsd ldrs: rdn 4th: sn wknd: t.o whn p.u bef 3 out* **50/1**
33-P **P** **Ballycracken (IRE)**[49] 1740 6-11-5 **112** BarryGeraghty —
(Nicky Henderson) *wknd 5th: t.o whn p.u bef 3 out* **10/1**[3]
5-5F **F** **Rajamand (FR)**[12] 2361 4-11-5 **112** NoelFehily 114
(Warren Greatrex) *hit 3rd: in rr: hdwy 4 out: chsng ldrs whn blndered 3 out: chsd ldrs next: disputing 7 l 3rd and no ch w ldng duo whn fell last* **11/4**[2]

5m 13.65s (-5.35) **Going Correction** -0.075s/f (Good) **16** Ran SP% **132.4**
Speed ratings (Par 107): **107,106,100,99,99 98,97,89,89,83 79,68,—,—,— —**
toteswingers:1&2 £7.50, 2&3 £30.90, 1&3 £13.60 CSF £27.96 CT £337.76 TOTE £3.30: £1.70, £2.20, £4.10, £3.70; EX 26.40 Trifecta £233.60 Part won. Pool of £315.71 - 0.63 winning units..
Owner John P McManus **Bred** J D Flood **Trained** Cheltenham, Gloucs

FOCUS
Plenty of runners but probably not the most competitive of races. The first two finished clear though and it is worth being positive about them. The third and fourth help set the level.

NOTEBOOK
Full Of Joy(IRE) ran well last time despite being beaten and, judging by market support, was expected to go one better, which he did by a narrow margin. It was a decent performance considering he lost his footing for a few strides on the home bend when making a move. (op 11-4 tchd 10-3 in places)
Vagrant Emperor(IRE), not seen since March 2009, ran a cracker and moved really strongly for much of the race. If he does not go backwards from this effort, races will be won with him. (op 15-2)
Mic Aubin(FR) had run over 3m3f on his previous outing. He probably ran as well as he was entitled to. (op 20-1)
Simply Wings(IRE) had been shaping like a stayer and ran with some credit, despite making little impact.
Rajamand(FR), up 4.5f in trip, was making a promising move when hitting three out. The jockey managed to get him back into some sort of position again, albeit well held in third, when he took a tired-looking fall at the last. He probably needs to go and win a novice hurdle at a minor course to get his confidence up. (op 10-3 tchd 7-2 in places)

2631 GPG NOVICES' CHASE (REGISTERED AS THE WORCESTER NOVICES' CHASE) GRADE 2 (18 fncs) 3m

3:15 (3:15) (Class 1) 4-Y-0+ **£14,708** (£5,625; £2,901; £1,532)

Form | | | | RPR
22-1 **1** **Aiteen Thirtythree (IRE)**[40] 1860 6-11-2 0 NoelFehily 153+
(Paul Nicholls) *lw: led 3rd: jnd fr 10th: hit 13th: travelling ok whn lft wl clr 14th: wnt rt 3 out and rdn next: pushed out* **13/2**[3]
1P-2 **2** *17* **Voramar Two**[16] 2285 7-11-2 0 (t) RichardJohnson 143+
(Philip Hobbs) *in tch: blnd 3rd: wl in tch in 3rd pl tl outpcd by ldng duo 13th: lft mod 2nd 14th: blnd 4 out: tried to cl run-in but nvr any ch* **8/1**
131- **3** *45* **Be There In Five (IRE)**[264] 4450 6-11-2 0 BarryGeraghty 112+
(Nicky Henderson) *in tch: j.big 4th and 5th: effrt to cl on ldrs 9th: no imp: wknd 12th: lft mod 3rd 14th: t.o* **5/1**[2]
1-11 **4** *32* **Swincombe Rock**[44] 1815 5-11-9 137 SamTwiston-Davies 70
(Nigel Twiston-Davies) *blnd 1st: j.rt 5th: sn wl bhd: t.o* **10/1**
1P-1 **F** **Tell Massini (IRE)**[28] 2057 6-11-6 0 PaddyBrennan —
(Tom George) *led to 3rd: styd trcking ldr: chal fr10th: upsides and travelling wl whn fell 14th: fatally injured* **8/11**[1]

6m 2.12s (-8.88) **Going Correction** -0.075s/f (Good) **5** Ran SP% **108.1**
Speed ratings (Par 115): **111,105,90,79,—**
CSF £44.80 TOTE £4.80: £2.00, £3.70; EX 36.20.
Owner Paul K Barber & The Stewart Family **Bred** Mrs Rosemary Ross **Trained** Ditcheat, Somerset

FOCUS
This race regularly produces a decent sort, so the winner is one worth following. He looks a smart novice.

NOTEBOOK
Aiteen Thirtythree(IRE) has always had a good reputation but took a while to get off the mark over hurdles after a couple of disappointing efforts. Representing a stable with a fine record in this contest, his jockey sent him off in front and the pair put up a bold show of jumping and stamina. He did get a bit tired in the end, but was also possibly idling a touch as well. However, he had such a big advantage that he had more than enough in hand to hang on, and looks every inch a RSA Chase candidate, although connections seemed to suggest he won't be aimed in that direction. The Hennessy next year appeared to be in their thoughts. (tchd 7-1)
Voramar Two finished well beaten on his chasing debut at Exeter but shaped a bit better in this, although he probably would not have finished second had Tell Massini not fallen. (op 15-2 tchd 7-1)
Be There In Five(IRE) just got the better of Aiteen Thirtythree at this course over hurdles when last seen in March, but never got into contention on his chasing debut. This seemed a little disappointing so he will be better judged after another start. (op 4-1)
Swincombe Rock, giving weight away to all of his rivals, got behind early and was never a factor. He had made hard work of it at Huntingdon, but against this calibre of rival, he was never going to get back into it, especially as he showed a tendency to jump to his right at some of his fences. (op 8-1)
Tell Massini(IRE) was in the process of running really well when coming down at the fifth-last. The winner of four of his six outings under rules, he was sadly put down due to his injuries. (op 10-11 tchd evens in places)

2632 FESTIVAL RACING ON COURSE BOOKMAKERS STANDARD OPEN NATIONAL HUNT FLAT RACE 2m 110y

3:50 (3:50) (Class 5) 4-6-Y-0 **£1,951** (£573; £286; £143)

Form | | | | RPR
2 **1** **Balding Banker (IRE)**[26] 2087 4-11-0 0 NoelFehily 120+
(Paul Nicholls) *lw: trckd ldr after 4f: led over 4f out: sn clr: pushed out fnl 2f: readily* **11/4**[2]
2 *10* **Gospel Preacher** 5-11-0 0 WayneHutchinson 111
(Alan King) *gd sort: scope: in rr: hdwy fr 4f out: styd on wl to take 2nd ins fnl 3f: nvr any ch w wnr* **9/1**
3 *9* **Fourovakind** 5-10-7 0 JeremiahMcGrath(7) 103
(Matt Hazell) *lw: str: in rr: stl plenty to do over 4f out: pushed along and hdwy over 3f out: tk 2nd ins fnl 2f and kpt on: nvr any threat* **80/1**
4 *13* **Flowerdew (IRE)** 5-11-0 0 BarryGeraghty 91
(Nicky Henderson) *lw: in tch: hdwy to dispute 2nd 4f out: nvr any ch w wnr and wknd ins fnl 3f* **11/2**[3]
5 *20* **No Obligation (IRE)** 5-11-0 0 RichardJohnson 73
(Brendan Powell) *tall: chsd ldrs tl wknd over 6f out* **33/1**
6 *10* **Nomansland (IRE)** 4-11-0 0 APMcCoy 73+
(Nicky Henderson) *athletic: in tch: hdwy 6f out to dispute 2nd 4f out: wknd ins fnl 3f: eased whn no ch fnl f* **8/11**[1]
05 **7** *7* **Ellie Wiggins**[16] 2295 4-10-0 0 NathanSweeney(7) 51
(Bob Buckler) *chsd ldr 4f: wknd 1/2-way* **66/1**
8 *1 1/4* **Next Man In (IRE)** 4-10-11 0 CharlieHuxley(3) 57
(Alan King) *sn bhd* **25/1**
9 *50* **Virginia Rose Wood (IRE)** 4-10-7 0 MattieBatchelor 5
(Peter Hedger) *b.bkwd: led: sn clr: hdd & wknd over 4f out* **100/1**

4m 7.00s (2.70) **Going Correction** -0.075s/f (Good)
WFA 4 from 5yo 7lb **9** Ran SP% **120.5**
Speed ratings: **90,85,81,74,65 60,57,56,33**
toteswingers:1&2 £3.70, 2&3 £27.10, 1&3 £15.60 CSF £26.93 TOTE £3.30: £1.10, £2.50, £11.00; EX 17.90 TRIFECTA Not won..
Owner Ian Axe & Potensis Limited **Bred** Peter And Ann Downes **Trained** Ditcheat, Somerset

FOCUS
A surprisingly small field for a Newbury bumper but the pace was reasonable. Not much to go on but arguably a step forward from the winner.

NOTEBOOK
Balding Banker(IRE) was a beaten favourite for an Ascot bumper on his only previous outing, but got into first place this time with a good display once in front. His jockey moved him towards the stands' rail on turning in and the pair came home strongly to win by a clear margin. (tchd 5-2 and 3-1)
Gospel Preacher, a half-brother to four Irish point winners, looks every inch a chaser in the making and showed plenty of ability here. This good-looking horse can win a bumper before jumping any obstacles. (op 12-1)
Fourovakind, a brother to a bumper winner, stayed on strongly past some much more fancied runners in the latter stages. He will need to prove this run was not a one off. (op 100-1)
Flowerdew(IRE), a half-brother to an Irish point winner, cost £52,000 last year at the sales and only showed a modicum of promise for the future. (op 7-1 tchd 5-1)
Nomansland(IRE) came in for a lot of market support on his debut, and he seemed full of himself before the off, noticeably when bucking on the way to the start. Held up in midfield, he was beaten surprisingly early when considering the apparent confidence, and now has plenty to prove. (op 4-5 tchd 5-6 in places)
T/Plt: £268.90 to a £1 stake. Pool of £60,028.67 - 162.93 winning tickets. T/Qpdt: £48.30 to a £1 stake. Pool of £4,883.59 - 74.81 winning tickets. ST

2329 TAUNTON (R-H)

Thursday, November 25

OFFICIAL GOING: Good
Rail on bends moved out adding 72m per circuit to race distances.
Wind: mild across Weather: cloudy with occassional snow flurries

2633 WELCOME TO RECIPROCAL ANNUAL MEMBERS (S) HURDLE (9 hdls) 2m 1f

12:40 (12:40) (Class 5) 4-Y-0+ **£2,055** (£599; £299)

Form | | | | RPR
4 **1** **If I Had Him (IRE)**[28] 2058 6-10-12 110 (p) AndrewTinkler 104
(George Baker) *trckd ldrs: rdn whn lft in ld 6th: kpt on: drvn out* **7/2**[2]
5332 **2** *1 3/4* **Dark Energy**[14] 2323 6-11-5 106 (t) JohnKington(3) 112
(Michael Scudamore) *hld up towards rr: stdy prog fr 5th: wnt 3rd after 3 out: sn rdn: chsd wnr bef last: kpt on: a being hld* **10/1**
3324 **3** *6* **Cortinas (GER)**[17] 2276 8-10-9 0 (t) PeterToole(3) 97
(Charlie Mann) *in tch: making hdwy whn lft 2nd and sltly hmpd 6th: rdn appr 2 out: fnd little: lost 2nd bef last: hung rt run-in* **6/1**
2060 **4** *25* **Try Cat**[14] 2329 4-10-5 99 (t) RhysFlint 67
(Philip Hobbs) *trckd ldr: losing pl whn lft 3rd 6th: wknd after 3 out: t.o* **13/2**

0 **5** *4 ½* **Cridda Boy**[23] 2137 4-10-5 0 (t) NathanSweeney(7) 70
(Simon Burrough) *hld up towards rr: sme hdwy u.p 6th: nvr on terms: wknd 3 out: t.o* **66/1**

-0PR **6** *2 ¾* **Border Castle**[14] 2326 9-10-12 0 NickScholfield 68
(Michael Blake) *mid-div: reminders after 4th: no ch fr after next: t.o* **5/1**[3]

-000 **7** *1 ¾* **Operachy**[30] 2021 5-10-7 78 TomO'Connor(5) 66
(James Frost) *mid-div: rdn after 6th: wknd after 3 out: t.o* **100/1**

8 *1* **Bless My Soul**[243] 7-10-5 0 MattGriffiths(7) 65
(Ron Hodges) *mid-div: rdn in rr after 4th: t.o* **20/1**

P-P0 **P** **Lethal Gun (IRE)**[30] 2021 8-10-5 60 (t) MrJBanks(7) —
(Richard Mitchell) *in tch: reminders after 4th: lost tch after next: t.o whn p.u bef 2 out* **150/1**

5610 **F** **Cruchain (IRE)**[19] 2213 7-11-2 118 RichieMcLernon(3) —
(Jonjo O'Neill) *led tl after 5th: regained ld and travelling wl whn fell heavily 6th* **10/3**[1]

P- **P** **May Boy**[388] 2043 4-10-7 0 IanPopham(5) —
(Ron Hodges) *a bhd: t.o whn p.u after 3 out* **100/1**

2006 **B** **Stir On The Sea (IRE)**[9] 2442 4-10-5 100 (b¹) TomO'Brien —
(James Frost) *trckd ldr: led after 4th: hdd after 5th: 3rd whn b.d next* **22/1**

4m 6.80s (-1.20) **Going Correction** -0.125s/f (Good)
WFA 4 from 5yo+ 7lb 12 Ran SP% **111.9**
Speed ratings (Par 103): **97,96,93,81,79 78,77,76,—,— —,—**
toteswingers:1&2 £7.00, 2&3 £4.70, 1&3 £4.90 CSF £33.32 TOTE £3.90: £1.70, £3.70, £1.10; EX 31.00.The winner was bought in for 6,800gns. Cruchain was claimed by Mrs S Mutch for £6000.
Owner Sir Alex Ferguson **Bred** Mrs J Morrissey **Trained** Whitsbury, Hants

FOCUS
A decent event for this grade, if ability alone was taken into account, but huge questions marks over the main protagonists made it a tricky contest for punters. The winner is rated 9lb off his Irish best.

NOTEBOOK
If I Had Him(IRE) won a couple of modest staying events on the level in the spring. He made a couple of minor errors on the way round and, having been left in front by the fall at the fourth last of favourite Cruchain, he battled on well enough from two out. This was his 15th start over hurdles, so he's probably not got a great deal of scope for improvement. He was bought in at the auction. (op 4-1)
Dark Energy had the strong gallop that he needs in order to get him settled. It was a commendable effort, as his penalty meant he was not well suited by conditions. This won't help with his handicap mark, and his preference for decent ground will limit his opportunities at this time of year. (op 9-1)
Cortinas(GER) as usual travelled strongly and was ridden nearer the pace than normal. Left chasing the winner after the carnage at the fourth last, he found very little from two out (as usual) and tamely faded away after the last. He was beaten when last contesting a hurdle in this grade back in the summer. (op 11-2 tchd 5-1)
Try Cat has been regressive over hurdles, and he wasn't really competitively involved in this after being left disputing third after the fourth-last carnage. (op 17-2)
Cridda Boy lacked experience having only his second start over hurdles, and although well beaten did show enough to suggest a small race could be within his capabilities. (op 50-1)
Border Castle won the Scottish Champion hurdle as recently as 2008, but didn't take to chasing and showed no zest here. Retirement probably beckons now. (op 11-2 tchd 9-2)
Cruchain(IRE) was sent off favourite, but is a very hard ride and, although still in front when crashing out at the fourth last, it was too early to say if it cost him the race. He was claimed for £6,000 after the race. (op 3-1)
Stir On The Sea(IRE) had vied for the lead having been keen in her first-time blinkers, but was on the retreat when exiting four out. (op 3-1)

2634 SUMMERFIELD DEVELOPMENTS "NATIONAL HUNT" NOVICES' HURDLE (10 hdls) 2m 3f 110y
1:10 (1:11) (Class 4) 4-Y-O+ **£4,110** (£1,198; £599)

Form RPR

14 **1** **Nicene Creed**[32] 1988 5-11-4 123 TomO'Brien 125
(Philip Hobbs) *trckd ldrs: disputing 2nd u.str.p appr 2 out: styd on run-in: led fnl stride* **9/4**[2]

3-40 **2** *shd* **Bally Legend**[22] 2145 5-10-7 0 IanPopham(5) 119
(Caroline Keevil) *trckd ldrs: challneged 3 out: rdn to ld bef next: styd on: ct fnl stride* **25/1**

2-1 **3** *4* **That'Ll Do**[32] 2000 5-10-13 0 MrRMahon(5) 122+
(Paul Nicholls) *trckd ldr: nt fluent 6th: led next: rdn and hdd appr 2 out: styd on same pce fr last* **4/6**[1]

00-6 **4** *32* **Graduation Night**[23] 2136 4-10-12 0 DarylJacob 87
(Jamie Snowden) *mid-div: rdn after 7th: wnt modest 4th after 3 out: nvr any ch w ldrs* **100/1**

5-66 **5** *3* **Reefer Beefer (IRE)**[14] 2331 5-10-12 0 AndrewTinkler 84
(Tony Newcombe) *struggling in rr 5th: nvr a factor* **100/1**

233- **6** *1* **Yukon Quest (IRE)**[228] 5158 5-10-12 0 GerardTumelty 83
(Alan King) *mid-div: rdn after 7th: wknd after 3 out* **12/1**[3]

00-0 **7** *17* **Mi Money**[23] 2142 5-10-2 0 (t) JohnKington(3) 61
(David Pipe) *nt fluent 2nd: reminders: mainly towards rr: t.o* **100/1**

1604 **8** *10* **My Brother Sylvest**[10] 2419 4-11-4 124 RhysFlint 65
(David Brace) *led tl 7th: sn rdn: wknd next: t.o* **16/1**

9 *¾* **Nosecond Chance (IRE)**[235] 4-10-9 0 PeterToole(3) 58
(Charlie Mann) *mid-div: hdwy after 6th: wknd 3 out: t.o* **25/1**

656 **10** *8* **Casper's Shadow (IRE)**[36] 1922 4-10-12 0 (t) JamieMoore 51
(Keith Goldsworthy) *trckd ldrs early: mid-div 3rd: rdn after 6th: sn wknd: t.o* **66/1**

0000 **11** *19* **Sheezatreasure (IRE)**[18] 2241 5-9-12 0 MarkQuinlan(7) 27
(James Evans) *struggling 5th: a towards rr: t.o* **150/1**

0-0 **12** *21* **Flora King**[49] 1749 5-10-12 0 (t) AidanColeman 15
(Anthony Honeyball) *a towards rr: t.o fr 7th* **80/1**

P **13** *21* **Flameproof (IRE)**[16] 2288 5-10-2 0 WayneKavanagh(3) —
(Caroline Keevil) *trckd ldr tl after 5th: wknd next: t.o* **100/1**

0-0P **P** **Shared Secret**[16] 2288 6-10-0 0 RachaelGreen(5) —
(Anthony Honeyball) *a towards rr: struggling 4th: t.o whn p.u after 7th* **100/1**

4m 41.0s (-5.00) **Going Correction** -0.125s/f (Good)
WFA 4 from 5yo+ 7lb 14 Ran SP% **120.4**
Speed ratings (Par 105): **105,104,103,90,89 88,82,78,77,74 67,58,50,—**
toteswingers:1&2 £9.60, 2&3 £6.10, 1&3 £1.50 CSF £54.72 TOTE £3.60: £1.10, £4.90, £1.10; EX 52.50.
Owner Mrs Diana L Whateley **Bred** Aylesfield Farms Stud Ltd **Trained** Withycombe, Somerset

FOCUS
A fair novices' hurdle which concerned only three from well before the home turn. The winner ran to his mark, with a big step up from the second.

NOTEBOOK
Nicene Creed, an expensive purchase, had won on his hurdling debut but disappointed behind Cue Card at Aintree. Always tracking the leaders, he was produced after the last and got there in the shadow of the post. He might have found the ground, which the jockeys reported as being softer than the official description of good, less than ideal, and he could be best put away now to wait for a sounder surface in the spring. (op 5-2)
Bally Legend, placed in bumpers, put up his best effort so far over hurdles on this step up in trip. He kicked on turning for home but came to the end of his tether after the last, and was caught on the line. He should be able to find compensation in a similar contest. (op 22-1)
That'Ll Do was sent off favourite in the strength of winning a no-contest on his hurdling debut. However, that was over 2m6f and the drop in trip on this sharp track looked to find him out for pace. He might have had an excuse however, as he stumbled leaving the back straight and was in trouble from that point.
Graduation Night was well beaten on his hurdling debut and finished some way back here, but did show some ability and looks the sort to find his level in handicaps after one more run.
My Brother Sylvest had the highest official rating but, after being headed early on the second circuit, dropped right away and probably needs a return to fast ground. (op 14-1)
Flameproof(IRE) Official explanation: jockey said mare hung left-handed

2635 JOHN HILLS MEMORIAL NOVICES' CHASE (12 fncs) 2m 110y
1:45 (1:45) (Class 4) 4-Y-O+ **£4,553** (£1,337; £668)

Form RPR

050- **1** **Clouseau (NZ)**[262] 4490 6-11-0 115 DarylJacob 115+
(Nick Williams) *trckd ldr: nt fluent 1st: narrow advantage briefly whn stmbld 3 out: shkn up to ld appr last: r.o: readily* **9/4**[3]

34-0 **2** *1 ½* **Arctic Ben (IRE)**[25] 2112 6-11-0 113 AndrewTinkler 107
(Henry Daly) *j. sltly lft: led: nt fluent 2nd: rdn and hanging lft whn hdd briefly 3 out: drvn whn hdd after 2 out: kpt on same pce* **2/1**[2]

1125 **3** *48* **Morning Sunshine (IRE)**[26] 2093 7-11-0 108 AdrianLane 73
(Donald McCain) *trckd ldng pair: j.lft: blnd 8th: sn rdn: wknd after next: t.o* **11/8**[1]

4m 18.4s (8.40) **Going Correction** +0.05s/f (Yiel) 3 Ran SP% **106.2**
Speed ratings (Par 105): **82,81,58**
CSF £6.38 TOTE £3.00; EX 4.80.
Owner The Gascoigne Brookes Partnership Iii **Bred** P J Kay & Mrs S L Kay **Trained** George Nympton, Devon

FOCUS
As tight a three-runner race as you will find, with the big question being who'd make the running as all three tend to be too keen and need a strongly run race. The winner was value for further and should go on to rate higher.

NOTEBOOK
Clouseau(NZ), a 1m winner in New Zealand, was making his chasing debut. He jumped perfectly adequately and his only meaningful error was when coming to lead a the tricky third-last, where he lost his hind legs on landing. Back in front going to the last, he unsurprisingly had too much toe for the runner-up. Life will be hard under a penalty in a similar contest, so it may be the handicap route that connections opt for. A sharp 2m looks imperative. Official explanation: trainer said, regarding apparent improvement in form, that the gelding was having its first run over fences. (op 15-8)
Arctic Ben(IRE) regularly spoils his chance by pulling too hard, so it was a good tactical move to allow him to bowl along in front. His jumping was careful (no bad thing) at times and he edged a little left to put himself right at times. He lacked the winner's turn of foot and was comfortably put in his place from the last. This was a step in the right direction, after his chasing debut when he made no show having been surprisingly made favourite in a handicap. He would be better suited to being held up in a larger field, too. Official explanation: jockey said gelding hung left-handed (op 7-4 tchd 13-8)
Morning Sunshine(IRE) had a bit to find on ratings, but was by far the most experienced over fences in the field. He was backed into favourite late on, but refused to settle and a couple of serious errors, particularly when on the retreat at the fourth last, meant he was well beaten turning out of the back straight. This wasn't his running and he is another more suited to a larger field. (op 15-8)

2636 AUDREY CHUDLEIGH MEMORIAL H'CAP HURDLE (10 hdls) 2m 3f 110y
2:20 (2:20) (Class 3) (0-135,133) 4-Y-O+ **£5,854** (£1,719; £859; £429)

Form RPR

-214 **1** **Organisateur (IRE)**[26] 2083 5-11-7 **133** IanPopham(5) 148+
(Paul Nicholls) *in tch: tk clsr order 5th: led and edgd rt last: r.o strly to assert fnl 120yds: readily* **10/3**[1]

/030 **2** *5* **Puerto Azul (IRE)**[26] 2081 6-10-3 **110** LeightonAspell 115+
(Oliver Sherwood) *hld up off main gp: latched on to gp after 5th: cl up 3 out: abt to mount chal whn hmpd by loose horse bef 2 out: rcvrd to chal for 2nd at the last: kpt on: nt gng pce of wnr* **10/1**

1503 **3** *6* **Cantabilly (IRE)**[6] 2502 7-10-3 **117** MattGriffiths(7) 116
(Ron Hodges) *hld up main gp: pckd 1st: hdwy 6th: led after 3 out: sn rdn: hdd and carried sltly rt last: kpt on same pce* **8/1**

20-3 **4** *1* **Wester Ross (IRE)**[43] 1608 6-10-10 **117** (p) MarkBradburne 114
(James Eustace) *trckd ldr: rdn and ev ch 2 out: keeping on at same pce whn lft 4th last* **8/1**

505- **5** *nk* **Special Occasion**[229] 5132 6-11-6 **127** TomO'Brien 125
(Caroline Keevil) *in tch: cl up 3 out: rdn after 2 out: styng on same pce whn sltly hmpd last* **14/1**

0-1U **6** *8* **U B Carefull**[161] 773 7-10-4 **118** MrPJTolman(7) 110
(Sirrell Griffiths) *hld up bhd: nt fluent 5th: clsd on main gp 3 out: sn rdn: one pce fr next* **16/1**

122- **7** *4 ½* **Raquel White**[218] 5316 6-10-13 **120** RhysFlint 107
(John Flint) *led: hit 3rd and 5th: rdn and hdd after 3 out: wknd after next* **15/2**[3]

563 **8** *58* **Consulate (IRE)**[14] 2333 6-10-8 **115** (p) DarylJacob 48
(Gordon Edwards) *chsd ldrs tl wknd after 3 out: t.o* **12/1**

F0/6 **9** *7* **Counting House (IRE)**[3] 2574 7-10-13 **120** TimmyMurphy 47
(Jim Old) *a detached in rr: t.o* **20/1**

24-2 **U** **Screaming Brave**[177] 566 4-10-8 **115** (t) JamieGoldstein —
(Sheena West) *hld up in tch: cl up and travelling ok whn blnd and uns rdr 7th* **7/1**[2]

355U **F** **Forest Rhythm (IRE)**[20] 2185 6-9-13 **109** WayneKavanagh(3) 107
(Seamus Mullins) *in tch: tk clsr orde 3 out: rdn bef next: styng on same pce in cl 4th whn fell last* **10/1**

4m 43.4s (-2.60) **Going Correction** -0.125s/f (Good)
WFA 4 from 5yo+ 7lb 11 Ran SP% **112.8**
Speed ratings (Par 107): **100,98,95,95,95 91,90,66,64,—,—**
toteswingers:1&2 £9.50, 2&3 £27.60, 1&3 £8.10 CSF £35.16 CT £243.64 TOTE £4.00: £1.70, £4.40, £3.40; EX 44.40.
Owner Mrs Angela Tincknell & W Tincknell **Bred** Wertheimer Et Frere **Trained** Ditcheat, Somerset

FOCUS
A steadily run race and plenty in with chances going to two out. The easy winner won with a lot in hand but the form is a bit suspect.

NOTEBOOK

Organisateur(IRE) readily put his mark on the race after the last, to claim his third course win. A break following three quick runs in the autumn certainly paid dividends. The handicapper will have his say, but this likeable type looks well capable of continuing his progressive profile. He's proven on contrasting ground conditions and will get further. (op 7-2 tchd 3-1)

Puerto Azul(IRE) was done no favours by the loose horse going to the second last, but in no way did this affect the result. He again travelled keenly (often his downfall) and is easily good enough to take a race off of this mark, but he looks as if he will need plenty to fall right for him. (tchd 9-1 and 11-1)

Cantabilly(IRE) usually runs well here and today was no exception. He is still 5lb above his Exeter winning mark in the autumn. (op 9-1 tchd 10-1)

Wester Ross(IRE) ran another solid race, but his lack of a change of gear saw he left behind between the last two flights. He probably needs dropping a few pounds, but has yet to totally convince he stays this far and hardly looks a winner waiting to happen. (op 17-2)

Special Occasion, a C&D winner last season when in the same yard as the winner, was beaten when hampered by the last-flight faller. He had travelled keenly during the race and showed he retains ability, and will come on for the run. (tchd 12-1 and 16-1)

U B Carefull was dropped right out and as usual was keen. His effort petered out going to two out and he has yet to convince he fully gets this trip. (op 12-1)

Raquel White set a decent tempo but weakened going to the second last as if her first run of the season was needed, rather than due to a lack of stamina. (op 11-2)

Forest Rhythm(IRE) travelled keenly but was held when coming down at the last. (op 14-1)

2637 P.A.S. SOUND & COMMUNICATIONS NOVICES' H'CAP HURDLE (12 hdls) 3m 110y

2:55 (2:55) (Class 4) (0-115,114) 4-Y-0+ **£4,110** (£1,198; £599)

Form				RPR
3244	**1**		**Prince Tom**[23] 2141 6-11-7 **114** IanPopham(5) (Paul Nicholls) *trckd ldrs: led appr 8th: rdn whn chal bypassing omitted 2 out: styd on wl to assert fr last: rdn out* **5/1**[2]	120+
/2-5	**2**	*4 ½*	**Massini Moon (IRE)**[15] 2314 6-10-1 **89** (b[1]) JamieMoore (Gary Moore) *mid-div: hdwy 8th: wnt 2nd next: sn rdn: chal bypassing omitted 2nd last: no ex fr last* **7/2**[1]	91
156P	**3**	*2 ¼*	**Petroupetrov (FR)**[10] 2420 7-10-9 **97** (v[1]) TomSiddall (Richard Phillips) *rn in snatches: trckd ldrs tl lost pl and shkn up after 5th: regained position 7th: hrd rdn after 10th: styd on same pce fr bypassed 2 out* **50/1**	97
06-0	**4**	*3 ¼*	**Witch's Hat (IRE)**[7] 2469 7-9-13 **92** (t) MichaelMurphy(5) (Jim Old) *hld up towards rr: hdwy after 8th: rdn after 10th: styd on same pce* **50/1**	90
3P5-	**5**	*16*	**The Hudnalls (IRE)**[244] 4869 9-10-9 **97** RhysFlint (Jim Old) *hld up towards rr: sme hdwy whn nt fluent 10th: sn rdn: wknd on long run bef last* **11/1**	80
-030	**6**	*½*	**Lost Glory (NZ)**[33] 1959 5-11-3 **108** RichieMcLernon(3) (Jonjo O'Neill) *hld up towards rr: hmpd 6th: rdn and sme hdwy after 10th: wknd bef bypassed 2 out* **8/1**	90
21	**7**	*2 ¾*	**Silver Accord (IRE)**[28] 2049 7-11-12 **114** LeightonAspell (Oliver Sherwood) *hld up towards rr: rdn whn bdly hmpd 10th: no ch after* **7/1**[3]	94
53-6	**8**	*6*	**Ready Or Not (IRE)**[28] 2049 7-10-13 **101** AndrewGlassonbury (Bob Buckler) *mid-div: rdn after 9th: wknd on long run after next* **10/1**	75
543	**9**	*16*	**Newyearsresolution (IRE)**[53] 1703 6-10-7 **95** DarylJacob (Nick Mitchell) *trckd ldrs: rdn whn mstke and hmpd 10th: sn wknd: t.o* **10/1**	55
4F14	**10**	*12*	**Pairc Na Gcapall (IRE)**[24] 2127 8-11-8 **113** (b) AlexMerriam(3) (Neil King) *led tl 8th: sn wknd: t.o* **18/1**	62
5-06	**11**	*20*	**Graylyn Ruby (FR)**[50] 1734 5-10-2 **93** WayneKavanagh(3) (Robin Dickin) *a towards rr: t.o fr after 10th* **12/1**	24
P52-	**F**		**Sawpit Solitaire**[258] 4569 5-11-2 **104** AidanColeman (Venetia Williams) *in tch: trcking ldrs whn fell 6th* **8/1**	—

6m 0.60s (-6.50) **Going Correction** -0.125s/f (Good) 12 Ran SP% **117.0**

Speed ratings (Par 105): **105,103,102,101,96 96,95,93,88,84 78,—**

CSF £22.97 CT £777.22 TOTE £6.90: £1.90, £1.60, £10.80; EX 30.00.

Owner Mrs Angela Tincknell & W Tincknell **Bred** W C Tincknell **Trained** Ditcheat, Somerset

FOCUS

An ordinary novice event. A step forward from the winner, wit the second and third setting the level.

NOTEBOOK

Prince Tom, a drifter in the market during the morning and on course, is an out-and-out galloper and his abundant stamina allowed him to see off the well backed runner-up on the run to the last. He was giving lumps of weight to his nearest rival. He shouldn't be too harshly dealt with by the handicapper for this initial success, and can handle softer ground. He should have a future over fences. (op 7-2)

Massini Moon(IRE), on his second start after a prolonged absence, and equipped with first-time blinkers, was well backed to build on the promise he showed at Huntingdon. He and the winner had the race to themselves up the straight and it was only going to the last he gave best. This was his first try at this trip and he just came up against a stronger stayer. He'll be reassessed for this, but can find a race. (op 6-1)

Petroupetrov(FR) ran in snatches, but it was a return to form having looked to fall out of love with chasing in his most recent runs. This was his first run in a visor and he's likely to remain hard to predict.

Witch's Hat(IRE) showed his first signs of ability in a tongue tie for the first time. He should be competitive in a similar novices' handicap off a similar mark, if reproducing this run.

The Hudnalls(IRE) ran perfectly adequately on his seasonal bow, on ground too quick and a trip that is his minimum. (op 12-1 tchd 9-1)

Lost Glory(NZ), backed on course, was badly hampered by the fall of Sawpit Solitaire with just over a circuit to run. He still travelled well enough until dropping away after three out. He has ability and probably found this trip a step too far. (op 12-1)

Silver Accord(IRE) was already in trouble when hampered at the last in the back straight. Up 9lb for his Fontwell win, he didn't give his running this time. (op 13-2)

Graylyn Ruby(FR) faded quickly halfway down the back straight. (op 11-1)

2638 TAP MEDICAL H'CAP CHASE (17 fncs) 2m 7f 110y

3:30 (3:30) (Class 4) (0-100,99) 4-Y-0+ **£4,553** (£1,337; £668; £333)

Form				RPR
/3P-	**1**		**Extra Bold**[550] 448 8-11-2 **96** StephenO'Donovan(7) (Emma Lavelle) *travelled wl: hld up: smooth hdwy to trck ldrs after 10th: led 12th: rdn after 3 out: hit last: drvn out* **7/2**[2]	109+
22-2	**2**	*2*	**Sir Winston (IRE)**[18] 2240 8-11-8 **95** DarylJacob (Victor Dartnall) *trckd ldrs: rdn appr 4 out: nt quite able to mount chal: styd on to go 2nd fr last: a being hld by wnr* **2/1**[1]	106
2601	**3**	*nk*	**Justabout**[14] 2332 7-11-1 **98** (tp) SClements(10) (Colin Tizzard) *disp ld tl chsd wnr fr 12th: rdn after 4 out: ch whn nodded on landing 4 out: styd on: no ex whn lost 2nd run-in* **8/1**	108
-P56	**4**	*16*	**Power Shared (IRE)**[19] 2217 6-11-4 **96** MichaelMurphy(5) (Pat Murphy) *hld up: hdwy 11th: rdn after 13th: wknd bef 2 out: dismntd after fin* **22/1**	93
3252	**5**	*18*	**Bollywood (IRE)**[14] 2332 7-10-9 **82** (t) TimmyMurphy (Alison Batchelor) *hld up: hdwy after 11th: rdn 4 out: wknd and j.lft fr 3 out* **8/1**	63
-350	**6**	*30*	**Terrible Tenant**[32] 1991 11-11-6 **96** JimmyDerham(3) (Seamus Mullins) *disp ld tl 11th: wknd after next: t.o* **16/1**	47
324/	**7**	*23*	**Ballyman (IRE)**[597] 4893 9-10-10 **83** JimmyMcCarthy (Jonathan Geake) *mstke 1st: blnd 13th: a in rr: t.o* **7/1**[3]	13
0163	**P**		**Outside Investor (IRE)**[7] 2483 10-10-8 **81** (b) LiamHeard (Patrick Rodford) *chsd ldrs: mstke 1st: rdn after 9th: bhd fr 11th: t.o whn p.u bef 13th* **28/1**	—
4404	**U**		**Swainson (USA)**[20] 2184 9-11-3 **90** (p) OwynNelmes (Helen Nelmes) *stmbld bdly on landing and uns rdr 1st* **33/1**	—
444-	**F**		**Mocho (IRE)**[289] 3949 9-11-12 **99** LiamTreadwell (Mrs H Parrott) *trcking ldrs whn fell 8th* **14/1**	—
3-56	**P**		**Machu Picchu (FR)**[32] 1992 8-11-11 **98** TomO'Brien (Jamie Snowden) *a in rr: mstke 11th: t.o whn p.u bef 4 out* **33/1**	—
P03P	**U**		**Rapid Return (IRE)**[14] 2332 7-10-2 **75** TomSiddall (Richard Phillips) *bhd whn swvd and uns rdr 8th* **22/1**	—

6m 12.3s (-2.30) **Going Correction** +0.05s/f (Yiel) 12 Ran SP% **120.9**

Speed ratings (Par 105): **105,104,104,98,92 82,75,—,—,— —,—**

toteswingers:1&2 £2.80, 2&3 £4.20, 1&3 £9.60 CSF £10.87 CT £52.14 TOTE £3.70: £1.30, £2.30, £2.60; EX 9.20.

Owner Miss Camilla Jenks **Bred** R Jenks **Trained** Wildhern, Hants

■ Stewards' Enquiry : S Clements 8-day ban: used whip with excessive frequency (Dec 9-16)

FOCUS

A competitive chase in which the tricky first fence in the straight caused plenty of grief. There is more to come from the winner, and the second is rated to his mark.

NOTEBOOK

Extra Bold is from a yard in fine form and the lengthy absence proved no barrier. He was always travelling strongly on his first start for these connections. His rider had little option but to allow him to take up the running with the best part of a circuit to run but he readily found enough after the last. He needs decent ground and, if whatever has caused him to be off the course for 18 months is behind him, he can win again. (op 11-4)

Sir Winston(IRE) won this last year off an 11lb lower mark, and despite mistakes kept battling on well here having been off the bridle from the fifth last. A commendable effort, but not one that will gain him any respite from the handicapper. (op 3-1 tchd 15-8)

Justabout was always up with the leaders and only gave best from the last. His small penalty for his C&D win was more than negated by his jockey's allowance. Should continue to go well before the ground deteriorates. (op 12-1)

Power Shared(IRE) is probably better over a shorter trip and ran one of his better races. Unfortunately he damaged a tendon, and he may not run again. (op 18-1 tchd 16-1)

Bollywood(IRE) was beaten in a weaker race here last time and was left behind turning for home. He doesn't make any great appeal as a future winner over fences. (op 17-2 tchd 9-1)

Terrible Tenant dropped away quickly having made most of the running for the first 2m. (op 14-1)

Ballyman(IRE), like the winner from a yard in good nick and returning from a long absence, made a blunder early on and was well beaten in the final mile. (op 12-1)

2639 SOUTHWEST-RACING.CO.UK MARES' H'CAP HURDLE (9 hdls) 2m 1f

4:00 (4:00) (Class 4) (0-110,110) 3-Y-0+ **£3,903** (£1,146; £573; £286)

Form				RPR
212	**1**		**Babilu**[18] 2242 5-11-3 **101** (p) TomO'Brien (Dai Burchell) *hld up towards rr: smooth hdwy fr 5th: ldng whn tried to duck out 2 out: kpt on fr last: rdn out* **9/2**[2]	109+
0-3R	**2**	*3 ¼*	**Posh Emily**[6] 2504 7-10-11 **102** (b[1]) MattGriffiths(7) (Ron Hodges) *disp ld tl 2nd: trckd ldrs: rdn after mstke 3 out: styd on to chse wnr bef last: a hld* **16/1**	104
2440	**3**	*8*	**Lucy's Perfect**[14] 2329 4-10-8 **97** (b) CO'Farrell(5) (David Pipe) *disp ld tl rdn after 3 out: blnd next: styd on same pce* **17/2**	92
4P-1	**4**	*½*	**Minnie Hill (IRE)**[6] 2504 6-10-12 **101** GilesHawkins(5) (Victor Dartnall) *disp ld: rdn and hdd whn hmpd appr 2 out: styd on same pce* **9/4**[1]	99+
00-6	**5**	*2*	**Bella Medici**[24] 2130 5-9-9 **84** oh11 (t) MichaelMurphy(5) (Pat Murphy) *mid-div tl dropped in rr u.p 6th: styd on again fr after 3 out: nvr gng pce to rch ldrs* **50/1**	76
2-62	**6**	*3 ¾*	**Ocean Transit (IRE)**[9] 2442 5-11-12 **110** DarylJacob (Richard Price) *mid-div: hdwy 5th: rdn after 3 out: sn btn* **5/1**[3]	98
0520	**7**	*7*	**Gulf Punch**[12] 2356 3-10-7 **109** (v[1]) JimmyDerham(3) (Milton Harris) *mid-div: rdn 3 out: sn btn* **9/1**	76
P000	**8**	*10*	**Rolanta (FR)**[14] 2329 5-10-0 **84** oh4 JamesDavies (James Frost) *t.k.h in rr: hdwy 3 out: sn rdn: wknd bef next* **40/1**	57
0-55	**9**	*17*	**Salybia Bay**[16] 2289 4-11-1 **99** NickScholfield (Andy Turnell) *hld up towards rr: hdwy appr 3 out: sn rdn: wknd bef next: t.o* **11/1**	57
124-	**10**	*16*	**Bundle Up**[216] 5359 7-11-8 **106** RhysFlint (John Flint) *trckd ldrs tl wknd 6th: t.o* **20/1**	49
10	**11**	*35*	**Clu Agus Cail (IRE)**[14] 2329 5-11-5 **103** TimmyMurphy (Alison Batchelor) *a detached in last: t.o* **14/1**	15

4m 10.0s (2.00) **Going Correction** -0.125s/f (Good)

WFA 3 from 4yo 15lb 4 from 5yo+ 7lb 11 Ran SP% **116.2**

Speed ratings (Par 105): **90,88,84,84,83 81,78,73,65,58 41**

toteswingers:1&2 £14.30, 2&3 £12.90, 1&3 £9.90 totesuper7: Win: Not won. Place: Not won. CSF £69.00 CT £592.63 TOTE £4.10: £1.20, £3.60, £4.00; EX 67.00.

Owner Mr & Mrs A J Mutch **Bred** Paul Wyatt Ranby Hall **Trained** Briery Hill, Blaenau Gwent

FOCUS

A modest mares' handicap hurdle, which was run in a slower time than the seller that opened the card. The winner was value for further.

NOTEBOOK

Babilu always travelled like the best horse in the race, but gave backers a major scare when she looked to try and duck out at the second last. Soon back on an even keel, she ran on well after that alarm. Connections said that this was out of character and she has been progressive this season. This drop in trip caused her no problem, and she copes with wetter ground. (tchd 4-1)

Posh Emily disgraced herself (refused to race) last time, but in blinkers for the first time she ran a solid enough race. She's only modest and two of her three wins have been in selling grade.

Lucy's Perfect could only muster the one pace from before two out and she will need a weak event to score. (op 9-1)

Minnie Hill(IRE) is due to go up 9lb in the near future after last week's easy win at Exeter, so connections were forced to run here. She faded tamely after being headed and hampered by the winner two out. She couldn't reproduce her seasonal debut win last season and will find life very hard now. (tchd 5-2)

Bella Medici ran her best race so far over hurdles from 11lb out of the handicap (not including jockey's allowance). She will be reassessed and still needs more before finding a race, but it was a forward step.

Ocean Transit(IRE) weakened after the third last and this was a disappointing run, with no obvious excuse. (op 9-2 tchd 11-2)

T/Jkpt: £9,742.10. Pool of £279,228.41 - 20.35 winning tickets. T/Plt: £59.00 to a £1 stake. Pool of £62,695.02 - 775.20 winning tickets. T/Qpdt: £24.80 to a £1 stake. Pool of £3,969.93 - 118.05 winning tickets. TM

2362 UTTOXETER (L-H)

Thursday, November 25

OFFICIAL GOING: Soft (heavy in places)

The final hurdle in the back straight was omitted on all circuits of all hurdle races.
Divided bends and hurdles moved out 4m to provide fresh ground.
Wind: light 1/2 against Weather: fine and sunny but cold

2640 PJD GROUP NOVICES' HURDLE (9 hdls 1 omitted) 2m
12:20 (12:21) (Class 4) 4-Y-0+ £2,211 (£649; £324; £162)

Form				RPR
1-2	1		**Silver Gypsy (IRE)**[27] 2068 5-10-5 0 (t) SeanQuinlan (Kim Bailey) *mde all: drew clr after 3 out: 19 l ahd last: eased towards fin* **2/7**[1]	99+
000	2	22	**Barrie Burn (IRE)**[15] 2307 4-10-12 0 DominicElsworth (Jonjo O'Neill) *t.k.h in rr: hdwy 5th: shkn up appr 2 out: styd on to take modest 2nd run-in* **66/1**	80+
6	3	hd	**Letmespeak (IRE)**[27] 2074 5-10-12 0 JasonMaguire (Donald McCain) *mid-div: hit 4th: reminders and hdwy next: chsd wnr 3 out: kpt on same pce run-in* **7/1**[2]	79
	4	4 ½	**Autumn Haze**[242] 5-10-12 0 PaulMoloney (Evan Williams) *w wnr: hit 5th: outpcd appr 3 out: kpt on one pce* **7/1**[2]	75
00-0	5	7	**South Stack**[25] 2109 5-10-12 0 AlanO'Keeffe (Michael Scudamore) *chsd ldrs: wknd between last 2* **80/1**	67
0-P6	6	14	**Sacco D'Oro**[12] 2362 4-10-2 0 CharlieStudd(3) (Michael Mullineaux) *mid-div: drvn and mstke 6th: sn wknd* **125/1**	46
	7	9	**Lordship (IRE)**[14] 6-10-12 0 AndrewThornton (Tony Carroll) *chsd ldrs: wknd appr 3 out* **66/1**	44
00	8	shd	**Daggerman**[15] 2307 5-10-5 0 HarryChalloner(7) (Barry Leavy) *in rr: bhd fr 6th* **100/1**	44
5	9	5	**Short Supply (USA)**[11] 2397 4-10-5 0 RobertWalford (Tim Walford) *in rr: bhd fr 6th: eased* **33/1**	32
0	10	shd	**Cluain Alainn (IRE)**[15] 2310 4-10-12 0 DaveCrosse (Ian Williams) *in rr: blnd 1st: reminders after 5th: sn bhd* **40/1**	39
0-06	11	24	**Frankie Falco**[10] 2419 4-10-12 0 JodieMogford (Giuseppe Fierro) *nt jump wl in rr: hung rt and bhd fr 5th: t.o* **100/1**	15
3/0	P		**Russian Music (USA)**[15] 2307 6-10-12 0 DougieCostello (Ian Williams) *chsd ldrs: reminders 6th: sn wknd: t.o whn p.u bef 2 out* **20/1**[3]	—
44	U		**Grey Gold (IRE)**[148] 869 5-10-12 0 JohnnyFarrelly (Richard Lee) *mid-div: mstke and uns rdr 2nd* **22/1**	—

4m 5.40s (10.20) **Going Correction** +0.75s/f (Soft)
WFA 4 from 5yo+ 7lb 13 Ran SP% **124.2**
Speed ratings (Par 105): **104,93,92,90,87 80,75,75,73,73 61,—,—**
toteswingers:1&2 £7.10, 2&3 £13.10, 1&3 £1.50 CSF £51.31 TOTE £1.20: £1.02, £11.60, £2.00.
Owner Mrs Tania D Yeomans **Bred** Mrs Clare Joyce **Trained** Andoversford, Gloucs

FOCUS
A novice hurdle that lacked strength in depth, and the easy winner stood out. She was value for further but still rated 10lb off his best. The second and fifth help set the standard.

NOTEBOOK
Silver Gypsy(IRE), beaten just a neck when well clear of the third on her only previous hurdles run, registered a comfortable first victory over jumps. She disputed the lead from the start and, once taking control in mid-race, was never seriously threatened. She drew well clear in the home straight and, while it would be unwise to get over-excited about the form of this event, should go well again under a penalty. (op 3-10 tchd 1-3)
Barrie Burn(IRE) had finished down the field on three previous runs and his presence in second puts the standard of this contest into perspective. He did much of his best work in the closing stages, however, and, judged on breeding, ought to stay longer trips. Official explanation: jockey said, regarding running and riding, that his orders were to get the gelding settled as it had not been finishing, but it was keen early off a slow pace and was unable to quicken end of back straight when leaders kicked for home, he felt it had run its best race and could be better suited by a longer trip.
Letmespeak(IRE), sixth of 15 in a bumper on his only previous outing, was well backed at each-way prices and justified the support. It was not all plain sailing, though, as he made a mistake at the fourth flight that cost him a fair bit of ground. He too stayed on nicely towards the finish but, if this is a true reflection of his ability, is clearly no star. (op 12-1)
Autumn Haze, making his hurdling debut after taking a two-finisher point-to-point, did just about enough to suggest he can win a modest race in this sphere. He tried to go with the winner in the early stages, even leading for a time, but tired late on. Given this effort, he may improve. (op 6-1)
Short Supply(USA) Official explanation: jockey said, regarding running and riding, that his orders were to jump off mid-division and ride race from there, the filly was holding its head unusually high, which made it difficult for him to push it out, adding that it had no more to give and allowed it to coast home in its own time.
Frankie Falco Official explanation: jockey said colt hung right

2641 BRIAN & BILL BIRTHDAY CELEBREATION BEGINNERS' CHASE (16 fncs) 2m 6f 110y
12:50 (12:50) (Class 4) 4-Y-0+ £2,862 (£840; £420; £209)

Form				RPR
0-5U	1		**Predictive (FR)**[12] 2363 7-11-2 130 JasonMaguire (Donald McCain) *mde all: drew clr 3 out: 8 l ahd last: heavily eased* **4/11**[1]	135+
4	2	7	**Three Chords (IRE)**[47] 1765 6-11-2 0 AndrewThornton (Caroline Bailey) *trckd ldrs: mstke 8th: wnt 2nd 10th: one pce fr 3 out* **20/1**	120
13-0	3	13	**Moorlands Teri**[32] 1986 7-10-9 0 DougieCostello (Tim Vaughan) *chsd ldrs: wknd appr 2 out* **6/1**[2]	105+
03-F	4	61	**Don't Tell Nina (IRE)**[16] 2299 6-11-2 0 DominicElsworth (Paul Webber) *chsd ldrs: lost grnd 6th: reminders 8th: sn bhd: hit 10th: t.o 4 out* **20/1**	46
F4P/	P		**Negus De Beaumont (FR)**[1006] 4084 9-11-2 0 GrahamLee (Ferdy Murphy) *in rr: bhd fr 4th: t.o 8th: p.u bef 11th* **12/1**[3]	—
/P-P	P		**The Client (IRE)**[43] 1830 9-10-9 39 JoeCornwall(7) (David Pearson) *sn bhd: drvn along 2nd: t.o 6th: p.u after 11th* **100/1**	—
3205	P		**Gothic Charm (IRE)**[10] 2420 8-11-2 104 (p) SeanQuinlan (Rachel Hobbs) *chsd wnr: reminders 6th and 8th: mstke and wknd 10th: sn bhd: t.o whn p.u after next* **16/1**	—

6m 11.1s (22.60) **Going Correction** +0.75s/f (Soft) 7 Ran SP% **111.7**
Speed ratings (Par 105): **90,87,83,61,—,—,—**
toteswingers:1&2 £4.80, 2&3 £8.30, 1&3 £1.10 CSF £9.96 TOTE £1.40: £1.20, £2.80; EX 10.20.
Owner Mr & Mrs Peter James Douglas **Bred** Michel Bourgneuf **Trained** Cholmondeley, Cheshire

FOCUS
Quite an interesting beginners' chase, despite the small field. The eased winner was 10lb off his best hurdles mark.

NOTEBOOK
Predictive(FR), twice a course winner over hurdles, was not hard-pressed to notch a first chasing success. He had unseated on his previous start but, apart from a slight mistake at the last, jumped impressively here. He led throughout, eased clear in the home straight and should win again. His owners sponsor races at Uttoxeter – including the first on this card - so it would no surprise to see him return at some stage. (op 8-13 tchd 4-6 in places)
Three Chords(IRE), a three-time point-to-point winner, had finished last of four in decent company on his one previous try over regulation fences, so this has to go down as an improvement. He was well beaten, however, despite figuring prominently from the outset, and will need to progress again in order to collect at this level. Handicap chases will probable afford him better opportunities in time. (tchd 16-1)
Moorlands Teri, a dual hurdles winner making her chasing debut, did enough to suggest she can score in this discipline, especially if she can be found suitable openings against her own sex. She jumped adequately in the main and was arguably entitled to get tired late on. (tchd 15-2)
Don't Tell Nina(IRE) had fallen on his chasing debut 16 days earlier and, while he was never in contention here, did at least complete. He had lost touch with the principals by four out, but kept plugging away gamely. (op 14-1)

2642 JOHN DRAISEY'S 80TH BIRTHDAY CELEBRATION NOVICES' HURDLE (12 hdls 2 omitted) 3m
1:25 (1:25) (Class 4) 4-Y-0+ £2,211 (£649; £324; £162)

Form				RPR
2	1		**My Boy Paddy (IRE)**[27] 2067 6-10-9 0 TomMolloy(3) (Nigel Twiston-Davies) *hld up towards rr: hdwy after 9th: wnt 2nd appr 2 out: led and hit last: drvn out* **4/9**[1]	119+
5-54	2	2 ½	**Definite Dawn (IRE)**[18] 2232 6-10-12 0 DougieCostello (Tim Vaughan) *w ldr: led 7th: hdd and hit last: kpt on same pce* **12/1**	111
0	3	29	**Duke Of Ormond (IRE)**[22] 2154 7-10-12 0 DaveCrosse (Anna Brooks) *chsd ldrs: wnt 2nd 9th: wknd appr 2 out* **66/1**	84
2	4	5	**Back Bob Back (IRE)**[27] 2069 5-10-12 0 DenisO'Regan (Tom George) *trckd ldrs: 4th and wkng whn hit 2 out* **11/2**[3]	79
00	5	2 ½	**Domoly (FR)**[20] 2192 7-10-12 0 GrahamLee (Ferdy Murphy) *hld up towards rr: effrt 9th: sn wknd* **50/1**	75
5251	6	1 ½	**Bled (FR)**[12] 2364 5-11-5 110 (b) JasonMaguire (Donald McCain) *led: drvn 4th: reminders and hdd 7th: lost pl appr 3 out* **9/2**[2]	80
06	7	22	**Hardwick Wood**[17] 2281 5-10-12 0 AndrewThornton (Caroline Bailey) *chsd ldrs: drvn 9th: sn wknd* **66/1**	51
00/	P		**Northorsouth**[1286] 336 8-10-12 0 RodiGreene (Bill Moore) *chsd ldrs: lost pl 5th: t.o 9th: p.u bef 2 out* **100/1**	—

6m 19.6s (14.40) **Going Correction** +0.75s/f (Soft) 8 Ran SP% **116.4**
Speed ratings (Par 105): **106,105,95,93,93 92,85,—**
toteswingers:1&2 £1.90, 2&3 £25.40, 1&3 £27.70 CSF £7.64 TOTE £1.60: £1.02, £2.50, £10.80; EX 8.00.
Owner Favourites Racing VII **Bred** Mrs Margaret Lucey **Trained** Naunton, Gloucs

FOCUS
A reasonable novices' hurdle, although just four appeared to hold realistic claims. The early pace was no more than steady. The winner was value for further, with the second to his mark.

NOTEBOOK
My Boy Paddy(IRE) was stepped up in trip after taking second in a decent 2m4f hurdle a month previously, and it appeared to sit him. Given a patient ride, he eased into contention approaching two out and jumped into the lead at the last. He was not entirely fluent at that final flight, but needed only to be pushed out to collect and, handled like this, should give another decent account when asked to carry a penalty. (op 8-13 tchd 2-5 and 4-6 in places)
Definite Dawn(IRE), fourth at Ffos Las on his latest start, probably ran to a similar level here. He was always near the head of affairs, leading from halfway until the winner swept past, and deserves to find a suitable opening. (op 8-1)
Duke Of Ormond(IRE), a modest Irish point-to-point winner, stepped up markedly on his only previous outing over hurdles. That said, he was still a long way behind the first two, and will need to make further progress in order to take one of these. (op 80-1)
Back Bob Back(IRE), a promising second on his only previous outing over hurdles, was rather disappointing. He raced in the first four throughout, but looked decidedly one-paced in the closing stages. (op 6-1)
Bled(FR), rated 110 after taking a handicap hurdle by 17 lengths on his most recent outing, was another to disappoint. He disputed the lead in the early stages, but was getting reminders before five from home and faded tamely from the home turn. (op 4-1 tchd 5-1)

2643 PEDLEY SCAFFOLDING H'CAP HURDLE (9 hdls 1 omitted) 2m
2:00 (2:01) (Class 5) (0-95,96) 4-Y-0+ £1,561 (£458; £229; £114)

Form				RPR
211	1		**Marino Prince (FR)**[3] 2583 5-11-10 96 7ex MarcGoldstein(3) (Jim Best) *hld up: hdwy 5th: lft in ld 2 out: clr last: drvn out* **11/10**[1]	99+
0P04	2	11	**Lady Of Ashcott**[22] 2149 4-10-0 58 (p) DougieCostello (Neil Mulholland) *chsd ldr: mstke 6th: outpcd appr next: lft 3rd 2 out: kpt on to take 2nd last 100yds* **14/1**	60
P/3-	3	9	**Imperial Royale (IRE)**[239] 4958 9-10-9 78 DaveCrosse (Patrick Clinton) *led: clr 4th to 6th: hdd appr 2 out: lft cl 2nd: 7 l 2nd last: wknd run-in: fin tired* **25/1**	59
512-	4	7	**Nous Voila (FR)**[272] 4284 9-11-5 95 KyleJames(7) (Alan Coogan) *chsd ldrs: lost pl 6th* **20/1**	68
3641	5	20	**Simone Martini (IRE)**[12] 2367 5-10-13 82 (vt) WarrenMarston (Milton Harris) *chsd ldrs: hit 4th: hrd drvn 6th: wknd appr next: sn bhd* **5/1**[3]	35
P04-	6	9	**South Bank (IRE)**[287] 3990 8-11-3 86 JohnnyFarrelly (Tim Vaughan) *towards rr: drvn 3rd: bhd and reminders 4th: t.o next* **12/1**	30
0121	F		**Lean Burn (USA)**[7] 2478 4-11-4 90 7ex DannyCook(3) (Barry Leavy) *hld up: stdy hdwy 5th: led appr 2 out: 6 l ahd whn fell heavily 2 out* **3/1**[2]	96+

4m 8.80s (13.60) **Going Correction** +0.75s/f (Soft)
WFA 4 from 5yo+ 7lb 7 Ran SP% **112.3**
Speed ratings (Par 103): **96,90,86,82,72 68,—**
toteswingers:1&2 £4.80, 2&3 £22.60, 1&3 £9.50 CSF £15.80 TOTE £2.30: £1.70, £5.60; EX 21.90.
Owner Miss J S Dollan **Bred** Newsells Park Stud Ltd **Trained** Lewes, E Sussex

FOCUS
A modest handicap hurdle, with the penalised top weight rated 96. Marino Prince is rated 10lb off his recent wins, with the faller rated as a 3l winner.

NOTEBOOK
Marino Prince(FR), successful at Hereford and Kempton this month and carrying a 7lb penalty, looked fortunate to complete his hat-trick. He eventually ran out a decisive winner, but would surely have been hard-pressed to overhaul penultimate-flight faller Lean Burn. He had the rest well beaten off, however, and, although he now faces a stiff rise from the handicapper, will probably continue to post decent efforts. (op 10-11 tchd 11-8 and 6-4 in places)

Lady Of Ashcott, whose previous form was largely uninspiring, posted easily her best effort of the season. Never too far off the pace, despite a couple of mid-race mistakes, she plugged on dourly in the closing stages. (op 25-1)
Imperial Royale(IRE) raced only once last season and, returning here from a 239-day layoff, made a bold bid to make all. He was clearly getting tired approaching two out, however, and, predictably, faded from that point on. (op 20-1 tchd 16-1)
Nous Voila(FR), a stone higher than when landing a Fakenham selling hurdle in February, was another to tire late on. That was no great surprise, as he was having his first run here for 272 days. (op 14-1)
Simone Martini(IRE), up 5lb since winning over C&D 12 days earlier, made an early mistake and was never able to mount a serious challenge thereafter. (op 7-1 tchd 9-2)
South Bank(IRE), making his seasonal debut after switching stables, was under pressure from an early stage. (op 8-1)
Lean Burn(USA), 2lb higher than when winning at Market Rasen a week earlier, might well have collected had he not fallen two out. He had a clear advantage - perhaps as much as six lengths - and seemingly plenty in left in the tank when coming down. (op 9-2 tchd 11-4)

2644 TRUCK TYRE SOLUTIONS H'CAP HURDLE (10 hdls 2 omitted) 2m 6f 110y
2:35 (2:36) (Class 4) (0-110,110) 4-Y-0+ **£2,211** (£649; £324; £162)

Form				RPR
/341	1		**Bellflower Boy (IRE)**[5] 2532 7-11-4 **109** 7ex................(tp) MrTWeston(7) (Dr Richard Newland) *hld up: hdwy to chse ldrs 7th: hrd drvn appr next: upsides 2 out: led narrowly last: styd on* **4/6**[1]	116+
1F-3	2	1 1/4	**Laborec (IRE)**[12] 2364 7-11-12 **110**.............................(p) DominicElsworth (Neil King) *chsd ldr: led 3 out: jnd next: hdd last: styd on same pce* **9/1**[3]	115
3-00	3	1 3/4	**Diktalina**[18] 2242 4-11-5 **110**.............................. OliverDayman(7) (Alison Thorpe) *in rr: hit 2nd: hdwy to chse ldrs 7th: wnt 3rd 2 out: 6 l down on 1st 2 last: kpt on* **25/1**	114
	4	14	**Clifton Pier (IRE)**[15] 2316 6-10-4 **88**.............................. JohnnyFarrelly (Mrs Prunella Dobbs, Ire) *led: mstke 2nd: hdd and hit 3 out: wknd and lost 3rd next* **9/2**[2]	81
3FF1	5	18	**Winged Farasi**[70] 1362 6-10-13 **97**.............................. TjadeCollier (Joanne Foster) *prom: reminders 6th: sn lost pl: bhd fr next* **11/1**	68
16/P	6	24	**Troys Run (IRE)**[12] 2364 7-10-11 **95**.............................. RodiGreene (Bill Moore) *prom: lost pl after 6th: sn bhd* **80/1**	42
-5P4	7	34	**Black Apache (IRE)**[17] 2275 6-11-4 **102**.........................(t) JasonMaguire (Donald McCain) *chsd ldrs: lost pl after 7th: sn bhd: t.o* **10/1**	15
0-PP	P		**Petroglyph**[12] 2364 6-10-10 **101**.............................. MrJMQuinlan(7) (Michael Quinlan) *in rr: drvn 5th: bhd fr next: t.o 7th: p.u bef next* **33/1**	—

5m 53.4s (22.50) **Going Correction** +0.75s/f (Soft)
WFA 4 from 6yo+ 8lb **8** Ran SP% **113.6**
Speed ratings (Par 105): **90,89,88,84,77 69,57,—**
toteswingers:1&2:£1.90, 2&3:£9.40, 1&3:£4.80 CSF £7.46 CT £78.51 TOTE £1.50: £1.10, £2.00, £3.10; EX 6.30.
Owner The Five Nations Partnership **Bred** Frank Sinnott **Trained** Claines, Worcs

FOCUS
Just a run-of-the-mill handicap hurdle, but several had claims. The early pace was very steady. The winner was rated a stone off his recent win over further.

NOTEBOOK
Bellflower Boy(IRE), carrying a 7lb penalty for his 21-length success at Huntingdon five days earlier, had to work a great deal harder to notch a follow up. Held up off the pace in the early stages, he had improved into third by three out and jumped upsides the runner-up at the last. His stamina proved the decisive factor on the run-in and, while his margin of victory was relatively small, it is fair to suggest that he would have been suited by a stronger gallop and a longer trip. Nonetheless, he may not find it easy to collect again from his future mark. (tchd 4-7and 8-11 in places)
Laborec(IRE) had been beaten a long way on his only previous outing this season, but had clearly come on for that run - here - and posted another admirable performance on a course that apparently suits him. Always close up, and in the lead three out, he stayed on resolutely to the line. (op 12-1)
Diktalina, whose rating had eased following two modest runs this season, now looks on a mark from which she can be competitive. Ridden patiently, she went third three out and battled on bravely thereafter. (op 16-1)
Clifton Pier(IRE), an Irish raider still looking for his initial win, tried to make all. He made a mistake at the second flight, but was still in front at the fourth last. He could not respond, though, when the first two overtook him shortly afterwards and looked one-paced late on. (op 6-1 tchd 13-2)
Winged Farasi, 5lb higher than when successful at Sedgefield in August, never threatened to add to that victory. He was third at one stage in mid-race, but faded in the closing stages. (op 10-1)

2645 SB WASTE MANAGEMENT & RECYCLING H'CAP CHASE (16 fncs) 2m 6f 110y
3:05 (3:08) (Class 5) (0-95,94) 4-Y-0+ **£1,999** (£620; £334)

Form				RPR
05P/	1		**Rebel Rock (IRE)**[648] 8-10-2 **70**.............................. PeterBuchanan (D P Keane, Ire) *in rr: hdwy whn mstke 10th: sn chsng ldr: led after 4 out: wl clr whn j. slowly last 2: nursed home* **3/1**[1]	97+
	2	6	**Glenturn (IRE)**[12] 2379 9-10-13 **81**.............................. JohnnyFarrelly (Mrs Prunella Dobbs, Ire) *in rr: hit 6th: bhd fr 9th: hdwy 4 out: wnt distant 2nd sn after 2 out: 15 l down last: kpt on* **5/1**[2]	90
P563	3	21	**Panthers Run**[16] 2301 10-10-0 **68** oh2.........................(t) DougieCostello (Jonathan Haynes) *chsd ldrs: outpcd 9th: wknd 3 out: lft dsitant 3rd appr last* **13/2**	56
-1P4	P		**Gunship (IRE)**[18] 2240 9-11-9 **94**.............................(b) DannyCook(3) (Cathy Hamilton) *chsd ldr: led 9th: sn clr: wknd and hdd after 4 out: distant 2nd and v tired whn blnd 2 out: t.o 4th whn p.u bef last* **6/1**[3]	—
6-04	P		**Aspolan (GER)**[14] 2332 7-11-2 **84**.............................(t) SeanQuinlan (Rachel Hobbs) *in rr: bhd fr 9th: t.o 4 out: p.u bef next* **10/1**	—
34-0	P		**Bearneen Boy (IRE)**[15] 2314 7-10-3 **71**.........................(p) RodiGreene (Neil King) *led: drvn 8th: hdd next: 3rd and wkng qckly whn blnd 11th: t.o next: p.u bef 4 out* **14/1**	—
5-45	P		**The Rustlin Rhino**[25] 2103 5-11-3 **85**.............................. JasonMaguire (Donald McCain) *nt jump wl: in rr: lost pl 8th: sn t.o: p.u after 10th* **3/1**[1]	—

6m 2.40s (13.90) **Going Correction** +0.75s/f (Soft) **7** Ran SP% **110.0**
Speed ratings (Par 103): **105,102,95,—,—,—,—**
CSF £17.04 CT £81.97 TOTE £3.70: £2.30, £2.80; EX 15.70.
Owner D Casey **Bred** Peter Breen **Trained** Higginstown, Co Kilkenny

FOCUS
A weak handicap that proved a real war of attrition. It was a fast time for the grade and the winner was value for a lot further, with the second to his mark.

NOTEBOOK
Rebel Rock(IRE), having his first run since taking a point-to-point 648 days earlier, came home clear of some very tired opposition. He was held up off the pace in the early stages, but had moved into third by halfway and was second at the fourth-last. He led at the next and, with most of his rivals virtually legless at that point, merely had to keep going to lift the prize. He may not be quick, but nobody could accuse him of lacking courage. Official explanation: trainer said, regarding apparent improvement in form, that the gelding had strengthened up having had a long lay-off and benefited from its subsequent point-to-point experience. (op 10-3 tchd 7-2 and 11-4)
Glenturn(IRE), an Irish raider with a 2008 Fairyhouse victory to his credit, also plugged on gamely, after racing in mid-division until out-slugging tiring rivals from the third last, although he never threatened to catch the winner. (op 13-2)
Panthers Run was racing from 2lb out of the handicap, but he stays at least this distance and, after racing in third for much of the journey, kept on at one pace in the closing stages. (op 6-1 tchd 15-2)
The Rustlin Rhino, making his chasing debut, was being pushed along as early as the fourth fence and never seemed to be enjoying himself. Official explanation: jockey said gelding never travelled (op 10-3 tchd 5-2)

2646 MUSICMAGPIE.CO.UK INTERMEDIATE OPEN NATIONAL HUNT FLAT RACE 2m
3:40 (3:40) (Class 6) 4-6-Y-0 **£1,301** (£382; £191; £95)

Form				RPR
0-2	1		**Poole Master**[12] 2368 5-10-11 0.............................. ChrisHonour(3) (David Pipe) *racd alone on inner: w ldr: led after 4f: drvn clr 7f out: rdn rt out* **6/4**[1]	110+
	2	4 1/2	**Railway Dillon (IRE)**[235] 5-11-0 0.............................. JasonMaguire (Donald McCain) *chsd ldrs: drvn to chse wnr 6f out: rdn 4f out: edgd lft and kpt on fnl 2f: no imp* **3/1**[2]	106+
	3	20	**Jan Jandura (IRE)**[192] 376 5-11-0 0.............................. JohnnyFarrelly (Tim Vaughan) *hld up: hdwy 6f out: drvn and hung lft over 3f out: sn wknd* **4/1**[3]	89
	4	7	**Just Benny (IRE)**[242] 5-11-0 0.............................. SeanQuinlan (Richard Phillips) *prom: drvn 7f out: hung lft and lost pl over 4f out* **33/1**	79
	5	3	**Aeneid**[438] 1442 5-11-0 0.............................. DougieCostello (Brian Rothwell) *prom: lost pl 7f out* **11/2**	76
	6	15	**Get Ready To Go (IRE)**[585] 6-11-0 0.............................. DenisO'Regan (Neil King) *prom: lost pl over 5f out: bhd fnl 4f* **10/1**	61
	7	123	**Charlie's Boy** 4-11-0 0.............................. DominicElsworth (Tobias B P Coles) *led 4f: lost pl 7f out: sn bhd: t.o 4f out* **12/1**	—

3m 58.2s (8.60) **Going Correction** +0.75s/f (Soft) **7** Ran SP% **120.1**
Speed ratings: **108,105,95,92,90 83,—**
toteswingers:1&2 £2.20, 2&3 £2.30, 1&3£2.60 CSF £6.74 TOTE £2.60: £1.90, £1.80; EX 7.90.
Owner G Thompson **Bred** Wood Farm Stud **Trained** Nicholashayne, Devon

FOCUS
An interesting finale featuring both proven bumper performers and well-bred newcomers to the discipline. Not an easy race to put a figure on but the winner is rated up 5lb on his recent course run.

NOTEBOOK
Poole Master, beaten only a short-head here when making his debut for this yard 12 days earlier, made all for a convincing success. He was slightly keen in the early stages - and his jockey seemed eager to keep him away from the others for as long as possible - but had settled by halfway and never looked likely to be headed. He has the size and scope to make a decent hurdler. (op 11-8 tchd 13-8 and 7-4 in places)
Railway Dillon(IRE) was bought for £25,000 after taking an Irish point-to-point in April, and did enough to suggest that was money wisely spent. He could not match the winner, but was second from a long way out and beat the rest comfortably. (op 7-2)
Jan Jandura(IRE), runner-up in a Roscommon bumper on his latest outing in May, gives the form a solid look. Held up early, he went third at halfway and maintained that position - albeit a long way adrift of the winner - all the way to the finish. (op 5-1 tchd 11-2)
Just Benny(IRE), pulled up in his only point-to-point, showed a glimpse of ability, but will need to improve to take an average race of this type. Official explanation: jockey said gelding hung badly left in straight
Aeneid, making his first appearance for these connections after two solid runs in Irish bumpers, was disappointing. He faded in the closing stages and may have needed this first run for 438 days. (op 15-2)
T/Plt: £17.90 to a £1 stake. Pool of £40,797.41 - 1,656.75 winning tickets. T/Qpdt: £14.90 to a £1 stake. Pool of £3,500.74 - 172.93 winning tickets. WG

2647 - 2653a (Foreign Racing) - See Raceform Interactive

2505 MUSSELBURGH (R-H)
Friday, November 26

OFFICIAL GOING: Good (good to firm in places; 6.2)
Rails on bends moved out 2m.
Wind: Fresh, against Weather: Cold, dry

2654 BALFOUR BEATTY ENGINEERING SERVICES CONDITIONAL JOCKEYS' H'CAP HURDLE (14 hdls) 3m 110y
12:10 (12:10) (Class 4) (0-100,98) 4-Y-0+ **£3,252** (£955; £477; £238)

Form				RPR
-610	1		**Buckstruther (IRE)**[14] 2351 8-10-10 **87**...................... NathanMoscrop(5) (Andrew Parker) *led to 1st: cl up: hdwy to chal 3 out: sn rdn: led run-in: styd on wl* **17/2**	90
/125	2	1 3/4	**Grand Art (IRE)**[94] 1362 6-11-6 **98**.............................(vt[1]) MrTomDavid(6) (Tim Vaughan) *hld up: smooth hdwy to ld 3 out: rdn bef last: hdd run-in: kpt on same pce* **13/2**	99
600/	3	6	**Harps Counsel (IRE)**[16] 2317 8-11-9 **95**...................... JamesO'Farrell (J K Magee, Ire) *j.lft: led 1st to 3 out: sn rdn: kpt on same pce fr next* **28/1**	93+
1233	4	2 3/4	**Auberge (IRE)**[28] 2080 6-11-8 **94**.............................. EwanWhillans (Dianne Sayer) *trckd ldrs: effrt 3 out: outpcd fr next* **4/1**[1]	88
-P05	5	1/2	**Vallani (IRE)**[14] 2353 5-10-8 **83**.............................. CampbellGillies(3) (Lucinda Russell) *nt fluent: trckd ldrs: outpcd and dropped to rr bef 3 out: rallied bef last: no imp run-in* **9/2**[2]	78+
5400	6	3/4	**Sambelucky (IRE)**[14] 2351 5-10-5 **80**.............................. KyleJames(3) (Keith Reveley) *hld up: drvn to improve bef 3 out: sn no imp* **5/1**[3]	71
4	7	shd	**Dickie Henderhoop (IRE)**[65] 1578 5-10-9 **87**.............. AlexanderVoy(6) (Lucy Normile) *hld up: outpcd 8th: effrt on outside after 3 out: plugged on fr last: no imp* **14/1**	78
2P50	8	1/2	**Kyber**[20] 2203 9-11-4 **98**.............................. PaulNorton(8) (Jim Goldie) *hld up: drvn bef 3 out: nvr able to chal* **16/1**	89
-0P0	9	2 1/4	**Sam Patch**[14] 2351 7-10-0 **80**.............................(t) CallumWhillans(8) (Donald Whillans) *mstkes: hld up in tch on outside: struggling after 3 out: btn whn hit last* **28/1**	68
-600	10	9	**Accordingtotheboss (IRE)**[20] 2208 5-10-13 **88**.......(p) FearghalDavis(3) (Nicky Richards) *prom: nt fluent 5th: rdn and wknd after 3 out* **6/1**	67

5m 50.6s (-6.10) **Going Correction** -0.475s/f (Good) **10** Ran SP% **112.4**
Speed ratings (Par 105): **90,89,87,86,86 86,86,86,85,82**
Tote Swingers: 1&2 £10.60, 1&3 £11.60, 2&3 £16.90 CSF £60.84 CT £1464.11 TOTE £10.80: £3.30, £2.20, £9.60; EX 82.70.
Owner Alastair and Rachel Bell **Bred** Mrs Rita Doocey **Trained** Ecclefechan, D'fries & G'way

The Form Book, Raceform Ltd, Compton, RG20 6NL

FOCUS
The ground seemed to be riding as advertised. This modest handicap hurdle was run at a pretty steady pace until it lifted on the approach to the final three flights. The form has an unsatisfactory look to it, although the first two did pull clear of the rest, most of whom finished in a heap. The race is rated around the first three.
NOTEBOOK
Buckstruther(IRE) could not adopt his favoured front-running role but he was always up with the pace before fighting on well to hold the runner-up. He has now won five of his last eight races, point-to-points included, and the easier ground may have contributed to a below-par at effort at Newcastle last time. Official explanation: trainer said, regarding apparent improvement in form, that the gelding was better suited by the faster ground. (op 9-1 tchd 15-2)
Grand Art(IRE)'s yard won this event two years ago with prolific scorer Little Shilling. Fitted with both a visor and a tongue tie for the first time on this return from three months off, he travelled noticeably well and looked set to collect when challenging two from home, but just looked to be outbattled by the winner. It might have been that his stamina for this trip was ebbing away, despite the steady tempo of the race. (op 9-2 tchd 7-1)
Harps Counsel(IRE) is a winning pointer in Ireland, and this handicap debut was his best effort so far over hurdles. Securing the early lead in the face of competition from the winner, he jumped out to his left for most of the way and could not hold on after trying to quicken things up on the home turn. (op 33-1)
Auberge(IRE) is a consistent mare and she appeared to give her running again back in fourth, but she has a modest strike rate and is now operating on a career-high mark. (op 7-2 tchd 10-3)
Vallani(IRE), who came in for support, was formerly trained by the late Peter Monteith. She lost her pitch and was the first in trouble when the pace lifted, but was staying on again. (op 6-1)
Dickie Henderhoop(IRE) Official explanation: jockey said gelding hung left
Accordingtotheboss(IRE) was soon left behind when the race began in earnest, and he does not look straightforward. (op 13-2 tchd 11-2)

2655 SALTIRE 2010 JUVENILE HURDLE (9 hdls) 2m
12:40 (12:40) (Class 4) 3-Y-O **£2,602** (£764; £382; £190)

Form				RPR
	1		**The Starboard Bow**[59] 3-10-12 0 PeterBuchanan (Lucinda Russell) *mde all: qcknd appr 3 out: edgd lft and styd on wl fr last* **2/1**[2]	104+
1102	**2**	1 ¾	**Meetings Man (IRE)**[28] 2078 3-11-7 122 AlexanderVoy(5) (Micky Hammond) *t.k.h: trckd ldrs: wnt 2nd 3 out: effrt and edgd rt after last: kpt on: hld towards fin* **11/8**[1]	115
2	**3**	10	**Makbullet**[44] 1825 3-10-9 0 JamesO'Farrell(3) (Michael Smith) *in tch: effrt whn hit 3 out: sn rdn and outpcd: no imp fr next* **9/1**[3]	93+
05	**4**	6	**Capricornus (USA)**[30] 2033 3-10-12 0 GrahamLee (Ferdy Murphy) *nt fluent on occasions: hld up: effrt bef 3 out: sn no imp* **14/1**	84
	5	1 ¾	**Sweet Caroline (IRE)**[252] 3-10-2 0 FearghalDavis(3) (Nicky Richards) *t.k.h: chsd wnr to 3 out: rdn and wknd fr next* **40/1**	75
24	**6**	6	**Almutaham (USA)**[33] 1984 3-10-12 96 PaddyAspell (James Moffatt) *hld up: drvn and outpcd bef 3 out: sn btn* **12/1**	76
	7	6	**I Got Music**[52] 3-10-5 0 JamesReveley (Keith Reveley) *hld up on outside: struggling bef 3 out: sn wknd* **12/1**	63
	8	20	**Barton Bounty**[69] 3-10-12 0 BrianHughes (Peter Niven) *hld up in tch: drvn bef 3 out: sn wknd* **66/1**	50

3m 45.3s (-3.10) **Going Correction** -0.475s/f (Good) **8** Ran SP% **111.4**
Speed ratings (Par 104): **88,87,82,79,78 75,72,62**
Tote Swingers: 1&2 £1.10, 1&3 £8.00, 2&3 £3.20 CSF £4.99 TOTE £2.60: £1.10, £1.10, £2.20; EX 5.60.
Owner John R Adam & Sons **Bred** Stratford Place Stud **Trained** Arlary, Perth & Kinross
FOCUS
Won by the very useful Carlito Brigante 12 months ago, this was a reasonable juvenile hurdle. It looked to be run at a decent pace but the time was slow compared with the later handicap and the form is suspect.
NOTEBOOK
The Starboard Bow ◆, an all-the-way winner, looks a useful recruit to this game. Twice successful on the Flat for Sylvester Kirk, and rated 78, he stays 2m in that sphere and will get further over hurdles. There is more to come from him after this taking victory, but on the debit side he looks a little headstrong and his jumping could be more polished. A suitable target could be the Scottish Triumph Hurdle here in February, which Carlito Brigante went on to win last season after taking this event. (op 11-4)
Meetings Man(IRE) set a reasonable standard on his surprise second (to a 100/1-shot) in a Listed race last time, but was saddled with a double penalty for his two wins. Keen behind the leaders through the first part of the race, he was outpaced by the winner two from home but rallied well after the last. This was a solid effort. (tchd 5-4 and 6-4)
Makbullet has left Howard Johnson's yard since his hurdles debut. He ran reasonably again here, if never reaching a threatening position, and gets the 2m well enough on a sharp track like this. (op 17-2 tchd 7-1)
Capricornus(USA) ran his best race so far over hurdles and his options now include handicaps. (tchd 12-1)
Sweet Caroline(IRE) was well held in a couple of Polytrack maidens for Barry Hills, the second of them back in March. She is out of an unraced half-sister to Champion Hurdle winner Sublimity and showed a bit of ability on this first try over hurdles, fading two from home after racing prominently. (op 33-1)
Almutaham(USA) made the frame on his first two tries over hurdles, but was ridden differently and was always in the rear division this time. Official explanation: vet said colt finished lame behind (tchd 11-1)

2656 WEATHERBYS PRINTING NOVICES' H'CAP CHASE (16 fncs) 2m 4f
1:15 (1:15) (Class 4) (0-105,105) 4-Y-0+ **£3,252** (£955; £477; £238)

Form				RPR
4335	**1**		**Storm Prospect**[20] 2203 7-11-0 93 (b) PeterBuchanan (Lucinda Russell) *cl up: wnt 2nd 8th: led 10th: mde rest: qcknd clr bef 4 out: unchal after* **10/3**[1]	106+
4450	**2**	15	**Heavenly Chorus**[20] 2208 8-11-2 95 JamesReveley (Keith Reveley) *led to 10th: effrt and rdn bef 4 out: one pce next: hld whn blnd last* **7/2**[2]	99+
06-6	**3**	2	**Apache Blue (IRE)**[204] 176 6-10-13 92 BrianHughes (John Wade) *nt fluent on occasions: midfield: effrt after 5 out: no imp fr next: lft 10 l 3rd 3 out* **4/1**[3]	91
346U	**4**	17	**Tranos (USA)**[14] 2352 7-10-11 90 (p) TomMessenger (Micky Hammond) *hld up: reminders 3rd: hdwy and prom 1/2-way: wknd after 5 out* **16/1**	72
0-50	**5**	2 ¾	**Papa Drew (IRE)**[17] 2302 6-10-0 79 CampbellGillies (Andrew Parker) *nt fluent in rr: struggling fr 9th: nvr on terms* **6/1**	58
460F	**P**		**Baaher (USA)**[7] 2510 6-11-12 105 WilsonRenwick (Jim Goldie) *hld up: struggling fnl circ: t.o whn p.u bef 4 out* **11/1**	—
3-60	**U**		**Devil Water**[26] 2107 7-11-2 102 NathanMoscrop(7) (James Ewart) *chsd ldr to 8th: cl up: rdn bef 4 out: 7 l 3rd and outpcd whn mstke and uns rdr next* **9/1**	101
PP-F	**P**		**Hard To Name**[18] 2270 7-10-1 80 BrianHarding (Alan Mactaggart) *nt fluent: bhd: struggling fnl circ: t.o whn p.u bef 4 out* **20/1**	—

5m 2.80s (1.60) **Going Correction** +0.225s/f (Yiel) **8** Ran SP% **108.6**
Speed ratings (Par 105): **105,99,98,91,90 —,—,—**
Tote Swingers: 1&2 £1.80, 1&3 £4.00, 2&3 £3.70 CSF £14.28 CT £40.74 TOTE £3.80: £1.40, £1.30, £1.50; EX 17.40.
Owner Mutual Friends **Bred** Mill House Stud **Trained** Arlary, Perth & Kinross
FOCUS
Few counted in this modest novice handicap, which was run at a good clip. The winner has long been on a fair mark and the second was below her best.
NOTEBOOK
Storm Prospect had not got his head in front in 21 races stretching back two and a half years, but had made the frame 11 times since that last win. He is pretty consistent and jumps soundly though, and was never in much danger after pulling clear turning into the home straight. This may have done his confidence some good, if not his handicap mark. (op 7-2)
Heavenly Chorus is usually held up, but adopted very different tactics on this return to fences and went out in front. Seen off by the winner from the home turn, she was no threat when walking through the last. (op 10-3 tchd 3-1)
Apache Blue(IRE), formerly with Howard Johnson, ran respectably on his chasing debut and is entitled to build on this first start since May. (op 6-1)
Tranos(USA) tends to get outpaced over 2m, but again failed to prove his stamina for this far. (op 11-1)
Devil Water, back up in trip for this second run after his summer break, was held in third place when parting company three from home. (op 8-1)

2657 EDINBURGH EVENING NEWS MAIDEN HURDLE (12 hdls) 2m 4f
1:50 (1:50) (Class 4) 4-Y-0+ **£2,602** (£764; £382; £190)

Form				RPR
30-F	**1**		**Jago River (IRE)**[28] 2075 4-11-0 0 BrianHughes (Howard Johnson) *trckd ldrs: wnt 2nd 5th: led gng wl 3 out: rdn last: hld on wl run-in* **6/4**[2]	105+
	2	¾	**Chocolate Caramel (USA)**[11] 8-11-0 0 GrahamLee (Richard Fahey) *in tch: effrt bef 3 out: ev ch next: nt fluent last: kpt on u.p* **13/2**[3]	103
56-0	**3**	½	**Return Perk (IRE)**[41] 1867 7-11-0 0 BarryKeniry (Jim Goldie) *t.k.h: chsd ldr to 5th: prom: effrt whn hit 2 out: rallied bef last: kpt on run-in: hld towards fin* **50/1**	103
-262	**4**	3 ½	**Mini Beck**[17] 2300 11-10-9 120 AlexanderVoy(5) (Sandy Thomson) *led: nt fluent 5th: rdn and hdd 3 out: outpcd fr next* **11/10**[1]	100
0	**5**	10	**Latin Connection (IRE)**[65] 1579 4-11-0 107 PeterBuchanan (S R B Crawford, Ire) *prom: effrt after 4 out: rdn and wknd after next* **20/1**	90
0/-0	**P**		**Bob Jackson (IRE)**[22] 2162 8-11-0 0 JohnnyFarrelly (Elliott Cooper) *bhd: lost tch after 5th: t.o whn p.u bef 7th* **100/1**	—

4m 41.4s (-10.10) **Going Correction** -0.475s/f (Good) **6** Ran SP% **108.7**
Speed ratings (Par 105): **101,100,100,99,95 —**
Tote Swingers: 1&2 £1.80, 1&3 £4.00, 2&3 £3.70 CSF £10.18 TOTE £2.70: £1.80, £2.40; EX 8.00.
Owner Andrea & Graham Wylie **Bred** P Byrne **Trained** Billy Row, Co Durham
FOCUS
They seemed to go a reasonable gallop in this ordinary maiden hurdle, and the time was decent, but all bar one were still in contention as they entered the home straight and the form may not prove entirely solid. The winner and fifth set the level.
NOTEBOOK
Jago River(IRE) was in second place when falling at the last on his hurdles debut at Wetherby, and the winner and runner-up in that contest have gone on to score since. Getting past his market rival two out, he had to work to hold off challengers on either side of him up the run-in and give his yard its third consecutive win in this event. (op 6-5)
Chocolate Caramel(USA) is a little long in the tooth to be trying hurdling, and he is rated only 58 on the Flat these days. He was less than fluent, but still had every chance and obviously has a bit of ability. (op 8-1 tchd 6-1)
Return Perk(IRE) showed a lot more than on his recent reappearance and rallied to briefly look a threat on the run-in. This was an encouraging effort, but it remains to be seen if this tall gelding is flattered by this. (op 40-1)
Mini Beck was the form pick, but after making the running again he could not counter when headed. The 11-y-o remains a maiden under rules. (op 6-4 tchd 7-4 in a place)
Latin Connection(IRE) seemed not to stay this longer trip. (tchd 18-1 and 25-1)

2658 JEDEN BUSINESS FLOORING H'CAP HURDLE (9 hdls) 2m
2:25 (2:28) (Class 4) (0-100,100) 3-Y-0+ **£3,252** (£955; £477; £238)

Form				RPR
0000	**1**		**Sheriff Hall (IRE)**[54] 1700 5-10-5 79 (t) JanFaltejsek (George Charlton) *trckd ldrs: led after 2nd: clr after next tl hit 2 out: hdd last: styd on wl u.p run-in to regain ld nr fin* **18/1**	91+
-621	**2**	hd	**Switched Off**[8] 2485 5-11-11 99 (p) DougieCostello (Ian Williams) *hld up in tch: hdwy after 4 out: effrt and led whn hit last: rdn: carried hd awkwardly and nt keen run-in: edgd lft and hdd nr fin* **9/4**[2]	111+
44-	**3**	3	**Whaston (IRE)**[15] 1520 5-11-2 90 BrianHughes (Pauline Robson) *prom: effrt bef 2 out: kpt on same pce run-in* **12/1**	98
0536	**4**	7	**Long Distance (FR)**[20] 2208 5-11-7 95 (v) CampbellGillies (Lucinda Russell) *bhd: nt fluent 5th: plenty to do bef 3 out: styd on strly fr last: nrst fin* **10/1**[3]	97
4-62	**5**	1 ¾	**Pillar Of Hercules (IRE)**[7] 2508 6-11-12 100 GrahamLee (Ferdy Murphy) *hld up: stdy hdwy and in tch whn hit 2 out: sn no imp* **15/8**[1]	102+
1-00	**6**	2	**Waterloo Corner**[20] 2208 8-11-11 99 KennyJohnson (Ray Craggs) *prom tl rdn and outpcd after 3 out: n.d after* **66/1**	97
06-0	**7**	3 ½	**Red Tanber (IRE)**[203] 191 7-10-6 80 AdrianLane (Bruce Mactaggart) *hld up: hdwy and in tch after 4 out: rdn and no ex fr next* **66/1**	75
2004	**8**	1 ¼	**Heart Of Dubai (USA)**[17] 2300 5-11-7 95 (p) BarryKeniry (Micky Hammond) *t.k.h: in tch: rdn and outpcd whn blnd 3 out: sn btn* **20/1**	90
0603	**9**	7	**Itstooearly**[20] 2208 7-11-2 90 PaddyAspell (James Moffatt) *bhd: struggling 1/2-way: nvr on terms* **33/1**	76
50-0	**10**	4 ½	**Heart O' The West (IRE)**[26] 2104 6-11-11 99 JamesReveley (Andrew Parker) *bhd: struggling 4th: nvr on terms* **50/1**	80
4302	**11**	3 ¾	**Bocciani (GER)**[33] 1997 5-11-2 93 JamesO'Farrell(3) (Dianne Sayer) *hld up in midfield on outside: hdwy after 4 out: rdn and wknd fr next* **28/1**	71
20PP	**12**	¾	**Overyou**[18] 2271 5-11-0 88 JohnnyFarrelly (Elliott Cooper) *hld up: struggling 1/2-way: nvr on terms* **14/1**	65
10P0	**13**	15	**Balnagore**[49] 1762 6-11-6 94 PeterBuchanan (Lucinda Russell) *led to after 2nd: lost pl whn hit 4th: sn struggling* **16/1**	56

2-40 **14** *31* **Tae Kwon Do (USA)**35 1953 4-11-4 **97**......................(p) AlexanderVoy(5) 28
(Julie Camacho) *w ldr: j. bdly lft first two: cl up tl rdn and wknd after 4 out* **50/1**

3m 38.6s (-9.80) **Going Correction** -0.475s/f (Good)
WFA 4 from 5yo+ 7lb **14** Ran SP% **118.2**
Speed ratings (Par 105): **105,104,103,99,99 98,96,95,92,89 88,87,80,64**
Tote Swingers: 1&2 £20.70, 1&3 £20.50, 2&3 £8.10 CSF £56.47 CT £528.87 TOTE £24.40: £5.40, £1.70, £3.20; EX 125.40.
Owner Mr & Mrs Raymond Anderson Green **Bred** Dorothy O'Keeffe **Trained** Stocksfield, Northumberland

FOCUS
Quite a competitive handicap hurdle, run at a sound pace and in a time more than four seconds inside the standard. The form should prove solid and it looks a race to be positive about. The winner improved to the level of his bumper form.

NOTEBOOK
Sheriff Hall(IRE) is usually held up but a change of tactics paid off. Still clear facing up to the last three flights, the game looked up when he was headed, but he took advantage of the runner-up's lack of application to get back up on the flat. The tongue tie had a beneficial effect on this scopey gelding, who should make a chaser. Official explanation: trainer said, regarding apparent improvement in form, that the gelding was better suited by making the running and the fitting of the first-time tongue strap. (op 16-1)
Switched Off was able to race off the same mark as when winning at Wincanton and was officially 8lb well in. He came through to lead at the last, which he flattened, but carried his head to one side on the run-in and wouldn't run on until he was headed, by which time it was too late. The impending weight rise may not prevent him from running well, but he is one to be wary of. (op 11-4)
Whaston(IRE), who has been in action on the AW lately, was making his handicap debut on only his third run over hurdles. He ran a pleasing race but lacked the pace of the first two from the final flight. (op 16-1)
Long Distance(FR), on whom a visor replaced cheekpieces, made good late progress under pressure. He is well handicapped if he ever gets things right and could be worth a try over 2m4f. (tchd 9-1)
Pillar Of Hercules(IRE) was another who was ahead of the handicapper, in his case by 5lb after his second over C&D last time. He travelled well off the pace as usual but although he made headway, fourth position was as close as he managed to reach. (op 2-1 tchd 7-4)
Waterloo Corner ran his best race of the season so far.
Red Tanber(IRE) was not discredited on his handicap debut after a break.
Heart Of Dubai(USA), who has been dropped 4lb, was not far behind the leaders when he was down on his nose three from home. (op 33-1)
Balnagore took his chance after appearing to receive a kick from another horse down at the start. (op 14-1)

2659 CLARKSON HILL GROUP PLC ST ANDREW'S DAY CHASE H'CAP (12 fncs) 2m
2:55 (2:55) (Class 3) (0-120,119) 4-Y-0+ **£6,505** (£1,910; £955; £477)

Form RPR
1012 **1** **Kosta Brava (FR)**20 2207 6-11-3 **110**............................. WilsonRenwick 118
(Howard Johnson) *t.k.h: trckd ldrs: hdwy to ld after 4 out: kpt on wl fr 2 out* **2/5**1
U6/6 **2** *7* **Kit Carson (IRE)**17 2301 10-10-0 **93** oh8............................ PaddyAspell 97
(R MacDonald) *t.k.h: cl up: hdwy to ld 7th: hdd after next: chal 4 out: hit and no ex fr 2 out* **22/1**
55 **3** *5* **The Cockney Squire (IRE)**20 2207 5-11-5 **112**........... PeterBuchanan 113+
(Lucinda Russell) *hld up in tch: drvn and outpcd 5 out: nt fluent next: no imp* **7/2**2
0FP **4** *9* **Follow The Sun (IRE)**10 2301 6-10-0 **93** oh3................... BrianHughes 84
(Peter Niven) *nt fluent: led to 7th: rallied to ld after next: hdd after 4 out: wknd after next* **10/1**3

4m 0.40s (8.00) **Going Correction** +0.225s/f (Yiel) **4** Ran SP% **107.1**
Speed ratings (Par 107): **89,85,83,78**
CSF £7.15 TOTE £1.40; EX 6.40.
Owner Andrea & Graham Wylie **Bred** Guy Blasco **Trained** Billy Row, Co Durham

FOCUS
A weak handicap chase for the grade, and not form to treat too positively. The winner has been rated to his mark.

NOTEBOOK
Kosta Brava(FR) was able to race from the same mark as when runner-up at Kelso and looked to face a straightforward task. He briefly appeared in trouble on the home turn and stumbled at the first up the straight, but led at the next and was well on top in the end. (op 1-3)
Kit Carson(IRE) ran creditably from 8lb out of the handicap on this second run back after a lengthy absence. He is well handicapped on his form in his younger days in Ireland for Charlie Swan, and to a lesser extent that for Martin Todhunter a couple of seasons ago. (op 20-1 tchd 25-1)
The Cockney Squire(IRE) took a long time to settle in last place and was left trailing by the other three before the straight, but was keeping on when it was all over. (tchd 4-1)
Follow The Sun(IRE), 3lb out of the handicap and running for only the second time over fences, made the running but did not last long when headed. (op 20-1)

2660 BORDER SAFEGUARD LTD MAIDEN OPEN NATIONAL HUNT FLAT RACE 2m
3:30 (3:30) (Class 5) 4-6-Y-0 **£1,951** (£573; £286; £143)

Form RPR
20-2 **1** **First Rock (IRE)**54 1702 4-11-2 0...................................... BrianHughes 102+
(Alan Swinbank) *t.k.h: cl up: led over 4f out: pushed out fr over 1f out* **8/11**1
5-0 **2** *1 3/4* **Big Sam**184 474 5-11-2 0... BarryKeniry 98
(Bruce Hellier) *hld up: hdwy over 3f out: chsd wnr ins fnl f: r.o* **33/1**
40 **3** *2 1/4* **Thurnham**14 2355 4-11-2 0... JamesReveley 96
(Keith Reveley) *hld up in tch: hdwy to chse wnr 3f out: rdn and edgd rt over 1f out: no ex and lost 2nd ins fnl f* **9/1**3
00 **4** *3 3/4* **Blazing Bay (IRE)**33 1989 5-10-9 0.................................. PaddyAspell 85
(James Moffatt) *t.k.h: trckd ldrs: rdn over 3f out: kpt on same pce fr 2f out* **16/1**
0 **5** *15* **Tobayornottobay**22 2167 4-10-2 0.............................. MrTomDavid(7) 70
(Bruce Hellier) *hld up: rdn 3f out: edgd rt and sn outpcd* **100/1**
6 *4* **Little Fifi** 5-10-9 0.. CampbellGillies 66
(Sandy Thomson) *bhd: drvn and outpcd 5f out: n.d after* **40/1**
6 **7** *10* **Pompan (IRE)**44 1824 4-11-2 0... GrahamLee 68+
(Peter Niven) *plld hrd: led at stdy gallop tl hdd over 4f out: wknd fr 3f out* **5/2**2
8 *58* **Plutonium (IRE)** 4-10-9 0... StevenGagan(7) 5
(Elliott Cooper) *in tch: outpcd 6f out: sn btn* **28/1**
0 **9** *6* **Lemon Queen (IRE)**22 2167 4-10-9 0............................. JohnnyFarrelly —
(Elliott Cooper) *t.k.h: cl up tl rdn and wknd over 4f out* **100/1**

3m 43.4s (0.60) **Going Correction** -0.475s/f (Good) **9** Ran SP% **113.2**
Speed ratings: **79,78,77,75,67 65,60,31,28**
Tote Swingers: 1&2 £5.40, 1&3 £2.00, 2&3 £11.90 CSF £38.00 TOTE £1.70: £1.02, £4.80, £2.40; EX 29.20.
Owner United Five Racing **Bred** K Molloy **Trained** Melsonby, N Yorks

FOCUS
An ordinary bumper. It was slowly run and the form was suspect.

NOTEBOOK
First Rock(IRE) was the pick on his previous form, finishing runner-up on two of his three previous starts although out of his depth in an Aintree Grade 2 in between. He won this comfortably enough after going on entering the straight and has the scope to make a go of things over hurdles. (op 4-5 tchd evens in places)
Big Sam, formerly with Martin Todhunter, was making his debut for a new yard after six months off. He travelled quite well towards the back and ran on nicely for second in the latter stages. (op 25-1)
Thurnham ran much better than he had at Newcastle a fortnight earlier. Easier ground and a greater emphasis on stamina will help his cause. (op 4-1)
Blazing Bay(IRE)'s two previous runs had been in better affairs that this at Aintree and this effort confirmed her limitations. (op 20-1)
Pompan(IRE) came in for support, but he failed to settle in front and showed evidence of a quirky side. (op 11-2)
T/Plt: £39.70 to a £1 stake. Pool of £45,224.37 - 829.86 winning tickets. T/Qpdt: £7.30 to a £1 stake. Pool of £3,977.07 - 402.60 winning tickets. RY

2626 NEWBURY (L-H)
Friday, November 26

OFFICIAL GOING: Good to soft (soft in places on hurdle course)
Both courses set wide increasing distances by about 40m per circuit.
Wind: Virtually nil Weather: Sunny

2661 Q ASSOCIATES JUVENILE HURDLE (8 hdls) 2m 110y
12:30 (12:30) (Class 3) 3-Y-0 **£6,505** (£1,910; £955; £477)

Form RPR
1 **Smad Place (FR)**130 3-10-12 0................................. WayneHutchinson 137+
(Alan King) *in tch: hdwy to cl on ldrs after 4 out: chsd ldr after 3 out: chal next: sn led: pushed clr appr last: easily* **8/1**3
1 **2** *27* **Dolatulo (FR)**20 2211 3-11-8 0.. APMcCoy 129+
(Paul Nicholls) *led: j. slowly 3rd and jnd tl after 4 out: drvn and jnd again whn blnd 2 out and hdd: no ch w wnr whn mstke last* **1/4**1
3 *13* **On Khee**43 3-10-5 0... TomScudamore 96+
(Hughie Morrison) *trckd ldrs: chsd ldr after 4 out: no imp and dropped to 3rd after 3 out: no ch after next* **7/1**2
4 *21* **Missionaire (USA)**35 3-10-12 0....................................... DenisO'Regan 82
(Tony Carroll) *in tch: sme hdwy to cl on ldrs after 4th: wknd bef next* **10/1**
0 **5** *6* **Lamps**16 2306 3-10-12 0... NickScholfield 77
(Michael Blake) *a in rr* **50/1**
6 **6** *44* **Professeur Emery (FR)**40 1882 3-10-12 0............................ NoelFehily 37
(Warren Greatrex) *trckd ldr: chal fr3rd to 4 out: wknd sn after: t.o* **16/1**
4 **7** *40* **Meglio Ancora**20 2211 3-10-12 0.. JamieMoore 1
(Jonathan Portman) *hit 4 out: a in rr and no ch after: t.o* **20/1**
P **Joan's Legacy**164 3-9-12 0.. MrJBanks(7) —
(Jimmy Fox) *j. slowly 2nd: sn t.o: p.u bef 3 out* **100/1**
P **Cuts Both Ways (USA)**228 3-10-12 0................................. TomO'Brien —
(Matthew Salaman) *a in rr: t.o whn p.u bef 3 out* **50/1**

4m 2.47s (-7.43) **Going Correction** -0.25s/f (Good) **9** Ran SP% **128.3**
Speed ratings (Par 106): **107,94,88,78,75 54,35,—,—**
Tote Swingers: 1&2 £1.10, 1&3 £4.10, 2&3 £1.20 CSF £12.06 TOTE £8.80: £1.70, £1.10, £1.70; EX 13.40 Trifecta £26.20 Pool: £931.59 - 26.30 winning units..
Owner Mrs Peter Andrews **Bred** Eric Aubree & Mme Maryse Aubree **Trained** Barbury Castle, Wilts

FOCUS
A well-run juvenile event which saw an easy winner, who looks a high-class recruit and is currently second in the juvenile rankings. The penalised second sets the level.

NOTEBOOK
Smad Place(FR) was making his British debut and this was his third outing over hurdles, having finished runner-up on his previous outing in July. He bided his time before making his move turning for home and it was clear in between the final two flights he was the one to be on. After making his way over to the stands' rail, which may well have been an advantage, he came right away after the last and looks a promising recruit to the juvenile division. He clearly stays well and the Grade 1 Future Champions Finale Hurdle at Chepstow on Welsh National day next month looks a viable target, which his trainer later confirmed to be his next port of call. He was later introduced into the ante-post betting for the Triumph Hurdle as short as 12/1 (Paddy Power).
Dolatulo(FR) hacked up when making it 2-2 over hurdles on his British debut for new connections at Sandown 20 days earlier and was all the rage to extend his yard's decent record in this race. He had not beaten much there, though, and was conceding upwards of 10lb all round here. He set out to make all again, but had to go off quicker this time and could've settled better. The writing was already on the wall for him prior to clouting the final flight, and he was laboured thereafter. He now has something to prove.
On Khee ◆, rated 75 on the level, was given a positive ride on this switch to hurdles and went well until feeling the pinch after two out. She ought to be winning on one of the smaller tracks.
Missionaire(USA) cost his new connections 25,000gns. He stayed well on the Flat and has won on testing ground, but was in trouble leaving the back straight here. The experience will not be lost on him.

2662 SANDERSON WEATHERALL BARBARA E BIRTHDAY NOVICES' H'CAP CHASE (15 fncs) 2m 2f 110y
1:00 (1:00) (Class 3) (0-125,125) 4-Y-0+ **£7,806** (£2,292; £1,146; £572)

Form RPR
14P- **1** **Little George (IRE)**242 4930 7-11-5 **118**.................... WayneHutchinson 130+
(Alan King) *hld up in rr: hdwy 11th: styng on whn nt fluent 3 out: tk 3rd next: styd on gamely run-in to ld fnl 75yds* **7/1**
-003 **2** *1 3/4* **Lordsbridge (USA)**25 2124 8-10-10 **109**......................... NickScholfield 118
(Andy Turnell) *hld up in rr: hdwy fr 10th: chsd ldr 3 out: chal next: sn led: styd on run-in: hdd and outpcd fnl 75yds* **25/1**
1216 **3** *1* **Mam Ratagan**34 1975 9-11-7 **123**.................................... PeterToole(3) 131
(Heather Main) *led tl jnd 2 out and sn hd: styd on wl run-in but nt quite pce of ldng duo* **22/1**
31-2 **4** *24* **Coup Royale (FR)**25 2127 6-11-2 **115**............................. AidanColeman 104
(Colin Tizzard) *trckd ldrs: wnt 2nd 10th: rdn and blnd 4 out: wknd after next: no ch whn mstke and stmbld last* **11/8**1
05/6 **5** *7* **Altilhar (USA)**25 2126 7-11-12 **125**.......................... AndrewGlassonbury 110+
(Gary Moore) *hit 1st: blnd 9th: hit 10th: a in rr* **66/1**
15P- **6** *11* **Llama Farmer**237 4990 5-11-10 **123**............................. DominicElsworth 93
(Paul Webber) *chsd ldrs: disp 2nd 11th: wknd after 4 out* **8/1**
04- **F** **Meneur (FR)**248 4800 8-10-6 **105**..................................... JamieMoore —
(Gary Moore) *chsd ldrs: hit 7th: blnd 9th: wknd 4 out: t.o whn fell last* **33/1**

5/1 **P** **Darby's Turn (IRE)**[23] 2153 8-11-12 **125**........................ WarrenMarston —
(Richard Phillips) *chsd ldr: hit 1st: mstke 10th: sn wknd: no ch whn hmpd next and p.u* **6/1**[3]

-1U3 **P** **Miss Sarenne (FR)**[181] 523 5-11-8 **121**.................................. APMcCoy —
(Nicky Henderson) *in tch: hdwy to chse ldrs fr 10th: wknd qckly 4 out: p.u bef next* **5/1**[2]

P-36 **F** **Alexander Beetle**[16] 2303 5-10-3 **102**................................ HaddenFrost —
(Henrietta Knight) *hit 5th: in tch: styng on bhd ldrs whn fell 11th* **20/1**

4m 37.76s (-6.24) **Going Correction** -0.25s/f (Good) **10** Ran SP% **114.1**
Speed ratings (Par 107): **103,102,101,91,88 84,—,—,—,—**
Tote Swingers: 1&2 £19.80, 1&3 £24.10, 2&3 £12.20 CSF £149.26 CT £3588.11 TOTE £8.20: £2.20, £4.80, £3.40; EX 118.30 TRIFECTA Not won..

Owner Ron George **Bred** Seamus Larkin **Trained** Barbury Castle, Wilts

FOCUS
A fair novices' handicap, run at a sound enough gallop. The first three came well clear. The winner

NOTEBOOK
Little George(IRE) was no more than modest over hurdles, but he has always looked more of a chaser in the making and he made a winning start to his new career, giving his yard a quick-fire double. He did things nicely under restraint through the race, but came under heavy pressure after making up ground around the home turn and looked held three out. His rider really got stuck into him thereafter, though, and just as the two leaders began to tire, he hit top gear on the run-in. That was likely down to this trip being on the sharp side and, well on top at the finish, he looks well up to defying a higher mark when faced with further in this sphere. (op 10-1)

Lordsbridge(USA) got a patient ride and looked to have been delivered with a winning challenge from the third-last. He looked to have done enough just after the last, but failed to sustain his effort when it mattered most. His jumping has markedly improved in two runs back over fences this term and he deserves to go one better again, but he is not an easy horse to catch right all the same. (op 20-1)

Mam Ratagan was given his usual positive ride and turned in a brave effort, finishing well clear of the remainder. He has yet to win a handicap, but does rates a decent benchmark for the race. (op 16-1 tchd 25-1)

Coup Royale(FR), very well backed, was 3lb higher than when second on his chase debut over 3m at Kempton 25 days earlier. He travelled nicely just off the pace, but hit the fourth-last and was unable to go with the principals thereafter. This trip was probably too sharp for him and he does remain open to some improvement over fences. (op 6-4)

Altilhar(USA) lacked fluency and came under pressure a long way out, before plugging on for a remote fifth. He could do with some further help from the handicapper and looks to need more practice. (op 50-1)

Llama Farmer deserves a mention. This imposing grey has always been regarded as a future chaser and shaped encouragingly until his lack of a run told on this debut over fences. He ought to benefit plenty for the outing. (tchd 9-1)

Darby's Turn(IRE) looked something of a reformed character when gamely opening his account over fences in a novice chase on his debut for new connections at Warwick 23 days earlier. He was left alone by the handicapper for that and, considering the third that day bolted up next time, it wasn't surprising to see him get well backed. He failed to settle early on, however, and that affected his usually sound jumping. It was apparent after the last on the back straight he was not on a going day and was well beat prior to being hampered at the next. He was later found to have finished distressed. Official explanation: jockey said gelding finished distressed (op 4-1 tchd 11-2 and 6-1 in a place)

Miss Sarenne(FR) had her chance before dropping out tamely on this first outing for 181 days. Something presumably went amiss. (op 4-1 tchd 11-2 and 6-1 in a place)

2663 SPORTINGBET.COM H'CAP HURDLE (12 hdls) 3m 110y
1:35 (1:35) (Class 2) (0-140,140) 4-Y-0+

£12,524 (£3,700; £1,850; £926; £462; £232)

Form RPR

0-22 **1** **Barafundle (IRE)**[6] 2523 6-11-2 **130**.................................... AlanO'Keeffe 139+
(Jennie Candlish) *trckd ldr: led 7th: rdn and pressed fr 3 out: styd on wl fr next: hrd rdn run-in: c clr fnl 100yds* **2/1**[1]

-14U **2** *7* **Miss Overdrive**[20] 2218 6-10-6 **120**.................................. NickScholfield 121
(Andy Turnell) *hld up in rr: hdwy 8th: pushed along and outpcd afrer 4 out: rallied and styd on wl after 3 out: chsd wnr and 1 l 2nd last: sn no ex and outpcd fnl 100yds* **16/1**

1-10 **3** *1 ¾* **Mostly Bob (IRE)**[30] 2035 7-10-11 **125**........................(t) RichardJohnson 125
(Philip Hobbs) *in tch: chsd ldrs fr 5th: hit 3 out: 4th last: styd on u.p to take 3rd fnl 75yds and gaining on 2nd cl home* **13/2**[3]

25-F **4** *1* **Galaxy Rock (IRE)**[33] 1985 6-11-1 **129**.................................. APMcCoy 129
(Jonjo O'Neill) *chsd ldrs: hit 8th: outpcd after 4 out: rallied next and chsd wnr 2 out tl appr last: no ex run-in and lost 3rd fnl 75yds* **20/1**

40-2 **5** *9* **Racing Demon (IRE)**[33] 1986 10-11-5 **133**........................ HaddenFrost 125
(Henrietta Knight) *led: tendency to jump rt: hdd 7th: styd chsng wnr to 3 out: wknd after next* **8/1**

22-0 **6** *4* **Quickbeam (IRE)**[13] 2360 8-11-2 **130**.............................. AidanColeman 118+
(Venetia Williams) *in tch: chsd ldrs fr 5th: rdn and hit 3 out: wknd fr next* **16/1**

1-0F **7** *13* **Estates Recovery (IRE)**[38] 1908 5-10-5 **119**.......................... RhysFlint 95
(Philip Hobbs) *chsd ldrs: hit 3rd: wknd fr 3 out: t.o* **40/1**

4-02 **8** *36* **Buena Vista (IRE)**[20] 2221 9-11-12 **140**......................(p) TomScudamore 83
(David Pipe) *rdn 4 out: a bhd: t.o* **12/1**

6-11 **9** *3 ¼* **Cotswold Charmer (IRE)**[23] 2154 5-9-12 **115**.... SamTwiston-Davies(3) 55
(Nigel Twiston-Davies) *blnd 1st: hld up in rr: mstke 5th: hdwy 4 out: chsng ldrs whn blnd 3 out and sn wknd: t.o* **9/2**[2]

1P04 **10** *19* **Markington**[19] 2235 7-11-0 **128**..(b) TomO'Brien 51
(Peter Bowen) *rdn and bhd fr 6th: t.o* **33/1**

4/U- **S** **Gala Evening**[41] 5211 8-10-11 **125**.................................... JasonMaguire —
(Jim Old) *in rr: t.o whn slipped up on flat after 4 out: fatally injured* **12/1**

FP2- **P** **Oscar Park (IRE)**[222] 5247 11-11-5 **133**............................. TimmyMurphy —
(David Arbuthnot) *hld up in rr: stdy hdwy to trck ldrs after 4 out: wknd and p.u bef next* **25/1**

6m 13.0s (4.70) **Going Correction** -0.25s/f (Good) **12** Ran SP% **117.1**
Speed ratings (Par 109): **82,79,79,78,76 74,70,59,58,51 —,—**
Tote Swingers: 1&2 £12.20, 1&3 £4.50, 2&3 £25.50 CSF £32.02 CT £181.88 TOTE £2.60: £1.10, £4.60, £2.50; EX 41.80 Trifecta £772.10 Part won. Pool: £1,0432.41 - 0.86 winning units..

Owner Mrs Judith Ratcliff **Bred** Donal Barnwell **Trained** Basford Green, Staffs

FOCUS
This is always a good staying handicap. It was run at just an average gallop with the first six pretty much upsides jumping the penultimate flight, but the form still makes sense.

NOTEBOOK
Barafundle(IRE) finished a clear second to the vastly improved Grand Crus in a very valuable handicap over brush hurdles at Haydock six days earlier. He was hiked up 7lb for that, but was able to race off the same mark on this quick reappearance, so had an obvious chance on paper. He proved somewhat free early on near the head of affairs and, after easily going to the front off the home bend, it was a case of what he would produce when off the bridle. He responded gamely and was always doing enough on the run-in. It was a deserved success and, although things will be tougher once assessed again after this race, he doesn't have many miles on the clock for his age. His in-form trainer will very likely give him a break now, and it wouldn't be at all surprising to see him return in a qualifier for the Pertemps Final at the Cheltenham Festival. (op 5-2 tchd 11-4 in places)

Miss Overdrive wasn't totally done with prior to unseating at the last on her previous outing at Wincanton and was 2lb lower this time. She travelled kindly off the pace, but came under pressure as the tempo became serious nearing the final bend. She stayed on gamely from three out, however, and this fully proves her effectiveness for the longer trip. It should rate a personal-best in defeat.

Mostly Bob(IRE) ◆ looked to be crying out for this step up in distance when reappearing at Haydock last month. His powerful stable has a decent record in this race and so it wasn't surprising to see him well backed earlier in the day off a 3lb lower mark. He emerged with his chance against the stands' rail after three out, but took an age to pick up and would've probably finished second had his rider got stuck into him a bit earlier, as he was staying on stoutly towards the finish. His turn looks to be nearing again. (op 11-2)

Galaxy Rock(IRE) had come to grief on his seasonal/chase debut last month. He shaped well under a positive ride back over hurdles and will likely be returning to chasing now his confidence should be restored, as he is held by the handicapper in this sphere. (op 25-1 tchd 18-1)

Racing Demon(IRE) was a creditable second off this mark on his seasonal return last month. He was able to dictate, but was a sitting duck for the winner and eventually paid for his early exertions before the final flight. His long losing run continues. (tchd 9-1 in places)

Quickbeam(IRE) shaped much more encouragingly on this second outing of the season, but is not a simple horse to place off his mark and has never won a handicap.

Cotswold Charmer(IRE) looked to have been handed a fair mark for his handicap debut. He made up his ground nicely from off the pace, but found little when asked for maximum effort and this proved beyond him at such an early stage in his career.

Oscar Park(IRE) Official explanation: vet said gelding pulled up lame right-fore

2664 FULLER'S LONDON PRIDE NOVICES' CHASE (REGISTERED AS THE BERKSHIRE NOVICES' STEEPLE CHASE) GRADE 2 (16 fncs) 2m 4f
2.10 (2.11) (Class 1) 4-Y-0+ **£14,708** (£5,625; £2,901; £1,532)

Form RPR

22-3 **1** **Cois Farraig**[27] 2082 5-11-1 0....................................... DominicElsworth 131+
(Paul Webber) *led to 5th: styd 2nd tl 7th: trckd ldrs: hmpd 11th: chal 12th: sn led: styd on wl fr 2 out: drvn out run-in* **10/1**[3]

10-1 **2** *2 ¾* **On Borrowed Wings (IRE)**[34] 1970 7-11-8 0................. TimmyMurphy 136
(Alan Fleming) *t.k.h: hld up in rr but in tch: mstke 3rd: nt fluent 5th: hdwy 8th: trckd ldrs 12th: chsd wnr after 3 out: no imp appr last: one pce* **22/1**

4F-F **3** *1 ½* **Celestial Halo (IRE)**[38] 1909 6-11-1 0..................................(t) NoelFehily 131+
(Paul Nicholls) *trckd ldrs: wnt 2nd 7th: lft in ld 11th: j. slowly next and sn hdd: styd 2nd tl blnd 3 out and lost position: reminder after next: styd on wl run-in: gng on cl home* **6/4**[2]

0P-0 **4** *7* **Erzen (IRE)**[202] 206 5-11-1 0.. AidanColeman 124+
(Venetia Williams) *chsd ldrs: hit 7th and 8th: hmpd 11th: wl there whn blnd 4 out: nvr a danger after but kpt on run-in* **66/1**

101- **F** **Spirit River (FR)**[254] 4674 5-11-1 0.................................. BarryGeraghty —
(Nicky Henderson) *trckd ldr: chal 3rd: led 5th tl fell 11th* **10/11**[1]

5m 9.90s (-2.10) **Going Correction** -0.25s/f (Good) **5** Ran SP% **107.3**
Speed ratings (Par 115): **94,92,92,89,—**
CSF £108.03 TOTE £11.50: £3.60, £2.30; EX 33.60.

Owner R V Shaw **Bred** T R Hewitt **Trained** Mollington, Oxon

FOCUS
Traditionally a strong Grade 2 novice event that has been won by some top chasers, including the likes of Denman, Jair Du Cochet and Bacchanal in the past decade. It was a funny race this year, however, and it is probably not worth getting carried away with the form after the favourite's fall and the hesitant jumping of the favourite. The winner is up 4lb on his Ascot figure.

NOTEBOOK
Cois Farraig came home to shed his maiden tag in style. Despite having failed to score under rules coming into this, he did have some decent placed form to his name and looked set for better things when finishing third on his seasonal/chase debut at Ascot last month. He did well to swerve Spirit River after that one came to grief at the 11th, but didn't appear to be going as well as Celestial Halo coming to the next fence. He jumped it a lot better, though, which saw him go to the front and he ran on gamely down the home straight. The experience should boost his confidence no end and, along with the classy Time For Rupert, his trainer clearly has a nice novice for the staying division this term. This race is often pre-cursor for the Grade 1 Feltham Novice Chase at Kempton on Boxing Day and that looks a logical next step for him. He has yet to race beyond this trip, but he is a half-brother to a 3m winner and his debut point success would suggest he ought to stay the longer trip on that sharper track. Whether he is up to winning there remains to be seen and his trainer may well keep him at a lower level, but this young chaser should be rating higher come what may at the end of the season. (op 8-1)

On Borrowed Wings(IRE) found Stratford too sharp yet still got up late on to make a winning start over fences there last month. He proved free under restraint early on, but got seriously involved from the top of the home straight and held every chance. This was a decent effort remembering he was conceding 8lb to his rivals and the Centenary Novices' Handicap at the Cheltenham Festival looks the race for him later on. (op 16-1 tchd 25-1)

Celestial Halo(IRE) was on a recovery mission having fallen on his chasing debut, when just getting on top, at Exeter last month. The step up in trip looked interesting for him, but he failed to convince that he enjoys jumping fences and it has to be considered disappointing he failed to collect after Spirit River's departure. He was looking in trouble prior to almost walking through the third-last, which ended any chance he may have held. The manner in which he was coming back at them on the run-in shows the engine is still there, and Paul Nicholls later said a return to hurdling at up to 3m is now on the cards. (tchd 13-8)

Erzen(IRE) ◆, having his first outing since leaving Nicky Henderson, lacked fluency on the back straight on this switch to chasing. This was a stiff ask first time up, though, and he wasn't at all disgraced as he boxed on in the home straight. He ought to come on plenty for the outing and take some beating next time, providing his sights are lowered as expected. (op 40-1)

Spirit River(FR), who looks all over a chaser, was having his first outing since winning at the Cheltenham Festival in March and was expected to take some beating on this chase debut for a leading stable that was bidding for a hat-trick in the race. He raced enthusiastically and had jumped accurately prior to meeting the 11th on an awkward stride and coming down. Looking at the way the race panned out it is fair to think he would've prevailed with a clear round and it's hoped this doesn't overly affect his confidence. A move to one of the smaller tracks should see him gain a confidence-boosting success. (op 11-10 tchd 5-4 in places)

2665 SPORTINGBET.COM H'CAP CHASE (FOR THE JIM JOEL MEMORIAL TROPHY) (13 fncs) 2m 1f

2:45 (2:45) (Class 2) (0-145,138) 4-Y-0+

£18,786 (£5,550; £2,775; £1,389; £693; £348)

Form				RPR
460-	1		**Aigle D'Or**253 4702 7-11-3 **129** APMcCoy (Nicky Henderson) *trckd ldrs fr 7th: chalng whn blnd 4 out: upsides again next: led 2 out travelling wl: drvn and styd on strly run-in* **13/2**	146+
3F-1	2	3 ¼	**Matuhi**7 2496 7-11-5 **131** 6ex (t) TomScudamore (David Pipe) *trckd ldr: led 7th: jnd fr 4 out: hdd 2 out: styd on u.p run-in but a hld* **3/1**2	143+
620-	3	4 ½	**First Point (GER)**223 5222 7-11-12 **138** BarryGeraghty (Nicky Henderson) *chsd ldrs: blnd 8th: trckd ldr next to 4 out: chal u.p next: styd on same pce u.p last* **12/1**	146
061-	4	2 ½	**Call Me A Legend**307 3597 6-11-0 **126** WayneHutchinson (Alan King) *towards rr: hmpd 6th: stl plenty to do 4 out: pckd next: styd on fr 2 out and kpt on run-in but nvr gng pce to rch ldrs* **10/1**	134+
1100	5	10	**Passato (GER)**13 2359 6-11-6 **137** (t) IanPopham(5) (Joanna Davis) *chsd ldrs to 8th: wknd next: no ch whn blnd last* **22/1**	137
1P-P	6	10	**Fighting Chance (IRE)**26 2112 10-11-4 **130** RichardJohnson (Richard Lee) *led: blnd and hdd 7th: blnd next: j. slowly and wknd 9th* **25/1**	119
142-	7	24	**Suntini (GER)**265 4444 8-11-5 **131** SamThomas (Emma Lavelle) *blnd 2nd: a towards rr: wl bhd fr 9th* **7/2**3	96
PP-0	B		**Perce Rock**14 2345 8-11-6 **135** RichieMcLernon(3) (Jonjo O'Neill) *mstke 1st: in rr tl hmpd and b.d 6th* **50/1**	—
635/	U		**Peplum (FR)**119 1143 7-10-5 **117** JamieMoore (Gary Moore) *in rr tl bdly hmpd and uns rdr 6th* **66/1**	—
20-3	F		**Rivaliste (FR)**14 2345 5-11-11 **137** NoelFehily (Paul Nicholls) *trckd ldrs tl fell 6th* **11/4**1	—

4m 4.54s (-8.46) **Going Correction** -0.25s/f (Good) **10** Ran SP% **115.7**

Speed ratings (Par 109): **109,107,105,104,99 94,83,—,—,—**

Tote Swingers: 1&2 £3.40, 1&3 £6.00, 2&3 £16.40 CSF £26.23 CT £230.49 TOTE £7.20: £2.20, £1.50, £3.50; EX 27.00 Trifecta £313.70 Pool: £1,030.43 - 2.43 winning units..

Owner John P McManus **Bred** S C Ecurie De Meautry **Trained** Upper Lambourn, Berks

FOCUS

This looked competitive, but the principals had it to themselves from the top of the home straight. It was run at a decent gallop, though, and the form still looks good rated around the runner-up. The winner produced a massive step up on his previous hurdles form.

NOTEBOOK

Aigle D'Or came into this with a very disappointing profile, having failed to convince in four outings in his first campaign over fences last season. He was resuming off a very good handicap mark, however, being 11lb lower than when narrowly denied in the Greatwood Handicap over hurdles in 2008. There was money for him late on and he belatedly resumed winning ways, completing the task in ready fashion. He got a confident ride and was going best of all turning for home. He wasn't clever four out, but it cost him no real momentum and he had matters in control nearing the final fence. It was probably case of him idling as the runner-up rallied late on, so he looks value for a bit further, and connections have done a great job to get him back firing. He should really go on from this now, despite a likely rise back up the handicap, and he does still have the option of novice events. (op 7-1 tchd 11-2)

Matuhi showed the real benefit of a change of scenery when running out a convincing winner on his debut for David Pipe at Ascot a week previously. He was officially 4lb ahead of the handicapper under his penalty and, despite not being able to dictate, ultimately made a bold bid to follow up. Returning to a bit further should suit ideally and there will still be other days for him this term. (tchd 7-2)

First Point(GER) gave a respectable account of himself under top weight on his return from a 223-day break. He only gave way in between the final two fences and, while he still has a little to learn in the jumping department, this is a display he can build on. (tchd 14-1)

Call Me A Legend ◆ was last seen thrashing Lordsbridge on her chase debut at Ascot back in January. She never seriously threatened, but was given a fairly considerate ride on her return and looks sure to come on a bundle for the run. She is one to be with next time out. (op 9-1 tchd 17-2)

Passato(GER) wasn't disgraced but the handicapper now looks firmly in charge. (op 25-1)

Fighting Chance(IRE) set off at a solid gallop, but spoilt his chance with two notable errors on the back straight. He at least completed here, but is another that currently looks weighted out of winning.

Suntini(GER), well backed, was taken off his feet from the start and this first outing for 265 days looked badly needed. (tchd 5-1 in a place)

Rivaliste(FR), who won on his debut for the stable on this card last year, was expected to come on for his seasonal return at Cheltenham a fortnight earlier. He was starting to get seriously involved prior to departing at the sixth, bringing down both Peplum and Perce Rock. (tchd 3-1)

2666 SIR CHARLES CLORE V CIR CHD 1984 "NATIONAL HUNT" MAIDEN HURDLE (8 hdls) 2m 110y

3:15 (3:16) (Class 3) 4-Y-0+ **£5,854** (£1,719; £859; £429)

Form				RPR
13-	1		**Kid Cassidy (IRE)**218 5351 4-11-0 APMcCoy (Nicky Henderson) *trckd ldrs: gng wl and chalng whn carried lft 2 out and sn led: lft clr last: easily* **13/8**1	137+
	2	15	**Tornado Bob (IRE)**196 326 5-11-0 JasonMaguire (Donald McCain) *chsd ldrs: wnt 2nd after 4 out: slt ld and hit next: wnt lft whn jnd 2 out and sn hdd: styd on same pce and no ch w wnr whn hmpd last and dropped to cl 3rd: rallied to regain 2nd fnl 75yds* **6/1**3	118+
14-3	3	1	**Ohio Gold (IRE)**23 2143 4-10-11 SamTwiston-Davies(3) (Colin Tizzard) *chsd ldrs: drvn to chal whn carried lft 2 out: sn outpcd: lft wl hld 2nd after last: outpcd into 3rd fnl 75yds* **15/8**2	115+
2-3	4	2 ½	**Merehead (FR)**48 1778 4-10-9 IanPopham(5) (Paul Nicholls) *in rr hit 4 out: hdwy appr next and sn in tch w ldrs: one pce next: kpt on again run-in* **10/1**	112+
22-3	5	13	**Featherbed Lane (IRE)**16 2310 5-11-0 TomScudamore (Anabel L M King) *trckd ldr 2nd: led after 4 out: narrowly hdd next: wknd 2 out* **20/1**	101
0140	6	4 ½	**Littledean Jimmy (IRE)**23 2143 5-10-7 CharlieWallis(7) (John O'Shea) *hld up in rr: hdwy appr 3 out: nvr gng pce to rch ldrs* **200/1**	95
P-0	7	16	**Robin Will (FR)**23 2143 5-11-0 NickScholfield (Paul Nicholls) *towards rr most of way* **50/1**	81
0	8	13	**Jam Tomorrow (FR)**22 2166 5-11-0 WayneHutchinson (Ian Williams) *chsd ldrs tl wknd after 4 out* **100/1**	69
31P-	9	3 ½	**Tiger Bay (IRE)**256 4636 6-11-0 (t) RichardJohnson (Noel Chance) *a in rr: no ch whn blnd last* **50/1**	66
0-	10	10	**Running Upthathill (IRE)**385 2099 6-11-0 AidanColeman (Venetia Williams) *in rr: no ch whn mstke 4 out* **66/1**	57
00	11	13	**Smoking (FR)**29 2056 4-11-0 GerardTumelty (Sean Curran) *in tch to 4 out* **200/1**	45
3	12	8	**Ratify**29 2059 6-11-0 LeightonAspell (Brendan Powell) *hit 3rd: bhd: no ch whn mstke 4 out* **66/1**	38
0-	13	13	**Slip Duty (IRE)**222 5256 8-10-7 AodhaganConlon(7) (Kate Buckett) *led tl hdd & wknd after 4 out* **200/1**	26
2-	F		**Dixie Bull (IRE)**241 4945 5-11-0 JimmyMcCarthy (Charles Egerton) *trckd ldrs: chal and carried rt 2 out: 2 l 2nd and hld by str travelling wnr whn fell last* **18/1**	122+
2-	U		**Somewhatinevitable (IRE)**221 5284 5-11-0 WillKennedy (Paul Webber) *mstke and uns rdr 1st* **16/1**	—

4m 10.31s (0.41) **Going Correction** -0.25s/f (Good)

WFA 4 from 5yo+ 7lb **15** Ran SP% **121.6**

Speed ratings (Par 107): **89,81,81,80,74 72,64,58,56,52 45,42,36,—,—**

Tote Swingers: 1&2 £3.40, 1&3 £1.70, 2&3 £4.50 CSF £12.07 TOTE £2.60: £1.40, £1.80, £1.20; EX 13.40 Trifecta £23.60 Pool: £12,75.86 - 39.91 winning units..

Owner John P McManus **Bred** Greenville House Stud And M Morgan **Trained** Upper Lambourn, Berks

FOCUS

A maiden where it paid to race handily, but the form still looks decent with the market principals coming to the fore. The impressive winner was vaslue for further and the faller is rated as a clear second.

NOTEBOOK

Kid Cassidy(IRE) won a junior bumper here on his debut and then showed improved form to finish third at the Punchestown Festival on his previous outing. His leading trainer has a good record in this event and he easily handed the stable successive wins in it, having saddled Bellvano to score last season. He did things easily through the race, but wasn't great three out and came under some pressure. As soon as Tony McCoy switched him to the inside nearing the next, though, he found his full stride and had the race in safe keeping coming to the last. He is bred to come into his own over fences down the line, but he will no doubt be rating higher over hurdles beforehand and it wouldn't be surprising to see him follow the same path as last year's winner by turning up next in the opening novice hurdle at Kempton on Boxing Day. That was won by Menorah last year and is usually always a warm race. (tchd 7-4 in a place)

Tornado Bob(IRE) ◆ was making his British debut for new connections and having his third outing since winning at the third attempt in an Irish bumper in May. It was quick ground that day, but he showed on his debut that he handles cut underfoot and, expected to get further this season, he got a positive ride. He was booked for third place prior to being left in second at the last, but was hampered there and would've been a clear second-best without that interference. He ought to improve nicely for the run and take a lot of beating next time out. (op 8-1)

Ohio Gold(IRE) shaped as though this drop back in trip may suit on his hurdling debut at Chepstow 23 days earlier and he was well backed here. He had every chance, but lacked the required turn of foot down the home straight and probably does need a slightly stiffer test. He is another that shouldn't be long in opening his account. (op 11-4)

Merehead(FR) had been beaten two lengths by the winner on his debut at this venue and the fact he got nowhere near him this time is an indication of how that rival has improved. He did fare best of those coming from off the pace on this switch to hurdling, however, and can be rated a little better than the bare form. (op 12-1)

Featherbed Lane(IRE) made his way to the front leaving the back straight and, although well beaten off from three out, ran his race. He goes some way to helping set the level.

Littledean Jimmy(IRE) Official explanation: vet said gelding lost right-fore shoe

Dixie Bull(IRE), fourth on debut in a bumper at Market Rasen in March, still looked green on this hurdling debut. He responded positively in the home straight, however, and looked sure to finish second before he guessed at the last flight. He evidently has a decent engine and ought to make amends next time, providing he comes out of this well enough. (op 16-1 tchd 20-1)

T/Jkpt: Not won. T/Plt: £270.00 to a £1 stake. Pool of £84,444.36 - 228.26 winning tickets. T/Qpdt: £36.90 to a £1 stake. Pool of £8,206.22 - 164.15 winning tickets. ST

2661 NEWBURY (L-H)

Saturday, November 27

OFFICIAL GOING: Good to soft (good in places on chase course)

Rail realignment increased distances by about 20m per circuit.

Wind: moderate behind Weather: white cloud

2667 SPORTINGBET.COM NOVICES' HURDLE (8 hdls) 2m 110y

11:55 (11:55) (Class 3) 4-Y-0+

£6,262 (£1,850; £925; £463; £231; £116)

Form				RPR
	1		**Act Of Kalanisi (IRE)**42 4-11-0 RichardJohnson (Dr Richard Newland) *sn trcking ldr: chal fr 3rd tl ld appr 3 out and nt fluent: rdn and wnt lft 2 out jnd last and blnd: sn hdd and 1 l down fnl 120yds: rallied gamely to ld again cl home* **9/1**	130+
	2	¾	**Secret World (IRE)**892 7-11-0 BarryGeraghty (Nicky Henderson) *trckd ldrs: wnt 2nd after 3 out: travelling wl whn qcknd to join wnr last and sn led: 1 l up fnl 120yds: sn rdn: no ex and hdd cl home* **5/2**2	126+
06-1	3	9	**Dona**17 2312 6-11-5 125 WayneHutchinson (Alan King) *wl in tch: rdn appr 3 out: wnt 3rd after: outpcd by ldng duo fr 2 out and wl hld whn nt fluent last: kpt on for clr 3rd* **2/1**1	124
06	4	10	**Lieutenant Miller**16 2328 4-11-0 AndrewTinkler (Nicky Henderson) *in rr tl hdwy appr 3 out: drvn and kpt on fr 2 out but nvr any ch w ldng trio* **40/1**	109
0-	5	8	**General Eliott (IRE)**48 4439 5-10-7 MrJBanks(7) (Frederick Sutherland) *in rr tl impr fr 3 out: styd on fr next and kpt on run-in but nvr any ch* **100/1**	102
0	6	10	**Fight Club (GER)**6 2540 9-11-0 DarylJacob (Bernard Llewellyn) *in tch: chsd ldrs 4 out: hit 3 out and sn wknd* **100/1**	96
0-	7	3 ½	**Shalambar (IRE)**40 4231 4-11-0 DenisO'Regan (Tony Carroll) *chsd ldrs: rdn appr 3 out and sn btn* **80/1**	90
6	8	2	**Teshali (IRE)**24 2145 4-11-0 TimmyMurphy (Paul Nicholls) *chsd ldrs tl wknd appr 3 out* **11/1**	88
	9	4	**Arbayoun (IRE)**34 2012 5-10-7 MrJamieJenkinson(7) (Frederick Sutherland) *a towards rr* **200/1**	84
0-00	10	20	**Eastern Supreme (IRE)**7 2512 5-11-0 (t) JasonMaguire (Kim Bailey) *led tl hdd appr 3 out: sn bhd: wknd qckly* **50/1**	69
	11	1 ¾	**Champs De Bleu (FR)** 7-11-0 AndrewGlassonbury (Gary Moore) *nvr beyond mid-div: wknd and j. slowly 3 out* **100/1**	65
	12	2	**Classic Vintage (USA)**21 4-11-0 LeightonAspell (Amanda Perrett) *sn chsng ldrs: rdn after 3 out: wknd next* **4/1**3	63

13 *50* **Lombok**[37] 4-11-0 0 .... JamieMoore 18
(Gary Moore) *j. slowly 2nd: sn towards rr: no ch whn j.rt 3 out: t.o* **33/1**

1 **14** *10* **Vesey Lodge (IRE)**[128] 1069 4-11-0 0 .... AlanO'Keeffe 9
(Jennie Candlish) *nvr jumping w much fluency: in tch early: wknd qckly bef 4th: t.o* **14/1**

P **15** *11* **Waldsee (GER)**[18] 2283 5-10-9 0 .... AnthonyFreeman(5) —
(Sean Curran) *j. modly in rr thrght: t.o* **200/1**

P **Opera Prince**[23] 5-11-0 0 .... LiamTreadwell —
(Lady Herries) *j. slowly 2nd: a in rr: t.o whn p.u bef 2 out* **100/1**

4m 4.30s (-5.60) **Going Correction** -0.50s/f (Good)
WFA 4 from 5yo+ 7lb **16** Ran SP% **120.4**
Speed ratings (Par 107): **93,92,88,83,79 75,73,72,70,61 60,59,36,31,26** —
toteswingers:1&2:£7.60, 1&3:£5.60, 2&3:£1.60 CSF £31.93 TOTE £10.20: £2.60, £2.30, £1.30; EX 46.90 Trifecta £59.20 Pool: £901.13 - 11.25 winning units..
Owner C E Stedman & Dr R D P Newland **Bred** Mrs Joan Keaney **Trained** Claines, Worcs

FOCUS
After the frost covers were removed the going was officially described as good to soft with soft places on the hurdles course. This has always been a high-class novice hurdle won by some very useful performers in recent seasons, most notably Albuhera, Marcel, Cockney Trucker and Finian's Rainbow. This year's line-up did not look the strongest on paper, but there were several recruits from the Flat and two of those fought out the finish. The early pace was steady, but the field came home well strung out. The time was ordinary but the first three all look well above average.

NOTEBOOK
Act Of Kalanisi(IRE) ◆, a dour stayer on the Flat, having won over 2m2f on soft, was making his hurdling debut for new connections. Given a positive ride by Richard Johnson, he pressed on turning for home, but the runner-up was cantering all over him between the last two and minor mistakes at those flights did not help. However, his stamina came into play under pressure and he battled back gamely to reclaim the advantage in the last 50 yards. He looks sure to win more good races and was quoted at 33-1 for the Supreme Novices' after this. However, he looks more likely to contest one of the races over longer trips if he gets to the Festival, and connections indicated he is likely to go up in both trip and class now. (op 11-1 tchd 12-1 in places)

Secret World(IRE) ◆, the winner of a division of the Wood Ditton on his debut back in 2006, was lightly raced for Jeremy Noseda and had not won since. Making his debut for his new yard after an absence of 892 days, he travelled well throughout, if a little keen early, but looked sure to win when moving upsides the winner after the penultimate flight. He asserted at the last but his lack of a recent outing seemed to find him out on the run-in, and he was outstayed by the winner near the line. Nevertheless, he looks a bright prospect, and a sounder surface or less-demanding track might suit him. (tchd 9-4 and 11-4)

Dona, the clear-cut winner of a modest handicap hurdle at Huntingdon, was the only previous scorer in the line-up. He made ground to chase the leaders into the straight, but was soon under pressure and could only keep on at one pace. Officially rated 125, he helps set the level of the form. (op 3-1 tchd 7-2 in places)

Lieutenant Miller, a stable companion of the runner-up and related to General Miller, was well beaten on both his starts in bumpers for which he started favourite. Making his hurdling debut, he stayed on from the rear and should be better for the experience.

General Eliott(IRE) was useful at around 1m on the Flat (Listed placed), and didn't appear to stay on his sole previous hurdles start. Sold relatively cheaply and making his debut for a new yard, he was another who was settled out the back before making steady headway in the straight. Well suited by soft ground, he should be able to build on this effort this winter.

Fight Club(GER), a 1m2f Group 2 winner in Germany on soft ground, started at long odds and pulled hard before being well beaten on his hurdling debut. He settled much better this time and moved into contention, appearing to be travelling well at the end of the back straight, before only keeping on at the one pace. He looks one to be interested in once qualified for handicaps.

Classic Vintage(USA), a very useful four-time Flat winner on everything from good to firm to soft, was making his hurdling debut, having finished fourth in the November Handicap on his last start on the Flat. He showed up well for a long way before fading in the straight. (op 7-2)

Vesey Lodge(IRE)'s rider reported that the gelding finished lame on his near fore. Official explanation: jockey said gelding finished lame left-fore (op 16-1)

2668 STANJAMES.COM FIGHTING FIFTH HURDLE GRADE 1 (8 hdls) 2m 110y
12:25 (12:28) (Class 1) 4-Y-0+ **£51,309** (£19,251; £9,639; £4,806; £2,412)

Form RPR

111- **1** **Peddlers Cross (IRE)**[231] 5123 5-11-7 151 .... JasonMaguire 161+
(Donald McCain) *trckd ldr: led after 3 out: jnd last: styd on strly to forge clr fnl 75yds* **9/4**[2]

225- **2** *1 ¼* **Starluck (IRE)**[256] 4660 5-11-7 160 .... TimmyMurphy 160
(Alan Fleming) *hld up in last: smooth hdwy 4th: effrt between last 2: chal run-in: no ex last 75yds* **7/1**[3]

311- **3** *6* **Binocular (FR)**[256] 4660 6-11-7 172 .... APMcCoy 156+
(Nicky Henderson) *hld up: wnt prom 4th: effrt between last 2: upsides last: wknd fnl 150yds* **5/6**[1]

14-P **4** *6* **Bygones Of Brid (IRE)**[10] 2447 7-11-7 142 .... GrahamLee 148
(Karen McLintock) *led: drvn 5th: hdd after 3 out: wl outpcd appr last* **66/1**

0111 **5** *17* **Nearby**[21] 2219 6-11-7 152 .... RichardJohnson 137+
(Philip Hobbs) *trckd ldng pair: effrt 3 out: stmbld landing next: sn wknd: eased whn bhd fnl 100yds* **10/1**

(-9.90) **Going Correction** -0.50s/f (Good) **5** Ran SP% **108.4**
Speed ratings: **103,102,99,96,88**
CSF £15.92 TOTE £3.10: £1.80, £2.40; EX 13.10.
Owner T G Leslie **Bred** Mrs A Delaney **Trained** Cholmondeley, Cheshire

FOCUS
A small but select field for this Grade 1 event, which was switched at short notice from Newcastle. Fears of a falsely run race evaporated as Bygones Of Brid set a respectable pace. The time was not especially quick, just over four seconds faster than the opening novice event, but the runners didn't begin to move until a couple of seconds after the tapes had risen, and they produced very fast finishing fractions. They soon raced in single file and although the field closed up on the home turn, the order didn't change until just after the third-last. Peddlers Cross looks sure to rate higher, Starluck was close to his best and Binocular is rated similar to his reappearance last year.

NOTEBOOK
Peddlers Cross(IRE) ◆ was unbeaten in four runs as a novice last term, culminating in the Neptune Investments at Cheltenham and the Mersey at Aintree, but was dropping in trip to take on seasoned 2m hurdlers on this reappearance. His trainer was positive beforehand, and the gelding took the eye in the preliminaries. Travelling strongly in second before leading after the first in the straight, he was firmly ridden between the final two flights and again came under the stick following a fine jump at the last, but responded most willingly and ran on strongly to repel first Binocular and then Starluck. He had no less than 21lb to find with Binocular on BHA ratings and, although the Nicky Henderson runner was not at his best, this still represented considerable improvement and there is surely further progress to come from him as he gains experience. Now a general 6-1 shot for the Stan James Champion Hurdle, he has a potent blend of speed and stamina and is surely a genuine Cheltenham contender. Connections have yet to map out a route to the festival, but the Haydock Champion Hurdle Trial in January may well come into consideration. (op 5-2 tchd 11-4 in places)

Starluck(IRE) has strengthened since last season in the opinion of his trainer and the grey, who has a decent record when fresh, ran a pleasing race. Held up in last before easing into third spot at the final flight, he only came off the bridle on the run-in as he went after the winner, who needed to find more to keep him at bay. (op 6-1 tchd 15-2 in places)

Binocular(FR) was a brilliant winner of the Champion Hurdle when last seen. He disappointed in the first half of last season, finishing only fifth to Go Native in this event at Newcastle before filling third, behind Go Native again and Starluck, in the Christmas Hurdle. He got it right on the day that really mattered, though, and everything looked in place for a big run here as he had pleased his trainer in his preparation and had 12lb in hand on both BHA figures and RPRs. He travelled smoothly in fourth, hurdling well as usual, before Tony McCoy started to push after the second-last. The favourite had every chance at the final flight, but appeared to blow up on the run-in and his rider was noticeably easier on his mount than the jockeys on the first two. While he was below his best, this still rates a satisfactory return with the Champion Hurdle in mind, but the emergence of Peddlers Cross and Menorah as serious contenders means he will face a stern challenge to retain his crown. He may well go for the Christmas Hurdle again. (op 10-11 tchd evens in places)

Bygones Of Brid(IRE) was pulled up in a Hexham novice chase first time out, but he was a smart novice hurdler last term. He performed a valuable role in setting a fair gallop and, although he was the first to come under pressure and was headed three from home, it was only on the approach to the final flight that he finally dropped away. This was a thoroughly creditable effort and connections must now decide whether to continue his chasing career.

Nearby, on whom Richard Johnson replaced conditional Chris Davies, has made great strides this season and was raised a further 7lb after completing a hat-trick in Wincanton's Elite Hurdle off 145 three weeks earlier. This represented by far his biggest test and he wasn't up to it, although he would not have been beaten quite so far had he had not been eased after stumbling two out. He will be hard to place in the short term as handicaps will be out from his current mark until the Totesport Trophy here in February. (tchd 11-1)

2669 SPORTINGBET.COM AMATEUR RIDERS' H'CAP CHASE (21 fncs) 3m 2f 110y
12:55 (12:56) (Class 3) (0-125,125)
4-Y-0+
£9,003 (£2,812; £1,405; £703; £351; £177)

Form RPR

14-1 **1** **Sarde (FR)**[9] 2476 6-11-2 122 .... (t) MrCGreene(7) 132+
(Kim Bailey) *hld up towards rr: hdwy 9th: dropped in rr 12th: in tch 16th: outpcd next: gd hdwy fr 4 out: drvn to chse ldr last: styd on to ld fnl 100yds: hld on wl* **9/2**[1]

4-64 **2** *1* **Noun De La Thinte (FR)**[15] 2343 9-11-1 121 .... MrJSherwood(7) 131
(Venetia Williams) *hit 1st: trckd ldrs: wnt 2nd 11th: hit 12th: led 16th: hdd 3 out: outpcd into 3rd last: rallied wl to retake 2nd fnl 50yds: gng on cl home* **8/1**

-00P **3** *2 ¾* **Carrickmines (IRE)**[7] 2522 8-11-4 120 .... (b1) MrTWeston(3) 129+
(Dr Richard Newland) *t.k.h in rr: blnd 1st and 7th: j. slowly 11th: blnd 13th: hdwy and hit 16th: qcknd to ld 3 out: 3 l clr after next: sn rdn: hdd and no ex fnl 100yds: lost 2nd fnl 50yds* **12/1**

5224 **4** *nk* **Pheidias (IRE)**[27] 2110 6-11-2 118 .... (p) MissGAndrews(3) 124
(Pam Sly) *sn trcking ldr: led 9th: hdd 16th: styd chsng ldrs tl outpcd appr last: rallied and styd on again fnl 100yds* **20/1**

P0-0 **5** *11* **Martys Mission (IRE)**[15] 2343 8-11-4 122 .... MrTJCannon(5) 120+
(Richard Rowe) *in tch whn hmpd and dropped in rr 10th: hdwy fr 17th and in tch 4 out: wknd fr next* **9/1**

1-53 **6** *½* **Son Histoire (FR)**[25] 2140 6-10-6 112 .... (b) MrTCheesman(7) 107
(Philip Hobbs) *in rr tl hdwy to chse ldrs fr 13th: wknd 4 out* **13/2**[3]

5132 **7** *6* **Sarahs Gift (IRE)**[21] 2214 7-10-9 108 .... (t) MrRMahon 102
(Lawney Hill) *led 2nd: hdd 9th: mstke 13th: styd in tch tl wknd 17th: no ch whn blnd 3 out* **8/1**

150- **8** *68* **Mill Side**[266] 4428 10-11-7 125 .... MrJHamer(5) 53
(Donald McCain) *sn chsng ldrs: blnd 16th: mstke 17th and wknd: no ch whn blnd 4 out* **6/1**[2]

6U-1 **U** **Rustarix (FR)**[15] 2343 9-11-4 124 .... MrJBanks(7) —
(Alan King) *t.k.h: in rr but in tch whn blnd and uns rdr 13th* **6/1**[2]

P-0F **U** **Scots Dragoon**[21] 2214 8-11-1 121 .... MrNdeBoinville(7) —
(Nicky Henderson) *led to 2nd: chsd ldrs: hit 12th: drvn and disputing cl 3rd whn mstke and uns rdr 14th* **12/1**

0042 **F** **Mzuri Bay**[40] 1903 5-9-11 103 .... (bt) MrTGarner(7) —
(Brendan Duke) *trckd ldrs: disputing cl 2nd whn fell 10th* **33/1**

6m 46.1s (-9.90) **Going Correction** -0.50s/f (Good) **11** Ran SP% **115.4**
Speed ratings (Par 107): **94,93,92,92,89 89,87,67,—,—** —
toteswingers:1&2:£14.00, 1&3:£22.40, 2&3:£33.60 CSF £39.97 CT £403.86 TOTE £5.10: £2.10, £2.50, £4.40; EX 40.60 Trifecta £921.80 Part won..
Owner Bill Ives **Bred** E A R L Haras De Nonant Le Pin **Trained** Andoversford, Gloucs
■ The first winner under rules in Britain for Charlie Greene.

FOCUS
This amateur riders' handicap chase, run over the full Hennessy trip, looked a competitive affair with a number of the runners coming into it in good form. The pace was sound and it produced a good finish. The form is ordinary for the track and pretty solid.

NOTEBOOK
Sarde(FR), whose wins had been at 2m6f, was given a good ride by his amateur, who stuck to the inside most of the way and did not make his effort until approaching the final fence over this longer trip. He landed running and, after getting past the leader, had enough in hand to hold off the rallying runner-up. His yard is in good form but this gelding is progressive now his foot problems appear to be behind him, and could win more good races this winter.

Noun De La Thinte(FR) ◆ is a game mare and signalled a return to form behind Rustarix at Cheltenham last time. Never far away, she kept battling and might have been closer had she not been short of room between the winner and third after the last. She deserves to pick up a race before long. (op 7-1)

Carrickmines(IRE) was in good form in the spring but had lost his way of late, and connections fitted blinkers for the first time after his poor effort the preceding weekend. He travelled really well in the headgear and looked the most likely winner when going on in the straight, but his efforts told after the last and he was run out of it. A drop to 3m and a sharper trip could see him back winning, providing the headgear continues to have the same effect. (op 16-1)

Pheidias(IRE) has appeared best suited by a sound surface around Fakenham up to now, but ran a fine race over this longer trip and on a stiffer track. He was never far away and was coming back at the first three after the last, so might find a suitable opportunity over the Christmas period at one of the Midlands tracks.

Martys Mission(IRE) had some decent form last autumn, including at this course, and was well backed. However, his chances were spoilt when he was hampered by the fall of Mzuri Bay at the tenth, and he did well to finish as close as fifth in the end. He has slipped down the handicap and will be aimed at the Kim Muir in the spring. (op 17-2 tchd 10-1)

Son Histoire(FR) could only keep on at the one pace in the straight. (op 8-1)

Sarahs Gift(IRE) was too keen on the first circuit and lost his place early on the second lap. He probably found the ground softer than ideal.

Mill Side spoilt his chances with several major jumping errors but was later reported to have bled. Official explanation: jockey said gelding bled from the nose (op 11-2)

Rustarix(FR) had not been asked for an effort when he unshipped his rider early on the second circuit. (op 11-2 tchd 13-2)

Scots Dragoon had already made an error and was being pushed along when losing his jockey midway down the back on the second circuit. (op 11-2 tchd 13-2)

2670 SPORTINGBET.COM NOVICES' H'CAP CHASE (FOR THE FULKE WALWYN TROPHY) (17 fncs) 2m 6f 110y

1:30 (1:30) (Class 3) (0-130,130) 4-Y-O+

£11,271 (£3,330; £1,665; £833; £415; £208)

Form				RPR
33-2	1		**Regal Approach (IRE)**[20] 2236 7-10-11 **115**..........(p) SeanQuinlan (Kim Bailey) *chsd ldrs: wnt 2nd 9th: upsides 3 out: led next: hdd appr last: j.rt: hrd rdn and styd on to ld last 50yds: hld on nr fin* **7/1**[2]	125+
0112	2	nk	**In The Zone (IRE)**[29] 2073 6-10-7 **114**.......... RichieMcLernon(3) (Jonjo O'Neill) *hld up towards rr: hdwy 12th: styd on wl fr 2 out: 4th last: wnt 2nd last 50yds: jst hld* **8/1**[3]	121
0-56	3	2 ¼	**Vino Griego (FR)**[15] 2348 5-11-9 **127**.......... JamieMoore (Gary Moore) *prom: chsd ldrs 9th: led appr last and wnt 2 l ahd: hung lft: hdd and no ex last 50yds* **20/1**	134+
05-3	4	3 ¾	**Stoney's Treasure**[22] 2184 6-10-9 **113**.......... WayneHutchinson (Alan King) *hld up towards rr: hdwy whn hit 8th: chsng ldrs 12th: hit 4 out: 5th last: kpt on same pce* **9/4**[1]	116+
1P-1	5	1 ½	**Bai Zhu (IRE)**[30] 2046 6-11-12 **130**.......... FelixDeGiles (Nicky Henderson) *w ldr: led 3rd: hdd 2 out: 3rd last: wknd last 50yds* **9/1**	130
-142	6	14	**Alderley Rover (IRE)**[23] 2165 6-11-7 **125**.......... JasonMaguire (Donald McCain) *nt jump wl in rr: j.rt: reminders after 2nd: sn bhd: sme hdwy 4 out: nvr on terms* **12/1**	114
4-3F	7	1 ¾	**Theophrastus (IRE)**[18] 2285 8-11-4 **122**.......... LiamTreadwell (Nick Gifford) *prom: lost pl 10th: bhd fr 12th* **25/1**	108
0-02	8	17	**Ballyegan (IRE)**[13] 2396 5-9-11 **108**.......... NathanSweeney(7) (Bob Buckler) *in rr-div: sme hdwy 8th: outpcd 12th: bhd whn j.lft 4 out* **14/1**	79
-123	9	36	**Job One (FR)**[67] 1570 7-10-10 **114**.......... HaddenFrost (Henrietta Knight) *led to 3rd: outpcd: lost pl and mstke 8th: sn bhd: t.o 4 out* **20/1**	52
6P-3	10	34	**Quintessentially (IRE)**[35] 1965 8-10-6 **110**..........(p) GrahamLee (Warren Greatrex) *chsd ldrs: rdn 10th: lost pl appr 4 out: sn bhd and eased: t.o* **33/1**	18
F21/	U		**Canalturn (FR)**[946] 5191 8-10-4 **115**.......... JakeGreenall(7) (Charles Egerton) *prom: hit 5th: lost pl 10th: mstke 12th: bhd whn blnd and uns rdr next* **10/1**	—
51/6	U		**Nodforms Paula (IRE)**[24] 2147 7-11-1 **119**.......... NickScholfield (Paul Nicholls) *in rr: drvn 8th: sn bhd: blnd and uns rdr 12th* **10/1**	—
P-34	U		**Prince Du Beury (FR)**[31] 2037 7-10-8 **112**..........(b¹) AndrewTinkler (Nicky Henderson) *w ldrs: wknd appr 4 out: j.lft next: 8th whn blnd and uns last* **28/1**	—
P04-	P		**Tafika**[260] 4568 6-10-6 **110**.......... DominicElsworth (Paul Webber) *in rr: bhd and drvn 2nd: blnd 4th: reminders and t.o 8th: p.u bef 11th* **25/1**	—

5m 41.6s (-8.70) **Going Correction** -0.50s/f (Good) **14** Ran SP% **120.5**
Speed ratings (Par 107): **95,94,94,92,92 87,86,80,68,56** —,—,—,—
toteswingers:1&2:£3.50, 1&3:£90.50, 2&3:£20.80 CSF £55.92 CT £1084.26 TOTE £9.00: £2.50, £2.00, £8.30; EX 72.50 Trifecta £613.00 Pool: £1,656.89 - 2.00 winning units..

Owner P J Vogt **Bred** N J Connors **Trained** Andoversford, Gloucs

■ Stewards' Enquiry : Sean Quinlan eight-day ban: used whip with excessive frequency (Dec 11-18)

FOCUS

A competitive novice handicap chase, and solid form if ordinary for the track. It proved a fair stamina test in the conditions and only the first five were serious players over the final four fences. The winner stepped up on his hurdles form with the second recorded a small personal best.

NOTEBOOK

Regal Approach(IRE) ◆ took time to master the front-running Bai Zhu and then, having got to the front two out, he pricked his ears and was headed going into the last. With something to run at again, he battled on most gamely to reclaim the lead on the run-in and hold off the runner-up. Gaining a belated first win, having made the frame 11 times previously without getting his head in front, he was helped by the return of cheekpieces and his stable continues in fine form. He will have more to offer back over 3m. (op 8-1 tchd 6-1)

In The Zone(IRE) was just denied a hat-trick at Uttoxeter but was 5lb higher here, putting him no less than 20lb above the mark he won off at Newton Abbot. Upped in trip, he lacked the pace to get to the leaders up the straight, but his rider persevered and he had moved into a share of fourth at the final fence. He had to be switched right on landing, and the manoeuvre arguably cost him victory as he was running on all the way to the line from there and went down narrowly. He is effective in even softer conditions and shapes as if he will stay 3m. (tchd 9-1 in a place)

Vino Griego(FR) ran his best race so far over fences and his jumping was more accomplished. After tracking the leading pair into the straight, he moved to the front jumping the last and looked in charge, but he idled in front and was cut down halfway up the run-in. He is certainly able enough, but there is a question over his attitude.

Stoney's Treasure, a solid favourite, ran his race with no apparent excuses bar a small mistake four from home, staying on for pressure without quite being able to get in a real challenge to the leaders. This was a sound run on only his second outing over fences. (tchd 5-2 and 2-1 in places)

Bai Zhu(IRE) represented a yard with a good record in this event and he ran a bold race under topweight, only headed two from home and still in there fighting at the last. This was just his second run over fences and it was pleasing to see him put in back-to-back good efforts. (tchd 17-2 and 10-1 and 12-1 in a place)

Alderley Rover(IRE) was struggling in rear from an early stage but stayed on past toiling rivals when it was all over. (op 11-1)

Quintessentially(IRE) performed respectably in the cheekpieces, but didn't see out the longer trip. (op 66-1)

Canalturn(FR), who was supported in the morning, was making his chase debut after more than two and a half years off the track and looked fit. However, he was beaten when he departed at the cross fence. (tchd 11-1 in a place)

Nodforms Paula(IRE) was already held when he fell at the last fence in the back straight. (tchd 11-1 in a place)

Prince Du Beury(FR) found 2m too sharp last time and he ran a better race in the blinkers, but his stamina gave way on the home turn and he was well adrift when refusing at the last. (tchd 11-1 in a place)

2671 SPORTINGBET.COM INTERMEDIATE HURDLE (LIMITED H'CAP) (REGISTERED AS THE GERRY FEILDEN HURDLE) (8 hdls) 2m 110y

2:00 (2:02) (Class 1) (0-145,145) 4-Y-O+

£14,252 (£5,347; £2,677; £1,335; £670; £335)

Form				RPR
40-1	1		**Tocca Ferro (FR)**[28] 2085 5-10-13 **134**.......... SamThomas (Emma Lavelle) *trckd ldr: qcknd to ld 2 out: drvn and r.o strly run-in* **7/2**[1]	146+
U13F	2	2 ¼	**Rebel Dancer (FR)**[49] 1766 5-10-4 **125** oh5..........(t) DougieCostello (Ian Williams) *hld up in rr: hdwy 3 out: trckd ldrs 2 out: chsd wnr last: kpt on u.p but a wl hld* **16/1**	132
4-25	3	2 ¼	**Olofi (FR)**[13] 2386 4-10-12 **133**.......... PaddyBrennan (Tom George) *in tch: chsd ldrs 3 out: rdn to chse wnr 2 out but no imp: lost 2nd at last: kpt on u.p to hold 3rd run-in* **7/2**[1]	138
23P-	4	hd	**The Betchworth Kid**[21] 4712 5-11-3 **138**.......... WayneHutchinson (Alan King) *in tch: styd on fr 3 out to chse ldrs 2 out: one pce last but kpt on to press for 3rd run-in tl no ex last strides* **9/2**[2]	143
1-00	5	14	**Ciceron (IRE)**[28] 2085 4-10-11 **132**.......... AidanColeman (Venetia Williams) *hld up towards rr: stdy hdwy fr 4 out to trck ldrs 3 out: rdn next and sn btn* **33/1**	125
-121	6	1	**Praxiteles (IRE)**[163] 768 6-10-6 **127**..........(t) TomScudamore (Rebecca Curtis) *poached 6 l ld fr s: styd in command tl drvn 3 out: hdd next and sn wknd* **14/1**	118
215-	7	4 ½	**Stormy Weather (FR)**[255] 4675 4-10-4 **125**..........(t) BrianHughes (Howard Johnson) *chsd ldrs: rdn 3 out: wknd qckly next* **11/2**[3]	112
35	8	5	**Kauto Relko (FR)**[23] 2164 6-10-4 **125** oh1.......... SeanQuinlan (Rachel Hobbs) *in rr tl hdwy after 4 out: in tch whn nt fluent and wknd 3 out* **28/1**	109
403F	9	5	**Forty Thirty (IRE)**[28] 2085 4-10-7 **128**.......... JamieGoldstein (Sheena West) *a towards rr: no ch fr 3 out* **40/1**	106
4-35	10	7	**Dr Livingstone (IRE)**[8] 2498 5-10-8 **129**..........(b) APMcCoy (Charles Egerton) *t.k.h: chsd ldrs early: in rr whn mstke 4 out: no ch after* **10/1**	101
100-	B		**Advisor (FR)**[224] 5220 4-10-7 **133**.......... IanPopham(5) (Paul Nicholls) *in rr but in tch whn bdly hmpd and b.d 4 out* **16/1**	—
5U-1	F		**Alegralil**[28] 2089 5-11-3 **145**.......... HenryBrooke(7) (Donald McCain) *wl in tch tl fell 4 out* **16/1**	—

3m 57.34s (-12.56) **Going Correction** -0.50s/f (Good)
WFA 4 from 5yo+ 7lb **12** Ran SP% **120.2**
Speed ratings (Par 111): **109,107,106,106,100 99,97,95,92,89** —,—
toteswingers:1&2:£10.70, 1&3:£24.00, 2&3:£34.00 CSF £57.73 CT £214.88 TOTE £4.10: £1.70, £3.80, £1.70; EX 48.50 Trifecta £439.10 Pool: £2,438.99 - 4.11 winning units..

Owner Mrs Sarah Prior and Tim Syder **Bred** Ian Kellitt Et Al **Trained** Wildhern, Hants

FOCUS

This long-established hurdle for horses in their second season is perhaps not quite as significant a race as it once was, but has nevertheless thrown up the high-class performers Tramantano and Afsoun in the last ten years. This year's line-up featured several with the potential to make their mark in decent handicaps later in the season, and the time was just over 2secs quicker than the earlier Fighting Fifth Hurdle. Tocca Ferro should go on to rate higher and the second is on the upgrade too.

NOTEBOOK

Tocca Ferro(FR) ◆ looked progressive when winning a Listed handicap at Ascot last month, even though he only just got home, and was 8lb higher here. He tracked the clear leader until going on travelling well at the second-last, and scored without being unduly troubled. He will go up again but looks sure to play a big part in races such as the Ladbroke at Ascot next month and the Totesport Gold Trophy here in February, with the latter the more likely target. (tchd 4-1)

Rebel Dancer(FR) did well on faster surfaces in the late summer, and had gone up 7lb after falling when giving the progressive Nearby a race at Bangor. Returning from a seven-week break, he was held up before staying on well to chase home the winner, although never looking as if he would get past. This was a good effort from 5lb out of the handicap, but he is sure to go up again despite having not won. (op 20-1)

Olofi(FR) has improved on his juvenile form this season, having finished fifth in the Greatwood Hurdle last time. He was never far away and had his chance, but the winner was clearly going the better two out and he could only keep on at the one pace under pressure. He helps set the level of the form. (op 9-2 tchd 5-1 in a place)

The Betchworth Kid was in good order on the Flat earlier this autumn and ran well again, although this trip probably does not play to his strengths over hurdles. He probably needs another half-mile or a race run at a really strong gallop at shorter. (op 4-1 tchd 5-1 in places)

Ciceron(IRE), a three-time scorer in the spring, was well behind today's winner at Ascot but ran better here. He looked set to get involved early in the straight but was left behind from two out. His record suggests good ground and a Flat track are his ideal conditions. (op 40-1)

Praxiteles(IRE) was allowed to get a clear lead at the start by a combination of the other jockeys holding their mounts back and the starter letting the field go. He maintained a clear advantage and his rider did his best to get a breather into his mount, but he was swept aside in the straight. (tchd 12-1)

Stormy Weather(FR) was close enough to the pace until fading from the third-last as if the run was needed. (op 6-1)

Alegralil was making headway when departing at the fifth, effectively bringing down Advisor.

2672 SPORTINGBET.COM LONG DISTANCE HURDLE (GRADE 2) (12 hdls) 3m 110y

2:30 (2:30) (Class 1) 4-Y-O+

£28,505 (£10,695; £5,355; £2,670; £1,340; £670)

Form				RPR
111-	1		**Big Buck's (FR)**[233] 5093 7-11-8 174.......... APMcCoy (Paul Nicholls) *hld up in rr but wl in tch off mod pce: clsd up 8th: tk narrow ld appr 2 out: qcknd run-in: easily* **2/7**[1]	160+
11-4	2	3	**Duc De Regniere (FR)**[28] 2090 8-11-0 154.......... BarryGeraghty (Nicky Henderson) *trckd ldrs in cl 4th off mod pce: wnt 2nd 3 out: chal 2 out: styd chsng wnr last and nt fluent: nvr any ch but styd on gamely for 2nd* **13/2**[2]	144
23-6	3	2 ½	**Arcalis**[203] 207 10-11-0 138.......... BrianHughes (Howard Johnson) *hld up in rr but in tch off mod pce: hdwy fr 2 out: drvn and styd on run-in: nvr any ch w wnr and no imp on 2nd fnl 120yds* **33/1**	142
23-0	4	4 ½	**Duke Of Lucca (IRE)**[35] 1967 5-11-0 148.......... RichardJohnson (Philip Hobbs) *disp cl 3rd off mod pce: rdn 3 out: outpcd fr 2 out* **14/1**	139
50-2	5	5	**Kayf Aramis**[28] 2090 8-11-0 148.......... PaddyBrennan (Nigel Twiston-Davies) *trckd ldr of mod pce: chal and nt fluent 6th: chal again after next tl led after 4 out: hdd appr 2 out and nt fluent: sn btn* **9/1**[3]	136
6224	6	72	**Spider Boy**[8] 2504 13-11-0 80..........(b) MrHGMiller (Zoe Davison) *set mod pce tl hdd after 4 out: sn wknd* **100/1**	69

6m 1.87s (-6.43) **Going Correction** -0.50s/f (Good) **6** Ran SP% **111.7**
Speed ratings (Par 115): **90,89,88,86,85 62**
toteswingers:1&2:£1.10, 1&3:£3.90, 2&3:£9.50 CSF £2.88 TOTE £1.40: £1.20, £2.00; EX 2.80.

Owner The Stewart Family **Bred** Henri Poulat **Trained** Ditcheat, Somerset

FOCUS

The no-hoper Spider Boy set a steady gallop in this Grade 2 and it wasn't a true test at the trip. Big Buck's was value for further and didn't need to be at his best. Duc De Regniere was 3lb off his top form and Arcalis ran well on this step up in trip.

The Form Book, Raceform Ltd, Compton, RG20 6NL

NOTEBOOK

Big Buck's(FR) unseated Sam Thomas at the last in the Hennessy two years ago and connections opted to switch him back to hurdles, and this trademark victory stretched his unbeaten record since to nine. Saddled with an 8lb penalty, he was 12lb and more clear of his rivals and he resumed where he left off last season with a very comfortable win, although he did not need to show anything like his best form. Held up by new jockey Tony McCoy, replacing the injured Ruby Walsh, he cruised into contention two from home, led at the last and had only to be shaken up to come clear on the flat. Following up last year's victory in this event, he joins Baracouda as a dual winner, while Inglis Drever was successful three years in a row. His next run is set to be in the Long Walk Hurdle at Ascot, a race he won when it was switched to Newbury last season, and whereas last year he didn't run again before the World Hurdle, he could be found a race in the new year this time. He is all class and the World Hurdle remains his to lose. (tchd 3-10 and 1-3 in places)

Duc De Regniere(FR) took this race two years ago, but there was no Big Buck's to contend with that day. Disappointing on his return at Wetherby, he presumably needed the run and this was an improvement, for all that he was outclassed by the winner on the run-in after moving through upsides to hold every chance. There was no disgrace in this and he remains a very smart performer, but winning opportunities may be hard to come by. (op 7-1)

Arcalis was placed in the County Hurdle at Cheltenham and the Scottish Champion Hurdle last spring to show that there is still life in him, and this first try at 3m represented a pleasing return to action. Only let down between the last two flights and running on for pressure, he stayed the trip well enough, albeit in a steadily-run race, but is another who will be tricky to place successfully in what is likely to be his final season. Barring a dead-heat, he has not won since taking the Fighting Fifth five years ago.

Duke Of Lucca(IRE) was just 2l behind Peddlers Cross in a Grade 2 novice hurdle at Aintree in the spring before finishing third at the top level at Punchestown, but he was well held off 148 in a handicap on his reappearance at Chepstow. Momentarily short of room on the turn into the straight as the leader dropped away, he was close enough three from home, but was soon outpaced as the first two asserted. This run was inconclusive as far as his stamina for this trip is concerned.

Kayf Aramis got to the front turning out of the back straight, but he was very quickly under pressure and had no answers when the first two home eased past him going into the second-last. He had finished ahead of Duc De Regniere at Wetherby, but was below that level here. (op 11-1)

2673 HENNESSY GOLD CUP CHASE (H'CAP) GRADE 3 (21 fncs) 3m 2f 110y

3:05 (3:08) (Class 1) 4-Y-0+

£99,767 (£37,432; £18,742; £9,345; £4,690; £2,345)

Form				RPR
11P-	**1**		**Diamond Harry**^{255} 4672 7-10-0 **156** oh4 DarylJacob (Nick Williams) *trckd ldr to 12th and again fr 16th tl slt ld after 17th: jnd and hit 4 out: asserted appr 2 out: styd on gamely u.p run-in* **6/1**^{2}	172+
121-	**2**	*1 1/4*	**Burton Port (IRE)**^{232} 5109 6-10-1 **157** oh4 ow1 BarryGeraghty (Nicky Henderson) *in tch: hdwy and nt fluent 12th: styng on to chse ldrs whn blnd 17th: rallied fr 4 out: drvn to chse wnr appr last: styd on gamely u.p but a jst hld* **15/2**^{3}	172+
U24-	**3**	*14*	**Denman (IRE)**^{220} 5322 10-11-12 **182** SamThomas (Paul Nicholls) *trckd ldrs: chal fr 17th: stl upsides but u.p 3 out: mstke next and sn dropped bk to 3rd: wknd bef last* **4/1**^{1}	182
05-2	**4**	*1/2*	**The Tother One (IRE)**^{28} 2091 9-9-9 **156** oh2 MrRMahon(5) (Paul Nicholls) *blnd 2nd: hit 5th and 7th: chsd ldrs 10th: in rr 14th: hit 16th and 17th: plenty to do 4 out: r.o fr 2 out: fin wl to take 4th nr fin* **28/1**	159
0P-F	**5**	*3/4*	**Niche Market (IRE)**^{21} 2221 9-9-9 **156** oh8 IanPopham(5) (Paul Nicholls) *chsd ldrs: rdn fr 17th: styd on fr 4 out to chse ldng trio next: nvr any ch and ct for 4th nr fin* **40/1**	154
42-6	**6**	*3 1/4*	**Carruthers**^{28} 2084 7-10-0 **156** oh1 MattieBatchelor (Mark Bradstock) *chsd ldrs: blnd 7th: wnt 2nd 12th to 16th: hit 17th: wknd after 4 out* **14/1**	155
P/1-	**7**	*4 1/2*	**Taranis (FR)**^{301} 3736 9-10-4 **160** (t) NickScholfield (Paul Nicholls) *chsd ldrs to 17th: wknd 4 out* **14/1**	152
11-1	**8**	*18*	**Weird Al (IRE)**^{27} 2105 7-10-0 **156** oh4 PaddyBrennan (Ian Williams) *towards rr tl hdwy 16th: in tch 17th but nvr quite rchd ldrs: wknd 4 out* **6/1**^{2}	131
-045	**9**	*13*	**Hills Of Aran**^{7} 2523 8-10-0 **156** oh11 JamieMoore (Keith Goldsworthy) *j. slowly 5th: hit 12th: a bhd* **100/1**	119
121-	**10**	*74*	**Silver By Nature**^{280} 4162 8-10-0 **156** PeterBuchanan (Lucinda Russell) *blnd 1st: hmpd 4th: a bhd: t.o* **25/1**	53
4F-2	**F**		**Madison Du Berlais (FR)**^{25} 2136 9-10-1 **157** (p) TomScudamore (David Pipe) *chsd ldrs: hit 3rd: fell next* **16/1**	—
1PP-	**P**		**Dream Alliance**^{231} 5127 9-9-9 **156** oh5 (p) GilesHawkins(5) (Philip Hobbs) *in tch early: in rr fr 10th: t.o and p.u bef 16th* **66/1**	—
F14/	**B**		**Neptune Collonges (FR)**^{624} 4444 9-10-8 **164** APMcCoy (Paul Nicholls) *mid-div whn bdly hmpd and b.d 4th* **14/1**	—
0P-0	**P**		**Barbers Shop**^{28} 2091 8-10-0 **156** (b^{1}) AndrewTinkler (Nicky Henderson) *in rr: brief effrt 17th: sn wknd: t.o whn p.u bef 2 out* **40/1**	—
14-2	**F**		**Big Fella Thanks**^{19} 2273 8-10-0 **156** oh5 GrahamLee (Ferdy Murphy) *in rr whn fell 3rd* **14/1**	—
/11-	**P**		**Pandorama (IRE)**^{334} 3133 7-10-0 **156** oh8 PCarberry (Noel Meade, Ire) *blnd 2nd: hmpd and in rr 4th: sn wl bhd: t.o whn p.u bef 8th* **8/1**	—
P4-0	**P**		**Razor Royale (IRE)**^{14} 2358 8-9-11 **156** oh10 SamTwiston-Davies(3) (Nigel Twiston-Davies) *in rr: sme prog 16th: wknd next: no ch whn hit 4 out: t.o whn p.u bef 2 out* **40/1**	—
UF-1	**F**		**Hey Big Spender (IRE)**^{19} 2273 7-10-0 **156** 4ex oh2 AidanColeman (Colin Tizzard) *slt ld: nt fluent 14th: hdd after 17th: sn wknd: no ch whn fell last* **25/1**	126

6m 27.81s (-28.19) **Going Correction** -0.50s/f (Good) **18** Ran SP% **124.9**
Speed ratings (Par 113): **121,120,116,116,116 115,113,108,104,82** —,—,—,—,— —,—,—
toteswingers:1&2:£10.30, 1&3:£8.50, 2&3:£10.50 CSF £48.48 CT £208.37 TOTE £7.20: £2.00, £2.60, £1.40, £6.10; EX 44.40 Trifecta £483.20 Pool: £73,679.61 - 112.82 winning units..

Owner Paul Duffy Diamond Partnership **Bred** Mrs A L Wood **Trained** George Nympton, Devon

FOCUS

The top pre-Christmas staying handicap chase, and a race in which Denman was bidding to make history by becoming the first three-time winner in the 54 runnings of the event. That gelding's presence in the line-up rather compressed the weights with only four others, including two of his stable companions and the 2008 winner Madison Du Berlais, in the handicap proper. Despite that there were several interesting second-season chasers lurking just out of the weights, and a couple of those fought out the finish. The pace was strong as is often the case and the time excellent, being over 18secs faster than the earlier amateurs' handicap over the trip and just over 0.7secs outside the course record. It has to go down as a very high-class renewal and Diamond Harry produced a big personal best. Like Burton Port, he is worth his place in the Gold Cup field. Denman is rated 2lb off his form in last year's race.

NOTEBOOK

Diamond Harry ◆ was a smart novice chaser last season, is well suited by soft ground and has a good strike-rate. Despite being 4lb out of the handicap, he was always in the first two and jumped much more convincingly than he did last season. It was clear early in the straight he was going better than his nearest challenger Denman, and he found more for pressure to hold off the runner-up, with whom he was 15lb better off compared with last year's fixed brush hurdle form. A horse with a record of 5-6 on this track, he might come back for the Aon Chase or go to Cheltenham for the trials meeting, although his trainer gave the impression that he could go straight to the Gold Cup without a previous run. The only concerns are that he needs the ground on the soft side and, although he has won twice at Cheltenham, he might be ideally suited by flatter tracks. (op 7-1 tchd 11-2)

Burton Port(IRE) ◆ had won five of his six starts over fences (his only defeat coming when runner-up in the RSA Chase). He was held up early and was making ground when crashing through the cross fence, which would have ended the chance of many. However, he recovered well and was the only danger to the winner from before the last fence, although he could never get close enough to trouble that rival. He has clearly improved for fences; he had been getting 15lb when beaten by Diamond Harry in the fixed brush final at Haydock at around this time last year, and it looks worth taking on the winner again at Cheltenham. (op 7-1)

Denman(IRE), the dual winner of this but 8lb higher than last season, ran another terrific race. He was unable to dominate as he did last year, but when he joined the winner after the cross fence an unprecedented third success looked possible. However, it was clear early in the straight that the younger horse was travelling the better, and he gradually faded from before the penultimate fence. Connections were delighted with his effort and he now looks likely to go straight for the Gold Cup. (op 9-2 tchd 5-1 in places)

The Tother One(IRE), a stable companion of the third, made a bad error at the second and put in several other untidy jumps. He was well back early in the straight, but rallied well again in the latter stages. He is more than capable of winning good races if he can be more fluent at his fences. (op 33-1)

Niche Market(IRE), third in this race last season, had to race from 8lb out of the handicap so was meeting Denman on the same terms. He put up another fine effort, being in the leading group until the principals asserted. The Welsh National over Christmas or one of the spring equivalents are likely to be his targets.

Carruthers, a useful front-runner who won here last December, was unable to get to the lead but still ran a creditable race, only fading out of contention in the straight. (op 16-1)

Taranis(FR) goes really well fresh and was given every chance, being held up before creeping into contention on the second circuit. He looked as though he might be involved turning for home, but he had no more to offer. (op 12-1)

Weird Al(IRE) was one of the few disappointments. A horse with an unblemished record over fences coming into this, he was close enough on the home turn, but the response from that point was less than seemed likely. He now has to prove he can compete at the top level. (op 13-2 tchd 7-1 in places)

Madison Du Berlais(FR) was another who fell early, bringing down Neptune Collonges. (tchd 9-1 in places)

Barbers Shop finished fourth in this last season but, with blinkers replacing cheekpieces, never got involved having been settled at the back. (tchd 9-1 in places)

Big Fella Thanks was the first to fall, departing at the third. He may now go for the Peterborough Chase. (tchd 9-1 in places)

Pandorama(IRE) made a bad early error, was then hampered when Madison Du Berlais came down, and was tailed off when pulled up after the first in the straight on the first circuit. (tchd 9-1 in places)

Hey Big Spender(IRE), yet another good novice last season whose wins included one at this meeting, forced the pace but clearly went a bit too fast, as he faded quickly once headed at the cross fence and was very tired when coming down at the last fence. (tchd 9-1 in places)

2674 SPORTINGBET.COM H'CAP CHASE (16 fncs) 2m 4f

3:40 (3:43) (Class 2) (0-145,145) 4-Y-0+

£25,048 (£7,400; £3,700; £1,852; £924; £464)

Form				RPR
P3-3	**1**		**Mount Oscar (IRE)**^{49} 1777 11-10-11 **133** (t) SamTwiston-Davies(3) (Colin Tizzard) *trckd ldrs: wnt handy 3rd at 3 out: led last: drew clr last 150yds* **11/2**^{3}	148+
32P-	**2**	*7*	**Pasco (SWI)**^{232} 5111 7-11-12 **145** APMcCoy (Paul Nicholls) *hld up in mid-div: hdwy 9th: trcking ldrs 11th: slt ld 2 out: hdd last: styd on same pce* **5/1**^{2}	152
0P-2	**3**	*2 3/4*	**Piraya (FR)**^{7} 2517 7-11-9 **142** (tp) TomScudamore (David Pipe) *w ldrs: led after 11th: hdd 2 out: kpt on one pce appr last* **15/2**	146
-611	**4**	*1 3/4*	**Working Title (IRE)**^{26} 2125 8-11-6 **139** BarryGeraghty (Nicky Henderson) *hld up in tch: hdwy to chse ldrs 11th: outpcd 4 out: styd on same pce to take n.d 4th betwen last 2* **4/1**^{1}	141
01-U	**5**	*9*	**Prince De Beauchene (FR)**^{19} 2273 7-11-7 **140** BrianHughes (Howard Johnson) *hld up in mid-div: hdwy to trck ldrs 11th: one pce fr 3 out: mstke and wknd last* **13/2**	135
-413	**6**	*23*	**Just Smudge**^{5} 2582 8-10-11 **130** AidanColeman (Venetia Williams) *in rr: bhd fr 10th* **25/1**	104
0P-6	**7**	*4 1/2*	**Bible Lord (IRE)**^{21} 2212 9-10-13 **132** NickScholfield (Andy Turnell) *mid-div: lost pl and hit 8th: sn bhd* **33/1**	103
-153	**8**	*3 1/4*	**Circus Of Dreams**^{18} 2293 7-10-3 **122** (v) LeightonAspell (Oliver Sherwood) *in rr: bhd fr 11th* **28/1**	89
PP-1	**9**	*5*	**Minella Theatre (IRE)**^{35} 1973 7-11-2 **135** HaddenFrost (Henrietta Knight) *lft in ld 1st: hdd next: hit 3rd: led 5th to 7th: drvn 10th: lost pl appr 4 out* **16/1**	97
4-03	**10**	*22*	**Tramantano**^{34} 1987 11-10-9 **128** (b) PaddyBrennan (Nigel Twiston-Davies) *in rr: blnd 7th: sme hdwy 11th: sn wknd: bhd whn mstke 3 out: t.o* **40/1**	70
UP-P	**P**		**Nozic (FR)**^{14} 2360 9-11-7 **140** LiamTreadwell (Nick Gifford) *mid-div: lost pl 10th: bhd whn p.u bef 4 out* **50/1**	—
-P05	**P**		**Pocket Aces (IRE)**^{15} 2345 8-10-2 **128** MrTJCannon(7) (Richard Rowe) *mid-div: blnd 7th and 9th: sn bhd: blnd bdly 4 out: t.o whn p.u bef 2 out* **14/1**	—
1P-4	**P**		**The Hollinwell**^{27} 2105 7-11-5 **138** GrahamLee (Ferdy Murphy) *nt jump wl and detached in last: bhd whn mstke 3rd: t.o whn reminders 9th: p.u bef 3 out* **16/1**	—
51B6	**F**		**Radetsky March (IRE)**^{69} 1557 7-10-9 **128** JasonMaguire (Mark Bradstock) *led: fell 1st* **50/1**	—
3122	**U**		**Alesandro Mantegna (IRE)**^{21} 2212 5-10-6 **125** (p) JamieMoore (Keith Goldsworthy) *w ldrs: led 2nd: stmbld on landing and hdd 5th: led 7th tl after 11th: wknd 3 out: 6th whn blnd and uns rdr last* **9/1**	114

4m 57.2s (-14.80) **Going Correction** -0.50s/f (Good) **15** Ran SP% **122.2**
Speed ratings (Par 109): **109,106,105,104,100 91,89,88,86,77** —,—,—,—,—
toteswingers:1&2:£4.20, 1&3:£7.60, 2&3:£9.40 CSF £32.29 CT £211.83 TOTE £6.60: £2.20, £2.30, £2.70; EX 35.30 Trifecta £137.30 Pool: £2,786.20 - 15.01 winning units..

Owner Mrs Jean R Bishop **Bred** P Hore **Trained** Milborne Port, Dorset

FOCUS

Quite a valuable handicap chase, and it was suitably competitive. Remarkably the first three home from 2009 filled the same positions again, the trio having things to themselves over the last three fences. The form looks solid with the first three pretty much reproducing last season's form.

NOTEBOOK

Mount Oscar(IRE), last year's winner, was back on the same mark, making him 6lb better off with the runner-up this time around, and 7lb better off with the third. Given a break since his promising return to the track at Chepstow, he improved on the home turn and led at the last before staying on strongly. The return to this shorter trip suited, and although he is rising 12 he looks to have plenty of life left in him. (op 7-1)

Pasco(SWI) ran a thoroughly creditable race under top-weight, just unable to resist his old rival's challenge from the final fence. He has yet to finish out of the first two in seven visits to Newbury and the valuable handicap chase at the early March meeting, in which he was second last year, could be ideal for him. (tchd 9-2 and 11-2 and 6-1 in places)

Piraya(FR) was a good second to the progressive Woolcombe Folly over 2m1f at Ascot last weekend and wore the same combination of aids. The return to this trip suited but, after moving to the front turning out of the back straight, he had to give best between the final two fences. (op 10-1)

Working Title(IRE) was on a hat-trick after two hurdling wins and was able to race off this 13lb lower chase mark. He could not race on with the leaders from the cross fence, but was staying on at the end and could be worth trying over further. (tchd 9-2 in places)

Prince De Beauchene(FR) ran a pleasing race over a trip perhaps on the sharp side for him. He will be suited by some mid-winter ground, but remains 8lb higher than for his one previous handicap win. (tchd 6-1 and 7-1)

Minella Theatre(IRE) was put up 10lb after his Stratford win, form subsequently boosted by the second and fourth. After racing up with the pace he faded on the entrance to the home straight. (tchd 14-1)

Alesandro Mantegna(IRE), raised 4lb after a close second at Sandown, did not jump out to the left as he had there. He ran well for a long way, but was tired when unseating his rider at the final fence.

T/Jkpt: Part won. £15,041.40 to a £1 stake. Pool £21,185.17 - 0.50 winning tickets. T/Plt: £69.40 to a £1 stake. Pool:£185,372.73 - 1,947.38 winning tickets T/Qpdt: £18.30 to a £1 stake. Pool:£13,598.75 - 547.05 winning tickets ST

2349 NEWCASTLE (L-H)
Saturday, November 27

2675 Meeting Abandoned - Snow

2554 TOWCESTER (R-H)
Saturday, November 27

2681 Meeting Abandoned - Frozen ground

2269 CARLISLE (R-H)
Sunday, November 28

2688 Meeting Abandoned - Frozen ground

2419 LEICESTER (R-H)
Sunday, November 28

2695 Meeting Abandoned - Frozen ground & snow

2702 - 2705a (Foreign Racing) - See Raceform Interactive

2570 FFOS LAS (L-H)
Monday, November 29

2706 Meeting Abandoned - Frost

2439 FOLKESTONE (R-H)
Monday, November 29

2712 Meeting Abandoned - Snow

Wind: modest, across Weather: snow flurries

2466 HEREFORD (R-H)
Tuesday, November 30

2719 Meeting Abandoned - Frozen track

AYR (L-H)
Wednesday, December 1

2726 Meeting Abandoned - Frozen track

CATTERICK (L-H)
Wednesday, December 1

2733 Meeting Abandoned - Snow

2426 PLUMPTON (L-H)
Wednesday, December 1

2740 Meeting Abandoned - Partially forzen track

2419 LEICESTER (R-H)
Thursday, December 2

2747 Meeting Abandoned - Frost & snow

2473 MARKET RASEN (R-H)
Thursday, December 2

2753 Meeting Abandoned - Snow

2480 WINCANTON (R-H)
Thursday, December 2

2759 Meeting Abandoned - Frozen ground

2209 SANDOWN (R-H)
Friday, December 3

2765 Meeting Abandoned - Snow

2604 CHEPSTOW (L-H)
Saturday, December 4

2771 Meeting Abandoned - Frozen track

2209 SANDOWN (R-H)
Saturday, December 4

2778 Meeting Abandoned - Snow

2610 WETHERBY (L-H)
Saturday, December 4

2784 Meeting Abandoned - Snow

2499 EXETER (R-H)
Sunday, December 5

OFFICIAL GOING: Good to soft (soft in places 6.9)

Wind: virtually nil Weather: dry

2791 EUROPEAN BREEDERS' FUND "NATIONAL HUNT" NOVICES' HURDLE (QUALIFIER) (7 hdls 1 omitted) 2m 1f
12:20 (12:21) (Class 4) 4-6-Y-O **£3,772** (£1,107; £553; £276)

Form					RPR
2-2	**1**		**The Reformer (IRE)**[29] 2216 5-10-12 0 HarrySkelton (Paul Nicholls) *mid-div: hdwy after 3rd: chal 3 out: sn rdn: narrow advantage last: styd on: drvn out* **5/2**[2]		118+
00-	**2**	*1 1/4*	**Shinrock Hill (IRE)**[276] 4411 6-10-5 0 MattGriffiths[(7)] (Philip Hobbs) *trckd ldr: led appr 3 out: rdn bef 2 out: narrowly hdd last whn pckd: styd on: hld towards fin* **100/1**		116
4-56	**3**	*nk*	**Grey Missile**[16] 2499 5-10-12 0 NickScholfield (Jeremy Scott) *trckd ldrs: rdn 3 out: styd on wout quite chalng ldng pair* **16/1**		116
1-	**4**	*9*	**Fontano (FR)**[230] 5283 4-10-9 0 AlexMerriam[(3)] (Emma Lavelle) *hld up towards rr: prog after 4th: rdn bef next: styd on same pce* **7/1**[3]		107
5	**5**	*17*	**Lobby Ludd**[32] 2143 5-10-12 0 RhysFlint (Philip Hobbs) *in tch: rdn appr 3 out: wknd bef 2 out* **50/1**		90
3-1	**6**	*1*	**Arthurian Legend**[32] 2145 5-11-5 0 TomO'Brien (Philip Hobbs) *in tch: rdn appr 3 out: sn wknd* **5/4**[1]		96
0	**7**	*1/2*	**Sulpius (GER)**[29] 2215 5-10-12 0 WillKennedy (Bob Buckler) *led tl rdn appr 3 out: sn wknd* **100/1**		89
2-P	**8**	*1 1/2*	**Ballestra (IRE)**[26] 2288 6-10-5 0 AidanColeman (Venetia Williams) *mid-div: rdn appr 3 out: sn wknd* **33/1**		80
0-55	**9**	*4 1/2*	**Reinriver**[13] 2577 4-10-5 0 TomScudamore (Brendan Powell) *a towards rr* **33/1**		77
	10	*5*	**Persian Present (IRE)** 4-10-12 0 JohnnyFarrelly (Sophie Leech) *mid-div tl after 4th* **150/1**		78
20	**11**	*3 3/4*	**Health Is Wealth (IRE)**[20] 2428 5-10-12 0 JoeTizzard (Colin Tizzard) *struggling 2nd: a in rr* **50/1**		74
10-	**12**	*1 1/4*	**Amroth Bay**[295] 4037 6-10-12 0 FelixDeGiles (Andrew Balding) *racd keenly: trckd ldrs: rdn appr 3 out: sn wknd* **9/1**		73
0-00	**13**	*8*	**Man Of Leisure**[11] 2607 6-10-7 0 KeiranBurke[(5)] (Nerys Dutfield) *trckd ldrs tl 4th: sn wknd* **200/1**		65
0	**14**	*19*	**Turf Legends (IRE)**[36] 2087 4-10-7 0 GilesHawkins[(5)] (Philip Hobbs) *struggling 2nd: a bhd* **100/1**		46

4m 11.1s (-4.40) **Going Correction** -0.125s/f (Good)

WFA 4 from 5yo+ 5lb **14 Ran SP% 115.3**

Speed ratings: **105,104,104,100,92 91,91,90,88,86 84,83,80,71**

toteswingers:1&2:£57.10, 1&3:£12.50, 2&3:£87.30 CSF £227.15 TOTE £2.40: £1.10, £11.50, £3.50; EX 175.10.

Owner C G Roach **Bred** Peter Murphy **Trained** Ditcheat, Somerset

FOCUS

A modest novice hurdle where three came clear.

NOTEBOOK
The Reformer(IRE), runner-up on both of his previous starts, moved smoothly just behind the leaders before making hard work of success. One got the impression that he started to doss once in front and is possibly value for a bit more than the winning margin. (op 9-4)
Shinrock Hill(IRE) ran a cracker on his first start for this stable after travelling strongly at the head of affairs. He looks certain to take something similar, especially if settling a bit better. (op 66-1)
Grey Missile appears to be getting better with racing and shapes like a horse that will stay further.
Fontano(FR), the winner of his only start in a bumper from The Reformer, was ridden patiently early and made some fair late progress. He is entitled to come on and may also stay a bit further. (op 4-1)
Lobby Ludd was far from disgraced on his second outing under rules and has something to build on. (op 66-1)
Arthurian Legend chased the leaders, but came under pressure on the home bend and was soon beaten. This was a long way below what he achieved on his hurdling debut. (op 7-4 tchd 6-5)

2792 EXETER HURDLE (LIMITED H'CAP) (7 hdls 1 omitted) 2m 1f
12:50 (12:50) (Class 2) 4-Y-O **£12,524** (£3,700; £1,850; £926)

Form RPR
33-4 **1** **Salontyre (GER)**[13] 2574 4-9-13 126 oh21.......(p) MissIsabelTompsett[(5)] 122
(Bernard Llewellyn) *trckd ldr: rdn appr 3 out: kpt on to take narrow ld last: styd on wl: rdn out* **22/1**
220- **2** *1 1/2* **Causeway King (USA)**[263] 4675 4-10-8 130................. RobertThornton 125
(Alan King) *led: looked to duck out 2nd: rdn after 2 out: narrowly hdd whn nt fluent last: no ex* **7/2[3]**
13-F **3** *9* **Sanctuaire (FR)**[21] 2386 4-11-10 146.................................... DarylJacob 131
(Paul Nicholls) *racd keenly: trckd ldrs: jnd ldr 3rd: rdn after 3 out: kpt on same pce: fdd appr last* **8/11[1]**
-005 **4** *5* **Ciceron (IRE)**[8] 2671 4-10-10 132...................................... AidanColeman 115
(Venetia Williams) *trckd ldr: rdn appr 3 out: wknd after 2 out* **10/3[2]**
4m 16.7s (1.20) **Going Correction** -0.125s/f (Good) **4** Ran SP% **107.6**
Speed ratings: **92,91,87,84**
CSF £83.40 TOTE £20.90; EX 28.60.
Owner Alex James **Bred** Gestut Wittekindshof **Trained** Fochriw, Caerphilly

FOCUS
A steadily run limited handicap. Suspect form.
NOTEBOOK
Salontyre(GER) managed to win, but how he did so on these terms is anyone's guess. He has proved to be a good sort at his level previously, but not many could have predicted this result against what looked some very useful rivals. It goes without saying that this performance must be treated with extreme caution for form purposes. Official explanation: trainer had no explanation for the apparent improvement in form. (op 25-1 tchd 28-1)
Causeway King(USA) got an easy lead, but had a good look at a couple of hurdles at about the halfway stage, causing his jockey, making his comeback after five months out, a few worrying moments. However, he kept going quite well and rallied bravely on his seasonal reappearance. (tchd 5-1)
Sanctuaire(FR), on his toes in the paddock again as he had been at Cheltenham, took a strong hold at the rear and refused to settle early. Wearing a noseband, he got to the heels of the leader before three out, but tended to duck in behind Causeway King when appearing to make his bid. It's entirely possible he got legless in the ground, but he does have plenty to prove now. (op 4-5 tchd 8-13)
Ciceron(IRE) raced kindly in behind, but found virtually nothing when asked to quicken. He probably doesn't want the ground so tacky. (op 3-1)

2793 HARRY DUTFIELD MEMORIAL NOVICES' CHASE (11 fncs 4 omitted) 2m 3f 110y
1:20 (1:20) (Class 2) 4-Y-O+ **£12,674** (£3,744)

Form RPR
11/3 **1** **Tarablaze**[25] 2303 7-11-0 135.. TomO'Brien 141+
(Philip Hobbs) *mde most: wnt sltly lft 4 out: 3 out and 2 out: wnt lft whn hit last: hdd: styd on u.str.p to ld fnl 50yds: drvn out* **4/11[1]**
3-14 **2** *1 3/4* **Hidden Keel**[21] 2387 5-11-0 0... PaddyBrennan 138
(Charlie Longsdon) *trckd wnr: pushed along 4 out: rdn after 3 out: led sn after last: hdd fnl 50yds: no ex* **2/1[2]**
4m 50.1s (-7.20) **Going Correction** -0.25s/f (Good) **2** Ran SP% **106.6**
Speed ratings (Par 109): **104,103**
TOTE £1.40.
Owner Mrs Diana L Whateley **Bred** Mrs S J Brasher **Trained** Withycombe, Somerset

FOCUS
The fences in the back straight were bypassed in all chases. Straightforward novice form.
NOTEBOOK
Tarablaze was novicey at some of his fences and jumped out to his left at a few, but even though he made a mistake at the final fence he rallied and ran on strongly up the stands' rail. There is little doubt he'll be better over further. (op 4-9)
Hidden Keel ◆ made a pleasing start to his chasing career and will no doubt find an opportunity soon. The horse has a fine record going left handed. (op 15-8)

2794 AXMINSTER CARPETS DEVON MARATHON H'CAP CHASE (14 fncs 8 omitted) 4m
1:50 (1:51) (Class 3) (0-120,119) 4-Y-O+ **£12,674** (£3,744; £1,872; £936; £468)

Form RPR
0-33 **1** **C'Monthehammers (IRE)**[28] 2248 7-11-10 117................. DavidEngland 134+
(Nigel Twiston-Davies) *mid-div: tk clsr order 12th: led appr 4 out: sn rdn: styd on wl: drvn out* **10/1**
/355 **2** *5* **Kitley Hassle**[26] 2286 8-10-7 100.......................................(b) HaddenFrost 110
(James Frost) *mid-div: rdn on long run after 9th: chsd wnr fr 4 out: styd on but a being hld* **10/1**
2P-4 **3** *17* **Minella Boys (IRE)**[25] 2305 8-11-12 119............................. FelixDeGiles 116
(Charlie Longsdon) *trckd ldrs: rdn appr 4 out: wknd 2 out* **6/1[2]**
0P-4 **4** *22* **Pancake (FR)**[25] 2311 7-11-2 109.......................................(b) TomO'Brien 91
(Philip Hobbs) *trckd ldr: led 4th: rdn and hdd appr 4 out: wknd 2 out* **17/2[3]**
044U **5** *8* **Ethiopia**[20] 2431 7-9-10 96.. NathanSweeney[(7)] 63
(Bob Buckler) *led tl 4th: chsd ldrs tl wknd on long run bef 4 out: t.o* **12/1**
1-00 **6** *52* **Omix D'Or (FR)**[15] 2532 8-11-7 114.................................. DavidDennis 34
(James Evans) *trckd ldrs: rdn on long run after 9th: wknd wl bef 4 out: t.o* **10/1**
243P **B** **Petite Margot**[21] 2395 11-11-4 111.................................. PaddyBrennan —
(Nigel Twiston-Davies) *mid-div: struggling towards rr whn b.d 9th* **17/2[3]**
P-0F **P** **Deep Quest**[16] 2503 11-11-3 110.......................................(t) RodiGreene —
(Simon Burrough) *a towards rr: hit 8th: struggling on long run after 9th: t.o whn p.u bef 2 out* **18/1**
3U-4 **F** **Helm (IRE)**[38] 2055 9-10-0 93... AidanColeman —
(Richard Rowe) *hld up towards rr: fell 9th: fatally injured* **5/1[1]**
631- **P** **Teeming Rain (IRE)**[271] 4498 11-11-12 119.......................(vt) APMcCoy —
(Jonjo O'Neill) *hld up towards rr: effrt to cl on long run after 9th: 5th but struggling whn nt fluent 4 out: sn p.u* **6/1[2]**
0P00 **P** **Au Courant (IRE)**[14] 2543 10-11-12 119.......................... JohnnyFarrelly —
(Sophie Leech) *mid-div: rdn on long run after 9th: sn wknd: p.u bef 4 out* **40/1**
2-51 **P** **Peut Etre Sivola (FR)**[21] 2395 7-11-10 117...............(vt) TomScudamore —
(David Pipe) *hld up towards rr: rdn on long run after 9th: wknd and p.u bef 4 out* **6/1[2]**
8m 14.4s (-14.30) **Going Correction** -0.25s/f (Good) **12** Ran SP% **123.2**
Speed ratings (Par 107): **107,105,101,96,94 81,—,—,—,— —,—**
toteswingers:1&2:£25.40, 1&3:£11.60, 2&3:£16.90 CSF £109.55 CT £666.76 TOTE £10.20: £3.70, £3.80, £2.50; EX 183.50.
Owner F J Mills & W Mills **Bred** Michael Shannon **Trained** Naunton, Gloucs

FOCUS
A marathon handicap run at a fair enough gallop, and unsurprisingly it was very hard work.
NOTEBOOK
C'Monthehammers(IRE) just about travelled the best for the longest and showed plenty of determination under pressure to claim victory. It was good performance on only his fourth start over fences and he has an entry in the Welsh National, so will presumably run there if getting in. (tchd 9-1 and 11-1)
Kitley Hassle, a four-time point winner in 2009, was taking a big step up in trip and proved to be a game rival from four out. He shapes like a thorough stayer. (op 16-1)
Minella Boys(IRE) was another to travel well for a long way before finding just the one pace. (op 5-1)
Pancake(FR) got to the lead quite early and appeared to enjoy himself until his stamina ebbed away. (op 16-1)
Helm(IRE) was out the back when sadly taking a fatal fall. (tchd 9-2)
Teeming Rain(IRE), who saves his best for this course, was quickly pulled up after hitting four out. (tchd 9-2)
Peut Etre Sivola(FR) does stay well, but looks too high in the weights and never threatened. (tchd 9-2)

2795 HERRINGSHOES.CO.UK CONDITIONAL JOCKEYS' NOVICES' H'CAP HURDLE (9 hdls 1 omitted) 2m 3f
2:20 (2:21) (Class 4) (0-100,99) 3-Y-O+ **£2,602** (£764; £382; £190)

Form RPR
0054 **1** **Hot Tottie (IRE)**[27] 2280 6-11-2 89.......................................(p) IanPopham 100+
(Jeremy Scott) *hld up but in tch: struggling to hold pl 6th: clsd on ldrs 3 out: led 2 out: styd on wl: rdn out* **11/8[1]**
40 **2** *12* **Holyrood**[13] 2583 4-11-6 99...(vt) MrTomDavid[(6)] 100
(Tim Vaughan) *trckd ldr: led 6th: rdn whn hdd 2 out: sn no ex* **8/1[3]**
5-00 **3** *9* **Trump Call (IRE)**[17] 2485 6-11-2 95............................ HarryChalloner[(6)] 85
(Venetia Williams) *hld up in tch: trckd ldrs 5th: rdn appr 3 out: fdd fr 2 out* **8/1[3]**
52P/ **4** *nk* **Kings Story (IRE)**[832] 1279 6-10-0 73 oh2......................... GilesHawkins 63
(Sophie Leech) *trckd ldrs: rdn after 6th: one pce and hld fr 3 out* **3/1[2]**
-P16 **5** *20* **Pistolet Dove (IRE)**[18] 2453 8-11-12 99......................... RichieMcLernon 69
(Sophie Leech) *t.k.h: hld up: hdwy to trck ldrs 3rd: rdn after 6th: wknd bef 3 out* **10/1**
4-40 **6** *53* **Uncle Bunge (IRE)**[30] 2185 4-11-9 96.......................................(t) DPFahy 13
(Liam Corcoran) *hld up but in tch: rdn appr 3 out: sn btn: hit 2 out* **8/1[3]**
P0 **P** **Sourchamp (FR)**[18] 2456 4-10-12 85.............................. MichaelMurphy —
(Arthur Whiting) *j.lft: led tl 6th: sn rdn and wknd: p.u bef next* **40/1**
4m 46.8s (4.10) **Going Correction** -0.125s/f (Good)
WFA 4 from 6yo+ 5lb **7** Ran SP% **112.0**
Speed ratings (Par 105): **86,80,77,77,68 46,—**
toteswingers:1&2:£3.10, 1&3:£3.40, 2&3:£5.70 CSF £12.35 CT £62.92 TOTE £2.50: £1.50, £2.30; EX 10.30.
Owner The Ten 2 One Gang **Bred** J P N Parker **Trained** Brompton Regis, Somerset

FOCUS
An ordinary contest that took little winning judged on these horse's recent efforts. The winner was well in on some previous form.
NOTEBOOK
Hot Tottie(IRE), who managed to settle this time, got outpaced as the tempo increased before finding her stride. The further she went, the better she looked and she won by a handy margin. Connections will surely be very eager to get her out before the handicapper can reassess her as she would escape a penalty, but obviously that may be tricky during the current cold spell. (op 6-4 tchd 5-4)
Holyrood, with a visor on this time, travelled strongly close to the lead and eased to the front after four out. Quietly ridden, he kept going but couldn't quicken when challenged by the winner. (op 6-1)
Trump Call(IRE), up in trip, made a forward move at around halfway and had his chance before weakening. (op 13-2)
Kings Story(IRE) attracted a lot of market support on his first outing since August 2008, but rarely looked like rewarding his supporters. That said, it was still a fair effort after a long absence. (op 6-1)
Pistolet Dove(IRE), back over hurdles, raced a bit keenly close to the leader early but dropped out before the home straight, looking an awkward ride at times. (op 15-2 tchd 11-1)

2796 CHILDREN'S HOSPICE SOUTH WEST NOVICES' H'CAP CHASE (11 fncs 7 omitted) 3m
2:50 (2:50) (Class 4) (0-105,102) 4-Y-O+ **£3,903** (£1,146; £573; £286)

Form RPR
5P14 **1** **Canal Bank (IRE)**[27] 2274 6-11-3 96.......................(p) RichieMcLernon[(3)] 108+
(Jonjo O'Neill) *hld up bhd ldrs: chal 3 out: led last: pushed out* **6/1**
-522 **2** *3/4* **Topless (IRE)**[13] 2573 9-11-4 101.................................(p) MarkQuinlan[(7)] 109
(Neil Mulholland) *led: rdn after 4 out: hdd last: styd on but no ex nr fin* **5/1[3]**
P-40 **3** *40* **Alteranthela (IRE)**[15] 2513 6-11-4 101............................ MrTJCannon[(7)] 73
(Richard Rowe) *w ldr: rdn on long run bef 4 out: readily hld whn lft 4th 3 out: wnt modest 3rd nr fin* **10/1**
5F0- **4** *nk* **Noble Aran (IRE)**[254] 4869 6-11-7 97............................... PaddyBrennan 69
(Nigel Twiston-Davies) *hld up bhd ldrs: rdn in cl 4th appr 4 out: wknd after 2 out: fin tired: lost 3rd nr finsh* **7/4[1]**
01-0 **5** *18* **Monn Royal (FR)**[28] 2243 6-11-5 102........................... HarryChalloner[(7)] 58
(Venetia Williams) *hld up bhd ldrs: nt fluent 6th: rdn on long run after 7th: wknd bef 4 out: t.o* **9/1**
023F **F** **Solitary Palm (IRE)**[15] 2513 7-11-7 102............................ IanPopham[(5)] —
(Brian Forsey) *trckd ldrs: effrt in cl 2nd whn pckd bdly 4 out: 4th and hld whn fell next* **9/2[2]**
504/ **P** **Elton**[586] 38 7-11-5 95.. TomO'Brien —
(Philip Hobbs) *trckd ldrs: mstke 1st: rdn and wknd wl after 7th: p.u bef 4 out* **11/1**
6m 13.8s (4.50) **Going Correction** -0.25s/f (Good) **7** Ran SP% **112.9**
Speed ratings (Par 105): **82,81,68,68,62 —,—**
toteswingers:1&2:£3.00, 1&3:£10.90, 2&3:£10.40 CSF £34.71 CT £292.62 TOTE £6.60: £2.90, £1.70; EX 21.40.
Owner John P McManus **Bred** Glenn Turley **Trained** Cheltenham, Gloucs

FOCUS
A novice handicap run at a steady gallop. The first pair came a long way clear.
NOTEBOOK
Canal Bank(IRE) must have had an off day at Carlisle last time as he won this quite comfortably under a confident ride. He ought to be capable of winning again if in the same mood next time. (op 5-1)
Topless(IRE) is a mainly consistent if frustrating performer. She was well ridden considering the way the race was run and was unlucky to meet the winner on a going day. (op 11-2 tchd 4-1)
Alteranthela(IRE) kept plugging away to narrowly gain third and could have probably done without the fences being bypassed. (tchd 14-1)
Noble Aran(IRE) travelled strongly, but got really tired in the latter stages. He is entitled to benefit from this after a break. (tchd 13-8)
Solitary Palm(IRE) was still in with a small chance when clipping four out. The jockey managed to gather his mount together, but the pair departed at the next. (op 13-2)
Elton Official explanation: trainer said gelding finished distressed (op 13-2)

2797 E B F "JUNIOR" STANDARD OPEN NATIONAL HUNT FLAT RACE 1m 5f
3:20 (3:21) (Class 5) 3-Y-O **£1,951** (£573; £286; £143)

Form RPR
4 **1** **It's A Gimme (IRE)**[28] 2237 3-10-12 0 APMcCoy 95+
(Jonjo O'Neill) *hld up: hdwy over 5f out: chal and edgd lft fr 2f out: led ins fnl f: styd on wl* **11/4**[2]
2 *2* **Kaylif Aramis** 3-10-12 0 PaddyBrennan 92
(Nigel Twiston-Davies) *mid-div: hdwy 6f out: rdn to ld 2f out: hdd ins fnl f: kpt on but no ex* **11/2**
3 *6* **What A Warrior (IRE)** 3-10-12 0 DavidEngland 85+
(Nigel Twiston-Davies) *hld up towards rr: rdn and styd on fr over 2f out: wnt 3rd ins fnl f: nvr threatened ldng pair* **14/1**
0 **4** *2* **Generous Bob**[47] 1913 3-10-9 0 WayneKavanagh(3) 82
(Seamus Mullins) *trckd ldr: rdn 3f out: sn one pce* **40/1**
5 *½* **Allez Les Rouges (IRE)** 3-10-12 0 FelixDeGiles 88+
(Andrew Balding) *racd keenly: led: rdn and hung bdly lft fr 3f out: hdd 2f out: continued to hang bdly lft and veered across crse fnl f: nvr able to rcvr* **5/2**[1]
6 *½* **Milarrow (IRE)** 3-10-12 0 JoeTizzard 81
(Colin Tizzard) *hld up towards rr: rdn over 3f out: styd on same pce* **8/1**
7 *1* **Saffron Sam** 3-10-12 0 AndrewGlassonbury 84+
(Simon Burrough) *trckd ldrs: rdn and mounting chal whn hmpd over 2f out: one pce after* **100/1**
8 *4 ½* **Glassawine** 3-10-12 0 TomScudamore 74
(David Pipe) *trckd ldrs: rdn 3f out: sn btn* **5/1**[3]
9 *27* **Jupiter Rex (FR)** 3-10-5 0 HarryChalloner(7) 38
(Venetia Williams) *prom for 6f: t.o* **14/1**
10 *19* **William Womble** 3-10-12 0 HaddenFrost 14
(James Frost) *mid-div tl wknd over 3f out* **66/1**

3m 14.1s (-2.60) **10** Ran SP% **116.7**
toteswingers:1&2:£4.80, 1&3:£7.70, 2&3:£7.70 CSF £18.35 TOTE £4.70: £1.70, £2.90, £5.30; EX 22.80.
Owner John P McManus **Bred** Gregg Stafford **Trained** Cheltenham, Gloucs
FOCUS
This could work out to be a fair race of its type. The fourth sets the level.
NOTEBOOK
It's A Gimme(IRE) improved on his debut effort behind Keys (who has won again since) to take this. It will be interesting to see if he goes over hurdles next or tries to carry a penalty in this sphere. (op 3-1 tchd 10-3)
Kaylif Aramis ◆, a brother to Kayf Aramis, made a highly satisfactory start to his career and drew clear of the remainder with the winner. He can find one of these. (op 9-2)
What A Warrior(IRE) looked distinctly inexperienced when asked to make an effort, so the way he finished was pleasing. He may, however, need more time. (op 16-1)
Generous Bob probably improved on his debut effort and is at least going in the right direction. (op 33-1)
Allez Les Rouges(IRE) ◆ was doing it all nicely until his rider asked for him to lengthen. For some reason the horse wanted to hang violently to his left, and it took all of the jockey's strength to get him to run between the wings of what would have been the last two hurdles. Once he had passed the last of those, his rider seemed to let him head to the stands' rail and he came home there. He would have gone very close had he kept a straighter line. Official explanation: jockey said gelding hung badly left in home straight (op 3-1)
Milarrow(IRE) made some nice late headway and should step up on this. (tchd 15-2)
Saffron Sam was almost run off the course by the errant Balding runner, but he looked to be held by that horse when it happened. (op 66-1)
T/Plt: £1,414.00 to a £1 stake. Pool:£68,376.43 - 35.30 winning tickets T/Qpdt: £19.70 to a £1 stake. Pool:£9,929.80 - 371.19 winning tickets TM

2547 KELSO (L-H)
Sunday, December 5
2798 Meeting Abandoned - Snow

2452 WARWICK (L-H)
Sunday, December 5
2805 Meeting Abandoned - Frost

2303 BANGOR-ON-DEE (L-H)
Monday, December 6
2812 Meeting Abandoned - Track frozen in parts

2654 MUSSELBURGH (R-H)
Monday, December 6
2818 Meeting Abandoned - Snow

2276 SOUTHWELL (L-H)
Monday, December 6
OFFICIAL GOING: Standard to slow
This Fibresand card, arranged at short notice, consisted of three Flat races followed by three bumpers.
Wind: Almost nil Weather: Sunny, cold

2824 TOTEPOOL A BETTER WAY TO BET "JUNIOR" STANDARD OPEN NATIONAL HUNT FLAT RACE 1m 6f (F)
2:20 (2:20) (Class 5) 3-Y-O **£1,712** (£499; £249)

Form RPR
1 **1** **Cinders And Ashes**[39] 2052 3-11-5 0 JasonMaguire 114+
(Donald McCain) *prom gng wl: smooth hdwy to ld centre over 2f out: drew clr fr over 1f out: eased towards fin: readily* **13/2**[3]
4 **2** *6* **Polurrian (IRE)**[26] 2315 3-10-12 0 JimmyMcCarthy 99
(Charles Egerton) *midfield: hdwy and prom over 4f out: effrt and chsd wnr wl over 1f out: kpt on fnl f: no imp* **13/2**[3]
4 **3** *11* **Main Beach**[13] 2597 3-10-12 0 DominicElsworth 86
(Tobias B P Coles) *t.k.h: trckd ldrs on ins: effrt over 2f out: edgd lft and wknd wl over 1f out* **17/2**
4 *2 ½* **Malibu Sun** 3-10-12 0 LeightonAspell 83
(Oliver Sherwood) *t.k.h: hld up in midfield: effrt and drvn over 3f out: hung lft and wknd wl over 1f out* **25/1**
23 **5** *1* **Bathcounty (IRE)**[26] 2315 3-10-12 0 TomO'Brien 82
(Barry Brennan) *led cl to ins rail to st: hdd over 2f out: sn rdn and outpcd* **7/2**[2]
6 *7* **Reai (IRE)** 3-10-12 0 APMcCoy 73
(Richard Fahey) *prom: rdn over 4f out: wknd over 2f out* **7/4**[1]
7 *¾* **Hopes Up** 3-10-5 0 DougieCostello 65
(Ian Williams) *plld hrd: hld up on outside: hdwy and prom after 6f: rdn and wknd over 3f out* **10/1**
0 **8** *3 ¾* **Roe Valley (IRE)**[26] 2315 3-10-7 0 BrianToomey(5) 68
(Linda Jewell) *hld up: hdwy and prom on ins over 3f out: sn rdn: wknd fr 2f out* **100/1**
9 *10* **Somervell** 3-10-12 0 RichieMcGrath 56
(Tim Easterby) *in tch on outside: stdy hdwy 1/2-way: rdn and wknd over 4f out* **22/1**
6 **10** *8* **Tild'Or Du Granit (FR)**[32] 2173 3-9-12 0 RobertKirk(7) 39
(James Evans) *t.k.h: cl up tl rdn and wknd fr 4f out* **66/1**
11 *8* **Indicco** 3-10-5 0 BrianHughes 30
(Ruth Carr) *cl up tl rdn and wknd over 3f out* **40/1**
12 *nse* **Glasson Lad (IRE)** 3-10-5 0 PaulGallagher(7) 37
(Ferdy Murphy) *hld up on ins: rdn over 6f out: struggling over 4f out* **33/1**
13 *15* **Sammy G** 3-10-5 0 SeanQuinlan 12
(Kim Bailey) *hld up: rdn and outpcd over 5f out: sn struggling: nvr on terms* **14/1**
14 *¾* **Stanroad** 3-10-12 0 KennyJohnson 18
(Robert Johnson) *t.k.h: hld up: hdwy on outside and in tch 1/2-way: wknd over 4f out* **100/1**

3m 18.8s (10.50) **Going Correction** +0.825s/f (Slow) **14** Ran SP% **128.6**
Speed ratings (Par 102): **103,99,93,91,91 87,86,84,79,74 69,69,61,60**
toteswingers:1&2:£10.40, 1&3:£15.60, 2&3:£11.60 CSF £49.82 TOTE £4.50: £1.50, £2.40, £4.80; EX 38.30.
Owner Racing Squirrels 2011 **Bred** Juddmonte Farms Ltd **Trained** Cholmondeley, Cheshire
FOCUS
This 'Junior' bumper was run at a sensible pace. This was a big step up from the winner, and he looks a useful performer for the division.
NOTEBOOK
Cinders And Ashes, a well-made type, carried a penalty after his narrow soft-ground debut success at Fontwell. He travelled best and, after taking charge, came right away for an impressive success. Clearly useful and from a top stable, he looks sure to make his mark in juvenile hurdle races. (op 11-2)
Polurrian(IRE), fourth first time out at Huntingdon, stepped up on that effort and finished clear second-best behind the easy winner. (op 15-2 tchd 8-1 and 11-2)
Main Beach, fourth first time at Lingfield, tended to race freely and will need to settle better if he is to progress. (op 8-1 tchd 7-1)
Malibu Sun kept on in his own time in the home straight and looks a real stayer. (op 20-1)
Bathcounty(IRE), one place ahead of Polurrian at Huntingdon, set the pace but soon weakened when put in his place by the winner. This was his third start and he does not look to be progressing. (op 6-1)
Reai(IRE), Flat bred, was under the pump fully half a mile from home and ultimately looked a non-stayer. He had clearly been showing something at home and may have to revert to maiden races over shorter on the Flat proper. (op 9-4 tchd 5-2)
Hopes Up took a keen grip. She made rapid headway on the wide outside to join the leaders at halfway but was on the retreat turning in. She will need to settle a lot better. (op 14-1)
Indicco Official explanation: jockey said filly lost its action

2825 BET TOTEPOOL TO SUPPORT YOUR SPORT MARES' STANDARD OPEN NATIONAL HUNT FLAT RACE 2m (F)
2:50 (2:50) (Class 5) 4-6-Y-O **£1,712** (£499; £249)

Form RPR
65- **1** **Tazzarine (FR)**[239] 5150 4-10-12 0 APMcCoy 94+
(Charles Egerton) *t.k.h: mde all towards ins rail: qcknd 1/2-way: rdn and styd on wl fr 2f out* **2/1**[2]
4-2 **2** *7* **Verde Goodwood**[188] 568 4-10-12 0 LeightonAspell 87
(Oliver Sherwood) *hld up: stdy hdwy 1/2-way: chsd wnr over 4f out: effrt and rdn over 2f out: no imp* **7/4**[1]
0 **3** *17* **Megan May**[47] 1927 4-10-12 0 DougieCostello 70
(Ian Williams) *cl up on ins: chsd wnr briefly bef 1/2-way: outpcd over 4f out: plugged on fnl 2f: nvr able to chal* **16/1**
4 *4* **Serenitatis (IRE)** 4-10-12 0 RichieMcGrath 66
(Tim Easterby) *prom: chsd wnr 1/2-way to over 4f out: rdn and wknd over 3f out* **9/2**[3]
0 **5** *9* **Luna Lightning**[20] 2445 6-10-12 0 MarkBradburne 57
(Linda Jewell) *prom: rdn and lost pl 1/2-way: sme late hdwy to pass btn horses in st: no ch w principals* **50/1**
0 **6** *5* **Matilda's Folly (IRE)**[12] 2616 5-10-12 0 BarryKeniry 52
(Ben Haslam) *hld up: drvn and outpcd over 4f out: sn struggling* **50/1**
0 **7** *6* **Quand Je Reve De Toi (FR)**[18] 2472 6-10-12 0 CharliePoste 46
(Mrs Pauline Harkin) *hld up on outside: struggling 6f out: sn btn* **16/1**
8 *29* **Primadora (IRE)** 4-10-12 0 (t) WarrenMarston 17
(Milton Harris) *t.k.h: hold up in tch: rdn and struggling 6f out: t.o* **10/1**

0 9 26 **Sally O'Malley (IRE)**[43] 1989 4-10-12 0.............................. AlanO'Keeffe —
(Charles Smith) *chsd wnr tl 7f out: sn struggling: t.o* **80/1**
4m 3.00s (17.50) **Going Correction** +0.825s/f (Slow) **9** Ran SP% **113.9**
Speed ratings: **89,85,77,75,70 68,65,50,37**
toteswingers:1&2:£2.00, 1&3:£5.20, 2&3:£4.50 CSF £5.74 TOTE £5.40: £1.70, £1.10, £2.80; EX 5.80.
Owner Bailey-Carvill Equine **Bred** Sandra Hosselet & Hubert Hosselet **Trained** Chaddleworth, Berks

FOCUS
A modest mares-only bumper, run at a very steady pace for the first 1m, and they came home strung right out. It has been rated around the third.

NOTEBOOK
Tazzarine(FR), who showed ability when sixth on her debut at Uttoxeter in March, disappointed on faster ground at Market Rasen the following month. Turned out in top trim, she quickened the pace setting out on to the final circuit and was soon out on her own. She only had to be kept going to win unchallenged, and clearly stays really well. (op 7-4 tchd 9-4)
Verde Goodwood, runner-up at Ffos Las on her second start in June, improved from the rear to go in pursuit of the winner exiting the back straight. Hard as she tried she was never going to get near her, but she did finish well clear of the remainder. (op 2-1)
Megan May, inclined to race keenly, stayed on to snatch a modest third. (op 14-1)
Serenitatis(IRE) chased the winner at halfway but tired markedly in the home straight. (op 5-1 tchd 4-1)

2826 BET TOTEPOOL ON ALL UK RACING STANDARD OPEN NATIONAL HUNT FLAT RACE 2m (F)
3:20 (3:20) (Class 5) 4-6-Y-O **£1,712** (£499; £249)

Form RPR
1 **Diocles (IRE)** 4-11-0 0.. JasonMaguire 115+
(Donald McCain) *in tch on ins: smooth hdwy over 4f out: c centre and led over 1f out: shkn up and drew clr fnl f: readily* **7/2**[3]
4 2 8 **Bunclody**[23] 2368 5-10-4 0.............................. SamuelWelton(10) 102
(George Moore) *w ldr on ins: led after 3f: rdn and hdd over 1f out: no ch w wnr* **3/1**[2]
1 3 4 ½ **Max Laurie (FR)**[15] 2560 5-11-4 0.............................. TomMolloy(3) 104
(Michael Banks) *hld up: stdy hdwy over 4f out: rdn over 3f out: kpt on same pce fr 2f out* **13/2**
4 ½ **Upthemsteps (IRE)**[246] 5-11-0 0.............................. DougieCostello 97
(Ian Williams) *t.k.h: set stdy pce 3f: w ldr: rdn and outpcd over 3f out: sn n.d* **6/1**
5 16 **Wait No More (IRE)**[212] 5-11-0 0.............................. AidanColeman 81
(Sarah Humphrey) *hld up in tch on outside: stdy hdwy over 5f out: rdn and outpcd 4f out: btn fnl 3f* **11/4**[1]
3- 6 11 **Mr Supreme (IRE)**[244] 5078 5-11-0 0.............................. RichieMcGrath 70
(Kate Walton) *trckd ldrs: rdn over 4f out: sn struggling* **9/1**
2-0 7 25 **Cloudy Joe (IRE)**[204] 355 4-10-11 0.............................. AdamPogson(3) 45
(Charles Pogson) *t.k.h: hld up: stdy hdwy on outside over 5f out: rdn and wknd fr 4f out* **14/1**
0- 8 9 **Flag Dancer**[226] 5391 4-10-7 0.............................. MattCrawley(7) 36
(Christine Dunnett) *t.k.h: trckd ldrs: rdn 1/2-way: struggling fnl 6f* **100/1**
3m 58.9s (13.40) **Going Correction** +0.825s/f (Slow)
WFA 4 from 5yo+ 5lb **8** Ran SP% **120.3**
Speed ratings: **99,95,92,92,84 79,66,62**
toteswingers:1&2:£3.60, 1&3:£5.50, 2&3:£4.60 CSF £15.36 TOTE £3.90: £2.00, £1.50, £2.30; EX 17.20.
Owner L G M Racing **Bred** Eric Watson **Trained** Cholmondeley, Cheshire

FOCUS
An ordinary bumper, run at a steady pace until the final 5f, yet the time was much faster than the preceding mares' race. It has been rated around the third in line with his Towcester win. The winner looks a good prospect.

NOTEBOOK
Diocles(IRE), out of a mare who stayed 3m, is not short on speed and he travelled strongly before cruising into contention. He certainly knew his job and, when shaken up, came right away for an easy debut success. He looks another potentially useful novice hurdling type for his powerful yard. (op 4-1)
Bunclody, in front when falling two out in an Irish point, had finished a well beaten fourth in a heavy-ground bumper at Uttoxeter last month. With his rider claiming the maximum 10lb, he set the pace and had all but the winner beaten off turning in. To his credit he stuck to his task in willing fashion. (op 7-2)
Max Laurie(FR), inclined to race wide, stayed on to claim a modest third spot. His first-time-out win came at Towcester, and he looks a real stayer. (op 7-1 tchd 8-1)
Upthemsteps(IRE), narrow winner of a maiden Irish point in April, was done for speed turning for home. (op 12-1)
Wait No More(IRE), another winner of a maiden point in Ireland in the spring, looks more of a potential chaser and was left for dead in the final half-mile. (tchd 7-2)
Mr Supreme(IRE), keen when a modest third first time at Wetherby in April, again would not settle and he too was left flat-footed on the final turn. (op 7-1)
T/Plt: £34.10 to a £1 stake. Pool:£74,604.20 - 1,595.46 winning tickets T/Qpdt: £4.80 to a £1 stake. Pool:£7,110.63 - 1,079.77 winning tickets RY

2390 FONTWELL (L-H)
Tuesday, December 7
2827 Meeting Abandoned - Frozen track

2598 SEDGEFIELD (L-H)
Tuesday, December 7
2834 Meeting Abandoned - Snow and frozen ground

2446 HEXHAM (L-H)
Wednesday, December 8
2840 Meeting Abandoned - Snow

2419 LEICESTER (R-H)
Wednesday, December 8
2847 Meeting Abandoned - Frozen track

2584 LUDLOW (R-H)
Thursday, December 9
2853 Meeting Abandoned - Track frozen in parts

2633 TAUNTON (R-H)
Thursday, December 9
2860 Meeting Abandoned - Track frozen in parts

2384 CHELTENHAM (L-H)
Friday, December 10

OFFICIAL GOING: Good
1st fence in back straight and 2nd fence in home straight omitted in all chase races. The cross-country race was abandoned due to frozen patches.
Wind: Virtually nil Weather: Overcast

2867 INJURED JOCKEYS' FUND OAKSEY HOUSE NOVICES' CHASE (15 fncs 2 omitted) 2m 5f
12:10 (12:40) (Class 2) 4-Y-0+ **£9,798** (£3,180; £1,792)

Form RPR
21-4 1 **Reve De Sivola (FR)**[28] 2348 5-11-0 0.............................. DarylJacob 140+
(Nick Williams) *nt fluent 1st and 2nd: in rr: hit 4th and reminder: hmpd 7th (water): hit 4 out: clsd on clr ldr appr 2 out and chal for 2nd: slt ld appr last: styd on wl u.p run-in* **3/1**[2]
0-F1 2 1 ¼ **Wishfull Thinking**[34] 2220 7-11-8 0.............................. RichardJohnson 149+
(Philip Hobbs) *lw: in tch: chsng ldrs whn bdly hmpd 7th (water): rcvrd 9th: wnt 2nd 10th: blnd 4 out: clsd on clr ldr appr 2 out: chal last: kpt on same pce u.p run-in* **8/1**
1-11 3 6 **Rebel Du Maquis (FR)**[29] 2330 5-11-8 148.............................. HarrySkelton 139+
(Paul Nicholls) *trckd ldr: chal 6th: led and lft wl clr 7th (water): blnd 11th: hit 4 out: wknd appr 2 out: hdd appr last: wknd run-in* **15/2**[3]
4-23 F **Othermix (FR)**[28] 2348 6-11-0 142.............................. (b) DougieCostello —
(Ian Williams) *lw: led: jnd 6th: narrowly hdd and fell 7th (water)* **15/2**[3]
01-F F **Spirit River (FR)**[14] 2664 5-11-0 0.............................. BarryGeraghty —
(Nicky Henderson) *j. slowly 1st: sltly hmpd 7th (water) and lft mod 2nd: hit 8th and 9th: wknd next: hit 4 out: wl bhd whn fell 3 out* **11/8**[1]
0-15 B **Radium (FR)**[26] 2384 5-11-5 147.............................. APMcCoy —
(Nicky Henderson) *in rr but in tch: hit 4th: wl there whn bdly hmpd and b.d 7th (water)* **12/1**
5m 15.18s (-4.22) **Going Correction** -0.05s/f (Good) **6** Ran SP% **109.4**
Speed ratings (Par 109): **106,105,103,—,— —**
Tote Swingers: 1&2:£3.70, 1&3:£3.20, 2&3:£2.60 CSF £23.52 TOTE £3.50: £1.70, £2.70; EX 27.10.
Owner Paul Duffy Diamond Partnership **Bred** Gilles Trapenard & Thomas Trapenard **Trained** George Nympton, Devon

FOCUS
The ground, which had been under frost covers since Sunday, was described as good all round, but riders in the first reported it to be nearer good to soft. This novice chase has been won in recent seasons by Weird Al, Tidal Bay, Calgary Bay and Exotic Dancer, and another quality field lined up this term. It was an eventful race, with an incident at the water jump having a significant impact, and the bare form should be treated with a degree of caution. Several of these remain smart prospects, however, including Reve De Sivola who was a stone off his hurdle form but can surely rate higher.

NOTEBOOK
Reve De Sivola(FR) did not always jump that well over hurdles and he made a noteworthy blunder on his chasing debut here last month, when fourth to Time For Rupert and a place behind Othermix. He was slow over the first couple of fences this time and dropped to the rear, but was safe enough afterwards. That said he looked an unlikely winner when last of the three still standing as they faced up to the final two fences, but he began to pick up from there as his stamina came into play, getting on top after the last. His trainer's string was held up more than most in the freeze and the gelding was not fully race-fit, so he can improve on what he did here. A dual Grade 1 winner over hurdles, he will be targeted at the new Jewson Novices' Chase over 2m4f at the Festival, when softer ground would be a plus. He should get 3m in time. (op 7-2)
Wishfull Thinking ◆ was a fortunate winner at Wincanton when left clear by the fall of Robinson Collonges. Fortune was not with him this time as he was badly hampered at the water, doing well to remain upright, and he deserves a lot of credit for getting as close as he did. After picking up the tiring leader in tandem with Reve De Sivola he was not quite able to get his head in front up the hill, but he was conceding 8lb to the winner, and is clearly a very useful novice. A step up to 3m should suit him. (op 7-1)
Rebel Du Maquis(FR) had made all in his two previous chases in this country, but Othermix took on the front-running role here. He was upsides with a lap to go and had just moved in front when the melee at the water jump left him in a very healthy lead. As late as the home turn he still looked to have an unassailable advantage, but he soon began to tire and the other pair passed him between the last two fences. This was a decent effort under his double penalty, but to an extent things were set up for him here. He has been described by his trainer as a spring horse so could well have a break now. (op 7-1 tchd 8-1)
Othermix(FR), 14l in front of today's winner last time, had the blinkers back and soon opened up a clear lead, but had been narrowly headed when falling at the water. Last year's Jewson handicap second had jumped well up to his point of departure. (tchd 5-4 and 6-4)
Spirit River(FR) had jumped well until coming down on his chasing debut at Newbury but was not so fluent this time. He was left in second place at the water, but the incident there seemed to unnerve him and he soon dropped last of the four still going. He was becomong increasingly remote, but was continuing in the hope of fourth prize, when he appeared to try to refuse and took a very heavy fall three out. His confidence is going to need some restoring now, and there is work to be done if he is to fulfil his obvious potential over fences. (tchd 5-4 and 6-4)

Radium(FR), disappointing behind Ghizao in a Listed race over 2m here last time, beat Othermix at Ascot but was 5lb worse off here. The Henderson second string, he was in touch when his old rival brought him down at the water jump, but seemed none the worse. (tchd 5-4 and 6-4)

2868 CASPIAN CAVIAR H'CAP HURDLE (8 hdls) 2m 1f

12:40 (1:16) (Class 3) (0-135,134) 3-Y-O+

£6,262 (£1,850; £925; £463; £231; £116)

Form RPR

1-11 **1** **L'Accordioniste (IRE)**[17] 2592 5-11-9 **131**.................. PaddyBrennan 139+
(Nigel Twiston-Davies) *lw: in tch: pushed along 3 out and lost pl: drvn and hdwy after 2 out but stl only 6th appr last: str run sn after and styd on to ld fnl 25yds: won gng away* **8/1**[3]

1216 **2** *1 ¾* **Praxiteles (IRE)**[13] 2671 6-11-3 **125**..............................(t) APMcCoy 130
(Rebecca Curtis) *hld up towards rr: hdwy appr 2 out: drvn to chal last: led u.str.p fnl 120yds: hdd and outpcd fnl 25yds* **8/1**[3]

34-0 **3** *hd* **Premier Dane (IRE)**[31] 2300 8-11-3 **125**.................. DougieCostello 129
(Nicky Richards) *hld up in tch: rdn and outpcd bef last: rallied run-in: fin wl to take 3rd cl home but no ch w wnr* **33/1**

-242 **4** *½* **Monetary Fund (USA)**[15] 2626 4-11-3 **125**.................. BarryGeraghty 130
(Nicky Henderson) *lw: in tch: chsd ldrs fr 4 out: hit 2 out: hrd rdn to chal last: led sn after: hdd u.p fnl 120yds: dropped bk to 4th: fnl 25yds* **9/2**[1]

/003 **5** *¾* **Higgy's Boy (IRE)**[34] 2213 5-11-1 **128**..............................(b) DavidBass(5) 131
(Nicky Henderson) *in rr: nt fluent 3rd and sn drvn along: hmpd 4 out: stl only 9th appr last: kpt on wl run-in: gng on cl home* **12/1**

-11P **6** *1 ¾* **Cockney Trucker (IRE)**[20] 2517 8-11-12 **134**.............. RichardJohnson 138+
(Philip Hobbs) *led: rdn and mstke last: sn hdd: wknd fnl 120yds* **14/1**

2-04 **7** *8* **Aather (IRE)**[41] 2085 5-11-3 **125**.................................. TimmyMurphy 120
(Alan Fleming) *lw: trckd ldrs tl pushed along and wknd bef last* **6/1**[2]

312- **8** *½* **Shoegazer (IRE)**[232] 5326 5-11-0 **125**..............................(t) DannyCook(3) 119
(David Pipe) *nt fluent 1st: in rr: hdwy appr last: no imp on ldrs and wknd run-in* **14/1**

631/ **9** *2 ¾* **Art Professor (IRE)**[749] 2330 6-11-5 **127**.................. AidanColeman 119
(Venetia Williams) *chsd ldrs: rdn 2 out: wknd bef last* **14/1**

05-5 **10** *½* **Special Occasion**[15] 2636 6-11-0 **127**.................. IanPopham(5) 118
(Caroline Keevil) *chsd ldrs: rdn bef 2 out: wknd bef last* **22/1**

01-0 **11** *8* **Hunterview**[62] 207 4-11-9 **131**..............................(b) TomScudamore 117
(David Pipe) *chsd ldrs: rdn appr 2 out: wknd sn after* **20/1**

20P- **12** *3 ¾* **My Shamwari (IRE)**[233] 5316 6-11-3 **125**.................. TomO'Brien 106
(Philip Hobbs) *in tch: rdn after 3 out: wknd and hit next* **10/1**

5124 **13** *10* **Hibiki (IRE)**[21] 2498 6-11-8 **130**..............................(p) DenisO'Regan 102
(Sarah Humphrey) *hit 1st: towards rr most of way* **20/1**

10/0 **14** *4* **Livvy Inn (USA)**[19] 2551 5-11-5 **127**.................. PeterBuchanan 95
(Lucinda Russell) *in tch: rdn 3 out: wknd next* **50/1**

05-2 **15** *14* **Ned Ludd (IRE)**[26] 2393 7-10-11 **122**..............(p) RichieMcLernon(3) 77
(Jonathan Portman) *chsd ldrs: rdn after 3 out: wknd bef next* **25/1**

00-F **16** *50* **Maucaillou (GER)**[27] 2360 7-11-4 **126**.................. WarrenMarston 36
(Martin Keighley) *hit 2nd: nt fluent 4th: t.o fr 4 out* **33/1**

/P0- **U** **Halla San**[167] 4154 8-11-5 **127**.................................. BrianHughes —
(Richard Fahey) *in tch whn mstke and uns rdr 4 out* **20/1**

4m 0.70s (-10.60) **Going Correction** -0.425s/f (Good)
WFA 4 from 5yo+ 5lb **17** Ran SP% **121.8**
Speed ratings (Par 107): **107,106,106,105,105 104,100,100,99,99 95,93,88,87,80 56,—**
Tote Swingers: 1&2 £3.40, 1&3 £80.20, 2&3 £188.60. CSF £61.98 CT £2026.09 TOTE £7.20: £1.80, £1.80, £6.10, £2.20; EX 73.70 TRIFECTA Not won..
Owner David Maxwell **Bred** J F C Maxwell **Trained** Naunton, Gloucs
■ Stewards' Enquiry : David Bass seven-day ban: used whip causing gelding to be wealed (Dec 26-Jan 1)

FOCUS
A competitive handicap hurdle run at a sound pace, and solid form. A massive step up from the winner who has obvious Festival credentials now.

NOTEBOOK
L'Accordioniste(IRE), who looks a chasing type, was hard at work in the pack at the top of the hill and although responding was still only sixth taking the final flight, but she ran on very strongly from there to win readily. Stretching her unbeaten record to four, following a bumper and a couple of novice hurdles, she was unexposed coming into this but was facing by far her stiffest test and was unproven on this sort of ground. She will obviously get further than this and the David Nicholson Mares' Hurdle, over 2m4f at the Festival, could be a suitable target if she continues to improve. (op 9-1 tchd 13-2)
Praxiteles(IRE) went off in front at Newbury but was ridden much more conservatively here, and the better ground was in his favour. He travelled strongly and improved to deliver his challenge at the last, but was cut down by the mare up the hill. (op 10-1)
Premier Dane(IRE) was another to run a solid race on this sounder surface and was staying on up the hill, suggesting a return to further will suit.
Monetary Fund(USA)'s yard has won this event with Spirit River and Jack The Giant in recent seasons. Runner-up at Newbury last time, in a race Spirit River also contested, he was 5lb higher here but ran another good race, even putting his head in front for a few strides after the last. (op 5-1 tchd 4-1)
Higgy's Boy(IRE) was off the bridle early on and looked pretty hard work, but his rider's efforts were rewarded to a degree as the gelding eventually stayed on up the hill from a good way back. He looks in need of further now. (op 11-1)
Cockney Trucker(IRE), reverting to hurdles, ran a big race under topweight and only relinquished his lead at the final flight, which he flattened. He went out to his right at most of the hurdles. (op 12-1)
Aather(IRE), fourth to the progressive Tocca Ferro last time, travelled well as usual and only faded on the approach to the final flight. He did finish in front of Hibiki on these 6lb better terms but is the type who needs things to drop right. (op 11-2 tchd 5-1)
Shoegazer(IRE) improved from the back after the second-last before his progress flattened out, and this was a satisfactory handicap debut over a trip too short for him. (tchd 20-1)
Art Professor(IRE) ran well for a long way on his first start for over two years, only fading between the final two flights. (tchd 16-1)
Special Occasion, whose head carriage was not too attractive, only weakened on the long run to the last. (op 25-1 tchd 33-1)

2869 CF ROBERTS ELECTRICAL + MECHANICAL SERVICES CONDITIONAL JOCKEYS' H'CAP CHASE (15 fncs 2 omitted) 2m 5f

1:15 (1:50) (Class 3) (0-125,125) 4-Y-O+

£6,262 (£1,850; £925; £463; £231; £116)

Form RPR

-612 **1** **Fine Parchment (IRE)**[19] 2544 7-11-2 **118**..............(t) PeterToole(3) 131+
(Charlie Mann) *lw: trckd ldrs: j. soundly: led after 3 out: clr last: rdn out* **17/2**

31F6 **2** *9* **Safari Adventures (IRE)**[34] 2204 8-11-9 **125**.............. CampbellGillies(3) 129
(Lucinda Russell) *led: hdd after 3 out: styd on same pce* **33/1**

3-21 **3** *1 ½* **Regal Approach (IRE)**[13] 2670 7-11-0 **121**..................(p) EdCookson(8) 125
(Kim Bailey) *hld up in midfield: hdwy to trck ldrs 10th: styd on same pce fr 3 out: hit next* **7/1**[2]

14-1 **4** *1 ¼* **Ravethebrave (IRE)**[24] 2441 6-11-6 **122**.................. CharlieHuxley(3) 123
(Alan King) *lw: trckd ldrs: effrt 3 out: styd on same pce* **10/1**

-451 **5** *3 ¾* **Holmwood Legend**[18] 2587 9-11-6 **122**.................. KeiranBurke(3) 120
(Patrick Rodford) *in rr-div: hdwy 4 out: one pce fr next* **16/1**

560P **6** *6* **Cullahill (IRE)**[26] 2395 8-10-11 **118**.................. NathanSweeney(8) 111
(Bob Buckler) *prom: outpcd 10th: kpt on fr 3 out* **25/1**

16-5 **7** *5* **Plein Pouvoir (FR)**[24] 2443 7-11-1 **117**.................. RTDunne(3) 107
(Venetia Williams) *chsd ldrs: 3rd whn pckd landing 3 out: wknd next* **12/1**

2434 **8** *1 ¼* **Knight Legend (IRE)**[20] 2531 11-11-4 **122**..................(t) HenryBrooke(5) 109
(Sarah Humphrey) *in rr: sme hdwy 3 out: nvr a factor* **33/1**

-040 **9** *4 ½* **Double Dizzy**[19] 2541 9-11-7 **120**..............................(bt) DonalDevereux 103
(Bob Buckler) *chsd ldrs: lost pl 7th: no threat after* **20/1**

1-53 **10** *13* **County Zen (FR)**[21] 2494 7-11-9 **125**.................. GilesHawkins(3) 96
(Philip Hobbs) *chsd ldrs: hit 2nd: lost pl 8th: t.o 11th* **16/1**

/6-5 **11** *29* **Patman Du Charmil (FR)**[27] 2374 8-11-1 **117**..............(b) TomMolloy(3) 62
(Nigel Twiston-Davies) *chsd ldrs: hit 8th: outpcd and lost pl 11th: sn bhd: t.o* **8/1**[3]

122- **12** *24* **Font**[507] 1020 7-11-9 **125**..............................(t) IanPopham(3) 49
(Paul Nicholls) *nt jump wl in rr: blnd 1st and 5th: bhd fr 4 out* **14/1**

U006 **P** **Factotum**[22] 2475 6-11-2 **123**.................................. GeraldQuinn(8) —
(Jonjo O'Neill) *in rr: sn drvn along: t.o 7th: p.u bef 4 out* **33/1**

0-42 **U** **Forty Five (IRE)**[37] 2148 8-11-1 **117**.................. RichieMcLernon(3) —
(Jonjo O'Neill) *in rr: mid-div whn mstke 9th: t.o whn blnd and uns rdr last* **8/1**[3]

0-36 **P** **Wolf Moon (IRE)**[27] 2357 7-11-10 **123**.................. DavidBass —
(Martin Keighley) *in rr: sn drvn along: bhd fr 7th: t.o whn p.u bef 2 out* **9/1**

04/2 **U** **Carrickboy (IRE)**[31] 2286 6-11-3 **122**.................. HarryChalloner(6) —
(Venetia Williams) *trckd ldrs: mstke 9th: handy 3rd whn blnd and uns rdr 4 out* **6/1**[1]

1453 **P** **Quell The Storm (FR)**[25] 2422 6-11-4 **122**..................(t) JakeGreenall(5) —
(Milton Harris) *mstkes: chsd ldrs: lost pl and blnd 10th: t.o whn p.u bef next* **66/1**

5m 17.5s (-1.90) **Going Correction** -0.05s/f (Good) **17** Ran SP% **123.7**
Speed ratings (Par 107): **101,97,97,96,95 92,90,90,88,83 72,63,—,—,— —,—**
Tote Swingers: 1&2 £181.70, 1&3 £7.00, 2&3 £136.60. CSF £272.95 CT £2085.17 TOTE £9.60: £2.20, £6.60, £1.70, £2.10; EX 380.90 Trifecta £977.10 Pool: £1,320.53 - 0.30 winning units..
Owner N W A Bannister **Bred** Timothy Considine **Trained** Upper Lambourn, Berks

FOCUS
There was only 8lb between the top and bottom weights in this conditionals' handicap. They went a good pace and the form should stand up. There is a case for rating the race a bit higher through the runner-up.

NOTEBOOK
Fine Parchment(IRE) ◆ led on the home turn and galloped on very strongly to slam his field in impressive style. An improved performer since the tongue-strap went on, he has won two of his last three and his defeat came over 3m1f. The drop back in trip suited, but he wasn't stopping at the end. Sure to take a hike in the weights for this, he jumped well and his trainer thinks he's the type for the Topham Trophy at Aintree in the spring. (op 10-1 tchd 8-1)
Safari Adventures(IRE) was all the better for a safe round at Kelso and he ran a bold race from the front off this 3lb lower mark, finding only the easy winner too good. His trainer has recently started stabling some horses with Michael Scudamore in Herefordshire, where conditions have not been as wintry as they have back home in Scotland.
Regal Approach(IRE) ◆ got off the mark with a gritty success at Newbury and he ran another thoroughly creditable race off his 6lb higher mark. A sound benchmark for this form, he has further progress in him back at 3m, which he stayed well over hurdles. (op 8-1)
Ravethebrave(IRE) stayed on from the third-last to go after the leaders but could not quite sustain his effort. This was a solid run on only his second start over fences, following his debut win at Folkestone. (op 9-1 tchd 8-1)
Holmwood Legend is pretty consistent and he ran well again, but a 4lb rise for his fortunate win at Ludlow took him to a career-high mark. He may still be worth trying over 3m again. (tchd 18-1)
Cullahill(IRE) did not arrive here in much form but ran creditably over a trip that is too short for him. (op 33-1)
Plein Pouvoir(FR) was appearing for only the third time since winning at Wincanton last Boxing Day, when 5lb higher. He improved to look a threat, but faded after pecking three from home. (op 16-1)
Font Official explanation: jockey said gelding had a breathing problem
Forty Five(IRE) was well beaten when parting company at the last, but is probably not one to give up on. He went up 5lb for his second at Chepstow but remains well handicapped compared with his hurdles mark. (op 13-2)
Carrickboy(IRE), runner-up to Royal Charm on his chasing debut, was always up with the pace and was still in contention when blundering away his rider at the fourth-last. (op 13-2)

2870 CITIPOST H'CAP HURDLE (12 hdls) 3m

1:50 (2:26) (Class 2) 4-Y-O+

£9,393 (£2,775; £1,387; £694; £346; £174)

Form RPR

11-0 **1** **Lush Life (IRE)**[26] 2387 5-11-2 **137**.................. BarryGeraghty 141+
(Nicky Henderson) *trckd ldrs: nt fluent 7th and 2 out: drvn to chal last: hrd rdn and styd on gamely to ld fnl 75yds* **8/1**[3]

5-52 **2** *1 ¼* **Barwell Bridge**[44] 2035 4-11-0 **135**..............................(t) DarylJacob 138+
(Warren Greatrex) *hld up in rr: stdy hdwy to trck ldrs appr 2 out: chal last: carried lft sn after: rallied u.p and kpt on to take 2nd last strides: no imp on wnr* **16/1**

-P62 **3** *nse* **Viking Blond (FR)**[27] 2360 5-10-13 **134**..............................(b) DavidEngland 137+
(Nigel Twiston-Davies) *led tl hdd after 2 out: rallied to take slt advantage appr last: sn jnd: edgd lft u.p sn after: edgd rt then hdd fnl 75yds: lost 2nd last strides* **14/1**

3-04 **4** *1 ¾* **Duke Of Lucca (IRE)**[13] 2672 5-11-12 **147**.................. RichardJohnson 147
(Philip Hobbs) *lw: chsd ldrs: wnt 2nd 4 out: rdn 2 out: one pce last: no imp whn hung rt run-in* **8/1**[3]

2-06 **5** *nk* **Quickbeam (IRE)**[14] 2663 8-10-7 **128**.................. AidanColeman 128
(Venetia Williams) *lw: chsd ldrs: rdn and kpt on fr 2 out: one pce run-in* **14/1**

31-5 **6** *4 ½* **Synchronised (IRE)**[21] 2500 7-11-8 **143**.................. APMcCoy 139+
(Jonjo O'Neill) *in rr: sltly hmpd and lost momentum 3 out: stl plenty to do after 2 out whn drvn: styd on wl appr last: fin strly: gng on cl home* **14/1**

-020 **7** *1 ½* **Buena Vista (IRE)**[14] 2663 9-11-5 **140**..............................(p) TomScudamore 136
(David Pipe) *in rr whn sltly hmpd 3 out and lost momentum: drvn and styd on fr 2 out: kpt on run-in: nt rch ldrs* **16/1**

13-2 **8** *3 ¾* **First Stream (GER)**[41] 2094 6-10-6 **127**.................. BrianHughes 120
(Howard Johnson) *in tch: nt fluent 3rd: chsd ldrs fr 3 out: wknd u.p bef last* **14/1**

-154 **9** *1* **Total Submission**[26] 2388 5-10-4 **125** .... WayneHutchinson 115
(Martin Keighley) *chsd ldrs: wnt 2nd 3 out: led after 2 out: hdd & wknd appr last* **16/1**

-110 **10** *25* **Solway Sam**[47] 1986 7-10-10 **131** .... RichieMcGrath 109+
(Lisa Harrison) *a in rr: no ch whn bdly hmpd 3 out* **16/1**

2354 **11** *7* **Raslan**[27] 2360 7-11-6 **144** .... (tp) DannyCook(3) 116+
(David Pipe) *chsd ldrs tl wkng and no ch whn bdly hmpd 3 out* **25/1**

3P1- **P** **Don't Push It (IRE)**[244] 5127 10-11-2 **140** .... MrAJBerry(3) —
(Jonjo O'Neill) *chsd ldrs to 7th: sn wknd: in rr whn hmpd and p.u 3 out* **25/1**

0-30 **B** **Afsoun (FR)**[21] 2498 8-11-5 **143** .... AlexMerriam(3) —
(Neil King) *in rr tl sme prog whn bdly hmpd and b.d 3 out* **66/1**

F-01 **F** **Superior Wisdom (IRE)**[21] 2500 10-10-11 **132** .... WillKennedy —
(Alex Hales) *lw: chsd ldrs: pushed along and styng on wl whn fell 3 out* **10/1**

6-61 **B** **Cross Kennon (IRE)**[27] 2360 6-11-3 **138** .... AlanO'Keeffe —
(Jennie Candlish) *lw: hld up in rr: stdy hdwy and clsng on ldrs whn bdly hmpd and b.d 3 out* **11/2**[1]

-115 **B** **Ackertac (IRE)**[27] 2360 5-10-6 **127** .... PaddyBrennan —
(Nigel Twiston-Davies) *in rr tl sme hdwy and styng on whn bdly hmpd and b.d 3 out* **6/1**[2]

6m 3.77s (2.77) **Going Correction** -0.425s/f (Good)
WFA 4 from 5yo+ 7lb **16** Ran SP% **120.4**
Speed ratings (Par 109): **78,77,77,76,76 75,74,73,73,64 62,—,—,—,— —**
Tote Swingers: 1&2 £17.10, 1&3 £26.70, 2&3 £40.20. CSF £124.80 CT £1773.69 TOTE £7.70: £2.10, £3.50, £2.90, £3.10; EX 133.10 Trifecta £1275.20 Pool: £1,723.35 - 0.63 winning units..
Owner Michael Buckley **Bred** Patrick T Brennan **Trained** Upper Lambourn, Berks

FOCUS

A competitive handicap hurdle, won in the last two years by high-class stayers Fair Along and Time For Rupert. There were seven in with a shout on the long run to the final flight and the form looks pretty sound, although the early pace was only steady. The fourth and fifth look the best guides.

NOTEBOOK

Lush Life(IRE) travelled well for a long way and showed a likeable attitude under pressure once securing the stands' rail after the last. He seemed to blow up over 2m5f on his reappearance at the Open meeting and clearly had sufficient stamina for this longer trip. He has a defeat of Menorah to his name from his novice season and is a very useful hurdler with more to offer. (op 15-2)
Barwell Bridge, another stepping up to 3m for the first time, looked a stayer when a never-nearer fifth in last season's Triumph Hurdle. Held up, he scythed through the field on the approach to the last and was carried left by the third on the run-in before coming back the other way, going down narrowly.
Viking Blond(FR) was put up 5lb for finishing second to Cross Kennon at the Open meeting. He ran a cracking race from the front and was coming back for more after the last, with the better ground not a hindrance to him. (op 12 1)
Duke Of Lucca(IRE), who ran here rather than in the Relkeel Hurdle on the second day of the meeting, represented a yard successful twice in this race in recent years. He ran a good race under topweight, putting aside any suspicions that he did not really get 3m. (op 10-1)
Quickbeam(IRE) improved at Newbury on what he had shown in Cross Kennon's race here on his reappearance, and was only edged out of the frame late on. He remains without a hurdles win since April 2008.
Synchronised(IRE) ran an encouraging race with his Welsh National prospects in mind. After getting behind he was staying on very nicely at the finish, and a proper Chepstow bog would enhance his credentials in the Christmas showpiece.
Buena Vista(IRE) was never quite able to make his presence felt. He won last season's Pertemps Final and that race looks the obvious target again.
First Stream(GER) ◆ made one jumping error but only faded out of contention going to the last. He did not quite get home but there is a decent race to be won with him over a little shorter. (op 12-1)
Total Submission, a lightly raced novice, ran well for a long way on this handicap debut and is another who is worth persevering with at this sort of trip.
Don't Push It(IRE), deserted by Tony McCoy for this first run since his Grand National win, will derive benefit from this pipe-opener over hurdles. All roads presumably lead to Aintree for him. (op 50-1)
Afsoun(FR) was not out of contention when put out of the race. (op 50-1)
Superior Wisdom(IRE), 7lb higher than when winning at Exeter, was the cause of a pile-up at the third-last, in the process of running well when stepping into the flight and coming down. (op 50-1)
Cross Kennon(IRE) had four of these behind him when winning a Listed event over slightly further here at the Open meeting, and was put up 8lb for that. After being held up as usual he had made steady progress to reach the heels of the leaders when he was brought down three out, but for which he would probably have been involved in the finish. (op 50-1)
Ackertac(IRE), fifth in Cross Kennon's Listed race, had nowhere to go in the melee three from home. (op 50-1)

2871 MAJORDOMO HOSPITALITY H'CAP CHASE (LISTED RACE) (19 fncs 2 omitted) 3m 1f 110y

2:25 (3:03) (Class 1) 4-Y-0+

£22,804 (£8,556; £4,284; £2,136; £1,072; £536)

Form RPR

4111 **1** **Midnight Chase**[27] 2358 8-11-3 **155** .... DougieCostello 167+
(Neil Mulholland) *led: hdd and blnd 3 out: rallied run-in: led last 75yds: all out* **11/4**[1]

02-1 **2** *nk* **Presenting Forever (IRE)**[50] 1932 6-10-0 **138** oh8 .... BrianHughes 148+
(Howard Johnson) *trckd ldrs: wnt 2nd 14th: led 3 out: 4 l clr last: drifted rt: hdd last 75yds: rallied and jst hld* **16/1**

B4-4 **3** *7* **Exmoor Ranger (IRE)**[41] 2084 8-10-7 **145** .... DenisO'Regan 149
(Victor Dartnall) *chsd ldrs: reminders 9th: outpcd 3 out: styd on same pce fr next* **11/1**

45-P **4** *1 1/4* **Knockara Beau (IRE)**[41] 2091 7-10-11 **149** .... JanFaltejsek 150
(George Charlton) *chsd ldrs: outpcd 15th: styd on fr 2 out* **12/1**

3-35 **5** *2 1/4* **From Dawn To Dusk**[27] 2358 11-10-6 **144** .... (t) RichardJohnson 143
(Philip Hobbs) *towards rr: hdwy whn j.rt 3 out: kpt on one pce* **10/1**

-666 **6** *1 3/4* **Irish Raptor (IRE)**[19] 2543 11-10-0 **138** oh10 .... DavidEngland 135
(Nigel Twiston-Davies) *mid-div: hdwy to chse ldrs 6th: one pce fr 4 out* **40/1**

PP-5 **7** *5* **Beat The Boys (IRE)**[62] 1777 9-10-3 **141** .... TimmyMurphy 135
(Nigel Twiston-Davies) *w ldrs: upsides 7th to 14th: wknd 2 out* **25/1**

33P- **8** *2* **Rare Bob (IRE)**[36] 2175 8-10-7 **145** .... PWFlood 138
(D T Hughes, Ire) *trckd ldrs: outpcd 4 out: no threat after* **12/1**

0105 **9** *3/4* **That's Rhythm (FR)**[41] 2091 10-10-4 **142** .... (v) GrahamLee 132
(Martin Todhunter) *nt fluent in rr: reminders 8th: sme hdwy 4 out: nvr nr ldrs* **25/1**

02P- **10** *13* **Faasel (IRE)**[237] 5223 9-10-1 **139** .... (b) TomScudamore 118
(David Pipe) *mid-div: reminders 11th: lost pl 13th* **10/1**

14/B **11** *1/2* **Neptune Collonges (FR)**[13] 2673 9-11-7 **164** .... MrRMahon(5) 142
(Paul Nicholls) *s.i.s: in rr: outpcd 14th: nvr on terms* **15/2**[2]

32-0 **12** *38* **Forest Pennant (IRE)**[34] 2221 8-9-9 **138** oh1 .... (b[1]) IanPopham(5) 82
(Paul Nicholls) *nt fluent in rr: t.o 12th* **20/1**

P/0- **13** *3/4* **Horner Woods (IRE)**[377] 2576 8-10-2 **140** .... AndrewTinkler 83
(Nicky Henderson) *hld up towards rr: sme hdwy 14th: sn drvn and wknd: hit 4 out* **8/1**[3]

2P-4 **14** *4 1/2* **Appleaday (IRE)**[34] 2214 9-10-0 **138** oh16 .... LiamTreadwell 77
(Paul Webber) *in rr: bhd fr 11th* **100/1**

3-P3 **15** *9* **Knowhere (IRE)**[28] 2343 12-10-0 **138** oh1 .... PaddyBrennan 69
(Nigel Twiston-Davies) *mstke 3rd: in rr: blnd 5th: bhd fr 10th* **20/1**

0F-F **P** **Palypso De Creek (FR)**[20] 2522 7-9-11 **138** oh2 ...... RichieMcLernon(3) —
(Charlie Longsdon) *lw: prom: reminders 9th: lost pl 11th: bhd fr 14th: t.o whn p.u bef 2 out* **10/1**

6m 28.3s (-9.90) **Going Correction** -0.05s/f (Good) **16** Ran SP% **127.1**
Speed ratings (Par 111): **113,112,110,110,109 109,107,106,106,102 102,90,90,89,86 —**
Tote Swingers: 1&2 £4.90, 1&3 £10.20, 2&3 £155.70. CSF £43.84 CT £448.74 TOTE £4.00: £1.40, £4.10, £2.90, £4.00; EX 73.30 Trifecta £571.20 Pool: £2,755.98 - 3.57 winning units..
Owner Lady Clarke **Bred** Conkwell Grange Stud Ltd **Trained** Burlescombe, Devon

FOCUS

This Listed chase has been won in the past decade by the likes of Mon Mome, Kingscliff and Marlborough, and this was another solid edition. Another step up from Midnight Chase, but he needs to improve another 10lb+ to have genuine Gold Cup prospects.

NOTEBOOK

Midnight Chase, making it six wins from his last seven starts, confirmed his relish for Cheltenham with a third successive win here this season. Going off in front, although not as far clear as when winning over an extended 3m3f at the Open meeting, he stumbled at the third-last and looked like he'd have to settle for second, but he landed running at the last and stayed on strongly against the inside rail to reclaim the lead. This was a very smart effort to defy a mark of 155 and connections understandably will target him at the Gold Cup, for which he is quoted at as low as 20/1. Set to run once more before March, he has more improvement to make if he is to trouble the big guns in the Gold Cup but his course record gives him each-way prospects. (op 7-2)
Presenting Forever(IRE), a Carlisle winner on his reappearance, was 8lb out of the weights here so effectively racing off 18lb higher. Going past the winner at the third-last, he was still several lengths to the good at the final fence, but hung to his right and was caught late on. Only six, he is clearly an improving young stayer. (op 20-1)
Exmoor Ranger(IRE) made a notable mistake four out but stayed on for a creditable third. His consistency does not win him much respite from the handicapper and he is now 10lb above his last winning mark. (op 14-1)
Knockara Beau(IRE) ran no race in the Charlie Hall, but apparently hurt a vertebra and suffered a fibrillating heart at Wetherby. He was consistent as a novice and put in a solid run, never far from the pace and sticking on. He is on a mark he is capable of winning off. (op 14-1 tchd 16-1)
From Dawn To Dusk had ground conditions more to suit that in Midnight Chase's race at the last meeting, but a mistake at the first ditch set him back and he could never reach a challenging position. (op 11-1)
Irish Raptor(IRE) ran respectably from 10lb out of the handicap. (tchd 50-1)
Beat The Boys(IRE) has become quite well handicapped and was still right there on the home turn before fading. (op 20-1)
Rare Bob(IRE), an Irish challenger, ran creditably with the cheekpieces left off but is proving hard to place since his Grade 1 win as a novice. (op 11-1 tchd 10-1)
Neptune Collonges(FR), who only reached the fourth on his comeback from injury in the Hennessy, had been dropped 10lb during his layoff. He was standing still when the tapes rose and could never get into the race, but the outing should have helped his fitness. (tchd 7-1 and 8-1)
Horner Woods(IRE), runner-up to Cooldine in the 2009 RSA Chase for Jessica Harrington, struggled to get to the leaders on this first run for a year and debut for the Henderson yard.

2872 GLENFARCLAS CROSS COUNTRY H'CAP CHASE (32 fncs) 3m 7f

() (Class 2) 5-Y-0+

£

2873 EBF "NATIONAL HUNT" NOVICES' HURDLE (QUALIFIER) (7 hdls 1 omitted) 2m 1f

3:35 (3:46) (Class 3) 4-6-Y-0

£6,262 (£1,850; £925; £463; £231; £116)

Form RPR

1- **1** **Prince Of Pirates (IRE)**[221] 114 5-10-12 0 .... APMcCoy 120+
(Nicky Henderson) *lw: racd in 2nd after 4 out: 3 l down and travelling wl whn lft clr 2 out: shkn up as 2nd clsd after last: readily* **5/2**[2]

40-5 **2** *3 3/4* **Robin De Creuse (FR)**[30] 2310 4-10-12 0 .... RichardJohnson 111+
(Philip Hobbs) *lw: in rr tl hdwy appr 2 out: styng on to press wnr whn mstke last: rallied run-in but a readily hld* **25/1**

6-45 **3** *11* **Thoresby (IRE)**[23] 2456 4-10-12 0 .... DarylJacob 103+
(Ben Case) *in rr tl hdwy after 3 out: styd on to chse wnr after 3 out: nvr any ch: wknd into wl hld 3rd bef last* **100/1**

/04- **4** *12* **Master Beau**[390] 2298 6-10-12 0 .... JanFaltejsek 91
(George Charlton) *lw: chsd ldrs: lft 2nd briefly 2 out: wknd bef last* **20/1**

4-04 **5** *3 3/4* **Richmond (FR)**[23] 2456 5-10-12 0 .... DougieCostello 86
(Ian Williams) *in rr: styng on whn hmpd 2 out: kpt on again run-in: nvr any threat* **50/1**

P-00 **6** *6* **Robin Will (FR)**[14] 2666 5-10-12 0 .... NickScholfield 81
(Paul Nicholls) *in rr tl mod prog fr 2 out* **80/1**

1-02 **7** *4* **Madame Jasmine**[29] 2331 5-10-5 0 .... ColinBolger 71
(Suzy Smith) *in rr tl sme prog appr last* **66/1**

54 **8** *7* **Ebony Diamond (IRE)**[21] 2495 6-10-12 0 .... PaulMoloney 71
(Charlie Mann) *in rr: sme hdwy whn hmpd 2 out: sn wknd* **66/1**

00-4 **9** *4* **Fun Guy**[29] 2331 5-10-12 0 .... AndrewGlassonbury 68
(Bob Buckler) *chsd ldr to 4 out: wknd after next* **66/1**

41-0 **10** *1 1/2* **Pere Blanc (IRE)**[18] 2577 5-10-12 0 .... TimmyMurphy 66
(David Arbuthnot) *a towards rr* **33/1**

0-4 **11** *7* **Drumlang (IRE)**[29] 2328 4-10-12 0 .... HaddenFrost 60
(Henrietta Knight) *chsd ldrs to 3 out* **66/1**

0 **12** *18* **Tanwood Boy (FR)**[23] 2456 6-10-12 0 .... AidanColeman 44
(Venetia Williams) *lw: a in rr* **100/1**

0-0 **13** *42* **Running Upthathill (IRE)**[14] 2666 6-10-12 0 .... SamThomas 6
(Venetia Williams) *a in rr: t.o* **100/1**

5 **14** *2 1/2* **Master Milan (IRE)**[34] 2215 4-10-12 0 .... DominicElsworth —
(Jonjo O'Neill) *bhd most of way: t.o* **66/1**

12- **F** **Al Ferof (FR)**[268] 4676 5-10-12 0 .... NoelFehily 123+
(Paul Nicholls) *lw: led: sn clr: 3 l up and gng wl whn fell 2 out* **4/7**[1]

52 **F** **Roper (IRE)**[40] 2109 5-10-9 0 .... RichieMcLernon(3) 86
(Jonjo O'Neill) *chsd ldrs: hit 4th: wknd fr 2 out: 5th and no ch whn fell last* **14/1**[3]

4m 5.58s (-5.72) **Going Correction** -0.425s/f (Good)
WFA 4 from 5yo+ 5lb **16** Ran SP% **124.1**
Speed ratings: **96,94,89,83,81 78,76,73,71,71 67,59,39,38,— —**
Tote Swingers: 1&2 £9.20, 1&3 £57.20, 2&3 £92.10. toteSuper 7: WIN: Not won. PLACE: Not won. CSF £62.74 TOTE £3.30: £1.30, £4.30, £18.20; EX 76.20 Trifecta £1036.90 Pool: £1,401.22 - 0.10 winning units..
Owner John P McManus **Bred** J R Curran **Trained** Upper Lambourn, Berks

FOCUS

This novice hurdle has been won by a string of high-class performers, with General Miller, Karabak, Calgary Bay, Tidal Bay and Noland the last five winners. This year's race attracted a couple of contenders with pretensions to stardom, but lacked strength in depth and the definite impression was that a number of these will be seen to better effect in lesser company on another day. The race was delayed by several minutes due to the setting sun. The winner is sure to rate higher but the ordinary time limits the rating.

NOTEBOOK

Prince Of Pirates(IRE), a bumper winner last term, was soon out after the favourite, and had closed to within three lengths when he was left in a clear lead two out. McCoy allowed the runner-up to close and things briefly looked interesting at the last, but the gelding soon asserted after being shaken up after the last. Whether he was a fortunate winner or not, he looks a very useful novice, and his next run will tell us more. (op 2-1)

Robin De Creuse(FR), who has the mke and shape of a chaser, emerged from the pack as a potential danger going to the last, but walked through the flight and was quickly put in his place on the run-in. This was a promising run, but it won't have helped his future handicap mark.

Thoresby(IRE) was never within striking distance of the winner or the faller, but found himself temporarily in second place after two out. This run confirmed that he has ability, and a race at one of the minor tracks should come his way.

Master Beau ◆ was a decent bumper perfomer and this was a pleasing hurdling debut after more than a year off. An ordinary novice hurdle in the north should soon be found for him.

Richmond(FR), a keen type, was hampered by the faller before keeping on and looks to be progressing now. (op 33-1)

Robin Will(FR), the favourite's stablemate, stayed on for sixth without ever being seen with a chance. There was promise in this run, which seemed a step up on his previous moderate efforts. Official explanation: jockey said, regarding running and riding, that his orders were to educate the gelding as it is a difficult ride at home, get it settled and get the steering right, adding that he asked for some effort after the 4th, felt it had a slight problem with its breathing coming down the hill and stayed on past tiring horses; trainer confirmed that it has been difficult to train having run off the course on its first run and been very keen subsequently, therefore the intention was to get it to finish. (op 100-1)

Madame Jasmine, who has the option of mares' races, gave a bit of encouragement.

Ebony Diamond(IRE), another hampered by Al Ferof, shaped with a bit of promise. (op 50-1)

Al Ferof(FR), runner-up to Cue Card in the Champion Bumper in March, looked a highly promising recruit to hurdling. Allowed a flyer as the tapes went up, he jinked into an early flight as if thinking about ducking out, but soon only had one serious pursuer. He was 3l to the good, and still travelling well, when he took a crunching fall at the second-last from which he looked fortunate to get up. The result was still in doubt at that stage, as the winner looked to be travelling just as well, but he would have been tough to get past. He should soon make amends if none the worse for this unfortunate experience, and a step up in trip will suit him. (op 5-6)

Roper(IRE), who shaped with promise when runner-up at Huntingdon, fell at the last after running another eye-catching race. (op 5-6)

T/Jkpt: Not won. T/Plt: £104.80 to a £1 stake. Pool:£186,960.91 - 1,301.38 winning tickets. T/Qpdt: £14.10 to a £1 stake. Pool:£13,400.84 - 699.15 winning tickets. ST

DONCASTER (L-H)

Friday, December 10

2874 Meeting Abandoned - Snow & frost

2867 CHELTENHAM (L-H)

Saturday, December 11

OFFICIAL GOING: Good to soft (good in places)

The first fence in the back straight was omitted on all circuits of all chase races due to the ground.

Wind: Virtually nil Weather: Overcast

2881 JENNY MOULD MEMORIAL H'CAP CHASE (13 fncs 1 omitted) 2m 110y

11:40 (11:40) (Class 2) 4-Y-0+

£12,524 (£3,700; £1,850; £926; £462; £232)

Form	Pos	Btn	Horse	Jockey	SP	RPR
01-1	**1**		**Woolcombe Folly (IRE)**[21] 2517 7-11-7 **154** (Paul Nicholls) *hld up in midfield: j. soundly: hdwy to chse ldrs 8th: wnt 2nd after 3 out: upsides 2 out: sn led: rdn clr run-in*	MrRMahon(5)	**4/1**[1]	172+
P-34	**2**	*6*	**Tanks For That (IRE)**[183] 709 7-10-7 **135** (Nicky Henderson) *trckd ldrs: j. soundly: led 7th: jnd 2 out: sn hdd and no ex*	BarryGeraghty	**9/1**	148
-021	**3**	*14*	**Fiendish Flame (IRE)**[31] 2304 6-11-3 **145** (Donald McCain) *led: j.lft 5th: blnd and hdd 7th: kpt on same pce fr 3 out*	JasonMaguire	**6/1**[3]	148
5-16	**4**	*3½*	**Cornas (NZ)**[39] 2138 8-11-8 **150** (Nick Williams) *in tch: styd on fr 4 out: tk n.d 4th 2 out*	DarylJacob	**8/1**	147
-030	**5**	*½*	**Tramantano**[14] 2674 11-10-0 **128** oh3 (Nigel Twiston-Davies) *in rr: hit 7th: hdwy 4 out: kpt on: nvr on terms*	PaddyBrennan	**25/1**	125
04-6	**6**	*3¾*	**Oh Crick (FR)**[27] 2385 7-11-6 **148** (Alan King) *mid-div: hdwy 8th: one pce fr 4 out: mstke 2 out*	RobertThornton	**5/1**[2]	142
2163	**7**	*2½*	**Mam Ratagan**[15] 2662 9-9-11 **128** oh3 (Heather Main) *trckd ldrs: hit 8th: wknd 2 out*	PeterToole(3)	**33/1**	119
-F42	**8**	*8*	**I'msingingtheblues (IRE)**[21] 2515 8-11-7 **152** (David Pipe) *stdd s: t.k.h in rr: sme hdwy 3 out: nvr on terms*	(t) DannyCook(3)	**16/1**	136
3-14	**9**	*1¾*	**Safari Journey (USA)**[29] 2345 6-11-2 **144** (Philip Hobbs) *mstkes in rr: nvr a factor*	(b) RichardJohnson	**9/1**	126
0422	**10**	*¾*	**Grand Lahou (FR)**[29] 2345 7-9-9 **130** (Tim Vaughan) *w ldrs: hmpd and j.lft 5th: 6th and wkng whn mstke 3 out*	MrTomDavid(7)	**16/1**	114
30-4	**11**	*1¾*	**Consigliere (FR)**[21] 2517 7-11-6 **148** (David Pipe) *in tch: hit 4th: lost pl 7th*	(bt) TomScudamore	**9/1**	128
06-F	**12**	*26*	**I'm Delilah**[35] 2206 8-10-10 **138** (Ferdy Murphy) *prom: 8th and outpcd whn blnd 4 out: sn lost pl: t.o 2 out*	GrahamLee	**16/1**	94
P-0B	**13**	*37*	**Perce Rock**[15] 2665 8-10-4 **135** (Jonjo O'Neill) *nt fluent in rr: hit 1st and 6th: bhd and reminders next: t.o 4 out*	RichieMcLernon(3)	**50/1**	58

4m 0.70s (-6.00) **Going Correction** -0.025s/f (Good) **13** Ran SP% **118.5**

Speed ratings (Par 109): **113,110,103,101,101 99,98,95,94,93 93,80,63**

toteswingers:1&2 £9.20, 2&3 £16.80, 1&3 £5.40 CSF £39.34 CT £217.06 TOTE £4.50: £2.30, £3.10, £2.30; EX 51.40 Trifecta £227.00 Pool: £1261.20 - 4.11 winning units..

Owner The Hon Mrs Townshend **Bred** Mrs M Doran **Trained** Ditcheat, Somerset

FOCUS

A decent handicap chase. They went a really good gallop and, interestingly, the time was 0.5secs quicker than that recorded by Master Minded in the Tingle Creek. Woolsombe Folly is up a stone+ on his recent win, helped by his rider's claim, and is a serious Champion Chase contender on this evidence.

NOTEBOOK

Woolcombe Folly(IRE) was being talked of as a live Champion Chase contender after this display. A ready winner off 142 on his reappearance at Ascot, he really needed to raise his game off 12lb higher in a better race, but this was only his fifth start over fences and he duly found the necessary improvement, staying on well to challenge the runner-up two out and getting well on top from the last. Now 4-5 as a chaser, his only defeat came when last of 12 in the Arkle which was just a few days after a nasty schooling accident at home. He can expect to find himself rated much higher now, and it will be fascinating to see where he goes next, with the Game Spirit at Newbury looking the likely aim. (tchd 9-2 in a place)

Tanks For That(IRE), off since disappointing off this mark at Aintree in the summer, prospered under an aggressive ride, but despite receiving a sizable amount of weight from the winner, he proved no match from before the last. (op 12-1)

Fiendish Flame(IRE) had gone up 5lb for winning a minor four-runner event at Bangor last time and ran well. He runs his race more often than not, but needs a good test at 2m and was just found wanting for pace against the front pair. (op 7-1 tchd 11-2)

Cornas(NZ), who finished lame when only sixth in the Haldon Gold Cup, did stay on, but never looked like winning and was probably a bit below his best. (op 12-1)

Tramantano bounced back from a couple of poor efforts, keeping on late from 3lb 'wrong'. (tchd 33-1 in a place)

Oh Crick(FR) was disappointing, failing to build on his reappearance effort, although it would be no surprise to see him come good again in the spring. (op 11-2 tchd 6-1 in a place)

Safari Journey(USA) failed to run up to his best, making mistakes. (op 11-1)

Consigliere(FR) was another to run below par. (tchd 17-2)

2882 JCB TRIUMPH HURDLE TRIAL (JUVENILE HURDLE) (8 hdls) 2m 1f

12:10 (12:14) (Class 2) 3-Y-0

£8,140 (£2,405; £1,202; £601; £300; £150)

Form	Pos	Btn	Horse	Jockey	SP	RPR
1	**1**		**Sam Winner (FR)**[28] 2356 3-11-7 146 (Paul Nicholls) *trckd ldrs: led after 2 out: pushed clr wl bef last: styd on strly run-in*	NoelFehily	**4/7**[1]	129+
511	**2**	*6*	**Pullyourfingerout (IRE)**[34] 2245 3-11-3 127 (Brendan Powell) *led tl after 1st: settled in bhd ldrs: travelling wl after 2 out: qcknd to chse wnr bef last: nvr on terms: and sn mstke: kpt on same pce*	APMcCoy	**16/1**	120
512	**3**	*4½*	**Akula (IRE)**[21] 2528 3-11-3 118 (Mark H Tompkins) *led after 1st: hdd 2nd: styd trcking ldr: hit 4 out: nt fluent 2 out and lost 2nd bef last whn no ch w wnr: one pce*	ColinBolger	**50/1**	116
	4	*4½*	**Red Sparky (IRE)**[20] 2561 3-11-0 0 (J Larkin, Ire) *chsd ldrs: blnd 4th: rdn and nt fluent 2 out: wknd wl bef last*	AELynch	**100/1**	109
1	**5**	*8*	**Pantxoa (FR)**[38] 2151 3-11-7 0 (Alan King) *plld hrd early in rr: hit 3rd: hdwy 3 out: chsd ldrs 2 out: wknd sn after*	RobertThornton	**10/1**	107
U2	**6**	*5*	**Tom Wade (IRE)**[51] 1935 3-11-0 0 (John Harris) *in rr: mstke and dropped off pce 3 out: gd hdwy appr 2 out but nvr on terms: wknd sn after*	CharliePoste	**100/1**	96
	7	*2*	**A Media Luz (FR)**[181] 3-10-7 0 (Nicky Henderson) *free to post: plld hrd: hit 1st: led 2nd: hdd after 2 out: sn btn: eased whn no ch run-in*	BarryGeraghty	**9/2**[2]	87+
04	**8**	*2*	**Horatio Caine (FR)**[28] 2356 3-11-0 0 (Nick Williams) *in tch tl outpcd and dropped in rr 4th: wl bhd after 3 out: styd on appr last: nvr any ch*	DarylJacob	**8/1**[3]	92+
	9	*17*	**Kayef (GER)**[79] 3-11-0 0 (Michael Scudamore) *chsd ldrs fr 3rd: rdn and wknd after 3 out*	TomScudamore	**80/1**	77
2	**10**	*3½*	**Killusty Fancy (IRE)**[19] 2570 3-11-0 0 (Dominic Ffrench Davis) *hit 1st: in tch 4 out: rdn after 3 out: wknd qckly and nt fluent 2 out*	MarkGrant	**100/1**	75
	11	*21*	**Blinka Me**[113] 3-11-0 0 (Alex Hales) *blnd 3 out: a bhd*	DenisO'Regan	**100/1**	55
0	**12**	*42*	**Green Art (IRE)**[28] 2356 3-11-0 0 (Tracey Barfoot-Saunt) *a bhd: t.o fr 4 out*	MrGBarfoot-Saunt	**200/1**	17

4m 8.88s (-2.42) **Going Correction** -0.075s/f (Good) **12** Ran SP% **115.6**

Speed ratings (Par 108): **102,99,97,94,91 88,87,86,78,77 67,47**

toteswingers:1&2 £3.90, 2&3 £18.50, 1&3 £12.60 CSF £12.11 TOTE £1.60: £1.10, £1.80, £5.60; EX 13.60 Trifecta £211.50 Pool: £2287.31 - 8.00 winning units..

Owner Mrs Angela Yeoman **Bred** Ecurie Winning **Trained** Ditcheat, Somerset

FOCUS

Not form to get carried away with, the second and third favourites both failing to meet with expectation, though Sam Winner put up another likeable performance in making it two from two since arriving from France. He is rated 12lb off his previous course win, with the sixth and time limiting factors.

NOTEBOOK

Sam Winner(FR) put up another likeable performance in making it two from two since arriving from France. An impressive 15l winner at last month's Open meeting, the son of Okawango didn't have to improve to take this, as things turned out, and he wasn't as impressive visually, but did have a penalty this time and still showed smart acceleration to go clear off the final bend. This seemed to cement his position at the top of the Triumph market (general 4-1 shot), and there's little doubt he sets the early-season standard, but there are plenty of cards still to be played, and whatever he does over hurdles, both his trainer and jockey believe he will be a better chaser, which isn't necessarily a plus when looking for a Triumph winner. The Supreme Novices' was mentioned also an option also, but we'll learn more after his next run, which is likely to come back here in January. (op 4-5)

Pullyourfingerout(IRE), an easy winner at Taunton on his second start who defied the penalty on soft ground at Market Rasen last time, faced a considerably stiffer task and was forced to take a lead. He travelled strongly under McCoy and stayed on well once headed for a clear second. He could end up in the Fred Winter. (tchd 14-1)

Akula(IRE), unable to defy a penalty at Huntingdon last time, seemed to improve markedly on previous achievements and may enjoy success down the handicap route later in the season. (op 40-1)

Red Sparky(IRE), well held on his debut at Navan, kept on late without seriously threatening and clearly has a future over hurdles, albeit at a lower level than this.

Pantxoa(FR), the only runner previously unbeaten, was looked over by the vet at the start and refused to settle early, which ultimately took its toll. He probably deserves another chance back down in grade. (tchd 11-1)

Tom Wade(IRE) ran better than his finishing position suggests and is going to be interesting for a handicap later in the season.

A Media Luz(FR), Group 3-placed over an extended 1m2f on the Flat, was weak in the market beforehand (free to post) and she refused to settle, being allowed to stride on at the second and giving herself no realistic chance of winning. She ended up well held and obviously deserves another chance, but needs to relax if she's to make it as a hurdler. (op 11-4)

Horatio Caine(FR) had finished a promising fourth to the winner over C&D last time, but made a couple of mistakes and found himself toiling from quite a way out. He still looks inexperienced and should come good at some stage. (op 10-1)

2883 DRS CONTRACTS NOVICES' CHASE (18 fncs 3 omitted) 3m 1f 110y
12:45 (12:45) (Class 2) 4-Y-0+

£9,393 (£2,775; £1,387; £694; £346; £174)

Form				RPR
22-1	**1**		**Time For Rupert (IRE)**[29] 2348 6-11-9 0 WillKennedy (Paul Webber) *trckd ldrs: j. soundly: wnt 2nd 5 out: led appr 2 out: styd on strly to forge clr run-in: v readily* **10/11**[1]	163+
-31F	**2**	8	**Chicago Grey (IRE)**[28] 2357 7-11-9 149 (t) PCarberry (Gordon Elliott, Ire) *in rr: hdwy 11th: hit 4 out: j.lft next: styd on to take 2nd last: no imp* **9/2**[2]	155
0-11	**3**	9	**Quinz (FR)**[22] 2497 6-11-9 144 RichardJohnson (Philip Hobbs) *w ldrs: led 4th: hdd appr 2 out: kpt on same pce run-in: eased towards fin* **6/1**[3]	150+
-211	**4**	14	**Robo (FR)**[25] 2436 5-11-9 134 DominicElsworth (Renee Robeson) *in rr: blnd bdly 12th: reminders 5 out: outpcd fr next: j.rt 3 out: wknd appr next: fatally injured* **14/1**	136
1142	**5**	5	**Balthazar King (IRE)**[28] 2357 6-11-9 140 TomO'Brien (Philip Hobbs) *led to 4th: chsd ldr: lost pl 3 out* **16/1**	129
13-3	**6**	7	**Cannington Brook (IRE)**[28] 2357 6-11-1 132 JoeTizzard (Colin Tizzard) *trckd ldrs: racd keenly: nt fluent 5th: wknd 4 out* **7/1**	117
252-	**P**		**Flight Leader (IRE)**[301] 4038 10-11-1 130 SamTwiston-Davies (Colin Tizzard) *in rr: lost tch and reminders 11th: t.o next: p.u bef 5 out* **33/1**	—
6/3	**P**		**Bentota (IRE)**[25] 2436 9-11-1 0 TomScudamore (Michael Scudamore) *in rr: p.u after 3rd: injured* **100/1**	—

6m 29.4s (-8.80) **Going Correction** -0.025s/f (Good) **8** Ran SP% **113.8**
Speed ratings (Par 109): **112,109,106,102,100 98,—,—**
toteswingers:1&2 £1.80, 2&3 £3.00, 1&3 £2.30 CSF £5.60 TOTE £1.90: £1.10, £1.80, £1.70; EX 5.20 Trifecta £13.80 Pool: £2112.22 - 112.86 winning units..

Owner Littlecote Racing Partnership **Bred** Robert O'Callaghan **Trained** Mollington, Oxon

FOCUS
This decent staying novice chase was run at a solid gallop and it represented a proper test. Things began to get really serious from five out and the form is straightforward. Time For Rupert looks a very strong candidate for the RSA Chase and the second posted a personal best.

NOTEBOOK
Time For Rupert(IRE) ◆ made it 2-2 since embarking on his chasing career and further cemented his position as favourite in the ante-post market for the RSA at the festival in March. He did the job in great style when winning a very classy event for the grade at this venue on his debut at the Open meeting last month, over a trip short of his best, and this was another flawless display back over his optimum distance. His only slight error came when reaching for the open ditch early on, but apart from that he again jumped with aplomb, especially over the last two fences. He had to go up a gear when asked to close on the clear leader Quinz after five out, but it was obvious coming to the third-last there was still plenty in the tank and he came right away when asked to seal the race. He is the real deal for chasing and he obviously loves this course, with form figures here now reading 12211. The RSA has often been won in the past by a novice that improved markedly on their previous hurdling form, but in recent years classier sorts have prevailed and this former 166-rated hurdler is the one they all have to beat if heading for that, as is expected. He was afterwards cut to a general 4-1 in most ante-post lists, with Paddy Power's standout at 9-2 soon getting snapped up. His trainer Paul Webber intends to give him one more outing before the festival, perhaps in the Argento Chase here. (op Evens tchd 5-6)

Chicago Grey(IRE) looked as though he was just about to land a hat-trick prior to coming down at the penultimate fence over C&D last month. He had won well here the time before and posted a personal-best effort in defeat here despite being no match for the classy winner. He still has a tendency to make the odd error, but gives this form a decent look and there will no doubt be other days for him. He has numerous options over the Christmas period, with the Welsh National being among then, but the Paddy Power Handicap at Leopardstown could be ideal should he turn out again this month. Longer term his trainer indicated the National Hunt Chase at the festival in March may be the race for him. (tchd 4-1)

Quinz(FR) has been in the form of his life since resuming over fences this season and arrived here after an easy success in a handicap off a mark of 130 at Ascot last month, for which he was officially hiked up a stone. He raced enthusiastically at the head of affairs and had opened up a decent advantage with five to jump. He was a sitting duck once the winner found his full stride and paid for his early exertions after the last, but this was still another decent performance. A flatter track is probably ideal for him and it will be interesting to see whether connections keep him to novice races or try their hand back in handicaps now. He could just be the sort for the valuable Grade 3 Racing Post Chase at Kempton in February. (op 13-2 tchd 11-2)

Robo(FR) had improved leaps and bounds in two outings over fences since joining current connections this term, winning both times at Fakenham. He was undone here by a blunder on the final circuit, where his rider did well to stay aboard, and wasn't able to show his best as a result. He collapsed after the winning line and the screens went up, and despite getting to his feet, sadly it later transpired he had suffered a fatal injury. (tchd 16-1)

Balthazar King(IRE) got a positive ride, but was unable to stay with them from four out and ran below his recent level. He is not simple to place now, but may appreciate a bit of a break. (tchd 20-1)

Cannington Brook(IRE) had finished one place behind Balthazar King over C&D on his chase/seasonal debut last month. Keen early, he again hit a flat spot at a crucial stage and failed to step up as may have been expected. A switch to one of the smaller tracks looks a good move for him and softer ground is probably what he wants. (op 8-1 tchd 9-1)

2884 UNICOIN HOMES RELKEEL HURDLE (GRADE 2) (10 hdls) 2m 4f 110y
1:20 (1:21) (Class 1) 4-Y-0+

£19,953 (£7,486; £3,748; £1,869; £938; £469)

Form				RPR
40-2	**1**		**Karabak (FR)**[21] 2516 7-11-2 161 APMcCoy (Alan King) *nt fluent 1st and 3rd: in tch 4th: hdwy fr 3 out to trck ldr 2 out: led wl bef last: hdd run-in: rallied gamely u.p to ld again fnl 120yds: styd on strly* **5/1**[2]	161+
-214	**2**	1 ¾	**Any Given Day (IRE)**[27] 2386 5-11-2 150 JasonMaguire (Donald McCain) *in rr: hit 4th: j. slowly 4 out: rdn and stl bhd after 3 out: stl plenty to do 2 out: rdn and str run sn after to chal last and sn led: hdd u.p fnl 120yds: styd on one pce* **10/1**	159
F-F3	**3**	4 ½	**Celestial Halo (IRE)**[15] 2664 6-11-6 165 (bt) HarrySkelton (Paul Nicholls) *chsd ldrs: rdn after 2 out: one pce and no imp on ldng duo whn nt fluent last* **10/1**	159
33-4	**4**	7	**Zaynar (FR)**[21] 2516 5-11-6 161 (b[1]) BarryGeraghty (Nicky Henderson) *trckd ldrs: drvn to ld 2 out: hdd wl bef last: sn btn* **4/1**[1]	152
1-40	**5**	nk	**Ashkazar (FR)**[21] 2516 6-11-6 152 TimmyMurphy (David Pipe) *j. slowly 3rd and stdd in rr: pushed along 4 out: hdwy to chse ldrs 2 out: sn rdn and no imp* **40/1**	153
0-25	**6**	2 ½	**Kayf Aramis**[14] 2672 8-11-2 148 (p) PaddyBrennan (Nigel Twiston-Davies) *in rr: pushed along fr 5th: rdn and hdwy fr 2 out: styd on u.p run-in whn swtchd rt: nvr gng pce to get into contention* **33/1**	145
1-33	**7**	1 ¼	**Restless Harry**[21] 2516 6-11-6 149 HenryOliver (Robin Dickin) *pressed ldr fr 3rd tl led after 3 out: hdd 2 out: hrd rdn and wknd wl bef last* **11/2**[3]	148
/1P-	**8**	2	**Sentry Duty (FR)**[56] 4701 8-11-2 160 AndrewTinkler (Nicky Henderson) *hld up in rr: hdwy and n.m.r after 2 out: nvr rchd ldrs: sn rdn and no imp* **8/1**	143
11-1	**9**	4	**Quartz De Thaix (FR)**[20] 2542 6-10-12 148 AidanColeman (Venetia Williams) *chsd ldrs to 2 out: wknd wl bef last* **8/1**	135
1-22	**10**	17	**Banjaxed Girl**[19] 2579 6-10-9 153 SamTwiston-Davies (Nigel Twiston-Davies) *led tl hdd after 3 out: wknd sn after next* **8/1**	126+
42-1	**11**	4	**Carlito Brigante (IRE)**[21] 2521 4-11-6 140 DNRussell (Gordon Elliott, Ire) *in rr but in tch: impr 3 out: drvn to chse ldrs appr 2 out: sn wknd* **20/1**	136+
611-	**12**	9	**Tail Of The Bank (IRE)**[280] 4446 7-10-12 124 LiamHeard (Laura Young) *chsd ldrs tl wknd after 3 out* **100/1**	107

4m 51.27s (-13.73) **Going Correction** -0.075s/f (Good)
WFA 4 from 5yo+ 6lb **12** Ran SP% **114.7**
Speed ratings (Par 115): **123,122,120,117,117 116,116,115,114,107 106,102**
toteswingers:1&2 £10.60, 2&3 £19.30, 1&3 £3.50 CSF £50.23 TOTE £3.90: £1.60, £3.60, £2.40; EX 53.10 Trifecta £606.10 Pool: £4316.55 - 5.27 winning units..

Owner John P McManus **Bred** Suc Cino Del Duca **Trained** Barbury Castle, Wilts

FOCUS
Zaynar was sent off at odds of 1-5 when winning the race last season, but this year's Relkeel Hurdle was a much more competitive affair. With a decent gallop on from the start, there were plenty of chances nearing the turn for home, but the class horses came clear from that point. Karabak was the form pick at the weights and is rated 4lb off his best, with a personal best from the runner-up. The next two were below their best.

NOTEBOOK
Karabak(FR) dug really deep on the run-in to gain an overdue and much-deserved success. Alan King's 7-y-o had finished runner-up for the second successive year in the Ascot Hurdle on his return last month, where he reversed form with old rival Zaynar when well held by Classy Silviniaco Conti. Connections opted to come here rather than take on Big Buck's again in the Long Walk Hurdle back there on Saturday, and the move paid off. He mastered Zaynar approaching the climb for home, but the runner-up came with a very strong challenge against the stands' rail at the last and momentarily looked like winning. Tony McCoy got stuck into him, though, and he was nicely on top at the finish. The winner clearly relished this stiffer test and, while he was well suited by the weights here, this should do his confidence a lot of good. His season will again revolve around another crack at Big Buck's in the World Hurdle here in March and, while it's hard to see him winning that, he is a stronger horse this year so is a good bet to make the places. He was trimmed to as short as 8-1 with William Hill in the ante-post betting, but was available at 14-1 with Bet365. (tchd 9-2)

Any Given Day(IRE), fourth in the Greatwood Hurdle here last month, got behind when his jumping became messy after flattening the flight passing the stands for the first time. He looked a hopeless cause three out, but found a second wind at the second-last and really motored up the home straight. It looked for a moment as though he would get on top, but the winner outstayed him near the finish. This rates a clear personal-best display from an improving 5-y-o and he is clearly now very much a graded performer. He is versatile as regards underfoot conditions, and the Aintree Hurdle at the Grand National meeting in April looks a viable end-of-term target. (op 11-1)

Celestial Halo(IRE) was back over hurdles having failed to take to chasing in two runs since returning this season. He had yet to prove himself over the longer distance, but was joint best in at the weights with the winner on official figures and had the blinkers back on to sharpen him up. He did things nicely on the inside through the race and held every chance turning for home, but couldn't sustain his effort up the rising finish. He was conceding 4lb to the first pair, and so officially ran to his mark of 165, but whether he gets this trip well enough to succeed over it at this sort of level remains open to some debate. (op 8-1)

Zaynar(FR) looked a horse with issues after hanging markedly in the home straight when unsuccessfully defending the Ascot Hurdle on his comeback last month. Headgear looked sure to be back on after that, and it was first-time blinkers rather than is usual cheekpieces that were chosen by connections. He raced much more enthusiastically as a result, back at a track he enjoys, and made a bold move after the penultimate flight but faded after being headed by Karabak. If anything, he paid for doing too much early in the blinkers, and it is still a little too early to be writing him off, but on recent evidence this is as good as he is these days. (tchd 7-2)

Ashkazar(FR), beaten out of sight in the Ascot Hurdle on his previous outing, looked as though he again wasn't on a going day through the early parts. The further he went the better he got, however, and this was a definite step back in the right direction. He still is not simple to place from his current mark, though. (op 50-1)

Kayf Aramis needs further and was faced with a stiff task, so wasn't at all disgraced.

Restless Harry, a a C&D winner as a novice, was expected to enjoy returning to this stiffer test after his gallant third in the Ascot Hurdle. He ultimately paid for doing too much on the front-end through the race, however, and was done with after two out. Connections may look to chasing for him after this. (op 7-1 tchd 5-1)

Sentry Duty(FR), last seen running a solid race in the Cesarewitch in October, won over this C&D on New Year's Day. He often goes best when fresh and began to get involved from well off the pace nearing three out. He flattened out when push came to shove though. (op 13-2)

Quartz De Thaix(FR), progressive at a lower level, was found out by the jump in grade. (tchd 9-1)

Banjaxed Girl, usually consistent, found this too tough an ask, but should still have run an awful lot better. (op 10-1)

Carlito Brigante(IRE) Official explanation: jockey said gelding had a breathing problem

2885 KEITH PROWSE HOSPITALITY TINGLE CREEK CHASE (GRADE 1) (13 fncs 1 omitted) 2m 110y
1:55 (1:55) (Class 1) 4-Y-0+

£34,206 (£12,834; £6,426; £3,204; £1,608; £804)

Form				RPR
14-1	**1**		**Master Minded (FR)**[21] 2515 7-11-7 178 NoelFehily (Paul Nicholls) *j. boldly: trckd ldng pair 3rd: str run to ld 2 out: drvn clr run-in* **10/11**[1]	173+
053-	**2**	8	**Petit Robin (FR)**[231] 5392 7-11-7 163 BarryGeraghty (Nicky Henderson) *t.k.h: trckd ldr: led after 9th: hdd 2 out: wknd fnl 100yds* **6/1**[3]	167
22-3	**3**	½	**Somersby (IRE)**[39] 2138 6-11-7 156 HaddenFrost (Henrietta Knight) *rrd over bkwards and uns rdr leaving paddock: hld up: outpcd whn mstke 9th: styd on fr 2 out: 4th last: fin wl* **13/2**	167
021-	**4**	12	**I'm So Lucky**[231] 5394 8-11-7 153 (t) TomScudamore (David Pipe) *led: quite keen: j.rt: hdd after 9th: swtchd rt to chse ldr 3 out: wknd appr last* **22/1**	156
11/1	**5**	¾	**Gauvain (GER)**[27] 2385 8-11-7 159 DarylJacob (Nick Williams) *chsd ldrs: outpcd whn hit 3 out: wknd appr next* **11/2**[2]	155
F-U5	**6**	2 ¾	**Mahogany Blaze (FR)**[27] 2385 8-11-7 148 (b) SamTwiston-Davies (Nigel Twiston-Davies) *towards rr: outpcd 9th: no ch after: kpt on fr 2 out* **40/1**	151

F4-3 **7** *7* **Kalahari King (FR)**[35] 2206 9-11-7 **164**........ GrahamLee 149
(Ferdy Murphy) *hld up in rr: hdwy 5th: rdn and lost pl 4 out: bhd and eased 2 out* **9/1**

-U64 **8** *6* **Oiseau De Nuit (FR)**[27] 2385 8-11-7 **146**........(b[1]) JoeTizzard 142
(Colin Tizzard) *in rr: outpcd 9th: bhd fr 3 out: wknd run-in* **66/1**

-PP5 **9** *dist* **Kinkeel (IRE)**[21] 2515 11-11-7 **82**........ EamonDehdashti 51
(Tony Carroll) *dropped to rr after 4th: bhd whn hit next: t.o 6th: eventually completed (btn 157 l)* **250/1**

4m 1.20s (-5.50) **Going Correction** -0.025s/f (Good) **9** Ran SP% **114.1**
Speed ratings: **111,107,107,101,101 99,96,93,47**
toteswingers:1&2 £3.20, 2&3 £5.30, 1&3 £1.40 CSF £6.83 TOTE £1.80: £1.10, £2.10, £2.10; EX 8.30 Trifecta £25.60 Pool: £5873.49 - 169.15 winning units..
Owner Clive D Smith **Bred** Marie-Christine Gabeur **Trained** Ditcheat, Somerset

FOCUS
It was a relief to everyone that this race was re-routed from last week's abandoned Sandown meeting (as was also the case in 2000). The prize-money may have been reduced, but the field was still a very strong one, even in the absence of dual winner of the race Twist Magic, and courtesy of I'm So Lucky and Petit Robin, the pace was a really decent one. Interestingly, though, the time was 0.5secs slower than that recorded by Woolcombe Folly in the opening handicap chase. Master Minded is rated in line with his best form of the past couple of seasons but still below the best of his old form. The next two both produced personal bests.

NOTEBOOK
Master Minded(FR) had enjoyed mixed fortunes since winning this in 2008, losing his Champion Chase crown earlier in the year when clearly below his best, but a breathing operation over the summer looked to have helped when putting in a faultless display on his reappearance at Ascot, and the only question here was whether he could reproduce it with just a 21-day break between races. The comprehensive answer was yes, as having wisely been kept back a bit from the pacesetters, he started to close running down the hill, responding to some exaggerated squeezing from Fehily, and swept into the lead at the second-last before powering clear. His effort in the straight was particularly pleasing, winging the last two fences and very much looking back to something like his brilliant best, re-establishing himself as the leading two-miler. The Victor Chandler at Ascot towards the end of January will be the winner's last stop before the festival and, assuming all goes well in the build-up to Cheltenham, he's sure to take the beating in his bid to win a third Champion Chase - best-priced 7-4. (tchd 11-10 and 6-5 in a place)
Petit Robin(FR) has a fine record fresh and Barry Geraghty was happy to ride him aggressively up on the pace with I'm So Lucky. The pair were duelling from some way out, but having mastered that rival, he than had to try and go again with the winner, which was always going to prove a near-impossible task. This wouldn't have been far off a career-best, which is another fillip for Master Minded, and connections will now head for the Game Spirit. (op 8-1)
Somersby(IRE) deserves a good deal of credit for running so well, considering he reared over on the walkway coming out on to the course and made a notable mid-race blunder, finishing strongly after the last, not quite getting up for second. Runner-up in last season's Arkle, he was being talked of as a Gold Cup horse over the summer but, beaten in the Haldon Gold Cup on his reappearance, his trainer was keen to turn attentions to a Champion Chase campaign. This run, however, seems to confirm he hasn't got the speed, so it now looks as though the Ryanair will be his target, a race he's sure to be a major player in. Interestingly his trainer will now look into getting him led out on to the course, as this wasn't an isolated incident. (tchd 11-2 and 7-1)
I'm So Lucky signed off with a good win at Sandown on his final outing and, having run well here in the past and already proven his ability over further, it was no surprise to see him ridden aggressively. He tried to tough it out down the hill, but couldn't race on with the front pair and finished quite tired in the end. This was a very satisfactory return and he could pick up a decent prize this season. (op 20-1)
Gauvain(GER) took his form to a new level when beating Forpadydeplasterer over C&D on his debut for Nick Williams, but there was more than a suspicion that he was flattered that day, and this run seemed to confirm he isn't up to the top level. (op 7-1)
Mahogany Blaze(FR) ran about as well as could have been expected (op 50-1)
Kalahari King(FR) was particularly disappointing as, although well held in a handicap at Kelso on his reappearance, he was expected to have improved significantly and had the form in the book to be in the scrap for scrap for second spot. (op 15-2 tchd 13-2)
Oiseau De Nuit(FR) failed to improve for the first-time blinkers. (op 50-1)

2886 VOTE A. P. GOLD CUP (HANDICAP CHASE) GRADE 3 (16 fncs 1 omitted) 2m 5f
2:30 (2:30) (Class 1) 4-Y-O+

£85,515 (£32,085; £16,065; £8,010; £4,020; £2,010)

Form RPR

U-25 **1** **Poquelin (FR)**[28] 2359 7-11-7 **163**........ IanPopham(5) 173
(Paul Nicholls) *trckd ldrs: hit 9th: led 2 out: sn rdn: jnd after last: styd on gamely and asserted fnl 100yds* **16/1**

41-6 **2** *1* **Great Endeavour (IRE)**[28] 2359 6-10-5 **142**........ TimmyMurphy 152
(David Pipe) *chsd ldrs: rdn after 4 out: styng on whn n.m.r bnd after 3 out: chsd wnr after 2 out and drvn upsides after last: no ex u.p and one pce fnl 100yds* **13/2**[2]

12-0 **3** *6* **Sunnyhillboy (IRE)**[28] 2359 7-9-13 **139**........ RichieMcLernon(3) 145
(Jonjo O'Neill) *in rr: drvn along 6th: hdwy appr 3 out: stl plenty to do: styd on wl fr 2 out and tk 3rd cl home: no imp on ldng duo* **9/1**

-562 **4** *½* **Calgary Bay (IRE)**[31] 2304 7-10-6 **143**........(p) HaddenFrost 147
(Henrietta Knight) *chsd ldrs: drvn along 4 out: one pce 2 out: styd on to chse ldng duo run-in: nvr any ch and lost 3rd cl home* **16/1**

6-11 **5** *11* **Little Josh (IRE)**[28] 2359 8-11-1 **155**........ SamTwiston-Davies(3) 151+
(Nigel Twiston-Davies) *led tl hdd and pckd 2 out: wknd bef last* **13/2**[2]

41-4 **6** *6* **Mad Max (IRE)**[28] 2359 8-11-6 **157**........ PCarberry 148
(Nicky Henderson) *chsd ldr to 2 out: wknd qckly and no ch whn blnd last* **10/1**

0-30 **7** *9* **Pigeon Island**[28] 2359 7-10-0 **137** oh4........(b) PaddyBrennan 121+
(Nigel Twiston-Davies) *in rr: hit 11th: hmpd 3 out: mod prog fr next* **33/1**

P-55 **8** *7* **Northern Alliance (IRE)**[17] 2621 9-10-5 **147**........ APHeskin(5) 125
(A J Martin, Ire) *chsd ldrs stl in tch whn bdly hmpd and wknd 3 out* **20/1**

-1F1 **9** *4 ½* **Robinson Collonges (FR)**[23] 2471 5-10-11 **148**........ NoelFehily 119
(Paul Nicholls) *in rr: pckd 5th: hdwy 8th: shkn up and styng on jst bhd ldrs whn blnd 3 out: sn wknd* **15/2**[3]

F-12 **10** *23* **Matuhi**[15] 2665 7-10-0 **137** oh2........(t) TomScudamore 91
(David Pipe) *chsd ldrs: blnd 4th: mstke 12th: wknd 4 out: no ch whn hmpd 3 out* **12/1**

-130 **11** *3 ¾* **Finger Onthe Pulse (IRE)**[28] 2359 9-10-10 **147**........(t) APMcCoy 92
(T J Taaffe, Ire) *rdn 11th: a in rr* **25/1**

40-1 **12** *1 ½* **Dave's Dream (IRE)**[29] 2345 7-10-11 **148**........ BarryGeraghty 92
(Nicky Henderson) *chsng ldrs: reminders after 4th: nvr really travelling after but stl chsng ldrs 8th: wknd fr 10th* **5/1**[1]

/F-4 **P** **Psycho (IRE)**[17] 2618 9-11-1 **152**........ DNRussell —
(A J Martin, Ire) *in tch whn mstke 8th: hit 11th: sn wknd: t.o whn p.u bef 3 out* **10/1**

PF0- **P** **Duers (IRE)**[59] 1837 8-10-0 **137** oh2........(p) AELynch —
(Paul Magnier, Ire) *a in rr: blnd 4 out: t.o whn p.u bef next* **66/1**

/1-2 **P** **Gonebeyondrecall (IRE)**[69] 1712 7-10-0 **137** oh1........(v[1]) PaulMoloney —
(N F Glynn, Ire) *in tch: wknd 10th: t.o whn p.u bef 2 out* **50/1**

-313 **F** **Noble Alan (GER)**[21] 2517 7-10-6 **143**........ BrianHarding —
(Nicky Richards) *in rr: mstke 4th: hdwy 11th: styng on wl and 3 l 5th whn fell 3 out* **16/1**

5m 10.26s (-9.14) **Going Correction** -0.025s/f (Good) **16** Ran SP% **123.6**
Speed ratings (Par 113): **116,115,113,113,108 106,103,100,98,90 88,88,—,—,—,—**
toteswingers:1&2 £40.80, 2&3 £20.40, 1&3 £67.80 CSF £114.92 CT £1020.64 TOTE £20.70: £3.80, £1.80, £2.50, £3.50; EX 166.30 Trifecta £1245.80 Pool: £28468.34 - 16.91 winning units..

Owner The Stewart Family **Bred** Georges Sandor And Eric Becq **Trained** Ditcheat, Somerset
■ Another change of title for this event, run recently as the Boylesports.com Gold Cup.

FOCUS
This very valuable and long-standing handicap is always a highly competitive race. It was as expected run at a decent gallop and the form looks rock-solid. A personal best from Poquelin under his claimer, the race rated around the second and third's C/D form from the festival.

NOTEBOOK
Poquelin(FR), winner of this last year, finished fifth under top weight in the Paddy Power Gold Cup on his return here last month, but stepped up big time on this better ground and became the first horse to register back-to-back wins in the race. He got a lovely trip just off the leaders and was ideally placed to strike turning for home. He found plenty from two out when asked for everything by his claiming rider and, while he wandered somewhat under maximum pressure, was always doing enough to fend off the runner-up. This was the 7-y-o's first success since winning it last season off an 11lb lower mark and, although he finished second in the Ryanair on his next outing after that, this should rate his best effort to date. Paul Nicholls, welcoming back his fourth winner on the card, later said his charge will now follow the same path as last term and be left off for a bid to go one better in the Ryanair in March. He was promoted to favouritism at around 6-1 with most firms in the ante-post market.
Great Endeavour(IRE) was a leading fancy for the Paddy Power last month, but his jumping let him down that day. He was given a similarly positive ride towards the outside of runners this time and jumped a lot more fluently on this sounder surface. He dug deep to rally off the home turn and looked as though he may master the winner coming to the last, but was unable to take advantage of the big weight concession on the run-in. This was much more like it again from last season's Byrne Group Plate victor. He finished nicely clear of the remainder, and it should be onwards and upwards for him now, despite a likely rise in the handicap. He may step up to 3m. (op 8-1)
Sunnyhillboy(IRE), on paper, ran right up to form. He finished second to Great Endeavour at the festival last season, and was one place behind him again when returning here last month. However, neither was near their best that day and while he improved markedly to finish third this time, things would have surely been different had he jumped more fluently early on as he got well behind. He still had plenty to do three out, but motored up the home straight as others were tiring and is clearly still at the right end of the weights. It may well prove that he is more of a 'spring' horse and no doubt connections will be eyeing another crack at the handicap at the festival in March. (tchd 10-1)
Calgary Bay(IRE), with cheekpieces back on, is a talented horse on his day and he ran a brave race back over this suitably longer trip on ground that suits. His turn isn't looking that far off again.
Little Josh(IRE) had plenty of these behind when readily winning the Paddy Power Gold Cup last month, and was bidding to become the fourth horse to do the double. He again set out to make all, but wasn't gifted an early lead and probably had to do a bit more than his rider ideally wanted. He was still in there fighting prior to clouting the second-last and losing any chance, but the suspicion is that his 9lb higher mark was just about to find him out. It was still another gallant effort. (op 7-1)
Mad Max(IRE), fourth in the Paddy Power, ran a sound race under a more positive ride yet was done with before the penultimate fence. (op 12-1)
Pigeon Island plugged on over a trip that stretches him and would've been a little closer without being hampered three out where Noble Alan departed.
Northern Alliance(IRE) fared best of the Irish raiders in eighth and would have been closer without being hampered.
Robinson Collonges(FR) came into this handicap debut as an unexposed novice. He made an early error out the back, but was taken a lot closer on the far side and looked a player out wide. He ultimately paid for that mid-race move, however, but is still only a 5-y-o and there will be other days for him. (op 6-1)
Matuhi failed to see out the longer trip in this hotter company.
Dave's Dream(IRE) was beaten well before the longer trip or his 11lb higher mark came into play. He just wasn't on a going day. Official explanation: jockey said gelding was never travelling (op 11-2 tchd 6-1 in a place)
Psycho(IRE) was badly let down by his jumping in this much bigger field. Official explanation: jockey said gelding made a mistake at the water jump and never travelled after (op 9-1)
Noble Alan(GER) was trying to stay on and wasn't neccessarily out of it when coming down. (op 9-1)

2887 STANJAMES.COM INTERNATIONAL HURDLE (GRADE 2) (8 hdls) 2m 1f
3:05 (3:06) (Class 1) 4-Y-O+

£85,515 (£32,085; £16,065; £8,010; £4,020; £2,010)

Form RPR

12-1 **1** **Menorah (IRE)**[27] 2386 5-11-4 162........ RichardJohnson 157+
(Philip Hobbs) *trckd ldrs: j.w: swtchd and led appr last: r.o strly: rdn clr run-in* **7/4**[1]

1-11 **2** *4 ½* **Cue Card**[29] 2344 4-11-4 160........ JoeTizzard 152
(Colin Tizzard) *trckd ldrs travelling strly: jnd ldrs 2 out: shkn up to ld between last 2: hdd appr last: styd on same pce run-in* **15/8**[2]

111 **3** *½* **Silviniaco Conti (FR)**[21] 2516 4-11-8 159........ NoelFehily 156
(Paul Nicholls) *chsd clr ldr: mstke 1st: led 3 out: hdd between last 2: kpt on same pce run-in* **5/2**[3]

1114 **4** *3 ¼* **Clerk's Choice (IRE)**[21] 2521 4-11-4 159........ TomMolloy 149
(Michael Banks) *hld up: hdwy to trck ldrs 4th: upsides between last 2: nt fluent last: edgd lft and fdd last 150yds* **20/1**

5 *2 ½* **Cristal Bonus (FR)**[27] 2418 4-11-8 152........ APMcCoy 150
(Evan Williams) *towards rr: hdwy to chse ldrs 3 out: drvn and one pce between last 2* **25/1**

1310 **6** *2* **Astracad (FR)**[27] 2386 4-11-0 140........ PaddyBrennan 140
(Nigel Twiston-Davies) *hld up: hdwy to chse ldrs 5th: one pce between last 2* **40/1**

141 **7** *10* **Nicene Creed**[16] 2634 5-11-0 123........ TomO'Brien 130
(Philip Hobbs) *led: clr after 1st tl after 5th: hdd next: wknd after 2 out* **66/1**

3/22 **8** *16* **Der Spieler (GER)**[36] 2197 5-11-0 143........ BarryGeraghty 114
(J G Coogan, Ire) *in rr: prom but drvn 5th: wknd 2 out: bhd whn nt fluent last* **50/1**

4413 **9** *12* **Liberty Seeker (FR)**[23] 2474 11-11-0 108........ MattCrawley 102
(John Harris) *in rr: in tch but drvn along 5th: lost pl appr 2 out: sn bhd* **250/1**

4m 3.50s (-7.80) **Going Correction** -0.075s/f (Good) **9** Ran SP% **114.6**
Speed ratings (Par 115): **115,112,112,111,109 109,104,96,91**
toteswingers:1&2 £1.10, 2&3 £1.10, 1&3 £1.30 CSF £5.23 TOTE £2.60: £1.30, £1.40, £1.30; EX 5.30 Trifecta £10.30 Pool: £7486.85 - 534.38 winning units..
Owner Mrs Diana L Whateley **Bred** Mrs E Grant And Miss Anna Brislane **Trained** Withycombe, Somerset
■ New sponsors for this event, traditionally known as the Bula.

FOCUS
The most eagerly awaited race of the day, with three potential stars clashing in a contest that has proved to be an excellent Champion Hurdle trial over the years. Philip Hobbs, responsible for Rooster Booster in 2002 (went on to win the Champion Hurdle), and Detroit City in 2006 (beaten favourite for the big one), had unearthed another serious contender in Menorah. The ordinary time limits the rating, and Memorah didn't need to improve on his Greatwood figure. Cue Card was up 2lb with Silviniaco Conto a bit off his Ascot form.

NOTEBOOK
Menorah(IRE) ◆, having won last season's Supreme Novices', put up a career-best when defying top weight in the Greatwood on his return, a race Hobbs also uses often for his Champion Hurdle contenders. He has had trouble in single-figure fields when there hasn't been much pace on in the past, so had stablemate Nicene Creed in as a pacemaker, but he was somewhat ignored in racing, taking such a clear early lead, and the race probably turned into more of a speed test than was ideal for his two market rivals, with the field having bunched right up at the top of the hill. That shouldn't detract, however, from what was a very impressive performance, stalking his rivals running down the hill and producing a serious gear change with minimal pressure applied to take it up on the run to the last, in the end staying on strongly for an emphatic success, one which now sees him reside atop many a Champion Hurdle list at a general 4-1. Like his trainer's previous winner of the Champion Hurdle, Rooster Booster, he's a strong-travelling type who doesn't want to hit the front too soon, loves Cheltenham, and seems to be getting better all the time, indeed even his jumping is very slick. Add to that the fact he already has a big-field festival win to his name (as had Rooster Booster), and he really does start to look the standout contender. It is unlikely he'll have another run before Cheltenham. (op 9-4)

Cue Card's participation had created most of the buzz surrounding the race, stepping out of novice company on only his third start over hurdles, and it was a good time for the 4-y-o to put any potential Champion Hurdle credentials to the test. His jumping seemed more fluent than it had done previously, and it was noticeable just how strongly he travelled, being the last one off the bridle and Joe Tizzard having to take a pull after two out, but it was clear turning in that he was going to have to come under pressure, something that had never happened previously, and he was unable to respond as Menorah raced past. It was good to see him tough it out for second, though, and it's almost certain he'd have learnt from this, the first 'proper' race he's had to date, so although beaten, his reputation is by no means diminished. Connections will make a decision about his Cheltenham target in the coming weeks, but for now, given his age, it would make a lot more sense to go down the novice route, with the Supreme seemingly favoured over the Neptune. He could go straight to the festival. (tchd 13-8 and 2-1 in a place)

Silviniaco Conti(FR) emerges with a great deal of credit, having attempted to concede 4lb to his two main rivals. A horse that has come from out of nowhere, putting in a stunning effort when beating Karabak in the Ascot Hurdle last time, he had a bit to prove on this drop in trip, having won the last twice over further, and perhaps in hindsight his rider would have tried to crank it up a bit earlier in an attempt to outstay his rivals, but there was no beating the winner regardless of how he'd been ridden, and the way he stayed on very much pointed to a return to further suiting. His trainer remains open-minded about the Champion, though, and he'll be given a break now before returning in another trial. Softer ground suits him ideally. (tchd 11-4)

Clerk's Choice(IRE), impressive in a 4-y-o event at the October meeting prior to disappointing in soft ground at Haydock, bounced back to give a more accurate reflection of his ability, although in the end he couldn't quite match the front trio. His previously questionable rating of 159 means handicaps are out, and he isn't up to championship standard, so he isn't going to be the easiest to place. (op 16-1 tchd 14-1)

Cristal Bonus(FR), Grade 1-placed in France on his final outing, rather harshly was asked to concede weight, along with the third, so the fact he managed to run so well on this British debut suggests he's a horse with a lot of class. Rated 152, placing him won't be easy either, but he's presumably been bought with chasing in mind next season. (op 20-1)

Astracad(FR), well behind Menorah when slightly disappointing in the Greatwood, had no right to get competitive against these, and didn't. He remains capable of better back in handicaps.

Nicene Creed is a useful prospect in his own right, so it's hoped this doesn't leave a mark.

2888 ALBERT BARTLETT NOVICES' HURDLE (REGISTERED AS THE BRISTOL NOVICES' HURDLE RACE) (GRADE 2) (12 hdls) 3m

3:40 (3:40) (Class 1) 4-Y-0+

£14,252 (£5,347; £2,677; £1,335; £670; £335)

Form				RPR
11	1		**Mossley (IRE)**[41] 2111 4-11-4 0 .... BarryGeraghty	142+
			(Nicky Henderson) *trckd ldrs: slt ld 2 out: travelling wl sn after: idled and jnd run-in: shkn up and styd on strly under hand driving fnl 120yds* **3/1**[1]	
3	2	1 ¼	**Join Together (IRE)**[39] 2142 5-11-0 0 .... DavidCottin	135
			(Paul Nicholls) *chsd ldrs tl hit 2 out and lost pl: rallied u.p last and chal sn after: kpt on: nt gng pce of wnr fnl 120yds* **14/1**	
421	3	2	**Teaforthree (IRE)**[19] 2571 6-11-4 130 .... APMcCoy	136
			(Rebecca Curtis) *chsd ldrs: chal 5th: styd front rnk and ev ch 2 out: stl upsides u.p after last: one pce into 3rd fnl 120yds* **13/2**[2]	
1-1	4	6	**Highland Valley (IRE)**[32] 2283 5-11-4 0 .... SamThomas	133+
			(Emma Lavelle) *nvr jumping w much fluency: in rr but in tch: drvn and hdwy appr 2 out: chsd ldrs sn after: nvr quite on terms: wknd last* **3/1**[1]	
41	5	6	**Old Wigmore (IRE)**[34] 2238 5-11-0 0 .... TomScudamore	120
			(Rebecca Curtis) *trckd ldrs: chal 6th: led 7th: narrowly hdd 2 out: wknd bef last* **20/1**	
25-1	6	hd	**Rif (FR)**[48] 1990 5-11-4 128 .... DenisO'Regan	124
			(Alex Hales) *in tch tl outpcd 7th: drvn and styd on fr 2 out: kpt on run-in: n.d* **22/1**	
4-21	7	7	**Golden Chieftain (IRE)**[17] 2607 5-11-4 0 .... JoeTizzard	119
			(Colin Tizzard) *plld hrd: led tl hdd 7th: styd pressing ldr to 3 out: wknd 2 out* **3/1**[1]	
1	8	nk	**Badgers Cove (IRE)**[19] 2584 6-11-4 0 .... CharliePoste	117
			(Robin Dickin) *in rr: rdn and sme hdwy after 4 out: wknd bef 2 out* **33/1**	
613-	P		**Galant Nuit (FR)**[268] 4703 6-11-0 132 .... GrahamLee	—
			(Ferdy Murphy) *in tch: in rr fr 4th: wknd quckly after 4 out: t.o whn p.u bef 2 out* **12/1**[3]	

6m 9.35s (8.35) **Going Correction** -0.075s/f (Good) **9** Ran SP% **114.7**
Speed ratings (Par 115): **83,82,81,79,77 77,75,75,—**
toteswingers:1&2 £7.80, 2&3 £5.10, 1&3 £7.30 CSF £45.46 TOTE £4.50: £2.20, £2.00, £1.70; EX 49.60 Trifecta £157.50 Pool: £2999.25 - 14.09 winning units..

Owner Michael Buckley **Bred** Pipe View Stud **Trained** Upper Lambourn, Berks

FOCUS
A Grade 2 staying novice hurdle that is usually won by a classy sort, and seven of this year's nine-strong field were last-time-out winners, so it was highly competitive. There was just a steady pace on, which resulted in five nearly upsides coming to the penultimate flight, but eventually the principals forged clear. Steps up from the first three, but not form to be confident about given the muddling nature of the race.

NOTEBOOK
Mossley(IRE) extended his unbeaten sequence to three and completed the task with a bit more in hand than the bare margin indicates. He did things easily through the race and appeared sure to win easily coming to the last as he was still swinging on the bridle. He was noticeably sweating under the saddle, however, and a sluggish leap at the last allowed the placed horses to close right up. Barry Geraghty still looked confident of getting him home in front up the run-in, though, and he never had to resort to the whip as he responded. It wasn't a severe test, but the winner obviously gets this longer trip and it's hard to assess just how high he may progress yet as a novice hurdler. This display puts him bang in contention for the Grade 1 Albert Bartlett over C&D at next year's festival. (old market op 4-1 new market)
Join Together(IRE), third on his hurdling debut at Exeter last month, was faced with a much stiffer task and proved friendless in the betting. The longer trip was much more to his liking and he posted a vastly improved effort under his accomplished French rider. He paid a compliment to his previous conqueror Court In Motion, and this former point winner should soon be off the mark. (old market op 14-1 new market)
Teaforthree(IRE), a chasing type, got off the mark over this trip at the second attempt over hurdles last month and had previous experience of this course having finished fourth in his final bumper outing in October. He was not surprisingly given a positive ride and turned in a game effort, stepping up again on his previous level. He helps to set the standard. (old market op 8-1 new market op 6-1)
Highland Valley(IRE) would've no doubt been closer had he jumped more fluently. This scopey 5-y-o shouldn't be fully judged on this effort. (old market op 7-2 new market)
Old Wigmore(IRE), stablemate of the third, dropped out after the third-last and would've probably been better off making this more of a test. (old market op 18-1 new market)
Rif(FR), off the mark at Towcester on his return in October, was a little out of his depth in this company. He still wasn't disgraced, though, considering more of a test would've suited. (new market)
Golden Chieftain(IRE) hacked up at Chepstow on his previous outing, but folded disappointingly from the second-last on this step up in class. He did take time to settle over this longer trip, however, and is another that shouldn't be judged too harshly on the back of this. (old market tchd 9-2 new market)
Galant Nuit(FR), a progressive chaser last term, had yet to win over hurdles. Connections were using this as a prep-race for the Welsh National and, pulling up after three out, it was later revealed he had struck into his heel and would have to miss out on the race. The Kim Muir in which he finished last season will again be his big target and connections are not afraid to head there fresh with him. (new market)
T/Jkpt: £3,033.90 to a £1 stake. Pool: £14,956.06 - 3.50 winning tickets. T/Plt: £43.90 to a £1 stake. Pool: £225,954.59 - 3,753.16 winning tickets. T/Qpdt: £14.60 to a £1 stake. Pool: £15,397.45 - 779.70 winning tickets. ST

DONCASTER (L-H)
Saturday, December 11
2889 Meeting Abandoned - Snow & frost

2591 LINGFIELD (L-H)
Saturday, December 11

OFFICIAL GOING: Standard
This card, consisting of an AW bumper and six Flat races, replaced the scheduled jumps card which was frozen off.
Wind: Almost nil Weather: Overcast

2896 DANIEL PITCHERS RICHMOND MAIDEN OPEN NATIONAL HUNT FLAT RACE 2m

11:50 (11:50) (Class 5) 4-6-Y-0 **£1,712** (£499; £249)

Form				RPR
	1		**Solaise (IRE)**[188] 5-10-9 0 .... MissLHorner[(5)]	88+
			(Liam Corcoran) *t.k.h: trckd ldr: led after 6f and injected pce: pressed over 3f out: sn kicked on again: rdn out* **20/1**	
	2	1 ¼	**Hackpenbay** 4-10-9 0 .... DavidBass[(5)]	87
			(Lawney Hill) *prom: chsd wnr 3f out: drvn to try to cl 2f out: hanging and nt qckn over 1f out* **15/2**	
	3	1 ¼	**Quix** 4-10-7 0 .... NathanSweeney[(7)]	86
			(Bob Buckler) *prom: pushed along 5f out: lost pl u.p over 3f out: rallied 2f out: wnt 3rd 1f out: kpt on* **6/1**[1]	
0	4	1 ¾	**Twentyten (IRE)**[35] 2222 5-10-7 0 .... MrJarrett[(7)]	84
			(Paul Henderson) *wl in rr: rdn 1/2-way: struggling bdly in last pair over 3f out: styd on strly fnl 2f: nrst fin* **100/1**	
0	5	1	**Absolution (IRE)**[31] 2309 4-11-0 0 .... AndrewThornton	83
			(Henrietta Knight) *t.k.h: trckd ldrs: rdn to chse ldng pair 2f out to 1f out: fdd* **10/1**	
06-0	6	¾	**Lilac Belle**[38] 2156 4-10-4 0 .... (t) ChrisHonour[(3)]	75
			(Alex Hales) *hld up in last pair: gng bttr than most whn hdwy into midfield 2f out: shkn up and kpt on ins fnl f* **25/1**	
4-	7	½	**Lost Two Stars (IRE)**[274] 4575 5-10-7 0 .... DaveCrosse	75
			(Colin Tizzard) *trckd ldrs: rdn over 5f out: cl enough 3f out: wknd over 1f out* **6/1**[1]	
	8	2 ¾	**Gdynia Baba (FR)** 6-10-11 0 .... MrSWalker[(3)]	79
			(Alison Batchelor) *hld up in midfield: dropped in rr and struggling over 3f out: modest late hdwy* **17/2**	
2	9	3 ¾	**Dark Ruby**[97] 1480 5-10-7 0 .... LeightonAspell	68
			(Les Hall) *hld up wl in rr: sme prog gng wl 3f out: shkn up and wknd over 1f out* **7/1**[3]	
0-0	10	½	**Top Bob (IRE)**[23] 2472 5-10-7 0 .... JimmyMcCarthy	68
			(David Arbuthnot) *t.k.h: hld up in last pair: pushed along over 4f out: sn no prog* **16/1**	
0	11	1 ¼	**Virginia Rose Wood (IRE)**[16] 2632 4-10-7 0 .... AndrewGlassonbury	66
			(Peter Hedger) *led in s: led at v slow pce for 6f: chsd wnr to 3f out: sn wknd* **100/1**	
	12	6	**Stays All Night (FR)** 4-10-11 0 .... MichaelMurphy[(3)]	67
			(Tim Vaughan) *hld up in midfield: rdn and effrt on outer over 3f out: chsd ldrs over 2f out: sn wknd* **15/2**	
	13	6	**Dakota Hues** 4-11-0 0 .... MattieBatchelor	61
			(Julia Feilden) *t.k.h: hld up in midfield: rdn and wknd over 3f out* **13/2**[2]	

3m 40.2s (2.20) **Going Correction** +0.075s/f (Slow) **13** Ran SP% **114.0**
Speed ratings: **97,96,95,94,94 94,93,92,90,90 89,86,83**
toteswingers:1&2 £27.60, 2&3 £12.30, 1&3 £26.90 CSF £153.17 TOTE £24.00: £8.70, £5.60, £2.20; EX 338.10.
Owner Balios Racing **Bred** J Costello **Trained** Charlton Adam, Somerset

FOCUS
This Polytrack bumper was salvaged when the rest of the planned jumps card was abandoned. It was slowly run until halfway and those held up towards the rear were at a real disadvantage. The form looks fairly weak.
NOTEBOOK
Solaise(IRE), given a good ride, was taken to the front with a circuit left and stepped up the gallop down the back. A winner on the last of his six starts in Irish points, the gelding willingly kept his pursuers at bay. He may have been flattered by this given that he had the run of the race, but should pay his way at an ordinary level over jumps. (op 14-1)
Hackpenbay, a half-brother to a winning pointer, was never far from the pace. He hung in behind the winner as his rider looked to switch him for a challenge but kept going well enough for second. (op 10-1)
Quix is out of an unraced half-sister to fair chaser Jimmy O'Dea, from the family of Champion Hurdle winners Morley Street and Granville Again. He lost a prominent position with 3f to run but stayed on again up the inside in the straight. (op 7-1)
Twentyten(IRE) had shown little in two Irish points and a bumper. After being shuffled back through the field on the second circuit he had only one horse behind him entering the home straight, but he finished fast from there, in the context of this race at any rate, to grab fourth.
Absolution(IRE), who was beaten a fair way on his debut at Bangor a month ago, travelled quite well and was third turning in before keeping on at the one pace. (op 14-1)
Lilac Belle plugged on from the back and will have to switch to hurdles now. (op 18-1)
Lost Two Stars(IRE) was unsuited by the nature of this race but she was still disappointing. She had caught the eye on her debut in the spring and needs a stiffer test. (op 7-2)

2433 FAKENHAM (L-H)
Sunday, December 12
2897 Meeting Abandoned - Snow

2526 HUNTINGDON (R-H)
Sunday, December 12
2904 Meeting Abandoned - Frozen areas in the back straight
The Peterborough Chase card, originally scheduled for the previous Thursday.

2911 - (Foreign Racing) - See Raceform Interactive

2404 CORK (R-H)
Sunday, December 12
OFFICIAL GOING: Soft

2912a O'CONNELL GROUP CORK STAYERS NOVICE HURDLE (GRADE 3) (13 hdls) 3m
12:50 (12:50) 4-Y-O+ **£17,256** (£5,044; £2,389; £796)

Form	Pos	Dist	Horse	Jockey	RPR
	1		**Mossey Joe (IRE)**227 73 7-11-0 (W J Austin, Ire) *racd keenly: restrained in rr: impr into 3rd 4 out: led after 3 out: drew clr appr next: nt extended: impressive* **12/1**	ADLeigh	139+
	2	9	**Fists Of Fury (IRE)**17 2652 6-11-0 (C Byrnes, Ire) *cl up in 2nd: chal 3 out: sn rdn and no imp: kpt on same pce fr 2 out* **9/2**3	DNRussell	126
	3	2	**Askanna (IRE)**28 2411 5-11-1 128 (Colin Bowe, Ire) *racd in 3rd: rdn and outpcd after 4 out: 5th bef st: styd on again fr last* **10/3**2	MrBO'Neill	125
	4	1 3/4	**Saville Row (IRE)**37 2198 5-11-0 (Mrs John Harrington, Ire) *led: slt mstke 4 out: rdn and hdd after 3 out: sn no ex: mod 4th after mstke last* **11/2**	RMPower	122
	5	hd	**Araucaria (IRE)**37 2196 6-10-12 (John E Kiely, Ire) *hld up in tch: impr into cl 4th after 4 out: rdn and no imp fr next: one pce* **11/8**1	AndrewJMcNamara	120
	6	21	**Down In Neworleans (IRE)**28 2408 5-11-0 (Ms Margaret Mullins, Ire) *trckd ldrs: several slt mstkes: dropped to rr 5 out: lost tch after 4 out* **12/1**	DEMullins	101

6m 3.60s (-28.50) **6** Ran SP% **114.1**
CSF £64.17 TOTE £12.90: £2.50, £3.50; DF 85.10.
Owner William Clifford **Bred** W Clifford **Trained** Cloughjordan, Co Tipperary
FOCUS
The third is a fairly solid guide to the level.
NOTEBOOK
Mossey Joe(IRE) ◆ was taking on four previous hurdle winners on this hurdling debut and the big 7-y-o turned in an extraordinary performance, scoring impressively despite pulling hard to beyond halfway. Sent to the front three out, he quickly went clear to win unchallenged. Trainer Willie Austin mentioned the Irish Grand National as a long-term target and he may have another run over hurdles before reverting to fences.
Fists Of Fury(IRE), successful over 2m2f at Thurles on his second start over hurdles last month, raced in second for most of the way but was found wanting when the winner went on three out. (op 13/2)
Askanna(IRE), whose rider was unable to claim his 5lb allowance because of the value of the race, was bidding for a fourth win over hurdles and tackling this trip for the first time since her second point-to-point win. She disappointed for the first time and, after tracking the leaders, she was being ridden along after four out and soon lost her place before staying on from two out. (op 5/2)
Saville Row(IRE), successful in a 2m6f maiden on his debut at Down Royal last month, made the running. He made a slight mistake four out and, after being headed at the third last, was well held in a battle for third when he fluffed the final hurdle. (op 13/2)
Araucaria(IRE), the winner of two bumpers and twice successful over hurdles at 2m4f, was going this distance for the first time. Held up, she was close enough if good enough after four out, but was unable to make any impression from before two out. (op 6/4)

2913 - 2916a (Foreign Racing) - See Raceform Interactive

AYR (L-H)
Monday, December 13
2917 Meeting Abandoned - Frozen track

2426 PLUMPTON (L-H)
Monday, December 13
OFFICIAL GOING: Good to soft (hdl 6.6, chs 7.2)
Wind: virtually nil Weather: murky, cold

2924 PANBET.COM JUVENILE HURDLE (9 hdls) 2m
12:35 (12:35) (Class 4) 3-Y-O **£2,397** (£698; £349)

Form	Pos	Dist	Horse	Jockey	RPR
	1		**Comedy Act**52 3-10-12 0 (Philip Hobbs) *trckd ldrs: wnt 2nd 4th: nt fluent 6th: clsd on ldr and mstke 6th: rdn to ld 2 out: styd on wl to draw clr flat* **2/5**1	RichardJohnson	111+
	2	5	**Mr Muddle**203 3-10-12 0 (Sheena West) *racd keenly: chsd ldrs tl led 2nd: hit 4th: clr whn mstke 6th: rdn and hdd 2 out: kpt on same pce flat* **66/1**	JamieGoldstein	104
02	3	1	**Omaruru (IRE)**40 2151 3-10-12 0 (Renee Robeson) *hld up wl in tch: hdwy after 5th: chsd ldng pair and rdn after 3 out: mstke next: styd on same pce between last 2* **7/1**2	MarkBradburne	102
34	4	1/2	**Ultravox (USA)**25 2466 3-10-12 110 (Jeremy Scott) *chsd ldrs: rdn after 3 out: styd on same pce fr 2 out* **16/1**	NickScholfield	103
6	5	19	**Bun Oir (USA)**37 2211 3-10-12 0 (Charlie Longsdon) *hld up wl in tch in rr: hdwy after 5th: chsd ldrs and rdn after 3 out: wknd qckly 2 out* **14/1**3	AndrewTinkler	87
5	6	2	**Balerina (FR)**37 2211 3-10-5 0 (Alan King) *in tch: hdwy to chse ldrs and mstke 5th: rdn and wknd after 6th: wl hld whn mstke 3 out* **14/1**3	RobertThornton	77
	7	nk	**Wulfrida (IRE)**74 3-10-5 0 (Alison Thorpe) *in tch towards rr: mstke 1st: blnd 3rd: j. awkwardly next: wknd 6th: wl btn fr next* **16/1**	DarylJacob	79
4	8	8	**Jewellery (IRE)**21 2570 3-9-12 0 (Alison Thorpe) *in tch in last trio tl struggling after 5th: wl btn after next* **100/1**	OliverDayman(7)	69
0	9	19	**Steely Bird**40 2151 3-10-5 0 (Richard Hawker) *racd keenly: led tl mstke and hdd 2nd: styd prom: j.lft 3rd: wkng and bhd whn mstke 6th: t.o fr 3 out* **100/1**	(p) MattGriffiths(7)	58
5	10	9	**Viviani (IRE)**23 2528 3-10-12 0 (Amanda Perrett) *w ldrs tl losing pl and mstke 5th: t.o fr 3 out* **14/1**3	(t) LeightonAspell	50
	11	23	**Wavertree Bounty**33 3-10-5 0 (John Ryan) *in tch tl wknd rapidly bef 3 out: t.o whn mstke 2 out* **66/1**	ColinBolger	23
00	P		**Green Art (IRE)**2 2882 3-10-7 0 (Tracey Barfoot-Saunt) *t.k.h: in tch tl dropped to in rr qckly 5th: sn t.o tl p.u 3 out: burst blood vessel* **100/1**	MrGBarfoot-Saunt(5)	—

3m 51.0s (-9.80) **Going Correction** -0.525s/f (Firm) **12** Ran SP% **121.6**
Speed ratings (Par 104): **103,100,100,99,90 89,89,85,75,71 59,—**
toteswingers:1&2 £23.30, 2&3 £59.30, 1&3 £2.60 CSF £53.96 TOTE £1.50: £1.10, £15.50, £1.60; EX 113.50.
Owner R A Green **Bred** Floors Farming & The Duke Of Devonshire **Trained** Withycombe, Somerset
FOCUS
A foggy day and the ground was officially advertised as good to soft. This opening juvenile event lacked any real strength in depth, but it was run at a fair gallop and the form should work out, with the first four coming clear. The winner looks a fair prospect.
NOTEBOOK
Comedy Act, formerly with Sir Mark Prescott, signed off on the Flat with a career-best second over 1m6f at Doncaster in October and is officially rated 87 in that sphere. Purchased for 125,000gns by his new connections, he was all the rage to make a winning debut over hurdles and duly obliged. He was only workmanlike and momentarily looked in trouble after a sticky jump three out, but to his credit he did all of his best work up the home straight. Some will crab his Triumph Hurdle credentials after this, but there is every chance this track wasn't really to his liking and he should be given a chance to see what he can do on more of a galloping circuit, especially when considering he stayed very well on the level. (op 4-9 after 4-7 in places tchd 1-2 in places)
Mr Muddle raced enthusiastically out in front and, despite not always being fluent, made a bold bid. He was a sitting duck coming to the last, but this rates a very pleasing debut effort and vastly more encouraging than his sole outing on the Flat back in May.
Omaruru(IRE) got going late on and ran close to the level of his second at Warwick 40 days earlier, so helps to set the standard. (op 11-2)
Ultravox(USA) rallied around the final turn and he too probably ran close to his previous level. Whether he is up to his current mark remains to be seen, but he is another benchmark for this form. (tchd 20-1)
Bun Oir(USA) was ridden more patiently, but was well held and has now gone backwards in two outings since joining the stable from Ireland. (tchd 12-1)
Wavertree Bounty Official explanation: vet said filly finished distressed

2925 PANBET.COM PLUMPTON RACES FREE BET TODAY "NATIONAL HUNT" NOVICES' HURDLE (12 hdls) 2m 5f
1:05 (1:05) (Class 4) 4-Y-O+ **£2,740** (£798; £399)

Form	Pos	Dist	Horse	Jockey	RPR
361	1		**Jetnova (IRE)**28 2428 5-11-5 113 (Alan King) *in tch in midfield: hdwy to chse ldrs bef 3 out: rdn wl bef next: mstke 2 out: ev ch u.p last: sn led: styd on wl* **16/1**	RobertThornton	126+
1-1	2	2 1/4	**Skint**37 2216 4-11-5 0 (Nicky Henderson) *trckd ldrs: swtchd rt bef 3 out: clr in ldng quartet and gng best after 3 out: led sn after next: rdn and rn green bef last: hdd sn after last: fnd little and nt gng pce of wnr fnl 150yds* **9/4**2	BarryGeraghty	124+
1	3	2	**On Trend (IRE)**34 2291 4-11-5 0 (Nick Gifford) *led: mstke 3rd and 5th: hrd pressed and hit 2 out: sn hdd: styd on same pce fr last* **10/1**	LiamTreadwell	123+
3	4	2 1/4	**Bunglasha Lady (IRE)**39 2168 5-10-5 0 (Warren Greatrex) *in tch: rdn and outpcd after 9th: n.m.r 3 out: rallied bef next: styd on steadily fr 2 out: nt gng pce to threaten ldrs* **8/1**3	WayneHutchinson	105+
3-33	5	7	**Aviador (GER)**28 2426 4-10-12 0 (Lucy Wadham) *in tch: hdwy to chse ldr and mstke 8th: ev ch and rdn 3 out: wknd next* **50/1**	LeightonAspell	107+
/0-4	6	5	**Half Cocked**42 2123 8-10-12 0 (Richard Rowe) *prom tl rdn and wknd sn after 3 out: wl hld fr next* **100/1**	AndrewThornton	101
22-1	7	3	**Amirico (IRE)**29 2396 5-11-5 0 (Venetia Williams) *t.k.h: hld up wl in tch: hdwy to trck ldrs bef 3 out: wknd qckly wl bef 2 out* **14/1**	AidanColeman	107
040/	8	8	**Rateable Value**247 6-10-12 0 (Colin Tizzard) *a towards rr: in tch tl wknd after 9th: wl btn after next* **100/1**	JoeTizzard	91
6-4	9	nk	**Newton Tonic**22 2560 5-10-12 0 (Alex Hales) *j.lft and nt a fluent: hld up in tch towards rr: hdwy 9th: rdn and wknd 3 out* **100/1**	TomO'Brien	91
01-	10	6	**Kind Of Easy (IRE)**252 5050 4-10-12 0 (Emma Lavelle) *j. novicey: a in rr: lost tch after 9th* **9/1**	SamThomas	88

1-12 **11** *16* **Brackloon High (IRE)**[20] 2594 5-11-5 131 .... RichardJohnson 78
(Noel Chance) *chsd ldr tl mstke 8th: rdn and losing pl rapidly whn mstke 3 out: t.o bef next* **15/8**[1]

40-2 **12** *81* **The Hon Tara**[42] 2130 6-10-5 0 ....(t) FelixDeGiles —
(Charlie Longsdon) *in tch tl dropped in rr 7th: blnd bdly next: sn t.o* **66/1**

5m 8.40s (-13.90) **Going Correction** -0.525s/f (Firm) **12** Ran SP% **114.7**
Speed ratings (Par 105): **105,104,103,102,99 97,96,93,93,91 85,54**
toteswingers:1&2 £8.30, 2&3 £5.20, 1&3 £14.70 CSF £52.09 TOTE £12.20: £3.10, £1.30, £2.70; EX 50.30.
Owner David Sewell **Bred** Paddy Kennedy **Trained** Barbury Castle, Wilts

FOCUS
An above-average novice hurdle for the track, which should produce winners. There was an average gallop on and the first three had it to themselves from two out. The first pair are on the upgrade.

NOTEBOOK
Jetnova(IRE) went off a very generous price considering he was off the mark over C&D on his previous outing, and he followed up with another gutsy performance. Having travelled nicely in midfield, he made a positive move on the final circuit, and his stamina really came into play when it mattered after the last. His official mark will now shoot up, but he is obviously improving nicely and promises to do better still when returned to 3m.
Skint ◆ also travelled sweetly, but still showed signs of inexperience when asked for an effort nearing the home straight. He looked the one to be on jumping the penultimate flight, but after coming to the stands' side thereafter he got outstayed by the winner. A slight drop back in trip should see him defy his penalty as this added experience ought to do him good, and he remains a useful prospect. (op 7-4 tchd 13-8)
On Trend(IRE) also came into this unbeaten, having won a point in Ireland and on his hurdling debut for connections at Lingfield last month. He again set off from the front over this extra distance, but wasn't allowed such an easy lead and could've jumped better. He still turned in a brave effort and had every chance, but was another that got outstayed up the rising finish. He gives the form a sound look. (op 12-1)
Bunglasha Lady(IRE) ◆ was up in trip after her third at Towcester, but appeared to find this contrasting track against her as she came under pressure a fair way out. She rallied strongly nearing the last, albeit too late in the day, and should be winning when back on a more demanding circuit over this sort of trip. (tchd 15-2)
Aviador(GER) made his move on the final lap and had his chance, but his stamina for the longer trip eventually ebbed away. He is another that ought to be off the mark when reverting to a sharper test and is now eligible for a mark. (op 66-1)
Amirico(IRE), a winner on his hurdling debut at Fontwell last month, dropped out rather tamely from three out and is obviously vulnerable under a penalty in this division.
Kind Of Easy(IRE) looked promising when beating a subsequent winner in a bumper at the second attempt on his final outing last term. The market suggested this seasonal return and first taste of hurdling would be needed, and he proved far too novicey to do himself justice. It wouldn't be surprising to see this half-brother to the classy Glencove Marina step up markedly next time out, providing he learns for the experience.
Brackloon High(IRE) the form pick, was up in trip and proved popular on his return to this venue. He was beat shortly after coming under pressure after four out, however, and ultimately failed to run his race. He has now got noticeably warm beforehand the last twice and, with Richard Johnson later reporting he stopped quickly, now has something to prove. Official explanation: jockey said gelding stopped quickly (op 5-2)

2926 PANBET.COM SUPPORTS VOTE MCCOY NOVICES' CHASE (12 fncs) 2m 1f
1:35 (1:36) (Class 3) 4-Y-0+

£6,262 (£1,850; £925; £463; £231; £116)

Form RPR

4-1R **1** **Medermit (FR)**[33] 2313 6-11-5 0 .... RobertThornton 148+
(Alan King) *hld up in tch: hdwy to chse ldr after 7th: mstke 9th: chal next: led 2 out: pushed clr bef last: in command flat: comf* **6/4**[1]

2-01 **2** *3 ¼* **Tullamore Dew (IRE)**[29] 2392 8-11-5 0 .... LiamTreadwell 144+
(Nick Gifford) *t.k.h: chsd ldr tl after 2nd: 3rd and pushed along whn mstke 3 out: styd on same pce between last 2: wnt 2nd fnl 50yds* **9/2**[3]

21- **3** *1* **Rackham Lerouge (FR)**[304] 4010 5-10-13 0 .... BarryGeraghty 135+
(Nicky Henderson) *racd keenly: j.w: led after 2nd: hdd and rdn 2 out: nt gng pce of wnr bef last: no ex flat and lost 2nd fnl 50yds* **7/2**[2]

631 **4** *36* **Potemkin (USA)**[36] 2233 5-11-5 125 ....(t) JamieMoore 109
(David Evans) *in tch in last pair: rdn after 7th: stl in tch tl wknd bef 3 out: lft poor 4th 2 out* **33/1**

4-0U **5** *¾* **Outside The Box**[18] 2626 6-10-13 0 .... TomSiddall 104
(Noel Chance) *led tl after 2nd: chsd ldr: mstke and lost pl 7th: wknd 9th: mstke 3 out: wl bhd whn j.rt and pckd last* **100/1**

200- **6** *9* **Sarando**[39] 4990 5-10-13 0 ....(t) DenisO'Regan 95
(Paul Webber) *chsd ldrs tl dropped in rr 3rd: nvr looked happy after: cajoled along after 6th: lost tch 8th: t.o bef 2 out* **16/1**

23/F **F** **American Trilogy (IRE)**[37] 2219 6-10-13 0 ....(b) NoelFehily 120+
(Paul Nicholls) *hld up in tch: hdwy 7th: mstke next: 4th and no imp u.p after 3 out: wl hld whn fell next* **7/2**[2]

4m 12.0s (-13.90) **Going Correction** -0.525s/f (Firm) **7** Ran SP% **112.4**
Speed ratings (Par 107): **111,109,109,92,91 87,—**
toteswingers:1&2 £2.60, 2&3 £2.20, 1&3 £2.70 CSF £8.71 TOTE £3.00: £2.00, £2.90; EX 9.50.
Owner The Dunkley & Reilly Partnership **Bred** Philippe Gasdoue **Trained** Barbury Castle, Wilts

FOCUS
This novice chase was won by Voy Por Ustedes in 2005 en-route to him winning the Arkle Trophy, and it was a very interesting affair this season. It was run at a sound gallop and the principals dominated from four out. Medermit was still a stone+ off his hurdles mark and there is a case for rating the form a few pounds higher.

NOTEBOOK
Medermit(FR) arrived with plenty to prove after refusing on his previous outing at Huntingdon when sent off from the front. He was unsurprisingly ridden with more restraint this time and got back to winning ways, as he was entitled to do considering he towered above his rivals on hurdle ratings. However, he again failed to really convince he is in love with chasing, tending to get in tight at his fences before making a bad mistake three out, and was workmanlike in winning. He showed a good attitude to get on top in the home straight and this should end any doubts about his temperament, but on the evidence so far he will struggle to reach such heights over fences as he did hurdles. Alan King declared he was very happy with his 6-y-o's effort and didn't rule out a step up in trip, which may well suit looking at the way he rallied here. The Arkle Trophy still hasn't been ruled out, but the new 2m4f Jewson Chase now looks a more likely target. (op 15-8 tchd 2-1 in a place)
Tullamore Dew(IRE) was a bloodless winner at odds of 1/5 on his chasing debut at Fontwell last month. This was obviously a lot tougher and he was the first of the principals to feel the pinch before hitting three out. He rallied after the last to grab the tiring third and left the clear impression he wants a stiffer test in this sphere. (tchd 4-1 and 5-1)
Rackham Lerouge(FR) ◆ was last seen opening his account over hurdles at Bangor in February and, despite his prolific profile, had plenty to find on form with the principals on this seasonal/chasing debut. He came in for good support, however, and it looked rounding the home turn as though he had the winner in some trouble. His lack of match practice told from the second-last, though, and he even lost second just before the line. It was a career-best from the likeable 5-y-o, and he ought to prove very hard to beat on his next assignment. (op 3-1)
Potemkin(USA) gained a confidence-boosting first success on his previous outing, but was outclassed in this field.
American Trilogy(IRE), the 2009 County Hurdle winner, who was saddled in the stable due to getting worked up, had fallen on his return from injury in the Elite Hurdle last month. He looked a player coming to four out, but was under the pump soon after and was well held prior to crashing out at the penultimate fence. His confidence will take some restoring after this experience. (op 4-1)

2927 PANBET.COM LOWER MARGINS BIGGER RETURNS H'CAP HURDLE (9 hdls) 2m
2:05 (2:07) (Class 4) (0-105,104) 3-Y-0+ **£2,397** (£698; £349)

Form RPR

1663 **1** **Swiss Art (IRE)**[21] 2586 4-11-8 100 .... DarylJacob 112+
(Nick Mitchell) *hld up in tch: hdwy to trck ldrs bef 3 out: clr w 2nd bef 2 out: led sn after 2 out: sn nudged along and readily drew clr: easily* **17/2**

3/34 **2** *4* **The Bishops Baby (IRE)**[34] 2289 7-11-0 99 .... MrTJCannon(7) 103
(Richard Rowe) *chsd ldrs: wnt 2nd 5th tl led bef 3 out: clr w wnr and rdn bef 2 out: hdd sn after 2 out: sn outpcd and no ch w wnr flat: kpt on* **7/1**

P-02 **3** *3 ½* **Olympian Boy (IRE)**[33] 2312 6-11-10 102 .... TomScudamore 102
(Anabel L M King) *led tl after 3 out: rdn and outpcd by ldng pair after 3 out: plugged on same pce u.p between last 2* **9/2**[2]

0/0- **4** *6* **Azione**[357] 3006 7-10-12 90 .... NickScholfield 85
(Rodney Farrant) *chsd ldr tl 5th: rdn and outpcd 3 out: one pce and wl btn bef next* **33/1**

6-0P **5** *4* **Keep Guessing**[35] 2280 7-11-5 97 .... WayneHutchinson 89
(Warren Greatrex) *reluctant to line up: hld up in tch: mstke 1st: reminders after 4th: outpcd bef 3 out: rallied u.p after 3 out: 5th and wl btn whn j.lft and mstke last* **20/1**

-100 **6** *1 ½* **Mauritino (GER)**[24] 2504 6-11-4 96 .... APMcCoy 86
(Jonjo O'Neill) *in tch in midfield: outpcd and lost pl bef 3 out: rdn and no prog wl bef 2 out* **10/3**[1]

5-23 **7** *2* **Himrayn**[188] 678 7-11-9 101 .... GerardTumelty 89
(Anabel L M King) *trckd ldrs tl rdn and wknd qckly after 3 out: wl btn whn hmpd and swtchd rt sn after last* **14/1**

005 **8** *13* **The Snatcher (IRE)**[28] 2419 7-11-0 92 .... WarrenMarston 69
(Richard Phillips) *nvr gng wl in rr: rdn along after 1st: lost tch wl bef 3 out* **22/1**

4502 **9** *1* **Bosamcliff (IRE)**[25] 2481 5-11-8 103 .... LeeStephens(3) 79
(David Evans) *in tch in midfield: reminders after 3rd: hit 5th and dropped in rr: lost tch after next* **6/1**[3]

4600 **10** *2 ¾* **Sommersturm (GER)**[33] 2312 6-10-12 90 .... DenisO'Regan 63
(Barney Curley) *hld up in tch in rr: pushed along after 4th: rdn and struggling after next: wl bhd bef 3 out* **10/1**

2-3P **11** *11* **Mega Watt (IRE)**[197] 541 5-11-12 104 .... AidanColeman 67
(Venetia Williams) *hld up in tch: hdwy to chse ldrs after 5th: wknd rapidly sn after 3 out: virtually p.u after 2 out* **6/1**[3]

3m 54.3s (-6.50) **Going Correction** -0.525s/f (Firm)
WFA 4 from 5yo+ 5lb **11** Ran SP% **120.7**
Speed ratings (Par 105): **95,93,91,88,86 85,84,78,77,76 70**
toteswingers:1&2 £9.40, 2&3 £7.50, 1&3 £7.10 CSF £67.09 CT £308.35 TOTE £11.10: £2.70, £2.40, £2.20; EX 91.20.
Owner Mrs Katrina Hitchins **Bred** John Yarr **Trained** Piddletrenthide, Dorset

FOCUS
A moderate handicap, run at a fair gallop. The winner stepped up and may do a bit better based on his best Flat form.

NOTEBOOK
Swiss Art(IRE) bounced back to winning ways on this debut for his new stable and did the job with a lot more in hand than the bare margin suggests. He was taken back through the early parts and made smooth headway as the race became to get really serious on the back straight. He was always going to pick up the second when asked to win the race, and looked a rejuvenated character with the headgear left off. His next outing will reveal more, but the recent change of scenery looks to have been of real benefit. (tchd 8-1 and 9-1)
The Bishops Baby(IRE), easy to back, got a positive ride and was the only one to give the winner a serious race when it mattered. She has evidently begun life in handicaps on a fair mark and may enjoy reverting to a stiffer test. (op 13-2 tchd 8-1)
Olympian Boy(IRE) set out to make all, but wasn't always that fluent and proved one-paced when headed. He rates the most sensible guide for the form. (tchd 5-1)
Azione, who has clearly had her problems, left the clear impression she would come on markedly for this return from a 357-day layoff. (op 25-1)
Keep Guessing was pulled up on his handicap debut at Southwell last month and proved somewhat reluctant to jump off here. He plugged on late and should be better off back over a stiffer test, but isn't one to rely on. (op 16-1)
Mauritino(GER), subject of a notable gamble, hadn't been at his best in two runs back after winning well off a 6lb lower mark in June. He had Tony McCoy aboard him for the first time, but any supporters knew their fate as he downed tools on the back straight. He plugged on again late and perhaps he needs a genuinely quick surface to shine. His trainer's representative later told the stewards that the gelding had made a noise. Official explanation: trainer's rep said gelding made a noise (op 13-2 tchd 3-1)
Bosamcliff(IRE) came under pressure a long way out and was later reported to have lost her right off-fore shoe. Official explanation: vet said mare lost right off-fore shoe (op 11-2)

2928 40% BETTER OFF ON BETFAIR SP H'CAP CHASE (18 fncs) 3m 2f
2:35 (2:35) (Class 4) (0-115,111) 4-Y-0+ **£3,252** (£955; £477; £238)

Form RPR

-132 **1** **Rey Nacarado (IRE)**[19] 2611 5-11-6 105 .... FelixDeGiles 120+
(Charlie Longsdon) *a travelling wl: hld up in tch: chsd ldr after 10th tl after 14th: wnt 2nd again next: led 2 out: wanting to hang lft: rdn clr bef last: r.o wl: comf* **4/1**[1]

5-21 **2** *4* **Rebel Melody (IRE)**[25] 2483 9-11-9 111 ....(bt) PeterToole(3) 119
(Charlie Mann) *mde most tl hdd and hit 2 out: styd on same pce after* **5/1**[2]

10-0 **3** *2 ¾* **Deep Pockets (IRE)**[40] 2147 11-11-7 111 .... IanPopham(5) 119+
(Caroline Keevil) *in tch: rdn whn blnd and lost pl 13th: styd on u.p after 3 out: wnt 3rd flat: no threat to ldng pair* **14/1**

P-14 **4** *2* **Digger Gets Lucky (IRE)**[20] 2595 8-11-5 104 .... LiamTreadwell 109
(Nick Gifford) *chsd ldrs: mstke 8th: wnt 3rd after 10th: wknd u.p 2 out: lost 3rd flat* **20/1**

-052 **5** *2* **Arnold Layne (IRE)**[28] 2420 11-11-3 102 .... AndrewThornton 104
(Caroline Bailey) *in tch: effrt to chse ldrs 12th: rdn to go 2nd after 14th tl next: outpcd u.p after 3 out: plugged on same pce after* **6/1**[3]

6-61 **6** *10* **Pacco (FR)**[22] 2557 7-11-11 110 ....(b) LeightonAspell 109+
(Oliver Sherwood) *hld up in last pair: hmpd 1st: hdwy 11th: in tch whn mstke 15th: rdn and no hdwy whn j.rt next: wl btn bef next* **8/1**

51-3 **7** *6* **Quartz Du Montceau (FR)**[46] 2050 6-10-7 95 ....(p) MarcGoldstein(3) 90
(Anna Newton-Smith) *in tch in midfield: dropped in rr and u.p after 12th: toiling bdly after next: plugged on: no ch fr 15th* **12/1**

322- **8** *8* **Tuskar Rock (FR)**253 5014 7-11-10 **109**.......................... AidanColeman 89
(Venetia Williams) *hld up in tch: hdwy 8th: chsd ldrs 12th: struggling and rdn bef 3 out: wknd u.p wl bef 2 out* **14/1**

-132 **9** *3 ¾* **High Oscar**28 2429 9-10-4 **96**.......................... MrTJCannon(7) 73
(Richard Rowe) *hld up in tch: hdwy to chse ldrs 12th: rdn and struggling whn mstke 15th: sn wknd* **7/1**

5034 **10** *39* **Skipper's Lad (IRE)**113 1348 8-11-6 **105**..........................(tp) JoeTizzard 47
(Colin Tizzard) *a in rr: hmpd 1st: j. slowly and rdn w no rspnse 10th: lost tch 13th: t.o* **25/1**

0-04 **11** *6* **Verasi**24 2497 9-11-0 **99**..........................(b) JamieMoore 35
(Gary Moore) *w ldr tl blnd 8th: lost 2nd and rdn after 10th: dropped in rr 13th: wl bhd after next: t.o* **14/1**

3403 **F** **Miller's Dawn**36 2240 6-10-12 **97**.......................... HaddenFrost —
(Henrietta Knight) *fell 1st* **8/1**

6m 43.2s (-7.50) **Going Correction** -0.525s/f (Firm) **12** Ran SP% **122.0**
Speed ratings (Par 105): **90,88,87,87,86 83,81,79,78,66 64,—**
toteswingers:1&2 £4.20, 2&3 £13.60, 1&3 £25.20 CSF £25.90 CT £262.85 TOTE £4.20: £1.30, £2.20, £6.80; EX 32.20.
Owner Runthatbymeagainagain **Bred** Sweet Wall **Trained** Over Norton, Oxon

FOCUS
A wide-open handicap that provided a proper test of stamina. The form looks sound with a big step up from the winner and the next two pretty much to their marks.

NOTEBOOK
Rey Nacarado(IRE) ◆ resumed winning ways with a dogged display on this second outing over fences. Second on his chasing debut 19 days earlier, this 5-y-o was stepping back up to the trip over which he registered his only previous success over hurdles three runs back, and it made all the difference. He is open to a fair bit more improvement in this sphere and can defy a higher mark. (op 11-2 tchd 6-1)
Rebel Melody(IRE) is a dour stayer and turned in a brave effort from the front, only getting picked off by the winner at the last. His 5lb rise for winning at Wincanton probably just found him out, but he remains in decent heart and rates a solid benchmark. (op 9-2 tchd 11-2)
Deep Pockets(IRE) is a dual C&D winner and this represents a definite step back in the right direction from the veteran. He could come on again for the outing. (op 11-1)
Digger Gets Lucky(IRE) was never far away towards the outside and had his chance on this further step up in trip.
Arnold Layne(IRE) failed to up his game when it mattered and has become a very tricky horse to win with. (op 7-1)
Pacco(FR) got back into the winner's enclosure when equipped with first-time blinkers at Towcester 22 days earlier. Patiently ridden, his jumping let him down after his jockey asked him to improve, and this was in keeping with his inconsistent profile. (op 7-1)

2929 PANBET.COM H'CAP HURDLE (14 hdls) 3m 1f 110y
3:10 (3:10) (Class 5) (0-95,95) 4-Y-0+ **£1,712** (£499; £249)

Form RPR

333- **1** **Gentleman Jimmy**231 17 10-11-9 **92**.......................... TomScudamore 99+
(Hughie Morrison) *chsd ldrs tl led bef 3 out: hld on wl u.p flat* **10/1**

2-52 **2** *nk* **Massini Moon (IRE)**18 2637 6-11-11 **94**..........................(b) JamieMoore 102+
(Gary Moore) *hld up in tch towards rr: stmbld bdly 6th: hdwy after next: chsd ldrs and mstke 3 out: rdn and ev ch last: nt qckn u.p and hld fnl 150yds* **7/2**1

054- **3** *4 ½* **The Red Laird**252 5055 7-11-9 **95**.......................... AlexMerriam(3) 98
(Neil King) *in tch: hdwy to chse ldrs 5th: rdn 3 out: styd on same pce fr 2 out: 3rd and btn whn mstke last* **20/1**

66-0 **4** *3 ¾* **Royaume Bleu (FR)**26 2452 5-11-2 **85**.......................... PaulMoloney 84
(Alex Hales) *plld hrd: hld up in tch in rr: hdwy 9th: chsd ldrs 3 out: rdn jst bef next: wknd between last 2* **4/1**2

-032 **5** *7* **Earl Of Thomond (IRE)**33 2314 5-11-4 **87**.......................... AndrewThornton 82
(Caroline Bailey) *led tl after 4th: styd prom: pressed ldrs bef 3 out: wknd u.p 2 out* **7/1**

3356 **6** *16* **Manadam (FR)**23 2532 7-11-6 **94**.......................... GemmaGracey-Davison(5) 72
(Anthony Middleton) *prom: rdn along fr 5th: wknd bef 11th: wl btn 3 out* **14/1**

/5F- **7** *12* **Unoitmakessense (IRE)**226 8-11-0 **90**.......................... MrWTelfer(7) 61
(Mrs Pauline Harkin) *hld up in tch: mstke 6th: outpcd after 11th: wknd sn after 3 out* **20/1**

1U-P **8** *28* **Prince Louis (FR)**29 2394 7-11-9 **95**..........................(t) PeterToole(3) 37
(Charlie Mann) *t.k.h: chsd ldrs tl led after 4th: hdd bef 3 out: sn wknd: t.o between last 2* **16/1**

0500 **9** *46* **Englishtown (FR)**23 2530 10-11-12 **95**..........................(p) APMcCoy —
(Jonjo O'Neill) *in tch in last trio: coaxed along and nt travelling fr 8th: lost tch 11th: wl t.o after next* **15/2**

033R **R** **Ramvaswani (IRE)**22 2558 7-11-0 **90**.......................... MrMMarris(7) —
(Neil King) *ref to r: tk no part* **50/1**

2-02 **P** **Tiger Line**19 2609 6-11-6 **89**.......................... WarrenMarston —
(Richard Phillips) *chsd ldrs tl dropped in rr u.p 9th: lost tch after next: wl t.o whn p.u 2 out* **5/1**3

6m 26.8s (-2.00) **Going Correction** -0.525s/f (Firm) **11** Ran SP% **116.3**
Speed ratings (Par 103): **82,81,80,79,77 72,68,59,45,— —**
toteswingers:1&2 £4.80, 2&3 £13.10, 1&3 £15.20 CSF £44.37 CT £698.22 TOTE £10.40: £3.00, £1.50, £7.90; EX 37.90.
Owner Burridge & Rutland **Bred** J G St Paul Burridge **Trained** East Ilsley, Berks
■ Stewards' Enquiry : Jamie Moore two-day ban: used whip with excessive frequency (Dec 28,30)

FOCUS
A very ordinary handicap and another open-looking race. There was just an average gallop on. The first two were both well in on their old form.

NOTEBOOK
Gentleman Jimmy was a market drifter on this return from a 231-day absence, but put his best foot forward off the home turn and came home a game winner. This was his first success since winning as a novice hurdler in 2006, and therefore his first win in a handicap. He has evidently done well for his time off the track and used to be rated a lot higher, so it will be interesting to see if he can build on this confidence booster. (op 7-1)
Massini Moon(IRE) proved popular after his improved second in first-time blinkers at Taunton 18 days previously, for which he was raised 5lb. He recovered from a bad mistake on the second lap and was delivered with every chance on the stands' side from two out, but ultimately the winner proved too resolute. He clearly has the talent to win a race, but isn't one for maximum faith and will probably go up again after this. (op 10-3 tchd 11-4)
The Red Laird, who won a bumper here in 2009, shaped encouragingly on this first run since April and looks sure to prove sharper next time out. It was just his second start in a handicap, although his ideal trip remains unknown.
Royaume Bleu(FR) hadn't shown a great deal since switching from the pointing field, but is bred to appreciate this sort of longer distance and was well backed. Keen early off the steady gallop, he made up his ground encouragingly on the final circuit, but his effort flattened out under pressure. This may have just stretched his stamina, and it can be considered an improved run. (op 11-2 tchd 6-1)
Earl Of Thomond(IRE) finished second off this mark when in front of the runner-up last time out, but failed to see out the longer trip like that rival. (op 8-1)
Tiger Line, up in trip, initially came under pressure around the seventh and it was clear soon after she was in trouble. Something presumably went amiss. (op 6-1 tchd 7-1)

2930 PANBET.COM NEW ACCUMULATOR BONUS H'CAP CHASE (14 fncs) 2m 4f
3:40 (3:40) (Class 5) (0-90,90) 4-Y-0+ **£2,602** (£764; £382; £190)

Form RPR

554/ **1** **Marias Rock**614 4904 8-11-0 **78**.......................... NickScholfield 87
(Jeremy Scott) *in tch: hdwy to chse ldrs after 8th: led 2 out: kpt on wl flat: drvn out* **8/1**

11-1 **2** *1* **Abbey Dore (IRE)**22 2555 7-11-2 **83**.......................... JimmyDerham(3) 91
(Seamus Mullins) *in tch: hdwy to chse ldrs after 11th: rdn bef 2 out: drvn and chsd wnr fnl 150yds: kpt on: a hld* **5/2**1

1F-4 **3** *3 ¼* **Fleur De Vassy**25 2470 6-11-12 **90**.......................... AidanColeman 95
(Venetia Williams) *j.lft: chsd ldr: mstke 1st: led 3 out: rdn and hdd next: stl pressing wnr last: wknd fnl 150yds* **3/1**2

P-F6 **4** *1* **Bobby Donald (IRE)**34 2292 8-11-4 **82**.......................... WarrenMarston 87
(Richard Phillips) *led: blnd 11th: hdd next: styd on same pce u.p fr 2 out* **20/1**

-044 **5** *15* **Loco Grande (IRE)**21 2575 5-11-10 **88**.......................... RichardJohnson 80
(Tim Vaughan) *mstkes: in tch in rr: hdwy 9th: mstke and rdn 11th: outpcd and wl hld whn hmpd and nt clr run after 3 out* **13/2**3

P-06 **6** *3* **Stop The Show (IRE)**186 695 9-11-5 **83**.......................... TomSiddall 72
(Richard Phillips) *in tch: pushed along and outpcd after 11th: plugged on same pce and no ch w ldrs fr next* **14/1**

-P0P **7** *7* **Brushford (IRE)**19 2608 6-11-5 **83**..........................(t) LeightonAspell 65
(Chris Gordon) *hld up in tch towards rr: mstke 2nd: hdwy 9th: wknd u.p 3 out* **33/1**

0U/3 **8** *4* **Oponce (FR)**34 2292 8-11-8 **86**.......................... WillKennedy 66
(Noel Chance) *chsd ldrs tl wknd qckly sn after 3 out: 6th and wl btn whn mstke and pckd next* **20/1**

0143 **9** *1 ¾* **Curragh Dancer (FR)**29 2390 7-10-10 **81**.......................... NathanSweeney(7) 58
(Paddy Butler) *dropped in rr after mstke 3rd: struggling and lost tch after 9th: wl btn fr next* **10/1**

1353 **10** *1 ¾* **Mujamead**25 2468 6-11-3 **86**..........................(p) LeeEdwards(5) 61
(Sally-Anne Wheelwright) *t.k.h: chsd ldrs: rdn along and lost pl after 9th: rallied to chse ldrs again 11th: wknd qckly sn after next* **16/1**

-04P **11** *28* **Aspolan (GER)**18 2645 7-10-9 **80**.......................... MrJMahot(7) 30
(Rachel Hobbs) *in tch in rr tl struggling u.p and lost tch after 9th: wl bhd fr next* **16/1**

5m 9.50s (2.20) **Going Correction** -0.525s/f (Firm) **11** Ran SP% **118.0**
Speed ratings (Par 103): **74,73,72,71,65 64,61,60,59,58 47**
toteswingers:1&2 £4.00, 2&3 £2.20, 1&3 £5.50 CSF £28.82 CT £75.74 TOTE £10.50: £3.00, £1.10, £1.70; EX 35.80.
Owner G T Lever **Bred** Mrs V M Withers **Trained** Brompton Regis, Somerset

FOCUS
This moderate handicap was run at a routine gallop and there were plenty in with a chance nearing three out, but the first four came clear thereafter. The winner is rated to the best of her hurdles form.

NOTEBOOK
Marias Rock was produced at her best on her return from a 614-day layoff, a fine training effort. She had failed to score in five previous outings, but this former winning pointer was having her first outing over regulation fences and it clearly proved a lot more to her liking. She doesn't have many miles on the clock for her age and is open to improvement in this sphere, but one will have to be wary of the bounce factor ahead of her next assignment.
Abbey Dore(IRE) was seeking a four-timer off a mark 20lb higher than when kicking off his winning sequence over 3m2f here in March. He made smooth headway from four out and was produced with every chance on the outside from two out, but was always being held by the gutsy winner. He rates the benchmark and may not be weighted out of winning again just yet. (op 11-4)
Fleur De Vassy proved free early on due to the lack of real pace on. She did things well through the race, though, and only gave way nearing the last, possibly on account of her refusal to settle. This was more like it on her second outing as a chaser and her trainer can place her to strike before long. (op 11-4)
Bobby Donald(IRE), soon in front, did well to keep on and finish so close after clouting the third-last fence. This was a lot more encouraging again and he is nicely treated at present on his previous best efforts. (op 16-1)
Loco Grande(IRE) clearly needs more practice over fences, but he is a little better than the bare form. (op 10-1)
T/Plt: £27.90 to a £1 stake. Pool of £81,840.64 - 2,135.39 winning tickets. T/Qpdt: £13.10 to a £1 stake. Pool of £6,296.87 - 353.19 winning tickets SP

2931 - 2936a (Foreign Racing) - See Raceform Interactive

CATTERICK (L-H)
Tuesday, December 14

OFFICIAL GOING: Good (good to soft in places; chs 7.6, hdl 8.0)
Wind: Light 1/2 against Weather: overcast, cold

2937 WENSLEY AMATEUR RIDERS' H'CAP HURDLE (10 hdls) 2m 3f
12:15 (12:15) (Class 4) (0-100,99) 3-Y-0+ **£2,186** (£677; £338; £169)

Form RPR

4006 **1** **Sambelucky (IRE)**18 2654 5-9-11 **77**.......................... MrRLindsay(7) 80
(Keith Reveley) *hld up in rr: hdwy 6th: trcking ldrs 3 out: styd on run-in: led nr fin* **15/2**

-015 **2** *nk* **What's Occurrin**23 2558 6-11-9 **99**.......................... MrMWalford(3) 102
(Tim Walford) *led: jnd last: hdd and no ex towards fin* **9/2**1

3020 **3** *3 ¼* **Bocciani (GER)**18 2658 5-10-13 **93**.......................... MissECSayer(7) 92
(Dianne Sayer) *chsd ldrs: one pce run-in* **25/1**

2620 **4** *¾* **Manoubi**27 2448 11-10-5 **85**.......................... MrCGreene(7) 84
(Martin Todhunter) *chsd ldrs: rdn after 3 out: one pce run-in* **12/1**

3-06 **5** *½* **Bob Will (IRE)**32 2351 5-10-9 **85**.......................... MrColmMcCormack(3) 83
(Chris Grant) *mid-div: styd on fr 2 out: kpt on wl run-in: nt rch ldrs* **15/2**

FF15 **6** *1 ¾* **Winged Farasi**19 2644 6-11-3 **97**.......................... MissJFoster(7) 93
(Joanne Foster) *chsd ldrs: one pce appr last* **25/1**

54-4 **7** *¾* **Taste The Wine (IRE)**15 2485 4-11-0 **94**.......................... MrRJWilliams(7) 92
(Bernard Llewellyn) *hld up in rr: gd hdwy to trck ldrs 6th: upsides 2 out: blnd last: wknd fnl 100yds* **11/2**2

-U22 **8** *4 ½* **Rossbrin (IRE)**213 336 5-10-6 **86**.......................... MrDHannig(7) 77
(Anna Brooks) *towards rr: styd on fr 3 out: nt rch ldrs* **7/1**3

1440 **9** *8* **Hoar Frost**69 1732 5-11-4 **98**.......................... MissGTutty(7) 81
(Karen Tutty) *in rr: sme hdwy appr 2 out: nvr on terms* **40/1**

650U **10** *3 ¾* **Samizdat (FR)**21 2603 7-10-5 **85**.......................... MissRobynGray(7) 64
(Dianne Sayer) *chsd ldrs: wknd 3 out* **20/1**

0054 **11** *5* **Toulouse Express (IRE)**21 2601 11-11-3 **97**..........................(p) MrTSpeke(7) 71
(Robert Johnson) *chsd ldrs: lost pl 3 out* **40/1**

-345 **12** *2* **Secret Desert**[26] 2478 4-10-9 **89** MrJRoche(7) 61
(Ferdy Murphy) *a in rr* **22/1**

101P **13** *3* **Mycenean Prince (USA)**[57] 1901 7-11-0 **92** MissPhillipaTutty(5) 61
(Karen Tutty) *in rr: bhd whn blnd 7th: t.o 2 out* **28/1**

-046 **14** *1* **Play The Rock (FR)**[22] 2589 7-9-7 **73** oh1 O-CdtJessicaLodge(7) 41
(Philip Kirby) *chsd ldrs: lost pl 7th* **12/1**

03-0 **15** *13* **Solway Flight**[52] 1962 7-11-0 **94** MrJSherwood(7) 49
(Lisa Harrison) *prom: drvn 5th: sn lost pl: bhd fr 2 out* **40/1**

6645 **P** **Railway Park (IRE)**[28] 2433 6-10-5 **85** MrOGarner(7) —
(John Wainwright) *chsd ldrs: drvn 5th: lost pl 7th: t.o 2 out: p.u appr last* **25/1**

4m 38.2s (-8.60) **Going Correction** -0.475s/f (Good)
WFA 4 from 5yo+ 5lb **16** Ran SP% **116.4**
Speed ratings (Par 105): **99,98,97,97,96 96,95,94,90,89 86,86,84,84,78** —
toteswingers:1&2:£7.60, 1&3:£53.80, 2&3:£39.00 CSF £34.37 CT £794.48 TOTE £10.40: £3.00, £1.40, £6.80, £3.90; EX 39.50.
Owner Maurice Foxton, JBP & DAG PArtnership **Bred** Barouche Stud Ireland Ltd **Trained** Lingdale, Redcar & Cleveland
■ A winner on his first ride under rules for Russell Lindsay.

FOCUS
This modest handicap for amateur riders was run at a fair gallop and few landed a serious blow from off the pace. The form is rated around the second and third.

NOTEBOOK
Sambelucky(IRE) just edged the verdict to hand his jockey a winner on his first ride under rules. Keith Reveley's 5-y-o was produced off the home turn and hit top gear on the run-in. It was his first success at the tenth time of asking, the drop back in trip helped, and he evidently likes this venue as he went close in a bumper here on his previous visit last year. (op 7-1 tchd 8-1)
What's Occurrin set off from the front and appreciated the return to this less demanding track. He gave his all under top weight and has to be considered unfortunate as he was well clear in second. (op 6-1)
Bocciani(GER) travelled well and returned to his best in defeat, but remains a maiden after 28 outings.
Manoubi went well for a long way under a positive ride, but has become hard to win with. (op 16-1)
Bob Will(IRE) again came in for support, but hit a flat spot at a crucial stage and it's not hard to see why he raced over 3m last time. (op 8-1 tchd 7-1)
Winged Farasi looked a player when making up his ground from off the pace, but couldn't go with the leaders from two out. (op 22-1)
Taste The Wine(IRE) was patiently ridden and began his move from four out. He looked a likely winner going to the last, but met it wrong and couldn't recover. (op 9-2)

2938 BUY YOUR 2011 ANNUAL BADGE TODAY MAIDEN CHASE (15 fncs) 2m 3f
12:45 (12:45) (Class 5) 4-Y-0+ **£1,951** (£573; £286; £143)

Form RPR

U-P3 **1** **Columbus Secret (IRE)**[20] 2615 5-11-0 0 JamesReveley 115+
(Keith Reveley) *hld up: hdwy to chse ldrs 7th: led 2 out: hld on wl towards fin* **66/1**

22-5 **2** *¾* **Time Out (IRE)**[27] 2450 7-10-7 110 NathanMoscrop(7) 112
(James Ewart) *chsd ldrs: led 4th to 6th: pckd 9th: styd on fr 3 out: wnt cl 2nd last: no ex fnl 75yds* **9/1**

4-25 **3** *10* **County Colours (IRE)**[59] 1867 5-11-0 0 BrianHughes 105+
(Howard Johnson) *t.k.h: j.rt: w ldrs: led 6th: hdd 2 out: wknd sn after last* **9/2**[3]

440- **4** *1* **Finlay**[348] 3189 7-11-0 0 JasonMaguire 101
(Donald McCain) *led 2nd: hdd 4th: lost pl 7th: bhd 10th: hdwy appr 3 out: hung rt and sn lost pl: j.rt last: kpt on* **14/1**

5 *2* **Lavally Legend (IRE)**[58] 1891 7-10-11 0 (t) PeterToole(3) 99
(John Anthony Staunton, Ire) *hld up in rr: hdwy to trck ldrs 8th: upsides 3 out: 4th and wkng whn hit last* **50/1**

P-45 **6** *12* **Earl Grez (FR)**[202] 468 5-10-7 0 KyleJames(7) 87
(Philip Kirby) *wnt prom 7th: outpcd 10th: wknd 3 out* **66/1**

4 **7** *9* **Mansonien L'As (FR)**[39] 2192 4-10-7 0 GrahamLee 71
(Ferdy Murphy) *chsd ldrs: outpcd 10th: lost pl 3 out* **16/1**

22-2 **8** *16* **Mr Syntax (IRE)**[32] 2350 6-11-0 0 RichieMcGrath 62
(Tim Fitzgerald) *led to 2nd: lost pl 7th: sn bhd: t.o 3 out* **3/1**[2]

0-43 **U** **Si Bien (FR)**[36] 2270 5-10-11 115 HarryHaynes(3) —
(James Ewart) *hld up: sme hdwy whn blnd and uns rdr 11th* **5/2**[1]

25-4 **U** **Four Strong Winds (IRE)**[30] 2400 6-10-11 117 RichieMcLernon(3) —
(Jonjo O'Neill) *towards rr: blnd and uns rdr 2nd* **6/1**

4m 44.1s (-4.70) **Going Correction** -0.475s/f (Good)
WFA 4 from 5yo+ 5lb **10** Ran SP% **113.5**
Speed ratings (Par 103): **90,89,85,85,84 79,75,68,—,—**
toteswingers:1&2:£19.70, 1&3:£21.50, 2&3:£5.40 CSF £559.30 TOTE £54.90: £8.60, £3.70, £1.50; EX 501.90.
Owner Richard Collins **Bred** W E McCluskey **Trained** Lingdale, Redcar & Cleveland

FOCUS
A moderate maiden chase that had an open look about it. There was an average gallop on and it proved a fairly eventful race. Not an easy race to put a figure on, with a massive step up from the winner.

NOTEBOOK
Columbus Secret(IRE) did enough to get off the mark at the fifth attempt. He had shown little coming into this and it's not easy to see where this big improvement came from. It was just his third outing over fences, though, and he is built like an old-fashioned chaser. The drop back from 3m also clearly proved much more up his street and he should be able to progress a little higher in this sphere. Official explanation: trainer said, regarding apparent improvement in form, that the gelding had been better suited by the drop in trip and better ground. (op 40-1)
Time Out(IRE) got a positive ride and did his best work from two out, finishing nicely clear in second. This was his second outing over fences and it was a definite step in the right direction, but a stiffer test over fences may be what he needs. (tchd 10-1)
County Colours(IRE) has largely disappointed since joining current connections and, after jumping out to his right at times on this switch to fences, his finishing effort was again limited due to him running freely. (op 6-1)
Finlay, making his seasonal return, is very much one of his yard's lesser lights but there was always a chance fences may bring out the best in him. He jumped too deliberately to land a blow, but was plugging on late and could build on this if brushing up his fencing. Official explanation: jockey said gelding hung right throughout (tchd 16-1)
Lavally Legend(IRE) crept into things off the home turn and looked sure to place at least. He failed to see it out when asked for his effort, though, and a drop back to 2m looks on the cards. (op 40-1)
Mr Syntax(IRE) refused to settle and jumped indifferently en-route to a well below-par display. Official explanation: trainer had no explanation for the poor form shown (op 7-2)
Si Bien(FR), the runner-up's better-fancied stablemate, had yet to be asked a question prior to falling at the penultimate fence on the back straight. (op 9-4 tchd 3-1)

2939 TURFTV NOVICES' HURDLE (10 hdls) 2m 3f
1:15 (1:15) (Class 4) 4-Y-0+ **£2,276** (£668; £334; £166)

Form RPR

1 **Lethal Glaze (IRE)**[38] 4-10-12 0 DougieCostello 122+
(Brian Ellison) *mid-div: hdwy to trck ldrs 6th: upsides 2 out: styd on to ld last 75yds: all out* **7/1**[3]

21 **2** *hd* **Moon Indigo**[31] 2375 4-11-5 123 BrianHughes 127
(Howard Johnson) *trckd ldrs: wnt 2nd 3rd: led appr 2 out: edgd lft and hdd run-in: no ex nr fin* **8/1**

-52 **3** *20* **Rival D'Estruval (FR)**[44] 2102 5-10-12 0 TimmyMurphy 105+
(Pauline Robson) *chsd ldrs: outpcd 2 out: 5th and wkng whn hmpd and lft modest 3rd last* **2/1**[1]

111F **4** *4* **Neptune Equester**[30] 2401 7-10-12 0 FearghalDavis 97+
(Brian Ellison) *chsd ldrs: drvn and outpcd 3 out: lft modest 5th last* **7/1**[3]

30-1 **5** *nk* **Carpincho (FR)**[35] 2297 6-11-5 0 DenisO'Regan 106+
(Sarah Humphrey) *nt fluent: led: hdd appr 2 out: sn wknd: lft modest 4th last* **7/2**[2]

6 *11* **Tinseltown**[161] 4-10-12 0 PaddyAspell 85
(Brian Rothwell) *hld up in rr: sme hdwy 7th: nvr nr ldrs* **150/1**

5-0 **7** *16* **Night In Milan (IRE)**[38] 2202 4-10-12 0 JamesReveley 69
(Keith Reveley) *rr-div: bhd fr 7th* **28/1**

2 **8** *3¾* **Chocolate Caramel (USA)**[18] 2657 8-10-12 0 AndrewTinkler 65
(Richard Fahey) *mid-div: outpcd 7th: no ch after* **33/1**

06 **9** *9* **A Patchy Dancer (IRE)**[24] 2525 5-10-12 0 HenryOliver 56
(Sue Smith) *a towards rr: bhd fr 7th* **100/1**

-662 **10** *5* **Ceasar's Return**[27] 2446 5-10-12 117 BarryKeniry 51
(George Moore) *rr-div: nvr on terms* **25/1**

0-F **11** *8* **Twice Lucky**[35] 2297 6-10-12 0 TjadeCollier 43
(Sue Smith) *in rr: bhd fr 6th* **100/1**

33-0 **12** *6* **Steel Edge (IRE)**[52] 1962 5-10-12 0 GrahamLee 37
(Ferdy Murphy) *rr-div: hdwy to chse ldrs 6th: lost pl 7th* **100/1**

543 **13** *1* **Mrs Eff**[21] 2598 4-10-5 0 RichieMcGrath 29
(Kate Walton) *sn bhd: t.o whn mstke 7th* **80/1**

56 **B** **Cygnet**[52] 1962 4-10-12 0 AdrianLane 117+
(Donald McCain) *hld up in rr: hdwy 6th: chsng ldrs appr 2 out: handy 4th and styng on whn b.d last* **40/1**

F **Omokoroa (IRE)**[53] 4-10-12 0 JasonMaguire 117+
(Donald McCain) *trckd ldrs: nt fluent 4th: jnd ldrs after 3 out: disp 2nd whn fell last* **8/1**

06 **P** **Beano Boy**[177] 800 5-10-12 0 BrianHarding —
(Brian Storey) *in rr: t.k.h early: bhd and drvn 5th: sn t.o: p.u after 3 out* **200/1**

4m 34.4s (-12.40) **Going Correction** -0.475s/f (Good)
WFA 4 from 5yo+ 5lb **16** Ran SP% **120.8**
Speed ratings (Par 105): **107,106,98,96,96 92,85,83,79,77 74,71,71,—,— —**
toteswingers:1&2:£10.20, 1&3:£4.60, 2&3:£4.50 CSF £59.13 TOTE £6.70: £2.40, £2.90, £1.30; EX 66.60.
Owner D Gilbert, A Marucci, M Lawrence **Bred** B Kennedy **Trained** Norton, N Yorks

FOCUS
This was an interesting enough novice hurdle. It was run at a solid gallop and, once again, it proved another race where the first two fought it out on the run-in. They can both rate a lot higher on hurdles form.

NOTEBOOK
Lethal Glaze(IRE) made a winning debut over hurdles on just his second outing for the stable that won the race last year, and completed the task in game fashion. He was a very useful handicapper at his best on the Flat and stamina was no worry for this new discipline, but he wasn't always easy to predict when previously with Richard Hannon. There was no faulting his attitude here, however, as he knuckled down really well in his battle with the penalised runner-up. His jumping was neat for a debutant and it wouldn't be at all surprising to see him defy a penalty if kept to this sort of company in the short term. (op 9-1)
Moon Indigo was narrowly off the mark at Wetherby a month earlier. He got a positive ride again and took up the running at the top of the home straight. Considering he signed off on the Flat with an official mark just 1lb inferior to the winner, this rates a decent effort under his penalty and he sets the standard. (op 15-2)
Rival D'Estruval(FR) was well backed, but proved one-paced off the home turn and was booked for fifth place prior to Donald McCain's duo coming to grief at the last. (op 5-2)
Neptune Equester was backed on this belated debut over hurdles. He got badly outpaced from the third-last, however, and blatantly needs a stiffer test. This should help restore his confidence. (op 11-2)
Carpincho(FR) had bolted up on his hurdling debut at Sedgefield last month and again set out to make all. He was a sitting duck off the home turn, though, and the run looked needed. (op 5-2, tchd 4-1 in a place)
Cygnet was in the process of running his best race to date when brought down by his stablemate. (op 16-1)
Omokoroa(IRE) was a similar type to the first pair on the level, and he too had become tricky to win with in that sphere. He made up his ground from three out and had every chance, but fell at the last. (op 16-1)

2940 CATTERICKBRIDGE.CO.UK H'CAP CHASE (19 fncs) 3m 1f 110y
1:45 (1:45) (Class 3) (0-120,119) 4-Y-0+ **£5,204** (£1,528; £764; £381)

Form RPR

P-43 **1** **Star Beat**[31] 2374 7-10-11 **104** (p) RichieMcGrath 124+
(Kate Walton) *led 4th: mde rest: drew clr appr 2 out: 10 l ahd last: eased run-in* **9/1**

-656 **2** *7* **Zitenka (IRE)**[31] 2374 8-11-7 **119** (b) JamesHalliday(5) 126+
(Tim Easterby) *chsd ldrs: wnt 2nd 6th: hit 14th: styd on same pce fr 3 out* **12/1**

-362 **3** *5* **Ballabrook (IRE)**[30] 2401 8-10-11 **104** JasonMaguire 104
(Donald McCain) *in rr: bhd whn mstke 14th: styd on wl fr 3 out: 5th last: kpt on wl to take 3rd run-in* **7/1**[3]

P531 **4** *1¾* **Top It All**[23] 2550 7-10-7 **100** TimmyMurphy 99
(Rose Dobbin) *chsd ldrs: blnd 6th: lost pl and reminders after 10th: hdwy and modest 5th after 4 out: one pce fr 2 out* **4/1**[1]

P000 **5** *7* **Keepitsecret (IRE)**[51] 1992 9-10-7 **103** RichieMcLernon(3) 93
(Jonjo O'Neill) *hld up in mid-div: stdy hdwy 11th: handy 3rd 4 out: j.rt and wknd 2 out* **25/1**

-450 **6** *5* **Top Dressing (IRE)**[59] 1871 9-11-9 **116** BrianHughes 101
(Howard Johnson) *mid-div: chsd ldrs 11th: wknd 15th* **33/1**

42-3 **7** *hd* **Work Boy**[26] 2476 9-11-1 **108** TjadeCollier 95
(Sue Smith) *chsd ldrs: reminders after 11th: 5th and outpcd whn blnd 4 out: sn wknd* **12/1**

3223 **8** *7* **More Equity**[23] 2550 8-10-11 **107** RyanMania(3) 85
(Dianne Sayer) *prom: hit 7th: outpcd 12th: no ch after* **14/1**

32/1 **9** *15* **Hernando's Boy**26 2474 9-11-3 **110** JamesReveley 73
(Keith Reveley) *in rr: mstke 8th: bhd fr 15th* **12/1**
P-P3 **10** *22* **Antonius Caesar (FR)**38 2214 7-10-11 **107** PeterToole(3) 48
(Alex Hales) *chsd ldrs: wknd qckly 4 out: sn bhd* **5/12**
4F-P **11** *11* **Carry Duff**27 2449 9-9-9 **95** ow2 PaulGallagher(7) 25
(Ferdy Murphy) *in rr: bhd whn mstke 15th* **40/1**
PP-3 **P** **Coldwells (IRE)**72 1697 10-10-0 **93** oh2 GrahamLee —
(Martin Todhunter) *chsd ldrs: mstke 1st: hit 8th: drvn 11th: lost pl 14th: t.o whn p.u bef 3 out* **16/1**
0/06 **P** **Cockleshell Road (IRE)**35 2299 7-11-7 **114** BrianHarding —
(Martin Todhunter) *in rr: drvn 11th: bhd whn p.u bef 13th: lame* **40/1**
-102 **F** **Baltic Pathfinder (IRE)**35 2298 6-10-11 **109** ShaneByrne(5) —
(Sue Smith) *led to 4th: w ldrs: fell 6th* **7/13**

6m 24.5s (-17.50) **Going Correction** -0.475s/f (Good) **14** Ran SP% **119.0**
Speed ratings (Par 107): **107,104,103,102,100 99,99,96,92,85 82,—,—,—**
toteswingers:1&2:£26.30, 1&3:£11.70, 2&3:£20.40 CSF £106.25 CT £803.59 TOTE £11.50: £3.30, £4.50, £2.10; EX 180.60.
Owner Blyth, Buttery, Tanfield and Wilson **Bred** P H Mathias **Trained** Middleham Moor, N Yorks

FOCUS
A wide-open staying handicap. There appeared to be an uneven gallop on, and few managed to get seriously involved. The easy winner was value for further and this rates a sizeable personal best.

NOTEBOOK
Star Beat proved easy to back, but that didn't stop him from running his rivals ragged under a positive ride. He was a beaten favourite in this contest last term, but has progressed since then and since joined a different trainer. Both his wins as a chaser have now been at this venue, but he did win elsewhere over hurdles and would have to be of serious interest should connections actually manage to find him an opportunity under a penalty. (op 7-1)
Zitenka(IRE) was behind the winner when sixth at Wetherby a month earlier and was beaten a similar distance here despite being 5lb better off. This was a little more encouraging, but he doesn't look one for maximum faith these days.
Ballabrook(IRE) was eating up the ground in the home straight and would've surely been better served by slightly more positive handling. This ground was just quick enough for him, though. (op 11-2)
Top It All was 5lb higher for winning at Kelso last month. He lost out by running in snatches nearing the final circuit, before running on again late, and perhaps the track wasn't for him. (op 5-1 tchd 11-2)
Keepitsecret(IRE) caught the eye with the way he travelled through the race and looked a player with four to jump. He couldn't sustain his effort in the home straight, but this was more like it again on his return from a 51-day break and a drop back in trip looks well worth a go as he is currently well handicapped on his previous best efforts.
Antonius Caesar(FR) dropped out from the fourth-last having gone with the winner up to that point and perhaps he needed the run. (op 6-1)

2941 RACINGUK.COM H'CAP HURDLE (12 hdls) 3m 1f 110y
2:15 (2:18) (Class 4) (0-110,110) 4-Y-0+ **£2,276** (£668; £334; £166)

Form RPR
2P-5 **1** **Sonara (IRE)**54 1929 6-10-0 **84** WilsonRenwick 91+
(Howard Johnson) *chsd ldrs: wnt 2nd 6th: led and blnd 2 out: hrd rdn and styd on run-in: all out* **13/23**
0-55 **2** *1* **Outlaw Tom (IRE)**21 2595 6-11-7 **108** (b1) PeterToole(3) 112
(Alex Hales) *trckd ldrs: wnt 3rd 8th: 3rd whn hit last: kpt on* **10/1**
6221 **3** *3 3/4* **Calypso Bay (IRE)**39 2183 4-11-6 **107** RichieMcLernon(3) 106+
(Jonjo O'Neill) *mid-div: outpcd 9th: kpt on fr 2 out: styd on to take n.d 3rd last 100yds* **11/22**
30-P **4** *1/2* **Allanard (IRE)**36 2271 6-10-0 **84** oh2 GrahamLee 83
(Martin Todhunter) *trckd ldrs: reminders 5th and 7th: sn lost pl: styd on appr 2 out: kpt on run-in* **28/1**
P6-6 **5** *1* **Melange (USA)**31 2373 4-10-12 **103** AlistairFindlay(7) 103+
(George Charlton) *led: hit 3 out: hdd next: 2nd last: edgd lft and wknd run-in* **16/1**
F-01 **6** *1 1/2* **Bardolet (IRE)**44 2103 7-10-9 **93** JamesReveley 92+
(Keith Reveley) *towards rr: lost pl 8th: wnt poor 4th 3 out: one pce whn hmpd and eased last 50yds* **9/21**
0U02 **7** *3/4* **Oniz Tiptoes (IRE)**31 2372 9-10-4 **88** (v) PaddyAspell 84
(John Wainwright) *in rr: hdwy 6th: lost pl after next and sn bhd: kpt on appr 2 out: styd on one pce* **12/1**
0-P0 **8** *8* **Stagecoach Opal**26 2477 9-10-12 **101** ShaneByrne(5) 89
(Sue Smith) *chsd ldrs: drvn and lost pl 8th: bhd fr 3 out* **33/1**
14-0 **9** *88* **Bene Lad (IRE)**38 2208 8-10-3 **87** TimmyMurphy —
(Jim Goldie) *prom: chsd ldrs 8th: wknd next: heavily eased 2 out: virtually p.u between last 2: t.o* **11/1**
-030 **10** *8* **Mardood**21 2603 5-10-5 **89** (p) DenisO'Regan —
(Chris Grant) *in rr: bhd fr 9th: t.o 2 out* **25/1**
01-1 **11** *22* **Wor Rom (IRE)**229 66 6-10-1 **92** ow1 MrNHalley(7) —
(Elliott Cooper) *in rr: t.o fr 8th: virtually p.u 2 out* **12/1**
0/P- **P** **Geeveem (IRE)**212 10-11-2 **107** ow2 MrMSeston(7) —
(Henry Hogarth) *in rr: bhd fr 4th: t.o 7th: p.u bef 8th* **50/1**
2P-2 **P** **Of Course (FR)**54 1929 8-11-6 **109** (p) PaulCallaghan(5) —
(Simon West) *in rr: hdwy to chse ldrs 6th: reminders next: lost pl 8th: t.o whn p.u after 3 out* **7/1**
P2-0 **F** **Double Default (IRE)**23 2549 9-11-7 **110** AlexanderVoy(5) —
(Martin Todhunter) *hld up towards rr: fell 6th* **40/1**
0F03 **P** **Solway Bee**66 1782 10-10-1 **88** HarryHaynes(3) —
(Lisa Harrison) *w ldrs: drvn 2nd: sn lost pl and bhd: t.o 7th: p.u bef next* **14/1**

6m 13.2s (-14.40) **Going Correction** -0.475s/f (Good)
WFA 4 from 5yo+ 7lb **15** Ran SP% **119.4**
Speed ratings (Par 105): **103,102,101,101,101 100,100,97,70,68 61,—,—,—,—**
toteswingers:1&2:£27.80, 1&3:£11.50, 2&3:£30.60 CSF £65.55 CT £386.28 TOTE £7.60: £2.90, £3.70, £1.90; EX 90.80.
Owner J Howard Johnson **Bred** Kevin Gaffney **Trained** Billy Row, Co Durham
■ Stewards' Enquiry : Wilson Renwick two-day ban: used whip with excessive frequency (Dec 28-29)
Alistair Findlay four-day ban: careless riding (Dec 28,30-Jan 1)

FOCUS
A moderate handicap and another race where it paid to race handily. Ordinary form.

NOTEBOOK
Sonara(IRE), who attracted support, was never far from the front and kicked for home nearing the penultimate flight. He wasn't clever at it, but still went clear from that point and, despite the runner-up closing, was always doing enough after the last. He saw out this longer trip really well and it was a first success over hurdles for him, ending a losing run that dated back to his last Flat win in 2007. (op 9-1 tchd 6-1)
Outlaw Tom(IRE), in first-time blinkers, had looked out of form over fences of late but he is a dour stayer and this was a lot better from him back over hurdles. The question is whether the headgear will continue to hold the desired effect. (op 16-1)
Calypso Bay(IRE) was whacked up 18lb for his clear-cut success over further at Fontwell last month. Easy to back, he hit a marked flat spot on the final circuit before staying on again with purpose all too late in the day. It looks as though he genuinely needs extreme distances to shine. (op 4-1)
Allanard(IRE), pulled up on his return last month, went in snatches nearing the final circuit. He was plugging on towards the finish and got the longer trip, but looks to have issues. (op 25-1)
Melange(USA) tired markedly in between the final two flights, but had run a brave race from the front prior to that and posted an improved effort. A slight drop back in trip can see him build on this. (op 20-1)
Bardolet(IRE), 6lb higher, lacked an extra gear when asked for his effort and may well have needed this return from a 44-day break. (tchd 4-1)
Oniz Tiptoes(IRE) plugged on from well off the pace without ever threatening. (op 10-1)

2942 RACING AGAIN ON 28TH DECEMBER H'CAP CHASE (12 fncs) 2m
2:45 (2:47) (Class 4) (0-105,105) 4-Y-0+ **£2,927** (£859; £429; £214)

Form RPR
4502 **1** **Heavenly Chorus**18 2656 8-11-0 **93** JamesReveley 107+
(Keith Reveley) *hld up: hdwy to trck ldrs 5th: styd on wl fr 2 out: led run-in: wnt clr: readily* **7/1**
213P **2** *6* **Emotive**66 1781 7-11-6 **99** CampbellGillies 104
(Barry Murtagh) *hld up: hdwy to trck ldrs 9th: led 2 out: hdd and no ex run-in* **25/1**
4-P2 **3** *2 1/2* **Northern Quest (IRE)**21 2601 9-11-7 **100** RobertWalford 102
(Henry Hogarth) *led 2nd: hdd 2 out: kpt on same pce run-in* **11/1**
2F-0 **4** *3/4* **Iris's Flyer**46 2080 8-10-5 **84** (p) BrianHughes 86
(Brian Rothwell) *chsd ldrs: mstke 3 out: kpt on same pce between last 2* **12/1**
6352 **5** *1 3/4* **Best Horse (FR)**35 2301 8-10-10 **89** GrahamLee 88
(Ferdy Murphy) *chsd ldrs: styd on same pce appr last: wknd towards fin* **8/1**
5/43 **6** *4 1/2* **Mighty Magnus (IRE)**21 2601 7-10-5 **84** FearghalDavis 82
(Martin Todhunter) *in rr: mstke 5th: hdwy 9th: sn chsng ldrs: wknd between last 2* **5/12**
0-30 **7** *3 1/4* **Saddlers Deal (IRE)**44 2107 5-11-11 **104** DenisO'Regan 98
(Chris Grant) *in rr: drvn 9th: kpt on fr 2 out* **11/23**
164- **8** *2* **Karingreason**259 4940 7-11-5 **105** MrColmMcCormack(7) 94
(Keith Reveley) *in rr: bhd fr 8th: kpt on fr 2 out* **12/1**
615P **9** *14* **Troodos Jet**35 2301 9-10-2 **81** (p) BrianHarding 56
(Dianne Sayer) *prom: lost pl 8th: bhd fr 3 out* **40/1**
5136 **10** *7* **Lindseyfield Lodge (IRE)**23 2550 9-11-2 **95** (p) KennyJohnson 63
(Robert Johnson) *w ldrs: lost pl 8th: bhd fr 3 out* **40/1**
30-3 **P** **Super Baby (FR)**38 2207 8-11-5 **105** (p) NathanMoscrop(7) —
(James Ewart) *led to 2nd: w ldrs: eased 3 out: bhd whn p.u bef last: lame* **7/21**
50 **F** **Forever Emo (IRE)**34 2303 7-10-10 **92** RichieMcLernon(3) 92
(Jonjo O'Neill) *in rr: hdwy to chse ldrs 9th: 6th and keeping on one pce whn fell last* **16/1**

3m 54.1s (-6.00) **Going Correction** -0.475s/f (Good) **12** Ran SP% **116.2**
Speed ratings (Par 105): **96,93,91,91,90 88,86,85,78,75 —,—**
toteswingers:1&2:£27.80, 1&3:£11.50, 2&3:£30.60 CSF £153.61 CT £1886.56 TOTE £6.60: £1.40, £8.20, £3.70; EX 140.40.
Owner The Mary Reveley Racing Club **Bred** Lady Jennifer Green And John Eyre **Trained** Lingdale, Redcar & Cleveland

FOCUS
A competitive handicap for the class, run at a fair gallop. There were nine in with a strong chance turning for home. The cosy winner is rated back to her best, with the second to her mark.

NOTEBOOK
Heavenly Chorus, a market drifter, returned to form when second at Musselburgh 18 days earlier and she went one better with a ready effort to give her stable a hat-trick on the card. She attempted to make all last time, but reverted to more patient tactics on this drop in trip and it paid off handsomely as she quickened up to lead at the last. It was her first win as a chaser at the 12th time of asking, and the manner of this success suggests she can add to her tally while in such form. (op 11-2)
Emotive had been pulled up on his last outing 66 days earlier, but has clearly come right back to form and this was much more in keeping with his usually consistent profile. He sets the level. (op 16-1 tchd 33-1)
Northern Quest(IRE) posted a solid effort from the front and he appreciated this return to better ground. He remains in good heart and is another benchmark for the form. (op 8-1)
Iris's Flyer got a positive ride and only tired out of things late in the day. This was a much-improved effort on his second run back with the cheekpieces back on, and a return to slightly further is what he wants. (op 10-1 tchd 9-1)
Best Horse(FR) made his move around the eighth fence and held every chance, but failed to really see it out after the last. (op 7-1)
Saddlers Deal(IRE) was well backed but never seriously figured. (op 8-1)
Super Baby(FR)'s rider was looking down from the home turn and pulled him up before the penultimate fence. He was later found to have finished lame. Official explanation: vet said gelding returned lame right-fore (op 9-2 tchd 100-30)

2943 BOOK RACECOURSE HOSPITALITY ON 01748 810165 INTERMEDIATE OPEN NATIONAL HUNT FLAT RACE 2m
3:15 (3:15) (Class 6) 4-6-Y-O **£1,370** (£399; £199)

Form RPR
1 **Little Hercules (IRE)** 4-11-4 0 BrianHughes 106+
(Howard Johnson) *hld up in rr: hdwy 5f out: styd on wl to ld fnl 150yds* **10/1**
2 **2** *1 1/4* **Fourjacks**23 2553 5-11-4 0 GrahamLee 104+
(Tim Easterby) *sn prom: drvn over 3f out: ev ch ins fnl f: no ex* **10/32**
2 **3** *3 1/4* **Dunowen Point (IRE)**66 1785 4-11-4 0 JasonMaguire 102+
(Donald McCain) *t.k.h in rr: hdwy 7f out: led over 1f out: hung bdly lft and hdd last 150yds* **15/81**
4 *1/2* **Crowning Jewel** 4-11-4 0 JamesReveley 101+
(Keith Reveley) *hld up: hdwy over 3f out: kpt on same pce appr fnl f* **14/1**
42 **5** *1/2* **Bunclody**8 2826 5-10-8 0 SamuelWelton(10) 100
(George Moore) *led after 2f: hdd over 1f out: one pce* **16/1**
43/ **6** *4* **Bogside (IRE)**594 53 6-11-4 0 JanFaltejsek 98+
(George Charlton) *w ldrs: hmpd and stmbld bnd after 7f: wknd over 1f out* **25/1**
3- **7** *shd* **Zaru (FR)**377 2639 4-11-1 0 HarryHaynes(3) 96
(James Ewart) *hld up in rr: hdwy 7f out: chsng ldrs 5f out: wknd over 1f out* **18/1**
8 *10* **Crafti Bookie (IRE)**225 4-10-8 0 BenjaminStephens(10) 86
(Sue Smith) *sn chsng ldrs: outpcd and lost pl 5f out* **40/1**
5 **9** *9* **Aeneid**19 2646 5-11-4 0 PaddyAspell 77
(Brian Rothwell) *sn prom: drvn along 5f out: sn lost pl* **50/1**
-2 **10** *14* **Pasture Bay (IRE)**209 399 4-11-4 0 TimmyMurphy 63
(George Charlton) *sn chsng ldrs: lost pl over 4f out* **6/13**

11 28 **Kyte** 5-10-13 0 .... ShaneByrne(5) 35
(Sue Smith) *in rr: bhd fnl 7f: t.o 2f out* **100/1**

12 63 **Milans Danielle (IRE)** 4-10-6 0 .... JamesHalliday(5) —
(Brian Storey) *led 2f: drvn and lost pl after 6f: sn bhd: t.o 4f out: virtually p.u over 1f out* **100/1**

23 R **High Hoylander**[32] 2355 4-11-4 0 .... HenryOliver —
(Sue Smith) *t.k.h: lost pl after 5f: hung rt and rn out bnd after 7f* **8/1**

3m 40.14s (-6.76) **Going Correction** -0.475s/f (Good) **13** Ran SP% **120.4**
Speed ratings: **97,96,94,94,94 92,92,87,82,75 61,30,—**
toteswingers:1&2:£10.20, 1&3:£8.40, 2&3:£2.00 CSF £42.82 TOTE £13.20: £3.60, £1.20, £1.80; EX 54.10.

Owner Andrea & Graham Wylie **Bred** Frank McKevitt **Trained** Billy Row, Co Durham

FOCUS
This bumper wasn't run at a bad gallop but there were seven nearly upsides 2f out. The principals eventually forged clear, though, and the form looks pretty sound.

NOTEBOOK
Little Hercules(IRE) showed a decent attitude when asked to seal the race and got his career off to a perfect start. He is certainly bred to make his mark when sent jumping, being from the family of Keen Leader, and there should be plenty more to come. (op 16-1)
Fourjacks finished second on his debut at Kelso and, despite again finding one too good on this sounder surface, gives this form a good look. He would probably be better off reverting to a stiffer track and can win one of these. (op 4-1 tchd 3-1)
Dunowen Point(IRE) was sent off at odds of 4-5 when touched off on his debut for connections at Hexham in October and again attracted support. He was again free early on, but emerged going well off the home turn and was in the right place when asked for everything. He hung towards the far rail under pressure, though, and still looked in need of the experience. He too helps to make this form look decent. (op 7-4 tchd 13-8)
Crowning Jewel ◆ is out of a dam who won a bumper and is a half-sister to the former high-class chasers Direct Route and Joe Mac. He got a patient ride and responded when coming under pressure 3f out, but was unable to find any extra from the furlong marker. This was a pleasing debut effort and it wouldn't be surprising to see him winning next time out. (tchd 12-1)
Bunclody improved when second on the Fibresand eight days earlier and ran another fair race from the front in this better company.
Bogside(IRE) showed enough to be of interest next time. (op 22-1)
Zaru(FR) shaped well on his return from a break. (op 12-1)
Pasture Bay(IRE), easy to back, steadily went backwards through the race and ran a long way below his debut form back in May. (tchd 7-1)
T/Plt: £688.70 to a £1 stake. Pool £54,813.87 - 58.10 winning tickets. T/Qpdt: £21.00 to a £1 stake. Pool £4,874.83 - 171.44 winning tickets WG

2439 FOLKESTONE (R H)
Tuesday, December 14

OFFICIAL GOING: Chase course - good to soft (6.6); hurdle course - soft (6.2)
Wind: Virtually nil Weather: bright and dry

2944 LADBROKES.COM NOVICES' HURDLE (8 hdls) 2m 1f 110y
12:35 (12:35) (Class 4) 3-Y-0+ **£3,425** (£998; £499)

Form RPR

1 **Extremely So**[87] 4-10-12 0 .... (t) PaulMoloney 115+
(Philip McBride) *hung lft thrght: chsd ldrs tl led after 3rd: mde rest: j.lft and slow 4th: rdn bef last: in command whn mstke last: kpt on* **50/1**

2 2 2 3/4 **American Ladie**[35] 2289 4-10-12 0 .... RobertThornton 109
(Alan King) *in tch: chsd wnr bef 2 out: clr w wnr and rdn ent st: no imp and hld whn j.big last* **7/4**[1]

6P/1 3 9 **Alarazi (IRE)**[29] 2419 6-11-12 111 .... DominicElsworth 116+
(Lucy Wadham) *plld hrd: hld up in rr: hdwy but stl plenty to do bef 2 out: wnt 3rd and rdn ent st: no prog and wl hld whn blnd last* **15/2**

0-64 4 8 **Graduation Night**[19] 2634 4-11-5 0 .... DarylJacob 99
(Jamie Snowden) *hld up towards rr: hdwy into midfield 3 out: mstke next: no threat to ldrs but plugged on steadily on long run to last: nvr trbld ldrs* **80/1**

5 3/4 **Alcalde**[171] 4-11-5 0 .... WillKennedy 101
(John Berry) *t.k.h: chsd ldrs: mstke 3rd: pressed ldrs bef 2 out: wknd on long run to last: wl btn whn mstke last* **12/1**

3-15 6 6 **Catspan (FR)**[35] 2296 4-11-5 0 .... APMcCoy 93
(Charles Egerton) *chsd ldr tl bef 2 out: wknd on long run to last: wl btn ent st* **6/1**[3]

1 7 3 1/4 **Camden (IRE)**[39] 2186 4-11-5 0 .... LeightonAspell 89
(Oliver Sherwood) *t.k.h: hld up wl in tch: j.lft 1st: hmpd 4th: wknd bef 2 out: eased bef last* **4/1**[2]

3-0 8 8 **Mr Chow (IRE)**[41] 2145 6-11-5 0 .... NoelFehily 81
(Warren Greatrex) *led: dived 2nd: hdd after 3rd: styd chsng ldrs tl wknd sn after 3 out* **22/1**

-300 9 16 **Bach To Back (IRE)**[22] 2577 5-11-5 0 .... PaddyBrennan 65
(Nigel Twiston-Davies) *hld up towards rr: mstke 3rd: struggling 6th: wl btn next: t.o bef last* **66/1**

10 17 **Saute**[60] 4-11-2 0 .... MarcGoldstein(3) 48
(Jim Best) *hld up in midfield: hdwy and in tch whn mstke 5th: sn rdn and struggling: t.o after 2 out* **10/1**

11 33 **Classic Port (FR)**[538] 6-11-5 0 .... ColinBolger 15
(Suzy Smith) *a bhd: lost tch after 5th: wl t.o 2 out* **50/1**

12 6 **Senses (USA)**[437] 4-11-5 0 .... TomScudamore 9
(David Pipe) *racd in midfield: mstke and dropped to rr 5th: lost tch next: wl t.o 2 out* **20/1**

6 P **Grey Cruzene (USA)**[29] 2432 4-11-2 0 .... CharlieStudd(3) —
(Chris Gordon) *racd wd: pckd 1st: bhd and lost tch after 3rd: wl t.o whn p.u 6th* **80/1**

4m 28.5s (-7.10) **Going Correction** -0.30s/f (Good)
WFA 4 from 5yo+ 5lb **13** Ran SP% **116.2**
Speed ratings (Par 105): **93,91,87,84,83 81,79,76,69,61 46,44,—**
toteswingers:1&2:£22.40, 1&3:£50.40, 2&3:£3.50 CSF £134.68 TOTE £63.20: £7.70, £1.40, £2.40; EX 425.40.

Owner N Davies **Bred** Kirtlington Stud And Gilridge Bloodstock **Trained** Newmarket, Suffolk

FOCUS
With no overnight frost, the going remained good to soft on the chase course, and soft on the hurdle course. An interesting novice hurdle full of unexposed sorts with potential, but it was the two fillies in the line-up who were the first two home. The cosy winner is rated in line with her best Flat form.

NOTEBOOK
Extremely So was a surprise winner, though she had proved herself able to handle these conditions when winning over 1m 3 1/2f on soft ground at Yarmouth in September. Ridden prominently with a circuit to go, she led jumping the second-last and kept finding more for pressure in the closing stages. This was a good run in a competitive race and she is likely to come on plenty. She had a tongue tie on for the first time. (op 66-1)
American Ladie went off a solid market leader for her in-form trainer. Having previously run well on the Flat in France on soft ground, she showed she had the stamina for this sort of trip when runner-up on her British debut in November over 2m 1/2f at Lingfield. This was another solid run and she should find a race before long. (op 11-8 tchd 15-8 in a place)
Alarazi(IRE), penalised for a soft-ground win at Leicester, was held up in rear, but made good headway down the back straight. He stayed on strongly in home straight to take third, despite a mistake at the last, suggesting a step up in trip will suit, and he looks to be progressing with experience. (op 11-2)
Graduation Night put in a much-improved performance, but whether he's able build on this performance remains to be seen. (op 100-1)
Alcalde, bought for 26,000gns from Mark Johnston, weakened when the leaders went for home. He probably found conditions too testing and is worth another chance in the spring on better ground. (op 14-1)
Catspan(FR), well supported, needs to improve his jumping as he seems to be a little slow in the air, but the market support suggests connections are confident in his abilities. (op 12-1 tchd 11-2)
Grey Cruzene(USA) Official explanation: jockey said gelding hung badly left throughout

2945 LADBROKESPOKER.COM BEGINNERS' CHASE (18 fncs) 3m 1f
1:05 (1:05) (Class 4) 4-Y-0+ **£3,903** (£1,146; £573; £286)

Form RPR

2230 1 **Triggerman**[38] 2221 8-11-1 132 .... RichardJohnson 137+
(Philip Hobbs) *in tch: chsd 7th: led 14th: mde rest: rdn and hung lft bef last: edging lft but kpt on wl flat: rdn out* **9/2**[3]

10-5 2 1 3/4 **Misstree Dancer**[20] 2606 6-10-5 0 .... DannyCook(3) 129
(Nick Mitchell) *t.k.h: in tch: chsd ldrs 7th: chsd wnr sn after 3 out: pressing wnr and j.lft 2 out: styd on same pce after: edging lft u.p flat* **8/1**

43-3 3 12 **Rear Gunner (IRE)**[28] 2441 8-11-1 113 .... (p) AndrewThornton 129+
(Diana Grissell) *mstkes: w ldrs: chsd ldr 5th: led and hit 7th: hdd 9th: w ldr and j.lft 11th: ev ch after 3 out: wknd next: wl hld whn hit last* **20/1**

41-5 4 9 **General Kutuzov (IRE)**[28] 2441 6-11-1 0 .... LiamTreadwell 117+
(Nick Gifford) *led tl 4th: j. slowly and dropped into midfield 6th: dropped to last and toiling after 12th: plugged on past btn horses fr 3 out: hmpd 2 out: wnt modest 4th last* **20/1**

10-4 5 3 3/4 **City Theatre (IRE)**[52] 1964 6-11-1 0 .... APMcCoy 114
(Jonjo O'Neill) *nt fluent: in tch: chsng ldng quartet and rdn whn j. slowly 13th: wknd u.p sn after 3 out* **4/1**[2]

6602 6 13 **Canni Thinkaar (IRE)**[28] 2441 9-10-10 113(b) GemmaGracey-Davison(5) 103
(Zoe Davison) *chsd ldr tl led 4th: hdd 7th: led again 9th tl 14th: wknd qckly u.p sn after 3 out* **28/1**

-244 7 8 **Pause And Clause (IRE)**[25] 2494 6-11-1 132 .... SamThomas 95
(Emma Lavelle) *nt fluent: hld up in tch: chsd 11th: rdn and fnd nil next: sn toiling and losing tch: wl bhd fr 15th: t.o* **5/2**[1]

05-2 P **Strategic Approach (IRE)**[22] 2580 8-11-1 0 .... NoelFehily —
(Warren Greatrex) *in tch towards rr: dropped to last 10th: rdn and short-lived effrt after 11th: lost tch next: wl bhd whn p.u 14th* **4/1**[2]

6m 22.1s (-13.70) **Going Correction** -0.30s/f (Good) **8** Ran SP% **110.8**
Speed ratings (Par 105): **109,108,104,101,100 96,93,—**
toteswingers:1&2:£5.50, 1&3:£6.70, 2&3:£21.90 CSF £35.58 TOTE £5.90: £1.70, £2.70, £7.20; EX 28.70.

Owner M G St Quinton **Bred** M J Roberts **Trained** Withycombe, Somerset

FOCUS
A decent novice chase and pretty solid form, with the winner and third setting the level.

NOTEBOOK
Triggerman had run some respectable races over fences this season prior to finding a Listed handicap too competitive last time, and he took advantage of the drop back in class. Despite being inclined to go left under pressure, he found enough and should gain some confidence from this. (op 5-1 tchd 4-1)
Misstree Dancer, an ex-pointer, has twice won on heavy ground over hurdles and looked an interesting recruit to chasing. She seemed suited by this stamina test and posted a good performance, showing enough to suggest she can find a race, particularly against her own sex. (op 14-1)
Rear Gunner(IRE) was prominent from an early stage, and this was a decent performance as he kept on, if rather one-paced, in the home straight. The first-time cheekpieces appear to have done no harm, and he may find opportunities at this sort of trip. (op 25-1)
General Kutuzov(IRE), stepping up in trip, lost his place early on the final circuit before staying on past beaten rivals, and might appreciate softer conditions. (op 16-1)
Pause And Clause(IRE) was much the best of these over hurdles but so far has been unable to replicate that ability over fences. He has struggled with his jumping, and it was hoped the longer trip may have helped him get into a better rhythm, but that was not the case. If connections persist over the larger obstacles, then he may be of more interest in handicaps, though a return to hurdling must now be on the cards. (op 100-30 tchd 7-2)
Strategic Approach(IRE) was disappointing, having made a pleasing enough chasing debut last time out. He clearly didn't run his race, being given reminders with over a circuit to go, and was pulled up some way from home. Official explanation: trainer said gelding was never jumping (op 3-1)

2946 LADBROKESBINGO.COM MAIDEN HURDLE (10 hdls) 2m 6f 110y
1:35 (1:37) (Class 4) 4-Y-0+ **£3,252** (£955; £477; £238)

Form RPR

1 1 **Global Power (IRE)**[29] 2432 4-11-0 0 .... LeightonAspell 120+
(Oliver Sherwood) *t.k.h: hld up in mdfield: mstke 1st: hdwy to trck ldrs 3 out: nt clr run and swtchd lft wl bef last: sn rdn to chse ldr: led last: styd on wl* **16/1**

3-42 2 2 3/4 **Super Villan**[37] 2238 5-11-0 114 .... MattieBatchelor 118
(Mark Bradstock) *chsd ldr tl led after 6th: j.lft 3 out: rdn bef last: hdd last: styd on same pce flat* **11/1**

4 3 4 1/2 **Double Whammy**[30] 2396 4-11-0 0 .... AndrewThornton 113
(Jamie Poulton) *chsd ldrs: mstke 7th: pressed ldrs after 3 out: drvn wl bef last: styd on same u.p st* **66/1**

16-4 4 3 **Awesome Freddie**[41] 2143 5-11-0 0 .... RobertThornton 111
(Alan King) *in tch in midfield: hdwy to chse ldrs after 6th: pressing ldrs and j.rt 2 out: wknd u.p bef last* **6/1**[3]

454- 5 1/2 **Red Mile (FR)**[261] 4916 5-11-0 0 .... SamThomas 112+
(Emma Lavelle) *hld up in tch in rr: hdwy into midfield after 6th: mstke 7th: rdn and outpcd sn after 2 out: rallied ent st: swtchd rt and plugged on same pce bef last* **14/1**

153- 6 11 **Sherwani Wolf (IRE)**[298] 4149 6-11-0 0 .... PaddyBrennan 102+
(Nigel Twiston-Davies) *in tch in midfield: hdwy to chse ldrs after 6th: pressing ldrs and rdn after 2 out: wknd ent st: wl btn and tired whn j. slowly last* **4/1**[2]

7 7 **Prince Of Valour (IRE)**[219] 4-11-0 0 .... DominicElsworth 92
(Lucy Wadham) *t.k.h: chsd ldrs: ev ch bef 2 out: rdn wl bef last: wknd qckly ent st* **66/1**

6 **8** *11* **Two Cloudy (IRE)**[31] 2368 4-10-11 0 MichaelMurphy(3) 81
(Pat Murphy) *hld up towards rr: clsd and in tch after 6th: wknd after 3 out: wl btn after next* **150/1**

21-2 **9** *nk* **Oscar Papa**[42] 2142 5-11-0 0 LiamTreadwell 92
(Nick Gifford) *in tch in midfield: hdwy to chse ldrs 7th: ev ch after 3 out: hmpd: mstke and lost pl next: sn rdn and btn: eased whn no ch bef last* **9/4**[1]

3/5- **10** *1 1/2* **Mr Bennett (IRE)**[351] 3123 7-11-0 0 TomScudamore 91
(David Pipe) *hld up towards rr: clsd and wl in tch after 6th: rdn and wknd qckly 2 out: wl bhd ent st: t.o* **8/1**

55-4 **11** *3/4* **Current Climate (IRE)**[35] 2291 6-11-0 0 JamieMoore 78
(Richard Rowe) *a towards rr: in tch: rdn and struggling 7th: lost tch 3 out: t.o* **100/1**

5-3 **12** *2 1/4* **Oddjob (IRE)**[37] 2231 6-11-0 0 WayneHutchinson 76
(Warren Greatrex) *in tch in midfield tl wknd qckly 3 out: t.o and eased bef last* **20/1**

05-3 **13** *3 1/4* **Bubbly Bruce (IRE)**[30] 2396 6-11-0 0 (t) NoelFehily 72
(Charlie Mann) *in tch in midfield: hdwy to chse ldrs after 6th: wnt 2nd and ev ch after 2 out: wknd qckly ent st: virtually p.u bef last: t.o* **9/1**

2-4 **P** **Gortenbuie (IRE)**[33] 2325 5-11-0 0 HaddenFrost —
(Henrietta Knight) *t.k.h: chsd ldrs tl wnt 2nd after 6th tl 3 out: sn fdd: wl btn and eased after next: wl t.o whn p.u last* **66/1**

3 **P** **Eternal City**[54] 1941 5-11-0 0 WillKennedy —
(Paul Webber) *led tl after 6th: sn rdn and losing pl: bhd and lost tch after next: wl t.o whn p.u 2 out* **100/1**

0 **P** **Another Round (IRE)**[23] 2560 6-11-0 0 AndrewGlassonbury —
(Laura Young) *a in rr: dropped to last and struggling u.p after 5th: wl t.o whn p.u 7th* **150/1**

5m 58.3s (-13.00) **Going Correction** -0.30s/f (Good)
WFA 4 from 5yo+ 6lb **16** Ran SP% **119.6**
Speed ratings (Par 105): **106,105,103,102,102 98,96,92,92,91 91,90,89,—,— —**
toteswingers:1&2:£4.10, 1&3:£29.30, 2&3:£89.80 CSF £173.24 TOTE £20.60: £2.90, £3.70, £16.90; EX 289.10.
Owner It Wasn't Us **Bred** R J Whitford **Trained** Upper Lambourn, Berks

FOCUS
A competitive maiden hurdle. The form looks sound enough and the winner should go on to rate higher.

NOTEBOOK
Global Power(IRE), is now 3-3 in all lifetime starts, having won a point, a bumper, and now a hurdle race. He clearly has the stamina for this sort of trip, and may possibly end up better over further, as his trainer feels that he's a real galloper. He appears to be a useful sort to have for staying hurdle races, though it must be expected that his real future lies over fences.
Super Villan kept finding for pressure in the straight but was beaten by one who saw out the trip that little better. He looks sure to pick up races with his aggressive front-running tactics. (op 14-1 tchd 10-1)
Double Whammy shaped with promise on his hurdling debut and this was an improvement. There should be more to come. (op 100-1)
Awesome Freddie was unable to quicken with the leaders when jumping the third from home. He stayed on one-paced in the home straight and this was a decent performance, as he is believed to need better ground. (op 9-1)
Red Mile(FR) stayed on quite well in the straight and is likely to continue improving over the winter, as he clearly has some ability. (op 16-1)
Sherwani Wolf(IRE) attracted market support in the morning, but disappointed on his return from a 298-day absence, tiring going to the last having been close enough turning for home. He's yet to convince over hurdles, this time failing to improve for a step up in trip, but he has the option of switching to handicaps. (op 3-1 tchd 9-2 in a place)
Prince Of Valour(IRE) was kept up the inner in an attempt to save ground on his first start under rules, but his best efforts previously have come on good or better ground.
Oscar Papa went off a solid favourite but was unable to build on his promising second to Emma Lavelle's Court In Motion last time out. This was a disappointing run as he faded quickly having been in contention at the penultimate flight. Official explanation: trainer said gelding never travelled (op 15-8)

2947 EASTWELL MANOR NOVICES' H'CAP CHASE (12 fncs) 2m
2:05 (2:06) (Class 5) (0-90,90) 4-Y-0+ **£2,797** (£821; £410; £205)

Form RPR

2/P- **1** **Jack's Lad (IRE)**[575] 369 11-11-1 **76** RichardJohnson 85
(Tim Vaughan) *bhd: mstke 3rd and 5th: hdwy to dispute 3rd and mstke 7th: rdn to chal after 3 out: led next: drvn and gd jump last: styd on wl* **11/4**[2]

60P4 **2** *3 1/2* **Watergate (IRE)**[22] 2583 4-11-9 **90** LeightonAspell 93+
(Richard Rowe) *led: sn clr: hdd and blnd 8th: led again and blnd 3 out: hdd next: no ex u.p and btn sn after last* **9/2**[3]

00-0 **3** *12* **Copper Sound**[32] 2348 6-11-10 **85** (tp) TomScudamore 81
(Michael Scudamore) *chsd ldr tl 5th: in tch after: cl 4th whn mstke 3 out: sn outpcd and drvn: wl hld and plugged on same pce fr next* **5/2**[1]

4014 **4** *1/2* **Isintshelovely (IRE)**[30] 2391 7-11-3 **78** (p) ColinBolger 72
(Chris Gordon) *in tch: rdn 6th: outpcd 8th: no threat to ldrs after 3 out: plugged on u.p between last 2* **12/1**

066 **5** *1/2* **Jack The Soldier (IRE)**[30] 2396 6-11-9 **87** CharlieStudd(3) 80
(Chris Gordon) *in tch in rr tl lost tch 7th: n.d after: plugged on fr 2 out* **11/2**

5U54 **6** *6* **Bold Pioneer (USA)**[30] 2392 7-10-3 **69** GemmaGracey-Davison(5) 60
(Zoe Davison) *t.k.h: hld up in rr early: hdwy to chse ldr 5th: led 8th: j.lft and mstke: next: hdd 3 out: wknd u.p bef 2 out: tired between last 2* **13/2**

4m 7.00s (-0.20) **Going Correction** -0.30s/f (Good)
WFA 4 from 6yo+ 5lb **6** Ran SP% **109.8**
Speed ratings (Par 103): **88,86,80,80,79 76**
toteswingers:1&2:£2.40, 1&3:£2.10, 2&3:£3.90 CSF £14.72 TOTE £2.50: £1.20, £2.10; EX 13.90.
Owner Batts, Vaughan, Mason & Johnson **Bred** Andrew Connolly **Trained** Aberthin, Vale of Glamorgan

FOCUS
A moderate novices' handicap chase with doubts surrounding most of the runners. The winner is rated to his best 2009 form.

NOTEBOOK
Jack's Lad(IRE) was produced to win after a 575-day-absence. Although fairly lightly raced, this was still a big ask and he was under pressure after the third from home, being forced wide around the bend. However, he jumped well in the home straight and was able to draw clear jumping the last. This was clearly the time to catch him and whether he can repeat the performance next time out is an unknown. (op 100-30)
Watergate(IRE), making his chasing debut, set off at a strong gallop in an attempt to make all. Despite a couple of mistakes down the back straight, he nevertheless kept battling on in the home straight and was only really beaten at the last. This was a vastly improved performance from a horse who has some potential, and he can win races from the front if able to sharpen up his jumping. (op 5-1 tchd 11-2)
Copper Sound returned in a hot chase at Cheltenham last time out after more than a year off and this was much more his level. He was never able to get competitive, however, and was under pressure a long way out, staying on one-paced. His best form is on a sounder surface. (tchd 9-4 and 11-4)
Isintshelovely(IRE) was said to have improved for the soft ground when winning at Fontwell in October, but that was over a much longer trip and so it wasn't surprising that she was outpaced early on his time. She is decent enough but a step up in trip is a must. (op 10-1 tchd 9-1)
Jack The Soldier(IRE) is an ex-pointer who had never run over this short a distance before, and is another who was quickly outpaced. He will be seen to better effect over a longer distance. (op 5-1 tchd 9-2)
Bold Pioneer(USA) was prominent with the runner-up, but made a number of mistakes, and despite being in touch turning for home, faded quite quickly.

2948 WEATHERBYS BANK H'CAP CHASE (15 fncs) 2m 5f
2:35 (2:35) (Class 3) (0-135,130) 4-Y-0+ **£7,806** (£2,292; £1,146; £572)

Form RPR

P/00 **1** **Only Vintage (USA)**[20] 2606 10-10-11 **115** RichardJohnson 133+
(Paul Henderson) *hld up in midfield on outer: clsd on ldrs 9th: wnt 2nd 12th: clr w ldr after 3 out: rdn to ld after 2 out: clr whn j.lft last: styd on wl* **25/1**

60-P **2** *7* **Regal Heights (IRE)**[19] 2629 9-11-4 **122** (p) NoelFehily 133
(Tom George) *chsd ldr tl led 5th: rdn and clr w eventual wnr after 3 out: hdd between last 2: btn last: plugged on same pce flat* **16/1**

11-0 **3** *7* **Chance Du Roy (FR)**[32] 2347 6-11-12 **130** TomO'Brien 135
(Philip Hobbs) *towards rr: mstke 6th: hdwy after 8th: drvn to chse ldng pair after 3 out: no imp fr 2 out* **7/1**

-P41 **4** *nk* **The Rainbow Hunter**[37] 2236 6-11-0 **125** EdCookson(7) 131+
(Andy Turnell) *hld up in rr: mstke 1st and 2nd: hdwy into midfield 8th: rdn after 3 out: disputing 3rd and hld whn mstke next: no prog after* **14/1**

06-0 **5** *8* **Theatre Dance (IRE)**[22] 2581 9-11-11 **129** DarylJacob 126
(David Arbuthnot) *towards rr: rdn and effrt after 3 out: styd on past btn horses fr 2 out: nvr trbld ldrs* **33/1**

6 *hd* **Roi De Rose (FR)**[443] 6-10-10 **114** (p) TomScudamore 110
(David Pipe) *chsd clr ldng trio: clsd and wl in tch 10th: 3rd and rdn 3 out: wknd wl bef next* **16/1**

21-1 **7** *3 1/2* **Midnight Haze**[33] 2324 8-11-10 **128** NickScholfield 121
(Kim Bailey) *led tl 5th: styd prom tl wknd bef 3 out: wl btn bef 2 out* **11/2**[3]

4/2U **8** *5* **Carrickboy (IRE)**[4] 2869 6-11-4 **122** AidanColeman 111
(Venetia Williams) *chsd ldrs: mstke 4th: j.lft: mstke and dropped to midfield next: hdwy to chse ldrs again 10th: wknd u.p bef 3 out* **7/2**[1]

P-66 **9** *6* **Buck The Legend (IRE)**[184] 735 8-11-7 **125** PaddyBrennan 108
(Nigel Twiston-Davies) *nvr gng wl and a towards rr: mstke 2nd: struggling after 10th: wl btn 3 out* **16/1**

-P2P **10** *11* **Victorias Groom (GER)**[23] 2541 8-11-10 **128** LeightonAspell 108
(Lucy Wadham) *chsd ldrs: wnt 2nd 6th tl 12th: sn wknd: wl bhd and eased between last 2: t.o* **22/1**

55-0 **11** *19* **Doctor Pat (IRE)**[66] 1769 6-11-3 **121** APMcCoy 77
(Jonjo O'Neill) *alway towards rr: rdn and no hdwy 10th: wl bhd 3 out: t.o* **14/1**

622F **12** *21* **Restezen D'Armor (FR)**[25] 2502 5-10-6 **110** (b) FelixDeGiles 47
(Charlie Longsdon) *t.k.h: hld up in rr: hdwy into midfield gng wl after 8th: rdn and struggling whn mstke 11th: wl bhd after 3 out: t.o: eased after last* **9/2**[2]

P05P **13** *8* **Pocket Aces (IRE)**[17] 2674 8-11-5 **123** AndrewThornton 53
(Richard Rowe) *racd in midfield: dropped to rr and struggling u.p 9th t.o bef 3 out* **14/1**

35/U **P** **Peplum (FR)**[18] 2665 7-10-13 **117** JamieMoore —
(Gary Moore) *a towards rr: struggling u.p whn blnd 10th: t.o after 3 out tl p.u last* **100/1**

453 **P** **Smack That (IRE)**[24] 2520 8-11-1 **122** (vt) JimmyDerham(3) —
(Milton Harris) *hld up in rr: stmbld bdly and lost tch 6th: detached last whn p.u bef 9th* **66/1**

5m 17.0s (-5.20) **Going Correction** -0.30s/f (Good) **15** Ran SP% **119.6**
Speed ratings (Par 107): **97,94,91,91,88 88,87,85,82,78 71,63,60,—,—**
toteswingers:1&2:£108.30, 1&3:£70.80, 2&3:£41.00 CSF £355.37 CT £3096.39 TOTE £44.30: £8.40, £7.50, £2.50; EX 356.70.
Owner D S Dennis **Bred** Max Morris And Isabel Morris **Trained** Rockbourne, Hants

FOCUS
This was run at a strong pace with a number of horses keen to lead. The winner is rated back to his best and the form has a solid look to it.

NOTEBOOK
Only Vintage(USA), ridden with some restraint, crept nicely into the race, joining the leaders three from home, before pulling away nicely in the home straight. He was able to take advantage of a nice mark, having once been rated 135 when with Henrietta Knight, but whether he can repeat the performance off higher is unknown. (op 22-1)
Regal Heights(IRE) has been falling down the handicap but still struggling recently and this was a much-improved performance. Taking up the lead early on, he stayed on all the way to the line. He can be a little hit-and-miss these days, so whether he can produce another good performance must be taken on trust. (op 20-1)
Chance Du Roy(FR) ran well off top-weight, though was never able to get competitive enough to challenge the eventual winner. He may have been unlucky to end up behind a couple of well-handicapped rivals, and it may be that he himself is still a little ahead of the handicapper. (op 17-2 tchd 9-1 and 13-2)
The Rainbow Hunter remains fairly unexposed over fences and this was a pleasing enough performance. He was left out at the back early on and looks a little one-paced, so may be seen to better effect over a longer trip. (op 16-1)
Theatre Dance(IRE) ran well on his seasonal reappearance recently after a lengthy absence, but was never able to get involved this time due to the strong early pace. He is another who is likely to improve for a step up in distance. (tchd 28-1)
Roi De Rose(FR), an interesting French recruit who had won his last three starts over fences in Switzerland, was making his first start for 443 days. He travelled well for a long way, just settled in behind the leaders, before seeming to run out of gas when turning for home. He was not given a hard time in the closing stages and looks sure to improve for the run. (op 12-1)
Midnight Haze has a tendency to jump right-handed and so was better suited going this way round. He was kept tight to the rail and helped to set the strong gallop, but may have been undone by the rise of 8lb for his win last time out. (op 5-1)
Carrickboy(IRE) was unlucky when unseating at Cheltenham four days previous, but was rather slow and ponderous in his jumping today, and it may be that the run came too soon for him. (op 4-1)

2949 LIPSCOMB.CO.UK H'CAP HURDLE (10 hdls) 2m 4f 110y
3:05 (3:06) (Class 4) (0-105,105) 3-Y-0+ **£3,252** (£955; £477; £238)

Form RPR

5-33 **1** **Prince Du Seuil (FR)**[24] 2530 7-11-12 **105** RobertThornton 118+
(Alan King) *confidently rdn: hld up in tch: hdwy to trck ldrs bef 2 out: clr w ldr and stl on bit bef last: rdn to assert flat: comf* **9/2**[2]

4421 **2** *6* **Kylenoe Fairy (IRE)**[28] 2442 6-11-12 **105**............................(t) APMcCoy 110
(Paul Henderson) *hld up in tch: chsd ldrs 6th: led gng wl 2 out: clr w eventual wnr after 2 out: rdn bef last: hdd flat: sn nt pce of wnr and btn* **6/1**[3]

2-12 **3** *13* **Lemon Silk (IRE)**[38] 2209 6-11-7 **105**................................ DavidBass(5) 96
(Alex Hales) *hld up in tch in rr: hdwy after 5th: chsd ldrs and rdn after 2 out: sn outpcd and no ch w ldng pair ent st: plugged on to go 3rd bef last* **4/1**[1]

436- **4** *2 ¾* **Jordan**[253] 5055 7-10-4 **90**.. MrTJCannon(7) 78
(Suzy Smith) *in tch in midfield: hdwy after 5th: chsd ldrs and rdn 2 out: wknd wl bef last: wl hld whn lft modest 4th last* **22/1**

0-5U **5** *1 ¾* **Island Jim (IRE)**[24] 2527 6-11-12 **105**........................... TomScudamore 92
(Charlie Longsdon) *in tch: hdwy to press ldrs 5th: led bef 3 out tl 2 out: sn u.p: wknd ent st: tired and lost 2 pls bef last* **25/1**

56-2 **6** *10* **Wheres Johnny**[29] 2430 9-11-6 **99**................................ MattieBatchelor 76
(Jamie Poulton) *in tch in rr: j. slowly 5th: clsd and wl in tch bef 3 out: rdn and wknd bef 2 out* **16/1**

5442 **7** *17* **Sail And Return**[30] 2390 6-10-8 **94**................................ JoshuaMoore(7) 55
(Philip Middleton) *w ldrs: ev ch 3 out: wknd rapidly sn after next: wl bhd and eased bef last: t.o* **15/2**

/04- **8** *1 ½* **Kadouchski (FR)**[13] 3023 6-11-11 **104**................................ WillKennedy 62
(John Berry) *hld up in tch: clsd 5th: chsd ldrs bef 3 out: wknd qckly 2 out: wl bhd and eased bef last* **14/1**

55-6 **9** *19* **Calusa Shadow**[22] 2577 6-11-10 **103**............................ RichardJohnson 42
(Philip Hobbs) *in tch towards rr: rdn after 5th: styd in tch tl btn bef 2 out: eased fr sn after 2 out: t.o* **7/1**

2-23 **10** *10* **The Hardy Boy**[30] 2394 10-10-12 **91**................................ NickScholfield 20
(Anna Newton-Smith) *chsd ldrs: rdn and wknd bef 2 out: wl bhd and eased bef last: t.o* **33/1**

05-P **11** *26* **Pull The Wool (IRE)**[23] 2554 6-10-11 **90**............................. LiamHeard —
(Laura Young) *w ldrs: mstke 4th: led next tl hdd bef 3 out: losing pl qckly whn mstke 3 out: wl t.o next* **66/1**

60/P **P** **Idris (GER)**[55] 1918 9-10-12 **94**.. CharlieStudd(3) —
(Philip Sharp) *in tch in midfield tl dropped to rr qckly bef 6th: sn t.o tl p.u last* **80/1**

-56P **P** **Machu Picchu (FR)**[19] 2638 8-11-2 **95**............................(v¹) DarylJacob —
(Jamie Snowden) *led 1st tl 5th: sn losing pl u.p: bhd and t.o whn p.u bef 3 out* **33/1**

PUR- **P** **Celian (FR)**[275] 4617 7-11-6 **102**...................................... AlexMerriam(3) —
(Neil King) *chsd ldrs tl dropped to rr and rdn after 4th: lost tch and j. slowly 6th: t.o whn p.u 2 out* **50/1**

50-0 **F** **Kaybeew**[223] 154 5-11-11 **104**.. PaddyBrennan 92
(Nigel Twiston-Davies) *hld up in tch in rr: hdwy 5th: chsd ldrs 3 out: rdn and wknd wl bef last: 4th and wl btn whn fell last* **16/1**

P-36 **B** **Twin Bud**[29] 2428 5-10-12 **94**.......................................(p) JimmyDerham(3) —
(Anna Newton-Smith) *hld up in rr whn b.d 1st* **20/1**

0F-0 **F** **Goring One (IRE)**[219] 216 5-11-7 **100**................................ FelixDeGiles —
(Anna Newton-Smith) *hld up in rr whn fell 1st* **33/1**

5m 31.1s (1.10) **Going Correction** -0.30s/f (Good) **17** Ran SP% **121.6**
Speed ratings (Par 105): **96,93,88,87,87 83,76,76,68,65 55,—,—,—,— —,—**
toteswingers:1&2:£4.30, 1&3:£4.00, 2&3:£4.90 CSF £28.36 CT £119.97 TOTE £6.50: £1.90, £1.90, £1.10, £6.80; EX 24.10.
Owner Mrs Peter Prowting **Bred** Paul-Louis Ravier **Trained** Barbury Castle, Wilts

FOCUS
This race ended up being all about the front two, who pulled well clear of the rest of the field, having gone a steady gallop early on. Steps up from the first two.

NOTEBOOK
Prince Du Seuil(FR) , like a number from the Alan King yard, appeared to be running off a handy enough mark based upon old form, and so it proved as he bolted up under a confident ride from Robert Thornton. Travelling best throughout, his jockey hadn't moved a muscle until after the last flight when he was shaken up to pull clear of the runner-up. His only other win came on soft ground, so it seems as though a bit of cut may be important to his chances. Having slipped to a mark of 105, he took full advantage, and if able to produce further performances as good as this, then he should be able to cope with any rise in mark. (op 5-1)
Kylenoe Fairy(IRE) has kept on improving this season and travelled as well as the winner for a long way, having taken it up two from home. However, she was being asked for an effort before the final flight and was unable to quicken when required. This was a good performance and there appears still to be plenty of improvement in her. She has performed well this season over both fences and hurdles, and is likely to continue being competitive alternating between the two. (op 11-2)
Lemon Silk(IRE) ended a lengthy losing run in October and appears to be at the top of his game, giving the form in behind a solid look. He was staying on round the bend and down the home straight, but was never able to get involved with the front two. He can be expected to continue running well in the coming months. (op 5-1)
Jordan was being ridden upon entering the back straight but kept finding for pressure and this was an improved performance which connections will hope he can build upon. (op 25-1)
Island Jim(IRE) travelled quite well for a long time, but was unable to go with the leaders when turning for home. He has tended to perform better on decent ground.
Calusa Shadow had only ever encountered good ground before today, but had run with some promise on his return after a lengthy absence in November. However, he struggled and is best watched if turned out on testing ground again. (op 6-1)
Kaybeew fell when tired at the last, but until that point had shaped a lot better than he has done for a while. (op 12-1)

2950 VOTE FOR A P MCCOY H'CAP CHASE (14 fncs 4 omitted) 3m 1f
3:35 (3:38) (Class 5) (0-90,90) 4-Y-O+ **£2,797** (£821; £410; £205)

Form RPR

3401 **1** **Pete The Feat (IRE)**[30] 2390 6-11-12 **90**............................ FelixDeGiles 98
(Anna Newton-Smith) *t.k.h: hld up in tch: rdn and effrt after 3 out: gd jump to ld next: drvn and 2 l clr last: hrd drvn fnl 100yds: jst lasted* **8/1**

04/3 **2** *nse* **Billy Murphy**[20] 2608 7-11-8 **86**...................................... MarkBradburne 94
(Paul Cowley) *prom: sltly outpcd 4 out: hdwy to press ldrs after 3 out: unable qck next: chsd wnr last: styd on wl u.p fnl 100yds: jst failed* **12/1**

3353 **3** *4* **Saddlewood (IRE)**[39] 2183 7-11-4 **82**.............................(tp) DarylJacob 87
(Jamie Snowden) *trckd ldrs: ev ch and pckd 3 out: sn led: hdd and rdn next: no ex and btn last* **9/2**[3]

P/F3 **4** *7* **Commanche Dawn**[30] 2391 8-10-0 **64** oh4......................... JamieMoore 63
(Gerry Enright) *hld up wl in tch in last trio: rdn and chsd ldrs after 3 out: wknd u.p sn after 2 out* **33/1**

3512 **5** *¾* **Rudinero (IRE)**[30] 2402 8-11-3 **84**............................(t) MichaelMurphy(3) 82
(Barry Brennan) *mostly chsd ldr tl led and blnd 3 out: sn hdd: wknd u.p sn after 2 out* **7/2**[1]

-B13 **6** *5* **Miss Fleur**[27] 2457 7-11-8 **89**... DannyCook(3) 83
(Nick Mitchell) *led and set stdy gallop: hdd and hit 3 out: sn unable qck u.p: wknd jst bef 2 out* **15/2**

/356 **7** *6* **Mister Virginian (IRE)**[47] 2051 11-11-3 **88**................(v¹) MrTJCannon(7) 75
(Chris Gordon) *in tch: reminder after 1st: rdn and dropped to last on long run to 5 out: wl btn after 3 out* **40/1**

4-22 **8** *7* **Sailor's Sovereign**[29] 2431 9-10-2 **69**..............(p) SamTwiston-Davies(3) 50
(Julian Smith) *hld up wl in tch: hdwy on long run to 5 out: chsng ldrs and nt fluent 4 out: wknd qckly sn after 2 out* **4/1**[2]

3-32 **9** *11* **Kiltimoney (IRE)**[30] 2394 10-10-1 **70**............................ GilesHawkins(5) 41
(Richard Mitchell) *chsd ldrs: blnd 7th: lost pl and struggling whn hit 5 out: wknd next: t.o* **5/1**

-P21 **10** *6* **Kappelhoff (IRE)**[30] 2394 13-10-12 **76**.......................(b) MattieBatchelor 42
(Lydia Richards) *in tch in rr: rdn along at times: mstke 9th and 11th: struggling bef 5 out: wl bhd after 3 out: t.o* **25/1**

6m 33.5s (-2.30) **Going Correction** -0.30s/f (Good) **10** Ran SP% **116.9**
Speed ratings (Par 103): **91,90,89,87,87 85,83,81,77,76**
toteswingers:1&2:£15.60, 1&3:£8.80, 2&3:£12.30; totesuper7: Win: Not won. Place: Not won. CSF £92.82 CT £487.67 TOTE £10.60: £3.60, £4.10, £1.40; EX 122.60.
Owner G J Larby & P J Smith **Bred** Michael O'Keeffe **Trained** Jevington, E Sussex

FOCUS
Due to low sun, both fences down the side of the course were bypassed. A moderate handicap, but a tight finish. The winner looks like being a better chaser than hurdler.

NOTEBOOK
Pete The Feat(IRE), successful over hurdles last time, was following up on his first start over fences, and this was a good performance off a 7lb higher mark. Jumping the last in front, he just idled a little allowing the runner-up to get within a nose. Nevertheless, he's clearly high on confidence and enjoying his racing. (op 9-1)
Billy Murphy is a lightly raced sort who had put up some decent performances three seasons ago, but hadn't been seen much since. Having run with some promise at Chepstow on his return from an absence last time out on soft ground, he was likely one to enjoy the conditions, and just left too much to do jumping the last. There are likely to be opportunities for him this season. (op 8-1)
Saddlewood(IRE) has yet to win, and despite travelling well for a long time, never looked like changing that. She looks exposed off her current mark, and she may be difficulty to place. (op 7-1)
Commanche Dawn had shown little previous form and did well to complete, having fallen on two of her last six hurdle starts. This was an improved performance from 4lb out the handicap. (op 25-1)
Rudinero(IRE) was prominent throughout and took it up three from home but was unable to quicken at the vital moment, perhaps finding the ground a little testing. (tchd 4-1)
Miss Fleur set the early pace and jumped well, but was unable to keep it up on the turn for home. (op 8-1 tchd 10-1)
T/Jkpt: Not won. T/Plt: £1,578.60 to a £1 stake. Pool:£87,801.66 - 40.60 winning tickets T/Qpdt: £344.00 to a £1 stake. Pool:£6,695.83 - 14.40 winning tickets. SP

2303 BANGOR-ON-DEE (L-H)
Wednesday, December 15

OFFICIAL GOING: Hurdle course - good (good to soft in places; 6.9); chase course - good to soft (6.1) (overall goingstick 6.5)
Wind: Nil Weather: Overcast

2951 DIRECT MORTGAGES NOVICES' CHASE (12 fncs) 2m 1f 110y
12:15 (12:15) (Class 4) 4-Y-0+ **£3,903** (£1,146; £573; £286)

Form RPR

5-02 **1** **Dan Breen (IRE)**[42] 2153 5-11-0 0................................ TomScudamore 144+
(David Pipe) *mde all: drew clr appr 2 out: over 16 l clr and wl in command whn blnd bdly last: gd rcvry: rdn briefly run-in: remained unchal* **3/1**[1]

0-U2 **2** *11* **Hollo Ladies (IRE)**[27] 2475 5-11-0 137................................ GrahamLee 128+
(Ferdy Murphy) *midfield: mstke 1st: hdwy 4th: wnt 2nd 7th: rdn appr 3 out: no ch w wnr sn after* **15/2**

21-1 **3** *5* **Gilbarry (IRE)**[46] 2088 5-11-7 134...................................... DenisO'Regan 136+
(Malcolm Jefferson) *chsd ldrs: disputing 2nd whn blnd 4 out: u.p after 3 out: no ch w wnr after and plugged on at one pce* **11/2**

-026 **4** *10* **Shadow Dancer (IRE)**[42] 2153 5-11-0 0................................ APMcCoy 115
(Jonjo O'Neill) *chsd ldr to 6th: wknd 4 out* **14/1**

-341 **5** *¾* **Mohayer (IRE)**[22] 2593 8-11-4 0................................ RichieMcLernon(3) 120
(Jonjo O'Neill) *hld up: hdwy 4 out: unable to go w ldrs fr next: sn wl btn* **28/1**

11-3 **6** *2 ¼* **Lord Villez (FR)**[28] 2447 6-10-7 116................................ PaulGallagher(7) 111
(Ferdy Murphy) *hld up: hdwy 7th: struggling appr 8th: bhd fr 4 out* **28/1**

13-1 **7** *10* **Mister Stickler (IRE)**[30] 2429 6-11-7 125...................... RobertThornton 115+
(Alan King) *hld up: rdn and hdwy appr 8th: wknd after 3 out: n.d whn nt fluent 2 out* **7/2**[3]

100- **8** *48* **Gus Macrae (IRE)**[249] 5128 6-11-0 0..............................(t) JasonMaguire 59
(Rebecca Curtis) *chsd ldrs: lost pl bef 7th: wl bhd fr 4 out: t.o* **10/3**[2]

2-PP **P** **Aboukir Bay (IRE)**[37] 2276 6-10-7 85............................(b) JoeCornwall(7) —
(John Cornwall) *bhd: struggling after 4th: t.o whn p.u bef 8th* **200/1**

4m 24.8s (2.70) **Going Correction** +0.30s/f (Yiel) **9** Ran SP% **111.5**
Speed ratings (Par 105): **106,101,98,94,94 93,88,67,—**
toteswingers:1&2:£7.40, 1&3:£5.10, 2&3:£28.00 CSF £24.34 TOTE £4.00: £1.60, £2.10, £1.30; EX 21.80.
Owner Stuart M Mercer **Bred** F Fitzgerald **Trained** Nicholashayne, Devon

FOCUS
An interesting novice chase which seemed to be run at a brisk pace, although the time was nearly 15 secs outside the standard. The winner is value for further and the form should work out with the third the best guide.

NOTEBOOK
Dan Breen(IRE) was a useful hurdler last term but had found Darby's Turn (pulled up since) too strong on his chase debut at Warwick. The experience was plainly not lost on him as he made all for an impressive win. He nearly threw it away with a bad blunder at the last, but was far enough clear for it not to matter and the error was an aberration in an otherwise neat round of jumping. It is likely that a number of his opponents found this too sharp a test, but he still looks a young chaser with a future. (op 7-2 tchd 4-1)
Hollo Ladies(IRE) was 10lb clear on adjusted official figures. He was left trailing by the winner from the third last, but stuck on to hold second, another solid effort. His win in the Future Champions Novices' Hurdle at Leopardstown last Christmas came over 2m, but he has been campaigned over further since and was runner-up over an extended 2m6f at Market Rasen. A return to around 2m4f should pay off. (op 8-1)
Gilbarry(IRE)'s Wetherby win, promising though it was, had identified the need for improvement in his jumping. Never far from the pace, a blunder at the final ditch soon had him on the retreat, but this was a fair effort under his penalty. (op 4-1)
Shadow Dancer(IRE) lost a prominent pitch with six to jump but plugged on to get the best of a four-way tussle for a remote fourth. Beaten further by Dan Breen than he had been at Warwick, he needs to go back up in trip. (op 16-1)
Mohayer(IRE) was well beaten under the penalty he picked up for finishing alone at Lingfield and all four of his wins, hurdles included, have come in heavy ground.

Mister Stickler(IRE), a Plumpton scorer on his chase debut, seemed to find things happening too quickly and was in trouble by halfway. This was disappointing, but it was reported that he had a breathing problem. Official explanation: jockey said gelding had a breathing problem (op 3-1 tchd 11-4)

Gus Macrae(IRE), the only chasing debutant on show, ran over hurdles at the big Cheltenham and Aintree fixtures last spring. He jumped soundly enough but was outpaced by the principals early on the final circuit and was steadily left behind from there. He needs to improve considerably on this but is another who will benefit from a longer trip. (op 9-2 tchd 3-1)

2952 DTM LEGAL H'CAP CHASE (15 fncs) 2m 4f 110y

12:45 (12:45) (Class 4) (0-105,104) 4-Y-0+ **£3,903** (£1,146; £573; £286)

Form RPR

2111 **1** **Douglas Julian**28 2450 8-11-4 **96**........ HenryOliver 111+
(Sue Smith) *chsd ldrs: handy 6th: niggled along fr 10th: led narrowly after 3 out: kpt responding for press: abt 1 l up whn lft abt 3 l clr last: styd on* **5/2**1

-52U **2** 1 ½ **One More Dinar**23 2585 7-10-0 **78** oh1........ RodiGreene 92+
(John Bryan Groucott) *prom: mstke 2nd: lost pl 3rd: remained in tch: effrt 3 out: chalng appr 2 out: abt 1 l down and ch whn blnd last: rallied towards fin but hld* **6/1**2

04/P **3** 15 **Walk Tall (IRE)**41 2170 7-11-3 **95**........ JasonMaguire 96
(Venetia Williams) *racd keenly: chsd ldr fr 2nd to 6th: remained handy: rdn to chal 2 out: wknd appr last* **7/1**3

13P- **4** 11 **Overlaw**238 5312 8-11-3 **95**........ DenisO'Regan 84
(Tom George) *led: hdd after 3 out: wknd 2 out* **9/1**

1053 **P** **Magnetic Pole**23 2587 9-11-7 **104**........(v) GilesHawkins(5) —
(Richard Lee) *towards rr: hdwy 8th: rdn appr 11th: wknd 4 out: t.o whn p.u bef 2 out* **10/1**

5P53 **P** **Hever Road (IRE)**30 2420 11-9-12 **83**........ JoeCornwall(7) —
(David Pearson) *bhd: pushed along appr 9th: nvr on terms: t.o whn p.u bef 2 out* **10/1**

/4-1 **P** **Optimum (IRE)**148 1049 8-11-6 **98**........ GrahamLee —
(Richard Ford) *hld up: hdwy appr 11th: no imp on ldrs: wknd bef 3 out: t.o whn p.u bef 2 out* **8/1**

354- **P** **Ours (FR)**278 4574 8-10-11 **92**........ PeterToole(3) —
(Mark Rimell) *handy tl wknd appr 3 out: t.o whn p.u bef 2 out* **9/1**

3412 **P** **Pistol Basc (FR)**32 2371 6-11-1 **100**........ PaulGallagher(7) —
(Ferdy Murphy) *midfield: dropped to rr 8th: sn pushed along: toiling after: t.o whn p.u bef 2 out* **7/1**3

5m 19.9s (10.80) **Going Correction** +0.30s/f (Yiel) **9** Ran SP% **117.2**
Speed ratings (Par 105): **91,90,84,80,—** —,—,—,—
toteswingers:1&2:£3.30, 1&3:£7.00, 2&3:£16.60 CSF £18.72 CT £93.96 TOTE £3.40: £2.00, £2.40, £2.20; EX 26.40.

Owner Mrs S Smith **Bred** A M Armitage **Trained** High Eldwick, W Yorks

FOCUS

An ordinary handicap chase. The four who completed were all in with a chance on the home turn. The runner-up is rated close to his best with the winner on the upgrade.

NOTEBOOK

Douglas Julian coped with a 12lb rise for his Hexham win to stretch his winning sequence to four, and is now two from two over fences. He looks quite an idle type and Henry Oliver was at him from some way out, but he gave the impression he had a bit in hand at the line and looks the type to make further progress. Softer ground and/or a stiffer test should suit. (op 7-2)

One More Dinar had to give best after a blunder at the last, but to his credit he was renewing his effort close home. Sure to be suited by the return to 3m, he remains a maiden, but has the ability to win races if his jumping holds up. (op 7-1)

Walk Tall(IRE) showed the benefit of last month's return from a lengthy lay-off and ran a pleasing race, only fading between the last two fences. He is another likely to benefit from 3m. (op 6-1)

Overlaw ◆ jumped well in front and had his field on the stretch, but could not hold on from the home turn. He can certainly be expected to come on for this first run since April and, although he is currently 12lb higher than when last successful, he is capable of winning again. (op 17-2)

Magnetic Pole Official explanation: jockey said gelding never travelled (tchd 17-2)

Optimum(IRE), a winner over hurdles at this venue when last seen in July, was never a serious factor on this chase debut. (tchd 17-2)

Pistol Basc(FR) was struggling at a relatively early stage and is better suited by a more galloping track, with Wetherby the venue for most of his best efforts these days. Official explanation: jockey said gelding ran flat (tchd 17-2)

2953 BANGORONDEERACES.CO.UK H'CAP CHASE (21 fncs) 3m 6f

1:15 (1:16) (Class 3) (0-120,119) 4-Y-0+ **£6,505** (£1,910; £955; £477)

Form RPR

0-51 **1** **Incentivise (IRE)**53 1968 7-11-6 **113**........ RobertThornton 121
(Richard Lee) *midfield: hdwy 14th: trckd ldrs 16th: wnt 2nd 17th: chalng appr 2 out: led after last: battled gamely to the line* **4/1**1

1-11 **2** hd **Gilsland (IRE)**32 2374 7-11-9 **116**........(v) JasonMaguire 124
(Donald McCain) *a.p: led 16th: rdn whn pressed appr 2 out: hdd narrowly after last: rallied u.p cl home: jst hld: collapsed fatally after r* **4/1**1

0-56 **3** 9 **Glebehall Bay (IRE)**23 2585 7-9-10 **96**........ HarryChalloner(7) 96
(Venetia Williams) *in tch: u.p after 10th: bhd 15th: stl plenty of work to do 4 out: tk mod 3rd appr last: no ch w ldrs* **9/1**

1U-4 **4** 17 **Ayemdee (IRE)**32 2366 7-10-12 **108**........ RichieMcLernon(3) 96
(Jonjo O'Neill) *hld up: j. slowly 7th: hdwy 11th: outpcd 16th: no imp after* **12/1**

1136 **5** 5 **Volcanic Rock (IRE)**48 2055 10-11-7 **114**........(t) APMcCoy 94
(John Anthony Staunton, Ire) *hld up: sme hdwy appr 14th: outpcd by ldrs bef 16th: no imp after* **11/2**2

20-3 **6** 30 **Pennek (FR)**31 2401 7-11-5 **119**........ KyleJames(7) 72
(Philip Kirby) *midfield: pushed along fr 4th: nvr travelling after: bhd after 13th: t.o* **15/2**3

-540 **P** **Silver Bay**39 2214 9-11-0 **107**........ LeightonAspell —
(Oliver Sherwood) *bhd: niggled along and outpcd bef 16th: p.u bef 4 out* **16/1**

0U3P **P** **September Moon**25 2532 12-9-9 **93** oh8........ GemmaGracey-Davison(5) —
(Michael Appleby) *led: hdd 6th: lost pl and struggling 8th: t.o whn p.u bef 16th* **33/1**

43PB **P** **Petite Margot**10 2794 11-11-4 **111**........ DavidEngland —
(Nigel Twiston-Davies) *prom: lost pl 8th: bhd 9th: t.o whn p.u bef 16th* **10/1**

-0PP **P** **Fine By Me (IRE)**27 2483 11-11-3 **113**........(b1) PeterToole(3) —
(Julian Smith) *trckd ldrs: blnd 15th: lost grnd qckly and wknd: t.o whn p.u bef 17th* **20/1**

3664 **U** **Shrewd Investor (IRE)**30 2420 10-10-7 **100**........(p) FearghalDavis —
(Henry Hogarth) *prom: led 6th: hdd 16th: 3rd abt 7 l off the pce whn blnd and uns rdr 4 out* **14/1**

7m 58.2s (3.20) **Going Correction** +0.30s/f (Yiel) **11** Ran SP% **114.2**
Speed ratings (Par 107): **107,106,104,100,98 90,**—,—,—,— —
toteswingers:1&2:£1.80, 1&3:£14.30, 2&3:£8.60 CSF £20.42 CT £133.92 TOTE £5.60: £2.00, £1.40, £2.80; EX 12.20.

Owner Ron Bartlett, F J Ayres & Jeff Hulston **Bred** Thomas Maher **Trained** Byton, H'fords

■ Stewards' Enquiry : Robert Thornton caution: used whip with excessive frequency.

FOCUS

A marathon handicap chase in which the first two came clear and are rated as having run slight personal bests. The form looks solid.

NOTEBOOK

Incentivise(IRE) gamely got the better of a protracted struggle with the runner-up to make a winning debut for the Richard Lee yard. Scoring for the first time away from Chepstow, he has abundant stamina and acts on much softer ground too. The minor 'Nationals', which have proliferated in recent seasons, look ideal races for him. (op 5-1)

Gilsland(IRE) was always up there, jumping boldly, and just missed out after a brave battle. Very sadly, this progressive gelding collapsed and died afterwards. (op 100-30, tchd 3-1 in places)

Glebehall Bay(IRE)'s jumping stood up better on this third run over fences and although he was never a threat to the front pair, he stayed on in encouraging fashion. He clearly has plenty of stamina. (op 10-1 tchd 11-1)

Ayemdee(IRE) is perhaps not straightforward but he ran a reasonable race on this step up in trip. The handicapper had dropped him since his last run but he is still 10lb higher than when completing a hat-trick a year ago.

Volcanic Rock(IRE), an Irish challenger, wore a tongue strap for the first time. He had no stamina concerns and ran his race with no obvious excuses. (op 6-1)

Fine By Me(IRE)'s hopes were ended by a shuddering blunder. (op 22-1)

Shrewd Investor(IRE), absent since May, ran well for a long way but looked held in third when parting company. (op 22-1)

2954 PARAMOUNT SECURITY "NATIONAL HUNT" NOVICES' HURDLE (9 hdls) 2m 1f

1:50 (1:51) (Class 4) 4-Y-0+ **£3,415** (£1,002; £501; £250)

Form RPR

1 **Backspin (IRE)**235 5402 5-10-12 0........ APMcCoy 124+
(Jonjo O'Neill) *a.p: lft cl 2nd 5th: led narrowly and stmbld 2 out: asserted last: styd on and in control after* **11/4**1

1-2 **2** 3 **Our Mick**31 2403 4-10-12 0........ JasonMaguire 118+
(Donald McCain) *led: hdd narrowly 2 out: sn rdn: no ex fnl 75yds* **4/1**2

3-32 **3** ½ **Flinty Bay (IRE)**33 2349 5-10-12 115........ DougieCostello 117
(Nicky Richards) *racd keenly: in tch: chsd ldrs 4 out: nt qckn bhd front pair appr last: styd on towards fin: nt quite pce to chal* **8/1**3

-002 **4** 14 **Sara's Smile**24 2547 4-10-2 0........ JohnKington(3) 98
(Donald McCain) *midfield: swvd to avoid casualties 5th: hdwy to chse ldrs 4 out: one pce u.p fr 2 out* **40/1**

3 **5** ¾ **Loch Ba (IRE)**39 2215 4-10-12 0........ HaddenFrost 103+
(Henrietta Knight) *trckd ldrs: pushed along and btn appr 2 out* **66/1**

4041 **6** 1 ¼ **Attaglance**27 2473 4-11-0 120........ JamesHalliday(5) 109
(Malcolm Jefferson) *midfield: sme hdwy 3 out: no imp on ldrs: nvr able to chal* **14/1**

40- **7** ½ **Briefcase (IRE)**314 3852 5-10-12 0........ DavidEngland 102
(Nigel Twiston-Davies) *hld up: hdwy into midfield 5th: outpcd fr 3 out* **100/1**

8 1 ½ **Sivola De Sivola (FR)** 4-10-12 0........ DenisO'Regan 101
(Tom George) *hld up: styd on fr 2 out: nvr rchd ldrs* **100/1**

34-4 **9** 11 **Lucky Sunny (IRE)**32 2362 7-10-12 0........ TomSiddall 91
(Richard Phillips) *racd keenly: hld up: sme prog 2 out: nvr on terms* **50/1**

5 **10** hd **Gentle Bob (IRE)**32 2365 5-10-9 0........ PeterToole(3) 90
(Tom George) *midfield: nt fluent 3 out and 2 out: nvr on terms w ldrs* **100/1**

45-5 **11** 1 ¼ **Takamaru (FR)**27 2482 4-10-12 0........ TomScudamore 89
(David Pipe) *in tch: pushed along and wknd 4 out* **25/1**

03 **12** 16 **Copsehill Girl (IRE)**98 1505 5-9-12 0........ TrevorWhelan(7) 68
(Ian Williams) *a bhd* **33/1**

13 11 **The Old Buccaneer (IRE)**1312 255 7-10-9 0........ RichieMcLernon(3) 65
(Jonjo O'Neill) *a bhd* **66/1**

13-1 **F** **High Benefit (IRE)**28 2456 5-10-12 0........ RobertThornton —
(Alan King) *prom: cl 2nd whn fell 5th* **11/4**1

00-0 **U** **Aitch Factor**21 2612 4-10-12 0........ FearghalDavis —
(Henry Hogarth) *hld up: overj. and uns rdr 1st* **200/1**

54 **U** **Renard D'Irlande (FR)**26 2499 5-10-5 0........ HarryChalloner(7) —
(Venetia Williams) *chsd ldrs tl hmpd and uns rdr 5th* **16/1**

4m 2.00s (-8.90) **Going Correction** -0.20s/f (Good) **16** Ran SP% **114.6**
Speed ratings (Par 105): **112,110,110,103,103 102,102,101,96,96 96,88,83,**—,— —
toteswingers:1&2:£3.10, 1&3:£5.30, 2&3:£3.80 CSF £12.25 TOTE £3.60: £1.50, £1.60, £2.60; EX 13.60.

Owner John P McManus **Bred** Brittas House Stud **Trained** Cheltenham, Gloucs

FOCUS

A year ago a division of this novice hurdle was won by Peddlers Cross, and the likes of Whiteoak, My Way De Solzen and Garde Champetre have also been successful in the past decade. This year's race may not have contained any stars but could well prove a fertile source of future winners, with the fourth and fifth setting the level.

NOTEBOOK

Backspin(IRE), who hails from a good jumping family, beat a big field in a Punchestown bumper in April on his sole start for Margaret Mullins. Running out a fluent winner on this first run for his powerful new connections, he looks a useful prospect but will be kept to a realistic level for now as he builds up experience. (op 5-2 tchd 3-1)

Our Mick, from the stable of Peddlers Cross and Whiteoak, both of whom won this race, made most of the running but could not hold off the winner between the last two flights. This was a pleasing hurdles debut and he should soon go one better. (op 9-2 tchd 7-2)

Flinty Bay(IRE) came home well for third and has now been placed on all four of his starts, the first of them a bumper, without getting his head in front. A stiffer test may well suit. (tchd 17-2)

Sara's Smile, the McCain second string, improved on what she showed when runner-up at Kelso and looks sure to win a little race, perhaps over a little further against her own sex.

Loch Ba(IRE), third to the promising Knight Pass in a Sandown bumper last month, made a pleasing debut over hurdles and is another who should make the grade.

Attaglance was never able to land a blow at the leaders but ran his race under the penalty. (op 16-1)

Briefcase(IRE) showed a bit of promise on this hurdles debut and may benefit from a step up in trip.

Sivola De Sivola(FR) showed a bit of promise on this debut.

Lucky Sunny(IRE), who raced keenly in rear again, shaped with a degree of promise but has stamina concerns. Official explanation: trainer's rep said gelding bled from the nose

Gentle Bob(IRE), a chasing type, hinted at ability.

High Benefit(IRE), successful at Warwick on her hurdling debut, was close up when taking a heavy fall at the fifth. (op 5-2, tchd 3-1 in a place)

2955 ALFA AGGREGATES H'CAP HURDLE (12 hdls) 3m
2:25 (2:25) (Class 3) (0-135,129) 4-Y-O+ **£7,155** (£2,101; £1,050; £524)

Form RPR

3411 **1** **Bellflower Boy (IRE)**[20] 2644 7-11-3 **120**..................(tp) TomScudamore 128+
(Dr Richard Newland) *towards rr: hdwy 7th: led 3 out: kpt up to work run-in* **7/1**

210 **2** ¾ **Silver Accord (IRE)**[20] 2637 7-10-10 **113**........................ LeightonAspell 119
(Oliver Sherwood) *hld up: hmpd 4th: hdwy 8th: chsd wnr appr 2 out: sn ev ch: styd on but a looked hld run-in* **9/1**

1260 **3** 9 **Worth A King'S**[24] 2542 4-10-12 **115**................................. JasonMaguire 115
(Donald McCain) *midfield: reminder after 3rd: hdwy appr 3 out: chsd ldrs 2 out: no ex fr last* **16/1**

34-0 **4** 6 **Sandofthecolosseum (IRE)**[33] 2347 5-10-10 **113**......... DougieCostello 107
(Alex Hales) *prom: led appr 4 out: hdd 3 out: rdn and wknd 2 out* **9/2**[2]

5-F4 **5** 23 **Galaxy Rock (IRE)**[19] 2663 6-11-12 **129**................................ APMcCoy 104
(Jonjo O'Neill) *in tch: chalng 4 out: wknd appr 2 out* **7/2**[1]

-004 **6** 7 **Fin Vin De Leu (GER)**[31] 2399 4-11-2 **122**.......................... PeterToole(3) 88
(Charlie Mann) *hld up: reminder after 3rd: hmpd 4th: hdwy 7th: rdn 8th: wknd 3 out* **11/1**

PP-P **7** 6 **Flintoff (USA)**[33] 2346 9-10-9 **112**.. RodiGreene 72
(Venetia Williams) *in rr: nt fluent 2nd: a rdn along: nvr on terms* **16/1**

1-56 **8** 5 **Munlochy Bay**[25] 2514 6-9-9 **105**...................................(p) MrLRPayter(7) 61
(Matt Sheppard) *hld up: struggling fr 7th: nt fluent 8th: nvr on terms* **13/2**[3]

001- **9** 7 **Beamazed**[309] 3955 6-10-10 **113**.. DenisO'Regan 62
(Malcolm Jefferson) *led: hdd appr 4 out: sn wknd* **11/1**

00-5 **10** 17 **Helens Vision**[25] 2514 7-10-3 **113**...................................... MarkQuinlan(7) 47
(James Evans) *trckd ldrs: lost pl bef 7th: struggling and n.d 4 out* **8/1**

1PPP **P** **Tisfreetdream (IRE)**[26] 2497 9-11-2 **122**..............(b[1]) RichieMcLernon(3) —
(Peter Pritchard) *trckd ldrs: lost pl 6th: wl bhd whn p.u bef 8th* **40/1**

13-P **F** **Leac An Scail (IRE)**[171] 844 9-10-12 **120**...................... ShaneByrne(5) —
(Sue Smith) *trckd ldrs tl fell 4th* **25/1**

5m 41.5s (-9.50) **Going Correction** -0.20s/f (Good)
WFA 4 from 5yo+ 7lb 12 Ran SP% **122.1**
Speed ratings (Par 107): **107,106,103,101,94 91,89,88,85,80** —,—
toteswingers:1&2:£19.10, 1&3:£7.60, 2&3:£30.50 CSF £70.86 CT £991.09 TOTE £8.30: £2.90, £3.30, £4.70; EX 86.30.
Owner The Five Nations Partnership **Bred** Frank Sinnott **Trained** Claines, Worcs

FOCUS

A fair handicap and the most valuable race of the day, this was run at a sound pace. The third and fourth help to set the level.

NOTEBOOK

Bellflower Boy(IRE) shrugged off an 11lb rise to supplement last month's wins at Huntingdon and Uttoxeter. The return to 3m suited and he appeared to win a little more easily than the fairly narrow margin would suggest, so a four-timer may not be out of the question. (op 15-2)

Silver Accord(IRE) emerged as the main threat to the winner off the home turn and went down fighting. Putting a below-par run behind him, this proved his stamina for 3m, on a fairly sharp track such as this at least.

Worth A King'S had been dropped 3lb since an uncharacteristically poor effort at Aintree. This was better and he seemed to get the 3m well enough.

Sandofthecolosseum(IRE) faded from the home turn. Ideally he needs more give underfoot, and he will not be seen to best effect until he goes chasing. (op 11-2)

Galaxy Rock(IRE) ran creditably under topweight but was the first of the leading five to crack. He remains 11lb higher than when last winning a year back. (op 5-1)

Beamazed, who has left Tim Walford since winning over an extended 3m3f at Sedgefield in February, should last longer next time. (op 12-1)

2956 NORTHERN RACING CLUB 30TH ANNIVERSARY CONDITIONAL JOCKEYS' H'CAP HURDLE (9 hdls) 2m 1f
3:00 (3:00) (Class 4) (0-100,99) 3-Y-O+ **£3,082** (£898; £449)

Form RPR

0623 **1** **Nouailhas**[38] 2244 4-10-11 **89**.. PeterHatton(5) 96+
(Reg Hollinshead) *racd keenly: hld up in midfield: hdwy to go prom 3rd: mstke and led 2 out: drew clr last: r.o wl* **7/1**

PP-4 **2** 6 **Vin Rose**[123] 1253 5-10-10 **83**.. PeterToole 84
(Mark Rimell) *hld up: hdwy appr 3 out: rdn to take 2nd bef last: no imp on wnr* **11/2**[3]

3454 **3** 3 **Sonic Anthem (USA)**[64] 1816 8-11-7 **94**......................... DonalDevereux 92
(John Mackie) *led: rdn and hdd 2 out: no ex last* **5/1**[2]

-542 **4** 5 **Present Your Case (IRE)**[30] 2425 5-11-5 **92**......................(t) DavidBass 86
(Ben Case) *midfield: hdwy 4 out: rdn whn chsd ldrs appr 2 out: sn one pce* **11/4**[1]

501F **5** nk **Petit Fleur**[25] 2530 8-11-7 **99**................................... StephenO'Donovan(5) 93
(Julian Smith) *hld up: hdwy 3 out: one pce and no imp fr 2 out* **8/1**

6P54 **6** 6 **Standing Order**[29] 2433 7-9-11 **73**...............................(t) HarryChalloner(3) 61
(Richard Ford) *in tch: effrt 3 out: wknd bef 2 out* **12/1**

0000 **7** 21 **Sheezatreasure (IRE)**[20] 2634 5-10-10 **86**.....................(p) RobertKirk(3) 55
(James Evans) *prom: nt fluent and lost pl 5th: nt fluent whn struggling 4 out: bhd after* **40/1**

06-0 **8** nk **Pezula**[214] 336 4-9-9 **73**.. PeterCarberry(5) 42
(Richard Phillips) *in tch: stmbld 3rd: rdn appr 5th: wknd 3 out* **16/1**

334 **9** ½ **Miss Miracle**[29] 2439 3-9-13 **89**.. RichieMcLernon(3) 44
(Jonjo O'Neill) *trckd ldrs: nt fluent 3rd: rdn and wknd 4 out* **11/2**[3]

6455 **10** 9 **Mad Professor (IRE)**[45] 2113 7-10-0 **79**......................(p) JoeCornwall(6) 39
(John Cornwall) *a bhd: struggling fr 5th: nvr on terms* **25/1**

4m 7.20s (-3.70) **Going Correction** -0.20s/f (Good)
WFA 3 from 4yo 13lb 4 from 5yo+ 5lb 10 Ran SP% **117.6**
Speed ratings (Par 105): **100,97,95,93,93 90,80,80,80,75**
toteswingers:1&2:£6.70, 1&3:£5.90, 2&3:£2.30 CSF £46.20 CT £212.53 TOTE £7.70: £2.90, £2.30, £2.00; EX 48.20.
Owner C W Wardle & Mrs J E Wardle **Bred** J D Graham **Trained** Upper Longdon, Staffs

FOCUS

A modest handicap for conditional jockeys. The time was over 5 secs slower than the earlier novice hurdle. The runner-up is rated close to form and sets the level.

NOTEBOOK

Nouailhas had been placed on his last two starts and a drop in trip saw him get off the mark on this sixth hurdles start. Despite carrying his head a little high, he found plenty to assert after a mistake two out. He holds an entry at Hereford next week and escapes a penalty for this. (op 8-1 tchd 13-2)

Vin Rose had not been seen for four months, but seems to go well fresh and the three who beat her last time out have all won since. She improved under a patient ride but was never a serious threat to the winner. (op 9-2)

Sonic Anthem(USA) made the running as usual but could not fend off the winner on the home turn. He is pretty consistent but his last win came back in the summer of 2008.

Present Your Case(IRE) did not travel quite as well over this shorter trip and was held off her 7lb higher mark. (op 4-1, tchd 9-2 in a place)

Petit Fleur was not discredited but is currently around a stone higher than when winning two starts back. (op 15-2 tchd 7-1)

Miss Miracle raced keenly on this handicap debut and was in trouble not long after halfway. (op 7-1)

2957 VOTE A.P. MCCOY IN BBC SPOTY INTERMEDIATE OPEN NATIONAL HUNT FLAT RACE 2m 1f
3:35 (3:40) (Class 5) 4-6-Y-O **£1,712** (£499; £249)

Form RPR

3 **1** **Avoca Promise (IRE)**[25] 2518 5-11-2 0......................... JimmyMcCarthy 108+
(Charles Egerton) *hld up in midfield: hdwy 5f out: led over 2f out: rn green: r.o wl fnl f* **4/1**[3]

1- **2** 2 **Raya Star (IRE)**[270] 4744 4-11-9 0.................................. RobertThornton 113
(Alan King) *hld up: hdwy 6f out: rdn over 2f out: chsd wnr over 1f out: styd on but unable to get to wnr* **3/1**[2]

3 2¼ **Knockalongi** 4-11-2 0.. APMcCoy 104
(Rebecca Curtis) *prom: led over 4f out: hdd over 2f out: kpt on same pce fr over 1f out* **8/1**

4 1 **Kings Lodge** 4-10-11 0.. DavidBass(5) 103
(Nicky Henderson) *in tch: green and outpcd over 6f out: hdwy over 3f out: chsd ldrs over 2f out: styd on same pce after* **9/4**[1]

5 3 **Mickytaker (IRE)**[226] 5-10-6 0...................................... PeterHatton(10) 102+
(Alan King) *hld up: hdwy into midfield 6f out: rdn over 2f out: one pce fr over 1f out* **16/1**

5 dht **Hayjack** 5-10-9 0... HarryChalloner(7) 101
(Venetia Williams) *midfield: pushed along 1/2-way: styd on fnl 2f: nt pce to chal ldrs* **40/1**

2 **7** 5 **Kent Street (IRE)**[33] 2355 5-10-6 0....................... BenjaminStephens(10) 96
(Sue Smith) *prom tl outpcd over 3f out: n.d after* **20/1**

8 4 **Cap Falco (IRE)** 5-10-11 0... GilesHawkins(5) 92
(Anabel L M King) *hld up in midfield: n.m.r 6f out: kpt on fr over 1f out: nt rch ldrs* **33/1**

3 **9** 4½ **Deciding Moment (IRE)**[34] 2328 4-11-2 0........................ LeightonAspell 89
(Ben De Haan) *in tch: effrt 4f out: wknd 2f out* **22/1**

10 2 **Stickaround** 5-10-9 0.. DenisO'Regan 80
(Malcolm Jefferson) *hld up: pushed along over 3f out: kpt on fnl 2f: nvr able to trble ldrs* **66/1**

11 1¼ **Spirit Of Barbados (IRE)** 4-11-2 0............................. TomScudamore 85
(David Pipe) *led: hdd after 2f: remained prom: rdn 4f out: wknd 3f out* **22/1**

12 3½ **So Fine (IRE)** 4-10-13 0.. RichieMcLernon(3) 82
(Anabel L M King) *midfield: struggling over 5f out: nvr a danger* **100/1**

13 ½ **Steeldrivinman** 4-11-2 0.. JasonMaguire 82
(Donald McCain) *racd keenly: prom: led after 2f: hdd over 4f out: wknd over 2f out* **11/1**

14 7 **Rascella Bay** 4-10-13 0... PeterToole(3) 76
(Charlie Mann) *trckd ldrs tl rdn and wknd over 4f out* **16/1**

15 2¾ **Commander Jet** 4-11-2 0.. JodieMogford 73
(Brian Baugh) *a bhd* **125/1**

0- **16** 37 **Escape Exit**[312] 3901 5-10-6 0...................................... CiaranMckee(10) 40
(Tom George) *trckd ldrs: pushed along 7f out: wknd 6f out: t.o* **100/1**

0 **17** 44 **Blantyre**[40] 2186 4-11-2 0.. HaddenFrost —
(Henrietta Knight) *broke loose bef r: midfield: rdn and wknd 5f out: t.o* **100/1**

3m 58.8s (-6.50) **Going Correction** -0.20s/f (Good) 17 Ran SP% **131.1**
Speed ratings: **107,106,105,104,103 103,100,98,96,95 95,93,93,90,88 71,50**
toteswingers:1&2:£8.40, 1&3:£17.30, 2&3:£10.20 CSF £16.43 TOTE £6.60: £2.20, £1.60, £3.70; EX 18.40.
Owner Bailey-Carvill Equine **Bred** Kenneth Parkhill **Trained** Chaddleworth, Berks

FOCUS

They went a reasonable gallop in this bumper, which should work out and produce a few winners.

NOTEBOOK

Avoca Promise(IRE) showed ability on his debut at Ascot and confirmed the decent impression on this second run. Surviving an anxious moment when stumbling in the back straight, he came through to win nicely. He may not be wholly straightforward, but has an engine and looks a scopey type.

Raya Star(IRE) ran well under the penalty he picked up when winning at Uttoxeter in the spring. Softer ground will help when he switches to hurdles. (op 11-2)

Knockalongi's trainer does well with her bumper horses and this one, a cheap buy, made a pleasing debut. (op 15-2)

Kings Lodge ◆ is out of a bumper winner who was a sister to the high-class hurdler Marello. He lost his place quite markedly before staying on, and will have learned plenty from this experience. (op 11-4 tchd 3-1 in places)

Mickytaker(IRE) won a 2m4f point in the spring and ran a creditable race on this rules debut. (op 50-1 tchd 33-1)

Hayjack is a half-brother to winning hurdler Shanxi Girl out of a prolific jumping mare. He stayed on nicely and should not let the family down. (op 50-1 tchd 33-1)

Cap Falco(IRE) cost £140,000 as a 3yo and, after appearing to be struggling, ultimately stayed on in pleasing fashion.

Deciding Moment(IRE), third at Ludlow on his debut, looked a threat on the home turn buit his effort soon fizzled out. (op 20-1)

Steeldrivinman Official explanation: jockey said gelding ran too free

T/Plt: £64.50 to a £1 stake. Pool:£57,946.94 - 655.00 winning tickets T/Qpdt: £12.10 to a £1 stake. Pool:£4,084.08 - 249.30 winning tickets DO

2667 NEWBURY (L-H)
Wednesday, December 15

OFFICIAL GOING: Good (good to soft in places)

Rails on chase course moved out adding 35m to advertised distances. Rails on hurdle course moved out adding 26m to advertised distances.

Wind: Virtually nil

2958 BLACKMORE BUILDING JUVENILE HURDLE (8 hdls) 2m 110y
11:55 (11:56) (Class 4) 3-Y-O **£3,903** (£1,146; £573; £286)

Form RPR

1 **Third Intention (IRE)**[165] 3-10-12 0....................................... JoeTizzard 114+
(Colin Tizzard) *chsd clr ldr: remained cl 2nd 2 out: drvn to chal last: led sn after: forged clr fnl 75yds* **16/1**

5 **2** *2 3/4* **Titan De Sarti (FR)**[32] 2356 3-10-12 0 BarryGeraghty 113+
(Nicky Henderson) *chsd ldrs: nt fluent 2nd to 4th: mstke 4 out: qcknd to trck ldr 3 out: led sn after: rdn and jnd last: hdd sn after: kpt on u.p tl no ex and one pce fnl 75yds* **15/8**[2]

3 *6* **Empire Levant (USA)**[181] 3-10-12 0 NoelFehily 110+
(Paul Nicholls) *chsd ldrs: disputing cl 3rd whn blnd 3 out: kpt on again fr next: tk 3rd last: edgd lft and green run-in: kpt on but nt a threat to ldng duo* **13/8**[1]

66 **4** *2 1/4* **Professeur Emery (FR)**[19] 2661 3-10-12 0 WayneHutchinson 104
(Warren Greatrex) *t.k.h: led: sn clr: c bk to field 3 out: hdd sn after: one pce appr last* **100/1**

1F3 **5** *10* **Whipperway (IRE)**[29] 2439 3-10-9 104 MarcGoldstein(3) 95
(Sheena West) *in tch: drvn to chse ldrs 3 out: nvr quite on terms: wknd fr 2 out* **33/1**

6 *4* **Looks Like Slim**[43] 3-10-12 0 DarylJacob 91
(Ben De Haan) *hld up in rr: stdy hdwy but nt a threat whn sltly hmpd 2 out: kpt on again run-in* **100/1**

03 **7** *nk* **Tatispout (FR)**[21] 2614 3-10-5 96 AndrewTinkler 84
(Charlie Longsdon) *mid-div: hdwy fr 4 out: in tch: next: nvr on terms and wknd fr 2 out* **50/1**

8 *25* **Langley**[98] 3-10-9 0 MichaelMurphy(3) 68
(Pat Murphy) *mid-div: hdwy 4 out: drvn and in tch 3 out but nvr on terms: gng lft and btn whn sltly hmpd 2 out* **50/1**

5R0 **9** *8* **Othello (IRE)**[87] 1545 3-10-5 0 MissJennyCarr(7) 61
(Jonjo O'Neill) *a towards rr* **150/1**

3003 **10** *1/2* **Dr Finley (IRE)**[29] 2438 3-10-12 105 (p) GerardTumelty 61
(Jeff Pearce) *in tch: rdn after 4 out: wknd next* **25/1**

11 *9* **Captain Cool (IRE)**[10] 3-10-12 0 DominicElsworth 52
(Richard Hannon) *chsd ldrs tl wknd 3 out* **40/1**

12 *7* **Rare Symphony (IRE)**[59] 3-10-5 0 RichardJohnson 39
(Philip Hobbs) *a towards rr: lost tch after 4 out* **9/2**[3]

13 *20* **Wild Geese (IRE)**[100] 3-10-9 0 CharlieHuxley(3) 28
(Jonathan Portman) *bhd fr 1/2-way* **80/1**

6 **14** *27* **Dream Spinner**[25] 2528 3-10-7 0 IanPopham(5) 4
(Dr Richard Newland) *blnd 3 out: a bhd* **50/1**

15 *15* **Time Square (FR)**[58] 3-10-12 0 (t) PaulMoloney —
(Tony Carroll) *hit 4th: blnd 3 out: a wl bhd* **100/1**

5 **F** **Dragon's Den (IRE)**[42] 2151 3-10-12 0 JamesDavies 91
(Chris Down) *in tch: rdn and no imp 3 out: 7th and no ch w ldrs whn fell 2 out* **50/1**

3m 57.31s (-12.59) **Going Correction** -0.425s/f (Good) **16** Ran SP% **118.9**
Speed ratings (Par 104): **112,110,107,106,102 100,100,88,84,84 80,76,67,54,47** —
toteswingers:1&2:£7.10, 1&3:£6.00, 2&3:£1.10 CSF £44.88 TOTE £17.50: £3.60, £1.20, £1.40; EX 54.80.
Owner Robert And Sarah Tizzard **Bred** Richard Klay And Dr M Klay **Trained** Milborne Port, Dorset

FOCUS
An intriguing contest that was run at a decent pace and produced a very good time. The fifth looks the best guide to the level.

NOTEBOOK
Third Intention(IRE) ◆, from a stable not associated with juvenile hurdlers, put up a decent performance. A winner over an extended 1m4f trip in Ireland, and a half-brother to winning Flat stayer Theola, he was always well placed and stayed on really strongly on his first run since July (he had also been gelded in that time) to get by the runner-up after being passed by him before two out. He announced himself as a creditable Triumph Hurdle candidate, although connections were reportedly pleasantly surprised by the way their horse performed in this.
Titan De Sarti(FR), representing a stable with a tremendous record in this contest, was sent off favourite to beat current Triumph Hurdle favourite Sam Winner on his British debut, but was beaten over 32l into fifth. His jumping early was far from fluent and he looked in trouble some way out, but he came back on the bridle up the home straight and got to the lead going well. His jumping improved the further he went, but he was unable to repel the winner after the final hurdle. (op 2-1 tchd 13-8)
Empire Levant(USA) ◆, highly regarded but said to be big and backward, was prominent in the Triumph Hurdle betting after showing good form on the Flat in France, and moved like a decent performer until walking through three out. He lost his place there, before staying on again, and showed more than enough to suggest he will be winning races before too long. (op 2-1 tchd 9-4)
Professeur Emery(FR) set a decent pace and did really well to keep on for fourth, especially as he'd been well beaten on his two previous attempts over hurdles.
Whipperway(IRE) kept plugging away and gives the race a guide considering she has an official mark.
Looks Like Slim made steady headway up the home straight to show some promise. (op 125-1)
Captain Cool(IRE) had plenty of racing on the Flat for this trainer, and collected a couple of victories, one at 1m2f and another at 1m6f. Seeming to want at least good ground in that sphere, he was prominent early but faded on turning into the home straight. (op 33-1)
Rare Symphony(IRE), twice a winner at up to 1m 1.5f on the Flat in Ireland, was without any headgear on her hurdling debut for Philip Hobbs (she wore something on four of her last five starts) and needed pushing leaving the back straight. She made no impression from that point onwards.
Time Square(FR) Official explanation: jockey said gelding ran too free

2959 BLUE SQUARE DONATE £5K TO RACING WELFARE NOVICES' CHASE (LIMITED H'CAP) (18 fncs) 3m

12:25 (12:26) (Class 3) (0-125,125)
4-Y-0+ **£5,854** (£1,719; £859; £429)

Form RPR

0/13 **1** **Major Malarkey (IRE)**[35] 2305 7-11-6 121 PaddyBrennan 135+
(Nigel Twiston-Davies) *chsd ldrs: blnd 14th: chsd ldr next: led last: hld on wl towards fin* **12/1**

P1-4 **2** *3/4* **Promising Anshan (IRE)**[222] 191 5-11-5 120 HarrySkelton 131
(Paul Nicholls) *hld up in mid-div: trckd ldrs 13th: upsides last: kpt on same pce fnl 75yds* **6/1**[2]

2-U2 **3** *1 3/4* **Ikorodu Road**[53] 1970 7-11-10 125 JohnnyFarrelly 135
(Martin Keighley) *w ldrs: led 5th: hdd last: hung lft and styd on same pce* **11/1**

13-3 **4** *14* **Double Pride**[32] 2363 6-11-2 117 WayneHutchinson 116
(Alan King) *hld up in rr: hdwy to trck ldrs 8th: hit 14th: one pce whn j.rt 2 out* **7/1**

42 **5** *nk* **Three Chords (IRE)**[20] 2641 6-10-9 110 AndrewThornton 107
(Caroline Bailey) *hld up towards rr: hdwy 13th: one pce whn j.rt 2 out* **25/1**

43-2 **6** *11* **Reblis (FR)**[35] 2311 5-10-10 111 (p) JamieMoore 98
(Gary Moore) *chsd ldrs: drvn 13th: wknd 3 out* **25/1**

320/ **7** *1 1/4* **Space Mission (IRE)**[663] 4042 8-11-0 115 DominicElsworth 103
(Paul Webber) *in rr: hdwy 15th: nvr on terms: 7th whn blnd 2 out* **25/1**

34-6 **8** *19* **Moleskin (IRE)**[43] 2140 7-11-7 122 DarylJacob 91
(Victor Dartnall) *chsd ldrs: wknd 4 out* **33/1**

34-P **9** *5* **Pliny (IRE)**[24] 2545 6-10-9 110 AidanColeman 74
(Venetia Williams) *w ldrs: wknd after 4 out* **33/1**

2164 **10** *11* **Alldunnandusted (IRE)**[29] 2441 6-10-9 113 JimmyDerham(3) 67
(Seamus Mullins) *nt fluent in rr: bhd fr 14th* **50/1**

-F51 **11** *1 1/2* **Near The Water (IRE)**[22] 2591 6-10-3 111 MrTJCannon(7) 64
(Richard Rowe) *in rr whn hmpd 1st: nt fluent: bhd fr 12th* **33/1**

-221 **12** *26* **Key Cutter (FR)**[23] 2580 6-11-7 122 (t) WillKennedy 51
(Paul Webber) *j.rt: led: mstke 3rd: hdd 5th: lost pl 14th: bhd whn blnd 2 out* **10/1**

110- **13** *8* **Topsham Belle (IRE)**[263] 4889 6-11-6 121 BarryGeraghty 43
(Nicky Henderson) *chsd ldrs: wknd 13th: bhd fr 4 out: t.o 2 out* **13/2**[3]

02-4 **P** **Mealagh Valley (IRE)**[195] 597 9-10-1 105 oh3.. SamTwiston-Davies(3) —
(Ben De Haan) *in rr: drvn 10th: bhd whn j.rt 14th: t.o whn p.u bef next* **28/1**

-452 **F** **Russian Song (IRE)**[26] 2502 6-10-6 107 JoeTizzard —
(Colin Tizzard) *in rr whn fell 1st* **9/1**

-103 **F** **Mostly Bob (IRE)**[19] 2663 7-11-10 125 (t) RichardJohnson —
(Philip Hobbs) *hld up in rr: smooth hdwy to trck ldrs 11th: ev ch whn fell 4 out* **11/2**[1]

5m 57.3s (-13.70) **Going Correction** -0.375s/f (Good) **16** Ran SP% **116.4**
Speed ratings (Par 107): **107,106,106,101,101 97,97,90,89,85 85,76,73,—,— —**
toteswingers:1&2:£16.00, 1&3:£35.30, 2&3:£70.70 CSF £72.51 CT £824.32 TOTE £11.50: £2.50, £2.10, £3.80, £2.00; EX 99.70.
Owner Baker Dodd & Cooke **Bred** Bill Ronayne **Trained** Naunton, Gloucs

FOCUS
A race won two years ago by Tricky Trickster, trained by this year's winning trainer, who is now three from three in this race, so this is a result worth following. The gallop seemed fair for the trip, but plenty held a chance turning in before three pulled nicely clear. The form looks solid rated around the third and fourth.

NOTEBOOK
Major Malarkey(IRE) ◆, 12lb higher than winning a novice handicap chase at Chepstow in November after a lengthy absence, made a couple of mistakes, the worst of which looked to be five out, but shows plenty of courage and kept putting his head down when his jockey asked for maximum effort. He is clearly a strong stayer and the National Hunt Chase at the festival in the preferred target this season. (op 14-1)
Promising Anshan(IRE) ◆, over 9l behind Mostly Bob when last on the course, and making his debut for Paul Nicholls, had an operation for his breathing since moving to Ditcheat. Tucked away in rear, he made his way through runners into a challenging position but could not force himself into a clear lead. This was a promising start to his chasing career under rules, and he'll no doubt be found the right opportunities by connections. (tchd 11-2 and 13-2)
Ikorodu Road ◆, trying 3m for the first time, had chasing experience and kept on really well after racing prominently. He had no problems with the distance and has plenty of scope for improvement. (op 10-1)
Double Pride, a well-related sort, showed more than enough to suggest he will be winning over fences before the end of the season.
Three Chords(IRE) ◆, a half-brother to L'Accordioniste, showed plenty of promise after travelling strongly for much of the contest.
Reblis(FR), with cheekpieces back on, was always thereabouts and plugged on. (tchd 33-1)
Space Mission(IRE) ◆, having his first run since February 2009, really caught the eye making progress from the rear and is one to be interested in next time. (op 40-1)
Topsham Belle(IRE) looked a fascinating contender on her chasing debut considering her lack of experience, but she appeared beaten a long way from home, and must rate a bit disappointing. It will be interesting to see whether she goes in against just her own sex next time. (op 9-2)
Mealagh Valley(IRE) Official explanation: vet said gelding pulled up lame (op 15-2)
Mostly Bob(IRE), making his chasing debut, finished a respectable third to Barafundle over this course and similar distance last time. He was still in with every chance when falling four out, and looks a nice prospect if his confidence isn't affected by this mishap. (op 15-2)

2960 FIRST GREAT WESTERN MAIDEN HURDLE (8 hdls) 2m 110y

12:55 (12:58) (Class 4) 4-Y-0+ **£3,903** (£1,146; £573; £286)

Form RPR

1 **Minella Class (IRE)**[276] 4627 5-11-0 0 BarryGeraghty 122+
(Nicky Henderson) *trckd ldrs: qcknd to chal travelling wl 2 out: led sn after: shkn up run-in: styd on strly* **4/1**[2]

2 *3 1/2* **Red Merlin (IRE)**[67] 5-11-0 0 PaddyBrennan 115+
(Donald McCain) *hld up towards rr: hdwy fr 4 out: trckd ldrs 4 out: styd on fr 2 out to chse wnr last: kpt on wl run-in but a readily hld* **5/1**[3]

3 **3** *6* **Pateese (FR)**[26] 2499 5-11-0 0 RichardJohnson 109
(Philip Hobbs) *slt ld after 1st: narrowly hdd 3rd: styd upsides tl narrow advantage 4 out: jnd 2 out: hdd sn after: lost 2nd last and sn outpcd* **14/1**

0-21 **4** *2* **Poole Master**[20] 2646 5-10-11 0 ChrisHonour(3) 107
(David Pipe) *trckd ldrs: ev ch and nt fluent 3 out: hanging lft appr next: outpcd sn after* **12/1**

113 **5** *3* **Kartanian (IRE)**[31] 2389 4-11-0 0 TomO'Brien 104
(Philip Hobbs) *chsd ldrs: rdn fr 3 out: styd on same pce fr next* **7/2**[1]

22- **6** *4 1/2* **Zarinski (IRE)**[389] 2430 4-11-0 0 RegisSchmidlin 100
(Nicky Henderson) *chsd ldrs: hit 2nd: stl wl there 3 out: rdn and one pce next: drvn and kpt on again run-in* **28/1**

7 *1/2* **Shootin The Breeze (IRE)** 5-10-11 0 DannyCook(3) 100
(David Pipe) *in rr: kpt on wl fr 2 out: styd on run-in but nvr any threat* **66/1**

8 *7* **Cotillion**[60] 4-11-0 0 WayneHutchinson 93
(Ian Williams) *in rr: hdwy after 4 out: nvr quite rchd ldrs: wknd fr 2 out* **5/1**[3]

4 **9** *4* **Kaolak (USA)**[53] 1962 4-11-0 0 JamesReveley 93+
(Keith Reveley) *in rr: hdwy appr 3 out: nvr quite on terms: wknd 2 out* **12/1**

6 **10** *2* **Drummers Drumming (USA)**[7] 2426 4-11-0 0 (t) MarkBradburne 88
(Charlie Morlock) *led tl after 1st: styd pressing ldrs: stl wl there 3 out: wknd fr next* **200/1**

0 **11** *3 3/4* **Free Falling**[5] 2289 4-10-7 0 WillKennedy 78
(Alastair Lidderdale) *in rr: sme prog fr 3 out* **150/1**

12 *2 3/4* **Clowance House**[459] 4-11-0 0 AidanColeman 82
(Venetia Williams) *pressed ldrs: ev ch 3 out: wknd sn after* **50/1**

4 **13** *11* **Admirable Duque (IRE)**[40] 2181 4-11-0 0 MarkGrant 72
(Dominic Ffrench Davis) *chsd ldrs to 3 out: wknd next* **150/1**

4-13 **14** *1 1/4* **Fountains Flypast**[38] 2241 6-10-9 0 (t) RachaelGreen(5) 71
(Anthony Honeyball) *chsd ldrs to 3 out* **16/1**

15 *1 1/2* **Non Dom (IRE)**[436] 4-11-0 0 JamieMoore 70
(Hughie Morrison) *in rr: hdwy to get in tch appr 4 out: wknd next* **20/1**

60-3 **16** *6* **Chervonet (IRE)**[29] 2440 4-11-0 0 (t) LiamTreadwell 64
(Nick Gifford) *a in rr* **150/1**

6-4 **17** *nk* **According**[44] 2122 4-11-0 0 AndrewTinkler 64
(Nicky Henderson) *pressed ldr 2nd: slt ld 3rd tl hdd 4 out: stl ev ch next: wknd bef 2 out* **33/1**

18 *3/4* **Highland Legacy**[54] 6-10-11 0 MarcGoldstein(3) 63
(Jim Best) *mstke 2nd: sn bhd* **66/1**

19 *58* **Cils Blancs (IRE)**[77] 4-10-7 0 .... JamesDavies 4
(Michael Scudamore) *a towards rr: t.o* **150/1**

03 **20** *14* **Attainable**[34] 2331 4-10-7 0 .... (t) RhysFlint —
(Jim Old) *a in rr: t.o* **150/1**

21 *11* **Louie's Lad**[41] 4-10-7 0 .... MrJackSalmon(7) —
(John Bridger) *in tch early: rdn and wknd 4 out: t.o* **250/1**

P **Lang Shining (IRE)**[45] 6-11-0 0 .... SamThomas —
(Jamie Osborne) *in rr: sme hdwy after 4 out: sn wknd: t.o whn p.u bef 2 out* **50/1**

4m 0.13s (-9.77) **Going Correction** -0.425s/f (Good) **22** Ran SP% **125.8**
Speed ratings (Par 105): **105,103,100,99,98 96,95,92,90,89 87,86,81,80,80 77,77,76,49,42 37,—**
toteswingers:1&2:£2.30, 2&3:£26.30, 1&3:£28.60 CSF £23.44 TOTE £3.90: £1.90, £2.10, £3.30; EX 23.10.
Owner Deal George Kelvin-Hughes Nicolson **Bred** Conna Stud **Trained** Upper Lambourn, Berks

FOCUS
A good race on paper, but the early pace wasn't strong, and the time was slower than the opening juvenile contest. There were, however, plenty of promising efforts, although most of the field were bunched together for a long time. The form looks solid enough and the race should produce winners.

NOTEBOOK
Minella Class(IRE) ◆, the winner of one of his three races under rules when trained in Ireland, was purchased by current connections for £95,000 in April, and that looks a good investment after the horse showed an impressive turn of foot. He has been bought to take on good horses, but one would imagine he'll kept to a modest level for now in order to gain more experience. (op 5-2)
Red Merlin(IRE) ◆, a very useful sort at up to 1m4f for Clive Cox on the Flat, cost new connections 58,000gns at the sales and looks a surefire future winner judged on this effort. (op 6-1 tchd 7-1)
Pateese(FR) ◆ showed promise on his hurdling debut at Exeter and more than built on that here, with another good effort after racing prominently. (op 16-1)
Poole Master kept on well on his first start over hurdles, despite hanging, and will no doubt be going closer next time if kept to a realistic level. (tchd 11-1)
Kartanian(IRE) ◆ showed plenty of ability in bumpers, so looked of obvious interest on his first outing over hurdles. A half-brother to Katiyra, a Group 2 winner on the Flat for John Oxx, he was close up but seemed to be caught a little one-paced in the final stages. That said, this was a pleasing hurdling debut. (op 9-2 tchd 5-1)
Zarinski(IRE) ◆ kept on and will be of some interest in handicap company, especially over further. (tchd 33-1)
Shootin The Breeze(IRE) ◆, reported to be a big individual who will make a 3m chaser in time, shaped really well and was a big eyecatcher. Whether he will be winning soon is debatable, but he certainly has a future. (op 50-1)
Cotillion, well beaten in the Cesarewitch when last on the racecourse, made late progress here after being held up. It goes without saying he'll need a stiffer test. (op 15-2)
Kaolak(USA), now with Keith Reveley after making his promising hurdling debut for John Ryan, ran another good race and should win any ordinary maiden. (op 16-1)
According dropped away before things got interesting and has lots to prove now. He is another that will probably find his level in handicaps. (op 25-1)

2961 POWERSOLVE ELECTRONICS GREATWOOD CHARITY H'CAP CHASE (15 fncs) 2m 2f 110y
1:30 (1:32) (Class 4) (0-115,115) 4-Y-0+ **£4,228** (£1,241; £620; £310)

Form RPR

3141 **1** **Rimini (FR)**[21] 2605 5-11-5 **108** .... PaulMoloney 118+
(David Rees) *prom: jnd ldrs 2 out: swtchd rt after last: styd on wl to ld nr fin* **6/1**[1]

3500 **2** *hd* **Coach Lane**[162] 919 9-11-2 **105** .... DarylJacob 114
(Nick Mitchell) *chsd ldrs: led 4 out: narrowly hdd last: regained ld last 100yds: hdd cl home* **25/1**

0032 **3** *3/4* **Lordsbridge (USA)**[19] 2662 8-11-9 **112** .... NickScholfield 120
(Andy Turnell) *mid-div: hdwy 10th: w ldrs 3 out: slt ld last: hdd run-in: no ex last 75yds* **8/1**

-34U **4** *5* **Prince Du Beury (FR)**[18] 2670 7-11-6 **109** .... AndrewTinkler 114
(Nicky Henderson) *hld up towards rr: stdy hdwy 10th: one pce fr 2 out: hit last* **14/1**

5300 **5** *2 3/4* **Mister Benedictine**[53] 1364 7-11-12 **115** .... (tp) DaveCrosse 118
(Brendan Duke) *mid-div: hdwy to chse ldrs 10th: 4th and wkng whn hit last* **50/1**

P02- **6** *14* **Royal Wedding**[271] 4719 8-11-10 **113** .... LiamTreadwell 101
(Nick Gifford) *rr-div: hdwy 10th: wknd appr 4 out* **28/1**

5P-2 **7** *3/4* **Strongbows Legend**[35] 2310 5-11-3 **106** .... FelixDeGiles 94
(Charlie Longsdon) *mid-div: hdwy to chse ldrs 10th: wknd after 4 out: mstke 2 out* **13/2**[2]

23-0 **8** *3* **Mister Matt (IRE)**[36] 2294 7-11-9 **112** .... HarrySkelton 97
(Bob Buckler) *in rr: hdwy 10th: outpcd 4 out: 6th whn j.lft last* **33/1**

04-F **9** *1 1/4* **Meneur (FR)**[19] 2662 8-10-13 **102** .... JamieMoore 86
(Gary Moore) *in rr: hdwy to chse ldrs 10th: wknd appr 2 out* **25/1**

P-P0 **10** *18* **Amble Forge (IRE)**[30] 2429 8-11-8 **111** .... JoeTizzard 79
(Colin Tizzard) *in rr: blnd 3rd: bhd fr 6th* **28/1**

6212 **11** *nse* **Nautical Approach (IRE)**[22] 2591 7-11-3 **106** .... (t) PaddyBrennan 74
(Alex Hales) *mid-div: lost pl 11th* **7/1**[3]

0P-0 **12** *nk* **Mokum (FR)**[188] 695 9-10-11 **100** .... WayneHutchinson 67
(Tony Carroll) *in rr: struggling 6th: nvr on terms* **33/1**

-143 **13** *nk* **Quipe Me Posted (FR)**[28] 2453 6-11-4 **107** .... SamThomas 74
(Jonjo O'Neill) *rr-div: sme hdwy 8th: outpcd 10th: in rr whn hmpd 3 out* **8/1**

2453 **14** *1 3/4* **Morestead (IRE)**[27] 2484 5-11-0 **106** .... (b) SamTwiston-Davies(3) 72
(Brendan Powell) *chsd ldrs: rdn 10th: lost pl and blnd 4 out* **14/1**

00P- **15** *1 1/4* **Signatory (USA)**[366] 2885 8-10-7 **106** .... GeraldQuinn(10) 70
(Jonjo O'Neill) *rr-div: hdwy 8th: lost pl 10th* **33/1**

-314 **U** **Festival Dreams**[47] 2073 5-9-13 **95** .... (p) DannyBurton(7) —
(Joanna Davis) *w ldrs: led 5th: blnd and hdd next: rdn and outpcd whn blnd and uns rdr 9th* **12/1**

-543 **F** **Marley Roca (IRE)**[36] 2298 6-11-4 **107** .... DominicElsworth —
(Paul Webber) *led: j.lft 1st: hdd 5th: led next: hdd 4 out: fading whn fell next* **8/1**

0136 **P** **Another Trump (NZ)**[40] 2184 6-11-11 **114** .... WillKennedy —
(Jonjo O'Neill) *in rr: bhd fr 7th: t.o 9th: p.u bef 11th* **25/1**

4m 40.4s (-3.60) **Going Correction** -0.375s/f (Good) **18** Ran SP% **123.7**
Speed ratings (Par 105): **92,91,91,89,88 82,82,80,80,72 72,72,72,71,71 —,—,—**
toteswingers:1&2:£38.80, 1&3:£6.00, 2&3:£22.60 CSF £152.41 CT £1229.28 TOTE £6.70: £1.80, £6.20, £2.10, £4.00; EX 256.50.
Owner D Rees **Bred** Haras D'Ecouves & Uplifting B'Stock Ltd **Trained** Clarbeston, Pembrokes

FOCUS
A fair handicap hurdle but solid form rated around the four immediately behind the winner.

NOTEBOOK
Rimini(FR), raised 10lb for winning by 8l on his previous outing at Chepstow, won three of his four starts in points, and showed a really good attitude to get on top in the final stages. He will go up the weights again, but should get further, which may help to offset a rise. (op 15-2)
Coach Lane, making his debut for this trainer, looked on a fair mark when considering the balance of his form, and put up a thoroughly likeable performance after racing prominently throughout. He responded well to pressure and went down fighting.
Lordsbridge(USA), up 3lb after finishing second over C&D last time, continues to run well, but just cannot get his head in front again, no matter how hard he tries. (op 9-1)
Prince Du Beury(FR), without blinkers this time, was down 4f in trip and kept on quite well without looking really dangerous. He has yet to win for current connections. (tchd 16-1)
Mister Benedictine, back over fences and with cheekpieces back on, hadn't won since May 2008, but ran well. A mistake at the last was enough to finish any chance he held. (op 40-1)
Royal Wedding, having his first run since March, kept on well after the last to pass a few horses. (op 25-1)
Strongbows Legend, making his chasing and handicap debut, showed a bit of promise last time and was nicely supported before the off. His jumping wasn't always fluent but he showed just enough to suggest he has the ability to get a first success. (op 7-1)
Nautical Approach(IRE), 10lb higher than his winning mark at Fakenham two starts previously, never got involved. (op 13-2 tchd 15-2)
Marley Roca(IRE) seems fairly weighted on his hurdles form, but was just starting to fade when coming down. (op 11-1)
Another Trump(NZ) Official explanation: jockey said gelding never travelled (op 11-1)

2962 COOLMATION H'CAP CHASE (21 fncs) 3m 2f 110y
2:05 (2:05) (Class 3) (0-130,130) 4-Y-0+ **£5,854** (£1,719; £859; £429)

Form RPR

/00- **1** **West End Rocker (IRE)**[353] 3083 8-11-11 **129** .... WayneHutchinson 140+
(Alan King) *in tch: hdwy to trck ldr 13th: styd front rnk: chal 17th: led 4 out: hrd drvn run-in: hld on all out* **12/1**

0-0U **2** *1 1/4* **Cornish Sett (IRE)**[33] 2343 11-11-0 **123** .... IanPopham(5) 131
(Caroline Keevil) *in tch tl dropped to rr 10th: hdwy 16th: hit 17th: dropped to rr and plenty to do fr 4 out: sltly hmpd and hdwy 2 out: str run after last to take 2nd fnl 30yds: nt rch wnr* **20/1**

31-P **3** *1 1/4* **Nicto De Beauchene (FR)**[45] 2106 9-11-7 **125** .... DarylJacob 134
(Victor Dartnall) *led tl hdd 8th: styd pressing ldr tl slt ld again fr 12th: styd strly pressed tl hdd 4 out: kpt on u.p run-in tl no ex and lost 2nd fnl 30yds* **11/1**

00-P **4** *1 1/4* **Officier De Reserve (FR)**[45] 2106 8-11-9 **127** .... AidanColeman 133
(Venetia Williams) *in tch: hdwy 15th: outpcd and mstke 4 out: rallied fr 2 out: stl plenty to do last: kpt on u.p run-in but nt rch ldng trio* **20/1**

0-05 **5** *4* **Martys Mission (IRE)**[18] 2669 8-10-7 **118** .... MrTJCannon(7) 120
(Richard Rowe) *in tch: chsd ldrs fr 12th: pressed ldrs 17th: wl there fr 4 out: sn rdn: styd on same pce fr 3 out* **6/1**[3]

03-P **6** *9* **Zacharova (IRE)**[32] 2358 7-11-5 **123** .... (b) SamThomas 120
(Venetia Williams) *in tch: rdn towards rr 15th: rallied and in tch 17th: wknd after 3 out* **25/1**

0PP- **7** *15* **Old Benny**[312] 3887 9-11-6 **127** .... (b) CharlieHuxley(3) 110+
(Alan King) *towards rr and j. slowly 8th: lost tch fr 16th: rdn next: wknd 4 out* **12/1**

-566 **U** **Lead On (IRE)**[32] 2358 9-11-11 **129** .... (b) TomO'Brien —
(Philip Hobbs) *in rr whn mstke and uns rdr 3rd* **12/1**

312/ **U** **Leading Contender (IRE)**[620] 4847 9-11-12 **130** .... RhysFlint 136
(Philip Hobbs) *in tch: hdwy 15th: drvn and styd on fr 4 out: 3 l 3rd and stl a ch whn mstke and uns rdr 2 out* **8/1**

P-PP **P** **Nozic (FR)**[18] 2674 9-11-12 **130** .... (v[1]) LiamTreadwell —
(Nick Gifford) *chsd ldrs: led 8th to 12th: styd pressing ldrs to 16th: wkng whn bdly hmpd 17th: sn wl bhd: t.o whn p.u bef 2 out* **40/1**

-0FU **F** **Scots Dragoon**[18] 2669 8-11-3 **121** .... BarryGeraghty —
(Nicky Henderson) *trckd ldrs fr 11th: upsides fr 14th tl wkng whn fell 17th* **10/1**

14-1 **F** **Eyre Square (IRE)**[33] 2354 7-10-8 **112** .... JamesReveley —
(Keith Reveley) *chsd ldrs: styng on to dispute 1/2 l 2nd whn fell 17th* **7/2**[1]

00P3 **F** **Carrickmines (IRE)**[18] 2669 8-11-3 **121** .... (b) RichardJohnson —
(Dr Richard Newland) *in rr: sme hdwy 12th but stl towards rr whn fell 14th* **11/2**[2]

6m 47.06s (-8.94) **Going Correction** -0.375s/f (Good) **13** Ran SP% **119.3**
Speed ratings (Par 107): **98,97,97,96,95 93,88,—,—,— —,—,—**
toteswingers:1&2:£62.20, 1&3:£54.20, 2&3:£32.10 CSF £224.32 CT £2708.26 TOTE £17.10: £3.70, £6.00, £3.90; EX 407.70.
Owner Barry Winfield & Tim Leadbeater **Bred** Ms P Kidd **Trained** Barbury Castle, Wilts

FOCUS
A race full of horses well handicapped if returning to their best form, but there weren't many lengths separating the runners as they left the back straight for the final time, and a big danger fell when in with every chance at the cross fence. Those in the frame behind the winner set the standard.

NOTEBOOK
West End Rocker(IRE), 6lb lower than when last seen on the racecourse back in December of last year, looks to be coming back to his best considering this performance. Settled in midfield, he moved up going really well over six fences out before finding plenty under pressure to get back on the winning trail. One would hope he can now progress again into the smart stayer he looked likely to make in his novice chase season. The trainer reported afterwards that he will give the winner a Grand National entry.
Cornish Sett(IRE) is not the most consistent of horses, useful though he can be at his best, but kept on past a couple of tiring rivals after the final fence. It's almost impossible to predict what he'll do next time. (tchd 22-1)
Nicto De Beauchene(FR), pulled up on his only start for this trainer since leaving the retired Alners, held a couple of positions in this, and ran much better than he had done at Carlisle. He's quite high in the weights but can be competitive. (tchd 12-1)
Officier De Reserve(FR) has been mainly disappointing since running respectably in the 2008 Welsh National, but had become fairly handicapped as a result. He needed some pushing along but wasn't beaten far. (op 14-1)
Martys Mission(IRE) looks a thorough stayer and probably wants even more of a test in this sort of grade. (op 13-2 tchd 5-1)
Zacharova(IRE), with blinkers back on, got himself behind at one stage but did keep going. (op 28-1)
Old Benny is well treated on his best form, and had been reportedly given a Hobday operation for a breathing problem. He showed signs of being a little quirky, but also did enough to suggest the ability is still there. (tchd 14-1)
Leading Contender(IRE), absent since finishing second to Don't Push It at Aintree back in April 2009, was 2lb lower than his last run but pulled hard early. He'd run a nice comeback race but looked held when unseating his jockey two out. (tchd 50-1)
Nozic(FR), visored for the first time, had been dropped 10lb since his last run, which means he is really well handicapped on his best form for Paul Nicholls. He was staying on when badly hampered by the fallen Eyre Square five out. (tchd 50-1)
Scots Dragoon seemed held when also coming down five out. (tchd 50-1)
Eyre Square(IRE) was still moving strongly when departing five from home. (tchd 50-1)

Carrickmines(IRE) had tagged himself into midfield, seemingly going quite well, when falling at the 14th. (tchd 50-1)

2963 EBF "NATIONAL HUNT" NOVICES' HURDLE (QUALIFIER) (10 hdls) 2m 3f

2:40 (2:44) (Class 4) 4-6-Y-O **£3,577** (£1,050; £525; £262)

Form				RPR
34-4	**1**		**Pride In Battle (IRE)**^{42} 2145 5-10-12 0 WayneHutchinson (Alan King) *trckd ldrs: chal 3 out: led last: edgd rt: styd on strly clsng stages* **15/2**	123
21-5	**2**	¾	**Cucumber Run (IRE)**^{31} 2389 5-10-12 0 BarryGeraghty (Nicky Henderson) *w ldrs: chal 3 out: hit last: no ex last 75yds* **13/8**^{1}	123
4-33	**3**	4	**Ohio Gold (IRE)**^{19} 2666 4-10-12 120 JoeTizzard (Colin Tizzard) *chsd ldrs: outpcd appr 2 out: styd on run-in to take 3rd last 100yds* **10/3**^{2}	119
1	**4**	5	**Court By Surprise (IRE)**^{38} 2241 5-11-5 0 SamThomas (Emma Lavelle) *w ldrs: led after 3rd: nt fluent and hdd last: wknd and lost 3rd last 100yds* **8/1**	125+
5-4	**5**	5	**Lord Liath (IRE)**^{25} 2518 4-10-9 0 CharlieHuxley$^{(3)}$ (Alan King) *hld up towards rr: hdwy appr 3 out: kpt on: nvr nr ldrs* **33/1**	110
33	**6**	4½	**Lexicon Lad (IRE)**^{52} 1989 5-10-12 0 PaddyBrennan (Tom George) *led tl after 3rd: w ldrs: wknd appr 2 out* **7/1**^{3}	106
40-	**7**	8	**Empire Builder (IRE)**^{269} 4757 4-10-12 0 AndrewThornton (Caroline Bailey) *hld up towards rr: stdy hdwy 7th: chsng ldrs appr next: wknd bef 2 out* **100/1**	99
3	**8**	4½	**No Secrets (IRE)**^{46} 2087 6-10-12 0 JamieMoore (Warren Greatrex) *trckd ldrs: t.k.h: 8th and wkng whn hit 3 out* **11/1**	99+
6-4	**9**	3¾	**Salut Honore (FR)**^{58} 1906 4-10-12 0 FelixDeGiles (Alex Hales) *hld up towards rr: bhd after 7th: nvr on terms* **150/1**	91
P-2	**10**	½	**Our Columbus (IRE)**^{32} 2365 6-10-9 0 SamTwiston-Davies$^{(3)}$ (Nigel Twiston-Davies) *chsd ldrs: rdn 7th: sn lost pl* **25/1**	91
	11	15	**Lady Kayf** 6-10-5 0 DaveCrosse (Mark Usher) *in rr: sme hdwy 7th: wknd next* **200/1**	70
30	**12**	6	**Ratify**^{19} 2666 6-10-12 0 AidanColeman (Brendan Powell) *in rr: bhd fr 3 out* **66/1**	72
24	**13**	7	**Willy Be Lucky (IRE)**^{30} 2432 4-10-9 0 JimmyDerham$^{(3)}$ (Seamus Mullins) *in rr: mstke 7th: bhd fr next* **100/1**	66
5	**14**	½	**Eldred (IRE)**^{52} 1989 4-10-12 0 AndrewTinkler (Nicky Henderson) *prom: drvn after 7th: wknd appr next* **33/1**	65
5	**15**	8	**No Obligation (IRE)**^{20} 2632 5-10-7 0 MrMMO'Connor$^{(5)}$ (Brendan Powell) *in rr: bhd fr 7th: t.o next* **150/1**	58
	16	72	**Stealing Time (IRE)**^{234} 5-10-9 0 MrAJBerry$^{(3)}$ (Jonjo O'Neill) *gave problems s and mounted trck: t.k.h in last: sme hdwy 6th: sn rdn and lost pl: bhd whn hung bdly rt bnd appr 3 out: sn t.o: eventually completed* **125/1**	—

4m 41.7s (-8.90) **Going Correction** -0.425s/f (Good)
WFA 4 from 5yo+ 5lb **16** Ran SP% **120.7**
Speed ratings: **101,100,99,96,94 92,89,87,86,85 79,77,74,73,70 40**
toteswingers:1&2:£3.70, 1&3:£4.90, 2&3:£2.20 CSF £19.96 TOTE £8.00: £2.30, £1.50, £1.50; EX 23.60.

Owner Mrs Elizabeth Pearce **Bred** Christopher Nicholson **Trained** Barbury Castle, Wilts

FOCUS

The early pace wasn't strong but the fancied horses came to the fore in the latter stages. A big step up from the winner but the third and fourth suggest the form is reasonable.

NOTEBOOK

Pride In Battle(IRE) had shown promise in both bumpers and his sole previous start over hurdles without winning, but after hugging the inside rail, found plenty under pressure to hold off the favourite. He shapes as though he'll get a bit further. (op 9-1 tchd 10-1)

Cucumber Run(IRE), making his hurdling debut, raced just in front of the winner early and was ideally placed to win, but was unable to get away from his rivals once in with every chance. He battled on but was always being held. (tchd 11-8 and 7-4 and 2-1 in places)

Ohio Gold(IRE) took a really keen grip early which may have not helped in the final stages, although he did keep on again to get third. (op 7-2 tchd 4-1)

Court By Surprise(IRE), the only horse giving weight away, led for much of the contest and wasn't disgraced once joined and passed. (tchd 9-1)

Lord Liath(IRE) ◆ shaped encouragingly on his hurdling debut after racing in rear early, and looks to need at least this distance.

Lexicon Lad(IRE), another to have his first outing over hurdles, showed more than enough after racing prominently to suggest he'll take something similar if not faced with anything out of the ordinary. (op 10-1 tchd 11-1)

2964 TOTESPORT.COM PETERBOROUGH CHASE (GRADE 2) (16 fncs) 2m 4f

3:10 (3:13) (Class 1) 4-Y-O+ **£17,404** (£6,718; £3,514; £1,903)

Form				RPR
54-3	**1**		**Tartak (FR)**^{53} 1958 7-11-0 147 (t) PaddyBrennan (Tom George) *led after 1st to 3rd: pressing ldr whn hit 7th: upsides fr next to 9th: chsd ldr again 12th: hit 4 out and dropped to 3rd next: lft 2nd 2 out: chal last: led u.p fnl 50yds* **11/4**^{2}	159+
11F/	**2**	½	**Breedsbreeze (IRE)**^{669} 3905 8-11-0 148 DarylJacob (Paul Nicholls) *hld up towards rr but in tch: hdwy 11th: chsd ldrs 4 out: chsd ldr 3 out: 1 l 2nd whn lft in ld 2 out: jnd last: sn rdn: hdd and no ex fnl 50yds* **11/2**	158+
53-0	**3**	28	**Herecomesthetruth (IRE)**^{43} 2138 8-11-10 155 ColinBolger (Chris Gordon) *in tch: chsd ldrs fr 11th: hit 12th: wknd 4 out: no ch whn lft poor 3rd 2 out* **33/1**	141
2-14	**4**	43	**Ollie Magern**^{46} 2091 12-11-4 147 SamTwiston-Davies (Nigel Twiston-Davies) *led 4th: jnd fr 7th: narrowly hdd 8th: wknd 12th: t.o* **20/1**	97
46-3	**U**		**Deep Purple**^{46} 2091 9-11-10 160 PaulMoloney (Evan Williams) *led 3rd to 4th: dropped to rr fr 11th: no ch whn bdly hmpd by loose horse and uns rdr 2 out* **4/1**^{3}	139
R3-2	**F**		**Twist Magic (FR)**^{43} 2138 8-11-10 175 SamThomas (Paul Nicholls) *led in and led tl after 1st: settled bhd ldrs: qckng to take slt ld fr 8th: 1 l ld and travelling wl whn fell 2 out: fatally injured* **9/4**^{1}	171
12P-	**P**		**Master Medic (IRE)**^{354} 3032 9-11-6 152 RobertWalford (Tim Walford) *a towards rr: wknd 8th: t.o whn p.u bef 10th* **8/1**	—

5m 2.45s (-9.55) **Going Correction** -0.375s/f (Good) **7** Ran SP% **111.6**
Speed ratings: **104,103,92,75,— —,—**
toteswingers:1&2:£3.80, 1&3:£11.90, 2&3:£22.80 CSF £17.36 TOTE £3.10: £1.80, £3.60; EX 17.10.

Owner Power Panels Electrical Systems Ltd **Bred** Francis Cottebrune & Colette Cottebrune **Trained** Slad, Gloucs

FOCUS

This contest was finally run, Huntingdon having been forced to abandon its re-scheduled meeting on Sunday. The winner is rated 5lb below his best with a small step up from the second.

NOTEBOOK

Tartak(FR), a classy novice who proved difficult to win with last season (his second to Deep Purple in this race being one of his better efforts), made mistakes when a well-beaten third in the Old Roan on his reappearance at Aintree, but was expected to have come on for that and he capitalised on the favourite's misfortune, getting up close home to snatch victory away from another Nicholls runner Breedsbreeze. The first-time tongue-tie was clearly a big help, and maybe he can now fulfil that earlier potential, although in all honesty, he didn't look entirely straightforward in getting past the runner-up, whom he had a significant fitness advantage over. The Melling Chase is again his long-term aim. (op 3-1 tchd 5-2)

Breedsbreeze(IRE) won the Grade 1 Feltham as a novice, but was forced to miss last season, having picked up a leg injury when falling on his latest outing in the Reynoldstown in February 2009. Considering he was expected to need the run, it was mightily encouraging to see him run such a big race, travelling well into contention and, having been gifted the lead, only the lack of a recent run costing him victory. It's hoped he goes the right way from this, and if he does, he should continue to contend in good races, with him also having the option of a return to 3m. (op 6-1 tchd 7-1)

Herecomesthetruth(IRE) couldn't race on with the principals down the straight, but is a smart performer on his day, especially when allowed to dominate, and RPRs suggests he prefers going the other way round, so isn't one to give write off just yet. (tchd 25-1)

Ollie Magern, who again ran his heart out when fourth in the Charlie Hall on his reappearance, gave it his best shot, but his legs won't carry him fast enough at this level these days, especially over this trip. (op 25-1)

Deep Purple, third in the Charlie Hall on his return, lost his position early and was in trouble a long way out. This clearly wasn't his true running, and perhaps a hard race at Wetherby has left its mark. (op 9-1 tchd 10-1)

Twist Magic(FR) was still in front and seemingly travelling well when he broke a rear fetlock in a fall two out. A five-time Grade 1 winner, this was a real tragedy. (op 9-1 tchd 10-1)

Master Medic(IRE), a rapidly progressive chaser at up to this trip until pulling up when out of his depth in the King George (final start for the Alners), was soon in trouble on this first start in a year and his rider was wise to pull him up. It's hoped he hasn't aggravated an old injury. (op 9-1 tchd 10-1)

2965 EBF KENTFORD RACING FILLIES' "JUNIOR" STANDARD OPEN NATIONAL HUNT FLAT RACE 1m 4f 110y

3:45 (3:45) (Class 5) 3-Y-O **£2,055** (£599; £299)

Form				RPR
	1		**Who's Afraid** 3-10-12 0 GerardTumelty (Alan King) *in tch: swtchd rt and styd on wl over 1f out: led last 75yds* **10/1**	94+
	2	1¼	**Young Mags (IRE)** 3-10-12 0 PaddyBrennan (Nigel Twiston-Davies) *w ldr: led over 4f out: hdd over 2f out: kpt on wl to take 2nd clsng stages* **11/2**^{2}	93
	3	½	**Tante Sissi (FR)**^{137} 3-10-12 0 WayneHutchinson (Alan King) *t.k.h in rr: stdy hdwy 4f out: led over 2f out: hdd last 75yds: no ex* **6/4**^{1}	92
20	**4**	4	**Pearl Mountain (IRE)**^{22} 2597 3-10-9 0 SamTwiston-Davies$^{(3)}$ (Jeff Pearce) *chsd ldrs: drvn over 3f out: chsng ldrs over 2f out: kpt on one pce* **18/1**	86
	5	4½	**Clyffe Top** 3-10-9 0 CharlieHuxley$^{(3)}$ (Jonathan Portman) *mid-div: drvn over 4f out: one pce fnl 2f* **50/1**	80
	6	2¼	**Cailin Maghnailbhe (IRE)** 3-10-12 0 DarylJacob (Seamus Mullins) *t.k.h in rr: hdwy 5f out: sn chsng ldrs: wknd 2f out* **25/1**	77
	7	2¼	**Dancing Teasel** 3-10-12 0 SamThomas (Emma Lavelle) *hld up in rr: kpt on fnl 3f: nvr a factor* **11/2**^{2}	74
	8	½	**County Hotel (IRE)** 3-10-12 0 TomO'Brien (Barry Brennan) *trckd ldrs: effrt over 2f out: sn wknd* **22/1**	73
0	**9**	¾	**Megagrace**^{35} 2315 3-10-12 0 JamieMoore (Gary Moore) *hld up in rr: nvr on terms* **8/1**^{3}	72
	10	2	**Willow The Rose** 3-10-12 0 AidanColeman (J R Jenkins) *trckd ldrs: effrt over 3f out: wknd 2f out* **14/1**	69
05	**11**	6	**Brambley**^{41} 2173 3-10-9 0 WayneKavanagh$^{(3)}$ (Seamus Mullins) *sn chsng ldrs: pushed along 5f out: lost pl 3f out* **66/1**	61
	12	9	**Karinga Madame** 3-10-12 0 AndrewThornton (Richard Rowe) *in rr: hdwy over 4f out: lost pl over 2f out* **50/1**	48
	13	10	**On The Raz** 3-10-9 0 ChrisHonour$^{(3)}$ (Jacqueline Retter) *led tl over 4f out: hung bdly lft and lost pl over 3f out: bhd fnl 2f* **66/1**	34

3m 10.8s (5.00) **13** Ran SP% **118.0**
toteswingers:1&2:£10.90, 1&3:£7.00, 2&3:£4.80; totesuper7: Win: Not won. Place: Not won. CSF £60.31 TOTE £13.40: £3.50, £2.70, £1.10; EX 58.20.

Owner Mr & Mrs Christopher Harris **Bred** Jethro Bloodstock **Trained** Barbury Castle, Wilts

FOCUS

A couple of nice fillies have won this race in the past, and this year's finish was nearly dominated by Alan King, but for punters, not the way round most seemed to expect. Not much to go on with the fourth and ninth offering some guidance.

NOTEBOOK

Who's Afraid, whose dam is a half-sister to the top-class Azertyuiop, was in midfield early before showing a good attitude once asked to quicken, and ran out a comfortable winner. If nothing else, considering her pedigree, she has made herself valuable for paddock purposes. (op 11-1)

Young Mags(IRE) ◆ raced prominently throughout and was another to show a fine attitude to pressure, as she got back past Tante Sissi after being headed by a few over 2f out. She looked both green and in need of further. (op 8-1)

Tante Sissi(FR) ◆, whose two seconds in French bumpers had been boosted by both winners, but mainly Toner D'Oudairies, who had taken a Grade 3 juvenile hurdle earlier on the day at Fairyhouse, raced keenly in rear and then got locked in a pocket before getting out. She looked likely to win when getting to the front in the latter stages, but didn't get home as well as the two in front of her. (op 13-8 tchd 11-8 and 7-4 in a place)

Pearl Mountain(IRE) probably returned to something resembling her debut second, and is a solid enough marker to the form. (op 16-1)

Clyffe Top, whose dam has produced winners, stayed on nicely in the final stages.

Cailin Maghnailbhe(IRE) ◆, a sister to Diva, a Flat and dual winner over hurdles, made a rapid move towards the front in the home straight but was unable to sustain her effort once there. However, it was a good first run and, considering her pedigree, she might be worth a try on the Flat. (op 22-1)

Dancing Teasel, whose winning relations have won over mainly sprinting trips, made a brief effort before only finding the one pace. (op 6-1)

T/Jkpt: Not won. T/Plt: £190.00 to a £1 stake. Pool:£64,632.03 - 248.30 winning tickets. T/Qpdt: £67.40 to a £1 stake. Pool:£4,618.42 - 50.68 winning tickets. ST

[2157] FAIRYHOUSE (R-H)

Wednesday, December 15

OFFICIAL GOING: Soft

This top-class meeting was originally scheduled for December 2nd, and postponed three times in all.

2966a BAR ONE RACING JUVENILE 3-Y-O HURDLE (GRADE 3) (10 hdls) 2m

11:50 (11:53) 3-Y-O **£17,256** (£5,044; £2,389; £796)

RPR

1 **Toner D'Oudairies (FR)**[40] 2195 3-10-9 .... DNRussell 120+
(Gordon Elliott, Ire) *trckd ldrs on outer: 5th 1/2-way: hdwy to chal 2 out: sn led and sent clr bef last: pushed out to maintain advantage run-in* **8/11**[1]

2 *2 1/2* **Kalann (IRE)**[11] 3-10-9 .... MDarcy 118+
(Sabrina J Harty, Ire) *in rr of mid-div: nt fluent 4th: pushed along to go 4th ent st: 3rd at last: kpt on wl run-in* **14/1**

3 *1 3/4* **Fearless Falcon (IRE)**[55] 1946 3-10-9 ....(b) KMDonoghue 116
(Adrian McGuinness, Ire) *a.p: 2nd 1/2-way: led 3 out: strly pressed next: sn hdd and no imp u.p: dropped to 3rd on run-in* **14/1**

4 *3* **Sailors Warn (IRE)**[45] 2115 3-10-9 .... AndrewJMcNamara 113
(E J O'Grady, Ire) *trckd ldrs in 4th: 3rd fr 4 out: wnt 2nd appr st: no imp after 2 out and dropped to 4th: kpt on one pce* **4/1**[2]

5 *14* **Days Ahead (IRE)**[32] 2380 3-10-13 ....(p) PCarberry 103
(Eoin Doyle, Ire) *chsd ldrs: 6th 1/2-way: drvn along in 5th ent st: no ex fr 2 out* **11/2**[3]

6 *1* **Walden Prince (IRE)** 3-10-9 .... BTO'Connell 98
(P F McEnery, Ire) *hld up in rr: sme hdwy appr st: mod 6th after 2 out: kpt on one pce* **50/1**

7 *3* **Captains Dilemma (IRE)**[25] 2535 3-10-9 ....(t) DJCondon 95
(T Hogan, Ire) *trckd ldrs on inner: 3rd 1/2-way: wknd appr st* **14/1**

8 *dist* **Cuckoo Hill**[161] 3-10-9 .... MPWalsh —
(Martin Brassil, Ire) *a bhd: rdn in rr bef 3 out: t.o* **50/1**

9 *1 1/2* **Ainm Spartacus (IRE)**[25] 2535 3-10-9 .... TJDoyle —
(Kieran Purcell, Ire) *led: jst hdd whn mstke 3 out: sn wknd: t.o* **20/1**

4m 1.50s (-10.50) **Going Correction** -0.25s/f (Good) **9** Ran SP% **122.0**
Speed ratings: **116,114,113,112,105 104,103,—,—**
CSF £14.25 TOTE £1.60: £1.10, £3.90, £3.50; DF 23.90.
Owner Gigginstown House Stud **Bred** Comte Michel De Gigou **Trained** Trim, Co Meath

FOCUS
Five of the nine runners were previous winners over hurdles. The form is sound with the race rated around the winner.

NOTEBOOK
Toner D'Oudairies(FR) ◆, a six-length winner at Down Royal on his previous start, confirmed the good impression created on that occasion with a comfortable win. Kept to the outside, he was in touch throughout and moved up three out before leading at the second last. Ridden clear before the final hurdle, he stayed on and was never in danger of being reeled in. Stan James went 25-1(from 33-1) for the Triumph Hurdle - Ladbrokes go 20-1 - and while that event looks an obvious target, trainer Gordon Elliott expressed reservations if the ground is any way quick. The Grade 2 Bord Na Mona Fire Magic Juvenile Hurdle at Leopardstown on December 26 is next for him as he jumped well and is regarded by his trainer as "a big staying type who will make a grand chaser". (op 8/11 tchd 4/5)
Kalann(IRE), winner of a 1m4f maiden at Dundalk 11 days previously, shaped well on what was his hurdling debut, making headway three out and staying on to go second in the closing stages having been ridden along in fourth approaching two out. (op 16/1)
Fearless Falcon(IRE) was put in his place by the winner, but kept on only to be run out of second place in the last 150 yards. (op 16/1)
Sailors Warn(IRE) was always close up and had every chance after going second three out, only to weaken between the last two hurdles. He stayed on again towards the finish. (op 9/2 tchd 7/2)
Days Ahead(IRE), a dual hurdles winner and never out of the first three in five attempts, was the only penalised runner. Held up in touch, he could make no headway from before two out. (op 5/1)

2967a BAR ONE RACING ROYAL BOND NOVICE HURDLE (GRADE 1) (10 hdls) 2m

12:20 (12:21) 4-Y-0+ **£46,017** (£13,451; £6,371; £2,123)

RPR

1 **Zaidpour (FR)**[32] 2382 4-11-7 .... PTownend 150+
(W P Mullins, Ire) *hld up on inner: cl 5th 3 out: smooth hdwy to chal whn mstke 2 out: sn rcvrd and effrtless prog to ld bef last: drew clr on the bridle run-in: impressive* **4/7**[1]

2 *12* **Pineau De Re (FR)**[28] 2461 7-11-10 .... BTO'Connell 133
(Philip Fenton, Ire) *trckd ldrs: 3rd 1/2-way: rdn fr 3 out: chalng at next whn mstke: kpt on one pce u.p to go mod 2nd run-in* **14/1**

3 *1 1/2* **Perfect Smile (IRE)**[50] 2026 5-11-10 131..............................(t) PCarberry 132
(Noel Meade, Ire) *trckd ldrs in 4th: hdwy to ld travelling wl after 3 out: pressed next: hdd bef last: no ch w wnr: kpt on one pce* **6/1**[2]

4 *13* **The Shepherd King (IRE)**[52] 2006 6-11-10 126............. BryanJCooper 119
(Thomas Cooper, Ire) *hld up in tch: prog into cl 4th travelling wl 3 out: pushed along bef next: sn no ex* **10/1**

5 *1/2* **Carloswayback (IRE)**[38] 2251 5-11-10 .... DNRussell 118
(Paul Nolan, Ire) *led or disp ld tl hdd 4th: dropped to rr whn mstke 4 out: no threat in st* **7/1**[3]

6 *dist* **Mount Helicon**[31] 2388 5-11-10 ....(t) JLCullen —
(T Hogan, Ire) *prom: led fr 4th tl hdd after 3 out: sn wknd: t.o* **16/1**

4m 1.70s (-10.30) **Going Correction** -0.25s/f (Good)
WFA 4 from 5yo+ 5lb **6** Ran SP% **112.1**
Speed ratings: **115,109,108,101,101** —
CSF £9.72 TOTE £1.30: £1.10, £2.90; DF 5.50.
Owner Mrs S Ricci **Bred** H H The Aga Khan's Studs Sc **Trained** Muine Beag, Co Carlow

FOCUS
Just the six runners, five of them coming out of maiden company. The pace was sensible and the ground was described as "beautiful" and "yielding to soft at worst" by two jockeys. If reputations were anything to go by, this was a strong renewal. The form is rated around the second and third.

NOTEBOOK
Zaidpour(FR) ◆ had been relegated to last place after half-a-mile, but his jockey had no concerns at all and he made up his ground effortlessly when it mattered. There was a risk of him being hemmed in around the home turn, but he could have lost many lengths and still won on the bridle. As novice performances go, this was as good as we have seen in Ireland in quite some time. Admittedly, the horse's half-brother Zaynar has not exactly gone on with age, but this fellow has far more toe in any case. Given that he is by Red Ransom, quicker ground really should not bother him, but he does seem very effective with ease. (op 8/11 tchd 8/15)
Pineau De Re(FR) excelled himself on his second run back after a long layoff. He outstayed the runner-up from the final flight and would have no problem tackling further, even though he raced quite keenly here. Connections will obviously be keen to avoid wherever the winner goes, but he has retained all his ability on this evidence. (op 10/1)
Perfect Smile(IRE) made a bold bid and looked to be going very well turning in, having travelled and jumped well in the main. It is hard to believe that he was left for dead by the winner, but he did nothing wrong and could well reverse form with the second next time. (op 9/2)
The Shepherd King(IRE) found this company too hot but was not disgraced. He travelled as well as the rest for a long way, but was perhaps a bit keen and had no more to give from the turn in. Official explanation: trainer said gelding scoped badly post-race (op 8/1)
Carloswayback(IRE) is held in very high regard but was the first beaten, a possible indication that the yard's horses are under-par. He is surely better than this. (op 13/2)
Mount Helicon was always likely to struggle over this trip and was out of his depth in any case.

2968a BAR ONE RACING HATTON'S GRACE HURDLE (GRADE 1) (12 hdls) 2m 4f

12:50 (12:52) 4-Y-0+ **£48,893** (£14,292; £6,769; £2,256)

RPR

1 **Hurricane Fly (IRE)**[236] 5380 6-11-10 166.............................. PTownend 164+
(W P Mullins, Ire) *settled in mid-div on inner: 5th 1/2-way: clsr 3 out: smooth hdwy to chal after 2 out: led early run-in: rdn to assert clsng stages* **11/4**[2]

2 *1 1/2* **Solwhit (FR)**[31] 2414 6-11-10 165.............................. DNRussell 161
(C Byrnes, Ire) *settled in mid-div: 6th 1/2-way: gd hdwy to trck ldrs 3 out: led early st: strly pressed appr last: hdd u.p early run-in: kpt on but nt match wnr* **1/1**[1]

3 *1 3/4* **Voler La Vedette (IRE)**[31] 2414 6-11-5 150.............................. AELynch 154
(C A Murphy, Ire) *in rr of mid-div: 8th 1/2-way: hdwy appr st: 5th 2 out: kpt on wl u.p on run-in wout rching principals* **8/1**[3]

4 *2* **Mourad (IRE)**[237] 5348 5-11-10 150.............................. MsKWalsh 157
(W P Mullins, Ire) *towards rr on outer: 9th 1/2-way: hdwy appr st: wnt 2nd briefly 2 out: no imp in 3rd bef last: kpt on one pce* **12/1**

5 *7* **Oscar Dan Dan (IRE)**[38] 2259 8-11-10 150..................... TimmyMurphy 150
(Thomas Mullins, Ire) *prom: 2nd 1/2-way: led briefly ent st: hdd u.p and no imp in 6th after 2 out: kpt on one pce* **20/1**

6 *hd* **Jumbo Rio (IRE)**[38] 2259 5-11-10 150..................... AndrewJMcNamara 150
(E J O'Grady, Ire) *trckd ldrs: 4th 1/2-way: chal briefly appr st: no ex fr 2 out* **20/1**

7 *3* **On The Way Out (IRE)**[73] 1711 7-11-10 141.............................. TJDoyle 147
(John E Kiely, Ire) *towards rr: sme hdwy appr st: mod 8th after 2 out: kpt on one pce* **66/1**

8 *2 1/2* **Powerstation (IRE)**[160] 1038 10-11-10 151.............................. NPMadden 144
(Eamonn O'Connell, Ire) *a towards rr: nvr a factor* **50/1**

9 *1 1/4* **Donnas Palm (IRE)**[31] 2414 6-11-10 155.............................. PCarberry 143
(Noel Meade, Ire) *mid-div on inner: 7th 1/2-way: clsr 3 out: rdn and no threat fr next* **14/1**

10 *16* **Aitmatov (GER)**[38] 2259 9-11-10 148..............................(bt) DJCondon 127
(Noel Meade, Ire) *led: strly pressed and hdd after 3 out: sn no ex and wknd* **33/1**

11 *28* **Summit Meeting**[40] 2197 5-11-10 143.............................. RMPower 99
(Mrs John Harrington, Ire) *chsd ldrs in 3rd: drvn along in 4th bef 3 out: sn wknd* **16/1**

5m 6.40s (-13.60) **Going Correction** -0.25s/f (Good) **11** Ran SP% **123.9**
Speed ratings: **117,116,115,114,112 112,110,109,109,102 91**
CSF £6.10 TOTE £3.80: £1.30, £1.20, £1.90; DF 5.00.
Owner George Creighton **Bred** Agricola Del Parco **Trained** Muine Beag, Co Carlow

FOCUS
Very hard to pick holes in this form, with the second, fourth and sixth good guides. There should be more to come from Hurricane Fly.

NOTEBOOK
Hurricane Fly(IRE) ◆ lacked the advantage of an outing this season and, unlike the runner-up, he was not previously a Grade 1 winner at this trip, which does put the form in a particularly strong perspective. He had a troubled campaign last year, but will be a serious Champion Hurdle contender if all stays well with him between now and March. He was cantering all over his rivals approaching the last and put the race to bed without too much fuss once asked to quicken. (op 100/30)
Solwhit(FR), with a winning return under his belt and reportedly not significantly held up by the weather, seemed to have plenty going for him. He travelled well, was given every chance to draw the sting from Hurricane Fly when sent into the lead early in the straight, and really there were no excuses in the end. He loses no caste in defeat and remains very near the top of the tree. (op 9/10)
Voler La Vedette(IRE) lent substance to the form with a staying-on third that saw her finish just a bit closer to Solwhit than at Punchestown in the middle of last month. Having finished third to Quevega in last season's David Nicholson she is clearly one of the best mares around, and the Cheltenham race is again the logical long-range target. (op 10/1)
Mourad(IRE) ran an admirable race on his first outing since taking third behind Quevega at Punchestown in the spring. Perhaps he is not going to be the easiest horse to place, since he is just a bit below the level of the very top hurdlers, but he provides further potency to the champion trainer's armoury. (op 16/1)
Oscar Dan Dan(IRE) won here 12 months ago but that was a much weaker contest. He showed up prominently until the heat was turned on and faded into fifth, well off the first four. (op 16/1)
Jumbo Rio(IRE) got closer to Oscar Dan Dan than when runner-up in the Lismullen Hurdle, and it was a fair enough effort, bearing in mind that his trainer had reported that the weather had been causing problems. (op 16/1)
On The Way Out(IRE) should continue to prosper when his sight are lowered again.

2970a JOHN DURKAN MEMORIAL PUNCHESTOWN STEEPLECHASE (GRADE 1) (16 fncs) 2m 4f

1:55 (1:56) 5-Y-0+ **£48,893** (£14,292; £6,769; £2,256)

RPR

1 **Tranquil Sea (IRE)**[34] 2339 8-11-10 157................. AndrewJMcNamara 161+
(E J O'Grady, Ire) *trckd ldr in 2nd: led bef 2 out: rdn to assert appr last: hld on u.p run-in* **5/2**[2]

2 *3/4* **J'y Vole (FR)**[238] 5322 7-11-5 156.............................. DJCondon 154
(W P Mullins, Ire) *hld up in rr: 6th 3 out: wnt 4th 2 out: landed in 2nd after last: kpt on wl run-in wout rching wnr* **4/1**[3]

3 *3/4* **Roberto Goldback (IRE)**[39] 2227 8-11-10 149.............................. RMPower 158
(Mrs John Harrington, Ire) *chsd ldrs in 3rd: drvn along appr 2 out: no imp on wnr bef last: kpt on u.p run-in* **13/2**

4 *1 1/2* **Glencove Marina (IRE)**[41] 2175 8-11-10 153.............................. PCarberry 157
(Eoin Griffin, Ire) *chsd ldrs: 5th 1/2-way: 4th 3 out: rdn and no imp in 5th after next: kpt on same pce run-in to regain 4th* **8/1**

5 *1/2* **Cooldine (IRE)**[238] 5322 8-11-10 160.............................. PTownend 156
(W P Mullins, Ire) *led: rdn and pressed after 3 out: hdd bef next: no imp in 4th at last: kpt on one pce* **9/4**[1]

6 4 **Trafford Lad**39 2226 8-11-10 147 AELynch 152
(Laurence James Butler, Ire) *hld up in rr: plld way into 4th bef 1/2-way: 5th 3 out: no imp u.p in st* **33/1**

7 9 **Coolcashin (IRE)**39 2226 9-11-10 138 TJDoyle 143
(Michael J Bowe, Ire) *chsd ldrs on inner: 6th 1/2-way: in tch 4 out: no ex u.p fr 2 out* **28/1**

P **Mossbank (IRE)**39 2226 10-11-10 151 DNRussell —
(Michael Hourigan, Ire) *chsd ldrs in 4th: dropped to rr bef 1/2-way: trailing after 4 out: p.u bef 2 out* **14/1**

5m 12.5s (-3.10) **Going Correction** -0.70s/f (Firm) **8** Ran SP% **116.8**
Speed ratings: **78,77,77,76,76 75,71,—**
CSF £13.79 TOTE £3.10: £1.60, £1.40, £2.00; DF 9.90.

Owner D Cox **Bred** Edward Curtin **Trained** Ballynonty, Co Tipperary
■ This race was switched from the twice abandoned Punchestwon meeting.

FOCUS
Three fences omitted. The standard is set around the fifth and seventh. The first five finished in a bunch and the time was slower than that of the Grade 1 novice chase.

NOTEBOOK
Tranquil Sea(IRE) ◆ confirmed the good impression that he had made in landing the Clonmel Oil Chase on his seasonal debut. It was a little surprising to see him displaced from the head of the market, but he belied any lack of confidence with a professional display to account for a mare who had finished a long way in front of him in last season's Ryanair. Edward O'Grady blames himself for his disappointing Cheltenham run last March, believing that the race came too soon after his previous outing. With that in mind, he may not appear again this time until returning for the same event. (op 2/1)

J'y Vole(FR) was well fancied on her seasonal debut here, and produced a solid effort, staying on well after being held up off the pace. This is probably close to her optimum trip, and she would not be out of place in the Ryanair in which she was a long-priced third last season. (op 9/2 tchd 7/2)

Roberto Goldback(IRE), running here in preference to the Hilly Way over a shorter trip, was never far from the pace and gave another creditable display following his third to The Nightingale on his seasonal debut at Down Royal. The second-season chaser still has a bit to find at Grade 1 level, but is a very capable sort who should be able to win a decent prize this season. (op 7/1)

Glencove Marina(IRE) got his career back on track with a Thurles win last month, but he was bound to find this a bit more demanding. However, he showed enough to prove that he is still a force to be reckoned with. (op 8/1 tchd 9/1)

Cooldine(IRE)'s rider tried to make his stamina count, but he was in trouble against the speedier types before the second-last. The run should set him up nicely for the Lexus at Leopardstown in just under a fortnight. (op 5/2)

Mossbank(IRE) Official explanation: jockey said saddle slipped

2971a BAR ONE RACING DRINMORE NOVICE CHASE (GRADE 1) (16 fncs) 2m 4f
2:30 (2:30) 4-Y-0+ **£46,017** (£13,451; £6,371; £2,123)

RPR

1 **Jessies Dream (IRE)**51 2017 7-11-10 136 TimmyMurphy 156
(Gordon Elliott, Ire) *trckd ldrs on inner: 5th 1/2-way: 3rd 4 out: hdwy to ld narrowly 2 out: jnd and strly pressed bef last where lft clr: kpt on wl run-in* **7/2**2

2 5 **Realt Dubh (IRE)**31 2412 6-11-10 PCarberry 151
(Noel Meade, Ire) *hld up in rr: 7th 4 out: gd hdwy on outer into cl 3rd bef 2 out: no imp appr last where lft 2nd: kpt on one pce* **9/2**3

3 hd **Head Of The Posse (IRE)**52 2008 7-11-10 139 DJCasey 151
(John E Kiely, Ire) *hld up: 6th 1/2-way: wnt 4th bef 4 out: cl up whn blnd 2 out: lft mod 3rd after last: kpt on run-in* **8/1**

4 24 **Bostons Angel (IRE)**40 2199 6-11-10 RMPower 127
(Mrs John Harrington, Ire) *trckd ldrs: 3rd 1/2-way: dropped to 6th bef 4 out: no ex u.p bef 2 out where lft mod 5th: lft distant 4th after last* **8/1**

5 3 ½ **Berties Dream (IRE)**32 2357 7-11-10 AELynch 124
(Paul John Gilligan, Ire) *prom early: dropped to rr 1/2-way: no threat fr 3 out* **20/1**

6 26 **Gold Cygnet (IRE)**31 2407 5-11-10 (t) PFMangan 98
(James Joseph Mangan, Ire) *a towards rr: mstke 5 out: t.o* **66/1**

F **Bob Lingo (IRE)**41 2174 8-11-10 130 MPWalsh —
(Thomas Mullins, Ire) *led: strly pressed fr 3 out: hdd early st: dropped to 5th whn fell 2 out* **33/1**

F **Mikael D'Haguenet (FR)**593 104 6-11-10 PTownend 158+
(W P Mullins, Ire) *trckd ldr in 2nd: disp briefly ent st: narrowly hdd 2 out: disp and appeared to be travelling best whn fell last* **6/4**1

B **Lucky William (IRE)**38 2263 6-11-10 123 AndrewJMcNamara —
(Thomas Cooper, Ire) *trckd ldrs: 4th 1/2-way: 5th 4 out: no imp in 6th whn b.d 2 out* **14/1**

5m 5.90s (-9.70) **Going Correction** -0.70s/f (Firm) **9** Ran SP% **118.5**
Speed ratings: **91,89,88,79,77 67,—,—,—**
CSF £20.34 TOTE £3.90: £1.40, £1.40, £1.80; DF 15.20.

Owner D A Johnson **Bred** Brian Doran **Trained** Trim, Co Meath
■ Gordon Elliott's first Grade 1 winner.

FOCUS
Three fences omitted. A vintage renewal of the race which served up a dramatic conclusion that would have - even on this glittering card - had everyone talking on the way home. The first two ran personal bests with the third setting the standard, with Jessies Dream in line with recent winners Trafford Lad and Pandorama. The time was much quicker than the John Durkan. Mikael D'Haguenet is rated as the winner in line with his hurdles best.

NOTEBOOK
Jessies Dream(IRE) ◆ would probably have finished second had his main rival stood up, but this was nonetheless a career-best performance that entitles him to strong consideration for the RSA Chase. Always going well, he had everything bar the favourite well-beaten coming to the last and, to his credit, he looked like he had a bit left after it. A lightly-raced horse, fences were always going to bring out the best in the son of Presenting and quotes of 20-1 for Cheltenham look more than fair, for all that he seems best with ease in the ground. (op 7/2 tchd 100/30)

Realt Dubh(IRE) was a little outclassed in the end but performed with credit. Carberry eased him into a challenging position turning in, but he was basically outpaced from there on. He might be worth stepping up further in trip.

Head Of The Posse(IRE) travelled well throughout but was also outpaced after blundering two out though he ran on again after that. This was only his third start over fences and he remains a high-class novice chaser, who would have no problem dropping back to 2m. (op 10/1)

Bostons Angel(IRE) had plenty on his plate here and was left behind. (op 10/1)

Berties Dream(IRE) has looked a shadow of his Cheltenham self over fences. He is not one to give up on just yet.

Mikael D'Haguenet(FR) ◆ surely would have won had he stayed up. There is always the worry about what he would have found off the bridle after such a mammoth layoff, but what is beyond doubt is how brilliantly he jumped here for his Irish chase debut. Moreover, he made not a semblance of a mistake at the last, only for his legs to give way on landing. Thankfully, he looked none the worse when he got up and the only worry is that it might leave a mental scar on him. Physically, it should be of no consequence and quotes of 7-1 for the RSA will tempt many. (op 11/8)

2972a O'CONNELL GROUP HILLY WAY STEEPLECHASE (GRADE 2) (13 fncs) 2m 1f
3:00 (3:00) 5-Y-0+ **£28,761** (£8,407; £3,982; £1,327)

RPR

1 **Golden Silver (FR)**38 2262 8-11-12 166 PTownend 165+
(W P Mullins, Ire) *hld up: 6th 1/2-way: wnt 3rd 2 out: smooth hdwy between horses to ld bef last: styd on wl to draw clr run-in* **4/6**1

2 4 ½ **Zaarito (IRE)**239 5303 8-11-4 148 RMPower 151
(C A Murphy, Ire) *trckd ldr in 2nd: chal fr 4 out: disp briefly after 2 out: no ch w wnr run-in: kpt on one pce u.p* **5/1**2

3 ½ **Kempes (IRE)**239 5303 7-11-12 149 DJCasey 159
(W P Mullins, Ire) *hld up towards rr: 7th 1/2-way: hdwy into 4th 2 out: lft 3rd after last: kpt on one pce* **16/1**

4 7 **Carthalawn (IRE)**38 2262 9-11-10 151 PCarberry 150
(Gordon Elliott, Ire) *chsd ldrs: 5th 1/2-way: rdn and no imp in 6th 2 out: lft 4th after last* **16/1**

5 4 **Scotsirish (IRE)**34 2339 9-11-10 153 EMullins 146
(W P Mullins, Ire) *chsd ldrs in 3rd: drvn along and no imp ent st: 7th 2 out: lft 5th after last* **11/1**

F **Osana (FR)**21 2618 8-11-4 147 (b) AndrewJMcNamara —
(E J O'Grady, Ire) *trckd ldrs: 4th 1/2-way: rdn in 5th 2 out: no imp whn fell last* **11/2**3

U **Let Yourself Go (IRE)**34 2339 8-11-7 149 SJHassett 157
(Adrian Maguire, Ire) *led: strly pressed fr 4 out: hdd u.p after 2 out: 3rd whn mstke and uns rdr last* **16/1**

P **Royal Choice (IRE)**74 1684 6-11-2 123 AELynch —
(Henry De Bromhead, Ire) *a bhd: t.o whn p.u bef last* **50/1**

4m 11.4s (-19.60) **Going Correction** -0.70s/f (Firm) **8** Ran SP% **120.0**
Speed ratings: **118,115,115,112,110 —,—,—**
CSF £5.20 TOTE £1.50: £1.02, £1.60, £4.10; DF 6.10.

Owner Mrs Violet O'Leary **Bred** Noel Pelat **Trained** Muine Beag, Co Carlow
■ This race was switched from the abandoned card at Cork three days earlier.

FOCUS
Two fences omitted. Golden Silver was a cosy winner and the form is sound enough, but limited a little by Let Yourself Go.

NOTEBOOK
Golden Silver(FR) ◆, a three-time winner at Grade 1 level and one of two in the line-up carrying a penalty, set up another clash with Big Zeb, to whom he finished second in the Fortria Chase at Navan last month, in the Paddy Power Dial-A-Bet Chase at Leopardstown (December 27) with a smoothly achieved victory here. Held up, he began to close after three out and went second two out. He was galloping over his rivals as he was sent to the front approaching the final fence and went away for an easy win. (op 5/6)

Zaarito(IRE), whose jumping often let him down in the past, made an encouraging start to his season. He raced in second place virtually throughout and had every chance from two out. Although no match for the winner from the final fence, he kept plugging away. (op 5/1 tchd 9/2)

Kempes(IRE), having his first run since landing a 3m1f Grade 1 novice at the Punchestown Festival, caught the eye. Held up, he jumped well and was staying on well in the closing stages. (op 12/1)

Carthalawn(IRE), third behind Big Zeb and Golden Silver in the Fortria Chase, ran a solid race until failing to make any headway from before two out.

Scotsirish(IRE), back in trip having run third behind Tranquil Sea over 2m4f on his reappearance at Clonmel last month, made a couple of mistakes and was done with once he fluffed four out. (op 9/1)

Let Yourself Go(IRE), runner-up to Tranquil Sea at Clonmel last month, is a confirmed front runner and he took them along at a good pace. Headed approaching the final fence, he was third when he blundered and unseated his rider. (op 14/1 tchd 20/1)

2969 - 2973a (Foreign Racing) - See Raceform Interactive

2791 EXETER (R-H)
Thursday, December 16

OFFICIAL GOING: Good to soft (chase 7.1, hurdle 7.5)
Rails on hurdle course moved out as far as possible adding 60yds per circuit to advertised distances.
Wind: quite strong against Weather: overcast with showers

2974 HAPPY CHRISTMAS MARES' NOVICES' HURDLE (10 hdls) 2m 3f
12:50 (12:50) (Class 4) 4-Y-0+ **£2,602** (£764; £382; £190)

Form RPR

1-21 **1** **Silver Gypsy (IRE)**21 2640 5-11-2 130 (t) JasonMaguire 128+
(Kim Bailey) *mde all: hmpd 1st: rdn and styd on strly fr 3 out: comf* **15/8**1

3 **2** 7 **Dun See Dee (IRE)**37 2288 6-10-10 0 TomScudamore 114
(Charlie Mann) *chsd wnr thrght: rdn appr 3 out: styd on but hld fr 2 out* **6/1**3

612F **3** 6 **Naughty Naughty**26 2514 5-10-11 115 MrMMO'Connor(5) 114
(Brendan Powell) *hld up towards rr: stdy prog fr 5th: rdn into 3rd appr 3 out: styd on same pce* **6/1**3

110- **4** 5 **Mizzurka**251 5114 6-10-10 0 APMcCoy 105+
(Bob Buckler) *in tch: wnt 3rd briefly appr 3 out: sn rdn: nt pce to chal: fading whn nt fluent last* **4/1**2

5 **5** 10 **Overnight Fame (IRE)**37 2288 6-10-10 0 PaddyBrennan 95
(Tom George) *in tch: blnd bdly 4th: rdn in cl 5th after 7th: wknd 2 out* **16/1**

4-U2 **6** 3 ¼ **Setter's Princess**23 2592 4-10-3 0 MattGriffiths(7) 93
(Ron Hodges) *trckd ldrs: rdn appr 3 out: wknd bef 2 out* **20/1**

52-5 **7** 1 **Tsarinova**221 230 5-10-10 0 WayneHutchinson 91
(Alan King) *mid-div: rdn after 7th: wknd bef next* **12/1**

6-43 **8** 1 ½ **Sapphire Rouge (IRE)**23 2592 4-10-7 0 JimmyDerham(3) 90
(Seamus Mullins) *mid-div: rdn appr 3 out: no imp* **40/1**

235 **9** 3 ½ **Lady Everywhere**28 2472 5-10-10 0 DarylJacob 87
(Nick Williams) *a towards rr* **40/1**

2-P0 **10** 1 ½ **Ballestra (IRE)**11 2791 6-10-5 0 RTDunne(5) 85
(Venetia Williams) *mid-div tl wknd appr 3 out* **100/1**

60P **11** 8 **Rolline (IRE)**37 2288 5-10-7 0 DonalDevereux(3) 78
(Stuart Kittow) *a towards rr* **200/1**

5-6 **12** 9 **Calico Rose**37 2288 6-10-10 0 DenisO'Regan 70
(Victor Dartnall) *mid-div tl wknd 7th* **33/1**

06 **13** *10* **Old Dungarvan Oak (IRE)**[21] 2627 4-10-10 0....... AndrewGlassonbury 61
(Gary Moore) *mid-div: rdn after 6th: sn wknd* **200/1**

U00 **14** *6* **Misstaysia (IRE)**[132] 1201 5-10-10 0.............................. RichardJohnson 55
(Henry Daly) *a towards rr* **100/1**

3-0 **15** *48* **Karinga Dream**[42] 2168 4-10-10 0....................................... SamThomas 12
(Venetia Williams) *a in rr: t.o* **40/1**

P **Marybelle**[2026] 8-10-10 0.. RhysFlint —
(Philip Hobbs) *chsd ldrs tl after 4th: sn bhd: t.o whn p.u bef 3 out* **80/1**

0-0 **P** **Just Lola**[219] 263 6-10-3 0.. MarkQuinlan(7) —
(Michael Blake) *prom: wandered and bmpd wnr 1st: chsd ldrs tl wknd after 6th: t.o whn p.u bef 3 out* **150/1**

-066 **F** **Catch The Rascal (IRE)**[25] 2554 4-10-10 0.................... TimmyMurphy 84
(Seamus Mullins) *a towards rr: little imp whn fell 2 out* **80/1**

4m 38.4s (-4.30) **Going Correction** -0.025s/f (Good)
WFA 4 from 5yo+ 5lb **18** Ran SP% **118.1**
Speed ratings (Par 105): **108,105,102,100,96 94,94,93,92,91 88,84,80,77,57** —,—,—
toteswingers:1&2:£3.70, 1&3:£3.50, 2&3:£6.00 CSF £11.79 TOTE £2.50: £1.10, £2.70, £2.40; EX 13.80.

Owner Mrs Tania D Yeomans **Bred** Mrs Clare Joyce **Trained** Andoversford, Gloucs

FOCUS

The going was officially described as good to soft, although the general consensus amongst riders was that it was a good bit softer, being described as 'hard work'. Quite a decent mares' novices' hurdle, albeit nowhere near as competitive as the field size suggested. Personal bests from the first two, and form that should work out.

NOTEBOOK

Silver Gypsy(IRE) readily defied the penalty picked up for winning at Uttoxeter last month. Up 3f in trip, she saw it out well, and is clearly at home in testing conditions, so can be expected to go in again over the winter. The mares' final at Newbury next year is presumably her long-term aim. (op 2-1)

Dun See Dee(IRE) has now run creditably on both starts since arriving from Ireland, and this former point winner is going to improve for 3m and fences in time. She'll win races. (tchd 11-2)

Naughty Naughty, the only other apart from the winner to have previously scored over hurdles, took a fall at Ascot last time and that may have knocked her confidence, as she failed to confirm previous course form with the runner-up and was probably a bit below her best. (op 5-1)

Mizzurka, a three-time bumper winner, including at Listed level, was disappointing on this first start over hurdles, although it did take a couple of runs for her to click last season, and it's likely she'll improve. (op 9-2 tchd 5-1)

Overnight Fame(IRE) made a notable blunder and can do better in time. (op 22-1 tchd 14-1)

2975 SOUTH-WEST RACING CLUB H'CAP CHASE (15 fncs) 2m 3f 110y

1:20 (1:24) (Class 3) (0-120,120) 4-Y-0+ **£6,505** (£1,910; £955; £477)

Form RPR

-312 **1** **Inside Dealer (IRE)**[28] 2484 6-11-5 **113**................................ JoeTizzard 129+
(Colin Tizzard) *trckd ldr: led after 11th: shkn up and in command whn hit 2 out: kpt on wl fr last* **3/1**[1]

P0-4 **2** *12* **Stradbrook (IRE)**[30] 2443 8-11-2 **110**.. APMcCoy 115
(Jonjo O'Neill) *hld up: hmpd 4th: prog 8th: rdn after 9th: styd on fr 4 out: chsd wnr 2 out: fdd fnl 100yds: jst hld on for 2nd* **6/1**[3]

-244 **3** *nse* **Maurisca (FR)**[40] 2209 5-11-0 **108**..................................(p) FelixDeGiles 118+
(Charlie Longsdon) *mid-div whn bdly hmpd 4th and lost pl: hdwy fr 9th: rdn to chse wnr after 4 out tl 2 out: nrly regained 2nd fnl stride* **5/1**[2]

-23 **4** *hd* **Darn Hot**[36] 2311 6-10-7 **104**.. ChrisHonour(3) 108
(Alex Hales) *hld up: hmpd 4th: rdn appr 4 out: styd on fr 3 out: fin wl to nrly snatch 2nd fnl strides* **8/1**

1-36 **5** *½* **Josear**[27] 2504 8-11-4 **112**.. SamThomas 114
(Chris Down) *trckd ldrs: rdn appr 4 out: styd on same pce* **25/1**

3/0- **6** *4* **Or Sing About (FR)**[590] 155 8-11-2 **113**............................... JimmyDerham(3) 112
(Seamus Mullins) *hld up towards rr: sme imp after 11th: sn rdn: no further imp fr 4 out* **33/1**

-041 **7** *17* **Manmoon (FR)**[22] 2604 7-9-12 **99** ow2...........................(t) MattGriffiths(7) 82
(Nigel Hawke) *mid-div: nt fluent 5th (water): trckd ldrs 8th: rdn appr 4 out: wknd after 4 out* **11/1**

2-40 **8** *¾* **Massini Sunset (IRE)**[26] 2529 10-10-0 **99**.................... GilesHawkins(5) 82
(Richard Mitchell) *mid-div whn hmpd 4th: sn in rr and pushed along: reminders after 7th: no ch fr 11th* **28/1**

-412 **9** *2½* **Present To You (IRE)**[41] 2181 5-11-12 **120**.................. RichardJohnson 111+
(Philip Hobbs) *hld up in mid-div: hdwy after 11th: effrt disputing cl 4th 4 out: wknd next* **13/2**

-150 **10** *1* **Rhum (FR)**[34] 2347 5-11-7 **115**.. PaddyBrennan 95
(Nigel Twiston-Davies) *trckd ldrs: mstke 10th: sn rdn: wknd after next* **9/1**

0-00 **11** *1* **Gaora Lane (IRE)**[30] 2443 9-11-9 **117**................................. DenisO'Regan 103
(Charlie Mann) *mid-div tl dropped to rr after 8th: u.p whn mstke 10th: nvr any ch after* **20/1**

12 *15* **Kap West (FR)**[411] 5-10-10 **104**... JohnnyFarrelly 69
(Laura Young) *led: blnd 9th: hdd after 11th: sn wknd: t.o* **80/1**

/1-P **F** **Direct Flight (IRE)**[216] 314 12-11-5 **118**.......................(t) IanPopham(5) —
(Jeremy Scott) *mid-div whn fell heavily 4th* **33/1**

4m 53.0s (-4.30) **Going Correction** -0.025s/f (Good) **13** Ran SP% **117.9**
Speed ratings (Par 107): **107,102,102,102,101 100,93,93,92,91 91,85,**—
toteswingers:1&2:£5.60, 1&3:£3.60, 2&3:£6.00 CSF £19.68 CT £88.24 TOTE £4.50: £1.70, £2.70, £1.30; EX 29.20.

Owner J M Dare, T Hamlin, J W Snook **Bred** B D Darrer **Trained** Milborne Port, Dorset

FOCUS

Just a modest handicap chase, but another step up from the progressive winner.

NOTEBOOK

Inside Dealer(IRE), who had been narrowly denied off 4lb lower at Wincanton the time before, was never far from the lead. He began to assert from three out, and stayed on in the manner of a horse who's likely to stay 3m in time. (tchd 10-3 and 7-2 in places)

Stradbrook(IRE), well held at Folkestone on his recent reappearance/return to fences, had been dropped 3lb and showed much-improved form, although in the end was clinging on for second. He could improve again and win a small race. (op 7-1 tchd 15-2)

Maurisca(FR) put up a really good effort considering how badly hampered he was at the fourth fence. Given time to recover by his rider, he gradually crept back into it and toughed it out well to just miss second. Having his first start of the season over fences, he can improve and is capable of winning off this mark. (op 13-2)

Darn Hot, another interfered with early, rallied well from the end of the back straight and kept on best she could without quite getting up for second. She's ideally suited by further than this. (op 7-1)

Josear showed improved form returned to fences, although he remains 7lb above his last winning mark. (op 20-1)

Or Sing About(FR) hasn't had much racing over the past couple of years, but his rating has come down as a result, and there was promise in this run. (op 40-1)

Massini Sunset(IRE) Official explanation: jockey said gelding never travelled

Present To You(IRE), straight into handicaps on this debut over fences, possibly found the ground too soft and deserves another chance. (op 6-1 tchd 11-2)

2976 A.P. MCCOY 15 TIMES CHAMPION JOCKEY GRADUATION CHASE (12 fncs) 2m 1f 110y

1:50 (1:52) (Class 2) 4-Y-0+ **£15,655** (£4,625; £2,312; £1,157; £577)

Form RPR

13-1 **1** **Royal Charm (FR)**[37] 2286 5-11-0 0...................................... DarylJacob 147+
(Paul Nicholls) *trckd ldrs: wnt 2nd at the 3rd: chal 3 out: 1/2 l down last: hrd rdn sn after: led fnl stride* **8/13**[1]

/1U- **2** *hd* **Leo's Lucky Star (USA)**[313] 3886 8-11-0 135.............(t) TomScudamore 145+
(David Pipe) *hld up in last pair: smooth hdwy to trck ldrs 8th: travelling wl whn chalng 3 out: led sn after 2 out: rdn after last: hdd fnl stride* **18/1**

00B- **3** *13* **Chapoturgeon (FR)**[252] 5097 6-11-7 150......................... TimmyMurphy 142+
(Paul Nicholls) *hld up in last pair: nt a fluent: struggling to hold pl after 8th: kpt on to snatch 3rd nr fin but no ch w front pair* **13/2**[3]

203- **4** *¾* **Sports Line (IRE)**[238] 5350 7-11-4 149............................. JasonMaguire 140+
(Donald McCain) *racd keenly: led: pressed fr 3 out: mstke 2 out: sn hdd: no ex: lost 3rd nr fin* **3/1**[2]

P-3P **5** *1¾* **Or Bleu (FR)**[21] 2629 8-11-7 124.................................... RichardJohnson 138
(Philip Hobbs) *chsd ldr tl 3rd: chsd ldrs: outpcd 8th: kpt on but nvr a threatened ldrs after* **28/1**

4m 19.6s (0.60) **Going Correction** -0.025s/f (Good) **5** Ran SP% **109.0**
Speed ratings (Par 109): **97,96,91,90,90**
CSF £10.37 TOTE £1.50: £1.10, £3.20; EX 8.10.

Owner Mrs Angela Tincknell & W Tincknell **Bred** Jean-Philippe Dubois **Trained** Ditcheat, Somerset

FOCUS

An interesting graduation chase that was run at a good clip thanks to Sports Line. Royal Charm improved to the level of his hurdles form, with a step up from the second.

NOTEBOOK

Royal Charm(FR) was under pressure early in the straight and briefly looked beaten, but he showed a gritty attitude to run down the strong-travelling runner-up close home. Previously 3-3 at the course, including a chase win on last month's debut, he again jumped well and the manner in which he stayed on suggests he may benefit from a return to further. He remains progressive and will presumably go up in grade now. (tchd 4-6 and 8-11 in places)

Leo's Lucky Star(USA), who'd have been better off with these in a handicap, has always been talented and he travelled like the best horse off the pace. Tom Scudamore will probably be wishing he had held on to him for longer, though, as having taken it up, he didn't seem to be doing much in front, and was eventually worn down. Rated 135, he can make his mark in decent handicaps if going on from this. (op 16-1)

Chapoturgeon(FR) would have found this trip on the sharp side and didn't jump all that fluently out of the ground, which would have been softer than ideal. He's another talented individual who, with a little assistance from the handicapper, will pop up again in a good handicap one day. (op 17-2)

Sports Line(IRE), twice Grade 1-placed as a novice for Willie Mullins, has a habit of racing freely and that was again the case here, being allowed to stride on, but never giving himself a chance of seeing it out in the ground. A mistake three out knocked the stuffing out of him, but he's likely to come on for it, will appreciate better ground, and could find himself on a decent mark for handicaps later in the season. (tchd 10-3)

Or Bleu(FR) had plenty on at the weights, but still offered little, as has been the case all too often for this disappointing sort. (op 33-1)

2977 SOUTH-WEST RACING CLUB H'CAP HURDLE (8 hdls) 2m 1f

2:20 (2:24) (Class 3) (0-130,130) 3-Y-0+ **£4,553** (£1,337; £668; £333)

Form RPR

531- **1** **Requin (FR)**[283] 4492 5-10-2 **106**...................................... DenisO'Regan 117+
(Victor Dartnall) *trckd ldr: led appr 3 out: rdn whn pressed last: drifted lft: styd on wl: drvn out* **7/1**[2]

3-41 **2** *½* **Salontyre (GER)**[11] 2792 4-10-2 **111** 7ex..........(p) MissIsabelTompsett(5) 122+
(Bernard Llewellyn) *in tch: clsd on ldrs after 5th: chal appr last: kpt on run-in: carried sltly lft: hld nr fin* **8/1**[3]

120- **3** *11* **Dream Esteem**[275] 4657 5-11-1 **119**.............................. TomScudamore 120
(David Pipe) *racd keenly in midfield: hdwy 5th: disputing 2nd whn rdn after 3 out: no ex appr last* **9/1**

PP-2 **4** *1* **Laustra Bad (FR)**[26] 2530 7-10-4 **113**.............................(tp) CO'Farrell(5) 114
(David Pipe) *trckd ldrs: rdn and ev ch 3 out: kpt on same pce fr next* **8/1**[3]

-562 **5** *1¼* **Prince Of Denial (IRE)**[29] 2456 6-10-5 **109**....................... PaddyBrennan 108
(Nigel Twiston-Davies) *mid-div: hdwy after 5th: effrt 3 out: styd on same pce* **8/1**[3]

66-5 **6** *2¼* **Johnny Mullen (IRE)**[32] 2393 7-10-4 **115**...................... MattGriffiths(7) 112
(Paul Henderson) *in tch: rdn after 5th: styd on same pce fr 3 out* **16/1**

3-32 **7** *¾* **Numide (FR)**[31] 2423 7-11-4 **122**.. SamThomas 118
(Rod Millman) *hld up bhd: sme prog into midfield appr 3 out: nvr trbld ldrs* **22/1**

016- **8** *1½* **Horsford (IRE)**[301] 4118 6-10-11 **115**.............................. JohnnyFarrelly 111+
(David Pipe) *led tl rdn appr 3 out: sn one pce* **33/1**

630/ **9** *7* **Cypress Grove (IRE)**[663] 4052 7-10-3 **107**.............. WayneHutchinson 96
(John Ryall) *nvr bttr than mid-div* **66/1**

-132 **10** *2¾* **Scoter Fontaine (FR)**[36] 2307 4-10-13 **117**............................ APMcCoy 103
(Rebecca Curtis) *trckd ldrs: rdn whn edgd lft appr 3 out: wknd 2 out* **11/4**[1]

-200 **11** *5* **Tobago Bay**[174] 838 5-11-2 **130**................................ JosephAkehurst(10) 112
(Gary Moore) *in tch tl rdn after 5th: wknd bef 3 out* **40/1**

3322 **12** *½* **Dark Energy**[21] 2633 6-10-8 **112**...(t) RhysFlint 93
(Michael Scudamore) *a towards rr* **33/1**

0-05 **13** *3¾* **Drussell (IRE)**[31] 2423 4-11-0 **118**.................................. MattieBatchelor 96
(Richard Phillips) *a towards rr* **66/1**

5-6F **14** *14* **Troubletimestwo (FR)**[40] 2213 4-10-11 **120**................... LeeEdwards(5) 85
(Tony Carroll) *mid-div tl wknd after 4th* **66/1**

62-0 **15** *3* **Amore Mio (GER)**[34] 2347 5-11-2 **120**................................ TomSiddall 82
(Richard Phillips) *a bhd* **18/1**

01-0 **16** *nk* **Puzzlemaster**[32] 2386 4-11-7 **125**...................................(t) RichardJohnson 87
(Hughie Morrison) *trckd ldrs: rdn after 5th: wknd bef 3 out* **16/1**

/0-0 **17** *11* **Wingman (IRE)**[27] 2498 8-11-6 **124**.......................... AndrewGlassonbury 76
(Gary Moore) *mid-div tl wknd appr 3 out* **18/1**

10-5 **P** **Don't Panic (IRE)**[23] 2596 6-10-5 **109**.............................. TimmyMurphy —
(Ron Hodges) *a towards rr: t.o whn p.u after 3 out* **28/1**

4m 12.4s (-3.10) **Going Correction** -0.025s/f (Good) **18** Ran SP% **125.4**
Speed ratings (Par 107): **106,105,100,100,99 98,98,97,94,92 90,90,88,81,80 80,75,**—
toteswingers:1&2:£11.40, 1&3:£11.80, 2&3:£16.10 CSF £59.45 CT £520.56 TOTE £8.70: £2.10, £2.60, £2.90, £2.70; EX 78.40.

Owner Exors of the Late P M De Wilde **Bred** Haras De Saint-Voir And Maurice Goin **Trained** Brayford, Devon

■ Stewards' Enquiry : Denis O'Regan three-day ban: careless riding (Dec 30-Jan 1)

FOCUS

This had looked an open handicap hurdle, but the front two ended up drawing clear. A big step forward from Requin to beat a well handicapped second, with the next two giving the form a solid look.

NOTEBOOK

Requin(FR), who had also been declared at Towcester, fended off the persistent runner-up after the last to make a winning debut for Victor Dartnall, having previously been with the Alners. Only a 5-y-o, he looks to have a bit about him in terms of scope, and it would be no surprise to see him add to his tally over hurdles before eventually going chasing. (op 8-1)

Salontyre(GER) caused a surprise when beating a few more high-profile names at the course latest, and was able to race off his correct mark this time, so was actually 14lb lower. It was therefore no surprise to see him emerge as a big threat to the winner, but having jumped the last, he was always just coming off worse. He's due to race off 15lb higher in future and things will obviously be a lot tougher. (op 11-1)

Dream Esteem travelled well in behind the pace, although perhaps a little too well, as when it came down to it, she didn't have sufficient gas left in the tank on this first start in 275 days. This was just her fourth start and she can still improve. (op 7-1 tchd 10-1)

Laustra Bad(FR) seems to have returned in decent form, although it's been almost three and a half years now since he last won a race. (op 11-1)

Prince Of Denial(IRE) didn't improve as expected for the switch to handicaps, although there's little doubt he'll be suited by a stiffer test in future. (op 13-2)

Johnny Mullen(IRE) is slipping in the weights and may be ready to win once stepped back up in trip. (tchd 14-1)

Scoter Fontaine(FR), switched to handicaps following just two runs, proved disappointing, dropping away without putting up much of a fight. (op 10-3 tchd 5-2 and 7-2 in places)

Puzzlemaster ran better than his finishing position suggests and will be of interest down the line once his mark has eased a tad.

2978 EUROPEAN BREEDERS' FUND/THOROUGHBRED BREEDERS' ASSOCIATION MARES' NOVICES' CHASE (15 fncs) 2m 3f 110y

2:50 (2:51) (Class 4) 4-Y-O+ **£4,228** (£1,241; £620; £310)

Form				RPR
0-31	**1**		**Sway (FR)**^{35} [2326] 4-10-12 0 ... APMcCoy (Jonjo O'Neill) *j. and travelled wl: cl up: chal 3 out: led sn after 2 out: drew clr: readily* **9/2**^{3}	129+
-054	**2**	*11*	**Bathwick Quest (IRE)**^{44} [2139] 6-10-12 112 ... TomScudamore (Brendan Powell) *led: rdn after 4 out: hdd sn after 2 out: kpt on but no ch w wnr* **33/1**	115
3135	**3**	*6*	**Amber Brook (IRE)**^{24} [2579] 9-10-12 0 ... PaddyBrennan (Nigel Twiston-Davies) *trckd ldrs: nudged along after 7th: rdn appr 4 out: styng on same pce whn lft 3rd and hmpd 2 out* **7/2**^{2}	113+
643	**4**	*11*	**The Wifes Pet (IRE)**^{38} [2278] 6-10-7 112 ... DavidBass$^{(5)}$ (Lawney Hill) *cl up: rdn whn squeezed up on bnd appr 4 out: wknd after 3 out: lft 4th next* **12/1**	100
30-2	**5**	*18*	**Cobbler's Queen (IRE)**^{41} [2182] 6-10-12 118 ... RichardJohnson (Henry Daly) *nt a fluent: hld up last but in tch: pushed along after 7th: rdn after 11th: nvr any imp: wknd bef 3 out* **8/1**	90
11P3	**6**	*26*	**Identity Parade (IRE)**^{25} [2552] 6-10-12 0 ... JasonMaguire (Donald McCain) *w ldr: hit 8th: rdn after 10th: bmpd on bnd bef 4 out: sn wknd* **14/1**	72
0-11	**F**		**Easter Legend**^{28} [2481] 6-11-10 0 ... SamThomas (Emma Lavelle) *hld up bhd ldrs: tk clsr order after 11th: nudged along and mounting chal whn fell 2 out* **5/4**^{1}	135

4m 55.3s (-2.00) **Going Correction** -0.025s/f (Good)
WFA 4 from 6yo+ 5lb **7** Ran SP% **113.3**
Speed ratings (Par 105): **103,98,96,91,84 74,—**
toteswingers:1&2:£12.60, 1&3:£2.40, 2&3:£15.90 CSF £90.06 TOTE £4.60: £2.60, £8.10; EX 101.00.

Owner John P McManus **Bred** Guy Cherel **Trained** Cheltenham, Gloucs

FOCUS

A good mares' novice chase contested by a trio of very useful hurdlers. The cosy winner is on the upgrade over fences, and the the second is rated to her hurdles mark.

NOTEBOOK

Sway(FR) jumped well and found plenty once in front, and certainly looked to be going better than the favourite when that one departed two out. She had got herself back on track when beating a fair sort at Ludlow latest, was again receiving the 4-y-o allowance and it would be a surprise were this to be the last of her victories as a novice. She's already shown she's capable of mixing it against the boys, but the mares' chase final at Newbury is presumably where she'll end up. (op 7-2)

Bathwick Quest(IRE), a 112-rated hurdler who was last of four on her chasing debut at the course, had clearly learnt from that and offered considerably more, albeit she was fortunate to inherit second.

Amber Brook(IRE), the best of these over hurdles, failed to complete in three points earlier in her career, and it looked worrying it had been left so late for her to go chasing, being almost ten. Her jumping was sound enough, but she lacked the pace over this trip, and in the end could only plod on down the straight. (op 4-1)

The Wifes Pet(IRE) was already under pressure when slightly squeezed on the final bend and she'll find easier opportunities. (op 16-1 tchd 18-1)

Cobbler's Queen(IRE) was soon detached in last and never got into it, failing to build on a promising debut behind Easter Legend. (op 7-1)

Identity Parade(IRE) did her best to rally, but was another beaten when receiving a bump. (op 16-1 tchd 12-1)

Easter Legend, shouldered with a double penalty following easy wins at Fontwell and Wincanton, didn't jump as well as she had previously, but was responding to pressure and trying to challenge when toppling over two out. She'd probably have been second, which would have been far from a disgrace conceding 12lb. (op 11-8)

2979 VOTE A.P. MCCOY FOR BBC SPORTS PERSONALITY NOVICES' CHASE (18 fncs) 3m

3:20 (3:21) (Class 4) 4-Y-O+ **£5,204** (£1,528; £764; £381)

Form				RPR
21-1	**1**		**Wymott (IRE)**^{36} [2303] 6-11-7 0 ... JasonMaguire (Donald McCain) *trckd ldr: led 3 out: rdn appr last: drifted sltly rt run-in: drvn out* **1/2**^{1}	148+
254	**2**	*½*	**Shalimar Fromentro (FR)**^{29} [2455] 4-10-7 0 ... DarylJacob (Nick Williams) *patiently rdn in last: stdy prog fr 14th: disp 3rd 4 out: sn rdn: wnt 2nd last: styd on after switching rt: fin wl* **28/1**	133+
2-21	**3**	*5*	**Adams Island (IRE)**^{33} [2363] 6-11-0 133 ...(p) AodhaganConlon$^{(7)}$ (Rebecca Curtis) *led tl rdn 3 out: styd chsng wnr tl last: no ex* **10/1**^{3}	142
112/	**4**	*10*	**Definity (IRE)**^{608} [5067] 7-11-0 0 ... HarrySkelton (Paul Nicholls) *racd keenly: cl up: rdn appr 4 out: styd on same pce* **3/1**^{2}	126
6124	**5**	*7*	**Frontier Dancer (IRE)**^{26} [2527] 6-11-7 128 ... PaddyBrennan (Nigel Twiston-Davies) *hld up: tk clsr order after 14th: effrt in 5th next: wknd bef 2 out* **40/1**	129
2-33	**6**	*29*	**John's Gift**^{44} [2141] 6-11-0 101 ... AndrewGlassonbury (Bob Buckler) *trckd ldrs: rdn appr 4 out: sn wknd: t.o* **66/1**	105
52-P	**7**	*1 ¼*	**Flight Leader (IRE)**^{5} [2883] 10-11-0 130 ... JoeTizzard (Colin Tizzard) *trckd ldr tl after 11th: dropped tamely away fr next: t.o* **28/1**	91
11P-	**8**	*31*	**Hopeful Start (IRE)**^{251} [5112] 6-11-0 0 ... APMcCoy (Jonjo O'Neill) *hld up but in tch: struggling 11th: wknd after 14th: t.o* **11/1**	64

6m 23.6s (14.30) **Going Correction** -0.025s/f (Good)
WFA 4 from 6yo+ 7lb **8** Ran SP% **119.9**
Speed ratings (Par 105): **75,74,73,69,67 57,57,47**
toteswingers:1&2:£3.90, 1&3:£2.40, 2&3:£13.80 CSF £20.69 TOTE £2.30: £1.10, £4.20, £2.00; EX 19.70.

Owner Trevor Hemmings **Bred** Mrs Mary Fennell **Trained** Cholmondeley, Cheshire

FOCUS

A decent novice chase which should produce winners. Wymott can rate higher on his hurdles form and the second is on the upgrade.

NOTEBOOK

Wymott(IRE) made hard work of this, being all out to hold on from 28-1 shot Shalimar Fromentro in the end. A Grade 2 winner as a novice over hurdles, he's held in high regard by his trainer, and got off to the perfect start at Bangor. This was expected to prove fairly straightforward, so having jumped well again, one would have liked to see him really stamp his authority, but he was unable to do so. It's possible he wasn't at his best on a day when conditions weren't overly pleasant, but he will need to raise his game once going up in grade. (op 8-15 tchd 4-7 and 8-13 in places)

Shalimar Fromentro(FR) ◆, well beaten over 2m on his chasing debut, improved dramatically for the step up in trip and some may argue he should have won, Daryl Jacob not being overly hard on him under a patient ride. It briefly looked as though he had the momentum to go past the winner after the last, but it wasn't to be this time. He looks to have a fair bit of scope and shouldn't be long in going one better. (op 33-1)

Adams Island(IRE) lacks the scope of the front pair, but he gave it a good go from the front and finished a clear third. (op 12-1)

Definity(IRE), rated one of Paul Nicholls' leading novice-chase prospects until injury struck last season, was very keen on this first start in 608 days, and it was no surprise to see him drop out of contention in the straight. There was definite promise in the run, though, and he should be a lot straighter next time. (op 10-3 tchd 7-2)

Frontier Dancer(IRE) doesn't looks capable of defying a penalty and may do better back in distance switched to handicaps.

John's Gift went well to a point in a race he was expected to struggle in, and there'll be easier opportunities for him.

Flight Leader(IRE) again offered little encouragement. (op 33-1)

Hopeful Start(IRE), a promising sort over hurdles who had beaten the third last season, was toiling a long way from the finish. That said, it would be no surprise to see him come good in handicaps later in the season. (op 16-1)

2980 WELCOME BACK ON NEW YEAR'S DAY AMATEUR RIDERS' H'CAP HURDLE (11 hdls) 2m 5f 110y

3:50 (3:53) (Class 4) (0-100,100) 4-Y-O+ **£2,498** (£774; £387; £193)

Form				RPR
342/	**1**		**Pocketwood**^{54} [4135] 8-11-9 **100** ... MissZoeLilly$^{(3)}$ (Alastair Lidderdale) *trckd ldrs on outer: led and wnt lft 3 out: wnt lft last 2: r.o strly to assert fr last* **11/2**^{2}	117+
0541	**2**	*4*	**Hot Tottie (IRE)**^{11} [2795] 6-11-1 **89** ...(p) MissIsabelTompsett (Jeremy Scott) *mid-div: hdwy after 8th: chal 2 out: rdn and ev ch last: edgd lft: kpt on but no ex towards fin* **5/2**^{1}	100
6/64	**3**	*13*	**Baby Car (FR)**^{29} [2452] 6-10-5 **86** ...(t) MrJBanks$^{(7)}$ (Noel Chance) *mid-div: blnd 1st: rdn and hdwy appr 3 out: styd on to take 3rd gng to last: no ch w front pair* **10/1**	85
35	**4**	*11*	**Low Delta (IRE)**^{128} [1232] 10-10-11 **90** ... MrPJTolman$^{(5)}$ (Michael Blake) *hld up towards rr: hdwy on outer 5th: rdn bef 3 out to chse ldrs: wknd after 2 out* **16/1**	79
3P42	**5**	*3*	**Elegant Olive**^{39} [2239] 7-10-4 **85** ... MrFTett$^{(7)}$ (Roger Curtis) *hld up towards rr: hdwy on outer 5th: rdn to chse ldrs 3 out: wknd after 2 out* **9/1**	72
P1-P	**6**	*2 ¼*	**Sea Saffron**^{226} [130] 9-11-9 **97** ... MrWBiddick (Susan Gardner) *hld up towards rr: hdwy fr 6th: rdn appr 3 out: wknd 2 out* **18/1**	82
0235	**7**	*1 ½*	**Coeur Brule (FR)**^{16} [2469] 4-11-6 **99** ... MrDavidTurner$^{(5)}$ (Sam Davison) *trckd ldrs: led 6th: rdn and hdd 3 out: sn wknd* **50/1**	82
4204	**8**	*1*	**Kilvergan Boy (IRE)**^{25} [2557] 6-11-2 **97** ... MrWTwiston-Davies$^{(7)}$ (Nigel Twiston-Davies) *trckd ldrs: rdn appr 3 out: sn wknd* **16/1**	79
5430	**9**	*nk*	**Newyearsresolution (IRE)**^{21} [2637] 6-11-2 **95** ... MrRGHenderson$^{(5)}$ (Nick Mitchell) *prom tl after 5th: struggling and hld in midfield whn mstke 8th* **20/1**	77
0-05	**10**	*1 ¼*	**French Leave (IRE)**^{27} [2504] 8-11-5 **93** ...(t) MrJoshuaGuerriero (Victor Dartnall) *in tch: rdn to chse ldrs appr 3 out: wknd bef 2 out* **12/1**	74
43F5	**11**	*16*	**Royial (FR)**^{45} [2134] 5-10-12 **93** ... MissCLBrown$^{(7)}$ (Seamus Mullins) *mid-div tl wknd appr 3 out* **40/1**	60
-30P	**12**	*5*	**Tarabela**^{25} [2558] 7-11-2 **97** ... MrDSymes-Meineck$^{(7)}$ (Gerald Ham) *mid-div: rdn appr 3 out: sn wknd* **50/1**	59
6-60	**13**	*2 ¾*	**Spot The Ball (IRE)**^{43} [2149] 5-11-0 **88** ... MrAJBerry (Jonjo O'Neill) *hld up bhd: drvn and hdwy fr 6th: chsd ldrs briefly gng to 3 out: wknd qckly* **8/1**^{3}	48
04-0	**14**	*2 ¾*	**Royal Chatelier (FR)**^{36} [2308] 5-11-2 **93** ... MrRWoollacott$^{(3)}$ (Michael Blake) *trckd ldrs: hit 7th: sn rdn: wknd after next* **25/1**	50
13-3	**15**	*10*	**Lightening Fire (IRE)**^{53} [1996] 8-10-4 **85** ...(b) MrRJWilliams$^{(7)}$ (Bernard Llewellyn) *mid-div tl wknd 8th* **12/1**	33
3506	**16**	*22*	**Terrible Tenant**^{21} [2638] 11-10-11 **92** ... MrKevinJones$^{(7)}$ (Seamus Mullins) *led tl 6th: grad fdd: t.o* **50/1**	20
60-P	**17**	*1*	**Red Perfection**^{29} [2452] 7-10-7 **88** ...(t) MrRHatch$^{(7)}$ (Tony Carroll) *a towards rr: t.o whn hmpd 3 out* **40/1**	15
00/6	**F**		**One And All (IRE)**^{37} [2283] 7-11-0 **93** ... MrDGPrichard$^{(5)}$ (Nigel Hawke) *mid-div: in rr whn fell 3 out* **28/1**	—

5m 45.3s (12.30) **Going Correction** -0.025s/f (Good)
WFA 4 from 5yo+ 6lb **18** Ran SP% **129.4**
Speed ratings (Par 105): **76,74,69,65,64 63,63,63,62,62 56,54,53,52,49 41,40,—**
toteswingers:1&2:£4.50, 1&3:£13.70, 2&3:£8.20; totesuper7: Win: Not won. Place: Not won. CSF £19.37 CT £142.57 TOTE £6.90: £1.60, £1.40, £3.10, £5.50; EX 21.30.

Owner The Sw1ft Buck Partnership **Bred** M J Lewin **Trained** Eastbury, Berks

■ Stewards' Enquiry : Mr R G Henderson two-day ban: used whip when out of contention (tbn)

FOCUS

The runners came home well strung out for this amateur riders' handicap hurdle. The winner is entitled to rate higher on Flat form and the second was well in on her recent course win.

NOTEBOOK

Pocketwood, a dual winner on the Flat this autumn, gives his running more often than not and didn't look badly treated at all on his old hurdles form. He met a stern challenge from the favourite, but galloped on relentlessly to score and his determined attitude is likely to lead to further success at a modest level. (op 6-1)

Hot Tottie(IRE), a recent course scorer, is due to race off 12lb higher in future. He was understandably made favourite but, having weaved her way through the field, found the winner too strong from the last. Although clear of the remainder, life will be tougher in future. (op 3-1)

Baby Car(FR), wearing a first-time tongue-tie, made some late headway and again left the impression he'll be more competitive upped to 3m. (op 9-1 tchd 11-1)

Low Delta(IRE), although back on a winning mark, gives the impression he's past his best. (tchd 20-1)
Elegant Olive was unable to build on her Hereford second on this drop in trip. (op 12-1)
Coeur Brule(FR) went for home a long way out and was always going to struggle to last.
Spot The Ball(IRE) stopped quickly and continues to offer limited encouragement. (op 17-2 tchd 9-1)
T/Plt: £51.90 to a £1 stake. Pool:£68,854.74 - 967.95 winning tickets T/Qpdt: £30.80 to a £1 stake. Pool:£3,851.76 - 92.40 winning tickets TM

2554 TOWCESTER (R-H)

Thursday, December 16

OFFICIAL GOING: Good to soft (soft in places) changing to soft after race 1 (12:40)

Wind: Strong across Weather: Rain turning to snow prior to the 6th race

2981 FREE BETS @ GG.COM NOVICES' HURDLE (11 hdls) 2m 5f

12:40 (12:47) (Class 3) 4-Y-0+ **£4,033** (£1,184; £592; £295)

Form RPR

02-0 **1** **De Forgotten Man (IRE)**[44] 2142 5-10-12 0 .... RobertThornton 109+
(Martin Keighley) *hld up: hdwy 5th: chsd ldr and hit 3 out: led next: drvn out* **7/1**

10 **2** *1* **Badgers Cove (IRE)**[5] 2888 6-11-4 0 .... CharliePoste 113
(Robin Dickin) *chsd ldrs: led 8th: rdn and hdd 2 out: styd on u.p* **7/2**[2]

6 **3** *nk* **Gunna Be A Devil (IRE)**[28] 2482 6-10-12 0 .... NickScholfield 107
(Jeremy Scott) *hld up: hdwy appr 8th: rdn after 2 out: styd on* **4/1**[3]

1-4U **4** *14* **Skipper Robin (FR)**[37] 2283 4-10-9 0 .... SamTwiston-Davies(3) 96
(Nigel Twiston-Davies) *chsd ldrs: rdn after 3 out: wknd bef last* **17/2**

5 *16* **Power Lord (IRE)**[270] 5-10-5 0 .... NathanSweeney(7) 80
(Bob Buckler) *hld up: drvn along after 5th: n.d: t.o* **66/1**

0- **6** *1* **Tim The Chair (IRE)**[292] 4301 5-10-5 0 .... StephenO'Donovan(7) 79
(Emma Lavelle) *chsd ldrs tl rdn and wknd 2 out: t.o* **16/1**

7 *28* **Lions In Law**[67] 6-10-5 0 .... MrTomDavid(7) 54
(Richard Hawker) *hld up: hdwy 5th: rdn and wknd after 8th: t.o* **25/1**

00-3 **8** *12* **Aeronautica (IRE)**[25] 2554 7-10-5 0 .... DominicElsworth 36
(Tor Sturgis) *hld up: mstke 6th: bhd fr 8th: t.o* **16/1**

/4-0 **9** *9* **Artic Pride (IRE)**[29] 2454 6-10-12 0 .... LeightonAspell 35
(Oliver Sherwood) *hld up: hdwy 5th: wknd 3 out: t.o* **25/1**

0 **10** *16* **Drink Up**[176] 833 6-10-12 0 .... AndrewThornton 20
(John O'Neill) *hld up: blnd 2nd: bhd fr 5th: t.o* **100/1**

P/ **P** **Supreme Oscar (IRE)**[683] 0000 7-10-5 0 .... MrJamieJenkinson(7) —
(Frederick Sutherland) *led to 8th: wknd bef next: t.o whn p.u bef 2 out* **200/1**

604 **P** **Just Unique**[33] 2365 6-10-9 0 .... PeterToole(3) —
(Mark Rimell) *uns rdr and got loose prior to the s: chsd ldr to appr 7th: sn wknd: t.o whn p.u bef 3 out* **100/1**

03 **P** **Duke Of Ormond (IRE)**[21] 2642 7-10-12 0 .... DaveCrosse —
(Anna Brooks) *hld up in tch: wknd 7th: t.o whn p.u bef 2 out* **40/1**

5-0 **P** **Ben The Horse (IRE)**[39] 2238 4-10-12 0 .... AndrewTinkler —
(Henry Daly) *chsd ldrs: drvn along after 3rd: lost pl 5th: sn t.o: p.u bef 7th* **40/1**

1 **P** **Stolen Thunder**[48] 2069 5-11-4 0 .... JamesDavies —
(Emma Lavelle) *prom tl rdn and wknd after 7th: t.o whn p.u bef 3 out* **3/1**[1]

0 **P** **Sam's Pride**[24] 2590 5-10-9 0 .... RichieMcLernon(3) —
(Peter Pritchard) *hld up: a in rr: bhd fr 6th: t.o whn p.u bef 3 out* **100/1**

5m 39.1s (11.90) **Going Correction** +0.15s/f (Yiel)
WFA 4 from 5yo+ 6lb **16** Ran SP% **119.5**
Speed ratings (Par 107): **83,82,82,77,71 70,60,55,52,45** —,—,—,—,— —
toteswingers:1&2:£6.80, 1&3:£7.50, 2&3:£4.60 CSF £30.30 TOTE £7.50: £3.60, £1.20, £2.20; EX 45.60.
Owner Mrs Peter Andrews **Bred** J Mangan **Trained** Condicote, Gloucs

FOCUS

After a delayed start there were just five still in contention at the third last flight. That was reduced to three at the next and, after a stirring battle, De Forgotten Man came out on top in a driving finish. Ordinary novice form.

NOTEBOOK

De Forgotten Man(IRE), an Irish maiden point winner in the past, took a soft-ground bumper here in February. Putting a poor run at Exeter on his return behind him, he slogged it out in the gamest possible fashion. He is clearly a real stayer and a longer term chasing prospect. (op 17-2)
Badgers Cove(IRE), another point winner, opened his account over hurdles at Ludlow last month. Out of his depth behind Mossley at Cheltenham five days earlier, he took it up before four out and went down fighting. He too looks a longer term chasing prospect. (op 10-3 tchd 3-1)
Gunna Be A Devil(IRE), a dual point winner in Ireland, improved from off the pace to join issue four out. He stuck on in willing fashion from the last and deserves to find an opening. (op 5-1 tchd 7-2)
Skipper Robin(FR), who took a bumper at Perth in April, ran his best race over hurdles on this third start but he will need to improve a fair bit more if he is to make his mark. (tchd 9-1)
Stolen Thunder, a wide-margin winner on his racecourse debut at Uttoxeter in October, dropped out some way from home after proving difficult to settle and was eventually pulled up. This was too bad to be true. Official explanation: jockey said gelding ran too free (op 10-3 tchd 4-1)

2982 FREE BETS @ GG.COM NOVICES' H'CAP CHASE (18 fncs) 3m 110y

1:10 (1:17) (Class 4) (0-105,102) 4-Y-0+ **£2,927** (£859; £429; £214)

Form RPR

-212 **1** **Aztec Treasure (NZ)**[23] 2595 6-11-9 102 .... RichieMcLernon(3) 119+
(Jonjo O'Neill) *hld up: mstke 11th: wnt handy 3rd next: hit 14th: trckd ldr next: led last: pushed out: comf* **5/2**[1]

5222 **2** *2* **Topless (IRE)**[11] 2796 9-11-11 101 .... (b[1]) DougieCostello 108
(Neil Mulholland) *led to 7th: led 10th: drvn 3 out: hdd sn after last: no ch w wnr* **11/2**[3]

-332 **3** *1 3/4* **Dromore Hill (IRE)**[22] 2608 6-10-12 88 .... (v) JimmyMcCarthy 93
(Charlie Morlock) *chsd ldrs: drvn along 3rd: dropped bk 14th: hdwy to chse ldng pair after 3 out: styd on wl run-in* **7/2**[2]

150- **4** *54* **Guydus (IRE)**[239] 5311 6-11-8 98 .... AidanColeman 49
(Venetia Williams) *in rr: hdwy 7th: reminders 12th: wknd 3 out: sn t.o* **16/1**

P-PP **P** **Raki Rose**[22] 2608 8-9-11 76 oh3 .... JohnKington(3) —
(Michael Scudamore) *sn trcking ldr: led 7th to 10th: 3rd and wkng whn blnd 3 out: t.o whn p.u bef next* **14/1**

333- **P** **Katalak (IRE)**[232] 49 7-11-10 100 .... WillKennedy —
(Jonathen de Giles) *chsd ldrs: lost pl after 7th: t.o whn p.u bef 9th* **28/1**

-F24 **P** **Mr Bond (IRE)**[22] 2605 7-11-0 90 .... NickScholfield —
(Andy Turnell) *mstkes in rr: blnd 10th: sn t.o: p.u bef 13th* **15/2**

3-60 **P** **Ready Or Not (IRE)**[21] 2637 7-11-3 100 .... NathanSweeney(7) —
(Bob Buckler) *blnd 1st: chsd ldrs 7th: wknd bef 3 out: t.o whn p.u bef 2 out* **8/1**

6P0- **P** **Quazy De Joie (FR)**[244] 5219 6-11-12 102 .... DominicElsworth —
(Jonjo O'Neill) *in rr: j.lft: t.o 13th: p.u bef 4 out* **11/1**

6m 52.4s (15.50) **Going Correction** +0.35s/f (Yiel) **9** Ran SP% **113.4**
Speed ratings (Par 105): **89,88,87,70,**— —,—,—,—
toteswingers:1&2:£2.30, 1&3:£2.60, 2&3:£3.30 CSF £16.82 CT £46.89 TOTE £4.10: £1.70, £1.10, £1.80; EX 12.70.
Owner John P McManus **Bred** W L Spring **Trained** Cheltenham, Gloucs

FOCUS

A modest 76-102 stayers' handicap and a real slog in the testing conditions, the ground was changed to soft after the opener. The easy winner was value for further and is on the upgrade, with the next two close to their marks.

NOTEBOOK

Aztec Treasure(NZ) survived one blunder before moving into the slipstream of the leader. He was clearly travelling much the best and had only to be nudged along to take charge at the last. He may not be entirely straightforward but he is talented when on one of his going days. (op 3-1 tchd 7-2)
Topless(IRE), whose sole win was over hurdles nearly four years ago, won the battle for the lead but it was clear turning for home that she was a mere sitting duck. (op 9-2 tchd 4-1 and 15-2)
Dromore Hill(IRE), who needs plenty of driving, took a remote third after three out. He made serious inroads on the run-in but is clearly not one to rely on. (tchd 11-4)
Guydus(IRE), making her chase debut on her first start since April, was struggling and being given reminders a long way from home. She stopped to nothing at the foot of the final hill. (op 12-1)
Mr Bond(IRE) Official explanation: jockey said gelding had a breathing problem

2983 HAYGAIN HAY STEAMERS H'CAP HURDLE (10 hdls) 2m 3f 110y

1:40 (1:47) (Class 3) (0-120,120) 4-Y-0+ **£4,098** (£1,203; £601; £300)

Form RPR

255F **1** **Grafite**[23] 2596 5-11-1 109 .... WarrenMarston 125+
(Milton Harris) *hld up: hdwy after 7th: led 2 out: clr whn hit last: styd on* **18/1**

43 **2** *8* **Mannlichen**[45] 2129 4-11-2 110 .... AidanColeman 117
(Venetia Williams) *chsd ldrs: led after 3 out: mstke and hdd next: styd on same pce* **16/1**

4-34 **3** *1 3/4* **Simply Wings (IRE)**[21] 2630 6-11-4 112 .... DougieCostello 116
(Richard Lee) *hld up: styd on appr 2 out: nt rch ldrs* **10/1**

F03- **4** *2 3/4* **Dinarius**[257] 4990 5-11-4 112 .... (p) PaulMoloney 113
(Alex Hales) *hld up: plld hrd: hdwy 6th: rdn appr 2 out: no ex* **12/1**

0332 **5** *15* **Tom O'Tara**[29] 2452 6-10-13 110 .... WayneKavanagh(3) 97
(Robin Dickin) *chsd ldrs tl led 5th: hdd 3 out: wknd bef next* **12/1**

352 **6** *1/2* **Taketimeout (IRE)**[32] 2397 5-11-2 113 .... RichieMcLernon(3) 100
(Jonjo O'Neill) *hld up: rdn appr 3 out: n.d* **12/1**

2-33 **7** *2 1/2* **Asturienne**[20] 2514 6-11-12 120 .... RobertThornton 103
(Alan King) *hld up in tch: wknd after 3 out* **11/2**[1]

-311 **8** *3* **Malindi Bay**[25] 2554 5-11-0 115 .... MrCGreene(7) 96
(Kim Bailey) *hld up in tch: led and mstke 3 out: sn hdd: wknd bef next* **6/1**[2]

5/P3 **9** *9* **Abstract Art (USA)**[28] 2471 7-11-10 118 .... AndrewThornton 89
(Rachel Hobbs) *hld up in tch: hit 6th: blnd 3 out: sn wknd* **100/1**

2-13 **10** *7* **Brixen (IRE)**[37] 2289 6-10-13 107 .... LeightonAspell 71
(Lucy Wadham) *led to 5th: wknd after 3 out* **9/1**

P0/0 **F** **Hoh Viss**[28] 2477 10-10-13 110 .... (b) AdamPogson(3) —
(Caroline Bailey) *chsd ldrs tl fell 3rd* **100/1**

30-5 **P** **Rock 'N' Roller (FR)**[26] 2530 6-10-10 104 .... JamieMoore —
(Gary Moore) *hld up: a in rr: t.o whn p.u bef last* **28/1**

0-0P **P** **Olympian (FR)**[32] 2393 8-11-2 117 .... JoshuaMoore(7) —
(Philip Middleton) *hld up: hdwy 7th: wknd 3 out: t.o whn p.u bef next* **25/1**

01/0 **P** **De Welsh Wizzard**[70] 1740 7-10-9 110 .... StephenO'Donovan(7) —
(Emma Lavelle) *hld up: hdwy 5th: wknd 3 out: t.o whn p.u bef last* **14/1**

3-03 **P** **Latin America (IRE)**[23] 2594 5-11-10 118 .... LiamTreadwell —
(Nick Gifford) *a in rr: t.o whn p.u bef 7th* **40/1**

43-2 **P** **Mac Aeda**[39] 2246 6-11-8 116 .... GrahamLee —
(Malcolm Jefferson) *hld up: rdn after 6th: wknd bef 3 out: t.o whn p.u bef 2 out* **10/1**

24 **P** **Causing Chaos (IRE)**[39] 2238 4-11-0 111 .... SamTwiston-Davies(3) —
(Nigel Twiston-Davies) *chsd ldrs: rdn after 6th: wknd after next: t.o whn p.u bef 2 out* **17/2**[3]

5m 8.90s (-0.70) **Going Correction** +0.15s/f (Yiel)
WFA 4 from 5yo+ 5lb **17** Ran SP% **121.0**
Speed ratings (Par 107): **107,103,103,102,96 95,94,93,90,87** —,—,—,—,— —,—
toteswingers:1&2:£60.50, 1&3:£83.00, 2&3:£38.90 CSF £265.59 CT £3034.96 TOTE £23.00: £4.70, £4.90, £2.70, £2.00; EX 508.00.
Owner J Dalton, C Shankland, D Dewbery **Bred** Mrs J L Egan **Trained** Herridge, Wiltshire

FOCUS

A 104-120 handicap hurdle run at a sound pace in the testing conditions and just two in it going to the second last flight. A big step forward from the easy winner and the next two are steadily progressive.

NOTEBOOK

Grafite, held in fourth when falling at the final flight at Lingfield on his handicap bow, moved up full of running going to three out. In front at the next, he was in total command when crashing through the final flight. That mistake was not enough to stop him winning, and the step up in trip/test of stamina clearly played to his strengths. (op 16-1)
Mannlichen, making his handicap bow on just his third start over hurdles, came there full of running to show ahead after three out but in the end was no match. He will appreciate a less stiff track and looks a ready-made winner. (op 14-1)
Simply Wings(IRE), settled well off the pace, moved closer three from home. He was soon outpaced by the first two before staying on in his own time. He will be suited by a return to 3m. (op 11-1)
Dinarius, having his first run since April, gave problems before the start, something he has done in the past. He stayed on from way off the pace, is suited by soft ground and going right-handed, but is clearly not trustworthy. (op 9-1)
Tom O'Tara, who steered a wide course, went on at halfway, but racing from an 11lb higher mark after his excellent runner-up finish at Warwick, he had no more to give after two out. (op 14-1)
Taketimeout(IRE), making his handicap debut, stayed on late in the day and looks to be still learning.
Asturienne, proven on bad ground around here, never threatened to enter the argument. (op 8-1)
Malindi Bay, chasing a hat-trick, shouldn't have had any obvious problems with conditions or the course, so one can only presume that the handicapper has her measure now. (op 11-2 tchd 13-2)
Brixen(IRE) made the early pace but dropped right away before the race developed. She didn't seem obviously suited by the step up in distance. (op 12-1 tchd 14-1)
De Welsh Wizzard travelled strongly for a lot of the race but stopped quickly once asked to get involved. (op 11-1)

Causing Chaos(IRE) still showed signs of inexperience and has plenty of time on his side to develop. (op 11-1)

2984 BROOKLANDS MEADOW BY TAYLOR WIMPEY H'CAP CHASE (16 fncs) 2m 6f

2:10 (2:18) (Class 3) (0-130,128) 4-Y-O+ **£5,703** (£1,684; £842; £421; £210)

Form RPR

-F21 **1** **Bobby Gee**[23] 2595 9-11-0 **116** ... TomO'Brien 135+
(Renee Robeson) *trckd ldrs: hit 6th: led 2 out: styd on wl run-in* **6/1**[1]

-505 **2** 7 **Mr Big (IRE)**[34] 2346 9-10-5 **110** ...(p) PeterToole(3) 121
(Charlie Mann) *led to 2nd: trckd ldrs: upsides 2 out: styd on same pce run-in* **13/2**[2]

04-6 **3** 4 1/2 **Rate Of Knots (IRE)**[36] 2305 7-10-8 **113** ... RichieMcLernon(3) 119+
(Jonjo O'Neill) *hld up towards rr: stdy hdwy whn hmpd 4 out: styd on fr 2 out: tk 3rd run-in* **15/2**

P-60 **4** 3 1/4 **Bible Lord (IRE)**[19] 2674 9-11-12 **128** ...(b[1]) NickScholfield 131
(Andy Turnell) *led 2nd: hdd 2 out: wknd run-in* **14/1**

U-1U **5** 4 1/2 **Rustarix (FR)**[19] 2669 9-11-8 **124** ... RobertThornton 122
(Alan King) *mid-div: wnt prom 9th: wknd 3 out* **7/1**[3]

6-P5 **6** 6 **The Vicar (IRE)**[21] 2629 7-10-10 **112** ...(p) HaddenFrost 105
(Henrietta Knight) *towards rr: mstke 2nd: hdwy 9th: mstke next: outpcd 12th* **14/1**

-642 **7** 15 **Noun De La Thinte (FR)**[19] 2669 9-11-9 **125** ... AidanColeman 112+
(Venetia Williams) *chsd ldrs: outpcd 12th: wknd 3 out* **9/1**

334- **8** 10 **Double Eagle**[300] 4147 8-11-2 **118** ... BrianHarding 85
(Donald McCain) *in rr: struggling 7th: bhd fr 12th* **10/1**

-3F0 **9** 15 **Theophrastus (IRE)**[19] 2670 8-11-3 **119** ... LiamTreadwell 71
(Nick Gifford) *mid-div: blnd and lost pl 7th: hdwy 9th: lost pl 12th* **8/1**

P-54 **10** 4 1/2 **Lorum Leader (IRE)**[39] 2249 9-10-10 **112** ... AndrewThornton 59
(Dr Richard Newland) *in rr: mstke 1st: bhd fr 9th* **14/1**

6-11 **F** **Ammunition (IRE)**[53] 1992 10-10-7 **112** ...(p) SamTwiston-Davies(3) —
(Nigel Twiston-Davies) *j.rt: w ldrs: mstke 8th: fell 4 out* **7/1**[3]

004P **P** **Nostringsattached (IRE)**[21] 2629 9-11-9 **125** ... DominicElsworth —
(Jonjo O'Neill) *in rr: bhd fr 7th: t.o 12th: p.u bef 12th* **50/1**

5m 56.4s (3.40) **Going Correction** +0.35s/f (Yiel) **12** Ran SP% **116.5**
Speed ratings (Par 107): **107,104,102,101,100 97,92,88,83,81** —,—
toteswingers:1&2:£9.70, 1&3:£15.10, 2&3:£15.50 CSF £44.81 CT £298.42 TOTE £6.80: £2.50, £1.30, £1.70; EX 53.80.

Owner The Oakley Partnership **Bred** W Ginzel And Mrs J Kehoe **Trained** Tyringham, Bucks

FOCUS
A competitive 110-128 handicap chase and a true test of stamina in the conditions. Solid-looking form, with another step forward from the winner.

NOTEBOOK
Bobby Gee, 6lb higher than when winning in ready fashion at Lingfield, travelled strongly and took this with the minimum of fuss. He is clearly going the right way. (tchd 7-1)
Mr Big(IRE), back over regulation fences and with the cheekpieces back on, travelled almost as well as the winner but was outspeeded over the final two fences. He is well worth another try over a fair bit further. (op 8-1)
Rate Of Knots(IRE), bidding to make it 3-3 around here, showed the benefit of her Carlisle return. Given a patient ride, she stayed on nicely after being hampered four from home. She loves testing ground and should be cherry-ripe next time. (op 11-1 tchd 13-2)
Bible Lord(IRE), suited by going right-handed, wore blinkers for the first time. Soon taking them along, he weakened on the run-in and seems to have lost the winning habit. (op 9-1)
Rustarix(FR), 4lb higher than his Cheltenham comeback success, didn't improve for the drop back in trip. (op 6-1 tchd 11-2 and 8-1)
The Vicar(IRE), dropping down the ratings, continues to under-perform.
Noun De La Thinte(FR), 4lb higher than when finishing runner-up at Newbury, is 13lb higher than for the last of her five victories last term. (op 7-1 tchd 10-1)
Ammunition(IRE), who tended to jump right, was still in the thick of things when departing four out. He was racing from a 5lb higher mark and was by no means done with racing over his favourite track. (op 6-1 tchd 15-2)

2985 TIPZONE @ GG.COM "NATIONAL HUNT" MAIDEN HURDLE (8 hdls) 2m

2:40 (2:46) (Class 4) 4-Y-O+ **£2,602** (£764; £382; £190)

Form RPR

4 **1** **Upthemsteps (IRE)**[10] 2826 5-10-12 0 ... DougieCostello 113+
(Ian Williams) *mde all: j.lft: shkn up appr last: styd on wl* **7/2**[1]

35-0 **2** 4 1/2 **Dune Shine**[36] 2307 5-10-12 0 ... DominicElsworth 107
(Oliver Sherwood) *hld up: hdwy 5th: chsd wnr 3 out: sn rdn: styd on same pce appr last* **11/2**[2]

44U **3** 7 **Grey Gold (IRE)**[21] 2640 5-10-12 0 ... JodieMogford 100
(Richard Lee) *hld up in tch: rdn after 3 out: styd on same pce appr last* **16/1**

4 1/2 **Baile Anrai (IRE)**[270] 6-10-9 0 ... MichaelMurphy(3) 100
(Ian Williams) *prom: nt fluent 3 out: sn rdn: styd on same pce appr last* **7/1**[3]

0 **5** 11 **Nosecond Chance (IRE)**[21] 2634 4-10-9 0 ... PeterToole(3) 90
(Charlie Mann) *chsd ldrs: rdn after 3 out: wknd bef last* **9/1**

00-0 **6** 9 **Everdon Brook (IRE)**[49] 2058 5-10-12 0 ... CharliePoste 82
(Ben Case) *hld up: hdwy after 5th: rdn and wknd appr 2 out: t.o* **25/1**

0-00 **7** 14 **Running Upthathill (IRE)**[6] 2873 6-10-12 0 ... AidanColeman 65
(Venetia Williams) *prom: rdn 3 out: sn wknd: t.o* **16/1**

0-00 **8** 8 **Deputy Dog (IRE)**[31] 2419 4-10-9 0 ... RichieMcLernon(3) 57
(Jonjo O'Neill) *hld up: j. slowly 4th: wknd after next: t.o* **14/1**

0- **9** 57 **Graylyn Amber**[271] 4742 5-10-2 0 ... WayneKavanagh(3) —
(Robin Dickin) *s.s: hld up: plld hrd: in rr whn hmpd 5th: sn bhd: t.o* **66/1**

00 **10** 6 **Filimoss**[25] 2554 5-10-5 0 ... GerardTumelty —
(Charlie Morlock) *hld up: bhd fr 3rd: t.o* **100/1**

0/ **P** **Lisa's Enigma**[776] 1929 7-10-12 0 ... WillKennedy —
(Shaun Harris) *got loose prior to the s: hld up: a in rr: t.o whn p.u bef 2 out* **100/1**

0 **B** **Be True (IRE)**[33] 2368 6-10-12 0 ... AdrianLane —
(Donald McCain) *prom: racd keenly: b.d after 5th* **8/1**

00-0 **B** **Flyford Prince**[170] 850 5-10-5 0 ... RobertKirk(7) —
(Tony Carroll) *hld up: hdwy whn b.d after 5th* **150/1**

06-0 **F** **Fifth Sea Lord (IRE)**[201] 514 5-10-12 0 ... MarkBradburne —
(Tom Gretton) *chsd ldrs: cl 3rd whn stmbld and fell after 5th* **100/1**

0 **P** **A Splash Of Green (IRE)**[68] 1778 5-10-12 0 ... JamieMoore —
(Jonathan Portman) *chsd ldrs: hit 2nd: blnd 3 out: sn wknd: t.o whn p.u bef next* **50/1**

P **Son Of Robain (FR)**[143] 4-10-12 0 ... LeightonAspell —
(Alison Batchelor) *hld up: hdwy 5th: wknd bef next: t.o whn p.u bef 2 out* **11/2**[2]

4m 15.7s (7.80) **Going Correction** +0.15s/f (Yiel) **16** Ran SP% **116.0**
Speed ratings (Par 105): **86,83,80,80,74 70,63,59,30,27** —,—,—,—,— —
toteswingers:1&2:£6.90, 1&3:£7.40, 2&3:£14.30 CSF £20.39 TOTE £5.60: £2.00, £2.40, £4.50; EX 27.20.

Owner The Ferandlin Peaches **Bred** Pat Coffey **Trained** Portway, Worcs

FOCUS
An ordinary maiden hurdle and quite a test in the conditions. The firfst three are rated in line with their bumper marks.

NOTEBOOK
Upthemsteps(IRE) has plenty of size and scope. Making virtually all, he steered a wide passage and his hurdling left something to be desired. He kept up the gallop in relentless fashion and will be well suited by a step up to 2m4f. (op 4-1 tchd 9-2 and 10-3)
Dune Shine, happy to bide his time, went in pursuit of the winner three out. He stuck to his guns but was unable to land a blow. This was a big improvement on his first try over hurdles. (op 9-1)
Grey Gold(IRE), fourth in two bumpers at Worcester, was in effect making his hurdling debut after departing early at Uttoxeter. He stuck on in his own time and looks a stayer in the making. (op 14-1)
Baile Anrai(IRE), a stablemate of the winner and successful in a maiden point in Ireland in March on his second start, stayed on on his own time up the final hill and will be suited by a much stiffer test. (op 5-1)
Nosecond Chance(IRE), another Irish maiden point winner, travelled strongly but didn't seem to get home. (op 11-1 tchd 8-1)
Be True(IRE), a half-brother to Snowy Morning, was still full of running when brought down on this hurdling debut. (op 7-1)

2986 RACING FORUM @ GG.COM H'CAP CHASE (12 fncs) 2m 110y

3:10 (3:10) (Class 4) (0-110,106) 4-Y-O+ **£2,927** (£859; £429; £214)

Form RPR

00-1 **1** **Irish Guard**[31] 2424 9-11-1 95 ... AndrewThornton 113+
(John O'Neill) *chsd ldrs 4th: led 7th: drew rt away fr 2 out: eased run-in* **12/1**

5-21 **2** 18 **Handtheprizeover**[25] 2559 5-11-3 100 ... PeterToole(3) 101+
(Ben Case) *in rr-div: hmpd and lost pl 5th: hdwy 9th: wnt 2nd appr 2 out: no ch w wnr* **9/4**[1]

PP-P **3** 2 **Organiz (FR)**[70] 1740 8-10-6 91 ... MrSWaley-Cohen(5) 88
(Robin Dickin) *hld up: hdwy to chas ldrs 4th: one pce whn hit 2 out* **14/1**

/2-4 **4** 16 **Riddleofthesands (IRE)**[43] 2148 6-11-9 106 ... SamTwiston-Davies(3) 85
(Nigel Twiston-Davies) *led: hdd 7th: wknd 2 out* **7/2**[2]

PP50 **5** 7 **Kinkeel (IRE)**[5] 2885 11-9-13 82 ... EamonDehdashti(3) 55
(Tony Carroll) *hld up: hdwy 6th: wknd appr 3 out* **18/1**

1-5P **P** **Devils River (IRE)**[23] 2591 8-11-2 96 ...(p) AndrewTinkler —
(Anna Brooks) *chsd ldrs: wknd 7th: bhd whn p.u bef 2 out* **16/1**

1-30 **P** **Karasakal (IRE)**[29] 2453 7-11-3 97 ... JamieMoore —
(Gary Moore) *in rr: bhd fr 8th: t.o whn p.u bef last* **16/1**

3530 **P** **Mujamead**[3] 2930 6-10-6 86 ...(p) TomMessenger —
(Sally-Anne Wheelwright) *mstke 5th: sn bhd: t.o whn p.u bef 3 out* **20/1**

31-4 **P** **Sawpit Supreme**[42] 2172 8-11-1 95 ... AidanColeman —
(Venetia Williams) *hdwy to chas ldrs 6th: wknd after 9th: bhd whn p.u bef 2 out* **13/2**[3]

-1F2 **F** **Owner Occupier**[22] 2605 5-11-6 100 ... ColinBolger —
(Chris Gordon) *chsd ldrs: fell 5th* **7/1**

4m 24.6s (8.50) **Going Correction** +0.35s/f (Yiel) **10** Ran SP% **115.0**
Speed ratings (Par 105): **94,85,84,77,73** —,—,—,—,—
toteswingers:1&2:£4.30, 1&3:£23.40, 2&3:£8.50 CSF £40.37 CT £392.99 TOTE £24.50: £5.50, £1.10, £6.00; EX 38.10.

Owner J G O'Neill **Bred** J G O'Neill **Trained** Stratton Audley, Oxon

FOCUS
A modest 82-106 handicap run in a snowstorm but a wide-margin, easy winner. He is rated back to the level of his 2009 course win.

NOTEBOOK
Irish Guard, raised 5lb after accounting for one other finisher at Leicester, made light of the conditions skipping clear over the last two and winning eased down. He was rated considerably higher in his prime and this looked something of a second coming. (op 16-1)
Handtheprizeover, raised 10lb after his C&D win on just his second start over fences, was knocked right back when badly hampered by the faller. He crept into the race to take second spot but the winner then ran clean away from him. Nevertheless he deserves credit for this. (op 11-4)
Organiz(FR), pulled up over hurdles on his first start for this stable, has won twice in points and has been placed in hunter chases but this is probably as good as he is now. (op 16-1)
Riddleofthesands(IRE), a keen type who has clearly had his problems, took them along but stopped to nothing at the foot of the final hill. (tchd 4-1)
Owner Occupier does not look a natural jumper and soon crashed out. (op 11-2)

2987 GG.COM MARES' STANDARD OPEN NATIONAL HUNT FLAT RACE 2m

3:40 (3:40) (Class 5) 4-6-Y-O **£1,626** (£477; £238; £119)

Form RPR

1 **Young Victoria** 4-10-12 0 ... CharliePoste 100
(Richard Lee) *a.p: chsd ldr 3f out: styd on to ld post* **33/1**

4 **2** hd **Addiction**[28] 2472 5-10-12 0 ... LeightonAspell 100
(Oliver Sherwood) *chsd ldrs: led over 1f out: sn rdn and edgd rt: hdd post* **8/1**

4 **3** 6 **Lady Hight (FR)**[42] 2167 4-10-12 0 ... AndrewTinkler 94
(Nicky Henderson) *hld up in tch: rdn over 2f out: styd on same pce* **3/1**[2]

4 1 1/2 **Accordingtoeileen (IRE)** 5-10-9 0 ... SamTwiston-Davies(3) 93
(Nigel Twiston-Davies) *hld up: hdwy 4f out: led 3f out: rdn and hdd over 1f out: no ex fnl f* **5/1**[3]

2 **5** 1 3/4 **Varkala (IRE)**[28] 2472 4-10-12 0 ... JimmyMcCarthy 93+
(Charles Egerton) *hld up: swvd lft 7f out: hdwy over 4f out: rdn over 2f out: sn outpcd* **9/4**[1]

1 **6** 14 **Dream Performance (IRE)**[68] 1771 5-11-5 0 ... GerardTumelty 85
(G C Maundrell) *hld up: reminders 10f out: outpcd 5f out: nvr nrr* **8/1**

5 **7** 1 **Lua De Itapoan**[22] 2616 5-10-12 0 ... DougieCostello 76
(Malcolm Jefferson) *hld up in tch: rdn over 3f out: sn wknd* **22/1**

8 1/2 **Psychosis** 5-10-12 0 ... JamesDavies 75
(Brendan Powell) *chsd ldrs: rdn over 4f out: sn wknd* **33/1**

4 **9** 8 **Charlotte's Ball (IRE)**[41] 2186 4-10-9 0 ow2 ... MrPYork(5) 69
(Raymond York) *led: rdn and hdd 3f out: sn wknd: t.o* **66/1**

10 3 3/4 **Mew Gull** 5-10-12 0 ... HaddenFrost 64
(Henrietta Knight) *hld up: hdwy 4f out: rdn and wknd over 2f out: t.o* **40/1**

11 5 **Star Shuil (IRE)** 5-10-12 0 ... WillKennedy 59
(David Arbuthnot) *hld up: hdwy over 4f out: rdn and wknd over 2f out: t.o* **16/1**

12 3 3/4 **Fashion Stakes** 4-10-12 0 ... CampbellGillies 55
(Chris Grant) *chsd ldrs: rdn and lost pl over 6f out: bhd fnl 4f: t.o* **33/1**

The Form Book, Raceform Ltd, Compton, RG20 6NL

13 *35* **Kearn's Girl (IRE)** 6-10-5 0 MrCGreene(7) 20
(Barry Brennan) *chsd ldr tl rdn and wknd over 3f out: t.o* **100/1**
14 *30* **Sharabosky** 6-10-12 0 AndrewThornton —
(Caroline Bailey) *hld up: a in rr: bhd fnl 4f: t.o* **50/1**
3 S **Hazy Dawn**28 2472 5-10-12 0 TomO'Brien —
(Michael Scudamore) *hld up: hdwy 7f out: prom when stmbld & fell 5f out* **18/1**

4m 14.5s (12.20) **Going Correction** +0.15s/f (Yiel)
WFA 4 from 5yo+ 5lb **15** Ran SP% **125.9**
Speed ratings: **75,74,71,71,70 63,62,62,58,56 54,52,34,19,—**
toteswingers:1&2:£64.90, 1&3:£17.50, 2&3:£7.40 CSF £278.26 TOTE £35.50: £7.20, £4.20, £1.40; EX 288.50.
Owner G D Thorp - R L Baker **Bred** R D And Mrs J S Chugg **Trained** Byton, H'fords
■ Stewards' Enquiry : Leighton Aspell caution: careless riding; one-day ban: careless riding (Dec 30)

FOCUS
A mares-only bumper run in a snowstorm and in the end a tight two-horse finish. Ordinary form, rated around the second, third and fifth.

NOTEBOOK
Young Victoria, jump bred on her dams's side, set sail for home at the foot of the final hill. Joined and crowded, she showed real battling qualities to hang on by the skin of her teeth. (op 50-1)
Addiction, 3l behind Varkala when they finished second and fourth respectively at Hereford a month ago, took on the winner 2f from home. She crowded and pushed that rival before going under by a whisker, the pair clear. (op 9-1)
Lady Hight(FR), only fourth when sent off favourite on her debut at Haydock six weeks earlier, came there looking a real threat but in the end could not match the first two. (op 11-4)
Accordingtoeileen(IRE), put to sleep at the back after giving away ground at the start, moved into the firing line turning for home but she hung left and in the end finished up on the chase track. (tchd 9-2)
Varkala(IRE) didn't seem to enjoy the best of passages and is well worth another chance. (op 11-4)
Hazy Dawn, who split Varkala and Addiction at Hereford, was poised when coming down on the bend just over half a mile out. (op 16-1)
T/Jkpt: Not won. T/Plt: £145.60 to a £1 stake. Pool:£74,386.47 - 372.71 winning tickets T/Qpdt: £76.60 to a £1 stake. Pool:£5,178.68 - 50.00 winning tickets CR

2988 - 2994a (Foreign Racing) - See Raceform Interactive

2512 ASCOT (R-H)
Friday, December 17
2995 Meeting Abandoned - Frost

2640 UTTOXETER (L-H)
Friday, December 17
3002 Meeting Abandoned - Snow

2512 ASCOT (R-H)
Saturday, December 18
3009 Meeting Abandoned - Frost

2519 HAYDOCK (L-H)
Saturday, December 18
3015 Meeting Abandoned - Snow

2349 NEWCASTLE (L-H)
Saturday, December 18
3021 Meeting Abandoned - Frost and snow

3028a, 3031a-3033a - (Foreign Racing) - See Raceform Interactive

2561 NAVAN (L-H)
Saturday, December 18

OFFICIAL GOING: Soft

3029a NAVAN NOVICE HURDLE (GRADE 1) (11 hdls) 2m 4f
1:15 (1:16) 4-Y-0+ **£43,141** (£12,610; £5,973; £1,991)

RPR
1 **Oscars Well (IRE)**34 2416 5-11-10 RMPower 148+
(Mrs John Harrington, Ire) *settled 4th: impr in 3rd 3 out: travelled wl to ld 2 out: kpt on strly fr bef last: easily* **9/4**2
2 *8* **Sweet Shock (GER)**49 2099 5-11-10 123 AELynch 137
(Michael O'Hare, Ire) *chsd ldrs in 3rd: impr to chal 3 out: sn rdn to ld: hdd 2 out: no ex: kpt on same pce* **4/1**3
3 *11* **Fully Funded (USA)**27 2562 5-11-10 PCarberry 126
(Noel Meade, Ire) *led: disp briefly 1/2-way: rdn and chal 3 out: sn hdd: no ex in 3rd 2 out: kpt on same pce* **7/4**1
4 *3/4* **Aughnacurraveel (IRE)**27 2562 6-11-10 122 MrMJO'Connor 125
(Garry Ducey, Ire) *hld up in rr: rdn in 5th 3 out: no imp in 4th 2 out: kpt on one pce* **4/1**3
5 *22* **He's Our Man (IRE)**24 2617 5-11-10 (t) JLCullen 103
(Patrick O Brady, Ire) *hld up in 5th: rdn in 4th 3 out: sn no ex and wknd* **20/1**
6 *dist* **Imperial Shabra (IRE)**24 2621 6-11-10 114 MWBowes —
(Patrick O Brady, Ire) *pressed ldr in 2nd: disp briefly 1/2-way: rdn and wknd ent st* **25/1**

4m 58.1s (-3.70) **6** Ran SP% **115.7**
CSF £12.29 TOTE £3.40: £2.10, £1.70; DF 17.40.
Owner Molley Malone Syndicate **Bred** Eugene O' Leary **Trained** Moone, Co Kildare
■ This Grade 1 was previously run as the Barry & Sandra Kelly Memorial.

FOCUS
Forecast favourite Hidden Cyclone was taken out because of the wintry conditions, which left the track only just raceable. The time was good and the form is rated around the runner-up. Easy winner Oscars Well built on his impressive maiden success.

NOTEBOOK
Oscars Well(IRE) looks very progressive and couldn't have done this any easier. Travelling well just behind the lead, he ranged up to challenge before the second-last, flew that flight and eased to the front. When his rider asked him to quicken he did that well and jumped the final flight equally well. He was impressive, but it was a sub-standard Grade 1 and we will probably learn a lot more about him if his intended target of a Grade 2 at Leopardstown in January is taken up as he will have to carry a penalty. (op 2/1)
Sweet Shock(GER), stepping up from handicap company into Grade 1, ran a fine race but lacked the class to cope with the winner. He was just being pushed along to stay in contention turning into the straight and he found a good bit but just wasn't good enough for this grade. (op 10/3)
Fully Funded(USA) ran nowhere near the form of his Monksfield Novice Hurdle win. He was ridden positively and briefly looked to have some of his rivals in trouble when going on before the straight but when he was challenged before the third last he folded. Rider and trainer said afterwards that he ran like a horse that blew up. (op 2/1 tchd 13/8)
Aughnacurraveel(IRE) was entitled to take his chance to see how he would fare in this company and the evidence of this and his run here in November suggests this is about as good as he is. Held up off the pace, he travelled well to a point but when the race really began in earnest turning into the straight he could make no impression. (op 6/1)
He's Our Man(IRE) was beaten turning into the straight.
Imperial Shabra(IRE) helped set the pace as he disputed for much of the way before weakening on the run to the straight. (op 20/1)

3030a PHILIPS ELECTRONICS TARA HURDLE (GRADE 2) (11 hdls) 2m 4f
1:50 (1:50) 4-Y-0+ **£24,159** (£7,061; £3,345; £1,115)

RPR
1 **Rigour Back Bob (IRE)**34 2411 5-11-8 138 AndrewJMcNamara 142+
(E J O'Grady, Ire) *chsd ldrs: 5th 1/2-way: rdn in 4th 3 out: styd on in 3rd last: r.o wl to ld run-in: kpt on strly cl home* **7/1**
2 *2 1/2* **Stonemaster (IRE)**239 5381 5-11-5 138 DNRussell 135
(D T Hughes, Ire) *chsd ldrs: 3rd 1/2-way: impr to chal 3 out: sn rdn to ld: chal 2 out: hdd bef last: kpt on in 3rd run-in: 2nd cl home* **11/4**2
3 *hd* **Alpine Glade (IRE)**66 1835 8-11-0 132 BMCash 130
(W McCreery, Ire) *hld up in rr: hdwy in 5th 3 out: impr to chal 2 out: rdn to ld bef last: hdd run-in: no ex: lost 2nd cl home* **6/1**3
4 *2 1/2* **Son Amix (FR)**24 2619 4-11-1 132 BryanJCooper 128
(Thomas Cooper, Ire) *chsd ldr in 2nd: disp fr 4th: led ent st: rdn and chal 3 out: sn hdd: no ex in 3rd 2 out: kpt on one pce* **5/2**1
5 *3 1/2* **Maggio (FR)**41 2260 5-11-5 (p) KMDonoghue 129
(Patrick Griffin, Ire) *chsd ldrs: 4th 1/2-way: rdn and dropped to rr ent st: no ex in 5th after 3 out: kpt on one pce* **25/1**
6 *7* **Aitmatov (GER)**3 2968 9-11-10 148 (bt) PCarberry 127
(Noel Meade, Ire) *led: disp fr 4th: rdn and hdd ent st: wknd fr 3 out* **5/2**1

5m 2.50s (0.70)
WFA 4 from 5yo+ 6lb **6** Ran SP% **114.4**
CSF £27.53 TOTE £6.20: £1.70, £2.30; DF 20.50.
Owner Gaticoma Syndicate **Bred** Michael Donohoe **Trained** Ballynonty, Co Tipperary

FOCUS
The progressive Stonemaster ran a slight personal best, with the runner-up rated to his best. The fifth potentially limits the form.

NOTEBOOK
Rigour Back Bob(IRE) stayed on strongly to win going away. Having shown little on his first two runs this season, he didn't really appear to be doing much more than going nowhere when the race began to take shape in the straight. However he started to really pick up after the second last and the more they went the stronger he galloped. Everything about him suggests he's a real stayer and the best won't be seen until he tackles 3m, an impression that was confirmed here. (op 6/1)
Stonemaster(IRE) made a pleasing reintroduction and he'll improve for stepping up in trip. Racing close enough to the pace, he went to the front early in the straight and kept battling away to get back up for second close home. He should benefit a good bit for this. (op 5/2)
Alpine Glade(IRE) was stepping up in trip and it seemed a simple case of her failing to stay. Held up, she moved through stylishly to get her head in front before the final flight but she was unable to cope with the winner's effort and just didn't get home up the hill. This suggests she's capable of a bold showing in a good race over 2m. (op 5/1)
Son Amix(FR) raced a bit keenly and would have benefited from a more generous pace. He was probably leading on sufferance for much of the contest and couldn't respond once headed after three out. (op 11/4 tchd 9/4)
Maggio(FR) kept on and ran a fine race on paper having tracked the pace for much of the journey. He looks likely to try and win a maiden hurdle. (op 22/1)
Aitmatov(GER) was on and off the bridle late in the race and dropped away quickly enough early in the straight. (op 3/1)

2269 CARLISLE (R-H)
Sunday, December 19
3034 Meeting Abandoned - Frozen course with severe snow/frost being forecast

2570 FFOS LAS (L-H)
Monday, December 20
3041 Meeting Abandoned - Snow

2633 TAUNTON (R-H)
Monday, December 20
3048 Meeting Abandoned - Snow

KEMPTON (A.W) (R-H)

Tuesday, December 21

OFFICIAL GOING: Standard to slow

Wind: nil Weather: dry, very cold

3054 DAY TIME, NIGHT TIME, GREAT TIME, STANDARD OPEN NATIONAL HUNT FLAT RACE 2m (P)

12:50 (12:50) (Class 6) 4-6-Y-O **£1,370** (£399; £199)

Form				RPR
1/	1		**Mintiverdi**[661] 4211 6-11-0 0 TomSiddall (Noel Chance) *t.k.h: hld up in tch on outer: rdn and hdwy over 2f out: chal ent fnl f: kpt on wl to ld nr fin* **12/1**	107
	2	hd	**Captain Kirkton (IRE)** 4-11-0 0 JamieMoore (Gary Moore) *trckd ldrs: wnt 2nd ent fnl 4f: rdn to ld over 1f out: kpt on wl tl hdd and no ex nr fin* **14/1**	107
	3	1	**Aldiva** 4-11-0 0 RobertThornton (Alan King) *hld up in tch: pushed along and hdwy to chse ldrs ent fnl 3f: wnt 3rd 1f out: kpt on fnl f: nt pce to rch ldng pair* **4/1**[2]	106
	4	2 1/4	**Our Golden Boy (IRE)** 4-11-0 0 DaveCrosse (Mark Usher) *hld up in tch: hdwy 4f out: rdn and unable qck over 2f out: styd on again fnl f: nt pce to rch ldrs* **66/1**	103
	5	3/4	**Basil Fawlty (IRE)** 5-11-0 0 WayneHutchinson (Warren Greatrex) *t.k.h: hld up in tch: rdn and outpcd over 2f out: rallied over 1f out: styd on steadily fnl f: gng on fin* **8/1**	103
510	6	1 1/2	**Spe Salvi (IRE)**[107] 1480 6-11-0 0 DarylJacob (David Arbuthnot) *t.k.h: hld up wl in tch: n.m.r and shuffled bk over 4f out: rallied and swtchd rt over 2f out: styd on same pce and no imp fnl f* **14/1**	101
2	7	2	**Lord Kennedy (IRE)**[75] 1749 5-11-0 0 DenisO'Regan (Alex Hales) *in tch: hdwy to chse ldr 11f out: led 8f out: rdn and hdd over 1f out: wknd fnl f* **15/2**	99
	8	3 1/2	**The Tracey Shuffle** 4-11-0 0 TomScudamore (David Pipe) *t.k.h: chsd ldr tl 11f out: styd chsng ldrs tl rdn and outpcd ent fnl 2f: wknd over 1f out* **5/1**[3]	96
	9	6	**Summerandlightning (IRE)** 4-10-7 0 JamesDavies (Mark Usher) *hld up in tch in rr of main gp: rdn and outpcd over 3f out: n.d fnl 3f* **66/1**	83
3	10	2 3/4	**Journeyman (IRE)**[226] 238 4-11-0 0 APMcCoy (Nicky Henderson) *in tch: rdn and wknd jst over 2f out* **15/8**[1]	87
0	11	116	**Charlie's Boy**[26] 2646 4-11-0 0 DominicElsworth (Tobias B P Coles) *led at stdy gallop tl 8f out: styd upsides ldr tl over 4f out: sn dropped to rr and lost tch: wl t.o over 2f out* **66/1**	—
	12	dist	**Generous Spender** 4-10-7 0 MrTJCannon(7) (Mrs H J Cobb) *rodeoing for 1f and immediately t.o* **50/1**	—

3m 44.9s (224.90) **12 Ran SP% 121.8**

Tote Swingers: 1&2 £28.50, 1&3 £20.30, 2&3 £7.10 CSF £170.56 TOTE £20.70: £3.30, £5.00, £1.50; EX 90.50.

Owner Mrs R F Greener **Bred** Mrs Rosemary F Greener **Trained** Upper Lambourn, Berks

■ Tom Siddall's first winner since his recent return from serious injury.

FOCUS

The opener was a regular bumper, but this card was otherwise framed for horses that have run over jumps, the first of its type. A similar meeting was programmed back in January but was scrapped when the turf course at Kempton thawed out. The track was power harrowed and rotavated to a depth of 10cm, and the ground was comparable to going the slow side of good on turf. The pace was very steady until it picked up approaching the home straight with around half a mile to run, and the form is unlikely to prove too solid. The winner, sixth and seventh are all pretty close to their marks.

NOTEBOOK

Mintiverdi was keen early on and trapped out wide for much of the trip, but she picked up well enough for pressure to get up in the last couple of strides. She had been sidelined since winning a turf bumper at this venue in February 2009, and did well to defy the penalty. Her target could be the listed mares' bumper at Sandown in March. (op 10-1)

Captain Kirkton(IRE) is from the family of high-class jumpers Celestial Gold and Fiveforthree. Fly-kicking in the straight on the first circuit, he travelled as well as any turning in but, after going on, was just pipped.

Aldiva's dam acted on Polytrack and won over hurdles for the King yard. A decent type, he was one of several who was staying on after being outpaced when the tempo lifted. He should make the grade.

Our Golden Boy(IRE), closely related to an Irish bumper/hurdle winner, was staying on well after being unable to hold his pitch when the pace quickened. (op 50-1)

Basil Fawlty(IRE) ◆ is a half-brother to a bumper winner and a winning hurdler. He was going on nicely at the finish and is one to keep an eye on after this promising start.

Spe Salvi(IRE), penalised for her win in the summer, showed no errant traits this time but was never able to mount a challenge.

Lord Kennedy(IRE) has left Seamus Mullins since finishing second at Worcester in October. Just avoiding a kick in the face from the runner-up early in the race, he led at halfway but could not hold on in the straight. (op 14-1)

The Tracey Shuffle, a brother to the yard's smart hurdler Mr Thriller, was well enough placed turning in but soon found himself on the retreat. (op 11-2)

Journeyman(IRE), third on his debut back in the spring but out with niggly problems since, failed to pick up when the race began to unfold. (op 13-8)

3055 BOXINGDAYRACES.CO.UK "JUMPERS' BUMPER" NATIONAL HUNT FLAT RACE 2m (P)

1:20 (1:21) (Class 4) 4-Y-0+ **£2,602** (£764; £382; £190)

Form				RPR
0-2	1		**Blue Monster (IRE)**[234] 93 6-11-0 0 APMcCoy (Nicky Henderson) *chsd ldrs: rdn to chse ldr ent fnl f: kpt on wl u.p to ld nr fin* **10/1**[3]	104
2-21	2	hd	**Dark Lover (GER)**[40] 2331 5-11-0 0 NoelFehily (Paul Nicholls) *t.k.h: hld up in tch in midfield: hdwy to trck ldrs 5f out: led over 2f out: rdn ent fnl 2f: pressed ins fnl f: hdd nr fin* **11/8**[1]	104
30-2	3	1 3/4	**Management (IRE)**[42] 2295 4-11-0 0 RobertThornton (Alan King) *t.k.h: hld up wl in tch in midfield: rdn to chse ldr 2f out: styd on same pce after: lost 2nd ent fnl f* **16/1**	102
	4	2 1/4	**Spanish Treasure (GER)**[245] 5304 4-11-0 0 NickScholfield (Andy Turnell) *t.k.h: hld up wl in tch in midfield: rdn and effrt jst over 2f out: kpt on same pce fr over 1f out* **2/1**[2]	100+
0-23	5	1 3/4	**Smooth Classic (IRE)**[66] 1860 6-11-0 0 WayneHutchinson (Warren Greatrex) *hld up wl in tch towards rr: hdwy to chse ldrs 4f out: pressed ldrs but unable qck whn rdn over 2f out: one pce and no threat to ldrs fr over 1f out* **12/1**	98
0612	6	6	**Tocatchaprince (IRE)**[29] 2583 4-11-0 0 (v) DaveCrosse (Milton Harris) *hld up wl in tch in last trio: rdn and unable qck over 2f out: plugged on same pce and no ch w ldrs fnl 2f* **33/1**	92
211-	7	2 1/4	**The Strawberry One**[239] 27 5-10-7 0 TimmyMurphy (David Arbuthnot) *led tl over 12f out: styd chsng ldr: rdn and ev ch wl over 2f out tl over 2f out: wknd qckly wl over 1f out* **10/1**[3]	83
5-	8	1 1/4	**Lambro River (IRE)**[273] 4801 5-11-0 0 LeightonAspell (Alison Batchelor) *t.k.h: chsd ldrs tl lost pl over 4f out: bhd and n.d fr wl over 2f out* **66/1**	89
0	9	1 3/4	**Viva Taipan (IRE)**[58] 1993 7-10-7 0 FelixDeGiles (Alex Hales) *hld up wl in tch in last trio: rdn and struggling over 3f out: n.d fr wl over 2f out* **100/1**	80
U5-6	10	nk	**Master Darcy**[230] 155 8-11-0 0 RichardJohnson (Laura Mongan) *chsd ldr after 2f tl led over 12f out: rdn and hdd over 2f out: sn wknd* **50/1**	86
0	11	9	**Champs De Bleu (FR)**[24] 2667 7-11-0 0 JamieMoore (Gary Moore) *t.k.h: chsd ldr for 2f: styd chsng ldrs tl wknd over 3f out: bhd over 2f out* **66/1**	77

3m 43.3s (223.30)

WFA 4 from 5yo+ 5lb **11 Ran SP% 116.1**

Tote Swingers: 1&2 £4.20, 1&3 £9.70, 2&3 £4.90 CSF £23.66 TOTE £6.90: £1.90, £1.40, £3.50; EX 20.70.

Owner N J Henderson **Bred** Tony Hickey **Trained** Upper Lambourn, Berks

FOCUS

This race was for horses which have never run on the Flat proper and which are eligible to run in novice hurdles. The pace was slightly better than for the opener and the time around a second and a half quicker but, as with all these races, the form is going to prove of dubious value. The first two are rated around 10lb off their best bumper figures.

NOTEBOOK

Blue Monster(IRE) showed ability in bumpers and was runner-up on his hurdling debut when last seen back in May. Sticking to the inside in the straight and the recipient of a strong ride from McCoy, he cut down the favourite close home. When he returns to hurdling he is likely to benefit from a longer trip. (op 15-2)

Dark Lover(GER) was second in both his bumpers before taking a novice hurdle. He travelled smoothly into the lead and the race looked his, but he was worn down. (op 7-4 tchd 15-8)

Management(IRE) has previous Polytrack experience having finished second in a Lingfield bumper six weeks ago, and appeared to give his running. (op 14-1)

Spanish Treasure(GER) cost £105,000 out of Eddie Hales's yard after winning a bumper at Punchestown in April. Held up, he did close in the straight without reaching the leaders. (op 5-2 tchd 15-8)

Smooth Classic(IRE) was a well beaten third in a 3m1f novice hurdle last time. He had his chance but, unsurprisingly, was unable to quicken up. (op 16-1)

The Strawberry One, a dual turf bumper winner, faded after making much of the running to the home straight. (op 6-1)

3056 PANORAMIC BAR AND RESTAURANT "JUMPERS' BUMPER" NATIONAL HUNT FLAT RACE 2m (P)

1:50 (1:50) (Class 4) 4-Y-0+ **£2,602** (£764; £382; £190)

Form				RPR
0-12	1		**Chain Of Command (IRE)**[44] 2233 7-11-0 0 WayneHutchinson (Warren Greatrex) *hld up in rr: hdwy into midfield 4f out: rdn to chse clr ldr jst over 2f out: led ent fnl f: kpt on wl* **11/2**[3]	107
35-4	2	1 1/2	**Alwaysonthemove**[226] 215 6-11-0 0 LeightonAspell (Laura Mongan) *t.k.h: hld up in midfield: lost pl and rr over 3f out: rallied ent fnl 2f: swtchd rt jst over 1f out: styd on wl u.p fnl f: wnt 2nd fnl 50yds: no threat to wnr* **50/1**	105
11	3	3/4	**Vertige Dore (FR)**[123] 1310 5-11-0 0 TimmyMurphy (Paul Nicholls) *t.k.h: hld up in midfield: outpcd and dropped towards rr over 3f out: rallied ent fnl 2f: kpt on fnl f to 3rd on post: no threat to wnr* **5/4**[1]	104
22	4	nse	**Sire De Grugy (FR)**[29] 2577 4-11-0 0 JamieMoore (Gary Moore) *t.k.h: hld up in last pair: hdwy to chse clr ldr ent fnl 3f: rdn and clsd on ldr jst over 2f out: ev ch ent fnl f: btn ins fnl f: wknd and lost 2 pls fnl 50yds* **5/2**[2]	104
4-33	5	hd	**Marleno (GER)**[38] 2362 4-11-0 0 (t) WarrenMarston (Milton Harris) *t.k.h: led: wnt clr over 11f out: rdn ent fnl 2f: hdd ent fnl f: styd on same pce after* **20/1**	104
04P-	6	5	**Snow Patrol**[317] 3911 9-10-7 0 CharlieWallis(7) (Nigel Dunger) *t.k.h: chsd ldr tl 7f out: rdn and no hdwy over 3f out: styd on same pce fr over 2f out* **100/1**	99
4305	7	2 1/2	**Pepporoni Pete (IRE)**[174] 866 9-10-11 0 (t) JimmyDerham(3) (Milton Harris) *t.k.h: hld up in midfield: hdwy and swtchd lft 5f out: chsd clr ldr briefly 4f out: wknd u.p over 2f out* **33/1**	97
	8	1 3/4	**As De Fer (FR)**[145] 4-10-9 0 RachaelGreen(5) (Anthony Honeyball) *t.k.h: chsd ldrs: wnt 2nd 7f out tl ent fnl 3f: sn wknd* **33/1**	95
52-4	9	1/2	**Shrewd Investment**[42] 2283 4-11-0 0 RobertThornton (Alan King) *t.k.h: prom in main gp: hung rt and lost pl over 4f out: no threat to ldrs after* **7/1**	94
/60-	10	113	**Solar Express**[317] 3910 5-10-7 0 MrJackSalmon(7) (John Bridger) *a towards rr: rdn and lost tch 6f out: wl t.o fnl 3f* **100/1**	—

3m 38.9s (218.90) **10 Ran SP% 115.5**

Tote Swingers: 1&2 £16.50, 1&3 £2.60, 2&3 £11.30 CSF £236.78 TOTE £8.00: £2.50, £9.10, £1.30; EX 131.90.

Owner Malcolm C Denmark **Bred** Miss Catherine McCaghey **Trained** Upper Lambourn, Berks

FOCUS

Runners in this must have run over hurdles but not on the Flat, and mustn't have won a Class 1 or 2 race. The eventual fifth set a strong pace and this was much the quickest race so far, and consequently a truer test of stamina. The second, fifth and sixth limit the rating.

NOTEBOOK

Chain Of Command(IRE) was suited by the decent tempo and came from last place to wear down the long-time leader. A winner over fences here in October, and rated 127 in that sphere by the BHA, he showed ability in bumpers two seasons ago and this was only the eighth race of his career. Well regarded by his trainer, he likes decent ground and is best going right-handed. (op 9-2)

Alwaysonthemove was third in a Polytrack bumper last term, but pulled hard and didn't get home when last appearing over hurdles in May. After losing his pitch, he stayed on stoutly up the inside rail for second.

Vertige Dore(FR) looked promising when winning over hurdles at Bangor, but that was four months ago and his trainer reported beforehand that the gelding was not fully wound up for this and would not have run over hurdles until mid-January. The favourite was duly found out, but he did stay on to shade third after hitting a flat spot. (op 7-4)

Sire De Grugy(FR) was runner-up in both a Sandown bumper, to the promising Knight Pass, and on his novice hurdle debut here. He looked set for second again after closing in tandem with the winner, but weakened inside the last. He is entered in the novice hurdle here on Boxing Day. (op 9-4 tchd 3-1)

Marleno(GER) has been Listed-placed in both a bumper and a novice hurdle, the latter at this course. This keen individual went out in front in a first-time tongue strap and was still clear turning into the straight, but he was gunned down approaching the furlong pole. (tchd 16-1)

3057 KEMPTON.CO.UK "JUMPERS' BUMPER" NATIONAL HUNT FLAT RACE (DIV I) 2m (P)

2:20 (2:20) (Class 4) 4-Y-0+ **£2,276** (£668; £334; £166)

Form RPR

102/ **1** **Giorgio Quercus (FR)**[612] 5076 5-11-0 0 APMcCoy 97+
(Nicky Henderson) *t.k.h: hld up in last pair: swtchd lft and gd hdwy over 2f out: led over 1f out: rdn clr 1f out: in command after: r.o wl* **7/4**[1]

6- **2** *1 1/4* **Bermuda Boy (FR)**[268] 4913 5-11-0 0 HarrySkelton 96
(Paul Nicholls) *t.k.h: hld up in tch: nt clr run and lost pl over 3f out: dropped to last and switching to outer over 2f out: hdwy u.p to chse wnr ins fnl f: r.o but nvr able to chal* **4/1**[2]

3 *3 1/2* **First Smash (GER)**[535] 862 5-11-0 0 WarrenMarston 93
(Milton Harris) *t.k.h: hld up in last pair tl gd hdwy over 3f out: rdn to ld ent fnl 2f: hdd over 1f out: nt pce of wnr ent fnl f: lost 2nd and wknd ins fnl f* **14/1**

3111 **4** *1/2* **National Trust**[27] 2610 8-10-11 0 AlanCreighton(3) 92
(Edward Creighton) *chsd ldrs: rdn and effrt over 2f out: kpt on same pce u.p fnl f* **7/1**[3]

45-0 **5** *3/4* **This Masquerade**[31] 2512 7-11-0 0 WayneHutchinson 91
(Warren Greatrex) *led: rdn and hdd ent fnl 2f: outpcd over 1f out: plugged on same pce and btn fnl f* **8/1**

3050 **6** *1 1/4* **Wade Farm Billy (IRE)**[17] 2209 6-11-0 0 JamieMoore 90
(Gary Moore) *hld up in tch towards rr: effrt and switching to inner 2f out: nvr enough room on rail and no hdwy fr over 1f out: nvr able to chal* **4/1**[2]

-005 **7** *2* **Little Roxy (IRE)**[50] 2135 5-10-4 0 MarcGoldstein(3) 81
(Anna Newton-Smith) *midfield: rdn and unable qck over 2f out: one pce and no threat to ldrs fnl 2f* **66/1**

50 **8** *1/2* **Aine's Delight (IRE)**[40] 2331 4-10-7 0 NickScholfield 81
(Andy Turnell) *t.k.h: hld up in tch towards rr: hdwy 4f out: chsd ldrs and rdn whn n.m.r over 2f out: sn outpcd and no threat to ldrs after* **25/1**

0-P0 **9** *10* **Master Paddy (IRE)**[34] 2456 6-11-0 0 AndrewThornton 78
(Andy Turnell) *t.k.h: chsd ldr tl over 2f out: sn wknd* **66/1**

503 **10** *1 3/4* **Sieglinde (FR)**[46] 2182 4-10-7 0 LeightonAspell 69
(Alison Batchelor) *t.k.h: chsd ldrs tl rdn and wknd wl over 2f out* **20/1**

3m 49.1s (229.10) **10 Ran SP% 118.2**

Tote Swingers: 1&2 £2.60, 1&3 £7.10, 2&3 £9.50 CSF £8.55 TOTE £3.40: £1.90, £1.50, £5.20; EX 12.60.

Owner Sir Robert Ogden **Bred** Daniel Chassagneux Et Al **Trained** Upper Lambourn, Berks

FOCUS

The stipulation for this event was that runners must have taken part in at least one hurdle race after 2008. They went a very steady pace and it turned into a sprint up the straight, with the time the slowest of the day. The seventh limits the form.

NOTEBOOK

Giorgio Quercus(FR), a useful juvenile hurdler two seasons ago, was sold by Million In Mind for £112,000 but remains in the same yard. He was held up at the back to settle him, but was switched out entering the straight and came with a smooth run to win stylishly. Already schooled over fences, he looks a nice chasing prospect. (op 9-4 tchd 5-2)

Bermuda Boy(FR) ◆ was trapped on the inside turning in and, although he was pulled out wide, the winner had taken first run on him. It probably didn't cost him victory and this was a promising effort from a horse who has had a breathing operation since his hurdles debut last spring. (tchd 7-2)

First Smash(GER), a winner on the Flat in Germany in his younger days, ran creditably from off the pace on this debut for the yard and first start since the summer of 2009. (op 12-1)

National Trust, who came here with a hat-trick of hurdles wins in selling/claiming company behind him, lacked a change of gear but wasn't disgraced. (op 5-1)

This Masquerade was fourth in a warm bumper on his debut last term but had not shown much in two efforts over hurdles. He reverted to front-running tactics and performed respectably. (op 10-1)

Wade Farm Billy(IRE) was a little disappointing after finishing a fair second in a 1m3f maiden at this track last month. (op 7-2)

3058 KEMPTON.CO.UK "JUMPERS' BUMPER" NATIONAL HUNT FLAT RACE (DIV II) 2m (P)

2:50 (2:50) (Class 4) 4-Y-0+ **£2,276** (£668; £334; £166)

Form RPR

00-B **1** **Advisor (FR)**[24] 2671 4-11-0 0 SamThomas 124
(Paul Nicholls) *chsd ldr: rdn to ld 1f out: hrd pressed ins fnl f: kpt on wl and holding rival whn jockey changed whip hand and edgd lft u.p nr fin* **8/1**

04-1 **2** *hd* **Eradicate (IRE)**[185] 207 6-10-9 0 DavidBass(5) 124
(Nicky Henderson) *in tch in last pair: niggled along 7f out: hdwy to chse ldrs 5f out: chsd ldng pair and hanging rt ent fnl 2f: swtchd lft over 1f out: chal u.p ins fnl f: looked hld whn pushed lft cl home* **5/4**[1]

0F-6 **3** *1 3/4* **Alsadaa (USA)**[23] 2085 7-11-0 0 RichardJohnson 122
(Laura Mongan) *led: rdn over 2f out: hdd 1f out: styd on same pce u.p after* **2/1**[2]

00- **4** *11* **Spiritual Guidance (IRE)**[327] 3694 7-11-0 0 WayneHutchinson 111
(Warren Greatrex) *t.k.h: hld up in tch in midfield: clr in ldng quartet and rdn over 2f out: wknd wl over 1f out* **25/1**

46-2 **5** *16* **Perception (IRE)**[33] 2480 4-10-7 0 RobertThornton 88
(Alan King) *chsd ldrs tl 5th and struggling ent fnl 3f: wl btn after* **9/2**[3]

6 **6** *12* **Good Buy Dubai (USA)**[36] 2421 4-10-11 0 AlanCreighton(3) 83
(Edward Creighton) *hld up in rr: struggling 4f out: wl bhd 3f: t.o* **66/1**

600 **7** *1 1/4* **Sablazo (FR)**[45] 2216 4-10-7 0 MrBJPoste(7) 82
(Andy Turnell) *in tch in last trio: struggling and wknd wl over 3f out: t.o* **66/1**

-550 **8** *25* **Salybia Bay**[26] 2639 4-10-7 0 NickScholfield 50
(Andy Turnell) *chsd ldrs tl 4f out: sn wknd: t.o fnl 2f* **50/1**

3m 37.6s (217.60) **8 Ran SP% 115.9**

Tote Swingers: 1&2 £2.80, 1&3 £3.10, 2&3 £1.60 CSF £18.71 TOTE £9.50: £2.30, £1.60, £1.10; EX 21.00.

Owner The Royal Ascot Racing Club **Bred** Kilboy Estate **Trained** Ditcheat, Somerset

FOCUS

Division II of the 2.20 and, for what it's worth, run over 11 seconds quicker. The first three were clear and the winner produced a good effort to beat a pair of decent rivals.

NOTEBOOK

Advisor(FR) got past long-timer leader Alsadaa then stuck his neck out bravely to repel Eradicate. He was brought down on his reappearance, but the breathing operation he had in the summer has benefited him and this 133-rated-hurdler will go for decent handicaps now, with a race back at Kempton on the 27th pencilled in. (op 9-1 tchd 10-1)

Eradicate(IRE) was Group-placed on the Flat for Mark Johnston and is the highest-rated of these over hurdles too, successful in the Swinton at Haydock back in May. He had stamina concerns on this first outing since the summer having failed to stay 2m in the Henry II Stakes, and looked held in third entering the final furlong. He responded to pressure from there, though, and pressed the winner to the line. Races like the Totesport Trophy and the County Hurdle will probably figure on his agenda in the new year. (op 6-5)

Alsadaa(USA) is currently rated 7lb superior to the winner over hurdles and he is a dual C&D scorer on the Flat. Going off in front as usual, he was never able to get clear and had to give best in the final furlong. (tchd 9-4 and 5-2 in places)

Spiritual Guidance(IRE) was unplaced in a bumper and a single maiden hurdle and had not run since January, so this was a decent effort. He obviously has ability.

Perception(IRE) is a dual C&D winner on the Flat proper and it was a little disappointing that she was beaten so comprehensively. (op 5-1 tchd 4-1)

3059 BISTRO PRICES FROM £42 "JUMPERS' BUMPER" NATIONAL HUNT FLAT RACE 2m (P)

3:20 (3:20) (Class 4) 5-Y-0+ **£2,602** (£764; £382; £190)

Form RPR

2-30 **1** **Free World (IRE)**[52] 2084 8-11-0 0 WayneHutchinson 128
(Warren Greatrex) *chsd ldr tl led 10f out: mde rest: rdn clr ent fnl f: in command fnl f: styd on wl* **14/1**

6114 **2** *4 1/2* **Working Title (IRE)**[24] 2674 8-11-0 0 APMcCoy 123
(Nicky Henderson) *t.k.h: hld up in tch: effrt and nt clr run over 2f out tl over 1f out: kpt on ins fnl f to snatch 2nd on post: no threat to wnr* **5/4**[1]

5024 **3** *nse* **Magic Sky (FR)**[30] 2541 10-10-7 0 JakeGreenall(7) 123
(Milton Harris) *t.k.h early: hld up in tch: rdn and outpcd over 3f out: swtchd rt and rallied u.p over 1f out: styd on wl fnl f: no threat to wnr* **25/1**

F-12 **4** *hd* **Harry Tricker**[41] 2313 6-11-0 0 (p) JamieMoore 123
(Gary Moore) *t.k.h: hld up wl in tch: rdn and effrt to chse clr wnr over 1f out: no imp fnl f: lost 2 pls nr fin* **11/4**[2]

3/FF **5** *1 1/4* **American Trilogy (IRE)**[8] 2926 6-11-0 0 HarrySkelton 122
(Paul Nicholls) *hld up in tch towards rr: hdwy 6f out: chsd ldrs and reminders over 3f out: styd on same pce u.p fr over 2f out* **4/1**[3]

56-4 **6** *2 1/2* **Enfant De Lune (FR)**[228] 194 6-11-0 0 RobertThornton 119
(Alan King) *t.k.h: hld up in midfield: hdwy to chse wnr over 3f out: rdn and nt pce of wnr ent fnl 2f: lost 2nd over 1f out: wknd fnl f* **12/1**

P2U- **7** *nse* **Dominican Monk (IRE)**[249] 5208 11-11-0 0 DarylJacob 119
(David Arbuthnot) *t.k.h: hld up in tch in rr: hdwy on outer ent fnl 3f: no prog and btn over 1f out* **16/1**

563- **8** *3 3/4* **Whatever Next (IRE)**[332] 3614 8-10-11 0 AlanCreighton(3) 115
(Edward Creighton) *led tl 10f out: chsd wnr after tl 6f out: wknd u.p over 2f out* **66/1**

34P- **9** *5* **Snake Charmer**[545] 809 7-11-0 0 (b) DaveCrosse 110
(Milton Harris) *chsd ldrs: wnt 2nd 6f out tl over 3f out: wknd u.p over 2f out* **33/1**

23-6 **10** *15* **She's Humble (IRE)**[36] 2429 8-10-10 0 ow3 AndrewThornton 91
(Linda Jewell) *in tch in rr: lost tch over 3f out* **66/1**

3-0P **11** *6* **Vinmix De Bessy (FR)**[206] 523 9-10-7 0 (p) JoshuaMoore(7) 89
(Gary Moore) *t.k.h early: hld up in tch: struggling and dropped to rr 4f out: lost tch 3f out* **33/1**

0/0- **12** *3/4* **Indian Spring (IRE)**[131] 1240 6-11-0 0 AndrewGlassonbury 88
(Gary Moore) *hld up in tch towards rr: lost tch over 3f out* **25/1**

3m 38.7s (218.70) **12 Ran SP% 127.9**

Tote Swingers: 1&2 £5.50, 1&3 £12.90, 2&3 £3.90 CSF £33.22 TOTE £12.90: £3.50, £1.10, £9.20; EX 40.40.

Owner Malcolm C Denmark **Bred** B Murphy **Trained** Upper Lambourn, Berks

FOCUS

A bumper for horses that have run over fences, and an interesting affair containing some decent sorts. The pace was just modest. The strongest race of the day, and a good effort from the winner.

NOTEBOOK

Free World(IRE) is a useful chaser at 2m4f-3m and he showed ability in bumpers a few seasons back. Never far away, he kicked a few lengths to the good entering the straight and was never in much danger of being caught, giving connections a double on the card. (op 16-1 tchd 20-1)

Working Title(IRE) was clear on BHA hurdles and chase figures and he won his only bumper. This represented an insufficent test of stamina but he ran creditably enough, just getting the best of a bunch finish for second. (op 7-4)

Magic Sky(FR), whose last run came over the big fences at Aintree, stayed on really well and almost snatched second. This was a pleasing trial for the Welsh National. (op 20-1)

Harry Tricker is two from two over fences this season, receiving the race from the stewards on the second occasion, and his trainer was anxious to get a run into him. The gelding looked set to finish second until tying up late on and should strip fitter. (tchd 5-2)

American Trilogy(IRE) had fallen on both runs since his comeback and this will have served as a useful confidence booster.

Enfant De Lune(FR) was a winner on the artifical track at Cagnes-Sur-Mer in his younger days. A fair chaser, he took a keen hold for a long way and lack of a recent run told as he faded out of the places late on. (op 10-1)

3060 CHRISTMAS AT KEMPTON "JUMPERS' BUMPER" NATIONAL HUNT FLAT RACE 2m (P)

3:50 (3:50) (Class 4) 4-Y-0+ **£2,602** (£764; £382; £190)

Form RPR

3-P1 **1** **Pepe Simo (IRE)**[45] 2210 6-11-0 0 SamThomas 120+
(Paul Nicholls) *hld up in tch: chsd ldr wl over 3f out: clr w ldr over 2f out: led on bit over 1f out: nudged along to assert ins fnl f: easily* **1/1**[1]

211/ **2** *1 1/4* **Noland**[742] 2695 9-11-0 0 NoelFehily 112
(Paul Nicholls) *w ldr tl led over 5f out: clr w wnr and rdn over 2f out: hdd over 1f out: nt gng pce of wnr ins fnl f* **11/4**[2]

-130 **3** *3* **Fountains Flypast**[6] 2960 6-10-9 0 RachaelGreen(5) 109
(Anthony Honeyball) *in tch towards rr: hdwy over 4f out: 4th and outpcd by ldng pair wl over 2f out: wnt 3rd ent fnl 2f: kpt on wl but nvr gng pce to trble ldrs* **16/1**

2350 **4** *6* **Caught By Witness (IRE)**[38] 2361 5-10-11 0 JimmyDerham(3) 103
(Milton Harris) *chsd ldrs: outpcd u.p wl over 2f out: lost 3rd and wl hld ent fnl 2f* **8/1**

00-3 **5** *12* **Dark Dancer**[80] 1680 6-10-7 0 RichardJohnson 84
(Laura Mongan) *hld up in tch in rr: hmpd after 2f: rdn and wknd over 3f out* **20/1**

6 *3/4* **Fringe Theatre** 4-11-0 0 JamieMoore 90
(Gary Moore) *t.k.h: hld up in tch in last trio: hmpd after 2f: rdn and wknd over 3f out* **25/1**

3-2P **7** *21* **Awesome George**[38] 2359 6-10-11 0 CharlieHuxley(3) 69
(Alan King) *hld up in tch: hmpd after 2f: rdn and wknd 4f out: t.o* **7/1**[3]

05 **8** *5* **Luna Lightning**[15] 2825 6-10-7 0 MarkBradburne 57
(Linda Jewell) *led tl over 5f out: lost pl u.p wl over 3f out: sn bhd: t.o* **100/1**

F-00 P **Toomuchinformation**[46] 2183 6-10-7 0..........................(p) FelixDeGiles —
(Anna Newton-Smith) *chsd ldrs tl lost action and p.u after 2f* **66/1**
3m 42.7s (222.70) **9** Ran SP% **117.3**
Tote Swingers: 1&2 £1.80, 1&3 £2.70, 2&3 £6.90. ToteSuper7: Win: not won Place: £54.30 CSF £3.73 TOTE £2.40: £1.70, £1.10, £2.50; EX 6.30.
Owner Highclere Thoroughbred Racing-Pepe Simo **Bred** Grange Stud **Trained** Ditcheat, Somerset

FOCUS
This was for horses that have never run in a conventional Flat race. Another steadily-run race, it provided a 1-2 for the Paul Nicholls stable. The winner was value for further but didn't need to be at his best.

NOTEBOOK
Pepe Simo(IRE), a winner of a beginners' chase last time, cruised up to his stablemate in the straight and won with a good deal in hand. This smart sort could return here next week for the Grade 2 Wayward Lad Novices' Chase, ground permitting. (op 5-4 tchd 11-8 in a place)
Noland was appearing on a racecourse for the first time since his win in the Grade 1 John Durkan Memorial Chase at Punchestown two years ago. He ran well too, stretching in the straight but ultimately finding his stable companion too strong. Paul Nicholls reported that the injury-plagued 9-y-o had not even had a racecourse gallop. The gelding could go to Cheltenham on New Year's Day. (op 9-4 tchd 3-1 in a place)
Fountains Flypast ◆, without the tongue tie for this quick reappearance, ran on nicely for third but was perhaps flattered by his proximity to the first two at the line. A return to 2m4f will suit him back over hurdles.
Caught By Witness(IRE) ran respectably in fourth and has a choice of hurdling engagements on Boxing Day. (op 12-1 tchd 15-2)
Fringe Theatre, who also held an entry in the opener, failed to settle on this racecourse debut.
Awesome George was hampered when a rival suffered an injury early on. (tchd 6-1 and 15-2)
T/Jkpt: Not won. T/Plt: £34.00 to a £1 stake. Pool £66,074.47 - 1,417.92 winning units T/Qpdt: £4.10 to a £1 stake. Pool £7,844.23 - 1,392.66 winning units SP

2466 HEREFORD (R-H)
Tuesday, December 21
3061 Meeting Abandoned - Frozen ground

2598 SEDGEFIELD (L-H)
Tuesday, December 21
3067 Meeting Abandoned - Frozen ground

2584 LUDLOW (R-H)
Wednesday, December 22
3074 Meeting Abandoned - Frost and snow

2654 MUSSELBURGH (R-H)
Wednesday, December 22
3081 Meeting Abandoned - Frozen in places

2824 SOUTHWELL (L-H)
Wednesday, December 22

OFFICIAL GOING: Standard to slow
Wind: Moderate 1/2 behind Weather: Fine and sunny but cold

3088 BIGGER WINS WITH SP+ AT TOTESPORT.COM STANDARD OPEN NATIONAL HUNT FLAT RACE 2m (F)
12:50 (12:51) (Class 6) 4-6-Y-O **£1,370** (£399; £199)

Form RPR
U6- 1 **Lombardy Boy (IRE)**[316] 3951 5-10-11 0.......................... TomMolloy(3) 99
(Michael Banks) *trckd ldrs: chal over 4f out: led over 2f out: rdn rt out* **6/1**[3]
2 *2* **Richie Rob** 4-10-9 0.......................... BrianToomey(5) 97
(Neville Bycroft) *mid-div: hdwy 7f out: drvn over 4f out: outpcd over 2f out: styd on to take 2nd last 75yds* **33/1**
3 *2 1/2* **Arctic Gunner**[597] 6-11-0 0.......................... JimmyMcCarthy 95
(G Deacon) *hld up: hdwy 7f out: drvn over 3f out: hung rt and one pce fnl 2f* **10/1**
4 *1/2* **Guess Again (IRE)** 5-11-0 0.......................... WayneHutchinson 94
(Warren Greatrex) *w ldr: led 8f out: hdd over 2f out: one pce over 1f out* **2/1**[2]
2 5 *7* **Inthesettlement**[31] 2546 5-10-7 0.......................... JasonMaguire 80
(Donald McCain) *t.k.h in rr: hdwy over 4f out: handy 3rd 3f out: sn rdn: wknd over 1f out* **8/11**[1]
5 6 *24* **Iznt Getting Court (IRE)**[61] 1955 4-11-0 0.......................... DougieCostello 63
(John Wainwright) *trckd ldrs: t.k.h: upsides over 4f out: lost pl over 3f out: sn bhd* **20/1**
7 *92* **Lady Gower** 4-10-4 0.......................... LeeStephens(3) —
(David Evans) *drvn to chse ldrs after 3f: reminders and lost pl after 7f: hdwy to chse ldrs over 6f out: lost pl over 4f out: sn wl bhd and t.o* **20/1**
0-0 8 *dist* **Flag Dancer**[16] 2826 4-10-7 0.......................... MattCrawley(7) —
(Christine Dunnett) *led: drvn and hdd 8f out: wknd qckly over 5f out: sn t.o and virtually p.u: eventually completed* **66/1**
4m 8.60s (23.10) **Going Correction** +1.50s/f (Slow)
WFA 4 from 5yo+ 5lb **8** Ran SP% **128.6**
Speed ratings: **102,101,99,99,96 84,38,—**
toteswingers: 1&2 £18.90. 1&3 £8.50, 2&3 £20.90. CSF £179.13 TOTE £7.40: £1.90, £16.90, £3.10; EX 115.90.
Owner M C Banks **Bred** P M Prior-Wandesforde **Trained** Waresley, Cambs

FOCUS
This was a conventional bumper to start with, run at a very steady pace. The favourite disappointed and the form looks weak.

NOTEBOOK
Lombardy Boy(IRE) had previous experience of the surface, in the process of staying on when unseating this rider here last January. Off since the following month, he galloped on determinedly down the centre of the track after leading entering the straight. His prospects of defying a penalty are limited. (op 7-1)
Richie Rob's pedigree did not look conclusive as far as his stamina was concerned, with Flat winners at up to 1m amongst his siblings, but his dam is out of a half-sister to Derby winner Shirley Heights. A cheap purchase as a yearling, he stayed on well down the outside once in line for home and certainly got the trip, albeit in this slowly run race.
Arctic Gunner was a first runner as a licensed trainer for Geoffrey Deacon, who has had plenty of success in point-to-points and hunter chases. This grey, out of an unraced half-sister to Supreme Novices' Hurdle winner Arctic Kinsman, was runner-up in a 2m5f point back in May 2009 on his sole start. He stayed on steadily and will be suited by soft ground and a longer trip over jumps. (op 12-1)
Guess Again(IRE), a half-brother to Grand Annual Chase winner St Pirran amongst others, made much of the running to the straight, but was run out of second spot at the furlong pole. (op 11-4 tchd 7-4)
Inthesettlement pulled hard when runner-up on her debut at Aintree and again took a keen grip in the first part of the race. She made smooth headway on the home turn but found little when let down in this deep surface. Getting her to settle is vital to her chances of success. (op 8-15)

3089 CALL TOTESPORT 0800 221 221 FOR SP+ "JUMPERS' BUMPER" NATIONAL HUNT FLAT RACE 2m (F)
1:20 (1:20) (Class 4) 4-Y-0+ **£2,602** (£764; £382; £190)

Form RPR
0-21 1 **First Rock (IRE)**[26] 2660 4-11-0 0.......................... BarryKeniry 112+
(Alan Swinbank) *trckd ldrs: t.k.h: led over 4f out: rdn clr 3f out: eased nr fin* **7/4**[1]
0 2 *11* **Saint Denis (FR)**[49] 2143 4-11-0 0.......................... DenisO'Regan 98
(Alex Hales) *trckd ldrs: pushed along after 7f: sn lost pl: kpt on to take modest 3rd over 2f out: wnt 2nd last 150yds* **8/1**
325 3 *2 1/4* **Dontupsettherhythm (IRE)**[44] 2281 5-10-11 0.......... AdamPogson(3) 96
(Charles Pogson) *trckd ldrs: wnt 2nd 4f out: wknd fnl f* **9/1**
0-4P 4 *3 1/4* **Lady Karinga**[63] 1914 5-10-4 0.......................... LeeStephens(3) 86
(David Evans) *trckd ldr: t.k.h: rdn and outpcd over 4f out: wnt mod 3rd over 3f out: one pce* **7/1**[3]
0P-0 5 *13* **Northwold**[52] 2111 6-11-0 0.......................... JimmyMcCarthy 80
(Christopher Kellett) *mid-div: drvn and outpcd 6f out: nvr a factor after* **66/1**
10-3 6 *3/4* **Pickworth (IRE)**[197] 684 5-10-7 0.......................... DougieCostello 72
(Philip Kirby) *in rr: sme hdwy 7f out: lost pl 5f out: sn bhd* **10/1**
F232 7 *19* **Flichity (IRE)**[30] 2584 5-11-0 0.......................... JasonMaguire 60
(Donald McCain) *hld up in rr: t.k.h: swtchd wd over 6f out: sn reminders: lost pl 5f out: sn bhd* **9/4**[2]
6-00 8 *26* **Sebennytos**[30] 2577 5-11-0 0.......................... WayneHutchinson 34
(Warren Greatrex) *led: hdd over 4f out: lost pl 3f out: sn bhd: t.o and eased 1f out* **25/1**
U0-4 9 *94* **Gabrielle Da Vinci**[224] 275 4-10-4 0.......................... TomMolloy(3) —
(David Evans) *in rr: struggling after 7f: t.o 6f out: virtually p.u: eventually completed* **33/1**
4m 3.00s (17.50) **Going Correction** +1.50s/f (Slow) **9** Ran SP% **118.1**
Speed ratings (Par 105): **116,110,109,107,101 100,91,78,31**
toteswingers: 1&2 £5.30. 1&3 £4.70, 2&3 £11.70. CSF £17.02 TOTE £2.00: £1.10, £2.50, £2.90; EX 25.00.
Owner United Five Racing **Bred** K Molloy **Trained** Melsonby, N Yorks

FOCUS
This was open to horses which have never run on the Flat proper and which are eligible for novice hurdles. The pace was quicker than for the opener and the time was over five seconds quicker.

NOTEBOOK
First Rock(IRE) was clear with his race won early in the home straight. He is a useful jumping prospect, but he carried his head high and idled in the latter stages, needing to be kept up to his work, and evidently has his quirks. His next run could be in a maiden hurdle back at Musselburgh on New Year's Day. (op 6-4 tchd 2-1 in a place)
Saint Denis(FR) showed a bit of ability in two Irish bumpers for Eddie Hales before finishing well beaten on his hurdling debut last month. He was fifth and going nowhere beginning the home turn but boxed on against the inside rail to take second. (op 10-1 tchd 12-1 and 14-1 in a place)
Dontupsettherhythm(IRE), a winning pointer, looked the last threat to the favourite turning out of the back straight but he was made to look very one-paced from there. (op 10-1 tchd 8-1)
Lady Karinga has made the frame in turf bumpers and a 3m novice hurdle, but this event was an inadequate test of stamina for her. (op 6-1)
Flichity(IRE), held up in last before being switched to the outer at halfway, made limited progress and soon dropped back beaten. Runner-up three times over hurdles, he is able but not straightforward, although he may not have faced the kickback here. (op 15-8)

3090 BET TOTEPOOL AT TOTESPORT.COM "JUMPERS' BUMPER" NATIONAL HUNT FLAT RACE 2m (F)
1:50 (1:50) (Class 4) 4-Y-0+ **£2,602** (£764; £382; £190)

Form RPR
6-60 1 **Cloudy Spirit**[32] 2514 5-10-7 0.......................... PaulMoloney 117+
(Reg Hollinshead) *hld up in rr: hdwy on outside to trck ldrs over 7f out: led over 4f out: styd on strly to forge 6 l clr jst ins fnl f: heavily eased fnl 75yds* **4/1**[2]
-534 2 *3* **River Dragon (IRE)**[45] 2246 5-11-0 0.......................... DougieCostello 111
(Neville Bycroft) *sn trcking ldrs: led 6f out: hdd over 4f out: styd on same pce* **12/1**
1143 3 *5* **Noble Scholar (IRE)**[35] 2446 5-11-0 0.......................... BarryKeniry 106
(Alan Swinbank) *hld up in rr: hdwy to chse ldrs 7f out: drvn 5f out: outpcd over 3f out: one pce* **5/1**[3]
0P-6 4 *10* **Quartano (GER)**[53] 2082 7-11-0 0.......................... PaddyBrennan 96
(Warren Greatrex) *trckd ldrs: chal over 4f out: outpcd over 3f out: wknd over 2f out* **5/2**[1]
2021 5 *2 1/4* **Pyracantha**[33] 2506 5-11-0 0.......................... RhysFlint 94
(Alan Swinbank) *chsd ldrs: pushed along after 7f: outpcd over 3f out: wknd fnl 2f* **5/2**[1]
/000 6 *38* **Patrick Dee**[30] 2577 5-10-7 0.......................... MattCrawley(7) 56
(Christine Dunnett) *led: hdd 6f out: sn rdn and lost pl: bhd fnl 3f* **66/1**
4-00 7 *60* **Calaficial (IRE)**[42] 2312 7-10-11 0.......................... AdamPogson(3) —
(Charles Pogson) *trckd ldr: t.k.h: reminders over 6f out: sn lost pl: t.o 4f out: virtually p.u: eventually completed* **33/1**
1246 8 *10* **Twentynineblack (FR)**[44] 2270 6-11-0 0.......................... JasonMaguire —
(Donald McCain) *hld up in rr: swtchd wd over 5f out: sn reminders and lost pl: t.o over 3f out: virtually p.u: eventually completed* **8/1**
4m 7.40s (21.90) **Going Correction** +1.50s/f (Slow) **8** Ran SP% **117.0**
Speed ratings (Par 105): **105,103,101,96,94 75,45,40**
toteswingers: 1&2 £7.70. 1&3 £4.60, 2&3 £3.10. CSF £51.22 TOTE £2.90: £1.30, £4.00, £1.20; EX 67.50.
Owner Mrs Norma Harris **Bred** Mrs Norma Harris **Trained** Upper Longdon, Staffs

FOCUS
Participants in this must have run over hurdles but not on the Flat, and cannot have won a Class 1 or 2 race. The pace looked reasonable but the time was over four seconds slower than that of the previous event.

NOTEBOOK
Cloudy Spirit is a fair hurdler, and finished sixth off a mark of 117 in a Listed handicap for mares at Cheltenham during the spring. Drawing clear in the straight before being eased with victory in the bag, she may go for a race over the brush hurdles at Haydock next week.
River Dragon(IRE) showed ability in bumpers for his previous yard. Reverting to the 'Flat' following his hurdles debut, he ran a creditable race, although in the end he was flattered to finish as close as he did to the mare.
Noble Scholar(IRE) gets 2m4f over hurdles and plugged on for a one-paced third. (op 4-1)
Quartano(GER) has a Listed bumper win in heavy ground to his name but has disappointed in his last few outings. Failing to get home after racing up with the pace, he has chase entries on Boxing Day.
Pyracantha won a Musselburgh handicap hurdle last time and was joint best-in with Cloudy Spirit on BHA hurdles figures, but did not see it out in this deep ground. He finished behind his longer-priced stablemate, but the trainer had warned before racing that some of his runners might need the outing. (op 11-4)
Twentyninebackblack(FR) ran a similar race to the yard's Flichity in the previous event. He has not shown much enthusiasm in any of his last three starts now.

3091 PLAY ROULETTE AT TOTESPORT.COM "JUMPERS' BUMPER" NATIONAL HUNT FLAT RACE 2m (F)
2:20 (2:20) (Class 4) 4-Y-0+ **£2,602** (£764; £382; £190)

Form RPR
150- **1** **Bivouac (UAE)**^{58} 4436 6-11-0 0 BarryKeniry 114+
(Alan Swinbank) *sn trcking ldrs: wnt 2nd on bit over 2f out: shkn up to ld over 1f out: sn wnt clr: v readily* **4/5**[1]
-040 **2** 3½ **Rawaaj**^{59} 1996 4-11-0 0 JasonMaguire 103
(Donald McCain) *led: hdd over 1f out: no ch w wnr* **12/1**
3-00 **3** 3¼ **Mr Chow (IRE)**^{8} 2944 6-11-0 0 WayneHutchinson 100
(Warren Greatrex) *t.k.h in midfield: drvn to chse ldrs over 4f out: kpt on same pce over 2f out: wnt 3rd 1f out* **5/1**[3]
2506 **4** 1¾ **Master Fong (IRE)**^{48} 2164 4-11-0 0 AdrianLane 98
(Donald McCain) *w ldr: one pce fnl 3f* **9/2**[2]
0606 **5** 7 **I'm In The Pink (FR)**^{14} 2330 6-11-0 0 (v) TimmyMurphy 91
(David Evans) *hld up towards rr: hdwy to trck ldrs 7f out: wknd wl over 1f out* **5/1**[3]
44 **6** 12 **Morocchius (USA)**^{22} 2282 5-10-11 0 AdamPogson(3) 79
(Charles Pogson) *trckd ldrs: t.k.h: lost pl over 2f out* **20/1**
204P **7** 26 **Wicklewood**^{36} 2438 4-10-7 0 (p) MattCrawley(7) 53
(Christine Dunnett) *in rr: pushed along after 6f: reminders over 8f out: lost pl over 5f out: sn bhd: t.o 3f out* **33/1**
532U **8** 20 **Peak Seasons (IRE)**^{36} 2434 7-11-0 0 JamieMoore 33
(Michael Chapman) *in tch in rr: drvn 6f out: lost pl over 4f out: sn bhd: t.o 3f out* **33/1**

4m 10.6s (25.10) **Going Correction** +1.50s/f (Slow)
WFA 4 from 5yo+ 5lb **8** Ran SP% **125.4**
Speed ratings (Par 105): **97,95,93,92,89 83,70,60**
toteswingers: 1&2 £3.80. 1&3 £2.20, 2&3 £10.80. CSF £14.29 TOTE £2.80: £1.50, £3.40, £1.30; EX 14.30.
Owner Mrs J M Penney **Bred** Darley **Trained** Melsonby, N Yorks

FOCUS
The conditions for this event were that runners must have taken part in at least one hurde race after 2008. It was a weakly contested race and the time was relatively slow.

NOTEBOOK
Bivouac(UAE) took a hold, but cruised into the lead and found plenty when let down. A winner four times on the Flat here this year, the first victory coming off 53, he is currently rated 76 and still has a bit to offer on this surface back at 1m4f-1m6f. Alternatively he remains unexposed over hurdles, and could go to Musselburgh in the New Year. (op 4-6)
Rawaaj showed little from a few tries on the Flat for Sir Michael Stoute and is a moderate hurdler. The bigger-priced of the McCain pair, he made the running and kept on surprisingly well. He may be worth running here from his current Flat mark of 62. (op 14-1)
Mr Chow(IRE), well held in a soft-ground novice hurdle recently, plugged on creditably enough from the home turn. (op 6-1)
Master Fong(IRE), a fair hurdler, tracked his stablemate but was left behind by the principals from the turn in. He might benefit from some headgear again. (op 6-1 tchd 13-2)
I'm In The Pink(FR) had not tackled further than an extended 1m4f on the Flat proper. He travelled quite well under a Murphy hold-up ride but did not have much left in the straight.
Morocchius(USA), who was taken steadily to post, is best at up to 1m and pulled too hard to last home.

3092 PLAY BLACKJACK AT TOTESPORT.COM "JUMPERS' BUMPER" NATIONAL HUNT FLAT RACE 2m (F)
2:50 (2:50) (Class 4) 5-Y-0+ **£2,602** (£764; £382; £190)

Form RPR
1-2P **1** **Den Of Iniquity**^{33} 2497 9-11-0 0 WayneHutchinson 142
(Warren Greatrex) *trckd ldrs: led over 4f out: rdn over 1f out: edgd lft: lasted home* **5/1**[3]
F/1- **2** ¾ **My Arch**^{67} 2446 8-11-0 0 BrianHughes 141
(Ollie Pears) *trckd ldrs: chal over 4f out: rdn over 2f out: kpt on ins fnl f: a jst hld* **15/8**[2]
5F-0 **3** 12 **Khachaturian (IRE)**^{32} 2523 7-11-0 0 AdrianLane 129
(Donald McCain) *w ldr: led after 3f: hrd rdn and hdd over 4f out: one pce fnl 3f* **7/1**
3355 **4** 28 **Always Bold (IRE)**^{51} 2125 5-11-0 0 JasonMaguire 101
(Donald McCain) *led 3f: w ldrs: reminders 7f out: rdn and lost pl over 4f out: hung lft and kpt on fnl f to take remote 4th clsng stages* **16/1**
36/1 **5** 2½ **Alfie Flits**^{31} 2548 8-11-0 0 BarryKeniry 98
(Alan Swinbank) *mid-div: hdwy to trck ldrs after 4f: drvn over 4f out: sn btn* **11/8**[1]
314 **6** 2¼ **Potemkin (USA)**^{9} 2926 5-11-0 0 (t) JamieMoore 96
(David Evans) *mid-div: hdwy on outside to chse ldrs over 6f out: lost pl over 4f out* **33/1**
1334 **7** 5 **Feeling Peckish (USA)**^{30} 2585 6-10-9 0 (t) GemmaGracey-Davison(5) 91
(Michael Chapman) *in rr: drvn after 7f: lost pl over 4f out* **100/1**
03/6 **8** 2¼ **Jubilee George**^{34} 2479 10-11-0 0 TomMessenger 89
(Christopher Kellett) *in rr: drvn after 6f: nvr on terms* **66/1**
-P00 **9** 11 **Orpen Wide (IRE)**^{22} 1953 8-11-0 0 JimmyMcCarthy 78
(Michael Chapman) *in rr: bhd and drvn 6f out* **40/1**
5020 **10** 34 **Bosamcliff (IRE)**^{9} 2927 5-10-7 0 (p) APMcCoy 37
(David Evans) *hld up in rr: hdwy after 4f: drvn 6f out: sn lost pl and bhd: t.o and eased fnl 2f* **10/1**

4m 10.6s (25.10) **Going Correction** +1.50s/f (Slow) **10** Ran SP% **128.9**
Speed ratings: **97,96,90,76,75 74,71,70,65,48**
toteswingers: 1&2 £3.30. 1&3 £7.30, 2&3 £3.60. CSF £16.43 TOTE £13.00: £2.90, £1.02, £2.30; EX 23.00.
Owner Malcolm C Denmark **Bred** David G Ford **Trained** Upper Lambourn, Berks
■ Stewards' Enquiry : Brian Hughes caution: used whip with excessive frequency.

FOCUS
The best race on the card, this was confined to horses that had run in at least one chase. The tempo was fair although the eventual time was only the same as that for the previous race.

NOTEBOOK
Den Of Iniquity held on grittily after drifting to the deeper ground on the inside under pressure. Representing connections successful twice on Kempton's similar card the previous day, this Listed bumper winner has been running over fences but could revert to hurdling now. (op 13-2)
My Arch, last seen finishing eighth in the Cesarewitch, is a thorough stayer and, after coming under pressure before the winner, he kept on stoutly all the way to the line. He is likely to run over hurdles next, and is in at Wetherby on Boxing Day. (tchd 2-1)
Khachaturian(IRE) made the running as usual but had no chance with the first two up the straight. The McCain horses were generally below par on this card. (op 6-1)
Always Bold(IRE) was beaten fully half a mile out. (tchd 14-1)
Alfie Flits was a classy Flat horse in his younger days and landed a beginners' chase a month ago. He appeared to hold strong claims, but had never run here before and was beaten a long way from home. He ran poorly on his one try on Polytrack too. (op 15-8 tchd 2-1 in a place)
Bosamcliff(IRE) Official explanation: trainer's rep said mare had a breathing problem

3093 PLAY BINGO AT TOTESPORT.COM "JUMPERS' BUMPER" NATIONAL HUNT FLAT RACE 2m (F)
3:20 (3:20) (Class 4) 4-Y-0+ **£2,602** (£764; £382; £190)

Form RPR
5-21 **1** **Priceless Art (IRE)**^{194} 718 5-11-0 0 BarryKeniry 125+
(Alan Swinbank) *trckd ldrs: smooth hdwy to ld 2f out: qcknd clr: v easily* **8/11**[1]
1116 **2** 11 **Scotsbrook Cloud**^{43} 2284 5-11-0 0 APMcCoy 107
(David Evans) *sn trcking ldrs: wnt 2nd over 2f out: styd on to take 2nd jst ins fnl f* **9/4**[2]
-004 **3** ¾ **Kayfton Pete**^{42} 2307 4-10-7 0 PeterHatton(7) 106
(Reg Hollinshead) *hld up: t.k.h: jnd ldrs 7f out: led over 3f out: hdd 2f out: kpt on same pce* **5/1**[3]
06-4 **4** 19 **Go On Be A Lady**^{43} 2301 7-10-7 0 RhysFlint 80
(Alan Swinbank) *set stdy pce: pushed along over 4f out: hdd over 3f out: sn outpcd and lost pl* **14/1**
5 4½ **Crabbies Court**^{233} 5-11-0 0 BrianHughes 83
(Lisa Williamson) *trckd ldr: outpcd over 2f out: sn lost pl and bhd* **50/1**

4m 14.3s (28.80) **Going Correction** +1.50s/f (Slow)
WFA 4 from 5yo+ 5lb **5** Ran SP% **114.0**
Speed ratings (Par 105): **88,82,82,72,70**
toteswinger: 1&2 £2.70. CSF £2.79 TOTE £1.50: £1.10, £1.10; EX 3.60.
Owner Matthew Green & David Manasseh **Bred** Lady Bamford **Trained** Melsonby, N Yorks

FOCUS
A weakly contested race, for horses that have never run on the Flat. It was the slowest event of the day and the five runners were closely bunched until the home turn.

NOTEBOOK
Priceless Art(IRE) completed a treble for the Alan Swinbank yard, sauntering clear of his toiling opponenents. Last seen taking a turf bumper in June, his second win in that sphere, he is set to go hurdling now and has the scope to do well at that game, but requires good ground. (op 1-2 tchd 4-5)
Scotsbrook Cloud, who completed a hurdles hat-trick before flopping on soft ground latest, stays well and got the better of a tussle for second. (tchd 2-1 and 5-2)
Kayfton Pete showed improved form in a novice hurdle last time and is sufficiently lightly raced to progress further. (op 8-1)
Go On Be A Lady, a stablemate of the winner, cut out the donkey work before weakening (tchd 12-1)
Crabbies Court, a maiden pointer, was well beaten on this rules debut. (op 40-1)
T/Plt: £301.20 to a £1 stake. Pool £59,675.46 - 144.59 winning units. T/Qpdt: £10.40 to a £1 stake. Pool £8,066.54 - 568.64 winning units. WG

2390 FONTWELL (L-H)
Sunday, December 26
3094 Meeting Abandoned - Frost

2526 HUNTINGDON (R-H)
Sunday, December 26
3100 Meeting Abandoned - Frozen track

2577 KEMPTON (R-H)
Sunday, December 26
3106 Meeting Abandoned - Frozen ground
Other races transferred to meeting on 27th December.

2473 MARKET RASEN (R-H)
Sunday, December 26
3110 Meeting Abandoned - Snow

2981 TOWCESTER (R-H)
Sunday, December 26
3116 Meeting Abandoned - Frost and snow

[2610]WETHERBY (L-H)
Sunday, December 26
3122 Meeting Abandoned - Frozen track

[2480]WINCANTON (R-H)
Sunday, December 26
3128 Meeting Abandoned - Snow

[2577]KEMPTON (R-H)
Monday, December 27
3135 Meeting Abandoned - Frozen ground

[2610]WETHERBY (L-H)
Monday, December 27
3141 Meeting Abandoned - Frozen ground

[2937]CATTERICK (L-H)
Tuesday, December 28
3147 Meeting Abandoned - Frost and snow

[2570]FFOS LAS (L-H)
Tuesday, December 28

OFFICIAL GOING: Good to soft (soft in places) changing to soft (good to soft in places) after race 2 (1.00)
Wind: light, across Weather: murky, dull

3153 WALTERS UK LTD NOVICES' HURDLE (11 hdls) 2m 6f
12:25 (12:25) (Class 4) 4-Y-0+ **£2,602** (£764; £382; £190)

Form RPR

1 **State Benefit (IRE)**[296] 5-10-12 0 AndrewTinkler 118
(Nicky Henderson) *chsd ldr tl led 3rd: rdn between last 2: hdd flat: battled on v gamely to ld again on post* **9/4**[1]

3 **2** *nse* **Iron Chancellor (IRE)**[51] 2238 5-10-12 0 RobertThornton 118
(Alan King) *in tch: chsd ldrs 8th: wnt 2nd bef next: rdn and ev ch 2 out: led narrowly flat: kpt on wl u.p flat tl hdd on post* **10/1**

3 *15* **Dovecote Wood**[325] 5-10-12 0 TomO'Brien 105
(Caroline Keevil) *chsd ldrs: chsng wnr whn reappeared 8th tl bef next: wknd 2 out* **10/1**

-342 **4** *3 ¼* **Father Probus**[51] 2241 4-10-12 0 PaddyBrennan 102
(Nigel Twiston-Davies) *chsd ldrs: clr in ldng sextet 8th: 4th and rdn bef 3 next: wknd bef 2 out* **14/1**

5 *9* **Viking Visitor (IRE)**[177] 900 5-10-9 0 RichieMcLernon(3) 94
(Jonjo O'Neill) *hld up in tch in midfield: clr in ldng sextet 8th: wknd after 3 out* **5/1**[3]

2- **6** *15* **Ardkilly Rebel (IRE)**[307] 4242 6-10-12 0 RichardJohnson 85+
(Philip Hobbs) *hld up in tch in midfield: clr in ldng sextet 8th: rdn whn blnd next: sn wknd* **5/2**[2]

5- **7** *2* **Rozolenn (FR)**[280] 4809 5-10-12 0 AidanColeman 79
(Venetia Williams) *chsd ldrs: 7th and wkng 8th: wl btn bef next: t.o* **50/1**

-000 **8** *½* **Boosha**[41] 2454 5-10-5 0 SeanQuinlan 71
(Rachel Hobbs) *a in rr: lost tch 6th: no ch 8th: t.o* **150/1**

4-00 **9** *24* **Artic Pride (IRE)**[12] 2981 6-10-12 0 LeightonAspell 57
(Oliver Sherwood) *in tch towards rr: struggling after 5th: t.o bef 3 out* **100/1**

10 *25* **Onthelips (IRE)** 6-10-12 0 DaveCrosse 34
(Amy Weaver) *a in rr: lost tch after 5th: t.o bef 3 out* **100/1**

00 **11** *nk* **Glenfly (IRE)**[56] 2142 5-10-12 0 RhysFlint 34
(Philip Hobbs) *in tch towards rr: struggling after 5th: t.o 8th* **100/1**

21-3 **12** *2 ¼* **Inga Bird**[53] 2181 5-10-5 0 JakeGreenall(7) 32
(Henry Daly) *led tl 3rd: chsng ldr after 5th: wl bhd whn reappeared 8th: t.o* **16/1**

0- **13** *11* **Rivermouth**[244] 53 5-10-12 0 WayneHutchinson 22
(Alan King) *in tch towards rr: pushed along and struggling after 5th: t.o 8th* **100/1**

14 *25* **Run To Fly (IRE)**[267] 5-10-6 0 ow1 MichaelByrne(7) —
(Peter Bowen) *a towards rr: wl t.o 8th* **150/1**

60P **15** *47* **John Sixteen (IRE)**[68] 1937 5-10-9 0 DonalDevereux(3) —
(Peter Bowen) *a in rr: wl t.o 8th* **200/1**

P **Dermey Bowler (IRE)**[258] 5190 7-10-9 0 MichaelMurphy(3) —
(Tim Vaughan) *in tch towards rr tl p.u and dismntd after 5th* **33/1**

ms (-318.00)
WFA 4 from 5yo+ 6lb **16** Ran SP% **117.4**
Tote Swingers: 1&2 £7.70, 1&3 £9.20, 2&3 £18.80 CSF £24.67 TOTE £4.20: £1.90, £3.30, £3.00; EX 21.20.
Owner Michael Buckley **Bred** Patrick Collins **Trained** Upper Lambourn, Berks

FOCUS
The cold weather relented to enable the first jumps action to be staged in Britain since 16th December. There had been 10mm of rain overnight and drizzle through the morning and jockeys reported the going to be soft and testing. Unfortunately there was also dense fog as the meeting began, rendering visibility very poor. A steady pace for much of the way with the race only developing from the home bend. Three broke clear at this stage until two forged clear in a battle to the line. The third and fourth set the level in a fair novice.

NOTEBOOK
State Benefit(IRE) ◆ had been prominent throughout and dug deep under pressure to just prevail. He had run away with an Irish point back in the spring, and his home work had been promising since switching to Nicky Henderson's yard and comfortably made the transition to racing under rules. From the limited evidence available it looks as if he will appreciate 3m. (op 2-1)
Iron Chancellor(IRE) ◆ pressed the winner all the way up the straight, went down fighting, and he made a significant step forward from his rules debut in early November. He has also come from the pointing sphere and may have taken a little longer to adjust but looks well up to winning races.
Dovecote Wood won his sole start as a pointer and ran respectably on this rules debut, so this son of Flakey Dove should improve for this experience and be winning in time. (op 11-1 tchd 8-1)
Father Probus went with the leading group as they entered the home straight, but he was soon left behind. This looked a stronger contest than his hurdling debut, when he was second, and the 4-y-o may need a stronger pace and a bit more time.
Viking Visitor(IRE), a former Irish point and bumper winner, made no impression on his hurdling debut, tracking the leaders before being left behind in the straight. (op 3-1)
Ardkilly Rebel(IRE), who was having his first run since February following the switch from David Pipe's yard, will need to improve on this effort. (op 9-2)
Dermey Bowler(IRE) Official explanation: jockey said gelding pulled up lame

3154 RONALD JESSETT 85TH BIRTHDAY H'CAP CHASE (13 fncs) 2m
1:00 (1:02) (Class 4) (0-115,114) 4-Y-0+ **£3,252** (£955; £477; £238)

Form RPR

3-33 **1** **Oscar Gogo (IRE)**[36] 2572 8-11-1 110 AdamWedge(7) 119+
(Evan Williams) *led tl hmpd by loose horse and hdd 5th: chsd ldr after tl rdn to ld and j.rt 2 out: r.o wl to forge clr last: rdn out* **17/2**

221 **2** *4* **Betabob (IRE)**[36] 2572 7-11-8 113 (tp) MichaelMurphy(3) 117
(Tim Vaughan) *t.k.h: hld up in rr: mstke 1st: hdwy to chse ldrs 9th: rdn and styd on same pce between last 2* **4/1**[2]

0-42 **3** *½* **Stradbrook (IRE)**[12] 2975 8-11-5 110 (b[1]) RichieMcLernon(3) 115
(Jonjo O'Neill) *hld up in last trio: hdwy to chse ldrs 8th: rdn and chsd wnr bef last: no imp and lost 2nd flat* **4/1**[2]

4 **4** *5* **Trooper Clarence**[51] 2236 6-11-3 105 PaulMoloney 107
(Evan Williams) *t.k.h: hld up in last trio: hdwy to chse ldrs whn blnd 10th: rallied 2 out: wnt lft and hit last: wknd flat* **22/1**

P433 **5** *7* **Good Old Days (IRE)**[51] 2243 11-10-13 101 JasonMaguire 96
(Kim Bailey) *t.k.h: chsd ldrs untl lft 2nd 4th: lft in ld next: hmpd by loose horse 6th: clr and mstke 9th: pressed next: rdn and hdd 2 out: sn wknd* **8/1**[3]

6 *7* **Yes Man (IRE)**[194] 775 5-10-9 100 DonalDevereux(3) 87
(Peter Bowen) *in tch in midfield: mstke 3rd: lost pl and rdn after 9th: wknd u.p bef 3 out* **12/1**

136P **7** *45* **Another Trump (NZ)**[13] 2961 6-11-1 113 GeraldQuinn(10) 59
(Jonjo O'Neill) *chsd ldrs: lft 3rd 4th: lost pl and dropped to rr after 8th: lost tch after next: t.o fr 3 out* **25/1**

1411 **U** **Rimini (FR)**[13] 2961 5-11-12 114 RichardJohnson —
(David Rees) *chsd wnr tl blnd bdly and uns rdr 4th* **7/4**[1]

4m 11.4s (6.40) **Going Correction** +0.175s/f (Yiel) **8** Ran SP% **113.9**
Speed ratings (Par 105): **91,89,88,86,82 79,56,—**
Tote Swingers: 1&2 £3.80, 1&3 £6.90, 2&3 £4.30 CSF £42.90 CT £157.69 TOTE £12.10: £3.10, £1.80, £1.10; EX 33.80.
Owner Mrs D McCabe **Bred** Vincent Holton **Trained** Llancarfan, Vale Of Glamorgan

FOCUS
A reasonably competitive handicap where previous C&D form played out once again. A step up from the winner who is rated to the best of his hurdles form.

NOTEBOOK
Oscar Gogo(IRE) adopted his customary prominent position but was outjumped at the first in the back straight and lost the lead, which may have proved beneficial as he was able to save his energy for a decisive surge from the home turn. He had been defeated by Betabob over C&D last month, but was better off at the weights this time and, with a 2lb lower mark also helping, he ran out a convincing winner. (op 8-1 tchd 10-1)
Betabob(IRE) took 26 attempts to gain his first win, over C&D last month, but was not so well treated this time round and could not reel in the winner. He needs to be held up and, though he made good progress down the back straight to have his chance, he could not reel in the more prominently-positioned winner in the soft conditions. (tchd 7-2 and 9-2)
Stradbrook(IRE) was keyed up beforehand in first-time blinkers but jumped a little carefully early in the race and, though he moved up to hold a chance, he was never quite getting there. His chasing form is some way below that he showed over hurdles. (op 10-3)
Trooper Clarence was moving up to challenge but hit the first in the home straight and lost valuable momentum. He won a couple of hurdles in the French provinces but has not reproduced that form in Britain yet, although on balance there was some encouragement to be gleaned here.
Good Old Days(IRE) jumped well to take up the lead at the first in the back straight but could not build on that advantage when getting hampered by the loose horse at the next, and eventually he weakened on ground softer than he likes.
Rimini(FR) was a warm order to continue his winning run this winter, but he got low at the third and unseated his jockey. (op 5-2)

3155 ISUZU MARES' H'CAP HURDLE (8 hdls) 2m
1:30 (1:30) (Class 4) (0-110,109) 3-Y-0+ **£2,602** (£764; £382; £190)

Form RPR

213- **1** **Real Treasure**[294] 4496 6-11-12 109 JasonMaguire 119+
(Kim Bailey) *w ldr tl led after 2nd: mde rest: clr and rdn 2 out: styd on wl flat: rdn out* **10/3**[1]

5345 **2** *5* **Can't Remember**[34] 2609 5-9-9 85 OliverDayman(7) 90
(Alison Thorpe) *chsd ldrs: wnt 2nd 3 out: rdn and kpt on same pce u.p fr bef 2 out* **10/1**

0604 **3** *6* **Try Cat**[33] 2633 4-10-13 96 (t) RichardJohnson 96
(Philip Hobbs) *chsd ldrs wnt 2nd bef 5th tl 3 out: rdn and wknd bef next* **10/1**

00-P **4** *3* **Cosavita (FR)**[83] 1726 5-11-3 100 PaulMoloney 97
(David Rees) *hld up in rr: hdwy and modest 6th after 5th: wnt 4th and rdn after 3 out: no imp on ldrs after* **25/1**

00-6 **5** *14* **Gilwen Glory (IRE)**[233] 231 7-11-8 105 DPFahy 89
(Evan Williams) *hld up in rr: mstke 2nd: lost tch 4th: n.d* **8/1**

/0-4 **6** *5* **Azione**[15] 2927 7-10-5 88 NickScholfield 68
(Rodney Farrant) *led tl after 2nd: chsd wnr tl bef 5th: wknd u.p wl bef 3 out* **9/2**[2]

3625 **7** *30* **Himayna**[60] 2072 6-10-13 99 MichaelMurphy(3) 52
(Tim Vaughan) *hld up in rr: lost tch 4th: t.o fr next* **12/1**

-550 **8** *1 ¼* **Reinriver**[23] 2791 4-11-2 99 TomScudamore 51
(Brendan Powell) *hld up in rr: j.big 1st: hdwy into midfield 3rd: chsd ldng trio 5th: wknd bef next: wl btn and eased after last: t.o* **9/1**

2342 **9** *9* **Josephine Malines**[36] 2586 6-11-8 105 (t) RhysFlint 49
(John Flint) *in tch in midfield: mstke 3rd: sn rdn and struggling: 7th and wl btn after 5th: t.o* **11/2**[3]

3-35 **10** 4 ½ **Laureate Des Loges (FR)**[68] 1936 6-11-4 **108**.............. JakeGreenall(7) 48
(Henry Daly) *hld up in rr: lost tch 4th: t.o fr next* **8/1**

3m 53.0s (4.00) **Going Correction** +0.425s/f (Soft)
WFA 4 from 5yo+ 5lb **10** Ran SP% **118.6**
Speed ratings (Par 105): **107,104,101,100,93 90,75,74,70,68**
Tote Swingers: 1&2 £8.80, 1&3 £9.20, 2&3 £4.60 CSF £37.29 CT £307.38 TOTE £4.50: £2.10, £1.60, £3.30; EX 31.20.
Owner The Real Partnership **Bred** M Massarella **Trained** Andoversford, Gloucs

FOCUS
Just a moderate mares' handicap but with two horses vying for the lead this was run at a sound pace. The winner should score again and the form is rated around the placed horses.

NOTEBOOK
Real Treasure, who was up there throughout, managed to keep up the gallop to wear down all potential challengers. This was also her first run since March, which shows just how strong her resurgent yard is at present. She looked fairly treated on her two previous hurdle runs, and should be able to reproduce her form when getting an all-out gallop on the soft ground she relishes. (op 7-2 tchd 4-1)
Can't Remember hung in there with the winner but was just run out of it from the last. She stuck to her task and made full use of her light weight, but she was just a bit outclassed. She is only moderate but is up to adding to her tally in a low-grade race. (op 12-1)
Try Cat was given every chance as she kept tabs on the winner until fading in the straight. This was a slight improvement on her previous efforts, on ground that was plenty soft enough, but overall she looks very moderate. (tchd 11-1)
Cosavita(FR), again racing without a tongue tie, plugged on but was never a threat. She has been sliding down the weights but still looks way below the winning form she showed in France in 2008. (op 28-1)
Gilwen Glory(IRE) was comprehensively beaten but may have needed her first run since May. (op 17-2)
Azione disputed the lead but was too keen and began to struggle half a circuit from home. (op 5-1)
Laureate Des Loges(FR) Official explanation: trainer said mare was unsuited by ground

3156 SAXTON DRILLING NOVICES' CHASE (15 fncs) 2m 3f 110y
2:05 (2:05) (Class 4) 4-Y-O+ **£3,577** (£1,050; £525; £262)

Form RPR
-112 **1** **Osric (IRE)**[59] 2088 7-11-2 0.. AndrewTinkler 134+
(Nicky Henderson) *t.k.h: a travelling wl: hld up in last pair: hdwy to trck ldng trio 7th: qcknd to chal 3 out: led next: in command last: rdn fnl 100yds: comf* **10/11**[1]

00-4 **2** 1 ½ **Squadron**[237] 155 6-11-2 0.. RobertThornton 132+
(Alan King) *j.rt: chsd ldrs tl lft 2nd 4th: led 12th: rdn whn j.rt and hdd 2 out: nt pce of wnr bef last: kpt on u.p but a hld flat* **7/2**[2]

2/1- **3** 3 ½ **A French Horse (FR)**[412] 2234 7-11-2 0......................... AidanColeman 130+
(Venetia Williams) *chsd ldrs: nt fluent 6th: effrt and ev ch 12th: no ex u.p after 2 out: 3rd and hld whn hit last* **6/1**[3]

22F3 **4** 6 **Blacktoft (USA)**[51] 2233 7-11-9 125.................................... PaulMoloney 130
(Evan Williams) *chsd ldr tl led 4th: hdd 12th: outpcd and swtchd rt 3 out: wknd bef next* **20/1**

3330 **P** **Akarshan (IRE)**[128] 1346 5-11-2 119..................................... TomO'Brien —
(Evan Williams) *hld up in last pair: lost tch and eased after 11th: t.o whn p.u next* **7/1**

12-4 **F** **Fahrisee (IRE)**[52] 2210 7-11-2 0.. DPFahy —
(Evan Williams) *t.k.h: hld up in tch: hmpd 4th: 5th whn fell 8th* **14/1**

5- **F** **Cruising Bye**[250] 5344 4-10-7 0.................................. RichieMcLernon(3) —
(Jonjo O'Neill) *j.rt: led tl j. bdly rt: blnd and hdd 4th: racd in last pair after: hmpd 8th: struggling whn fell 10th* **33/1**

5m 6.50s (0.50) **Going Correction** +0.175s/f (Yiel)
WFA 4 from 5yo+ 5lb **7** Ran SP% **115.8**
Speed ratings (Par 105): **106,105,104,101,— —,—**
Tote Swingers: 1&2 £1.40, 1&3 £1.10, 2&3 £3.90 CSF £4.87 TOTE £2.20: £1.40, £2.40; EX 5.50.
Owner Mr & Mrs R Kelvin Hughes **Bred** P Turley And Sons **Trained** Upper Lambourn, Berks

FOCUS
A reasonable novice chase and the form looks reliable rated around the first three.

NOTEBOOK
Osric(IRE) ◆ was quite keen on his first race for two months but he was ridden confidently, allowing his rivals to take each other on before making his move. He had to be driven right out, but effectively sealed the race with fluent jumps at the final two fences. He was a fair novice hurdler showing versatility regarding ground requirements and a turn of foot last season. He now looks on track to fulfil his potential over fences. (tchd 4-5 and Evens)
Squadron was the best of these over hurdles and reportedly had not done much schooling when beaten on his chasing debut back in May. He jumped adequately here, if tending to go right as he got tired but ran on again on the flat. He looks capable of winning over fences, without looking fully convincing as a chaser. (tchd 10-3 and 4-1)
A French Horse(FR) vied for the lead coming into the straight, and eventually paid for that effort as the market leaders came to the fore. He was not always the most resolute over hurdles, but ran an encouraging enough chasing debut here, especially as it was his first run for more than a year. (op 7-1)
Blacktoft(USA) was up against it given he was racing on softer ground over a longer trip than ideal, and the penalty for a fast-ground novice chase win in the summer did not help. After racing up with the lead he was outpaced in the closing stages. (op 18-1)
Akarshan(IRE) jumped slowly and could never get on terms with the leading group, eventually pulling up before the home straight. (op 12-1)

3157 WALTERS UK LTD H'CAP CHASE (17 fncs) 2m 5f
2:40 (2:40) (Class 3) (0-130,130) 5-Y-O **£6,337** (£1,872; £936; £468; £234)

Form RPR
1 **Royal Tune (FR)**[31] 5-11-6 **124**.. JacquesRicou 148+
(G Macaire, France) *in tch: hdwy to join ldr 9th: bmpd next and 13th: led bef 14th: sn clr and in command: v easily* **4/1**[1]

-332 **2** 17 **Plunkett (IRE)**[42] 2436 7-10-8 **112**....................................... PaulMoloney 116
(Evan Williams) *hld up in rr: stdy hdwy 12th: wnt 3rd but no ch w wnr 3 out: pressing for 2nd whn n.m.r last: kpt on to go 2nd flat* **11/2**[2]

-604 **3** 1 ¼ **Bible Lord (IRE)**[12] 2984 9-11-8 **126**.............................(b) NickScholfield 131+
(Andy Turnell) *j.rt: led: j.rt and bmpd wnr 10th and 13th: hdd bef 14th: sn outpcd and btn whn mstke 14th: lost 2nd flat* **8/1**

16-3 **4** 14 **Emergency Exit (IRE)**[66] 1973 7-11-4 **122**.......................... RichardJohnson 112
(Philip Hobbs) *hld up in rr: blnd 7th: hdwy to chse ldrs 12th: wknd bef 14th: lost 3rd 3 out* **11/2**[2]

44-3 **5** 6 **Wheels Up (IRE)**[39] 2503 9-10-13 **120**..............................(t) MrAJBerry(3) 105
(Jonjo O'Neill) *hld up in rr: clsd and in tch 8th: chsd ldrs 12th: wknd qckly after next: t.o* **16/1**

1F42 **6** 34 **Moulin De La Croix**[40] 2470 6-10-8 **115**............(t) SamTwiston-Davies(3) 69
(Nigel Twiston-Davies) *chsd ldrs tl wknd u.p 13th: t.o fr 2 out* **7/1**[3]

0-PP **P** **Ordre De Bataille (FR)**[47] 2324 8-10-3 **107**.................... AndrewTinkler —
(Henry Daly) *chsd ldrs: wknd u.p after 13th: wl bhd whn p.u last* **20/1**

0F-P **P** **Mr Robert (IRE)**[114] 1486 9-11-5 **130**................................ AdamWedge(7) —
(Evan Williams) *in tch in midfield: rdn and struggling 12th: wl bhd whn p.u 14th* **33/1**

/4-3 **P** **Our Bob (IRE)**[54] 2165 8-11-9 **127**......................................(t) TomO'Brien —
(Philip Hobbs) *chsd ldr tl after 8th: mstke next: hit 10th and lost pl: t.o whn p.u 14th* **7/1**[3]

04PP **P** **Nostringsattached (IRE)**[12] 2984 9-11-2 **123**.......... RichieMcLernon(3) —
(Jonjo O'Neill) *hld up in rr: clsd and in tch after 8th: struggling 10th: bhd and losing tch whn p.u 12th* **25/1**

-550 **P** **Award Winner**[43] 2429 7-10-13 **117**................................ JimmyMcCarthy —
(Brendan Powell) *in tch in midfield: lost pl after 8th: t.o whn p.u 13th* **33/1**

B11- **P** **Afistfullofpebbles**[334] 3699 6-10-11 **125**...................... GeraldQuinn(10) —
(Jonjo O'Neill) *in tch in midfield tl dropped towards rr 9th: lost tch next: wl t.o whn p.u 13th* **9/1**

5m 31.7s (1.70) **Going Correction** +0.175s/f (Yiel) **12** Ran SP% **117.3**
Speed ratings: **103,96,96,90,88 75,—,—,—,— —,—**
Tote Swingers: 1&2 £6.10, 1&3 £7.70, 2&3 £11.10 CSF £25.33 CT £166.53 TOTE £5.30: £1.70, £2.20, £3.10; EX 27.80.
Owner Mme Patrick Papot **Bred** Mme B Gabeur **Trained** Les Mathes, France

FOCUS
A competitive field put firmly in their place by the runaway French raider. This was Guillaume Macaire's first runner in Britain for nearly three years, and he once again showed astute placing to resume the winning thread in emphatic style. The form could be rated higher and the winner can score again.

NOTEBOOK
Royal Tune(FR) moved to the fore in the back straight but was angled wider after getting bumped as Bible Lord jumped to the right, but it was immaterial after the home turn as the winner quickened clear in a matter of strides, and increased the advantage all the way to the line. The manner of the victory may not have helped his future handicap mark, but it connections clearly have a decent weapon for future overseas raids.He had been well beaten by former stablemate Long Run in November 2009 but has done well since, largely in the French provinces. His trainer explained that the decision to race in Britain was taken because the races in France are not long enough. Eventually he will be stepped up to 3m, and on this run he will easily stay that far, so we can expect to see him plunder more races in Britain in due course. (op 9-2)
Plunkett(IRE) has dropped in the ratings to be on a reasonable mark for his handicap debut, and he attracted some market support. He ran well and stuck to the task without ever threatening the winner. However, off a similar mark he looks capable of returning to winning ways. (op 15-2)
Bible Lord(IRE) is not exactly consistent but held a good chance off a diminishing handicap mark, and the blinkers that helped towards a rejuvenation at Towcester last time had been retained. He jumped out to the right, bumping the winner at one stage and on this evidence might be better racing the other way around.
Emergency Exit(IRE) saved ground against the inside rail but could only stay on at one pace. He had not improved on his Wincanton novice chase win on his British debut, but had excuses, and this run on soft ground suggests he might be getting back on track, though he could do with some leniency from the handicapper. (op 15-2)
Wheels Up(IRE) travelled well round the final bend but did not get home. He is capable of winning more races, especially in less-testing conditions, and is on a reasonable mark.
Moulin De La Croix faced a stiff task in stronger company, and was beginning to struggle from the back straight. (op 6-1)
Our Bob(IRE) Official explanation: jockey said gelding was distressed

3158 EILEEN REES BIRTHDAY MAIDEN HURDLE (8 hdls) 2m
3:15 (3:15) (Class 4) 3-Y-O+ **£2,602** (£764; £382; £190)

Form RPR
3 **1** **Pilgreen (FR)**[66] 1974 5-11-6 0.. PaulMoloney 105+
(Evan Williams) *hld up in tch in rr: hdwy 5th: pressed ldrs 2 out: hung lft between last 2: led last: kpt hanging lft but styd on wl flat* **7/2**[2]

1- **2** 2 **Master Fiddle**[273] 4945 5-11-6 0.. AndrewTinkler 107+
(Nicky Henderson) *t.k.h: hld up in tch: hdwy to ld gng wl whn blnd bdly and hdd 3 out: rallied to press ldrs whn hit next: chsd wnr sn after last: kpt on* **6/4**[1]

3 2 ¼ **Nemo Spirit (IRE)**[80] 5-11-6 0... RichardJohnson 102
(Tim Vaughan) *mde most tl hdd and lft in ld again 3 out: hdd next: styd on same pce u.p fr last* **4/1**[3]

2-30 **4** 1 ¼ **Quiet Whisper (IRE)**[36] 2577 4-10-13 0.......................... MrCGreene(7) 100
(Kim Bailey) *t.k.h: hld up wl in tch: hdwy to press ldr bef 3 out: lft 2nd 3 out: led next: hdd last: wknd u.p fnl 150yds* **66/1**

-140 **5** 4 **Dipity Doo Dah**[51] 2246 6-10-6 0.................................... MichaelByrne(7) 92+
(Peter Bowen) *hld up in tch in last pair: hdwy into midfield 3 out: rdn bef next: pushed along and kpt on same pce between last 2: eased fnl 75yds* **66/1**

03-3 **6** 6 **Seren Cwmtudu (IRE)**[60] 2068 6-10-13 0............................ TomO'Brien 84
(Evan Williams) *in tch: rdn and struggling whn hit 3 out: wknd u.p bef next* **9/1**

7 ½ **King's Realm (IRE)**[67] 3-10-7 0... DarylJacob 77
(Alison Thorpe) *t.k.h: hld up in tch: rdn after 5th: wknd bef 2 out* **50/1**

02 **8** nse **Well Hello There (IRE)**[50] 2282 4-11-3 0................. RichieMcLernon(3) 90
(Jonjo O'Neill) *hld up in tch: pushed along and effrt to chse ldr after 5th: wknd after next* **10/1**

4-04 **9** 1 ¼ **Original Prankster (IRE)**[54] 2166 5-11-6 0..................... PaddyBrennan 89
(Nigel Twiston-Davies) *in tch in midfield: struggling u.p after 5th: wknd bef next* **40/1**

0 **10** nk **Jomade (IRE)**[226] 355 4-11-6 0.. SeanQuinlan 89
(Kim Bailey) *hld up in tch in rr: mstke 2nd: j. slowly next: hdwy after 4th: rdn and no hdwy after 5th: nvr trbld ldrs* **33/1**

3 **11** 7 **Bishophill Jack (IRE)**[41] 2456 4-11-6 0............................ JasonMaguire 84
(Kim Bailey) *w ldrs: ev ch whn blnd 5th: wknd u.p after next* **12/1**

40 **12** nse **Jewellery (IRE)**[15] 2924 3-9-9 0 ow2.............................. OliverDayman(7) 64
(Alison Thorpe) *w ldrs tl rdn and wknd bef 3 out* **100/1**

13 6 **Sustainability (IRE)** 5-10-13 0.................................. HarryChalloner(7) 77
(Venetia Williams) *in tch towards rr: struggling u.p after 5th: wl btn next* **66/1**

5-02 **14** 3 **Dune Shine**[12] 2985 5-11-6 0.. DominicElsworth 74
(Oliver Sherwood) *t.k.h: hld up in tch towards rr: mstke 4th: rdn and struggling after 5th: wl btn whn swtchd lft 2 out* **33/1**

15 3 **Major Potential (USA)**[822] 4-11-6 0................................ AidanColeman 72
(Venetia Williams) *chsd ldrs: rdn bef 3 out: wknd rapidly 3 out: wl bhd whn mstke 2 out* **100/1**

3 **16** 13 **Sorcillera**[56] 2137 4-10-13 0.. RhysFlint 53
(John Flint) *t.k.h: w ldr tl wknd rapidly bef 3 out: mstke 3 out: wl bhd next: t.o* **16/1**

3m 59.8s (10.80) **Going Correction** +0.425s/f (Soft)
WFA 3 from 4yo 13lb 4 from 5yo+ 5lb **16** Ran SP% **131.6**
Speed ratings (Par 105): **90,89,87,87,85 82,82,81,81,81 77,77,74,73,71 65**
Tote Swingers: 1&2 £4.00, 1&3 £5.60, 2&3 £4.30 CSF £9.90 TOTE £6.00: £1.90, £1.80, £1.50; EX 18.10.

Owner Exors of the Late P M De Wilde **Bred** Earl Detouillon Raphael & Frederique **Trained** Llancarfan, Vale Of Glamorgan

FOCUS
Four horses battled it out up the straight in a reasonable maiden. The time was slow though and the form is rated around the winner, fourth and fifth.

NOTEBOOK
Pilgreen(FR) was tapped for speed down the back but gradually responded to his jockey's urgings, and it eventually paid off as he came with a decisive late charge. He had shown some promise without ever threatening at Stratford in October and was well backed to improve on that run. This was a creditable performance on ground that may have been as soft as he can handle, and he looks capable of staying further than this. (op 8-1)
Master Fiddle surged to the lead travelling supremely well turning in, but he took off too early at the first in the home straight and landed on all fours. That shook his confidence for the next, and it was only approaching the last that he recovered any momentum. The son of Fiddling The Facts obviously needs to improve his jumping but assuming he does he looks a good prospect. (op 11-8 tchd 7-4)
Nemo Spirit(IRE) ran a sound race on his hurdling debut, racing up with the pace until just fading near the finish. He had lost his way somewhat on the Flat, but the switch to jumping with Tim Vaughan's yard might have sparked a revival. (op 9-2)
Quiet Whisper(IRE) was still right there up until the last, running much better than his odds suggested he would. This was his best run over hurdles and, with the stable in such good form at the moment, it would be no surprise to see him placed to win soon.
Bishophill Jack(IRE) might have been able to stay up with the lead for longer had he not dived at the fourth-last. (op 16-1)

3159 DAVIES CHEMISTS LTD "NEWCOMERS" MARES' STANDARD OPEN NATIONAL HUNT FLAT RACE 2m

3:50 (3:50) (Class 6) 3-5-Y-0 **£1,431** (£420; £210; £104)

Form	Pos	Dist	Horse	Jockey	RPR
	1		**Genstone Trail** 4-11-5 0	RobertThornton	95+
			(Alan King) *hld up in tch: trckd ldrs gng best over 3f out: pushed ahd over 1f out: rn green and rdn ins fnl f: kpt on* **11/8**[1]		
	2	2 ½	**Bathwick Junior** 3-10-6 0	RhysFlint	75
			(John Flint) *chsd ldrs: rdn and effrt to chal 4f out: led 3f out tl over 1f out: styd on same pce ins fnl f* **11/1**		
	3	½	**Cresswell Melody (IRE)** 3-10-1 0	RachaelGreen(5)	74
			(Anthony Honeyball) *led and set stdy gallop: rdn and qcknd ent fnl 4f: hdd: rn green and hung lft 3f out: swtchd rt and tried to rally jst over 1f out: kpt on* **6/1**[3]		
	4	5	**Astralogical (IRE)** 5-11-5 0	WayneHutchinson	82
			(Alan King) *pressed ldr tl rdn and unable qck wl over 3f out: outpcd and bhd whn edgd rt over 2f out: plugged on same pce after* **15/2**		
	5	¾	**Goodtimes A'Coming** 4-11-5 0	RichardJohnson	81
			(Noel Chance) *hld up in tch in last: shkn up and effrt 4f out: rdn over 2f out: btn over 1f out: wknd fnl f* **2/1**[2]		

4m 7.10s (23.70) **Going Correction** +0.425s/f (Soft)
WFA 3 from 4yo+ 13lb **5** Ran SP% **109.8**
Speed ratings (Par 101): **70,68,68,66,65**
ToteSuper7: Win: not won Place: £26.90. CSF £15.94 TOTE £2.10: £1.30, £5.30; EX 19.20.
Owner Mickleton Racing Club **Bred** Mrs S C Welch **Trained** Barbury Castle, Wilts

FOCUS
No form to go on, but some astute yards represented in this mares' bumper and the winner can rate higher.

NOTEBOOK
Genstone Trail was momentarily restrained off the heels of the leaders around the final turn, but she was briefly outpaced as the dash for home began, though she soon got into her stride and stayed on strongest. She is related to 2m4f jumpers like Stoneys Treasure, and on this performance she also looks likely to need further in time. (op 6-4 tchd 11-10)
Bathwick Junior made the first bid for home off the final bend but was outstayed near the finish. This was a good run especially as the stable do not have many bumper runners. (op 12-1 tchd 10-1)
Cresswell Melody(IRE) was a bit keen in the early lead, but after wandering a little in the straight she stayed on again near the finish. (op 7-1)
Astralogical(IRE), the less-fancied of the Alan King runners, is related to some 2m4f jumpers, so it was disappointing to see her the first to capitulate. (op 4-1)
Goodtimes A'Coming, from a yard with a strong bumper record, did not get home on the ground and was somewhat disappointing. (op 5-2 tchd 11-4)
T/Jkpt: £7,100.00 to a £1 stake. Pool:£10,000 - 1 winning ticket. T/Plt: £35.70 to a £1 stake. Pool:£97,980 - 1,997.94 winning tickets. T/Qpdt: £5.10 to a £1 stake. Pool:£7,781 - 1,123.74 winning tickets. SP

2419 LEICESTER (R-H)

Tuesday, December 28

3160 Meeting Abandoned - Frost and snow

3088 SOUTHWELL (L-H)

Tuesday, December 28

OFFICIAL GOING: Standard to slow
Wind: ALMOST NIL Weather: Ovecast

3166 TOTEPLACEPOT STANDARD OPEN NATIONAL HUNT FLAT RACE 2m (F)

12:50 (12:50) (Class 6) 3-6-Y-0 **£1,370** (£399; £199)

Form	Pos	Dist	Horse	Jockey	RPR
	1		**Oscara Dara (IRE)** 5-11-6 0	TimmyMurphy	115+
			(Alan Fleming) *a.p: chsd ldr over 2f out: led on bit over 1f out: sn clr* **9/2**[2]		
2	2	10	**Hackpenbay**[17] 2896 4-11-6 0	SamThomas	100
			(Lawney Hill) *led: rdn and hdd over 1f out: wknd ins fnl f* **11/2**		
	3	1 ¼	**Anychancedave (IRE)** 3-10-7 0	BarryKeniry	86
			(Alan Swinbank) *chsd ldrs: rdn over 4f out: styd on same pce fnl 3f* **9/4**[1]		
6	4	5	**Lights Of Broadway (IRE)**[40] 2472 4-10-13 0	MarkGrant	87
			(Barry Brennan) *prom: rdn and lost pl over 4f out: n.d after* **25/1**		
	5	hd	**Sous Mix (FR)** 4-11-6 0	DenisO'Regan	94
			(Michael Easterby) *prom: chsd ldr over 4f out tl rdn over 2f out: wknd over 1f out* **5/1**[3]		
	6	2 ¾	**Hot Head** 3-10-4 0	RichardKilloran(3)	78
			(Tim Vaughan) *prom: pushed along over 7f out: rdn over 4f out: wknd over 3f out* **11/2**		
0	7	6	**Bit Of A Clown (IRE)**[49] 2295 4-11-6 0	AndrewThornton	85
			(Caroline Bailey) *hld up: hdwy over 7f out: wknd over 4f out* **100/1**		
6	8	3 ¾	**Jersey Joe (IRE)**[58] 2108 3-10-7 0	FearghalDavis	68
			(Brian Ellison) *hld up: rdn over 4f out: wknd over 3f out* **14/1**		
2-00	9	19	**Cloudy Joe (IRE)**[22] 2826 4-11-3 0	AdamPogson(3)	62
			(Charles Pogson) *chsd ldr tl rdn over 4f out: wknd over 3f out: t.o* **33/1**		
0	10	¾	**Glasson Lad (IRE)**[22] 2824 3-10-7 0	GrahamLee	49
			(Ferdy Murphy) *hld up: a in rr: t.o* **100/1**		
	11	¾	**Needwood Ridge** 3-10-7 0	DavidDennis	48
			(Frank Sheridan) *hld up: a in rr: t.o* **50/1**		
	12	8	**Smart Song** 5-10-13 0	PaulGallagher(7)	53
			(Ferdy Murphy) *hld up: a in rr: bhd fnl 4f: t.o* **33/1**		

3m 57.7s (12.20) **Going Correction** +0.375s/f (Slow)
WFA 3 from 4yo+ 13lb **12** Ran SP% **116.7**
Speed ratings: **84,79,78,75,75 74,71,69,60,59 59,55**
Tote Swingers: 1&2 £8.70, 1&3 £3.90, 2&3 £2.70 CSF £27.63 TOTE £4.20: £2.00, £1.70, £1.30; EX 35.30.
Owner BG Racing Partnership **Bred** Tom And P Phelan **Trained** Beare Green, Surrey

FOCUS
The opening bumper was run at a very steady pace until the final half mile and in the end an impressive wide-margin winner. He is value for further but the form is ordinary rated around the second and fourth.

NOTEBOOK
Oscara Dara(IRE), well backed in the morning, travelled very strongly. He moved up on to the heels of the leader turning for home, and in the end sprinted clear. The opposition was weak and he lacks a bit of scope but he could hardly have made a better start. (op 4-1 tchd 5-1)
Hackpenbay, runnner-up in a Polytrack bumper on his debut two weeks earlier, took them along but was swept aside in a matter of strides when the winner was sent about his business. (op 4-1 tchd 6-1)
Anychancedave(IRE), a big newcomer, was hard at work as soon as the pace increased. He stuck to his task and will have learnt from this but he looks to have more stamina than basic speed. (op 2-1 tchd 5-2)
Lights Of Broadway(IRE), beaten 25 lengths when sixth on her debut at Hereford, fared a fraction better this time but will need to improve a good deal to make her mark.
Sous Mix(FR) travelled strongly as far as the home turn. She may have needed this. (op 9-1)
Hot Head, whose dam finished runner-up in the Park Hill Stakes in these colours, was being pushed along before the pace increased and, despite being a son of Selkirk, he looks basically slow. The market was seemingly expecting a better performance from a horse whose 2-y-o half-brother won his only racecourse start at this track in November. (op 14-1 tchd 5-1)
Smart Song Official explanation: trainer said gelding finished lame on his right-fore leg

3167 TOTESWINGER "JUMPERS' BUMPER" NATIONAL HUNT FLAT RACE 2m (F)

1:20 (1:20) (Class 4) 4-Y-0+ **£2,602** (£764; £382; £190)

Form	Pos	Dist	Horse	Jockey	RPR
-211	1		**Priceless Art (IRE)**[6] 3093 5-11-0 0	BarryKeniry	117
			(Alan Swinbank) *a.p: chsd ldr 1/2-way: rdn to chal over 2f out: led 1f out: edgd lft: all out* **2/11**[1]		
40-6	2	hd	**Jack The Gent (IRE)**[34] 2612 6-11-0 0	DougieCostello	117
			(George Moore) *led: rdn and hdd 1f out: styd on gamely* **20/1**		
20-0	3	19	**Easton Clump**[34] 2607 7-11-0 0	MarkGrant	98
			(Dominic Ffrench Davis) *chsd ldrs: rdn over 4f out: wknd wl over 3f out* **20/1**		
	4	10	**Next Exit (IRE)**[289] 5-10-7 0	MrTomDavid(7)	88
			(Tim Vaughan) *hld up: hdwy 10f out: rdn and wknd over 4f out* **6/1**[2]		
0040	5	¾	**Beau D'Argent**[37] 2547 4-10-0 0	PaulGallagher(7)	80
			(Ferdy Murphy) *sn bhd: sme hdwy u.p 5f out: nvr on terms* **66/1**		
-442	6	49	**Ouest Eclair (FR)**[42] 2438 5-11-0 0	GrahamLee	38
			(Ferdy Murphy) *sn pushed along in rr: bhd fr 1/2-way: t.o* **13/2**[3]		
	7	hd	**Royal Crystal**[282] 7-10-7 0	(t) PaddyAspell	31
			(James Turner) *plld hrd: trckd ldr 2f: remained handy tl rdn and wknd 6f out: t.o* **66/1**		
00-0	8	nk	**Erin Dancer (IRE)**[67] 1951 5-10-4 0	TonyKelly(10)	38
			(Ferdy Murphy) *a bhd: t.o* **28/1**		
00-P	9	20	**Sheepclose (IRE)**[34] 2612 5-11-0 0	DenisO'Regan	18
			(Michael Easterby) *chsd ldr after 2f tl 1/2-way: wknd 7f out: t.o* **33/1**		
060	10	14	**Are Olive**[60] 2075 7-10-7 0	RobertWalford	—
			(Tim Walford) *hld up: lost tch fnl 9f: sn t.o* **50/1**		

3m 52.7s (7.20) **Going Correction** +0.375s/f (Slow)
WFA 4 from 5yo+ 5lb **10** Ran SP% **133.1**
Speed ratings (Par 105): **97,96,87,82,82 57,57,57,47,40**
Tote Swingers: 1&2 £3.40, 1&3 £4.60, 2&3 £51.60 CSF £13.30 TOTE £1.10: £1.02, £4.80, £5.20; EX 9.30.
Owner Matthew Green & David Manasseh **Bred** Lady Bamford **Trained** Melsonby, N Yorks

FOCUS
A strong gallop and the time was over 5secs quicker than the opener. The winner is rated below his previous course win and the race is rated around the third to fifth.

NOTEBOOK
Priceless Art(IRE) was an easy winner on the all-bumper card here a week earlier, but this did not work out according to plan. The winner of three bumpers, he escaped a penalty and was sent off at prohibitive odds. It looked plain sailing when he moved up smoothly on to the heels of the leader leaving the back straight but, once in line for home, he was soon under strong pressure and only gained the upper hand near the line. He had made a deep impression on this rider last week and this may have come too soon. After a short break he will make his hurdling debut as soon as his trainer can find some decent ground for him. (op 1-5 after early 1-4 in a place)
Jack The Gent(IRE), well beaten sixth in a novices' hurdle at Wetherby in November on his first start for almost a year, set a good pace and battled back in brave fashion. Just denied in the end, he finished a long way clear of the remainder and, now his breathing problem has been sorted out, he can surely make his mark over hurdles. (op 22-1)
Easton Clump, a close second in a Newbury bumper a year ago for a different yard, has achieved little in two starts over hurdles since and was readily out-speeded by the first two in the final half-mile. (op 16-1)
Next Exit(IRE), winner of an Irish maiden point in March on his second start, is described as 'uncomplicated'. He was under strong pressure before the home turn and looks a stayer.
Beau D'Argent kept on in her own time and will appreciate 3m back over hurdles. (op 80-1)
Ouest Eclair(FR) was soon under pressure to keep up. He is rated 93 over hurdles and seemed not to take to the Fibresand surface. (op 7-1)
Royal Crystal Official explanation: jockey said mare had no more to give, having run too free in the early stages

3168 TOTEQUADPOT "JUMPERS' BUMPER" NATIONAL HUNT FLAT RACE 2m (F)

1:55 (1:55) (Class 4) 4-Y-0+ **£2,602** (£764; £382; £190)

Form	Pos	Dist	Horse	Jockey	RPR
P-4P	1		**The Hollinwell**[31] 2674 7-11-0 0	GrahamLee	111
			(Ferdy Murphy) *mde virtually all: rdn over 1f out: styd on gamely* **12/1**		

345 **2** *hd* **Natural Spring**[38] 2526 5-10-7 0 .... DenisO'Regan 104
(Suzy Smith) *prom: lost pl 1/2-way: hdwy over 5f out: rdn to chse wnr fnl f: r.o* **14/1**

-601 **3** *2 3/4* **Cloudy Spirit**[6] 3090 5-10-7 0 .... SamThomas 101
(Reg Hollinshead) *hld up: hdwy over 6f out: rdn over 3f out: styd on same pce fnl f* **5/2**[2]

10-0 **4** *3 1/2* **Preuty Boy (FR)**[52] 2209 5-11-0 0 .... TimmyMurphy 105
(Alan Fleming) *chsd ldrs: rdn over 5f out: outpcd 4f out: styd on u.p fr over 1f out* **8/1**[3]

/6-P **5** *nk* **Wardington Lad**[37] 2558 8-10-7 0 .... KyleJames(7) 104
(Michael Appleby) *trckd ldrs: racd keenly: rdn and ev ch over 3f out: wknd over 1f out* **66/1**

5-13 **6** *1/2* **Ballybriggan (IRE)**[45] 2361 6-11-0 0 .... DougieCostello 104
(John Quinn) *hld up: hdwy over 6f out: rdn 2f out: wknd fnl f* **7/4**[1]

3150 **7** *3 3/4* **Barron Watlass (IRE)**[39] 2506 6-10-4 0 .... SamuelWelton(10) 100
(George Moore) *hld up in tch: jnd ldrs over 4f out: rdn and wknd over 1f out* **50/1**

-620 **8** *16* **Ring For Time**[196] 756 7-10-7 0 .... (p) WillKennedy 77
(John Flint) *prom: lost pl 1/2-way: wknd over 6f out* **14/1**

F-64 **9** *11* **Charingworth (IRE)**[66] 1956 7-10-7 0 .... PaulGallagher(7) 73
(Ferdy Murphy) *hld up in tch: rdn over 6f out: sn wknd: t.o* **25/1**

1433 **10** *13* **Noble Scholar (IRE)**[6] 3090 5-11-0 0 .... BarryKeniry 60
(Alan Swinbank) *hld up: pushed along 10f out: bhd fr 1/2-way: t.o* **12/1**

3m 52.1s (6.60) **Going Correction** +0.375s/f (Slow) **10** Ran SP% **112.1**
Speed ratings (Par 105): **98,97,96,94,94 94,92,84,79,72**
Tote Swingers: 1&2 £18.30, 1&3 £3.20, 2&3 £6.50 CSF £157.15 TOTE £13.90: £3.60, £3.00, £1.50; EX 146.70.
Owner Mr And Mrs Neil Iveson **Bred** E R Hanbury **Trained** West Witton, N Yorks

FOCUS
An ordinary contest with the third, fourth, sixth and seventh fairly close to their marks.

NOTEBOOK
The Hollinwell looked a chaser going places but the occasion seemed to get to him and he was pulled up after breaking a blood-vessel at the Cheltenham Festival. He jumped badly and was pulled up at Newbury last month but here he enjoyed himself in front, racing with the choke out. He had to battle hard but did just enough in the end. Connections will be hoping that his jumping comes back together given some decent ground, and with him it might be a case of the smaller the field the better, as he is happiest setting his own pace. (op 8-1)
Natural Spring, fifth at Huntingdon on her hurdling bow last month, elected to race wide and was the final challenger. She was just held in the end and looks sure to improve and take a mares-only novices' hurdle. (op 12-1)
Cloudy Spirit, a decisive winner in the end here a week ago, again gave a good account of herself but was simply not good enough on the day. Connections are eyeing the 'fixed brush' races at Haydock this winter. (op 11-4 tchd 3-1 in places)
Preuty Boy(FR), winner of a handicap hurdle over 2m6f at Plumpton in February from a mark of 112, stayed on after getting badly tapped for toe on the home turn. This should put him spot-on for a return to hurdling. (op 12-1 tchd 14-1)
Wardington Lad, a bumper winner four years ago, had been pulled up over hurdles at Towcester on his return five weeks previously. He seemed to run well above himself but would be very well treated if he can reproduce this effort back over hurdles.
Ballybriggan(IRE), third over hurdles at Cheltenham from a mark of 124 seven weeks earlier, came there looking a real threat but his effort petered out in the final furlong, and he may well have needed this after the freeze-up. (tchd 6-4)
Noble Scholar(IRE), third behind Cloudy Spirit here last week, ran badly and was virtually pulled up leaving the back straight. Official explanation: jockey said gelding ran flat (op 9-1)

3169 TOTEEXACTA "JUMPERS' BUMPER" NATIONAL HUNT FLAT RACE 2m (F)
2:30 (2:30) (Class 4) 4-Y-0+ **£2,602** (£764; £382; £190)

Form RPR

121 **1** **Recession Proof (FR)**[35] 2594 4-11-0 0 .... DougieCostello 124
(John Quinn) *mde all: shkn up over 1f out: styd on wl* **7/2**[2]

50-1 **2** *2 1/2* **Bivouac (UAE)**[6] 3091 6-11-0 0 .... BarryKeniry 122
(Alan Swinbank) *hld up in tch: chsd wnr 4f out: rdn over 2f out: styd on same pce fnl f* **4/1**[3]

34-P **3** *4 1/2* **Nodform William**[41] 2448 8-11-0 0 .... BrianHughes 117
(Karen McLintock) *chsd ldrs: rdn over 4f out: styd on same pce fnl 2f* **80/1**

-U22 **4** *nk* **Hollo Ladies (IRE)**[13] 2951 5-11-0 0 .... GrahamLee 117
(Ferdy Murphy) *prom: rdn over 4f out: styd on one pce fnl 2f* **17/2**

10-2 **5** *4* **Bothy**[44] 2386 4-11-0 0 .... FearghalDavis 113
(Brian Ellison) *hld up in tch: rdn over 4f out: wknd 2f out* **2/1**[1]

1502 **6** *5* **J'Adhere (FR)**[40] 2485 5-10-7 0 .... MrTomDavid(7) 108
(Tim Vaughan) *hld up: hdwy over 6f out: rdn over 3f out: sn wknd* **33/1**

P0-P **7** *4* **Borero (FR)**[34] 2611 7-11-0 0 .... PaddyAspell 104
(Michael Easterby) *hld up: rdn over 6f out: nvr trbld ldrs* **150/1**

31/3 **8** *1 3/4* **Best Prospect (IRE)**[37] 2551 8-11-0 0 .... (vt) DenisO'Regan 102
(Michael Dods) *hld up: hdwy 1/2-way: rdn and wknd over 3f out* **16/1**

0315 **9** *nk* **Divers (FR)**[46] 2348 6-10-7 0 .... PaulGallagher(7) 102
(Ferdy Murphy) *hld up: hdwy 1/2-way: rdn over 5f out: sn wknd* **33/1**

00-0 **10** *15* **Yetholm (USA)**[38] 2530 5-11-0 0 .... (p) WillKennedy 87
(John Flint) *chsd wnr tl rdn 4f out: wknd over 3f out: t.o* **100/1**

2-3P **11** *1 1/2* **Vodka Brook (IRE)**[45] 2374 7-11-0 0 .... RobertWalford 85
(Tim Walford) *mid-div: pushed along 11f out: lost pl 1/2-way: bhd fnl 6f: t.o* **25/1**

-336 **12** *3/4* **Nodforms Violet (IRE)**[45] 2361 6-11-0 0 .... BrianHarding 84
(Karen McLintock) *hld up: pushed along 10f out: bhd fr 1/2-way: t.o* **20/1**

0-65 **13** *71* **Veronicas Boy**[39] 2508 4-11-0 0 .... (v) TimmyMurphy 13
(George Moore) *chsd ldrs: rdn and wknd over 7f out: t.o* **80/1**

1-F4 **14** *29* **Bogside Theatre (IRE)**[37] 2551 6-9-11 0 .... SamuelWelton(10) —
(George Moore) *hdwy to go prom 13f out: rdn and wknd over 6f out: t.o* **12/1**

3m 48.2s (2.70) **Going Correction** +0.375s/f (Slow) **14** Ran SP% **118.3**
Speed ratings (Par 105): **108,106,104,104,102 99,97,96,96,89 88,88,52,38**
CSF £16.48 TOTE £5.80: £1.70, £1.40, £16.10; EX 19.60.
Owner Mrs Vanessa J Stone **Bred** N P Bloodstock Ltd & Morton Bloodstock **Trained** Settrington, N Yorks

FOCUS
A competitive 'jumpers bumper' run at a sound pace, the time was much quicker than the preceding three races, but in the end it developed into a match. the form is rated around the third, sixth and seventh.

NOTEBOOK
Recession Proof(FR), a winner at Carlisle and Lingfield from three starts over hurdles, made every yard. He dug deep and stayed on much too well for the runner-up in the end. There will be plenty of good opportunities for him back over hurdles in the New Year, with the Tote Gold Trophy at Newbury in February the immediate target. (tchd 3-1)
Bivouac(UAE), a winner four times on the Flat here this year, took a bumper at the replacement fixture six days earlier. He moved up travelling strongly to track the winner 3f out but was very much second best at the line. He is likely to return to hurdling next and should be able to take a handicap. (op 10-3 tchd 3-1)
Nodform William, who has clearly had his problems, has twice failed to justify favouritism in selling company over hurdles on his last three starts. He seemed to run well above himself here.
Hollo Ladies(IRE) stuck on after getting outpaced and will return to novice chases in good heart. (op 9-1 tchd 10-1 and 8-1)
Bothy, runner-up behind Menorah in the Greatwood at Cheltenham, was under strong pressure and making little impact leaving the back straight. The Fibresand surface was presumably not to his liking. (op 3-1)

3170 BET TOTEPOOL ON ALL UK RACING "JUMPERS' BUMPER" NATIONAL HUNT FLAT RACE 2m (F)
3:05 (3:05) (Class 4) 5-Y-0+ **£2,602** (£764; £382; £190)

Form RPR

00-1 **1** **Palomar (USA)**[52] 1609 8-11-0 0 .... FearghalDavis 116
(Brian Ellison) *hld up and bhd: hdwy 1/2-way: led on bit over 3f out: rdn over 1f out: hung lft ins fnl f: styd on* **5/2**[1]

3-31 **2** *1 1/4* **Riguez Dancer**[34] 2613 6-11-0 0 .... GrahamLee 115
(Ferdy Murphy) *hld up: hdwy 0ver 9f out: chsd ldr 6f out: ev ch over 3f out: sn rdn: styd on same pce ins fnl f* **5/2**[1]

3340 **3** *2 1/2* **Feeling Peckish (USA)**[6] 3092 6-11-0 0 .... (t) AndrewGlassonbury 112
(Michael Chapman) *hld up: hdwy over 6f out: outpcd over 3f out: styd on u.p fr over 1f out* **250/1**

1/ **4** *2* **Sole Bonne Femme (IRE)**[239] 126 8-11-0 0 .... WillKennedy 110
(Gerard Butler) *prom: lost pl 1/2-way: hdwy over 5f out: sn rdn: outpcd over 3f out: rallied over 1f out: one pce ins fnl f* **66/1**

4-30 **5** *10* **Kalahari King (FR)**[17] 2885 9-10-7 0 .... PaulGallagher(7) 100
(Ferdy Murphy) *hld up: hdwy 10f out: rdn over 5f out: sn wknd* **8/1**[3]

4-P4 **6** *hd* **Bygones Of Brid (IRE)**[31] 2668 7-11-0 0 .... TimmyMurphy 100
(Karen McLintock) *prom tl rdn and wknd over 4f out* **11/4**[2]

3214 **7** *1 1/2* **Film Festival (USA)**[42] 2436 7-10-11 0 .... DannyCook(3) 98
(Brian Ellison) *led: rdn and hdd over 3f out: wknd over 2f out* **20/1**

3-60 **8** *nk* **Leslingtaylor (IRE)**[44] 2386 8-11-0 0 .... DougieCostello 98
(John Quinn) *trckd ldrs: racd keenly: rdn and wknd over 3f out* **10/1**

610- **9** *18* **Tora Bora (GER)**[253] 5271 8-10-7 0 .... (p) MissCLWills(7) 80
(Brendan Powell) *sn pushed along and prom: rdn and wknd 6f out: t.o* **100/1**

0/5 **10** *13* **Quinola Des Obeaux (FR)**[38] 2527 6-11-0 0 .... (t) DavidDennis 67
(Frank Sheridan) *chsd ldrs: lost pl 12f out: bhd fr 1/2-way: t.o* **33/1**

6-44 **11** *29* **Go On Be A Lady**[0] 3093 7-10-7 0 .... BarryKeniry 31
(Alan Swinbank) *sn pushed along in rr: bhd fnl 12f: t.o* **50/1**

3m 51.5s (6.00) **Going Correction** +0.375s/f (Slow) **11** Ran SP% **116.6**
Speed ratings: **100,99,98,97,92 92,91,91,82,75 61**
Tote Swingers: 1&2 £2.60, 1&3 £71.70, 2&3 £28.00 CSF £8.56 TOTE £4.30: £1.60, £1.30, £21.60; EX 12.20.
Owner Koo's Racing Club **Bred** Juddmonte Farms Inc **Trained** Norton, N Yorks

FOCUS
Another interesting event and again it boiled down to a two-horse race at the business end. The first two were rated below their best with the fourth setting the level.

NOTEBOOK
Palomar(USA) has turned over a new leaf since joining Brian Ellison's yard. After a valuable handicap hurdle success at Market Rasen, he ran with credit in both the Cesarewitch and the November Handicap. Dropped in at the start and sticking to the inside route, in the end he had too much foot for Riguez Dancer. He is still something of a character but is just the type to make a bold bid in one of the more valuable handicap hurdles this winter. Suited by going right-handed the Imperial Cup will be a tempting target. (op 2-1)
Riguez Dancer, who took a handicap chase at Wetherby last month, is proven on this surface from his Flat-racing days. He looked a major threat to the winner turning in but lacked the speed to seriously trouble him. Nevertheless this was a sound effort, and he should enjoy further success returned to fences. (op 9-2)
Feeling Peckish(USA), beaten over 50 lengths here last week, stands up well to a busy schedule and seemed to run way above himself. (op 200-1)
Sole Bonne Femme(IRE), having his first outing for this yard and his first start since May, has been let down by his jumping over fences in Ireland.
Kalahari King(FR) kept on in his own time after getting outpaced leaving the back straight. The workout will have put him spot-on for a return to fences in the New Year. (op 15-2 tchd 6-1)
Bygones Of Brid(IRE), who didn't take to fences at the first attempt, had finished fourth in the Fighting Fifth Hurdle at Newbury. He didn't shine here, looking a bit ring-rusty after the freeze-up. (op 7-2)
Leslingtaylor(IRE), another who has proved a grand servant, was back in action after a six-week break and he ran as if it was needed. Official explanation: jockey said gelding lost his action in the home straight (op 8-1 tchd 13-2)

3171 BET TOTEPOOL ON ALL IRISH RACING "JUMPERS' BUMPER" NATIONAL HUNT FLAT RACE 2m (F)
3:35 (3:35) (Class 4) 4-Y-0+ **£2,602** (£764; £382; £190)

Form RPR

13-P **1** **Lightening Rod**[37] 2542 5-10-11 0 .... MrOGreenall(3) 130
(Michael Easterby) *hld up and bhd: hdwy over 5f out: led over 1f out: r.o wl* **9/2**[2]

3-03 **2** *3 1/2* **Moorlands Teri**[33] 2641 7-10-0 0 .... (t) MrTomDavid(7) 119
(Tim Vaughan) *chsd ldrs: rdn over 4f out: styd on to go 2nd nr fin* **20/1**

-211 **3** *hd* **First Rock (IRE)**[6] 3089 4-11-0 0 .... BarryKeniry 126
(Alan Swinbank) *trckd ldrs: plld hrd: led 12f out: rdn and hdd over 1f out: styd on same pce: lost 2nd nr fin* **5/6**[1]

1261 **4** *2 1/4* **Sheriff Hutton (IRE)**[52] 2204 7-11-0 0 .... RobertWalford 124
(Tim Walford) *trckd ldr: plld hrd: rdn over 2f out: ev ch over 1f out: no ex ins fnl f* **15/2**

6024 **5** *20* **Panama Canal (IRE)**[40] 2475 5-10-11 0 .... AdamPogson(3) 104
(Charles Pogson) *prom: rdn over 4f out: wknd over 2f out* **40/1**

56 **6** *17* **St Enoder**[158] 1086 5-10-7 0 .... SamThomas 80
(Brendan Powell) *mid-div: effrt over 6f out: sn wknd: t.o* **100/1**

11P- **7** *14* **Poker De Sivola (FR)**[255] 5223 7-11-0 0 .... GrahamLee 73
(Ferdy Murphy) *chsd ldrs: pushed along 10f out: rdn and wknd over 5f out: t.o* **11/2**[3]

0 **8** *3 1/2* **Tee Shot (IRE)**[36] 2576 4-10-11 0 .... RichardKilloran(3) 69
(Tim Vaughan) *a bhd: t.o fr 1/2-way* **100/1**

2/ **9** *hd* **China House (IRE)**[981] 5122 7-11-0 0 .... BrianHughes 69
(Lisa Williamson) *plld hrd: led 4f: chsd ldrs: rdn and wknd 6f out: t.o* **22/1**

40 **10** *16* **Mansonien L'As (FR)**[14] 2938 4-10-7 0 .... PaulGallagher(7) 53
(Ferdy Murphy) *hld up and a bhd: t.o fnl 7f* **100/1**

PP/6 11 2 **Borderhopper**[41] 2446 6-10-4 0 TonyKelly(10) 51
(Ferdy Murphy) *a bhd: t.o fr 1/2-way* **100/1**

3m 46.8s (1.30) **Going Correction** +0.375s/f (Slow) **11** Ran SP% **115.4**
Speed ratings (Par 105): **111,109,109,108,98 89,82,80,80,72 71**
Tote Swingers: 1&2 £13.60, 1&3 £3.10, 2&3 £4.90 CSF £85.67 TOTE £4.40: £1.80, £3.10, £1.10; EX 101.50.
Owner N W A Bannister **Bred** Millsec Limited **Trained** Sheriff Hutton, N Yorks

FOCUS
Plenty of dead wood in this concluding bumper. The first two are rated in line with their hurdles form with the fourth and fifth pretty much to their marks.

NOTEBOOK
Lightening Rod, a dual bumper winner and successful in a handicap hurdle at Kelso in March from a mark of 115, still looked as if the outing might be needed on his second start after his summer break. Dropped in at the start and taking the bypass route, he came there travelling very strongly and won going away in the end. He has plenty of foot and will be very interesting back over hurdles. (tchd 5-1)
Moorlands Teri, a dual bumper winner and twice successful over hurdles, had finished third in a 2m6f novices' chase at Uttoxeter last month. She is regarded as a long-distance chaser in the making, so this was a notable effort. (op 14-1)
First Rock(IRE) was keen and pulled himself to the front before halfway. Winner of a bumper at Musselburgh and again here last week, he was unpenalised here and will make his debut over hurdles when the weather relents. (op 10-11 tchd Evens)
Sheriff Hutton(IRE), another on the keen side, took a handicap chase over 2m6f at Kelso last month from a mark of 129. This will have put him spot-on for the resumption. (tchd 7-1)
Poker De Sivola(FR), winner of the 4m National Hunt Chase at Cheltenham in March, was struggling to keep up soon after halfway and eventually completed in his own time. His long-term target this time is the Scottish National, and he is likely to be seen over hurdles during the winter months. (op 7-1 tchd 5-1)
T/Plt: £9.30 to a £1 stake. Pool:£64,411 - 5,05.66 winning tickets. T/Qpdt: £7.00 to a £1 stake. Pool:£5,670 - 591.36 winning tickets. CR

3172 - 3173a (Foreign Racing) - See Raceform Interactive

[542]LEOPARDSTOWN (L-H)

Tuesday, December 28

OFFICIAL GOING: Soft to heavy changing to heavy after race 1 (12:20)

3174a BALLYMALOE COUNTRY RELISH FORT LENEY NOVICE CHASE (GRADE 1) (17 fncs) 3m

1:25 (1:25) 4-Y-0+ **£43,141** (£12,610; £5,973; £1,991)

RPR

1 **Bostons Angel (IRE)**[13] 2971 6-11-10 RMPower 143
(Mrs John Harrington, Ire) *a.p: 3rd 1/2-way: hdwy on inner to ld briefly ent st: narrowly hdd bef last: regained ld early run-in: kpt on wl u.p* **14/1**

2 3/4 **Quito De La Roque (FR)**[12] 2992 6-11-10 DNRussell 142
(C A Murphy, Ire) *chsd ldrs: 5th 1/2-way: slt mstke 7 out: 4th whn nt fluent 2 out: rdn and no imp in 5th at last: styd on wl u.p clsng stages: nt rch wnr* **10/3**[2]

3 1 1/2 **Western Charmer (IRE)**[33] 2649 8-11-10 AELynch 141
(D T Hughes, Ire) *a.p: 2nd 1/2-way: 3rd and rdn ent st: kpt on one pce u.p run-in* **20/1**

4 1 **Thegreatjohnbrowne (IRE)**[44] 2413 6-11-10 PCarberry 140
(Noel Meade, Ire) *led and attempted to make all: hdd briefly ent st: rallied to narrowly ld again bef last: hdd and edgd rt u.p run-in: no ex clsng stages* **3/1**[1]

5 1 1/2 **Chicago Grey (IRE)**[17] 2883 7-11-10 147 (t) DJCondon 138
(Gordon Elliott, Ire) *hld up towards rr on inner: mstke 4 out: wnt 5th bef 2 out: drvn along in 4th appr last: no imp u.p run-in* **5/1**

6 21 **Head Of The Posse (IRE)**[13] 2971 7-11-10 139 MPWalsh 117
(John E Kiely, Ire) *hld up in rr: mstke 4 out: drvn along in 6th 2 out: sn no ex* **9/2**[3]

7 dist **Elysian Rock**[33] 2647 6-11-10 133 BarryGeraghty —
(M F Morris, Ire) *trckd ldrs: 4th 1/2-way: no ex appr 2 out: wknd: t.o* **12/1**

8 22 **Quadrillon (FR)**[38] 2533 6-11-10 PTownend —
(W P Mullins, Ire) *a towards rr: 7th 1/2-way: no ex fr 3 out: t.o* **7/1**

P **Healys Bar (IRE)**[44] 2413 6-11-10 PWFlood —
(Oliver McKiernan, Ire) *mid-div on outer: 6th 1/2-way: no ex appr 2 out: sn wknd: p.u bef last* **25/1**

6m 33.9s (-0.10) **Going Correction** +0.275s/f (Yiel) **9** Ran SP% **118.4**
Speed ratings: **111,110,110,109,109 102,—,—,—**
CSF £63.79 TOTE £18.20: £4.30, £1.80, £6.80; DF 142.60.
Owner E A P Scouller **Bred** P A D Scouller **Trained** Moone, Co Kildare
■ This Grade 1 was run most recently as the Knight Frank Novices' Chase.

FOCUS
This was a below-average Grade 1 and bookmaker reaction with a view to the RSA Chase was predictably tempered. They finished fairly close up and there is no star among them. The pace was sensible but two out-and-out stayers fought out the finish. It has been rated through the runner-up and third in line with the best view of their hurdles form.

NOTEBOOK
Bostons Angel(IRE) clearly needed this type of stamina test to be seen to best effect and stayed at it best. He looked to have no more than an outside chance on form but he produced a solid performance that happened to be good enough. Never far off the pace, he just kept galloping and had everything beaten up the run-in, only for the runner-up to press him strongly close home. He handles better ground but, with a view to Cheltenham, he looks comfortably inferior to some other RSA candidates. (op 16/1)
Quito De La Roque(FR) would have gotten up in a few more strides. He travelled well in midfield but made a slight mistake at a crucial stage, and took a while to get going afterwards. He basically has one pace and kept finding it when his rivals were tiring up the run-in. He kept finding from the last but the line just came too soon. (op 7/2)
Western Charmer(IRE) was another who looked a bit below the class required here but he ran a cracker. Always close-up, he kept on all the way to the line and appreciated the step up to 3m.
Thegreatjohnbrowne(IRE) had jumped really well until the last flight on the first circuit and his jumping was not as fluent thereafter. He tended to jump a little to his right and paid the price when getting tired. If he had jumped as well as he can, he may well have won. (op 11/4)
Chicago Grey(IRE) made a major mistake at the fourth that didn't help, but he never really looked like winning. (op 4/1)
Head Of The Posse(IRE) was very disappointing, and he was beaten after two out before finding little. This trip may stretch his stamina. (op 5/1)
Elysian Rock probably found this company a bit hot but still ran below his best.
Quadrillon(FR) ran a shocker. (op 8/1)

Healys Bar(IRE) was out of his depth. Official explanation: jockey said gelding made a bad mistake 3 out and was pulled up

3175a WOODIESDIY.COM CHRISTMAS HURDLE (GRADE 2) (12 hdls) 3m

2:00 (2:00) 4-Y-0+ **£25,884** (£7,566; £3,584; £1,194)

RPR

1 **Mourad (IRE)**[13] 2968 5-11-6 156 PTownend 156+
(W P Mullins, Ire) *hld up towards rr: cl 7th travelling wl appr 2 out: smooth hdwy early st: 2nd and poised to chal bef last: led early run-in and pushed out to assert* **7/4**[1]

2 2 **Powerstation (IRE)**[13] 2968 10-11-8 150 BarryGeraghty 154
(Eamonn O'Connell, Ire) *a.p: trckd ldr in 2nd tl led at 1/2-way: rdn and strly pressed appr last: hdd early run-in: no ch w wnr and kpt on same pce* **12/1**

3 2 1/2 **Rigour Back Bob (IRE)**[10] 3030 5-11-8 143 AndrewJMcNamara 152
(E J O'Grady, Ire) *mid-div: 6th 1/2-way: pushed along appr 2 out: wnt 4th u.p bef last: kpt on one pce run-in* **9/1**

4 5 **Oscar Dan Dan (IRE)**[13] 2968 8-11-10 150 DNRussell 149
(Thomas Mullins, Ire) *led: hdd 1/2-way: remained prom tl rdn and lost pl 2 out: no imp in 8th ent st: rallied u.p fr bef last: kpt on one pce* **9/1**

5 1/2 **Shinrock Paddy (IRE)**[59] 2095 6-11-10 143 (t) APCawley 148
(Paul Nolan, Ire) *trckd ldrs on inner: 4th 1/2-way: 5th bef 2 out: wnt 2nd briefly u.p early st: sn no imp and wknd run-in* **6/1**[3]

6 1 1/4 **Moskova (IRE)**[37] 2565 7-10-12 136 PCarberry 135
(Paul Nolan, Ire) *in rr: rdn along in 9th 3 out: sme hdwy fr next: mod 6th bef last: kpt on one pce* **25/1**

7 1 1/4 **Mossey Joe (IRE)**[16] 2912 7-11-6 AELynch 142
(W J Austin, Ire) *settled in mid-div on inner: 5th 1/2-way: slt mstke 3 out: cl 3rd travelling wl next: sn rdn and no ex fr early st* **10/3**[2]

8 5 **Rick (FR)**[33] 2648 6-11-3 131 PWFlood 134
(D T Hughes, Ire) *mid-div: hdwy on outer to go 2nd 4 out: rdn appr st: sn no ex* **12/1**

P **Garrai Ard (IRE)**[500] 950 7-10-12 (t) TPTreacy —
(Laurence James Butler, Ire) *a bhd: t.o whn p.u bef last* **100/1**

P **Summit Meeting**[13] 2968 5-11-3 143 RMPower —
(Mrs John Harrington, Ire) *trckd ldrs: 3rd 1/2-way: 6th 3 out: rdn and no ex appr next: bhd whn p.u bef last* **12/1**

6m 24.6s (6.60) **Going Correction** +0.20s/f (Yiel) **10** Ran SP% **121.6**
Speed ratings: **97,96,95,93,93 93,92,91,—,—**
CSF £26.36 TOTE £2.60: £1.10, £2.90, £2.20; DF 16.10.
Owner Teahon Consulting Limited **Bred** His Highness The Aga Khan's Studs S C **Trained** Muine Beag, Co Carlow

FOCUS
It has been rated around the third, fifth and seventh to their latest form, with the runner-up running slightly better then when successful in this race in 2009.

NOTEBOOK
Mourad(IRE) turned for home going ominously well and took over from leader Powerstation soon after the last to register a comfortable victory, the sixth of his career. On this evidence he's fully entitled to be aimed at the Ladbrokes World Hurdle in March. He coped admirably on this testing surface again but his trainer reckons he's probably better on better ground. (op 13/8)
Powerstation(IRE) ran a cracker on ground that was totally against him. He held the call at halfway and away from the penultimate flight, and had most of his rivals in trouble when they straightened for home, with the exception of the comfortable winner. Placed in each of his four visits to the Cheltenham Festival, he showed much improvement from his seasonal return at Thurles and, when he encounters some nicer ground, he could well be knocking on the door again. (op 14/1)
Rigour Back Bob(IRE) had returned to winning ways over 2m4f at Navan in the Tara Hurdle after a couple of disappointing efforts, and he ran a creditable race back over 3m in his first start over this distance since taking a Grade 3 event at the Punchestown Festival last April. The distress signals went up when the tempo increased leaving the back straight and he had no more to offer on the run to the last in this testing ground, but he's probably more effective these days on a sounder surface. (op 8/1)
Oscar Dan Dan(IRE) took them along at a moderate clip, which was fully understandable considering ground conditions, before the runner-up took over. Last season's Hatton's Grace winner looked a spent force running away from the second-last but he somehow managed a second wind and kept on again under pressure in the straight. (op 8/1)
Shinrock Paddy(IRE) was fitted with a tongue-tie for the first time but his race was run when they straightened for home. (op 13/2)
Moskova(IRE) was out the back before she began to make some inroads when the race unfolded, and she plugged on without threatening from the second-last. On this evidence she will appreciate even further. (op 33/1)
Mossey Joe(IRE) was a warm order before racing, bidding to extend his unbeaten sequence to five following his impressive Grade 3 novice hurdle win over this trip at Cork on his seasonal debut. He didn't race as keenly as when winning impressively that day, and leaving the back straight was still travelling, but he emptied quickly when the gun was put to his head turning in. This was a big step up in class and the ground probably didn't help his cause, but time could well prove he's better than this form. (op 7/2 tchd 4/1)
Rick(FR) raced prominently for a time and went second midway down the back, but he was fighting a losing battle after leaving the back straight.
Summit Meeting Official explanation: trainer said gelding made a respiratory noise in running

3176a LEXUS CHASE (GRADE 1) (17 fncs) 3m

2:35 (2:35) 5-Y-0+ **£82,300** (£25,221; £11,946; £3,982; £1,327)

RPR

1 **Pandorama (IRE)**[31] 2673 7-11-10 148 PCarberry 169+
(Noel Meade, Ire) *trckd ldrs on inner: 6th 1/2-way: hdwy into 2nd bef 4 out: nt fluent 3 out: 3rd at next: travelled best early st to ld at last: drew clr run-in* **7/2**[1]

2 6 **Money Trix (IRE)**[324] 3928 10-11-10 DNRussell 163
(Nicky Richards) *mid-div: 7th 1/2-way: mstke 10th: 6th 3 out: rdn in 5th ent st: kpt on u.p clsng stages wout threatening wnr* **7/1**[3]

3 3/4 **Joncol (IRE)**[51] 2262 7-11-10 160 APCawley 162
(Paul Nolan, Ire) *trckd ldrs on outer: 5th 1/2-way: pushed along in 4th after 2 out: no imp on wnr run-in: kpt on one pce* **5/1**[2]

4 2 1/2 **Glencove Marina (IRE)**[13] 2970 8-11-10 153 BarryGeraghty 160
(Eoin Griffin, Ire) *trckd ldrs: 4th 1/2-way: 3rd 4 out: 2nd after next: drvn along in 3rd appr last: no imp u.p run-in* **16/1**

5 4 1/2 **The Listener (IRE)**[416] 2139 11-11-10 AndrewJMcNamara 155
(Nick Mitchell) *attempted to make all: slt mstke 4 out: strly pressed after 2 out: hdd u.p whn slow at last: no ex run-in and wknd* **10/1**

6 9 **J'y Vole (FR)**[13] 2970 7-11-5 153 DJCondon 141
(W P Mullins, Ire) *towards rr whn mstke 1st: hld up: wnt 7th bef 4 out: 6th after 2 out: no ex appr last* **7/1**[3]

7 12 **Vic Venturi (IRE)**[262] 5127 10-11-10 158 (p) PWFlood 134
(D T Hughes, Ire) *towards rr: nvr a factor* **25/1**

8	7	**Siegemaster (IRE)**[37] 2565 9-11-10 145 .....(p) RLoughran (D T Hughes, Ire) *prom: mstke 6th: 3rd 1/2-way: sn lost pl: no ex fr 4 out* **33/1**	127
9	dist	**Notre Pere (FR)**[37] 2543 9-11-10 149 ..... AELynch (J T R Dreaper, Ire) *a towards rr: niggled along after 1/2-way: trailing fr 5 out: t.o* **14/1**	—
10	4	**Mossbank (IRE)**[13] 2970 10-11-10 151 ..... APHeskin (Michael Hourigan, Ire) *a towards rr: t.o* **50/1**	—
U		**Kempes (IRE)**[13] 2972 7-11-10 154 ..... APMcCoy (W P Mullins, Ire) *hld up towards rr: 9th 4 out: 8th and in tch whn blnd and uns rdr 2 out* **9/1**	—
P		**Cooldine (IRE)**[13] 2970 8-11-10 158 ..... PTownend (W P Mullins, Ire) *prom: 2nd 1/2-way: blnd 6 out: 4th 4 out: rdn and no ex in 7th ent st: eased and p.u bef last* **7/2**[1]	—

6m 30.0s (-4.00) **Going Correction** +0.275s/f (Yiel) 12 Ran SP% **126.5**
Speed ratings: **117,115,114,113,112 109,105,103,—,— —,—**
CSF £30.48 TOTE £3.70: £1.60, £2.50, £2.60; DF 30.20.
Owner R J Bagnall **Bred** P Carmody **Trained** Castletown, Co Meath

FOCUS
A top-class novice during a truncated novice campaign last season, Pandorama showed no ill-effects from a disappointing seasonal debut in the Hennessy at Newbury with an emphatic victory in this Grade 1 contest, and is clearly top class. The runner-up and third set a solid standard and have been rated as running to the same level as when placed in this race last year.

NOTEBOOK
Pandorama(IRE) ◆ gave his supporters a moment of anxiety with an awkward jump at the third-last, but ultimately asserted strongly on the run-in, drawing clear of those scrambling for the minor money. It was a fine performance for a horse making only a fifth appearance over fences, and the logical step will be to return for the Hennessy, at \n\x\x the same venue, before a possible tilt at the Cheltenham Gold Cup. In that regard, the ground is likely to be a major consideration, given his clear preference for soft. (op 6/1)
Money Trix(IRE) took the runner-up spot for the second year in a row, a grand display on his first start since a below-par run in the Hennessy at this venue in February. He stayed on stoutly having been under pressure from a long way out. (op 7/1 tchd 13/2)
Joncol(IRE) ◆ showed the anticipated improvement from his seasonal debut over an inadequate trip in the Fortria. With the stable beginning to click back into form, he could make a bold bid for a repeat of his Hennessy win. (op 9/2)
Glencove Marina(IRE) did not quite get home on his first attempt over the trip but ran a perfectly respectable race and will be worth another chance at the distance on better ground. He has had more than his share of problems, but remains a force to be reckoned with, perhaps at a grade lower than this. (op 16/1 tchd 20/1)
The Listener(IRE), a former winner of this race, ensured that it was a good test, trying to make all. He ran out of steam on the run-in but that can easily be forgiven, seeing that it was his first run after a long layoff. He has a fine record on Irish soil, and will presumably return for the Hennessy, which he won in 2008. (op 9/1)
J'y Vole(FR) was ridden to get the trip but failed to pick up when it mattered.
Kempes(IRE) was not too far off the pace when unseating his rider at the second-last.
Cooldine(IRE) was the big disappointment of the race. He was well placed to four out but was soon struggling in the straight as the race unfolded. He was eased and pulled up.

3177 - 3180a (Foreign Racing) - See Raceform Interactive

2459 LIMERICK (R-H)
Tuesday, December 28
OFFICIAL GOING: Soft to heavy (heavy in places)

3181a DORANS PRIDE NOVICE HURDLE (GRADE 3) (13 hdls) 2m 6f
1:35 (1:36) 4-Y-0+ **£16,393** (£4,792; £2,269; £756)

			RPR
1		**Knockfierna (IRE)**[15] 2932 5-10-12 ..... NPMadden (C Byrnes, Ire) *racd 3rd: prog to ld and rdn ent st: strly pressed fr last: all out* **2/1**[1]	128
2	shd	**Start Me Up (IRE)**[47] 2337 6-11-0 116 ..... DJCasey (C F Swan, Ire) *racd 4th: wnt 2nd 2 out: sn rdn: strly pressed wnr fr last: kpt on wl: jst failed* **7/2**[3]	130
3	13	**Ballinahow Lady (IRE)**[48] 2320 5-10-9 97 ..... JLCullen (David M O'Brien, Ire) *led: hdd fr 7th: rdn and no imp on ldrs fr 3 out: kpt on one pce* **12/1**	112
4	9	**Saville Row (IRE)**[16] 2912 5-11-0 ..... ADLeigh (Mrs John Harrington, Ire) *racd 2nd: led fr 7th: rdn after 3 out: hdd ent st: wknd bef 2 out* **3/1**[2]	108
F		**Carloswayback (IRE)**[13] 2967 5-11-0 ..... APCrowe (Paul Nolan, Ire) *hld up in last: cl up last whn fell 3 out* **3/1**[2]	—

6m 2.10s (362.10) 5 Ran SP% **113.2**
CSF £9.67 TOTE £2.30: £1.20, £1.80; DF 8.60.
Owner Mrs Karina Healy **Bred** Mrs K Healy **Trained** Ballingarry, Co Limerick

FOCUS
One wonders what sort of a race it would have turned into but for an incident at the third-last when Carloswayback fell. It has been rated around the runner-up and third.

NOTEBOOK
Knockfierna(IRE) ◆ completed the hat-trick of victories here in ultra-tough fashion. Racing close enough to a gradually increasing pace, she was in front turning into the straight, pinged the final two flights and really responded strongly when joined and, indeed, very briefly headed by the runner-up. She seems to be improving all the time. (op 7/4 tchd 9/4)
Start Me Up(IRE), who the more he steps up in trip the more he seems to improve, raced just off the pace, travelled well to track them into the straight and when it developed into a battle he wasn't found wanting. He just didn't jump the final flight quite as well as the winner and, in a race where the margin of defeat was so little, it may have made all the difference. (op 7/2 tchd 10/3)
Ballinahow Lady(IRE) did a good job of helping to set the gallop and she kept battling for as long as she was able, but in the end wasn't good enough.
Saville Row(IRE) hasn't really progressed from his debut victory at Down Royal in November. He tried to increase the pace early on the final circuit, and succeeded to a degree, but he'd run out of steam by the second-last.
Carloswayback(IRE) ◆, held up at the back, closed up travelling well but then stumbled and fell after the third-last flight. No questions had been asked of him at that stage. (op 5/2 tchd 9/4)

3182 - 3185a (Foreign Racing) - See Raceform Interactive

2547 KELSO (L-H)
Wednesday, December 29
3186 Meeting Abandoned - Frost and snow.

2958 NEWBURY (L-H)
Wednesday, December 29
OFFICIAL GOING: Good to soft (soft in places)
Owing to poor visibility, official times were only available for three of the eight races. Rails moved adding 18m to chase course and 40m to hurdles course.
Wind: Nil Weather: Fog

3193 BATHWICK TYRES SUPPORTS HEROS ANDOVER NOVICES' CHASE (FOR THE HALLOWE'EN TROPHY) (15 fncs) 2m 2f 110y
12:00 (12:00) (Class 3) 4-Y-O+ **£5,854** (£1,719; £859; £429)

Form				RPR
0-21	1		**Ghizao (GER)**[45] 2384 6-11-10 0 ..... TimmyMurphy (Paul Nicholls) *trckd ldrs whn in view fr 4th: stl chsng ldrs whn in view fr 10th: chal 4 out: led appr next: drvn and styd on strly run-in* **11/4**[2]	160+
1-22	2	4 ½	**Captain Chris (IRE)**[45] 2384 6-11-0 0 .....(t) RichardJohnson (Philip Hobbs) *in ld whn in view 4th: stl ldng whn bk in view 10th: mstke 11th: wnt rt and jnd 4 out: hdd appr next and dropped to 3rd: rallied run-in to re-take 2nd cl home but no ch w wnr* **13/8**[1]	147+
	3	nk	**Surfing (FR)**[188] 834 4-11-4 143 ..... APMcCoy (Nicky Henderson) *chsng ldrs whn in view 4th: stl front rnk whn bk in view 10th: chsd wnr 3 out: no imp last: one pce and lost 2nd cl home* **11/2**[3]	149
0-23	4	14	**Balzaccio (FR)**[39] 2527 5-11-0 135 ..... RobertThornton (Alan King) *chsng ldrs whn in view fr 10th: rdn 4 out: wknd fr next* **14/1**	134
4P-1	5	10	**Little George (IRE)**[33] 2662 7-11-6 127 ..... WayneHutchinson (Alan King) *in tch whn in view fr 4th: wknd fr 11th* **14/1**	130
	6	35	**Lucky To Be (FR)**[31] 2702 4-11-4 0 ..... JacquesRicou (G Macaire, France) *in rr 4th and again whn in view fr 10th: t.o* **7/1**	106
522F	7	27	**Sonning Star (IRE)**[37] 2582 6-11-0 121 ..... LeightonAspell (Nick Gifford) *in rr whn in view 4th and again 10th: t.o* **125/1**	67
20-0	8	12	**Babysitter (IRE)**[74] 1863 7-10-11 0 ..... RichieMcLernon(3) (Jonjo O'Neill) *in rr whn in view 4th and again whn in view 10th: t.o* **80/1**	56
-031	F		**Dee Ee Williams (IRE)**[37] 2578 7-11-6 140 .....(v) LiamTreadwell (Nick Gifford) *led whn in view 1st: chsng ldrs whn in view again 4th and stl wl in tch whn bk in view and fell 10th* **10/1**	—

4m 39.66s (-4.34) **Going Correction** -0.05s/f (Good)
WFA 4 from 5yo+ 5lb 9 Ran SP% **117.1**
Speed ratings (Par 107): **107,105,104,99,94 80,68,63,—**
totoswingers:1&2:£1.70, 1&3:£3.00, 2&3:£3.40 CSF £8.15 TOTE £3.80: £1.50, £1.20, £2.20; EX 8.00.
Owner The Johnson & Stewart Families **Bred** Baron G Von Ullman **Trained** Ditcheat, Somerset

FOCUS
This isn't a race that has produced an Arkle winner in recent years, although you can hardly knock 2004 winner Kauto Star's achievements over further, and Big Buck's was runner-up in 2007. There is a chance this could be a stronger renewal, however, as a result of the recent bleak spell of weather. The visibility for this contest was really poor. The form looks solid with the cosy winner up 5lb on his recent win.

NOTEBOOK
Ghizao(GER) ◆ leapt to the head of the betting in some places for the Arkle after his performance at Cheltenham last time, his second start over fences, and shortened even further when taking this under top weight. He didn't appear to make any mistakes when the runners could be seen and kept on strongly after the last to record a decisive victory. Predictably, the bookmakers were swift to cut him for the Arkle, for which he was made a general 6/1 shot. He heads straight to that race now. (tchd 3-1 in places)
Captain Chris(IRE), beaten 10l by Ghizao last time on his chasing debut but 10lb better off here, had been given a breathing operation since that Cheltenham effort (said to have gurgled there during the race) and was soon at the head of affairs here. He appeared to jump to his right at both the fourth and third last before disappearing into the fog, which saw him lose the lead, but he did rally under pressure after the final fence and managed to get into second close to the line. He may well want 2m4f this season, so the new race at the festival in March, the Jewson Novices' Chase, might be his best option. (op 15-8 tchd 2-1 in a place)
Surfing(FR) ◆ won one of his three starts over fences in France, all at Auteuil, the latest of them in a 2m2f 4-y-o chase in May on very soft ground. Easy in the market despite positive remarks, he didn't seem to make any mistakes when in view, after racing prominently, and ran as though he needed this after a lengthy break. He remains an interesting prospect but one can't be sure yet what his ideal distance will be. (tchd 6-1)
Balzaccio(FR) had run nicely in a couple of chases over slightly further, and was far from disgraced against this better calibre of rival. It will be interesting to see in what direction connections go with him now. (op 16-1)
Little George(IRE) won a novice handicap on his chasing debut, so this was a completely different mission against some talented individuals. The second string for Alan King on jockey bookings, he was noted as being on his toes prior to the off, and slightly keen in the race, but probably ran up to the level that could have been expected. (op 16-1)
Lucky To Be(FR) has been running respectably in French graded chases, notably behind the exciting Kauto Stone, and came from a stable that had a winner at Ffos Las the previous day. A half-brother to the illustrious Master Minded, he was always in rear and reportedly bled from the nose. (tchd 13-2)
Dee Ee Williams(IRE) didn't quite hit the heights forecast for him early in his career, but got off the mark over fences last time (his second try at chasing after three runs in the 09/10 season) at Kempton in a first-time visor, admittedly in a small field, where he ended up being the only finisher. He was chasing the leaders when coming down at the tenth. It was too far out to know what would have happened, but he wasn't being asked any questions at that stage. (op 12-1 tchd 14-1)

3194 HAPPY BIRTHDAY LAURA JUVENILE HURDLE (8 hdls) 2m 110y
12:30 (12:30) (Class 3) 3-Y-O **£4,878** (£1,432; £716; £357)

Form				RPR
3-52	1		**Grandouet (FR)**[46] 2356 3-11-8 136 ..... APMcCoy (Nicky Henderson) *trckd ldrs: wnt 2nd 3 out: led travelling smoothly wl bef 2 out: c clr on bit run-in: v easily* **11/10**[1]	143+
0	2	4 ½	**A Media Luz (FR)**[18] 2882 3-10-5 0 ..... AndrewTinkler (Nicky Henderson) *stdd and hld up in rr: hdwy to trck ldrs 3 out: chsd wnr appr next: sn rdn: effrt last but no imp: easily outpcd run-in but wl clr of 3rd* **7/1**[3]	116+
	3	18	**Mark Twain (IRE)**[73] 3-10-12 0 ..... JasonMaguire (Kim Bailey) *hit 1st: in rr: stl bhd whn mstke 3 out: hdwy fr 2 out but stl 5th jumping last: styd on to take wl hld 3rd cl home* **20/1**	107+
0	4	1	**L'Eminence Grise (IRE)**[53] 2211 3-10-12 0 ..... DarylJacob (Nick Williams) *hit 1st: chsd ldr to 3 out: outpcd appr 2 out: wknd sn after: lost 3rd cl home* **20/1**	105
5112	5	8	**Pullyourfingerout (IRE)**[18] 2882 3-11-8 132 .....(t) DougieCostello (Brendan Powell) *led to hdd wl bef 2 out: wknd sn after* **4/1**[2]	111+

0 **6** *15* **Langley**[14] 2958 3-10-9 0 MichaelMurphy(3) 84
(Pat Murphy) *in rr but in tch: mstke then hmpd 3 out: no ch whn wnt lft 2 out* **100/1**
7 *2 1/4* **Knockdolian (IRE)**[58] 3-10-12 0 TimmyMurphy 86
(Roger Charlton) *in rr but in tch: nt fluent 2nd: sme prog whn bdly hmpd 3 out: no ch after: wnt lft last* **18/1**
10 **F** **Domtaline (FR)**[61] 2078 3-10-13 0 IanPopham(5) —
(Paul Nicholls) *trcking ldrs: gng ok and disputing 2 1/2 l 2nd whn fell 3 out* **4/1**[2]

4m 12.75s (2.85) **Going Correction** +0.45s/f (Soft) **8** Ran SP% **115.9**
Speed ratings (Par 106): **111,108,100,99,96 89,88,—**
toteswingers:1&2:£2.90, 1&3:£3.30, 2&3:£65.80 CSF £9.72 TOTE £2.40: £1.10, £2.50, £4.30; EX 7.30.
Owner Simon Munir **Bred** Dominique Le Baron **Trained** Upper Lambourn, Berks

FOCUS
Previous renewals of this contest have been taken by Fred Winter types, if they make the Cheltenham festival, so it remains to be seen how high a rank this winner will get to. The early pace was far from frenetic, and saw most of the field hold a semblance of a chance turning in. Not an easy race to put a figure on but the winner is an obvious Triumph Hurdle contender.

NOTEBOOK
Grandouet(FR) ran much better on his second British outing when chasing home Sam Winner, albeit 15l behind but giving him 8lb, and that gelding went on to win again. He bolted up here after travelling to the front easily. Quotes for the Triumph Hurdle were soon forthcoming, but a couple of notes of caution should be taken on board. Firstly, his owner has a few options with juvenile hurdlers, and it's might also be worth noting that he was beaten 11l off level weights by Dolatulo in France, now trained by Paul Nicholls and also owned by Simon Munir. (op 10-11 tchd 6-5)
A Media Luz(FR) ◆ was a bitter disappointment on her debut after coming to the course with some classy French Flat form in Group company. She was much too keen on her hurdling debut but this was completely different, as she appeared to settle better after starting off at the back. Travelling strongly, she seemed to come there cruising when in view down the home straight but was ultimately put in her place by the winner, despite getting lots of weight. However, this was much better and she can go on to prove she has a future over hurdles, and may develop into a likely type for the Fred Winter if getting a win under her belt. (op 15-2)
Mark Twain(IRE), a fair sort on the Flat, made a highly encouraging start over hurdles, staying on from the rear to make ground throughout the final 2f. (op 25-1 tchd 16-1)
L'Eminence Grise(IRE), fancied but out the back on his only previous start, shaped much better here and does at least look to be going in the right direction. (op 25-1)
Pullyourfingerout(IRE), runner-up to Sam Winner on that horse's second British outing, was ridden by Tony McCoy last time but did have a tongue-tie back on for this. In the lead early, his jockey tried to kick on turning in, and headed to the stands' rail, but he was unable to get clear and was soon one-paced. The ground may have been softer than he wants considering his previous efforts. (tchd 7-2 and 9-2)
Knockdolian(IRE), a modest sort at up to 1m4f on the Flat for the same trainer, was making some ground when badly hampered by the faller. (op 25-1 tchd 16-1)
Domtaline(FR) bolted up in what looked an ordinary contest on his first run for Paul Nicholls but was easily beaten when sent for a Listed event at Wetherby in late October - the jockey reported that the gelding wasn't travelling after a mile. Absent since and a little keen early here, he was still in with a chance when tripping over three out. (op 5-1 tchd 11-2)

3195 BATHWICK TYRES SUPPORTS HEROS MANDARIN GRADUATION CHASE (18 fncs) 3m
1:00 (1:01) (Class 2) 4-Y-0+ **£16,262** (£4,775; £2,387; £1,192)

Form RPR
0/1- **1** **Pride Of Dulcote (FR)**[434] 1850 7-11-4 147 NickScholfield 158
(Paul Nicholls) *in ld 2nd and again whn bk in view 8th: and again whn bk in view 14th: jnd whn bk in view fnl 75yds: hld on gamely: all out:* **7/2**[2]
115- **2** *hd* **Punchestowns (FR)**[287] 4672 7-11-7 158 APMcCoy 161
(Nicky Henderson) *racing in cl 4th 2nd: trcking ldr and travelling wl whn bk in view 14th: chalng u.p whn bk in view fnl 75yds: no ex last strides* **4/11**[1]
P-36 **3** *40* **Tatenen (FR)**[39] 2517 6-11-7 140 LeightonAspell 125
(Richard Rowe) *trckd ldrs 2nd: disputing 2nd whn bk in view 8th: wkng whn bk in view 14th: t.o* **25/1**
0450 **4** *9* **Hills Of Aran**[32] 2673 8-11-7 144 RhysFlint 117
(Keith Goldsworthy) *w ldr whn in view 2nd: disputing 2nd whn bk in view 8th: wl bhd whn bk in view 14th: t.o* **16/1**[3]

ms (-371.00) **4** Ran SP% **105.3**
CSF £5.30 TOTE £3.00; EX 5.80.
Owner Mrs Angela Yeoman **Bred** Scea Marais Des Pictons **Trained** Ditcheat, Somerset

FOCUS
The two previous winners were the useful staying chasers Gone To Lunch and Carruthers and this year's renewal, despite the small field, looked another decent and intriguing contest, with all the runners rated 140 or more. The two horses returning from injury dominated the market and produced a close race, although due to the fog closing in, very little was visible. The first two are high-class chasers.

NOTEBOOK
Pride Of Dulcote(FR), a high-class novice hurdler two seasons ago, had been an easy winner on his chasing debut 14 months previously but sustained a leg injury and had been absent since. He made much of the running and, after being headed by the favourite having apparently made a mistake at the last, he battled back to regain the advantage near the line. He should come on considerably for the outing, and is quoted at 25/1 for the Gold Cup. It will be interesting to see where he goes next, with the Irish Hennessy one of several options. (op 3-1)
Punchestowns(FR), the highest rated in the line-up and winner of a Grade 1 at 2m4f last season, had finished well beaten in RSA Chase after chipping a bone on his hock. Sent off at odds-on, he was travelling well enough on the heels of the winner turning for home and held a slight advantage after the last, only to be run out of it near the line. He will have to improve on this if he is to be considered a serious Gold Cup contender, and might be given the chance to prove himself in the Aon Chase back here in February. (op 4-9 tchd 1-3)
Tatenen(FR) has been disappointing since making a good start over fences and was the lowest-rated runner. He came under pressure and dropped away from the last on the far side. (op 16-1)
Hills Of Aran, a dual winner in the summer on a sound surface, was being niggled with a circuit to go and was left behind going down the far side. The ground probably did not suit. (tchd 14-1)

3196 HEROS "ALL HORSES DESERVE A FUTURE" INTRODUCTORY HURDLE (8 hdls) 2m 110y
1:35 (1:35) (Class 3) 4-Y-0+ **£5,009** (£1,480; £740; £370; £184; £92)

Form RPR
11-1 **1** **Rock On Ruby (IRE)**[45] 2389 5-11-0 0 (t) HarrySkelton 138+
(Paul Nicholls) *in ld whn in view after 2nd: in ld whn in view appr 3 out: in ld and drvn whn bk in view fnl 50yds: styd on wl* **4/1**[3]
51-1 **2** *6* **Megastar**[40] 2495 5-11-5 0 JamieMoore 137+
(Gary Moore) *in tch whn in view after 1st: chsng ldrs whn bk in view appr 3 out: chsng wnr but no imp u.p whn bk in view fnl 50yds* **2/1**[2]
13-1 **3** *6* **Kid Cassidy (IRE)**[33] 2666 4-11-5 0 APMcCoy 132
(Nicky Henderson) *in tch whn in view after 1st: shkn up and hdwy whn bk in view appr 3 out: chsng ldng duo but no ch whn bk in view fnl 50yds* **11/8**[1]
1-1 **4** *5* **Muldoon's Picnic (IRE)**[59] 2109 4-11-5 0 JasonMaguire 129
(Kim Bailey) *chsng ldrs whn in view after 1st: chsng wnr and rdn whn bk in view appr 3 out: one pce in 4th whn bk in view fnl 50yds* **11/1**
2 **5** *15* **Buddy Holly**[25] 1832 5-11-0 0 WillKennedy 109
(Violet M Jordan) *in tch whn in view after 1st: stl in tch whn bk in view appr 3 out: wl bhd whn bk in view fnl 50yds* **66/1**
06-4 **6** *1 3/4* **Soleil D'Avril (FR)**[49] 2310 4-11-0 0 RobertThornton 107
(Alan King) *chsng ldrs whn in view after 1st: rdn and stl wl there whn bk in view appr 3 out: wl btn whn bk in view fnl 50yds* **40/1**
00 **7** *14* **Sulpius (GER)**[24] 2791 5-10-7 0 NathanSweeney(7) 95
(Bob Buckler) *chsng wnr whn in view after 1st: rdn and losing position whn bk in view appr 3 out: wl btn whn bk in view fnl 50yds* **200/1**
25 **8** *1* **Fiddlededee (IRE)**[55] 2168 5-10-4 0 RichieMcLernon(3) 87
(Jonjo O'Neill) *in rr whn in view after 1st: in rr whn bk in view appr 3 out: wl bhd whn bk in view fnl 50yds* **40/1**
9 *10* **Decoy (FR)**[134] 4-11-5 0 TomScudamore 90
(David Pipe) *chsng ldrs whn in view after 1st: stl in tch whn bk in view appr 3 out: wl btn whn bk in view fnl 50yds* **20/1**
00 **10** *1 1/4* **Champs De Bleu (FR)**[8] 3055 7-10-7 0 JoshuaMoore(7) 84
(Gary Moore) *in rr whn in view after 1st: in rr whn bk in view appr 3 out and wl bhd whn bk in view fnl 50yds* **200/1**
0 **11** *14* **That'lldoboy (FR)**[50] 2283 4-11-0 0 NickScholfield 71
(Paul Nicholls) *in rr whn in view after 1st: in rr whn bk in view appr 3 out: wl bhd whn bk in view fnl 50yds* **100/1**
2 **12** *31* **Charles**[80] 1799 4-11-0 0 SeanQuinlan 43
(Kim Bailey) *in rr whn in view after 1st: in rr whn bk in view appr 3 out: wl bhd whn bk in view fnl 50yds* **100/1**

ms (-249.90) **12** Ran SP% **117.9**
toteswingers:1&2:£1.70, 1&3:£1.10, 2&3:£1.30 CSF £12.46 TOTE £4.60: £1.30, £1.60, £1.20; EX 11.80.
Owner The Festival Goers **Bred** John O'Dwyer **Trained** Ditcheat, Somerset

FOCUS
Good horses win this race as such as Dave's Dream, Khyber Kim and Duc De Regniere prove. However, no-one had the slightest idea what happened in this, as visibility was extremely limited. This was smart novice form nevertheless.

NOTEBOOK
Rock On Ruby(IRE) ◆, the winner of three of his four starts in bumpers, including a Listed contest at Cheltenham on his final attempt in that sphere, won by a comfortable margin after setting off in front. It's impossible to know what he did during the contest, but is obviously an exciting prospect. The jockey felt Rock On Ruby will get 2m4f quite easily and the Neptune Novices' Hurdle looks his best option should he head to Cheltenham in March. (op 11-2 tchd 6-1)
Megastar ◆ looked a horse with a massive future over hurdles judged on his effort at Ascot back in mid-November, and followed Rock On Ruby home. It probably wasn't a bad effort giving 5lb away to the winner. (op 5-2)
Kid Cassidy(IRE), bidding to give Nicky Henderson his fourth consecutive winner of this race, won easily over C&D on his hurdling debut but appeared to pull very hard in the early stages. He then seemed to lose his position down the side of the course when emerging from the fog, before appearing to run on inside the final half a furlong. (op 11-10 tchd 6-4 and 13-8 in places)
Muldoon's Picnic(IRE), unbeaten in one bumper and one maiden hurdle coming into this, finished a decent fourth after appearing to race prominently and clearly has his share of ability. (op 10-1)
Buddy Holly had shown some aptitude for hurdling at Wetherby - he has run twice since on the Flat.
Decoy(FR), a 10l winner of his only start over hurdles for John Hammond in France after winning one of his seven outings on the Flat, is a half-brother to the ill-fated 2010 Albert Bartlett runner-up Najaf, and will presumably be capable of better in time, possibly over further. (op 16-1)

3197 SPORTINGBET SUPPORTS HEROS CHARITY CHALLOW NOVICES' HURDLE GRADE 1 (10 hdls) 2m 5f
2:10 (2:10) (Class 1) 4-Y-0+ **£19,953** (£7,486; £3,748; £1,869; £938; £469)

Form RPR
1 **1** **Backspin (IRE)**[14] 2954 5-11-7 0 APMcCoy 147+
(Jonjo O'Neill) *trcking ldrs whn in view bef 1st and after 3rd: chalng whn in view again appr 3 out: clr whn in view again fnl 50yds: pushed out* **5/1**[3]
F2-1 **2** *8* **Court In Motion (IRE)**[57] 2142 5-11-7 132 SamThomas 140
(Emma Lavelle) *in rr whn in view bef 1st and after 3rd: hdwy to trck ldrs whn bk in view appr 3 out: styng on to chse wnr but no imp whn bk in view fnl 50yds* **5/1**[3]
12-F **3** *1 3/4* **Al Ferof (FR)**[19] 2873 5-11-7 0 HarrySkelton 138
(Paul Nicholls) *in rr whn in view bef 1st and after 3rd: hdwy to chse ldrs whn bk in view appr 3 out: one pce u.p whn bk in view fnl 50yds* **5/2**[2]
3-12 **4** *2 1/4* **For Non Stop (IRE)**[45] 2387 5-11-7 135 DarylJacob 136+
(Nick Williams) *chsng ldrs whn in view bef 1st and after 3rd: slt ld whn bk in view appr 3 out but sn jnd: styng on same pce and no ch w ldrs whn bk in view fnl 50yds* **9/4**[1]
012 **5** *3* **Tullyraine (IRE)**[66] 1990 6-11-7 132 PaddyBrennan 133
(Nigel Twiston-Davies) *chsng ldrs whn in view bef 1st and after 3rd: rdn to stay prom whn bk in view appr 3 out: one pce 5th whn bk in view fnl 50yds* **33/1**
2122 **6** *70* **Youralltalk (IRE)**[42] 2454 6-11-7 113 JamieMoore 70
(Keith Goldsworthy) *chsng ldrs whn in view bef 1st: in slt ld whn bk in view after 3rd: wkng and no ch whn bk in view appr 3 out: t.o* **66/1**
1 **7** *1/2* **Act Of Kalanisi (IRE)**[32] 2667 4-11-7 0 RichardJohnson 70
(Dr Richard Newland) *chsng ldrs whn in view bef 1st and after 3rd: stl wl there and pushed along whn bk in view appr 3 out: wl bhd whn bk in view fnl 50yds: t.o* **7/1**
2 **P** **Top Benefit (IRE)**[37] 2571 8-11-7 0 JasonMaguire —
(Keith Goldsworthy) *in ld whn in view bef 1st: in tch whn bk in view after 3rd: no ch whn bk in view bef 3 out: p.u* **100/1**

5m 21.22s (2.22) **Going Correction** +0.45s/f (Soft)
WFA 4 from 5yo+ 6lb **8** Ran SP% **110.6**
Speed ratings (Par 117): **113,109,109,108,107 80,80,—**
toteswingers:1&2:£3.30, 1&3:£1.40, 2&3:£1.40 CSF £27.52 TOTE £5.60: £1.60, £1.80, £1.40; EX 34.80 Trifecta £129.20 Pool: £1385.52 - 7.93 winning units..
Owner John P McManus **Bred** Brittas House Stud **Trained** Cheltenham, Gloucs

FOCUS
This Grade 1 has been won by several that have gone on to be high-class chasers in recent seasons, most notably Denman and this season's Hennessy winner Diamond Harry. This year's race looked an interesting contest, with several stepping up in trip and others dropping back from 3m. The pace did not appear strong early on but the first four in the market filled the frame, although not in the right order betting-wise. A big step up from the winner but he is still below the level that will be required at Cheltenham.

NOTEBOOK

Backspin(IRE) ◆ beat three subsequent winners when taking his bumper at Punchestown in April and won at Bangor on his first start for current connections. Up in trip and grade, and tackling soft ground for the first time, he was always travelling well and came away to win in decisive fashion. He looks a really good prospect and was quoted at 10/1 for the Neptune Novices' Hurdle at the Festival, although he is shorter for the Albert Bartlett over 3m. (op 6-1)

Court In Motion(IRE) was placed in a bumper here on his debut, and the first seven from that contest have all won at least once since. He got off the mark over hurdles at the third attempt upped to this trip last time and, after travelling well, stayed on without troubling the winner. (op 6-1)

Al Ferof(FR), a dual bumper winner and runner-up in Cheltenham Festival bumper, was leading when taking a heavy fall on his hurdling debut at Cheltenham. Trying the trip for the first time, he moved up threateningly off the home bend but did not appear to sustain his effort. (op 9-4 tchd 11-4 in places)

For Non Stop(IRE), the winner of a novices' handicap at Chepstow, had run well against a handicap good thing and subsequent winner at Cheltenham over this trip. He was sent off favourite on the basis of that performance against a subsequent winner who is now rated in the high 150s, and had the highest rating of those with marks. Never far away, he was upsides the winner three out but faded out of the placings after the last. Perhaps the trip on this ground proved too much, especially as he was reported to have missed work due to the bad weather. (op 5-2 tchd 11-4 in places)

Tullyraine(IRE), runner-up in an Irish point and a winner over 3m on his hurdling debut, was dropping in trip and up in grade. He did not run too badly and will appreciate a return to further. (op 40-1)

Act Of Kalanisi(IRE), a resolute stayer on the Flat and a winner on his debut over hurdles on this track over 2m, looked likely to appreciate the step up in trip but, after being close up turning in, he dropped right away in the straight. (op 15-2 tchd 8-1)

3198 NORTH FARM STUD "THE HOME OF HEROS" NOVICES' H'CAP CHASE (17 fncs) 2m 6f 110y

2:45 (2:45) (Class 3) (0-130,129) 4-Y-O+ **£5,854** (£1,719; £859; £429)

Form				RPR
0-52	**1**		**Misstree Dancer**[15] 2945 6-11-3 **120** ... HarrySkelton (Nick Mitchell) *chsng ldrs whn in view 7th and again appr 4 out: reported to be 2nd whn lft in ld last: drvn whn bk in view fnl 50yds* **16/1**	133
4-14	**2**	*1*	**Ravethebrave (IRE)**[19] 2869 6-11-5 **122** ... RobertThornton (Alan King) *chsng ldrs whn in view after 7th and appr 4 out: chsng wnr and no imp whn bk in view fnl 50yds* **9/1**	133
P414	**3**	*5*	**The Rainbow Hunter**[15] 2948 6-11-0 **124** ... EdCookson(7) (Andy Turnell) *chsng ldrs whn in view after 7th and again appr 4 out: one pce in 3rd whn bk into view fnl 50yds* **12/1**	130
1-42	**4**	*2 ¾*	**Promising Anshan (IRE)**[14] 2959 5-11-4 **126** ... MrRMahon(5) (Paul Nicholls) *disputing ld whn in view after 2nd and after 7th: rdn but stl wl there whn bk in view appr 4 out: no imp on ldrs whn bk in view fnl 50yds* **3/1**[1]	130
4252	**5**	*nk*	**Swing Bill (FR)**[47] 2343 9-11-7 **127** ... DannyCook(3) (David Pipe) *chsng ldrs whn in view after 2nd and after 7th: pressing ldrs whn bk in view approachng 4 out: no ch u.p whn bk in view fnl 50yds* **15/2**	131
1122	**6**	*11*	**In The Zone (IRE)**[32] 2670 6-10-13 **119** ... RichieMcLernon(3) (Jonjo O'Neill) *in tch whn in view after 2nd and after 7th: rdn and one pce whn bk in view appr 4 out: wl btn whn bk in view fnl 50yds* **9/1**	113
20-2	**7**	*shd*	**Tarateeno**[40] 2501 7-11-4 **124** ... MichaelMurphy(3) (Pat Murphy) *chsng ldrs whn in view after 7th: rdn and no imp whn bk in view appr 4 out: no ch whn bk in view fnl 50yds* **16/1**	118
-213	**8**	*2 ½*	**Regal Approach (IRE)**[19] 2869 7-11-4 **121** ... (p) JasonMaguire (Kim Bailey) *chsng ldrs whn in view after 2nd and after 7th: rdn whn bk in view bef 4 out: bhd whn bk in view fnl 50yds* **5/1**[2]	112
64-1	**9**	*dist*	**Ashfield's Dream**[52] 2248 6-11-10 **127** ... PaulMoloney (Evan Williams) *in rr whn in view after 2nd and after 7th: wl bhd whn bk in view appr 4 out and t.o whn bk in view fnl 50yds* **12/1**	—
542P	**F**		**Federstar (GER)**[38] 2544 8-10-12 **118** ... JimmyDerham(3) (Milton Harris) *in rr whn in view after 7th: reportedly fell bef 4 out* **40/1**	—
5/65	**P**		**Altilhar (USA)**[33] 2662 7-11-3 **120** ... (b) JamieMoore (Gary Moore) *a in rr whn in view: p.u* **40/1**	—
6-32	**P**		**Psi (USA)**[39] 2529 5-10-7 **110** ... (p) AndrewGlassonbury (Gary Moore) *in rr whn in view after 7th: p.u* **25/1**	—
-U23	**U**		**Ikorodu Road**[14] 2959 7-11-12 **129** ... JohnnyFarrelly (Martin Keighley) *slt ld whn in view after 2nd and after 7th: stl slt ld and rdn whn bk in view appr 4 out: reported 2 l ahd whn uns rdr last* **7/1**[3]	142+
5P-6	**P**		**Llama Farmer**[33] 2662 5-11-3 **120** ... DominicElsworth (Paul Webber) *in tch whn in view after 7th: bhd whn in view bef 4 out and p.u* **20/1**	—
21-P	**F**		**Flanagan (IRE)**[55] 2171 6-10-12 **115** ... AidanColeman (Venetia Williams) *in rr whn in view after 7th: reportedly fell bef 4 out* **33/1**	—

ms (-350.30) **15** Ran SP% **129.5**

toteswingers:1&2:£48.60, 1&3:£64.00, 2&3:£46.00 CSF £155.30 CT £1826.82 TOTE £24.00: £6.80, £3.60, £5.70; EX 189.10.

Owner Mrs Sarah Faulks **Bred** Mr And Mrs N Faulks **Trained** Piddletrenthide, Dorset

FOCUS

A fair and competitive handicap chase with the first two on the upgrade.

NOTEBOOK

Misstree Dancer, who had shown promise on her chasing debut under rules last time, prevailed after racing prominently, although was seemingly a lucky winner, as she made a mistake two out before being left in front at the final fence - Harry Skelton did say afterwards that he felt his mount would have fought all the way to the line had Ikorodu Road stayed upright. A dual point-to-point winner, she will get a bit further and handles better ground considering those two successes between the flags, so she is one to watch for during the spring in a decent handicap. (op 18-1)

Ravethebrave(IRE) emerged as the winner's biggest threat after looking to be going well turning into the home straight, but couldn't get to her. (op 8-1)

The Rainbow Hunter looked high in the weights on his two successes in handicap company, but did hold Regal Approach on their meeting at Ffos Las, and confirmed that form. The jockey reported afterwards that his mount wants 3m and better ground. (op 25-1)

Promising Anshan(IRE), a place in front of Ikorodu Road earlier this month, was under strong pressure leaving the back straight but wasn't beaten too far in the end. (op 7-2 tchd 4-1 in places)

Swing Bill(FR), down in distance, looked to have every chance when in view and seemed to run his race.

Regal Approach(IRE), in front of Ravethebrave on his previous outing, won a C&D handicap in November off a 6lb lower mark. He moved into contention going strongly but dropped out in this ground. (op 13-2)

Ashfield's Dream ◆ looked potentially fairly treated after winning on his chasing debut (the third has won since) but was pulling very hard in rear when he could be seen. He is probably better than his final position suggests, but his jockey said afterwards the race wasn't run quickly enough for his mount. (op 10-1)

Ikorodu Road, taking a drop in trip after running well at this course over 3m last time, was matched at short prices on the exchanges and, after making much of the running, was reported to be about 2l in front at the last when coming down. (op 8-1)

3199 A.P. WINS SPORTS PERSONALITY LONG WALK HURDLE GRADE 1 (12 hdls) 3m 110y

3:20 (3:20) (Class 1) 4-Y-O+ **£22,638** (£8,594; £4,354; £2,230; £1,170)

Form				RPR
11-1	**1**		**Big Buck's (FR)**[32] 2672 7-11-7 174 ... APMcCoy (Paul Nicholls) *trcking ldrs whn in view after 2nd: and after 5th: slt ld whn in view after 4 out: cl 2nd whn bk in view appr 3 out but travelling wl: in ld on bit whn in view again fnl 50yds* **2/13**[1]	167+
-000	**2**	*6*	**Lough Derg (FR)**[39] 2516 10-11-7 140 ... (v) TomScudamore (David Pipe) *led and clr whn in view after 2nd: stl clr whn in view after 5th: narrowly hdd whn in view after 4 out: led again whn in view bef next: all out to hold 2nd whn in view fnl 50yds: no ch w wnr* **40/1**	155
-330	**3**	*hd*	**Restless Harry**[18] 2884 6-11-7 149 ... HenryOliver (Robin Dickin) *chsng ldrs whn in view after 2nd: disputing 2nd whn in view after 5th: rdn and outpcd whn in view appr 3 out: rallied u.p whn in view fnl 50yds: nt quite get up for 2nd: no ch w wnr* **12/1**[3]	155
-256	**4**	*20*	**Kayf Aramis**[18] 2884 8-11-7 148 ... (p) PaddyBrennan (Nigel Twiston-Davies) *chsng ldrs whn in tch after 5th: rdn and no ch whn bk in view appr 3 out* **33/1**	137
-30B	**5**	*25*	**Afsoun (FR)**[19] 2870 8-11-7 143 ... AlexMerriam (Neil King) *in rr but in tch whn in view after 5th: rdn and bhd whn in view appr 3 out: t.o whn in view fnl 50yds* **100/1**	114
1-42	**P**		**Duc De Regniere (FR)**[32] 2672 8-11-7 154 ... AndrewTinkler (Nicky Henderson) *in tch whn in view after 5th: rdn and wkng whn in view after 4 out: reportedly p.u bef 2 out* **9/1**[2]	—

ms (-368.30) **6** Ran SP% **110.7**

toteswingers:1&2:£2.70, 1&3:£1.40, 2&3:£5.90 CSF £10.64 TOTE £1.10: £1.10, £6.80; EX 12.50.

Owner The Stewart Family **Bred** Henri Poulat **Trained** Ditcheat, Somerset

FOCUS

This race was cancelled when the weather curtailed racing a week before Christmas, but it was the second season in a row that the contest had been moved to Newbury due to the abandonment of Ascot. Big Buck's was value for further with Lough Derg back to his best 2010 form.

NOTEBOOK

Big Buck's(FR) emerged from the fog easily going clear and won in the manner one would expect from a horse head and shoulders above his contemporaries. This told us little we didn't already know about him, and he remains in imperious form. It's difficult to see where the danger is going to come from in his bid to retain the World Hurdle in March, as a look at his market rivals for that race don't look anywhere good enough to trouble him all things being equal, and it's a little surprising to see his odds not even shorter than they currently are. Only the possibility of Long Run returning to hurdles or an appearance by dual David Nicholson winner Quevega would give that race some serious interest at the moment. He will now head to the Cleeve Hurdle at Cheltenham on the 29th January. (op 1-6 tchd 1-5 in places)

Lough Derg(FR), who has also won this race before, albeit at Ascot, gained a decent advantage as they jumped off but looked to be struggling leaving the back straight, so it was a surprise to see him still challenging the winner turning into the home straight. He hasn't gone close for a long time, so he either holds the form down or bounced back to something closer to his best. The former seems more likely.

Restless Harry, who tracked the leader upsides the winner for much of the way, got outpaced early in the straight but was making ground with every stride in the latter stages and would have been second in a few more strides.

Kayf Aramis seemingly never got involved. (op 28-1)

Afsoun(FR) was going well leaving the back straight but faded. (op 66-1)

Duc De Regniere(FR) was struggling a long way out and was most disappointing. (op 17-2)

3200 HELP HEROS - HELP HORSES CHARITY STANDARD OPEN NATIONAL HUNT FLAT RACE 2m 110y

3:50 (3:51) (Class 5) 4-6-Y-O **£1,626** (£477; £238; £119)

Form				RPR
	1		**African Broadway (IRE)**[255] 4-11-2 0 ... JohnnyFarrelly (David Pipe) *w ldrs whn in view after 2f: slt ld whn in view again 6f out: clr whn in view again fnl 30yds* **50/1**	119+
	2	*16*	**Cresswell Bramble** 6-10-9 0 ... TimmyMurphy (Keith Goldsworthy) *chsng ldrs whn in view 6f out: chsng wnr and no ch whn in view fnl 30yds* **33/1**	96
-1	**3**	*½*	**Batonnier (FR)**[231] 284 4-11-9 0 ... RobertThornton (Alan King) *in rr whn in view after 2f: improving whn in view 6f out: styng on to press for 2nd whn in view fnl 30yds* **8/1**[3]	109
6-	**4**	*hd*	**Presenting Ace (IRE)**[314] 4123 4-11-2 0 ... TomScudamore (David Pipe) *in tch whn in view after 2f: styng on whn in view 6f out: styng on to press for 3rd whn in view fnl 30yds* **14/1**	102
	5	*6*	**Airdrie (IRE)**[229] 4-11-2 0 ... AndrewThornton (Henrietta Knight) *in ld whn in view after 2f: narrowly hdd whn in view 6f out: one pce whn bk in view fnl 30yds* **40/1**	96
	6	*8*	**Wiesentraum (GER)** 4-11-2 0 ... LeightonAspell (Lucy Wadham) *in rr but styng on whn in view 6f out: one pce whn in view fnl 30yds* **40/1**	88
	7	*¾*	**Paddy The Hare (IRE)** 5-11-2 0 ... RichardJohnson (Dr Richard Newland) *in rr whn in view after 2f: styng on whn in view 6f out: no ch w ldrs whn in view fnl 30yds* **20/1**	88
	8	*5*	**Accordingtojodie (IRE)**[123] 1414 4-11-9 0 ... APMcCoy (Nicky Henderson) *chsng ldrs whn in view after 2f: chalng whn in view 6f out: no ch whn bk in view fnl 30yds* **13/8**[1]	90
6	**9**	*6*	**Get Ready To Go (IRE)**[34] 2646 6-11-2 0 ... DenisO'Regan (Neil King) *chsng ldrs whn in view 6f out: no ch whn in view fnl 30yds* **100/1**	77
	10	*½*	**Airmen's Friend (IRE)** 4-10-13 0 ... PeterToole(3) (Charlie Mann) *chsng ldrs whn in view after 2f: stl in tch but pushed along whn in view 6f out: no ch whn in view fnl 30yds* **33/1**	76
00	**11**	*28*	**Kidajo**[44] 2432 4-11-2 0 ... DaveCrosse (Roger Curtis) *mid-div whn in view 6f out: no ch whn in view fnl 30yds* **200/1**	48
6-	**12**	*½*	**Another Dimension (IRE)**[254] 5283 4-10-9 0 ... CharlieWallis(7) (Nigel Dunger) *in tch whn in view 6f out: no ch whn in view fnl 30yds* **80/1**	48
	13	*nk*	**Numbercruncher (IRE)** 4-11-2 0 ... DougieCostello (Brendan Powell) *in tch whn in view 6f out: no ch whn in view fnl 30yds* **66/1**	47
0	**14**	*1 ¾*	**Menepresents (IRE)**[56] 2156 5-10-9 0 ... HaddenFrost (Henrietta Knight) *in tch whn in view 6f out: no ch whn in view fnl 30yds* **100/1**	38

360- **15** *shd* **Keltic Crisis (IRE)**[334] 3732 6-11-2 0 JimmyMcCarthy 45
(Jonathan Geake) *in rr whn in view 6f out: no ch whn in view fnl 30yds* **100/1**
16 *3* **Leath Acra Mor (IRE)** 4-11-2 0 JasonMaguire 42
(Ian Williams) *in rr whn in view 6f out: in rr whn in view fnl 30yds* **66/1**
200- **17** *nse* **Padre Eterno**[275] 4932 5-11-2 0 DominicElsworth 42
(Heather Main) *in rr whn in view 6f out: no ch whn in view fnl 30yds* **100/1**
18 *3 ½* **Suspect (GER)** 4-10-11 0 MrRMahon(5) 39
(Paul Nicholls) *in tch whn in view after 2f: chsng ldrs whn in view 6f out: wl bhd whn in view fnl 30yds* **3/1**[2]
0 **19** *¾* **Go On Arch (IRE)**[45] 2389 4-11-2 0 PaddyBrennan 38
(Nigel Twiston-Davies) *chsng ldrs whn in view 6f out: wl bhd whn in view fnl 30yds* **8/1**[3]
4 **20** *21* **El Padrino (IRE)**[53] 2215 5-11-2 0 LiamTreadwell 17
(Nick Gifford) *rdn and wkng whn in view 6f out: wl bhd whn in view fnl 30yds* **16/1**

ms (-244.30) **20** Ran SP% **124.0**
toteswingers:1&2:£141.20, 1&3:£57.50, 2&3:£18.00 CSF £1231.11 TOTE £57.50: £13.40, £9.50, £3.20; EX 1582.10.
Owner A E Frost **Bred** Joseph Power **Trained** Nicholashayne, Devon

FOCUS
Visibility for the concluding race on the card was virtually zero, so it was impossible to gauge accurately what happened. The winner is probably a decent 4yo.

NOTEBOOK
African Broadway(IRE) showed promise in a couple of Irish points in April (still in the lead when falling on the first occasion and narrowly beaten the second time). Subject of reasonably positive comments in a stable tour, he came home a wide-margin winner from what looked a decent field. Johnny Farrelly reported afterwards that his mount is a stayer in the making, and he was pleased how he stuck to the task while being on his own down the home straight. (op 40-1)
Cresswell Bramble, a half-sister to Cresswell Bubbles, who made a winning bumper debut for this yard, got up for second and Timmy Murphy reported she was green and will improve.
Batonnier(FR) was a well-backed favourite when winning a bumper at Fontwell (1m6f on good ground) despite showing signs of inexperience, and did enough here under a penalty to get third. He is probably a decent type. (tchd 15-2)
Presenting Ace(IRE), having his first start for David Pipe, shaped with some promise in what was a decent Ffos Las bumper last season, and probably improved on that here. He can win something similar.
Airdrie(IRE), fourth and second twice in three starts between the flags in Ireland earlier in year, will surely do better with time. (op 33-1)
Wiesentraum(GER), a half-brother to 2m2f chase winner Wiesenfurst, pleased his rider, who said afterwards that he felt his horse would have more to come. (op 33-1)
Paddy The Hare(IRE), a brother to his stable's 2m3f-2m4f hurdle winner Good Old Thyme, could be seen travelling nicely turning back in and might be capable of more. (tchd 16-1)
Accordingtojodie(IRE) justified favouritism in a small field at Galway (2m on good to firm ground) in August for Thomas Mullins, and was then sold to join Nicky Henderson's stable. Racing prominently, he was disappointing considering his starting price but the ground here was very different to the one he was successful on, so should be given another chance. (op 6-4 tchd 11-8)
Suspect(GER) has a smart German Flat pedigree (his dam is a half-sister to top-class 1m4f performer Shirocco, and 10.5f-2m Group winner Subiaco) but was well beaten. His jockey reported afterwards that his mount was very green and clueless, but he also felt that something may have been amiss with his mount, as he'd shown plenty at home. (op 4-1, tchd 9-2 in places)
Go On Arch(IRE) didn't run too badly when making his debut behind Rock On Ruby in a Listed bumper at Cheltenham, but seemingly ran below that sort of form in this. (op 15-2)
T/Jkpt: Part won. £7,100.00 to a £1 stake. Pool: £10,000.00 - 0.50 winning tickets. T/Plt: £74.60 to a £1 stake. Pool: £108,288.43 - 1,058.58 winning tickets T/Qpdt: £54.10 to a £1 stake. Pool: £5,376.05 - 73.44 winning tickets ST

3201 - 3202a (Foreign Racing) - See Raceform Interactive

3172 LEOPARDSTOWN (L-H)
Wednesday, December 29
OFFICIAL GOING: Heavy

3203a PADDYPOWERPOKER.COM FUTURE CHAMPIONS NOVICE HURDLE (GRADE 1) (8 hdls) 2m
12:50 (12:50) 4-Y-0+ **£46,017** (£13,451; £6,371; £2,123)

RPR
1 **First Lieutenant (IRE)**[56] 2159 5-11-10 DNRussell 145
(M F Morris, Ire) *trckd ldr in 2nd: tk clsr order appr 2 out: sn rdn to chal: led last: kpt on wl u.p: all out* **16/1**
2 *nk* **Zaidpour (FR)**[14] 2967 4-11-7 PTownend 142+
(W P Mullins, Ire) *trckd ldrs in 3rd: tended to jump sltly rt: 3 l down and pushed along ent st: rdn after last: no imp tl r.o wl last 100yds* **1/4**[1]
3 *½* **Hidden Cyclone (IRE)**[52] 2260 5-11-10 AndrewJMcNamara 145
(John Joseph Hanlon, Ire) *attempted to make all: t.k.h early: rdn and strly pressed fr 2 out: hdd whn slt mstke last: kpt on u.p* **5/1**[2]
4 *4 ½* **Perfect Smile (IRE)**[14] 2967 5-11-10 132 (t) PCarberry 140
(Noel Meade, Ire) *hld up in tch: cl 4th appr 2 out: sn rdn and one pce* **14/1**[3]
5 *7* **Hazeymm (IRE)**[14] 2969 7-11-10 124 BarryGeraghty 133
(E J O'Grady, Ire) *hld up in tch: cl 5th appr 2 out: sn no ex* **33/1**

4m 2.70s (-4.80) **Going Correction** -0.15s/f (Good)
WFA 4 from 5yo+ 5lb **5** Ran SP% **112.2**
Speed ratings: **106,105,105,103,99**
CSF £22.69 TOTE £9.50: £2.70, £1.02; DF 23.30.
Owner Gigginstown House Stud **Bred** Mrs Mary O'Connor **Trained** Fethard, Co Tipperary

FOCUS
A small, but altogether select field for this race. The pace was sensible, even if the race was won in a time eight seconds faster than Hurricane Fly in the day's big race. The fifth limits the level.

NOTEBOOK
First Lieutenant(IRE) ◆ showed just why he is held in such high regard. Quite probably a Gold Cup horse in time, he disappointed at Fairyhouse in November but that run was all wrong. He wants further than this, but was cleverly ridden and had the upper hand most of the way up the straight. What was most encouraging was how he stuck his neck out all the way up the run-in, showing a resolution that will stand him in good stead. It would be no surprise if connections were wary of taking, what his trainer calls, "a horse for next year" to Cheltenham, but if he did go, it would be for something like the Neptune. He has a cracking future ahead of him.
Zaidpour(FR), monstrously impressive in the Royal Bond, did not look the same horse here. His trainer predictably said post-race that this contest came too soon. That is probably true, and there are two points to consider: he was never travelling as well here as he had at Fairyhouse and he also was probably given too much to do in a tactical race. His rider never hit him until well after the last, and he arguably should have been more vigorous between the last two flights. Official explanation: jockey said gelding jumped right down the back straight and was unable to pick up when asked for his effort approaching the 2nd last hurdle (op 30/100)
Hidden Cyclone(IRE) was able to dictate his own pace, which considerably helped his cause, and his jumping is consistent with a horse who will be seen to best effect when tackling fences. This was a cracking effort for a horse who wants further and still looks inexperienced, and he'll return to Leopardstown at the Hennessy meeting over 2m4f. (op 4/1)
Perfect Smile(IRE) gives the form solidity. He travelled well but predictably just could not pick up superior horses over this trip. He appeals as a horse worth trying over further. (op 14/1 tchd 12/1)
Hazeymm(IRE) was outclassed but not disgraced in the circumstances.

3204a PADDY POWER DIAL-A-BET CHASE (GRADE 1) (11 fncs) 2m 1f
1:20 (1:21) 5-Y-0+ **£57,522** (£16,814; £7,964; £2,654)

RPR
1 **Big Zeb (IRE)**[52] 2262 9-11-12 174 BarryGeraghty 165+
(C A Murphy, Ire) *cl up in 3rd: j.w: 2nd fr 3 out: disp ld travelling best 2 out: led ent st: 3l clr after last: hrd rdn and one pce last 100yds: all out* **1/1**[1]
2 *1 ¾* **Golden Silver (FR)**[14] 2972 8-11-12 166 PTownend 163+
(W P Mullins, Ire) *trckd ldr in 2nd: 3rd 3 out: in tch stl travelling wl after 2 out: slt mstke last: drvn out and kpt on wl wout ever threatening wnr* **15/8**[2]
3 *1* **Scotsirish (IRE)**[14] 2972 9-11-12 152 DJCondon 162
(W P Mullins, Ire) *led: rdn and jnd 2 out: hdd ent st: rdr lost whip appr last: kpt on same pce run-in* **22/1**
4 *6* **Captain Cee Bee (IRE)**[60] 2096 9-11-12 158 MPWalsh 157
(Edward P Harty, Ire) *hld up in rr: nt fluent 3rd: rdn and no imp fr 2 out: kpt on same pce* **7/2**[3]

4m 24.9s (2.90) **Going Correction** -0.075s/f (Good) **4** Ran SP% **111.4**
Speed ratings: **90,89,88,85**
CSF £3.50 TOTE £1.40; DF 2.90.
Owner Patrick Joseph Redmond **Bred** Lyle Buttimer **Trained** Gorey, Co Wexford

FOCUS
With Arkle winner Sizing Europe stepping up in trip this term, the three best 2m chasers on these shores lined up for an intriguing renewal of this contest. The front-running third was not beaten far and sets the standard.

NOTEBOOK
Big Zeb(IRE) ◆ maintained his superiority over Golden Silver and, although the winning margin was being reduced on the run-in, Geraghty always appeared to have matters under control after the last. Settled in behind Scotsirish and Golden Silver, Big Zeb never touched a twig throughout and made ground on his opponents in the air. A big jump at the second-last took him upsides Scotsirish and Geraghty kicked for home rounding the final bend, where he took three lengths out of the field. He pinged the last but didn't stretch right away from Golden Silver as one might have expected. However, given Murphy's comments after the race, that the winner had missed an important piece of work in the cold snap, he could be excused for failing to do so. The Tied Cottage Chase is next on the horizon. (op 5/4)
Golden Silver(FR) didn't jump as well as he can and, although he got to within a length and a half of the winner, he never looked like overturning the favourite. He would have preferred a stronger gallop, is a top performer in his own right and will mop up the races that Big Zeb doesn't appear in at home. (op 7/4)
Scotsirish(IRE) ◆ ran a cracker and may have even finished closer had his jockey not lost his whip rounding the final bend. (op 25/1 tchd 20/1)
Captain Cee Bee(IRE) was the big disappointment but he hated the ground and a line should be put through this. He will return to his best on a livelier surface. (op 3/1)

3205a PADDYPOWER.COM IPHONE APP FESTIVAL HURDLE (GRADE 1) (8 hdls) 2m
1:55 (1:55) 4-Y-0+ **£51,769** (£15,132; £7,168; £2,389)

RPR
1 **Hurricane Fly (IRE)**[14] 2968 6-11-10 166 PTownend 164+
(W P Mullins, Ire) *trckd ldr in 2nd: cl up travelling wl fr 2 out: led on bridle last: drew clr: nt extended: impressive* **8/11**[1]
2 *2* **Solwhit (FR)**[14] 2968 6-11-10 165 DNRussell 157+
(C Byrnes, Ire) *trckd ldrs in 3rd: slt mstke at 3rd: cl up travelling wl fr 2 out: effrt on inner whn nt fluent last: swtchd and kpt on u.p run-in: no ch w wnr* **6/4**[2]
3 *shd* **Luska Lad (IRE)**[54] 2197 6-11-10 150 AndrewJMcNamara 157
(John Joseph Hanlon, Ire) *led: rdn and strly pressed fr 2 out: hdd last: kpt on same pce u.p* **20/1**
4 *2* **Thousand Stars (FR)**[213] 546 6-11-10 163 MsKWalsh 154
(W P Mullins, Ire) *hld up in tch: 4th and rdn after 2 out: kpt on wout threatening first* **16/1**[3]
5 *10* **Won In The Dark (IRE)**[39] 2516 6-11-10 148 PCarberry 144
(Sabrina J Harty, Ire) *s.i.s and hld up: plld hrd 1/2-way: 4th appr 2 out: sn no ex and wknd* **40/1**

4m 10.8s (3.30) **Going Correction** -0.15s/f (Good) **5** Ran SP% **111.0**
Speed ratings: **85,83,83,82,77**
CSF £2.21 TOTE £1.80: £1.02, £1.40; DF 2.40.
Owner George Creighton **Bred** Agricola Del Parco **Trained** Muine Beag, Co Carlow

FOCUS
The winning time was very slow, 13sec slower than the maiden over the C&D, and the third and fourth finished far too close for comfort. The first two are clearly capable of better than this bare form suggests.

NOTEBOOK
Hurricane Fly(IRE) won even more emphatically than he had done in the Hatton's Grace two weeks earlier, when he was having his first outing of the season and Solwhit already had a run under his belt. Trainer Willie Mullins had been slightly concerned by the possibility that the race might come a bit soon, but any such fears proved groundless. Most bookmakers now have him as the favourite for the Champion Hurdle in March and it is hard to argue with that assessment on this performance.
Solwhit(FR) delayed his challenge until far later than in in his previous meetings with Hurricane Fly at Punchestown and Fairyhouse, but it failed to work as the slow pace did not really play to his strengths, but such was Hurricane Fly's supremacy that it hardly made a difference. (op 7/4)
Luska Lad(IRE) has won plenty of races, but he gave perhaps the best performance of his career in defeat, setting a steady pace and sticking to his task under pressure when headed. He has looked best going right-handed in the past, so this was especially praiseworthy.
Thousand Stars(FR) can build on this first run after a break. (op 14/1 tchd 12/1)
Won In The Dark(IRE) was found wanting after failing to settle effectively on ground that would not have been ideal.

3206a PADDY POWER CHASE (GRADE B) (EXTENDED H'CAP) (17 fncs) 3m
2:30 (2:30) (0-145,144) 5-Y-0+
£94,513 (£32,300; £15,486; £5,398; £3,716; £2,035)

RPR
1 **Majestic Concorde (IRE)**[59] 1123 7-11-9 144 MrRPMcNamara 158
(D K Weld, Ire) *a.p: 2nd fr 1/2-way: led fr 4 out: clr appr last: styd on wl u.p* **33/1**

2 2 1/2 **Becauseicouldntsee (IRE)**[34] 2648 7-11-0 135............ MissNCarberry 146
(N F Glynn, Ire) *trckd ldrs: 7th appr 1/2-way: 5th 4 out: 3rd 3 out: 2nd and rdn after 2 out: styd on wl wout ever getting to wnr* 9/1[2]

3 6 **Pomme Tiepy (FR)**[38] 2565 7-10-7 128.......................... PTownend 133+
(W P Mullins, Ire) *hld up towards rr: hdwy 3 out: 13th after 2 out: styd on wl to go mod 3rd after last* 10/1[3]

4 1 3/4 **Agus A Vic (IRE)**[65] 2018 9-9-13 123........................(tp) APThornton(3) 126
(Patrick Martin, Ire) *hld up: prog after 4 out: 9th after 2 out: rdn and styd on* 16/1

5 shd **Catch Me (GER)**[34] 2647 8-11-6 141...................... AndrewJMcNamara 144
(E J O'Grady, Ire) *in tch: 6th 1/2-way: 9th 4 out: 8th after 3 out: kpt on u.p fr 2 out* 16/1

6 3/4 **Ambobo (USA)**[249] 5400 10-10-12 133..............................(t) MPWalsh 135+
(Martin Brassil, Ire) *towards rr: prog into 14th 2 out: styd on fr bef last* 33/1

7 1 3/4 **Stormin Exit (IRE)**[38] 2541 7-10-6 127.......................... JamesReveley 128
(Jim Goldie) *trckd ldrs on inner: 6th 1/2-way: prog 5 out: 2nd briefly 4 out: 6th 3 out: kpt on same pce u.p* 16/1

8 1/2 **Old Si (IRE)**[48] 2341 7-9-8 120..................................(b) BryanJCooper(5) 120
(D T Hughes, Ire) *prom: 3rd bef 1/2-way: 7th after 4 out: kpt on same pce fr next* 33/1

9 1 1/4 **Beautiful Sound (IRE)**[46] 2379 8-9-10 117.......................... MsKWalsh 116
(Gordon Elliott, Ire) *mid-div: 9th after 1/2-way: 7th 4 out: 5th and rdn after next: 4th appr last: no ex run-in* 5/1[1]

10 3 **Will Jamie Run (IRE)**[38] 2565 9-10-2 123.......................... RLoughran 119
(John C McConnell, Ire) *prom: disp ld 4th and 5th: 3rd 6 out: rdn and lost pl 4 out: 8th 2 out: kpt on same pce* 50/1

11 1 1/2 **Leanne (IRE)**[62] 2063 8-10-9 130.................................... RCColgan 124
(W Harney, Ire) *led and disp: hdd 4 out: 4th u.p 2 out: no ex fr last* 16/1

12 3 **Stewarts House (IRE)**[38] 2565 8-10-7 128............................ PWFlood 119
(A L T Moore, Ire) *prom on outer: 3rd after 1/2-way: 2nd 2 out: sn rdn: mod 3rd and no imp whn slt mstke last: wknd* 25/1

13 10 **Jered (IRE)**[14] 2973 8-11-2 137.. PCarberry 118
(Noel Meade, Ire) *hld up in rr: sme prog 3 out: 12th 2 out: no ex bef last* 22/1

14 3 **Skippers Brig (IRE)**[382] 2832 9-11-4 139.......................... BrianHarding 117
(Nicky Richards) *mid-div: 10th 1/2-way: no ex fr bef 4 out* 10/1[3]

15 21 **A New Story (IRE)**[48] 2338 12-10-12 133.......................... SGMcDermott 90
(Michael Hourigan, Ire) *in rr of mid-div: no ex fr 3 out: trailing bef last* 40/1

16 8 **The Burrow Vic (IRE)**[90] 1656 7-9-10 117............................ APCawley 66
(D E Fitzgerald, Ire) *hld up: mstke 8th: bhd fr 5 out* 16/1

17 nk **Got Attitude (IRE)**[38] 2565 7-10-5 126.................................. RMPower 76
(Mrs John Harrington, Ire) *mid-div on inner: bad mstke 5th: no ex fr 3 out* 33/1

P **Undergraduate (IRE)**[48] 2341 8-10-2 123 ow2...................... MJFerris —
(Michael E O'Callaghan, Ire) *hld up towards rr: p.u bef last* 33/1

P **Streets Of Gold (IRE)**[59] 2117 8-10-6 127..........................(bt) APCrowe —
(C Roche, Ire) *in rr of mid-div: no imp fr 4 out: p.u bef last* 14/1

P **Dancing Hero (IRE)**[41] 2489 9-10-1 122................................ DJCasey —
(Thomas Foley, Ire) *in tch on outer to 1/2-way: wknd 5 out: p.u bef 3 out* 20/1

F **Clan Tara (IRE)**[382] 2853 8-11-3 138..................................(t) DNRussell —
(Paul Nolan, Ire) *mid-div on inner tl fell 5 out* 10/1[3]

P **Venalmar**[56] 2158 8-10-7 128.. BarryGeraghty —
(M F Morris, Ire) *mid-div: 9th and rdn 3 out: sn no ex: p.u bef last* 9/1[2]

P **Hangover (IRE)**[52] 2256 8-10-6 130.................................... NJO'Shea(3) —
(Conor O'Dwyer, Ire) *in rr of mid-div: mstke 7 out: no ex fr 4 out: p.u bef last* 16/1

P **Oscar Looby (IRE)**[48] 2339 7-10-9 137..........................(tp) TCCarroll(7) —
(Noel Meade, Ire) *mid-div: 11th 1/2-way: mstkes 7 out and 6 out: no ex fr 3 out: p.u bef last* 25/1

U **Follow The Plan (IRE)**[55] 2175 7-11-2 144........................ PFMangan(7) —
(Oliver McKiernan, Ire) *mstke and uns rdr 1st* 33/1

P **Bohemian Lass (IRE)**[59] 2117 7-9-8 120.......................... IJMcCarthy(5) —
(T Hogan, Ire) *mid-div to 1/2-way: p.u bef 8 out* 33/1

P **Across The Bay (IRE)**[38] 2565 6-10-11 132......................(b1) DJCondon —
(Noel Meade, Ire) *in tch: 9th 1/2-way: lost pl 8 out: p.u bef 6 out* 20/1

P **Away We Go (IRE)**[16] 2934 7-10-11 135............................ PTEnright(3) —
(Timothy Cleary, Ire) *hld up: sme prog 6 out: 10th 4 out: rdn and wknd next: p.u bef last* 33/1

6m 25.4s (-8.60) **Going Correction** -0.075s/f (Good) 28 Ran SP% **155.4**
Speed ratings: **111,110,108,107,107 107,106,106,106,105 104,103,100,99,92 89,89,—,—,— —,—,—,**
CSF £322.72 CT £3289.85 TOTE £33.50: £7.30, £2.20, £2.80, £5.10; DF 518.20.
Owner Dr R Lambe **Bred** Martin Donovan **Trained** The Curragh, Co Kildare

FOCUS
The third has been rated to the best of her 2009-10 form, with the runner-up to a personal best on his handicap debut.

NOTEBOOK
Majestic Concorde(IRE) jumped well throughout, led four out and was ridden clear before the final fence. He stayed on well on the flat and has a range of targets in 2011, including the Chester Cup and another tilt at the Galway Plate, while trainer Dermot Weld might also enter him for the John Smith's Grand National.
Becauseicouldntsee(IRE), runner-up in the National Hunt Chase at Cheltenham in March and having only his second run since, having finished fourth over hurdles on his previous start, was never far off the leaders and arrived into second place after two out. Unable to get to the winner approaching the final fence, he kept plugging away. (op 10/1)
Pomme Tiepy(FR) ◆ has failed to win over fences since the 2007-2008 season, when she was successful five times. She had shown signs of a return to form when fifth in the Troytown Chase last month and she again indicated that there is a decent handicap to be won with her with another decent effort here. Held up, she crept steadily through the field from three out and stayed on for third on the run-in. (op 10/1 tchd 11/1)
Agus A Vic(IRE), back from a break and with cheekpieces fitted for the first time, began a forward move four out and stayed on steadily from two out to be nearest at the finish.
Catch Me(GER), let down by his jumping in the past, performed creditably and, having lost touch four out, was coming back at the leaders from two out and just missed out on fourth place.
Ambobo(USA), having his first run of the season, made an encouraging return and was putting in good work from two out, finishing the race well.
Stormin Exit(IRE) kept to the inner and tracked the leaders, going second briefly four out. After losing his place, he kept on without posing a real threat.
Beautiful Sound(IRE) headed the market on what was only his third start over racecourse fences. Raised 10lb for his last win, he looked like getting into serious contention when closing on the leaders three out, having appeared to get a bit outpaced early on. He began to weaken nearing the last and tired on the run-in. (op 6/1)
Venalmar made a forward move to track the leaders before three out but began to beat a retreat soon afterwards, and was well out of contention when he was pulled up before the final fence. Official explanation: jockey said gelding never travelled particularly well and was pulled up (op 10/1)
Bohemian Lass(IRE) Official explanation: trainer said mare scoped badly post-race (op 10/1)

3208a PADDYPOWER.COM FUTURE CHAMPIONS (PRO/AM) INH FLAT RACE (GRADE 2) 2m
3:35 (3:35) 4-7-Y-0 **£16,393** (£4,792; £2,269; £756)

RPR

1 **Jim Will Fix It (IRE)**[48] 2342 5-12-0..................................(t) MrSRByrne 126
(Seamus Roche, Ire) *a.p: led bef 1/2-way: drvn along and edgd clr early st: 3 l advantage 1f out: strly pressed whn drifted rt cl home: all out to hold on* 8/1

2 shd **Mississippi River (IRE)**[45] 2410 5-12-0...................... MrRPMcNamara 126
(John E Kiely, Ire) *trckd ldrs in 4th: prog into 2nd 3f out: 3rd and rdn early st: no imp tl r.o wl ins fnl f: jst failed* 2/1[1]

3 2 **Valleymount (IRE)**[59] 2121 4-11-6................................ MissNCarberry 116
(F Flood, Ire) *hld up: 8th 4f out: hdwy into 4th ent st: rdn and kpt on fr 2f out* 4/1[3]

4 1/2 **Rebel Fitz (FR)**[65] 2019 5-12-0.................................... MrMJO'Connor 124
(Michael Winters, Ire) *trckd ldrs in 5th: impr into 3rd 4f out: 2nd early st: sn rdn and no imp: kpt on same pce ins fnl f* 7/2[2]

5 9 **Shannon Spirit (IRE)**[287] 4676 5-12-0.............................. MrJTCarroll 115
(T Hogan, Ire) *hld up in rr: prog into 7th 4f out: mod 5th and no imp st* 8/1

6 4 **Bayross (IRE)**[53] 2229 5-12-0.. MrJPSullivan 111
(J Larkin, Ire) *trckd ldrs in 6th: rdn 4f out: sn lost tch* 33/1

7 4 **Sydney Des Pictons (FR)**[266] 5092 4-11-11.................... MrMJO'Hare 104
(C A McBratney, Ire) *towards rr: rdn and no imp fr 4f out* 10/1

8 3 **Bandra Bullet (IRE)**[54] 2201 4-11-11................................ MsLO'Neill 101
(John C McConnell, Ire) *trckd ldrs in 3rd: 2nd 5f out: rdn and wknd over 3f out* 25/1

9 15 **True Character (IRE)**[11] 3033 4-11-11........................ MissKHarrington 86
(Mrs John Harrington, Ire) *hld up in tch: 7th 1/2-way: 5th 4f out: no ex bef st* 12/1

10 21 **Narrandera (IRE)**[48] 2342 7-12-0.................................... MrMJScallan 68
(J A Berry, Ire) *led: hdd bef 1/2-way: drvn along and wknd over 5f out: trailing whn eased ent st: t.o* 66/1

4m 0.70s (-1.20) **Going Correction** -0.15s/f (Good)
WFA 4 from 5yo+ 5lb 10 Ran SP% **122.8**
Speed ratings: **97,96,95,95,91 89,87,85,78,67**
CSF £25.48 TOTE £11.70: £3.50, £1.80, £1.20; DF 36.80.
Owner Ms Marie Robinson **Bred** Mr Seamus Roche **Trained** Hugginstown, Co Kilkenny
■ Stewards' Enquiry : Mr S R Byrne severe caution: used whip with excessive frequency

FOCUS
A race in which all bar one of the runners were previous winners. Decent form, rated around the sixth.

NOTEBOOK
Jim Will Fix It(IRE) produced a thoroughly game effort. Sent to the front before halfway, he was ridden clear over a furlong out and stayed on under pressure. He drifted right towards the finish and was all out to hold on. (op 8/1 tchd 9/1)
Mississippi River(IRE) tracked the leaders and went second 3f out. Third and under pressure over 2f out, he challenged on the inside and, when the winner drifted away from him late on, he stayed on well under pressure and just failed to get up. (op 5/2)
Valleymount(IRE), successful on similar ground at Cork last month, was held up and began to make headeway leaving the back straight. Fourth into the straight, he kept on steadily all the way to the line. (op 9/2)
Rebel Fitz(FR) had beaten Mississippi River into second place at Galway in October and raced in touch throughout here, going second early in the straight and having every chance before failing to raise any extra over the final furlong. (op 3/1 tchd 4/1)
Shannon Spirit(IRE), a seven-length winner on his debut at Thurles in January, had not run since finishing in rear in the Weatherbys Champion Bumper at Cheltenham in March. Held up in rear, he made progress over 4f out but could make no further headway having been only a moderate fifth on the final bend.
T/Jkpt: @8,025.30. Pool of @21,401.00 - 2 winning units. T/Plt: @16.60. Pool of @30,323.00 - 1363.98 winning units. II

3207 - 3209a (Foreign Racing) - See Raceform Interactive

3179 LIMERICK (R-H)
Wednesday, December 29

OFFICIAL GOING: Soft to heavy (heavy in places)

3210a GREENMOUNT PARK NOVICE CHASE (GRADE 2) (14 fncs) 2m 3f 120y
12:35 (12:35) 4-Y-0+ **£23,008** (£6,725; £3,185)

RPR

1 **Mr Cracker (IRE)**[52] 2255 5-11-6 130.................................. APHeskin 151
(Michael Hourigan, Ire) *sn led and mde virtually all: j.w: in command whn lft wl clr 2 out: styd on wl: easily* 9/4[2]

2 dist **C'Est Ca**[35] 2620 6-11-6.. EMullins 126
(W P Mullins, Ire) *led tl slow 1st and hdd: slow again 2nd: sn 3rd: rdn along fr 5 out: no imp on ldrs fr next: lft remote 2nd 2 out* 5/1

3 dist **Kakagh (IRE)**[60] 2098 6-11-6 123.............................. MrDerekO'Connor —
(W Harney, Ire) *a last: struggling and rdn along fr 5th: trailing fr 1/2-way: lft remote 3rd 2 out* 11/4[3]

F **The Hurl (IRE)**[41] 2486 7-11-6.. NPMadden 139
(M F Morris, Ire) *racd 2nd on outer: rdn along in 2nd fr 3 out: no imp on wnr whn fell next* 2/1[1]

5m 7.70s (307.70) 4 Ran SP% **107.4**
CSF £11.77 TOTE £2.60; DF 14.60.
Owner Gigginstown House Stud **Bred** R Jenks **Trained** Patrickswell, Co Limerick

FOCUS
The winner has been rated as a 12-length winner over the favourite, who fell two out.

NOTEBOOK
Mr Cracker(IRE) had everything bar the favourite beaten at the third-last and was well in control when that one fell two out. He's earned a step up in class after this effort. (op 5/2)
C'Est Ca recovered after a couple of early mistakes but, when the pace began to increase markedly in the back straight, he began to struggle and was soon beaten.
Kakagh(IRE) could never go the pace at any point. (op 9/4)
The Hurl(IRE) was the only horse to make a race of it with the winner most of the way, and he jumped almost as well. The pace eventually started to tell on him as they descended to the straight and he was beaten when taking a tired fall at the second-last. Happily both horse and rider were unscathed.

3211 - 3216a (Foreign Racing) - See Raceform Interactive

2519 HAYDOCK (L-H)

Thursday, December 30

3217 Meeting Abandoned - Frozen track

2633 TAUNTON (R-H)

Thursday, December 30

OFFICIAL GOING: Good to soft (good in places; 9.2)

Rails on hurdle course moved out adding about 72 metres per circuit to advertised distances.

Wind: mild across Weather: overcast but dry

3224 TOTEPLACEPOT (S) HURDLE (9 hdls) 2m 1f
12:45 (12:45) (Class 5) 4-Y-0+ **£2,055** (£599; £299)

Form	Pos	Dist	Horse / Details	Jockey	RPR
6065	1		**I'm In The Pink (FR)**[8] 3091 6-11-5 116 (v) (David Evans) *hld up in mid-div: tk clsr order 6th: led appr last: pushed clr* **7/4**[1]	APMcCoy	118+
62	2	4 ½	**Perfect Reward**[37] 2596 6-11-1 115 (Gary Moore) *trckd ldrs: rdn after 3 out: led 2 out: hdd bef last: sn hld: kpt on same pce* **15/8**[2]	JoshuaMoore(7)	115
6043	3	6	**Try Cat**[2] 3155 4-10-5 96 (t) (Philip Hobbs) *led: nt fluent 6th: rdn and hdd appr 2 out: styd pressing for 2nd tl fdd flat* **3/1**[3]	RichardJohnson	94+
P0	4	5	**Tiger Breeze (USA)**[41] 2499 4-10-5 0 (Bob Buckler) *hld up in last pair: hdwy to join ldrs after 5th: rdn and ev ch after 3 out: wknd bef next* **50/1**	NathanSweeney(7)	95
02	5	25	**Primera Rossa**[24] 2421 4-10-5 0 (J S Moore) *trckd ldrs: pckd 4th: rdn and wknd after 3 out: t.o* **11/1**	WillKennedy	65
0-00	6	12	**Sir Clad**[38] 2590 4-10-9 0 (t) (Claire Dyson) *trckd ldrs: rdn after 5th: wknd after next: t.o* **100/1**	TommyPhelan(3)	61
0	7	1 ¾	**Bless My Soul**[35] 2633 7-10-5 0 (Ron Hodges) *prom tl hit 4th: in tch tl wknd 6th: t.o* **28/1**	MattGriffiths(7)	59
0/	8	53	**King Of Magic**[1176] 1645 6-10-5 0 (Bill Turner) *mid-div tl rdn 5th: sn bhd: t.o* **50/1**	MarkQuinlan(7)	11
0P/0	P		**Barodine**[63] 793 7-10-12 83 (Ron Hodges) *nudged along in rr after 3rd: lost tch fr after 5th: t.o whn p.u after 3 out* **40/1**	NickScholfield	—

4m 8.10s (0.10) **Going Correction** -0.10s/f (Good)
WFA 4 from 6yo+ 5lb **9 Ran SP% 115.3**
Speed ratings (Par 103): **95,92,90,87,75 70,69,44,—**
toteswingers:1&2:£1.10, 1&3:£1.40, 2&3:£1.20 CSF £5.39 TOTE £3.40: £1.50, £1.40, £1.10; EX 5.90.The winner was bought in for 5,200gns.
Owner B J Mould **Bred** Mme Catherine Auniac **Trained** Pandy, Monmouths

FOCUS
An ordinary seller, run in a relatively slow time. Less than half the field could be seriously considered on the form they had shown over hurdles, and it wasn't a big surprise to see the first three home finish in betting order. The winning rider reported after the race that the going rode good to soft.

NOTEBOOK
I'm In The Pink(FR), fifth in a recent Southwell jumpers' bumper, tracked his market rival throughout and was easily on top after the final flight. He wins in his turn but doesn't seem the most reliable of horses. (op 2-1)
Perfect Reward looked the most obvious candidate on his best form but he made a couple of minor jumping errors and was easily held once passed. (op 6-4)
Try Cat, making a quick reappearance after running at Ffos Las, led for most of the contest and kept on respectably when joined. There is a little race in her, especially as she is settling a little better. (op 7-2 tchd 4-1)
Tiger Breeze(USA) deserves a mention for shaping with some promise down in grade.

3225 TOTEEXACTA FLEXI BETTING NOVICES' HURDLE (9 hdls) 2m 1f
1:15 (1:15) (Class 4) 3-Y-0+ **£4,110** (£1,198; £599)

Form	Pos	Dist	Horse / Details	Jockey	RPR
60-1	1		**Iolith (GER)**[59] 2122 5-11-12 116 (Alan King) *in tch: hdwy to ld appr 2 out: shkn up and r.o strly fr last: readily* **10/3**[2]	WayneHutchinson	115+
	2	7	**Spirit Is Needed (IRE)**[82] 4-11-5 0 (Milton Harris) *mid-div: hdwy whn swtchd lft on bnd after 3 out: sn rdn: styd on to go 2nd run-in: no ch w wnr* **25/1**	WarrenMarston	99
1322	3	2	**Crystal Rock (IRE)**[47] 2361 5-11-12 121 (Nicky Henderson) *trckd ldr: rdn whn ev ch 2 out: one pce whn lost 2nd run-in* **15/8**[1]	APMcCoy	104
	4	2	**Reginaldinho (UAE)**[133] 4-11-5 0 (Venetia Williams) *trckd ldr: blnd 1st: rdn after 3 out: 2 l 2nd whn stmbld bdly last: nt rcvr and lost 2 pls flat* **40/1**	AidanColeman	98+
	5	¾	**Ange Guerrier (FR)**[436] 5-11-5 0 (Paul Nicholls) *hld up towards rr: prog into midfield 6th: rdn after 3 out: styd on same pce* **5/1**[3]	HarrySkelton	95
60	6	1 ¼	**Hawkaller**[41] 2493 5-11-0 0 (Anthony Honeyball) *led tl rdn appr 2 out: styd chsng ldrs tl fdd fr last* **100/1**	RachaelGreen(5)	93
23-0	7	1 ½	**Shammick Boy (IRE)**[47] 2368 5-11-5 0 (Victor Dartnall) *nvr fluent: mid-div: hmpd 1st: rdn after 6th: one pce fr after 3 out* **20/1**	AndrewGlassonbury	92
4	8	3	**Swinging Hawk (GER)**[39] 2540 4-11-5 0 (Ian Williams) *hld up towards rr: sme imp into midfield 3 out: sn rdn: no further imp whn mstke 2 out* **5/1**[3]	DougieCostello	89
	9	6	**Cool Strike (UAE)**[103] 4-11-5 0 (Alex Hales) *mid-div: rdn whn hmpd on bnd after 3 out: wknd bef next* **16/1**	PaddyBrennan	84
4	10	10	**E Street Boy**[211] 589 4-11-5 0 (David Pipe) *a towards rr* **28/1**	TomScudamore	75
0	11	7	**Our Flora**[82] 1768 5-10-5 0 (Kim Bailey) *a towards rr* **125/1**	MrCGreene(7)	61
5450	12	1 ½	**Superior Knight**[43] 2456 6-11-5 0 (t) (James Evans) *a towards rr* **200/1**	DavidDennis	67
50	13	1 ¾	**Master Milan (IRE)**[20] 2873 4-11-2 0 (Jonjo O'Neill) *in tch: tk clsr order 6th: sn rdn: wknd after 3 out* **100/1**	RichieMcLernon(3)	65
	14	hd	**Peqeno Diablo (IRE)**[63] 2061 5-11-7 0 (Claire Dyson) *trckd ldrs tl rdn after 3 out: sn wknd* **22/1**	IanPopham(5)	72

4m 8.70s (0.70) **Going Correction** -0.10s/f (Good)
WFA 4 from 5yo+ 5lb **14 Ran SP% 119.2**
Speed ratings (Par 105): **94,90,89,88,88 87,87,85,82,78 74,74,73,73**
toteswingers:1&2:£36.00, 1&3:£1.90, 2&3:£20.60 CSF £84.46 TOTE £4.60: £2.00, £6.20, £1.30; EX 227.10.
Owner Favourites Racing XI **Bred** Gestut Schlenderhan **Trained** Barbury Castle, Wilts

FOCUS
A fair contest considering the BHA ratings of the two that had won, which contained a few interesting unexposed types. The early gallop looked ordinary and the winning time was slower than the seller. The form has been given a downbeat rating but might have been rated higher.

NOTEBOOK
Iolith(GER) landed an ordinary affair at Kempton in early November (next three home haven't advertised the form) but improved on that with a decent display. He was one of many that took a strong hold under restraint, so it was pleasing to see him find so much for pressure. Group 3-placed on the Flat in Germany, a gelding operation appears to have transformed him over hurdles and he should have more to come. Connections suggested afterwards that their horse may have one more run and then go to the Supreme Novices' Hurdle. (op 11-4)
Spirit Is Needed(IRE) caught the eye with the way he travelled in behind and put up a solid display on his hurdling debut. Very useful on the Flat, his new connections look to have nice prospect. (op 20-1)
Crystal Rock(IRE) set a fair level for this considering he had already been given an official rating of 121. Returning to novice company after running in handicaps on his previous four starts, but this has to be counted a little disappointing considering he had the run of the race just behind the leader. (op 11-4)
Reginaldinho(UAE) was fresh and keen on his first outing since August, a 1m4f race at Clairefontaine for Manfred Hofer. A winner over 1m4f and 1m6f in Germany, he probably would have been second had he not slipped after clipping the final hurdle.
Ange Guerrier(FR), who was bought for £85,000 following his last Flat effort in 2009, had been given a breathing operation in the summer and then suffered an attack of colic, so was entitled to need this. Another to be keen early towards the rear of the field, and hampered by the runner-up rounding the final bend, he made a satisfactory debut but nothing more. (op 11-2 tchd 6-1)
Hawkaller enjoyed an easy lead and wasn't beaten far, especially when you consider that his rider was far from hard on him after jumping the final hurdle.
Shammick Boy(IRE) disappointed connections on his return to action, in a bumper, but kept on in pleasing style here after still looking a bit green. A step up in trip may help him. (op 16-1)
Swinging Hawk(GER) caught the eye at Aintree on his hurdling debut but failed by a long way to reproduce that sort of effort in this. (op 9-2)
Cool Strike(UAE) was very useful on the Flat for Andrew Balding, usually wearing a visor, so it was slightly surprising that he only cost new connections £20,000. Racing in midfield, he was starting to stay on, but was another hampered by Spirit Is Needed on the final bend. Considering he acted so well on quick ground on the Flat, he is one to keep an eye out for later on in the season. (op 18-1 tchd 20-1)
E Street Boy didn't really get involved but one has the suspicion that he can develop into a fair sort in time, as he was making some progress from the rear in the final stages.

3226 TOTESUPER7 NOVICES' H'CAP CHASE (14 fncs) 2m 3f
1:50 (1:50) (Class 5) (0-95,95) 4-Y-0+ **£2,740** (£798; £399)

Form	Pos	Dist	Horse / Details	Jockey	RPR
4/P3	1		**Walk Tall (IRE)**[15] 2952 7-11-7 89 (Venetia Williams) *in tch: trckd ldrs 7th: rdn to chal whn stmbld 3 out: remained pressing ldrs: led sn after last: styd on: drvn out* **4/1**[2]	AidanColeman	102+
-0F5	2	1 ¼	**Chilla Cilla**[42] 2468 7-10-8 76 (t) (Anthony Honeyball) *hld up: smooth hdwy 4 out: trckd ldrs next: tk narrow advantage sn after 2 out: rdn whn hdd sn after last: styd on same pce* **11/1**	NickScholfield	85
23-F	3	5	**Douryna**[36] 2605 7-11-9 91 (Colin Tizzard) *trckd ldrs: led briefly 7th: mstke next: rdn appr 3 out: hdd sn after 2 out: no ex whn mstke last* **3/1**[1]	JoeTizzard	98+
F0-4	4	19	**Noble Aran (IRE)**[25] 2796 6-11-12 94 (Nigel Twiston-Davies) *mid-div: hdwy 8th: rdn and ev ch after 4 out: hld whn stmbld next: wknd 2 out* **9/2**[3]	PaddyBrennan	84+
0322	5	1	**Fongoli**[44] 2434 4-10-3 77 (b) (Brendan Powell) *led: hit 1st: reminders: hdd briefly 7th: hdd next: sn drvn: no ch fr 4 out* **8/1**	MattieBatchelor	59
2-26	6	10	**Remember Bampi**[210] 594 6-11-5 90 (tp) (Simon Burrough) *pushed along after 6th: hit 8th: a towards rr: t.o* **12/1**	JimmyDerham(3)	70
-032	7	½	**Corredor Sun (USA)**[57] 2152 4-11-4 95 (p) (Nigel Twiston-Davies) *chsd ldrs: rdn along fr after 7th: wknd bef 4 out: t.o* **6/1**	SamTwiston-Davies(3)	66
/060	8	33	**Red Law (IRE)**[42] 2482 6-11-9 94 (Mark Gillard) *hld up and a towards rr: t.o* **33/1**	TommyPhelan(3)	41
15-0	P		**Delcombe**[57] 2144 9-10-8 83 ow3 (Richard Mitchell) *hld up: hit 7th: struggling whn hit 10th: sn wknd: p.u bef 3 out: dismntd: lame* **16/1**	SClements(7)	—

4m 57.3s (0.80) **Going Correction** -0.025s/f (Good)
WFA 4 from 6yo+ 5lb **9 Ran SP% 113.4**
Speed ratings (Par 103): **97,96,94,86,85 81,81,67,—**
toteswingers:1&2:£9.50, 1&3:£3.80, 2&3:£8.70 CSF £44.87 CT £148.24 TOTE £3.80: £1.30, £3.00, £1.90; EX 57.00.
Owner Trevor Hemmings **Bred** Peter O'Keeffe **Trained** Kings Caple, H'fords

FOCUS
A moderate but competitive-looking handicap. The winner is rated better than the bare result and to the level of his best hurdles form.

NOTEBOOK
Walk Tall(IRE) didn't run too badly at Bangor on his previous outing, his second outing after a lengthy break due to tendon problems, and built on that performance with a tidy success, even after stumbling three from home. One would imagine that he should be capable of winning again now that he has got his head in front. (tchd 3-1 and 9-2)
Chilla Cilla, who was due to be ridden by Rachael Green, was given a patient ride and came with a sweeping effort down the home straight to give the winner lots to think about between the final two fences. She wasn't able to get past the winner, but still put up what looked to be her best performance. (op 9-1 tchd 12-1)
Douryna would have gone close on her chasing debut (her first start for this stable) but for falling at the last at Chepstow - winner of that contest has gone on to win at Newbury since. She moved easily during the race but didn't find a lot at the end and also jumped a few fences a bit slowly. (op 9-4)
Noble Aran(IRE) didn't appear to get home over 3m at Exeter last time, so the drop in trip at this sharper course didn't come as a surprise. He needed stoking along quite early, as if the pace of the contest was a stride too quick for him, but his jockey kept him going and, indeed, appeared to briefly look behind him for dangers shortly after jumping the last fence in the back straight. However, the response he got from his mount was minimal and he came home at the one pace. (op 5-1)
Red Law(IRE) Official explanation: jockey said gelding had a breathing problem

Delcombe Official explanation: jockey said gelding pulled up lame

3227 TOTESWINGER FLEXI BETTING MARES' NOVICES' HURDLE (10 hdls) 2m 3f 110y

2:25 (2:25) (Class 4) 4-Y-O+ **£4,110** (£1,198; £599)

Form RPR

4403 **1** **Lucy's Perfect**[35] 2639 4-10-10 97................................(b) TomScudamore 113+
(David Pipe) *led 1st: rdn after 3 out: sn hrd pressed: wnt rt and hdd last: rallied v gamely to regain ld nr fin* **14/1**

10-4 **2** *nk* **Mizzurka**[14] 2974 6-10-10 0.................................. APMcCoy 114+
(Bob Buckler) *nt a fluent: prom: rdn to chal after 3 out: led last: 1 1/2 clr sn after: no ex whn ct nr fin* **11/4**[3]

4-1 **3** *10* **Semi Colon (FR)**[42] 2472 4-10-10 0.................................. AndrewTinkler 103
(Nicky Henderson) *mid-div: hdwy 6th: rdn in cl 3rd after 3 out: sn one pce* **7/4**[1]

4-0 **4** *20* **Lost Two Stars (IRE)**[19] 2896 5-10-10 0.............................. JoeTizzard 85
(Colin Tizzard) *towards rr: struggling 6th: wnt modest 4th after 3 out: nvr on terms w ldrs* **33/1**

3-00 **5** *17* **Karinga Dream**[14] 2974 4-10-10 0.................................. AidanColeman 70
(Venetia Williams) *pushed along fr 5th: rdn next: a towards rr: t.o* **80/1**

65-1 **6** *1 ¾* **Tazzarine (FR)**[24] 2825 4-10-10 0.................................. JimmyMcCarthy 68
(Charles Egerton) *chsd ldrs: hit 5th: rdn after next: wknd bef 3 out: t.o* **12/1**

0/0 **7** *33* **Molly Round (IRE)**[41] 2499 6-10-7 0.............................. DonalDevereux(3) 38
(Grant Cann) *led tl 1st: chsd ldrs tl lost pl 4th: sn in rr: t.o* **150/1**

00 **8** *1 ½* **Sun Des Mottes (FR)**[54] 2216 4-10-10 0.............................. TimmyMurphy 37
(David Pipe) *racd keenly: sn prom: nt fluent 2nd: wknd bef 7th: t.o* **50/1**

200- **9** *11* **Chilli Rose**[259] 5196 5-10-10 115.................................. WayneHutchinson 27
(Alan King) *mid-div: trckd ldrs 3rd: rdn after 6th: wknd next: t.o* **9/4**[2]

-244 **10** *10* **Hill Forts Gloria (IRE)**[35] 2627 5-10-7 100.............. WayneKavanagh(3) 18
(Seamus Mullins) *a towards rr: t.o fr after 7th* **66/1**

/P-P **P** **Dark Haven**[43] 2456 7-10-10 0.................................. LiamTreadwell —
(James Evans) *a bhd: t.o whn p.u after 3 out* **150/1**

6 **P** **Piggy Back (IRE)**[39] 2546 4-10-7 0.............................. RichieMcLernon(3) —
(Jonjo O'Neill) *mid-div: hrd rdn on bnd after 5th: sn dropped to rr: t.o whn p.u bef 7th* **66/1**

4m 46.2s (0.20) **Going Correction** -0.10s/f (Good) **12** Ran SP% **118.6**
Speed ratings (Par 105): **95,94,90,82,76 75,62,61,57,53 —,—**
toteswingers:1&2:£9.10, 1&3:£6.90, 2&3:£1.90 CSF £53.67 TOTE £15.00: £2.50, £1.30, £1.50; EX 42.30.
Owner Avalon Surfacing Ltd **Bred** Avalon Surfacing Ltd & East Burrow Farm **Trained** Nicholashayne, Devon

FOCUS

A moderate mares' hurdle but featuring several unexposed types, and a three-horse race according to the market. However, only two of them were amongst the trio that drew clear towards the end of the back straight and there was a surprise result. A big step up from the winner who is rated in line with the best of her Flat form.

NOTEBOOK

Lucy's Perfect, a 1m2f Flat winner on good ground, had put up some fair efforts over hurdles but had a lot to find on official ratings. Given a positive ride, she looked beaten when the runner-up went clear after the last. However, she battled back under pressure and got up near the line.

Mizzurka, a three-time bumper winner, including at Listed level, on soft ground last season, had been slightly disappointing on her hurdling debut. She was not that fluent at her hurdles here but looked sure to win when going on taking the last and quickly went clear on the flat. However, she then seemed to idle and looked as if she tried to duck out at the paddock gate inside the last half-furlong, and the momentum lost by the hesitation probably cost her the race. She clearly has enough ability to win her share at this level, but she is certainly not totally straightforward and has something to prove now. (tchd 5-2)

Semi Colon(FR), a soft-ground bumper winner on her previous start, travelled well into contention on this hurdling debut. However, she came under pressure leaving the back straight and was soon left behind by the principals. (op 15-8 tchd 2-1)

Lost Two Stars(IRE), a half-sister to Herecomesthetruth, was making her hurdling debut following a couple of fair efforts in bumpers. She stayed on past beaten rivals and should be better for the experience.

Tazzarine(FR), the winner of a Fibresand bumper on her third start, showed up early on this hurdling debut but ended up well beaten. (op 14-1)

Chilli Rose, a good-ground bumper winner and placed at up to 2m4f on soft ground over hurdles, finished distressed when well beaten at Huntingdon last February and has not looked the same since. She was in trouble a long way from home here. (op 11-4)

3228 STEVE LOGAN MEMORIAL (COUNTY CONTRACTORS) H'CAP HURDLE (9 hdls) 2m 1f

3:00 (3:00) (Class 3) (0-120,120) 3-Y-O+ **£5,854** (£1,719; £859; £429)

Form RPR

-335 **1** **Marleno (GER)**[9] 3056 4-10-12 106................................(t) WarrenMarston 114+
(Milton Harris) *patiently rdn in rr: pushed along and hdwy after 3 out: chalng whn hit 2 out: led bef last: rdn and r.o wl* **20/1**

20-3 **2** *1 ¾* **Dream Esteem**[14] 2977 5-11-12 120.............................. TomScudamore 123
(David Pipe) *mid-div: hdwy 3 out to chse ldrs: sltly outpcd appr 2 out: styd on fr last: wnt 2nd nr fin* **7/1**[3]

-402 **3** *shd* **Bally Legend**[35] 2634 5-11-8 116.................................. TomO'Brien 120
(Caroline Keevil) *mid-div: hdwy to trck ldrs after 4th: disp 2nd 3 out: rdn whn sltly outpcd appr 2 out: styd on again fr last* **9/1**

22-4 **4** *¾* **Bold Addition (FR)**[47] 2361 5-11-5 118.......................... IanPopham(5) 120
(Paul Nicholls) *in tch: tk clsr order 6th: disp 2nd 3 out: rdn and ev ch appr 2 out: kpt on same pce* **3/1**[1]

5/5P **5** *nk* **Ruthenoise (FR)**[53] 2242 5-11-7 115.............................. AndrewTinkler 117
(Nicky Henderson) *prom: led 5th: rdn and edgd rt after 2 out: hdd bef last: kpt on but no ex fr last: lost 3 pls nr fin* **33/1**

-214 **6** *13* **Niceonefrankie**[202] 710 4-11-7 115.............................. AidanColeman 105
(Venetia Williams) *mid-div: rdn and hdwy to chse ldrs 3 out: wknd after 2 out* **33/1**

02/3 **7** *1 ¼* **Tuanku (IRE)**[41] 2498 5-11-4 119.............................. PeterHatton(7) 108
(Alan King) *mid-div: rdn after 4th: nvr gng pce to threaten ldrs* **10/1**

400- **8** *18* **Kings Troop**[68] 4563 4-10-12 106.............................. WayneHutchinson 79
(Alan King) *rdn after 6th: a towards rr: t.o* **13/2**[2]

2000 **9** *2 ¾* **American World (FR)**[37] 2596 6-10-13 110.......................... MrAJBerry(3) 80
(Brendan Powell) *mid-div tl 6th: t.o* **100/1**

-003 **10** *27* **George Nympton (IRE)**[38] 2577 4-11-10 118....................(b) DarylJacob 64
(Nick Williams) *led tl 5th: wknd after next: t.o* **18/1**

-033 **11** *2 ¾* **Superius (IRE)**[67] 1998 5-10-13 107.............................. SamThomas 51
(Emma Lavelle) *in tch: rdn after 6th: wknd next: t.o* **20/1**

U-33 **12** *13* **Just One Thing (IRE)**[51] 2294 5-10-13 107.......................... PaulMoloney 39
(Evan Williams) *t.k.h: trckd ldrs: wknd bef 6th: t.o* **33/1**

0-53 **P** **Super Kenny (IRE)**[35] 2626 4-11-9 117.............................. APMcCoy —
(Nicky Henderson) *a towards rr: rdn and wknd 3 out: bhd whn p.u bef 2 out* **3/1**[1]

5360 **P** **What An Oscar (IRE)**[35] 2630 5-10-7 104.......... SamTwiston-Davies(3) —
(Nigel Twiston-Davies) *sn t.o: p.u after 4th* **40/1**

4m 4.80s (-3.20) **Going Correction** -0.10s/f (Good)
WFA 4 from 5yo+ 5lb **14** Ran SP% **122.0**
Speed ratings (Par 107): **103,102,102,101,101 95,94,86,85,72 71,65,—,—**
toteswingers:1&2:£35.60, 1&3:£37.10, 2&3:£13.40 CSF £149.24 CT £1376.88 TOTE £30.20: £6.40, £3.20, £2.50; EX 207.60.
Owner Pet Necessities Partnership **Bred** L Paulick **Trained** Herridge, Wiltshire

FOCUS

This appeared to be run at a strong gallop and was the fastest of the races over the trip. A step up from the easy winner and form to be fairly positive about.

NOTEBOOK

Marleno(GER) was given a completely different ride when shaping nicely in a recent jumpers' bumper, but proved he can get the job done after being held up early. He looks capable of winning again if things fall right for him, even after being reassessed, as the fitting of a tongue-tie appears to have had a positive effect. (op 22-1 tchd 25-1)

Dream Esteem, who ran respectably in this year's Supreme Novices' Hurdle, shaped with promise on her comeback at Exeter and again here, albeit looking in the grip of the handicapper. (op 13-2 tchd 6-1)

Bally Legend, down in trip on his handicap debut, was only narrowly beaten at this course last time and should be found a winning opportunity soon, if maintaining this level of form. (op 12-1)

Bold Addition(FR) showed promise on his return to action at the end of last month but was one paced in this after holding every chance. He is lightly raced, so can be given another chance. (op 4-1)

Ruthenoise(FR), who had also raced keenly on her two most recent starts, did well to finish as close as she did as the gallop she'd help set appeared strong.

Kings Troop didn't show a lot when last over hurdles during the 09/10 season (he did win a couple on the Flat his year for this stable) and once again here. (op 9-2)

George Nympton(IRE), with the blinkers retained, dropped away at a fairly early stage having set a strong gallop. (op 20-1)

Super Kenny(IRE) ran well on his handicap debut at Newbury in a conditional jockeys' race on his previous start, but failed miserably to build on that here. He never made any meaningful impression. (op 7-2)

3229 TOTETRIFECTA FLEXI BETTING CONDITIONAL JOCKEYS' H'CAP HURDLE (10 hdls) 2m 3f 110y

3:30 (3:31) (Class 2) 4-Y-O+ **£12,674** (£3,744; £1,872; £936; £468)

Form RPR

32 **1** **Dynaste (FR)**[48] 2347 4-10-6 130.................................. CO'Farrell(3) 100
(David Pipe) *mde all: 4 l clr 2 out: sn rdn: jst hld on: all out* **5/2**[1]

2141 **2** *shd* **Organisateur (IRE)**[35] 2636 5-11-9 147.............................. IanPopham(3) 155
(Paul Nicholls) *mid-div: hdwy 7th: disp 2nd appr 2 out: sn rdn: 2 ¼ l down last: kpt on wl fnl 100yds: jst failed* **8/1**[3]

2424 **3** *7* **Monetary Fund (USA)**[20] 2868 4-10-4 128.................. RichardKilloran(3) 130
(Nicky Henderson) *hld up towards rr: hdwy fr 6th: rdn to chse wnr after 3 out: styd on same pce fr after next* **12/1**

-403 **4** *15* **Gilded Age**[43] 2455 4-10-1 130.............................. PeterHatton(8) 119
(Alan King) *hld up towards rr: rdn and sme hdwy appr 3 out: wnt modest 4th flat* **25/1**

2002 **5** *½* **Dantari (IRE)**[68] 1967 5-10-6 130.................................. DPFahy(3) 118
(Evan Williams) *chsd ldr tl 5th: rdn 3 out: wknd bef next* **16/1**

11P6 **6** *hd* **Cockney Trucker (IRE)**[20] 2868 8-10-10 134.................. GilesHawkins(3) 122
(Philip Hobbs) *trckd ldrs: jnd ldr 5th tl rdn after 3 out: wknd bef last* **10/1**

31/0 **7** *hd* **Art Professor (IRE)**[20] 2868 6-9-12 125.......................... HarryChalloner(6) 113
(Venetia Williams) *dwlt: sn in tch: rdn bef 3 out: wknd sn after* **16/1**

-253 **8** *11* **Olofi (FR)**[33] 2671 4-10-12 133.................................. PeterToole 114+
(Tom George) *in tch: trckd ldrs 5th: rdn after 3 out: wknd bef next* **9/2**[2]

20-2 **9** *4* **Causeway King (USA)**[25] 2792 4-10-6 130.................. CharlieHuxley(3) 104
(Alan King) *chsd ldrs tl wknd after 3 out* **28/1**

3-B2 **10** *3 ½* **Gifted Leader (USA)**[56] 2164 5-10-5 126.......................(t) MichaelMurphy 97
(Ian Williams) *pushed along after 5th: a towards rr* **25/1**

-314 **11** *nk* **Pennellis (FR)**[35] 2626 6-10-1 122.......................... SamTwiston-Davies 93
(Paul Nicholls) *mid-div: rdn after 7th: rdn after 3 out to chse ldrs: wknd qckly bef next* **10/1**

U-P1 **12** *62* **Darstardly Dick (IRE)**[88] 1706 7-10-1 125..................(b) MattGriffiths(3) 40
(Victor Dartnall) *nvr travelling or fluent: a last: t.o* **40/1**

2000 **B** **Tobago Bay**[14] 2977 5-10-0 129.............................. JosephAkehurst(8) —
(Gary Moore) *mid-div whn b.d 7th* **100/1**

0-30 **P** **Westlin' Winds (IRE)**[68] 1956 4-10-10 136.......................... JakeGreenall(5) —
(Charles Egerton) *nvr travelling in rr: t.o whn p.u bef 2 out* **20/1**

55F1 **F** **Grafite**[14] 2983 5-10-1 122.................................. RichieMcLernon —
(Milton Harris) *hld up towards rr: making hdwy whn fell 7th* **14/1**

4m 39.1s (-6.90) **Going Correction** -0.10s/f (Good)
WFA 4 from 5yo+ 5lb **15** Ran SP% **121.5**
Speed ratings (Par 109): **109,108,106,100,99 99,99,95,93,92 92,67,—,—,—**
toteswingers:1&2:£3.70, 1&3:£8.10, 2&3:£13.30 CSF £21.08 CT £210.75 TOTE £3.60: £1.80, £1.70, £3.80; EX 23.00 Trifecta £93.00 Pool of £717.73 - 5.71 winning units..
Owner A J White **Bred** Paul Chartier **Trained** Nicholashayne, Devon
■ Colin O'Farrell's first winner since coming over from Ireland.

FOCUS

Taunton was rewarded with a strong contest for such a decent winner's prize. It was hard to rule any of these out before the off, but the field thinned out going down the back straight and not many got involved in the latter stages. The well-on winner is rated close to his latest level, with a step up from the progressive second.

NOTEBOOK

Dynaste(FR)'s chance was there for all to see after trying to give weight to Aegean Dawn at Cheltenham. He was given a no-nonsense ride when clearly fancied to capitalise on what could have been a fair mark (although it was 11lb higher than last time), and the jockey should take plenty of credit for this success, as he kicked on rounding the final bend and was strong in the saddle to hold on by a narrow margin. (op 11-4)

Organisateur(IRE), 14lb higher for a win over C&D in November, clearly loves his trips to Taunton, as a 1112 record shows. He made his way through runners to threaten the winner coming to the last, but possibly found the concession of lots of weight too much after Dynaste had poached a lead. (op 15-2 tchd 7-1)

Monetary Fund(USA) has developed into a consistent hurdler and ran well until tiring after jumping two out. A combination of the extra distance and his handicap mark probably stopped him finishing any closer.

Gilded Age ran on through beaten horses down the home straight. (op 22-1)

Dantari(IRE) was never far away but failed to get home. His last winning handicap mark was 119, so he needs to ease down the weights to have an obvious chance. (op 18-1)

Cockney Trucker(IRE) looked a bit free early and faded. He has yet to win in handicap company. (op 11-1)

Olofi(FR) looked worth a try over this sort of distance but ran as though he didn't stay, even on this sharp track. (op 11-2)

3230 TOTEPOOL A BETTER WAY TO BET H'CAP CHASE (14 fncs 3 omitted) 2m 7f 110y

4:00 (4:01) (Class 4) (0-105,105) 4-Y-0+ **£4,553** (£1,337; £668; £333)

Form				RPR
P00/	**1**		**Sultan Fontenaille (FR)**[810] 1660 8-11-9 **102**...........(tp) TomScudamore (David Pipe) *hld up bhd: hdwy on long run bef 10th: led sn after 2 out: styd on wl: rdn out* **4/1**[2]	114+
-020	**2**	*1 ¾*	**Ballyegan (IRE)**[33] 2670 5-11-5 **105**........................... NathanSweeney(7) (Bob Buckler) *hld up towards rr: midfield 6th: rdn to chse ldr after 3 out: ev ch 2 out: styd on but no ex fr last* **33/1**	113
35-5	**3**	*hd*	**Aconitum (GER)**[38] 2585 5-11-3 **96**.............................(v) DougieCostello (Neil Mulholland) *led tl 6th: chsd ldr tl outpcd 3 out: plenty to do whn mstke 2 out: styd on strly fr last: jst failed to snatch 2nd* **14/1**	105+
6-4P	**4**	*nse*	**Lavenoak Lad**[199] 749 10-11-1 **101**..............................(t) MattGriffiths(7) (Simon Burrough) *mid-div: rdn and hdwy on long run to 10th: led 3 out: hdd 2 out: styd on but no ex* **40/1**	108
2-22	**5**	*½*	**Sir Winston (IRE)**[35] 2638 8-11-2 **95**.................................... DarylJacob (Victor Dartnall) *mid-div tl mstke and lost pl 4th: hdwy on long run to 10th: rdn to chse ldrs after 3 out: styd on same pce fr 2 out* **10/3**[1]	105+
50P1	**6**	*1 ¼*	**Foxesbow (IRE)**[42] 2479 6-11-6 **99**.. APMcCoy (Jonjo O'Neill) *in tch: rdn to chse ldrs on long run to 2 out: styd on same pce* **9/1**	104
/4-4	**7**	*3*	**Shacklesborough (IRE)**[63] 2059 6-11-5 **103**................... MrRMahon(5) (Paul Nicholls) *slowly away: sn chsng ldrs: rdn bef 3 out: one pce fr 2 out* **9/2**[3]	106
-22P	**8**	*1 ¼*	**River Indus**[211] 586 10-11-5 **105**.............................. JoshuaMoore(7) (Bob Buckler) *prom: hit 3rd: led 7th tl 3 out: sn rdn: outpcd on long run bef next* **33/1**	108
-5PF	**9**	*22*	**Backfromthebrink (IRE)**[67] 1991 6-11-9 **102**.................. WillKennedy (Paul Webber) *in tch: slow 10th: struggling whn mstke 3 out: sn wknd* **50/1**	89
P434	**10**	*7*	**Me Julie**[38] 2573 7-10-11 **90**... NickScholfield (Arthur Whiting) *trckd ldrs: led 6th tl next: chsd ldrs tl wknd 3 out* **20/1**	66
6013	**11**	*16*	**Justabout**[35] 2638 7-11-5 **98**...(tp) JoeTizzard (Colin Tizzard) *t.o fr 5th* **9/1**	59
04P-	**F**		**This Way (IRE)**[257] 5230 8-11-12 **105**...................(t) AndrewGlassonbury (John Ryall) *hld up towards rr: fell 7th* **40/1**	—
234	**P**		**Darn Hot**[14] 2975 6-11-8 **104**... ChrisHonour(3) (Alex Hales) *hld up towards rr: hmpd 7th: sn t.o: p.u bef 10th* **13/2**	—

6m 10.9s (-3.70) **Going Correction** -0.025s/f (Good) **13** Ran SP% **118.7**
Speed ratings (Par 105): **105,104,104,104,104 103,102,102,95,92 87,—,—**
toteswingers:1&2:£28.60, 1&3:£17.50, 2&3:£52.80 CSF £132.16 CT £1697.87 TOTE £4.80: £2.10, £12.00, £3.50; EX 174.50.
Owner D R Mead **Bred** Mme Henri Devin **Trained** Nicholashayne, Devon

FOCUS
A moderate but competitive handicap chase in which plenty had a chance but this was a case of gamble landed. The form is rated around the fourth and there should be more to come from the winner.

NOTEBOOK
Sultan Fontenaille(FR), a winner over hurdles and fences on a sound surface at shorter trips, had been absent since October 2008. Having his first run for a new yard, he was a morning gamble and justified the support with an ultimately cosy victory, having been held up travelling well. This was a fine training performance. (tchd 7-2)
Ballyegan(IRE), a point winner and placed over hurdles on heavy ground, had been beaten a long way on his chasing debut but ran much better having been held up. He should be capable of winning a similar race.
Aconitum(GER) had finished well beaten on his only start over fences - without the usual visor - last time. With the headgear reapplied, he made the early running before losing his place on the second lap, only to rally in the straight and, despite pecking at the penultimate fence, finished best of all. He is another who can win races over fences at this level, especially when the ground is more testing. (op 20-1)
Lavenoak Lad, a C&D winner in 2007, stays a lot further and appreciates soft ground. His rider tried to put his stamina to good use by kicking on down the back for the last time, but he could not shake off his rivals and was run out of the places late on. A return to further and softer ground will be in his favour. (op 50-1)
Sir Winston(IRE) beat Lavenoak Lad when gaining his only chasing win over C&D in November 2009. He was sent off favourite but, after a mistake on the first circuit, took time to work his way back into contentio, and then could not find any extra in the straight. (op 4-1 tchd 3-1)
Foxesbow(IRE), a winner at 3m on good and 2m4f on easy ground over fences, had been raised 5lb for his last success. Back from a six-week break, he rallied after losing his place on the second circuit but could not change gear again in the straight. (op 15-2 tchd 7-1)
Shacklesborough(IRE), a former pointer and good-ground bumper winner, had been well held in two runs over hurdles. Making his chasing debut, he was always prominent but made a few novicey jumps and tired in the closing stages. (tchd 5-1)
River Indus, a C&D winner who appears to handle any ground, had not been seen since pulling up in June. He was involved in the pacemaking for a long way before fading from the end of the back straight. The run should bring him on.
Darn Hot Official explanation: jockey said mare never travelled
T/Jkpt: Not won. T/Plt: £31.10 to a £1 stake. Pool:£105,725.70 - 2,479.53 winning tickets T/Qpdt: £24.20 to a £1 stake. Pool:£6,697.69 - 204.20 winning tickets TM

3231 - 3238a (Foreign Racing) - See Raceform Interactive

3201 LEOPARDSTOWN (L-H)

Thursday, December 30

OFFICIAL GOING: Chase course - heavy; hurdle course - soft to heavy

3239a BORD NA MONA FIRE MAGIC JUVENILE HURDLE (GRADE 2) (8 hdls) 2m

1:00 (1:00) 3-Y-0 **£28,761** (£8,407; £3,982; £1,327)

			RPR
1		**Sailors Warn (IRE)**[15] 2966 3-10-12 .... AndrewJMcNamara (E J O'Grady, Ire) *hld up in tch: 7th 3 out: smooth hdwy next: led travelling best bef last: sn rdn clr: easily* **12/1**	131+
2	*3 ½*	**Fearless Falcon (IRE)**[15] 2966 3-10-12 ....(b) KMDonoghue (Adrian McGuinness, Ire) *a.p: cl 2nd fr 4 out: led 3 out: rdn and strly pressed fr 2 out: hdd bef last: kpt on u.p* **16/1**	124
3	*2*	**Accidental Outlaw (IRE)**[47] 2380 3-10-12 .... MPWalsh (Charles O'Brien, Ire) *trckd ldrs in 4th: 5th 3 out: dropped to 8th whn slt mstke 2 out: 6th appr last: styd on* **10/1**	122+
4	*3 ½*	**Toner D'Oudairies (FR)**[15] 2966 3-11-1 .... DNRussell (Gordon Elliott, Ire) *trckd ldrs: 4th fr 1/2-way: rdn after 2 out: 3rd and no imp last: one pce* **6/4**[1]	122
5	*2*	**Kalann (IRE)**[15] 2966 3-10-12 .... MDarcy (Sabrina J Harty, Ire) *hld up in tch: cl 8th 3 out: prog next: 5th and rdn st: one pce* **7/2**[2]	117
6	*2*	**Kristal Komet (IRE)**[14] 2988 3-10-7 .... PTownend (Tracey Collins, Ire) *cl up: led narrowly 4th: hdd bef 3 out: 2nd 2 out: sn rdn and lost pl: one pce* **14/1**	110
7	*10*	**What A Charm (IRE)**[60] 3-10-7 .... PWFlood (A L T Moore, Ire) *sn led: slt mstke and hdd 4th: remained cl up: 3rd whn slt mstke 2 out: wknd bef st* **9/2**[3]	100
8	*8*	**Narima (GER)**[39] 2561 3-10-7 .... BryanJCooper (Mervyn Torrens, Ire) *in tch: 6th 1/2-way: cl 5th appr 2 out: sn rdn and wknd* **25/1**	92
9	*8*	**Days Ahead (IRE)**[15] 2966 3-10-12 ....(p) JRBarry (Eoin Doyle, Ire) *mid-div on outer: mstke 2nd: 9th and drvn along 3 out: sn wknd* **25/1**	89
10	*9*	**Al Dafa (USA)**[37] 2600 3-10-12 ....(b[1]) PCarberry (Gordon Elliott, Ire) *a bhd: trailing fr bef 3 out* **33/1**	80

4m 2.20s (-5.30) **Going Correction** +0.025s/f (Yiel) **10** Ran SP% **120.4**
Speed ratings: **114,112,111,109,108 107,102,98,94,90**
CSF £176.16 TOTE £15.20: £2.80, £3.00, £2.30; DF 176.30.
Owner Patrick Wilmott **Bred** Mrs Claire Doyle **Trained** Ballynonty, Co Tipperary

FOCUS
It's highly unlikely there was a Triumph Hurdle winner among these. It has been rated through the third to his best.

NOTEBOOK
Sailors Warn(IRE), a consistent sort on the Flat, is crucially ground-versatile with a view to Cheltenham. Moreover, he travelled with ease here on his third hurdling start and tanked into contention between the last two flights. He might not have beaten much but the manner was impressive. He jumped better than he did at Fairyhouse and is clearly getting the hang of hurdling. He is a best-priced 25-1 for the Triumph Hurdle with Totesport and Stan James. (op 14/1)
Fearless Falcon(IRE) put in a fine effort. Winner of an ordinary Thurles maiden in October, he was well held in third behind Toner D'Oudairies at Fairyhouse but reversed that form here. He is very consistent. (op 20/1)
Accidental Outlaw(IRE), an ordinary maiden on the Flat, has developed into quite a useful hurdler. He may be a Fred Winter horse as he handles better ground and stayed on well. (op 14/1)
Toner D'Oudairies(FR) had been Ireland's best 3-y-o hurdler up until this race, so it is not an endorsement of the quality of the country's juvenile hurdlers that his trainer describes him as "slow". He looked that here, well and truly outpaced from the second-last. He did not jump as proficiently as he can and is probably better than this. Official explanation: vet said gelding was blowing post-race (op 5/4)
Kalann(IRE), winner of a weak AW maiden less than a month ago, failed to build on his Fairyhouse effort. He already looks in need of further and lacks a turn of foot. (op 7/2 tchd 4/1)
Kristal Komet(IRE) ran a decent race but is not up to this level. (op 16/1)
What A Charm(IRE) was very disappointing. She had jumped quite well until the fourth but went out like a light after the second-last. Considering how well she stays on the Flat and how superior in that code she is to all of these, it was disappointing, but she is worth another chance.

3241a BORD NA MONA WITH NATURE NOVICE CHASE (GRADE 1) (11 fncs) 2m 1f

2:00 (2:00) 4-Y-0+ **£51,769** (£15,132; £7,168; £2,389)

			RPR
1		**Realt Dubh (IRE)**[15] 2971 6-11-12 .... PCarberry (Noel Meade, Ire) *trckd ldrs: mostly 3rd: cl 5th 3 out: smooth hdwy after 2 out: 2nd and clsng whn lft in ld last: styd on wl* **10/1**[3]	146
2	*5*	**Noble Prince (GER)**[64] 2041 6-11-12 .... BarryGeraghty (Paul Nolan, Ire) *trckd ldrs in 6th: cl up 3 out: rdn next: 4th early st: lft 3rd last: styd on* **5/1**[2]	141+
3	*hd*	**Torphichen**[14] 2991 5-11-12 .... AndrewJMcNamara (E J O'Grady, Ire) *racd wd: 6th 1/2-way: prog into 4th 4 out: 3rd and rdn 2 out: sn chal: lft 2nd at last: kpt on same pce u.p* **10/1**[3]	141
4	*5*	**Loosen My Load (IRE)**[46] 2384 6-11-12 .... AELynch (Henry De Bromhead, Ire) *cl up in 2nd: disp ld briefly 3 out: 2nd and rdn 2 out: sn outpcd: lft mod 4th fr last* **12/1**	136
5	*½*	**Mikael D'Haguenet (FR)**[15] 2971 6-11-12 .... PTownend (W P Mullins, Ire) *trckd ldrs: 3rd bef 1/2-way: dropped to 5th whn slt mstke 4 out: 4th and drvn along 2 out: 6th and one pce st: lft mod 5th fr last* **4/7**[1]	135
6	*dist*	**Gates Of Rome (IRE)**[46] 2412 6-11-12 .... DNRussell (C A Murphy, Ire) *trckd ldrs: 5th early: dropped towards rr 5 out: wknd after next: t.o* **40/1**	—
7	*28*	**Pay The Bounty**[40] 2533 7-11-12 128.. PTEnright (Robert Tyner, Ire) *a bhd: rdn and wknd bef 5 out: completely t.o* **50/1**	—
F		**Saludos (IRE)**[53] 2263 6-11-12 .... RMPower (Mrs John Harrington, Ire) *led: jnd briefly 3 out: led again bef 2 out: sn rdn: strly pressed whn fell last* **10/1**[3]	145

4m 21.6s (-0.40) **Going Correction** +0.30s/f (Yiel) **8** Ran SP% **119.7**
Speed ratings: **112,109,109,107,106 —,—,—**
CSF £62.10 TOTE £9.90: £1.80, £1.20, £2.00; DF 31.10.
Owner D J Sharkey **Bred** R Hartigan **Trained** Castletown, Co Meath

FOCUS
This did not go to script and it provided two main talking points, a disappointing run by the favourite and a debate about what would have transpired if the front-running Saludos had not fallen at the last. The first three have all been rated close to their previous best chase form.

NOTEBOOK
Realt Dubh(IRE) was probably about to assert when his chief rival Saludos departed at the last. He had disappointed Noel Meade with his jumping when second to Jessies Dream in the Drinmore but was polished in that area this time. He is set to return to the venue for the Arkle. (op 8/1)
Noble Prince(GER), having only his second run over fences, emerged with credit on this step up in class from a beginners' chase win at Punchestown in October. His winning form over hurdles was over 2m4f and he looks more than likely to improve when stepping up in distance, having stayed on well on the run-in to snatch second.
Torphichen ran a solid race, suggesting that there are probably good races to be won with him.
Loosen My Load(IRE) weakened from two out, with the ground probably not to to his liking. He had a few soft touches when initially sent over fences and now has a fair bit to prove at this level.
Mikael D'Haguenet(FR) was a major disappointment. He dropped off the pace with a slight mistake four out and failed to raise his effort under pressure from two out. For the moment the jury is out on the former novice hurdling star. (op 8/13)
Saludos(IRE) looks a useful long-term prospect. He had made a spirited effort but looked vulnerable between the last two fences and was being pressed by the winner when falling at the last. (op 10/1 tchd 9/1)

The Form Book, Raceform Ltd, Compton, RG20 6NL

3240 - 3251a (Foreign Racing) - See Raceform Interactive

[2640] UTTOXETER (L-H)

Friday, December 31

OFFICIAL GOING: Heavy (4.1)

Common bends and hurdles positioned on outside adjacent to fences. Final hurdle in the back straight omitted on all circuits of all hurdle races.

Wind: Nil Weather: Overcast

3252 FOINAVON ASSET MANAGEMENT MAIDEN HURDLE (DIV I) (10 hdls 2 omitted) 2m 4f 110y

12:10 (12:10) (Class 5) 4-Y-0+ **£1,561** (£458; £229; £114)

Form			Horse	Jockey	RPR
	1		**Maxdelas (FR)**[319] 4-11-0 125	PaddyBrennan	113+
			(Nigel Twiston-Davies) *trckd ldrs: chalng 3 out: led 2 out: drew clr after last: eased down towards fin*	7/2[2]	
2	**2**	*3*	**Railway Dillon (IRE)**[36] 2646 5-11-0 0	JasonMaguire	105
			(Donald McCain) *led: rdn and hdd 2 out: kpt on but no ch w wnr fr last*	11/4[1]	
4	**3**	*½*	**Coolbeg (IRE)**[51] 2309 4-11-0 0	SamThomas	106+
			(Tom George) *midfield: clsd to trck ldrs whn mstke 3 out: nt qckn bef 2 out: styd on run-in: nt quite gng pce to mount serious chal*	14/1	
1	**4**	*2*	**Havingotascoobydo (IRE)**[122] 1448 5-11-0 0	WarrenMarston	103
			(Martin Keighley) *hld up: hdwy appr 7th: nt fluent 2 out: styd on same pce*	9/2[3]	
005	**5**	*10*	**El Diego (IRE)**[52] 2283 6-11-0 0	DarylJacob	92
			(Jamie Snowden) *hld up: styd on steadily fr 2 out: nvr able to rch ldrs*	20/1	
5-50	**6**	*1 ½*	**Takamaru (FR)**[16] 2954 4-11-0 0	TomScudamore	91
			(David Pipe) *hld up: pushed along and hdwy appr 3 out: one pce frrom 2 out*	15/2	
	7	*9*	**Opera Og (IRE)**[278] 4-11-0 0	AidanColeman	85
			(Venetia Williams) *prom: chalng 3 out: wknd appr last*	9/2[3]	
0-06	**8**	*19*	**Everdon Brook (IRE)**[15] 2985 5-11-0 0	CharliePoste	63
			(Ben Case) *in rr: nt fluent 2nd: pushed along after 7th: sme hdwy whn nt fluent 3 out: dropped away 2 out*	66/1	
50	**P**		**Pagan Lightning (USA)**[44] 2446 5-10-11 0	JamesO'Farrell(3)	—
			(Dianne Sayer) *in tch: lost pl 6th: t.o whn p.u bef 2 out*	100/1	
0P	**P**		**Brockton Scrumpy**[48] 2363 5-10-11 0	CharlieHuxley(3)	—
			(Lisa Williamson) *prom: wknd appr 3 out: wl bhd whn p.u bef 2 out: dismntd: lame*	150/1	

5m 40.6s (36.60) **Going Correction** +1.425s/f (Heav) **10** Ran SP% **111.6**

Speed ratings (Par 103): **87,85,85,84,81 80,77,69,—,—**

toteswingers:1&2: £1.40, 2&3: £5.20, 1&3: £10.30 CSF £13.05 TOTE £4.30: £1.30, £1.20, £4.20; EX 5.30.

Owner Million In Mind Partnership **Bred** Jean-Pierre Laberou & Mme Yvette Laberou **Trained** Naunton, Gloucs

FOCUS

Racing was given the green light at the early morning inspection but conditions were very testing and described as deep and sticky, with stamina at a premium. A maiden hurdle run at a very steady pace but only two were seriously involved after the second-last flight. The winner was the pick on his French form and should rate higher.

NOTEBOOK

Maxdelas(FR) ◆, placed twice over hurdles in the French Provinces last winter, moved up travelling easily and, sent clear on the run-in, won easing up, value for at least double the official margin. He looks a decent prospect and connections will step him up in class next time to see if they have a Cheltenham prospect on their hands. (op 3-1 tchd 11-4)

Railway Dillon(IRE) took them along at a steady pace but it was clear once in line for home that the winner was travelling much the better. He looks to just stay and, though nothing out of the ordinary, he should be able to find a similar event stepped up to 3m. (op 3-1)

Coolbeg(IRE), fourth in a Bangor bumper in November on his debut, showed ability on his first try over hurdles and might do better in less testing conditions. (tchd 12-1)

Havingotascoobydo(IRE), a heavy-ground Irish maiden point winner, had not run since taking a fast-ground bumper at Newton Abbot in August. Given a patient ride, he seemed to fall in a hole going to three out before sticking on again at the finish, and he may have needed it after his absence. (op 4-1)

El Diego(IRE) has shown gradual improvement in four starts over hurdles now and this dual Flat winner would be better off in low-grade handicaps. (op 18-1)

Takamaru(FR), given a patient ride on his second start over hurdles, is another whose future may lie in handicaps in due course. (op 9-1 tchd 7-1)

Opera Og(IRE), bought for 60,000gns after being left clear when taking an Irish maiden point in May, is quite a big type. He tired once in line for home and should be capable of a fair bit better in due course. (op 6-1)

Brockton Scrumpy Official explanation: jockey said gelding lost its action; vet said gelding was lame

3253 FOINAVON ASSET MANAGEMENT MAIDEN HURDLE (DIV II) (10 hdls 2 omitted) 2m 4f 110y

12:40 (12:40) (Class 5) 4-Y-0+ **£1,561** (£458; £229; £114)

Form			Horse	Jockey	RPR
2	**1**		**Tornado Bob (IRE)**[35] 2666 5-11-0 0	JasonMaguire	122+
			(Donald McCain) *trckd ldrs: led 5th: clr after 7th: overj. and stmbld on landing 3 out: j. path appr 2 out: wl in command whn mstke last: eased down towards fin*	1/1[1]	
12	**2**	*13*	**Herdsman (IRE)**[41] 2525 5-11-0 0	TomO'Brien	101+
			(Philip Hobbs) *trckd ldrs: wnt 2nd 6th: no imp on wnr fr bef 3 out: mstke 2 out: plugged on: no ch*	13/8[2]	
42-2	**3**	*4 ½*	**Wood Yer (IRE)**[99] 1593 4-11-0 0	PaddyBrennan	95
			(Nigel Twiston-Davies) *nt fluent: in midfield: outpcd after 7th: styd on fr 2 out: nt rch front 2*	13/2[3]	
3	**4**	*15*	**Jan Jandura (IRE)**[36] 2646 5-10-7 0	MrTomDavid(7)	82
			(Tim Vaughan) *racd keenly: in tch: nt fluent 7th: outpcd appr 3 out: wl btn after*	10/1	
0/P6	**5**	*3 ¼*	**Lindengrove**[61] 2111 5-10-11 0	TommyPhelan(3)	76
			(Claire Dyson) *led: hdd 5th: remained handy tl wknd 3 out*	66/1	
6-0	**6**	*2 ¾*	**Saffron Lord**[54] 2238 5-11-0 0	TomSiddall	73
			(Martin Keighley) *in tch: wknd 7th: n.d whn mstke 3 out*	66/1	
00	**7**	*10*	**Tanwood Boy (FR)**[21] 2873 6-11-0 0	AidanColeman	63
			(Venetia Williams) *racd keenly: hld up: hdwy 7th: nt rch ldrs: wknd 3 out*	66/1	
0-00	**8**	*41*	**Monty's Revenge (IRE)**[60] 2123 5-11-0 0	WarrenMarston	22
			(Martin Keighley) *racd keenly: prom tl wknd appr 7th*	80/1	
00-	**9**	*2 ¼*	**Brainwave (IRE)**[412] 2275 5-10-11 0	RichieMcLernon(3)	20
			(Jonjo O'Neill) *hld up: rdn after 6th: nvr on terms: t.o*	33/1	
00/P	**P**		**Murfreesboro**[50] 2323 7-11-0 0	WillKennedy	—
			(Alan Jones) *hld up: struggling 6th: t.o whn p.u after 7th: dismntd*	66/1	
5	**P**		**Crabbies Court**[9] 3093 5-11-0 0	BrianHughes	—
			(Lisa Williamson) *rrd over in pre parade ring: a bhd: struggling 7th: t.o whn p.u bef 3 out*	100/1	

5m 41.9s (37.90) **Going Correction** +1.425s/f (Heav)

WFA 4 from 5yo+ 6lb **11** Ran SP% **121.7**

Speed ratings (Par 103): **84,79,77,71,70 69,65,49,49,—,—**

toteswingers:1&2: £1.10, 2&3: £3.00, 1&3: £2.20 CSF £3.03 TOTE £1.90: £1.30, £1.10, £1.40; EX 3.10.

Owner Mrs Diana L Whateley **Bred** Christopher Maye **Trained** Cholmondeley, Cheshire

FOCUS

The second division of the maiden hurdle and again the pace was very steady until the winner went for home four out. The winner is on the upgrade and the third helps with the level.

NOTEBOOK

Tornado Bob(IRE) ◆, runner-up in a 2m maiden hurdle at Newbury in November on his first start for this yard, went on racing keenly with a circuit to go and, despite getting two of the final three flights wrong, came home virtually alone, eased down near the line. He is still regarded as immature and, likely to prefer less testing conditions, will be given another outing at this level to improve his jumping before he moves up in grade. He looks a fine longer term prospect. (op 6-4 tchd 13-8 and 7-4 in places)

Herdsman(IRE), who took a bumper at Aintree in October on his debut, had chased home a highly rated McCain novice at Haydock the following month. He tried to close on the winner on the run round to three out but was never going to trouble him and blundered at the penultimate flight. He may not appreciate conditions as testing as this. (op 6-4 tchd 11-10)

Wood Yer(IRE), absent since finishing runner-up at Perth in September on his first try over hurdles, was making hard work of it with a full circuit to go. He kept on to take a modest third spot but is clearly a real stayer and another who will appreciate much less testing conditions.

Jan Jandura(IRE), who took a keen hold, tired in the home straight and blundered at the last. He too needs much better ground. (op 11-1)

Tanwood Boy(FR), well beaten on his first two starts, shaped much better until tiring in the home straight. By no means knocked about, he looks a likely sort for handicaps.

3254 MUSIC MAGPIE BEGINNERS' CHASE (18 fncs) 3m

1:10 (1:10) (Class 4) 4-Y-0+ **£2,941** (£888; £457; £242)

Form			Horse	Jockey	RPR
12-2	**1**		**Glenwood Knight (IRE)**[44] 2447 7-11-0 122	JasonMaguire	127+
			(Donald McCain) *led appr 2nd: overj. and stmbld 11th: sn hdd: regained ld next: drew clr fr 3 out: eased down towards fin*	1/1[1]	
0/	**2**	*9*	**Not So Prudent (IRE)**[278] 6-11-0 0	PaddyBrennan	111
			(Nigel Twiston-Davies) *hld up: wnt 3rd appr 11th: lost tch w front pair after 14th: styd on fr 2 out: tk 2nd run-in: no ch w wnr*	28/1	
2-32	**3**	*2*	**Silent Cliche (IRE)**[37] 2615 6-11-0 124	BrianHughes	110
			(Howard Johnson) *led: hdd appr 2nd: remained prom: lft in ld after 11th: hdd 12th: continued to press wnr tl rdn and btn appr 3 out: lost 2nd run-in*	5/2[2]	
1P-0	**4**	*63*	**Hopeful Start (IRE)**[15] 2979 6-10-11 0	RichieMcLernon(3)	46
			(Jonjo O'Neill) *hld up: blnd 12th: sn lft wl bhd: t.o*	17/2	
-066	**P**		**Love Of Tara**[39] 2579 8-10-7 0	WarrenMarston	—
			(Martin Keighley) *prom: dropped in rr 11th: struggling fr next: t.o whn p.u bef 3 out*	11/2[3]	

6m 54.6s (39.50) **Going Correction** +1.85s/f (Heav) **5** Ran SP% **107.9**

Speed ratings (Par 105): **108,105,104,83,—**

CSF £18.14 TOTE £2.20: £1.50, £5.40; EX 28.90.

Owner Peter Knight & Jon Glews **Bred** Edward And Joseph McCormack **Trained** Cholmondeley, Cheshire

FOCUS

An ordinary beginners' chase turned into a procession by the eased down winner, who is rated to his mark.

NOTEBOOK

Glenwood Knight(IRE), rated 122 over hurdles, had finished runner-up over 2m on his first try over fences at Hexham in November. He made a complete hash of the first fence on the final circuit and, forging clear from four out, met the second-last wrong. A fine leap at the last showed that stamina was not an issue, and he looks just the type his excellent trainer does so well with. He could be an Aintree type in time. (tchd 10-11 and 11-10 in a place)

Not So Prudent(IRE), who showed little in two starts in points, was very novicey early on. A remote third setting out on to the final circuit, he kept on to take a flattering second spot at the last. He looks a real stayer. (op 20-1 tchd 33-1)

Silent Cliche(IRE), rated 122 over hurdles, had finished runner-up at Wetherby on his first start over regulation fences. An Irish maiden point winner, he tried to lay it down to the winner but was readily beaten off and in the end lost second. (op 3-1)

Hopeful Start(IRE), rated 134 over hurdles, has shown little in two starts over fences now and was already struggling badly when making an horrendous mistake seven out. (op 8-1 tchd 9-1)

3255 A & S ENTERPRISES H'CAP HURDLE (8 hdls 2 omitted) 2m

1:40 (1:44) (Class 5) (0-95,95) 3-Y-0+ **£1,561** (£458; £229; £114)

Form			Horse	Jockey	RPR
0-00	**1**		**Smokey George**[58] 2149 5-10-10 **79**	JasonMaguire	93+
			(Kim Bailey) *midfield: hdwy 4th: wnt 2nd 3 out: led 2 out: drew clr after last: easily*	11/1	
005	**2**	*15*	**Illysantachristina**[54] 2231 7-10-11 **87**	MattGriffiths(7)	87
			(Bernard Llewellyn) *midfield: hdwy after 5th: led appr 3 out: rdn and hdd 2 out: no imp on wnr after last*	33/1	
000	**3**	*7*	**Dramatic Jewel (USA)**[40] 2540 4-11-2 **85**	PeterBuchanan	76
			(Lucinda Russell) *midfield: hdwy 4th: chalng 3 out: nt qckn bef 2 out: wknd appr last*	14/1	
P042	**4**	*1 ¼*	**Lady Of Ashcott**[36] 2643 4-10-1 **70**	(p) RodiGreene	60
			(Neil Mulholland) *prom: rdn and outpcd after 5th: tried to rally u.p 3 out: no imp fr 2 out*	8/1[3]	
060	**5**	*4 ½*	**Hardwick Wood**[36] 2642 5-10-13 **85**	(b[1]) AdamPogson(3)	72
			(Caroline Bailey) *racd keenly: prom: mstke 4th: rdn appr 3 out: wknd bef 2 out*	25/1	
-P66	**6**	*13*	**Sacco D'Oro**[36] 2640 4-10-13 **85**	CharlieStudd(3)	58
			(Michael Mullineaux) *hld up: niggled along 3 out: nvr rchd chalng position*	66/1	
4000	**7**	*3*	**Django Reinhardt**[32] 2467 4-11-0 **90**	MrDavidTurner(7)	60
			(Sam Davison) *midfield: rdn and wknd appr 3 out*	22/1	
/3-3	**8**	*hd*	**Imperial Royale (IRE)**[36] 2643 9-10-9 **78**	DaveCrosse	47
			(Patrick Clinton) *sn prom: rdn and wknd after 5th*	8/1[3]	
PPP	**9**	*¾*	**Petroglyph**[36] 2644 6-11-5 **95**	(p) MrJMQuinlan(7)	64
			(Michael Quinlan) *hld up: struggling after 5th: nvr on terms*	7/1[2]	
50U0	**10**	*8*	**Samizdat (FR)**[17] 2937 7-10-6 **82**	MissECSayer(7)	43
			(Dianne Sayer) *prom tl wknd appr 3 out*	10/1	
02FF	**11**	*38*	**Beauchamp Viking**[40] 2559 6-10-9 **85**	(t) NathanSweeney(7)	8
			(Simon Burrough) *hld up bhd: nvr threatened*	22/1	

6000 **12** ½ **Sommersturm (GER)**18 2927 6-11-1 **84**............................ PaulMoloney 6
(Barney Curley) *hld up: rdn appr 5th: nvr on terms* **7/1**2

0P00 **13** *10* **Sarah's Boy**42 2499 5-10-13 **82**................................(tp) TomScudamore —
(David Pipe) *led: rdn and hdd appr 3 out: sn wknd* **10/3**1

5R00 **P** **Othello (IRE)**16 2958 3-9-10 **85**................................ MissJennyCarr(7) —
(Jonjo O'Neill) *a bhd: t.o after 4th: p.u bef 2 out* **14/1**

4m 16.5s (21.30) **Going Correction** +1.425s/f (Heav)
WFA 3 from 4yo 13lb 4 from 5yo+ 5lb **14** Ran SP% **118.0**
Speed ratings (Par 103): **103,95,92,91,89 82,81,81,80,76 57,57,52,—**
toteswingers:1&2: £101.70, 2&3: £87.70, 1&3: £28.90 CSF £331.24 CT £5015.47 TOTE £12.50: £4.30, £9.30, £3.30; EX 435.20.
Owner Mrs Penny Perriss **Bred** J F Perriss **Trained** Andoversford, Gloucs

FOCUS
A moderate handicap hurdle run at a true pace after two false starts, and they were dispatched in very ragged fashion at the third attempt. There were just two in serious consideration at the second-last flight. A massive step up from the easy winner and the next two are on the upgrade.

NOTEBOOK
Smokey George, well beaten on his handicap debut two months earlier, travelled very strongly in the ground. Sent to the front two out, he came readily clear. Now he has come to hand this slow learner might well be capable of defying a higher mark. (op 12-1)
Illysantachristina, a modest point winner in the spring, had shown little in three starts over hurdles. Making her handicap debut, she went on three from home but in the end proved no match. (op 28-1)
Dramatic Jewel(USA), another making his handicap debut, had shown little in three previous starts. He was left trailing by the first two over the final three flights. (op 12-1)
Lady Of Ashcott, a well beaten runner-up her latest when out of the handicap, had to race from a 12lb higher mark this time. (op 15-2 tchd 9-1)
Hardwick Wood, a point winner, wore blinkers on his handicap debut and was readily outpaced. (op 28-1 tchd 22-1)
Sommersturm(GER), from a yard always to be feared when the money is down, started at a much shorter price than his recent form entitled him to and was well beaten by halfway. (op 9-2)
Sarah's Boy, who had shown next to nothing in four previous tries over hurdles, started favourite on his handicap bow but, after making the running, he went out like a light going to three out and trailed in tailed off in last. (op 4-1 tchd 11-4)

3256 HAPPY BIRTHDAY MICK JAMES H'CAP HURDLE (10 hdls 2 omitted) 2m 4f 110y
2:10 (2:10) (Class 4) (0-110,110) 3-Y-O+ **£2,341** (£687; £343; £171)

Form RPR

P41/ **1** **Supreme De Paille (IRE)**649 4653 8-11-8 **106**.............. PaddyBrennan 127+
(Nigel Twiston-Davies) *midfield: hdwy 7th: lft in ld 3 out: clr after 2 out: easily* **7/1**3

2 *13* **Sun Tzu (IRE)**161 1088 6-11-7 **105**................................. TomScudamore 101
(Dr Richard Newland) *a.p: ev ch appr 3 out: no ch w wnr fr after 2 out* **10/1**

13-1 **3** *23* **Ban Uisce (IRE)**46 2430 5-11-2 **107**................................ MarkQuinlan(7) 80
(Neil Mulholland) *trckd ldrs: rdn appr 3 out: sn btn: plugged on at one pce after* **85/40**1

352P **4** *2½* **I Can Run Can You (IRE)**99 1592 4-10-3 **90**........... RichieMcLernon(3) 61
(Jonjo O'Neill) *hld up: hdwy to chse ldrs 7th: rdn and wknd appr 3 out* **12/1**

5004 **5** *7* **Swiss Guard**136 1278 4-10-10 **101**.......................... MrMatthewBarber(7) 65
(Tim Vaughan) *hld up: hdwy 6th: sn chsd ldrs: wknd after 3 out* **25/1**

000 **6** *103* **Me Fein**51 2310 6-10-8 **92**.. PaulMoloney —
(Barney Curley) *hld up: hdwy 6th: rdn and wknd appr 6th: t.o* **11/1**

1P00 **P** **Deep Reflection**43 2475 10-11-6 **104**............................ WarrenMarston —
(Martin Keighley) *prom: rdn after 5th: lost pl 6th: t.o whn p.u bef 3 out* **25/1**

33-0 **F** **Timetoring**58 2147 8-11-2 **105**..........................(p) MissIsabelTompsett(5) —
(Bernard Llewellyn) *led: over 1 l ahd whn fell 3 out* **4/1**2

P **Piment D'Estruval (FR)**454 1610 7-10-11 **102**.............. MrTomDavid(7) —
(Tim Vaughan) *midfield: bhd fr 6th: t.o whn p.u bef 3 out* **25/1**

6/0- **P** **True Blue Saga (IRE)**291 4656 5-11-2 **107**......................(t) MrEDavid(7) —
(Tim Vaughan) *midfield: nt fluent 2nd: pushed along and wknd after 7th: t.o whn p.u bef 3 out* **33/1**

/P-F **P** **Palm Reader (IRE)**61 2104 7-11-12 **110**.......................... JasonMaguire —
(Donald McCain) *prom: reminders after 6th: lost pl bef 7th: t.o whn p.u bef 3 out* **9/1**

5m 45.3s (41.30) **Going Correction** +2.10s/f (Heav)
WFA 4 from 5yo+ 6lb **11** Ran SP% **114.1**
Speed ratings (Par 105): **105,100,91,90,87 —,—,—,—,— —**
toteswingers:1&2: £7.40, 2&3: £6.40, 1&3: £4.10 CSF £67.77 CT £198.41 TOTE £6.60: £2.50, £3.40, £1.20; EX 88.10.
Owner Terry Evans **Bred** John Mounsey **Trained** Naunton, Gloucs

FOCUS
A competitive 90-110 handicap hurdle run at what seemed a sound pace, but the time was very slow. Not easy form to pin down but the winner appeared to take a big step up. The favourite was 20lb+ off his recent win.

NOTEBOOK
Supreme De Paille(IRE), absent since getting off the mark at Huntingdon in March 2009, was making his handicap debut. He travelled very strongly and looked to be going best when the long-time leader departed three out. In the end he cruised home and is clearly much better than the 106 he ran from here. (op 13-2 tchd 6-1)
Sun Tzu(IRE), a mover on the morning line, had won an Irish maiden hurdle on heavy ground almost two years ago. Absent since falling in a chase in July, he has since been bought by this trainer for just £4,500. He was left in front three from home but was soon left for dead by the winner. (op 6-1)
Ban Uisce(IRE), who is proven in this ground, had won under this rider on his return at Plumpton. Raised 7lb, he was driven along to keep up early on the final circuit and was left a modest third three from home. Connections might now be tempted to send him chasing. (op 11-4 tchd 2-1 and 3-1 in a place)
I Can Run Can You(IRE), absent for 99 days after being pulled up, made very hard work of it, and a forward move after four out was very short-lived. (op 11-1)
Swiss Guard was making his handicap bow after four months on the sidelines. He moved up four from home but in this ground he tired badly from the next. (tchd 28-1)
Timetoring, dropping back to his best trip, made the running but had been joined when crashing out three from home. He would most likely have finished third. (op 5-1)

3257 CONGRATULATIONS TO A P MCCOY H'CAP CHASE (12 fncs) 2m
2:40 (2:40) (Class 4) (0-115,110) 4-Y-0+ **£2,915** (£861; £430; £215; £107)

Form RPR

103- **1** **Mallusk (IRE)**277 4928 5-11-9 **107**.................................... JasonMaguire 125+
(Kim Bailey) *a.p: gng wl whn chalng 4 out: led 2 out: rdn appr last: styd on wl to draw clr run-in* **3/1**2

553 **2** *10* **The Cockney Squire (IRE)**35 2659 5-11-12 **110**.......... PeterBuchanan 119
(Lucinda Russell) *led: rdn appr 3 out: hdd 2 out: n.d to wnr after last* **5/1**3

53F- **3** *4½* **Quintero (FR)**280 4865 6-11-12 **110**.................................... PaulMoloney 114
(Evan Williams) *in tch: nt fluent 8th: rdn and btn appr 2 out: plugged on at one pce after* **6/1**

3-13 **4** *7* **Abey M'Boy**46 2429 7-11-9 **107**.. LeightonAspell 112+
(Oliver Sherwood) *hld up: blnd bdly 6th: clsd to chse ldrs 4 out: no imp after 2 out: mstke last: eased whn btn run-in* **6/4**1

-P23 **5** *9* **Northern Quest (IRE)**17 2942 9-11-2 **100**....................... RobertWalford 88
(Henry Hogarth) *trckd ldrs tl wknd appr 3 out* **15/2**

5044 **6** *5* **Petrosian**50 2326 6-11-1 **106**...(p) HarryChalloner(7) 92
(Lisa Williamson) *hld up in tch: nt fluent 4th: pushed along 7th: lost tch after 8th: t.o* **33/1**

4m 23.2s (27.60) **Going Correction** +1.85s/f (Heav) **6** Ran SP% **110.7**
Speed ratings (Par 105): **105,100,97,94,89 87**
toteswingers:1&2: £2.80, 2&3: £3.10, 1&3: £2.30 CSF £17.43 TOTE £3.10: £1.60, £2.80; EX 18.60.
Owner A N Solomons **Bred** Mrs Christine Kelly **Trained** Andoversford, Gloucs

FOCUS
A 100-110 handicap chase and again the pace was sound in the testing conditions. The easy winner was up a stone+ on his ordinary y hurdles form.

NOTEBOOK
Mallusk(IRE), a giant of a horse, was making his chasing bow from his hurdle-race mark of 107 on his first start since March. He jumped soundly and, taking charge three from home, came readily clear in the end. He is already a better chaser than he was a hurdler and should continue to climb the ladder, especially if faced with a stiffer test. (tchd 11-4)
The Cockney Squire(IRE), having just his third start over fences, took them along but in the end proved no match. (op 6-1 tchd 7-1)
Quintero(FR), absent since falling when upsides in a novices' handicap hurdle in March, has undergone a wind operation since. Another making his chasing bow, he ran as if he was in need of it. (op 9-2)
Abey M'Boy blundered badly and lost his place at the first fence on the final circuit. He worked his way back into contention four out but was a tired third when making another mistake at the final fence. His jumping will need to improve if he is to progress. (op 2-1)

3258 DIGIBET.COM H'CAP HURDLE (12 hdls 2 omitted) 3m
3:10 (3:13) (Class 5) (0-95,95) 4-Y-0+ **£1,561** (£458; £229; £114)

Form RPR

UR-P **1** **Celian (FR)**17 2949 7-11-12 **95**.. MarkBradburne 108+
(Neil King) *mainly disp ld tl def advantage 8th: clr fr 2 out: styd on wl* **12/1**

P-51 **2** *21* **Ukrainian Star (IRE)**44 2457 7-10-12 **81**.....................(p) WarrenMarston 70
(Martin Keighley) *disp ld tl hit 8th: continued to chse wnr: rdn appr 3 out: no imp fr bef 2 out* **2/1**1

U020 **3** *3¾* **Oniz Tiptoes (IRE)**17 2941 9-11-5 **88**..............................(v) PaddyAspell 72
(John Wainwright) *hld up: rdn along after 6th: kpt on to take 3rd 2 out: nvr a danger* **4/1**2

44-3 **4** *21* **Paradise Expected**230 336 7-11-9 **95**...................... RichardKilloran(3) 58
(Tim Vaughan) *in tch: rdn after 9th: wl outpcd by front pair after: lost 3rd and wl btn 2 out* **15/2**

0-00 **5** *13* **Carys's Lad**51 2314 7-11-2 **85**.. LeightonAspell 35
(Michael Mullineaux) *hld up: struggling after 9th: nvr on terms w ldrs* **8/1**

05-P **6** *30* **Chit Chat**246 59 5-10-13 **85**...................................... RichieMcLernon(3) 5
(Jonjo O'Neill) *midfield: reminders after 7th: struggling whn mstke 9th: t.o* **13/2**3

0-4P **P** **Quay Meadow (IRE)**39 2589 8-10-13 **87**....................... AlexanderVoy(5) —
(John Norton) *hld up: niggled along fr after 5th: t.o whn p.u bef 3 out* **8/1**

00-3 **P** **Glamorous Gg**48 2365 5-10-13 **85**.............................. MichaelMurphy(3) —
(Ian Williams) *prom: reminders after 4th: lost pl 8th: struggling after: t.o whn p.u bef 2 out* **12/1**

6m 57.3s (52.10) **Going Correction** +2.10s/f (Heav) **8** Ran SP% **116.0**
Speed ratings (Par 103): **97,90,88,81,77 67,—,—**
CSF £38.07 CT £117.66 TOTE £15.10: £4.00, £1.02, £1.90; EX 50.40.
Owner Across The Pond Partnership **Bred** Olivier Delegue **Trained** Newmarket, Suffolk

FOCUS
A modest 81-95 stayers' handicap hurdle and just two in contention fully four flights from home. The winner is rated to the level of his best chase form with the runner-up 20lb off his recent form on better ground.

NOTEBOOK
Celian(FR) had failed to complete in four outings including over fences since taking a 2m4f handicap at Huntingdon a year ago from a 1lb lower mark. He went head-to-head with the runner-up before gaining the upper hand three out. Driven well clear, in the end he was able to virtually walk over the line. He clearly appreciates mud underfoot. (op 20-1)
Ukrainian Star(IRE), who took a low-grade handicap chase over 3m2f at Warwick in November from this mark, tended to race with the choke out in the first-time cheekpieces. After looking to be travelling best he suddenly came under strong pressure going to three out and the winner soon left him for dead. Stamina ought not to have been an issue. (op 3-1)
Oniz Tiptoes(IRE), proven over extreme distances in bad ground, is something of a moody individual. He kept on in his own time in the home straight without ever threatening to enter the argument. (tchd 7-2 and 9-2)
Paradise Expected was having her first start since May and it was almost certainly needed. (op 5-1)

3259 GRAHAM GOODE'S COMMENTATING SWANSONG MAIDEN OPEN NATIONAL HUNT FLAT RACE 2m
3:40 (3:41) (Class 6) 4-6-Y-0 **£1,301** (£382; £191; £95)

Form RPR

604/ **1** **Just Cloudy**619 5137 6-11-2 0... SamThomas 105+
(Anthony Honeyball) *hld up: hdwy 3f out: led over 1f out: hrd pressed wl ins fnl f: styd on and plld out more towards fin* **5/1**

2 *1¾* **Monbeg Dude (IRE)**341 5-11-2 0.................................. TomScudamore 101
(Michael Scudamore) *a.p: rdn and nt qckn whn drifted rt over 1f out: styd on to take 2nd towards fin* **4/1**2

3 **3** *¾* **Heliopsis (IRE)**79 1824 5-11-2 0..................................... AidanColeman 100+
(Venetia Williams) *trckd ldrs: led 1/2-way: rdn and hdd over 1f out: kpt on u.p tl no ex towards fin* **2/1**1

4 *1¾* **Kaffie**251 5-10-9 0... SeanQuinlan 91
(Kim Bailey) *in tch: effrt to chal fr over 2f out: styd on same pce ins fnl f* **9/2**3

3 **5** *28* **Miss Hippy (IRE)**39 2576 5-10-4 0............................ MrMMO'Connor(5) 63
(Milton Harris) *hld up: hdwy over 4f out: rdn 3f out: wknd over 2f out* **16/1**

6 *16* **Bally Gunner** 5-11-2 0.. DaveCrosse 54
(Roger Curtis) *hld up in tch: hdwy 1/2-way: rdn and wknd over 2f out* **40/1**

54 **7** *56* **Qualitee**40 2546 5-10-4 0.. IanPopham(5) —
(Claire Dyson) *led: hdd 1/2-way: wknd over 5f out: t.o* **14/1**

0 **8** *4½* **Generals Love (IRE)**40 2560 4-11-2 0............................ JasonMaguire —
(Donald McCain) *racd keenly: prom: lost pl over 6f out: toiling after: t.o* **16/1**

The Form Book, Raceform Ltd, Compton, RG20 6NL

9 1 1/4 **Master Conor (IRE)**[251] 4-11-2 0 .... RobertWalford —
(Henry Hogarth) *hld up in tch: pushed along and dropped to rr 7f out: t.o* **25/1**

4m 22.1s (32.50) **Going Correction** +2.10s/f (Heavy) **9** Ran SP% **112.9**
Speed ratings: **102,101,100,99,85 77,49,47,47**
toteswingers:1&2: £3.70, 2&3: £2.60, 1&3: £3.80 CSF £24.67 TOTE £6.50: £1.70, £1.50, £1.20; EX 27.70.
Owner Alvin Trowbridge **Bred** D Timmis **Trained** Seaborough, Dorset

FOCUS
A bumper run at a very steady pace to past halfway and four were still bang in contention with 2f left to run. Ordinary form, with a step up from the winner.

NOTEBOOK
Just Cloudy looked fit and well on his first start since April 2009 and his first outing for this trainer. Patiently ridden, he made stealthy headway going into the home turn. After taking charge he tended to hang fire and had to be driven right out. (tchd 4-1)
Monbeg Dude(IRE), who changed hands for £12,000 after taking a maiden Irish point in January, came back for more in the closing stages and clearly stays really well. (op 6-1 tchd 13-2)
Heliopsis(IRE) wouldn't settle and went on soon after halfway. He looked to be travelling strongly but came up short in the end. He will need to accept restraint a lot better if he is to progress. (op 6-4)
Kaffie, placed in two points in the spring, is not that big. She came there to have every chance and will appreciate an extra half mile over hurdles. (op 7-1)
T/Jkpt: Not won. T/Plt: £196.20 to a £1 stake. Pool of £76,575.76 - 284.85 winning tickets. T/Qpdt: £133.40 to a £1 stake. Pool of £5,519.40 - 30.60 winning tickets. DO

2452 WARWICK (L-H)
Friday, December 31

OFFICIAL GOING: Soft (good to soft in places)
Wind: Almost Nil Weather: Overcast

3260 COVENTRY TELEGRAPH CONDITIONAL JOCKEYS' H'CAP HURDLE (12 hdls) 3m 1f
12:50 (12:50) (Class 4) (0-105,104) 4-Y-0+ **£2,740** (£798; £399)

Form RPR
54-3 **1** **The Red Laird**[18] 2929 7-11-5 **97** .... GilesHawkins 101+
(Neil King) *led to 5th: led after 7th: rdn appr 2 out: hit last: styd on u.p* **9/2**[1]
-022 **2** 2 1/4 **Filippo Lippi (IRE)**[158] 1094 5-11-0 **100** .... GeraldQuinn(8) 102
(Jonjo O'Neill) *hld up in tch: chsd wnr 8th: ev ch 3 out: sn rdn: styd on same pce flat* **14/1**
33-1 **3** 1 **Gentleman Jimmy**[18] 2929 10-11-7 **99** .... IanPopham 99
(Hughie Morrison) *chsd ldrs: rdn after 3 out: styd on to go 3rd nr fin* **13/2**
-P61 **4** nk **Monsieur Cadou (FR)**[43] 2469 5-11-10 **102** .... SamTwiston-Davies 102
(Tom George) *chsd ldrs: rdn appr 2 out: styd on same pce flat: lost 3rd nr fin* **5/1**[2]
2226 **5** 2 1/4 **Nobby Kivambo (IRE)**[36] 2630 5-11-10 **102** ....(p) MrMMO'Connor 100
(Brendan Powell) *sn prom: rdn after 3 out: styd on same pce* **14/1**
0211 **6** shd **Chico Time (IRE)**[47] 2402 9-11-7 **104** ....(p) StephenO'Donovan(5) 103
(Norma Twomey) *hld up: hdwy after 7th: rdn 3 out: styd on same pce* **8/1**
P-23 **7** 3 **Mic Aubin (FR)**[36] 2630 7-11-12 **104** .... TomMolloy 102+
(Giles Smyly) *hld up: sme hdwy after 8th: sn outpcd: n.d after* **11/2**[3]
52-F **8** 59 **Sawpit Solitaire**[36] 2637 5-11-6 **104** .... HarryChalloner(6) 39
(Venetia Williams) *chsd wnr tl led 5th: hdd after 7th: wknd 9th* **16/1**
04P0 **P** **Aspolan (GER)**[18] 2930 7-10-3 **86** ....(p) PeterCarberry(5) —
(Rachel Hobbs) *hld up: sme hdwy after 7th: sn wknd: t.o whn p.u bef 2 out* **33/1**
403F **P** **Miller's Dawn**[18] 2928 6-11-5 **97** .... DonalDevereux —
(Henrietta Knight) *prom: rdn appr 7th: wkng whn hmpd next: t.o whn p.u bef 2 out* **16/1**
-32 **P** **Bear Dancing (IRE)**[56] 2192 6-11-6 **101** .... CampbellGillies(3) —
(Lucinda Russell) *chsd ldrs: lost pl 5th: bhd fr next: t.o whn p.u bef 2 out* **17/2**
-450 **F** **Balustrade (IRE)**[47] 2396 4-11-8 **100** .... RichardKilloran —
(Chris Gordon) *hld up: in rr whn fell 8th* **40/1**

6m 23.4s (-4.10) **Going Correction** -0.175s/f (Good)
WFA 4 from 5yo+ 7lb **12** Ran SP% **115.7**
Speed ratings (Par 105): **99,98,97,97,97 96,96,77,—,— —,—**
toteswingers:1&2: £16.80, 2&3: £19.20, 1&3: £7.00 CSF £63.99 CT £408.83 TOTE £5.20: £2.20, £3.10, £2.40; EX 104.70.
Owner The Red Laird Partnership **Bred** Mrs P B E Beaton **Trained** Newmarket, Suffolk

FOCUS
The ground was predominantly soft. This was no more than an ordinary staying handicap hurdle and, while the pace was fair, there were still six with a chance at the third-last. Some in-form sorts fought out the finish and the form is solid enough.

NOTEBOOK
The Red Laird won a bumper on testing ground, so these conditions were ideal, and he was well supported to break his duck over hurdles. He showed on his previous start that stamina is his strong suit and, given a positive ride, kept on gamely to gain a gritty success. He's still relatively lightly raced over hurdles and may improve a little more. (op 7-1)
Filippo Lippi(IRE) has yet to win over hurdles, but ran a solid enough race on his first outing since the summer. His previous best efforts were all on better ground, but he proved here he acts on soft, and though frustrating and costly to follow, he has the ability to win a race. (op 11-1)
Gentleman Jimmy was closely weighted with the winner on their form at Plumpton, and ran creditably once again, but he didn't help his cause by racing a touch freely early on. (op 6-1 tchd 5-1)
Monsieur Cadou(FR) was on a 7lb higher mark than when winning at Hereford on his previous start, but seemed to run up to that form and clearly stays 3m well enough. (tchd 9-2)
Mic Aubin(FR) is better than the bare form, as he was hampered when Balustrade fell at the fifth from home. (op 6-1)

3261 WHITSON BLOODSTOCK LTD NOVICES' H'CAP HURDLE (9 hdls) 2m 3f
1:20 (1:20) (Class 4) (0-100,100) 3-Y-0+ **£2,740** (£798; £399)

Form RPR
-631 **1** **Eastwell Smiles**[141] 1048 6-11-3 **91** ....(bt) RichardJohnson 103+
(Richard Phillips) *mde all: clr 2nd: nt fluent 5th: rdn whn nt fluent last: all out* **6/1**[3]
-045 **2** nse **Richmond (FR)**[21] 2873 5-11-12 **100** .... DougieCostello 112+
(Ian Williams) *hld up: hdwy appr 5th: chsd wnr 3 out: jst over 4 l down next: hit last: rdn flat: styd on wl: could nt quite get up* **11/4**[1]
0/2 **3** 24 **The Gripper (IRE)**[43] 2469 6-11-0 **95** .... PeterCarberry(7) 82
(Rachel Hobbs) *hld up in tch: racd keenly: rdn after 6th: wknd next* **11/1**
-605 **4** 12 **Not A Bob (IRE)**[63] 2070 5-11-0 .... MrAJBerry(3) 66
(Jonjo O'Neill) *hld up: bhd fr 5th: t.o* **14/1**
-051 **5** 1 1/4 **Moscow Mischief**[40] 2547 6-11-12 **100** .... CampbellGillies 74
(Lucinda Russell) *chsd ldrs tl wknd appr 5th: t.o* **14/1**
5-60 **6** 4 1/2 **No Woman No Cry**[58] 2154 5-11-0 **88** .... JoeTizzard 57
(Colin Tizzard) *hld up: pushed along 4th: wknd next: t.o* **14/1**
0-50 **7** 2 **Beau Lake (IRE)**[36] 2630 6-11-5 **100** .... MrTJCannon(7) 67
(Suzy Smith) *chsd wnr to 5th: wknd 3 out: t.o* **6/1**[3]
6000 **8** 7 **Le Roi Max (FR)**[39] 2583 6-10-11 **88** .... SamTwiston-Davies(3) 48
(Nigel Twiston-Davies) *hld up: a in rr: blnd 2 out: t.o* **14/1**
1006 **9** 2 **Mauritino (GER)**[18] 2927 6-11-8 **96** ....(t) APMcCoy 54
(Jonjo O'Neill) *hld up in tch: chsd wnr 5th tl wknd 3 out: t.o* **4/1**[2]
0/P0 **P** **Dareios (GER)**[61] 2111 5-10-7 **84** .... DonalDevereux(3) —
(John Mackie) *hld up: bhd fr 4th: t.o whn p.u bef 4 out* **40/1**
04-F **P** **Wham Bang**[214] 556 6-11-0 **88** .... SeanQuinlan —
(Robin Mathew) *chsd ldrs tl wknd bef 5th: t.o whn p.u bef 2 out* **80/1**
0-00 **P** **Midnight Trix**[53] 2281 4-10-6 **80** .... FelixDeGiles —
(Alex Hales) *hld up: hdwy appr 4th: wknd qckly bef next: t.o whn p.u bef 2 out* **28/1**

4m 36.7s (-6.00) **Going Correction** -0.175s/f (Good)
WFA 4 from 5yo+ 5lb **12** Ran SP% **117.4**
Speed ratings (Par 105): **105,104,94,89,89 87,86,83,82,— —,—**
toteswingers:1&2: £5.40, 2&3: £6.70, 1&3: £15.00 CSF £22.87 CT £180.01 TOTE £3.90: £1.40, £1.90, £3.30; EX 27.80.
Owner Mrs S J Harvey **Bred** Old Mill Stud **Trained** Adlestrop, Gloucs

FOCUS
A 0-100 novice handicap hurdle run at a decent gallop, and the first two finished a long way clear of the rest. Both produced steps up and the form could be rated 10lb+ higher.

NOTEBOOK
Eastwell Smiles, who was 9lb higher than when winning at Bangor in the summer, put up a game effort. Without a run since August, he was given a positive ride and picked up well when pressed after a mistake at the last. A left-handed track is ideal for him, as he was jumping that way for most of the race, but he'll face a further rise up the weights after this, and may now head for the sales. (op 13-2)
Richmond(FR), a bumper winner in testing ground in France in 2009, was well backed to win on his handicap debut. He'd shown promise in ordinary novice events, and kept on in good style from the second-last to finish a long way clear of the remainder. He'll win a race on his favoured soft ground, but by finishing so far clear of the rest, his handicap mark will take a knock. (op 2-1)
The Gripper(IRE) came out best of the others, but could never land a serious blow. (op 8-1)
Not A Bob(IRE), who was never travelling, finished well beaten in fourth. (op 16-1 tchd 12-1)
Moscow Mischief was struggling a long way out. (op 12-1 tchd 16-1)
Mauritino(GER), tried here in a tongue tie, ran better than his finishing position, for three out he looked a real danger to the winner, but then weakened quickly. He needs better ground and probably a shorter trip. (op 8-1)

3262 JADE AND ADAM TYLER NEW YEAR NOVICES' CHASE (12 fncs) 2m
1:50 (1:50) (Class 4) 4-Y-0+ **£3,332** (£1,034; £557)

Form RPR
-213 **1** **Rock Noir (FR)**[51] 2304 5-11-7 0 .... APMcCoy 150+
(Jonjo O'Neill) *hld up: hdwy 6th: jnd ldr 3 out: led on bit after next: canter* **9/4**[3]
5-15 **2** 7 **Keki Buku (FR)**[40] 2542 7-11-0 0 .... RichardJohnson 128
(Philip Hobbs) *chsd ldr: nt fluent 5th: led after next: rdn and hdd after 2 out: sn outpcd* **11/8**[1]
6U-3 **3** 5 **Qozak (FR)**[59] 2139 6-11-0 0 ....(t) NickScholfield 125
(Paul Nicholls) *led tl after 6th: chsd ldr fr ther tl 3 out: sn rdn: styd on same pce* **15/8**[2]

4m 0.80s (-4.80) **Going Correction** -0.175s/f (Good) **3** Ran SP% **107.7**
Speed ratings (Par 105): **105,101,99**
CSF £5.53 TOTE £2.10; EX 3.10.
Owner John P McManus **Bred** Scea Terres Noires **Trained** Cheltenham, Gloucs

FOCUS
An interesting and potentially classy novice chase and, despite the small field, the gallop was fair. The easy winner was value for further and is closing in on the level of his best French hurdles form.

NOTEBOOK
Rock Noir(FR), who had Qozak well behind him when making a winning debut over fences at Exeter, put a very disappointing effort at Bangor behind with an easy win. Although he took a little time to warm up to his task, he came through strongly to join issue after the third-last, and drew right away to win without being asked any sort of question. Considering he was giving 7lb to his two rivals, it was a decent effort, though that is tempered a little by a niggling doubt as to whether his two rivals ran to their hurdling marks. That said, Rock Noir remains an interesting young chaser. (op 7-4 tchd 6-4)
Keki Buku(FR) jumped well in the main, and a mile from home he looked the likely winner, so it was therefore rather disappointing the way he was brushed aside so easily by the winner. The pair were together, both seemingly going well three out, but soon after it became a one-sided contest and in the end he struggled to hold on to second spot. The winner seemed far too good for him, but on the evidence of his jumping here and his hurdles form he'll have no trouble in winning over fences in slightly lesser grade. (op 9-4 after early 5-2 in places)
Qozak(FR) was rather disappointing on his first run over fences, and once again he didn't appear to run up to his best hurdles form. He tends to jump right, so a return to a right-handed track will suit him, but the doubt remains as to whether he's going prove as good over fences as he was over hurdles. (op 13-8)

3263 AMBER SECURITY H'CAP CHASE (18 fncs) 3m 110y
2:20 (2:20) (Class 4) (0-115,115) 4-Y-0+ **£3,577** (£1,050; £525; £262)

Form RPR
5052 **1** **Mr Big (IRE)**[15] 2984 9-11-4 **110** ....(p) PeterToole(3) 123+
(Charlie Mann) *led tl after 1st: a.p: chsd ldr 12th: led appr 2 out: sn rdn: styd on gamely* **5/1**[2]
4-63 **2** hd **Rate Of Knots (IRE)**[15] 2984 7-11-10 **113** .... APMcCoy 126+
(Jonjo O'Neill) *hld up: hit 2nd: hdwy appr 12th: chal 2 out: sn rdn swtchd lft flat: styd on u.p* **11/4**[1]
0525 **3** 15 **Arnold Layne (IRE)**[18] 2928 11-10-12 **101** .... AndrewThornton 97
(Caroline Bailey) *led after 1st: hdd next: remained handy tl lost pl 4th: hdwy appr 12th: wknd 3 out* **5/1**[2]
63-0 **4** 3 1/2 **Whatever Next (IRE)**[10] 3059 8-11-6 **109** .... TimmyMurphy 103
(Edward Creighton) *hld up: hdwy 5th: rdn and wknd appr 2 out* **12/1**
223- **5** 7 **Rapid Increase (IRE)**[256] 5281 7-10-13 **112** .... GeraldQuinn(10) 98
(Jonjo O'Neill) *chsd ldrs: led bef 2nd: sn hdd: remained handy: pushed along 8th: wknd 4 out* **18/1**
-1U5 **6** 3/4 **Double The Trouble**[56] 2184 9-11-5 **108** .... NickScholfield 100+
(Andy Turnell) *hld up: racd keenly: hdwy 5th: led 8th: clr whn blnd 11th: hdd and wkng whn blnd 2 out* **25/1**
-536 **7** 8 **Son Histoire (FR)**[34] 2669 6-11-6 **109** ....(b) RhysFlint 88
(Philip Hobbs) *prom: lost pl 4th: bhd whn hit 9th: sn lost tch* **15/2**[3]
-P30 **8** 39 **Antonius Caesar (FR)**[17] 2940 7-11-2 **105** ....(p) TomO'Brien 43
(Alex Hales) *prom: mstke and lost pl 4th: bhd fr 11th: t.o* **8/1**

P3P- **9** *nk* **Freeze Up (IRE)**[283] 4806 8-11-11 **114**........................... RichardJohnson 51
(Philip Hobbs) *trckd ldrs: led 2nd to 8th: wknd appr 12th: t.o* **9/1**

0-PP **P** **Evella (IRE)**[43] 2470 6-11-9 **115**.. AlexMerriam(3) —
(Neil King) *hld up: hdwy 3rd: lost pl 9th: t.o whn p.u bef 12th* **14/1**

6m 24.1s (-2.90) **Going Correction** -0.175s/f (Good) **10** Ran SP% **116.3**
Speed ratings (Par 105): **97,96,92,91,88 88,85,73,73,—**
CSF £19.88 CT £72.57 TOTE £5.60: £1.70, £1.50, £2.10; EX 14.00.
Owner Mark Hunter & Hugh Villiers **Bred** Philip Gould **Trained** Upper Lambourn, Berks
■ Stewards' Enquiry : Peter Toole nine-day ban: used whip with excessive frequency forcing gelding to return wealed (Jan 14-20)

FOCUS
The early pace was ordinary, but it increased markedly going out onto the final circuit and ended up a fair test. Most of these were fairly exposed and the first two, who came clear, could struggle a bit depending on what the handicapper makes of the form.

NOTEBOOK
Mr Big(IRE), last in the Pardubuice in October, ran his best race since when second last time at Towcester, where Rate Of Knots was more than 4l behind him in third. There was much less between them this time, the pair battling it out from the second-last. The winner goes well for inexperienced riders, and is likely to head for a race like the Royal Artillery Gold Cup, which he won last season. (op 9-2 tchd 11-2)
Rate Of Knots(IRE) hasn't won since February 2009 but, although she was struggling from a fair way out, she only just failed to end that sequence. She had a hard race, so might need a break, but she left the impression she can find a similar race, probably on a stiffer track. (op 7-2)
Arnold Layne(IRE) is not the force of old, having suffered from all sorts of problems in the past few years, but he ran creditably enough over a trip shorter than ideal. He's certainly fairly treated at present, and left the impression he can pick up a small race given a more severe test of stamina. (op 6-1)
Whatever Next(IRE) was having his first run over fences of the season and, though he was feeling the pinch nearly a mile from home, he ran well enough to suggest there is a little race in him. (tchd 10-1)
Rapid Increase(IRE) shaped as though the run was needed. Official explanation: jockey said gelding had a breathing problem (op 16-1 tchd 20-1)
Double The Trouble ran much better than his finishing position. Keen early, he was several lengths clear when he made a terrible mistake at the 11th, but to his credit he was still in contention three out and was still in third when he made another error at the last. He's worth noting when dropped back in trip. (tchd 22-1)
Evella(IRE) Official explanation: trainer said mare bled from nose

3264 EUROPEAN BREEDERS' FUND MARES' "NATIONAL HUNT" NOVICES' HURDLE (11 hdls) 2m 5f
2:50 (2:52) (Class 4) 4-Y-0+ **£2,927** (£859; £429; £214)

Form RPR

3-12 **1** **Alverstone**[36] 2627 7-11-5 119.. APMcCoy 125+
(Lawney Hill) *led to 2nd: chsd ldr tl led again appr 6th: j.lft 2 out: rdn out* **11/8**[1]

-224 **2** *4 1/2* **Way Back When**[52] 2288 5-10-7 108........................ MrSWaley-Cohen(5) 114
(Alan King) *hld up: hdwy appr 7th: chsd wnr 3 out: rdn after next: styd on same pce last* **13/2**[3]

-504 **3** *27* **Genny Wren**[41] 2526 4-10-12 0.. JimmyMcCarthy 90
(Renee Robeson) *mid-div: hdwy appr 7th: sn wknd: lft remote 3rd last: t.o* **25/1**

2-0 **4** *6* **Blazing Empress**[58] 2156 5-10-5 0.. MrMEnnis(7) 83
(Sarah Humphrey) *plld hrd: led 2nd: hit 4th: hdd bef 6th: chsd wnr to 3 out: sn wknd: t.o* **100/1**

6-12 **5** *33* **Midnight Macarena**[41] 2526 5-10-12 0........................ DominicElsworth 48
(Lucy Wadham) *chsd ldrs tl wknd 8th: t.o* **9/2**[2]

40-0 **6** *20* **Francesa**[57] 2168 5-10-12 0.. RichardJohnson 28
(Henry Daly) *hld up: a in rr: bhd fr 7th: t.o* **50/1**

40/ **7** *15* **Starlet Mandy (IRE)**[964] 234 7-10-9 0............... SamTwiston-Davies(3) 13
(Nigel Twiston-Davies) *hld up: bhd fr 7th: t.o* **33/1**

240/ **P** **Midsummer Legend**[680] 4018 6-10-5 0............... StephenO'Donovan(7) —
(Norma Twomey) *hld up: a in rr: bhd fr 7th: t.o whn p.u bef last* **100/1**

22-3 **U** **Good Faloue (FR)**[41] 2526 5-10-9 107........................... AlexMerriam(3) —
(Neil King) *hld up: blnd and uns rdr 6th* **15/2**

5-13 **P** **Annimation (IRE)**[36] 2627 6-11-2 110........................... JimmyDerham(3) —
(Seamus Mullins) *chsd ldrs tl wknd after 3 out: t.o whn p.u bef last* **14/1**

3115 **F** **Alpine Breeze (IRE)**[39] 2571 4-11-12 120........................ TimmyMurphy 121
(Don Cantillon) *hld up: hdwy appr 7th: 5 l 3rd and btn whn fell last* **8/1**

50-U **F** **Lady Karabaya**[63] 2068 5-10-12 0.. HaddenFrost —
(Henrietta Knight) *hld up in tch: fell 7th* **33/1**

5m 13.6s (-1.40) **Going Correction** -0.175s/f (Good) **12** Ran SP% **116.8**
Speed ratings (Par 105): **95,93,83,80,68 60,54,—,—,— —,—**
toteswingers:1&2: £2.60, 2&3: £15.90, 1&3: £23.40 CSF £10.06 TOTE £3.00: £1.80, £1.40, £4.20; EX 11.10.
Owner The Freudians **Bred** Mrs M L Luck **Trained** Aston Rowant, Oxon

FOCUS
Quite a competitive mares' novice hurdle, but the gallop was only ordinary. The first two and the faller ran pretty much to their marks.

NOTEBOOK
Alverstone, a dual bumper winner, made it two from four over hurdles and looks the sort who will fare even better when she goes over fences. She had the run of the race in what was something of a tactical affair, but even so, she ran out a decisive winner. As the penalties accumulate, winning will get harder for her, but back over 3m, she might well hold her own in better grade. (tchd 13-8)
Way Back When, rated 108 and receiving 7lb from the 119-rated winner, ran up to form, and though she's been expensive to follow, there was little wrong with this performance, and she'll find easier races. (op 8-1 tchd 6-1)
Genny Wren kept on to finish a well-beaten third, and is likely to find easier opportunities in small handicaps. Considering she raced keenly for the first half of the race.
Blazing Empress, considering she raced keenly for the first half of the race, was far from disgraced, and she is another who is likely to do better in small handicaps.
Alpine Breeze(IRE), who was sweating up beforehand, raced a touch keenly, and while her rivals chose the outside route down the far side, she was kept to the inner. She was running a solid race for she was in third, but held, when she took a crashing fall at the final flight. With her penalties, she is not easy to place. (op 9-1 tchd 15-2)

3265 TURFTV H'CAP CHASE (17 fncs) 2m 4f 110y
3:20 (3:22) (Class 4) (0-105,105) 4-Y-0+ **£3,252** (£955; £477; £238)

Form RPR

4003 **1** **Silver Dollars (FR)**[40] 2555 9-10-12 **91**.. DarylJacob 102
(David Arbuthnot) *a.p: rdn to ld flat: styd on wl u.p* **7/2**[1]

40/0 **2** *nk* **Rateable Value**[18] 2925 6-11-0 **93**.. JoeTizzard 105+
(Colin Tizzard) *led to 3rd: led again 5th: j.rt last 2 fences: rdn: hdd and rdr dropped off side rein flat: r.o gamely* **8/1**

-P5P **3** *3* **Michigan D'Isop (FR)**[64] 2055 10-11-6 **99**.............. AndrewGlassonbury 107
(John Ryall) *chsd ldr: led 3rd to 5th: chsd ldr: chal 11th to 4 out: sn rdn: no ex last* **7/1**[3]

-5U2 **4** *6* **Pacha D'Oudairies (FR)**[39] 2587 7-11-12 **105**............ DominicElsworth 108
(Michael Blake) *hld up: hdwy 11th: lost pl next: rallied 13th: wknd after 2 out* **17/2**

2120 **5** *17* **Nautical Approach (IRE)**[16] 2961 7-11-12 **105**.................(t) TomO'Brien 93+
(Alex Hales) *hld up in tch: lost pl 5th: last whn blnd 9th: hdwy 5 out: wknd next* **9/2**[2]

0P-0 **6** *hd* **Signatory (USA)**[16] 2961 8-11-11 **104**.. APMcCoy 89
(Jonjo O'Neill) *hld up: hdwy appr 11th: rdn and wknd after 3 out* **9/1**

P505 **7** *19* **Kinkeel (IRE)**[15] 2986 11-9-13 **81** oh2 ow2................ EamonDehdashti(3) 47
(Tony Carroll) *prom to 14th: t.o* **12/1**

40-P **F** **Ironical (IRE)**[235] 249 6-11-0 **96**........................... SamTwiston-Davies(3) —
(Nigel Twiston-Davies) *chsd ldrs: rdn and lost pl whn fell 11th* **7/2**[1]

5m 23.2s (2.20) **Going Correction** -0.175s/f (Good) **8** Ran SP% **114.5**
Speed ratings (Par 105): **88,87,86,84,77 77,70,—**
toteswingers:1&2: £5.80, 2&3: £19.00, 1&3: £5.00 CSF £30.96 CT £184.94 TOTE £4.90: £1.40, £2.70, £2.40; EX 39.60.
Owner A R Parrish **Bred** Daniel Moine **Trained** Compton, Berks

FOCUS
An ordinary 0-105 handicap chase run at an ordinary gallop. There was not much recent form to go on.

NOTEBOOK
Silver Dollars(FR)'s previous wins have all been on better ground. Although he was keen early on, he stayed on well to score in a driving finish, but the form is unlikely to prove anything special. (op 9-2)
Rateable Value, who didn't show a great deal in bumpers or over hurdles earlier in his career, and failed to win when tried pointing earlier in 2010, turned in a career-best on his first run over regulation fences. This is probably his trip, and though the form is nothing special and he tended to race quite keenly, he's open to improvement. (tchd 13-2)
Michigan D'Isop(FR) was a bit mulish in the preliminaries, and is not the most reliable of performers, but ran one of his better races. (op 9-2)
Pacha D'Oudairies(FR) may well have just needed this after a break. (op 8-1 tchd 9-1)
Nautical Approach(IRE) lost any chance he had with a bad error at the ninth. (op 6-1)
Signatory(USA) was again disappointing. (op 13-2)
Kinkeel(IRE) has yet to regain his best form this season but is becoming well handicapped. (op 16-1)

3266 WHITSON BLOODSTOCK LTD STANDARD OPEN NATIONAL HUNT FLAT RACE 2m
3:50 (3:50) (Class 6) 4-6-Y-0 **£1,507** (£439; £219)

Form RPR

1 **Shuil Royale (IRE)** 5-11-0 0.. DarylJacob 109+
(David Arbuthnot) *trckd ldrs: wnt 2nd 2f out: led ins fnl f: r.o* **5/1**[3]

41- **2** *1 1/2* **Cresswell Crusader**[307] 4301 6-11-2 0........................ RachaelGreen(5) 113
(Anthony Honeyball) *led: rdn over 1f out: hdd and unable qck ins fnl f* **5/2**[1]

3 *1* **Tempest River (IRE)** 4-10-7 0.. CharliePoste 98
(Ben Case) *sn prom: rdn over 2f out: styd on* **40/1**

4 *1 3/4* **Tales To Tell (IRE)**[257] 5-11-0 0................................ RobertThornton 103
(Alan King) *prom: rdn over 4f out: styd on same pce ins fnl f* **7/2**[2]

4 **5** *nse* **Five Rivers (IRE)**[55] 2222 4-11-0 0........................ WayneHutchinson 103
(Warren Greatrex) *hld up: hdwy 9f out: rdn over 2f out: no ex ins fnl f* **6/1**

6 *nk* **Miss Milborne** 4-10-7 0.. JoeTizzard 96
(Colin Tizzard) *prom: outpcd over 4f out: rallied over 2f out: styd on* **12/1**

7 *3 1/4* **Sunny Ledgend**[242] 5-10-7 0.. MrSWDrinkwater(7) 101
(Andrew J Martin) *chsd ldr tl rdn over 2f out: wknd ins fnl f* **12/1**

0 **8** *13* **Next Man In (IRE)**[36] 2632 4-10-11 0........................ CharlieHuxley(3) 87
(Alan King) *hld up: hdwy u.p 1/2-way: wknd over 4f out* **40/1**

10/ **9** *7* **Dizzy Whizz**[775] 2236 6-11-0 0.. TimmyMurphy 80
(Murty McGrath) *prom: lost pl 12f out: n.d after* **16/1**

10 *2* **Cider Lolly** 4-10-4 0.. SamTwiston-Davies(3) 71
(Colin Tizzard) *chsd ldrs tl rdn and wknd over 3f out* **28/1**

6 **11** *2 1/4* **Farewellatmidnight**[58] 2156 4-10-7 0.. TomO'Brien 68
(Alex Hales) *hld up: hdwy 12f out: wknd over 4f out* **20/1**

0 **12** *1 1/4* **San Salito (FR)**[41] 2518 4-10-11 0.. TomMolloy(3) 74
(Giles Smyly) *hld up: sme hdwy over 6f out: sn wknd* **100/1**

13 *3* **Bushlark** 4-10-7 0.. JimmyMcCarthy 64
(Renee Robeson) *hld up: nvr on terms* **66/1**

14 *8* **Perjury** 6-10-7 0.. TomSiddall 56
(Robin Mathew) *hld up: a in rr: bhd fr 1/2-way: t.o* **100/1**

4 **15** *8* **Full Ov Beans**[185] 855 6-10-7 0.. MrJEngland(7) 55
(Michael Gates) *hld up: a in rr: bhd fr 1/2-way: t.o* **33/1**

0 **16** *36* **Commander Jet**[16] 2957 4-11-0 0.. JodieMogford 19
(Brian Baugh) *hld up: a in rr: bhd fr 1/2-way: t.o* **100/1**

4 **P** **Toomyvara (IRE)**[246] 60 6-11-0 0.. LiamTreadwell —
(Nick Gifford) *prom: pushed along 1/2-way: wknd over 6f out: t.o whn p.u over 1f out* **40/1**

3m 52.1s (1.20) **Going Correction** -0.175s/f (Good)
WFA 4 from 5yo+ 5lb **17** Ran SP% **125.9**
Speed ratings: **90,89,88,87,87 87,86,79,76,75 73,73,71,67,63 45,—**
toteswingers:1&2: £8.20, 2&3: £91.10, 1&3: £100.00 CSF £17.12 TOTE £7.90: £2.30, £1.50, £10.60; EX 31.30.
Owner Phil Fry **Bred** Greenville House Stud And M Morgan **Trained** Compton, Berks

FOCUS
A decent gallop to this bumper, but with only eight lengths between the first seven the form is unlikely to be anything special. The runner-up did set a decent standard though.

NOTEBOOK
Shuil Royale(IRE) is a 5-y-o with plenty of scope, and considering how keen he ran, and how green he appeared, he did well to win. It took him an age to drop the bit, and even longer before he really put his head down and raced, so it would be no surprise if he were not a fair bit better than the bare form. However, he'll probably need to improve if he's to win under a penalty. (op 8-1)
Cresswell Crusader, whose Chepstow bumper win in February had worked out well, ran a sound enough race on his first start since under his penalty. He may come on for the run, but he's always going to be vulnerable having to give weight away. (op 4-1)
Tempest River(IRE) kept on to finish third, shaping well on her debut, and she'll find easier opportunities in mares' events. (op 50-1)
Tales To Tell(IRE), winner of an Irish point-to-point, will be suited by a stiffer track. (tchd 10-3)
Five Rivers(IRE) again ran creditably, but will need to raise his game to win a bumper. (op 4-1)
Miss Milborne shaped with a degree of promise on her debut. (op 11-1)
Toomyvara(IRE) Official explanation: jockey said gelding lost his action
T/Plt: £40.90 to a £1 stake. Pool of £79,810.22 - 1,423.63 winning tickets. T/Qpdt: £10.20 to a £1 stake. Pool of £5,781.60 - 417.40 winning tickets. CR

3267, 3269a-3281a - (Foreign Racing) - See Raceform Interactive

2411 PUNCHESTOWN (R-H)

Friday, December 31

OFFICIAL GOING: Soft to heavy

3268a IRISH STALLION FARMS EUROPEAN BREEDERS FUND LOMBARDSTOWN MARES NOVICE CHASE (GRADE 3) (12 fncs) 2m

12:45 (12:45) 4-Y-0+ £22,146 (£6,473; £3,066; £1,022)

RPR

1 **Blazing Tempo (IRE)**[50] 2340 6-11-4 PTownend 143+
(W P Mullins, Ire) *trckd ldrs: 3rd travelling wl appr 4 out: led 2 out: asserted bef last: styd on wl: easily* 9/10[1]

2 4 **Cool Quest (IRE)**[50] 2340 6-10-11 KTColeman 131
(Terence O'Brien, Ire) *trckd ldrs in 3rd: mstke 1st: 2nd fr 1/2-way: chal and led briefly early st: hdd 2 out and sn no imp on wnr: kpt on same pce* 9/2[2]

3 7 **Tramp Stamp (IRE)**[64] 2064 6-10-11 PCarberry 124
(Matthieu Palussiere, Ire) *hld up in rr: in tch travelling wl 4 out: pushed along after next: rdn to go 4th after 2 out: kpt on one pce wout threatening principals* 8/1

4 2 **Coscorrig (IRE)**[152] 1156 8-11-1 120 PWFlood 128
(D T Hughes, Ire) *racd keenly towards rr on outer: 6th 1/2-way: wnt 4th travelling wl bef 4 out: 3rd whn mstke 2 out: no imp whn mstke again last* 16/1

5 3 1/2 **No One Tells Me**[57] 2174 5-10-11 MJBolger 119
(Mrs John Harrington, Ire) *trckd ldr in 2nd: mstke and lost pl 7th: 5th appr 4 out: u.p in 7th early st: kpt on one pce* 9/1

6 5 **Inch Native (IRE)**[207] 672 8-10-11 AndrewJMcNamara 114
(Denis Paul Murphy, Ire) *chsd ldrs on inner: 4th 1/2-way: 6th appr 4 out: drvn along after 3 out: no ex fr next* 20/1

7 3 **Back Of The Pack (IRE)**[61] 2119 8-11-4 134 MDarcy 118
(Colin Kidd, Ire) *led: niggled along appr 4 out: strly pressed next and hdd ent st: no ex fr 2 out* 11/2[3]

4m 17.3s (3.40) 7 Ran SP% 118.0
CSF £6.06 TOTE £1.80: £1.50, £2.50; DF 6.00.
Owner Mrs S Ricci **Bred** W Austin **Trained** Muine Beag, Co Carlow

FOCUS
The time was slow in comparison with the beginners' chase, and it has been rated through the runner-up.

NOTEBOOK
Blazing Tempo(IRE), dropping down in trip after her chasing debut win at Clonmel in November, jumped much better on this occasion and put up a more impressive overall performance. She travelled well behind the leaders, was clearly going best from four out, led two out and quickly asserted to win comfortably. She will be entered for some of the big novice chases, although trainer Willie Mullins is favouring keeping her to mares' races in the more immediate future. (op 10/11 tchd 4/5)
Cool Quest(IRE), runner-up to Blazing Tempo at Clonmel and meeting her 7lb better here for a beating of 1 3/4l, recovered from a mistake at the first and was always close up. Sent to the front after three out, she kept on but could make no impression on the winner, who jumped past her at the second-last fence.
Tramp Stamp(IRE), who had just been headed by eventual winner Cool Quest when falling at the final fence on her chasing debut at Clonmel in October, made headway from behind after four out. Driven along after three out, she kept on without posing any real threat.
Coscorrig(IRE), having her first run since joining Dessie Hughes, is a C&D winner on fast ground. Often a front-runner in the past, she was held up and raced quite keenly. She looked held in third when fluffing two out and was making no impression when she made another mistake at the final fence. (op 14/1)
No One Tells Me, a three-time winner over hurdles and in against her own sex for the first time over fences at her third attempt, raced in second place and was still prominent when she pecked at the seventh fence. She lost touch soon afterwards and kept on from two out without posing any sort of threat. (op 9/1 tchd 10/1)

2937 CATTERICK (L-H)

Saturday, January 1

3282 Meeting Abandoned - Frozen track

2881 CHELTENHAM (L-H)

Saturday, January 1

OFFICIAL GOING: Good to soft
Wind: Virtually nil Weather: Overcast

3288 NEPTUNE INVESTMENT MANAGEMENT NOVICES' HURDLE (10 hdls) 2m 4f 110y

12:20 (12:20) (Class 3) 4-Y-0+

£6,262 (£1,850; £925; £463; £231; £116)

Form RPR

21-1 1 **Bobs Worth (IRE)**[40] 2577 6-11-8 0 BarryGeraghty 142+
(Nicky Henderson) *in tch: hdwy to trck ldrs 3 out: qcknd to chal between horses after 2 out: led wl bef last: rdn and styd on strly fnl 120yds* 3/1[1]

2-14 2 2 1/4 **Rose Of The Moon (IRE)**[48] 2389 6-11-2 0 NickScholfield 133+
(Milton Harris) *hit 3rd: in tch 4th: rdn and towards rr 3 out: hit next and plenty to do whn drvn and hdwy wl bef last: styd on wl run-in to take 2nd fnl 100yds: clsng on wnr nr fin but a readily hld* 12/1

4-11 3 1 3/4 **Habbie Simpson**[45] 2454 6-11-12 126 RobertThornton 140
(Alan King) *in tch: chsd ldrs fr 4 out: chal 2 out: wnt 2nd and rdn wl bef last: no imp on wnr run-in and outpcd into 3rd fnl 100yds* 11/1

0- 4 14 **On His Own (IRE)**[290] 4676 7-11-2 0 BrianHughes 119
(Howard Johnson) *w ldr: hit 4th: blnd 6th: stl upsides whn hit 2 out: wknd bef last* 16/1

5 3 3/4 **Barbatos (FR)**[103] 5-11-2 0 DougieCostello 114
(Ian Williams) *chsd ldrs: rdn 3 out: lost pl next: styd on again run-in but nvr any ch* 50/1

3106 6 shd **Astracad (FR)**[21] 2887 5-11-12 140 PaddyBrennan 124
(Nigel Twiston-Davies) *in tch fr 4th: chsd ldrs and rdn after 3 out: stl wl there next: wknd bef last* 7/2[2]

7 3 3/4 **Saint Are (FR)**[193] 5-11-12 0 AidanColeman 122
(Tim Vaughan) *chsd ldrs: hit 5th: j. slowly 6th: sn rdn: wknd after 2 out* 100/1

1540 8 nk **Total Submission**[22] 2870 6-11-8 125 WarrenMarston 117
(Martin Keighley) *mde most tl hdd & wknd wl bef last* 50/1

-210 9 9 **Golden Chieftain (IRE)**[21] 2888 6-11-8 0 JoeTizzard 111
(Colin Tizzard) *in rr: rdn and j. slowly 5th: blnd next: bmpd whn virtually t.o 2 out: styd on run-in and kpt on cl home but nvr any ch* 14/1

11-1 10 1 1/2 **Safran De Cotte (FR)**[52] 2307 5-11-8 0 RichardJohnson 109
(Henry Daly) *towards rr but in tch whn hit 3rd: wknd fr 3 out: wl bhd whn blnd last* 11/1

3-10 11 1 1/4 **Heez A Cracker (FR)**[48] 2387 5-11-8 118 DarylJacob 109+
(Emma Lavelle) *chsd ldrs to 3 out* 20/1

04-4 12 5 **Master Beau**[22] 2873 7-11-2 0 JanFaltejsek 96
(George Charlton) *chsd ldrs to 4 out: wknd after next* 33/1

3-4 13 30 **Easter Meteor**[43] 2493 5-11-2 0 SamThomas 69
(Emma Lavelle) *j. slowly 1st: in rr: j. slowly 5th and next: hdwy to chse ldrs 3 out: sn wknd* 17/2[3]

53- 14 15 **The White Admiral (IRE)**[301] 4452 6-11-2 0 AndrewTinkler 55
(Nicky Henderson) *in rr: hdwy 4 out: wknd qckly next* 33/1

1 F **Lethal Glaze (IRE)**[18] 2939 5-11-8 0 APMcCoy 125+
(Brian Ellison) *hld up in rr: hit 1st: hdwy 3 out: styng on wl to dispute 3 l 4th whn fell 2 out* 11/1

5m 2.27s (-2.73) **Going Correction** +0.25s/f (Yiel) 15 Ran SP% 118.5
Speed ratings (Par 107): **115,114,113,108,106 106,105,105,101,101 100,98,87,81,—**
toteswingers: 1&2 £38.10, 1&3 £13.60, 2&3 £10.10. CSF £36.40 TOTE £3.80: £1.80, £4.80, £3.60; EX 58.70 Trifecta £563.30 Part won. Pool: £761.32 - 0.20 winning units..
Owner The Not Afraid Partnership **Bred** Mrs L Eadie **Trained** Upper Lambourn, Berks

FOCUS
Following a dry night the going was given as good to soft, with the jockeys reporting it to be a bit dead. The early pace didn't look hectic. This looked a good novice hurdle on paper and is likely to produce its fair share of winners. Bobs Worth is a smart novice and obvious Festival material.

NOTEBOOK
Bobs Worth(IRE), along with On His Own, travelled best throughout and, whereas the latter appeared to blow up, he saw his race out strongly and showed improved form for the step up in trip. His pedigree had suggested as much, and, as this was just his second start over hurdles, there's surely even better to come, although there will have to be, for his price for the Neptune (largely unchanged at 16-1, with bigger available on Betfair) to contract. (tchd 11-4 and 10-3 in places)
Rose Of The Moon(IRE) ◆, running over hurdles for the first time, wasn't always the most fluent towards the rear of the field, and he had to be niggled along to keep in touch, but stamina is clearly his thing and he passed most of the field to run on best of all for second. He should be winning races once upped to 3m. (op 11-1)
Habbie Simpson really picked up running down the hill and got himself bang in contention at the second-last. He couldn't live with the strong travelling winner from the last but it was a good effort giving him 4lb, and there wouldn't a great deal between them strictly on the ratings. (op 12-1)
On His Own(IRE), who has plenty of size about him, was last seen finishing well beaten in the Champion Bumper here in March, is another bred to stay well. He made a few mistakes but, along with the winner, travelled best to the second-last. Lack of a recent run told from there, but he shaped like a good horse and on this evidence he'll soon be winning races. (op 20-1)
Barbatos(FR), debuting for his new stable having run well in his one start at Auteuil back in September, ran a sound race and might be one for handicaps in due course.
Astracad(FR) was a bit disappointing. This was a drop in class for him having taken on Menorah in his last two starts. It might just be that he needs genuine good ground to be seen at his best. (op 9-2)
Total Submission, more exposed than most in the field, took them along and was still there turning in, but he couldn't stay with the classier types up the hill. (op 40-1)
Safran De Cotte(FR) didn't help his cause by failing to settle. (op 10-1)

3289 CHELTENHAM & THREE COUNTIES CLUB HURDLE (10 hdls) 2m 4f 110y

12:55 (12:55) (Class 2) 4-Y-0+

£12,524 (£3,700; £1,850; £926; £462; £232)

Form RPR

114- 1 **Oscar Whisky (IRE)**[291] 4657 6-11-4 146 BarryGeraghty 163+
(Nicky Henderson) *in tch: nt fluent 6th: smooth hdwy 2 out: led on bit bef last: shkn up and qcknd clr last 100yds: eased nr fin: readily* 3/1[2]

2142 2 7 **Any Given Day (IRE)**[21] 2884 6-11-8 159 JasonMaguire 159
(Donald McCain) *hld up: niggled along to improve bef 2 out: rdn: hdwy and ev ch appr last: outpcd fnl 100yds* 7/2[3]

-F33 3 6 **Celestial Halo (IRE)**[21] 2884 7-11-8 160 (bt) HarrySkelton 153
(Paul Nicholls) *t.k.h: pressed ldr: chal 4th: led next: hdd bef last: sn outpcd* 9/2

0-21 4 3 3/4 **Karabak (FR)**[21] 2884 8-11-12 161 APMcCoy 154
(Alan King) *trckd ldrs: nt fluent 6th: hdwy to press ldr after 3 out: rdn after next: cl up tl edgd lft and wknd fr last* 2/1[1]

-044 5 3 **Duke Of Lucca (IRE)**[22] 2870 6-11-4 149 RichardJohnson 143
(Philip Hobbs) *trckd ldrs: nt fluent 2nd: rdn and outpcd after 2 out: n.d after* 11/1

-303 6 9 **Barizan (IRE)**[42] 2521 5-11-12 140 PaulMoloney 142
(Evan Williams) *led to 5th: rdn and lost pl after 3 out: sn struggling* 33/1

50-0 7 6 **Secret Dancer (IRE)**[43] 2498 6-11-4 131 SamThomas 131
(Alan Jones) *hld up: nt fluent 4th and 3 out: rdn and wknd fr next* 66/1

5m 0.50s (-4.50) **Going Correction** +0.25s/f (Yiel) 7 Ran SP% 111.5
Speed ratings (Par 109): **118,115,113,111,110 107,104**
toteswingers: 1&2 £2.20, 1&3 £1.70, 2&3 £6.00. CSF £13.46 TOTE £3.90: £2.00, £2.40; EX 11.40.
Owner Walters Plant Hire Ltd **Bred** Stephanie Hanly **Trained** Upper Lambourn, Berks

FOCUS
Just 7lb separated five of these seven on adjusted official ratings, and that was reflected in a competitive betting heat. Barizan has blazed in the past, but although he disputed the lead here, he was ridden more conservatively over this longer trip, and the early pace appeared just fair. Cozy winner Oscar Whisky was value for further and this puts him on the fringes of the Champion Hurdle picture. Any Given Day is rated to the level of his recent C/D run.

NOTEBOOK
Oscar Whisky(IRE), last seen finishing fourth in the Supreme, announced himself a possible player in the Champion Hurdle with a taking display. Bar an error at the fifth-last, his jumping was good and, not only did he travel strongly, but he picked up really well when Barry Geraghty, who didn't have to get serious with him, asked him to quicken up on the run-in. Clearly he was only beating staying types here and it will be different taking on the genuine two-milers, and he does have a bit to find with the likes of Menorah on Supreme Novices' form, but he's improving and a best price of 16-1 for the Champion looks about right for the time being. The Welsh Champion Hurdle, which has long been his target, is up next, and that might tell us more. Nicky Henderson completely ruled out the possibility of stepping up to 3m with him, so the World Hurdle is not under consideration. (op 9-4)

Any Given Day(IRE) reversed last month's C&D form with Karabak on 4lb better terms. Not for the first time his jumping wasn't great, but he does stay particularly well and he ran on strongly up the hill. He was just unfortunate to bump into a rival with a lot more speed than him at the finish. (op 9-2 tchd 5-1)
Celestial Halo(IRE) raced a bit keenly while disputing the lead but he still looked to have his chance turning in, only to be soon left behind. His best days appear to be behind him and he looks likely to remain a hard horse to place. (tchd 4-1)
Karabak(FR) was under pressure but still had his chance to play a hand on the turn in. He didn't find a great deal, though, and was eventually well held. It's possible the ground was more testing than he likes - the winning time was 9.23sec slower than when he won the Relkeel Hurdle. (op 5-2)
Duke Of Lucca(IRE) had some good form as a novice but he was up against it at these weights. He probably didn't run far off his rating, though. (op 12-1)
Barizan(IRE), no doubt concerned to preserve his stamina, wasn't ridden as positively from the front as we have seen in the past, but his best races have been run when forcing a strong pace, so that took away his biggest asset. He's just a difficult horse to place off his current mark. (op 25-1)
Secret Dancer(IRE) faced a stiff task at the weights and was towards the back of the field throughout. (op 40-1)

3290 RACEODDS H'CAP CHASE (21 fncs 1 omitted) 3m 2f 110y
1:30 (1:30) (Class 2) (0-145,145) 5-Y-0+

£9,393 (£2,775; £1,387; £694; £346; £174)

Form RPR
13-6 **1** **Blazing Bailey**[63] 2090 9-11-0 **133** RobertThornton 151+
(Alan King) *in tch: chsd ldrs fr 14th: wnt cl 2nd 4 out: chal 3 out: drvn clr appr bypassed fnl fence: styd on strly* **11/1**
43-0 **2** *11* **Richard's Sundance (IRE)**[50] 2343 9-11-3 **136** HarrySkelton 144
(Victor Dartnall) *chsd ldr to 9th and styd pressing for 2nd tl 4 out: rallied to chse wnr at bypassed fnl fence but nvr any ch* **16/1**
0-P4 **3** *1 1/2* **Officier De Reserve (FR)**[17] 2962 9-10-7 **126** AidanColeman 133
(Venetia Williams) *in tch: hit 6th: lost position 9th: hdwy 13th: styng on to chse ldrs whn hit 3 out: kpt on appr bypassed fnl fence but nvr any ch w wnr* **8/1**[3]
5-21 **4** *6* **Buffalo Bob (IRE)**[37] 2629 8-11-1 **134** JasonMaguire 134
(Kim Bailey) *led: nt fluent 3rd: rdn 4 out: jnd next: narrowly hdd sn after: wknd into 4th at bypassed fnl fence* **4/1**[1]
0-30 **5** *2 1/2* **Character Building (IRE)**[49] 2358 11-11-7 **140** DougieCostello 143+
(John Quinn) *in tch: dropped to rr 14th: rdn 16th and rallied 4 out: chsd ldrs after next but nvr quite on terms: wknd bef bypassed fnl fence* **14/1**
1-2P **6** *6* **Brooklyn Brownie (IRE)**[168] 1020 12-11-2 **140** JamesHalliday[(5)] 133
(Malcolm Jefferson) *a front rnk rdn 4 out: wknd after next and no ch appr bypassed fnl fence* **33/1**
3F-F **7** *5* **Maljimar (IRE)**[41] 2543 11-11-9 **142** DarylJacob 132
(Nick Williams) *j. slowly 2nd: in rr: hdwy 15th styd on to chse ldrs 4 out: wknd 2 out and no ch at pypassed fnl fence* **12/1**
4-14 **8** *2 3/4* **Etxalar (FR)**[42] 2522 8-10-8 **127** CampbellGillies 116
(Lucinda Russell) *in tch: hit 13th: rdn and wknd 4 out: mstke next and wl bhd at bypassed fnl fence* **20/1**
4-00 **9** *3 1/4* **Dashing George (IRE)**[41] 2541 9-10-9 **128** (p) TomScudamore 114
(Dr Richard Newland) *chsng ldrs whn blnd 1st and rdr lost iron: styd pressed ldrs and wnt 2nd 10th tl appr 4 out: sn hrd drvn: wknd after next and no ch bypassed fnl fence* **14/1**
0FP- **10** *14* **My Will (FR)**[252] 5395 11-11-3 **143** MrJBarber[(7)] 113
(Paul Nicholls) *nvr jumping w much fluency after mstkes 4th and 5th: wl bhd whn blnd 3 out* **16/1**
00-6 **P** **Joe Lively (IRE)**[50] 2346 12-11-12 **145** (p) JoeTizzard —
(Colin Tizzard) *trckd ldrs tl fatally injured and p.u sn after 12th* **18/1**
-P30 **P** **Knowhere (IRE)**[22] 2871 13-11-1 **137** SamTwiston-Davies[(3)] —
(Nigel Twiston-Davies) *pushed along to stay in tch 5th: drvn 9th: wknd and mstke 16th: t.o whn p.u after 3 out* **20/1**
0-03 **P** **Il Duce (IRE)**[42] 2531 11-10-8 **127** (b) JimmyMcCarthy —
(Alan King) *in rr tl hdwy to get in tch fr 8th: wknd 16th: t.o whn p.u after 3 out* **22/1**
566U **P** **Lead On (IRE)**[17] 2962 10-10-10 **129** RhysFlint —
(Philip Hobbs) *hit 3rd and bhd: no ch whn hit 15th: blnd next: t.o whn p.u bef 18th* **33/1**
P2P0 **F** **Victorias Groom (GER)**[18] 2948 9-10-7 **126** DominicElsworth —
(Lucy Wadham) *mid-div whn fell 12th* **33/1**
/12- **P** **The Sliotar (IRE)**[327] 3941 10-11-5 **138** RichardJohnson —
(Philip Hobbs) *hit 4th: mstke next: sn bhd: rdn and no ch fr 10th: t.o whn p.u bef 3 out* **9/1**
40-5 **P** **Qhilimar (FR)**[50] 2343 7-10-3 **125** (b) RichieMcLernon[(3)] —
(Alan Jones) *in rr hit 6th and 7th: wl bhd 10th: mstke 12th: p.u bef next* **13/2**[2]

6m 57.87s (4.07) **Going Correction** +0.475s/f (Soft) **17** Ran SP% **123.5**
Speed ratings: **112,108,108,106,105 104,102,101,100,96** —,—,—,—,— —,—
toteswingers: 1&2 £27.30, 1&3 £9.30, 2&3 £21.80. CSF £157.10 CT £1489.49 TOTE £14.10: £2.50, £4.90, £2.20, £1.50; EX 253.60 Trifecta £748.70 Part won. Pool: £1,011.87 - 0.20 winning units..
Owner Three Line Whip **Bred** A M Tombs **Trained** Barbury Castle, Wilts
■ Stewards' Enquiry : Harry Skelton one-day ban: used whip with excessive frequency (Jan 16)

FOCUS
A good handicap, but one made up mostly of exposed types. Blazing Bailey is rated up a stone on his previous chase form but was a 160+ hurdler at best. The runner-up is better than his mark with the third up a few pounds on his recent efforts.

NOTEBOOK
Blazing Bailey, a former high-class hurdler, was having just his fifth start over fences and running in a handicap for the first time. He took on some fair novices last season, including Burton Port, and with his stable in better form this time around there was always a chance that he'd been let in lightly off a mark of 133. Despite hanging right for much of the race, he travelled well, jumped perfectly soundly and stayed on strongly up the hill for an easy win. He'll go up a fair bit for this, but there should be further improvement to come, and as he stays so well the Scottish National and/or bet365 Gold Cup look natural longer-term targets. (op 12-1)
Richard's Sundance(IRE) looked on a good mark based on his success at Wincanton last January, but he'd been well beaten in three starts since. This was a return to form and he should be able to win something similar. (tchd 20-1 in a place)
Officier De Reserve(FR), dropped 1lb despite running well at Newbury last time, rewarded Aidan Coleman's perseverance and put up another solid effort.
Buffalo Bob(IRE) had an 8lb higher mark to overcome but for a long way he looked to have every chance of doing just that, as he generally jumped well out in front. However, he looked to be done for stamina over this longer trip. (op 11-2 tchd 6-1 in places)
Character Building(IRE) ran a shocker here in November, but this was more encouraging, especially as he was badly hampered by the fall of Victorias Groom. That said, he remains above his last winning mark. (op 16-1 tchd 20-1 in a place)
Brooklyn Brownie(IRE) is another who ran no sort of race on his previous start but showed more sparkle this time. He's still 5lb higher than his last winning mark, though, which leaves things a bit tricky.
Maljimar(IRE) got round this time and was bang there in the hunt for a place turning in, but he weakened quickly from there. He might have needed the run and can last longer next time. (op 10-1)
Etxalar(FR) didn't jump particularly well but kept going. (op 16-1)
My Will(FR) enters retirement now.
Joe Lively(IRE), who had a good record here, sadly broke a hind leg when hampered with a circuit to go. (op 7-1 tchd 15-2)
The Sliotar(IRE), debuting for a new stable, is a lightly raced 10-y-o ando has gone well fresh in the past. His novice form tied in closely with Blazing Bailey, but he jumped poorly here and was never a threat. (op 7-1 tchd 15-2)
Qhilimar(FR) was another whose jumping let him down. (op 7-1 tchd 15-2)

3291 TIGMI TRAVEL DIPPER NOVICES' CHASE GRADE 2 (17 fncs) 2m 5f
2:00 (2:03) (Class 1) 5-Y-0+

£14,252 (£5,347; £2,677; £1,335; £670; £335)

Form RPR
1522 **1** **Hell's Bay (FR)**[37] 2628 9-11-4 143 JoeTizzard 156+
(Colin Tizzard) *t.k.h: hld up on ins: smooth hdwy to trck ldrs after 11th: led gng wl bef 2 out: mstke and rdn last: hld on wl run-in* **16/1**
-1R1 **2** *3/4* **Medermit (FR)**[19] 2926 7-11-4 0 RobertThornton 155+
(Alan King) *hld up: smooth hdwy and prom after 11th: cl up whn pckd 3 out: chal on bit bef next: rdn after 2 out: kpt on run-in: hld towards fin* **9/2**[3]
1-41 **3** *22* **Reve De Sivola (FR)**[22] 2867 6-11-7 0 DarylJacob 140
(Nick Williams) *nt fluent: in tch: drvn and outpcd 4 out: hit next: plugged on fr 2 out to take 3rd run-in: no ch w first two* **4/1**[2]
P-12 **4** *1* **Have You Seen Me (IRE)**[47] 2427 8-11-0 139 TomMolloy 129
(Nigel Twiston-Davies) *t.k.h: cl up: led 2nd: hdd bef 2 out: sn btn: lost modest 3rd run-in* **28/1**
13-1 **5** *7* **Master Of The Hall (IRE)**[43] 2494 7-11-4 141 BarryGeraghty 128
(Nicky Henderson) *hld up: hdwy on outside and prom whn blnd 10th: sn rcvrd: gng wl 3 out: disputing 3rd and outpcd whn mstke next: sn btn* **13/2**
-311 **6** *9* **Sway (FR)**[16] 2978 5-10-2 0 APMcCoy 106
(Jonjo O'Neill) *hld up: hdwy and in tch 9th: pushed along 13th: swtchd to outside whn pckd 3 out: sn btn* **11/2**
2-31 **7** *1 1/4* **Cois Farraig**[36] 2664 6-11-7 134 DominicElsworth 120
(Paul Webber) *nt fluent in midfield: dropped to rr whn hit 10th: sn struggling: no ch whn j.rt and blkd 3 out* **22/1**
-23F **8** *6* **Othermix (FR)**[22] 2867 7-11-0 142 (bt) DougieCostello 108
(Ian Williams) *trckd ldrs: rdn after 13th: wknd fr 3 out* **20/1**
00-F **9** *1/2* **Mr Thriller (FR)**[50] 2348 6-11-0 0 TomScudamore 115
(David Pipe) *mstkes: cl up: hit and lost pl 11th: sn struggling: no ch fr 3 out* **7/2**[1]
1135 **10** *6* **Billie Magern**[49] 2357 7-11-7 137 PaddyBrennan 116
(Nigel Twiston-Davies) *in tch: lost pl whn mstke 10th: outpcd whn blnd 12th: no ch whn bmpd 3 out* **50/1**
21-3 **F** **Sang Bleu (FR)**[37] 2628 5-10-9 0 HarrySkelton —
(Paul Nicholls) *nt fluent in rr 1st: fell 3rd* **28/1**
0-21 **P** **Simarian (IRE)**[215] 550 6-11-0 130 PaulMoloney —
(Evan Williams) *nt fluent: midfield: dropped to rr 6th: sn struggling: t.o whn p.u bef 4 out* **80/1**
213- **U** **Ranjobaie (FR)**[294] 4589 6-11-0 0 AidanColeman —
(Venetia Williams) *hld up: blnd and uns rdr 8th* **40/1**

5m 21.6s (2.20) **Going Correction** +0.475s/f (Soft)
WFA 5 from 6yo+ 4lb **13** Ran SP% **116.6**
Speed ratings: **114,113,105,104,102 98,98,96,95,93** —,—,—
toteswingers: 1&2 £13.20, 1&3 £22.20, 2&3 £4.60. CSF £80.92 TOTE £24.00: £4.50, £2.40, £2.20; EX 127.60 Trifecta £331.80 Pool: £1,807.31 - 4.03 winning units..
Owner A G Fear & A J Norman **Bred** James Patrick Kelly **Trained** Milborne Port, Dorset

FOCUS
A really competitive renewal, run in a good time, 0.93sec quicker than the decent handicap that followed, and a nice boost for both the Arkle second-favourite Finian's Rainbow and RSA Chase favourite Time For Rupert. The runner-up is closing in on his hurdles best and the third is still a stone+ off his hurdles form.

NOTEBOOK
Hell's Bay(FR), who'd finished runner-up to two of the market leaders for the novice chases at the festival in his previous two starts, got his reward and gave connections some compensation for the loss of Joe Lively in the previous race. A two-horse race from the second-last, he made a mistake at the last which gave the runner-up a chance to close, but he was always just holding that rival off. He was given quotes around the 14-1 mark for the Jewson Kauto Star Novices' Chase, the new race at the festival, and that looks the obvious target on this showing. (tchd 14-1)
Medermit(FR) appreciated the step up in trip and ran a cracker in defeat given his relative lack of chasing experience compared with the winner. He's another for whom the Jewson looks the natural target, and he tops the market for the time being at 10-1, the thinking no doubt being that he has more scope to improve further than Hell's Bay. On this evidence he should be able to find a graded race en-route. (tchd 4-1 and 5-1 in places)
Reve De Sivola(FR), who again didn't jump well, but saw his stamina come into play late on and picked up an unlikely third close home. He had been due to be aimed at the Jewson, but perhaps connections will have a rethink now. (op 11-2)
Have You Seen Me(IRE) took them along at a decent gallop and ran well on this step up in class. This was just his third outing over fences and, while outclassed by the first two, has the makings of a nice handicap type.
Master Of The Hall(IRE) raced towards the outer for much of the race and had every chance turning in, but he was soon left behind by the first two. However, he was one of the least experienced chasers in the field, and he travelled well enough to suggest he can win more races. (op 9-2 tchd 7-1 in places)
Sway(FR) was a rare ride for Tony McCoy at 10st 2lb, but he was able to do the weight owing to a bout of, in his words, 'man flu' since Christmas. The mare found this competition a bit hot, but will no doubt find further success against her own sex. (tchd 9-2 and 6-1 in places)
Cois Farraig made costly mistakes, and was in trouble some way from home. (op 20-1)
Othermix(FR) ran well for a long way until hitting the wall. A sounder surface suits him better. (tchd 25-1)
Mr Thriller(FR)' s jockey reported that the gelding was never travelling or jumping. Official explanation: jockey said gelding never travelled or jumped (op 9-2)

3292 VICTORCHANDLER.COM CHASE H'CAP GRADE 3 (17 fncs) 2m 5f
2:35 (2:35) (Class 1) 5-Y-0+

£22,804 (£8,556; £4,284; £2,136; £1,072; £536)

Form RPR
4-31 **1** **Tartak (FR)**[17] 2964 8-11-8 **149** (t) PaddyBrennan 159+
(Tom George) *hit 3rd: in tch: chsd ldrs fr 10th: mstke 3 out: rdn and rallied fr 2 out: styd on wl u.p to chse ldr fnl 100yds: r.o gamely to ld fnl 25yds* **7/1**[3]

21-1 **2** 3/4 **Carole's Legacy**[40] 2579 7-11-0 **141** .... BarryGeraghty 148+
(Nicky Henderson) *trckd ldrs: chal fr 8th: lft disputing ld 11th: led 13th: jnd fr 4 out but kpt slt advantage tl hdd last: rallied gamely to ld again sn after: hdd and nt qckn fnl 25yds* **7/2**[1]

-U56 **3** 3 **Mahogany Blaze (FR)**[21] 2885 9-11-3 **147**......(b) SamTwiston-Davies(3) 151
(Nigel Twiston-Davies) *mid-div: improving whn sltly hmpd 11th: hdwy 13th: chal fr 4 out and remained upsides tl rdn to take narrow ld last: hdd sn after: no ex and dropped to 3rd fnl 100yds* **25/1**

F420 **4** 2 1/2 **I'msingingtheblues (IRE)**[21] 2881 9-11-7 **148**...........(t) TomScudamore 149
(David Pipe) *hld up towards rr: hit 6th: stdy hdwy on ins 4 out: trcking ldrs travelling wl appr 2 out: rdn sn after: no ex run-in: wknd fnl 120yds* **25/1**

F-0P **5** 13 **Can't Buy Time (IRE)**[49] 2359 9-11-1 **142**........ APMcCoy 132
(Jonjo O'Neill) *in tch fr 7th: hmpd 11th hdwy to trck ldrs 13th: rdn 3 out: wknd next* **10/1**

0-31 **6** 6 **Mister McGoldrick**[42] 2531 14-11-1 **142**........ DominicElsworth 127
(Sue Smith) *chsd ldrs to 12th: wknd 3 out* **16/1**

5-P4 **7** 5 **Knockara Beau (IRE)**[22] 2871 8-11-7 **148**........ JanFaltejsek 130+
(George Charlton) *mid-div whn hit 6th: in rr 8th: mstke 10th: nvr in contention after* **7/1**[3]

F-1F **8** 5 **Hey Big Spender (IRE)**[35] 2673 8-11-11 **152**........ JoeTizzard 129
(Colin Tizzard) *blnd 1st: in rr and nvr really travelling fr 7th and no ch after* **9/1**

6-3P **9** 1 **Door Boy (IRE)**[49] 2359 8-10-9 **136**........ BrianHughes 113
(Howard Johnson) *chsd ldrs: drvn to chal 4 out: wknd after next* **25/1**

2210 **10** 1 **Quito Du Tresor (FR)**[50] 2345 7-10-5 **132**........ CampbellGillies 117+
(Lucinda Russell) *in rr: hit 13th: sme hdwy whn sprawled on landing 3 out: nt rcvr* **33/1**

-622 **11** 3 1/4 **Five Dream (FR)**[43] 2496 7-10-3 **135**........(b) MrRMahon(5) 108
(Paul Nicholls) *sn in rr: mstke 8th and no ch after: mstke 4 out: blnd next* **11/1**

6-50 **12** *nse* **Patman Du Charmil (FR)**[22] 2869 9-10-0 **127** oh13........ DavidEngland 97
(Nigel Twiston-Davies) *w ldr tl after 4th: styd disputing 2nd tl lft in slt ld 11th: jnd next: mstke and hdd 13th: wknd qckly* **66/1**

-010 **P** **Moon Over Miami (GER)**[41] 2541 10-10-8 **135**.............(t) PaulMoloney —
(Charlie Mann) *sn bhd: hmpd 11th: t.o whn p.u bef 13th* **33/1**

/1-0 **F** **Taranis (FR)**[35] 2673 10-11-12 **153**........(t) NickScholfield 138
(Paul Nicholls) *in tch: chsd ldrs fr 8th: wl there and rdn 13th: 5 l 6th and btn whn fell 2 out* **5/1**[2]

1-05 **F** **Pickamus (FR)**[42] 2517 8-10-10 **137**........ RichardJohnson —
(Henry Daly) *mde most tl 1 l whn fell 11th* **20/1**

5m 22.53s (3.13) **Going Correction** +0.475s/f (Soft) **15** Ran SP% **120.9**
Speed ratings: **113,112,111,110,105 103,101,99,99,98 97,97,—,—,—**
toteswingers: 1&2 £6.30, 1&3 £32.40, 2&3 £41.40 CSF £30.03 CT £596.66 TOTE £7.00: £2.80, £2.20, £7.60; EX 26.20 Trifecta £1236.70 Pool: £26,406.14 - 15.80 winning units..
Owner Power Panels Electrical Systems Ltd **Bred** Francis Cottebrune & Colette Cottebrune **Trained** Slad, Gloucs

FOCUS
A high-class handicap chase and as usual a competitive event. The pace appeared sound and it produced a good finish, but the time was just under a second slower than the preceding Grade 2 novice chase. Tartak took advantage of a good mark but his best runs have been at Aintree and Carole's Legacy improved to the level of his best hurdles form.

NOTEBOOK
Tartak(FR), who won the rearranged Peterborough Chase in a first-time tongue-tie on his previous start, had not previously won at this course in four attempts but had run well. With the tongue-strap on again, he disproved the theory that he only wins on flat tracks by overcoming an early mistake to finish best of all up the hill, snatching the prize from the game runner-up. He is now confirming the promise he showed as a novice chaser two years ago, and will return here for the Ryanair Chase at the festival, with the Ascot Chase beforehand and the Melling Chase at Aintree afterwards. (tchd 15-2)
Carole's Legacy is a consistent performer, mainly in mares' races over hurdles and fences, and stays further. Left in front towards the end of the back straight, she gamely fought off several challenges over the last three fences but could not resist the winner's late run. She deserves to pick up a similar contest and the Ladbroke Trophy back here at the end of the month might be a suitable target. (op 9-2 tchd 5-1 in places)
Mahogany Blaze(FR) gained his last win at this track back in April 2008 but had contested mainly graded races since and posted some creditable efforts. Making his handicap debut over fences, he ran really well, leading over the last before tiring up the hill. He has plenty of similar races to run in at this level and could well pick up one of them. (op 20-1)
I'msingingtheblues(IRE), all of whose wins over fences had been on flat tracks, had finished well beaten on both runs over fences here over 2m but was trying his longest trip. He was travelling best of all on the heels of the leaders three out but had nothing in reserve from the penultimate fence, and was probably beaten by lack of stamina for the uphill finish.
Can't Buy Time(IRE) won this last year off 1lb lower but had shown little since. This was more like it, even if he could not get involved in the finish. (op 9-1 tchd 17-2)
Mister McGoldrick benefited from a drop in the weights to win a veterans' chase at Huntingdon last time but was up 5lb, and was unable to trouble the principals in this better race. (op 12-1)
Knockara Beau(IRE) stays well, likes soft ground and had run well without winning on all four previous visits here. However, he lost his place going away from the stands and only ran on past beaten horses up the hill. (op 10-1)
Hey Big Spender(IRE), a C&D winner here last January, was 14lb higher this time but made an early mistake and was always out the back. If the plan was to hold him up, it did not suit. (op 8-1 tchd 15-2)
Door Boy(IRE) had failed to finish on both previous tries here but ran well and had every chance three out before stopping quickly. Something might have been amiss. (op 22-1)
Quito Du Tresor(FR), a winner at up to 2m4f, had gained all his successes on good ground and flat tracks. He got in touch with the leaders at the top of the hill before dropping away again.
Taranis(FR), a course winner over 3m1f here last January following an absence of over two years, was clear of the rest in sixth but held when falling. (op 11-2 tchd 6-1 in place)
Pickamus(FR), a useful novice last year who had gained all his wins on flat tracks, was 7lb higher than for his last success. He made the running and jumped with plenty of enthusiasm before departing when still in front at the last fence going away from the stands. (op 11-2 tchd 6-1 in place)

3293 SKYBET.COM H'CAP HURDLE (12 hdls) 3m
3:10 (3:10) (Class 2) 4-Y-0+
£9,393 (£2,775; £1,387; £694; £346; £174)

Form RPR

-405 **1** **Ashkazar (FR)**[21] 2884 7-11-12 **152**........ TimmyMurphy 161
(David Pipe) *hld up on ins: stdy hdwy into 4th pl but plenty to do 2 out: effrt and led run-in: styd on strly* **20/1**

31-3 **2** 3 1/4 **Junior**[49] 2358 8-10-3 **134**........(b) COFarrell(5) 140+
(David Pipe) *cl up: led 6th: hrd pressed fr 3 out: rdn bef next: hdd run-in: kpt on same pce* **11/2**[3]

110- **3** 3 3/4 **Chartreux (FR)**[288] 4712 6-10-6 **132**........ TomScudamore 136+
(David Pipe) *in tch: smooth hdwy bef 3 out: chal bef 2 out to bef last: no ex u.p* **7/1**

6-FF **4** 3/4 **Gwanako (FR)**[49] 2359 8-10-7 **140**........ MrDGPrichard(7) 142
(Paul Nicholls) *hld up: drvn and outpcd appr 3 out: rallied after next: styd on run-in: nrst fin* **28/1**

111 **5** 3/4 **Kilcrea Kim (IRE)**[40] 2574 6-10-6 **132**........ RichardJohnson 135+
(Philip Hobbs) *hld up in midfield on ins: stdy hdwy whn hmpd after 3 out: chsng ldng pair whn nt fluent next: sn rdn: rallied whn hit last: no ex run-in* **9/2**[2]

15P- **6** 15 **Mobaasher (USA)**[259] 5223 8-11-5 **145**........ AidanColeman 133
(Venetia Williams) *hld up: drvn along after 3 out: sme hdwy after next: nvr able to chal* **33/1**

0-40 **7** 17 **According To Pete**[42] 2523 10-9-13 **130**........ JamesHalliday(5) 103
(Malcolm Jefferson) *prom: rdn along after 4 out: wknd after next* **33/1**

P11- **8** 3/4 **Ringaroses**[182] 5113 10-10-11 **140**........(t) RichieMcLernon(3) 112
(Jonjo O'Neill) *in tch: drvn and outpcd bef 3 out: rallied appr next: wknd after 2 out* **25/1**

0-25 **9** 3/4 **Racing Demon (IRE)**[36] 2663 11-10-7 **133**........ HaddenFrost 104
(Henrietta Knight) *in tch tl rdn and wknd after 3 out* **33/1**

0200 **10** 1 3/4 **Buena Vista (IRE)**[22] 2870 10-11-0 **140**........(p) JoeTizzard 113
(David Pipe) *bhd: struggling bef 3 out: nvr on terms* **33/1**

1U-3 **11** 7 **King's Legacy (IRE)**[48] 2387 7-10-0 **131**........ MrRMahon(5) 96
(Paul Nicholls) *hld up: blnd bdly 2nd: rdn bef 3 out: nvr on terms* **4/1**[1]

P1-P **12** 5 **Don't Push It (IRE)**[22] 2870 11-11-0 **140**........ APMcCoy 99
(Jonjo O'Neill) *racd wd in rr: struggling 4 out: nvr on terms* **14/1**

P623 **13** 1 1/4 **Viking Blond (FR)**[22] 2870 6-10-12 **138**........(b) PaddyBrennan 108+
(Nigel Twiston-Davies) *trckd ldrs: rdn along whn bdly hmpd and lost pl qckly after 3 out: nt rcvr* **9/1**

00-6 **14** 18 **Sarando**[19] 2926 6-10-4 **130**........(t) DominicElsworth 71
(Paul Webber) *in tch tl rdn and wknd after 3 out* **40/1**

P-02 **15** 22 **Le Beau Bai (FR)**[43] 2500 8-10-10 **143**........ JakeGreenall(7) 105+
(Richard Lee) *t.k.h: cl up: hit 4 out: rdn and wknd after next* **16/1**

-2P1 **16** *nk* **Den Of Iniquity**[10] 3092 10-10-3 **129**........ DarylJacob 50
(Warren Greatrex) *mstke 1st: nt fluent: in tch on outside tl wknd after 4 out* **12/1**

3540 **17** 25 **Raslan**[22] 2870 8-11-4 **144**........(tp) GerrySupple 43
(David Pipe) *led to 6th: lost pl qckly after next: sn no ch* **66/1**

5m 59.1s (-1.90) **Going Correction** +0.25s/f (Yiel) **17** Ran SP% **124.1**
Speed ratings (Par 109): **113,111,110,110,110 105,99,99,99,98 96,94,94,88,80 80,72**
toteswingers: 1&2 £46.50, 1&3 £35.40, 2&3 £7.00. CSF £120.70 CT £876.04 TOTE £35.10: £5.60, £1.80, £2.10, £7.50; EX 203.20 Trifecta £1088.60 Pool: £2,648.08 - 1.80 winning units..
Owner D A Johnson **Bred** H H The Aga Khan's Studs Sc **Trained** Nicholashayne, Devon

FOCUS
A triumph for David Pipe, as he saddled the first three home from five runners. A surprise personal best for Ashkazar but he may be a shade flattered. The runner-up was 3l off his best with a step forward from the unexposed third.

NOTEBOOK
Ashkazar(FR), one of five runners for his trainer, was not the one expected to deliver according to the betting. With the leading duo taking each other on from some way out, the race was eventually set up for a closer, and he finished best of all to grab an unlikely victory. He's clearly improved for the step up to 3m for the first time, and this brings in the possibility that he might now be aimed at the World Hurdle, although a more realistic target would surely be the Pertemps Handicap, as he showed here that he has no trouble carrying a big weight.
Junior, who is fabulously versatile, ran another fantastic race in defeat, especially as he and his stablemate Chartreux went at it from some way out, eventually slitting each other's throats. Quicker ground won't hurt him in future. (op 7-1)
Chartreux(FR) ◆ looked a potential blot on the handicap as he was unexposed having had just two previous starts over hurdles, including one in Grade 1 company. While he was beaten, it's fair to assume he is indeed a well-handicapped horse, as he looked the most likely winner running down the hill, but couldn't shake off the bang in-form Junior, and eventually the pair beat each other up and set it up for a closer. (tchd 15-2)
Gwanako(FR), back over hurdles in search of a confidence-booster, got just that, and was another beneficiary of the battle up front helping to set things up for those ridden more patiently.
Kilcrea Kim(IRE) arrived here chasing a four-timer. Although hampered at the top of the hill, he looked to be in a good position running down the hill, stalking the duelling pair from the Pipe stable, but he could never quite bridge the gap in the straight. While he got the trip all right, he didn't look to improve for it. (op 11-2 tchd 4-1 in places)
Mobaasher(USA) has run well fresh in the past so it would be dangerous to assume he'll come on a bundle for this.
According To Pete, although seventh, was again beaten a long way, and probably needs even more help from the handicapper.
Ringaroses looked fit enough for this return to action but eventually faded from the bottom of the hill. (op 22-1 tchd 20-1)
King's Legacy(IRE) was the disappointment of the race. He blundered badly early on in the race and then raced a bit keenly, and was never a real threat. His form behind Grands Crus here last time out looks solid, and it wouldn't be at all surprising to see him bounce back from this. (tchd 7-2)
Viking Blond(FR) Official explanation: jockey said gelding suffered interference in running

3294 E B F "HIGH SHERIFF OF GLOUCESTERSHIRE'S" "JUNIOR" STANDARD OPEN NATIONAL HUNT FLAT RACE (LISTED) 1m 6f 110y
3:45 (3:45) (Class 1) 4-Y-0 **£8,478** (£3,174; £1,586; £792)

Form RPR

11 **1** **Keys (IRE)**[39] 2597 4-11-2 0........ PaddyBrennan 114+
(Roger Charlton) *hld up in mid-div: smooth hdwy to trck ldrs 3 out: slt ld on bit over 1f out but strly chal: rdn ins fnl f: narrowly hdd fnl 100yds: carried rt: rallied and led again last stride* **3/1**[1]

11 **2** *shd* **Cinders And Ashes**[26] 2824 4-11-2 0........ JasonMaguire 114+
(Donald McCain) *in tch: chsd ldrs 3 out: drvn and qcknd to chal 1f out: edgd rt u.p and slt ld fnl 100yds: hdd last stride* **6/1**[3]

3 3 1/4 **Trozulon (FR)**[173] 4-11-2 0........ BarryGeraghty 110+
(Nicky Henderson) *hld up in tch: rdn: one pce and n.m.r over 2f out: rallied and r.o wl to take 3rd wl ins fnl f but no ch w ldng duo* **13/2**

41 **4** 3/4 **It's A Gimme (IRE)**[27] 2797 4-11-2 0........ APMcCoy 109
(Jonjo O'Neill) *in rr but in tch: stdy hdwy over 3f out: drvn to take 3rd over 1f out but no imp on ldng duo: one pce into 4th wl ins fnl f* **14/1**

1 **5** 6 **Cousin Khee**[74] 1913 4-11-2 0........ TomScudamore 102
(Hughie Morrison) *chsd ldrs: slt ld over 3f out: rdn 2f out: hdd over 1f out: wknd fnl f* **4/1**[2]

1 **6** 3/4 **Zama Zama**[45] 2458 4-11-2 0........ AndrewTinkler 101
(Nicky Henderson) *chsd ldrs: rdn and outpcd over 3f out: drvn and hung lft wl over 1f out: styd on again ins fnl f* **10/1**

2 **7** 1 **Kuilsriver (IRE)**[55] 2237 4-10-12 0........(t) DarylJacob 96
(Alison Thorpe) *mde most tl hdd over 3f out: sn rdn: wknd 2f out* **40/1**

5 **8** 6 **Allez Les Rouges (IRE)**[27] 2797 4-10-12 0........ RichardJohnson 89
(Andrew Balding) *in rr but in tch: hdwy over 2f out: nvr quite rchd ldrs and one pce sn after* **25/1**

3 **9** *1* **Revani**[45] 2458 4-10-12 0 HarrySkelton 88
(Nick Mitchell) *disp ld to 1/2-way: rdn over 3f out: wknd over 2f out* **100/1**

3 **10** *1 3/4* **What A Warrior (IRE)**[27] 2797 4-10-9 0 SamTwiston-Davies(3) 85
(Nigel Twiston-Davies) *chsd ldrs: rdn 3f out: sn btn* **18/1**

11 *2 1/4* **Jojabean (IRE)** 4-10-12 0 RobertThornton 83
(Alan King) *in rr but in tch: pushed along over 3f out: nvr gng pce to get into contention* **12/1**

1 **12** *1/2* **Broughtons Star**[52] 2315 4-11-2 0 TimmyMurphy 86
(Willie Musson) *t.k.h: hld up in rr and racd towards outside: gng ok over 3f out: pushed along and sn dropped away* **16/1**

2 **13** *1 1/4* **Cardinal Rose**[45] 2458 4-10-9 0 RichieMcLernon(3) 81
(Jonjo O'Neill) *towards rr most of way* **40/1**

2 **14** *13* **Kaylif Aramis**[27] 2797 4-10-12 0 AidanColeman 65
(Nigel Twiston-Davies) *towards rr fr 1/2-way* **33/1**

15 *3/4* **Sole Survivor (FR)** 4-10-12 0 DominicElsworth 64
(Paul Webber) *chsd ldrs to 3f out* **16/1**

0 **16** *3* **Saffron Sam**[27] 2797 4-10-12 0 NickScholfield 61
(Simon Burrough) *chsd ldrs tl wknd ins fnl 3f* **66/1**

3m 33.7s (213.70) **16** Ran SP% **127.2**
toteswingers: 1&2 £8.70, 1&3 £12.00, 2&3 £15.00. CSF £20.72 TOTE £4.20: £2.00, £2.60, £3.50; EX 17.90 Trifecta £97.90 Pool: £1,248.17 - 9.42 winning units..
Owner Seasons Holidays **Bred** B Hurley **Trained** Beckhampton, Wilts
■ Stewards' Enquiry : Jason Maguire one-day ban: careless riding (Jan 16)

FOCUS
A really interesting junior bumper featuring seven last-time-out winners, and it was fought out by the two dual winners in the race. Although the early pace wasn't great and there were plenty in with a chance running down the hill, the right horses eventually came clear and the form looks really strong for the grade, rated around the runner-up and the fifth to the tenth. A stewards' enquiry was called, as the first two bumped into each other more than once on the run-in, but most of the blame lay with Cinders And Ashes, and the result was always going to stand.

NOTEBOOK
Keys(IRE) was impressive at Lingfield last time and showed here he can handle dead turf as well. There's no doubt that he'll be seen to better effect on quicker ground as his prime asset is a turn of foot. He battled well to regain the lead after being headed, and he still has to show that 2m will suit as well, but he could well have a hand to play in the Champion Bumper back here in March, for which he's been given general quotes of 16-1. He won't run again beforehand. (op 11-4)
Cinders And Ashes, like the winner chasing a hat-trick in this sphere, ran a sound race and only went down narrowly. He's also likely to be aimed at the Champion Bumper now, although there's always the option of going to Aintree. (op 13-2 tchd 7-1)
Trozulon(FR) ◆ did best of the Henderson pair. Winner of a 1m4f AQPS firm-ground maiden in the French Provinces back in July, he's out of a half-sister to Juveigneur and shaped well on his debut for his new stable, staying on strongly at the finish. He shouldn't have any trouble with a step up to 2m. (op 8-1)
It's A Gimme(IRE), who's out of a half-sister to Commanche Court, finished nicely clear of the rest and looks the type to do well once sent jumping. (op 12-1 tchd 10-1)
Cousin Khee failed to uphold his trainer's great record in this race, but he still didn't run badly, and perhaps a return to quicker ground will see him improve. (op 5-1)
Zama Zama, who has a fair bit of size about him, was the lesser-fancied of the Henderson pair, didn't settle that well early on, but stayed on again after getting outpaced. A stronger-run race would have probably suited him. (op 12-1)
Kuilsriver(IRE) did best of those without a previous win to their names. He'd finished second off levels to Keys at Ffos Las on his previous start, and their performances here show how much Roger Charlton's gelding has improved in the interim.
T/Jkpt: Not won. T/Plt: £156.20 to a £1 stake. Pool of £194,585.09 - 1909.03 winning tickets. T/Qpdt: £27.00 to a £1 stake. Pool of £16,151.34 - 442.50 winning tickets. ST

2974 EXETER (R-H)

Saturday, January 1

OFFICIAL GOING: Good to soft
Rail on hurdles course moved out as far as possible increasing advertised distances by about 50yds per circuit.
Wind: Virtually nil Weather: Overcast but dry

3295 THURLESTONE HOTEL "NATIONAL HUNT" NOVICES' HURDLE (10 hdls) 2m 3f
12:40 (12:40) (Class 4) 5-Y-0+ **£2,602** (£764; £382; £190)

Form RPR

2-3 **1** **Filbert (IRE)**[53] 2291 5-10-12 0 TomO'Brien 119
(Philip Hobbs) *trckd ldrs: rdn to ld after 3 out: wnt sltly rt next: styd on: drvn out* **9/1**

5-45 **2** *1* **Lord Liath (IRE)**[17] 2963 5-10-12 0 WayneHutchinson 118
(Alan King) *mid-div: hdwy after 7th: rdn to chse ldng pair 3 out: pressed wnr fr last but a being jst hld: styd on* **5/1**[2]

11 **3** *2* **Mr Hudson (IRE)**[60] 2136 6-11-0 0 IanPopham(5) 124
(Paul Nicholls) *prom: led 5th: rdn and hdd after 3 out: sltly hmpd 2 out: swtchd lft: styd on same pce* **8/11**[1]

63 **4** *19* **Gunna Be A Devil (IRE)**[16] 2981 7-10-12 0 JohnnyFarrelly 99
(Jeremy Scott) *hld up towards rr: stdy prog fr 5th: rdn into 4th 3 out: nvr trbld ldrs* **14/1**

5 *5* **Rooftop Rainbow (IRE)**[272] 7-10-9 0 DannyCook(3) 94
(Linda Blackford) *led tl 5th: chsd ldrs: rdn after 7th: wknd fr 3 out* **66/1**

5-61 **6** *5* **Accordintolawrence (IRE)**[43] 2499 5-11-5 0 FelixDeGiles 99
(Charlie Longsdon) *trckd ldrs: rdn after 7th: wknd 3 out* **11/2**[3]

2-4P **7** *2* **Gortenbuie (IRE)**[18] 2946 6-10-12 0 AndrewThornton 88
(Henrietta Knight) *mid-div: rdn after 7th: wknd bef 3 out* **50/1**

00 **8** *2 3/4* **Otter Mist**[38] 2607 6-10-7 0 GilesHawkins(5) 86
(Victor Dartnall) *trckd ldrs: rdn after 7th: grad fdd* **100/1**

0 **9** *8* **Flying Award (IRE)**[41] 2560 7-10-12 0 WillKennedy 78
(Susan Gardner) *racd wd: mid-div: rdn after 7th: sn wknd* **100/1**

50 **10** *1/2* **No Obligation (IRE)**[17] 2963 6-10-7 0 MrMMO'Connor(5) 78
(Brendan Powell) *trckd ldrs: rdn after 7th: sn wknd* **125/1**

6 **11** *9* **Lariat Sam (IRE)**[42] 2518 6-10-9 0 CharlieHuxley(3) 70
(Alan King) *mid-div: pushed along after 4th: wknd after 6th* **50/1**

0 **12** *2 1/4* **Mighty Monty**[42] 2518 6-10-12 0 AndrewGlassonbury 68
(Victor Dartnall) *prom: rdn appr 3 out: sn wknd* **100/1**

0/0- **13** *1 1/4* **Red Rock (FR)**[308] 4309 6-10-12 0 SeanQuinlan 67
(Tor Sturgis) *a towards rr* **100/1**

0 **14** *23* **Fresher Fishing (IRE)**[41] 2560 7-10-5 0 MattGriffiths(7) 46
(Victor Dartnall) *a towards rr: wknd 5th: t.o* **80/1**

0-P **P** **Midnight Paradise**[60] 2137 5-9-12 0 (t) MarkQuinlan(7) —
(Neil Mulholland) *mid-div: hit 5th: sn struggling: t.o whn p.u bef 3 out* **100/1**

P **Silver Sutton** 8-10-5 0 NathanSweeney(7) —
(Bob Buckler) *struggling in rr 4th: t.o whn p.u bef 7th* **125/1**

4m 42.3s (-0.40) **Going Correction** +0.025s/f (Yiel) **16** Ran SP% **119.8**
Speed ratings: **101,100,99,91,89 87,86,85,82,81 78,77,76,67,— —**
toteswingers: 1&2 £4.60, 1&3 £3.10, 2&3 £2.20. CSF £53.23 TOTE £9.40: £2.70, £1.80, £1.10; EX 63.70.
Owner R Triple H **Bred** Micheal Woodlock **Trained** Withycombe, Somerset
■ Stewards' Enquiry : Wayne Hutchinson one-day ban: used whip with excessive frequency (Jan 16)

FOCUS
A card which featured six hurdle races and a bumper following the abandonment of three scheduled chases in the wake of the severe frost and snow before Christmas. The rails were placed as wide as possible to ensure fresh ground but the jockeys reported it was riding 'dead'. This opening contest may well produce a decent performer - previous winners include Racing Demon, Lodge Lane and Tataniano, who all went on to much better things. The first three should all progress as they pulled right away from the rest of the field in the final half-mile. The form has been rated through the third.

NOTEBOOK
Filbert(IRE) had received a form boost just before the off, when Bobs Worth, who had beaten him into second in a Kempton bumper in April, won a decent-looking contest at Cheltenham. Always in a handy position just behind the leaders, he was produced by Tom O'Brien three from home to gradually assert under a strong drive. He impressed with his attitude as he found plenty when challenged at the last, and he looks a decent chaser in the making.
Lord Liath(IRE) raced in mid-division for most of the contest and challenged strongly when asked for his effort two out. He briefly looked like he would go past the winner jumping the last, but he was always held thereafter. This represents a further step up from the promise he showed at Newbury in a similar contest last month, and more improvement should come when he steps up in trip. After the race, Wayne Hutchinson received a one-day ban for excessive use of the whip. (op 11-2)
Mr Hudson(IRE), who took the scalp of Madison du Berlais on his previous hurdle start, raced prominently throughout and tried to kick clear rounding the home turn. He soon came under pressure when joined by the winner three from home although, to his credit, he stayed on all the way to the line. This was a solid effort under his penalty and he looks worth another chance, especially over longer trips. (tchd 4-5 and 5-6 in places)
Gunna Be A Devil(IRE) stayed on past beaten horses after being outpaced into the home turn. (op 12-1)
Rooftop Rainbow(IRE), a former pointer, made most of the running, but he was headed and quickly went backwards five from home. He then knuckled badly at the third last but still ran back on into a clear fifth place. He deserves plenty of credit for this effort. (op 80-1)
Accordintolawrence(IRE), who won his only previous hurdle start over 2f shorter at this course in November, was feeling the pinch before the home straight and he plodded home at the same pace thereafter. (op 6-1)

3296 ROYAL CASTLE HOTEL NOVICES' HURDLE (8 hdls) 2m 1f
1:15 (1:15) (Class 4) 4-Y-0+ **£2,602** (£764; £382; £190)

Form RPR

6-2 **1** **Bermuda Boy (FR)**[11] 3057 6-11-0 0 IanPopham(5) 111+
(Paul Nicholls) *trckd ldrs: nudged along after 3 out to chse ldr: chal last: upsides whn lft w def advantage run-in: rdn out* **13/8**[1]

50 **2** *1 1/2* **Gentle Bob (IRE)**[17] 2954 6-11-5 0 WayneHutchinson 109
(Tom George) *mid-div: hdwy after 5th: rdn whn wnt 3rd 2 out: styng on whn lft 2nd run-in* **66/1**

00 **3** *4* **That'lldoboy (FR)**[3] 3196 5-11-5 0 AndrewThornton 106
(Paul Nicholls) *mid-div: hdwy after 5th: rdn after 2 out: styng on same pce whn lft 3rd run-in* **25/1**

- **4** *13* **Wild Rhubarb**[553] 6-10-12 0 LiamTreadwell 86
(Jonjo O'Neill) *in tch: rdn whn lost pl after 5th: styd on fr last: wnt 4th nr fin* **12/1**[3]

000/ **5** *1/2* **Magic Marmalade (IRE)**[231] 8-11-0 0 GilesHawkins(5) 94
(Philip Hobbs) *led tl 4th: chsd ldrs: rdn after 5th: styd on same pce fr next: lft 4th briefly last* **14/1**

6 **6** *3 1/4* **Valley View (IRE)**[64] 2067 5-11-2 0 MrAJBerry(3) 90
(Jonjo O'Neill) *in tch: rdn after 5th: one pce fr 3 out* **16/1**

300- **7** *nk* **Just Tootsie**[268] 5102 7-11-2 0 DannyCook(3) 91
(Nick Mitchell) *prom: led 4th tl next: rdn bef 3 out: styd chsng ldrs tl wknd 2 out* **28/1**

06 **8** *1 1/4* **Fight Club (GER)**[22] 2667 10-11-0 0 MissIsabelTompsett(5) 89
(Bernard Llewellyn) *hld up towards rr: sme prog into midfield 3 out: no further imp fr next* **16/1**

60 **9** *8* **Calusa Catrina (IRE)**[40] 2577 6-10-5 0 ChrisDavies(7) 74
(Philip Hobbs) *a towards rr* **50/1**

0002 **10** *2* **Barrie Burn (IRE)**[37] 2640 5-11-5 0 WillKennedy 80
(Jonjo O'Neill) *a towards rr* **12/1**[3]

11 *2 3/4* **Lady From Ige (IRE)**[97] 7-10-12 0 RodiGreene 70
(Neil Mulholland) *racd keenly: mstke 3 out: a towards rr* **33/1**

50- **12** *1* **Gulf Of Aqaba (USA)**[321] 4055 5-11-5 0 DaveCrosse 76
(Ian Williams) *mid-div: hit 2nd: rdn after 5th: wknd 3 out* **33/1**

13 *2* **Special Cuvee**[28] 5-10-12 0 OliverDayman(7) 74
(Alison Thorpe) *mid-div tl wknd 3 out* **80/1**

00 **14** *9* **Cluain Alainn (IRE)**[37] 2640 5-11-2 0 MichaelMurphy(3) 66
(Ian Williams) *mid-div tl wknd after 5th* **40/1**

500 **15** *59* **Vico Road (IRE)**[47] 2419 6-11-5 0 JohnnyFarrelly 13
(Jonjo O'Neill) *mid-div tl 4th: sn bhd: t.o* **80/1**

4 **R** **Piroulet (FR)**[51] 2322 5-11-5 0 TomO'Brien 109
(Philip Hobbs) *racd keenly: trckd ldrs: led 5th: rdn after 3 out: drifted rt w narrow advantage whn jockey failed to ntice upcoming rails and crashed through* **15/8**[2]

4m 18.3s (2.80) **Going Correction** +0.025s/f (Yiel) **16** Ran SP% **128.2**
Speed ratings (Par 105): **94,93,91,85,85 83,83,82,79,78 76,76,75,71,43 —**
toteswingers: 1&2 £20.70, 1&3 £21.40, 2&3 £156.70. CSF £144.89 TOTE £2.90: £1.20, £12.80, £7.20; EX 106.10.
Owner Charles Whittaker & Sylvia Mizel **Bred** Douglas McIntyre **Trained** Ditcheat, Somerset
■ Stewards' Enquiry : Tom O'Brien twelve-day ban: took wrong course (Jan 15-26)

FOCUS
An ordinary novices' hurdle with some late drama. The form is rated through the winner, who should go on to rate higher.

NOTEBOOK
Bermuda Boy(FR) was challenging Piroulet when left clear on the run-in, although he did need to be driven out strongly to repel a late challenge from the runner-up. He travelled extremely well on the heels of the leaders for most of the contest, and this effort confirmed the promise he had shown in a Kempton bumper just before Christmas. He may well be able to defy a penalty. (op 6-4 tchd 7-4)
Gentle Bob(IRE) had shown little in two previous hurdle starts but he stayed on strongly under pressure in the final 2f to grab a clear second place. He looks well worth a try over further following this pleasing effort.

That'Ildoboy(FR), a stablemate of the winner, travelled keenly and carried his head awkwardly in the home straight, but he still posted a far more encouraging effort following two disappointing previous runs over hurdles. He could be one to take from this race as he appears to be getting the hang of things. (op 33-1 tchd 18-1)
Wild Rhubarb ran an eyecatching race on this hurdling debut. A stayer on the Flat, she already looks in need of much further as she was never sighted with a chance until running on strongly after the last. (op 10-1)
Magic Marmalade(IRE), a former pointer, took them along at a good clip for most of the way, and stuck to his task reasonably well once headed three from home. (tchd 12-1)
Piroulet(FR), who had just been joined by the winner at the last, failed to straighten up having jumped that obstacle and crashed through the rails dolling off the inside of the track halfway up the run-in. Tom O'Brien had his whip in the correct hand but he had his head down as he was trying to squeeze a final effort out of his mount, so he may just have lost his bearings slightly, although, in his defence, Piroulet was hanging badly to his right for most of the home straight and still looked a bit green. However, the stewards took a dim view and gave the jockey a 12-day ban for taking the wrong course. (op 3-1)

3297 BILLY WILLIAMS MEMORIAL NOVICES' H'CAP HURDLE (12 hdls) 2m 7f 110y
1:45 (1:45) (Class 4) (0-100,100) 4-Y-0+ **£2,602** (£764; £382; £190)

Form RPR
50P- **1** **Crank Hill**[279] 4915 9-11-4 **99**.................................. NathanSweeney(7) 103+
(Bob Buckler) *mde all: j.rt at times: pushed along after 8th: rdn after 9th: styd on strly fr 3 out: mstke last: hung lft run-in: rdn out* **11/1**
606 **2** *6* **Brunette'Sonly (IRE)**[39] 2592 6-11-1 **89**...................... AndrewThornton 85
(Seamus Mullins) *racd keenly: in tch: wnt 3rd after 9th: styd on same pce: wnt 2nd nr fin* **16/1**
5-60 **3** *½* **Calusa Shadow**[18] 2949 7-11-12 **100**.................................. TomO'Brien 99+
(Philip Hobbs) *trckd ldrs: wnt 2nd after 9th: chalng whn bad mstke 3 out: sn rdn: hld fr next: no ex whn lost 2nd nr fin* **6/1**
4-00 **4** *6* **Royal Chatelier (FR)**[16] 2980 6-11-2 **90**............................ FelixDeGiles 82
(Michael Blake) *in tch: hrd rdn fr 7th: one pce fr 3 out* **10/1**
/643 **5** *18* **Baby Car (FR)**[16] 2980 7-10-12 **86**....................................(t) WillKennedy 59
(Noel Chance) *hld up in tch: disp 2nd 7th tl rdn after 9th: wknd 3 out* **13/8**[1]
-104 **6** *19* **Musical Wedge**[44] 2469 7-11-7 **98**................................ TommyPhelan(3) 54
(Claire Dyson) *trckd wnr tl rdn after 7th: chsd ldrs tl rdn and wknd after 9th* **4/1**[2]
402 **7** *11* **Holyrood**[27] 2795 5-11-4 **99**..(vt) MrTomDavid(7) 45
(Tim Vaughan) *trckd ldrs: chsd wnr 7th tl rdn after 9th: wknd bef 3 out* **5/1**[3]

6m 9.70s (10.70) **Going Correction** +0.025s/f (Yiel) **7** Ran SP% **112.4**
Speed ratings (Par 105): **83,81,80,78,72 66,62**
toteswingers: 1&2 £12.80, 1&3 £8.10, 2&3 £9.60. CSF £139.80 TOTE £15.20; £4.70, £5.90; FX 194.80.
Owner Strictly Come Racing **Bred** Mrs P Badger **Trained** Henley, Somerset

FOCUS
A moderate staying novices' hurdle run in commemoration of a former local trainer. The pace was steady but they appeared to finish pretty tired. The winner had slipped to a good mark and there was a step up from the second.

NOTEBOOK
Crank Hill, better known as a chaser, was making his first appearance over hurdles since April 2008 and having his first start since March. He made all the running and, although being pushed along before four out, kept finding for pressure and was clear before the last. He hit that flight and got tired on the run-in but was never in danger of defeat. He was well treated on his best form and the absence of headgear did not appear to make much difference. (op 8-1)
Brunette'Sonly(IRE) was taking a big step up in trip on this handicap debut. She was keen early and, after a brief effort down the far side, looked like dropping away before rallying in the straight. She can build on this if settling better.
Calusa Shadow had not built on his hurdling debut and had been dropped 3lb following his handicap debut. He made headway travelling like the winner turning in, but hit the third last and had no more to offer. (tchd 11-2)
Royal Chatelier(FR) was under pressure soon after halfway but rallied to chase the leaders into the straight only to have nothing left from the second-last. This was still his best effort for this yard so far. (op 9-1)
Baby Car(FR) was held up but, after briefly looking to get involved at the end of the back straight, faded pretty tamely. The rider later reported that the gelding had a breathing problem. Official explanation: jockey said gelding had a breathing problem (op 15-8)
Musical Wedge has not built on his handicap debut and dropped away after showing up for most of the trip. (op 9-2)
Holyrood tracked the leaders from the start but was beaten turning for home and may not have stayed on this dead ground. (tchd 9-2)

3298 BATHWICK TYRES H'CAP HURDLE (8 hdls) 2m 1f
2:15 (2:16) (Class 2) 4-Y-0+ **£8,238** (£2,433; £1,216; £608; £304)

Form RPR
132- **1** **Salden Licht**[56] 5194 7-11-12 **142**.............................. WayneHutchinson 155+
(Alan King) *travelled wl for most of way: mid-div: smooth hdwy after 5th to trck ldr 3 out: led last: readily* **2/1**[1]
225- **2** *1 ½* **Sir Kezbaah (IRE)**[281] 4871 7-10-3 **119**............................... FelixDeGiles 125
(Jeremy Scott) *trckd ldrs: rdn appr 3 out: styd on to go 2nd run-in: no ch w wnr* **9/1**
1-00 **3** *1 ¾* **Hunterview**[22] 2868 5-10-8 **127**..................................(b) DannyCook(3) 131
(David Pipe) *led: rdn after 3 out: hdd appr last: no ex whn lost 2nd towards fin* **8/1**[3]
145- **4** *3 ¼* **Alfie Spinner (IRE)**[273] 4990 6-10-11 **127**........................... WillKennedy 129
(Nick Williams) *trckd ldr tl rdn appr 3 out: styd on same pce* **9/1**
1212 **5** *2 ½* **Karasenir (IRE)**[63] 2092 5-11-1 **131**..................................... TomO'Brien 132+
(Philip Hobbs) *trckd ldrs: rdn appr 3 out: styd on same pce* **5/1**[2]
-320 **6** *2* **Numide (FR)**[16] 2977 8-10-5 **121**.. JohnnyFarrelly 118
(Rod Millman) *hld up: hdwy after 5th: mstke 3 out: sn rdn: styd on same pce* **25/1**
-412 **7** *1 ½* **Salontyre (GER)**[16] 2977 5-10-5 **126**................(p) MissIsabelTompsett(5) 122
(Bernard Llewellyn) *sn nudged along towards rr but in tch: nt pce to get involved fr 3 out* **12/1**
110- **8** *34* **Open Day (IRE)**[290] 4675 5-10-13 **132**................................ MrAJBerry(3) 98
(Jonjo O'Neill) *mid-div: awkward 2nd: struggling next: sn in rr: t.o* **20/1**
4P-1 **9** *12* **Warne's Way (IRE)**[48] 2393 8-10-7 **123**.........................(b) LiamTreadwell 78
(Brendan Powell) *nt pce to sit promly: sn towards rr: t.o* **20/1**
0-B1 **10** *19* **Advisor (FR)**[11] 3058 5-10-12 **133**..................................... IanPopham(5) 71
(Paul Nicholls) *mid-div: little short of room 1st: rdn after 5th: sn btn: eased after 3 out: t.o* **5/1**[2]
2/U- **11** *7* **Optimus Maximus (IRE)**[252] 5393 6-10-6 **125**..........(t) TommyPhelan(3) 56
(Claire Dyson) *bhd fr 4th: t.o* **50/1**

4m 10.9s (-4.60) **Going Correction** +0.025s/f (Yiel) **11** Ran SP% **120.8**
Speed ratings (Par 109): **111,110,109,107,106 105,105,89,83,74 71**
toteswingers: 1&2 £4.40, 1&3 £4.00, 2&3 £10.60. CSF £20.24 CT £125.32 TOTE £3.10: £1.70, £3.90, £2.80; EX 25.30 Trifecta £159.20 Pool: £438.96 - 2.04 winning units..
Owner Dai Griffiths **Bred** Gestut Wittekindshof **Trained** Barbury Castle, Wilts

FOCUS
They went a decent pace in this good handicap, which probably played into the hands of the eventual winner, who never came off the bridle. He was value for further with the next three close to their marks.

NOTEBOOK
Salden Licht ◆, who was last seen running a creditable fifth in the November Handicap at Doncaster, simply outclassed his rivals despite giving lumps of weight away and ultimately won in the manner of a very good horse. He was always travelling supremely well in the mid-division and ranged up to take over from the second last, after which he was ridden out with hands and heels. The margin of victory certainly flatters his nearest pursuers and it will be interesting to see how the handicapper reacts. His next target is the Totesport Trophy at Newbury in February, depending on what the assessor does, and on this showing he looks to have claims, as he will enjoy the fast pace they tend to go in that race. (op 5-2 tchd 15-8)
Sir Kezbaah(IRE), whose new trainer has a decent record in handicap hurdles at this course, ran encouragingly after a long absence and he looks well up to winning a handicap on this showing. He was always prominent and found plenty for pressure in the home straight. (op 8-1)
Hunterview set out to make all and he was still two lengths in front and travelling fairly comfortably as they came into the home straight. However, the distress signals went out from the second last as the winner came upsides and he eventually lost second place in the dying strides. This was still an encouraging effort and similar tactics could pay dividends next time.
Alfie Spinner(IRE) was in the front rank throughout but was never able to mount a serious challenge. On this evidence, he needs to be stepped back up in trip. (tchd 10-1)
Karasenir(IRE) was another to race prominently, but he was fairly one-paced when the race began in earnest, while his jumping wasn't as fluent as some of the others. He may need slightly quicker ground to show his best. (op 7-1)
Numide(FR) briefly looked a danger on the wide outside at the third last but his effort soon petered out following a mistake. His best days are clearly behind him but his new yard might find a small race for him on this evidence. (op 20-1)

3299 BATHWICK TYRES PLYMOUTH H'CAP HURDLE (10 hdls) 2m 3f
2:50 (2:50) (Class 4) (0-115,115) 4-Y-0+ **£3,252** (£955; £477; £238)

Form RPR
0-43 **1** **Mic's Delight (IRE)**[38] 2607 7-11-9 **112**.................. AndrewGlassonbury 130+
(Victor Dartnall) *in tch: mstke 6th: rdn to ld 2 out: styd on wl: rdn out* **5/1**[1]
16-0 **2** *7* **Horsford (IRE)**[16] 2977 7-11-11 **114**..............................(t) JohnnyFarrelly 125+
(David Pipe) *led tl rdn after 3 out: sn hld by wnr but kpt on for clr 2nd* **6/1**[2]
2-60 **3** *19* **Ceepeegee (IRE)**[44] 2482 6-11-2 **115**.............................. SClements(10) 110
(Colin Tizzard) *mid-div: hdwy 7th: sn rdn: wnt 3rd 3 out but no ch w ldng pair* **33/1**
/1-5 **4** *4 ½* **Max Bygraves**[50] 2347 8-11-7 **110**.. SeanQuinlan 99
(Kim Bailey) *mid-div: rdn in 5th after 7th: wknd 2 out* **5/1**[1]
4-02 **5** *1* **Point West (IRE)**[38] 2607 7-11-7 **115**................................. IanPopham(5) 103
(Nick Mitchell) *hld up bhd: pushed along 5th: rdn after 7th: styd on past btn horses fr 3 out: nvr trbld ldrs* **12/1**
-050 **6** *nk* **Drussell (IRE)**[16] 2977 5-11-10 **113**........................... WayneHutchinson 100
(Richard Phillips) *hld up towards rr: rdn after 7th: styd on past btn horses horses: nvr trbld ldrs* **40/1**
P-24 **7** *5* **Laustra Bad (FR)**[16] 2977 8-11-7 **113**...........................(tp) DannyCook(3) 98
(David Pipe) *trckd ldrs: rdn after 7th: hld whn lost 3rd 3 out: wknd 2 out* **15/2**
2-00 **8** *6* **Amore Mio (GER)**[16] 2977 6-11-12 **115**................................ TomSiddall 92
(Richard Phillips) *rdn after 4th: a in rr* **40/1**
0 **9** *16* **As De Fer (FR)**[11] 3056 5-11-6 **114**................................ RachaelGreen(5) 77
(Anthony Honeyball) *prom tl rdn after 7th: sn wknd: t.o* **40/1**
3005 **10** *7* **Mister Benedictine**[17] 2961 8-11-10 **113**........................(tp) DaveCrosse 70
(Brendan Duke) *mid-div: rdn after 4th: wknd 6th: t.o* **40/1**
03-4 **11** *1 ¾* **Dinarius**[16] 2983 6-11-9 **112**..(p) TomO'Brien 67
(Alex Hales) *poor s: a in rr: t.o* **10/1**
02-5 **12** *9* **Castlerock**[69] 1988 7-11-4 **110**.. MrAJBerry(3) 57
(Jonjo O'Neill) *mid-div: rdn after 7th: wknd next: eased: t.o* **7/1**[3]
/P30 **P** **Abstract Art (USA)**[16] 2983 8-11-10 **113**..................... AndrewThornton —
(Rachel Hobbs) *poor s: a bhd: t.o whn p.u bef 3 out* **28/1**
4234 **P** **Murcar**[129] 1364 6-11-4 **114**.. OliverDayman(7) —
(Alison Thorpe) *in tch: rdn 5th: sn wknd: t.o whn p.u bef 3 out* **20/1**
3400 **P** **Woodmore (IRE)**[42] 2529 7-11-7 **110**.................................. FelixDeGiles —
(Charlie Longsdon) *trckd ldrs: rdn 7th: sn wknd: p.u bef 3 out* **20/1**
1211 **P** **Just The Job (IRE)**[51] 2327 7-11-0 **110**.......................... MarkQuinlan(7) —
(Neil Mulholland) *trckd ldrs: losing pl whn rdn after 4th: sn in rr: t.o whn p.u bef 3 out* **7/1**[3]

4m 39.0s (-3.70) **Going Correction** +0.025s/f (Yiel) **16** Ran SP% **126.8**
Speed ratings (Par 105): **108,105,97,95,94 94,92,89,83,80 79,75,—,—,— —**
toteswingers: 1&2 £10.80, 1&3 £58.80, 2&3 £66.40. CSF £33.30 CT £907.09 TOTE £6.70: £1.80, £1.80, £8.70, £1.70; EX 50.60 Trifecta £211.10 Part won. Pool: £285.32 - 0.64 winning units..
Owner The Higos Hopefuls **Bred** Mrs Anne Caplice **Trained** Brayford, Devon

FOCUS
A wide-open handicap, with the 16 runners separated by just 5lb on official ratings. A couple of runners were left around 10l at the start. Yet again, those who raced prominently fared best, although for the second race in succession the horse who tried to make all was eventually run out of it. The time was decent and it is probably worth being positive about the form.

NOTEBOOK
Mic's Delight(IRE), who had been working on the beach during the bad weather, stayed on strongly to win going away on his handicap debut and just his third start over hurdles. He raced prominently throughout and, although he needed to be kept up to his work for the last half-mile, he was always getting the better of the argument with the long-time leader. He briefly wandered around on the approach to the final flight and looked a tired horse at the line but he did respond to all of his rider's urgings. He looks like making a decent staying chaser in time. (op 11-2)
Horsford(IRE) adopted bold front-running tactics and they almost paid off. He tried to kick on as they entered the home straight and poached a 2l lead, but the winner had him covered. Nevertheless, he kept plugging away to finish a clear second best. (op 9-1)
Ceepeegee(IRE) ran better than he had done on his previous two starts this season. He made up some ground on the home bend and, while he never made any inroads on the front two, he stayed on nicely in the final 2f to grab third place. (op 40-1)
Max Bygraves, having just his second outing since September 2009, probably ran to a similar level than when finishing fifth in a hot Cheltenham handicap at the Paddy Power meeting in November. He is entitled to progress again and he may be tried over fences next. (op 11-2)
Point West(IRE) made late progress to run on past some beaten rivals. He had finished in front of the winner at Chepstow on his most recent start but was never seen with a chance. He needs further.
Drussell(IRE) made some eyecatching late progress and he could be another who may benefit from a step up in trip.

Laustra Bad(FR) faded badly in the last 3f, having looked like making the frame at one point. This was a retrograde step following two encouraging efforts, and on this evidence he doesn't look like ending his long losing run any time soon. (op 8-1)

3300 NICK VAUX H'CAP HURDLE (11 hdls) 2m 5f 110y

3:25 (3:25) (Class 5) (0-95,93) 4-Y-0+ **£2,055** (£599; £299)

Form RPR

4/3- **1** **Spanish Cruise (IRE)**[425] [2034] 7-11-8 **92** .... DannyCook(3) 97+
(David Pipe) *ducked lft at s and rdr lost both irons tl after 1st: nt a fluent: led tl 2nd: led after 5th: rdn and narrowly hdd 3 out: styd upsides u.str.p: kpt st to ld fnl stride* **11/10**[1]

1-P6 **2** *½* **Sea Saffron**[16] [2980] 10-11-5 **93** .... MarkQuinlan(7) 96
(Susan Gardner) *trckd ldrs: rdn to chal after 8th: tk narrow advantage 3 out: hld on to v narrow advantage u.str.p tl drifted lft and hdd fnl stride* **7/1**[3]

0-62 **3** *37* **Acosta**[42] [2532] 7-10-7 **77** .... (b) EamonDehdashti(3) 46
(Dr Jeremy Naylor) *hmpd s: nvr travelling or fluent in last: wl t.o 7th: got gng in home st to snatch modest 3rd fnl strides: t.o* **7/1**[3]

4300 **4** *1¾* **Newyearsresolution (IRE)**[16] [2980] 7-11-4 **92** .... SClements(7) 60
(Nick Mitchell) *prom: led 2nd tl after 5th: prom: rdn after 7th: sn btn: regained modest 3rd after 2 out: lost 3rd fnl strides: t.o* **16/1**

F/14 **5** *nk* **Cash Back**[192] [826] 11-11-6 **92** .... RachaelGreen(5) 59
(Anthony Honeyball) *trckd ldrs: rdn after 7th: sn btn: pressed for modest 3rd fr 3 out: no ex fr last: t.o* **11/2**[2]

3-55 **6** *10* **Immense (IRE)**[42] [2532] 7-11-7 **91** .... (tp) MichaelMurphy(3) 49
(Ian Williams) *trckd ldrs: rdn after 8th: wnt 3rd 3 out but no ch w ldng pair: wknd sn after: t.o* **15/2**

-P00 **7** *9* **Our Little Dreamer (IRE)**[48] [2390] 7-11-3 **84** .... TomO'Brien 34
(Jeremy Scott) *trckd ldrs tl pushed along after 5th: sn in rr: t.o* **20/1**

/65- **P** **Floradora Do**[259] 9-10-0 **74** .... MattGriffiths(7) —
(Ron Hodges) *towards rr: wknd 6th: t.o after 4 out and sn p.u* **28/1**

5m 41.4s (8.40) **Going Correction** +0.025s/f (Yiel) **8** Ran SP% **113.9**
Speed ratings (Par 103): **85,84,71,70,70 66,63,—**
toteswingers: 1&2 £2.90, 1&3 £2.50; 2&3 £5.70. CSF £9.67 CT £36.90 TOTE £1.90: £1.40, £2.20, £2.20; EX 8.80.
Owner The Chosen Few **Bred** Gainsborough Stud Management Ltd **Trained** Nicholashayne, Devon
■ Stewards' Enquiry : Mark Quinlan one-day ban: used whip with excessive frequency (Jan 16)
Danny Cook one-day ban: used whip with excessive frequency (Jan 16)

FOCUS

A moderate handicap hurdle but another success for the Pipe stable with a gambled-on runner returning from a long absence. A real battle developed between the principals, who finished a long way ahead of the rest. The first two are rated close to form.

NOTEBOOK

Spanish Cruise(IRE) had not been seen since running third on his chasing debut in November 2009, having had tendon trouble. However, he was clearly fit enough and, after helping to make the running throughout, battled on gamely to get up again virtually on the line under a vigorous ride. That does not tell the whole story however, as the gelding tried to whip round as the tapes went up and, but for colliding with another runner, would have unseated his jockey. However, Cook sat tight and jumped the first hurdle without stirrups, so deserves plenty of credit for this success. (op 10-11)

Sea Saffron, a winner over fences at this track, came through to challenge in the straight and looked to be holding the winner until drifting left and getting caught on the line. He was clear of the rest and can gain compensation over hurdles before returning to fences. (op 8-1)

Acosta ran on past beaten rivals to take third. However, he was being ridden and looked less than enthusiastic with a circuit to go, so looks one to be wary of. (tchd 13-2)

Newyearsresolution(IRE) would have been an appropriate winner and made a bold bid from the front. He was well beaten in the end but might be the sort who will make his mark on better ground in the summer. (op 20-1)

Cash Back, whose best form under rules has been on fast ground during the summer, was returning from over six months off and did not perform badly. (op 7-1 tchd 15-2 and 5-1)

Immense(IRE) seems to stay well but, after chasing the leaders into the straight, weakened quite quickly and was eased before the final flight. (op 13-2 tchd 8-1)

3301 BATHWICK TYRES TAUNTON MAIDEN OPEN NATIONAL HUNT FLAT RACE 2m 1f

4:00 (4:03) (Class 6) 4-6-Y-O **£1,370** (£399; £199)

Form RPR

21- **1** **Glitzy D'Ocala (FR)**[271] [5035] 6-11-5 0 .... TomO'Brien 120+
(Philip Hobbs) *trckd ldrs early: midfield 1/2-way: hdwy 6f out: led over 1f out: styd on strly: comf* **7/2**[2]

22 **2** *15* **Billy Merriott (IRE)**[51] [2335] 5-11-0 0 .... IanPopham(5) 108+
(Paul Nicholls) *sn trcking ldr: led 3f out: sn rdn: hdd over 1f out: sn hld by wnr* **6/1**

4 **3** *6* **Golden Gael**[59] [2156] 5-10-12 0 .... WillKennedy 94
(Jeremy Scott) *led for 5f: trckd ldrs: rdn over 3f out: styd on fnl 2f: wnt 3rd ins fnl f* **14/1**

02 **4** *¾* **Bardolf (IRE)**[41] [2560] 5-11-5 0 .... WayneHutchinson 100
(Alan King) *mid-div: struggling 1/2-way: styd on fnl 3f: wnt 3rd briefly ent fnl f* **9/2**[3]

5 *2¼* **Champagne Rosie** 5-10-5 0 .... NathanSweeney(7) 91
(Bob Buckler) *mid-div: rdn over 3f out: styd on fnl 2f* **33/1**

2 **6** *2½* **Morgan's Bay**[232] [319] 6-11-5 0 .... SamThomas 98+
(Tom George) *plld hrd early: trckd ldrs: rdn 3f out: wandered 2f out: styd on same pce* **5/2**[1]

7 *1* **Gypsy Moth (IRE)** 5-10-7 0 .... GilesHawkins(5) 88
(Caroline Keevil) *green early in rr: hdwy fr 1/2-way: trckd ldrs 7f out: rdn to chse ldng pair 3f out: wknd ent fnl f* **25/1**

8 *6* **Ronnie Ronalde (IRE)** 6-11-2 0 .... DannyCook(3) 90
(Nick Mitchell) *trckd ldr: led after 4f: rdn and hdd 3f out: swtchd lft: wknd ent fnl f* **9/1**

9 *13* **Romany Quest** 4-10-7 0 .... AndrewGlassonbury 66
(Linda Blackford) *a towards rr* **66/1**

4 **10** *2* **Unnecessary Xpense**[45] [2458] 4-10-4 0 .... JohnKington(3) 64
(Michael Scudamore) *a towards rr* **50/1**

11 *45* **Russian Genie (IRE)** 5-10-5 0 .... MattGriffiths(7) 29
(Victor Dartnall) *trckd ldrs tl 1/2-way: sn bhd: t.o* **16/1**

6 **12** *15* **Wosayu**[51] [2335] 5-10-9 0 .... SClements(10) 22
(Colin Tizzard) *mid-div: rdn over 3f out: sn wknd: t.o* **50/1**

13 *1¾* **Colonial Harry** 4-10-0 0 .... MarkQuinlan(7) 9
(Neil Mulholland) *mid-div: rdn 5f out: sn wknd: t.o* **25/1**

14 *32* **See You Sunday** 6-10-9 0 .... WayneKavanagh(3) —
(Seamus Mullins) *a towards rr: lost tch 1/2-way: t.o* **50/1**

4m 13.9s (5.10) **Going Correction** +0.025s/f (Yiel)
WFA 4 from 5yo+ 11lb **14** Ran SP% **123.8**
Speed ratings: **89,81,79,78,77 76,76,73,67,66 45,37,37,22**
toteswingers: 1&2 £6.80, 1&3 £13.50, 2&3 £14.00. CSF £24.34 TOTE £6.70: £2.60, £1.70, £6.50; EX 28.60.
Owner Miss I D Du Pre **Bred** David Darme **Trained** Withycombe, Somerset

FOCUS

A fair bumper with some reasonable previous form amongst the runners. A step up from the winner and the next three give the form a pretty solid look.

NOTEBOOK

Glitzy D'Ocala(FR) ◆, whose rider was kicked at the start, only qualified for this as he had been subsequently disqualified after winning a bumper at Chepstow in the spring due to having a prohibited substance in his urine sample. He gained compensation in fine style though, cruising through to take the lead halfway up the straight and coming right away. He looks a decent jumping prospect. (op 7-1)

Billy Merriott(IRE) has now been runner-up on all three bumper starts but did nothing wrong, as he was beaten by a superior rival. He has one more chance in this grade before going hurdling. (op 4-1 tchd 7-2)

Golden Gael showed promise on her debut and did the same here, although giving the impression that she will be seen to better effect once switched to hurdles and racing over longer trips.

Bardolf(IRE) ran well last time on soft ground at Towcester. He looked short of pace and should do better over further. (op 13-2)

Champagne Rosie made a promising debut for a yard running back into form and can be expected to know more next time. (op 28-1)

Morgan's Bay, who cost £100,000 when bought out of Henry Daly's yard following his debut, was too keen under restraint in the early stages and paid for it once the race began in earnest. (tchd 11-4)

Gypsy Moth(IRE), a half-sister to a bumper winner from the family of Spartan Missile, was clueless and pushed along in the early stages on this debut. However, she eventually got the hang of things and was chasing the leaders early in the straight before her exertions took their toll. She clearly has ability and can improve a fair amount with this under her belt.

Ronnie Ronalde(IRE) is related to a couple of decent stayers over hurdles and fences and ran a promising race on this racecourse debut, disputing the lead for a long way before tiring in the straight. He will be better for the run and looks sure to make a chaser in time. (op 11-2)

T/Plt: £166.50 to a £1 stake. Pool of £65,615.61 - 287.63 winning tickets. T/Qpdt: £156.20 to a £1 stake. Pool of £194,585.09 - 1909.03 winning tickets. TM

2433 FAKENHAM (L-H)

Saturday, January 1

OFFICIAL GOING: Good to soft changing to soft after race 2 (12.30).

Fresh ground all way round on hurdles track but impact on distances not notified.
Wind: Virtually nil Weather: Overcast

3302 NEW YEAR'S DAY MAIDEN HURDLE (DIV I) (9 hdls) 2m

12:00 (12:00) (Class 5) 4-Y-0+ **£1,712** (£499; £249)

Form RPR

224 **1** **Sire De Grugy (FR)**[11] [3056] 5-11-5 0 .... JamieMoore 136+
(Gary Moore) *nt a fluent: chsd clr ldr: clsd to ld bef 6th: clr and in command fr next: mstke last: eased flat: v easily* **4/9**[1]

-335 **2** *19* **Aviador (GER)**[19] [2925] 5-11-5 0 .... LeightonAspell 116+
(Lucy Wadham) *prom in main gp: chsd wnr fr 6th: struggling whn hit next: wl hld after* **7/2**[2]

43-0 **3** *15* **Lap Of Honour (IRE)**[63] [2092] 7-11-5 105 .... GrahamLee 104
(Ferdy Murphy) *hld up in rr: hdwy 5th: chsd ldng pair and rdn 3 out: sn wknd: wl btn whn mstke 2 out* **20/1**

00 **4** *13* **Goodwood Starlight (IRE)**[38] [2607] 6-11-2 0 .... (t) MarcGoldstein(3) 89
(Jim Best) *plld hrd: hld up in rr: hdwy into 7th 6th: no ch w ldrs whn j.rt next: wnt poor 4th last: n.d: t.o* **33/1**

-00 **5** *1½* **Mister New York (USA)**[43] [2122] 6-11-5 0 .... MarkBradburne 87
(Noel Chance) *racd off the pce in midfield: nt fluent 2nd: clsd and in tch 6th: wknd u.p bef next: t.o 2 out* **28/1**

2 **6** *2½* **Glorybe (GER)**[49] [2370] 5-10-12 0 .... TomMessenger 78
(Chris Bealby) *t.k.h: hld up in rr: mstke 1st: pushed along and hdwy after 5th: rdn and wknd bef 3 out: t.o 2 out* **8/1**[3]

7 *31* **Dancing Belle**[28] 6-10-9 0 .... AlexMerriam(3) 50
(J R Jenkins) *a in rr: hmpd 1st and 3rd: rdn and struggling after 5th: t.o fr next* **80/1**

05 **8** *1* **Rumballina**[46] [2439] 4-9-9 0 ow2 .... MrRichardCollinson(7) 39
(Amy Weaver) *racd off the pce in midfield: mstke 3rd: rdn and lost pl after 5th: t.o fr next* **66/1**

446 **9** *21* **Morocchius (USA)**[10] [3091] 6-11-2 102 .... AdamPogson(3) 38
(Charles Pogson) *led: virtually bolted into clr ld after 1st: hanging and j.rt 4th: hdd bef 6th: wkng qckly whn hit 6th: t.o next* **33/1**

04P0 **10** *11* **Wicklewood**[10] [3091] 5-10-12 89 .... (p) MattCrawley(7) 28
(Christine Dunnett) *a in rr: dropped to last and rdn w no rspnse 4th: t.o fr 6th* **50/1**

4m 16.2s (10.80) **Going Correction** +0.975s/f (Soft)
WFA 4 from 5yo+ 11lb **10** Ran SP% **121.4**
Speed ratings (Par 103): **112,102,95,88,87 86,71,70,60,54**
toteswingers: 1&2 £1.40, 1&3 £6.10, 2&3 £4.10. CSF £2.35 TOTE £1.60: £1.02, £1.20, £3.40; EX 3.00.
Owner The Preston Family & Friends **Bred** La Grugerie **Trained** Lower Beeding, W Sussex

FOCUS

Underfoot conditions were officially good to soft, with the ground expected to ride 'dead' by the clerk of the course. Few could be given a realistic chance in this opening event, an ordinary maiden hurdle. A step up from the winner with the second and fourth helping to set the level.

NOTEBOOK

Sire De Grugy(FR), who had made the first four in his last two starts at Kempton, took advantage of a marked drop in class to notch a smooth success. In second place early on, he led four hurdles out and was never challenged thereafter. He did not have a great deal to beat and was clumsy at the final flight, but should collect again at some stage. Connections rate him a decent prospect for chasing next term. (op 2-5 tchd 4-11 and 1-2 in places)

Aviador(GER), dropped in trip after seeming to find 2m5f too far last time, made the frame for the fifth time in six starts. He has the ability to register a victory, but may need to make the switch to handicaps in order to find a suitable opening. (op 9-2)

Lap Of Honour(IRE) had fair form last season, but had disappointed on his reappearance. This effort was therefore an improvement, as he stayed on gamely towards the finish, but it did not indicate he will be breaking his duck in the immediate future. (tchd 18-1)

Goodwood Starlight(IRE), whose Flat mark reached 87 at one stage, had shown little on his two previous hurdles outings. He hinted at slightly more here, staying on late after being held up early on, but will need to progress a good deal to take one of these. (op 50-1)

Mister New York(USA), without the blinkers he had been wearing recently, failed to show significant improvement for the lack of headgear. He was always in about the same position.

Morocchius(USA) had disappointed on his debut for this stable ten days earlier and, after bolting clear at the start and running keenly until overtaken in mid-race, soon faded out of contention.

3303 HAPPY NEW YEAR (S) HURDLE (11 hdls) 2m 4f
12:30 (12:30) (Class 5) 4-Y-0+ **£2,055** (£599; £299)

Form RPR

143F **1** **Celticello (IRE)**[40] 2588 9-11-2 122 MrJMQuinlan(7) 118+
(Michael Quinlan) *hld up in tch: pushed along to chse ldng pair after 3 out: wnt 2nd after next: led bef last: in command and rdn out flat* **15/8**[1]

4340 **2** 2½ **Knight Legend (IRE)**[22] 2869 12-10-13 110 (t) MrMEnnis(7) 112
(Sarah Humphrey) *t.k.h: chsd ldrs tl wnt 2nd after 5th: led 8th: hdd and rdn bef last: sn btn: styd on same pce flat* **4/1**[3]

4130 **3** 9 **Liberty Seeker (FR)**[21] 2887 12-11-2 108 MattCrawley(7) 109
(John Harris) *hld up wl in tch: hdwy to join ldr 3 out: rdn bef next: wknd between last 2* **9/1**

1114 **4** 13 **National Trust**[11] 3057 9-11-5 120 KyleJames(7) 99
(Edward Creighton) *led: hdd 8th: rdn bef next: wknd u.p bef 2 out* **11/4**[2]

0/0F **5** 2¼ **Hoh Viss**[16] 2983 11-11-3 110 (b) AdamPogson(3) 90
(Caroline Bailey) *t.k.h: chsd ldr tl after 5th: styd handy tl wknd u.p bef 3 out* **16/1**

430- **6** 7 **Mymateeric**[64] 4231 5-11-6 108 GerardTumelty 84
(Jeff Pearce) *nt fluent: in rr: reminders after 1st: clsd and in tch 8th: wknd u.p bef next* **15/2**

B **P** **Humbel Times (IRE)**[43] 2493 7-11-3 0 AlexMerriam(3) —
(Neil King) *mstkes: in tch: mstke and reminder 5th: struggling and blnd 7th: lost tch u.p bef next: t.o whn hit 2 out: p.u sn after* **25/1**

5m 28.3s (15.70) **Going Correction** +0.975s/f (Soft) **7** Ran SP% **112.9**
Speed ratings (Par 103): **107,106,102,97,96 93,—**
toteswingers: 1&2 £2.90, 1&3 £1.90, 2&3 £4.70. CSF £9.66 TOTE £3.20: £1.70, £2.50; EX 12.40.The winner was bought in for 6,000gns.
Owner Thomas Mann **Bred** P D Savill **Trained** Newmarket, Suffolk

FOCUS
This looked quite competitive for the grade. The winner was the form pick and the next two were close to their marks.

NOTEBOOK
Celticello(IRE), back over hurdles after falling in a chase last time out, seemed to enjoy the switch. Ridden patiently, he eased into third place before two out and jumped ahead at the last. His stable is back in decent nick after a lean spell and, as he was the form pick, this victory was no great surprise, even if an official rating of 122 probably flatters him. (op 13-8 tchd 2-1)
Knight Legend(IRE), reverting to hurdles after some solid runs in handicap chases, also appreciated these smaller obstacles. Never far away, he ran on gamely towards the finish without seriously threatening to overhaul the winner. (tchd 9-2)
Liberty Seeker(FR), taking a massive drop in class after contesting a Grade 2 event three weeks previously, ran creditably. He was in the first three from halfway and lost touch with the principals only in the home straight. (op 8-1)
National Trust, winner of three on his last four outings, set out to make all. He was headed at halfway, though, and, despite staging a brief rally, could not quicken when the first three changed gear on the home turn. (op 7-2 tchd 5-2)
Mymateeric, whose career record coming here stood at 1-33, was well backed at double-figure odds. He ran disappointingly, however, getting a reminder as early as the second flight and failing to respond when niggled along from halfway. (op 16-1 tchd 7-1)

3304 NEW YEAR'S DAY MAIDEN HURDLE (DIV II) (9 hdls) 2m
1:05 (1:05) (Class 5) 4-Y-0+ **£1,712** (£499; £249)

Form RPR

05 **1** **Nosecond Chance (IRE)**[16] 2985 5-11-2 0 PeterToole(3) 102+
(Charlie Mann) *in tch in midfield: hdwy to chse ldr after 6th: rdn to ld after 2 out: clr and mstke last: drvn out* **4/1**[1]

6U **2** 4 **All For Free (IRE)**[49] 2362 5-11-2 0 JimmyDerham(3) 95+
(Milton Harris) *hld up in tch in last trio: rdn and outpcd after 6th: modest 7th next: 5th and styng on last: r.o flat to go 2nd nr fin: no threat to wnr* **9/2**[2]

-000 **3** ¾ **Deputy Dog (IRE)**[16] 2985 5-10-9 0 GeraldQuinn(10) 95
(Jonjo O'Neill) *in tch: rdn after 6th: 6th and outpcd u.p sn after 3 out: rallied u.p bef last: styd on to go 3rd flat: no threat to wnr* **17/2**

06-0 **4** 1½ **Uncle Ant (IRE)**[52] 2310 6-11-5 0 JamieMoore 95
(Paul Webber) *mstkes: t.k.h: led: clr w wnr after 3 out: rdn and hit 2 out: hdd wl bef last: one pce u.p and btn last: lost 2 pls towards fin* **28/1**

0-00 **5** shd **Erin Dancer (IRE)**[4] 3167 6-11-5 0 GrahamLee 93
(Ferdy Murphy) *hld up in tch in last trio: hdwy after 5th: chsd ldng pair bef 3 out: rdn and outpcd bef 2 out: plugged on same pce between last 2: lost 2 pls flat* **20/1**

20 **6** 12 **Ultimate Quest (IRE)**[28] 2512 6-11-5 0 MarkBradburne 83
(Michael Chapman) *chsd ldrs: mstke 2nd: wnt 2nd 6th tl bef next: wknd u.p after 3 out* **5/1**[3]

45 **7** 22 **Mister Fantastic**[47] 2426 5-10-12 0 MissCareyWilliamson(7) 59
(Sarah Humphrey) *t.k.h: chsd ldr: mstke 2nd: lost 2nd 6th: sn wknd: t.o fr 2 out* **12/1**

8 15 **Farmers Glory**[155] 4-10-4 0 AlexMerriam(3) 32
(Neil King) *chsd ldrs tl short of room bnd bef 5th and lost pl: rdn and wknd after 6th: t.o fr 2 out* **25/1**

9 6 **Mangham (IRE)**[5] 6-11-5 0 LeightonAspell 48+
(David Brown) *hld up in tch: hmpd: stmbld and veered bdly rt 6th: sn lost pl and bhd bef next: rallied to go modest 4th after 3 out: wknd rapidly next: t.o and virtually p.u flat* **8/1**

P **Rumble Of Thunder (IRE)**[96] 5-11-5 0 RichieMcGrath —
(Kate Walton) *t.k.h: hld up in tch: dropped to rr after 5th: wl btn 3 out: bhd and p.u last* **5/1**[3]

P **Ericaceous**[212] 4-9-10 0 ow3 (t) MrMMarris(7) —
(Christine Dunnett) *hld up in tch in last trio: stmbld 1st: hdwy to chse ldrs 3rd tl after 5th: bhd whn bdly hmpd and lost tch next: p.u bef 3 out* **100/1**

4m 26.8s (21.40) **Going Correction** +0.975s/f (Soft)
WFA 4 from 5yo+ 11lb **11** Ran SP% **113.9**
Speed ratings (Par 103): **85,83,82,81,81 75,64,57,54,— —**
toteswingers: 1&2 £4.40, 1&3 £4.50, 2&3 £7.70. CSF £20.58 TOTE £6.60: £2.50, £2.40, £2.40; EX 26.90.
Owner Hugh Villiers **Bred** Michael And Mrs B C Lenihan **Trained** Upper Lambourn, Berks
■ Stewards' Enquiry : Gerald Quinn ten-day ban: in breach of rule (B) 59.4, insufficient effort (Jan 15-24)

FOCUS
This looked significantly weaker than the first leg that opened the card. The winner is on the upgrade and the form probably doesn't amount to much.

NOTEBOOK
Nosecond Chance(IRE), a point winner with two previous hurdle runs on his cv, justified support after elbowing his way to the head of the betting. He was no better than a workmanlike winner, though, needing to be hard-ridden from the final flight to maintain the lead had taken shortly after the second-last. Handicaps will probably be on the cards for him now, as he might well struggle under a penalty in novices' events. (op 6-1)
All For Free(IRE), a bumper winner in Ireland but previously unimpressive over hurdles, stayed on well in the closing stages and, judged on this run, may benefit from a longer trip. His future also appears to be in handicaps. (op 13-2)
Deputy Dog(IRE) had shown glimmers of previous form, in bumpers and over hurdles, and this was arguably his best effort. Never too far off the pace, he stayed on late to grab third near the line. (op 11-1 tchd 8-1)
Uncle Ant(IRE), with little to recommend him on previous performances, set out to make all. The fact that was still in front two flights from home and then managed to fill fourth despite getting tired on the run-in puts this form into perspective. (tchd 22-1)
Erin Dancer(IRE), tailed off on his latest run over hurdles, is another whose presence in the first five suggests this was a moderate contest. (op 12-1)
Rumble Of Thunder(IRE)'s rider reported the gelding ran too free. Official explanation: jockey said gelding ran to free (op 9-2 tchd 4-1)

3305 NORTH NORFOLK AMATEUR RIDERS' H'CAP CHASE (16 fncs) 2m 5f 110y
1:35 (1:35) (Class 4) (0-100,100) 5-Y-0+ **£2,498** (£774; £387; £193)

Form RPR

022 **1** **Flying Squad (UAE)**[38] 2604 7-11-0 95 (t) MrCGreene(7) 112+
(Milton Harris) *hld up in tch: hdwy to trck ldrs after 11th: wnt 2nd 2 out: pushed ahd between last 2: in command and pushed out flat: comf* **5/2**[1]

U/30 **2** 2½ **Oponce (FR)**[19] 2930 9-10-1 82 MrJBanks(7) 91
(Noel Chance) *chsd ldrs: wnt 2nd after 11th: led 13th tl rdn and hdd between last 2: styd on same pce u.p after* **6/1**

3403 **3** 23 **Feeling Peckish (USA)**[4] 3170 7-9-10 77 (t) MrTBellamy(7) 63
(Michael Chapman) *chsd ldr tl led 3rd tl 7th: styd prom: rdn whn mstke 11th: lft 4th and sltly hmpd 13th: wknd bef 2 out: lft modest 3rd last* **11/4**[2]

123/ **4** 11 **Investment Affair (IRE)**[948] 509 11-11-1 96 MrMEnnis(7) 77
(Sarah Humphrey) *t.k.h: chsd ldrs: mstke 9th: lft 2nd 13th tl 2 out: sn wknd u.p: lft poor 4th last* **8/1**

P065 **P** **Muntami (IRE)**[47] 2422 10-11-5 100 MrMMarris(7) —
(John Harris) *a in rr: mstke 1st: j. slowly 4th: lost tch after 11th: t.o fr 3 out tl p.u last* **28/1**

0-3P **F** **Captain Smoothy**[47] 2420 11-10-7 88 MrRichardCollinson(7) 97
(Neil King) *led tl 3rd: chsd ldr tl led again 7th: hdd and blnd bdly 13th: rallied u.p to chse ldng pair after 2 out: no imp and wl hld whn fell last* **3/1**[3]

5m 58.5s (16.70) **Going Correction** +0.90s/f (Soft) **6** Ran SP% **109.1**
Speed ratings: **105,104,95,91,— —**
toteswingers: 1&2 £2.20, 1&3 £1.40, 2&3 £2.60. CSF £16.22 TOTE £2.50: £2.00, £2.40; EX 13.60.
Owner Mrs Denise Hopkins **Bred** Darley **Trained** Herridge, Wiltshire

FOCUS
A moderate event. The cosy winner was value for further and is rated to his best.

NOTEBOOK
Flying Squad(UAE), runner-up on both his previous chasing starts, comfortably broke his duck in the discipline here. Always travelling smoothly, he was held up early on, but began to make eyecatching progress at the fourth-last. He quickened decisively from two out and, by the final fence, held a healthy lead. He deserved this victory, but might find it hard to follow up if the handicapper raises his rating significantly. (op 3-1)
Oponce(FR), having his third outing after a long absence, ran creditably. He travelled sweetly for much of the journey, taking the lead four out and staying on gamely thereafter, but could not muster the finishing zip of the winner. (op 11-2 tchd 5-1)
Feeling Peckish(USA), third in a jumpers' bumper at Southwell just four days earlier, ran in snatches. He was keen early on, but made a mistake at halfway and then had to be niggled along to stay with the leaders. Only the final fence fall of Captain Smoothy secured him third spot. (op 3-1 tchd 5-2)
Muntami(IRE)'s rider reported the gelding's saddle slipped. Official explanation: jockey said saddle slipped (op 20-1 tchd 33-1)
Captain Smoothy, making his first appearance for a new stable, can be considered unlucky not to have gained a significant placing. He cut out a lot of the running and, despite getting tired late on, was still in third when falling at the last. (op 20-1 tchd 33-1)

3306 WELCOME TO 2011 H'CAP HURDLE (11 hdls) 2m 4f
2:10 (2:10) (Class 3) (0-125,122) 4-Y-0+ **£5,529** (£1,623; £811; £405)

Form RPR

P-51 **1** **I'Ve Been Framed (IRE)**[42] 2530 7-11-9 119 (p) MarkBradburne 125+
(Neil King) *chsd ldr tl led 5th: mde rest: clr and drvn whn hit 2 out: hrd pressed and mstke last: edgd rt u.p but hld on gamely flat: all out* **4/1**[1]

3504 **2** hd **Caught By Witness (IRE)**[11] 3060 6-11-7 120 JimmyDerham(3) 125+
(Milton Harris) *hld up in rr: hdwy to chse ldrs 8th: swtchd lft and hdwy between horses to chse clr wnr bef 2 out: sn drvn: clsd and chal last: edgd rt u.p and a jst hld flat* **11/2**[3]

0111 **3** 11 **Amuse Me**[57] 2185 5-10-9 115 GeraldQuinn(10) 110
(Jonjo O'Neill) *mstkes: chsd ldrs: wnt 2nd 6th tl after 3 out: wknd u.p and wnt lft next* **9/2**[2]

3356 **4** 1½ **Decision**[22] 2312 5-9-10 99 AdamWedge(7) 92
(Lawney Hill) *chsd ldrs: drvn and no hdwy after 3 out: 4th and btn whn hmpd next: plugged on same pce after* **12/1**

223/ **5** 3 **Super Directa (GER)**[644] 4755 7-11-4 114 LeightonAspell 102
(Lucy Wadham) *in tch in midfield: wknd bef 3 out: eased between last 2: lft 5th last* **7/1**

230- **6** 24 **Bureaucrat**[344] 3586 9-11-10 120 (p) RichieMcGrath 84
(Kate Walton) *in tch in midfield tl rdn and wknd bef 3 out* **25/1**

0000 **7** 4½ **Tarvini (IRE)**[50] 2347 6-11-10 120 (p) GerardTumelty 80
(Jonjo O'Neill) *a in rr: detached in last and rdn after 5th: lost tch fr 7th: t.o fr 3 out* **25/1**

12-0 **8** 79 **Anak (IRE)**[38] 2606 5-11-12 122 (b[1]) JamieMoore 3
(Jim Best) *chsd ldrs tl rdn along and grad lost pl fr 4th: bhd 6th: lost tch next: wl t.o bef 3 out* **14/1**

4-53 **P** **Slew Charm (FR)**[39] 2596 9-11-0 117 (t) MrJBanks(7) —
(Noel Chance) *hld up in tch: 5th and rdn bef 3 out: wknd wl bef 2 out: stl 5th but wl btn whn p.u last: dismntd* **15/2**

-640 **P** **Charingworth (IRE)**[4] 3168 8-11-5 115 GrahamLee —
(Ferdy Murphy) *hld up in tch: rdn and wknd bef 3 out: wl bhd whn p.u 2 out* **9/1**

-354 **P** **Horseshoe Reef (AUS)**[40] 2580 8-10-13 112 (p) AlexMerriam(3) —
(Jamie Snowden) *led tl 5th: rdn and lost pl next: lost tch after 7th: t.o whn p.u 3 out* **28/1**

P **Schumpters Lad (IRE)**179 923 6-11-7 **120** PeterToole(3) —
(Charlie Mann) *hld up in tch: hdwy to chse ldrs 7th: 4th and rdn 3 out: wknd rapidly: wl btn whn p.u next* **14/1**

5m 28.4s (15.80) **Going Correction** +0.975s/f (Soft) **12** Ran SP% **120.0**
Speed ratings (Par 107): **107,106,102,101,100 91,89,57,—,— —,—**
toteswingers: 1&2 £7.20, 1&3 £2.30, 2&3 £4.90. CSF £26.38 CT £105.00 TOTE £6.10: £1.90, £2.40, £1.70; EX 43.50.
Owner Mr & Mrs A Whyte P Edwards C Appleton **Bred** Mrs Patricia Kelly-Furey **Trained** Newmarket, Suffolk

FOCUS
A competitive event in which few could be confidently discounted. The first two finished clear and are seemingly on the upgrade.

NOTEBOOK
I'Ve Been Framed(IRE), raised 6lb since scoring at Huntingdon in late November, shrugged off the extra with a game success. Second early on and in front before halfway, he made virtually all the rest of the running. He was challenged strongly by the runner-up at the final flight but, even though he may just have been headed at that point, he battled on resolutely and was edging away at the line. He is sure to take another hit from the handicapper after this success and that may well make life tougher for him. (op 9-2 tchd 5-1)
Caught By Witness(IRE), a bumper winner over 2m 2f, seemed to appreciate stepping up to this trip. Ridden patiently early on, he made progress before the third-last and joined the winner at the final flight. He fought hard to grab a decisive advantage, but could not quite land the spoils. (op 7-1)
Amuse Me lined up bidding for a four-timer, but was 16lb higher than when scoring at Fontwell last time and the extra proved his undoing. He was always close to the pace, but unable to stay with the first two in the home straight. (tchd 4-1 and 5-1 in places)
Decision is still a maiden, but did enough here to suggest he is no lost cause. In the first half-dozen throughout, he posted a creditable effort. (op 16-1)
Super Directa(GER) ◆, returning after a 644-day absence, definitely hinted at better to come. Another close to the pace from the outset, he was still battling on towards the finish, even though his chance of a first-three placing had disappeared.

3307 WENSUM H'CAP CHASE (12 fncs) 2m 110y
2:45 (2:45) (Class 5) (0-95,90) 5-Y-O+ **£2,055** (£599; £299)

Form RPR
0043 **1** **Lukie Victor (IRE)**38 2604 10-11-4 **87** AdamWedge(7) 99
(Evan Williams) *pressed ldr: mstke 6th: rdn along briefly next: rdn to ld and j.lft 9th: hdd and drvn 2 out: rallying and pressing ldr whn lft wl clr last* **15/8**1

-000 **2** *22* **Zepnove (IRE)**42 2514 5-11-7 **90** (p) AlexMerriam(3) 76
(Neil King) *a in rr and nvr looked happy: rdn and lost tch after 7th: lft duelling for poor 3rd bef 2 out: lft 2nd and hmpd last* **8/1**

32U0 **3** *7* **Peak Seasons (IRE)**10 3091 8-10-12 **74** JamieMoore 57
(Michael Chapman) *chsd ldrs: mstke 3rd: jnd ldrs 7th: drvn and struggling next: wl btn 3 out: lft poor 3rd and hmpd last* **4/1**3

3525 **P** **Best Horse (FR)**18 2942 9-11-12 **88** GrahamLee —
(Ferdy Murphy) *t.k.h: led tl 9th: 3rd and fdd rapidly whn rdn after next: p.u bef 2 out* **10/3**2

3-FF **F** **Gavroche Gaugain (FR)**46 2434 7-11-2 **85** PaulGallagher(7) 97+
(Ferdy Murphy) *hld up in tch: trckd ldrs whn mstke 9th: rdn to ld 2 out: 2 l clr between last 2: pressed again whn fell heavily last* **4/1**3

4m 36.4s (19.80) **Going Correction** +0.90s/f (Soft)
WFA 5 from 7yo+ 3lb **5** Ran SP% **109.0**
Speed ratings: **89,78,75,—,—**
CSF £14.75 TOTE £2.50: £1.60, £4.90; EX 24.00.
Owner R E R Williams **Bred** Miss Georgina Behan **Trained** Llancarfan, Vale Of Glamorgan

FOCUS
A poor contest. The winner is rated tpo form and the faller was heading for a personal best.

NOTEBOOK
Lukie Victor(IRE), who lined up without a win since 2008, was arguably a fortunate scorer. He disputed the lead from the outset, so nobody can begrudge him this success, but he seemed booked for second when Gavroche Gaugain fell heavily at the last. What can be said about the winner is that he jumped adequately throughout and was still responding to driving at that final obstacle. (op 11-4 after early 3-1 in places)
Zepnove(IRE), making her chasing debut after a series of disappointing efforts over hurdles, took advantage of others' misfortunes or inadequacies to grab second. She was held up in last place for much of the journey and never in serious contention. (op 9-1 tchd 10-1)
Peak Seasons(IRE), whose last win was in April 2009, was another ridden patiently. He looked woefully one-paced in the closing stages, though, and this run brings his current losing sequence to 29. (op 3-1)
Gavroche Gaugain(FR) had fallen on both his previous outings this season and, with another fall against his name, he will look an unappealing betting medium next time out. He can be considered unlucky here, however, as he was challenging strongly when hitting the deck at the final fence.

3308 HOLT H'CAP HURDLE (13 hdls) 2m 7f 110y
3:20 (3:20) (Class 4) (0-110,109) 4-Y-O+ **£2,602** (£764; £382; £190)

Form RPR
3206 **1** **Phare Isle (IRE)**50 2347 6-11-10 **107** CharliePoste 117+
(Ben Case) *a gng wl: in tch: chsd ldr after 10th: rdn to ld after 3 out: drawing wl clr whn hit 2 out: heavily eased after last* **7/2**1

51-0 **2** *12* **Days Of Pleasure (IRE)**60 2141 6-11-5 **109** (p) MrTJCannon(7) 102
(Chris Gordon) *mde most tl hdd and rdn bef 10th: 4th and wl outpcd bef 3 out: plugged on between last 2 to go 2nd last: no ch w wnr* **12/1**

6-61 **3** *3 ¾* **Along Came Rosie**50 2353 7-11-7 **104** FearghalDavis 94
(Andrew Crook) *hld up in tch: effrt to chse ldrs after 9th: rdn and outpcd next: 3rd and wl btn after 3 out: sltly hmpd and mstke next* **15/2**

41 **4** *7* **Lastroseofsummer (IRE)**43 2505 5-11-3 **107** MattCrawley(7) 92
(Rae Guest) *t.k.h: chsd ldrs tl led bef 10th: hdd and rdn bef 3 out: no ch w wnr 2 out: lost 2 pls fr last* **7/2**1

P-11 **5** *7* **Prince Massini (IRE)**59 2144 10-11-1 **105** AdamWedge(7) 80
(Evan Williams) *w ldrs tl rdn and wknd bef 3 out: wl btn 2 out* **4/1**2

2-0P **6** *72* **Art Exhibition (IRE)**55 2247 6-11-7 **107** (bt) PeterToole(3) 10
(Charlie Mann) *w ldrs tl dropped to rr and rdn w no rspnse 9th: wl t.o after next* **20/1**

-341 **P** **Little Carmela**47 2425 7-11-12 **109** MarkBradburne —
(Neil King) *bhd and nvr gng wl: rdn and lost tch after 5th: t.o fr 7th tl p.u 10th* **8/1**

4426 **P** **Ouest Eclair (FR)**4 3167 6-10-10 **93** GrahamLee —
(Ferdy Murphy) *hld up in rr: clsd and in tch 9th: wknd qckly u.p next: t.o whn p.u bef last* **11/2**3

6m 35.8s (29.40) **Going Correction** +0.975s/f (Soft) **8** Ran SP% **115.2**
Speed ratings (Par 105): **90,86,84,82,80 56,—,—**
toteswingers: 1&2 £10.00, 1&3 30.50, 2&3 £18.80. CSF £42.83 CT £296.73 TOTE £4.40: £1.40, £4.50, £2.70; EX 79.90.
Owner Nicholson Family Moore Moore & Kendrick **Bred** Maurice Harrington **Trained** Edgcote, Northants
■ Stewards' Enquiry : Mr T J Cannon four-day ban: careless riding (tbn)

FOCUS
A competitive finale featuring four last-time-out winners, and a step up from the winner.

NOTEBOOK
Phare Isle(IRE), sixth in a red-hot Cheltenham conditional riders' handicap on his previous start, found this company a great deal easier to deal with. Always handy, he was in third at halfway and took second four out. He shot into a clear lead before the second-last and, despite making a meal of that flight, notched a comfortable success. A rise in his rating seems inevitable after this, but several of his rivals were below-par, so whether he can shrug off a rise remains to be seen. Connections believe, in any event, that he will not be at his best until he tackles fences. (op 9-2)
Days Of Pleasure(IRE), wearing first-time cheekpieces for this second outing of the season, appeared to benefit from the headgear. This display was not up to the standard he achieved when score at Fontwell in April, but it can be counted a good deal better than his seasonal reappearance. (op 16-1)
Along Came Rosie, making her handicap debut after landing a maiden hurdle at Newcastle in mid-November, did not do enough to prove conclusively that she is on a reasonable mark. That said, however, she was far from disgraced and still relatively lightly raced. (tchd 7-1 and 8-1)
Lastroseofsummer(IRE), another making her handicap debut, in her case after collecting a maiden hurdle at Musselburgh six weeks previously, got left behind in the closing stages. She had figured prominently for much of the race though, and should not be written off just yet. (op 3-1)
Prince Massini(IRE) lined up on a hat-trick, after wins at Uttoxeter and Chepstow, but failed to show his form. He was in contention four out, but soon lost touch with the leaders and faded rather tamely late on. (tchd 9-2)
Art Exhibition(IRE) has been slipping down the ratings, but his performance here did not suggest that his mark has yet reached a level from which he can be competitive. His sole win, at Fontwell in 2008, is becoming a distant memory. (tchd 18-1 and 25-1)
Little Carmela's rider reported the mare was never travelling.\n\x\x \n\x\x Official explanation: jockey said mare was never travelling (op 15-2 tchd 17-2)
T/Plt: £18.50 to a £1 stake. Pool of £42,897.67 - 1,691.55 winning tickets. T/Qpdt: £11.10 to a £1 stake. Pool of £2,935.70 - 194.60 winning tickets. SP

2654 MUSSELBURGH (R-H)
Saturday, January 1
3309 Meeting Abandoned - Frozen track

3316 - 3329a (Foreign Racing) - See Raceform Interactive

AYR (L-H)
Sunday, January 2
OFFICIAL GOING: Good to soft (good in places; 7.4)
Common bend after winning post.
Wind: Almost nil Weather: Dull, cold

3330 EUROPEAN BREEDERS' FUND "NATIONAL HUNT" NOVICES' HURDLE (QUALIFIER) (11 hdls) 2m 4f
12:20 (12:20) (Class 4) 4-7-Y-O **£2,602** (£764; £382; £190)

Form RPR
011 **1** **Lively Baron (IRE)**59 2166 6-11-8 0 JasonMaguire 117+
(Donald McCain) *trckd ldr: hit 4 out: nt fluent whn outpcd next: rallied after 2 out: styd on wl run-in: led nr fin* **5/4**1

10-5 **2** *1 ½* **Kings Grey (IRE)**51 2349 7-11-2 0 JamesReveley 107
(Keith Reveley) *midfield: stdy hdwy after 4 out: effrt bef 2 out: led after last: kpt on: hdd nr fin* **12/1**

P-12 **3** *¾* **Sunarri (IRE)**42 2545 7-11-1 120 AlistairFindlay(7) 112
(Jane Walton) *t.k.h early and j. sltly rt on occasions: led: hit 3rd: rdn 2 out: hdd after last: kpt on* **3/1**2

3-6 **4** *½* **Mr Supreme (IRE)**27 2826 6-11-2 0 RichieMcGrath 106
(Kate Walton) *hld up: hdwy after 4 out: rdn and styd on wl fr last: nrst fin* **66/1**

666 **5** *½* **Bertie Milan (IRE)**57 2202 6-11-2 0 TomMessenger 105
(Sue Bradburne) *prom: drvn along and outpcd bef 3 out: plugged on fr next* **66/1**

0 **6** *2 ¾* **And The Man**56 2246 5-10-6 0 StephenMulqueen(10) 102
(Nicky Richards) *hld up: hit 4 out: hdwy bef 3 out: styd on steadily fr next: nvr nr to chal* **66/1**

6 **7** *8* **Under The Stars (IRE)**50 2375 6-11-2 0 FearghalDavis 94
(Nicky Richards) *t.k.h early: prom: nt fluent 1st: effrt after 4 out: outpcd fr next* **80/1**

03-4 **8** *7* **Miss Abbey**44 2505 7-10-9 0 GrahamLee 80
(Jim Goldie) *midfield: hdwy after 4 out: rdn and wknd fr next* **14/1**

5 **9** *nk* **King Sandor (IRE)**58 2192 6-11-2 0 DougieCostello 87
(Nicky Richards) *hld up: pushed along bef 3 out: nvr rchd ldrs* **80/1**

-4 **10** *4* **Kingsmoss (IRE)**127 1412 6-11-2 114 (p) BarryKeniry 83
(J J Lambe, Ire) *trckd ldrs tl rdn and wknd appr 3 out* **10/1**3

00 **11** *2* **Artic Night (FR)**39 2612 5-11-2 0 WilsonRenwick 81
(Nicky Richards) *bhd: pushed along 4 out: nvr on terms* **125/1**

02-4 **12** *nse* **Forcefield**43 2525 5-10-9 0 MissLAlexander(7) 81
(N W Alexander) *midfield: dropped to rr fr 3rd: n.d fnl circ* **80/1**

336 **13** *6* **Moufatango (FR)**56 2246 5-11-2 0 BrianHarding 78
(Nicky Richards) *hld up towards rr: outpcd whn mstke 4 out: sn btn* **50/1**

041- **14** *18* **Lesanda**341 3679 5-10-9 0 BrianHughes 50
(Richard Fahey) *hld up in midfield: rdn after 4 out: sn wknd* **40/1**

21- **15** *43* **Tanzanite Bay**262 5199 6-10-9 0 PeterBuchanan 7
(Lucinda Russell) *in tch: shortlived effrt bef 6th: wknd next: t.o* **11/1**

0-00 **F** **Scotswell**42 2552 5-10-9 0 GaryRutherford(7) 80
(Harriet Graham) *in tch on outside: nt fluent and outpcd 6th: rallied 4 out: wknd bef next: btn whn fell 2 out* **200/1**

4m 54.0s (-18.00) **Going Correction** -1.025s/f (Hard) **16** Ran SP% **115.1**
Speed ratings: **95,94,94,93,93 92,89,86,86,84 84,84,81,74,57** —
toteswingers: 1&2 £6.70, 1&3 £2.80, 2&3 £5.90 CSF £16.89 TOTE £2.10: £1.10, £2.60, £1.70; EX 16.10.
Owner Trevor Hemmings **Bred** Michael Gowen **Trained** Cholmondeley, Cheshire

FOCUS
The track was passed fit after a morning inspection and the ground was officially good to soft, though the clerk of the course expected it to ride 'quite dead'. Racing began with a fair novices' hurdle. The pace was not especially strong.

NOTEBOOK
Lively Baron(IRE), successful over brush hurdles at Haydock last time, just managed to notch a follow-up under his penalty. Always close to the pace, he seemed to be travelling sweetly until needing to be nudged along three out and thereafter had to work hard. He looked beaten at the final flight, which he jumped in third, but battled on gamely to get his head in front close home. (op 11-10)

Kings Grey(IRE) ◆, successful in a Huntingdon bumper last season, ran a cracker on his second start over hurdles and, given that he is a big, sturdy horse, has obvious scope for improvement. Much of his best work was done in the latter half of the race and he should soon take one of these, possibly over a slightly longer trip. Chasing will ultimately be his game, though. (op 11-1)
Sunarri(IRE), second off a mark of 113 in an Aintree handicap on his latest outing, helps to give a guide to the level of this form. It should be noted, however, that his hurdling was not entirely fluent and he jumped out to the right on several occasions. (op 11-2)
Mr Supreme(IRE), making his hurdles debut, did enough to suggest he can collect at some stage. He stayed on late, having been held up in rear in the early stages, and seems likely to appreciate a step up in trip.
Bertie Milan(IRE), dropped in distance after fading late on over 2m6f last time, fared better here. Never too far off the pace, he plugged on gamely in the home straight. (op 50-1)
And The Man Official explanation: vet said gelding was distressed post race; jockey said, regarding running and riding, his instructions were to get the gelding settled into a nice rhythm and put the gelding in the race leaving the back straight. The trainer confirmed these instructions adding that the gelding was very backward.
Under The Stars(IRE) hinted at better to come. He was prominent early on and lost touch with the principals only in the closing stages. (tchd 100-1)
Forcefield Official explanation: jockey said gelding was unsuited by going

3331 VICTORCHANDLER.COM MAIDEN HURDLE (9 hdls) 2m

12:50 (12:53) (Class 5) 4-Y-0+ **£1,951** (£573; £286; £143)

Form RPR

23-6 **1** **Darna**[91] 1702 5-11-5 0 JanFaltejsek 111+
(William Amos) *trckd ldr most of way tl chal 3 out: led next: pushed along and styd on strly run-in: readily* **11/1**

0-02 **2** 2 1/4 **Rupert Lamb**[39] 2612 5-11-5 0 BrianHughes 110+
(Howard Johnson) *trckd ldrs: blnd 5th: sn rcvrd: shkn up and qcknd to dispute cl 2nd 2 out: sn chsng wnr: rdn and effrt last: nvr quite on terms: one pce run-in* **10/11**[1]

40 **3** 10 **Kaolak (USA)**[18] 2960 5-11-5 0 JamesReveley 100
(Keith Reveley) *led: jnd 3 out: hdd next: sn outpcd by ldng duo: styd on one pce* **9/2**[2]

0 **4** 2 1/2 **Drum Bustible (IRE)**[42] 2553 7-11-5 0 DougieCostello 97
(J J Lambe, Ire) *disp 2nd: hit 3rd: chal 3 out: rdn and wknd bef next* **66/1**

5 3 1/4 **Fortuni (IRE)**[96] 5-11-5 0 WilsonRenwick 95
(Rose Dobbin) *trckd ldrs: wknd fr 3 out: no ch whn hit last* **15/2**[3]

50-0 **6** 9 **Hole In One (IRE)**[51] 2353 5-10-12 0 CampbellGillies 78
(Lucinda Russell) *chsd ldrs tl wknd 3 out: no ch whn hit 2 out* **66/1**

4-P **7** 2 1/4 **Northern Flame (IRE)**[57] 2202 6-11-5 0 PaddyAspell 82
(N W Alexander) *in tch to 4 out: n.d after* **125/1**

44- **8** shd **Checklow (USA)**[288] 4730 6-11-2 0 JamesO'Farrell(3) 82
(Howard Johnson) *in tch to 4 out: n.d after* **12/1**

0-64 **9** 7 **Scarvagh Rose**[42] 2547 6-10-12 0 GrahamLee 68
(Rose Dobbin) *hit 1st: in rr: sn in mid-div: hdwy to get in tch 5th: wknd after 4 out* **25/1**

3-60 **10** 4 **Fightstar (FR)**[57] 2202 7-11-5 0 PeterBuchanan 71
(Lucinda Russell) *in tch early: bhd fr 1/2-way* **50/1**

11 nk **Ulysees (IRE)**[64] 2824 12-11-5 0 RichieMcGrath 71
(Jim Goldie) *in rr tl sme hdwy after 4 out: sn wknd* **50/1**

12 hd **Suburbia (USA)**[130] 5-10-12 0 (t) MrGJCockburn(7) 70
(Lucinda Russell) *a in rr* **125/1**

0 **13** 4 1/2 **Parc Des Princes (USA)**[44] 2509 5-11-5 0 FearghalDavis 66
(Nicky Richards) *rdn 5th: a bhd* **50/1**

P6- **14** 17 **Mississippian (IRE)**[6] 827 7-11-5 0 JasonMaguire 49
(Rose Dobbin) *t.k.h: hit 3rd: blnd 4th: a bhd* **40/1**

P4- **15** 6 **Haulage Lady (IRE)**[282] 4875 5-10-12 0 BrianHarding 36
(Karen McLintock) *a in rr* **200/1**

16 15 **Mr Lu**[44] 6-11-5 0 BarryKeniry 28
(Jim Goldie) *hit 4th: blnd 2 out: a wl bhd* **100/1**

3m 46.79s (-16.31) **Going Correction** -1.025s/f (Hard) **16** Ran SP% **116.6**
Speed ratings (Par 103): **99,97,92,91,90 85,84,84,80,78 78,78,76,67,64 57**
toteswingers: 1&2 £5.30, 1&3 £14.70, 2&3 £4.00 CSF £20.56 TOTE £23.50: £5.30, £1.10, £1.10; EX 31.70.
Owner J L Gledson **Bred** L Fuller **Trained** Broadhaugh, Scottish Borders
■ Stewards' Enquiry : Jason Maguire jockey failed to report gelding ran to free: £140 fine

FOCUS
Just a run-of-the-mill maiden hurdle. The pace was not overly-strong and racing prominently appeared to be an advantage.

NOTEBOOK
Darna, in the first three on both bumper outings last term but a beaten favourite on his reappearance, made an encouraging hurdling debut. Always in the first three, he went to the front before the third-last and galloped on resolutely all the way home. Challenged strongly by the runner-up from the final flight, he showed a commendable attitude and should win again. (op 12-1 tchd 10-1)
Rupert Lamb, second in a novice event at Wetherby late in November, made a couple of costly mistakes and, probably as a consequence, could not quite match the winner in the closing stages. He has the raw ability to take one of these, but will need to sharpen up his jumping. (op 11-10)
Kaolak(USA), not disgraced in hurdle events at Aintree and Newbury this season, again ran creditably. He went off in front, settling better than he had on his previous outings, and was still at the head of affairs approaching three out. He began to tire from that point and was losing ground on the first two in he closing stages, but is beginning to learn to relax and ought to notch a success at some stage. (op 6-1)
Drum Bustible(IRE) made a moderately encouraging hurdles debut, racing in the first half dozen throughout. Handicapping will probably be his game, once he is qualified. (op 50-1)
Fortuni(IRE), successful from a mark of 85 on the Flat in midsummer, was another making his hurdles debut and he too performed sufficiently well to offer some encouragement for the future. He was losing ground at the finish, but should progress from this first outing for 96 days. (op 5-1)

3332 WATCH LIVE RACING AT VICTORCHANDLER.COM BEGINNERS' CHASE (18 fncs) 2m 5f

1:20 (1:21) (Class 4) 5-Y-0+ **£2,865** (£889; £479)

Form RPR

-002 **1** **Elzahann (IRE)**[44] 2507 9-10-7 0 GrahamLee 108+
(Ferdy Murphy) *led: mstke 5 out: hdd after next: outpcd fr 2 out: 9 l down whn lft 33 l clr last* **3/1**[3]

5026 **2** 24 **Rossini's Dancer**[57] 2203 6-11-0 95 TomMessenger 81
(Sue Bradburne) *mstkes: prom: rdn and outpcd 5 out: sn btn: 33 l down whn lft 2nd last* **20/1**

2-16 **3** 35 **Cool Mission (IRE)**[56] 2235 7-11-0 0 JasonMaguire 49
(Donald McCain) *prom: j. slowly 5th: outpcd after 10th: lost tch fr 13th: lft remote 3rd last* **6/5**[1]

6 **F** **Golfer's Crossing (IRE)**[58] 2191 8-11-0 0 PeterBuchanan 44
(Lucinda Russell) *in tch: outpcd fr 6th: lost tch 10th: no ch whn fell last* **16/1**

05-F **F** **The Knoxs (IRE)**[51] 2350 8-11-0 0 BrianHughes 130+
(Howard Johnson) *pressed ldr: chal 1/2-way: led gng wl after 4 out: drew clr fr 2 out: 9 l in front and gng strly whn fell last* **5/2**[2]

5m 31.0s (-11.00) **Going Correction** -0.55s/f (Firm) **5** Ran SP% **109.7**
Speed ratings: **98,88,75,—,—**
toteswingers: 1&2 Not won. CSF £36.71 TOTE £4.50: £3.40, £5.30; EX 27.10.
Owner Ian Allan Todd **Bred** Denis Cummins **Trained** West Witton, N Yorks

FOCUS
An interesting contest, featuring a couple of smart former hurdlers, and it came to a dramatic conclusion.

NOTEBOOK
Elzahann(IRE), beaten just half a length on her chasing bow at Musselburgh in November, was a fortunate winner. She made much of the early running, racing keenly, so can hardly be crabbed for effort. She looked booked for a well-beaten second place, though, until The Knoxs came down at the final fence, because she was starting to get left behind as that unlucky chasing debutant quickened the pace. (old market op 11-4 new market)
Rossini's Dancer, whose jumping has been indifferent since he was sent chasing, lacked fluency again here. He was slow over several fences early on and, after racing in a distant third on the final circuit, took second only after The Knoxs fell. (new market)
Cool Mission(IRE), making his chasing bow after three wins over hurdles, did not look entirely happy over fences. He was cautious at a few, laboured at others, and will need to improve on this if he is to notch a first victory over larger obstacles. (old market op 11-8 new market op 11-8)
Golfer's Crossing(IRE), an Irish point winner in 2008, was never in contention. Always towards the rear, he looked short of pace throughout and fell at the last. (old market op 11-4 new market)
The Knoxs(IRE), twice successful over hurdles in the first half of last season, can be counted an unfortunate loser. He jumped well for the most part, even extravagantly on occasion, and was clear when falling heavily at the final fence. (old market op 11-4 new market)

3333 PLAY POKER AT VICTORCHANDLER.COM H'CAP CHASE (17 fncs) 2m 4f

1:55 (1:55) (Class 3) (0-130,126) 5-Y-0+ **£5,073** (£1,489; £744; £372)

Form RPR

1-PP **1** **Sagalyrique (FR)**[53] 2305 7-11-9 123 (t) JasonMaguire 136+
(Donald McCain) *hld up: hdwy on ins 1/2-way: chsng ldrs 5 out: rdn and outpcd after next: rallied 2 out: hrd rdn to ld run-in: styd on wl* **8/1**

0-34 **2** 3/4 **Premier Sagas (FR)**[56] 2248 7-11-4 118 BrianHarding 131+
(Nicky Richards) *cl up: led gng wl 2 out: rdn last: hdd run-in: hld nr fin* **5/1**[2]

1F62 **3** 5 **Safari Adventures (IRE)**[23] 2869 9-11-12 126 CampbellGillies 133
(Lucinda Russell) *led: rdn 4 out: hdd 2 out: kpt on same pce fr last* **11/2**[3]

132- **4** 10 **Mirage Dore (FR)**[287] 4754 8-11-12 126 WilsonRenwick 123
(Rose Dobbin) *hld up: hdwy and in tch 1/2-way: rdn after 5 out: no imp fr 3 out* **12/1**

50/0 **5** 1/2 **Lampion Du Bost (FR)**[10] 2341 12-10-8 108 RichieMcGrath 107
(Jim Goldie) *nt fluent on occasions: hld up: blnd 12th: sn outpcd: styd on fr 2 out: n.d* **8/1**

3U13 **6** 2 1/4 **Or De Grugy (FR)**[57] 2204 9-11-6 125 AlexanderVoy(5) 120
(Sue Bradburne) *trckd ldrs tl rdn and wknd fr 3 out* **10/1**

U-02 **7** 2 **Raysrock (IRE)**[42] 2551 9-11-7 121 PeterBuchanan 117
(Lucinda Russell) *cl up: mstke 8th: rdn 5 out: wknd fr next* **13/2**

14-4 **8** 1 **Fortysecond Street (IRE)**[71] 1957 7-11-9 123 BrianHughes 120+
(Howard Johnson) *nt fluent on occasions: prom: effrt after 5 out: wknd after next* **9/2**[1]

-P31 **9** 20 **Columbus Secret (IRE)**[19] 2938 6-10-12 112 JamesReveley 94
(Keith Reveley) *mstkes in rr: struggling 12th: sn btn* **11/1**

41/P **P** **Role On (IRE)**[42] 2549 9-11-3 120 EwanWhillans(3) —
(Rose Dobbin) *towards rr: struggling 12th: btn whn mstke 3 out: p.u bef next* **33/1**

5m 8.10s (-14.80) **Going Correction** -0.55s/f (Firm) **10** Ran SP% **113.8**
Speed ratings: **107,106,104,100,100 99,98,98,90,—**
toteswingers: 1&2 £10.50, 1&3 £12.60, 2&3 £7.60 CSF £47.59 CT £239.26 TOTE £6.10: £2.50, £2.20, £2.20; EX 59.70.
Owner Sir Robert Ogden **Bred** Scea Des Marais **Trained** Cholmondeley, Cheshire

FOCUS
This looked fiercely competitive and, not surprisingly, there was a tight finish.

NOTEBOOK
Sagalyrique(FR) was fitted with a first-time tongue-tie after being pulled up on both his previous outings this season and it appears to have made a significant difference to his level of performance. In rear early on, this April Bangor winner made progress from halfway and had worked his way into second at the final fence. He stayed on strongly up the run-in and was edging away from the runner-up close home. Official explanation: trainer said, regarding apparent improvement in form shown, gelding was suited by the application of a tongue tie for the first time
Premier Sagas(FR) was dropped in trip after seeming to find 2m6f at Market Rasen too far on his latest start and, although he was outpointed in the final strides, he saw out this shorter distance well enough. He was always in the first two and deserves to notch a victory in the near future.
Safari Adventures(IRE), second in a conditionals' event at Cheltenham three weeks previously and officially rated 126, looks a feasible marker for the form. He took on his usual role, making the pace from the outset, and plugged on gamely even after he was headed following the second-last. (op 9-2 tchd 4-1)
Mirage Dore(FR), making his handicap chase debut and returning from a 287-day layoff, ran a cracker. Always chasing the leaders, he tried hard to defy joint top weight and should improve for the outing. (tchd 14-1)
Lampion Du Bost(FR), making only his second appearance since 2008, also hinted at better to come. He overtook several rivals in the second half of the race and clearly still retains plenty of ability. (op 12-1)
Or De Grugy(FR), 5lb higher than when registering his fourth Kelso success in October, seemed to find the extra too much. All his best runs have come at the borders' venue, however, so he could not confidently be dismissed as badly handicapped if he goes back there. (op 11-1)

3334 BET LIVE AT VICTORCHANDLER.COM H'CAP HURDLE (11 hdls) 2m 4f

2:25 (2:26) (Class 3) (0-135,128) 4-Y-0+ **£4,228** (£1,241; £620; £310)

Form RPR

366- **1** **Diklers Oscar (IRE)**[261] 5205 8-10-13 115 JamesReveley 124+
(Keith Reveley) *hld up in rr: gd hdwy appr 4 out: drvn and styd on appr 3 out: chal last: slt ld sn after: drvn out* **5/2**[1]

3360 **2** 2 3/4 **Nodforms Violet (IRE)**[5] 3169 7-10-13 118 RyanMania(3) 123
(Karen McLintock) *in tch: hit 5th: hdwy 4 out: chsd ldr 3 out: chal 2 out: led bef last: hdd sn after and styd on same pce* **8/1**

-601 **3** 7 **Stopped Out**[42] 2549 6-11-9 125 RichieMcGrath 123
(Kate Walton) *chsd clr ldr tl led wl bef 3 out: sn rdn: jnd next: hdd bef last: outpcd by ldng duo run-in* **7/1**[3]

0-00 **4** 2 3/4 **Culcabock (IRE)**[49] 2386 11-11-6 122 CampbellGillies 116
(Lucinda Russell) *in tch: hdwy after 4 out: drvn to dispute 2nd 3 out: wknd fr next* **16/1**

1-00 **5** 1 **Chester Lad**[43] 2523 6-11-8 124 JanFaltejsek 117
(George Charlton) *chsd ldrs: hit 5th and 6th: rdn 3 out and mstke: wknd next* **16/1**

04/P **6** *8* **Bywell Beau (IRE)**65 2076 12-10-13 **122**....................(t) AlistairFindlay(7) 108
(George Charlton) *led: t.k.h and sn clr: hdd wl bef 3 out: sn btn: hit 2 out* **33/1**

0003 **7** *¾* **Daytime Dreamer (IRE)**63 2104 7-9-9 **102** oh1.......... JamesHalliday(5) 87
(Martin Todhunter) *in tch: rdn 3 out: no ch after* **16/1**

06-4 **8** *2½* **Grandad Bill (IRE)**44 2506 8-11-5 **121**.............................. BarryKeniry 103
(Jim Goldie) *hit 3rd: in rr: rdn 4 out: nvr gng pce to rch ldrs* **8/1**

64-4 **9** *8* **Ascendant**73 1931 5-11-2 **118**.. BrianHughes 95
(Howard Johnson) *chsd ldrs: nt fluent 2nd: hit 4th: rdn 4 out: wknd bef next* **14/1**

1F-0 **10** *4½* **Toshi (USA)**42 2551 9-11-12 **128**.. GrahamLee 98
(Jim Goldie) *in rr: hdwy on ins appr 3 out: sn rdn and wknd* **25/1**

23-0 **11** *19* **Glingerbank (IRE)**42 2549 11-11-6 **122**............................ BrianHarding 73
(Nicky Richards) *a in rr* **14/1**

2603 **12** *1¼* **Worth A King'S**18 2955 5-10-13 **115**............................... JasonMaguire 64
(Donald McCain) *nt fluent 1st: in tch 5th: sn pushed along and lost tch* **13/2**2

0/00 **13** *16* **Livvy Inn (USA)**23 2868 6-11-7 **123**............................ PeterBuchanan 56
(Lucinda Russell) *hit 3rd and 4 out: a towards rr* **28/1**

4m 52.06s (-19.94) **Going Correction** -1.025s/f (Hard) **13** Ran SP% **117.8**
Speed ratings (Par 107): **98,96,94,93,92 89,89,88,84,83 75,75,68**
toteswingers: 1&2 £14.20, 1&3 £12.30, 2&3 £19.30 CSF £22.20 CT £126.56 TOTE £4.20: £1.80, £3.80, £2.80; EX 37.60.
Owner The Thoughtful Partnership **Bred** William O'Keeffe **Trained** Lingdale, Redcar & Cleveland

FOCUS
Another competitive contest, even though it featured only one last-time-out winner, and the pace was strong.

NOTEBOOK
Diklers Oscar(IRE), making her seasonal bow after a 261-day layoff, scored cleverly under a well-judged ride. Held up in rear early on, she eased into mid-division at halfway and went fourth with three to jump. She was then delivered to hit the front at the final flight and, despite drifting right in the closing stages, appeared to have a fair bit in hand at the line. She is sure to take a rise in the ratings for this, but looks to be progressive. How many more races she has may depend on the weather, though, as she is due to retire to the paddocks after being covered in the spring. (op 4-1)
Nodforms Violet(IRE), sixth off a mark 1lb higher at Cheltenham in November, seems the ideal marker for this form. Always close to the front of the pack that chased clear early leader Bywell Beau, she went second two out but was unable to match the winner's finishing speed. (op 7-1)
Stopped Out was 7lb higher than when winning over 2m6f at Kelso in November and made a bold bid to overcome the rise in his rating. Second in the early stages and in front three out, where Bywell Beau faded, he stayed on gamely. (op 9-1)
Culcabock(IRE) invariably reserves his best for races of this type - big field/decent pace - and posted a sound effort. He still appears to have a race in him, even though now into the veteran stage of his career. (op 18-1)
Chester Lad, disappointing in two starts over 3m this season, fared a lot better here, figuring in the first half-dozen throughout. This is his trip. (op 20-1)
Bywell Beau(IRE), making only his second appearance since 2009, did enough to suggest he retains enough ability to be competitive in this grade. He went off in front - and was perhaps 15 lengths clear in mid-race - setting a healthy pace before predictably fading in the closing stages. (op 28-1 tchd 25-1)
Toshi(USA) Official explanation: jockey said gelding failed to stay trip
Worth A King'S Official explanation: jockey said gelding was never travelling

3335 PLAY CASINO AT VICTORCHANDLER.COM H'CAP HURDLE (9 hdls) 2m
3:00 (3:00) (Class 4) (0-115,115) 4-Y-0+ **£2,471** (£725; £362; £181)

Form RPR

15P- **1** **Cunning Clarets (IRE)**261 5207 6-11-7 **110**......................... BrianHughes 120+
(Richard Fahey) *hld up in tch: smooth hdwy to chse clr ldr after 4 out: led and hit 2 out: rdn and edgd rt run-in: r.o* **9/1**3

0251 **2** *2* **Blenheim Brook (IRE)**46 2446 6-11-12 **115**.................. PeterBuchanan 121
(Lucinda Russell) *chsd clr ldr to after 4 out: rdn and outpcd bef next: rallied after 2 out: chsd wnr run-in: r.o* **7/2**2

4245 **3** *nk* **Rain Stops Play (IRE)**81 1829 9-10-6 **105**........... StephenMulqueen(10) 111
(Nicky Richards) *hld up: hdwy bef 3 out: rdn and kpt on fr last: nrst fin* **20/1**

0001 **4** *1¾* **Sheriff Hall (IRE)**37 2658 6-10-0 **89** oh1.............................(t) JanFaltejsek 93
(George Charlton) *led: clr fr 3rd to 3 out: hdd next: kpt on same pce u.p fr last* **7/2**2

0203 **5** *8* **Bocciani (GER)**19 2937 6-10-2 **94**............................... JamesO'Farrell(3) 92
(Dianne Sayer) *in tch: nt fluent 4 out: rdn and outpcd after next: no imp fnl 2* **12/1**

4-P3 **6** *1¼* **Nodform William**5 3169 9-11-2 **105**.. GrahamLee 102+
(Karen McLintock) *nt fluent: chsd ldrs: drvn and outpcd fr 3 out* **10/3**1

33-0 **7** *11* **Pokfulham (IRE)**44 2508 5-11-4 **107**.................................... BarryKeniry 91
(Jim Goldie) *bhd: hit 5th: rdn next: nvr rchd ldrs* **12/1**

340- **8** *½* **Sydney Cove (IRE)**430 1965 5-10-11 **100**.......................... FearghalDavis 83
(William Amos) *midfield: outpcd whn nt fluent 4 out: n.d after* **28/1**

200- **9** *13* **Soprano (GER)**332 3624 9-11-0 **103**................................. KennyJohnson 73
(Jim Goldie) *bhd: outpcd 1/2-way: nvr on terms* **20/1**

60FP **10** *21* **Baaher (USA)**37 2656 7-10-12 **108**.................................. PaulNorton(7) 57
(Jim Goldie) *bhd: struggling bef 4 out: nvr on terms* **20/1**

P-3P **11** *7* **Also Jo**46 2448 8-10-8 **97**... BrianHarding 39
(William Amos) *nt fluent: midfield: struggling bef 4 out: sn btn* **22/1**

33/0 **P** **Geojimali**42 2551 9-10-11 **100**... JamesReveley —
(Jim Goldie) *bhd: struggling 1/2-way: t.o whn p.u bef 3 out* **33/1**

3m 44.6s (-18.50) **Going Correction** -1.025s/f (Hard) **12** Ran SP% **117.9**
Speed ratings (Par 105): **105,104,103,102,98 98,92,92,86,75 72,—**
toteswingers: 1&2 £6.90, 1&3 £21.80, 2&3 £12.90 CSF £36.77 CT £626.96 TOTE £12.40: £5.10, £1.20, £1.10; EX 40.70.
Owner The Matthewman One Partnership **Bred** J Donnelly **Trained** Musley Bank, N Yorks

FOCUS
Just a moderate handicap hurdle, but several had reasonable claims. The pace was decent.

NOTEBOOK
Cunning Clarets(IRE) was returning from an absence of 261 days, but he looked fit beforehand and notched a snug victory. Patiently ridden early on while Sheriff Hall established a clear lead, he moved into fourth at halfway and was second two out. He went to the front approaching the final flight and, despite making an error there, he was always in command. The handicapper will have a say now, but there is probably more to come. (tchd 10-1)
Blenheim Brook(IRE), successful in a novice event at Hexham in mid-November, has clearly been given a mark from which he can be competitive. In front briefly in the early stages, he raced in second once Sheriff Hall took up the baton and then galloped on gamely right to the finish. (op 3-1)
Rain Stops Play(IRE), second over 2m4f at Sedgefield in September, posted another commendable effort. He was held up towards the rear early on, but made up a good deal of ground in the second half of the race and looked as if a return to a longer trip would be in his favour. (op 14-1)
Sheriff Hall(IRE), raised 9lb for his Musselburgh win, was soon in a clear lead and was only collared two out. (op 9-2 tchd 5-1)

Bocciani(GER) lined up still a maiden after 28 tries, but ran creditably and is evidently no lost cause. He might well make the breakthrough, indeed, if the handicapper gives him encouragement by lowering his rating a little. (op 10-1)
Nodform William, third in a jumpers' bumper three days earlier and plausibly treated on his best form, was rather disappointing. He figured in the first three in the early stages, but seemed to lack a change of gear in the home straight. (op 4-1)
Also Jo in the first half-dozen throughout but one-paced late on, probably found the ground slightly too quick. He thrives when it is heavy.\n (op 20-1)

3336 BEST ODDS GUARANTEED AT VICTOR CHANDLER NOVICES' H'CAP HURDLE (12 hdls) 3m 110y
3:30 (3:31) (Class 5) (0-95,95) 4-Y-0+ **£1,781** (£519; £259)

Form RPR

03-5 **1** **Too Cool To Fool (IRE)**235 287 8-11-3 **86**........................ GrahamLee 92+
(Jim Goldie) *hld up in tch on ins: effrt bef 2 out: led last: drvn out* **8/1**

54-0 **2** *1¾* **Aghill (IRE)**65 2080 7-11-12 **95**.................................... JasonMaguire 98
(Rose Dobbin) *led to 2nd: cl up: ev ch fr 4 out: led briefly appr last: kpt on same pce run-in* **8/1**

6F-2 **3** *2¾* **Border Flora**55 2271 6-11-10 **93**...................................... FearghalDavis 93
(William Amos) *in tch: hdwy and ev ch 2 out to last: kpt on same pce run-in* **6/1**2

-00P **4** *2¼* **Yes Mate**40 2602 7-9-7 **69** oh2.................................. HenryBrooke(7) 68
(Dianne Sayer) *prom: led 4 out to appr last: no ex run-in* **40/1**

P055 **5** *5* **Vallani (IRE)**37 2654 6-10-12 **81**................................... PeterBuchanan 74
(Lucinda Russell) *hld up towards rr: outpcd 8th: rallied 2 out: kpt on run-in: nvr rchd ldrs* **7/1**3

2P-5 **6** *1¼* **Paddys Honour (IRE)**55 2271 8-11-10 **93**..................... CampbellGillies 85
(Lucinda Russell) *trckd ldrs: drvn bef 3 out: no ex fr next* **16/1**

0-P4 **7** *nk* **Allanard (IRE)**19 2941 7-11-1 **84**..............................(p) DougieCostello 75
(Martin Todhunter) *midfield: pushed along fr 7th: drvn bef 3 out: sn outpcd* **7/1**3

00-0 **8** *1½* **Ontrack (IRE)**239 209 7-11-4 **87**................................. WilsonRenwick 77
(Rose Dobbin) *in tch: rdn fr 1/2-way: outpcd fr 3 out* **20/1**

5-U4 **9** *2* **Sundown Trail (IRE)**56 2250 6-11-4 **87**........................... BrianHarding 76
(Nicky Richards) *hld up: stdy hdwy 8th: effrt bef 3 out: wknd bef next* **11/1**

-500 **10** *4* **Soldiers Tree (IRE)**63 2103 6-10-11 **80**......................(p) TomMessenger 64
(Sue Bradburne) *bhd and reminders after 3rd: hdwy to trck ldrs 7th: rdn bef 4 out: wknd fr next* **22/1**

-016 **11** *16* **Bardolet (IRE)**19 2941 8-11-10 **93**................................... JamesReveley 71+
(Keith Reveley) *hld up: blnd 8th: effrt bef 3 out: wknd bef next* **4/1**1

33/P **12** *10* **Spirit Calling (IRE)**46 2448 10-11-3 **93**...................... MrGJCockburn(7) 51
(Lucinda Russell) *hld up: stdy hdwy on outside 1/2-way: rdn and wknd fr 4 out* **20/1**

0-0P **13** *49* **Samaret**63 2103 6-9-7 **69** oh11.................................. GaryRutherford(7) —
(Harriet Graham) *bhd: struggling fr 7th: t.o* **50/1**

F-42 **P** **Little Wizard (IRE)**222 456 9-11-3 **93**........................ AlistairFindlay(7) —
(George Charlton) *cl up: led 2nd: hit and hdd 4 out: lost pl qckly and p.u bef next* **20/1**

PP-P **P** **Bombie Boy**58 2190 6-9-10 **70** oh5 ow1....................(b) JamesHalliday(5) —
(Brian Storey) *in tch: lost pl 1/2-way: struggling whn p.u bef 7th* **100/1**

6m 8.40s (-23.40) **Going Correction** -1.025s/f (Hard) **15** Ran SP% **119.7**
Speed ratings (Par 103): **96,95,94,93,92 91,91,91,90,89 84,81,65,—,—**
toteswingers: 1&2 £10.40, 1&3 £6.70, 2&3 £6.70 CSF £64.21 CT £418.20 TOTE £6.80: £2.30, £2.90, £2.00; EX 81.90.
Owner J S Goldie **Bred** Simon Young **Trained** Uplawmoor, E Renfrews
■ Stewards' Enquiry : Tom Messenger five-day ban: excessive use of whip (16th-20th January)

FOCUS
A modest finale, with the top weight rated 95, but still competitive on paper.

NOTEBOOK
Too Cool To Fool(IRE), who lined up a maiden and was returning from a 235-day layoff, notched his stable's first victory since the big freeze set in. Held up in touch in the early stages, he went fourth two out and improved into second approaching the last. From there onwards, he showed creditable resolution and was inching away from the runner-up in the dying strides. He clearly has abundant stamina. (op 9-1)
Aghill(IRE), seventh off a 4lb higher mark over 2m6f at Wetherby last time out, seemed to appreciate this slight drop in grade. Always in the leading group, he got the front at the final flight before being outpaced by the winner on the run-in. (op 10-1)
Border Flora, runner-up on his first outing for 11 months at Carlisle in November, again posted a solid display. This was a new trip for her and she appeared to handle it well. (op 5-1)
Yes Mate had shown little previously in a variety of disciplines and his presence in fourth seemingly puts the form into perspective. He raced close to the pace from the outset, but could not find a change of gear in the closing stages. (tchd 50-1)
Vallani(IRE), fifth when rated 2lb higher at Musselburgh in late November, filled the same position here. It is hard to escape the conclusion from these two efforts that she needs some help with her rating. (op 9-1)
Paddys Honour(IRE), having only his second run since July 2009, did enough to suggest he can still be competitive at this level. He lost ground on the leaders in the closing stages, but may still find some improvement having been so lightly raced in recent seasons.
Bardolet(IRE) Official explanation: trainer had no explanation for the poor form shown
Little Wizard(IRE) Official explanation: jockey said gelding lost his action but returned sound
T/Plt: £70.50 to a £1 stake. Pool: £58,633.48. 606.77 winning tickets. T/Qpdt: £75.30 to a £1 stake. Pool: £3,157.09. 31.00 winning tickets. RY

2944 FOLKESTONE (R-H)
Sunday, January 2

OFFICIAL GOING: Chase course - soft (6.3); hurdle course - heavy (5.4)
Wind: Virtually nil Weather: Dry, cloudy, brighter spells

3337 LADBROKES.COM CONDITIONAL JOCKEYS' H'CAP CHASE (FOR THE TED LONG CHALLENGE CUP) (15 fncs) 2m 5f
12:45 (12:45) (Class 5) (0-90,89) 5-Y-0+ **£2,397** (£698; £349)

Form RPR

-6P5 **1** **Wasntme (IRE)**39 2608 8-10-4 **67**..............................(tp) MrMMO'Connor 72+
(Colin Tizzard) *led tl outj. and hdd 2nd: w ldr tl led again 8th: hdd 3 out: rdn to ld again bef next: forged clr and wandered last: kpt on: rdn out* **11/4**3

1430 **2** *3½* **Curragh Dancer (FR)**20 2930 8-11-4 **81**................................ DavidBass 80
(Paddy Butler) *in tch: mstke 6th: rdn along after 9th: hdwy on inner to ld 3 out: drvn and hdd bef next: outpcd 2 out: chsd wnr between last 2: swtchd lft and kpt on same pce flat* **13/2**

1U5 **3** *6* **Russellstown Boy (IRE)**39 2605 11-11-4 **89**............(p) AdamWedge(8) 82
(Evan Williams) *w ldr tl led 2nd: hdd 8th: dived 10th: ev ch 3 out: sn outpcd u.p: 4th and btn next: plugged on to go 3rd flat* **9/4**2

/P-1 4 3/4 **Jack's Lad (IRE)**19 2947 12-10-12 81 .... MrTomDavid(6) 72
(Tim Vaughan) *t.k.h: in tch: mstke 11th: jnd ldrs and mstke next: stl ev ch and rdn bef 2 out: wknd qckly u.p between last 2: fdd flat* **7/4**1

5m 34.3s (12.10) **Going Correction** -0.20s/f (Good) **4** Ran SP% **107.1**
Speed ratings: **68,66,64,64**
CSF £16.10 TOTE £3.90; EX 15.00.
Owner Lydden Racing **Bred** Oliver Power **Trained** Milborne Port, Dorset

FOCUS
A low-grade race, but the pace was fair and all four were still in with a chance as they jumped the third last in a line.

NOTEBOOK
Wasntme(IRE) disputed the lead throughout, and though he did not jump all that fluently early on he showed some tenacity to see it out best. He has been tried over a variety of trips but is often too slow to make much of an impact, but he goes well in soft ground and had the advantage of a light weight here. (op 7-2)
Curragh Dancer(FR) struggled when attempting chasing at Plumpton last month, but coped better over these easier fences, although his jumping was still far from fluent, especially at the ditches. He was the first to come under pressure on the final circuit, but rallied to move into a challenging position, although that effort may have cost him at the finish. He looks capable of winning another small race but does not look a natural chaser. (op 15-2 tchd 6-1)
Russellstown Boy(IRE) jumped best of the field but was forced four-deep around the final bend and was the first to crack. His sole win came over a similar trip in testing ground at Uttoxeter in October but he has not been able to reproduce that form off a 10lb higher mark subsequently. (op 5-2 tchd 11-4 and 2-1)
Jack's Lad(IRE) won over 2m here three weeks ago on his return from a 575-day absence and had been raised 5lb since. He travelled well and moved up to challenge at the second last, but did not get home, and it looked more a question of stamina reserves emptying rather than any bounce factor. (op 5-4)

3338 LADBROKESPOKER.COM MARES' NOVICES' H'CAP HURDLE (8 hdls) 2m 1f 110y
1:15 (1:15) (Class 4) (0-100,100) 4-Y-0+ **£1,918** (£559; £279)

Form RPR
00-6 **1** **Time To Think**52 2329 6-11-0 88 .... JimmyDerham(3) 94+
(Seamus Mullins) *mde all: gng best after 2 out: rdn clr bef last: idling and j. slowly last: jnd flat: fnd ex u.p towards fin* **11/4**1
60-F **2** *nk* **Here's The Key (FR)**48 2424 7-11-5 90 ....(t) DenisO'Regan 91
(Paul Webber) *chsd ldrs tl pushed along and lost pl after 3rd: last and looked wl btn u.p 3 out: styd on past btn horses ent st: 7 l 3rd and clsng last: chal flat: no ex and hld towards fin* **5/1**
066F **3** *9* **Catch The Rascal (IRE)**17 2974 5-11-3 91 .... WayneKavanagh(3) 83
(Seamus Mullins) *in tch: chsd ldng pair after 3 out: rdn after: stl in tch ent st: no imp bef last: hld whn mstke last* **16/1**
5500 **4** *3 3/4* **Salybia Bay**12 3058 5-11-5 97 ....(b1) MrBJPoste(7) 86
(Andy Turnell) *chsd wnr: clr w wnr after 2 out: stl pressing wnr and drvn ent st: wknd bef last: lost 2 pls and mstke last* **20/1**
665 **5** *10* **Galant Star (FR)**40 2592 5-11-6 91 .... AndrewGlassonbury 70
(Gary Moore) *hld up in tch: hdwy after 3rd: 4th and mstke 2 out: sn rdn and wknd: wl hld whn j.rt last* **7/1**
3-60 **6** *1/2* **She's Humble (IRE)**12 3059 9-10-12 90 .... JoshuaMoore(7) 68
(Linda Jewell) *chsd ldrs tl rdn and wknd bef 2 out* **11/1**
333 **P** **Bari Bay**50 2367 5-10-1 72 ....(b) AidanColeman —
(Michael Blake) *hld up in rr: clsd and in tch 5th: wknd 2 out: wl btn whn eased ent st: t.o whn p.u last* **4/1**2
3532 **P** **Doyenne Dream**47 2435 4-11-3 100 .... MarkBradburne —
(James Eustace) *in tch in last trio: rdn and no rspnse after 3rd: lost tch next: t.o whn p.u 5th* **9/2**3

4m 42.4s (6.80) **Going Correction** +0.15s/f (Yiel)
WFA 4 from 5yo+ 11lb **8** Ran SP% **113.0**
Speed ratings (Par 105): **80,79,75,74,69 69,—,—**
toteswingers: 1&2 £5.20, 1&3 £15.40, 2&3 £8.70 CSF £16.76 CT £180.05 TOTE £4.40: £1.70, £2.40, £3.20; EX 22.20.
Owner Mrs Fay Hewett **Bred** M E R Allsopp **Trained** Wilsford-Cum-Lake, Wilts
■ Stewards' Enquiry : Denis O'Regan four-day ban: excessive use of whip (16th-19th Jan)

FOCUS
A very moderate race with the long-time leader looking set to grind it out, until a storming late charge from out of the pack produced a dramatic finish.

NOTEBOOK
Time To Think led from the start and gradually wore down her rivals one by one until she forged a clear advantage going to the last. However, she was beginning to tire and idle a bit on the flat, but managed to find enough to repel a late challenge near the line. Her six-length sixth at Taunton in November was arguably the best form on offer, and she was able to build on that seasonal reappearance to exploit her stamina on this testing ground. Connections intend to keep her over hurdles for the time being but ultimately she is set for chasing. (op 10-3 tchd 7-2)
Here's The Key(FR) never looked happy on the ground and had up to 15 lengths to find turning in, but she charged up the straight to nearly catch the winner on the line. By making up so much ground in these conditions she showed she has enough ability to break her maiden before too long. (op 13-2)
Catch The Rascal(IRE) has taken a while to show anything in bumpers and hurdles to date, but she showed a bit more on her handicap debut here, making some late progress after being held up early. However, she still needs to improve to make any impact off her current mark. (op 12-1)
Salybia Bay raced prominently in first-time blinkers but did not get home in the testing conditions. (op 12-1)
Galant Star(FR) was making some progress when losing valuable momentum with a mistake at the last in the back straight, and her effort petered out. She will need some leniency from the handicapper to make an impression. (op 6-1)
Bari Bay was unable to capitalise on her light weight. (op 6-1)
Doyenne Dream was never travelling and pulled up after coming under pressure. Connections thought that she might be coming into season, which would explain the poor run. Official explanation: jockey said filly was never going (op 6-1)

3339 LADBROKESBINGO.COM MAIDEN CHASE (12 fncs) 2m
1:50 (1:50) (Class 5) 5-Y-0+ **£2,397** (£698; £349)

Form RPR
FP-2 **1** **Ballybach (IRE)**64 2081 7-11-0 0 .... SamThomas 120+
(Nick Gifford) *chsd ldrs: wnt 2nd 7th tl mstke 3 out: rallied and pushed into ld bef 2 out: j.rt and bmpd rival 2 out: outj. and hdd last: kpt hanging rt but kpt on to ld fnl 50yds: forged ahd nr fin* **4/5**1
3-0B **2** *1* **Fiftyonefiftyone (IRE)**40 2593 7-11-0 120 .... LeightonAspell 114
(Oliver Sherwood) *chsd clr ldr: clsd 5th: lost 2nd 7th tl chsd wnr again 3 out: rdn and led briefly bef 2 out: stl ev ch whn bmpd 2 out: drvn and gd jump to ld again last: hdd and no ex fnl 50yds* **11/4**2
5-4U **3** *17* **Four Strong Winds (IRE)**19 2938 7-10-11 117 ....(p) RichieMcLernon(3) 100+
(Jonjo O'Neill) *led: sn clr: hdd after 3 out: sn wknd: hld on for modest 3rd towards fin* **6/1**3
P-06 **4** *nk* **Raspbary**41 2583 5-10-7 94 .... JimmyDerham(3) 94
(Seamus Mullins) *j.lft and novicey in rr: struggling 8th: mstke and rdr lost iron next: 4th and wl btn 2 out: plugged on and pressing for 3rd towards fin* **18/1**
0 **5** *64* **Stealing Time (IRE)**18 2963 6-10-4 0 ....(b1) GeraldQuinn(10) 33
(Jonjo O'Neill) *a in rr: j.lft 6th: wnt lft and mstke next: sn lost tch: t.o fr 3 out* **25/1**

4m 3.70s (-3.50) **Going Correction** -0.20s/f (Good)
WFA 5 from 6yo+ 3lb **5** Ran SP% **105.6**
Speed ratings: **100,99,91,90,58**
CSF £3.15 TOTE £1.70: £1.10, £1.80; EX 3.00.
Owner Michael O'Shea **Bred** Michael Barron **Trained** Findon, W Sussex

FOCUS
The ratings of the first three suggested this was a reasonable maiden chase, with the main protagonists battling it out all the way up the straight.

NOTEBOOK
Ballybach(IRE) was set to mount a challenge when leaving his hind legs in the ditch in the back straight, and that made him jump carefully at the final two, but he had a bit more in hand than his main challenger. He was rated 120 over hurdles and that looks fair enough for his new chasing career, although he will need some more experience over fences to realise that level. (op 10-11, after 11-10 in a place tchd evens in places)
Fiftyonefiftyone(IRE) raced a bit keenly as he hugged the inside rail throughout, but he served up a challenge right to the line. He does have a tendency to expend too much energy too early, but he does have enough ability to win over fences, although he may not have reached his mark of 120 yet, and perhaps a tongue-tie could help him see it out. (op 5-2 tchd 9-4)
Four Strong Winds(IRE) has been held up in previous races, but this time he tore off in the lead and although he did not jump that soundly he did well to maintain the lead until the home turn. This shows he has some ability, though his jumping needs to improve. (op 9-2)
Raspbary ran as well as could be expected on his chasing debut considering he was outclassed. (op 16-1)
Stealing Time(IRE) jumped slowly and was struggling with a circuit to go. (op 33-1 tchd 22-1)

3340 LADBROKES.COM ON YOUR MOBILE NOVICES' HURDLE (10 hdls) 2m 6f 110y
2:20 (2:20) (Class 4) 5-Y-0+ **£1,918** (£559; £279)

Form RPR
30 **1** **No Secrets (IRE)**18 2963 7-10-12 0 .... WayneHutchinson 123+
(Warren Greatrex) *w ldr tl led 5th: mde rest: rdn and styd on wl to draw clr bef last: comf* **15/2**
-346 **2** *13* **Yabora (FR)**49 2388 6-10-12 122 ....(p) RichardJohnson 111
(Charlie Longsdon) *chsd ldrs: trckd ldr after 2 out: pressing wnr and rdn ent st: btn bef last: mstke last: hld on for 2nd cl home* **13/8**1
54-5 **3** *nk* **Red Mile (FR)**19 2946 6-10-12 0 .... SamThomas 112+
(Emma Lavelle) *hld up in tch in rr: hdwy after 8th: rdn sn after 3 out: chsd ldng pair ent st: no imp and no ch w wnr after: plugged on and pressing for 2nd cl home* **9/2**3
0600 **4** *16* **Downe Payment (IRE)**48 2428 6-9-12 0 .... MissHGrissell(7) 86
(Diana Grissell) *racd wd: led tl 5th: styd prom tl wknd on long run between last 2* **200/1**
5 *2 1/2* **Faith Keeper (IRE)**272 6-10-12 0 .... PaddyBrennan 91
(Nigel Twiston-Davies) *in tch: chsd ldrs 7th: rdn sn after 2 out: wknd u.p wl bef last* **16/1**
0-6 **6** *1 1/2* **Tim The Chair (IRE)**17 2981 6-10-5 0 .... StephenO'Donovan(7) 90
(Emma Lavelle) *chsd ldrs: wnt 2nd after 5th tl wknd u.p after 2 out* **33/1**
7 *31* **Traffic Chaos (IRE)**71 6-10-12 0 .... DenisO'Regan 58
(Charlie Mann) *in tch: mstke 3rd: struggling and rdn whn j. slowly and sltly hmpd 8th: lost tch next: t.o after 2 out* **20/1**
0 **8** *6* **Saute**19 2944 5-10-9 0 .... MarcGoldstein(3) 52
(Jim Best) *racd wd: t.k.h: hld up in tch: mstke 1st: lost pl 6th: hmpd 8th: lost tch next: wl t.o after 2 out* **33/1**
0 **9** *20* **Highland Legacy**18 2960 7-10-5 0 .... AshleyBird(7) 32
(Jim Best) *in tch towards rr: pushed along and struggling after 7th: lost tch after next: wl t.o after 3 out* **50/1**
11 **F** **Global Power (IRE)**19 2946 5-11-5 0 .... LeightonAspell —
(Oliver Sherwood) *hld up in tch towards rr: hdwy 6th: cl 6th and travelling wl whn stmbld: slipped and fell 8th* **5/2**2
P **P** **Son Of Robain (FR)**17 2985 5-10-12 0 .... DominicElsworth —
(Alison Batchelor) *in tch in rr: rdn and toiling after 5th: lost tch next: t.o whn p.u 7th* **66/1**

6m 6.30s (-5.00) **Going Correction** +0.15s/f (Yiel) **11** Ran SP% **117.1**
Speed ratings: **110,105,105,99,98 98,87,85,78,—,—**
toteswingers: 1&2 £2.80, 1&3 £7.30, 2&3 £2.20 CSF £19.95 TOTE £8.90: £3.20, £1.10, £2.10; EX 24.80.
Owner Malcolm C Denmark **Bred** Seamus Murphy **Trained** Upper Lambourn, Berks

FOCUS
A reasonable novice hurdle for the track.

NOTEBOOK
No Secrets(IRE) set a good gallop from the outset, and gradually wore down the challengers, and when looking like he would have to battle to fend off the challenge of the favourite, he kept going to stretch further clear. He had weakened on his previous two outings, in a bumper and a hurdle, but they had been better races than this and on faster ground. Ridden prominently on this testing ground he came into his element. Connections might look to run him under a penalty at another small track before he eventually goes chasing. (tchd 7-1 and 8-1)
Yabora(FR), in first-time cheekpieces, was poised to challenge from the home turn and looked likely to go on, but he tired disappointingly up the straight. This was an easier task than the Grade 2 company he faced at Cheltenham seven weeks ago, but this ex-French gelding seems to prefer better ground than this. (op 5-2)
Red Mile(FR) kept on at one pace but could make no real impact. He is gradually improving and could pick up a race so long as his proximity to the 122-rated favourite is not taken too literally. (op 4-1)
Downe Payment(IRE) disputed the lead until fading in the home straight, but plugged on. (op 150-1)
Faith Keeper(IRE), runner-up in a maiden point-to-point, could do no more than plug on at one pace, but should improve for this effort. (op 11-1 tchd 10-1)
Global Power(IRE), winner of a maiden hurdle over C&D last month, was still travelling well up with the pace when slithering on landing in the back straight. (tchd 9-4)

3341 LIPSCOMB (S) H'CAP HURDLE (10 hdls) 2m 6f 110y
2:55 (2:56) (Class 5) (0-90,90) 4-Y-0+ **£1,918** (£559; £279)

Form RPR
0445 **1** **Loco Grande (IRE)**20 2930 6-11-10 88 ....(p) RichardJohnson 103+
(Tim Vaughan) *chsd ldr 3rd: mstke 2 out: sn led: rdn and in command ent st: mstke last: tired but kpt on gamely: rdn out* **6/4**1
5455 **2** *9* **Vacario (GER)**58 2183 7-11-4 85 ....(t) TommyPhelan(3) 90
(Mark Gillard) *nt a fluent: in tch in rr: outpcd by ldng pair 7th: wnt modest 3rd bef 3 out: clsd u.p 2 out: chsd wnr wl bef last: no imp and btn ent st* **5/1**3

354 **3** *30* **Low Delta (IRE)**[17] 2980 11-11-12 **90**............................ DominicElsworth 65
(Michael Blake) *hld up in tch in rr: outpcd and struggling after 7th: 4th and wl btn bef 2 out: plugged on to go poor 3rd after last* **4/1**[2]

4-0P **4** *4* **Bearneen Boy (IRE)**[38] 2645 8-10-0 **64** oh2.................(b) AidanColeman 35
(Neil King) *led: mstke 3 out: blnd next: sn hdd & wknd u.p: wl btn ent st: lost 3rd after last* **5/1**[3]

P300 **P** **Lucky Pearl**[41] 2589 10-10-10 **81**....................................(p) MrTomDavid(7) —
(Tim Vaughan) *chsd ldr tl 3rd: j. slowly and reminders 6th: outpcd by ldng pair and u.p next: lost tch 3 out: wl t.o whn p.u after next* **15/2**

540- **P** **Bridge Of Fermoy (IRE)**[272] 5038 6-10-10 **74**....... AndrewGlassonbury —
(Daniel O'Brien) *in tch in rr: rdn and lost tch rapidly after 6th: sn t.o: p.u 3 out* **16/1**

6m 22.3s (11.00) **Going Correction** +0.15s/f (Yiel) 6 Ran SP% **111.0**
Speed ratings (Par 103): **83,79,69,68,—** —
toteswingers: 1&2 £2.40, 1&3 £3.70, 2&3 £1.90 CSF £9.30 TOTE £2.40: £1.80, £2.50; EX 11.10.There was no bid for the winner.
Owner The Runthatbymeagain Partnership **Bred** Martyn J McEnery **Trained** Aberthin, Vale of Glamorgan

FOCUS
This was run at a fair pace and all were tired by the home turn.

NOTEBOOK
Loco Grande(IRE) went with the leader as they began to stretch clear on the final circuit, and although he put in some untidy down the back straight, he had most in reserve and dug deep for a clear-cut victory. He had shown only moderate form since his juvenile win in February 2009, but he had been rated much higher last season and, with cheekpieces applied once more, he was very well backed for this. (op 3-1)
Vacario(GER) was unable to go with the leaders on the final circuit, but as they began to tire he made up some ground, although he was never able to make any real impression on the winner. He is generally consistent but has been on the go for quite a while and might just lack the freshness to make the most of a sliding handicap mark. (op 4-1)
Low Delta(IRE), held up early, plugged on but was never a threat. He handles testing ground so may have been expected to do a bit better. (op 10-3)
Bearneen Boy(IRE), back in blinkers today, took the field along at an honest pace before tiring round the final bend. He has looked on the downgrade since his return from a lengthy absence and this was not his favoured ground, but this was a small step in the right direction. (op 9-2)
Lucky Pearl's best form has been on faster ground. (op 6-1)

3342 EASTWELL MANOR BEGINNERS' CHASE (18 fncs) 3m 1f
3:25 (3:25) (Class 5) 5-Y-0+ **£2,397** (£698; £349)

Form RPR

14-3 **1** **Peveril**[43] 2523 7-11-0 0.. AndrewTinkler 143+
(Nicky Henderson) *a travelling wl: chsd ldr 8th: upsides and gng wl 15th: led next: clr and in command whn wnt lft last 2: eased towards fin: easily* **4/6**[1]

3-36 **2** *5* **Cannington Brook (IRE)**[22] 2883 7-11-0 128....................... JoeTizzard 133
(Colin Tizzard) *j.lft: led: hdd and mstke 3 out: sn outpcd by wnr: kpt on same pce u.p and a hld after* **15/8**[2]

P-5P **3** *104* **Lord Generous**[43] 2523 7-11-0 0....................................(p) PaddyBrennan —
(Nigel Twiston-Davies) *chsd ldr tl mstke 11th: dropped to last and rdn 11th: lost tch after next: t.o whn mstke 15th: lft poor 3rd next* **12/1**[3]

/0-6 **F** **Or Sing About (FR)**[17] 2975 9-10-11 113.................... JimmyDerham(3) —
(Seamus Mullins) *in tch in rr: wnt 3rd 11th: rdn and outpcd by ldng pair after next: lost tch and tailing off whn mstke 15th: j.lft and fell next* **66/1**

-F45 **U** **Galaxy Rock (IRE)**[18] 2955 7-10-11 0....................... RichieMcLernon(3) —
(Jonjo O'Neill) *in tch tl blnd and uns rdr 4th* **20/1**

6m 23.5s (-12.30) **Going Correction** -0.20s/f (Good) 5 Ran SP% **108.7**
Speed ratings: **111,109,—,—,—**
toteswingers: 1&2 £1.70 CSF £2.30 TOTE £1.60: £1.10, £1.10; EX 2.20.
Owner Trevor Hemmings **Bred** R D And Mrs J S Chugg **Trained** Upper Lambourn, Berks

FOCUS
There was an impressive success in this beginners' chase from a potentially decent novice chaser.

NOTEBOOK
Peveril took a while to get into a rhythm over the fences on this tight track, but by the final circuit he was cruising as he duelled with the eventual second. He showed a tendency to jump out to the left, especially over the final two fences, but was never in danger and came home for a comfortable success. He was a smart novice hurdler last season, progressing to be fourth in the conditionals' hurdle at the Cheltenham Festival and ending the season on a rating of 140. That performance is all the more meritorious as he is all over a three-mile chaser and should continue to progress over fences. Connections think he is a nice sort and it is possible that he could make it to the RSA chase at this year's festival. (op 8-13 tchd 4-7, tchd 4-5 in a place and 8-11 in places)
Cannington Brook(IRE) gallantly stuck to the task but was just outclassed by the winner. He had shown promise on his chasing debut at Cheltenham in November, and although he failed to build on that next time, this showed he was back on track. His jumping was still somewhat novicey out in front, but he should be up to winning over fences on slightly faster ground. (op 9-4, tchd 5-2 in a place)
Lord Generous carried his head slightly to one side and ran in snatches, and overall he does not look as good as he did a year ago. (op 11-1)
Or Sing About(FR) began to struggle with about 2m left to go. (op 50-1)
Galaxy Rock(IRE) landed steeply over the fourth and gave his jockey no chance. (op 50-1)

3343 THOMAS SMITH BIRTHDAY H'CAP HURDLE (8 hdls) 2m 1f 110y
3:55 (3:55) (Class 4) (0-105,102) 4-Y-0+ **£2,055** (£599; £299)

Form RPR

-P02 **1** **Zelos Diktator**[25] 1101 5-10-6 **89**.................................(p) JoshuaMoore(7) 92
(Gary Moore) *chsd ldrs: effrt and ev ch 2 out: rdn to ld wl bef last: forged ahd ent st: hung lft bef last: hrd pressed last: edgd lft u.p but kpt on flat* **5/1**[2]

5026 **2** *1 3/4* **J'Adhere (FR)**[5] 3169 6-11-12 **102**.................................. RichardJohnson 103
(Tim Vaughan) *racd wd: hld up in tch in rr: smooth hdwy on outer 3 out: w ldrs next: nudged along and sltly outpcd ent st: rdn to chal last: styng on same pce whn short of room and swtchd rt flat* **5/4**[1]

0-P0 **3** *13* **Celtic Ballad (IRE)**[58] 2185 5-10-9 **85**.................................. JoeTizzard 73
(Colin Tizzard) *led: mstke 4th: hdd after next: wknd u.p 2 out: 6th and wl btn ent st: plugged on to go modest 3rd last* **17/2**

1F2F **4** *6* **Owner Occupier**[17] 2986 6-11-2 **92**.................................. ColinBolger 74
(Chris Gordon) *chsd ldr tl led after 5th: mstke next: hdd wl bef last: wknd u.p ent st* **9/1**

04-0 **5** *3 1/4* **Kadouchski (FR)**[19] 2949 7-11-11 **101**................................ WillKennedy 80
(John Berry) *chsd ldrs: mstke 5th: sn rdn: wknd sn after 2 out* **5/1**[2]

250/ **6** *3 3/4* **Carmond (GER)**[630] 4955 7-10-13 **89**.............................. LeightonAspell 64
(Oliver Sherwood) *hld up in tch: hdwy to chse ldrs 4th: taken wd after 3 out: wknd sn after next* **15/2**[3]

4m 40.3s (4.70) **Going Correction** +0.15s/f (Yiel) 6 Ran SP% **110.1**
Speed ratings (Par 105): **84,83,77,74,73 71**
toteswingers: 1&2 £1.10, 1&3 £4.70, 2&3 £3.00 CSF £11.68 TOTE £5.70: £3.10, £1.20; EX 6.00.

Owner G A Jackman **Bred** The Duke Of Roxburghe's Stud **Trained** Lower Beeding, W Sussex

FOCUS
Just a steady early pace, but the ground had cut up considerably by the last and they struggled home, with the front two pulling clear in a protracted slow-motion battle for the stands' rail.

NOTEBOOK
Zelos Diktator was a bit green on his first start over jumps since being claimed out of a Perth seller in July by Gary Moore, but his jockey gave him plenty of time and, in a determined effort to claim the fresh ground on the outer in the home straight, he gamely held off the challenge of the favourite. He had run respectably on the AW since his last outing over jumps, and has reportedly strengthened up in the interim, so although he had not performed well on testing ground in the past, with cheekpieces re-applied he was able to make the most of a reasonable mark. (op 11-2 tchd 9-2)
J'Adhere(FR) can pull hard but although he was keen he settled a bit better at the rear of the field. Moving up to challenge on fresh ground wide round the final turn, he tried to grab the favoured stands' rail but did not have enough to pick off the winner. He won a bumper in testing conditions at this track, but overall seems to prefer better going. (op 6-4 tchd 6-5, after 7-4 in places)
Celtic Ballad(IRE) faded markedly after helping to set the early pace. He has been given a chance by the handicapper, but the absence of a tongue-tie this time might not have helped in the soft ground. (op 10-1)
Owner Occupier, reverting to hurdles after a couple of falls over fences this winter, raced prominently until capitulating in the straight. (op 7-1 tchd 10-1)
Kadouchski(FR) did not stay 2m4f in testing ground at this track last time, and once again did not seem to cope with the conditions. (tchd 6-1)
Carmond(GER), having his first start for Oliver Sherwood and his first outing since tailing off on his chase debut last April, is potentially well handicapped if able to build on this tune-up. (op 5-1)
T/Plt: £29.20 to a £1 stake. Pool: £53,858.44. 1,343.21 winning tickets. T/Qpdt: £3.70 to a £1 stake.Pool: £4,879.59. 959.30 winning tickets. SP

2924 PLUMPTON (L-H)
Sunday, January 2

OFFICIAL GOING: Good to soft (hdl 6.4; chs 6.7)
Wind: Almost nil Weather: Cloudy becoming fine

3344 ATTHERACES.COM FREE REPLAYS NOVICES' HURDLE (9 hdls) 2m
12:35 (12:35) (Class 4) 4-Y-0+ **£2,055** (£599; £299)

Form RPR

1 **1** **Gibb River (IRE)**[53] 2310 5-11-12 0... APMcCoy 138+
(Nicky Henderson) *trckd ldng pair: wnt 2nd 6th: led sn after 3 out: steadily drew clr: hit last: easily* **6/4**[1]

2 **2** *7* **Mr Muddle**[20] 2924 4-10-7 0... JamieGoldstein 108
(Sheena West) *led: mstke 4th: clr w three others fr 5th: nt fluent next: drvn and hdd sn after 3 out: kpt on but no ch w wnr* **7/2**[2]

1 **3** *3* **Extremely So**[19] 2944 5-11-5 0..(t) PaulMoloney 115
(Philip McBride) *trckd ldng trio: wl clr of rest after 5th: effrt 3 out: wnt 3rd bef next: kpt on same pce* **11/2**[3]

0 **4** *15* **Non Dom (IRE)**[18] 2960 5-11-5 0.................................... TomScudamore 102
(Hughie Morrison) *hld up in last trio: wl bhd fr 5th in main pack: prog fr next: styd on stdy fr 3 out to take 4th last: nt wout promise* **18/1**

60 **5** *5* **Teshali (IRE)**[36] 2667 5-11-5 0... TimmyMurphy 98
(Paul Nicholls) *pressed ldr to 6th: wknd rapidly 3 out: lost remote 4th last* **16/1**

6 *8* **Fireitfromye (IRE)**[333] 3839 6-11-5 0.................................... DarylJacob 92
(Alan Fleming) *in tch tl outpcd after 4th: mstke next: wl bhd fr in 7th pl after 6th: no real prog fr 3 out* **10/1**

5 **7** *1 1/2* **Alcalde**[19] 2944 5-11-5 0... WillKennedy 90
(John Berry) *chsd ldrs: blnd 4th: outpcd bef next: disp remote 5th pl fr 6th: wknd 2 out* **10/1**

0 **8** *4 1/2* **The Old Buccaneer (IRE)**[18] 2954 8-11-5 0.................. LiamTreadwell 84
(Jonjo O'Neill) *nvr beyond midfield: lft bhd fr 5th: t.o after and no real prog* **100/1**

4 **9** *7* **Yesyoucan (IRE)**[82] 1817 6-10-12 0................................ MrTJCannon(7) 78
(Alan Fleming) *t.k.h: hld up in midfield: outpcd after 4th: wl bhd in 8th after 6th: no prog* **33/1**

0 **10** *5* **Brave Enough (USA)**[66] 2047 4-10-7 0................................ HaddenFrost 62
(Roger Curtis) *lost pl 3rd and sn wl in rr: t.o fr 6th* **250/1**

11 *6* **Benozzo Gozzoli**[180] 5-11-5 0...................................... AndrewThornton 68
(Seamus Mullins) *mstkes: t.k.h: in tch to 4th: sn wl bhd: t.o fr 6th* **125/1**

1P-0 **12** *7* **Tiger Bay (IRE)**[37] 2666 7-11-5 0......................................(t) TomSiddall 62
(Noel Chance) *hld up in last trio: wl bhd fr 5th: t.o* **80/1**

0 **13** *9* **Lombok**[36] 2667 5-11-5 0.. JamieMoore 54
(Gary Moore) *hld up in rr: j. violently rt fr 5th: prog to dispute remote 5th pl at 6th: wknd 3 out: alarming jumps last 2* **66/1**

F **Perfect Shot (IRE)**[83] 5-11-5 0.. DaveCrosse —
(Jim Best) *hld up: in last trio whn fell 2nd* **33/1**

3m 54.4s (-6.40) **Going Correction** -0.25s/f (Good)
WFA 4 from 5yo+ 11lb 14 Ran SP% **117.7**
Speed ratings (Par 105): **106,102,101,93,91 87,86,84,80,78 75,71,67,—**
toteswingers: 1&2 £2.50, 1&3 £3.00, 2&3 £3.90 CSF £6.21 TOTE £2.30: £1.10, £1.90, £2.30; EX 8.50.
Owner Corbett Stud **Bred** Scuderia Pieffegi Sas **Trained** Upper Lambourn, Berks

FOCUS
Paul Moloney described the ground as very dead on returning after this opening novice hurdle. Very few got into this.

NOTEBOOK
Gibb River(IRE) had no trouble defying a penalty and won has he liked. Always travelling strongly, he didn't jump the last that well, but at no point did McCoy have to go for him and the 5-y-o cruised home. He handled quicker going on turf so shouldn't be inconvenienced by spring ground, and it'll be interesting to see where he goes next, as he shapes like he'll stay further. His connections expect him to jump a fence in time. (op 11-10 tchd 13-8 in a place)
Mr Muddle, sent off a big price when runner-up here on his hurdling debut, showed that to be no fluke with another sound effort in defeat. He tried his best to get the winner off the bridle and, while failing to do that, at least beat the rest well enough. There is probably a little race to be won with him. (op 4-1)
Extremely So, the only mare in the field, was a bit keen early but she stalked the leading trio and picked up a place when Teshali dropped out. She never threatened the winner, though, and is likely to remain vulnerable under her penalty. (op 6-1 tchd 13-2)
Non Dom(IRE) ◆ caught the eye staying on for fourth having been held up way off the pace. He was a fair performer on the Flat and looks an interesting sort for handicaps on quicker ground after one more run. (op 20-1 tchd 16-1)

The Form Book, Raceform Ltd, Compton, RG20 6NL

Teshali(IRE) is another who'll be suited by quicker ground. He found conditions too testing here but has now had the required three runs for a mark, and he could be a different proposition in the spring. (op 20-1)

3345 AT THE RACES SKY 415 NOVICES' CHASE (12 fncs) 2m 1f

1:05 (1:06) (Class 3) 5-Y-0+ **£6,319** (£1,907; £982; £520)

Form RPR

-012 **1** **Tullamore Dew (IRE)**[20] 2926 9-11-4 0........................ LiamTreadwell 138+
(Nick Gifford) *mde all: shkn up whn hrd pressed after 3 out: 2 l up and styng on wl whn lft clr 2 out: pushed out* **1/1**[1]

45P- **2** *7* **Norman The Great**[166] 2296 7-10-12 0........................ RobertThornton 124
(Alan King) *trckd ldng pair: cl enough 4 out: outpcd after next: pushed along whn lft 5 l 2nd 2 out: no imp* **12/1**[3]

53P **3** *22* **Smack That (IRE)**[19] 2948 9-11-4 117........................(vt) DaveCrosse 114
(Milton Harris) *hld up last: nt fluent 4th: effrt after 8th: easily outpcd fr 3 out: lft modest 3rd and sltly hmpd 2 out* **40/1**

402 **4** *16* **King Ozzy (IRE)**[54] 2293 7-11-4 120........................(t) WarrenMarston 100
(Martin Keighley) *pressed wnr: mstke 6th: nt fluent next: lost 2nd pl after 8th and sn wknd: lft poor 4th 2 out* **16/1**

02/1 **F** **Giorgio Quercus (FR)**[12] 3057 6-10-12 0........................ APMcCoy 128+
(Nicky Henderson) *hld up in 4th: nt fluent 3rd: mstke 6th: prog to trck wnr after 8th: pushed up to chal after 3 out: 2 l down and appeared to be hld whn fell 2 out* **11/8**[2]

4m 20.85s (-5.05) **Going Correction** -0.25s/f (Good) **5** Ran SP% **108.1**
Speed ratings: **101,97,87,79,—**
CSF £11.25 TOTE £2.50: £1.90, £2.40; EX 6.80.
Owner Give Every Man His Due **Bred** Michael Daly **Trained** Findon, W Sussex

FOCUS

A good little novice chase.

NOTEBOOK

Tullamore Dew(IRE), whose second to Medermit over this C&D last time had been given a nice boost when Alan King's grey ran so well in the Dipper Chase at Cheltenham the previous day, put up a fine round of jumping. Soon sent to the front, he made every yard, and while the result was in some doubt when they turned into the straight and Giorgio Quercus drew up alongside, it's probably fair to say he was still the likelier winner. He deserves a step up in class now, and his sure-footed jumping should hold him in good stead. The Centenary Novices' Handicap Chase (the old Jewson) at the Festival might be under consideration for him, and he'll have one more run beforehand. (op 11-8)
Norman The Great was fortunate to finish second, but he travelled and jumped well in the main and posted a very respectable effort on his chasing debut. Better ground will likely help him in future. (op 14-1 tchd 10-1)
Smack That(IRE), who was held up, is fully exposed and was up against it in this company.
King Ozzy(IRE), ridden prominently, began to lose his place from the fourth-last. He too faced a stiff task at the weights. (op 18-1 tchd 20-1)
Giorgio Quercus(FR), a useful hurdler who has always been seen as a chaser in the making, took a jumpers' bumper last time out on his return from a lengthy absence, and promised to be a big threat on his debut over fences in receipt of 6lb from the favourite. He didn't settle early, though, and didn't pay his fences enough respect either, making several minor errors before eventually clipping the top of the second-last and coming down. He was bang in contention at the time and clearly has the ability to win a similar race if getting his act together. (op Evens tchd 6-4 in places)

3346 ATTHERACES.COM E B F "NATIONAL HUNT" NOVICES' HURDLE (QUALIFIER) (12 hdls) 2m 5f

1:40 (1:40) (Class 3) 4-7-Y-0 **£2,927** (£859; £429; £214)

Form RPR

-216 **1** **Mister Hyde (IRE)**[49] 2387 6-11-12 123........................ APMcCoy 130+
(Jonjo O'Neill) *mstke 1st: cl up: wnt prom 7th: led 9th: drew clr after 2 out: 4 l up last: v comf* **15/8**[1]

4 **2** *2 ¾* **Charming Lad (IRE)**[66] 2051 6-11-3 0........................ PeterToole[(3)] 115
(Charlie Mann) *in tch: jnd ldrs 7th: rdn in 5th pl after 3 out: styd on to take 2nd last: no ch w wnr* **40/1**

1-1 **3** *3* **Carribs Leap (IRE)**[72] 1951 6-11-12 0........................ JimmyMcCarthy 118
(Charles Egerton) *prom: chsd ldr 5th to 8th: styd cl up: rdn after 3 out: kpt on same pce* **9/1**

4 *1* **Invictus (IRE)**[294] 5-11-6 0........................ RobertThornton 112+
(Alan King) *trckd ldrs: wnt prom 8th: cl up 3 out: rdn next: disp 2nd 2 out: one pce after* **10/3**[3]

2 **5** *26* **Water Garden (FR)**[58] 2186 5-11-6 0........................ TimmyMurphy 88
(Paul Nicholls) *hld up in last pair: sme prog into midfield 8th: outpcd by ldrs next: nudged along and no prog after* **9/1**

6-40 **6** *1 ¼* **Salut Honore (FR)**[18] 2963 5-11-6 0........................ FelixDeGiles 90
(Alex Hales) *hld up in last pair: mstke 2nd: sme prog into midfield 8th: outpcd by ldrs next: nudged along and no prog after* **100/1**

7 *34* **Ballinhassig (IRE)**[287] 6-10-13 0........................ MrTJCannon[(7)] 56
(Sarah Wall) *in tch in rr to 8th: sn bhd: t.o fr next* **100/1**

41-0 **8** *6* **Dusky Bob (IRE)**[62] 2123 6-11-6 0........................ LiamTreadwell 51
(Nick Gifford) *a in rr: lost tch fr 8th: t.o next* **33/1**

5-40 **9** *13* **Current Climate (IRE)**[19] 2946 7-11-6 0........................ JamieMoore 39
(Richard Rowe) *mstke 5th and dropped to last: struggling next: t.o* **80/1**

00-0 **10** *34* **Duffy Moon**[81] 1821 7-11-6 0........................(t) GerardTumelty 9
(Charlie Morlock) *nt jump wl: pressed ldr to 5th: sn lost pl: wknd 8th: t.o* **150/1**

2-01 **F** **De Forgotten Man (IRE)**[17] 2981 6-11-9 116..... SamTwiston-Davies[(3)] —
(Martin Keighley) *prom: hit 6th: rdn after 8th: struggling in 6 l 6th whn fell 3 out* **25/1**

21 **F** **Time For Spring (IRE)**[43] 2512 7-11-12 122........................ TomO'Brien 114
(Charlie Longsdon) *led: nt fluent 8th: mstke and hdd next: w wnr 3 out: lost pl next: 7 l 5th whn fell last* **11/4**[2]

5m 15.9s (-6.40) **Going Correction** -0.25s/f (Good) **12** Ran SP% **117.6**
Speed ratings: **102,100,99,99,89 89,76,73,68,55 —,—**
toteswingers: 1&2 £50.80, 1&3 £4.90, 2&3 £65.10 CSF £81.27 TOTE £2.20: £1.10, £6.40, £3.60; EX 86.10.
Owner Bensaranat Club & Ocean Trailers Ltd **Bred** Mrs Catherine Kenneally **Trained** Cheltenham, Gloucs

FOCUS

A decent novice hurdle, and the market told the story, as by far the strongest of the front three in the betting was the winner.

NOTEBOOK

Mister Hyde(IRE) landed a gamble in good style, with McCoy able to ease up after jumping the last with a clear lead. In hindsight the gelding may have found the race coming too soon when only sixth to Grands Crus at Cheltenham last time (third run in 18 days), but he put up a career-best here following a 49-day break. The final of this series is likely to be in connections' minds, but he looks a likely sort for the Coral Cup too, although at present no bookmaker quotes him. He'll probably stay further in time as well. (op 7-2)
Charming Lad(IRE) didn't run up to market expectations on his hurdling debut at Fontwell, but this was far more encouraging. An Irish point winner, he again travelled kindly but had more left for the finish this time. He should be able to find something similar. (op 66-1)
Carribs Leap(IRE), winner of his previous three starts, in a point, a bumper and a novice hurdle, bypassed the Challow Hurdle for this, and put up a sound effort under his penalty. Clearly his future lies over fences. (op 6-1)
Invictus(IRE), who changed hands for £162,000 after winning an Irish point in March, jumped one or two a bit big, but there was plenty to like about this hurdling debut and he looks sure to improve for the experience. (op 3-1)
Water Garden(FR), debuting over hurdles, was given a patient ride. Having threatened to get into contention down the back, he then dropped away from the third-last. (op 13-2)
Time For Spring(IRE), another who bypassed the Challow, made much of the running but had dropped back to fifth when tipping up at the final flight. (op 3-1 tchd 10-3)

3347 AT THE RACES SUSSEX NATIONAL (HANDICAP CHASE) (20 fncs) 3m 5f

2:10 (2:10) (Class 3) (0-130,127) 5-Y-0+

£9,393 (£2,775; £1,387; £694; £346; £174)

Form RPR

P-43 **1** **Minella Boys (IRE)**[28] 2794 9-11-4 **119**........................(tp) FelixDeGiles 137+
(Charlie Longsdon) *patiently rdn: prog to trck ldrs 13th: wnt 2nd 3 out: sn rdn: led last: drvn out* **8/1**

111- **2** *2 ¼* **Master Overseer (IRE)**[364] 3278 8-11-7 **122**................ TomScudamore 138+
(David Pipe) *disp ld fr 2nd tl gained def advantage 16th: drvn 4 out: kpt on wl tl hdd and no ex last* **9/2**[1]

-51P **3** *17* **Peut Etre Sivola (FR)**[28] 2794 8-11-2 **117**....................(v) JohnnyFarrelly 118
(David Pipe) *racd wd: patiently rdn: prog to join ldrs 13th: wnt cl 3rd 3 out: sn rdn: wknd bef next* **16/1**

-212 **4** *6* **Rebel Melody (IRE)**[20] 2928 10-10-9 **113**....................(bt) PeterToole[(3)] 108
(Charlie Mann) *disp ld fr 2nd tl 16th: sn u.p: lost 2nd and wknd 3 out* **7/1**[3]

15-2 **5** *10* **Kawagino (IRE)**[49] 2395 11-11-10 **125**........................ AndrewThornton 119+
(Seamus Mullins) *prom on inner: blnd bdly 13th and dropped to rr: nvr able to rcvr* **11/1**

2121 **6** *2 ¾* **The Ferbane Man (IRE)**[175] 951 7-11-3 **118**..................(p) DarylJacob 101
(Tim Vaughan) *led to 2nd: trcking ldrs whn blnd bdly 5th: toiling in rr fr 7th: wl bhd fr 16th* **14/1**

-055 **7** *hd* **Martys Mission (IRE)**[18] 2962 9-10-8 **116**..................... MrTJCannon[(7)] 101
(Richard Rowe) *trckd ldrs: wl there whn nt fluent 14th: sn u.p: cl up 16th: steadily wknd* **8/1**

P/F3 **P** **Pass Me By**[49] 2395 12-10-12 **113**........................ DavidEngland —
(Suzy Smith) *in tch in midfield: hmpd 6th: u.p and wkng 14th: p.u bef 16th* **20/1**

0-03 **U** **Deep Pockets (IRE)**[20] 2928 12-10-5 **111**........................ IanPopham[(5)] —
(Caroline Keevil) *mstke 1st: last whn j. awkwardly and uns rdr 2nd* **12/1**

2U-5 **P** **Noble Bily (FR)**[43] 2529 10-10-3 **107**........................ AlexMerriam[(3)] —
(Neil King) *nt a fluent: in tch in rr to 11th: sn bhd: t.o whn p.u bef 15th* **5/1**[2]

46F3 **P** **Whataboutya (IRE)**[56] 2249 10-11-0 **115**........................(p) APMcCoy —
(Jonjo O'Neill) *w.w in rr: shkn up 14th: sn wknd and eased: p.u bef 16th* **16/1**

60P6 **F** **Cullahill (IRE)**[23] 2869 9-10-8 **116**........................ NathanSweeney[(7)] —
(Bob Buckler) *mstke 1st: in rr tl fell 7th* **16/1**

/1-4 **F** **Hunters Ploy (IRE)**[55] 2273 9-11-9 **127**.............. SamTwiston-Davies[(3)] —
(Nigel Twiston-Davies) *trckd ldrs: disputing 3rd whn fell heavily 9th* **20/1**

3F00 **P** **Theophrastus (IRE)**[17] 2984 9-11-0 **115**....................(p) LiamTreadwell —
(Nick Gifford) *tended to jump rt: rousted along to go prom 3rd: terrible blunder 6th and dropped to last pair: t.o whn p.u bef 15th* **20/1**

7m 27.1s (-12.90) **Going Correction** -0.25s/f (Good) **14** Ran SP% **124.2**
Speed ratings: **107,106,101,100,97 96,96,—,—,— —,—,—,—**
toteswingers: 1&2 £15.00, 1&3 £49.20, 2&3 £10.80 CSF £45.15 CT £564.56 TOTE £9.30: £3.00, £2.20, £6.60; EX 48.60.
Owner Miss Penny Zygmant **Bred** James J Phelan **Trained** Over Norton, Oxon

FOCUS

A competitive handicap chase.

NOTEBOOK

Minella Boys(IRE), recording his first chase success under rules, stays all day and appreciated the testing conditions, while the return of the tongue-tie and application of cheekpieces for the first time clearly had a positive effect too. The Midlands National looks a suitable target for him.
Master Overseer(IRE) hadn't been seen since rallying to win this event 12 months earlier, but he was produced in peak form in a repeat bid and went very close to doing so off a 6lb higher mark. Hopefully, he can build on this. (op 7-2 tchd 5-1 and 11-2 in a place)
Peut Etre Sivola(FR) left a poor run at Exeter behind him and returned to the sort of form which saw him run out a clear winner of the Southern National on his previous start. The softer the ground the better it is for him. (tchd 18-1)
Rebel Melody(IRE) was up there throughout and ran a solid race, but he needs to find some improvement from somewhere to win off his current mark. (op 8-1)
Kawagino(IRE) was 7lb better off with Peut Etre Sivola compared with when he was beaten six lengths by the Pipe horse at Fontwell, but he was beaten further by that rival this time, a bad blunder knocking him right back. (op 16-1)
The Ferbane Man(IRE), running in a handicap for the first time, ran as though he might have needed this first outing since July. (op 12-1 tchd 16-1)
Pass Me By Official explanation: jockey said gelding was never travelling (op 6-1)
Noble Bily(FR) simply didn't jump well enough. (op 6-1)

3348 ATTHERACES.COM BE A VIRTUAL OWNER H'CAP HURDLE (9 hdls) 2m

2:45 (2:46) (Class 4) (0-110,110) 4-Y-0+ **£2,055** (£599; £299)

Form RPR

213P **1** **Manshoor (IRE)**[42] 2558 6-11-3 **101**........................ APMcCoy 108
(Lucy Wadham) *racd wd: led to 2nd: styd w ldrs: led after 3 out and drvn 5 l clr next: all out* **8/1**

-420 **2** *2* **Beside The Fire**[50] 2361 6-11-5 **106**..................... SamTwiston-Davies[(3)] 110
(Colin Tizzard) *cl up: lost pl and then blnd 6th: sn rdn in 8th pl: rallied bef 2 out: styd on to take 2nd flat: nt rch wnr* **5/1**[2]

0522 **3** *2 ½* **Lepido (ITY)**[58] 2185 7-11-8 **106**........................(v) JamieMoore 108
(Gary Moore) *racd wd: cl up: rdn to chse ldng pair 3 out: sn outpcd: drvn to chse wnr bef last: kpt on but lost 2nd flat* **6/1**[3]

6-26 **4** *1 ½* **Wheres Johnny**[19] 2949 10-11-1 **99**........................(t) MattieBatchelor 100
(Jamie Poulton) *led 2nd to 5th: outpcd and drvn 3 out: styd on same pce again fr 2 out* **20/1**

/342 **5** *2 ½* **The Bishops Baby (IRE)**[20] 2927 8-10-12 **103**............. MrTJCannon[(7)] 101
(Richard Rowe) *w ldrs: led 5th: drvn and hdd after 3 out: wknd after 2 out* **14/1**

1F35 **6** *4* **Whipperway (IRE)**[18] 2958 4-10-5 **104**........................ AlexMerriam[(3)] 88
(Sheena West) *cl up: lost pl bef 6th: rdn and outpcd 3 out: plugged on one pce after* **11/1**

00-1 **7** *1* **Black Phantom (IRE)**[60] 2149 5-11-2 **100**........................ NickScholfield 94
(Andy Turnell) *cl up on inner: sing to be outpcd in 4th whn blnd 3 out: n.d after* **8/1**

235 **8** *shd* **Denton Ryal**[18] 2294 4-10-7 **103**................ JamieGoldstein 85
(Sheena West) *racd wd: hld up in last trio: in tch at rr of main gp bef 3 out: sn outpcd: shkn up and wnt wl btn 6th briefly 2 out* **16/1**

2304 **9** *4 ½* **Sweet World**[52] 2333 7-11-7 **110**................ MissIsabelTompsett(5) 100
(Bernard Llewellyn) *t.k.h: hld up in last trio: in tch at rr of main gp bef 3 out: sn outpcd: nvr nr ldrs after* **16/1**

03-6 **10** *14* **Diamond Eclipse (IRE)**[45] 2469 5-10-7 **91**................ DarylJacob 75+
(Nick Williams) *hld up: stdy prog 5th: n.m.r bnd bef next: gng wl enough bef 3 out: sn wknd rapidly* **8/1**

0 **11** *13* **Arbayoun (IRE)**[36] 2667 6-10-3 **90**................ RichardKilloran(3) 60
(Frederick Sutherland) *a in last trio: lost tch w rest fr 5th: no ch fr next* **40/1**

02-3 **P** **Quetzal (IRE)**[62] 2128 6-11-5 **103**................ RobertThornton —
(Alan King) *wl in tch: pushed along to chse ldrs 6th: rdn and btn 3 out: wknd and p.u bef next* **7/2**[1]

3m 59.1s (-1.70) **Going Correction** -0.25s/f (Good)
WFA 4 from 5yo+ 11lb 12 Ran SP% **120.5**
Speed ratings (Par 105): **94,93,91,91,89 87,87,87,84,77 71,—**
toteswingers: 1&2 £12.20, 1&3 £9.30, 2&3 £7.50 CSF £49.31 CT £263.75 TOTE £10.30: £3.00, £1.70, £2.20; EX 71.70.
Owner Tim Wood **Bred** Liberty Road Stables **Trained** Newmarket, Suffolk

FOCUS
This looked quite an open race on paper.

NOTEBOOK
Manshoor(IRE) came away from the rest in the straight and only had to be kept up to his work to score. Tony McCoy took the ride in place of 7lb conditional Matt Crawley, who was apparently unwell, and that probably accounted for the market move for him beforehand, as he looked to have plenty on his plate having been dropped just 1lb since being put up 12lb for winning at Towcester in October. The testing ground clearly caused him no bother. Official explanation: trainer said, regarding the apparent improvement in form shown, gelding was better suited by the good to soft ground (op 11-1 tchd 15-2)
Beside The Fire got outpaced but then rallied to well to come back and take second on the run-in. This was a drop in class for him and there was a nice bit of promise to be taken from it, although it looks as though he could really do with a step up in trip. (op 11-2)
Lepido(ITY) put up another solid effort in defeat, but his problem is that the handicapper knows where he stands with him now. (op 15-2 tchd 5-1)
Wheres Johnny ran a better race with the tongue-tie fitted for the first time, but he remains on a losing run stretching back the best part of three years now. (op 22-1)
The Bishops Baby(IRE), at the head of affairs for a long way, didn't run badly, but perhaps better ground will suit her. (op 12-1 tchd 16-1)
Black Phantom(IRE), 15lb higher than for his Chepstow win, stuck towards the inner on the more poached ground, which can't have helped. (tchd 15-2)
Quetzal(IRE) was disappointing on the most testing ground he has so far encountered. Official explanation: jockey said gelding stopped quickly (op 3-1 tchd 11-4)

3349 AT THE RACES VIRGIN 534 H'CAP CHASE (14 fncs) 2m 4f
3:15 (3:15) (Class 4) (0-105,100) 5-Y-0+ **£2,602** (£764; £382; £190)

Form RPR

0410 **1** **Manmoon (FR)**[17] 2975 8-11-2 **97**................(t) MattGriffiths(7) 105+
(Nigel Hawke) *led 3rd to 5th and fr 8th: jnd and lft 3 l clr 4 out: drvn out* **16/1**

3324 **2** *1 ½* **Romney Marsh**[47] 2444 10-10-6 **80**................ HaddenFrost 88+
(Roger Curtis) *hld up: hmpd bnd after 6th: prog 8th: wnt 3rd after 10th: lft 2nd next: drvn and nt qckn fr 2 out* **9/1**

230 **3** *22* **The Hardy Boy**[19] 2949 11-11-3 **91**................ NickScholfield 77
(Anna Newton-Smith) *led to 3rd: led 5th to 8th: outpcd after 10th: lft 3rd next: grad lost grnd* **8/1**

5144 **4** *20* **Sumdancer (NZ)**[40] 2591 9-11-7 **100**................ IanPopham(5) 68
(Michael Madgwick) *cl up: nt fluent 2nd: stmbld bdly bnd after 6th: mstke 8th: rdn 10th: struggling after: wknd 2 out* **12/1**

4663 **5** *3* **Maximix**[40] 2591 8-11-7 **95**................(v[1]) JamieMoore 61
(Gary Moore) *tk little interest in rr: rdn 6th: blnd next: lost tch u.str.p 9th: tk remote 5th last* **15/2**[3]

P-41 **6** *10* **Ere Alfie (IRE)**[58] 2184 7-11-10 **98**................(p) DarylJacob 55
(Nick Williams) *in tch: nt fluent 9th: sn pushed along: struggling after next: no prog 3 out: wknd next: fin v tired* **6/4**[1]

1320 **P** **High Oscar**[20] 2928 10-11-1 **96**................ MrTJCannon(7) —
(Richard Rowe) *in tch: j. slowly 4th: drvn and no rspnse after 8th: t.o whn p.u bef 10th* **9/2**[2]

200 **U** **Health Is Wealth (IRE)**[28] 2791 6-11-9 **97**................ DaveCrosse —
(Colin Tizzard) *trckd ldrs: mstke 3rd: wnt 2nd 10th: upsides gng strly whn blnd and uns rdr next (4 out)* **8/1**

5m 11.3s (4.00) **Going Correction** -0.25s/f (Good) 8 Ran SP% **115.7**
Speed ratings: **82,81,72,64,63 59,—,—**
toteswingers: 1&2 £19.70, 1&3 £13.60, 2&3 £6.40 CSF £144.76 CT £1246.04 TOTE £21.40: £4.50, £3.80, £2.90; EX 166.40.
Owner D R Mead, G C Board **Bred** Olivier Delegue **Trained** Woolminstone, Somerset

FOCUS
An ordinary handicap chase.

NOTEBOOK
Manmoon(FR), despite being 4lb higher than for his last win at Chepstow in November, was still well handicapped on the best of his form from last winter, and he appreciated the drop in grade having contested a class 3 race at Exeter last time. He was, however, helped by the failure of his main rivals to run their races. (op 14-1)
Romney Marsh last won over fences in March 2007, but she ran well here considering she was hampered at around halfway. (op 10-1)
The Hardy Boy, who won this race back in 2007, has a good record at this track, but it's unlikely he'd have been placed had Health Is Wealth stood up. (op 17-2 tchd 15-2)
Sumdancer(NZ), best when ridden more positively than he was here, stumbled badly on the turn out of the back straight and was always struggling thereafter. (op 10-1)
Maximix ran poorly in the first-time visor.
Ere Alfie(IRE) was well below his best and perhaps needs to be ridden more aggressively to be seen at his best. (tchd 11-8)
Health Is Wealth(IRE) ◆, a winning pointer making his chasing debut under rules, was upsides the winner and going well when coming down at the fourth-last. He would surely have been involved in the finish had he not fallen, and can be competitive off his current mark if this tumble doesn't leave a mental scar. (op 9-1 tchd 10-1)

3350 ATTHERACES.COM EXCLUSIVE HUGH TAYLOR H'CAP HURDLE (12 hdls) 2m 5f
3:45 (3:45) (Class 5) (0-90,89) 4-Y-0+ **£1,541** (£449; £224)

Form RPR

06-0 **1** **Arctic Flow**[208] 684 7-9-11 **63** oh26................ WayneKavanagh(3) 71
(Caroline Keevil) *led 3rd to 4th: lft in ld next: drvn 4 l clr after 2 out: hld on* **40/1**

-024 **2** *1 ¾* **Crystal Prince**[66] 2049 7-11-7 **89**................(tp) IanPopham(5) 95
(Charlie Longsdon) *hld up: prog fr 8th: wnt cl 4th 3 out: drvn to chse wnr 2 out: styd on: nvr able to chal* **9/2**[3]

0050 **3** *15* **Little Roxy (IRE)**[12] 3057 6-10-5 **68**................ FelixDeGiles 63
(Anna Newton-Smith) *hld up in tch: prog 9th: chsd wnr 3 out to 2 out: wknd* **6/1**

0-06 **4** *19* **Whitcombe Spirit**[49] 2390 6-11-8 **85**................(b[1]) MattieBatchelor 65
(Jamie Poulton) *prom: pressed wnr 6th: mstkes 8th and next: lost 2nd 3 out: sn wknd: mstke last* **14/1**

-604 **5** *25* **Form And Beauty (IRE)**[45] 2468 9-10-2 **70**.....(p) MissIsabelTompsett(5) 23
(Bernard Llewellyn) *mstkes: last tl prog and prom after 5th: sn dropped to rr after: struggling 9th: t.o* **9/1**

4P-6 **U** **Snow Patrol**[12] 3056 10-10-3 **73**................ CharlieWallis(7) —
(Nigel Dunger) *led to 3rd: led 4th tl blnd bdly and uns rdr 5th* **4/1**[2]

6126 **P** **Tocatchaprince (IRE)**[12] 3055 5-11-2 **79**................(v) DaveCrosse —
(Milton Harris) *reminder after 1st: in tch: hmpd 5th: prog to press ldng pair whn mstke 9th: wknd rapidly: t.o whn p.u bef 2 out: lame* **10/3**[1]

00-F **P** **Sir John**[41] 2589 5-11-8 **85**................ APMcCoy —
(Jonjo O'Neill) *in tch: shkn up and wknd rapidly 8th: t.o whn p.u bef 3 out* **9/2**[3]

5m 21.8s (-0.50) **Going Correction** -0.25s/f (Good) 8 Ran SP% **112.8**
Speed ratings (Par 103): **90,89,83,76,66 —,—,—**
toteswingers: 1&2 £28.50, 1&3 £21.40, 2&3 £4.60 CSF £206.90 CT £1255.96 TOTE £46.90: £6.30, £2.40, £3.10; EX 321.10.
Owner Mrs C J Dunn **Bred** Mrs H R Dunn **Trained** Blagdon, Somerset

FOCUS
A shock result to this handicap.

NOTEBOOK
Arctic Flow was something of a shock winner from 26lb out of the weights. It was hard to argue with the handicapper's assessment beforehand, considering that the mare had never before finished within 74l of the winner in six previous starts in bumpers and novice hurdles. However, there was a little bit of money for her on her handicap debut and first start since June, and clearly there were those that suspected she was quite a bit better than she had shown in the past. Her trainer, who later claimed the mare had been 'insultingly handicapped' is now 4-11 at this track. Official explanation: trainer said, regarding apparent improvement in form shown, mare was suited by ground, was weak and immature and hass strengthed up over the summer. (tchd 50-1)
Crystal Prince, whose only previous win in 36 starts under either code came here last January, was having his first start since late October and stuck to his task well enough. (op 11-2)
Little Roxy(IRE) stuck more towards the inside, where the ground was more poached. (op 7-1)
Whitcombe Spirit eventually paid for racing keenly early in the first-time blinkers. (op 12-1 tchd 16-1)
Tocatchaprince(IRE) was hampered by Snow Patrol when that one unseated his rider at the fifth, then blundered badly at the ninth and soon beat a retreat. Official explanation: trainer said gelding finished lame (op 3-1)
Sir John was struggling from some way out. (op 3-1)
T/Jkpt: Not won. T/Plt: £138.50 to a £1 stake. Pool: £82,321.53. 433.75 winning tickets. T/Qpdt: £96.80 to a £1 stake. Pool £6,439.19. 49.20 winning tickets. JN

3351 - 3352a (Foreign Racing) - See Raceform Interactive

[2617] NAAS (L-H)
Sunday, January 2

OFFICIAL GOING: Soft (soft to heavy in places)

3353a SLANEY NOVICE HURDLE (GRADE 2) (11 hdls) 2m 4f
1:25 (1:25) 5-Y-0+ **£21,012** (£6,142; £2,909; £969)

RPR

1 **Gagewell Flyer (IRE)**[42] 2564 7-11-3................ EMullins 139+
(W P Mullins, Ire) *mde all: rdn and kpt on wl fr bef last* **6/1**

2 *4* **Fists Of Fury (IRE)**[21] 2912 7-11-3................ AndrewJMcNamara 135
(C Byrnes, Ire) *chsd ldr in 2nd: rdn bef 2 out: no ex and kpt on same pce fr bef last* **8/1**

3 *1 ¾* **Pineau De Re (FR)**[18] 2967 8-11-3................ BTO'Connell 133
(Philip Fenton, Ire) *settled bhd ldrs: 4th 1/2-way: hdwy into 3rd 4 out: rdn bef 2 out: no ex bef last: kpt on same pce* **4/1**[2]

4 *1* **Sizing Mexico (IRE)**[45] 2490 6-11-3................ AELynch 132
(Henry De Bromhead, Ire) *chsd ldr in 3rd: pushed along in 4th 4 out: rdn and no ex next: kpt on same pce* **11/2**

5 *dist* **Bishopsfurze (IRE)**[21] 2913 6-11-3................ PTownend —
(W P Mullins, Ire) *hld up in last: bdly hmpd 4 out: sn no imp* **6/4**[1]

F **Si C'Etait Vrai (FR)**[64] 2097 5-11-0................ PWFlood —
(D T Hughes, Ire) *settled bhd ldrs: 5th 1/2-way: fell 4 out* **5/1**[3]

4m 51.1s (-9.80) 6 Ran SP% **117.4**
CSF £50.01 TOTE £7.90: £2.30, £3.20; DF 113.30.
Owner Clipper Logistics Group Ltd **Bred** Mrs Jacinta McGeough **Trained** Muine Beag, Co Carlow

FOCUS
An interesting race no doubt, the character of which was altered very much at the fourth-last flight. A fair step up from the winner, with the thir rated in line with his Zaidpour form.

NOTEBOOK
Gagewell Flyer(IRE) looks very much to be coming into his own now and would have been a very difficult horse for his stable companion to beat. Setting out to make all, he dominated at a steady enough pace and jumped really well. Once Emmet Mullins asked him to stretch turning into the straight he responded most readily and drew clear between the last two, staying on strongly up the hill. He had the run of the race but it was a very taking performance in every aspect and he's clearly very useful. (op 7/1 tchd 8/1)
Fists Of Fury(IRE) had given vain chase to Mossey Joe over 3m at Cork last month and may appreciate stepping back up to that sort of trip. He raced a bit keenly and was content to sit behind the winner, but his relative lack of pace was exposed when the winner quickened up. He did stay on to pretty decent effect. (op 12/1 tchd 14/1)
Pineau De Re(FR) wasn't suited by the was the race was run. He raced too keenly and his tendency to jump to his right meant that his rider was only able to get a bit of cover quite sporadically. He still appeared to be travelling very well turning in but found little enough off the bridle.
Sizing Mexico(IRE) has a chance of proving the best of these over half a mile further. The stop-start nature of the gallop probably didn't suit him and he wasn't really travelling from the third-last, but he did stick at it. One would imagine he's unlikely to run over a trip as short as this again. (op 6/1)
Bishopsfurze(IRE) made a mistake anyway, but the evasive action he had to take at the fourth-last to avoid the faller Si C'Etait Vrai, who came down right in front of him, completely ended his chance. Official explanation: jockey said gelding jumped poorly and made a bad mistake four from home (op 11/8 tchd 5/4)

3354 - 3357a (Foreign Racing) - See Raceform Interactive

3330 AYR (L-H)

Monday, January 3

OFFICIAL GOING: Good (good to soft in places; (hdl 7.6, chs 7.7)

Common bend used after winning post. Inner chase rail out 5m, inner hurdle rail out 7m.

Wind: Breezy, half against Weather: Cloudy, sunny spells

3358 VICTORCHANDLER.COM JUVENILE HURDLE (9 hdls) 2m

12:30 (12:30) (Class 4) 4-Y-O **£1,951** (£573; £286; £143)

Form RPR

1 **1** **First Fandango**[42] 2570 4-10-12 0 (t) MrTomDavid(7) 110+
(Tim Vaughan) *trckd ldrs: effrt and drvn bef 3 out: led run-in: edgd lft and hld on wl u.p* **5/4**[1]

4 **2** *hd* **Vosges (FR)**[47] 2451 4-10-9 113 HarryHaynes(3) 101+
(James Ewart) *led at decent gallop: rdn bef 3 out: hung rt fr next: hdd run-in: rallied towards fin: jst hld* **11/1**

5 **3** *shd* **Sweet Caroline (IRE)**[38] 2655 4-10-5 0 FearghalDavis 94+
(Nicky Richards) *hld up in tch: stdy hdwy to trck ldrs bef 3 out: effrt after next: hrd rdn and ev ch run-in: kpt on: hld nr fin* **33/1**

0 **4** *5* **I Got Music**[38] 2655 4-10-5 0 JamesReveley 88
(Keith Reveley) *hld up: pushed along 4 out: hdwy after next: styd on fnl 2: nrst fin* **33/1**

054 **5** *2* **Capricornus (USA)**[20] 2655 4-10-12 92 GrahamLee 93
(Ferdy Murphy) *nt fluent on occasions: hld up: hdwy and prom whn hit 3 out: rdn and no imp fr next* **50/1**

1 **6** *1 1/2* **The Starboard Bow**[38] 2655 4-11-5 0 PeterBuchanan 98
(Lucinda Russell) *w ldr: rdn bef 3 out: no ex after next* **85/40**[2]

7 *1* **Kingdom Of Munster (IRE)**[90] 4-10-12 0 BrianHughes 90
(Richard Fahey) *hld up: stdy hdwy to trck ldrs whn mstke 3 out and next: sn rdn and btn* **12/1**

8 *54* **Stanley Bridge**[170] 4-10-12 0 BrianHarding 36
(Barry Murtagh) *bhd: lost tch 4th: eased whn no ch fr 3 out* **250/1**

P **9** *hd* **Kai Broon (IRE)**[47] 2451 4-10-12 0 CampbellGillies 36
(Lucinda Russell) *midfield: struggling 4th: eased whn no ch fnl 3* **50/1**

5 **F** **Penny Bazaar**[41] 2600 4-10-2 0 RyanMania(3) —
(Dianne Sayer) *bhd: outpcd whn fell 4th* **250/1**

P **Baralaka**[90] 4-10-12 0 WilsonRenwick —
(Rose Dobbin) *prom: j. slowly and outpcd 4th: struggling and p.u after next* **7/1**[3]

3m 52.5s (-10.60) **Going Correction** 0.060/f (Hard) **11** Ran SP% **115.0**

Speed ratings: **88,87,87,85,84 83,83,56,56,—,—**

toteswingers: 1&2 £5.50, 1&3 £11.80, 2&3 £36.20 CSF £15.71 TOTE £2.40: £1.10, £2.30, £6.60; EX 13.10.

Owner Mrs M Findlay **Bred** Aylesfield Farms Stud Ltd **Trained** Aberthin, Vale of Glamorgan

■ Stewards' Enquiry : Mr Tom David 6-day ban: excessive use of the whip (Jan 17-22)

FOCUS

A juvenile hurdle run at a furious pace but with slow finishing fractions. The form is rated around the first two.

NOTEBOOK

First Fandango, rated 79 on the Flat, followed up his Ffos Las win with his young rider good value for his 7lb claim. He is not a fluent jumper yet but showed real battling qualities, although it was a very close run thing in the end. Connections have one eye on the Fred Winter at Cheltenham. (op 7-4)

Vosges(FR), placed twice in France, has obviously improved for his Hexham fourth. He set the pace jumping soundly having already been schooled over fences, and battled back like a lion on the run-in. He will be suited by 2m4f but clearly has the ability to win over two. (op 12-1 tchd 8-1)

Sweet Caroline(IRE), out of a half-sister to the Champion Hurdle winner Sublimity, had finished a well beaten fifth behind The Starboard Bow first time over hurdles at Musselburgh. She just missed out in the end and can surely add to her stud value by finding a race. (op 25-1)

I Got Music, just 46 on the Flat, had finished a distant seventh in The Starboard Bow's race at Musselburgh. She shaped a lot better here, staying on nicely on the run-in, and is the type for modest handicaps later on. (op 22-1)

Capricornus(USA), rated 77 on the level and already 92 over hurdles, had finished fourth in that Musselburgh race. He is the type to improve when the better ground comes next spring. (op 40-1)

The Starboard Bow, 78 on the Flat, couldn't dominate this time and did not reproduce his Musselburgh form. (op 15-8 tchd 9-4)

Kingdom Of Munster(IRE), rated 64 on the Flat, showed ability on his first try over hurdles. (op 11-1)

Baralaka, best of these on the Flat with a rating of 87, cost £36,000. He stopped to nothing at the first flight in the back straight and was soon pulled up. Something was clearly amiss and he was later reported to have been distressed. Official explanation: trainer said gelding finished distressed (op 8-1)

3359 BET LIVE AT VICTORCHANDLER.COM NOVICES' CHASE (12 fncs) 2m

1:00 (1:00) (Class 4) 5-Y-O+ **£3,252** (£955; £477; £238)

Form RPR

-121 **1** **Wind Shuffle (GER)**[159] 1114 8-11-0 0 RichieMcGrath 135+
(Jim Goldie) *mde all: rdn and hrd pressed fr 3 out: kpt on gamely u.p run-in: all out* **6/1**

510- **2** *nse* **Nafaath (IRE)**[270] 5094 5-10-10 0 BrianHughes 132+
(Howard Johnson) *pressed wnr: hit 5 out: nt fluent next: effrt and chal 3 out: edgd lft: kpt on wl u.p fr last: jst failed* **11/8**[1]

1-36 **3** *18* **Lord Villez (FR)**[19] 2951 7-11-0 116 GrahamLee 116
(Ferdy Murphy) *prom: hdwy to trck ldrs bef 4th: rdn and outpcd bef 4 out: sn n.d* **6/1**

-43U **4** *5* **Si Bien (FR)**[20] 2938 6-10-11 115 HarryHaynes(3) 113
(James Ewart) *hld up: stdy hdwy whn hit 6th: nt fluent and outpcd next: n.d after* **7/2**[2]

61F **5** *31* **Saveiro (FR)**[74] 1930 7-11-7 121 BarryKeniry 87
(Alan Swinbank) *chsd ldrs: nt fluent 3rd: nt fluent and lost pl next: sn outpcd: lost tch fr 5 out* **9/2**[3]

3m 54.7s (-16.00) **Going Correction** -0.725s/f (Firm)

WFA 5 from 6yo+ 3lb **5** Ran SP% **111.1**

Speed ratings: **111,110,101,99,83**

CSF £15.52 TOTE £6.20: £2.10, £1.10; EX 20.00.

Owner Mrs S Bruce & Mrs L Mackay **Bred** Gestut Elsetal **Trained** Uplawmoor, E Renfrews

FOCUS

A much better than average novices' chase and the pace was very strong. Just two in it from four out and it was a desperately close call in the end. The winner is rated in line with his best Flat form.

NOTEBOOK

Wind Shuffle(GER), 123 over hurdles and a multiple winner on the Flat, took to fences like a duck to water. He would not be denied and hung on by the skin of his teeth. He is sure to enjoy further success. (op 4-1 tchd 13-2)

Nafaath(IRE), a smart Flat horse in Ireland, took a while to recover from the gelding operation. Rated 140 over hurdles after slamming Saveiro here in March, he took on the winner but made quite a serious mistake five out. Upsides from the next, he only just missed out in the end. He should take high rank in the 2m novice chase division. (tchd 13-8)

Lord Villez(FR), rated just 116, was inclined to race quite freely. He was left behind going to four out but, like so many of his stablemates, he will improve and make his mark in the spring. (op 13-2)

Si Bien(FR), 112 over hurdles, is a keen type and wore a gag. After hitting a couple of fences in the back straight he was soon out of contention. Much easier opportunities will come his way. (op 9-2)

Saveiro(FR) took a heavy fall on his last start. He didn't look to enjoy himself at all here and was well behind from five out. (op 11-2 tchd 4-1)

3360 PLAY LIVE CASINO AT VICTORCHANDLER.COM H'CAP CHASE (17 fncs) 2m 4f

1:35 (1:35) (Class 5) (0-95,94) 5-Y-O+ **£1,951** (£573; £286; £143)

Form RPR

1 **Schindlers Society (IRE)**[79] 1878 8-11-12 94 (p) BrianHughes 104+
(J J Lambe, Ire) *hld up: nt fluent 5th: stdy hdwy and in tch 1/2-way: chsd ldr 4 out: effrt bef 2 out: led last: edgd lft run-in: drvn out* **6/1**[3]

P-3P **2** *2* **Coldwells (IRE)**[20] 2940 11-11-2 84 JamesReveley 93+
(Martin Todhunter) *cl up: led 5th: 3 l clr whn blnd 3 out: rdn next: hdd last: kpt on same pce run-in* **12/1**

U/24 **3** *15* **Festival King (IRE)**[92] 1697 9-11-10 92 BrianHarding 85
(Pauline Robson) *in tch on outside: hdwy to chse ldr 9th to 12th: outpcd after next: rallied to chse clr ldrs last: no imp* **5/1**[2]

-U64 **4** *5* **Seek The Truth (IRE)**[52] 2354 8-10-9 77 TomMessenger 67
(Sue Bradburne) *trckd ldrs: effrt bef 3 out: outpcd whn pckd next: sn btn* **9/2**[1]

-404 **5** *7* **Prince Tam**[58] 2207 7-11-1 83 (p) CampbellGillies 65
(Lucinda Russell) *hld up: stdy hdwy and prom 10th: rdn 3 out: wknd bef next* **16/1**

-052 **6** *34* **Dark Gentleman**[46] 2479 8-10-9 77 TjadeCollier 24
(Evelyn Slack) *hld up in tch: outpcd whn checked 10th: sn struggling: t.o* **5/1**[2]

1P-3 **7** *3 3/4* **Something Silver**[52] 2352 10-11-9 91 (v) RichieMcGrath 34
(Jim Goldie) *led to 5th: cl up tl wknd 10th: sn btn* **6/1**[3]

24-6 **F** **Native Coll**[64] 2103 11-11-1 83 GrahamLee —
(N W Alexander) *in tch: drvn and outpcd after 8th: rallied next: 5th and in tch whn fell 10th* **7/1**

/00- **P** **Oleolat (FR)**[267] 5139 9-11-10 92 (t) JanFaltejsek —
(William Amos) *in tch: drvn and outpcd 1/2-way: wknd 10th: t.o whn p.u bef 5 out* **10/1**

5m 9.50s (-13.40) **Going Correction** -0.725s/f (Firm) **9** Ran SP% **112.0**

Speed ratings: **97,96,90,88,85 71,70,—,—**

toteswingers: 1&2 £9.90, 1&3 £3.60, 2&3 £3.30 CSF £68.91 CT £382.40 TOTE £6.70: £1.80, £3.70, £1.60; EX 56.70.

Owner Mrs Orla Cleary-O'Kane **Bred** John Mulcahy **Trained** Dungannon, Co. Tyrone

FOCUS

A low-grade 77-94 handicap chase run at a true gallop and the finish fought out by two horses that came into this on the back of being pulled up last time. There is a case for rating the form a bit higher.

NOTEBOOK

Schindlers Society(IRE), pulled up lame early on at Downpatrick in October a week after finishing runner-up at Fairyhouse, was having just his seventh start over fences. He went in pursuit of the leader four out and a better jump at the final fence sealed the issue, giving his Irish-based trainer a welcome winner in Scotland. He carries his head high and has his own way of doing things. (op 13-2)

Coldwells(IRE) went on with a circuit to go and jumped really well. Pulled up on three of her previous four starts, she held a 3l lead when making a serious error three out. Outjumped at the last, she is 7lb below her hurdle-race mark and her sole success in 33 starts now came over 3m two years ago now. (op 14-1)

Festival King(IRE), hard at work five out on his first start for three months, was left behind by the first two going to the next. He has managed just one win after a dozen starts over fences now. (op 9-2 tchd 4-1)

Seek The Truth(IRE), a mover on the morning line, was 8lb below his last winning mark over 3m at Newcastle over a year ago. He was readily tapped for toe from four out. (op 5-1 tchd 11-2)

Prince Tam, 0-8 over fences, was stepping up in trip but was found sadly lacking in the home straight. (op 20-1)

Dark Gentleman couldn't dominate and his jumping suffered. He was struggling badly setting out on to the final circuit. (op 11-2)

Something Silver, who likes it round here, lost the lead with a circuit to go and seemed to sulk. (op 11-2 tchd 5-1)

3361 BET NOW AT VICTORCHANDLER.COM H'CAP CHASE (19 fncs) 3m 1f

2:05 (2:05) (Class 4) (0-115,115) 5-Y-O+ **£3,252** (£955; £477; £238)

Form RPR

4-1F **1** **Eyre Square (IRE)**[19] 2962 8-11-9 112 JamesReveley 125+
(Keith Reveley) *trckd ldrs: cl 2nd and gng wl whn lft in ld last: pushed out run-in* **7/4**[1]

5314 **2** *1 1/2* **Top It All**[20] 2940 8-10-11 100 WilsonRenwick 107
(Rose Dobbin) *prom: blnd and rdr lost iron briefly 7th: pushed along after 5 out: hdwy 3 out: sn rdn: lft cl 2nd last: kpt on run-in: nt rch wnr* **6/1**[3]

4- **3** *12* **On Gossamer Wings (IRE)**[51] 2379 7-10-8 97 (p) BrianHughes 96+
(J J Lambe, Ire) *led to 6th: led 11th tl hdd after 2 out: cl 3rd whn hmpd by faller last: no ex* **22/1**

11P **4** *1* **Sotovik (IRE)**[56] 2272 10-11-7 113 EwanWhillans(3) 109
(Alistair Whillans) *cl up: led 6th: hit 8th: hdd 11th: nt fluent 14th: rdn and outpcd fr 3 out* **11/1**

0F6/ **5** *1* **Raining Horse (FR)**[645] 4781 9-11-4 110 HarryHaynes(3) 106
(James Ewart) *hld up: hdwy to trck ldrs 5th: nt fluent 7th: effrt and wnt 2nd briefly bef 3 out: outpcd fr next: hld whn lft 4th last* **12/1**

6/6P **6** *19* **Banoge (IRE)**[55] 2298 9-11-1 104 GrahamLee 88
(Rose Dobbin) *hld up: rdn after 5 out: wknd fr next: t.o* **12/1**

3P-P **P** **Waterski**[52] 2354 10-10-1 93 RyanMania(3) —
(Jean McGregor) *in tch: lost pl 2nd: blnd and struggling 11th: t.o whn p.u after 14th* **16/1**

-511 **F** **Isla Pearl Fisher**[58] 2203 8-10-8 97 PaddyAspell 107+
(N W Alexander) *hld up: nt fluent 13th: hdwy to ld after 2 out: jst in front and rdn whn fell last* **7/2**[2]

60-0 **U** **Flaming Thistle (IRE)**[58] 2203 7-10-7 96 FearghalDavis —
(Nicky Richards) *hld up: mstke 13th: wknd 5 out: t.o whn swvd to avoid jockey and uns rdr after last* **12/1**

6m 33.7s (-16.20) **Going Correction** -0.725s/f (Firm) **9** Ran SP% **114.5**

Speed ratings: **96,95,91,91,91 84,—,—,—**

toteswingers: 1&2 £3.50, 1&3 £4.80, 2&3 £28.40 CSF £13.13 CT £168.42 TOTE £3.40: £1.30, £2.80, £6.70; EX 12.20.

Owner John Wade **Bred** William Neville **Trained** Lingdale, Redcar & Cleveland

■ Stewards' Enquiry : Wilson Renwick one-day ban: used whip with excessive frequency (Jan 17)

FOCUS

A depleted field for this 93-113 handicap chase and again the pace was sound. There is p[robably better to come from the cosy winner. The second produced a small chase best and the faller was heading for similar.

NOTEBOOK

Eyre Square(IRE), still in contention when falling late on at Newbury, was having just his seventh start over fences and was able to run from a mark 7lb below his hurdle rating. Well backed and a grand, big type, he travelled strongly. Tapped for toe for a few strides four out, he was upsides when handed the advantage at the final fence. He won cosily and is open to further improvement so he must be kept on the right side. Connections think he may make a Scottish National horse in time. (tchd 2-1 and 9-4 in places)

Top It All, having just his fourth start over fences, was another tapped for toe four out. He kept on to be handed second spot at the last, and is another open to improvement. (op 15-2)

On Gossamer Wings(IRE) helped set the pace but was fourth and held when hampered at the final fence. Apparently all this ex-pointer does is just stay. (op 25-1)

Sotovik(IRE), pulled up when attempting a hat-trick at Carlisle, was back after a two-month break but, after helping force the pace, he was left behind from two out. (op 9-1)

Raining Horse(FR), absent for getting on for two years, went well for a long way and hopefully his problems are behind him. (op 11-1)

Isla Pearl Fisher, a winner at Carlisle and Kelso, form that has worked out well, had a 6lb rise to overcome. Given a patient ride, he moved up five out and, level two out, held a narrow advantage when he crashed out at the final fence. The winner looked to be travelling just the stronger but he deserves to find consolation. (op 4-1)

3362 PLAY POKER AT VICTORCHANDLER.COM H'CAP HURDLE (12 hdls) 3m 110y

2:40 (2:40) (Class 4) (0-115,115) 4-Y-O+ **£2,602** (£764; £382; £190)

Form				RPR
0-20	**1**		**Arctic Court (IRE)**[43] 2545 7-11-7 **110** .... RichieMcGrath (Jim Goldie) *hld up: stdy hdwy 1/2-way: effrt 3 out: led bef last: kpt on strly run-in* **8/1**[3]	118+
-4U0	**2**	3 ¾	**Oil Burner**[47] 2448 6-10-11 **100** .... JamesReveley (William Amos) *hld up: stdy hdwy 8th: effrt bef 3 out: styd on to go 2nd towards fin: no ch w wnr* **7/1**[2]	101
2-13	**3**	nk	**Ballymacduff (IRE)**[43] 2549 7-11-5 **108** .... (t) JanFaltejsek (George Charlton) *t.k.h: cl up: led 5th: clr after 4 out: rdn bef 2 out: hdd bef last: kpt on same pce run-in: lost 2nd towards fin* **5/1**[1]	109
2230	**4**	½	**More Equity**[20] 2940 9-10-10 **102** .... RyanMania[(3)] (Dianne Sayer) *prom: effrt bef 3 out: kpt on same pce run-in* **10/1**	102
-P26	**5**	9	**Delightfully (FR)**[47] 2448 7-10-7 **103** .... (v) MrGJCockburn[(7)] (Lucinda Russell) *hld up: blnd 4th: hdwy and in tch 4 out: rdn and no imp fr next* **9/1**	94
P5-6	**6**	27	**Wild Cane Ridge (IRE)**[58] 2205 12-11-12 **115** .... (b) WilsonRenwick (Rose Dobbin) *led to 5th: cl up: rdn 4 out: blnd next and sn wknd* **10/1**	86
4423	**7**	3 ½	**Devotion To Duty (IRE)**[43] 2545 5-11-11 **114** .... PeterBuchanan (Lucinda Russell) *nt fluent on occasions: towards rr: rdn bef 4 out: nvr on terms* **7/1**[2]	78
0-42	**8**	2 ¾	**What A Dream**[43] 2552 5-11-5 **108** .... FearghalDavis (William Amos) *t.k.h early: hld up: hdwy and in tch 8th: rdn and wknd after next* **7/1**[2]	71
-23P	**9**	15	**Proficiency**[102] 1596 6-10-7 **96** .... (v) PaddyAspell (Sue Bradburne) *cl up: blnd 8th: wknd fr next* **16/1**	39
2-0F	**P**		**Double Default (IRE)**[20] 2941 10-11-7 **110** .... GrahamLee (Martin Todhunter) *hld up: rdn along 7th: no imp whn blnd 4 out: wknd and p.u bef next* **22/1**	—
0PP-	**P**		**Quws Law (IRE)**[289] 4733 9-11-7 **110** .... (t) CampbellGillies (Lucinda Russell) *in tch on outside: struggling 8th: sn btn: t.o whn p.u bef next* **20/1**	—
35-P	**P**		**Prideus (IRE)**[43] 2548 7-11-12 **115** .... (t) BrianHughes (Brian Storey) *midfield: struggling 1/2-way: t.o whn p.u bef 3 out* **40/1**	—
3-1	**P**		**Torta Nel Cielo**[43] 2552 7-11-3 **109** .... HarryHaynes[(3)] (James Ewart) *prom: hit 5th: nt fluent 7th: sn struggling: t.o whn p.u bef 4 out* **8/1**[3]	—

6m 4.80s (-27.00) **Going Correction** -0.95s/f (Hard) **13** Ran SP% **122.0**

Speed ratings (Par 105): **105,103,103,103,100 92,90,90,85,— —,—,—**

toteswingers: 1&2 £10.30, 1&3 £6.80, 2&3 £8.40 CSF £63.51 CT £316.26 TOTE £11.90: £3.20, £3.10, £2.30; EX 85.30.

Owner Mr & Mrs Raymond Anderson Green **Bred** Paul Doyle **Trained** Uplawmoor, E Renfrews

■ Stewards' Enquiry : Graham Lee £140.00 fine: arrived late into parade ring

Mr G J Cockburn £140.00 fine: arrived late into parade ring

Richie McGrath £140.00 fine: arrived late into parade ring

FOCUS

A competitive 94-115 handicap hurdle and eight still in contention turning for home. Fair form with the first two improving.

NOTEBOOK

Arctic Court(IRE), whose effort came under the microscope when seventh on his final start here last term in March, seemed to relish this test of stamina. He went in pursuit of the leader three out and, landing in front at the final flight, in the end won going away. He looks open to further improvement. Official explanation: trainer could offer no explination as to improved perfomance (op 7-1)

Oil Burner, who seemed to take a kick on the shoulder before the start, looks quite a keen sort. Working his way into it, he stayed on in good style from the last to snatch second place near the line. He too looks open to further improvement. (op 11-1)

Ballymacduff(IRE) took it up with a circuit to go and stepped up the pace. He had all but the winner held three from home but in the end had to settle for third spot. He deserves to find another opening. (tchd 9-2 and 6-1)

More Equity, whose last three starts have been over fences, was back over hurdles off 4lb higher than for her last hurdle-race success which was a year and a half ago now. (op 14-1)

Delightfully(FR) is only small and wore a visor this time. She never really entered the argument. (op 11-1)

Wild Cane Ridge(IRE) took them along but was getting tapped for toe when blundering three out. (op 12-1 tchd 14-1)

Devotion To Duty(IRE) didn't seem to last out this longer trip.

Quws Law(IRE) Official explanation: trainer said gelding had a breathing problem

Prideus(IRE) Official explanation: trainer said gelding scoped dirty post race

3363 BEST ODDS GUARANTEED AT VICTOR CHANDLER H'CAP HURDLE (9 hdls 2 omitted) 2m 4f

3:10 (3:11) (Class 5) (0-90,90) 4-Y-O+ **£1,951** (£573; £286; £143)

Form				RPR
4-00	**1**		**Bene Lad (IRE)**[20] 2941 9-11-9 **87** .... RichieMcGrath (Jim Goldie) *mde all: qcknd bef 2 out: kpt on wl fr last* **6/1**	94+
0061	**2**	1 ¼	**Sambelucky (IRE)**[20] 2937 6-11-5 **83** .... JamesReveley (Keith Reveley) *hld up: hdwy bef omitted 3 out: rdn and sltly outpcd 2 out: rallied to chse wnr run-in: kpt on fin* **3/1**[1]	86
004/	**3**	3 ½	**Classic Henri**[644] 4801 7-10-10 **74** .... BrianHarding (Barry Murtagh) *in tch: hdwy bef 3 out (usual 4 out): effrt and chsd wnr bef 2 out to run-in: no ex* **50/1**	74
0-04	**4**	3	**Winter Alchemy (IRE)**[58] 2208 6-11-1 **89** .... StephenMulqueen[(10)] (Nicky Richards) *hld up: rdn and outpcd after 3 out (usual 4 out): rallied between last 2: nvr able to chal* **7/2**[2]	85
6204	**5**	1 ¼	**Manoubi**[20] 2937 12-11-2 **85** .... JamesHalliday[(5)] (Martin Todhunter) *chsd wnr tl rdn and no ex bef 2 out* **9/1**	80
40-P	**6**	4	**Ravensbill (IRE)**[52] 2351 9-11-7 **85** .... CampbellGillies (William Amos) *hld up: rdn after 3 out (usual 4 out): no imp fr 2 out* **40/1**	76
-0P6	**7**	9	**Transact (IRE)**[56] 2271 6-10-6 **70** .... GrahamLee (Martin Todhunter) *trckd ldrs tl rdn and wknd bef 2 out* **9/1**	52
-065	**8**	3 ½	**Bob Will (IRE)**[20] 2937 6-11-2 **85** .... AlexanderVoy[(5)] (Chris Grant) *t.k.h: trckd ldrs tl rdn and wknd bef omitted 3 out* **11/2**[3]	64
2/5-	**9**	½	**Crackerjack Lad (IRE)**[571] 672 8-11-12 **90** .... PeterBuchanan (Lucinda Russell) *hld up: stdy hdwy and in tch 6th: rdn and wknd bef 2 out* **12/1**	68
600-	**P**		**Shadow Boxer**[303] 4433 6-11-3 **81** .... WilsonRenwick (Donald Whillans) *bhd: struggling bef 5th: t.o whn p.u bef next* **16/1**	—

4m 58.8s (-13.20) **Going Correction** -0.95s/f (Hard) **10** Ran SP% **114.9**

Speed ratings (Par 103): **88,87,86,84,84 82,79,77,77,—**

toteswingers: 1&2 £4.90, 1&3 £27.20, 2&3 £11.60 CSF £24.53 CT £820.27 TOTE £9.80: £3.30, £2.00, £12.00; EX 16.20.

Owner Mr & Mrs Raymond Anderson Green **Bred** Greenville House Stud And M Morgan **Trained** Uplawmoor, E Renfrews

■ A 440/1 treble for Jim Goldie and Richie McGrath.

FOCUS

A modest 70-90 handicap hurdle and an all-the-way winner completing a treble for trainer Jim Goldie and jockey Richard McGrath. Ordinary form, the winner back to his 2008 best.

NOTEBOOK

Bene Lad(IRE), whose two most recent victories early last year were over fences, had been virtually pulled up when tailed off on his return over 3m at Catterick. Racing with real enthusiasm, he had shaken off all but the runner-up two out and was never seriously challenged. He is a keen sort who will now revert to fences. (op 7-1)

Sambelucky(IRE), given a patient ride, was racing from a 6lb higher mark than his Catterick success. He stayed on really well on the run-in but is slightly flattered to get so close to the idling winner. He clearly stays really well. (tchd 10-3)

Classic Henri, who showed little in three starts over hurdles when last seen almost two years ago, moved up travelling strongly to chase the winner. Hard as he tried he could not land a serious blow. Hopefully he will come out of this all right. (op 33-1)

Winter Alchemy(IRE), stepping up in trip, stayed on in his own time in the home straight. He doesn't have too many miles on the clock and may be better suited by more give underfoot. (tchd 10-3)

3364 PLAY CASINO AT VICTORCHANDLER.COM "JUNIOR" STANDARD OPEN NATIONAL HUNT FLAT RACE 1m 6f

3:40 (3:40) (Class 6) 4-Y-O **£1,370** (£399; £199)

Form				RPR
2	**1**		**Close House**[54] 2315 4-10-12 0 .... GrahamLee (Karen McLintock) *mde all: hrd pressed fnl half m: kpt on wl u.p to assert wl ins fnl f* **8/13**[1]	102
	2	1 ¼	**Koultas King (IRE)** 4-10-5 0 .... MrTomDavid[(7)] (Tim Vaughan) *trckd ldrs: effrt and disp ld 4f out: kpt on u.p: hld towards fin* **5/1**[2]	101
	3	19	**Porridge** 4-10-12 0 .... CampbellGillies (Lucinda Russell) *prom: outpcd over 4f out: no imp fnl 3f* **9/1**	78
	4	22	**Samstown** 4-10-12 0 .... PeterBuchanan (Lucinda Russell) *prom: rdn and outpcd over 4f out: sn btn* **13/2**[3]	51
0	**5**	10	**Playing Truant (IRE)**[64] 2108 4-10-9 0 .... HarryHaynes[(3)] (James Ewart) *cl up tl wknd over 5f out* **33/1**	39
	6	25	**Miss Fernietickles** 4-9-12 0 .... GaryRutherford[(7)] (Harriet Graham) *in tch: struggling over 5f out: sn btn: t.o* **33/1**	2
	7	39	**Jilly Anne** 4-10-0 0 .... MissLHorner[(5)] (Chris Grant) *bhd: lost tch 1/2-way: t.o* **28/1**	—

3m 16.0s (196.00) **7** Ran SP% **111.3**

toteswingers: 1&2 £1.10, 1&3 £2.20, 2&3 £5.50 CSF £3.69 TOTE £1.80: £1.10, £3.40; EX 4.70.

Owner Alan Lamont **Bred** Allan Munnis **Trained** Ingoe, Northumberland

FOCUS

An uncompetitive 'junior bumper' but the first two went head-to-head from soon after halfway. It seemed a strange decision to bypass the damaged third-last hurdle rather than remove the flights and run between the wings. The winner is rated to his debut mark.

NOTEBOOK

Close House, beaten a whisker first time at Huntingdon, is quite a big type. He answered his rider's every call and was on top at the line. He looks essentially a stayer and the first two finished a long way clear. (tchd 4-6)

Koultas King(IRE), much smaller than the winner, had come out on top in a seven-horse gallop on the Polytrack at Wolverhampton. He knew his job and went toe to toe with the winner, but had to admit defeat near the finish. He had a very tough introduction. (op 6-1 tchd 9-2)

Porridge, jump bred, took a remote third ahead of his stablemate. (op 10-1 tchd 17-2)

Samstown, a newcomer, hung badly right as he tired in the closing stages. (op 8-1)

T/Jkpt: £50,795.70 to a £1 stake. Pool: £71,543.37. 1.00 winning tickets. T/Plt: £81.20 to a £1 stake. Pool: £70,532.80. 633.88 winning tickets. T/Qpdt: £30.40 to a £1 stake. Pool: £5,243.54. 127.60 winning tickets. RY

2466 HEREFORD (R-H)

Monday, January 3

OFFICIAL GOING: Soft

Third fence after the winning post and final fence in back straight (open ditch) omitted in all chases.

Wind: Nil Weather: Overcast

3365 LINDLEY CATERING "NATIONAL HUNT" MAIDEN HURDLE (DIV I) (8 hdls) 2m 1f

12:20 (12:20) (Class 5) 4-Y-O+ **£1,821** (£534; £267; £133)

Form				RPR
1-2	**1**		**Whoops A Daisy**[61] 2156 5-10-12 0 .... APMcCoy (Nicky Henderson) *a.p: led after 3 out: pressed tl r.o to draw clr and wl in command run-in* **10/3**[3]	122+

21 **2** *5* **Charminster (IRE)**[44] 2525 5-11-5 0 JasonMaguire 126+
(Donald McCain) *a.p: chalng 2 out: rdn between last 2: jinked lft and no ex after last* **5/4**[1]
6/22 **3** *17* **Gurtacrue (IRE)**[61] 2145 6-11-5 129 PaulMoloney 107
(Evan Williams) *led: hdd after 3 out: stl ev ch 2 out: sn rdn and wknd* **5/2**[2]
02-P **4** *7* **Ballagio (IRE)**[57] 2241 6-11-5 0 HarrySkelton 100
(Paul Nicholls) *midfield: hdwy to trck ldrs 3 out: nt fluent 2 out: sn rdn and btn* **20/1**
410- **5** *8* **Behindcloseddoors (IRE)**[269] 5121 5-11-5 0 SeanQuinlan 91
(Kim Bailey) *racd keenly: in tch: rdn 2 out: sn wknd* **33/1**
4500 **6** *1 1/4* **Superior Knight**[4] 3225 7-11-5 0 DavidDennis 90
(James Evans) *midfield: outpcd after 3 out: no imp after* **200/1**
0-56 **7** *4* **Another Kate (IRE)**[40] 2607 7-10-12 0 SamThomas 79
(David Richards) *prom tl rdn and wknd 2 out* **14/1**
00 **8** *2* **High Kite (IRE)**[44] 2518 5-11-5 0 HaddenFrost 84
(Henrietta Knight) *midfield: wl outpcd fr 3 out* **66/1**
24 **9** *2* **Thornton Alice**[40] 2616 6-10-12 0 WarrenMarston 75
(Richard Phillips) *a bhd* **66/1**
0-00 **10** *3/4* **Benny The Swinger (IRE)**[57] 2241 6-11-5 0 AndrewThornton 81
(Henrietta Knight) *midfield: rdn appr 2 out: dropped away between last 2* **66/1**
6 **11** *nk* **Matrow's Lady (IRE)**[46] 2466 4-10-0 0 RodiGreene 62
(Neil Mulholland) *j. slowly 2nd: a bhd* **66/1**
3000 **12** *6* **Bach To Back (IRE)**[20] 2944 6-11-5 0 PaddyBrennan 75
(Nigel Twiston-Davies) *hld up: struggling fr 3 out: nvr on terms* **100/1**
00 **13** *14* **Jam Tomorrow (FR)**[38] 2666 6-11-5 0 DougieCostello 61
(Ian Williams) *midfield: wknd 3 out* **125/1**
00-P **P** **Rahotep (FR)**[61] 2143 6-11-5 0 AndrewTinkler —
(Henry Daly) *a bhd: struggling 2 out: t.o whn p.u bef last* **150/1**

4m 3.10s (3.70) **Going Correction** +0.325s/f (Yiel)
WFA 4 from 5yo+ 11lb **14** Ran SP% **119.4**
Speed ratings (Par 103): **104,101,93,90,86 86,84,83,82,81 81,78,72,—**
toteswingers: 1&2 £1.10, 1&3 £1.60, 2&3 £1.50 CSF £7.85 TOTE £4.70: £1.10, £1.40, £1.50; EX 12.00.
Owner Let's Live Racing **Bred** N J Henderson And Mrs S A Aston **Trained** Upper Lambourn, Berks

FOCUS
Deployment of covers enabled the course to survive its 8.30am inspection. Racing took place on going described as soft officially, and as "really dead" and "hard work" by riders after the opener. Three dominated the market of division one of the maiden hurdle, with two of those finishing well clear at the end of a race run at a fair gallop in the conditions. The form looks fairly sound with the winner stepping up on her bumper efforts.

NOTEBOOK
Whoops A Daisy gave a most accomplished round of jumping at this first attempt, and looked to have the measure of the runner-up some way out even before his late waywardness. The mares' finale at Newbury looks a feasible target if connections' assertion that she will stay further still proves well founded. (op 7-2 tchd 4-1)
Charminster(IRE) ◆ had the edge on jumping experience over the winner having landed his sole Irish point, but he'd looked green late on the first of his two bumper starts and ran around after the final flight here, too. This was still an entirely creditable hurdling debut, and he will have more to offer as he develops physically and mentally. (op 11-8 tchd 6-4 and 13-8 in places)
Gurtacrue(IRE), a well-supported dual Irish point scorer, raced as prominently throughout here as when taking a 2m4f bumper last June, so it's likelier the inadequacy of this trip rather than racing tactic prevented him taking a greater hand late on. A mark of 129 may overestimate his achievements under rules to date, but 2m4f-3m handicaps can see him in a better light. (op 3-1)
Ballagio(IRE), outpaced late on behind Whoops A Daisy in a Bangor bumper two starts back, shaped far better than on his hurdling debut over 2m3f here last time. There ought to be an ordinary handicap in him at least. \n\x\x \bBehindcloseddoors\p was too effervescent early on to last home. That was the case on his debut last season before landing a bumper five days later, though, so he can be fancied to race more kindly if turned out quickly again after this first start since April.\n (tchd 22-1)
Behindcloseddoors(IRE) ◆ was too effervescent early on to last home. That was the case on his debut last season before landing a bumper five days later, though, so he can be fancied to race more kindly if turned out quickly again after this first start since April.
Another Kate(IRE) is yet to reproduce her best bumper form over hurdles, though a switch to mares-only company may assist.

3366 LINDLEY CATERING "NATIONAL HUNT" MAIDEN HURDLE (DIV II) (8 hdls) 2m 1f
12:50 (12:50) (Class 5) 4-Y-0+ **£1,821** (£534; £267; £133)

Form RPR
4 **1** **Spanish Treasure (GER)**[13] 3055 5-11-5 0 NickScholfield 129+
(Andy Turnell) *midfield: hdwy 5th: led after 2 out: r.o wl to pull away fnl 100yds* **7/2**[1]
1 **2** *2 1/2* **Kells Belle (IRE)**[239] 237 5-10-12 0 AndrewTinkler 117
(Nicky Henderson) *midfield: hdwy 3 out: chalng fr 2 out: nt qckn fnl 100yds* **7/2**[1]
3 *2 3/4* **Sollim (FR)**[271] 4-10-7 0 APMcCoy 109
(Paul Nicholls) *midfield: hdwy 4th: chalng 2 out: nt qckn u.p appr last: no ex fnl 100yds* **5/1**[2]
4 **4** *9* **Baile Anrai (IRE)**[18] 2985 7-11-5 0 DougieCostello 112
(Ian Williams) *trckd ldrs: led after 3 out: hdd after 2 out: wknd appr last* **12/1**
2000 **5** *12* **Great Hero**[47] 2456 6-11-5 0 SeanQuinlan 102
(Richard Phillips) *in rr: hdwy into midfield whn blnd 2 out: nvr able to get to ldrs* **125/1**
1303 **6** *5* **Fountains Flypast**[13] 3060 7-11-0 0 RachaelGreen(5) 96
(Anthony Honeyball) *hld up: pushed along appr 5th: hdwy to chse ldrs 3 out: cl up whn nt fluent 2 out: sn wknd* **5/1**[2]
4-P0 **7** *1/2* **Fidelor (FR)**[47] 2454 5-11-5 0 WillKennedy 94
(Henry Daly) *led: hdd after 3 out: wknd after 2 out* **125/1**
P425 **8** *2 1/2* **Freckle Face**[46] 2466 4-10-0 110 MattGriffiths(7) 81
(Bill Turner) *bhd: pushed along appr 5th: hdwy to chse ldrs after 3 out: wknd after 2 out* **25/1**
P/60 **9** *15* **Jayjay Valentine**[45] 2499 8-11-5 0 DenisO'Regan 77
(Victor Dartnall) *prom tl wknd after 3 out* **50/1**
6-00 **10** *3* **Beau Colonel (FR)**[42] 2577 5-11-5 0 AndrewThornton 74
(Henrietta Knight) *hld up: struggling fr 3 out: nvr on terms* **150/1**
0024 **11** *10* **Sara's Smile**[19] 2954 5-10-12 98 JasonMaguire 57
(Donald McCain) *trckd ldrs tl rdn and wknd after 3 out* **12/1**
-156 **12** *10* **Catspan (FR)**[20] 2944 5-11-5 0 JimmyMcCarthy 54
(Charles Egerton) *prom tl wknd 3 out* **20/1**
54 **13** *29* **Just Dave (IRE)**[58] 2216 5-11-5 0 PaulMoloney 25
(Evan Williams) *in tch to 5th: bhd after 3 out: t.o* **8/1**[3]
0- **P** **Lombardy Breeze (IRE)**[611] 120 6-11-5 0 HaddenFrost —
(Henrietta Knight) *midfield: wknd appr 5th: t.o whn p.u bef 2 out* **100/1**

4m 2.10s (2.70) **Going Correction** +0.325s/f (Yiel)
WFA 4 from 5yo+ 11lb **14** Ran SP% **118.1**
Speed ratings (Par 103): **106,104,103,99,93 91,91,89,82,81 76,72,58,—**
toteswingers: 1&2 £2.20, 1&3 £2.70, 2&3 £2.50 CSF £14.61 TOTE £4.70: £1.90, £2.00, £2.50; EX 16.80.
Owner M Tedham **Bred** M Beining **Trained** Broad Hinton, Wilts

FOCUS
Another solidly enough run contest in the dead going, and a winning time a second inside that of the opening division. The form looks solid and the winner should go on to rate higher.

NOTEBOOK
Spanish Treasure(GER), conqueror of six subsequent winners in a Punchestown bumper on debut, and heavily supported, took a little time to warm to the task but made up the ground very easily when asked approaching two out, and dug in deep to maintain his advantage from that point. An appearance in a Kempton jumpers' bumper 13 days earlier had put him spot on for this, and the Black Sam Bellamy gelding is held in high regard by Andrew Turnell, although he is unlikely to be aimed too high for the time being. (op 5-1)
Kells Belle(IRE) ◆, a market drifter, had to concede race-fitness to the winner on this first start since taking her sole bumper at Worcester in May, but a couple of novicey leaps on the way round probably played a bigger role in her eventual defeat. She can improve for the experience, and a mares' novice at the least should prove a formality. (op 2-1 tchd 9-2)
Sollim(FR) hadn't found the necessary turn of foot to go closer in his two hurdles starts at Auteuil previously, and nor did he here. It's still early days with him, though, especially as he looks more an embryonic chasing type, and he can be found an opening this winter. (op 9-2 tchd 4-1)
Baile Anrai(IRE) played his hand sooner than any of those to finish in front of him but was soon outsped, as perhaps befits an Irish point winner who'd found 2m in soft at Towcester on the sharp side last time. There are handicaps to be won with him over further. (op 14-1 tchd 16-1 and 10-1)
Fountains Flypast delivered less than had seemed likely half a mile out and disappointed on this third run in quick succession. (op 6-1)
Just Dave(IRE), although not racing as keenly as in either bumper start, already looked in trouble by halfway. He may not have cared for this softest surface he has encountered. Official explanation: jockey said gelding was never travelling (op 17-2 tchd 10-1)

3367 LINDLEY CATERING H'CAP HURDLE (8 hdls) 2m 1f
1:20 (1:21) (Class 5) (0-95,95) 4-Y-O+ **£1,821** (£534; £267; £133)

Form RPR
0402 **1** **Rawaaj**[12] 3091 5-11-2 **85** JasonMaguire 97+
(Donald McCain) *trckd ldrs: chalng 2 out: sn led: rdn appr last: styd on wl to draw clr run-in* **11/8**[1]
-000 **2** *4* **Man Of Leisure**[29] 2791 7-11-0 **88** KeiranBurke(5) 96
(Nerys Duffield) *a.p: led after 4th: nt fluent 5th: hdd after 2 out: rdn bef last: styd on same pce run-in* **50/1**
P050 **3** *9* **Bright Decision**[40] 2607 5-11-3 **86** (p) DaveCrosse 85
(Joanna Davis) *a.p: niggled along after 4 th: rdn and ch 2 out: outpcd by front pair bef last: no imp after* **8/1**[3]
-000 **4** *5* **Gallimaufry**[45] 2499 5-10-7 **76** RodiGreene 69
(Neil Mulholland) *in rr: pushed along after 3rd: toiling bef 3 out: kpt on modly appr last: nvr on terms w ldrs* **14/1**
P-40 **5** *1 1/4* **Born To Be Wilde (IRE)**[40] 2609 6-11-4 **94** MrJEngland(7) 86
(Evan Williams) *hld up: hdwy after 3rd: sn prom: rdn and wknd after 2 out* **14/1**
525- **6** *1 1/2* **Golden Button (IRE)**[253] 4 6-11-12 **95** (t) TomSiddall 85
(Kim Bailey) *racd keenly: hld up in tch: trckd ldrs gng wl 3 out: rdn and wknd appr last* **11/4**[2]
-P00 **7** *41* **Master Paddy (IRE)**[13] 3057 7-10-4 **73** (b[1]) NickScholfield 22
(Andy Turnell) *racd keenly: hld up: hdwy to chse ldng bunch after 3 out: rdn and wknd after 2 out: t.o* **14/1**
P2P- **8** *70* **Little Rort (IRE)**[268] 5136 12-10-1 **77** MissCBoxall(7) —
(Simon Lewis) *led: hdd after 4th: mstke 5th: wknd appr 3 out: t.o* **25/1**
-4RP **P** **Orpen Bid (IRE)**[66] 2068 6-10-3 **75** (p) CharlieStudd(3) —
(Michael Mullineaux) *prom: wknd after 4th: t.o 3 out: p.u bef 2 out* **18/1**

4m 7.90s (8.50) **Going Correction** +0.325s/f (Yiel) **9** Ran SP% **111.0**
Speed ratings (Par 103): **93,91,86,84,83 83,63,31,—**
toteswingers: 1&2 £18.10, 1&3 £3.40, 2&3 £18.10 CSF £52.68 CT £396.01 TOTE £1.90: £1.10, £9.60, £2.00; EX 62.90.
Owner Tim & Miranda Johnson Partnership **Bred** Shadwell Estate Company Limited **Trained** Cholmondeley, Cheshire

FOCUS
An uninspiring assortment, and a winning time over 6secs slower than the quicker of the two maiden hurdles. The winner didn'r run to the mark promised by his Southwell bumper run.

NOTEBOOK
Rawaaj, like the winner of the previous race last seen in a jumpers' bumper, didn't travel with too much willing until finally securing at least a share of the lead after halfway, and it took until the final flight for him to put a comfortable margin between himself and the rest. Pretty modest over a variety of trip and going types previously, he holds an entry in a Southwell conditionals' handicap on Wednesday, and it wouldn't surprise to see him honour that or another engagement very soon before reassessment. (op 6-4 tchd 13-8)
Man Of Leisure shaped with a bit more purpose around the least galloping course he has tried over hurdles to date, though he was already starting to lose the argument when going right at the last. His opening handicap mark here hadn't looked at all generous, but this effort offers a little more hope and he could find a bad selling handicap.
Bright Decision, a handicap debutant, fared better in first-time cheekpieces but looked to get outpaced soon after leaving the back straight. Future hopes may rest in him seeing out trips around 2m4f better than he had done in novice company previously. (op 9-1)
Gallimaufry, related to two 3m chase scorers, and out of a mare from the same family as two Grand National winners, needs a big step up in trip on the evidence of this staying-on but never dangerous fourth. (op 11-1 tchd 10-1)
Golden Button(IRE)'s mark looked more realistic than some on this handicap bow, but she's still to convince fully as a stayer of this trip over hurdles. (op 5-2)

3368 LINDLEY CATERING BEGINNERS' CHASE (15 fncs 4 omitted) 3m 1f 110y
1:55 (1:55) (Class 4) 5-Y-O+ **£2,602** (£764; £382; £190)

Form RPR
4-22 **1** **Pearlysteps**[44] 2527 8-10-7 136 JakeGreenall(7) 140+
(Henry Daly) *a.p: led 10th: jnd after 12th: mstke 2 out: rdn between last 2: mstke last: edgd lft run-in: styd on wl and in command fnl 50yds* **5/4**[1]
1426 **2** *2 1/4* **Alderley Rover (IRE)**[37] 2670 7-11-0 125 JasonMaguire 137
(Donald McCain) *hld up in tch: clsd 11th: upsides after 12th: rdn appr last: no ex fnl 50yds* **7/2**[3]
122- **3** *10* **Aldertune (IRE)**[323] 4054 7-11-0 0 HarrySkelton 126
(Paul Nicholls) *hld up: wnt cl 3rd 12th: rdn appr 2 out: sn wknd* **11/4**[2]
0-45 **4** *37* **City Theatre (IRE)**[20] 2945 7-11-0 0 APMcCoy 91
(Jonjo O'Neill) *chsd ldr: lft in ld 7th: hdd 10th: nt fluent 12th: wknd 3 out: sn eased whn wl btn* **11/2**

-302 **5** *15* **Brimley**[46] 2471 8-10-11 88 LeeStephens(3) 76
(Ann Price) *led: mstke and hdd 7th: dropped to last pl 9th: sn struggling: t.o bef 11th* **66/1**

6m 32.1s (0.30) **Going Correction** +0.325s/f (Yiel) **5** Ran SP% **110.2**
Speed ratings: **112,111,108,96,92**
toteswingers: 1&2 £4.60 CSF £6.19 TOTE £2.20: £1.30, £1.30; EX 3.90.
Owner The Glazeley Partnership **Bred** W P Jenks **Trained** Stanton Lacy, Shropshire
■ Jake Greenall's first winner since turning conditional.

FOCUS
A decent beginners' chase for the track. The winner ran pretty much to his mark but should go on to rate higher.

NOTEBOOK
Pearlysteps had nothing of the likes of Wymott or Golan Way in opposition this time, and the Alflora gelding duly opened his account over fences at the third attempt. Outjumped two out but pretty tidy otherwise, the response under pressure was very pleasing, and although eventually driven out by Jake Greenall, he didn't particularly look to be coming to the end of his tether late on. More galloping tracks than this suited him best over hurdles and should do so in this discipline too, and he should be able to make a mark in good staying handicap chases in due course. (op 11-8 tchd 6-4)
Alderley Rover(IRE)'s jumping technique unravelled somewhat in a Newbury handicap last time out but let him down to any noticeable extent just once at halfway here. He got better the further he was sent over hurdles, and similarly looks well worth keeping to this sort of trip in his current vocation. A return to a drier surface wouldn't inconvenience, either. (op 4-1)
Aldertune(IRE) took to fences well enough at this first time of asking, but was the first of the three market leaders to come under pressure and might just have needed this after 11 months away. Although his stamina petered out stepped up to 3m on his final hurdling start, it would not surprise to see this relative of Midlands National heroine Miss Orchestra need longer trips in due course. (tchd 5-2)
City Theatre(IRE), as at Folkestone last time, threw in a significant error just as the race was starting to develop and was never in the hunt after that. He remains capable of better if he can only cut out the mistakes. (tchd 5-1 and 6-1)
Brimley achieved little in finishing a 46l second over an extended 2m5f here last time, and was a spent force following a mistake before halfway. (op 50-1)

3369 LINDLEY CATERING NOVICES' H'CAP HURDLE (13 hdls) 3m 2f
2:25 (2:25) (Class 5) (0-95,102) 4-Y-0+ **£1,821** (£534; £267; £133)

Form RPR
P5-5 **1** **The Hudnalls (IRE)**[39] 2637 10-11-12 95 RhysFlint 100
(Jim Old) *a.p: rdn to ld appr last: styd on: on top cl home* **7/2**[3]
3-01 **2** *2* **Not Talking (IRE)**[52] 2351 8-10-5 74 DougieCostello 78
(John Quinn) *in tch: led after 2 out: hdd appr last: rallied briefly run-in: nt qckn cl home* **6/4**[1]
2500 **3** *24* **Easement**[44] 2532 8-11-12 95 (v) JimmyMcCarthy 74
(Charlie Morlock) *prom: led 10th: hdd after 2 out: wknd appr last* **16/1**
R-P1 **4** *8* **Celian (FR)**[3] 3258 8-12-2 102 7ex AlexMerriam(3) 73
(Neil King) *led: mstke and hdd 10th: remained prom tl wknd after 2 out* **3/1**[2]
5 *3/4* **Gleannacreim (IRE)**[100] 1618 8-10-13 85 RichardKilloran(3) 55
(Tim Vaughan) *hld up in rr: effrt to chse ldrs 2 out: dropped out sn after* **7/1**
PP46 **6** *49* **The Walnut Tree (IRE)**[40] 2608 10-9-7 69 oh22 MissCBoxall(7) —
(Simon Lewis) *hld up in tch: pushed along appr 10th: wknd bef 2 out: t.o* **66/1**
5F-0 **P** **Unoitmakessense (IRE)**[21] 2929 9-11-7 90 CharliePoste —
(Mrs Pauline Harkin) *mstkes: hld up: rdn after 8th: t.o 10th: p.u bef 2 out* **11/1**

6m 48.5s (16.80) **Going Correction** +0.325s/f (Yiel) **7** Ran SP% **115.4**
Speed ratings (Par 103): **87,86,79,76,76 61,—**
toteswingers: 1&2 £1.10, 1&3 £9.60, 2&3 £5.40 CSF £9.71 TOTE £3.30: £2.20, £1.10; EX 9.70.
Owner Chris Jenkins **Bred** Dunmanway Breeding Club **Trained** Barbury Castle, Wilts

FOCUS
Not much pace on in this poor long-distance contest, and the field was still pretty well bunched with a circuit to travel. The first two came clear and the winner is rated to his C/D best, with the runner-up to his mark.

NOTEBOOK
The Hudnalls(IRE) entered the race still a maiden, his nearest miss having come when a neck second off this mark in a C&D 0-100 handicap just over a year earlier, and as on that occasion he derived the benefit of his seasonal reappearance. The ordinary early fractions wouldn't necessarily have suited a horse with stamina in abundance, and something more severe (whether that's a longer course, stronger gallop or even deeper going) wouldn't go amiss. (op 4-1)
Not Talking(IRE)'s win off 10lb lower at Newcastle last time had been recorded over 2f shorter, albeit whilst running into the teeth of a gale that rendered it a desperate test. He too, then, may have liked a greater emphasis on stamina here, but he gave his all in defeat and remains relatively unexposed in 3m plus contests. \n\x\x \bEasement\p offered little once ridden and headed, and is still to reproduce the effort that nearly reaped him a selling-hurdle win on better ground in September.\n (op 11-8 tchd 13-8)
Easement offered little once ridden and headed, and is still to reproduce the effort that nearly reaped him a selling-hurdle win on better ground in September.
Celian(FR), although it looked a facile victory at the time, may still have been feeling the effects of his race in another 0-95 handicap at Uttoxeter just three days earlier (3m, heavy) and couldn't raise another effort once deprived of the lead. His next outing should tell us more as to whether that win really does herald a lasting revival of fortunes. (op 4-1)
Gleannacreim(IRE)'s forward move proved short-lived, but present connections haven't had him for long and it wouldn't surprise to see them place him to advantage at some point this winter. Official explanation: jockey said gelding hung badly right (op 13-2 tchd 6-1)
Unoitmakessense(IRE) was an all-or-nothing jumper in British points last season (three wins and three crashes out from six runs), and his jumping fell to bits from halfway here. (op 10-1)

3370 LINDLEY CATERING FIRST FOR CONFERENCES H'CAP HURDLE (11 hdls) 2m 6f 110y
3:00 (3:00) (Class 4) (0-115,115) 4-Y-0+ **£2,927** (£859; £429; £214)

Form RPR
-011 **1** **Salpierre (IRE)**[47] 2452 6-11-10 113 APMcCoy 126+
(Jonjo O'Neill) *a.p: led 8th: pressed briefly last: styd on and in command fnl 50yds* **5/2**[1]
0-13 **2** *3* **Victors Serenade (IRE)**[55] 2284 6-11-8 111 SamThomas 116
(Anthony Honeyball) *trckd ldrs: j.lft 6th: wnt 2nd appr last: sn ev ch: nt qckn fnl 50yds* **4/1**[2]
34-0 **3** *4 1/2* **Double Eagle**[18] 2984 9-11-8 111 (p) JasonMaguire 111
(Donald McCain) *led: hdd 8th: rdn after 3 out: outpcd after 2 out: styd on to take 3rd after last but no imp on front 2* **8/1**[3]
4 *2* **Stonethrower (IRE)**[264] 5187 6-11-9 115 (t) RichardKilloran(3) 113
(Tim Vaughan) *hld up: hdwy 3 out: chalng 2 out: nt qckn bef last: fdd run-in* **16/1**
-644 **5** *1/2* **Graduation Night**[20] 2944 5-11-4 107 DarylJacob 105
(Jamie Snowden) *midfield: hdwy 7th: chsd ldrs 3 out: outpcd after 2 out: kpt on but n.d fr last* **16/1**
0-50 **6** *1/2* **Vin De Roy (FR)**[47] 2454 6-11-7 110 SeanQuinlan 109+
(Rachel Hobbs) *midfield: hmpd 6th: hdwy 7th: rdn whn chsng ldrs after 3 out: outpcd after 2 out: nt fluent last whn btn* **20/1**
30/0 **7** *16* **Cypress Grove (IRE)**[18] 2977 8-11-2 105 WayneHutchinson 86
(John Ryall) *in rr: pushed along 3 out: nvr able to get on terms* **16/1**
0-P4 **8** *1/2* **Knight Woodsman**[44] 2532 7-10-7 99 AlexMerriam(3) 80
(Neil King) *midfield: pushed along after 7th: wknd after 3 out* **10/1**
11-5 **9** *10* **Willandrich (IRE)**[60] 2161 9-11-2 108 MichaelMurphy(3) 79
(Ian Williams) *midfield: hdwy to trck ldrs after 4th: wknd after 3 out* **14/1**
0321 **10** *1 1/2* **Henry Hook (IRE)**[43] 2558 7-11-12 115 (p) DenisO'Regan 84
(Victor Dartnall) *hld up: nt fluent 5th: pushed along after 3 out: nvr on terms* **8/1**[3]
-003 **11** *2 1/2* **Diktalina**[24] 2644 5-11-1 111 OliverDayman(7) 78
(Alison Thorpe) *prom: hmpd 6th: rdn and wknd appr 3 out* **16/1**
2122 **12** *25* **Jump Up**[85] 1795 5-10-11 100 RhysFlint 42
(Keith Goldsworthy) *trckd ldrs: hmpd 6th: wknd 8th: t.o* **16/1**
-102 **P** **Tin Pot Man (IRE)**[57] 2235 5-11-0 110 (t) MrJEngland(7) —
(Evan Williams) *in rr: nt fluent 5th: sn struggling: mstke 3 out: t.o whn p.u after 2 out* **20/1**

5m 37.9s (-0.10) **13** Ran SP% **125.5**
toteswingers: 1&2 £3.50, 1&3 £4.00, 2&3 £8.00 CSF £13.79 CT £71.84 TOTE £3.80: £2.20, £1.50, £3.20; EX 13.10.
Owner F Gillespie **Bred** Mrs Mary Furlong **Trained** Cheltenham, Gloucs

FOCUS
A respectable race for the grade, though there suddenly didn't appear to be many still in with chances from three out. The e winner continues to look progressive and is better than the bare result. Several riders hedged their bets as to where the best ground was.

NOTEBOOK
Salpierre(IRE) was kept widest for much of the way, which had the added advantage of giving a gelding still prone to the odd mistake a better sight of his hurdles. Briefly closed down by the runner-up turning for home, the partnership quickly put the matter beyond doubt in a few strides to land the hat-trick. Versatile regarding going types and capable of staying further yet, he remains one to keep on-side. (op 3-1)
Victors Serenade(IRE) repeated the habit evident at Exeter last time of jumping markedly left at least once, but failed in no other regard, just running into a more progressive rival. He can find another race on this evidence and is well worth a try left-handed (yet to go that way round in seven career starts). (op 6-1)
Double Eagle, sporting first-time cheekpieces, fared best of those to help cut out the early pace and didn't curl up despite being outpaced from the penultimate flight. He remains feasibly treated over hurdles having placed off up to 122 in the past, and something can come his way whilst remaining so, possibly over slightly further. (op 11-1)
Stonethrower(IRE) looked a threat with half a mile to go, soon after which the lack of a recent run told on this first effort since April and debut for Tim Vaughan. Further may suit judged on one-paced late efforts at up to 2m6f in Ireland previously, with all going types coming alike, and he can land a small handicap in the coming weeks. (op 14-1)
Graduation Night, stepped back up to 2m6f for this handicap debut, could use further still on this evidence.
Henry Hook(IRE)'s prospects of following up a Towcester win off 10lb lower in November were done no favours by a couple of sticky mid-race jumps. (tchd 7-1)

3371 LINDLEY GROUP H'CAP CHASE (12 fncs 4 omitted) 2m 5f 110y
3:30 (3:30) (Class 4) (0-115,113) 5-Y-0+ **£2,667** (£783; £391; £195)

Form RPR
P42- **1** **Brenin Cwmtudu**[252] 17 8-10-8 102 AdamWedge(7) 113+
(Evan Williams) *midfield: hdwy 5th: wnt 2nd 8th: led after 2 out: edgd lft run-in: drvn out and styd on* **17/2**
P-20 **2** *1 1/4* **Strongbows Legend**[19] 2961 6-11-4 105 AndrewTinkler 114+
(Charlie Longsdon) *hld up: hdwy after 7th: hmpd 8th: effrt after 9th: chsd wnr appr last: no imp on run-in* **5/1**[2]
45-F **3** *9* **Western Whisky (FR)**[51] 2366 9-11-5 106 (p) JodieMogford 104
(Richard Lee) *bhd: reminders after 6th: rdn 9th: styd on fr 2 out: tk 3rd fnl stride: nvr threatened front 2* **12/1**
314U **4** *nse* **Festival Dreams**[19] 2961 6-10-8 95 (b) DaveCrosse 96+
(Joanna Davis) *prom: led 4th: blnd 9th: rdn and hdd after 2 out: wknd last* **16/1**
46-4 **5** *23* **Supreme Keano (IRE)**[40] 2611 9-11-9 110 (p) APMcCoy 90
(Jonjo O'Neill) *j.rt thrght: prom: mstke 8th: wknd appr 2 out* **5/2**[1]
500P **6** *17* **Tyup Pompey (IRE)**[53] 2324 10-11-5 109 LeeStephens(3) 67
(Ann Price) *led: hdd 4th: remained handy tl wknd after 9th* **40/1**
315- **7** *1 3/4* **Cesium (FR)**[263] 5195 6-11-12 113 PaddyBrennan 69
(Tom George) *midfield: hdwy to chse ldrs 5th: wknd after 9th* **14/1**
2040 **8** *2* **Kilvergan Boy (IRE)**[18] 2980 7-10-4 94 SamTwiston-Davies(3) 48
(Nigel Twiston-Davies) *trckd ldrs: lost pl 8th: mstke 9th: toiling after* **9/1**
P-00 **9** *2 1/2* **Mokum (FR)**[19] 2961 10-10-11 98 WayneHutchinson 49
(Tony Carroll) *a bhd: pckd 5th: nvr on terms* **33/1**
31F4 **10** *17* **High Jack (IRE)**[47] 2453 9-11-7 108 NickScholfield 42
(Andy Turnell) *trckd ldrs: lost pl 5th: hit 6th: n.d after* **20/1**
0-11 **P** **Irish Guard**[18] 2986 10-11-9 110 AndrewThornton —
(John O'Neill) *hld up: hdwy into midfield 5th: wknd 9th: t.o whn p.u bef 3 out* **8/1**
452F **P** **Russian Song (IRE)**[19] 2959 7-11-6 107 JoeTizzard —
(Colin Tizzard) *hld up: hit 4th: blnd 6th: bhd whn p.u bef 7th* **11/2**[3]

5m 27.6s (7.60) **Going Correction** +0.325s/f (Yiel) **12** Ran SP% **122.6**
Speed ratings: **99,98,95,95,86 80,80,79,78,72 —,—**
toteswingers: 1&2 £15.30, 1&3 £22.60, 2&3 £44.60 CSF £52.72 CT £525.99 TOTE £15.60: £3.30, £2.70, £3.60; EX 71.20.
Owner T Hywel Jones **Bred** Mrs C J C Bailey **Trained** Llancarfan, Vale Of Glamorgan
■ Stewards' Enquiry : Dave Crosse caution; excessive use of whip

FOCUS
The pace looked fair from the outset in this moderate handicap, and very few were still meaningfully involved with half a mile to travel. Reasonable form for the level, with a chase personal best from the winner.

NOTEBOOK
Brenin Cwmtudu had more in hand than the official verdict having idled a touch up the run-in, and his passage throughout the race hadn't been the most untroubled either (hampered at least once). His record in races after an absence more than two months now reads: 61413131, including all four career victories, and an adequate break after this race will likely prove the most fundamental factor to his chances of following up. (op 9-1 tchd 8-1)
Strongbows Legend is still only eight races into his career and betrayed his inexperience over fences on occasions (rider reported gelding had jumped left afterwards). He appeared to cope well with the 3f step up in trip though, and he can find a comparable contest if the jumping goes the right way from here. Official explanation: jockey said gelding hung left handed (op 11-2)

Western Whisky(FR), a Ludlow soft-ground 3m winner, found this on the sharp side and was nearest at the finish. Confidence will at least have been restored after his haphazard display at Uttoxeter last time.
Festival Dreams, who unseated behind Strongbows Legend at Newbury last time, eventually faded after crashing through the fourth-last. Safe enough when winning at Uttoxeter in October, he's become a bit of a risky proposition since. (op 20-1)
Supreme Keano(IRE) entered the race 6lb below the mark he placed twice off at Haydock and Ffos Las this time last year, and was the subject of warm support. Already in receipt of a reminder after three fences, however, backers soon knew their fate as errors started to creep in, and it may be that courses with longer straights where he can sort his jumping out better are an absolute must for him nowadays. Official explanation: jockey said gelding hung and jumped right handed (op 4-1)
High Jack(IRE) (op 18-1)
Irish Guard's handicap chase record off marks of 100 or higher now reads: PFP8P, so a raise of 20lb for two wins before Christmas has probably rendered another victory in the short term unlikely. (op 6-1 tchd 5-1)
Russian Song(IRE) pulled up sharply after major blunder just after the stands. (op 6-1 tchd 5-1)

3372 LINDLEY GROUP STANDARD OPEN NATIONAL HUNT FLAT RACE 2m 1f
4:00 (4:00) (Class 6) 4-6-Y-O **£1,301** (£382; £191; £95)

Form RPR
5 **1** **Hayjack**[19] 2957 6-11-5 0 SamThomas 110+
(Venetia Williams) *a.p: led 6f out: rdn over 1f out: r.o wl to draw clr ins fnl f* **16/1**
3 **2** *3 ¾* **Dineur (FR)**[53] 2335 5-11-5 0 WayneHutchinson 106+
(Alan King) *racd keenly: hld up in rr: hdwy after 5f: effrt to chse ldrs over 2f out: wnt 2nd over 1f out: nt qckn and no imp on wnr ins fnl f* **9/2**[3]
6 **3** *2 ¼* **Theatrical Star**[50] 2389 5-11-5 0 JoeTizzard 104+
(Colin Tizzard) *in tch: upsides and gng wl 6f out: ev ch 2f out: rdn over 1f out and nt qckn: one pce fnl f* **11/8**[1]
4 *14* **Hoare Abbey (IRE)** 5-11-5 0 PaddyBrennan 90
(Tom George) *hld up: hdwy to trck ldrs 6f out: rdn over 2f out: sn btn* **5/2**[2]
5 *4* **Tickle Me (IRE)** 5-11-5 0 HaddenFrost 86
(Henrietta Knight) *prom tl pushed along and wknd over 2f out* **16/1**
0-0 **6** *11* **Russian Conquest**[239] 238 5-10-9 0 DarrenO'Keeffe[(10)] 75
(Seamus Mullins) *racd keenly: midfield: hdwy after 5f: lost pl 1 m out: wl outpcd 4f out: n.d after* **50/1**
7 *10* **Crystal Cliche** 6-10-12 0 DarylJacob 58
(Julian Smith) *hld up: struggling 5f out: nvr on terms* **100/1**
0-0 **8** *hd* **Victory Bay**[169] 1029 6-11-5 0 NickScholfield 65
(Simon Burrough) *hld up: outpcd 4f out: nvr on terms* **100/1**
9 *5* **Great Kicker (IRE)** 6-11-5 0 HarrySkelton 60
(Paul Nicholls) *racd keenly: handy: effrt 4f out: wknd 3f out* **8/1**
0-00 **10** *59* **Castle Legend**[50] 2389 6-10-12 0 MissCBoxall[(7)] 1
(Simon Lewis) *racd keenly: led: hdd 6f out: rdn and wknd 5f out: t.o* **100/1**

4m 10.6s (16.80) **Going Correction** +0.325s/f (Yiel) **10** Ran SP% **116.7**
Speed ratings: **73,71,70,63,61 56,51,51,49,21**
CSF £86.70 TOTE £8.90: £2.30, £1.70, £1.20; EX 42.00.
Owner James Hayman-Joyce & HJ Racing **Bred** P R And Mrs J F Emery **Trained** Kings Caple, H'fords

FOCUS
Very little in the way of pace on here, and the field remained closely grouped until past halfway. There was something of a sprint finish. The first three are probably all above average.

NOTEBOOK
Hayjack, always well placed, coped best with the sprint finish that ensued and powered up the home turn to emulate his dam in landing a contest in this sphere. This may not represent a huge leap up on the form of his debut fifth in a well-run Bangor contest a month earlier, but this nice, big jumping type is likely to come into his own granted a longer trip and obstacles in any event. (op 9-1)
Dineur(FR) ◆, who refused to settle on debut at Taunton, was already over-keen in the paddock on this occasion, and carried that out onto the course with him. That he was still able to keep meaningfully involved until the final furlong having pulled so hard early on either says a fair bit for him, or less for most of those he beat. Either way, he is certainly capable of better in this sphere once learning to relax. (op 4-1 tchd 7-2)
Theatrical Star, green pitched straight into Listed company at Cheltenham on his debut, wasn't entirely settled early on either but calmed down sooner than the runner-up. Although a brother to one bumper winner in Alegralil, he does look in need of a trip and hurdles now. (op 2-1)
Hoare Abbey(IRE) is out of a bumper winner who has already produced two scorers in this sphere herself, but having received a waiting ride seemed to be struggling to make up the ground some way before the turn for home. He may still be a touch weak and can prove better than this. (op 3-1 tchd 9-4)
Great Kicker(IRE)'s half-brother Kicks For Free won his first two bumpers for Paul Nicholls, but there didn't seem any major confidence in him going the first step to emulating that (did drift to 11-1 at one point), and he never looked about to respond sufficiently for pressure once it was applied. (op 7-1 tchd 11-1)
T/Plt: £5.30 to a £1 stake. Pool: £60,808.90. 8,294.01 winning tickets. T/Qpdt: £4.00 to a £1 stake. Pool: £3,844.58. 698.15 winning tickets. DO

2896 LINGFIELD (L-H)
Monday, January 3

OFFICIAL GOING: Heavy (chs 3.4, hdl 3.6)
Wind: Nil Weather: Overcast

3373 HAXTED CONDITIONAL JOCKEYS' H'CAP CHASE (14 fncs) 2m 4f 110y
1:10 (1:12) (Class 4) (0-105,96) 5-Y-O+ **£2,808** (£818; £409)

Form RPR
-400 **1** **Massini Sunset (IRE)**[18] 2975 11-11-7 **96** (b) SClements[(5)] 108+
(Richard Mitchell) *mde all: set sedate pce to 1/2-way: pushed along and wl in command fr 3 out: drew further clr flat* **11/2**[3]
/02- **2** *8* **Quilver Tatou (FR)**[273] 5040 7-11-9 **96** (t) PeterToole[(3)] 99
(Charlie Mann) *chsd wnr: nt fluent 5th: 6th and 8th: shkn up and no imp after 3 out: wl hld whn mstke last* **7/4**[1]
4011 **3** *1 ¾* **Pete The Feat (IRE)**[20] 2950 7-11-12 **96** RichieMcLernon 97
(Anna Newton-Smith) *bmpd 1st: hld up in 3rd: rdn on long run after 11th: effrt to dispute 2nd whn mstke 3 out: wl btn after* **7/4**[1]
14P- **4** *17* **Flashy Conquest**[369] 3179 9-10-6 **76** MrMMO'Connor 69+
(Colin Tizzard) *often j.rt: hld up last: mstke 4th: struggling after 11th: brief rally 3 out: wl btn whn mstke next* **9/2**[2]

5m 33.1s (14.90) **Going Correction** +0.40s/f (Soft) **4** Ran SP% **106.3**
Speed ratings: **87,83,83,76**
CSF £15.01 TOTE £6.80; EX 18.40.
Owner Mr And Mrs Andrew May **Bred** Gerard O'Keeffe **Trained** Piddletrenthide, Dorset

FOCUS
The late withdrawal of Fleur De Vassy made this conditional jockeys' chase a little less competitive but it was run at a sensible pace in the conditions. Sound form, the winner taking advantage of a good mark.

NOTEBOOK
Massini Sunset(IRE) bounced back to form in decent fashion after some lacklustre efforts so far this term. With the blinkers reapplied coupled with the change of tactics, he ran out a very comfortable winner. He was racing off his lowest mark for nearly three years but clearly remains capable on his day, and should not been too harshly reassessed after this. (op 9-2)
Quilver Tatou(FR) racing with a tongue-tie that saw him step up on any previous hurdle form when runner-up on his chasing debut in April, ran a solid enough race on his return to action but could not match the winner's pace from the last. He can find a similar opportunity before long. (op 2-1)
Pete The Feat(IRE) looked to have a golden opportunity to complete his hat-trick off a 6lb higher mark but he came under pressure after the fourth-last and, although he rallied going to three out, which he clouted, he could only keep on at the same pace. He can remain competitive in similar heats. (op 15-8)
Flashy Conquest came in for some support for the in-form Tizzard camp after over a year off. He was rather rusty at his obstacles with his jumping to the right getting progressively worse. He was still in with a shout turning in, but lack of a recent outing was his undoing in these conditions. (op 4-1 tchd 5-1)

3374 MARSH GREEN NOVICES' HURDLE (10 hdls) 2m 3f 110y
1:45 (1:47) (Class 4) 4-Y-O+ **£2,329** (£678; £339)

Form RPR
2 **1** **Captain Kirkton (IRE)**[13] 3054 5-11-6 0 JamieMoore 123+
(Gary Moore) *trckd ldrs: jnd them 3 out: led bef next: pushed along and drew rt away bef last: quite impressive* **11/2**[3]
42-2 **2** *17* **Raduis Bleu (FR)**[55] 2291 6-11-6 114 RobertThornton 108+
(Alan King) *hld up in tch: prog to join ldrs 3 out: shkn up to chal bef 2 out: fnd nil and sn btn* **5/6**[1]
0 **3** *8* **Prince Of Valour (IRE)**[20] 2946 5-11-6 0 DominicElsworth 99
(Lucy Wadham) *hld up in tch: nt fluent 4th: prog on outer 7th: rdn to take 3rd 2 out: no imp after: wl hld whn mstke last* **15/2**
6P **4** *6* **Grey Cruzene (USA)**[20] 2944 5-11-6 0 ColinBolger 92
(Chris Gordon) *disp ld tl bef 2 out: styd on inner and sn wknd: no ch whn mstke last* **200/1**
1- **5** *9* **Gorgehous Lliege (FR)**[287] 4792 5-11-6 0 AidanColeman 83
(Venetia Williams) *trckd ldrs: cl up whn nt fluent 3 out: sn rdn: wknd bef 2 out and styd on inner: bttr for r* **10/1**
0 **6** *3 ½* **Lions In Law**[18] 2981 7-10-13 0 MarkQuinlan[(7)] 80
(Richard Hawker) *disp ld to 6th: sn rdn: wknd after next: sn bhd* **66/1**
4-46 **7** *4 ½* **Cloudy Wager**[44] 2526 6-10-13 0 FelixDeGiles 68
(Anna Newton-Smith) *hld up in last: lost tch 6th: latched on to bk of field next: dropped away again next* **33/1**
110 **8** *14* **Zakeeta (IRE)**[23] 2356 4-10-12 117 LeightonAspell 69+
(Oliver Sherwood) *fractious preliminaries and kpt away fr others at s: disp ld to 3 out: rdn and wknd rapidly bef next: heavily eased* **9/2**[2]
5-0 **9** *54* **Lambro River (IRE)**[13] 3055 6-10-13 0 MrSHanson[(7)] 7
(Alison Batchelor) *mstke 4th: sn dropped to last and lost tch: wl t.o* **66/1**
0P- **P** **Sahara Sunshine**[85] 4257 6-10-13 0 (t) RichardJohnson —
(Laura Mongan) *in tch to 6th: wknd after next: t.o 3 out: last whn p.u bef last* **66/1**

5m 12.2s (5.50) **Going Correction** +0.30s/f (Yiel)
WFA 4 from 5yo+ 11lb **10** Ran SP% **116.9**
Speed ratings (Par 105): **101,94,91,88,85 83,81,76,54,—**
toteswingers: 1&2 £1.30, 1&3 £5.60, 2&3 £2.60 CSF £10.93 TOTE £6.60: £1.70, £1.10, £2.60; EX 12.80.
Owner Miss Gill Arthur **Bred** Hugh O'Connor **Trained** Lower Beeding, W Sussex

FOCUS
An uncompetitive novice hurdle, but an impressive performance in the conditions from the winner. He looks a smart novice, with the second setting a fair standard.

NOTEBOOK
Captain Kirkton(IRE) travelled strongly throughout, and only had to be shaken up going to the last to sprint clear and score with any amount in hand. He had clearly benefited from an AW bumper run last month when second and showing plenty of promise, and jumped well on this hurdling debut. Held in some regard by connections and having a good jumping pedigree, (dam a sister to Celestial Gold), he has a bright future. He will now go for another novice with connections eyeing a possible crack at the EBF Final at Sandown. (op 9-2)
Raduis Bleu(FR) ran another solid race and travelled as well as the winner before clipping the second last, but he could not match the winner's superior pace. He has run creditably over fences and hurdles and was just unlucky to bump into such a promising sort, but with the yard in fine form he will go one better sooner rather than later. (tchd 10-11, Evens in places and 4-5 in places)
Prince Of Valour(IRE) ran well for a long way on his debut for new connections last month and had clearly come on for the run. He stayed on well enough in the straight to suggest he can find an opening over hurdles before switching his attention to fences. (op 10-1 tchd 11-1)
Grey Cruzene(USA) ran a very respectable race after trying to make all. This was a much better effort than on his hurdling debut and he can only build upon this.
Gorgehous Lliege(FR) had landed a touch in Plumpton bumper last season and shaped with promise on this hurdling debut. He has plenty of potential and will improve for the outing. (op 15-2 tchd 13-2)
Zakeeta(IRE) was kept well away from the others at the start and this dual hurdle winner was again a little disappointing, dropping away tamely turning in. (op 7-1)
Sahara Sunshine was reported to have a breathing problem. Official explanation: trainer siad mare had a breathing problem

3375 HOLTYE H'CAP CHASE (12 fncs) 2m
2:15 (2:15) (Class 4) (0-115,113) 5-Y-O+ **£2,808** (£818; £409)

Form RPR
4P-6 **1** **Babe Heffron (IRE)**[240] 213 10-11-5 **106** TomScudamore 120+
(Tom George) *led at fast pce: hdd 3rd: chsd ldr: clsd to ld again 3 out: steadily drew away: pushed out* **9/4**[1]
F510 **2** *8* **Near The Water (IRE)**[19] 2959 7-11-9 **110** LeightonAspell 114
(Richard Rowe) *hld up in last pair and wl off the pce: effrt fr 9th: wnt 4th bef 3 out: no imp tl styd on fr last to take 2nd nr fin* **7/2**[3]
P0-1 **3** *¾* **Baseball Ted (IRE)**[45] 2503 9-11-5 **106** RichardJohnson 109
(Charlie Longsdon) *led 3rd and maintained str pce: 5 l clr 7th: hdd 3 out: sn no ch w wnr: wknd and lost 2nd nr fin* **11/2**
02/ **4** *1 ½* **Kasimali (IRE)**[295] 4633 8-11-2 **103** JamieMoore 105
(Gary Moore) *pushed along in last pair early and wl off the pce: effrt to go 3rd bef 3 out: one pce and no imp after* **8/1**
5030 **5** *26* **Sieglinde (FR)**[13] 3057 5-9-11 **95** MrSHanson[(7)] 67
(Alison Batchelor) *chsd clr ldng pair to 6th: lft in 3rd pl again 8th to 9th: sn wknd: t.o* **16/1**

-423 **6** *5* **Stradbrook (IRE)**[6] 3154 9-11-6 **110**........................ RichieMcLernon(3) 101+
(Jonjo O'Neill) *hld up in 4th: trckd clr ldng pair 6th: abt 6 l down and gng wl enough whn stmbld bdly on landing 8th lost all ch: tried to rally bef 3 out: eased bef next: t.o* **11/4**[2]

4m 13.5s (5.70) **Going Correction** +0.40s/f (Soft)
WFA 5 from 7yo+ 3lb **6** Ran SP% **112.0**
Speed ratings: **101,97,96,95,82 80**
toteswingers: 1&2 £4.20, 1&3 £1.70, 2&3 £1.60 CSF £10.75 TOTE £4.30: £1.80, £2.10; EX 11.80.
Owner Simon Clarke & David Thorpe **Bred** D And Mrs Noonan **Trained** Slad, Gloucs

FOCUS
An ordinary handicap run at a good clip, and easy form to rate.

NOTEBOOK
Babe Heffron(IRE), after battling for the lead early, was wisely restrained back to allow the leader to bowl along at a good pace, and had plenty left in the tank to draw clear after regaining the lead three out. A market mover in the morning and proven in testing conditions, he had a lot going for him as he had also slipped to a favourable mark with the stable hitting form. Obviously, he will find life more difficult after being reassessed but he has been a good servant to the yard since joining them and can continue to pay his way. (op 5-2)
Near The Water(IRE) was a C&D winner in November and can be forgiven his run over 3m in better race at Newbury last time. Although, this was another respectable effort he never got involved from the rear until staying on in the straight to snatch second nearing the finish. (op 9-2)
Baseball Ted(IRE) returned to form, on debut for this yard, at Exeter in November but, after running freely in the lead, he had little more to offer when headed in the straight and was a spent force when failing to hold on to the runner-up spot nearing the finish. (op 7-2)
Kasimali(IRE), on his first run for 295 days and on his debut for Gary Moore, could only stay on at the same pace in the straight. Most of his form has been over further than the minimum in Ireland, and he will be seen in a truer light when upped in trip with this run under his belt. (op 7-1)
Stradbrook(IRE) was on the heels of the leaders when making a hash of five out and was soon beaten. (op 7-2)

3376 TANDRIDGE MAIDEN HURDLE (8 hdls) 2m 110y
2:50 (2:50) (Class 5) 4-Y-0+ **£2,055** (£599; £299)

Form RPR
00-2 **1** **Shinrock Hill (IRE)**[29] 2791 7-11-5 117........................ RichardJohnson 116+
(Philip Hobbs) *mde all at stdy pce: shkn up whn pressed after 2 out: styd on wl flat* **8/11**[1]

60 **2** *3 ½* **Remember Now (IRE)**[63] 2122 5-11-0 0........................ DavidBass(5) 113+
(Nicky Henderson) *t.k.h: hld up in 4th: effrt after 3 out: chsd wnr 2 out: cl enough last: shkn up and no ex* **4/1**[2]

0-5 **3** *10* **General Eliott (IRE)**[37] 2667 6-11-2 0........................ TomMolloy(3) 103
(Frederick Sutherland) *settled in last: nt fluent 1st: sme prog on outer after 3 out: wnt 4th 2 out: nt pce to threaten: shkn up and tk 3rd last: kpt on* **11/2**[3]

4 *10* **Time Book (IRE)**[405] 5-11-5 0........................ JamieMoore 95
(Gary Moore) *trckd ldng pair: wnt 2nd 3 out to next: sn wknd* **10/1**

50P- **5** *4* **Beat The Devil**[388] 2815 5-11-2 0........................ PeterToole(3) 89
(Tom George) *hld up in last pair: effrt after 5th: shkn up after 3 out: no prog bef next: wknd* **50/1**

36 **6** *3 ½* **Mut'Ab (USA)**[63] 2129 6-10-12 0........................ JoshuaMoore(7) 87
(Gary Moore) *hld up in 6th: chsd ldng trio 3 out: wkng whn mstke next* **16/1**

66 **7** *43* **Good Buy Dubai (USA)**[13] 3058 5-11-5 0........................ TimmyMurphy 42
(Edward Creighton) *trckd wnr to 5th: wkng whn mstke next: sn t.o* **50/1**

4m 15.7s (1.60) **Going Correction** +0.30s/f (Yiel) **7** Ran SP% **112.2**
Speed ratings (Par 103): **108,106,101,96,95 93,73**
toteswingers: 1&2 £1.10, 1&3 £1.50, 2&3 £3.70 CSF £3.90 TOTE £1.70: £1.10, £2.50; EX 4.20.
Owner R S Brookhouse **Bred** P J Fenton **Trained** Withycombe, Somerset

FOCUS
An ordinary novice hurdle run at a steady pace. Not an easy race to put a figure on, it has been rated through the winner to his previous best.

NOTEBOOK
Shinrock Hill(IRE) was found a good opportunity to build upon the promise shown when chasing home The Reformer last month at odds of 100-1. He failed to go on from Irish point success when with David Pipe last season but has posted two respectable efforts now for Philip Hobbs. He looks as though he will stay further and has the stamp of a chaser, so connections have plenty of options for the 7-y-o. (op 8-13 tchd 5-6)
Remember Now(IRE) had only shown modest form in two previous runs in similar contests but this was a step in the right direction. A half-brother to Binocular, he clearly has some ability and is beginning to learn to settle. He travelled well when challenging going to two out but, when asked, his effort soon flattened out. A handicap looks within his compass as he now qualifies for a mark. (op 5-1 tchd 7-2)
General Eliott(IRE) retains most of his ability on the Flat and travelled well into the race here entering the straight but, as with the runner-up, his effort soon petered out in the conditions. He looks capable of finding an opening judged on this and his fair fifth in a competitive novice at Newbury last time. (op 7-1 tchd 15-2 and 5-1)
Time Book(IRE) won his last of four runs over middle-distances on the Flat and conditions were probably testing enough for him here but this was a promising effort nonetheless. (op 9-1)

3377 LINGFIELDPARK.CO.UK H'CAP CHASE (18 fncs) 3m
3:20 (3:20) (Class 5) (0-95,95) 5-Y-0+ **£2,055** (£599; £299)

Form RPR
-P22 **1** **Hobb's Dream (IRE)**[50] 2391 7-9-13 **75**........................(p) MarkQuinlan(7) 93+
(Neil Mulholland) *a gng wl: in tch: prog 11th: led 13th: mde most after: drew clr fr 3 out: pushed out* **4/1**[2]

P0-P **2** *13* **Quazy De Joie (FR)**[18] 2982 7-11-8 **94**........................(t) RichieMcLernon(3) 100
(Jonjo O'Neill) *hld up in tch: mstke 6th and reminders: prog 12th: rdn 15th: chsd wnr 3 out: sn lft bhd* **7/1**

P0P0 **3** *½* **Brushford (IRE)**[21] 2930 7-10-11 **80**........................(t) LeightonAspell 85
(Chris Gordon) *cl up on inner: jnd ldrs 13th: chsd wnr 15th to 3 out: sn outpcd* **12/1**

4/32 **4** *¾* **Billy Murphy**[20] 2950 8-11-7 **90**........................ MarkBradburne 96
(Paul Cowley) *nt a fluent: chsd ldrs: pushed along 10th: rdn to stay in tch whn mstke 15th: outpcd fr 3 out: kpt on* **9/2**[3]

/F34 **5** *13* **Commanche Dawn**[20] 2950 9-10-0 **69** oh9........................ JamieMoore 60
(Gerry Enright) *settled in last: blnd 4th: rdn fr 10th: sn lost tch: tried to plug on bef 3 out: no real prog after* **16/1**

1-21 **6** *1* **Portrait Royale (IRE)**[48] 2444 9-11-12 **95**........................ FelixDeGiles 89+
(Anna Newton-Smith) *trckd ldng pair to 11th: lost pl and rdn 13th: tried to rally after 15th: hld whn mstke 3 out: wknd 2 out: eased* **11/4**[1]

-320 **7** *17* **Kiltimoney (IRE)**[20] 2950 11-10-0 **69**........................ TomScudamore 57+
(Richard Mitchell) *w ldr: mstke 6th: lost pl 11th: rallied and w ldrs again 13th: drvn and wkng whn sprawled on landing 3 out: eased* **15/2**

-P03 **P** **Wide Receiver (IRE)**[43] 2557 8-10-9 **78**........................(v) GerardTumelty —
(Charlie Morlock) *mde most to 12th: wknd rapidly 14th: t.o whn p.u bef 3 out* **11/1**

6-0P **P** **Peter Sent**[60] 2172 9-11-8 **94**........................ PeterToole(3) —
(Tom George) *cl up gng wl: hmpd 6th: led 12th tl hdd and mstke next: wl on terms after 14th: wknd rapidly and mstke 15th: t.o whn p.u bef 3 out* **20/1**

6m 31.0s (7.30) **Going Correction** +0.40s/f (Soft) **9** Ran SP% **115.8**
Speed ratings: **103,98,98,98,93 93,87,—,—**
toteswingers: 1&2 £10.50, 1&3 £43.80, 2&3 £43.80 CSF £32.30 CT £309.07 TOTE £3.80: £1.30, £3.30, £4.80; EX 44.50.
Owner John & Jeanette Hobbs & P J Proudley **Bred** Mrs A R Mulholland **Trained** Burlescombe, Devon

FOCUS
A low-grade staying handicap. A small personal best from the winner with the fourth the best guide.

NOTEBOOK
Hobb's Dream(IRE) finished full of running to draw right away from the rest of the field and record a very easy success. He travelled well all the way and had everything off the bridle going to three out. He holds few secrets and life will become tough after the handicapper assesses this performance. (op 5-1)
Quazy De Joie(FR) was well-in based on his seconds here and at Warwick with the tongue-tie back on after pulling up on his reappearance. Apart from a mistake two out his jumping was sound enough, and he ran respectably, although never having any chance with the winner. (tchd 15-2)
Brushford(IRE) has been struggling to recapture his form this term but this was a better effort stepping up in distance. He has slipped to a mark below that of his last successful one and had his chance here, but could only muster the same pace from three out. (op 14-1)
Billy Murphy acts in the conditions and had solid claims here based on his two runs after returning to action following 19 months off. He was struggling from a fair way out and could never land a blow. (op 5-1 tchd 11-2)
Commanche Dawn was another who was struggling in the back straight and could never get involved.
Portrait Royale(IRE) was up another 5lb for her recent Folkestone success and was well supported to add to her fine record, but was under pressure going to five out. She did rally three out but had little more to offer from two out and might be in the grip of the handicapper. (op 5-2 tchd 9-4 and 3-1)
Kiltimoney(IRE) was still fighting it out for a place when slipping on landing three out. (op 8-1)

3378 BREATHE SPA AT MARRIOTT LINGFIELD H'CAP HURDLE (8 hdls) 2m 110y
3:50 (3:50) (Class 4) (0-110,110) 4-Y-0+ **£2,329** (£678; £339)

Form RPR
30-U **1** **Rosoff (IRE)**[239] 219 9-10-5 **89**........................(p) RichardJohnson 98+
(Laura Mongan) *hld up: mstke 4th: prog to ld bef 2 out: styd on wl* **7/1**[2]

40-1 **2** *3 ½* **Oscar Prairie (IRE)**[48] 2440 6-11-10 **108**........................(t) LeightonAspell 114+
(Warren Greatrex) *cl up: chal bef 2 out: chsd wnr after: no imp last* **4/9**[1]

4-P0 **3** *26* **Sebastiano (FR)**[41] 2596 8-11-9 **110**........................ EamonDehdashti(3) 90
(Gary Moore) *led to 3rd: pushed along 5th: led after 3 out tl bef next: wknd* **11/1**

6125 **4** *¾* **Just Beware**[48] 2442 9-10-11 **100**........................(p) GemmaGracey-Davison(5) 80
(Zoe Davison) *racd wd: led 3rd tl after 3 out: upsides bef 2 out: wknd* **10/1**

-665 **P** **Reefer Beefer (IRE)**[39] 2634 6-11-2 **100**........................ RobertThornton —
(Tony Newcombe) *mstkes: t.o fr 5th: p.u bef 2 out* **8/1**[3]

4m 16.7s (2.60) **Going Correction** +0.30s/f (Yiel) **5** Ran SP% **110.3**
Speed ratings (Par 105): **105,103,91,90,—**
CSF £11.29 TOTE £11.00: £3.70, £1.02; EX 18.40.
Owner Mrs P J Sheen **Bred** G Coppola **Trained** Epsom, Surrey

FOCUS
Only a small field and fairly uncompetitive, but it produced a bit of a shock. The winner is rated back to something like his best.

NOTEBOOK
Rosoff(IRE), returning from eight months off, looked in trouble briefly when awkward four out but he found enough resolve to take up the running in the straight, staying on strongly for a ready success. He was well-in on his form of two years ago and likes the conditions, which connections have been waiting for, but it will remain to be seen if he can go on from this. (op 9-1)
Oscar Prairie(IRE) was coming here off the back of a success of an ordinary novice hurdle at Folkestone. He had his chance turning in but was made to look very one-paced by the winner after two out, and might have been better suited by forcing an even stronger gallop. (op 1-2 after 4-6 in places, tchd 4-7 in places)
Sebastiano(FR) is suited by conditions but got very tired after holding every chance going to two out. (op 9-1)
Just Beware, back up in the weights, also had little more to give after holding her chance turning in (op 8-1 tchd 11-1)
Reefer Beefer(IRE) was never particularly fluent at his obstacles and was struggling from a long way out. (tchd 15-2)
T/Plt: £87.60 to a £1 stake.Pool: £53,947.18. 449.31 winning tickets. T/Qpdt: £12.70 to a £1 stake. Pool: £4,085.84. 236.70 winning tickets. JN

3379 - 3385a (Foreign Racing) - See Raceform Interactive

2419 LEICESTER (R-H)
Tuesday, January 4

OFFICIAL GOING: Hurdle course - soft (good to soft in places; 6.4) chase course - good (good to firm in places, soft on flat crossings; 8.2)
Wind: Light behind Weather: Overcast

3386 WIDMERPOOL NOVICES' HURDLE (DIV I) (8 hdls) 2m
12:50 (12:50) (Class 4) 4-Y-0+ **£1,886** (£553; £276; £138)

Form RPR
1 **Credit Swap**[94] 6-11-5 0........................ AidanColeman 121+
(Venetia Williams) *hld up in tch: tk clsr order 3 out: led last: rdn and r.o wl: eased nr fin* **4/1**[3]

P/13 **2** *4 ½* **Alarazi (IRE)**[21] 2944 7-11-12 118........................ DominicElsworth 119
(Lucy Wadham) *hld up: hdwy 4th: chsd ldr next: led appr 2 out: rdn and hdd last: styd on same pce flat* **11/4**[1]

0-2 **3** *3 ½* **Marching Song (USA)**[141] 284 5-11-5 0........................ NickScholfield 109
(Andy Turnell) *hld up: hdwy appr 2 out: wnt 3rd and mstke last: styd on same pce* **11/1**

1 **4** *4* **Dance For Julie (IRE)**[35] 1018 4-10-7 0........................ BarryKeniry 92
(Ben Haslam) *led 2nd: hdd appr 2 out: wknd bef last* **10/3**[2]

5 *2 ¾* **Desert Cry (IRE)**[108] 5-11-5 0........................ JasonMaguire 102
(Donald McCain) *trckd ldrs: racd keenly: wknd appr last* **7/1**

05 **6** *1 ½* **Cridda Boy**[40] 2633 5-10-12 0........................(t) NathanSweeney(7) 99
(Simon Burrough) *hld up in tch: nt fluent 4th: wknd 3 out* **150/1**

1 **7** *7* **Break The Chain**[57] 2282 5-11-12 0........................ AndrewThornton 100
(Caroline Bailey) *trckd ldrs: rdn after 3 out: sn wknd* **7/1**

60- **8** *2 ½* **Golden Dream (IRE)**[394] 2738 7-11-5 0........................ SamThomas 90
(Caroline Bailey) *hld up: rdn after 5th: a in rr* **40/1**

P5-0 **9** *11* **Valid Point (IRE)**[62] 2145 5-11-5 0 .... RhysFlint 79
(Jim Old) *prom tl rdn and wknd after 3 out: t.o* **40/1**
65 **10** *9* **Gtaab**[64] 2122 5-11-5 0 .... DenisO'Regan 70
(Paul Webber) *led to 2nd: chsd ldr to 5th: rdn and wknd bef next: t.o* **16/1**
000 **11** *4 ½* **Body Gold (ARG)**[57] 2281 8-11-2 0 .... SamTwiston-Davies(3) 65
(Nigel Twiston-Davies) *hld up: bhd fr 3rd: t.o* **80/1**
6000 **12** *14* **Sablazo (FR)**[14] 3058 5-10-12 0 .... MrBJPoste(7) 51
(Andy Turnell) *chsd ldrs: rdn after 5th: wknd bef next: t.o* **100/1**

3m 51.5s (-9.50) **Going Correction** -0.40s/f (Good)
WFA 4 from 5yo+ 11lb **12** Ran SP% **116.7**
Speed ratings (Par 105): **107,104,103,101,99 98,95,94,88,84 81,74**
Tote Swingers: 1&2 £3.70, 1&3 £13.30, 2&3 £5.40 CSF £15.42 TOTE £3.80: £1.10, £2.20, £3.70; EX 20.00.
Owner M J Pilkington **Bred** Jeremy Green And Sons **Trained** Kings Caple, H'fords

FOCUS
An interesting novices' hurdle featuring several unexposed types and a couple of useful ex-Flat performers. Credit Swap is promising and the race should produce winners.

NOTEBOOK
Credit Swap was having his first run for new connections and first start since winning the Cambridgeshire. He picked up well from off the pace and settled the issue after the last, recording an ultimately comfortable success. He looks sure to go on to better things given his favoured soft ground. He was given a 33/1 quote for the Supreme Novices' Hurdle. (tchd 5-1)
Alarazi(IRE), who had scored over C&D in November, set the standard off 118. Sent off favourite, he raced much closer to the pace than on his previous start but, after leading early in the straight, was no match for the potentially classy winner. (op 3-1)
Marching Song(USA), returning from a break since running on the Flat in August, was held up before making good headway to reach the heels of the leaders at the penultimate flight. He had no more to offer from that point, but the outing should bring him on. (op 12-1 tchd 10-1)
Dance For Julie(IRE) was well backed follow up her winning hurdling debut back in the summer. She raced up with the pace until fading early in the straight and, although a soft-ground winner on the Flat, she may appreciate better ground in this discipline. (op 5-1)
Desert Cry(IRE) was a useful Flat performer in Italy but was too keen early on this hurdling debut for new connections. In the circumstances this was not a bad effort, and he can build on this if settling better. (op 9-2)
Cridda Boy ran his best race over hurdles so far on this third start and, now qualified for a handicap mark, can find his level in that sphere.
Break The Chain was having his first run since winning on his debut on a sound surface in November. He proved far less effective on this softer going. (op 13-2)

3387 WIDMERPOOL NOVICES' HURDLE (DIV II) (8 hdls) 2m
1:20 (1:20) (Class 4) 4-Y-0+ **£1,886** (£553; £276; £138)

Form RPR
2-31 **1** **Frascati Park (IRE)**[46] 2493 7-11-12 132 .... PaddyBrennan 101+
(Nigel Twiston-Davies) *mde all: clr tl 2 out: styd on* **8/15**[1]
14/5 **2** *1 ¾* **Araldur (FR)**[242] 191 7-11-5 140 .... RobertThornton 122+
(Alan King) *a.p: chsd wnr and mstke 4th: cl enough 2 out: styd on same pce flat* **11/4**[2]
230 **3** *20* **High Hoylander**[21] 2943 5-11-5 0 .... HenryOliver 102
(Sue Smith) *hld up and bhd: hdwy 3 out: wnt 11 l 3rd next: sn wknd* **25/1**
06 **4** *4* **Mayolynn (USA)**[55] 2310 5-11-0 0 ow2 .... AndrewThornton 93
(Caroline Bailey) *chsd ldr to 4th: remained handy tl rdn and wknd appr 2 out* **50/1**
0 **5** *8* **Cruise Control**[14] 2322 5-11-5 0 .... GerardTumelty 90
(Richard Price) *hld up: nvr on terms: t.o* **66/1**
460 **6** *7* **Rhyton (IRE)**[93] 1696 4-10-7 0 .... AdrianLane 71
(Donald McCain) *hld up: hdwy appr 5th: wknd next: t.o* **66/1**
0-0 **7** *4* **Shalambar (IRE)**[38] 2667 5-11-5 0 .... WayneHutchinson 79
(Tony Carroll) *chsd ldrs tl wknd 5th: t.o* **25/1**
8 *8* **Speed Dating**[94] 5-11-5 0 .... DougieCostello 71
(John Quinn) *mid-div: hdwy appr 5th: rdn and wknd after 3 out: t.o* **7/1**[3]
500 **9** *hd* **Aine's Delight (IRE)**[14] 3057 5-10-12 0 .... NickScholfield 64
(Andy Turnell) *hld up: plld hrd: mstke 2nd: hdwy 5th: wknd bef next: t.o* **66/1**

3m 51.3s (-9.70) **Going Correction** -0.40s/f (Good)
WFA 4 from 5yo+ 11lb **9** Ran SP% **118.5**
Speed ratings (Par 105): **108,107,97,95,91 87,85,81,81**
Tote Swingers: 1&2 £1.10, 1&3 £3.20, 2&3 £2.90 CSF £2.33 TOTE £1.80: £1.02, £1.10, £6.20; EX 2.40.
Owner Barry Connell **Bred** J Mangan **Trained** Naunton, Gloucs
■ Stewards' Enquiry : Andrew Thornton three-day ban: jockey weighed in 2lb heavy (Jan 18-20)

FOCUS
This second division looked less competitive after several withdrawals. They bet 25-1 bar three and it was a match between the market leaders in the straight. The winner is rated 10lb off his previous best.

NOTEBOOK
Frascati Park(IRE) who had previously finished placed in four Grade 2s, followed up his Ascot success in determined style. He coped with the drop in trip, making all the running and finding more when challenged at the second-last. These two successes should boost his confidence for a step back up in grade, and he will go for a 2m3½f handicap hurdle back at Ascot later in the month. (op 8-13 tchd 4-6 in places)
Araldur(FR), a Grade 2 winner over fences back in 2008, had run creditably on his first try over hurdles in May. A much bigger individual than the winner, he loomed up looking a big danger in the straight, but his jumping was not as slick as that rival and he was always being held from the penultimate flight. This should help put him right for a return to fences. (tchd 3-1)
High Hoylander, a keen sort who had been placed in two of his three bumpers, again took a good hold on this hurdling debut. He ran on from the rear without troubling the principals and can do better in time. (op 28-1)
Mayolynn(USA) ran creditably on this third start over hurdles and now qualifies for a mark. She can do better in handicaps against her own sex. (op 33-1)
Speed Dating, a four-time winner at up to 1m4f on the Flat, tracked the leaders until dropping away tamely in the straight on this hurdling debut. He looked in need of this outing but is probably better suited by a sounder surface in any case. (tchd 13-2)

3388 HAPPY 18TH BIRTHDAY GEORGINA STEVENSON H'CAP CHASE (15 fncs) 2m 4f 110y
1:50 (1:50) (Class 5) (0-90,90) 5-Y-0+ **£2,055** (£599; £299)

Form RPR
324P **1** **Autumn Red (IRE)**[62] 2155 11-11-12 90 .... (tp) DenisO'Regan 101+
(Paul Webber) *chsd ldrs: lost pl bef 2nd: cajoled along in rr tl hdwy 11th: drvn to ld fnl 75yds* **7/1**[3]
4423 **2** *nk* **Monty's Moon (IRE)**[122] 1468 9-10-5 69 .... (b) AidanColeman 79
(Rachel Hobbs) *hld up: hdwy u.p appr 3 out: drvn to ld flat: hdd fnl 75yds* **4/1**[1]
P36U **3** *4* **Phar Again (IRE)**[44] 2555 8-10-13 80 .... (vt) TommyPhelan(3) 87
(Claire Dyson) *a.p: chsd ldr 7th: led 2 out: rdn and hdd flat: styd on same pce* **8/1**
1-61 **4** *13* **Guns Of Love (IRE)**[54] 2334 9-11-2 80 .... CharliePoste 75
(Robin Dickin) *chsd ldr: led 3rd: nt fluent 10th: rdn and hdd 2 out: wknd last* **15/2**
5050 **5** *5* **Kinkeel (IRE)**[4] 3265 12-10-10 77 .... EamonDehdashti(3) 69+
(Tony Carroll) *hld up: nt fluent 3rd: hdwy after 5th: wknd appr last* **12/1**
0-03 **6** *1 ¾* **Copper Sound**[21] 2947 7-11-4 82 .... (tp) TomScudamore 70
(Michael Scudamore) *led to 3rd: chsd ldr: nt fluent 6th (water): mstke next: wknd 11th* **7/1**[3]
-143 **7** *10* **Reelwill (FR)**[44] 2559 6-10-11 75 .... TomMessenger 51
(Chris Bealby) *prom: rdn appr 4 out: wknd bef next: t.o* **7/1**[3]
U/P5 **8** *19* **Byways Boy**[44] 2555 8-10-13 77 .... (b[1]) AndrewThornton 34
(Caroline Bailey) *chsd ldrs tl wknd 9th: t.o* **16/1**
0P05 **P** **Kercabellec (FR)**[51] 2402 13-9-7 64 oh3 .... JoeCornwall(7) —
(John Cornwall) *prom: lost pl 5th: hdwy 9th: mstke and wknd 11th: t.o whn p.u bef next* **25/1**
F24P **F** **Mr Bond (IRE)**[19] 2982 8-11-9 87 .... NickScholfield —
(Andy Turnell) *hld up: hdwy to go 4 l 3rd and gng wl whn fell 3 out* **11/2**[2]

5m 13.2s (-5.70) **Going Correction** -0.40s/f (Good) **10** Ran SP% **113.2**
Speed ratings: **94,93,92,87,85 84,81,73,—,—**
Tote Swingers: 1&2 £4.30, 1&3 £11.30, 2&3 £7.90 CSF £35.09 CT £228.10 TOTE £10.00: £2.20, £1.60, £3.10; EX 36.00.
Owner Dodson & Partners **Bred** Liam Ryan **Trained** Mollington, Oxon
■ Stewards' Enquiry : Denis O'Regan five-day ban: jockey used whip excessivly causing gelding to be wealed (Jan 20-24)

FOCUS
As is often the case here, the ground was riding much faster on the chase course than the hurdles track. An open contest judging from the market, and a race of changing fortunes. The winner is rated in line with his 2010 best.

NOTEBOOK
Autumn Red(IRE), with cheekpieces replacing the blinkers he has been wearing of late, never looked to be going that well and was at the back for most of the way. Only seventh jumping three out, he stayed on as the leaders tired and got to the front on the run-in, despite drifting left, to gain a belated first success. His rider subsequently got a five-day ban as the vet reported after the race that the horse was marked. (op 8-1)
Monty's Moon(IRE), having his first start since September, was held up at the back but had to be ridden to make ground from the home turn. He had every chance at the last, but could not find a change of gear on the flat. (op 5-1)
Phar Again(IRE), with a visor replacing the cheekpieces he has been wearing in recent runs, showed plenty of enthusiasm and got to the front before the last. However, he was soon challenged and had nothing more to offer. This trip and a sound surface seems to suit him best. (tchd 15-2)
Guns Of Love(IRE), 8lb higher for his win at Taunton in November, made much of the running but ran out of stamina from the second-last. A drop back to the minimum trip will be in his favour. (op 13-2)
Kinkeel(IRE) ran reasonably but was hesitant at several fences after an early mistake.
Copper Sound lost a prominent early position and never got back into contention. (op 8-1 tchd 17-2)
Mr Bond(IRE) was probably the unlucky horse of the race. Held up early, he was making good headway in front of the principals when taking a heavy fall at the last ditch, three out. The way he was travelling suggests he would have won had he stood up. (tchd 6-1)

3389 LOUGHBOROUGH MARES' MAIDEN HURDLE (10 hdls) 2m 4f 110y
2:20 (2:20) (Class 4) 4-Y-0+ **£2,192** (£639; £319)

Form RPR
5-55 **1** **Bianco Fuji**[67] 2068 6-11-4 0 .... LeightonAspell 121+
(Oliver Sherwood) *hld up: hdwy 7th: led 2 out: clr last: styd on wl* **12/1**
5-0 **2** *9* **Victoria Rose (IRE)**[56] 2288 6-10-11 0 .... NathanSweeney(7) 110+
(Simon Burrough) *hld up: hdwy 4th: rdn appr 3 out: j.rt next: blnd last: styd on same pce: wnt 2nd fnl 75yds* **66/1**
32 **3** *2* **Dun See Dee (IRE)**[19] 2974 7-11-4 119 .... APMcCoy 108+
(Charlie Mann) *led and nt fluent 1st: hdd 6th: led again bef 3 out: rdn and hdd next: wknd flat: lost 2nd fnl 75yds* **4/7**[1]
23-2 **4** *3* **Empress Orchid**[53] 2353 6-11-4 104 .... JasonMaguire 104
(Donald McCain) *prom: rdn after 3 out: wknd bef last* **5/1**[2]
5 *7* **Kings Queen (IRE)**[279] 5-11-4 0 .... PaddyBrennan 96
(Tom George) *hld up: hdwy 4th: chsd ldr 3 out: wknd after next* **12/1**
00 **6** *16* **Free Falling**[20] 2960 5-11-4 0 .... WillKennedy 80
(Alastair Lidderdale) *chsd ldrs: rdn 7th: wknd bef 3 out: t.o* **50/1**
0-36 **7** *11* **Pickworth (IRE)**[13] 3089 6-10-11 0 .... KyleJames(7) 69
(Philip Kirby) *hld up: mstke 1st: hit 6th: wknd appr 3 out: t.o* **33/1**
0 **8** *20* **M'Lady Rousseur (IRE)**[44] 2554 5-11-4 0 .... TomMessenger 49
(Chris Bealby) *hld up: mstke 2nd: a in rr: wknd after 7th: t.o* **100/1**
60P0 **9** *11* **Rolline (IRE)**[19] 2974 6-11-1 0 .... DonalDevereux(3) 38
(Stuart Kittow) *chsd ldrs: led 5th: hdd & wknd appr 3 out* **100/1**
50 **10** *10* **Melua Maid (IRE)**[67] 2067 9-11-4 0 .... TjadeCollier 28
(Sue Smith) *chsd ldrs: pushed along 3rd: lost pl after next: sn wl bhd: t.o* **66/1**
3000 **11** *4 ½* **Restless Harriet**[44] 2556 5-10-8 0 .... ChristopherWard(10) 24
(Robin Dickin) *hld up: rdn after 4th: sn bhd: t.o* **100/1**
54 **P** **Rahaala (IRE)**[58] 2245 4-10-5 0 .... DougieCostello —
(Lucy Wadham) *hld up: nt fluent: mstke 2nd: hdwy and mstke 7th: sn rdn: wknd bef next: t.o whn j.v.slowly last: sn p.u* **7/1**[3]
0P **P** **Congella**[41] 2612 6-11-4 0 .... RobertWalford —
(Tim Walford) *mid-div: hdwy 3rd: wknd 7th: t.o whn p.u bef next* **100/1**

5m 17.2s (-7.50) **Going Correction** -0.40s/f (Good)
WFA 4 from 5yo+ 12lb **13** Ran SP% **120.1**
Speed ratings (Par 105): **98,94,93,92,90 83,79,72,67,64 62,—,—**
Tote Swingers: 1&2 £27.20, 1&3 £4.40, 2&3 £8.80 CSF £535.78 TOTE £13.90: £3.90, £17.80, £1.10; EX 491.60.
Owner P K Gardner **Bred** P K Gardner **Trained** Upper Lambourn, Berks

FOCUS
A modest mares' maiden hurdle and something of a surprise result. A step up from the winner but she should go on to rate higher.

NOTEBOOK
Bianco Fuji, a half-sister to the yard's useful Argento Luna amongst others, was having just her second start over hurdles. She was a little keen under restraint early, but made her ground in good style and soon had the race in the bag after jumping ahead two out. The longer trip probably helped, and presumably her target will be the mares' finale at Newbury, a race her sibling won in 2009. (op 10-1)
Victoria Rose(IRE), whose dam stayed well, had shown ability behind Mizzurka in a bumper last season. This was much better than her hurdling debut and she can win handicaps, possibly over further, in time.
Dun See Dee(IRE), a bumper winner who had today's runner-up miles behind on their hurdling debuts, had built on that since. Sent off at odds-on, she made the running but her jumping was far from fluent and, although responding to pressure early in the straight, she had no more to offer from the penultimate flight. Official explanation: vet said mare finished lame (op 8-13 tchd 8-15)

Empress Orchid, placed in two bumpers and two hurdles prior to this, travelled well in behind the leaders but could not pick up under pressure. Possibly this softer surface was not in her favour. (op 9-2)

Kings Queen(IRE), an Irish point winner, moved into contention travelling well early in the straight but then got tired. She was keen early on this first start since March, so should come on for the run and be less fresh next time. (tchd 16-1)

3390 HIGHFIELDS NOVICES' CHASE (15 fncs) 2m 4f 110y

2:50 (2:50) (Class 4) 5-Y-0+ **£2,602** (£764; £382; £190)

Form				RPR
-142	1		**Hidden Keel**[30] 2793 6-11-0 129 PaddyBrennan (Charlie Longsdon) *led after 1st: mde rest: blnd 4 out: lft clr after next: nt fluent last: easily* **5/2**[2]	150+
F-22	2	8	**Fredo (IRE)**[46] 2494 7-11-0 133 TomScudamore (Ian Williams) *prom: chsd wnr 4th tl mstke 11th: wknd after 4 out: wnt mod 2nd flat* **7/2**[3]	133
212-	3	6	**Great Reason**[287] 4801 7-11-0 0 APMcCoy (Nicky Henderson) *prom: chsd wnr 11th: 3 l 2nd whn blnd bdly 3 out: sn wknd: lost 2nd flat* **9/4**[1]	130+
610-	4	6	**Swansbrook (IRE)**[297] 4589 8-11-0 0 RobertThornton (Alan King) *hld up: hdwy 8th: wnt 3rd 4 out: wknd next* **9/1**	120
0-PF	5	10	**Alderluck (IRE)**[64] 2125 8-11-0 0 LiamTreadwell (Nick Gifford) *hld up: bhd fr 7th* **8/1**	112
-321	6	6	**Kellystown Lad (IRE)**[42] 2599 8-11-7 126 GrahamLee (Ferdy Murphy) *hld up and bhd: pushed along after 5th: hdwy 9th: rdn and wknd bef 4 out* **10/1**	113
35	P		**Canticle**[47] 2475 6-11-0 0 TomMessenger (Chris Bealby) *led tl after 1st: nt fluent next: chsd wnr to 4th: wknd 8th: t.o whn p.u bef 3 out* **66/1**	—

5m 5.40s (-13.50) **Going Correction** -0.40s/f (Good) 7 Ran SP% **113.3**
Speed ratings: **109,105,103,101,97 95,—**
Tote Swingers: 1&2 £2.80, 1&3 £2.00, 2&3 £1.30 CSF £11.85 TOTE £3.50: £2.60, £3.30; EX 11.30.
Owner Mrs Peter Matthey & John F Horn **Bred** Mrs M J Matthey **Trained** Over Norton, Oxon

FOCUS

An interesting novices' chase featuring some useful types and run 7.8secs faster than the earlier handicap. Hidden Keel looks a smart novice and winners should come out of the race.

NOTEBOOK

Hidden Keel, a bumper winner and twice successful over hurdles, built on his chasing debut last time with a fine front-running display. He was pretty fluent at his fences and, despite a mistake at the first in the straight, he had all his rivals in trouble at that point and was able to take it easy after the third horse made an error at the last ditch. His trainer has high hopes of him, and he looks a good prospect if he can go on from this. (op 11-4 tchd 3-1)

Fredo(IRE) had come up against very decent sorts in his two previous runs over fences and probably met another here. His jumping could have been better but he stayed on well up the straight, suggesting a return to longer trips will be in his favour. He should not be too long getting off the mark. (op 10-3 tchd 4-1)

Great Reason was a fair hurdler despite not having had much racing so far. He travelled well for much of the way, but was struggling to reel in the winner when making a hash of the last ditch. His rider was not hard on him afterwards, as the gelding was found to have bled from the nose. He is another who should win chases this season if none the worse. Official explanation: trainer's rep said gelding bled from the nose (op 11-4 tchd 3-1)

Swansbrook(IRE), a soft-ground hurdles winner last year, was making his chasing debut on his first start since March. He was settled off the pace and never really got involved, but showed enough to suggest an aptitude for fences. He will appreciate softer ground in future. (op 10-1)

Kellystown Lad(IRE), the only previous winner over fences in the line-up, had a tough task under his penalty and never got competitive having been held up. (op 8-1)

3391 CHARLES STREET NOVICES' H'CAP CHASE (18 fncs) 2m 7f 110y

3:20 (3:20) (Class 4) (0-115,112) 5-Y-0+ **£2,602** (£764; £382; £190)

Form				RPR
425	1		**Three Chords (IRE)**[20] 2959 7-11-10 **110** AndrewThornton (Caroline Bailey) *hld up in tch: led after 3 out: drvn out* **9/4**[1]	122+
04-P	2	2 ¾	**Tafika**[38] 2670 7-11-7 **107** DominicElsworth (Paul Webber) *chsd ldrs: outpcd appr 4 out: rallied bef 2 out: wnt 2nd flat: styd on* **14/1**	113
-144	3	¾	**Digger Gets Lucky (IRE)**[22] 2928 9-11-3 **103** LiamTreadwell (Nick Gifford) *prom: mstke 3rd: lost pl 7th: nt fluent 9th (water): hdwy fr 2 out: styd on: wnt 3rd towards fin* **13/2**[3]	110
-355	4	2 ½	**Papa Caruso**[42] 2599 7-11-10 **110** TjadeCollier (Sue Smith) *a.p: chsd ldr and pckd 11th: rdn appr 4 out: no ex flat* **13/2**[3]	114
6-04	5	nk	**Witch's Hat (IRE)**[40] 2637 8-10-6 **92** (t) RhysFlint (Jim Old) *chsd ldrs: rdn 12th: outpcd 14th: rallied appr last: styd on* **12/1**	95
-351	6	16	**Persian Gates (IRE)**[58] 2250 7-11-0 **100** TomMessenger (Chris Bealby) *hld up: racd keenly: hdwy 7th: chsd ldr 4 out: sn rdn: wknd appr last* **9/1**	90
006-	7	23	**Simply Strong (IRE)**[312] 4282 7-11-5 **105** (t) DenisO'Regan (Charlie Mann) *sn prom: led 4th: hdd after 3 out: wknd qckly after next: t.o* **20/1**	77+
-4F0	8	9	**Mister Watzisname (IRE)**[59] 2214 9-11-12 **112** (t) FelixDeGiles (Charlie Longsdon) *hld up and bhd: mstke 9th (water): t.o* **20/1**	67
0-15	9	nse	**De Bansha Man (IRE)**[77] 1912 6-11-4 **107** SamTwiston-Davies[(3)] (Nigel Twiston-Davies) *led to 4th: chsd ldrs tl rdn and wknd 4 out: t.o* **9/2**[2]	62
33-P	10	nk	**Katalak (IRE)**[19] 2982 8-10-10 **96** (t) WillKennedy (Jonathen de Giles) *hld up: wknd 13th: t.o* **28/1**	50

5m 54.4s (-9.60) **Going Correction** -0.40s/f (Good) 10 Ran SP% **112.9**
Speed ratings: **100,99,98,98,97 92,84,81,81,81**
Tote Swingers: 1&2 £5.10, 1&3 £3.40, 2&3 £16.50 CSF £30.32 CT £177.75 TOTE £3.20: £1.90, £6.40, £1.50; EX 34.50.
Owner Mrs C Aldridge & R Juleff **Bred** J F C Maxwell **Trained** Brixworth, Northants

FOCUS

A modest but competitive-looking novices' handicap chase. A personal best from the winner with the third and fourth giving the form a bit of substance.

NOTEBOOK

Three Chords(IRE), a three-time point winner, had shown promise in his two previous races over fences this season. Settled early, he came through to lead three out travelling strongly, and scored in straightforward fashion. He should be able to build on this. (tchd 5-2)

Tafika has been relatively lightly raced, but improved considerably on his chasing debut last time. After racing up with the pace, he dropped back on the home turn but got a second wind in the straight to chase home the winner. He should be up to winning a similar contest. (tchd 16-1)

Digger Gets Lucky(IRE) has had plenty of experience over fences, including scoring on soft ground. He was another to lose his place and looked well beaten on the home turn, but rallied well on the climb to the line. (op 6-1 tchd 7-1)

Papa Caruso got into contention on the second circuit, but was under pressure some way from home and had nothing in reserve in the latter stages. (op 7-1 tchd 8-1)

Witch's Hat(IRE), whose best effort over hurdles was on his previous start when a tongue tie was fitted, ran well on this chasing bow. He was another who lost his place at the end of the back straight before coming again. (op 16-1)

Simply Strong(IRE), who won an Irish point on fast ground, made the running jumping well, but got tired once headed at the last ditch. (tchd 16-1)

De Bansha Man(IRE) dropped away disappointingly having been prominent for a long way. It may be that he needs a flat track to show his best form. Official explanation: trainer's rep said gelding was unsuited by the good (good to firm in places) ground (tchd 4-1)

3392 FIELD FARM H'CAP HURDLE (10 hdls) 2m 4f 110y

3:50 (3:50) (Class 4) (0-100,99) 4-Y-0+ **£2,329** (£678; £339)

Form				RPR
-001	1		**Smokey George**[4] 3255 6-10-13 **86** 7ex JasonMaguire (Kim Bailey) *hld up: hdwy appr 3 out: led on bit bef 2 out: easily* **1/1**[1]	104+
3542	2	2 ¾	**Be My Light (IRE)**[47] 2478 5-10-13 **91** (p) DavidBass[(5)] (Charlie Longsdon) *chsd ldr: ev ch 2 out: sn rdn: styd on same pce last* **6/1**[3]	96
555	3	13	**Cloudy Dawn**[156] 1149 6-10-5 **78** HenryOliver (Sue Smith) *led: hit 4th: nt fluent 6th: rdn and hdd bef 2 out: sn wknd* **7/1**	70
3400	4	2 ½	**Apache Chant (USA)**[59] 2209 7-11-12 **99** WayneHutchinson (Tony Carroll) *chsd ldrs: lost pl after 6th: wknd 3 out* **11/1**	89
P5P3	5	2 ½	**Winter Holly**[50] 2425 5-10-12 **85** RobertWalford (Tim Walford) *prom: lost pl after 4th: hdwy 7th: wknd appr 3 out* **25/1**	73
0325	6	12	**Earl Of Thomond (IRE)**[22] 2929 6-11-0 **87** AndrewThornton (Caroline Bailey) *hld up: hdwy 7th: sn rdn: wknd after next* **4/1**[2]	67
124-	7	39	**Home She Goes (IRE)**[325] 4043 9-11-6 **96** AdamPogson[(3)] (Charles Pogson) *hld up: hdwy 4th: wknd after 3 out: t.o* **14/1**	42
-PPP	8	40	**Aboukir Bay (IRE)**[20] 2951 7-10-5 **85** (bt) JoeCornwall[(7)] (John Cornwall) *hld up: hdwy 3rd: rdn and wknd after 3 out: t.o* **40/1**	—

5m 27.0s (2.30) **Going Correction** -0.40s/f (Good) 8 Ran SP% **118.1**
Speed ratings (Par 105): **79,77,73,72,71 66,51,36**
Tote Swingers: 1&2 £2.60, 1&3 £3.50, 2&3 £5.90 CSF £8.38 CT £29.41 TOTE £2.70: £1.50, £1.30, £4.00; EX 7.60.
Owner Mrs Penny Perriss **Bred** J F Perriss **Trained** Andoversford, Gloucs

FOCUS

A moderate handicap hurdle run nearly ten seconds slower than the earlier mares' hurdle. The winner was well in and value for a lot further.

NOTEBOOK

Smokey George was an easy winner at Uttoxeter just four days previously, and he repeated the trick over this longer distance under a 7lb penalty. Settled out the back early, he came through travelling strongly before drawing away going to the final flight. The hat-trick is a distinct possibility and he has further entries in the next few days which he may take up, as he is due to rise 20lb in the handicap from the weekend. (tchd 11-10 in palces)

Be My Light(IRE) was never far away and was the only one to give the winner any sort of race. She could be of interest in a mares' race at around this trip. (op 11-2 tchd 9-2)

Cloudy Dawn, a former point winner making his handicap debut over hurdles, forced the pace and tried to kick on from the home turn. However, once headed going to two out, he was soon beaten. (op 10-1)

Apache Chant(USA) lost his place at the end of the back straight before running on again past beaten horses. He has yet to score in 20 starts over hurdles now. (op 14-1)

Earl Of Thomond(IRE) looked a major player, but was being pushed along before the end of the back straight and might have found the ground softer than ideal. (op 9-2 tchd 7-2)

T/Jkpt: Not won. T/Plt: £22.70 to a £1 stake. Pool: £82,864 - 2,653.46 winning tickets. T/Qpdt: £16.40 to a £1 stake. Pool: £5,778 - 260.70 winning tickets. CR

3166 SOUTHWELL (L-H)

Wednesday, January 5

OFFICIAL GOING: Good to soft (soft in places; 7.3)

Golf Club bend 5yds inside and bend into home straight 5yds outside the line raced on November 8th.

Wind: moderate 1/2 against Weather: rain and breezy

3393 STARSPORTSBET.CO.UK NOVICES' CHASE (13 fncs) 2m

12:40 (12:40) (Class 4) 5-Y-0+ **£2,732** (£848; £456)

Form				RPR
P1-4	1		**Hold Fast (IRE)**[76] 1930 7-11-0 0 BrianHughes (Howard Johnson) *trckd ldrs: lft 2nd 3rd: led 5th: jnd 3 out: styd on u.p run-in: hld on wl towards fin* **6/1**[2]	130+
210-	2	nk	**Bellvano (GER)**[292] 4711 7-11-0 0 APMcCoy (Nicky Henderson) *t.k.h: chsd wnr 9th: upsides on bit whn pckd 3 out: stmbld landing next: sn drvn: 1 l down last: no ex clsng stages* **1/5**[1]	132+
-0U5	3	50	**Outside The Box**[23] 2926 7-11-0 0 TomSiddall (Noel Chance) *j.rt: t.k.h: led to 5th: lost pl 4 out: sn t.o* **66/1**	79
2F34	U		**Blacktoft (USA)**[8] 3156 8-11-0 125 AdamWedge[(7)] (Evan Williams) *w ldr: bmpd 1st: blnd and uns rdr 3rd* **16/1**[3]	—

4m 18.3s (8.30) **Going Correction** +0.65s/f (Soft) 4 Ran SP% **105.0**
Speed ratings: **105,104,79,—**
CSF £7.94 TOTE £4.80; EX 9.80.
Owner Andrea & Graham Wylie **Bred** R J Whitford **Trained** Billy Row, Co Durham

FOCUS

An interesting novice chase run at a steady gallop but with very fast finishing fractions. It produced a surprise winner who is rated to his best hurdles figure, with Bellvano, undone by mistakes, a stone off but capable of rating much higher.

NOTEBOOK

Hold Fast(IRE) built on his chasing debut at Carlisle in October to outbattle the well backed odds-on favourite. A winner of two of his three starts over hurdles over further, he jumped neatly and found plenty for pressure. He looks a fair prospect and should improve for a step up in trip. (op 13-2)

Bellvano(GER) looked to have been found a good opportunity to make a winning debut, but it did not work out that way. Racing enthusiastically, he travelled the better turning in, but a mistake at the second-last stopped his momentum and he was unable to pass the game winner. He is sure to learn from this, will improve for the run and should be able to go one better next time. (op 2-11)

Outside The Box showed up well for a long way before struggling to go with the front two after four out. He jumped right throughout and may appreciate a drop in class and racing the other way around.

Blacktoft(USA) had plenty of previous chasing experience and led early before unseating his rider at the third fence. He will need to bounce back from this. (tchd 18-1)

3394 BET TOTE DIRECT AT STAR SPORTS BEGINNERS' CHASE (19 fncs) 3m 110y

1:10 (1:11) (Class 4) 5-Y-O+ **£2,667** (£783; £391; £195)

Form RPR

U224 **1** **Hollo Ladies (IRE)**[8] 3169 6-11-0 137 GrahamLee 132+
(Ferdy Murphy) *trckd ldrs: jnd ldr 15th: led and stmbld landing 2 out: styd on run-in: all out* **9/4**[2]

31-3 **2** *hd* **Be There In Five (IRE)**[41] 2631 7-11-0 0 APMcCoy 131
(Nicky Henderson) *led: jnd 15th: hdd appr 2 out: upsides last: styd on: jst hld* **6/5**[1]

-030 **3** *39* **Global Flyer**[54] 2347 7-11-0 110 AndrewThornton 96
(Caroline Bailey) *in last: reminders 9th: outpcd 12th: wnt modest 4th 15th: kpt on to take distant 3rd last* **33/1**

210P **4** *5* **Quo Video (FR)**[74] 1966 7-11-0 0 RichardJohnson 91
(Tim Vaughan) *w ldrs: wknd 4 out: lost distant 3rd last* **12/1**

12-3 **5** *54* **Milans Man (IRE)**[61] 2191 6-11-0 0 BrianHughes 43
(Howard Johnson) *w ldrs: hit 8th: drvn 13th: reminders next: sn lost pl and bhd: t.o 4 out* **4/1**[3]

6m 47.3s (21.30) **Going Correction** +0.65s/f (Soft) **5** Ran SP% **106.9**
Speed ratings: **91,90,78,76,59**
CSF £5.28 TOTE £2.90: £1.80, £1.30; EX 4.80.

Owner Martin Bourke **Bred** J C Fagan **Trained** West Witton, N Yorks

FOCUS
A fair beginners' chase for the course produced a head-bobbing finish. The first two are rated pretty much in line with their hurdles form.

NOTEBOOK
Hollo Ladies(IRE), a Grade1-winning hurdler in Ireland, had finished runner-up on his previous two outings over fences, but went one better with a game victory. Travelling strongly just off the pace, he jumped well and closed on the long-time leader entering the straight, after pecking on landing at the second last, before outbattling the runner-up after the last. He is improving with experience, handled the step up to 3m well and may be able to defy a penalty before being stepped up in class. (op 11-4)

Be There In Five(IRE), a 138-rated hurdler, had disappointed on his chase debut at Newbury in November but showed improved form here, jumping boldly and quite big at some of the fences. He took the field along and just failed to hold off the winner, but should be able to land a similar contest. (op Evens)

Global Flyer was making his chasing debut and looked to be struggling down the back, before running on to take third. He will improve for the run but may need a drop in grade to be competitive. (tchd 40-1)

Quo Video(FR) was another making his chasing debut having been pulled up in Grade 2 novice hurdle company at Chepstow in October. He attacked his fences and looked to be going well before fading when the pace increased. (op 14-1 tchd 16-1 and 10-1)

Milans Man(IRE) failed to build on his first outing over fences, and was soon struggling after a mistake at the eighth. (op 7-2 tchd 3-1)

3395 OPEN A STAR SPORTS ACCOUNT ON 08000 521 321 H'CAP CHASE (19 fncs) 3m 110y

1:40 (1:40) (Class 4) (0-115,115) 5-Y-O+ **£2,667** (£783; £391; £195)

Form RPR

0-55 **1** **Raise You Five (IRE)**[48] 2470 7-11-4 107 APMcCoy 116+
(Jonjo O'Neill) *trckd ldrs: hit 13th: led 3 out: hrd rdn run-in: all out* **8/1**

4-P0 **2** *nk* **Pliny (IRE)**[21] 2959 7-11-2 105 AidanColeman 114+
(Venetia Williams) *trckd ldrs: led 4 out: sn hdd: rallied and upsides whn hit 2 out: kpt on wl: jst hld* **4/1**[3]

5322 **3** *16* **Dallas Bell**[54] 2354 9-10-8 100 EwanWhillans(3) 93
(Alistair Whillans) *in rr: shkn up 5th: hdwy to chse ldrs 14th: outpcd 3 out: kpt on to take modest 3rd last* **11/4**[1]

-66P **4** *3/4* **Daldini**[53] 2374 9-11-7 110 TjadeCollier 104
(Sue Smith) *led to 4 out: outpcd 2 out: kpt on clsng stages* **10/1**

3-F4 **5** *2 1/2* **Don't Tell Nina (IRE)**[41] 2641 7-11-7 110 DominicElsworth 101
(Paul Webber) *trckd ldrs: led after 4 out: hdd next: wknd fr 2 out* **33/1**

-000 **6** *9* **Gaora Lane (IRE)**[20] 2975 10-11-6 112 PeterToole(3) 96
(Charlie Mann) *j.lft: chsd ldrs: wknd 4 out: sn bhd* **9/1**

3-11 **F** **Roseneath (IRE)**[59] 2249 7-11-12 115 (p) DenisO'Regan —
(Alex Hales) *in rr: blnd 7th: j.rt 9th: hdwy to chse ldrs 12th: lost pl: hmpd and fell 4 out* **10/3**[2]

6U04 **P** **Phoenix Des Mottes (FR)**[50] 2437 8-9-10 92 JoeCornwall(7) —
(John Cornwall) *in rr: hmpd 9th: bhd and reminders 12th: sn t.o: p.u bef 2 out* **22/1**

0245 **U** **Panama Canal (IRE)**[8] 3171 6-11-1 107 AdamPogson(3) —
(Charles Pogson) *t.k.h: trckd ldrs: hit 10th: outpcd whn blnd and uns rdr 15th* **12/1**

6m 50.3s (24.30) **Going Correction** +0.65s/f (Soft) **9** Ran SP% **114.9**
Speed ratings: **87,86,81,81,80 77,—,—,—**
Tote Swingers: 1&2 £5.60, 1&3 £2.60, 2&3 £3.20 CSF £40.86 CT £111.14 TOTE £5.40: £2.20, £1.90, £1.20; EX 41.50.

Owner John P McManus **Bred** Mrs Mary O'Connor **Trained** Cheltenham, Gloucs

FOCUS
A competitive handicap chase. The winner produced a big step up on her previous chase form but this was a tricky race to rate.

NOTEBOOK
Raise You Five(IRE) got off the mark over fences, showing a game attitude to just hold off the runner-up in another thrilling finish. Twice a winner over hurdles, she had shown little in her two starts over fences, but looked to be on an interesting mark. Having jumped slowly down the back, she travelled powerfully on the outside and responded well to pressure after the last. She may be open to further improvement. Official explanation: regarding apparent improvement in form trainer said mare benefited from racing over a longer trip (op 13-2 tchd 6-1)

Pliny(IRE), who attracted market support, was another unexposed over fences and travelled nicely up with the pace before just failing to pass the winner. This was a much improved run and there may be more to come, although the handicapper will have his say. (op 5-1 tchd 11-2)

Dallas Bell, a runner-up on his last two starts, and up 4lb for his latest effort, looked to be struggling before running on, albeit one paced, to take third. The handicapper looks to have him in his grasp. (tchd 3-1)

Daldini, a C&D winner last February, took the field along before failing to quicken once the pace increased. (tchd 12-1)

Don't Tell Nina(IRE) improved on his recent form before fading late on. He may need a drop in trip. (op 28-1)

Roseneath(IRE) failed to complete the hat-trick following wins at Huntingdon and Market Rasen. Up 5lb for the latest win, he was held up and never jumped with any fluency before departing at the last in the back straight. (op 5-2)

3396 BETFAIR CONDITIONAL JOCKEYS' TRAINING SERIES H'CAP HURDLE (13 hdls) 3m 110y

2:10 (2:10) (Class 5) (0-90,93) 4-Y-O+ **£1,541** (£449; £224)

Form RPR

-034 **1** **Dancing Daffodil**[52] 2390 6-10-1 68 ChristopherWard(8) 77
(Robin Dickin) *in tch: chsd ldrs 9th: wnt cl 2nd appr 2 out: styd on to ld last 100yds* **6/1**

0011 **2** *1 3/4* **Smokey George**[1] 3392 6-11-12 93 14ex EdCookson(8) 100
(Kim Bailey) *hld up in rr: stdy hdwy to trck kldrs 9th: led on bit appr 2 out: drvn between last 2: hdd and no ex run-in* **5/6**[1]

U4/3 **3** *55* **Talesofriverbank**[54] 2351 8-10-5 69 CallumWhillans(5) 27
(Alistair Whillans) *in rr: drvn 3rd: reminders 6th: kpt on fr 3 out: tk remote 3rd run-in* **5/1**[3]

0F4P **4** *3 1/2* **No More Whispers (IRE)**[42] 2608 6-11-7 85 (p) JakeGreenall(5) 39
(Evan Williams) *led: drvn 9th: hdd appr 2 out: sn wknd* **25/1**

0P-2 **5** *31* **Flaming Breeze (IRE)**[66] 2103 6-11-9 85 PaulGallagher(3) 11
(Henry Hogarth) *chsd ldrs: drvn 9th: wknd 3 out: sn bhd* **9/2**[2]

0006 **6** *39* **A P Ling**[30] 2556 4-9-10 74 TrevorWhelan(5) —
(Christopher Kellett) *mstke 1st: hdwy racing wd to chse ldrs 4th: drvn and lost pl 9th: t.o sn after 3 out* **50/1**

4-P4 **P** **Ortega (FR)**[48] 2479 9-10-11 76 (p) JoeCornwall(6) —
(John Cornwall) *in tch: drvn 9th: wknd rapidly 3 out: wl t.o whn p.u bef next* **33/1**

P0-5 **P** **Dancing Legend**[240] 249 5-11-4 80 KyleJames(3) —
(Peter Hiatt) *tk fierce hold: trckd ldrs: sddle sn slipped: p.u after 1st* **66/1**

6m 44.1s (36.60) **Going Correction** +1.075s/f (Soft)
WFA 4 from 5yo+ 13lb **8** Ran SP% **113.9**
Speed ratings (Par 103): **84,83,65,64,54 42,—,—**
Tote Swingers: 1&2 £1.90, 1&3 £2.70, 2&3 £2.40 CSF £11.73 CT £26.65 TOTE £5.80: £1.30, £1.10, £1.60; EX 15.00.

Owner John & Margaret Cooper & Law & Disorder **Bred** Mrs C M Dickin **Trained** Atherstone on Stour, Warwicks

■ Stewards' Enquiry : Paul Gallagher eight-day ban: improper use of whip (tba)

FOCUS
A moderate handicap. The winner improved to the level of her course bumper win.

NOTEBOOK
Dancing Daffodil, back up to 3m, got off the mark at the ninth time of asking over hurdles in impressive fashion. Travelling strongly, she loomed up towards the outside of the course and had more left in the tank than the odds-on favourite in the final stages. (op 7-1 tchd 8-1)

Smokey George was looking to complete a hat-trick following victories at Uttoxeter last week and Leicester the previous day, but found this one race too many. Under a double penalty, he was held up well off the pace and travelled kindly before making his effort on the run to the last, but he failed to quicken with the winner. This was still a fair effort on his third run in a short period of time, but he is due to go up another 6lb at the weekend, which will make his life even harder. (op Evens tchd 4-5 and 11-10 in a place)

Talesofriverbank, 4lb higher than when third on her return from a break at Newcastle latest, ran a solid race without threatening the front two. (op 7-2)

No More Whispers(IRE), wearing first-time cheekpieces, led for a long way but came under pressure down the back and was readily held. (op 20-1)

Flaming Breeze(IRE), off since finishing second in October, may have needed the run, but was ultimately a bit disappointing. (op 5-1 tchd 6-1)

3397 HAPPY NEW YEAR FROM STAR SPORTS H'CAP HURDLE (9 hdls) 2m

2:40 (2:40) (Class 5) (0-95,95) 4-Y-O+ **£1,541** (£449; £224)

Form RPR

-P66 **1** **Bromhead (USA)**[66] 2114 5-11-5 88 [1] JamesReveley 98+
(Kevin Morgan) *hld up: smooth hdwy to go handy 2nd 3 out: led appr next: shkn up and wnt clr between last 2: eased nr fin* **11/2**[3]

-340 **2** *8* **River Rhapsody (IRE)**[63] 2149 5-10-13 82 PaulMoloney 83
(Evan Williams) *chsd ldrs: pushed along 4th: chsd wnr appr 2 out: no imp* **5/2**[2]

4440 **3** *5* **Silver Steel (FR)**[99] 1645 8-11-12 95 (t) GrahamLee 92
(Richard Ford) *chsd ldrs: rdn 3 out: one pce appr next* **7/1**

4543 **4** *1 1/2* **Sonic Anthem (USA)**[21] 2956 9-11-10 93 RhysFlint 87
(John Mackie) *w ldr: led 4th: hdd appr 2 out: one pce* **2/1**[1]

-P4F **5** *32* **Wishes Or Watches (IRE)**[50] 2434 11-9-11 69 oh3 SamTwiston-Davies(3) 44
(John Upson) *in rr: drvn and outpcd 7th: sn bhd: t.o* **12/1**

12-P **P** **My Les**[14] 2070 5-11-11 94 (b[1]) MattieBatchelor —
(Jim Best) *nt jump wl and j.rt-handed: chsd ldrs: blnd 3rd: reminders next: lost pl and bhd 5th: t.o 3 out: p.u bef next* **8/1**

-P40 **P** **Cherokee Story**[46] 2526 5-11-11 94 (b) TomMessenger —
(Chris Bealby) *led to 4th: sn drvn: wknd 3 out: sn bhd: t.o whn p.u bef last* **33/1**

4m 18.2s (21.10) **Going Correction** +1.075s/f (Soft) **7** Ran SP% **111.5**
Speed ratings (Par 103): **90,86,83,82,66 —,—**
Tote Swingers: 1&2 £3.50, 1&3 £6.10, 2&3 £3.10 CSF £19.13 TOTE £8.60: £2.90, £2.10; EX 20.30.

Owner K A Morgan **Bred** Grovendale, K Nikkel And S Robertson **Trained** Newmarket, Suffolk

FOCUS
A modest handicap hurdle that produced an easy winner who showed improved form. The next two were close to their marks.

NOTEBOOK
Bromhead(USA) bounced back to form impressively. Always travelling strongly, he cruised to the front turning into the home straight and won eased down. In a first-time hood, and just 4lb higher than his previous winning mark, this was an improved effort, albeit in a poor contest. (op 8-1)

River Rhapsody(IRE), third on his seasonal debut at Sedgefield but disappointing since, ran a fair race without ever threatening the winner. (op 10-3)

Silver Steel(FR) was supported in the market on his first start over hurdles since February 2009 but was beaten off before coming to the second-last fence. (op 5-1)

Sonic Anthem(USA) is on a lengthy losing run and continues to struggle to get his head in front. (tchd 15-8)

Wishes Or Watches(IRE) failed to challenge on his first start over hurdles since November 2009. (tchd 14-1)

3398 SOUTHWELL "NATIONAL HUNT" MAIDEN HURDLE (9 hdls) 2m

3:10 (3:11) (Class 5) 4-Y-O+ **£1,541** (£449; £224)

Form RPR

1-1 **1** **Problema Tic (FR)**[236] 319 5-11-5 0 APMcCoy 125+
(Nicky Henderson) *trckd ldr: led appr 2 out: clr last: comf* **8/13**[1]

5-64 **2** *3 1/4* **Smart Freddy**[44] 2577 5-11-0 0 DavidBass(5) 115
(Lawney Hill) *trckd ldrs: 4 l 2nd whn mstke last: no ch w wnr* **16/1**

2-3 **3** *5* **Timesawastin (IRE)**[69] 2056 5-11-5 0 PaulMoloney 112
(Evan Williams) *led: hung bdly lft and hdd appr 2 out: 3rd and wkng whn hit last* **3/1**[2]
0-23 **4** *25* **Management (IRE)**[15] 3055 5-11-5 0 RobertThornton 87
(Alan King) *chsd ldrs: rdn 3 out: wknd appr next* **11/2**[3]
50 **5** *6* **Midnight Molly**[59] 2237 4-10-0 0 JamieMoore 63
(John Spearing) *in rr: drvn and hdwy to chse ldrs 5th: outpcd 3 out: wknd appr next* **100/1**
5-00 **6** *8* **Night In Milan (IRE)**[22] 2939 5-11-5 0 JamesReveley 74
(Keith Reveley) *hld up: wnt prom 4th: lost pl after 5th: bhd fr 3 out* **66/1**
0-40 **7** *6* **Fun Guy**[26] 2873 6-11-5 0 AndrewGlassonbury 69
(Bob Buckler) *chsd ldrs to 6th: sn lost pl* **100/1**
26- **8** *18* **Kensix Star (IRE)**[283] 4912 5-11-5 0 BrianHughes 53
(Howard Johnson) *chsd ldrs: wknd 6th* **33/1**
0- **9** *27* **Lucky Lukey**[430] 2025 5-11-5 0 RichieMcGrath 29
(Richard Ford) *hld up in rr: bhd fr 5th: t.o 2 out* **100/1**
20 **10** *41* **Charles**[7] 3196 5-11-5 0 JasonMaguire —
(Kim Bailey) *in rr: bhd whn j. slowly 4th: t.o whn j.rt 6th* **25/1**

4m 12.8s (15.70) **Going Correction** +1.075s/f (Soft)
WFA 4 from 5yo+ 11lb **10** Ran SP% **119.4**
Speed ratings (Par 103): **103,101,98,86,83 79,76,67,53,33**
Tote Swingers: 1&2 £4.50, 1&3 £1.50, 2&3 £5.00 CSF £12.71 TOTE £1.02: £1.02, £3.20, £2.00; EX 13.70.
Owner Sir Robert Ogden **Bred** Julien Merienne & Mrs Maryvonne Merienne **Trained** Upper Lambourn, Berks

FOCUS
This maiden hurdle produced an impressive winner, value for further, and the first three pulled well clear of the remainder. The time was good compared with the earlier handicap.

NOTEBOOK
Problema Tic(FR), two from two in bumpers last year, maintained his unbeaten record to score on his hurdling debut. Highly regarded by his top trainer, he looks a nice prospect and won in the manner of a good horse. He will no doubt be stepping up in grade and should be winning more races. (op 4-6 tchd 8-11)
Smart Freddy, a fair fourth behind a stablemate of the winner last time, ran a race full of credit. He came under pressure turning for home before running on strongly to grab second, and should be capable of winning a similar contest.
Timesawastin(IRE), fourth on debut for this yard at Stratford in October, travelled kindly and looked booked for at least second before hanging badly left on turning into the home straight. He also should be up to winning if keeping straighter under pressure. Official explanation: jockey said gelding was unsteerable down the home straight (tchd 7-2)
Management(IRE) failed to live with the front three but did the best of the remainder. He may want a step up in trip. (op 13-2 tchd 5-1)
Midnight Molly never featured but did hint at having some ability.

3399 SOUTHWELL-RACECOURSE.CO.UK STANDARD OPEN NATIONAL HUNT FLAT RACE 2m
3:40 (3:40) (Class 6) 4-6-Y-0 **£1,370** (£399; £199)

Form RPR
1 **1** **Knight Pass (IRE)**[60] 2215 5-11-12 0 WayneHutchinson 128+
(Warren Greatrex) *trckd ldrs: led on bit 2f out: qcknd clr fnl f: smoothly* **1/2**[1]
2 *4* **Gores Island (IRE)** 5-11-5 0 RichardJohnson 107
(Noel Chance) *hld up towards rr: t.k.h: gd hdwy over 4f out: chsd wnr over 1f out: no imp* **16/1**
3 *5* **Victor Leudorum (IRE)** 4-10-4 0 PeterToole(3) 90
(Charlie Mann) *mid-div: hdwy to chse ldrs over 3f out: wnt 3rd over 1f out: kpt on same pce* **28/1**
31 **4** *1* **Avoca Promise (IRE)**[21] 2957 6-11-12 0 APMcCoy 108
(Charles Egerton) *mid-div: hdwy over 4f out: chsng ldrs 2f out: kpt on one pce* **3/1**[2]
5 *¾* **Scales (IRE)** 5-11-5 0 GrahamLee 100
(Malcolm Jefferson) *hld up in mid-field: hdwy 7f out: sn trcking ldrs: fdd over 1f out* **33/1**
6 *½* **Cool Steel (IRE)** 5-11-5 0 RobertThornton 100
(Alan King) *in rr: hdwy after 6f: chsng ldrs over 3f out: fdd over 1f out* **16/1**
7 *½* **Mootabar (IRE)** 4-10-7 0 BarryKeniry 87
(Chris Fairhurst) *s.i.s: hdwy after 4f: chsng ldrs over 4f out: wknd over 1f out* **66/1**
3 **8** *½* **Quix**[25] 2896 5-10-12 0 NathanSweeney(7) 99
(Bob Buckler) *racd wd: led: hung lft and hdd 2f out: sn wknd* **33/1**
0 **9** *6* **North Brook (IRE)**[236] 319 6-11-2 0 EwanWhillans(3) 93
(Alistair Whillans) *chsd ldrs: drvn 5f out: sn wknd* **14/1**
0 **10** *4½* **Colorado Kid (IRE)**[45] 2553 5-11-5 0 BrianHughes 88
(Howard Johnson) *chsd ldrs: reminders 5f out: lost pl over 3f out* **66/1**
2 **11** *2* **Fill The Power (IRE)**[208] 718 5-11-5 0 HenryOliver 86
(Sue Smith) *chsd ldrs: lost pl 8f out* **14/1**[3]
0 **12** *1½* **Crafti Bookie (IRE)**[22] 2943 5-10-9 0 Zachery-JamesGaughan(10) 85
(Sue Smith) *mid-div: outpcd after 6f: bhd and reminders 7f out* **100/1**
13 *3½* **Malenfant** 4-10-0 0 JakeGreenall(7) 69
(Michael Easterby) *rr-divsion: hdwy 7f out: sn chsng ldrs: lost pl over 2f out* **50/1**
0 **14** *dist* **Powder King**[56] 2315 4-10-7 0 TomMessenger —
(Chris Bealby) *stdd s: t.k.h: hdwy to chse ldr after 3f: lost pl 7f out: t.o 3f out: eventually completed* **100/1**

4m 10.3s (18.80) **Going Correction** +1.075s/f (Soft)
WFA 4 from 5yo 11lb 5 from 6yo 3lb **14** Ran SP% **127.3**
Speed ratings: **96,94,91,91,90 90,90,89,86,84 83,82,81,—**
Tote Swingers: 1&2 £5.00, 1&3 £9.30, 2&3 £19.90 CSF £12.75 TOTE £1.50: £1.40, £2.90, £6.50; EX 17.00.
Owner Malcolm C Denmark **Bred** D J Fitzpatrick **Trained** Upper Lambourn, Berks

FOCUS
This bumper looked like a match considering the market, but the odds-on favourite completely outclassed his rivals.

NOTEBOOK
Knight Pass(IRE) was the subject of some strong market support after making a big impression at Sandown on debut, and built on that effort to defy a penalty in impressive fashion. Travelling ominously well throughout, he eased to the front 1f from home before showing a nice turn of foot to put the race to bed. Warren Greatrex reported afterwards that the jockey said it was no more than a piece of work for Knight Pass and that the horse is all class. Cheltenham is the objective, for which he is challenging for favouritism, but he may run before as there is a Listed bumper at Newbury in February that he could go for. (op 4-7 tchd 8-13)
Gores Island(IRE) made a pleasing debut to run on under pressure. He should improve for the outing and ought to prove competitive in bumpers or over hurdles. (tchd 18-1)
Victor Leudorum(IRE) ran a race full of promise. His trainer has a 15% strike-rate in bumpers and he should be able to improve on this. (op 33-1)
Avoca Promise(IRE) improved from his first run to take a Bangor bumper last time but struggled to land a blow under a penalty here. He came under pressure down the back straight and responded gamely, but may struggle while carrying a penalty in bumpers and looks in need of further. (tchd 11-4)
Scales(IRE) ran a solid race on debut. He kept on for pressure and should be able to step up on this for a yard who excel in this sphere.
Fill The Power(IRE) failed to build on his previous second at Market Rasen. (op 16-1 tchd 20-1)
T/Plt: £69.00 to a £1 stake. Pool: £61,564.81 - 650.82 winning tickets. T/Qpdt: £6.50 to a £1 stake. Pool: £7,596.68 - 853.25 winning tickets. WG

2526 HUNTINGDON (R-H)
Thursday, January 6
OFFICIAL GOING: Good to soft (good in places; hdl 7.4; chs 7.7)
Wind: Virtually nil Weather: Overcast, dry after light rain earlier

3400 WILLIAMHILL.COM CONDITIONAL JOCKEYS' H'CAP HURDLE (12 hdls) 3m 2f
12:40 (12:41) (Class 5) (0-90,90) 4-Y-0+ **£2,055** (£599; £299)

Form RPR
P425 **1** **Elegant Olive**[21] 2980 8-11-7 85 DavidBass 87
(Roger Curtis) *in tch in rr: chsd ldrs 9th: rdn and ev ch after 3 out: led next: hit last: edgd lft but hld on wl u.p flat* **10/3**[2]
5P43 **2** *¾* **Jacarado (IRE)**[45] 2589 13-9-9 67 (v) ChristopherWard(8) 68
(Robin Dickin) *travelled wl: chsd ldrs tl wnt 2nd 6th: led 8th: rdn and forged clr w wnr after 3 out: hdd and j.lft 2 out: kpt on same pce flat* **5/1**
3-40 **3** *1½* **A Fistful Of Euros**[64] 2144 7-11-6 90 DannyBurton(6) 89
(Chris Down) *t.k.h early: chsd ldr tl 6th: styd prom: rdn but stl ev ch whn mstke 3 out: styd on same pce u.p between last 2* **12/1**
-PPP **4** *10* **Raki Rose**[21] 2982 9-10-5 69 (v[1]) CO'Farrell 61
(Michael Scudamore) *led tl 8th: sn rdn along but styd w ldr: wknd u.p bef 2 out: wl hld whn mstke last* **4/1**[3]
0-P6 **5** *4½* **Honourable Dreamer (IRE)**[60] 2244 6-11-0 81 (t) RichieMcLernon(3) 67
(Jonjo O'Neill) *t.k.h early: hld up in tch: mstke 6th: clsd after next: rdn and wkng whn hit 3 out: wl btn bef next* **6/1**
0006 **6** *34* **Patrick Dee**[15] 3090 6-10-5 72 MattCrawley(3) 27
(Christine Dunnett) *in tch: j. slowly 3rd: rdn and wknd qckly after 9th: t.o whn mstke last* **22/1**
2P/4 **7** *53* **Kings Story (IRE)**[32] 2795 7-10-7 71 (p) RichardKilloran —
(Sophie Leech) *in tch: rdn along after 7th: wknd 9th: t.o after next* **3/1**[1]

6m 34.2s (11.30) **Going Correction** -0.175s/f (Good) **7** Ran SP% **111.1**
Speed ratings (Par 103): **75,74,74,71,69 59,43**
toteswingers: 1&2 £3.10, 1&3 £4.80, 2&3 £7.90. CSF £19.13 CT £167.62 TOTE £3.20: £2.50, £1.80; EX 13.50.
Owner Collective Dreamers **Bred** Edward Crow **Trained** Lambourn, Berks
■ Stewards' Enquiry : Christopher Ward caution: use of whip

FOCUS
Only one previous winner in the line-up, and that was over fences, so clearly a weak contest. the frist three are rated pretty much bang on their marks.

NOTEBOOK
Elegant Olive had at least proved that she stayed and found just enough when getting to the lead to gain a first success. Whether she can progress from this is debatable, but she can remain competitive in this sort of grade over extended trips. (op 9-4)
Jacarado(IRE), the only previous winner in the field, cruised throughout the race and made the winner fight for her victory as they edged clear. He can still win races against lowly opposition. (op 13-2)
A Fistful Of Euros, dropped 5lb since her last outing but up significantly in trip, seemed to improve a little on previous efforts, but was still comfortably held. (tchd 16-1)
Raki Rose, in a first-time visor, hardly had form figures to inspire but was handed an easy lead. However, he quickly came under pressure when joined, and although he kept on, there wasn't a lot left in the locker in the home straight. (op 6-1)
Honourable Dreamer(IRE), tried in a tongue-tie and raised significantly in distance, was made to look very one-paced. (op 13-2)
Patrick Dee, who had done all of his racing over hurdles at about 2m, didn't get home. (op 16-1 tchd 25-1)
Kings Story(IRE), back in cheekpieces, was one of the first beaten when the tempo increased. (tchd 7-2)

3401 WILLIAM HILL - HOME OF BETTING JUVENILE NOVICES' HURDLE (8 hdls) 2m 110y
1:10 (1:13) (Class 4) 4-Y-0 **£2,276** (£668; £334; £166)

Form RPR
1 **Tony Star (FR)**[116] 4-10-12 0 RichardJohnson 108+
(Philip Hobbs) *hld up in rr: hmpd 1st: stdy hdwy after 3rd: ev ch whn mstke 3 out: led after 2 out: j.rt last: kpt on wl u.p flat* **13/2**[3]
2 *½* **Paintball (IRE)**[87] 4-10-12 0 TomScudamore 108+
(Charlie Longsdon) *hld up in tch: hdwy to chse ldrs after 5th: led: blnd and hdd 2 out: stl ev ch and pushed rt last: kpt on u.p but a jst hld flat* **4/1**[1]
01 **3** *2½* **Pepite Rose (FR)**[51] 2439 4-10-12 121 AidanColeman 103
(Venetia Williams) *chsd ldrs: gd jump to ld 4th: rdn and hdd 2 out: stl ev ch whn pushed rt last: no ex and btn fnl 100yds* **4/1**[1]
023 **4** *nk* **Omaruru (IRE)**[24] 2924 4-10-12 118 MarkBradburne 102
(Renee Robeson) *chsd ldrs: rdn and sltly outpcd bef 2 out: rallied u.p last: styd on wl flat: nt rch ldrs* **9/1**
52 **5** *¾* **Dhaafer**[43] 2614 4-10-12 0 RobertThornton 103
(Alan King) *chsd ldr tl 4th: styd prom: outpcd jst bef 2 out: rdn and styd on same pce between last 2: 4th and hld whn nt fluent last* **9/2**[2]
56 **6** *¾* **Balerina (FR)**[24] 2924 4-10-5 0 (p) WayneHutchinson 95
(Alan King) *hld up in tch: hdwy to chse ldrs after 3 out: pushed and unable qck 2 out: 5th and hld whn mstke last* **33/1**
6 **7** *1* **Looks Like Slim**[22] 2958 4-10-12 0 DarylJacob 100
(Ben De Haan) *hld up in tch: hdwy into midfield bef 3 out: 7th and no imp whn mstke 2 out: pushed along and kpt on flat: nvr trbld ldrs* **16/1**
8 *7* **Second Brook (IRE)**[93] 4-10-5 0 PeterHatton(7) 95
(Reg Hollinshead) *bhd: mstke 3rd: detached last after 3rd: stl 15th 3 out: styd on past horses bef next: kpt on flat: nvr trbld ldrs* **100/1**
9 *12* **Goodison Park**[57] 4-9-12 0 MrJMQuinlan(7) 74
(Michael Quinlan) *in tch: rdn and struggling bef 3 out: wl hld whn hmpd last* **40/1**
10 *5* **Lucky Breeze (IRE)**[88] 4-10-5 0 FelixDeGiles 71
(Ed de Giles) *nt jump wl: hld up in tch in rr: rdn and wknd after 5th* **20/1**
11 *10* **Lajidaal (USA)**[124] 4-10-12 0 JamieMoore 66
(Gary Moore) *in tch towards rr: rdn and struggling 5th: wl btn 3 out: t.o* **20/1**

12 3 **Grams And Ounces**[100] 4-10-12 0 DaveCrosse 63
(Amy Weaver) *hld up in tch in rr: hdwy 5th: rdn and btn bef 3 out: wknd bef 2 out: t.o* **33/1**

0 **13** 1 **Rare Symphony (IRE)**[22] 2958 4-10-5 0 TomO'Brien 55
(Philip Hobbs) *in tch: rdn and struggling after 5th: wl btn next: t.o* **12/1**

0 **14** 2 3/4 **Farmers Glory**[5] 3304 4-10-9 0 AlexMerriam(3) 59
(Neil King) *w ldrs tl wknd rapidly bef 3 out: t.o between last 2* **250/1**

15 1/2 **Mater Mater**[57] 4-10-5 0 TomMessenger 51
(Caroline Bailey) *t.k.h: in tch: j. awkwardly 2nd: lost pl bef 4th: rdn and lost tch 5th: t.o* **100/1**

2 **16** 9 **Molon Labe (IRE)**[50] 2451 4-10-12 0 JamesReveley 81+
(Tom Tate) *j.lft: led tl j.lft and hdd 4th: wknd 3 out: wl btn whn blnd bdly last: virtually p.u flat: t.o* **12/1**

3m 52.8s (-2.10) **Going Correction** -0.175s/f (Good) **16** Ran SP% **123.0**
Speed ratings: **97,96,95,95,95 94,94,90,85,82 78,76,76,75,74 70**
toteswingers: 1&2 £6.40, 1&3 £4.70, 2&3 £5.00. CSF £31.49 TOTE £5.30: £1.80, £1.90, £1.70; EX 35.50.
Owner Thurloe 51 **Bred** Jean-Paul Doucet **Trained** Withycombe, Somerset
■ Stewards' Enquiry : Peter Hatton 14-day ban: schooling in public

FOCUS
Plenty of runners for this juvenile event, and despite a number of horses finishing close up, this was probably a decent contest with the first two capable of rating a lot higher. The pace was steady.

NOTEBOOK
Tony Star(FR) ◆, a half-brother to Secant Star, won the second of his two starts in French bumpers (1m3f) back in September, and got his hurdling career off to the perfect start. His jumping wasn't always fluent, which is understandable, and a slight mistake at the last threatened his chance, but he found plenty when gathered together and looks a useful prospect. (op 8-1)
Paintball(IRE) ◆, a useful sort at his best on the Flat for William Muir at about 1m2f, was sold for 70,000gns and made a highly encouraging start to his hurdling career. An error two out may have cost him victory, and he shaped like a sure-fire winner in the near future. (tchd 7-2 and 9-2)
Pepite Rose(FR), officially rated 121, easily won at Folkestone last time. Her hurdling technique saw her stand out at the head of affairs, and she kept on gamely when challenged. She seems sure to win more races. (op 9-2 tchd 5-1)
Omaruru(IRE) hadn't been running too badly since going over hurdles and helps to give the race some shape. He has plenty of size and should get even stronger with time. (op 8-1)
Dhaafer ◆ came through to have every chance but looked one-paced in the latter stages. His performances suggest he wants further and/or a stiffer course. (op 4-1)
Balerina(FR) ◆ showed much more than on her two previous tries over hurdles with cheekpieces fitted for the first time. She, like her stablemate in fifth, has the option of handicaps now and would be of some interest in that company under their ideal conditions.
Looks Like Slim ◆ once again made pleasing late headway and looks to have the ability to win something in time. (op 12-1)
Second Brook(IRE) ◆, a moderate maiden on the Flat for this trainer, put in a strange run, as he got detached quite early, admittedly after hitting a couple of hurdles hard but without stopping his momentum significantly, and didn't get involved until running through some tiring horses late on. He never had a chance with the principals and it didn't looked the best judged ride by his claiming jockey. The stewards duly enquired into the performance, suspending the rider for 14 days under Rule (B)59.2 (intentionally failed to ensure horse is run on its merits), fined the trainer £3,000 under Rule (C)45 (duty to ensure best possible placing), and also banned Second Brook for 40 days. Peter Hatton said his instructions were to give the horse an educational ride, something confirmed by the stable's representative, who also stated the horse had been given a wind operation since his previous run on the Flat. Official explanation: 40-day ban: schooling in public (Jan 11 - 19 Feb) rider said regarding the running and riding, that his instructions were to give the horse an educational ride as he has run on the flat and may be keen. The trainer's representative stated that he agreed that those were his instructions as the horse has had a wind operation since it last ran on the flat.

3402 WILLIAMHILL.COM NOVICES' H'CAP CHASE (16 fncs) 2m 4f 110y
1:40 (1:41) (Class 5) (0-95,95) 5-Y-0+ **£2,276** (£668; £334; £166)

Form RPR

P235 **1** **Normandy Landings**[45] 2575 8-10-10 **79** (p) DougieCostello 86+
(Neil Mulholland) *chsd ldr 2nd tl 10th: wnt 2nd again 11th: led 3 out: pushed clr and in command next: idled bdly flat: pushed along and a doing enough* **3/1**[1]

0665 **2** 1 1/2 **Jack The Soldier (IRE)**[23] 2947 7-10-12 **84** CharlieStudd(3) 88
(Chris Gordon) *chsd ldrs: mstke 5th: wnt 2nd 10th tl 11th: 4th and outpcd u.p after 3 out: rallied to chse wnr between last 2: kpt on u.p flat as wnr idled but nvr able to chal* **13/2**

4033 **3** 3 1/4 **Feeling Peckish (USA)**[5] 3305 7-10-8 **77** (t) AndrewGlassonbury 78
(Michael Chapman) *chsd ldr tl 2nd: rdn along and outpcd 11th: drvn bef 3 out: wnt 3rd last: no imp flat* **5/1**[3]

50 **4** 15 **Bajan Sunshine (IRE)**[100] 1646 10-10-0 **69** (v[1]) JamesDavies 60
(Gary Brown) *hld up in tch in last trio: pushed along and hdwy to chse ldng trio 11th: rdn to chse wnr after 2 out: no imp and hld whn j.lft 2 out: wknd qckly bef last* **12/1**

0/U3 **5** 56 **Quintus (FR)**[74] 1995 7-11-7 **90** TomMessenger 52+
(Chris Bealby) *led: blnd 10th: mstke 12th: hdd and hit 3 out: wknd and dropped to last next: virtually p.u flat: t.o* **9/2**[2]

1-4P **F** **Sawpit Supreme**[21] 2986 9-11-9 **92** AidanColeman —
(Venetia Williams) *fell 1st* **8/1**

0-65 **P** **Rester Vrai (FR)**[51] 2436 6-10-5 **81** JoeCornwall(7) —
(John Cornwall) *hld up in tch in last trio: rdn and struggling 11th: losing tch whn blnd bdly next and immediately p.u* **8/1**

005 **P** **Domoly (FR)**[42] 2642 8-11-12 **95** LeightonAspell —
(Alison Batchelor) *t.k.h: hld up in tch in last trio: mstke 7th: losing tch whn mstke 12th: tailing off whn p.u 3 out* **10/1**

5m 13.1s (7.80) **Going Correction** +0.45s/f (Soft) **8** Ran SP% **112.2**
Speed ratings: **103,102,101,95,74** —,—,—
toteswingers: 1&2 £3.40, 1&3 £3.60, 2&3 £6.40. CSF £21.98 CT £92.07 TOTE £4.00: £2.20, £2.50, £1.10; EX 21.60.
Owner Mrs H R Cross **Bred** Mrs H R Cross **Trained** Burlescombe, Devon

FOCUS
A very ordinary contest in which few could be faniced. The winner was well handicapped on his best form over shorter.

NOTEBOOK
Normandy Landings has plenty of experience over fences but came into this a maiden under all codes after plenty of tries. However, despite getting to the front plenty early enough, he managed to hold off all challengers. (op 4-1)
Jack The Soldier(IRE), who reportedly got worked up in the paddock, didn't show a great deal on his chasing debut under rules at Folkestone (2m) and was readily held despite running on strongly after the last. (op 4-1)
Feeling Peckish(USA) was another to keep on after getting outpaced. (op 11-2 tchd 13-2)
Bajan Sunshine(IRE), fitted with a visor for the first time, was up 4f in distance and came with a promising effort to chase Normandy Landings before fading quickly once in the home straight. (op 10-1)
Quintus(FR), now trying 2m4f, set off at a good pace and was allowed an easy lead. He appeared to enjoy himself when in the clear but stopped quickly once joined. (op 11-2)
Rester Vrai(FR), dropping in trip after finishing well beaten over 3m on his first run over fences, was well behind when his jockey pulled him up. (op 16-1)
Domoly(FR), making his chasing/handicap debut for new connections after leaving Ferdy Murphy, was beaten early. (op 16-1)

3403 WILLIAMHILL.COM "NATIONAL HUNT" NOVICES' HURDLE (8 hdls) 2m 110y
2:10 (2:12) (Class 4) 4-Y-0+ **£2,602** (£764; £382; £190)

Form RPR

1-52 **1** **Cucumber Run (IRE)**[22] 2963 6-11-5 0 BarryGeraghty 120+
(Nicky Henderson) *hld up in tch: clsd to trck ldrs after 4th: chsd ldr 3 out: shkn up to ld after 2 out: in command last: comf* **4/6**[1]

3151 **2** 6 **Mr Jay Dee (IRE)**[82] 1867 6-11-5 0 MattCrawley(7) 119+
(Lucy Wadham) *chsd ldrs: mstke 1st: clsd on ldr bef 4th: led after 4th: blnd next: rdn bef 2 out: hdd sn after 2 out: btn whn mstke last: styd on same pce flat* **16/1**

030 **3** 2 3/4 **Tatispout (FR)**[22] 2958 4-10-0 96 AndrewTinkler 89
(Charlie Longsdon) *hld up wl bhd: gd hdwy 5th: wnt 3rd and rdn between last 2: kpt on same pce flat* **33/1**

5-05 **4** 2 3/4 **This Masquerade**[16] 3057 8-11-5 0 JamieMoore 105
(Warren Greatrex) *chsd clr ldr: clsd bef 4th: lost 2nd 3 out: wknd bef next* **66/1**

00-4 **5** 9 **Spiritual Guidance (IRE)**[16] 3058 8-11-5 0 WayneHutchinson 97
(Warren Greatrex) *hld up wl off the pce towards rr: gd hdwy after 4th: chsd ldrs after next: rdn and wknd 3 out* **33/1**

0-05 **6** 20 **South Stack**[42] 2640 6-11-5 0 TomScudamore 79
(Michael Scudamore) *t.k.h early: hld up wl bhd: gd hdwy 5th: no imp bef 3 out: wnt modest 6th last* **100/1**

-453 **7** 3 1/4 **Thoresby (IRE)**[27] 2873 5-11-5 0 DarylJacob 79
(Ben Case) *chsd ldrs: clsd bef 4th: rdn and wknd bef 3 out: t.o* **16/1**

0-P0 **8** 9 **Sheepclose (IRE)**[9] 3167 6-10-12 0 JakeGreenall(7) 68
(Michael Easterby) *t.k.h: hld up wl bhd: pushed along after 3rd: lost tch 5th: sme late hdwy: n.d: t.o* **100/1**

1-00 **9** 2 **Pere Blanc (IRE)**[27] 2873 6-11-5 0 TimmyMurphy 66
(David Arbuthnot) *hld up wl bhd: lost tch after 5th: nvr trbld ldrs: t.o* **40/1**

3-1F **10** 1/2 **High Benefit (IRE)**[22] 2954 6-11-5 0 RobertThornton 79+
(Alan King) *hld up in midfield: hdwy to chse ldrs 5th: rdn and wknd qckly 3 out: t.o* **11/4**[2]

U-05 **11** hd **Fairynuff**[43] 2612 7-11-5 0 RichieMcGrath 65
(Kate Walton) *racd in midfield: n.m.r on inner and pushed along after 3rd: mstke next: wknd 5th: t.o* **66/1**

/05- **12** 9 **Star King (IRE)**[406] 2527 6-11-5 0 HaddenFrost 57
(Henrietta Knight) *hld up in midfield: j.rt 1st: clsd and in tch 4th: wknd next: t.o* **100/1**

2-U **13** 10 **Somewhatinevitable (IRE)**[41] 2666 6-11-5 0 WillKennedy 48
(Paul Webber) *t.k.h: in tch in main gp: clsd and chsd ldrs 4th: rdn next: wknd qckly bef 3 out: t.o* **14/1**[3]

5 **14** 2 1/4 **Automaticman (IRE)**[56] 2328 5-11-5 0 RichardJohnson 46
(Henry Daly) *a bhd: lost tch 5th: t.o* **50/1**

05 **15** 18 **Absolution (IRE)**[26] 2896 5-11-5 0 AndrewThornton 30
(Henrietta Knight) *t.k.h early: chsd ldrs tl lost pl rapidly 4th: wl t.o after next: pushed out flat* **100/1**

0-0 **P** **Medicine Man (IRE)**[61] 2216 7-11-5 0 JasonMaguire —
(Ben De Haan) *led and sn clr: c bk to field bef 4th: hdd after 4th: sn dropped out: t.o whn p.u 3 out* **80/1**

3m 49.0s (-5.90) **Going Correction** -0.175s/f (Good)
WFA 4 from 5yo+ 11lb **16** Ran SP% **123.5**
Speed ratings (Par 105): **106,103,101,100,96 86,85,81,80,80 79,75,70,69,61** —
toteswingers: 1&2 £4.80, 1&3 £8.30, 2&3 £21.60. CSF £14.70 TOTE £1.70: £1.10, £2.60, £5.80; EX 12.20.
Owner The Goblyns **Bred** Miss Nicola Ann Adams **Trained** Upper Lambourn, Berks

FOCUS
This looked an uncompetitive contest, but it was strongly run and the fastest time over the trip. The cosy winner was value for further.

NOTEBOOK
Cucumber Run(IRE) was taking a drop in trip after a promising performance at Newbury. Always close up, he was well positioned throughout and came home quite an easy winner once getting to the front. The way he kept on suggests that he is well worth another try over further in time, and is no doubt worth a try at a slightly higher level. (tchd 8-11)
Mr Jay Dee(IRE), sold for 22,500gns out of the Alan Swinbank stable since his last start, comfortably won a Kelso maiden in October and appeared to run up to his best here after being given a prominent ride. He hit three out quite hard but kept on well thereafter, and he looks an above-average sort. (op 20-1)
Tatispout(FR) looked interesting getting at least 19lb from most of the field, and probably ran as well as she was entitled to. She was been under restraint towards the rear, and may make more progress if settling a little better. (op 28-1)
This Masquerade had run respectably in Kempton jumpers' bumper on his previous outing and showed a modicum of promise here.
Spiritual Guidance(IRE), one place behind his stablemate, like him had run respectably in a jumpers' bumpers at Kempton latest, and showed a little promise here. (op 40-1)
High Benefit(IRE) travelled quite strongly in midfield but faded quickly once under strong pressure. Something may have been amiss with her considering the way her jockey eased off. (op 3-1)

3404 WILLIAM HILL - HOME OF BETTING H'CAP CHASE (12 fncs) 2m 110y
2:40 (2:42) (Class 5) (0-90,88) 5-Y-0+ **£2,276** (£668; £334; £166)

Form RPR

2-0P **1** **Lerida**[62] 2194 9-10-13 **75** (p) BrianHarding 82+
(Sharon Watt) *chsd ldr tl led after 5th: mde rest: hld on wl u.p flat* **11/2**[2]

-002 **2** 1 1/4 **Mamba (GER)**[49] 2468 9-10-5 **67** JamesDavies 74+
(Chris Down) *hld up in last pair: reminder after 5th: hdwy next: chsd ldrs and barging match w rival bef 2 out: kpt on u.p to chse wnr fnl 50yds* **4/1**[1]

0FP4 **3** 1 **Follow The Sun (IRE)**[41] 2659 7-11-12 **88** BrianHughes 92
(Peter Niven) *hld up in last pair: hdwy 5th: chsd ldrs and barging match w rival bef 2 out: stl on bit and chal last: rdn and unable qck flat: wknd fnl 50yds* **13/2**[3]

5P42 **4** 1/2 **Rince Donn (IRE)**[46] 2559 9-10-11 **80** MrTGarner(7) 84
(Roger Curtis) *hld up in tch: chsd wnr and rdn after 3 out: styd on same pce flat* **4/1**[1]

2U03 **5** 11 **Peak Seasons (IRE)**[5] 3307 8-10-12 **74** AndrewGlassonbury 69
(Michael Chapman) *chsd ldrs: wnt 2nd 9th: ev ch 3 out: rdn and wknd bef next* **11/2**[2]

4550 **6** 33 **Mad Professor (IRE)**[22] 2956 8-10-0 **69** (b) JoeCornwall(7) 48
(John Cornwall) *chsd ldrs: w ldr after 5th tl 9th: wknd after next: t.o* **12/1**

6P53 **P** **Colliers Court**[56] 2334 14-11-5 **88**................................ HarryChalloner(7) —
(Lisa Williamson) *led tl hdd and rdn after 5th: sn dropped to last and lost tch: t.o whn p.u next* **8/1**

3/60 **P** **Jubilee George**[15] 3092 11-11-9 **85**................................ TomMessenger —
(Christopher Kellett) *in tch: lost pl and j. slowly 4th: blnd 8th: wknd after 3 out: t.o whn p.u last* **10/1**

4m 20.8s (10.60) **Going Correction** +0.45s/f (Soft) **8** Ran SP% **112.0**
Speed ratings: **93,92,91,91,86 71,—,—**
toteswingers: 1&2 £4.50, 1&3 £4.90, 2&3 £3.60. CSF £27.20 CT £143.76 TOTE £5.40: £1.70, £1.20, £3.00; EX 28.30.
Owner Famous Five Racing **Bred** Worksop Manor Stud **Trained** Brompton-on-Swale, N Yorks

FOCUS
With the top weight a 14-y-o officially rated 88, it's fair to say this contest didn't take a great deal of winning. The winner ran to his mark with chase bests from the next two.

NOTEBOOK
Lerida was always prominent and showed a fine attitude under pressure to win his first race since October 2008. His two previous runs this season were poor, although connections reported afterwards they thought the horse would have won last time (pulled up at Hexham) had he not pulled a shoe off. (op 13-2)
Mamba(GER) appears to have improved since going over fences, and should be capable of winning something off such a lower mark if getting into races. (op 7-2 tchd 9-2)
Follow The Sun(IRE), who raced prominently or led the last two times he had run over fences, travelled strongly throughout at the rear and it looked a matter of time before he got to the front considering the way he was going in the home straight, but his jockey delayed his effort for as long as he could and the horse found less than expected off the bridle. (op 8-1)
Rince Donn(IRE), without a tongue-tie this time, was produced to have every chance but could never get to the front. (op 7-2)
Colliers Court appeared to down tools quickly once challenged for the lead. Official explanation: trainer said gelding finished distressed (op 15-2 tchd 7-1)
Jubilee George Official explanation: £140 fine: entered the parade ring after the signal to mount had been given (op 15-2 tchd 7-1)

3405 WILLIAM HILL - HOME OF BETTING NOVICES' HURDLE (10 hdls) 2m 4f 110y
3:10 (3:10) (Class 4) 4-Y-0+ **£2,276** (£668; £334; £166)

Form			RPR

1B6F **1** **Radetsky March (IRE)**[40] 2674 8-11-6 0.......................... JasonMaguire 125+
(Mark Bradstock) *mde all: clr 7th: in command whn j.lft last 2: easily* **20/1**

2 *12* **Faultless Feelings (IRE)**[252] 74 5-11-6 0.................... RichardJohnson 112
(Philip Hobbs) *in tch in midfield: rdn to chse ldng trio 3 out: wnt 3rd but no ch w wnr after 3 out: kpt on to go 2nd flat* **8/1**[3]

3 *1* **Cheney Manor**[221] 6-10-13 0................................ MrNdeBoinville(7) 113+
(Nicky Henderson) *chsd ldrs: chsd clr ldr 7th: rdn and no imp whn blnd 2 out: lost 2nd flat* **9/2**[2]

4 **4** *3 1/4* **Kingsmere**[60] 2241 6-11-6 0................................ AndrewTinkler 108
(Henry Daly) *hld up in tch towards rr: rdn and effrt bef 3 out: wnt modest 4th bef 2 out: j.lft last: kpt on but no ch w wnr* **9/1**

5-30 **5** *8* **Oddjob (IRE)**[23] 2946 7-11-6 0................................ JamieMoore 101
(Warren Greatrex) *t.k.h: hld up in tch: rdn and lost pl after 6th: no ch w wnr but plugged on again after 3 out* **50/1**

40-0 **6** *3 1/4* **Empire Builder (IRE)**[22] 2963 5-11-6 0...................... AndrewThornton 98
(Caroline Bailey) *t.k.h hld up in midfield early: dropped to rr after 5th: pushed along and hdwy into midfield bef 3 out: sn no imp: plugged on* **16/1**

2-10 **7** *6* **Amirico (IRE)**[24] 2925 6-11-12 0................................ AidanColeman 99
(Venetia Williams) *chsd ldrs: 3rd: rdn and struggling bef 3 out: lost 3rd and wknd qckly bef 2 out* **8/1**[3]

1-0 **8** *10* **Custer Of The West (IRE)**[62] 2186 6-11-6 0........... WayneHutchinson 83
(Alan King) *t.k.h: hld up in tch: wknd bef 3 out: t.o* **50/1**

0-P **9** *10* **Sunday Sharpner (IRE)**[69] 2069 5-11-6 0.................. JimmyMcCarthy 74
(Renee Robeson) *in tch towards rr: rdn and wknd wl bef 3 out: t.o* **150/1**

P **10** *1* **Norwich Well (IRE)**[58] 2291 6-11-6 0.......................... LeightonAspell 74
(Oliver Sherwood) *in tch in rr: rdn and struggling 7th: wl btn next: t.o* **100/1**

1135 **11** *1/2* **Kartanian (IRE)**[22] 2960 5-11-6 0................................ TomO'Brien 83
(Philip Hobbs) *in tch: 5th and rdn after 7th: wl btn after next: t.o* **6/4**[1]

341P **12** *4* **Little Carmela**[5] 3308 7-11-5 109............................(p) DougieCostello 69
(Neil King) *mstke 1st: chsd ldr tl after 5th: dropped to rr after 6th: lost tch next: t.o* **25/1**

5-00 **13** *35* **Lambro River (IRE)**[3] 3374 6-11-6 0.............................. TimmyMurphy 38
(Alison Batchelor) *in tch in rr: j.lft 5th: mstke next: sn lost tch: t.o* **150/1**

23-5 **P** **Mister Chancer (IRE)**[60] 2241 6-11-6 0.......................... RobertThornton —
(Alan King) *chsd ldrs: wnt 2nd after 5th tl 7th: wknd bef next: mstke 3 out: wl btn whn eased and p.u 2 out* **11/1**

0P- **P** **Whatshallwedo**[291] 4765 6-11-6 0.................................. LiamHeard —
(Chris Down) *t.k.h: in tch: mstke 5th: lost tch qckly 7th: wl t.o whn p.u 2 out* **150/1**

4m 52.9s (-6.10) **Going Correction** -0.175s/f (Good) **15** Ran SP% **120.1**
Speed ratings (Par 105): **104,99,99,97,94 93,91,87,83,83 83,81,68,—,—**
toteswingers: 1&2 £18.70, 1&3 £12.50, 2&3 £12.50. CSF £167.57 TOTE £21.70: £4.90, £5.40, £1.30; EX 270.40.
Owner P J D Pottinger **Bred** Ms J Finn **Trained** Letcombe Bassett, Oxon

FOCUS
This had looked a good contest on paper but few got into it. The fourth and sixth are the best guides and the winner, a 130+ chaser at best, may be capable of rating higher over hurdles.

NOTEBOOK
Radetsky March(IRE), back over hurdles after running over fences since April 2008, went straight into the lead and stayed there, virtually unchallenged. It was a good, positive ride by Jason Maguire, which deserved to be rewarded, and he will be dangerous under a penalty if allowed an easy time of it in front again. (op 22-1)
Faultless Feelings(IRE), not beaten far on his only Irish start under rules, won a 2m4f maiden point (started 4-7 fav for that) and did the better of the two Hobbs representatives. He stayed on nicely after coming under pressure a long way out and is entitled to be straighter next time after a lengthy break. (op 10-1)
Cheney Manor, a wide-margin 2m5f point winner for this jockey last May on good to firm ground, showed plenty of promise but may have found the ground a bit too soft. A mistake two out ended his chances. (op 4-1 tchd 5-1)
Kingsmere, the winner of one of his two points, shaped with some promise on his hurdling debut and kept on here after being held up. He is probably one for handicaps. (op 8-1)
Oddjob(IRE) appeared to run better than he had last time and is certainly bred to do well over jumps, being a brother to Ground Ball and half-brother to Mr Pointment.
Empire Builder(IRE) has run two fair races since joining this stable, and one would imagine he'll find his level in handicaps. (op 14-1)
Amirico(IRE) won an ordinary contest on his hurdling debut (form hasn't worked out particularly well) and is seemingly being found out under his penalty. (op 9-1)
Kartanian(IRE) was up in trip after running with promise on his hurdling debut at Newbury, but hit a flat spot down the back straight and was a disappointment. He should be given another chance to prove this effort all wrong considering his earlier profile, as there is a chance he wants better ground. Official explanation: trainer said gelding ran flat (op 7-4 tchd 15-8)

3406 WILLIAMHILL.COM STANDARD OPEN NATIONAL HUNT FLAT RACE 1m 6f
3:40 (3:43) (Class 6) 4-6-Y-0 **£1,370** (£399; £199)

Form			RPR

2 **1** **Ericht (IRE)**[47] 2518 5-11-5 0.. BarryGeraghty 120+
(Nicky Henderson) *a gng wl: in tch: smooth hdwy to ld over 2f out: readily drew clr over 1f out: v easily* **1/2**[1]

2 *7* **Majorica King (FR)** 5-11-5 0.. LeightonAspell 107+
(Oliver Sherwood) *hld up in tch towards rr: hdwy 5f out: rdn to chse wnr 2f out: no ch w wnr but kpt on wl for 2nd* **16/1**

3 *3 1/2* **Evans Wood** 4-10-0 0..(t) JakeGreenall(7) 90
(Michael Easterby) *t.k.h: hld up in tch in rr: hdwy to chse ldrs 4f out: rdn wl over 1f out: no ch w wnr after but kpt on fnl f* **66/1**

4 *1 3/4* **Raifteiri (IRE)** 4-10-4 0.. AlexMerriam(3) 88
(Neil King) *in tch: chsd ldrs 4f out: rdn and unable qck over 2f out: no ch w wnr but kpt on again fnl f* **66/1**

5 *nk* **Johnny Owen (IRE)** 5-11-5 0.. APMcCoy 100
(David Brace) *hld up in tch: hdwy to chse ldrs over 4f out: drvn and nt pce of wnr wl over 1f out: kpt on same pce after* **9/2**[2]

6 *1 1/2* **Military Precision (IRE)** 5-11-5 0.......................... WayneHutchinson 98
(Warren Greatrex) *chsd ldr tl rdn over 2f out: lost 2nd 2f out and sn outpcd: wl hld ent fnl f* **8/1**[3]

0 **7** *6* **Hopes Up**[31] 2824 4-10-0 0.. DougieCostello 73
(Ian Williams) *led tl rdn and hdd over 2f out: wknd over 1f out* **66/1**

8 *5* **In Vigo (IRE)** 4-10-7 0.. PaulMoloney 73
(William Jarvis) *t.k.h: hld up in tch in midfield: wknd over 3f out* **20/1**

204 **9** *12* **Pearl Mountain (IRE)**[22] 2965 4-10-0 0.......................... GerardTumelty 52
(Jeff Pearce) *chsd ldrs: rdn along 6f out: wknd wl over 3f out* **33/1**

0 **10** *2* **Tango Master**[57] 2315 4-10-4 0.................................. RichardKilloran(3) 56
(Mouse Hamilton-Fairley) *in tch towards rr: rdn 5f out: wknd 4f out* **125/1**

11 *hd* **Marksman** 4-10-7 0.. JamesDavies 56
(George Margarson) *t.k.h: hld up in tch in midfield: hdwy to chse ldrs over 6f out: wknd over 3f out* **50/1**

0 **12** *34* **Stays All Night (FR)**[26] 2896 5-11-5 0.......................... RichardJohnson 27
(Tim Vaughan) *t.k.h: hld up in tch in rr: wknd over 4f out: wl btn and eased fnl f: t.o* **100/1**

13 *2* **Seventh Hussar** 5-11-5 0.. HaddenFrost 25
(Henrietta Knight) *chsd ldrs tl rdn: hung lft and btn over 2f out: virtually p.u after: t.o* **50/1**

6 **14** *2* **Rebel Flag (IRE)**[44] 2597 4-10-7 0.................................. TomMessenger 10
(Chris Bealby) *chsd ldrs tl wknd qckly 5f out: t.o* **66/1**

15 *1 3/4* **It's A Killer** 6-11-5 0.. AndrewThornton 20
(Richard Rowe) *t.k.h: hld up in tch in rr: lost tch 5f out: t.o* **66/1**

3m 16.9s (-3.10) **15** Ran SP% **122.7**
toteswingers: 1&2 £4.70, 1&3 £25.30, 2&3 £77.30. CSF £10.70 TOTE £1.60: £1.10, £3.10, £19.30; EX 11.90.
Owner Mrs Christopher Hanbury **Bred** Mrs M McDonagh **Trained** Upper Lambourn, Berks

FOCUS
Not much previous form to go on in this bumper and probably not much strength in depth, but the winner should rate higher and win more races.

NOTEBOOK
Ericht(IRE) finished second at Ascot to an enterprisingly ridden winner, but made no mistake in this after racing wide on the course throughout. He came right away at the end and gained some quotes for the Cheltenham Champion Bumper as a result, but connections seemed to favour a bid at the Aintree version in April instead. (op 8-15 tchd 8-13)
Majorica King(FR), a £22,000 half-brother to Flat/jump winners, and wearing a noseband for his debut, made good late headway and shapes as though he'll win a bumper if given a realistic opportunity. (op 20-1)
Evans Wood, who was wearing a tongue-tie on his debut, kept on really well down the home straight to show promise, and was making ground throughout the final 2f. (op 100-1)
Raifteiri(IRE), who is related to seven winners at 1m2f-plus, notably US Grade 2 winner Nazirali, fetched just £8,000 in November but looks well worth the money judged on this performance.
Johnny Owen(IRE), wearing a noseband on his debut, had a good pedigree for the Flat, being a brother to the useful 7f winner Picture Perfect, and was a 40,000euros yearling. Never far from the winner for much of the race, he showed signs of greenness and can improve for the run. (tchd 5-1)
Military Precision(IRE) has a decent Flat pedigree, and cost 15,000euros as 3-y-o. He travelled enthusiastically near the head of the chasing bunch but failed to pick up strongly when under pressure. (op 10-1)
Seventh Hussar Official explanation: jockey said gelding lost a shoe
T/Jkpt: Not won. T/Plt: £77.60 to a £1 stake. Pool: £66,522.80 - 625.05 winning tickets. T/Qpdt: £34.60 to a £1 stake. Pool: £5,090.00 - 108.60 winning tickets. SP

2584 LUDLOW (R-H)
Thursday, January 6
3407 Meeting Abandoned - Frozen track

3414 - (Foreign Racing) - See Raceform Interactive

2647 THURLES (R-H)
Thursday, January 6
OFFICIAL GOING: Hurdle course - yielding; chase course - soft

3415a BEAMISH STOUT PHIL SWEENEY MEMORIAL CHASE (GRADE 3) (13 fncs) 2m 2f
1:05 (1:05) 5-Y-0+ **£15,969** (£4,668; £2,211)

RPR

1 **Psycho (IRE)**[26] 2886 10-11-10 150.................................. PCarberry 154
(A J Martin, Ire) *trckd ldr in 2nd: chal fr 3 out: brought towards stands' side and led after 2 out: pushed out to assert run-in: kpt on wl* **5/2**[2]

2 *2 1/2* **Quiscover Fontaine (FR)**[258] 5379 7-11-3 142.......................... PTownend 144
(W P Mullins, Ire) *trckd ldrs: racd wd thrght: nt fluent 6 out: tk clsr order fr 4 out: pushed along fr 2 out: wnt 2nd at last: kpt on same pce but nt match wnr* **3/1**[3]

3	9	**Let Yourself Go (IRE)**[22] 2972 9-11-10 150 .... SJHassett (Adrian Maguire, Ire) *led: strly pressed fr 3 out: rdn and hdd after next: dropped to 3rd at last: no ex run-in* **7/4**[1]	142
F		**Clan Tara (IRE)**[8] 3206 9-11-3 138 .... (t) DNRussell (Paul Nolan, Ire) *trckd ldrs whn fell 3rd* **7/2**	—

4m 40.0s (-2.60) **4** Ran SP% **112.2**
CSF £10.16 TOTE £2.90; DF 16.00.
Owner Exors Of The Late C H McClure **Bred** J Mangan **Trained** Summerhill, Co. Meath

FOCUS
The winner looked better than ever in beating the smart runner-up, but the favourite was below par.

NOTEBOOK
Psycho(IRE) was able to track the favourite while jumping well at an even pace. Easing to the front between the final two fences, he didn't have to show an inordinate burst of speed to see them off. It was the ideal confidence booster after his setback. (op 2/1)
Quiscover Fontaine(FR) ran well and gives plenty of encouragement for the remainder of the season. He jumped well enough, was caught out a bit for pace at the top of the straight and pecked slightly on landing at the second last. He picked up and stayed on without having the speed of the winner. (op 10/3 tchd 5/2)
Let Yourself Go(IRE) went out in front as he normally does, but his best chance was to try to turn this into more of a stamina test and put the winner's jumping under pressure. This he never did and it was disappointing to see his challenge tamely fade. (op 7/4 tchd 2/1)

2951 BANGOR-ON-DEE (L-H)
Friday, January 7
3421 Meeting Abandoned - Snow

2390 FONTWELL (L-H)
Friday, January 7

OFFICIAL GOING: Heavy (soft in the odd place; 5.2)
The second fence down the back was omitted for all chases. Rail movement added 30yds per circuit on both courses.
Wind: virtually nil becoming medium across Weather: bright spells after earlier rain, raing for last three races

3428 DOCKER HUGHES MEMORIAL NOVICES' HURDLE (13 hdls) 3m 3f
1:00 (1:01) (Class 4) 5-Y-O+ **£2,016** (£592; £296; £147)

Form				RPR
0-46	1		**Half Cocked**[25] 2925 9-10-12 103 .... AndrewThornton (Richard Rowe) *chsd ldr tl led after 1st: mde rest: clr after 9th: drew wl clr after 3 out: v easily* **11/1**	121+
3213	2	18	**Saintly Lady (IRE)**[44] 2606 6-10-9 113 .... (p) DonalDevereux(3) (Peter Bowen) *chsd ldrs: wnt 3rd after 9th: chsd clr wnr u.p bef 2 out: no imp and wl hld between last 2* **9/4**[2]	96
-542	3	87	**Definite Dawn (IRE)**[43] 2642 7-10-12 120 .... APMcCoy (Tim Vaughan) *in tch in midfield: reminders after 5th and 7th: chsd wnr after 9th: drvn and no hdwy after 3 out: 3rd and v tired next: virtually p.u between last 2: t.o* **15/8**[1]	56
0/66	4	19	**Front Street (IRE)**[46] 2571 7-10-9 0 .... MichaelMurphy(3) (Pat Murphy) *hld up in tch in rr: lost tch qckly 9th: wl t.o fr next* **80/1**	—
2F-P	P		**War Of The World (IRE)**[174] 1020 9-10-7 0 .... MrTomDavid(5) (Tim Vaughan) *in tch in rr: nt fluent 2nd: lost tch after 9th: t.o bef 3 out tl p.u 2 out* **14/1**	—
2-21	P		**Acrai Rua (IRE)**[201] 797 8-10-12 115 .... PaulMoloney (Evan Williams) *in tch in rr: struggling and lost tch 8th: wl t.o whn p.u bef 10th* **4/1**[3]	—
03P	P		**Duke Of Ormond (IRE)**[22] 2981 8-10-12 0 .... (p) DaveCrosse (Anna Brooks) *chsd ldng pair: reminders after 5th: mstke next: more reminders after 7th: lost tch rapidly after 9th: t.o whn p.u next* **66/1**	—
4P4	P		**Lady Karinga**[16] 3089 6-10-5 0 .... JamieMoore (David Evans) *t.k.h early: led tl after 1st: chsd wnr after tl lost pl rapidly after 9th: t.o whn p.u bef next* **14/1**	—

7m 20.5s (27.70) **Going Correction** +1.175s/f (Heavy) **8** Ran SP% **109.9**
Speed ratings: **105,99,73,68,**—,—,—,—
Tote Swingers: 1&2 £6.30, 1&3 £5.20, 2&3 £1.20 CSF £34.28 TOTE £14.50: £2.40, £1.10, £1.50; EX 27.50.
Owner Richard Rowe Racing Partnership **Bred** Mrs P Nicholson **Trained** Sullington, W Sussex

FOCUS
A modest marathon novice hurdle where underfoot conditions played a big part. The going was officially heavy and the jockeys were very keen to emphasise just how testing conditions were. The winner produced a massive step up in the desperate ground.

NOTEBOOK
Half Cocked ◆ ran out an easy winner. One would never have guessed that this lightly raced sort was taking a considerable step up in trip, having never attempted further than 2m5f, as he thrived on the stamina test. Connections believe the ground to be key and may look at a race such as the Sussex National to target with him. If able to dominate like today, there appears little doubt he will be winning good races. (op 9-1)
Saintly Lady(IRE) is a very consistent mare who again appeared to again run her race, which suggests that the winner was not overly flattered. Handling the conditions and trip, she is in good heart and can find further opportunities in this class. (tchd 15-8)
Definite Dawn(IRE) was beaten a distance in third and was giving out distress signals with two circuits still to go. He should have enjoyed today's conditions, but was clearly below par and better can be expected next time. (op 7-4)
Front Street(IRE) probably prefers better ground, but may have a chance over staying distances.
War Of The World(IRE) travelled well for a long way on his reappearance after 174 days' absence, and should come on for this next time when he is likely to return to chasing. (op 12-1 tchd 16-1)
Acrai Rua(IRE) looked to hate this ground. (op 12-1 tchd 16-1)

3429 HARDINGS CATERING NOVICES' CHASE (14 fncs 2 omitted) 2m 6f
1:30 (1:30) (Class 4) 5-Y-O+ **£2,932** (£910; £490)

Form				RPR
50-0	1		**Quantitativeeasing (IRE)**[56] 2348 6-11-0 0 .... APMcCoy (Nicky Henderson) *trckd ldng pair: wnt 2nd after 11th: upsides ldr and stl on bit 3 out: led last: nudged clr flat: v easily* **8/11**[1]	137+
4-10	2	6	**Fruity O'Rooney**[48] 2523 8-11-7 0 .... JamieMoore (Gary Moore) *led: jnd and rdn 3 out: hdd last: nt pce of wnr flat: kpt on* **7/4**[2]	136+
4P6-	3	2 ¾	**Straw Bear (USA)**[377] 3031 10-11-0 0 .... LiamTreadwell (Nick Gifford) *nt a fluent: hld up in tch in last: wnt 3rd after 11th: no prog between last 2 and btn last* **12/1**[3]	121
PP31	P		**Prescelli (IRE)**[46] 2573 7-11-0 117 .... (p) TimmyMurphy (Keith Goldsworthy) *w ldr: rdn after 10th: rdn and dropped to last after next: wl btn whn mstke 2 out: p.u last* **20/1**	—

6m 13.0s (30.00) **Going Correction** +1.40s/f (Heav) **4** Ran SP% **106.7**
Speed ratings: **101,98,97,**—
CSF £2.38 TOTE £1.50; EX 2.80.
Owner John P McManus **Bred** Mrs C A Moore **Trained** Upper Lambourn, Berks

FOCUS
The second fence down the back was omitted for all chases. A fair novice chase with a couple of useful sorts. The easy winner handled the ground best of all and has been rated in line with his best hurdles form, but still a long way shy of what will be needed at Cheltenham.

NOTEBOOK
Quantitativeeasing(IRE) won this race in the manner of a good horse as he jumped well throughout and was never asked for any real effort as he cruised to victory. This was a much easier assignment for this formerly useful hurdler than his chase debut in November and was a good bit of placing by his trainer, as it allowed the gelding to get into a nice jumping rhythm and build his confidence. He eased past the leader after the last and clearly enjoyed the heavy ground, on which he has previously thrived. The new Jewson over 2m4f at the Cheltenham Festival looks an obvious target, for which he is a general 16-1 chance. He looks to have a promising chase career ahead of him. (tchd 4-5 and 5-6 in places)
Fruity O'Rooney slipped on landing six from home and his jockey did well to stay aboard. Despite being under pressure from then onwards, he kept finding more and proved himself as a very game sort. Under a penalty this was a good effort and he will surely win again soon if able to put in a clear round of jumping. (op 2-1)
Straw Bear(USA) was returning from a 377-day absence and looked more assured over fences than he has done before. Careful over the first couple of obstacles, he grew in confidence and put in a better round. Though unable to go with the eventual winner when he quickened away, he should come on for the run and connections will look for a beginners chase for him to get off the mark over fences. (tchd 14-1)
Prescelli(IRE) looked out of her depth here, beaten a long way from home, and is likely to be sent back handicapping. (op 12-1)

3430 HARDINGS CATERING NOVICES' H'CAP HURDLE (9 hdls) 2m 2f 110y
2:00 (2:00) (Class 5) (0-95,98) 4-Y-O+ **£1,599** (£496; £152)

Form				RPR
6311	1		**Eastwell Smiles**[7] 3261 7-12-1 98 7ex .... (bt) RichardJohnson (Richard Phillips) *mde all: clr after 1st: drew wl fr 6th: v easily* **8/11**[1]	105+
0-P4	2	49	**Autumm Spirit**[53] 2425 7-10-10 82 .... (t) WayneKavanagh(3) (Robin Dickin) *chsd ldrs: chsd clr wnr bef 4th: rdn and btn after 3 out: v tired after 2 out: t.o* **10/1**[3]	40
0-40	3	21	**Broadway Star (FR)**[191] 860 8-11-12 95 .... (t) APMcCoy (Tim Vaughan) *chsd wnr tl bef 4th: rdn and dropped to 4th after 5th: sn lost tch and t.o fr next* **6/5**[2]	32
000/	P		**Tecktal (FR)**[132] 4952 8-10-2 78 .... GarethThomas(7) (Pat Phelan) *chsd ldrs: j.rt 1st: 3rd and wkng whn mstke 6th: t.o whn p.u bef 2 out* **12/1**	—
-000	P		**Dalrymple (IRE)**[32] 2583 5-10-8 84 .... (t) MattCrawley(7) (Michael Madgwick) *bhd: sltly hmpd 1st: sn rdn along and nvr gng wl after: lost tch after 5th: wl t.o whn p.u 2 out* **25/1**	—

4m 58.4s (24.10) **Going Correction** +1.35s/f (Heav) **5** Ran SP% **107.1**
Speed ratings (Par 103): **103,82,73,**—,—
CSF £7.54 TOTE £1.60: £1.30, £3.00; EX 3.70.
Owner Mrs S J Harvey **Bred** Old Mill Stud **Trained** Adlestrop, Gloucs

FOCUS
A weak event. The winner confirmed the merit of his improved Warwick run but nothing else got home.

NOTEBOOK
Eastwell Smiles had been found a decent opportunity and racked up a hat-trick. Leading from start to finish, Richard Johnson, on his only ride of the day, set a fair early pace which had his rivals in trouble with more than a circuit to go. The winner thrived on the stamina test, pulling further clear the further he went. Due to go up another 3lb, even that may not be enough, as he looks a fair sort who can win his share of races at this lowly level and over longer trips. (op 5-6 and 10-11 in a place)
Autumm Spirit had shown little so far, but was the only one to give the winner any sort of race. She perhaps struggled with the stamina test and may need better ground to get competitive as the trip should have suited. (op 9-1 tchd 11-1)
Broadway Star(FR) was having his first run for his new trainer. He should come on for the outing, though is likely to be seen to better effect on decent ground. (tchd 9-4 and 11-4)
Tecktal(FR) has shown little in her previous attempts over hurdles, but this was her first run over the obstacles in 635 days, so she may come on a little for the experience. (op 9-1)
Dalrymple(IRE) was outpaced from the off and looks difficult to place. (op 9-1)

3431 HARDINGS CATERING H'CAP CHASE (16 fncs 3 omitted) 3m 2f 110y
2:30 (2:30) (Class 4) (0-105,104) 5-Y-O+ **£3,177** (£1,155)

Form				RPR
1-12	1		**Abbey Dore (IRE)**[25] 2930 8-10-5 86 .... JimmyDerham(3) (Seamus Mullins) *a gng wl: hld up in tch: hdwy to chse ldrs after 6th: wnt 2nd after 12th: pushed ahd bef last: sn in command: comf* **85/40**[1]	105+
2222	2	18	**Topless (IRE)**[22] 2982 10-11-11 103 .... (b) DougieCostello (Neil Mulholland) *chsd ldr tl gd jump to ld 2nd: mde most after tl rdn and hdd bef last: sn btn* **13/2**	99
1P-4	P		**Herald Angel (FR)**[54] 2401 8-11-5 104 .... (t) CDTimmons(7) (Barry Brennan) *in tch in rr: niggled along after 6th: hdwy into midfield 10th: chsd ldng trio 12th: struggling next: wnt modest 3rd wl bef 3 out: sn lost tch: t.o whn p.u last* **16/1**	—
10-5	P		**Absolute Shambles**[110] 1550 7-11-0 92 .... (t) ColinBolger (Chris Gordon) *led tl outj. and hdd 2nd: reminders after next and steadily lost pl: bhd 10th: losing tch whn p.u after next* **20/1**	—
-403	P		**Alteranthela (IRE)**[33] 2796 7-11-6 98 .... LeightonAspell (Richard Rowe) *in tch: lost pl and rr whn rdn along 6th: mstke 11th: sn lost tch: p.u bef next* **9/1**	—
/003	P		**Bob Casey (IRE)**[61] 2236 9-11-8 100 .... TimmyMurphy (Keith Goldsworthy) *chsd ldr 3rd: mstke 8th: lost 2nd after 11th: rdn and struggling whn mstke next: sn lost tch: t.o whn p.u 3 out* **10/1**	—
1-30	P		**Quartz Du Montceau (FR)**[25] 2928 7-11-0 92 .... (p) FelixDeGiles (Anna Newton-Smith) *chsd ldrs: mstke 5th: rdn 10th: dropped to last and struggling u.p 12th: t.o whn p.u 3 out* **11/2**[3]	—
3-F3	P		**Douryna**[8] 3226 8-10-13 91 .... JoeTizzard (Colin Tizzard) *hld up in tch: hdwy into midfield after 8th: rdn and fdd rapidly after 11th: tailing off whn p.u bef next* **4/1**[2]	—

7m 34.9s (33.80) **Going Correction** +1.40s/f (Heav) **8** Ran SP% **110.5**
Speed ratings: **105,99,**—,—,—,—,—,—
Tote Swingers: 1&2 £10.30 CSF £15.41 TOTE £4.10: £2.10, £1.80; EX 12.70.
Owner Dr & Mrs Peter Leftley **Bred** Dermot Day **Trained** Wilsford-Cum-Lake, Wilts

FOCUS
Only two got home in this moderate staying handicap. The winner produced a big step up but the form could be 5lb+ out either way.

NOTEBOOK

Abbey Dore(IRE) ended up an easy winner, completing his fourth victory in his last five starts, off a 3lb higher mark than his creditable second last time out at Plumpton. Held up early on, he crept nicely into the race before jumping into the lead two out and pulling clear of the runner-up. Sure to receive a hike in the weights, he is still on the upgrade and has more races in him. (op 5-2 tchd 2-1 and 11-4 in a place)

Topless(IRE) set a strong pace and had all bar the winner well beaten off. This was another game performance and she sets a decent enough standard, but she does herself no favours as she needs a drop in the handicap to give her a chance of winning. She is too consistent for her own good. (op 4-1)

Herald Angel(FR) has won over this trip before but on good ground so this was a respectable enough effort and he can be effective off his current mark on a better surface. (op 17-2)

Absolute Shambles Official explanation: jockey said gelding was never travelling and pulled up (op 17-2)

Bob Casey(IRE) ran reasonably for quite a way, but he didn't see out the trip as well as expected. (op 17-2)

Douryna seemed outpaced from an early stage and despite early signs of promise over fences, she hasn't yet looked like fulfilling it. (op 17-2)

3432 HARDINGS CATERING H'CAP HURDLE (11 hdls) 2m 6f 110y

3:00 (3:00) (Class 5) (0-95,94) 4-Y-0+ **£1,561** (£458; £229; £114)

Form RPR

3452 **1** **Can't Remember**[10] 3155 6-10-10 **85** .... OliverDayman(7) 93+
(Alison Thorpe) *hld up in tch: trckd ldrs 6th: led jst bef 3 out: rdn bef next: forged ahd bef last: tired but kpt on gamely flat* **9/2**[3]

36-4 **2** *15* **Jordan**[24] 2949 8-10-13 **88** .... MrTJCannon(7) 83
(Suzy Smith) *in tch: chsd ldrs 7th: ev ch 3 out: sn clr w wnr and rdn: wknd between last 2: btn whn mstke last* **13/8**[1]

-060 **3** *8* **Chouromanesco (FR)**[191] 863 8-11-10 **92** .... MattieBatchelor 77
(Mark Bradstock) *t.k.h: hld up in last pair: hdwy to press ldr 3rd: ev ch 3 out: sn wknd* **8/1**

650- **4** *28* **Hazy Bay**[260] 5326 6-11-7 **89** .... AndrewThornton 57
(Michael Roberts) *led tl hdd jst bef 3 out: mstke 3 out and sn lost tch: t.o next* **14/1**

U220 **P** **Rossbrin (IRE)**[24] 2937 6-11-3 **85** .... AndrewTinkler —
(Anna Brooks) *in tch: dropped to last and rdn after 7th: lost tch bef 3 out: t.o whn p.u 2 out* **2/1**[2]

6m 28.5s (46.00) **Going Correction** +1.35s/f (Heavy) **5** Ran SP% **107.4**
Speed ratings (Par 103): **74,68,66,56,**—
CSF £11.97 TOTE £3.50: £1.10, £1.40; EX 7.00.
Owner Tristar **Bred** R C And Mrs A J Long **Trained** Bronwydd Arms, Carmarthens

FOCUS

A very weak handicap. Surprisingly, given the ground, the form makes plenty of sense.

NOTEBOOK

Can't Remember was the only horse in the field to have won over hurdles and had been a decent runner-up off this mark in a better race last time out at Ffos Las. She looked in a little bit of trouble with a circuit still to go but kept on finding more in the back straight to put herself in contention. Jumping the second-last best, she was able to quicken away, though she may struggle with a rise in mark as she doesn't win all too often. (op 10-3 tchd 3-1)

Jordan was certain to act in the ground, but having been out-jumped at the second-last was only able to stay on one-paced. Well supported, this was a decent run and she is one to respect if running in easy ground next time out. (op 2-1 tchd 6-4)

Chouromanesco(FR) was making his handicap debut after a 191-day absence and ran fairly well for some way. He should come on for the run and can find opportunities in this class. (op 7-1 tchd 17-2)

Hazy Bay looked to be travelling well but seemed to stop quickly halfway down the back straight. (op 9-1)

3433 HARDINGS CATERING H'CAP CHASE (13 fncs 2 omitted) 2m 4f

3:30 (3:30) (Class 4) (0-115,115) 4-Y-0+ **£2,862** (£840; £420; £209)

Form RPR

6 **1** **Roi De Rose (FR)**[24] 2948 7-11-9 **112** .... (p) TomScudamore 129+
(David Pipe) *chsd ldrs: wnt 2nd after 7th: led 9th: mde rest: gng clr whn hit 3 out: styd on wl: comf* **15/8**[1]

-365 **2** *12* **Josear**[22] 2975 9-11-9 **112** .... SamThomas 114+
(Chris Down) *chsd ldrs: wnt 3rd after 9th: rdn and no hdwy whn j.lft 3 out: chsd clr wnr bef next: kpt on but no imp* **7/1**[3]

P-P1 **3** *7* **Sordid Secret (IRE)**[218] 597 8-10-13 **102** .... PaulMoloney 94
(Evan Williams) *in tch towards rr: mstke 5th: pushed along and struggling after 8th: lost tch wl bef 3 out: wnt modest 3rd 2 out* **8/1**

4530 **4** *8* **Morestead (IRE)**[23] 2961 6-11-2 **105** .... (b) LeightonAspell 92
(Brendan Powell) *led tl hdd and mstke 9th: wknd qckly next: wl btn bef 3 out* **8/1**

-5U5 **5** *19* **Island Jim (IRE)**[24] 2949 7-10-13 **102** .... (t) PaddyBrennan 78+
(Charlie Longsdon) *racd off the pce in midfield: mstke 4th: clsd and chsd ldrs 7th: mstke 9th: chsd wnr bef next: btn 3 out: sn fdd: eased after last* **5/1**[2]

-450 **P** **Commemoration Day (IRE)**[47] 2541 10-11-5 **115** ....(b) JoshuaMoore(7) —
(Gary Moore) *a bhd: rdn along and nvr travelling after: lost tch u.p 8th: t.o whn p.u 10th* **14/1**

5002 **P** **Coach Lane**[23] 2961 10-11-6 **109** .... DarylJacob —
(Nick Mitchell) *chsd ldrs: wknd rapidly 10th: t.o next tl p.u 2 out* **5/1**[2]

4500 **P** **Lidjo De Rouge (FR)**[63] 2184 12-9-13 **95** .... MrDGPrichard(7) —
(Paul Henderson) *a in rr: lost tch after 8th: t.o after 10th tl p.u last* **12/1**

5m 36.5s (29.20) **Going Correction** +1.40s/f (Heavy) **8** Ran SP% **117.2**
Speed ratings (Par 105): **97,92,89,86,78** —,—,—
Tote Swingers: 1&2 £4.90, 1&3 £3.80, 2&3 £10.60 CSF £16.24 CT £86.82 TOTE £2.70: £1.20, £1.70, £2.70; EX 17.80.
Owner A Wichser **Bred** Ernst Iten **Trained** Nicholashayne, Devon

FOCUS

A moderate handicap and another clear-cut winner in Roi De Rose, who is rated up a stone+ on his recent Britsih debut.

NOTEBOOK

Roi De Rose(FR) ◆, an impressive winner, had put in an eyecatching effort on his British debut last time out and clearly improved from that run. An economical jumper, he was ridden prominently and seemed to enjoy the decent gallop that was set. Despite a mistake three out, he pulled clear of the field and looks the sort sure to thrive over 3m. He is obviously quite well thought of as he went off a well backed favourite and seems likely to be able to handle a rise in mark. He is one to keep a close eye on in the coming months. (op 9-4 tchd 5-2 in a places)

Josear ran well, creeping into the race to join the leaders four from home, but may require a drop in mark to become competitive again as 112 looks a little on the high side. (op 15-2 tchd 8-1)

Sordid Secret(IRE) was a long way back for most of the race, but enjoyed the stamina test and stayed on well. An ex-Irish point winner, she is certainly worth stepping back up to 3m over which she won last time out, and should come on plenty for the run after this 218-day absence.

Morestead(IRE) has achieved two of his three career wins here, but all of them have come on good ground or faster. He led the field for a long time but his early exertions took their toll as he faded down the back. The way he kept on though suggests he is worth another chance when back on a better surface. (op 11-1 tchd 12-1)

Island Jim(IRE) was the subject of some good early market support and took up the running with just under a circuit to go. He just didn't appear to see out the trip, even taking into account the heavy conditions, and may improve for a step down in distance. (op 15-2)

3434 HARDINGS CATERING STANDARD OPEN NATIONAL HUNT FLAT RACE 2m 2f 110y

4:00 (4:00) (Class 6) 4-6-Y-0 **£1,370** (£399; £199)

Form RPR

1 **Arbeo (IRE)** 5-11-6 0 .... SamThomas 110+
(Diana Grissell) *a travelling wl: hld up in tch: jnd ldr on bit over 2f out: led jst over 1f out: sn drew wl clr: v easily* **8/1**

0- **2** *10* **Blazing Bolte**[529] 1064 6-10-13 0 .... JamieGoldstein 86
(Sheena West) *in tch: rdn and struggling over 3f out: styd on again fr over 1f out: wnt 2nd ins fnl f: no ch w wnr* **20/1**

04 **3** *3 1/4* **Twentyten (IRE)**[27] 2896 6-11-6 0 .... APMcCoy 90
(Paul Henderson) *chsd ldrs: wnt 2nd over 5f out: led over 3f out: jnd and rdn ent fnl 2f: hdd jst over 1f out: sn btn: lost 2nd ins fnl f* **5/1**[3]

1- **4** *6* **There And Then**[331] 3979 5-11-3 0 .... DarrenO'Keeffe(10) 92
(Seamus Mullins) *in tch towards rr: rdn 6f out: hdwy to chse ldrs over 4f out: wknd over 2f out* **7/2**[1]

5 *22* **Brass Tax (IRE)**[251] 5-11-6 0 .... JimmyMcCarthy 62
(Charlie Morlock) *in tch in midfield: rdn and wknd 3f out: wl bhd fnl f: t.o* **12/1**

0 **6** *11* **Psychosis**[22] 2987 6-10-13 0 .... JamesDavies 44
(Brendan Powell) *chsd ldrs tl wknd over 4f out: wl bhd fnl f: t.o* **20/1**

7 *13* **Oscar The Myth (IRE)** 5-11-6 0 .... DarylJacob 38
(Jamie Snowden) *in tch tl wknd over 4f out: t.o over 1f out* **10/1**

8 *2 3/4* **Lord Richie (IRE)** 5-11-3 0 .... MichaelMurphy(3) 35
(Pat Murphy) *w ldr on inner tl over 4f out: hung lft and wknd rapidly over 2f out: t.o and virtually p.u fnl f* **33/1**

02 **9** *nk* **Tenby Jewel (IRE)**[46] 2576 6-11-6 0 .... TimmyMurphy 35
(Keith Goldsworthy) *led tl over 3f out: wknd rapidly over 2f out: virtually p.u fnl f: t.o* **4/1**[2]

4 **P** **Ice 'N' Easy (IRE)**[52] 2445 5-11-6 0 .... AndrewThornton —
(Richard Rowe) *in tch tl lost tch qckly 7f out: wl t.o whn p.u 1f out* **11/2**

0 **P** **Lady Gower**[16] 3088 5-10-13 0 .... JamieMoore —
(David Evans) *sn bhd and nvr gng wl: t.o whn p.u 1/2-way* **50/1**

4m 52.7s (24.00) **Going Correction** +1.35s/f (Heavy)
WFA 4 from 5yo 11lb 5 from 6yo 3lb **11** Ran SP% **116.6**
Speed ratings: **103,98,97,94,85 81,75,74,74,**— —
Tote Swingers: 1&2 £21.90, 1&3 £8.60, 2&3 £8.80. Totesuper7: WIN: Not won. PLACE: £72.90 - 7 winning units. CSF £158.19 TOTE £11.40: £2.90, £4.90, £1.70; EX 142.60.
Owner Nigel & Barbara Collison **Bred** William J O'Doherty **Trained** Brightling, E Sussex

FOCUS

A tricky bumper to assess, but there was a taking winner who was value for further and should win more races. There were steps up from the next two.

NOTEBOOK

Arbeo(IRE) was an impressive winner who looks a nice prospect for connections. This 22,000euros buy travelled impressively throughout and was caused no problems at all by the testing conditions (op 12-1)

Blazing Bolte hadn't been seen on a racecourse for 529 days, but this was an encouraging performance as she stayed on strongly down the home straight to take second. She is sure to come on greatly for the run and is likely to thrive at staying trips. (op 25-1)

Twentyten(IRE) improved from his last run and is another who looks to have some ability. He kept on one-paced in the closing stages and appeared to enjoy the heavy underfoot conditions. (tchd 9-2)

There And Then was in trouble with a circuit to go and in the end did well to get so close to the leaders as he kept finding more in the home straight. Under a penalty it was a good effort, though he does look as though a step up in trip should suit when he goes hurdling. (op 3-1 tchd 4-1)

Brass Tax(IRE) looks as though he may turn out a decent long-term proposition. (op 14-1)

T/Jkpt: £3,216.20 to a £1 stake. Pool: £40,769 - 9 winning tickets. T/Plt: £7.80 to a £1 stake. Pool: £79,503 - 7,362.08 winning tickets. T/Qpdt: £3.10 to a £1 stake. Pool: £5,451.00 - 1,283.06 winning tickets. SP

2604 CHEPSTOW (L-H)

Saturday, January 8

OFFICIAL GOING: Soft (heavy in places)

This meeting was rearranged after being snowed off on December 27th.

Wind: medium across Weather: bright, light cloud

3435 GET BEST ODDS GUARANTEED AT CORAL.CO.UK BEGINNERS' CHASE (18 fncs) 3m

12:35 (12:35) (Class 4) 5-Y-0+ **£3,903** (£1,146; £573; £286)

Form RPR

10-5 **1** **Silver Kate (IRE)**[59] 2303 8-10-7 0 .... AidanColeman 137+
(David Richards) *mde most tl 7th: j. ahd again next: drew clr w rival after 14th: rdn bef 2 out: nt fluent last: hdd flat: battled on v gamely to ld again nr fin* **2/1**[2]

P-22 **2** *nk* **Voramar Two**[44] 2631 8-11-0 0 .... (t) TomO'Brien 143
(Philip Hobbs) *in tch: chsd wnr bef 14th: rdn to chal 2 out: led narrowly flat: hdd and no ex nr fin* **13/8**[1]

0-20 **3** *25* **Tarateeno**[10] 3198 8-10-11 120 .... MichaelMurphy(3) 126+
(Pat Murphy) *hld up in tch: trcking ldrs and stl travelling wl whn slipped on landing and lost pl 11th: rallied to chse ldrs after 13th: wknd after next: lft modest 3rd 2 out* **9/1**

1P1- **4** *62* **Whats Up Woody (IRE)**[303] 4530 6-11-0 0 .... BrianHughes 56
(Howard Johnson) *w wnr 3rd tl led 7th tl 8th: styd w wnr tl wknd qckly bef 14th: t.o fr 3 out: t.o whn lft 4th 2 out* **8/1**[3]

-032 **F** **Moorlands Teri**[11] 3171 8-10-2 0 .... (t) MrTomDavid(5) 107
(Tim Vaughan) *in tch: pushed along bef 13th: 3rd and wknd u.p after 14th: disputing 3rd and wl btn whn fell 2 out* **22/1**

1-54 **U** **General Kutuzov (IRE)**[25] 2945 7-11-0 0 .... LiamTreadwell —
(Nick Gifford) *t.k.h: chsd ldrs tl blnd bdly and uns rdr 13th* **10/1**

4 **P** **Sunsalve (IRE)**[219] 602 7-11-0 0 .... (t) APMcCoy —
(Rebecca Curtis) *nt fluent: in tch in rr: struggling 11th: tailing off whn p.u 13th* **16/1**

6m 16.2s (-5.80) **Going Correction** +0.075s/f (Yiel) **7** Ran SP% **111.9**
Speed ratings: **112,111,103,82,**— —,—
Tote Swingers: 1&2 £1.02, 1&3 £5.60, 2&3 £5.80 CSF £5.68 TOTE £3.10: £1.80, £1.30; EX 7.50.
Owner David M Richards **Bred** Patrick J Hannon **Trained** Llantilio Crossenny,Monmouths

FOCUS

This fair staying beginners' chase was run at an average tempo and the two market leaders dominated from the fifth-last. The winner can probably match her hurdles best of 142 over fences and the second ran to his mark.

NOTEBOOK

Silver Kate(IRE) jumped far too deliberately on her chasing debut at Bangor in November, but she loves this track and put in a vastly improved effort to get off the mark. Very well backed, she was soon at the head of affairs and had clearly benefited from intensive schooling at home as she jumped neatly. She looked vulnerable as the runner-up loomed up off the home turn, but kept responding to pressure and refused to go down in a driving finish after the last. This 141-rated hurdler is now 3-4 at the course and should go on from this as a chaser now. (op 10-3 tchd 7-2)

Voramar Two ◆ has now found one too good on his three outings over fences, but he gave his all in defeat under a strong ride and has to be considered unfortunate to have bumped into the winner. He certainly deserves a change of fortune and probably does want a slightly sounder surface. (op 6-4 tchd 7-4)

Tarateeno spoilt his chance with a bad mistake at the 11th. He is a dour stayer and did his best to get back into contention, but was always up against it thereafter. A return to handicaps or move to one of the smaller tracks looks best for him. (op 8-1)

Whats Up Woody(IRE) won two of his four outings over hurdles last term and had conditions in his favour for this chasing debut after a 303-day absence. He did things nicely through the race under a positive ride, but ultimately paid for being too enthusiastic. The run should bring him on a bundle. (tchd 15-2)

General Kutuzov(IRE) proved free early on and disappointingly departed at the 13th fence. (op 9-1 tchd 8-1)

3436 CORAL FUTURE CHAMPIONS FINALE JUVENILE HURDLE (GRADE 1) (8 hdls) — 2m 110y

1:10 (1:11) (Class 1) 4-Y-O

£19,953 (£7,486; £3,748; £1,869; £938; £469)

Form	Pos	Dist	Horse / Trainer / Comment	Jockey	RPR
311	**1**		**Marsh Warbler**^{46} 2600 4-11-0 139 (Brian Ellison) *w ldr tl led bef 5th: hdd next: sn led again: rdn bef 2 out: styng on strly and gd jump last: in command flat: rdn out* **8/1^{3}**	FearghalDavis	140+
	2	*2¾*	**Houblon Des Obeaux (FR)**^{77} 4-11-0 0 (Venetia Williams) *in tch: effrt to press ldrs after 4th: led 5th: sn hdd: drvn 3 out: styd on same pce between last 2* **20/1**	AidanColeman	137
1	**3**	*¾*	**Smad Place (FR)**^{43} 2661 4-11-0 0 (Alan King) *t.k.h early: hld up wl in tch: effrt to press ldrs bef 5th: rdn and outpcd 3 out: rallied last: kpt on flat but no threat to wnr* **9/4^{2}**	WayneHutchinson	138+
11	**4**	*2¾*	**Sam Winner (FR)**^{28} 2882 4-11-0 146 (Paul Nicholls) *trckd ldrs: jnd ldrs bef 5th: rdn and swtchd lft after 2 out: fnd little u.p: wknd last* **8/13^{1}**	APMcCoy	134
12	**5**	*10*	**Dolatulo (FR)**^{43} 2661 4-11-0 137 (Paul Nicholls) *hld up wl in tch: 5th and struggling bef 3 out: wknd 2 out* **12/1**	HarrySkelton	124
4623	**6**	*19*	**Royal And Ancient (IRE)**^{35} 2306 4-11-0 111 (Milton Harris) *in tch in rr: mstke 4th: rdn and struggling bef next: wl bhd fr 3 out* **100/1**	(tp) DaveCrosse	105
26	**7**	*17*	**Kalamill (IRE)**^{56} 2356 4-11-0 0 (Shaun Lycett) *nt a fluent: led: j. slowly and reminder 2nd: hdd after 4th: sn wknd: t.o between last 2* **66/1**	(t) DenisO'Regan	88
	F		**Flighty Frances (IRE)**^{87} 4-10-7 0 (John Flint) *mstkes: in tch tl wknd bef 5th: bhd whn fell 3 out* **100/1**	WillKennedy	—

4m 9.50s (-1.10) **Going Correction** -0.10s/f (Good) **8** Ran SP% **119.7**

Speed ratings: **98,96,96,95,90 81,73,—**

Tote Swingers: 1&2 £13.80, 1&3 £2.00, 2&3 £9.40 CSF £105.03 TOTE £10.20: £1.80, £3.20, £1.10; EX 131.20 Trifecta £613.40 Part won. Pool of £828.97 - 0.70 winning units..

Owner Dan Gilbert & Kristian Strangeway **Bred** Darley **Trained** Norton, N Yorks

FOCUS

This has been a pretty weak race by Grade 1 standards in recent years and, despite some decent sorts having prevailed, it has failed to produce a Triumph Hurdle winner since Mysilv scored way back in 1993. Marsh Warbler produced a step up but would need to improve again to win the Triumph. Houblon Des Obeaux improved markedly on his French form, Smad Place ran to his debut level while Sam Winner still heads the juvenile rankings.

NOTEBOOK

Marsh Warbler ran out a decisive winner and caused a shake-up to the Triumph market. He had proved a revelation since getting on soft ground and looked decent in winning twice since his debut third for connections in November. He was given his usual positive ride and being able to race on the front-end on just an ordinary gallop proved right up his street. As the dash for home developed from the fourth-last flight he quickened neatly to go clear nearing the last and a decent leap there sealed it. Brian Ellison's 4-y-o was promoted to near the top of the betting for the Triumph, and Betfred and Totesport were most impressed in going as short as 8-1, which made him their new favourite. That looks worth holding fire on, however, as despite being open to more improvement, this was hardly the test that race will provide at a contrasting Cheltenham in March. He did score on quick ground on the Flat, but how his stamina will hold out there will have to be taken on trust. It may well prove that this was his big day.

Houblon Des Obeaux(FR) ◆ was making his British debut for new connections having scored once from seven previous outings over hurdles in France. He posted a massive run, holding every chance, and looking right at home on the deep surface. No doubt his previous experience was an advantage here, but he is bred for further and there is a strong chance a better pace would have been more to his liking. He ought to have little trouble defying a penalty back in ordinary juvenile company before having another crack at something more valuable. (op 22-1)

Smad Place(FR), whose yard won two of the last three runnings of this race, was an impressive debut winner at Newbury on his previous outing. He looked the one that was most inconvenienced by the ordinary gallop, however, as he lacked a change of gear when the tempo quickly lifted in the home straight. He was keeping on again towards the finish and bookmaker reaction to ease him for the Triumph could be worth taking a look at, as he should really prove more at home on that stiffer track. Coral went 20-1. (op 2-1, tchd 5-2 in places)

Sam Winner(FR) was all the rage to make it 3-3 since coming over from France. Paul Nicholls has a miserable record in this event, however, and this 4-y-o ran a long way below the level of his previous wins. He was in trouble from three out and was eased from about 4-1 to a general 10-1, still near the top of the Triumph market. His connections were quick to blame the tacky ground and perhaps returning to Cheltenham could always spark a revival, but his ability to act on the likely quicker surface come March would be of some concern. (op 8-11)

Dolatulo(FR) was the second string of Nicholls and had proved no match when trying to concede a penalty to Smad Place at Newbury last time out. He was keen in the preliminaries here and ridden with much greater restraint through the race, which saw him refuse to settle. He was never seriously in the hunt and is clearly headstrong, but the suspicion is that we may yet to have seen the best of him. (op 14-1)

3437 CORAL WELSH NATIONAL (HANDICAP CHASE) GRADE 3 (22 fncs) — 3m 5f 110y

1:45 (1:49) (Class 1) 5-Y-O+

£45,608 (£17,112; £8,568; £4,272; £2,144; £1,072)

Form	Pos	Dist	Horse / Trainer / Comment	Jockey	RPR
1-56	**1**		**Synchronised (IRE)**^{29} 2870 8-11-6 **150** (Jonjo O'Neill) *in tch on outer: hdwy to chse ldrs after 17th: j.lft and mstke 19th and j.lft after: wnt 2nd and led next: styd on strly to draw clr flat* **5/1^{2}**	APMcCoy	165+
23-P	**2**	*2¾*	**Giles Cross (IRE)**^{56} 2358 9-10-2 **132** (Victor Dartnall) *led: drew clr and dived 19th: hdd and rdn 2 out: no ex and btn flat: kpt on* **12/1**	HarrySkelton	143
-24U	**3**	*9*	**I'moncloudnine (IRE)**^{48} 2543 8-10-3 **133** (Neil Mulholland) *chsd ldrs: mstke 3rd: rdn and mstke 18th: wknd and hit 2 out: hld on for 3rd cl home* **16/1**	DougieCostello	135
F-04	**4**	*½*	**Ballyfitz**^{49} 2523 11-10-4 **134** (Nigel Twiston-Davies) *chsd ldrs 2nd tl 5th: styd prom: j.lft and bmpd rival 13th: lost pl next: rallied to chse ldrs 18th: 5th and wkng whn mstke 3 out: kpt on flat and pressing for 3rd nr fin* **8/1^{3}**	(p) DavidEngland	136
11-2	**5**	*11*	**Maktu**^{65} 2163 9-10-3 **136** (Pat Murphy) *t.k.h: chsd ldrs on outer: wnt 2nd 5th tl bef 3 out: sn wknd: 4th and btn whn mstke 3 out* **9/2^{1}**	MichaelMurphy(3)	129+
-211	**6**	*hd*	**Watamu Bay (IRE)**^{50} 2501 8-10-12 **147** (Paul Nicholls) *in tch towards rr: rdn after 11th: struggling and lost pl next: 13th and wl btn bef 18th: styd on fr 3 out: no ch w ldrs* **8/1^{3}**	MrRMahon(5)	137
21-0	**7**	*1½*	**Silver By Nature**^{42} 2673 9-11-12 **156** (Lucinda Russell) *in tch in midfield: hdwy and wl in tch after 17th: lft 6th next: sn rdn and wknd* **18/1**	PeterBuchanan	144
10-5	**8**	*nk*	**Ballyfoy (IRE)**^{49} 2512 10-10-6 **136** (Jamie Poulton) *in tch towards rr: struggling and mstke 16th: rallied u.p and bk in tch after next: wknd 18th* **20/1**	MattieBatchelor	124
4-43	**9**	*3½*	**Exmoor Ranger (IRE)**^{29} 2871 9-11-1 **145** (Victor Dartnall) *hld up in tch in rr: mstke 5th: hdwy after 11th: blnd 13th: rdn and wknd bef 18th* **16/1**	DenisO'Regan	129
-000	**10**	*2¼*	**Dashing George (IRE)**^{7} 3290 9-10-0 **130** oh2 (Dr Richard Newland) *hld up in tch in rr: hdwy 1/2-way: wl in tch after 17th: wkng whn hmpd next: wl btn 3 out* **33/1**	(b^{1}) LiamTreadwell	112
2 P0	**11**	*1*	**Flight Leader (IRE)**^{23} 2979 11-10-0 **130** (Colin Tizzard) *chsd ldrs: pushed along 15th: rdn and struggling whn blnd 19th: sn wknd* **50/1**	AidanColeman	111
U-42	**P**		**Royal Rosa (FR)**^{48} 2543 12-10-2 **132** (Howard Johnson) *in tch towards rr: mistke 10th and 11th and dropped to rr: lost tch 15th: t.o whn p.u 3 out* **25/1**	(p) BrianHughes	—
0243	**P**		**Magic Sky (FR)**^{18} 3059 11-9-9 **132** (Milton Harris) *hld up in rr: prog to trck ldrs 1/2-way: wkng whn hmpd 18th: wl bhd whn p.u last* **28/1**	JakeGreenall(7)	—
PP-P	**P**		**Dream Alliance**^{42} 2673 10-11-7 **151** (Philip Hobbs) *nt a fluent: a towards rr: lost tch 14th: t.o whn p.u 17th* **28/1**	(p) TomO'Brien	—
PP-0	**P**		**Old Benny**^{24} 2962 10-10-0 **130** oh3 (Alan King) *in tch in midfield: rdn and struggling 16th: lost tch after next: t.o whn p.u 3 out* **14/1**	(b) WayneHutchinson	—
0UU-	**P**		**Arbor Supreme (IRE)**^{48} 2565 9-10-10 **143** (W P Mullins, Ire) *in tch towards rr: j. slowly 12th: wknd 16th: wl bhd whn p.u 18th* **16/1**	RichieMcLernon(3)	—
2-02	**P**		**Dance Island (IRE)**^{49} 2522 8-10-7 **137** (Ben Case) *in tch: mstke 14th: pushed along and hdwy next: chsd ldrs after 17th: blnd next: sn wknd: wl bhd whn p.u 19th* **10/1**	CharliePoste	—
32-F	**F**		**Bench Warrent (IRE)**^{55} 2395 8-9-11 **130** (Charlie Mann) *chsd ldr tl 2nd: styd chsng ldrs: 6th and struggling whn fell 18th* **20/1**	(p) PeterToole(3)	—

7m 53.7s (4.70) **Going Correction** +0.075s/f (Yiel) **18** Ran SP% **128.6**

Speed ratings (Par 113): **96,95,92,92,89 89,89,89,88,87 87,—,—,—,— —,—,—**

Tote Swingers: 1&2 £22.50, 1&3 £30.60, 2&3 £49.70 CSF £60.99 CT £931.25 TOTE £6.30: £2.40, £3.70, £3.90, £2.70; EX 89.00 Trifecta £1984.50 Pool of £15849.81 - 5.91 winning units..

Owner John P McManus **Bred** Mrs Noreen McManus **Trained** Cheltenham, Gloucs

FOCUS

There wasn't much of a gallop on, so despite the gruelling test that meant it was a race where it paid to race handily. The form still looks strong with two old rivals coming clear, however. Synchronised is a high-class stayer on this sort of ground and Giles Cross posted a personal best, with I'moncloudnine close to his mark.

NOTEBOOK

Synchronised(IRE) was having his first run back over fences since winning the Midlands National last season and he followed up that victory with another ready effort off a 7lb higher mark. He had scored on his only previous visit here in 2009 over 3m, when also beating Giles Cross, and had the ground very much in his favour. He did have plenty of weight, but showed when becoming the first horse to win the Uttoxeter marathon carrying more than 11st that weight was not such a big issue to him. He was given a very well-judged ride by Tony McCoy - who has now been successful in all of the big National races - and went to the front with plenty in the tank after two out. He was in no serious danger thereafter and this was no doubt his most assured round of jumping over fences to date, so he appears to be learning with experience on that front. The winner will now take another rise in the handicap and it is not certain where he will run next, although connections are tempted by the Grand National just yet. Leaving Aintree for another year would perhaps be a wise move as he is still only an 8-yo, but looking at his jumping this time he could well take to the fences there. Ground is important to his cause, however, as he is no doubt at his best when the mud is flying and it usually rides nearer good in the National each April. He could be backed for that as big as 20-1 in the ante-post market after the race. He does have the option of reverting to hurdling as he is currently rated 7lb lower in that sphere and did show at Cheltenham on his previous outing there could be a race for him over the smaller jumps. (op 9-2)

Giles Cross(IRE), pulled up on his seasonal debut, had finished a distant and very tired third on 9lb worse terms to the winner in the Midlands National on his final outing last season. He likes it out in front and is a dual course winner, so it wasn't surprising to see him bounce back to his best with ground conditions in his favour. He wasn't done many favours by his old rival at the last, but it made no real difference to the result. He could be just the sort for the Irish National this season, providing it rides soft at Fairyhouse in April, and is another for whom a crack at the Grand National next term looks on the cards. (tchd 14-1)

I'moncloudnine(IRE) ◆ ran a gallant race under a positive ride. He failed to see it out like the first pair on this first outing beyond 3m1f, but it was much better again from him and he still looks weighted to win when eased in distance.

Ballyfitz was up there early on. He hit a flat spot at a crucial stage, but rallied in the home straight and it's not hard to see why connections reached for some headgear. He is weighted to find a race, but is not one to completely trust. (op 12-1)

Maktu, whose trainer won this with Supreme Glory in 2001, ran a nice race in defeat on his return in November and had been laid out for this event. Well backed, he had his chance but ultimately paid for running too enthusiastically. He is better than this on his day and, while it wouldn't be at all surprising to see him back for another crack next season, there ought to be a nice pot in him before that long. (op 11-2)
Watamu Bay(IRE) finished runner-up on his chasing debut for his current stable here on his comeback, but had improved markedly to win the last twice and he too had his ground for this handicap debut. He posted a sound effort without every threatening over this stiffer test considering he had plenty of weight for a novice. The best of him has probably still to be seen. (op 9-1)
Silver By Nature did his best to get involved off the home turn, but was held soon after and his 20lb higher mark this time was too much for him. (op 16-1)
Dream Alliance has shown nothing since winning the race last season and has now been pulled up in four subsequent outings, so an honourable retirement may well beckon. (op 9-1 tchd 12-1)
Dance Island(IRE) was fancied to run a big race, but he came under heavy pressure before the home turn and something may have been amiss. (op 9-1 tchd 12-1)

3438 CORAL.CO.UK H'CAP CHASE (16 fncs) 2m 3f 110y
2:20 (2:24) (Class 2) 5-Y-0+ **£10,408** (£3,056; £1,528; £763)

Form RPR
1-03 **1** **Chance Du Roy (FR)**[25] 2948 7-10-9 **130** TomO'Brien 144+
(Philip Hobbs) *chsd ldrs: effrt to chse clr ldr 13th: rdn to ld next: faltered between last 2: hit last: edgd lft u.p flat: hld on gamely: all out* **11/2**[3]
-3P5 **2** ¾ **Or Bleu (FR)**[23] 2976 9-9-12 **124** GilesHawkins(5) 137+
(Philip Hobbs) *j.rt: led: clr whn hit 9th and 10th: pushed clr again 13th: hdd next: swtchd rt and rallied to press wnr flat: hld towards fin* **17/2**
1-U5 **3** 9 **Prince De Beauchene (FR)**[42] 2674 8-11-3 **138** BrianHughes 143
(Howard Johnson) *chsd ldrs: mstke and lost pl 9th: rallied after 11th: 4th and outpcd by ldrs 13th: no ch w ldng pair 3 out: wnt 3rd last* **3/1**[1]
-PPP **4** 3¾ **Nozic (FR)**[24] 2962 10-10-9 **130** (v) LiamTreadwell 129
(Nick Gifford) *chsd ldr: outpcd 12th: lost 2nd next: wknd 3 out: lost 3rd last* **18/1**
0-06 **5** 4 **Chief Yeoman**[77] 1967 11-10-8 **129** AidanColeman 124
(Venetia Williams) *racd off the pce in midfield: clsd and in tch: rdn and struggling after 11th: no threat to ldrs after: plugged on u.p fr 3 out* **20/1**
0-40 **6** 11 **Consigliere (FR)**[28] 2881 8-11-12 **147** (b) JohnnyFarrelly 134
(David Pipe) *racd off the pce in midfield: clsd and chsd ldrs 8th: rdn and wkng whn blnd 3 out: wl btn after* **8/1**
0-3F **7** 3 **Rivaliste (FR)**[43] 2665 6-10-11 **137** MrRMahon(5) 118
(Paul Nicholls) *t.k.h: hld up off the pce in last trio: rdn and effrt after 12th: no prog and wl btn 3 out* **11/2**[3]
6121 **8** 2 **Fine Parchment (IRE)**[29] 2869 8-10-6 **130** (t) PeterToole(3) 109
(Charlie Mann) *chsd ldrs tl rdn and wknd after 12th: wl btn 3 out* **9/2**[2]
2-6P **9** 2½ **Karanja**[50] 2500 12-10-6 **127** (tp) WayneHutchinson 104
(Simon Burrough) *a in rr: lost tch 10th: no ch fr next: t.o* **40/1**
0202 **P** **Nikola (FR)**[48] 2541 10-10-7 **128** PaddyBrennan —
(Nigel Twiston-Davies) *racd off the pce in midfield: dropped to rr and struggling 8th: lost tch 10th: t.o whn p.u 12th* **16/1**
3P3 **P** **Smack That (IRE)**[6] 3345 9-9-7 **121** oh4 (vt) JakeGreenall(7) —
(Milton Harris) *j.rt: bhd: lost tch 8th: t.o whn p.u 10th* **50/1**

5m 7.90s (-3.40) **Going Correction** +0.075s/f (Yiel) **11** Ran SP% **115.9**
Speed ratings: **109,108,105,103,102 97,96,95,94,—** —
Tote Swingers: 1&2 £3.30, 1&3 £4.10, 2&3 £3.80 CSF £49.79 CT £166.23 TOTE £6.30: £1.90, £3.40, £1.60; EX 28.80 Trifecta £174.90 Pool: £1058.93 - 4.48 winning units..
Owner Miss I D Du Pre **Bred** Jean, Raymond And Jean-Claude Campos **Trained** Withycombe, Somerset

FOCUS
A fair handicap, run at a sound enough gallop and another race where it proved hard to land a serious blow from off the pace. It saw a 1-2 for trainer Phillip Hobbs as his pair drew right away from their rivals in the home straight. A big step up from Chance Du Roy to beat his well handicapped stablemate.

NOTEBOOK
Chance Du Roy(FR) just came out on top. He travelled really well and looked sure to win comfortably when taking over from his stablemate. However, he wasn't clever at the last and was probably idling on the run-in as his rider had to get serious with him. This was just his fifth outing as a chaser and there should be some more to come now his confidence will be boosted. (op 8-1)
Or Bleu(FR) ◆ was given a very positive ride and turned in a game effort in defeat to finish a clear second-best. He rallied bravely after the last and his jumping was better in the main here, so despite going back up for this he could well end his losing run next time out. (op 9-1)
Prince De Beauchene(FR) lacked the tactical pace to land a telling blow then it mattered and looks to want stepping back up in trip. (op 10-3 tchd 7-2)
Nozic(FR) came into this with everything to prove having been pulled up on his last four starts, but posted a much more encouraging effort. He is very well handicapped, so it is hoped he can build on this. (op 25-1 tchd 16-1)
Consigliere(FR), with the tongue-tie left off, was in the process of running an improved race prior to getting the fourth-last wrong and would have probably placed but for that. (op 7-1)
Rivaliste(FR) was laboured from off the pace and perhaps he was remembering his heavy fall at Newbury last time out. (op 5-1 tchd 6-1)
Nikola(FR) Official explanation: jockey said gelding was unsuited by the going soft (heavy in places)

3439 WATCH UK & IRISH RACING AT CORAL.CO.UK MAIDEN HURDLE (11 hdls) 2m 4f
2:50 (2:54) (Class 4) 5-Y-0+ **£2,602** (£764; £382; £190)

Form RPR
1 **Our Father (IRE)** 5-11-0 0 TimmyMurphy 118+
(David Pipe) *hld up in last trio: stdy prog after 7th: trckd ldrs on inner bef 2 out: produced to ld between last 2: pushed clr last: comf* **9/1**
0 **2** 4 **Cotillion**[24] 2960 5-10-11 0 MichaelMurphy(3) 111
(Ian Williams) *in tch in midfield: mstke 5th: pushed along and hdwy after 7th: chsd ldrs 3 out: led next: rdn and hdd between last 2: kpt on but nt pce of wnr last* **9/2**[2]
2-34 **3** 6 **Merehead (FR)**[43] 2666 5-11-0 0 HarrySkelton 107
(Paul Nicholls) *t.k.h: hld up in midfield: mstke 1st: hdwy to chse ldrs after 7th: mstke next: chsd ldr 3 out tl next: hung lft and wknd between last 2* **3/1**[1]
0B **4** 1¼ **Be True (IRE)**[23] 2985 7-10-11 0 JohnKington(3) 106+
(Donald McCain) *chsd ldrs: hung rt bnd after 4th: led and mstke 8th: hit next: rdn and hdd 2 out: wknd between last 2* **50/1**
3-FP **5** 1¼ **Seymour Eric**[56] 2365 6-11-0 0 JohnnyFarrelly 103
(Michael Scudamore) *in tch: hdwy to chse ldng pair after 7th: pressing ldrs next: wknd u.p 2 out* **80/1**
-424 **6** 9 **Pontyates**[90] 1799 6-11-0 0 TomO'Brien 94
(Peter Bowen) *in tch in midfield: rdn and wknd 8th: no ch fr next: plugged on* **66/1**
6 **7** shd **Rockabilly (FR)**[72] 2058 6-11-0 0 PaddyBrennan 93
(Nigel Twiston-Davies) *led: hit 3rd: hdd 8th: mstke and wknd qckly next* **25/1**
3-4P **8** 1¼ **Big Knickers**[80] 1922 6-10-7 0 DougieCostello 85
(Neil Mulholland) *in tch: lost pl and dropped towards rr 7th: plugged on same pce and no ch w ldrs fr next* **33/1**
1-20 **9** 3½ **Oscar Papa**[25] 2946 6-11-0 0 LiamTreadwell 89
(Nick Gifford) *w ldr: mstke 6th: wknd qckly 3 out: sn wl btn: eased between last 2* **3/1**[1]
00 **10** 2¼ **Saute**[6] 3340 5-10-7 0 (p) AshleyBird(7) 86
(Jim Best) *chsd ldrs: mstke and losing pl 6th: wknd bef 8th* **100/1**
5 **11** 2¾ **Mickytaker (IRE)**[24] 2957 6-11-0 0 WayneHutchinson 84
(Alan King) *in tch in midfield: mstke 8th: sn wknd and wl btn next* **15/2**
-560 **12** 1 **Another Kate (IRE)**[5] 3365 7-10-7 0 AidanColeman 76
(David Richards) *t.k.h: chsd ldrs tl wknd qckly bef 8th: eased flat* **16/1**
1 **13** 19 **The Merry Giant (IRE)**[234] 412 5-11-0 0 APMcCoy 64
(Rebecca Curtis) *a towards rr: pushed along after 6th: lost tch 8th: wl bhd and eased flat* **7/1**[3]
P/P **14** 38 **Supreme Oscar (IRE)**[23] 2981 8-11-0 0 MattieBatchelor 26
(Frederick Sutherland) *mstkes and j.lft: a bhd: lost tch 6th: wl t.o after next* **150/1**
P **Ostaadi**[562] 5-11-0 0 DPFahy —
(Bernard Llewellyn) *mstkes in rr: lost tch 6th: wl t.o after next tl p.u 2 out* **50/1**

5m 5.50s (3.70) **Going Correction** -0.10s/f (Good) **15** Ran SP% **123.4**
Speed ratings: **88,86,84,83,83 79,79,78,77,76 75,75,67,52,—**
Tote Swingers: 1&2 £6.20, 1&3 £3.90, 2&3 £4.40 CSF £49.57 TOTE £10.40: £2.90, £2.00, £1.60; EX 70.50.
Owner D A Johnson **Bred** P Tierney **Trained** Nicholashayne, Devon

FOCUS
This should work out to be a fair novice hurdle. It was run at a routine gallop and there were plenty in with a chance from the fourth-last, but eventually they finished fairly strung out. The winenr should go on to rate higher.

NOTEBOOK
Our Father(IRE) ◆ proved easy enough to back for this debut and, after refusing to settle under early restraint, it looked a case of him going to need the initial experience. However, the further he went the better he got and he arrived on the scene going easily nearing the third-last. Kept more towards the inside for his challenge, he found plenty when eventually asked to win the race and ran out a taking debut winner. He is bred to get further and jump a fence, but clearly has some speed and at this stage comes into the "could be anything" category. It will be fascinating to see how he fares under a penalty (op 5-1)
Cotillion ◆ finished fifth to subsequent Tolworth winner Minella Class on his hurdling debut at Newbury last time and was solid in the betting here. He moved nicely and held every chance, but couldn't live with the winner when it mattered. The longer trip was more to his liking, though, and he shouldn't be long in going one better.
Merehead(FR) was bidding to enhance his yard's fine record in this event and met support. He got involved off the home turn and looked a big player, but flattened out when push came to shove. Dropping back in trip looks on the cards. (op 9-2 tchd 5-1)
Be True(IRE) was brought down on his debut over hurdles last time, but didn't show much before that and so this was a much improved performance. This half-brother to Snowy Morning is clearly on an upwards curve and is one to look out for next time.
Seymour Eric went well for a long way and this was his first completion over hurdles at the third time of asking. He should build on this and shapes as though he will get further. (op 66-1)
Oscar Papa was well backed to return to form, but he came under heavy pressure off the home turn and disappointed again. Official explanation: jockey said gelding was never travelling (op 9-2)
The Merry Giant(IRE) was easy to back for this switch to hurdling after a 234-day break and looked uneasy on the ground. (op 6-1)

3440 CORAL.CO.UK H'CAP HURDLE (12 hdls) 3m
3:25 (3:26) (Class 3) (0-135,130) 4-Y-0+ **£4,553** (£1,337; £668; £333)

Form RPR
513- **1** **Universal Soldier (IRE)**[294] 4724 6-11-7 **125** HarrySkelton 146+
(Lawney Hill) *in tch: trckd ldr gng wl after 8th: led next: sn wl clr: easily* **16/1**
-P01 **2** 15 **Stow**[45] 2606 6-10-13 **117** AidanColeman 120
(Venetia Williams) *chsd ldrs: rdn and outpcd bef 9th: chsd clr wnr bef 3 out: no imp: plugged on to hold 2nd* **5/1**[2]
-PU6 **3** 1½ **Heathcliff (IRE)**[45] 2606 9-11-9 **127** (b) CharliePoste 127
(Richard Lee) *in tch on outer: rdn and dropped to rr 6th: wl bhd after 8th: styd on past btn horses u.p fr 3 out: wnt 3rd flat: no ch w wnr* **20/1**
14U2 **4** 2 **Miss Overdrive**[43] 2663 7-10-11 **122** MrBJPoste(7) 121
(Andy Turnell) *in tch towards rr: mstke 7th: no ch w wnr but sme hdwy after 9th: mstke 3 out: disputing modest 3rd and mstke 2 out: styd on same pce after* **12/1**
6200 **5** 4½ **Ring For Time**[11] 3168 8-11-0 **118** (p) WillKennedy 112
(John Flint) *in tch in midfield: rdn and no hdwy bef 9th: no ch w wnr but ch of 3rd 2 out: wknd bef last* **33/1**
40-6 **6** 6 **Sullumo (GER)**[50] 2500 8-11-9 **130** PeterToole(3) 118
(Charlie Mann) *hld up in tch in midfield: rdn and rdn bef 9th: sn no ch w wnr: disputing modest 3rd bef 2 out: wknd between last 2* **25/1**
112/ **7** 2¾ **Jokers Legacy (IRE)**[643] 4875 9-11-6 **124** (t) DougieCostello 109
(Tim Vaughan) *in tch in midfield: mstke 3rd: rdn and no hdwy 9th: 7th and wl hld whn mstke 3 out* **20/1**
0-46 **8** 1¼ **Maraafeq (USA)**[55] 2393 7-11-0 **125** MrJSherwood(7) 109
(Venetia Williams) *in tch: chsd ldrs after 7th: struggling u.p next: wknd qckly bef 3 out* **50/1**
PF-4 **9** 13 **Jaunty Journey**[69] 2106 8-11-7 **125** PaddyBrennan 99
(Nigel Twiston-Davies) *chsd ldr: mstke 4th: pushed into ld 8th: hdd and drvn next: sn wknd: t.o* **5/1**[2]
5042 **10** 4 **Caught By Witness (IRE)**[7] 3306 6-11-4 **125** RichieMcLernon(3) 92
(Milton Harris) *hld up in rr: mstke 2nd: hdwy 6th: chsd ldrs after 8th: wknd qckly bef 3 out: t.o* **14/1**
4010 **11** 3¾ **Thelobstercatcher**[49] 2523 7-11-7 **125** (p) TomO'Brien 88
(Peter Bowen) *in tch tl lost pl and dropped to rr 6th: lost tch bef 9th: t.o* **10/1**
23-0 **12** 16 **Money Order (IRE)**[62] 2235 9-11-12 **130** APMcCoy 77
(Brendan Powell) *hld up in tch in rr: mstke 4th: wknd bef 9th: t.o and eased flat* **7/1**[3]
0-44 **13** 2¾ **Made In Japan (JPN)**[48] 2544 11-11-8 **126** (p) DavidEngland 70
(Nigel Twiston-Davies) *led: hit 3rd: hdd 8th: drvn and dropped out qckly bef 9th: t.o fr 2 out* **33/1**
43P- **14** 24 **Magnifico (FR)**[315] 4298 10-10-11 **115** (p) JodieMogford 35
(Nikki Evans) *chsd ldrs: mstke 5th: lost pl fr next: wl t.o fr 9th* **40/1**
151- **P** **Bertie May**[328] 4054 9-11-7 **125** WayneHutchinson —
(Kevin Bishop) *in tch in midfield: lost pl and reminder 6th: lost tch 8th: t.o whn p.u next* **14/1**

26/2 **P** **Vagrant Emperor (IRE)**[44] 2630 8-11-8 126 TimmyMurphy —
(Emma Lavelle) *in tch in midfield: wknd bef 9th: wl bhd whn p.u 2 out* **9/2**[1]

1/P- **P** **Woody Waller**[82] 2437 6-11-8 129 JamesO'Farrell(3) —
(Howard Johnson) *in tch in midfield: lost pl and bhd 7th: lost tch next: t.o and p.u 9th* **66/1**

3-21 **P** **Humbel Ben (IRE)**[207] 756 8-11-1 119 LiamTreadwell —
(Alan Jones) *a in rr: lost tch 6th: p.u next* **28/1**

6m 9.90s (-9.90) **Going Correction** -0.10s/f (Good) **18** Ran SP% **128.6**
Speed ratings (Par 107): **112,107,106,105,104 102,101,101,96,95 94,88,87,79,— —,—,—**
Tote Swingers: 1&2 £13.50, 1&3 £60.40, 2&3 £19.80 CSF £89.90 CT £1671.37 TOTE £24.40: £5.00, £1.90, £5.10, £3.70; EX 187.10.

Owner Lindie Donaldson & Regan King **Bred** John McAleese **Trained** Aston Rowant, Oxon

FOCUS
What looked to be a wide-open staying handicap was turned into a procession by the winner, who produced a massive step up. The form looks solid enough.

NOTEBOOK
Universal Soldier(IRE) could hardly have won any easier on his debut for new connections. He showed fair ability when winning once from three outings over hurdles for Nicky Henderson, but this was a vast improvement and he could have been called the winner a long way out. His new connections believe he has strengthened up for his recent time off the track and he had obviously begun life in handicaps on a decent mark. A hike in the weights is now inevitable, but he has very few miles on the clock and further improvement looks on the cards. He also has the size to jump fences and so that could be an option this season.

Stow was 5lb higher than when back to winning ways over C&D with a last-gasp display 45 days earlier. He couldn't go with the winner when that rival asserted, but kept on to finish nicely clear in second and gives the form a decent look. (op 6-1)

Heathcliff(IRE) ◆ won this race off a 23lb lower mark in 2008. He was never seriously competitive, but motored home from off the pace to grab third and this was another step back in the right direction. (op 16-1)

Miss Overdrive plugged on from off the pace and probably found the ground too demanding over this trip, so didn't run badly.

Ring For Time kept to her task under pressure in the home straight and posted an improved display on just her second outing for the yard. She can find easier assignments.

Jaunty Journey was well backed on this switch from chasing and was given a positive ride. He was a sitting duck for the winner turning for home, however, and faded tamely from three out. (tchd 9-2)

Made In Japan(JPN) Official explanation: jockey said gelding was unsuited by ground soft (heavy in places)

Vagrant Emperor(IRE) was up 9lb for his narrow miss at Newbury when returning from injury. He had stamina to prove for this longer trip and he was in trouble a fair way out. Perhaps the bounce factor came into play and the ground may also have been against him, but his stable is going through a bit of a quiet period. Official explanation: jockey said gelding was unsuited by ground soft (heavy in places) (op 5-1)

3441 NEW BET IN PLAY SERVICE AT CORAL.CO.UK STANDARD OPEN NATIONAL HUNT FLAT RACE 2m 110y
3:55 (3:57) (Class 6) 4-6-Y-0 **£1,301** (£382; £191; £95)

Form RPR

12 **1** **Saint Luke (IRE)**[122] 1510 6-11-12 0 APMcCoy 112
(Peter Bowen) *racd wd: mde virtually all: rdn over 2f out: clr w rival over 1f out: hld on u.p fnl f* **4/5**[1]

2 *hd* **Noble Perk** 6-11-5 0 JodieMogford 105
(Adrian Wintle) *in tch: effrt to press wnr over 3f out: rdn and drew clr w wnr over 1f out: kpt on wl fnl f: jst hld* **11/1**

3-0 **3** *8* **Don't Hang About**[48] 2560 6-11-5 0 JohnnyFarrelly 97
(Richard Mitchell) *w ldr: styd on inner and hung bdly lft 4f out: stl pressing ldrs tl wknd over 1f out* **10/1**

05 **4** *19* **Radmores Oscar**[47] 2576 5-10-12 0 CharlieWallis(7) 78
(John O'Shea) *in tch in last pair tl wknd 4f out: wl btn over 2f out* **20/1**

5 *13* **Beat All Out**[76] 6-11-5 0 TomO'Brien 65
(Dai Burchell) *chsd ldrs tl rdn and wknd over 2f out: wl btn over 1f out* **4/1**[2]

6 *23* **Ledbury Star (IRE)** 5-11-5 0 TimmyMurphy 42
(Matt Sheppard) *racd wd: hld up in tch: pushed along and btn 4f out: sn wl bhd: eased fnl f: t.o* **13/2**[3]

4m 15.2s (10.20) **Going Correction** -0.10s/f (Good)
WFA 5 from 6yo 3lb **6** Ran SP% **111.1**
Speed ratings: **72,71,68,59,53 42**
Tote Swingers: 1&2 £2.30, 1&3 £1.20, 2&3 £13.60 CSF £10.58 TOTE £1.60: £1.10, £6.40; EX 13.90.

Owner Saith O Ni & Ednyfed & Elizabeth Morgan **Bred** Joseph O'Dwyer **Trained** Little Newcastle, Pembrokes

FOCUS
An ordinary bumper, run at a steady gallop and the first pair dominated from 3f out.

NOTEBOOK
Saint Luke(IRE) got back to winning ways and landed strong support, but needed all of Tony McCoy's strength to score. He did get a little warm beforehand which cannot have helped and, remembering he was conceding 7lb to the second, showed a very good attitude at the business end. This former point winner is well regarded by his trainer and should appreciate getting back on some better ground when going hurdling. A longer trip will suit in that sphere. (op 4-6)

Noble Perk very nearly made a winning debut. He got tapped for toe around 4f out, but responded positively for pressure thereafter and only just lost out at the finish. This was his stable's first runner in a bumper and it obviously rates a very pleasing effort. (op 14-1)

Don't Hang About ran poorly on his comeback at Towcester, but this was more like it again and he returned to the sort of form that saw him finish third over C&D last term. (op 8-1 tchd 13-2)

Radmores Oscar was doing his best work late in the day and should appreciate racing over further when sent hurdling. (op 14-1)

Beat All Out cost his new connections £20,000 and met support on this debut. He looked a threat at the top of the home straight, but couldn't quicken when asked for his effort and, looking at his form between the flags, needs a sounder surface to shine. (op 5-1)

Ledbury Star(IRE), bred to stay well over jumps, was a market mover for his debut. He was the first beaten, however. Official explanation: jockey said gelding ran green (op 14-1)

T/Jkpt: Not won. T/Plt: £247.30 to a £1 stake. Pool of £134,602.91 - 397.19 winning tickets. T/Qpdt: £61.00 to a £1 stake. Pool of £10,245.46 - 124.10 winning tickets. SP

2209 SANDOWN (R-H)
Saturday, January 8

OFFICIAL GOING: Chase course - soft (heavy in placs) hurdle course - heavy
Wind: Brisk, against Weather: Cloudy early but soon fine and sunny

3442 32RED.COM MARES' HURDLE (LISTED RACE) (8 hdls 1 omitted) 2m 4f
1:00 (1:00) (Class 1) 4-Y-0+
£9,121 (£3,422; £1,713; £854; £428; £214)

Form RPR

-220 **1** **Banjaxed Girl**[28] 2884 7-11-4 153 SamTwiston-Davies 144+
(Nigel Twiston-Davies) *mde all: urged along after 3 out: nt fluent 2 out: clr last: all out* **6/4**[1]

02-5 **2** *2 1/2* **Alasi**[63] 2218 7-11-0 130 DominicElsworth 136+
(Paul Webber) *mstke 1st: hld up in last pair: prog and mstke 3 out: chsd wnr 2 out: no imp last: kpt on* **20/1**

-211 **3** *3/4* **Silver Gypsy (IRE)**[23] 2974 6-11-0 135 (t) SeanQuinlan 135+
(Kim Bailey) *chsd wnr: hit 3rd: rdn and lost 2nd 2 out: kpt on u.p after last* **11/4**[2]

1211 **4** *12* **Synthe Davis (FR)**[107] 1588 6-11-0 130 RichardJohnson 123
(Laura Mongan) *cl up: nt fluent 5th and next: wl in tch bef 2 out: sn wknd* **15/2**

0-42 **5** *10* **Mizzurka**[9] 3227 7-11-0 110 AndrewGlassonbury 114
(Bob Buckler) *sloppy rnd of jumping: trckd ldrs: rdn and stl in tch bef 2 out: sn wknd* **12/1**

U-1F **6** *32* **Alegralil**[42] 2671 6-11-8 145 JasonMaguire 87
(Donald McCain) *a in last pair: rdn whn nt fluent 3 out: sn lost tch: t.o* **9/2**[3]

5m 14.0s (8.30) **Going Correction** +0.425s/f (Soft) **6** Ran SP% **109.1**
Speed ratings (Par 111): **100,99,98,93,89 77**
Tote Swingers: 1&2 £1.20, 1&3 £11.70, 2&3 £3.30 CSF £25.87 TOTE £2.50: £1.40, £6.00; EX 31.30.

Owner Jill Scott John Phillips Sarah MacEchern **Bred** R D Chugg And J R H Fowler **Trained** Naunton, Gloucs

FOCUS
The meeting had to pass a morning inspection and conditions were clearly testing, as the jockeys confirmed. The opener was run in a time no less than 32sec outside the RP standard, despite the pace appearing to be reasonable. This was only the second running of this Listed event, the first having been in 2008; the meeting has been lost to the weather since. Banjaxed Girl was the form pick but was clearly below her best, with the fifth helping to set the level.

NOTEBOOK
Banjaxed Girl came here needing to put an uncharacteristic below-par run behind her, albeit one when taking on the males in Cheltenham's Relkeel Hurdle. Going out in front as usual, she came under pressure turning out of the back straight and looked vulnerable, but galloped on with typical gameness to grind out victory. She was 12lb clear on adjusted BHA ratings and was below her best but can be forgiven that in the conditions. Her target remains the David Nicholson Hurdle at the Cheltenham Festival. (op 13-8 tchd 7-4)

Alasi ran Banjaxed Girl close at Cheltenham in April but had 19lb to find with her old rival on these terms. Sharper for her reappearance at Wincanton two months ago, she moved into second place two out, where she lost little momentum despite a nod on landing, but couldn't quicken up in the ground from there. She did close the gap towards the line but it was more a case of the winner tying up.

Silver Gypsy(IRE) had been beaten only by the progressive subsequent handicap winner L'Accordioniste in three runs over hurdles, but this represented a marked rise in grade. Proven in heavy ground, she ran her race but weakened between the last two flights. Her jumping had been less than fluent at times. (op 9-4)

Synthe Davis(FR) was on the upgrade in the summer and autumn, landing back-to-back Fontwell novice events when last seen. Faced with very different ground on this rise in class, she was not disgraced but had run her race by the second-last. (op 6-1 tchd 8-1)

Mizzurka, a Listed bumper winner at this venue last spring, was the least experienced hurdler in this line-up. She had the worst chance on official figures and was struggling before the home turn, although she did fleetingly attempt to rally. The ground should not have posed her too many problems. (op 20-1)

Alegralil, a faller last time, had won in this grade first time out at Wetherby but was always in rear here and failed to pick up when asked. The ground seems an obvious excuse. Official explanation: jockey said mare was never travelling (op 6-1 tchd 13-2 in a place)

3443 32RED POKER JUVENILE HURDLE (7 hdls 1 omitted) 2m 110y
1:30 (1:31) (Class 4) 4-Y-0 **£2,602** (£764; £382; £190)

Form RPR

1 **Music Of The Moor (IRE)**[95] 4-10-12 0 JamesReveley 118+
(Tom Tate) *hld up in last early: stdy prog fr 4th: wnt 2nd bef 2 out: clsd to ld and blnd last: briefly hdd but sn forged ahd* **8/1**

05 **2** *1 1/4* **Lamps**[43] 2661 4-10-12 0 DominicElsworth 114
(Michael Blake) *lost pl rapidly bef 3rd and sn wl in rr: sme hdwy after 3 out but stl only modest 7th bef next: styd on strly after: tk 2nd nr fin and clsd on wnr* **66/1**

664 **3** *2 1/2* **Professeur Emery (FR)**[24] 2958 4-10-12 114 JasonMaguire 111+
(Warren Greatrex) *led at str pce and spreadeagled field fr 3rd: stl clr after 3 out: c bk fr next: hdd last but briefly lft in ld: no ex and lost 2nd nr fin* **11/2**[2]

0 **4** *21* **Kayef (GER)**[28] 2882 4-10-12 0 AlanO'Keeffe 92
(Michael Scudamore) *chsd ldng pair: u.p after 3 out: wl hld whn mstke 2 out: wknd and lost 3rd last* **66/1**

55 **5** *2* **Ibn Hiyyan (USA)**[45] 2614 4-10-12 0 GrahamLee 88
(Ferdy Murphy) *hld up in rr: prog fr 4th: chsng ldrs in 6th bef 2 out but nt on terms: no imp after* **50/1**

1 **6** *16* **Comedy Act**[26] 2924 4-11-5 0 RichardJohnson 89+
(Philip Hobbs) *chsd ldr: j. slowly 3rd and 4th: wknd bef 2 out: blnd last: virtually p.u* **1/1**[1]

7 *49* **Sea Change (IRE)**[89] 4-10-12 0 TomScudamore 23
(David Pipe) *settled midfield: rdn fr 3rd and sn struggling: wl t.o after 3 out* **6/1**[3]

0 **8** *3 3/4* **Zambuka (FR)**[51] 2466 4-10-5 0 MarkGrant 13
(Barry Brennan) *mstkes: prom to 3 out: sn wknd rapidly: t.o* **100/1**

9 *1 1/2* **Usquaebach**[17] 4-10-5 0 ColinBolger 11
(Pat Phelan) *mstkes: in rr fr 3rd: wl t.o after 3 out* **66/1**

10 *24* **Terra Bleu (IRE)**[89] 4-10-7 0 MrMMO'Connor(5) —
(Milton Harris) *j. terribly: sn in last pair: blnd 4th and rdr lost irons: wl t.o* **100/1**

4 **P** **Missionaire (USA)**[43] 2661 4-10-12 0 SamThomas —
(Tony Carroll) *prom whn blnd 1st: mstke next: in rr fr 3rd: t.o whn p.u bef 2 out* **14/1**

P **Whitby Jack**[219] 4-10-12 0 JamieMoore —
(Gary Moore) *mstkes: chsd ldrs: wknd after 3 out: wl bhd in 7th whn mstke 2 out: p.u bef last* **10/1**

4m 14.7s (7.50) **Going Correction** +0.425s/f (Soft) **12** Ran SP% **115.0**
Speed ratings: **99,98,97,87,86 78,55,54,53,42** —,—
Tote Swingers: 1&2 £93.30, 1&3 £6.10, 2&3 £44.40 CSF £385.89 TOTE £9.10: £2.10, £20.20, £1.60; EX 834.70.
Owner The Ivy Syndicate **Bred** Snig Elevage **Trained** Tadcaster, N Yorks

FOCUS
This became a searching test for these juveniles in the ground and the form should not be taken literally. The winner is better than the bare result and the type to rate higher. The eventual third set a brisk pace but the time was nearly 28sec outside the standard, not a bad time for the grade despite slow finishing fractions.

NOTEBOOK
Music Of The Moor(IRE), a 1m4f winner on the Flat and currently rated 81 in that sphere, is proven in heavy ground and his yard does well with their relatively few jumpers. Sensibly held up right out the back, and hampered at the second, he made steady progress, still on the bridle when the rest of the field were hard at work. He was still cruising when taking it up before the last, but it proved deceptive as he blundered there, losing his lead, and had to work a bit to move back in front again. Clearly a decent juvenile, he has been given quotes of 25-1 for the Triumph Hurdle but is unlikely to encounter testing conditions should he run there.
Lamps was well beaten on his first two starts over hurdles but did finish a place ahead of Professeur Emery at Newbury. He was a remote seventh turning into the home straight but soon began to stay on and finished fast to grab second on the run-in. He is very likely flattered by this, but on this evidence would benefit from a step up in trip.
Professeur Emery(FR) made the running again and settled after the second. He had all bar the winner beaten turning in but was cut down between the last two flights before finding himself briefly back in front on the run-in. Second-best on merit, he hurdled nicely and is well up to winning a similar event. (op 6-1 tchd 7-1)
Kayef(GER) won over 1m4f on the Flat in the French provinces and faced a stiff task behind Sam Winner and company on his hurdling debut at Cheltenham. He was well beaten but there was promise in this performance.
Ibn Hiyyan(USA) showed modest form in his first two hurdle runs and was well beaten here, but he wasn't disgraced and will be eligible for handicaps now. (tchd 40-1)
Comedy Act was the only previous hurdling winner on show and gave away 7lb all round. After chasing the clear leader he was a spent force two from home. The ground was against him and his jumping was not as slick as it might have been. (tchd 10-11 and 11-1 in places)
Sea Change(IRE), another with a BHA Flat rating of 81, was well beaten on this hurdles bow and debut for the yard and, as he did on the Flat, showed an unattractive head carriage. (op 8-1)
Whitby Jack, although eventually pulled up, did show a glimmer of encouragement. He was the subject of favourable reports and probably deserves another chance on better ground. (op 8-1)

3444 32RED.COM H'CAP CHASE (22 fncs) 3m 110y
2:05 (2:09) (Class 2) (0-145,144) 5-Y-0+
£9,393 (£2,775; £1,387; £694; £346; £174)

Form				RPR
1-P3	**1**		**Nicto De Beauchene (FR)**[24] 2962 10-10-7 **125**... AndrewGlassonbury (Victor Dartnall) *mde most fr 2nd: rdn and styd on wl to draw clr fr 3 out* **15/2**[3]	143+
016P	**2**	*16*	**Quattrocento (FR)**[48] 2544 7-10-3 **121**...(v) JamieMoore (Peter Bowen) *sn prom: pressing whn mstke 15th: rdn to go 2nd after 4 out: no imp on wnr fr next* **33/1**	126
12/U	**3**	*9*	**Leading Contender (IRE)**[24] 2962 10-10-12 **130**... RichardJohnson (Philip Hobbs) *settled wl in rr: mstke 12th: prog fr next: chsd ldrs 17th: kpt on to take 3rd 3 out: no imp after* **8/1**	125
3-52	**4**	*7*	**Youngstown (IRE)**[51] 2476 8-10-4 **122**... BrianHarding (Donald McCain) *prom: chsd wnr 17th tl after 4 out: wknd into 4th fr 3 out* **7/2**[1]	108
314-	**5**	*20*	**Soixante (IRE)**[282] 4969 8-10-9 **127**...(p) HaddenFrost (Henrietta Knight) *pressed ldrs to 16th: wkng whn mstke 4 out: sn bhd* **33/1**	95
46P-	**6**	*40*	**Ma Yahab**[266] 5223 10-10-8 **126**... SamThomas (Venetia Williams) *in tch in rr: sltly hmpd 9th: mstke 12th: sn dropped away: t.o whn j. bdly lft 18th* **16/1**	52
00-4	**7**	*4 ½*	**South O'The Border**[60] 2286 9-10-11 **132**... SamTwiston-Davies(3) (Nigel Twiston-Davies) *in tch: blnd 9th: sn dropped to rr and u.p: t.o fr 16th* **25/1**	54
-S00	**P**		**Eric's Charm (FR)**[56] 2358 13-11-12 **144**... LeightonAspell (Oliver Sherwood) *wl in tch in midfield: losing grnd whn mstkes 14th and next: sn wl bhd: poor 7th whn p.u bef 3 out* **25/1**	—
20-2	**U**		**Far More Serious (IRE)**[50] 2497 11-11-0 **132**... TomScudamore (Charlie Longsdon) *in tch in rr whn mstke and uns rdr 6th* **9/1**	—
P-40	**U**		**Appleaday (IRE)**[29] 2871 10-10-4 **122**... DominicElsworth (Paul Webber) *trckd ldrs: mstke 12th: 7th and in tch whn blnd and uns rdr next* **8/1**	—
1-10	**P**		**Midnight Haze**[25] 2948 9-10-10 **128**... JasonMaguire (Kim Bailey) *led to 2nd: w ldr to 13th: wkng whn blnd 4 out: poor 6th whn p.u bef next: b.b.v* **4/1**[2]	—
/0-0	**P**		**Horner Woods (IRE)**[29] 2871 9-11-4 **136**... BarryGeraghty (Nicky Henderson) *hld up last: detached at 12th: prog to v modest 8th at 17th and appeared gng wl enough: p.u bef 19th (4 out)* **9/1**	—
0P-4	**P**		**Fortification (USA)**[51] 2482 8-10-12 **135**...(p) MattGriffiths(5) (Michael Blake) *in tch: wnt prom 11th: lft bhd fr 14th: poor 7th whn blnd 17th: t.o in 6th whn p.u bef last* **25/1**	—

6m 37.0s (9.20) **Going Correction** +0.60s/f (Soft) **13** Ran SP% **119.5**
Speed ratings: **109,103,101,98,92 79,78,**—,—,— —,—,—
Tote Swingers: 1&2 £75.80, 1&3 £5.30, 2&3 £26.30 CSF £230.52 CT £2024.71 TOTE £8.20: £2.80, £11.60, £3.70; EX 245.30 TRIFECTA Not won..
Owner Exors of the Late P M De Wilde **Bred** Raymond Bellanger **Trained** Brayford, Devon

FOCUS
Several non-runners, but this still had the look of a competitive handicap on paper. The first chase of the day, it proved a real stamina test and was run in a time 36 sec outside the standard. A personal best from the winner and there is a case for rating the race a few pounds higher.

NOTEBOOK
Nicto De Beauchene(FR) made a lot of the running and stayed on strongly to slam his field, having put in a fine round of jumping. Trained by Robert and Sally Alner prior to this season, he is a brother to their Welsh National winner Miko De Beauchene, and although he will be up in the weights for this he may have further improvement in him over marathon trips, having never tackled further than an extended 3m2f. (op 8-1)
Quattrocento(FR) delayed the race when requiring adjustments to his tack. He disappointed last time at Aintree but bounced back with a much better effort and kept on willingly once giving chase to the winner four out. Most of his form has been on much faster ground but he handled the conditions well.
Leading Contender(IRE) ◆ is a dour stayer, as proved by his second to Don't Push It in a fast-run handicap at Aintree two seasons ago. Having just his second run since, he showed he retains all his ability and there is a decent race to be won with him. This was only his sixth run over fences. (tchd 9-1)
Youngstown(IRE)'s second to Sarde at Market Rasen has been franked since by the winner going in again. He ran well for a long way on this rise in grade before his stamina in this ground began to wane. (op 6-1)
Soixante(IRE) faded after a mistake at the last down the far side. This was a satisfactory first run since April and he is worth another try over this trip on less testing ground. (op 25-1)
Eric's Charm(FR) was runner-up in this race when it was last held three years ago. Running here rather than in the Welsh National, it does appear his best days are behind him now. (op 17-2 tchd 8-1)
Midnight Haze, who was well supported, was up with the winner for a long way but his exertions told and he dropped away before pulling up. He is a winner over a furlong more in heavy ground but has been found wanting from this mark on his last two starts. It transpired that he had broken a bled from the nose. Official explanation: jockey said gelding bled from nose (op 17-2 tchd 8-1)
Horner Woods(IRE) has shown little since finishing second to Cooldine in the 2009 RSA Chase, but he has been lightly raced during that period and has been coming down the weights. His former handler Jessica Harrington still has an input into his training and it may be premature to write him off. (op 17-2 tchd 8-1)

3445 32RED HURDLE (A NOVICES' HURDLE) (REGISTERED AS THE TOLWORTH HURDLE) GRADE 1 (7 hdls 1 omitted) 2m 110y
2:40 (2:42) (Class 1) 4-Y-0+ **£17,103** (£6,417; £3,213; £1,602; £804)

Form				RPR
1	**1**		**Minella Class (IRE)**[24] 2960 6-11-7 0... BarryGeraghty (Nicky Henderson) *trckd ldr: led on long run after 3 out: gng bttr than rivals bef next: clr last: drvn rt out* **6/4**[1]	143+
1-12	**2**	*7*	**Megastar**[10] 3196 6-11-7 139... JamieMoore (Gary Moore) *trckd ldng pair: rdn to chse wnr bef 2 out: 3 l down whn nt fluent 2 out: wl hld after: mstke last* **9/2**[3]	137+
2-41	**3**	*3 ½*	**Toubab (FR)**[49] 2519 5-11-7 144... SamThomas (Paul Nicholls) *hld up: chsd ldng trio fr 3rd: rdn to go 3rd bef 2 out: no imp after* **2/1**[2]	132
10	**4**	*8*	**Act Of Kalanisi (IRE)**[10] 3197 5-11-7 0... RichardJohnson (Dr Richard Newland) *led: mstke 3rd: hdd on long run after 3 out: grad wknd* **14/1**	127
2	**5**	*28*	**Red Merlin (IRE)**[24] 2960 6-11-7 0... JasonMaguire (Donald McCain) *nt fluent 1st: last fr 3rd: rdn after 3 out: sn wknd* **8/1**	104+

4m 13.8s (6.60) **Going Correction** +0.425s/f (Soft) **5** Ran SP% **109.3**
Speed ratings (Par 117): **101,97,96,92,79**
CSF £8.46 TOTE £2.70: £1.60, £2.30; EX 10.10.
Owner Deal George Kelvin-Hughes Nicolson **Bred** Conna Stud **Trained** Upper Lambourn, Berks

FOCUS
The first running of the Tolworth under the 32Red banner. It looked an up-to-scratch field for this Grade 1 novice contest, despite the total prize fund for the race dropping by £20,000 since it last beat the weather three years ago. The pace was ordinary and the time was just less than a second quicker than the earlier juvenile hurdle. A big step up from Minella Class, but still a stone off what is likely to be required at Cheltenham, and Megastar is rated in line with his previous hurdles best.

NOTEBOOK
Minella Class(IRE) was quickly upped in grade after creating a big impression on his British debut at Newbury. Travelling well before quickening approaching the final two flights, he was soon in command, although he had to be kept up to his work in the gruelling conditions. Stamina was never going to prove a serious problem, as he made the frame in three Irish points over 3m, two of them in heavy ground. He handles better ground too and is clearly a classy performer. His trainer is inclined to aim him at the 2m5f Neptune Investement Management Hurdle at Cheltenham, rather than the shorter Supreme Novices'. (op 11-8)
Megastar's trainer had expressed his concerns over the ground beforehand and, in the circumstances, the big 6yo ran another pleasing race. His jumping has not been that fluent in his three runs so far and an awkward jump two out ended his hopes here, but he stuck on for second despite finding underfoot conditions against him. He reportedly returned with cuts to his legs and will be given a break now, after two runs in ten days, but the Supreme Novices' remains on the agenda. (op 5-1 tchd 6-1)
Toubab(FR)'s trainer had won the last three runnings of this race to take place, with Breedsbreeze, Silverburn and Noland. This one, impressive against three opponents in a Listed event at Haydock, looked a threat turning in but did not pick up out of the ground and could only plug on from the second-last. The most experienced hurdler in the field, he had 5lb in hand of Megastar on official figures but was below par in the conditions. (tchd 7-4)
Act Of Kalanisi(IRE) was found out in this grade in the Challow at Newbury, where he ought to have stayed the trip based on his Flat exploits. Making the running, he flattened the third flight and was quickly relegated to fourth on the long run round to the home straight. He needs his sights lowering. (op 16-1 tchd 18-1 and 20-1 in places)
Red Merlin(IRE) made a pleasing hurdles debut when runner-up to Minella Class at Newbury, but clearly did not match that form on this different ground. He had won in heavy conditions on the Flat in the autumn and, although he lacked the hurdling experience of his rivals, this was disappointing. (op 10-1 tchd 15-2 and 11-1 in places)

3446 32RED H'CAP CHASE (13 fncs) 2m
3:15 (3:15) (Class 2) 5-Y-0+
£12,524 (£3,700; £1,850; £926; £462; £232)

Form				RPR
-164	**1**		**Cornas (NZ)**[28] 2881 9-11-2 **148**... LeightonAspell (Nick Williams) *a in ldng quartet: cl 3rd fr 6th: chal 3 out: rdn to ld next: styd on wl* **14/1**	156+
2-1F	**2**	*2 ¾*	**Tchico Polos (FR)**[56] 2359 7-11-6 **157**...(t) IanPopham(5) (Paul Nicholls) *pressed ldr: led 9th: drvn and hdd 2 out: kpt on same pce* **7/1**[3]	161
4-66	**3**	*½*	**Oh Crick (FR)**[28] 2881 8-10-13 **145**... RobertThornton (Alan King) *settled midfield: mstke 3rd: chsng ldrs in 6th after 10th but nt on terms: styd on fr next: wnt 3rd last: kpt on* **9/1**	150
-312	**4**	*1 ½*	**Riguez Dancer**[11] 3170 7-10-0 **132** oh3... GrahamLee (Ferdy Murphy) *trckd ldrs: wl in tch in 4th after 10th: rdn and one pce after 3 out* **8/1**	134
1U-2	**5**	*5*	**Leo's Lucky Star (USA)**[23] 2976 9-10-8 **140**...(t) TomScudamore (David Pipe) *hld up in last trio: stdy prog fr 7th: trckd ldrs after 10th gng wl enough: shkn up after 3 out: nt qckn* **5/1**[2]	138
0213	**6**	*14*	**Fiendish Flame (IRE)**[28] 2881 7-10-13 **145**... JasonMaguire (Donald McCain) *led: hdd and mstke 9th: stl upsides 3 out: wkng whn mstke 2 out* **7/2**[1]	132+
30-2	**7**	*3 ¾*	**Free World (FR)**[68] 2126 7-11-6 **152**... SamThomas (Paul Nicholls) *blnd 3rd and dropped to last: nt a fluent after: struggling fr 8th: sn no ch* **10/1**	136+
4204	**8**	*2 ¾*	**I'msingingtheblues (IRE)**[7] 3292 9-10-13 **148**...(t) DannyCook(3) (David Pipe) *t.k.h: hld up in last trio: struggling and no prog 8th: wl bhd after 10th* **8/1**	125

121- **9** *4* **French Opera**^{266} [5221] 8-11-12 **158**.................................. BarryGeraghty 131
(Nicky Henderson) *chsd ldng pair: mstke 3rd: lost pl qckly 7th: wl bhd after 10th (4 out)* **5/1**^{2}

4m 10.0s (8.20) **Going Correction** +0.60s/f (Soft) **9** Ran SP% **116.0**
Speed ratings: **103,101,101,100,98 91,89,87,85**
Tote Swingers: 1&2 £20.50, 1&3 £11.90, 2&3 £47.60 CSF £107.76 CT £940.37 TOTE £16.30: £4.10, £2.10, £2.50; EX 147.70 Trifecta £476.00 Pool: £714.13 - 1.11 winning units..
Owner The Gascoigne Brookes Partnership Iii **Bred** D P And Mrs K C Fleming **Trained** George Nympton, Devon

FOCUS
The first running of this event, and high-class handicap form. Cornas is rated back to his old best with a personal best from Tchico Polos. The pace was relatively sound.

NOTEBOOK
Cornas(NZ) travelled nicely just off the gallop and saw it out well once leading on the home turn. A classy chaser on his day, he has acquitted himself well in Graded company over the past few seasons and this was his first handicap win. It was also his first taste of heavy ground and he got through it well. (op 16-1)
Tchico Polos(FR) was up there all the way and this was a highly creditable effort off 4lb higher than when winning the Haldon Gold Cup earlier in the season. He is proven over further and handled the conditions well. (op 13-2)
Oh Crick(FR), two places behind Cornas on his latest start at Cheltenham, stayed on for third. He has dropped around a stone since the spring but remains 6lb above his last winning mark, in the Red Rum Chase at Aintree two seasons back. (op 11-1)
Riguez Dancer, runner-up in a jumpers' bumper last time, is proven in testing conditions and ran a solid race from 3lb out of the weights. (op 9-1)
Leo's Lucky Star(USA) looked a threat at the Pond Fence before fading. It could be that he is best caught fresh. (tchd 6-1)
Fiendish Flame(IRE), a place ahead of Cornas when third to Woolcombe Folly at Cheltenham, had winning form over hurdles in heavy ground. He made the running as usual but was on the retreat when blundering two out. (op 9-2)
Free World(FR) is usually consistent, but was without the tongue tie for this drop back in trip and was always struggling after an early mistake. (op 17-2)
French Opera was successful in four of his five starts last term, the defeat coming when second in the Grand Annual off 4lb lower than he was here. He has a good record first time out but dropped away tamely down the back and, while the ground is a plausible excuse, he may not prove easy to place this term. It was officially confirmed that he was unsuited by the ground. Official explanation: jockey said gelding was unsuited by soft, heavy in places (op 9-2 tchd 4-1 and 11-2 in places)

3447 32RED H'CAP HURDLE (7 hdls 1 omitted) 2m 110y
3:45 (3:49) (Class 2) (0-145,145) 4-Y-0+
£9,393 (£2,775; £1,387; £694; £346; £174)

Form RPR
1-62 **1** **Mille Chief (FR)**^{50} [2400] 5-11-12 **145**.................................. RobertThornton 158+
(Alan King) *trckd ldrs: cl up 3 out: smooth prog to chal 2 out: led last: pushed clr: quite impressive* **10/3**^{2}
1P-0 **2** *6* **Sophies Trophy (IRE)**^{55} [2387] 6-10-6 **125**..........................(t) ColinBolger 128
(Pat Phelan) *w ldrs: led 3rd: drvn 2 out: hdd last: kpt on wl but no ch w wnr* **25/1**
00P- **3** *6* **Zazamix (FR)**^{274} [5119] 6-9-9 **119** oh2.................................. DavidBass$^{(5)}$ 117
(Nicky Henderson) *trckd ldrs: lost pl 4th: sn pushed along: rallied u.p into 4th 2 out: no ch w ldrs but styd on to take 3rd nr fin* **9/4**^{1}
460- **4** *1½* **Kudu Country (IRE)**^{262} [5308] 5-10-5 **124**......................... JamesReveley 122+
(Tom Tate) *trckd ldrs: cl 3rd and clr of rest whn mstke 2 out: wknd after last* **12/1**
1160 **5** *1½* **Tiger O'Toole (IRE)**^{163} [1133] 6-10-11 **130**........................ JasonMaguire 124
(Evan Williams) *hld up in last trio: rdn after 3 out: kpt on fr 2 out: nvr any danger* **33/1**
-30P **6** *3* **Westlin' Winds (IRE)**^{9} [3229] 5-11-1 **134**........................ TomScudamore 125
(Charles Egerton) *w ldrs tl hrd rdn and fdd bef 2 out* **18/1**
-555 **7** *1* **Ultimate**^{49} [2521] 5-10-9 **131**.................................. DannyCook$^{(3)}$ 122
(Brian Ellison) *hld up in last pair: nt fluent 3rd: shkn up after 3 out: plugged on but nvr a threat* **11/1**
1-3 **8** *nse* **Valento**^{217} [633] 6-10-1 **120**.................................. SeanQuinlan 110
(Kim Bailey) *hld up in rr: rdn bef 2 out: plugged on but nvr a threat* **25/1**
126- **9** *12* **Rollwiththepunches**^{263} [5299] 6-11-0 **133**..........................(t) GrahamLee 111
(Philip McBride) *led to 3rd: styd prom: drvn bef 2 out: sn wknd* **20/1**
6233 **10** *3½* **Heron Bay**^{48} [2542] 7-10-1 **123**.................................(p) DonalDevereux$^{(3)}$ 97
(Peter Bowen) *hld up in rr: rdn and struggling after 3 out: no ch fr next* **8/1**
223- **11** *38* **First Avenue**^{357} [3464] 6-10-2 **121**..........................(p) AndrewGlassonbury 57
(Gary Moore) *hld up in rr: sme prog after 3 out: no hdwy whn mstke 2 out: wkng rapidly whn mstke last: t.o* **20/1**
0-00 **P** **Wingman (IRE)**^{23} [2977] 9-10-0 **119** oh2.............................. JamieMoore —
(Gary Moore) *mstkes 1st and 2nd: sn lost pl: last after next: sn t.o: p.u after 3 out* **13/2**^{3}

4m 10.5s (3.30) **Going Correction** +0.425s/f (Soft) **12** Ran SP% **119.7**
Speed ratings (Par 109): **109,106,103,102,101 100,100,100,94,92 74,—**
Tote Swingers: 1&2 £25.10, 1&3 £2.10, 2&3 £19.20 CSF £89.68 CT £228.97 TOTE £4.20: £1.70, £7.00, £2.00; EX 109.40 Trifecta £777.70 Part won. Pool: £1051.05 - 0.50 winning units..
Owner McNeill Family **Bred** Earl Ecurie Delbart & Classic Breeding **Trained** Barbury Castle, Wilts

FOCUS
This decent handicap hurdle was, unsurprisingly, the quickest of the three C&D races. There was a false start initially. Impressive winner Mille Chief is entitled to take his chance in the Champion Hurdle on this evidence and the form looks solid.

NOTEBOOK
Mille Chief(FR) put in a high-class performance off a mark of 145, cruising up to the leader two from home and quickening away on the flat for a very easy win. He faced a stiff task against the well-in Aegean Dawn at Ascot and went up 9lb for that, but proved himself still well handicapped here. Set to go for the Totesport Trophy at Newbury next month, he will obviously have to go on the shortlist after this, and deservedly he will be given a Champion Hurdle entry too. (op 3-1 tchd 7-2)
Sophies Trophy(IRE) was put in his place by the easy winner from the final flight, but this was still a pleasing effort. The return of a tongue strap appeared a big help, and the drop in trip suited in this ground. (op 20-1)
Zazamix(FR), 2lb out of the weights and getting 26lb from the winner, lost his pitch before the home turn and was only fifth over the final flight before staying on. This was a satisfactory return to action but it remains to be seen if he can build on it. (op 11-4)
Kudu Country(IRE) had no ground concerns and ran his race but was held in third when blundering two out. He should come on for this first appearance since the spring. (tchd 11-1 and 14-1)
Tiger O'Toole(IRE) ◆ had not been seen since the Galway Hurdle in the summer and all his form has been on better ground, so there was definite promise in this staying-on performance. (op 22-1)
Westlin' Winds(IRE) ran better than of late. (op 25-1 tchd 16-1)
Ultimate, on whom a change of tactics did not work out, has had a wind operation since his last run. (op 12-1 tchd 9-1)
Wingman(IRE) has become very well handicapped, racing off 5lb lower than when beating subsequent Champion Hurdle winner Punjabi in the 2008 Totesport Trophy, but was one of the first beaten. (op 11-1)
T/Plt: £850.00 to a £1 stake. Pool of £109,336.74 - 93.89 winning tickets. T/Qpdt: £77.70 to a £1 stake. Pool of £10,001.99 - 95.20 winning tickets. JN

2480 WINCANTON (R-H)
Saturday, January 8

OFFICIAL GOING: Soft (good to soft in places; hdl 6.6; chs 6.8)
Wind: quite strong behind Weather: cloudy but dry

3448 HIGOS INSURANCE GLASTONBURY NOVICES' HURDLE (DIV I) (11 hdls) 2m 6f
12:45 (12:45) (Class 4) 4-Y-0+ **£2,276** (£668; £334; £166)

Form RPR
F21- **1** **Buck Mulligan**^{265} [5251] 6-11-6 0.. PaulMoloney 123+
(Evan Williams) *mid-div: hdwy appr 3 out: led 2 out: clr last: comf* **8/1**^{3}
0-3 **2** *8* **Round Tom (FR)**^{62} [2232] 6-11-6 0.................................. DarylJacob 112
(Paul Nicholls) *prom in chsng gp: clsd on ldr 7th: rdn after 3 out: styd on same pce fr next: wnt 2nd bef last: no ch w wnr* **7/1**^{2}
13 **3** *4½* **On Trend (IRE)**^{26} [2925] 5-11-12 123............................... WarrenMarston 114
(Nick Gifford) *prom in chsng gp: clsd on ldr after 6th: led 3 out: rdn and hdd whn hit 2 out: no ex whn lost 2nd bef last* **9/4**^{1}
4 *hd* **Sum Laff (IRE)**^{635} 7-11-6 0.. AndrewTinkler 106
(Charlie Mann) *mid-div: hdwy 3 out: sn rdn: styd on same pce* **8/1**^{3}
30 **5** *2* **Bishophill Jack (IRE)**^{11} [3158] 5-11-6 0................................ TomSiddall 104
(Kim Bailey) *mid-div tl lost pl and drvn in rr after 5th: sme prog after 3 out: styd on same pce fr next* **22/1**
0-6 **6** *½* **Troy Tempest (IRE)**^{49} [2512] 6-10-13 0................. StephenO'Donovan$^{(7)}$ 105
(Emma Lavelle) *hld up towards rr: hdwy appr 3 out: rdn bef 2 out: grad fdd* **10/1**
5-3 **7** *1¾* **Ace High**^{67} [2136] 7-11-6 0.. JoeTizzard 105+
(Victor Dartnall) *hld up towards rr: rdn after 3 out: no imp* **9/4**^{1}
0-03 **8** *36* **Easton Clump**^{11} [3167] 8-11-6 0.................................. GerardTumelty 66
(Dominic Ffrench Davis) *chsd ldrs in main gp: mstke 2nd: led appr 7th: nt fluent whn hdd 3 out: sn rdn: wknd bef next* **50/1**
000 **9** *5* **Glenfly (IRE)**^{11} [3153] 6-11-6 0.. RhysFlint 61
(Philip Hobbs) *chsd ldrs in main gp: rdn after 3 out: sn wknd* **80/1**
000 **10** *98* **Sun Des Mottes (FR)**^{9} [3227] 5-10-13 0.............................. GerrySupple —
(David Pipe) *led: sn wl clr: hdd bef 7th: wknd qckly: sn wl t.o* **80/1**
00 **U** **Dig Guns (IRE)**^{322} [4100] 7-10-13 0.............................. MrTGarner$^{(7)}$ —
(Warren Greatrex) *chsd clr ldr: awkward 1st and 2nd and rdr lost iron briefly both times: wnt rt and uns rdr 4th* **66/1**

5m 14.4s (-12.10) **Going Correction** -0.45s/f (Good) **11** Ran SP% **115.6**
Speed ratings (Par 105): **104,101,99,99,98 98,97,84,82,47** —
Tote Swingers: 1&2 £8.10, 1&3 £8.50, 2&3 £6.30 CSF £59.53 TOTE £8.60: £2.30, £2.00, £1.50; EX 35.80.
Owner L Fell **Bred** Peter Botham **Trained** Llancarfan, Vale Of Glamorgan

FOCUS
The going had eased a touch to soft, good to soft in places. This was just a modest novice hurdle, but the winner is a 130+ chaser and should have more to offer over hurdles.

NOTEBOOK
Buck Mulligan, off since winning a novice chase for the yard in the spring, smoothly moved into contention and could be called the winner rounding the final bend. Winning with a fair bit in hand, he is clearly a useful prospect with more to come over both hurdles and fences.
Round Tom(FR), third in an ordinary event at Ffos Las on his hurdles debut, was no match for the winner but clearly has the ability to win, with 3m on better ground likely to suit. (op 6-1)
On Trend(IRE), the only previous hurdles winner, was conceding weight all round and came up short, as he had done when filling the same position at Plumpton on his previous run. (op 5-2 tchd 11-4)
Sum Laff(IRE), narrow winner of a point in April, made a promising debut, just missing out on third. He should improve for the experience. (op 15-2 tchd 9-1)
Bishophill Jack(IRE) stayed on again having lost his position and will be of interest for low-grade handicaps. (op 33-1)
Ace High jumped slowly and found little for pressure. He had shaped promisingly at Exeter and, with plenty of size about him, may just need more time. Better ground may help. (op 11-4)

3449 HIGOS THATCHED INSURANCE NOVICES' H'CAP HURDLE (8 hdls) 2m
1:15 (1:17) (Class 4) (0-110,109) 4-Y-0+ **£2,602** (£764; £382; £190)

Form RPR
0/02 **1** **Arrayan**^{50} [2504] 6-10-5 **93**.. CO'Farrell$^{(5)}$ 106+
(David Pipe) *mid-dvision: hdwy 3 out: rdn appr 2 out: led appr last: kpt on wl* **9/4**^{1}
2-42 **2** *2¼* **Royale's Charter**^{76} [2003] 5-11-5 **102**.................................. DarylJacob 112+
(Nick Williams) *t.k.h: prom: rdn to ld 2 out: hdd bef last: kpt on but sn hld* **9/2**^{2}
053 **3** *9* **Silver Roque (FR)**^{54} [2419] 5-11-7 **104**.......................... AndrewThornton 105
(Henrietta Knight) *mid-div: hdwy 3 out: ev ch 2 out: sn rdn: kpt on same pce* **15/2**
-4P0 **4** *7* **The Grifter**^{51} [2482] 9-11-5 **105**.................................. RichardKilloran$^{(3)}$ 101
(John Ryall) *led: mstke 3 out: rdn and hdd whn nt fluent 2 out: hung rt and fdd sn after* **12/1**
0/05 **5** *3* **Wise Hawk**^{51} [2485] 6-10-9 **92**.. JamesDavies 84
(Chris Down) *trckd ldrs: hit 3 out: rdn bef next: fdd appr last* **18/1**
4-05 **6** *½* **Peveril Pandora**^{50} [2499] 8-10-12 **95**............................(t) MarkBradburne 85
(Jimmy Fox) *hld up towards rr: hdwy 3 out: sn rdn: one pce fr next* **7/1**^{3}
504F **7** *nk* **Art Man**^{45} [2605] 8-10-4 **90**..(t) WayneKavanagh$^{(3)}$ 80
(James Frost) *towards rr: nudged along after 3rd: rdn whn in tch after 3 out: wknd next* **28/1**
2365 **8** *1¼* **Sansili**^{59} [2308] 4-10-3 **98**.. RhysFlint 75
(Peter Bowen) *trckd ldrs: rdn after 5th: wknd bef 2 out* **10/1**
0-6P **9** *9* **Commit To Memory**^{44} [2630] 6-10-7 **90**.............................. RodiGreene 70
(Jimmy Fox) *prom tl dropped to midfield 2nd: drvn after next: sn in rr: nvr a factor after* **40/1**
33-5 **10** *4½* **Gunslinger (FR)**^{178} [823] 6-11-7 **104**................................ PaulMoloney 84
(Michael Scudamore) *hld up bhd: hdwy 3 out: rdn and wknd bef next* **11/1**
00-4 **11** *½* **Across The Straits (FR)**^{54} [2430] 7-10-9 **95**................ JimmyDerham$^{(3)}$ 70
(Jonathan Geake) *hld up towards rr: nt fluent 3rd: hdwy 3 out: stmbld on bnd sn after and lost any ch: wknd next* **16/1**

3m 42.5s (-6.40) **Going Correction** -0.45s/f (Good)
WFA 4 from 5yo+ 11lb **11** Ran SP% **115.4**
Speed ratings (Par 105): **98,96,92,88,87 87,86,86,81,79 79**
Tote Swingers: 1&2 £2.70, 1&3 £3.60, 2&3 £5.30 CSF £12.79 CT £64.13 TOTE £3.10: £1.60, £2.00, £1.20; EX 10.20.

Owner Mrs Angela Tincknell & W Tincknell **Bred** West Stow Stud Ltd **Trained** Nicholashayne, Devon

FOCUS
An ordinary novices' handicap hurdle but the first three are on the upgrade.

NOTEBOOK
Arrayan, backed when showing much-improved form on his handicap debut at Exeter on his previous start, comes from a yard in good form and he stayed on strongly from the last to win with a bit in hand. Having only his fifth start over hurdles, he is clearly on the up and looks capable of winning again. (op 2-1 tchd 15-8)
Royale's Charter had run well at the course last time and he put in another sound effort from a mark of 102. Clear of the third, he shouldn't be long in winning something similar. (op 4-1)
Silver Roque(FR) got a little better with each start in novice hurdles and this scopey individual moved well for a long way on this switch to handicaps. There are races to be won with him, especially once he goes over fences. (op 8-1)
The Grifter was readily swept aside and isn't going to be the easiest to win with, already being a 9yo. (op 20-1)
Across The Straits(FR) Official explanation: jockey said gelding had clipped heels and stumbled on the final bend

3450 HIGOS INSURANCE STREET NOVICES' H'CAP CHASE (21 fncs) 3m 1f 110y
1:50 (1:57) (Class 4) (0-110,110) 5-Y-0+ **£4,553** (£1,337; £668; £333)

Form RPR
6-04 **1** **Honourable Arthur (IRE)**[66] 2146 8-10-9 **93**......(p) DarylJacob 105
(Victor Dartnall) *trckd ldrs: jnd ldr 13th: led next: rdn whn hrd pressed fr after 4 out: styd on gamely fr last: drvn out* **3/1**[1]
313 **2** *1* **Dunkelly Castle (IRE)**[66] 2146 7-11-12 **110**...... AndrewTinkler 122
(Roger Curtis) *hld up in last pair: hdwy into cl 3rd after 17th: chalng whn pckd 3 out: sn rdn w ev ch: pckd last: styd on but no ex* **4/1**[3]
3-26 **3** *9* **Reblis (FR)**[24] 2959 6-11-4 **109**......(p) JoshuaMoore[(7)] 112
(Gary Moore) *cl up: rdn along after 16th: jnd wnr after next: ev ch tl nt fluent 2 out: styd on same pce* **7/2**[2]
F-0F **4** *21* **Goring One (IRE)**[25] 2949 6-11-2 **100**...... AndrewThornton 86+
(Anna Newton-Smith) *led 3rd: nt fluent 13th: hdd next: styd chsng ldrs tl wknd appr 3 out: mstke 2 out* **18/1**
22-0 **5** *14* **Tuskar Rock (FR)**[26] 2928 8-11-2 **107**...... HarryChalloner[(7)] 74
(Venetia Williams) *led tl 3rd: trckd ldr: pushed along after 12th: wknd after 4 out: t.o* **13/2**
1640 **6** *16* **Alldunnandusted (IRE)**[24] 2959 7-11-7 **108**...... JimmyDerham[(3)] 59
(Seamus Mullins) *trckd ldrs: rdn whn stmbld 4 out: wknd bef next: t.o* **10/1**
34-1 **P** **Beware Chalk Pit (IRE)**[54] 2431 7-10-12 **96**...... JimmyMcCarthy —
(Jonathan Geake) *hld up in last pair: blnd 3rd: disputing cl 4th whn mstke 17th: wknd sn after next: p.u bef 3 out* **4/1**[3]

6m 48.9s (9.40) **Going Correction** -0.25s/f (Good) **7** Ran SP% **114.9**
Speed ratings: **75,74,71,65,61 56,—**
Tote Swingers: 1&2 £3.20, 1&3 £2.20, 2&3 £3.60 CSF £15.92 CT £42.84 TOTE £4.20: £2.30, £3.30; EX 16.10.
Owner Miss A Woolley **Bred** Mrs Neta O Connor **Trained** Brayford, Devon

FOCUS
A modest but open contest. The early pace was a steady one, but it still proved a good test in the conditions. The winner improved to the level of his best hurdles form.

NOTEBOOK
Honourable Arthur(IRE), wearing cheekpieces for the first time, travelled much more sweetly than he had previously and kept finding for pressure when strongly pressed in the straight. He is a fine-looking sort and, with the promise of more to come on a faster surface, looks capable of winning again. (op 7-2)
Dunkelly Castle(IRE), third in a decent race at Chepstow last time, having previously won at Worcester, moved nicely into contention and looked the likeliest winner coming to three out, but his jumping wasn't the slickest over the last few fences and he was always being held from the last. (op 13-2)
Reblis(FR) ran well without being able to match the front pair late on. He is yet to win over fences. (tchd 4-1)
Goring One(IRE), a faller last time, made a couple of mistakes but at least got round. (tchd 25-1)
Beware Chalk Pit(IRE), racing off just 2lb higher than when winning at Plumpton, wasn't helped by an early mistake and his fate was sealed by another error when trying to close late on. (op 11-4)

3451 HIGOS INSURANCE WELLS NOVICES' CHASE (17 fncs) 2m 5f
2:25 (2:25) (Class 3) 5-Y-0+ **£5,854** (£1,719; £859; £429)

Form RPR
110- **1** **The Minack (IRE)**[274] 5112 7-10-12 0...... NickScholfield 140+
(Paul Nicholls) *trckd ldr: pckd 6th: led narrowly 3 out: shkn up to assert last: readily* **5/4**[1]
36-1 **2** *3 ¾* **Bouggler**[54] 2427 6-11-4 0...... PaulMoloney 143+
(Emma Lavelle) *trckd ldrs: led 12th: rdn whn narrowly hdd after pecking 4: remained w ev ch tl hit 2 out: no ex* **5/2**[2]
-4F2 **3** *4 ½* **Rougham**[58] 2326 5-10-7 0...... RhysFlint 126
(Philip Hobbs) *led tl narrowly hdd whn pckd 12th: rdn in cl 3rd after 5 out: styd on same pce fr 3 out* **13/2**
01P- **4** *8* **Lord Ragnar (IRE)**[269] 5182 8-10-12 0...... AndrewTinkler 125+
(Nicky Henderson) *nt particularly fluent 1st 4 fences: cl up: struggling 13th: wknd bef 3 out* **5/1**[3]
-053 **P** **Persian Run (IRE)**[81] 1908 7-10-12 119...... JoeTizzard —
(Colin Tizzard) *in tch tl pce qcknd 10th: sn wl bhd: p.u bef 4 out* **40/1**

5m 19.2s (-6.00) **Going Correction** -0.25s/f (Good)
WFA 5 from 6yo+ 4lb **5** Ran SP% **105.5**
Speed ratings: **101,99,97,94,—**
CSF £4.43 TOTE £1.80: £1.20, £2.10; EX 4.40.
Owner C G Roach **Bred** Kenilworth House Stud **Trained** Ditcheat, Somerset

FOCUS
A decent little novice chase that saw a smart debut effort from The Minack, who is expected to take high rank this season by Paul Nicholls. The first two are both rated around 7lb their bset hurdles marks.

NOTEBOOK
The Minack(IRE) is expected to take high rank this season by Paul Nicholls. A triple scorer over hurdles before finding Grade 1 company too much too soon at Aintree on his final start, he jumped fluently on this first start over fences and could be called the winner a long way out. He didn't shake off the runner-up immediately, but a good jump two out pretty much sealed the win and, considering this was his first start in 274 days, it's reasonable to expect improvement. He'll presumably be considered for both the Jewson and RSA at the festival and he looks a bright prospect. (op 7-4 tchd 11-10)
Bouggler, rated 148 over hurdles, had made a workmanlike winning debut over fences at Plumpton and looked vulnerable here under a penalty. He tried to kick on, but the winner always had the move covered and he was outmatched from the second-last. (op 15-8)
Rougham, beaten by a useful mare at Ludlow on his previous start, tried to rally after being headed and perhaps 3m on good ground will prove his optimum. (op 6-1)
Lord Ragnar(IRE), rated 129 over hurdles, took a while to warm to the fences and never threatened the principals, but there will be other days for him. (op 9-2 tchd 7-1)
Persian Run(IRE), although pulled up, isn't one to give up on just yet. He will be of interest down the line in handicaps. (op 33-1)

3452 HIGOS.CO.UK INSURANCE SERVICES H'CAP HURDLE (10 hdls) 2m 4f
3:00 (3:00) (Class 3) (0-135,135) 4-Y-0+ **£6,505** (£1,910; £955; £477)

Form RPR
5-U4 **1** **Sparrow Hills (IRE)**[55] 2393 7-9-10 **112**...... RobertKirk[(7)] 119+
(Steven Dixon) *led tl 4th: led 6th: styd on gamely fr 2 out: drvn out* **16/1**
4P-1 **2** *1 ¼* **Gold Reef**[63] 2209 8-10-6 **122**...... PeterHatton[(7)] 126
(Alan King) *mid-div: hdwy 3 out: rdn bef next: styd on wl to go 2nd sn after last but nvr quite gng to reel in wnr* **8/1**
-522 **3** *2 ¼* **Five Star Wilsham (IRE)**[60] 2284 7-10-8 **117**...... NickScholfield 119
(Jeremy Scott) *t.k.h: trckd ldrs: effrt 2 out: cl 2nd but hung lft appr last: no ex run-in* **7/2**[1]
0-FU **4** *1 ¼* **Dansimar**[51] 2481 7-11-2 **130**...... RTDunne[(5)] 132
(Venetia Williams) *trckd ldrs: rdn appr 2 out: short of room appr last: styd on* **28/1**
-350 **5** *2 ½* **Dr Livingstone (IRE)**[42] 2671 6-11-3 **126**......(t) JimmyMcCarthy 124
(Charles Egerton) *hld up towards rr: rdn and stdy prog after 3 out: nt pce to get on terms but styd on fr next: nrst fin* **20/1**
15-0 **6** *hd* **Red Harbour (IRE)**[49] 2523 7-10-13 **129**...... MrDGPrichard[(7)] 128
(Paul Nicholls) *mid-div: hdwy appr 3 out: ev ch 2 out: sn rdn: hung lft and fdd run-in* **9/2**[2]
3-14 **7** *1 ¼* **Paint The Clouds**[54] 2428 6-10-8 **117**...... DarylJacob 114
(Warren Greatrex) *mid-div: rdn after 3 out: styd on same pce fr next* **10/1**
211 **8** *3* **Get It On (IRE)**[62] 2246 6-11-3 **126**...... PaulMoloney 123+
(Evan Williams) *hld up towards rr: gd hdwy after 3 out: cl up whn hit 2 out: sn rdn: hld whn hit last: fdd* **9/1**
4212 **9** *11* **Kylenoe Fairy (IRE)**[25] 2949 7-9-12 **110**......(t) JimmyDerham[(3)] 93
(Paul Henderson) *mid-div: hdwy 3 out: effrt bef next: wkng whn hit last* **7/1**[3]
4P-0 **10** *12* **Snake Charmer**[18] 3059 8-10-6 **115**......(b) DaveCrosse 86
(Milton Harris) *prom tl after 3 out: t.o* **33/1**
32/6 **11** *7* **Russian Epic**[81] 1911 7-9-12 **110**......(t) CPGeoghegan[(3)] 74
(Philip Hobbs) *trckd ldrs: pckd 5th: jnd wnr whn hit 3 out: sn rdn: wknd bef next* **10/1**
0000 **12** *53* **Tarvini (IRE)**[7] 3306 6-9-12 **117**......(p) GeraldQuinn[(10)] 28
(Jonjo O'Neill) *lost tch 5th: t.o* **50/1**
55UF **P** **Forest Rhythm (IRE)**[44] 2636 7-9-11 **109**......(t) WayneKavanagh[(3)] —
(Seamus Mullins) *t.k.h: trckd ldrs: led 4th tl rn wd on bnd appr 6th: wknd after 7th: t.o whn p.u bef 2 out* **25/1**
-33P **P** **Accordingtoemandem (IRE)**[55] 2387 7-10-13 **122**......(t) JoeTizzard —
(Ian Williams) *mid-div tl after 4th: nvr travelling towards rr after: p.u bef 2 out* **20/1**

4m 44.2s (-12.60) **Going Correction** -0.45s/f (Good) **14** Ran SP% **119.8**
Speed ratings (Par 107): **107,106,105,105,104 104,103,102,97,93 90,69,—,—**
Tote Swingers: 1&2 £52.90, 1&3 £14.80, 2&3 £3.00 CSF £126.21 CT £560.56 TOTE £24.30: £7.40, £2.40, £1.60; EX 272.30 TRIFECTA Not won..
Owner S Dixon **Bred** Ged Quain **Trained** Winterslow, Wilts

FOCUS
A competitive handicap hurdle. The winner was well in on his 2009 best and is rated back to that sort of level, and the form in general is sound.

NOTEBOOK
Sparrow Hills(IRE) ground it out well under pressure. Things didn't really work out for him over fences last season but, returning after a short break, he looks back on the right track. (op 18-1)
Gold Reef, 7lb higher than when winning at Sandown, ran every bit as well, chasing home the winner without ever looking likely to get to him. (op 15-2)
Five Star Wilsham(IRE) was found out late on, having raced keenly through the early stages. (op 5-1)
Dansimar, back over hurdles after an unsuccessful spell over fences, ran well enough without suggesting she's ready to win off this mark. (op 22-1)
Dr Livingstone(IRE) made some late headway and ran with a bit more promise in the tongue-tie.
Red Harbour(IRE), well backed, has been a bit disappointing in two starts this season and is left with a bit to prove. (op 11-2 tchd 6-1)
Get It On(IRE) may have made his ground too quickly as his finishing effort was weak on this return to handicaps. (op 8-1)
Forest Rhythm(IRE) Official explanation: jockey said gelding hung left

3453 HIGOS INSURANCE SERVICES H'CAP CHASE (17 fncs) 2m 5f
3:30 (3:30) (Class 2) (0-145,142) 5-Y-0+
£12,524 (£3,700; £1,850; £926; £462; £232)

Form RPR
1U5- **1** **Fistral Beach (IRE)**[280] 4988 8-11-1 **131**...... NickScholfield 146+
(Paul Nicholls) *j. sltly lft at times: trckd ldr: pckd 3rd: led 13th: in command fr 3 out: styd on wl* **7/2**[1]
6111 **2** *4* **I'm A Legend**[51] 2484 9-9-13 **122**......(p) MarkQuinlan[(7)] 130
(Neil Mulholland) *mid-div: hdwy after 10th: cl 3rd 4 out: rdn to chse wnr fr next: styd on but a being hld* **7/1**[3]
0-P2 **3** *10* **Regal Heights (IRE)**[25] 2948 10-10-6 **122**......(p) AndrewThornton 121
(Tom George) *in tch: tk clsr order 10th: hit 12th: rdn after next: ev ch 4 out: styd on same pce fr next* **6/1**[2]
0400 **4** *3 ¾* **Double Dizzy**[29] 2869 10-9-7 **116**......(t) NathanSweeney[(7)] 110
(Bob Buckler) *chsd ldrs: rdn 13th: styd on same pce fr 4 out* **10/1**
P-33 **5** *2 ½* **Le Burf (FR)**[50] 2497 10-10-8 **127**...... TomMolloy[(3)] 124+
(Giles Smyly) *hld up towards rr: hit 2nd: creeping clsr whn pckd bdly 13th: sn rdn: styng on same pce whn awkward 2 out: nvr threatened ldrs* **12/1**
3-31 **6** *10* **Mount Oscar (IRE)**[42] 2674 12-11-12 **142**......(t) JoeTizzard 124
(Colin Tizzard) *mid-div: reminders after 8th: sn towards rr: no ch fr 12th* **10/1**
1142 **7** *10* **Working Title (IRE)**[18] 3059 9-10-12 **138**...... JeremiahMcGrath[(10)] 110
(Nicky Henderson) *mid-div: hdwy 10th: rdn in cl 4th whn pckd 4 out: sn wknd* **7/1**[3]
5-00 **8** *16* **Doctor Pat (IRE)**[25] 2948 7-10-2 **118**...... BarryKeniry 74
(Jonjo O'Neill) *a bhd: t.o* **25/1**
211- **9** *21* **Bradford Boris**[303] 4538 7-10-3 **119**...... DarylJacob 54
(Nick Williams) *racd freely: led: hit 11th: hdd 13th: wknd after next: t.o* **6/1**[2]
-22P **P** **Pavillon Bleu (FR)**[50] 2500 8-10-9 **125**...... RhysFlint —
(Philip Hobbs) *nvr travelling in rr: t.o whn p.u after 4 out* **12/1**
1446 **P** **North Island (IRE)**[62] 2232 9-10-7 **123**......(p) AndrewTinkler —
(Peter Bowen) *chsd ldrs tl 10th: sn wknd: t.o whn p.u bef 13th* **66/1**

5m 14.9s (-10.30) **Going Correction** -0.25s/f (Good) **11** Ran SP% **114.7**
Speed ratings: **109,107,103,102,101 97,93,87,79,—,—**
Tote Swingers: 1&2 £4.10, 1&3 £3.20, 2&3 £10.50 CSF £28.06 CT £141.60 TOTE £3.20: £1.40, £1.90, £3.50; EX 28.90 Trifecta £108.10 Pool: £416.59 - 2.85 winning units..
Owner C G Roach **Bred** P E Clinton **Trained** Ditcheat, Somerset

FOCUS
An open-looking handicap chase run in a decent time. A step forward from the cosy winner who can probably rate higher.
NOTEBOOK
Fistral Beach(IRE) drew clear from the third-last and won in the style of a horse with more to offer. Off since disappointing in heavy ground at Haydock last spring, he had earlier looked a progressive handicap chaser and made light of a mark of 131 on this seasonal return. He tended to go left at a few of his fences, so won't have any trouble going back left-handed, and he may have a big handicap in him this season. (op 3-1 tchd 11-4)
I'm A Legend, chasing a four-timer, had gone up a further 7lb, leaving him on a career-high mark, but he ran another stormer, staying on to finish well clear of the third. There was no disgrace in losing out to the unexposed winner. (tchd 13-2)
Regal Heights(IRE) is well weighted on his old form and the way he's running at present suggests he may be able to take advantage at some stage. (op 7-1 tchd 8-1)
Double Dizzy is back on a good mark and he is likely to get his head in front before the season's out. (op 12-1)
Le Burf(FR) did well considering the notable blunder he made. He stayed on again afterwards, but his winning chance had well and truly gone. (tchd 16-1)
Bradford Boris, progressive last season, ended up well held but should improve for this first outing in 303 days. (op 7-1)

3454 HIGOS INSURANCE GLASTONBURY NOVICES' HURDLE (DIV II) (9 hdls 2 omitted) 2m 6f
4:05 (4:09) (Class 4) 4-Y-0+ **£2,276** (£668; £334; £166)

Form				RPR
111-	1		**Ballabriggs (IRE)**[296] 4703 10-11-6 140 ... AdrianLane *(Donald McCain) trckd ldrs: hung sltly lft on stable bnd: chal on long run after 2 out: led narrowly sn after last(usually 2nd last): squeezed up chalrs by-passing omitted last: styd on: rdn out* **10/3**[2]	123+
-333	2	2 ¾	**Ohio Gold (IRE)**[24] 2963 5-11-6 120 ... JoeTizzard *(Colin Tizzard) racd keenly in midfield: bdly hmpd 5th: chal 2 out (was 3 out): ev ch fr last tl bdly squeezed up by-passing omitted last: no ch after* **5/4**[1]	122+
-322	3	4	**Zakatal**[79] 1941 5-11-6 120 ... (bt[1]) RhysFlint *(Philip Hobbs) trckd ldrs: hit 2nd: jnd ldr whn hit 2 out: rdn to ld bef last: hdd on long run-in: bdly hmpd by-passing omitted last hurdle: no ex* **13/2**[3]	118+
-006	4	2 ¾	**Robin Will (FR)**[29] 2873 6-11-6 0 ... NickScholfield *(Paul Nicholls) patiently rdn in rr: hdwy 2 out: effrt appr last: styd on same pce* **10/1**	113
-235	5	1	**Smooth Classic (IRE)**[18] 3055 7-11-6 115 ... DarylJacob *(Warren Greatrex) disp ld tl after 2 out: sn rdn: styd on same pce fr last* **7/1**	111
500	6	6	**No Obligation (IRE)**[7] 3295 6-11-1 0 ... MrMMO'Connor[(5)] *(Brendan Powell) hld up towards rr: rdn and little imp fr after 2 out(was 3 out)* **100/1**	105
000	7	12	**Smoking (FR)**[43] 2666 5-11-6 0 ... GerardTumelty *(Sean Curran) hld up towards rr: rdn bef 2 out (was 3 out) grad fdd* **100/1**	93
00	8	72	**Quiet Alice**[51] 2482 6-10-13 0 ... RodiGreene *(Neil Mulholland) mid-div tl struggling 6th: sn bhd* **200/1**	14
0-00	9	dist	**Contentwithmyluck (IRE)**[72] 2056 5-11-6 0 ... MarkBradburne *(Tom Gretton) disp ld tl wknd after 7th: sn wl t.o* **150/1**	—
114	F		**Natureofthebeast (IRE)**[47] 2584 6-11-12 123 ... PaulMoloney *(Evan Williams) disputing ld whn fell 5th: fatally injured* **12/1**	—

5m 18.8s (-7.70) **Going Correction** -0.45s/f (Good) **10** Ran SP% **113.3**
Speed ratings (Par 105): **96,95,93,92,92 90,85,59,—,—**
Tote Swingers: 1&2 £2.80, 1&3 £2.60, 2&3 £1.60 CSF £7.98 TOTE £3.40: £1.10, £1.30, £2.10; EX 10.60.
Owner Trevor Hemmings **Bred** Mrs S L Jackson **Trained** Cholmondeley, Cheshire
■ Stewards' Enquiry : Adrian Lane five-day ban; careless riding (22nd-26th Jan)
FOCUS
The fatal fall Natureofthebeast suffered with a circuit to go led to the final flight being bypassed and the front three came close together as they struggled to round it on the long run-in, Zakatal getting squeezed out and being the worst affected. The first three are all rated withing a few pounds of their pre-race marks but there are doubts over the form. The flight on the stable bend was also omitted due to the low sun.
NOTEBOOK
Ballabriggs(IRE), off since winning the Kim Muir from a mark of 140, was previously winless over hurdles, but this much-improved sort travelled like a classy sort and stayed on well on the long run-in. He was the least affected by the barging that took place rounding the bypassed last, holding his ground and making it difficult for the other two, and his campaign will continue to be geared towards the Grand National. (op 7-2 tchd 9-2 in places)
Ohio Gold(IRE), badly hampered when Natureofthebeast came down, was able to recover and came to hold every chance in the straight. He was virtually level rounding the bypassed last when squeezed up and had no chance after, but there will be other days for him. (op 13-8 tchd 11-10)
Zakatal had looked rather paceless previously, but he did much better in the blinkers and was still in there fighting when squeezed and hampered by the front pair. That ended his chance, but there will be probably be other days for him. (op 5-1)
Robin Will(FR) is clearly talented, but he doesn't look the most straightforward and reportedly is still immature. He travelled well enough off the steady gallop before staying on and could be one to look for in handicaps. (op 8-1)
Smooth Classic(IRE) should also find it easier going in handicaps. (op 8-1 tchd 6-1)
T/Plt: £16.00 to a £1 stake. Pool of £66,503.64 - 3,024.43 winning tickets. T/Qpdt: £11.00 to a £1 stake. Pool £3,769.36 - 252.70 winning tickets. TM

3455 - 3462a (Foreign Racing) - See Raceform Interactive

2598 SEDGEFIELD (L-H)
Sunday, January 9
3463 Meeting Abandoned - Frost

3470a-3471a, 3476a (Foreign Racing) - See Raceform Interactive

3238 LEOPARDSTOWN (L-H)
Sunday, January 9
OFFICIAL GOING: Hurdle course - soft (soft to heavy in places), chase course - soft to heavy (heavy in places)

3472a TOTE PICK SIX KILLINEY NOVICE CHASE (GRADE 2) (14 fncs) 2m 5f
1:20 (1:26) 5-Y-0+ **£21,012** (£6,142; £2,909)

			RPR
1		**Magnanimity (IRE)**[57] 2378 7-11-5 ... DNRussell *(D T Hughes, Ire) led: slow at 1st and 2nd: sn hdd: led again bef 5th: strly pressed and drvn along after 2 out: kpt on wl u.p run-in* **9/4**[2]	148
2	¾	**Jessies Dream (IRE)**[25] 2971 8-11-12 147 ... TimmyMurphy *(Gordon Elliott, Ire) trckd ldrs in 3rd: 2nd fr 9th: nt fluent 4 out: poised to chal fr 2 out: drifted rt at last: fnd little u.p run-in: kpt on but nt match wnr* **4/9**[1]	154+
3	dist	**Elysian Rock**[12] 3174 7-11-5 133 ... BarryGeraghty *(M F Morris, Ire) prom: led after 2nd tl hdd bef 5th: j.rt thrght: dropped to 3rd at 9th: wknd bef 4 out: t.o* **9/1**[3]	—

5m 46.3s (1.30) **Going Correction** +0.35s/f (Yiel) **3** Ran SP% **110.0**
Speed ratings: **79,78,—**
CSF £3.93 TOTE £3.00; DF 5.20.
Owner Gigginstown House Stud **Bred** Thomas Foy **Trained** The Curragh, Co Kildare
FOCUS
The first two hunted round and the runner-up looked to have a lot in the tank approaching the last, but could not peg back the winner, who is gradually progressive.
NOTEBOOK
Magnanimity(IRE) went to the front at about halfway and so well was he jumping and potentially so well does he stay that Russell went for his race at the second-last. He had three lengths in hand when putting in a big jump at the final fence and from there he pulled out enough to beat a classier and better horse in the runner-up and favourite. His trainer described him as a solid 3m chasing type and fences really do seem to have brought out the best in him. If he got soft ground or maybe worse at Cheltenham he wouldn't be far from anybody's RSA Chase shortlist. First and foremost though, this was Russell at his best. (op 5/2)
Jessies Dream(IRE) just didn't jump as well as the winner and the rider was inviting trouble by apparently being happy sitting a couple of lengths off the leader jumping the last. Predictably, the horse jumped to his right and lost even more ground, ground he made up gradually on the run to the line to be beaten less than a length. The ground may well have been a reason for his fiddly jumping but it's certainly a race that he should have won. (op 4/9 tchd 1/2)
Elysian Rock ran no race at all, jumping to his right almost the whole way and dropping away from about the fifth-last. He's probably a better horse going right-handed but that wouldn't entirely explain what was a poor effort.

3473a TOTE PICK SIX EVERY SUNDAY LEOPARDSTOWN H'CAP CHASE (GRADE A) (14 fncs) 2m 5f
1:50 (1:57) 5-Y-0+ **£42,025** (£12,284; £5,818; £1,939)

			RPR
1		**Rare Bob (IRE)**[30] 2871 9-11-10 145 ... (b[1]) PWFlood *(D T Hughes, Ire) led: sn clr: reduced advantage 2 out: kpt on wl u.p fr bef last* **10/1**	157
2	2	**Got Attitude (IRE)**[11] 3206 8-10-4 125 ... (p) RMPower *(Mrs John Harrington, Ire) chsd clr ldr mainly 2nd: mstke 4 out: clsr fr 2 out: no imp u.p appr last where mstke: kpt on one pce* **16/1**	134
3	½	**Organisedconfusion (IRE)**[25] 2973 6-10-5 126 ... APCawley *(A L T Moore, Ire) hld up in rr: hdwy into 6th 2 out: wnt 3rd u.p appr last: no imp and kpt on one pce run-in* **8/1**[3]	135
4	nk	**Dooneys Gate (IRE)**[275] 5111 10-11-7 142 ... MrPWMullins *(W P Mullins, Ire) towards rr: pushed along and trailing 1/2-way: sme hdwy into 8th appr st: 4th at last: kpt on one pce* **12/1**	150
5	13	**Jered (IRE)**[11] 3206 9-11-0 135 ... APMcCoy *(Noel Meade, Ire) chsd ldrs: 6th 1/2-way: clsr in 5th 2 out: no imp in 6th whn mstke at last: kpt on one pce* **8/1**[3]	130
6	½	**Silent Creek (IRE)**[10] 3249 9-10-1 122 ... (b) APCrowe *(C Roche, Ire) chsd ldrs: 5th 1/2-way: 3rd 4 out: rdn ent st: no imp and dropped to 5th at last: no ex run-in* **4/1**[1]	117
7	1 ¾	**Conem (IRE)**[10] 3249 11-10-2 123 ... ADLeigh *(W J Austin, Ire) mid-div: 8th 1/2-way: blnd 4 out: kpt on one pce in st* **9/1**	116
8	shd	**Jayo (FR)**[25] 2973 8-11-7 142 ... PTownend *(W P Mullins, Ire) mid-div: 7th 1/2-way: 6th 4 out: rdn and no ex ent st* **4/1**[1]	135
9	11	**Follow The Plan (IRE)**[11] 3206 8-11-9 144 ... TJDoyle *(Oliver McKiernan, Ire) chsd ldrs: mstke 4th: 3rd 1/2-way: drvn along in 4th 2 out: no ex in st: btn whn eased run-in* **14/1**	126
10	7	**Askmeroe (IRE)**[247] 192 8-9-5 117 oh1 ... APHeskin[(5)] *(A J Martin, Ire) in rr of mid-div: 9th 1/2-way: 8th whn mstke 2 out: no ex in st* **10/1**	92
P		**Paco Jack (IRE)**[22] 3031 7-10-9 130 ... (tp) PCarberry *(P J Rothwell, Ire) a towards rr: p.u bef 3 out* **33/1**	—
P		**Venalmar**[11] 3206 9-10-7 128 ... BarryGeraghty *(M F Morris, Ire) chsd clr ldr: 4th 1/2-way: drvn along bef 5 out: sn no ex and wknd: p.u bef 3 out* **13/2**[2]	—

5m 39.1s (-5.90) **Going Correction** +0.35s/f (Yiel) **12** Ran SP% **126.9**
Speed ratings: **92,91,91,90,85 85,85,85,80,78 —,—**
CSF £162.91 CT £1368.61 TOTE £9.90: £3.50, £3.60, £2.20; DF 129.50.
Owner D A Syndicate **Bred** Don Hadden **Trained** The Curragh, Co Kildare
■ Stewards' Enquiry : R M Power severe caution: used whip with excessive frequency
FOCUS
The front-running Rare Bob is getting closer to his smart form, and the standard is solid around the placed horses.
NOTEBOOK
Rare Bob(IRE) did the job from the front in this competitive handicap under his big weight. First-time blinkers and being allowed to lead seemed to be key here and he dictated and dominated with a really good round of jumping. He went on again at the second-last and held that advantage at the final fence, keeping up the gallop against some strong finishers. He may well go for the Ryanair Chase and better ground won't inconvenience him. (op 9/1 tchd 11/1)
Got Attitude(IRE) didn't jump well on this ground but kept his position throughout and managed to overcome a particularly bad mistake at the third-last to keep going in gutsy fashion all the way to the line. He's another horse that should improve greatly on better ground and that should lead to an improvement in his jumping as well.
Organisedconfusion(IRE) made his ground from off the pace but wasn't done any real favours by being forced to race widest of all coming out of the back straight and that cost him some of the momentum he was building up. In fairness he kept going from the final fence without really threatening to make an impression on the winner and there should be a good handicap in him.

Dooneys Gate(IRE) was held up well off the pace and began to run on from before the second-last. His run did just flattened out after the last but a good handicap chase is within his compass. (op 10/1)
Jered(IRE) ran a creditable race in the conditions. He wasn't making any real impression when blundering at the last but did keep on again. (op 9/1)
Silent Creek(IRE)'s effort petered out from the second-last after closing up with some semblance of a chance. (op 6/1)
Jayo(FR) raced just off the pace most of the way but never really threatened from the turn out of the back straight. (op 7/2 tchd 5/1)

3474a MCR HURDLE (EXTENDED H'CAP) (GRADE B) (8 hdls) 2m

2:25 (2:28) (0-145,134) 4-Y-0+

£51,724 (£16,379; £7,758; £2,586; £1,724; £862)

RPR

1 **Final Approach**25 2969 5-10-9 123 PTownend 141+
(W P Mullins, Ire) *trckd ldrs: 7th 1/2-way: gd hdwy on inner to ld ent st: slt mstke last: kpt on wl run-in* **6/1**2

2 2 **Call The Police (IRE)**399 2742 8-10-8 123 EMullins(3) 139
(W P Mullins, Ire) *trckd ldrs: 9th 1/2-way: 6th 3 out: rdn to go 3rd at last: kpt on u.p wout rching wnr* **16/1**

3 1 **Mutadarek**12 3177 10-9-5 108 (p) SJGray(5) 123+
(Ms Joanna Morgan, Ire) *towards rr: hdwy on outer appr 2 out: 8th appr last: kpt on wl run-in* **25/1**

4 shd **Northern Alliance (IRE)**29 2886 10-10-6 123 APHeskin(5) 138
(A J Martin, Ire) *chsd ldrs: 5th 1/2-way: cl 3rd 2 out: 2nd at last: no ex u.p run-in* **33/1**

5 1 **Wilde Wit Pleasure (IRE)**10 3246 8-10-12 124 (tp) JMAllen 138
(Sean O O'Brien, Ire) *in rr of mid-div: sme hdwy appr 2 out: 10th ent st: kpt on u.p fr bef last* **50/1**

6 2 1/2 **Asigh Pearl (IRE)**25 2969 7-10-10 122 6ex DJCondon 133
(Noel Meade, Ire) *mid-div: hdwy 3 out: cl 6th at next: 4th whn mstke last: no imp and kpt on one pce* **20/1**

7 3/4 **Prima Vista**12 3177 6-10-13 125 15ex PCarberry 136
(Noel Meade, Ire) *mid-div: 9th 3 out: hdwy to join issue next: 4th u.p early st: no ex run-in* **7/2**1

8 1 1/4 **Alpine Eagle (IRE)**119 1513 7-11-3 134 MJBolger(5) 143
(Mrs John Harrington, Ire) *chsd ldrs: 8th 1/2-way: hdwy into 2nd after 3 out: no ex in st and dropped to 6th at last* **25/1**

9 nk **Fosters Cross (IRE)**25 2969 9-11-7 133 DNRussell 142
(Thomas Mullins, Ire) *mid-div: kpt on in st wout threatening* **25/1**

10 2 1/2 **Belord (GER)**63 2252 8-10-4 116 KTColeman 123
(John J Walsh, Ire) *towards: sme hdwy appr 2 out: kpt on in st* **18/1**

11 3/4 **Capellanus (IRE)**12 3177 5-10-7 121 AndrewJMcNamara 125
(E J O'Grady, Ire) *mid-div: 10th 1/2-way: rdn and no imp fr 2 out* **9/1**

12 1/2 **Montan (FR)**25 2969 7-10-3 115 NPMadden 120
(A J Martin, Ire) *mid-div best* **20/1**

13 4 1/2 **Tijuana Dancer (IRE)**12 3177 7-10-1 113 TimmyMurphy 114
(A J Martin, Ire) *chsd ldrs on inner: 8th 3 out: rdn and no ex ent st* **13/2**3

14 3/4 **Slieveardagh (IRE)**12 3177 7-11-3 134 PFMangan(5) 134
(E J O'Grady, Ire) *prom: 4th on inner 1/2-way: hdwy to ld 3 out: hdd u.p early st: sn no ex and wknd* **33/1**

15 1 1/4 **Lancetto (FR)**84 1896 6-11-0 126 BarryGeraghty 125
(James J Hartnett, Ire) *mid-div: no threat fr 2 out* **16/1**

16 19 **Vital Plot (USA)**12 3177 7-10-9 124 (bt) BTO'Connell(3) 104
(S Weld, Ire) *nvr a factor* **50/1**

17 1 **Mosstown (IRE)**8 3318 5-10-7 121 RMPower 98
(Mrs John Harrington, Ire) *mid-div: no threat fr 2 out* **33/1**

18 17 **Mr Clyde (IRE)**28 2915 8-10-1 113 JRBarry 75
(Patrick J Flynn, Ire) *a towards rr* **50/1**

19 1 1/2 **Casey Top (IRE)**106 1617 8-10-8 125 (t) BryanJCooper(5) 85
(Leonard Whitmore, Ire) *prom: led 4 out: hdd next: no ex bef 2 out: wknd* **25/1**

20 3 1/2 **Prince Of Fire (GER)**46 2620 6-10-9 121 APMcCoy 78
(C F Swan, Ire) *prom: 3rd on outer 1/2-way: drvn along bef next: sn no ex: wknd* **12/1**

21 4 **Mubrook (USA)**46 2621 6-10-0 112 TPTreacy 65
(E J O'Grady, Ire) *a towards rr: nvr a factor* **14/1**

22 19 **New Phase (IRE)**56 2405 7-11-7 133 MrRPMcNamara 67
(D K Weld, Ire) *trckd ldrs: 6th 1/2-way: no ex appr 2 out: wknd: eased whn btn in st: t.o* **14/1**

23 dist **Whodoyouthink (IRE)**25 2969 6-11-2 128 PWFlood —
(Oliver McKiernan, Ire) *a bhd: completely t.o* **14/1**

P **Un Hinged (IRE)**8 3318 11-10-9 128 (t) TCCarroll(7) —
(John J Coleman, Ire) *a bhd: p.u bef last* **40/1**

P **Island Oscar (IRE)**12 3177 7-10-5 117 (p) DJCasey —
(Paul A Roche, Ire) *a bhd: p.u bef 2 out* **50/1**

P **Some Slam (IRE)**36 241 6-10-8 120 AELynch —
(David Marnane, Ire) *led: hdd 4 out: sn no ex and wknd: p.u bef 3 out* **20/1**

3m 54.2s (-13.30) **Going Correction** -0.50s/f (Good) **26** Ran SP% **153.3**
Speed ratings: **113,112,111,111,110 109,109,108,108,107 106,106,104,104,103 93,93,84,84,82 80,70,—,—,EM**
CSF £98.92 CT £2376.68 TOTE £9.00: £2.40, £4.30, £3.60, £7.60; DF 191.80.
Owner Douglas Taylor **Bred** D Taylor **Trained** Muine Beag, Co Carlow
■ The winning owner is the Managing Director of the race sponsors.

FOCUS
Another competitive edition, but something that the race lacked this year in contrast to most runnings were some genuine hard-luck stories. The unexposed first two, both trained by Willie Mullins, ran personal bests, the standard set around the next four.

NOTEBOOK
Final Approach, when racing on the Flat for another stable, looked like a bridle horse on more than one occasion. That's something he couldn't be accused of now as he ran out a very easy winner of this contest after finding plenty off the bridle. Held up just off the pace, he did get a nice run up the inside when it counted but he didn't come off the bridle to get to the front early in the straight and quickened up when asked. This was a smart performance by a horse definitely ahead of the handicapper and how much more he can improve is something that will become evident, but he looks a horse from whom there could be plenty more to come. (op 8/1)
Call The Police(IRE), having his first run for the stable having won twice previously for John McConnell, raced quite handily most of the way. He just didn't have the initial pace to hold on to a challenging position coming out of the back straight but kept going strongly under pressure from the last without making an impression on his stable companion. He looks like a horse that will stay further and one wonders whether he could make up into a Coral Cup horse.
Mutadarek was held up well off the pace and wasn't helped by the fact that he had to race almost widest of all to make his challenge. He came late as he normally does and finished well but one would imagine the winner would have pulled out a bit more had he been really challenged.
Northern Alliance(IRE) is very well in over hurdles compared to his mark over fences but he showed his versatility with this big run over a trip well short of his best. Never far from the pace and jumping well, he was just run out of the placings from the final flight by speedier horses but evidence like this more than suggests he could win a nice handicap over a more appropriate trip.
Wilde Wit Pleasure(IRE) wasn't held up a long way off the pace and with him it seemed more a case of him taking a while to get going. He kept on well under pressure over a trip maybe slightly short of his optimum and he's looking more like a horse with a reasonable pot in him.
Asigh Pearl(IRE) fared best of the Noel Meade horses. She made some ground from off the pace before they turned out of the back straight but was under pressure to hold her place before the turn in. In the circumstances she kept going quite well. (op 16/1)
Prima Vista made quite rapid and very smooth headway to join issue with the leaders on the outside at the second-last but his effort did flatten out considerably running to the final flight. (op 4/1)
Alpine Eagle(IRE) had a stiff task under his weight but only faded from the last.
Belord(GER) ran on from quite a way back in the straight.
Tijuana Dancer(IRE) was reasonably well positioned three out on the inside before fading. (op 8/1)
Prince Of Fire(GER) travelled well in the leading group for much of the race before fading inside the final half mile. (op 10/1)
Whodoyouthink(IRE) Official explanation: jockey said gelding was unable to lie up in the early stages and may need a step up in trip on better ground.

3475a PERTEMPS H'CAP HURDLE (12 hdls) 3m

3:00 (3:00) 4-Y-0+ **£13,448** (£3,931; £1,862; £620)

RPR

1 **Across The Bay (IRE)**11 3206 7-9-13 123 DJCondon 136
(Noel Meade, Ire) *a.p: hdwy to dispute 2 out: rdn to ld appr last: kpt on u.p run-in* **20/1**

2 1 3/4 **Son Amix (FR)**22 3030 5-10-0 133 BryanJCooper(5) 140
(Thomas Cooper, Ire) *settled bhd ldrs: 7th 1/2-way: 5th 2 out: wnt 2nd bef last: no imp on wnr run-in: kpt on u.p* **8/1**3

3 1 1/2 **The Bishop Looney (IRE)**56 2406 7-10-0 124 DJCasey 134
(T J Nagle Jr, Ire) *a.p: 3rd 1/2-way: hdwy to dispute briefly 2 out: 3rd u.p appr last: kpt on one pce run-in* **8/1**3

4 2 **Sivota (IRE)**45 2648 7-10-9 133 (t) PTownend 141
(W P Mullins, Ire) *hld up towards rr: hdwy appr 2 out: wnt 5th bef last: kpt on wout rching ldrs* **8/1**3

5 2 **Shane Rock**11 3207 6-9-10 120 oh8 SWFlanagan 126
(M F Morris, Ire) *a.p: 4th 1/2-way: led briefly bef 2 out: sn hdd u.p and dropped to 4th bef last: kpt on one pce* **25/1**

6 1/2 **Four Chimneys (IRE)**9 3271 10-10-1 125 (b) ADLeigh 130
(W J Austin, Ire) *towards rr: hdwy fr 4 out: wnt 6th appr st: no imp u.p fr bef last: kpt on one pce* **16/1**

7 3/4 **Summit Meeting**12 3175 6-11-5 143 (t) RMPower 147
(Mrs John Harrington, Ire) *towards rr: hdwy appr 2 out: 7th appr last: kpt on one pce* **16/1**

8 3 1/2 **Saville Row (IRE)**12 3181 6-9-12 122 TPTreacy 123
(Mrs John Harrington, Ire) *chsd ldrs: 9th 1/2-way: no imp u.p fr 2 out: kpt on one pce* **25/1**

9 1/2 **Ambobo (USA)**11 3206 11-9-10 120 (t) NPMadden 120
(Martin Brassil, Ire) *in rr of mid-div: sme hdwy appr 2 out: no imp u.p fr early st: kpt on one pce* **7/1**2

10 1/2 **Queiros Bleu (FR)**86 1853 7-10-4 128 AELynch 128
(Henry De Bromhead, Ire) *towards rr: kpt on one pce wout threatening fr 2 out* **20/1**

11 10 **The Shepherd (IRE)**11 3207 7-10-6 130 PCarberry 120
(Gordon Elliott, Ire) *trckd ldrs: 5th 1/2-way: pushed along after 3 out: no ex appr st* **9/4**1

12 2 1/2 **Silk Affair (IRE)**260 5401 6-9-8 123 APHeskin(5) 110
(Patrick J Flynn, Ire) *chsd ldrs: 8th 1/2-way: no threat fr 2 out* **16/1**

13 2 1/2 **Qualviro (FR)**52 2487 7-9-10 120 oh3 (p) TJDoyle 105
(J H Culloty, Ire) *led: drvn along after 3 out: hdd and dropped to 4th u.p next: sn no ex and wknd* **33/1**

14 1/2 **Hold The Pin (IRE)**11 3207 12-9-10 120 (t) PWFlood 104
(A J Martin, Ire) *nvr a factor* **25/1**

15 3/4 **Oscar Dan Dan (IRE)**12 3175 9-11-10 148 DNRussell 132
(Thomas Mullins, Ire) *mid-div on outer: no ex fr 3 out: wknd* **10/1**

16 3 **Baron De Feypo (IRE)**11 3207 13-9-7 120 oh5 DGHogan(3) 101
(Patrick O Brady, Ire) *chsd ldrs on inner: 6th 1/2-way: no ex and wknd after 3 out* **33/1**

17 30 **I Hear A Symphony (IRE)**57 2376 9-9-11 121 RCColgan 72
(J J Lambe, Ire) *nvr a factor: wknd fr 3 out: t.o* **25/1**

18 4 **Duroob**11 3207 9-9-3 120 oh11 BRDalton(7) 67
(Patrick O Brady, Ire) *a bhd: t.o* **50/1**

U **Prince Rudi (IRE)**56 2406 9-9-10 123 (b) RJMolloy(3) —
(S T Nolan, Ire) *uns rdr at s* **16/1**

6m 18.2s (0.20) **Going Correction** -0.50s/f (Good) **19** Ran SP% **142.0**
Speed ratings: **79,78,77,77,76 76,76,75,74,74 71,70,69,69,69 68,58,56,—**
CSF £179.06 CT £1447.99 TOTE £40.60: £7.20, £2.40, £2.30, £2.40; DF 551.80.
Owner Scotch Piper Syndicate **Bred** Noel McLoughlin **Trained** Castletown, Co Meath

FOCUS
It has been rated around the first four.

NOTEBOOK
Across The Bay(IRE), reverting to hurdles after running two stinkers over fences (pulled up in Troytown and Paddy Power handicap chases) and minus the blinkers he wore in the second of those races, was racing off a mark 7lb lower than his chase rating. After racing prominently throughout in a race in which the pace to beyond halfway was moderate, he disputed the lead two out before forging ahead before the final hurdle from where he was always doing enough to hold off the runner-up. Trainer Noel Meade said of the winner: "He seemed to lose his bottle over fences and you could see very early in the race that he was really loving being back over hurdles. He could end up running in the final of this series at Cheltenham, depending on the ground. He loves it soft."
Son Amix(FR), a consistent performer who had finished out of the frame only once in nine previous attempts over hurdles, was trying a new trip and appeared to get the distance well. Always tracking the leaders, he was ridden to go second before the final hurdle and kept on up the run-in without quite getting to the winner.
The Bishop Looney(IRE), a winner over the trip, was prominent all the way and was vying for the lead two out. Unable to raise his game for pressure approaching the final hurdle, he kept plugging away. (op 10/1)
Sivota(IRE), stepping up in trip, was having his first run in a handicap since scoring over 2m4f at the Punchestown festival in April. Racing off a 25lb higher mark here, he was held up at the back of the field before making steady progress from before two out. He stayed on all the way to the line without ever looking like taking a serious hand in the finish. (op 7/1 tchd 13/2)
Shane Rock had finished in mid-division over the C&D on his previous start last month. He produced a better effort here and, having been close up throughout, he went to the front before two out befoe finding no extra when headed between the last two hurdles.

The Shepherd(IRE) was on a hat-trick after wins over the trip at Clonmel and here. Up 9lb for the second of those victories, he tracked the leaders but was driven along after three out and was soon done with. He was reported to be lame behind after the race. Official explanation: vet said gelding was lame behind post-race (op 5/2)

3224 TAUNTON (R-H)

Monday, January 10

OFFICIAL GOING: Good to soft (soft in places; 7.1)

Rails on bends moved out adding 37m per circuit on both courses.

Wind: Strong, half-across. Weather: Heavy rain from 2.15

3477 HAPPY NEW YEAR CLAIMING HURDLE (9 hdls) 2m 1f

1:15 (1:15) (Class 5) 4-Y-0+ £2,055 (£599; £299)

Form RPR

3P **1** **Chrysander**[60] 2324 9-11-8 110 (vt) PaulMoloney 115+
(Evan Williams) *trckd ldr: led appr 2 out: styd on wl: drifted rt flat: rdn out* **13/2**[3]

-660 **2** *3* **Cockatoo (USA)**[51] 2529 8-11-6 0 (b) JamieMoore 109
(Gary Moore) *trckd ldrs: rdn after 3 out: styd on same pce fr next: wnt 2nd run-in* **28/1**

0651 **3** *2 1/4* **I'm In The Pink (FR)**[11] 3224 7-11-8 120 (v) TimmyMurphy 111+
(David Evans) *in tch: hmpd 1st: rdn appr 2 out: chalng for 2nd whn wnt lft and hit last: styd on same pce* **7/4**[1]

2555 **4** *3/4* **Marodima (FR)**[49] 2586 8-11-12 120 (p) DarylJacob 113
(Jamie Snowden) *led: rdn and hdd appr 2 out: styd on same pce* **15/2**

3040 **5** *1 3/4* **Sweet World**[8] 3348 7-11-2 110 MissIsabelTompsett[(5)] 106
(Bernard Llewellyn) *mid-div: hdwy after 6th: wnt 3rd after 3 out: rdn after 2 out: no ex fr last* **13/2**[3]

6 *20* **Starburst**[34] 6-10-12 0 JimmyMcCarthy 81
(Brendan Powell) *a towards rr* **50/1**

4/1- **7** *3/4* **Cursum Perficio**[619] 88 9-11-0 105 (t) GilesHawkins[(5)] 85
(Richard Lee) *mid-div: mstke 6th: hit 3 out: rdn after 3 out: sn wknd* **25/1**

P04 **8** *1 1/2* **Tiger Breeze (USA)**[11] 3224 5-11-6 0 AndrewGlassonbury 85
(Bob Buckler) *a towards rr* **66/1**

00 **9** *1 3/4* **Bless My Soul**[11] 3224 8-11-0 0 (t) MattGriffiths[(5)] 82
(Ron Hodges) *rdn after 6th: a towards rr* **100/1**

0000 **10** *3/4* **Rolanta (FR)**[46] 2639 6-10-12 78 HaddenFrost 75
(James Frost) *hld up: sme hdwy 3 out: sn rdn: wknd bef 2 out* **150/1**

00 **11** *9* **Steely Bird**[28] 2924 4-10-9 0 (p) NickScholfield 64
(Richard Hawker) *bhd fr 6th: t.o* **150/1**

3050 **P** **Pepporoni Pete (IRE)**[20] 3056 10-11-8 118 (t) WarrenMarston —
(Milton Harris) *in tch: rdn after 3 out: sn eased and p.u* **10/3**[2]

U **Yourgolftravel Com**[86] 6-11-7 0 DannyCook[(3)] 97
(David Pipe) *t.k.h in rr: sme prog into 6th after 3 out: rdn and no further imp fr next: blnd and uns rdr last* **16/1**

4m 7.90s (-0.10) **Going Correction** -0.075s/f (Good)
WFA 4 from 5yo+ 11lb 13 Ran SP% **116.8**
Speed ratings (Par 103): **97,95,94,94,93 83,83,82,82,81 77,—,—**
Tote Swingers:1&2:£5.60, 2&3:£2.80, 1&3:£2.80 CSF £157.18 TOTE £10.50: £2.30, £4.00, £1.40; EX 68.10.
Owner R E R Williams **Bred** Darley **Trained** Llancarfan, Vale Of Glamorgan

FOCUS

An ordinary claimer run at an uneven gallop and the form looks fair enough. The winner is rated to his 2009 mark.

NOTEBOOK

Chrysander flopped back over fences without headgear on his latest outing, but had been given a break since and was equipped with a visor for the first time since his Flat career. He resumed winning ways with a ready effort on ground that suits back over hurdles, in a grade he is clearly superior to on his day. This should do his confidence a lot of good and his success would suggest the ground wasn't riding too bad. (op 6-1)

Cockatoo(USA) ◆, who extended his record to 0-10 over fences last time, looked interesting back over hurdles on his first outing in this lower grade. He proved friendless in the betting ring and can be quirky, but posted a much more encouraging display. There should be one of these within his compass. (op 20-1)

I'm In The Pink(FR) won over C&D in a seller on his return to hurdling 11 days earlier, but has never been the most reliable and this was tougher. He had his chance and likely ran close enough to his previous level, though still below his best. (op 13-8 tchd 6-4, tchd 15-8 and 2-1 in places)

Marodima(FR) posted a definite a step back in the right direction under his usual positive ride. (tchd 8-1)

Sweet World met support and posted a much better effort, but didn't help his cause by running freely. He has only one win from 29 outings over hurdles to his name. (op 9-1 tchd 6-1)

Cursum Perficio Official explanation: jockey said gelding blew up

Pepporoni Pete(IRE) came in for decent support back over hurdles, but didn't settle with the cheekpieces again absent and eventually pulled up with something going amiss. Official explanation: trainer said, jockey reported that he felt there was something wrong with gelding's back. (op 4-1 tchd 9-2)

3478 ENTER THE RACECARD COMPETITION NOVICES' HURDLE (9 hdls) 2m 1f

1:45 (1:45) (Class 3) 4-Y-0+ £4,110 (£1,198; £599)

Form RPR

6-13 **1** **Dona**[44] 2667 7-11-9 125 RobertThornton 127+
(Alan King) *trckd ldrs: rdn after 3 out: swtchd lft bef next: chal last: led sn after and bmpd: kpt on: drvn out* **7/2**[2]

6 **2** *1 1/4* **Ladies Dancing**[33] 2137 5-11-4 0 JamesDavies 119
(Chris Down) *in tch: tk clsr order 6th: led after 3 out: sn rdn: hung lft and hdd sn after last: kpt on but no ex nr fin* **66/1**

2 **3** *7* **Secret World (IRE)**[44] 2667 8-11-4 0 BarryGeraghty 115+
(Nicky Henderson) *mid-div: hdwy 5th to trck ldrs: cl 3rd travelling okay whn nt fluent 2 out: sn rdn: fnd little* **4/9**[1]

0 **4** *6* **Decoy (FR)**[12] 3196 5-11-9 0 DannyCook[(3)] 115
(David Pipe) *hld up towards rr: sme prog u.p into 6th after 3 out: styd on past btn horses: nvr threatened ldrs* **16/1**

5 *hd* **Old Way (IRE)**[483] 5-11-4 0 AidanColeman 107
(Venetia Williams) *trckd ldrs: rdn after 3 out: styd on same pce* **20/1**

01-P **6** *19* **Reverend Green (IRE)**[33] 315 5-11-4 0 LiamHeard 96+
(Chris Down) *led: nt fluent 5th: rdn and hdd after 3 out: wknd next* **40/1**

21- **7** *3 3/4* **Thunderstorm (IRE)**[396] 2786 6-11-4 0 TomO'Brien 87
(Philip Hobbs) *trckd ldrs early: settled in midfield 4th: rdn after 3 out: wknd bef next* **9/1**[3]

00 **8** *8* **Jomade (IRE)**[13] 3158 5-11-4 0 SeanQuinlan 79
(Kim Bailey) *mid-div: hdwy 5th: rdn and wknd 3 out* **100/1**

0 **9** *11* **Persian Present (IRE)**[36] 2791 5-11-4 0 JohnnyFarrelly 69
(Sophie Leech) *in tch tl 5th: sn bhd: t.o* **200/1**

00 **10** *7* **Turf Legends (IRE)**[36] 2791 5-10-13 0 GilesHawkins[(5)] 63
(Philip Hobbs) *mid-div tl after 5th: sn bhd* **150/1**

0- **11** *2 1/4* **Empty Scabbard**[317] 4309 7-11-4 0 DarylJacob 61
(Ron Hodges) *a towards rr* **150/1**

12 *5* **Draco Boy**[458] 4-10-6 0 NickScholfield 45
(Andy Turnell) *a bhd* **200/1**

0 **P** **Light Dragoon**[54] 2456 6-11-4 0 PaulMoloney —
(Evan Williams) *trckd ldr: rdn and wknd after 3 out: p.u sn after last: fatally injured* **50/1**

0 **P** **William Womble**[36] 2797 4-10-6 0 HaddenFrost —
(James Frost) *a bhd: t.o fr 5th: p.u bef 3 out* **200/1**

4m 4.30s (-3.70) **Going Correction** -0.075s/f (Good)
WFA 4 from 5yo+ 11lb 14 Ran SP% **121.8**
Speed ratings (Par 107): **105,104,101,98,98 89,87,83,78,75 74,71,—,—**
Tote Swingers:1&2:£54.80, 2&3:£25.40, 1&3:£1.02 CSF £190.14 TOTE £3.10: £1.10, £14.20, £1.10; EX 196.20.
Owner The Hallowed Turf Partnership **Bred** A Lestorte & D Lamarque **Trained** Barbury Castle, Wilts

FOCUS

Not a bad novice hurdle, rated around the winner to his mark. The second improved to what could be expected from his best Flat form, but the third was well below his Newbury figure.

NOTEBOOK

Dona dug deep to resume winning ways under his penalty. He was comfortably held by Secret World on identical terms at Newbury on his last outing in November, but with that rival failing to find anything for pressure he was fully entitled to take this. He deserves credit for responding as he did after coming off the bridle considering this track probably wasn't ideal for him. As such he can be rated a little better than the bare margin and remains on an upwards curve. He could well return here for a valuable novice event later this month.

Ladies Dancing ◆ posted a creditable effort on the AW last month and ran a big race on this return to hurdling, improving markedly on the level of his debut at Exeter. He really shouldn't be long in going one better if maintaining this form.

Secret World(IRE) has to rate as disappointing, but he was sent off far too short in the betting. Now an 8-y-o, he's had problems travelling to the course in the past, which have been well documented, but he was clearly expected to get off the mark. He moved best of all, but wasn't clever two out and his fate was sealed soon after. This leaves him with a good bit to prove, but it is too soon to be writing him off. (op 1-2)

Decoy(FR) was conceding weight all round. This was better than his British debut last month, but a stiffer test looks to be what he wants. He is one to keep an eye on. (op 20-1)

Old Way(IRE), a useful maiden on the Flat in France, was making his hurdling debut for new connections after a long absence. He turned in a pleasing effort and is another here that looks to want further.

Thunderstorm(IRE) looked promising in bumpers last year, but the betting screamed that he would need the run on his hurdling debut and so it proved as he was in trouble before the home turn. He too should improve for further and leave this behind in due course. (op 8-1)

3479 OXYGEN CREATIVE DESIGN AND WEB DEVELOPMENT NOVICES' LIMITED H'CAP CHASE (17 fncs) 2m 7f 110y

2:15 (2:15) (Class 3) (0-135,132) 5-Y-0+ £6,851 (£1,997; £999)

Form RPR

2-31 **1** **Shakalakaboomboom (IRE)**[49] 2582 7-11-1 128 BarryGeraghty 140+
(Nicky Henderson) *hld up but in tch: hdwy to join ldr 12th: nt fluent 3 out: shkn up to ld appr last: asserted run-in: pushed out* **2/1**[1]

3121 **2** *3 1/4* **Inside Dealer (IRE)**[25] 2975 7-10-12 125 JoeTizzard 130
(Colin Tizzard) *trckd ldr: led briefly 9th: led 12th: rdn holding narrow advantage after 3 out: hdd appr last: no ex* **7/2**[2]

0-42 **3** *12* **Squadron**[13] 3156 7-10-12 125 RobertThornton 120
(Alan King) *trckd ldrs: hit 4th: rdn after 12th: cl up whn mstke 3 out: styd on same pce fr next* **9/2**[3]

0-20 **4** *1/2* **Earth Planet (IRE)**[59] 2343 9-10-7 125 (bt[1]) MrRMahon[(5)] 119
(Paul Nicholls) *trckd ldrs: rdn appr 3 out: styd on same pce fr 2 out* **15/2**

0P6F **5** *4 1/2* **Cullahill (IRE)**[8] 3347 9-10-5 118 oh2 HarrySkelton 108
(Bob Buckler) *chsd ldrs: nt fluent 4th: rdn after 4 out: one pce fr next* **12/1**

2243 **6** *40* **Gee Dee Nen**[56] 2427 8-10-11 124 JamieMoore 93+
(Gary Moore) *led: hdd briefly 9th: hdd 12th: rdn after next: sn btn* **22/1**

2301 **F** **Triggerman**[27] 2945 9-11-5 132 TomO'Brien 133
(Philip Hobbs) *chsd ldrs: pckd 1st: pushed along fr 5th: dropped to last but in tch after 10th: rallied after 4 out: ev ch whn fell 3 out* **5/1**

6m 6.60s (-8.00) **Going Correction** -0.15s/f (Good) 7 Ran SP% **114.2**
Speed ratings: **107,105,101,101,100 86,—**
Tote Swingers:1&2:£3.20, 2&3:£2.40, 1&3:£3.30 CSF £9.82 CT £27.00 TOTE £2.80: £2.00, £2.10; EX 9.70.
Owner Liam Breslin **Bred** Godfrey Moylan **Trained** Upper Lambourn, Berks

FOCUS

A decent novice handicap for the class and another step forward from the winner. The runner-up is also on the upgrade.

NOTEBOOK

Shakalakaboomboom(IRE) ◆, up in trip, followed up his initial success over fences at Kempton off a 9lb higher mark with a ready display and has really come into his own since going chasing this season. He was ridden confidently and did things sweetly through the race, but eventually had to work to fight off the runner-up. He was well on top at the finish, however, and this experience should really see him go forward again. It also proves his versatility for underfoot conditions and a bold bid for the hat-trick is expected, despite another likely rise. (tchd 9-4)

Inside Dealer(IRE) ◆ was 12lb higher and another with stamina to prove. He too was ridden confidently and travelled nicely, before locking horns with the winner in the home straight. He was ultimately put in his place, but finished a clear second-best and improved again in defeat. He can go in again. \n\x\x \bSquadron\p looked likely to relish this step back up in trip for the first time as a chaser and was feasibly treated back in a handicap. He hit a flat spot before making an error three out, though, and perhaps he needs better ground over this trip. (op 5-1)

Squadron looked likely to relish this step back up in trip for the first time as a chaser and was feasibly treated back in a handicap. He hit a flat spot before making an error three out, though, and perhaps he needs better ground over this trip. (tchd 5-1)

Earth Planet(IRE) was equipped with first-time blinkers and back on suitably softer ground. He never seriously threatened, though, and remains hard to win with. (op 8-1 tchd 7-1)

Triggerman was off the mark over fences on his previous outing. Conceding weight all round, he didn't jump that fluently looked in trouble when going in snatches on the final circuit. However, he was in the process of rallying and appeared booked for third but for falling in the home straight. It's hoped this doesn't overly dent his confidence. (op 9-2)

3480 EUROPEAN BREEDERS' FUND MARES' "NATIONAL HUNT" NOVICES' HURDLE (9 hdls 1 omitted) 2m 3f 110y

2:45 (2:45) (Class 4) 4-Y-0+ £3,425 (£998; £499)

Form RPR

3-36 **1** **Seren Cwmtudu (IRE)**[13] 3158 7-11-3 0 PaulMoloney 112+
(Evan Williams) *trckd ldr: led 7th: rdn bypassing omitted 2 out: hung lft run-in: drvn out* **5/1**

0-10 **2** *1* **Violin Davis (FR)**[49] 2577 5-11-3 0 HarrySkelton 110
(Paul Nicholls) *trckd ldr: rdn to chse wnr bypassing omitted 2 out: swtchd rt sn after last: kpt on but no ex nr fin* **15/2**

0-4P **3** *29* **Some Secret**[62] 2288 6-11-3 0 JamesDavies 84
(Chris Down) *mid-div: rdn whn blnd 3 out: plugged on past btn horses fr bypassed 2 out but nvr any ch* **50/1**

0 **4** *4* **China Sky (IRE)**[240] 333 6-11-3 0 BarryGeraghty 80
(Nicky Henderson) *hld up: reminders after 4th: hdwy 6th: rdn and wknd after 3 out: t.o* **4/1**[3]

0-UF **5** *1 1/2* **Lady Karabaya**[10] 3264 6-11-3 0 HaddenFrost 81
(Henrietta Knight) *trckd ldrs: rdn after 3 out: sn wknd: t.o* **28/1**

5106 **6** *8* **Spe Salvi (IRE)**[20] 3054 7-11-3 0 DarylJacob 72
(David Arbuthnot) *mid-div: rdn after 6th: wknd after 3 out: t.o* **7/2**[2]

-604 **7** *1 3/4* **Definitley Lovely**[67] 2168 6-11-3 0 PaddyBrennan 70
(Nigel Twiston-Davies) *led tl 7th: sn rdn: wknd after next: t.o* **9/4**[1]

00-0 **8** *37* **Betty Browneyes**[61] 2310 6-11-3 0 JoeTizzard 37
(Tom George) *trckd ldrs: rdn after 7th: sn wknd: t.o* **100/1**

-430 **U** **Sapphire Rouge (IRE)**[25] 2974 5-10-10 0 MrKevinJones(7) 74
(Seamus Mullins) *struggling after 5th: a towards rr: poor 6th whn jinked and uns rdr last* **18/1**

00 **P** **Our Flora**[11] 3225 6-10-10 0 MrCGreene(7) —
(Kim Bailey) *a towards rr: lost tch fr after 5th: t.o whn p.u after 2 out* **100/1**

4m 44.8s (-1.20) **Going Correction** -0.075s/f (Good) **10** Ran SP% **114.1**
Speed ratings (Par 105): **99,98,87,85,84 81,80,66,—,—**
Tote Swingers:1&2:£7.20, 2&3:£29.40, 1&3:£29.40 CSF £40.11 TOTE £4.50: £1.60, £1.80, £6.50; EX 52.30.

Owner T Hywel Jones **Bred** Mrs C J C Bailey **Trained** Llancarfan, Vale Of Glamorgan

FOCUS
An average mares-only novice hurdle where the first pair dominated from three out. The winner is rated back to her Uttoxeter mark.

NOTEBOOK
Seren Cwmtudu(IRE) failed to improve as many expected when upped in trip at Ffos Las 13 days earlier, but she showed her true colours this time with a fairly ready effort to get off the mark. Given a positive ride, she took it up nearing the home turn and was always doing enough to repel the runner-up when it mattered, despite still showing signs of inexperience. This imposing mare should come into her own when sent chasing, but looks open to further improvement in this sphere now she has got her head in front. (op 9-2)
Violin Davis(FR) ◆ was disappointing on her hurdling debut at Kempton in November, but was back against her own sex and ran a lot more encouragingly. She ought to be placed to go one better in something similar before long. (op 13-2 tchd 8-1)
Some Secret fared best of the remainder in third and turned her most encouraging effort since narrowly failing in a bumper on her debut in 2009. Handicaps should present her with easier opportunities. (op 66-1)
China Sky(IRE), Best Mate's half-sister, was an expensive failure on her debut last year but she proved easy to back for this introduction to hurdling and first outing since. She was never going that well and, being by Definite Article, perhaps quicker ground is required. (op 3-1)
Spe Salvi(IRE), well backed, had steering problems in bumpers and again tried to duck out going round the paddock bend on this switch to hurdles. She was in trouble shortly after going out onto the back straight and clearly has some issues, but is another for whom the ground may not have suited. (op 6-1)
Definitley Lovely was expected to enjoy the longer trip and met strong support. Having set out to make all, however, she folded tamely on the far side and something may have gone amiss. (op 11-4, tchd 3-1 in places)

3481 SOUTHWEST-RACING.CO.UK H'CAP HURDLE (9 hdls) 2m 1f
3:15 (3:15) (Class 4) (0-115,115) 4-Y-0+ **£3,425** (£998; £499)

Form RPR

5F-P **1** **Henry King (IRE)**[68] 2148 7-11-11 **114** (t) AndrewGlassonbury 120
(Victor Dartnall) *led 2nd: mde rest: rdn and hrd pressed fr after 2 out: drifted lft run-in: kpt on gamely: all out* **10/1**

22 **2** *1/2* **American Ladie**[27] 2944 5-11-10 **113** RobertThornton 119
(Alan King) *trckd ldrs: rdn for str chal fr after 2 out: ev ch run-in: kpt on* **4/1**[2]

0-42 **3** *3 3/4* **The Chazer (IRE)**[52] 2499 6-11-4 **112** GilesHawkins(5) 116+
(Richard Lee) *mid-div: hdwy after 5th: rdn to chse ldng pair appr 2 out: styd on same pce* **4/1**[2]

3351 **4** *4 1/2* **Marleno (GER)**[11] 3228 5-11-11 **114** (t) WarrenMarston 114
(Milton Harris) *hld up bhd: hdwy 3 out: rdn to chse ldng trio next: styng on same pce whn nt fluent last* **15/2**[3]

6212 **5** *6* **Switched Off**[45] 2658 6-11-4 **107** (p) DougieCostello 100
(Ian Williams) *in tch: rdn after 3 out: sn one pce* **7/2**[1]

-3R2 **6** *1 1/4* **Posh Emily**[46] 2639 8-11-0 **108** MattGriffiths(5) 100
(Ron Hodges) *hld up towards rr: rdn after 6th: styd on steadily fr after 3 out: nvr threatened ldrs* **33/1**

524 **7** *1/2* **Sun Quest**[48] 2596 7-10-9 **105** RobertKirk(7) 98
(Steven Dixon) *led tl 2nd: chsd ldrs: rdn after 3 out: sn one pce* **11/1**

3P6P **8** *2 3/4* **Chilbury Hill (IRE)**[64] 2243 8-10-5 **94** LiamHeard 84
(Kevin Bishop) *mid-div: hdwy after 4th to trck ldrs: rdn after 3 out: wknd after 2 out* **50/1**

4 **9** *9* **Mariinsky (GER)**[197] 847 5-11-1 **111** CDTimmons(7) 92
(Tim Vaughan) *in tch: rdn after 5th: wknd after 3 out* **40/1**

3-13 **10** *6* **Ban Uisce (IRE)**[10] 3256 6-10-11 **107** MarkQuinlan(7) 83
(Neil Mulholland) *trckd ldrs: rdn after 6th: wknd after 3 out* **8/1**

3240 **11** *11* **Watch Out**[51] 2530 7-10-10 **99** (tp) JimmyMcCarthy 65
(Dai Burchell) *a towards rr: t.o* **66/1**

146 **12** *17* **Potemkin (USA)**[3] 3092 6-11-4 **110** (t) LeeStephens(3) 60
(David Evans) *mid-div tl wknd 3 out: t.o* **66/1**

4315 **13** *20* **Nothing Is Forever (IRE)**[33] 2333 7-10-12 **101** (p) DarylJacob 33
(Liam Corcoran) *mid-div tl wknd 3 out: t.o* **28/1**

0043 **14** *shd* **Kayfton Pete**[19] 3093 5-11-3 **113** PeterHatton(7) 45
(Reg Hollinshead) *mid-div tl 6th: sn wl bhd: t.o* **33/1**

15 *27* **Hail Caesar (IRE)**[118] 1523 5-11-12 **115** PaulMoloney 23
(Evan Williams) *trckd ldrs tl 6th: sn bhd: t.o* **14/1**

4m 4.20s (-3.80) **Going Correction** -0.075s/f (Good) **15** Ran SP% **125.9**
Speed ratings (Par 105): **105,104,103,100,98 97,97,95,91,88 83,75,66,66,53**
Tote Swingers:1&2:£11.00, 2&3:£3.60, 1&3:£18.80 CSF £50.72 CT £195.16 TOTE £11.30: £4.00, £1.30, £2.00; EX 72.60.

Owner Mrs C Barber **Bred** M Conaghan **Trained** Brayford, Devon

■ Stewards' Enquiry : Andrew Glassonbury caution: used whip with excessive frequency.

FOCUS
An open handicap. There was a fair gallop on, but it wasn't easy to get involved from off the pace and it was another race where two came clear in a tight finish. The first two both produced steps forward.

NOTEBOOK
Henry King(IRE), pulled up on his chase debut last time, finally got his head in front over jumps and displayed a likeable attitude in the process. He was soon sent to the front and travelled kindly, but looked a little vulnerable at the top of the home straight. He kept finding for pressure, however, and wasn't going to be denied after the last. The addition of a first-time tongue tie looks to have made the difference and he could have more to offer now, as he will still look fairly treated after a rise in the handicap. (op 8-1)
American Ladie ◆, making her handicap debut, has now found one too good on her three outings for Alan King. However, there was plenty to like about this improved effort and, well clear of the rest in second, looks well up to going one better despite a likely rise.
The Chazer(IRE) ◆ still looked fairly treated off an 8lb higher mark for finishing second at Exeter last time out. He ran another decent race in defeat, but would surely have been better off under a more prominent ride. There should be an opening for him in the coming weeks. (op 6-1)
Marleno(GER) relished being ridden with restraint when winning here last time and was 8lb higher. He made up a lot of ground on the far side, but eventually that effort took its toll. (op 9-1 tchd 7-1)
Switched Off had his chance, but was anchored by his new 8lb higher mark. (op 4-1 tchd 10-3)
Posh Emily went in snatches early on, but was noted staying on stoutly all too late in the home straight.

3482 ORCHARD RESTAURANT H'CAP CHASE (16 fncs 1 omitted) 2m 7f 110y
3:45 (3:45) (Class 4) (0-115,115) 5-Y-0+ **£4,110** (£1,198; £599)

Form RPR

110- **1** **Sona Sasta (IRE)**[271] 5184 8-11-0 **106** DannyCook(3) 134+
(David Pipe) *led tl bmpd 2nd: led 5th: drew wl clr after 13th: v easily* **4/5**[1]

-006 **2** *18* **Omix D'Or (FR)**[36] 2794 9-11-8 **111** (p) DavidDennis 113
(James Evans) *prom: bmpd 2nd: rdn to chse wnr after 13th: sn no ch* **12/1**

-540 **3** *8* **Lorum Leader (IRE)**[25] 2984 10-10-13 **109** (b) MrTWeston(7) 104
(Dr Richard Newland) *trckd ldrs: rdn after 13th but sn no ch: wnt modest 3rd 3 out* **9/1**

0PP- **4** *25* **Aberdeen Park**[8] 2241 9-10-13 **105** LeeStephens(3) 82
(David Evans) *led 2nd tl 5th: rdn and losing pl whn hmpd on bnd after 10th: no ch fr 12th: lost modest 3rd 3 out* **50/1**

2-13 **P** **Take It There**[49] 2573 9-11-11 **114** (t) FelixDeGiles —
(Alastair Lidderdale) *in tch tl wknd 13th: t.o whn p.u on long run to 3 out* **8/1**[3]

1P6F **P** **Marc Of Brilliance (USA)**[51] 2513 8-11-5 **115** JoshuaMoore(7) —
(Gary Moore) *hld up: blnd 4th: wknd 13th: p.u on long run to 3 out* **40/1**

4P-F **P** **This Way (IRE)**[11] 3230 9-11-2 **105** (t) AndrewGlassonbury —
(John Ryall) *nt a fluent: a towards rr: t.o whn p.u after 13th* **18/1**

210F **P** **Builteoir (IRE)**[64] 2236 9-10-0 **96** MrJEngland(7) —
(Evan Williams) *hld up: blnd 2nd: bhd whn blnd bdly 7th (broke fence): sn wl t.o: p.u after 11th* **22/1**

1-PF **P** **Flanagan (IRE)**[12] 3198 7-11-12 **115** AidanColeman —
(Venetia Williams) *in tch: reminders after 10th: wknd after 13th: t.o whn p.u on long run to 3 out* **4/1**[2]

6m 16.4s (1.80) **Going Correction** +0.125s/f (Yiel) **9** Ran SP% **118.4**
Speed ratings: **102,96,93,85,— —,—,—,—**
Tote Swingers:1&2:£3.90, 2&3:£20.30, 1&3:£3.30 CSF £11.77 CT £57.82 TOTE £1.70: £1.02, £3.80, £3.10; EX 13.30.

Owner R S Brookhouse **Bred** Michael Larkin **Trained** Nicholashayne, Devon

■ The fourth-last fence was bypassed.

FOCUS
A moderate staying handicap won by a highly progressive chase debutant. He produced a step up and was value for further.

NOTEBOOK
Sona Sasta(IRE) ◆ ran his rivals ragged on this seasonal and handicap debut, jumping like a professional in the main. He confirmed himself a dour stayer when winning back-to-back handicaps over hurdles last season, and wasn't suited by lively ground at Cheltenham on his final outing. The ground was up his street here, though, and the way he put the race to bed a long way out gave him the look of a very well handicapped horse. A hike in the weights is now forthcoming, and rightly so, but connections will surely be tempted to run him under a penalty. The bounce factor would be of some concern should that prove the case and he currently holds no future entries, but he would no doubt be a warm order. Whatever the case plenty more should be heard of him over fences this season. (tchd 5-6 and 10-11 in places)
Omix D'Or(FR) had lost his form since resuming this season, but this was better again in first-time cheekpieces and he goes some way to helping set the level of the form. (op 14-1)
Lorum Leader(IRE) is well handicapped at present and he looked a possible danger going out onto the back straight. However, he seemed to down tools around five out and only plugged on thereafter. (op 7-1)
Aberdeen Park, who refused to race on the AW last time, had the visor removed for this return to chasing. She looked to be on a going day when taking them along on, but went in snatches going out onto the final circuit and rapidly lost ground. (op 40-1)
Take It There was beaten well before stamina became an issue for this longer trip. (op 9-1)
This Way(IRE) Official explanation: jockey said gelding had a breathing problem (op 9-1)
Flanagan(IRE) met support, but had fallen on his chasing debut last month and jumping was again the big issue here. (op 9-1)

3483 STAPLE FITZPAINE H'CAP HURDLE (11 hdls 1 omitted) 3m 110y
4:15 (4:15) (Class 4) (0-115,115) 4-Y-0+ **£3,425** (£998; £499)

Form RPR

6-44 **1** **Awesome Freddie**[27] 2946 6-11-12 **115** RobertThornton 119+
(Alan King) *mid-div: hdwy after 7th: rdn to chse ldr 2 out: led sn after last: edgd rt: styd on wl: rdn out* **10/3**[1]

03U **2** *1 1/4* **Deep Pockets (IRE)**[8] 3347 12-11-2 **110** IanPopham(5) 113
(Caroline Keevil) *disp ld: rdn into clr ld appr 2 out: hung lft and hdd run-in: styd on but no ex* **12/1**

5-32 **3** *4* **Devon Native (IRE)**[51] 2514 8-11-3 **113** DannyBurton(7) 111
(Chris Down) *trckd ldrs: rdn and ev ch sn after 3 out: styd on same pce fr next* **7/2**[2]

541P **4** *2* **Mtpockets (IRE)**[57] 2395 6-11-7 **110** DougieCostello 109+
(Neil Mulholland) *in tch: nudged along at times: tk clsr order 7th: rdn after 3 out: cl 4th whn mstke 2 out: no ex* **8/1**[3]

300 **5** *1 1/4* **Ratify**[26] 2963 7-10-9 **98** AidanColeman 93
(Brendan Powell) *trckd ldrs: jnd ldr after 8th: rdn and ev ch after 3 out: styd on same pce fr next* **28/1**

211P **6** *17* **Just The Job (IRE)**[9] 3299 7-11-0 **110** MarkQuinlan(7) 90
(Neil Mulholland) *mid-div: rdn after 8th: wknd after 3 out* **16/1**

2116 **7** *8* **Chico Time (IRE)**[10] 3260 10-10-8 **104** (p) StephenO'Donovan(7) 80
(Norma Twomey) *disp ld tl rdn after 8th: wknd after 3 out* **10/1**

0F04 **8** *13* **Giovanna**[51] 2514 10-11-11 **114** (t) WarrenMarston 75
(Richard Phillips) *mid-div tl wknd appr 3 out: t.o* **9/1**

56P3 **9** *1/2* **Petroupetrov (FR)**[46] 2637 8-10-11 **100** (v) TomSiddall 61
(Richard Phillips) *mid-div tl wknd after 8th: t.o* **16/1**

2104 **10** *3 1/4* **Royal Kicks (FR)**[49] 2582 10-10-9 **105** MrTJCannon(7) 63
(Suzy Smith) *in tch tl wknd after 8th: t.o* **10/1**

F221 **P** **Cannon Fire (FR)**148 1259 10-10-13 109 MrJEngland(7) —
(Evan Williams) *a bhd: t.o whn p.u after 2 out* **20/1**
1-PF **P** **Direct Flight (IRE)**25 2975 13-11-4 107 (t) NickScholfield —
(Jeremy Scott) *sn towards rr: t.o 5th: p.u bef 8th* **40/1**
220- **U** **Daraz Rose (IRE)**289 4888 10-10-12 108 (t) MrCGreene(7) —
(Barry Brennan) *a towards rr: t.o fr 8th: wnt lft and uns rdr 2 out* **40/1**
5-1 **P** **Norisan**244 267 7-10-11 100 (t) PaddyBrennan —
(Alan Jones) *a bhd: t.o whn p.u after 8th* **14/1**

6m 9.50s (2.40) **Going Correction** +0.20s/f (Yiel) **14** Ran SP% **123.8**
Speed ratings (Par 105): **104,103,102,101,101 95,93,89,88,87** —,—,—,—
Tote Swingers:1&2:£11.60, 2&3:£24.60, 1&3:£4.80. totesuper7: Win Not won; Place £590.80. CSF £43.03 TOTE £4.00: £1.20, £4.90, £1.20; EX 51.50.
Owner Mrs Gwen Meacham & Mr & Mrs D Thornhill **Bred** Alan Briscoe And Mrs Gwen Meacham **Trained** Barbury Castle, Wilts
■ The final flight was bypassed.

FOCUS
A moderate staying handicap in which the winner was another big improver for his in-form yard.

NOTEBOOK
Awesome Freddie made it third time lucky over hurdles with a gusty effort on this handicap debut. He was saddled with top weight and had yet to run over this far, but was open to the most improvement in this field. He moved sweetly into contention and stuck his head down when asked to master the runner-up, looking all about stamina in the process. He will jump a fence, but there should be improvement in him over hurdles before then. (op 7-2 tchd 3-1)
Deep Pockets(IRE) unseated over fences last time, but had shown improved form on his penultimate outing. He ran a gallant race from the front on this return to hurdling and was only just held, but didn't help his cause by drifting to the stands' side on the run-in. This veteran certainly deserves to find another opening. (op 14-1 tchd 16-1)
Devon Native(IRE) had been placed on her two previous outings this term and was 4lb higher than when staying on dourly over 2m6f at Ascot in November. Well backed, she had her chance but failed to see out this longer trip that well on the ground. There is surely a race to be won with her this season back on a sounder surface. (op 11-2)
Mtpockets(IRE) was pulled up on her chasing debut last time so this was obviously a step back in the right direction. Her win under rules in October came over 3m3f.
Ratify ◆ went well for a long way under bottom weight on this handicap debut and looks one to side with when racing on some better ground. (tchd 33-1)
Direct Flight(IRE) Official explanation: jockey said gelding never travelled
T/Jkpt: Not won. T/Plt: £32.40 to a £1 stake. Pool:£73,443.03. 1,654.07 winning tickets. T/Qpdt: £32.90 to a £1 stake. Pool:£5,023.53. 112.80 winning tickets. TM

2981 TOWCESTER (R-H)

Monday, January 10

OFFICIAL GOING: Soft (6.9)
Flight down hill omitted all hurdles. Final open ditch omitted all chases. Shared bends and hurdles track dolled out to widest point.
Wind: Brisk, across. Weather: Overcast

3484 LADBROKES GOT THE FEELING, GET THE APP JUVENILE HURDLE (7 hdls 1 omitted) 2m
12:55 (12:55) (Class 4) 4-Y-0 **£2,602** (£764; £382; £190)

Form RPR
344 **1** **Ultravox (USA)**28 2924 4-10-5 115 NathanSweeney(7) 112+
(Jeremy Scott) *t.k.h early: trckd ldrs: wnt 2nd 3rd: led 3 out: sn clr: drvn out* **2/1**1
46 **2** *29* **Miereveld**7 1498 4-10-12 0 (b) FearghalDavis 83
(Brian Ellison) *led: hdd 3 out: sn no ch w wnr: tired whn hit last: jst hld on for poor 2nd* **12/1**
0 **3** *½* **King's Realm (IRE)**13 3158 4-10-5 0 OliverDayman(7) 84
(Alison Thorpe) *chsd ldrs: hmpd 4 out: dropped bk to mod 3rd after 3 out: styd on to cl on tiring 2nd cl home but nvr any ch w wnr* **9/1**
3 **4** *13* **Kitty Koo (IRE)**25 2211 4-10-0 0 LeeEdwards(5) 62
(Tony Carroll) *t.k.h: chsd ldrs tl wknd sn after 3 out* **20/1**
55 **5** *nse* **Rare Malt (IRE)**37 2435 4-10-2 0 JimmyDerham(3) 62
(Milton Harris) *a in rr: lost tch fr 3 out* **14/1**
2 **P** **Harry Hunt**53 2466 4-10-12 122 (v1) JodieMogford —
(Graeme McPherson) *hit 1st: t.k.h: chsd ldrs tl wknd 3 out: t.o whn p.u after 2 out* **3/1**2
6236 **F** **Royal And Ancient (IRE)**2 3436 4-10-12 111 (t) DaveCrosse —
(Milton Harris) *trckd ldrs: disputing 1 l 2nd and gng okay whn fell 4 out* **7/2**3
001 **P** **Baggsy (IRE)**23 2556 4-10-12 93 MattieBatchelor —
(Julia Feilden) *hit 1st and 3rd: a wl bhd: t.o 4 out: p.u bef 2 out* **33/1**

4m 17.95s (10.05) **Going Correction** +0.65s/f (Soft) **8** Ran SP% **112.6**
Speed ratings: **100,85,85,78,78** —,—,—
Tote Swingers:1&2:£27.90, 2&3:£20.50, 1&3:£5.10 CSF £26.02 TOTE £4.70: £1.10, £4.70, £4.20; EX 26.30.
Owner Jonathan Harvey **Bred** Hascombe Stud **Trained** Brompton Regis, Somerset

FOCUS
Testing conditions underfoot, so as usual for this track stamina was at a premium. This was an ordinary juvenile hurdle and in the end a severe test. A step up from the winner but not form to get carried away with.

NOTEBOOK
Ultravox(USA), a well-beaten fourth when Harry Hunt was runner-up at Hereford in November, improved on that effort when fourth behind Comedy Act at Plumpton last month. A decent type, he came right away up the final hill and clearly stays really well. (op 5-2)
Miereveld, busy and a winner on the Fibresand at Southwell since two uninspiring efforts over hurdles in the autumn, took them along at a sound pace in the conditions. He was clear second jumping the last but was out on his feet at the line. (tchd 14-1)
King's Realm(IRE), a winner over 2m on Lingfield's Polytrack surface in October, was messed about by the faller. He showed clear third best going to two out and would have snatched second spot in a few more strides. He clearly stays really well. (op 15-2)
Kitty Koo(IRE), a poor plater on the Flat, had finished a staying-on third at Sandown on her debut over hurdles but she seemed to find these conditions beyond her.
Rare Malt(IRE) was another who found this test too much. (op 22-1 tchd 25-1)
Harry Hunt, having his seventh start and fitted with a visor this time, doesn't look a battler and was well behind when pulled up. Official explanation: jockey said gelding ran too free (op 5-1)
Royal And Ancient(IRE), out of his depth in the Finale at Chepstow two days earlier, had not been asked a question when crashing out. (op 5-1)

3485 LADBROKES ROULETTE NOVICES' HURDLE (10 hdls 2 omitted) 3m
1:25 (1:25) (Class 4) 5-Y-0+ **£2,602** (£764; £382; £190)

Form RPR
102 **1** **Badgers Cove (IRE)**25 2981 7-11-5 122 CharliePoste 113
(Robin Dickin) *mde virtually all: jnd fr 6th and stl hrd pressed whn u.p 2 out: asserted bef last: styd on wl* **7/4**1
55 **2** *3½* **Overnight Fame (IRE)**25 2974 7-10-5 0 DenisO'Regan 95
(Tom George) *trckd wnr fr 5th: styd on along the inner and chal fr 6th: disp ld appr 2 out: rdn sn after: outstyd appr last whn swtchd lft: one pce run-in* **85/40**2
5 **3** *8* **Power Lord (IRE)**25 2981 6-10-5 0 NathanSweeney(7) 93
(Bob Buckler) *in tch: impr fr 6th: rdn and no imp fr 3 out: styd on to take wl hld 3rd fnl flight* **66/1**
5-04 **4** *11* **Emperor Charlie**50 2552 7-10-12 0 GrahamLee 88+
(Ferdy Murphy) *in rr whn blnd and reminders 5th: hdwy next: lft in cl 3rd 4 out: rdn next: wknd 2 out: lost wl hld 3rd fnl flight* **10/1**
/0U4 **5** *33* **Belmore Baron**58 2375 9-10-12 0 HenryOliver 49
(Sue Smith) *in rr: hdwy 6th: wknd 3 out* **25/1**
3-05 **6** *21* **Inkberrow Rose (IRE)**50 2554 7-10-5 0 MarkBradburne 21
(Tom Gretton) *bhd fr 6th: t.o* **33/1**
0 **7** *dist* **Ballinhassig (IRE)**8 3346 6-10-5 0 MrWRussell(7) —
(Sarah Wall) *prom early: bhd fr 6th: sn t.o* **150/1**
520- **P** **Upham Atom**271 5184 8-10-12 107 LiamTreadwell —
(Kate Buckett) *chsd wnr to 5th: rdn 3 out: sn btn: wl hld 5th whn p.u bef last* **10/1**
UP/P **P** **Iris Mary (IRE)**208 766 10-10-2 0 SamTwiston-Davies(3) —
(Shaun Lycett) *a in rr: t.o whn p.u bef 4 out* **150/1**
-114 **F** **Pure Anticipation (IRE)**86 1860 6-10-12 115 RichardJohnson —
(Tim Vaughan) *trckd ldrs: disputing 1 l 3rd and travelling okay whn fell 4 out* **4/1**3
-000 **P** **Cloudy Joe (IRE)**13 3166 5-10-9 0 AdamPogson(3) —
(Charles Pogson) *a in rr: t.o whn p.u bef 4 out* **100/1**

6m 42.32s (27.32) **Going Correction** +0.65s/f (Soft) **11** Ran SP% **117.1**
Speed ratings: **80,78,76,72,61 54,37**,—,—,— —
Tote Swingers:1&2:£1.50, 2&3:£13.90, 1&3:£17.60 CSF £5.69 TOTE £1.90: £1.10, £1.30, £14.50; EX 8.50.
Owner E R C Beech & B Wilkinson **Bred** Miss Lillian Barry **Trained** Atherstone on Stour, Warwicks
■ Stewards' Enquiry : Charlie Poste two-day ban: careless riding (Jan 24-25)

FOCUS
A severe test for these novice hurdlers. Ordinary form, with the first two rated to their marks.

NOTEBOOK
Badgers Cove(IRE), who took the middle route, kept up the gallop in most determined fashion and gained the upper hand going to the final flight. He has a soft-ground knee action and, a winning pointer, should make an even better staying chaser next term. He's clearly going the right way and his spring target will be the EBF Final at Sandown. (op 5-2, tchd 11-4 in places)
Overnight Fame(IRE) never left the inside. An Irish maiden point winner, she took on the winner but was getting the worst of the argument when forced to switch going to the final flight. She clearly stays really well and ought to take a mares' only race at least. (op 3-1 tchd 10-3)
Power Lord(IRE), well behind the winner here three weeks ago, showed a fair bit more, staying on to take third at the final flight. Stamina is clearly his forte.
Emperor Charlie ◆, from the family of Amberleigh House, shaped better than his final position indicates. Given a patient ride, he took a clear third before tiring. He will be of interest in a low-grade handicap in less testing conditions. (op 9-1)
Pure Anticipation(IRE) took the by-pass route but looked to be just starting to struggle when hitting the deck four from home. She may not want conditions so testing. (op 11-4 tchd 9-2)

3486 LADBROKESPOKER.COM NOVICES' CHASE (11 fncs 1 omitted) 2m 110y
1:55 (1:55) (Class 4) 5-Y-0+ **£4,332** (£1,575)

Form RPR
21-3 **1** **Rackham Lerouge (FR)**28 2926 6-11-0 132 APMcCoy 128+
(Nicky Henderson) *mde all: j.lft 5th: c clr fr sole rival 2 out: comf* **1/4**1
024 **2** *9* **King Ozzy (IRE)**8 3345 7-11-7 120 (t) RichardJohnson 123
(Martin Keighley) *chsd wnr thrght and a wl there: j.big 5th: stl travelling okay appr 2 out: sn drvn and outpcd* **16/1**3
-363 **U** **Lord Villez (FR)**7 3359 7-11-0 116 GrahamLee —
(Ferdy Murphy) *racd in cl 3rd: nt fluent 6th: 1 l off 2nd and gng okay whn blnd and uns rdr 3 out* **11/2**2
-064 **F** **Raspbary**8 3339 5-10-7 94 JimmyDerham(3) —
(Seamus Mullins) *a in 4th: in tch and gng okay whn fell 6th* **40/1**

4m 26.55s (10.45) **Going Correction** +0.45s/f (Soft)
WFA 5 from 6yo+ 3lb **4** Ran SP% **103.7**
Speed ratings: **93,88**,—,—
CSF £4.04 TOTE £1.10; EX 3.20.
Owner Mrs Judy Wilson **Bred** Gerard Ferte **Trained** Upper Lambourn, Berks

FOCUS
Only two of these completed and the easy winner didn't need to improve on his Plumpton run.

NOTEBOOK
Rackham Lerouge(FR), winner of three AQPS bumpers in France and successful in a novices' hurdle at Bangor in February, is already rated 132 after finishing a highly respectable third behind Medermit on his chasing bow last month. Tending to jump left-handed, he had it in the bag two out and had only to be kept up to his work. A half-brother to Punchestowns, he should continue to progress especially going left-handed. (op 3-10 tchd 1-3, after early 4-11 in a place)
King Ozzy(IRE), 20lb inferior to the winner over hurdles, had already had five starts over fences, earning a rating of 120. Conceding the winner 7lb, he put a poor effort at Plumpton a week earlier behind him. (op 12-1 tchd 10-1)
Lord Villez(FR), inclined to race keenly, had not been asked a question in third when giving his rider little chance three out. (op 9-2 tchd 4-1)

3487 BET IN PLAY AT LADBROKES NOVICES' HURDLE (8 hdls 2 omitted) 2m 3f 110y
2:25 (2:30) (Class 4) 5-Y-0+ **£2,602** (£764; £382; £190)

Form RPR
1-3 **1** **Bottman (IRE)**78 2003 6-10-12 0 APMcCoy 120+
(Tim Vaughan) *trckd ldr: upsides fr 5th tl drvn ahd wl bef bypassed 2nd last fight: styd on wl* **7/2**3
53 **2** *6* **Redbridge Flyer (IRE)**68 2145 7-10-12 0 RichardJohnson 114
(Philip Hobbs) *led: jnd fr 5th: hdd wl bef bypassed 2nd last fight: wl hld whn hit last* **3/1**2
4-60 **3** *4½* **Morcambe**54 2454 6-10-12 0 AndrewTinkler 109
(Nicky Henderson) *chsd ldrs: rdn and no imp after 3 out: one pce appr bypassed 2nd last flight* **16/1**

35 **4** *12* **Loch Ba (IRE)**[26] 2954 5-10-12 0.......................... DominicElsworth 98
(Henrietta Knight) *uns rdr coming on to crse and got loose: ct s: in rr: hdwy 5th: hit 3 out and lost position: sme hdwy fr bypassed 2nd last flight: lft 4th last* **6/1**

42F **5** *14* **See You Jack**[51] 2530 6-10-12 114.......................... AndrewThornton 83
(Caroline Bailey) *chsd ldrs: hit 3 out: sn wknd and no ch appr bypassed 2nd last flight* **5/2**[1]

6 *3/4* **Valsfirth (IRE)**[995] 8-10-12 0.......................... JasonMaguire 82
(Donald McCain) *in tch: hit 5th: rdn 3 out: wknd wl bef bypassed 2nd last flight* **10/1**

5-05 **7** *hd* **Robertewenutter**[67] 2166 7-10-12 0.......................... HenryOliver 82
(Sue Smith) *chsd ldrs to 3 out: wknd sn after* **33/1**

0-5P **P** **Dancing Legend**[5] 3396 5-10-2 80.......................... SamTwiston-Davies(3) —
(Peter Hiatt) *in rr whn p.u bef 3rd* **100/1**

0-00 **P** **Duffy Moon**[8] 3346 7-10-12 0..........................(t) GerardTumelty —
(Charlie Morlock) *a in rr: t.o 5th: p.u bef last* **200/1**

00- **P** **Rich Live (FR)**[312] 4405 6-10-9 0.......................... AlexMerriam(3) —
(Lady Anne Connell) *a in rr: t.o whn p.u bef last* **100/1**

000 **P** **Action Hawk (GER)**[48] 2594 7-10-12 0.......................... DenisO'Regan —
(Ben Pollock) *a in rr: t.o 5th: p.u bef last* **250/1**

030 **F** **Copsehill Girl (IRE)**[26] 2954 6-10-5 0.......................... WayneHutchinson —
(Ian Williams) *in tch: chsd ldrs and rdn 3 out: poor 4th whn fell last* **28/1**

050 **P** **Ellie Wiggins**[46] 2632 5-9-12 0.......................... NathanSweeney(7) —
(Bob Buckler) *in rr whn p.u and crashed through rail appr 3rd* **80/1**

50 **P** **Gun And More**[63] 2281 6-10-12 0.......................... TjadeCollier —
(Sue Smith) *blnd and bhd 4th: t.o whn p.u after 5th* **150/1**

5m 22.6s (13.00) **Going Correction** +0.65s/f (Soft) **14** Ran SP% **116.2**
Speed ratings: **100,97,95,91,85 85,85,—,—,— —,—,—,—**
Tote Swingers:1&2:£2.30, 2&3:£13.00, 1&3:£4.90 CSF £14.05 TOTE £3.80: £1.50, £1.90, £4.40; EX 17.30.
Owner The Oxymorons **Bred** M Cahill **Trained** Aberthin, Vale of Glamorgan
■ As well as the flight down the hill, the second-last flight was bypassed.

FOCUS
A severe test in the conditions and the first three finished some way clear. Ordinary novice form.

NOTEBOOK
Bottman(IRE), a bumper winner who has needed plenty of time, started odds on when making his hurdling bow at Wincanton in October, but was found to have an infection after finishing a well-beaten third. He kept close tabs on the leader and stayed on strongly to forge clear despite a tendency to jump left-handed. He clearly stays really well and will make a chaser in time. (op 5-1 tchd 13-2)
Redbridge Flyer(IRE), who has changed stables since finishing third at Chepstow in November, took them along at a sound pace but was hard at work fully half a mile from home. It was soon clear that he was only going to finish second best, but he ought to be able to go one better at some stage this winter. (tchd 5-2)
Morcambe is a late-developing type. He stuck to the inner and kept on in his own time up the final hill. There ought to be a bit better to come, especially in less testing conditions. (op 14-1 tchd 18-1)
Loch Ba(IRE), happy to sit off the pace, was hard at work at the normal third-last and looks to just stay. (op 4-1)
See You Jack was under pressure and going nowhere at the foot of the final hill and probably did not handle the very testing conditions. (op 3-1 tchd 9-4)
Dancing Legend Official explanation: jockey said saddle slipped

3488 LADBROKES MOBILE MASTERS H'CAP CHASE (14 fncs 2 omitted) 2m 6f
2:55 (2:59) (Class 3) (0-135,130) 5-Y-0+ **£6,505** (£1,910; £955; £477)

Form RPR

221 **1** **Flying Squad (UAE)**[9] 3305 7-9-11 104 oh2..........................(t) JimmyDerham(3) 118+
(Milton Harris) *hld up in rr: hmpd 6th: hdwy 8th: trckd ldrs bypassed 3rd last: led gng smoothly wl bef 2 out: eased nr fin* **4/1**[2]

0202 **2** *2 1/2* **Ballyegan (IRE)**[11] 3230 6-9-8 105.......................... NathanSweeney(7) 112
(Bob Buckler) *chsd ldrs: chsd wnr appr last but nvr any ch: styd on same pce* **7/2**[1]

5-31 **3** *2 3/4* **Mohi Rahrere (IRE)**[73] 2073 8-10-10 114.......................... RichardJohnson 117
(Barry Leavy) *in rr: hit 4th: blnd 7th: styd on appr 2 out: tk 3rd last and kpt on to cl on 2nd nr fin but nvr any ch w wnr* **4/1**[2]

5-25 **4** *11* **Kawagino (IRE)**[8] 3347 11-11-7 125.......................... AndrewThornton 117
(Seamus Mullins) *j. slowly 1st and 2nd: in tch fr 5th: hit 10th and in rr: kpt on again appr 2 out but nvr any threat* **17/2**

-052 **5** *2 3/4* **Camden George (IRE)**[54] 2449 10-10-7 111.......................... TjadeCollier 101
(Sue Smith) *chsd ldr: led 7th: jnd fr 10th: hdd wl bef 2 out and sn wknd* **8/1**[3]

11-P **6** *16* **Afistfullofpebbles**[13] 3157 7-11-2 123.......................... RichieMcLernon(3) 97
(Jonjo O'Neill) *in tch tl rdn and bhd fr 9th* **25/1**

3-PF **7** *3 1/2* **Leac An Scail (IRE)**[26] 2955 10-11-4 122.......................... HenryOliver 92
(Sue Smith) *hit 2nd: chsd ldrs: blnd 6th: wknd 11th* **40/1**

PP-P **P** **Kilbeggan Blade**[61] 2305 12-11-7 125..........................(v[1]) JasonMaguire —
(Robin Dickin) *led to 7th: w ldr fr 9th tl wknd after bypassed 3rd last: t.o whn p.u bef last* **18/1**

4-35 **F** **Wheels Up (IRE)**[13] 3157 10-11-0 118..........................(t) APMcCoy —
(Jonjo O'Neill) *trcking ldrs whn hmpd and fell 6th* **12/1**

FP-1 **P** **Andrew Nick (IRE)**[221] 599 9-10-9 118.......................... DavidBass(5) —
(Matt Hazell) *bhd and j. slowly 5th: t.o whn p.u bef 11th* **28/1**

-3P0 **P** **Vodka Brook (IRE)**[13] 3169 8-11-12 130..........................(p) RobertWalford —
(Tim Walford) *chsd ldrs tl blnd 10th: nt rcvr: t.o whn p.u bef 11th* **12/1**

5m 58.77s (5.77) **Going Correction** +0.45s/f (Soft) **11** Ran SP% **114.2**
Speed ratings: **107,106,105,101,100 94,93,—,—,— —**
Tote Swingers:1&2:£4.80, 2&3:£6.40, 1&3:£6.30 CSF £18.10 CT £58.50 TOTE £3.80: £1.60, £1.20, £1.60; EX 20.40.
Owner Mrs Denise Hopkins **Bred** Darley **Trained** Herridge, Wiltshire

FOCUS
Quite a valuable handicap chase. The pace was sound and there were just four in with a chance going to two out. A step up from the winner, and solid form.

NOTEBOOK
Flying Squad(UAE), who opened his account on just his third start over fences at Fakenham on New Year's Day, defied a 9lb higher mark (2lb out of the weights). Confidently ridden, he moved up on the bridle a mile from home and after taking charge he had only to be kept up to his work to score in decisive fashion. There is even better to come from this promising young chaser. (op 6-1 tchd 7-2)
Ballyegan(IRE), considered unlucky when runner-up behind a leniently treated, gambled-on rival at Taunton on just his second chase start, went down fighting. He clearly appreciates testing conditions. (op 4-1)
Mohi Rahrere(IRE), absent since winning from a 10lb lower mark at on his chasing debut at Uttoxeter in October, has gone well fresh and came here on the back of a recent workout at Wolverhampton. He was badly let down by his jumping and looked like being pulled up when tailed off at halfway. Although then making up a deal of ground under a persistent ride to move into fourth spot going to two out, he could make no more inroads on the run-in. A late developer, he can surely find another race when his jumping comes up to scratch. (op 9-2)
Kawagino(IRE), better going left-handed, ran a moody sort of race. (op 10-1 tchd 11-1)
Camden George(IRE) helped force the pace but he struggled to keep up at the foot of the final hill and lost two places on the run-in. Despite a declining mark he has not won for almost two years now. (op 13-2)

3489 BEST ODDS GUARANTEED AT LADBROKES.COM MAIDEN HURDLE (7 hdls 1 omitted) 2m
3:25 (3:25) (Class 4) 4-Y-0+ **£1,951** (£573; £286; £143)

Form RPR

25 **1** **Buddy Holly**[12] 3196 6-11-5 0.......................... WillKennedy 118+
(Violet M Jordan) *trckd ldrs: wnt 2nd 3 out: led appr 2 out: r.o strly* **9/2**[2]

33 **2** *12* **Pateese (FR)**[26] 2960 6-11-5 120.......................... RichardJohnson 112+
(Philip Hobbs) *led: jnd fr 4th tl after 4 out: hmpd by loose horse appr 3 out: hdd appr 2 out and sn no ch w wnr but clr 2nd best* **4/7**[1]

00- **3** *23* **World Watch (IRE)**[291] 4846 6-11-5 0.......................... MarkBradburne 81
(Tom Gretton) *hld up in rr: stdy hdwy fr 3 out: styd on fr next but nvr any ch w ldng duo* **100/1**

033/ **4** *3 3/4* **Okafranca (IRE)**[455] 4301 6-11-5 105.......................... RhysFlint 77
(Jim Old) *in rr tl mod prog after 3 out* **14/1**

500 **5** *7* **Master Milan (IRE)**[11] 3225 5-11-5 0.......................... APMcCoy 70
(Jonjo O'Neill) *pressed ldr: chal 4th to 4 out: wknd 3 out* **28/1**

06 **6** *10* **Tippering (IRE)**[59] 2349 6-11-5 0.......................... TjadeCollier 60
(Sue Smith) *pushed along fr 2nd and chsd ldrs: wknd appr 3 out* **6/1**[3]

05/0 **7** *15* **Golbelini**[62] 2289 6-10-12 0.......................... WayneHutchinson 38
(Martin Keighley) *in rr: sme hdwy 3 out: nvr rchd ldrs: wknd 2 out: no ch whn blnd last* **33/1**

0-40 **8** *13* **Drumlang (IRE)**[31] 2873 5-11-5 0.......................... DominicElsworth 32
(Henrietta Knight) *bhd most of way* **20/1**

0-F0 **9** *3/4* **Twice Lucky**[27] 2939 7-11-5 0.......................... HenryOliver 32
(Sue Smith) *bhd fr 1/2-way* **100/1**

0-0 **10** *58* **Slip Duty (IRE)**[45] 2666 9-10-12 0.......................... AodhaganConlon(7) —
(Kate Buckett) *chsd ldrs to 4 out* **100/1**

0- **11** *nse* **Semah George**[296] 4742 5-11-5 0.......................... TomMessenger —
(John Holt) *bhd fr 1/2-way* **100/1**

0 **U** **Major Potential (USA)**[13] 3158 5-11-5 0.......................... SamThomas —
(Venetia Williams) *blnd and uns rdr 1st* **80/1**

0/ **U** **Backstreet Billy (IRE)**[630] 5124 7-11-5 0.......................... DenisO'Regan —
(Richard Lee) *in rr tl stdy hdwy to trck ldrs 3 out: wknd bef next: tired and no ch whn blnd and uns rdr last* **40/1**

4m 16.3s (8.40) **Going Correction** +0.65s/f (Soft) **13** Ran SP% **121.6**
Speed ratings (Par 105): **105,99,87,85,82 77,69,63,62,33 33,—,—**
Tote Swingers:1&2:£1.10, 2&3:£38.60, 1&3:£45.60 CSF £7.55 TOTE £4.10: £2.10, £1.02, £33.20; EX 8.80.
Owner EDS Roofing Supplies Ltd **Bred** R J & S A Carter **Trained** Quainton, Bucks

FOCUS
Plenty of deadwood and just four still in with a chance when there was a dramatic incident approaching the third-last flight. It was the fastest of the races over this trip and there may be more to come from the winner.

NOTEBOOK
Buddy Holly, rated 65 on the Flat, had run with credit on his two previous starts over hurdles. He was 6l ahead with the race in the bag when he made a mistake at the final flight. A 1m2f performer on the level, he proved his stamina here and could run in a handicap at Cheltenham next. (op 4-1)
Pateese(FR), third at Exeter and at Newbury behind Minella Class, was setting sail for home when knocked broadsides by a loose horse just before three out. There is no knowing how much it took out of him and in the end he was no match, eased down near the line. A dual Flat winner in France, he deserves another chance. (op 8-13 tchd 8-11)
World Watch(IRE), well held in two bumpers, was a rank outsider on his first start for ten months. He stayed on in his own time from way off the pace and there should be better to come, especially when stepped up in trip. Official explanation: jockey said, regarding running and riding, that his orders were to settle the gelding, which has run too free in the past, and do his best, adding that he was able to settle and get it relaxed, jumping nicely however, it did show signs of racing keenly downhill, the leaders quickened away in the back straight and he felt it prudent in order to achieve the best possible placing he rode sympathetically to achieve third place.
Okafranca(IRE), tailed off when last seen on the Flat 15 months ago, was placed twice over hurdles from three starts two seasons ago. Already rated 105, low-grade handicaps now beckon. (op 16-1)
Master Milan(IRE), a fast-ground Irish point winner, helped force the pace but stopped to nothing at the foot of the final hill. This was his third start over hurdles and he is a likely type for handicaps on much better ground in the spring.
Tippering(IRE) was another in the firing line for a long way. He looks as though he needs more time, but is not without ability. (op 7-1)

3490 LADBROKES.COM H'CAP HURDLE (7 hdls 1 omitted) 2m
3:55 (3:55) (Class 3) (0-125,125) 4-Y-0+ **£4,553** (£1,337; £668; £333)

Form RPR

P-10 **1** **Warne's Way (IRE)**[9] 3298 8-11-8 121.......................... LeightonAspell 132+
(Brendan Powell) *trckd ldrs tl lost pl and dropped to rr 4th: gd hdwy after 3 out to ld wl bef next: drvn wl clr last* **14/1**

40-2 **2** *14* **Call It On (IRE)**[56] 2419 5-10-9 108.......................... JamesReveley 104
(Philip Kirby) *in rr tl hdwy after 3 out: styd on fr 2 out to take wl hld 2nd after last* **9/1**

-626 **3** *1 1/4* **Ocean Transit (IRE)**[46] 2639 6-11-0 113.......................... APMcCoy 110+
(Richard Price) *chsd ldrs: led 3 out: hdd wl bef next: no ch but stl 2nd whn blnd last: wknd into 3rd sn after* **8/1**

F-42 **4** *9* **Daring Origyn (FR)**[62] 2283 6-10-11 117..........................(t) JakeGreenall(7) 104
(Richard Lee) *chsd ldrs: rdn 3 out: wknd bef 2 out* **9/2**[2]

-6F0 **5** *6* **Troubletimestwo (FR)**[25] 2977 5-10-11 115.......................... LeeEdwards(5) 95
(Tony Carroll) *in rr: rdn appr 3 out: mod prog u.p appr 2 out* **50/1**

1-24 **6** *4* **Je Ne Sais Plus (FR)**[72] 2089 7-11-2 115.......................... DenisO'Regan 95+
(Tom George) *hld up in rr: hdwy whn blnd 4 out: nt rcvr* **9/2**[2]

3325 **7** *3 1/4* **Tom O'Tara**[25] 2983 7-10-0 109.......................... ChristopherWard(10) 86+
(Robin Dickin) *hit 1st: in rr tl hdwy 3 out: styng on whn n.m.r bnd appr 2 out: fnd little and sn no ch* **4/1**[1]

F6-2 **8** *18* **Tahiti Pearl (IRE)**[67] 2162 7-10-6 105.......................... HenryOliver 60
(Sue Smith) *chsd ldrs: hit 3rd and sn bhd* **14/1**

F1F- **9** *4* **Reindeer Dippin**[352] 3597 9-11-12 125.......................... JasonMaguire 76
(Donald McCain) *led tl hdd 4 out: wknd after 3 out: eased whn no ch appr 2 out* **11/1**

-0PP **10** *15* **Olympian (FR)**[25] 2983 9-10-6 112..........................(b[1]) JosephAkehurst(7) 48
(Philip Middleton) *mid-div: gd hdwy fr 3rd to ld 4 out: hdd 3 out and sn wknd* **20/1**

2146 **11** *35* **Niceonefrankie**[11] 3228 5-11-1 114.......................... SamThomas 15
(Venetia Williams) *chsd ldrs to 4 out: wknd after next: no ch whn blnd last* **7/1**[3]

/U-0 **12** *7* **Optimus Maximus (IRE)**[9] 3298 6-11-4 120..............(t) TommyPhelan(3) 14
(Claire Dyson) *chsd ldrs to 4 out: wknd* **40/1**

4m 18.58s (10.68) **Going Correction** +0.65s/f (Soft) **12** Ran SP% **120.8**
Speed ratings (Par 107): **99,92,91,86,83 81,80,71,69,61 44,40**
Tote Swingers:1&2:£23.90, 2&3:£9.60, 1&3:£6.40 CSF £134.09 CT £1093.93 TOTE £14.60: £6.30, £2.80, £3.00; EX 265.50.
Owner Nigel Stafford **Bred** Mrs Ann Kennedy **Trained** Upper Lambourn, Berks

FOCUS
A competitive handicap hurdle and in the end a relatively unfancied wide-margin winner. There is a case for rating the form a few pounds higher.

NOTEBOOK
Warne's Way(IRE), without the blinkers this time, is not easy to predict. Suited by the mud, he was 6lb higher than for his narrow Fontwell success two outings ago. Badly outpaced at one stage, after taking charge he came right away going to the final flight. The problem is he doesn't seem to run two races alike. (op 16-1)
Call It On(IRE), runner-up in a novices' event at Leicester in November on his first start for this yard, stayed on up the final hill to snatch second spot. Rated 85 on the Flat, he's potentially well treated on just 108 and connections reckon much less testing conditions will suit him a fair bit better.
Ocean Transit(IRE), absent since running below par at Taunton in November, was well held when he blundered at the last. Connections feared beforehand that she may need the outing after the freeze-up.
Daring Origyn(FR) was hard at work some way from home and proved one-paced. This trip even on a track as testing as this is on the short side for him. (op 11-2)
Troubletimestwo(FR) is now attractively handicapped but he needs much better ground than he encountered here.
Je Ne Sais Plus(FR), absent for ten weeks, was on the back foot after a mistake four out.
Tom O'Tara, ridden by a 10lb claimer, looks a tricky ride. Dropped in at the start, he made a mistake at the first. Taken wide, he then hung when left short of room on the bend going to two out. (op 15-2)
Niceonefrankie Official explanation: jockey sais gelding stopped quickly
T/Plt: £18.50 to a £1 stake. Pool:£55,999.06. 2,203.30 winning tickets. T/Qpdt: £3.30 to a £1 stake. Pool:£3,988.63. 879.92 winning tickets. ST

[3386] LEICESTER (R-H)

Tuesday, January 11

OFFICIAL GOING: Hurdle course - heavy (soft in places); chase course - good to soft (good in places; heavy on the flat crossings)
Wind: Fresh behind Weather: Overcast

3491 NOMAD NOVICES' HURDLE (DIV I) (8 hdls) 2m
1:00 (1:00) (Class 4) 4-Y-O+ **£1,951** (£573; £286; £143)

Form RPR
04 **1** **Non Dom (IRE)**[9] 3344 5-11-5 0.. JamieMoore 111
(Hughie Morrison) *hld up: hdwy 5th: chsd ldr 2 out: led last: drvn out* **10/3**[2]
0 **2** *3 ¼* **Clowance House**[27] 2960 5-11-5 0.................................. AidanColeman 109+
(Venetia Williams) *a.p: chsd ldr appr 3 out: led bef next: rdn and hdd whn mstke last: no ex flat* **4/1**[3]
00 **3** *4* **Bit Of A Clown (IRE)**[14] 3166 5-11-5 0......................... AndrewThornton 104
(Caroline Bailey) *led: rdn and hdd appr 2 out: wknd flat* **100/1**
65 **4** *16* **Bun Oir (USA)**[29] 2924 4-10-7 114.................................... AndrewTinkler 76
(Charlie Longsdon) *hld up: hdwy 5th: wknd bef next* **11/2**
U0F **5** *12* **Goodtimetoby (IRE)**[48] 2607 8-11-5 0............................ CharliePoste 78
(Richard Lee) *hld up: hdwy appr 3 out: rdn and wknd bef next: t.o* **100/1**
0 **6** *10* **Pegeno Diablo (IRE)**[12] 3225 6-11-7 0............................ IanPopham(5) 73
(Claire Dyson) *chsd ldr tl nt fluent 3rd: rdn and wknd after 5th: t.o* **33/1**
3600 **7** *½* **Kilcommon Pride (IRE)**[48] 2607 6-11-5 0........................ HaddenFrost 65
(Roger Curtis) *hld up: a in rr: rdn and wknd 5th: t.o* **125/1**
6 **8** *2 ¾* **Ezdiyaad (IRE)**[109] 1603 7-11-5 0.............................(t) LeightonAspell 63
(Kevin Morgan) *chsd ldrs: wnt 2nd 4th tl appr 3 out: rdn and wknd sn after: t.o* **15/2**
9 *49* **Any Given Moment (IRE)**[99] 5-11-5 0............................ JasonMaguire 14
(Donald McCain) *chsd ldrs: j.lft 1st: rdn appr 5th: wknd bef next: t.o* **11/4**[1]
0-0 **10** *8* **Mandalay Prince**[62] 2310 7-11-5 0.................................. TimmyMurphy 6
(Willie Musson) *a bhd: t.o* **100/1**
3 **P** **First Smash (GER)**[21] 3057 6-11-5 0............................ WarrenMarston —
(Milton Harris) *hld up: rdn appr 5th: sn wknd: t.o whn p.u bef next* **9/1**

4m 0.80s (-0.20) **Going Correction** +0.05s/f (Yiel)
WFA 4 from 5yo+ 11lb **11** Ran SP% **113.6**
Speed ratings (Par 105): **102,100,98,90,84 79,79,78,53,49** —
toteswingers:1&2: £3.20, 2&3: £15.50, 1&3: Not won. CSF £16.70 TOTE £2.60: £1.10, £2.60, £13.50; EX 22.10.
Owner Raymond Tooth **Bred** Mrs Ann Kennedy **Trained** East Ilsley, Berks

FOCUS
The going had changed following 6mm of overnight rain, with it riding heavy, soft in places on the hurdles track and good to soft, good in places on the chase course. The first division of an ordinary novice hurdle and not form to get carried away with. The first two are entitled to rate higher on their Flat form.

NOTEBOOK
Non Dom(IRE), who made some eyecatching late headway at Plumpton last time, had work to do if he was to turnaround debut form with the runner-up (finished 14l adrift), but he was backed as though a big run was expected and, having travelled well, he eventually got on top from the last. He clearly stays the trip well and, although he'll have more on under a penalty, he should enjoy more success in handicaps down the line. (op 5-1)
Clowance House, who ran well until fitness began to tell on his hurdles debut at Newbury, went on coming to two out, but the winner always seemed to have him in his sights and he was unable to confirm the form. He should pick up a small race on this evidence. (op 7-2)
Bit Of A Clown(IRE), well beaten in a couple of AW bumpers, had the run of things in front, but kept going better than expected given his 100-1 odds, and he clearly has a future. (op 150-1)
Bun Oir(USA) should do better once handicapping on a sounder surface. (op 9-1)
Goodtimetoby(IRE), who had failed to complete in two of his three previous starts, moved quite nicely into a chasing position up the straight, but he couldn't follow through with his effort. This was his best effort to date. (op 125-1)
Ezdiyaad(IRE), wearing a first-time tongue-tie, was backed beforehand but he failed to improve as expected, the drop in trip not helping having raced freely early on. (op 6-1 tchd 8-1 in places)
Any Given Moment(IRE), a progressive sort on the Flat, had joined a top yard. He was never really going and it's probable the ground played its part in his performance. Therefore, he's worth another chance. Official explanation: jockey said gelding never travelled (op 2-1)
Mandalay Prince Official explanation: jockey said gelding was unsuited by the heavy (soft in places) ground
First Smash(GER) was disappointing considering he had shaped quite well in a 'jumpers' bumper' on his debut for the yard. He too warrants another chance back on better ground, though. (tchd 10-1)

3492 HOSE THORNS H'CAP CHASE (15 fncs) 2m 4f 110y
1:30 (1:30) (Class 5) (0-90,90) 5-Y-O+ **£1,951** (£573; £286; £143)

Form RPR
36U3 **1** **Phar Again (IRE)**[7] 3388 8-10-13 80........................(vt) TommyPhelan(3) 90
(Claire Dyson) *chsd ldr to 9th: remained handy: rdn after 11th: chsd ldr 2 out: led last: drvn out* **9/2**[3]
P-U4 **2** *3* **Killfinnan Castle (IRE)**[75] 2048 8-10-8 72.......................(p) WillKennedy 80
(Violet M Jordan) *hld up: hdwy 9th: pckd 11th: led appr 3 out: rdn and hdd last: styd on same pce flat* **9/1**
0600 **3** *9* **Red Law (IRE)**[12] 3226 7-11-5 90.................................... MrPJTolman(7) 91
(Mark Gillard) *hld up: hdwy 10th: sn rdn: wknd flat* **33/1**
504 **4** *8* **Bajan Sunshine (IRE)**[5] 3402 10-10-5 69............................ JamesDavies 62
(Gary Brown) *hld up in tch: rdn appr 4 out: wknd last* **16/1**
42-2 **5** *6* **Bertenbar**[255] 95 7-11-1 79.. AndrewThornton 66
(Henrietta Knight) *trckd ldrs: wnt 2nd 9th tl rdn after 3 out: wknd bef last* **7/2**[2]
P-P3 **6** *¾* **Organiz (FR)**[26] 2986 9-11-6 89................................ MrSWaley-Cohen(5) 79
(Robin Dickin) *hld up: mstke 7th: hdwy 4 out: hmpd next: wknd 2 out: hit last* **12/1**
0505 **7** *31* **Kinkeel (IRE)**[7] 3388 12-10-8 75................................ EamonDehdashti(3) 33
(Tony Carroll) *prom: pushed along 6th: sn lost pl: bhd fr 9th: t.o* **33/1**
2P34 **P** **Whatcanisay**[48] 2608 12-10-5 69.................................(t) HaddenFrost —
(James Frost) *hld up: mstke 3rd: bhd fr 5th: t.o whn p.u bef 8th* **9/1**
F3-6 **P** **Ajzal (IRE)**[250] 183 7-11-3 81......................................(b) FelixDeGiles —
(Ed de Giles) *led tl appr 3 out: sn wknd: hit 2 out: t.o whn p.u bef next* **12/1**
52U2 **U** **One More Dinar**[27] 2952 8-11-4 82................................ MarkBradburne —
(John Bryan Groucott) *chsd ldrs: disputing 4th whn blnd and uns rdr 8th* **11/4**[1]

5m 19.9s (1.00) **Going Correction** -0.05s/f (Good) **10** Ran SP% **114.2**
Speed ratings: **96,94,91,88,86 85,74,—,—,—**
toteswingers:1&2: £14.60, 2&3: £30.20, 1&3: £12.60 CSF £43.47 CT £1166.75 TOTE £4.20: £2.00, £3.40, £4.40; EX 43.70.
Owner B and S Vaughan **Bred** Mrs J Wilkinson **Trained** Cleeve Prior, Worcs
■ Stewards' Enquiry : Tommy Phelan four-day ban: used whip with excessive frequency (Jan 25-28)

FOCUS
A moderate handicap chase. The winner is rated in line with his recent C&D win.

NOTEBOOK
Phar Again(IRE), whose only previous chase win came at this course, shaped more promisingly returned here last week and built on that with a workmanlike win. Consistency hasn't been his strong point in the past, however, so don't bank on him to give his best next time. (op 11-2 tchd 6-1)
Killfinnan Castle(IRE), just 1lb above his last win, raised his game in the first-time cheekpieces and ran easily his best race of the season so far. (tchd 17-2)
Red Law(IRE) improved dramatically on his chasing debut effort at Taunton, despite still appearing to be plenty high enough in the weights. He hasn't had many chances and may progress again. (op 16-1)
Bajan Sunshine(IRE) had run an improved race just five days earlier and was far from discredited once again. (op 12-1)
Bertenbar looked to need this return from a 255-day absence. (tchd 4-1)
Whatcanisay Official explanation: jockey said gelding never travelled (op 8-1)
Ajzal(IRE), having his first start since leaving Tom George, went well for a long way in front but couldn't sustain it in the straight. (op 8-1)
One More Dinar set the standard, but he's had trouble with his jumping in the past and he unseated Mark Bradburne following a blunder at the eighth. (op 8-1)

3493 DOVE (S) HURDLE (10 hdls) 2m 4f 110y
2:00 (2:00) (Class 5) 4-Y-O+ **£1,626** (£477; £238; £119)

Form RPR
F-32 **1** **Laborec (IRE)**[47] 2644 8-11-6 113..............................(p) DominicElsworth 115
(Neil King) *hld up: hdwy 4th: chsd ldr 6th: led 2 out: drvn out* **6/4**[1]
P30P **2** *10* **Abstract Art (USA)**[10] 3299 8-11-6 108.........................(p) AidanColeman 107+
(Rachel Hobbs) *led 2nd: clr whn hit 5th: rdn and hdd 2 out: wknd flat* **25/1**
44P2 **3** *½* **Pocket Too**[7] 2558 8-10-13 105..(p) MrJBanks(7) 104
(Matthew Salaman) *hld up: hdwy 7th: rdn after 3 out: styd on same pce fr next* **9/2**[2]
-F41 **4** *38* **Earth Magic (IRE)**[67] 2188 11-11-9 129............................. PaulMoloney 69
(Evan Williams) *led to 2nd: chsd ldr: mstke 3rd: lost 2nd 6th: rdn and wknd next: t.o* **5/1**[3]
0235 **5** *13* **Captain Becket**[63] 2284 8-11-9 95...................................... HaddenFrost 56
(James Frost) *hld up: sme hdwy 7th: sn wknd: t.o* **40/1**
3402 **6** *1 ¼* **Knight Legend (IRE)**[10] 3303 12-11-3 110..............(t) CharlieHuxley(3) 53
(Sarah Humphrey) *prom tl rdn and wknd appr 3 out: t.o* **9/2**[2]
P00P **7** *26* **Deep Reflection**[11] 3256 11-11-6 100........................(p) JimmyDerham(3) 29
(Martin Keighley) *hld up: hdwy 7th: sn rdn and wknd: t.o* **33/1**
-040 **8** *18* **Verasi**[29] 2928 10-11-3 92.......................................(b) EamonDehdashti(3) 8
(Gary Moore) *hld up: mstke 3rd: sn given reminders: bhd fr 5th: t.o* **20/1**
/0F5 **P** **Hoh Viss**[10] 3303 11-11-3 104...(b) AdamPogson(3) —
(Caroline Bailey) *chsd ldrs tl wknd appr 5th: t.o whn p.u bef 7th* **40/1**
/0-0 **P** **Indian Spring (IRE)**[21] 3059 7-11-6 119.........................(b) JamieMoore —
(Gary Moore) *hld up: rdn 6th: wknd next: t.o whn p.u bef 3 out* **16/1**
-006 **P** **Sir Clad**[12] 3224 5-11-3 0..(t) TommyPhelan(3) —
(Claire Dyson) *chsd ldrs: pushed along 3rd: wknd after next: t.o whn p.u bef last* **200/1**

5m 22.7s (-2.00) **Going Correction** +0.05s/f (Yiel) **11** Ran SP% **115.8**
Speed ratings (Par 103): **105,101,101,86,81 81,71,64,—,— —**
toteswingers:1&2: £8.40, 2&3: not won, 1&3: £2.20 CSF £47.37 TOTE £2.80: £1.10, £5.90, £4.00; EX 35.30.The winner was bought in for 5,000gns.
Owner Robert Bothway **Bred** Aidan McGrath **Trained** Newmarket, Suffolk

FOCUS
The form of this reasonable selling hurdle is rated through the winner and third to their marks.

NOTEBOOK
Laborec(IRE) finished well on top. Runner-up in a handicap hurdle at Uttoxeter latest, he briefly looked in trouble early in the straight, but it was clear from after two out that he had the runner-up's move covered. He's a decent sort at this level who's capable of winning again. (op 2-1)
Abstract Art(USA) had looked promising a couple of seasons back and the drop in grade/application of cheekpieces enabled him to show a bit of form. He raced enthusiastically in a clear lead and looked to be full of running still at the top of the straight, but eventually emptied out. (op 33-1)
Pocket Too never looked like winning, but he kept grinding away and nearly caught the runner-up. (op 5-1)

Earth Magic(IRE), who went off at a bigger price than expected, produced a rather tame effort, quickly being brushed aside. Considering he had won in similar ground last time, he should have done better. (op 4-1 tchd 13-2)

Knight Legend(IRE) failed to give his running on ground that would have been too soft. (op 4-1)

3494 GROBY NOVICES' H'CAP CHASE (12 fncs) 2m
2:30 (2:30) (Class 4) (0-115,115) 5-Y-0+ £2,602 (£764; £382; £190)

Form RPR

-224 1 **Anquetta (IRE)**[61] 2330 7-11-7 **115** DavidBass(5) 134+
(Nicky Henderson) *a.p: hit 6th: led after 4 out: rdn and swished tail flat: styd on* **5/1**[2]

4401 2 2 3/4 **Bedarra Boy**[54] 2468 5-10-7 **100** DarylJacob 109
(David Arbuthnot) *hld up: hdwy after 8th: ev ch last: styd on same pce flat* **11/2**[3]

-12F 3 8 **Red Rouble (IRE)**[52] 2529 6-11-9 **112** PaddyBrennan 119+
(Nigel Twiston-Davies) *prom: rdn 7th: styd on same pce fr 2 out* **2/1**[1]

-F65 4 16 **Iona Days (IRE)**[61] 2322 6-11-2 **105** HaddenFrost 96
(Henrietta Knight) *led to 2nd: led 3rd to next: chsd ldrs tl rdn and wknd 2 out* **6/1**

6 5 3/4 **Yes Man (IRE)**[14] 3154 6-10-5 **97** (v[1]) DonalDevereux(3) 89
(Peter Bowen) *plld hrd and sn prom: led 4th: pckd next: hdd after 4 out: sn rdn: wknd next* **16/1**

P534 6 2 **Marc Aurele (IRE)**[57] 2422 6-11-2 **108** (t) JimmyDerham(3) 96
(Milton Harris) *hld up in tch: dropped in rr 3rd: hdwy appr 4 out: wknd bef 2 out* **10/1**

P-6P 7 18 **Llama Farmer**[13] 3198 6-11-12 **115** (p) DominicElsworth 87
(Paul Webber) *chsd ldrs tl wknd 7th: t.o* **8/1**

36P0 8 23 **Another Trump (NZ)**[14] 3154 7-11-6 **109** APMcCoy 61
(Jonjo O'Neill) *hld up: mstke 2nd: j. slowly and bhd fr 4th: t.o* **12/1**

0000 9 7 **Shalamiyr (FR)**[47] 2626 6-11-5 **108** RhysFlint 53
(Philip Hobbs) *chsd ldr: led 2nd to next: remained handy: rdn appr 4 out: wknd 3 out: t.o* **33/1**

4m 5.40s (-2.80) **Going Correction** -0.05s/f (Good)
WFA 5 from 6yo+ 3lb **9** Ran SP% **116.4**
Speed ratings: **105,103,99,91,91 90,81,69,66**
toteswingers:1&2: £7.60, 2&3: £3.90, 1&3: £1.90 CSF £33.36 CT £72.63 TOTE £3.90: £1.20, £1.40, £1.70; EX 25.80.
Owner The Ten From Seven **Bred** Gerry Martin **Trained** Upper Lambourn, Berks

FOCUS
Quite an open novices' handicap chase. The first two are on the upgrade.

NOTEBOOK
Anquetta(IRE), making his handicap debut following just the two runs in novice chases, seemed fairly weighted off a mark of 115 and, despite swishing his tail under pressure, he always looked to be doing enough from the last. He remains capable of better. (tchd 11-2)

Bedarra Boy, raised 5lb having made a successful chasing debut at Hereford in November, moved nicely into contention and threw down a strong challenge to the winner, but was always coming off second best. He should win more races as a chaser, especially back on better ground. (op 5-1 tchd 6-1)

Red Rouble(IRE), off since falling when favourite at Huntingdon in November, jumped soundly enough but was found wanting for pace on this drop to 2m. (op 9-4 tchd 5-2)

Iona Days(IRE), off for two months and now switching to fences, went well to a point and should improve for the experience. His trainer isn't in the best of form either at present. (op 15-2)

3495 NOMAD NOVICES' HURDLE (DIV II) (8 hdls) 2m
3:00 (3:00) (Class 4) 4-Y-0+ £1,951 (£573; £286; £143)

Form RPR

2-35 1 **Featherbed Lane (IRE)**[46] 2666 6-11-5 0 APMcCoy 115+
(Anabel L M King) *hld up: hdwy 5th: led appr last: drvn out* **6/5**[1]

1 2 4 1/2 **The Cockney Mackem (IRE)**[110] 1599 5-11-5 0 PaddyBrennan 110+
(Nigel Twiston-Davies) *a.p: nt fluent 4th: led 3 out: hit next: rdn and hdd appr last: styd on same pce flat* **6/4**[2]

50 3 13 **Art Broker (IRE)**[51] 2540 5-10-12 0 JakeGreenall(7) 98+
(Henry Daly) *chsd ldrs: ev ch whn hit 2 out: sn rdn: wknd flat* **10/1**[3]

0P4 4 1 1/4 **Chase Gate**[49] 2594 6-11-5 0 HaddenFrost 95
(James Frost) *chsd ldr tl led appr 3 out: sn hdd: wknd bef next* **25/1**

00/ 5 nk **Bold Adventure**[5] 3659 7-11-5 0 LeightonAspell 94
(Willie Musson) *hld up: hdwy 5th: wknd after 3 out* **16/1**

00 6 12 **Bridge Street Boy**[237] 412 6-11-5 0 RichardJohnson 82
(Richard Lee) *hld up: wknd 3 out: t.o* **66/1**

7 36 **Jordaura**[78] 5-11-5 0 TomMessenger 46
(John Holt) *hld up: mstke 4th: wknd 3 out: t.o* **22/1**

6-0F 8 40 **Fifth Sea Lord (IRE)**[26] 2985 6-11-5 0 AndrewThornton 6
(Tom Gretton) *led tl hdd & wknd appr 3 out: t.o* **100/1**

000P 9 3 1/4 **Action Hawk (GER)**[1] 3487 7-11-5 0 JamesDavies 3
(Ben Pollock) *chsd ldrs tl rdn and wknd appr 3 out: t.o* **200/1**

4m 0.90s (-0.10) **Going Correction** +0.05s/f (Yiel) **9** Ran SP% **111.6**
Speed ratings (Par 105): **102,99,93,92,92 86,68,48,46**
toteswingers:1&2: £1.10, 2&3: £3.90, 1&3: £1.80 CSF £3.07 TOTE £3.90: £1.60, £1.02, £1.40; EX 3.90.
Owner Mrs Roz Wyles & Aiden Murphy **Bred** Sweetmans Bloodstock **Trained** Wilmcote, Warwicks

FOCUS
A straight match on paper in this ordinary novice hurdle. The first two are rated in line with their bumper form.

NOTEBOOK
Featherbed Lane(IRE) took over at the head of the market before the race and stayed on best from the last under McCoy. He looks to have a bit of physical scope and should really come into his own once upped in trip, so can probably defy a penalty before going handicapping. (op 13-8 tchd 11-10)

The Cockney Mackem(IRE), off since winning a moderate Perth bumper in September, has plenty of size about him, but his lack of jumping experience told late and he was unable to match the winner from the last. There was enough promise in this, though, to think he'll be winning something similar once upped in trip. (op 11-10 tchd 13-8)

Art Broker(IRE) was unable to race on with the front pair in the end, a mistake two out ending his hopes. He'll be of interest once sent handicapping. (tchd 9-1)

Chase Gate ran better than his finishing suggests and is another likely type for handicaps. (op 40-1)

Bold Adventure has been in form on the Flat and will appreciate a sounder surface. (op 12-1)

Jordaura, useful up to 1m on the Flat, was weak in the market and never got into it. His stamina is going to remain an issue. (op 25-1 tchd 20-1)

3496 LEICESTER ANNUAL MEMBERS NOVICES' CHASE (18 fncs) 2m 7f 110y
3:30 (3:30) (Class 3) 5-Y-0+ £4,553 (£1,337; £668; £333)

Form RPR

10-0 1 **Topsham Belle (IRE)**[27] 2959 7-10-6 117 AndrewTinkler 117+
(Nicky Henderson) *hld up in tch: nt fluent: reminders after 5th: drvn along 14th: outpcd 4 out: rallied appr last: rdn to ld fnl 100yds: styd on* **13/2**

F2-1 2 1/2 **Teddy's Reflection (IRE)**[52] 2513 8-11-5 122 HaddenFrost 127
(Henrietta Knight) *chsd ldr to 5th: wnt 2nd again 10th: led 2 out: rdn and hdd fnl 100yds: styd on same pce* **6/1**[3]

0-21 3 17 **Phidippides (IRE)**[50] 2588 7-11-5 0 PaulMoloney 117
(Evan Williams) *led: hit 11th: rdn and hdd 2 out: wknd last* **4/7**[1]

5P-2 4 25 **Sandynow (IRE)**[50] 2588 6-10-13 0 RichardJohnson 93
(Henry Daly) *prom: mstke 1st: chsd ldr 5th to 8th: nt fluent 9th and next: ev ch 4 out: rdn and wknd after next: j. slowly last: t.o* **11/2**[2]

6m 6.80s (2.80) **Going Correction** -0.05s/f (Good) **4** Ran SP% **106.7**
Speed ratings: **93,92,87,78**
CSF £33.46 TOTE £7.70; EX 18.40.
Owner Fortnum Racing **Bred** Ardobrien Stud Ltd **Trained** Upper Lambourn, Berks

FOCUS
An intriguing novice chase. The winner is rated in line with the best of her hurdles form.

NOTEBOOK
Topsham Belle(IRE), disappointing on her chasing debut, was expected to do well this season switched to fences and she got herself back on track with a battling victory. It didn't look promising as she was last and receiving reminders over a circuit from home, but as her stamina kicked in down the straight she came strongly and her light weight clearly made a difference. For a daughter of Presenting, she handles testing conditions very well and it would be a surprise were she not to add to this in 2011. (tchd 8-1)

Teddy's Reflection(IRE), successful off 115 at Ascot in November - his trainer's last winner - jumped on two out and looked likely to score, but he started to look vulnerable on the run-in and was eventually worn down. He'll probably come on for this and can win again over fences. (op 5-1)

Phidippides(IRE), off the mark in easy fashion when beating Sandynow over 2m4f at Ludlow latest, is held in very high regard by his trainer, but this ground would have been plenty soft enough for him and, following a notable blunder at the 11th, his confidence appeared to go at his fences. (tchd 4-6)

Sandynow(IRE) stopped quickly in the straight, but he looked a promising sort over hurdles and will probably come good once sent handicapping in time. (op 13-2 tchd 9-2)

3497 CHIEFTAIN H'CAP HURDLE (8 hdls) 2m
4:00 (4:00) (Class 4) (0-105,103) 4-Y-0+ £2,602 (£764; £382; £190)

Form RPR

1233 1 **Dormouse**[53] 2504 6-11-9 **100** (p) APMcCoy 102
(Anabel L M King) *a.p: rdn after 3 out: lft upsides next: rdr dropped whip after 2 out: led flat: jst hld on* **2/1**[1]

P661 2 nse **Bromhead (USA)**[6] 3397 5-11-4 **95** 7ex LeightonAspell 98
(Kevin Morgan) *hld up: hdwy appr 5th: lft in ld 2 out: hit last: rdn and hdd flat: styd on* **7/2**[2]

F520 3 9 **Whereveryougoigo (IRE)**[51] 2545 5-11-11 **102** (v[1]) RichardJohnson 96
(Peter Bowen) *prom: rdn appr 3 out: wkng whn lft 3rd next* **5/1**[3]

U-5F 4 8 **Istron Bay**[48] 2605 9-11-5 **96** JodieMogford 85+
(Richard Lee) *hld up: in rr whn mstke 4th: hit 2 out: n.d* **28/1**

0045 5 15 **Swiss Guard**[11] 3256 5-11-1 **99** MrMatthewBarber(7) 69
(Tim Vaughan) *led to 4th: rdn after next: stmbld appr 3 out: wknd bef next: t.o* **14/1**

/0-P 6 16 **True Blue Saga (IRE)**[11] 3256 6-11-2 **100** (t) MrEDavid(7) 54
(Tim Vaughan) *hld up: rdn appr 5th: wknd next: t.o* **50/1**

7 8 **Bell Harbour (IRE)**[558] 853 9-11-11 **102** PaulMoloney 48
(Evan Williams) *chsd ldrs tl wknd after 5th: t.o* **25/1**

4U-5 8 19 **Double Handful (GER)**[242] 315 5-11-12 **103** AidanColeman 30
(Venetia Williams) *chsd ldrs: rdn appr 3 out: wknd bef next: t.o* **15/2**

360- U **Rushwee (IRE)**[309] 4489 9-11-5 **103** MattCrawley(7) 105+
(Lucy Wadham) *chsd ldr 2nd tl led 4th: hit 3 out: 2 l ahd whn blnd and uns rdr 2 out* **15/2**

4m 2.80s (1.80) **Going Correction** +0.05s/f (Yiel) **9** Ran SP% **111.7**
Speed ratings (Par 105): **97,96,92,88,80 72,68,59,—**
toteswingers:1&2: 2.30, 2&3: £3.60, 1&3: £2.30. totesuper7: Win: Not won. Place: £183.10 CSF £9.15 CT £28.30 TOTE £3.60: £1.30, £1.10, £3.30; EX 10.70.
Owner Aiden Murphy **Bred** Deerfield Farm **Trained** Wilmcote, Warwicks

FOCUS
An ordinary handicap hurdle but the form makes sense. The first two are rated to form and the unseater was heading towards a personal best.

NOTEBOOK
Dormouse, whose rider dropped his whip soon after the second-last, did remarkably well to get up in a driving finish and make it a double on the day for Anabel King, who hadn't sent out a winner since last September. A horse who had previously reserved his best form for sounder surfaces, he had been comfortably held off this mark of late, but the market spoke for him and he toughed it out well. He shouldn't go up too much, but further progress will be required if he's to go in again. (op 7-2)

Bromhead(USA), last week's Southwell winner, gave his running again and the hood has clearly turned his fortunes around. He wasn't helped by the winner edging into him close home and should continue to give a good account. (tchd 10-3 and 4-1 in places)

Whereveryougoigo(IRE), backed beforehand in the first-time visor, made only limited headway and was fortunate to grab fourth. (op 8-1 tchd 9-2)

Istron Bay, a faller over fences latest, never got into it but this should have helped his confidence. (op 18-1)

Double Handful(GER) showed disappointingly little and has plenty of prove. (op 13-2 tchd 8-1)

Rushwee(IRE) was in front and apparently finding for pressure when he dived at the second-last and unseated his rider. (op 4-1)

T/Plt: £135.60 to a £1 stake. Pool of £68,761.52 - 370.01 winning tickets. T/Qpdt: £13.00 to a £1 stake. Pool £6,161.77 - 348.14 winning tickets. CR

2349 NEWCASTLE (L-H)
Tuesday, January 11

OFFICIAL GOING: Soft (good to soft in places) changing to soft (heavy in places) after race 1 (12.40)

The two fences going away from the stands were omitted in all chases due to low sun.

Wind: Breezy, half behind Weather: Cloudy, sunny spells

3498 MEYER TIMBER.COM MARES' NOVICES' HURDLE (9 hdls 2 omitted) 2m 4f
12:40 (12:41) (Class 4) 4-Y-0+ £2,016 (£592; £296; £147)

Form RPR

00-6 1 **Fentara**[248] 209 6-11-2 0 RobertWalford 99
(Tim Walford) *hld up in midfield: stdy hdwy appr 3 out: effrt and led last 75yds: kpt on wl* **33/1**

3-22 2 hd **Aneyeforaneye (IRE)**[48] 2616 5-10-11 0 JamesHalliday(5) 99
(Malcolm Jefferson) *led: hit 5th: blnd and hdd 3 out: rallied and disp ld last 100yds: kpt on: jst hld* **3/1**[1]

-613 **3** 2 **Along Came Rosie**[10] 3308 7-11-1 104 PaulGallagher(7) 106+
(Andrew Crook) *cl up: led 3 out: 5 l clr last: sn rdn: wknd and hdd last 75yds* **5/1**[3]

125- **4** 11 **Its Teescomponents (IRE)**[289] 4911 9-11-2 105 JamesReveley 87
(Keith Reveley) *sn stdd in midfield: outpcd 1/2-way: plugged on fr 3 out: nvr able to chal* **4/1**[2]

5430 **5** 1 1/4 **Mrs Eff**[28] 2939 5-11-2 0 BrianHughes 88
(Kate Walton) *hld up: hdwy and in tch bef 3 out: sn outpcd: no imp whn blnd last* **40/1**

2F **6** 8 **Sophonie (FR)**[49] 2598 5-11-2 110 GrahamLee 79
(Ferdy Murphy) *t.k.h: hld up: hdwy and prom 6th: rdn 3 out: wknd bef next* **3/1**[1]

7 17 **Etoile Ardente**[304] 7-10-13 0 HarryHaynes(3) 64
(James Ewart) *chsd ldr to 6th: rdn and sn struggling* **66/1**

-000 **8** 68 **Bach Street Girl (IRE)**[51] 2554 7-11-2 80 TomSiddall 2
(Lynn Siddall) *in tch to 4th: rdn and struggling fr next: t.o* **250/1**

5F **P** **Penny Bazaar**[8] 3358 4-9-10 0 HenryBrooke(7) —
(Dianne Sayer) *bhd: lost tch 4th: p.u bef next* **250/1**

000- **P** **Mocha (FR)**[275] 5144 6-10-9 0 NathanMoscrop(7) —
(James Ewart) *hld up: hdwy and in tch 6th: rdn and wknd bef next: t.o whn p.u after 2 out* **66/1**

0-05 **P** **Betty's Run**[217] 679 9-11-2 64 PaddyAspell —
(Lynn Siddall) *trckd ldrs tl wknd 4th: t.o whn p.u after 2 out* **250/1**

00-5 **P** **Izzy Bella**[95] 1758 5-11-2 0 WilsonRenwick —
(Sue Bradburne) *in tch tl wknd fr 4th: t.o whn p.u bef 3 out* **80/1**

3-03 **P** **Allbarkanobite**[48] 2616 6-11-2 0 RichieMcGrath —
(Kate Walton) *hld up: hdwy and in tch after 6th: rdn and wknd 3 out: t.o whn p.u bef last* **20/1**

43-2 **P** **Hannah Jacques (IRE)**[82] 1934 6-11-2 0 DougieCostello —
(Nicky Richards) *hld up in midfield: nt fluent 6th: sn rdn: wknd bef 3 out: t.o whn p.u after next* **8/1**

0- **P** **Lady Chorister**[301] 4669 6-10-11 0 PaulCallaghan(5) —
(Simon West) *nt fluent in rr: lost tch 4th: t.o whn p.u bef next* **200/1**

5m 33.3s (12.20) **Going Correction** +0.575s/f (Soft)
WFA 4 from 5yo+ 12lb **15** Ran SP% **113.8**
Speed ratings (Par 105): **98,97,97,92,92 89,82,55,—,— —,—,—,—**
toteswingers:1&2: £13.90, 2&3: £4.60, 1&3: £18.50 CSF £125.40 TOTE £38.30: £4.80, £1.30, £2.70; EX 224.20.
Owner Mrs E Dixon **Bred** Mrs A E And Miss S J Dixon **Trained** Sheriff Hutton, N Yorks

FOCUS
An ordinary contest. The winner stepped up on her bumper form.

NOTEBOOK
Fentara had shown limited ability over hurdles to date, but seemed to relish the step up in trip and handled the conditions to record her first victory. Having come under pressure down the back straight, she stayed on gamely for pressure between the last two hurdles and out-fought the runner-up after the last. This was her first start for 248 days, so there may be more improvement to come. (op 50-1)
Aneyeforaneye(IRE), runner-up on her previous three bumper starts, took the field along at a fair pace and again had to settle for second. She led turning into the straight, but was headed by the eventual third before rallying late on. She is sure to improve for the experience on this hurdles debut. (tchd 11-4 and 10-3 and 7-2 in a place)
Along Came Rosie looked the winner (traded 1.01 on Betfair) jumping the last, but tied up badly in the testing conditions to finish an extremely tired third. She ran with credit under her penalty, but will appreciate better ground.
Its Teescomponents(IRE) was having her first start for 289 days and is sure to improve for the run on this return to hurdles. (op 7-2)
Mrs Eff struggled to quicken when the pace lifted and stayed on at the one pace. (op 50-1)
Sophonie(FR) fell when going well at Sedgefield last time, but failed to improve on that here. Having travelled strongly off the pace, she failed to pick up and is becoming a little disappointing. Official explanation: trainer's rep said mare failed to stay (tchd 7-2)
Lady Chorister Official explanation: jockey said mare ran green

3499 STP CONSTRUCTION BEGINNERS' CHASE (14 fncs 4 omitted) 3m
1:10 (1:12) (Class 4) 5-Y-0+ **£2,439** (£716; £358; £178)

Form RPR

6-10 **1** **Captain Americo (IRE)**[52] 2523 9-11-0 125 NickScholfield 131+
(James Ewart) *mde all: blnd 7th: rdn clr after 3 out: hit next: kpt on run-in: all out* **11/10**[1]

4P/P **2** 2 1/4 **Negus De Beaumont (FR)**[47] 2641 10-11-0 115 GrahamLee 125
(Ferdy Murphy) *chsd ldng pair: reminders 9th: rdn and outpcd appr 4 out: styd on to take 2nd last: kpt on same pce* **33/1**

/21 **3** nk **Dove Hill (IRE)**[64] 2269 8-11-0 0 BrianHughes 125+
(Howard Johnson) *w wnr: rdn and hit 3 out: kpt on same pce run-in* **9/4**[2]

-44P **4** 78 **Almond Court (IRE)**[60] 2353 8-10-7 74 KennyJohnson 39
(Robert Johnson) *sn bhd: blnd 3rd: sme hdwy 8th: wknd next: lft t.o 5th bef 4 out: lft distant 3rd bef next* **200/1**

324/ **P** **Steady Tiger (IRE)**[628] 5168 9-11-0 0 FearghalDavis —
(Nicky Richards) *hld up: mstke 6th: hit 8th: wknd next: t.o whn p.u bef 4 out* **8/1**

11-0 **P** **Mister Marker (IRE)**[95] 1759 7-11-0 120 BrianHarding —
(Nicky Richards) *in tch: drvn 10th: sn wknd: poor 4th whn nt fluent next: p.u bef 3 out* **5/1**[3]

6m 43.7s (21.20) **Going Correction** +0.725s/f (Soft) **6** Ran SP% **109.6**
Speed ratings: **93,92,92,66,—** —
toteswingers:1&2: £4.30, 2&3: £4.70, 1&3: £1.80 CSF £25.32 TOTE £2.10: £1.10, £9.60; EX 28.50.
Owner M Tedham **Bred** Paddy Molloy **Trained** Langholm, Dumfries & G'way

FOCUS
A fair beginners' chase, ran at a steady gallop. The two cross fences were omitted due to the low-lying sun. The cosy winner can probably rate higher.

NOTEBOOK
Captain Americo(IRE) got off the mark over fences at the sixth attempt with a fine front-running display. He jumped neatly bar making a serious error at the fence in front of the stands, but recovered well to land a cosy success. A useful staying hurdler, he made good use of his previous chasing experience and connections are hopeful he will improve on this. (op 11-8 tchd 6-4)
Negus De Beaumont(FR) was pulled up on his first start for 33 months at Uttoxeter last time, but built on that to finish a credible second. Having come under pressure down the back straight, he stayed on nicely up the home straight, jumping boldly to nick second after the last. He may land a minor race. (op 22-1 tchd 40-1)
Dove Hill(IRE) won the second of his two hurdle starts and made an encouraging chasing debut. He jumped well in the main and should build on this and win a race of this nature. (op 2-1 tchd 15-8)
Almond Court(IRE) was held up and struggled to get competitive having made a bad mistake at the third fence. (op 100-1)
Steady Tiger(IRE), returning from a 628-day absence, was making his chasing debut and struggled before being pulled up. He will improve both for fitness and experience. (op 13-2 tchd 6-1)
Mister Marker(IRE) was having his second chase start and was again disappointing, being pulled up on this step up in trip. (op 13-2 tchd 6-1)

3500 SPORTPOOL.CO.UK H'CAP HURDLE (8 hdls 1 omitted) 2m
1:40 (1:41) (Class 4) (0-115,115) 4-Y-0+ **£2,016** (£592; £296; £147)

Form RPR

0306 **1** **The Magic Bishop**[74] 2080 6-10-4 98 JamesHalliday(5) 109+
(Malcolm Jefferson) *prom: ev ch whn blnd 3 out: led whn hit next: sn hrd pressed: styd on wl run-in* **18/1**

-P01 **2** 1/2 **Rolecarr (IRE)**[67] 2190 8-10-6 95 AdrianLane 103
(Ann Hamilton) *prom: effrt and ev ch 2 out: kpt on run-in: hld last 75yds* **15/2**[3]

35-2 **3** 7 **Malin Bay (IRE)**[244] 289 6-11-8 111 FearghalDavis 112
(Nicky Richards) *hld up: pushed along 4 out: hdwy bef next: kpt on run-in: nt gng pce of first two* **12/1**

63-1 **4** 1 **Viscount Rossini**[7] 2247 9-11-2 112 (b) PeterCarberry(7) 112
(Steve Gollings) *in tch: effrt bef 3 out: kpt on same pce fr next* **8/1**

15-0 **5** 3/4 **Agglestone Rock**[10] 1155 6-11-10 113 JamesReveley 112
(Philip Kirby) *hld up: hdwy bef 3 out: rdn and no imp fr next* **4/1**[1]

1500 **6** 4 **Barron Watlass (IRE)**[14] 3168 7-11-2 105 (p) BarryKeniry 101
(George Moore) *t.k.h: hld up: rdn bef 3 out: kpt on fr next: no imp* **11/1**

-062 **7** 7 **Bollin Ruth**[164] 727 9-10-8 100 EwanWhillans(3) 88
(Donald Whillans) *hld up: outpcd 4 out: sme late hdwy: nvr on terms* **33/1**

-5F2 **8** shd **Leith Walk (IRE)**[64] 2275 8-9-12 97 CallumWhillans(10) 85
(Donald Whillans) *hld up in midfield: effrt after 4 out: no imp fr next* **16/1**

P-06 **9** 1 1/2 **Cranky Corner**[63] 2300 7-11-7 110 TjadeCollier 97
(Sue Smith) *t.k.h: hld up: hdwy and in tch bef 3 out: wknd bef next* **11/1**

34-5 **10** 1/2 **Otto Quercus (FR)**[90] 1831 6-10-13 102 BrianHughes 89
(John Wade) *led tl hdd bef 2 out: sn rdn and wknd* **33/1**

F26- **11** 1 1/4 **Colour Clash**[296] 4752 8-11-12 115 WilsonRenwick 100
(Rose Dobbin) *in tch tl rdn and wknd bef 2 out* **16/1**

3-P0 **12** 3/4 **Quicuyo (GER)**[51] 2551 8-11-3 109 RyanMania(3) 93
(James Ewart) *cl up tl rdn and wknd fr 3 out* **6/1**[2]

1500 **13** 11 **Ardesia (IRE)**[143] 1328 7-10-2 91 BrianHarding 64
(Tina Jackson) *cl up: struggling after 4 out: sn lost pl* **28/1**

3-10 **14** 9 **Hi Dancer**[9] 2076 8-11-0 113 SeveBrumpton(10) 77
(Ben Haslam) *hld up in midfield: effrt after 4 out: wknd fr next* **25/1**

100- **15** 5 **Sendali (FR)**[76] 4578 7-11-5 108 DenisO'Regan 67
(James Bethell) *hld up: rdn bef 3 out: nvr on terms* **18/1**

3-F5 **16** 3 3/4 **Luso's Lad (IRE)**[73] 2092 7-11-9 115 JamesO'Farrell(3) 70
(Howard Johnson) *hld up: pushed along bef 3 out: sn btn* **28/1**

PP0 **P** **Bob's Dream (IRE)**[51] 2551 9-11-7 110 (t) CampbellGillies —
(William Amos) *in tch tl wknd bef 3 out: t.o whn p.u bef next* **50/1**

4m 17.2s (7.20) **Going Correction** +0.575s/f (Soft) **17** Ran SP% **122.4**
Speed ratings (Par 105): **105,104,101,100,100 98,94,94,94,93 93,92,87,82,80 78,—**
toteswingers:1&2: £39.10, 2&3: £7.90, 1&3: £46.60 CSF £138.72 CT £1715.21 TOTE £23.50: £5.20, £1.40, £2.70, £2.10; EX 251.00.
Owner P Nelson **Bred** Peter Nelson **Trained** Norton, N Yorks

FOCUS
A wide-open looking handicap hurdle. The form is sound with the winner rated back to the level of his Wetherby second.

NOTEBOOK
The Magic Bishop, a running-on sixth at Wetherby latest, improved on that effort to run out a game winner. Tracking the pace, he handled the testing conditions best of all and out-fought the runner-up on the run-in to record his first career success. (op 20-1)
Rolecarr(IRE), up 13lb for a wide-margin win at Hexham on his last start, ran another solid race, just failing to match the winner in the closing stages. He relishes heavy conditions and continues to improve, although the handicapper will have his say. (op 9-1 tchd 10-1)
Malin Bay(IRE) was returning from a 244-day layoff and ran a race full of promise on just his fourth start over hurdles. He is sure to improve for the outing and remains of interest in this grade.
Viscount Rossini, a winner at Market Rasen on his last hurdle start, had a 7lb penalty for that victory and struggled to match the front three. He may struggle off this mark, but remains a consistent type. (op 10-1)
Agglestone Rock, rated 22lb higher over fences, was held up and struggled to land a blow back over hurdles, staying on at the one pace. He looks on a decent mark, but again disappointed and a return to chasing looks likely. (op 7-2 tchd 9-2)
Quicuyo(GER) ran well for a long way before failing to pick up turning for home. (op 7-1 tchd 11-2)

3501 S V RUTTER H'CAP CHASE (14 fncs 4 omitted) 3m
2:10 (2:10) (Class 4) (0-105,104) 5-Y-0+ **£2,439** (£716; £358; £178)

Form RPR

P-33 **1** **Star Player (IRE)**[64] 2274 9-11-12 104 (t) DenisO'Regan 120
(Chris Grant) *w ldrs: led 5th: mde rest jumping soundly: styd on gamely fr 2 out* **9/2**[1]

F **2** 3 **Arctic Mick (IRE)**[48] 2622 10-11-5 97 AELynch 110
(Michael O'Hare, Ire) *hld up in rr: hdwy to trck ldrs 8th: wnt 2nd 4 out: styd on same pce between last 2* **7/1**[3]

2045 **3** 15 **Manoubi**[8] 3363 12-10-7 85 JamesReveley 85
(Martin Todhunter) *chsd ldrs: wnt 2nd 10th: stmbld landing next: wknd fr 3 out* **9/2**[1]

2P-2 **4** 11 **Seeking Power (IRE)**[67] 2193 10-10-10 95 MissLAlexander(7) 85
(N W Alexander) *lost pl and mstke 3rd: drvn 8th: outpcd next: kpt on fr 4 out: nvr a factor* **9/2**[1]

4P-0 **5** 6 **Sammy Spiderman**[64] 2274 8-11-7 99 BrianHarding 82
(Alistair Whillans) *hld up: hdwy 8th: lost pl and hit 10th* **9/1**

-355 **P** **Master Sebastian**[64] 2274 12-11-6 98 PeterBuchanan —
(Lucinda Russell) *mde most to 5th: wknd after 9th: sn bhd: t.o whn p.u bef 4 out* **8/1**

664U **P** **Shrewd Investor (IRE)**[27] 2953 11-11-7 99 (p) RobertWalford —
(Henry Hogarth) *w ldrs: drvn 9th: sn lost pl and bhd: t.o whn p.u bef 4 out* **6/1**[2]

023- **P** **Shelomoh (IRE)**[283] 4984 10-11-9 101 PaddyAspell —
(James Turner) *chsd ldrs: drvn 9th: sn wknd: t.o 6th whn p.u bef 2 out* **14/1**

6m 36.9s (14.40) **Going Correction** +0.725s/f (Soft) **8** Ran SP% **109.1**
Speed ratings: **105,104,99,95,93** —,—,—
toteswingers:1&2: £4.40, 2&3: £9.00, 1&3: £6.50 CSF £32.21 CT £133.97 TOTE £5.30: £2.50, £1.10, £2.40; EX 30.70.
Owner Steve Wilson **Bred** Mrs Hugh Baird **Trained** Newton Bewley, Co Durham

FOCUS
A competitive handicap chase. There may be more to come from the winner who was rated 130 at his peak.

NOTEBOOK
Star Player(IRE), third at Carlisle latest, put in a fine round of jumping to run out a clear-cut winner. After grabbing the lead with a circuit to go, his jockey gradually wound it up from the front to score a hard-fought win. The gelding looks to have recovered from the injury that kept him out for 21 months and may have more to come. (op 4-1)
Arctic Mick(IRE), a faller in two of his five previous chases, ran a solid race. Held up, he travelled strongly before struggling to see out the trip in the conditions. He may appreciate a drop in trip, but remains a maiden and may need a drop in the weights. (tchd 13-2)
Manoubi, fifth at Ayr over hurdles on his last start, ran a fair race back over fences. Held up towards the rear, he chased the leader before a mistake four out ended his chances. He may need a drop in class. (op 6-1)
Seeking Power(IRE) blundered at the third fence and struggled to get competitive thereafter. He stayed on one-paced to claim fourth. (op 5-1)
Sammy Spiderman was unable to land a blow. (op 8-1 tchd 10-1)

3502 ESH GROUP H'CAP HURDLE (11 hdls 2 omitted) 2m 6f
2:40 (2:42) (Class 4) (0-105,105) 4-Y-0+ **£2,016** (£592; £296; £147)

Form | | | | RPR
3-51 **1** | | **Too Cool To Fool (IRE)**[9] 3336 8-11-0 **93** 7ex. GrahamLee | 96
(Jim Goldie) *prom: hit 3rd: effrt and drvn 2 out: sn ev ch: styd on u.p to ld nr fin* **4/1**[1]
-003 **2** ¾ **Mister Pete (IRE)**[32] 2448 8-11-2 **100** (p) AlexanderVoy(5) 102
(Chris Grant) *led: rdn 2 out: sn hrd pressed: kpt on run-in: hdd nr fin* **12/1**
1-10 **3** 5 **Wor Rom (IRE)**[28] 2941 7-10-4 **90** (p) MrNHalley(7) 87
(Elliott Cooper) *prom: effrt bef 3 out: kpt on same pce fr next* **16/1**
U3-4 **4** 3 **What A Steel (IRE)**[51] 2545 7-10-12 **94** EwanWhillans(3) 89
(Alistair Whillans) *hld up: hdwy and prom bef 2 out: no ex fr last* **6/1**[3]
000- **5** 32 **Bubbly Breeze (IRE)**[265] 5311 6-10-11 **90** BrianHarding 52
(Pauline Robson) *t.k.h: in tch tl rdn and wknd fr 3 out* **33/1**
3-62 **6** 2½ **Charlie Bucket**[51] 2549 8-11-2 **105** CallumWhillans(10) 65
(Donald Whillans) *hld up: rdn 7th: nvr on terms* **8/1**
P-F **7** 3¾ **Thatlldoforme**[51] 2549 9-11-5 **98** DenisO'Regan 54
(Alistair Whillans) *hld up: hdwy and in tch bef 3 out: sn rdn and wknd* **17/2**
-433 **8** 38 **Lukey Luke**[64] 2271 8-10-1 **80** PaddyAspell —
(James Turner) *in tch tl rdn and wknd bef 3 out* **9/2**[2]
63-5 **9** 3¼ **Quacity (FR)**[102] 1664 7-11-12 **105** PeterBuchanan 20
(Lucinda Russell) *hld up: hdwy and prom 7th: wknd after next* **12/1**
4-06 **10** 3½ **Young Buddy**[55] 2450 6-10-11 **95** (p) JamesHalliday(5) 6
(Malcolm Jefferson) *chsd ldrs: nt fluent 6th: rdn and wknd after 4 out* **10/1**
0540 **11** 11 **Toulouse Express (IRE)**[28] 2937 12-11-1 **94** KennyJohnson —
(Robert Johnson) *bhd: struggling after 6th: nvr on terms* **100/1**
000- **12** 32 **Qbuster (IRE)**[306] 4534 10-11-7 **100** (t) NickScholfield —
(Sharon Watt) *hld up: stdy hdwy 6th: wknd fr 4 out* **22/1**
2-U3 **P** **Cosmetic**[49] 2603 6-10-0 **79** oh1 WilsonRenwick —
(Howard Johnson) *pressed ldr: hit 4th: lost 2nd 4 out: sn wknd: t.o whn p.u next* **14/1**
-650 **P** **Goffa Crag**[51] 2552 7-11-10 **103** FearghalDavis —
(Nicky Richards) *bhd: struggling bef 7th: t.o whn p.u bef 3 out* **33/1**
6m 4.00s (28.00) **Going Correction** +0.575s/f (Soft) 14 Ran SP% **122.3**
Speed ratings (Par 105): **72,71,69,68,57 56,54,41,39,38 34,23,—,—**
toteswingers:1&2 £9.30, 2&3: £44.00, 1&3: £10.20 CSF £50.98 CT £712.89 TOTE £4.30: £2.10, £4.30, £6.50; EX 52.00.
Owner J S Goldie **Bred** Simon Young **Trained** Uplawmoor, E Renfrews

FOCUS
A moderate handicap hurdle produced a thrilling finish, with the first four pulling well clear. Ordinary form with another step forward from the winner.

NOTEBOOK
Too Cool To Fool(IRE) returned from a break to bounce back to form at Ayr latest (3m), and followed up in brave fashion under a 7lb penalty. Dropping back in trip, he travelled powerfully before joining the long-time leader at the last and showing a willing attitude to hold off the runner-up. He is clearly in good heart. (op 6-1 tchd 13-2 in a place)
Mister Pete(IRE), third at Hexham in November on his last jumps start, led the field coming down to the last and just failed to match the winner on the run-in. He deserves a lot of credit and this was a game effort, although the handicapper will have his say. (op 8-1)
Wor Rom(IRE) had the cheekpieces back on and built on his reappearance at Catterick to run a solid race, staying on strongly for pressure without threatening the front two. A step back up in trip looks likely. (op 14-1)
What A Steel(IRE) was held up on this step up in trip and having made steady headway through the field, he was never dangerous. He may prefer a drop back in distance, but ran a fair race. (op 8-1)
Lukey Luke was disappointing. Held up, he never threatened. Official explanation: trainer said gelding was unsuited by the soft (heavy in places) ground (op 7-1)

3503 FREEBETTING.CO.UK H'CAP CHASE (12 fncs 4 omitted) 2m 4f
3:10 (3:13) (Class 5) (0-95,92) 5-Y-0+ **£1,593** (£467; £233; £116)

Form | | | | RPR
13-3 **1** **Do It For Dalkey**[67] 2189 9-11-6 **86** PeterBuchanan 98+
(Lucinda Russell) *hld up: wnt prom 5th: chsd ldr appr next: led appr 4 out: styd on to draw clr between last 2* **5/2**[1]
P-P2 **2** 6 **Jeringa**[49] 2602 12-11-12 **92** (b) BrianHughes 96
(John Wade) *led to 3rd: led 7th: hdd appr 4 out: one pce fr 2 out* **11/2**[3]
2P-5 **3** ½ **Paddys Unyoke (IRE)**[67] 2189 10-11-1 **88** GaryRutherford(7) 94
(Stuart Coltherd) *chsd ldrs: reminders 9th: outpcd and mstke 4 out: kpt on one pce fr 2 out* **20/1**
-50P **4** 4½ **Apache Brave (IRE)**[63] 2301 8-10-0 **66** oh7 (b) RobertWalford 65
(Henry Hogarth) *in rr: wnt prom 8th: drvn 10th: sn outpcd: kpt on fr 2 out: wnt modest 4th last* **28/1**
-3P2 **5** 5 **Coldwells (IRE)**[8] 3360 11-11-4 **84** JamesReveley 82
(Martin Todhunter) *w ldrs: wknd fr 3 out* **3/1**[2]
F-04 **6** 26 **Iris's Flyer**[28] 2942 9-11-4 **84** (p) PaddyAspell 52
(Brian Rothwell) *hld up towards rr: sme hdwy 8th: drvn 10th: lost pl bef next: sn bhd* **8/1**
1252 **U** **Stolen Light (IRE)**[65] 2250 10-11-12 **92** (b) FearghalDavis —
(Andrew Crook) *prom: lost pl and 6th whn blnd and uns rdr 4 out* **10/1**
0536 **U** **Ice Image (IRE)**[138] 1378 9-11-0 **87** (t) AlistairFindlay(7) 86
(George Charlton) *in rr: wnt prom 5th: lost pl 8th: hdwy 4 out: 4th and one pce whn blnd and uns rdr 2 out* **8/1**
5m 48.5s (21.30) **Going Correction** +0.725s/f (Soft) 8 Ran SP% **108.5**
Speed ratings: **86,83,83,81,79 69,—,—**
toteswingers:1&2: £2.80, 2&3: £13.60, 1&3: £9.20 CSF £15.16 CT £190.08 TOTE £2.70: £2.10, £1.60, £5.70; EX 16.40.
Owner G S Brown **Bred** G Brown **Trained** Arlary, Perth & Kinross

FOCUS
A modest handicap chase. The winner was up 10lb on his best hurdles form and should go on to rate higher.

NOTEBOOK
Do It For Dalkey, a beaten favourite when third at Hexham on his seasonal debut, improved on that effort to land a cosy victory. Jumping beautifully throughout, he travelled kindly and simply out-jumped his rivals down the straight. This was just his second chase start and there looks to be plenty of further improvement to come. (tchd 11-4)
Jeringa second off this mark over further at Sedgefield latest, took the field along early and stayed on one-paced to hold second. He handled the drop in trip well, but would be suited by a return to further. (op 7-1 tchd 5-1)
Paddys Unyoke(IRE) showed improved form. After tracking the leaders, he was unable to match the winner before staying on at the same pace. (tchd 22-1)
Apache Brave(IRE) was held up early and never threatened from 7lb out of the handicap. (op 25-1)
Coldwells(IRE), second off this mark at Ayr earlier this month, proved very disappointing. Outpaced turning for home, she weakened badly and this was not her true running. Better ground may help her.
Ice Image(IRE) looked held in fourth when unseating his rider at the second-last. (op 12-1)

3504 E.B.F./DBS MARES' STANDARD OPEN NATIONAL HUNT FLAT RACE (QUALIFIER) 2m
3:40 (3:41) (Class 6) 4-7-Y-O **£1,301** (£382; £191; £95)

Form | | | | RPR
1 **1** **Zhakiera Spirit**[48] 2616 5-11-10 0 BrianHughes 118+
(Howard Johnson) *t.k.h: in tch: smooth hdwy to ld over 4f out: qcknd clr fr over 2f out: v easily* **4/5**[1]
4 **2** 34 **Serenitatis (IRE)**[36] 2825 5-11-3 0 RichieMcGrath 72
(Tim Easterby) *cl up: led briefly 5f out: no ch w wnr fr over 2f out* **12/1**
3 ¾ **Looby Magoodle** 5-10-12 0 BrianToomey(5) 71
(Richard Fahey) *hld up: pushed along 6f out: plugged on same pce fr 3f out* **6/1**[3]
0-5 **4** 1¼ **Cool Water**[230] 474 6-11-3 0 GrahamLee 70
(John Wade) *t.k.h: hld up: drvn and outpcd over 4f out: n.d after* **33/1**
0 **5** 22 **Heather Glen (IRE)**[68] 2167 5-11-3 0 TjadeCollier 48
(Sue Smith) *trckd ldrs tl rdn and wknd fr over 4f out* **18/1**
0 **6** 10 **Fashion Stakes**[26] 2987 5-11-3 0 CampbellGillies 38
(Chris Grant) *prom: lost pl after 6f: drvn whn stmbld bdly over 5f out: no ch after* **66/1**
7 8 **High Expectation** 4-10-5 0 NickScholfield 18
(James Ewart) *hld up: hdwy on outside 1/2-way: rdn and wknd fr over 3f out* **3/1**[2]
0 **8** 10 **A Beat So Far**[53] 2511 5-11-3 0 KennyJohnson 20
(Robert Johnson) *led to 5f out: sn rdn and btn* **80/1**
0 **9** 28 **Mordetta Road**[48] 2616 6-11-3 0 PaddyAspell —
(James Turner) *cl up: lost pl over 6f out: lost tch fnl 4f* **66/1**
4m 12.4s (8.00) **Going Correction** +0.575s/f (Soft)
WFA 4 from 5yo+ 11lb 9 Ran SP% **115.0**
Speed ratings: **103,86,85,85,74 69,65,60,46**
totswingers:1&2: £3.70, 2&3: £5.60, 1&3: £2.30 CSF £12.40 TOTE £2.50: £1.10, £3.90, £1.10; EX 9.50.
Owner Andrea & Graham Wylie **Bred** Pleasure Palace Racing **Trained** Billy Row, Co Durham

FOCUS
Probably just an ordinary contest overall but a very impressive winner who looks well up to the standard of a typical winner of Sandown's Listed mares' bumper.

NOTEBOOK
Zhakiera Spirit made a winning debut at Wetherby in November, and made it two from two with an effortless success. Travelling ominously she cruised to the front and put the race to bed, without her rider ever moving a muscle. This was an impressive performance under a penalty, and while it is difficult to know what she has beaten, she looks a classy mare. Connections are targeting the Listed mares' bumper at Sandown for this sister to the very useful hurdler Megastar. (op 4-6 tchd 5-6)
Serenitatis(IRE), fourth on the AW on her debut at Southwell, showed some ability, knuckling down to win the race for second.
Looby Magoodle, a half-sister to bumper winner Barnie Magoogle, made a fair debut just losing out in her battle to finish second. She will improve for the experience. (op 5-1)
Cool Water hinted at some ability in two bumper start to date and probably ran her race here. (op 28-1)
High Expectation, well supported in the market, was disappointing and should improve for the run. Her pedigree suggests she will be better over obstacles. (op 5-1)
T/Jkpt: Not won. T/Plt: £89.90 to a £1 stake. Pool of £69,931.05 - 567.78 winning tickets. T/Qpdt: £26.90 to a £1 stake. Pool of £6,414.96 - 176.18 winning tickets. RY

DONCASTER (L-H)
Wednesday, January 12

OFFICIAL GOING: Good (8.4)
The third-last fence was omitted in both chases - ground under repair.
Wind: moderate 1/2 against Weather: fine

3505 YORKSHIRE RADIO SUPPORTS YORKSHIRE RACING NOVICES' HURDLE (DIV I) (10 hdls) 2m 3f 110y
12:35 (12:35) (Class 4) 4-Y-0+ **£2,055** (£599; £299)

Form | | | | RPR
0-62 **1** **Jack The Gent (IRE)**[15] 3167 7-11-6 100 BarryKeniry 124
(George Moore) *led 1st: narrowly hdd 3 out: styd on to ld last 150yds: all out* **33/1**
2 hd **Loose Preformer (IRE)**[284] 5-11-6 0 BarryGeraghty 124
(Nicky Henderson) *chsd ldrs: reminders after 7th: narrow ld 3 out: hdd run-in: kpt on: no ex nr fin* **7/4**[2]
1-14 **3** 1¾ **Muldoon's Picnic (IRE)**[14] 3196 5-11-12 128 JasonMaguire 129
(Kim Bailey) *hld up in mid-div: hdwy 6th: sn trcking ldrs: rdn 3 out: nt fluent next: styd on same pce run-in* **11/8**[1]
3452 **4** 14 **Natural Spring**[15] 3168 6-10-13 0 DenisO'Regan 104+
(Suzy Smith) *chsd ldrs: wknd appr 2 out* **8/1**[3]
5 7 **Moscow Chancer (IRE)**[311] 5-11-6 0 PaddyBrennan 104
(Tom George) *chsd ldrs: effrt 3 out: hung bdly rt and wknd between last 2* **40/1**
3253 **6** 7 **Dontupsettherhythm (IRE)**[21] 3089 6-11-3 0 AdamPogson(3) 97
(Charles Pogson) *j.rt: led to 1st: chsd ldrs: wknd fr 3 out* **100/1**
56B **7** 4 **Cygnet**[29] 2939 5-11-6 115 AdrianLane 94
(Donald McCain) *hld up in rr: hdwy 7th: 6th and btn whn mstke 2 out* **14/1**
0F-P **8** 19 **No Tears (IRE)**[81] 1963 8-11-6 0 RobertThornton 76
(Alan King) *hld up in rr: sme hdwy 7th: wknd appr next* **50/1**
0405 **9** 3 **Beau D'Argent**[15] 3167 5-10-13 0 GrahamLee 66
(Ferdy Murphy) *hld up in rr: sme hdwy 7th: nvr nr ldrs* **150/1**
0-00 **10** 10 **Jaques Vert (FR)**[54] 2509 5-11-6 0 RichieMcGrath 64
(Robert Wylie) *hld up in rr: hdwy 5th: lost pl after 7th* **100/1**

40 **11** *1 ¾* **Piroulet (FR)**[11] 3296 5-11-6 0 .... RichardJohnson 63
(Philip Hobbs) *chsd ldrs: lost pl and heavily eased after 7th* **12/1**
/0-0 **12** *5* **Froggy Lane**[67] 2202 8-11-6 0 .... JimmyMcCarthy 58
(Simon West) *chsd ldrs: wknd 6th: bhd whn blnd 3 out* **200/1**
5-10 **13** *4* **Ben Cee Pee M (IRE)**[92] 1812 6-11-6 0 .... LeightonAspell 55
(Oliver Sherwood) *a in rr: bhd fr 7th* **50/1**
0 **14** *79* **Master Conor (IRE)**[12] 3259 5-11-6 0 .... RobertWalford —
(Henry Hogarth) *in rr and drvn 4th: t.o 7th: eventually completed* **150/1**

4m 40.3s (-11.00) **Going Correction** -0.35s/f (Good) course record **14** Ran SP% **117.0**
Speed ratings (Par 105): **108,107,107,101,98 96,94,86,85,81 80,78,77,45**
toteswingers:1&2:£14.90, 1&3:£10.60, 2&3:£1.50 CSF £92.25 TOTE £27.70: £4.50, £1.30, £1.10; EX 160.40.
Owner J B Wallwin **Bred** P O'Connor **Trained** Middleham Moor, N Yorks

FOCUS
The ground was described as "dead" and "nearer good to soft than good" by jockeys in the first, but the time was 5.3sec outside the RP standard so conditions cannot have been too testing. The first three finished clear in what looked a fair novice hurdle. The form looks quite solid.

NOTEBOOK
Jack The Gent(IRE) has reportedly had his breathing looked into and he ran an improved race when bustling up the warm favourite Priceless Art in a jumpers' bumper at Southwell, the pair well clear. He made a lot of the running on this return to hurdles and battled on willingly to force his way back in front on the run-in. This big, scopey sort looks a real chasing type for next season. (tchd 28-1)
Loose Preformer(IRE), bought for £80,000 after winning a maiden point in April, is out of an unraced half-sister to his connections' high-class jumper Bacchanal. He took a narrow lead three from home, but could never shake off the more experienced winner and just missed out. A slight rise in trip will help and he should not be long in winning a novice hurdle. (tchd 15-8)
Muldoon's Picnic(IRE) was the form pick after his fourth behind very useful pair Rock On Ruby and Megastar at Newbury. The ground should have suited and he ran his race, but under his penalty he was just held by the first two over the final two flights. (op 6-4)
Natural Spring, in common with the winner, finished second in a Southwell jumpers' bumper recently. She stayed on without posing a threat and has the ability to win a novice hurdle, perhaps over a little further against her own sex. (op 10-1)
Moscow Chancer(IRE) showed ability on his debut in an Irish point in the spring and ran with reasonable promise on this rules debut, only weakening going to the second-last then hanging away from the stick. (op 66-1)
Dontupsettherhythm(IRE) ran creditably again on this return to hurdling.
Cygnet, who showed improvement latest prior to being brought down at the final flight, ran his race back in seventh and looks the type for handicaps.
Piroulet(FR) was disappointing, failing to pick up when brought under pressure, and he could have been remembering his unfortunate experience at Exeter. (op 11-1)

3506 YORKSHIRE RADIO SUPPORTS YORKSHIRE RACING NOVICES' HURDLE (DIV II) (10 hdls) 2m 3f 110y
1:05 (1:07) (Class 4) 4-Y-O+ **£2,055** (£599; £299)

Form RPR
1 **Drive Time (USA)**[547] 6-11-6 0 .... BrianHughes 126+
(Howard Johnson) *w ldrs: n.m.r and swtchd lft appr 3 out: hit 2 out: led appr last: styd on wl last 100yds* **7/1**
4 **2** *3 ¾* **Brunswick Gold (IRE)**[59] 2403 6-11-6 0 .... APMcCoy 122+
(Steve Gollings) *led 2nd: hdd appr last: styd on same pce run-in* **10/3**[2]
4-1 **3** *2* **Thanks For Coming**[244] 304 5-11-6 0 .... BarryGeraghty 119
(Nicky Henderson) *trckd ldrs: t.k.h: chal 3 out: styd on same pce between last 2* **5/1**[3]
00-5 **4** *13* **The Laodicean**[72] 2123 5-11-6 0 .... RobertThornton 107
(Alan King) *hld up in rr: hdwy 7th: chsng ldrs next: wknd between last 2* **11/2**
30-6 **5** *2 ½* **Mister Wall Street (FR)**[77] 2038 6-11-6 107 .... GrahamLee 106
(Ferdy Murphy) *hld up towards rr: hdwy 7th: sn chsng ldrs: 5th and wkng whn mstke 2 out* **16/1**
6 *4 ½* **Mizen Station (IRE)**[66] 6-11-6 0 .... LeightonAspell 103
(Oliver Sherwood) *prom: wknd appr 2 out* **16/1**
60 **7** *1 ¾* **Get Ready To Go (IRE)**[14] 3200 7-11-6 0 .... DenisO'Regan 100
(Neil King) *prom: outpcd appr 3 out: grad wknd* **100/1**
5 **8** *nk* **Bollin Felix**[52] 2540 7-11-6 0 .... RichieMcGrath 102
(Tim Easterby) *nt fluent: chsd ldrs: rdn appr 3 out: sn wknd* **9/4**[1]
060 **9** *36* **A Patchy Dancer (IRE)**[29] 2939 6-11-6 0 .... HenryOliver 67
(Sue Smith) *prom: lost pl and mstke 5th: sn bhd: sme hdwy appr 3 out: nt a factor* **100/1**
00 **10** *14* **Mind Shower (IRE)**[60] 2375 5-11-6 0 .... PaddyAspell 54
(Robert Wylie) *t.k.h in midfield: wknd after 7th: sn bhd* **200/1**
P-05 **11** *15* **Northwold**[21] 3089 7-11-6 0 .... JimmyMcCarthy 40
(Christopher Kellett) *led to 2nd: lost pl 6th: sn bhd* **200/1**
12 *65* **Sendefaa (IRE)**[830] 6-10-13 0 .... DavidEngland —
(Michael Gates) *t.k.h in rr: bhd fr 7th: t.o next* **150/1**
0-0 **P** **Escape Exit**[28] 2957 6-11-6 0 .... PaddyBrennan —
(Tom George) *in rr: hit 6th: t.o whn p.u bef 3 out* **100/1**
10 **P** **Vicpol (ITY)**[67] 2215 5-11-6 0 .... DougieCostello —
(Tom Gretton) *in rr: drvn 5th: sn bhd: t.o whn p.u bef 3 out* **33/1**

4m 41.0s (-10.30) **Going Correction** -0.35s/f (Good) course record **14** Ran SP% **117.7**
Speed ratings (Par 105): **106,104,103,98,97 95,95,94,80,74 68,42,—,—**
toteswingers:1&2:£5.50, 1&3:£6.60, 2&3:£4.60 CSF £30.70 TOTE £8.90: £2.00, £1.50, £2.60; EX 42.70.
Owner Andrea & Graham Wylie **Bred** Centennial Farms Mgmt Co , Inc **Trained** Billy Row, Co Durham
■ Stewards' Enquiry : A P McCoy caution: careless riding.

FOCUS
Division two was run in a time 0.7sec slower than the first division and looks of a similar standard. The winner can rate higher on his Flat form.

NOTEBOOK
Drive Time(USA) won both his starts over 1m6f on the Flat in 2009 for Jim Bolger, beating the Group 1-placed Red Rock Canyon in the second of them, but has reportedly had his share of problems since coming over from Ireland. Never far from the pace and travelling best on this debut over hurdles, he asserted after a good leap at the final flight. He looks a decent recruit and can progress to better things in this sphere. (op 11-2 tchd 5-1)
Brunswick Gold(IRE) ran a big race from the front, grabbing the stands' rail in the straight but just lacking the pace of the winner from the last. Likely to come on for the run, he should win a similar race and will make a chaser further down the line. (op 9-2)
Thanks For Coming ♦, winner of a modest Ludlow bumper back in May, ran pleasingly on this first try over hurdles, keeping on up the run-in after the first two had pulled away from him. He still showed signs of inexperience and should have learned plenty from the run. (op 4-1 tchd 6-1)
The Laodicean was well held by the principals in the end, but this still looked a step up on his one previous try over hurdles. (op 7-1)
Mister Wall Street(FR) appeared to give his running back in fifth and now might be the time to try him in a handicap. (op 20-1)
Mizen Station(IRE) changed hands for a reported £30,000 after a winning debut between the flags in Ireland two months ago. On what he showed here he will be suited by a return to 3m. (op 14-1)
Get Ready To Go(IRE) showed nothing in a pair of bumpers last season but was a winning pointer in Ireland and he was by no means discredited on this hurdles debut.
Bollin Felix promised to appreciate this rise in trip but dropped away disappointingly from the home turn. Still missing the headgear he wore regularly on the Flat, he does not look the most athletic of jumpers. (op 5-2)

3507 ATTEYS SOLICITORS JUVENILE HURDLE (8 hdls) 2m 110y
1:40 (1:41) (Class 4) 4-Y-O **£2,397** (£698; £349)

Form RPR
1 **1** **Local Hero (GER)**[49] 2614 4-11-5 0 .... APMcCoy 125+
(Steve Gollings) *trckd ldrs: wnt 2nd on bit appr 3 out: sltly hmpd 2 out: led sn after 2 out: easily* **1/4**[1]
30 **2** *2 ¾* **Franklino (FR)**[55] 2466 4-10-12 0 .... RobertThornton 105
(Alan King) *hld up: hdwy to trck ldrs appr 3 out: tk 2nd towards fin: no ch w wnr* **5/1**[2]
3 *nk* **Eltheeb**[91] 4-10-12 0 .... BarryKeniry 105
(George Moore) *trckd ldrs: led after 4th: j.lft 2 out: sn hdd: j.lft last: lost 2nd nr fin* **12/1**[3]
4 *39* **Aim'Ees Star**[48] 4-9-12 0 .... MrMMarris(7) 59
(John Harris) *t.k.h in last: bhd fr 5th: t.o whn mstke last* **250/1**
5 *48* **Minortransgression (USA)**[6] 4-10-12 0 ....(t) JasonMaguire 18
(David Evans) *w ldr: rdn after 5th: sn lost pl and bhd: t.o 2 out* **28/1**
F **Clear Alternative (IRE)**[135] 4-10-5 0 .... MrJBanks(7) —
(Terry Clement) *reluctant ldr: led after 4th: 4th and wkng whn fell heavily 3 out* **100/1**

4m 12.1s (7.40) **Going Correction** -0.35s/f (Good) **6** Ran SP% **109.2**
Speed ratings: **69,67,67,49,26** —
toteswingers:1&2:£1.02, 1&3:£1.20, 2&3:£1.50 CSF £1.87 TOTE £1.50: £1.10, £1.40; EX 2.00.
Owner P J Martin **Bred** Gestut Evershorst **Trained** Scamblesby, Lincs

FOCUS
The horses stood still for several seconds after the tapes rose and the resultant pace was very steady, so this is muddling form. The time, for what it's worth, was 18secs outside the standard. The first three finished a long way clear. The winner was value for further and looks a decent novice.

NOTEBOOK
Local Hero(GER) made it two from two over hurdles with a very comfortable success and was value for a considerably wider margin of victory, but what he actually achieved is questionable. He jumped well again, bar diving at the second-last when looming upsides the leader, and was able to coast home on the run-in. With further progress almost guaranteed, he could be a Cheltenham horse, and the Triumph and the Fred Winter are both possibilities, but he'll be given more experience before his trainer decides on which route to take with him. He is set to go to Cheltenham for the Finesse Hurdle at the end of the month (op 2-7 tchd 3-10 and 1-3 in a place)
Franklino(FR) sweated up in the preliminaries, as he had first time over hurdles at Aintree. He could not go with the first two when they started racing in the straight, but did pick up well after the last to run past the third. A truer gallop will suit and he is eligible for handicaps after this. (op 4-1)
Eltheeb, a winner over 1m2f for John Dunlop on the Flat, is currently rated 69 at that game. Sent on at halfway, he quickened things up once into the straight but the favourite was much too strong for him from the second-last. He jumped out to the left more than once. (op 14-1)
Aim'Ees Star was a poor maiden plater on the Flat and will have stamina problems if persevered with over hurdles. (op 200-1)
Minortransgression(USA) Official explanation: jockey said and confirmed by trainer's rep that gelding had a breathing problem

3508 1STSECURITYSOLUTIONS.CO.UK NOVICES' CHASE (17 fncs 1 omitted) 3m
2:15 (2:17) (Class 3) 5-Y-O+ **£4,553** (£1,337; £668; £333)

Form RPR
-213 **1** **Adams Island (IRE)**[27] 2979 7-10-12 133 ....(p) AodhaganConlon(7) 142+
(Rebecca Curtis) *mde all: j. soundly: drvn 3 l ahd last: edgd lft last 100yds: kpt on* **7/2**[3]
103F **2** *1 ¼* **Mostly Bob (IRE)**[28] 2959 8-10-13 125 ....(t) RichardJohnson 134+
(Philip Hobbs) *chsd ldng pair: hit 13th and next: sn outpcd: rallied to go 2nd last: edgd lft: n.m.r and swtchd rt nr fin* **5/2**[1]
10-3 **3** *6* **Lake Legend**[62] 2330 7-10-13 0 .... WayneHutchinson 128
(Alan King) *chsd ldng pair: reminders 12th: chsd wnr 4 out: wknd last* **11/4**[2]
0-12 **4** *10* **On Borrowed Wings (IRE)**[47] 2664 8-11-5 138 .... TimmyMurphy 126
(Alan Fleming) *hld up in detached last: nt fluent: shkn up 11th: nvr on terms* **11/4**[2]
0021 **5** *37* **Elzahann (IRE)**[10] 3332 9-10-12 0 .... GrahamLee 98
(Ferdy Murphy) *j.rt: w ldr: hit 6th: wknd and hit 4 out: wl bhd fr 2 out* **20/1**

6m 0.80s (-11.20) **Going Correction** -0.35s/f (Good) **5** Ran SP% **108.9**
Speed ratings: **105,104,102,99,86**
CSF £12.51 TOTE £3.60: £1.80, £1.90; EX 12.20.
Owner Naughty Boys Partnership **Bred** Robert Finnegan **Trained** Newport, Dyfed
■ Stewards' Enquiry : Aodhagan Conlon two-day ban: careless riding (Jan 26-27)

FOCUS
An interesting event contested by some useful novices. The time was respectable, just under three seconds outside the standard. Another chase best from the winner.

NOTEBOOK
Adams Island(IRE), third to a promising pair at Exeter last time, was one of two penalised runners here and he added to his Uttoxeter win, making most and staying on stoutly. He appeared to slip into the first fence but put in a good round of jumping otherwise. All his previous form had come in soft conditions, but this better surface was not a problem to him. (tchd 4-1)
Mostly Bob(IRE) jumped the last back in third but was in the process of coming home well when having to switch as the winner edged across and tightened him up. The line would just have come too soon for him in any case, but the clear round will have done him good and a similar race over this trip should soon be found for him. (op 11-4)
Lake Legend was upped in trip for this second venture over fences. After hitting a flat spot before the straight he chased the winner over the final line of obstacles, but he lacked the pace to get in a challenge and was run out of second from the last. The 3m may have just stretched him. (op 3-1)
On Borrowed Wings(IRE) was 5lb clear on BHA figures following his second of four finishers in a Grade 2 novice at Newbury. Held up as usual, he was rather careful at a number of his fences and it was apparaent with six to jump that he was struggling to make any impression on the principals. He is better than this and the longer trip did not seem to be the problem. Official explanation: trainer had no explanation for the poor form shown (tchd 5-2)
Elzahann(IRE) was a fortunate winner at Ayr and she was not up to this stiffer task, fading up the home straight. All her wins have come on left-handed tracks but she showed a tendency to jump to her right here. (op 16-1)

3509 HOLMES RIGBY H'CAP HURDLE (10 hdls) 2m 3f 110y
2:50 (2:50) (Class 4) (0-115,115) 4-Y-O+ **£2,055** (£599; £299)

Form RPR
/450 **1** **Wild Desert (FR)**[60] 2361 6-11-4 107 .... RobertThornton 118+
(Alan King) *w ldrs: led appr 7th: styd on strly fr 2 out: drvn out* **9/2**[1]

1/5- **2** 4 ½ **China Gold**612 2468-11-10 **113** .... WayneHutchinson 117
(Alan King) *prom: hdwy to chse wnr 2 out: styd on same pce* **7/1**
32/0 **3** ¾ **Burnt Oak (UAE)**60 2373 9-11-11 **114** .... BarryKeniry 118+
(Chris Fairhurst) *hld up in rr: hdwy 7th: chsng ldrs next: wnt 3rd betweew last 2: styd on same pce* **8/1**
3-2P **4** 3 ½ **Mac Aeda**27 2983 7-11-12 **115** .... GrahamLee 116
(Malcolm Jefferson) *chsd ldrs: styd on same pce appr 2 out: hit last* **6/1**3
366- **5** ¾ **The Panama Kid (IRE)**259 44 7-11-7 **115** .... JamesHalliday(5) 114
(Malcolm Jefferson) *prom: kpt on one pce appr 2 out* **14/1**
-102 **6** 7 **Montoya's Son (IRE)**91 1829 6-11-12 **115** .... BrianHughes 108
(Howard Johnson) *chsd ldrs: wnt 2nd 3 out: wknd fr next* **10/1**
230 **7** ¾ **Himrayn**30 2927 8-10-10 **99** .... GerardTumelty 91
(Anabel L M King) *prom: chsng ldrs 3 out: wknd between last 2* **20/1**
-405 **8** 29 **Pie At Midnight**55 2473 5-11-3 **106** .... JasonMaguire 72
(Donald McCain) *t.k.h in midfield: effrt appr 3 out: sn rdn and wknd* **20/1**
6-65 **9** ¾ **Melange (USA)**29 2941 5-10-7 **103** ....(t) AlistairFindlay(7) 69
(George Charlton) *led: hdd appr 7th: lost pl appr next* **5/1**2
-060 **10** 3 ½ **Takaatuf (IRE)**54 2508 5-11-2 **105** .... DenisO'Regan 68
(John Hellens) *in rr: hdwy 6th: lost pl appr 3 out* **66/1**
22P- **11** 9 **Irish Symphony (IRE)**259 51 7-11-3 **109** .... CharlieHuxley(3) 63
(John Mackie) *t.k.h: trckd ldrs: lost pl appr 3 out* **25/1**
-353 **12** 6 **Helieorbea**16 2421 5-11-0 **103** ....(p) TimmyMurphy 52
(Alan Brown) *w ldrs: hung rt wknd appr 3 out* **25/1**
0/P- **P** **King Killone (IRE)**276 11-11-1 **104** .... RobertWalford —
(Henry Hogarth) *in rr: drvn 4th: sn bhd: t.o whn p.u bef 3 out* **100/1**
23/- **U** **Crop Walker (IRE)**761 2741 9-11-2 **105** .... RichieMcGrath —
(Kate Walton) *hld up in mid-div: lost pl after 3rd: bhd fr 7th: t.o whn blnd and uns rdr 2 out* **16/1**
-650 **F** **Veronicas Boy**15 3169 5-10-3 **102** ....(b1) SamuelWelton(10) —
(George Moore) *mid-div: fell 4th* **12/1**

4m 41.7s (-9.60) **Going Correction** -0.35s/f (Good) course record **15** Ran SP% **121.8**
Speed ratings (Par 105): **105,103,102,101,101 98,98,86,86,84 81,78,—,—,—**
toteswingers:1&2:£6.20, 1&3:£7.90, 2&3:£13.30 CSF £33.49 CT £251.75 TOTE £6.30: £2.40, £2.20, £3.20; EX 16.60.
Owner Whites Of Coventry & Stephen Dunn **Bred** Wertheimer Et Frere **Trained** Barbury Castle, Wilts

FOCUS
An ordinary handicap hurdle run in a time slightly slower than the two divisions of the novice hurdle that opened the card. Alan King sent out a one-two. The winner produced a big step up on his previous form and the nest two are very well in on their old marks.

NOTEBOOK
Wild Desert(FR) came into this a lightly raced maiden over hurdles, but had run well when eighth to a stablemate in a competitive novice handicap at Cheltenham's Open meeting and was racing off the same mark here. Never far from the pace, he was already in command when stuttering into each of the last two flights and scored emphatically. The longer trip helped and he could have further progress in him. (op 5-1)
China Gold provided trainer Alan King with a one-two, keeping on well without unduly troubling the winner. Sidelined since May 2009 due to a minor tendon injury, this was a pleasing return to action and he should come on for it. He ought to get a bit further too. (op 6-1 tchd 5-1)
Burnt Oak(UAE) had run well after an absence at Wetherby and he showed the benefit of that outing as he stayed on well for third over this longer trip. He looks on a fair mark at present. (op 7-1 tchd 13-2)
Mac Aeda ◆ was pulled up on his handicap debut and this was more like it. He was coming home well after the last and a step up in trip can pay dividends. (op 17-2)
The Panama Kid(IRE), in the same ownership as the fourth, ran a satisfactory first race since last spring. He has proved hard to win with, but the handicapper had dropped him 5lb and he also has the option of reverting to chasing, for which he still qualifies as a novice.
Montoya's Son(IRE) has been in the news after it was found that a banned anabolic steroid had been given to him in 2009. Making his handicap debut after a three-month break, he looked a threat at the first flight in the home straight, but found little when let down and faded a little tamely. Without the tongue strap he was fitted with last time, he is likely to switch to chasing soon. (op 8-1)
Himrayn was sharper for his reappearance a month ago and he showed up well until fading two from home. (tchd 25-1)
Melange(USA) was expected to be suited by the drop back in trip, but he weakened badly after making the running. (op 6-1)
Helieorbea Official explanation: jockey said gelding hung right-handed home straight

3510 ALPHAFEEDS.COM H'CAP CHASE (17 fncs 1 omitted) 3m
3:25 (3:25) (Class 4) (0-110,110) 5-Y-O+ **£2,740** (£798; £399)

Form RPR
-1U5 **1** **La Pantera Rosa (IRE)**49 2611 8-11-4 **102** ....(p) BarryKeniry 114+
(Micky Hammond) *w ldr: led 3rd: hit 11th: styd on gamely fr 2 out* **10/1**
1-5F **2** 1 ¾ **Quel Bruere (FR)**53 2529 7-11-8 **106** ....(t) JodieMogford 113
(Graeme McPherson) *chsd ldrs: chsd wnr 3 out: upsides next: kpt on same pce run-in* **25/1**
2-30 **3** hd **Work Boy**29 2940 10-11-8 **106** .... TjadeCollier 113
(Sue Smith) *led to 3rd: chsd wnr: reminders after 10th: outpcd 3 out: styd on between last 2: kpt on same pce run-in* **9/2**2
5- **4** 6 **Crack At Dawn (IRE)**45 10-10-11 **95** ....(b1) DavidEngland 97
(Michael Gates) *chsd ldrs: wnt 2nd 10th: edgd lft after 4 out: wknd last* **80/1**
34U4 **5** 3 ½ **Prince Du Beury (FR)**28 2961 8-11-11 **109** .... AndrewTinkler 107
(Nicky Henderson) *hld up: hmpd 2nd: hdwy 11th: drvn appr 4 out: one pce: wknd 2 out* **9/2**2
11-1 **6** 42 **Palos Conti (FR)**75 2079 8-11-12 **110** .... DougieCostello 92+
(Tim Pitt) *hld up in rr: effrt 11th: wknd after 4 out: bhd and heavily eased 2 out: t.o* **6/5**1
540P **P** **Silver Bay**28 2953 10-11-1 **99** .... LeightonAspell —
(Oliver Sherwood) *blnd and lost pl 2nd: nt jump wl detached in last after: bhd fr 10th: t.o whn p.u bef 12th* **11/2**3

6m 12.7s (0.70) **Going Correction** -0.35s/f (Good) **7** Ran SP% **111.4**
Speed ratings: **86,85,85,83,82 68,—**
toteswingers:1&2:£7.80, 1&3:£9.70, 2&3:£19.40 CSF £156.71 CT £1249.20 TOTE £10.70: £4.50, £11.60; EX 147.10.
Owner Thomas,Hattie,Gabby,Paul & Vicky Snook **Bred** A W Buller **Trained** Middleham Moor, N Yorks
■ Stewards' Enquiry : Tjade Collier one-day ban: used whip with excessive frequency (Jan 26)

FOCUS
Just a modest handicap chase but they appeared to go a reasonable gallop. The winner rates a personal best.

NOTEBOOK
La Pantera Rosa(IRE) saw it out determinedly up the straight but was tying up after the last as the placed horses bore down on him. Suited by decent ground, he goes well fresh and appreciated the seven-week break since his last run. (op 9-1 tchd 11-1)
Quel Bruere(FR) ran a solid race, but never quite looked like pegging back the winner and gave the impression that the return of a visor might pay off.
Work Boy was the first to come off the bridle, but he eventually responded to pressure and was closing at the line. A stiffer track will suit and he is not handicapped out of things at present. (op 7-1 tchd 15-2)
Crack At Dawn(IRE), third in a resticted point-to-point in November, was contesting his first handicap chase and ran well for a long way in the change of headgear. (op 66-1)
Prince Du Beury(FR) could never land a blow after being held up but seemed to see out the trip well enough, albeit on this relatively easy track. (tchd 4-1)
Palos Conti(FR) was held up and never able to get involved. He was bidding for a four-timer but was raised 12lb to a career-high mark after his Wetherby win, where La Pantera Rosa was beaten in second when unseating at the last. Dougie Costello reported that his mount ran flat. Official explanation: jockey said gelding ran flat (tchd 11-8)
Silver Bay was expected to be suited by the trip and track, but he almost came down at the first ditch and his jumping went to pot afterwards. (op 5-1 tchd 9-2)

3511 SIGNATURE STANDARD OPEN NATIONAL HUNT FLAT RACE 2m 110y
3:55 (3:55) (Class 6) 4-6-Y-O **£1,370** (£399; £199)

Form RPR
3 **1** **Knockalongi**28 2957 5-11-5 0 .... APMcCoy 113+
(Rebecca Curtis) *trckd ldrs: chal 7f out: wnt 2nd over 4f out: led over 1f out: styd on wl fnl f* **11/4**2
22 **2** 2 ¾ **Fourjacks**29 2943 6-11-5 0 .... GrahamLee 110
(Tim Easterby) *led tl over 7f out: led 5f out: hdd over 1f out: styd on same pce* **7/2**3
3 5 **Hinton Indiana** 6-11-5 0 .... BarryGeraghty 106
(Nicky Henderson) *sn trcking ldrs: wnt n.d 3rd over 2f out: one pce* **13/8**1
0 **4** 2 ½ **Red Rocco (IRE)**54 2511 4-10-7 0 .... BarryKeniry 91
(George Moore) *in rr: drvn 6f out: kpt on fnl 3f: one pce: wnt modest 4th over 1f out* **80/1**
5 6 **Venitzia (IRE)** 5-11-5 0 .... BrianHughes 98+
(Howard Johnson) *t.k.h in mid-div: hdwy to chse ldrs 5f out: edgd rt 3f out: sn wknd* **6/1**
-20 **6** 6 **Pasture Bay (IRE)**29 2943 5-11-5 0 .... TimmyMurphy 93
(George Charlton) *hld up in rr: hdwy 5f out: chsng ldrs 3f out: wknd 2f out* **40/1**
3 **7** 7 **Shan Blue (IRE)**97 1749 6-10-12 0 .... LKasl(7) 89
(Steve Gollings) *hld up: hdwy 7f out: sn chsng ldrs: hung lft and lost pl over 2f out* **33/1**
8 nk **Silent Snow (IRE)** 6-11-0 0 .... JamesHalliday(5) 86
(Malcolm Jefferson) *in rr: drvn along after 6f: nvr on terms* **66/1**
0 **9** 8 **Cap Falco (IRE)**28 2957 6-11-5 0 .... RichardJohnson 82
(Anabel L M King) *hld up in rr: drvn along 9f out: bhd fnl 5f* **20/1**
0 **10** 2 ¼ **Grey Assassin**54 2511 4-10-0 0 .... KyleJames(7) 65
(Simon West) *prom: drvn 7f out: lost pl over 4f out* **100/1**
63 **11** 8 **Alta Rock (IRE)**164 1153 6-11-5 0 .... TjadeCollier 69
(Sue Smith) *sn trcking ldr: led over 7f out tl 5f out: lost pl over 3f out: sn bhd* **80/1**

3m 55.2s (-3.90) **Going Correction** -0.35s/f (Good)
WFA 4 from 5yo 11lb 5 from 6yo 3lb **11** Ran SP% **116.4**
Speed ratings: **95,93,91,90,87 84,81,81,77,76 72**
toteswingers:1&2:£2.00, 1&3:£2.50, 2&3:£2.30 CSF £12.17 TOTE £3.80: £1.60, £1.10, £1.90; EX 13.30.
Owner Peter Neary **Bred** R Hollinshead **Trained** Newport, Dyfed

FOCUS
This had the look of a fair bumper, from which winners should emerge. The first two pulled clear with the second setting a decent standard.

NOTEBOOK
Knockalongi had made a promising debut at Bangor, two places ahead of subsequent winner Hayjack. He impressed with his attitude as he saw off the runner-up's sustained challenge and looks the type to enjoy further success, although defying a penalty in this sphere may prove difficult. (op 5-2 tchd 10-3)
Fourjacks has finished second on all three starts now and gives a good indication of the form's value. He can go one better should connections opt to run him in one last bumper. (op 4-1 tchd 9-2)
Hinton Indiana is a half-brother to fairly useful hurdler Hinton Thunderbolt. He will have learned from this debut experience and a bumper should come his way should connections take that route with him. (op 9-4)
Red Rocco(IRE) came in for support on his Musselburgh debut and he stepped up on what he showed there, staying on quite nicely for fourth. (tchd 66-1)
Venitzia(IRE) is out of an unraced half-sister to useful chasers Samuel Wilderspin and Fourth In Line and was the subject of favourable reports, but he lacked the pace of the leaders when the race to the line developed. (op 5-1 tchd 9-2 and 13-2)
Pasture Bay(IRE) has ability and finished closer to Fourjacks than he had at Catterick. (op 33-1)
Shan Blue(IRE) did not build on his debut effort behind Knockalongi at Bangor and is going to need time. (op 28-1)
T/Jkpt: Not won. T/Plt: £79.90 to a £1 stake. Pool:£76,852.71 - 701.67 winning tickets T/Qpdt: £35.80 to a £1 stake. Pool:£5,395.96 - 111.40 winning tickets WG

2547 KELSO (L-H)
Wednesday, January 12
3512 Meeting Abandoned - Frozen track

2937 CATTERICK (L-H)
Thursday, January 13
OFFICIAL GOING: Good to soft (good in places; chs 7.6; hdl 7.7)
Wind: nil Weather: Mild, bright and sunny

3519 YORKSHIRE4X4.COM ADVENTURE ACTIVITIES JUVENILE MAIDEN HURDLE (8 hdls) 2m
12:50 (12:50) (Class 5) 4-Y-O **£2,055** (£599; £299)

Form RPR
3 **1** **Mark Twain (IRE)**15 3194 4-11-0 0 .... JasonMaguire 116+
(Kim Bailey) *trckd ldr: led 2 out: sn rdn clr: easily* **9/4**1
42 **2** 13 **Call To Arms (IRE)**64 2306 4-10-11 111 .... DonalDevereux(3) 100+
(Peter Bowen) *led: hdd narrowly whn nt fluent 2 out: sn no match wnr* **11/4**2
0 **3** 2 ¼ **Kingdom Of Munster (IRE)**10 3358 4-11-0 0 .... BrianHughes 96
(Richard Fahey) *hld up: nt fluent 5th: hdwy to go 3rd appr 2 out: sn no further imp* **7/1**
3 **4** 1 ½ **Anaya**54 2528 4-10-4 0 .... SamTwiston-Davies(3) 88
(David Bourton) *trckd ldrs: rdn after 3 out: sn one pce: hld in 4th whn mstke last* **4/1**3

0 **5** *8* **Admission**[56] 2466 4-11-0 0..........(t) JohnnyFarrelly 86
(Sophie Leech) *hld up: hdwy to trck ldrs appr 4th: rdn after 3 out: wknd appr next* **25/1**

6 *3 3/4* **Lil Ella (IRE)**[92] 1833 4-10-7 0.......... TomSiddall 78
(Patrick Holmes) *nt fluent: in tch: wknd after 3 out* **6/1**

2 **7** *20* **Bateau Bleu**[34] 1324 4-11-0 0.......... BarryKeniry 63
(Ben Haslam) *in tch: nt fluent 5th: wknd after 3 out* **33/1**

P **Young Firth**[79] 4-11-0 0.......... PaddyAspell —
(John Norton) *trckd ldrs: rdn and wknd qckly after 3 out: p.u bef 2 out* **200/1**

P **Pont De Nuit**[32] 4-11-0 0.......... CampbellGillies —
(Tracy Waggott) *midfield: wknd qckly after 3 out: p.u bef 2 out* **100/1**

P **Presidium Galaxy**[192] 4-10-7 0.......... GrahamLee —
(George Moore) *hld up: reminders after 3rd and sn lost tch: p.u bef 4th* **100/1**

3m 52.7s (0.20) **Going Correction** 0.0s/f (Good) **10** Ran SP% **113.5**
Speed ratings: **99,92,91,90,86 84,74,—,—,—**
toteswingers:1&2 £2.20, 2&3 £4.20, 1&3 £3.70 CSF £8.42 TOTE £3.50: £1.40, £1.10, £2.50; EX 6.90.

Owner Mrs David Johnson **Bred** Barouche Stud Ireland Ltd **Trained** Andoversford, Gloucs

FOCUS
A modest juvenile hurdle run at a sound pace. The easy winner was value for further and can rate higher, but this was not a strong race.

NOTEBOOK
Mark Twain(IRE), rated 74 on the Flat, had finished a well-beaten third in a much stronger event at Newbury. He kept tabs on the leader and, after taking charge, quickly went clear for a very comfortable eased-down victory. He will find it much tougher under a penalty and will need to make big strides to earn a place in the Fred Winter line-up. (op 15-8)

Call To Arms(IRE), rated 75 on the level and already 111 over hurdles, had chased home subsequent Finale winner Marsh Warbler at Bangor. He set the pace but was readily overwhelmed by the winner. He will struggle in handicap company. (tchd 3-1)

Kingdom Of Munster(IRE), who showed a glimmer of ability on his first try over hurdles at Ayr, is rated 64 on the Flat and may have to drop to selling or claiming company. (op 5-1)

Anaya, rated just 52 on the level, was well held when she blundered at the last. She's basically plating-class. (op 13-2)

Admission, rated 95 on the Flat, was reported to have a breathing problem when well beaten on his hurdling debut at Hereford and he stopped to nothing here going to two out. (op 16-1)

Lil Ella(IRE) did not jump fluently and was soon making hard work of it. (op 12-1)

3520 WAKEFIELD BEGINNERS' CHASE (14 fncs 1 omitted) 2m 3f
1:20 (1:20) (Class 4) 5-Y-0+ **£2,602** (£764; £382; £190)

Form RPR

121/ **1** **Glencree (IRE)**[633] 5113 7-11-0 0.......... BrianHughes 124+
(Howard Johnson) *midfield: hdwy appr 8th: led ninth: pckd bdly on landing 5 out: retained narow ld: 3 l clr last: drvn run-in: all out* **7/2**[1]

0215 **2** *nse* **Pyracantha**[22] 3090 6-11-0 0.......... BarryKeniry 122
(Alan Swinbank) *prom: rdn 3 out: kpt on wl u.p run-in: jst failed* **11/2**

363U **3** *1 3/4* **Lord Villez (FR)**[3] 3486 7-11-0 116.......... GrahamLee 121
(Ferdy Murphy) *midfield on inner: hit 4th: hdwy to trck ldrs 8th: rdn to chse wnr after 3 out: kpt on* **5/1**[3]

61P- **4** *23* **Arctic Wings (IRE)**[78] 5393 7-10-9 0.......... LeeEdwards(5) 100
(Tony Carroll) *trckd ldrs: t.k.h initially: rdn after 4 out: wknd 3 out* **12/1**

1P21 **5** *3/4* **Front Of House (IRE)**[66] 2281 9-11-0 0.......... DominicElsworth 100
(Ben Haslam) *hld up: hit 8th: kpt on after 4 out: nvr threatened ldrs* **4/1**[2]

31-6 **6** *3* **Humbie (IRE)**[239] 396 7-11-0 0.......... RichieMcGrath 97
(Pauline Robson) *hld up: hit 4 out: kpt on after 3 out: n.d* **6/1**

50-0 **7** *12* **Carters Rest**[55] 2508 8-11-0 0.......... DenisO'Regan 87
(Chris Grant) *trckd ldrs: wknd after 4 out* **50/1**

400 **8** *9* **Mansonien L'As (FR)**[16] 3171 5-10-6 0.......... LaurentBouldoires(3) 75
(Ferdy Murphy) *hld up: mstke 9th: n.d* **100/1**

5-63 **9** *nk* **Stick Together**[56] 2477 8-10-2 0.......... JamesHalliday(5) 70
(Malcolm Jefferson) *j. slowly in rr: a bhd* **10/1**

0/ **10** *1/2* **Knocklayde Euro (IRE)**[14] 3233 7-11-0 103..........(p) WilsonRenwick 76
(J J Lambe, Ire) *prom: led 6th: hdd 9th: remained prom tl wkng appr 3 out* **66/1**

055- **11** *3/4* **The Only Way**[276] 5166 8-10-7 90.......... CampbellGillies 69
(Chris Grant) *led: blnd 2nd: hdd 6th: lost tch after 9th* **100/1**

64-0 **U** **Karingreason**[30] 2942 8-10-7 104.......... JamesReveley —
(Keith Reveley) *midfield whn hmpd and uns rdr 2nd* **16/1**

4m 45.4s (-3.40) **Going Correction** -0.175s/f (Good)
WFA 5 from 6yo+ 3lb **12** Ran SP% **116.7**
Speed ratings: **100,99,99,89,89 87,82,79,79,78 78,—**
toteswingers:1&2 £4.70, 2&3 £8.00, 1&3 £3.70 CSF £22.99 TOTE £4.90: £1.90, £2.20, £2.10; EX 37.90.

Owner Andrea & Graham Wylie **Bred** P J Doyle **Trained** Billy Row, Co Durham

■ Stewards' Enquiry : Brian Hughes caution: used whip with excessive frequency.

FOCUS
A beginners' chase run at a sound pace and just three were in serious contention from the third-last. Fair novice form for the track.

NOTEBOOK
Glencree(IRE), rated 125 over hurdles and absent with a leg problem since winning for a second time at Hexham in April 2009, travelled strongly in midfield. After a scare five out he went on at the next and looked in total command until tying up on the run-in. At the line there was nothing to spare, but provided this Irish point winner is none the worse he looks sure to improve and enjoy further success. (op 9-2)

Pyracantha, a winner of a bumper and two hurdle races, the latest at Musselburgh in November, is now rated 122. Fit after an outing three weeks earlier in a bumper at Southwell, he was never far way. Tending to jump right-handed, he was 3l down at the last and only just failed to get up. He is sure to go one better. (op 7-1)

Lord Villez(FR), making a quick reappearance, stuck to his guns and looks sure to make his mark at a modest level in due course, given decent ground. (op 4-1)

Arctic Wings(IRE), rated 122 over hurdles, made a satisfactory chasing debut on his return to action. (op 10-1)

Front Of House(IRE), after an early mistake, stayed on in encouraging fashion on his chasing bow. He prefers slightly better ground. (op 9-2)

Humbie(IRE), rated 115 over hurdles, is from the family of Denman. Inclined to be a bit keen, he kept on late in the day on his first start since May and can do better over further in time. (tchd 11-2)

Carters Rest, out of sorts since his shock win in a bumper at Ayr in 2009, gave some encouragement on just his second start for this yard and his chasing debut. (op 40-1)

3521 CATTERICKBRIDGE.CO.UK NOVICES' HURDLE (8 hdls) 2m
1:50 (1:51) (Class 4) 4-Y-0+ **£2,081** (£611; £305; £152)

Form RPR

F1 **1** **Danceintothelight**[57] 2451 4-11-0 0.......... BarryKeniry 109+
(Micky Hammond) *mde all: racd keenly: rdn after 2 out: j.lft last: hrd rdn run-in: hld on all out* **9/2**[2]

2 *hd* **Shadows Lengthen**[46] 5-10-12 0.......... JakeGreenall(7) 114+
(Michael Easterby) *midfield: rdn and outpcd after 3 out: stl only 7th 2 out: gd hdwy to go 2nd last: kpt on strly run-in: jst failed* **8/1**

23 **3** *8* **Dunowen Point (IRE)**[30] 2943 5-11-5 0.......... JasonMaguire 108+
(Donald McCain) *j.lft: trckd ldrs: rdn and ev ch 2 out: sn one pce: lost 2nd last: wknd run-in* **7/4**[1]

4 *1 1/2* **Gentleman Jeff (USA)**[88] 1896 7-11-12 0.......... DenisO'Regan 111
(Chris Grant) *trckd ldrs: rdn appr 2 out: sn one pce* **11/1**

5342 **5** *1 1/2* **River Dragon (IRE)**[11] 3090 6-11-0 0.......... BrianToomey(5) 103
(Neville Bycroft) *trckd ldrs: rdn after 3 out: one pce after 2 out* **5/1**[3]

0 **6** *3/4* **Speed Dating**[9] 3387 5-11-5 0.......... DougieCostello 102
(John Quinn) *midfield: hdwy to chse ldrs after 3 out: no further imp after 2 out* **16/1**

-064 **7** *2 1/4* **Tale Of Tanganyika (FR)**[55] 2509 5-11-5 0.......... GrahamLee 102
(John Wade) *midfield on outer: hdwy to trck ldrs after 3 out: hit 2 out: sn wknd* **5/1**[3]

-360 **8** *17* **Pickworth (IRE)**[9] 3389 6-10-5 0.......... KyleJames(7) 78
(Philip Kirby) *in tch: mstke 3 out: rdn and sn wknd* **50/1**

0 **9** *10* **Dirleton (IRE)**[97] 1764 5-11-5 0.......... RichieMcGrath 76
(George Charlton) *hld up: n.d* **50/1**

10 *17* **Napoletano (ITY)**[77] 5-11-5 0.......... KennyJohnson 61
(Robert Johnson) *hld up: mstke 4th: a bhd* **150/1**

0 **11** *1 1/4* **Royal Crystal**[16] 3167 8-10-12 0..........(t) PaddyAspell 53
(James Turner) *hld up in midfield: lost tch after 5th* **200/1**

12 *19* **Aldaado (IRE)**[10] 5-11-5 0.......... TomSiddall 42
(Paul Midgley) *nt fluent: a in rr* **150/1**

P **Daredevil Dan**[269] 5-11-5 0.......... BrianHarding —
(Tina Jackson) *hld up: a bhd: p.u bef 2 out* **66/1**

06 **U** **Matilda's Folly (IRE)**[38] 2825 6-10-2 0.......... SeveBrumpton(10) —
(Ben Haslam) *hld up: mstke and uns rdr 1st* **250/1**

0 **P** **Plutonium (IRE)**[48] 2660 5-10-12 0.......... StevenGagan(7) —
(Elliott Cooper) *in rr: j. slowly 2nd: sn t.o: p.u bef 4th* **150/1**

3m 49.4s (-3.10) **Going Correction** 0.0s/f (Good)
WFA 4 from 5yo+ 11lb **15** Ran SP% **121.5**
Speed ratings (Par 105): **107,106,102,102,101 101,99,91,86,77 77,67,—,—,—**
toteswingers:1&2 £9.70, 2&3 £4.60, 1&3 £3.10 CSF £40.85 TOTE £4.70: £1.70, £4.10, £1.90; EX 56.60.

Owner Roland Roper **Bred** Mrs David Low **Trained** Middleham Moor, N Yorks

FOCUS
A competitive novices' hurdle in which seven were still in contention two out, and in the end a pat on the back for the juvenile brigade. Another step up from the winner, and fair form.

NOTEBOOK
Danceintothelight, a winner on the Flat here, ought to have won both his previous starts over hurdles. He bowled along in front and in the end did just enough. Rated just 65 on the level, he has certainly taken well to hurdling. (op 4-1 tchd 5-1)

Shadows Lengthen, rated 93 at his peak on the AW after six successive wins last winter, has not been in the same form this time. Well supported, he came from off the pace and, but for flattening the final flight, might well have got there. Losses are only lent. (tchd 7-1)

Dunowen Point(IRE), placed when favourite in two starts in bumpers, tended to jump left-handed. He came there travelling strongly and jumped the second-last on the heels of the winner but again he came up short. (op 2-1)

Gentleman Jeff(USA), a winner twice on the Flat and once over hurdles in Ireland, changed hands for £12,000. Absent since October, he ran without his usual blinkers this time. (op 9-1)

River Dragon(IRE), whose last two outings have been on the AW at Southwell, will have a better chance in low-grade handicaps after one more start. (tchd 11-2)

Speed Dating, successful three times on the Flat last year, showed a fair bit more than on his first try over hurdles a week earlier but he too may be seen to better effect in handicap company in due course.

Tale Of Tanganyika(FR), who didn't build on his debut success in bumper company, was well held when he made a mess of the second-last, and he has something to prove now. (op 11-1)

3522 WATT FENCES NORTH YORKSHIRE GRAND NATIONAL H'CAP CHASE (FOR THE DENYS SMITH CHALLENGE TROPHY) (23 fncs) 3m 6f
2:20 (2:20) (Class 3) (0-130,130) 5-Y-0+
£4,383 (£1,295; £647; £324; £161; £81)

Form RPR

-254 **1** **General Hardi**[61] 2374 10-10-11 **115**.......... DenisO'Regan 124
(John Wade) *hld up: outpcd after 16th: stl only 7th 3 out: styd on strly after 2 out: led nr fin* **16/1**

-400 **2** *1/2* **According To Pete**[12] 3293 10-11-7 **125**..........(p) GrahamLee 135+
(Malcolm Jefferson) *midfield on inner: hdwy to trck ldrs 16th: rdn and outpcd appr 3 out: rallied after 2 out: led last: kpt on but hdd nr fin* **9/2**[1]

-431 **3** *4* **Star Beat**[30] 2940 8-10-12 **116**..........(p) RichieMcGrath 124+
(Kate Walton) *led: drvn after 3 out: hdd last: no ex run-in* **7/1**[2]

13-2 **4** *4 1/2* **Heez A Steel (IRE)**[253] 162 10-11-3 **128**.......... AlistairFindlay(7) 131
(George Charlton) *trckd ldrs: lost pl after nt fluent 6 out and next: kpt on again after 3 out* **40/1**

U114 **5** *1* **Quinder Spring (FR)**[53] 2550 7-10-4 **108**.......... PeterBuchanan 108
(Lucinda Russell) *prom: stl 2nd 3 out: wknd appr last* **10/1**

121F **6** *2 1/4* **Overquest**[62] 2354 9-10-6 **110**.......... JohnnyFarrelly 109
(Elliott Cooper) *hld up in midfield: trckd ldrs 16th: hdwy on outer to hold ev ch after 4 out: wknd after 3 out* **7/1**[2]

6562 **7** *35* **Zitenka (IRE)**[30] 2940 9-10-11 **120**..........(b) JamesHalliday(5) 101+
(Tim Easterby) *hld up: hdwy to trck ldrs after 10th: rdn 6 out: wknd after 4 out* **10/1**

52-2 **8** *17* **Rambling Minster**[68] 2205 13-11-12 **130**.......... MrColmMcCormack(7) 88
(Keith Reveley) *mstkes: hld up: a towards rr* **8/1**[3]

6-1F **P** **Newman Des Plages (FR)**[53] 2543 10-11-2 **125**.......... AlexanderVoy(5) —
(Martin Todhunter) *midfield: rn in snatches: lost pl after 7th and nvr rcvrd: p.u bef 17th* **25/1**

15U- **P** **Ya I Know (IRE)**[289] 4938 10-9-12 **105** oh3 ow1..........(tp) CharlieHuxley(3) —
(Sarah Humphrey) *midfield: reminders after 8th: wknd after 15th: p.u bef 3 out* **16/1**

-432 **P** **Cast Iron Casey (IRE)**[68] 2204 9-11-1 **119**.......... WilsonRenwick —
(Howard Johnson) *midfield on outer: rdn after 6 out and sn wknd: t.o whn p.u bef 3 out* **9/1**

32-R **F** **Bay Cherry (IRE)**[74] 2106 9-11-7 **125** BrianHughes —
(Howard Johnson) *midfield: fell 2nd* **17/2**

/1-P **P** **Palace Merano (FR)**[74] 2106 8-11-8 **126** (p) JasonMaguire —
(Donald McCain) *prom on outer: blnd 10th: sn lost pl: t.o whn p.u bef 4 out* **40/1**

4-3 **P** **On Gossamer Wings (IRE)**[10] 3361 7-9-7 **104** oh7...(p) HenryBrooke(7) —
(J J Lambe, Ire) *prom: hit 10th: wknd after 6 out: mstke 4 out: p.u bef 3 out* **25/1**

7m 41.8s (-11.20) **Going Correction** -0.175s/f (Good) course record **14** Ran SP% **117.3**
Speed ratings: **107,106,105,104,104 103,94,89,—,— —,—,—,—**
toteswingers:1&2 £39.60, 2&3 £5.40, 1&3 £27.00 CSF £83.97 CT £559.83 TOTE £18.40: £4.50, £2.10, £2.50; EX 126.50.
Owner John Wade **Bred** Mrs A Yearley **Trained** Mordon, Co Durham

FOCUS
A 104-130 stayers' handicap chase and a severe test of stamina. There were four in serious contention two out but in the end the winner came from behind to get up on the line. Solid handicap form.

NOTEBOOK
General Hardi, winner of just two of his previous 23 outings over fences, was 11lb higher than for his last success over this trip in the Durham National at Sedgefield in April. Picking up ground early on the final circuit, he had plenty to do when just fifth two out but really knuckled down to pull it out of the fire near the line. It was his first outing for two months and, considering the freeze-up, connections deserve full marks.
According To Pete, who has won from a 7lb higher mark in the past, was back over fences. Fitted with cheekpieces for the first time, he travelled as sweet as a nut round the inner. He looked nailed on when landing in front at the last only to miss out near the line. (op 11-2)
Star Beat, who loves to dominate, was 12lb higher than for his all-the-way success here a month ago. He stepped up the gallop at the first fence on the final circuit but in the end the first two saw out this extended trip the better. (op 13-2, tchd 15-2 in a place)
Heez A Steel(IRE), having just his fourth start over fences on his first outing since May, made a couple of mistakes at a crucial stage. He stuck to his guns in the home straight and deserves credit for this.
Quinder Spring(FR), unbeaten in six starts in points last year, travelled strongly but seemed to be found out by lack of fitness over the final three fences. The best of him has yet to be seen under Rules. (op 9-1)
Overquest, 13lb higher than for his last success at Carlisle in November, didn't get home after looking a major threat on the turn for home. (op 15-2 tchd 6-1)
Rambling Minster was taken off his feet on this better ground and made jumping errors. (op 13-2 tchd 9-1)
Newman Des Plages(FR) Official explanation: jockey said gelding never travelled

3523 LEEDS H'CAP HURDLE (10 hdls) 2m 3f
2:50 (2:52) (Class 4) (0-105,105) 4-Y-0+ **£2,081** (£611; £305; £152)

Form RPR

60 **1** **San Deng**[61] 2372 9-10-1 **90** JoeColliver(10) 98
(Micky Hammond) *mid-div: hmpd bnd after 3rd: styd on wl appr 2 out: led appr last: kpt on wl* **28/1**

05 **2** *1 1/2* **Latin Connection (IRE)**[48] 2657 5-11-0 **100** MrBGCrawford(7) 107
(S R B Crawford, Ire) *in rr: gd hdwy 3 out: styd on to chal whn hit last: no ex* **50/1**

2035 **3** *1 3/4* **Bocciani (GER)**[11] 3335 6-10-12 **94** JamesO'Farrell(3) 98
(Dianne Sayer) *chsd ldrs: ev ch 2 out: styd on same pce run-in* **20/1**

-006 **4** *18* **Waterloo Corner**[48] 2658 9-11-6 **99** KennyJohnson 88
(Ray Craggs) *chsd ldrs: hit 6th: led appr 2 out: hdd appr last: sn wknd* **33/1**

03-0 **5** *2 1/4* **King Mak**[56] 2477 9-11-9 **102** DougieCostello 88
(Marjorie Fife) *w ldrs: wknd after 3 out* **16/1**

4-P2 **6** *7* **Imperial Breeze (IRE)**[68] 2223 6-11-7 **100** BrianHughes 79
(J J Lambe, Ire) *trckd ldrs: led after 3 out: rdn and hdd appr next: wknd between last 2* **16/1**

0030 **7** *hd* **Daytime Dreamer (IRE)**[11] 3334 7-11-8 **101** GrahamLee 80
(Martin Todhunter) *w ldrs: led appr 6th: hdd after 3 out: sn wknd* **14/1**

053- **8** *1/2* **Shifting Gold (IRE)**[12] 4665 5-11-5 **103** (bt) BrianToomey(5) 84
(Kevin Ryan) *hld up in mid-div: hdwy 6th: w ldrs 3 out: wknd next* **9/2**[2]

22 **9** *5* **Everaard (USA)**[196] 713 5-11-1 **94** RichieMcGrath 68
(Kate Walton) *w ldrs: reminders after 5th: wknd next* **14/1**

0-3P **10** *8* **Super Baby (FR)**[30] 2942 9-11-5 **101** (p) HarryHaynes(3) 68
(James Ewart) *mid-div: hdwy 6th: lost pl next* **14/1**

1P-0 **11** *2 1/2* **Gwyre (IRE)**[89] 1870 5-11-7 **100** BrianHarding 65
(Tim Easterby) *chsd ldrs: drvn 3 out: sn wknd* **33/1**

2453 **12** *nse* **Rain Stops Play (IRE)**[11] 3335 9-11-2 **105** StephenMulqueen(10) 70
(Nicky Richards) *hld up in rr: nt fluent: hdwy 6th: wknd after 3 out* **8/1**[3]

6-P5 **13** *3/4* **Wardington Lad**[16] 3168 9-11-0 **100** KyleJames(7) 64
(Michael Appleby) *w ldrs: lost pl 7th* **12/1**

44-P **14** *2 3/4* **Perfectus (IRE)**[57] 2448 7-10-8 **92** JamesHalliday(5) 54
(Malcolm Jefferson) *in rr: gd hdwy 6th: chsng ldrs 3 out: wknd appr next* **8/1**[3]

6032 **15** *54* **Barbarian**[51] 2603 5-10-13 **92** FearghalDavis 5
(Alan Brown) *in rr: reminders 4th: bhd fr 7th* **14/1**

000P **16** *24* **Front Rank (IRE)**[53] 2551 11-11-5 **105** MissECSayer(7) —
(Dianne Sayer) *nt fluent in rr: wl bhd and reminders 4th: sn t.o* **66/1**

0152 **P** **What's Occurrin**[30] 2937 7-11-10 **103** RobertWalford —
(Tim Walford) *led tl appr 6th: lost pl next: hit 3 out: t.o whn p.u bef 2 out* **4/1**[1]

4m 44.1s (-2.70) **Going Correction** 0.0s/f (Good) **17** Ran SP% **124.1**
Speed ratings (Par 105): **105,104,103,96,95 92,92,91,89,86 85,85,85,83,61 51,—**
toteswingers:1&2 £127.70, 2&3 £67.20, 1&3 £122.20 CSF £996.92 CT £24800.42 TOTE £54.00: £7.30, £9.60, £6.40, £8.10; EX 2234.70.
Owner Belarus Partnership **Bred** N C D Horn **Trained** Middleham Moor, N Yorks
■ Joe Colliver's first winner.

FOCUS
A highly competitive 90-105 handicap hurdle, and in the end the first three came well clear. The winner showed a return to form, with surprise improvement from the second.

NOTEBOOK
San Deng, from a stable that has been in good form since the resumption, had gone almost two years since his sole previous success. Overcoming early interference, he stayed on in really good style under his young rider, aboard his first winner, to take charge on the run-in. He stays further and the strong gallop played into his hands. Official explanation: trainer said, regarding apparent improvement in form, that the gelding benefited from a drop in handicap mark and the jockey's 10lb allowance. (op 40-1 tchd 25-1)
Latin Connection(IRE), an Irish challenger making his handicap bow, had failed to complete in three of his previous six starts. He had worked his way upsides when hitting the last and then had to settle for second best. (op 40-1)
Bocciani(GER), who can be tricky at the start, is a long-standing maiden under both codes. This must go down as his best effort over hurdles so far. (op 28-1)
Waterloo Corner, 3lb higher than for his last success, went on but his stamina seemed to give out completely going to the last.
King Mak, without a win for nearly three years, is better suited by fences these days. (op 20-1)
Imperial Breeze(IRE), another Irish raider, travelled really strongly but, after going on, found little for pressure on his handicap bow. This was his first worthwhile form. (op 20-1)
Daytime Dreamer(IRE) failed to see it out after showing ahead early on the final circuit. (op 16-1 tchd 12-1)
Shifting Gold(IRE), kept busy on the AW, was another who seemed to find his stamina stretched to breaking point after holding every chance. (op 4-1 tchd 5-1)
What's Occurrin, on the back of a couple of good efforts, didn't enjoy an uncontested lead and seemed to drop everything before eventually calling it a day. Official explanation: trainer had no explanation for the poor form shown (tchd 9-2)

3524 W. L. AND HECTOR CHRISTIE MEMORIAL TROPHY (NOVICES' H'CAP CHASE) (12 fncs) 2m
3:20 (3:20) (Class 4) (0-115,112) 5-Y-0+ **£2,602** (£764; £382; £190)

Form RPR

5021 **1** **Heavenly Chorus**[30] 2942 9-10-13 **102** MrColmMcCormack(7) 115+
(Keith Reveley) *hld up: hdwy after 3 out: led last: drvn clr run-in* **7/2**[2]

20/2 **2** *4* **Blackpool Billy (IRE)**[53] 2548 9-11-12 **108** GrahamLee 118+
(Ferdy Murphy) *hld up on outer: hdwy after 8th: trckd ldrs after 4 out: led on bit bef 2 out: hdd whn blnd 2 out: nt fluent last: kpt on run-in* **3/1**[1]

-456 **3** *1/2* **Earl Grez (FR)**[30] 2938 6-10-9 **98** KyleJames(7) 104
(Philip Kirby) *trckd ldrs: led 7th: hdd appr 2 out: sn regained ld: hdd last: no ex fnl 100yds: lost 2nd nr fin* **33/1**

40F3 **4** *2 3/4* **Grand Award**[56] 2479 6-11-4 **100** JasonMaguire 105
(Donald McCain) *midfield: hit 2nd: hdwy to trck ldrs appr 3 out: mstke last: kpt on same pce* **4/1**[3]

P-0F **5** *3/4* **Peachey Moment (USA)**[62] 2352 6-11-2 **98** FearghalDavis 101
(Nicky Richards) *hld up: nt fluent 4th: hdwy to trck ldrs after 4 out: rdn after 3 out: sn one pce* **25/1**

0/3- **6** *5* **Waterloo Road (IRE)**[317] 4369 8-11-10 **106** BrianHughes 104
(Howard Johnson) *trckd ldrs: led 6th: hdd 7th: stl ev ch bef 2 out: wknd appr last* **15/2**

15-0 **7** *1* **Overbranch**[242] 353 8-10-12 **99** (b) JamesHalliday(5) 97
(Malcolm Jefferson) *midfield: rdn 3 out: sn no imp* **12/1**

0044 **8** *2 1/2* **Monsieur Jourdain (IRE)**[51] 2599 5-11-12 **112** (p) RichieMcGrath 103
(Tim Easterby) *in tch: trckd ldrs 7th: wknd after 4 out: hld whn mstke 3 out* **14/1**

0446 **9** *2 1/2* **Petrosian**[13] 3257 7-10-12 **101** (p) HarryChalloner(7) 95
(Lisa Williamson) *w ldr: led 5th: hdd 6th: sn rdn and lost pl: 7th whn mstke last* **50/1**

1360 **10** *20* **Lindseyfield Lodge (IRE)**[30] 2942 10-10-12 **94** (p) KennyJohnson 69
(Robert Johnson) *led: hdd 5th: wknd 7th* **66/1**

-42P **F** **Little Wizard (IRE)**[11] 3336 9-10-11 **93** JanFaltejsek —
(George Charlton) *prom: fell 3rd* **8/1**

3m 57.3s (-2.80) **Going Correction** -0.175s/f (Good) **11** Ran SP% **114.7**
Speed ratings: **100,98,97,96,96 93,93,91,90,80 —**
toteswingers:1&2 £3.40, 2&3 £30.90, 1&3 £56.20 CSF £14.20 CT £290.01 TOTE £3.80: £1.20, £1.10, £5.70; EX 11.90.
Owner The Mary Reveley Racing Club **Bred** Lady Jennifer Green And John Eyre **Trained** Lingdale, Redcar & Cleveland

FOCUS
A modest 93-108 2m handicap chase, and in the end a ready and progressive winner. The second is better than the bare result.

NOTEBOOK
Heavenly Chorus, raised 9lb after opening her account over fences here last month, is jumping really well now and, having swept to the front, scored with something in hand. Clearly in great heart, she should continue to give a good account of herself at this level. (op 5-2)
Blackpool Billy(IRE), almost put out of the contest at an early stage, travelled very strongly. He was ahead when making a mess of the second-last and in the end found the winner too strong. Rated 108, 8lb below his hurdle-race mark, he has plenty of potential if he keeps right. (op 11-4 tchd 5-2)
Earl Grez(FR), making his handicap debut on just his second start over fences, ran by far his best race to date. (op 40-1)
Grand Award, who survived an early blunder, was on the heels of the first three when repeating the error at the final fence. He is proving very hard to win with. (op 5-1)
Peachey Moment(USA), on the same mark as when falling on his second start for this stable, still has plenty to learn about jumping fences but he shaped better and is by no means a forlorn hope. (tchd 20-1)
Waterloo Road(IRE), a remote third on his chasing debut here in March, was having just his second start over fences. He stopped to nothing two out and almost certainly needed the outing. (op 6-1 tchd 8-1)

3525 HUDDERSFIELD STANDARD NATIONAL HUNT FLAT RACE (CONDITIONALS & AMATEURS) 2m
3:50 (3:50) (Class 6) 4-6-Y-O **£1,370** (£399; £199)

Form RPR

1 **Broadbackbob (IRE)**[61] 6-10-12 0 MrBGCrawford(7) 102+
(S R B Crawford, Ire) *dropped in s: hld up: smooth hdwy fr 5f out: chal over 2f out: led wl over 1f out: rdn clr: comf* **4/1**[2]

1 **2** *3 3/4* **Little Hercules (IRE)**[30] 2943 5-11-9 0 RyanMania(3) 104+
(Howard Johnson) *midfield: hdwy to trck ldrs over 3f out: rdn to chal 2f out: kpt on: no match wnr* **11/8**[1]

5 **3** *1* **Brave Spartacus (IRE)**[62] 2355 5-11-5 0 CampbellGillies 94
(Chris Grant) *led: rdn whn hdd wl over 1f out: kpt on one pce* **25/1**

4 *3* **Perfect Ending (IRE)** 4-10-4 0 EwanWhillans(3) 79
(Richard Fahey) *trckd ldrs: rdn over 3f out: kpt on* **7/1**[3]

5 *2 3/4* **Capital Venture (IRE)** 5-11-2 0 HarryHaynes(3) 88
(James Ewart) *hld up: rdn and outpcd over 6f out: kpt on fnl 3f: nrst fin* **10/1**

6 *5* **Alleged Vanity (IRE)** 5-11-2 0 CharlieHuxley(3) 83
(Chris Grant) *midfield: rdn over 3f out: kpt on same pce* **40/1**

6- **7** *1* **Yorkshire Knight (IRE)**[508] 1295 6-11-2 0 DonalDevereux(3) 82
(Peter Bowen) *hld up: hdwy on outer 7f out: rdn over 4f out: kpt on same pce* **11/1**

1-0 **8** *1 1/4* **Silvers Spirit**[50] 2616 5-10-12 0 MrColmMcCormack(7) 81
(Keith Reveley) *hld up: rdn over 5f out: sn no imp* **50/1**

5- **9** *2* **The Giggler (IRE)**[312] 4466 5-10-12 0 JakeGreenall(7) 79
(Alan Swinbank) *prom: rdn over 3f out: wknd 2f out* **10/1**

6 **10** *16* **Alpha One (IRE)**[53] 2553 5-11-0 0 AlexanderVoy(5) 63
(Chris Grant) *chsd ldrs: rdn over 7f out: wknd 5f out* **100/1**

11 *10* **Go Teescomponents** 4-10-0 0 MrRLindsay(7) 41
(Keith Reveley) *green: a in rr* **14/1**

0 **12** *18* **Ben Brierley**[64] 2309 4-10-2 0 JamesHalliday(5) 23
(Bruce Hellier) *hld up: n.d* **100/1**

13 *8* **Stitched Up (IRE)** 5-10-12 0 .... HenryBrooke(7) 27
(Tim Walford) *trckd ldrs: wknd over 3f out* **66/1**

3m 49.8s (2.90) **Going Correction** 0.0s/f (Good)
WFA 4 from 5yo+ 11lb **13** Ran SP% **119.5**
Speed ratings: **92,90,89,88,86 84,83,83,82,74 69,60,56**
toteswingers:1&2 £2.30, 2&3:£5.60, 1&3:£8.20 CSF £9.55 TOTE £4.80: £1.40, £1.02, £4.70; EX 11.60.
Owner S R B Crawford **Bred** Kevin Kerrigan **Trained** Larne, Co Antrim

FOCUS
A run-of-the-mill bumper run at a steady pace to past halfway and in the end a most convincing gambled-on winner. He is rated in line with his best Irish form.

NOTEBOOK
Broadbackbob(IRE), placed in three points and fourth in a Leopardstown bumper, was well supported. Dropped in at the start, he moved up on the bridle to to take charge but in the end his rider left nothing to chance. He will now go hurdling.
Little Hercules(IRE), who accounted for two solid rivals when making a winning debut here last month, was hampered on the bend leaving the back straight. He had every chance but in the end the winner was simply too strong.
Brave Spartacus(IRE), whose rider was keen to make the running, kept on surprisingly well. He may need 2m4f over hurdles.
Perfect Ending(IRE), a half-brother to the stable's Group winner Anna Pavlova, made a satisfactory debut but he looks to lack a gear or two.
Capital Venture(IRE), inclined to be a shade keen going to post, is from the family of Menorah. He stayed on when it was all over and there should be a bit better to come.
Alleged Vanity(IRE) showed a glimmer on his debut.
Yorkshire Knight(IRE) was having his first start since flopping when sent off favourite on his debut in August 2009.
T/Jkpt: Not won. T/Plt: £383.60 to a £1 stake. Pool of £57,685.22 - 109.75 winning tickets.
T/Qpdt: £358.30 to a £1 stake. Pool of £3,631.72 - 7.50 winning tickets. AS

3365 HEREFORD (R-H)
Thursday, January 13

OFFICIAL GOING: Heavy
Wind: Light behind Weather: Overcast

3526 LINDLEY CATERING NOVICES' HURDLE (8 hdls) 2m 1f
1:10 (1:10) (Class 4) 4-Y-0+ **£2,016** (£592; £296; £147)

Form RPR
44U3 **1** **Grey Gold (IRE)**28 2985 6-11-5 0 .... JodieMogford 125+
(Richard Lee) *chsd ldrs: led 3 out: sn clr: wandered into 2 out: easily* **10/3**2

6- **2** *25* **Milo Milan (IRE)**413 2536 6-11-5 0 .... CharliePoste 93
(Richard Lee) *hld up: hdwy appr 5th: rdn to go 13 l 2nd 2 out: sn wknd* **50/1**

0 **3** *3/4* **Spinning Waters**79 2021 5-11-0 0 .... MrBMoorcroft(5) 91
(Dai Burchell) *hld up: hdwy u.p 3 out: wknd bef next: wnt 3rd post* **50/1**

66 **4** *nse* **Valley View (IRE)**12 3296 5-11-5 0 .... APMcCoy 91
(Jonjo O'Neill) *hld up: hdwy 3 out: wknd bef next: lost 3rd post* **9/2**3

5 *30* **Togiak (IRE)**103 4-10-4 0 .... DannyCook(3) 49
(David Pipe) *hld up: hdwy appr 5th: rdn and wknd after 3 out: t.o* **2/1**1

65 **6** *8* **Shoudhavenownbettr (IRE)**52 2588 7-10-12 0 ....(p) MrJMRidley(7) 53
(Matt Sheppard) *bhd fr 3rd: t.o whn hmpd 5th* **100/1**

0 **7** *1/2* **Senses (USA)**30 2944 5-11-0 0 .... CO'Farrell(5) 53
(David Pipe) *chsd ldrs tl rdn and wknd after 3 out: t.o* **15/2**

8 *7* **Jacko's Boy**264 8-11-5 0 .... WarrenMarston 46
(Martin Keighley) *prom: chsd ldr 4th tl led next: hdd 3 out: rdn and wknd bef next: t.o* **12/1**

00 **9** *4* **Eddie Boy**72 2137 5-11-5 0 .... WillKennedy 42
(Rebecca Curtis) *chsd ldr tl led after 2nd: hdd 5th: rdn and wknd after 3 out: t.o* **28/1**

0U **10** *2* **Major Potential (USA)**3 3489 5-11-5 0 .... AidanColeman 40
(Venetia Williams) *chsd ldrs tl rdn and wknd after 3 out: t.o* **40/1**

11 *6* **Caddie Master (IRE)** 5-11-2 0 .... RichieMcLernon(3) 34
(Jonjo O'Neill) *hld up: drvn along after 5th: a bhd: t.o* **50/1**

5P- **12** *42* **Bay Central (IRE)**315 4399 7-10-12 0 .... MrJEngland(7) —
(Evan Williams) *led tl after 2nd: wknd appr 3 out: t.o* **33/1**

0/P **13** *19* **Su Bleu (IRE)**239 406 9-11-2 0 .... JimmyDerham(3) —
(Milton Harris) *bhd fr 3rd: t.o* **100/1**

14 *1 3/4* **Little Buddy**56 4-10-4 0 .... PeterToole(3) —
(Richard Price) *a in rr: t.o whn blnd 6th* **200/1**

05 **F** **Cruise Control**9 3387 5-11-5 0 .... GerardTumelty 61
(Richard Price) *chsd ldrs tl rdn and wknd after 3 out: t.o whn fell last* **14/1**

F **Fraamtaaztiic**450 4-9-11 0 .... WayneKavanagh(3) —
(Ron Hodges) *mid-div: wknd after 4th: t.o whn fell next* **150/1**

4m 15.0s (15.60) **Going Correction** +0.775s/f (Soft)
WFA 4 from 5yo+ 11lb **16** Ran SP% **118.6**
Speed ratings (Par 105): **94,82,81,81,67 63,63,60,58,57 54,35,26,25,— —**
toteswingers:1&2 £12.00, 2&3 £23.30, 1&3 not won. CSF £159.91 TOTE £3.50: £1.10, £18.70, £9.20; EX 191.60.
Owner Mrs M A Boden **Bred** James Keegan And Jeff Hamilton **Trained** Byton, H'fords

FOCUS
This didn't look the most competitive novice hurdle, and the testing conditions soon thinned the field out. The winner produced a massive step up.

NOTEBOOK
Grey Gold(IRE) ◆ was fancied by connections to run well and duly bolted up after being in the right place at the right time down the back straight. He bounded clear once in front and was never going to be caught by toiling rivals, and was probably aided by his ability to handle conditions much better than others. (op 11-2)
Milo Milan(IRE), having his first run for Richard Lee, is viewed as a long-term chasing prospect, so this was a pleasing first try over hurdles.
Spinning Waters was one of a few in this that did best on quick ground when racing on the Flat, so this wasn't a bad effort after becoming one-paced. (op 40-1)
Valley View(IRE) hadn't been within hailing distance of a winner in two starts under rules, and upheld that trend here after racing in rear for most of the contest. (op 4-1 tchd 5-1)
Togiak(IRE) looked a potentially decent recruit, as he has a mark of 92 on the Flat. Having his first start since leaving Ed Dunlop for 120,000gns, he made a promising move at around halfway but failed to pick up when asked to get on terms. Reported to lack size, he had run well in soft on the Flat, but the majority of his best form was on a sound surface. (op 15-8 tchd 6-4)
Senses(USA) ◆, who was heavily backed, showed plenty of ability on the Flat for Jeremy Noseda on decent ground, so one would imagine that this 81-rated Flat horse by Rahy will have far better prospects on less demanding ground later in the season. (op 16-1 tchd 20-1 and 7-1)

3527 LINDLEY CATERING H'CAP CHASE (18 fncs 1 omitted) 3m 1f 110y
1:40 (1:40) (Class 5) (0-95,95) 5-Y-0+ **£1,626** (£477; £238; £119)

Form RPR
P221 **1** **Hobb's Dream (IRE)**10 3377 7-10-6 82 7ex ....(p) MarkQuinlan(7) 102+
(Neil Mulholland) *hld up: hdwy 7th: lft 2nd 10th: led appr 3 out: sn clr: j.lft last two: easily* **11/4**1

550- **2** *24* **Huckleberry (IRE)**278 5133 9-9-11 69 oh2 ....(p) PeterToole(3) 59
(James Unett) *prom: chsd ldr 7th tl led 10th: hdd appr 3 out: wkng whn j.lft last two* **14/1**

-225 **3** *2 3/4* **Sir Winston (IRE)**14 3230 9-11-12 95 .... DarylJacob 85
(Victor Dartnall) *hld up: hmpd 2nd: hdwy 9th: hmpd next: wknd 3 out* **5/1**3

50-4 **4** *3/4* **Guydus (IRE)**28 2982 7-11-9 92 .... AidanColeman 79
(Venetia Williams) *hld up: reminders after 3rd: hmpd 10th: hdwy 14th: wknd 4 out* **28/1**

P-51 **5** *10* **Cold Harbour**52 2575 7-11-5 95 .... MrJEngland(7) 80
(Evan Williams) *led to 3rd: chsd ldrs: hmpd 10th: j.lft 12th: hit next: wknd 4 out: t.o* **18/1**

44U5 **6** *4 1/2* **Ethiopia**39 2794 8-11-4 94 .... NathanSweeney(7) 66
(Bob Buckler) *hld up and a bhd: t.o* **14/1**

-036 **7** *32* **Copper Sound**9 3388 7-10-13 82 ....(p) RhysFlint 22
(Michael Scudamore) *prom tl wknd appr 14th: t.o* **40/1**

5-34 **8** *26* **Ballymorn (IRE)**53 2555 7-11-3 86 .... HaddenFrost —
(Henrietta Knight) *prom: lost pl 8th: rallied 12th: wknd appr 14th t.o* **33/1**

3-62 **P** **Sir Peter (IRE)**53 2557 9-11-9 92 ....(p) RichardJohnson —
(Henry Daly) *hld up: bhd fr 6th: t.o whn p.u bef 4 out* **5/1**3

/P-1 **F** **Shannons Boy (IRE)**50 2608 9-11-8 91 ....(t) CharliePoste —
(Richard Lee) *chsd ldr tl led 3rd: hdd and fell 10th* **9/2**2

04-6 **F** **South Bank (IRE)**49 2643 9-10-13 82 ....(v1) SamThomas —
(Tim Vaughan) *hld up: fell 2nd* **9/1**

6m 54.2s (22.40) **Going Correction** +0.775s/f (Soft) **11** Ran SP% **115.6**
Speed ratings: **96,88,87,87,84 83,73,65,—,— —**
toteswingers:1&2 £12.10, 2&3 £14.10, 1&3 £2.70 CSF £38.46 CT £184.67 TOTE £2.60: £1.10, £8.30, £2.30; EX 53.80.
Owner John & Jeanette Hobbs & P J Proudley **Bred** Mrs A R Mulholland **Trained** Burlescombe, Devon

FOCUS
Not many of these came into this at the top of their game, so while this was a solid race for the level, the form is weak. The winner produced another step forward. The fence past the stands was bypassed on the second circuit.

NOTEBOOK
Hobb's Dream(IRE), raised 7lb for a wide-margin success at Lingfield but due to go up a further 9lb from the weekend, won with plenty in hand after racing prominently. She is clearly effective in these conditions at a lowly level, but will obviously find things difficult now she heads up the handicap. (op 10-3 tchd 5-2)
Huckleberry(IRE) went clear with the winner halfway down the back straight on their final circuit, but didn't get home, looking tired after the second-last. (op 12-1 tchd 16-1)
Sir Winston(IRE) is well above his only winning handicap mark and never really looked like getting to the front. (op 7-2)
Guydus(IRE) was well beaten on her chasing/seasonal debut in the middle of December, so this looked a bit better, although her rider was pushing her along a long way from home. (op 18-1)
Cold Harbour lost his place after racing handily, but rallied to some extent to get into contention for a place leaving the back straight for the final time. (op 22-1)
Shannons Boy(IRE), absent since making a winning return to the racecourse in late November, and 9lb higher, looked to be going nicely when falling at the tenth. (op 16-1)
South Bank(IRE) unfortunately took a very heavy fall. (op 16-1)

3528 LINDLEY CATERING MAIDEN HURDLE (11 hdls) 2m 6f 110y
2:10 (2:10) (Class 5) 5-Y-0+ **£1,561** (£458; £229; £114)

Form RPR
1 **Minella Stars (IRE)**312 6-11-0 0 .... HarrySkelton 113+
(Paul Nicholls) *hld up: hdwy 4th: led after 2 out: sn rdn: j.big last: drvn out* **10/11**1

6-45 **2** *3 1/2* **Grey Wulff (IRE)**50 2607 6-11-0 0 .... SamThomas 106
(Emma Lavelle) *chsd ldrs: lost pl after 6th: hdwy 8th: outpcd after 3 out: rallied appr last: r.o to go 2nd post: nt trble wnr* **8/1**

22 **3** *hd* **Railway Dillon (IRE)**13 3252 6-11-0 0 .... AdrianLane 107
(Donald McCain) *chsd ldrs: led 3 out: hdd next: sn rdn: styd on* **9/2**3

5 **4** *3 1/2* **Gallant Oscar (IRE)**61 2368 5-10-7 0 .... AodhaganConlon(7) 104
(Rebecca Curtis) *plld hrd and prom: lost pl 6th: hdwy after next: led 2 out: sn rdn and hdd: wknd flat* **20/1**

3 **5** *5* **Nemo Spirit (IRE)**16 3158 6-11-0 0 .... RichardJohnson 98
(Tim Vaughan) *hld up in tch: mstke 1st: rdn and wknd appr 2 out* **7/2**2

0-66 **6** *nk* **Tim The Chair (IRE)**11 3340 6-10-7 0 .... StephenO'Donovan(7) 97
(Emma Lavelle) *led to 3 out: wknd appr 2 out* **40/1**

7 *6* **Inca Cave (IRE)**334 6-10-9 0 .... KeiranBurke(5) 92
(Patrick Rodford) *chsd ldrs: j. bit 5th: rdn and wknd appr 2 out* **100/1**

0 **8** *1 3/4* **Bennys Mist (IRE)**64 2309 5-11-0 0 .... AidanColeman 91
(Venetia Williams) *hld up: mstkes 2nd and 6th: hdwy 8th: rdn and wknd appr 2 out* **100/1**

0 **9** *64* **Rathconrath (FR)**75 2087 6-11-0 0 .... WayneHutchinson 25
(Althea Barclay) *prom tl rdn and wknd after 3 out: t.o* **100/1**

00-0 **10** *1* **Mister Concussion**53 2560 7-11-0 0 .... MarkGrant 24
(Peter Jones) *hld up: wkng whn blnd 8th: t.o* **100/1**

0PP/ **P** **The Chisholm (IRE)**256 9-11-0 0 ....(bt1) JodieMogford —
(Adrian Wintle) *prom: dropped in rr 4th: bhd fr 6th: t.o whn p.u bef 2 out* **50/1**

5m 54.4s (16.40) **Going Correction** +0.775s/f (Soft) **11** Ran SP% **117.0**
Speed ratings: **102,100,100,99,97 97,95,94,72,72 —**
toteswingers:1&2 £7.30, 2&3 £3.70, 1&3 £2.00 CSF £9.20 TOTE £2.70: £1.20, £1.90, £1.10; EX 11.30.
Owner Mrs Johnny de la Hey **Bred** Michael Dixon **Trained** Ditcheat, Somerset

FOCUS
The pace throughout the early stages was understandably modest. The bare form is only ordinary but the winner should go on to rate higher.

NOTEBOOK
Minella Stars(IRE), a dual winner form three starts in Irish points, made a winning start under rules in good style. A nice-looking type, built to jump a fence, he moved up wide of the field before doing enough when asked to quicken to go clear. He can probably carry a penalty in a similar type of race, but will no doubt make his name as a chaser in the future. (op 13-8 tchd 7-4 in places)
Grey Wulff(IRE) is now eligible for handicaps and should find his level in them if reproducing this sort of effort. The further he went, the closer he got to the winner, so a step up in trip or stiffer course will no doubt suit. (tchd 11-1)

Railway Dillon(IRE) had shown ability on both his previous starts, the latter being his hurdling debut at Uttoxeter, and gave the impression he was still a bit green here under pressure. He looked like dropping away at one stage but found more and kept on. (op 11-4)
Gallant Oscar(IRE), up 6f in distance for his hurdling debut, looked booked for second turning in but was passed by two horses after the final hurdle, despite not appearing to weaken significantly. (op 16-1 tchd 22-1)
Nemo Spirit(IRE) shaped with promise at Ffos Las on his first try over hurdles, and handled soft on the Flat, but never got involved here. (tchd 4-1)
Tim The Chair(IRE) ran well for a long time towards the head of the field before finding just the one pace. (op 33-1)
Inca Cave(IRE) kept on and hinted at better to come. (tchd 80-1)
Bennys Mist(IRE) also suggested he is capable of better.

3529 LINDLEY CATERING GROUP H'CAP HURDLE (11 hdls) 2m 6f 110y
2:40 (2:40) (Class 4) (0-115,114) 4-Y-0+ **£2,016** (£592; £296; £147)

Form RPR
0/23 **1** **The Gripper (IRE)**[13] 3261 7-10-0 **95** PeterCarberry(7) 102+
(Rachel Hobbs) *a.p: chsd ldr 8th: led appr 2 out: rdn bef last: styd on wl* **7/1**[2]
-343 **2** 2 ¾ **Simply Wings (IRE)**[28] 2983 7-11-12 **114** RobertThornton 119+
(Richard Lee) *hld up: hdwy 4th: j. slowly and lost pl 7th: hdwy 3 out: chsd wnr next: rdn and ev ch last: unable qck flat* **11/4**[1]
5665 **3** 10 **Mauricetheathlete (IRE)**[79] 2023 8-10-0 **95** MrNSlatter(7) 90
(Martin Keighley) *chsd ldrs: lost pl 4th: rallied 7th: wknd appr 2 out* **20/1**
P-P0 **4** 3 **Flintoff (USA)**[29] 2955 10-11-3 **105** (b) AidanColeman 96
(Venetia Williams) *sn drvn along and prom: lost pl after 3rd: r.o flat: nt trble ldrs* **15/2**[3]
P-51 **5** ½ **Najca De Thaix (FR)**[50] 2609 10-11-4 **106** JamieMoore 97
(John Spearing) *led: rdn and hdd appr 2 out: wknd bef last* **8/1**
/PP0 **6** 22 **Krackatara**[72] 2141 9-11-1 **110** MissLGardner(7) 79
(Susan Gardner) *hld up: hdwy appr 8th: rdn and wknd after 3 out: t.o* **33/1**
P-3P **7** 8 **Doctor Disny**[53] 2557 8-10-8 **96** (b[1]) SeanQuinlan 57
(Kim Bailey) *prom tl rdn and wknd appr 2 out: t.o* **12/1**
32-1 **8** 40 **Silver Footnote**[61] 2365 6-11-2 **104** SamThomas 25
(Emma Lavelle) *chsd ldr to 8th: sn rdn: wknd after next: t.o* **11/4**[1]
F5-P **9** 3 **Pearl (IRE)**[40] 2574 7-11-1 **103** (tp) DarylJacob 21
(Alison Thorpe) *hld up: racd wd: hdwy 7th: rdn and wknd after 3 out: t.o* **16/1**
4214 **P** **Be Ashored**[99] 1730 6-11-0 **105** RichardKilloran(3) —
(Tim Vaughan) *hld up: drvn along appr 6th: bhd fr next: t.o whn p.u bef 2 out* **18/1**

5m 52.7s (14.70) **Going Correction** +0.775s/f (Soft) **10** Ran SP% **115.3**
Speed ratings (Par 105): **105,104,100,99,99 91,88,75,73,—**
CSF £26.90 CT £370.30 TOTE £9.70: £4.10, £1.30, £9.70; EX 33.90.
Owner The Hobb's Choice Partnership **Bred** John J Hughes **Trained** Hanley Swan, Worcs

FOCUS
An ordinary handicap. A step up from the winner to beat the progressive runner-up.

NOTEBOOK
The Gripper(IRE), up in trip, attracted some market support and, after travelling strongly throughout, kept going strongly enough under pressure to hold on. (op 10-1 tchd 13-2)
Simply Wings(IRE), another up in distance, was given a patient ride and his rider seemed keen to keep his mount in behind for as long as possible, probably because of the weight concession. However, the winner didn't stop and he failed to get past. (op 10-3)
Mauricetheathlete(IRE) plugged on to claim third, but doesn't have a lot of strong form and didn't look an easy ride. (op 28-1)
Flintoff(USA), dropped 7lb since his last run, needed pushing along from almost the time the tapes flew across, and never held any hope of winning. (op 12-1)
Najca De Thaix(FR), raised 14lb for a 16l victory at Chepstow, hasn't been the most consistent during his career and dropped out after being joined leaving the back straight. (op 13-2 tchd 6-1)
Silver Footnote, up in trip again, was far less exposed than his rivals but ran a shocker. He was going nicely heading towards four out but found little shortly after it. Something was presumably amiss. Official explanation: jockey said gelding stopped quickly (op 9-4 tchd 3-1)

3530 LINDLEY H'CAP HURDLE (13 hdls) 3m 2f
3:10 (3:10) (Class 5) (0-90,90) 4-Y-0+ **£1,561** (£458; £229; £114)

Form RPR
-512 **1** **Ukrainian Star (IRE)**[13] 3258 8-11-3 **81** (tp) WarrenMarston 91+
(Martin Keighley) *chsd ldrs: racd wd: led 3rd to 5th: led 8th: rdn after 3 out: styd on wl u.p* **6/1**[2]
036- **2** 12 **Saulty Max (IRE)**[311] 4493 7-11-8 **86** PaddyBrennan 89+
(Nigel Twiston-Davies) *hld up: hdwy and mstke 7th: chsd wnr 10th: rdn after 2 out: wknd flat* **6/1**[2]
3566 **3** 16 **Manadam (FR)**[31] 2929 8-11-7 **90** MattGriffiths(5) 78
(Anthony Middleton) *hld up: hdwy after 8th: rdn and wknd appr 2 out: mstke last* **16/1**
2125 **4** 16 **Heezagrey (IRE)**[67] 2239 8-10-3 **74** MarkQuinlan(7) 40
(James Evans) *hld up: drvn along after 6th: nvr on terms: t.o* **5/1**[1]
-623 **5** hd **Acosta**[12] 3300 7-10-8 **75** (b) EamonDehdashti(3) 41
(Dr Jeremy Naylor) *chsd ldrs tl rdn and wknd after 3 out: t.o* **13/2**[3]
4552 **5** dht **Vacario (GER)**[11] 3341 7-11-0 **85** (t) MrPJTolman(7) 51
(Mark Gillard) *prom tl rdn and wknd after 3 out: t.o* **16/1**
2P-0 **7** 49 **Little Rort (IRE)**[10] 3367 12-10-6 **77** MissCBoxall(7) —
(Simon Lewis) *prom tl wknd 8th: t.o* **66/1**
-P4P **P** **Fourpointone**[60] 2402 10-11-4 **82** (p) RhysFlint —
(Michael Scudamore) *chsd ldrs: rdn after 6th: wknd 8th: t.o whn p.u bef 3 out* **22/1**
-001 **P** **Woodlands Gem (IRE)**[52] 2589 9-10-13 **80** (bt) RichieMcLernon(3) —
(Peter Pritchard) *mid-div: dropped in rr 4th: bhd fr next: t.o whn p.u bef 7th* **10/1**
36/P **P** **Queen Musa**[50] 2609 9-10-3 **70** (v[1]) WayneKavanagh(3) —
(Dr Jeremy Naylor) *mid-div: drvn along after 5th: wknd 7th: t.o whn p.u bef 9th* **50/1**
6/P6 **P** **Troys Run (IRE)**[49] 2644 8-11-7 **85** AndrewGlassonbury —
(Bill Moore) *chsd ldrs: rdn after 9th: wknd next: t.o whn p.u bef 3 out* **50/1**
4PP- **P** **Photogenique (FR)**[495] 1383 8-11-1 **82** MichaelMurphy(3) —
(Rob Summers) *hld up: sme hdwy u.p after 8th: sn wknd: t.o whn p.u bef 3 out* **50/1**
5 **P** **Gleannacreim (IRE)**[10] 3369 8-11-4 **85** RichardKilloran(3) —
(Tim Vaughan) *hld up: a in rr: drvn along 6th: t.o whn p.u bef 2 out* **25/1**
0P3- **P** **Castlemaine Vic (IRE)**[463] 1652 8-11-7 **85** (b[1]) RichardJohnson —
(Adrian Wintle) *hld up: rdn after 8th: sn wknd: t.o whn p.u bef 3 out* **5/1**[1]
4-FP **P** **Wham Bang**[13] 3261 7-11-5 **83** (p) SeanQuinlan —
(Robin Mathew) *led to 3rd: led 5th to 8th: sn rdn and wknd: t.o whn p.u bef 3 out* **66/1**
000- **P** **Border Lad**[272] 5216 7-10-10 **74** DarylJacob —
(Alison Thorpe) *hld up: hdwy 8th: wknd appr 3 out: t.o whn p.u bef next* **16/1**
-000 **P** **Running Upthathill (IRE)**[28] 2985 7-10-10 **74** AidanColeman —
(Venetia Williams) *hld up: hdwy 6th: wknd qckly after 8th: t.o whn p.u bef 10th* **10/1**

7m 3.80s (32.10) **Going Correction** +0.775s/f (Soft) **17** Ran SP% **128.1**
Speed ratings (Par 103): **81,77,72,67,67 67,52,—,—,— —,—,—,—,— —,—**
toteswingers:1&2 £11.80, 2&3 £28.30, 1&3 £24.10 CSF £42.44 CT £570.79 TOTE £5.50: £1.50, £2.10, £5.60, £2.20; EX 44.20.
Owner The Class Act Partnership **Bred** Mrs G O'Connell **Trained** Condicote, Gloucs

FOCUS
A moderate handicap hurdle and a real slog. The winner improved to his chase mark with the form rated through the second.

NOTEBOOK
Ukrainian Star(IRE) was supposed to wear a tongue-tie for the first time as well as the cheekpieces, but connections couldn't get the breathing aid on him and the stewards were informed well before the off. However, that didn't stop him winning a war of attrition after being handy throughout. (op 11-2 tchd 9-2)
Saulty Max(IRE), without cheekpieces on her first run after a lengthy absence, hadn't been tried over this far before but appeared to get the distance without a problem. She was well clear of the third. (op 11-2 tchd 5-1)
Manadam(FR), like most, never threatened to get anywhere the leading two. (op 22-1)
Heezagrey(IRE), who isn't an easy ride, managed to motivate himself just in time to grab fourth in a three-way photo. (op 15-2 tchd 8-1)
Woodlands Gem(IRE), up 8lb for her narrow Ludlow success, was pushed along after jumping the first and was one of the first beaten. (op 16-1)
Troys Run(IRE) Official explanation: vet said gelding bled from the nose (op 16-1)
Castlemaine Vic(IRE) contracted in price markedly but showed nothing in first-time blinkers. (op 16-1)

3531 SIS LIVE NOVICES' H'CAP CHASE (12 fncs) 2m
3:40 (3:41) (Class 3) (0-125,125) 5-Y-0+ **£4,553** (£1,337; £668; £333)

Form RPR
3-01 **1** **Cadoudalas (FR)**[71] 2148 8-11-5 **118** RichardJohnson 134+
(Richard Lee) *led to 2nd: led next: mstke 8th: clr 2 out: styd on wl: eased towards fin* **4/1**[2]
-331 **2** 9 **Oscar Gogo (IRE)**[16] 3154 9-11-4 **117** PaulMoloney 122
(Evan Williams) *a.p: chsd wnr 2 out: sn rdn and no imp* **8/1**
50-1 **3** 4 ½ **Clouseau (NZ)**[49] 2635 7-11-4 **117** DarylJacob 119+
(Nick Williams) *hld up: hdwy 4th: blnd 7th: chsd wnr 3 out to next: styd on same pce* **8/1**
5033 **4** 2 **Cantabilly (IRE)**[49] 2636 8-10-11 **115** MattGriffiths(5) 114
(Ron Hodges) *bhd: styd on fr 3 out: nvr on terms* **25/1**
0264 **5** 29 **Shadow Dancer (IRE)**[29] 2951 6-11-7 **120** APMcCoy 89
(Jonjo O'Neill) *hld up: wknd fr 8th: t.o* **3/1**[1]
40P4 **6** 8 **Adajal (IRE)**[52] 2587 8-11-1 **117** (t) RichieMcLernon(3) 78
(Jonjo O'Neill) *prom: lost pl 4th: drvn along 7th: wknd next: t.o* **66/1**
0542 **7** 1 ¾ **Bathwick Quest (IRE)**[28] 2978 7-11-2 **115** LeightonAspell 74
(Brendan Powell) *chsd ldrs tl wknd appr 3 out: t.o* **14/1**
6-2F **P** **Lord Singer (FR)**[51] 2593 6-11-5 **118** JamieMoore —
(Gary Moore) *plld hrd: led 2nd to 3rd: chsd ldr tl rdn and wknd 3 out: blnd next: sn p.u* **7/1**[3]
U **Symphonick (FR)**[102] 5-11-2 **119** NickScholfield —
(Paul Nicholls) *hld up: mstkes 2nd and 5th: hdwy 8th: disputing 5 l 4th and styng on whn blnd and uns rdr next* **3/1**[1]

4m 12.4s (8.80) **Going Correction** +0.775s/f (Soft)
WFA 5 from 6yo+ 3lb **9** Ran SP% **116.7**
Speed ratings: **109,104,102,101,86 82,81,—,—**
toteswingers:1&2 £3.00, 2&3 £7.20, 1&3 £10.70 CSF £36.13 CT £245.93 TOTE £4.20: £1.20, £1.60, £3.20; EX 31.50.
Owner Six To Five Against G D Thorp, R L Baker **Bred** Mme Evelyne Van Haaren **Trained** Byton, H'fords

FOCUS
This was by far the most competitive race of the day, as virtually all of these could be given a chance of winning. Solid form, with the first three on the upgrade.

NOTEBOOK
Cadoudalas(FR) ◆ had already beaten Oscar Gogo when winning at Chepstow in November. He went off quickly in front along with Lord Singer and considering Gary Moore's horse was shaken off a long way out, Richard Johnson's mount deserves plenty of credit for keeping on so well in the testing ground. The horse looks progressive and is one to follow. (op 6-1)
Oscar Gogo(IRE), 7lb higher for his win in handicap company at Ffos Las, can lead but couldn't here and was forced to settle in. He tried to get on terms but made no impression. (op 13-2)
Clouseau(NZ) made a winning debut over fences in a three-runner contest at Taunton in November (absent since) and moved nicely here until clouting the seventh. He still managed to get back into contention, but that earlier mistake probably took its toll in the latter stages, and he couldn't make much impression from two out. (op 5-1)
Cantabilly(IRE) got well behind before running on through rivals as they tired.
Shadow Dancer(IRE), making his handicap debut over fences, didn't get involved after being held up. (op 5-1)
Symphonick(FR), the winner of a French 4-y-o chase for Guillaume Macaire over 2m1f in heavy ground, travelled strongly under restraint, but his jumping wasn't always perfect and eventually cost him, as he hit four out and unseated his jockey. He was making some ground at the time, but it was much too far out to know what would have happened had the partnership stayed intact. (op 10-3 tchd 7-2)

3532 LINDLEY CATERING H'CAP HURDLE (8 hdls) 2m 1f
4:10 (4:10) (Class 5) (0-95,100) 4-Y-0+ **£1,626** (£477; £238; £119)

Form RPR
/021 **1** **Arrayan**[5] 3449 6-11-13 **100** 7ex CO'Farrell(5) 124+
(David Pipe) *trckd ldr: led and hit 2nd: clr after 2 out: eased flat* **4/5**[1]
0002 **2** 11 **Man Of Leisure**[10] 3367 7-11-1 **88** KeiranBurke(5) 96
(Nerys Dutfield) *led to 2nd: chsd wnr: ev ch 3 out: rdn and wknd after next* **11/2**[2]
0213 **3** 7 **Monsieur (FR)**[56] 2467 11-11-3 **85** HarrySkelton 85
(Carroll Gray) *hld up: hdwy 4th: rdn and wknd after 2 out* **7/1**[3]
-6UF **4** ¾ **Thievery**[53] 2559 10-10-10 **78** RichardJohnson 76
(Henry Daly) *hld up: hdwy appr 2 out: nvr on terms* **16/1**
6-F0 **5** 19 **Arthurian (IRE)**[53] 2558 6-10-3 **78** (bt) MrTGarner(7) 57
(Anthony Middleton) *chsd ldrs: rdn and lost pl 3rd: sn bhd: t.o* **20/1**
4420 **6** 16 **Sail And Return**[30] 2949 7-11-5 **94** (t) JoshuaMoore(7) 57
(Philip Middleton) *chsd ldrs: hit 5th: wknd appr 2 out: t.o* **7/1**[3]
0000 **7** 15 **Sheezatreasure (IRE)**[29] 2956 6-10-9 **84** (p) MarkQuinlan(7) 32
(James Evans) *prom: mstke 3rd: sn rdn and rdr dropped whip: bhd fr 5th: blnd 3 out: t.o* **50/1**

00-0 **8** *97* **Kielder Rise**[59] 2425 7-11-3 **85**.. PaulMoloney —
(Evan Williams) *prom: lost pl after 2nd: bhd fr 4th: t.o* **33/1**
500 **P** **Don Jose (USA)**[64] 2307 8-11-6 **88**.................................... CharliePoste —
(Richard Lee) *hld up: hdwy 4th: wknd appr 3 out: t.o whn p.u bef next* **25/1**

4m 20.1s (20.70) **Going Correction** +0.775s/f (Soft) **9** Ran SP% **115.3**
Speed ratings (Par 103): **82,76,73,73,64 56,49,4,—**
toteswingers:1&2 £13.70, 2&3 £7.90, 1&3 £1.02. totesuper7: Win: Not won. Place: Not won. CSF £5.65 CT £18.67 TOTE £1.90: £1.10, £1.60, £1.30; EX 7.50.
Owner Mrs Angela Tincknell & W Tincknell **Bred** West Stow Stud Ltd **Trained** Nicholashayne, Devon

FOCUS
A modest handicap hurdle and a race that revolved around the winner. He was well in on his Wincanton victory but this looks another step forward.

NOTEBOOK
Arrayan gained a comfortable success at Wincanton five days previously. Ridden in confident style, he had everything brushed aside turning in and won easily, but he is due to go up a further 5lb. (op 4-6 tchd 5-6)
Man Of Leisure, 2lb higher in the future, raced keenly on the inside and kept on in the style of a horse that can take a handicap on a sharp track. (op 7-1)
Monsieur(FR) is a low-grade performer who rarely wins. (op 9-1 tchd 13-2)
Thievery, who looked of some interest on his first outing over hurdles since November 2006, couldn't get on terms after racing towards the rear. (op 14-1 tchd 11-1)
T/Plt: £75.90 to a £1 stake. Pool of £73,103.87 - 702.36 winning tickets. T/Qpdt: £13.80 to a £1 stake. Pool of £6,027.92 - 321.80 winning tickets. CR

3533 - 3539a (Foreign Racing) - See Raceform Interactive

3400 HUNTINGDON (R-H)
Friday, January 14

OFFICIAL GOING: Soft (chs 6.4, hdl 5.9)
The final fence in the back straight was omitted in all chases.
Wind: blustery Weather: overcast but very mild

3540 CROMWELL STAND CONDITIONAL JOCKEYS' H'CAP HURDLE (10 hdls) 2m 5f 110y
12:40 (12:41) (Class 5) (0-95,95) 4-Y-0+ **£2,055** (£599; £299)

Form RPR
0041 **1** *1* **Dancing Daffodil**[9] 0006 0-9-12 **76** 7ex.................... ChristopherWard(0) 77+
(Robin Dickin) *abt to take wrong crse bef 1st but luckily kpt in by a rival: bhd: plodded on fr 3 out: fin 5th: awrdd r* **5/2**[1]
0/05 **2** *2 3/4* **Giollacca (IRE)**[72] 2144 7-10-7 **76**.. TomMolloy 76+
(Graeme McPherson) *hmpd bef 1st but one of only three to take correct crse: hld up in rr tl clsd 7th: wknd 2 out: mstke last: fin 6th: plcd 2nd* **11/2**[3]
001- **3** *dist* **Sovereign Spirit (IRE)**[12] 2662 9-11-3 **86**..................(tp) RichardKilloran —
(Chris Gordon) *tk wrong crse and p.u bef 1st but retracd and continued several fs bhd: ref to jump flattened fnl hurdle tl rdr fnlly bmpd him over: fin 8th: plcd 3rd* **12/1**
0066 **D** *87* **Patrick Dee**[8] 3400 6-10-0 **72**.. MattCrawley(3) —
(Christine Dunnett) *tk wrong crse bef 1st: prom tl rdn and wknd qckly bef 7th: t.o bef 2 out: fin 7th: disqualified* **80/1**
00-6 **D** *2* **Mr Tingle**[72] 2150 7-11-4 **95**.. PeterCarberry(8) 98+
(Richard Phillips) *tk wrong crse bef 1st: trckd ldrs: 4th and rdn whn mstke 3 out: rallied to press ldrs and blnd last: kpt on again flat: fin 3rd: disqualified* **7/2**[2]
0000 **D** *1 3/4* **Boosha**[17] 3153 6-11-9 **92**.. SamTwiston-Davies 90
(Rachel Hobbs) *tk wrong crse bef 1st: prom: nt fluent 4th: no ex after 2 out: 4th and btn whn blnd last: fin 4th: disqualified* **12/1**
2246 **D** *1 1/4* **Spider Boy**[48] 2672 14-10-8 **80**......................(b) GemmaGracey-Davison(3) 81
(Zoe Davison) *tk wrong crse bef 1st: led: rdn bef 7th: hdd 2 out: ev ch last: plugged on gamely: fin 2nd, 1 1/4l: disqualified* **14/1**
4021 **D** **Rawaaj**[11] 3367 5-11-1 **92** 7ex.. HenryBrooke(8) 94
(Donald McCain) *tk wrong crse bef 1st: pressed ldr: rdn to ld 2 out: all out: fin 1st: disqualified* **11/2**[3]
PP **P** **Laureus (GER)**[92] 1840 8-9-11 **69**.............................. NathanSweeney(3) —
(Rachel Hobbs) *stdd s: plld v hrd: tk wrong crse bef 1st: p.u bef 2nd* **50/1**
050 **P** **Rumballina**[13] 3302 4-10-2 **84**......................................(p) MrMMO'Connor —
(Amy Weaver) *tk wrong crse bef 1st: prom: shkn up after 5th: t.o and mstke 6th: p.u next* **66/1**
-005 **P** **Karinga Dream**[15] 3227 5-11-5 **94**................................ HarryChalloner(6) —
(Venetia Williams) *tk wrong crse bef 1st: prom tl rdn and lost pl after 5th: t.o and p.u 2 out* **14/1**

(-310.60) course record
WFA 4 from 5yo+ 12lb **11** Ran SP% **115.0**
Tote Swingers: 1&2 £5.40, 1&3 £2.90, 2&3 £22.10 CSF £16.55 CT £137.22 TOTE £3.10: £1.10, £2.30, £6.50; EX 17.70.
Owner John & Margaret Cooper & Law & Disorder **Bred** Mrs C M Dickin **Trained** Atherstone on Stour, Warwicks
■ Stewards' Enquiry : Gemma Gracey-Davison 15-day ban: 12 days for taking wrong course (Jan 28-Feb 8), three days for not pulling up having knowingly taken wrong course (Feb 9-11)
Nathan Sweeney 12-day ban: taking wrong course (Jan 28-Feb 8)
Henry Brooke 15-day ban: 12 days for taking wrong course (Jan 28-Feb 8), three days for not pulling up having knowingly taken wrong course (Feb 9-11)
Peter Carberry 15-day ban: 12 days for taking wrong course (Jan 28-Feb 8), three days for not pulling up having knowingly taken wrong course (Feb 9-11)
Matt Crawley 15-day ban: 12 days for taking wrong course (Jan 28-Feb 8), three days for not pulling up having knowingly taken wrong course (Feb 9-11)
Mr M M O'Connor 15-day ban: 12 days for taking wrong course (Jan 28-Feb 8), three days for not pulling up having knowingly taken wrong course (Feb 9-11)
Sam Twiston-Davies 15-day ban: 12 days for taking wrong course (Jan 28-Feb 8), three days for not pulling up having knowingly taken wrong course (Feb 9-11)
Harry Challoner 15-day ban: 12 days for taking wrong course (Jan 28-Feb 8), three days for not pulling up having knowingly taken wrong course (Feb 9-11)

FOCUS
This moderate opening handicap for conditional riders developed into a very messy affair before the runners had even jumped the first hurdle. There was confusion as the early leaders set off to the first flight on the chase course, which is separated by a false rail. That saw eight in the wrong, with only Dancing Daffodil and Giollacca steering the correct route, although Sovereign Spirit also eventually found his way. They both sat off the pace as the race developed in front of them and failed to land a significant blow on their rivals. However, after the subsequent stewards' enquiry the majority were disqualified and Dancing Daffodil, who finished fifth, was awarded the race. Not form to dwell on.

NOTEBOOK
Dancing Daffodil, who finished fifth, was awarded the race. She was 6lb well in under her penalty for getting off the mark over further at Southwell last time and was solid in the market here. The drop back in trip was against her as the race unfolded, but she did lose momentum when switching course early on and still gave her all. That said, she was a very fortunate winner. (op 11-4)
Giollacca(IRE) also lost some momentum in the early drama, but after trying to get involved on the far side she flattened out and probably needs an even stiffer test. (op 7-1)
Rawaaj, who took a walk in the market, came home in front of those that took the incorrect route and has to rate as unfortunate not to have followed up. (op 16-1)
Spider Boy, a game veteran, was second best on merit. (op 16-1)
Mr Tingle, well backed, was racing over a suitably longer trip and would have very likely led them home had he not made crucial mistakes. His turn shouldn't be far off. (op 16-1)

3541 BRAMPTON H'CAP CHASE (14 fncs 2 omitted) 2m 4f 110y
1:10 (1:10) (Class 4) (0-100,96) 5-Y-0+ **£2,602** (£764; £382; £190)

Form RPR
0031 **1** **Silver Dollars (FR)**[14] 3265 10-11-11 **95**.............................. DarylJacob 105+
(David Arbuthnot) *wnt 3rd at 5th and 2nd at 8th: led on ins bef 2 out: sn drew wl clr* **2/1**[2]
3P-4 **2** *18* **Overlaw**[30] 2952 9-11-8 **92**.. PaddyBrennan 92+
(Tom George) *led and sn 6 l clr: rn wd and hdd bef 2 out: sn v tired: heavily eased flat* **6/4**[1]
15/P **3** *22* **Randolph O'Brien (IRE)**[72] 2155 11-11-9 **96**...... SamTwiston-Davies(3) 66
(Nigel Twiston-Davies) *wnt 3rd at 9th: mstke 10th: rdn 11th: btn whn hit next: sn t.o* **4/1**[3]
P05P **4** *22* **Kercabellec (FR)**[10] 3388 13-9-7 **70** oh9.......................... JoeCornwall(7) 18
(John Cornwall) *taken down v early: chsd ldr: hit 5th: relegated 3rd whn hit 7th: last fr 10th: t.o next* **28/1**
23/4 **F** **Investment Affair (IRE)**[13] 3305 11-11-8 **92**.................. AidanColeman —
(Sarah Humphrey) *fell 1st* **13/2**

5m 27.6s (22.30) **Going Correction** +0.975s/f (Soft) **5** Ran SP% **110.1**
Speed ratings: **96,89,80,72,—**
CSF £5.67 TOTE £2.10: £1.30, £1.40; EX 5.80.
Owner A R Parrish **Bred** Daniel Moine **Trained** Compton, Berks

FOCUS
An ordinary handicap chase, run at a sound gallop. The winner is rated to his mark.

NOTEBOOK
Silver Dollars(FR) followed up his narrow success at Warwick a fortnight previous with a decisive display. He was 4lb higher, but does enjoy going this way around and could have been called the winner turning into the home straight. He is now due for a break and another likely rise will obviously make things tougher, but he is very much at the top of his game. (tchd 15-8 and 9-4)
Overlaw was very well backed on this return to a right-handed circuit and he took them along at a solid pace. He began to wilt nearing the home turn, though, and found this trip too demanding under such tactics. (tchd 13-8)
Randolph O'Brien(IRE) was another that came in for support reverting to a right-handed track. He was beginning to feel the pinch prior to mistakes at the final two on the far side that ended his chance. (op 11-2)
Kercabellec(FR), 9lb out of the weights, wasn't fluent and predictably got detached. (op 18-1)

3542 EUROPEAN BREEDERS' FUND "NATIONAL HUNT" NOVICES' HURDLE (QUALIFIER) (8 hdls) 2m 110y
1:40 (1:41) (Class 4) 4-7-Y-0 **£2,927** (£859; £429; £214)

Form RPR
1 **Spirit Son (FR)**[116] 5-11-12 0.. BarryGeraghty 141+
(Nicky Henderson) *hld up in midfield: smooth effrt to chse ldr 3 out: led on bit bef next: easily* **8/13**[1]
0 **2** *2 1/2* **Sivola De Sivola (FR)**[30] 2954 5-11-2 0........................... PaddyBrennan 120
(Tom George) *midfield: effrt after 5th: last of three gng clr 2 out: sn rdn: tk 2nd shortly after last and kpt on but no ch w wnr* **10/1**[3]
4-21 **3** *4* **Palace Jester**[51] 2612 6-11-8 122... APMcCoy 123+
(Jonjo O'Neill) *chsd ldr: led bef 3 out: hdd and hit 2 out: rdn and outpcd between last two: sn lost 2nd and wknd flat* **2/1**[2]
0003 **4** *15* **Deputy Dog (IRE)**[13] 3304 5-10-13 0......................... RichieMcLernon(3) 103+
(Jonjo O'Neill) *chsd ldrs: u.p 5th: btn after 3 out: mstke next: plodded on* **50/1**
5 **5** *7* **Airdrie (IRE)**[16] 3200 5-11-2 0.. AndrewThornton 98+
(Henrietta Knight) *prom: nt fluent 3 out: one pce next: wknd and mstke last* **25/1**
10-5 **6** *2* **Behindcloseddoors (IRE)**[11] 3365 5-11-2 0.................... SeanQuinlan 92
(Kim Bailey) *chsd ldrs: rdn whn nt fluent 3 out: sn lost tch* **28/1**
-040 **7** *2 1/2* **Original Prankster (IRE)**[17] 3158 6-10-13 0...... SamTwiston-Davies(3) 90
(Nigel Twiston-Davies) *chsd ldrs: rdn and lost tch after 3 out* **50/1**
P-00 **8** *30* **Tiger Bay (IRE)**[12] 3344 7-11-2 0.......................................(t) WillKennedy 60
(Noel Chance) *mounted outside paddock: set stdy pce: rdn and hdd bef 3 out: fdd bdly: t.o* **100/1**
0 **9** *nse* **Bumblebee (IRE)**[55] 2518 6-11-2 0............................ WayneHutchinson 59
(Warren Greatrex) *towards rr: t.o 3 out* **40/1**
60 **10** *6* **Upper Deck (IRE)**[57] 2473 6-11-2 0................................ WarrenMarston 53
(Richard Phillips) *j. poorly in rr: lost tch 4th: sn t.o* **150/1**
0 **11** *4* **Malenfant**[9] 3399 4-9-11 0.. JakeGreenall(7) 37
(Michael Easterby) *j. v poorly and wl bhd: rdr lost iron 1st: lost tch 4th: sn t.o* **100/1**
0-0 **P** **Graylyn Amber**[29] 2985 6-10-6 0................................ WayneKavanagh(3) —
(Robin Dickin) *t.k.h in rr: lost tch after 5th: hopelessly t.o whn p.u 2 out* **150/1**
00 **P** **Blantyre**[30] 2957 5-11-2 0.. HaddenFrost —
(Henrietta Knight) *sn bhd: wkng whn mstke 4th: stopped to nil and t.o whn mstke 5th: p.u next* **150/1**

3m 58.9s (4.00) **Going Correction** +0.525s/f (Soft)
WFA 4 from 5yo+ 11lb **13** Ran SP% **122.0**
Speed ratings: **111,109,107,100,97 96,95,81,81,78 76,—,—**
Tote Swingers: 1&2 £2.90, 2&3 £1.10 CSF £9.03 TOTE £1.70: £1.10, £1.50, £1.10; EX 9.50.
Owner Michael Buckley **Bred** Anne Baudrelle & Jean-Marc Baudrelle **Trained** Upper Lambourn, Berks

FOCUS
This novice event saw three backed pretty much to the exclusion of their rivals and they duly dominated in the home straight. All of them can rate higher this season and the form should work out. The smart winner was value for further.

NOTEBOOK
Spirit Son(FR) arrived with a lofty reputation on this British debut for his new connections having won on debut in a Listed event over 2m2f at Auteuil in September. He was all the rage despite conceding weight to a progressive 122-rated rival in Palace Jester and he completed the task with a taking performance. He was niggled to make his move after three out, but it was apparent turning for home he was the one to be on and he ultimately put the race to bed with plenty left in the tank. He is an imposing 5-y-o and fences will surely bring out the very best of him in due course, but plenty more should be heard about him over hurdles in the meantime. (op 1-2 tchd 4-6 in places)

Sivola De Sivola(FR) got the hang of things late in the day when eighth behind subsequent Tolworth winner Backspin on his debut last month. He again got going late in the day here, but finished his race very encouragingly and this represents vastly improved form. He will appreciate stepping up in trip and looks a sure-fire winner in the coming weeks. (op 12-1 tchd 9-1)

Palace Jester, readily off the mark at Wetherby in November, was ridden positively and went well. He couldn't raise his game when the winner loomed up, though, and probably paid late on for his early exertions. This was still another good effort under his penalty, but now may be the time to step him up in trip and he is a decent benchmark. (op 9-4 tchd 15-8)

Deputy Dog(IRE) wasn't always fluent. He kept to on post his best effort, however, and is another that can get off the mark when faced with a stiffer test.

Airdrie(IRE) has plenty of size about him and shaped with promise on his debut at Newbury last month. He didn't jump that well on this switch to hurdles, but again showed ability and is one to keep an eye on with a view to going chasing in due course. (tchd 28-1)

Behindcloseddoors(IRE) was well held, but did move nicely through the race until coming under pressure after hitting three out and this was better. He is one for handicaps. (op 33-1)

3543 HUNTINGDON AUDI A1 NOVICES' CHASE (16 fncs) 2m 4f 110y

2:10 (2:11) (Class 3) 5-Y-0+ **£4,664** (£1,448; £779)

Form				RPR
601/	1		**Mr Gardner (IRE)**665 4607 8-10-12 0 .... BarryGeraghty (Nicky Henderson) *j.w: mde all: drew clr fr 2 out: won v decisively* **1/2**1	150+
111/	2	32	**Patsy Finnegan**662 4678 9-10-12 0 .... RobertThornton (Alan King) *chsd wnr: pushed along and wknd bef 2 out: eased last* **3/1**2	125+
000	3	86	**Bemused (IRE)**66 2291 6-10-12 0 .... AndrewThornton (Simon Earle) *j.lft in last: lost tch 3rd: continued although wl over a fence bhd on fnl circ and inherited 3rd bef 2 out* **40/1**	32
00P/	P		**Platin Grounds (GER)**1014 4869 9-10-12 0 .... PaddyBrennan (Nigel Twiston-Davies) *pressed ldng pair tl fdd qckly 3 out: sn eased and t.o: remote 3rd whn p.u next* **6/1**3	—

5m 17.2s (11.90) **Going Correction** +0.975s/f (Soft) **4** Ran SP% **108.4**
Speed ratings: **116,103,71,—**
CSF £2.50 TOTE £1.50; EX 2.60.

Owner Mr & Mrs R Kelvin Hughes **Bred** J P King **Trained** Upper Lambourn, Berks

FOCUS

Three interesting novice chase prospects here, each of them returning from injury layoffs. The winner was a high-class novice hurdler two years ago and should prove at least as good over fences.

NOTEBOOK

Mr Gardner(IRE) looked a star in the making when slamming Fistral Beach in a maiden hurdle at Newbury in March 2009, but he unfortunately picked up a tendon injury afterwards and this was his first outing since. A very big horse, he has always been thought of as a chaser in the making and did win his sole outing between the flags in Ireland prior to joining his powerful connections. That was on soft ground, so this surface was not a worry and he was heavily backed. He completed the task with an impressive display and put in some bold leaps, in particular at the very first fence. He had the race sewn up before three out and has obviously resumed in great heart. Stepping up in trip should really be more to his liking over fences, but he isn't slow and it will be fascinating to see how he is campaigned for the remainder of the season. (op 8-15)

Patsy Finnegan had won his last three outings over hurdles, but he too picked up a tendon injury and was returning for this chase debut after a layoff just three days shy of the winner's. Officially rated 121 as a hurdler, he did his best to keep tabs with the winner through the race, but didn't prove such a natural as that rival. He was in trouble around three out, but kept to his task and should come on a bundle for the experience. (op 7-2)

Platin Grounds(GER) is rated 130 over hurdles and was making his chase debut after a whopping 1014-day absence. He was allowed to find his feet and jumped sufficiently, but was legless when in rear coming out of the back straight. He was sensibly pulled up before the home straight. (op 5-1)

3544 TURFTV H'CAP CHASE (10 fncs 2 omitted) 2m 110y

2:40 (2:40) (Class 4) (0-100,97) 5-Y-0+ **£2,665** (£827; £445)

Form				RPR
3-1P	1		**Desperate Dex (IRE)**79 2034 11-11-2 97 .... TonyKelly(10) (Ferdy Murphy) *nt gng wl early: urged along 3rd: 4th but outpcd at 5th: 15 l bhd at next: clsd after 3 out: 4 l 3rd and cajoled along fr 2 out tl last: c wd flat and passed plodding rivals cl home* **3/1**2	102
-614	2	1 3/4	**Guns Of Love (IRE)**10 3388 9-10-9 80 .... CharliePoste (Robin Dickin) *chsd ldr tl led 7th: rdn and racing v idly fr bef 2 out: plugged on tl collared nr fin* **13/8**1	83
06-4	3	1/2	**Kirbys Glen (IRE)**247 276 9-10-7 83 .... KeiranBurke(5) (Patrick Rodford) *3rd but outpcd at 5th: clsd to go 2nd after 3 out: pressed ldr w ev ch 2 out tl nt qckn fnl 100yds* **7/2**3	86
PPP0	P		**Aboukir Bay (IRE)**10 3392 7-10-7 85 .... (bt) JoeCornwall(7) (John Cornwall) *pushed along fr 2nd: nt fluent 3rd: lost tch bef 5th: t.o 3 out: p.u next* **14/1**	—
04U0	P		**Jumpjack Flint**58 2456 5-11-6 95 .... FelixDeGiles (Charlie Longsdon) *led and abt 6 l clr: hanging and rdn into fences: hdd u.p and mstke 7th: downed tools: t.o and p.u 2 out* **9/2**	—

4m 26.4s (16.20) **Going Correction** +0.975s/f (Soft) **5** Ran SP% **110.2**
Speed ratings: **100,99,98,—,—**
CSF £8.66 TOTE £2.20: £1.20, £1.60; EX 5.10.

Owner Crossed Fingers Partnership **Bred** Sir Anthony Scott **Trained** West Witton, N Yorks
■ Tony Kelly's first winner under rules.

FOCUS

A very tricky handicap. The winner is rated in line with last season's C&D win, and the next two are rated to their marks.

NOTEBOOK

Desperate Dex(IRE) reportedly ran flat when pulled up at Haydock on his return from a break in November, and things didn't look good for his supporters here as he began to run in snatches after jumping the second fence. He began to take interest again leaving the back straight and made up significant ground, but he wasn't clever two out. That looked to be an end of his chance, but as the placed horses began to wilt after the last he picked up again and ultimately won going away. This veteran clearly has his quirks and his inexperienced rider - gaining a first win under rules - deserves the plaudits, but he has now scored on four of his last six outings. (op 9-4 tchd 7-2)

Guns Of Love(IRE) was solid in the betting back down in trip. He looked the one to be on when taking it up on the back straight, but began to make heavy weather of things nearing the home straight. He kept to his task, but was tired after the last and this ground was no doubt softer than he cares for. He helps to put the form into some perspective. (op 7-4 tchd 6-4)

Kirbys Glen(IRE) attracted some support and, ridden with more patience than is often the case, held every chance. He was done with after the last, though, and remains a maiden under rules. (op 9-2)

Jumpjack Flint, making his chase and handicap debuts, remains one to avoid at all costs. (op 6-1 tchd 4-1)

3545 RACING UK MARES' NOVICES' H'CAP HURDLE (8 hdls) 2m 110y

3:10 (3:10) (Class 4) (0-100,100) 4-Y-0+ **£2,276** (£668; £334; £166)

Form				RPR
-000	1		**Roxane Bruere (FR)**68 2244 6-9-4 73 .... (t) ChristopherWard(10) (Robin Dickin) *trckd ldrs: 3rd whn nt fluent 4th: led after 3 out: clr fr last: kpt on one pce* **7/1**	77+
-P42	2	3 1/4	**Autumm Spirit**7 3430 7-10-6 82 .... (t) WayneKavanagh(3) (Robin Dickin) *unruly and mounted outside paddock: rdr lost iron 1st: prom: led 4th tl after 3 out: 3rd next: regained 2nd flat but nt rch wnr* **9/1**	84
P-42	3	5	**Vin Rose**30 2956 6-10-12 85 .... AidanColeman (Mark Rimell) *hld up: effrt 5th: wnt 2nd 2 out: rdn and nrly 3 l down and no imp whn blnd last* **11/4**1	84+
5-33	4	11	**Sally's Idea**56 2505 5-11-3 97 .... MrJHamer(7) (Donald McCain) *t.k.h in ld: hdd 4th: hit next: hit 3 out: sn lost tch* **3/1**2	84
2013	5	8	**Lady Pacha**59 2435 4-10-7 97 .... BrianToomey(5) (Tim Pitt) *bhd: rdn bef 4th: j. slowly 5th: struggling 3 out* **4/1**3	62
532P	6	17	**Doyenne Dream**12 3338 4-11-1 100 .... FelixDeGiles (James Eustace) *immediately pushed along: bhd: hrd rdn bef 4th: nt keen: struggling 3 out* **5/1**	63

4m 6.40s (11.50) **Going Correction** +0.525s/f (Soft)
WFA 4 from 5yo+ 11lb **6** Ran SP% **110.8**
Speed ratings (Par 105): **93,91,89,83,80 72**
Tote Swingers: 1&2 £5.10, 1&3 £3.70, 2&3 £3.50 CSF £58.44 CT £205.44 TOTE £7.80: £5.80, £10.30; EX 64.50.

Owner R E Hill **Bred** Herve Durandet **Trained** Atherstone on Stour, Warwicks

FOCUS

A weak mares' novice handicap, run in a slow time. The winner is rated back to her best.

NOTEBOOK

Roxane Bruere(FR) had shown little previously, including on her handicap debut last time out, but she was well backed and opened her account with a ready effort. She travelled best of all and took it up going well rounding the home bend under her conditional rider, who was completing a double having taken the right course aboard Dancing Daffodil in the controversial opener. She wasn't fully extended to win and a first-time tongue tie clearly worked the oracle. Connections later reasoned that a crossed noseband and possibly going right handed was responsible for the much-improved showing. Official explanation: trainer said regarding apperent improvement that the application of a tongue tie, cross nose band and possibly the right handed-track had helped. (op 9-1 tchd 10-1)

Autumm Spirit, a distant second to an in-form rival last time, kept on to give her yard a 1-2. This was a lot more encouraging and she could build on it back over a slightly stiffer test, providing she can maintain this form. (tchd 10-1)

Vin Rose, well backed, began to be niggled three out, yet responded. She was looking held by the winner prior to hitting the last, however, and probably found the ground against her. (op 85-40 tchd 15-8)

Sally's Idea was sent out into a clear early lead, but that was reduced going out onto the back straight and she was in trouble around three from home. She is another for whom the ground was probably too demanding. (op 7-2)

3546 PETERBOROUGH CHASE RESTAURANT STANDARD OPEN NATIONAL HUNT FLAT RACE 2m 110y

3:40 (3:40) (Class 6) 5-6-Y-0 **£1,370** (£399; £199)

Form				RPR
	1		**Hit The Headlines (IRE)** 5-11-0 0 .... BarryGeraghty (Nicky Henderson) *hld up towards outer: clsd gng wl 3f out: led over 2f out: clr and pushed along over 1f out: impressive* **11/10**1	121+
	2	9	**Diamond Sweeper (IRE)** 5-11-0 0 .... RobertThornton (Alan King) *bhd on outer: effrt 4f out: rdn to chse wnr vainly fnl 300yds: promising* **9/2**2	107+
0	3	6	**Sunny Ledgend**14 3266 6-10-7 0 .... MrSWDrinkwater(7) (Andrew J Martin) *racd keenly: led at decent pce tl hdd over 2f out: no ch w principals but kpt on gamely in wl hld 3rd fnl f* **33/1**	101
	4	nse	**Howard's Legacy (IRE)** 5-11-0 0 .... AidanColeman (Venetia Williams) *hld up in tch: effrt 4f out: ev ch over 2f out: wknd over 1f out* **25/1**	101+
	5	18	**Piece Of Magic**306 6-10-0 0 .... JakeGreenall(7) (Michael Easterby) *prom: gng wl 3f out: ev ch tl fdd bdly fnl 2f* **15/2**	83
6	6	3 1/4	**Wiesentraum (GER)**16 3200 5-11-0 0 .... LeightonAspell (Lucy Wadham) *hld up and bhd: effrt 5f out: lost tch 3f out: poor 6th st* **17/2**	83
	7	7	**Turtlethomas (IRE)**272 5-10-9 0 .... DavidBass(5) (Lawney Hill) *chsd ldrs: rdn and rn green over 3f out: sn lost tch: poor 7th st* **14/1**	76
3-	8	35	**Sir Cool (IRE)**270 5283 5-11-0 0 .... APMcCoy (Tor Sturgis) *prom tl fdd rapidly 3f out: t.o* **13/2**3	38
0	9	3 1/2	**North Stack**77 2074 5-11-0 0 .... RhysFlint (Michael Scudamore) *last after 4f: lost tch 4f out: sn t.o* **150/1**	34
00	10	nk	**Topthorn**55 2518 5-11-0 0 .... WillKennedy (Martin Bosley) *bhd: rdn and lost tch 4f out: sn t.o* **150/1**	34
	11	91	**Just Richie (IRE)** 6-11-0 0 .... NickScholfield (Arthur Whiting) *last and struggling after 4f: a long way bhd fr 1/2-way: fin eventually* **125/1**	—
0	P		**Carbis Bay**60 2432 5-10-9 0 .... (p) GemmaGracey-Davison(5) (Zoe Davison) *t.k.h: w ldr tl stopped to nil after 6f: sn p.u* **150/1**	—

3m 53.7s (4.60) **Going Correction** +0.525s/f (Soft)
WFA 5 from 6yo 3lb **12** Ran SP% **117.7**
Speed ratings: **110,105,102,102,94 92,89,73,71,71 28,—**
Tote Swingers: 1&2 £3.20, 1&3 £9.80, 2&3 £20.60 CSF £5.86 TOTE £1.90: £1.10, £1.80, £6.40; EX 7.70.

Owner Michael Buckley **Bred** Richard O' Hara **Trained** Upper Lambourn, Berks

FOCUS

Somewhat unusually for a race of this nature there was a decent gallop on and it produced an impressive debut winner, who scored in a good time and looks a smart prospect. The first four came clear.

NOTEBOOK

Hit The Headlines(IRE) ◆ came right away from his rivals from 2f out, handing his trainer/rider a treble from three runners on the card, and looks a horse with a very bright future. A 5-y-o with bundles of scope, his dam is from the same family as smart 2m chaser Dempsey and has already produced this season's useful Irish novice chaser Lastoftheleaders, who also won a bumper and over hurdles. He initially ran green when asked for an effort, but responded kindly turning for home and was soon in command. He certainly appeals as the sort to defy a penalty and this may well tempt Nicky Henderson into looking at the Champion Bumper at the Cheltenham Festival. (op 6-5 tchd 5-4, 6-4 in places)

Diamond Sweeper(IRE) ◆, a half-brother to dual bumper winner Giordano Bruno, hails from a top yard and didn't go unbacked for his racecourse debut. He proved distinctly green and became outpaced on the back straight, but got better the further he went. He stayed on to finish a clear second-best and should go close on his next assignment. (op 8-1)

Sunny Ledgend improved a deal on his debut seventh at Warwick last month and fared best of those with previous experience. He started off in points and left the clear impression here that he needs a stiffer test. (op 28-1)
Howard's Legacy(IRE) was patiently ridden and moved up going sweetly nearing the home turn. He was found out in the final 2f, but is sure to improve for the initial experience. A longer trip will be to his liking over jumps. (op 20-1)
Piece Of Magic was unbeaten in two points on good ground and was something of a market springer on this bumper debut. She looked sure to place nearing the home turn, but found very little once push came to shove and perhaps the ground was against her. Official explanation: trainer said filly finished distressed (tchd 13-2)
Sir Cool(IRE) split subsequent hurdle winners on his debut at Kempton last season and was making his debut for new connections with the assistance of Tony McCoy. Ridden prominently, he wilted coming out of the back straight, probably on account of the more testing surface. (op 11-2 tchd 5-1)
Carbis Bay Official explanation: jockey said gelding lost his action and hung badly left
T/Plt: £81.30 to a £1 stake. Pool: £50,620.39. 454.05 winning tickets. T/Qpdt: £51.50 to a £1 stake. Pool: £3,440.65. 49.40 winning tickets. IM

2654 MUSSELBURGH (R-H)
Friday, January 14

OFFICIAL GOING: Good to soft (soft in places)
Wind: Breezy, against Weather: Cloudy, bright

3547 COUNTRY REFRESHMENTS MAIDEN HURDLE (9 hdls) 2m
12:50 (12:50) (Class 4) 4-Y-0+ **£1,951** (£573; £286; £143)

Form				RPR
5	1		**King Fingal (IRE)**[71] 2162 6-11-5 0 DougieCostello (John Quinn) *t.k.h: prom: effrt and lft cl 2nd 2 out: ev ch whn lft in ld last: rdn out* **5/2**[2]	113+
403	2	4 ½	**Kaolak (USA)**[12] 3331 5-11-5 0 JasonMaguire (Keith Reveley) *pressed ldr: led 3 out: jst hdd whn lft in ld next: jst in front whn blnd and hdd last: kpt on same pce run-in* **9/2**[3]	113+
051-	3	17	**Wyse Hill Teabags**[307] 4582 6-11-5 0 RichieMcGrath (Jim Goldie) *nt fluent on occasions: midfield: effrt bef 3 out: plugged on fr next to take modest 3rd run-in: no ch w first two* **16/1**	91
-236	4	hd	**Dr Flynn (IRE)**[66] 2296 6-11-5 0 WilsonRenwick (Howard Johnson) *hld up: hdwy and in tch after 4 out: rdn and outpcd fr next* **20/1**	90
5	5	5	**Fortuni (IRE)**[12] 3331 5-11-5 0 GrahamLee (Rose Dobbin) *trckd ldrs tl rdn and outpcd 3 out: lft modest 3rd next: sn no ex* **8/1**	85
20	6	11	**Chocolate Caramel (USA)**[31] 2939 9-11-5 0 BrianHughes (Richard Fahey) *hld up: shkn up bef 3 out: nvr rchd ldrs* **50/1**	75
	7	½	**Cool Baranca (GER)**[84] 5-10-9 0 RyanMania(3) (Dianne Sayer) *hld up towards rr: outpcd after 4 out: n.d after* **125/1**	67
0-50	8	3	**Darkan Road**[63] 2355 6-11-5 0 JanFaltejsek (George Charlton) *bhd: j.rt and blkd 2nd: rdn after 4 out: nvr on terms* **66/1**	71
	9	3	**Royal Willy (IRE)**[84] 5-11-0 0 MissLHorner(5) (Chris Grant) *bhd: outpcd 1/2-way: sn btn* **33/1**	68
	10	3 ¾	**The Galloping Shoe**[160] 6-11-2 0 EwanWhillans(3) (Alistair Whillans) *t.k.h: hld up: pushed along after 4 out: nvr on terms* **14/1**	64
5	11	44	**Barello Road**[56] 2511 5-10-12 0 CampbellGillies (Lucinda Russell) *in tch: nt fluent and lost pl 3rd: struggling fr next: t.o* **100/1**	13
0	12	¾	**Suburbia (USA)**[12] 3331 5-11-5 0 (t) PeterBuchanan (Lucinda Russell) *midfield: struggling 4 out: wknd bef next: t.o* **125/1**	19
1	F		**Aikman (IRE)**[246] 311 7-11-2 0 HarryHaynes(3) (James Ewart) *led tl hit and hdd 3 out: rallied and regained ld whn fell next* **9/4**[1]	116+
	F		**Sobrando Lodge (IRE)**[69] 2229 6-11-5 0 DenisO'Regan (Mark Michael McNiff, Ire) *in tch: rdn and outpcd bef 3 out: sn wknd: no ch whn fell last* **28/1**	64

3m 46.5s (-1.90) **Going Correction** +0.075s/f (Yiel) **14** Ran SP% **118.4**
Speed ratings (Par 105): **107,104,96,96,93 88,87,86,84,83 61,60,—,—**
Tote Swingers: 1&2 £3.20, 1&3 £18.60, 2&3 £11.40 CSF £13.49 TOTE £2.70: £1.50, £1.30, £4.00; EX 15.20.
Owner King Fingal Partnership **Bred** The Lavington Stud **Trained** Settrington, N Yorks

FOCUS
An interesting opener to the card with a number of unexposed sorts in this maiden hurdle. What looked like proving a tight three-way finish was ended by the fall of Aikman at the second-last. He is rated as the winner, and the first two both posted big steps up.

NOTEBOOK
King Fingal(IRE) was well supported in the market and was able to take advantage of Aikman's fall two out by pulling clear of the eventual runner-up after the final flight. He clearly enjoys some cut in the ground and looks the sort to take higher order in the hurdling ranks. (op 7-2)
Kaolak(USA) ◆ had won off 92 on the Flat, but there were concerns about his ability to see out the trip in the testing conditions. In the end he saw it out well enough and was just unlucky to meet a better horse on the day. He is improving with every run and is sure to be winning soon. (op 11-2 tchd 4-1)
Wyse Hill Teabags ran well for a long way and was unlucky to be hampered after the second last by Aikman when the horse got up. He probably needed the run after a 307-day absence and is sure to come on for it, especially if running on good ground on which he had previously won a bumper. (op 12-1)
Dr Flynn(IRE) was just out-battled for third, but this was an improved effort and he should again come on for the experience. (op 18-1)
Fortuni(IRE) was prominent but weakened after the last and couldn't see out the trip in the conditions. He will be better on decent ground.
The Galloping Shoe Official explanation: jockey said gelding bled from the nose
Aikman(IRE) ◆ had every chance when falling at the second-last. Having travelled well, he arguably looked the most likely winner but dived at the hurdle. This was nevertheless a good run and he remains a nice prospect. (tchd 11-4)
Sobrando Lodge(IRE) fell at the last having run okay until tiring. (tchd 11-4)

3548 COUNTRY REFRESHMENTS BEGINNERS' CHASE (18 fncs) 3m
1:20 (1:20) (Class 4) 5-Y-0+ **£3,252** (£955; £477; £238)

Form				RPR
0-4	1		**On His Own (IRE)**[13] 3288 7-11-2 0 BrianHughes (Howard Johnson) *led to 12th: cl up: str chal and rdn 4 out: hit 2 out and last: led run-in: drvn and asserted towards fin* **4/9**[1]	123+
43P/	2	1	**Nine De Sivola (FR)**[636] 5079 10-11-2 127 GrahamLee (Ferdy Murphy) *cl-up: led 12th: hrd pressed fr 4 out: sn rdn: hdd run-in: hld towards fin* **7/2**[2]	118
0262	3	18	**Rossini's Dancer**[12] 3332 6-11-2 95 PaddyAspell (Sue Bradburne) *trckd ldrs: mstkes 8th and next: outpcd 13th: plugged on fr 2 out: no ch w first two* **28/1**	102
/5-4	4	7	**Posh Bird (IRE)**[69] 2224 8-10-9 110 AELynch (I R Ferguson, Ire) *trckd ldrs tl rdn and wknd bef 4 out* **7/1**[3]	88
5000	P		**Soldiers Tree (IRE)**[12] 3336 6-11-2 0 (p) TomMessenger (Sue Bradburne) *in tch: rdn 8th: lost tch fr 10th: p.u 13th* **100/1**	—

6m 14.1s (10.70) **Going Correction** +0.575s/f (Soft) **5** Ran SP% **108.4**
Speed ratings: **105,104,98,96,—**
CSF £2.45 TOTE £1.30: £1.50, £1.90; EX 3.50.
Owner Andrea & Graham Wylie **Bred** Ms Margaret Treacy **Trained** Billy Row, Co Durham
■ Stewards' Enquiry : Brian Hughes one-day ban: used whip in the incorrect place (Jan 28)

FOCUS
An uncompetitive beginners' chase. The winner is rated close to the level of his best hurdles form and the second is rated 140+ at his best over fences.

NOTEBOOK
On His Own(IRE) was well supported into 4-9 and though he won, it was only after a thrilling duel in the home straight with Nine De Sivola. He was able to set his own pace early on and it was a steady one in these testing conditions. He looked to have the measure of the runner-up, but novicey mistakes at the final two fences kept giving his rival a chance and he was only able to draw clear in the final yards. Prior to that he had actually jumped very well on his chasing debut and, seen as still a "big baby" at home, he is certain to come on for the experience. Clearly well regarded, he looks a lovely prospect. (tchd 4-6 in places)
Nine De Sivola(FR) is as experienced as they come in beginners' chases, having already had 18 previous chase runs, but he has still been unable to win any of them. He out-jumped the winner most of the way and this was a good effort after a 636-day absence, for which he will come on a bundle. A step up in trip is certain to suit and a race like the Scottish National, in which he was runner-up in 2007, looks the target. (tchd 3-1 and 4-1)
Rossini's Dancer was under pressure with a circuit still to travel but plugged on well to take a distant third. He faced a tough ask at the weights and may be of more interest if sent handicapping. (op 16-1)
Posh Bird(IRE) travelled well for a long way but emptied turning for home. Her first chase under rules, she may find better opportunities in mares'-only races. (op 13-2 tchd 11-2)
Soldiers Tree(IRE) was off the bridle more than a circuit from home and showed nothing.

3549 COUNTRY REFRESHMENTS H'CAP CHASE (16 fncs) 2m 4f
1:50 (1:50) (Class 4) (0-110,101) 5-Y-0+ **£3,903** (£1,146; £573; £286)

Form				RPR
0063	1		**Nelliedonethat (IRE)**[52] 2602 11-11-2 91 CampbellGillies (Lucinda Russell) *led to 2nd: cl up: led 6th: mde rest: drew clr fr 4 out: eased run-in* **4/1**[2]	110+
0-04	2	15	**Guns And Butter (IRE)**[62] 2371 9-11-11 100 WilsonRenwick (Rose Dobbin) *trckd ldrs: pushed along fnl circ: rallied to chse (clr) wnr 3 out: kpt on fr next: no imp* **8/1**	103+
UF-4	3	2	**Lahib The Fifth (IRE)**[66] 2298 11-11-10 99 FearghalDavis (Nicky Richards) *hld up: rdn along 1/2-way: hdwy after 5 out: plugged on fr 2 out: nvr rchd ldrs* **22/1**	99
-300	4	1 ¾	**Saddlers Deal (IRE)**[31] 2942 6-11-12 101 DenisO'Regan (Chris Grant) *cl up: chsd wnr 10th to 3 out: wknd fr next* **4/1**[2]	98
13P2	5	½	**Emotive**[31] 2942 8-11-11 100 RichieMcGrath (Barry Murtagh) *hld up: stdy hdwy 11th: rdn and wknd bef 4 out* **8/1**	97
0P-P	6	7	**Golden Globe (IRE)**[58] 2450 9-11-4 100 PaulGallagher(7) (Ferdy Murphy) *hld up: mstke and drvn 9th: struggling fr 11th* **20/1**	90
-60U	7	11	**Devil Water**[49] 2656 8-11-4 100 NathanMoscrop(7) (James Ewart) *hld up: pushed along 11th: sn btn* **10/1**	79
0-41	P		**Cybora (FR)**[56] 2510 9-11-10 99 GrahamLee (Ferdy Murphy) *led 2nd to 6th: w ldr tl mstke 9th: struggling after next: t.o whn p.u bef 4 out* **7/2**[1]	—
3/P0	P		**Spirit Calling (IRE)**[12] 3336 10-11-11 100 (p) PeterBuchanan (Lucinda Russell) *cl up: rdn and wknd bef 9th: t.o whn p.u bef 4 out* **7/1**[3]	—

5m 13.6s (12.40) **Going Correction** +0.575s/f (Soft) **9** Ran SP% **115.1**
Speed ratings: **98,92,91,90,90 87,83,—,—**
Tote Swingers: 1&2 £6.60, 1&3 £15.90, 2&3 £30.90 CSF £35.62 CT £622.60 TOTE £5.80: £2.50, £2.40, £4.60; EX 38.30.
Owner Kelso Members Lowflyers Club **Bred** Miss Katie Thorner And Joseph Kent **Trained** Arlary, Perth & Kinross

FOCUS
An ordinary handicap chase, but an impressive winner who was value for further and is rated back to form.

NOTEBOOK
Nelliedonethat(IRE) put up a magnificent display of jumping and ran out an easy winner. Taking up the running with more than a circuit to run, he had his rivals in trouble a long way from home. Foot perfect in the home straight, he made good use of his stamina having won over 3m here before, and is likely to be just as effective over a longer trip. (op 5-1)
Guns And Butter(IRE) had disappointed on his last two starts, but this was a vast improvement as he seemed to enjoy the testing conditions. On this show he is worth a step up in trip. (op 15-2 tchd 7-1)
Lahib The Fifth(IRE) was under pressure with a fair way to go, but was another who stayed on well and enjoyed the conditions. He should come on for the run and needs a stamina test these days. (op 18-1)
Saddlers Deal(IRE) was ridden prominently but in the conditions was unable to quicken with the winner. The trip appeared to cause no real problem and so a return to the better ground on which he ran a promising seasonal reappearance will suit. (op 5-1)
Emotive looked like running a big race as he travelled ominously through the field down the back straight, but was only able to stay on one-paced. He is a consistent sort who seemingly ran his race, but may need a drop back down the handicap. (op 7-1 tchd 6-1)
Golden Globe(IRE) had been pulled up on his last two starts so finishing was an improvement, but he needs 2m. (tchd 22-1)
Cybora(FR) Official explanation: trainer said mare was unsuited by ground good to soft (soft in places)
Spirit Calling(IRE) Official explanation: jockey said gelding had a breathing problem

3550 COUNTRY REFRESHMENTS JUVENILE HURDLE (FOR THE TOM MCCONNELL MEMORIAL TROPHY) (9 hdls) 2m
2:20 (2:20) (Class 4) 4-Y-0 **£1,951** (£573; £286; £143)

Form				RPR
42	1		**Vosges (FR)**[11] 3358 4-10-12 113 DougieCostello (James Ewart) *led: hdd and rdn bef 2 out: rallied u.p to ld run-in: styd on wl* **6/4**[2]	105
23	2	1 ½	**Makbullet**[49] 2655 4-10-9 98 JamesO'Farrell(3) (Michael Smith) *chsd ldrs: smooth hdwy to ld bef 2 out: rdn bef last: edgd rt and hdd run-in: kpt on: hld nr fin* **5/1**[3]	103+
14	3	5	**Dance For Julie (IRE)**[10] 3386 4-10-12 0 BarryKeniry (Ben Haslam) *trckd wnr: effrt and ev ch whn nt fluent 3 out: sn rdn: wknd appr last* **11/8**[1]	99

0545 4 34 **Capricornus (USA)**[11] 3358 4-10-12 92 GrahamLee 84
(Ferdy Murphy) *nt fluent: in tch: rdn after 4 out: wknd fr next* 12/1

3m 53.7s (5.30) **Going Correction** +0.075s/f (Yiel) 4 Ran SP% 106.5

Speed ratings: **89,88,85,68**

CSF £8.21 TOTE £2.60; EX 5.40.

Owner A Humbert N A Sperling & Mrs L Drew **Bred** Mme Henri Devin **Trained** Langholm, Dumfries & G'way

FOCUS

A small but competitive juvenile hurdle. The first three ran pretty much to their marks.

NOTEBOOK

Vosges(FR) has made a pleasing start to his British career and won in a good manner here, having been headed before the final flight. Battling back after the last, he jumped well and looks the sort to make a nice chaser in the long-term. Connections are confident he will be able to defy a penalty, and he looks sure to be winning plenty of races now he is off the mark. (op 5-4)

Makbullet had stamina doubts coming into this having been a winning sprinter on the Flat, but in the end appeared to see out the trip well, just being undone in the closing stages. He travelled best throughout the race and jumped nicely, but good ground is likely to bring the best out of him in the future. (op 13-2)

Dance For Julie(IRE) was disappointing having been well backed into favouritism. For a long time she looked a possible winner, but turning for home she was unable to go the pace. She remains a nice sort, but her only win came on good ground and the suspicion is that she needs a better surface. (op 6-4 tchd 13-8)

Capricornus(USA) had been previously beaten by both the front two and never looked like reversing that. A longer trip may bring out some improvement. (op 9-1)

3551 COUNTRY REFRESHMENTS (S) HURDLE (9 hdls) 2m

2:50 (2:50) (Class 5) 4-Y-0+ **£1,951** (£573; £286; £143)

Form				RPR
3-00	1		**Pokfulham (IRE)**[12] 3335 5-11-5 107 (v) GrahamLee (Jim Goldie) *cl up: effrt bef 3 out: ev ch next: edgd rt whn nt fluent last: styd on u.p to ld nr fin* 11/4[2]	113
60P-	2	hd	**Lennon (IRE)**[281] 5097 11-11-5 0 BrianHughes (Howard Johnson) *j.lft: led: rdn 2 out: hung lft run-in: hdd nr fin* 8/13[1]	113
0/	3	17	**Lakil House (IRE)**[328] 11-11-0 112 (p) CO'Farrell(5) (Jason Cairns, Ire) *trckd ldrs: rdn and outpcd bef 3 out: no ex whn hit next* 17/2[3]	97
	4	18	**Danehillsundance (IRE)**[171] 7-11-5 0 (t) BarryKeniry (Philip Kirby) *hld up: outpcd after 4 out: n.d after* 14/1	78
4005	5	nse	**King's Chorister**[114] 1574 5-11-5 66 (t) BrianHarding (Barry Murtagh) *hld up: hdwy and in tch after 4 out: wknd fr next* 100/1	78
305-	6	17	**Wee Sonny (IRE)**[15] 3233 5-11-5 96 JamesO'Farrell(3) (Liam Lennon, Ire) *prom untl rdn and wknd fr 4 out* 28/1	64
P6-0	7	3/4	**Mississippian (IRE)**[12] 3331 7-10-12 0 MrAdamNicol(7) (Rose Dobbin) *t.k.h early: hld up: struggling 1/2-way: nvr on terms* 50/1	60
/55-	P		**Autumn Harvest**[131] 2623 7-11-2 90 RyanMania(3) (William Young) *t.k.h: hdwy and prom 3rd: wknd 4 out: p.u bef next* 40/1	—
0	P		**Mr Lu**[12] 3331 6-11-5 0 RichieMcGrath (Jim Goldie) *bhd: hit 1st: struggling fr 4th: t.o whn p.u 4 out* 66/1	—

3m 48.2s (-0.20) **Going Correction** +0.075s/f (Yiel) 9 Ran SP% 116.1

Speed ratings (Par 103): **103,102,94,85,85 76,76,—,—**

Tote Swingers: 1&2 £1.60, 1&3 £1.80, 2&3 £2.10 CSF £4.94 TOTE £2.70: £1.10, £1.10, £2.00; EX 10.10.No bid for the winner.

Owner Ambrose Turnbull **Bred** Killian Farm **Trained** Uplawmoor, E Renfrews

FOCUS

Another tight finish in which the front two pulled well clear of the rest. An ordinary seller in which the winner ran to his mark.

NOTEBOOK

Pokfulham(IRE) won only his second race in 27 career starts, wearing a visor for the first time over hurdles, which seemed to do the trick. Never in front until the final few yards, this was a game effort to keep on past the favourite. The drop in class on a course he has run well at previously should give him confidence, and he can be stepped back up in class. He was retained without a bid. (op 3-1)

Lennon(IRE) had easily the best chance on the figures and should have won, but idled in the closing stages and gave the impression that he isn't the most game of horses. Allowed to set the pace, he looked sure to pull clear turning for home but seemed unwilling. He clearly retains some ability and may benefit from more patient riding nowadays. (op 4-6 tchd 8-11)

Lakil House(IRE) was a distant third, but finished well clear of the rest and put in a good run, having not been seen since a point-to-point in February. He probably needs more of a trip than this, and can improve for it. (op 9-1)

Danehillsundance(IRE) was making his hurdles debut. Rated 84 on the Flat, he may be seen with better effect on better ground. (op 16-1)

King's Chorister was coming back from a break of 114 days and had the headgear removed.

3552 COUNTRY REFRESHMENTS KILMANY CUP H'CAP CHASE (18 fncs) 3m

3:20 (3:20) (Class 3) (0-120,120) 5-Y-0+ **£6,505** (£1,910; £955; £477)

Form				RPR
511F	1		**Isla Pearl Fisher**[11] 3361 8-10-3 97 PaddyAspell (N W Alexander) *hld up: hdwy 5 out: effrt and led bef last: kpt on strly run-in* 7/2[1]	110+
/243	2	5	**Festival King (IRE)**[11] 3360 9-10-0 94 oh2 BrianHarding (Pauline Robson) *trckd ldrs: led 3 out to bef last: sn rdn: kpt on same pce run-in* 11/1	103+
1-52	3	9	**Bally Wall (IRE)**[67] 2269 8-11-5 113 AELynch (I R Ferguson, Ire) *hld up in tch: mstke and lost pl 3rd: rallied bef 11th: outpcd bef 4 out: plugged on fnl 2: nt pce of first two* 9/2[3]	114+
/342	4	6	**Lockstown**[54] 2550 8-11-0 108 GrahamLee (Ann Hamilton) *trckd ldrs: drvn and outpcd 3 out: no imp fr next* 4/1[2]	102
4506	5	11	**Top Dressing (IRE)**[31] 2940 10-11-5 113 (p) BrianHughes (Howard Johnson) *cl up: effrt after 5 out: wknd bef 2 out* 25/1	97
2-34	6	6	**Go Silver Bullet (FR)**[187] 947 10-11-12 120 PeterBuchanan (Lucinda Russell) *led to 3 out: rdn and wknd fr next* 25/1	98
3623	7	27	**Ballabrook (IRE)**[31] 2940 9-10-10 104 JasonMaguire (Donald McCain) *hld up: j.lft 8th and next: rdn 5 out: wknd bef next* 5/1	67
00-0	P		**Soprano (GER)**[12] 3335 9-10-9 103 KennyJohnson (Jim Goldie) *nt fluent: bhd and detached: clsd briefly after 12th: wknd next: t.o whn p.u bef 2 out* 40/1	—
-P21	P		**New Shuil (IRE)**[56] 2507 7-10-13 107 DenisO'Regan (John Wade) *hld up in midfield: rdn and outpcd after 5 out: sn btn: t.o whn p.u bef 2 out* 9/2[3]	—

6m 13.0s (9.60) **Going Correction** +0.575s/f (Soft) 9 Ran SP% 113.7

Speed ratings: **107,105,102,100,96 94,85,—,—**

Tote Swingers: 1&2 £7.60, 1&3 £5.90, 2&3 £10.00 CSF £37.93 CT £174.65 TOTE £3.00: £1.10, £6.10, £1.30; EX 44.60.

Owner Mrs J E B Gammell **Bred** Mrs D Marshall **Trained** Kinneston, Perth & Kinross

FOCUS

A wide-open looking handicap chase run at a good pace. The winner is rated in line with his Ayr fall.

NOTEBOOK

Isla Pearl Fisher, due to go up 4lb following a last-fence fall last time, took advantage of his old mark to jump upsides the leader two out and run out a good winner. He may now be given a short break and brought back for a race at the Scottish Grand National meeting.

Festival King(IRE) made a mistake two out that put paid to his chances. He tended to jump left-handed most of the way and will possibly be better served going that way round, but this better after a couple of disappointing runs. A drop back in grade may assist.

Bally Wall(IRE) made a bad mistake early on and was under pressure from then onwards, so did well to stay on for third. He is already due to be dropped 2lb, which should help.

Lockstown jumped well, but may have too much on his plate now off a mark of 108.

Top Dressing(IRE) ran better than of late and may have been assisted by the re-application of cheekpieces.

Go Silver Bullet(FR) made the running but perhaps struggled for fitness in this relatively testing ground after a 187-day absence. He should come on for the run and may be dropped back in trip.

Ballabrook(IRE) Official explanation: trainer said gelding was unsuited by track

3553 COUNTRY REFRESHMENTS INTERMEDIATE OPEN NATIONAL HUNT FLAT RACE 2m

3:50 (3:50) (Class 5) 4-6-Y-O **£1,626** (£477; £238; £119)

Form				RPR
41	1		**Jukebox Melody (IRE)**[61] 2403 5-11-12 0 GrahamLee (Malcolm Jefferson) *t.k.h: prom: hdwy 7f out: led over 2f out: pushed out fnl f* 7/4[1]	110+
	2	2	**Pyjama Game (IRE)** 5-11-5 0 WilsonRenwick (Rose Dobbin) *midfield: rdn over 4f out: hdwy to chse wnr over 1f out: edgd rt fnl f: kpt on* 8/1[3]	101
403	3	4 1/2	**Thurnham**[49] 2660 5-11-5 0 DenisO'Regan (Keith Reveley) *hld up: effrt and pushed along 6f out: styd on fnl 2f: no imp* 9/1	96
0	4	nk	**Dizzy River (IRE)**[246] 311 6-11-5 0 RichieMcGrath (George Charlton) *hld up: stdy hdwy over 6f out: outpcd 4f out: kpt on fr 2f out: no imp* 8/1[3]	96
	5	1 1/2	**Think Green** 5-10-12 0 BrianHarding (James Ewart) *trckd ldrs: effrt and drvn over 2f out: kpt on same pce over 1f out* 8/1[3]	87
0-	6	5	**Shannagarry (IRE)**[272] 5227 5-11-5 0 JanFaltejsek (George Charlton) *t.k.h: cl up: led 1/2-way to over 1f out: sn wknd* 16/1	89
0-4	7	2 3/4	**Jacks Grey**[55] 6-11-5 0 JasonMaguire (I R Ferguson, Ire) *hld up: stdy hdwy over 5f out: rdn and wknd fr 2f out* 9/2[2]	86
	8	1	**Beyond The Tweed** 5-10-12 0 NathanMoscrop(7) (James Ewart) *in tch: hdwy 1/2-way: effrt and ev ch 3f out: wknd fr 2f out* 50/1	85
00	9	7	**Knockando**[63] 2355 6-11-5 0 PeterBuchanan (Lucinda Russell) *cl up: rdn over 5f out: wknd fr 3f out* 25/1	78
0	10	52	**Isla Patriot**[246] 311 5-11-5 0 PaddyAspell (N W Alexander) *hld up: struggling 1/2-way: t.o* 100/1	26
	11	16	**Bowmore Rock (IRE)** 6-10-12 0 MrDRFox(7) (Mark Michael McNiff, Ire) *hld up: hung lft fr 1/2-way: struggling 4f out: virtually p.u fnl 2f* 28/1	10
00	12	3/4	**Over The Clyde**[54] 2553 6-11-2 0 RyanMania(3) (William Young) *in tch: lost pl after 6f: lost tch fnl 6f* 125/1	10
0	13	34	**Milans Danielle (IRE)**[31] 2943 5-10-12 0 BrianHughes (Brian Storey) *led to 1/2-way: sn lost pl and struggling: t.o* 100/1	—

3m 46.5s (3.70) **Going Correction** +0.075s/f (Yiel) 13 Ran SP% 115.8

Speed ratings: **93,92,89,89,88 86,84,84,80,54 46,46,29**

Tote Swingers: 1&2 £5.00, 1&3 £3.10, 2&3 £10.80 CSF £15.10 TOTE £2.40: £1.20, £4.10, £1.10; EX 19.20.

Owner Richard Collins **Bred** Finbar Leahy **Trained** Norton, N Yorks

FOCUS

A moderate bumper. The third is the best guide and the winner looks a smart prospsct.

NOTEBOOK

Jukebox Melody(IRE) defied a penalty to run out a comfortable winner of this weak looking bumper, despite racing very keen. He is bred to be suited by further and can do better again, but he must learn to settle. (op 15-8 tchd 13-8)

Pyjama Game(IRE) cost 46,000euros and ran with promise on his racecourse debut. He looks to a have a bumper in him. (op 9-1)

Thurnham put in a good run as he stayed on from the rear to good effect. He is sure to be suited by a step up in trip when sent hurdling and didn't seem unduly inconvenienced by the conditions. (op 6-1)

Dizzy River(IRE) was another who stayed on well in the later stages and ran well on only his second start after a 246-day absence. He looks to have some promise.

Think Green travelled well for a long time but was unable to go with the leaders. She looks a little one-paced. (op 11-1)

Shannagarry(IRE) ran better than on his debut, but faded in the closing stages and didn't appear to truly see out the trip in the conditions. (op 25-1)

Jacks Grey had previously shown some promise, but despite travelling well couldn't quicken with the leading group.

Beyond The Tweed stayed on one-paced. (op 40-1)

Bowmore Rock(IRE) Official explanation: jockey said gelding hung left throughout

T/Jkpt: £2,185.90 to a £1 stake. Pool: £47,720.68. 15.50 winning tickets. T/Plt: £39.90 to a £1 stake. Pool: £53,302.52. 974.62 winning tickets. T/Qpdt: £34.10 to a £1 stake. Pool: £3,887.24. 84.30 winning tickets. RY

2577 KEMPTON (R-H)

Saturday, January 15

OFFICIAL GOING: Good to soft (soft in places)

A bumper card and a 358-1 five-timer for Nicky Henderson, including the Christmas Hurdle and a 1-2 in the King George.

3554 WILLIAM HILL JUVENILE HURDLE (8 hdls) 2m

11:50 (11:51) (Class 4) 4-Y-O **£3,252** (£955; £477; £238)

Form				RPR
	1		**Kazzene (USA)**[214] 4-10-12 0 (p) APMcCoy (David Pipe) *t.k.h towards rr: nt fluent 3rd and 5th: stdy hdwy after 3 out: drvn to take slt ld and mstke last: drvn out* 11/4[3]	106+

20 **2** *1 1/2* **Kuilsriver (IRE)**[14] 3294 4-10-12 0....(t) JasonMaguire 102
(Alison Thorpe) *led fr 2nd to 4th: led sn after: mstke and hdd next: rdn and lost pl after 3 out: plenty to do u.p next: styd on wl appr last: r.o to take 2nd fnl 30yds* **33/1**

3 *2* **Brampour (IRE)**[153] 4-10-12 0.... HarrySkelton 100+
(Paul Nicholls) *t.k.h: in tch: drvn to chse ldr and 1 l down whn lft in narrow ld 2 out: u.p and nt fluent whn hdd last: styd on same pce and lost 2nd fnl 30yds* **13/8**[1]

26 **4** *2* **Finch Flyer (IRE)**[105] 1674 4-10-12 0.... AndrewGlassonbury 99
(Gary Moore) *chsd ldrs: lft disputing cl 2nd whn hit 2 out: wknd u.p last* **100/1**

31 **5** *3/4* **Jolly Roger (IRE)**[56] 2528 4-11-5 120.... RhysFlint 105
(John Flint) *led to 2nd: led again 4th: sn hdd: led next: rdn and hdd 2 out: sn wknd* **11/1**

6 *7* **Cuckoo Rock (IRE)**[29] 4-10-9 0.... RichieMcLernon(3) 92
(Jonathan Portman) *chsd ldrs: rdn 3 out: mstke and wknd next* **100/1**

7 *3 1/2* **Mavalenta (IRE)**[50] 4-10-5 0.... PaddyBrennan 81
(Nigel Twiston-Davies) *chsd ldrs: rdn 3 out: wknd appr next* **33/1**

20 **8** *26* **Killusty Fancy (IRE)**[35] 2882 4-10-12 0.... MarkGrant 64
(Dominic Ffrench Davis) *t.k.h: chsd ldrs tl wknd 3 out* **40/1**

9 *18* **New Code**[24] 4-10-12 0.... JamieMoore 48
(Gary Moore) *sn bhd* **22/1**

U **Aldorable**[59] 4-10-5 0.... ColinBolger —
(Roger Teal) *nt fluent 1st: a towards rr: t.o whn blnd and uns rdr 2 out* **100/1**

02 **F** **A Media Luz (FR)**[17] 3194 4-10-5 0.... BarryGeraghty 103+
(Nicky Henderson) *t.k.h: stdd in rr: stdy hdwy 3 out: 1 l ld and travelling wl whn fell 2 out* **5/2**[2]

4m 6.57s (6.57) **Going Correction** +0.025s/f (Yiel) 11 Ran SP% **117.3**
Speed ratings: **84,83,82,81,80 77,75,62,53,—,—**
toteswingers: 1&2 £19.90, 1&3 £1.20, 2&3 £17.50. CSF £81.51 TOTE £3.60: £1.60, £5.30, £1.60; EX 74.80 Trifecta £495.00 Pool: £749.28 - 1.12 winning units..

Owner Terry Neill **Bred** Hopewell Investments LLC **Trained** Nicholashayne, Devon

FOCUS
Some of these are well regarded, but it was a messy affair, with the field only getting going a couple of seconds after the tape went up and the pace steady, resulting in several of these racing keenly. The visual impression was backed up by a poor time and the proximity of some outsiders who had previously run to only a moderate level clearly limits the form. Faller A Media Luz was set to win, while the first and third should rate higher.

NOTEBOOK
Kazzene(USA) failed to settle and didn't jump that well on occasions either, indeed he got much too high at the third last, after which he was forced widest of all into the straight, and in managing to win he provided further evidence that the bare form is not particularly strong. However, while running to only a modest level, this can still be classed as a pleasing start considering the improvement he should make in due course when a stronger gallop will help him settle and jump better. He had cheekpieces fitted, and he apparently also wore them in France, but he displayed a game attitude. It's likely he'll be entered in both the Triumph Hurdle and Supreme Novices'. (tchd 9-4 and 3-1)
Kuilsriver(IRE) is one of those whose proximity could be used to knock the form, having shown only limited form (top RPR 100) in two bumper starts, but this was clearly a pleasing hurdles debut. He was ridden positively, but with the benefit of hindsight may have been better setting a stronger gallop, as he lost his position when lacking the pace of some of these after being steadied into three out, before staying on strongly in the straight. (op 50-1)
Brampour(IRE), runner-up in a 1m7f Listed race in France when last seen in August, pulled hardest of all, so it was no surprise he faded late on. His trainer expects much better when the gelding is faced with quicker ground and a stronger gallop, and doubtless he'll show improved form, but he's still impossible to fancy for the Triumph Hurdle, which remains the plan. (op 15-8 tchd 2-1)
Finch Flyer(IRE) is another whose proximity limits the form. Rated 55 on the Flat, he was tailed off in blinkers at Fontwell last time, and prior to that had recorded an RPR of just 89 when runner-up at the same track on his hurdling debut.
Jolly Roger(IRE) had little chance under the penalty he picked up for winning at Huntingdon and was duly well held. (op 14-1)
A Media Luz(FR), wearing earplugs for the second time, was going best approaching two out, looking the likely winner, but she stepped at the hurdle and went down. She was one of those who had been keen enough early on, just as on her hurdling debut at Cheltenham (before improved effort at Newbury), so it's possible she wouldn't have found as much as had looked likely, but whatever, she'll be capable of better in a stronger-run race. She was said to be fine afterwards, but will have to prove this hasn't left a mental scar. (op 2-1)

3555 WILLIAM HILL NOVICES' CHASE (12 fncs) 2m
12:20 (12:20) (Class 2) 5-Y-0+ **£8,799** (£2,622; £1,327; £680; £355)

Form RPR
1 **1** **Nadiya De La Vega (FR)**[59] 2455 5-10-8 0.... BarryGeraghty 136+
(Nicky Henderson) *trckd ldr: hit 7th: j. into ld 4 out: 3 l up whn blnd 2 out and rdr lost iron: drvn and hld on wl run-in* **4/7**[1]

-P11 **2** *1* **Pepe Simo (IRE)**[25] 3060 7-11-5 0.... SamThomas 144+
(Paul Nicholls) *hld up: hdwy bef 4 out: wnt 2nd appr 3 out: 1 1/2 l down whn nt fluent last: chal run-in: a jst hld towards fin* **4/1**[2]

-435 **3** *19* **Sambulando (FR)**[54] 2572 8-11-0 122....(t) PaddyBrennan 123
(Tom George) *led: hdd 4 out: wknd appr 3 out: tk remote 3rd appr last* **66/1**

00-0 **4** *11* **Gus Macrae (IRE)**[31] 2951 7-11-0 0....(t) APMcCoy 114
(Rebecca Curtis) *trckd ldrs: wknd appr 3 out: lost 3rd bef last* **25/1**

031F **5** *12* **Dee Ee Williams (IRE)**[17] 3193 8-11-5 140....(v) LiamTreadwell 111
(Nick Gifford) *j.lft: trckd ldrs: rdn after 5 out: wknd after 4 out* **13/2**[3]

62-U **P** **Quasar D'Oudairies (FR)**[54] 2578 7-11-0 120.... JasonMaguire —
(Nick Williams) *hld up: lost tch qckly after 5th: p.u bef 7th* **20/1**

-121 **P** **Chain Of Command (IRE)**[25] 3056 8-11-5 127.... JamieMoore —
(Warren Greatrex) *racd keenly: hld up: wknd qckly after 5 out: t.o whn p.u bef 3 out* **14/1**

4m 2.30s (4.30) **Going Correction** +0.025s/f (Yiel)
WFA 5 from 7yo+ 3lb 7 Ran SP% **113.8**
Speed ratings: **90,89,80,74,68 —,—**
toteswingers: 1&2 £1.50, 1&3 £7.10, 2&3 £29.80. CSF £3.38 TOTE £1.50: £1.10, £2.20; EX 3.20.

Owner Million In Mind Partnership **Bred** Haras de la Vega **Trained** Upper Lambourn, Berks

FOCUS
Nicky Henderson had taken the previous two runnings of this race, with Royals Darling and Mad Max, and he completed a hat-trick. The winner was the form pick but a bit below his Warwick level. Decent novice chase form.

NOTEBOOK
Nadiya De La Vega(FR) made a mistake at the seventh and also dived at the second last, a blunder that looked to cause her rider to lose an iron, but she dug deep under pressure, jumped the final fence really well and held off the runner-up with what looked to be a bit up her sleeve. She was clipped in to 20-1 for the Arkle, but her rider was of the opinion that she'll be suited by a step up in trip, and the new 2m4f Jewson Novices Chase, looks like it will be more her thing (14-1 opening show). (op 8-13 tchd 4-6 in places)
Pepe Simo(IRE) ran a fine race in defeat considering he was giving the winner 11lb. He didn't jump the final fence as well as the mare but battled on well while always looking just about held. Paul Nicholls reckons a fast-run race will see him to best effect, and has the Grand Annual in mind. (op 7-2)
Sambulando(FR) faced a stiff task but for the most part jumped better than he has in the past. He should find things easier back in handicap company.
Gus Macrae(IRE) was still with the first two at the top of the straight but was soon beaten off. Nevertheless, this was a far more encouraging performance, and he's another who appeals as a likely type to win in handicap company in due course.
Dee Ee Williams(IRE), who was beaten a long way in this race last year as well, still tends to jump out to his left. He's a difficult horse to place as he's near a career-high mark over hurdles and isn't as good over fences. Official explanation: trainer said gelding finished distressed (op 9-1)
Quasar D'Oudairies(FR) Official explanation: vet said gelding pulled up lame
Chain Of Command(IRE) Official explanation: trainer said gelding pulled up distressed

3556 WILLIAM HILL NOVICES' HURDLE (10 hdls) 2m 5f
12:50 (12:50) (Class 3) 4-Y-0+ **£4,553** (£1,337; £668; £333)

Form RPR
1 **Chablais (FR)**[307] 6-11-2 0.... BarryGeraghty 136+
(Nicky Henderson) *trckd ldrs: hit 3rd and 5th: nt fluent 3 out and led sn after: travelling wl 2 out: rdn and styd on strly fnl 100yds* **15/8**[1]

132 **2** *1* **Sybarite (FR)**[62] 2388 5-11-2 0.... PaddyBrennan 133+
(Nigel Twiston-Davies) *chsd ldrs: hit 5th and 3 out: rdn sn after: styd on to go 2nd after 2 out: nt fluent last: styd on strly to cl on wnr run-in but no imp fnl 100yds* **13/2**

2-21 **3** *9* **The Reformer (IRE)**[41] 2791 6-11-8 121.... HarrySkelton 128
(Paul Nicholls) *in tch: chsd ldrs 7th: drvn to chse wnr appr 2 out: no imp and dropped bk to 3rd sn after: sn no ch w ldng duo* **6/1**[3]

-115 **4** *15* **Firm Order (IRE)**[54] 2581 6-11-12 117.... WillKennedy 117
(Paul Webber) *pressed ldrs: chal 4 out: led 3 out: hdd sn after: wknd next* **20/1**

0-15 **5** *3 3/4* **Made In Time (IRE)**[57] 2493 6-11-8 0....(t) APMcCoy 112+
(Rebecca Curtis) *hld up in rr: hdwy 6th: trckd ldrs fr 4 out: rdn after next: wknd fr 2 out* **10/3**[2]

4- **6** *6* **Credit Crunched (IRE)**[430] 2234 6-11-2 0.... SamThomas 98
(Alan King) *in rr: hdwy and hit 4 out: rdn next: wknd bef 2 out* **33/1**

3602 **7** *20* **Nodforms Violet (IRE)**[13] 3334 7-11-2 123.... RichardJohnson 92+
(Karen McLintock) *sn in tch: rdn 4 out: wknd and hit next* **14/1**

4-6 **8** *2* **Just Josie**[53] 2594 5-10-9 0.... JamieGoldstein 68
(Sheena West) *in tch to 6th* **150/1**

241- **9** *shd* **Midnight Prayer**[277] 5179 6-11-2 0.... RobertThornton 75
(Alan King) *in tch: blnd 5th: no ch after: blnd 2 out* **7/1**

34- **10** *1 1/2* **Mudita Moment (IRE)**[320] 4358 6-10-11 0.... IanPopham(5) 73
(Anna Brooks) *chsd ldrs to 4 out* **66/1**

00 **11** *1/2* **Whispering Jack**[57] 2493 6-11-2 0.... JasonMaguire 73
(Charlie Mann) *bhd most of way* **100/1**

00 **12** *4* **Highland Legacy**[13] 3340 7-10-9 0....(p) AshleyBird(7) 69
(Jim Best) *chses ldrs to 6th: sn in rr* **100/1**

5 **13** *3 1/4* **Cleaver**[53] 2594 10-11-2 0.... LiamTreadwell 66
(Lady Herries) *t.k.h: j. modly towards rr thrght* **40/1**

/P0- **14** *4 1/2* **Big Bertie (IRE)**[277] 5173 7-11-2 0.... RodiGreene 61
(Anna Newton-Smith) *mde most tl hdd 3 out: wknd qckly* **100/1**

223 **15** *4* **Arthur's Pass**[206] 833 7-11-2 0.... RhysFlint 57
(Tom George) *chsd ldrs to 3 out: wknd next* **50/1**

16 *dist* **Lucius Fabeo (IRE)** 7-10-13 0.... MarcGoldstein(3) —
(Anna Newton-Smith) *hit 1st: a wl bhd: t.o fr 1/2-way* **125/1**

000 **P** **Sulpius (GER)**[17] 3196 6-11-2 0.... AndrewGlassonbury —
(Bob Buckler) *chsd ldrs: rdn 6th: sn wknd: t.o whn p.u bef 3 out* **100/1**

5m 23.16s (-0.84) **Going Correction** +0.025s/f (Yiel) 17 Ran SP% **123.7**
Speed ratings (Par 107): **102,101,98,92,91 88,81,80,80,79 79,78,76,75,73 —,—**
toteswingers: 1&2 £3.20, 1&3 £3.70, 2&3 £6.50. CSF £14.35 TOTE £3.00: £1.50, £1.90, £2.70; EX 12.80 Trifecta £50.80 Pool: £750.25 - 10.91 winning units..

Owner Mr & Mrs R Kelvin Hughes **Bred** Mme Albert & Mlle Sandra Hosselet **Trained** Upper Lambourn, Berks

FOCUS
This looked a quality novice hurdle on paper. It produced an impressive winner who looks a smart recruit, and with the runner-up providing a good guide, the form looks solid. It should produce plenty of winners.

NOTEBOOK
Chablais(FR), who cost £260,000 at the sales, made the best start possible to his career under Rules, travelling strongly throughout and quickening up well from the second last to put the race to bed. He was closed down by the runner-up on the run-in, but always had plenty in hand, and his trainer suggested it was probably just a case of him being in front for longer than he'd want. While undoubtedly a chaser in the making, he stated his case for the Neptune at Cheltenham here, and the 20-1 with Boylesports looks a perfectly fair price. (op 2-1 tchd 9-4 in places)
Sybarite(FR), runner-up in a Grade 2 hurdle at Cheltenham on his hurdling debut back in November, wasn't always the most fluent of jumpers, but he kept on well for pressure to close down the idling winner on the run-in. He helps set the level of the race, and looks the type that will appreciate returning to a stiffer track. (op 6-1 tchd 11-2)
The Reformer(IRE) ran well under his penalty on this half-mile step up in distance, and certainly saw the trip out well enough. He remains open to improvement, and might find more success down the handicap route. (op 13-2 tchd 15-2)
Firm Order(IRE) faced a stiff task under his double penalty and really could not have been expected to have done any better than he did, especially as his best form has come on quicker ground. (tchd 25-1)
Made In Time(IRE) travelled strongly to the turn into the straight, but when Tony McCoy went for him there wasn't anything there, and with nothing to gain he allowed his mount to coast home. He'll be of more interest once switched to handicaps. (op 9-2)
Credit Crunched(IRE) ◆ ran well on his return from a 430-day absence. Lack of a run eventually caught up with him but he showed more than enough to suggest he'll be of interest in handicaps after one more run. (op 25-1)
Nodforms Violet(IRE), put up 5lb for finishing second at Ayr last time, has an official mark of 123. He bumped into a few more progressive types here, but should be capable of remaining competitive back at a lesser level. (op 12-1)
Midnight Prayer, who has some useful bumper form to his name, was still there until the turn out of the back straight. Returning from a nine-month absence, he's another who's entitled to come on for the outing. (tchd 13-2 and 15-2)
Whispering Jack Official explanation: jockey said gelding hung left

Sulpius(GER) Official explanation: jockey said gelding lost a front shoe

3557 WILLIAM HILL H'CAP HURDLE (8 hdls) 2m

1:20 (1:23) (Class 3) (0-135,134) 4-Y-0+ **£4,553** (£1,337; £668; £333)

Form				RPR
220/	1		**Ski Sunday**[238] 5078 6-11-11 **133**........(t) APMcCoy (Lawney Hill) *t.k.h early: trckd ldrs on outer: rdn and hdwy to ld 2 out: kpt on wl to pull clr run-in* **4/1**[2]	146+
1-12	2	6	**Skint**[33] 2925 5-11-3 **125**........ BarryGeraghty (Nicky Henderson) *trckd ldrs: hdwy to chal 2 out: sn rdn: kpt on but no match wnr* **3/1**[1]	133+
4-06	3	2	**Karky Schultz (GER)**[61] 2423 6-10-9 **117**........ PaddyBrennan (James Eustace) *led: rdn whn hdd 2 out: edgd lft appr last: kpt on run-in* **40/1**	122
040-	4	1	**Zanir (FR)**[280] 5128 7-11-7 **134**........ IanPopham(5) (Tom George) *midfield: trckd ldrs: rdn appr 2 out: kpt on* **16/1**	139
-040	5	1 1/4	**Aather (IRE)**[36] 2868 6-10-12 **125**........ COFarrell(5) (Alan Fleming) *midfield: hdwy to trck ldrs 3 out: rdn appr 2 out: kpt on same pce* **8/1**	128
31/	6	11	**Samsons Son**[71] 4152 7-10-11 **119**........ RobertThornton (Alan King) *in tch on inner: nt fluent 4 out: trckd ldrs 3 out: rdn bef 2 out: sn one pce* **5/1**[3]	114
61-1	7	3 3/4	**Via Galilei (IRE)**[51] 2626 6-10-8 **116**........ JamieMoore (Gary Moore) *hld up in midfield: hdwy to chse ldrs after 3 out: rdn and sn no further imp* **8/1**	108
52-2	8	3/4	**Souter Point (USA)**[226] 590 5-10-8 **119**........ RichardKilloran(3) (Nicky Henderson) *midfield: hdwy to chse ldrs after 3 out: wknd appr 2 out* **20/1**	108
/1-6	9	1 1/4	**Simply Blue**[57] 2498 7-11-1 **123**........ AndrewGlassonbury (Simon Burrough) *midfield: rdn after 3 out: sn no imp* **16/1**	111
1444	10	15	**William Hogarth**[54] 2572 6-11-3 **125**........(p) JasonMaguire (Keith Goldsworthy) *w ldr: rdn bef 4 out: wknd qckly after next* **14/1**	99
000B	11	1 3/4	**Tobago Bay**[16] 3229 6-10-7 **125**........ JosephAkehurst(10) (Gary Moore) *chsd ldrs: rdn bef 4 out: lost pl bef next: sn wknd* **80/1**	98
40	12	6	**Alhaque (USA)**[57] 2498 5-10-5 **116**........ EamonDehdashti(3) (Gary Moore) *hld up: a bhd* **100/1**	83
2121	13	2 1/2	**Babilu**[51] 2639 6-10-5 **113**........(p) RichardJohnson (Dai Burchell) *racd keenly: hld up: brief hdwy 3 out: sn no further imp* **12/1**	78
	14	6	**Big Robert**[58] 2489 7-10-9 **117**........(p) TimmyMurphy (Matt Sheppard) *hld up on outer: rdn after 3 out: sn no hdwy* **20/1**	77
6-56	15	11	**Johnny Mullen (IRE)**[30] 2977 8-10-0 **113**........ MattGriffiths(5) (Paul Henderson) *hld up: rdn whn mstke 3 out: sn wknd* **16/1**	63
02-0	16	4 1/2	**Top Mark**[51] 2626 9-11-1 **123**........ GerardTumelty (Alan King) *hld up: a in rr* **66/1**	69

3m 56.5s (-3.50) **Going Correction** +0.025s/f (Yiel) **16** Ran SP% **131.6**
Speed ratings (Par 107): **109,106,105,104,103 98,96,96,95,88 87,84,82,79,74 72**
toteswingers: 1&2 £3.00, 1&3 £81.20, 2&3 £31.10. CSF £17.33 CT £456.66 TOTE £5.20: £1.80, £1.60, £6.80, £5.90; EX 16.00 Trifecta £1267.10 Part won. Pool: £1,712.36 - 0.80 winning units..

Owner Scarlet Pimpernel **Bred** New England, Stanley House & Mount Coote Studs **Trained** Aston Rowant, Oxon

FOCUS

A decent handicap hurdle run at a fair pace. The time was creditable, being only 2.90 seconds slower than Binocular managed in the Christmas Hurdle later on the card. Solid form, with the winner back to his Aintree mark as a juvenile.

NOTEBOOK

Ski Sunday, formerly a smart juvenile hurdler for Tim Vaughan, running second in both the Fred Winter and an Aintree Grade 1, hadn't been seen since finishing runner-up on the Flat for Nicky Henderson last May. However, there was good money for him as he made his return for another new trainer, and the support was fully justified, the 6-y-o running out a convincing winner to take Tony McCoy's record for Lawney Hill to 4-7. This was apparently his first start over hurdles since losing his left eye in an accident, but the handicapper had been kind, letting him in off a mark 10lb lower than when last seen jumping, and he took full advantage. His partial blindness compromised his chance to an extent, as he was purposely kept towards the outside of runners, meaning he was keen early without cover, and it's to his credit he found so much for pressure. Racing in a tongue-tie for the first time since falling in 2008, he looked in a bit of trouble early in the straight, with the runner-up appearing to be going the better of the pair, but the way he kept responding to pressure was quite taking. The obvious race now is the County Hurdle. (op 3-1 tchd 9-2 in places)

Skint looked the winner before managing only second over 2m5f at Plumpton on his previous start, and it was the same story this time over a much shorter trip. It was slightly disappointing that he found less than had looked likely, even though he was beaten by a well-handicapped rival, and he needs to see his race out better if he's to make significant progress. (op 4-1)

Karky Schultz(GER), returning from a two-month break, stuck on well when headed, a game effort behind two better treated rivals. (tchd 50-1)

Zanir(FR) ran well under top weight after an absence of 280 days and is obviously entitled to come on for this. (op 20-1 tchd 22-1)

Aather(IRE) is not a strong finisher, but this was a respectable effort. (op 9-1 tchd 7-1)

Samsons Son should have been okay fitness-wise having run on the Flat in November, but he still shaped as though this first hurdles start since February 2009 was needed. He came off the bridle after three out, but stuck on and should improve. (op 8-1)

Via Galilei(IRE), up 8lb for his November Newbury win, disappointed and has yet to show his best form over hurdles going right-handed. (op 9-1 tchd 10-1)

3558 WILLIAM HILL - HOME OF BETTING H'CAP CHASE (16 fncs) 2m 4f 110y

1:55 (1:57) (Class 3) (0-135,129) 5-Y-0+

£7,514 (£2,220; £1,110; £555; £277; £139)

Form				RPR
2-1P	1		**Polyfast (FR)**[182] 1020 8-11-12 **129**........ BarryGeraghty (Nicky Henderson) *trckd ldrs: wnt 2nd 12th: rdn 3 out: styd on u.p fr 2 out to chal last: slt ld sn after: hrd rdn: edgd rt: hld on all out* **9/2**[2]	139
F623	2	hd	**Safari Adventures (IRE)**[13] 3333 9-11-9 **126**........ CampbellGillies (Lucinda Russell) *led: rdn appr 3 out: stl slt ld last: narrowly hdd sn after: kpt on gamely u.p: pushed lft cl home: jst failed* **8/1**	136
610F	3	1/2	**Cruchain (IRE)**[51] 2633 8-10-10 **113**........ WillKennedy (Dai Burchell) *in rr: hit 7th: hdwy 10th: chsd ldrs 12th: outpcd in 3rd appr 3 out: styd on wl fr 2 out: drvn to chal last: kpt on wl run-in: no ex whn carried rt cl home* **12/1**	126+
-301	4	35	**Free World (IRE)**[25] 3059 9-11-5 **122**........ JamieMoore (Warren Greatrex) *trckd ldr: chal 9th: drvn along 10th: hit 11th: lost 2nd next: wknd 4 out* **5/1**[3]	100
6361	5	10	**Ursis (FR)**[62] 2400 10-11-5 **122**........ RhysFlint (Steve Gollings) *in tch: rdn after 7th and 9th: hit next: wknd appr 4 out* **8/1**	91
5-22	6	8	**Its Crucial (IRE)**[56] 2531 11-11-0 **117**........ PaddyBrennan (Nigel Twiston-Davies) *in rr: hit 2nd: 6th and 10th: lost tch 12th* **9/1**	79
6043	7	1 3/4	**Bible Lord (IRE)**[18] 3157 10-11-7 **124**........(b) MarkGrant (Andy Turnell) *trckd ldrs: mstke 1st: hit 5th and 10th: wknd and blnd 12th: no ch whn blnd 4 out* **4/1**[1]	84
16-5	R		**The Snail**[69] 2234 8-11-7 **124**........ PaulMoloney (Evan Williams) *ref to r* **8/1**	—
1-0F	P		**Drybrook Bedouin**[231] 525 9-11-2 **119**........ HarrySkelton (Nick Mitchell) *hit 4th: in rr and hit 8th: rdn 10th: hmpd 11th and wknd: t.o 4 out: p.u bef 2 out* **20/1**	—
1425	F		**Jimbatai (IRE)**[66] 2305 8-10-12 **118**........ DannyCook(3) (Barry Leavy) *chsd ldrs fr 7th: blnd 8th: pushed along to dispute 4 l 4th whn fell 11th* **8/1**	—

5m 15.9s (-3.60) **Going Correction** +0.025s/f (Yiel) **10** Ran SP% **120.6**
Speed ratings: **107,106,106,93,89 86,85,—,—,—**
toteswingers: 1&2 £3.30, 1&3 £35.10, 2&3 £33.50. CSF £41.91 CT £413.09 TOTE £4.70: £2.00, £2.20, £5.70; EX 31.50 Trifecta £953.00 Pool: £1,717.22 - 1.33 winning units..

Owner W J Brown **Bred** Patrick Boiteau **Trained** Upper Lambourn, Berks

FOCUS

A competitive handicap. A step up from Polyfast on his C&D form last season, with the second to his best.

NOTEBOOK

Polyfast(FR), who saved ground on the inner most of the way round, was switched to challenge the leader rounding the turn into the straight and, although still marginally down jumping the last, he responded to pressure to just edge ahead close home. He has a history of going well fresh, indeed he won over this C&D on his reappearance last season, so an absence since July was of no concern, especially with his stable in such cracking form, and he probably wouldn't be the type to back if returned to the track too soon. The Festival Plate would be his race if going to the festival, but it's worth noting that he's done all his winning on sharp tracks. (tchd 4-1)

Safari Adventures(IRE) made a bold bid to make every yard of the running, and came up only narrowly short. Happier going this way round (tends to jump right-handed), the problem for him is that he'll now go up in the weights for losing. (op 15-2)

Cruchain(IRE), debuting for his new stable having been claimed out of a selling hurdle last time out, rallied after getting outpaced by the first two turning in. He's on a good mark judged on his best form and looks worth keeping on side. (op 14-1 tchd 16-1)

Free World(IRE)'s trainer had suggested he would make the running, as he did for a long way when winning a jumpers' bumper on the Polytrack last time. In the event, however, Safari Adventures wanted it more and he had to settle for a position tracking the pace. Faster ground suits him better anyway. (tchd 11-2)

Ursis(FR), 7lb higher for his latest win at Market Rasen, was given a reminder approaching the winning post first time round, and he never really got into a rhythm. (op 8-1 tchd 10-1)

Bible Lord(IRE) didn't jump well enough. (tchd 11-2 in a place)

Jimbatai(IRE) had made a mistake at the fence prior to his departure and had already come under pressure too. (op 10-1 tchd 11-1)

3559 WILLIAMHILL.COM CHRISTMAS HURDLE (GRADE 1) (8 hdls) 2m

2:25 (2:26) (Class 1) 5-Y-0+

£42,757 (£16,042; £8,032; £4,005; £2,010; £1,005)

Form				RPR
11-3	1		**Binocular (FR)**[49] 2668 7-11-7 171........ APMcCoy (Nicky Henderson) *trckd ldr: led gng wl bef 2 out: shkn up bef last: kpt on wl run-in* **13/8**[1]	164+
1-21	2	3 3/4	**Overturn (IRE)**[150] 1133 7-11-7 159........ JasonMaguire (Donald McCain) *led: rdn whn hdd bef 2 out: kpt on but no match for wnr* **7/1**	160
25-2	3	2 1/4	**Starluck (IRE)**[49] 2668 6-11-7 160........ TimmyMurphy (Alan Fleming) *in tch on outer: trckd ldrs 3 out: rdn bef 2 out: kpt on one pce* **3/1**[3]	158
121-	4	7	**Khyber Kim**[280] 5125 9-11-7 167........ PaddyBrennan (Nigel Twiston-Davies) *hld up: hdwy to get in tch 3 out: sn rdn and outpcd: 8 l down in 4th whn hit last* **5/2**[2]	153
4-02	5	74	**Bocamix (FR)**[56] 2521 5-11-7 130........ FearghalDavis (Andrew Crook) *hld up: mstke 1st: wknd qckly after 4 out: t.o* **100/1**	77
16-1	6	20	**Escort'men (FR)**[98] 1775 5-11-7 149........ SamThomas (Paul Nicholls) *hld up: hit 1st: rdn bef 3 out: sn wknd: t.o* **12/1**	57

3m 53.6s (-6.40) **Going Correction** +0.025s/f (Yiel) **6** Ran SP% **112.8**
Speed ratings (Par 117): **117,115,114,110,73 63**
toteswingers: 1&2 £2.70, 1&3 £1.30, 2&3 £3.80. CSF £13.70 TOTE £2.00: £1.20, £3.90; EX 13.20.

Owner John P McManus **Bred** Elie Lellouche **Trained** Upper Lambourn, Berks

■ This season's Christmas Hurdle was rearranged after Kempton's Boxing Day meeting was abandoned due to frost and snow.

FOCUS

A field of nine were originally due to line up, but Barizan, Oscar Whisky and Sanctuaire all failed to make the rearranged running. Despite the small field, this was still a quality edition. The pace set was fast and the time was 2.90 seconds quicker than earlier handicap won by 133-rated Ski Sunday. Binocular was still 6lb off his Champion Hurdle mark but this still rates the top 2m hurdle performance of the season so far. Overturn confirmed the merit of his Irish run, with Starluck to his mark.

NOTEBOOK

Binocular(FR) ◆ kept Overturn honest from the off and such simple tactics proved most effective, getting in a good rhythm and jumping superbly throughout. This was particularly encouraging with his Champion Hurdle prospects in mind considering he managed only a laboured third in this race in 2009, before going on to win at Cheltenham, and he's building nicely towards another peak performance in March. He's likely to have his final prep in the Contenders Hurdle at Sandown, a race he won last year. (op 9-4)

Overturn(IRE) was reported to have finished distressed when last seen tailed off in the Ebor in August, but he returned with a terrific front-running effort. He was hassled throughout by a superior rival, yet kept on well around a track that plays to his strengths. He's entitled to come on for this and is probably also worth his place at Cheltenham, where his presence as a pace angle would help his stablemate. Before then he could go for the Kingwell Hurdle at Wincanton. (op 13-2 tchd 15-2 and 8-1 in places)

Starluck(IRE) wasn't ideally suited by this turning into a decent stamina test. He ran with credit, but has his limitations. His connections are said to be toying with the idea of stepping him up to 2m4f, reasoning that the trip might help a horse who only has limited burst off the bridle. (tchd 10-3 in places)

Khyber Kim had been off since winning the Aintree Hurdle last April, and although he's won when fresh in the past, he found things happening too quickly for him on his belated return. Last year's Champion Hurdle runner-up should come on a good deal for this, but there's talk of him being given an entry in the World Hurdle this time. He's not sure to run in that race, but the idea is it may provide him with his best chance of winning a championship event at Cheltenham. (op 11-4)

Bocamix(FR) was outclassed.

Escort'men(FR) was having only his fifth start over hurdles in Britain. He hit the first quite hard, and although recovering to a point, he was the first beaten. Official explanation: jockey said gelding stopped quickly (op 8-1)

3560 WILLIAM HILL KING GEORGE VI CHASE GRADE 1 (18 fncs) 3m

3:00 (3:00) (Class 1) 5-Y-O+

£102,618 (£38,502; £19,278; £9,612; £4,824; £2,412)

Form RPR

13-3 **1** **Long Run (FR)**63 2359 6-11-10 162 MrSWaley-Cohen 180+
(Nicky Henderson) *trckd ldrs: wnt 2nd 7th: led 3 out: drvn clr sn after: comf* **9/2**2

5F-1 **2** *12* **Riverside Theatre**75 2126 7-11-10 160 BarryGeraghty 171+
(Nicky Henderson) *stdd in rr 4th: hdwy 9th: blnd 13th: rdn appr 3 out: styd on to take 2nd after 2 out: kpt on but nvr any ch w wnr* **10/1**3

1F-1 **3** *7* **Kauto Star (FR)**70 2226 11-11-10 190 (t) APMcCoy 169+
(Paul Nicholls) *trckd ldr 2nd to 7th: styd rr there: nt fluent 12th: rdn 4 out: one pce u.p next but styd on to chse wnr and wl hld whn blnd bdly 2 out and wknd into 3rd* **4/7**1

3-14 **4** *5* **Nacarat (FR)**56 2524 10-11-10 158 PaddyBrennan 161+
(Tom George) *led: nt fluent 6th: hdd 3 out: wkng and wl hld in 4th whn blnd 2 out* **14/1**

01-3 **5** *39* **Planet Of Sound**56 2524 9-11-10 163 (t) RichardJohnson 122
(Philip Hobbs) *in rr tl sme hdwy and hit 12th: wknd qckly 4 out* **20/1**

F-2F **6** *10* **Madison Du Berlais (FR)**49 2673 10-11-10 157 (p) DannyCook 113
(David Pipe) *chsd ldrs: j. slowly 3rd: hit 9th and in rr next: t.o fr 12th* **40/1**

1-4F **P** **Albertas Run (IRE)**56 2515 10-11-10 168 DougieCostello —
(Jonjo O'Neill) *chsd ldrs: pushed along fr 10th: wknd 12th: t.o whn p.u bef 13th* **33/1**

22-2 **P** **Forpadydeplasterer (IRE)**62 2385 9-11-10 167 RobertThornton —
(Thomas Cooper, Ire) *in rr: nt fluent 3rd: rdn 10th: wknd and p.u bef 12th* **14/1**

13-1 **P** **The Nightingale (FR)**70 2227 8-11-10 167 SamThomas —
(Paul Nicholls) *in tch: chsng ldrs whn hit 8th: blnd 10th: wknd fr 13th: t.o whn p.u bef 2 out* **16/1**

6m 3.04s (-11.96) **Going Correction** +0.025s/f (Yiel) **9** Ran SP% **120.3**
Speed ratings (Par 117): **120,116,113,112,99 95,—,—,—**
toteswingers: 1&2 £3.40, 1&3 £1.50, 2&3 £2.20. CSF £47.28 CT £62.39 TOTE £4.90: £1.70, £3.10, £1.02; EX 44.10 Trifecta £97.80 Pool: £15,449.40 - 116.79 winning units..
Owner Robert Waley-Cohen **Bred** Mrs Marie-Christine Gabeur **Trained** Upper Lambourn, Berks
■ A combination of frost and snow prevented this season's King George from taking place on Boxing Day.

FOCUS

The race's prestige was threatened by the BHA's surprising decision not to allow new entries, an issue highlighted by Imperial Commander's absence. The original field was reduced by two, with Ollie Magern and Sizing Europe absent. Long Run outjumped and outstayed his rivals and rates a high-class winner of the race, which was run in a good time, with no reason to doubt worth of form, even though the second, third and fourth all lost ground through errors.

NOTEBOOK

Long Run(FR), equipped with earplugs for the first time, wasn't great over the first but was always going well for his amateur, who himself produced an accomplished display, and this was a high-class performance from the supremely talented, relative youngster. An exciting ex-French runner, this was the sort of performance he promised when taking the 2009 Feltham by 13l. He had suffered defeats when well fancied on his last two starts, both at Cheltenham, finishing the last campaign with a disappointing third in the RSA, but his effort in the Paddy Power Gold Cup on his reappearance was a career-best according to RPRs. The margin of victory may flatter him, but he seemed likely to win with authority even before the favourite's key mistake. The obvious question now is can he prove as effective at Cheltenham in the Gold Cup? There's a major stat against him, though - no 6-y-o has won the Gold Cup since Mill House in 1963. (op 13-2)

Riverside Theatre was 4-4 here (two over hurdles, two over fences), but he was up significantly in grade and trip after a 2m4f graduation chase win here last time. He kept on into second behind his stablemate without ever posing a serious threat, and his rider felt he got the distance. This rates another personal best. (op 12-1)

Kauto Star(FR) was bidding for an unprecedented fifth straight victory in the race. However, it was clear from some way out he was not at his brilliant best. Usually such an exuberant jumper, he got in closer than ideal to the majority of his fences and was running in snatches from an early stage. Well and truly off the bridle after the fourth-last, rounding the final bend in a laboured third, he had just moved into second approaching two out, but was still struggling to make any impression on the winner when ploughing through that fence, almost forcing Tony McCoy over his head. This was a good 20lb below his 2009 form and it seems probable that he's now past his best, but it needs pointing out that some of his trainer's horses are not running as well as usual, and he was also said to have bled. A third win in the Cheltenham Gold Cup remains the target, and he is unlikely to be seen in the interim. Official explanation: trainer said gelding was found to have bled from the nose (tchd 4-6 in places, 8-13 in places and 8-15 in places)

Nacarat(FR) seemed to set a more sensible pace than when beaten 40l in this race last year, so a bit better could have been expected. He could be aimed at the Ryanair Chase, and while he has a poor record at Cheltenham his trainer believes he is better equipped to cope now.

Planet Of Sound suffered a breathing problem in last season's Ryanair and that issue seemed to resurface, with connections reporting he 'choked'. He had benefited from a tongue-tie since last Cheltenham, but it didn't help this time. Official explanation: trainer said gelding had a breathing problem (op 18-1 tchd 16-1)

Madison Du Berlais(FR) was runner-up in this last season, but he had fallen on his last two chasing starts and offered nothing. (op 33-1)

Albertas Run(IRE)'s jockey apparently thought the gelding had gone wrong behind, and he was reportedly stiff and sore on his return home. (op 16-1)

Forpadydeplasterer(IRE) reportedly scoped dirty afterwards. (op 16-1)

The Nightingale(FR), well backed ante-post before drifting on course, made a couple of mistakes on this step up in class and trip. He reportedly finished distressed and was found to be suffering from a fibrillating heart Official explanation: trainer said, that on return, vet found gelding to be suffering from atrial fibrillation. (op 16-1)

3561 WILLIAMHILL.COM LANZAROTE HURDLE H'CAP (10 hdls) 2m 5f

3:35 (3:36) (Class 2) 4-Y-O+

£28,179 (£8,325; £4,162; £2,083; £1,039; £522)

Form RPR

23-0 **1** **James De Vassy (FR)**56 2523 6-11-2 144 WillKennedy 149+
(Nick Williams) *in tch: gd hdwy to chal appr 2 out: hmpd but led 2 out: sn rdn: kpt on wl* **8/1**3

1412 **2** *2* **Organisateur (IRE)**16 3229 6-11-7 154 IanPopham(5) 157+
(Paul Nicholls) *in tch: trckd ldrs 3 out: hdwy to chal whn edgd bdly lft 2 out: sn chsd wnr: kpt on wl run-in: lost 2nd nr fin* **20/1**

0-11 **3** *½* **Palomar (USA)**18 3170 9-10-5 133 FearghalDavis 134
(Brian Ellison) *hld up: hdwy to chse ldrs after 3 out: rdn to go 2nd bef last: kpt on but lost 2nd nr fin* **9/1**

20-3 **4** *8* **First Point (GER)**50 2665 8-10-10 138 BarryGeraghty 133+
(Nicky Henderson) *midfield on outer: hdwy to trck ldrs 3 out: ev ch whn sltly hmpd 2 out: wknd appr last* **14/1**

0025 **5** *¾* **Dantari (IRE)**16 3229 6-10-2 130 PaulMoloney 122
(Evan Williams) *w ldr: led bef 5th: hdd 3 out: wknd after 2 out* **28/1**

1-10 **6** *2¼* **Quartz De Thaix (FR)**35 2884 7-11-6 148 SamThomas 140
(Venetia Williams) *trckd ldrs: led 3 out: rdn whn hdd 2 out: 6 l down in 4th whn hit last: wknd run-in* **25/1**

-250 **7** *5* **Racing Demon (IRE)**14 3293 11-10-2 130 HaddenFrost 116
(Henrietta Knight) *midfield: trckd ldrs 4 out: rdn and wknd appr 2 out* **33/1**

1212 **8** *½* **Drill Sergeant**56 2519 6-10-0 128 (t) TimmyMurphy 117+
(Donald McCain) *trckd ldrs: rdn but stl ev ch whn mstke 2 out: wknd after* **14/1**

/12- **9** *1½* **Like Minded**407 2695 7-9-12 131 MrRMahon(5) 115
(Paul Nicholls) *trckd ldrs on outer: wknd appr 2 out* **13/2**2

-065 **10** *3¾* **Chief Yeoman**7 3438 11-9-9 128 RTDunne(5) 110
(Venetia Williams) *midfield: rdn bef 3 out: sn no imp* **28/1**

4504 **11** *shd* **Hills Of Aran**17 3195 9-10-13 141 (p) RhysFlint 121
(Keith Goldsworthy) *hld up on outer: a towards rr* **40/1**

-522 **12** *25* **Barwell Bridge**36 2870 5-10-11 139 (t) JasonMaguire 97
(Warren Greatrex) *hld up: nvr threatened* **10/1**

3P-4 **13** *16* **The Betchworth Kid**49 2671 6-10-10 138 RobertThornton 91
(Alan King) *midfield: mstke 3rd: nt fluent next: rdn and lost pl whn hit 4 out: wknd after next* **3/1**1

115B **14** *6* **Ackertac (IRE)**36 2870 6-10-0 128 oh1 PaddyBrennan 66
(Nigel Twiston-Davies) *hld up: a towards rr* **12/1**

2000 **15** *73* **Buena Vista (IRE)**14 3293 10-10-7 140 (b) CO'Farrell(5) 12
(David Pipe) *led narrowly: hdd bef 5th: wknd qckly appr 4 out: t.o* **50/1**

4-03 **P** **Premier Dane (IRE)**36 2868 9-10-1 129 DougieCostello —
(Nicky Richards) *hld up on inner: a bhd: p.u bef 2 out* **40/1**

U211 **F** **Songe (FR)**70 2212 7-10-12 140 RichardJohnson 122
(Charlie Longsdon) *hld up: hdwy to chse ldrs 3 out: wkng in 9th whn fell 2 out* **12/1**

-P46 **U** **Bygones Of Brid (IRE)**18 3170 8-11-0 142 APMcCoy —
(Karen McLintock) *prom on outer whn mstke and uns rdr 5th* **16/1**

1-40 **P** **Al Co (FR)**69 2235 6-10-0 131 RichieMcLernon(3) —
(Jonjo O'Neill) *midfield: reminders after 3rd and sn lost pl: t.o whn p.u bef 2 out* **33/1**

5m 17.6s (-6.40) **Going Correction** +0.025s/f (Yiel) **19** Ran SP% **131.4**
Speed ratings (Par 109): **113,112,112,109,108 107,105,105,105,103 103,94,88,85,58 —,—,—,—**
toteswingers: 1&2 £44.60, 1&3 £10.60, 2&3 £34.30. CSF £167.96 CT £1508.07 TOTE £8.00: £2.60, £4.70, £3.30, £3.60; EX 231.70 Trifecta £3318.10 Pool: £16,441.93 - 4.60 winning units..
Owner Jakeman, Barrett, Booth & Ferrand **Bred** Green Hill Farm **Trained** George Nympton, Devon
■ Stewards' Enquiry : Richie McLernon one-day ban: used whip without giving gelding time to respond (Jan 29)

FOCUS

The winning time was 5.56sec quicker than that recorded by Chablais in winning the novice hurdle earlier on the card. There weren't that many unexposed horses in this line-up, and the overall form doesn't look too hot, although it still rates solid handicap form. The first two were better than the bare result.

NOTEBOOK

James De Vassy(FR) was one of only a few who could still be expected to be on the up, having run only four times last season but finished fourth in the Greatwood and third in the Coral Cup in two of those starts. Although disappointing on his reappearance, he was entitled to have come on for that, and he travelled through this race like a good horse. Despite being bumped by Organisateur approaching the second last, it didn't halt his momentum that much and he soon quickened up approaching the final flight, which he jumped well. He could drop back half a mile for the Totesport Trophy (best price 25-1 with Boylesports) next, and shouldn't be too inconvenienced by the shorter trip, especially if the ground is testing, but he'll surely find something better treated than him. Cheltenham will apparently be skipped if the ground looks likely to come up too lively. Official explanation: trainer said, regarding apparent improvement in form, that he was disappointed with the gelding's last run - which was its first of the season - and it had come on for it. (op 10-1)

Organisateur(IRE) looked to face a stiff task under top-weight off a mark of 154 but he has improved with every start this winter and this was another career best. Another rise in the weights will make things even more difficult, though, and he might be worth trying out in a conditions event somewhere.

Palomar(USA), winner of a jumpers' bumper at Southwell last time out, had no problem with the longer trip and ran a sound race off an 8lb higher mark than when last successful over hurdles. (op 17-2 tchd 8-1)

First Point(GER), representing the bang in-form Nicky Henderson stable, looked to have no more than an outsider's chance on paper, but nothing from the yard can be discounted at present and he actually swung into the straight looking to be going best of all. However, he'd raced wide the whole way round, and perhaps that eventually cost him. (op 12-1)

Dantari(IRE) seems likely to continue to struggle to win similarly competitive handicaps. (op 25-1)

Drill Sergeant, wearing a tongue-tie for the first time, was interesting in that he was a lightly raced novice carrying a low weight against largely exposed rivals. Normally a horse who likes to get on with it, he was restrained this time and was far too keen on this step up in trip. He hit the second last and tired quickly from there, but he's not one to give up on, especially when he looks likely to get his own way in front. (tchd 16-1 in a place)

Like Minded had been off the track since finishing second in a Grade 2 novice event at Sandown in December 2009. He's likely to go chasing next, but his trainer had expected him to be competitive in this final start over hurdles off what looked a fair mark. However, he was in trouble from the turn out of the back straight and ran as though the outing was needed. (op 7-1)

The Betchworth Kid put his nose in the turf following a bad mistake at the third flight and never really recovered. Further blunders followed, and this really was a bad day at the office. (op 7-2)

3562 WILLIAM HILL NOVICES' H'CAP CHASE (18 fncs) 3m

4:05 (4:07) (Class 3) (0-120,119) 5-Y-O+ **£6,505** (£1,910; £955; £477)

Form RPR

3-33 **1** **Rear Gunner (IRE)**32 2945 9-11-8 115 (p) AndrewThornton 128+
(Diana Grissell) *mde all: clr fr 10th: blnd 13th: stdd and jnd 4 out: sn drvn clr again: styd on strly fr 3 out: readily* **13/2**3

4-60 **2** *6* **Moleskin (IRE)**31 2959 8-11-10 117 (p) AndrewGlassonbury 125
(Victor Dartnall) *trckd wnr fr 3rd: drvn and styd on to chal 4 out: sn outpcd by wnr and no chnce fr next: hit 2 out but kpt on wl for clr 2nd* **11/1**

1321 **3** *14* **Rey Nacarado (IRE)**33 2928 6-11-2 114 DavidBass(5) 110
(Charlie Longsdon) *chsd ldrs: wnt 3rd 7th: drvn to chal 4 out: sn rdn and no ex: wknd into wl hld 3rd appr 3 out* **13/8**1

-313 **4** *29* **Mohi Rahrere (IRE)**5 3488 8-11-4 114 DannyCook(3) 82
(Barry Leavy) *in rr: hit 5th: hdwy 9th: hit 10th: blnd 12th: sn wknd: t.o* **15/2**

006P **5** *79* **Factotum**36 2869 7-11-12 119 APMcCoy 16
(Jonjo O'Neill) *a bhd: lost tch fr 1/2-way: t.o* **33/1**

0-6F U Or Sing About (FR)[13] 3342 9-11-0 110 (p) JimmyDerham(3) —
(Seamus Mullins) chsd ldrs: rdn 8th: wknd 10th: t.o whn veered bdly lft 2 out: veered bdly lft again: tried to refuse and uns rdr at last 50/1
26-F P Arturo Uno (IRE)[56] 2513 8-11-4 111 PaddyBrennan —
(Nigel Twiston-Davies) hit 1st and 5th: a in rr: t.o whn p.u after 9th 7/1
03-1 P Mallusk (IRE)[15] 3257 6-11-10 117 JasonMaguire —
(Kim Bailey) in tch: blnd 3rd: towards rr whn blnd 9th: p.u sn after 11/4[2]
6m 16.98s (1.98) **Going Correction** +0.025s/f (Yiel) **8** Ran SP% **115.6**
Speed ratings: **97,95,90,80,54** —,—,—
toteswingers: 1&2 £8.90, 1&3 £2.80, 2&3 £6.20. CSF £70.71 CT £169.75 TOTE £8.50: £1.80, £2.80, £1.10; EX 73.20 Trifecta £216.90 Pool: £961.52 - 3.28 winning units..
Owner Cockerell Cowing Racing **Bred** Cockerell Cowing Racing **Trained** Brightling, E Sussex

FOCUS
An ordinary race to close a marathon card, but a good ride from Andrew Thornton, who made it a real test. Arguably another step forward from the winner.

NOTEBOOK
Rear Gunner(IRE) was able to get a breather in down the far side, allowing the others to close up, but then kicked on again and dourly saw out the trip to record his first win over fences. The cheekpieces, which he was wearing for the second time, appear to have helped, and his jumping was better this time. (op 15-2)
Moleskin(IRE), wearing cheekpieces for the first time, ran his best race so far over fences, but the winner had been given a canny ride and he couldn't quite close him down in the straight. He should be able to find a little race. (op 9-1 tchd 8-1)
Rey Nacarado(IRE), 9lb higher for his Plumpton success, still looked the one to beat, but he wasn't up to defying it. Having had only three starts over fences, though, he's still capable of further improvement. (tchd 3-1 in a place)
Mohi Rahrere(IRE), making a quick reappearance after finishing third at Towcester earlier in the week, struggled with his jumping on this sharper track. (op 6-1)
Arturo Uno(IRE) Official explanation: jockey said gelding never travelled (op 9-4 tchd 7-2)
Mallusk(IRE) looked to be taken out of his comfort zone by the pace of the race, and mistakes followed. He'll appreciate a return to a stiffer track where they go slower early. Official explanation: jockey said gelding never travelled (op 9-4 tchd 7-2)
T/Jkpt: £2,028.50 to a £1 stake. Pool: £10,000.00 -3.50 winning tickets. T/Plt: £27.10 to a £1 stake. Pool: £132,209.19 - 3,554.64 winning tickets. T/Qpdt: £11.90 to a £1 stake. Pool: £10,534.27 - 650.00 winning tickets. AS

3260 WARWICK (L-H)
Saturday, January 15
OFFICIAL GOING: Heavy (soft in places; chs 5.1, hdl 4.6)
Wind: Strong behind Weather: Overcast

3563 TOTEPLACEPOT NOVICES' H'CAP HURDLE (8 hdls) 2m
12:40 (12:40) (Class 4) (0-110,110) 4-Y-0+ **£2,927** (£859; £429; £214)

Form RPR
32-0 **1** **Lively Fling (USA)**[77] 2081 5-11-9 **107** AidanColeman 119+
(Venetia Williams) chsd ldrs: led after 3 out: rdn and hdd bef next: 1 l down and styng on whn lft clr last 3/1[1]
064 **2** 16 **Mayolynn (USA)**[11] 3387 5-10-11 **95** AndrewThornton 91
(Caroline Bailey) chsd ldr tl led 5th: rdn and hdd after 3 out: sn wknd: lft 2nd last 15/2
00-0 **3** 27 **The Lemonpie (GER)**[118] 1548 6-10-10 **94** DaveCrosse 63
(Milton Harris) plld hrd: led: clr 2nd tl hdd 5th: wknd after next: blnd 2 out: lft 3rd last: t.o 25/1
U26 **4** 1 1/4 **Tom Wade (IRE)**[35] 2882 4-10-4 **107** MattCrawley(7) 63
(John Harris) hld up: rdn 5th: sn wknd: t.o 6/1[3]
0006 **5** 3 1/2 **Me Fein**[15] 3256 7-10-4 **88** DenisO'Regan 52
(Barney Curley) hld up: bhd fr 4th: t.o 12/1
-200 **6** 1 1/4 **Carbon Print (USA)**[47] 2322 6-10-13 **97** (t) FelixDeGiles 60
(James Evans) hld up: bhd fr 4th: t.o 33/1
5- **7** 33 **Fletch And Lenny (IRE)**[69] 7-11-1 **99** JodieMogford 29
(Adrian Wintle) hld up: bhd fr 4th: t.o 40/1
411U **P** **Rimini (FR)**[18] 3154 6-11-11 **109** LeightonAspell —
(David Rees) chsd ldrs tl rdn and wknd after 3 out: t.o whn p.u bef last: dismntd 7/2[2]
2-F2 **F** **Highway Code (USA)**[63] 2362 5-11-12 **110** (t) CharliePoste 122+
(Richard Lee) hld up in tch: blnd 3 out: led bef next: 1 l clr and rdn whn fell last 7/2[2]
3m 57.5s (1.00) **Going Correction** +0.20s/f (Yiel)
WFA 4 from 5yo+ 11lb **9** Ran SP% **112.4**
Speed ratings (Par 105): **105,97,83,82,81 80,64,**—,—
Tote Swingers: 1&2 £7.20, 1&3 £8.10, 2&3 £25.60 CSF £24.34 CT £461.82 TOTE £3.70: £1.40, £2.00, £9.10; EX 23.20.
Owner John Nicholls (Trading) Ltd **Bred** George Strawbridge Jr **Trained** Kings Caple, H'fords

FOCUS
This was an ordinary novice handicap hurdle, but they went a good pace in the conditions thanks to The Lemonpie and the field finished very well spread out. The riders' description of the conditions ranged from "soft" to "dead and hard work". A big step up from the winenr who rates as dead-heating with the faller.

NOTEBOOK
Lively Fling(USA), not seen since losing a shoe on his Ascot reappearance in October, was travelling well when taking it up rounding the home bend but he appeared to be getting the worst of the argument when presented with the race at the last. (op 7-2 tchd 11-4)
Mayolynn(USA), making her handicap debut after showing a hint of ability on her third start over hurdles, was always up there but had little response when headed by the winner starting the turn for home and she was third-best on merit. (op 7-1)
The Lemonpie(GER), disappointing over hurdles since arriving from Germany, appeared to do far too much early in the ground and looked sure to drop right out when headed before three out, but he found stamina reserves from somewhere to regain a distant third.
Tom Wade(IRE), making his handicap debut after facing an impossible task at Cheltenham last time, never figured and needs better ground. (op 8-1)
Fletch And Lenny(IRE) Official explanation: jockey said gelding hung right-handed
Rimini(FR), 9lb higher than when successful on his last hurdles start in October but off a 5lb lower mark than over fences, was there with every chance jumping three out but then stopped to nothing. Official explanation: vet said gelding was lame behind (op 3-1)

Highway Code(USA) looked to be holding Lively Fling when he stepped at the final flight and paid the penalty. Making his handicap debut in a first-time tongue-tie, he had already run a couple of decent races in heavy ground and although off the bridle just after halfway, he responded to the pressure to hit the front approaching two out before disaster struck. He deserves compensation.

3564 TOTESPORT 0800 221 221 NOVICES' CHASE (18 fncs) 3m 110y
1:10 (1:10) (Class 2) 5-Y-0+ **£10,888** (£3,744)

Form RPR
2542 **1** **Shalimar Fromentro (FR)**[30] 2979 5-10-8 131 DarylJacob 132+
(Nick Williams) hld up in tch: chsd ldr appr 2 out: 4 l down and rdn whn lft clr last 2/1[2]
-102 **2** 5 **Fruity O'Rooney**[8] 3429 8-11-5 130 JoshuaMoore 136
(Gary Moore) led to 8th: chsd ldr tl rdn appr 2 out: styd on same pce: lft 2nd last 14/1[3]
4-31 **F** **Peveril**[13] 3342 7-11-5 0 AndrewTinkler 148
(Nicky Henderson) chsd ldr tl led 8th: rdn appr 2 out: 4 l clr whn fell last 8/15[1]
6m 35.1s (8.10) **Going Correction** +0.35s/f (Yiel)
WFA 5 from 7yo+ 5lb **3** Ran SP% **105.2**
Speed ratings: **101,99,**—
CSF £11.86 TOTE £1.90; EX 5.00.
Owner Mrs Jane Williams **Bred** F Meslin **Trained** George Nympton, Devon

FOCUS
The absence of Wayward Prince because of the heavy ground took much of the interest away from this novice chase, but as in the opener the race took a dramatic twist at the final obstacle, this time with tragic consequences. The winner is on the upgrade.

NOTEBOOK
Shalimar Fromentro(FR), getting 5lb more than weight for age from his two penalised rivals, ran a blinder against the smart Wymott at Exeter last month, but he was never going to win this, especially as his jumping wasn't as polished as the other pair, until he was presented with the race at the final fence. (op 85-40 tchd 9-4)
Fruity O'Rooney tried to make all, but he was in trouble when the favourite put pressure on him jumping the five fences down the far side on the final circuit and had been shaken off before two out. (op 9-1)
Peveril had put in a very professional round of jumping for most of this contest, being bold on some occasions and clever on others, and seemed to have the race in the bag when he failed to take off at the last, taking a horrible and fatal fall. (op 4-7 tchd 4-6 in places)

3565 TOTEPOOL H'CAP CHASE (FOR THE EDWARD COURAGE CUP) (12 fncs) 2m
1:40 (1:40) (Class 3) (0-135,134) 5-Y-0+ **£6,505** (£1,910; £955; £477)

Form RPR
61-4 **1** **Call Me A Legend**[50] 2665 7-11-4 **126** WayneHutchinson 141+
(Alan King) hld up: hdwy 8th: led appr last: rdn clr flat 11/8[1]
010P **2** 8 **Moon Over Miami (GER)**[14] 3292 10-11-12 **134** (t) DarylJacob 139
(Charlie Mann) hld up: hdwy 5th: led 7th to 2 out: sn rdn: rdr lost iron briefly on landing over last: no ex flat 8/1
0-14 **3** 11 **Pret A Thou (FR)**[56] 2520 8-11-4 **133** HarryChalloner(7) 129
(John Bryan Groucott) chsd ldrs: led after 2nd: hdd 6th: wknd appr 2 out: lft 3rd last 5/1[3]
5346 **4** 29 **Prince Des Marais (FR)**[52] 2613 8-10-12 **120** (t) AndrewThornton 84
(Caroline Bailey) hld up in tch: wknd 6th: t.o 22/1
P-P6 **P** **Fighting Chance (IRE)**[50] 2665 11-11-3 **125** DenisO'Regan —
(Richard Lee) led tl after 2nd: chsd ldrs tl wknd 8th: t.o whn p.u bef 3 out 17/2
/12- **U** **Silk Drum (IRE)**[245] 4434 6-11-10 **132** BrianHughes 137
(Howard Johnson) chsd ldrs: led 6th to next: led 2 out: sn rdn and hdd: disputing 2nd and looked hld whn blnd and uns rdr last 10/3[2]
4m 7.40s (1.80) **Going Correction** +0.35s/f (Yiel) **6** Ran SP% **107.8**
Speed ratings: **109,105,99,85,**— —
Tote Swingers: 1&2 £1.50, 1&3 £6.30, 2&3 £4.40 CSF £11.32 TOTE £2.10: £1.90, £2.80; EX 10.50.
Owner Mrs K Holmes **Bred** D And Mrs Holmes **Trained** Barbury Castle, Wilts

FOCUS
With a few who like to force the pace in this field, a decent pace was always likely. Fair form with the winner on the upgrade.

NOTEBOOK
Call Me A Legend ◆ was returning from ten months off due to a fractured pelvis when an eyecatching fourth at Newbury in November, and duly stepped up from that. She looked to have blown it with a blunder three out having moved up to slipstream the leaders, but she rallied to sneak up the inside into the lead between the last two fences. She got close to the last, but was still able to pull clear on the run-in. The winner is due to be retired to the paddocks at the end of the season, but has the Grand Annual as a possible target before that happens. (op 7-4 tchd 5-4)
Moon Over Miami(GER), who normally takes on better rivals, was in front just after halfway but could do little when the winner appeared on his inside between the last two fences. (op 13-2 tchd 6-1)
Pret A Thou(FR) handles the ground and normally likes to lead, but he was given no peace up front and was already on the retreat when a mistake five out ended his hopes. (op 9-2 tchd 11-2)
Fighting Chance(IRE) had run poorly on three occasions since completing a hat-trick in the middle of last winter and he dropped right out just after halfway here. He is still to show that he handles ground as soft as this. (op 3-1 tchd 11-4, 7-2 in places)
Silk Drum(IRE), not seen since winning on the Flat at Doncaster last May and having only his third start over fences, was always up there and was still battling for second when a bad blunder at the last sent his rider to the floor. (op 3-1 tchd 11-4, 7-2 in places)

3566 PERTEMPS H'CAP HURDLE (SERIES QUALIFIER) (12 hdls) 3m 1f
2:10 (2:10) (Class 2) 5-Y-0+ **£8,456** (£2,483; £1,241; £620)

Form RPR
5P-6 **1** **Mobaasher (USA)**[14] 3293 8-11-7 **142** (t) AidanColeman 148+
(Venetia Williams) hld up: hdwy appr 8th: rdn to ld and j.lft last: styd on u.p 12/1
45-4 **2** 1 1/2 **Alfie Spinner (IRE)**[14] 3298 6-10-6 **127** DarylJacob 129
(Nick Williams) led to 4th: remained handy: led appr 2 out: rdn and hdd bef last: styd on same pce flat 9/2[1]
-5F4 **3** 2 1/4 **Sangfroid**[57] 2500 7-10-7 **128** LeightonAspell 130
(Nick Williams) hld up: hdwy appr 8th: hmpd next: outpcd after 3 out: rallied bef last: rdn and no imp flat 14/1
4F-2 **4** 13 **Micheal Flips (IRE)**[101] 1731 7-11-12 **147** NickScholfield 138+
(Andy Turnell) chsd ldrs: rdn after 3 out: mstke next: wkng whn blnd last 14/1
-530 **5** 3/4 **County Zen (FR)** [36] 2869 8-10-2 **128** GilesHawkins(5) 114
(Philip Hobbs) chsd ldrs tl led 7th: rdn and hdd appr 2 out: wknd bef last 25/1
42PF **6** 17 **Federstar (GER)**[17] 3198 9-10-7 128 DaveCrosse 97
(Milton Harris) hld up: hdwy 6th: rdn and wknd appr 2 out: t.o 25/1
PU63 **7** 8 **Heathcliff (IRE)**[7] 3440 9-10-6 127 (v) DenisO'Regan 88
(Richard Lee) sn pushed along in rr: bhd and drvn along 6th: t.o 9/2[1]
P-16 **8** 1/2 **The Shy Man** [56] 2523 8-9-13 127 PeterCarberry(7) 88
(G M Moore) prom: lost pl 6th: rallied next: rdn and wknd appr 2 out 5/1

0-40 **9** *30* **South O'The Border**[7] 3444 9-10-5 **129**..........(p) SamTwiston-Davies(3) 60
(Nigel Twiston-Davies) *chsd ldrs: j. slowly 1st: led 4th to 7th: rdn after next: wknd 4 out: t.o* **22/1**

P0-U **P** **Halla San**[36] 2868 9-10-1 **127**.. BrianToomey(5) —
(Richard Fahey) *hld up in tch: racd keenly: wknd qckly after 7th: t.o whn p.u bef next* **33/1**

066P **P** **Love Of Tara**[15] 3254 9-10-4 **125**................................ WayneHutchinson —
(Martin Keighley) *prom tl wknd after 7th: t.o whn p.u bef 2 out* **25/1**

3-20 **P** **First Stream (GER)**[36] 2870 7-10-6 **127**..........................(b) BrianHughes —
(Howard Johnson) *hld up: wknd appr 8th: sn t.o: p.u bef 2 out* **12/1**

-311 **F** **Kauto The Roc (FR)**[54] 2581 7-9-7 **121** oh1...................... PeterHatton(7) —
(Alan King) *hld up: hdwy 4th: mstke next: cl 3rd whn fell 9th* **7/1**[3]

2061 **P** **Phare Isle (IRE)**[14] 3308 6-10-0 **121** oh1............................ CharliePoste —
(Ben Case) *hld up in tch: rdn and wknd bef 8th: t.o whn p.u bef 2 out* **10/1**

6m 30.1s (2.60) **Going Correction** +0.20s/f (Yiel) **14** Ran SP% **122.2**
Speed ratings: **103,102,101,97,97 91,89,89,79,— —,—,—,—**
Tote Swingers: 1&2 £6.60, 1&3 £19.70, 2&3 £13.70 CSF £63.02 CT £789.32 TOTE £17.00: £4.40, £2.20, £5.50; EX 69.90 Trifecta £341.30 Part won. Pool: £461.25 - 0.40 winning units..
Owner Seasons Holidays **Bred** Brushwood Stable **Trained** Kings Caple, H'fords

FOCUS
A fiercely competitive handicap on paper, but the significance of the form of this race is likely to emerge later on. The winner posted his best figure since 2008.

NOTEBOOK
Mobaasher(USA), who stays all day, had the tongue-tie back on and looked the likely winner some way out as he seemed to be running all over his rivals. He did hit a flat spot turning in, but was sent to the front jumping two out and although he pricked his ears and seemed to doss coming to the last, he had done enough by then. He is likely to head for the final at the festival. (tchd 11-1)
Alfie Spinner(IRE) ◆ remains 12lb higher than when last successful in a handicap, but had been shaping as though a thorough test of stamina would suit him and so it proved, especially as he was rallying at the line having lost the advantage jumping the second-last. He remains totally unexposed as a staying hurdler. (op 11-2)
Sangfroid usually runs well in defeat and this staying-on effort was another creditable performance, but he is just 1-21 over hurdles so can hardly be supported with any confidence. (tchd 16-1)
Micheal Flips(IRE), back over hurdles after an adequate chasing debut on his seasonal reappearance at Towcester in October, had never run over as far as this under rules, and although he was travelling almost as well as the winner coming to the home turn, his stamina appeared to give out as he blundered his way over the last two hurdles.
County Zen(FR), back over hurdles for the first time since winning off 5lb lower at Newbury last March, had also never run over this far before, but he ran really well in a handy position until weakening over the final two flights. He can win again back over shorter. (op 22-1)
Federstar(GER) has had an unhappy time of it over fences recently and is still 8lb higher than when completing a hat-trick over hurdles in the spring, but he wasn't totally disgraced on this occasion.
Heathcliff(IRE) is an out-and-out stayer who handles the ground and even this may have been an inadequate test, but he ran a thoroughly moody race here, dropping himself out in a detached last and never figuring. Official explanation: jockey said gelding never travelled (op 11-2)
The Shy Man(IRE) showed up until weakening on the turn for home, but has paid dearly in the weights for his wide-margin success on his return to hurdles at Aintree in October. (op 9-1)
Kauto The Roc(FR) was bidding for a hat-trick off a 9lb higher mark, but his ability to go in the ground was the big question. Unfortunately we don't know how he would have fared as he came down four out when still in the mix. (op 6-1)

3567 NEPTUNE INVESTMENT MANAGEMENT LEAMINGTON NOVICES' HURDLE (GRADE 2) (11 hdls) 2m 5f
2:45 (2:45) (Class 1) 5-Y-0+

£14,252 (£5,347; £2,677; £1,335; £670; £335)

Form RPR

2-12 **1** **Court In Motion (IRE)**[17] 3197 6-11-7 135...................... AidanColeman 147+
(Emma Lavelle) *hld up: hdwy 6th: led after 3 out: sn clr: canter* **6/4**[1]

11F4 **2** *21* **Neptune Equester**[32] 2939 8-11-0 0................................ DenisO'Regan 114+
(Brian Ellison) *hld up: drvn along 7th: hdwy 3 out: wkng whn 2nd appr 2 out: mstke last* **25/1**

1-10 **3** *5* **Safran De Cotte (FR)**[14] 3288 5-11-4 0.......................... LeightonAspell 111
(Henry Daly) *hld up: hdwy whn blnd 3 out: nt rcvr* **16/1**

212 **4** *1* **Moon Indigo**[32] 2939 5-11-4 130.. BrianHughes 110
(Howard Johnson) *chsd ldrs tl wknd 8th* **11/1**

111 **5** *15* **Mossley (IRE)**[35] 2888 5-11-7 145................................... AndrewTinkler 103
(Nicky Henderson) *chsd ldrs: drvn along after 8th: wknd appr 2 out: t.o* **9/4**[2]

3611 **6** *3 3/4* **Jetnova (IRE)**[33] 2925 6-11-4 128.............................. WayneHutchinson 91
(Alan King) *chsd ldr: mstke 2nd: pushed along 7th: wknd after 3 out: t.o* **7/1**[3]

1 **P** **Maxdelas (FR)**[15] 3252 5-11-0 125.......................... SamTwiston-Davies —
(Nigel Twiston-Davies) *led and sn clr: hdd & wknd after 3 out: t.o whn p.u after next* **8/1**

61 **P** **Lamb's Cross**[113] 1600 5-11-4 0...................................... DavidEngland —
(Nigel Twiston-Davies) *hld up: a in rr: t.o whn p.u bef 7th* **50/1**

5m 20.2s (5.20) **Going Correction** +0.20s/f (Yiel) **8** Ran SP% **114.4**
Speed ratings: **98,90,88,87,82 80,—,—**
Tote Swingers: 1&2 £21.90, 1&3 £10.40, 2&3 £44.70 CSF £38.15 TOTE £2.60: £1.30, £4.00, £2.90; EX 49.80 Trifecta £421.70 Part won. Pool: £569.88 - 0.72 winning units..
Owner N Mustoe **Bred** Peter O'Reilly **Trained** Wildhern, Hants

FOCUS
A decent line-up for this Grade 2 novice hurdle and Maxdelas made sure it was a proper test in the conditions. Another step up from Court In Motion but all the others were out on their feet.

NOTEBOOK
Court In Motion(IRE), who had finished runner-up in the Challow Hurdle at Newbury last month, moved into the race in the final mile as though he had just joined in, and once cruising to the front after three out was able to saunter clear without ever coming off the bridle. Highly regarded by connections, he will now head for the Albert Bartlett at the festival, for which he was immediately cut to a top-priced 8-1 alongside his Newbury conqueror Backspin, provided there is enough cut in the ground. (op 7-4 tchd 2-1)
Neptune Equester, a three-time winner over fences last year and a well-beaten fourth on his hurdling debut at Catterick last month, eventually plugged on for a remote second. At least this should have set him up nicely for a return to fences if connections wish. (op 28-1 tchd 33-1)
Safran De Cotte(FR) is proven in the ground, but he was disappointing at Cheltenham on New Year's Day, and although he ran on from the rear to finish third, he was never really in the race. (op 20-1)
Moon Indigo, taking a big step up in class and unproven on ground this soft, was comfortably seen off and achieved little in finishing a remote fourth. (op 12-1 tchd 10-1)
Mossley(IRE), previously unbeaten in two hurdles and a bumper, stays well and was the one to beat on adjusted official ratings, but even he had to concede that conditions were too testing over the last couple of flights. Official explanation: jockey said gelding stopped very quickly (op 2-1 tchd 15-8)
Maxdelas(FR) made sure it was a proper test in the conditions, although he eventually paid for doing so. (op 7-1 tchd 9-1)
Lamb's Cross Official explanation: jockey said gelding was unsuited by the heavy (soft in places) ground (op 7-1 tchd 9-1)

3568 TOTESPORT.COM CLASSIC CHASE (H'CAP) (GRADE 3) (22 fncs) 3m 5f
3:20 (3:22) (Class 1) 5-Y-0+

£34,206 (£12,834; £6,426; £3,204; £1,608; £804)

Form RPR

00-1 **1** **West End Rocker (IRE)**[31] 2962 9-10-11 **133**........... WayneHutchinson 148+
(Alan King) *hld up in tch: mstke 10th: led 3 out: mstke next: drvn out* **10/1**

-431 **2** *3/4* **Minella Boys (IRE)**[13] 3347 9-10-4 **126**..........................(tp) FelixDeGiles 139
(Charlie Longsdon) *hld up: hdwy 12th: chsd wnr appr 2 out: styd on u.p* **4/1**[1]

-511 **3** *8* **Incentivise (IRE)**[31] 2953 8-9-9 **122** oh1......................... GilesHawkins(5) 129
(Richard Lee) *hld up: blnd 16th: hdwy 18th: rdn after 3 out: styd on same pce whn hit last* **9/1**

-020 **4** *3/4* **Le Beau Bai (FR)**[14] 3293 8-10-10 **139**........................... JakeGreenall(7) 145
(Richard Lee) *hld up: hdwy 16th: rdn after 3 out: no ex last* **11/2**[2]

6420 **5** *14* **Noun De La Thinte (FR)**[30] 2984 10-9-9 **124**.............. MrJSherwood(7) 115
(Venetia Williams) *chsd ldrs: rdn after 16th: wknd appr 2 out* **33/1**

00-0 **6** *8* **Comply Or Die (IRE)**[70] 2221 12-11-12 **148**.................(b) JohnnyFarrelly 138+
(David Pipe) *chsd ldr tl led 6th to 3 out: wkng whn mstke last* **33/1**

F211 **7** *20* **Bobby Gee**[30] 2984 10-10-4 **126**... LeightonAspell 89
(Renee Robeson) *prom: pckd 8th: wknd 16th: t.o* **9/1**

/F3P **P** **Pass Me By**[13] 3347 12-9-11 **122** oh10...................... WayneKavanagh(3) —
(Suzy Smith) *chsd ldrs: lost pl 6th: sn drvn along: hit 15th: t.o whn p.u bef next* **100/1**

5P-1 **P** **Hello Bud (IRE)**[55] 2543 13-11-3 **142**................(t) SamTwiston-Davies(3) —
(Nigel Twiston-Davies) *led to 6th: remained handy tl rdn and wknd appr 16th: t.o whn p.u bef 3 out* **16/1**

243P **P** **Magic Sky (FR)**[7] 3437 11-10-9 **131**.................................... CharliePoste —
(Milton Harris) *hld up and a bhd: slipped bnd appr 3rd: t.o whn p.u bef 16th* **40/1**

-26U **P** **Picture In The Sky (IRE)**[54] 2580 10-10-0 **122** oh7........(p) SeanQuinlan —
(Susan Nock) *a in rr: pushed along 8th: t.o whn p.u bef 11th* **50/1**

3/2- **P** **Companero (IRE)**[432] 2186 11-11-4 **140**............................... BrianHughes —
(Howard Johnson) *chsd ldrs: hit 12th and 14th: sn rdn: wknd appr 16th: t.o whn p.u bef 18th* **12/1**

3-02 **P** **Richard's Sundance (IRE)**[14] 3290 9-11-1 **137**............... DenisO'Regan —
(Victor Dartnall) *chsd ldrs tl wknd appr 3 out: j. slowly next: sn p.u* **15/2**[3]

-P43 **P** **Officier De Reserve (FR)**[14] 3290 9-10-4 **126**...........(b[1]) AidanColeman —
(Venetia Williams) *hld up in tch: rdn: wknd and p.u bef 16th* **15/2**[3]

-331 **P** **C'Monthehammers (IRE)**[41] 2794 8-10-3 **125**................. DavidEngland —
(Nigel Twiston-Davies) *hld up: a in rr: drvn along 10th: blnd 14th: t.o whn p.u bef 16th* **17/2**

7m 41.4s (0.40) **Going Correction** +0.35s/f (Yiel) **15** Ran SP% **123.4**
Speed ratings: **113,112,110,110,106 104,98,—,—,— —,—,—,—,—**
Tote Swingers: 1&2 £18.70, 1&3 £20.20, 2&3 £10.20 CSF £50.85 CT £388.71 TOTE £11.60: £4.00, £2.30, £3.60; EX 70.50 Trifecta £1228.40 Part won. Pool: £1,660.07 - 0.93 winning units..

Owner Barry Winfield & Tim Leadbeater **Bred** Ms P Kidd **Trained** Barbury Castle, Wilts
■ Stewards' Enquiry : Felix De Giles three-day ban: used whip with excessive frequency without giving gelding time to respond (Jan 29-31)

FOCUS
A highly competitive handicap chase and a severe test of stamina in the conditions. Only seven of the 15 runners managed to complete but the form looks solid. The winner is verging on Grand National class.

NOTEBOOK
West End Rocker(IRE) had been put up 4lb for his successful on his return from a year off at Newbury last month (couple of subsequent winners behind) and he duly followed up in game style. He was pulled up in the 2009 Scottish National in his only previous try beyond 3m2f, but it was a different story here and he was travelling particularly well when jumping to the front three from home. He had to be kept up to his work to hold off the runner-up, but he looks better than ever just now and still doesn't have that many miles on the clock for a chaser of his age. He may be aimed at the National. (tchd 17-2)
Minella Boys(IRE), 7lb higher than when taking the Sussex National over this trip at Plumpton earlier this month when sporting first-time cheekpieces, attracted plenty of market support beforehand and although off the bridle some way out, stuck to his guns and was coming back for more at the line. He may well go up again for this, but remains at the top of his game. (op 8-1)
Incentivise(IRE), successful over 3m6f at Bangor last month, was 9lb higher in his bid for a hat-trick. He ran really well and had every chance turning for home despite being under strong pressure, but looked held when uprooting the last. (op 11-1 tchd 12-1)
Le Beau Bai(FR), back over fences after a couple of spins over hurdles, was given a very patient ride and looked likely to figure when creeping closer a mile from home, but he soon came under pressure, and though he stayed on he was never getting there quickly enough. (tchd 5-1)
Noun De La Thinte(FR) finished around 40l behind Bobby Gee at Towcester last month, but although she reversed that form she was ridden along and going nowhere a good 6f from home.
Comply Or Die(IRE), the 2008 Grand National winner, had the blinkers back on and ran a much better race here, providing a bold sight in making much of the running until out-jumped by the winner three out. There still seems to be some life in the veteran.
Bobby Gee, proven in the ground but raised 10lb in his bid for a hat-trick, appeared not to stay. (op 8-1 tchd 10-1)
Picture In The Sky(IRE) Official explanation: jockey said gelding never travelled

3569 BET TOTEPOOL AT TOTESPORT.COM "NEWCOMERS" STANDARD OPEN NATIONAL HUNT FLAT RACE 2m
3:55 (3:56) (Class 6) 4-5-Y-0 **£1,507** (£439; £219)

Form RPR

1 **Russe Blanc (FR)** 4-10-7 0.. CharliePoste 96+
(Richard Lee) *hld up: hdwy 12f out: led over 1f out: drvn out* **14/1**

2 *2 1/4* **Roll The Dice (IRE)** 5-11-0 0.................................... GilesHawkins(5) 105
(Philip Hobbs) *led at stdy pce: hdd over 2f out: rdn and ev ch fr over 1f out: no ex towards fin* **9/2**[3]

3 *3 3/4* **Perazzi George (IRE)** 5-11-5 0..................................... LeightonAspell 101
(Chris Gordon) *hld up: rdn over 6f out: hdwy over 3f out: styd on same pce* **50/1**

4 *hd* **Cold Knight** 5-11-5 0.. WayneHutchinson 101
(Alan King) *hld up: hdwy over 5f out: led over 2f out to over 1f out: no ex ins fnl f: lost 3rd nr fin* **13/8**[1]

5 *2 1/4* **Rich Buddy** 5-11-5 0.. SeanQuinlan 99
(Richard Phillips) *hld up: hdwy 12f out: wknd over 1f out* **14/1**

6 *24* **Rowlestone Lad** 4-10-7 0... GerardTumelty 63
(Richard Price) *hld up: hdwy 1/2-way: wknd 4f out: t.o* **66/1**

7 *17* **Semelay (FR)** 5-11-5 0.. LiamHeard 58
(Laura Young) *chsd ldrs tl wknd over 4f out: t.o* **100/1**

8 *9* **Red Shuttle** 4-10-0 0 MrJMQuinlan(7) 37
(Michael Quinlan) *hld up in tch: racd keenly: rdn and wknd over 3f out: t.o* **20/1**

9 *6* **Atlantic Pearl** 5-11-5 0 JohnnyFarrelly 43
(David Pipe) *chsd ldrs tl wknd 4f out: t.o* **15/8**[2]

10 *nk* **Sharinga** 4-9-7 0 PeterHatton(7) 23
(Reg Hollinshead) *prom tl wknd over 4f out: t.o* **25/1**

4m 22.0s (31.10) **Going Correction** +0.20s/f (Yiel)
WFA 4 from 5yo 11lb **10** Ran SP% **117.4**
Speed ratings: **30,28,27,26,25 13,5,—,—,—**
Tote Swingers: 1&2 £5.70, 1&3 £24.90, 2&3 £19.90 CSF £73.42 TOTE £15.30: £3.20, £1.90, £6.60; EX 66.50.
Owner Mark Jackson **Bred** B De La Motte Saint-Pierre & Jean-Francois Lambert **Trained** Byton, H'fords

FOCUS
None of these had ever seen the racecourse before, under rules or otherwise. The runners stood still for a good ten seconds at the start before breaking into a canter and the pace didn't pick up significantly until after halfway. As a result the form is hard to quantify.

NOTEBOOK
Russe Blanc(FR), sold for £8,000 last spring and a half-brother to two winners on the Flat in France, came off the bridle when the pace picked up around six furlongs from home. To his credit he stuck at it, forging his way to the front passing the two-furlong pole and keeping on for a game victory. The form may not amount to much, but he has a good attitude. (op 11-1)
Roll The Dice(IRE), a £40,000 3yo and a half-brother to three winning pointers, very much had the run of the race out in front, but he battled back gamely once headed and appears to have a future. (op 6-1)
Perazzi George(IRE), who cost 1,500 euros as a 4yo and is out of a sister to a bumper/hurdles/chase winner, moved up menacingly on the outside turning in before his effort flattened out. This was an encouraging enough start. (op 33-1)
Cold Knight, out of a half-sister to the 1994 Supreme Novices' Hurdle winner Arctic Kinsman, looked a big danger when moving up into a challenging position racing down the back straight and was just about in front starting up the home straight, but he couldn't go through with it and tired in the last furlong. (op 5-2 tchd 11-4)
Rich Buddy, a £27,000 3yo and a half-brother to a couple of winners over hurdles, made some late progress to pull well clear of the others and he should improve. (op 16-1 tchd 11-1)
Atlantic Pearl, who cost £24,000 as a 3yo and is out of a half-sister to the smart Hobbs Hill, was expected to do better but, having been handy from the start, he came off the bridle and weakened tamely when the tempo increased after halfway. (op 13-8 tchd 6-4)
T/Plt: £269.20 to a £1 stake. Pool: £70,301.21 - 190.63 winning tickets. T/Qpdt: £22.30 to a £1 stake. Pool: £5,637.57 - 186.50 winning tickets. CR

2610 WETHERBY (L-H)

Saturday, January 15

OFFICIAL GOING: Soft (good to soft in places; chs 6.1, hdl 6.4)
Wind: Strong 1/2 behind Weather: Overcast, light rain, very blustery

3570 WETHERBY RACECOURSE & CONFERENCE CENTRE H'CAP HURDLE (9 hdls) 2m 110y

12:30 (12:30) (Class 4) (0-110,110) 4-Y-0+ **£1,951** (£573; £286; £143)

Form				RPR
60-U	**1**		**Rushwee (IRE)**[4] 3497 9-11-5 **103** DominicElsworth	110+
			(Lucy Wadham) *t.k.h: wnt prom 5th: chsd ldr appr 3 out: led 2 out: j.rt last: rdn clr* **7/4**[1]	
2-60	**2**	*5*	**Last Of The Bunch**[67] 2300 6-11-9 **107** BarryKeniry	108
			(Alan Swinbank) *led to 2 out: styd on same pce* **7/1**	
3-03	**3**	*7*	**Lap Of Honour (IRE)**[14] 3302 7-11-4 **102** GrahamLee	96
			(Ferdy Murphy) *hld up in rr: effrt appr 3 out: lft modest 3rd 2 out: one pce* **3/1**[2]	
0055	**4**	*3 ¾*	**Teenage Idol (IRE)**[55] 2549 7-11-5 **110** MissECSayer(7)	100
			(Evelyn Slack) *chsd ldr: drvn after 6th: hung rt and wknd 2 out* **4/1**[3]	
110	**F**		**Turf Trivia**[78] 2078 4-10-13 **109** PeterBuchanan	87
			(George Moore) *chsd ldrs: pushed along after 6th: disputing 3rd whn fell heavily 2 out* **7/1**	

4m 11.1s (15.30) **Going Correction** +0.925s/f (Soft)
WFA 4 from 6yo+ 11lb **5** Ran SP% **106.4**
Speed ratings (Par 105): **101,98,95,93,—**
CSF £12.23 TOTE £2.90: £1.50, £3.10; EX 14.30.
Owner Mr & Mrs J Timmons **Bred** Michael Doyle **Trained** Newmarket, Suffolk

FOCUS
The ground was described by the jockeys as riding rather dead and a bit holding. An ordinary handicap where the winner confirmed the merit of his unlucky Leicester run.

NOTEBOOK
Rushwee(IRE) gained quick compensation having looked certain to score at Leicester earlier in the week before unseating his rider. Always travelling strongly, in a race where there was not much depth, he did this with the minimum of fuss but will obviously find life more difficult when reassessed. (op 2-1)
Last Of The Bunch had some fair novice form last season but has been struggling since switching to handicaps. Although this was a fair front-running performance, he is on a mark that appears to be high enough. (op 11-2)
Lap Of Honour(IRE), on a reasonable mark of 102 on his handicap debut, could only stay on at the same pace in the straight but should be capable of winning off a similar mark. (tchd 10-3 in a place)
Teenage Idol(IRE) came in for a little support dropping back in trip, but had little more to offer from three out and was comfortably beaten. (tchd 7-2 and 9-2)
Turf Trivia, a winner of two juveniles already this season, was the first to come under pressure turning out of the back straight but, to his credit, was sticking to the task well, although looking held, before taking a crashing fall two out. (op 6-1 tchd 11-2)

3571 ANDY DICKINSON LAS VEGAS FUNNY MONEY NOVICES' CHASE (16 fncs) 2m 4f 110y

1:00 (1:01) (Class 3) 5-Y-0+ **£4,553** (£1,337; £668; £333)

Form				RPR
2P-1	**1**		**Alvarado (IRE)**[99] 1759 6-11-4 0 WilsonRenwick	147+
			(Howard Johnson) *trckd ldrs: led 4 out: j.rt next: hung lft between last 2: 5 l ahd whn blnd bdly last: drvn out* **5/2**[2]	
-222	**2**	*3*	**Fredo (IRE)**[11] 3390 7-10-9 130 MichaelMurphy(3)	133
			(Ian Williams) *chsd ldrs: led appr 4 out: sn hdd: kpt on run-in* **7/4**[1]	
1-11	**3**	*8*	**Smuglin**[58] 2475 8-10-11 134 BrianHarding	126
			(Donald McCain) *led: hdd appr 4 out: hit 2 out: wknd last* **7/2**[3]	
6/15	**4**	*49*	**Alfie Flits**[24] 3092 9-11-4 135 BarryKeniry	82
			(Alan Swinbank) *nt fluent: chsd ldrs: reminders 6th: blnd next: outpcd 9th: sn lost tch: hit 11th: t.o after 13th* **7/1**	
3-U1	**P**		**Sibenek (IRE)**[68] 2272 7-11-4 122 GrahamLee	—
			(Martin Todhunter) *in last: nt fluent 8th: lost pl next: t.o 12th: p.u bef next* **9/1**	

5m 21.1s (13.30) **Going Correction** +0.575s/f (Soft) **5** Ran SP% **109.7**
Speed ratings: **97,95,92,74,—**
CSF £7.53 TOTE £3.60: £1.50, £1.20; EX 6.70.
Owner Andrea & Graham Wylie **Bred** P R Joyce **Trained** Billy Row, Co Durham
■ Stewards' Enquiry : Michael Murphy one-day ban: used whip without giving gelding time to respond (Jan 29)
Wilson Renwick three-day ban: used whip in incorrect place (Jan 29-31)

FOCUS
An interesting novice chase in which the front three drew well clear of the remainder turning out of the back straight. The winner is on the upgrade and looks a smart novice.

NOTEBOOK
Alvarado(IRE) made a pleasing start to his chasing career when winning at Carlisle and followed up in decent fashion here. Travelling and jumping well for most of the way, he was well in command before blundering through the last. Connections have no solid plans for him but believe he will be better suited going right-handed. (op 7-2 tchd 4-1)
Fredo(IRE), a fair staying handicap hurdler on his day, has been runner-up over fences four times now but has been unlucky to have bumped into some useful types. He ran another solid race but would have appreciated a longer trip and his turn will come. (op 15-8)
Smuglin has been in good form since joining this stable and ran respectably in defeat again. She was staying on at the same pace before clouting two out, but she is a genuine mare and should find plenty of opportunities to add to her tally. (op 2-1)
Alfie Flits was receiving reminders from an early stage and was never jumping with any fluency before losing touch with the principals turning out of the back straight. (tchd 11-2)
Sibenek(IRE), a winner of a handicap chase at Carlisle, was always going to find it more difficult back in this company and was under pressure a long way out before pulling up turning in and will be of more interest back in handicap company. (op 14-1 tchd 8-1)

3572 EUROPEAN BREEDERS' FUND "NATIONAL HUNT" NOVICES' HURDLE QUALIFIER (11 hdls) 2m 4f

1:30 (1:30) (Class 4) 4-7-Y-0 **£2,602** (£764; £382; £190)

Form				RPR
	1		**Trustan Times (IRE)**[104] 5-11-2 0 AdrianLane	127+
			(Tim Easterby) *in tch: hdwy 7th: jnd ldrs after next: led 3 out: hit next: wandered between last 2: drvn out* **20/1**	
4-1	**2**	*3 ¼*	**Yurok (IRE)**[76] 2102 7-11-8 0 TjadeCollier	124+
			(Sue Smith) *chsd ldrs: wnt 2nd 7th: rdn appr 3 out: wnt 2nd between last 2: nt fluent last: kpt on* **9/4**[2]	
1-22	**3**	*5*	**Our Mick**[31] 2954 5-10-13 0 JohnKington(3)	114+
			(Donald McCain) *trckd ldr: t.k.h: nt jump wl: led 6th: hdd 3 out: 4 l 2nd whn mstke 2 out: wknd between last 2* **10/11**[1]	
/35-	**4**	*13*	**Candleford**[300] 4757 6-10-13 0 RyanMania(3)	101+
			(Sally Hall) *mid-div: lost pl after 7th: styd on fr 2 out* **100/1**	
20	**5**	*6*	**Fill The Power (IRE)**[10] 3399 5-11-2 0 HenryOliver	93
			(Sue Smith) *in rr: hdwy 8th: one pce fr next* **80/1**	
01-6	**6**	*12*	**Comeragh King**[62] 2403 7-11-2 0 PeterBuchanan	81
			(Tim Fitzgerald) *in tch: outpcd 8th: wknd appr 2 out* **40/1**	
425	**7**	*10*	**Bunclody**[32] 2943 6-11-2 0 BarryKeniry	71
			(George Moore) *in tch: wnt modest 4th 8th: wknd 2 out* **20/1**	
3-64	**8**	*6*	**Mr Supreme (IRE)**[13] 3330 6-11-2 0 RichieMcGrath	65
			(Kate Walton) *prom: lost pl after 7th* **11/1**[3]	
5	**9**	*6*	**Wait No More (IRE)**[40] 2826 6-10-13 0 AlexMerriam(3)	61
			(Sarah Humphrey) *chsd ldrs: lost pl after 7th* **50/1**	
0	**10**	*21*	**Ben Trovato (IRE)**[56] 2518 5-10-9 0 StephenO'Donovan(7)	38
			(John Upson) *nt fluent in rr: mstke 2nd: reminders next: sn bhd: t.o 6th* **200/1**	
0-0	**11**	*12*	**Rivermouth**[18] 3153 6-11-2 0 JimmyMcCarthy	26
			(Alan King) *mid-div: outpcd and lost pl 7th: sn bhd: t.o* **66/1**	
	12	*19*	**Indian Snow (IRE)** 6-10-13 0 EwanWhillans(3)	7
			(William Amos) *in rr: blnd 1st: bhd whn mstke 6th: t.o 3 out* **100/1**	
40-P	**13**	*10*	**Nothing Ventured**[52] 2612 6-11-2 0 MichaelMcAlister	—
			(John Norton) *in rr: bhd fr 5th: t.o 3 out* **200/1**	
50	**P**		**Aeneid**[32] 2943 6-11-2 0 (t) PaddyAspell	—
			(Brian Rothwell) *in rr: drvn 3rd: bhd whn mstke 6th: t.o whn p.u bef 3 out* **100/1**	
33	**P**		**Milano Supremo (IRE)**[104] 1702 6-11-2 0 (t) GrahamLee	—
			(Chris Grant) *mid-div: lost pl 7th: t.o whn p.u bef 3 out* **18/1**	
4-13	**P**		**Bow Badger**[62] 2397 5-11-5 119 JamesO'Farrell(3)	—
			(Howard Johnson) *led: t.k.h and hung rt: j.rt: hdd 6th: wknd qckly 8th: 10th whn p.u bef next* **16/1**	
	P		**Shoal Bay Dreamer** 5-10-9 0 BrianHarding	—
			(Dianne Sayer) *in rr: blnd 2nd: sn bhd: t.o 5th: p.u bef next* **150/1**	

5m 13.1s (13.60) **Going Correction** +0.925s/f (Soft) **17** Ran SP% **123.9**
Speed ratings: **109,107,105,100,98 93,89,86,84,76 71,63,59,—,— —,—**
Tote Swingers: 1&2 £8.10, 1&3 £12.10, 2&3 £1.10 CSF £66.26 TOTE £29.30: £5.00, £1.20, £1.10; EX 113.90.
Owner Mrs M E Armitage & Peter Armitage **Bred** David Gordon **Trained** Great Habton, N Yorks

FOCUS
An interesting novice hurdle and the form ought to hold up with the three principals looking promising sorts who drew well clear of the rest of the field off a decent pace. The winner was value for further and this was a decent novice for the track.

NOTEBOOK
Trustan Times(IRE), an impressive Irish point-to-point winner, won this in a decent manner and looks one to keep on side for the future. He was rather green after taking up the running after three out but stayed on stoutly to run out a deserved winner. Although being kept up to his work, he was comfortably in control before a less-than-fluent jump at the last and probably won with a little more in hand than the winning margin suggests. The form looks solid and with connections feeling he would need this after being held up in his preparation, there should be plenty more to come. (op 16-1)
Yurok(IRE) is a definite improver for the future and this was another decent effort. He stayed on well in the straight and might have had the winner pulling out more had he not met the last wrong, although admittedly so did the winner. He is a big, scopey sort who looks to have a bright future. (op 3-1 tchd 2-1)
Our Mick was a well-supported favourite off the back of some useful bumper form before chasing home the very promising Backspin on hurdling debut last time. The step up in trip was expected to suit and he ran a solid enough race, but the winner had his measure from three out before a tired mistake two out claimed any chance he had of hanging on to the runner-up spot and he was ultimately outstayed. (tchd 11-10, tchd 6-5 in a place)
Candleford had only modest form to his name, but put in a respectable effort, although never troubling the principals.
Fill The Power(IRE) was another who showed promise on this hurdling debut without troubling the leaders.
Milano Supremo(IRE) Official explanation: vet said gelding finished distressed

Bow Badger Official explanation: jockey said gelding hung right

3573 YORKSHIRE RACING CLUB REMEMBERS JOE DYER H'CAP CHASE (13 fncs) 2m

2:00 (2:03) (Class 3) (0-135,133) 5-Y-0+ **£3,168** (£936; £468; £234; £117)

Form RPR

16-0 **1** **Lease Lend**78 2077 8-11-12 **133**....(tp) RichieMcGrath 145
(Tim Easterby) *hld up: hdwy 9th: chsd ldr next: led and lft clr last: drvn out* **8/1**

6-46 **2** 22 **Enfant De Lune (FR)**25 3059 7-10-9 **116**.... JimmyMcCarthy 106
(Alan King) *chsd ldrs: hmpd 1st: one pce fr 4 out: lft 15 l 2nd last* **5/2**1

050- **3** 2 ¼ **Open De L'Isle (FR)**287 4986 9-10-8 **115**.... BrianHarding 103
(James Ewart) *nt fluent: chsd ldrs: lost pl 6th: sme hdwy 4 out: lft 5th last: kpt on to take 3rd fnl 100yds* **9/1**

1-56 **4** 2 ¾ **Ockey De Neulliac (FR)**56 2520 9-11-2 **123**.... GrahamLee 108
(Ferdy Murphy) *in rr: hmpd 1st: mstke 8th: kpt on fr 3 out: lft modest 3rd whn hit last* **12/1**

-025 **5** 4 **Et Maintenant (FR)**55 2541 9-11-1 **122**.... PeterBuchanan 103
(Lucinda Russell) *chsd ldrs: lost pl after 9th: sn bhd: t.o 3 out: no ch after* **11/2**2

0-43 **6** ½ **Folk Tune (IRE)**57 2510 8-10-1 **115**....(t) KyleJames(7) 96
(John Quinn) *hld up in mid-div: hdwy to chse ldrs 5th: outpcd next: j.lft after: lost poor 3rd last: wknd* **16/1**

1042 **7** 1 ¾ **Viable**52 2613 9-11-1 **122**.... WarrenMarston 101
(Pam Sly) *hdwy to chse ldrs 5th: lost pl 9th: sn bhd: t.o 3 out: no ch after* **14/1**

-311 **F** **Kilkenny All Star (IRE)**68 2276 10-11-1 **122**.... DominicElsworth —
(Sue Smith) *chsng ldr whn fell 1st* **6/1**3

-221 **U** **Lord Larsson**64 2350 8-10-13 **120**....(t) BarryKeniry 129
(Malcolm Jefferson) *led: clr 4th: hdd whn blnd bdly and uns rdr last: fatally injured* **8/1**

3m 59.9s (4.10) **Going Correction** +0.575s/f (Soft) **9** Ran SP% **110.7**
Speed ratings: **112,101,99,98,96 96,95,—,—**
Tote Swingers: 1&2 £7.40, 1&3 £18.60, 2&3 £5.50 CSF £27.67 CT £175.48 TOTE £11.90: £3.00, £1.40, £3.20; EX 37.70 Trifecta £134.10 Part won. Pool: £181.35 - 0.63 winning units..
Owner C H Stevens **Bred** Lord Halifax **Trained** Great Habton, N Yorks

FOCUS
A proper gallop for this 2m handicap chase had the field strung out at an early stage, and the time was fast. Another step forward from the winner.

NOTEBOOK
Lease Lend had been well below-par on his last two starts after having a decent time ahead of the handicapper last season and was racing here off only 1lb higher than when scoring over 2m5f at Haydock. The strong pace would have suited him now dropped back in trip and he travelled well throughout under a confident ride before being left well clear at the last. He acts well around here and is a very likeable performer, but his future lies in the grasp of the handicapper. Official explanation: trainer had no explanation for the apparent improvement in form (op 9-1 tchd 10-1)
Enfant De Lune(FR) tried his best to mix it up the front but got outpaced by the leader going down the back straight and was soundly beaten when left a modest second at the last. (op 11-4 tchd 9-4 and 3-1 in a place)
Open De L'Isle(FR) requires testing conditions and ran well enough after an absence of 287 days and looks to be on a reasonable mark compared to his hurdles rating. (op 8-1)
Ockey De Neulliac(FR) has not found his form yet but is capable on his day and never got involved here. (op 17-2)
Kilkenny All Star(IRE) has been in great form but crashed out heavily at the first. (op 11-2 tchd 5-1)
Lord Larsson, on a mark of 120 for this handicap debut after scoring at Newcastle last time, led the field a merry dance and turned out of the back straight with a commanding advantage. He had been headed when blundering and unseating his rider at the last but would have been a clear second. Unfortunately, he suffered a fatal injury. (op 11-2 tchd 5-1)

3574 TOTESPORT IRISH DAY - SATURDAY 5TH FEBRUARY H'CAP CHASE (16 fncs) 2m 4f 110y

2:35 (2:36) (Class 4) (0-115,115) 5-Y-0+ **£1,951** (£573; £286; £143)

Form RPR

-436 **1** **Border Reiver**64 2354 7-10-7 **96**....(t) RichieMcGrath 107+
(Tim Easterby) *trckd ldrs: wnt 2nd 3 out: led next: drvn out* **9/2**3

-5F2 **2** 4 ½ **Dawn Ride (IRE)**63 2374 10-11-12 **115**....(p) BarryKeniry 121+
(Micky Hammond) *hld up: hdwy to trck ldrs 12th: effrt appr next: handy 3rd whn hit 2 out: kpt on fr 2 out: to take 2nd nr fin* **8/1**

P-61 **3** ½ **Babe Heffron (IRE)**12 3375 10-11-12 **115**.... WilsonRenwick 121
(Tom George) *led 2nd: hdd 2 out: kpt on same pce: 4 l 2nd whn blnd last: lost 2nd nr fin* **13/2**

U3/2 **4** 16 **Innominate (IRE)**59 2450 9-10-7 **96**....(p) PeterBuchanan 85
(Lucinda Russell) *led to 2nd: chsd ldrs: wknd appr 2 out* **6/1**

6-12 **5** 5 **Deuteronomy (IRE)**63 2366 10-10-13 **102**.... GrahamLee 89
(John Wade) *chsd ldrs: reminders and lost pl 7th: chsng ldrs 10th: 4th whn hmpd and stmbld landing 4 out: sn lost pl and bhd* **7/2**2

102F **6** 7 **Baltic Pathfinder (IRE)**32 2940 7-11-6 **109**.... HenryOliver 90
(Sue Smith) *stdd s: t.k.h: hdwy to trck ldrs 4th: hit 8th and reminders: rdn 11th: sn lost pl and mstke next: sn bhd* **10/1**

-113 **P** **Ocarina (FR)**64 2354 9-11-7 **110**....(p) BrianHarding —
(James Ewart) *rn in snatches: reminders 3rd: in rr whn reminders 7th: sme hdwy next: hit 9th: bhd fr 11th: t.o whn p.u bef 3 out* **3/1**1

5m 22.9s (15.10) **Going Correction** +0.575s/f (Soft) **7** Ran SP% **113.2**
Speed ratings: **94,92,92,86,84 81,—**
Tote Swingers: 1&2 £15.90, 1&3 £7.60, 2&3 £8.70 CSF £37.11 TOTE £6.80: £2.90, £2.90; EX 39.90.
Owner C H Stevens **Bred** M H Easterby **Trained** Great Habton, N Yorks

FOCUS
An ordinary but open 2m4f handicap chase run at a decent pace. The winner was very well in on his best 2009 form and the next two ran to their marks.

NOTEBOOK
Border Reiver had a few questions to answer after some recent efforts, but answer them he did, running out a deserved winner to complete a treble on the day for Tim Easterby. The strong pace played to his strengths now dropped back in trip after blundering away his chance last time. He is well treated on the pick of his form, but he will have to string some results together to make more appeal. Official explanation: trainer said, regarding apparent improvement in form, that the gelding had benefited from a long break of 64-days. (op 7-1)
Dawn Ride(IRE) is a course specialist but could never quite lay down a serious challenge and just stayed on in the straight. He is weighted up to his best. (op 6-1)
Babe Heffron(IRE) found a good opportunity when returning to winning ways last time and set out to make this a decent test. He had little more to offer when headed and the 9lb rise might be enough to anchor him. (op 5-1)
Innominate(IRE) is another who appears to be well treated on past form but remains a maiden. He was under pressure turning in before a costly mistake three out ended any chance he held. (op 15-2)
Deuteronomy(IRE) was receiving reminders from an early stage and put in a very laboured effort for a consistent performer. He did rally to have a chance going to four out but weakened soon after. (op 10-3)
Ocarina(FR) ran no sort of race after never travelling in the rear. Official explanation: jockey said gelding never travelled (op 4-1)

3575 BUY YOUR TICKETS ONLINE AT WETHERBYRACING.CO.UK H'CAP HURDLE (13 hdls) 3m 1f

3:10 (3:10) (Class 3) (0-135,129) 4-Y-0+ **£2,602** (£764; £382; £190)

Form RPR

5534 **1** **Lackamon**59 2446 6-10-1 **104**.... TjadeCollier 127+
(Sue Smith) *w ldr: led 6th: wnt wl clr bef 3 out: 17 l ahd last: heavily eased* **9/1**

1P-U **2** 14 **Double Expresso**57 2507 7-11-9 **129**.... JamesO'Farrell(3) 130+
(Howard Johnson) *trckd ldrs: lost pl and reminders 5th: chsd ldrs 8th: modest 2nd 3 out: no ch w wnr* **11/1**

05P5 **3** 2 ½ **Terenzium (IRE)**58 2477 9-10-7 **110**....(p) BarryKeniry 107
(Micky Hammond) *in rr: drvn and lost tch 7th: t.o 10th: poor 5th and styd on 2 out: tk 3rd run-in* **20/1**

-005 **4** 2 ¼ **Chester Lad**13 3334 6-11-4 **121**.... JanFaltejsek 117
(George Charlton) *hld up: hdwy 8th: hit next: outpcd appr 3 out: lft modest 4th whn hit 2 out* **12/1**

2121 **5** ¾ **Corso Palladio (IRE)**84 1959 9-10-12 **118**....(p) DonalDevereux(3) 112
(Peter Bowen) *trckd ldrs: one pce fr 3 out: fdd run-in* **9/2**3

0044 **6** 43 **Parlesotho (FR)**54 2579 8-10-11 **117**.... TomMolloy(3) 68
(Ben Case) *chsd ldrs: shkn up 4th: lost pl 9th: sn bhd: t.o* **7/2**2

31-0 **F** **Benbane Head (USA)**84 1967 7-11-11 **128**.... WarrenMarston 122
(Martin Keighley) *trckd ldrs: wnt 2nd 7th to 3 out: 4th and wl hld whn fell 2 out* **11/4**1

-4P1 **P** **The Hollinwell**18 3168 8-11-9 **126**.... GrahamLee —
(Ferdy Murphy) *led: hdd 6th: j.lft and reminders next: wknd afterr 8th: bhd and eased 10th: t.o whn p.u bef next* **5/1**

6m 46.7s (30.20) **Going Correction** +0.925s/f (Soft) **8** Ran SP% **114.5**
Speed ratings (Par 107): **88,83,82,82,81 68,—,—**
Tote Swingers: 1&2 £17.40, 2&3 £5.40 CSF £97.19 CT £1914.87 TOTE £8.70: £2.00, £3.80, £3.40; EX 94.20 TRIFECTA Not won..
Owner Mrs S Smith **Bred** W P Jenks **Trained** High Eldwick, W Yorks

FOCUS
A good pace for this staying handicap hurdle. The winner produced a massive step up and was value for a lot further.

NOTEBOOK
Lackamon ran away for an easy success after sitting prominently throughout. A point-to-point and bumper winner who has shaped as though he would improve with the step to 3m after some respectable efforts over shorter, he started life in handicap company off a mark of 104. He made full use of his light weight and galloped his rivals into the ground. He will not be lightly treated for this performance by the handicapper but he is only a six-year-old with plenty of scope for further improvement with connections also having the option to switch his attention to fences. (op 14-1)
Double Expresso had created a good impression in the novice ranks last season and was returning to hurdles after unseating over fences last time. He was getting reminders embarking on the final circuit and could never get on terms with the winner but stayed on to go second in the home straight. He will, no doubt, be back over fences before long. (op 9-1 tchd 8-1)
Terenzium(IRE) stayed on past beaten horses in the home straight but was never competitive. (tchd 16-1)
Chester Lad also ran on past beaten rivals. (op 18-1)
Corso Palladio(IRE) was an interesting contender but was slightly disappointing after chasing the leaders for much of the way and folding rather tamely going to two out. (op 15-2)
Benbane Head(USA), on his second run back since injury, had been up there for a long way but was a beaten fourth when taking a nasty fall two out. (op 2-1 tchd 3-1)

3576 BOOK ONLINE AND SAVE @ WETHERBYRACING.CO.UK FILLIES' "JUNIOR" STANDARD OPEN NATIONAL HUNT FLAT RACE 1m 5f

3:45 (3:45) (Class 6) 4-Y-0 **£1,267** (£369; £184)

Form RPR

1 **Newdane Dancer (IRE)** 4-10-7 0.... RyanMania(3) 93
(Howard Johnson) *trckd ldrs: pushed along 6f out: styd on to ld over 1f out: hld on towards fin* **5/1**3

1 **2** ½ **Doynosaur**72 2173 4-11-3 0.... BarryKeniry 99
(Mrs K Burke) *trckd ldrs: hmpd bnd 6f out: sn drvn: edgd rt over 1f out: styd on wl to snatch 2nd towards fin* **9/2**2

2 **3** hd **Young Mags (IRE)**31 2965 4-10-7 0.... TomMolloy(3) 93+
(Nigel Twiston-Davies) *sn led: hung bdly lft bnd over 4f out: hung lft and hdd over 1f out: no ex last 100yds* **4/6**1

4 6 **Skiddaw Secret** 4-10-10 0.... RichieMcGrath 84
(John Weymes) *t.k.h: led early: trckd ldrs: wknd 2f out* **33/1**

5 2 ¼ **Tobetall** 4-10-5 0.... JamesHalliday(5) 81
(Malcolm Jefferson) *trckd ldrs: hung lft and wknd over 2f out* **25/1**

3 **6** 22 **Reveal The Light**72 2173 4-10-10 0.... PaddyAspell 53
(Garry Woodward) *hld up in rr: hdwy after 6f: lost pl over 3f out: sn bhd* **12/1**

7 38 **Cottam Chocolate** 4-10-7 0.... JamesO'Farrell(3) 3
(Alan Lockwood) *in rr: drvn after 4f: lost tch over 5f out: t.o fnl 4f* **50/1**

3m 28.8s (208.80) **7** Ran SP% **111.3**
Tote Swingers: 1&2 £4.20, 2&3 £1.10 CSF £25.60 TOTE £7.10: £2.60, £2.60; EX 33.10.
Owner Andrea & Graham Wylie **Bred** Spratstown Stud A T **Trained** Billy Row, Co Durham
■ Stewards' Enquiry : Tom Molloy three-day ban: used whip with excessive frequency in incorrect place (Jan 29-31)

FOCUS
No real pace early on for this fillies' bumper for four-year-olds, but the front three look capable of going on from this. Not an easy race to put a figure on.

NOTEBOOK
Newdane Dancer(IRE), from the family of Direct Route, had to dig deep to land the spoils after a prolonged tussle in the straight. A nice type who showed a willing attitude, she can only build on this experience. (op 15-2 tchd 8-1)
Doynosaur had to defy a penalty for her debut success and with another few strides might well have done so, as she was staying on strongly when switched to the near-side rails inside the final furlong. She is a big filly who is progressing nicely and should be a nice prospect when sent hurdling. (op 4-1 tchd 7-2)
Young Mags(IRE) had run well when second on her debut and did her best to make all, but was not the most straightforward in the straight when coming under pressure before giving best in the final furlong and losing second on the line. (op 4-5)
Skiddaw Secret ran with a degree of promise but, after sitting prominently, she could only keep on at the same pace in the straight. (op 22-1)
Tobetall raced in touch but had no more to offer from over a furlong out. (op 14-1)
Reveal The Light had only been beaten by less than two lengths by the runner-up at Towcester and will have to bounce back after this effort, where she was well-beaten from a fair way out. Official explanation: jockey said filly was in season (op 9-1)

T/Plt: £235.20 to a £1 stake. Pool: £50,932.65 - 158.04 winning tickets. T/Qpdt: £84.80 to a £1 stake. Pool: £4,079.77 - 135.60 winning tickets. WG

3577a, 3580a-3583a - (Foreign Racing) - See Raceform Interactive

3351 NAAS (L-H)

Saturday, January 15

OFFICIAL GOING: Soft to heavy (heavy in places)

3578a LIMESTONE LAD HURDLE (GRADE 3) (10 hdls) 2m 3f
1:05 (1:06) 5-Y-0+ **£15,409** (£4,504; £2,133; £711)

RPR

1 **Shinrock Paddy (IRE)**[18] 3175 7-11-10 143 (t) APCawley 152+
(Paul Nolan, Ire) *trckd ldrs: 3rd 1/2-way: prog after 3 out: cl 2nd and pushed along early st: led 2 out: rdn clr last: kpt on u.p* **5/1**

2 2 1/2 **Donnas Palm (IRE)**[31] 2968 7-11-8 155 PCarberry 147+
(Noel Meade, Ire) *hld up towards rr: 8th and pushed along after 3 out: 7th 2 out: styd on wl u.p fr bef last* **2/1**[1]

3 shd **Stonemaster (IRE)**[15] 3270 6-11-3 139 DNRussell 142
(D T Hughes, Ire) *trckd ldrs: 6th 4 out: prog after 3 out: 4th and rdn 2 out: styd on fr last* **9/2**[3]

4 nk **On The Way Out (IRE)**[12] 3380 8-10-13 140 PTownend 138
(John E Kiely, Ire) *hld up towards rr: hdwy 4 out: 4th 3 out: kpt on same pce fr next* **4/1**[2]

5 1/2 **Prince Rudi (IRE)**[6] 3475 9-10-13 123 (p) RJMolloy 137
(S T Nolan, Ire) *racd wd: prog 1/2-way: led bef 4 out: strly pressed 3 out: hdd ent st: one pce fr 2 out* **33/1**

6 3 **Lucky William (IRE)**[15] 3270 7-10-13 133 BryanJCooper 134
(Thomas Cooper, Ire) *trckd ldrs: 6th 1/2-way: prog into 3rd 4 out: 2nd after 3 out: led narrowly ent st: hdd 2 out: no ex bef last* **9/1**

7 1 **Vic Venturi (IRE)**[18] 3176 11-10-13 PWFlood 133
(D T Hughes, Ire) *prom: 2nd 1/2-way: 4th 4 out: lost pl 3 out: one pce* **20/1**

8 13 **Aitmatov (GER)**[28] 3030 10-11-8 145 (bt) DJCondon 129
(Noel Meade, Ire) *led: hdd bef 3rd: dropped to rr and wknd bef 4 out* **16/1**

9 7 **Made In Taipan (IRE)**[15] 3270 9-10-13 AndrewJMcNamara 113
(Thomas Mullins, Ire) *prom: led fr 3rd: hdd bef 4 out: wknd fr 3 out* **12/1**

4m 59.2s (7.60) **9** Ran SP% **119.5**
CSF £16.49 TOTE £5.80: £1.50, £1.50, £1.90; DF 21.90.
Owner Barry Connell **Bred** Cecil Ashe **Trained** Enniscorthy, Co. Wexford

FOCUS
The winning time was slower than the maiden hurdle over the C&D. The winner showed improved form, while Donnas Palm ran well against a pace bias.

NOTEBOOK
Shinrock Paddy(IRE) in the end just proved that bit more straightforward than the rest of his opposition. Racing prominently for much of the journey, he was struggling a bit when the pace quickened before the straight but when coming back on an even keel and challenging at the second last, he looked the likely winner. He responded fully when asked to go and win his race and galloped to the line. The Boyne Hurdle at Navan next month looks the most likely target now. (op 9/2)
Donnas Palm(IRE) is a horse that hasn't always been the easiest to read on occasions in the past and ran a strange race here. Held up at the back of a pace that increased only gradually, he was struggling and going nowhere turning into the straight, but then picked up after the last and came home strongly. (op 9/4)
Stonemaster(IRE) is a strong galloping horse that stays well and will make a smashing chaser. He just didn't have the pace to challenge early in the straight, despite having travelled well turning in, and just stayed on from the second last. It was a good run from a horse that should make his mark over fences next season. (op 9/2 tchd 4/1)
On The Way Out(IRE) travelled well behind the lead most of the way and still appeared to be full of running turning in but he just found little when asked initially and then stayed on again. (op 7/2)
Prince Rudi(IRE) ran a very fair race considering his rating. He stays well and was just tapped for tactical speed early in the straight having gone to the front well over half a mile from the finish. He came wide into the straight and in the end kept going well at one pace, but it was quite a smart effort.
Lucky William(IRE) travelled strongly to the front early in the straight but stopped pretty quickly when coming under pressure. (op 10/1)

3579a WOODLANDS PARK 100 CLUB NOVICE CHASE (GRADE 2) (16 fncs) 3m
1:35 (1:35) 5-Y-0+ **£22,413** (£6,551; £3,103)

RPR

1 **Quito De La Roque (FR)**[18] 3174 7-11-5 DNRussell 152+
(C A Murphy, Ire) *trckd ldrs in 3rd: niggled along bef 5 out: rdn 3 out: hdwy into 2nd and chal after 2 out: led bef last: lft clr: styd on wl* **11/10**[1]

2 14 **Western Charmer (IRE)**[18] 3174 9-11-5 PWFlood 140+
(D T Hughes, Ire) *led: hdd after 3rd: remained prom: 2nd and drvn along 3 out: rallied u.p next: no ex whn lft mod 2nd fr last* **6/1**[3]

3 dist **Slippers Percy (IRE)**[9] 3414 9-11-5 DGHogan —
(Denis Gerard Hogan, Ire) *trckd ldrs in mod 4th: reminders 5 out: mstke 4 out: sn no ex: lft remote 3rd fr last: t.o* **20/1**

F **Royal De La Thinte (FR)**[15] 3269 6-11-5 (t) AELynch —
(J T R Dreaper, Ire) *cl up: led after 3rd: j.w tl mstke 4 out: edgd clr after 3 out: rdn and strly pressed after 2 out: hdd whn fell last* **7/4**[2]

P **Gran Torino (IRE)**[7] 3455 6-11-5 PCarberry —
(Noel Meade, Ire) *sn trailing in rr: slow 2nd: slt mstke 5th: completely t.o whn p.u after 3 out* **10/1**

6m 54.8s (6.70) **5** Ran SP% **112.1**
CSF £8.21 TOTE £2.40: £2.00, £1.70; DF 7.20.
Owner Gigginstown House Stud **Bred** Robert Mongin **Trained** Gorey, Co Wexford

FOCUS
Quito De La Roque had already taken it up when left clear and continues to improve.

NOTEBOOK
Quito De La Roque(FR) had no real right to win but his toughness and reserves of stamina finally got him home. Tracking the two leaders, his jumping didn't stand up against some of the leaps being put in, especially by the leader, but he managed to hang in there. When jumping the second last only a length adrift there was little doubt about which horse would stay the best on this deep ground. He's a dour stayer that can't have it soft enough and a wet spring could lead to his picking up a big prize. (op 5/4 tchd 1/1)
Western Charmer(IRE) certainly jumps well. The trailblazing leader didn't get too much on him with some of his more extravagant jumps, but in the end this fellow got a bit tired from the last and it would seem that his run at Leopardstown may have taken a bit more out of him than it did the winner. Fourteen lengths separated them today compared to one-and-a-half lengths at Christmas. He's still very decent and looks good enough to pick up a nice race before long. (op 11/2)
Slippers Percy(IRE) went with the pace for as long as he could but lost touch with the three leaders from about a mile out.
Royal De La Thinte(FR) couldn't have impressed more with his jumping. He attacks his fences with relish and is extremely fluent. It may not have helped him though that he was brought wide into the straight and he did forfeit valuable ground by doing so, but in fairness the winner had taken his measure when he took an unlucky fall at the last. (op 6/4)
Gran Torino(IRE) never jumped and was trailing from a very early stage. He was completely tailed off when pulled up before the home straight. (op 6/4)

3153 FFOS LAS (L-H)

Sunday, January 16

OFFICIAL GOING: Soft (heavy in places; 6.1)
Open ditch on the far side of the track omitted in both chases.
Wind: Strong across Weather: Raining

3584 LINCWEAR MAIDEN HURDLE (DIV I) (11 hdls) 2m 6f
1:00 (1:00) (Class 5) 4-Y-0+ **£1,626** (£477; £238; £119)

Form RPR

2 1 **Carlicue (IRE)**[85] 1963 6-11-5 0 (t) DarylJacob 121+
(Paul Nicholls) *led to 8th: led again bef next: styd on wl* **4/5**[1]

6-06 2 4 1/2 **Saffron Lord**[16] 3253 6-11-5 0 TomSiddall 114
(Martin Keighley) *a.p: chsd wnr 2 out: rdn and mstke last: styd on same pce* **150/1**

336 3 3 1/2 **Lexicon Lad (IRE)**[32] 2963 6-11-5 0 PaddyBrennan 111
(Tom George) *hld up: mstke 4th: hdwy 6th: ev ch 3 out: mstke next: no ex last* **9/2**[2]

3 4 3 **Duneen Point (IRE)**[55] 2571 7-11-5 119 SamThomas 107
(Tim Vaughan) *hld up: hdwy after 5th: rdn appr 3 out: wknd bef last* **16/1**

3 5 10 **Roalco De Farges (FR)**[59] 2482 6-11-5 0 RichardJohnson 100+
(Philip Hobbs) *prom: led 8th: sn hdd: mstke 3 out: wknd next* **14/1**

63 6 67 **Letmespeak (IRE)**[52] 2640 6-11-5 0 AdrianLane 30
(Donald McCain) *prom: rdn and lost pl after 5th: sn bhd: t.o* **80/1**

-240 7 1/2 **Railway Diva (IRE)**[53] 2607 7-10-12 0 PaulMoloney 23
(Evan Williams) *hld up: hdwy appr 6th: wknd after 8th: t.o* **100/1**

P 8 60 **Ostaadi**[8] 3439 5-11-5 0 (p) DPFahy —
(Bernard Llewellyn) *chsd ldr tl rdn 7th: sn wknd: t.o* **80/1**

30 P **Journeyman (IRE)**[26] 3054 5-11-5 0 APMcCoy —
(Nicky Henderson) *hld up: hdwy after 5th: wknd bef 7th: t.o whn p.u bef 2 out* **15/2**[3]

4 P **Tales To Tell (IRE)**[16] 3266 6-11-5 0 RobertThornton —
(Alan King) *chsd ldrs: lost pl after 5th: wknd 8th: t.o whn p.u bef 3 out* **17/2**

60P0 P **John Sixteen (IRE)**[19] 3153 6-11-2 0 DonalDevereux[(3)] —
(Peter Bowen) *hld up: reminders after 4th: rdn and wknd after 5th: t.o whn p.u bef 3 out* **200/1**

5m 44.4s (26.40) **Going Correction** +0.925s/f (Soft) **11** Ran SP% **113.2**
Speed ratings (Par 103): **89,87,86,85,81 57,56,35,—,— —**
toteswingers: 1&2 £30.60, 1&3 £2.00, 2&3 £56.20. CSF £159.63 TOTE £2.20: £1.70, £20.90, £1.10; EX 81.90.
Owner Potensis Limited **Bred** Sean Donnelly **Trained** Ditcheat, Somerset

FOCUS
There had been 3mm of rain during the previous 24hrs, and further rain falling as the meeting began led to a change in the going to soft, heavy in places. The ground certainly looked to be pretty testing for this maiden hurdle, an impression later confirmed by the jockeys.

NOTEBOOK
Carlicue(IRE), wearing a first-time tongue-tie, set a decent standard on his Chepstow second, travelled well the whole way round and stayed on strongly from the second-last to win well. Clearly stamina is his forte and this former heavy ground point-to-point winner will only benefit from a return to 3m. (op 11-10)
Saffron Lord stepped up massively on his previous two hurdling attempts and is now eligible for a mark. His connections will no doubt be hoping the handicapper doesn't take the form at face value. (op 100-1)
Lexicon Lad(IRE) improved on his hurdling debut at Newbury but, as he's by Presenting, one would have to believe that he'll be better suited to being back on quicker ground. (op 5-1 tchd 4-1)
Duneen Point(IRE) has been given quite a stiff mark based on his previous three starts over hurdles, so perhaps this will encourage the handicapper to drop him a pound or two. (op 11-1)
Roalco De Farges(FR) ran well enough to the turn into the straight, but then weakened right out, and he may do better back on a sounder surface. (op 20-1 tchd 22-1)

3585 LINCWEAR MAIDEN HURDLE (DIV II) (11 hdls) 2m 6f
1:30 (1:30) (Class 5) 4-Y-0+ **£1,626** (£477; £238; £119)

Form RPR

3/60 1 **King Of Dubai**[53] 2607 6-11-5 0 RhysFlint 117+
(John Flint) *hld up: hdwy 6th: led appr 2 out: clr last: eased towards fin* **66/1**

2P 2 4 **Top Benefit (IRE)**[18] 3197 9-11-5 0 SamThomas 108
(Keith Goldsworthy) *led: hit 4th and next: sn hdd: remained handy: rdn and hit 3 out: styd on same pce last* **15/2**[2]

3 3 hd **Junior Jack**[228] 589 6-11-5 0 WarrenMarston 110+
(Martin Keighley) *hld up in tch: led 6th: mstke 8th: nt fluent 3 out: hdd and hit next: no ex last* **8/1**[3]

5 4 15 **Rooftop Rainbow (IRE)**[15] 3295 7-11-5 0 NickScholfield 91
(Linda Blackford) *prom: lost pl after 5th: n.d after* **40/1**

2- 5 1 1/4 **Bringewood Moll**[394] 2957 8-10-5 0 MrJSherwood[(7)] 83
(John Needham) *chsd ldrs tl rdn and wknd appr 3 out* **50/1**

14- 6 2 1/2 **Fishoutofwater (IRE)**[281] 5129 7-11-5 0 APMcCoy 90+
(Rebecca Curtis) *hld up: nt fluent 1st: blnd 3rd: hdwy 6th: eased appr 3 out* **4/9**[1]

0 7 14 **Run To Fly (IRE)**[19] 3153 6-11-2 0 DonalDevereux[(3)] 74
(Peter Bowen) *chsd ldrs tl wknd appr 8th: t.o* **100/1**

222- 8 2 1/2 **Major Payne (IRE)**[505] 1333 7-11-5 0 AdrianLane 73
(Donald McCain) *hld up: rdn after 5th: mstke next: hdwy appr 8th: sn rdn and wknd: t.o* **15/2**[2]

34 9 30 **Jan Jandura (IRE)**[16] 3253 6-11-5 0 RichardJohnson 41
(Tim Vaughan) *sn prom: led after 5th: hdd next: rdn and wknd after 8th: t.o* **20/1**

0 10 37 **Little Frano (IRE)**[64] 2368 7-10-12 0 MichaelByrne[(7)] 4
(Peter Bowen) *chsd ldrs tl wknd 8th: t.o* **100/1**

5m 46.1s (28.10) **Going Correction** +0.925s/f (Soft) **10** Ran SP% **116.5**
Speed ratings (Par 103): **85,83,83,78,77 76,71,70,59,46**
toteswingers: 1&2 £16.30, 1&3 £26.40, 2&3 £3.90. CSF £470.60 TOTE £50.60: £6.70, £1.70, £2.60; EX 193.40.
Owner Brian Jones **Bred** A Smith **Trained** Kenfig Hill, Bridgend

FOCUS
The winning time was 1.7sec slower than the first division. There was a turn-up here, with 6

NOTEBOOK
King Of Dubai coped with conditions better than the rest and won relatively easily. His previous form left him with plenty to find strictly on the book, but he had hinted on more than one occasion in the past, both in a bumper at Plumpton and over hurdles at Hereford that he was crying out for a proper test of stamina. His future depends on how the handicapper rates this race. Official explanation: trainer said, regarding apparent improvement in form, that the gelding was better suited by the heavier ground. (op 50-1)
Top Benefit(IRE), a three-time point-to-point winner, was out of his depth in the Challow Hurdle last time out but ran much better returned to a more realistic level. (op 9-1)
Junior Jack ran well in these testing conditions considering he'd been off the track since June, and he should come on for this hurdling debut. (op 7-1)
Rooftop Rainbow(IRE) stayed on from well off the pace to take fourth and looks like he could do with going 3m plus already.
Fishoutofwater(IRE), who had useful bumper form last season, was sent off a short price on his hurdling debut, but his jumping was poor throughout and McCoy wasn't hard on him once it was clear he wasn't going to be playing a hand in the finish. It's back to school for him. Official explanation: jockey said gelding was unsuited by the soft (heavy in places) ground (op 4-7)

3586 ASHBURNHAM BEGINNERS' CHASE (16 fncs 2 omitted) 3m
2:05 (2:05) (Class 4) 5-Y-O+ **£3,252** (£955; £477; £238)

Form RPR
F45U **1** **Galaxy Rock (IRE)**[14] 3342 7-11-0 0 ....(b1) APMcCoy 129+
(Jonjo O'Neill) *led after 1st: hdd after 10th: led again after 4 out: clr whn blnd and rdr dropped whip last: easily* **2/1**[1]
-P00 **2** *6* **Flight Leader (IRE)**[8] 3437 11-11-0 124 .... JoeTizzard 111+
(Colin Tizzard) *chsd ldrs: nt fluent early: drvn along 9th: sn outpcd: styd on to go 2nd flat* **85/40**[2]
/0-4 **3** *2 1/4* **Mortimers Cross**[64] 2363 10-10-7 114 .... MrJSherwood(7) 113+
(John Needham) *chsd ldrs: led after 10th: j. slowly 12th: sn rdn: hdd after next: blnd 2 out: sn wknd: j. slowly last: lost 2nd flat* **8/1**
-163 **4** *2* **Cool Mission (IRE)**[14] 3332 7-10-11 0 .... JohnKington(3) 106
(Donald McCain) *led: hdd after 1st: chsd wnr to 9th: sn rdn: wkng whn mstke 4 out* **13/2**[3]
P-64 **5** *14* **Winterwood (IRE)**[69] 2278 8-11-0 118 ....(p) SamThomas 98+
(Tim Vaughan) *hld up: hit 8th: bhd fr next* **10/1**
4P **6** *37* **Sunsalve (IRE)**[8] 3435 7-10-7 0 ....(t) AodhaganConlon(7) 53
(Rebecca Curtis) *prom tl wknd 9th: t.o* **20/1**
0U- **U** **Theballyedmondchap (IRE)**[320] 4375 7-11-0 0 .... PaulMoloney —
(Evan Williams) *hld up: bhd whn hit 5th: t.o whn blnd and uns rdr 7th* **10/1**

6m 38.8s (15.80) **Going Correction** +0.425s/f (Soft) **7** Ran SP% **112.7**
Speed ratings: **90,88,87,86,81 69,—**
toteswingers: 1&2 £1.30, 1&3 £3.10, 2&3 £3.80. CSF £6.74 TOTE £3.00: £1.60, £2.00; EX 6.70.
Owner Michael & John O'Flynn **Bred** Arctic Tack Stud **Trained** Cheltenham, Gloucs

FOCUS
The open ditch in the back straight was omitted.

NOTEBOOK
Galaxy Rock(IRE) had fallen and unseated in his previous two starts over fences, but he had blinkers on for the first time here and was a well-backed favourite. Although he got in close at the last and gave his backers a bit of a fright, he jumped well in the main, and if the headgear continues to have a positive effect he has the potential to win a decent staying handicap over fences. His wins over hurdles came on better ground than this, so quicker conditions should help him. (op 3-1)
Flight Leader(IRE) was also well supported, but his jumping wasn't anywhere near as good as the winner's. He lost ground at almost every fence, but his bottomless stamina kicked in up the straight and he ran on for second late on. (op 5-2 tchd 2-1)
Mortimers Cross doesn't mind these conditions and he jumped better than at Uttoxeter. He'll be of more interest in handicap company. (op 17-2)
Cool Mission(IRE), whose best performance over hurdles came at Perth on good to firm, probably found the ground too testing. (op 5-1 tchd 7-1)

3587 PORSCHE CARDIFF H'CAP HURDLE (10 hdls) 2m 4f
2:40 (2:40) (Class 3) (0-130,130) 4-Y-O+ **£4,228** (£1,241; £620; £310)

Form RPR
3206 **1** **Numide (FR)**[15] 3298 8-11-2 120 .... JohnnyFarrelly 124
(Rod Millman) *hld up: hdwy after 3 out: rdn flat: r.o to ld post* **25/1**
311/ **2** *shd* **Phardessa**[694] 4053 10-10-9 113 .... TomSiddall 118
(Richard Phillips) *hld up: hdwy 7th: rdn to ld flat: hung rt: hdd post* **50/1**
25-2 **3** *2* **Sir Kezbaah (IRE)**[15] 3298 7-11-5 123 .... NickScholfield 125
(Jeremy Scott) *prom: lost pl 6th: rallied appr 2 out: rdn and swtchd lft flat: styd on* **11/4**[1]
0-00 **4** *2 3/4* **Yetholm (USA)**[19] 3169 6-10-6 110 ....(p) RhysFlint 111+
(John Flint) *chsd ldrs: led appr 3 out: blnd last: hdd and unable qck flat* **22/1**
-331 **5** *nk* **Prince Du Seuil (FR)**[33] 2949 8-11-0 118 .... RobertThornton 118
(Alan King) *hld up: hdwy 7th: mstke 3 out: sn rdn: styd on same pce appr last* **6/1**[3]
1320 **6** *10* **Scoter Fontaine (FR)**[31] 2977 5-10-13 117 .... APMcCoy 109+
(Rebecca Curtis) *hld up: hdwy appr 5th: wknd bef last* **5/1**[2]
0460 **7** *1/2* **Ravati (IRE)**[200] 861 5-9-10 105 .... MissLHorner(5) 93
(Peter Brookshaw) *hld up: hdwy after 6th: wknd appr 2 out* **33/1**
3505 **8** *3 1/4* **Dr Livingstone (IRE)**[8] 3452 6-11-6 124 ....(bt) JimmyMcCarthy 109
(Charles Egerton) *hld up: hdwy 6th: wknd after next* **20/1**
0-21 **9** *2 3/4* **Shinrock Hill (IRE)**[13] 3376 7-11-0 118 .... RichardJohnson 100
(Philip Hobbs) *chsd ldrs: led 7th: hdd bef next: wknd 2 out: eased bef last* **5/1**[2]
13-1 **10** *nk* **Real Treasure**[19] 3155 7-11-2 120 .... SeanQuinlan 104
(Kim Bailey) *chsd ldr tl led 6th: blnd and hdd next: wknd appr 3 out* **20/1**
/2-5 **11** *6* **Mae Cigan (FR)**[244] 372 8-10-7 111 .... GerardTumelty 87
(Michael Blanshard) *hld up: rdn after 7th: a in rr* **25/1**
S-00 **12** *8* **Stripe Me Blue**[52] 2626 9-10-8 112 .... LeightonAspell 80
(Peter Jones) *hld up: hdwy 5th: rdn and wknd after next: t.o* **22/1**
-21P **13** *2* **Simarian (IRE)**[15] 3291 6-11-5 130 .... AdamWedge(7) 96
(Evan Williams) *led to 6th: sn rdn: wknd appr 3 out: t.o* **33/1**
-221 **14** *18* **Gambo (IRE)**[114] 1603 5-10-9 113 .... PaulMoloney 61
(Evan Williams) *hld up: plld hrd: hdwy appr 5th: wknd bef 3 out: t.o* **11/1**

5m 3.00s (14.00) **Going Correction** +0.925s/f (Soft) **14** Ran SP% **120.7**
Speed ratings (Par 107): **109,108,108,107,106 102,102,101,100,100 97,94,93,86**
toteswingers: 1&2 £82.60, 1&3 £19.30, 2&3 £25.60. CSF £863.69 CT £4491.65 TOTE £25.30: £5.50, £6.00, £1.70; EX 841.80.
Owner Midd Shire Racing **Bred** S C E A Haras De Manneville **Trained** Kentisbeare, Devon

FOCUS
A competitive handicap in bad conditions, and the finish was fought out by two outsiders.

NOTEBOOK
Numide(FR) was undoubtedly well handicapped on his best form when with Gary Moore, but it's some time since he showed that sort of ability, and this step up in trip wasn't sure to suit. However, he has always liked testing ground and he got the trip well, staying on strongly from the back of the field to get up on the line. Now that he's proved his stamina connections might have a few more options. (op 22-1)
Phardessa hadn't been seen out since February 2009, but she handles bottomless ground really well and was produced fit enough to run her race on her reappearance. A little unlucky to be chinned on the line having hung right on the run-in, she should be capable of winning a similar race, although a quick return will bring the bounce factor into the equation.
Sir Kezbaah(IRE), runner-up to Salden Licht at Exeter on his debut for his new stable last time, won in similar conditions to these last year. He looks to have run right up to form and is the best guide to the level of the race. (op 10-3 tchd 5-2 and 7-2 in places)
Yetholm(USA) led them into the straight and was still in front when he flattened the final flight, which halted his momentum. He looks on a mark he can win off. (op 20-1)
Prince Du Seuil(FR), put up 13lb for winning at Folkestone last time, found his new mark beyond him, but wasn't disgraced. (op 11-2 tchd 5-1)
Scoter Fontaine(FR) weakened out of it in the straight, failing to improve for the step up in trip. (op 6-1 tchd 7-1 in places)
Shinrock Hill(IRE) failed to build on the promise of his maiden hurdle win at Lingfield on this handicap debut. (op 9-2)

3588 MARUBENI KOMATSU H'CAP CHASE (16 fncs 2 omitted) 3m
3:15 (3:15) (Class 3) (0-135,125) 5-Y-O+ **£5,204** (£1,528; £764; £381)

Form RPR
U15 **1** **Sweden (IRE)**[72] 2191 7-10-9 108 .... PaulMoloney 121+
(Evan Williams) *hld up: hdwy 5th: led and hung lft after 2 out: drvn out* **10/3**[3]
0-6F **2** *6* **Pak Jack (FR)**[56] 2543 11-11-9 122 .... SeanQuinlan 130
(Richard Phillips) *a.p: chsd ldr 8th: led 10th: rdn and hdd after 2 out: styd on same pce flat* **20/1**
3-00 **3** *8* **Money Order (IRE)**[8] 3440 9-11-5 121 .... RichieMcLernon(3) 125+
(Brendan Powell) *hld up: blnd 1st: mstke 6th: hdwy 9th: rdn appr 4 out: wknd 2 out* **17/2**
/1P- **4** *18* **Kildonnan**[324] 4283 12-11-6 119 .... RhysFlint 104
(Jim Old) *chsd ldrs: mstkes 4th and 12th: rdn and wknd 3 out* **7/1**
2313 **P** **Sporting Rebel (IRE)**[61] 2443 11-11-7 120 .... HaddenFrost —
(James Frost) *led to 1st: chsd ldr tl rdn 8th: sn lost pl: bhd and drvn along 9th: p.u after next: b.b.v* **3/1**[2]
314/ **P** **Tamadot (IRE)**[700] 3943 9-11-12 125 .... RichardJohnson —
(Philip Hobbs) *chsd ldrs: lost pl 3rd: hmpd next: hdwy 5th: nt fluent 10th: wknd and p.u bef 4 out* **9/4**[1]
F1-P **P** **Costa Courta (FR)**[67] 2305 9-11-12 125 .... JimmyMcCarthy —
(Charlie Morlock) *led 1st: hdd and mstke 10th: rdn after 12th: wknd and p.u bef next* **11/1**

6m 29.0s (6.00) **Going Correction** +0.425s/f (Soft) **7** Ran SP% **115.0**
Speed ratings: **107,105,102,96,— —,—**
toteswingers: 1&2 £7.40, 1&3 £5.00, 2&3 £18.30. CSF £53.65 CT £522.61 TOTE £3.40: £1.40, £5.50; EX 53.90.
Owner Mr & Mrs William Rucker **Bred** Patrick Condon **Trained** Llancarfan, Vale Of Glamorgan

FOCUS
Nothing like the 0-135 class 3 chase advertised, given that the top-weight was rated 10lb below the ceiling.

NOTEBOOK
Sweden(IRE), despite having been reported by his rider as being unsuited by the heavy going when disappointing at Hexham last time, coped perfectly well with the bottomless ground he encountered here on his handicap debut. Apparently it was gluey at Hexham, but the rain had loosened the turf here. Anyway, clearly he's not short of stamina, and this lightly raced former point winner can rate higher. (op 11-4)
Pak Jack(FR) isn't normally one to be with in a finish, and once again, for the 11th time in his 32-race career, he found one too good. (op 14-1)
Money Order(IRE) made a really bad mistake at the first which almost brought him to a halt, so in the circumstances he did well to be anywhere near at the finish. He's not badly handicapped over fences. (op 8-1 tchd 7-1 and 9-1)
Kildonnan won first time out last season so his absence wasn't a huge concern beforehand, but he weakened in the straight in the manner of a horse that needed the run. (op 13-2 tchd 15-2)
Sporting Rebel(IRE) was disappointing as he was struggling with a circuit to run. It turned out he had broken a blood vessel. Official explanation: jockey said gelding bled from the nose (op 3-1)
Tamadot(IRE) probably needed the outing, having been off the track for 700 days. (op 3-1)

3589 THREE CLIFFS H'CAP HURDLE (12 hdls) 3m
3:45 (3:45) (Class 4) (0-110,110) 4-Y-O+ **£2,602** (£764; £382; £190)

Form RPR
0-65 **1** **Gilwen Glory (IRE)**[19] 3155 8-10-11 102 .... AdamWedge(7) 108+
(Evan Williams) *hld up: hdwy 7th: rdn after next: led and hit last: styd on wl* **16/1**
2213 **2** *3/4* **Calypso Bay (IRE)**[33] 2941 5-11-9 107 .... APMcCoy 113+
(Jonjo O'Neill) *hld up: hdwy 8th: chsd ldr 3 out: led and hit next: hdd last: styd on u.p* **11/4**[1]
4202 **3** *3 1/2* **Beside The Fire**[14] 3348 6-11-12 110 .... JoeTizzard 110
(Colin Tizzard) *a.p: led 3 out: hdd next: rdn and hung rt flat: styd on same pce* **10/1**
2265 **4** *1 1/4* **Nobby Kivambo (IRE)**[16] 3260 6-10-13 102 ....(p) MrMMO'Connor(5) 102
(Brendan Powell) *led: rdn and hdd 3 out: styd on same pce appr last* **18/1**
5-51 **5** *6* **The Hudnalls (IRE)**[13] 3369 10-11-2 100 .... RhysFlint 94
(Jim Old) *chsd ldrs: pushed along 6th: outpcd next: rallied 9th: styd on same pce fr 3 out* **9/1**
0055 **6** *11* **El Diego (IRE)**[16] 3252 7-11-2 105 .... DavidBass(5) 87
(Jamie Snowden) *hld up: rdn after 7th: nvr on terms* **25/1**
2 **7** *1 1/4* **Sun Tzu (IRE)**[16] 3256 7-11-0 105 .... MrTWeston(7) 87
(Dr Richard Newland) *prom: mstke 4th: rdn and mstke 3 out: sn wknd* **12/1**
3-13 **8** *3 3/4* **Gentleman Jimmy**[16] 3260 11-11-3 101 .... RichardJohnson 82+
(Hughie Morrison) *chsd ldr to 9th: rdn and wknd bef next* **8/1**
-506 **9** *3 1/2* **Takamaru (FR)**[16] 3252 5-11-4 102 .... JohnnyFarrelly 76
(David Pipe) *mid-div: dropped to rr 3rd: hdwy 8th: rdn and wknd bef 3 out* **5/1**[2]
2332 **10** *3 1/4* **Quedillac (FR)**[98] 1796 7-11-5 108 .... MrTomDavid(5) 78
(Tim Vaughan) *hld up: hdwy after 8th: led briefly appr 3 out: sn rdn and wknd* **33/1**
3-0F **11** *nk* **Timetoring**[16] 3256 9-11-2 105 ....(p) MissIsabelTompsett(5) 75
(Bernard Llewellyn) *hld up in tch: jnd ldrs 9th: rdn and wknd after 3 out* **16/1**

040/ **12** *nk* **Sea Diva (IRE)**[638] 5079 11-11-3 **108**....................(p) AodhaganConlon(7) 78
(Rebecca Curtis) *hld up: pushed along after 5th: drvn along 7th: wknd after next* **11/2**[3]

6m 20.7s (33.70) **Going Correction** +0.925s/f (Soft) **12** Ran SP% **120.4**
Speed ratings (Par 105): **80,79,78,78,76 72,72,70,69,68 68,68**
toteswingers: 1&2 £22.90, 1&3 £38.50, 2&3 £6.00. CSF £62.14 CT £485.79 TOTE £22.40: £5.40, £2.50, £2.30; EX 105.60.
Owner Keith And Sue Lowry **Bred** R Jenks **Trained** Llancarfan, Vale Of Glamorgan

FOCUS
An ordinary handicap.

NOTEBOOK
Gilwen Glory(IRE) was under pressure some way out but her rider's persistence paid off, she kept responding, and in the end wore down the favourite close home. She was entitled to have come on for her recent return from a seven-month absence, and she was undoubtedly well handicapped on her best form, even before accounting for her rider's 7lb claim.
Calypso Bay(IRE) was given a patient ride and delivered with his challenge at the second-last. He couldn't quite hold off the winner, but it was a decent effort on ground which was almost certainly much softer than ideal. (op 7-2 tchd 4-1 in places after early 9-2)
Beside The Fire was taking a big step up in trip but he'd shaped as though it would suit, and he got it well. He can probably find a similar race. (op 17-2)
Nobby Kivambo(IRE) kept plugging away and ran a respectable race, but he remains a maiden and the handicapper knows where he stands with him. He helps set the level of the race. (op 20-1)
The Hudnalls(IRE), who was sixth in this race last year off the same mark, didn't finish much closer to the winner this time around. (tchd 10-1)
Takamaru(FR) was disappointing on his handicap debut. (op 10-3)
Sea Diva(IRE) wasn't travelling from an early stage and never threatened to get involved on her debut for her new stable. (op 10-1)

3590 E.B.F./DBS MARES' STANDARD OPEN NATIONAL HUNT FLAT RACE (QUALIFIER) 2m
4:20 (4:20) (Class 5) 4-7-Y-O **£1,712** (£499; £249)

Form				RPR
4	**1**		**Kaffie**[16] 3259 6-11-2 0.......... SeanQuinlan *(Kim Bailey) chsd ldr tl led 6f out: rdn over 1f out: styd on* **8/1**[3]	104+
35	**2**	*1*	**Miss Hippy (IRE)**[16] 3259 6-11-2 0.......... WarrenMarston *(Milton Harris) hld up: hdwy u.p over 5f out: chsd wnr ins fnl f: styd on* **50/1**	101
3	**3**	*½*	**Dream Function (IRE)**[74] 2156 6-11-2 0..........(t) RichardJohnson *(Philip Hobbs) a.p: chsd wnr 4f out: rdn over 1f out: styd on* **3/1**[2]	100
3	**4**	*7*	**Queen's Bay**[138] 1448 5-11-2 0.......... JoeTizzard *(Colin Tizzard) chsd ldrs: outpcd over 4f out: styd on u.p fr over 1f out* **22/1**	93
2	**5**	*2 ¼*	**Cresswell Bramble**[18] 3200 7-11-2 0.......... RhysFlint *(Keith Goldsworthy) led: hdd 6f out: rdn and wknd over 2f out* **3/1**[2]	91
6-	**6**	*½*	**Lucky Mix**[302] 4729 5-11-2 0.......... RobertThornton *(Alan King) hld up: hdwy 10f out: rdn and wknd over 2f out* **10/1**	90
1	**7**	*26*	**Monnow Made (IRE)**[56] 2546 6-11-9 0.......... APMcCoy *(Charles Egerton) trckd ldrs: rdn over 4f out: wknd over 3f out: t.o* **15/8**[1]	81+
	8	*¾*	**Bringewood Bunny** 7-10-9 0.......... MrJSherwood(7) *(John Needham) hld up: rdn and wknd over 7f out: t.o* **25/1**	64
	9	*7*	**Ravanchi** 7-10-13 0.......... JamesO'Farrell(3) *(Peter Brookshaw) chsd ldrs 9f: t.o* **66/1**	57
	10	*27*	**Lady Dixton** 5-10-9 0.......... CDTimmons(7) *(Tim Vaughan) hld up: wknd over 6f out: t.o* **40/1**	30
	11	*14*	**Classy Crewella** 5-11-2 0.......... WillKennedy *(Brian Eckley) hld up: rdn and wknd 1/2-way: t.o* **66/1**	16

3m 59.0s (15.60) **Going Correction** +0.925s/f (Soft)
WFA 5 from 6yo+ 3lb **11** Ran SP% **120.6**
Speed ratings: **110,109,109,105,104 104,91,91,87,74 67**
toteswingers: 1&2 £7.20, 1&3 £6.50, 2&3 £16.40. totesuper7: WIN: Not won. PLACE: £281.80 - 3 winning units. CSF £353.43 TOTE £8.30: £2.30, £6.40, £1.90; EX 511.90.
Owner D H Morgan **Bred** Miss Marie Steele **Trained** Andoversford, Gloucs

FOCUS
Nothing more than a fair mares' bumper.

NOTEBOOK
Kaffie, for whom there was a bit of money beforehand and Kim Bailey's mare, had finished fourth in similar conditions at Uttoxeter last time and stayed on strongest to get off the mark at the second attempt. She still looked a bit green here, is open to further improvement, and will now be aimed at the final of the series at Sandown on March 12. (op 14-1)
Miss Hippy(IRE) stayed on past beaten horses to be nearest at the finish. She finished 28l behind Kaffie at Uttoxeter last time but narrowed the gap between them to a length here. (op 66-1 tchd 40-1)
Dream Function(IRE), wearing a tongue-tie for the first time, was racing on much softer ground than she encountered on her debut. She's a sister to Captain Chris, who has a preference for a decent surface, so these conditions may well have been far from ideal. (op 15-8 tchd 10-3)
Queen's Bay is out of a mare who won a 3m3f chase, and the way she has stayed on in both her bumper starts to date suggests that she too will be seen to best effect when faced with a real test of stamina. (op 20-1 tchd 25-1)
Cresswell Bramble didn't get home after making much of the running, perhaps as a result of finding the ground too testing. (op 5-1)
Monnow Made(IRE) wasn't up to defying a penalty in the conditions. Official explanation: jockey said mare was unsuited by the soft (heavy in places) ground (op 5-2)
T/Jkpt: Not won. T/Plt: £595.90 to a £1 stake. Pool: £92,252.43 - 113.00 winning tickets. T/Qpdt: £122.60 to a £1 stake. Pool: £8,882.58 - 53.60 winning tickets. CR

3591a, 3593a - (Foreign Racing) - See Raceform Interactive

3316 FAIRYHOUSE (R-H)
Sunday, January 16

OFFICIAL GOING: Heavy

3592a TOTE PICK SIX MARES NOVICE HURDLE (LISTED RACE) (10 hdls) 2m 2f
1:10 (1:12) 4-Y-0+ **£14,008** (£4,094; £1,939; £646)

			RPR
1		**Our Girl Salley (IRE)**[18] 3202 6-11-7.......... BarryGeraghty *(Mrs Prunella Dobbs, Ire) settled bhd ldrs: 6th 1/2-way: cl in 4th ent st: impr to chal 2 out: led bef last: rdn and kpt on wl run-in* **2/5**[1]	132
2	*¾*	**Belle Brook (IRE)**[10] 3418 7-11-4.......... DNRussell *(Michael Cullen, Ire) chsd ldrs: 4th 1/2-way: cl in 3rd ent st: impr to ld bef 2 out where chal: rdn and hdd bef last: kpt on: nt match wnr run-in* **20/1**	128
3	*4*	**Lonesome Dove (IRE)**[18] 3202 6-11-4 116.......... DJCasey *(C F Swan, Ire) chsd ldrs: 5th 1/2-way: hdwy to chal in 2nd ent st: rdn in 3rd 2 out: no ex bef last: kpt on same pce* **20/1**	124
4	*1 ¼*	**Stephanie Kate (IRE)**[18] 3211 5-11-2.......... DGHogan *(C F Swan, Ire) hld up towards rr: cl in 6th bef 2 out: rdn in 5th 2 out: no ex bef last: kpt on same pce* **12/1**	121
5	*¾*	**Wood Lily (IRE)**[15] 3316 5-11-2.......... RMPower *(Mrs John Harrington, Ire) hld up towards rr: cl in 6th ent st: rdn into 4th 2 out: no ex bef last: kpt on same pce* **10/1**[3]	120
6	*9*	**Araucaria (IRE)**[18] 3202 7-11-7.......... AndrewJMcNamara *(John E Kiely, Ire) led: rdn and chal ent st: hdd bef 2 out: no ex and wknd* **5/1**[2]	116
7	*22*	**Catcherinscratcher (IRE)**[18] 3212 6-11-0.......... AELynch *(Henry De Bromhead, Ire) chsd ldr in 2nd: cl up fr 3 out: rdn and wknd ent st* **16/1**	87
P		**Midnight Socialite (IRE)**[17] 3251 7-11-0..........(t) JLCullen *(T Hogan, Ire) chsd ldrs: 3rd 1/2-way: mstke 5 out: sn rdn and wknd: p.u after 3 out* **25/1**	—

4m 47.3s (-2.10) **Going Correction** +0.20s/f (Yiel) **8** Ran SP% **124.1**
Speed ratings: **112,111,109,109,109 105,95,—**
CSF £15.10 TOTE £1.40: £1.02, £4.30, £5.50; DF 15.00.
Owner Mrs Ann S O'Neill **Bred** John Salley **Trained** Dunganstown, Co Wicklow

FOCUS
The form looks solid enough, with the runner-up seemingly improving and the third/fourth running to form.

NOTEBOOK
Our Girl Salley(IRE) extended her winning sequence to five and made it three from three over hurdles although she had to work harder for victory than had looked likely when she went to the front between the last two hurdles. Held up in a race run at quite a decent pace, she closed on the outside after three out and was on terms over the second-last. Sent to the front soon afterwards, she stayed on when asked to raise her game after the last although the runner-up was coming back at her towards the finish. She will be entered for the novice hurdles and the David Nicholson Mares' Hurdle at the Cheltenham Festival. Paddy Power cut Our Girl Salley two points to 10-1 for the mares' event. She remains 10-1 with Stan James and is the same price with Sean Graham. (op 1/2)
Belle Brook(IRE), winner of a 2m maiden at Thurles ten days previously, has raced over longer trips than this and she gave the impression here that a return to longer distances will suit. Always in touch, she went to the front two out and stayed on quite well in the closing stages after being headed by the winner between the last two hurdles. (op 16/1)
Lonesome Dove(IRE), fifth behind Our Girl Salley over 2m4f at Leopardstown last month having won a maiden over that trip at Clonmel on her previous start, had every chance. She went second approaching two out but could raise no extra under pressure in third between the last two hurdles.
Stephanie Kate(IRE), winner of a 2m maiden at Limerick last month when she beat Darwins Fox, who won at Naas on Saturday, was held up before beginning her effort approaching two out. Soon ridden, she kept on without posing a serious threat. (op 10/1)
Wood Lily(IRE), a decisive winner over 2m here on her hurdling debut early this month, was held up in rear and began to close after three out. Fourth two out, she could make little impression approaching the final hurdle but stayed on. (op 8/1)
Midnight Socialite(IRE) Official explanation: vet said mare was found to have burst a blood vessel post-race

3594a TOTE PICK SIX NORMANS GROVE CHASE (GRADE 2) (13 fncs) 2m 1f
2:15 (2:16) 5-Y-0+ **£21,012** (£6,142; £2,909; £969)

			RPR
1		**Golden Silver (FR)**[18] 3204 9-11-12 166.......... PTownend *(W P Mullins, Ire) trckd ldr in mod 2nd: slt mstke and niggled 3 out: clsd bef 2 out: led appr last: pushed out run-in and kpt on strly: comf* **2/11**[1]	166+
2	*5 ½*	**Rubi Light (FR)**[17] 3249 6-11-7 143.......... AELynch *(Robert Alan Hennessy, Ire) led and clr: reduced advantage bef 2 out: rdn and hdd appr last: no ex and kpt on same pce* **8/1**[2]	150
3	*2 ½*	**Let Yourself Go (IRE)**[10] 3415 9-11-7 148.......... SJHassett *(Adrian Maguire, Ire) settled in last early: 3rd bef 5th: poor 3rd 5 out: rdn and kpt on same pce ent st: sme late hdwy fr bef last* **9/1**[3]	148
4	*dist*	**Tally Em Up (IRE)**[63] 2406 8-11-5 129..........(t) DNRussell *(P J Rothwell, Ire) racd 3rd early: dropped to last bef 5th: wknd bef 4 out: t.o* **33/1**	—

4m 25.3s (-5.70) **Going Correction** -0.15s/f (Good) **4** Ran SP% **108.7**
Speed ratings: **107,104,103,—**
CSF £2.45 TOTE £1.10; DF 2.60.
Owner Mrs Violet O'Leary **Bred** Noel Pelat **Trained** Muine Beag, Co Carlow

FOCUS
Golden Silver was value for at least double the winning margin and didn't need to be at his best.

NOTEBOOK
Golden Silver(FR) eventually won easily enough and ultimately showed his class in the testing conditions. Sitting at one stage about 15 lengths off the runner-up, he did close but with the runner-up showing no signs of stopping at the third-last a few distress signals did go out. However, Townend didn't panic, knew he was on a very high-class horse, and in the end he just edged closer and closer and proved too good from the final fence. If his trainer was hoping for an easy race, that didn't quite materialise. (op 1/6)
Rubi Light(FR) was allowed an uncontested lead. Jumping and galloping is his game, he did that to terrific effect, but in the prevailing conditions it was inevitable that he was going to tire somewhat. It was still a fine effort and the handicapper's reaction will be interesting. (op 10/1 tchd 12/1)
Let Yourself Go(IRE) likes to race prominently, but he was held up on this occasion. He was staying on at the finish and how well the change of tactics worked is very hard to say as he finished about as close to the winner as he was entitled to. (op 15/2)
Tally Em Up(IRE) was predictably out of her depth but €1100 for turning up was worth the effort.

3595 - 3597a (Foreign Racing) - See Raceform Interactive

3302 FAKENHAM (L-H)
Monday, January 17

OFFICIAL GOING: Soft changing to heavy after race 2 (1:55)
Wind: virtually nil Weather: rain

3598 HEMPTON BEGINNERS' CHASE (18 fncs) 3m 110y
1:25 (1:25) (Class 5) 5-Y-0+ **£2,332** (£724; £389)

Form				RPR
-PPP	**1**		**Evella (IRE)**[17] 3263 7-10-4 115.......... AlexMerriam(3) *(Neil King) mde all: lft clr 12th: wl clr and in n.d bef 3 out: pushed out* **14/1**	125+
P-00	**2**	*21*	**Snake Charmer**[9] 3452 8-11-0 0..........(v) DaveCrosse *(Milton Harris) nt jump wl and numerous blunders: chsd ldrs: reminder 6th: lft disputing 2nd and hmpd 12th: wnt clr 2nd 2 out: no imp and wl hld whn blnd last* **15/2**[3]	117+
330P	**3**	*5*	**Akarshan (IRE)**[20] 3156 6-10-7 119.......... AdamWedge(7) *(Evan Williams) in tch: mstke 2nd: lft disputing 2nd 12th: no hdwy and wl btn bef 3 out: last fr next* **8/1**	106

-332 **P** **Night Orbit**[15] 2278 7-11-0 124 SamThomas —
(Julia Feilden) *blnd bdly and rdr lost iron briefly 1st: last and nvr jumping or gng wl after: reminders 6th: nvr any rspnse: losing tch whn blnd bdly 14th and immediately p.u* **11/10**[1]

0046 **F** **Fin Vin De Leu (GER)**[33] 2955 5-10-9 0 (p) JamesDavies —
(Charlie Mann) *chsd wnr tl fell 12th* **5/2**[2]

7m 6.80s (31.10) **Going Correction** +1.325s/f (Heav)
WFA 5 from 6yo+ 5lb **5** Ran SP% **105.7**
Speed ratings: **103,96,94,—,—**
CSF £86.23 TOTE £12.50: £4.30, £4.00; EX 58.90.
Owner Mrs S M Richards **Bred** Donal Boyle **Trained** Newmarket, Suffolk

FOCUS
After persistent rain conditions were very testing. A weak beginners' chase and an abject performance from the favourite. The easy winner is rated to the level of his hurdles mark.

NOTEBOOK
Evella(IRE), a 115-rated hurdler, had pulled up on her two previous tries over fences, having bled from the nose second time at Warwick on New Year's Eve. She gave her rivals a jumping lesson and making light of the testing conditions, was out on her own throughout the final circuit. What she actually achieved is open to doubt, but at least she proved she is back in good health. (op 10-1)
Snake Charmer, back over fences, made numerous jumping errors and probably achieved very little. (op 14-1)
Akarshan(IRE), who had jumped poorly in two previous starts over fences, chased the winner early on the final circuit, but in the end seemed to find this trip beyond him. (op 11-2 tchd 5-1)
Night Orbit, fit after a recent outing on the AW, looked to have been found a good opportunity after being placed on each of his three previous starts over fences. He made a bad blunder at the first and had lost touch with over a circuit to go. After another blunder five out he was pulled up. Presumably he was unable to handle the bad ground but even so there must be a question mark over him now. Official explanation: trainer had no explanation for ther poor form shown (op 3-1 tchd 7-2 and 9-4)
Fin Vin De Leu(GER), rated 120 over hurdles and proven in soft ground, was on the heels of the winner when falling at the last with a circuit to go on his chasing debut. (op 3-1 tchd 7-2 and 9-4)

3599 JANUARY MAIDEN HURDLE (11 hdls) 2m 4f
1:55 (1:56) (Class 5) 4-Y-0+ **£1,951** (£573; £286; £143)

Form RPR

10 **1** **Camden (IRE)**[34] 2944 5-11-5 0 LeightonAspell 115+
(Oliver Sherwood) *mde virtually all: drew clr w rival after 7th: rdn 3 out: tired but forged ahd ent st: v tired but kpt plugging on gamely flat* **7/1**[3]

2 *10* **Silicium (FR)** 5-11-5 0 APMcCoy 110+
(Nicky Henderson) *trckd ldrs: mstke 5th: drew clr w wnr and mstke 8th: stl on bit 3 out: shkn up after next: rdn and btn ent st: sn v tired: eased flat* **4/6**[1]

00-3 **3** *53* **Chicklemix**[65] 2370 5-10-12 0 WarrenMarston 45
(Pam Sly) *t.k.h: chsd wnr tl 7th: losing tch w ldng pair whn mstke next: t.o 3 out: plodded on to hold poor 3rd flat: fin tired* **14/1**

0-30 **4** *hd* **Chervonet (IRE)**[33] 2960 5-11-5 0 (t) LiamTreadwell 52
(Nick Gifford) *in tch: reminders after 3rd: lost tch after 7th: t.o whn mstke next: plodded on: tired but pressing poor for 3rd flat* **50/1**

2-3U **5** *13* **Good Faloue (FR)**[17] 3264 6-10-9 107 AlexMerriam(3) 32
(Neil King) *in tch in midfield: rdn after 4th: a struggling after: lost tch 7th: wl t.o bef 3 out: hmpd last: fin tired* **7/2**[2]

162- **6** *74* **Fairview Sue**[281] 5150 7-10-12 0 JodieMogford —
(Graeme McPherson) *hld up in tch towards rr: hdwy after 4th: 4th and losing tch whn mstke 8th: t.o next: stl 4th but v tired whn blnd last: walked home* **16/1**

206 **P** **Ultimate Quest (IRE)**[16] 3304 6-11-5 105 DaveCrosse —
(Michael Chapman) *in tch: rdn and struggling after 4th: mstke next: t.o whn p.u after 7th* **50/1**

6-P0 **P** **Kirkum (IRE)**[81] 2054 6-10-12 0 MissCareyWilliamson(7) —
(Diana Weeden) *bhd: whn mstke 1st and reminders: sn detached: t.o fr 3rd tl p.u 6th* **150/1**

00/ **P** **Frosty Spring**[253] 8-10-9 0 CharlieStudd(3) —
(David Thompson) *in tch: rdn and lost pl qckly 4th: t.o after next tl p.u after 7th* **100/1**

0-0 **P** **Agapanthus (GER)**[68] 2310 6-11-5 0 DarylJacob —
(Barney Curley) *t.k.h: hld up in rr on outer: reminder and hdwy after 5th: j.lft 6th: 7th and wkng whn dived lft next: t.o whn p.u 3 out* **50/1**

0P-0 **P** **Mr Valentino (IRE)**[58] 2530 6-11-0 100 (t) DavidBass(5) —
(Lawney Hill) *in tch in midfield: mstke 3rd: sn rdn and struggling: lost tch 5th: t.o whn p.u 7th* **25/1**

00 **P** **Farmers Glory**[11] 3401 4-10-0 0 MrMMarris(7) —
(Neil King) *bhd rdn and lost tch after 4th: t.o whn mstke 6th: p.u next* **100/1**

5m 44.1s (31.50) **Going Correction** +1.65s/f (Heav)
WFA 4 from 5yo+ 12lb **12** Ran SP% **119.6**
Speed ratings (Par 103): **103,99,77,77,72 42,—,—,—,— —,—**
toteswingers:1&2:£2.40, 1&3:£8.80, 2&3:£4.70 CSF £12.48 TOTE £5.20: £1.40, £1.10, £2.70; EX 18.80.
Owner T D J Syder **Bred** Fran Kavanagh **Trained** Upper Lambourn, Berks

FOCUS
Conditions looked even more testing on the hurdle-race track. Just seven still going with a circuit to go and after one more flight just two still going at racing pace. The winner improved to the level of her bumper win.

NOTEBOOK
Camden(IRE), who showed a low head carriage in the early stages, made every yard on just his second start over hurdles. A point and bumper winner, he clearly stays really well and, keeping up the gallop, fought off his sole challenger going to the final flight. He will need time to recover from this war of attrition. (tchd 15-2)
Silicium(FR), a big newcomer, travelled smoothly on the heels of the leader and looked to be travelling much the better when upsides three out. He came under pressure on the run round to the final flight and tired badly. He too will need time to recover but looked much the best prospect and can surely gain compensation. (op 4-5 tchd 5-6 and 8-13)
Chicklemix, a soft-ground bumper winner, was having her second start over hurdles and was left behind from four out. She too seemed to struggle to handle the desperate underfoot conditions.
Chervonet(IRE), soon driven along and reckoned a slow learner, kept on in his own time to secure a remote fourth spot on the run-in. (op 66-1)
Good Faloue(FR), another soft-ground bumper winner, was having his seventh start over hurdles and was soon under pressure to keep up. (tchd 9-2)
Fairview Sue, who showed fair form in bumpers, was having her first start since April. She was a tired third when making a mistake at the first flight on the final circuit and was clinging on to fourth when almost falling at the last. She walked up the run-in and can do much better in due course.
Frosty Spring Official explanation: trainer said mare was unsuited by the heavy (soft in places) ground
Mr Valentino(IRE) Official explanation: trainer said gelding was unsuited by the heavy (soft in places) ground

3600 TOTE NOVICES' CHASE (16 fncs) 2m 5f 110y
2:30 (2:30) (Class 3) 5-Y-0+ **£3,252** (£955; £477)

Form RPR

400- **1** **Mamlook (IRE)**[205] 5099 7-10-12 0 APMcCoy 139+
(David Pipe) *trckd ldr tl after 12th: stl cl 3rd whn mstke next: rdn to ld last: kpt on wl flat: rdn out* **6/5**[2]

0121 **2** *3/4* **Tullamore Dew (IRE)**[15] 3345 9-11-8 0 LiamTreadwell 146+
(Nick Gifford) *led: qcknd gallop after 11th: rdn bef 2 out: hdd and blnd last: kpt on wl but unable qck flat* **4/5**[1]

0 **3** *3/4* **Maringo Bay (IRE)**[73] 2181 6-10-12 0 DarylJacob 134+
(Charlie Mann) *j.lft: t.k.h: hld up in tch in last: mstke 11th: effrt on inner to press ldr after 12th: stl ev ch between last 2: mstke and one pce last* **20/1**[3]

6m 7.10s (25.30) **Going Correction** +1.325s/f (Heav) **3** Ran SP% **105.8**
Speed ratings: **107,106,106**
CSF £2.55 TOTE £1.90; EX 3.50.
Owner P A Deal & G Lowe **Bred** Peter Jones And G G Jones **Trained** Nicholashayne, Devon

FOCUS
A fascinating novice chase run at a sound pace in the conditions and all three runners were abreast going to the final fence. The form is rated through the second and Mamlook was a stone off his hurdles mark.

NOTEBOOK
Mamlook(IRE), the Chester Cup winner, had been absent since the Northumberland Plate in June. Looking in top trim despite fears about the ground, he jumped like an old hand. Travelling very strongly, he went on going to the last and was asked to do just enough. He has a rating of 143 over hurdles and was in receipt of 10lb from the runner-up, rated just 139. He should take high rank. (op 10-11)
Tullamore Dew(IRE), who would have met the winner on much better terms in a handicap hurdle, has taken really well to fences. He set a sensible pace, but had just been headed when he made his only error at the final fence. He fought back gamely and deserves full marks. (op Evens)
Maringo Bay(IRE) had shown little in his first start over hurdles in November. Jumping left-handed in the early stages, he travelled strongly and moved upsides five out. Still level at the last, this highly-rated maiden Irish pointer looks sure to win races especially if going the other way round. (tchd 16-1)

3601 FAKENHAM "NATIONAL HUNT" NOVICES' HURDLE (9 hdls) 2m
3:00 (3:00) (Class 4) 4-Y-0+ **£1,951** (£573; £286; £143)

Form RPR

6U2 **1** **All For Free (IRE)**[16] 3304 5-11-4 0 WarrenMarston 107+
(Milton Harris) *t.k.h: chsd ldrs: gd jump to chse ldr 5th: led next: rdn between last 2: out-j. runner-up and in command last: eased towards fin* **7/2**[3]

43 **2** *9* **Lady Hight (FR)**[32] 2987 5-10-11 0 APMcCoy 94+
(Nicky Henderson) *racd wd: t.k.h: chsd ldrs: mstke 1st: wnt 2nd 5th: clr w wnr next: j.lft and mstke 2 out: styng on same pce whn mstke and btn last: eased towards fin* **11/4**[2]

1512 **3** *12* **Mr Jay Dee (IRE)**[11] 3403 6-11-11 124 LeightonAspell 93
(Lucy Wadham) *j.rt: led tl 6th: j.rt and hdd 5th: 3rd and struggling whn mstke next: wl btn 2 out* **1/1**[1]

00 **4** *21* **The Old Buccaneer (IRE)**[15] 3344 8-11-1 0 RichieMcLernon(3) 62
(Jonjo O'Neill) *chsd ldr tl 5th: lost pl qckly bnd after 6th: wl btn after next* **10/1**

0 **5** *4 1/2* **Onthelips (IRE)**[20] 3153 7-11-4 0 DaveCrosse 58
(Amy Weaver) *racd wd: in tch in last trio: flashed tail and hdwy after 5th: rdn and btn after next* **100/1**

-335 **6** *7* **Float My Boat**[174] 1099 5-11-1 0 AlexMerriam(3) 51
(Sean Regan) *in tch in last trio: rdn and wknd after 5th: wl bhd bef 2 out: t.o* **33/1**

0-24 **7** *34* **Meridiem**[64] 2397 7-11-1 0 ChrisHonour(3) 17
(Sean Regan) *t.k.h: hld up in tch: dropped to rr after 4th: lost tch bef 3 out: t.o* **50/1**

4m 39.5s (34.10) **Going Correction** +2.225s/f (Heav) **7** Ran SP% **113.9**
Speed ratings (Par 105): **103,98,92,82,79 76,59**
toteswingers:1&2:£1.90, 1&3:£1.60, 2&3:£1.10 CSF £13.67 TOTE £2.90: £1.90, £2.00; EX 16.80.
Owner J Zambuni **Bred** Edward Sexton **Trained** Herridge, Wiltshire

FOCUS
A modest novice hurdle and the pace was very steady until going to three out. The winner improved towards the level of his Irish bumper form.

NOTEBOOK
All For Free(IRE), who raced keenly due to the lack of pace, went on four from home and soon stepped up the gallop. The better jump at the last sealed it and he was able to ease off near the line. A bumper winner in Ireland, he is going the right way over hurdles for this yard. (op 4-1 tchd 9-2)
Lady Hight(FR), another to race keenly, went in pursuit of the winner and looked a real threat when making a mistake two out. She was about three lengths down when not fluent at the last and that sealed her fate. She finished some way clear of the third and looks sure to find a race. (op 15-8 tchd 3-1 and 10-3 in places)
Mr Jay Dee(IRE), a bumper and maiden hurdle winner for another yard, had finished runner-up at Huntingdon on his only previous start for this stable. Connection were worried about how he would handle the conditions and his jumping was not up to scratch, and he was readily left behind when the pace increased. (op 11-10)
The Old Buccaneer(IRE), placed in an Irish bumper on his debut over three years ago, had shown nothing in two previous recent starts for this stable. A son of Turtle Island, he was expected to relish the conditions and came in for market support, but he was left well behind after four out. (op 28-1)

3602 SCULTHORPE H'CAP CHASE (18 fncs) 3m 110y
3:30 (3:30) (Class 3) (0-120,120) 5-Y-0+ **£3,168** (£936; £468; £234; £117)

Form RPR

11-2 **1** **Ray Mond**[62] 2443 10-11-6 **117** AlexMerriam(3) 133+
(Neil King) *j.rt: mde all: mstke 3rd: hit 9th: blnd 14th: drew clr and in command after 3 out: kpt on wl: eased towards fin* **11/2**

0521 **2** *10* **Mr Big (IRE)**[17] 3263 10-11-5 **118** (p) DavidBass(5) 121+
(Charlie Mann) *chsd wnr thrght: blnd 14th: rdn and struggling after 15th: mstke next: plugged on same pce and wl hld after* **11/4**[2]

2211 **3** *12* **Flying Squad (UAE)**[7] 3488 7-10-12 **109** 7ex (t) JimmyDerham(3) 100
(Milton Harris) *hld up in rr: mstke 9th: clsd and in tch after 13th: wnt 3rd next: btn after 3 out: mstke next* **11/8**[1]

2244 **4** *7* **Pheidias (IRE)**[51] 2669 7-11-3 **118** (p) MissGAndrews(7) 102
(Pam Sly) *in tch in last pair: clsd 10th: mstke 13th: sn rdn along: hit next: 4th and no imp 3 out: j. slowly and wl btn next* **9/2**[3]

4/ **5** 53 **El Jo (IRE)**610 363 10-11-7 **120** .... GilesHawkins(5) 48
(Martin Bosley) *chsd ldng pair tl blnd and dropped to last 12th: sn rdn: blnd 14th: lost tch next: t.o between last 2* **16/1**

7m 10.3s (34.60) **Going Correction** +1.575s/f (Heavy) **5** Ran SP% **108.2**
Speed ratings: **107,103,99,97,80**
CSF £20.11 TOTE £5.30: £2.20, £2.70; EX 13.60.
Owner A White **Bred** Mrs A Gordon And M Rodda **Trained** Newmarket, Suffolk

FOCUS
A competitive 109-120 stayers' handicap chase run at a sound pace in the conditions. Another step forward from the prolific winner, with the second rated to his mark.

NOTEBOOK
Ray Mond, having his first start for this trainer, won his last five starts last spring starting off from a mark of 73 and rising to 103. Rated 117, he raced with real enthusiasm out in front and jumping very accurately on the whole he had it in the bag two out. He should continue to prove hard to beat at this sort of level. (op 4-1 tchd 6-1)
Mr Big(IRE), 8lb higher than his Warwick success, was hard at work four out and soon proved no match. He now attempts a repeat success in next month's Royal Artillery Gold Cup at Sandown. (op 3-1 tchd 2-1)
Flying Squad(UAE), in effect 5lb higher than his convincing Towcester success on just his fifth start over fences, didn't show the same dash here. It was his second outing in eight days on bad ground and it may well have come too soon. He is well worth another chance. (tchd 5-4 and 13-8 and 7-4 in places)
Pheidias(IRE), twice a winner here in novice company last spring, was already struggling when he made a mistake five out and he does not appreciate conditions as testing as he encountered. (op 11-2 tchd 6-1)

3603 EAST DEREHAM H'CAP HURDLE (13 hdls) 2m 7f 110y
4:00 (4:09) (Class 5) (0-95,95) 4-Y-0+ **£1,951** (£573; £286; £143)

Form RPR
-4P3 **1** **Sweet Seville (FR)**6 994 7-11-12 **95** .... LeightonAspell 105+
(Terry Clement) *r wd: hld up in tch: hdwy to ld sn after 3 out: rdn after next: kpt on flat* **16/1**
4451 **2** 1 1/4 **Loco Grande (IRE)**15 3341 6-11-12 **95** .... (p) APMcCoy 103
(Tim Vaughan) *racd wd: led tl after 2nd: styd prom tl led again and j.lft 9th: mstke 3 out: sn hdd and rdn: swtchd to ins and pressing wnr again bnd bef last: kpt on same pce flat* **7/4**1
PPP0 **3** 22 **Petroglyph**17 3255 7-11-2 **92** .... MrJMQuinlan(7) 77
(Michael Quinlan) *hld up in tch: trckd ldrs after 9th: rdn and wknd bef 2 out: 3rd and wl btn whn blnd last* **5/2**2
BP **4** 1 1/4 **Humbel Times (IRE)**16 3303 7-9-7 **69** .... MrRichardCollinson(7) 53
(Neil King) *s.i.s: hld up in tch: hdwy to chse ldrs 8th: pressed ldrs bef 3 out: rdn and wknd qckly bef 2 out* **12/1**
-050 **5** 16 **Just Dan**62 2433 5-9-12 **70** .... (v1) CharlieStudd(3) 38
(David Thompson) *chsd ldr tl after 1st: styd prom tl wknd qckly 3 out* **11/1**
33RR **6** 61 **Ramvaswani (IRE)**6 2929 8-11-4 **90** .... AlexMerriam(3) —
(Neil King) *rel to r and slowly away: sn rcvrd and led after 2nd: rdn along fr 6th: hdd 9th: dropped out qckly next and sn t.o* **22/1**
-126 **P** **Hurricane Electric (IRE)**57 2558 6-11-8 **91** .... JodieMogford —
(Graeme McPherson) *chsd ldrs tl lost pl and dropped to last after 9th: losing tch whn mstke next: sn p.u* **3/1**3

6m 57.5s (51.10) **Going Correction** +2.225s/f (Heavy) **7** Ran SP% **116.2**
Speed ratings (Par 103): **103,102,95,94,89 69,—**
toteswingers:1&2:£3.60, 1&3:£6.90, 2&3:£2.30 CSF £47.18 CT £98.84 TOTE £20.20: £4.90, £2.20; EX 34.20.
Owner Rick Dale **Bred** R & E Bamford Limited **Trained** Newmarket, Suffolk
■ Owls Fc (100/1, unruly at s) & No More Whispers (13/2, rider injured at s) were withdrawn. Deduct 10p in the £ under R4.

FOCUS
Plenty of drama at the start of this low-grade handicap hurdle, which was run at a very steady pace until the final circuit. The winner is inconsistent but this was a good effort.

NOTEBOOK
Sweet Seville(FR), with her third trainer in a year and a half, was fighting fit after three outings on the AW. She stole a march on all but the runner-up and did more than enough on the run-in. She started life in handicap company from over a stone higher mark but this is her level. (old market tchd 20-1, new market op 12-1)
Loco Grande(IRE), penalised for his wide-margin success in selling company at Folkestone, ran from a mark of 95 but he has won off 101 in the dim and distant past. He saved precious ground by sticking to the inner on the home turn but had to give best in the end. He will be higher in the ratings when his revised mark kicks in at the weekend. (old market op 5-2 tchd 15-8, new market op 13-8 tchd 6-4)
Petroglyph was a winner three times last season, the final success from a 9lb higher mark. Pulled up four times and well beaten twice in six starts since, he travelled nicely but was left for dead by the first two from three out. (old market tchd 7-2, new market op 9-4)
Humbel Times(IRE), pulled up in a seller here on New Year's Day, started slowly and looks devoid of ability. (old market op 20-1 tchd 22-1 and 14-1, new market op 10-1 tchd 8-1)
Hurricane Electric(IRE), who came in for support, was having his second start after a summer break and was losing touch with a full circuit to go before eventually pulling up. It was not just the ground that accounted for this very poor effort. Official explanation: trainer said gelding was unsuited by the heavy (soft in places) ground (old market op 11-4 tchd 4-1, new market op 5-2)
T/Plt: £261.60 to a £1 stake. Pool:£56,112.67 - 156.57 winning tickets T/Qpdt: £11.50 to a £1 stake. Pool:£5,558.96 - 355.30 winning tickets SP

3344 PLUMPTON (L-H)
Monday, January 17

OFFICIAL GOING: Heavy (chs 3.3, hdl 3.5)
First fence in the back straight omitted on all circuits of the chase course; damaged ground. Hurdles track set up to outer winter line.
Wind: Almost nil Weather: Overcast, raining race 4

3604 RANA RISK MANAGEMENT NOVICES' HURDLE (9 hdls) 2m
1:10 (1:10) (Class 4) 4-Y-0+ **£2,055** (£599; £299)

Form RPR
2 **1** **Not Til Monday (IRE)**18 1660 5-11-4 0 .... TimmyMurphy 121+
(J R Jenkins) *w ldr: clr of rest fr 5th: led next: drew away after 3 out: 20 l up next: easily* **4/1**2
1-00 **2** 10 **Dusky Bob (IRE)**15 3346 6-11-4 0 .... AndrewThornton 100
(Nick Gifford) *sn settled to chse clr ldrs: outpcd fr 6th and pushed along: rallied after 3 out to take modest 2nd next* **20/1**
40-0 **3** 1/2 **Briefcase (IRE)**33 2954 6-11-4 0 .... PaddyBrennan 102+
(Nigel Twiston-Davies) *hld up bhd clr ldrs: disputing 4th whn blnd 5th: outpcd fr next: rallied to press for modest 2nd fr 2 out* **5/1**3
60 **4** 1/2 **Two Cloudy (IRE)**34 2946 5-11-1 0 .... (t) MichaelMurphy(3) 99
(Pat Murphy) *hld up in rr: only 8th at 6th and wl off the pce: pushed along and prog fr 3 out: pressed for a pl fr 2 out: mstke last: kpt on* **16/1**
60 **5** 10 **Drummers Drumming (USA)**13 2960 5-11-4 0 .... (t) JimmyMcCarthy 88
(Charlie Morlock) *hld up in midfield: lost pl after 5th: only 9th next and wl bhd: styd on steadily bef 2 out: nt disgracd* **50/1**
25 **6** 6 **Koup De Kanon (FR)**59 2495 5-10-11 0 .... StephenO'Donovan(7) 82
(Emma Lavelle) *hld up in detached last: stl only 7th at 6th and wl off the pce: rapid prog after: wnt 2nd briefly bef 2 out: no ch and exertions sn told* **9/4**1
7 25 **Ceannline (IRE)**204 5-10-11 0 .... AidanColeman 50
(Venetia Williams) *trckd ldng pair: nt fluent 2nd: clr of rest after 5th: wnt 2nd after 3 out: sn wknd rapidly: no ch whn mstke last* **7/1**
6P4 **8** 13 **Grey Cruzene (USA)**14 3374 5-11-4 0 .... ColinBolger 44
(Chris Gordon) *w ldrs to 2nd: sn dropped to rr and nt gng wl: t.o in last fr 6th* **14/1**
0-00 **9** 14 **Citrus Mark**86 1974 6-11-4 0 .... WillKennedy 30
(Paul Webber) *led: clr w wnr 5th: hdd next: wknd rapidly and lost 2nd sn after 3 out* **66/1**
55- **P** **Birthday Star (IRE)**408 2337 9-10-11 0 .... JoshuaMoore(7) —
(Linda Jewell) *t.k.h: hld up and a wl in rr: t.o 3 out: p.u bef next* **100/1**
P **Guarino (GER)**563 7-11-4 0 .... JamieMoore —
(Gary Moore) *t.k.h: hld up: prog to chse clr ldrs 6th: 4th and trying to cl next: sn wknd rapidly: p.u bef 2 out* **7/1**
U **Dulce Domum**158 5-10-11 0 .... HaddenFrost —
(Roger Curtis) *a in rr: 11th and wl bhd whn mstke and uns rdr 6th* **100/1**

4m 12.7s (11.90) **Going Correction** +0.875s/f (Soft) **12** Ran SP% **115.2**
Speed ratings (Par 105): **105,100,99,99,94 91,79,72,65,— —,—**
toteswingers:1&2:£15.00, 1&3:£4.20, 2&3:£12.00 CSF £77.85 TOTE £5.00: £2.10, £3.90, £1.80; EX 66.30.
Owner The Three Honest Men **Bred** G J King **Trained** Royston, Herts

FOCUS
Following heavy overnight rain the meeting was in some doubt, and the ground was very testing. There was a headwind in the home straight. The easy winner was the form pick but this was a big step up.

NOTEBOOK
Not Til Monday(IRE) ran the field ragged, helping force a strong early pace and pulling clear down the back straight. He had shown some promise on his first two hurdle runs, and his selling second at Hexham was the best form on offer here, but this still looks an improvement. He seems happiest when in front and is probably best kept left-handed as he had a slight tendency to jump out that way. A step up in trip looks likely to suit in time. (op 11-4)
Dusky Bob(IRE) had finished fourth behind Cue Card on his first bumper run and won a subsequent bumper, but had not previously been able to transfer that ability to hurdles. He seemed to handle the ground well enough and is likely to be kept at 2m.
Briefcase(IRE) made a bad mistake at around halfway so did well to recover and finish strongly. His 100-1 seventh behind subsequent Grade 1 winner Backspin in December was one of the better pieces of form on offer and, if able to put in a clear round, he can find races. (op 11-2)
Drummers Drumming(USA) has shown little, but stayed on at the one pace and may have a chance if sent handicapping.
Koup De Kanon(FR) was disappointing as he was just not good enough to get near the winner. (op 11-4 tchd 3-1 in a place)

3605 SIS LIVE NOVICES' CHASE (12 fncs 2 omitted) 2m 4f
1:40 (1:40) (Class 3) 5-Y-0+ **£6,262** (£1,850; £925; £463)

Form RPR
0-60 **1** **Sarando**16 3293 6-10-12 126 .... (t) WillKennedy 139+
(Paul Webber) *led to 4th: led again after 8th: rdn and pressed whn pckd bdly 2 out: sn drew clr* **6/1**3
13-U **2** 12 **Ranjobaie (FR)**16 3291 6-10-12 0 .... AidanColeman 128+
(Venetia Williams) *hld up in 3rd: wnt 2nd after 3 out and looked to be gng best: pckd 2 out: immediately btn* **85/40**2
-124 **3** 8 **Have You Seen Me (IRE)**16 3291 8-11-1 139 .... TomMolloy(3) 125+
(Nigel Twiston-Davies) *mstke 1st: pressed wnr: led 4th tl after 8th: upsides whn blnd 4 out: lost 2nd and btn after 3 out* **1/1**1
4-10 **4** 45 **Ashfield's Dream**19 3198 7-11-4 127 .... PaulMoloney 78
(Evan Williams) *a last: pushed along and lost tch on long run fr 8th: t.o whn j. slowly 4 out and next* **9/1**

5m 29.1s (21.80) **Going Correction** +1.05s/f (Soft) **4** Ran SP% **106.3**
Speed ratings: **98,93,90,72**
CSF £18.00 TOTE £7.20; EX 18.60.
Owner Eight Men & A Hoss **Bred** Juddmonte Farms Ltd **Trained** Mollington, Oxon

FOCUS
An interesting novice chase run at a steady pace. The first two are rated in line with their hurdles form with the third below his best.

NOTEBOOK
Sarando put in a good front-running performance as he out-jumped his rivals and ran out an easy winner. A previous winner on heavy ground, the step back in trip to 2m4f seemed ideal, especially as he was able to set his own pace. He may have one run beforehand, but the Centenary Novice Chase at Cheltenham looks the target as this qualifies him for a £60,000 bonus if he wins a chase at the Festival. (op 11-2 tchd 7-1)
Ranjobaie(FR) travelled well for a long way and looked likely to throw down a decent challenge entering the home straight, but found nothing when asked for an effort. His wins have all come on much better going than this and he can be more competitive on a sounder surface. He will be better served going right-handed. (op 13-8 tchd 6-4)
Have You Seen Me(IRE) made a bad mistake four out that put paid to his chances. He seemed to settle better this time though and, if able to put in a clear round, can find further opportunities at this level. (op 11-8 tchd 10-11 and 6-4 in a place)
Ashfield's Dream never got involved and connections will worry that he is not building on his promising start to the campaign, just like last season. (op 15-2 tchd 12-1)

3606 OPEN A STAR SPORTS ACCOUNT ON 08000 521321 H'CAP CHASE (10 fncs 2 omitted) 2m 1f
2:10 (2:10) (Class 5) (0-95,93) 5-Y-0+ **£1,626** (£477; £238; £119)

Form RPR
-606 **1** **She's Humble (IRE)**15 3338 9-11-12 **93** .... AndrewThornton 102+
(Linda Jewell) *mde all: abt 4 l clr fr 3 out: urged along at last: tired flat but hld on wl* **15/2**
P4F5 **2** 1 3/4 **Wishes Or Watches (IRE)**12 3397 11-9-11 **67** oh3 SamTwiston-Davies(3) 72
(John Upson) *hld up in last pair: prog to chse wnr 7th: abt 4 l down and no imp fr 3 out: kpt on flat* **10/1**
0305 **3** 20 **Sieglinde (FR)**14 3375 5-11-3 **87** .... TimmyMurphy 69
(Alison Batchelor) *hld up last: nt fluent 2nd: outpcd fr 6th: plugged on to take v modest 3rd 2 out* **12/1**

-F64 **4** *5* **Bobby Donald (IRE)**[35] 2930 9-11-1 **82**........................ RichardJohnson 62
(Richard Phillips) *cl up: j. awkwardly 2nd: drvn in 4th after 6th and sn struggling: n.d fr 4 out* **6/4**[1]

P6-4 **P** **Ede's**[61] 156 11-10-10 **77**.. ColinBolger —
(Pat Phelan) *chsd ldrs: wnt 2nd 5th to next: sn u.p: losing grnd on front pair whn mstke 4 out: wknd and lost 3rd 2 out: p.u bef last* **9/2**[3]

0431 **P** **Lukie Victor (IRE)**[16] 3307 10-11-10 **91**.............................. PaulMoloney —
(Evan Williams) *chsd wnr: mstke 4th: wknd rapidly next: t.o last fr 6th: p.u bef 3 out* **3/1**[2]

4m 42.4s (16.50) **Going Correction** +1.05s/f (Soft)
WFA 5 from 9yo+ 3lb **6** Ran SP% **111.7**
Speed ratings: **103,102,92,90,—** —
toteswingers:1&2:£10.00, 1&3:£6.30, 2&3:£8.50 CSF £66.26 TOTE £8.90: £4.40, £8.20; EX 74.90.
Owner Valence Racing Too **Bred** Pat Jones **Trained** Sutton Valence, Kent

FOCUS
Another front-running winner in this weak handicap chase. The front two pulled well clear and are rated to their marks.

NOTEBOOK
She's Humble(IRE) set a steady pace and stayed on all the way to the line. She was 1lb lower than when second over C&D in April 2009 and seemed to thrive on the ground, although conditions meant that she was right at the limit of her stamina. She may struggle with a rise in the weights, especially if running on better ground. (tchd 10-1)
Wishes Or Watches(IRE) was running from 3lb out of the handicap, and put in a game performance as he kept on and shaped as if he might appreciate a return to further. He fell on his last chase start, so should gain confidence from this. (op 14-1 tchd 9-1)
Sieglinde(FR) wasn't particularly fluent at her fences and needs to improve if she is to win her first race. (op 11-1)
Bobby Donald(IRE) has now failed to win in 19 career starts and probably needs further. (op 9-4)
Lukie Victor(IRE) Official explanation: trainer's rep had no explanation for the poor form shown

3607 STAR SPORTS BET - THE GENTLEMAN'S BOOKMAKER E B F MARES' "NATIONAL HUNT" NOVICES' HURDLE (12 hdls) 2m 5f
2:40 (2:41) (Class 4) 4-Y-0+ **£2,397** (£698; £349)

Form RPR

233P **1** **Rith Bob (IRE)**[69] 2288 8-11-3 107....................................... PaulMoloney 113+
(David Rees) *nt a fluent: mde all: drew away fr 9th: over 20 l up fr 2 out: eased flat* **7/2**[3]

-460 **2** *16* **Cloudy Wager**[14] 3374 6-11-3 0... FelixDeGiles 86
(Anna Newton-Smith) *mostly chsd wnr: rdn and lft bhd after 9th: all out to hold 2nd nr fin* **9/1**

0-F2 **3** *1 ¼* **Here's The Key (FR)**[15] 3338 7-11-3 95............................(t) WillKennedy 84
(Paul Webber) *in tch: rdn in 4th after 9th: sn outpcd: wnt 3rd 2 out: kpt on to press for 2nd nr fin* **13/5**[2]

2-04 **4** *7* **Blazing Empress**[17] 3264 6-11-3 0.................................... AidanColeman 79
(Sarah Humphrey) *t.k.h: cl up: rdn in 3rd fr 9th: sn lft bhd by wnr: wknd 2 out* **11/2**

/5P- **5** *64* **Saltara**[347] 3844 7-10-12 0... MrMMO'Connor[(5)] 13
(Mark Bradstock) *stdd s: hld up in detached last early: in tch to 1/2-way: t.o fr 9th: nowhere nr fnl flight as wnr fin* **25/1**

-125 **6** *1 ½* **Midnight Macarena**[17] 3264 6-11-3 0.........................(t) RichardJohnson 11
(Lucy Wadham) *nt a fluent: in tch to 8th: wl bhd next: t.o and nowhere nr fnl flight as wnr fin* **5/2**[1]

050 **7** *31* **Brambley**[33] 2965 4-10-2 0... WayneKavanagh[(3)] —
(Seamus Mullins) *in tch: mstke 8th and wknd: t.o next: remote 5th whn mstke last: walked in* **33/1**

F **P** **Sonus Weld (IRE)**[77] 2130 6-10-10 0.............................(p) MrHGMiller[(7)] —
(Paddy Butler) *led in s and reluctant to jump off: in tch to 5th: wknd rapidly next: t.o whn p.u bef 8th* **66/1**

050 **P** **Luna Lightning**[27] 3060 7-11-3 0...................................... JamieMoore —
(Linda Jewell) *j.rt 1st: in tch to 5th: sn struggling: wkng rapidly whn p.u after 8th* **100/1**

5m 39.0s (16.70) **Going Correction** +0.875s/f (Soft)
WFA 4 from 6yo+ 12lb **9** Ran SP% **113.2**
Speed ratings (Par 105): **103,96,96,93,69 68,57,—,—**
toteswingers:1&2:£6.70, 1&3:£2.40, 2&3:£7.50 CSF £31.79 TOTE £3.10: £1.10, £2.50, £1.30; EX 20.00.
Owner D Rees **Bred** George Ward **Trained** Clarbeston, Pembrokes

FOCUS
A moderate contest. The easy winner was value for further and is rated back to her best.

NOTEBOOK
Rith Bob(IRE) got off the mark under rules on her 12th attempt with a comfortable front-running win. A beaten favourite on her three previous starts, she had been running well enough without winning, but seemed to thrive on the ground and pulled clear. She seems to enjoy going this way round and, on better ground, is likely to appreciate a step up in trip. She is likely to be kept in mares' novice hurdle company. (op 5-2 tchd 9-4)
Cloudy Wager put in her best performance so far as she stayed on at the one pace. The step up in trip seemed to help, but it remains to be seen whether she can build upon it, or whether this was just a flash in the pan. (op 8-1)
Here's The Key(FR) stayed on well in the closing stages, seemingly enjoying the trip, but may just have had too much to do at the weights. In the circumstances this was a good run, but she is likely to find life easier back in handicaps. (op 7-2 tchd 5-2)
Blazing Empress again failed to settle early on, which gave her no chance of being able to see out the trip in these conditions. She jumped well enough though and, if she can settle from the off, she probably has the ability to make her mark at this level. (op 7-1)
Midnight Macarena was sent off favourite, but needs a better surface than this and was never able to get involved. Her jockey reported that she was never travelling. Official explanation: jockey said mare never travelled (op 11-4 tchd 9-4)

3608 REVELSTOKE WINE COMPANY H'CAP CHASE (12 fncs 2 omitted) 2m 4f
3:10 (3:10) (Class 4) (0-110,104) 5-Y-0+ **£2,602** (£764; £382; £190)

Form RPR

4001 **1** **Massini Sunset (IRE)**[14] 3373 11-11-5 **104**...................(b) SClements[(7)] 120+
(Richard Mitchell) *trckd ldr: led 4th: mde rest: drew clr fr 4 out: in no real danger after: pushed out* **11/1**

04P- **2** *8* **Master D'Or (FR)**[314] 4497 11-11-5 **97**............................... PaulMoloney 105
(Sophie Leech) *settled last: shkn up after 7th: prog fr next: rdn and styd on to take 2nd bef 2 out: briefly threatened to cl: no imp bef last* **33/1**

02/4 **3** *16* **Kasimali (IRE)**[14] 3375 8-11-10 **102**..................................... JamieMoore 94
(Gary Moore) *settled in 8th: mstke 2nd: u.p fr 6th: prog to chse ldrs 8th: lft bhd bef 4 out: tk modest 3rd last* **9/4**[1]

2303 **4** *29* **The Hardy Boy**[15] 3349 11-10-11 **89**............................. AndrewThornton 52
(Anna Newton-Smith) *chsd ldng pair: rdn and hld whn mstke 4 out: wknd next: t.o* **15/2**

4F00 **5** *18* **Mister Watzisname (IRE)**[13] 3391 9-11-11 **103**..............(t) FelixDeGiles 48
(Charlie Longsdon) *in tch to 7th: wknd next: wl t.o bef 4 out* **10/1**

3/4F **P** **Investment Affair (IRE)**[3] 3541 11-11-0 **92**.................... AidanColeman —
(Sarah Humphrey) *a in rr: rdn and wknd after 7th: p.u after next* **10/1**

4101 **F** **Manmoon (FR)**[15] 3349 8-11-4 **101**................................(t) MattGriffiths[(5)] —
(Nigel Hawke) *led: mstke 2nd: hdd 4th: chsd wnr after: lft bhd fr 4 out: wknd and lost 2nd bef 2 out: 4th and v tired whn fell last: winded* **4/1**[2]

1444 **P** **Sumdancer (NZ)**[15] 3349 9-11-4 **99**.............................. MarcGoldstein[(3)] —
(Michael Madgwick) *chsd ldrs: mstke 4th: struggling u.p on long run after 8th: sn wknd: blnd 4 out: scrambled over next and p.u* **14/1**

FP-P **P** **Rouge Et Blanc (FR)**[75] 2148 6-11-3 **102**..................... PeterCarberry[(7)] —
(Oliver Sherwood) *in tch: rdn and struggling in 6th on long run after 8th: no prog after: wl bhd whn p.u bef 2 out* **7/1**[3]

5m 30.3s (23.00) **Going Correction** +1.275s/f (Heav) **9** Ran SP% **111.2**
Speed ratings: **105,101,95,83,76** —,—,—,—
toteswingers:1&2:£18.60, 1&3:£6.80, 2&3:£5.70 CSF £239.04 CT £1073.45 TOTE £15.90: £3.30, £10.10, £1.50; EX 188.40.
Owner Mr And Mrs Andrew May **Bred** Gerard O'Keeffe **Trained** Piddletrenthide, Dorset

FOCUS
A modest contest. The easy winner is back to the level of his 2008 win over C&D.

NOTEBOOK
Massini Sunset(IRE) defied an 8lb rise to run out a good winner of this competitive handicap chase. The return of blinkers and front-running tactics have worked wonders and have now brought him two consecutive victories, both in heavy ground. He may struggle with a further rise in the weights, but remains in good heart and is likely to continue running his race. (op 8-1 tchd 12-1)
Master D'Or(FR) was held up early on, but began to stay on down the back straight and put in his best performance for a while. He has a good record around Plumpton and could come on massively for this first run in 314 days. He would be of interest back round here in a similar sort of race. (op 25-1)
Kasimali(IRE) was a well-backed favourite but came off the bridle with more than a circuit to go, giving him no chance on this testing ground. In the end it was a good ride from Jamie Moore to get him up for third on only his second start for his new yard and the early money suggests that he is expected to have a win in him. (op 7-4)
The Hardy Boy is a six-time C&D winnner and had a chance on his best form, but at his age, he probably found the ground too testing. His record around here is good and he is so consistent that he might still be interesting back on a better surface. (op 8-1)
Mister Watzisname(IRE) is dropping quickly down the handicap, but has now failed to win for three years and remains 0-18 in chases. (op 11-1 tchd 12-1)

3609 STARSPORTSBET.CO.UK H'CAP CHASE (15 fncs 3 omitted) 3m 2f
3:40 (3:41) (Class 5) (0-90,88) 5-Y-0+ **£1,626** (£477; £238; £119)

Form RPR

-066 **1** **Stop The Show (IRE)**[35] 2930 10-11-4 **80**.......................... RichardJohnson 88+
(Richard Phillips) *patiently rdn: in tch: prog after 11th to trck ldrs: led sn after 3 out: drvn and styd on wl* **4/1**[1]

B136 **2** *3 ¼* **Miss Fleur**[34] 2950 8-11-9 **88**.. DannyCook[(3)] 92
(Nick Mitchell) *cl up: led 11th to 4 out: chal again next: chsd wnr after: one pce bef last* **6/1**

5044 **3** *½* **Bajan Sunshine (IRE)**[6] 3492 10-10-2 **64**....................(t) MattieBatchelor 68
(Gary Brown) *t.k.h: hld up last: stdy prog fr 11th: led 4 out: hdd and nt qckn sn after 3 out: kpt on again flat* **7/1**

R60- **4** *14* **Zimbabwe (FR)**[313] 4521 11-11-0 **76**.................................(p) DavidDennis 68
(Nigel Hawke) *w ldrs: led 6th to 8th: cl up but rdn after 11th: nt qckn 4 out: sn lft bhd* **16/1**

-30P **5** *15* **Quartz Du Montceau (FR)**[10] 3431 7-11-8 **87**(p) SamTwiston-Davies[(3)] 62
(Anna Newton-Smith) *w ldrs: cl up after 11th but drvn: steadily wknd fr 4 out* **11/2**[3]

3560 **6** *10* **Mister Virginian (IRE)**[34] 2950 12-10-12 **81**...............(v) MrTJCannon[(7)] 46
(Chris Gordon) *cl up: led 8th: blnd 10th: hdd next: wknd 4 out* **16/1**

3200 **P** **Kiltimoney (IRE)**[14] 3377 11-10-6 **68**.............................. JohnnyFarrelly —
(Richard Mitchell) *in tch: mstke 2nd: drvn 11th: wknd rapidly and p.u bef next (4 out)* **7/1**

F345 **U** **Commanche Dawn**[14] 3377 9-10-0 **62** oh5.......................... JamieMoore —
(Gerry Enright) *blnd 2nd and 8th: last whn blnd and uns rdr next* **5/1**[2]

000P **P** **Seaview Lad (IRE)**[54] 2608 8-10-2 **64**...............(b[1]) AndrewGlassonbury —
(Bob Buckler) *mde most to 6th: lost pl qckly 8th: t.o whn p.u after 11th* **11/1**

7m 25.8s (35.10) **Going Correction** +1.275s/f (Heav) **9** Ran SP% **111.4**
Speed ratings: **97,96,95,91,86 83,—,—,—**
toteswingers:1&2:£9.10, 1&3:£6.10, 2&3:£6.80 CSF £27.14 CT £156.58 TOTE £3.90: £1.40, £1.50, £2.10; EX 36.20.
Owner The Adlestrop Club **Bred** M Doran **Trained** Adlestrop, Gloucs

FOCUS
A weak handicap chase. The winner was down to a good mark and the next two ran to their marks.

NOTEBOOK
Stop The Show(IRE) had the services of Richard Johnson for the first time and it was a good ride to get this horse over the line for his first career win over fences. He looked on a handy enough mark and the way he kept finding more in the closing stages suggests that a small rise shouldn't pose too many problems as he has run well off higher. (tchd 7-2 and 9-2)
Miss Fleur had failed to build upon her November win at Lingfield, but this was a much better showing under top weight in these testing conditions. She may need a further drop back down the handicap to give her a chance of winning. (op 15-2)
Bajan Sunshine(IRE) hasn't won since 2006, but he seemed to enjoy the step up in trip and was staying on well enough at the end to suggest that he is worth keeping at this sort of distance. (op 8-1)
Zimbabwe(FR) was returning from a 313-day absence and should come on for the run, but he is getting no younger and hasn't won for four years. (op 14-1)
Quartz Du Montceau(FR) was just 1lb higher than his C&D win last season, but was outpaced down the back straight and ran poorly. (op 9-2)
Commanche Dawn jumped poorly and is not one to back with any confidence. (op 9-2)

3610 STAR SPORTS LAY A BET H'CAP HURDLE (9 hdls) 2m
4:10 (4:10) (Class 4) (0-100,100) 4-Y-0+ **£2,055** (£599; £299)

Form RPR

-264 **1** **Wheres Johnny**[15] 3348 10-11-11 **99**...........................(t) MattieBatchelor 100
(Jamie Poulton) *chsd ldr to 5th: sn u.p: rallied to take 2nd after 3 out: chal last: led nr fin: jst hld on* **4/1**[3]

0-U1 **2** *shd* **Rosoff (IRE)**[14] 3378 9-11-8 **96**................................(p) RichardJohnson 97
(Laura Mongan) *hld up in 4th: chsd ldng pair after 3 out: rdn next: clsd to chal flat: jst failed* **11/10**[1]

-P00 **3** *½* **Like Ice**[57] 2558 6-11-5 **100**.. JosephAkehurst[(7)] 100
(Philip Middleton) *hld up last: prog 6th: led 3 out: hrd rdn and hdd nr fin* **20/1**

0-P4 **4** *13* **Cosavita (FR)**[20] 3155 6-11-10 **98**......................................(t) PaulMoloney 85
(David Rees) *trckd ldng pair: led 6th: hdd and fnd nil 3 out: steadily fdd* **2/1**[2]

1254 **5** 4 **Just Beware**[14] 3378 9-11-4 **97**....................(p) GemmaGracey-Davison(5) 80
(Zoe Davison) *led at stdy pce: blnd 5th: hdd next: wknd u.p fr 3 out* **14/1**
4m 27.5s (26.70) **Going Correction** +1.10s/f (Heav) **5** Ran SP% **112.4**
Speed ratings (Par 105): **77,76,76,70,68**
CSF £9.43 TOTE £5.90: £1.70, £1.80; EX 9.50.
Owner C J S Racing Partnership **Bred** T J Armour **Trained** Telscombe, E Sussex

FOCUS
The closest finish of the day. Ordinary handicap form, the winner to his recent C&D mark.

NOTEBOOK
Wheres Johnny got the verdict on the nod and this was a game performance from a horse who was off the bridle a long way from home. Twice a previous course winner, this was his first win in three years and he appears to save his best efforts for round here. (op 9-2 tchd 5-1 in a place)
Rosoff(IRE) won over C&D off 1lb lower in 2008 and came here off the back of a win in a similar race at Lingfield. He was unable to quicken entering the home straight, but stayed on one-paced in the closing stages suggesting that, despite all his wins coming over 2m, a slight step up in trip may help. (op Evens tchd 5-6 and 6-5 in places)
Like Ice seemed to enjoy the drop back to 2m, having previously failed to convince over further. (tchd 25-1)
Cosavita(FR) looks like she needs a further drop in the handicap. (op 11-4 tchd 3-1)
Just Beware has tended to run best on a sounder surface. (op 12-1)
T/Jkpt: Not won. T/Plt: £1,435.00 to a £1 stake. Pool:£74,111.07 - 37.70 winning tickets T/Qpdt: £116.30 to a £1 stake. Pool:£7,282.82 - 46.30 winning tickets JN

3337 FOLKESTONE (R-H)
Tuesday, January 18

OFFICIAL GOING: Heavy
Hurdle rail moved in onto fresh ground reducing races by about 40yds per circuit.
Wind: virtually nil Weather: bright and sunny

3611 BETFAIR RACING EXCELLENCE CONDITIONAL JOCKEYS' TRAINING SERIES H'CAP HURDLE (8 hdls) 2m 1f 110y
1:40 (1:41) (Class 5) (0-85,85) 4-Y-0+ **£1,918** (£559; £279)

Form RPR
-064 **1** **Whitcombe Spirit**[16] 3350 6-11-2 **80**....................(b) JeremiahMcGrath(5) 86
(Jamie Poulton) *hld up towards rr and travelled wl: stdy hdwy 4th: jnd ldrs 2 out: pushed ahd ent st: clr last: kpt on flat: pushed out* **25/1**
0-1P **2** 1 ¼ **Chestnut Ben (IRE)**[112] 1647 6-10-11 **73**..................... JoshuaMoore(3) 78
(Gary Brown) *hld up in tch: hdwy to chse ldrs 5th: wnt 2nd 2 out: sn ev ch tl rdn and outpcd ent st: rallied u.p to chse wnr bef last: tired but kpt on flat* **7/1**[3]
P-6U **3** 13 **Snow Patrol**[16] 3350 10-10-9 **73**............................. StephenO'Donovan(5) 65
(Nigel Dunger) *chsd ldrs: wnt 2nd after 3 out: led next: rdn and hdd ent st: sn wknd* **8/1**
1342 **4** 2 ½ **Quam Celerrime**[66] 2367 6-11-1 **77**................................. MattGriffiths(3) 67
(Roger Curtis) *bhd: pushed along and struggling after 3rd: hdwy into modest 7th 2 out: plugged on to go 4th flat: nvr trbld ldrs* **5/1**[1]
-0P4 **5** 3 ¼ **Bearneen Boy (IRE)**[16] 3341 8-9-12 **62**........................ TrevorWhelan(5) 48
(Neil King) *led: reminders after 3rd: more reminders after next: nt fluent and drvn 3 out: hdd next: wknd on long run to last* **5/1**[1]
4335 **6** 4 ½ **Catholic Hill (USA)**[57] 2583 6-11-3 **81**..........................(b) PeterHatton(5) 63
(Mark Gillard) *hld up in rr: stdy hdwy on outer 4th: chsd ldrs and mstke 2 out: chsd ldng trio and rdn on long run between last 2: wknd ent st* **10/1**
-655 **7** 1 ¼ **Keyneema**[68] 2334 9-11-3 **79**.......................................(p) PeterCarberry(3) 60
(Cathy Hamilton) *chsd ldrs: rdn and wknd bef 2 out: btn whn nt clr run on inner on long run between last 2: no ch whn j.lft last* **15/2**
6F-3 **8** 12 **Doctored**[64] 2430 10-11-3 **79**...................................(p) AodhaganConlon(3) 48
(Daniel O'Brien) *in tch towards rr: rdn and struggling after 3rd: lost tch bef 3 out: t.o between last 2* **13/2**[2]
00P- **P** **Tifernati**[318] 4439 7-9-10 **63** ow1.................................. JosephAkehurst(8) —
(Gary Moore) *in tch: chsd ldrs 4th: rdn and wknd qckly sn after 2 out: wl bhd whn p.u last* **10/1**
40-P **P** **Bridge Of Fermoy (IRE)**[16] 3341 6-10-7 **69**.............(p) PaulGallagher(3) —
(Daniel O'Brien) *chsd ldrs: rdn 5th: wknd bef 2 out: t.o whn p.u last* **66/1**
055/ **P** **Hungry For More**[700] 3987 7-11-7 **85**............................. JakeGreenall(5) —
(Mark Hoad) *hld up in rr: mstke 1st: hdwy 3rd: pushed along and struggling next: wknd 5th: bhd whn p.u 2 out* **40/1**
5-P0 **P** **Pull The Wool (IRE)**[35] 2949 7-11-9 **85**...................... NathanSweeney(3) —
(Laura Young) *hld up in tch in midfield: rdn after 5th: wknd bef 2 out: t.o whn p.u last* **25/1**
4055 **P** **Keckerrockernixes (IRE)**[65] 2390 5-10-12 **81**........... DonovanEldin(10) —
(Richard Rowe) *in tch: mstke 2nd: reminders and lost pl bef next: bhd and toiling 4th: t.o 3 out tl p.u next* **16/1**
0000 **P** **Rolanta (FR)**[8] 3477 6-11-0 **78**.. ChrisDavies(5) —
(James Frost) *t.k.h: chsd ldr tl after 3 out: sn wknd: wl bhd whn p.u last* **80/1**
4m 48.6s (13.00) **Going Correction** +1.075s/f (Soft) **14** Ran SP% **119.0**
Speed ratings (Par 103): **103,102,96,95,94 92,91,86,—,— —,—,—,—**
Tote Swingers: 1&2 £39.00, 1&3 £36.00, 2&3 £20.40 CSF £186.14 CT £1551.48 TOTE £29.80: £6.70, £2.40, £3.40; EX 231.60.
Owner Telscombe Racing **Bred** Wood Hall Stud Limited **Trained** Telscombe, E Sussex
■ Jerry McGrath's first winner as a professional.
■ Stewards' Enquiry : Trevor Whelan one-day ban: used whip with excessive frequency (Feb 1)

FOCUS
A wide-open handicap, confined to conditional riders, in which they went an ordinary gallop. Modest form, with a well handicapped winner.

NOTEBOOK
Whitcombe Spirithad yet to win a race of any description coming into this, but had been dropped another 5lb in the handicap and was reverting to a sharper test. He settled a lot better and caught the eye with the way he travelled through the race. It was apparent as he hit the front turning for home he would take some beating and this was a much-improved display on ground that clearly suits. Whether he can build on this remains to be seen, but he would escape a penalty if turning out quickly. (op 28-1)
Chestnut Ben(IRE) showed his true colours again for the return to softer ground, but even he found this too demanding. A clear second-best, he still looks weighted to find another race. (op 9-2)
Snow Patrol does go well on heavy ground and this was better again, but his best trip these days is open to debate. (op 11-1)
Quam Celerrime is another that needs testing ground to shine, but he was never going well after getting behind from the start on this return from a 66-day break. (op 6-1)
Bearneen Boy(IRE) set out to make all, but his fate was obvious coming out of the back straight and this ground probably was not for him. (op 11-2 tchd 6-1)
Doctored had a back problem over Christmas and looked a troubled horse here as he was never going. (op 7-1 tchd 6-1)

3612 PALMARSH PRIMARY SCHOOL RACING TO SCHOLL NOVICES' H'CAP CHASE (12 fncs) 2m
2:10 (2:11) (Class 4) (0-105,105) 5-Y-0+ **£2,602** (£764; £382; £190)

Form RPR
/3-5 **1** **Jeczmien (POL)**[56] 2591 8-11-1 **94**................................(t) LiamTreadwell 104+
(Nick Gifford) *j.w: t.k.h: led 3rd: mde most after: hmpd by loose horse bef 6th: pushed along between last 2: rdn flat: edgd lft but kpt on gamely towards fin* **16/1**
-30P **2** ½ **Karasakal (IRE)**[33] 2986 8-10-13 **92**..................................... JamieMoore 99
(Gary Moore) *hld up in tch: wnt 3rd 6th: chsd wnr sn after 3 out: rdn after next: kpt on u.p towards fin* **8/1**[3]
P-24 **3** 14 **Vic's World (IRE)**[216] 761 9-11-2 **95**................................... HaddenFrost 88
(James Frost) *led tl 3rd: w ldr after tl sn after 3 out: wknd u.p bef next* **7/1**[2]
02-2 **4** 50 **Quilver Tatou (FR)**[15] 3373 7-11-3 **96**.............................(t) PaulMoloney 69
(Charlie Mann) *in tch: blnd and dropped to last 6th: nvr gng wl after: nit next: rdn and detached whn mstke 9th: lost tch 2 out: j.lft last: eased flat: t.o* **4/7**[1]
2-S0 **U** **Nomadic Warrior**[66] 2373 6-11-2 **95**........................ AndrewGlassonbury —
(John Holt) *in tch tl blnd and uns rdr 3rd* **7/1**[2]
4m 21.3s (14.10) **Going Correction** +0.775s/f (Soft) **5** Ran SP% **105.6**
Speed ratings: **95,94,87,62,—**
CSF £101.43 TOTE £17.30: £6.20, £4.60; EX 36.30.
Owner Mrs R Gifford **Bred** Sk Golejewko Sp Z O O **Trained** Findon, W Sussex

FOCUS
A very weak handicap. Not an easy race to put a figure on but the winner is rated to the best of his hurdles form.

NOTEBOOK
Jeczmien(POL), who won one of Austria's most prestigious races over 1m in 2007, showed massively improved form to land his first success over jumps. The taxing surface was a real concern beforehand and he proved friendless in the betting. His chance also looked to be compromised early on as he pulled his way to the front, but he did jump accurately. He was still going best at the top of the home straight and, despite tiring near the finish, was always doing enough on the run-in. This success is made more meritorious as he was continually messed about by the loose horse and he could well be about to come good for connections, as getting on some better ground should suit ideally. (op 10-1 tchd 18-1)
Karasakal(IRE) easily won a weak handicap over hurdles here in 2009, but this was just his fourth outing since and he had yet to convince as a chaser. He was 6lb lower than when winning, though, and this was by far his best effort over fences to date. He doesn't look the most willing, but his canny trainer can place him to go one better. (op 13-2)
Vic's World(IRE), still a maiden under rules, was done with off the home turn on her return from a 216-day break. She doesn't want this ground, though, and wasn't given a hard time over the last two fences. (op 11-2)
Quilver Tatou(FR) was the one to beat on the level of his two previous outings over fences and proved all the rage in the market. His jumping was iffy at Lingfield last time, however, and it was jumping that found him again here. He too probably wants a sounder surface and a stiffer test, but appears one to have reservations about. Official explanation: trainer's rep said gelding never travelled or jumped with any fluency (op 4-6 tchd 8-15)

3613 WESTENHANGER JUVENILE MAIDEN HURDLE (8 hdls) 2m 1f 110y
2:40 (2:41) (Class 4) 4-Y-0 **£1,918** (£559; £279)

Form RPR
0233 **1** **Lady Willa (IRE)**[27] 2485 4-10-2 91.............................. TommyPhelan(3) 105+
(Mark Gillard) *w ldr: drew wl clr of field 2 out: pushed ahd ent st: rdn bef last: tired and blnd last: v tired and hung lft flat: hung on grimly: all out* **14/1**
22 **2** 3 **Mr Muddle**[4] 3344 4-10-12 119... JamieGoldstein 106
(Sheena West) *led: drew wl clr w wnr 2 out: rdn and hdd ent st: lft w ch last: v tired and no ex flat* **10/11**[1]
40 **3** 22 **Meglio Ancora**[53] 2661 4-10-9 0................................. RichieMcLernon(3) 84
(Jonathan Portman) *in tch: pushed along bef 3 out: 5th and wl btn 2 out: plugged on between last 2 to go modest 3rd sn after last* **15/2**[3]
0 **4** 3 **Goodison Park**[12] 3401 4-9-12 0.................................... MrJMQuinlan(7) 74
(Michael Quinlan) *hld up in tch: hdwy after 5th: wnt 3rd bef 2 out: rdn and no hdwy sn after 2 out: wl btn and tired ent st: lost 3rd sn after last* **10/1**
0 **5** 58 **Knockdolian (IRE)**[20] 3194 4-10-12 0............................. TimmyMurphy 23
(Roger Charlton) *trckd ldng pair tl wknd rapidly jst bef 2 out: wl t.o between last 2* **11/4**[2]
6 8 **Don Stefano**[509] 4-10-8 0 ow1....................................... TomO'Connor(5) 16
(Bill Turner) *in tch in rr: pushed along after 4th: wknd u.p bef 2 out: wl t.o between last 2: mstke and veered bdly lft last* **80/1**
7 12 **Polo Springs**[512] 4-9-12 0..(t) MarkQuinlan(7) —
(Bill Turner) *hld up in tch: hdwy to chse ldrs after 3rd: struggling whn blnd and pckd 3 out: sn wknd: wl t.o between last 2* **66/1**
4m 52.2s (16.60) **Going Correction** +1.075s/f (Soft) **7** Ran SP% **109.3**
Speed ratings: **95,93,83,82,56 53,47**
Tote Swingers: 1&2 £4.20, 1&3 £4.20, 2&3 £2.20 CSF £26.04 TOTE £14.00: £3.50, £1.70; EX 30.10.
Owner T J C Seegar **Bred** Simon Keswick **Trained** Holwell, Dorset

FOCUS
An ordinary juvenile event, dominated by the first pair.The winner improved to the level of her hurdles form with the second close to his mark.

NOTEBOOK
Lady Willa(IRE) finally shed her maiden tag on this return to hurdling and completed the task gamely. She had hit the frame in three of her four previous runs in this sphere, but had shown little back on the level recently and this ground was a big concern for her. She handled it best of all, however, and deserves credit for keeping on as she did after making a mess of the final flight. (op 12-1)
Mr Muddle flopped on his AW debut four days earlier, but proved popular on this return to a discipline he had shown improved form in on his two previous outings. He wasn't left alone in front, though, and this surface ultimately saw him find another one too good. The run came soon enough for him, however, and there is little doubt he can open his account when reverting to better ground. (op 6-4)
Meglio Ancora, uneasy in the betting, wasn't always fluent and hit a flat spot from halfway. He merely plugged on at his own pace thereafter, but at least now has the option of handicaps. (op 10-1 tchd 11-1 and 7-1)
Goodison Park was nigh on impossible to fancy on previous form, but she still met support and this was more encouraging. (op 16-1)

The Form Book, Raceform Ltd, Compton, RG20 6NL

Knockdolian(IRE) was bitterly disappointing. Perhaps the ground was to blame, but he stopped quickly when asked for an effort and presumably something went amiss. (op 11-8)

3614 EASTWELL MANOR H'CAP CHASE (15 fncs) 2m 5f

3:10 (3:10) (Class 5) (0-95,95) 5-Y-0+ **£2,397** (£698; £349)

Form				RPR
0113	**1**		**Pete The Feat (IRE)**[15] 3373 7-11-12 **95** FelixDeGiles (Anna Newton-Smith) *hld up in tch: gd jump and hdwy 11th: hit 3 out: chsd ldr bef next: pushed into ld last: kpt on u.p flat* **11/4**[2]	105+
P34P	**2**	2 ¼	**Whatcanisay**[7] 3492 12-10-0 **69** (bt[1]) HaddenFrost (James Frost) *j.w: led: rdn bef 2 out: drvn and hdd last: no ex flat: wknd fnl 100yds* **11/1**	75
6P51	**3**	2 ¼	**Wasntme (IRE)**[16] 3337 8-10-2 **71** (tp) HarrySkelton (Colin Tizzard) *chsd ldrs: wnt 2nd bef 11th tl after 3 out: rdn and outpcd bef 2 out: plugged on same pce u.p between last 2* **3/1**[3]	75
3533	**4**	6	**Saddlewood (IRE)**[35] 2950 8-10-13 **82** (tp) DarylJacob (Jamie Snowden) *chsd ldr tl bef 11th: mstke next: pushed along and btn bef 2 out* **5/2**[1]	80
POU6	**5**	17	**Oncle Kid (FR)**[63] 2443 9-11-12 **95** JamieMoore (Paul Henderson) *in tch: pushed along after 9th: mstke 11th: wknd u.p after 3 out: wl btn and eased flat* **7/1**	89+
3-PO	**P**		**Katalak (IRE)**[14] 3391 8-11-4 **87** (t) LiamTreadwell (Jonathen de Giles) *a last: pushed along 9th: lost tch 12th: hit next: t.o whn p.u 2 out* **11/1**	—

5m 48.4s (26.20) **Going Correction** +0.775s/f (Soft) **6** Ran SP% **109.4**
Speed ratings: **81,80,79,77,70** —
Tote Swingers: 1&2 £6.50, 1&3 £2.40, 2&3 £6.20 CSF £26.85 TOTE £3.30: £2.30, £4.40; EX 37.90.

Owner G J Larby & P J Smith **Bred** Michael O'Keeffe **Trained** Jevington, E Sussex

FOCUS
An open little handicap. It was run at a fair gallop and the form could be rated higher.

NOTEBOOK
Pete The Feat(IRE) got back to winning ways with a game success on his return to this venue. He came unstuck when bidding for a hat-trick at Lingfield 15 days earlier, but was a gutsy winner on his chase debut here last month and it was again his attitude that won him the day this time. Another likely rise will make his life harder again, but he is versatile regards trip and is obviously still on an upwards curve. (tchd 3-1)

Whatcanisay has gone without success since 2007 and had pulled up in two of his last four outings. The application of first-time blinkers brought about a much more enthusiastic effort from the front, however, and there is clearly still some petrol left in the tank. Whether the headgear will work so well next time is the worry, though. (op 12-1 tchd 16-1)

Wasntme(IRE) was still well handicapped on his previous best efforts despite being 4lb higher than when resuming winning ways over C&D 16 days previously. He felt the pinch turning for home, but kept on and rates the most sensible guide for the form. (tchd 11-4 and 10-3)

Saddlewood(IRE) appeared to have decent claims of reversing her last-time-out form with the winner on 5lb terms as this drop back in trip was expected to help. She was in trouble turning out of the back straight, however, and as a horse that has had trouble with her wind perhaps the ground was to blame. She remains a maiden. Official explanation: jockey said mare never travelled (op 10-3)

3615 FOLKESTONE-RACECOURSE.CO.UK H'CAP CHASE (16 fncs 2 omitted) 3m 1f

3:40 (3:41) (Class 4) (0-110,108) 5-Y-0+ **£2,740** (£798; £399)

Form				RPR
-616	**1**		**Pacco (FR)**[36] 2928 8-11-12 **108** (b) LeightonAspell (Oliver Sherwood) *in tch: hdwy to join ldr bef 3 out: led next: drvn clr bef last: styd on wl* **11/2**	123+
0/02	**2**	7	**Rateable Value**[18] 3265 7-11-0 **96** JoeTizzard (Colin Tizzard) *w ldr tl led bef 14th: hdd 2 out: sn rdn: btn last: tired fnl 100yds* **5/2**[2]	106+
-216	**3**	6	**Portrait Royale (IRE)**[15] 3377 9-10-12 **94** FelixDeGiles (Anna Newton-Smith) *pressed ldrs: j.rt and sltly outpcd 15th: drvn and no hdwy bef 2 out: wknd between last 2* **9/4**[1]	96
FOOP	**4**	hd	**Theophrastus (IRE)**[16] 3347 9-11-8 **104** LiamTreadwell (Nick Gifford) *t.k.h: hld up in tch: hdwy to chse ldrs 14th: rdn and wknd 2 out* **5/1**[3]	107
3-04	**5**	71	**Whatever Next (IRE)**[18] 3263 9-11-10 **106** TimmyMurphy (Edward Creighton) *j.rt: mde most tl bef 14th: wkng whn sltly hmpd 15th: wl btn and eased after next: t.o* **7/1**	37
P-06	**P**		**Signatory (USA)**[18] 3265 9-11-0 **99** (t) RichieMcLernon[(3)] (Jonjo O'Neill) *chsd ldrs tl dropped to last and rdn 15th: sn lost tch: t.o whn p.u 2 out* **18/1**	—

6m 51.7s (15.90) **Going Correction** +0.775s/f (Soft) **6** Ran SP% **109.2**
Speed ratings: **105,102,100,100,78** —
Tote Swingers: 1&2 £1.30, 1&3 £3.20, 2&3 £1.20 CSF £19.04 TOTE £5.60: £3.30, £3.00; EX 18.90.

Owner Ray And Marian Elbro **Bred** Mme Brigitte Ricous **Trained** Upper Lambourn, Berks

FOCUS
The second fence after the winning post was omitted on both circuits due to low sun. A tricky staying handicap, run at an average gallop and it saw the first pair lock horns from three out. A personal best from the winner.

NOTEBOOK
Pacco(FR) bounced back to his best in a race that really brought out his strengths. He has never been the easiest to predict, but found the race run to suit this time and his superior stamina saw him run out a ready winner. He is the type to defy a likely rise if able to maintain this current mood. (op 9-2 tchd 4-1)

Rateable Value ◆ posted a career-best when going down narrowly to Silver Dollars at Warwick 18 days earlier and that one has since scored again. He did things nicely on this step up in trip and gave his all, but the winner outstayed him. There is surely a race for him in the coming weeks. (op 11-4 tchd 3-1)

Portrait Royale(IRE), a dual C&D winner, was in trouble around four out. She tried her best to stay involved from that point, but the ground just looked that bit too demanding for her. (op 11-4)

Theophrastus(IRE) had been dropped 11lb after pulling up on his latest outing in first-time cheekpieces and he met support with the headgear abandoned. Despite running freely he posted a more encouraging effort, but is another that ideally wants a sounder surface. (op 13-2 tchd 9-2)

Whatever Next(IRE) dropped out tamely from the fifth-last and remains below par. (op 5-1 tchd 9-2)

Signatory(USA) remains one to avoid. (op 16-1 tchd 14-1 and 20-1)

3616 LIPSCOMB.CO.UK MARES' MAIDEN OPEN NATIONAL HUNT FLAT RACE 2m 1f 110y

4:10 (4:12) (Class 6) 4-6-Y-0 **£1,370** (£399; £199)

Form				RPR
0-	**1**		**Madame Allsorts**[341] 3995 6-11-2 0 TimmyMurphy (Willie Musson) *hld up wl off the pce in last pair: stdy hdwy 7f out: stl 7th 5f out: chsd ldng trio and styd on inner ent st: chsd clr ldr and pushed along wl over 1f out: led ins fnl f: kpt on* **11/1**	103+
6	**2**	4 ½	**Miss Milborne**[18] 3266 5-11-2 0 JoeTizzard (Colin Tizzard) *t.k.h: chsd ldrs: wnt 2nd over 4f out: led over 2f out and sn clr: rn green and hung lft over 1f out: hdd ins fnl f: sn btn* **5/1**[2]	100+
2	**3**	9	**Bathwick Junior**[21] 3159 4-10-5 0 RhysFlint (John Flint) *hld up towards rr: hdwy 1/2-way: chsd ldrs 5f out: rdn and outpcd wl over 2f out: chsd clr wnr briefly 2f out: one pce and wl hld after* **6/1**[3]	78
25	**4**	16	**Varkala (IRE)**[33] 2987 5-11-2 0 JimmyMcCarthy (Charles Egerton) *in tch: chsd ldrs 7f out: rdn and wknd over 3f out: wl btn ent st: plugged on* **5/1**[2]	75
0-	**5**	9	**Tinabianca (FR)**[273] 5301 5-10-13 0 JimmyDerham[(3)] (Seamus Mullins) *led: hdd and rdn over 2f out: sn wknd* **7/1**	64
	6	1 ½	**Bach To Front (IRE)** 6-11-2 0 GerardTumelty (Sarah Wall) *in tch: pushed along and struggling over 5f out: rdn and wknd over 3f out* **80/1**	63
0-	**7**	3	**Queen's Forest (IRE)**[274] 5284 6-10-9 0 StephenO'Donovan[(7)] (Emma Lavelle) *taken down early: t.k.h: sn chsng ldr: lost 2nd over 4f out: wknd qckly over 3f out:* **15/2**	60
40	**8**	47	**Charlotte's Ball (IRE)**[33] 2987 5-10-11 0 MrPYork[(5)] (Raymond York) *chsd ldrs tl wknd qckly 5f out: wl t.o fnl 3f* **33/1**	13
5	**9**	14	**Clyffe Top**[34] 2965 4-10-2 0 RichieMcLernon[(3)] (Jonathan Portman) *in tch tl rdn and wknd 5f out: wl t.o over 2f out* **12/1**	—
0	**10**	124	**Dance Til Midnight**[82] 2052 4-10-5 0 JamieMoore (Richard Rowe) *in tch tl dropped to rr and toiling 1/2-way: wl t.o fnl 5f* **66/1**	—
	11	2	**Keara** 6-10-13 0 AlexMerriam[(3)] (Amy Weaver) *in tch tl dropped to rr and rdn 9f out: sn toiling bdly: wl t.o fnl 6f* **33/1**	—
	P		**Well Chilled** 6-11-2 0 LeightonAspell (Peter Winkworth) *bhd: pushed along and toiling over 8f out: lost tch 1/2-way: tailing off whn p.u 7f out* **9/2**[1]	—

4m 45.7s (20.50) **Going Correction** +1.075s/f (Soft)
WFA 4 from 5yo 11lb 5 from 6yo 3lb **12** Ran SP% **114.7**
Speed ratings: **97,95,91,83,79 79,77,57,50,—** —,—
Tote Swingers: 1&2 £21.90, 1&3 £9.30, 2&3 £15.10 CSF £62.00 TOTE £9.30: £2.30, £3.10, £1.80; EX 82.90.

Owner R D Musson **Bred** R And R Musson **Trained** Newmarket, Suffolk

FOCUS
This mares' bumper was another wide-open looking affair. There was a routine gallop on and again underfoot conditions played a big part. The second and third set the level.

NOTEBOOK
Madame Allsorts got on top late in day having been given a very patient ride and opened her account at the second attempt. It appeared on the back straight as though the ground was against her, but she picked up steadily from then on and obviously stays well. (op 8-1)

Miss Milborne was one of the form choices after her debut sixth at Warwick 18 days earlier. She travelled best through the race and looked 2f out as though she would collect. However, she ran distinctly green and hung over to the stands' side in the final furlong. That allowed the winner to get on top and really she threw this away. She is not the first horse to have done this here, though. Official explanation: jockey said saddle slipped (op 9-2 tchd 4-1 and 11-2)

Bathwick Junior, third on her debut at Ffos Las last month, was faced with a stiffer test and was ridden with much more restraint. She again displayed an engine to make up her ground on the far side, but ultimately paid for those exertions. (op 11-2 tchd 13-2)

Varkala(IRE) hit a marked flat spot on the back straight before plugging on again down the home straight. She doesn't look that straightforward. (op 6-1 tchd 7-1)

Tinabianca(FR) was sent off at 7/1 in the Goffs Land Rover Bumper on her debut at Punchestown last year and was better than the bare form there. She was making her British debut for a new yard that won the race last season and attracted support, but after setting out to make all she tired off the home bend. (op 5-1 tchd 9-2)

Bach To Front(IRE) is bred to get further and showed definite ability on her debut. (op 66-1 tchd 100-1)

Queen's Forest(IRE), a mare with scope, ran too free on her debut last term and it was a similar story again on this seasonal return. She has ability, but will not realise her potential until consenting to settle. (op 9-1 tchd 11-1)

Well Chilled, whose sister Well Refreshed has placed in bumpers for these connections, was subject of a big gamble. She was never seriously in the hunt from off the pace and got pulled up with something looking amiss. (op 5-1 tchd 7-2)

T/Plt: £791.50 to a £1 stake. Pool:£72,543.25 - 66.90 winning tickets T/Qpdt: £13.90 to a £1 stake. Pool:£6,278.00 - 33.65 winning tickets SP

3393 SOUTHWELL (L-H)

Tuesday, January 18

OFFICIAL GOING: Good to soft (soft in places; 7.1)

Golf Club rail 5yds inside line raced on Jan 5th and bend into straight 5yds inside line raced on in November. 3m races reduced by 90yds, 2m4f by 60yds.

Wind: moderate 1/2 behind Weather: fine and sunny

3617 SOUTHWELL-RACECOURSE.CO.UK H'CAP CHASE (16 fncs) 2m 4f 110y

1:00 (1:00) (Class 4) (0-115,114) 5-Y-0+ **£2,927** (£859; £429; £214)

Form				RPR
-500	**1**		**Patman Du Charmil (FR)**[17] 3292 9-11-9 **114** (b) SamTwiston-Davies[(3)] (Nigel Twiston-Davies) *mde all: styd on wl fr 3 out: eased towards fin* **5/1**[3]	126+
P4-P	**2**	5	**Porta Vogie (IRE)**[258] 158 9-10-11 **102** TomMolloy[(3)] (Graeme McPherson) *in rr: hit 8th: hdwy 10th: chsng ldrs 12th: wnt 2nd after 4 out: kpt on same pce fr next: no imp* **5/1**[3]	110
U04P	**3**	24	**Phoenix Des Mottes (FR)**[13] 3395 8-9-7 **88** JoeCornwall[(7)] (John Cornwall) *chsd ldrs: wnt 2nd 4th: outpcd after 4 out: tk remote 3rd next* **33/1**	73
4U-	**4**	22	**King Jack**[301] 4800 9-11-11 **113** (p) WarrenMarston (Richard Phillips) *chsd ldrs: hit 5th: wnt 2nd 4 out: wknd rapidly appr next: sn bhd* **6/1**	79
3652	**5**	3	**Josear**[11] 3433 9-11-8 **110** SamThomas (Chris Down) *chsd ldrs: hit 3rd: reminders 9th: j. slowly and lost pl next: sn bhd: t.o 3 out* **10/3**[1]	73

P-PP **6** *1 ½* **Waterski**[15] 3361 10-10-0 **88** oh1 .... RobertWalford 50
(Jean McGregor) *in tch: drvn 7th: reminders next: lost pl after 9th: bhd fr 12th: t.o 3 out* **14/1**

0423 **7** *23* **Tifoso (FR)**[41] 2450 6-10-7 **95** .... (v) BrianHughes 36
(Richard Guest) *j.rt: in tch: 4th whn blnd 11th: lost pl and 5th whn mstke 4 out: t.o next: fatally injured* **7/2**[2]

P **Tooman Lane (IRE)**[297] 4906 7-11-10 **112** .... TomSiddall —
(Patrick Holmes) *in rr: bhd fr 12th: t.o whn p.u after 4 out* **10/1**

5m 24.3s (9.30) **Going Correction** +0.375s/f (Yiel) **8** Ran SP% **111.6**
Speed ratings: **97,95,85,77,76 75,75,—**
Tote Swingers: 1&2 £5.70, 1&3 £10.60, 2&3 £13.90 CSF £29.01 CT £720.84 TOTE £4.40: £1.40, £2.00, £3.10; EX 33.70.
Owner H R Mould **Bred** Mme Guilhaine Le Borgne **Trained** Naunton, Gloucs

FOCUS
The ground was officially described as good to soft, good in places, with the soft places by the second-last fence and around the winning post. This was a fair handicap chase run at a sound gallop. the winner posted his best figure since October 2009.

NOTEBOOK
Patman Du Charmil(FR) has contested better races previously and was 24lb lower than he was two years ago. He registered a comprehensive victory with enthusiastic jumping and a good front-running ride from his jockey. (tchd 9-2)
Porta Vogie(IRE) came in for late money on this reappearance and jumped well in the main, but couldn't match the winner's pace between the final two fences. The front two came well clear of the remainder, indicating they may be ahead of the handicapper. (op 11-1)
Phoenix Des Mottes(FR) has often been inconsistent but saves his best for this track, and although beaten some way by the front two, this was an improved effort. (op 25-1)
King Jack, 3lb higher than when winning at Huntingdon last season, jumped boldly but weakened in the straight looking like he needed the run on this seasonal bow. (op 9-2)
Josear was well beaten, and connections reported that the run came too soon after his recent second at Fontwell. Official explanation: trainer's rep said race came too soon for gelding (op 3-1 tchd 11-4)

3618 SOUTHWELL GOLF CLUB JUNIOR MEMBERS H'CAP CHASE (13 fncs) 2m
1:30 (1:30) (Class 5) (0-90,90) 5-Y-O+ **£1,626** (£477; £238; £119)

Form RPR

FP43 **1** **Follow The Sun (IRE)**[12] 3404 7-11-11 **89** .... BrianHughes 99
(Peter Niven) *hld up in rr: gd hdwy appr 3 out: wnt cl 2nd last: styd on to ld nr fin* **8/1**[3]

-0P1 **2** *hd* **Lerida**[12] 3404 9-11-2 **80** .... (p) BrianHarding 90
(Sharon Watt) *led 2nd: kpt on wl fr 3 out: hdd towards fin* **11/2**[2]

5050 **3** *1 ¾* **Kinkeel (IRE)**[7] 3492 12-10-8 **75** .... EamonDehdashti(3) 84
(Tony Carroll) *chsd ldrs: outpcd appr 3 out: styd on between last 2: 4th and nt fluent last: kpt on run-in* **8/1**[3]

530P **4** *3 ¾* **Mujamead**[33] 2986 7-11-0 **83** .... (p) LeeEdwards(5) 89
(Sally-Anne Wheelwright) *led to 2nd: chsd ldr tl wknd last* **20/1**

15P0 **5** *7* **Troodos Jet**[35] 2942 10-10-12 **79** .... RyanMania(3) 78
(Dianne Sayer) *chsd ldrs: wknd appr 3 out* **25/1**

5506 **6** *1* **Mad Professor (IRE)**[12] 3404 8-9-8 **65** .... (b) JoeCornwall(7) 63
(John Cornwall) *mid-div: blnd 7th: lost pl 4 out* **50/1**

230- **7** *10* **Ravenscar**[422] 2453 13-10-7 **74** ow1 .... AdamPogson(3) 65
(Charles Pogson) *chsd ldrs: wknd 4 out: eased between last 2* **12/1**

U035 **8** *10* **Peak Seasons (IRE)**[12] 3404 8-10-6 **70** .... DaveCrosse 50
(Michael Chapman) *in rr: drvn 6th: bhd fr next: t.o 3 out* **25/1**

PP24 **9** *8* **Alaskan Prince (IRE)**[80] 2088 6-11-9 **87** .... JanFaltejsek 60
(Peter Salmon) *chsd ldrs: lost pl 9th: sn bhd: t.o 3 out* **10/1**

0022 **P** **Mamba (GER)**[12] 3404 9-10-5 **69** .... JamesDavies —
(Chris Down) *nvr gng: last and drvn along 3rd: t.o 6th: p.u bef next* **9/2**[1]

54-P **P** **Ours (FR)**[34] 2952 9-11-12 **90** .... (t) AidanColeman —
(Mark Rimell) *towards rr: mstke 5th: bhd fr 4 out: t.o whn p.u bef next* **9/2**[1]

3U53 **P** **More Shennanigans**[58] 2548 10-10-6 **70** .... AdrianLane —
(Jean McGregor) *in rr: reminder s5th: bhd fr next: t.o 8th: p.u bef 4 out* **9/1**

4m 14.6s (4.60) **Going Correction** +0.375s/f (Yiel) **12** Ran SP% **115.2**
Speed ratings: **103,102,102,100,96 96,91,86,82,— —,—**
Tote Swingers: 1&2 £7.00, 1&3 £18.10, 2&3 £13.60 CSF £48.75 CT £365.74 TOTE £4.90: £2.50, £2.20, £2.40; EX 33.70.
Owner Francis Green Racing Ltd **Bred** Ronnie O'Leary **Trained** Barton-le-Street, N Yorks

FOCUS
A moderate handicap chase rated through the runner-up.

NOTEBOOK
Follow The Sun(IRE) finished 2 1/4l behind Lerida at Huntingdon last time, but turned the tables this time with a 4lb pull in the weights. This was a good, patient ride by Brian Hughes, who delivered the 7-y-o as late as possible after jumping the last. There may be more to come now he's got his head in front under rules. (op 5-1)
Lerida set a sensible pace throughout and battled on well under pressure once narrowly headed, only going down by a narrow margin. He could win again from this mark. (op 7-1)
Kinkeel(IRE) often mixes it in the highest grade, but at this more realistic level he ran well in defeat and at this course he is always respected (two wins from five starts).
Mujamead ran better than in his previous efforts as he settled well during the race. He may need to be dropped a few pounds to gain a victory over fences.
Troodos Jet appreciated the pace up front which helped him get close to the leaders approaching the last, but he never looked like winning. (tchd 28-1)
Mamba(GER) ran no sort of race, with trainer Chris Down suggesting this came too soon after her recent run at Huntingdon where she split Follow The Sun and Lerida. Official explanation: trainer's rep said race came too soon for mare (op 4-1)

3619 SOUTHWELL-RACECOURSE.CO.UK H'CAP HURDLE (9 hdls) 2m
2:00 (2:00) (Class 5) (0-90,89) 4-Y-O+ **£1,712** (£499; £249)

Form RPR

P666 **1** **Sacco D'Oro**[18] 3255 5-11-3 **83** .... CharlieStudd(3) 91+
(Michael Mullineaux) *hld up in rr: stdy hdwy 3 out: trckd ldr next: led between last 2: smoothly* **20/1**

-053 **2** *3 ¾* **Pinewood Legend (IRE)**[65] 2398 9-11-3 **80** .... (b) BrianHughes 84
(Peter Niven) *led tl after 2nd: w ldr: led 5th: hit 2 out: hdd between last 2: no ch w wnr* **3/1**[1]

/055 **3** *9* **Wise Hawk**[10] 3449 6-11-12 **89** .... (t) JamesDavies 84
(Chris Down) *chsd ldrs: one pce fr 2 out* **5/1**

-004 **4** *15* **Prize Fighter (IRE)**[56] 2603 9-11-7 **84** .... TomSiddall 65
(Lynn Siddall) *t.k.h in rr: hdwy 5th: sn trcking ldrs: hung rt and lost pl bnd appr 3 out* **9/2**[3]

0PP0 **5** *18* **Overyou**[53] 2658 6-11-7 **84** .... (p) JohnnyFarrelly 65
(Elliott Cooper) *chsd ldrs: drvn 6th: handy 3rd whn j. bdly rt 2 out: modest 4th whn heavily eased appr last* **9/2**[3]

333P **6** *1* **Bari Bay**[16] 3338 5-10-9 **72** .... (b) NickScholfield 36
(Michael Blake) *in rr: dropped bk 3rd: bhd fr 5th: t.o 3 out* **7/2**[2]

5-60 **7** *4 ½* **Solo Choice**[38] 480 5-11-8 **85** .... RichieMcGrath 45
(Ian McInnes) *w ldr: blnd 1st: mstke 2nd: sn led: hdd 5th: lost pl after 3 out: sn t.o* **18/1**

4m 6.30s (9.20) **Going Correction** +0.60s/f (Soft) **7** Ran SP% **110.3**
Speed ratings (Par 103): **101,99,94,87,78 77,75**
Tote Swingers: 1&2 £4.70, 1&3 £9.60, 2&3 £3.80 CSF £74.87 TOTE £14.70: £3.50, £1.60; EX 85.70.
Owner Paul D'Amato **Bred** Knight's Bloodstock **Trained** Alpraham, Cheshire

FOCUS
There was a minor upset in this weak handicap hurdle, run at a modest gallop. A big hurdles best from the winner but the form does make sense.

NOTEBOOK
Sacco D'Oro, a maiden on the Flat and over jumps, got stuck in the mud at Uttoxeter last month, but clearly appreciated this better ground, winning with the minimum amount of fuss. This wasn't a good race, though, so the form may be questionable. Official explanation: trainer said, regarding apparent improvement in form, that it was a poor race and the mare seemed better suited by the good to soft ground (op 28-1 tchd 33-1 and 16-1)
Pinewood Legend(IRE) looked the winner entering the straight but couldn't quicken when asked. He is now running into form after needing his seasonal reappearance in November.
Wise Hawk, fitted with a tongue-tie, settled well but was no match for the first two. He may need some help from the handicapper in due course. (op 6-1 tchd 9-2)
Prize Fighter(IRE) was 11lb lower than when second at Doncaster a year ago, but has been regressive since. (op 10-3)
Bari Bay was well backed but proved disappointing. (op 4-1 tchd 9-2)
Solo Choice seems to have gone backwards since a promising second on his hurdling debut at Sedgefield. (op 25-1 tchd 28-1)

3620 SOUTHWELL NOVICES' HURDLE (9 hdls) 2m
2:30 (2:30) (Class 4) 4-Y-O+ **£2,211** (£649; £324; £162)

Form RPR

1 **1** **Bear's Affair (IRE)**[97] 1824 5-11-4 0 .... APMcCoy 125+
(Nicky Henderson) *trckd ldrs: smooth hdwy to chal 2 out: sn led: easily* **8/13**[1]

20-4 **2** *3 ½* **Basford Bob (IRE)**[61] 2473 6-11-4 0 .... AlanO'Keeffe 113+
(Jennie Candlish) *t.k.h: sn trcking ldrs: hit 6th: outpcd 2 out: styd on run-in: tk 2nd nr fin* **6/1**[3]

104U **3** *nk* **Ashammar (FR)**[58] 2548 6-11-11 124 .... (t) WillKennedy 119
(Paul Webber) *hld up towards rr: hdwy 6th: styd on to take 2nd last: kpt on same pce* **10/1**

2330 **4** *3* **Heron Bay**[10] 3447 7-11-8 123 .... (p) DonalDevereux(3) 117
(Peter Bowen) *w ldr: led appr 2 out: hdd after 2 out: 3rd whn nt fluent last: fdd* **7/2**[2]

40- **5** *19* **The Quantum Kid**[297] 4891 7-11-4 0 .... CharliePoste 93
(Robin Dickin) *led tl appr 2 out: wknd between last 2* **50/1**

05 **6** *¾* **First Spirit**[32] 2282 5-10-8 0 .... WayneKavanagh(3) 84
(Robin Dickin) *chsd ldrs: wknd 3 out: 7th whn mstke next* **66/1**

566 **7** *1* **St Enoder**[21] 3171 6-10-11 0 .... SamThomas 83
(Brendan Powell) *chsd ldrs: wknd 3 out* **80/1**

0 **8** *6* **Lava Steps (USA)**[9] 607 5-11-4 0 .... RodiGreene 85
(Paul Midgley) *mid-div: mstke 5th: wknd appr 3 out* **150/1**

9 *1 ¼* **Warren Bank**[176] 6-11-1 0 .... TomMolloy(3) 84
(Mary Hambro) *t.k.h in rr: nvr on terms* **100/1**

350- **10** *9* **Smudger**[282] 5158 6-11-4 0 .... HenryOliver 76
(Sue Smith) *hld up in rr: hdwy 4th: lost pl and mstke 6th* **40/1**

0000 **11** *19* **Why So Serious**[80] 2092 5-11-4 0 .... JanFaltejsek 59
(Peter Salmon) *chsd ldrs: lost pl 6th: mstke next: sn bhd* **150/1**

0-0P **12** *10* **Just Lola**[33] 2974 7-10-11 0 .... NickScholfield 43
(Michael Blake) *mid-div: lost pl 6th: bhd whn j.rt 2 out* **150/1**

13 *2 ½* **Sanctuary**[76] 5-11-4 0 .... JohnnyFarrelly 47
(Michael Scudamore) *j. poorly in rr: bhd fr 4th* **40/1**

5 **P** **Dispol Diva**[66] 2370 5-10-11 0 .... TomSiddall —
(Paul Midgley) *in rr: j.rt 3rd: sn bhd: t.o whn j. bdly rt 5th: sn p.u* **80/1**

4m 6.50s (9.40) **Going Correction** +0.60s/f (Soft) **14** Ran SP% **121.3**
Speed ratings (Par 105): **100,98,98,96,87 86,86,83,82,78 68,63,58,—**
Tote Swingers: 1&2 £2.50, 1&3 £2.90, 2&3 £9.80 CSF £5.17 TOTE £1.80: £1.20, £2.00, £2.20; EX 6.10.
Owner G B Barlow **Bred** T J Whitley **Trained** Upper Lambourn, Berks

FOCUS
An ordinary novice hurdle dominated by the front four in the market. The easy winner was value for further and the form makes sense.

NOTEBOOK
Bear's Affair(IRE) stepped up on his bumper victory at Uttoxeter with a likeable display on his hurdling bow. He was keen whilst tracking the leaders, but once settled by McCoy smoothly put the race to bed despite not liking the tacky ground. Being by Presenting, he will surely continue to improve on faster ground in the future. (op 1-2)
Basford Bob(IRE) came on for his seasonal reappearance at Market Rasen in November, staying on well to grab second. Considering how hard he pulled, this was a good performance and will do better over further. (op 7-1)
Ashammar(FR), another who pulled hard, reverted back to hurdles after not taking to fences and put in a much better display in this sphere. He was pipped for second, but again should appreciate further. (op 12-1)
Heron Bay bounced back from a poor showing at Sandown recently, finishing fourth. The sounder surface helped considerably. (op 4-1 tchd 3-1)
The Quantum Kid looked like causing a shock coming into the straight, but his effort was short-lived. (op 66-1)
First Spirit continues to improve with her jumping, but was one-paced in the straight.
Smudger, back after a 282-day absence, looked in need of the run. (op 80-1)
Just Lola Official explanation: trainer said mare had a breathing problem
Sanctuary Official explanation: jockey said gelding jumped poorly

3621 PLAY GOLF AT SOUTHWELL GOLF CLUB H'CAP HURDLE (13 hdls) 3m 110y
3:00 (3:02) (Class 4) (0-115,111) 4-Y-O+ **£2,341** (£687; £343; £171)

Form RPR

5341 **1** **Lackamon**[3] 3575 6-11-12 **111** 7ex .... TjadeCollier 133+
(Sue Smith) *trckd ldrs: led appr 2 out: wnt clr between last 2: easily* **2/1**[1]

10-0 **2** *12* **Tora Bora (GER)**[21] 3170 9-10-8 **93** .... (p) SamThomas 94
(Brendan Powell) *led: jnd 3 out: hdd appr next: kpt on: no ch w wnr* **12/1**

-506 **3** *2* **Vin De Roy (FR)**[15] 3370 6-11-10 **109** .... SeanQuinlan 110
(Rachel Hobbs) *chsd ldrs: mstke 9th: one pce appr 2 out* **12/1**

001- **4** *13* **Master Eddy**[298] 4869 11-11-12 **111** .... DavidEngland 98
(Shaun Lycett) *chsd ldrs: wknd after 3 out* **20/1**

-103 **5** *shd* **Wor Rom (IRE)**[7] 3502 7-9-12 **90** .... (p) MrNHalley(7) 77
(Elliott Cooper) *chsd ldrs: drvn 9th: lost pl 3 out* **5/1**[3]

1-54 **6** 1 ¼ **Max Bygraves**[17] 3299 8-11-8 **107** JasonMaguire 94
(Kim Bailey) *hld up in mid-div: chsd ldrs 6th: wknd and modest 3rd 2 out: 4th last: tired bdly run-in* **7/2**[2]

42-3 **7** 34 **Bring On The Judge (IRE)**[71] 2269 8-11-9 **111**. SamTwiston-Davies(3) 66
(Nigel Twiston-Davies) *t.k.h in rr: hit 8th: lost pl next: bhd and eased 2 out: t.o whn blnd last* **8/1**

5P00 **P** **Osolomio (IRE)**[55] 2606 8-11-5 **104** (t) AlanO'Keeffe —
(Jennie Candlish) *in rr: lost pl 7th: sn bhd: t.o whn p.u bef 9th* **20/1**

0-22 **P** **Radmores Revenge**[55] 2606 8-11-3 **109** CharlieWallis(7) —
(John O'Shea) *towards rr: drvn 7th: sn wknd: t.o whn p.u bef 9th: lame* **18/1**

5-P3 **P** **The Portonion (IRE)**[75] 2166 7-11-9 **108** DougieCostello —
(Malcolm Jefferson) *in rr: outpcd 9th: sn bhd: t.o whn blnd 6th: sn p.u* **28/1**

6m 26.5s (19.00) **Going Correction** +0.60s/f (Soft) **10** Ran SP% **117.0**
Speed ratings (Par 105): **93,89,88,84,84 83,73,—,—,—**
Tote Swingers: 1&2 £13.20, 1&3 £8.90, 2&3 £49.00 CSF £25.43 CT £235.15 TOTE £3.70: £1.70, £3.60, £2.70; EX 41.20.

Owner Mrs S Smith **Bred** W P Jenks **Trained** High Eldwick, W Yorks

FOCUS
An average 0-115 handicap hurdle for the class, with the top weight 4lb below the ceiling. Another step up from the winner with the next two close to their marks.

NOTEBOOK
Lackamon, carrying a 7lb penalty for an easy success over 3m1f at Wetherby, cruised to victory. Stamina is clearly his forte and he is well handicapped at present. He will go up in the weights but in this form he could defy another rise. (op 15-8 tchd 13-8)

Tora Bora(GER) showed the benefit of a recent AW bumper run with a good front-running display. He could not stay with the winner over the final two flights but ran with credit.\n (op 22-1 tchd 28-1)

Vin De Roy(FR) settled well and showed improvement with this step up in trip. Now he's shown that he can stay this far, connections have more options. (op 14-1)

Master Eddy often needs his seasonal reappearance so it was encouraging to see him run well. All his wins have come at Newbury in March, so connections may have a race in mind. (op 25-1)

Max Bygraves was well backed, but may need a slower-run race at this distance to truly see out the trip. He was later reported to have a breathing problem Official explanation: trainer's rep said gelding had a breathing problem (op 4-1 tchd 9-2)

Radmores Revenge Official explanation: trainer said gelding finished lame

3622 MEMBERSHIP OF SOUTHWELL GOLF CLUB H'CAP HURDLE (9 hdls 2 omitted) 2m 4f 110y

3:30 (3:30) (Class 5) (0-90,90) 4-Y-O+ **£1,626** (£477; £238; £119)

Form RPR

-006 **1** **Night In Milan (IRE)**[13] 3398 5-11-12 **90** JamesReveley 105+
(Keith Reveley) *hld up: stdy hdwy normal 4 out: w ldr next: hmpd by loose horse appr nromal 2 out: hung lft appr omitted last: sn led narrowly: hld on wl towards fin* **15/2**

52P4 **2** ½ **I Can Run Can You (IRE)**[18] 3256 5-11-10 **88** APMcCoy 98
(Jonjo O'Neill) *t.k.h: trckd ldrs: drvn along w a circ to go: led appr normal 2 out: hdd narowly sn after omitted last: no ex towards fin* **9/2**[2]

0-60 **3** 18 **Celts Espere**[233] 538 8-10-10 **74** WayneHutchinson 68
(Chris Bealby) *in rr: styd on and lft modest 4th 2 out: wnt 3rd appr omitted last* **14/1**

060 **4** 16 **King Benny (IRE)**[180] 1066 7-11-10 **88** (p) JohnnyFarrelly 70
(Elliott Cooper) *led: hdd appr normal 2 out: wknd qckly appr omitted last* **5/1**[3]

3450 **5** 16 **Secret Desert**[35] 2937 5-11-8 **86** GrahamLee 51
(Ferdy Murphy) *in rr: sme hdwy normal 4 out: sn wknd* **16/1**

5553 **P** **Cloudy Dawn**[14] 3392 6-11-0 **78** HenryOliver —
(Sue Smith) *w ldr: drvn circ to go: wknd normal 4 out: t.o whn p.u bef normal 2 out* **4/1**[1]

3004 **P** **Galant Eye (IRE)**[61] 2467 12-10-2 **73** DannyBurton(7) —
(Chris Down) *chsd ldrs: reminders circ to go: sn wknd: t.o whn p.u bef 2 out* **11/1**

4P0P **P** **Aspolan (GER)**[18] 3260 8-11-3 **81** (b1) SeanQuinlan —
(Rachel Hobbs) *in rr: chsd ldrs 5th: wknd normal 7th: sn bhd: t.o whn p.u bef normal 2 out* **16/1**

-005 **F** **Carys's Lad**[18] 3258 8-10-13 **80** CharlieStudd(3) —
(Michael Mullineaux) *in rr: fell 2nd* **20/1**

00P/ **U** **L'Apprenti Sorcier (FR)**[1106] 3302 8-10-8 **72** (t) MattieBatchelor —
(Joanna Davis) *towards rr whn j. v big and uns rdr 1st* **40/1**

6-00 **P** **Pezula**[34] 2956 5-10-6 **70** WarrenMarston —
(Richard Phillips) *mid-div: sme hdwy normal 3 out: wknd qckly and wl bhd whn p.u bef normal 2 out* **40/1**

5424 **U** **Present Your Case (IRE)**[34] 2956 6-11-7 **90** (t) DavidBass(5) —
(Ben Case) *mid-div: sme hdwy normal 3 out: 4th and one pce whn blnd and uns rdr next (normal 2 out)* **11/2**

5m 21.5s (10.80) **Going Correction** +0.60s/f (Soft) **12** Ran SP% **118.4**
Speed ratings (Par 103): **103,102,95,89,83 —,—,—,—,— —,—**
Tote Swingers: 1&2 £9.40, 1&3 £26.40, 2&3 £24.80 CSF £41.12 CT £466.52 TOTE £6.40: £2.10, £2.10, £3.60; EX 34.60.

Owner Richard Collins **Bred** Commandant Brendan Healy **Trained** Lingdale, Redcar & Cleveland

FOCUS
The final flight was bypassed on the last two circuits. A weak handicap hurdle but it produced a good finish. A big step forward from the winner but he was value for further.

NOTEBOOK
Night In Milan(IRE) won this with a bit in hand, as despite being hampered by a loose horse and hanging left, he was much too good for the runner-up. This was the 5-y-o's handicap debut, up in trip for a trainer who excels with this type. There should be more to come. Official explanation: trainer said, regarding apparent improvement in form, that the gelding jumped conventional hurdles poorly in its earlier starts but, but apperared to be better suited by the brush hurdles and was suited by the step up in trip. (op 12-1 tchd 7-1)

I Can Run Can You(IRE) kept the straighter line on the run-in but may be flattered to end up close to the winner with the former running green. The two pulled well clear and he can gain compensation off a similar mark. (op 7-2)

Celts Espere looked in need of the run after a 233-day absence. (op 16-1)

King Benny(IRE) cut out the early running but paid for his freeness in the straight. (op 7-2)

Cloudy Dawn never travelled with any enthusiasm and was disappointing. (op 6-1)

Present Your Case(IRE) remains a maiden and was well beaten when unseating at the last. (op 6-1)

3623 SOUTHWELL MARES' MAIDEN OPEN NATIONAL HUNT FLAT RACE 2m

4:00 (4:01) (Class 6) 4-6-Y-O **£1,370** (£399; £199)

Form RPR

1 **Baby Shine (IRE)**[93] 5-10-11 0 MattCrawley(7) 113+
(Lucy Wadham) *hld up in mid-div: smooth hdwy 6f out: wnt 2nd over 2f out: shkn up to ld appr fnl f: styd on wl: eased towards fin* **2/1**[1]

2 4 ½ **Florafern** 6-11-1 0 CharlieHuxley(3) 104+
(Oliver Sherwood) *chsd ldrs: 3rd and outpcd 2f out: styd on to take 2nd last 75yds* **14/1**

5 **3** 2 ¼ **Cue To Cue**[75] 2167 5-11-4 0 JamesReveley 103
(Keith Reveley) *led: hdd appr fnl f: kpt on same pce* **7/2**[3]

3S **4** 6 **Hazy Dawn**[33] 2987 6-11-4 0 WayneHutchinson 97
(Michael Scudamore) *w ldrs: chal over 4f out: wknd fnl 2f* **28/1**

5 nk **Sharlene's Quest (IRE)** 5-10-13 0 CO'Farrell(5) 97
(V J Hughes) *trckd ldrs: drvn over 4f out: outpcd over 2f out: kpt on fnl f* **50/1**

2 **6** 1 **Victrix Gale (IRE)**[209] 833 5-11-4 0 APMcCoy 96
(Nicky Henderson) *trckd ldrs: pushed along 6f out: hung rt and fdd fnl 2f* **9/4**[2]

0 **7** 24 **Stickaround**[34] 2957 6-11-4 0 GrahamLee 74
(Malcolm Jefferson) *in rr: drvn 7f out: sn lost pl and bhd* **66/1**

0 **8** 10 **Star Shuil (IRE)**[33] 2987 6-11-4 0 JasonMaguire 65
(David Arbuthnot) *t.k.h towards rr: effrt 6f out: sn lost pl and bhd* **33/1**

9 hd **Tinagenic (FR)** 5-11-4 0 WarrenMarston 65
(Seamus Mullins) *trckd ldrs: drvn 5f out: wknd over 3f out: 7th whn eased 2f out* **16/1**

5 **10** 4 **Goodtimes A'Coming**[21] 3159 5-11-4 0 RichardJohnson 61
(Noel Chance) *hld up towards rr: drvn and sme hdwy 4f out: sn wknd* **14/1**

11 16 **Poetic Beat** 6-11-4 0 RobertThornton 47
(Seamus Durack) *in rr: drvn 7f out: sn lost pl and bhd* **33/1**

0 **12** dist **Summerandlightning (IRE)**[28] 3054 5-11-4 0 JamesDavies —
(Mark Usher) *in rr: sn drvn along: reminders 7f out: sn lost pl and bhd: hopelessly t.o over 3f out: eventually completed* **100/1**

00 **13** 3 ½ **Sally O'Malley (IRE)**[43] 2825 5-11-4 0 AlanO'Keeffe —
(Charles Smith) *racd wd: lost pl after 5f: sn wl bhd: hopelessly t.o fnl 8f: eventually completed* **200/1**

4m 0.50s (9.00) **Going Correction** +0.60s/f (Soft) **13** Ran SP% **119.8**
Speed ratings: **101,98,97,94,94 93,81,76,76,74 66,51,50**
Tote Swingers: 1&2 £12.50, 1&3 £4.10, 2&3 £16.10 CSF £31.03 TOTE £3.10: £1.10, £2.90, £1.50; EX 35.20.

Owner P A Philipps,T S Redman & Mrs L Redman **Bred** Kevin Francis O'Donnell **Trained** Newmarket, Suffolk

FOCUS
Just an ordinary mares' bumper but it yielded an impressive and well above average winner.

NOTEBOOK
Baby Shine(IRE), successful in a 3m Irish point, put that experience to good use with a taking display on her debut under rules. Extremely well backed, she quickened past her rivals after travelling powerfully throughout and will be aimed at the Listed mares' bumper at Sandown on March 12. (op 7-2)

Florafern, whose trainer does well in this sphere, stayed on best but too late in the day. She is a half-sister to four winning hurdlers up to 3m so evidently will be seen in better light up in distance, but could pick up a bumper en route. (op 8-1 tchd 7-1)

Cue To Cue couldn't quicken in the tacky ground after leading for a long way. She could be one to keep an eye on with a sounder surface underfoot. (op 4-1 tchd 10-3)

Hazy Dawn stayed on moderately in the straight, but showed improvement from her first two races. (op 25-1)

Sharlene's Quest(IRE) performed with credit and will come on for the run. (op 100-1 tchd 40-1)

Victrix Gale(IRE) got loose before her debut when second in a bumper at Worcester but couldn't build on that promise here. Being by Presenting she will appreciate better ground than she got on this occasion. (op 7-4 tchd 11-4)

T/Jkpt: Not won. T/Plt: £294.20 to a £1 stake. Pool:£67,968.30 - 167.46 winning tickets T/Qpdt: £23.20 to a £1 stake. Pool:£7,378.17 - 234.50 winning tickets WG

3193 NEWBURY (L-H)

Wednesday, January 19

OFFICIAL GOING: Soft (heavy in places)

Wind: virtually nil Weather: Bright and Sunny

3624 BERKSHIRE STAND BOOKSHOP JUVENILE HURDLE (8 hdls) 2m 110y

1:00 (1:00) (Class 4) 4-Y-O **£2,602** (£764; £382; £190)

Form RPR

1 **Cedre Bleu (FR)**[126] 4-10-12 0 SamThomas 123+
(Paul Nicholls) *trckd ldr: hit 3rd: led appr 3 out: shkn up and styd on strly fr after 2 out: drew clr flat* **10/3**[2]

52 **2** 10 **Titan De Sarti (FR)**[35] 2958 4-10-12 0 BarryGeraghty 113
(Nicky Henderson) *trckd ldrs: wnt 2nd 3 out: sn rdn: no ex and hld by wnr fr after next* **1/2**[1]

3441 **3** 9 **Ultravox (USA)**[9] 3484 4-10-12 115 NathanSweeney(7) 112
(Jeremy Scott) *j.rt at times: led: nt fluent 1st: rdn and hdd appr 3 out: one pce and comf hld whn blnd 2 out* **9/1**[3]

4 32 **Lapin Garou (FR)** 4-10-12 0 DarylJacob 78
(Nick Williams) *trckd ldrs: struggling whn hit 3 out: wknd next* **16/1**

4m 10.2s (0.30) **Going Correction** +0.225s/f (Yiel) **4** Ran SP% **105.6**
Speed ratings: **108,103,99,84**
CSF £5.49 TOTE £3.70; EX 6.90.

Owner Paul K Barber & D A Johnson **Bred** G F A Du Hoguenet **Trained** Ditcheat, Somerset

FOCUS
A race won by subsequent Triumph Hurdle winner Detroit City in 2006, but this was a disappointing turn-out numerically, possibly due to the ease in the ground.

NOTEBOOK
Cedre Bleu(FR) ◆, representing an interesting ownership combination, made a perfect start to his British career with a smooth success - he had finished third at 27-1 in a Listed Auteuil hurdle on his last start in France. A horse with plenty of size and scope, he raced prominently and arguably got first run on his market rival, gaining enough of an advantage to remain clear. Predictably, he drew quotes for the Triumph Hurdle, but Paul Nicholls said afterwards that his horse is likely to have one more run this season, in something similar to this, and go chasing next term. (op 9-2 tchd 3-1)

Titan De Sarti(FR) set a good standard when considering his previous outing over C&D, but he was disappointing in this and never got close enough to the winner to make him work. There is still room for improvement in his jumping, and he may possibly be suited by a stronger pace and better ground in future. (op 8-15 tchd 4-9, 4-7 in places)
Ultravox(USA), a wide-margin winner at Towcester, looked to face a tall order under his penalty against a couple of potentially decent types and was readily held. (op 13-2 tchd 10-1)
Lapin Garou(FR), having his first taste of racecourse action, was green and didn't show a great deal, but he deserves another chance. (op 12-1)

3625 ZENERGI NOVICES' CHASE (13 fncs) 2m 1f
1:30 (1:31) (Class 3) 5-Y-0+ **£4,189** (£1,432)

Form RPR
15-1 **1** **Finian's Rainbow (IRE)**55 2628 8-11-4 156 BarryGeraghty 156+
(Nicky Henderson) *mde virtually all: rchd for 4th: lft wl clr 3 out: unchal* **2/13**1
0-00 **2** *51* **Babysitter (IRE)**21 3193 8-10-12 0 APMcCoy 110
(Jonjo O'Neill) *led tl 1st: sn chsng ldrs: nudged along fr 4th: outpcd fr 8th: lft modest 2nd 3 out* **12/1**3
11-0 **F** **Tail Of The Bank (IRE)**39 2884 8-10-12 0 LiamHeard 131+
(Laura Young) *sn trcking wnr: coming u.p and 3 l down whn fell heavily 3 out* **9/1**2
4m 17.3s (4.30) **Going Correction** +0.225s/f (Yiel) **3** Ran SP% **104.3**
Speed ratings: **98,74,—**
CSF £2.29 TOTE £1.10; EX 1.70.
Owner Michael Buckley **Bred** J O'Keeffe **Trained** Upper Lambourn, Berks

FOCUS
This race hadn't been run since Big Buck's won in 2008, and all three renewals had gone to the favourite, so it wasn't a surprise to see Finian's Rainbow continue that trend with an authoritative display. He jumped into the lead shortly after the first and put in a pleasing display thereafter, a mistake at the third the only concern.

NOTEBOOK
Finian's Rainbow(IRE) won in authoritative style. He jumped into the lead shortly after the first and put in a pleasing display thereafter, a mistake at the fourth the only concern. If there is one tiny nagging doubt about him going on to win the Arkle, it would be that he does seem to jump perfectly well but low, so wouldn't want to meet a fence wrong at speed. It is also true that he hasn't beaten many horses in his two starts (subsequent Grade 2 winner Hell's Bay wouldn't have been suited by a the small-field contest he won on his chasing debut), so it can easily be argued that his relatively short price for the Arkle (best-priced 6-1) is based on hype rather than substance at the moment. He will have another run before making his way to Cheltenham, possibly in Warwick's Kingmaker or Kempton's Pendil, and remains an exciting prospect. (op 1-7 tchd 1-6, 1-5 in a place)
Babysitter(IRE) never got into any sort of challenging position. (op 11-1 tchd 10-1)
Tail Of The Bank(IRE) ◆ was in the process of running a blinder on his chasing debut when coming down three out. If his confidence isn't knocked by the fall, he looks certain to win any ordinary novice event. (op 11-1)

3626 RUTLAND ANTIQUE CENTRE BAKEWELL NOVICES' HURDLE (10 hdls) 2m 3f
2:05 (2:05) (Class 4) 5-Y-0+ **£2,602** (£764; £382; £190)

Form RPR
4-41 **1** **Pride In Battle (IRE)**35 2963 6-11-5 126 RobertThornton 132+
(Alan King) *tended to jump lft: trckd ldr: led narrowly whn pckd 3 out: rdn after 2 out: styd on wl to assert fr last: rdn out* **11/8**1
B6F1 **2** *2 1/2* **Radetsky March (IRE)**13 3405 8-11-5 126 APMcCoy 125
(Mark Bradstock) *led: narrowly hdd 3 out: sn rdn: kpt on gamely pressing wnr: no ex fr last* **2/1**2
1 **3** *3/4* **Penny Max (IRE)**64 2445 5-10-12 0 SamThomas 116
(Emma Lavelle) *racd keenly: hld up in last pair: hdwy whn nt fluent 5th: rdn in 4th appr 3 out: edgd rt: styd on: nt gng pce to chal* **4/1**3
4 *11* **Ravastree (IRE)**80 5-10-12 0 WayneHutchinson 107+
(Alan King) *in tch: rdn after 7th: hld whn mstke next: wnt 4th bef last but nvr any ch w ldrs* **12/1**
5 *15* **Amaury De Lusignan (IRE)**73 5-10-12 0 JamieMoore 100+
(Gary Moore) *racd keenly: trckd ldrs: rdn appr 3 out: wknd after 2 out: lost 4th bef last* **25/1**
4 **6** *76* **Autumn Haze**55 2640 6-10-12 0 PaulMoloney 14
(Evan Williams) *trckd ldrs tl dropped to last pair after 4th: rdn after 7th: wknd bef next: t.o* **20/1**
P **Sunley Peace**1187 7-10-12 0 AndrewGlassonbury —
(Gary Moore) *nt a fluent: hld up: pckd 1st: rdn after 7th: sn wknd: p.u bef 3 out* **33/1**
4m 52.3s (1.70) **Going Correction** +0.225s/f (Yiel) **7** Ran SP% **114.7**
Speed ratings: **105,103,103,99,92 60,—**
toteswingers:1&2 £1.90, 2&3 £1.10, 1&3 £1.10 CSF £4.49 TOTE £1.80: £1.60, £1.50; EX 5.60.
Owner Mrs Elizabeth Pearce **Bred** Christopher Nicholson **Trained** Barbury Castle, Wilts

FOCUS
A race won in the past by some decent types like the Nicky Henderson (who wasn't represented this year) trio of Mad Max, Wogan and Trabolgan, so this winner is a name to keep an eye out for when going over fences.

NOTEBOOK
Pride In Battle(IRE) ◆ landed a race over C&D on his previous outing (form has worked out well) and showed plenty of courage under pressure here to keep going. One got the impression that he won with a bit more in hand than the winning distance suggested, and he will be given a couple of entries at the Cheltenham Festival, as connections feel he'll be far from disgraced. However, a decision about what race, if any, he heads for won't be made until he has another run sometime in February. He'll make a chaser in time. (op 6-4 tchd 13-8)
Radetsky March(IRE), who won by a wide margin on his return to hurdling, didn't go off at the same speed he had done at Huntingdon and couldn't shake off his rivals as a result. One couldn't fault his bravery, however, because he kept responding to McCoy and ran on to take second. (op 3-1 tchd 10-3)
Penny Max(IRE) ◆ showed he has a future over hurdles with a solid first effort over them. He shaped as though 2m4f and further won't be a problem. (op 10-3 tchd 3-1)
Ravastree(IRE), the winner of an Irish point last October, who cost connections £65,000 a month later, made a promising debut, albeit well beaten, and should be of some interest next time. (tchd 11-1)
Amaury De Lusignan(IRE), runner-up on his sole start in an Irish point last November, showed plenty of ability until the latter stages but may need better ground to be seen as his best.

3627 EUROPEAN BREEDERS' FUND/THOROUGHBRED BREEDERS' ASSOCIATION MARES' NOVICES' CHASE (16 fncs) 2m 4f
2:40 (2:40) (Class 4) 5-Y-0+ **£3,332** (£1,034; £557)

Form RPR
3F-4 **1** **Kerada (FR)**74 2218 7-10-12 0 BarryGeraghty 136+
(Nicky Henderson) *j.w: prom: led 3rd: hdd after 11th tl after next: in command and styd on wl fr 2 out* **5/4**2
-330 **2** *6* **Asturienne**34 2983 7-10-12 0 RobertThornton 128+
(Alan King) *chsd ldrs: reminder after 9th: rdn after 12th: styd on to chse wnr after 3 out: a being hld* **6/1**3
3116 **3** *20* **Sway (FR)**18 3291 5-11-6 137 APMcCoy 125
(Jonjo O'Neill) *led tl 3rd: kpt pressing wnr: led after 11th tl after next: rdn after 4 out: lost 2nd after next: wknd after 2 out* **1/1**1
/P-5 **P** **Fillyofthevalley**55 2627 8-10-12 0 MarkGrant —
(Peter Jones) *chsd ldrs tl wknd after 12th: t.o whn mstke 3 out: p.u bef next* **100/1**
5m 11.2s (-0.80) **Going Correction** +0.225s/f (Yiel) **4** Ran SP% **109.7**
Speed ratings: **110,107,99,—**
TOTE £2.20; EX 5.50.
Owner Turf Club 2010 **Bred** E A R L La Croix Sonnet **Trained** Upper Lambourn, Berks

FOCUS
An interesting mares' contest despite the small field.

NOTEBOOK
Kerada(FR) ◆ is a useful sort over hurdles but looks likely to make into a better chaser judged on this performance. A strong-looking mare, she jumped well under a positive ride and won by a healthy margin. She will head for the final of this series if maintaining this level of form.ooks likely to make into a better chaser judged on this performance. A strong-looking mare, she jumped well under a positive ride and won by a healthy margin. She will head for the finale of this series if maintaining this level of form. (tchd 11-8, 6-4 in places)
Asturienne, the lowest-rated of the three with a chance here over hurdles, made a pleasing chasing debut and has the finale of this series as her target, all being well. (op 9-2 tchd 7-1)
Sway(FR), comfortably held in a hot Grade 2 novice chase last time, looked the one to beat, despite a double penalty, but ruined her chance with poor jumping, which is surprising considering the experience edge she had over her rivals. (op 5-4)

3628 M AND C CARPETS H'CAP CHASE (15 fncs) 2m 2f 110y
3:15 (3:15) (Class 4) (0-115,115) 5-Y-0+ **£2,602** (£764; £382; £190)

Form RPR
5/UP **1** **Peplum (FR)**36 2948 8-11-11 114 JamieMoore 130+
(Gary Moore) *trckd ldrs: pushed along after 3 out: led bef last: drew clr run-in: readily* **50/1**
-402 **2** *8* **Flaming Gorge (IRE)**61 2503 6-11-12 115 DarylJacob 124+
(Nick Williams) *led tl 5th: lft in ld 8th: rdn whn narrowly hdd after 11th: led again sn after 3 out: hdd bef last: styd on: no ex* **6/1**3
5-34 **3** *4 1/2* **Stoney's Treasure**53 2670 7-11-10 113 RobertThornton 120+
(Alan King) *in tch: trcking ldrs whn hmpd 8th: jnd ldr next: led 11th tl stmbld 3 out: sn rdn: styd on same pce* **11/8**1
6-43 **4** *1/2* **The Boss (IRE)**63 2454 6-11-4 107 NickScholfield 110
(Jeremy Scott) *hld up: hdwy after 11th: rdn after 4 out: styd on same pce fr next* **7/2**2
3F-3 **5** *14* **Quintero (FR)**19 3257 7-11-6 109 PaulMoloney 101
(Evan Williams) *trckd ldrs: hit 4th: struggling towards rr 8th: clsd on ldrs u.p 4 out: wknd after 3 out* **12/1**
-P00 **6** *2 1/4* **Amble Forge (IRE)**35 2961 9-11-4 107 (t) JoeTizzard 94
(Colin Tizzard) *hld up: rdn appr 4 out: wknd after 3 out* **25/1**
0000 **7** *1* **American World (FR)**20 3228 7-11-12 115 APMcCoy 101
(Brendan Powell) *prom: rdn after 11th: wknd after 4 out* **25/1**
6026 **P** **Canni Thinkaar (IRE)**36 2945 10-11-5 113(b) GemmaGracey-Davison(5) —
(Zoe Davison) *nt a fluent: towards rr whn mstke 7th: lost tch 9th: p.u after next* **28/1**
-134 **U** **Abey M'Boy**19 3257 8-11-2 105 LeightonAspell 99
(Oliver Sherwood) *hld up: sme hdwy after 11th: sn rdn: styng on same pce in 5th whn mstke: stmbld and uns rdr last* **7/1**
0 **F** **Kap West (FR)**34 2975 6-10-8 97 JohnnyFarrelly —
(Laura Young) *prom: led 5th tl fell 8th* **20/1**
4m 45.6s (1.60) **Going Correction** +0.225s/f (Yiel) **10** Ran SP% **116.7**
Speed ratings: **105,101,99,99,93 92,92,—,—,—**
toteswingers:1&2 £11.90, 2&3 £3.20, 1&3 £32.30 CSF £309.96 CT £716.04 TOTE £108.30: £21.20, £1.90, £2.00; EX 367.20.
Owner Patrick Wilmott **Bred** Dr Vet Hubert Favre & Laurent Favre **Trained** Lower Beeding, W Sussex

FOCUS
The early pace had looked respectable but that may have been deceiving, as virtually the whole field looked to hold some sort of chance heading to the fourth last. One got the impression that it turned into a sprint.

NOTEBOOK
Peplum(FR), dropping in class, won in decisive style but quite what this performance adds up to his debateable - he surprised connections, who weren't expecting this at all. It was the first time he had completed since moving to Gary Moore, so a follow up is far from certain when considering all of his Irish form as well.
Flaming Gorge(IRE) shaped with promise on his chasing debut in mid-November and confirmed that with a sound effort in this. He is worth a try back over 2m. (op 13-2 tchd 7-1)
Stoney's Treasure, dropping 4f in trip, held every chance on turning in but lost valuable momentum when landing steeply after three out. He'll probably be better over further, as he was outpaced heading to the final fence. (op 7-4 tchd 15-8 in places)
The Boss(IRE) ◆ had shown some promise despite being well-beaten in a couple of novice hurdles, and attracted market support on his chasing debut under rules. The winner of a 3m point the previous January, he looked to be ridden for a turn of foot and became outpaced as the tempo increased. A more prominent ride would have helped his cause. (op 5-1)
Quintero(FR) looks to want further. (op 11-1)
Amble Forge(IRE) looked to have run up a bit light. (op 20-1)
Abey M'Boy, who looked very fit beforehand, appeared to be going well but didn't find as much as looked likely when the rider asked for more. (op 16-1)
Kap West(FR) was on his toes beforehand. (op 16-1)

3629 MC SEAFOODS H'CAP CHASE (FOR THE HARWELL TROPHY) (18 fncs) 3m
3:50 (3:50) (Class 3) (0-125,125) 5-Y-0+ **£4,553** (£1,337; £668; £333)

Form RPR
10-1 **1** **Sona Sasta (IRE)**9 3482 8-10-11 113 7ex DannyCook(3) 131+
(David Pipe) *j.rt thrght: mde all: shkn up and in command fr 2 out: readily* **5/6**1
4143 **2** *7* **The Rainbow Hunter**21 3198 7-11-4 124 EdCookson(7) 132+
(Andy Turnell) *hld up: stdy prog fr 9th to trck wnr after 13th: rdn after 14th: nvr able to mount chal: styd on wl to draw clr of remainder: hld fr 2 out: hung rt run-in* **11/1**3
F-22 **3** *8* **Vamizi (IRE)**78 2140 8-11-4 122 MrMMO'Connor(5) 121
(Mark Bradstock) *prom: hmpd 6th: rdn after 13th: no ch w front pair fr 4 out: styd on same pce* **8/1**2
-40U **4** *3 1/4* **Appleaday (IRE)**11 3444 10-11-9 122 LiamTreadwell 117
(Paul Webber) *mid-div: hit 9th: rdn after 13th: no ch fr 4 out: styd on past btn horses fr 2 out* **12/1**

624- **5** *1 ½* **Trigger The Light**[281] 5174 10-11-3 **116**.................... WayneHutchinson 111+
(Alan King) *chsng ldrs whn blnd bdly and lost pl 11th: no ch fr 4 out: styd on past btn horses fr 2 out* **20/1**

2P0F **6** *12* **Victorias Groom (GER)**[18] 3290 9-11-12 **125**................ LeightonAspell 106
(Lucy Wadham) *chsd ldrs: rdn after 14th: disptuted 3rd but no ch fr 4 out: wknd 2 out* **20/1**

250P **7** *2 ¼* **Ginolad (AUS)**[198] 911 11-11-4 **117**................................ AidanColeman 94
(Venetia Williams) *mid-div: hdwy 9th: rdn and wknd after 13th* **33/1**

51-P **8** *4 ½* **Bertie May**[11] 3440 9-11-0 **113**.. DarylJacob 86
(Kevin Bishop) *chsd ldrs early: squeezed up and lost pl bef 3rd: towards rr: hdwy after 14th: sn rdn: no ch fr next: wknd 2 out* **16/1**

53-0 **9** *1* **Wind Instrument (IRE)**[67] 2358 10-11-11 **124**.............. RobertThornton 96
(Alan King) *chsd ldrs: rdn 13th: wknd after next* **12/1**

16P2 **10** *nk* **Quattrocento (FR)**[11] 3444 7-11-8 **121**............................(v) JamieMoore 92
(Peter Bowen) *hld up towards rr: hdwy fr 11th: cl up whn stmbld 13th: sn rdn: wknd 4 out* **14/1**

31-P **P** **Teeming Rain (IRE)**[45] 2794 12-11-5 **118**..........................(vt) APMcCoy —
(Jonjo O'Neill) *nudged along in rr fr 7th: nt fluent 8th (water): slow next: sn lost tch: p.u bef 13th* **25/1**

6m 15.6s (4.60) **Going Correction** +0.225s/f (Yiel) **11** Ran SP% **118.2**
Speed ratings: **101,98,96,94,94 90,89,88,87,87** —
toteswingers:1&2 £4.70, 2&3 £8.10, 1&3 £3.50 CSF £10.51 CT £49.93 TOTE £2.00: £1.40, £2.80, £1.90; EX 14.80.

Owner R S Brookhouse **Bred** Michael Larkin **Trained** Nicholashayne, Devon

FOCUS
An easy success for the well-handicapped favourite.

NOTEBOOK
Sona Sasta(IRE) was given an uncomplicated ride towards the head of affairs and found more than enough despite a high head carriage. Due to race off a 13lb higher mark from the weekend, he will probably bid to bring up the hat-trick fairly soon. (op 8-11 tchd evens in places)
The Rainbow Hunter, up in trip, attracted market support at long odds and travelled strongly throughout. He got to the leader going well but couldn't get past. Connections were unlucky to bump into a horse a long way in front of the handicapper. (op 16-1 tchd 10-1)
Vamizi(IRE) raced up with the pace early and responded to pressure after the final fence to hold the closing Appleaday. Official explanation: vet said gelding lost a shoe (op 10-1)
Appleaday(IRE) lost his position down the back straight, but rallied and ran on in the final stages. (op 10-1 tchd 9-1)
Trigger The Light ◆, without the blinkers he had worn on his last three starts, would have played a bigger part had he not made a bad blunder at the eleventh. It was a pleasing return to action, for which he looked fit enough beforehand, and he should be competitive off this sort of mark over fences if his jumping holds out. (op 16-1)
Bertie May Official explanation: trainer said gelding choked
Quattrocento(FR) Official explanation: vet said gelding lost a shoe

3630 PASHMINA UK "JUNIOR" STANDARD OPEN NATIONAL HUNT FLAT RACE — 1m 4f 110y
4:20 (4:21) (Class 6) 4-Y-O **£1,370** (£399; £199)

Form RPR

1 **Tour D'Argent (FR)** 4-10-12 0.. BarryGeraghty 97+
(Nicky Henderson) *travelled wl: in tch: eased upsides over 2f out: sn tk narrow advantage: pushed clr ins fnl f: readily* **10/11**[1]

6 **2** *4* **Milarrow (IRE)**[45] 2797 4-10-12 0.. JoeTizzard 86
(Colin Tizzard) *trckd ldr: rdn to chal over 3f out: stl upsides wnr ent fnl f: a fighting losing battle: jst hld on to 2nd* **12/1**[3]

3 *shd* **Oscar Flyer (IRE)** 4-10-12 0... RichardJohnson 86
(Tim Vaughan) *mid-div: rdn and stdy prog fr 4f out: styd on: jst failed to snatch 2nd* **12/1**[3]

0 **4** *6* **Glassawine**[45] 2797 4-10-9 0... DannyCook(3) 78
(David Pipe) *led: rdn and hdd 2f out: styd on same pce* **16/1**

5 *10* **Hamilton Hill** 4-10-12 0... JamieMoore 64
(Terry Clement) *towards rr: pushed along 6f out: stdy prog fr 4f out tl wknd over 1f out* **20/1**

6 *nk* **Gleann Eagas (IRE)** 4-10-12 0.. SamThomas 63
(Emma Lavelle) *hld up towards rr: effrt but nvr on terms w ldrs over 3f out: wknd over 1f out* **14/1**

0 **7** *½* **Kala Patthar**[63] 2458 4-10-9 0................................ SamTwiston-Davies(3) 63
(Colin Tizzard) *mid-div: rdn and hdwy to chse ldrs 4f out: wknd over 1f out* **20/1**

0 **8** *14* **The De Thaix (FR)**[70] 2309 4-10-12 0................................. CharliePoste 43
(Robin Dickin) *chsd ldrs tl wknd over 3f out* **50/1**

42 **9** *9* **Polurrian (IRE)**[44] 2824 4-10-12 0.................................... JimmyMcCarthy 30
(Charles Egerton) *chsd ldrs: rdn over 4f out: wknd over 2f out* **7/2**[2]

00 **10** *19* **Roe Valley (IRE)**[44] 2824 4-10-12 0................................ LeightonAspell 4
(Linda Jewell) *t.k.h: hld up towards rr: effrt over 3f out: wknd over 2f out* **100/1**

11 *nk* **Queen's Pawn (IRE)** 4-10-8 0 ow1...................................... MrPYork(5) 4
(Raymond York) *rdn 6f out: a towards rr* **100/1**

3m 6.20s (0.40) **11** Ran SP% **116.0**
toteswingers:1&2 £7.00, 2&3 £13.80, 1&3 £4.90. totesuper7: Win: Not won. Place: Not won. CSF £12.64 TOTE £2.00: £1.10, £2.90, £2.10; EX 17.00.

Owner Michael Buckley **Bred** Haras De Saint-Voir **Trained** Upper Lambourn, Berks

FOCUS
A fair-looking bumper.

NOTEBOOK
Tour D'Argent(FR), whose dam was a multiple winner of non-thoroughbred races in France, was slightly on his toes beforehand and travelled powerfully in behind runners before coming with his effort over 1f out. He didn't lengthen as might have been expected, but still looks promising, although connections won't aim too high this season. His trainer is now 3-3 in this race. (op Evens)
Milarrow(IRE), on his toes in the paddock, was a little disappointing on his Exeter debut, but upheld the form with Glassawine with a keeping-on effort.
Oscar Flyer(IRE), a half-brother to a couple of winners, displayed plenty of ability on his first outing and will do even better over further judged by the way he kept on. (tchd 14-1)
Glassawine, on his toes beforehand, was handed an uncontested lead, and definitely shaped better than he had done on debut even allowing for the early advantage he held. (op 10-1)
Hamilton Hill is related to a few winners and caught the eye just in behind those who fought out the finish. (op 22-1)
Polurrian(IRE), who is a bit on the leg, had experience on his side but was readily brushed aside down the home straight. He might be better suited by quicker ground on turf. (op 9-2 tchd 10-3)
T/Plt: £32.00 to a £1 stake. Pool of £44,226.69 - 1,006.99 winning tickets. T/Qpdt: £6.10 to a £1 stake. Pool of £4,129.48 - 494.80 winning tickets. TM

[3498] NEWCASTLE (L-H)
Wednesday, January 19

OFFICIAL GOING: Soft (heavy in places; good to soft in last 1f; chs 5.4, hdl 5.1)
The two cross fences after the winning post were omitted in all chases due to a low sun. The flight after the post was omitted in the last three hurdle races.
Wind: Slight, half against Weather: Cloudy, bright

3631 LA TAXIS H'CAP HURDLE (9 hdls) — 2m
12:40 (12:40) (Class 5) (0-95,95) 4-Y-0+ **£1,561** (£458; £229; £114)

Form RPR

0P60 **1** **Transact (IRE)**[16] 3363 6-10-0 **69** oh3................................(p) GrahamLee 75
(Martin Todhunter) *in tch: effrt and pushed along whn hit 3 out: rallied: ev ch run-in: styd on u.p to ld towards fin* **9/1**[3]

34/3 **2** *nk* **Sundae Best (IRE)**[56] 2610 7-11-12 **95**.............................. BrianHughes 101
(Howard Johnson) *trckd ldrs: hdwy to ld bef 3 out: rdn bef next: kpt on run-in: hdd towards fin* **12/1**

5444 **3** *3 ½* **Devils Delight (IRE)**[67] 2367 9-9-9 **74**............................ JamesSmith(10) 76
(James Moffatt) *hld up: hdwy and prom bef 2 out: sn rdn: kpt on same pce run-in* **9/2**[2]

-640 **4** *18* **Scarvagh Rose**[17] 3331 6-11-9 **92**................................... WilsonRenwick 76
(Rose Dobbin) *hld up: stdy hdwy and in tch 3 out: hit and wknd next* **14/1**

2-06 **5** *3 ¾* **Pete**[70] 2308 8-11-6 **92**.. EwanWhillans(3) 72
(Barry Murtagh) *hld up: smooth hdwy to trck ldrs bef 3 out: rdn and wknd next* **14/1**

0003 **6** *2 ¾* **Dramatic Jewel (USA)**[19] 3255 5-11-2 **85**...................... PeterBuchanan 63
(Lucinda Russell) *hld up towards rr: drvn and outpcd 1/2-way: rallied bef 3 out: no further imp fr next: lame* **3/1**[1]

04/0 **7** *2 ¼* **Miss Champagne (IRE)**[66] 2398 8-10-0 **69** oh4................. PaddyAspell 44
(Andrew Wilson) *trckd ldrs tl rdn and wknd after 3 out* **33/1**

4101 **8** *10* **Janal (IRE)**[75] 2194 8-10-1 **77**.. GaryRutherford(7) 42
(Stuart Coltherd) *in tch: outpcd bef 4 out: n.d after* **9/1**[3]

-60P **9** *5* **Hair Of The Dog**[192] 948 7-10-0 **69**.............................. CampbellGillies 29
(William Amos) *t.k.h: cl up: led bef 4 out to bef next: wknd bef 2 out* **9/1**[3]

-3P0 **10** *15* **Also Jo**[17] 3335 8-11-10 **93**.. JamesReveley 38
(William Amos) *cl up: ev ch 4 out: wknd bef next* **10/1**

P-62 **11** *7* **Bubses Boy**[75] 2188 5-11-6 **89**.. KennyJohnson 27
(Robert Johnson) *bhd and detached: no ch fr 1/2-way* **40/1**

55-P **12** *12* **Autumn Harvest**[5] 3551 7-11-4 **90**..............................(p) RyanMania(3) 16
(William Young) *led to bef 4 out: wknd qckly bef next* **00/1**

0 **P** **Ulysees (IRE)**[17] 3331 12-11-12 **95**................................... RichieMcGrath —
(Jim Goldie) *mstkes in rr: struggling 4th: t.o whn p.u bef 3 out* **20/1**

4m 15.5s (5.50) **Going Correction** +0.425s/f (Soft) **13** Ran SP% **114.9**
Speed ratings (Par 103): **103,102,101,92,90 88,87,82,80,72 69,63,**—
toteswingers:1&2 £12.40, 2&3 £11.20, 1&3 £9.50 CSF £103.06 CT £551.10 TOTE £10.20: £3.70, £3.80, £1.80; EX 116.40.

Owner P G Airey **Bred** Dr Paschal Carmody **Trained** Orton, Cumbria

FOCUS
No rain but some heavy frosts since the meeting here a week ago and the ground was described as 'very holding' and 'hard work'. A low-grade 69-95 handicap hurdle and just five were still in contention two out.

NOTEBOOK
Transact(IRE), having his third start since returning to this yard, has come down a stone since his handicap debut and had to race from 3lb out of the handicap. After an error three out, he dug deep to show ahead near the line. He wore cheekpieces for the first time, and this looks his trip. (op 11-1)
Sundae Best(IRE) looked to have been given a stiff mark on his handicap bow after finishing a well-beaten third in a claimer on his return. After taking charge, he was only edged out near the finish. (op 10-1)
Devils Delight(IRE), 4lb higher than her sole win in 27 previous attempts at Sedgefield almost a year ago, had a bit to do after an error four out and she looks weighted to the limit. (op 11-2)
Scarvagh Rose, making her handicap debut, dropped away over the last two flights and may just have needed this. (op 16-1)
Pete, who scored twice in 2009, disappointed on his chase debut and then showed little on his return to hurdling. He travelled strongly, but weakened badly late on. He ran without his usual tongue-tie. (op 16-1)
Dramatic Jewel(USA), who seemed to turn in an improved effort when third behind a subsequent winner at Uttoxeter, was never travelling and came under strong pressure before the halfway mark.He was later found to be lame behind. (op 10-3)

3632 MK PARTNERSHIP BEGINNERS' CHASE (11 fncs 2 omitted) — 2m 110y
1:10 (1:10) (Class 4) 5-Y-0+ **£2,499** (£775; £417)

Form RPR

43U4 **1** **Si Bien (FR)**[16] 3359 6-11-0 115.. GrahamLee 116+
(James Ewart) *nt fluent: t.k.h: lft 2nd fr 2nd: effrt and chal whn lft 22 l clr 4 out: 18 l up whn blnd 2 out: shkn up and hld on run-in* **11/8**[2]

2 *1 ¾* **Cloonawillin Lady (IRE)**[332] 8-10-0 0........................... StevenGagan(7) 94
(Elliott Cooper) *chsd ldrs: outpcd fr 4th: lft 22 l 2nd 4 out: styd on wl fr last: nt rch wnr* **50/1**

P0-P **3** *34* **Byron Bay**[57] 2603 9-11-0 0...(p) KennyJohnson 71
(Robert Johnson) *bhd: lost tch bef 4th: lft poor 3rd 4 out* **100/1**

2-42 **F** **Degas Art (IRE)**[66] 2399 8-11-0 0.. BrianHughes —
(Howard Johnson) *cl up: lft in ld 2nd: jnd whn fell 4 out* **5/6**[1]

0/50 **U** **Quinola Des Obeaux (FR)**[22] 3170 7-11-0 112..............(t) DavidDennis —
(Frank Sheridan) *led tl pckd and uns rdr 2nd* **10/1**[3]

4m 31.3s (10.20) **Going Correction** +0.425s/f (Soft) **5** Ran SP% **108.7**
Speed ratings: **93,92,76**,—,—
CSF £27.94 TOTE £2.20: £1.50, £5.10; EX 23.00.

Owner Whistlejacket Partnership **Bred** Mme Ursula Roder & Haras De Preaux **Trained** Langholm, Dumfries & G'way

FOCUS
A weak but incident-packed beginners' chase.

NOTEBOOK
Si Bien(FR)'s jumping was poor and his rider deserves full marks. Left in a long lead four out, he almost went two out and in the end scrambled to hold on. His jumping was poor even before he was left in front and he will need to brush up considerably in that department if he is to progress. (op 6-4 tchd 5-4)
Cloonawillin Lady(IRE), 1-11 in Irish points and having her first outing for almost a year, was left over 20l second four out. Still 15l down two out, she was fast catching the flagging winner at the line. Quite what she actually achieved on the day is open to doubt. (op 40-1)
Byron Bay, who showed next to nothing in two starts over fences last season, has achieved little both over hurdles and on the Flat since. His school round put some money into his owners account. Official explanation: trainer said gelding had a breathing problem

Degas Art(IRE), a smart juvenile hurdler, had already run four times over fences failing to complete on two occasions. He held a narrow advantage when crashing out four from home. The way the race panned out he must have taken a deal of beating, but even so he has plenty to prove. (op Evens tchd 11-10)

3633 MALONE & SONS NOVICES' HURDLE (12 hdls 1 omitted) 3m
1:40 (1:40) (Class 3) 5-Y-0+ **£3,642** (£1,069; £534; £267)

Form				RPR
	1		**Soll**[297] 6-10-12 0 ... DougieCostello (John Quinn) *trckd ldrs: led 4 out: rdn and styd on strly to go clr fr 2 out* **4/1**[2]	116+
5-00	2	10	**Willie Hall**[59] 2552 7-10-12 0 ... CampbellGillies (William Amos) *hld up in tch: stdy hdwy and cl up 3 out: rdn and lft 5 l 2nd next: no imp whn hit last* **9/1**	101+
50-	3	1 ¾	**Foxes Delight (IRE)**[266] 42 7-10-6 0 ow1 ...(t) AlistairFindlay(7) (Jane Walton) *trckd ldrs: hit 7th: outpcd bef 4 out: rallied and lft modest 3rd 3 out: plugged on: no imp* **200/1**	96
05-0	4	1 ¾	**Mannered**[98] 1829 6-10-5 0 ... MrJohnDawson(7) (John Wade) *hld up: stdy hdwy and in tch after 4 out: rdn and one pce after next* **50/1**	93
60-0	5	2 ¼	**Frontier Boy (IRE)**[80] 2102 7-10-5 0 ... NathanMoscrop(7) (James Ewart) *nt fluent: hld up: effrt bef 4 out: no imp fr next* **33/1**	91
2516	6	39	**Bled (FR)**[55] 2642 6-11-4 110 ...(b) JasonMaguire (Donald McCain) *cl up: rdn 1/2-way: wknd fr 4 out: t.o* **6/1**	58
56-1	7	6	**Rupin (FR)**[90] 1928 6-11-1 0 ... RyanMania(3) (Howard Johnson) *led to 4 out: rdn and wknd fr next: t.o* **11/2**	52
P6-	8	39	**Digg Whitaker**[297] 4907 6-10-12 0 ... PeterBuchanan (John Wade) *hld up: struggling 8th: sn btn: t.o* **50/1**	7
6620	F		**Ceasar's Return**[36] 2939 6-10-12 113 ... BarryKeniry (George Moore) *trckd ldrs: rdn 4 out: rallied to chse wnr bef next: 3 l down and one pce whn fell 2 out* **9/2**[3]	101
060-	U		**Hawaii Klass**[314] 4536 6-10-2 0 ... CallumWhillans(10) (Donald Whillans) *mstke and uns rdr 1st* **33/1**	—
4U02	B		**Oil Burner**[16] 3362 6-10-12 100 ... JamesReveley (William Amos) *hld up in tch: stdy hdwy after 4 out: lft 6 l 3rd and one pce whn b.d 2 out* **11/4**[1]	101
0P	P		**Smart Command (IRE)**[67] 2375 7-10-2 0 ... TonyKelly(10) (Ferdy Murphy) *bhd and sn struggling: t.o whn p.u 4 out* **100/1**	—

6m 29.9s (15.90) **Going Correction** +0.425s/f (Soft) **12** Ran SP% **115.8**
Speed ratings: **90,86,86,85,84 71,69,56,—,— —,—**
toteswingers:1&2 £10.20, 2&3 £29.50, 1&3 £29.50 CSF £36.76 TOTE £5.30: £1.90, £2.60, £19.50; EX 47.80.
Owner Derrick Mossop **Bred** D Mossop **Trained** Settrington, N Yorks

FOCUS
A modest stayers' novice hurdle that was a real test in the conditions and produced a winner of some potential.

NOTEBOOK
Soll, game winner of an Irish maiden point in March, is a giant of a horse. He looked in command when left clear two out but in the end had to be kept right up to his work. This is his ground and this potential chaser will improve fitness wise for the outing. (op 6-1)
Willie Hall, a bumper winner here, had been beaten a long way in two previous outings over hurdles. He moved into contention four out but was well held in fourth when left second two out. He put in a very tired jump at the last and will appreciate a less stiff test on much better ground. (op 10-1 tchd 11-1)
Foxes Delight(IRE), a very moderate winning pointer and an erratic jumper, was last seen over hurdles almost a year ago. Struggling to keep up over 1m out, his stamina enabled him to secure a remote third spot two out. He just stays.
Mannered, having his second start over hurdles, may be seen to better light in modest stayers' handicaps later on.
Bled(FR), given reminders with a circuit to go, stopped to nothing four out. His official mark of 110 flatters him. (tchd 11-2)
Rupin(FR), who took a very weak event at Carlisle in October, was another to help force the pace but he too stopped to nothing in the final straight. (op 9-2 tchd 4-1)
Ceasar's Return, driven five out, was in pursuit of the winner but seemingly held when he took a heavy fall two out. (op 4-1)
Oil Burner, a free-going sort, moved up looking a real danger but the needle was on empty when he was brought down at the penultimate flight. He would not want ground as testing as he encountered here. (op 4-1)

3634 PARKLANDS GOLF COURSE H'CAP CHASE (16 fncs 2 omitted) 3m
2:15 (2:15) (Class 3) (0-130,130) 5-Y-0+ **£4,553** (£1,337; £668; £333)

Form				RPR
1/51	1		**Cavers Glen**[59] 2544 9-10-10 114 ... BrianHarding (Alistair Whillans) *hld up in tch: stdy hdwy bef 5 out: effrt and led 3 out: 8 l clr last: kpt on wl* **5/1**[2]	123+
4/03	2	4 ½	**See You There (IRE)**[63] 2449 12-10-10 114 ...(t) PeterBuchanan (Lucinda Russell) *trckd ldrs: chal fr 1/2-way: mstke 5 out: rdn and outpcd 3 out: styd on wl fr last: tk 2nd last stride* **25/1**	115
PP0-	3	hd	**Morgan Be**[291] 4980 11-10-11 115 ... RichieMcGrath (Kate Walton) *mstkes: towards rr: stdy hdwy bef 5 out: kpt on to chse (wnr) last: kpt on same pce run-in: lost 2nd last stride* **17/2**	117
66P4	4	1 ¾	**Daldini**[14] 3395 9-10-0 104 oh1 ... TjadeCollier (Sue Smith) *led: hit 9th: rdn and hdd 3 out: kpt on same pce after next* **9/2**[1]	104
P-2F	P		**Minster Shadow**[59] 2543 12-11-6 124 ...(v) CampbellGillies (Chris Grant) *hld up towards rr: drvn along whn mstke 9th: sn struggling: t.o whn p.u 5 out* **9/1**	—
P/P2	P		**Negus De Beaumont (FR)**[8] 3499 10-10-11 115 ... GrahamLee (Ferdy Murphy) *nt fluent in rr: struggling 1/2-way: t.o whn p.u bef 5 out* **5/1**[2]	—
12-0	P		**Fiftyfive Degrees (IRE)**[74] 2205 10-10-8 112 ...(p) TimmyMurphy (Pauline Robson) *blkd 1st: prom: drvn 1/2-way: rallied: wknd bef 11th: t.o whn p.u bef 4 out* **5/1**[2]	—
U136	P		**Or De Grugy (FR)**[17] 3333 9-11-2 125 ... AlexanderVoy(5) (Sue Bradburne) *cl up tl rdn and wknd after 9th: t.o whn p.u 5 out* **16/1**	—
1F-6	P		**Captain Tidds (IRE)**[71] 2293 10-11-5 123 ... SeanQuinlan (Richard Phillips) *mstkes in rr: struggling fr 9th: t.o whn p.u 5 out* **8/1**[3]	—
3P0P	F		**Vodka Brook (IRE)**[9] 3488 8-11-5 130 ...(b[1]) MrMWalford(7) (Tim Walford) *trckd ldrs: rdn bef 4 out: mstke and outpcd 3 out: wl btn whn fell heavily last: fatally injured* **14/1**	120

6m 28.1s (5.60) **Going Correction** +0.425s/f (Soft) **10** Ran SP% **116.2**
Speed ratings: **107,105,105,104,— —,—,—,—,—**
toteswingers:1&2 £36.40, 2&3 £25.80, 1&3 £17.90 CSF £106.41 CT £1040.76 TOTE £4.20: £1.50, £5.70, £4.10; EX 87.00.
Owner John & Liz Elliot, A Brunton, P Copeland **Bred** J J Elliot **Trained** Newmill-On-Slitrig, Borders

FOCUS
A 104-130 stayers' handicap and a war of attrition in the glue pot ground.

NOTEBOOK
Cavers Glen, 11lb higher than when accounting for a subsequent good winner at Aintree in November, sensibly wanted nothing to do with the hectic early pace. Working his way into contention on the final circuit, he went on travelling much the strongest and was able to ease off near the line. This was a fine training feat after the lengthy freeze-up and connections are now looking at the Eider Chase over 4m here next month. (op 4-1 tchd 11-2)
See You There(IRE), 8lb below his last win over two years ago, deserves credit because he raced upsides throughout in a race run at a very strong pace. This may be as good as the old boy is now. (op 22-1)
Morgan Be, out of sorts last season, has come down a stone as a result. Clattering his way round, his stamina enabled him to fight it out for a modest second place on the run-in. (op 12-1 tchd 8-1)
Daldini found himself involved in a three-way battle for the lead and it took its toll in the end. His last success, almost a year ago now, came from a 14lb higher mark and his turn will surely come again. (tchd 4-1)
Negus De Beaumont(FR) was reported to have finished distressed. Official explanation: trainer said gelding finished distressed (op 11-2)
Vodka Brook(IRE), who seemed to lose his way after his good third at Carlisle in October on his first outing for this yard, stopped to nothing after an error three out and was a remote and tired fifth when sadly taking a fatal fall at the final fence. (op 11-2)

3635 BOOKER CASH & CARRY CONDITIONAL JOCKEYS' H'CAP HURDLE (10 hdls 1 omitted) 2m 4f
2:50 (2:56) (Class 4) (0-105,105) 4-Y-0+ **£2,016** (£592; £296; £147)

Form				RPR
1/04	1		**Kings Guard (IRE)**[63] 2448 8-10-6 88 ... EwanWhillans(3) (Alistair Whillans) *t.k.h: trckd ldrs: effrt 3 out: led last: drvn clr run-in* **5/2**[1]	97+
-0FP	2	6	**Double Default (IRE)**[16] 3362 10-11-12 105 ... JamesHalliday (Martin Todhunter) *cl up: led 3 out to last: kpt on same pce u.p run-in* **20/1**	107
-001	3	4 ½	**Bene Lad (IRE)**[16] 3363 9-11-1 94 ... CampbellGillies (Jim Goldie) *nt fluent on occasions: led to 3 out: drvn and outpcd fr next* **10/3**[2]	94+
0-00	4	11	**Euro American (GER)**[63] 2448 11-11-5 98 ... RyanMania (Rose Dobbin) *hld up: stdy hdwy to trck ldrs 3 out: rdn and wknd next* **8/1**	89
0-P6	5	17	**Ravensbill (IRE)**[16] 3363 9-10-2 81 ... FearghalDavis (William Amos) *hld up in tch: outpcd 5th: rallied 4 out: wknd bef next* **10/1**	50
-02P	6	2 ¼	**Tiger Line**[37] 2929 7-10-4 89 ... PeterCarberry(6) (Richard Phillips) *hld up towards rr: drvn and outpcd 6th: sn struggling* **4/1**[3]	56
00-P	7	15	**Archdale Lady (IRE)**[103] 1760 7-9-9 79 oh1 ... HenryBrooke(5) (Ferdy Murphy) *hld up in tch: stdy hdwy and cl up 1/2-way: wknd after 4 out* **25/1**	31
3/0-	8	12	**Robbie Dye**[616] 295 9-10-3 90 ... CallumWhillans(8) (Donald Whillans) *hld up: struggling bef 4 out: sn btn* **12/1**	30
0300	P		**Mardood**[36] 2941 6-10-6 88 ...(p) AlexanderVoy(3) (Chris Grant) *trckd ldrs tl rdn and wknd after 6th: p.u after next* **12/1**	—

5m 31.4s (10.30) **Going Correction** +0.425s/f (Soft) **9** Ran SP% **115.8**
Speed ratings (Par 105): **96,93,91,87,80 79,73,68,—**
toteswingers:1&2 £6.60, 2&3 £11.30, 1&3 £2.40 CSF £48.12 CT £170.82 TOTE £3.70: £1.30, £5.00, £1.70; EX 66.20.
Owner J D Wright **Bred** James J Donohoe **Trained** Newmill-On-Slitrig, Borders

FOCUS
A modest 79-105 conditional jockeys' handicap hurdle. The pace was sound and there were just four in with a shout from three out.

NOTEBOOK
Kings Guard(IRE), absent for a year and a half after opening his account from an 8lb lower mark over 3m at Carlisle, ran with the choke out. After a good tussle he came out on top on the run-in and will be even better back over further. (op 11-4 tchd 3-1)
Double Default(IRE), a dual winner for another yard in 2007, has failed to complete four times in seven starts since. He travelled strongly and, after taking charge, went down fighting. At least he is back on song. (op 28-1 tchd 33-1)
Bene Lad(IRE), 7lb higher than his Ayr success, took them along at a good clip but had no more to give two out. A dual winner over fences, now may be the right time to revert to the major obstacles. (op 11-4 tchd 7-2)
Euro American(GER), a dual course winner, the latest from a 31lb higher mark almost five years ago now, doesn't have time on his side now. This was a slightly more encouraging run but this may be the limit of his ability now. (tchd 7-1)
Tiger Line ran disappointingly for no obvious reason for a second time and there must be reservations about her now. (tchd 7-2)

3636 S.V. RUTTER LTD BEST WISHES FOR 2011 H'CAP CHASE (14 fncs 2 omitted) 2m 4f
3:25 (3:26) (Class 5) (0-90,93) 5-Y-0+ **£1,552** (£458; £229; £114; £57)

Form				RPR
0526	1		**Dark Gentleman**[16] 3360 8-10-12 77 ... RyanMania(3) (Evelyn Slack) *mde all: clr 1/2-way: rdn and 4 l up last: hld on wl run-in* **20/1**	89+
/436	2	nk	**Mighty Magnus (IRE)**[36] 2942 8-11-7 83 ... JamesReveley (Martin Todhunter) *hld up: stdy hdwy bef 5 out: wnt 8 l 2nd next: effrt and 4 l down last: kpt on run-in* **8/1**[3]	92
-550	3	12	**Teenando (IRE)**[213] 804 11-11-5 81 ... HenryOliver (Sue Smith) *cl up: wnt 2nd 9th to 4 out: sn outpcd: no imp fr next* **16/1**	80
U644	4	2 ¾	**Seek The Truth (IRE)**[16] 3360 8-10-12 74 ... GrahamLee (Sue Bradburne) *prom: lft 2nd and hmpd 8th: sn drvn: outpcd next: no imp fr 4 out* **4/1**[2]	70
4045	5	36	**Prince Tam**[16] 3360 7-11-4 80 ...(p) CampbellGillies (Lucinda Russell) *hld up: hmpd 8th: struggling fr next: btn bef 4 out* **20/1**	38
P-00	6	hd	**Glengap (IRE)**[231] 578 8-10-2 71 ... StevenGagan(7) (Elliott Cooper) *hld up in tch: hmpd and outpcd 8th: struggling fr next: t.o* **33/1**	29
5633	P		**Panthers Run**[55] 2645 11-10-4 66 ...(t) DougieCostello (Jonathan Haynes) *hld up: struggling 9th: sn btn: t.o whn p.u bef 4 out* **14/1**	—
4-6F	F		**Native Coll**[16] 3360 11-11-0 83 ... MissLAlexander(7) (N W Alexander) *chsd clr ldr: fell 8th* **9/1**	—
P-53	P		**Paddys Unyoke (IRE)**[8] 3503 10-11-12 88 ... BrianHarding (Stuart Coltherd) *prom: lost pl and reminders bef 4th: struggling bef 7th: t.o whn p.u bef next* **12/1**	—
3-31	P		**Do It For Dalkey**[8] 3503 9-12-3 93 7ex ... PeterBuchanan (Lucinda Russell) *towards rr: hdwy and in tch 4th: struggling after 9th: t.o whn p.u bef 4 out* **11/8**[1]	—

5m 43.2s (16.00) **Going Correction** +0.425s/f (Soft) **10** Ran SP% **115.9**
Speed ratings: **85,84,80,78,64 64,—,—,—,—**
toteswingers:1&2 £21.60, 2&3 £19.80, 1&3 £24.60 CSF £165.39 CT £2626.26 TOTE £24.90: £2.50, £1.70, £3.20; EX 112.70.
Owner A Slack **Bred** A Slack **Trained** Hilton, Cumbria

FOCUS
A low grade handicap chase and again the pace was sound in the holding ground.
NOTEBOOK
Dark Gentleman, runner-up from a 3lb lower mark at Market Rasen in November, was unable to dominate when sulking and well beaten at Ayr next time. Here, though, he had his own way out in front and just did enough after jumping the last with a 4l advantage. (op 18-1 tchd 25-1)
Mighty Magnus(IRE), stepping up in trip on just his third start for this yard after a lengthy spell on the sidelines, went in pursuit of the winner four out. He was closing on the run-in, but was never going to quite get there. That elusive first win is hopefully just around the corner. (op 9-1 tchd 15-2)
Teenando(IRE), whose three career wins come in testing conditions at Carlisle, the latest from a 12lb higher mark almost two years ago, had conditions to suit but these days he is not the most fluent of jumpers. (op 12-1)
Seek The Truth(IRE), another who has slipped to a lenient mark, dropped right out four from home and does not appreciate conditions as testing as he encountered here. (op 11-2)
Do It For Dalkey, penalised for his C&D success a week earlier, did not jump fluently and dropped right out 1m from home. This was only the 9-y-o's third start over fences and it almost certainly came too soon on the back of his success. (op 15-8 tchd 2-1)

3637 GOSFORTH DECORATING & BUILDING SERVICES MARES' MAIDEN HURDLE (8 hdls 1 omitted) 2m
4:00 (4:01) (Class 4) 4-Y-0+ **£2,016** (£592; £296; £147)

Form				RPR
3-24	1		**Empress Orchid**[15] 3389 6-11-2 105 JasonMaguire (Donald McCain) *mde all: pushed clr bef last: eased run-in* 4/5[1]	104+
240	2	4 ½	**Thornton Alice**[16] 3365 6-11-2 0 SeanQuinlan (Richard Phillips) *hld up: hdwy and prom bef 3 out: effrt next: wnt 2nd run-in: kpt on: no ch w wnr* 8/1[3]	91
41-0	3	2 ¾	**Lesanda**[17] 3330 5-11-2 0 BrianHughes (Richard Fahey) *prom: hdwy to chse wnr bef 3 out: effrt next: lost 2nd run-in: no ex* 14/1	89
50	4	14	**Short Supply (USA)**[15] 2640 5-11-2 0 RobertWalford (Tim Walford) *chsd wnr: lost 2nd whn hit 3 out: wknd fr next* 20/1	76
P-P4	5	10	**Roll Over Rose (IRE)**[68] 2353 6-11-2 100 CampbellGillies (William Amos) *trckd ldrs tl rdn and wknd bef 3 out* 10/3[2]	66
	6	2 ½	**Chichina (USA)**[38] 4-10-5 0 (p) PaddyAspell (Tracy Waggott) *in tch tl rdn and wknd bef 3 out* 100/1	51
0-06	7	2 ¼	**Tchikita (FR)**[68] 2353 8-10-9 95 NathanMoscrop[(7)] (James Ewart) *mstkes: towards rr: struggling after 4 out: btn next* 20/1	60
50	8	2 ½	**Seminal Moment**[59] 2547 5-10-13 0 EwanWhillans[(3)] (William Amos) *midfield: struggling after 4 out: sn btn* 100/1	57
00	9	5	**Zefooha (FR)**[12] 2370 7-11-2 0 PeterBuchanan (Tim Walford) *hld up towards rr: struggling 4 out: sn btn* 33/1	52
P/	10	3 ¾	**Princess Aliuska**[60] 5029 6-10-13 0 JohnKington[(3)] (Charles Smith) *hld up: struggling 4 out: sn btn* 100/1	48
	11	5	**Drumlargan Girl (IRE)**[261] 128 6-11-2 0 JamesReveley (Martin Todhunter) *prom: nt fluent 4 out: wknd bef next* 28/1	43
0	12	84	**Another Mystery**[62] 2473 6-10-13 0 RyanMania[(3)] (Evelyn Slack) *wnt rt s and rel to r: t.o thrght* 200/1	—
	P		**Maybeme**[17] 5-10-11 0 BrianToomey[(5)] (Neville Bycroft) *a bhd: struggling 1/2-way: t.o whn p.u 2 out* 50/1	—

4m 27.7s (17.70) **Going Correction** +0.425s/f (Soft)
WFA 4 from 5yo+ 11lb **13** Ran SP% **117.8**
Speed ratings (Par 105): **72,69,68,61,56 55,54,52,50,48 45,3,—**
toteswingers:1&2 £11.80, 2&3 £7.90, 1&3 £2.80 CSF £7.24 TOTE £2.30: £1.30, £2.50, £1.70; EX 11.80.
Owner W Bromley & Mrs L King **Bred** Robin Smith **Trained** Cholmondeley, Cheshire

FOCUS
A typically weak mares' maiden hurdle with plenty of deadwood. No one wanted to make it and they stood still for about seven seconds when the tapes went across.
NOTEBOOK
Empress Orchid, placed in three starts in bumper company, would have opened her account over an extra 4f here two starts ago but for tying up on the run-in. Her hurdling has improved and with no-one wanting to make it, she was soon taking them along. She went clear on the run-in and won easing down. Connections will no doubt be seeking more of the same under a penalty. (op 8-11 tchd 10-11)
Thornton Alice, who changed hands for £5,000 after finishing runner-up on her debut in a Wetherby bumper, showed little on her first start over hurdles. She crept her way into the race but in the end she is flattered by the margin of defeat.
Lesanda, winner of a soft-ground bumper at Sedgefield, showed little on her first try over hurdles after a year on the sidelines. She showed a lot more here and there may be a little more to come. (op 12-1)
Short Supply(USA), a winner three times on the level, the latest coming since her second try over hurdles, showed a fair bit more, but she was tired and on the retreat when clouting the second last. She may do better in modest handicap company on less testing ground in the spring.
Roll Over Rose(IRE), fourth when Empress Orchid was a luckless runner-up here over an extra 4f in November, was hard at work and going nowhere once in line for home. She may well have needed this after the freeze up. (op 4-1 tchd 3-1)
Zefooha(FR) is another who may fare better in modest handicap company on much better ground in due course.
T/Jkpt: Not won. T/Plt: £1,991.70 to a £1 stake. Pool of £63,708.19 - 23.35 winning tickets. T/Qpdt: £268.30 to a £1 stake. Pool of £6,419.79 - 17.70 winning tickets. RY

2584 LUDLOW (R-H)
Thursday, January 20
3638 Meeting Abandoned - Frost

3477 TAUNTON (R-H)
Thursday, January 20
OFFICIAL GOING: Good to soft (soft in places; 6.9)
Rails moved on bends increasing distances by circa 50m per circuit.
Wind: virtually nil Weather: bright and sunny

3645 JAYS/GG BIRTHDAY NOVICES' HURDLE (9 hdls) 2m 1f
1:30 (1:30) (Class 4) 4-Y-0+ **£3,425** (£998; £499)

Form				RPR
3-00	1		**Shammick Boy (IRE)**[21] 3225 6-11-4 0 AndrewGlassonbury (Victor Dartnall) *mde all: nt fluent 3rd: styd on strly fr 2 out: unchal: comf* 9/1[3]	120+
1	2	10	**Credit Swap**[16] 3386 6-11-10 0 AidanColeman (Venetia Williams) *mid-div: hdwy after 5th: wnt 2nd after 3 out: rdn bef next: kpt on but no imp on comfortable wnr* 4/7[1]	115+
6-21	3	4	**Bermuda Boy (FR)**[19] 3296 6-11-5 0 IanPopham[(5)] (Paul Nicholls) *in tch: trckd ldrs 4th: rdn after 3 out: styd on same pce* 3/1[2]	111
-100	4	10	**Ben Cee Pee M (IRE)**[8] 3505 6-11-4 0 LeightonAspell (Oliver Sherwood) *hld up towards rr: rdn and stdy prog fr 3 out: wnt 4th 2 out: styd on same pce* 66/1	96
21-0	5	4 ½	**Thunderstorm (IRE)**[10] 3478 6-11-4 0 RhysFlint (Philip Hobbs) *in tch: rdn after 6th: nvr any imp on ldrs* 12/1	92
00	6	4	**Mr Bachster (IRE)**[62] 2499 6-10-11 0 EdGlassonbury[(7)] (Victor Dartnall) *mid-div: hdwy 6th to trck ldrs: rdn whn hit 3 out: wknd next* 100/1	90
/0-0	7	9	**Red Rock (FR)**[19] 3295 6-11-4 0 DarylJacob (Tor Sturgis) *hld up towards rr: blnd 2 out and last: nvr any real imp on ldrs* 150/1	83
U	8	1 ¾	**Yourgolftravel Com**[10] 3477 6-11-1 0 (t) DannyCook[(3)] (David Pipe) *a towards rr* 50/1	79
0	9	11	**Lady From Ige (IRE)**[19] 3296 7-10-11 0 RodiGreene (Neil Mulholland) *a towards rr* 100/1	62
00	10	2	**Senses (USA)**[7] 3526 5-11-4 0 JohnnyFarrelly (David Pipe) *mid-div: rdn after 6th: sn btn* 50/1	67
000	11	1	**Jomade (IRE)**[10] 3478 5-11-4 0 SeanQuinlan (Kim Bailey) *chsd ldrs tl after 4th: sn towards rr* 100/1	66
4	12	6	**Time Book (IRE)**[17] 3376 5-11-4 0 JamieMoore (Gary Moore) *mid-div: trckd ldrs 4th: rdn after 3 out: fdd fr next* 25/1	61
0-0	13	6	**Mac Beattie**[62] 2499 5-11-4 0 PaulMoloney (Evan Williams) *trckd ldrs tl wknd 3 out* 100/1	55
0B-	14	13	**Monopole (IRE)**[515] 1294 7-11-4 0 GerrySupple (David Pipe) *mid-div tl wknd bef 3 out* 100/1	44

4m 8.90s (0.90) **Going Correction** +0.175s/f (Yiel) **14** Ran SP% **121.2**
Speed ratings (Par 105): **104,99,97,92,90 88,84,83,78,77 77,74,71,65**
toteswingers:1&2:£4.40, 1&3:£5.50, 2&3:£1.10 CSF £15.16 TOTE £11.80: £2.40, £1.10, £1.10; EX 24.30.
Owner First Brayford Partnership **Bred** Miss D Flanagan **Trained** Brayford, Devon

FOCUS
A race won by decent sorts in the past, like Ghizao, so this may have been a good contest. A big step forward from the winner under a positive ride.
NOTEBOOK
Shammick Boy(IRE) stole this under a great ride by Andrew Glassonbury. A horse that shaped as though further than this 2m1f would suit last time, he was sent into an easy lead and then injected some pace at the start of the second circuit, gaining himself a nice advantage and getting a few rivals off the bridle. His rider wisely kept something in reserve and the pair out-ran their rivals down the home straight. He looks a useful sort now his running style has been sorted out, and has the shape to jump fences in the future. (op 10-1)
Credit Swap got the job done on his hurdling debut at Leicester, despite being weak in the market, but was far from impressive. He ran a similar race here under his penalty, as he made hard work of making ground under pressure and just couldn't get to the front. A slightly stiffer test or further may suit. (op 8-15 tchd 1-2 and 8-13)
Bermuda Boy(FR) raced enthusiastically at the head of the chasing pack, but came under pressure after jumping the last hurdle in the back straight and made little impression from that point. Official explanation: jockey said that the gelding hung right handed. (op 4-1)
Ben Cee Pee M(IRE), down in trip, ran his best race over hurdles and is one to keep an eye out for in a low-grade handicap on much quicker ground.
Thunderstorm(IRE) ◆'s beaten distance doesn't do him justice. He looks to have more than enough ability to win something in due course.

3646 SHOREDITCH H'CAP CHASE (19 fncs) 3m 3f
2:00 (2:00) (Class 4) (0-110,113) 5-Y-0+ **£4,110** (£1,198; £599)

Form				RPR
5125	1		**Rudinero (IRE)**[37] 2950 9-10-0 83 (t) MichaelMurphy[(3)] (Barry Brennan) *mid-div: trckd ldr fr 5th: led 15th tl next: sn rdn: 3 l down whn lft wl clr 3 out* 6/1	96
22P0	2	16	**River Indus**[21] 3230 11-11-2 103 JoshuaMoore[(7)] (Bob Buckler) *chsd ldrs: awkward 4th: rdn appr 13th: plugged on: no ch fr 4 out: lft modest 2nd next* 20/1	101
-4P4	3	nk	**Lavenoak Lad**[21] 3230 11-11-0 101 (t) NathanSweeney[(7)] (Simon Burrough) *in tch: rdn after 12th: plugged on fr 4 out: lft modest 3rd next* 14/1	97
5360	4	25	**Son Histoire (FR)**[20] 3263 7-11-12 106 (b) RichardJohnson (Philip Hobbs) *led: blnd bdly 10th: hdd 15th: sn rdn: wknd 4 out: lft poor 4th next: t.o* 10/1	82
-121	5	7	**Abbey Dore (IRE)**[13] 3431 8-11-4 101 JimmyDerham[(3)] (Seamus Mullins) *in tch: rdn after 12th: sn no ch: t.o* 9/2[2]	69
-243	6	4	**Reland (FR)**[59] 2585 6-11-8 102 PaddyBrennan (Nigel Twiston-Davies) *chsd ldrs: rdn whn mstke 13th: wknd after next: t.o* 6/1	68
5-53	7	10	**Aconitum (GER)**[21] 3230 6-11-2 96 (v) DougieCostello (Neil Mulholland) *nvr travelling or fluent: sn detached: t.o* 4/1[1]	56
43-P	8	23	**Wizard Of Edge**[98] 1843 11-11-1 95 TimmyMurphy (Ron Hodges) *prom early: chsd ldrs fr 5th: nt fluent 7th: struggling and lost tch 12th: t.o* 16/1	29
1160	F		**Chico Time (IRE)**[10] 3483 10-10-11 98 (b) StephenO'Donovan[(7)] (Norma Twomey) *slowly away: in rr whn fell heavily 2nd* 16/1	—
-563	F		**Glebehall Bay (IRE)**[36] 2953 8-11-2 96 AidanColeman (Venetia Williams) *chsd ldrs: rdn appr 13th: mstke 14th: led after 4 out: 3 l clr whn fell next* 11/2[3]	113+

7m 13.3s (9.90) **Going Correction** +0.425s/f (Soft) **10** Ran SP% **114.4**
Speed ratings: **102,97,97,89,87 86,83,76,—,—**
toteswingers:1&2:£38.00, 1&3:£31.40, 2&3:£31.90 CSF £105.82 CT £1597.08 TOTE £7.60: £4.30, £4.40, £2.90; EX 166.10.
Owner David Gibbons **Bred** A J Keane And Stephen Ryan **Trained** Lambourn, Berks

FOCUS
This looked an open contest. Ordinary form, with a personal best from Rudinero and from faller Glebehall Bay, who has been rated a 4l winner.
NOTEBOOK
Rudinero(IRE) had come well clear with Glebehall Bay down the back straight and was left with a big advantage when that horse fell three out. He was nicely backed throughout the day and is a fair sort at his level over staying trips. (op 7-1)
River Indus, up in trip, needed driving along even earlier than Glebehall Bay and proved to be thoroughly one-paced. (op 18-1)
Lavenoak Lad got behind and never figured. (op 12-1)
Son Histoire(FR), dropped 3lb since his last outing, set a fair pace but found little once joined. (op 9-1 tchd 17-2)
Abbey Dore(IRE) has been winning plenty of low-grade events but was 15lb higher than for his last win/run. Ridden patiently, he never looked like getting on terms. (op 4-1)

Reland(FR) travelled strongly just in behind the leaders and was making ground until hitting the 13th. (op 7-1)

Aconitum(GER) didn't look in the best of moods at the start and during the race. (op 9-2)

Chico Time(IRE), back over fences and with blinkers replacing cheekpieces, started slowly, didn't jump the first with any enthusiasm and ploughed through the second after taking off far too early, sending her rider to the floor. (op 6-1 tchd 5-1)

Glebehall Bay(IRE) came off the bridle a long way out but Aidan Coleman never gave up and forced his mount to the front after four out. The pair looked all set to hold on until landing far too steeply at the next. (op 6-1 tchd 5-1)

3647 EUROPEAN BREEDERS' FUND "NATIONAL HUNT" NOVICES' HURDLE (QUALIFIER) (10 hdls) — 2m 3f 110y

2:30 (2:30) (Class 4) 4-7-Y-0 — **£3,425** (£998; £499)

Form	Pos	Dist	Horse / Trainer / Comment	SP	RPR
2-F3	1		**Al Ferof (FR)**[22] 3197 6-11-5 0 HarrySkelton (Paul Nicholls) *trckd ldrs: led 5th: drew wl clr fr 7th: unextended*	1/7[1]	121+
4-0	2	20	**His Lordship**[251] 319 7-11-5 0 NickScholfield (Grant Cann) *mid-div: hdwy to chse wnr after 6th: rdn and no ch w wnr fr 3 out: styd on same pce*	25/1	98
	3	8	**Kim Tian Road (IRE)**[158] 1268 5-10-9 0 RichieMcLernon(3) (Martin Hill) *hld up towards rr: hdwy fr 6th: rdn to chal for 2nd fr 3 out but no ch w wnr: blnd last*	14/1[2]	89+
4/0-	4	27	**Barton Cliche**[628] 120 6-11-5 0 DougieCostello (Neil Mulholland) *trckd ldrs: rdn and wknd sn after 3 out: t.o*	25/1	67
	5	10	**Kadalkin (FR)**[262] 5-11-5 0 LiamHeard (Nigel Hawke) *mid-div: rdn whn hit 3 out: sn wknd: t.o*	40/1	58
0	6	2½	**Ronnie Ronalde (IRE)**[19] 3301 6-11-0 0 IanPopham(5) (Nick Mitchell) *hld up towards rr: nvr any real imp: wknd after 3 out: t.o*	22/1	55
0P	7	12	**Another Round (IRE)**[37] 2946 7-11-2 0 (b[1]) MarcGoldstein(3) (Laura Young) *led: wnt rt 2nd: hdd 5th: chsd wnr: mstke next: wknd 7th: t.o*	100/1	44
-4P0	8	2	**Big Knickers**[12] 3439 6-10-7 0 MrMMO'Connor(5) (Neil Mulholland) *a towards rr: t.o fr 7th*	18/1[3]	36
0-	9	12	**Sir Ocus**[347] 3915 5-11-5 0 JoeTizzard (Colin Tizzard) *mid-div: rdn appr 7th: sn wknd: t.o*	18/1[3]	32
0/0P	10	3¼	**Tanners Emperor**[78] 2143 7-11-2 0 TommyPhelan(3) (Claire Dyson) *chsd ldrs tl after 4th: sn in rr: t.o*	100/1	29
0	11	3½	**Dapple Prince (IRE)**[83] 2074 6-11-5 0 DarylJacob (Tom Gretton) *a towards rr: t.o fr 7th*	100/1	26
0-PP	P		**Midnight Paradise**[19] 3295 5-10-5 0 (tp) MarkQuinlan(7) (Neil Mulholland) *w ldrs: pushed along fr 4th: wknd bef 6th: t.o whn p.u bef 7th*	100/1	—

4m 47.6s (1.60) **Going Correction** +0.175s/f (Yiel) 12 Ran SP% **123.1**

Speed ratings: **103,95,91,81,77 76,71,70,65,64 62,—**

toteswingers:1&2:£3.00, 1&3:£2.10, 2&3:£39.30 CSF £11.60 TOTE £1.10: £1.02, £4.50, £1.90; EX 6.00.

Owner J Hales **Bred** J Rauch & G Chenu **Trained** Ditcheat, Somerset

FOCUS

A Ferof stood out in an otherwise weak novice hurdle. He was value for further but is rated a stone+ off his best form.

NOTEBOOK

Al Ferof(FR) got to the lead with over a circuit to go and won easily against some very moderate performers. His confidence will have been boosted, and he is likely to have one more race before being aimed at the Neptune Hurdle in March. (op 1-8 tchd 2-13)

His Lordship had run respectably on his racecourse debut, and chased Al Ferof home on his first run over hurdles. (op 33-1)

Kim Tian Road(IRE), having her first run since leaving Ireland, kept plugging away for third and was a country mile in front of the remainder.

3648 THURLBEAR H'CAP CHASE (12 fncs) — 2m 110y

3:00 (3:00) (Class 4) (0-115,115) 5-Y-0+ — **£4,110** (£1,198; £599)

Form	Pos	Dist	Horse / Trainer / Comment	SP	RPR
4012	1		**Bedarra Boy**[9] 3494 5-10-10 **102** DarylJacob (David Arbuthnot) *hld up in tch: trckd ldrs after 5th: blnd 8th: led 4 out: clr whn mstke 2 out: comf*	6/4[1]	117+
P/P-	2	15	**Stoway (FR)**[439] 2130 9-11-7 **110** JodieMogford (Richard Lee) *chsd ldrs: struggling whn lft 4th 4 out: lft modest 3rd 3 out: wnt 2nd run-in: no ch w wnr*	12/1	109
0-13	3	2½	**Baseball Ted (IRE)**[17] 3375 9-11-3 **106** RichardJohnson (Charlie Longsdon) *led tl 2nd: chsd ldr: rdn after 4 out: jst lost 2nd whn lft clr 2nd 3 out: wknd after 2 out: lost 2nd run-in*	11/4[2]	105
002P	4	46	**Coach Lane**[13] 3433 10-11-6 **109** HarrySkelton (Nick Mitchell) *chsd ldrs: pushed along fr 5th: rdn whn blnd bdly 7th: sn no ch: t.o*	10/1	77
550P	5	3	**Award Winner**[23] 3157 8-11-7 **113** RichieMcLernon(3) (Brendan Powell) *in tch: rdn after 6th: wknd 4 out: t.o*	25/1	63
0334	F		**Cantabilly (IRE)**[7] 3531 8-11-7 **115** MattGriffiths(5) (Ron Hodges) *hld up: rdn and hdwy fr 8th: jst gone 2 l 2nd and styng on whn fell 3 out*	5/1[3]	114
U/40	U		**Paquet Cadeau (FR)**[61] 2530 8-11-7 **110** AndrewTinkler (Henry Daly) *led whn rchd for 2nd: hdd whn blnd and uns rdr 4 out*	10/1	—

4m 17.7s (7.70) **Going Correction** +0.425s/f (Soft)

WFA 5 from 8yo+ 3lb 7 Ran SP% **113.1**

Speed ratings: **98,90,89,68,66 —,—**

toteswingers:1&2:£14.50, 1&3:£1.40, 2&3:£4.30 CSF £18.37 TOTE £2.90: £1.90, £4.60; EX 22.50.

Owner P M Claydon **Bred** Mickley Stud & E Kent **Trained** Compton, Berks

FOCUS

An ordinary contest. The winner was value for further and the faller was heading for his mark.

NOTEBOOK

Bedarra Boy looked interesting off bottom weight and was left in front leaving the back straight when Paquet Cadeau departed. Running for a stable in great form, his rider did well to sit a bad mistake two out before steering his mount home for an easy success. (op 9-4)

Stoway(FR), absent since pulling up for Charlie Longsdon back in November 2009, jumped big and boldly close up before losing his place down the back straight. However, his rider didn't give up and the pair ran on strongly to snatch second place. His best form, when he was at his peak, came over at least 2m4f. (op 9-1)

Baseball Ted(IRE) raced up with the pace but had no change of gear. (op 5-2 tchd 9-4)

Cantabilly(IRE) didn't run too badly in a much better contest last time, and was keeping on here when coming down three from home. (tchd 11-2)

Paquet Cadeau(FR), back over fences after two poor attempts over hurdles, was still in with every chance when unseating his rider four out. He had taken a couple of chances earlier but couldn't get away with his final one. (tchd 11-2)

3649 MEYERTIMBER.COM H'CAP HURDLE (9 hdls) — 2m 1f

3:30 (3:30) (Class 2) (0-145,145) 4-Y-0+ — **£10,276** (£2,995; £1,498)

Form	Pos	Dist	Horse / Trainer / Comment	SP	RPR
0054	1		**Ciceron (IRE)**[46] 2792 5-10-7 **126** AidanColeman (Venetia Williams) *trckd ldrs: led sn after 2 out: sn rdn: drifted lft run-in: jst hld on: all out*	8/1	131+
2125	2	hd	**Karasenir (IRE)**[19] 3298 5-10-11 **130** RichardJohnson (Philip Hobbs) *led after 2nd: rdn and hdd after 2 out: swtchd lft after last: rallied wl fnl 100yds: jst hld*	5/1	136+
00-2	3	8	**Tito Bustillo (FR)**[75] 2219 6-11-3 **136** NickScholfield (Paul Nicholls) *trckd ldrs: jnd ldrs after 4th: mstke 6th: ev ch appr 2 out: rdn bef last: nt pce of ldrs: drifted rt flat*	9/4[1]	134
-440	4	1¼	**Benfleet Boy**[62] 2498 7-11-1 **134** LeightonAspell (Brendan Powell) *led tl after 2nd: w ldr: rdn after 3 out: styd on same pce fr next*	16/1	130
-131	5	4½	**Dona**[10] 3478 7-10-13 **132** 7ex RobertThornton (Alan King) *trckd ldrs: rdn after 6th: outpcd after 3 out*	9/2[3]	124
1332	6	10	**Sircozy (IRE)**[75] 2213 5-10-3 **122** (p) JamieMoore (Gary Moore) *hld up but in tch: pushed along after 5th: rdn after 6th: wknd 2 out*	11/1	106
3-F3	7	2½	**Sanctuaire (FR)**[46] 2792 5-11-12 **145** DarylJacob (Paul Nicholls) *hld up last but in tch: tk str hold: short lived effrt after 3 out: wknd bef next*	4/1[2]	128

4m 6.90s (-1.10) **Going Correction** +0.175s/f (Yiel) 7 Ran SP% **110.9**

Speed ratings (Par 109): **109,108,105,104,102 97,96**

toteswingers:1&2:£10.20, 1&3:£12.20, 2&3:£2.30 CSF £44.24 TOTE £11.70: £4.50, £2.70; EX 48.20.

Owner Tony Verrier **Bred** Haras Du Mezeray And Skymarc Farms **Trained** Kings Caple, H'fords

FOCUS

Despite there being a confirmed front-runner taking part, the early pace looked far from quick and the field was close up with four to jump.

NOTEBOOK

Ciceron(IRE) hadn't been running well for a while, but was 6lb lower than when last seen and running for a stable very much back in form. It remains to be seen what he is capable of when going up in the weights again, as he was being reeled in by the runner-up with every stride. (op 9-1)

Karasenir(IRE) is unexposed as a handicapper and showed a good attitude under pressure to rally after being caught flat footed. (op 11-2 tchd 6-1)

Tito Bustillo(FR), absent since a fair effort in Wincanton's Elite Hurdle in early November, was defending a two from two record at this course but ran disappointingly. He was under pressure before jumping two out and was made to look one-paced. (op 2-1)

Benfleet Boy, who was second in this last season, was always close up but couldn't quicken.

Dona has been in great form this season, and had risen from an official mark off 110 to 132 in just three outings. A C&D winner last time, he appeared to find this company too hot. (op 5-1 tchd 4-1)

Sanctuaire(FR) once again took a fierce hold in rear and continues to frustrate. However, he may go down the weights again and would be an interesting horse if aimed at one of the handicaps at Cheltenham in March, when he will get a strong gallop to chase. (tchd 7-2 and 9-2 in places)

3650 SOUTHWEST-RACING.CO.UK H'CAP CHASE (14 fncs) — 2m 3f

4:00 (4:00) (Class 4) (0-110,107) 5-Y-0+ — **£3,425** (£998; £499)

Form	Pos	Dist	Horse / Trainer / Comment	SP	RPR
00/5	1		**Magic Marmalade (IRE)**[19] 3296 8-11-4 **99** RichardJohnson (Philip Hobbs) *trckd ldrs: hit 2nd: pckd next: rdn after 3 out: swtchd rt bef last: swtchd lft run-in: str run fnl 75yds to ld fnl strides*	11/1	108+
00/1	2	½	**Sultan Fontenaille (FR)**[21] 3230 9-11-12 **107** (tp) JohnnyFarrelly (David Pipe) *hld up bhd ldrs: pushed along briefly bef 8th: chalng whn pckd 3 out: sn drvn: narrow advantage whn hit next: hdd sn after last: rallied fnl 75yds to regain 2nd fnl strides*	10/11[1]	117+
53/1	3	nk	**Golden Duck (IRE)**[76] 2187 11-11-10 **105** DarylJacob (Nick Williams) *disp ld: hdd 4 out: regained narrow advantage 3 out: hdd 2 out: sn rdn: led again sn after last: no ex whn lost 2 pls fnl strides*	7/2[2]	113
200U	4	12	**Health Is Wealth (IRE)**[18] 3349 6-11-2 **97** JoeTizzard (Colin Tizzard) *trckd ldrs: led 4 out: rdn and hdd next: wknd after 2 out*	9/2[3]	95
5223	5	32	**Lepido (ITY)**[18] 3348 7-11-12 **107** (v) JamieMoore (Gary Moore) *trckd ldrs: hit 2nd: rdn after 4 out: wknd after 3 out*	9/1	86
3P-	P		**Colonel Arthur (IRE)**[478] 1570 10-11-6 **104** (t) RichieMcLernon(3) (Sophie Leech) *disp ld tl rdn appr 8th: stopped rapidly: p.u bef 9th*	50/1	—

5m 2.20s (5.70) **Going Correction** +0.425s/f (Soft) 6 Ran SP% **113.1**

Speed ratings: **105,104,104,99,86 —**

toteswingers:1&2:£3.30, 1&3:£4.00, 2&3:£1.20 CSF £23.28 TOTE £10.10: £3.20, £1.50; EX 24.40.

Owner Racing Magic **Bred** Michael McEvoy **Trained** Withycombe, Somerset

FOCUS

Not many runners but a thrilling finish fought out by three horses. A good effort from the winner who's rated up a stone on his recent hurdles run.

NOTEBOOK

Magic Marmalade(IRE) was quickly switched to fences on his second outing for Phillip Hobbs (he had been consistent in points) and travelled strongly for a long time. However, he looked booked for third coming to the last before finding extra and winning in determined style. A half-brother to the staying chaser Notabotheronme, also trained by Phillip Hobbs, he should get further and ought to follow up if given a realistic target. Official explanation: trainer's wife said, regarding the running and riding, the gelding had been running well in point-to-points and was having its first run over fences for the yard, having been with them for three months (op 12-1 tchd 10-1)

Sultan Fontenaille(FR), 5lb higher than when winning on his first start for David Pipe over 4.5f further, got his nose in front close to the line but was passed in the final strides by the winner. (op Evens tchd 11-10)

Golden Duck(IRE), 10lb higher than when successful at Fontwell in early November after a lengthy absence, looked almost certain to win after going about a length up after jumping the final fence, but his two closest rivals responded in admirable style and he lost two positions in the final stages. (op 9-2)

Health Is Wealth(IRE) stopped quickly the moment his rider asked for more. With hindsight, Joe Tizzard would have been better off kicking his mount on when seemingly going well heading to three out. (op 4-1)

Colonel Arthur(IRE) Official explanation: vet said that the gelding had bled from the nose

3651 P.A.S. SOUND & COMMUNICATIONS MAIDEN OPEN NATIONAL HUNT FLAT RACE — 2m 1f

4:30 (4:30) (Class 5) 4-6-Y-0 — **£2,055** (£599; £299)

Form	Pos	Dist	Horse / Trainer / Comment	SP	RPR
32	1		**Divine Folly (IRE)**[66] 2432 6-10-13 0 DavidBass(5) (Lawney Hill) *mde all: styd on wl fnl 2f: rdn out*	2/1[2]	94+

2 4 ½ **Bathwick Brave (IRE)** 4-10-7 0 JohnnyFarrelly 80+
(David Pipe) *mid-div: trckd ldrs 1/2-way: rdn to chse wnr 3f out: styd on but a being hld* **15/8**[1]

0- 3 4 ½ **Vincentian (IRE)**[286] 5121 6-11-4 0 DarylJacob 85
(David Arbuthnot) *trckd ldrs: rdn 4f out: styd on fnl 2f but unable to mount chal* **7/2**[3]

P0- 4 1 **How's My Friend**[272] 5368 6-11-4 0 NickScholfield 84
(Grant Cann) *mid-div: hdwy 5f out: rdn over 4f out: styd on fnl 2f: nvr trbld ldrs* **20/1**

6-0 5 9 **Another Dimension (IRE)**[22] 3200 5-11-4 0 TimmyMurphy 75
(Nigel Dunger) *mid-div tl dropped to rr after 8f: sn pushed along: styd on again fnl 3f* **16/1**

4 6 ¾ **Prince Of King**[86] 2025 6-11-4 0 JamieMoore 75
(Helen Nelmes) *mid-div: rdn to chse ldng trio 3f out: styd on same pce* **20/1**

0 7 ½ **Lynford Nakita**[233] 568 5-10-6 0 IanPopham(5) 67
(Caroline Keevil) *hld up towards rr: sme late prog: nvr any danger* **80/1**

8 1 **Ashbourne Folly (IRE)** 5-11-4 0 RobertThornton 73
(Bob Buckler) *disp ld tl over 7f out: sn pushed along: wknd over 4f out* **12/1**

0 9 5 **Dani (IRE)**[78] 2156 5-10-11 0 AidanColeman 61
(Mark Rimell) *trckd ldrs: rdn 4f out: wknd over 2f out* **40/1**

10 8 **Little Ms Piggie** 5-10-4 0 NathanSweeney(7) 53
(Simon Burrough) *mid-div tl 4f out* **50/1**

0 11 8 **Crystal Cliche**[17] 3372 6-10-11 0 GerardTumelty 45
(Julian Smith) *in tch tl over rdn 4f out* **125/1**

12 12 **Jovial Starry Nite** 6-10-11 0 HarrySkelton 33
(Carroll Gray) *mid-div tl 5f out* **125/1**

0-0 13 16 **Tenitemsplustoast**[256] 237 5-10-13 0 KeiranBurke(5) 24
(Patrick Rodford) *chsd ldrs tl over 4f out: t.o* **100/1**

14 26 **Landscape Lad** 6-10-13 0 MattGriffiths(5) —
(Ron Hodges) *t.k.h: hld up towards rr: hdwy to join ldrs after 5f: wknd 6f out: t.o* **50/1**

4m 17.2s (14.80) **Going Correction** +0.175s/f (Yiel)
WFA 4 from 5yo+ 11lb **14 Ran SP% 123.6**
Speed ratings: **72,69,67,67,63 62,62,62,59,55 52,46,38,26**
toteswingers:1&2:£2.70, 1&3:£3.60, 2&3:£7.80 CSF £5.93 TOTE £2.30: £1.20, £1.50, £1.40; EX 5.50.
Owner Mrs Helen Mullineux **Bred** Daryl Deacon **Trained** Aston Rowant, Oxon

FOCUS
This was run at an early dawdle, as is usual in this type of event. The winner was the form pick but is rated below his best.

NOTEBOOK
Divine Folly(IRE) had run well in a couple of bumpers previously and, after being ridden positively here, he bounded clear once asked to quicken and won nicely. The plan is to have one more run in a bumper before being put away. (op 11-4)
Bathwick Brave(IRE), who cost £30,000 in December, travelled like a good horse but looked to be undone by experience on his racecourse debut. He should be good enough to win something similar. (op 2-1)
Vincentian(IRE) looked like going backwards at one point down the back straight, but he kept on well after a reminder or two to hold every chance turning in. Unfortunately, the first two kicked on again and he was unable to make any impression.
How's My Friend has plenty of size and will no doubt do better in time.
T/Plt: £87.40 to a £1 stake. Pool:£75,874.70 - 633.73 winning tickets T/Qpdt: £45.10 to a £1 stake. Pool:£5,381.22 - 88.16 winning tickets TM

3519 CATTERICK (L-H)
Friday, January 21
3652 Meeting Abandoned - Frost

3435 CHEPSTOW (L-H)
Friday, January 21
3659 Meeting Abandoned - Frost

2547 KELSO (L-H)
Friday, January 21
3666 Meeting Abandoned - Frost

2512 ASCOT (R-H)
Saturday, January 22
OFFICIAL GOING: Good to soft (soft in places; hdl 7.0, chs 7.2)
Wind: Almost nil Weather: Overcast, drizzly

3672 ROSLING KING LLP NOVICES' LIMITED H'CAP CHASE (16 fncs) 2m 3f
12:40 (12:40) (Class 3) (0-135,130) 5-Y-O+ **£9,505** (£2,808; £1,404; £702; £351)

Form RPR

4F23 1 **Rougham**[14] 3451 5-11-2 **130** RhysFlint 138
(Philip Hobbs) *j. boldy: led and one of a pair given clr ld: jnd after 10th: kicked on again next: hrd pressed 2 out: jnd again last: battled on wl to hold on* **9/2**[2]

1121 2 ½ **Osric (IRE)**[25] 3156 8-11-5 **129** BarryGeraghty 141
(Nicky Henderson) *lw: allowed two ldrs including wnr a clr advantage and hld up in 4th: wnt 3rd 8th: blnd 10th: chsd wnr 12th: chal 2 out: upsides last: battled on: a jst hld* **13/8**[1]

3-10 3 19 **Mister Stickler (IRE)**[38] 2951 7-11-1 **125** WayneHutchinson 122+
(Alan King) *allowed 2 ldrs a clr s: hld up in 5th: prog to go 3rd whn blnd 4 out: cl enough next: wknd after 2 out* **5/1**[3]

0323 4 12 **Lordsbridge (USA)**[38] 2961 9-9-12 **115** EdCookson(7) 101
(Andy Turnell) *j.lft: hld up in last and allowed 2 ldrs a clr advantage: struggling fr 11th: nvr a factor* **9/2**[2]

1245 5 2 ½ **Frontier Dancer (IRE)**[37] 2979 7-11-4 **128** PaddyBrennan 111
(Nigel Twiston-Davies) *lw: chsd wnr and allowed clr advantage over rest: mstkes 6th and 7th: chal after 10th: lost 2nd 12th and struggling: wknd 4 out* **8/1**

3216 6 1 **Kellystown Lad (IRE)**[18] 3390 8-11-1 **125** GrahamLee 106
(Ferdy Murphy) *allowed 2 ldrs clr s: chsd them to 8th: dropped to last after 10th: t.o 3 out: fin w a flourish* **10/1**

4m 47.5s (0.50) **Going Correction** -0.175s/f (Good)
WFA 5 from 6yo+ 3lb **6 Ran SP% 111.3**
Speed ratings: **91,90,82,77,76 76**
toteswingers:1&2 £2.00, 2&3 £4.50, 1&3 £5.00 CSF £12.63 CT £35.20 TOTE £6.10: £2.90, £1.50; EX 11.30 Trifecta £46.60 Pool of £745.60 - 11.84 winning units..
Owner Mr & Mrs James Wigan **Bred** Mrs James Wigan & London TB Services Ltd **Trained** Withycombe, Somerset

FOCUS
An unsatisfactory start, with the winner stealing several lengths at the start, and few got into this novice handicap chase. The first two are on the upgrade and the form could be rated up to 6lb higher.

NOTEBOOK
Rougham went off at a decent clip and only the favourite Osric was able to challenge him in the straight. It looked for a moment as though the market leader had his number, but as he had done for much of the contest, produced bold leaps at each of the last two fences and had enough momentum to hold on, with the pair coming close on the run-in. He had finished third behind the potentially smart The Minack at Wincanton last time, and he looks the right type for the Centenary Novice Handicap Chase (formerly the Jewson) at the festival. (op 11-2 tchd 6-1)
Osric(IRE)'s rider attracted some criticism following the race, with it argued he had the 8-y-o too far out of his ground, but this free-going sort, who had been keen to post, needs restraining, and he was delivered in plenty of time to challenge. He stayed on without being able to get past the determined winner, and would be another likely type for the Centenary. (tchd 7-4)
Mister Stickler(IRE) had won on his chasing debut off 7lb lower prior to disappointing effort in a novice at Bangor latest. A mistake four out may have taken more out of him than it had looked here, as his finishing effort was rather tame. (op 6-1)
Lordsbridge(USA) is a tricky horse to win with and, having been held up, jumping left, he came under pressure and couldn't get close. (op 4-1)
Frontier Dancer(IRE), who chased the winner early, hasn't built on a successful start over fences, failing to improve for the switch to handicaps. (op 9-1)
Kellystown Lad(IRE) ran poorly at Leicester last time and only started to run on here once the race was over. He may be a different proposition over 3m. (op 9-1)

3673 ASCOT ANNUAL BADGEHOLDERS' JUVENILE HURDLE (9 hdls) 2m
1:15 (1:15) (Class 3) 4-Y-O **£4,383** (£1,295; £647; £324; £161; £81)

Form RPR

-521 1 **Grandouet (FR)**[24] 3194 4-11-8 145 BarryGeraghty 130+
(Nicky Henderson) *lw: hld up in tch: trckd ldrs fr 6th: smooth effrt after 3 out to ld between last 2: easily* **4/9**[1]

1230 2 6 **Two Kisses (IRE)**[70] 2356 4-11-1 123 APMcCoy 113+
(Brendan Powell) *led at decent pce: mstke 6th: rdn and hdd between last 2: no ch w wnr* **11/1**[3]

60 3 3 ¼ **Looks Like Slim**[16] 3401 4-10-12 0 WayneHutchinson 106
(Ben De Haan) *t.k.h early: hld up in tch: mstke 4th: cl up 3 out: outpcd next: kpt on to win battle for 3rd* **20/1**

04 4 nk **L'Eminence Grise (IRE)**[24] 3194 4-10-12 0 DarylJacob 105
(Nick Williams) *cl up in 3rd: outpcd after 3 out: kpt on again fr last* **20/1**

5 15 **Magic Prospect (FR)**[218] 4-10-9 0 PeterToole(3) 93
(Charlie Mann) *chsd ldr: mstke 4th: lost 2nd bef 2 out: wkng whn mstke last* **20/1**

6 1 ¾ **Ostentation**[85] 4-10-12 0 ColinBolger 91
(Roger Teal) *w'like: lw: hld up in last pair: mstke 6th: jst in tch 3 out: sn outpcd: mstke 2 out: kpt on* **66/1**

P 7 7 **Whitby Jack**[14] 3443 4-10-12 0 JamieMoore 83
(Gary Moore) *wl in tch: pushed along after 3 out: sn outpcd: eased whn no ch last* **33/1**

8 33 **Plenty Pocket (FR)**[138] 4-10-7 0 IanPopham(5) 79+
(Paul Nicholls) *t.k.h: hld up in tch: wknd sn after 3 out: t.o* **7/2**[2]

9 17 **Singapore Storm (FR)** 4-10-12 0 PaddyBrennan 38
(Tom George) *rangy: nt jump wl: a last: struggling fr 6th: wl t.o* **50/1**

3m 47.6s (-1.40) **Going Correction** -0.05s/f (Good) **9 Ran SP% 120.5**
Speed ratings: **101,98,96,96,88 87,84,67,59**
toteswingers:1&2 £1.10, 2&3 £18.40, 1&3 £6.80 CSF £6.04 TOTE £1.50: £1.10, £1.90, £4.40; EX 5.70 Trifecta £43.30 Pool of £1489.75 - 25.43 winning units..
Owner Simon Munir **Bred** Dominique Le Baron **Trained** Upper Lambourn, Berks

FOCUS
An uncompetitive juvenile hurdle. The pace was a decent one, though, thanks to the runner-up. The easy winner was value for further but below the level of his Newbury win.

NOTEBOOK
Grandouet(FR) reportedly thrives on racing and has been a marked improver since wearing earplugs, building on his Cheltenham second to Sam Winner with back-to-back victories, and there's the promise of better to come. In what looks another weak year, the winner has been promoted to favourite for the Triumph Hurdle, and perhaps he'll cement his position at the head of the market in next month's Adonis (next target; connections won it with Soldatino last year), but at this stage, considering what he's actually beaten, the 7-1 (Paddy Power, William Hill) looks skinny. (op 1-2 tchd 4-7 in a place, 8-15 in places and 1-2 in places)
Two Kisses(IRE), although flattered, finished an awful lot closer to the winner than she had done at Cheltenham in November and has clearly benefited from a 70-day break. She was on her toes beforehand, but showed enough to suggest she can win again. (op 12-1)
Looks Like Slim ◆ travelled well before coming off the bridle and staying on again. He should continue to improve and it will be disappointing if he doesn't pick up a race of two.
L'Eminence Grise(IRE), who appears to be making physical improvement, finished a good bit closer to the winner than he had done at Newbury. He'll be an interesting one for handicaps down the line. (op 25-1)
Magic Prospect(FR), a lightly made sort who had fair form on the Flat in France (well beaten in the Queen's Vase latest), ended up well held, but he offered some hope and should improve. (op 25-1)
Ostentation, useful at about 1m on the Flat, never reached a challenging position, but he was keeping on late and should learn from this experience.
Whitby Jack isn't one to give up on just yet and should do better in handicaps later in the year. (op 28-1)
Plenty Pocket(FR)'s trainer's pre-race comments suggested he would be in need of the experience, and he did race keenly so expect better next time. Official explanation: jockey said gelding had a breathing problem (op 10-3 tchd 4-1)

Singapore Storm(FR) was green and noisy in the paddock.

3674 1942 WAS A VINTAGE YEAR MARES' HURDLE (REGISTERED AS THE WARFIELD MARES' HURDLE RACE) GRADE 2 (13 hdls) 3m

1:50 (1:50) (Class 1) 4-Y-0+

£22,804 (£8,556; £4,284; £2,136; £1,072; £536)

Form					RPR
-111	1		**Sparky May**[58] 2627 6-11-0 138 (Patrick Rodford) *t.k.h: hld up in rr: prog fr 5th: plld way through to ld 9th: clr next: hrd rdn after 2 out: kpt on gamely* **7/1**[3]	KeiranBurke	149+
1-12	2	4	**Carole's Legacy**[21] 3292 7-11-5 150 (Nicky Henderson) *lw: trckd ldrs: chsd wnr bef 10th: drvn bef 2 out: kpt on: no real imp* **1/1**[1]	BarryGeraghty	150
2-52	3	10	**Alasi**[14] 3442 7-11-0 136 (Paul Webber) *t.k.h early: hld up in rr: stdy prog fr 8th: chsd ldng pair after 10th: mstke next (3 out) whn in tch: fdd 2 out* **12/1**	WillKennedy	135
-121	4	49	**Alverstone**[22] 3264 8-11-0 120 (Lawney Hill) *swtg: disp ld at decent pce: hdd and stmbld 9th: wknd bef next: eased: t.o* **10/1**	(t) APMcCoy	91
-P41	5	22	**Fit To Drive**[77] 2214 9-11-0 124 (Brendan Powell) *disp ld at gd pce: hit 6th hrd: hdd 9th: wkng whn blnd next: t.o* **50/1**	(t) TomScudamore	71
-111	6	11	**L'Accordioniste (IRE)**[43] 2868 6-11-0 141 (Nigel Twiston-Davies) *lw: terrible rnd of jumping: trckd ldrs: in tch whn anther mstke 8th: sn struggling: t.o* **10/3**[2]	PaddyBrennan	61
P-12	P		**Gold Reef**[14] 3452 8-11-0 125 (Alan King) *hld up in rr: lost tch after 8th: sn t.o: p.u bef 2 out* **14/1**	RobertThornton	—
-361	P		**Seren Cwmtudu (IRE)**[12] 3480 7-11-0 117 (Evan Williams) *a in rr: lost tch after 6th: t.o whn p.u after 8th* **50/1**	PaulMoloney	—

5m 47.5s (-8.50) **Going Correction** -0.05s/f (Good) **8 Ran SP% 113.0**
Speed ratings (Par 115): **112,110,107,91,83 80,—,—**
toteswingers:1&2 £2.40, 2&3 £4.40, 1&3 £8.10 CSF £14.60 TOTE £9.10: £2.30, £1.10, £2.80; EX 14.50 Trifecta £262.20 Pool of £5084.80 - 14.35 winning units..
Owner Bill Muddyman **Bred** Ruxley Holdings Ltd **Trained** Ash, Somerset

FOCUS
This Grade 2 mares' hurdle proved a good test and only three mattered from the third-last flight. Another step up from the winner who looks a top-class novice.

NOTEBOOK
Sparky May ran out a brave winner and extended her unbeaten record over hurdles to four on this first venture outside of novice company. She tanked to the front around five out and attained a clear advantage soon after. This was her first outing over the trip, though, and having taken a keen hold through the race, it wasn't surprising to see her tire a little from the penultimate flight. Her attitude when under maximum pressure was spot on, however, and she was always just doing enough to repel the runner-up. This rates another career-best, on ground that was probably soft enough, and it is hard to gauge just how good she is at this stage. The David Nicholson Mares' Hurdle at the Cheltenham Festival, for which she'll pick up a penalty, is the target and, while Quevega will prove a very tough nut to crack, this 6-y-o should be accorded respect if turning up. Her trainer reported she would definitely come on for the run. (op 13-2 tchd 8-1 in places)
Carole's Legacy is a solid benchmark for this form. Conceding weight all round, she came under pressure a fair way out and, although she again gave her all, the winner had gone beyond recall in the home straight. She may just have been feeling the effects of a tough race over fences at Cheltenham on New Year's Day and again lost nothing in defeat. The David Nicholson Mares' Hurdle, a race she was second in last season, remains her likely swansong before heading off to the paddocks, and she ought to make a wonderful broodmare. (op 5-4 tchd 11-8 in places)
Alasi returned to form at Sandown a fortnight earlier in Listed company behind old rival Banjaxed Girl. She kept on steadily from off the pace, but she too had stamina to prove and didn't help her chance of fully seeing out the trip by racing enthusiastically. She deserves to get her head back in front. (tchd 14-1)
Alverstone had got herself warm beforehand. She wasn't helped by being taken on for the lead and her fate was apparent a long way out. (op 11-1 tchd 16-1 in a place)
Fit To Drive, back to winning ways over fences last time, wasn't particularly fluent on this return to hurdling and paid for doing too much early on. (op 40-1)
L'Accordioniste(IRE) was stepping up from 2m1f on this debut in graded company, but is a half-sister to a 3m winner and had a good chance on paper. Her hurdling badly let her down, however, and she wasn't on a going day. It was felt something was amiss with her and it's too soon to be writing her off. Official explanation: jockey said mare never travelled (op 3-1 tchd 7-2)
Seren Cwmtudu(IRE) Official explanation: jockey said mare lost its action

3675 VICTOR CHANDLER CHASE (REGISTERED AS THE CLARENCE HOUSE STEEPLE CHASE) GRADE 1 (13 fncs) 2m 1f

2:25 (2:25) (Class 1) 5-Y-0+

£59,146 (£22,281; £11,151; £5,575; £2,793; £1,396)

Form					RPR
4-11	1		**Master Minded (FR)**[42] 2885 8-11-7 178 (Paul Nicholls) *trckd ldrs: prog and gd jump on outer to ld 9th: 4 l clr after 3 out and looked in full control: shkn up after 2 out: pressed after last: drvn and jst hld on* **4/7**[1]	APMcCoy	171
2-33	2	shd	**Somersby (IRE)**[42] 2885 7-11-7 162 (Henrietta Knight) *lw: w ldrs: rdn to chse wnr 3 out: no imp bef next: kpt on and only 2 l down last: clsd flat: jst failed* **8/1**[2]	HaddenFrost	171
1-46	3	20	**Mad Max (IRE)**[42] 2886 9-11-7 155 (Nicky Henderson) *lw: trckd ldng pair: led 3rd to 7th: sn rdn: in tch 4 out: wknd after next* **8/1**[2]	(t) DavidBass	154
-305	4	1 3/4	**Kalahari King (FR)**[25] 3170 10-11-7 162 (Ferdy Murphy) *hld up in rr: lost tch w ldrs fr 7th: disputing modest 6th whn nrly carried off crse by loose horse after 9th: poor 7th next: styd on wl fr 2 out* **25/1**	GrahamLee	158+
1/15	5	8	**Gauvain (GER)**[42] 2885 9-11-7 159 (Nick Williams) *hld up last: j. slowly 3rd: j.lft 5th: wl bhd after: kpt on fr 3 out: nvr a factor* **20/1**	DarylJacob	150+
21-4	6	7	**I'm So Lucky**[42] 2885 9-11-7 153 (David Pipe) *led to 3rd: led 7th to next: wknd qckly fr 3 out* **33/1**	(t) TomScudamore	138
-1F2	7	7	**Tchico Polos (FR)**[14] 3446 7-11-7 158 (Paul Nicholls) *blnd 1st: chsd ldrs: lost tch w them fr 7th: wknd fr 4 out* **25/1**	(t) IanPopham	134
124-	8	31	**Crack Away Jack**[391] 3082 7-11-7 149 (Emma Lavelle) *lw: j. v awkwardly 2nd whn already wl in rr: nvr on terms: t.o fr 8th* **14/1**[3]	WayneHutchinson	104
53-2	F		**Petit Robin (FR)**[42] 2885 8-11-7 163 (Nicky Henderson) *trckd ldrs: cl 5th and gng wl whn fell 9th* **8/1**[2]	BarryGeraghty	—

4m 4.90s (-10.10) **Going Correction** -0.175s/f (Good) **9 Ran SP% 119.0**
Speed ratings: **116,115,106,105,101 98,95,80,—**
toteswingers:1&2 £2.20, 2&3 £7.70, 1&3 £2.80 CSF £5.93 TOTE £1.40: £1.10, £2.40, £2.70; EX 6.50 Trifecta £34.30 Pool of £11259.41 - 242.32 winning units..
Owner Clive D Smith **Bred** Marie-Christine Gabeur **Trained** Ditcheat, Somerset
■ A third straight win in the race for Paul Nicholls.

FOCUS
The early pace was a good one, I'm So Lucky and then Mad Max, egged on by Somersby, ensuring it was a proper test at the distance. As a result, the winning time was very credible, just 0.90secs outside standard. Master Minded is rated 3lb off his season's best, with the form rated around the first two.

NOTEBOOK
Master Minded(FR), having gone on when the pace slowed down the far side, became tired, and a little lonely out in front, and in the end just held on under an all-out drive from McCoy. Interestingly, the champion jockey later admitted he had given the winner a "bad" ride, so it would probably be unwise to take a dim view of this display, especially taking into account the form of the stable and the ground, which would have been testing enough considering he's had breathing difficulties in the past. On the whole, he has looked back to very near his best this season, and he'll be freshened up now before attempting to regain his Champion Chase crown - for which his odds have lengthened slightly. (op 4-6)

Somersby(IRE) produced a career best. Last season's Arkle runner-up, who had reared over backwards on the walkway prior to finishing third to Master Minded at Cheltenham last month, was seen to much better effect under a positive ride, and found himself as the only one able to stay within challenging distance of the winner. It became clear from the second-last that he was still in with a shout, and actually traded at odds-on in running after the last when it looked extremely likely he would run down the favourite. It wasn't to be, however, and connections, who had originally stated the Ryanair would be his festival target, now have to decide whether to jump ship again, and go for the Queen Mother, as under a similarly positive ride he would hold strong place claims.

Mad Max(IRE), who had Somersby 9l behind when winning over 2m4f on good ground at Aintree last spring, had found his stamina stretched in two starts at about 2m5f at Cheltenham this season, and the return to a flatter track with a first-time tongue-tie was expected to make a difference. He was faced with competition for the lead, though, and despite doing his best, was unable to race on with the front pair. Rated 155, there's probably no race for him at Cheltenham, so Aintree and/or Punchestown will likely be his main aim now. (op 10-1)

Kalahari King(FR) would have been third but for almost being carried off the course by a riderless Petit Robin. Third in last season's Champion Chase, he'd have outside place claims once again but would be a surprise winner come March. Perhaps the Ryanair will be a more viable alternative.

Gauvain(GER) was always struggling, jumping slowly, and again seemed to confirm his surprise Cheltenham win over Forpadydeplasterer in November was a one-off. (tchd 18-1)

I'm So Lucky took them along at a good clip early, but as had been the case behind the winner at Cheltenham last time, he was unable to maintain it. (tchd 50-1 in a place)

Crack Away Jack was interesting on this return from 391 days off, but he looked a bit rusty and wasn't given a hard time. This former Champion Hurdle fourth could be of interest in a handicap at Cheltenham, as he came into this rated just 149.

Petit Robin(FR) still appeared to be travelling well when he fell heavily and suffered a shoulder injury which required surgery. (tchd 9-1)

3676 BET WITH YOUR MOBILE AT VICTORCHANDLER.COM HOLLOWAY'S HURDLE (LIMITED H'CAP) GRADE 2 (11 hdls) 2m 3f 110y

2:55 (3:01) (Class 1) 4-Y-0+

£22,804 (£8,556; £4,284; £2,136; £1,072; £536)

Form					RPR
1605	1		**Tiger O'Toole (IRE)**[14] 3447 6-10-5 129 (Evan Williams) *hld up last: mstke 5th: prog fr 8th: stl plenty to do after 3 out: sustained hdwy fr next: clsd to ld flat: drvn out* **40/1**	PaulMoloney	137+
121/	2	1/2	**Walkon (FR)**[660] 4825 6-11-10 148 (Alan King) *lw: hld up in rr: stdy prog fr 7th: rdn and effrt after 3 out: chsd ldr next: clsd bef last: led briefly flat: r.o: hld nr fin* **12/1**	RobertThornton	155+
0002	3	2 1/2	**Lough Derg (FR)**[24] 3199 11-11-10 148 (David Pipe) *lw: led to 3rd: led again 6th: kicked on fr 8th: 4 l clr bef 2 out: pressed whn mstke last: sn hdd and no ex* **8/1**	(v) TomScudamore	155+
120-	4	11	**Notus De La Tour (FR)**[289] 5094 5-11-3 141 (David Pipe) *hld up wl in rr: pushed along and sme prog fr 8th: rchd 6th after 3 out: stl pushed along and nvr on terms* **3/1**[1]	APMcCoy	136
1/3-	5	3 3/4	**Shalone**[406] 2834 7-11-3 141 (Alan King) *hld up towards rr: blnd 5th: effrt 8th but no imp on ldrs next: wl btn 7th: bef 2 out* **14/1**	WayneHutchinson	134+
11-	6	1 1/4	**Soldatino (FR)**[309] 4710 5-11-10 148 (Nicky Henderson) *free to post: hld up in rr: nt fluent 3rd: t.k.h downhill fr 5th: cl up after 3 out gng wl: 4th and btn whn hmpd 2 out* **11/2**[2]	BarryGeraghty	142+
-101	7	hd	**Warne's Way (IRE)**[12] 3490 8-10-3 130 (Brendan Powell) *settled in rr: reluctant and dropped to last 5th: sn t.o: stl last after 3 out: r.o fr next* **25/1**	(v) RichieMcLernon(3)	120
-311	8	1/2	**Frascati Park (IRE)**[18] 3387 7-10-9 133 (Nigel Twiston-Davies) *tended to jump lft: pressed ldr: led 3rd to 6th: mstke 8th and lost pl: wl btn after 3 out* **6/1**[3]	PaddyBrennan	127+
	9	13	**Sire Collonges (FR)**[276] 5-10-4 128 oh1 (Paul Nicholls) *nt a fluent: a towards rr: struggling after 8th: no ch after 3 out* **8/1**	DarylJacob	110+
P46U	10	22	**Bygones Of Brid (IRE)**[7] 3561 8-11-4 142 (Karen McLintock) *prom: rdn after 7th: sn lost pl: wl bhd after 3 out: t.o* **20/1**	GrahamLee	100
0P-1	11	4 1/2	**Spear Thistle**[68] 2423 9-10-2 129 (Charlie Mann) *prom: chsd ldr briefly after 8th: sn wknd: wl bhd after 3 out: t.o* **50/1**	(p) SamTwiston-Davies(3)	83
-B10	12	61	**Advisor (FR)**[21] 3298 5-10-0 129 (Paul Nicholls) *hld up towards rr: rdn and wknd after 7th: wl bhd after 3 out: virtually p.u* **28/1**	(b1) IanPopham(5)	28
P-02	F		**Sophies Trophy (IRE)**[14] 3447 6-10-5 129 (Pat Phelan) *lw: trckd ldrs: cl up 3 out: sn u.p: abt 7 l 5th and wl hld whn fell 2 out* **12/1**	(t) ColinBolger	120
1130	F		**Lucaindubai (IRE)**[70] 2361 5-9-13 128 oh5 (Evan Williams) *prom: chsd ldr bef 3 out and cl up: sn drvn: 4 l down and abt to lose 2nd whn fell heavily 2 out* **22/1**	DavidBass(5)	123

4m 44.4s (-3.60) **Going Correction** -0.05s/f (Good) **14 Ran SP% 119.7**
Speed ratings (Par 115): **105,104,103,99,97 97,97,97,91,83 81,56,—,—**
toteswingers:1&2 £114.80, 2&3 £20.20, 1&3 £92.30 CSF £429.12 CT £4212.46 TOTE £67.60: £13.80, £4.60, £3.00; EX 882.90 Trifecta £5130.00 Pool of £21496.59 - 3.70 winning units..
Owner Ms S Howell **Bred** Mrs Jayne M Gollings **Trained** Llancarfan, Vale Of Glamorgan

FOCUS
A cracking handicap which saw the return of some classy performers. There was a solid early pace on before things slowed up a little going into the back straight and it lifted again when Lough Derg kicked on coming out of Swinley Bottom. The winner is rated up 1lb but still below the level of what will be needed in the totesport Trophy. Walkon is rated to his Triumph Hurdle mark.

NOTEBOOK
Tiger O'Toole(IRE) came from last to first and knuckled down gamely to prevail close home. He ran somewhat in snatches out the back early on, but the generous pace helped him and he began to hit top gear from two out. A decent leap at the last saw him land running and really his rider emerges with plenty of credit. His best form had come on better ground, but he caught the eye when fifth in testing conditions behind Mille Chief at Sandown on his return from a break a fortnight earlier and had clearly come on a good deal for that. This was his first success beyond 2m1f and there is every reason to believe he is still capable of improving further on this career-best display. His odds were slashed from 66-1 to around 16-1 for the Totesport Trophy, for which he'll pick up a 5lb penalty and, while he would have more on his plate, the nature of that race would very likely suit him. (op 66-1)
Walkon(FR) was having his first outing since running away with a Grade 1 as a juvenile at Aintree in April 2009 and thrilled connections, who switched him here following the abandonment of Haydock, where he was due to take on Peddlers Cross. Up to this trip for the first time, the market suggested the run would be needed and he proved somewhat fresh early on, but as the race progressed he improved. Having looked the winner when taking the measure of Lough Derg, the concession of 19lb to the runner-up, who came even later, proved just beyond him, but it was a blinding comeback and his engine clearly remains intact. He ought to come on plenty, and connections are entitled to look at the Champion Hurdle, although the Grade 1 Aintree Hurdle over 2m4f really looks the race for him. He could run in the totesport Trophy. (op 10-1)
Lough Derg(FR) was bidding for a third win in the race and ran a blinder, but he couldn't cope with the two finishers after making a mess of the final flight. (op 9-1 tchd 10-1)
Notus De La Tour(FR), up in trip, was the subject of a big morning gamble and looked the stable's best hope of a fourth consecutive success in the race. He lost out by hitting something of a flat spot on this first run since last April, though, and looked in need of the run. It wouldn't be surprising to see him improve a good deal and the Totesport Trophy is probably next up for him. (op 11-4 tchd 7-2)
Shalone has had his problems and this was his first outing for 406 days. He is entitled to come on a bundle and remains an interesting horse, so it's hoped he remains sound. (op 11-1)
Soldatino(FR) was having his first run back since winning the Triumph Hurdle and was reported to have had a tricky preparation. He proved easy to back and was very keen to post. Those exertions likely found him out in the home straight and, on the evidence thus far, last season's juveniles were just an ordinary bunch. However, there was plenty to like about the way he moved through the race before stamina became an issue, and the suspicion is that he might not have peaked yet. (op 5-1 tchd 13-2 and 7-1 in places)
Frascati Park(IRE) had belatedly come good as a hurdler the last twice, including over this course and distance. He attracted support for his handicap debut and wasn't disgraced, but is most effective when allowed his own way in front. (op 8-1 tchd 11-2)
Sire Collonges(FR) looked to have been given a fair mark for this British/handicap debut. He was never a serious player, but this imposing 5yo looks all over a future chaser and ought to benefit a deal for this experience. (tchd 17-2)
Sophies Trophy(IRE) could well win when reverting to 2m if none the worse for this. (op 20-1)
Lucaindubai(IRE) was running a personal best prior to departing. (op 20-1)

3677 VICTORCHANDLER.COM H'CAP CHASE (17 fncs) 2m 5f 110y
3:30 (3:34) (Class 2) 5-Y-0+

£43,834 (£12,950; £6,475; £3,241; £1,617; £812)

Form				RPR
-363	**1**		**Tatenen (FR)**[24] 3195 7-10-13 **137** AndrewThornton (Richard Rowe) *mostly j.w: cl up: led 10th gng strly: nt fluent 12th: clr 13th: rdn 2 out: drew further away after: impressive* **22/1**	154+
112	**2**	*16*	**I'm A Legend**[14] 3453 9-9-8 **125** (p) MarkQuinlan(7) (Neil Mulholland) *hld up in midfield: mstke 8th: prog to chse wnr after 12th: blnd next: no imp after 3 out: jst hung on for 2nd* **11/2**[3]	130+
1F/2	**3**	*shd*	**Breedsbreeze (IRE)**[38] 2964 9-11-7 **150** IanPopham(5) (Paul Nicholls) *lw: mstke and stmbld 1st: sn last: sme prog fr 10th: rchd 4th 3 out but nowhere nr ldrs: kpt on fr next: nrly snatched 2nd* **3/1**[1]	155+
P-23	**4**	*8*	**Piraya (FR)**[56] 2674 8-11-4 **142** (tp) TomScudamore (David Pipe) *chsd ldrs: rdn and struggling fr 11th: wl bhd fr 14th: kpt on again fr 2 out* **7/2**[2]	137
0-10	**5**	*4 ½*	**Edgbriar (FR)**[70] 2359 9-11-5 **143** (p) APMcCoy (Paul Webber) *cl up bhd ldrs: disp 2nd fr 13th and clr of rest next: wknd rapidly 2 out* **10/1**	134
0-50	**6**	*1 ¼*	**The Sawyer (BEL)**[70] 2359 11-10-11 **142** NathanSweeney(7) (Bob Buckler) *narrow ldr at str pce to 10th: sn lost pl and wl in rr: no ch fr 14th* **8/1**	131
P-10	**7**	*17*	**Minella Theatre (IRE)**[56] 2674 8-10-9 **133** HaddenFrost (Henrietta Knight) *a towards rr: jst in tch but rdn 11th: struggling fr next: no ch fr 14th* **18/1**	108
1-65	**8**	*¾*	**Soulard (USA)**[85] 2077 8-10-8 **132** PaddyBrennan (Tom George) *lw: w ldr at fast pce: chsd wnr fr 10th tl mstke 12th: sn wknd* **14/1**	105
-05F	**9**	*1*	**Pickamus (FR)**[21] 3292 8-10-13 **137** AndrewTinkler (Henry Daly) *pressed ldr's fast pce: lost pl rapidly 10th: toiling in rr fr 12th* **16/1**	109
F-03	**10**	*nk*	**Panjo Bere (FR)**[63] 2515 8-11-1 **146** JoshuaMoore(7) (Gary Moore) *wl in rr: nt golng wl fr 6th: toiling in last 8th: rapid prog u.p to go 4th at 13th: sn no hdwy: wknd again 3 out* **12/1**	118
U563	**U**		**Mahogany Blaze (FR)**[21] 3292 9-11-8 **149** (b) SamTwiston-Davies(3) (Nigel Twiston-Davies) *lw: 10th whn blnd and uns rdr 4th* **14/1**	—

5m 14.6s (-11.40) **Going Correction** -0.175s/f (Good) **11** Ran SP% **119.3**
Speed ratings: **113,107,107,104,102 102,95,95,95,95** —
toteswingers:1&2 £19.40, 2&3 £2.50, 1&3 £20.90 CSF £143.16 CT £480.07 TOTE £31.90: £6.90, £1.90, £1.70; EX 208.00 Trifecta £589.20 Pool of £2879.67 - 3.61 winning units..
Owner The Stewart Family **Bred** Olivier Tricot **Trained** Sullington, W Sussex

FOCUS
This was always going to be strongly run, with so many front-runners in opposition. The winner is rated to this season's Kempton level, but was a 158 horse at his peak.

NOTEBOOK
Tatenen(FR), under a fine ride from Andrew Thornton, was able to win his first race since joining Richard Rowe. A faller when favourite for the Arkle in 2009, the winner has become very well handicapped and, although he hadn't built on a promising return in two subsequent outings, there were excuses, and he really grabbed this race by the scruff of the neck down the far side. Winning easily from a mark of 137, he will find himself back in the mid to high 140s now, but can still be a player in something like the Festival Plate. (op 20-1)
I'm A Legend, denied a four-timer at Wincanton last time, again gave his running off a new career-high mark and gutted it out well for second. (tchd 13-2)
Breedsbreeze(IRE), who ran a stormer on his return from a lengthy absence at Newbury last month, was a bit weak in the market and probably lost his race over the first few fences, blundering at the first and then jumping hesitantly. To his credit, he did stay on well down the straight, and a return to 3m looks in order now. The William Hill at the festival is probably his race. (op 9-4 tchd 7-2)
Piraya(FR) plugged on best he could, but never looked like winning. (op 6-1 tchd 10-3)
Edgbriar(FR) ended up well held and doesn't look up to winning from this mark. (op 11-1 tchd 12-1)
The Sawyer(BEL), who's registered six of his eight career wins in the month of January, including this race last year off 12lb lower, doesn't look up to winning off his current mark either. (op 9-1)

3678 EUROPEAN BREEDERS' FUND "NATIONAL HUNT" NOVICES' HURDLE (QUALIFIER) (11 hdls) 2m 3f 110y
4:05 (4:08) (Class 3) 4-7-Y-0

£5,009 (£1,480; £740; £370; £184; £92)

Form				RPR
13	**1**		**Poungach (FR)**[64] 2493 5-11-2 0 DarylJacob (Paul Nicholls) *lw: trckd ldrs: smooth prog to go 2nd after 3 out: led sn after 2 out: cruised clr* **3/1**[2]	139+
301	**2**	*8*	**No Secrets (IRE)**[20] 3340 7-11-8 0 WayneHutchinson (Warren Greatrex) *mde most: rdn after 3 out: hdd sn after 2 out: kpt on wl but no match for wnr* **13/2**[3]	134+
5-02	**3**	*15*	**Victoria Rose (IRE)**[18] 3389 6-10-2 0 NathanSweeney(7) (Simon Burrough) *trckd ldng trio: pushed along 7th: lost pl next: struggling in 7th after 3 out: rallied last: kpt on to take 3rd fnl strides* **33/1**	107
1-13	**4**	*½*	**Carribs Leap (IRE)**[20] 3346 6-11-12 118 APMcCoy (Charles Egerton) *pressed ldr: rdn 3 out: lost 2nd bef next: steadily wknd: lost 3rd last strides* **12/1**	123
-123	**5**	*3 ½*	**Frontier Spirit (IRE)**[68] 2428 7-11-5 117 SamTwiston-Davies(3) (Nigel Twiston-Davies) *trckd ldrs: cl up and rdn 3 out: outpcd bef next: disp modest 3rd last: fdd* **22/1**	116
1-2	**6**	*¾*	**Master Fiddle**[25] 3158 6-11-2 0 BarryGeraghty (Nicky Henderson) *str: lw: trckd ldrs in 6th: cl up 3 out: sn u.p: wknd bef next* **6/4**[1]	109
7	*nk*	**Wise Move (IRE)** 5-10-11 0 DavidBass(5) (Nicky Henderson) *settled in rr and rn green: in tch to 8th: sn wl adrift of ldrs: poor 8th after 3 out and pushed along: styd on w sme effect after last: nt wout promise* **20/1**	111+
1-4	**8**	*hd*	**Fontano (FR)**[48] 2791 5-10-13 0 AlexMerriam(3) (Emma Lavelle) *hld up in rr: sme prog fr 8th: no nrr than 6th after 3 out: no hdwy after* **9/1**	110
/33-	**9**	*57*	**Well Refreshed**[325] 4391 7-11-2 0 WillKennedy (Peter Winkworth) *hld up in last pair: struggling to stay in tch fr 6th: t.o bef 3 out: blnd last* **66/1**	58
20	**10**	*9*	**Lord Kennedy (IRE)**[32] 3054 6-11-2 0 GrahamLee (Alex Hales) *in tch to 7th: wknd rapidly next: t.o after 3 out* **66/1**	50
1/	**P**		**Suburban Bay**[794] 2297 6-11-2 0 RobertThornton (Alan King) *hld up in rr: stl at bk of main gp 7th but appeared gng wl enough: wknd next: t.o whn p.u bef 2 out* **16/1**	—
10-0	**P**		**Amroth Bay**[48] 2791 7-11-2 0 HaddenFrost (Andrew Balding) *t.k.h: pressed ldrs to 8th: wknd rapidly: poor 9th whn p.u bef 2 out* **66/1**	—
50	**P**		**Eldred (IRE)**[38] 2963 5-11-2 0 AndrewTinkler (Nicky Henderson) *settled midfield: dropped in rr and rdn 7th: t.o whn p.u bef 3 out* **100/1**	—
0	**P**		**Airmen's Friend (IRE)**[24] 3200 5-11-2 0 PaulMoloney (Charlie Mann) *swtg: hld up in last pair: lost tch 5th: wl t.o and eased 7th: p.u bef 2 out* **100/1**	—

4m 43.7s (-4.30) **Going Correction** -0.05s/f (Good) **14** Ran SP% **120.4**
Speed ratings: **106,102,96,96,95 94,94,94,71,68** —,—,—,—
toteswingers:1&2 £4.00, 2&3 £34.10, 1&3 £25.80 CSF £21.78 TOTE £4.30: £1.60, £2.70, £6.40; EX 21.40 Trifecta £533.90 Pool of £2251.42 - 3.12 winning units..
Owner Donlon, Doyle, MacDonald & Webb **Bred** Gheorghe Codre **Trained** Ditcheat, Somerset

FOCUS
Just a fair novice hurdle. The winner was up a stone on his course run and looks a smart novice. The form is solid and the race should throw up plenty of winners.

NOTEBOOK
Poungach(FR) ◆ travelled strongly and readily asserted having gone on after two out. A fine, big sort, he had clearly learned a lot from November's hurdling debut third at the course and looked much more the finished article. His future lies over 3m, but he's clearly got the speed for this trip and, whilst thought to be on the fringes of Cheltenham class by Nicholls, he's inclined to miss it with him and instead go to Aintree. Whatever he does as a hurdler, it should be eclipsed once sent chasing. (op 7-2 tchd 11-4 and 4-1 in a place)
No Secrets(IRE) travelled well under a positive ride and finished clear of the remainder. He can win again and is another future chaser. (op 8-1 tchd 10-1 in a place)
Victoria Rose(IRE) ◆ confirmed the promise of her last-time-out Leicester second, again staying on well late and just getting up for third. She'll be winning in mares' only company back over a longer trip.
Carribs Leap(IRE) looked vulnerable under his 10lb penalty and, having been kicked into the lead by McCoy, was unable to hold on down the straight. (tchd 14-1)
Frontier Spirit(IRE) will find life easier in handicaps. (op 25-1)
Master Fiddle failed to build on the promise of his Ffos Las second, being beaten before stamina became an issue over this longer trip. (op 11-8 tchd 15-8)
Wise Move(IRE) ◆, making his debut over hurdles, comes from a family that includes plenty of winners. He stayed on late, having run green and struggled for the first half of the race, so he should learn a lot. (op 16-1)
Suburban Bay, off since winning a junior bumper in November 2008, travelled well up to a point, but that lack of an outing told in the end.
Amroth Bay Official explanation: jockey said gelding hung left
Eldred(IRE) looked lean.
T/Jkpt: Not won. T/Plt: £18.50 to a £1 stake. Pool of £161,866.12 - 6,374.97 winning tickets. T/Qpdt: £11.10 to a £1 stake. Pool of £10,388.97 - 687.36 winning tickets. JN

2519 HAYDOCK (L-H)
Saturday, January 22
3679 Meeting Abandoned - Frost

3448 WINCANTON (R-H)
Saturday, January 22

OFFICIAL GOING: Soft (good to soft in places; hdl 6.6, chs 6.4)
Wind: mild across Weather: overcast and cold

3686 BATHWICK TYRES YEOVIL H'CAP HURDLE (8 hdls) 2m
1:40 (1:41) (Class 3) (0-120,120) 4-Y-0+ **£4,878** (£1,432; £716; £357)

Form				RPR
P-14	**1**		**Minnie Hill (IRE)**[58] 2639 7-10-8 **109** EdGlassonbury(7) (Victor Dartnall) *chsd ldrs: led appr 2 out: sn rdn: styd on wl fr ast: drvn out* **4/1**[2]	113+

U-20 **2** *1½* **King's Revenge**[54] 2347 8-11-2 **117**...........................(b) PeterCarberry(7) 120
(Shaun Lycett) *in tch: rdn to chse wnr 2 out: ch last: kpt on but no ex* **14/1**

3 *2¼* **Tenor Nivernais (FR)**[145] 4-10-13 **118**............................ AidanColeman 109+
(Venetia Williams) *mid-div: hdwy after 3 out: rdn to chse ldng pair next: styd on but nt pce to chal* **7/1**[3]

5UFP **4** *3½* **Forest Rhythm (IRE)**[14] 3452 7-10-10 **107**.............. WayneKavanagh(3) 105
(Seamus Mullins) *hld up towards rr: rdn and stdy prog 3 out: styd on fr next: nrst fin* **40/1**

41 **5** *1¼* **If I Had Him (IRE)**[58] 2633 7-11-2 **110**.........................(v[1]) LeightonAspell 107
(George Baker) *mid-div: hdwy after 3 out: rdn to chse ldrs next: styd on same pce* **22/1**

P6P0 **6** *8* **Chilbury Hill (IRE)**[12] 3481 8-9-9 **94** oh1........................ GilesHawkins(5) 84
(Kevin Bishop) *hld up towards rr: styd on past btn horses fr 2 out: nvr nrr* **20/1**

2-44 **7** *3* **Bold Addition (FR)**[23] 3228 6-11-7 **120**............................ MrRMahon(5) 109
(Paul Nicholls) *trckd ldrs: led after 3 out: sn rdn: hdd appr next: sn wknd* **7/2**[1]

52FP **8** *1¾* **Russian Song (IRE)**[19] 3371 7-10-13 **107**..........................(p) JoeTizzard 92
(Colin Tizzard) *sn struggling towards rr: sme late prog past btn horses* **25/1**

3210 **9** *nse* **Henry Hook (IRE)**[19] 3370 7-11-7 **115**.................(p) AndrewGlassonbury 100
(Victor Dartnall) *a towards rr* **20/1**

2/30 **10** *2¼* **Tuanku (IRE)**[23] 3228 6-11-6 **117**.................................. CharlieHuxley(3) 100
(Alan King) *in tch: rdn after 3 out: wknd next* **10/1**

122U **11** *3¾* **Alesandro Mantegna (IRE)**[56] 2674 6-11-8 **116**...........(p) SamThomas 99
(Keith Goldsworthy) *mid-div: mstke 2nd: wknd 3 out* **10/1**

2/60 **12** *3½* **Russian Epic**[14] 3452 7-10-12 **106**..............................(t) RichardJohnson 86
(Philip Hobbs) *mid-div: rdn after 3 out: sn btn* **16/1**

P-00 **13** *13* **Prince Pippin (IRE)**[77] 2209 5-11-1 **112**.....................(t) MarcGoldstein(3) 77
(Michael Madgwick) *trckd ldr: led briefly after 3 out: sn rdn: wknd next* **40/1**

10-5 **14** *1¾* **Haarth Sovereign (IRE)**[252] 331 7-11-3 **111**............(t) TomMessenger 74
(Lawney Hill) *in tch: effrt after 3 out: wknd next* **12/1**

3243 **15** *9* **Cortinas (GER)**[58] 2633 9-10-7 **104**............................(t) TommyPhelan(3) 59
(Claire Dyson) *led tl after 3 out: sn wknd* **50/1**

0-50 **P** **Helens Vision**[38] 2955 8-11-4 **112**.................................... LiamTreadwell —
(James Evans) *mid-div tl 3rd: sn bhd: t.o whn p.u bef 2 out* **18/1**

3m 37.6s (-11.30) **Going Correction** -0.525s/f (Firm)
WFA 4 from 5yo+ 11lb **16** Ran SP% **123.0**
Speed ratings (Par 107): **107,106,105,103,102 98,97,96,96,95 93,91,85,84,79** —
Tote Swingers: 1&2 £26.40, 1&3 £11.60, 2&3 £29.40 CSF £53.74 CT £392.81 TOTE £5.80: £1.70, £4.80, £2.00, £8.80; EX 86.80.
Owner Mrs L M Northover **Bred** John Dineen **Trained** Brayford, Devon

FOCUS
A really competitive handicap. A personal best from the winner, with the second's best run since 2008.

NOTEBOOK
Minnie Hill(IRE) travelled strongly up with the pace throughout and showed a pleasing attitude under pressure to do enough. She appears to like this course (2 wins now from 3 starts) and, as this came off a career-high mark, seems to be improving. (op 7-1)
King's Revenge was always close up and fought on well when asked to go with Minnie Hill. He had little chance last time he was seen over hurdles behind Aegean Dawn at Cheltenham (he had one run on the AW since), but probably ran to the sort of level he did for this jockey the previous time over C&D. (op 16-1 tchd 20-1)
Tenor Nivernais(FR) looked fascinating on his first start in Britain and travelled strongly for a long way. He became outpaced turning in and seemed no threat, but he found a bit more and started to run on again. He either needed the run after a lengthy break or is in need of further (tchd 8-1)
Forest Rhythm(IRE) hadn't completed on his last three starts, so this was a lot better. He is at his best on a sound surface.
If I Had Him(IRE), wearing a visor for the first time, won a seller on his last start and shaped creditably here. He looked in need of further. (op 16-1)
Chilbury Hill(IRE) didn't run too badly, albeit well held. (op 33-1 tchd 18-1)
Bold Addition(FR) pulled hard and found little. (op 3-1)

3687 BATHWICK TYRES H'CAP CHASE (21 fncs) 3m 1f 110y
2:10 (2:11) (Class 3) (0-135,132) 5-Y-0+

£10,645 (£3,145; £1,572; £787; £392; £197)

Form RPR

-0U2 **1** **Cornish Sett (IRE)**[38] 2962 12-11-6 **126**.......................... NickScholfield 136+
(Caroline Keevil) *chsd ldrs: led narrowly 3 out: sn rdn and hrd pressed: styd on wl run-in: drvn out* **10/1**

-424 **2** *1* **Promising Anshan (IRE)**[24] 3198 6-11-1 **126**.................. MrRMahon(5) 135+
(Paul Nicholls) *chsd ldrs: jnd ldrs 12th: led 17th: rdn and hdd after 4 out: regained ld briefly bef next: remained upsides wnr: ev ch last: no ex* **11/2**[2]

6-05 **3** *11* **Theatre Dance (IRE)**[39] 2948 10-11-7 **127**...................... TimmyMurphy 128+
(David Arbuthnot) *hld up: hdwy after 17th: rdn after 4 out: j.lft last 3: wnt 3rd whn mstke 2 out: styd on but no ch w ldng pair* **5/1**[1]

-P10 **4** *5* **Darstardly Dick (IRE)**[23] 3229 8-11-2 **122**..........(b) AndrewGlassonbury 116
(Victor Dartnall) *mid-div: hdwy fr 15th: ev ch 4 out: sn rdn: styd on same pce fr next* **18/1**

0-2U **5** *¾* **Far More Serious (IRE)**[14] 3444 11-11-12 **132**.................. FelixDeGiles 131
(Charlie Longsdon) *in tch: jnd ldrs 16th: rdn to ld briefly appr 3 out: 4th and hld whn bdly hmpd 2 out* **10/1**

61-2 **6** *10* **Briery Fox (IRE)**[253] 314 13-11-5 **132**.................. JakeGreenall(7) 118
(Henry Daly) *stmbld bdly 1st: nvr really travelling after: a towards rr* **28/1**

0340 **7** *3¾* **Skipper's Lad (IRE)**[40] 2928 9-9-7 **106** oh5..........(b) MrRGHenderson(7) 87
(Colin Tizzard) *disp ld most of way tl rdn to chse ldrs after 16th: wknd after 3 out* **50/1**

20-0 **8** *4½* **Notabotheronme (IRE)**[71] 2343 9-10-1 **112**..............(p) GilesHawkins(5) 89
(Philip Hobbs) *a towards rr* **12/1**

51P3 **9** *58* **Peut Etre Sivola (FR)**[20] 3347 8-10-10 **116**.................(v) JohnnyFarrelly 40
(David Pipe) *mid-div: effrt after 16th: wknd after 4 out: t.o* **8/1**

0062 **F** **Omix D'Or (FR)**[12] 3482 9-10-5 **111**.................................(p) DavidDennis —
(James Evans) *led: blnd 11th: hdd after 16th: fell next: fatally injured* **9/1**

301F **F** **Triggerman**[12] 3479 9-11-12 **132**.................................. RichardJohnson —
(Philip Hobbs) *in tch: pushed along fr 15th: rdn after 4 out: styng on in cl enough 4th whn fell 3 out* **7/1**[3]

2113 **P** **Flying Squad (UAE)**[5] 3602 7-10-1 **110**...................(t) JimmyDerham(3) —
(Milton Harris) *a in rr: bhd whn p.u bef 3 out* **8/1**

6m 33.8s (-5.70) **Going Correction** -0.225s/f (Good) **12** Ran SP% **113.3**
Speed ratings: **99,98,95,93,93 90,89,87,70,**— —,—
Tote Swingers: 1&2 £13.40, 1&3 £19.20, 2&3 £4.40 CSF £62.68 CT £309.01 TOTE £10.40: £3.00, £2.20, £2.00; EX 81.80.
Owner Peter Hart **Bred** J F C Maxwell **Trained** Blagdon, Somerset

FOCUS
The pace looked sound for the distance, but two were left well clear in the latter stages. The winner is enjoying a resurgence and the second posted a personal best.

NOTEBOOK
Cornish Sett(IRE) is undoubtedly fairly handicapped, but it sometimes appears his mind needs to be fully focused on the task in hand to be at his best. Today was a good day for him, as he was always going well in behind and things fell right for him in front. He cruised into the lead turning in but was made to work harder than looked likely for victory. His form at class 3 level and lower is very consistent. (op 17-2)
Promising Anshan(IRE), back up in distance, was less exposed than most of his rivals and ran a fine race after being close up throughout. He looked far from comfortable close to the line (his head came up and so did his tail), but you couldn't fault his resolution before that happened, and something may well have gone amiss late on. (op 5-1)
Theatre Dance(IRE), another back up in trip, was ridden with restraint and made little impression. A mistake two out made little difference. (op 13-2)
Darstardly Dick(IRE), well beaten in a strong handicap hurdle on his last run, didn't pose a serious threat and is possibly better in smaller fields. (op 14-1)
Far More Serious(IRE), still well above his highest winning mark, looked to have every chance but found only the one-pace before three out. He was held when Theatre Dance cannoned into him at the second-last fence. (op 9-1)
Briery Fox(IRE), having his first outing since May, was keen early and will no doubt be straighter for this run. (op 25-1)
Triggerman was beginning to stay on when coming to grief at the third-last fence. He was far from beaten at the time and may well have troubled the front two had he stayed upright. (op 6-1)

3688 BATHWICK TYRES DORCHESTER H'CAP HURDLE (11 hdls) 2m 6f
2:50 (2:51) (Class 3) (0-125,125) 4-Y-0+ **£4,878** (£1,432; £716; £357)

Form RPR

-U41 **1** **Sparrow Hills (IRE)**[14] 3452 7-10-11 **117**.......................... RobertKirk(7) 120
(Steven Dixon) *a.p: led 3 out: rdn and briefly hdd appr 2 out: hdd narrowly run-in: kpt on gamely to regain ld fnl strides* **14/1**

P-32 **2** *hd* **Lupanar (IRE)**[61] 2581 7-10-9 **118**........................(p) JosephAkehurst(10) 121
(Gary Moore) *mid-div: hdwy after 3 out: chal sn after next: sn rdn: tk narrow advantage run-in: hdd fnl strides* **25/1**

12-0 **3** *½* **Shoegazer (IRE)**[43] 2868 6-11-12 **125**...........................(t) JohnnyFarrelly 127
(David Pipe) *hld up towards rr: gd hdwy 3 out: sn rdn: styd on wl to have ev ch run-in: no ex nr fin* **10/1**

F-44 **4** *nk* **Busker Royal**[231] 633 8-11-8 **124**............................ RichardKilloran(3) 126
(Nicky Henderson) *mid-div: hdwy after 3 out: rdn next: styd on to hold ev ch sn after last: no ex nr fin* **20/1**

-430 **5** *1¾* **Boomtown Kat**[81] 2141 7-10-9 **111**.......................... EamonDehdashti(3) 111
(Karen George) *chsd ldrs: rdn after 3 out: ch next: wnt rt last: no ex* **66/1**

5223 **6** *1* **Five Star Wilsham (IRE)**[14] 3452 7-11-4 **117**................ NickScholfield 117
(Jeremy Scott) *mid-div: hdwy after 8th: rdn into narrow advantage briefly appr 2 out: ev ch last: no ex* **13/2**[2]

4440 **7** *nk* **William Hogarth**[7] 3557 6-11-6 **122**.........................(p) CharlieHuxley(3) 121
(Keith Goldsworthy) *mid-div: hdwy after 3 out: rdn to chse ldrs next: wnt rt last: styd on same pce* **40/1**

31-1 **8** *2½* **Requin (FR)**[37] 2977 6-11-8 **121**.............................. AndrewGlassonbury 118
(Victor Dartnall) *rdn after 3 out: nvr bttr than mid-div* **9/1**

4023 **9** *nk* **Bally Legend**[23] 3228 6-11-3 **119**............................... WayneKavanagh(3) 116
(Caroline Keevil) *in tch: effrt after 3 out: one pce fr next* **8/1**[3]

3R26 **10** *4* **Posh Emily**[12] 3481 8-10-3 **107**.................................. MattGriffiths(5) 100
(Ron Hodges) *hld up towards rr: sme late prog: nvr a factor* **50/1**

0FUF **11** *1¼* **Scots Dragoon**[38] 2962 9-10-11 **120**.................. JeremiahMcGrath(10) 112
(Nicky Henderson) *prom: rdn after 3 out: one pce fr next* **40/1**

30 **12** *nk* **Valento**[14] 3447 6-11-5 **118**.. JasonMaguire 110
(Kim Bailey) *a towards rr: hdwy after 3 out: rdn bef next: edgd rt and no further imp* **33/1**

2-13 **13** *½* **That'Ll Do**[58] 2634 6-11-2 **120**.. MrRMahon(5) 111
(Paul Nicholls) *mid-div: hdwy on outer after 3 out: sn rdn: wknd bef last* **6/1**[1]

634 **14** *¾* **Gunna Be A Devil (IRE)**[21] 3295 7-10-11 **115**.............. GilesHawkins(5) 106
(Jeremy Scott) *hld up towards rr: effrt after 3 out but nvr on terms w ldrs* **14/1**

-323 **15** *3½* **Devon Native (IRE)**[12] 3483 8-10-7 **113**........................ DannyBurton(7) 100
(Chris Down) *led tl 3 out: sn btn* **16/1**

4-53 **16** *2¾* **Red Mile (FR)**[20] 3340 6-10-13 **112**...................................... SamThomas 97
(Emma Lavelle) *in tch tl dropped in rr and struggling 7th: nvr a danger after* **9/1**

-603 **17** *¾* **Ceepeegee (IRE)**[21] 3299 6-11-0 **113**.................................... JoeTizzard 97
(Colin Tizzard) *mid-div tl dropped in rr 6th: nt a danger after* **50/1**

-460 **18** *shd* **Maraafeq (USA)**[14] 3440 7-11-8 **121**............................... AidanColeman 105
(Venetia Williams) *in tch: rdn after 3 out: wknd bef 2 out* **16/1**

-022 **19** *18* **Romance Dance**[201] 910 8-10-9 **108**............................. LeightonAspell 76
(Sophie Leech) *mid-div tl wknd after 3 out: t.o* **50/1**

0-34 **20** *5* **Wester Ross (IRE)**[18] 2636 7-11-4 **117**.........................(p) FelixDeGiles 81
(James Eustace) *a towards rr: t.o* **50/1**

2005 **21** *31* **Ring For Time**[14] 3440 8-11-2 **115**..(p) RhysFlint 51
(John Flint) *mid-div tl wknd after 7th: t.o* **16/1**

5m 14.2s (-12.30) **Going Correction** -0.525s/f (Firm) **21** Ran SP% **124.6**
Speed ratings (Par 107): **101,100,100,100,100 99,99,98,98,97 96,96,96,96,94 93,93,93,86,85 73**
Tote Swingers: 1&2 £35.40, 1&3 £53.20 CSF £330.28 CT £3646.57 TOTE £19.70: £4.50, £5.20, £2.50, £7.00; EX 252.90.
Owner S Dixon **Bred** Ged Quain **Trained** Winterslow, Wilts

FOCUS
Despite the huge field, the gallop early looked far from strong, and quite a few took a strong hold. They finished in a heap and the form is ordinary.

NOTEBOOK
Sparrow Hills(IRE), 5lb higher after winning at this course over 2m4f last time, raced prominently and showed a willing attitude under pressure. The move to Steven Dixon's stable has appeared to rejuvenate the horse, and Sparrow Hills is still lightly raced for his age and capable of more. (op 18-1)
Lupanar(IRE) had gone close on his previous two starts and was only narrowly denied again. The cheekpieces have had a positive effect on him, despite him losing the lead towards the end.
Shoegazer(IRE), stepped back up in trip again, travelled strongly in rear and made a positive move when the tempo lifted. He looked a big danger as he moved through but his big weight looked to take its toll after the final hurdle. Johnny Farrelly appeared to stop riding for a few strides close to the winning line but, thankfully for him, it made no difference to the final outcome. Official explanation: caution: used whip with excessive frequency. (op 17-2 tchd 8-1)
Busker Royal, having his first run since last June, can go well fresh and shaped nicely. He met bits of trouble while buried away in midfield and was possibly unlucky not be a bit closer despite having every chance. (op 18-1)
Boomtown Kat ◆, a previous C&D winner, shaped with lots of promise on his first outing since early November, and is worth considering next time on quicker ground.

Five Star Wilsham(IRE) should have finished much closer to the winner judged on their meeting last time, but he pulled hard early and may not have got home as a result. (op 9-1)
William Hogarth, beaten a long way a week previously at Kempton, kept on but was made to look one-paced. (op 50-1)
Requin(FR) was one of the least exposed in the field but hit a serious flat spot and could only run on towards the end. (op 6-1)
Bally Legend, taking a big step up in trip, stayed on but never looked dangerous.
That'Ll Do, having only his fourth start under rules, and first in a handicap, was beaten before the race got really competitive. (op 7-1)

3689 BATHWICK TYRES TAUNTON H'CAP CHASE (17 fncs) 2m 5f
3:25 (3:25) (Class 3) (0-130,130) 5-Y-O+ **£6,337** (£1,872; £936; £468; £234)

Form				RPR
6-33	1		**Bugsy's Boy**[92] 1952 7-10-4 **115**.....(p) TrevorWhelan(7) (George Baker) *chsd ldrs: disp fr 10th: outrt ldr after 4 out: kpt on wl: rdn out* **12/1**	125+
4515	2	1 1/4	**Holmwood Legend**[43] 2869 10-11-4 **122**..... FelixDeGiles (Patrick Rodford) *in tch: rdn to chse ldrs after 13th: chsd wnr 3 out: styd on but no ex fr last* **6/1**[3]	131+
6-34	3	16	**Emergency Exit (IRE)**[25] 3157 8-11-2 **120**..... RichardJohnson (Philip Hobbs) *hld up: hit 3rd: mstke 5th: hdwy after 13th: wnt 3rd 3 out: sn rdn: no ch w ldng pair fr next* **9/1**	117+
61	4	2 1/4	**Roi De Rose (FR)**[15] 3433 7-11-4 **122**.....(p) JohnnyFarrelly (David Pipe) *led: pckd 8th: rdn and hdd after 4 out: fdd fr next* **2/1**[1]	113
4004	5	4	**Double Dizzy**[14] 3453 10-10-10 **114**.....(t) AndrewGlassonbury (Bob Buckler) *chsng ldrs whn blnd bdly 4th: struggling in rr 9th: nvr a threat after* **9/1**	103
1530	6	1 1/4	**Circus Of Dreams**[56] 2674 8-11-3 **121**.....(v) LeightonAspell (Oliver Sherwood) *in tch: rdn after 4 out: lft 5th 3 out: wknd next: blnd last* **16/1**	110
-335	F		**Le Burf (FR)**[14] 3453 10-11-7 **125**..... LiamTreadwell (Giles Smyly) *in tch: mstke 11th: rdn after 13th: one pce and hld in 5th whn fell 3 out* **7/2**[2]	—
/P0-	P		**Qrackers (FR)**[406] 2830 7-11-12 **130**..... AidanColeman (Venetia Williams) *in tch: trckd ldrs 6th: rdn and wknd after 4 out: p.u bef 2 out* **20/1**	—
11-0	P		**Bradford Boris**[14] 3453 7-10-12 **119**..... JimmyDerham(3) (Nick Williams) *prom: nt fluent 6th: dropped to rr qckly 10th: t.o whn p.u bef 4 out* **7/1**	—

5m 16.7s (-8.50) **Going Correction** -0.225s/f (Good) **9** Ran SP% **120.7**
Speed ratings: **107,106,100,99,98 97,—,—,—**
Tote Swingers: 1&2 £14.80, 1&3 £6.70, 2&3 £16.80 CSF £85.75 CT £694.68 TOTE £14.40: £3.00, £2.70, £2.60; EX 87.40.
Owner Seaton Partnership **Bred** Mrs R S Evans **Trained** Whitsbury, Hants

FOCUS
A fair-looking contest run in a decent time. Improvement from the first two.

NOTEBOOK
Bugsy's Boy, off the track since late October, had cheekpieces on for the first time over Jumps (he wore them plenty of times on the Flat), and they may have made the difference, as he jumped and travelled beautifully before keeping on well over the final three fences. He seems to act in most ground. (op 16-1 tchd 18-1)
Holmwood Legend gave chase to the winner down the home straight but would have almost certainly still been beaten had he not clipped the top of two out. (op 8-1)
Emergency Exit(IRE), disappointing since his win on his first start for this stable in January of last year over C&D, made jumping errors, so gave himself no chance of getting involved. (op 8-1)
Roi De Rose(FR), raised 10lb after a really impressive performance at Fontwell, was readily held once the winner kicked away from him going to three from home. (op 9-4 tchd 5-2 and 11-4 in places)
Le Burf(FR), who was below his last winning mark after slipping down the weights, got behind and was making no impression when falling three out. (op 4-1 tchd 10-3)
Qrackers(FR) ◆, dropped 10lb since his last run over fences back in December 2009, had never run over this far before and was without his usual tongue-tie, but shaped nicely and will be of some interest down in distance and with the aid refitted. (op 4-1 tchd 10-3)
Bradford Boris didn't show a lot of his seasonal reappearance and dropped away alarmingly here down the back straight. (op 4-1 tchd 10-3)

3690 BATHWICK TYRES SALISBURY NOVICES' CHASE (17 fncs) 2m 5f
4:00 (4:00) (Class 3) 5-Y-O+ **£5,529** (£1,623; £811; £405)

Form				RPR
FF61	1		**Forget It**[82] 2124 6-10-12 117..... AndrewGlassonbury (Gary Moore) *hld up: smooth hdwy to trck ldr after 13th: led sn after 3 out: pushed clr fr next: readily* **12/1**	124+
140-	2	6	**Lady Bling Bling**[283] 5184 10-10-5 109..... MarkGrant (Peter Jones) *trckd ldrs: led sn after 8th: mstke 4 out: rdn whn mstke 3 out: sn hdd: kpt on but sn hld by wnr* **33/1**	112+
/2U0	3	10	**Carrickboy (IRE)**[39] 2948 7-10-12 120..... AidanColeman (Venetia Williams) *trcking ldrs whn v bdly hmpd and virtually b.d 8th (rdr lost irons): bhd: hdwy after 13th: effrt 3 out: fading whn lft 3rd next* **10/3**[2]	118+
6-02	4	1 1/4	**Horsford (IRE)**[21] 3299 7-10-12 117.....(t) JohnnyFarrelly (David Pipe) *trckd ldrs: hit 11th: rdn and ev ch 4 out: wknd next: lft 4th 2 out* **9/4**[1]	107
021F	5	18	**Mud Monkey**[61] 2587 7-10-12 120.....(t) SamThomas (Claire Dyson) *led tl 4th: cl up: bdly hmpd 8th: rdn after 13th: wknd after next: wnt bdly lft 2 out: t.o* **5/1**[3]	96
504-	6	2 1/4	**Speed Bonnie Boat**[359] 3697 8-9-12 115..... JakeGreenall(7) (Henry Daly) *chsd ldrs tl 7th: rdn after 8th: in rr fr 10th: t.o* **18/1**	83
-0B2	P		**Fiftyonefiftyone (IRE)**[20] 3339 7-10-12 120..... LeightonAspell (Oliver Sherwood) *trckd ldrs: led 4th: mstke 7th: wnt rt: hdd and bmpd next: rdn after 11th: wknd after 4 out: bhd whn p.u bef 2 out* **14/1**	—
P31P	P		**Prescelli (IRE)**[15] 3429 7-10-5 117.....(p) RhysFlint (Keith Goldsworthy) *in tch: mstke 8th: sn pushed along: lost tch fr 10th: t.o whn p.u bef 4 out* **16/1**	—
U	F		**Symphonick (FR)**[9] 3531 5-10-8 119..... NickScholfield (Paul Nicholls) *hld up: hit 7th: hdwy 12th: rdn after 4 out: pckd next: 3rd and hld whn fell 2 out* **13/2**	110+

5m 23.8s (-1.40) **Going Correction** -0.225s/f (Good)
WFA 5 from 6yo+ 4lb **9** Ran SP% **112.3**
Speed ratings: **93,90,86,86,79 78,—,—,—**
Tote Swingers: 1&2 £47.50, 1&3 £8.30, 2&3 £35.70 CSF £262.99 TOTE £9.90: £3.30, £4.30, £1.50; EX 220.50.
Owner The Cockpit Crew **Bred** Mrs J Chandris **Trained** Lower Beeding, W Sussex

FOCUS
A 0-120 novice chase, run at an average gallop. The winner is rated up 5lb on his previous chase win.

NOTEBOOK
Forget It made it 2-2 since going chasing and ran out a ready winner. He had fallen in two of his three outings over hurdles after winning in that sphere last season, but his jumping is so much better over fences and he obviously stays well. His trainer does well with this sort of performer and a bold bid for the hat-trick should be expected. (op 10-1)
Lady Bling Bling, returning from 283-day break, ran a blinder under a positive ride, and would have given the winner more of a fight had she not blundered three out. She should only improve. (op 28-1)
Carrickboy(IRE)'s rider performed miracles to stay aboard after he got badly hampered the eighth fence and, while he did well enough to finish third in the circumstances, his jumping continues to be less than convincing. (op 7-2 tchd 3-1)
Horsford(IRE), placed in both his Irish points, came in for support on this switch to fences. He had his chance, but was disappointingly one-paced in the home straight and perhaps he wants dropping back in trip. Official explanation: jockey said gelding jumped poorly (op 11-4 tchd 3-1 in places)
Mud Monkey was too free for his own good through the early parts. (tchd 6-1)
Fiftyonefiftyone(IRE) Official explanation: jockey said gelding hung left-handed (op 7-1 tchd 6-1)
Symphonick(FR) looked a threat four out, but was toiling before he departed. (op 7-1 tchd 6-1)

3691 BATHWICK TYRES BRIDGWATER "NATIONAL HUNT" NOVICES' HURDLE (8 hdls) 2m
4:30 (4:31) (Class 4) 4-Y-O+ **£2,602** (£764; £382; £95; £95)

Form				RPR
05	1		**Furrows**[61] 2590 6-11-4 0..... LeightonAspell (Oliver Sherwood) *hld up bhd: stdy prog after 3 out: wnt 2 l 2nd whn mstke last: sn rdn: styd on strly towards fin: led fnl stride* **66/1**	93+
0-56	2	nk	**Behindcloseddoors (IRE)**[8] 3542 5-11-4 0..... JasonMaguire (Kim Bailey) *led: rdn after 2 out: 2 l clr last: ct fnl stride* **25/1**	91
155-	3	2 1/2	**Ramses De Marcigny (FR)**[303] 4846 6-10-13 0..... MrRMahon(5) (Paul Nicholls) *in tch: mstke 1st: wnt rt 2nd: rdn after 3 out: styd on same pce* **7/2**[2]	89
606	4	3/4	**Hawkaller**[23] 3225 6-10-13 0..... RachaelGreen(5) (Anthony Honeyball) *trckd ldrs: wnt 2nd after 3 out: mstke next: sn rdn: hit last: kpt on same pce* **7/1**	90
020	4	dht	**Tenby Jewel (IRE)**[15] 3434 6-11-1 0..... CharlieHuxley(3) (Keith Goldsworthy) *mid-div: hdwy after 3 out: rdn and hung rt after next: styd on* **66/1**	88
40	6	2 1/2	**Cap Elorn (FR)**[59] 2607 5-11-4 0..... HarrySkelton (Paul Nicholls) *hld up towards rr: rdn and hdwy after 3 out: styd on same pce fr next* **16/1**	87
00-3	7	1 1/4	**Joker Choker (IRE)**[74] 2295 6-11-1 0..... RichardKilloran(3) (Nicky Henderson) *hld up towards rr: hdwy 3 out: rdn to chse ldrs next: styd on same pce fr last* **14/1**	86
5-60	8	9	**Calico Rose**[37] 2974 7-10-11 0..... AndrewGlassonbury (Victor Dartnall) *rdn after 3 out: nvr bttr than mid-div* **16/1**	70
051	9	2 1/2	**Nosecond Chance (IRE)**[21] 3304 5-11-8 117..... PeterToole(3) (Charlie Mann) *in tch: rdn appr 2 out: wknd last* **11/2**[3]	81
05	10	2	**Direct Flo (IRE)**[61] 2570 4-10-0 0..... SeanQuinlan (Kim Bailey) *a towards rr* **100/1**	54
0-06	11	7	**Russian Conquest**[19] 3372 5-11-1 0..... WayneKavanagh(3) (Seamus Mullins) *hit 2 out: a towards rr* **100/1**	66
60	12	1 1/2	**Wosayu**[21] 3301 5-11-4 0..... JoeTizzard (Colin Tizzard) *mid-div: rdn after 5th: btn whn mstke 3 out* **100/1**	65
600	13	5	**Calusa Catrina (IRE)**[21] 3296 6-10-4 0..... ChrisDavies(7) (Philip Hobbs) *mid-div: rdn after 3 out: sn wknd* **50/1**	53
000/	14	5	**Honest**[675] 4571 8-11-1 0..... EamonDehdashti(3) (Karen George) *struggling 4th: a towards rr* **100/1**	56
/0-0	15	8	**Steptoe**[252] 327 6-11-4 0..... FelixDeGiles (Nicky Henderson) *mid-div: hdwy into 3rd after 3 out: rdn and wknd qckly bef next* **28/1**	49
6	16	2 1/2	**Otis Tarda (IRE)**[107] 1748 5-10-13 0..... RhysFlint(5) (Philip Hobbs) *racd keenly: trckd ldrs: rdn after 3 out: sn wknd* **40/1**	46
40	17	34	**E Street Boy**[23] 3225 5-11-4 0..... JohnnyFarrelly (David Pipe) *struggling 5th: a towards rr: t.o* **50/1**	16
3-16	18	6	**Arthurian Legend**[48] 2791 6-11-11 0..... RichardJohnson (Philip Hobbs) *trckd ldrs: mstke 3rd: rdn after 3 out: wknd qckly: t.o* **9/4**[1]	17

3m 44.7s (-4.20) **Going Correction** -0.525s/f (Firm)
WFA 4 from 5yo+ 11lb **18** Ran SP% **119.9**
Speed ratings (Par 105): **89,88,87,87,87 85,85,80,79,78 75,74,71,69,65 64,47,44**
Tote Swingers: 1&2 £41.10, 1&3 £39.10, 2&3 £42.00 CSF £1200.58 TOTE £77.50: £16.30, £7.10, £2.40; EX 2570.20.
Owner Furrows Ltd **Bred** John Coward & Mrs Rachael Downey **Trained** Upper Lambourn, Berks

FOCUS
This weak novice hurdle was run at a modest gallop and there was a turn up with the first pair being sent off at odds of 66/1 and 25/1 respectively. The first two improved but this isn't form to get carried away with.

NOTEBOOK
Furrows made smooth headway from off the pace and looked likely to win nicely coming to the last, but he made a mess of it. To his credit he picked up again and was narrowly on top where it mattered. This half-brother to his stable's moderate chaser Abey M'boy will be jumping fences down the line, but should be open to improvement in this sphere beforehand.
Behindcloseddoors(IRE) made a bold bid to lead all the way and showed much-improved form. He deserves to go one better. (tchd 28-1)
Ramses De Marcigny(FR) proved easy to back on this seasonal and hurdling debut. He jumped well in the main, but looks to be crying out for a longer trip. (op 3-1 tchd 4-1)
Hawkaller lost out with two messy jumps over the final two flights, but this was a clear personal-best effort. (op 15-2 tchd 6-1 after 12-1 in a lpace)
Tenby Jewel(IRE)caught the eye with the way he travelled through the race and posted a pleasing hurdling debut. A stiffer test should suit ideally. (op 15-2 tchd 6-1 after 12-1 in a lpace)
Cap Elorn(FR) ◆ was doing his best work late in the day and is one to side with over a stiffer test. (op 33-1)
Joker Choker(IRE) had every chance on this switch to hurdling and, despite being one of his trainer's lesser lights, can be placed to strike as he gains experience. (op 9-1 tchd 16-1)
Nosecond Chance(IRE) struggled to see out the race under his penalty. (op 8-1 tchd 9-2)
Arthurian Legend dropped out alarmingly on the far side. Something surely must have been amiss. (op 5-2 tchd 11-4)

T/Plt: £2,001.90 to a £1 stake. Pool of £114,300.73 - 41.68 winning tickets. T/Qpdt: £314.20 to a £1 stake. Pool of £6,328.24 - 14.90 winning tickets. TM

2473 MARKET RASEN (R-H)

Sunday, January 23

OFFICIAL GOING: Chase course - good to soft (good in places; 5.9); hurdle course - good (good to soft in places; 6.5)

Rails on innermost line reducing circuit distance by 48yds.

Wind: moderate 1/2 against Weather: overcast, damp and cool, shower after race 3

3692 WATCH RACING UK ON SKY CHANNEL 432 NOVICES' HURDLE (10 hdls) 2m 3f

1:20 (1:20) (Class 4) 4-Y-0+ **£2,602** (£764; £382; £190)

Form / RPR

1-11 **1** **Problema Tic (FR)**[18] 3398 5-11-12 0 APMcCoy 132+
(Nicky Henderson) *trckd ldrs: upsides whn nt fluent 2 out: slt ld last: styd on to assert clsng stages* **10/11**[1]

0 **2** 1 ½ **Saint Are (FR)**[22] 3288 5-11-12 0 RichardJohnson 124
(Tim Vaughan) *chsd ldrs: lft in ld bnd after 5th: hdd last: no ex fnl 100yds* **5/1**[3]

34P/ **3** ½ **Wistow**[695] 4171 7-10-12 0 SeanQuinlan 110
(Pam Sly) *mid-div: hdwy 6th: handy 3rd and nt fluent 2 out: styd on run-in* **50/1**

0 **4** 15 **Cool Strike (UAE)**[24] 3225 5-11-5 0 SamThomas 101
(Alex Hales) *in tch: drvn and outpcd after 3 out: no threat after: tk modest 4th last* **40/1**

6/3- **5** 2 ¾ **Hudibras (IRE)**[431] 2361 7-11-2 0 PeterToole(3) 98
(Charlie Mann) *chsd ldrs: hit 7th: hrd drvn and outpcd next: wknd between last 2* **14/1**

6 2 ½ **Maraased**[267] 6-11-5 0 RhysFlint 96
(Steve Gollings) *trckd ldrs: t.k.h: outpcd and hung lft bnd appr 2 out: sn wknd* **80/1**

06 **7** 31 **Speed Dating**[10] 3521 5-11-5 0 DougieCostello 65
(John Quinn) *mid-div: hdwy 6th: drvn 3 out: sn wknd and bhd* **25/1**

0 **8** 10 **Practice Round (IRE)**[78] 2215 5-11-2 0 RichieMcLernon(3) 55
(Jonjo O'Neill) *chsd ldrs: lost pl after 7th: sn bhd* **100/1**

9 ¾ **Tait's Clock (IRE)** 5-11-5 0 RichieMcGrath 54
(Jonjo O'Neill) *nt fluent in rr: bhd fr 7th* **80/1**

6 **10** 2 ½ **Glory Nights**[235] 589 7-11-5 0 LiamTreadwell 52
(Dr Richard Newland) *nt fluent in rr: bhd fr 6th: t.o 3 out* **80/1**

11 5 **Look Officer (USA)**[40] 5-10-9 0 (t) AdamPogson(3) 40
(Mandy Rowland) *hld up in rr: hdwy 7th: wknd appr 2 out: fin lame* **150/1**

P **12** 17 **Maybeme**[4] 3637 5-10-7 0 BrianToomey(5) 23
(Neville Bycroft) *j.lft and nt fluent: in rr: sme hdwy 6th: sn wknd* **200/1**

50 **13** 15 **King Sandor (IRE)**[21] 3330 6-11-5 0 BrianHarding 15
(Nicky Richards) *nt fluent in rr: reminders after 3rd: bhd fr 6th: t.o 3 out* **100/1**

0-22 **R** **Dear Sam (GER)**[66] 2473 6-11-5 115 TomScudamore —
(Steve Gollings) *led: hung bdly lft and rn out bnd after 5th* **5/2**[2]

2303 **U** **High Hoylander**[19] 3387 5-11-5 0 HenryOliver —
(Sue Smith) *hld up towards rr: mstke and uns rdr 4th* **33/1**

4m 28.6s (-10.80) **Going Correction** -0.30s/f (Good) **15** Ran SP% **122.3**
Speed ratings (Par 105): **110,109,109,102,101 100,87,83,83,82 79,72,66,—,—**
Tote Swingers: 1&2 £1.90, 1&3 £18.60, 2&3 £31.90 CSF £6.09 TOTE £1.70: £1.40, £1.50, £10.60.
Owner Sir Robert Ogden **Bred** Julien Merienne & Mrs Maryvonne Merienne **Trained** Upper Lambourn, Berks

FOCUS
The course passed a morning inspection and the ground was described as good to soft, good in places. The surface certainly appeared to be riding sound enough in this opening novice hurdle, which was run at a decent tempo.

NOTEBOOK
Problema Tic(FR) came out on top near the finish and followed up his Southwell success with a little more authority than the bare margin suggests. He did well to pick up again after hitting two out and the longer trip helped his cause. Now unbeaten in four career outings, he obviously has a bit of class but things will be tougher from here on. (op 4-7 tchd Evens)
Saint Are(FR), despite being well beaten on his British debut at Cheltenham on New Year's Day, still ran encouragingly there, and this former French winner rates a good benchmark for the form. He can land one of these before going handicapping. (op 15-2)
Wistow made a pleasing comeback effort and her proximity should not be used to drag this form down too much. (op 66-1)
Cool Strike(UAE) ran a much more encouraging race than his hurdling debut 24 days earlier and the better ground helped. He shaped as though even further is what he wants.
Hudibras(IRE) moved nicely in mid-field, but found just the one pace and tired in the home straight. He ought to come on a good deal for the run. (op 20-1 tchd 22-1)
Look Officer(USA) Official explanation: vet said mare pulled up lame right-fore
Dear Sam(GER), who was well backed, ran out on the turn going out on to the far side and ended up on the chase course. He got warm beforehand and again proved free out in front. It was clear shortly before he veered off the course that his rider was having trouble and this leaves him with lots to prove. (op 4-1)

3693 MARKETRASENRACES.CO.UK CONDITIONAL JOCKEYS' H'CAP HURDLE (10 hdls) 2m 5f

1:50 (1:50) (Class 4) (0-115,115) 4-Y-0+ **£2,602** (£764; £382; £190)

Form / RPR

4004 **1** **Apache Chant (USA)**[19] 3392 7-10-3 95 (p) LeeEdwards(3) 98
(Tony Carroll) *in rr: hdwy 3 out: short of room appr next: chal appr last: edgd rt and kpt on to ld last 100yds: all out* **14/1**

-066 **2** ½ **Farmers Cross (IRE)**[65] 2506 7-10-4 101 TonyKelly(8) 103
(Ferdy Murphy) *hld up in rr: gd hdwy 6th: led and hmpd by loose horse appr 2 out: hdd last 100yds: crowded and no ex* **14/1**

3-44 **3** 3 **What A Steel (IRE)**[12] 3502 7-10-1 93 EwanWhillans(3) 94+
(Alistair Whillans) *trckd ldrs: t.k.h: drvn 3 out: short of room appr next: hung lft and one pce appr last* **9/2**[1]

-020 **4** 4 ½ **Madame Jasmine**[44] 2873 6-10-9 98 RichieMcLernon 93
(Suzy Smith) *chsd ldrs: lft cl 2nd 3 out: one pce fr next* **13/2**[2]

4-43 **5** 1 ½ **Tricky Tree (IRE)**[71] 2375 5-11-3 106 CPGeoghegan 101+
(Pam Sly) *chsd ldrs: drvn whn hmpd 3 out: one pce 6th whn j.lft and mstke last* **25/1**

0P3F **6** 1 **Carrickmines (IRE)**[39] 2962 9-11-8 111 (b) FearghalDavis 104
(Dr Richard Newland) *in rr: gd hdwy 7th: chsng ldrs after next: upsides whn hit 2 out: wknd last* **14/1**

1-50 **7** 2 ½ **Willandrich (IRE)**[20] 3370 9-11-3 106 MichaelMurphy 103+
(Ian Williams) *chsd ldrs: keeping on whn bdly hmpd appr 2 out: nt rcvr* **10/1**

-123 **8** hd **Lemon Silk (IRE)**[40] 2949 7-11-2 105 DavidBass 94
(Alex Hales) *in rr: drvn and sme hdwy 3 out: nvr nr ldrs* **13/2**[2]

06- **9** 8 **Very Edgy (IRE)**[328] 4357 7-11-7 110 (p) TomMolloy 91
(Charles Egerton) *in rr: drvn 6th: sn bhd: sme hdwy appr 2 out: sn wknd* **16/1**

5024 **10** nse **Hippodrome (IRE)**[66] 2477 9-10-8 100 (p) MattCrawley(3) 81
(John Harris) *mid-div: lost pl 3 out* **33/1**

-206 **11** 4 **Life Long (IRE)**[67] 2454 7-10-11 100 CharlieHuxley 77
(Anabel L M King) *in rr: drvn 5th: wl bhd fr3 out* **28/1**

6-20 **12** 9 **Tahiti Pearl (IRE)**[13] 3490 7-11-0 106 ow1 ShaneByrne(3) 94+
(Sue Smith) *mde most to 7th: lft in ld next: hdd and wkng whn bdly hmpd appr 2 out: eased* **33/1**

U- **13** 1 ½ **Be Definite (IRE)**[421] 2564 7-11-12 115 PeterToole 82
(Tom George) *in rr: bhd fr 3 out* **33/1**

-4U4 **14** 1 ½ **Skipper Robin (FR)**[38] 2981 5-11-4 110 SamTwiston-Davies(3) 75
(Nigel Twiston-Davies) *chsd ldrs: hung rt and lost pl after 3 out* **20/1**

F2/4 **15** 2 ½ **Carndonagh (IRE)**[75] 2296 7-11-3 109 JamesHalliday(3) 74
(Malcolm Jefferson) *chsd ldrs: pckd 3rd: lost pl 3 out* **12/1**

4 **U** **Stonethrower (IRE)**[20] 3370 6-11-6 115 (t) MrTomDavid(6) —
(Tim Vaughan) *w ldr: led 7th: blnd and uns rdr next* **7/1**[3]

5m 4.00s (-4.80) **Going Correction** -0.30s/f (Good) **16** Ran SP% **120.9**
Speed ratings (Par 105): **97,96,95,93,93 93,92,91,88,88 87,83,83,82,81 —**
Tote Swingers: 1&2 £67.10, 1&3 £27.90, 2&3 £6.00 CSF £176.88 CT £1026.20 TOTE £10.40: £2.60, £4.00, £1.90, £1.80; EX 203.80.
Owner M S Cooke **Bred** Cliveden Stud Ltd **Trained** Cropthorne, Worcs

FOCUS
This moderate handicap was run at an ordinary gallop, and that resulted in a host with chances coming to the penultimate flight.

NOTEBOOK
Apache Chant(USA) got on top where it mattered, finally shedding his maiden tag at the 28th attempt. The better ground evidently helped, as did the return of cheekpieces, and he would escape a penalty if turning out quickly. He holds two entries this week.
Farmers Cross(IRE) ◆ was given a well-judged ride in defeat and rates a typical improver from his stable. He can gain compensation if found another race on similar ground next time. (op 12-1)
What A Steel(IRE)'s stable had a double at Newcastle last week and was well backed. He travelled sweetly into contention under bottom weight, but failed to see it out that well and may prefer dropping in trip. (op 11-2)
Madame Jasmine held every chance on her handicap debut, but is another who may be better off reverting to a sharper test. (op 9-2 tchd 7-1)
Tricky Tree(IRE), another handicap debutant, looks to be crying out for a stiffer test. (op 33-1)
Willandrich(IRE) deserves another chance as he wasn't suited by the lack of an early gallop and was still in there fighting prior to being hampered. (op 12-1 tchd 9-1)
Skipper Robin(FR) Official explanation: jockey said gelding hung right in straight
Stonethrower(IRE) unseated three out when still going okay and continued loose, which caused a bit of mayhem as things got tight in the home straight.

3694 DIGIBET.COM BEGINNERS' CHASE (14 fncs) 2m 6f 110y

2:20 (2:22) (Class 4) 5-Y-0+ **£3,252** (£955; £477; £238)

Form / RPR

0P4 **1** **Quo Video (FR)**[18] 3394 7-11-0 0 (t) RichardJohnson 140+
(Tim Vaughan) *led: narrowly hdd 4 out: led again next: hit 2 out: styd on strly: eased towards fin* **20/1**

4262 **2** 5 **Alderley Rover (IRE)**[20] 3368 7-11-0 132 JasonMaguire 137+
(Donald McCain) *trckd ldrs: hit 9th: slt ld 4 out: hit next and hdd: styd on same pce fr 2 out* **2/1**[2]

P-15 **3** 65 **Sergeant Pink (IRE)**[67] 2455 5-10-9 0 (p) TomScudamore 64
(Steve Gollings) *nt fluent and rn in snatches: chsd ldrs: shkn up 4th: pushed along 7th: outpcd and lost pl next: t.o 3 out: tk remote 3rd last* **8/1**[3]

065P **4** 24 **Muntami (IRE)**[22] 3305 10-10-7 100 MattCrawley(7) 45
(John Harris) *chsd ldrs: drvn 7th: outpcd and lost pl next: t.o last whn j. slowly 4 out: tk distant 4th last* **100/1**

1-32 **5** 64 **Be There In Five (IRE)**[18] 3394 7-11-0 138 APMcCoy —
(Nicky Henderson) *nt fluent and j.lft: chsd ldrs: drvn 10th: wknd appr 3 out: blnd 2 out: distant 3rd whn j.v.slowly and tried refuse last: hacked up run-in to complete hopelessly t.o* **4/6**[1]

5m 41.6s (-4.40) **Going Correction** -0.30s/f (Good)
WFA 5 from 7yo+ 4lb **5** Ran SP% **110.2**
Speed ratings: **95,93,70,62,40**
CSF £60.82 TOTE £19.80: £4.30, £1.80; EX 41.50.
Owner Folly Road Racing Partners (1996) **Bred** Dominique Clayeux & Haras De Saint-Voir **Trained** Aberthin, Vale of Glamorgan

FOCUS
There wasn't much pace in this modest beginners' chase and the form looks worth treating with a degree of caution.

NOTEBOOK
Quo Video(FR) relished getting back on quicker ground and opened his account over fences at the second attempt with a ready display. He was given a positive ride from the front and did things best of all through the race. He momentarily looked in trouble coming to three out, but the runner-up made another error there and he went clear. He made his only mistake when hitting the next, but a decent leap at the last sealed the race. The addition of a first-time tongue tie clearly helped and he can improve on this, but a sound surface is important to his cause. (tchd 16-1)
Alderley Rover(IRE) posted his best effort as a chaser at Hereford last time out and registered his only win over hurdles on good ground, so he had plenty going for him. Not for the first time, he lacked fluency over his fences, though, and was done with after hitting the third-last. (op 15-8 tchd 9-4)
Sergeant Pink(IRE) was not on a going day. (tchd 7-1)
Muntami(IRE) was outclassed but at least completed this time.
Be There In Five(IRE) had the winner a long way behind when touched off at Southwell 18 days earlier. His fate was apparent before the home turn here, however, and he was booked for a distant third prior to trying to refuse at the last. Perhaps going this way round was not for him, but he now has it to prove. Official explanation: vet ssid gelding finished distressed (op 4-5 tchd 10-11)

3695 GET RACING UK IN YOUR PUB 08703518834 H'CAP CHASE (14 fncs) 2m 6f 110y

2:55 (2:56) (Class 4) (0-115,113) 5-Y-0+ **£3,252** (£955; £477; £238)

Form / RPR

0P16 **1** **Foxesbow (IRE)**[24] 3230 7-10-12 99 APMcCoy 111+
(Jonjo O'Neill) *trckd ldrs: wnt 2nd 10th: hung rt and led 2 out: drvn rt out: all out* **5/1**[1]

0525 **2** ½ **Camden George (IRE)**[13] 3488 10-11-7 108 TjadeCollier 118
(Sue Smith) *chsd ldrs 7th: styd on fr 4 out: tk 4th next: 4 l 2nd last: styd on: a jst hld* **8/1**[2]

34P **3** 3 1/4 **Darn Hot**[24] 3230 7-11-0 **104**............ ChrisHonour(3) 112
(Alex Hales) *in tch: drvn and 3rd 4 out: one pce whn hit last* **14/1**
5403 **4** 1 3/4 **Lorum Leader (IRE)**[13] 3482 10-11-5 **106**............(b) LiamTreadwell 112
(Dr Richard Newland) *chsd ldrs: led after 7th: hdd 2 out: one pce* **10/1**
-000 **5** 25 **Mokum (FR)**[20] 3371 10-10-7 **94**............ WayneHutchinson 77
(Tony Carroll) *in rr: mstke and reminders 7th: sme hdwy 10th: nvr on terms* **10/1**
04P3 **6** hd **Phoenix Des Mottes (FR)**[5] 3617 8-9-8 **88**............ JoeCornwall(7) 71
(John Cornwall) *chsd ldrs: wknd 4 out* **25/1**
4-0U **7** 4 1/2 **Karingreason**[10] 3520 8-11-3 **104**............ PhilKinsella 83
(Keith Reveley) *in rr: sme hdwy 9th: wknd 4 out* **22/1**
11P4 **8** 3 **Sotovik (IRE)**[20] 3361 10-11-8 **112**............ EwanWhillans(3) 88
(Alistair Whillans) *prom: outpcd 8th: bhd fr 10th* **16/1**
-630 **9** 1 3/4 **Stick Together**[10] 3520 8-11-3 **109**............(b) JamesHalliday(5) 83
(Malcolm Jefferson) *in rr: reminders and bhd fr 7th: t.o 4 out* **33/1**
5400 **10** 20 **Toulouse Express (IRE)**[12] 3502 12-10-10 **97**............(v) KennyJohnson 53
(Robert Johnson) *hld up in rr: bhd fr 8th: t.o 9th: j.rt last: virtually p.u* **33/1**
P145 **F** **Thai Vango (IRE)**[77] 2249 10-11-8 **112**............ SamTwiston-Davies(3) —
(Nigel Twiston-Davies) *in rr: reminders 7th: bhd whn fell 9th* **10/1**
-5F2 **P** **Quel Bruere (FR)**[11] 3510 7-11-5 **106**............(vt) JodieMogford —
(Graeme McPherson) *mde most: hit 6th: reminders next: sn hdd: lost pl 9th: t.o whn mstke 3 out: p.u bef next* **9/1**[3]
2301 **P** **You Know Yourself (IRE)**[71] 2371 8-11-3 **109**............ ShaneByrne(5) —
(Sue Smith) *towards rr whn leather broke: rdr lost iron and p.u bnd after s* **5/1**[1]
15-0 **P** **Cesium (FR)**[20] 3371 6-11-12 **113**............ JasonMaguire —
(Tom George) *chsd ldrs: hit 2nd: j.rt next: drvn 4th: lost pl and p.u bef next* **12/1**
245U **P** **Panama Canal (IRE)**[18] 3395 6-11-1 **105**............ AdamPogson(3) —
(Charles Pogson) *sn trcking ldrs: wknd qckly appr 3 out: 7th whn p.u bef 2 out* **25/1**

5m 36.1s (-9.90) **Going Correction** -0.30s/f (Good) **15** Ran SP% **119.9**
Speed ratings: **105,104,103,103,94 94,92,91,91,84 —,—,—,—,—**
Tote Swingers: 1&2 £8.80, 1&3 £16.40, 2&3 £29.40 CSF £41.72 CT £528.42 TOTE £4.90: £1.20, £4.10, £3.20; EX 52.80.
Owner John P McManus **Bred** Mrs Eleanor Hadden **Trained** Cheltenham, Gloucs
■ Stewards' Enquiry : Tjade Collier caution: used whip with excessive frequency.

FOCUS
A wide-open handicap, run at a sound gallop.

NOTEBOOK
Foxesbow(IRE) resumed winning ways under typically strong handling from the champion jockey. He was never far away and got asked for everything after jumping three out. He was on top at the next, but wanted to hang under pressure and badly idled on the run-in. That allowed the runner-up to close near the finish, but McCoy got stuck into him and the line just came in time. He clearly isn't the most straightforward but is in decent form and may be able to defy a higher mark. (tchd 11-2)
Camden George(IRE) was doing his best work too late in the day. This was better again from him and his form figures at the course read 12222, so he rates a sound benchmark for the form. (op 7-1)
Darn Hot got into the race around four out and had her chance but just looked held by the handicapper. (tchd 16-1)
Lorum Leader(IRE) showed more enthusiasm under a positive ride and tired out of it only late on. He is well handicapped on his previous best efforts but is not easy to catch right. (op 11-1)
You Know Yourself(IRE) was up 8lb for winning on his chase debut last time, but departed before the first here due to his tack going wrong. He took an age to pull up. Official explanation: jockey said stirrup leather broke (op 11-2)
Cesium(FR) Official explanation: jockey said gelding never travelled (op 11-2)
Panama Canal(IRE) Official explanation: trainer said gelding had a breathing problem (op 11-2)

3696 MIDDLE RASEN H'CAP HURDLE (8 hdls) 2m 1f
3:25 (3:26) (Class 4) (0-115,115) 4-Y-0+ **£2,602** (£764; £382; £190)

Form RPR
00-3 **1** **Quite The Man (IRE)**[109] 1734 6-11-2 **105**............ GrahamLee 114+
(Malcolm Jefferson) *hld up in midfield: hdwy to trck ldrs 3 out: lft in ld appr next: drvn out* **8/1**
-323 **2** 1 1/2 **Flinty Bay (IRE)**[39] 2954 6-11-12 **115**............ DougieCostello 120+
(Nicky Richards) *trckd ldrs: lft cl 2nd 2 out: styd on same pce last 100yds* **4/1**[2]
10/3 **3** hd **Fujin Dancer (FR)**[51] 2308 6-10-3 **99**............ MissHBethell(7) 105+
(Brian Ellison) *in rr: hdwy appr 2 out: 4th last: str run fnl 150yds: fin wl* **20/1**
5-25 **4** 2 1/4 **Texas Holdem (IRE)**[67] 2448 12-11-4 **110**............ JamesO'Farrell(3) 112
(Michael Smith) *in rr: hdwy 5th: lft handy 3rd appr 2 out: kpt on on same pce* **9/1**
1405 **5** 7 **Dipity Doo Dah**[26] 3158 7-10-4 **100**............ MichaelByrne(7) 95
(Peter Bowen) *in rr: hdwy after 3 out: hit next and one pce* **16/1**
3-40 **6** 1 1/4 **Dinarius**[22] 3299 6-11-9 **112**............(p) JimmyMcCarthy 105
(Alex Hales) *in rr: sme hdwy 2 out: nvr on terms* **20/1**
3-14 **7** nse **Viscount Rossini**[12] 3500 9-11-2 **112**............(b) PeterCarberry(7) 106
(Steve Gollings) *chsd ldrs: outpcd and lost pl after 3 out: kpt on run-in* **14/1**
0/ **8** 9 **Silent Jo (JPN)**[59] 2653 9-10-11 **103**............ RichieMcLernon(3) 89
(Jonjo O'Neill) *mid-div: shkn up 2nd: drvn and lost pl 4th: in rr whn reminders next: bhd whn eased clsng stages* **33/1**
3352 **9** 8 **Aviador (GER)**[22] 3302 5-11-5 **108**............ LeightonAspell 84
(Lucy Wadham) *led to 4th: lost pl appr 2 out: bhd whn eased run-in* **7/1**[3]
2331 **10** 10 **Dormouse**[12] 3497 6-11-5 **108**............(p) TomScudamore 74
(Anabel L M King) *w ldr: led 4th: hdd after 3 out: wknd appr next: bhd whn eased run-in* **9/1**
22-6 **F** **Zarinski (IRE)**[39] 2960 5-11-8 **111**............ APMcCoy —
(Nicky Henderson) *w ldrs: led after 3 out: broke leg: hdd and fell appr 2 out: fatally injured* **5/2**[1]
2P-0 **F** **Irish Symphony (IRE)**[11] 3509 7-11-0 **106**............ CharlieHuxley(3) —
(John Mackie) *hld up towards rr whn fell 3rd* **33/1**

4m 3.60s (-3.10) **Going Correction** -0.30s/f (Good) **12** Ran SP% **120.1**
Speed ratings (Par 105): **95,94,94,93,89 89,89,85,81,76 —,—**
Tote Swingers: 1&2 £5.50, 1&3 £7.90, 2&3 £9.50 CSF £39.44 CT £626.73 TOTE £9.10: £3.10, £1.80, £5.20; EX 34.90.
Owner Boundary Garage (Bury) Limited **Bred** Cathy Doran **Trained** Norton, N Yorks

FOCUS
Not a bad handicap for the class, with a fair gallop.

NOTEBOOK
Quite The Man(IRE), on his handicap debut, got on top near the final flight and somewhat belatedly opened his account over hurdles at the fifth attempt. He had become a bit disappointing since going jumping but has always had the scope to do better and is clearly coming good. Fences will bring the best out of him, but there should be improvement in this sphere, especially over a stiffer test.
Flinty Bay(IRE) ran some solid races in novice company and again went well on this switch to a handicap. He may just come on for the run and is up to scoring off this sort of mark. (tchd 9-2)
Fujin Dancer(FR) ◆ was eating up the ground after the final flight and was a big eye-catcher on his return to hurdling. He is not the easiest to get right, but there is surely another race to be won with him on similar ground before long. (op 22-1 tchd 25-1)
Texas Holdem(IRE) travelled well in mid-field but laboured when push came to shove and wants a stiffer test. This veteran's last success was back in 2006. (op 14-1)
Zarinski(IRE) unsurprisingly proved popular on this handicap debut over hurdles with the ground in his favour. He was bang there and still travelling well prior to going wrong and coming down nearing the penultimate flight, sadly with fatal results. (op 2-1 tchd 11-4 and 3-1 in places)

3697 RACING AGAIN TUESDAY 8TH FEBRUARY H'CAP HURDLE (10 hdls) 2m 3f
3:55 (3:55) (Class 5) (0-95,95) 4-Y-0+ **£2,055** (£599; £299)

Form RPR
50-2 **1** **Scrum V**[75] 2302 7-11-9 **92**............ PaddyAspell 92+
(John Davies) *prom: drvn to chse ldrs 3 out: upsides last: sn led: edgd rt: all out* **9/2**[2]
3650 **2** shd **Sansili**[15] 3449 4-10-8 **92**............(p) DonalDevereux(3) 80+
(Peter Bowen) *trckd ldrs: led appr 2 out: hdd sn after last: rallied: carried rt: jst hld* **10/3**[1]
6250 **3** 3 3/4 **Himayna**[26] 3155 7-11-12 **95**............ RichardJohnson 96+
(Tim Vaughan) *led: hit 4th and 3 out: hdd after 3 out: keeping on same pce whn hit last* **6/1**
32P5 **4** 1/2 **Galley Slave (IRE)**[68] 2438 6-10-13 **89**............ KyleJames(7) 88
(Michael Chapman) *t.k.h in rr: effrt 3 out 4th and one pce last* **9/1**
-620 **5** 5 **Bubses Boy**[4] 3631 5-11-6 **89**............ KennyJohnson 87
(Robert Johnson) *t.k.h in rr: hdwy after 7th: drvn appr 2 out: one pce* **25/1**
645P **6** 2 1/2 **Railway Park (IRE)**[40] 2937 7-11-0 **83**............(tp) GrahamLee 81
(John Wainwright) *chsd ldrs: rdn 3 out: wknd between last 2* **13/2**
0-26 **7** 16 **Friends Of Tina (IRE)**[74] 2314 8-11-6 **89**............(p) WillKennedy 85
(Alex Hales) *chsd ldrs: reminders 6th: hrd drvn 3 out: lost pl appr next* **5/1**[3]
00-0 **8** 2 1/2 **Benluna (IRE)**[72] 2349 7-11-0 **86**............ EwanWhillans(3) 82
(Alistair Whillans) *t.k.h: trckd ldrs: hit 3 out: wknd appr next* **8/1**
PP0P **9** 8 **Aboukir Bay (IRE)**[9] 3544 7-9-8 **70**............(bt) JoeCornwall(7) 65
(John Cornwall) *chsd ldrs: lost pl afterr 6th: bhd fr 3 out* **28/1**

4m 36.1s (-3.30) **Going Correction** -0.30s/f (Good)
WFA 4 from 5yo+ 11lb **9** Ran SP% **114.0**
Speed ratings (Par 103): **94,93,92,92,90 89,82,81,77**
Tote Swingers: 1&2 £4.90, 1&3 £4.50, 2&3 £3.20 CSF £20.07 CT £89.42 TOTE £5.70: £2.10, £1.10, £2.70; EX 21.60.
Owner J J Davies **Bred** Paddy Byrne **Trained** Piercebridge, Durham
■ Stewards' Enquiry : Paddy Aspell caution: careless riding.

FOCUS
An ordinary handicap, run at an average gallop.

NOTEBOOK
Scrum V, returning from a 75-day absence, went to the front jumping the final flight and knuckled down gamely to fend off Sansili's renewed challenge. The pair came close late on and he edged into the second, which resulted in a stewards' inquiry. It was a very close verdict but still looked the right result and this his first success at the eighth time of asking. The sounder surface looked to make the difference and it was just his second outing in a handicap. (tchd 5-1)
Sansili, in first-time cheekpieces, has always looked as though a stiffer test was what he needed and duly posted his best effort to date on this step up in trip. He didn't do much when initially sent to the front but, to his credit, was coming right back near the finish and deserves to get off the mark. (op 7-2)
Himayna attempted to make all and, despite not always being fluent, gave way only on the run-in. The better ground suited and it was a sound effort under top weight. (op 13-2 tchd 5-1 and 7-1 in places)
Galley Slave(IRE) got going late in the day and put up a more encouraging display, but still looks to need some respite from the handicapper. (tchd 8-1)
Friends Of Tina(IRE) never looked happy. (op 9-2 tchd 4-1)
T/Jkpt: Not won. T/Plt: £99.80 to a £1 stake. Pool of £78,064.48 - 570.68 winning tickets. T/Qpdt: £27.10 to a £1 stake. Pool of £4,923.06 - 134.35 winning tickets. WG

[3484]TOWCESTER (R-H)
Sunday, January 23

OFFICIAL GOING: Soft (heavy in places; 7.1) (tacky & holding)
Hurdles course doled out wide. Chase and Hurdles course on shared bends. Flight of hurdles down the hill omitted on all circuits due to bad ground.
Wind: Fresh, half-behind Weather: Overcast

3698 GG.COM TIPZONE NOVICES' HURDLE (10 hdls 2 omitted) 3m
1:30 (1:31) (Class 4) 5-Y-0+ **£2,602** (£764; £382; £190)

Form RPR
-132 **1** **Victors Serenade (IRE)**[20] 3370 6-11-4 115............ AidanColeman 124+
(Anthony Honeyball) *hld up in tch: led after 3 out: clr whn mstke next: eased towards fin* **2/1**[1]
52 **2** 10 **Bounds And Leaps**[63] 2554 6-10-5 0............ JohnnyFarrelly 96
(Michael Scudamore) *prom: chsd ldr 4th to 7th: rdn after 3 out: styd on same pce wnt 2nd again after next* **9/2**[3]
14 **3** 8 **Havingotascoobydo (IRE)**[23] 3252 6-10-12 0............ WarrenMarston 100+
(Martin Keighley) *hld up: hdwy after 3rd: led appr 7th: mstke 3 out: sn hdd: wknd next* **3/1**[2]
4-31 **4** 13 **The Red Laird**[23] 3260 8-10-9 103............ AlexMerriam(3) 85
(Neil King) *led to appr 7th: sn rdn: wknd appr 2 out: blnd last: t.o* **5/1**
0 **5** 13 **Inca Cave (IRE)**[10] 3528 6-10-7 0............ KeiranBurke(5) 69
(Patrick Rodford) *hld up: reminders after 4th: hdwy u.p 6th: wknd appr 3 out: t.o* **25/1**
502 **6** 10 **Gentle Bob (IRE)**[22] 3296 6-10-12 113............ PaddyBrennan 61
(Tom George) *hld up: hdwy 5th: blnd 3 out: sn wknd: t.o* **8/1**
00 **7** 21 **Ben Trovato (IRE)**[8] 3572 5-10-5 0............ MrCGreene(7) 38
(John Upson) *hld up: bhd fr 4th: t.o* **250/1**
0 **8** 2 1/4 **Traffic Chaos (IRE)**[21] 3340 6-10-12 0............ DarylJacob 36
(Charlie Mann) *prom tl wknd 6th: t.o* **25/1**
000/ **9** 131 **Abitofargybargy (IRE)**[790] 2412 9-10-12 0............ GerardTumelty —
(Richard Price) *chsd ldr to 4th: wknd after next: t.o* **100/1**
0/P- **P** **Anyauldiron (IRE)**[623] 247 8-10-12 0............ FelixDeGiles —
(Charlie Longsdon) *chsd ldrs: blnd 3rd: wknd appr 7th: t.o whn p.u bef 2 out* **40/1**
0-00 **P** **Flag Dancer**[32] 3088 5-10-5 0............ MrMMarris(7) —
(Christine Dunnett) *hld up: rdn after 3rd: t.o whn p.u after 5th* **250/1**

P **Colleens Pride (IRE)** 8-10-5 0 .... AndrewTinkler —
(Jonjo O'Neill) *hld up: plld hrd: stmbld sn after s: sn p.u* 40/1
6m 37.0s (22.00) **Going Correction** +0.675s/f (Soft) 12 Ran SP% **118.7**
Speed ratings: **90,86,84,79,75 72,65,64,—,— —,—**
Tote Swingers: 1&2 £1.90, 1&3 £2.40, 2&3 £5.80 CSF £11.20 TOTE £2.80: £1.10, £1.70, £1.80; EX 13.60.
Owner Michael & Angela Bone **Bred** Thomas Horgan **Trained** Seaborough, Dorset

FOCUS
Very tacky and holding ground, making for a real test of stamina through the card. This very modest novice event was run no less than 48 seconds outside the standard.

NOTEBOOK
Victors Serenade(IRE), who has been running well in handicaps, was carrying a penalty but ran out a wide-margin winner on this return to novice company. In front turning into the home straight, he was already drawing clear when he dived at the second-last. Towcester's hill suited him well but there may be a little more improvement in him on left-handed tracks. (op 9-4)
Bounds And Leaps was runner-up over 2m5f here on her hurdling debut two months ago. She saw out the trip better than most on this first run against male opponents, but was no match for the winner. (op 17-2)
Havingotascoobydo(IRE) was soon on the retreat after a blunder three from home. He has won a 3m Irish point in heavy going but didn't truly see this out in the bad ground. (op 9-4 tchd 10-3)
The Red Laird took a Warwick handicap last time and escaped a penalty as it was a conditionals' race. A well-beaten eighth in this event last year, he faded after making a lot of the running. (tchd 4-1 and 11-2)
Gentle Bob(IRE) was runner-up over 2m1f at Exeter on New Year's Day, and he didn't see out this considerably longer trip in the conditions. He is not one to write off. (tchd 7-1)

3699 SIS H'CAP CHASE (12 fncs) 2m 110y
2:00 (2:00) (Class 5) (0-95,93) 5-Y-0+ **£1,951** (£573; £286; £143)

Form				RPR
0503	1		**Kinkeel (IRE)**[5] 3618 12-9-13 **69** .... EamonDehdashti(3) (Tony Carroll) *a.p: drvn along after 7th: led flat: rdn and hung lft: styd on u.p* 9/2[3]	82+
026P	2	2	**Duke Of Malfi**[79] 2194 8-11-12 **93** .... (p) PeterBuchanan (Lucinda Russell) *led to 5th: led again appr 2 out: sn rdn: hdd flat: swtchd rt: styd on same pce* 9/2[3]	103
0360	3	10	**Copper Sound**[10] 3527 7-10-6 **73** .... (vt) AndrewTinkler (Michael Scudamore) *chsd ldr tl led 5th: rdn and hdd appr 2 out: wknd flat* 3/1[2]	72
P466	4	2 ½	**The Walnut Tree (IRE)**[20] 3369 10-10-1 **68** oh20 ow1 .... MarkGrant (Simon Lewis) *prom: lost pl after 4th: hdwy appr 6th: rdn after 3 out: wknd last* 16/1	66
/6P-	P		**Suprendre Espere**[581] 771 11-10-0 **67** oh5 .... TomMessenger (Christopher Kellett) *bhd fr 3rd: t.o whn p.u bef 6th* 18/1	—
-P36	P		**Organiz (FR)**[12] 3492 9-10-13 **85** .... MrSWaley-Cohen(5) (Robin Dickin) *chsd ldrs: blnd 5th: rdn and wknd after 3 out: t.o whn p.u bef next* 11/4[1]	—
PP54	P		**Wiesenfurst (GER)**[75] 2292 7-10-13 **85** .... (tp) TomO'Connor(5) (John Berwick) *chsd ldrs: rdn and dropped in rr after 3rd: bhd fr 5th: t.o whn p.u bef 2 out* 7/1	—

4m 26.1s (10.00) **Going Correction** +0.675s/f (Soft) 7 Ran SP% **111.7**
Speed ratings: **103,102,97,96,— —,—**
Tote Swingers: 1&2 £1.80, 1&3 £3.70, 2&3 £4.80 CSF £23.92 TOTE £5.00: £2.60, £2.60; EX 10.40.
Owner Group 1 Racing (1994) Ltd **Bred** Roland Rothwell **Trained** Cropthorne, Worcs
■ Stewards' Enquiry : Eamon Dehdashti caution: careless riding; one-day ban: used whip with excessive frequency (Feb 6)

FOCUS
A low-grade handicap chase, but the form looks to make sense.

NOTEBOOK
Kinkeel(IRE) appeared in trouble at one stage, but he rallied going to the last and was in command when he veered over to the paddock exit on the run-in. This remarkably durable chaser, who has a fine completion record in a long career over fences, was 6lb lower than when third at Southwell on Tuesday and took full advantage. (op 10-3)
Duke Of Malfi ran creditably under topweight but was held when the winner went across him on the run-in. He has dropped to 3lb below his last winning mark. (op 3-1 tchd 5-1)
Copper Sound, down a further 9lb, was dropping in trip and trying a visor in place of cheekpieces. Winner of a bumper in heavy ground, he showed up until fading between the last two fences. (op 9-2)
The Walnut Tree(IRE) was last of the four to complete but not beaten that far despite being a long way out of the weights. (op 25-1)
Organiz(FR), who had plenty of form in deep ground in his younger days in France, is another who has been given some help by the handicapper. He did well to stay on his feet when slithering on landing at the fifth and remained in touch until weakening at the foot of the final hill. (op 7-2)

3700 ODDSANYWHERE.COM H'CAP CHASE (18 fncs) 3m 110y
2:30 (2:30) (Class 5) (0-90,90) 5-Y-0+ **£1,951** (£573; £286; £143)

Form				RPR
P0/2	1		**Atherstone Hill (IRE)**[67] 2457 9-10-11 **78** .... (v) WayneKavanagh(3) (Robin Dickin) *chsd ldr tl led 5th: hdd 7th: led again next: rdn appr 2 out: styd on* 5/2[1]	99+
	2	16	**The Real Rupee (IRE)**[17] 3416 8-10-10 **77** .... (p) JimmyDerham(3) (Conor O'Dwyer, Ire) *led to 5th: led 7th to next: hit 11th: ev ch 3 out: sn rdn: wknd last* 8/1	83
65-P	3	13	**Thunder Child**[262] 173 11-10-7 **76** .... (t) MattGriffiths(5) (Simon Burrough) *hld up: hdwy 6th: ev ch 3 out: sn rdn and wknd: wnt 3rd towards fin* 20/1	68
0443	4	1 ¾	**Bajan Sunshine (IRE)**[6] 3609 10-10-0 **64** .... (t) JamesDavies (Gary Brown) *hld up: hdwy 14th: rdn to go 3rd 2 out: wknd bef last: lost 3rd towards fin* 9/2[3]	54
F-43	5	15	**Fleur De Vassy**[41] 2930 7-11-12 **90** .... AidanColeman (Venetia Williams) *chsd ldrs: j. slowly 2nd: ev ch 3 out: rdn and wknd bef next: t.o* 10/3[2]	70
5606	6	2 ¾	**Mister Virginian (IRE)**[6] 3609 12-11-3 **81** .... (v) ColinBolger (Chris Gordon) *prom: lost pl and pushed along 6th: wknd 12th: t.o* 40/1	54
3242	7	31	**Romney Marsh**[21] 3349 10-11-4 **82** .... HaddenFrost (Roger Curtis) *chsd ldrs: pushed along 3rd: drvn along after 11th: wknd 14th: t.o* 8/1	24
-220	P		**Sailor's Sovereign**[40] 2950 10-10-3 **67** .... (p) GerardTumelty (Julian Smith) *hld up: hdwy 6th: rdn appr 3 out: sn wknd: t.o whn p.u bef last* 7/1	—

6m 57.2s (20.30) **Going Correction** +0.675s/f (Soft) 8 Ran SP% **111.8**
Speed ratings: **94,88,84,84,79 78,68,—**
Tote Swingers: 1&2 £7.20, 1&3 £17.60, 2&3 £16.50 CSF £21.56 CT £315.11 TOTE £3.80: £1.40, £3.00, £5.00; EX 25.90.
Owner Colin & Co **Bred** William Deacon **Trained** Atherstone on Stour, Warwicks
■ Stewards' Enquiry : Matt Griffiths four-day ban: used whip with excessive frequency without giving gelding time to respond (Feb 6-9)

FOCUS
A moderate and slowly run handicap chase.

NOTEBOOK
Atherstone Hill(IRE) jumped soundly and galloped on willingly enough to record his first career victory. He had been an encouraging runner-up at Warwick in November on his return from a break and he handled this worse ground well. Connections are keen to bring him back to Towcester. (op 7-2)
The Real Rupee(IRE), an Irish challenger, had never finished nearer than seventh from a limited number of career outings, so this was a step forward. His jumping was sketchy at times.
Thunder Child, a former hunter chaser, was fitted with a first-time tongue-tie on this debut for the Burrough yard. He weakened on the final turn but plugged on to salvage third. (tchd 18-1 and 25-1)
Bajan Sunshine(IRE), who could never quite reach the leaders having been given a hold-up ride. (op 11-2)
Fleur De Vassy looked to be going as well as any facing up to the final hill, but her big weight told over this longer trip and she stopped quickly. (op 5-2 tchd 9-4)

3701 JAMES "THE PICKLE" WHITE'S 30TH BIRTHDAY NOVICES' HURDLE (7 hdls 1 omitted) 2m
3:05 (3:05) (Class 3) 4-Y-0+ **£3,252** (£955; £477; £238)

Form				RPR
143	1		**Pret A Thou (FR)**[8] 3565 8-11-2 125 .... HarryChalloner(7) (John Bryan Groucott) *mde all: rdn appr 2 out: styd on gamely* 11/4[3]	129+
5	2	2 ¼	**Old Way (IRE)**[13] 3478 5-11-4 0 .... AidanColeman (Venetia Williams) *chsd wnr 2nd: rdn appr 2 out: hit last: styd on same pce* 9/4[1]	122+
6-40	3	31	**Newton Tonic**[41] 2925 6-11-4 0 .... FelixDeGiles (Alex Hales) *chsd ldrs tl wknd after 3 out: t.o* 6/1	91
0	4	½	**Caddie Master (IRE)**[10] 3526 5-11-1 0 .... MrAJBerry(3) (Jonjo O'Neill) *hld up: nvr on terms: t.o* 14/1	90
43	5	8	**Coolbeg (IRE)**[23] 3252 5-11-4 0 .... PaddyBrennan (Tom George) *prom tl rdn and wknd after 3 out: t.o* 5/2[2]	82
00	6	13	**Drink Up**[38] 2981 7-11-4 0 .... AndrewThornton (John O'Neill) *chsd ldrs tl wknd appr 3rd: t.o* 25/1	69
0/PP	7	111	**Murfreesboro**[23] 3253 8-11-1 0 .... RichardKilloran(3) (Alan Jones) *hld up: a in rr: t.o whn hit last* 100/1	—
P-	P		**Dudley Docker (IRE)**[61] 1900 9-10-11 0 .... MrMMarris(7) (Daniel O'Brien) *sddle slipped and p.u after 2nd* 66/1	—

4m 18.8s (10.90) **Going Correction** +0.675s/f (Soft) 8 Ran SP% **113.3**
Speed ratings (Par 107): **99,97,82,82,78 71,—,—**
Tote Swingers: 1&2 £1.40, 1&3 £2.80, 2&3 £2.70 CSF £9.46 TOTE £3.90: £1.40, £1.10, £1.80; EX 11.90.
Owner C J Tipton **Bred** Mme Robert Jeannin **Trained** Bourton, Shropshire

FOCUS
This was a weak novice hurdle for the grade, but it was run at a fair pace in the conditions.

NOTEBOOK
Pret A Thou(FR), gained his seventh career win, making all as in all his previous successes, had been unable to dominate in two runs back over fences since his successful hurdling debut at Uttoxeter. He will find things tougher under a double penalty in novice hurdles. (op 5-2 tchd 3-1)
Old Way(IRE) showed promise on his hurdles debut and backed that up with an encouraging effort. He came off the bridle in second turning for home, but refused to give way and kept the winner up to his work. His turn should come. (op 5-2 tchd 15-8)
Newton Tonic, who played up down at the start, was well held in third but showed more than he had on his hurdling debut. He ran respectably in a bumper on a previous visit to Towcester. (op 10-1)
Caddie Master(IRE) stayed on from well back and would have been third with slightly further to go. He is going to need a longer trip, and maybe better ground. (tchd 12-1)
Coolbeg(IRE) could not build on his Uttoxeter third and the drop back in distance was perhaps not what he wanted. (op 2-1)
Murfreesboro Official explanation: jockey said gelding was unsuited by the soft (heavy in places) ground
Dudley Docker(IRE) Official explanation: jockey said saddle slipped

3702 GG.COM ALERTS BEGINNERS' CHASE (18 fncs) 3m 110y
3:35 (3:35) (Class 4) 5-Y-0+ **£2,665** (£827; £445)

Form				RPR
3P-3	1		**Chamirey (FR)**[61] 2599 8-11-0 0 .... (b) TimmyMurphy (Donald McCain) *mde all: nt a fluent: clr fr 6th: wnt rt last: easily* 8/15[1]	118+
0-04	2	27	**Preuty Boy (FR)**[26] 3168 6-11-0 0 .... JohnnyFarrelly (Alan Fleming) *hld up: hdwy 9th: chsd wnr 14th: wknd 3 out* 10/1	75
P-P6	3	4	**Jolly Boys Outing (IRE)**[243] 466 8-10-7 0 .... MrBJPoste(7) (Rosemary Gasson) *w.r.s: bhd: hdwy and in tch 5th: wknd 12th: wnt 3rd appr 2 out: j.rt last* 33/1	71
P	P		**Buffalo Creek (FR)**[65] 2493 7-11-0 0 .... DarylJacob (Giles Smyly) *chsd ldrs wkng whn blnd 12th: t.o whn p.u bef 3 out* 8/1[3]	—
0/2	P		**Not So Prudent (IRE)**[23] 3254 7-11-0 0 .... PaddyBrennan (Nigel Twiston-Davies) *prom: chsd wnr 7th to 14th: wknd 3 out: t.o whn j. slowly 2 out: sn p.u* 4/1[2]	—

6m 59.6s (22.70) **Going Correction** +0.675s/f (Soft) 5 Ran SP% **108.4**
Speed ratings: **90,81,80,—,—**
CSF £6.15 TOTE £1.30: £1.10, £2.10; EX 6.70.
Owner Sir Robert Ogden **Bred** Mme Marie-France Graffard **Trained** Cholmondeley, Cheshire

FOCUS
A decidedly uncompetitive beginners' chase, run in a time a couple of seconds slower than the earlier handicap.

NOTEBOOK
Chamirey(FR) had been a beaten favourite on his chasing debut at Sedgefield in November, but was expected to be suited by this step back up in trip and the return of blinkers. Making all and sticking to the best ground on the inner, he jumped well enough and was in no danger from a long way out, winning in bloodless fashion. This will have done his confidnce no harm and he will be ready for a more taxing assignment next. (op 4-7 tchd 1-2)
Preuty Boy(FR), whose hurdles win last term came under Timmy Murphy, was well beaten back in second on this chasing debut. This trip probably stretches his stamina. (op 8-1)
Jolly Boys Outing(IRE), a former hunter chaser, almost refused to race and started a long way behind the others. The modest pace allowed him to get back in touch and it looked briefly as if he might finish a remote second. (op 25-1)
Not So Prudent(IRE) could not step up on his Uttoxeter second, weakening quickly three from home after receiving a more prominent ride. (op 7-2)

3703 RACING FORUM @ GG.COM AMATEUR RIDERS' H'CAP HURDLE (9 hdls 1 omitted) 2m 3f 110y
4:05 (4:05) (Class 5) (0-90,90) 4-Y-0+ **£1,873** (£581; £290; £145)

Form				RPR
0/00	1		**Molly Round (IRE)**[24] 3227 7-10-7 71 .... MrSWaley-Cohen (Grant Cann) *chsd ldr tl led 5th: hdd next: led again 3 out: drvn out* 6/1	87+

6-01 **2** 2 3/4 **Arctic Flow**[21] 3350 7-10-0 69 .... MrRGHenderson(5) 82
(Caroline Keevil) *a.p: ev ch appr 2 out: rdn bef last: styd on same pce flat* **4/1**[2]

-601 **3** 27 **Queenstown Lad**[70] 2391 6-10-5 76 .... MrJSherwood(7) 62
(Gary Brown) *prom: pushed along after 5th: wknd appr 2 out* **9/2**[3]

543 **4** 1/2 **Low Delta (IRE)**[21] 3341 11-11-0 85 .... MrCGreene(7) 71
(Michael Blake) *hld up: hdwy 3 out: wknd bef next* **7/1**

600- **5** 16 **Jack Rio (IRE)**[308] 4769 6-10-2 73 .... MrDSymes-Meineck(7) 43
(Laura Young) *hld up: sme hdwy after 3 out: wknd bef next: t.o* **40/1**

P-00 **6** 10 **Little Rort (IRE)**[10] 3530 12-9-13 70 .... MissCBoxall(7) 30
(Simon Lewis) *mid-div: hdwy after 4th: wkng whn mstke 3 out: t.o* **25/1**

01-0 **7** 11 **Sovereign Spirit (IRE)**[9] 3540 9-11-1 86 ....(t) MissAmyAppleton(7) 35
(Chris Gordon) *racd keenly: hdwy and mstke 2nd: wknd 3 out: t.o* **12/1**

-0P0 **P** **Everyman**[66] 2469 7-11-5 90 .... MrJamieJenkinson(7) —
(John Bryan Groucott) *in rr: bhd fr 4th: t.o whn p.u bef next* **33/1**

0-P0 **P** **Red Perfection**[38] 2980 8-10-12 83 ....(t) MrRHatch(7) —
(Tony Carroll) *chsd ldrs: rdn after 5th: wknd 3 out: t.o whn p.u bef next* **25/1**

0-PP **P** **Bridge Of Fermoy (IRE)**[5] 3611 6-9-12 69 .... MrJPearce(7) —
(Daniel O'Brien) *mid-div: bhd fr 5th: t.o whn p.u bef 2 out* **40/1**

05P- **P** **Septos**[272] 16 7-10-6 75 .... MrMPrice(5) —
(Richard Price) *mid-div: pushed along and lost pl 4th: sn bhd: t.o whn p.u bef 2 out* **25/1**

006 **P** **Free Falling**[19] 3389 5-11-8 89 ....(v) MissZoeLilly(3) —
(Alastair Lidderdale) *chsd ldrs: lost pl after 4th: bhd fr next: t.o whn p.u bef 2 out* **18/1**

0066 **P** **A P Ling**[18] 3396 4-9-7 76 oh6 .... MrTGarner(7) —
(Christopher Kellett) *hld up: hdwy appr 5th: wknd bef 3 out: t.o whn p.u bef last* **50/1**

-45P **P** **The Rustlin Rhino**[59] 2645 6-11-2 85 .... MrJHamer(5) —
(Donald McCain) *led: blnd 4th: mstke and hdd next: led again 6th to 3 out: sn wknd: t.o whn p.u bef last* **7/2**[1]

5m 20.9s (11.30) **Going Correction** +0.675s/f (Soft)
WFA 4 from 5yo+ 11lb **14** Ran SP% **121.5**
Speed ratings (Par 103): **104,102,92,91,85 81,77,—,—,— —,—,—,—**
Tote Swingers: 1&2 £6.30, 1&3 £5.20, 2&3 £5.70 CSF £29.00 CT £121.86 TOTE £7.90: £2.50, £2.50, £1.90; EX 33.50.
Owner Andrew Kavanagh **Bred** Andrew Kavanagh **Trained** Cullompton, Devon.

FOCUS
A weak handicap for amateur riders, run on the worst of the ground. The first two came a long way clear.

NOTEBOOK
Molly Round(IRE) had been well beaten in all her previous starts, but she was making her handicap debut off a lowly mark and had the services of the most accomplished jockey in the race. A half-sister to former very useful novice hurdler Our Bob, she was always in the front rank and stayed on well. Official explanation: trainer said, regarding apparent improvement in form, that the mare appeared suited by the drop in class and being able to race prominently. (op 15-2)
Arctic Flow was effectively only 6lb higher than when winning from a long way out of the weights at Plumpton. She loomed up going well on the turn, but could not quite get past a tough opponent. This half-sister to River Indus finished a long way clear of the remainder and is still on the upgrade. (tchd 7-2 and 9-2)
Queenstown Lad was 12lb higher than when winning from out of the handicap at Fontwell. That was over 3m3f and he plugged on for a distant third after a couple of jumping errors. (op 5-1 tchd 11-2)
Low Delta(IRE)'s only win came in this race two years ago, when he was 5lb higher. Held up and kept to the less poached ground, he stayed on and nearly grabbed third. (op 6-1)
Jack Rio(IRE) was adrift in last place for much of the way before making late progress past beaten rivals under her inexperienced rider. (tchd 33-1)
Bridge Of Fermoy(IRE) Official explanation: jockey said gelding lost a front shoe (op 9-2)
Free Falling Official explanation: jockey said filly never travelled (op 9-2)
The Rustlin Rhino didn't jump too well on his return to hurdles. Stopping quickly before the final hill, he is proving costly to follow. Official explanation: jockey said gelding stopped very quickly (op 9-2)
T/Plt: £51.00 to a £1 stake. Pool of £85,235.32 - 1,219.96 winning tickets. T/Qpdt: £24.90 to a £1 stake. Pool of £5,020.20 - 148.91 winning tickets. CR

3704 - (Foreign Racing) - See Raceform Interactive

3470 LEOPARDSTOWN (L-H)
Sunday, January 23

OFFICIAL GOING: Soft

3705a FRANK WARD SOLICITORS ARKLE NOVICE CHASE (GRADE 1) (11 fncs) 2m 1f
1:45 (1:45) 5-Y-0+ **£44,827** (£13,103; £6,206; £2,068)

RPR

1 **Realt Dubh (IRE)**[24] 3241 7-11-12 146 .... PCarberry 156+
(Noel Meade, Ire) *settled bhd ldrs: 5th 1/2-way: hdwy in 3rd 3 out: lft 2nd 2 out: travelled wl ent st: led bef last: rdn and chal last: disp run-in: jst prevailed cl home* **5/2**[1]

2 shd **Noble Prince (GER)**[24] 3241 7-11-12 141 .... BarryGeraghty 156
(Paul Nolan, Ire) *settled bhd ldrs: 4th 1/2-way: lft 3rd 2 out: rdn ent st: styd on to chal last: disp run-in: no ex cl home* **3/1**[2]

3 10 **Mr Cracker (IRE)**[25] 3210 6-11-12 137 .... DNRussell 146
(Michael Hourigan, Ire) *led: hdd bef 2 out: lft in ld again 2 out: rdn ent st: hdd bef last: no ex and kpt on same pce* **7/1**

4 14 **Shirley Casper (IRE)**[14] 3471 10-11-7 114 .... PWFlood 127
(D T Hughes, Ire) *mstke 1st: hld up in last: 5th 3 out: lft 4th 2 out: rdn and no imp: kpt on one pce* **33/1**

5 dist **Saludos (IRE)**[24] 3241 7-11-12 138 .... RMPower —+
(Mrs John Harrington, Ire) *chsd ldr in 2nd: 3rd 5 out where slt mstke: mstke 3 out and dropped in rr: wknd and t.o* **5/1**[3]

U **Flat Out (FR)**[15] 3455 6-11-12 .... EMullins —
(W P Mullins, Ire) *trckd ldrs in 3rd: 2nd 5 out: impr to ld bef 2 out where bad mstke and uns rdr* **3/1**[2]

4m 14.8s (-7.20) **Going Correction** -0.70s/f (Firm) **6** Ran SP% **110.7**
Speed ratings: **88,87,83,76,— —**
CSF £10.35 TOTE £2.00: £1.20, £3.10; DF 11.80.
Owner D J Sharkey **Bred** R Hartigan **Trained** Castletown, Co Meath
■ Stewards' Enquiry : P Carberry caution: used whip improperly

FOCUS
The winner and runner-up have been rated as running small personal bests.

NOTEBOOK
Realt Dubh(IRE) had jumped pretty well while tracking the pace, took over going to the last and then rallied very strongly on the run-in when he was challenged and when it appeared he was going to be outstayed. It was a display which showed this horse's resolution to its fullest extent. He looks likely to go for the Arkle and has most of the attributes that one could ask for. He jumps, travels, stays and has the stomach for a battle. He may find one or two too good but, all things being equal, his opponents will know they have been in a race. (op 9/4 tchd 11/4)
Noble Prince(GER) had to be stoked along from about the third-last but was then delivered with what looked a perfectly timed challenge. When hitting the front one would have expected him to stay on that bit better than the runner-up and it was maybe a shade surprising that he was outbattled. It also leaves a slight question about what his best trip really is. (op 4/1)
Mr Cracker(IRE) tried to stretch them from the second-last. It didn't work out against this calibre of opposition, but it was a perfectly fair effort over a trip short of his best and connections will have a far better idea now of how good a horse they have. There's nothing really to suggest that he didn't run up to his mark. (op 7/1 tchd 15/2)
Shirley Casper(IRE) should come more into her own in the spring. She closed up to track the leaders coming out of the back straight, but wasn't good enough to improve her position from two out.
Saludos(IRE) was put to the test and he does get a bit low at one or two. He made a bad blunder three out which ended his chance, and his rider said afterwards that the horse burst a blood vessel. Official explanation: trainer said gelding was found to have a burst blood vessel post-race which was confirmed by the vet (op 9/2 tchd 11/2)
Flat Out(FR) produced a terrific jump at the third-last that brought him alongside the lead, and he was arguably travelling best of all when he took off half a stride too soon at the following fence and paid the penalty. (op 5/2)

3706a RYAN'S EVENT CLEANERS H'CAP CHASE (GRADE C) (12 fncs) 2m 3f
2:15 (2:17) (0-140,131) 5-Y-0+ **£16,250** (£4,750; £2,250; £750)

RPR

1 **By The Hour (IRE)**[38] 2993 8-10-1 111 .... PTEnright 124
(Robert Tyner, Ire) *mid-div: hdwy into 6th 4 out: impr to chal ent st: rdn to ld appr last: j. sltly lft last: drifted lft u.p run-in: kpt on wl* **16/1**

2 1 1/2 **Questions Answered (IRE)**[24] 3249 6-10-6 123 .... RJJones(7) 135
(E McNamara, Ire) *chsd ldrs: 5th 1/2-way: hdwy into 2nd 3 out: chal next: led ent st: rdn and narrowly hdd appr last: kpt on: drifted lft u.p run-in: sltly hmpd clsng stages* **9/4**[1]

3 3 **Deal Done (FR)**[60] 2618 7-11-7 131 ....(p) PWFlood 140
(D T Hughes, Ire) *chsd ldrs: 3rd 1/2-way: cl up 6 out: led 3 out: strly pressed next: hdd ent st: cl 3rd last: hmpd run-in: no ex and kpt on same pce* **20/1**

4 1/2 **Conem (IRE)**[14] 3473 11-10-12 122 .... BarryGeraghty 130+
(W J Austin, Ire) *hld up towards rr: late hdwy in mod 7th ent st: 5th last: kpt on run-in* **10/1**

5 7 **Diophas (GER)**[24] 3242 8-10-8 118 .... AndrewJMcNamara 119
(E J O'Grady, Ire) *mid-div: hdwy in 6th 2 out: lft 4th: rdn and no ex ent st: kpt on one pce* **11/1**

6 17 **Top Of The Rock (IRE)**[24] 3242 8-10-12 127 ....(p) MJBolger(5) 111
(Mrs John Harrington, Ire) *chsd ldrs: 4th 1/2-way: rdn in 9th 3 out: lft 6th 2 out: mod 5th ent st: no imp on ldrs: kpt on one pce* **12/1**

7 3 **Stormin Exit (IRE)**[25] 3206 8-11-2 126 .... JamesReveley 107
(Jim Goldie) *chsd ldrs: 7th 1/2-way: lost pl 4 out where 11th: rdn into mod 6th ent st: kpt on one pce* **6/1**[3]

8 5 **Erritt Lake (IRE)**[70] 2413 8-10-4 119 .... BryanJCooper(5) 95
(D T Hughes, Ire) *prom early: sn chsd ldrs: 6th 1/2-way: rdn and no ex appr 2 out: kpt on one pce* **11/2**[2]

9 5 1/2 **Clew Bay Cove (IRE)**[24] 3249 11-10-7 117 ....(t) APCrowe 88
(C A Murphy, Ire) *towards rr for most: no imp in mod 9th ent st: kpt on one pce* **16/1**

10 13 **Paddy O Dee**[23] 3279 6-9-13 109 .... SWJackson 67
(P J Rothwell, Ire) *chsd ldrs early: sn mid-div: towards rr 1/2-way: nvr a factor after* **33/1**

11 1/2 **Rookery Rebel (IRE)**[10] 3533 9-10-1 111 .... DGHogan 68
(C W J Farrell, Ire) *mid-div: mstke 3rd: sn towards rr: nvr a factor after* **20/1**

12 5 1/2 **Puddencullinan (IRE)**[21] 3352 9-9-13 109 .... TJDoyle 61
(John Brassil, Ire) *sn led and disp: cl 2nd 1/2-way: rdn in 4th 3 out: sn no ex and wknd* **25/1**

13 16 **I Hear A Symphony (IRE)**[14] 3475 9-11-4 128 ....(t) RCColgan 64
(J J Lambe, Ire) *hld up towards rr: sme hdwy in 10th 4 out: rdn whn hmpd 2 out: wknd* **20/1**

U **Idarah (USA)**[24] 3242 8-10-10 125 .... APHeskin(5) —
(Paul Cashman, Ire) *uns rdr 3rd* **14/1**

F **Arklow Ger (IRE)**[24] 3242 9-10-8 118 .... APCawley —
(Paul Nolan, Ire) *prom: narrow ld 1/2-way: hdd 3 out: 3rd whn fell 2 out* **9/1**

B **Penny's Bill (IRE)**[194] 980 9-10-13 123 ....(t) SWFlanagan —
(Miss Elizabeth Doyle, Ire) *mid-div: 8th 1/2-way: hdwy in 6th 3 out: 5th whn b.d next* **10/1**

4m 46.8s (-18.00) **Going Correction** -0.70s/f (Firm) **16** Ran SP% **144.2**
Speed ratings: **109,108,107,106,103 96,95,93,91,85 85,83,76,—,— —**
CSF £59.78 CT £826.42 TOTE £27.60: £4.10, £1.60, £3.90, £2.60; DF 164.30.
Owner Who Are The Five Syndicate **Bred** Tony And Maggie Erangey **Trained** Kinsale, Co Cork
■ Stewards' Enquiry : R J Jones three-day ban: careless riding (Feb 9-10, 12)

FOCUS
The form looks sound enough rated around the winner, second and fourth.

NOTEBOOK
By The Hour(IRE) could hardly have been an obvious fancy but ran out a snug winner. Winner of a weak Sligo contest in September, she shaped well in the Cork National but disappointed at Gowran and came here on the back of a dire effort at Clonmel. Clearly back to her best, she seemed to relish the big field and a good gallop seems to be significant for her. She jumped to her left at the last, hampering the runner-up somewhat, but it was insignificant. She may come back to Leopardstown for the 2m5f handicap on Hennessy day and is one to keep on-side in big fields. Official explanation: trainer said, regarding the apparent improvement in form shown, that mare appeared to lose interest when equipped with cheekpieces last time and these were left off this time.
Questions Answered(IRE) is a likeable sort who enjoys his racing and gives his all. He looked likely to win after a cracking jump two out, but the winner was soon travelling better. He remains well treated and probably wants a bit further ideally. (op 3/1 tchd 10/3)
Deal Done(FR), winner of a beginners' chase in March, gave a bold bid off top-weight. He was hemmed in by the second up the run-in and can be rated slightly better than the bare form.
Conem(IRE) likes Leopardstown and ran on really well from the last. He probably remains just a shade high in the weights.
Diophas(GER) ran a fair race, but is hard to win with. (op 12/1)
Stormin Exit(IRE) seemed to have every chance. (op 11/2)
Erritt Lake(IRE) seems potentially well treated, but he was one of the first niggled and this was disappointing. (op 6/1)
Arklow Ger(IRE) ran a little freely and was probably in some trouble when exiting. (op 10/1)

Penny's Bill(IRE) was not out of the equation at the time. (op 10/1)

3707a BHP INSURANCES IRISH CHAMPION HURDLE (GRADE 1) (8 hdls) 2m
2:45 (2:49) 4-Y-0+ **£61,637** (£18,017; £8,534; £2,844)

RPR

1 **Hurricane Fly (IRE)**[25] 3205 7-11-10 166 PTownend 168+
(W P Mullins, Ire) *trckd ldr in 2nd: chal ent st: travelled wl to ld bef last: rdn and kpt on wl run-in: comf* **4/9**[1]

2 3 ½ **Solwhit (FR)**[25] 3205 7-11-10 164 DNRussell 164
(C Byrnes, Ire) *chsd ldrs in 3rd: rdn to chal ent st: 2nd bef last where slt mstke: kpt on u.p: no ex run-in* **3/1**[2]

3 2 **Thousand Stars (FR)**[25] 3205 7-11-10 156 MsKWalsh 161
(W P Mullins, Ire) *led: slt mstke 4th: rdn and chal ent st: hdd bef last: no ex and kpt on same pce* **14/1**

4 9 **Voler La Vedette (IRE)**[39] 2968 7-11-5 154 BarryGeraghty 148
(C A Murphy, Ire) *settled 4th: slt mstke 4 out: rdn and no imp bef 2 out: kpt on one pce* **9/1**[3]

5 dist **Sublimity (FR)**[20] 3380 11-11-10 153 (t) AELynch —
(Robert Alan Hennessy, Ire) *hld up in last: mstke 3 out: rdn and wknd bef next: t.o* **25/1**

3m 52.1s (-15.40) **Going Correction** -0.425s/f (Good) **5** Ran SP% **114.8**
Speed ratings: **121,119,118,113,—**
CSF £2.42 TOTE £2.00: £1.02, £1.40; DF 2.80.

Owner George Creighton **Bred** Agricola Del Parco **Trained** Muine Beag, Co Carlow

FOCUS
The front-running third has been rated back to his questionable best, with the runner-up rated to last season's best (when winning this).

NOTEBOOK
Hurricane Fly(IRE) beat Solwhit for the fourth time in a row. They covered the distance more than six seconds quicker than the runners in the opening maiden hurdle which certainly wasn't run at a crawl. It was as close to Champion Hurdle pace as the winner has gone without having run in one. Early in the race Hurricane Fly had a tendency to jump right and there were a couple of hurdles that he didn't pay too much respect to. In his defence, though, his jumping is significantly better when he starts to race and concentrates more. He also has enough speed to get himself back into a race should he make an early mistake. If one leaves that slight worry aside, he seems to have everything one would hope to see in a potential champion hurdler. He travels well, has more than one change of gear, and stays well. One would think he could be ridden from more or less anywhere in a race to boot. There are no real lines of form to tie him in with the Binoculars of this world, but there's no doubt that he's good enough to have a leading chance at Cheltenham. (op 4/9 tchd 1/2)

Solwhit(FR) chose to track the winner once again as he did at Christmas, but at the pace they went it didn't make any difference and he tried to kick at the right time. He just wasn't good enough, but he kept galloping to the line and one couldn't fault his effort in any way. It underlines him not being good enough to win the Champion Hurdle, but he could be good enough to get into the placings. (op 10/3)

Thousand Stars(FR) was headed between the final two flights and, although he continued to find, he just wasn't good enough. One would imagine he's good enough to go very close in a race like the Red Mills Hurdle.

Voler La Vedette(IRE) never got into the race and ran below her best. (op 12/1)

Sublimity(FR) isn't anywhere near this level any more. A fairly serious mistake three out didn't do anything for his cause, but it would have been hard to imagine him finishing anywhere other than a well-beaten last of the five. (op 25/1 tchd 33/1)

3708a SYNERGY SECURITY SOLUTIONS NOVICE HURDLE (GRADE 2) (10 hdls) 2m 4f
3:20 (3:23) 5-Y-0+ **£22,133** (£6,469; £3,064; £1,021)

RPR

1 **Hidden Cyclone (IRE)**[25] 3203 6-11-6 AndrewJMcNamara 144+
(John Joseph Hanlon, Ire) *chsd ldrs early: led 5th: rdn to assert bef last where slt mstke: kpt on wl run-in* **7/4**[1]

2 2 **Ballyhaunis**[66] 2489 6-11-3 131 (t) PTownend 137
(W P Mullins, Ire) *settled bhd ldrs: hdwy in 3rd 2 out: rdn in 2nd and no imp bef last: kpt on same pce* **3/1**[3]

3 3 **Si C'Etait Vrai (FR)**[21] 3353 5-11-0 DNRussell 131
(D T Hughes, Ire) *chsd ldr in 2nd: slt mstke 1st: rdn to chal ent st: no ex in 3rd bef last: kpt on same pce* **11/4**[2]

4 5 **Fully Funded (USA)**[36] 3029 6-11-8 PCarberry 134
(Noel Meade, Ire) *led: hdd 5th: 3rd 1/2-way: pushed along 3 out: rdn in last and no ex 2 out: kpt on one pce* **7/1**

5 27 **Carloswayback (IRE)**[26] 3181 6-11-3 BarryGeraghty 102
(Paul Nolan, Ire) *hld up in rr early: hdwy into 3rd 5 out: rdn in 4th 2 out: no ex and wknd: eased bef last* **8/1**

4m 59.4s (-7.00) **Going Correction** -0.425s/f (Good) **5** Ran SP% **111.6**
Speed ratings: **97,96,95,93,82**
CSF £7.54 TOTE £2.70: £1.60, £1.70; DF 7.80.

Owner Mrs A F Mee **Bred** Ronald O'Neill **Trained** Bagenalstown, Co Carlow

FOCUS
The time was good and the fourth is the guide to the level.

NOTEBOOK
Hidden Cyclone(IRE) took it up a long way out, a tactically astute move considering the horse just wanted to get on with it. He put in some quick jumps thereafter and it was really impressive how he put the race beyond question between the last two. He was a shade messy at the last, but was probably idling a bit at the time and gave the impression he was only doing enough. This horse is going to the very top and shapes as though he will get further. His trainer reckons chasing will improve him and he has the potential to be a Gold Cup horse in time. With regard to Cheltenham, he was introduced by Paddy Power at 12-1 for the Neptune Management Novices' Hurdle. If one could be sure he would run that would be a fine bet, as good ground is no problem to him. However, his trainer's reluctance to take the festival route is understandable in view of his future over fences, which will be tackled later this year, all being well. (op 7/4 tchd 15/8)

Ballyhaunis is no mug, but he was outclassed by the winner. He had every chance to use his Flat-race speed and reel in Hidden Cyclone from two out, but he simply could not pick up. He is going the right way and this seems his ideal trip. (op 11/4)

Si C'Etait Vrai(FR) was surprisingly short in the market, a measure of his home reputation. He had little experience taking on the likes of Hidden Cyclone, but ran a decent race and is another who will not be long hurdling. To be beaten 5l was no disgrace and he is still learning. (op 11/4 tchd 5/2)

Fully Funded(USA) was always likely to struggle and Paul Carberry tried to dictate before he was headed by the winner. The Grade 2 he won earlier this term was not strong and this is probably as good as he is. (op 7/1 tchd 8/1)

Carloswayback(IRE) once again was disappointing. Held in high esteem at home, he did not jump too well early on but briefly looked a threat at the third-last. He was soon beaten and stopped as if something was amiss. It is hard to know what to make of him.

3709a NEW TOTE DAILY DOUBLE H'CAP HURDLE (10 hdls) 2m 4f
3:50 (3:51) (81-123,122) 5-Y-0+ **£8,625** (£2,000; £875; £500)

RPR

1 **Glam Gerry (IRE)**[24] 3243 7-11-3 113 MPWalsh 130+
(C A Murphy, Ire) *mid-div: hdwy in 6th 3 out: rdn into 4th ent st: led appr last: kpt on wl u.p run-in* **7/1**[3]

2 ½ **Bruach Na Mara (IRE)**[25] 3207 8-10-13 114 BryanJCooper[(5)] 129
(W Harney, Ire) *mid-div early: 7th 1/2-way: hdwy into 3rd after 3 out: chal 2 out: led ent st: rdn and hdd appr last: no ex and kpt on same pce run-in* **9/1**

3 2 ½ **Golan Guy (IRE)**[78] 2224 6-10-3 99 PTownend 112
(A J Martin, Ire) *mid-div: hdwy into 9th 2 out: rdn in 7th ent st: styd on in 3rd last: no ex run-in: kpt on same pce* **9/1**

4 2 ½ **Mubrook (USA)**[14] 3474 6-11-0 110 (p) AndrewJMcNamara 120
(E J O'Grady, Ire) *chsd ldrs: 6th 1/2-way: rdn in 5th 2 out: kpt on same pce in 4th last: no ex run-in* **6/1**[1]

5 4 **Ring Street Roller (IRE)**[20] 3379 11-10-5 106 (p) MJBolger[(5)] 112
(W McCreery, Ire) *chsd ldrs: 8th 1/2-way: rdn in 10th 2 out: styd on to 7th last: no imp: kpt on same pce* **12/1**

6 2 ½ **Action Master**[8] 3581 5-11-1 114 (p) RLoughran 115
(D T Hughes, Ire) *mid-div: hdwy in 7th 3 out: cl 4th 2 out: rdn to chal ent st: no ex bef last where 5th: kpt on same pce* **25/1**

7 2 ½ **Falcon Island**[15] 3460 6-11-2 112 RMPower 113
(Mrs John Harrington, Ire) *mid-div: hdwy into 7th 2 out: rdn in 8th ent st: no ex in 6th last: kpt on same pce* **8/1**

8 3 ½ **Ephorus (USA)**[22] 3323 6-11-0 110 (p) JLCullen 108
(John Joseph Hanlon, Ire) *mid-div: 9th 1/2-way: rdn in 7th bef 2 out: no ex in 11th 2 out: kpt on one pce st* **7/1**[3]

9 1 ½ **Mister Farmer (FR)**[22] 3319 10-10-0 96 (t) NPMadden 92
(Martin Brassil, Ire) *towards rr: rdn in 14th bef 2 out: no imp: kpt on one pce st* **12/1**

10 1 ¼ **Grandad Bill (IRE)**[21] 3334 8-11-7 117 JamesReveley 112
(Jim Goldie) *led: hdd 3rd: 2nd 1/2-way: rdn and no ex 3 out: sn lost pl: 13th bef 2 out: kpt on one pce* **16/1**

11 7 **Kirbybroguelantern (IRE)**[8] 3581 10-10-10 113 (tp) RJJones[(7)] 101
(T Hogan, Ire) *chsd ldrs: 3rd 1/2-way: 2nd 3 out: chal 2 out: rdn in 3rd ent st: no ex and wknd* **33/1**

12 4 ½ **Tally Em Up (IRE)**[7] 3594 8-10-2 105 (tp) DJBates[(7)] 88
(P J Rothwell, Ire) *towards rr for most: nvr a factor* **20/1**

13 nk **Talkin' Tough (IRE)**[22] 3318 9-10-10 111 EJO'Connell[(5)] 94
(B R Hamilton, Ire) *chsd ldr: led 3rd: rdn and chal 2 out: hdd ent st: wknd* **16/1**

14 ½ **Brave Betsy (IRE)**[25] 3207 9-11-2 112 DJCondon 94
(Ms Joanna Morgan, Ire) *in rr of mid-div: hdwy into 8th 2 out: rdn in 10th and no ex ent st: wknd* **20/1**

15 1 ½ **Empire Theatre (IRE)**[25] 3207 7-11-3 113 (t) PCarberry 94
(Noel Meade, Ire) *chsd ldrs early: 10th 1/2-way: wknd 4 out* **16/1**

16 14 **Politeo (FR)**[25] 3207 5-11-1 119 APHeskin[(5)] 83
(Paul Nolan, Ire) *chsd ldrs: 4th 1/2-way: rdn and wknd bef 2 out* **13/2**[2]

17 19 **Mission Possible (IRE)**[10] 3533 10-10-6 102 DJCasey 50
(P J Rothwell, Ire) *a towards rr* **25/1**

18 dist **Hoopy (IRE)**[23] 3271 9-11-0 115 (tp) KMDonoghue[(5)] —
(Gordon Elliott, Ire) *chsd ldrs: 5th 1/2-way: wknd appr 3 out: t.o* **25/1**

P **Pom Flyer (FR)**[174] 1172 11-10-13 109 BarryGeraghty —
(F Flood, Ire) *towards rr: p.u after 5th* **20/1**

5m 8.00s (1.60) **Going Correction** -0.425s/f (Good) **19** Ran SP% **145.5**
Speed ratings: **79,78,77,76,75 74,73,71,71,70 67,66,65,65,65 59,51,—,—**
CSF £74.30 CT £616.07 TOTE £8.00: £2.40, £2.20, £3.10, £2.20; DF 97.10.
Owner Barry Connell **Bred** Ardobrien Stud Ltd **Trained** Gorey, Co Wexford

FOCUS
The runner-up sets the standard.

NOTEBOOK
Glam Gerry(IRE) did the job well. Something of an eye-taker on his final maiden start at Leopardstown over Christmas, he was given a confident ride and clearly appreciated stepping up to this trip. He looked as if he was always holding the runner-up in the final furlong and 3m should not be a problem to him. He can win again off his new mark. (op 6/1)
Bruach Na Mara(IRE) went down fighting. His consistency cannot be faulted and he is also versatile as regards trip. Three miles might be ideal for him and he deserves a handicap win. (op 12/1)
Golan Guy(IRE) looked as if he was travelling best coming down to the last, but was rather one-paced. He tends to find little off the bridle but is good enough to win off this mark. (op 9/1 tchd 10/1)
Mubrook(USA) had every chance. He got the trip well and this is probably as good as he is, though he still has time on his side. (op 8/1)
Ring Street Roller(IRE) kept on well from off the pace.
Ephorus(USA) struggled to win a weak race at Tramore last time and was always likely to find this much more demanding. He will probably go chasing sooner rather than later.
Pom Flyer(FR) Official explanation: jockey said gelding pulled up lame

3570 WETHERBY (L-H)
Monday, January 24
OFFICIAL GOING: Good to soft (soft in places)

3711 TURFTV.CO.UK JUVENILE MAIDEN HURDLE (9 hdls) 2m 110y
12:55 (12:55) (Class 5) 4-Y-O **£1,541** (£449; £224)

Form RPR

1 **Tigre D'Aron (FR)**[44] 4-11-0 0 BrianHughes 117+
(Howard Johnson) *mde all: drvn 3 out: kpt on run-in: jst hld on* **4/9**[1]

2 nse **High Ransom**[99] 4-10-7 0 BarryKeniry 110+
(Micky Hammond) *chsd ldrs: wnt 2nd 6th: styd on to chal last: kpt on wl towards fin: jst hld* **11/1**[3]

0 3 21 **Grams And Ounces**[18] 3401 4-11-0 0 DougieCostello 98
(Amy Weaver) *chsd ldrs: 3rd and one pce whn blnd 2 out* **33/1**

4 3 **White Diamond**[91] 4-10-2 0 JamesHalliday[(5)] 90+
(Malcolm Jefferson) *nt fluent: chsd ldrs: outpcd 4th: kpt on to take modest 4th appr 3 out: one pce* **7/1**[2]

5 8 **Royal Holiday (IRE)**[39] 4-11-0 0 FearghalDavis 87
(Brian Ellison) *in rr: bhd whn reminders 6th: nvr on terms* **33/1**

P4 **6** *2 ½* **Petrocelli**[101] 1699 4-11-0 0 ... JamesReveley 86
(Wilf Storey) *hld up in rr: hdwy appr 3 out: 5th 2 out: sn wknd* **66/1**

246 **7** *2 ½* **Almutaham (USA)**[59] 2655 4-11-0 96 ... PaddyAspell 83
(James Moffatt) *mid-div: pushed along 3rd: bhd fr 6th* **28/1**

6 **8** *6* **Lil Ella (IRE)**[11] 3519 4-10-7 103 ... TomSiddall 70
(Patrick Holmes) *chsd wnr to 6th: wknd appr 3 out: bhd whn mstke 2 out* **16/1**

P **High Rolling**[28] 4-11-0 0 ... RichieMcGrath —
(Tim Easterby) *in rr: nt fluent 2nd: bhd and reminders 6th: t.o whn p.u bef 2 out* **16/1**

4m 1.30s (5.50) **Going Correction** +0.475s/f (Soft) **9** Ran SP% **112.7**
Speed ratings: **106,105,96,94,90 89,88,85,—**
toteswingers:1&2:£2.70, 1&3:£6.40, 2&3:£19.90 CSF £5.76 TOTE £1.50: £1.10, £2.70, £5.40; EX 6.20.

Owner Andrea & Graham Wylie **Bred** Marc Trinquet And Olivier Trinquet **Trained** Billy Row, Co Durham

■ Stewards' Enquiry : Barry Keniry one-day ban: used whip in incorrect place (Feb 7)
Brian Hughes one-day ban: used whip in incorrect place (Feb 7)

FOCUS
An ordinary-looking juvenile contest, although the winner could prove decent. the form should work out.

NOTEBOOK
Tigre D'Aron(FR), runner-up on his only start in France over hurdles, is a nice, strong-looking sort who went straight into the lead - he employed similar tactics for his previous connections. It seemed sure he'd win comfortably at one point heading into the home straight, but was made to work really hard by the runner-up and only narrowly prevailed. He is probably better than he showed and has the size to make a chaser. (op 4-7 tchd 8-13 in places)
High Ransom, arguably a disappointing maiden on the Flat for Michael Jarvis, but a sister to 2005 Arkle Chase winner Contraband, took a keen hold under restraint and looked to have little chance of making any impact when coming under strong pressure a long way out. However, she responded to the urgings of her rider and almost got up. She appeared to have quite a pronounced knee action. (op 10-1 tchd 12-1)
Grams And Ounces ran better than he had done on his hurdling debut, albeit in a lesser race, and has the size to win over hurdles. (op 28-1)
White Diamond, a fair sort on the Flat in Ireland for previous connections, doesn't look the biggest and, although travelling strongly for quite some time, never looked like getting into a challenging position. (op 8-1)

3712 WETHERBY RACECOURSE H'CAP CHASE (16 fncs) 2m 4f 110y
1:25 (1:25) (Class 5) (0-95,95) 5-Y-O+ **£1,712** (£499; £249)

Form RPR

-P40 **1** **Allanard (IRE)**[22] 3336 7-11-1 84 ...(p) JamesReveley 99+
(Martin Todhunter) *blnd 3rd: trckd ldrs 7th: clumsy and led 12th: wnt clr 3 out: 20 l ld at last: eased clsng stages* **5/2**[1]

633P **2** *13* **Panthers Run**[5] 3636 11-10-0 69 oh3 ...(t) DougieCostello 66
(Jonathan Haynes) *led: hdd 12th: kpt on to take distant 2nd sn after 2 out* **9/2**[3]

-440 **3** *1 ¾* **Go On Be A Lady**[27] 3170 8-11-3 86 ...(p) BarryKeniry 81
(Alan Swinbank) *chsd ldrs: outpcd 10th: kpt on fr 2 out: tk 3rd last* **6/1**

50P4 **4** *11* **Apache Brave (IRE)**[13] 3503 8-10-0 69 oh9 ...(b) RobertWalford 59
(Henry Hogarth) *chsd ldrs: hit 6th: chsd wnr 4 out: 15 l 2nd whn blnd 2 out: wknd qckly run-in* **11/4**[2]

00-0 **5** *19* **Qbuster (IRE)**[13] 3502 10-11-12 95 ...(t) BrianHarding 63
(Sharon Watt) *in tch: hit 2nd: hit 7th and reminders: lost pl and hit 12th* **10/1**

F-P0 **6** *39* **Carry Duff**[41] 2940 10-10-12 91 ... TonyKelly[(10)] 24
(Ferdy Murphy) *in rr: drvn 7th and sn lost pl: bhd fr 10th: t.o 4 out* **15/2**

5m 18.0s (10.20) **Going Correction** +0.575s/f (Soft) **6** Ran SP% **108.6**
Speed ratings: **103,98,97,93,85 71**
toteswingers:1&2:£2.10, 1&3:£3.00, 2&3:£3.20 CSF £13.14 TOTE £2.90: £1.30, £1.70; EX 13.60.

Owner E Ron Madden **Bred** R Madden **Trained** Orton, Cumbria

FOCUS
A weak 69-95 handicap chase but in the end an easy winner of some potential, who is rated a stone better than his hurdles form.

NOTEBOOK
Allanard(IRE), making his chasing debut from his hurdle-race mark of 84, made a jumping error at the final fence in the back straight both times. He came clear and won easing down, value for at least 20 lengths. This was his first career win on his 11th start and he is clearly a much better chaser than he was a hurdler. He has the potential to be competitive, even from a guaranteed much higher mark. (op 10-3)
Panthers Run, whose sole previous success in 27 previous starts was at Hexham over a year ago, set the pace but was readily left for dead by the winner. (tchd 4-1)
Go On Be A Lady, in first-time cheekpieces, was having just her third start over fences. She stuck to her guns in the closing stages and will be better suited by 3m. (op 11-2 tchd 13-2)
Apache Brave(IRE), 9lb out of the handicap, came in for support on the morning line. As usual he made jumping errors and weakened in the straight. (op 10-3)
Qbuster(IRE), who looked on a stiff mark for his handicap debut, made jumping errors and was beaten off long before the final turn. (op 9-1)

3713 GORACING.CO.UK H'CAP HURDLE (13 hdls) 3m 1f
2:00 (2:00) (Class 4) (0-115,114) 4-Y-0+ **£1,951** (£573; £286; £143)

Form RPR

0-P0 **1** **Borero (FR)**[27] 3169 8-10-10 105 ... JakeGreenall[(7)] 113
(Michael Easterby) *in tch: drvn 7th: outpcd 10th: hdwy next: wnt 2nd between last 2: led last: rdn out* **17/2**

P-P0 **2** *3* **Arctic Echo**[72] 2372 12-11-0 105 ...(t) MichaelMurphy[(3)] 110
(Rob Summers) *chsd ldrs: reminders 7th: led 10th: hdd last: no ex* **50/1**

2-01 **3** *8* **Monogram**[107] 1783 7-11-12 114 ... BrianHughes 115+
(Howard Johnson) *trckd ldrs: led 7th: wnt 2nd appr 3 out: rdn and hit 2 out: wandered: hung rt and wknd last* **5/2**[1]

-044 **4** *4 ½* **Emperor Charlie**[14] 3485 7-11-3 105 ... GrahamLee 99
(Ferdy Murphy) *hld up in rr: hdwy 8th: rdn 10th: sn wl outpcd: kpt on fr 2 out* **8/1**[3]

4-03 **5** *½* **Double Eagle**[21] 3370 9-11-9 111 ...(p) JasonMaguire 107+
(Donald McCain) *j.rt: led to 7th: led 9th to next: wknd 2 out* **7/2**[2]

6P30 **6** *12* **Petroupetrov (FR)**[14] 3483 8-10-12 100 ...(v) TomSiddall 87
(Richard Phillips) *w ldrs: led 7th: hdd 9th: wknd appr 3 out* **14/1**

5P53 **7** *nk* **Terenzium (IRE)**[9] 3575 9-11-7 109 ...(p) BarryKeniry 91
(Micky Hammond) *in rr: reminders 7th: sn lost tch* **11/1**

41P4 **8** *¾* **Mtpockets (IRE)**[14] 3483 6-11-7 109 ... DougieCostello 91
(Neil Mulholland) *w ldrs: drvn 7th: sn lost pl* **7/2**[2]

-050 **9** *3 ½* **Robertewenutter**[14] 3487 7-10-9 97 ... HenryOliver 76
(Sue Smith) *prom: outpcd 10th: sn lost pl* **28/1**

6m 33.2s (16.70) **Going Correction** +0.475s/f (Soft) **9** Ran SP% **115.1**
Speed ratings (Par 105): **92,91,88,87,86 83,82,82,81**
toteswingers:1&2:£46.20, 1&3:£6.10, 2&3:£17.00 CSF £267.37 CT £1366.48 TOTE £11.20: £2.90, £12.30, £1.40; EX 642.20.

Owner N W A Bannister & M J R Bannister **Bred** Eric Becq **Trained** Sheriff Hutton, N Yorks

FOCUS
A fair handicap hurdle run at a reasonable pace. The fourth sets the level in a reasonable handicap.

NOTEBOOK
Borero(FR) landed what appeared to be a decent gamble, having been available at 33/1 in the morning. He was being shoved along for much of the final circuit and looked set to finish well back, but began to pick up in the home straight and forged clear once leading at the last. Reverting to hurdles, he had shown little for this yard previously but has reportedly had treatment for a bad back, and had become well handicapped on his old form for Charlie Mann. Official explanation: trainer said, regarding apparent improvement in form, that the gelding had lost its confidence over fences and benefited from the return to hurdles. (op 10-1)
Arctic Echo is another who has been eased in the handicap and ran a better race in the first-time tongue tie. He looked in command two out but was worn down on the long run to the final flight.
Monogram, making his handicap debut, travelled best and looked set for a comfortable win turning in, but his stamina soon began to ebb away and he did not find much when let down. Reported by his rider to have hung right, he remains a decent prospect. He could switch to chasing now. Official explanation: jockey said gelding hung right-handed in straight (op 3-1)
Emperor Charlie, another in a handicap for the first time, stayed on late after being outpaced by the leaders down the far side. (op 7-1)
Double Eagle, the long-time leader, showed a tendency to jump out to his right. (tchd 10-3 and 4-1)
Mtpockets(IRE)'s rider reported the mare was never travelling. Official explanation: jockey said mare never travelled (op 4-1)

3714 TOTESPORT.COM IRISH DAY - SATURDAY 5TH FEBRUARY NOVICES' CHASE (16 fncs) 2m 4f 110y
2:35 (2:37) (Class 3) 5-Y-0+ **£3,332** (£1,034; £557)

Form RPR

10-4 **1** **Alfie Sherrin**[75] 2303 8-10-12 0 ... APMcCoy 130+
(Jonjo O'Neill) *trckd ldrs: lft handy 2nd and sltly hmpd 7th: upsides 10th: shkn up to ld between last 2: wnt easily clr run-in: eased fnl 50yds: impressive* **13/8**[2]

31-3 **2** *7* **Knockavilla (IRE)**[86] 2088 8-11-4 125 ... BrianHughes 120
(Howard Johnson) *led: rdn 4 out: hit 2 out: sn hdd: 3 l down whn mstke last* **13/2**[3]

10-6 **3** *49* **Sir Tantallus Hawk**[71] 2399 7-10-12 0 ... BarryKeniry 80
(Alan Swinbank) *nt jump wl in last: j.rt and mstke 3rd: blnd 5th: outpcd 8th: lost tch and mstke 11th: t.o 4 out* **9/1**

2-21 **F** **Glenwood Knight (IRE)**[24] 3254 8-11-4 135 ... JasonMaguire —
(Donald McCain) *trckd ldr: upsides 4th: fell 7th* **11/10**[1]

5m 21.9s (14.10) **Going Correction** +0.575s/f (Soft) **4** Ran SP% **109.0**
Speed ratings: **96,93,74,—**
CSF £10.44 TOTE £2.40; EX 7.10.

Owner John P McManus **Bred** Mrs J L Egan **Trained** Cheltenham, Gloucs

FOCUS
A very decent novices' chase but much of the interest was lost when Uttoxeter winner Glenwood Knight crashed out at the last with a circuit to go. The first two are rated below previous marks.

NOTEBOOK
Alfie Sherrin, who had to sidestep the stricken Glenwood Knight, is rated 147 over hurdles and was bought for £110,000 out of Paul Nicholls' stable in August. He is apparently not easy to train but travelled like a very good horse here, jumping soundly and galloping all over his only serious rival. He put it to bed in a matter of strides when sent on and was able to ease right off. He has the potential to climb high up the novice chase tree and the Jewson could be a likely spring target. (op 6-4 tchd 11-8, 15-8 in a place)
Knockavilla(IRE), disappointing on his return here after a six-month break, is a 125-rated hurdler. He led the winner on sufferance and was no match when he repeated his error two out at the last. (op 5-1 tchd 15-2)
Sir Tantallus Hawk, a 132-rated hurdler, jumped with no confidence on his first try over fences and, after a third serious jumping error five out, he eventually completed in his own time. He will need a big drop in grade to regain his confidence. (tchd 17-2)
Glenwood Knight(IRE), a grand type, is rated 135 over hurdles already, a stone above his hurdle mark. Hopefully he will bounce back from this out of character tumble. He should make a fine staying chaser in time. (op 6-4)

3715 "ENJOY THE CRAIC" ON SATURDAY 5TH FEBRUARY NOVICES' HURDLE (9 hdls) 2m 110y
3:10 (3:10) (Class 4) 4-Y-0+ **£1,951** (£573; £286; £143)

Form RPR

2 **1** **A Bridge Too Far (IRE)**[63] 2590 5-11-4 0 ... APMcCoy 113+
(Paul Webber) *trckd ldrs: led 5th: styd on wl run-in: drvn out* **2/1**[1]

2 *2 ¾* **Ubi Ace**[132] 5-11-4 0 ... RobertWalford 109
(Tim Walford) *trckd ldrs: jnd wnr appr 3 out: styd on same pce run-in* **14/1**

P **3** *8* **Rumble Of Thunder (IRE)**[23] 3304 5-11-4 0 ... RichieMcGrath 102
(Kate Walton) *w ldrs: led 4th: hdd next: outpcd appr 3 out: styd on between last 2: tk modest 3rd sn after last* **50/1**

F **4** *2 ¾* **Omokoroa (IRE)**[41] 2939 5-11-4 0 ... JasonMaguire 100
(Donald McCain) *nt fluent: chsd ldrs: rdn appr 3 out: wknd appr last* **2/1**[1]

51-P **5** *6* **Chief Bucaneer (IRE)**[261] 214 8-11-10 0 ... JanFaltejsek 101
(George Charlton) *chsd ldrs: outpcd appr 3 out: kpt on fr 2 out* **11/1**[3]

00 **6** *2* **Whiskey Ridge (IRE)**[227] 718 5-11-4 0 ... HenryOliver 92
(Sue Smith) *chsd ldrs: drvn 6th: outpcd appr next: kpt on fr 2 out* **100/1**

5- **7** *¾* **Mytara**[301] 4932 6-10-11 0 ... SeanQuinlan 85
(Pam Sly) *t.k.h towards rr: mstke 2nd: kpt on fr 3 out: nvr on terms* **16/1**

6 **8** *nk* **Tinseltown**[8] 2939 5-11-4 0 ... PaddyAspell 94+
(Brian Rothwell) *t.k.h in midfield: hdwy 5th: chsng ldrs 3 out: 4th and btn whn mstke 2 out: 6th whn hit last* **40/1**

0-46 **9** *nk* **Harris Hawk**[73] 2355 6-10-11 0 ... MrJohnDawson[(7)] 93
(John Wade) *mid-div: nt fluent: kpt on fr 3 out: nvr a factor* **50/1**

540/ **10** *14* **Northern Cross (IRE)**[636] 34 7-11-4 0 ... BrianHughes 80
(Howard Johnson) *chsd ldrs: rdn appr 3 out: 7th and wkng whn blnd 2 out* **33/1**

4 **11** *3* **Danehillsundance (IRE)**[10] 3551 7-11-4 0 ... BarryKeniry 75
(Philip Kirby) *nvr betrter than mid-div: wknd 3 out* **50/1**

12 *7* **Red Valerian Two (IRE)**[23] 4-10-2 0 ... MrMMO'Connor[(5)] 58
(George Moore) *a towards rr: bhd fr 3 out* **100/1**

13 *3 ¾* **Sweet Sugar (FR)**[231] 5-11-4 0 ... GrahamLee 66
(Ferdy Murphy) *hld up in midfield: effrt appr 3 out: sn wknd* **8/1**[2]

00 **14** *2 ¾* **Lava Steps (USA)**[6] 3620 5-11-4 0 ... TomSiddall 63
(Paul Midgley) *led: hdd 4th: lost pl after 6th* **100/1**

0-0U **15** *12* **Aitch Factor**[40] 2954 5-11-4 0 PhilKinsella 52
(Henry Hogarth) *a towards rr: wl bhd fr 3 out* **100/1**
06U **16** *7* **Matilda's Folly (IRE)**[11] 3521 6-10-11 0 AndrewThornton 39
(Ben Haslam) *t.k.h in rr: bhd fr 3 out: hit last* **200/1**
06P **17** *6* **Beano Boy**[41] 2939 6-10-13 0 JamesHalliday(5) 41
(Brian Storey) *in rr: wl bhd fr 6th* **150/1**
18 *35* **Salto Des Mottes (FR)** 5-11-4 0 DougieCostello 9
(Neil Mulholland) *in rr: wl bhd fr 6th t.o: virtually p.u run-in* **50/1**

4m 1.70s (5.90) **Going Correction** +0.475s/f (Soft)
WFA 4 from 5yo+ 11lb **18** Ran SP% **117.0**
Speed ratings (Par 105): **105,103,99,98,95 94,94,94,94,87 86,82,81,79,74 70,68,51**
toteswingers:1&2:£8.50, 1&3:£28.40, 2&3:£70.40 CSF £32.30 TOTE £3.60: £1.50, £4.00, £13.00; EX 37.20.
Owner R C Moody **Bred** William O'Keeffe **Trained** Mollington, Oxon

FOCUS
A big field of mainly unexposed horses, although some with form on the Flat and over fences.

NOTEBOOK
A Bridge Too Far(IRE), making his hurdling debut having been runner-up in a bumper in November, was ridden positively and, after going on down the far side, asserted from the penultimate flight. Connections believe he will be suited by further. He was subsequently sent to the Doncaster sales where he was bought by Donald McCain for £65,000.
Ubi Ace ◆, a Flat winner at up to 1m4f, made an encouraging debut and was the only one to give the winner a race. He should be up to winning a similar contest before long. (op 9-1)
Rumble Of Thunder(IRE), another decent Flat performer, put a disappointing hurdling debut behind him. Always in the front rank, he was staying on again in the latter stages. (op 40-1)
Omokoroa(IRE) had fallen when running well on his hurdling debut and performed with credit here. He may be of more interest once qualified for a mark.
Chief Bucaneer(IRE), a C&D winner in the spring, ran reasonably under his penalty on his first start since May. (op 12-1)
Matilda's Folly(IRE) Official explanation: jockey said, regarding running and riding, that his orders were to settle the mare early stages give it a good view of the hurdles and do his best, it was keen early but became tired latterly, was very green, became unbalanced and made a mistake at the last through tiredness.

3716 WETHERBYRACING.CO.UK H'CAP CHASE (18 fncs) 3m 1f
3:40 (3:40) (Class 4) (0-110,110) 5-Y-0+ **£1,999** (£620; £334)

Form RPR
-303 **1** **Work Boy**[12] 3510 10-11-3 **106** ShaneByrne(5) 117+
(Sue Smith) *chsd ldrs: reminders 5th: led after next: hdd 11th: lft in ld next: rdn appr 4 out: 2 l ahd whn mstke 2 out: kpt on: all out* **3/1**[2]
64UP **2** *1 1/2* **Shrewd Investor (IRE)**[13] 3501 11-10-8 **92** (p) PhilKinsella 96
(Henry Hogarth) *w ldr: led 3rd: hdd 9th: hmpd 12th: chsd wnr 4 out: styd on same pce fr 2 out: nvr able to chal and a jst hld* **6/1**
0156 **3** *30* **Seize**[113] 1697 9-11-12 **110** PaddyAspell 92
(James Moffatt) *chsd ldrs: hmpd 8th and 12th: lft 2nd 12th: wknd appr 4 out: sn bhd* **17/2**
1U51 **F** **La Pantera Rosa (IRE)**[12] 3510 8-11-8 **106** (p) BarryKeniry —
(Micky Hammond) *chsd ldrs: reminders 9th: led 11th: fell next* **7/2**[3]
F-05 **P** **Blazing Diva (IRE)**[73] 2354 8-11-6 **104** GrahamLee —
(Sandy Thomson) *led to 3rd: reminders and led 9th: hit next and sn hdd: 4th and weakning whn blnd 13th: t.o whn p.u after next* **7/1**
P141 **F** **Canal Bank (IRE)**[50] 2796 7-11-1 **102** (p) RichieMcLernon(3) —
(Jonjo O'Neill) *trckd ldrs: fell 8th* **9/4**[1]

6m 28.0s (18.60) **Going Correction** +0.575s/f (Soft) **6** Ran SP% **115.3**
Speed ratings: **93,92,82,—,— —**
toteswingers:1&2:£3.90, 1&3:£5.20, 2&3:£4.60 CSF £21.05 TOTE £3.80: £2.10, £4.30; EX 28.10.
Owner Mrs S Smith **Bred** Mrs M Parker **Trained** High Eldwick, W Yorks

FOCUS
A modest 92-110 handicap chase and a disappointing turn-out after the freeze-up. A fair pace but two of the leading fancies ended up on the ground. The winner is value for further and rated to his mark.

NOTEBOOK
Work Boy, closely matched with La Pantera Rosa on Doncaster running, was left in charge when that one departed. He made very hard work of it under a forceful if untidy ride but after a mistake two out he did just enough. His rating cannot go up much and this big horse should continue to give account of himself at this level. (op 11-4)
Shrewd Investor(IRE), without a win for nearly two years and pulled up on his previous outing two weeks earlier, went in pursuit of the winner four out. He was just two lengths down when Workboy clouted two out but, as hard as he tried, he could not quite get on level terms. (op 8-1)
Seize, absent since October and having his first run for this yard, stopped to nothing four out. (op 8-1 tchd 15-2)
La Pantera Rosa(IRE), raised 4lb for his Doncaster success, has never been the safest of jumpers. He had just assumed command when hitting the deck seven out. (op 2-1 tchd 5-2)
Canal Bank(IRE), improved under this rider since being fitted with cheekpieces, was 6lb higher than for his Exeter success. He crashed out at the second last with a full circuit to go. (op 2-1 tchd 5-2)

3717 FOLLOW WETHERBY RACECOURSE ON FACEBOOK RACING EXCELLENCE "HANDS AND HEELS" H'CAP HURDLE (11 hdls) 2m 4f
4:15 (4:16) (Class 5) (0-90,88) 4-Y-0+ **£1,541** (£449; £224)

Form RPR
0604 **1** **King Benny (IRE)**[6] 3622 7-11-12 **88** PeterCarberry 93+
(Elliott Cooper) *hld up: smooth hdwy to trck ldrs 8th: led last: drvn out* **13/2**[3]
5P55 **2** *2 3/4* **Cute N You Know It**[73] 2351 8-9-11 **62** (p) TonyKelly(3) 64
(Andrew Crook) *w ldrs: upsides 3 out: kpt on same pce appr last: crowded run-in: tk 2nd nr fin* **10/1**
4606 **3** *1/2* **Rhyton (IRE)**[20] 3387 4-10-12 **86** HenryBrooke 76
(Donald McCain) *chsd ldrs: led 8th: hdd last: edgd rt: kpt on same pce* **11/1**
00 **4** *5* **Some Catch (IRE)**[61] 2612 5-10-0 **62** oh4 MrJMQuinlan 61+
(Elliott Cooper) *hld up in rr: hdwy to chse ldrs whn mstke 7th: chsng ldrs 3 out: one pce fr next* **9/2**[2]
0612 **5** *1 1/4* **Sambelucky (IRE)**[21] 3363 6-11-8 **87** MrRLindsay(3) 82
(Keith Reveley) *hld up: wnt prom 6th: sn pushed along: drvn 8th: wknd and one pce fr 2 out* **2/1**[1]
0603 **6** *1* **Chouromanesco (FR)**[17] 3432 8-11-12 **88** (p) AodhaganConlon 83
(Mark Bradstock) *hld up in rr: hdwy 7th: chsng ldrs next: sn drvn: one pce fr 2 out* **10/1**
5P0/ **7** *6* **Kyathos (GER)**[638] 10 10-10-5 **70** MrGRSmith(3) 61
(David Thompson) *chsd ldrs: wknd 2 out* **66/1**
3-30 **8** *2 1/4* **Lightening Fire (IRE)**[39] 2980 9-11-4 **83** (b) MrRJWilliams(3) 74
(Bernard Llewellyn) *nt fluent: led 2nd: hdd 8th: wknd between last 2* **10/1**
-05P **9** *35* **Betty's Run**[13] 3498 9-9-11 **62** oh1 MrCGreene(3) 18
(Lynn Siddall) *in rr: mstke 5th: lost pl next: bhd fr 8th: t.o next* **80/1**
6030 **10** *3/4* **Itstooearly**[59] 2658 8-11-6 **87** MrJBelbin(5) 42
(James Moffatt) *in rr: jnd ldrs 7th: lost pl appr 3 out: sn bhd: t.o* **14/1**
P-00 **P** **Oscar Trial (IRE)**[103] 1822 9-10-2 **64** JakeGreenall —
(Sharon Watt) *led to 2nd: drvn 6th: wknd next: sn bhd: t.o whn p.u bef 3 out* **12/1**

5m 19.8s (20.30) **Going Correction** +0.475s/f (Soft)
WFA 4 from 5yo+ 12lb **11** Ran SP% **117.5**
Speed ratings (Par 103): **78,76,76,74,74 73,71,70,56,56 —**
toteswingers:1&2:£6.50, 1&3:£7.60, 2&3:£8.10 CSF £69.47 CT £708.07 TOTE £9.20: £2.50, £3.10, £2.50; EX 47.70.
Owner Tom McNicholas **Bred** Glenn Turley **Trained** Brigham, Cumbria

FOCUS
A very moderate "hands and heels" hurdle for conditionals and amateurs. The early pace was very steady and the form is moderate.

NOTEBOOK
King Benny(IRE) looked the stable first string on jockey bookings but it was his stable companion who attracted the money. However, he was always going best with his rider sticking to the inside the whole way. He was held onto as long as possible in the straight but, once he hit the front just before the last, he quickly came clear. This was a bad race but he looks capable of improvement, and might be turned out again quickly. (op 11-2)
Cute N You Know It goes well on this track and ran another good race over a trip that is on the short side for her. A return to 3m will be in her favour. (op 17-2)
Rhyton(IRE), a 1m4f Flat winner but lightly raced and well beaten over jumps prior to this, ran his best race for current connections, leading early in the straight and only weakening once headed by the winner. (op 12-1 tchd 14-1)
Some Catch(IRE), who had shown nothing in four previous starts, was 4lb out of the weights on this handicap debut but was backed in to second favourite. However, after being held up she was struggling to get into contention at the end of the back straight, and never looked like playing a major part. It was at least an improved effort. (op 17-2)
Sambelucky(IRE), a winner under this rider last month, was 10lb higher and never figured having been held up. (tchd 9-4)
Chouromanesco(FR) got involved leaving the back straight but faded once the principals committed. (op 14-1)
T/Jkpt: £3,309.20 to a £1 stake. Pool:£371,478.38 - 79.70 winning tickets T/Plt: £106.70 to a £1 stake. Pool:£69,615.08 - 476.14 winning tickets T/Qpdt: £65.00 to a £1 stake. Pool:£4,285.13 - 48.75 winning tickets WG

3491 LEICESTER (R-H)
Tuesday, January 25

OFFICIAL GOING: Hurdle course - soft (heavy in places); chase course - good (soft on the flat crossings)
Wind: Light behind Weather: Overcast

3718 CROXTON PARK NOVICES' HURDLE (DIV I) (10 hdls) 2m 4f 110y
1:10 (1:10) (Class 4) 4-Y-0+ **£2,276** (£668; £334; £166)

Form RPR
21 **1** **Tornado Bob (IRE)**[25] 3253 6-11-12 130 JasonMaguire 142+
(Donald McCain) *mde all: clr last: easily* **1/1**[1]
-452 **2** *8* **Lord Liath (IRE)**[24] 3295 5-11-5 0 RobertThornton 118
(Alan King) *chsd ldrs: rdn after 7th: wnt 2nd appr 2 out: wknd bef last* **11/4**[2]
21-1 **3** *1* **Glitzy D'Ocala (FR)**[24] 3301 6-11-5 0 RichardJohnson 116
(Philip Hobbs) *chsd wnr tl rdn appr 2 out: sn wknd* **11/4**[2]
4-40 **4** *2 3/4* **Lucky Sunny (IRE)**[41] 2954 8-11-5 0 SeanQuinlan 113+
(Richard Phillips) *hld up: racd keenly: nt fluent 1st: hdwy 7th: wknd and eased appr 2 out* **50/1**
066 **5** *35* **Tippering (IRE)**[15] 3489 6-11-5 0 TjadeCollier 78
(Sue Smith) *prom: pushed along after 3rd: sn lost pl: hdwy bef 5th: wknd 7th: t.o* **80/1**
00- **6** *1/2* **Kauto Cyreo (FR)**[289] 5158 6-11-0 0 IanPopham(5) 78
(Claire Dyson) *prom: racd keenly: wknd appr 7th: t.o* **150/1**
0-20 **7** *6* **The Hon Tara**[43] 2925 7-10-12 0 (t) FelixDeGiles 65
(Charlie Longsdon) *hld up: hdwy 4th: wknd after next: t.o* **80/1**
636- **8** *16* **Group Leader (IRE)**[232] 4678 5-10-12 115 TimBailey(7) 56
(J R Jenkins) *hld up: effrt after 7th: sn wknd: t.o* **40/1**[3]

5m 24.5s (-0.20) **Going Correction** +0.30s/f (Yiel) **8** Ran SP% **110.9**
Speed ratings (Par 105): **112,108,108,107,94 94,91,85**
toteswingers:1&2 £1.10, 2&3 £1.10, 1&3 £1.90 CSF £3.90 TOTE £2.60: £1.10, £1.02, £1.70; EX 4.90.
Owner Mrs Diana L Whateley **Bred** Christopher Maye **Trained** Cholmondeley, Cheshire

FOCUS
While this novice event was robbed by the defection of Champion Court, it was still an interesting clash between the three market leaders. They went an average gallop and only four mattered from the home turn. It has been rated around the second to his Exeter mark.

NOTEBOOK
Tornado Bob(IRE) hacked up in bad ground when off the mark at Uttoxeter 25 days earlier and confirmed himself an improver with another clear-cut success under a penalty. He was unsurprisingly given a positive ride and outstayed his rivals in ground that obviously holds no fears. It must be remembered his Irish bumper win was on quick ground, though, so his versatility on that front will prove very useful for connections in placing him for the remainder of the season. Jumping fences will ultimately be more his game next term, but he is fully entitled to take his chance in something more valuable now. (tchd 11-10 tchd 6-5 in places)
Lord Liath(IRE) ◆ posted an improved effort when third at Exeter last time and probably improved again here, but found the winner too strong in the stamina department over the slightly stiffer test. He should be winning before long. (op 5-2 tchd 3-1)
Glitzy D'Ocala(FR) showed a liking for testing ground when hacking up on his debut for the stable in an Exeter bumper 24 days previously. He kept tabs on the winner, but began to feel the pinch from three out and possibly paid for running somewhat freely over the longer trip. (op 7-2)

Lucky Sunny(IRE), up in trip, was given a curious ride. He appeared to race awkwardly out the back early, but made up ground easily in the back straight and had his chance turning for home. His rider was anything but hard on him, though, and he would have surely been placed under more vigorous handling. The stewards enquired into his running and riding and the jockey explained his orders were to drop him in and pass horses late on. He said his mount was again keen early on and he felt he was emptying on the heavy ground in the home straight. He also added the horse had bled in the past and, after some deliberation, the officials took no further action. Official explanation: jockey said, regarding running and riding, that his orders were to drop the gelding in, get it relaxed, and aim to pass horses towards the end, but it was very keen early and when put into the race in the home straight behind leaders it began to empty on the heavy ground, he therefore felt it prudent to hold it together in closing stages. (op 40-1)

3719 CROXTON PARK NOVICES' HURDLE (DIV II) (10 hdls) 2m 4f 110y

1:40 (1:40) (Class 4) 4-Y-O+ **£2,276** (£668; £334; £166)

Form RPR

13 **1** **Extremely So**[23] 3344 5-11-5 117 ....(t) PaulMoloney 105+
(Philip McBride) *chsd ldrs: led after 2nd: j.lft next: rdn and hdd appr 2 out: looked btn whn lft clr after 2 out: all out* **3/1**[2]

0-06 **2** *3 ¼* **Empire Builder (IRE)**[19] 3405 5-11-5 0 .... AndrewThornton 98
(Caroline Bailey) *led after 1st: hdd after next: chsd ldrs tl rdn and outpcd after 3 out: lft 14 l 2nd next: styd on u.p flat* **9/1**[3]

0-P0 **3** *½* **Sunday Sharpner (IRE)**[19] 3405 5-11-5 0 .... JimmyMcCarthy 98
(Renee Robeson) *hld up: hdwy appr 3 out: lft 3rd next: kpt on u.p* **80/1**

000 **4** *3 ¾* **Highland Legacy**[10] 3556 7-11-5 0 ....(p) DaveCrosse 95
(Jim Best) *prom: drvn along after 4th: styd on same pce fr 3 out* **50/1**

00 **5** *17* **Crafti Bookie (IRE)**[20] 3399 5-11-5 0 .... HenryOliver 79
(Sue Smith) *led tl after 1st: chsd ldrs tl wknd appr 3 out* **80/1**

6 *18* **Baan (USA)**[455] 8-11-5 0 .... FelixDeGiles 59
(James Eustace) *hld up: hdwy after 6th: rdn and wknd appr 2 out: t.o* **28/1**

604P **7** *15* **Just Unique**[40] 2981 7-11-2 0 .... PeterToole[(3)] 44
(Mark Rimell) *plld hrd and prom: lost pl 6th: bhd fr next: t.o* **100/1**

00- **8** *35* **Bloodyburn Bay (IRE)**[291] 5122 7-11-5 0 .... JodieMogford 9
(Graeme McPherson) *hld up: bhd fr 5th: t.o* **100/1**

0 **9** *4* **Lucius Fabeo (IRE)**[10] 3556 7-11-5 0 .... NickScholfield 5
(Anna Newton-Smith) *mid-div: rdn and dropped in rr bef 5th: bhd fr next: t.o* **100/1**

4 **U** **Invictus (IRE)**[23] 3346 5-11-5 0 .... RobertThornton 115+
(Alan King) *hld up in tch: led appr 2 out: gng clr whn rdr lost iron: horse jinked rt and uns rdr after 2 out* **4/7**[1]

P **Areuwitmenow (IRE)**[108] 6-11-5 0 .... AndrewTinkler —
(Charlie Longsdon) *hld up: j. slowly 5th: rdn and wknd bef 7th: t.o whn p.u bef 2 out* **14/1**

5m 30.7s (6.00) **Going Correction** +0.30s/f (Yiel) **11** Ran SP% **116.2**
Speed ratings (Par 105): **100,98,98,97,90 83,78,64,63,—,—**
toteswingers:1&2 £4.40, 2&3 £9.90, 1&3 £10.00 CSF £28.01 TOTE £2.90: £1.10, £2.30, £18.00; EX 36.80.
Owner N Davies **Bred** Kirtlington Stud And Gilridge Bloodstock **Trained** Newmarket, Suffolk

FOCUS
This was much weaker than the first division. The winner has been rated 10lb off her best, with the second to his mark.

NOTEBOOK
Extremely So had just been mastered prior to being left in front and came home for a second success from just three outings over hurdles. She obviously rates a very lucky winner, however. (op 5-2)
Empire Builder(IRE) hit a flat spot before keeping on again late in the day and proved his stamina. Handicaps will present better options for him, though. (op 14-1)
Sunday Sharpner(IRE) had shown little coming into this race, but this was a step in the right direction and he now qualifies for a handicap mark.
Highland Legacy looked quirky, but this was better from him and no doubt he will fare better in handicaps.
Bloodyburn Bay(IRE) Official explanation: jockey said gelding hung left
Invictus(IRE) ◆, heavily backed, jinked and unseated Robert Thornton at the penultimate flight. He had just taken over at that stage but, with the race at his mercy, Thornton lost his right iron which appeared to be the cause of the horse jinking and he fell off. He should be considered a winner without a penalty next time out. (op 4-6)
Areuwitmenow(IRE) Official explanation: jockey ssid gelding hung left throughout (op 4-6)

3720 BROOK CONDITIONAL JOCKEYS' H'CAP CHASE (15 fncs) 2m 4f 110y

2:10 (2:10) (Class 5) (0-95,90) 5-Y-O+ **£2,276** (£668; £334; £166)

Form RPR

6U31 **1** **Phar Again (IRE)**[14] 3492 8-11-9 **87** ....(vt) IanPopham 102+
(Claire Dyson) *a.p: chsd ldr 4 out: rdn after 2 out: led flat: drvn out* **7/2**[1]

4-PP **2** *5* **Ours (FR)**[7] 3618 9-11-12 **90** .... PeterToole 100
(Mark Rimell) *led to 2nd: led again 4th: nt fluent next: rdn and hdd flat: styd on same pce* **12/1**

5062 **3** *2 ¼* **Donald Will Do (IRE)**[71] 2424 11-10-7 **76** .... JakeGreenall[(5)] 83
(Caroline Bailey) *led 2nd to 4th: chsd ldr to 4 out: rdn appr last: no ex flat* **8/1**

24PF **4** *12* **Mr Bond (IRE)**[21] 3388 8-11-4 **87** .... EdCookson[(5)] 85+
(Andy Turnell) *hld up: hdwy 7th: blnd 11th: rdn and wknd 2 out* **11/2**[2]

P432 **5** *8* **Jacarado (IRE)**[19] 3400 13-10-5 **77** ....(v) ChristopherWard[(8)] 64
(Robin Dickin) *hld up in tch: outpcd 10th: rallied appr 4 out: sn wknd* **11/2**[2]

6652 **6** *dist* **Jack The Soldier (IRE)**[19] 3402 7-11-9 **87** .... RichardKilloran —
(Chris Gordon) *chsd ldrs: cl 3rd whn blnd 6th (water): sn bhd: t.o* **15/2**

5066 **7** *37* **Mad Professor (IRE)**[7] 3618 8-9-9 **65** ....(b) JoeCornwall[(6)] —
(John Cornwall) *a in rr: bhd fr 6th: t.o* **28/1**

40/P **P** **Mickwell Bay**[78] 2277 10-10-3 **67** .... BrianToomey —
(Tim Pitt) *hld up: bhd fr 7th: t.o whn p.u bef 4 out* **12/1**

0F52 **F** **Chilla Cilla**[26] 3226 8-11-3 **81** ....(t) RichieMcLernon —
(Anthony Honeyball) *hld up: hmpd 2nd: blnd next: mstke 8th: fell next* **6/1**[3]

62-0 **P** **Quelclasse (FR)**[259] 266 7-11-10 **88** ....(t) SamTwiston-Davies —
(Jamie Snowden) *prom: rdn 10th: wknd after next: t.o whn p.u bef 4 out* **20/1**

5m 19.7s (0.80) **Going Correction** -0.05s/f (Good) **10** Ran SP% **113.7**
Speed ratings: **96,94,93,88,85 72,58,—,—,—**
toteswingers:1&2 £7.80, 2&3 £11.90, 1&3 £3.80 CSF £42.93 CT £311.87 TOTE £3.90: £2.00, £3.80, £2.00; EX 42.00.
Owner B and S Vaughan **Bred** Mrs J Wilkinson **Trained** Cleeve Prior, Worcs
■ Stewards' Enquiry : Ian Popham two-day ban: used whip with excessive frequency (Feb 8-9)

FOCUS
An open handicap, run at a good gallop. The winner was a 120+ horse at his peak and may be still capable of better.

NOTEBOOK
Phar Again(IRE) followed up his C&D success a fortnight earlier with a gutsy effort. He was 7lb higher and consistency has never been his strong suit, but it was clear he arrived here in good heart and his initial win in 2008 did come off an 18lb higher mark. With that in mind he should not be discounted when going for the hat-trick. (op 9-2 tchd 10-3)
Ours(FR) showed his true colours again and only got picked off by the winner late on. Slightly more patient tactics could pay off next time providing he maintains this form, as he is weighted to strike at present. (op 20-1)
Donald Will Do(IRE) is not easy to predict, but likes this venue and was second in the race last term. He posted one of his better efforts, but is not certain to build on it next time. (op 10-1)
Mr Bond(IRE)'s jumping was again the big issue and he remains winless. (op 6-1 tchd 13-2)
Jacarado(IRE) was 10lb higher for finishing second last time out and found this too sharp. (op 9-2)
Jack The Soldier(IRE)'s jumping let him down. (op 13-2)
Chilla Cilla's jumping her badly let her down before she departed. (op 4-1)

3721 EUROPEAN BREEDERS' FUND MARES' "NATIONAL HUNT" NOVICES' HURDLE (8 hdls) 2m

2:40 (2:40) (Class 4) 4-Y-O+ **£3,903** (£1,146; £573; £286)

Form RPR

30-6 **1** **Lifestyle**[80] 2222 5-11-2 0 .... BarryGeraghty 121+
(Nicky Henderson) *hld up in tch: racd keenly: led appr and hit 2 out: clr last: easily* **2/1**[2]

0-21 **2** *12* **Risaala**[66] 2526 5-11-1 122 .... MissGAndrews[(7)] 112+
(Pam Sly) *trckd ldrs: plld hrd: led after 4th: hdd 3 out: styd on same pce appr last* **10/11**[1]

0-06 **3** *7* **Francesa**[25] 3264 6-11-2 0 .... RichardJohnson 97
(Henry Daly) *hld up in tch: rdn and wknd appr 2 out* **14/1**

03 **4** *10* **Alexander Road (IRE)**[96] 1934 6-11-2 0 .... JasonMaguire 87
(Donald McCain) *chsd ldrs: j.lft 1st: rdn appr 5th: wknd 3 out* **8/1**[3]

00-0 **5** *nk* **Argentia**[65] 2554 6-11-2 0 .... AndrewThornton 87
(Lucy Wadham) *led tl after 4th: led again 3 out: rdn: hdd & wknd bef next* **33/1**

540 **6** *10* **Qualitee**[25] 3259 6-11-2 0 .... DaveCrosse 79
(Claire Dyson) *prom: blnd 3 out: sn wknd: t.o* **100/1**

5/00 **7** *15* **Golbelini**[15] 3489 6-11-2 0 .... WarrenMarston 62
(Martin Keighley) *hld up: rdn and wknd after 5th: t.o* **40/1**

6-06 **8** *10* **Lilac Belle**[45] 2896 5-11-2 0 ....(t) FelixDeGiles 52
(Alex Hales) *hld up: hdwy appr 3 out: rdn and wknd bef next: t.o* **40/1**

330- **9** *28* **Alfie's Pearl**[348] 3995 6-10-13 0 .... AdamPogson[(3)] 24
(Charles Pogson) *a in rr: bhd fr 5th: t.o* **28/1**

4m 3.60s (2.60) **Going Correction** +0.30s/f (Yiel) **9** Ran SP% **115.8**
Speed ratings (Par 105): **105,99,95,90,90 85,77,72,58**
toteswingers:1&2 £1.40, 2&3 £3.30, 1&3 £4.60 CSF £4.20 TOTE £2.20: £1.20, £1.10, £2.60; EX 4.50.
Owner The Turf Club & David Ford **Bred** David G Ford **Trained** Upper Lambourn, Berks

FOCUS
This was basically a two-horse race. The impressive winner has been rated up a stone on her best bumper form.

NOTEBOOK
Lifestyle ◆ was very closely matched with the runner-up in bumpers last term, but had disappointed on her last two outings in that sphere and proved weaker in the betting despite getting 6lb. Despite wearing a crossed noseband she took time to settle and wasn't always fluent, but there was a lot to like about the way she finished her race on the demanding surface. She ought to go on from this now and the final of this series could be on her agenda. (op 13-8)
Risaala was readily off the mark over 2m4f when last seen 66 days earlier, and was strongly supported to follow up. She spoilt her cause over this sharper test by refusing to settle, however, and was firmly put in her place late on. (op 11-8)
Francesa kept on under maximum pressure to post her most encouraging effort as a hurdler to date. She ought to get further and can find her feet in handicaps. (op 16-1)
Alexander Road(IRE) proved easy to back for this switch to hurdling and she too lacked fluency. Stepping up in trip is what she wants.
Golbelini Official explanation: trainer's rep said mare was stiff post-race

3722 DICK CHRISTIAN NOVICES' CHASE (12 fncs) 2m

3:10 (3:10) (Class 3) 5-Y-O+ **£4,553** (£1,337; £668; £333)

Form RPR

2/1F **1** **Giorgio Quercus (FR)**[23] 3345 6-10-12 0 .... BarryGeraghty 134+
(Nicky Henderson) *trckd ldr: racd keenly: led 7th: qcknd clr flat: comf* **4/6**[1]

20-1 **2** *6* **Thumbs Up**[241] 518 6-11-4 0 .... JasonMaguire 125
(Donald McCain) *hld up: mstke 2nd: hdwy 8th: chsd wnr 3 out: ev ch 2 out: rdn appr last: outpcd flat* **9/2**[3]

5-50 **3** *¾* **Special Occasion**[46] 2868 7-10-7 125 .... IanPopham[(5)] 117
(Caroline Keevil) *chsd ldrs: shkn up after 8th: styd on same pce last* **4/1**[2]

5/1P **4** *4 ½* **Darby's Turn (IRE)**[60] 2662 9-11-4 125 .... WarrenMarston 120
(Richard Phillips) *led to 7th: rdn after 3 out: no ex last* **10/1**

4m 8.90s (0.70) **Going Correction** -0.05s/f (Good) **4** Ran SP% **107.3**
Speed ratings: **96,93,92,90**
toteswingers:1&2 £8.40, 2&3 £56.40, 1&3 £36.10 CSF £4.00 TOTE £1.60; EX 2.90.
Owner Sir Robert Ogden **Bred** Daniel Chassagneux Et Al **Trained** Upper Lambourn, Berks

FOCUS
This novice chase appeared a decent opportunity for the winner. It has been rated around the third and fourth.

NOTEBOOK
Giorgio Quercus(FR) ran out a convincing winner. He would have at least run the useful Tullamore Dew very close with a clear round on his chasing debut last time out, but he paid more respect to his fences here. He again failed to settle and it momentarily looked in between the final two fences as though he may pay the price, but his response was impressive. He has bundles of pace and there is every chance he can rate much higher in this division if learning to settle better. (op 8-13)
Thumbs Up was last seen scoring first time up over fences at Cartmel in May 2010. He proved easy enough to back for this return and was a little ring-rusty early on. He was a live threat to the winner nearing the last, but was conceding 6lb to that rival and was put in his place thereafter. There should be another one of these for him before he switches to handicaps as a chaser. (tchd 11-2)
Special Occasion responded to pressure around four out, but was done with from the second-last. This was a respectable effort on his chasing debut over a trip short of his best. (op 6-1)
Darby's Turn(IRE), who reportedly ran flat when pulled up at Newbury in November, proved far too keen on this return to novice company. He was in trouble as a result from the fourth-last fence. (op 7-1 tchd 13-2 and 12-1)

3723 SIS+ H'CAP CHASE (18 fncs) 2m 7f 110y

3:40 (3:40) (Class 4) (0-100,99) 5-Y-O+ **£3,252** (£955; £477; £238)

Form RPR

P300 **1** **Antonius Caesar (FR)**[25] 3263 8-11-3 **97** .... PeterCarberry[(7)] 116
(Alex Hales) *led to 7th: led again next: rdn out* **13/2**[3]

40-4 **2** 4½ **Finlay**42 2938 8-11-12 **99**......(t) JasonMaguire 115+
(Donald McCain) *hld up: hdwy 14th: chsd wnr 2 out: rdn flat: styd on same pce* **6/1**2

0-P2 **3** 11 **Quazy De Joie (FR)**22 3377 7-11-7 **94**......(t) APMcCoy 99
(Jonjo O'Neill) *hld up in tch: hmpd 3rd: lost pl 5th: hdwy 13th: rdn after 14th: wknd appr last* **5/2**1

P53P **4** 2¼ **Hever Road (IRE)**41 2952 12-10-1 **81**...... JoeCornwall(7) 84
(David Pearson) *prom: rdn 4 out: wknd after 2 out* **16/1**

0000 **5** 60 **Glenfly (IRE)**17 3448 6-11-3 **90**...... RichardJohnson 51
(Philip Hobbs) *hld up: rdn and hung rt after 7th: hdwy 10th: wknd after 2 out: j. slowly last: t.o* **8/1**

06-0 **6** 7 **Simply Strong (IRE)**21 3391 7-11-7 **97**......(t) PeterToole(3) 31
(Charlie Mann) *chsd ldrs tl wknd 4 out: t.o* **11/1**

-0F4 **7** 1 **Goring One (IRE)**17 3450 6-11-5 **92**...... AndrewThornton 25
(Anna Newton-Smith) *hld up: bhd fr 7th: t.o* **12/1**

24P1 **8** 11 **Autumn Red (IRE)**21 3388 11-11-10 **97**......(bt) DenisO'Regan 19
(Paul Webber) *chsd ldr: led 7th to next: remained handy: shkn up 11th: wknd appr 4 out: t.o* **8/1**

03PU **P** **Rapid Return (IRE)**61 2638 8-10-2 **75**...... SeanQuinlan —
(Richard Phillips) *prom: pushed along 12th: wknd next: t.o whn p.u bef 4 out* **20/1**

3034 **F** **Not So Sure Dick (IRE)**89 2046 6-11-12 **99**...... AndrewTinkler —
(George Baker) *hld up: hdwy 9th: fell 11th* **8/1**

5m 59.6s (-4.40) **Going Correction** -0.05s/f (Good) **10** Ran SP% **116.2**
Speed ratings: **105,103,99,99,79 76,76,72,—,—**
toteswingers:1&2 £9.40, 2&3 £6.10, 1&3 £3.00 CSF £45.72 CT £123.95 TOTE £9.80: £3.10, £2.30, £1.90; EX 52.30.
Owner Hyzakite Racing **Bred** Haras Des Sablonnets **Trained** Wardington, Oxon

FOCUS
An ordinary staying handicap, run at a fair gallop. The winner was very well handicapped and has been rated 7lb off the pick of his 2010 runs here.

NOTEBOOK
Antonius Caesar(FR) made all and finally ended his losing run. He has been in-and-out since his last win in April 2009, but is happiest these days when allowed to dominate and he saw it out really well under strong handling from his talented young rider. After a likely rise for this, he will still look well treated on his old form, but has never backed up wins before. Official explanation: trainer said, regarding apparent improvement in form, that the gelding is inconsistent and was probably helped by coming down in the weights. (tchd 7-1)
Finlay, well backed up in trip, travelled easily into the home straight and appeared the most likely winner. His jumping when it mattered was poor, though, and he probably paid for running with the choke out early on. He remains winless. (op 11-2 tchd 13-2)
Quazy De Joie(FR) came under heavy pressure from three out and is not a simple horse to catch right. (op 7-2)
Hever Road(IRE), pulled up last time, looked a player turning for home but failed to see it out that well.
Glenfly(IRE) was making his chase and handicap debuts. He proved laboured through the race, but this was still a bit more encouraging and dropping back in trip may suit. (op 15-2 tchd 7-1)

3724 HUMBERSTONE H'CAP HURDLE (10 hdls) 2m 4f 110y
4:10 (4:10) (Class 4) (0-110,110) 4-Y-0+ **£2,276** (£668; £334; £166)

Form RPR

-515 **1** **Najca De Thaix (FR)**12 3529 10-11-7 **105**...... JamieMoore 121+
(John Spearing) *chsd ldrs: led 3rd: clr 2 out: easily* **9/1**

2-23 **2** 17 **Wood Yer (IRE)**25 3253 5-11-5 **103**...... PaddyBrennan 95
(Nigel Twiston-Davies) *mid-div: drvn along 5th: hdwy u.p 7th: wkng whn wnt mod 2nd 2 out* **6/1**2

4P23 **3** 6 **Pocket Too**14 3493 8-11-7 **105**......(p) PaulMoloney 88
(Matthew Salaman) *prom: rdn after 7th: wknd next* **8/1**

-P00 **4** 5 **Fidelor (FR)**22 3366 5-11-10 **108**...... RichardJohnson 89
(Henry Daly) *chsd ldrs: rdn after 3 out: wkng whn mstke next* **28/1**

0030 **5** 2 **Diktalina**22 3370 5-11-5 **110**...... OliverDayman(7) 86
(Alison Thorpe) *prom: rdn after 7th: wknd 3 out* **18/1**

0-10 **6** 4 **Black Phantom (IRE)**23 3348 5-11-1 **99**...... NickScholfield 71
(Andy Turnell) *hld up in tch: rdn and wknd after 7th* **10/1**

33/4 **7** 16 **Okafranca (IRE)**15 3489 6-11-4 **102**...... RhysFlint 58
(Jim Old) *hld up: a towards rr: rdn and wknd after 7th: t.o* **12/1**

00P0 **8** 64 **Deep Reflection**14 3493 11-10-8 **95**......(v) JimmyDerham(3) —
(Martin Keighley) *a in rr: bhd and rdn 5th: t.o* **33/1**

000- **P** **Final Veto**284 5207 8-10-11 **95**...... HenryOliver —
(Sue Smith) *chsd ldrs tl rdn and wknd 7th: t.o whn p.u bef 3 out* **11/1**

-5F4 **P** **Istron Bay**14 3497 9-10-7 **91**......(p) JodieMogford —
(Richard Lee) *mstke 2nd: a in rr: bhd fr 5th: t.o whn p.u bef 2 out* **16/1**

1/4 **P** **Sole Bonne Femme (IRE)**28 3170 9-11-11 **109**......(p) WillKennedy —
(Gerard Butler) *led to 3rd: chsd ldr tl mstke 6th: sn rdn: wknd bef next: t.o whn p.u bef 2 out* **16/1**

50/6 **P** **Carmond (GER)**23 3343 7-9-13 **86**...... CharlieHuxley(3) —
(Oliver Sherwood) *hld up: hdwy 4th: rdn and wknd 7th: t.o whn p.u bef 2 out* **12/1**

-000 **P** **Amore Mio (GER)**24 3299 6-11-12 **110**...... WarrenMarston —
(Richard Phillips) *a in rr: t.o whn p.u bef 3 out* **7/1**3

142- **F** **Seasonselite**364 3670 6-10-11 **95**...... AidanColeman —
(Venetia Williams) *trckd ldrs: racd keenly: fell 6th* **5/1**1

-5PP **P** **Dancing Legend**15 3487 5-10-0 **84** oh4...... SeanQuinlan —
(Peter Hiatt) *mstke 3rd: a in rr: t.o whn p.u bef 3 out* **66/1**

5m 29.7s (5.00) **Going Correction** +0.30s/f (Yiel) **15** Ran SP% **122.3**
Speed ratings (Par 105): **102,95,93,91,90 89,82,58,—,— —,—,—,—,—**
toteswingers:1&2 £4.40, 2&3 £6.50, 1&3 £12.40. totesuper7: Win: Not won. Place: £268.40 CSF £62.72 CT £462.66 TOTE £13.30: £4.20, £1.90, £3.50; EX 41.10.
Owner Peter Kelsall **Bred** Michel Bourgneuf And Danielle Paulhac **Trained** Kinnersley, Worcs

FOCUS
A weak handicap which proved very hard work for the majority on such ground. The winner was well treated on the best of his 2008 form but this still rates a personal best.

NOTEBOOK
Najca De Thaix(FR) relished the underfoot conditions and ran out a bloodless winner. He has won two of his last three races, but it's hoped the handicapper doesn't take this form too literally, and his best option is probably to turn out under a penalty. (op 8-1)
Wood Yer(IRE) proved an incredibly hard ride for Paddy Brennan, who deserves plenty of credit for getting him home in second. He is not straightforward, but this ground didn't look to be for him. (op 8-1)
Pocket Too, third in a claimer here last time, hit his usual flat spot before plugging on again. He goes some way to putting the form into perspective. (op 12-1)
Fidelor(FR) went well for a long way on this switch to a handicap and will be of greater interest when getting on some better ground. (op 33-1)
Seasonselite, making her handicap debut, again ran with the choke out on this return from a layoff. She was still to be asked a serious question prior to taking a heavy fall. (op 7-2 tchd 11-2)
T/Plt: £39.40 to a £1 stake. Pool of £64,808.69 - 1,197.87 winning tickets. T/Qpdt: £10.70 to a £1 stake. Pool of £5,380.60 - 369.00 winning tickets. CR

2598 SEDGEFIELD (L-H)
Tuesday, January 25

OFFICIAL GOING: Good to soft (good in places; goingstick: chs 6.3; hdl 6.6)
Wind: light across

3725 JOHN WADE SKIP HIRE "NATIONAL HUNT" NOVICES' HURDLE (QUALIFIER) (8 hdls) 2m 1f
1:00 (1:00) (Class 4) 4-Y-0+ **£2,081** (£611; £305; £152)

Form RPR

212 **1** **Charminster (IRE)**22 3365 5-11-4 0...... GrahamLee 125+
(Donald McCain) *trckd clr ldr: clsd after 4 out: led bef 2 out: sn clr: easily* **2/9**1

30 **2** 17 **Shan Blue (IRE)**13 3511 6-11-4 0...... TomScudamore 105+
(Steve Gollings) *sn in clr ld: nt so far clr 4 out: hdd bef 2 out: mstke 2 out: sn nt match wnr* **33/1**

1-03 **3** 3 **Tiptoeaway (IRE)**68 2473 6-11-4 0...... BrianHarding 101
(Tim Easterby) *in tch: reminders after 3rd: wnt 3rd 4 out: rdn after 3 out: kpt on* **7/1**2

01-6 **4** 26 **Arrow Barrow (IRE)**65 2552 6-10-11 0...... MrJohnDawson(7) 78
(John Wade) *in tch: mstke 3rd: hit next: rdn after 4 out and sn one pce: wl hld in 4th whn mstke last* **16/1**3

000 **5** 6 **Velvet Vic (IRE)**67 2509 5-11-4 0...... PaddyAspell 72
(Richard Guest) *nt fluent: in tch: rdn after 4 out: wknd after next* **100/1**

00 **6** 6 **Another Mystery**6 3637 6-10-8 0...... RyanMania(3) 60
(Evelyn Slack) *hld up: n.d* **200/1**

20 **7** ¾ **Middlebrook (IRE)**74 2355 6-11-4 0...... JamesReveley 66
(Peter Niven) *in tch: rdn after 3 out: wknd appr 2 out* **33/1**

0600 **8** ½ **A Patchy Dancer (IRE)**13 3506 6-10-13 0...... ShaneByrne(5) 66
(Sue Smith) *racd keenly: hld up: n.d* **100/1**

9 17 **Quelle Chance (IRE)** 5-11-4 0...... BrianHughes 50
(Howard Johnson) *hld up: a towards rr* **20/1**

0/4- **P** **Rats**602 572 8-11-4 0...... PeterBuchanan —
(Alan Kirtley) *a bhd: p.u bef 2 out* **100/1**

0 **P** **Stitched Up (IRE)**12 3525 5-11-4 0...... RobertWalford —
(Tim Walford) *hld up: a bhd: p.u bef 2 out* **100/1**

4m 6.00s (-0.90) **Going Correction** +0.20s/f (Yiel) **11** Ran SP% **115.3**
Speed ratings (Par 105): **110,102,100,88,85 82,82,82,74,— —**
toteswingers:1&2 £7.10, 2&3 £5.40, 1&3 £1.20 CSF £16.24 TOTE £1.30: £1.02, £4.30, £1.10; EX 10.40.
Owner T G Leslie **Bred** Raymond Cahalane **Trained** Cholmondeley, Cheshire

FOCUS
A weak novice hurdle. The fifth limits the level, although the race could be rated 9lb higher through the third and fourth.

NOTEBOOK
Charminster(IRE) ◆, probably unsuited by soft ground on his hurdles debut at Hereford, travelled like a classy sort returned to better ground and had the race under wraps from two out. He has still looked green on occasions, but should continue to improve as he gains experience and can defy a penalty. (op 3-10)
Shan Blue(IRE), a winning pointer who shaped well on his first start in bumpers, clearly appreciated the switch to hurdles and, although no match for the winner, he held on well for second. He'll appreciate a longer trip and can win something similar.
Tiptoeaway(IRE) is improving with experience over hurdles, and this future chaser will be of interest once faced with a stiffer test. He is probably one to look out for in handicaps. (op 6-1)
Arrow Barrow(IRE), down in trip having faded on his hurdles debut, lacked the pace to get involved and is another who may be more of a handicap prospect.

3726 COLLINS SEAFOODS MAIDEN CHASE (QUALIFIER) (PART OF COLLINS SEAFOODS YOUNG CHASERS SERIES) (21 fncs) 3m 3f
1:30 (1:30) (Class 4) 5-Y-0+ **£2,798** (£868; £467)

Form RPR

1 **Radharc Na Mara (IRE)**28 3183 7-10-7 0...... RichieMcGrath 108+
(J T R Dreaper, Ire) *hld up: hit 8th: trckd ldrs 11th: lft in narrow ld 5 out: 1 l up whn lft wl clr next: eased towards fin* **7/2**2

4000 **2** 31 **Mansonien L'As (FR)**12 3520 5-10-9 0...... GrahamLee 75
(Ferdy Murphy) *hld up: rdn and lost tch after 15th: lft in remote 2nd 4 out* **20/1**

44P4 **3** 36 **Almond Court (IRE)**14 3499 8-10-7 74...... KennyJohnson 41
(Robert Johnson) *hld up: bhd fr 14th: lft in distant 3rd 4 out* **50/1**

00/P **F** **Riskier**81 2192 6-10-7 0...... MrJohnDawson(7) —
(John Wade) *led: racd keenly: 2 l up and stl gng wl whn fell 5 out* **28/1**

-323 **F** **Silent Cliche (IRE)**25 3254 7-11-0 124...... BrianHughes —
(Howard Johnson) *in tch: reminders 9th: hit 10th: wnt 2nd 11th: 1 l down whn bdly hmpd and fell 4 out* **4/7**1

02 **F** **Kalulushi (IRE)**77 2297 6-11-0 0...... BrianHarding —
(Donald McCain) *trckd ldr: 5 l down in 4th whn fell 6 out* **8/1**3

7m 18.1s (29.10) **Going Correction** +0.825s/f (Soft)
WFA 5 from 6yo+ 5lb **6** Ran SP% **107.2**
Speed ratings: **89,79,69,—,— —**
toteswingers:1&2 £4.40, 2&3 £9.90, 1&3 £10.00 CSF £41.28 TOTE £3.30: £1.90, £6.40; EX 31.20.
Owner Mrs O E Matthews **Bred** Eugene Matthews **Trained** Kilsallaghan, Co Dublin

FOCUS
An eventful contest, with the jumping of most the runners going to pieces down the back straight. The first two have been rated in line with their previous chase form.

NOTEBOOK
Radharc Na Mara(IRE), who travelled strongly throughout, improved for this first try at a marathon trip and can probably defy a penalty under similar conditions. (op 5-2)
Mansonien L'As(FR), very fortunate to finish second, hasn't shown much since arriving from France, but she is only five. (tchd 22-1)
Riskier, pulled up on his hurdles debut, looked much more at home over fences and was still going well enough when getting the fifth from home wrong. It is hoped his confidence isn't affected too severely. (op 8-11 tchd 4-5)
Silent Cliche(IRE) was still very much in contention when the winner impeded him jumping four out. Whether he'd have won or not remains to be seen, but it is likely he wouldn't have been far away. (op 8-11 tchd 4-5)

Kalulushi(IRE) was yet another casualty, although it's unlikely he'd have been winning. (op 8-11 tchd 4-5)

3727 COLLINS SEAFOODS H'CAP HURDLE (8 hdls) 2m 1f
2:00 (2:00) (Class 5) (0-90,90) 4-Y-O+ **£1,561** (£458; £229; £114)

Form RPR
5026 **1** **Authentic Act (IRE)**[77] 2302 7-11-0 **78** JamesReveley 84+
(Martin Todhunter) *hld up: rdn and hdwy after 3 out: sn chsng ldrs: led bef last: kpt on* **5/1**[3]
0055 **2** 2½ **King's Chorister**[11] 3551 5-10-2 **66** (t) BrianHarding 72+
(Barry Murtagh) *in tch on inner: hdwy to hold ev ch 2 out: sn rdn: kpt on* **13/2**
01P0 **3** ½ **Mycenean Prince (USA)**[42] 2937 8-11-12 **90** PhilKinsella 92
(Karen Tutty) *prom: rdn and lost pl after 3 out: styd on again after 2 out: wnt 3rd run-in* **28/1**
45P6 **4** 5 **Railway Park (IRE)**[2] 3697 7-11-5 **83** (tp) PaddyAspell 81
(John Wainwright) *led narrowly: rdn whn hdd bef last: no ex run-in* **12/1**
0U00 **5** ¾ **Samizdat (FR)**[25] 3255 8-10-10 **77** RyanMania(3) 76
(Dianne Sayer) *chsd ldrs: rdn and outpcd appr 2 out: kpt on again run-in* **4/1**[2]
0532 **6** 1½ **Pinewood Legend (IRE)**[7] 3619 9-11-2 **80** (bt) BrianHughes 77
(Peter Niven) *trckd ldrs: chal on bit after 3 out: rdn appr 2 out: wknd bef last* **3/1**[1]
4RPP **7** nk **Orpen Bid (IRE)**[22] 3367 6-10-4 **71** CharlieStudd(3) 67
(Michael Mullineaux) *hld up in tch: rdn appr 2 out: sn no imp* **33/1**
40-0 **8** 46 **Fantastic Morning**[240] 532 7-10-5 **69** LeightonAspell 23
(Violet M Jordan) *midfield: hit 3 out: sn rdn and wknd qckly* **7/1**
-532 **P** **Mister Fizzbomb (IRE)**[95] 1949 8-11-4 **85** (v) HarryHaynes(3) —
(John Wainwright) *hld up: bhd after 4th: t.o whn p.u bef 2 out* **14/1**
0-06 **P** **Just Maddie**[65] 2547 7-11-9 **87** GrahamLee —
(Rayson Nixon) *in tch on outer: reminders after 3rd: wknd qckly after 3 out: t.o whn p.u bef next* **16/1**

4m 11.6s (4.70) **Going Correction** +0.20s/f (Yiel) **10** Ran SP% **114.1**
Speed ratings (Par 103): **96,94,94,92,91 91,91,69,—,—**
toteswingers:1&2 £7.40, 2&3 £23.00, 1&3 £6.60 CSF £36.96 CT £818.78 TOTE £4.10: £1.50, £3.00, £6.00; EX 44.20.
Owner Mr & Mrs Ian Hall **Bred** Gestut Ammerland **Trained** Orton, Cumbria

FOCUS
A low-grade handicap hurdle, rated around the winner to his mark.

NOTEBOOK
Authentic Act(IRE), a C&D winner on good to firm last May, found the ground too soft for him last time, but he had earlier run well off a similar mark and stayed on best here. The short break had clearly done him good. (tchd 9-2)
King's Chorister, still a maiden over hurdles, ran his best race since last spring, but once again found something too strong when it mattered. (op 6-1)
Mycenean Prince(USA) remains 7lb higher than when winning in September, but this was at least better than his recent efforts. (op 20-1 tchd 18-1)
Railway Park(IRE), pulled up at Market Rasen just two days earlier, seemed well suited to a front-running ride, but remains a maiden. (op 14-1)
Pinewood Legend(IRE) had returned to form at Southwell the time before, so with the tongue-tie back on it was surprising to see him stop the way he did. (op 7-2)

3728 JOHN WADE DEMOLITION H'CAP HURDLE (10 hdls) 2m 4f
2:30 (2:33) (Class 5) (0-90,97) 4-Y-O+ **£1,561** (£458; £229; £114)

Form RPR
5310 **1** **Sea Cliff (IRE)**[110] 1745 7-11-11 **89** JohnnyFarrelly 91
(Andrew Crook) *prom: led bef 2 out: sn rdn: drvn and hld on wl run-in* **14/1**
04/3 **2** ½ **Classic Henri**[22] 3363 7-10-10 **74** BrianHarding 77
(Barry Murtagh) *hld up in tch: hdwy to trck ldrs after 3 out: chal 2 out: kpt on: a jst hld run-in* **8/1**[2]
0061 **3** 1¼ **Night In Milan (IRE)**[7] 3622 5-11-12 **97** 7ex MrColmMcCormack(7) 100+
(Keith Reveley) *hld up in rr: hdwy but stl plenty to do appr 2 out: rdn and wnt 3rd bef last: kpt on run-in* **11/10**[1]
0P00 **4** ½ **Sam Patch**[60] 2654 8-10-3 **77** (t) CallumWhillans(10) 77
(Donald Whillans) *chsd ldrs: rdn after 3 out: kpt on* **20/1**
3600 **5** 12 **Lindseyfield Lodge (IRE)**[12] 3524 10-11-4 **82** (p) KennyJohnson 74
(Robert Johnson) *led: hdwy appr 2 out: sn wknd* **40/1**
250P **6** 9 **Freedom Flying**[163] 1259 8-11-5 **90** KyleJames(7) 71
(Lee James) *chsd ldrs on inner: rdn after 4 out: wknd after 3 out* **40/1**
5PP- **7** nk **Hazy Oaks**[275] 12 8-11-6 **84** RichieMcGrath 65
(Kevin M Prendergast) *trckd ldrs on outer: hit 4 out: rdn after 3 out: wknd appr 2 out* **12/1**[3]
005F **8** ¾ **Carys's Lad**[7] 3622 8-10-13 **80** CharlieStudd(3) 60
(Michael Mullineaux) *midfield: rdn after 3 out: sn no imp* **18/1**
6000 **9** 6 **Accordingtotheboss (IRE)**[60] 2654 6-11-6 **84** (t) FearghalDavis 59
(Nicky Richards) *nt fluent: hld up: n.d* **8/1**[2]
0320 **10** 2 **Barbarian**[12] 3523 5-11-7 **90** (b) JamesHalliday(5) 63
(Alan Brown) *prom: wknd after 3 out* **20/1**
03P- **11** nk **Formedable (IRE)**[279] 5318 9-11-2 **80** LeightonAspell 53
(Violet M Jordan) *hld up in tch: hit 3 out: sn wknd* **16/1**
F243 **12** 13 **Political Pendant**[101] 1873 10-10-11 **78** RyanMania(3) 39
(Rayson Nixon) *rel to r: hld up: a towards rr* **8/1**[2]
40-0 **13** 7 **Sadler's Cove (FR)**[245] 459 13-10-7 **74** (tp) JamesO'Farrell(3) 29
(J K Magee, Ire) *hld up: a bhd* **50/1**
000- **14** 13 **Ruby Queen (IRE)**[275] 8 9-10-11 **75** PaddyAspell 18
(Geoffrey Harker) *midfield on inner: lost pl after 4 out: mstke next and sn wl bhd* **40/1**

5m 4.40s (11.70) **Going Correction** +0.20s/f (Yiel) **14** Ran SP% **125.3**
Speed ratings (Par 103): **84,83,83,83,78 74,74,74,71,71 70,65,62,57**
toteswingers:1&2 £5.90, 2&3 £4.20, 1&3 £7.80 CSF £118.11 CT £230.16 TOTE £18.80: £4.40, £1.70, £1.40; EX 97.70.
Owner Andy Hulme **Bred** G W Robinson **Trained** Middleham Moor, N Yorks

FOCUS
A modest handicap hurdle rated around the fourth.

NOTEBOOK
Sea Cliff(IRE), 6lb higher than when winning at Worcester in September, was a flop back there next time but he appreciated running without any form of headgear this time, and saw it out well having taken over two out. (op 10-1)
Classic Henri has twice run well since returning from a lengthy absence and can pick up something similar off this mark.
Night In Milan(IRE), the one to beat under a penalty, was given an ill-judged ride, being ridden too far out of his ground. Although he didn't want to hit the front too soon, he was given a ridiculous amount to do and never actually looked like winning. A fine, big sort, his future lies over fences but he can win again over hurdles first. Official explanation: jockey said, regarding running and riding, that his orders were to drop the gelding out to get it settled and jumping, then make the effort from halfway and do his best. (op 6-4 tchd 13-8)
Sam Patch put up a much more encouraging display. (op 25-1)

3729 ROFLOW H'CAP HURDLE (13 hdls) 3m 3f 110y
3:00 (3:01) (Class 4) (0-100,95) 4-Y-O+ **£2,081** (£611; £305; £152)

Form RPR
-062 **1** **Midnight Diamond (IRE)**[77] 2290 8-10-3 **72** (b) TomScudamore 103+
(Tim Vaughan) *mde all: clr fr 9th: unchal: v easily* **9/2**[2]
0-00 **2** 40 **Ontrack (IRE)**[23] 3336 7-11-2 **85** WilsonRenwick 77
(Rose Dobbin) *hld up: hdwy after 4 out: hit 3 out but sn wnt 2nd: nvr threatened wnr* **8/1**
500 **3** 3¼ **Melua Maid (IRE)**[21] 3389 9-10-2 **81** NathanCook(10) 67
(Sue Smith) *in tch on inner: wnt 3rd bef 2 out: n.d* **40/1**
0203 **4** 1½ **Oniz Tiptoes (IRE)**[25] 3258 10-11-3 **86** (v) PaddyAspell 71
(John Wainwright) *hld up: rdn and outpcd after 4 out: wnt 4th 2 out: n.d* **8/1**
/60- **5** 11 **Easter Vic**[329] 4366 10-10-13 **85** HarryHaynes(3) 60
(Robert Goldie) *hld up: a in rr* **50/1**
U-3B **6** 25 **Greenandredparson (IRE)**[23] 3351 8-11-2 **92** JeremiahMcGrath(7) 44
(Patrick Griffin, Ire) *midfield: brief hdwy after 4 out: wknd after 3 out* **8/1**
00/3 **7** 11 **Harps Counsel (IRE)**[60] 2654 9-11-9 **95** JamesO'Farrell(3) 37
(J K Magee, Ire) *trckd clr ldr: lost 2nd after 3 out: wknd qckly* **16/1**
40P- **P** **Beau Peak**[450] 2020 12-9-5 **70** CallumWhillans(10) —
(Donald Whillans) *hld up: a in rr: p.u bef 3 out* **80/1**
-4PP **P** **Quay Meadow (IRE)**[25] 3258 9-10-11 **85** (p) AlexanderVoy(5) —
(John Norton) *in tch: rdn and lost pl after 8th: t.o whn p.u bef 3 out* **33/1**
0P-0 **R** **French Ties (IRE)**[69] 2452 9-11-7 **90** (p) AlanO'Keeffe —
(Jennie Candlish) *hld up: jinked lft and rn out 4th* **7/2**[1]
P-56 **P** **Paddys Honour (IRE)**[23] 3336 8-11-7 **90** PeterBuchanan —
(Lucinda Russell) *midfield: lost pl and wknd after 3 out: t.o whn p.u bef last* **8/1**
F-23 **P** **Border Flora**[23] 3336 6-11-10 **93** FearghalDavis —
(William Amos) *hld up: bmpd 5th and sn lost pl: p.u bef 6th* **11/2**[3]

6m 54.1s (2.10) **Going Correction** +0.20s/f (Yiel) **12** Ran SP% **114.7**
Speed ratings (Par 105): **105,93,92,92,89 81,78,—,—,— —,—**
toteswingers:1&2 £8.40, 2&3 £56.40, 1&3 £36.10 CSF £38.28 CT £1264.92 TOTE £5.00: £1.90, £3.40, £7.30; EX 46.20.
Owner J Phillips & J Mordecai **Bred** Illuminatus Investments **Trained** Aberthin, Vale of Glamorgan

FOCUS
Virtually nothing got into this apart from the winner. He has been rated back to the level of his best form in 2007/08.

NOTEBOOK
Midnight Diamond(IRE) was in a clear lead some way from the finish and galloped on remorselessly for an easy success. The fitting of a visor looks to have been the making of him, but he can expect the handicapper to take action for such an authoritative display. Connections will presumably try to get him out under a penalty. (op 6-1 tchd 4-1)
Ontrack(IRE) looked a potential improver and he boxed on best of the remainder for second. (op 9-1)
Melua Maid(IRE) had previously offered little under rules, so this keeping-on third will no doubt have pleased connections.
Oniz Tiptoes(IRE) never got close enough to challenge. (op 7-1)
Harps Counsel(IRE) travelled well to a point and could be worth another chance. (tchd 18-1)
French Ties(IRE), last year's winner, took his rider by surprise when jinking and running out at the fourth. (op 10-3 tchd 3-1, 4-1 in a place)
Border Flora, was the disappointment of the race having been running well prior to this. (op 10-3 tchd 3-1, 4-1 in a place)

3730 DIGIBET.COM H'CAP CHASE (13 fncs) 2m 110y
3:30 (3:30) (Class 4) (0-115,112) 5-Y-O+ **£2,602** (£764; £382; £190)

Form RPR
-060 **1** **Cranky Corner**[14] 3500 7-11-2 **107** ShaneByrne(5) 115+
(Sue Smith) *trckd ldrs: tk cl order 8th: led 4 out: rdn appr 2 out: kpt on wl* **4/1**[3]
0121 **2** 2½ **Kosta Brava (FR)**[60] 2659 7-11-12 **112** WilsonRenwick 119+
(Howard Johnson) *racd keenly: in tch on inner: chsd wnr 2 out: rdn and ev ch whn hit last: no further imp run-in* **3/1**[1]
-FFF **3** 6 **Gavroche Gaugain (FR)**[24] 3307 7-10-3 **89** GrahamLee 92+
(Ferdy Murphy) *hld up in tch: hdwy to chse ldrs 3 out: rdn bef 2 out: hld in 3rd whn mstke last* **7/2**[2]
-015 **4** 2¾ **Cocoa Key (IRE)**[67] 2506 7-11-2 **102** PaddyAspell 102
(Richard Guest) *w ldr: led 6th: hdd 4 out: rdn after 3 out: wknd after 2 out* **13/2**
0262 **5** 2¾ **J'Adhere (FR)**[23] 3343 6-10-12 **105** CDTimmons(7) 104
(Tim Vaughan) *racd keenly: hld up in tch: hit 4th: rdn 3 out and sn no imp* **7/2**[2]
4-52 **6** 32 **I'm Your Man**[251] 403 12-10-6 **95** (p) RyanMania(3) 62
(Evelyn Slack) *led: hdd 6th: rdn 4 out: wknd bef next* **9/1**

4m 20.1s (11.50) **Going Correction** +0.825s/f (Soft) **6** Ran SP% **112.8**
Speed ratings: **105,103,101,99,98 83**
toteswingers:1&2 £2.60, 2&3 £2.20, 1&3 £4.00 CSF £16.85 TOTE £4.80: £3.40, £2.00; EX 19.60.
Owner Trevor Hemmings **Bred** A R Bromley **Trained** High Eldwick, W Yorks

FOCUS
A moderate contest rated around the runner-up to his mark.

NOTEBOOK
Cranky Corner had been a disappointment over hurdles, considering he was a useful bumper horse, but there was always a chance the switch to fences would bring the best out of him and he kept pulling out more, having hit the front leaving the back. On this evidence he'll stay a bit further and it will be interesting to see whether he can maintain this level of form. (op 9-2 tchd 5-1 and 7-2)
Kosta Brava(FR) had only gone up 2lb for his latest success and he briefly looked like running down the winner, but in the end the 5lb weight concession made the difference. (op 2-1 tchd 7-2)
Gavroche Gaugain(FR), a faller on each of his three previous starts over fences, twice when holding a winning chance, at least completed this time and can build on it. (op 5-1)
Cocoa Key(IRE) ran well to a point on this first start over fences. (op 7-1 tchd 5-1)
J'Adhere(FR) was disappointing and showed little. (op 9-2 tchd 5-1)

3731 COLLINS SEAFOODS 'NEWCOMERS' STANDARD OPEN NATIONAL HUNT FLAT RACE 2m 1f
4:00 (4:00) (Class 6) 4-5-Y-O **£1,301** (£382; £191; £95)

Form RPR
1 **Matthew Riley (IRE)** 4-10-7 0 RichieMcGrath 106+
(Kate Walton) *trckd ldrs on outer: led 4f out: rdn clr over 1f out: comf* **16/1**
2 13 **Edmund (IRE)** 4-10-7 0 BrianHughes 91
(Howard Johnson) *trckd ldrs: rdn over 3f out: kpt on: wnt 2nd nr fin* **12/1**

3 *nk* **Street Dance (IRE)** 5-11-4 0.......... LeightonAspell 102
(Don Cantillon) *hld up in rr: hdwy fr over 6f out: trckd ldrs 3f out: rdn to go 2nd over 1f out: wknd fnl 100yds: lost 2nd nr fin* **5/1**[2]
4 *nse* **Bygones Sovereign (IRE)** 5-11-4 0.......... GrahamLee 102
(Karen McLintock) *led: rdn whn hdd 4f out: kpt on same pce* **5/1**[2]
5 *2 ½* **Powerful Ambition (IRE)** 5-11-4 0.......... FearghalDavis 100
(Brian Ellison) *w ldr: rdn and outpcd over 4f out: kpt on fnl 3f* **5/2**[1]
6 *20* **Tartan Tiger (IRE)** 5-11-4 0.......... DougieCostello 82
(John Quinn) *trckd ldrs: wknd over 3f out* **11/2**[3]
7 *5* **Angel Sun (FR)** 5-10-8 0.......... TonyKelly(10) 77
(Ferdy Murphy) *hld up: rdn over 6f out: sn no imp* **12/1**
8 *1 ¼* **Soul Bid (IRE)** 5-11-4 0.......... CampbellGillies 76
(Chris Grant) *midfield on inner: rdn over 6f out: wknd over 4f out* **33/1**
9 *17* **Pekan Two** 5-11-4 0.......... BrianHarding 61
(John Hellens) *hld up: n.d* **50/1**
10 *13* **Wind Prospect** 5-11-4 0.......... KennyJohnson 49
(Ray Craggs) *racd keenly: in tch on outer: wknd over 3f out: eased* **100/1**
11 *32* **Port View (IRE)** 5-10-11 0.......... MrJohnDawson(7) 20
(John Wade) *hld up: a towards rr* **33/1**
12 *14* **Edieskaia (IRE)** 5-10-11 0.......... CDTimmons(7) 8
(Tim Vaughan) *midfield: reminders 1/2-way: wknd over 6f out* **9/1**

4m 0.70s (-0.60) **Going Correction** +0.20s/f (Yiel)
WFA 4 from 5yo 11lb **12** Ran SP% **117.4**
Speed ratings: **109,102,102,102,101 92,89,89,81,75 60,53**
toteswingers:1&2 £11.20, 2&3 £9.50, 1&3 £11.10 CSF £188.54 TOTE £22.50: £3.30, £2.40, £2.30; EX 153.20.
Owner Mr and Mrs Paul Chapman **Bred** Miss Yvonne Prendiville **Trained** Middleham Moor, N Yorks

FOCUS
Probably just a moderate bumper. Not much to go on form-wise, but the second, third, fourth and fifth are from the right stables and the winner is probably above average.

NOTEBOOK
Matthew Riley(IRE) travelled well before running right away from his field down the straight. A likeable son of Dr Massini, it will be interesting to see how he gets on under a penalty before going hurdling. (op 12-1)
Edmund(IRE), from a yard that does well in this sphere, was a negative in the market but he stayed on well to take second and should improve. (op 9-1)
Street Dance(IRE) moved well enough into contention, but was unable to stay on as strongly as the winner. This was a promising start. (op 9-2)
Bygones Sovereign(IRE) stayed on again having been outpaced and should stay further over hurdles. (tchd 11-2)
Powerful Ambition(IRE) looked one of the more interesting ones and was backed accordingly, but he became readily outpaced when the tempo quickened and clearly needs a stiffer test. (op 7-2)
T/Plt: £131.80 to a £1 stake. Pool of £60,224.38 - 333.48 winning tickets. T/Qpdt: £44.40 to a £1 stake. Pool of £5,016.60 - 83.50 winning tickets. AS

3732 - 3738a (Foreign Racing) - See Raceform Interactive

3540 HUNTINGDON (R-H)
Wednesday, January 26

OFFICIAL GOING: Good to soft (soft in places) changing to soft on hurdle course after race 1 (1.15) changing to soft on chase course after race 3 (2.15)
Light half-behind Light rain

3739 HUNTINGDON AUDI A1 NOVICES' HURDLE (DIV I) (8 hdls) 2m 110y
1:15 (1:16) (Class 4) 4-Y-0+ **£2,276** (£668; £334; £166)

Form RPR
P- 1 **Nobunaga**[362] 3715 6-11-4 0.......... AidanColeman 119+
(Venetia Williams) *a.p: chsd ldr after 3rd to 5th: led 2 out: drvn out* **66/1**
4/52 2 *hd* **Araldur (FR)**[22] 3387 7-11-4 125.......... RobertThornton 120+
(Alan King) *a.p: nt fluent 4th: chsd ldr and nt fluent next: chal 2 out: sn rdn: r.o* **7/4**[1]
0-52 3 *11* **Robin De Creuse (FR)**[47] 2873 5-11-4 0.......... RichardJohnson 111
(Philip Hobbs) *led to 2 out: blnd and no ex last* **4/1**[3]
4 *16* **Alystar (IRE)**[816] 5-10-11 0.......... BarryGeraghty 87
(Nicky Henderson) *prom: racd keenly: wknd after 3 out* **7/1**
41 5 *8* **Spanish Treasure (GER)**[23] 3366 5-11-11 0.......... NickScholfield 95
(Andy Turnell) *chsd ldr tl after 3rd: remained handy tl rdn and wknd appr 2 out: t.o* **5/2**[2]
6 *1* **Prince Of Dreams**[96] 4-10-7 0.......... FelixDeGiles 76
(Ed de Giles) *plld hrd and prom: mstke 3rd: wknd appr 3 out: t.o* **100/1**
-003 7 *5* **Mr Chow (IRE)**[35] 3091 7-11-4 0.......... WayneHutchinson 81
(Warren Greatrex) *hld up: nvr on terms: t.o* **28/1**
8 *¾* **Kayaan**[91] 4-10-7 0.......... WarrenMarston 69
(Pam Sly) *hld up: n.d: t.o* **40/1**
0P-P 9 *19* **Whatshallwedo**[20] 3405 6-11-4 0.......... LiamHeard 63
(Chris Down) *prom tl wknd appr 3 out: t.o* **250/1**
10 *11* **Fourth In Line (IRE)**[113] 1718 7-11-4 0.......... GerardTumelty 53
(Anabel L M King) *hld up: j. slowly 4th: a in rr: t.o* **150/1**
00 11 *23* **Lombok**[24] 3344 5-11-4 0.......... JamieMoore 33
(Gary Moore) *hld up: bhd fr 5th: t.o whn j.rt 2 out* **100/1**
F **Ptolomeos**[82] 3384 8-10-11 0.......... MrMMarris(7) —
(Sean Regan) *s.s: hld up: plld hrd: a bhd: t.o whn blnd 3 out: fell next* **200/1**
-5P0 F **Bahr Nothing (IRE)**[76] 2322 5-11-4 0.......... AndrewTinkler —
(Henry Daly) *hld up: hmpd and fell 2nd* **200/1**
303U U **High Hoylander**[3] 3692 5-11-4 0.......... HenryOliver —
(Sue Smith) *hld up: plld hrd: j.rt 2nd: hdwy 5th: sn wknd: blnd and uns rdr 3 out* **22/1**

4m 12.6s (17.70) **Going Correction** +0.575s/f (Soft)
WFA 4 from 5yo+ 11lb **14** Ran SP% **113.2**
Speed ratings (Par 105): **81,80,75,68,64 63,61,61,52,47 36,—,—,—**
toteswingers:1&2 £20.60, 2&3 £2.00, 1&3 £33.00 CSF £176.78 TOTE £31.90: £3.40, £1.10, £1.70; EX 240.90.
Owner The Risky Partnership **Bred** Millsec Limited **Trained** Kings Caple, H'fords

FOCUS
There was a farcical start here, but the form still looks fair.

NOTEBOOK
Nobunaga pulled off a shock 66-1 victory with a taking display on only his second hurdling start. Always coasting along up with the pace, he ran on determinedly to thwart the persistent second. He won in testing conditions on the Flat in Ireland and, interestingly, had been a 4-1 chance on his hurdling debut. Although things didn't go right that day, he looked a useful individual in beating a 125-rated hurdler (and 150 chaser) into second here. (op 50-1)
Araldur(FR), a Grade 2 chase winner, finished second to the 132-rated Frascati Park at Leicester on his seasonal reappearance, was well backed to come on for that. He jumped slowly at a couple of flights, but battled on gamely to be narrowly denied close home. Alan King is aiming to win a couple of races over the smaller obstacles this season before reverting to chasing next season. (op 85-40 tchd 13-8)
Robin De Creuse(FR) pinched an early lead and ran a solid race before hitting the final flight. His turns is not looking that far off. (op 7-2 tchd 9-2)
Alystar(IRE), a 200,000euros yearling, was an interesting hurdling newcomer for the bang in-form Nicky Henderson yard. On her toes beforehand and keen during the race, she stayed on adequately into fourth. She can step up on this promising introduction judged on this good effort. (op 6-1)
Spanish Treasure(GER), penalised for impressing in a decent novice event at Hereford, looked to run below that form, with possibly this race coming too soon on worse ground. Andy Turnell reported the horse to have bled during the race, so he can be given another chance to confirm the impression created on his debut on better ground. Official explanation: trainer said gelding had bled (tchd 9-4)

3740 HUNTINGDON AUDI A1 NOVICES' HURDLE (DIV II) (8 hdls) 2m 110y
1:45 (1:48) (Class 4) 4-Y-0+ **£2,276** (£668; £334; £166)

Form RPR
1 **Buckie Boy (IRE)**[177] 5-11-4 0.......... BarryGeraghty 114+
(Nicky Henderson) *a.p: led appr 2 out: rdn and edgd lft flat: r.o* **11/2**
2 *1 ¼* **Cozy Tiger (USA)**[22] 6-11-4 0.......... LeightonAspell 112+
(Willie Musson) *hld up: hdwy appr 3 out: rdn to chse wnr last: r.o* **7/2**[2]
3 *3 ¾* **Yvonne Evelyn (USA)**[476] 6-10-11 0.......... RobertThornton 101
(Alan King) *prom: rdn after 3 out: styd on same pce fr next* **14/1**
60 4 *½* **Ezdiyaad (IRE)**[15] 3491 7-11-4 0.......... (t) PaulMoloney 107
(Kevin Morgan) *hld up: racd keenly: hdwy appr 3 out: rdn bef next: styd on same pce* **14/1**
0-23 5 *6* **Marching Song (USA)**[22] 3386 5-11-4 0.......... NickScholfield 109+
(Andy Turnell) *hld up: hdwy appr 3 out: chsd wnr 2 out: 3rd and looking hld whn blnd last: nt rcvr* **5/2**[1]
2-U0 6 *9* **Somewhatinevitable (IRE)**[20] 3403 6-11-4 0.......... DenisO'Regan 93
(Paul Webber) *hld up: hdwy and hit 2 out: nvr nr to chal* **17/2**
0-45 7 *nk* **Spiritual Guidance (IRE)**[20] 3403 8-11-4 0.......... WayneHutchinson 93
(Warren Greatrex) *prom: blnd 5th: rdn and wknd appr 2 out* **4/1**[3]
0-0P 8 *nk* **Graylyn Amber**[12] 3542 6-10-11 0.......... CharliePoste 84
(Robin Dickin) *unruly to post: led: hdd & wknd appr 2 out* **150/1**
3356 9 *4* **Float My Boat**[9] 3601 5-11-1 0.......... AlexMerriam(3) 87
(Sean Regan) *hld up: wknd after 5th* **150/1**
0U0 10 *8* **Major Potential (USA)**[13] 3526 5-11-4 0.......... AidanColeman 79
(Venetia Williams) *chsd ldrs tl wknd 3 out* **50/1**
0-0 11 *11* **Lureyno**[106] 1812 5-11-4 0.......... (p) JimmyMcCarthy 74
(Renee Robeson) *hld up: mstke 4th: n.d: t.o* **100/1**
0 12 *39* **Wavertree Bounty**[44] 2924 4-10-3 0 ow3.......... ColinBolger 14
(John Ryan) *chsd ldr tl wknd appr 3 out: t.o* **66/1**
13 *1 ½* **Mr Madeit (IRE)** 5-11-4 0.......... AndrewThornton 28
(Caroline Bailey) *mid-div: blnd and lost pl 4th: sn bhd: t.o* **40/1**
0-0 14 *16* **Crackerjac Boy (USA)**[70] 2456 6-11-4 0.......... WarrenMarston 12
(Richard Phillips) *hld up: bhd fr 3rd: t.o* **100/1**

4m 7.20s (12.30) **Going Correction** +0.575s/f (Soft)
WFA 4 from 5yo+ 11lb **14** Ran SP% **119.2**
Speed ratings (Par 105): **94,93,91,91,88 84,84,84,82,78 73,54,54,46**
toteswingers:1&2 £3.40, 2&3 £23.30, 1&3 £32.80 CSF £25.27 TOTE £4.50: £1.50, £1.40, £2.90; EX 17.60.
Owner North South Partnership **Bred** John Kirby **Trained** Upper Lambourn, Berks

FOCUS
This second division of the novice hurdle was run at a steady gallop.

NOTEBOOK
Buckie Boy(IRE), once a winner from 12 starts on the Flat, at times looked an awkward customer in that sphere, but showed a willing attitude for this change of code, winning with some ease. Nicky Henderson is a master at transforming Flat recruits into jumpers and seems to have a nice handicap prospect in due course. (op 7-2)
Cozy Tiger(USA), a progressive handicapper on the AW this season, ran a highly encouraging race on this hurdling debut. He jumped fluently in the main, and appreciated the increasingly testing going (ran well on sole Flat start on soft). He can pick up an average novice hurdle under similar conditions. (op 9-2 tchd 5-1)
Yvonne Evelyn(USA) stayed on well from the last to fight it out for third, jumping nicely to deserve that spot, and can use this experience to good use. (op 10-1)
Ezdiyaad(IRE) raced freely, but still posted a creditable effort and is one for handicaps. (op 16-1)
Marching Song(USA) was beaten before hitting the last and is another for whom handicaps will present better opportunities. (op 9-4 tchd 3-1)
Somewhatinevitable(IRE) Official explanation: jockey said gelding hung badly left-handed
Spiritual Guidance(IRE) was tailed off in a C&D novice event recently but shaped more encouragingly this time, staying on well when the race was over. He has now qualified for handicaps. (op 13-2)
Mr Madeit(IRE) Official explanation: jockey said gelding suffered interference first flight in back straight

3741 RACING UK NOVICES' H'CAP CHASE (19 fncs) 3m
2:15 (2:15) (Class 4) (0-105,101) 5-Y-0+ **£2,602** (£764; £382; £190)

Form RPR
-041 1 **Honourable Arthur (IRE)**[18] 3450 8-11-12 **101**.......... (p) DenisO'Regan 120+
(Victor Dartnall) *a.p: chsd ldr 11th: 4 l down whn lft in ld 15th: hmpd by loose horse bef 2 out: clr last: hmpd again by loose horse nr fin: comf* **7/2**[2]
3622 2 *9* **Timpo (FR)**[65] 2585 8-11-9 **98**.......... RichardJohnson 101
(Henry Daly) *chsd ldr: j.rt 9th and 10th: lost 2nd pl next: outpcd 14th: lft 3rd next: rallied after 2 out: wnt 2nd and j.rt last: no imp* **9/4**[1]
4-34 3 *24* **Rileyev (FR)**[63] 2604 6-11-3 **92**.......... AidanColeman 75
(Venetia Williams) *hld up: hdwy 12th: blnd next: lft 2nd 15th: rdn and ev ch bef 2 out: wknd appr last: t.o* **6/1**
60-0 4 *22* **Golden Dream (IRE)**[22] 3386 7-11-11 **100**.......... SamThomas 65
(Caroline Bailey) *chsd ldrs to 11th: t.o* **11/2**[3]
P-4P U **Herald Angel (FR)**[19] 3431 8-10-9 **91**.......... (t) CDTimmons(7) —
(Barry Brennan) *prom: j. slowly and lost pl 2nd: in rr fr then: lost tch after 12th: t.o whn blnd and uns rdr last* **11/2**[3]
3005 U **Ratify**[16] 3483 7-11-8 **97**.......... LeightonAspell —
(Brendan Powell) *led: clr 11th: 4 l ahd whn blnd and uns rdr 15th* **7/1**

6m 34.1s (23.80) **Going Correction** +0.75s/f (Soft) **6** Ran SP% **110.5**
Speed ratings: **90,87,79,71,—,—**
toteswingers:1&2 £1.10, 2&3 £2.40, 1&3 £5.20 CSF £11.86 TOTE £3.10: £1.70, £2.00; EX 6.00.

Owner Miss A Woolley **Bred** Mrs Neta O Connor **Trained** Brayford, Devon

FOCUS
An ordinary staying handicap and slightly suspect form.

NOTEBOOK

Honourable Arthur(IRE) put in the best jumping display of the six runners, fencing boldly throughout, and took up the running after the leader unseated down the back straight. He ran out a convincing winner, and clearly the cheekpieces, which he wore for the first time when successful at Wincanton last time, have had a beneficial effect. He can prove competitive from a higher mark. (op 3-1 tchd 11-4)

Timpo(FR) has been a fairly consistent horse but finds it hard to win. He jumped right at some of his fences and, although he found for pressure to stay on for second, he made little impression on the winner. (tchd 11-4)

Rileyev(FR) was quietly fancied on the back of his fourth at Chepstow, a race from which the three ahead of him have won since, but continues to look a weak finisher. He is sliding down the ratings but may yet need more help from the handicapper. (op 13-2)

Herald Angel(FR) never got into the race from the rear and parted company with his jockey at the last. (op 8-1)

Ratify was running a good race in front before throwing his jockey off halfway round. He is unexposed over fences and is one to note in a similar race if allowed a useful lead. (op 8-1)

3742 PERTEMPS H'CAP HURDLE (QUALIFIER) (12 hdls) 3m 2f

2:45 (2:45) (Class 2) 5-Y-O+ **£8,238** (£2,433; £1,216; £608; £304)

Form | | | | RPR

1632 **1** **Mr Moonshine (IRE)**[80] 2248 7-10-8 **120** .... HenryOliver 135+
(Sue Smith) *mde all: clr after 9th: 17l ahd last: eased flat* **16/1**

-61B **2** *4* **Cross Kennon (IRE)**[47] 2870 7-11-12 **138** .... AlanO'Keeffe 137
(Jennie Candlish) *hld up: rdn after 8th: styd on to go 2nd last: nvr nrr* **11/2**[2]

0111 **3** *1* **Salpierre (IRE)**[23] 3370 6-10-13 **125** .... APMcCoy 124+
(Jonjo O'Neill) *chsd wnr 3rd: nt fluent 5th: rdn after 9th: wknd appr 2 out: lost 2nd last* **3/1**[1]

2132 **4** *nse* **Saintly Lady (IRE)**[19] 3428 6-9-12 **113** ....(p) DonalDevereux[(3)] 111
(Peter Bowen) *chsd ldrs: lost pl 8th: kpt on u.p appr last* **20/1**

-511 **5** *9* **I'Ve Been Framed (IRE)**[25] 3306 7-10-13 **125** ....(p) RichardJohnson 116
(Neil King) *hld up in tch: rdn after 9th: wknd bef next* **10/1**

311F **6** *1 ½* **Kauto The Roc (FR)**[11] 3566 7-10-8 **120** .... RobertThornton 108
(Alan King) *hld up: sme hdwy appr 8th: rdn after next: wknd bef 3 out* **7/1**[3]

P012 **7** *2 ¾* **Stow**[18] 3440 6-10-6 **118** .... AidanColeman 103
(Venetia Williams) *chsd ldrs: rdn after 7th: wknd bef next* **10/1**

42/1 **8** *37* **Pocketwood**[41] 2980 9-10-3 **115** .... FelixDeGiles 63
(Alastair Lidderdale) *hld up: rdn and wknd appr 8th: t.o* **12/1**

4-10 **9** *hd* **Moghaayer**[65] 2581 6-10-8 **120** .... BarryGeraghty 68
(Nicky Henderson) *hld up: a in rr: bhd fr 8th: t.o* **12/1**

0-66 **10** *11* **Sullumo (GER)**[18] 3440 8-10-10 **125** ....(b[1]) PeterToole[(3)] 62
(Charlie Mann) *prom tl wknd after 8th: t.o* **16/1**

0-10 **F** **Go Amwell**[47] 2581 8-9-13 **114** ....(v) MarcGoldstein[(3)] —
(J R Jenkins) *hld up: hdwy to go 7 l 3rd whn fell 3 out* **66/1**

6/2P **P** **Vagrant Emperor (IRE)**[18] 3440 8-11-0 **126** .... SamThomas —
(Emma Lavelle) *hld up in tch: mstke 9th: rdn and wknd bef next: p.u bef last* **14/1**

-201 **P** **Arctic Court (IRE)**[23] 3362 7-10-5 **117** .... TimmyMurphy —
(Jim Goldie) *hld up: hit 7th: wknd next: t.o whn p.u bef 3 out* **7/1**[3]

6m 37.8s (14.90) **Going Correction** +0.575s/f (Soft) **13** Ran SP% **123.6**
Speed ratings: **100,98,98,98,95 95,94,82,82,79 —,—,—**
toteswingers:1&2 £36.00, 2&3 £4.20, 1&3 £22.40 CSF £106.55 CT £348.09 TOTE £19.00: £4.30, £2.10, £1.60; EX 180.80.
Owner Mrs S Smith **Bred** T McIlhagga **Trained** High Eldwick, W Yorks

FOCUS

A competitive-looking handicap, but the winner ran them ragged from the front and rates value for a lot further.

NOTEBOOK

Mr Moonshine(IRE), a point winner in heavy ground over 3m, had a light weight for this handicap debut and won with authoritative ease. Henry Oliver rode a good race from the outset, dictating matters early on and coasting to victory over several previous winners. He is worth more than the winning margin suggests, having been eased right down, and is unexposed over longer trips with stamina clearly his forte. The Pertemps Final at Cheltenham could be on the agenda (20-1 with Paddy Power) after a guaranteed hike up in the weights, although he would need some ease in the ground to feature.

Cross Kennon(IRE), unlucky to be brought down at Cheltenham last time out when 8lb higher than when winning at that course previously, confirmed his upward curve with a good display from a long way back. He stayed on particularly well in the straight when asked for maximum effort and will continue to be competitive from this mark judged on this. He will be aimed at the final of the series at Cheltenham (20-1 with Paddy Power). (op 6-1 tchd 13-2)

Salpierre(IRE), raised a whopping 35lb since his winning spree began at Southwell in November, ran with credit considering his weight and the fact he took a good grip for some way, and is another likely to continue to improve with racing. (op 11-4 tchd 4-1)

Saintly Lady(IRE) is a consistent mare but finds it hard to win. She responded for pressure more than she usually does, which was encouraging. (op 16-1)

Arctic Court(IRE) Official explanation: trainer's rep had no explanation for the poor form shown

3743 HUNTINGDON NOVICES' CHASE (19 fncs) 3m

3:15 (3:16) (Class 3) 5-Y-O+ **£4,553** (£1,337; £668; £333)

Form | | | | RPR

3-15 **1** **Master Of The Hall (IRE)**[25] 3291 7-11-4 137 .... BarryGeraghty 148+
(Nicky Henderson) *hld up: hdwy 13th: chsd ldr 3 out: led 2 out: styd on wl* **2/1**[2]

-PF5 **2** *6* **Alderluck (IRE)**[22] 3390 8-10-12 0 .... LiamTreadwell 134+
(Nick Gifford) *led to 5th: chsd ldr: pckd 9th and 13th: led appr 3 out: hdd next: styng on same pce whn mstke last* **22/1**

620- **3** *nse* **Helpston**[312] 4739 7-10-12 0 .... DavidEngland 130
(Pam Sly) *chsd ldr 2nd: led 5th: hdd 11th: outpcd 15th: rallied 3 out: rdn bef next: hung rt and no ex flat* **15/2**

23F0 **4** *38* **Othermix (FR)**[25] 3291 7-10-12 140 ....(bt) APMcCoy 98
(Ian Williams) *hld up: rdn 15th: wknd after 3 out: t.o* **9/2**[3]

-222 **5** *15* **Voramar Two**[18] 3435 8-10-12 140 ....(t) RichardJohnson 102+
(Philip Hobbs) *nt fluent: chsd ldrs: j. slowly 2nd: led 11th: hit 13th: hdd appr 3 out: rdn and wknd sn after: t.o* **11/10**[1]

6m 24.0s (13.70) **Going Correction** +0.75s/f (Soft) **5** Ran SP% **115.2**
Speed ratings: **107,105,104,92,87**
CSF £28.45 TOTE £2.50: £1.10, £13.60; EX 32.20.
Owner Martin Landau & Jonathan Duffy **Bred** Sweetmans Bloodstock **Trained** Upper Lambourn, Berks

FOCUS

A good little novice chase and a very useful winner.

NOTEBOOK

Master Of The Hall(IRE) answered any stamina doubts in emphatic style, winning at a canter. He settled well throughout the race, jumping exuberantly, while most of his rivals made errors. He is now two from three in chases, the only defeat coming in the hot Grade 2 Dipper Novices' at Cheltenham earlier in the month. (op 7-4 tchd 9-4)

Alderluck(IRE) jumped better than on his chasing debut but was playing for second from a fair way out. He did knuckle down well to pressure, though, and looks to have a good future in handicaps down the line. (op 20-1 tchd 25-1)

Helpston defied a 312-day absence for this seasonal and chasing debut to finish a respectable third. Well backed before the off, he jumped well in the main and, with plenty of size about him, could go on from this. A quick reappearance may bring the bounce factor into the equation, though. (op 14-1)

Othermix(FR), second in the Jewson at Cheltenham last term, had plenty to find with the winner on their recent Cheltenham run, and was firmly put in his place this time around. He didn't jump fluently and possibly didn't like the testing ground. (op 6-1 tchd 4-1)

Voramar Two jumped sketchily for the majority of the race, looking far from enthusiastic. This was a step down from his previous good efforts over fences, and it could have been down to not liking the testing conditions. Official explanation: trainer's rep said gelding had a breathing problem (op 5-4 tchd 6-4)

3744 TURFTV H'CAP HURDLE (10 hdls) 2m 5f 110y

3:45 (3:45) (Class 4) (0-115,115) 4-Y-O+ **£2,602** (£764; £382; £190)

Form | | | | RPR

-100 **1** **Heez A Cracker (FR)**[25] 3288 5-11-12 **115** .... WayneHutchinson 124+
(Emma Lavelle) *trckd ldrs: racd keenly: led appr 2 out: blnd last: rdn out* **5/1**[2]

P-06 **2** *3* **Crazy Eyes (IRE)**[65] 2581 6-11-6 **112** ....(t) PeterToole[(3)] 116
(Charlie Mann) *hld up: hdwy appr 3 out: rdn whn hit last: styd on to go 2nd nr fin: nt rch wnr* **11/1**

2-22 **3** *¾* **Raduis Bleu (FR)**[23] 3374 6-11-11 **114** .... RobertThornton 116
(Alan King) *led: rdn and hdd appr 2 out: no ex flat: lost 2nd towards fin* **6/1**[3]

410- **4** *9* **Good For Blue (IRE)**[318] 4618 8-11-9 **112** .... RichardJohnson 105
(Richard Phillips) *hld up: nt fluent 2nd: hdwy appr 3 out: wknd bef last* **25/1**

025- **5** *7* **Premier Des Marais (FR)**[599] 627 8-11-4 **107** .... JamieMoore 93
(Gary Moore) *hld up: hdwy appr 7th: wknd after 3 out* **20/1**

42F5 **6** *1 ¼* **See You Jack**[16] 3487 6-11-10 **113** .... AndrewThornton 98
(Caroline Bailey) *chsd ldr tl after 5th: rdn and wknd 3 out* **22/1**

-03P **7** *7* **Latin America (IRE)**[41] 2983 6-11-10 **113** ....(p) LiamTreadwell 92
(Nick Gifford) *prom: chsd ldr after 5th tl rdn 3 out: wknd bef next* **33/1**

020 **8** *15* **Well Hello There (IRE)**[29] 3158 5-11-5 **108** .... APMcCoy 89+
(Jonjo O'Neill) *trckd ldrs: rdn appr 7th: wknd after 3 out: eased bef last* **9/2**[1]

5224 **9** *½* **Talenti (IRE)**[14] 912 8-10-9 **108** ....(t) KielanWoods[(10)] 72
(Charlie Longsdon) *hld up in tch: mstkes 1st and 6th: wknd next* **9/1**

-3P0 **10** *1* **Mega Watt (IRE)**[44] 2927 6-10-13 **102** .... AidanColeman 63
(Venetia Williams) *hld up: hdwy after 5th: rdn and wknd appr 3 out* **16/1**

-411 **11** *14* **Red Not Blue (IRE)**[241] 539 8-11-3 **106** .... GerardTumelty 53
(Simon Earle) *mid-div: hdwy 5th: wknd 3 out* **8/1**

15-P **12** *6* **Chaim (IRE)**[83] 2171 9-11-12 **115** .... LeightonAspell 56
(Lucy Wadham) *hld up: a in rr: bhd fr 7th: t.o* **14/1**

0P-0 **P** **Bally Conn (IRE)**[85] 2141 9-10-13 **102** .... SamThomas —
(Martin Hill) *prom: reminders after 4th: wknd 6th: t.o whn p.u bef 3 out* **12/1**

50/0 **P** **Cathedral Rock (IRE)**[81] 2209 9-11-5 **115** ....(b) MrJonathanBailey[(7)] —
(Ms A E Embiricos) *hld up: hdwy on outside appr 6th: rdn and wknd bef next: t.o whn p.u bef 2 out* **40/1**

/100 **P** **Dakota Boy (IRE)**[65] 2581 9-11-4 **107** ....(t) DenisO'Regan —
(Alex Hales) *hld up: a in rr: bhd fr 7th: t.o whn p.u bef 2 out* **14/1**

5m 25.5s (14.90) **Going Correction** +0.575s/f (Soft) **15** Ran SP% **123.8**
Speed ratings (Par 105): **95,93,93,90,87 87,84,79,79,78 73,71,—,—,—**
toteswingers:1&2 £23.30, 2&3 £12.50, 1&3 £15.20 CSF £56.24 CT £347.59 TOTE £8.90: £3.80, £3.40, £1.10; EX 71.70.
Owner Gdm Partnership **Bred** Henrietta Charlet & Daniel Charlesworth **Trained** Wildhern, Hants
■ Stewards' Enquiry : Robert Thornton one-day ban: careless riding (Feb 9)

FOCUS

Another competitive handicap hurdle, this time for 0-115 rated horses.

NOTEBOOK

Heez A Cracker(FR), well backed, ran out an impressive winner, showing a good burst of pace over the final two flights and seeing out the trip in good fashion. The 5-y-o had his sights lowered after being set stiff tasks at Cheltenham since winning a novice event at Kempton. Interestingly, Emma Lavelle said her gelding would appreciate a flat track after his latest start, a comment comprehensively confirmed here. He could be competitive after a rise in the weights. (op 13-2 tchd 15-2 and 8-1 in places)

Crazy Eyes(IRE) stayed on best of all besides the winner, thrusting down the straight, clearly running better than most in the testing conditions. He is coming to hand steadily this term and, although running well on bad going here, will be better on spring ground. (op 12-1)

Raduis Bleu(FR) has been a model of consistency for connections but paid for making the running at a decent clip here. He may need to drop a couple more pounds to get his head in front, but at least he is genuine. (tchd 11-2 and 13-2)

Good For Blue(IRE) shaped well after nearly a year off the track and should come on plenty for this. (tchd 28-1)

Premier Des Marais(FR) ◆ caught the eye emptying late on after travelling powerfully. He will benefit from a drop in trip. (op 18-1)

See You Jack showed encouraging signs back at this track. He was second in a novice event here in October and may need even more of a stamina test to shine. (op 20-1)

Well Hello There(IRE) was up in trip for this handicap debut, but was laboured leaving the back straight and proved disappointing. (tchd 4-1 and 5-1)

3745 HUNTINGDON AUDI A5 "NATIONAL HUNT" NOVICES' H'CAP HURDLE (10 hdls) 2m 4f 110y

4:15 (4:15) (Class 4) (0-105,104) 4-Y-O+ **£2,397** (£698; £349)

Form | | | | RPR

5422 **1** **Be My Light (IRE)**[22] 3392 5-10-6 **94** ....(p) KielanWoods[(10)] 106+
(Charlie Longsdon) *hld up in tch: led appr 3 out: rdn out* **9/1**

2P42 **2** *1* **I Can Run Can You (IRE)**[8] 3622 5-10-10 **88** .... APMcCoy 98+
(Jonjo O'Neill) *hld up: hdwy after 6th: hdd bef 3 out: rdn and ev ch last: hung lft towards fin: styd on* **7/4**[1]

04-0 **3** *11* **King Of Leon (FR)**[255] 353 7-11-8 **100** .... SamThomas 101+
(Emma Lavelle) *hld up: hdwy 7th: wknd appr last* **9/2**[2]

0-63 **4** *4 ½* **Mr Tingle**[12] 3540 7-10-10 **95** .... PeterCarberry[(7)] 90
(Richard Phillips) *hld up: hdwy appr 3 out: rdn and wknd next* **8/1**[3]

-500 **5** *7* **Beau Lake (IRE)**[26] 3261 7-10-11 **96** .... MrTJCannon[(7)] 84
(Suzy Smith) *hld up: hit 4th: hdwy appr 7th: rdn and wknd after 3 out* **33/1**

P614 **6** *½* **Monsieur Cadou (FR)**[26] 3260 6-11-9 **104** .... SamTwiston-Davies[(3)] 91
(Tom George) *hld up: hdwy appr 6th: rdn and wknd after 3 out* **9/1**

P422 **7** *8* **Autumm Spirit**[12] 3545 7-10-0 **81** ....(t) WayneKavanagh[(3)] 60
(Robin Dickin) *chsd ldrs tl wknd appr 3 out: t.o* **14/1**

6004 **8** *15* **Downe Payment (IRE)**[24] 3340 6-10-7 **92** .... MissHGrissell[(7)] 56
(Diana Grissell) *prom tl wknd 6th: t.o* **28/1**

0-40 **9** *6* **Forty Knights**[66] 2558 6-10-11 **96** MrRHawkins(7) 54
(Chris Down) *hld up: hdwy 5th: rdn and wknd after next: t.o* **66/1**

-P40 **10** *13* **Knight Woodsman**[23] 3370 7-11-0 **95** (p) AlexMerriam(3) 40
(Neil King) *led: mstke 4th: hdd 6th: wknd bef next: t.o* **22/1**

5203 **11** *54* **Whereveryougoigo (IRE)**[15] 3497 5-11-10 **102** (v) RichardJohnson —
(Peter Bowen) *mid-div: hdwy 5th: rdn and wknd after next: t.o* **22/1**

-522 **P** **Massini Moon (IRE)**[44] 2929 7-11-3 **102** (b) JoshuaMoore(7) —
(Gary Moore) *prom: rdn and wknd after 5th: t.o whn p.u bef 7th* **10/1**

P500 **P** **Bobbisox (IRE)**[67] 2514 6-11-3 **95** (p) DenisO'Regan —
(Alex Hales) *chsd ldrs: reminders after 3rd: wknd 7th: t.o whn p.u bef 2 out* **33/1**

5m 8.40s (9.40) **Going Correction** +0.575s/f (Soft) **13** Ran SP% **120.9**
Speed ratings (Par 105): **105,104,100,98,96 95,92,87,84,79 59,—,—**
toteswingers:1&2 £6.90, 2&3 £9.10, 1&3 £19.00. totesuper7: Win: Not won. Place: Not won. CSF £24.38 CT £85.53 TOTE £7.80: £3.00, £1.60, £1.80; EX 37.30.
Owner Foxtrot NH Racing Partnership IV **Bred** Mrs L Suenson-Taylor **Trained** Over Norton, Oxon
■ Kielan Woods's first winner in Britain, to go with three in Ireland.

FOCUS
A moderate novice handicap.

NOTEBOOK
Be My Light(IRE) had run well in similar conditions at Leicester last time out and, with the cheekpieces kept on to help her concentrate, put in a thoroughly likeable performance. Charlie Longsdon reported she will have a break after this war of attrition, but could win again if making use of the useful claim from the jockey.
I Can Run Can You(IRE) finished close to a handicap good thing at Southwell recently, but maybe this race came too soon. Narrowly denied in the straight, he is at least in good form but may need a rest after this stamina test. (op 2-1 tchd 9-4)
King Of Leon(FR) was on course for a well-backed victory coming into the straight before lacking for race fitness from two out. The way he travelled was highly encouraging and he will be better suited by faster ground. (op 7-2 tchd 5-1)
Mr Tingle, disqualified last time for taking the wrong course, probably needs better ground and remains open to further improvement in handicaps. (tchd 17-2)
T/Jkpt: Not won. T/Plt: £49.60 to a £1 stake. Pool of £66,802.75 - 981.90 winning tickets. T/Qpdt: £13.10 to a £1 stake. Pool of £4,398.57 - 247.01 winning tickets. CR

3547 MUSSELBURGH (R-H)

Wednesday, January 26

OFFICIAL GOING: Good (good to firm in places in home straight)
Stands bend moved out 4m and bottom bend out 2m.
Wind: nil Weather: Cloudy, cold

3746 TOTEPOOL A BETTER WAY TO BET NOVICES' HURDLE (DIV I) (9 hdls) 2m

1:05 (1:05) (Class 4) 4-Y-0+ **£1,626** (£477; £238; £119)

Form RPR

3-22 **1** **Silverlord (FR)**[27] 3231 7-11-11 122 (t) JasonMaguire 118+
(Gordon Elliott, Ire) *in tch on inner: hdwy to chse ldr 3 out: ev ch 2 out: drvn and kpt on strly run-in: led nr fin* **6/4**[2]

4032 **2** *shd* **Kaolak (USA)**[12] 3547 5-11-4 116 JamesReveley 110+
(Keith Reveley) *trckd ldrs: hdwy to ld 4 out: rdn after 2 out: kpt on: ct nr fin* **11/10**[1]

3 *5* **Raleigh Quay (IRE)**[100] 4-10-7 0 BarryKeniry 94
(Micky Hammond) *trckd ldrs: rdn after 3 out: hit 2 out: kpt on run-in* **9/1**[3]

0600 **4** *3/4* **Takaatuf (IRE)**[14] 3509 5-11-4 100 GrahamLee 104
(John Hellens) *midfield on inner: hit 3 out: rdn and hdwy bef 2 out: kpt on run-in* **40/1**

0 **5** *11* **Cool Baranca (GER)**[12] 3547 5-10-8 0 RyanMania(3) 87
(Dianne Sayer) *trckd ldr: racd keenly: rdn 3 out: wknd appr last* **40/1**

6-00 **6** *5* **Jersey Boys**[88] 2092 5-11-4 0 BrianHughes 88
(Howard Johnson) *hld up: racd keenly: hdwy after 4 out: rdn and no further imp after 3 out* **50/1**

4 **7** *1 1/2* **Via Archimede (USA)**[182] 1114 6-11-4 0 PeterBuchanan 88
(Lucinda Russell) *led: hdd 4 out: wknd after 3 out* **33/1**

PF0- **8** *2 1/4* **Lisbon Lion (IRE)**[198] 4576 6-11-4 0 PaddyAspell 85
(James Moffatt) *hld up: racd keenly: n.d* **100/1**

9 *1 1/2* **Northern Acres**[116] 5-11-4 0 WilsonRenwick 83
(Sue Bradburne) *midfield: hdwy to chse ldrs 4 out: wknd 2 out* **100/1**

00 **10** *3 3/4* **Parc Des Princes (USA)**[24] 3331 5-11-4 0 BrianHarding 79
(Nicky Richards) *hld up in midfield: racd keenly: rdn after 3 out: wknd after 2 out* **100/1**

00 **11** *2 1/4* **Dirleton (IRE)**[13] 3521 5-11-4 0 RichieMcGrath 77
(George Charlton) *hld up: n.d* **66/1**

00 **12** *12* **Davy Boy Legend (IRE)**[66] 2552 8-11-1 0 EwanWhillans(3) 65
(Josie Ross) *hld up: a towards rr* **66/1**

13 *25* **Lambrini Lace (IRE)**[40] 6-10-4 0 HarryChalloner(7) 33
(Lisa Williamson) *j.lft: hld up on outer: a towards rr* **100/1**

3m 50.6s (2.20) **Going Correction** -0.275s/f (Good)
WFA 4 from 5yo+ 11lb **13** Ran SP% **114.3**
Speed ratings (Par 105): **83,82,80,80,74 72,71,70,69,67 66,60,47**
toteswingers:1&2 £1.02, 2&3 £5.60, 1&3 £7.40 CSF £3.24 TOTE £2.80: £1.10, £1.10, £1.20; EX 3.00.
Owner Miss Stephanie Swift **Bred** Delsol Farm Inc **Trained** Trim, Co Meath

FOCUS
The betting made this a two-horse contest and punters were proved correct, although not quite the way round most expected. The early pace was slow.

NOTEBOOK
Silverlord(FR), winner of a Down Royal maiden hurdle in heavy ground on his previous start when left in the lead, lost his place down the back straight but came with a strong run from two out to get up close to the line. (op 5-4)
Kaolak(USA), runner-up over C&D almost two weeks previously, is starting to become a little disappointing, not only because he was beaten at short odds, but he cruised into the lead going well and had every chance to lengthen clear, giving none of his rivals any chance of catching him, but couldn't get away. (op 6-5)
Raleigh Quay(IRE) ◆, who had a 2-2 record at this course on the Flat, made an encouraging start to his hurdling career and is one to watch if returned to this track. (op 10-1 tchd 12-1 in a place)
Takaatuf(IRE) is only officially rated 100 and ran with credit, so puts the form in some perspective. (op 50-1)
Cool Baranca(GER) ran better than she had done over C&D last time and may have a small handicap in her. (tchd 50-1)
Jersey Boys Official explanation: jockey said gelding ran too free

3747 BET TOTEPOOL ON ALL UK RACING MARES' NOVICES' HURDLE (12 hdls) 2m 4f

1:35 (1:35) (Class 4) 4-Y-0+ **£1,951** (£573; £286; £143)

Form RPR

-222 **1** **Aneyeforaneye (IRE)**[15] 3498 5-11-0 0 GrahamLee 104+
(Malcolm Jefferson) *hld up in tch: racd keenly: hdwy after 4 out: chsd ldr whn hit 3 out: nt fluent last: kpt on strly run-in: led nr fin* **11/4**[1]

0-11 **2** *nk* **Lovey Dovey (IRE)**[228] 732 7-11-0 0 DougieCostello 102+
(Simon West) *w ldr: led after 3rd: rdn after 2 out: kpt on run-in: hdd nr fin* **7/2**[2]

0240 **3** *3 1/2* **Sara's Smile**[23] 3366 5-11-0 97 JasonMaguire 98
(Donald McCain) *trckd ldrs: chsd wnr after 3 out: kpt on* **7/1**[3]

4 *1* **Streamtown (IRE)**[13] 3539 7-11-0 0 CampbellGillies 97
(S R B Crawford, Ire) *hld up: stl plenty to do appr 3 out: hdwy to chse ldrs 2 out: kpt on* **25/1**

3-40 **5** *10* **Miss Abbey**[24] 3330 7-11-0 0 (t) JamesReveley 87
(Jim Goldie) *hld up: rdn after 3 out: sn no imp* **14/1**

23P0 **6** *7* **Proficiency**[23] 3362 6-10-9 93 (v) AlexanderVoy(5) 81
(Sue Bradburne) *trckd ldrs on inner: lost pl after 4 out: wknd after 3 out* **50/1**

7 *7* **Brave Beauty (IRE)**[20] 3418 7-11-0 0 TomScudamore 75
(Gordon Elliott, Ire) *trckd ldrs: racd keenly: hit 4th: nt fluent 7th: outpcd after 4 out: wknd after 3 out* **7/2**[2]

0515 **8** *2 1/2* **Moscow Mischief**[26] 3261 7-11-6 98 PeterBuchanan 77
(Lucinda Russell) *led to 3rd: remained prom: wknd appr 3 out* **20/1**

53 **9** *21* **Sweet Caroline (IRE)**[23] 3358 4-10-2 0 FearghalDavis 38
(Nicky Richards) *trckd ldrs: racd keenly: wknd qckly appr 3 out* **7/1**[3]

4m 44.4s (-7.10) **Going Correction** -0.275s/f (Good)
WFA 4 from 5yo+ 12lb **9** Ran SP% **113.3**
Speed ratings (Par 105): **103,102,101,101,97 94,91,90,82**
toteswingers:1&2 £4.40, 2&3 £5.40, 1&3 £6.10 CSF £12.17 TOTE £2.70: £1.50, £2.20, £4.50; EX 16.50.
Owner Mrs J U Hales & Mrs L M Joicey **Bred** Walter Connors **Trained** Norton, N Yorks

FOCUS
Probably only a fair race of its type at best, but a few of these looked to have some untapped potential, so may turn out to be a bit better than the bare form suggests.

NOTEBOOK
Aneyeforaneye(IRE) ◆ got up in the final strides to mug the race from the runner-up. It was a good performance by the winner, however, as she took a fierce hold in the early stages and seemed most unlikely to find enough to get home. Indeed, she got caught one-paced before two out, but made up the ground and ended a run of second places. (op 3-1 tchd 5-2 and 10-3 in a place)
Lovey Dovey(IRE) ◆ has a really good winning profile and shaped nicely on her hurdling debut. She looked to have fought off all rivals down the home straight but couldn't quite hold on. Her turn isn't far away. (op 11-4)
Sara's Smile, back against mares, ran much better than she had done on her last couple of outings and kept on well for pressure. (op 9-1)
Streamtown(IRE) was ridden patiently and never quite got on terms. It was a good start to her hurdling career and, as a previous point winner, she ought to stay further. (op 20-1 tchd 18-1)
Brave Beauty(IRE), up 4f in distance, attracted support in the market (possibly due to the stable having the previous winner on the card) but was easily held. (op 5-1)
Sweet Caroline(IRE), trying 2m4f for the first time, was weak in the market and reportedly played up before the start. She moved well when the pace was even but dropped out quickly when asked to quicken. Official explanation: jockey said filly ran too free (op 13-2 tchd 6-1)

3748 BOOGIE IN THE MORNING CONDITIONAL JOCKEYS' H'CAP CHASE (18 fncs) 3m

2:05 (2:05) (Class 4) (0-100,98) 5-Y-0+ **£3,252** (£955; £477; £238)

Form RPR

4-02 **1** **Aghill (IRE)**[24] 3336 7-11-7 **98** HenryBrooke(5) 109+
(Rose Dobbin) *hld up: hdwy to trck ldrs 9th: rdn and outpcd after 5 out: bk in contention 3 out: rdn to go 2nd 2 out: kpt on run-in: led nr fin* **11/2**

1-66 **2** *1/2* **Copper's Gold (IRE)**[115] 1701 7-11-4 **93** (v[1]) CampbellGillies(3) 100
(Lucinda Russell) *prom: lft in front after 10th: rdn after 4 out: kpt on: ct nr fin* **4/1**[3]

1U23 **3** *40* **Archie's Wish**[74] 2371 7-10-12 **84** JamesHalliday 61
(Micky Hammond) *hld up: hdwy to trck ldrs 12th: chal 4 out: rdn 3 out: wknd qckly appr last* **7/2**[2]

-012 **4** *21* **Not Talking (IRE)**[23] 3369 8-10-2 **77** KyleJames(3) 23
(John Quinn) *in tch: j.lft 4th and again 12th: wknd after 5 out* **10/3**[1]

0-00 **F** **Froggy Lane**[14] 3505 8-11-0 **89** AlexanderVoy(3) —
(Simon West) *racd keenly hld up: hit 1st: hung lft and racd wd bnd after 2nd: hdwy to ld 3rd: rn wd and hdd bnd after 10th: cl up whn blnd and fell 6 out* **50/1**

5-20 **P** **King Penda (IRE)**[97] 1929 8-11-7 **96** FearghalDavis(3) —
(Nicky Richards) *racd keenly: led to 3rd: trckd ldr: rdn and wknd after 5 out: p.u bef 3 out* **11/2**

-505 **P** **Papa Drew (IRE)**[61] 2656 7-10-3 **75** HarryHaynes —
(Andrew Parker) *hld up: blnd 9th: sn struggling: p.u bef 4 out* **7/1**

6m 6.25s (2.85) **Going Correction** +0.20s/f (Yiel) **7** Ran SP% **110.5**
Speed ratings: **103,102,89,82,—,—,—**
toteswingers:1&2 £4.70, 2&3 £1.60, 1&3 £3.10 CSF £26.13 TOTE £5.50: £3.70, £1.10; EX 19.80.
Owner J Kelly **Bred** J B Kerr **Trained** South Hazelrigg, Northumbria

FOCUS
Low-grade stuff but competitive.

NOTEBOOK
Aghill(IRE), making his chasing debut under rules but a former winning pointer, travelled nicely for most of the race and found plenty for pressure to get up after the final fence. He clearly has plenty of stamina. (op 4-1 tchd 6-1)
Copper's Gold(IRE), with a visor on instead of blinkers, gained a couple of wins over fences early last year including this race off an official mark of 77, and made a bold bid to repeat that success. A good jump at the last seemed likely to seal it for him but he lost out in a tight finish. (op 5-1)
Archie's Wish, up 4f in trip, stays well but looked tired after two out and was readily outpaced heading to the final fence. (op 9-2)
Not Talking(IRE) was hardly being given a stiff introduction to fences, but gave the impression that he will appreciate stronger handling in the future. (tchd 7-2)
King Penda(IRE) pulled hard on his chasing debut and was a disappointment. (op 10-1)

Papa Drew(IRE), a half-brother to Thyestes Chase winner Priests Leap, was beaten early. (op 10-1)

3749 TOTEPOOL A BETTER WAY TO BET NOVICES' HURDLE (DIV II) (9 hdls) 2m
2:35 (2:35) (Class 4) 4-Y-0+ £1,626 (£477; £238; £119)

Form				RPR
4	1		**Waldvogel (IRE)**[252] 397 7-11-4 0 DougieCostello (Nicky Richards) *hld up in tch on inner: hit first: hdwy 3 out: chsd ldr after 2 out: led after last: kpt on wl* 20/1	122+
1F	2	1 1/4	**Aikman (IRE)**[12] 3547 7-11-1 0 HarryHaynes(3) (James Ewart) *w ldr: led narrowly after 4 out: rdn after 3 out: hit last: hdd sn after: kpt on: a hld by wnr* 11/4[2]	121+
43/6	3	5	**Bogside (IRE)**[43] 2943 7-11-4 0 JanFaltejsek (George Charlton) *trckd ldrs on outer: hdwy to chal appr 3 out: stl ev ch last: no ex run-in* 33/1	115
0-65	4	3 1/2	**Mister Wall Street (FR)**[14] 3506 6-11-4 106 GrahamLee (Ferdy Murphy) *midfield on inner: hdwy to trck ldrs 4 out: rdn after 3 out: kpt on same pce* 5/1[3]	110
55	5	7	**Fortuni (IRE)**[12] 3547 5-11-4 0 (t) WilsonRenwick (Rose Dobbin) *midfield: trckd ldrs after 4 out: rdn after 3 out: wknd appr last* 8/1	103
-000	6	10	**The Tiddly Tadpole**[66] 2553 6-10-11 0 HenryBrooke(7) (Simon West) *racd keenly in midfield: rdn and edgd lft bef 2 out: hit 2 out: wknd after* 200/1	96
	7	1	**Battle Honour**[163] 4-10-7 0 PaddyAspell (Sue Bradburne) *hld up: hdwy to chse ldrs 4 out: wknd 3 out* 100/1	81
25	8	shd	**Red Merlin (IRE)**[18] 3445 6-11-4 0 JasonMaguire (Donald McCain) *nt fluent: trckd ldrs: mstke 4 out and sn lost pl: btn whn hmpd bef 2 out* 5/4[1]	95
1	9	15	**Dica (FR)**[68] 2509 5-11-8 0 JamesO'Farrell(3) (Patrick Griffin, Ire) *led narrowly: hdd after 4 out: wknd appr 3 out* 16/1	84
50P	10	18	**Pagan Lightning (USA)**[26] 3252 6-10-11 0 MissECSayer(7) (Dianne Sayer) *a in rr* 200/1	59
	11	16	**Sports Model (IRE)** 5-11-4 0 BrianHughes (Howard Johnson) *midfield: lost pl after 3rd: bhd after* 40/1	43
0-50	12	13	**Bullring (FR)**[24] 1201 5-11-4 0 JamesReveley (Peter Niven) *in tch on outer: rdn after 4 out: sn wknd* 100/1	30

3m 43.1s (-5.30) **Going Correction** -0.275s/f (Good)
WFA 4 from 5yo+ 11lb 12 Ran SP% **117.9**
Speed ratings (Par 105): **102,101,98,97,93 88,88,88,80,71 63,57**
toteswingers:1&2 £11.00, 2&3 £21.10, 1&3 £39.40 CSF £75.38 TOTE £25.10: £3.80, £2.00, £9.40; EX 80.60.
Owner Craig Bennett **Bred** Gestut Ravensberg **Trained** Greystoke, Cumbria

FOCUS
The second division of the novices' hurdle, which looked much better that the first on paper, was run in a quicker time, and produced plenty of potentially nice horses.

NOTEBOOK
Waldvogel(IRE) ◆, absent since being beaten at evens in a modest Kelso novice last May, crept through rivals to steadily get into contention and was a comfortable winner once changing gear. He has the potential to win a good contest over hurdles on the best of his Flat form, but one would want to see him repeat this sort of effort before being confident about his future. (op 16-1)
Aikman(IRE) ◆ has lots of ability and almost made up for an unfortunate mishap on his latest start. Always prominent, he looks a useful type and could improve for going over further considering he is a three-time point-to-point winner. (op 5-2 tchd 3-1)
Bogside(IRE) ◆, a horse with plenty of size and substance, looked a potential winner as he moved into contention before keeping on in good style. It was a fine start to his hurdling career and he has plenty of scope.
Mister Wall Street(FR) is exposed as a hurdler but ran another respectable race. (op 15-2 tchd 9-2)
Fortuni(IRE) ◆, with a tongue-tie on for the first time, is now eligible for handicaps and will be of some interest in that sphere if returning to the best of his Flat form for Sir Mark Prescott. (op 10-1)
The Tiddly Tadpole ◆ doesn't look devoid of ability but is possibly a bit wayward. (op 250-1)
Red Merlin(IRE) faced what looked to be his easiest task so far over hurdles but jumped moderately and put himself out of contention as a result when the tempo lifted. Official explanation: trainer had no explanation for the poor form shown (tchd 6-4)
Dica(FR), who hadn't been out since making a successful hurdling debut over C&D back in mid-November, raced up with pace but became one-paced before three out. (op 20-1)

3750 COSMIC CASE H'CAP HURDLE (14 hdls) 3m 110y
3:05 (3:05) (Class 4) (0-110,108) 4-Y-0+ £3,252 (£955; £477; £238)

Form				RPR
220	1		**Everaard (USA)**[13] 3523 5-10-11 93 (p) RichieMcGrath (Kate Walton) *trckd ldrs on inner: hdwy to ld 2 out: sn rdn: clr last: drvn out towards fin* 9/1	102+
0555	2	3/4	**Vallani (IRE)**[24] 3336 6-10-0 82 oh2 PeterBuchanan (Lucinda Russell) *trckd ldrs: rdn and outpcd 4 out: styd on again after 2 out: wnt 2nd last: kpt on strly towards fin* 15/2[3]	87
0-0P	3	9	**Soprano (GER)**[12] 3552 9-11-1 97 (p) GrahamLee (Jim Goldie) *hld up towards inner: hdwy into 4th appr 3 out: rdn bef 2 out: kpt on one pce: wnt 3rd run-in* 20/1	93
P-51	4	1 1/2	**Sonara (IRE)**[43] 2941 7-10-7 89 WilsonRenwick (Howard Johnson) *led narrowly tl 5th: remained prom: led again 4 out: rdn whn hdd 2 out: wknd after last* 7/2[1]	85
UP1-	5	1/2	**Grand Union (IRE)**[279] 5334 7-10-11 100 MrJohnDawson(7) (John Wade) *prom: chal 3 out: sn rdn: wknd after last* 11/1	95
2304	6	5	**More Equity**[23] 3362 9-11-3 102 RyanMania(3) (Dianne Sayer) *trckd ldrs: hit 9th: rdn after 4 out: wknd after 3 out* 8/1	91
	7	29	**Western Bound (IRE)**[906] 1106 10-11-4 100 JasonMaguire (Gordon Elliott, Ire) *hld up: hdwy into midfield appr 4 out: rdn bef 3 out: sn wknd* 8/1	60
052	8	shd	**Latin Connection (IRE)**[13] 3523 5-11-3 106 (t) MrBGCrawford(7) (S R B Crawford, Ire) *racd keenly: w ldr out wd: led after 5th: hdd 4 out: wknd appr 3 out: blnd 2 out* 14/1	66
430	9	2 3/4	**Twentypoundluck (IRE)**[24] 3351 6-11-1 100 JamesO'Farrell(3) (Andrew Crook) *hld up: rdn after 4 out: a in rr* 14/1	57
-133	P		**Ballymacduff (IRE)**[23] 3362 7-11-12 108 JanFaltejsek (George Charlton) *prom and keen: sddle slipped after 5th: p.u bef 7th* 4/1[2]	—

5m 46.2s (-10.50) **Going Correction** -0.275s/f (Good) 10 Ran SP% **112.6**
Speed ratings (Par 105): **105,104,101,101,101 99,90,90,89,—**
toteswingers:1&2 £8.80, 2&3 £18.60, 1&3 £26.80 CSF £72.23 CT £1304.87 TOTE £14.70: £5.00, £4.20, £4.90; EX 103.90.
Owner Tennant, Sharpe & Boston **Bred** F & F Investments **Trained** Middleham Moor, N Yorks
■ Stewards' Enquiry : Richie McGrath one-day ban: used whip without giving gelding time to respond (Feb 9)

FOCUS
A poor contest.

NOTEBOOK
Everaard(USA), taking a big step up in trip, had cheekpieces back on and gained a first victory over hurdles. He had put up a couple of fair performances but, on the whole, had looked unpredictable and is not one to trust to reproduce this again next time. Official explanation: trainer said, regarding apparent improvement in form, that the gelding had been suited by the re-application of cheek pieces. (op 15-2 tchd 7-1)
Vallani(IRE), running from 2lb out of the handicap, hit a flat spot well before the third-last hurdle, but she never gave up and was gaining on Everaard with every stride as the winning line approached. (op 8-1)
Soprano(GER) was backed at long prices (Jim Goldie trained the mare for which the race was named after) and plugged on for an honourable third. (op 33-1 tchd 18-1)
Sonara(IRE), 5lb higher than when winning at Catterick in the middle of December, didn't find a great deal off the bridle after racing prominently and just stayed on. (tchd 10-3)
Grand Union(IRE) ◆, off since beating Ballymacduff at Perth in April of last year, came with a promising effort down the home straight but proved to be one-paced when in with every chance. He should progress from this run and be of interest next time. (op 12-1)
Western Bound(IRE), having his first run for this trainer after a huge absence, made some ground as the pace increased but that effort was short-lived. (op 10-1 tchd 11-1)
Latin Connection(IRE) Official explanation: jockey said gelding ran too free
Ballymacduff(IRE), 8lb above his only winning mark, and with his usual tongue-tie left off, was pulled up early after his jockey's saddle slipped. Official explanation: jockey said saddle slipped (op 7-2 tchd 9-2)

3751 BETFAIR.COM/PAULNICHOLLS H'CAP CHASE (16 fncs) 2m 4f
3:35 (3:35) (Class 3) (0-120,119) 5-Y-0+ £6,505 (£1,910; £955; £477)

Form				RPR
6-61	1		**Tyrone House (IRE)**[78] 2298 7-11-4 111 JamesReveley (John Wade) *hld up: hdwy to trck ldrs 6 out: wnt 2nd after 5 out: led 3 out: sn rdn: kpt on* 12/5[1]	121+
-313	2	2 3/4	**Persian Prince (IRE)**[245] 473 11-9-10 96 ow1 MrJohnDawson(7) (John Wade) *prom: led 7th: rdn whn hdd 3 out: kpt on: a hld by wnr* 7/1	102
F3-0	3	11	**Or D'Oudairies (FR)**[256] 330 9-11-0 107 GrahamLee (Ferdy Murphy) *hld up: blnd 3rd: mstke 11th: hdwy after 5 out: wnt 3rd 3 out: kpt on one pce* 7/1	105+
4361	4	4 1/2	**Border Reiver**[11] 3574 7-10-10 103 (t) RichieMcGrath (Tim Easterby) *trckd ldrs: lost pl 10th: styd on again to chse ldrs after 5 out: nt fluent 4 out: wknd after next* 9/2[2]	94
346	5	11	**Go Silver Bullet (FR)**[12] 3552 10-11-12 119 PeterBuchanan (Lucinda Russell) *prom: lost pl 4th: midfield: wknd after 6 out* 11/2[3]	100
1/PP	6	15	**Role On (IRE)**[24] 3333 9-11-8 115 WilsonRenwick (Rose Dobbin) *midfield: hdwy to trck ldrs 9th: wknd appr 4 out* 16/1	86
4403	U		**Silver Steel (FR)**[21] 3397 8-10-4 104 (vt[1]) HarryChalloner(7) (Richard Ford) *hld up: hdwy whn blnd 9th: hmpd and uns 6 out* 16/1	—
-253	F		**County Colours (IRE)**[43] 2938 6-11-0 107 BrianHughes (Howard Johnson) *led narrowly: blnd and hdd 7th: in cl 2nd whn fell 6 out* 7/1	—

5m 1.33s (0.13) **Going Correction** +0.20s/f (Yiel) 8 Ran SP% **112.2**
Speed ratings: **107,105,101,99,95 89,—,—**
toteswingers:1&2 £3.90, 2&3 £6.70, 1&3 £4.80 CSF £18.92 CT £100.59 TOTE £2.80: £1.02, £1.80, £3.50; EX 14.60.
Owner John Wade **Bred** Michael Martin Sheehan **Trained** Mordon, Co Durham

FOCUS
There was plenty of pace on from the start, and trainer John Wade would have been enjoying the final stages as his pair fought out the finish.

NOTEBOOK
Tyrone House(IRE), 6lb higher than when winning at Sedgefield on his previous outing, was held up while others raced keenly and came through at just the right time to claim a second victory in a row. He should get further. (op 3-1 tchd 9-4)
Persian Prince(IRE), off since last May, raced freely from the outset, so kept on surprisingly well in the latter stages. Despite being 11, he looks more than capable of winning again soon, especially when the ground is on the quick side. (tchd 8-1)
Or D'Oudairies(FR), having his first run since May, and making his debut for Ferdy Murphy, wasn't wearing the tongue-tie he had been running in. Held up with the winner at the rear, he shaped respectably without being really dangerous. (op 6-1)
Border Reiver, raised 7lb for winning at Wetherby, had every chance but ran as though the handicapper has his measure. (tchd 5-1)
Silver Steel(FR), with a visor tried for the first time, was behind County Colours when he came to grief and gave Harry Challoner no chance of staying in the saddle when trying to avoid the faller. (tchd 8-1)
County Colours(IRE), making his handicap debut, wasn't beaten when taking a crashing fall six out. (tchd 8-1)

3752 WATCH RACING UK ONLINE AT RACINGUK.COM STANDARD OPEN NATIONAL HUNT FLAT RACE 2m
4:05 (4:05) (Class 6) 4-6-Y-0 £1,626 (£477; £238; £119)

Form				RPR
	1		**Felix Yonger (IRE)**[27] 3244 5-11-4 0 BrianHughes (Howard Johnson) *trckd ldr: rdn to ld narrowly over 2f out: sn drvn: hld on wl towards fin* 13/8[1]	103+
2	2	1 1/4	**D'Gigi**[68] 2511 5-10-11 0 JamesReveley (Keith Reveley) *hld up: hdwy over 2f out: rdn to hold ev ch ins fnl f: kpt on: jst hld towards fin* 8/1[3]	94+
	3	shd	**Distime (IRE)**[101] 5-11-4 0 DougieCostello (John Quinn) *led: drvn whn hdd narrowly over 2f out: stl ev ch ins fnl f: kpt on* 7/4[2]	101
6	4	nk	**Way To Finish**[68] 2511 5-11-4 0 PaddyAspell (James Moffatt) *hld up: smooth hdwy over 2f out: rdn to hold ev ch jst ins fnl f: kpt on* 50/1	101
	5	2 1/2	**De Vine Memory** 4-10-0 0 GrahamLee (Peter Niven) *in tch: rdn over 2f out: hung rt over 1f out: kpt on ins fnl f* 33/1	81
5-02	6	1/2	**Big Sam**[61] 2660 6-11-4 0 BarryKeniry (Bruce Hellier) *hld up in tch: rdn over 2f out: kpt on ins fnl f: nrst fin* 12/1	98
04	7	1	**Dizzy River (IRE)**[12] 3553 6-11-4 0 RichieMcGrath (George Charlton) *trckd ldr on inner: rdn over 2f out: wknd ins fnl f* 12/1	97
	8	9	**Civil Unrest (IRE)** 5-11-1 0 HarryHaynes(3) (James Ewart) *prom: rdn wl over 3f out: sn wknd* 14/1	90
	9	16	**Pas Trop Tard (FR)** 4-10-2 0 AlexanderVoy(5) (James Ewart) *midfield on outer: rdn over 6f out: wknd over 3f out: eased* 50/1	68

3m 48.0s (5.20) **Going Correction** -0.275s/f (Good)
WFA 4 from 5yo+ 11lb 9 Ran SP% **114.5**
Speed ratings: **76,75,75,75,73 73,73,68,60**
toteswingers:1&2 £3.10, 2&3 £2.50, 1&3 £2.00 CSF £15.17 TOTE £3.50: £1.50, £1.10, £1.20; EX 10.50.

Owner Andrea & Graham Wylie **Bred** J Brophy **Trained** Billy Row, Co Durham
■ Stewards' Enquiry : Brian Hughes one-day ban: used whip down the shoulder in the forehand (Feb 9)
FOCUS
This looked a decent contest and it produced a thrilling finish.
NOTEBOOK
Felix Yonger(IRE) showed plenty of ability for Anthony Mullins on his one start in Ireland, and went one better than on his debut for Howard Johnson. He kept on strongly and has a pleasing attitude. (op 6-4 tchd 2-1)
D'Gigi, a half-sister to Butler's Cabin, made steady progress into contention and battled on bravely to confirm the promise of her debut, which had come over C&D. (op 12-1)
Distime(IRE), who won a maiden Irish point last October, raced prominently and showed a good attitude to rally once joined. (op 15-8 tchd 13-8 and 2-1 in a place)
Way To Finish ◆ got much closer to D'Gigi than he had done on their respective debuts, and caught the eye with the way he travelled into a challenging position.
De Vine Memory wasn't disgraced on her first outing and should improve. (op 40-1)
Big Sam made a little late progress after getting outpaced turning in. (op 10-1 tchd 9-1)
T/Plt: £266.90 to a £1 stake. Pool of £51,120.22 - 139.80 winning tickets. T/Qpdt: £185.80 to a £1 stake. Pool of £3,415.69 - 13.60 winning tickets. AS

3753 - 3759a (Foreign Racing) - See Raceform Interactive

3584 FFOS LAS (L-H)
Thursday, January 27

OFFICIAL GOING: Good to soft (soft in places)
Weather: Overcast and cold.

3760 GLYN ABBEY MAIDEN HURDLE (8 hdls) 2m
1:20 (1:20) (Class 4) 4-Y-0+ **£2,602** (£764; £382; £190)

Form				RPR
332	1		**Pateese (FR)**[17] 3489 6-11-4 120 RichardJohnson (Philip Hobbs) *lft trcking ldr 2nd: sn lft in ld: kicked clr after 3 out: styd on wl* **6/4**[1]	112+
-220	2	3 ¾	**Ballinteni**[75] 2361 9-11-4 110 JoeTizzard (Colin Tizzard) *prom: chsd ldr 4th: pushed along and lost pl after next: rdn and rallied 2 out: chsd wnr last: r.o flat* **14/1**	109
00-	3	5	**James Pollard (IRE)**[49] 2240 6-11-4 0 (t) JamesDavies (Bernard Llewellyn) *hld up in rr: hdwy 5th: chsd wnr 2 out tl one pce fr last* **100/1**	105
1406	4	4 ½	**Littledean Jimmy (IRE)**[62] 2666 6-10-11 0 CharlieWallis(7) (John O'Shea) *midfield: hdwy 4th: wnt 2nd after next tl one pce fr 2 out* **66/1**	100
	5	1	**Street Entertainer (IRE)**[109] 4-10-2 0 CO'Farrell(5) (David Pipe) *midfield: shkn up after 5th: outpcd by ldrs bef next: styd on fr 2 out* **16/1**	88
0/P-	6	3	**Bestowed**[11] 827 6-10-13 0 MrTomDavid(5) (Tim Vaughan) *chsd ldrs tl one pce fr 2 out* **125/1**	96
	7	2	**Maadraa (IRE)**[559] 6-11-4 0 DPFahy (Bernard Llewellyn) *in tch: trckd ldrs fr 4th: rdn after next: one pce fr 3 out* **50/1**	95
0	8	¾	**Special Cuvee**[26] 3296 5-10-11 0 OliverDayman(7) (Alison Thorpe) *in tch: rdn bef 3 out: kpt on one pce* **100/1**	94
1-05	9	5	**Thunderstorm (IRE)**[7] 3645 6-11-4 0 TomO'Brien (Philip Hobbs) *in rr div fr 2nd: pushed along after 5th: kpt on same pce fr next* **12/1**	89
	10	hd	**The Hague**[147] 5-11-4 0 SamThomas (Tim Vaughan) *hld up in rr: hdwy and in tch 5th: wknd appr 2 out* **25/1**	89
5	11	17	**Mr One Too (IRE)**[68] 2525 6-11-4 0 JasonMaguire (Keith Goldsworthy) *bhd fr 2nd: j. slowly 4th and sn lost tch: t.o* **50/1**	74
231-	12	19	**Di Kaprio (FR)**[327] 4429 5-11-4 0 PaulMoloney (Evan Williams) *trckd ldr: lft in ld 2nd tl bdly hmpd and carried wd on bnd by loose horse bef next: styd prom tl wknd after 5th: t.o* **7/2**[2]	57
5	13	31	**Ange Guerrier (FR)**[28] 3225 6-11-4 0 HarrySkelton (Paul Nicholls) *hld up in rr: mod hdwy 4th: rdn after next: sn wl bhd: t.o* **4/1**[3]	29
00	U		**Stays All Night (FR)**[21] 3406 5-10-11 0 CDTimmons(7) (Tim Vaughan) *led and racd keenly: hit 1st: blnd and uns rdr next* **150/1**	—

3m 55.3s (6.30) **Going Correction** +0.525s/f (Soft)
WFA 4 from 5yo+ 11lb **14 Ran SP% 115.2**
Speed ratings (Par 105): **105,103,100,98,97 96,95,95,92,92 83,74,58,—**
toteswingers:1&2 £1.90, 2&3 £36.80, 1&3 £23.80 CSF £24.02 TOTE £2.50: £1.02, £4.70, £12.40; EX 17.40.
Owner The Test Valley Partnership **Bred** Zakaria Hakam **Trained** Withycombe, Somerset
FOCUS
The ground was changed to good to soft, soft in places prior to racing. This opening maiden was a modest event and it was run at an average gallop. The form is rated through the winner.
NOTEBOOK
Pateese(FR) was given a sensibly positive ride and readily got his head in front over hurdles at the fourth time of asking. He got bogged down at Towcester last time when beaten at odds-on, but was hampered there and this rates a deserved success. Things will be tougher under a penalty, though. (op 13-8 tchd 5-4 and 7-4 in places)
Ballinteni was well beaten on his handicap debut in this sphere at Cheltenham in November, but his previous second at Kempton was a good effort and he returned to near his best here. He rates the benchmark, but is clearly vulnerable in novice company. (op 9-1)
James Pollard(IRE) had not shown a lot in two previous outings as a hurdler, but won a handicap on the Flat here last year and this was an encouraging display. He is now eligible for a mark.
Littledean Jimmy(IRE) looked a big player turning for home and, while he dropped out where it mattered, this was by far his most encouraging effort over hurdles. He is one to side with when revering to a sounder surface. (op 100-1)
Street Entertainer(IRE) rather lost his way on the Flat, but has joined a top yard for his new career and this was something of an eye-catching debut. He could step up on this nicely next time out. (tchd 14-1)
Di Kaprio(FR), making his hurdling debut for new connections, was fresh early on and was left in front when Stays All Night unseated at the first. He had no chance when that one carried him off the first bend when loose and, while he recovered, that certainly didn't help his cause. The run will not be lost on him. Official explanation: jockey said gelding ran too freely and suffered interference (op 4-1)
Ange Guerrier(FR) was free on his hurdling debut last month and again failed to settle early on this time. He never threatened to land a serious blow and now has plenty to prove. (op 9-2 tchd 5-1)

3761 KOMATSU MINING MAIDEN HURDLE (DIV I) (9 hdls 1 omitted) 2m 4f
1:50 (1:50) (Class 4) 4-Y-0+ **£2,276** (£668; £334; £166)

Form				RPR
3-63	1		**Doctor Foxtrot (IRE)**[82] 2209 6-11-5 118 (b) RichardJohnson (Philip Hobbs) *trckd ldrs: hmpd 2nd: mstke 7th: sn drvn: chsd ldr bef 2 out: led sn after last: hld on wl* **5/1**	117+
	2	½	**Rangitoto (IRE)**[361] 6-11-5 0 SamThomas (Paul Nicholls) *trckd ldrs: led 6th: wnt clr bypassing next: hrd drvn after 2 out: hdd sn after last: kpt on: jst hld* **4/1**[3]	116+
1220	3	18	**Jump Up**[24] 3370 5-11-5 95 JamieMoore (Keith Goldsworthy) *trckd ldr tl lft in ld 2nd: jnd 5th: hdd next: sn rdn and outpcd by ldrs: plugged on* **33/1**	100+
42	4	nk	**Charming Lad (IRE)**[25] 3346 6-11-2 115 PeterToole(3) (Charlie Mann) *prom: rdn after 7th: sn chsng ldr: wknd appr 2 out* **3/1**[2]	97
	5	1 ¾	**Mr Moss (IRE)**[257] 6-11-5 0 PaulMoloney (Evan Williams) *towards rr: hmpd 2nd: hdwy bef 3 out: sn u.p and one pce* **28/1**	95
250	6	3 ¼	**Fiddledee (IRE)**[29] 3196 6-10-9 0 RichieMcLernon(3) (Jonjo O'Neill) *hld up in rr: modest hdwy after 7th: sn outpcd by ldrs* **14/1**	85
340	7	41	**Jan Jandura (IRE)**[11] 3585 6-10-12 0 CDTimmons(7) (Tim Vaughan) *in rr: hdwy 5th: rdn aftter 7th: sn wknd: t.o* **66/1**	55
P0	8	7	**Ostaadi**[11] 3584 5-11-5 0 (p) DPFahy (Bernard Llewellyn) *in tch tl wknd bef 3 out: t.o* **100/1**	49
1	9	28	**Lucky Landing (IRE)**[75] 2368 5-11-5 0 JasonMaguire (Donald McCain) *trckd ldrs: disp ld 5th to 6th: hrd rdn after next: sn hung rt and wknd qckly: t.o* **2/1**[1]	24
1020	10	1 ¼	**Thomas Bell (IRE)**[85] 2145 7-10-12 0 CharlieWallis(7) (John O'Shea) *midfield: rdn after 6th: wknd bef 3 out: t.o* **100/1**	23
	F		**The Humbel Monk (IRE)**[285] 9-11-5 0 JoeTizzard (Lucy Jones) *led tl fell 2nd* **80/1**	—
	P		**Fair Rome** 7-10-12 0 TomO'Brien (Peter Bowen) *a in rr: wl bhd fr 4th: t.o whn p.u after 7th* **66/1**	—

4m 58.9s (9.90) **Going Correction** +0.525s/f (Soft) **12 Ran SP% 114.3**
Speed ratings (Par 105): **101,100,93,93,92 91,75,72,61,60 —,—**
toteswingers:1&2 £7.90, 2&3 £41.10, 1&3 £28.30 CSF £24.15 TOTE £5.70: £2.70, £2.20, £6.20; EX 31.20.
Owner Dr V M G Ferguson **Bred** Highfort Stud **Trained** Withycombe, Somerset
■ Stewards' Enquiry : Richard Johnson one-day ban: used whip with excessive frequency (Feb 10)
FOCUS
The first pair came a long way clear in this first division of the 2m4f maiden. Ordinary form, rated through the winner and third to their marks. The third-last flight was bypassed on the final circuit.
NOTEBOOK
Doctor Foxtrot(IRE) belatedly got his head in front at the 12th attempt under very strong handling from Richard Johnson. He ran as well as ever when equipped with first-time blinkers in a handicap at Sandown on his previous outing last year and a reproduction of that form proved good enough. It's not hard to see why he wears blinkers, but he deserves extra credit here as he was badly hampered at the second. He should pay his way back in handicaps. (tchd 7-1)
Rangitoto(IRE) ◆, a notable market drifter, was an impressive winner of an Irish point in this month last year. He took it up going strongly around four out and went clear off the home turn. However, he idled badly going to two out, and by the time he picked up again when the winner came at him it was too late. He would have very likely scored had his rider held onto him for longer and he looks a nice horse in the making. (op 10-3)
Jump Up got badly outpaced before the home turn, but was eating up the ground late on and this was a step back in the right direction. He helps set the level and looks well worth a chance back over further. Official explanation: jockey said gelding hung badly (tchd 40-1)
Charming Lad(IRE) was gambled on to improve on his Plumpton second 25 days earlier, but he was laboured from three out and probably wants better ground. (op 5-2 tchd 2-1)
Mr Moss(IRE), a good-ground point winner prior to joining connections last year, caught the eye getting into the race late on and should come on a bundle. (op 25-1)
Fiddledee(IRE), up in trip, is one to look out for in handicaps in due course. (op 16-1 tchd 20-1)
Lucky Landing(IRE), who handled heavy ground when winning his bumper in November, was disappointing on this hurdling debut and he now has a bit to prove. (op 11-4)

3762 KOMATSU MINING MAIDEN HURDLE (DIV II) (10 hdls) 2m 4f
2:25 (2:25) (Class 4) 4-Y-0+ **£2,276** (£668; £334; £166)

Form				RPR
	1		**Storming Gale (IRE)**[312] 5-11-5 0 JasonMaguire (Donald McCain) *trckd ldr to 4th: styd prom: led appr 2 out: sn qcknd clr: easily* **6/1**	120+
2	2	3 ½	**Alla Svelta (IRE)**[86] 2137 5-11-5 0 PaulMoloney (Evan Williams) *hld up bhd ldrs: wnt 2nd and rdn after 2 out: r.o flat: no ch w wnr* **5/1**[3]	110+
3223	3	6	**Zakatal**[19] 3454 5-11-5 120 (bt) RichardJohnson (Philip Hobbs) *a.p: trckd ldr 4th: led 7th: hdd appr 2 out: sn rdn and one pce* **10/3**[2]	104
35	4	3 ¼	**Nemo Spirit (IRE)**[14] 3528 6-11-5 0 (t) SamThomas (Tim Vaughan) *led to 7th: rdn and one pce fr 3 out: hld in 4th whn mstke last* **15/2**	105+
/0-4	5	8	**Don't Turn Bach (IRE)**[71] 2454 7-11-5 0 HarrySkelton (Paul Nicholls) *hld up in rr: hdwy 6th: sn trcking ldrs: rdn and wknd appr 2 out* **9/4**[1]	96+
000	6	6	**Whispering Jack**[12] 3556 6-11-2 0 PeterToole(3) (Charlie Mann) *in tch: shkn up 3 out: sn one pce* **40/1**	89
04/1	7	9	**Just Cloudy**[27] 3259 7-11-0 0 RachaelGreen(5) (Anthony Honeyball) *racd wd towards rr: hit 2nd: nt fluent 5th: hdwy u.p 7th: wknd 3 out* **10/1**	81
00	8	6	**Little Frano (IRE)**[11] 3585 7-10-12 0 MichaelByrne(7) (Peter Bowen) *midfield: dropped in rr 4th: lost tch w ldrs after 7th* **100/1**	75
00	9	15	**Flying Award (IRE)**[26] 3295 7-10-12 0 MarkQuinlan(7) (Susan Gardner) *chsd ldrs tl wknd qckly after 7th: t.o* **100/1**	62
00	10	3 ¼	**Run To Fly (IRE)**[11] 3585 6-11-5 0 TomO'Brien (Peter Bowen) *in tch tl wknd after 7th: t.o* **100/1**	59
40/0	11	9	**Starlet Mandy (IRE)**[27] 3264 8-10-9 0 SamTwiston-Davies(3) (Nigel Twiston-Davies) *a in rr: lost tch after 7th: t.o* **50/1**	44
360	12	41	**Naughtyatiz (IRE)**[81] 2231 5-10-12 0 OliverDayman(7) (Debra Hamer) *a bhd: lost tch after 7th: t.o* **125/1**	14

5m 0.40s (11.40) **Going Correction** +0.525s/f (Soft) **12 Ran SP% 113.8**
Speed ratings (Par 105): **98,96,94,92,89 87,83,81,75,74 70,54**
CSF £34.57 TOTE £5.50: £1.40, £2.60, £1.20; EX 38.90.
Owner T G Leslie **Bred** Peter O'Keeffe **Trained** Cholmondeley, Cheshire
FOCUS
The second division of the 2m4f maiden and it was run at an ordinary gallop. The easy winner was value for further and can rate higher.
NOTEBOOK
Storming Gale(IRE) ◆ was last seen getting off the mark at the second time of asking between the flags in Ireland 312 days previously, and he ran out an impressive winner on this hurdling debut for his powerful new connections. There was a lot to like about the manner in which he went about his business and he had plenty in hand at the finish. It will be fascinating to see where he turns up next. (op 7-2)

Alla Svelta(IRE) ◆ posted another encouraging effort, and has now bumped into one on both his outings over hurdles. He still ran green when initially asked for his effort and perhaps this ground was soft enough for him, but he still saw out the extra distance well. He should be winning before long. (op 11-2)
Zakatal set the standard, but he has struggled to see out his race at every distance he has been tried over now and remains very hard to win with. (op 3-1)
Nemo Spirit(IRE), equipped with a first-time tongue tie, set out to make all back in trip but was done with from two out. He is not one to give up on with a view to going handicapping. (op 12-1)
Don't Turn Bach(IRE) was laboured on his hurdling debut in November, but he travelled much more sweetly this time and looked sure to be in the shake-up going to three out. He found nothing when push came to shove, though, and looks a horse that may have an issue. (op 11-4 tchd 3-1)
Whispering Jack shaped more encouragingly and wasn't given too hard a time when his chance had gone. He can surely find his feet when switching to handicaps. Official explanation: jockey said gelding hung left-handed (op 50-1)

3763 E.B.F./T.B.A. MARES' NOVICES' CHASE (18 fncs) 3m

3:00 (3:00) (Class 4) 5-Y-0+ **£3,903** (£1,146; £573; £286)

Form RPR
F-41 **1** **Kerada (FR)**[8] 3627 7-11-4 0 .... AndrewTinkler 136+
(Nicky Henderson) *hld up tl hdwy to trck ldr 3rd: hit 9th: led 13th: drew clr fr 4 out: eased flat* **4/11**[1]
0-25 **2** *21* **Cobbler's Queen (IRE)**[42] 2978 7-10-12 113 .... RichardJohnson 114
(Henry Daly) *led 1st: mstke 9th: hdd 13th: lft bhd by wnr fr 4 out: kpt on for mod 2nd* **7/1**[2]
1P36 **3** *16* **Identity Parade (IRE)**[42] 2978 7-10-12 115 .... JasonMaguire 101
(Donald McCain) *led to 1st: blnd 4th and sn dropped to rr: wnt mod 3rd 14th: sn rdn and wknd* **8/1**[3]
032F **4** *22* **Moorlands Teri**[19] 3435 8-10-7 0 .... (t) MrTomDavid(5) 89
(Tim Vaughan) *a in rr: j. slowly and reminders 4th: mstke 10th: slow again 12th: wknd and lost tch 14th: t.o* **8/1**[3]

6m 23.9s (0.90) **Going Correction** +0.30s/f (Yiel) 4 Ran SP% **108.0**
Speed ratings: **110,103,97,90**
CSF £3.44 TOTE £1.40; EX 3.40.
Owner Turf Club 2010 **Bred** E A R L La Croix Sonnet **Trained** Upper Lambourn, Berks

FOCUS
An uncompetitive mares' novices' chase. The easy winner is rated in line with her best hurdles form.

NOTEBOOK
Kerada(FR) made it 2-2 since embarking on a chase career with an easy success. The winner still has something to learn about jumping fences, but she only made her chase debut at Newbury eight days earlier and there is little doubt she can rate higher in this sphere. This also conclusively proves her stamina for the trip, which gives her more options, but the final of this series (2m6f110yds) will most probably be her big target. She finished third in the hurdle equivalent last season and needs one more run over fences to qualify. (tchd 1-3 and 2-5)
Cobbler's Queen(IRE) ran more encouragingly again, but was never going to stick with old rival Kerada, who is officially rated 9lb her superior over hurdles, in the home straight. She can be placed to strike in due course. (tchd 13-2)
Identity Parade(IRE) set out to make all, but some errant jumps saw her go backwards and she was in trouble a good way out. She needs more practice in this sphere. (op 9-1)
Moorlands Teri jumped worst of all and perhaps her fall at Chepstow 19 days earlier had taken its toll.

3764 JEFF'S FOLLY H'CAP HURDLE (12 hdls) 3m

3:35 (3:35) (Class 4) (0-110,109) 4-Y-0+ **£3,252** (£955; £477; £238)

Form RPR
0-0F **1** **Kaybeew**[44] 2949 6-11-4 104 .... SamTwiston-Davies(3) 112+
(Nigel Twiston-Davies) *in tch: hdwy 6th: hit 3 out: sn led: rdn appr last: hld on wl u.p* **14/1**
1216 **2** *1 ½* **The Ferbane Man (IRE)**[25] 3347 7-11-11 108 .... (p) RichardJohnson 113
(Tim Vaughan) *in tch: hdwy 7th: rdn to go 2nd 2 out: clsd on wnr appr last: no ex towards fin* **3/1**[2]
0222 **3** *12* **Filippo Lippi (IRE)**[27] 3260 6-11-3 103 .... RichieMcLernon(3) 98
(Jonjo O'Neill) *w ldrs: rdn bef 3 out: kpt on same pce fr 2 out* **5/1**[3]
114- **4** *¾* **Choumakeur (FR)**[546] 1095 9-10-8 96 .... (bt) CO'Farrell(5) 92+
(David Pipe) *prom: tended to run-in snatches: hit 8th: rdn bef 3 out: sn one pce* **2/1**[1]
U-32 **5** *1* **Corlande (IRE)**[64] 2610 11-11-12 109 .... (b) JasonMaguire 102
(Donald McCain) *led: rdn 9th: hdd after 3 out: wkng whn j.rt 2 out* **10/1**
614- **6** *20* **Amazing Valour (IRE)**[471] 1733 9-10-10 93 .... (b) TomO'Brien 67
(Peter Bowen) *in tch tl rdn and wknd 9th: t.o* **9/1**
102P **7** *34* **Tin Pot Man (IRE)**[24] 3370 5-11-5 109 .... (t) MrJEngland(7) 53
(Evan Williams) *prom tl lost pl 4th: rdn 7th: t.o fr 9th* **11/1**
0U46 **P** **Stafford Charlie**[64] 2609 5-10-5 95 .... (v) CharlieWallis(7) —
(John O'Shea) *s.s: hld up in last pl: lost tch 8th: t.o whn p.u bef next* **28/1**

6m 13.4s (26.40) **Going Correction** +0.525s/f (Soft) 8 Ran SP% **112.5**
Speed ratings (Par 105): **77,76,72,72,71 65,53,—**
CSF £55.29 CT £243.19 TOTE £34.30: £6.70, £2.30, £1.10; EX 89.70.
Owner Roberts Green Whittall-Williams Savidge **Bred** C E Whiteley **Trained** Naunton, Gloucs

FOCUS
This moderate staying handicap was run at an ordinary gallop and the first five were closely bunched turning for home. The first pair drew clear from the penultimate flight and the winner showed big improvement.

NOTEBOOK
Kaybeew got the better of The Ferbane Man in a battling finish to score. This was a welcome return to form and a deserved first success over hurdles for the 6-y-o, who had fallen at the last hurdle on his previous outing. It was also a very welcome winner for the yard. Official explanation: trainer said, regarding apparent improvement in form, that the gelding had benefited from the step up in trip. (op 11-1)
The Ferbane Man(IRE) responded gamely to pressure from three out and momentarily looked like getting on top on the run-in, but the winner pulled out that bit extra at the business end. He is currently rated 8lb lower over hurdles and is a likeable performer. (op 4-1 tchd 5-2)
Filippo Lippi(IRE), 3lb higher, began to feel the pinch rounding the home bend and was done with before two out. He remains a maiden. (op 9-2)
Choumakeur(FR) was returning from a 546-day layoff, but hails from a stable with few peers when getting one ready after an absence. He may have enjoyed more of a test, but the run really looked as if it would do him good. (op 9-4 tchd 5-2)
Corlande(IRE) made a bold bid from the front and could come on for the run. However, he is not easy to win with. (op 17-2 tchd 8-1)

3765 BARRY WALTERS CATERING NOVICES' H'CAP CHASE (17 fncs) 2m 5f

4:05 (4:05) (Class 4) (0-115,113) 5-Y-0+ **£3,252** (£955; £477; £238)

Form RPR
00 **1** **As De Fer (FR)**[26] 3299 5-11-5 110 .... SamThomas 124+
(Anthony Honeyball) *led: hit 1st: hdd 3rd: clsd on ldr 11th: led bef 4 out: sn clr: 10 l up whn lft wl in command 2 out: eased flat* **10/1**
0/6F **2** *27* **One And All (IRE)**[42] 2980 8-9-11 89 .... MattGriffiths(5) 76
(Nigel Hawke) *in tch: dropped in rr 12th: t.o next: remote 5th whn mstke 3 out: styd on fr next: wnt poor 2nd last* **15/2**
-4U3 **3** *4* **Four Strong Winds (IRE)**[25] 3339 7-11-8 112 .... RichieMcLernon(3) 95
(Jonjo O'Neill) *in tch: mstkes 3rd and 5th: shkn up bef 4 out: no imp on ldrs: briefly lft in poor 2nd after 2 out* **9/1**
4-02 **4** *17* **Arctic Ben (IRE)**[63] 2635 7-11-12 113 .... RichardJohnson 81
(Henry Daly) *racd keenly tl hdwy to ld 3rd: sn 7 l clr: reeled in 11th: hdd bef 4 out: wknd qckly* **4/1**[2]
0-44 **5** *18* **Noble Aran (IRE)**[28] 3226 7-10-2 92 .... SamTwiston-Davies(3) 44
(Nigel Twiston-Davies) *in rr: nt fluent: labouring fr 6th: t.o fr 13th* **5/1**[3]
3322 **U** **Plunkett (IRE)**[30] 3157 8-11-9 110 .... PaulMoloney 116
(Evan Williams) *towards rr: in tch: hdwy 12th: chsd wnr bef 4 out: 10 l down and hld whn blnd bdly 2 out: rdr unbalanced and eventually uns* **11/8**[1]

5m 45.1s (15.10) **Going Correction** +0.30s/f (Yiel)
WFA 5 from 7yo+ 4lb 6 Ran SP% **109.6**
Speed ratings: **83,72,71,64,57 —**
toteswingers:1&2 £8.80, 2&3 £8.80, 1&3 £4.80 CSF £70.19 TOTE £8.50: £2.20, £3.10; EX 59.80.
Owner Midd Shire Racing **Bred** Didier Leviel **Trained** Seaborough, Dorset

FOCUS
A tricky handicap, run at a sound early gallop, although the time was moderate. The winner did it well but this was not much of a race.

NOTEBOOK
As De Fer(FR) went to the front going strongly rounding the home turn and could have been called the winner soon after. He ultimately scored easily and this was a massive improvement on his chasing debut. A hike in the handicap is now inevitable, but this former French winner remains unexposed. He would also have to be of serious interest if turned out under a penalty, as he had anything but a hard race. (op 12-1)

One And All(IRE), who attracted support, didn't look a straightforward ride but was doing his best work towards the finish. (op 16-1)

Four Strong Winds(IRE) failed to convince he wanted this step up in trip. (op 7-1 tchd 10-1)

Arctic Ben(IRE) did his chances of getting home over this far little good by again running with the choke out. (tchd 7-2 and 9-2)

Noble Aran(IRE) was beaten a mile out and remains one to swerve. (op 9-2 tchd 6-1)

Plunkett(IRE), second again over the C&D last month, was heavily backed but was well held in second prior to unseating some way after the penultimate fence. His rider didn't look happy with him as he tried to make up ground nearing the final bend and perhaps something was amiss, but the ground was probably not for him in any case. (op 5-4 tchd Evens)

3766 BURCHELL'S TRANSPORT STANDARD OPEN NATIONAL HUNT FLAT RACE 2m

4:40 (4:42) (Class 5) 4-6-Y-0 **£1,712** (£499; £249)

Form RPR
1 **Ballytober**[96] 5-11-4 0 .... RichardJohnson 108+
(Philip Hobbs) *set mod pce: jnd 4f out: rdn 3f out: styd on strly ins fnl f* **2/1**[1]
2 *3* **Grand Vision (IRE)** 5-11-4 0 .... TimmyMurphy 104+
(Don Cantillon) *trckd ldrs: pushed along and sltly outpcd over 3f out: styd on wl to go 2nd ins fnl f wout threatening wnr* **10/3**[2]
3 *1 ½* **Karinga Dancer** 5-11-4 0 .... HarrySkelton 103
(Paul Nicholls) *trckd wnr: chal 4f out: hrd drvn 2f out: no ex and lost 2nd ins fnl f* **11/1**
4 *3* **Allerton (IRE)** 4-10-4 0 .... SamTwiston-Davies(3) 89
(Nigel Twiston-Davies) *hld up in rr: hdwy 3f out: styd on same pce fnl 2f* **6/1**[3]
4-2 **5** *1 ¾* **Forever Waining (IRE)**[77] 2328 5-11-4 0 .... TomO'Brien 98
(Peter Bowen) *chsd ldrs: rdn over 3f out: sn one pce* **8/1**
6 *5* **Ballyrock (IRE)**[263] 5-11-4 0 .... SamThomas 95
(Tim Vaughan) *in tch: jnd ldrs 1/2-way: rdn and wknd 5f out* **8/1**
6 **7** *14* **Benheir (IRE)**[258] 319 5-11-4 0 .... AndrewTinkler 79
(Henry Daly) *midfield: hdwy 7f out: rdn 4f out: sn wknd* **20/1**
26- **8** *7* **Cody Wyoming**[327] 4429 5-11-4 0 .... JoeTizzard 72
(Heather Main) *hld up in rr: rdn over 4f out: sn wknd* **12/1**
06 **9** *12* **Oscar Sierra (IRE)**[79] 2295 5-10-13 0 .... MrTomDavid(5) 60
(Tim Vaughan) *hld up: wknd over 5f out: t.o* **33/1**

3m 53.7s (10.30) **Going Correction** +0.525s/f (Soft)
WFA 4 from 5yo 11lb 9 Ran SP% **116.6**
Speed ratings: **95,93,92,91,90 87,80,77,71**
toteswingers:1&2 £1.80, 2&3 £10.70, 1&3 £11.10 totesuper7: Win: Not won. Place: Not won. CSF £8.63 TOTE £3.80: £2.00, £1.30, £4.20; EX 11.80.

Owner Mrs Diana L Whateley **Bred** Mrs C J Berry **Trained** Withycombe, Somerset

FOCUS
This probably wasn't a bad bumper, but it was run at a crawl and most proved keen as a result. The winner should go on to rate higher.

NOTEBOOK
Ballytober, an Irish maiden point winner in October, was purchased for £85,000 and made just about all to make a winning start for connections. He was ideally placed when things began to get serious in the home straight, and responded to pressure when it mattered. His dam is from the family of Liberthine and Long Run, and he ought to come on for the run. A longer trip will be required once he goes jumping. (op 5-2 tchd 15-8)

Grand Vision(IRE) was well backed and hails from a yard that is always to be respected in this sphere. He was badly caught out by the steady gallop, however, and looks sure to win one of these granted more of a test. (op 4-1)

Karinga Dancer, said to be very backward by his leading trainer, only cracked inside the final 2f and posted an encouraging debut. He ought to come on plenty for the experience. (op 9-1 tchd 12-1)

Allerton(IRE), related to numerous winners over jumps, was doing some good late work and she is another that should improve for the initial experience. (op 8-1)

Forever Waining(IRE), second at Ludlow last time out, failed to pick up that well on this ground but still helps to set the level of the form. (op 13-2)

T/Plt: £1,027.80 to a £1 stake. Pool of £60,685.99 - 43.10 winning tickets. T/Qpdt: £252.80 to a £1 stake. Pool of £4,886.41 - 14.30 winning tickets. RL

[3563]WARWICK (L-H)

Thursday, January 27

OFFICIAL GOING: Good to soft (soft in places)

Wind: moderate against Weather: overcast and chilly

3767 RACING UK JUVENILE MAIDEN HURDLE (8 hdls) 2m

1:10 (1:10) (Class 4) 4-Y-O **£2,602** (£764; £382; £190)

Form RPR

525 **1** **Dhaafer**[21] 3401 4-11-0 117 RobertThornton 114+
(Alan King) *prom: 2nd and rdn 3 out: led bef next: styd on stoutly flat* **5/1**[2]

2 *5* **Head Hunted**[110] 4-11-0 0 PaddyBrennan 108+
(Charlie Mann) *prom: led 5th: rdn and hung rt bef 2 out: sn hdd: btn whn hit last* **8/1**[3]

34 **3** *9* **Kitty Koo (IRE)**[17] 3484 4-10-2 97 LeeEdwards(5) 92
(Tony Carroll) *chsd ldrs: rdn 3 out: outpcd by ldng pair bef 2 out where wnt modest 3rd: kpt on wout chalng: j.lft last* **66/1**

4 *12* **Sir Pitt**[115] 4-11-0 0 DarylJacob 87
(Alison Thorpe) *prom: lost pl after 3rd: no ch w ldrs after 3 out: 15 l 5th whn nt fluent next* **20/1**

0 **5** *6* **Blinka Me**[47] 2882 4-11-0 0 DenisO'Regan 82
(Alex Hales) *plld hrd in ld: hdd and j. slowly 5th: wknd next* **66/1**

2 **6** *shd* **Paintball (IRE)**[21] 3401 4-11-0 0 TomScudamore 84
(Charlie Longsdon) *t.k.h: pressed ldrs: rdn after 3 out: dropped out tamely bef next* **6/5**[1]

7 *9* **True To Form (IRE)**[117] 4-11-0 0 GerardTumelty 74
(George Baker) *chsd ldrs: pushed along 4th: lost tch 3 out* **5/1**[2]

5 **8** *7* **Togiak (IRE)**[14] 3526 4-11-0 0 HaddenFrost 67
(David Pipe) *midfield: pushed along whn mstke 5th: sn struggling: t.o* **12/1**

0 **9** *5* **Terra Bleu (IRE)**[19] 3443 4-10-9 0 MrMMO'Connor(5) 63
(Milton Harris) *a bhd: labouring bef 4th: t.o 3 out* **150/1**

60 **10** *10* **Tild'Or Du Granit (FR)**[52] 2824 4-10-0 0 RobertKirk(7) 47
(James Evans) *a wl bhd: labouring bef 4th: t.o 3 out* **150/1**

0 **11** *6* **Jupiter Rex (FR)**[53] 2797 4-11-0 0 AidanColeman 48
(Venetia Williams) *cumbersme: last whn j. bdly rt 3rd: continued wl bhd: t.o 3 out* **66/1**

06 **12** *3/4* **Langley**[29] 3194 4-10-11 0 (t) MichaelMurphy(3) 48
(Pat Murphy) *midfield: rdn 5th: sn fdd: t.o* **80/1**

13 *13* **Mutanaker**[126] 4-11-0 0 FelixDeGiles 36
(Ed de Giles) *bhd fr 4th: t.o 3 out* **25/1**

20 **U** **Molon Labe (IRE)**[21] 3401 4-11-0 0 JamesReveley —
(Tom Tate) *j. slowly in midfield: wknd 5th: remote 9th whn j. violently lft and uns rdr 2 out* **28/1**

3m 53.8s (-2.70) **Going Correction** -0.05s/f (Good) **14** Ran SP% **116.7**
Speed ratings: **104,101,97,91,88 87,83,79,77,72 69,69,62,—**
toteswingers:1&2 £17.40, 2&3 £78.80, 1&3 £8.40 CSF £40.01 TOTE £7.10: £1.90, £2.40, £5.40; EX 37.80.
Owner Simon Munir **Bred** Shadwell Estate Company Limited **Trained** Barbury Castle, Wilts

FOCUS

Some interesting newcomers made this look a race full of potential, but none of them came up to scratch and an experienced sort proved too good. The winner can probably rate higher over further.

NOTEBOOK

Dhaafer, already with an official mark of 117, had shown more than enough to win an ordinary contest, but this seemed a better performance than previous attempts. He showed an enthusiastic attitude once in front and can win again when given a test. (op 9-2)

Head Hunted, a 1m6f winner for David Simcock in August, attracted market support and ran a cracker on his hurdling debut. A leggy sort, he got tired in the latter stages but stayed on well enough to suggest he will have no trouble landing something similar. (op 14-1)

Kitty Koo(IRE) should easily be a better hurdler than she was on the Flat, but may need further and/or a stiffer course to collect a victory. (op 100-1)

Sir Pitt, twice a winner for John Gosden at Southwell on the Flat, is a staying type and kept on well after getting behind. (op 16-1)

Paintball(IRE) had finished comfortably in front of Dhaafer at Huntingdon, so this was disappointing. However, he is worth another chance, especially on quicker ground. Official explanation: jockey said gelding stopped quickly (op 6-4 tchd 11-10)

True To Form(IRE), who won four races in a row for Sir Mark Prescott on the AW in the autumn at about 1m, pulled much too hard from the outset to have anything left at the end of the contest. His trainer indicated beforehand that this race was more about education for his horse, and better can be expected in the future. (op 9-2 tchd 11-2)

3768 MOLSON COORS CUSTOMERS H'CAP CHASE (20 fncs) 3m 2f

1:40 (1:40) (Class 4) (0-110,115) 5-Y-0+ **£2,927** (£859; £429; £214)

Form RPR

02-F **1** **Shaking Hands (IRE)**[70] 2483 7-11-10 106 (bt) TomScudamore 127+
(David Pipe) *prom: led 10th: jnd 14th: hdd and blnd 3 out: drvn up on inner to ld bef next: cajoled clr after: all out* **7/2**[1]

1443 **2** *10* **Digger Gets Lucky (IRE)**[23] 3391 9-11-9 105 LiamTreadwell 117+
(Nick Gifford) *midfield: hit 7th: hdwy 11th: jnd wnr 14th: lft 3 l clr briefly 3 out: rdn and hdd bef next: sn outpcd but remained wl clr of rest* **9/1**

5253 **3** *20* **Arnold Layne (IRE)**[27] 3263 12-11-5 101 AndrewThornton 93
(Caroline Bailey) *chsd ldrs: rdn bef 14th: outpcd next: plodding on in 27 l 3rd 2 out* **9/2**[2]

2-05 **4** *5* **Tuskar Rock (FR)**[19] 3450 8-11-5 101 AidanColeman 89
(Venetia Williams) *chsd ldrs: rdn befe 14th: sn struggling* **16/1**

P-44 **5** *10* **Pancake (FR)**[53] 2794 8-11-12 108 (b) RhysFlint 87
(Philip Hobbs) *midfield but j. modly and nvr looking happy: lost tch bef 14th: t.o* **12/1**

0320 **6** *14* **Corredor Sun (USA)**[28] 3226 5-10-7 94 (p) DavidEngland 55
(Nigel Twiston-Davies) *prom: mstke 6th: rdn bef 14th: 3rd but fading whn hit 3 out: t.o* **16/1**

3552 **7** *2 1/4* **Kitley Hassle**[53] 2794 9-11-6 102 (b) HaddenFrost 66
(James Frost) *midfield: outpcd 10th: t.o fr 14th* **17/2**

P4PP **8** *17* **Fourpointone**[14] 3530 10-10-0 82 (p) SamJones 31
(Michael Scudamore) *sn labouring: t.o fr 10th* **25/1**

160F **9** *44* **Chico Time (IRE)**[7] 3646 10-11-2 98 (p) MarkGrant —
(Norma Twomey) *j.rt and immediately lost tch: t.o fr 8th: plugged rnd eventually* **25/1**

1P/6 **P** **Sexy Rexy (IRE)**[84] 2171 10-11-10 106 PaddyBrennan —
(Nigel Twiston-Davies) *nt fluent and sn struggling bdly: t.o whn crashed over 11th and p.u* **16/1**

P1-1 **P** **Kathleens Pride (IRE)**[79] 2284 11-11-8 104 CharliePoste —
(Robin Dickin) *sn bhd: t.o 7th: p.u 9th* **7/1**

/600 **P** **Jayjay Valentine**[24] 3366 8-11-1 97 DenisO'Regan —
(Victor Dartnall) *led at fast pce and sn had plenty in trble: nt fluent 9th: hit 10th and hdd: 6th and fading whn blnd 13th: t.o and p.u next* **13/2**[3]

6m 45.5s (-7.20) **Going Correction** -0.15s/f (Good)
WFA 5 from 7yo+ 5lb **12** Ran SP% **119.8**
Speed ratings: **105,101,95,94,91 86,86,80,67,— —,—**
toteswingers:1&2 £12.30, 2&3 £5.00, 1&3 £4.40 CSF £36.02 CT £144.40 TOTE £4.50: £1.20, £4.30, £2.00; EX 54.50.
Owner Brocade Racing **Bred** Robert McCarthy **Trained** Nicholashayne, Devon

FOCUS

This was run at a good gallop. Little bar the first two got into the race with a winning chance. The winner is looking progressive.

NOTEBOOK

Shaking Hands(IRE) and the runner-up bounded clear from a relatively early stage. Plenty of plaudits go to the winner, who showed lots of courage here after lying winded for a while last time when falling at Wincanton. He had proven stamina and kept plugging away to regain the lead after being headed. (op 3-1)

Digger Gets Lucky(IRE) didn't have a lot of staying form in his record, so it wasn't surprising that he didn't get home as well as his rival. That said, this effort proves he does stay extended distances, which should given connections more options. (op 12-1)

Arnold Layne(IRE) was a remote third. (op 11-2)

Pancake(FR) showed no interest from an early stage but was made to get round under a strong ride from Rhys Flint. He is well handicapped but needs to show more enthusiasm. (op 10-1 tchd 14-1)

Kathleens Pride(IRE) Official explanation: jockey said gelding never travelled; vet said gelding was found to have a slightly irregular heart beat (op 8-1)

Jayjay Valentine, making his chasing debut under rules, set a strong pace. He jumped quickly and efficiently for a circuit but soon got tired and dropped out once joined. (op 8-1)

3769 100% BRITISH BARLEY H'CAP CHASE (12 fncs) 2m

2:15 (2:16) (Class 4) (0-110,109) 5-Y-0+ **£2,927** (£859; £429; £214)

Form RPR

33F4 **1** **Folie A Deux (IRE)**[82] 2217 9-11-12 109 (t) APMcCoy 113
(Dr Richard Newland) *rn in snatches: j. deliberately 5th and lost pl: last whn j. slowly 8th and lost tch: drvn along on inner bef 2 out where 7 l down: stl had to pass five at last where fnlly responding to urgings: led 50yds out: amazing ride* **9/4**[1]

4563 **2** *1/2* **Earl Grez (FR)**[14] 3524 6-10-11 101 KyleJames(7) 104
(Philip Kirby) *tended to jump and edge rt: prom: rdn 3 out: drvn ahd after next: kpt on tl ct cl home* **5/1**

0FP5 **3** *2* **Playing With Fire (IRE)**[77] 2329 7-11-6 103 CharliePoste 106+
(Robin Dickin) *pressed ldrs: rdn and looked wkng 3 out: rallied bef last where ev ch briefly: nt qckn flat* **7/2**[2]

016 **4** *1* **Roc De Guye (FR)**[64] 2605 6-10-2 92 RobertKirk(7) 92
(James Evans) *hld up in tch: effrt 3 out: rdn next: cl 3rd 2 out: 4th at last: nt qckn after* **17/2**

3-51 **5** *3 1/4* **Jeczmien (POL)**[9] 3612 8-11-4 101 7ex (t) LiamTreadwell 99
(Nick Gifford) *led: j.rt 4th: hrd pressed and nt fluent 3 out: hdd after next: remained w ch tl wknd flat* **9/2**[3]

U21 **6** *3 1/4* **Carrig An Uisce (IRE)**[79] 2294 10-11-1 103 (p) IanPopham(5) 98
(Anna Brooks) *hld up in tch: effrt 3 out: tried to chal next but nvr looked wnr: hit last and wknd* **10/1**

4m 10.4s (4.80) **Going Correction** -0.15s/f (Good) **6** Ran SP% **107.5**
Speed ratings: **82,81,80,80,78 77**
toteswingers:1&2 £3.70, 2&3 £4.20, 1&3 £3.90 CSF £12.61 TOTE £3.70: £2.90, £2.90; EX 9.70.
Owner G Carstairs **Bred** Lord James Beresford **Trained** Claines, Worcs

FOCUS

An extraordinary race due to the exceptional riding ability of Tony McCoy and proof, if any was needed, of why he is the master of his profession. Ordinary form and they finished in a heap.

NOTEBOOK

Folie A Deux(IRE), having his first start for this trainer, likes to get on with things but was dropped in (as per the jockey's instructions) and started to struggle down the back straight, so much so that he dropped quite a few lengths off the back of his rivals and was matched at 1000 for £142 on Betfair. However, the champion failed to give up and got his mount back to have a chance two out. It still took plenty of strength to get Folie A Deux to the front, but he did so in time and claimed a remarkable victory. (tchd 11-4)

Earl Grez(FR) was looking to build on his performance last time and did so, but bumped into a jockey in no mood to lose. (op 11-2)

Playing With Fire(IRE) showed plenty of ability on her first run over fences, and shaped as though a step up in trip should be within her range. (op 5-1)

Roc De Guye(FR), off since a bad run at Chepstow in November, stayed on off a low weight and can make an impact in a lesser contest. (op 11-1 tchd 14-1)

Jeczmien(POL), raised 7lb for winning at Folkestone, was allowed an easy lead but couldn't respond when the pack closed in. (op 7-2 tchd 3-1)

Carrig An Uisce(IRE), making his chasing debut, got tired but wasn't beaten a long way. (op 9-1 tchd 17-2)

3770 MEYERTIMBER.COM NOVICES' CHASE (17 fncs) 2m 4f 110y

2:50 (2:50) (Class 3) 5-Y-0+ **£4,553** (£1,337; £668)

Form RPR

10-1 **1** **The Minack (IRE)**[19] 3451 7-11-4 0 NickScholfield 146+
(Paul Nicholls) *settled last: clsd and lft 2nd at 12th: shkn up to ld 2 out: rdn and rather idle flat: a looked best* **1/4**[1]

-234 **2** *1 1/4* **Balzaccio (FR)**[29] 3193 6-10-12 135 RobertThornton 136
(Alan King) *racd in 2nd pl: mstke 11th: chal and lft in ld next: rdn 3 out: hdd next: ev ch whn hit last: kpt on but hld after* **4/1**[2]

-5P3 **3** *111* **Lord Generous**[25] 3342 7-10-12 0 (p) PaddyBrennan —
(Nigel Twiston-Davies) *led and 5 l clr early: j.rt 9th: reminder after 10th: rdn whn terrible mstke 12th and hdd: continued t.o: climbed next: trotted in* **8/1**[3]

5m 15.2s (-5.80) **Going Correction** -0.15s/f (Good) **3** Ran SP% **111.1**
Speed ratings: **105,104,—**
CSF £1.90 TOTE £1.20; EX 1.90.
Owner C G Roach **Bred** Kenilworth House Stud **Trained** Ditcheat, Somerset

FOCUS

This was a two-horse race from some way out. The Minack is rated to his hurdles mark.

NOTEBOOK

The Minack(IRE), who had a handler down at the start, pull out plenty to remain unbeaten over fences. The suspicion is that the winner is much better than the result suggests, as he was dossing in front. His connections plan to take in the Reynoldstown Novices' Chase on the 19th February at Ascot before assessing whether he should be aimed at Cheltenham. The RSA Chase is the obvious target but he also appeals as one to keep an eye on for a handicap at the festival, especially if headgear was tried, because a big field and strong pace may ideally suit. (op 2-5)

Balzaccio(FR) deserves a victory over fences but, considering his mark, may need to stay in novice company to collect one. (op 3-1 tchd 9-2)

Lord Generous was never really travelling with any fluency before making a shocking blunder at the 12th. (op 11-1 tchd 14-1)

3771 MOLSON COORS H'CAP HURDLE (12 hdls) 3m 1f
3:25 (3:25) (Class 3) (0-130,122) 4-Y-0+ **£3,903** (£1,146; £573; £286)

Form RPR

0100 1 **Thelobstercatcher**[19] 3440 7-11-8 **121**....................(v[1]) DonalDevereux(3) 128+
(Peter Bowen) *cl up: led 5th: drew clr on bit bef 2 out: unchal after: racd awkwardly flat: eased fnl 100yds* **25/1**

03U2 2 2 ½ **Deep Pockets (IRE)**[17] 3483 12-10-13 **114**........................ IanPopham(5) 115
(Caroline Keevil) *led tl 5th: remained prom: rdn 3 out: outpcd in 7 l 2nd whn hit next: flattered by proximity to wnr* **14/1**

P-40 3 2 ½ **Saphire Night**[64] 2606 10-11-2 **119**................................(t) JakeGreenall(7) 118
(Tom George) *trckd ldrs: 4th and rdn and outpcd 3 out: styd on fr next: hung lft: unable to chal* **33/1**

3424 4 7 **Father Probus**[30] 3153 5-11-4 **114**.................................... PaddyBrennan 106
(Nigel Twiston-Davies) *plld hrd and several positions and looked awkward ride: effrt 8th: disp 2nd and hrd drvn 3 out: wknd next* **22/1**

/5-0 5 21 **Mr Bennett (IRE)**[44] 2946 8-11-7 **117**........................... TomScudamore 95
(David Pipe) *hld up and bhd: effrt after 7th: drvn next: sn outpcd: 25 l 5th 2 out* **17/2**

0-21 6 9 **Full Of Joy (IRE)**[63] 2630 6-11-7 **117**...................................... APMcCoy 92
(Jonjo O'Neill) *racd wd: hld up in bunch: short-lived effrt 8th: btn after next: t.o* **2/1**[1]

-552 7 15 **Outlaw Tom (IRE)**[44] 2941 7-11-2 **112**..........................(b) DenisO'Regan 64
(Alex Hales) *nvr bttr than midfield: drvn and lost tch bef 8th: t.o 3 out* **7/1**[2]

512- 8 11 **Broughton Green (IRE)**[335] 4282 10-11-10 **120**...................... RhysFlint 62
(Jim Old) *nvr bttr than midfield: hit 8th: rdn and sn btn: t.o 3 out* **28/1**

PPPP 9 23 **Tisfreetdream (IRE)**[43] 2955 10-11-7 **117**..........................(p) TomSiddall 38
(Peter Pritchard) *midfield: drvn 8th: lost tch and j. slowly next: t.o 3 out* **50/1**

102 10 2 ½ **Silver Accord (IRE)**[43] 2955 8-11-10 **120**........................ LeightonAspell 39
(Oliver Sherwood) *bhd: rdn and lost tch bef 8th: t.o 3 out* **10/1**

/0P- P **Gritti Palace (IRE)**[357] 3843 11-10-3 **99**............................ CharliePoste —
(John Upson) *prom briefly: sn downed tools and last by 5th: t.o 7th: bumbled on tl fnlly p.u after 3 out* **50/1**

0222 F **Vivarini**[7] 2574 7-11-6 **116**.. RobertThornton —
(John O'Shea) *midfield: 10 l 7th and outpcd whn fell 3 out* **12/1**

P **Danderry (IRE)**[421] 2659 7-11-10 **120**.................................... AidanColeman —
(Lawney Hill) *dropped in rr and rdn after 7th: lost tch bef next: t.o and p.u 2 out* **15/2**[3]

/231 P **The Gripper (IRE)**[14] 3529 7-9-13 **102**.......................... PeterCarberry(7) —
(Rachel Hobbs) *prom: mstke 4th: sn p.u: fatally injured* **8/1**

6m 21.4s (-6.10) **Going Correction** -0.05s/f (Good) **14** Ran SP% **121.2**
Speed ratings (Par 107): **107,106,105,103,96 93,88,85,77,77 —,—,—,—**
toteswingers:1&2 £60.20, 2&3 £60.20, 1&3 £30.10 CSF £317.19 CT £11018.91 TOTE £27.30: £6.80, £3.90, £9.70; EX 443.50.
Owner G A Moore **Bred** J H Ray, M Mulholland & A M Varmen **Trained** Little Newcastle, Pembrokes

FOCUS
A fair handicap. The easy winner is rated back to the level of his Chepstow form.

NOTEBOOK
Thelobstercatcher, an unpredictable type, was wearing a visor for the first time. Held up early, he cruised through to take up the running plenty early enough and rarely looked like being caught. He started to idle from two out but had enough in hand to hang on, clearly relishing the testing ground. Official explanation: trainer's rep said, regarding apparent improvement in form, that the gelding appeared to be suited by wearing a first time visor.
Deep Pockets(IRE), who finished over 50l behind Thelobstercatcher at Chepstow in early November, ran well last time and gives the contest a fairly reliable marker. He raced prominently and plugged on for pressure. (tchd 12-1)
Saphire Night, still above her highest winning mark, was another to stay on at the one pace without ever threatening to win.
Father Probus, making his handicap debut, wasn't disgraced but didn't get seriously involved. (tchd 20-1 and 25-1)
Mr Bennett(IRE), making his handicap debut, got behind but stayed on when it was all too late. He might do better in staying chases in due course. (op 15-2)
Full Of Joy(IRE), raised 12lb for a narrow victory at Newbury, didn't always jump fluently and made little impact. Official explanation: jockey had no explanation for the poor form shown (op 5-2 tchd 11-4)
Danderry(IRE) Official explanation: vet said gelding had mucus coming from its nose

3772 WARWICK RACECOURSE FOR CONFERENCES H'CAP CHASE (17 fncs) 2m 4f 110y
3:55 (3:59) (Class 4) (0-110,110) 5-Y-0+ **£2,927** (£859; £429; £214)

Form RPR

-4PF 1 **Sawpit Supreme**[21] 3402 9-10-8 **92**................................. AidanColeman 100+
(Venetia Williams) *bhd: nt fluent 8th: effrt and rdn after 3 out: wnt 2nd bef next: styd on gamely to ld fnl 100yds: edgd clr* **10/1**

1U56 2 3 **Double The Trouble**[27] 3263 10-11-8 **106**.......................... NickScholfield 112
(Andy Turnell) *racd keenly in ld: mstke 13th: rdn 2 out: hdd and nt qckn fnl 100yds* **15/2**

-145 3 7 **Brimham Boy**[71] 2453 9-11-7 **105**.................................(t) WarrenMarston 106
(Martin Keighley) *racd keenly in 2nd: mstke 7th: lost 2nd and blnd 13th: btn bef 2 out: plugged on gamely* **6/1**[3]

2323 4 ¾ **Prophete De Guye (FR)**[77] 2324 8-11-9 **107**.................. LeightonAspell 107
(James Evans) *plld hrd in rr: mstkes: hdwy 12th: outpcd and mstke 3 out: kpt on to dispute 7 l 3rd at last: no ex* **4/1**[2]

0-12 5 10 **Oscar Prairie (IRE)**[24] 3378 6-11-12 **110**.................(t) WayneHutchinson 99
(Warren Greatrex) *j. in v novicey fashion: chsd ldrs: rdn bef 11th: lost tch and mstke 14th* **11/4**[1]

0303 6 14 **Global Flyer**[22] 3394 7-11-12 **110**................................. AndrewThornton 87
(Caroline Bailey) *j. slowly 1st and 9th: midfield: struggling fr 12th* **14/1**

F63 7 1 ¾ **Gentleman Anshan (IRE)**[66] 2588 7-11-0 **105**... MissHannahWatson(7) 80
(Rosemary Gasson) *t.k.h in rr: qckcnd 11th: wnt 2nd and chal 13th tl 3 out: fdd bdly bef next and sn eased* **25/1**

-52P 8 11 **Oranger (FR)**[243] 525 9-10-11 **102**.......................... MrSWDrinkwater(7) 67
(Andrew J Martin) *dropped bk last and rdn after 10th: t.o* **11/1**

44-F P **Mocho (IRE)**[63] 2638 10-11-1 **99**...................................... LiamTreadwell —
(Mrs H Parrott) *cl up tl mstke 10th: sn lost pl: t.o and p.u 2 out* **9/1**

2-25 F **Bertenbar**[16] 3492 7-10-0 **84** oh8.. HaddenFrost —
(Henrietta Knight) *3rd whn fell 3rd* **8/1**

5m 19.4s (-1.60) **Going Correction** -0.15s/f (Good) **10** Ran SP% **121.8**
Speed ratings: **97,95,93,92,89 83,83,78,—,—**
toteswingers:1&2 £27.10, 2&3 £12.00, 1&3 £14.10 CSF £86.16 CT £500.82 TOTE £25.90: £9.00, £2.00, £1.90; EX 78.20.
Owner David A Hunt **Bred** J T Jones **Trained** Kings Caple, H'fords
■ Stewards' Enquiry : Warren Marston one-day ban: careless riding (Feb 10)

FOCUS
An ordinary handicap chase. The winner is rated to the level of her hurdles form.

NOTEBOOK
Sawpit Supreme got no further than the first fence on her previous start but, after being settled in behind, was produced at the right time here to win comfortably. She is open to a bit more improvement but may struggle to win off a much higher mark. (tchd 12-1)
Double The Trouble is fairly treated and ran really well despite taking a strong hold throughout. A return to a much quicker surface will see him difficult to beat in this sort of mood. (op 8-1 tchd 7-1)
Brimham Boy still above his highest winning mark, was never far away and was another to keep on surprisingly well considering how keenly he raced. (op 5-1 tchd 13-2)
Prophete De Guye(FR) moved strongly under restraint, as he can do, and made a respectable return to action. (op 9-2 tchd 7-2)
Oscar Prairie(IRE), having his first run over fences, was beaten at 4-9 on his previous start (tongue-tied for the first time) and dropped out here before the race took shape. He can improve his jumping and will be of more interest when doing so. (op 3-1 tchd 7-2)

3773 RACING UK INTERMEDIATE OPEN NATIONAL HUNT FLAT RACE 2m
4:25 (4:28) (Class 6) 5-6-Y-0 **£1,507** (£439; £219)

Form RPR

1 **Hildisvini (IRE)**[40] 3033 5-10-12 0... FelixDeGiles 110+
(Charlie Longsdon) *led in s: t.k.h trcking ldrs: wnt 4th and rdn and rn green st: edgd rt but styd on to ld fnl 100yds: sn clr* **16/1**

1 2 2 **Young Victoria**[42] 2987 5-10-5 0.................................. JakeGreenall(7) 108
(Richard Lee) *prom: led 1/2-way: drvn and edgd lft and then hung rt over 1f out: rn green and hdd and no ex fnl 100yds* **12/1**

3 3 **Dreamers Of Dreams (IRE)** 6-10-12 0.......................... LeightonAspell 106
(Don Cantillon) *hld up in midfield: effrt 4f out: wnt 2nd and chal briefly st: squeezed by wnr over 1f out and edgd lft: nt qckn ins fnl f* **4/1**[2]

4 hd **Themilanhorse (IRE)** 5-10-12 0................................... NickScholfield 105
(Paul Nicholls) *towards rr on outside: effrt 4f out: last of five w ch st: n.m.r 1f out: kpt on steadily ins fnl f* **15/2**

3 5 4 ½ **Secret Past (IRE)**[67] 2560 6-10-12 0.................................. BrianHughes 102
(Karen McLintock) *led at mod pce tl 1/2-way: 3rd and rdn st: wknd over 1f out* **9/1**

6 6 **Motou (FR)** 6-10-12 0.. WarrenMarston 97
(Richard Phillips) *hld up: effrt 4f out: 8th and btn st* **33/1**

7 4 ½ **Old Style (IRE)** 6-10-12 0.. AlanO'Keeffe 92
(Jennie Candlish) *racd wd and plld hrd in last tl hdwy 1/2-way: pressed ldrs briefly over 3f out: sn btn* **25/1**

8 nk **All For Cash** 6-10-5 0.. MrJSherwood(7) 91
(Kim Bailey) *green and bdly outpcd 1/2-way: plugged on in clsng stages wout threatening* **28/1**

2 9 nk **Gospel Preacher**[63] 2632 6-10-12 0............................ RobertThornton 91
(Alan King) *plld hrd in midfield: effrt 4f out: 6th and wkng st* **11/4**[1]

10 8 **One For Lou (IRE)** 5-10-9 0...................................... MichaelMurphy(3) 84
(Ian Williams) *nvr trbld ldrs: btn 5f out* **5/1**[3]

11 3 **Bluemoonandstars (IRE)**[284] 6-10-5 0........................ TrevorWhelan(7) 81
(George Baker) *prom: drvn 4f out: sn btn: modest 7th st* **16/1**

6 12 5 **Bally Gunner**[27] 3259 6-10-12 0... HaddenFrost 77
(Roger Curtis) *bhd: short-lived effrt 7f out* **100/1**

13 1 ¼ **Handford Henry (IRE)** 5-10-12 0.................................... DavidEngland 76
(John Holt) *hld up and wl bhd: nvr on terms* **100/1**

14 24 **Willard** 5-10-7 0... LeeEdwards(5) 54
(Tony Carroll) *plld hrd: nvr on terms: t.o fnl 3f* **50/1**

15 3 ¼ **Thank The Groom** 5-10-12 0.. WillKennedy 51
(Martin Bosley) *struggling 6f out: t.o fnl 3f* **100/1**

16 2 ¾ **Nik Nak Too** 5-10-9 0.. JimmyDerham(3) 49
(Seamus Mullins) *in rr early: t.o fnl 3f* **33/1**

00 17 4 **Radmores Sam Evans**[74] 2389 6-10-12 0............................ DaveCrosse 45
(John O'Shea) *prom tl lost pl 7f out: t.o* **50/1**

18 4 ½ **Spieder Bay** 6-9-12 0.. RobertKirk(7) 34
(James Evans) *t.k.h and cl up early: t.o fnl 4f* **66/1**

3m 52.3s (1.40) **Going Correction** -0.05s/f (Good) **18** Ran SP% **126.1**
Speed ratings: **94,93,91,91,89 86,83,83,83,79 78,75,74,62,61 59,57,55**
toteswingers:1&2 £11.90, 2&3 £17.40, 1&3 £21.20 CSF £190.30 TOTE £19.40: £3.60, £1.80, £2.10; EX 112.80.
Owner J S Wall **Bred** Sean Wickham **Trained** Over Norton, Oxon

FOCUS
Lots of unraced horses made this look an interesting contest, so it was slightly disappointing to see two previously raced horses fight out the finish. The fifth sets the level.

NOTEBOOK
Hildisvini(IRE), runner-up on his final outing in Ireland, travelled nicely in behind after needing to be led in and fought on for pressure to gain a success on his first outing for Charlie Longsdon. The horse shapes like a stayer.
Young Victoria was unconsidered when winning on her debut, but proved that effort was no fluke with a good performance under a penalty. She clearly relishes plenty of ease in the ground. (tchd 11-1)
Dreamers Of Dreams(IRE) attracted market support and had every chance turning in before steadily weakening. From a decent jumping family, he should be straighter for this effort. (op 5-1 tchd 10-3)
Themilanhorse(IRE) was one of the last to come off the bridle but didn't pick up when asked for maximum effort. (op 6-1 tchd 8-1)
Motou(FR), who never made the racecourse for Nicky Henderson, took plenty of driving but made an encouraging debut.
Gospel Preacher had run encouragingly at Newbury but failed to reproduce that performance on different ground after taking a keen hold. (tchd 10-3)
T/Jkpt: Not won. T/Plt: £861.70 to a £1 stake. Pool of £59,864.11 - 50.71 winning tickets. T/Qpdt: £81.60 to a £1 stake. Pool of £4,680.83 - 42.40 winning tickets. IM

3774 - 3777a (Foreign Racing) - See Raceform Interactive

3533 THURLES (R-H)
Thursday, January 27

OFFICIAL GOING: Hurdle course - soft to heavy; chase course - soft

3778a MATTY RYAN MEMORIAL KINLOCH BRAE CHASE (GRADE 2) (14 fncs) 2m 4f
3:20 (3:20) 6-Y-0+ **£25,215** (£7,370; £3,491; £1,163)

RPR

1 **Follow The Plan (IRE)**[18] 3473 8-11-3 **142**........................... PFMangan 152
(Oliver McKiernan, Ire) *hld up towards rr: 7th 4 out: 6th next: 4th and hdwy 2 out: r.o wl ins fnl f to ld cl home* **25/1**

2 nk **Roberto Goldback (IRE)**43 2970 9-11-8 156 RMPower 157
(Mrs John Harrington, Ire) *trckd ldrs: 5th 1/2-way: impr into 2nd after 5 out: chal 3 out: sn led: rdn and strly pressed fr 2 out: kpt on wl u.p: hdd cl home* 9/2

3 3 **J'y Vole (FR)**30 3176 8-11-3 153 PTownend 149
(W P Mullins, Ire) *hld up in tch: prog into 5th 4 out: 4th next: 2nd and chal after 2 out: no ex ins fnl f* 7/4[1]

4 9 **Newmill (IRE)**24 3380 13-11-8 EFPower 147
(James Daniel Dullea, Ire) *hld up in rr: 6th and hdwy 4 out: 3rd next: 2nd and rdn to chal bef 2 out: sn no ex* 16/1

5 4 1/2 **Leanne (IRE)**29 3206 9-10-12 128 RCColgan 130
(W Harney, Ire) *prom: lft in ld 7th: strly pressed 3 out: sn hdd: no ex fr 2 out* 25/1

6 3 **Trafford Lad**43 2970 9-11-3 147 (t) AELynch 132
(Laurence James Butler, Ire) *trckd ldrs on outer: 5th 5 out: 3rd briefly next: no ex fr 3 out* 12/1

7 19 **Glencove Marina (IRE)**30 3176 9-11-6 155 BarryGeraghty 116
(Eoin Griffin, Ire) *chsd ldrs: mstke 1st: 4th u.p 5 out: wknd 3 out: eased after 2 out* 7/2[2]

8 1 1/4 **Psycho (IRE)**21 3415 10-11-6 152 PCarberry 115
(A J Martin, Ire) *prom: lft 2nd at 7th: 3rd after 5 out: wknd bef next: eased fr 2 out* 4/1[3]

F **Mossbank (IRE)**30 3176 11-11-3 145 (p) DNRussell —
(Michael Hourigan, Ire) *led tl fell 7th* 28/1

5m 16.8s (-11.40) **9** Ran SP% **121.5**
CSF £140.03 TOTE £48.60: £8.00, £1.90, £1.02; DF 226.30.
Owner Redgap Partnership **Bred** Patrick Sheehan **Trained** Rathcoole, Co Dublin

FOCUS
The final fence was bypassed. The winner is rated right back to his novice best.

NOTEBOOK
Follow The Plan(IRE), off the track for a year after Cheltenham in 2009 and without showing a trace of his best form since, was fully on his game here. A couple of mistakes on the far side notwithstanding, he crept into the race from the turn out of the back straight and from the top of the straight he stayed on resolutely and galloped to the line while squeezing through a gap on the inside which wasn't made any wider by the runners having to bypass the final fence. Trainer Oliver McKiernan said afterwards he had no future plans for the horse. (op 50/1)
Roberto Goldback(IRE) had to play second fiddle again and deserves to win a nice race. He jumped well and got to the front before what was effectively the final fence. One would imagine that bypassing the final fence might just have inconvenienced him marginally more than the winner. (op 11/2)
J'y Vole(FR) didn't run up to her best and one wonders whether that run in the Lexus left more of a mark than might have been originally thought. She was sticky at a couple of fences and despite travelling well coming to what was effectively the final fence she couldn't get past the runner-up and her effort flattened out late on. (op 15/8 tchd 2/1)
Newmill(IRE) ran as well as could have been expected in his quest for a third win in this race. Held up in rear, he closed up on the outside before the turn into the straight and had every chance. He just faded on the long run from the final fence but it was a perfectly respectable effort.
Leanne(IRE) was left in front by the fall of Mossbank with a circuit to go but ran out of steam before the turn into the straight and came home at the one pace.
Trafford Lad is well below the level he was as a novice although he wasn't totally disgraced here.
Glencove Marina(IRE) didn't jump well and was a spent force coming out of the back. Official explanation: vet said gelding was found to be lame post-race (op 10/3 tchd 4/1)
Psycho(IRE) ran no race whatsoever, weakening away quite quickly from the fourth-last. (op 7/2)

3779a ASK & GETAWAY COOLMORE NATIONAL HUNT SIRES EUROPEAN BREEDERS FUND MARES NOVICE CHASE (GRADE 3)
(14 fncs) 2m 4f
3:50 (3:50) 5-Y-0+ **£23,814** (£6,961; £3,297; £1,099)

RPR

1 **For Bill (IRE)**14 3534 8-10-11 (t) PCarberry 142+
(Michael Winters, Ire) *trckd ldrs in 4th: prog into 2nd after 1/2-way: led 3 out: rdn clr after 2 out: styd on wl: comf* 5/2[2]

2 5 **Blazing Tempo (IRE)**27 3268 7-11-5 PTownend 143+
(W P Mullins, Ire) *trckd ldrs: 4th 1/2-way: 3rd 4 out: impr into cl 2nd after next: slt mstke 2 out: sn rdn and no imp: kpt on same pce fr last* 7/4[1]

3 1 **Cool Quest (IRE)**27 3268 7-10-11 KTColeman 133+
(Terence O'Brien, Ire) *mod 2nd: tk clsr order fr 4th: 3rd after 1/2-way: 4th 4 out: no imp fr next: lft 3rd 2 out: kpt on* 12/1[3]

4 28 **Gentle Alice (IRE)**30 3183 7-10-11 DJCondon 104
(Daniel G Murphy, Ire) *hld up: prog into 5th 1/2-way: no ex fr 3 out: lft remote 4th fr 2 out* 14/1

5 12 **Miss Pepperpot (IRE)**161 1303 7-10-11 MPWalsh 92
(F Flood, Ire) *mid-div: 6th 6 out: no imp whn mstke 4 out: lft remote 5th fr 2 out* 66/1

6 13 **Lady Shanakill (IRE)**30 3183 7-10-11 (t) PFMangan 79
(James Joseph Mangan, Ire) *hld up: sme prog into 7th 6 out: no ex fr 4 out* 50/1

7 14 **Twelfth Of Never (IRE)**11 3593 8-10-11 SWFlanagan 65
(Miss Elizabeth Doyle, Ire) *chsd ldrs: 6th early: lost tch fr bef 6 out* 80/1

8 23 **Aura About You (IRE)**278 5397 8-10-11 BarryGeraghty 42
(Paul Nolan, Ire) *a bhd: wknd 6 out: t.o* 25/1

9 3 **Back Of The Pack (IRE)**26 3327 9-11-3 135 MDarcy 45
(Colin Kidd, Ire) *chsd ldrs in 5th: drvn along 1/2-way: dropped to 8th 6 out: sn no ex and wknd: t.o* 16/1

P **Inch Native (IRE)**27 3268 9-10-11 JLCullen —
(Denis Paul Murphy, Ire) *a bhd: trailing 6 out: p.u bef 5 out* 50/1

F **Morning Supreme (IRE)**24 3384 8-10-11 EMullins —
(W P Mullins, Ire) *led and clr: reduced advantage fr 5th: hdd whn slt mstke 3 out: 3rd u.p whn fell 2 out* 5/2[2]

5m 20.8s (-7.40) **11** Ran SP% **124.2**
CSF £8.03 TOTE £3.40: £1.70, £1.30, £2.90; DF 9.00.
Owner Donal Sheahan **Bred** Mrs Margaret Lacy **Trained** Kanturk, Co Cork
■ Stewards' Enquiry : K T Coleman five-day ban: mistook the winning post (Feb 10, 12-13, 16-17)

FOCUS
Although she was getting a fair bit of weight from the previous winners in this race, this was a really good performance from For Bill and especially rider Paul Carberry who had never sat on the mare before and was only drafted in late to ride her following Davy Russell's fall in the previous contest. The form is rated around the second and third.

NOTEBOOK
For Bill(IRE) jumped really well for Carberry and once getting her head in front before the straight she found plenty and won going away. It was a fine performance from an admirable mare and she may now go to Limerick for a similar contest in March. (op 7/4)
Blazing Tempo(IRE) was giving 8lb to the winner which may have been an impossible task. However, she travelled into the race like a dream to track For Bill into the straight and looked the likely winner. She hit the second-last, though, and emptied out quickly enough after that. It was a fine effort and there may not be a lot to choose between her and For Bill at level weights. (op 9/4)
Cool Quest(IRE) ran a controversial race which got her rider in trouble. She ran in snatches, racing prominently but losing her place before the turn into the straight and then picking up again after the second-last. She was flying home when her rider eased down having mistaken the winning post and this prevented her getting up for second place. (op 14/1)
Gentle Alice(IRE) was tracking the pace before turning into the straight but couldn't make an impression once the winner took over.
Miss Pepperpot(IRE) wasn't disgraced and kept on reasonably well having been handy most of the way.
Morning Supreme(IRE) went off in front but she had a tendency to jump to her left and could never dominate. She did fight back when headed before the straight but was starting to run on empty when coming down at the second-last, horse and rider returning unscathed. (op 3/1)

3780 - (Foreign Racing) - See Raceform Interactive

3505 DONCASTER (L-H)
Friday, January 28

OFFICIAL GOING: Good (good to firm in places; 8.9)
Third fence after the winning line omitted in all chase races; ground under repair.
Wind: light 1/2 against Weather: fine and sunny, cold

3781 SKYBET.COM NOVICES' HURDLE (DIV I) (8 hdls) 2m 110y
12:50 (12:50) (Class 4) 5-Y-0+ **£1,986** (£579; £289)

Form RPR

2-40 1 **Solis**74 2423 5-10-2 108 JoeColliver(10) 114+
(Micky Hammond) *mid-div: drvn and hdwy appr 3 out: hmpd 2 out: led last: styd on wl* 16/1[3]

4-00 2 2 **Exotic Man (FR)**76 2375 6-10-5 0 MrJohnDawson(7) 111
(John Wade) *t.k.h in rr: hdwy 5th: chal last: styd on same pce* 100/1

4-13 3 hd **Semi Colon (FR)**29 3227 5-10-5 0 AndrewTinkler 103
(Nicky Henderson) *chsd ldrs: led 3 out: hdd last: no ex* 11/4[1]

51 4 6 **King Fingal (IRE)**14 3547 6-11-5 0 DougieCostello 111
(John Quinn) *chsd ldrs: hit 5th: drvn next: wknd appr last* 11/4[1]

5 nk **Yorgunnabelucky (USA)**139 5-10-12 0 WayneHutchinson 105
(Alan King) *prom: effrt appr 3 out: hmpd 2 out: wknd appr last* 4/1[2]

6 11 **Akbabend**112 5-10-12 0 JasonMaguire 96+
(Charlie Mann) *chsd ldr: hit 4th: upsides whn j.lft 3 out and next: wknd and j.lft last* 25/1

2 7 9 **Spirit Is Needed (IRE)**29 3225 5-10-12 0 WarrenMarston 84
(Milton Harris) *t.k.h: trckd ldrs: lost pl after 5th* 11/4[1]

8 13 **Udaya Klum** 8-10-12 0 HenryOliver 71
(Sue Smith) *chsd ldrs: lost pl appr 3 out: sn bhd: j. bdly lft last* 33/1

00 9 hd **Lindoro**68 2540 6-10-7 0 BrianToomey(5) 71
(Kevin M Prendergast) *led: j.rt: clr 4th: hdd 3 out: wkng whn hit next* 200/1

4050 10 42 **Beau D'Argent**16 3505 5-10-5 0 GrahamLee 22
(Ferdy Murphy) *in rr: drvn 4th: sn bhd: t.o 3 out* 100/1

0P 11 1 **A Splash Of Green (IRE)**43 2985 6-10-9 0 RichieMcLernon(3) 28
(Jonathan Portman) *in rr: bhd fr 4th: t.o 3 out* 150/1

3m 58.7s (-6.00) **Going Correction** -0.55s/f (Firm) **11** Ran SP% **115.8**
Speed ratings: **92,91,90,88,88 82,78,72,72,52 52**
toteswingers:1&2:£24.30, 1&3:£4.60, 2&3:£58.00 CSF £912.77 TOTE £20.60: £2.80, £16.10, £1.40; EX 761.40.
Owner J McAllister **Bred** The Lavington Stud **Trained** Middleham Moor, N Yorks

FOCUS
The ground was riding "pretty quick" according to jockeys in the first, an ordinary novice hurdle for the track. The third and fourth set the level.

NOTEBOOK
Solis had work to do turning in and was carried wide at the second-last, but came with a steady run in the centre of the track under his inexperienced rider to win a shade comfortably. Sold out of John Quinn's yard after a disappointing handicap debut on soft ground, he had caught the eye at Wetherby the time before. He may get a bit further. (op 18-1)
Exotic Man(FR), patiently ridden, improved to have every chance up the stands' rail and belied his big price. This half-brother to the top-class Exotic Dancer was quickly let go by Sir Robert Ogden and Paul Nicholls and had not shown much in two starts for his current owner-trainer, but obviously has ability.
Semi Colon(FR) was always in the front rank chasing the clear leader and ran a sound race on this first outing against the males. She won't mind returning to a bit further. (tchd 3-1)
King Fingal(IRE) could never quite work his way into a challenging position, but looked to run his race and seems a decent guide to the form. (op 7-2)
Yorgunnabelucky(USA) ◆ was a useful middle-distance Flat performer for Mark Johnston and remains in the same ownership. He lost momentum when hampered two out but was staying on in pleasing fashion late on, and has a future at this game. (tchd 9-2)
Akbabend, another ex-Mark Johnston inmate, showed up for a long way on this hurdles debut but began to jump out to his left when weakening. He wore headgear on his last few starts on the Flat and doesn't look straightforward. (op 22-1)
Spirit Is Needed(IRE) had run well on his hurdling debut but was disappointing here, dropping out of contention before the home turn. Official explanation: trainer had no explanation for the poor form shown (tchd 3-1 and 7-2 in a place)

3782 PEGLER YORKSHIRE CONDITIONAL JOCKEYS' H'CAP HURDLE (8 hdls) 2m 110y
1:20 (1:21) (Class 4) (0-100,98) 4-Y-0+ **£2,329** (£678; £339)

Form RPR

0-00 1 **Shalambar (IRE)**24 3387 5-11-9 97 LeeEdwards(3) 106+
(Tony Carroll) *trckd ldrs: upsides whn hit 5th: styd on to ld last 150yds: all out* 6/1[3]

0211 2 hd **Rawaaj**14 3540 5-11-6 94 JohnKington(3) 101
(Donald McCain) *trckd ldrs: upsides sn after last: no ex nr fin* 7/1

-065 3 2 3/4 **Pete**9 3631 8-11-7 92 EwanWhillans 96
(Barry Murtagh) *in rr-div: hdwy 5th: slt ld between last 2: hdd run-in: kpt on same pce* 10/1

2133 4 1 **Monsieur (FR)**15 3532 11-10-11 85 MattGriffiths(3) 88
(Carroll Gray) *hld up in rr: t.k.h: hdwy on ins 3 out: chsng ldrs between last 2: styd on same pce run-in* 20/1

6041 5 1/2 **King Benny (IRE)**4 3717 7-11-5 95 7ex GeraldQuinn(5) 99
(Elliott Cooper) *trckd ldrs: effrt appr 3 out: styd on same pce fr 2 out* 9/2[1]

462 6 nk **Miereveld**18 3484 4-11-2 98 (b) FearghalDavis 90
(Brian Ellison) *trckd ldrs: hung rt appr 3 out: narrow ld 2 out: hdd between last 2: one pce* 16/1

555 7 1 1/2 **Rare Malt (IRE)**18 3484 4-10-5 92 (p) JakeGreenall(5) 82
(Milton Harris) *hld up in rr: hdwy appr 3 out: kpt on: nvr threatened ldrs* 20/1

-P50 8 2 **Wardington Lad**15 3523 9-11-8 96 KyleJames(3) 95
(Michael Appleby) *in rr: drvn and sme hdwy appr 3 out: kpt on fr 2 out: nvr nr ldrs* 33/1

30-5 **9** 3 3/4 **It's A Date**[72] 2452 6-11-7 **95**..........(p) CharlieHuxley(3) 91
(Alan King) *chsd ldrs: led appr 3 out: hdd next: wknd appr last and mstke* **5/1**[2]

5P-0 **10** 1 1/2 **Won More Night**[67] 2583 9-10-12 **83**..........(t) IanPopham 77
(Martin Keighley) *mid-div: effrt appr 3 out: nvr a factor* **28/1**

5434 **11** 1/2 **Sonic Anthem (USA)**[23] 3397 9-11-7 **92**.......... DonalDevereux 85
(John Mackie) *led after 1st: hdd appr 3 out: sn lost pl* **10/1**

0044 **12** 5 **Prize Fighter (IRE)**[10] 3619 9-10-13 **84**.......... JamesHalliday 72
(Lynn Siddall) *hld up in rr: sme hdwy 3 out: wknd sn after next* **18/1**

5000 **13** 11 **Ardesia (IRE)**[17] 3500 7-11-1 **89**.......... AlexanderVoy(3) 66
(Tina Jackson) *chsd ldrs: hit 4th: sn outpcd: lost pl appr 3 out* **28/1**

- **14** 1 3/4 **Gilt Free (IRE)**[623] 329 9-11-3 **96**.......... TrevorWhelan(8) 71
(George Baker) *in rr: hdwy 5th: wknd after 3 out* **16/1**

2166 **15** 36 **Royal Flynn**[66] 2603 9-10-9 **90**..........(p) JamesRobinson(10) 29
(Kate Walton) *in rr: bhd whn hit 5th: t.o next* **16/1**

0P-5 **P** **Beat The Devil**[25] 3376 5-11-7 **92**.......... GilesHawkins —
(Tom George) *mid-div: blnd bdly 3rd: lost pl and rdr lost irons tl after next: bhd whn p.u bef 3 out* **25/1**

3m 52.9s (-11.80) **Going Correction** -0.55s/f (Firm)
WFA 4 from 5yo+ 11lb **16** Ran SP% **125.9**
Speed ratings (Par 105): **105,104,103,103,102 102,102,101,99,98 98,96,90,90,73** —
toteswingers:1&2:£12.00, 1&3:£17.30, 2&3:£17.10 CSF £45.00 CT £429.13 TOTE £8.50: £2.10, £2.70, £2.90, £4.20; EX 34.50.
Owner B J Millen **Bred** His Highness The Aga Khan's Studs S C **Trained** Cropthorne, Worcs

FOCUS
Quite a competitive conditionals' handicap, run at a decent pace. The time was nearly six seconds quicker than the earlier novice hurdle and the form looks solid. Thw winner is entitled to rate higher still on his old flat form.

NOTEBOOK
Shalambar(IRE) was making his handicap debut after three unplaced runs behind some useful novices. He was soon under pressure after a mistake four out, but battled on well to force his head in front on the run-in. He was quite useful on the Flat in Ireland for Michael Halford, and may have a little more improvement in him. Official explanation: trainer said, regarding apparent improvement in form, that the gelding was better suited by the faster going. (op 9-2 tchd 4-1)
Rawaaj, thrown out after taking the wrong course latest, responded to pressure to deliver a sustained challenge and remains in top form. (op 15-2 tchd 8-1)
Pete showed ahead between the last two and, while he couldn't hold on, this was something of a return to form. The type who travels well, he is still without the tongue strap he wore regularly in the past. (op 9-1 tchd 11-1)
Monsieur(FR), who gave one or two problems at the start, stayed on well from the back of the field. He is in decent heart currently and acts on most types of ground. (op 22-1)
King Bonny(IRE), a winner at Wetherby in the week, ran a fair race considering he was hampered at an early flight. He remains quite well treated on his old form in Ireland. (op 6-1)
Miereveld, a lightly raced novice making his handicap debut on better ground, could not hold on after showing briefly in front. (op 14-1)
Rare Malt(IRE), another handicap debutante, was keeping on at the end. (op 25-1)
Beat The Devil Official explanation: jockey said gelding made a mistake at third and never travelled thereafter

3783 SKYBET.COM NOVICES' HURDLE (DIV II) (8 hdls) 2m 110y
1:55 (1:56) (Class 4) 5-Y-0+ **£1,986** (£579; £289)

Form RPR

6/2- **1** **Whispering Death**[133] 1752 9-10-12 0.......... WilsonRenwick 115
(Howard Johnson) *hld up: hdwy to trck ldrs 4th: effrt 2 out: chal last: rdn and edgd lft: led fnl strides: all out* **12/1**

-233 **2** shd **Milgen Bay**[67] 2584 5-10-12 117.......... SamJones 115
(Oliver Sherwood) *w ldr: led sn after 5th: sn drvn: hdd narrowly last: r.o: jst hld* **11/2**[3]

411 **3** shd **Andhaar**[75] 2397 5-11-12 125.......... RichardJohnson 129
(Steve Gollings) *trckd ldrs: upsides 3 out: narrow ld last: hdd and ex last strides* **7/2**[2]

4 5 **Brunston**[83] 5-10-12 0.......... AndrewTinkler 110
(Nicky Henderson) *trckd ldrs: upsides 3 out: rdn and wkng whn j.lft last* **4/6**[1]

5 75 **Okalydokely (IRE)**[534] 1043 7-10-9 0.......... JamesO'Farrell(3) 35
(Andrew Crook) *t.k.h: led hdd after 5th: lost pl and j.lft next: sn wl bhd: wl t.o* **100/1**

0 **6** 8 **Perjury**[28] 3266 7-10-5 0.......... SeanQuinlan 20
(Robin Mathew) *nt fluent: w ldrs: lost pl 5th: bhd fr next: wl t.o* **150/1**

0 **7** 10 **Drop The Hammer**[76] 2370 5-10-5 0.......... GrahamLee 10
(David O'Meara) *nt fluent: j. slowly and lost pl 3rd: sn reminders: t.o next* **28/1**

8 56 **Dennis Doyle (IRE)** 5-10-7 0.......... GilesHawkins(5) —
(Tom George) *nt fluent in last: sn bhd: t.o 4th: eventually completed* **40/1**

U **December**[62] 5-10-9 0.......... AlexMerriam(3) —
(Christine Dunnett) *t.k.h towards rr: trckd ldrs 4th: wknd appr 2 out: wl t.o and disputing 6th whn j.rt and uns rdr last* **100/1**

000 **U** **Artic Night (FR)**[26] 3330 5-10-12 0.......... FearghalDavis —
(Nicky Richards) *hld up in mid-div: mstke and uns rdr 1st* **66/1**

3m 52.1s (-12.60) **Going Correction** -0.55s/f (Firm) **10** Ran SP% **115.3**
Speed ratings: **107,106,106,104,69 65,60,34,—,—**
toteswingers:1&2:£1.80, 1&3:£2.20, 2&3:£2.50 CSF £71.20 TOTE £12.50: £2.10, £1.60, £1.60; EX 40.10.
Owner J Howard Johnson **Bred** Milton Park Stud **Trained** Billy Row, Co Durham

FOCUS
This looked the stronger of the two divisions, and that was backed up by a time. The first four came a mile clear and there was a fine finish. The winner is rated to his 2009 mark.

NOTEBOOK
Whispering Death, lightly raced over hurdles, had not been seen since a run on the Flat in September. Travelling strongly in the slipstream of the favourite in the straight and only coming off the bridle when switched to the stands' rail between the last two flights, he ran on well on the flat to shade a three-way photo. The Johnson yard won both divisions of this novice hurdle in 2009, one of them with the smart Quwetwo. (op 9-1 tchd 17-2)
Milgen Bay was the first of the four principals to be brought under pressure, but stayed on willingly and had his head in front just the wrong side of the line. His turn should not be delayed long and a step back up in trip ought to suit. (op 9-2)
Andhaar had every chance and was just denied the hat-trick. This was a fine effort under a double penalty and the jumping problems which hindered him earlier in the season look to have been ironed out. (op 11-4 tchd 4-1)
Brunston, winner of the Newbury Spring Cup for Roger Charlton last year, was well backed. He jumped nicely on this hurdles debut and held every chance on the run down to the final flight, but was the first of the front four to crack. There was not a great deal wrong with this effort and he should come on for the run. (op Evens tchd 11-10 in a place)

Dennis Doyle(IRE) Official explanation: jockey said gelding ran green

3784 SIMPSON MILLAR NOVICES' H'CAP CHASE (17 fncs 1 omitted) 3m
2:30 (2:30) (Class 3) (0-125,125) 5-Y-0+ **£5,204** (£1,528; £764; £381)

Form RPR

03F2 **1** **Mostly Bob (IRE)**[16] 3508 8-11-12 **125**..........(t) RichardJohnson 140+
(Philip Hobbs) *hld up in mid-div: hdwy 5th: trcking ldrs 8th: led 11th: j.rt last 4: drew clr fr 3 out: drvn out: eased towards fin* **3/1**[1]

-4F1 **2** 8 **Frankie Anson (IRE)**[153] 1402 7-11-7 **120**.......... DougieCostello 126
(Micky Hammond) *hit 1st: in rr: hdwy 8th: chsng ldrs 11th: 3rd and rdn whn hit 4 out: chsd wnr next: no imp* **14/1**

-202 **3** 10 **Strongbows Legend**[25] 3371 6-10-10 **109**.......... AndrewTinkler 105
(Charlie Longsdon) *in rr: mstke 10th: hdwy 13th: wnt modest 3rd 2 out* **8/1**

1F5 **4** 3 3/4 **Saveiro (FR)**[25] 3359 7-11-7 **120**.......... BarryKeniry 110
(Alan Swinbank) *hld up: hdwy 8th: hit 11th: one pce whn hit 4 out* **33/1**

-36P **5** 3/4 **Wolf Moon (IRE)**[49] 2869 8-11-7 **120**.......... WarrenMarston 110
(Martin Keighley) *w ldrs: lost pl 11th: sn bhd: kpt on fr 2 out* **12/1**

0/33 **6** 2 **Mexican Pete**[71] 2475 11-11-10 **123**.......... DaveCrosse 111
(Ian Williams) *mid-div: trckd ldrs 7th: wknd 3 out* **40/1**

5241 **7** 3 1/2 **Ovthenight (IRE)**[79] 2311 6-10-8 **114**.......... MissGAndrews(7) 98
(Pam Sly) *in rr: reminders after 7th: wl bhd fr 9th: t.o 12th* **20/1**

-262 **8** 3 1/4 **Sonny Mullen (IRE)**[69] 2513 7-11-5 **118**.......... JasonMaguire 100
(Kim Bailey) *led: hdd 11th: wknd 3 out* **3/1**[1]

0215 **P** **Elzahann (IRE)**[16] 3508 9-10-13 **112**.......... GrahamLee —
(Ferdy Murphy) *mstkes: chsd ldrs: j.rt 3rd: blnd 6th: reminders after next: sn bhd: p.u bef 10th* **20/1**

3-34 **P** **Double Pride**[44] 2959 7-11-4 **117**..........(b[1]) WayneHutchinson —
(Alan King) *prom: blnd bdly 2nd and rdr briefly lost irons: lost pl 10th: mstke next: t.o 12th: p.u bef 4 out: bled fr nose* **4/1**[2]

1111 **U** **Douglas Julian**[44] 2952 9-10-5 **104**.......... HenryOliver —
(Sue Smith) *chsd ldrs: drvn 9th: outpcd whn hit 13th: modest 7th whn blnd and uns rdr 3 out* **15/2**[3]

5m 47.6s (-24.40) **Going Correction** -0.85s/f (Firm) course record **11** Ran SP% **122.1**
Speed ratings: **107,104,101,99,99 98,97,96,—,— —**
toteswingers:1&2:£5.60, 1&3:£8.10, 2&3:£9.80 CSF £41.95 CT £317.72 TOTE £4.30: £1.60, £4.70, £3.30; EX 40.20.
Owner Favourites Racing XXVI **Bred** Mrs Mary Gallagher **Trained** Withycombe, Somerset

FOCUS
A competitive novice handicap, and sound form. The winner is on the upgrade and looks a decent novice.

NOTEBOOK
Mostly Bob(IRE) put up a very taking performance under topweight, clearing right away up the straight for his first win over fences. He jumped nicely, if out to his right in the latter stages, and looks a progressive chaser who will get a bit further too. (op 7-2)
Frankie Anson(IRE), previously with Alan Swinbank, chased the winner in vain over the final three fences. This was a decent effort, although he gives the impression that he is not wholly straightforward. (op 12-1 tchd 11-1)
Strongbows Legend, 4lb higher than when second at Hereford, put in some untidy jumps but stayed on quite well for third. He got the 3m well enough. (op 15-2 tchd 17-2)
Saveiro(FR), another going into unknown territory stamina-wise, plugged on for a well-held fourth. (op 28-1)
Wolf Moon(IRE) dropped right out of contention down the back before staying on again when it was all over. (op 10-1 tchd 9-1)
Mexican Pete faded and might not quite have seen it out. (op 33-1)
Sonny Mullen(IRE) jumped well enough but could not hold off the challengers in the straight. (op 15-2)
Double Pride was reported to have bled from the nose. Official explanation: trainer's rep said gelding bled from the nose (tchd 7-2)
Douglas Julian, going for a fifth successive win, and a hat-trick over fences, was an additional 8lb higher and was in trouble some way before finally unseating. (tchd 7-2)

3785 SKYSPORTS.COM/RACING JUVENILE HURDLE (8 hdls) 2m 110y
3:05 (3:06) (Class 3) 4-Y-0 **£4,228** (£1,241; £620; £310)

Form RPR

3 **1** **Empire Levant (USA)**[44] 2958 4-10-12 0.......... HarrySkelton 118+
(Paul Nicholls) *t.k.h: hdwy to join ldr 3 out: led on bit next: drvn and styd on run-in* **4/6**[1]

10 **2** 2 1/4 **Palawi (IRE)**[26] 2356 4-11-4 0.......... DougieCostello 121
(John Quinn) *led: clr after 1st to 5th: hdd 2 out: swtchd lft: kpt on same pce run-in* **10/3**[2]

P0 **3** 34 **Kai Broon (IRE)**[25] 3358 4-10-12 0.......... CampbellGillies 81
(Lucinda Russell) *chsd clr ldrs: outpcd 3 out: sn wknd: j.lft last* **66/1**

302 **4** 2 **Franklino (FR)**[16] 3507 4-10-12 107.......... WayneHutchinson 79
(Alan King) *trckd ldrs: drvn appr 3 out: sn wknd* **9/2**[3]

00P **5** 3 1/2 **Farmers Glory**[11] 3599 4-10-9 0.......... AlexMerriam(3) 76
(Neil King) *in rr: mstke 2nd: sme hdwy appr 3 out: sn wknd* **150/1**

6 42 **Cabal**[165] 4-10-2 0.......... JamesO'Farrell(3) 26
(Andrew Crook) *chsd ldrs: lost pl 5th: t.o and eased 2 out: virtually p.u* **28/1**

3m 53.5s (-11.20) **Going Correction** -0.55s/f (Firm) **6** Ran SP% **106.9**
Speed ratings: **104,102,86,86,84 64**
toteswingers:1&2:£1.40, 1&3:£5.10, 2&3:£7.40 CSF £2.90 TOTE £1.70: £1.20, £1.30; EX 3.30.
Owner Sir A Ferguson,G Mason,R Wood & P Done **Bred** Haras Du Mezeray S A **Trained** Ditcheat, Somerset
■ Stewards' Enquiry : James O'Farrell three-day ban: weighed in 2lb heavy (Feb 12-13)

FOCUS
The first two drew a long way clear and are decent juveniles, but the race lacked any depth. The time compared favourably with the earlier races over the trip. The winner is rated similar to his Newbury level.

NOTEBOOK
Empire Levant(USA) confirmed the impression of his promising debut at Newbury. He travelled up well before easing to the front, but had to be kept up to his work to hold off the persistent runner-up. The type to make a nice chaser in time, he is useful but maybe not up to Triumph Hurdle class. (op 8-13)
Palawi(IRE), another with scope, faced more realistic opposition after finishing down the field behind the likes of Sam Winner and Grandouet at Cheltenham. Racing in a clear lead until being closed down before the straight, he did not give up when headed by the winner and this was a good effort conceding 6lb. (op 7-2 tchd 3-1)
Kai Broon(IRE) was left trailing by the principals in the straight, but clung on for a remote third. (op 50-1)

Franklino(FR) is proving disappointing, but may need further. (op 5-1 tchd 11-2)

3786 R.A. BEAVER H'CAP CHASE (14 fncs 1 omitted) 2m 3f

3:40 (3:41) (Class 3) (0-130,128) 5-Y-0+ **£5,204** (£1,528; £764; £381)

Form RPR

-PP1 **1** **Sagalyrique (FR)**26 3333 7-11-12 **128**..........(tp) JasonMaguire 140+
(Donald McCain) *w ldr: led 8th: drvn clr 2 out: rdn out* **11/4**2

45-0 **2** *5* **Double Vodka (IRE)**69 2520 10-11-6 **122**.......... JamesReveley 128
(Chris Grant) *chsd ldrs: wnt modest 2nd 3 out: hit next: kpt on same pce: no imp* **16/1**

5512 **3** *2* **Kack Handed**67 2572 8-10-12 **114**.......... RichardJohnson 117
(Henry Daly) *j.rt: led: hdd 8th: kpt on same pce fr 3 out* **4/1**3

164- **4** *6* **Professor Higgins (IRE)**329 4417 8-11-6 **122**.......... WilsonRenwick 120
(Howard Johnson) *trckd ldrs: chsd wnr 4 out: wknd 2 out* **9/4**1

-534 **5** *29* **Russian Flag (FR)**70 2496 8-11-9 **128**.......... AlexMerriam(3) 96
(Neil King) *chsd ldrs: hit 9th and next: lost pl appr 4 out* **11/1**

22-0 **6** *55* **Font**49 2869 8-11-9 **125**..........(t) HarrySkelton 38
(Paul Nicholls) *trckd ldrs: reminders 10th: 5th and lost pl whn hit next: sn bhd: eased 2 out: wl t.o: virtually p.u* **7/1**

2-03 **7** *½* **Le Roi Rouge (FR)**81 2272 9-11-7 **123**.......... GrahamLee 36
(Ferdy Murphy) *in last: mstke 4th: sn bhd: blnd and reminders 6th: t.o next: eased appr 4 out: eventually completed* **8/1**

4m 39.0s (-10.00) **Going Correction** -0.85s/f (Firm) course record **7** Ran SP% **115.3**
Speed ratings: **87,84,84,81,69 46,45**
toteswingers:1&2:£9.10, 1&3:£3.00, 2&3:£9.70 CSF £39.49 TOTE £4.00: £2.70, £6.60; EX 53.20.
Owner Sir Robert Ogden **Bred** Scea Des Marais **Trained** Cholmondeley, Cheshire

FOCUS
A fair handicap chase. The winner is on the upgrade and the next two set the level.

NOTEBOOK
Sagalyrique(FR), who delivered a fluent round of jumping, showed with a definite lead turning for home and saw it out well to follow up his Ayr win. Improved since being fitted with a tongue tie, he had the cheekpieces back in place too. (op 10-3)
Double Vodka(IRE) stuck to his task willingly but was always being held by the winner. This was a big improvement on his reappearance effort and he gave the impression he might stay a little further. (op 12-1)
Kack Handed jumped out to his right again. Held together when headed, he seemed to get the longer trip well enough. (op 9-2 tchd 5-1)
Professor Higgins(IRE) looked a big threat early in the straight but could not sustain his effort. It may be that he needed this first run since March, but he won first time out last term and a more likely explanation is that he does not truly see out this trip. (op 11-4 tchd 3-1)
Russian Flag(FR) dropped away after successive mistakes and remains out of sorts. (op 17-2)
Font was quickly left toiling and has plenty to prove. (op 13-2 tchd 11-2)

3787 SHEFFIELD INSULATIONS E B F "NATIONAL HUNT" NOVICES' HURDLE (QUALIFIER) (4 hdls 6 omitted) 2m 3f 110y

4:10 (4:15) (Class 3) 4-7-Y-0 **£4,651** (£1,365; £682; £341)

Form RPR

1-15 **1** **King Of The Night (GER)**77 2344 7-11-7 0.......... IanPopham(5) 132+
(Paul Nicholls) *hld up: t.k.h: hdwy 1/2-way: wnt 2nd gng wl omitted 2 out: shkn up to ld omitted last: pushed out* **7/2**2

0-42 **2** *1 ½* **Basford Bob (IRE)**10 3620 6-11-2 0.......... AlanO'Keeffe 120
(Jennie Candlish) *hld up in rr: hdwy appr omitted 3 out: styd on to take 2nd last 150yds: no real imp* **13/2**3

-621 **3** *2 ½* **Jack The Gent (IRE)**16 3505 7-11-8 125.......... BarryKeniry 124
(George Moore) *t.k.h and overshot s: led: shkn up appr omitted 3 out: hdd omitted last: kpt on same pce* **7/2**2

-113 **4** *2 ¾* **Rudanphast (IRE)**124 1623 6-11-8 117.......... RichardJohnson 121
(Peter Bowen) *chsd ldr: j.rt 1st (normal 4th): drvn omitted 3 out: one pce* **10/1**

0-61 **5** *3 ¾* **Cavite Beta (IRE)**78 2325 5-11-7 0.......... DavidBass(5) 121
(Nicky Henderson) *trckd ldrs: t.k.h: effrt omitted 3 out: fdd appr omitted last* **6/4**1

35-4 **6** *15* **Candleford**13 3572 6-10-13 0.......... RyanMania(3) 98
(Sally Hall) *sn prom: drvn and outpcd appr omitted 3 out: grad wknd* **28/1**

7 *2 ¼* **Maxford Lass**349 4050 6-10-9 0.......... DougieCostello 87
(John Quinn) *t.k.h: trckd ldrs: wknd omitted 3 out* **100/1**

000 **8** *19* **Barnack**65 2612 5-11-2 0.......... WarrenMarston 75
(Pam Sly) *hld up in rr: lost pl after normal 4 out: sn bhd* **100/1**

4-22 **9** *4 ½* **Verde Goodwood**53 2825 5-10-9 0.......... SamJones 64
(Oliver Sherwood) *hld up: in rr and drvn normal 4 out: sn bhd* **33/1**

000P **10** *3 ½* **Cloudy Joe (IRE)**18 3485 5-10-13 0.......... AdamPogson(3) 67
(Charles Pogson) *t.k.h: sn trcking ldrs: lost pl after normal 4 out: sn bhd* **100/1**

50P **11** *13* **Gun And More**18 3487 6-10-11 0.......... HenryOliver(5) 54
(Sue Smith) *t.k.h: trckd ldrs: lost pl 3rd (normal 6th) sn bhd: t.o appr omitted 3 out* **150/1**

4m 27.9s (-23.40) **Going Correction** -0.975s/f (Hard) course record **11** Ran SP% **116.9**
Speed ratings: **107,106,105,104,102 96,95,88,86,85 79**
CSF £25.41 TOTE £3.70: £1.60, £1.70, £1.30; EX 28.50.
Owner Mr & Mrs G Calder **Bred** Gestut Norina **Trained** Ditcheat, Somerset

FOCUS
Part novice hurdle and part jumpers' bumper, with the three flights in the home straight omitted on both circuits because of a low sun. The pace was very steady and the form has to be taken with a large pinch of salt, but some decent novices lined up and the first six have all been rated within 5lb of their pre-race marks.

NOTEBOOK
King Of The Night(GER) was a ready winner of his hurdles debut at Cheltenham but was found out behind Cue Card in Grade 2 company there last time. Closing down the long-time leader nicely before being pushed out to assert, he could be ready for a step back up in grade. (tchd 10-3)
Basford Bob(IRE), a bumper winner, stayed on from the back of the field to grab second late on. He is perhaps not the easiest of rides but is well capable of making his mark over hurdles. (op 5-1)
Jack The Gent(IRE), who overshot the start on the way to post, was bidding to follow up a recent C&D win. Setting the pace, he kicked in the straight and soon had most of his pursuers in trouble, but was eventually cut down. He will surely make a name for himself over fences in time. (op 9-2 tchd 11-2)
Rudanphast(IRE) ran creditably on this first start since September, but couldn't quicken up in the straight. (op 12-1)
Cavite Beta(IRE), who missed an engagement in the Challow Hurdle over Christmas because of the testing ground, also failed to quicken. (op 7-4 tchd 5-4)
Maxford Lass, out of a half-sister to Racing Post Chase winner Simon, showed a glimmer of promise on this British and hurdling debut.
T/Plt: £96.30 to a £1 stake. Pool:£74,188.75 - 561.99 winning tickets T/Qpdt: £12.80 to a £1 stake. Pool:£6,358.36 - 365.63 winning tickets WG

3428 FONTWELL (L-H)

Friday, January 28

OFFICIAL GOING: Good to soft (soft in places; 6.3)
Rail realignment increased chases by 60yds per circuit and hurdles by 80yds per circuit.
Wind: mild across Weather: sunny and bright

3788 FOLLOW CHANCELLOROFTHEFORMCHECKER.CO.UK AT CHELTENHAM BEGINNERS' CHASE (15 fncs) 2m 4f

1:00 (1:00) (Class 4) 5-Y-0+ **£3,252** (£955; £477; £238)

Form RPR

12/4 **1** **Definity (IRE)**43 2979 8-11-0 0.......... NickScholfield 134+
(Paul Nicholls) *j.w: mde all: pushed along after 3 out: styd on wl: pushed out* **4/7**1

P6-3 **2** *6* **Straw Bear (USA)**21 3429 10-11-0 0.......... APMcCoy 130
(Nick Gifford) *trckd ldrs: trckd wnr fr after 6th: rdn after 3 out: a being hld: hit last: no ex fnl 75yds* **9/4**2

10P- **3** *77* **L'Homme De Nuit (GER)**21 4330 7-11-0 0..........(t) DenisO'Regan 60
(Jim Best) *nt fluent early: hld up: no ch w ldrs fr 10th: wnt modest 3rd run-in* **33/1**

4 *nk* **Paddy The Yank (IRE)**279 8-10-11 0.......... DannyCook(3) 59
(Richard Mitchell) *trckd ldrs tl lost tch fr 10th: lost modest 3rd run-in* **100/1**

4U45 **P** **Prince Du Beury (FR)**16 3510 8-11-0 108.......... DarylJacob —
(Jamie Snowden) *w wnr tl slow jump 6th: rdn after next: sn bhd: p.u bef 11th: lame* **10/1**3

5m 22.4s (15.10) **Going Correction** +1.00s/f (Soft) **5** Ran SP% **107.4**
Speed ratings: **109,106,75,75,—**
CSF £2.17 TOTE £1.70: £1.10, £1.10; EX 2.00.
Owner C G Roach **Bred** Kenilworth House Stud **Trained** Ditcheat, Somerset

FOCUS
A small field, but an interesting beginners' chase that turned into a match between the market leaders. There is a case for rating the form up to 7lb higher.

NOTEBOOK
Definity(IRE) put in a professional round of jumping to run out a comfortable winner, using his stamina to string out the field. A decent seasonal re-appearance at Exeter in a hot race had proved that he retained ability and, though this trip was probably short of his best, he was a class above his rivals. He may next run in the Reynoldstown at Ascot or come back here for a 2m6f race that the stable won in 2006 with Star De Mohaison. He remains an exciting chasing prospect and has entries in both the RSA and the Jewson Chase. (op 8-13 tchd 4-6)
Straw Bear(USA) is not a natural at his fences, but this was another solid jumping performance at a trip that probably stretches his stamina. His absence away from racing appears to have re-ignited his enthusiasm and connections can find a beginners' chase to get off the mark. (tchd 2-1)
L'Homme De Nuit(GER) was making his first jumps appearance for 334 days and may come on for the run. (op 25-1)
Paddy The Yank(IRE) jumped adequately on his debut under rules but looks slow.
Prince Du Beury(FR) was too deliberate at his fences and is now 0-23. He was later reported to be lame on his right hind. Official explanation: vet said gelding pulled up lame right-hind (op 9-1 tchd 17-2)

3789 CHANCELLOROFTHEFORMCHECKER.CO.UK ADJUSTED FORM RATINGS "NATIONAL HUNT" NOVICES' HURDLE (9 hdls) 2m 2f 110y

1:30 (1:30) (Class 4) 4-Y-0+ **£2,016** (£592; £296; £147)

Form RPR

-616 **1** **Accordintolawrence (IRE)**27 3295 5-11-2 0.......... KielanWoods(10) 123
(Charlie Longsdon) *trckd ldrs: rdn after 2 out: swtchd lft jst bef last: led run-in: edgd rt: drvn out* **7/1**

6- **2** *2 ¼* **Cottage Acre (IRE)**562 959 8-11-5 0.......... PaddyBrennan 116+
(Tom George) *cl up: led appr 2 out: rdr dropped whip jst bef last: hdd sn after: sn squeezed up and swtchd lft: kpt on but no ex* **40/1**

013 **3** *5* **Pepite Rose (FR)**22 3401 4-10-7 118.......... AidanColeman 97
(Venetia Williams) *trckd ldrs: ev ch appr 2 out: sn rdn: kpt on same pce* **11/4**2

-51F **4** *¾* **Kaituna (IRE)**68 2554 5-11-5 0.......... LeightonAspell 109
(Oliver Sherwood) *led: rdn and hdd appr 2 out: styd on same pce* **15/2**

5 *7* **Cousin Maggie (IRE)**285 7-10-12 0.......... JimmyMcCarthy 97
(Brendan Powell) *trckd ldrs: rdn 3 out: c wd on bnd sn after: fdd after next* **40/1**

006 **6** *20* **Mr Bachster (IRE)**8 3645 6-10-12 0.......... EdGlassonbury(7) 85
(Victor Dartnall) *mid-div: rdn and lost tch appr 3 out* **66/1**

464- **7** *12* **Mossini (IRE)**324 4517 6-11-5 0.......... JamieMoore 74
(Gary Moore) *a towards rr* **40/1**

00 **8** *1 ¾* **Mighty Monty**27 3295 6-11-5 0.......... DenisO'Regan 72
(Victor Dartnall) *a towards rr* **33/1**

000 **9** *2 ½* **Champs De Bleu (FR)**30 3196 8-11-5 0.......... AndrewGlassonbury 70
(Gary Moore) *mid-dvision: nudged along after 5th: wknd after next* **100/1**

000 **10** *1 ½* **Kidajo**30 3200 5-11-5 0.......... HaddenFrost 69
(Roger Curtis) *mid-div tl wknd 6th* **100/1**

0 **11** *1 ¾* **Oscar The Myth (IRE)**21 3434 5-11-5 0.......... DarylJacob 67
(Jamie Snowden) *hmpd 1st: a towards rr* **100/1**

44 **U** **Baile Anrai (IRE)**25 3366 7-11-5 0.......... TomScudamore 104
(Ian Williams) *w ldr tl rdn after 3 out: hld in cl 7th whn bdly hmpd and uns rdr 2 out* **5/1**3

-1P0 **U** **Bad Sir Brian (IRE)**67 2577 6-11-5 0.......... LiamTreadwell —
(Nick Gifford) *mid-div whn blnd bdly and uns rdr 6th* **66/1**

1-2 **F** **Raya Star (IRE)**44 2957 5-11-5 0.......... RobertThornton 116+
(Alan King) *mid-div: blnd 1st: hdwy 6th: pushed along and disputing cl 2nd whn fell 2 out* **9/4**1

5m 1.40s (27.10) **Going Correction** +1.00s/f (Soft)
WFA 4 from 5yo+ 11lb **14** Ran SP% **114.6**
Speed ratings (Par 105): **82,81,78,78,75 67,62,61,60,59 59,—,—,—**
toteswingers:1&2:£39.30, 1&3:£6.00, 2&3:£26.40 CSF £230.96 TOTE £6.00: £2.00, £6.60, £1.70; EX 227.70.
Owner Johnnie Lightfoot **Bred** James Lacy **Trained** Over Norton, Oxon
■ Stewards' Enquiry : Kielan Woods two-day ban: careless riding (Feb 11-12)

FOCUS
A competitive novice hurdle run at a steady pace. After a stewards' inquiry involving the first two, the result remained unaltered. Favourite Raya Star fell two out when seemingly travelling best. The time was relatively slow but the form is given the benefit of the doubt.

NOTEBOOK
Accordintolawrence(IRE) was running under a penalty and swooped late to put his flop last time out behind him. Despite cutting the runner-up off in the closing stages, he still won comfortably and looks a nice prospect. (op 10-1 tchd 6-1)

Cottage Acre(IRE) was a dual point winner in Ireland and was having his first run for 562 days. This was a good effort and he looks the sort to be winning his fair share of races. His jockey lost his whip after the last. (tchd 33-1 and 50-1)
Pepite Rose(FR) was receiving both age and sex allowances and set the standard, giving the form a solid look. She was prominent for a long time and seemingly ran her race, just tiring in the closing stages. (tchd 5-2)
Kaituna(IRE) led for a long way and kept on at the one pace, showing that her confidence was unaffected by her fall last time out. She is likely to be suited by better ground. (op 10-1 tchd 11-1)
Cousin Maggie(IRE) was making her rules debut and shaped as though she might appreciate further. (op 33-1)
Baile Anrai(IRE) was running a good race before being brought down by the favourite and is another who is likely to enjoy further. (op 6-1)
Raya Star(IRE) fell two out when seemingly travelling best and looking certain to be involved in the finish. The race was thrown wide open leaving four in with a chance at the last. (op 6-1)

3790 OTHER NATIONALS PROJECT AT CHANCELLOROFTHEFORMCHECKER.CO.UK H'CAP CHASE (16 fncs) 2m 6f
2:05 (2:07) (Class 5) (0-90,90) 5-Y-0+ **£1,593** (£467; £233; £116)

Form RPR
404U **1** **Swainson (USA)**[64] 2638 10-11-5 **90** JoshuaMoore[(7)] 100+
(Helen Nelmes) *trckd ldrs: led after 9th: styd on gamely fr 3 out: rdn out* **33/1**
003P **2** *3 ¾* **Bob Casey (IRE)**[21] 3431 9-11-9 **87** RhysFlint 94
(Keith Goldsworthy) *led: hit 9th: sn hdd: chsd wnr: rdn after 4 out: kpt on but a being hld fr next* **4/1**[2]
0242 **3** *1 ¼* **Crystal Prince**[26] 3350 7-11-7 **85** (tp) FelixDeGiles 89
(Charlie Longsdon) *hld up: hdwy after 11th: wnt 3rd after 4 out: sn rdn: styd on same pce fr next* **8/1**
54/1 **4** *13* **Marias Rock**[46] 2930 9-11-8 **86** NickScholfield 78
(Jeremy Scott) *trckd ldrs: rdn after 12th: one pce fr 4 out* **7/2**[1]
P210 **5** *15* **Kappelhoff (IRE)**[45] 2950 14-10-11 **75** (b) LeightonAspell 57
(Lydia Richards) *hld up: pushed along after 10th: sme brief hdwy next: wknd 4 out* **14/1**
4-34 **6** *6* **Paradise Expected**[28] 3258 8-11-6 **87** RichardKilloran[(3)] 65
(Tim Vaughan) *trckd ldrs tl 10th: sn struggling: wknd 4 out* **14/1**
500P **P** **Lidjo De Rouge (FR)**[21] 3433 12-11-12 **90** JamieMoore —
(Paul Henderson) *trckd ldrs tl struggling after 7th: bhd fr 11th: p.u after 4 out* **25/1**
-U42 **U** **Killfinnan Castle (IRE)**[17] 3492 8-10-12 **76** (p) WillKennedy —
(Violet M Jordan) *hld up: blnd whn uns rdr 4th* **7/2**[1]
4232 **P** **Monty's Moon (IRE)**[24] 3388 9-10-11 **75** (b) AidanColeman —
(Rachel Hobbs) *trckd ldr: hit 5th: wknd 11th: t.o whn p.u after 4 out: b.b.v* **7/1**[3]
0003 **P** **Bemused (IRE)**[14] 3543 6-10-0 **64** GerardTumelty —
(Simon Earle) *a in last: slow 5th: mstke 12th: p.u bef next* **20/1**

6m 14.2s (31.20) **Going Correction** +1.00s/f (Soft) **10** Ran SP% **112.9**
Speed ratings: **83,81,81,76,71 68,—,—,—,—**
toteswingers:1&2:£34.50, 1&3:£20.60, 2&3:£13.30 CSF £157.49 CT £1181.92 TOTE £42.40: £5.10, £1.60, £3.30; EX 116.50.
Owner T M W Partnership **Bred** Palides Investments N V Inc & Hair 'Em Corporation **Trained** Warmwell, Dorset

FOCUS
A weak handicap chase, rated through the second to his previous chase best.

NOTEBOOK
Swainson(USA) put in a game performance off top weight. Taking it up with a circuit to go, he kept finding more when asked for an effort and jumped well at the final few fences. An awkward head carriage after the last showed how tired he was, but he still kept running on all the way to the line. This was only his second win in 17 starts at a trip that was probably right at the limit of his stamina, and it remains to be seen whether he can repeat the performance. (op 28-1)
Bob Casey(IRE) stayed on at the one pace for a creditable second on only his third chase start, and may be suited by further. He was not fluent at his fences, but should come on for the experience. (op 5-1)
Crystal Prince travelled ominously well for a long time and looked ready to throw down a challenge turning for home, but found little when asked for an effort. This was an improvement on what he had previously achieved over fences, but he has now won only once from 29 starts, which is a concern. (op 9-1 tchd 15-2)
Marias Rock struggled to get involved off an 8lb higher mark than for her win last time out, but she has not had a lot of recent racing and is worth another chance. (tchd 10-3)
Kappelhoff(IRE) is a three-time C&D winner, but this run was probably as good as he is these days, and he is getting no younger. (op 12-1 tchd 11-1 and 16-1)
Paradise Expected looked on an attractive mark but never got involved. (op 12-1 tchd 16-1)
Monty's Moon(IRE) Official explanation: vet said gelding bled when scoped

3791 CHANCELLOR OF THE FORMCHECKER H'CAP HURDLE (11 hdls) 2m 6f 110y
2:40 (2:42) (Class 4) (0-105,105) 4-Y-0+ **£2,016** (£592; £296; £147)

Form RPR
450F **1** **Balustrade (IRE)**[28] 3260 5-11-7 **100** ColinBolger 105+
(Chris Gordon) *mid-div: hdwy fr after 8th: rdn to chse ldrs after 3 out: led appr last: edgd rt: drvn out* **50/1**
-36B **2** *1* **Twin Bud**[45] 2949 6-10-12 **94** (p) JimmyDerham[(3)] 96
(Anna Newton-Smith) *uns rdr and galloped loose to s: hld up towards rr: hdwy fr 8th: rdn to chse ldrs after 3 out: wnt 2nd run-in: drifted lft: styd on* **16/1**
6-42 **3** *4* **Jordan**[21] 3432 8-10-2 **88** MrTJCannon[(7)] 87
(Suzy Smith) *trckd ldrs: led 3 out: rdn next: hdd bef last: rallying whn squeezed out on rails run-in: hld after* **12/1**
-130 **4** *3* **Ban Uisce (IRE)**[18] 3481 6-11-12 **105** (p) RobertThornton 100
(Neil Mulholland) *hld up towards rr: hdwy after 7th: rdn to chse ldrs after 3 out: styd on same pce fr next* **7/1**[3]
350 **5** *shd* **The Clyda Rover (IRE)**[71] 2482 7-11-5 **98** JamieMoore 93
(Helen Nelmes) *mid-div: hdwy 7th: ev ch 3 out: sn rdn: one pce fr next* **22/1**
50-4 **6** *13* **Hazy Bay**[21] 3432 6-10-7 **86** ow3 AndrewThornton 70
(Michael Roberts) *racd wdst: trckd ldrs tl lost pl after 7th: mstke next: sn rdn: styd on fr after 3 out but nvr bk on terms* **33/1**
2355 **7** *1 ¾* **Captain Becket**[17] 3493 8-11-2 **95** HaddenFrost 77
(James Frost) *trckd ldrs: rdn after 3 out: fdd appr last* **33/1**
0004 **8** *15* **Boosha**[14] 3540 6-10-13 **92** AidanColeman 60
(Rachel Hobbs) *mid-div: hdwy 4th: led after 7th: rdn and hdd 3 out: sn wknd: t.o* **14/1**
P-60 **9** *21* **Dawn At Sea**[87] 2141 9-10-13 **102** (p) ThomasFlint[(10)] 52
(John Flint) *a towards rr: t.o* **16/1**
6-04 **10** *4 ½* **Royaume Bleu (FR)**[46] 2929 6-10-6 **85** FelixDeGiles 30
(Alex Hales) *uns rdr and galloped loose to s: mid-div tl wknd after 8th: t.o* **5/1**[2]
-050 **11** *3 ¾* **French Leave (IRE)**[43] 2980 9-11-0 **93** (t) DenisO'Regan 35
(Victor Dartnall) *in tch: blnd 2nd: rdn after 7th: wknd after next: t.o* **9/1**
5304 **12** *16* **Morestead (IRE)**[21] 3433 6-11-10 **103** (b) LeightonAspell 31
(Brendan Powell) *led tl after 7th: sn rdn: wknd next: t.o* **25/1**
/3-1 **13** *18* **Spanish Cruise (IRE)**[27] 3300 7-11-9 **102** TomScudamore 14
(David Pipe) *chsd ldrs: rdn after 6th: wknd after next: t.o* **10/3**[1]
00-0 **14** *½* **Just Tootsie**[27] 3296 7-10-13 **95** DannyCook[(3)] 6
(Nick Mitchell) *trckd ldrs tl 7th: sn struggling: bhd fr next: t.o: b.b.v* **10/1**
P00/ **P** **Milan Deux Mille (FR)**[665] 4840 9-11-0 **93** (t) GerrySupple —
(David Pipe) *a bhd: losing tch whn p.u bef 7th* **20/1**
4512 **P** **Loco Grande (IRE)**[11] 3603 6-11-2 **95** (p) SamThomas —
(Tim Vaughan) *mid-div whn stmbld bdly 4th: towards rr whn mstke 6th: lost tch after next: t.o whn p.u bef last* **5/1**[2]

6m 2.30s (19.80) **Going Correction** +1.00s/f (Soft) **16** Ran SP% **134.9**
Speed ratings (Par 105): **105,104,103,102,102 97,97,91,84,82 81,76,69,69,— —**
toteswingers:1&2:£73.60, 1&3:£76.50, 2&3:£64.90 CSF £721.87 CT £9846.63 TOTE £75.50: £13.10, £4.50, £1.80, £2.60; EX 1458.50.
Owner L Gilbert **Bred** His Highness The Aga Khan's Studs S C **Trained** Morestead, Hants
■ Stewards' Enquiry : Colin Bolger two-day ban: careless riding (Feb 11-12)

FOCUS
A modest handicap and a big step up from the winner.

NOTEBOOK
Balustrade(IRE) put in a vastly improved performance and kept on gamely in the closing stages. He had shown some promise in the autumn but struggled on testing ground in two runs since. Decent going is clearly key to him and he is going the right way.
Twin Bud was held up in rear and thrived on the stamina test, as she stayed on well and looked to have timed her run to perfection, but just couldn't get to the winner. She still might have improvement in her and may appreciate further. (op 14-1)
Jordan is a consistent sort who runs her race and did so again, but was unlucky to be cut up by the winner after the last, though this didn't affect the result. She can remain competitive off this mark at this level. (op 14-1)
Ban Uisce(IRE) travelled well for a long way and put in a good run off top weight, but perhaps needs a drop down the handicap in order to be winning again. (op 16-1)
The Clyda Rover(IRE) is a lightly raced sort and looked to take it up entering the home straight but tired quickly. He stayed on well at the one pace and may be suited by even further. (op 28-1 tchd 20-1)
Hazy Bay still looks on too high of a mark. (op 40-1)
Captain Becket travelled well for a long way but is better on a sounder surface. (op 40-1)
Spanish Cruise(IRE) Official explanation: jockey said gelding never travelled
Just Tootsie Official explanation: trainer's rep said gelding bled
Loco Grande(IRE) Official explanation: jockey said gelding ran flat

3792 CHANCELLOROFTHEFORMCHECKER.CO.UK CHAMPION JOCKEY OF FONTWELL H'CAP CHASE (13 fncs) 2m 2f
3:15 (3:15) (Class 5) (0-95,94) 5-Y-0+ **£1,951** (£573; £286; £143)

Form RPR
-14P **1** **Randjo (FR)**[78] 2334 6-11-10 **90** DenisO'Regan 110+
(Victor Dartnall) *chsd ldrs: led 9th: drew wl clr after 4 out: mstke last: comf* **9/2**[3]
6550 **2** *20* **Keyneema**[10] 3611 9-11-3 **86** (b[1]) DannyCook[(3)] 83
(Cathy Hamilton) *in tch: wnt 4th after 7th: rdn after 9th: wnt 2nd after 3 out: nvr any ch w wnr* **11/1**
0P03 **3** *4 ½* **Brushford (IRE)**[25] 3377 7-10-13 **79** LeightonAspell 72
(Chris Gordon) *nvr travelling in rr: reminders fr 6th: wl t.o after 9th: styd on fr after 2 out to snatch 3rd fnl stride* **7/2**[2]
3034 **4** *nse* **The Hardy Boy**[11] 3608 11-11-9 **89** NickScholfield 82
(Anna Newton-Smith) *chsd ldrs tl after 7th: no ch fr next: styd on again fr after 3 out* **18/1**
-655 **5** *6* **Littleton Aldor (IRE)**[65] 2604 11-10-5 **78** (b[1]) MrPJTolman[(7)] 68
(Mark Gillard) *j.rt: led: sn clr: hdd 9th: sn rdn: kpt chsng ldrs tl wknd after 2 out* **20/1**
4F52 **P** **Wishes Or Watches (IRE)**[11] 3606 11-9-11 **66** oh2 PeterToole[(3)] —
(John Upson) *in tch tl after 7th: sn bhd: t.o whn p.u bef 2 out* **6/1**
6635 **P** **Maximix**[26] 3349 8-11-2 **92** (v) JosephAkehurst[(10)] —
(Gary Moore) *sn struggling to go pce: hit 3rd: t.o 5th: p.u after 7th* **14/1**
P-42 **P** **Overlaw**[14] 3541 9-11-12 **92** PaddyBrennan —
(Tom George) *chsd ldrs: ev ch 4 out: sn rdn and hld: wknd rapidly and abt to lose 2nd whn p.u bef 3 out: b.b.v* **10/3**[1]
0-P0 **P** **Tinalliat (FR)**[227] 758 8-10-11 **77** (t) PaulMoloney —
(David Rees) *in tch: pckd bdly 2nd: wknd after 6th: t.o whn p.u bef 8th* **16/1**
064F **P** **Raspbary**[18] 3486 5-11-8 **94** JimmyDerham[(3)] —
(Seamus Mullins) *sn struggling in rr: p.u bef 5th: dismntd* **12/1**

5m 9.00s (34.30) **Going Correction** +1.00s/f (Soft)
WFA 5 from 6yo+ 3lb **10** Ran SP% **116.4**
Speed ratings: **63,54,52,52,49 —,—,—,—,—**
toteswingers:1&2:£13.70, 1&3:£4.50, 2&3:£12.80 CSF £51.94 CT £193.37 TOTE £4.20: £1.80, £3.70, £1.70; EX 77.50.
Owner Exors of the Late P M De Wilde **Bred** Denis Fontaine **Trained** Brayford, Devon

FOCUS
A strongly run handicap chase.

NOTEBOOK
Randjo(FR) had made a good impression when winning on his chasing debut in May but had struggled since. He bounced back to form running out an easy winner, taking the running up halfway down the back straight before pulling well clear. The removal of headgear is a key factor as he jumped well and looks likely to have more races in him, perhaps back over the minimum trip as he appears to have the speed for 2m. Official explanation: trainer said, regarding apparent improvement in form, that the gelding ran too keenly in a first-time visor last time. (op 13-2 tchd 7-1)
Keyneema stayed on from the rear, but was passing tired horses and is perhaps flattered by the result. The first-time blinkers seem to have helped and he would be of interest back over 2m, a trip at which both his wins have come. (op 12-1)
Brushford(IRE) also stayed on from a long way back, emphasising the strong early pace set. (op 4-1 tchd 9-2)
The Hardy Boy is much better at Plumpton than anywhere else, but jumped well. (op 16-1)
Littleton Aldor(IRE), in first-time blinkers, still jumped markedly to his right. (op 18-1)
Overlaw pulled up before the third-last when in the mix and is reported to have bled. Official explanation: jockey said gelding stopped quickly and pulled up; vet said gelding bled when scoped (op 7-2)

Raspbary Official explanation: jockey said gelding lost its action and pulled up (op 7-2)

3793 BIG JIM BOOKMAKERS, THE CHANCELLOR'S CHOICE H'CAP HURDLE (9 hdls) 2m 2f 110y

3:50 (3:50) (Class 4) (0-115,115) 4-Y-0+ **£2,016** (£592; £296; £147)

Form				RPR
-020	1		**Dune Shine**[31] 3158 6-11-2 **105**........ LeightonAspell (Oliver Sherwood) *hld up towards rr: stdy prog fr 6th: rdn appr 2 out: styd on wl fr last: led fnl 100yds: rdn out* **20/1**	112+
3425	2	1	**The Bishops Baby (IRE)**[26] 3348 8-10-7 **103**........ MrTJCannon(7) (Richard Rowe) *hld up towards rr: smooth hdwy after 6th: led travelling wl 2 out: sn rdn: edgd lft and hdd fnl 100yds: no ex* **10/1**	107
-P03	3	3	**Sebastiano (FR)**[25] 3378 8-11-5 **108**........(p) JamieMoore (Gary Moore) *mid-div: hdwy after 5th: travelling wl whn bdly hmpd by loose horse on bnd after 3 out: sn rcvrd: rdn and ev ch next: styd on same pce* **16/1**	113+
5240	4	nk	**Sun Quest**[18] 3481 7-10-8 **104**........ RobertKirk(7) (Steven Dixon) *disp ld: mstke 6th: rdn after 3 out: hdd bef next: styd on same pce* **6/1**[2]	106
-240	5	2	**Laustra Bad (FR)**[27] 3299 8-11-10 **113**........(tp) TomScudamore (David Pipe) *chsd ldrs: rdn whn hmpd on bnd after 3 out: styd on same pce* **6/1**[2]	113
11P6	6	16	**Just The Job (IRE)**[18] 3483 7-10-10 **106**........ MarkQuinlan(7) (Neil Mulholland) *mid-div tl outpcd after 6th* **12/1**	91
31/F	7	7	**No To Trident**[92] 2054 6-11-2 **105**........(p) RhysFlint (John Flint) *trckd ldrs: chalng whn mstke 3 out: sn rdn: wknd next* **6/1**[2]	89+
50-0	8	23	**Oh No Not Harry (FR)**[266] 191 6-11-7 **110**........ RobertThornton (Ian Williams) *hld up towards rr: mstke 3rd: rdn and hdwy after 3 out: wknd next* **8/1**[3]	68
2641	9	3/4	**Wheres Johnny**[11] 3610 10-10-10 **106** 7ex........(t) JeremiahMcGrath(7) (Jamie Poulton) *nudged along after 3rd: a towards rr* **22/1**	63
P166	P		**Bolton Hall (IRE)**[4] 1936 9-11-5 **115**........(bt) JoshuaMoore(7) (Keith Goldsworthy) *prom tl drvn after 5th: sn bhd: t.o whn p.u bef last* **33/1**	—
1P	P		**Norisan**[18] 3483 7-10-10 **99**........(t) SamThomas (Alan Jones) *nvr travelling: sn t.o: p.u bef 2 out* **25/1**	—
13P1	P		**Manshoor (IRE)**[26] 3348 6-11-5 **108**........ APMcCoy (Lucy Wadham) *disp ld tl rdn appr 3 out: wknd qckly: p.u bef 2 out* **7/2**[1]	—
F356	U		**Whipperway (IRE)**[26] 3348 4-10-0 **104**........ MarcGoldstein(3) (Sheena West) *trcking ldrs whn blnd bdly and uns rdr 2nd* **9/1**	—

4m 52.5s (18.20) **Going Correction** +1.00s/f (Soft)
WFA 4 from 6yo+ 11lb **13** Ran SP% **124.8**
Speed ratings (Par 105): **101,100,99,99,98 91,88,78,78,— —,—,—**
toteswingers:1&2:£24.50, 1&3:£43.50, 2&3:£33.50 CSF £206.81 CT £3299.51 TOTE £23.10: £6.40, £3.30, £5.20; EX 133.70.
Owner Mobile Distribution Solutions Ltd **Bred** Karen Roydon Racing Ltd **Trained** Upper Lambourn, Berks

FOCUS

A competitive handicap hurdle, and solid-looking form.

NOTEBOOK

Dune Shine seemed to enjoy the cut in the ground as he ran out a game winner, staying on all the way in the home straight. This was only his fifth career start and he seems the sort to continue improving, shaping as though a further stamina test will suit in time. Official explanation: trainer's rep said, regarding apparent improvement in form, that the gelding did not appear quite right when returning from it's previous run. (op 22-1)

The Bishops Baby(IRE) looked the winner from a long way out, travelling all over the field and appeared to have the race won after the last (hitting 1.02 on Betfair), but drifted left and was collared in the dying strides. She has been running well enough without winning, and should find an opportunity soon, perhaps on a sounder surface.

Sebastiano(FR) was hampered by a loose horse round the top bend and was forced wide. In the circumstances it was an excellent run to recover and stay on for third. First-time cheekpieces seem to have helped produce this return to form. (op 18-1)

Sun Quest is now two from 36 starts and probably needs to drop further down the handicap. (op 8-1)

Laustra Bad(FR) hasn't won since April 2007, looks one-paced and will struggle to find an opportunity. (op 8-1)

Norisan Official explanation: jockey said gelding never travelled (op 4-1 tchd 9-2)

Manshoor(IRE) stopped quickly and clearly failed to run his race. Official explanation: jockey said gelding never travelled (op 4-1 tchd 9-2)

3794 VISIT CHANCELLOROFTHEFORMCHECKER.CO.UK DAILY STANDARD OPEN NATIONAL HUNT FLAT RACE 1m 6f

4:20 (4:20) (Class 6) 4-6-Y-0 **£1,370** (£399; £199)

Form				RPR
	1		**Beattie Green** 4-10-0 0........ PaddyBrennan (Stuart Kittow) *cl up: led 4f out: sn clr: v easily* **8/1**	110+
	2	6	**Jumps Road** 4-10-7 0........ JoeTizzard (Colin Tizzard) *prom: led over 6f out: hdd 4f out: sn rdn: kpt on but nt pce of easy wnr* **9/1**	104
	3	17	**Magnifique Etoile** 4-10-7 0........ FelixDeGiles (Charlie Longsdon) *trckd ldrs tl outpcd over 3f out: wknd over 1f out* **15/2**	83
	4	1	**Time Do (FR)** 4-10-7 0........ TomO'Brien (Caroline Keevil) *led tl over 6f out: outpcd over 3f out: wknd over 1f out* **20/1**	82
-13	5	4	**Batonnier (FR)**[30] 3200 5-11-11 0........ RobertThornton (Alan King) *hld up last but wl in tch: hdwy 5f out: sn rdn: wknd 4f out* **15/8**[1]	95
	6	6	**Caunay** 4-10-0 0........ MarkQuinlan(7) (Neil Mulholland) *cl up tl wknd over 4f out* **33/1**	70
3	7	17	**Victor Leudorum (IRE)**[23] 3399 4-10-4 0........ PeterToole(3) (Charlie Mann) *trckd ldrs tl wknd 5f out: t.o* **5/1**[3]	50
	8	8	**Tieptiep (FR)** 4-10-2 0........ MrRMahon(5) (Paul Nicholls) *cl up tl lost pl 1/2-way: last but in tch: rdn 6f out: wknd 5f out: t.o* **9/2**[2]	40
	9	41	**Milton Hill** 4-10-7 0........ MarkGrant (Dominic Ffrench Davis) *in tch tl rdn 5f out: sn wknd: t.o* **66/1**	—

3m 44.5s (13.40) **9** Ran SP% **111.7**
toteswingers:1&2:£8.40, 1&3:£7.90, 2&3:£9.30 CSF £72.63 TOTE £10.70: £2.70, £2.30, £2.60; EX 86.80.
Owner Stuart Kittow **Bred** Manor Farm Packers Ltd **Trained** Blackborough, Devon

FOCUS

An interesting bumper with eight newcomers in a race won last year by Cue Card. The impressive winner is the type to rate higher.

NOTEBOOK

Beattie Green was an impressive winner of a race won 12 months before by Cue Card. She was kept wide by Paddy Brennan, who was an eye-catching booking, and travelled strongly. She quickened in the home straight pulling well clear in the manner of a nice horse. She looks a lovely prospect. (op 12-1)

Jumps Road was a drifter before the off, but defied markets expectations to run a decent race. He led for a long way keeping on well enough and can find a race. (op 11-2)

Magnifique Etoile was a little keen early on and needs to settle better, but should come on for the experience. (op 8-1 tchd 13-2)

Time Do(FR) kept on at the one pace and looks likely to need a stamina test. (op 16-1)

Batonnier(FR) ran okay giving so much weight away. (op 2-1 tchd 9-4)

Victor Leudorum(IRE) was disappointing and never got involved. (tchd 9-2 and 11-2)

T/Jkpt: Not won. T/Plt: £1,341.80 to a £1 stake. Pool:£73,247.89 - 39.85 winning tickets T/Qpdt: £410.40 to a £1 stake. Pool:£6,100.68 - 11.00 winning tickets TM

2533 GOWRAN PARK (R-H)

Friday, January 28

OFFICIAL GOING: Soft

Third time lucky for this meeting, originally scheduled for January 20th.

3796a GALMOY HURDLE (GRADE 2) (13 hdls) 3m

1:45 (1:45) 5-Y-0+ **£21,012** (£6,142; £2,909; £969)

			RPR
1		**Mourad (IRE)**[31] 3175 6-11-8 156........ PTownend (W P Mullins, Ire) *trckd ldrs in mod 4th: tk clsr order bef 3 out: smooth hdwy to ld after 2 out: sn drew clr: nt extended: impressive* **4/9**[1]	167+
2	6	**Moskova (IRE)**[31] 3175 8-10-12 133........ RMPower (Paul Nolan, Ire) *in rr: rdn 5 out: prog into 5th appr 3 out: styd on to go mod 2nd fr bef last* **25/1**	147
3	3	**Oscar Dan Dan (IRE)**[19] 3475 9-11-10 145........ PCarberry (Thomas Mullins, Ire) *hld up in 5th: last and rdn 3 out: kpt on to go mod 3rd after last* **14/1**	156
4	1/2	**Jumbo Rio (IRE)**[28] 3270 6-11-10 149........ AndrewJMcNamara (E J O'Grady, Ire) *mod 3rd: tk clsr order bef 3 out: short of room briefly 2 out: no imp fr bef last: one pce* **7/1**[3]	156
5	8	**Powerstation (IRE)**[31] 3175 11-11-8 151........ BarryGeraghty (Eamonn O'Connell, Ire) *cl 2nd: nt fluent 6 out: pushed along fr bef 3 out: wknd 2 out: sn eased* **11/2**[2]	148
6	15	**Footy Facts (IRE)**[30] 3207 11-11-3 139........ PTEnright (Robert Tyner, Ire) *led: strly pressed fr 3 out: hdd after 2 out: sn no ex and wknd* **14/1**	126

6m 17.1s (-11.80) **6** Ran SP% **114.3**
CSF £13.60 TOTE £1.20: £1.10, £6.50; DF 17.50.
Owner Teahon Consulting Limited **Bred** His Highness The Aga Khan's Studs S C **Trained** Muine Beag, Co Carlow

FOCUS

The easy winner progressed again and looks a World Hurdle player, with the next three rateed close to their marks.

NOTEBOOK

Mourad(IRE) ◆, successful over the same trip at Leopardstown last month, followed up here with another Grade 2 success and one that was very easily achieved. Held up in touch in a race run at a good pace, he closed before two out and led between the last two hurdles, going six lengths clear into the final hurdle before appearing to win with plenty in hand. The winner is unlikely to run again before the Ladbrokes World Hurdle for which he is 8-1 with the sponsors and Stan James, who make him 4-1 (from 7-1) in their 'without Big Buck's' market. (op 8/15)

Moskova(IRE), sixth behind Mourad at Leopardstown on her previous start, reversed placings with a couple of other rivals from that race. She raced in rear and was being pushed along soon after halfway. She made headway from three out and went second before the final hurdle without ever posing a threat to Mourad. She is to be covered in the near future. (op 22/1)

Oscar Dan Dan(IRE), fourth in the race Mourad won at Leopardstown before running moderately in the Pertemps qualifier at that same track, was held up and made his effort on the outside approaching two out. A Grade 1 winner over 2m4f last season, he was unable to raise his effort before the final hurdle.

Jumbo Rio(IRE) has useful form at 2m and 2m4f but had fallen in last year's French Champion Hurdle on his only previous attempt beyond 2m4f. He raced in third place, and after closing three out he was done with by the second-last hurdle. (op 13/2)

Powerstation(IRE), second in this race a year ago, had been beaten only two lengths when runner-up to Mourad in the Christmas Hurdle at Leopardstown's Christmas meeting. He raced upsides the front-running Footy Facts for much of the journey before weakening from two out. Now 11, he is more effective on better ground than the tacky conditions he encountered here. (op 11/2 tchd 6/1)

3798a CONNOLLY'S RED MILLS THYESTES H'CAP CHASE (GRADE A) (16 fncs) 3m

2:55 (2:55) 5-Y-0+ **£50,431** (£14,741; £6,982; £2,327)

			RPR
1		**Siegemaster (IRE)**[31] 3176 10-11-7 145........(b) DNRussell (D T Hughes, Ire) *trckd ldrs: 7th 6 out: 6th and prog after 4 out: 3rd 2 out: led appr last: kpt on wl u.p whn strly pressed cl home* **16/1**	162
2	3/4	**The Midnight Club (IRE)**[283] 5303 10-11-2 140........ EMullins (W P Mullins, Ire) *hld up: sme prog on outer whn bad mstke 6 out: 11th 4 out: 8th and hdwy appr 3 out: 5th 2 out: 2nd after last: styd on wl* **6/1**[2]	156
3	3	**Ballytrim (IRE)**[30] 3207 10-11-0 138........ RMPower (W P Mullins, Ire) *hld up: 13th bef 4 out: 9th and prog bef 3 out: 4th 2 out: 2nd bef last: kpt on same pce* **33/1**	151
4	3 1/2	**Alpha Ridge (IRE)**[28] 3269 9-10-11 135........(t) BarryGeraghty (Paul Nolan, Ire) *a.p: led and disp fr 7th: edgd clr after 4 out: strly pressed 2 out: hdd appr last: no ex* **9/2**[1]	145+
5	1/2	**Bella Mana Mou (IRE)**[20] 3461 9-9-12 122........(t) NPMadden (Michael Cullen, Ire) *hld up: hdwy after 4 out: mod 2nd appr 3 out: chal after next: no ex appr last* **20/1**	131+
6	1 1/4	**Pomme Tiepy (FR)**[30] 3206 8-10-6 130........ PTownend (W P Mullins, Ire) *hld up towards rr: hdwy 4 out: 7th appr 3 out: kpt on same pce u.p fr next* **6/1**[2]	138
7	6	**Selection Box (IRE)**[29] 3233 10-9-13 128........ EJO'Connell(5) (C A McBratney, Ire) *trckd ldrs: prog into mod 4th 6 out: 3rd next: rdn fr 4 out: no ex fr 3 out* **25/1**	130
8	1 3/4	**Telenor**[298] 5067 8-10-13 137........(t) AELynch (J T R Dreaper, Ire) *mid-div: 8th 6 out: no imp fr 4 out: kpt on same pce* **10/1**	137
9	9	**Whinstone Boy (IRE)**[27] 3327 10-11-1 139........ SWFlanagan (James Joseph Mangan, Ire) *led: hdd 7th: 3rd 5 out: 2nd and prog 4 out: no ex fr 3 out* **12/1**	130

10 1 3/4 **Will Jamie Run (IRE)**[30] 3206 10-9-6 121 .... CDMaxwell(5) 111
(John C McConnell, Ire) *prom: 2nd early: 4th 1/2-way: 5th whn mstke 6 out: no ex fr 4 out* **25/1**

11 25 **Hangover (IRE)**[30] 3206 9-10-0 129 ....(p) APHeskin(5) 94
(Conor O'Dwyer, Ire) *prom: cl 2nd 1/2-way: disputing ld whn pckd bdly 8 out: hdd 5 out: wknd after 4 out* **8/1**[3]

P **Cane Brake (IRE)**[28] 3271 12-10-13 137 ....(p) DJCasey —
(Conor O'Dwyer, Ire) *a towards rr: p.u bef 3 out* **25/1**

P **Miss Mitch (IRE)**[89] 2117 10-10-13 137 .... AndrewJMcNamara —
(P A Fahy, Ire) *trckd ldrs: 5th 1/2-way: wkng whn mstke 6 out: p.u bef 4 out* **16/1**

P **Stewarts House (IRE)**[30] 3206 9-9-13 128 ....(t) KMDonoghue(5) —
(A L T Moore, Ire) *trckd ldrs in 6th: bad mstke 5th: wknd 5 out: p.u bef 3 out* **12/1**

P **Good Fella (IRE)**[298] 5065 10-9-13 123 .... MFMooney —
(Patrick Mooney, Ire) *sn trailing in rr: p.u bef 3 out* **33/1**

P **Agus A Vic (IRE)**[30] 3206 10-9-10 123 ....(tp) APThornton(3) —
(Patrick Martin, Ire) *towards rr: prog into 9th 6 out: 4th briefly appr 3 out: sn no ex: p.u bef last* **9/1**

P **Hume River (IRE)**[27] 3320 9-9-11 121 ....(bt1) TPTreacy —
(Mrs John Harrington, Ire) *chsd ldrs: 6th bef 1/2-way: lost pl bef 6 out: p.u bef 4 out* **25/1**

P **Across The Bay (IRE)**[19] 3475 7-10-6 130 .... PCarberry —
(Noel Meade, Ire) *hld up: p.u bef 8 out* **14/1**

6m 15.7s (-3.30) **18** Ran SP% **136.8**
CSF £113.83 CT £3226.69 TOTE £20.70: £3.90, £1.40, £10.10, £1.80; DF 192.30.
Owner Gigginstown House Stud **Bred** Col W B Mullins **Trained** The Curragh, Co Kildare

FOCUS

A memorable finish to a renewal more than worthy of the track's showcase race. They went a strong gallop and the form should stand up well. The winner improved slightly on last year's third in this.

NOTEBOOK

Siegemaster(IRE) was probably entitled to be a little shorter in the betting here, considering he was running off just 1lb higher than when third in this race last year and he has generally been holding his form. He was always well placed, game when he hit the front, and was always holding the runner-up. The blinkers seem to help the winner. Once reassessed, he will probably be between a rock and a hard place in terms of races to run in, but he is probably worth another tilt at the Irish National. The Aintree equivalent in 2012 is on the agenda, too.

The Midnight Club(IRE) is probably the one to take out of the race with a view to the future. This horse is not far off Grade 1 class and would surely have won but for a crucial mistake. His lack of a recent run was probably not a huge drawback given who trains him, but this was a performance worthy of great credit and he must be considered a leading player for the Aintree National. He seems to have a preference for deep ground, but he got away with it at Cheltenham when third in last season's Jewson. He was cut to a general 20-1 co-favourite for the National after the race. (op 8/1)

Ballytrim(IRE) is a dour stayer, and with that in mind he looked like he may master them all when he got so close by the second-last. He bounced back to form here and will presumably be aimed at the Irish National.

Alpha Ridge(IRE), remarkably backed at 1-6 in running, disputed a pace that inevitably had him running out of steam late on. He jumped a little left at times but generally quite boldly, and it is hard to fault this performance. (op 6/1)

Bella Mana Mou(IRE), pulled up in her last three handicap chases, was accordingly hard to fancy, but she bounced back to her best. She looked a big danger turning in, but her run just petered out. She is probably too high in the weights to win a big pot.

Pomme Tiepy(FR) looked a vulnerable favourite and she was in trouble quite a way out. She ran on but will be hard to place now and has gone a long time without winning. (op 5/1)

Selection Box(IRE) looked a threat five out but soon had no more to give.

Telenor ◆ almost certainly will be appreciably better for the outing and ran a creditable enough race. It may serve to get him dropped a couple of pounds in the handicap, and he remains of interest ahead of the Irish National. (op 11/1)

Whinstone Boy(IRE) was always liable to struggle off his mark in his bid to win back-to-back renewals, especially as he could not get a soft lead.

Agus A Vic(IRE) Official explanation: vet said gelding was found to have lost a front shoe in running

Across The Bay(IRE) Official explanation: jockey said gelding never travelled throughout

3797 - 3801a (Foreign Racing) - See Raceform Interactive

3288 CHELTENHAM (L-H)

Saturday, January 29

OFFICIAL GOING: Good to soft (good in places)

Wind: Moderate behind Weather: Overcast

3802 JCB TRIUMPH HURDLE TRIAL (JUVENILE HURDLE) (GRADE 2) (8 hdls) 2m 1f

12:55 (12:55) (Class 1) 4-Y-O

£12,827 (£4,812; £2,409; £1,201; £603; £301)

Form RPR

11 **1** **Local Hero (GER)**[17] 3507 4-11-4 129 .... APMcCoy 132+
(Steve Gollings) *trckd ldrs: hit 4 out: nt fluent 2 out: drvn and styd on wl to chal whn nt fluent last: styd on gamely u.p to ld fnl 50yds: kpt on strly* **15/8**[1]

1 **2** 2 **Third Intention (IRE)**[45] 2958 4-11-4 0 .... JoeTizzard 128+
(Colin Tizzard) *t.k.h: w ldr tl led 2 out travelling wl: shkn up and jnd last: drvn and kpt on wl run-in: hdd and one pce fnl 50yds* **5/2**[2]

3 2 3/4 **Indian Daudaie (FR)**[83] 2266 4-11-7 0 .... HarrySkelton 129+
(Paul Nicholls) *in tch: chsd ldrs fr 3 out: nt fluent next and sn rdn: nt pce of ldng duo appr last but kpt on run-in* **5/1**[3]

5123 **4** 11 **Akula (IRE)**[49] 2882 4-11-4 125 .... RichardJohnson 118+
(Mark H Tompkins) *led tl hdd 2 out: wknd after and no ch w ldng trio whn mstke last* **10/1**

31 **5** 5 **Mark Twain (IRE)**[16] 3519 4-11-0 134 ....(t) SeanQuinlan 108
(Kim Bailey) *chsd ldrs: rdn after 3 out: wknd and pckd 2 out: no ch whn pckd last* **10/1**

1 **6** 3 1/2 **Maoi Chinn Tire (IRE)**[92] 2078 4-11-7 0 .... AlanO'Keeffe 110
(Jennie Candlish) *in rr: nt fluent 4th: hdwy to chse ldrs 3 out: hit next and wknd sn after* **9/1**

4 **7** 36 **Lapin Garou (FR)**[10] 3624 4-11-0 0 .... DarylJacob 71
(Nick Williams) *in rr: nt fluent 2nd: nt fluent 4 out: hdwy to cl on ldrs next: rdn: nt fluent and wknd 2 out* **25/1**

4m 14.15s (2.85) **Going Correction** +0.25s/f (Yiel) **7** Ran SP% **112.0**
Speed ratings: **103,102,100,95,93 91,74**
toteswingers:1&2:£1.50, 1&3:£1.60, 2&3:£2.30 CSF £6.65 TOTE £2.50: £1.80, £2.10; EX 5.80.
Owner P J Martin **Bred** Gestut Evershorst **Trained** Scamblesby, Lincs
■ This event was previously known as the Finesse Hurdle.

FOCUS

This juvenile Grade 2 has lived up to its title in recent seasons with Katchit having gone on to win the Triumph Hurdle, and Walkon, Franchoek and Akilak all finishing placed following their victories here. There was plenty of interest amongst the runners in this year's field and it produced a terrific finish. The winner is rated a bit better than the bare result but is still a stone or more off an ordinary Triumph Hurdle winner. A step up from the second and the third should improve.

NOTEBOOK

Local Hero(GER), a middle-distance Flat winner who had won both his previous starts over hurdles, retained his unbeaten record in game fashion. He did well to score considering he made several mistakes, the worst at the fifth, and an awkward jump at the last looked to have cost him the race. However, he battled back and won with something in reserve. He was quoted at 14-1 for the Triumph afterwards and will be suited by the likely stronger gallop in that race. There is nothing wrong with his attitude but he will need to jump better to win at the festival. (op 7-4, 13-8 and 2-1 and 9-4 in a place)

Third Intention(IRE), a fast-ground middle-distance Flat winner in Ireland who stayed on well to take a Newbury juvenile hurdle on his debut, was very keen in the early stages. He committed for home off the bend but the winner looked to have his measure going to the last. However, he jumped it much better than his rival and went clear, only to be run down in the last half-furlong. The impression was that he might well reverse this form given a stronger gallop, and he is quoted at 16-1 for the Triumph following this. (op 3-1 tchd 10-3 in places)

Indian Daudaie(FR), a hurdles winner in France and runner-up in a Grade 1 at Auteuil before joining current connections, ran well on this British debut on ground arguably quicker than he prefers. He was not beaten far by the front pair, though, and was giving them both weight, so this was creditable. However, his trainer has plenty of other, arguably stronger, candidates for the Triumph and it will be no surprise if he goes to the Fred Winter instead. (tchd 9-2, 11-2 and 6-1 in a place)

Akula(IRE), a winner at Ludlow, provided a guide to the relative merits of these, having finished third to Triumph Hurdle second-favourite Sam Winner over C&D in December. He made much of the running and was only beaten off going to the last, where he made a bad mistake. As a result, he was beaten further by the winner here. (op 12-1)

Mark Twain(IRE), a 1m winner on the Flat and third to Triumph Hurdle favourite Grandouet on his hurdling debut at Newbury, was an easy winner at Catterick next time. Wearing a first-time tongue tie, he was under pressure on the turn downhill to three out and finished well held. On this evidence, his official rating of 134 looks on the high side. (op 9-1)

Maoi Chinn Tire(IRE), a three-time winner at 6f and 7f on the Flat and all-weather, caused a 200-1 surprise when running away with the Listed Wensleydale Hurdle on his hurdling debut with the current Triumph Hurdle favourite well behind. Having his first outing since, he travelled well enough under restraint but found nothing up the hill. His stamina probably ran out on this stiffer course and tacky ground, and he could do better on a flatter track and faster going in the spring. (op 10-1 tchd 12-1)

Lapin Garou(FR), a French-bred who was well beaten on his hurdling debut at Newbury, had to improve considerably on that to feature here and was well beaten. He looks to need more time. (op 22-1 tchd 20-1)

3803 TIMEFORM NOVICES' H'CAP CHASE (17 fncs) 2m 5f

1:30 (1:30) (Class 2) 5-Y-O+

£12,524 (£3,700; £1,850; £926; £462; £232)

Form RPR

5-1F **1** **The Giant Bolster**[78] 2348 6-11-12 **140** .... RodiGreene 148+
(David Bridgwater) *hmpd and in rr 1st: hit 7th: rdn 10th: hdwy next: drvn 13th: lost pl 4 out: disputing 5th next: rallied sn after: rdn to chal last: sn led: drvn out* **5/1**[2]

-563 **2** 2 1/4 **Vino Griego (FR)**[63] 2670 6-11-2 **130** .... JamieMoore 137+
(Gary Moore) *chsd ldrs: hit 7th: chal 8th tl blnd 11th: chal 12th: blnd 3 out: chal last: sn led: hdd after last: kpt on same pce* **7/1**

-221 **3** 1 1/4 **Pearlysteps**[26] 3368 8-11-3 **138** .... JakeGreenall(7) 141
(Henry Daly) *chsd ldrs: hit 7th and 10th: blnd 11th: hit 3 out: rallied fr next: chsng ldrs whn hit last: one pce* **8/1**

-521 **4** 2 3/4 **Misstree Dancer**[31] 3198 7-11-0 **128** .... HarrySkelton 129
(Nick Mitchell) *slt advantage but a hrd pressed: rdn 4 out: stmbld 2 out and hdd: wknd last* **9/1**

2-11 **5** 1 **Diamond Brook (IRE)**[71] 2502 6-10-7 **121** .... DarylJacob 121
(Nick Williams) *pressed ldr tl mstke 10th: wknd and no ch whn hit 4 out: mstke 2 out* **6/1**

1134 **6** 11 **Cootehill (IRE)**[84] 2220 7-11-2 **130** .... PaddyBrennan 122
(Nigel Twiston-Davies) *hit 2nd: chsd ldrs: chal fr 4th tl hit 12th: wknd and hit 3 out* **20/1**

-311 **7** 25 **Shakalakaboomboom (IRE)**[19] 3479 7-11-6 **134** .... BarryGeraghty 110
(Nicky Henderson) *in rr but in tch: hit 4th: nt fluent 6th: chsd ldrs 9th: wknd bef 3 out* **5/2**[1]

-142 **F** **Ravethebrave (IRE)**[31] 3198 7-11-1 **129** .... RobertThornton —
(Alan King) *fell 1st* **11/2**[3]

5m 29.5s (10.10) **Going Correction** +0.525s/f (Soft) **8** Ran SP% **113.3**
Speed ratings: **101,100,99,98,98 94,84,—**
toteswingers:1&2:£7.40, 1&3:£11.80, 2&3:£19.90 CSF £38.41 CT £273.31 TOTE £5.70: £2.20, £2.60, £3.20; EX 38.70 Trifecta £132.40 Pool £649.91 - 3.63 winning units..
Owner Simon Hunt **Bred** Gestut Fahrhof **Trained** Icomb, Gloucs
■ Stewards' Enquiry : Rodi Greene two-day ban: used whip with excessive frequency (Feb 12-13)
Jamie Moore two-day ban: used whip with excessive frequency (Feb 12-13)

FOCUS

A really interesting novices' handicap chase that proved a dour test in the ground, which was clearly stamina-sapping and certainly softer than the official description. The first two are rated better than the bare result and in line with their best hurdles form.

NOTEBOOK

The Giant Bolster ◆, off since falling behind Time For Rupert at the course in November, had earlier made a successful chase debut, and he deserves a huge amount of credit for defying top-weight. Soon on the back foot following slow jumps at each of the first two fences (also slightly hampered), he was never travelling particularly well, Rodi Greene having to keep him up to his work, but it was clear from three out that he still had plenty of running left in him and, having closed and been switched before the last, it was he who came up the hill best. On this evidence 3m is going to suit over fences and it would be no surprise to see him take his chance in the RSA, having finished a very good sixth at 200-1 in the Neptune last term. Alternatively, there's the new Centenary novice handicap (formerly the Jewson). (op 7-1 tchd 9-2)

Vino Griego(FR) continues to be a nearly horse. A fine-looking animal with plenty of size, and ability to match, he jumped really well for much of the race, but just when looking to have seized control, he nodded badly on landing three out, and in the end was outstayed. He hasn't won since his novice hurdle over a year ago and perhaps it would be in the horse's interests to gain a confidence-boosting victory in a minor novice chase at one of the lesser tracks. (op 17-2)

Pearlysteps, winner of a Hereford beginners' chase, rallied having lost his position and was close enough coming to the last, but could find no extra. This was a satisfactory start in handicaps.

Misstree Dancer, a winner at Newbury latest, gave it a bold shot off an 8lb higher mark. She can win again back against her own sex. (tchd 11-1)

Diamond Brook(IRE) had achieved little in two wins at Exeter (lucky winner first time; scraped home latest), and he was beaten a long way out here from 2lb higher. (op 13-2 tchd 11-2 and 7-1 in a place)

Cootehill(IRE) would have found this ground too soft. (op 16-1)

Shakalakaboomboom(IRE), whose two wins over fences had come on flat, right-handed tracks, was up another 6lb and never looked like completing the hat-trick, being niggled with a circuit to run, and ended up well held. He probably needs to go back right-handed. (op 11-4)

3804 MURPHY GROUP CHASE (H'CAP) (GRADE 3) (17 fncs) 2m 5f

2:00 (2:00) (Class 1) 5-Y-0+

£22,804 (£8,556; £4,284; £2,136; £1,072; £536)

Form RPR

-F12 **1** **Wishfull Thinking**[50] 2867 8-11-3 **148**.........................(t) RichardJohnson 160+
(Philip Hobbs) *j.w: trckd ldrs: led travelling wl 13th: in command fr after 3 out: styd on strly: rdn out* **9/2**[1]

5624 **2** *3 ½* **Calgary Bay (IRE)**[49] 2886 8-10-12 **143**............................. HaddenFrost 152
(Henrietta Knight) *in tch: wnt 2nd 14th: ev ch 3 out: sn rdn: styd on but hld fr next* **11/2**[3]

U1-5 **3** *11* **Bakbenscher**[89] 2126 8-10-9 **140**.................................... RobertThornton 145+
(Alan King) *hld up: hit 3rd: disputing cl 3rd whn nt fluent 4 out: sn rdn: styd on same pce fr next: awkward on landing last and nrly uns rdr* **10/1**

-506 **4** *16* **The Sawyer (BEL)**[7] 3677 11-10-8 **139**............................... WillKennedy 123
(Bob Buckler) *chsd ldrs tl rdn whn outpcd after 13th: sn no ch: wnt modest 4th at the last* **16/1**

-115 **5** *7* **Little Josh (IRE)**[49] 2886 9-11-10 **155**.............................. PaddyBrennan 135
(Nigel Twiston-Davies) *led tl 13th: rdn whn hit 3 out: sn wknd: lost modest 4th at the last* **13/2**

-214 **6** *13* **Buffalo Bob (IRE)**[28] 3290 8-10-3 **134**................................ SeanQuinlan 103
(Kim Bailey) *chsd ldr tl 10th: chsd ldrs: rdn after 12th: mstke 14th: sn btn: t.o* **5/1**[2]

0B-3 **7** *16* **Chapoturgeon (FR)**[44] 2976 7-11-5 **150**.......................... TimmyMurphy 101
(Paul Nicholls) *hld up: veered lft on path after 5th: sme hdwy 10th: rdn after 13th: wknd after 3 out: t.o* **10/1**

6-21 **8** *23* **Drever Route (IRE)**[108] 1828 8-10-0 **131** oh3.................... BrianHughes 61
(Howard Johnson) *hld up towards rr: rdn after 11th: wknd after 4 out: t.o* **10/1**

11/2 **P** **Noland**[39] 3060 10-11-12 **157**.. APMcCoy —
(Paul Nicholls) *chsd ldrs early: dropped to 6th at the 4th: struggling whn nt fluent 9th (water) and next: bhd fr after 11th: p.u bef 4 out* **13/2**

P-F6 **U** **Atouchbetweenacara (IRE)**[70] 2524 10-10-6 **137**.......... AidanColeman —
(Venetia Williams) *towards rr whn virtually fell and uns rdr 8th* **14/1**

5m 23.4s (4.00) **Going Correction** +0.525s/f (Soft) **10** Ran SP% **116.7**
Speed ratings: **113,111,107,101,98 93,87,78,—,—**
toteswingers:1&2:£6.00, 1&3:£5.30, 2&3:£14.10 CSF £30.16 CT £236.31 TOTE £4.70: £2.40, £2.30, £3.00; EX 35.70 Trifecta £294.00 Pool £2,145.88 - 5.40 winning units..

Owner Mrs Diana L Whateley **Bred** Cobhall Court Stud **Trained** Withycombe, Somerset

■ This event was most recently known as the Betfair Trophy.

FOCUS

A high-class and competitive handicap chase typical of races run at around this trip on the track, and the time was nearly 7secs faster than the preceding novices' handicap. The winner produced a big step forward in the first-time tongue tie and is obvious festival material, and the second was close to his best

NOTEBOOK

Wishfull Thinking ◆ is a useful novice chaser who won a Grade 2 at Wincanton before running Reve De Sivola, whom he was giving 8lb, to just over a length over C&D in December, having been badly hampered at the water. Wearing a first-time tongue tie on his handicap debut over fences, he travelled well and his jumping put his more experienced rivals to shame. He went on at the top of the hill and was always holding his nearest rival thereafter. He is likely to have several options if returning here for the festival, with the Jewson, RSA Chase and possibly the Festival Plate amongst them, and looks a major contender for the first-named. (op 5-1 tchd 11-2 in a place)

Calgary Bay(IRE), a C&D winner here back in 2009, stays further but ran well again over C&D in December. He also travelled well and was the only serious challenger to the winner from three out. He kept trying and could have a similar race in him, particularly around here, if maintaining his form. (op 7-1)

Bakbenscher ◆, a dual chase winner but one who has gained most of his wins on sharp or flat tracks, again made mistakes but ran well on this first start since the beginning of November. He might appreciate a return to softer ground than this.

The Sawyer(BEL) was bidding to complete a hat-trick in the race, but had not scored since winning here last year and had finished mostly well beaten. Despite that and the fact that he had dropped in the weights of late, he was still racing off a mark 5lb higher than in 2010, and in this contest was struggling at the top of the hill. He did, however, stay on in the closing stages for fourth.

Little Josh(IRE), a game all-the-way winner of the Paddy Power in November, was raised 9lb for that and finished behind Calgary Bay over C&D in December. Meeting that rival on the same terms, he got an uncontested lead early, but was taken on by the winner at the top of the hill and gradually faded.

Buffalo Bob(IRE) has won at up to 3m but looked to be found out for stamina over 3m2f here last time despite running well. However, he did not jump that fluently and is another who is likely to appreciate softer going than this, and possibly a return to further. (op 7-1)

Chapoturgeon(FR) won the Jewson at the festival over this C&D back in 2009. He had not won since, though, and has had jumping problems. He looked somewhat reluctant early before making a short-lived effort at the top of the hill. He needs some help from the handicapper and possibly the aid of headgear.

Drever Route(IRE) proved he stayed this sort of trip when scoring at Wetherby in October, but had not been seen since and was 9lb higher in a better race. He never got competitive. (op 9-1 tchd 12-1 in a place)

Noland, a high-class chaser and hurdler in his time - he won the Supreme Novices' Hurdle and finished third in the Arkle Trophy on this track - returned from two years off to finish second in a jumpers' bumper at Kempton before Christmas. However, he lost his place after racing prominently early and was pulled up near the top of the hill. He could be retired. (tchd 16-1 in a place)

Atouchbetweenacara(IRE), lightly raced and well beaten since scoring over C&D in April 2009, made an horrendous error going away from the stands, giving his jockey no chance. (tchd 16-1 in a place)

3805 ARGENTO CHASE (REGISTERED AS THE COTSWOLD CHASE) (GRADE 2) (21 fncs) 3m 1f 110y

2:30 (2:30) (Class 1) 5-Y-0+ **£51,309** (£19,251; £9,639; £4,806; £2,412)

Form RPR

4/B0 **1** **Neptune Collonges (FR)**[50] 2871 10-11-0 162..................... APMcCoy 171
(Paul Nicholls) *mde all: rdn 4 out: clr whn given breather after 3 out: rdn and stl clr 2 out: hrd rdn and fading run-in: hld on all out* **11/2**

4-32 **2** *1 ¼* **Tidal Bay (IRE)**[70] 2524 10-11-0 166................................... BrianHughes 171
(Howard Johnson) *hld up in 4th: rdn and hdwy fr 3 out: chsd wnr wl bef 2 out but stl plenty to do: styd on wl as wnr fdd run-in: fin strly but a hld* **5/2**[2]

15-2 **3** *30* **Punchestowns (FR)**[31] 3195 8-11-5 158.......................... BarryGeraghty 151
(Nicky Henderson) *trckd wnr fr 5th tl hit 15th and lost position: styd on again to go 2nd 4 out: rdn and no imp sn after and nt fluent 3 out: wknd and lost 2nd wl bef 2 out* **11/10**[1]

5-24 **4** *4 ½* **The Tother One (IRE)**[63] 2673 10-11-0 152......................(p) DarylJacob 141
(Paul Nicholls) *chsd wnr to 5th: nt fluent 6th: wnt 2nd again 15th but nvr any ch: dropped to 3rd 4 out: sn wknd* **5/1**[3]

-2F6 **5** *2 ½* **Madison Du Berlais (FR)**[14] 3560 10-11-0 149........(p) TomScudamore 137
(David Pipe) *hit 6th: a in last: lost tch fr 4 out* **14/1**

6m 48.78s (10.58) **Going Correction** +0.525s/f (Soft) **5** Ran SP% **114.9**
Speed ratings: **104,103,94,93,92**
CSF £20.47 TOTE £6.10: £2.00, £1.70; EX 21.50.

Owner J Hales **Bred** G A E C Delorme Freres **Trained** Ditcheat, Somerset

FOCUS

A very informative running of this Gold Cup trial, with one pretender's bubble well and truly burst, and a former star seeing his flame reignited. Runner-up Tidal Bay, although a moody performer, can be used as the benchmark to the form. Neptune Collonges was rated 178 at his peak but things went his way here, while Punchestowns faced a stiff task at the weights but was still disappointing.

NOTEBOOK

Neptune Collonges(FR) was quickly sent into the lead by McCoy and never gave it up. Although the likeable grey hadn't shown up in a handicap off 164 here last time, little went right that day (forced to be held up following very slow start) and, being a three-time Grade 1-winning chaser (also third and fourth in two Gold Cups), it was no surprise to see him stay out in front. McCoy, keen to make use of his jumping/stamina, pressed on a long way from home and, despite the enigmatic Tidal Bay chasing him up the hill, he always looked like holding on. Clearly still capable of very high-class form, he's only ten, and it wouldn't be the biggest surprise were he to put up another good show back here in March - although his trainer was keen to state this may have been his 'Gold Cup'. The Grand National is also under consideration. (op 7-1)

Tidal Bay(IRE), who, according to RPRs, recorded a career-best when bustling up Imperial Commander at Haydock, often runs well here and Brian Hughes was doing his best to 'kid' him along throughout the contest. Although given a lot to do to the naked eye, that's the way he has to be ridden, and as was the case at Haydock, he was closing with every stride at the line. He deserves to take his chance in the Gold Cup and, providing there's a good gallop on, he'd hold strong place claims at the very least. (tchd 11-4)

Punchestowns(FR) was disappointing,, although there was a suspicion beforehand that this would prove more of a test than he cares for. A beaten favourite in last season's RSA (returned with a chipped bone in his hock), he had reportedly come on appreciably for his reappearance effort, but jumping was put under the spotlight by the winner, and he simply didn't jump fluently enough. It would be no surprise to see him go for the World Hurdle now, a race he was runner-up in two years ago, although his trainer is adamant that he still needed this and will go for the Gold Cup. (op 5-4 tchd 11-8 in places)

The Tother One(IRE) didn't jump well enough and was disappointing, considering the smaller field and first-time cheekpieces were expected to bring about improvement. (op 11-2)

Madison Du Berlais(FR), subject to a change of tactics, never got out of last and remains below his best. The Haydock Grand National trial will be next.

3806 NEPTUNE INVESTMENT MANAGEMENT NOVICES' HURDLE (REGISTERED AS CLASSIC NOVICES' HURDLE RACE) (GRADE 2) (10 hdls) 2m 4f 110y

3:05 (3:07) (Class 1) 4-Y-0+**£14,252** (£5,347; £2,677; £1,335; £670; £335)

1-11 **1** **Bobs Worth (IRE)**[28] 3288 6-11-12 140........................... BarryGeraghty 153+
(Nicky Henderson) *a wl in tch: trckd ldrs 3 out: carried rt wl bef 2 out but pressed ldr sn after: led wl bef last: jnd run-in: drvn: edge lft and asserted fnl 120yds: won gng away* **7/2**[2]

1-11 **2** *2 ¼* **Rock On Ruby (IRE)**[31] 3196 6-11-12 0..........................(t) HarrySkelton 150+
(Paul Nicholls) *hld up towards rr but in tch: hdwy to trck ldrs fr 6th: disputing 2nd whn clipped 2 out: rallied to press wnr last and upsides sn after: edgd lft and outpcd u.p and rdr dropped whip fnl 120yds* **6/1**[3]

-113 **3** *9* **Habbie Simpson**[28] 3288 6-11-9 139............................. RobertThornton 137
(Alan King) *in tch: rdn to chse ldrs after 3 out: styd on u.p fr next: tk wl hld 3rd cl home* **9/1**

11 **4** *nk* **Backspin (IRE)**[31] 3197 6-11-12 150....................................... APMcCoy 140
(Jonjo O'Neill) *trckd ldrs: led 6th: rdn and jnd after 2 out: hdd wl bef last: wknd run-in: lost 3rd cl home* **11/8**[1]

42 **5** *9* **Brunswick Gold (IRE)**[17] 3506 6-11-5 0................................. RhysFlint 123
(Steve Gollings) *hld up in rr but in tch: hdwy 3 out: hrd drvn and no imp on ldrs next: wknd sn after* **50/1**

3332 **6** *1 ½* **Ohio Gold (IRE)**[21] 3454 5-11-5 120....................................... JoeTizzard 124+
(Colin Tizzard) *led at mod early pce: hit 3rd: hdd 6th: stmbld 3 out: wknd next* **33/1**

02 **7** *1* **Sivola De Sivola (FR)**[15] 3542 5-11-5 0........................ TomScudamore 122
(Tom George) *a towards rr: nt fluent 5th: bhd whn hit 4 out and 3 out: effrt sn after: nvr on terms and sn no ch* **33/1**

142 **8** *4 ½* **Rose Of The Moon (IRE)**[28] 3288 6-11-5 0...................... JakeGreenall 117
(Milton Harris) *hit 3rd: sn bhd: hit 5th: rdn and effrt 3 out: nvr on terms and sn btn* **16/1**

21 **9** *10* **Champion Court (IRE)**[76] 2388 6-11-12 0.................... WarrenMarston 123+
(Martin Keighley) *chsd ldrs: wnt 2nd 3 out: hung rt wl bef 2 out and wknd qckly sn after* **11/1**

1 **P** **Drive Time (USA)**[17] 3506 6-11-9 0.................................... BrianHughes —
(Howard Johnson) *chsd ldr: led 4th to 6th: wknd qckly fr 3 out: t.o whn p.u bef next* **20/1**

5m 24.85s (19.85) **Going Correction** +0.25s/f (Yiel) **10** Ran SP% **115.4**
Speed ratings (Par 115): **72,71,67,67,64 63,63,61,57,—**
toteswingers:1&2:£2.90, 1&3:£7.10, 2&3:£7.20 CSF £23.66 TOTE £4.70: £1.90, £1.80, £2.30; EX 22.30 Trifecta £106.80 Pool £16,445.16 - 113.89 winning units..

Owner The Not Afraid Partnership **Bred** Mrs L Eadie **Trained** Upper Lambourn, Berks

FOCUS

The best novice hurdle run at this sort of distance in Britain this season and, although the pace was an unsatisfactory one, the right horses dominated in the straight.

NOTEBOOK

Bobs Worth(IRE), who won with more in hand than the official margin suggested over C&D latest, briefly appeared to be going least well of the 'big' three, and wasn't helped when Champion Court carried him wide as they turned to race down the hill, but he quickly picked up and jumped level with the favourite at the second-last. With that one backing out of it, he was left with Rock On Ruby to see off, and what was most pleasing about his performance was the way he picked up again on the climb to the line. He appears to have all the qualities needed to win at the Cheltenham Festival and is understandably clear at the head of the Neptune market (best-priced 5-1), the one note of caution being his trainer's particularly poor record in that event. (op 9-2)

Rock On Ruby(IRE), previously undefeated over hurdles, was stepping up in trip having won in the mist at Newbury last time, and he probably travelled best throughout the race. It could have been expected that he'd outpace the winner having challenged at the last, but he simply couldn't stay on as well and the fact his rider dropped his whip made no difference to the result. Perhaps a return to 2m in the Supreme will suit. (op 5-1)

Habbie Simpson, 4l behind the winner over C&D latest, stayed on well to take third off the favourite. Clearly progressive, he could be of some interest in the Coral Cup. (tchd 10-1)

Backspin(IRE), previously undefeated and looking the one to beat following his cosy victory in the Grade 1 Challow hurdle over Christmas (ridden more prominently than the placed runners that day), travelled strongly throughout under Tony McCoy, who allowed him to bowl into a narrow lead, but he was quickly seen off by the winner from two out. He was hanging under pressure and it would be no surprise were he to show himself better than this in time. (tchd 6-4 and 13-8 in places)

Brunswick Gold(IRE) ran about as well as could have been expected, reversing last-time-out form with Drive Time, and he'll find much easier opportunities. (tchd 66-1)

Ohio Gold(IRE) was a reluctant leader early and ended up well beaten. He'll find easier opportunities. (tchd 66-1 in a place)

Sivola De Sivola(FR) was having only his third start and it showed. He's open to a fair bit of improvement. (op 40-1)

Rose Of The Moon(IRE) split the first and third at the course last time, but he was re-routed here late after Doncaster was called off, and clearly wasn't at his best.

Champion Court(IRE), winner of a relatively weak Grade 2 over C&D in November, is an impressive-looking sort who tanked through the race without cover. It was disconcerting to see him hang right off the bend starting out downhill, but it was only his second start over hurdles (fourth in all), and he deserves another chance. Official explanation: jockey said gelding hung right-handed (op 10-1 tchd 9-1)

Drive Time(USA), a ready winner at Doncaster on his debut, stopped quickly and clearly failed to give his running. It may be that there was something amiss. Official explanation: jockey said gelding was unsuited by the good to soft (good in places) ground (op 16-1)

3807 REWARDS4RACING CLEEVE HURDLE (GRADE 2) (12 hdls) 3m

3:35 (3:39) (Class 1) 5-Y-O+

£22,804 (£8,556; £4,284; £2,136; £1,072; £536)

Form				RPR
2-11	**1**		**Grands Crus (FR)**[70] 2523 6-11-4 158 (t) TomScudamore	171+
			(David Pipe) *travelled strly thrght: hld up towards rr: smooth hdwy 8th: led 2 out: sn clr: impressive* **2/1**[1]	
-P40	**2**	*10*	**Knockara Beau (IRE)**[28] 3292 8-11-0 145 JanFaltejsek	149
			(George Charlton) *trckd ldr: led 7th: rdn and hdd 2 out: sn hld by wnr: styd on same pce* **33/1**	
3303	**3**	*hd*	**Restless Harry**[31] 3199 7-11-4 148 HenryOliver	155
			(Robin Dickin) *chsd ldrs: rdn whn sltly outpcd after 3 out: styd on again after 2 out: jst failed to snatch 2nd* **7/1**	
P-61	**4**	*¾*	**Mobaasher (USA)**[14] 3566 8-11-0 149 (tp) AidanColeman	148
			(Venetia Williams) *hld up towards rr: rdn and stdy prog fr after 3 out: styd on fr last: nt rch ldrs* **14/1**	
2F2-	**5**	*7*	**Bensalem (IRE)**[282] 5348 8-11-0 153 RobertThornton	144
			(Alan King) *mid-div: hdwy after 9th to trck ldrs: rdn after 2 out: styd on same pce* **11/2**[2]	
3-63	**6**	*14*	**Arcalis**[63] 2672 11-11-0 143 BrianHughes	129
			(Howard Johnson) *hld up towards rr: rdn after 3 out: styd on past btn horses: nvr a danger* **33/1**	
5	**7**	*3 ¼*	**Cristal Bonus (FR)**[49] 2887 5-11-8 152 APMcCoy	134
			(Evan Williams) *hld up towards rr: rdn after 3 out: little imp* **20/1**	
2564	**8**	*6*	**Kayf Aramis**[31] 3199 9-11-0 145 (p) PaddyBrennan	121
			(Nigel Twiston-Davies) *chsd ldrs tl 3 out: no ch after* **33/1**	
00-1	**9**	*2*	**Fair Along (GER)**[91] 2090 9-11-8 158 (p) RhysFlint	127
			(Philip Hobbs) *led tl 7th: rdn and ev ch after 3 out: wknd next* **16/1**	
-FF4	**10**	*11*	**Gwanako (FR)**[28] 3293 8-11-0 140 NickScholfield	109
			(Paul Nicholls) *in tch: rdn after 3 out: wknd after next* **25/1**	
5040	**11**	*¾*	**Hills Of Aran**[14] 3561 9-11-0 138 (p) JamieMoore	109
			(Keith Goldsworthy) *in tch: rdn after 8th: in rr fr next* **100/1**	
1-FF	**12**	*15*	**Spirit River (FR)**[50] 2867 6-11-4 152 BarryGeraghty	99
			(Nicky Henderson) *racd wd: mid-div: hdwy after 7th to trck ldrs: rdn after 3 out: wknd after 2 out: eased* **15/2**	
4122	**13**	*½*	**Organisateur (IRE)**[14] 3561 6-10-9 159 IanPopham(5)	95
			(Paul Nicholls) *mid-div: struggling whn mstke 9th: rdn after 3 out: wknd next* **6/1**[3]	
4P31	**P**		**Sweet Seville (FR)**[12] 3603 7-10-7 105 TimmyMurphy	—
			(Terry Clement) *sn struggling in rr: lost tch 6th: p.u bef next* **200/1**	

6m 3.60s (2.60) **Going Correction** +0.25s/f (Yiel) **14** Ran SP% **118.7**

Speed ratings: **105,101,101,101,99 94,93,91,90,86 86,81,81,—**

toteswingers:1&2:£79.50, 1&3:£4.10, 2&3:£59.10 CSF £85.77 TOTE £3.40: £1.60, £9.80, £2.70; EX 100.90 Trifecta £1315.60 Pool £5,333.78 - 3.00 winning units..

Owner Roger Stanley & Yvonne Reynolds III **Bred** Jean-Marie Prost Alamartine **Trained** Nicholashayne, Devon

■ Stewards' Enquiry : Jan Faltejsek two-day ban: used whip with excesive frequency (Feb 12-13)
Henry Oliver caution: used whip with excesive frequency.

FOCUS

A Grade 2 that has been won by the likes of Big Buck's and Inglis Drever in recent seasons. This year's line-up featured a big field comprising some trying to prove their credentials as World Hurdle contenders, some established sorts at this level, and several returning to hurdles after racing mainly over fences of late. It was turned into a procession by the rapidly progressive Grands Crus who was value for 18l and looks a serious threat to Big Buck's in the World Hurdle. His RPR of 171 is the best by a hurdler this season. The form appears solid.

NOTEBOOK

Grands Crus(FR) ◆, who is rapidly progressive, turned this into a procession. David Pipe's gelding had made a big impression when winning here and then following up at Haydock over 3m, but was stepping up in grade. However, despite being keen under restraint for more than a circuit, he cruised into contention and, when Tom Scudamore let out an inch of rein after the second-last, he bounded clear and destroyed a good field without coming off the bridle. He certainly looks a credible challenger to Big Buck's in the World Hurdle, especially on a line through restless Harry, and the bookmakers tend to agree, making him as short as 3-1 in places. (op 5-2 tchd 11-4 in places)

Knockara Beau(IRE) has been racing over fences since May 2009, but was a decent hurdler in the past and enjoyed this return to the smaller obstacles. He took over in front with a circuit to go and kept galloping, although no match for the winner, all the way to the line. He has reportedly had a muscle problem which he has been treated for, and may come back here for the festival with the William Hill Trophy the likely target. (op 28-1)

Restless Harry, a tough and genuine sort who has won twice around here over shorter, finished third to Big Buck's in the rescheduled Long Walk Hurdle at Newbury. He ran his usual game race, sticking on up the hill after looking beaten. (op 9-1)

Mobaasher(USA) raced over fences last year, but returned to hurdles this season and won a Warwick handicap earlier in the month. With cheekpieces added to the tongue tie he wore then, he was held up before running on and looks a major contender for the Pertemps Final (for which he qualified at Warwick), if connections opt to go there. (op 16-1)

Bensalem(IRE) ◆, a winner over an extended 2m5f here in the past, ran well in a Grade 1 at Punchestown when returning to hurdles in April. Having suffered colic subsequently, this was first run since and he performed with plenty of credit, only fading late on. He should come on a good deal for the outing. (op 9-2)

Arcalis is getting on now but ran well tried at 3m in Newbury's Long Distance Hurdle. He likes this track and, although looking well held running down the hill, kept on up the rising ground.

Cristal Bonus(FR), placed in a Grade 1 on heavy ground in France, ran well behind Menorah in a Grade 2 over 2m1f here before Christmas. Stepping up in trip, he never really got competitive and is likely to return to shorter in future.

Fair Along(GER) goes well here and was having his first run since winning the West Yorkshire Hurdle in October. He led for a circuit and was still there at the bottom of the hill before fading. He will appreciate slightly better ground. (op 14-1)

Gwanako(FR), another better known as a chaser, ran a decent race returned to hurdles over C&D at the last meeting and did so again. He could well pick up a handicap if kept over hurdles. (tchd 28-1)

Spirit River(FR) won a handicap at 2m1f before taking the Coral Cup at last season's festival. He had fallen on both starts over fences this season, and was up in trip and grade for this return to hurdles. He showed up for a fair way before fading and, although he may not have stayed, this was a little disappointing. (op 6-1)

Organisateur(IRE), a consistent sort and runner-up in the Lanzarote Hurdle last time, was up in trip and grade here and never figured. That said, his best form has been on sharp tracks, so he can be given another chance. (op 7-1)

3808 STELLAR FOOTBALL "END OF TRANSFER WINDOW" H'CAP HURDLE (8 hdls) 2m 1f

4:10 (4:12) (Class 2) 4-Y-O+ **£9,757** (£2,865; £1,432; £715)

Form				RPR
1/00	**1**		**Art Professor (IRE)**[30] 3229 7-10-5 **122** AidanColeman	132
			(Venetia Williams) *trckd ldrs: led 2 out: narrowly hdd sn after: hrd drvn to ld again bef last: narrowly hdd fnl 100yds: styd on gamely to ld again last stride* **8/1**	
/132	**2**	*shd*	**Alarazi (IRE)**[25] 3386 7-10-1 **118** TimmyMurphy	129+
			(Lucy Wadham) *hld up in rr: impr appr 2 out: drvn and stl only 5th sn after: str run to chse wnr whn nt fluent last: sn rcvrd to chal and slt ld fnl 100yds: hdd last stride* **11/1**	
1P66	**3**	*8*	**Cockney Trucker (IRE)**[30] 3229 9-11-3 **134** RichardJohnson	138
			(Philip Hobbs) *tendency to jump rt: led tl narrowly hdd 4th: styd chsng ldrs tl outpcd 2 out: rallied appr last and styd on to take 3rd appr last but no imp on ldng duo* **9/1**	
4-12	**4**	*3 ¾*	**Eradicate (IRE)**[39] 3058 7-11-7 **143** DavidBass(5)	143
			(Nicky Henderson) *chsd ldrs: rdn and effrt after 2 out: nvr quite on terms: wknd last and hung lft u.p run-in* **14/1**	
0-00	**5**	*1 ¾*	**Secret Dancer (IRE)**[28] 3289 6-10-13 **130** WillKennedy	128
			(Alan Jones) *in rr: hdwy appr 2 out: sn one pce kpt on again run-in* **12/1**	
0405	**6**	*¾*	**Aather (IRE)**[14] 3557 6-10-3 **125** CO'Farrell(5)	122
			(Alan Fleming) *hld up in rr: stdy hdwy after 3 out: nvr quite rchd ldrs and one pce after 2 out* **7/1**[2]	
0-32	**7**	*2 ¼*	**Dream Esteem**[30] 3228 6-10-5 **122** TomScudamore	117
			(David Pipe) *chsd ldrs: led after 3 out: narrowly hdd 2 out: led again sn after: hdd bef last: sn wknd* **15/2**[3]	
43F1	**8**	*3 ¼*	**Celticello (IRE)**[28] 3303 9-9-12 **122** MrJMQuinlan(7)	114
			(Michael Quinlan) *in rr tl sme hdwy after 3 out: nvr rchd ldrs and btn after 2 out* **25/1**	
-B20	**9**	*6*	**Gifted Leader (USA)**[30] 3229 6-10-6 **123** DarylJacob	110
			(Ian Williams) *towards rr most of way* **25/1**	
5P-1	**10**	*8*	**Cunning Clarets (IRE)**[27] 3335 6-10-0 **117** PaddyBrennan	105+
			(Richard Fahey) *in rr: mstke 4 out: hdwy 3 out: chsd ldrs 2 out: sn wknd* **9/2**[1]	
04	**11**	*8*	**Decoy (FR)**[19] 3478 5-10-7 **127** DannyCook(3)	99
			(David Pipe) *chsd ldrs tl wknd 3 out* **25/1**	
-342	**12**	*23*	**Tanks For That (IRE)**[49] 2881 8-11-6 **137** BarryGeraghty	89
			(Nicky Henderson) *pressed ldr: led 4th: hdd after 3 out: styd wl there tl wknd qckly after 2 out* **8/1**	
23-0	**13**	*3*	**First Avenue**[21] 3447 6-10-1 **118** (p) JamieMoore	67
			(Gary Moore) *in rr: in tch whn j. slowly 4th: wknd 3 out* **25/1**	
130-	**14**	*17*	**Nomecheki (FR)**[316] 4716 9-10-13 **130** LiamTreadwell	64
			(Nick Gifford) *a in rr: t.o after 3 out* **20/1**	
100-	**P**		**Fushe Jo**[316] 4711 7-11-0 **131** BrianHughes	—
			(Howard Johnson) *nt fluent 1st: wknd qckly and p.u after 3 out* **25/1**	
4034	**P**		**Gilded Age**[30] 3229 5-10-10 **127** (b1) RobertThornton	—
			(Alan King) *chsd ldrs tl rdn and wknd qckly after 4 out: t.o whn p.u after next* **16/1**	

4m 10.5s (-0.80) **Going Correction** +0.25s/f (Yiel) **16** Ran SP% **127.2**

Speed ratings (Par 109): **111,110,107,105,104 104,103,101,98,95 91,80,79,71,— —**

toteswingers:1&2:£25.00, 1&3:£22.20, 2&3:£21.70 CSF £87.40 CT £801.30 TOTE £10.10: £2.90, £2.30, £2.70, £3.80; EX 83.00 Trifecta £508.70 Pool £2,108.17 - 3.06 winning units..

Owner Jeremy Hancock **Bred** Castleton Group **Trained** Kings Caple, H'fords

■ Stewards' Enquiry : Aidan Coleman three-day ban: used whip with excesive frequency (Feb 12-14)

FOCUS

A wide-open handicap hurdle that provided a gripping finish. The winne is rated back to his 2008 form and the runner-up may have more to come.

NOTEBOOK

Art Professor(IRE) had clearly been in need of a couple of runs back from two years off and found himself on a mark 5lb lower than when last winning. Coming in for late support, he was never far from the pace, travelling kindly and, having gone on turning in, battled back well to shade it in a head-bobber. He shouldn't go up much and can probably win again. His rider received a ban for excessive use of the whip. (op 10-1)

Alarazi(IRE) ◆, having only his sixth start over hurdles, looked potentially well treated on this handicap debut and he was produced to challenge approaching the last, at which he wasn't particularly fluent, and then, having edged into the lead, was cruelly denied on the line. He was formerly smart on the Flat in Ireland and should be capable of winning a decent handicap hurdle. (op 10-1 tchd 9-1)

Cockney Trucker(IRE) battled back in typically game fashion, but just lacked the gears of the front pair. (op 12-1)

Eradicate(IRE) is still 11lb higher than when winning the Swinton last spring, so this was an encouraging effort. (op 12-1)

Secret Dancer(IRE), useful on his day, showed enough to make him of future interest, keeping on late. (op 14-1 tchd 16-1 in a place)

Aather(IRE) never got close enough to challenge. (op 9-1)

Dream Esteem raced on with the winner, but could find no extra from before the last. (op 13-2 tchd 8-1)

Cunning Clarets(IRE), up 7lb, dropped away having briefly made a forward move. (op 13-2)

Tanks For That(IRE) stopped quickly and was disappointing. (op 13-2)

Nomecheki(FR), off since finishing eighth in the Grand Annual, was very keen early on and showed little, but deserves a chance to leave this form behind returned to fences. Official explanation: jockey said gelding stopped quickly (op 16-1)

Gilded Age Official explanation: jockey said gelding stopped quickly

T/Jkpt: £48,362.50 to a £1 stake. Pool:£68,116.26 - 1.00 winning ticket T/Plt: £268.60 to a £1 stake. Pool:£222,021.02 - 603.20 winning tickets T/Qpdt: £29.40 to a £1 stake. Pool:£16,978.21 - 426.47 winning tickets ST

3781 DONCASTER (L-H)

Saturday, January 29

3809 Meeting Abandoned - Frozen track

Sky Bet Chase meeting.

3252 UTTOXETER (L-H)

Saturday, January 29

OFFICIAL GOING: Chase course - heavy; hurdle course - soft

Hurdles moved to fresh ground 6-8m off inside rail. Divided bends with chases on outside. Final flight in the back straight omitted on all circuits in hurdles.

Wind: Light behind Weather: Overcast

3816 UTTOXETER MARES' NOVICES' HURDLE (9 hdls 1 omitted) 2m

1:05 (1:06) (Class 4) 4-Y-0+ £2,211 (£649; £324; £162)

Form RPR

-241 **1** **Empress Orchid**[10] 3637 6-11-6 109 JasonMaguire 108+
(Donald McCain) *mde all: rdn clr appr last: eased towards fin* **8/13**[1]

6- **2** *11* **Saoma (FR)**[451] 2061 5-11-0 0 LeightonAspell 90
(Lucy Wadham) *a.p: chsd wnr appr 2 out: sn rdn: styd on same pce* **9/2**[2]

U000 **3** *1 1/2* **Misstaysia (IRE)**[44] 2974 6-11-0 0 AndrewThornton 90
(Henry Daly) *hld up: plld hrd: hdwy after 6th: styd on same pce fr 2 out: blnd last* **16/1**[3]

-241 **4** *24* **Diamond MM (IRE)**[112] 1780 5-11-6 0 DPFahy 74
(Alison Thorpe) *chsd wnr tl mstke 3 out: blnd and wknd next: t.o* **9/2**[2]

00 **5** *72* **Go Ruby Go**[231] 731 7-11-0 0 JamesReveley —
(Kevin Morgan) *hld up: mstke 2nd: hdwy 4th: wknd after 6th: t.o* **33/1**

5406 **P** **Qualitee**[4] 3721 6-10-11 0 TommyPhelan(3) —
(Claire Dyson) *hld up: p.u bef 3rd: sddle slipped* **33/1**

4m 8.60s (13.40) **Going Correction** +0.95s/f (Soft)
WFA 4 from 5yo+ 11lb 6 Ran SP% **110.0**
Speed ratings (Par 105): **104,98,97,85,49** —
toteswingers:1&2:£1.02, 1&3:£1.90, 2&3:£4.40 CSF £3.73 TOTE £1.70: £1.10, £2.70; EX 4.00.
Owner W Bromley & Mrs L King **Bred** Robin Smith **Trained** Cholmondeley, Cheshire

FOCUS
An uncompetitive and weak mares' novice hurdle. The easy winner is rated to he best.

NOTEBOOK
Empress Orchid built on her victory at Newcastle with a comfortable win. Allowed to set her own pace, she quickened entering the home straight, pulling well clear. She looks a nice sort and should have improvement in her, shaping as though further may suit. Connections expect her to make a chaser in time. (op 4-6)
Saoma(FR), returning from a 451-day absence, ran with some promise and can be expected to come on for the run. (op 4-1)
Misstaysia(IRE) was held up and made a couple of jumping mistakes, but needs to settle better to give herself a chance. (tchd 12-1)
Diamond MM(IRE) made a bad mistake three out that put paid to her chances, but looked to already be struggling under a penalty. (op 11-2)
Go Ruby Go was too keen early on and needs to settle better.
Qualitee's saddle slipped before the third flight and was pulled up. Official explanation: jockey said saddle slipped (op 40-1)

3817 E.B.F./TBA MARES' NOVICES' CHASE (16 fncs) 2m 6f 110y

1:35 (1:37) (Class 4) 5-Y-0+ £3,252 (£955; £477; £238)

Form RPR

PPP1 **1** **Evella (IRE)**[12] 3598 7-11-1 124 AlexMerriam(3) 134+
(Neil King) *mde all: clr 2 out: shkn up appr last: styd on* **15/8**[2]

-113 **2** *14* **Smuglin**[14] 3571 8-11-4 132 JasonMaguire 126+
(Donald McCain) *chsd wnr: pushed along after 3rd: drvn along fr 7th: wkng whn blnd last* **5/6**[1]

24-0 **3** *43* **Home She Goes (IRE)**[25] 3392 9-10-9 0 AdamPogson(3) 80
(Charles Pogson) *chsd ldrs tl wknd 9th: t.o fr next* **20/1**

-F23 **4** *32* **Here's The Key (FR)**[12] 3607 7-10-12 95 (t) DenisO'Regan 39
(Paul Webber) *chsd ldrs to 8th: t.o fr 10th* **13/2**[3]

6m 26.7s (38.20) **Going Correction** +1.70s/f (Heav) 4 Ran SP% **107.4**
Speed ratings: **101,96,81,70**
CSF £3.98 TOTE £3.30; EX 5.40.
Owner Mrs S M Richards **Bred** Donal Boyle **Trained** Newmarket, Suffolk

FOCUS
An uncompetitive mares' novices' chase, rated around the first two.

NOTEBOOK
Evella(IRE) made all to run out a cosy winner of this mares' novices' chase. Boosted by her win last time out at Fakenham, she out-jumped her rivals at every fence and had them struggling with more than a circuit to go. Finding plenty when asked to quicken, she is in good form and seems the sort to run up a sequence. The mares' final at Newbury may be a long-term target. (op 5-2)
Smuglin was under pressure from Jason Maguire almost from the off, jumping low at her fences. Receiving strong reminders with more than a circuit to go, she did to her credit stay on a little, but this was not her running. She is reported to have hated the ground and it is too soon to write her off. Official explanation: jockey said mare was unsuited by the heavy ground (op 8-13 tchd 4-7)
Home She Goes(IRE) faced a tough ask on her chasing debut, but jumped adequately and can find an easier race. (tchd 25-1)
Here's The Key(FR) looked well out of her depth and unconvincing at her fences. (op 9-1 tchd 10-1)

3818 PJD GROUP (S) HURDLE (10 hdls 2 omitted) 2m 4f 110y

2:05 (2:07) (Class 5) 4-7-Y-0 £1,561 (£458; £229; £114)

Form RPR

0612 **1** **Big Talk**[19] 2556 4-10-4 103 (v) MrSWDrinkwater(7) 101+
(David Bridgwater) *prom: lost pl after 2nd: hdwy 6th: led appr and j.rt last: all out* **6/1**

22FP **2** *1/2* **King Of Castile**[132] 1555 7-11-9 110 (p) LiamHeard 111
(Barry Leavy) *prom: chsd ldr 7th: led next: rdn and hdd bef last: rallied and ev ch flat: unable qck nr fin* **9/2**[3]

04 **3** *11* **I Got Music**[26] 3358 4-10-0 0 JamesReveley 77
(Keith Reveley) *chsd ldrs: rdn appr 3 out: wknd bef last* **3/1**[2]

6513 **4** *nse* **I'm In The Pink (FR)**[19] 3477 7-11-9 116 (v) LeeStephens(3) 104+
(David Evans) *prom: ev ch 2 out: sn rdn and wknd* **9/2**[3]

5 *22* **Mekong Miss**[71] 5-10-8 0 ow1 MrPYork(5) 68
(Raymond York) *hld up: hdwy 3 out: wknd next: t.o* **33/1**

622 **6** *7* **Perfect Reward**[30] 3224 7-11-5 115 JoshuaMoore(7) 74
(Gary Moore) *led to appr 5th: chsd ldrs: rdn bef 3 out: wknd next: t.o* **11/4**[1]

3034 **7** *15* **Nicky Nutjob (GER)**[75] 2421 5-10-12 100 (p) CharlieWallis(7) 52
(John O'Shea) *hld up: hdwy 3rd: led appr 5th: blnd 7th: hdd 3 out: sn wknd: t.o* **16/1**

5m 33.0s (29.00) **Going Correction** +0.95s/f (Soft)
WFA 4 from 5yo+ 12lb 7 Ran SP% **111.1**
Speed ratings: **82,81,77,77,69 66,60**
toteswingers:1&2:£3.60, 1&3:£3.30, 2&3:£7.40 CSF £31.13 TOTE £9.20: £4.60, £5.40; EX 57.90.The winner was bought in for 6,000gns
Owner Deauville Daze Partnership **Bred** Miss K Rausing **Trained** Icomb, Gloucs
■ Stewards' Enquiry : Mr S W Drinkwater one-day ban: used whip without giving gelding time to respond (tba)

FOCUS
A wide-open selling hurdle, with all the field holding a chance entering the home straight. the second sets the level.

NOTEBOOK
Big Talk battled back in the dying strides to get up. Hugging the rail all the way round he seemed to thrive on the stamina test, shaping as though further will suit in time. He was also a little big at some of his hurdles, suggesting that chasing is where his long-term future will lie. (op 8-1)
King Of Castile was having his first run for Barry Leavy, and the change of environment appears to have re-ignited his enthusiasm for racing. He can be expected to come on for the run and can be competitive at this level. (op 7-1)
I Got Music was receiving age and sex allowances, and stayed on well enough. (tchd 11-4)
I'm In The Pink(FR) travelled best of all and looked to be coming with a winning run two out, but emptied in the closing stages and is better over 2m. (op 4-1 tchd 5-1)
Mekong Miss showed some promise on her hurdling debut and may find an opportunity at this level on better ground. (op 40-1)
Perfect Reward seemed to suffer for setting the pace at various stages. (op 5-2 tchd 9-4)
Nicky Nutjob(GER) may also have done too much too soon. (tchd 14-1)

3819 RICHARD WILCOXSON MEMORIAL NOVICES' H'CAP CHASE (16 fncs) 2m 5f

2:35 (2:38) (Class 4) (0-100,100) 5-Y-0+ £3,252 (£955; £477; £238)

Form RPR

-220 **1** **Mister Wiseman**[87] 2146 9-11-8 96 (p) DavidDennis 111
(Nigel Hawke) *mde all: clr 10th: rdn appr 2 out: styd on wl* **7/1**

5U24 **2** *5* **Pacha D'Oudairies (FR)**[29] 3265 8-11-12 100 DenisO'Regan 110
(Michael Blake) *prom: chsd ldr 11th: rdn appr last: no ex flat* **9/2**

P5P4 **3** *18* **Delgany Gunner**[81] 2290 7-9-10 75 oh25 ow1 (vt) GilesHawkins(5) 66
(Ben Pollock) *in rr: bhd and rdn 8th: wnt 3rd nr fin: nvr nrr* **10/1**

-212 **4** *1 3/4* **Handtheprizeover**[44] 2986 6-11-12 100 LeightonAspell 89
(Ben Case) *hld up: hdwy 12th: wknd next* **11/4**[1]

3/24 **5** *43* **Innominate (IRE)**[14] 3574 9-11-4 92 (p) PeterBuchanan 38
(Lucinda Russell) *chsd wnr to 11th: wknd next: t.o* **4/1**[3]

14U4 **P** **Festival Dreams**[26] 3371 6-11-7 95 (b) DaveCrosse —
(Joanna Davis) *chsd ldrs: mstkes 7th and 8th: wknd and p.u bef 12th* **7/2**[2]

00P0 **P** **Action Hawk (GER)**[18] 3495 7-10-0 74 oh22 (tp) JamesDavies —
(Ben Pollock) *sn pushed along in rr: bhd and rdn 8th: t.o whn p.u bef next* **66/1**

5m 56.1s (32.60) **Going Correction** +1.70s/f (Heav) 7 Ran SP% **110.2**
Speed ratings: **105,103,96,95,79** —,—
toteswingers:1&2:£3.60, 1&3:£14.60, 2&3:£7.10 CSF £35.59 TOTE £5.80: £2.80, £3.00; EX 36.00.
Owner D R Mead **Bred** Mrs D Thomson **Trained** Woolminstone, Somerset

FOCUS
An ordinary novices' handicap chase. A seasonal best from the winner, but still 5lb off his old mark.

NOTEBOOK
Mister Wiseman put up a game front-running performance and made every yard for only his second win in 33 career starts and his first over fences. Returning from an 87-day absence, he jumped wonderfully and kept finding for pressure. If able to get an easy lead again, he will be difficult to peg back. (op 6-1)
Pacha D'Oudairies(FR) has been slowly dropping down the handicap and looked poised to challenge, having travelled nicely into the race, but was unable to find for pressure. He looks one-paced and may find an opportunity over a longer trip. (op 4-1 tchd 7-2)
Delgany Gunner was running from way out of the handicap, but stayed on well to take third. His jumping was sound, but his form suggests he may struggle to replicate it. (op 16-1)
Handtheprizeover travelled well, but struggled to get home in the testing conditions and is better suited by 2m. (op 7-2)
Innominate(IRE) failed to run any race at all. (op 9-2)
Festival Dreams Official explanation: jockey said gelding never travelled; trainer's rep said gelding returned distressed
Action Hawk(GER) Official explanation: jockey said gelding had a breathing problem

3820 WEATHERBYS BLOODSTOCK INSURANCE NOVICES' H'CAP HURDLE (9 hdls 1 omitted) 2m

3:10 (3:16) (Class 3) (0-125,118) 4-Y-O+ £3,802 (£1,123; £561; £280; £140)

Form RPR

2-30 **1** **Pegasus Prince (USA)**[77] 2375 7-11-2 108 JamesReveley 120+
(Keith Reveley) *hld up: hdwy 2 out: rdn to ld fnl 75yds: r.o* **8/1**

2512 **2** *1 3/4* **Blenheim Brook (IRE)**[27] 3335 6-11-12 118 PeterBuchanan 128
(Lucinda Russell) *chsd ldrs: led appr last: rdn and hdd fnl 75yds* **7/2**[1]

26-0 **3** *18* **Colour Clash**[18] 3500 8-11-1 112 AlexanderVoy(5) 105
(Rose Dobbin) *chsd ldrs: led appr 2 out: hdd & wknd bef last* **13/2**

2-01 **4** *3 1/4* **Lively Fling (USA)**[14] 3563 5-11-11 117 SamThomas 108
(Venetia Williams) *prom: drvn along fr 5th: wknd appr 2 out* **11/2**[3]

236F **5** *2 3/4* **Royal And Ancient (IRE)**[19] 3484 4-10-8 111 (t) DaveCrosse 86
(Milton Harris) *hld up: rdn after 6th: wknd bef next* **11/1**

0-U1 **6** *22* **Rushwee (IRE)**[14] 3570 9-11-5 111 LeightonAspell 75
(Lucy Wadham) *prom tl rdn and wknd 3 out: t.o* **7/1**

0F64 **7** *2 1/4* **My Viking Bay (IRE)**[69] 2554 7-10-7 106 CharlieWallis(7) 68
(John O'Shea) *hld up: rdn and wknd appr 3 out: t.o* **22/1**

425F **8** *21* **Jimbatai (IRE)**[14] 3558 8-11-4 110 LiamHeard 51
(Barry Leavy) *prom: lost pl 5th: sn bhd: t.o* **11/1**

3111 **P** **Eastwell Smiles**[22] 3430 7-11-1 107 (bt) JohnnyFarrelly —
(Sophie Leech) *led: hdd & wknd appr 2 out: t.o whn p.u bef last* **9/2**[2]

4m 7.40s (12.20) **Going Correction** +0.95s/f (Soft)
WFA 4 from 5yo+ 11lb 9 Ran SP% **113.7**
Speed ratings (Par 107): **107,106,97,95,94 83,82,71,**—
toteswingers:1&2:£15.50, 1&3:£7.60, 2&3:£5.20 CSF £36.32 CT £193.64 TOTE £10.60: £2.80, £1.50, £2.10; EX 40.00.
Owner John Wade **Bred** Liberty Road Stables **Trained** Lingdale, Redcar & Cleveland

FOCUS
A competitive handicap hurdle run at a decent gallop. The winner is on the upgrade and there may be more to come, while the second is rated to form.
NOTEBOOK
Pegasus Prince(USA) was able to use his proven stamina to pinch the race after the last. Given a 77-day break, he put two below-par efforts behind him to score over a trip that is probably short of his best. (op 10-1)
Blenheim Brook(IRE) ◆ looked to have the race in the bag, but perhaps got to the front a little too soon. He remains on an upward curve and can remain competitive off this mark. (tchd 4-1)
Colour Clash seemed to have come on for his seasonal re-appearance, travelling well for a long way, but it may just be that this run will have put him perfect. (tchd 11-2 and 7-1)
Lively Fling(USA) seemed to struggle with a 10lb rise for his win last time out and, though further improvement cannot be discounted, he may have to much on his plate. (op 5-1)
Royal And Ancient(IRE) stayed on well on his handicap debut and seems to have enough some ability. (op 12-1 tchd 10-1)

3821 A & S ENTERPRISES H'CAP CHASE (16 fncs) 2m 6f 110y
3:45 (3:46) (Class 4) (0-115,115) 5-Y-0+ **£3,332** (£1,034; £557)

Form RPR
4P-2 **1** **Master D'Or (FR)**12 3608 11-10-8 **97** PaulMoloney 111
(Sophie Leech) *hld up: hdwy and mstke 4 out: led appr 2 out: rdn out* **8/1**
0P5/ **2** 3 1/4 **El Zorro**792 2482 10-11-4 **110** AlexMerriam(3) 120
(Neil King) *hld up in tch: chsd ldr 12th: led after 3 out: rdn and hdd bef next: styd on same pce last* **12/1**
4034 **3** 14 **Lorum Leader (IRE)**6 3695 10-10-10 **106** (b) MrTWeston(7) 104
(Dr Richard Newland) *w ldr tl led 4th: hdd after 3 out: wknd next* **4/1**2
316/ **P** **Zed Candy (FR)**25 2894 8-11-12 **115** PeterBuchanan —
(Richard Ford) *hld up: hdwy 10th: wknd appr 4 out: t.o whn p.u bef last* **20/1**
50-3 **P** **Open De L'Isle (FR)**14 3573 9-11-8 **114** HarryHaynes(3) —
(James Ewart) *hld up: hdwy 9th: rdn after next: wknd 12th: t.o whn p.u after 3 out* **9/1**
-P56 **P** **The Vicar (IRE)**44 2984 8-11-5 **108** (p) AndrewThornton —
(Henrietta Knight) *led: j.rt 3rd: hdd next: remained handy tl rdn after 8th: sn wknd: t.o whn p.u bef 12th* **6/1**3
23-5 **P** **Rapid Increase (IRE)**29 3263 8-10-13 **112** GeraldQuinn(10) —
(Jonjo O'Neill) *chsd ldrs: rdn after 10th: wknd 12th: t.o whn p.u bef 3 out* **14/1**
4233 **P** **Supreme Plan (IRE)**67 2595 8-11-10 **113** (tp) JasonMaguire —
(Kim Bailey) *prom: chsd ldr 9th to 12th: mstke 4 out: sn wknd: p.u bef next* **11/4**1
4-04 **P** **Sandofthecolosseum (IRE)**45 2955 6-11-9 **112** DenisO'Regan —
(Alex Hales) *prom: lost pl 4th: bhd fr 6th: t.o whn p.u bef 4 out* **7/1**
6m 26.6s (38.10) **Going Correction** +1.70s/f (Heav) **9** Ran SP% **113.7**
Speed ratings: **101,99,95,—,— —,—,—,—**
toteswingers:1&2:£34.10, 1&3:£11.90, 2&3:£10.10 CSF £92.54 CT £439.80 TOTE £10.10: £2.20, £4.00, £1.80; EX 114.00.
Owner C J Leech **Bred** Mr And Mrs Michel Vaultier **Trained** Kingsbridge, Devon
FOCUS
A fair handicap chase, but the conditions found out most of these. The winner has been rated in line with his 2008/9 form.
NOTEBOOK
Master D'Or(FR) ran out a ready winner. Staying on down the back, he took it in the home straight, pulling clear before idling a little in the closing stages. A winner off 13lb higher over hurdles in 2009, he looked to have a decent chance at the weights, especially after a creditable second last time out, and so it proved. He is likely to be able to handle a rise in mark. (op 7-1 tchd 13-2)
El Zorro was returning from a 792-day-absence and can be expected to come on plenty for the run. He travelled well for a long time and came to challenge, but just emptied in the testing ground. He has low mileage for a 10-year-old and can find a race. (op 14-1)
Lorum Leader(IRE) set the pace for a long time and seemed to again benefit from the blinkers, which he has now worn for three consecutive starts. This was a decent effort, but he has failed to win since November 2009. (op 5-1)
Zed Candy(FR) had never previously gone further than 2m and never looked likely to get the trip here. (op 16-1 tchd 22-1)
Supreme Plan(IRE) is now 0-13 under rules. (op 16-1 tchd 22-1)

3822 BANNER MARQUEES H'CAP HURDLE (10 hdls 2 omitted) 2m 4f 110y
4:20 (4:20) (Class 4) (0-105,105) 4-Y-0+ **£2,081** (£611; £305; £152)

Form RPR
-056 **1** **Inkberrow Rose (IRE)**19 3485 7-10-1 **83** (p) TommyPhelan(3) 85
(Tom Gretton) *chsd ldrs: rdn appr 2 out: r.o wl to ld towards fin* **9/2**3
0-46 **2** 1 1/4 **Azione**32 3155 8-10-5 **84** LeightonAspell 85
(Rodney Farrant) *led: hdd briefly 7th: rdn appr last: hdd towards fin* **13/2**
-004 **3** shd **Royal Chatelier (FR)**28 3297 6-10-9 **88** DenisO'Regan 90+
(Michael Blake) *hld up in tch: rdn after 3 out: sn outpcd: rallied appr last: r.o wl* **11/2**
0-61 **4** 1 1/2 **Fentara**18 3498 6-11-12 **105** RobertWalford 106+
(Tim Walford) *chsd ldrs: chal 3 out: mstke next: sn rdn: no ex nr fin* **3/1**2
351- **5** 7 **Equity Release (IRE)**507 1416 10-11-5 **101** (t) AdamPogson(3) 94
(Louise Davis) *hld up: hdwy appr 3 out: rdn and wknd flat* **14/1**
03PP **6** 57 **Duke Of Ormond (IRE)**22 3428 8-11-3 **96** (p) CharliePoste 31
(Anna Brooks) *chsd ldr: reminder after 3rd: led briefly 7th: sn drvn along: wknd 3 out: t.o* **16/1**
20 **U** **Sun Tzu (IRE)**13 3589 7-11-5 **105** (b) MrTWeston(7) —
(Dr Richard Newland) *hld up: blnd and uns rdr 6th* **5/2**1
5m 26.6s (22.60) **Going Correction** +0.95s/f (Soft) **7** Ran SP% **113.0**
Speed ratings (Par 105): **94,93,93,92,90 68,—**
toteswingers:1&2:£9.60, 1&3:£4.50, 2&3:£6.30 CSF £32.02 CT £162.17 TOTE £7.30: £2.80, £5.10; EX 40.10.
Owner Alan S Clarke **Bred** R R Clarke **Trained** Inkberrow, Worcestershire
■ Stewards' Enquiry : Tommy Phelan two-day ban: used whip with excessive frequency (Feb 12-13)
FOCUS
A thrilling handicap hurdle where three horses besides the winner traded below 1.5 in-running. A big hurdles best from the winner, with the next two close to their marks.
NOTEBOOK
Inkberrow Rose(IRE) got her head up in the dying strides and seems to have been revitalised by first-time cheekpieces. She travelled well, appreciating the stamina test, and may even get further. Official explanation: trainer said, regarding apparent improvement in form, that the mare didn't stay 3m last time and has possibly benefited from the first-time cheek pieces. (op 11-2)
Azione shaped well at Plumpton two runs back after a year-long absence and travelled well here, seeing out the trip comfortably. She seems to retain her ability, should come on again for the run and can pick up races. (op 8-1)
Royal Chatelier(FR) came from a fair way back, but just had too much to do after the last. He remains lightly raced and will be suited by a strong pace, as stamina appears his forte. (op 13-2 tchd 7-1)
Fentara looked on a fair enough mark on handicap debut and appeared to run her race. She seems suited by this sort of trip and can find opportunities at this level. (op 9-4 tchd 7-2)
Equity Release(IRE) travelled supremely entering the home straight and looked the most likely winner, but found nothing and faded disappointingly. He is likely to be dropped back to 2m where he will be suited by decent ground. (op 10-1)
T/Plt: £471.50 to a £1 stake. Pool:£75,866.31 - 117.45 winning tickets T/Qpdt: £135.20 to a £1 stake. Pool:£5,520.42 - 30.20 winning tickets CR

3823 - 3829a (Foreign Racing) - See Raceform Interactive

3598 FAKENHAM (L-H)
Sunday, January 30

OFFICIAL GOING: Good to soft (good in places; 7.6)
Fresh ground all the way round on both courses but impact on distances not known.
Wind: virtually nil Weather: overcast, dry

3830 COLKIRK MARES' NOVICES' HURDLE (11 hdls) 2m 4f
1:55 (1:55) (Class 4) 4-Y-0+ **£3,252** (£955; £477; £238)

Form RPR
60 **1** **Farewellatmidnight**30 3266 5-11-2 0 JimmyMcCarthy 93+
(Alex Hales) *t.k.h: hld up: lft 3rd at 1st: chsd clr ldr 5th: clsd bef 3 out: mstke next: rdn and squeezed through on inner to ld bef last: kpt on u.p flat* **7/1**2
0 **2** 2 **Mater Mater**24 3401 4-10-4 0 TomMessenger 78
(Caroline Bailey) *racd keenly: j.rt: led: lft wl clr 1st: j.rt and hit 3 out and next: rdn and hdd bef last: kpt on same pce flat* **12/1**
P **3** 143 **Ericaceous**29 3304 4-10-4 0 (t) JamieMoore —
(Christine Dunnett) *lft chsng clr ldr 1st tl 5th: a 3rd after: losing tch and j.rt 7th: t.o and nursed home fr next* **25/1**
P **4** 52 **Colleens Pride (IRE)**7 3698 8-10-6 0 GeraldQuinn(10) —
(Jonjo O'Neill) *a last: nvr jumping fluently: rdn and nt keen after 3rd: lost tch 6th: wl t.o after next* **11/1**3
2-1F **U** **Line Freedom (FR)**66 2627 6-11-8 0 AndrewTinkler —
(Nicky Henderson) *uns rdr 1st* **1/10**1
5m 19.8s (7.20) **Going Correction** +0.50s/f (Soft)
WFA 4 from 5yo+ 12lb **5** Ran SP% **123.3**
Speed ratings (Par 105): **105,104,—,—,—**
CSF £68.37 TOTE £15.60: £2.90, £10.10; EX 24.30.
Owner Mrs J Way **Bred** Mrs J Way **Trained** Wardington, Oxon
FOCUS
This was an extra meeting to make up for an earlier abandoned fixture during the big freeze in December. There was fresh ground all the way round on both courses but impact on distances is not known. The winner is rated to her bumper mark.
NOTEBOOK
Farewellatmidnight looked clear second-best on paper, but the early departure of Line Freedom allowed her to open her account at the first time of asking over hurdles. She beat three very moderate rivals, however, and this form does not amount to much. She made her move two from home, but her jockey had to get fairly serious with her to maintain the advantage. (op 15-2)
Mater Mater was sent straight to the front by Tom Messenger and at one point she held an advantage of about ten lengths, despite her tendency to jump to the right throughout. She tired only from the second-last and she stuck to her task well once headed. (tchd 14-1)
Ericaceous was tailed off from about halfway and offered no encouragement whatsoever.
Line Freedom(FR) was sent off at 1-10 as her form was head and shoulders above anything else on offer, but she failed to pick up at the first and her jockey was catapulted out of the side door in what looked a fairly soft unseat. (tchd 1-12)

3831 WENSUM NOVICES' HURDLE (9 hdls) 2m
2:25 (2:25) (Class 4) 4-Y-0+ **£3,168** (£936; £468; £234; £117)

Form RPR
50 **1** **Alcalde**28 3344 5-11-4 0 RhysFlint 112+
(John Berry) *j.lft at times: chsd ldng trio tl lft cl 3rd 5th: chsd ldr after next: led 3 out: mstke next: clr and in command last: comf* **9/2**3
10 **2** 12 **Break The Chain**26 3386 5-11-11 0 AndrewThornton 110+
(Caroline Bailey) *chsd ldng pair tl lft 2nd 5th tl next: rdn to chse wnr after 3 out: no imp and btn whn hit last* **7/2**2
-240 **3** 19 **Meridiem**13 3601 7-11-1 0 ChrisHonour(3) 83
(Sean Regan) *hld up wl off the pce in last quartet: mstke 4th: wnt poor 4th after 5th: no imp: wnt 3rd after 2 out: nvr trbld ldrs* **66/1**
6U21 **4** 28 **All For Free (IRE)**13 3601 5-11-11 **122** WarrenMarston 73+
(Milton Harris) *t.k.h: chsd ldr tl lft in ld 5th: hit and hdd 3 out: sn drvn and dropped out: 4th and wl btn sn after next: t.o: burst blood vessel* **7/4**1
00 **5** 1 3/4 **Practice Round (IRE)**7 3692 5-11-4 0 DougieCostello 56
(Jonjo O'Neill) *a wl off the pce in last quartet: lost tch 5th: t.o* **16/1**
0-0P **6** 2 1/2 **Agapanthus (GER)**13 3599 6-11-4 0 DenisO'Regan 54
(Barney Curley) *hld up wl off the pce in last quartet: j.lft 1st: rdn and hmpd 5th: sn lost tch: t.o fr next* **16/1**
0 **7** 19 **Tait's Clock (IRE)**7 3692 5-11-4 0 LiamTreadwell 37
(Jonjo O'Neill) *mstkes: a in rr and nvr on terms: t.o after 5th* **33/1**
24/ **U** **Laterly (IRE)**108 2739 6-11-4 0 TomScudamore —
(Steve Gollings) *led: clr tl blnd bdly and uns rdr 5th* **7/2**2
4m 9.20s (3.80) **Going Correction** +0.50s/f (Soft) **8** Ran SP% **115.2**
Speed ratings (Par 105): **110,104,94,80,79 78,68,—**
toteswingers:1&2:£3.00, 1&3:£26.30, 2&3:£20.50 CSF £21.24 TOTE £3.00: £1.70, £1.10, £7.20; EX 17.80.
Owner The Alhambra Partnership **Bred** Miss K Rausing And Mrs S Rogers **Trained** Newmarket, Suffolk
FOCUS
A modest novice hurdle where jumping played an important part. Not the strongest of races, with the favourite well below form.
NOTEBOOK
Alcalde, a three-time winner on the Flat, had not made much impression on two previous hurdles starts, albeit in slightly better company, but travelled well throughout here. He went on when the favourite blundered three out and was always holding the runner-up. This should give him confidence and he will carry on over hurdles, although might have a run or two back on the Flat in the spring. (tchd 7-2)
Break The Chain, a winner on good ground on his debut, never seemed to be travelling that comfortably but went in pursuit of the winner after three out. He was seen off from the home turn though, and a return to genuine good ground is likely to be in his favour. (op 4-1)
Meridiem was never involved having been held up. He now qualifies for a handicap mark, though.
All For Free(IRE), a C&D winner having his third successive run at the track, chased the leader until left in front with a circuit to go, but was not travelling as well as the winner when he flattened the third-last and it knocked the stuffing out of him. He was subsequently reported to have bled. Official explanation: trainer said gelding bled from the nose (op 5-2)

Laterly(IRE)showed promise over hurdles more than two years ago but had raced on the Flat since. He set off in front and was still clear when losing his hind legs at the hurdle in front of the stands with a circuit to go, and decanting his rider. (op 11-4 tchd 5-2)

3832 HEMPTON H'CAP CHASE (18 fncs) 3m 110y
2:55 (2:55) (Class 3) (0-135,132) 5-Y-O+ **£6,285** (£1,873; £948; £486; £254)

Form				RPR
4251	1		**Three Chords (IRE)**[26] 3391 7-10-12 118 AndrewThornton (Caroline Bailey) *a travelling wl: chsd ldrs: wnt 2nd after 14th: led 2 out: pushed clr wl bef last: stdd into last and slt mstke: urged along and readily fnd ex whn pressed flat* **3/1**[1]	133+
2-FF	2	1 3/4	**Bench Warrent (IRE)**[22] 3437 8-11-6 129 (p) PeterToole(3) (Charlie Mann) *chsd ldr tl 3rd: styd handy tl chsd ldr again after 8th: led 13th: jnd and mstke 3 out: sn rdn: hdd next: nt pce of wnr between last 2: gd jump and pressed wnr sn after last: no ex fnl 150yds* **6/1**	136
2PF6	3	19	**Federstar (GER)**[15] 3566 9-10-7 116 JimmyDerham(3) (Milton Harris) *hld up in tch in rr: stmbld on landing 12th: sn rdn along and struggling: wnt modest 3rd bef 2 out: plugged on but no threat to ldrs* **10/1**	106
4205	4	nk	**Noun De La Thinte (FR)**[15] 3568 10-10-9 122 MrJSherwood(7) (Venetia Williams) *chsd ldrs: wnt 2nd 3rd tl after 8th: styd chsng ldrs tl rdn and struggling after 14th: wl btn 3 out* **11/2**[3]	115
-1U5	5	24	**Rustarix (FR)**[45] 2984 10-11-3 123 RobertThornton (Alan King) *in tch: pushed along 10th: rdn along and hdwy to chse ldrs whn mstke 12th: wkng whn mstke 15th: wl btn next: t.o* **13/2**	101
1-21	P		**Ray Mond**[13] 3602 10-11-3 126 AlexMerriam(3) (Neil King) *led: mstke 4th and 9th: hdd 13th: wknd qckly 3 out: wl bhd whn p.u between last 2* **10/3**[2]	—
F-FP	U		**Palypso De Creek (FR)**[51] 2871 8-11-12 132 TomSiddall (Charlie Longsdon) *tried to refuse and uns rdr 1st* **13/2**	—

6m 26.5s (-9.20) **Going Correction** -0.175s/f (Good) 7 Ran SP% **113.5**
Speed ratings: **107,106,100,100,92** —,—
toteswingers:1&2:£4.50, 1&3:£5.60, 2&3:£13.00 CSF £20.77 CT £156.96 TOTE £5.20: £3.00, £3.10; EX 24.00.
Owner Mrs C Aldridge & R Juleff **Bred** J F C Maxwell **Trained** Brixworth, Northants

FOCUS
This was a competitive handicap despite the small field. The presence of confirmed front-runner Ray Mond ensured that there was a decent pace throughout. Another step up from the winner, who was value for further.

NOTEBOOK
Three Chords(IRE), by far the most unexposed runner in the field, recorded a fairly comfortable win, although the eventual margin of victory was far less emphatic than looked likely at one point. Always travelling well, he raced in mid-division in the early part of the race, but once Bench Warrent took over at the head of affairs, he went with that one and the pair drew a mile clear of the remainder. He cruised into the lead as they rounded the far turn and quickly established a five-length advantage as they approached the last, but a slow jump at that fence meant that he came under strong driving on the run-in, although he quickly asserted again once his chief rival got upsides. This was another encouraging display and he should be able to defy another rise, although he has the option of novice chases under a double penalty. (op 11-4)
Bench Warrent(IRE), a faller on both his starts this term, including the Welsh National three weeks previously, took over from Ray Mond at the sixth-last and he and the eventual winner gradually forged clear from that point onwards. He came under strong pressure two out and looked to be dropping away, but from there he responded well to his rider's urgings to get back to within two lengths at the line. This was a solid effort and this dour stayer will appreciate stepping back up in trip. (op 13-2 tchd 7-1 and 11-2)
Federstar(GER) was back over fences after running reasonably well over hurdles at Warwick earlier this month. This was a fairly encouraging display, although he never remotely looked like taking a hand in the finish. (op 14-1)
Noun De La Thinte(FR), who ran well over 3m5f in a better race at Warwick last time on ground that was far too soft for her, was slightly disappointing on this occasion. She never travelled with any fluency and made several mistakes as she gradually lost touch with the leaders from the third last. She may need a short break. (op 5-1 tchd 9-2 and 6-1)
Rustarix(FR) was struggling from a long way out. (op 8-1)
Ray Mond was headed six from home and was pulled up at the final fence having become tailed off. Perhaps the handicapper has finally caught up with him after a sequence of six wins and a second place in his previous seven runs. Official explanation: jockey said gelding stopped quickly and pulled up (op 6-1)
Palypso De Creek(FR) put on the brakes approaching the first fence and his jockey had no option but to jump off. This was his fourth non-completion in a row and he is becoming very frustrating after a promising start to his British career. (op 6-1)

3833 PUDDING NORTON MAIDEN HURDLE (11 hdls) 2m 4f
3:25 (3:25) (Class 4) 4-Y-O+ **£3,252** (£955; £477; £238)

Form				RPR
0420	1		**Caught By Witness (IRE)**[22] 3440 6-11-5 125 (t) WarrenMarston (Milton Harris) *in tch: chsd ldr after 7th: led 3 out: sn rdn clr: blnd bdly 2 out: in n.d after: mstke last: eased flat* **4/6**[1]	106+
-0	2	7	**Alonso De Guzman (IRE)**[84] 2246 7-11-5 0 (t) RichardJohnson (Tim Vaughan) *racd keenly: mstkes: chsd ldr tl led 3rd: hdd 3 out: rdn and nt pce of wnr bef next: wl hld after but plugged on to hold 2nd* **5/1**[2]	94+
-406	3	6	**Salut Honore (FR)**[28] 3346 5-11-5 0 SamJones (Alex Hales) *hld up in tch: wnt 3rd after 7th: rdn and no hdwy after next: mstke 3 out: plugged on same pce after* **18/1**	90
600	4	6	**Get Ready To Go (IRE)**[18] 3506 7-11-5 0 DougieCostello (Neil King) *j.rt at times: led mstke 2nd: hdd 3rd: chsd ldr tl after 7th: 4th and toiling u.p next: wl btn 3 out* **10/1**	84
50	5	24	**Uncle Keef (IRE)**[71] 2512 5-11-5 0 AndrewTinkler (Nicky Henderson) *in tch in midfield: nt fluent 6th: rdn whn mstke next: sn struggling: 5th and wl btn bef 3 out: t.o* **11/2**[3]	62
	6	34	**Sunny Spells**[31] 6-11-5 0 ColinBolger (Julia Feilden) *in tch in midfield: lost tch after 7th: t.o bef 3 out* **12/1**	29
0660	P		**Patrick Dee**[16] 3540 6-11-5 64 JamieMoore (Christine Dunnett) *chsd ldrs: lost pl after 5th: lost tch rapidly after 7th: t.o whn p.u bef 3 out* **100/1**	—
BP4	P		**Humbel Times (IRE)**[13] 3603 7-11-2 64 AlexMerriam(3) (Neil King) *a wl bhd: rdn and no rspnse after 3rd: lost tch 6th: t.o whn p.u bef 8th* **50/1**	—
-00P	P		**Flag Dancer**[7] 3698 5-10-12 0 (p) MrMMarris(7) (Christine Dunnett) *chsd ldrs: mstke 2nd: lost pl after next: bhd and losing tch 5th: t.o whn p.u bef 7th* **150/1**	—
	P		**Maccool (IRE)**[16] 5-11-5 0 DenisO'Regan (Barney Curley) *a in rr: mstke 3rd: struggling 5th: wl bhd whn p.u bef 8th* **33/1**	—

5m 19.9s (7.30) **Going Correction** +0.50s/f (Soft) 10 Ran SP% **120.6**
Speed ratings (Par 105): **105,102,99,97,87 74**,—,—,—,—
toteswingers:1&2:£2.50, 1&3:£4.20, 2&3:£7.90 CSF £4.77 TOTE £1.90: £1.10, £1.90, £3.10; EX 6.30.
Owner Nic Allen **Bred** Denis Duggan And Mrs Margaret Duggan **Trained** Herridge, Wiltshire

FOCUS
An uncompetitive maiden hurdle. The winner was again well below his best but still good enough.

NOTEBOOK
Caught By Witness(IRE) stood out on form and duly got off the mark at the seventh attempt over hurdles, making up for a narrow defeat over C&D on New Year's Day. He had to be ridden clear after three out but was always in control from that point. Milton Harris was planning to enter him for the Martin Pipe conditionals' race at Cheltenham but the rider reported he felt the gelding had a problem, possibly with his back, and the trainer will have him checked out first. (op 8-13 tchd 4-7)
Alonso De Guzman(IRE), a fair middle-distance/stayer on the Flat, was wearing a tongue-tie for the first time and did much better than on his hurdling debut in November. However, after making much of the running, he had no answer when the favourite went for home. (op 15-2)
Salut Honore(FR) ran his best race so far over hurdles and now qualifies for a handicap mark. (op 20-1)
Get Ready To Go(IRE), a former Irish point winner, made the early running and stayed prominent until losing his pitch on the last circuit. He did keep on again in the closing stages and looks worth trying at 3m. (op 9-1 tchd 8-1)
Uncle Keef(IRE) got into contention at around halfway but dropped away on the last lap. He now qualifies for handicaps, and will probably need good ground to make an impression in that sphere. (tchd 5-1)

3834 TOFTREES H'CAP CHASE (12 fncs) 2m 110y
3:55 (3:55) (Class 3) (0-125,122) 5-Y-O+ **£5,079** (£1,549; £809; £439)

Form				RPR
-2FP	1		**Lord Singer (FR)**[17] 3531 6-11-4 114 JamieMoore (Gary Moore) *urged along to jump off: mde all and racd keenly after 1st: rdn after 2 out: styd on wl and in command bef last* **3/1**[2]	124+
3464	2	8	**Prince Des Marais (FR)**[15] 3565 8-11-8 118 (t) AndrewThornton (Caroline Bailey) *chsd ldrs: 3rd and rdn after 3 out: plugged on same pce between last 2: wnt 2nd nr fin* **9/1**	121
-462	3	1/2	**Enfant De Lune (FR)**[15] 3573 7-11-6 116 RobertThornton (Alan King) *chsd wnr thrght: rdn along and j.lft 2 out: no ex u.p and btn between last 2: lost 2nd nr fin* **7/2**[3]	118
5346	4	9	**Marc Aurele (IRE)**[19] 3494 6-10-6 105 (t) JimmyDerham(3) (Milton Harris) *chsd ldng pair tl 6th: struggling and rdn along after next: no prog and wl hld fr 3 out* **5/1**	102
0P0	F		**Vinmix De Bessy (FR)**[40] 3059 10-11-9 122 (p) EamonDehdashti(3) (Gary Moore) *j. slowly 1st: racd in last pair tl fell 3rd* **22/1**	—
2625	F		**J'Adhere (FR)**[5] 3730 6-10-9 105 RichardJohnson (Tim Vaughan) *plld hrd: hld up in last and many mstkes: hmpd 3rd: effrt but stl plenty to do whn blnd 9th: no hdwy and wl btn in last whn fell last* **2/1**[1]	102

4m 19.1s (2.50) **Going Correction** -0.175s/f (Good) 6 Ran SP% **111.6**
Speed ratings: **87,83,83,78**,— —
CSF £26.44 TOTE £3.90: £2.30, £3.30; EX 25.80.
Owner The Winning Hand **Bred** Eric Blondel **Trained** Lower Beeding, W Sussex

FOCUS
They went a good pace in this ordinary contest, but very few got into it. The winner is rated to his best.

NOTEBOOK
Lord Singer(FR) was sent into an early lead and was never headed. He raced very keenly in the early part of the race, but his jockey did well to restrain him and he simply kept finding more, especially in the back straight when Enfant de Lune briefly came to his quarters. Moore kicked again approaching the last and he eventually won going away. He jumped boldly throughout and clearly relished going left-handed again - his career record going this way round is now 3-6, while he is 0-4 going right-handed. (op 5-2)
Prince Des Marais(FR) got up for second place in the shadows of the post. He raced in third place for most of the contest but was never able to get anywhere near the eventual winner. He still looks quite high in the handicap but will enjoy running on faster ground in the spring. (tchd 7-1)
Enfant De Lune(FR) was the only one to serve it up to the winner and was unlucky to lose second place near the finish. He briefly looked a threat to Lord Singer as they jumped the second-last but simply could not reduce the deficit from that point, and he paid for that extra effort on the run-in. He deserves a change of luck. (op 11-4)
Marc Aurele(IRE), another who prefers quicker ground, won twice over hurdles for Paul Nicholls last year, making virtually all both times. He has been held up on his last four starts over fences, and perhaps a return to forcing tactics will bring about some improvement. (op 7-1 tchd 15-2)
J'Adhere(FR) came in for plenty of support but he was never able to land a blow. He was hampered by the fall of Vinmix de Bessy at the third fence, but he jumped poorly throughout and when Richard Johnson asked for an effort there was minimal response. He eventually took a tired fall at the last when well held. This was a second disappointing run over fences but he too may improve for slightly quicker ground. (op 11-4)

3835 FAKENHAM STANDARD OPEN NATIONAL HUNT FLAT RACE 2m
4:25 (4:25) (Class 6) 4-6-Y-O **£1,370** (£399; £199)

Form				RPR
	1		**All That Remains (IRE)**[119] 6-11-4 0 RhysFlint (Steve Gollings) *t.k.h: chsd ldr: jnd ldr 4f out: rdn to ld ent st: clr 1f out: kpt on u.p ins fnl f* **11/4**[2]	107
3	2	3/4	**Tealissio**[233] 718 5-11-4 0 DougieCostello (Lucy Wadham) *in tch: trckd ldng pair 4f out: rdn over 2f out: kpt on wl ins fnl f: wnt 2nd nr fin* **12/1**	106
32	3	nk	**Dineur (FR)**[27] 3372 5-11-4 0 RobertThornton (Alan King) *t.k.h: hld up in tch: hdwy to ld after 3f: jnd 4f out: rdn over 2f out: hdd ent st: rallied u.p ins fnl f: lost 2nd nr fin* **4/1**[3]	106
4	4	17	**Kings Lodge**[46] 2957 5-11-4 0 AndrewTinkler (Nicky Henderson) *t.k.h: hld up in tch: trckd ldrs 1/2-way: rdn and wknd qckly 3f out* **1/1**[1]	93
0	5	7	**Peintre Ster (IRE)**[81] 2315 4-10-4 0 AlexMerriam(3) (Neil King) *led for 3f: styd handy: rdn 6f out: wknd wl over 3f out* **80/1**	73
	6	10	**Ammo Away** 5-11-4 0 RichardJohnson (Tim Vaughan) *in tch: rdn and outpcd 5f out: t.o fnl 3f* **25/1**	75
	7	44	**Major Kirk** 4-10-2 0 ow2 (p) MrAWilliams(7) (Terry Clement) *in tch in rr: rdn and lost tch qckly over 5f out: wl t.o fnl 4f* **100/1**	27

4m 13.8s (14.00) **Going Correction** +0.50s/f (Soft)
WFA 4 from 5yo+ 11lb 7 Ran SP% **110.4**
Speed ratings: **85,84,84,75,72 67,45**
toteswingers:1&2:£3.10, 1&3:£1.60, 2&3:£3.10 CSF £30.30 TOTE £4.80: £2.10, £3.00; EX 33.20.
Owner P J Martin **Bred** Eoin, Patrick And Cian O'Connor **Trained** Scamblesby, Lincs

FOCUS
A fair bumper in which the early pace was very steady. The time was slow and the form is suspect.

NOTEBOOK
All That Remains(IRE), bought for £64,000 after beating two subsequent dual winners in an Irish point, was making his debut under rules having not shown much at home, but travelled well over this much shorter trip before asserting off the home turn. He had to be driven out but should come on for the run, and is likely to appreciate a stiffer test in future. (op 5-1)

Tealissio, having his first start since finishing third in a bumper back in June, gradually crept into contention and finished well without being able to reel in the winner. He is another who should benefit from the outing. (op 15-2)
Dineur(FR), who looked open to improvement when placed on his two previous starts, took up the running after half a mile to ensure a more sensible gallop. He kept battling under pressure but was just run out of it. He is likely to benefit from further over hurdles in time. (op 3-1)
Kings Lodge failed to build on the promise of his debut, being under pressure fully half a mile from home, but did not look at home on the track. He can be given another chance on a more conventional course. Official explanation: jockey said gelding was unsuited by the track (tchd 5-6)
T/Plt: £265.90 to a £1 stake. Pool:£61,575.10 - 168.99 winning tickets T/Qpdt: £34.10 to a £1 stake. Pool:£7,125.94 - 154.40 winning tickets SP

[3526]HEREFORD (R-H)

Sunday, January 30

OFFICIAL GOING: Soft (good to soft in places; chs 6.3, hdl 6.1)
Final fence omitted on all circuits of the chase course; under repair.
Wind: Nil Weather: A few bright spells but cold

3836 EUROPEAN BREEDERS' FUND "NATIONAL HUNT" NOVICES' HURDLE (QUALIFIER) (10 hdls) 2m 4f

1:35 (1:35) (Class 4) 4-7-Y-O £2,016 (£592; £296; £147)

Form RPR
-521 1 **Cucumber Run (IRE)**[24] 3403 6-11-8 124 .... APMcCoy 136+
(Nicky Henderson) *trckd ldrs: wnt 2nd appr 3 out: upsides 2 out: led bef last: readily drew clr run-in* **4/5**[1]
3-40 2 4 **Easter Meteor**[29] 3288 5-11-2 0 .... SamThomas 123+
(Emma Lavelle) *a.p: led appr 3 out: jnd 2 out: hdd between last 2: u.p whn mstke last: no ex run-in* **7/2**[2]
1P 3 11 **Stolen Thunder**[45] 2981 6-11-8 0 .... WayneHutchinson 116+
(Emma Lavelle) *j.lft: hld up: pushed along appr 7th and stdy hdwy: chsd clr ldrs bef 3 out: wnt 3rd after 2 out: no imp on front pair* **16/1**
00 4 19 **Bennys Mist (IRE)**[17] 3528 5-11-2 0 .... AidanColeman 91
(Venetia Williams) *midfield: pushed along after 6th: chsd clr ldrs appr 3 out: nvr able to threaten* **20/1**
34-0 5 shd **Mudita Moment (IRE)**[15] 3556 6-10-11 0 .... IanPopham(5) 91
(Anna Brooks) *midfield: stdy hdwy to chse clr ldrs appr 3 out: no imp: wknd after 2 out* **40/1**
3 6 10 **Dovecote Wood**[33] 3153 6-11-2 0 .... TomO'Brien 86+
(Caroline Keevil) *led: mstke 7th: hdd appr 3 out: wknd bef 2 out* **9/2**[3]
006 7 11 **Bridge Street Boy**[19] 3495 6-11-2 0 .... JodieMogford 70
(Richard Lee) *midfield: pushed along 7th: nvr on terms w ldrs* **100/1**
1-4 8 7 **There And Then**[23] 3434 5-11-2 0 .... BarryKeniry 63
(Seamus Mullins) *midfield: struggling after 6th: bhd after* **25/1**
00-P 9 3 ¼ **Rich Live (FR)**[20] 3487 6-10-13 0 .... SeanQuinlan(3) 60
(Lady Anne Connell) *trckd ldrs: pushed along after 6th: wknd bef 3 out* **125/1**
054 10 2 **Radmores Oscar**[22] 3441 5-10-9 0 .... CharlieWallis(7) 58
(John O'Shea) *rdn after 3rd: a bhd* **100/1**
6 11 19 **Ledbury Star (IRE)**[22] 3441 5-11-2 0 .... DavidDennis 39
(Matt Sheppard) *a bhd: struggling 5th: t.o* **100/1**
03-U P **Roman Landing**[266] 223 7-11-2 0 .... CharliePoste —
(Peter Pritchard) *midfield: struggling 3 out: t.o whn p.u bef last* **150/1**
006- F **Mr Windmill**[282] 5370 5-11-2 0 .... RodiGreene —
(Lisa Williamson) *prom: rdn and lost pl bef 4th: struggling and bhd whn fell 6th* **100/1**
60-P P **Solo Roma (IRE)**[260] 337 7-11-2 0 .... (p) WillKennedy —
(Violet M Jordan) *hld up: struggling 6th: t.o whn p.u bef 7th* **150/1**
04 P **Generous Bob**[56] 2797 4-10-1 0 .... WayneKavanagh(3) —
(Seamus Mullins) *midfield: pushed along after 6th: sn bhd: t.o whn p.u last* **50/1**
0 P **Just Richie (IRE)**[16] 3546 6-11-2 0 .... NickScholfield —
(Arthur Whiting) *midfield: rdn after 3rd: lost pl 4th: t.o 6th: p.u bef 7th* **150/1**

5m 2.50s (7.00) **Going Correction** +0.40s/f (Soft)
WFA 4 from 5yo+ 12lb 16 Ran SP% **121.6**
Speed ratings: **102,100,96,88,88 84,79,77,75,75 67,—,—,—,— —**
toteswingers:1&2:£1.20, 1&3:£5.00, 2&3:£7.60 CSF £3.58 TOTE £1.70: £1.10, £1.40, £4.10; EX 4.70.
Owner The Goblyns **Bred** Miss Nicola Ann Adams **Trained** Upper Lambourn, Berks

FOCUS
An uncompetitive novice hurdle, with the front two in the market drawing clear. The ground on the hurdles track seemed considerably tackier. The cosy winner is on the upgrade.

NOTEBOOK
Cucumber Run(IRE), off the mark over hurdles at Huntingdon last time out, moved smoothly throughout under McCoy and stayed on well to go clear from before the last. He currently has a rating of 124 and connections are probably best advised to go down the handicap route with him now. (op 8-11 tchd 5-6)
Easter Meteor, who drew 11 lengths clear of the remainder, returned to the sort of form shown on his first couple of starts and is a winner waiting to happen, especially once he goes handicapping. (tchd 10-3)
Stolen Thunder ran as though something was amiss when pulling up at Towcester and, although well held in third, did enough to make him of interest for staying hurdles. He should come into his own once chasing. (op 22-1)
Bennys Mist(IRE) ran his most promising race to date and will be of interest once handicapping. (op 25-1)
Mudita Moment(IRE) Official explanation: vet said gelding finished distressed
Dovecote Wood proved disappointing, dropping right away having made a lot of the running. (op 6-1 tchd 4-1 and 15-2 in a place)

3837 LINDLEY CATERING NOVICES' H'CAP HURDLE (11 hdls) 2m 6f 110y

2:05 (2:05) (Class 5) (0-95,95) 4-Y-O+ £1,561 (£458; £229; £114)

Form RPR
03-3 1 **Constant Cupid (IRE)**[73] 2469 7-11-1 84 .... (v) JodieMogford 95+
(Graeme McPherson) *prom: led 6th: mstke 3 out: wnt clr appr last: easily* **9/2**[1]
-403 2 7 **Broadway Star (FR)**[23] 3430 8-11-4 92 .... (t) MrTomDavid(5) 92+
(Tim Vaughan) *in tch: wnt 2nd 8th: mstke 3 out: u.p and wl outpcd by wnr appr last: no ch after* **15/2**
-000 3 10 **Artic Pride (IRE)**[33] 3153 7-11-0 83 .... LeightonAspell 72
(Oliver Sherwood) *midfield: stdy hdwy 5th: hdwy 3 out: chsd clr ldrs appr 2 out: plugged on one pce and no imp* **5/1**[2]
/P65 4 4 ½ **Lindengrove**[30] 3253 6-11-1 87 .... TommyPhelan(3) 69
(Claire Dyson) *prom: led 4th: hdd 6th: rdn and wknd after 3 out* **16/1**
0-30 5 4 **Aeronautica (IRE)**[45] 2981 8-11-0 83 .... WayneHutchinson 61
(Tor Sturgis) *midfield: sme hdwy u.p 3 out: no imp on ldrs: wl btn 2 out* **6/1**[3]
6435 6 3 ¼ **Baby Car (FR)**[29] 3297 7-11-3 86 .... (t) WillKennedy 60
(Noel Chance) *hld up: effrt 3 out but no imp on ldrs: wknd 2 out* **6/1**[3]
3025 7 24 **Brimley**[27] 3368 8-11-9 95 .... LeeStephens(3) 45
(Ann Price) *led: hdd 4th: remained prom tl rdn and wknd after 7th* **12/1**
00-6 8 59 **Acquisitive (FR)**[260] 327 5-11-12 95 .... PaddyBrennan —
(Nigel Twiston-Davies) *chsd ldrs: j.rt 5th: mstke 3 out: sn wknd: t.o* **8/1**
651/ P **Lescer's Lad**[675] 4731 14-10-7 83 .... (t) JeremiahMcGrath(7) —
(Mrs A M Woodrow) *hld up: wl bhd whn p.u bef 8th* **25/1**
05F P **Kilbready Star (IRE)**[84] 2243 11-11-2 85 .... CharliePoste —
(Peter Pritchard) *a bhd: t.o 8th: p.u bef last* **22/1**
4U0P P **Jumpjack Flint**[16] 3544 5-11-6 92 .... (t) DannyCook(3) —
(David Pipe) *a bhd: t.o 3 out: p.u bef 2 out* **12/1**

5m 45.0s (7.00) **Going Correction** +0.40s/f (Soft) 11 Ran SP% **115.8**
Speed ratings (Par 103): **103,100,97,95,94 93,84,64,—,— —**
toteswingers:1&2:£5.60, 1&3:£3.90, 2&3:£7.80 CSF £37.89 CT £175.17 TOTE £4.90: £1.10, £5.10, £2.90; EX 40.00.
Owner David Du Croz **Bred** Mrs Christine Kelly **Trained** Upper Oddington, Gloucs

FOCUS
Most of these were in trouble a long way out. The form is rated around the second and third.

NOTEBOOK
Constant Cupid(IRE), off since showing improved form at the course in November, had his field in trouble a long way from the finish and is clearly improving. It would be no surprise to see him turned out under a penalty. (op 5-1 tchd 11-2)
Broadway Star(FR), who found the heavy ground no good for him last time, ran considerably better here and is one to keep on side once granted drier conditions. (op 12-1)
Artic Pride(IRE) had offered little previously over hurdles, but the switch to handicaps was always likely to bring about an improved effort. There's room for improvement in his jumping, but still showed enough to suggest he could win a small race over 3m. (op 6-1)
Lindengrove showed a bit more on this handicap debut. (tchd 14-1)
Baby Car(FR), who was reported to have a breathing problem latest, again ran as though all was not well. Official explanation: vet said gelding has a breathing problem (tchd 11-2)
Acquisitive(FR) stopped very quickly on this handicap debut. (op 7-1)

3838 LINDLEY CATERING NOVICES' CHASE (10 fncs 2 omitted) 2m

2:35 (2:35) (Class 3) 5-Y-O+ £4,553 (£1,337; £668; £333)

Form RPR
-011 1 **William's Wishes (IRE)**[76] 2422 6-11-8 139 .... PaulMoloney 139+
(Evan Williams) *mde all: easily wnt clr after last: unchal* **8/13**[1]
0U53 2 7 **Outside The Box**[25] 3393 7-10-12 113 .... WillKennedy 114+
(Noel Chance) *chsd wnr thrght: pushed along and outpcd after last: sn no ch* **14/1**
-002 3 23 **Babysitter (IRE)**[11] 3625 8-10-12 0 .... APMcCoy 89
(Jonjo O'Neill) *j.lft a few times: chsd ldrs: struggling and outpcd 8th: plugged on for poor 3rd* **3/1**[2]
-21P 4 2 ¼ **Humbel Ben (IRE)**[22] 3440 8-10-12 0 .... PaddyBrennan 88
(Alan Jones) *hld up: hit 3rd: carried wd 6th: sn swtchd rt: struggling 8th: nvr a factor* **6/1**[3]
5 23 **Medellin (IRE)**[168] 1262 7-10-7 0 ow2 .... SClements(7) 78+
(Liam Corcoran) *hld up: wnt 3rd at 5th: mstke 8th: j.lft whn outpcd by ldrs 2 out: wknd last* **50/1**

4m 9.80s (6.20) **Going Correction** +0.575s/f (Soft) 5 Ran SP% **109.8**
Speed ratings: **107,103,92,90,79**
CSF £9.01 TOTE £2.10: £1.10, £4.80; EX 8.10.
Owner Mrs D E Cheshire **Bred** Mrs M O'Driscoll **Trained** Llancarfan, Vale Of Glamorgan

FOCUS
The fence in the straight was bypassed in all chase races. An easy win, as expected, for William's Wishes, who was value for further but is a stone+ off being an Arkle candidate at this stage.

NOTEBOOK
William's Wishes(IRE), who had been due to run at Doncaster the previous day, made it 3-3 over fences, the result never being in doubt. He jumped quickly out in front and readily opened up a clear lead on touching down after what was actually the last fence. Given an Arkle entry earlier in the week, his trainer doesn't feel he's quite up to championship grade and is also concerned about his relative lack of size, so he's likely to go down the handicap route. (op 4-9 tchd 4-6)
Outside The Box ran a race full of promise with handicaps in mind, although it remains to be seen in whether he's harmed his future mark in finishing so close. (op 16-1 tchd 18-1 and 12-1)
Babysitter(IRE) tended to jump out to his left and needs a longer trip in handicaps to be seen at his best. (op 4-1)
Humbel Ben(IRE) never got involved o this chasing debut, but should do better in time. (op 10-1)

3839 LINDLEY CATERING H'CAP HURDLE (8 hdls) 2m 1f

3:05 (3:05) (Class 5) (0-90,90) 4-Y-O+ £1,561 (£458; £229; £114)

Form RPR
6P30 1 **Galantos (GER)**[94] 2049 10-10-11 82 .... JoshuaMoore(7) 92+
(Helen Nelmes) *in tch: led 2 out: abt 3 l clr appr last: a doing enough towards fin* **14/1**
6045 2 1 ½ **Form And Beauty (IRE)**[28] 3350 9-9-9 64 .... IanPopham(5) 70
(Bernard Llewellyn) *hld up in midfield: hdwy 3 out: wnt 2nd and abt 3 l down appr last: styd on u.p run-in: no further imp fnl strides* **10/1**
0052 3 15 **Illysantachristina**[30] 3255 8-11-6 89 .... MattGriffiths(5) 80
(Bernard Llewellyn) *hld up in rr: hdwy 5th: chsd ldrs after 3 out: ev ch 2 out: wknd bef last* **6/1**
-04P 4 ¾ **Stage Right**[84] 2244 10-10-9 73 .... MarkGrant 63
(Simon Lewis) *prom: rdn and outpcd appr 5th: rallied 2 out but no imp on ldrs* **66/1**
-P03 5 7 **Celtic Ballad (IRE)**[28] 3343 5-11-7 85 .... JoeTizzard 68
(Colin Tizzard) *prom tl rdn and wknd appr 2 out* **12/1**
0001 6 2 **Roxane Bruere (FR)**[16] 3545 6-10-3 77 .... (t) ChristopherWard(10) 61
(Robin Dickin) *hld up: hdwy appr 4th: led bef 3 out: hdd 2 out: wknd bef last* **11/2**[3]
0000 7 2 ½ **Sun Des Mottes (FR)**[22] 3448 5-10-11 75 .... TimmyMurphy 54
(David Pipe) *hld up and bhd: stdy hdwy into midfield 3 out: sn rdn and no imp: wl btn* **7/2**[1]
6000 8 5 **Kilcommon Pride (IRE)**[19] 3491 6-11-10 88 .... HaddenFrost 62
(Roger Curtis) *hld up: rdn 3 out: nvr on terms w ldrs* **80/1**
0424 9 8 **Lady Of Ashcott**[30] 3255 5-9-12 69 .... (p) MarkQuinlan(7) 35
(Neil Mulholland) *midfield: rdn 4th: wknd 3 out* **9/2**[2]
6006 10 5 **Echo Dancer**[73] 2467 5-10-13 87 .... (t) JoshWall(10) 48
(Trevor Wall) *hld up: hdwy into midfield 5th: wknd bef 2 out* **40/1**
431P 11 10 **Lukie Victor (IRE)**[13] 3606 10-10-12 81 .... (v) DavidBass(5) 32
(Evan Williams) *j.lft: led: hdd 4th: remained cl up tl rdn and wknd appr 2 out* **11/1**
004P 12 41 **Galant Eye (IRE)**[12] 3622 12-10-1 72 .... DannyBurton(7) —
(Chris Down) *in tch: rdn briefly early on: lost pl 4th: bhd after* **25/1**

P-50 **13** *hd* **Empire Seeker (USA)**[90] 2131 6-11-8 **86**........................ JasonMaguire —
(Heather Main) *midfield: struggling and dropped bhd 4th: t.o* **20/1**
PPP **P** **Laureus (GER)**[16] 3540 8-10-5 **69**.. RodiGreene —
(Rachel Hobbs) *plld hrd: hld up: hdwy u.p into midfield 3 out: wknd 2 out: t.o whn p.u bef last* **40/1**
060/ **P** **Driving Miss Suzie**[998] 160 7-11-5 **90**......................... MrPJTolman(7) —
(Debra Hamer) *prom: led 4th: hdd appr 3 out: wknd bef 2 out: t.o whn p.u bef last* **33/1**

4m 10.3s (10.90) **Going Correction** +0.40s/f (Soft) **15** Ran SP% **121.0**
Speed ratings (Par 103): **90,89,82,81,78 77,76,74,70,68 63,44,43,—,—**
toteswingers:1&2:£19.10, 1&3:£26.80, 2&3:£11.40 CSF £138.22 CT £945.18 TOTE £21.40: £7.10, £5.60, £3.70; EX 149.00.
Owner Mrs C Knowles **Bred** R Zimmer **Trained** Warmwell, Dorset

FOCUS
A very moderate handicap hurdle. The winner stepped up on recent runs and was rated 100+ in the past.

NOTEBOOK
Galantos(GER), off since October, had previously failed to win in 15 attempts over hurdles, but he held on well having gone to the front before the second-last. Now ten, it remains to be seen whether he can defy much of a rise. (tchd 12-1)
Form And Beauty(IRE) ran easily his best race over hurdles to date (run a couple of decent races off higher marks over fences), and may be able to win a race after all. (op 16-1)
Illysantachristina, an improved second on her recent handicap debut, had gone up 2lb and failed to quite run up to that level. (op 5-1 tchd 13-2)
Stage Right, off for 84 days, plugged on again having been outpaced. (op 50-1)
Roxane Bruere(FR), up 4lb for winning at Huntingdon, made good headway to lead, but had little in reserve for the business end. (op 6-1)
Sun Des Mottes(FR), who had shown little previously over hurdles (often racing too freely), proved popular on this handicap debut and Timmy Murphy gave her an exaggerated hold-up ride. However, although she settled better than in the past, she never got close enough to challenge and continues to look a short runner. Official explanation: trainer's rep had no explanation for the poor form shown (op 11-4 tchd 9-4)

3840 LINDLEY CATERING GROUP H'CAP HURDLE (10 hdls) 2m 4f
3:35 (3:35) (Class 4) (0-115,114) 4-Y-0+ **£2,016** (£592; £296; £147)

Form RPR
432 **1** **Mannlichen**[45] 2983 5-11-12 **114**.. AidanColeman 129+
(Venetia Williams) *in tch: a travelling wl: led appr 3 out: effrtlessly drew clr bef last: v easily* **11/4**[1]
6P06 **2** *15* **Chilbury Hill (IRE)**[8] 3686 8-9-11 **90**............................. GilesHawkins(5) 83
(Kevin Bishop) *hld up: hdwy 3 out: outpcd after 2 out: kpt on to take 2nd last: no ch w wnr* **9/2**[3]
1/0P **3** *2 ½* **De Welsh Wizzard**[45] 2983 8-10-10 **105**........................ JoshuaMoore(7) 96
(Emma Lavelle) *chsd ldrs: rdn bef 3 out: sn outpcd: styd on same pce fr bef last whn chalng for pls* **14/1**
0005 **4** *2 ¾* **Great Hero**[27] 3366 6-11-12 **114**... SeanQuinlan 104+
(Richard Phillips) *hld up in midfield: sltly hmpd 7th: hdwy sn after: ev ch fr 3 out tl rdn and outpcd after 2 out: no ex after last* **22/1**
6661 **5** *14* **Sacco D'Oro**[12] 3619 5-10-1 **92**.. CharlieStudd(3) 66
(Michael Mullineaux) *hld up: hdwy 6th: outpcd bef 2 out: nvr a danger* **11/1**
5-33 **6** *10* **Molanna View (IRE)**[90] 2123 6-11-4 **106**........................... SamThomas 70
(Emma Lavelle) *midfield: hdwy after 7th: chsng ldrs whn nt fluent 3 out: wknd appr 2 out* **7/2**[2]
0-2P **7** *3 ½* **Winchester Red**[209] 911 9-10-12 **107**...................(t) MrJEngland(7) 67
(Evan Williams) *led: hdd appr 3 out: wknd bef 2 out* **20/1**
40 **8** *7* **Marlinsky (GER)**[20] 3481 5-11-2 **109**............................. MrTomDavid(5) 62
(Tim Vaughan) *hld up: sme hdwy appr 3 out: no imp on ldrs: wknd bef 2 out* **16/1**
2445 **9** *16* **Mangonel**[73] 2480 7-9-9 **88** oh6.......................................(v) IanPopham(5) 25
(Stuart Howe) *prom tl rdn and wknd after 3 out* **16/1**
500P **10** *50* **Freddy's Star (IRE)**[80] 2333 9-11-3 **112**........................ DannyBurton(7) —
(Gerald Ham) *in tch: rdn and wknd 7th: bhd after: t.o* **33/1**
-P60 **11** *25* **Lucky Dancer**[147] 1477 6-10-12 **100**...............................(t) PaulMoloney —
(Evan Williams) *hld up: struggling after 6th: t.o* **12/1**

5m 5.80s (10.30) **Going Correction** +0.40s/f (Soft) **11** Ran SP% **113.6**
Speed ratings (Par 105): **95,89,88,86,81 77,75,73,66,46 36**
toteswingers:1&2:£3.60, 1&3:£6.20, 2&3:£12.10 CSF £14.76 CT £143.19 TOTE £4.10: £1.90, £1.60, £5.10; EX 15.80.
Owner Graham Mezzone **Bred** Miss K Rausing **Trained** Kings Caple, H'fords

FOCUS
This proved nothing more than a hack round for favourite Mannlichen. He is on the upgrade and there should be more to come.

NOTEBOOK
Mannlichen, who was perfectly placed throughout under Aidan Coleman, hacked round for an easy success. Runner-up off 4lb lower on his handicap debut at Towcester, he handled the chopped-up ground better than anything else and won in the style of a horse capable of mixing it at a higher level. It'll be interesting to see where he goes next, with the conditionals' handicap hurdle at Cheltenham looking a possible aim. (op 5-2)
Chilbury Hill(IRE), backed beforehand, stayed on best in the battle for second. (op 13-2)
De Welsh Wizzard, the Emma Lavelle second string according to the betting, was a bit keen early and kept on surprisingly well. This was his best run since returning from an absence. (op 16-1 tchd 12-1)
Great Hero didn't quite last home, but it was still a step forward. (tchd 25-1)
Sacco D'Oro Official explanation: jockey said mare was unsuited by the soft (good to soft in places) ground
Molanna View(IRE) was beaten soon after a mistake three out on this handicap debut. His action suggests good ground is needed. (op 3-1)

3841 LINDLEY CATERING H'CAP CHASE (12 fncs 2 omitted) 2m 3f
4:05 (4:05) (Class 3) (0-135,134) 5-Y-0+ **£4,553** (£1,337; £668; £333)

Form RPR
4220 **1** **Grand Lahou (FR)**[50] 2881 8-11-2 **129**........................... MrTomDavid(5) 138+
(Tim Vaughan) *mde all: rdn whn pressed fnl 200yds: a doing enough towards fin* **6/1**[2]
0P-P **2** *1* **Saphir Des Bois (FR)**[275] 78 7-11-11 **133**...................... TomO'Brien 140
(Peter Bowen) *chsd wnr thrght: rdn and tried to chal fnl 200yds: kpt on u.p: hld towards fin* **3/1**[1]
402P **3** *16* **Postmaster**[113] 1777 9-11-4 **133**....................................(t) CDTimmons(7) 123
(Tim Vaughan) *midfield: hdwy to chse ldrs after 6th: rdn and outpcd by front 2 fr bef last* **14/1**
3415 **4** *14* **Mohayer (IRE)**[46] 2951 9-10-12 **123**......................... RichieMcLernon(3) 101
(Jonjo O'Neill) *hld up: blnd 4th: hdwy to chse ldrs 8th: wknd bef 2 out* **15/2**[3]
00P6 **5** *7* **Tyup Pompey (IRE)**[27] 3371 10-10-0 **108** oh1 ow3........ LeeStephens(3) 80
(Ann Price) *in tch: outpcd whn swvd to avoid faller 8th: n.d after* **16/1**
1-40 **6** *½* **Tempting Paradise (IRE)**[208] 919 8-10-0 **108** oh1.......... PaulMoloney 77
(Evan Williams) *chsd ldrs: lost pl bef 6th: outpcd and n.d after* **8/1**
-P6P **7** *4 ½* **Fighting Chance (IRE)**[15] 3565 11-10-12 **120**.................. JodieMogford 84
(Richard Lee) *a bhd: wl outpcd after 5th* **16/1**
00F3 **8** *7* **Enlightenment (IRE)**[72] 2496 11-11-7 **134**......................... DavidBass(5) 91
(Evan Williams) *hld up: toiling fr bef 8th: t.o* **14/1**
122- **F** **R De Rien Sivola (FR)**[506] 1422 6-11-5 **127**....................(t) HarrySkelton —
(Paul Nicholls) *hld up: hdwy 6th: 4th whn fell 8th* **3/1**[1]

4m 54.3s (7.60) **Going Correction** +0.575s/f (Soft) **9** Ran SP% **112.3**
Speed ratings: **107,106,99,93,91 90,88,85,—**
toteswingers:1&2:£6.70, 1&3:£8.10, 2&3:£24.50 CSF £24.36 CT £238.09 TOTE £7.70: £2.80, £1.80, £3.30; EX 24.60.
Owner Oceans Racing **Bred** Jean-Pierre Hebrard **Trained** Aberthin, Vale of Glamorgan

FOCUS
Few got into this handicap chase, and once R De Rien Sivola came down, it was clear only two could win. The first two are rated pretty much to their marks.

NOTEBOOK
Grand Lahou(FR), runner-up over 2m at Cheltenham in November off the same mark, saw this longer trip out better than expected, always holding the runner-up in the final 100 yards. He has to be ridden positively like this and could return to Cheltenham next month for the Grand Annual. (op 11-2)
Saphir Des Bois(FR), due to run in the abandoned Sky Bet Chase the previous day, looked of strong interest in this weaker event on debut for Peter Bowen. Although not that big, he jumps soundly enough, but was maybe just found out by the lack of a recent run, proving unable to get past on the long run-in. (op 7-2, tchd 4-1 in places)
Postmaster ran well up to a point on this debut for connections, but couldn't race on with the front pair. (op 12-1)
Mohayer(IRE) never got into it and doesn't look capable of winning off this mark. (op 8-1)
Fighting Chance(IRE) Official explanation: jockey said gelding never travelled
R De Rien Sivola(FR) looked potentially well treated on this return from a lengthy absence, and she was travelling smoothly until coming down at the eighth. It's hoped this doesn't affect her confidence with the future in mind. (op 11-4)

3842 LINDLEY CATERING INTERMEDIATE NATIONAL HUNT FLAT RACE (CONDITIONALS AND AMATEURS RACE) 2m 1f
4:35 (4:35) (Class 6) 4-6-Y-O **£1,301** (£382; £191; £95)

Form RPR
1 **Mono Man (IRE)** 5-10-13 0.. DavidBass(5) 117+
(Nicky Henderson) *a.p: led 2f out: drew clr over 1f out: readily* **1/1**[1]
0- **2** *17* **Cocacobana (IRE)**[333] 4384 6-10-8 0........................... KillianMoore(10) 97
(Graeme McPherson) *midfield: hdwy to ld 6f out: rdn and hdd 2f out: no ch w wnr fnl f: jst hld on for 2nd* **40/1**
3 *nk* **Gizzit (IRE)** 5-10-11 0... EdGlassonbury(7) 97
(Karen George) *hld up: hdwy to go prom after 5f: lost pl and outpcd 6f out: rallied 3f out: styd on ins fnl f to press runner-up cl home* **33/1**
4 **4** *7* **Accordingtoeileen (IRE)**[45] 2987 6-10-4 0........ MrWTwiston-Davies(7) 83
(Nigel Twiston-Davies) *prom: rdn 3f out: sn outpcd: plugged on at one pce fnl 2f* **13/2**
6 **5** *3 ¼* **Carlos Gardel**[81] 2309 6-11-4 0.....................................(t) CampbellGillies 86
(Mark Rimell) *prom tl rdn and wknd over 2f out* **66/1**
4 **6** *¾* **Our Golden Boy (IRE)**[40] 3054 5-10-11 0......................... MrCGreene(7) 86
(Mark Usher) *trckd ldrs tl wknd over 4f out* **16/1**
7 *4 ½* **Native Art (IRE)** 6-10-11 0... MrRMcDowall(7) 81
(Rachel Hobbs) *hld up: struggling 5f out: styd on fnl 2f: nvr able to chal* **40/1**
8 *1* **Rock And Ska (FR)** 6-10-11 0..(t) RobertKirk(7) 80
(James Evans) *hld up: effrt on wd outside over 3f out but no imp on ldrs* **66/1**
9 *hd* **No Through Road** 4-10-2 0.. CO'Farrell(5) 69
(Michael Scudamore) *led: hdd 6f out: wknd over 2f out* **80/1**
10 *16* **Waywood Princess** 6-10-4 0.............................. MrJamieJenkinson(7) 57
(John Bryan Groucott) *hld up: struggling 5f out: nvr on terms* **100/1**
0 **11** *6* **Paddy The Hare (IRE)**[32] 3200 6-10-11 0........................ MrTWeston(7) 58
(Dr Richard Newland) *hld up: hdwy after 6f: wknd 3f out* **11/2**[3]
12 *nk* **Roses Legend** 6-10-13 0.. MrTomDavid(5) 58
(Reginald Brown) *plld hrd: prom: lost pl after 5f: rdn and in tch over 5f out: wknd 3f out* **25/1**
3 **13** *shd* **Aldiva**[40] 3054 5-11-1 0.. CharlieHuxley(3) 58
(Alan King) *in tch: rdn 4f out: sn wknd* **5/1**[2]
14 *11* **Scottys** 5-10-13 0... IanPopham(5) 47
(Rachel Hobbs) *hld up: struggling 5f out: t.o* **28/1**
0 **15** *19* **Summer De Baune (FR)**[80] 2328 6-10-13 0...............(t) LeeEdwards(5) 28
(John Bryan Groucott) *midfield: rdn and wknd over 7f out: t.o* **80/1**

4m 5.80s (12.00) **Going Correction** +0.40s/f (Soft)
WFA 4 from 5yo 11lb 5 from 6yo 3lb **15** Ran SP% **122.8**
Speed ratings: **87,79,78,75,74 73,71,71,71,63 60,60,60,55,46**
toteswingers:1&2:£21.00, 1&3:£33.60, 2&3:£22.50 CSF £67.45 TOTE £1.90: £1.20, £4.50, £13.00; EX 74.20.
Owner Mrs Christopher Hanbury **Bred** Mrs E Costelloe **Trained** Upper Lambourn, Berks

FOCUS
Yet another winner for the in-form Nicky Henderson stable. Mono Man impressed but this is not an easy race to put a figure on.

NOTEBOOK
Mono Man(IRE), a son of Old Vic, gradually drew clear for an easy success. The state of the ground didn't make it easy for him, but he clearly has plenty of ability and it'll be interesting to see how he fares under a penalty. (op 10-11)
Cocacobana(IRE) had been off 11 months but still managed to improve on his sole previous effort. (op 66-1)
Gizzit(IRE), related to several winners, shaped with plenty of promise, rallying having lost his position, and should improve.
Accordingtoeileen(IRE) proved one-paced under pressure and is likely to want further over hurdles. (op 8-1)
Paddy The Hare(IRE) was unable to build on his debut effort (op 13-2 tchd 7-1 and 5-1)
Aldiva hadn't been beaten far at Kempton on debut, but was unable to confirm that promise. (op 9-2 tchd 6-1)

T/Jkpt: Part won. £7,100.00 to a £1 stake. Pool:£10,000.00 - 0.50 winning tickets. T/Plt: £58.50 to a £1 stake. Pool:£82,220.99 - 1,025.34 winning tickets T/Qpdt: £40.90 to a £1 stake. Pool:£4,633.91 - 83.70 winning tickets DO

3455 PUNCHESTOWN (R-H)

Sunday, January 30

OFFICIAL GOING: Soft (cross-country chase (1.20) abandoned due to frost)

Cross-country race (race 1) abandoned due to frozen track. Willie Mullins sent out a 952-1 five-timer, with Paul Townend aboard four of them.

3844a BOYLESPORTS.COM TIED COTTAGE CHASE (GRADE 2) (11 fncs) 2m
1:50 (1:50) 5-Y-0+ £22,413 (£6,551; £3,103; £1,034)

RPR

1 **Golden Silver (FR)**14 3594 9-11-12 166 PTownend 171+
(W P Mullins, Ire) *hld up in rr: nt fluent 2nd and 3rd: 4th and no imp after 3 out: hdwy after 2 out: 2nd and chal fr last: styd on wl to ld cl home* **3/1**2

2 ½ **Big Zeb (IRE)**32 3204 10-11-12 174 BarryGeraghty 170
(C A Murphy, Ire) *settled in 4th: impr into 2nd 4 out: led 3 out: strly pressed fr last: kpt on u.p: hdd cl home* **4/6**1

3 7 **Sizing Europe (IRE)**85 2226 9-11-12 160 AELynch 166
(Henry De Bromhead, Ire) *trckd ldrs in 3rd: cl 2nd after 5 out: slt mstke 4 out: drvn along after 3 out: no imp after 2 out: 3rd and no ex appr last* **4/1**3

4 8 **Scotsirish (IRE)**32 3204 10-11-10 157 DJCondon 153
(W P Mullins, Ire) *racd in 2nd: led 4 out: hdd next: 4th and no ex after 2 out* **25/1**

5 21 **Changing Course (IRE)**79 2346 9-11-4 119 (b) MDarcy 126
(Henry De Bromhead, Ire) *led: clr early: nt fluent 5th: drvn along 5 out: hdd & wknd bef next* **150/1**

4m 3.80s (-10.10) **Going Correction** -0.40s/f (Good) 5 Ran SP% **109.5**
Speed ratings: **109,108,105,101,90**
CSF £5.69 TOTE £8.80: £1.02, £1.90; DF 12.70.
Owner Mrs Violet O'Leary **Bred** Noel Pelat **Trained** Muine Beag, Co Carlow

FOCUS
Big Zeb still remains the one to beat at Cheltenham despite this reverse. Golden Silver produced a personal best, with Sizing Europe rated to his Arkle mark.

NOTEBOOK
Golden Silver(FR) finally got the better of the Champion Chase winner for the first time in five attempts having traded at 90-1 in running at one stage. Early on he didn't seem to want to know. His jumping was sticky and he was somewhat detached from the field. It wasn't a dissimilar performance in a way from his win at Fairyhouse two weeks previously when it took him quite some time to pick up against inferior opposition. Here he again failed to even start picking up until about half a mile from the finish but the momentum he built up from before the turn into the straight proved unstoppable as the race worked out. He looks likely to go to Cheltenham, although his trainer may look for another race beforehand. His two previous runs at Prestbury Park have been very unhappy experiences. This time promises to be better, but his victory here was a product of circumstance more than anything and doesn't represent a changing of the guard. (op 7/2)
Big Zeb(IRE) has fulfilled all his potential since Barry Geraghty took over the ride, but he may well want this one back. He was happy to sit just behind the gallop set by pacemaker Changing Course and produced two huge leaps at the fourth-last and third-last which carried him to the front. Geraghty probably expected Sizing Europe to carry him into the race further than he did, but he couldn't and Big Zeb was left to make the best of his way home a bit earlier than was desirable and was unable in the end to cope with the momentum built up by the winner. Perhaps letting him pop the last as he did contributed to his defeat as well, but there was no dishonour in this defeat, and he definitely remains the one to beat at Cheltenham. (op 8/13)
Sizing Europe(IRE) jumped well and took it up four out. Once the runner-up outjumped him at the third-last, though, the distress signals were out and he was beaten after the second-last. The drawing board will require some revisiting after this effort, and if Cheltenham is still on the agenda it would be no surprise to see him aimed at the Ryanair Chase.
Scotsirish(IRE) finished just about as close as might have been expected.
Changing Course(IRE) dropped away as expected.

3846a MOSCOW FLYER NOVICE HURDLE (GRADE 2) (9 hdls) 2m
2:50 (2:55) 5-Y-0+ £22,418 (£6,556; £3,107; £1,038)

RPR

1 **Gagewell Flyer (IRE)**28 3353 7-11-8 PTownend 146+
(W P Mullins, Ire) *mde all: rdn clr after 2 out: nt fluent last: strly pressed clsng stages: kpt on wl* **13/8**1

2 nk **Earlson Gray (FR)**240 6-11-2 EMullins 140+
(W P Mullins, Ire) *trckd ldrs in 5th: stl travelling wl after 2 out: 4th st: mod 2nd appr last: r.o strly u.p: jst failed* **16/1**

3 10 **Tornedo Shay (IRE)**15 3580 6-11-2 AndrewJMcNamara 129
(T J O'Mara, Ire) *trckd ldrs in 3rd: nt jump wl: rdn bef 2 out: no imp: kpt on same pce* **3/1**2

4 2 **Joe Smooth**22 3459 5-11-0 (t) DNRussell 125
(Noel Meade, Ire) *trckd ldrs in 4th: smooth hdwy after 3 out: 2nd after 2 out: sn rdn and no imp* **6/1**

5 4 **Byerley Bear (IRE)**27 3382 6-11-2 AELynch 123+
(Henry De Bromhead, Ire) *hld up in rr: pckd 2nd: sme prog after 3 out: no imp fr next* **11/2**3

6 ½ **Seafield (IRE)**70 2562 6-11-2 (t) APCawley 123+
(Paul Nolan, Ire) *hld up in 6th: rdn 3 out: no ex fr next* **14/1**

7 3 **Big Game Hunter (IRE)**22 3461 5-11-0 125 (p) BarryGeraghty 118
(M F Morris, Ire) *racd in 2nd: rdn 3 out: wknd after 2 out* **8/1**

3m 59.0s (-11.00) **Going Correction** -0.70s/f (Firm) 7 Ran SP% **116.4**
Speed ratings: **99,98,93,92,90 90,89**
CSF £28.33 TOTE £2.40: £1.70, £8.50; DF 29.50.
Owner Clipper Logistics Group Ltd **Bred** Mrs Jacinta McGeough **Trained** Muine Beag, Co Carlow

FOCUS
A steady pace only began to pick up 3f out and the winner was best positioned. Hold-up horses were disadvantaged.

NOTEBOOK
Gagewell Flyer(IRE) completed a hat-trick here by making all. Dropped back to 2m following his Grade 2 win over 2m4f at Naas early this month in an effort to give him experience jumping at speed, he had to give weight to his six rivals and jumped well apart from a sloppy leap at the final hurdle. He went away from his rivals when asked to raise his effort before two out, but was being reeled in by the runner-up towards the finish. Willie Mullins confirmed the Neptune Investment Management Novices' Hurdle at the festival as the winner's target. (op 7/4 tchd 6/4)
Earlson Gray(FR), a stablemate of the winner, was making his Irish debut having run 20 times (ten times over hurdles) in France, where he was once successful over fences. His performance here was encouraging, and while he was bought with chasing in mind, he should be capable of winning over hurdles. Held up, he was fifth two out before closing to go second approaching the final hurdle. He stayed on well from the last and was just held. (op 12/1)
Tornedo Shay(IRE), the winner of three bumpers and a maiden hurdle over this trip, raced close up despite being less than fluent at a few hurdles. Ridden in third two out, he was unable to raise his game thereafter. (op 5/2 tchd 7/2)
Joe Smooth, winner of a maiden over the C&D early this month, was held up and made a forward move before two out. Second briefly off the final bend, he was soon under pressure and unable to make any impression. (op 6/1 tchd 11/2)
Byerley Bear(IRE), winner of a bumper and a maiden at Cork, was having only his second run over hurdles. Held up in rear, he made some headway after four out but was unable to make any impression from before two from home. (op 5/1 tchd 6/1)

3845 - 3849a (Foreign Racing) - See Raceform Interactive

3358 AYR (L-H)

Monday, January 31

OFFICIAL GOING: Good (chase 8.0; hurdle 8.1)

Rails on both courses out 7m from innermost line.
Wind: Fresh, half against Weather: Cloudy

3850 BET LIVE AT VICTORCHANDLER.COM NOVICES' HURDLE (9 hdls) 2m
1:15 (1:20) (Class 4) 4-Y-0+ £2,602 (£764; £382; £190)

Form RPR

3-61 1 **Darna**29 3331 5-11-11 0 CampbellGillies 125+
(William Amos) *led to bef 4th: cl up: led and edgd to stands' rail 3 out: rdn after next: kpt on wl run-in* **2/1**1

5 2 2¼ **Desert Cry (IRE)**27 3386 5-11-4 0 JasonMaguire 113
(Donald McCain) *t.k.h early: chsd ldrs: effrt and chsd wnr after 3 out: kpt on fr last: no imp* **3/1**2

6/5- 3 7 **Vivaldi (IRE)**86 2225 6-11-13 124 (p) EJO'Connell(5) 121
(J J Lambe, Ire) *hld up in midfield: stdy hdwy 1/2-way: effrt bef 3 out: kpt on same pce fr next* **9/1**

4 8 **Proud Times (USA)**58 5-11-4 0 BarryKeniry 102
(Alan Swinbank) *nt fluent: hld up in tch: hdwy bef 3 out: outpcd whn hit next: sn no ex* **3/1**2

34-1 5 2¼ **Freddie Brown**257 399 7-11-4 0 JanFaltejsek 101+
(George Charlton) *t.k.h: cl up: led bef 4th to 3 out: wknd after next* **13/2**3

000U 6 11 **Artic Night (FR)**3 3783 5-11-4 0 FearghalDavis 88
(Nicky Richards) *prom: rdn after 4 out: wknd fr next* **40/1**

/43- 7 8 **Cabbyl Doo**564 973 8-11-4 0 PaddyAspell 81
(James Moffatt) *midfield: hdwy and prom 4th: rdn and wknd fr 3 out* **33/1**

400- 8 10 **Agricultural**258 3690 5-10-13 76 AlexanderVoy(5) 72
(Lucy Normile) *towards rr: drvn along 1/2-way: nvr on terms* **50/1**

00-0 9 13 **Monsoon Music (IRE)**75 2446 7-11-4 0 PeterBuchanan 60
(Lucinda Russell) *prom: lost pl 4th: n.d after* **66/1**

10 4 **Saga Surprise (FR)**250 487 6-11-4 0 (t) MichaelMcAlister 56
(Maurice Barnes) *nt fluent in rr: struggling 1/2-way: nvr on terms* **66/1**

0 11 19 **Farmer Henry**83 2297 7-11-4 0 TomMessenger 39
(Sandy Forster) *nt fluent: bhd: struggling after 4th: nvr on terms* **100/1**

06P0 12 14 **Beano Boy**7 3715 6-11-4 0 RichieMcGrath 27
(Brian Storey) *sn towards rr: struggling after 4th: sn btn* **200/1**

0-0 13 2¾ **King Puc**75 2446 6-11-1 0 EwanWhillans(3) 24
(Barry Murtagh) *nt fluent in rr: no ch fr 4th* **66/1**

14 1¼ **Officer Mor (USA)**118 5-11-1 0 RyanMania(3) 23
(Evelyn Slack) *nt fluent on occasions: towards rr: struggling 1/2-way: sn btn* **80/1**

15 10 **Arikinui**707 6-10-4 0 GaryRutherford(7) 7
(Stuart Coltherd) *hld up towards rr: struggling 4th: sn btn* **66/1**

16 6 **Lucky Belle (IRE)**258 4-9-7 0 PaulGallagher(7) —
(William Young) *midfield: struggling after 4th: sn btn* **66/1**

0-P0 P **Paul Revere (IRE)**71 2552 7-11-4 0 BrianHarding —
(Nicky Richards) *hld up in midfield: hit and wknd 4th: t.o whn p.u bef 3 out* **66/1**

3m 49.7s (-13.40) **Going Correction** -0.725s/f (Firm)
WFA 4 from 5yo+ 11lb 17 Ran SP% **125.7**
Speed ratings (Par 105): **104,102,99,95,94 88,84,79,73,71 61,54,53,52,47 44,—**
toteswingers:1&2:£4.10, 1&3:£6.30, 2&3:£6.30 CSF £8.19 TOTE £4.00: £1.50, £1.60, £2.40; EX 11.00.
Owner J L Gledson **Bred** L Fuller **Trained** Broadhaugh, Scottish Borders

FOCUS
There was no real strength in depth to this opening novice hurdle and, with it being run at a fair gallop, the form looks straightforward. The first two are on the upgrade and the race could be rated higher.

NOTEBOOK
Darna followed up his C&D success 29 days earlier with a gutsy effort under his penalty. He set out to make all, but was taken on by the free-going Freddie Brown and looked vulnerable as the race developed in the home straight. He refused to let the runner-up past from two out, however, and is worth rating a little better than the bare margin. Things will be tougher under a double penalty in this division, but he may improve for a longer trip and he should make a nice novice chaser next term. (op 11-4)
Desert Cry(IRE), too keen on his hurdling debut at Leicester, again took time to settle yet the generous gallop helped on that front. This quicker ground also proved more suitable for him and he was going best of all three out, but ultimately the winner outstayed him. His trainer can place him to win one of these on similar ground as he was a clear second-best. (op 11-4)
Vivaldi(IRE), back from an 86-day break, was never a serious threat. He did his best work late on under his double penalties and, off a mark of 124, rates the benchmark. (op 8-1 tchd 7-1)
Proud Times(USA) is a dual winner over 1m4f on the AW and rated 86 in that sphere. He jumped well enough, but shaped as though a stiffer test will be for him over hurdles. (op 7-2)
Freddie Brown was having his first outing since winning a quick-ground bumper at Kelso last May. He spoilt his chance by failing to settle on this hurdling debut, but showed plenty and looks sure to improve for the outing. (op 7-1 tchd 6-1)
Paul Revere(IRE) Official explanation: trainer said gelding finished distressed

3851 VICTORCHANDLER.COM "NATIONAL HUNT" NOVICES' HURDLE (11 hdls) 2m 4f
1:45 (1:50) (Class 4) 4-Y-0+ £2,602 (£764; £382; £190)

Form RPR

11-1 1 **Ballabriggs (IRE)**23 3454 10-11-12 140 JasonMaguire 130+
(Donald McCain) *trckd ldrs: j. soundly: led on bit 3 out: shkn up appr last: styd on strly: eased towards fin* **11/10**1

22-3 2 5 **Yes Tom (IRE)**32 3232 6-11-5 0 DougieCostello 117+
(R T J Wilson, Ire) *t.k.h: trckd ldrs: wnt 2nd last: kpt on: no imp* **3/1**2

0-52 3 4½ **Kings Grey (IRE)**29 3330 7-11-5 0 JamesReveley 113
(Keith Reveley) *hld up in rr: wnt prom 5th: chsng ldrs whn hit 8th: 2nd whn hit 2 out: kpt on same pce appr last* **4/1**3

6F 4 6 **Golfer's Crossing (IRE)**29 3332 8-11-5 0 CampbellGillies 107
(Lucinda Russell) *led tl appr 3 out: wknd appr last* **66/1**

-40 5 2½ **Kingsmoss (IRE)**29 3330 6-11-5 114 (p) BrianHughes 104
(J J Lambe, Ire) *mid-div: chsd ldrs 8th: fdd appr 3 out* **20/1**

212/ **6** *3 ¼* **Vivona Hill**[699] 4274 7-11-5 0 BarryKeniry 100
(Alan Swinbank) *hld up in mid-div: mstke 4th: hdwy to trck ldrs next: wknd 3 out: bttr for r* **16/1**

2-40 **7** *½* **Forcefield**[29] 3330 5-10-12 0 MissLAlexander(7) 100
(N W Alexander) *mstke 1st: hdwy to chse ldrs 8th: wknd appr next* **100/1**

3360 **8** *15* **Moufatango (FR)**[29] 3330 5-11-5 0 BrianHarding 89
(Nicky Richards) *chsd ldrs: outpcd and reminders 8th: lost pl appr next: sn bhd: t.o* **66/1**

000 **9** *10* **Knockando**[17] 3553 6-11-5 0 PeterBuchanan 77
(Lucinda Russell) *in rr: nt fluent 7th: nvr on terms* **50/1**

5-0 **10** *11* **Collyns Avenue**[71] 2552 8-11-5 0 GrahamLee 68
(Shelley Johnstone) *prom: drvn after 5th: lost pl after 7th* **50/1**

0-1 **11** *1 ¾* **Cheatingsideoftown (IRE)**[183] 1153 5-11-5 0 TomMessenger 66
(Sue Bradburne) *chsd ldrs: wknd appr 3 out* **33/1**

F- **12** *10* **Lewlaur Supreme (IRE)**[350] 4071 8-11-5 0 RichieMcGrath 57
(Jim Goldie) *t.k.h in rr: hdwy on wd outside 6th: sn chsng ldrs: wknd appr 8th* **66/1**

P **13** *18* **Shoal Bay Dreamer**[16] 3572 5-10-9 0 RyanMania(3) 34
(Dianne Sayer) *in rr: drvn 7th: sn bhd* **200/1**

20-2 **14** *29* **Murrell (IRE)**[95] 2058 6-11-5 0 PhilKinsella 15
(Henry Hogarth) *nt fluent in rr: bhd fr 6th: t.o 3 out* **25/1**

-500 **15** *6* **Darkan Road**[17] 3547 6-11-5 0 JanFaltejsek 9
(George Charlton) *mid-div: wnt prom 5th: lost pl 7th: bhd fr 3 out: t.o* **66/1**

00P/ **P** **Minnigaff (IRE)**[1395] 11-11-0 0 AlexanderVoy(5) —
(George Foster) *w ldrs: lost pl and eased 5th: sn p.u* **100/1**

03 **P** **Howizee**[94] 2075 5-11-5 0 (t) MichaelMcAlister —
(Maurice Barnes) *in rr: nt fluent 3rd: drvn 6th: sn bhd: t.o whn p.u bef 3 out* **25/1**

4m 59.1s (-12.90) **Going Correction** -0.725s/f (Firm) **17** Ran SP% **126.3**
Speed ratings (Par 105): **96,94,92,89,88 87,87,81,77,72 72,68,61,49,47 —,—**
toteswingers:1&2:£2.40, 1&3:£2.20, 2&3:£3.10 CSF £4.18 TOTE £2.30: £1.20, £1.30, £1.20; EX 6.00.
Owner Trevor Hemmings **Bred** Mrs S L Jackson **Trained** Cholmondeley, Cheshire

FOCUS
A relatively uncompetitive novices' hurdle that could be rated higher, with the third to his mark.

NOTEBOOK
Ballabriggs(IRE) was defying a penalty picked up for winning at Wincanton latest. Running over hurdles to protect his chase rating with a view towards the Grand National, he's shown himself to be very useful indeed and it would be no surprise were connections to give him his chance in the Albert Bartlett, being as he was a festival winner last year. However, the Grimthorpe Chase was mentioned after the race as a likely target. (tchd 6-5 and 5-4 in a place)
Yes Tom(IRE), who promises to be suited by the step up to 3m, stayed on well for second and it's surely only a matter of time before he picks up one of these. (op 7-2)
Kings Grey(IRE) also shapes as though a stiffer test will suit. He'll be interesting also in handicaps down the line. (tchd 7-2)
Golfer's Crossing(IRE), back over hurdles, was eventually outstayed, but showed enough to suggest he can win races.
Vivona Hill, returning from a 699-day absence, shaped with any real promise. He should be straighter next time. (op 14-1)
Minnigaff(IRE) Official explanation: jockey said gelding never travelled and hung left-handed

3852 BEST ODDS GUARANTEED AT VICTOR CHANDLER NOVICES' CHASE (17 fncs) 2m 4f
2:15 (2:20) (Class 4) 5-Y-O+ **£3,252** (£955; £477; £238)

Form RPR

-342 **1** **Premier Sagas (FR)**[29] 3333 7-11-0 121 BrianHarding 130+
(Nicky Richards) *t.k.h: led to 3rd: cl up: led gng wl bef 2 out: clr bef last: rdn and r.o wl* **5/4**[1]

3-61 **2** *4 ½* **Benny Be Good**[83] 2299 8-11-7 127 JamesReveley 130+
(Keith Reveley) *cl up: drvn and outpcd 5 out: rallied 3 out: chsd (clr) wnr last: styd on: no imp* **5/2**[2]

6-F2 **3** *6* **Catch Bob (IRE)**[83] 2299 7-11-0 123 GrahamLee 123+
(Ferdy Murphy) *nt fluent: hld up in tch: mstkes 5th and 8th: hdwy to ld after 11th: hdd bef 2 out: no ex and lost 2nd last* **5/1**[3]

0/53 **4** *5* **Ballycolin**[73] 2507 8-11-0 103 PeterBuchanan 114
(I A Duncan, Ire) *prom: drvn and outpcd 12th: no imp fr 3 out* **16/1**

24/P **5** *1 ½* **Steady Tiger (IRE)**[20] 3499 9-11-0 0 FearghalDavis 113
(Nicky Richards) *hld up: hdwy and prom whn hit 5 out: rdn and sn outpcd: n.d after* **16/1**

6665 **6** *25* **Bertie Milan (IRE)**[29] 3330 6-11-0 0 TomMessenger 95
(Sue Bradburne) *towards rr: outpcd after 11th: struggling fr 5 out: t.o* **20/1**

1-0P **7** *20* **Mister Marker (IRE)**[20] 3499 7-11-0 120 DougieCostello 72
(Nicky Richards) *hld up: outpcd 11th: struggling fnl 5: t.o* **14/1**

0/0- **P** **Pericam**[274] 6-10-11 0 RyanMania(3) —
(Simon Waugh) *t.k.h: mstkes: led 3rd to after 11th: blnd next: lost tch 5 out: p.u bef next* **40/1**

5m 10.1s (-12.80) **Going Correction** -0.725s/f (Firm) **8** Ran SP% **114.4**
Speed ratings: **96,94,91,89,89 79,71,—**
toteswingers:1&2:£1.10, 1&3:£2.40, 2&3:£2.00 CSF £4.86 TOTE £2.40: £1.10, £1.40, £1.50; EX 5.20.
Owner David Wesley Yates **Bred** Edgar Van Haaren **Trained** Greystoke, Cumbria

FOCUS
Not many could be given a chance in this. the winner is rated to form as is the third.

NOTEBOOK
Premier Sagas(FR), runner-up to a subsequent winner in a handicap here last time, who came out well on top. It briefly looked as though he had a fight on his hands to get past Catch Bob, but the further he went the stronger he became, and it'll be interesting to see him over 3m returning to handicaps. (op 6-5)
Benny Be Good, penalised for scoring at Sedgefield, never looked like winning, but did stick on valiantly (confirming last-time-out form with Catch Bob), and he'll do better in future under a more positive ride, as he stays this sort of trip well. (op 11-4)
Catch Bob(IRE) made mistakes, but it looked turning in as though he was in with a good chance of winning. However, he was untidy at the third from home, and had no more to give from before the last. (tchd 11-2)
Ballycolin, a point winner who ran well in a novice chase at Musselburgh latest, was down 4f in trip and didn't have the pace. (op 20-1 tchd 22-1)
Steady Tiger(IRE) finished well held but at least offered a bit of hope for the future. (op 20-1 tchd 22-1)

3853 PLAY CASINO AT VICTORCHANDLER.COM H'CAP CHASE (18 fncs) 2m 5f
2:50 (2:55) (Class 4) (0-105,105) 5-Y-O+ **£3,252** (£955; £477; £238)

Form RPR

2432 **1** **Festival King (IRE)**[17] 3552 9-11-1 94 BrianHarding 105+
(Pauline Robson) *j.w: mde all: clr 3 out: rdn and kpt on wl run-in* **11/2**[2]

F-43 **2** *5* **Lahib The Fifth (IRE)**[17] 3549 11-11-5 98 FearghalDavis 103
(Nicky Richards) *hld up in midfield: blnd 4th: hdwy 11th: effrt 4 out: chsd (clr) wnr last: kpt on: no imp* **16/1**

3223 **3** *2 ½* **Dallas Bell**[26] 3395 9-11-4 100 EwanWhillans(3) 104
(Alistair Whillans) *cl up: effrt bef 4 out: one pce fr 2 out: hld whn blnd and lost 2nd last* **8/1**

320 **4** *8* **Soul Magic (IRE)**[80] 2351 9-9-13 85 GaryRutherford(7) 81
(Harriet Graham) *prom: rdn whn hit 5 out: no imp fr next* **25/1**

322U **5** *4 ½* **Hasper**[214] 872 13-10-7 89 RyanMania(3) 83
(Sandy Forster) *trckd ldrs tl rdn and wknd after 4 out* **20/1**

6/05 **6** *2 ¼* **Lampion Du Bost (FR)**[29] 3333 12-11-12 105 RichieMcGrath 98
(Jim Goldie) *hld up: hdwy and pushed along whn blnd 13th: drvn and no imp bef 4 out* **6/1**[3]

-125 **7** *10* **Deuteronomy (IRE)**[16] 3574 10-11-7 100 DenisO'Regan 85
(John Wade) *trckd ldrs: outpcd 11th: struggling whn blnd 13th: wknd* **15/2**

3P25 **8** *18* **Coldwells (IRE)**[20] 3503 11-10-9 88 JamesReveley 62
(Martin Todhunter) *trckd ldrs: lost pl 1/2-way: struggling fr 11th* **9/1**

F-63 **9** *6* **Garleton (IRE)**[96] 2036 10-11-6 104 (t) AlexanderVoy(5) 62
(Maurice Barnes) *hld up: sn pushed along: outpcd whn blnd 13th: sn wknd* **11/1**

0F1- **P** **Seven Is Lucky (IRE)**[303] 4983 9-11-5 98 GrahamLee —
(Jim Goldie) *bhd: struggling fnl circ: t.o whn p.u bef 4 out* **15/2**

030 **P** **Appeal Denied (IRE)**[80] 2351 9-9-7 79 PaulGallagher(7) —
(Sandy Forster) *mstkes: towards rr: shortlived effrt 1/2-way: struggling fnl circ: wl btn whn p.u bef 13th* **28/1**

1 **P** **Schindlers Society (IRE)**[28] 3360 8-11-7 100 (p) BrianHughes —
(J J Lambe, Ire) *hld up: reminders 7th: struggling 11th: sn btn: t.o whn p.u bef 4 out* **9/2**[1]

5m 30.5s (-11.50) **Going Correction** -0.725s/f (Firm) **12** Ran SP% **118.8**
Speed ratings: **92,90,89,86,84 83,79,72,70,— —,—**
toteswingers:1&2:£22.70, 1&3:£5.10, 2&3:£24.80 CSF £84.02 CT £708.48 TOTE £4.70: £1.60, £5.80, £2.80; EX 88.00.
Owner Mr & Mrs Raymond Anderson Green **Bred** Patrick Boudengen **Trained** Kirkharle, Northumberland
■ Stewards' Enquiry : Richie McGrath caution: used whip without giving gelding time to respond.

FOCUS
Few got into this and the form is ordinary, although it could be rated a few pounds higher.

NOTEBOOK
Festival King(IRE) jumped enthusiastically under a positive ride and made every yard. Back to near his best when runner-up off this mark at Musselburgh latest, the 9-y-o was winning for only the second time over fences, but these tactics clearly suited and he should go in again. (op 5-1)
Lahib The Fifth(IRE), 3lb higher than when last winning, kept on without getting close enough to seriously challenge. This was his best effort in a while. (op 20-1)
Dallas Bell gave his running while again suggesting this mark is beyond him. (op 10-1)
Soul Magic(IRE), 5lb higher than when losing out narrowly over hurdles in October, wasn't without some promise on this debut over fences.
Lampion Du Bost(FR) should have done better considering the promise with which he shaped latest. (tchd 13-2)
Schindlers Society(IRE), who won over the C&D last time out, was never travelling and proved very disappointing. Official explanation: trainer had no explanation for the poor form shown

3854 PLAY POKER AT VICTORCHANDLER.COM H'CAP CHASE (12 fncs) 2m
3:25 (3:30) (Class 4) (0-115,115) 5-Y-O+ **£3,252** (£955; £477; £238)

Form RPR

-P00 **1** **Quicuyo (GER)**[20] 3500 8-11-4 110 (t) RyanMania(3) 127+
(James Ewart) *chsd clr ldr: clsd 1/2-way: led 4 out: drew clr after next* **11/2**[3]

F0-F **2** *9* **Tartan Snow**[75] 2450 11-10-6 102 GaryRutherford(7) 113+
(Stuart Coltherd) *hld up: blnd bdly 3rd: pushed along bef 5 out: hdwy 3 out: styd on to take 2nd nr fin: no ch w wnr* **33/1**

5532 **3** *1 ½* **The Cockney Squire (IRE)**[31] 3257 6-11-7 110 PeterBuchanan 119+
(Lucinda Russell) *plld hrd: led and clr to 7th: hung rt and hdd 4 out: kpt on same pce fr next: lost 2nd towards fin* **5/1**[2]

0/22 **4** *12* **Blackpool Billy (IRE)**[18] 3524 9-11-10 113 GrahamLee 111
(Ferdy Murphy) *hld up in tch: blnd 6th: rdn after 5 out: no imp fr next* **11/10**[1]

0-00 **5** *shd* **Carters Rest**[18] 3520 8-10-13 102 DenisO'Regan 99
(Chris Grant) *hld up: outpcd bef 5 out: sn drvn: nvr able to chal* **8/1**

-6U5 **6** *4* **Pamak D'Airy (FR)**[68] 2613 8-11-5 108 PhilKinsella 100
(Henry Hogarth) *prom: rdn and outpcd whn hit 4 out: sn wknd* **8/1**

42PF **7** *nk* **Little Wizard (IRE)**[18] 3524 9-9-12 93 ow1 AlistairFindlay(7) 86
(George Charlton) *hld up: outpcd whn blnd 7th: sn btn* **8/1**

PP-P **8** *32* **Quws Law (IRE)**[28] 3362 9-11-12 115 (t) CampbellGillies 78
(Lucinda Russell) *prom tl lost pl after 3rd: struggling fr 1/2-way: t.o* **25/1**

3P-P **P** **Arc Warrior (FR)**[92] 2107 7-11-2 105 (t) RichieMcGrath —
(Andrew Parker) *bhd: outpcd 4th: j.v.slowly and p.u next* **33/1**

3m 57.0s (-13.70) **Going Correction** -0.725s/f (Firm) **9** Ran SP% **122.7**
Speed ratings: **105,100,99,93,93 91,91,75,—**
toteswingers:1&2:£19.70, 1&3:£4.90, 2&3:£15.70 CSF £150.08 CT £974.86 TOTE £7.50: £2.20, £7.70, £1.60; EX 268.70.
Owner Dennis J Coppola **Bred** Stiftung Gestut Fahrhof **Trained** Langholm, Dumfries & G'way

FOCUS
Another race in which it paid to be prominent. The form is rated around the first two.

NOTEBOOK
Quicuyo(GER) tracked the early leader before taking a narrow advantage at the first in the straight and gradually extended it for a fourth course victory. Well beaten over hurdles on his recent debut for the yard, his best efforts had previously come in heavy ground, but he travelled strongly in the tongue-tie on this sounder surface and won with plenty of authority. On this evidence, he can win again. (op 6-1)
Tartan Snow stayed on from well back to take second, but as has often been the case with this iffy jumper, a bad early blunder cost him his chance.
The Cockney Squire(IRE) failed to settle in the lead and, as a consequence, had little left for the finish. (op 9-2)
Blackpool Billy(IRE) was notably disappointing, making mistakes and failing to reproduce the form shown on either start since returning. (op 11-8 tchd 6-4)
Carters Rest improved on his initial effort over fences, keeping on late. (op 9-1 tchd 10-1)
Little Wizard(IRE) Official explanation: vet said gelding bled from the nose

3855 WATCH LIVE RACING AT VICTORCHANDLER.COM H'CAP HURDLE (9 hdls) 2m
4:00 (4:05) (Class 4) (0-105,105) 4-Y-O+ **£2,602** (£764; £382; £190)

Form RPR

0554 **1** **Teenage Idol (IRE)**[16] 3570 7-11-9 105 RyanMania(3) 118+
(Evelyn Slack) *trckd ldrs: led bef 3 out: clr next: eased run-in* **7/1**[3]

3-50 **2** *9* **Quacity (FR)**[20] 3502 7-11-9 **102** PeterBuchanan 105
(Lucinda Russell) *prom: drvn bef 3 out: chsd (clr) wnr run-in: r.o* **8/1**
-000 **3** *2 3/4* **Jaques Vert (FR)**[19] 3505 5-11-9 **102** PaddyAspell 102
(Robert Wylie) *hld up: hdwy on outside bef 3 out: sn rdn: kpt on fr last: no imp* **16/1**
/2-5 **4** *2 3/4* **Beverly Hill Billy**[71] 2551 7-11-2 **102** PaulGallagher(7) 100
(Sandy Forster) *cl up: led 4 out to bef next: no ex fr 2 out* **8/1**
0506 **5** *1 1/2* **Daniel's Dream**[200] 999 11-10-0 **79** oh9 (tp) GrahamLee 76
(John Dixon) *cl up: rdn bef 3 out: outpcd fr next* **50/1**
0434 **6** *3/4* **Inner Voice (USA)**[82] 2319 8-11-0 **98** (p) EJO'Connell(5) 94
(J J Lambe, Ire) *midfield: drvn bef 3 out: plugged on fr last: nvr able to chal* **12/1**
PP0P **7** *5* **Bob's Dream (IRE)**[20] 3500 9-11-9 **102** (t) CampbellGillies 94
(William Amos) *midfield: effrt u.p bef 3 out: sn outpcd* **25/1**
44-3 **8** *6* **Whaston (IRE)**[41] 2658 6-11-2 **95** BrianHughes 83
(Pauline Robson) *prom: hit 4 out: effrt bef next: sn wknd* **9/2**[1]
5-P0 **9** *7* **Autumn Harvest**[12] 3631 7-9-13 **83** (p) JamesHalliday(5) 63
(William Young) *led to 4 out: rdn and wknd after next* **33/1**
0P **10** *5* **Ulysees (IRE)**[12] 3631 12-10-6 **85** RichieMcGrath 62
(Jim Goldie) *nt fluent in rr: struggling 1/2-way: nvr on terms* **33/1**
40-0 **11** *2 1/2* **Sydney Cove (IRE)**[29] 3335 5-11-5 **98** FearghalDavis 71
(William Amos) *midfield: drvn and outpcd 1/2-way: n.d after* **18/1**
052- **12** *48* **Super Ally (IRE)**[311] 4863 6-10-10 **89** BrianHarding 19
(Andrew Parker) *hld up: rdn 1/2-way: btn bef 3 out* **8/1**
B100 **13** *9* **No Supper (IRE)**[86] 2208 7-11-0 **100** MrJBewley(7) 22
(George Bewley) *midfield: drvn bef 3 out: wknd bef next* **14/1**
0-15 **P** **Emirate Isle**[69] 2603 7-11-2 **95** (p) DenisO'Regan —
(Brian Storey) *midfield: outpcd 1/2-way: sn btn: p.u bef 3 out* **5/1**[2]
535- **C** **Ergo (FR)**[269] 2445 7-11-0 **103** JamesSmith(10) —
(James Moffatt) *bhd: struggling bef 4 out: no ch whn carried out next* **25/1**
2333 **P** **Rafta (IRE)**[154] 1427 5-11-7 **100** PhilKinsella —
(Linda Perratt) *a bhd: struggling fr 1/2-way: t.o whn p.u bef 3 out* **10/1**
-600 **P** **Bunacurry**[80] 2349 6-10-8 **92** AlexanderVoy(5) —
(Barry Murtagh) *hld up: rdn bef 4 out: sn btn: t.o whn p.u bef 3 out* **50/1**

3m 49.9s (-13.20) **Going Correction** -0.725s/f (Firm) **17** Ran SP% **132.8**
Speed ratings (Par 105): **104,99,98,96,96 95,93,90,86,84 82,58,54,—,— —,—**
toteswingers:1&2:£17.10, 1&3:£31.70, 2&3:£45.00 CSF £63.96 CT £903.07 TOTE £8.80: £2.10, £2.80, £5.40, £2.80; EX 70.10.
Owner A Slack **Bred** Mrs J Ryan And Mrs John M Weld **Trained** Hilton, Cumbria

FOCUS
An open handicap hurdle that was run at a decent clip. The winner is rated back to last year's form backed up by the fourth and fifth.

NOTEBOOK
Teenage Idol(IRE), who had previously failed to win a handicap, travelled much the best into the straight and was never going to be caught, having begun to assert from three out. He'll need to progress again if he's to defy much of a rise. Incidentally, with this winner jockey Ryan Mania rode out his claim. (op 8-1)
Quacity(FR) ran better returned to 2m, although the way he boxed on for second certainly indicates he needs a stiffer test. (op 10-1)
Jaques Vert(FR), making his handicap debut, stayed on from the rear in the manner of a horse with more to offer, especially once faced with a stiffer test again. (op 14-1)
Beverly Hill Billy was never far away and had his chance, but couldn't race on with the winner and slowly faded. (op 10-1)
Daniel's Dream shaped surprisingly well given he was 9lb 'wrong' and returning from 200 days off.
Bob's Dream(IRE) once again put in a weak finishing effort. (op 20-1)
Emirate Isle Official explanation: jockey said gelding was unsuited by the good ground

3856 BET NOW AT VICTORCHANDLER.COM STANDARD NATIONAL HUNT FLAT RACE (CONDITIONAL AND AMATEUR) 2m
4:30 (4:35) (Class 6) 4-6-Y-0 **£1,370** (£399; £199)

Form RPR
3 **1** **Anychancedave (IRE)**[34] 3166 4-10-2 0 ow2 JeremiahMcGrath(7) 104+
(Alan Swinbank) *hld up: hdwy over 3f out: led over 1f out: pushed clr* **3/1**[1]
5- **2** *9* **Inoogoo (IRE)**[289] 5227 6-11-1 0 RyanMania(3) 107+
(George Bewley) *cl up: led over 3f out: hung lft and hdd over 1f out: sn no ex* **8/1**
0-4 **3** *8* **Four Fiddlers (IRE)**[71] 2553 6-10-11 0 MissLAlexander(7) 100
(N W Alexander) *hld up: hdwy and prom over 6f out: effrt 3f out: sn one pce* **40/1**
3-0 **4** *8* **Zaru (FR)**[48] 2943 5-11-1 0 HarryHaynes(3) 93
(James Ewart) *led to over 3f out: rdn and outpcd fnl 2f* **9/2**[3]
004 **5** *1* **Blazing Bay (IRE)**[66] 2660 6-10-4 0 MrJBelbin(7) 85
(James Moffatt) *bhd: pushed along 1/2-way: sme late hdwy: nvr on terms* **20/1**
6 *4* **Gris Lord (IRE)**[32] 3237 6-10-11 0 MrCCully(7) 88
(R T J Wilson, Ire) *prom: rdn over 5f out: wknd over 2f out* **10/3**[2]
7 *2 1/4* **Al Gregg (IRE)** 5-10-11 0 MrJCreswell(7) 86
(I A Duncan, Ire) *hld up: struggling over 5f out: btn fnl 3f* **25/1**
5 **8** *44* **Scales (IRE)**[26] 3399 5-10-13 0 JamesHalliday(5) 47
(Malcolm Jefferson) *in tch: struggling over 5f out: lost tch ent st: t.o* **3/1**[1]
000 **9** *21* **Over The Clyde**[17] 3553 6-10-11 0 MrRWilson(7) 28
(William Young) *bhd: lost tch fr 1/2-way: t.o* **200/1**
10 *nk* **Aye Well** 6-11-1 0 1 EwanWhillans(3) 28
(Elliott Cooper) *prom: struggling 6f out: t.o* **28/1**
S **Wotsurpoison** 4-10-2 0 AlexanderVoy(5) —
(Lucy Normile) *t.k.h: hld up: broke down after 3f: fatally injured* **28/1**

3m 45.0s (-15.70) **Going Correction** -0.725s/f (Firm)
WFA 4 from 5yo 11lb 5 from 6yo 3lb **11** Ran SP% **120.8**
Speed ratings: **110,105,101,97,97 95,93,71,61,61 —**
toteswingers:1&2:£3.40, 1&3:£15.60, 2&3:£25.40 CSF £26.29 TOTE £4.40: £1.40, £2.20, £6.40; EX 24.90.
Owner DavidManasseh,TitusBramble,LeeCattermole **Bred** Lowland Enterprises **Trained** Melsonby, N Yorks
■ Stewards' Enquiry : Jeremiah McGrath three-day ban: weighed in 2lb heavy (Feb 14-16)

FOCUS
Two pulled clear in what looked a modest bumper and the fourth and fifth help set the level.

NOTEBOOK
Anychancedave(IRE), from a yard that does well in this sphere, improved markedly on his debut third, when possibly unsuited by the Fibresand at Southwell, getting well on top late having taken a while to hit top gear. He's going to stay further over hurdles, but may be able to defy a penalty first.
Inoogoo(IRE) is the one to take from the race. He travelled supremely well and looked all over the winner when going clear, but the lack of a run since April may have ultimately told. This was a promising start for his new trainer and he looks a horse to be interested in next time. (op 9-1)
Four Fiddlers(IRE) kept plugging away and will probably require 3m over hurdles. It's doubtful whether he's up to winning a bumper. (op 33-1)
Zaru(FR) is another who won't be winning until he's jumping. (op 4-1)
Gris Lord(IRE) failed to match the form he showed at Down Royal last time. (op 7-2)
Scales(IRE) stopped quickly and was unable to build on a promising first effort. (op 7-2)
T/Jkpt: Not won. T/Plt: £38.20 to a £1 stake. Pool:£89,929.20 - 1,716.48 winning tickets T/Qpdt: £20.50 to a £1 stake. Pool:£6,787.69 - 243.90 winning tickets RY

2584 LUDLOW (R-H)
Monday, January 31
3857 Meeting Abandoned - Frozen track

3611 FOLKESTONE (R-H)
Tuesday, February 1
OFFICIAL GOING: Chase course - good hurdle course - soft
Wind: virtually nil Weather: dull, light rain

3864 BET ON TONIGHTS FOOTBALL AT TOTESPORT.COM "NATIONAL HUNT" NOVICES' HURDLE (8 hdls) 2m 1f 110y
2:10 (2:10) (Class 4) 4-Y-0+ **£1,918** (£559; £279)

Form RPR
2241 **1** **Sire De Grugy (FR)**[31] 3302 5-11-10 131 JamieMoore 125+
(Gary Moore) *t.k.h: trckd ldng pair tl cruised ahd bef 2 out: c wl clr after 2 out: eased flat: nt extended* **2/9**[1]
6 **2** *16* **Fireitfromye (IRE)**[30] 3344 6-11-3 0 DarylJacob 92
(Alan Fleming) *w ldr tl led 3rd: hdd after 3 out: rdn and no ch w wnr wl bef last: kpt on to hold 2nd* **10/1**[3]
4/ **3** *1 3/4* **Keepthebooton (IRE)**[675] 4760 8-11-3 0 WillKennedy 90
(Noel Chance) *hld up in tch: mstke 5th: rdn along to go 3rd: no ch w wnr wl bef last: plugged on* **33/1**
04 **4** *39* **Caddie Master (IRE)**[9] 3701 5-11-3 0 APMcCoy 75+
(Jonjo O'Neill) *led tl 3rd: styd upsides ldr tl bef 2 out: wknd wl bef last: t.o* **16/1**
00- **5** *41* **Premier Article (IRE)**[384] 3418 6-11-0 0 EamonDehdashti(3) 10
(Gary Moore) *hld up in tch: bdly hmpd 4th: rallied and in tch again after next: rdn and no rspnse after 2 out: wknd qckly wl bef last and sn t.o* **100/1**
5-42 **F** **Alwaysonthemove**[42] 3056 7-11-3 0 LeightonAspell —
(Laura Mongan) *t.k.h: hld up wl in tch: blnd bdly 3rd: 5th whn fell next* **13/2**[2]

4m 33.5s (-2.10) **Going Correction** -0.125s/f (Good) **6** Ran SP% **114.1**
Speed ratings (Par 105): **99,91,91,73,55 —**
toteswingers:1&2 £1.20, 2&3 £6.80, 1&3 £4.10 CSF £3.91 TOTE £1.10: £1.10, £2.50; EX 3.20.
Owner The Preston Family & Friends **Bred** La Grugerie **Trained** Lower Beeding, W Sussex

FOCUS
No strength-in-depth to this novice hurdle, but the short-priced winner justified the market confidence with aplomb. The second has been rated to his mark.

NOTEBOOK
Sire De Grugy(FR), second to subsequent Grade 2 winner Bobs Worth on his hurdling debut in November, and with a subsequent soft-ground win under his belt, was the one to beat. He pulled hard for over a circuit, but even as he was being restrained, his jumping was fluent and economical. He relaxed once allowed to stride on and coasted into a definitive lead, brushing aside his rivals effortlessly. He is a big stamp of a horse and connections stressed that he must have soft ground, so his future target could be a handicap at Taunton or the Dovecote at Kempton. (op 1-5)
Fireitfromye(IRE) made little impression on his hurdling debut last month, but that is turning out to be a hot race, producing three subsequent winners already, and his second in an Irish bumper suggests he has some ability. After disputing the lead for much of the way, he was readily outclassed once the winner sailed by, though this was a step in the right direction. (op 12-1)
Keepthebooton(IRE), having his first outing since March 2009, got outpaced from the second-last, but plugged on and should come on for this run. (op 25-1)
Caddie Master(IRE), ridden up with the lead this time, after staying on from off the pace in the mud at Towcester last week, was leaden-legged from the home turn, but now qualifies for handicaps. (op 20-1)
Alwaysonthemove has yet to make an impact over hurdles and came down as the pace began to quicken. (op 7-1)

3865 40 LIVE FOOTBALL MARKETS AT TOTESPORT.COM MAIDEN CHASE (15 fncs) 2m 5f
2:40 (2:40) (Class 5) 5-Y-0+ **£2,397** (£698; £349)

Form RPR
42 **1** **Native Gallery (IRE)**[78] 2428 6-11-0 0 DarylJacob 114+
(Ben De Haan) *chsd ldr tl led 10th: rdn and asserted between last 2: pushed out: comf* **10/11**[1]
5/3- **2** *9* **Swift Lord (IRE)**[356] 3972 6-11-0 0 JamieMoore 107+
(Gary Moore) *hld up in tch: chsd ldng pair and mstke 10th: wnt 2nd 3 out: effrt and pressed wnr 2 out: unable qck and btn bef last: eased fnl 75yds* **7/4**[2]
P0-0 **3** *54* **Big Bertie (IRE)**[17] 3556 7-11-0 0 AndrewThornton 59
(Anna Newton-Smith) *led: nt fluent 7th: hdd and mstke 10th: stl ev ch whn mstke 12th: 3rd and wkng whn blnd next: sn lost tch w ldng pair: hld on for 3rd fnl 75yds: t.o* **40/1**
/33- **4** *hd* **No More Prisoners (IRE)**[75] 2491 11-10-9 93 (tp) MissLHorner(5) 49
(Liam Corcoran) *hld up in rr: hdwy into midfield 7th: lost tch w ldng trio 11th: t.o after 3 out: plugged on and pressing for poor 3rd fnl 75yds* **17/2**[3]
00 **5** *27* **Ballinhassig (IRE)**[22] 3485 6-10-7 0 MrTJCannon(7) 22
(Sarah Wall) *in tch in rr tl struggling after 8th: lost tch after next: t.o fr 12th* **100/1**
4P0 **6** *1/2* **Karingabay Queen**[74] 2495 6-10-0 0 (b) MrBJPoste(7) 14
(Kevin Tork) *chsd ldrs: mstke and nrly uns rdr 2nd: styd chsng ldrs tl wknd 10th: 5th and losing tch whn mstke 12th: t.o whn j.lft last 2* **66/1**
7 *28* **Pipes A'Calling**[1402] 10-10-4 0 CharlieHuxley(3) —
(Sarah Humphrey) *mstkes: j.big 1st: alway towards rr: rdn and lost tch 8th: t.o fr next* **33/1**

5m 26.3s (4.10) **Going Correction** +0.10s/f (Yiel) **7** Ran SP% **107.1**
Speed ratings: **96,92,72,71,61 61,50**
toteswingers:1&2 £1.02, 2&3 £20.20, 1&3 £25.70 CSF £2.47 TOTE £1.50: £1.10, £1.50; EX 3.00.
Owner William A Tyrer **Bred** M O'Dowd **Trained** Lambourn, Berks

FOCUS
Only two with any discernible ability, and they finished a distance clear of the remainder off a slow early pace. The first two have been rated in line with their hurdles form.

NOTEBOOK
Native Gallery(IRE) disputed the lead throughout, jumped efficiently and stayed on best. The winner of two points in Ireland, he had shown some potential when narrowly beaten in a novice hurdle at Plumpton when last seen in November and looks capable enough over fences, especially as he is not overly big. Connections might revert to hurdles next to make the most of a reasonable mark. (op 11-10 tchd 11-8 and 5-6)
Swift Lord(IRE), having his first run in almost a year, was keen on his reappearance but made good progress before the final bend to chase home the winner. He has some ability, as he showed when winning an Irish bumper, and again in a strong novice hurdle at Ludlow a year ago, but his jumping will need to improve if he is to make any impact over fences. (op 11-8 tchd 6-5)
Big Bertie(IRE) was in the process of running a much-improved race on this chasing debut until he hit the 12th, which caused him to lose confidence and drop away. (tchd 50-1)
No More Prisoners(IRE) just lost out in the battle for a distant third, but he was 0-24 over jumps when trained in Ireland and will need to improve for his new stable. Official explanation: jockey said gelding made a noise (op 10-1 tchd 8-1)

3866 GET LIVE FOOTBALL STATS AT TOTESPORT.COM NOVICES' HURDLE (10 hdls) 2m 6f 110y
3:10 (3:11) (Class 4) 4-Y-O+ **£1,918** (£559; £279)

Form RPR
0-15 **1** **Carpincho (FR)**[49] 2939 7-11-12 0 APMcCoy 135+
(Sarah Humphrey) *a travelling wl: hld up towards rr: gd hdwy 7th: jnd ldrs on bit 3 out: led ent st: nudged clr bef last: v easily* **4/1**[2]
43 **2** 6 **Double Whammy**[49] 2946 5-11-5 116 DominicElsworth 116
(Jamie Poulton) *in tch towards rr: outpcd 7th: modest 8th 3 out: styd on steadily fr next: wnt 4th ent st: lft 3rd and hmpd last: kpt on dourly to go 2nd towards fin: no ch w wnr* **17/2**[3]
323- **3** 1 3/4 **Knighton Combe**[311] 4890 11-11-5 0 DarylJacob 116+
(Jamie Snowden) *in tch: chsd ldrs 5th: wnt prom 8th: led sn after 2 out: rdn and hdd ent st: btn whn lft 2nd last: lost 2nd towards fin* **9/1**
2- **4** 14 **O Malley's Oscar (IRE)**[318] 4744 6-11-5 0 ColinBolger 100
(Suzy Smith) *chsd ldrs tl pushed along and wknd sn after 2 out: lft modest 4th last* **28/1**
02 **5** 11 **Saint Denis (FR)**[41] 3089 5-11-5 0 WillKennedy 89
(Alex Hales) *chsd ldrs: wnt 2nd after 6th: dived 8th: led next: hdd and rdn sn after 2 out: wknd qckly wl bef last* **25/1**
0-65 **6** 58 **Venetian Lad**[78] 2428 6-11-5 0 LeightonAspell 31
(Lydia Richards) *hld up in tch in rr: sme hdwy after 7th: wknd after next: t.o wl bef last* **40/1**
U **7** 20 **Dulce Domum**[15] 3604 5-10-12 0 DaveCrosse —
(Roger Curtis) *in tch in rr: rdn and struggling after 6th: lost tch after next: wl t.o after 3 out* **150/1**
000 **8** 11 **Saute**[24] 3439 5-10-9 0 (p) AshleyBird[(10)] —
(Jim Best) *in tch tl dropped in rr and rdn along after 6th: lost tch 8th: wl t.o after 3 out* **100/1**
02 **U** **Cotillion**[24] 3439 5-11-5 0 DougieCostello 119
(Ian Williams) *t.k.h: hld up in tch towards rr: hdwy to chse ldrs 8th: ev ch 2 out: rdn and nt gng pce of wnr bef last: 2nd and btn whn mstke: stmbld and uns rdr last* **11/4**[1]
-461 **P** **Half Cocked**[25] 3428 9-11-12 120 AndrewThornton —
(Richard Rowe) *led: mstke 8th: hdd next: sn dropped out: t.o whn p.u last* **11/4**[1]
P **The Crafty Cuckoo (IRE)**[339] 6-11-5 0 JamieMoore —
(Emma Lavelle) *chsd ldr tl after 5th: sn lost pl: bhd whn p.u 2 out* **9/1**
-062 **P** **Saffron Lord**[16] 3584 6-11-5 119 (t) TomSiddall —
(Martin Keighley) *in tch tl wknd after 6th: bhd whn p.u 3 out* **16/1**

6m 0.70s (-10.60) **Going Correction** -0.125s/f (Good) **12** Ran SP% **121.1**
Speed ratings (Par 105): **108,105,105,100,96 76,69,65,—,— —,—**
toteswingers:1&2 £13.80, 2&3 £5.00, 1&3 £4.50 CSF £37.38 TOTE £3.50: £1.60, £2.90, £4.00; EX 50.70.
Owner W D Glover & P Chapman **Bred** Patrice Perraud **Trained** West Wratting, Cambs

FOCUS
A competitive event with several jostling for position in the back straight, but in the end only the winner truly saw out the trip in the soft ground. The race has been rated through the second to his C&D mark.

NOTEBOOK
Carpincho(FR) travelled well, made a move three-wide around the home turn and stayed on better than the rest for a comfortable success. He had some decent bumper form last season and ran away from a modest field on his hurdling debut. He flopped next time, but was back to form here, and connections had secured the services of Tony McCoy to help him defy his penalty. He looks quite decent, especially when fresh, and will reportedly be tackling fences before too long. (op 9-2)
Double Whammy, third over C&D in December, looked outclassed down the back but came home strongly. With the stable in good form at present, he might be able to go one better in the near future. (op 11-1 tchd 8-1)
Knighton Combe, making his hurdling debut at the age of 11, was competitive in the leading bunch as the race got serious before just getting run out of it in the straight. A multiple winner over fences last season, he looks on course to add to his tally. (op 8-1)
O Malley's Oscar(IRE), an ex-pointer who showed ability when last seen in a bumper last March, made some progress in the back straight before blowing up, and should come on for this run. (op 33-1)
Saint Denis(FR), off the mark over a longer trip at Fontwell last month, was up with the leaders, but had no answer as the pace lifted down the back. The drop in trip and his penalty proved too much here. (op 22-1)
Cotillion travelled well to challenge for the lead coming into the straight, but his stamina began to empty and he was a tired horse when buckling after the last and dumping his jockey. (op 2-1 tchd 3-1)
Half Cocked Official explanation: vet said gelding finished lame right-fore (op 2-1 tchd 3-1)
The Crafty Cuckoo(IRE) Official explanation: trainer said gelding choked (op 2-1 tchd 3-1)

3867 MORE LIVE FOOTBALL BETTING AT TOTESPORT.COM H'CAP CHASE (18 fncs) 3m 1f
3:40 (3:40) (Class 5) (0-90,90) 5-Y-O+ **£2,397** (£698; £349)

Form RPR
050 **1** **Ilewin Tom**[153] 1450 8-10-0 64 oh5 JamieMoore 84+
(Gary Brown) *hld up in tch: clsd to trck ldrs gng wl 13th: led 2 out: pushed wl clr between last 2: eased flat: v easily* **10/1**
30P5 **2** 18 **Quartz Du Montceau (FR)**[15] 3609 7-11-5 86 (p) PeterToole[(3)] 80
(Anna Newton-Smith) *chsd ldrs: wnt 2nd 11th: led 15th: out j. and hdd sn after next: sn rdn and ld again bef next: hdd 2 out: sn btn* **5/1**[3]
/302 **3** 16 **Oponce (FR)**[31] 3305 9-11-9 87 WillKennedy 67
(Noel Chance) *hld up in tch: clsd to press ldrs 13th: mstke 15th: gd jump next and sn led: rdn and hdd bef next: sn wknd* **9/2**[2]
0-5P **4** 3/4 **Absolute Shambles**[25] 3431 7-11-10 88 ColinBolger 67
(Chris Gordon) *led: mstke and hdd 8th: led again after next tl hdd 15th: wknd qckly next* **11/2**
345U **5** 4 **Commanche Dawn**[15] 3609 9-9-9 66 oh7 ow2 MrTJCannon[(7)] 39
(Gerry Enright) *j.lft and several slow jumps: a bhd: lost tch 13th: t.o fr 3 out* **9/1**
5121 **6** 20 **Ukrainian Star (IRE)**[19] 3530 8-11-7 85 (p) WarrenMarston 52
(Martin Keighley) *chsd ldr tl led 8th tl after next: mstke 11th: sn pushed along: wknd u.p 15th: tailing off whn blnd 2 out* **11/8**[1]

6m 40.5s (4.70) **Going Correction** +0.10s/f (Yiel)
WFA 5 from 7yo+ 3lb **6** Ran SP% **111.4**
Speed ratings: **96,90,85,84,83 77**
toteswingers:1&2 £4.90, 2&3 £4.40, 1&3 £18.20 CSF £55.46 CT £252.21 TOTE £15.70: £8.80, £3.40.
Owner Tom Segrue **Bred** T J Segrue **Trained** East Garston, Berks

FOCUS
A very moderate handicap chase. The winner was well in on old form but has been rated as recording a personal best here.

NOTEBOOK
Ilewin Tom, patiently ridden early, made good progress in the back straight to battle for the lead, and extended his advantage from the home turn. He gained his sole previous victory following a wind operation in May 2009, but had been nowhere near that form since. However, back down to that winning mark of just 59 meant he was getting upwards of 21lb from his rivals and that proved decisive. He had reportedly improved for having had another wind operation and a break. Official explanation: trainer said, regarding apparent impriovement in form, that the gelding had benefitted from a break and a wind operation. (op 16-1)
Quartz Du Montceau(FR) ran his race but had been up with the pace for most of the way and was vulnerable to a late finisher. He was also back down to his last winning mark but has just a moderate conversion record. (op 8-1)
Oponce(FR) looked to be about to build on the ability he showed last time as he swooped at the end of the back straight, but his effort was short-lived. He was stepping up in trip, but the lightly-raced gelding stopped as if his breathing or another ailment was troubling him. (op 7-2 tchd 5-1)
Absolute Shambles ballooned several fences and needed to be driven into others, and would appreciate a return to faster ground. (op 6-1 tchd 7-1 and 5-1)
Commanche Dawn has been in good form this winter but was the first to crack and this was far from his true running. (op 13-2 tchd 6-1 and 12-1)
Ukrainian Star(IRE) Official explanation: trainer said, regarding running, that the gelding ran flat

3868 SIS LIVE H'CAP HURDLE (8 hdls) 2m 1f 110y
4:10 (4:10) (Class 4) (0-110,108) 4-Y-O+ **£2,055** (£599; £299)

Form RPR
4252 **1** **The Bishops Baby (IRE)**[4] 3793 8-11-0 103 MrTJCannon[(7)] 106+
(Richard Rowe) *hld up in last pair: clsd and in tch 3rd: stl last: gng wl whn swtchd lft bef last: rdn to chal flat: r.o wl to ld towards fin* **7/2**[2]
2462 **2** nk **Spider Boy**[18] 3540 14-9-8 83 oh2 ow1 (b) MrHGMiller[(7)] 86
(Zoe Davison) *led: pressed and rdn after 2 out: hdd and bmpd sn after last: sn led again: battled on wl tl hdd and no ex towards fin* **11/1**
P033 **3** 2 1/2 **Sebastiano (FR)**[4] 3793 8-11-12 108 (p) JamieMoore 109
(Gary Moore) *hld up in midfield: clsd 3rd: chal ent st: rdn bef last: led and hung sn after last: sn hdd and one pce* **9/2**[3]
0641 **4** 2 3/4 **Whitcombe Spirit**[14] 3611 6-10-5 87 (b) DominicElsworth 85
(Jamie Poulton) *hld up off the pce in last pair: clsd 3rd: trckd ldrs after 2 out: rdn and one pce bef last* **3/1**[1]
-U12 **5** 2 **Rosoff (IRE)**[15] 3610 9-11-1 97 (p) RhysFlint 93
(Laura Mongan) *chsd ldr tl 2nd: wnt 2nd again 4th: ev ch after 2 out tl pushed along and fnd nil bef last: btn whn hung lft flat* **8/1**
5005 **6** 10 **Master Milan (IRE)**[22] 3489 5-10-13 95 APMcCoy 81
(Jonjo O'Neill) *chsd ldr 2nd tl 4th: styd chsng ldrs tl lost pl but stl in tch bef 2 out: wknd bef last* **3/1**[1]

4m 41.6s (6.00) **Going Correction** -0.125s/f (Good) **6** Ran SP% **109.8**
Speed ratings (Par 105): **81,80,79,78,77 73**
toteswingers:1&2 £3.70, 2&3 £3.00, 1&3 £3.10 CSF £34.41 TOTE £4.10: £1.20, £6.80; EX 37.70.
Owner Richard Rowe Racing Partnership **Bred** David And Mrs Gillian Nevin **Trained** Sullington, W Sussex

FOCUS
An ordinary, but tight-looking handicap. The winner scored under a fine ride and has been rated in line with her recent run, with the runner-up to his season's best.

NOTEBOOK
The Bishops Baby(IRE) had been in front a little too soon when second at Fontwell four days earlier and was ridden with exaggerated waiting tactics this time, swooping very late after travelling well. It was another advertisement of her young rider's skills. (op 10-3 tchd 4-1)
Spider Boy put up a gallant effort, setting the pace and finding extra to fight off the challenge of Sebastiano, only to be collared on the line. He might have lost a bit of pace, but remains admirably consistent. (op 9-1 tchd 8-1 and 12-1)
Sebastiano(FR) looked a little unlucky when getting hampered by a loose horse at Fontwell but he was unable to reverse placings with The Bishops Baby. He did not settle off the slow pace and that may have cost him, as he threw down a strong challenge but was outbattled by the rallying second. (tchd 4-1)
Whitcombe Spirit won a weaker contest over C&D a fortnight ago, but was outclassed here. (op 7-2)
Rosoff(IRE) relishes testing conditions, so although he was up there until the turn in, he could not go with them as the pace quickened. (op 5-1)
Master Milan(IRE) was backed into joint-favouritism for his handicap debut but he began to struggle on the final circuit and may be better on faster ground. (op 9-2 tchd 11-4)

3869 SAGA INSURANCE H'CAP CHASE (12 fncs) 2m
4:40 (4:40) (Class 4) (0-110,105) 5-Y-O+ **£2,602** (£764; £382; £190)

Form RPR
664 **1** **Valley View (IRE)**[19] 3526 5-11-1 96 APMcCoy 106+
(Jonjo O'Neill) *hld up in tch: wnt 2nd 3 out: upsides ldr and travelling wl bef next: j.big 2 out: pushed ahd after last: pushed out: comf* **4/5**[1]
F2F4 **2** 1 1/4 **Owner Occupier**[30] 3343 6-11-0 100 MrTJCannon[(7)] 109
(Chris Gordon) *led: rdn bef 2 out: hdd after last: styd on same pce fnl 150yds* **8/1**[3]
-S0U **3** hd **Nomadic Warrior**[14] 3612 6-11-2 95 TomMessenger 104
(John Holt) *hld up in last pair: 5th and rdn whn mstke 3 out: wnt 3rd bef next: no imp tl styd on wl u.p fnl 150yds: pressing for 2nd nr fin: no threat to wnr* **33/1**
134U **4** 11 **Abey M'Boy**[13] 3628 8-11-10 103 LeightonAspell 102
(Oliver Sherwood) *hld up in last pair: rdn and effrt after 3 out: no prog and wl hld between last 2* **3/1**[2]
4-F0 **5** 10 **Meneur (FR)**[48] 2961 9-11-3 96 JamieMoore 84
(Gary Moore) *t.k.h: chsd ldrs: cl 3rd 3 out: wknd u.p bef next* **8/1**[3]

/P26 **6** 2 3/4 **Zhukov (IRE)**[74] 2494 9-11-5 **105**........................ MrBJPoste(7) 90
(Kevin Tork) *chsd ldrs: rdn and wknd after 3 out: wl btn next* **28/1**
6061 **7** 2 3/4 **She's Humble (IRE)**[15] 3606 9-11-4 **97**........................ AndrewThornton 79
(Linda Jewell) *racd wd: w ldr tl 8th: dropped to rr next: wknd 3 out: wl bhd next* **10/1**

4m 6.60s (-0.60) **Going Correction** +0.10s/f (Yiel)
WFA 5 from 6yo+ 1lb **7** Ran SP% **118.3**
Speed ratings: **105,104,104,98,93 92,91**
toteswingers:1&2 £2.80, 2&3 £22.60, 1&3 £7.30 CSF £8.82 CT £127.37 TOTE £2.00: £1.10, £4.70; EX 12.60.
Owner John P McManus **Bred** Michael Barry **Trained** Cheltenham, Gloucs

FOCUS
A moderate handicap which saw a progressive winner. The second has been rated as improving a touch on his previous best chase form.

NOTEBOOK
Valley View(IRE) ◆ had shown little in three novice hurdles this season, but the market had assessed him on the promise of his victory in his sole Irish point last year, and as a consequence he looked well handicapped for the switch to chasing. Travelling well, he stalked the leaders, and although he had to battle to overcome the second, the result was never really in doubt. There should be more opportunities to come from this base rating. (op 5-4)
Owner Occupier disputed a good pace and only went down under a fight. He jumped better than of late and looks on reasonable mark to go one better. (op 9-1 tchd 10-1 and 7-1)
Nomadic Warrior was having just his second race over fences, having unseated his rider at the third on his first attempt. He came home strongly from the last, but had never been going quite well enough to get involved any earlier.
Abey M'Boy could never get involved, but stayed on a bit towards the finish. (op 10-3)
Meneur(FR) was in touch and looked to be going quite well, but he faded tamely from the home turn and looks worthy of his tumbling handicap mark. (op 15-2 tchd 13-2)
T/Plt: £371.10 to a £1 stake. Pool of £64,154.44 - 126.17 winning tickets. T/Qpdt: £253.60 to a £1 stake. Pool of £4,490.39 - 13.10 winning tickets. SP

3645 TAUNTON (R-H)
Tuesday, February 1

OFFICIAL GOING: Good to soft (good in places)
Rail on bend moved adding 27m to advertised distances.
Wind: mild across Weather: sunny with patchy cloud

3870 TIMEFORM BETFAIR RACING CLUB CONDITIONAL JOCKEYS' H'CAP HURDLE (12 hdls) 3m 110y
1:50 (1:50) (Class 5) (0-90,90) 4-Y-0+ £2,397 (£698; £349)

Form RPR
5003 **1** **Easement**[29] 3369 8-11-9 **90**........................(v) JoshuaMoore(3) 95+
(Charlie Morlock) *disp ld tl outrt ldr after 8th: rdn after 3 out: styd on wl: rdn out* **6/1**[2]
-606 **2** 1 3/4 **No Woman No Cry**[32] 3261 6-10-12 **84**........................(p) SClements(8) 85
(Colin Tizzard) *mid-div: rdn and hdwy after 8th: styng on same pce whn lft 2nd bef 2 out: a being hld by wnr* **12/1**
/50- **3** 3/4 **Normally**[455] 2051 7-11-2 **90**........................ ThomasFlint(10) 91
(John Flint) *prom tl outpcd after 8th: styd on again fr 2 out: wnt 3rd run-in* **4/1**[1]
-403 **4** shd **A Fistful Of Euros**[26] 3400 7-11-6 **90**........................ DannyBurton(6) 90
(Chris Down) *t.k.h: prom tl 9th: sn rdn to chse ldrs: styd on same pce fr after 3 out* **9/1**[3]
3P0F **5** 4 **Inchloch**[71] 2585 9-11-12 **90**........................(t) IanPopham 86
(Claire Dyson) *hld up towards rr: stdy prog fr 8th: rdn 3 out: styd on same pce fr next* **25/1**
005P **6** 1 1/4 **Karinga Dream**[18] 3540 5-11-4 **85**........................ RTDunne(3) 80
(Venetia Williams) *mid-div: hdwy 8th: sn rdn: styd on same pce fr 2 out* **9/1**[3]
00-P **7** 9 **Border Lad**[19] 3530 7-10-6 **70**........................ RichardKilloran 56
(Alison Thorpe) *hld up towards rr: rdn after 8th: little imp: nvr a factor* **16/1**
01BP **8** 4 1/2 **Lansdowne Princess**[86] 2240 9-11-2 **80**........................ DavidBass 65
(Gerald Ham) *hld up towards rr: hit 4th: hdwy after 8th: rdn to chse ldrs after 3 out: wkng whn mstke 2 out* **14/1**
5663 **9** 3/4 **Manadam (FR)**[19] 3530 8-11-4 **85**........................ MattGriffiths(3) 66
(Anthony Middleton) *reminders fr 1st: a towards rr* **6/1**[2]
400 **10** 1 **Jewellery (IRE)**[35] 3158 4-10-9 **90**........................ EdGlassonbury(5) 58
(Alison Thorpe) *rdn after 9th: a towards rr* **20/1**
/03- **11** nk **That's For Sure**[343] 4220 11-10-11 **78**........................(tp) AodhaganConlon(3) 57
(Debra Hamer) *mid-div tl wknd after 9th* **10/1**
-050 **12** 1 1/4 **Northwold**[20] 3506 7-10-8 **72**........................ TomMolloy 50
(Christopher Kellett) *a bhd* **40/1**
06 **13** 1 1/4 **Lions In Law**[29] 3374 7-11-6 **89**........................ ChrisDavies(5) 66
(Richard Hawker) *mid-div tl wknd after 9th* **22/1**
546/ **P** **Merry Storm (IRE)**[668] 4856 12-10-6 **70**........................(t) DonalDevereux —
(Lisa Day) *trckd ldrs tl rdn after 7th: wknd after next: t.o whn p.u after 3 out* **20/1**
-P0P **P** **Pull The Wool (IRE)**[14] 3611 7-11-1 **79**........................ RichieMcLernon —
(Laura Young) *trckd ldrs: jnd wnr 9th: rdn and ev ch briefly after 3 out: styng on same pce in 2nd whn p.u bef next: dismntd* **33/1**

6m 5.50s (-1.60) **Going Correction** -0.225s/f (Good)
WFA 4 from 5yo+ 11lb **15** Ran SP% **121.0**
Speed ratings (Par 103): **93,92,92,92,90 90,87,86,85,85 85,85,84,—,—**
toteswingers:1&2 £18.30, 2&3 £17.20, 1&3 £8.70 CSF £67.55 CT £327.97 TOTE £7.20: £2.50, £3.40, £2.30; EX 78.20.
Owner W R Morlock **Bred** C A Cyzer **Trained** Upper Lambourn, Berks
■ Stewards' Enquiry : Matt Griffiths seven-day ban: used whip in incorrect place causing gelding to be wealed (Feb 15 -21)
Danny Burton six-day ban: used whip with excessive frequency (Feb 15-20)

FOCUS
A modest and wide-open handicap hurdle, run at a steady gallop. The first two have been rated as recording small personal bests.

NOTEBOOK
Easement, well backed in the market, built on his third at Hereford latest to land his first career success. Always travelling kindly up with the pace, he led turning for home and landed a cosy win despite a mistake at the last. He showed a game attitude but may struggle off a higher mark. (op 17-2 tchd 11-2)
No Woman No Cry, sporting first-time cheekpieces, improved for this return to further, running on for second. He crept into the race, finishing strongly up the straight, and can remain competitive off this mark. (op 14-1)
Normally was well supported in the market on this return from a 455-day absence. He ran a fair race, plugging on having been outpaced running down the back, and should improve for the run. He should be competitive in this grade. (op 11-2 tchd 6-1)
A Fistful Of Euros raced keenly and took the field along before struggling down the back, but found for pressure and rallied turning for home. She may need a drop in the weights to get her head in front. (op 8-1)
Inchloch ran a solid race on this return to hurdles, without ever threatening the winner. (tchd 28-1)
Karinga Dream ran an okay race on this step up in trip. (op 10-1)
Manadam(FR) was disappointing and never raced with any enthusiasm (op 13-2)
Pull The Wool(IRE) was going well when pulled up lame before the second last. Official explanation: jockey said mare returned lame (op 25-1)

3871 BETFAIR.COM/PAULNICHOLLS NOVICES' CHASE (14 fncs) 2m 3f
2:20 (2:20) (Class 4) 5-Y-0+ £4,453 (£1,298; £649)

Form RPR
U-33 **1** **Qozak (FR)**[32] 3262 7-11-0 0........................(t) NickScholfield 144+
(Paul Nicholls) *a.p: led 9th: drew clr after 4 out: readily* **11/2**
-152 **2** 10 **Keki Buku (FR)**[32] 3262 8-11-0 0........................(t) RichardJohnson 134
(Philip Hobbs) *hld up: nt fluent 6th: stdy hdwy fr after next: rdn after 4 out: wnt 2nd 2 out: no ch w wnr* **5/2**[1]
5420 **3** 11 **Bathwick Quest (IRE)**[19] 3531 7-10-7 112........................ TomScudamore 115
(Brendan Powell) *led tl 9th: pressed wnr tl after 4 out: lost 2nd 2 out: styd on same pce* **40/1**
-503 **4** 7 **Special Occasion**[7] 3722 7-10-11 125........................ IanPopham(3) 115
(Caroline Keevil) *in tch: rdn after 7th: outpcd fr next: no ch after* **14/1**
10-4 **5** 9 **Swansbrook (IRE)**[28] 3390 8-11-0 0........................ RobertThornton 109
(Alan King) *hld up: hit 5th: struggling after 7th: nvr able to get on terms* **8/1**
0-3P **6** 2 1/2 **Tasheba**[73] 2523 6-11-0 0........................ BarryGeraghty 107+
(Nicky Henderson) *chsd ldng pair tl after 4 out: wkng whn hit 3 out* **3/1**[2]
30P0 **7** 43 **Tarabela**[47] 2980 8-10-7 0........................ JohnnyFarrelly 54
(Gerald Ham) *t.o fr 7th* **150/1**
P/3- **8** shd **Reymysterio (IRE)**[246] 10-10-9 0........................ KeiranBurke(5) 60
(Patrick Rodford) *j.lft: sn struggling in rr: hit 7th: sn t.o* **150/1**
P-04 **9** 6 **Hopeful Start (IRE)**[32] 3254 7-10-11 0........................ RichieMcLernon(3) 54
(Jonjo O'Neill) *in tch after 8th: sn wknd: t.o* **33/1**
3-U2 **P** **Ranjobaie (FR)**[15] 3605 6-11-0 0........................ AidanColeman —
(Venetia Williams) *in tch: nt fluent 5th: hit 8th: wknd qckly and p.u after next* **4/1**[3]

4m 43.0s (-13.50) **Going Correction** -0.225s/f (Good) **10** Ran SP% **113.4**
Speed ratings: **105,100,96,93,89 88,70,70,67,—**
toteswingers:1&2 £4.50, 2&3 £7.40, 1&3 £12.90 CSF £19.75 TOTE £5.30: £1.70, £1.30, £3.70; EX 18.90.
Owner The Stewart Family & Paul K Barber **Bred** Ivan Dumont **Trained** Ditcheat, Somerset

FOCUS
An interesting novice chase, featuring some useful types, that was run at a good gallop. The winner has been rated to the best of his hurdles form.

NOTEBOOK
Qozak(FR) put in a professional round of jumping to both outclass and outstay his rivals. Given a positive ride, he was always up with the pace and stayed on nicely to land a cosy first chase success. He looks a progressive sort and appreciated the step up in trip to make it 4-4 around here. He should win more races over fences Official explanation: trainer said, regarding apparent improvement in form, that the gelding appeared better suited by going right-handed. (op 5-1)
Keki Buku(FR) finished ahead of the winner at Warwick latest, but failed to confirm that form. Held up, he jumped soundly, but had too much ground to make up on the winner and ran on to finish a clear second. He may land a minor race. (op 9-4 tchd 11-4)
Bathwick Quest(IRE) was able to adopt her favoured front-running tactics and set a good end-to-end gallop before tiring in the straight. (op 50-1)
Special Occasion probably ran his race, without ever seriously getting involved. (op 18-1)
Swansbrook(IRE) failed to build on his chase debut, making the odd jumping error. (op 17-2)
Tasheba was disappointing on his chase debut, but may improve for the experience. (op 7-2)
Ranjobaie(FR), who isn't the biggest, made several jumping errors before being pulled up. Official explanation: jockey said gelding never travelled; vet said gelding lost a shoe and struck into itself (tchd 5-1)

3872 BETFAIR IPHONE & ANDROID APP NOVICES' HURDLE (9 hdls) 2m 1f
2:50 (2:51) (Class 4) 4-Y-0+ £3,768 (£1,098; £549)

Form RPR
-001 **1** **Shammick Boy (IRE)**[12] 3645 6-11-10 0........................ DenisO'Regan 135+
(Victor Dartnall) *mde most: rdn whn mstke and hdd last: hrd drvn and rallied wl fnl 75yds: led line* **13/8**[1]
23 **2** shd **Secret World (IRE)**[22] 3478 8-11-3 129........................ BarryGeraghty 126
(Nicky Henderson) *trckd ldr in clr 2nd: rdn after 2 out: led sn after last: hrd drvn: hdd line* **5/2**[2]
3 **3** 18 **Rock Of Deauville (IRE)**[75] 2466 4-10-7 0........................ HarrySkelton 100+
(Paul Nicholls) *mid-div of chsng gp: stdy prog fr 5th: wnt 3rd 3 out: rdn after 2 out: sn outpcd* **6/1**
4 13 **Qalinas (FR)**[94] 4-10-7 0........................ TomScudamore 84
(David Pipe) *mid-div of chsng gp: rdn bef 3 out: wnt modest 4th appr 2 out: nvr any ch w ldrs* **7/2**[3]
03 **5** 22 **Spinning Waters**[19] 3526 5-11-3 0........................ TomO'Brien 72
(Dai Burchell) *mid-div tl wknd 3 out: t.o* **40/1**
P **6** 3 3/4 **Guarino (GER)**[15] 3604 7-11-3 0........................ AndrewGlassonbury 70
(Gary Moore) *chsd clr ldrs rdn after 3 out: sn wknd: t.o* **80/1**
7 2 **Mission Complete (IRE)** 5-11-0 0........................ RichieMcLernon(3) 66
(Jonjo O'Neill) *mid-div of chsng gp tl wknd 6th: t.o* **50/1**
0 **8** 8 **Mick's Dancer**[83] 2310 6-11-3 0........................ SeanQuinlan 58
(Richard Phillips) *hit 1st: a towards rr: t.o* **80/1**
9 10 **Fran's Folly** 5-10-3 0........................ MarkQuinlan(7) 41
(Neil Mulholland) *chsd clr ldrs: hit 3rd: wknd after 5th: t.o* **100/1**
5 **10** 24 **Johnny Owen (IRE)**[26] 3406 5-11-3 0........................ JohnnyFarrelly 24
(David Brace) *a towards rr: t.o* **40/1**
0-00 **11** 7 **Victory Bay**[29] 3372 6-11-3 0........................(t) NickScholfield 17
(Simon Burrough) *a towards rr: t.o* **150/1**
0-0 **12** 6 **Sir Ocus**[12] 3647 5-11-3 0........................ JoeTizzard 11
(Colin Tizzard) *a towards rr: t.o* **66/1**
P- **13** 79 **Stellar Cause (USA)**[370] 2884 5-11-3 0........................(t) RodiGreene —
(Nick Ayliffe) *chsd clr ldrs early: t.o fr 5th* **150/1**

4m 0.60s (-7.40) **Going Correction** -0.225s/f (Good)
WFA 4 from 5yo+ 9lb **13** Ran SP% **116.3**
Speed ratings (Par 105): **99,98,90,84,74 72,71,67,62,51 48,45,8**
toteswingers:1&2 £2.10, 2&3 £3.10, 1&3 £3.20 CSF £5.70 TOTE £2.10: £1.02, £1.50, £2.50; EX 7.60.
Owner First Brayford Partnership **Bred** Miss D Flanagan **Trained** Brayford, Devon

FOCUS
A decent novice hurdle that produced a thrilling finish, with the first two pulling well clear. The second has been rated back to his mark, and the third to his Hereford run.

NOTEBOOK

Shammick Boy(IRE) showed a game attitude to just outbattle Secret World in a tight finish. Having taken the field along at a sound gallop, he found plenty for pressure, and once headed after the last, rallied to get up in the dying strides. This was a useful performance under a penalty and he looks a nice prospect who should continue to improve and will stay further. (op 2-1)

Secret World(IRE) travelled like the winner and touched 1.04 in-running on Betfair, before being nailed on the line. He has now been beaten in his three hurdle starts and is becoming expensive to follow. He should land a similar event, though, and may appreciate better ground. (op 2-1)

Rock Of Deauville(IRE), third at Hereford on debut, travelled strongly to chase the leaders into the straight, but couldn't quicken with the front two. He may improve again and could find a minor race. (tchd 13-2)

Qalinas(FR) failed to get competitive on this first start for connections. He struggled to narrow the gap on the front three, but should improve for a longer trip. (tchd 4-1)

Spinning Waters finished best of the remainder and now qualifies for handicaps. (op 50-1)

Stellar Cause(USA) Official explanation: trainer said gelding had been struck into

3873 FOLLOW PAUL NICHOLLS ON FACEBOOK AND TWITTER H'CAP CHASE (14 fncs) 2m 3f

3:20 (3:20) (Class 5) (0-95,95) 5-Y-0+ **£2,740** (£798; £399)

Form RPR

2RP- **1** **Marsh Court**[297] 5136 8-11-10 **93** AidanColeman 102+
(Jamie Snowden) *hld up: stdy hdwy fr 7th: led after 2 out: in command whn awkward last: comf* **9/1**

65 **2** *6* **Yes Man (IRE)**[21] 3494 6-11-9 **95** (v) DonalDevereux(3) 99
(Peter Bowen) *sn led: rdn whn hit 3 out: hdd after 2 out: no ex* **8/1**

F52F **3** *16* **Chilla Cilla**[7] 3720 8-10-12 **81** (t) NickScholfield 70
(Anthony Honeyball) *hld up: hmpd 3rd: stdy hdwy fr 8th: rdn in 4th whn hmpd on bnd appr 3 out: sn wnt 3rd: no ch w ldng pair* **5/1**[3]

2U2U **4** *2 ¾* **One More Dinar**[21] 3492 8-10-13 **82** RodiGreene 70
(John Bryan Groucott) *trckd ldrs: lft 2nd 8th: stmbld 2 strides after 4 out: sn rdn and lost 2nd: wkng whn mstke 2 out: hit last* **4/1**[2]

000 **5** *18* **Bless My Soul**[22] 3477 8-10-12 **86** (t) MattGriffiths(5) 52
(Ron Hodges) *in tch tl 10th: sn bhd: t.o* **14/1**

6003 **6** *1* **Red Law (IRE)**[21] 3492 7-10-9 **85** (t) MrPJTolman(7) 50
(Mark Gillard) *nt fluent: prom whn slow jump 1st: reminders: in tch whn hmpd 8th: rdn: wknd 10th: t.o* **7/2**[1]

006- **U** **Drumbeater (IRE)**[314] 4821 11-10-2 **78** MarkQuinlan(7) —
(Bernard Scriven) *hld up: blnd 5th: pushed along whn blnd bdly and uns rdr 9th* **14/1**

022P **P** **Mamba (GER)**[14] 3618 9-10-0 **69** (p) JamesDavies —
(Chris Down) *in tch: pckd bdly 3rd: pushed along 6th: t.o fr 8th: p.u bef 4 out* **7/1**

P-10 **F** **Killowenabbey (IRE)**[92] 2131 7-11-5 **95** (tp) AodhaganConlon(7) —
(Debra Hamer) *trckd ldr tl stmbld bdly 3 strides after 8th and fell* **14/1**

4m 53.1s (-3.40) **Going Correction** -0.225s/f (Good) 9 Ran SP% **112.5**

Speed ratings: **98,95,88,87,80 79,—,—,—**

toteswingers:1&2 £7.00, 2&3 £8.40, 1&3 £3.60 CSF £75.27 CT £399.08 TOTE £7.10: £2.40, £3.70, £1.20; EX 52.60.

Owner Mrs P De W Johnson **Bred** Mrs P De W Johnson **Trained** Ebbesbourne Wake, Wilts

FOCUS

A competitive handicap chase. The second has been rated as improving to the level of his hurdles form.

NOTEBOOK

Marsh Court was well supported early in the market on this return from 297 days off and duly landed the money. Jumping well throughout, she chased the long-time leader and led going to the last to land a comfortable victory. She can improve for the outing and should be competitive off her new mark. (op 15-2)

Yes Man(IRE) took the field along for much of the way, but could not match the winner when it mattered. This was an improved effort and he seemed to enjoy himself out in front. (op 10-1)

Chilla Cilla fell on her latest start and was ridden patiently. Travelling nicely, she wasn't given a hard time once beaten and should build on this with her confidence boosted. (tchd 9-2 and 11-2)

One More Dinar unseated on his last start and didn't jump fluently again. Under pressure down the back, he stayed on at the one pace. (op 7-2)

Bless My Soul never threatened on this chasing debut. (op 20-1)

Red Law(IRE) jumped poorly and will need to improve in that department to figure. (op 10-3 tchd 3-1)

Drumbeater(IRE) jumped right throughout and unseated his rider at the ninth. (tchd 13-2)

Mamba(GER) was always struggling and pulled up before four out. (tchd 13-2)

Killowenabbey(IRE) stumbled and came down after the eighth. He was tracking the leader at the time. (tchd 13-2)

3874 40% BETTER OFF ON BETFAIR SP H'CAP HURDLE (9 hdls) 2m 1f

3:50 (3:50) (Class 3) (0-135,129) 4-Y-0+ **£6,851** (£1,997; £999)

Form RPR

-063 **1** **Karky Schultz (GER)**[17] 3557 6-11-1 **118** PaddyBrennan 125
(James Eustace) *prom: led 3 out: rdn and hdd bef next: rallied v gamely u.str.p after last: led nr fin* **14/1**

1-10 **2** *nk* **Via Galilei (IRE)**[17] 3557 6-10-5 **115** JoshuaMoore(7) 123+
(Gary Moore) *hld up towards rr: smooth hdwy fr 5th: led appr 2 out: sn rdn: kpt on: no ex whn hdd nr fin* **7/1**[3]

3 **3** *1 ¼* **Tenor Nivernais (FR)**[10] 3686 4-10-6 **119** AidanColeman 115+
(Venetia Williams) *chsd ldrs: riidden after 3 out: cl 3rd at the last: kpt on but no ex* **2/1**[1]

1-60 **4** *21* **Simply Blue**[17] 3557 7-11-3 **120** AndrewGlassonbury 104
(Simon Burrough) *mid-div: hdwy after 6th: rdn after 3 out: wnt 4th but no ch w ldrs whn hit 2 out* **25/1**

F-P1 **5** *½* **Henry King (IRE)**[22] 3481 7-11-6 **123** (t) DenisO'Regan 107
(Victor Dartnall) *sn led: hdd 3 out: sn rdn: wknd bef next* **9/1**

1211 **6** *2 ½* **Sir Frank (IRE)**[184] 1148 6-11-10 **127** TomScudamore 108
(David Pipe) *mid-div: rdn after 6th: wknd bef 2 out* **14/1**

0P-0 **7** *1* **My Shamwari (IRE)**[53] 2868 7-11-5 **122** RichardJohnson 102
(Philip Hobbs) *awkward 1st: hld up towards rr: sme prog 6th: wknd after 3 out* **5/1**[2]

-202 **8** *16* **King's Revenge**[10] 3686 8-11-3 **120** (b) JasonMaguire 84
(Shaun Lycett) *mid-div tl 5th: sn struggling in rr: t.o* **12/1**

0-20 **9** *nk* **Causeway King (USA)**[33] 3229 5-11-12 **129** RobertThornton 93
(Alan King) *chsd ldrs: rdn after 5th: wknd after next: t.o* **20/1**

6263 **10** *3* **Ocean Transit (IRE)**[22] 3490 6-10-4 **112** (p) DavidBass(5) 73
(Richard Price) *nvr travelling: constantly rdn: a in rr: t.o* **12/1**

605 **11** *13* **Teshali (IRE)**[30] 3344 5-10-5 **108** (t) TimmyMurphy 56
(Paul Nicholls) *racd wd: mid-div: hdwy after 5th: rdn after 3 out: sn wknd: t.o* **11/1**

6F05 **12** *2* **Troubletimestwo (FR)**[22] 3490 5-10-5 **113** LeeEdwards(5) 59
(Tony Carroll) *mid-div: pushed along 3rd: bhd after next: t.o* **33/1**

600- **P** **Picot De Say**[235] 2710 9-11-0 **117** AndrewTinkler —
(Adrian Wintle) *struggling 5th: a in rr: t.o: whn p.u after 3 out* **33/1**

1210 **F** **Babilu**[17] 3557 6-10-8 **111** (p) TomO'Brien —
(Dai Burchell) *mid-div: trcking ldrs and travelling wl enough whn fell 6th* **25/1**

3m 57.0s (-11.00) **Going Correction** -0.225s/f (Good)

WFA 4 from 5yo+ 9lb 14 Ran SP% **127.9**

Speed ratings (Par 107): **107,106,106,96,96 94,94,86,86,85 79,78,—,—**

toteswingers:1&2:£20.60 2&3:£7.30 1&3:£12.10 CSF £109.38 CT £288.21 TOTE £16.00: £3.80, £2.50, £1.30; EX 176.40.

Owner Harold Nass **Bred** B Fassbender **Trained** Newmarket, Suffolk

FOCUS

An open-looking handicap hurdle. The winner has been rated as recording a small personal best, and the third rated to his recent debut for this yard.

NOTEBOOK

Karky Schultz(GER) built on his recent third at Kempton to run out a brave winner, rallying once headed in the run-in. He showed a willing attitude off this 1lb higher mark and looks likely to progress again. (tchd 12-1)

Via Galilei(IRE) disappointed on his last start, but returned to form to just be denied. He travelled like the winner, but couldn't quite hold on. This was an improved effort on his third handicap start, and there may be more to come. (op 17-2)

Tenor Nivernais(FR) travelled strongly and had every chance, but couldn't quicken with the first two. Twice a winner in France, he should continue to be competitive in this sort of race, with a stiffer test likely to suit. (op 11-4)

Simply Blue has been edging down the handicap and ran his race, but finished a distant fourth. He may need to drop a few pounds more. (tchd 28-1)

Henry King(IRE) made the early running, but faded once coming under pressure down the back straight. (op 8-1)

Sir Frank(IRE), making his handicap debut on this first start for connections, is likely to appreciate better ground. (op 12-1)

My Shamwari(IRE) was well backed in the market but could never get on terms. (op 17-2)

Teshali(IRE), weak in the market, was disappointing on his handicap debut. (op 15-2)

3875 READ PAUL NICHOLLS EXCLUSIVELY ON BETFAIR H'CAP CHASE (12 fncs) 2m 110y

4:20 (4:20) (Class 5) (0-95,86) 5-Y-0+ **£2,740** (£798; £399)

Form RPR

6142 **1** **Guns Of Love (IRE)**[18] 3544 9-11-6 **80** CharliePoste 91+
(Robin Dickin) *mde all: styd on wl fr 3 out: rdn out* **5/2**[1]

30P4 **2** *5* **Mujamead**[14] 3618 7-11-4 **83** (p) LeeEdwards(5) 90+
(Sally-Anne Wheelwright) *trckd ldrs: rdn whn lost pl and stmbld bdly 4 out: styd on again fr 2 out: wnt 2nd at the last: readily hld by wnr* **11/2**[3]

P424 **3** *1 ¾* **Rince Donn (IRE)**[26] 3404 9-11-6 **80** HaddenFrost 83
(Roger Curtis) *trckd ldrs: cl 2nd and rdn whn mstke 3 out: lost 2nd bef last: styd on same pce* **11/2**[3]

2FF0 **4** *nse* **Beauchamp Viking**[8] 3255 7-11-8 **85** (t) JimmyDerham(3) 88
(Simon Burrough) *hld up: hdwy to trck ldrs 8th: sn rdn: styd on same pce fr 3 out* **11/2**[3]

6-43 **5** *2 ¼* **Kirbys Glen (IRE)**[18] 3544 9-11-3 **82** KeiranBurke(5) 85
(Patrick Rodford) *trckd wnr: pckd 3rd: pushed along after 7th: rdn after 4 out: lost 2nd bef next: styd on same pce* **3/1**[2]

0-00 **6** *8* **Betty Browneyes**[22] 3480 6-11-12 **86** (t) PaddyBrennan 83
(Tom George) *trcking ldrs whn blnd 5th: in tch: rdn after 4 out: one pce fr next* **14/1**

6P-P **P** **Suprendre Espere**[9] 3699 11-10-2 **62** (b) RodiGreene —
(Christopher Kellett) *hld up: pushed along after 5th: lost tch fr next: t.o whn p.u bef 3 out* **20/1**

4m 12.6s (2.60) **Going Correction** -0.225s/f (Good) 7 Ran SP% **111.2**

Speed ratings: **84,81,80,80,79 75,—**

toteswingers:1&2 £2.70, 2&3 £4.30, 1&3 £2.5 CSF £15.74 TOTE £4.30: £2.60, £2.10; EX 19.20.

Owner Whoops 72! **Bred** Pat O'Rourke **Trained** Atherstone on Stour, Warwicks

FOCUS

A trappy handicap chase. The winner has recorded a small personal best, with the third in line with his recent form.

NOTEBOOK

Guns Of Love(IRE) led from pillar to post to land a gutsy success. Jumping nicely out in front, he ground his rivals into the ground to continue his recent good form. He has now won three of his last six and should remain of interest despite a rise in the weights. (op 9-4)

Mujamead, a fair fourth at Southwell latest, stayed on strongly for pressure after the last to grab second. He showed a good attitude but may need a drop in the weights. (op 6-1)

Rince Donn(IRE) has struggled to get his head in front and again found a couple to good. He travelled and jumped okay, but a mistake three out ended his chance. (op 5-1)

Beauchamp Viking was under pressure very early on, but kept responding for his jockey to stay on down the straight. A mistake at the second last didn't help his cause and he may appreciate racing over further. (op 13-2 tchd 7-1 and 5-1)

Kirbys Glen(IRE) was disappointing and failed to reverse form with the winner at revised weights. He may be better than this, but remains a maiden. (op 4-1)

Suprendre Espere didn't jump well enough to get involved. (op 22-1 tchd 18-1)

3876 EBF/DBS MARES STANDARD OPEN NATIONAL HUNT FLAT RACE (QUALIFIER) 2m 1f

4:50 (4:50) (Class 5) 4-7-Y-0 **£2,055** (£599; £299)

Form RPR

1 **Kentford Grey Lady** 5-11-2 0 SamThomas 111+
(Emma Lavelle) *hld up towards rr: smooth hdwy fr over 7f out: led 2f out: sn clr: easily* **16/1**

2 *4 ½* **Definite Artist (IRE)** 5-11-2 0 AidanColeman 102
(Venetia Williams) *mid-div: hdwy 1/2-way: rdn to ld briefly jst over 2f out: kpt on: sn no ch w easy wnr* **8/1**[3]

3 *1 ¾* **Pyleigh Lass** 5-10-13 0 IanPopham(3) 100
(Jeremy Scott) *mid-div: rdn whn outpcd 4f out: styd on again fnl 2f: wnt 3rd ins fnl f* **66/1**

25 **4** *2* **Cresswell Bramble**[16] 3590 7-10-9 0 JoshuaMoore(7) 98
(Keith Goldsworthy) *led tl rdn over 2f out: styd on same pce* **14/1**

1 **5** *5* **Wassailing Queen**[90] 2156 5-11-9 0 JoeTizzard 101+
(Colin Tizzard) *prom: rdn 5f out: one pce fnl 3f* **7/4**[1]

40 **6** *¾* **Long Row**[87] 2222 5-11-2 0 TimmyMurphy 92
(Stuart Howe) *hld up towards rr: racd wd: rdn over 3f out: swtchd lft over 2f out: styd on: nvr trbld ldrs* **66/1**

2 **7** *nk* **Bellaboosh (IRE)**[268] 230 5-11-2 0 BarryGeraghty 92
(Nicky Henderson) *trckd ldrs: rdn over 5f out: one pce fnl 3f* **11/4**[2]

1 **8** *½* **Who's Afraid**[48] 2965 4-10-13 0 RobertThornton 88
(Alan King) *trckd ldrs: effrt 3f out: wknd wl over 1f out* **8/1**[3]

9 *6* **Top Rose** 5-11-2 0 CharliePoste 85
(Robin Dickin) *hld up towards rr: rdn and hdwy over 6f out: wknd over 2f out* **66/1**

10 *2 ¼* **Diamond Smiles** 4-10-6 0 (t) DenisO'Regan 73
(Paul Webber) *mid-div: rdn over 6f out: wknd 2f out* **9/1**

4 **11** *nse* **Astralogical (IRE)**35 3159 6-11-2 0 WayneHutchinson 83
(Alan King) *trckd ldrs: rdn and ev ch 4f out tl 3f out: sn wknd* **40/1**
12 *2* **Our Double Diamond** 6-11-2 0 NickScholfield 81
(Jeremy Scott) *hld up towards rr: midfield 1/2-way: rdn over 3f out: wknd over 2f out* **66/1**
13 *83* **Luccombe Rose** 6-10-11 0 DavidBass(5) —
(Lawney Hill) *trckd ldrs tl 1/2-way: t.o fnl 5f* **20/1**

4m 3.80s (1.40) **Going Correction** -0.225s/f (Good)
WFA 4 from 5yo+ 9lb **13** Ran SP% **121.0**
Speed ratings: **87,84,84,83,80 80,80,80,77,76 76,75,36**
toteswingers:1&2 £33.10, 2&3 £114.30, 1&3 £76.20. totesuper7: Win: Not won. Place: Not won. CSF £134.90 TOTE £19.00: £4.80, £3.40, £11.30; EX 114.70.
Owner D I Bare **Bred** D I Bare **Trained** Wildhern, Hants

FOCUS
This mares' bumper was run at a steady gallop and produced an impressive winner. She should go on to rate higher, while the fourth, sixth and seventh set the level.

NOTEBOOK
Kentford Grey Lady travelled powerfully before quickening away from her rivals to land an easy debut success. This well-bred mare showed a nice turn of foot and looks a bright prospect who should stay further once hurdling.
Definite Artist(IRE) ran a fine race on debut, travelling nicely up with the pace. She can build on this experience and go close in similar company. (op 11-1)
Pyleigh Lass ran a big race on her debut, running on really strongly in the last furlong. She will appreciate a step up in trip. (op 100-1)
Cresswell Bramble seemed to run her race and has shown some ability in her three starts without looking like winning. (op 16-1)
Wassailing Queen, successful in a similar contest at Warwick latest, raced keenly and struggled under her penalty. She helps rate the form. (op 9-4)
Bellaboosh(IRE) didn't quicken when asked for her effort and this must rate as a poor run. She may be better than this. (op 9-4 tchd 3-1)
Who's Afraid, winner of a 'junior' fillies' bumper at Newbury, was also disappointing, just staying on at the one pace. (op 13-2 tchd 9-1)
T/Jkpt: Not won. T/Plt: £69.80 to a £1 stake. Pool of £100,573.61 - 1,051.68 winning tickets. T/Qpdt: £14.30 to a £1 stake. Pool of £7,044.37 - 364.42 winning tickets. TM

3718 LEICESTER (R-H)
Wednesday, February 2

OFFICIAL GOING: Hurdle course - heavy (soft in places; 7.9). chase course - good (soft on the flat course crossings; 6.6)
Wind: Moderate, across Weather: Overcast

3877 EUROPEAN BREEDERS' FUND "NATIONAL HUNT" NOVICES' HURDLE QUALIFIER (10 hdls) 2m 4f 110y
2:00 (2:00) (Class 4) 4-7-Y-0 **£3,903** (£1,146; £573; £286)

Form RPR
-431 **1** **Mic's Delight (IRE)**32 3299 7-11-8 122 DenisO'Regan 134+
(Victor Dartnall) *w ldr: led 4 out: nt fluent 3 out: rdn after 2 out: hit last: sn hdd: drvn and kpt on wl to ld again nr fin* **9/4**1
11F **2** *½* **Global Power (IRE)**31 3340 5-11-8 0 LeightonAspell 132+
(Oliver Sherwood) *hld up in midfield: hdwy after 6th: hit 3 out: rdn to chse wnr bef next: led narrowly after last: kpt on but hdd nr fin* **9/2**
5F1F **3** *10* **Grafite**34 3229 6-11-5 122 MrCGreene(7) 125
(Milton Harris) *hld up: hdwy bef 4 out: chsd ldrs 3 out: rdn to go 3rd 2 out: kpt on but no threat to ldng pair* **16/1**
44-2 **4** *1½* **Bless The Wings (IRE)**81 2375 6-11-2 0 RobertThornton 115
(Alan King) *hld up in midfield: trckd ldrs on outer 4 out: rdn 3 out: sn one pce: hld whn hit last* **9/1**
5 **5** *4½* **Barbatos (FR)**32 3288 5-11-2 0 DougieCostello 110
(Ian Williams) *led narrowly: hdd 4 out: sn rdn: wknd after 3 out* **4/1**3
-103 **6** *30* **Safran De Cotte (FR)**18 3567 5-11-8 120 RichardJohnson 95
(Henry Daly) *hld up: racd keenly: hdwy bef 6th: trckd ldrs 4 out: rdn and wknd qckly after 3 out* **7/2**2
21F **7** *21* **Time For Spring (IRE)**31 3346 7-11-12 122 FelixDeGiles 88
(Charlie Longsdon) *trckd ldrs on inner: wknd qckly after 3 out* **14/1**
8 *12* **The Musical Guy (IRE)** 5-11-2 0 PaddyBrennan 66
(Nigel Twiston-Davies) *trckd ldr: racd keenly: nt fluent 2nd and 6th: hit 4 out: wknd qckly after 3 out* **66/1**
0-00 **9** *20* **Rivermouth**18 3572 6-11-2 0 WayneHutchinson 26
(Alan King) *hld up: reminders after 4th: lost tch after 5th: t.o* **150/1**
000 **10** *32* **Haydens Mount**75 2499 6-11-2 0 HaddenFrost —
(James Frost) *trckd ldrs on outer: nt fluent 5th: wknd after next: t.o* **250/1**
0P-0 **P** **Newgatehopeful**237 693 7-10-9 0 (t) MrJohnWilley(7) —
(Mark Campion) *midfield: wknd after 6th: t.o whn p.u bef 2 out* **250/1**
P **Speakers Corner** 5-11-2 0 PaulMoloney —
(Barney Curley) *nt fluent: hld up: rdn after 4th: sn bhd: t.o whn p.u bef 3 out* **66/1**

5m 25.9s (1.20) **Going Correction** +0.075s/f (Yiel) **12** Ran SP% **118.2**
Speed ratings: **100,99,96,95,93 82,74,69,62,49** —,—
toteswingers: 1&2 £3.10, 1&3 £12.90, 2&3 £9.60 CSF £12.98 TOTE £4.30: £1.80, £2.60, £5.60; EX 17.00.
Owner The Higos Hopefuls **Bred** Mrs Anne Caplice **Trained** Brayford, Devon

FOCUS
A good novice event with five penalised runners. They went an average sort of gallop and there were plenty of chances turning for home, but the first pair came well clear from two out. It looked hard work

NOTEBOOK
Mic's Delight(IRE) followed up his Exeter success on New Year's Day with another gutsy effort on this return to novice company, and provided another winner for his in-form trainer/rider combination. The ground was no trouble to him and he showed a great attitude when it mattered, again looking a real stayer in the making. A switch to fences will no doubt bring out the best of him next season, but connections will now aim him at the final of this series at Sandown next month. (op 11-4)
Global Power(IRE) was creeping into the race prior to falling in his quest to extend his unbeaten sequence to four at Folkestone last time, and he very nearly resumed winning ways here. He too clearly stays very well and deserves to get his head back in front. (op 7-2)
Grafite got going late on after being set a fair bit to do on this return from handicap company. He was held from two out, but was in turn clear of the remainder in third and rates a fair benchmark. (op 12-1)
Bless The Wings(IRE), second on his hurdling debut 81 days earlier, travelled nicely into contention but tired out of it after the penultimate flight. He should get off the mark when reverting to better ground. (tchd 8-1)
Barbatos(FR) looked to do plenty through the early stages in a share of the lead and that cost him in the home straight. He has the scope to rate a fair bit higher once tackling fences. (op 5-1 tchd 11-2)
Safran De Cotte(FR) proved disappointing on this drop in class. He looked a big player four out, but didn't help his rider under pressure and now has something to prove. (op 9-2 tchd 5-1)
Time For Spring(IRE) lacked an extra gear when it mattered, but this should help restore his confidence and handicaps probably now beckon for him. (op 16-1)

3878 THRUSSINGTON H'CAP CHASE (15 fncs) 2m 4f 110y
2:30 (2:30) (Class 4) (0-110,110) 5-Y-0+ **£2,602** (£764; £382; £190)

Form RPR
5U55 **1** **Island Jim (IRE)**26 3433 7-11-2 100 (t) AndrewTinkler 108
(Charlie Longsdon) *trckd ldrs: w ldrs after 5th: led 9th: hdd narrowly 4 out: led again last: drvn out* **13/2**3
1F40 **2** *2¾* **High Jack (IRE)**30 3371 9-11-8 106 NickScholfield 112
(Andy Turnell) *led 2nd tl 4th: remained prom: ev ch fr 4 out: kpt on run-in* **11/1**
-11P **3** *1¼* **Irish Guard**30 3371 10-11-9 107 AndrewThornton 114+
(John O'Neill) *racd on outer: led 4th tl 9th: led again 4 out: hdd whn nt fluent last: one pce run-in* **8/1**
4P36 **4** *1¾* **Phoenix Des Mottes (FR)**10 3695 8-9-8 85 JoeCornwall(7) 89
(John Cornwall) *hld up towards rr: hdwy appr 4 out: kpt on: nrst fin* **14/1**
0005 **5** *1½* **Mokum (FR)**10 3695 10-10-10 94 WayneHutchinson 96
(Tony Carroll) *in tch: reminders after 8th: outpcd after 11th: kpt on again after 4 out* **6/1**2
-F45 **6** *11* **Don't Tell Nina (IRE)**28 3395 7-11-4 102 DominicElsworth 94
(Paul Webber) *midfield: nt fluent 6th: j.rt 10th: lost pl 11th: a struggling after* **6/1**2
053P **7** *3½* **Magnetic Pole**49 2952 10-10-13 102 (v) GilesHawkins(5) 91
(Richard Lee) *hld up in midfield: nt fluent 8th and 9th: nvr in contention* **12/1**
-243 **8** *6* **Vic's World (IRE)**15 3612 9-10-9 93 HaddenFrost 80
(James Frost) *midfield: rdn whn nt fluent 2 out: wknd bef last* **8/1**
-045 **P** **Whatever Next (IRE)**15 3615 9-11-3 101 AidanColeman —
(Edward Creighton) *led tl 2nd: blnd 4th: wknd after 10th: t.o whn p.u bef 2 out* **17/2**
5102 **P** **Near The Water (IRE)**30 3375 7-11-12 110 LeightonAspell —
(Richard Rowe) *hld up: a bhd: t.o whn p.u bef 4 out* **5/1**1

5m 18.0s (-0.90) **Going Correction** +0.075s/f (Yiel) **10** Ran SP% **114.0**
Speed ratings: **104,102,102,101,101 97,95,93**,—,—
toteswingers: 1&2 £10.50, 1&3 £13.80, 2&3 £13.90 CSF £72.15 CT £577.98 TOTE £11.00: £2.40, £3.00, £1.70; EX 90.10.
Owner D Adam M Coates G Swire Mrs S Mounsey **Bred** Joe Colfer **Trained** Over Norton, Oxon

FOCUS
A moderate handicap where it paid to race handily.

NOTEBOOK
Island Jim(IRE) shed his maiden tag with a gutsy effort. He pulled his way to the front early on and looked vulnerable three out, but kept on most gamely thereafter. The better ground here has to go down as having had the desired effect. Official explanation: trainer said, regarding the apparent improvement in form, that the gelding had benefited from wearing a tongue strap for only the second time, and had appreciated today's better ground. He also stated that last time out when wearing a tongue strap for the first time, he had not got home in the heavy ground (op 15-2 tchd 8-1)
High Jack(IRE) was always up there and, despite hitting three out, went down fighting. This was a definite return to form back on more suitable ground.
Irish Guard was pulled up last time, but that was when bidding for a hat-trick. He was kept wide throughout and appeared the most likely winner when asked to win the race. An error at the last cost him momentum, though, and he was held thereafter. He helps to set the level. (tchd 15-2)
Phoenix Des Mottes(FR) was never seriously on terms, but did by far the best of those coming from off the pace, and posted one of his better efforts. A return to further should suit, but consistency isn't his strong point. (op 18-1)
Mokum(FR) went in snatches from a fairly early stage and proved hard work for his rider. (op 7-1)
Near The Water(IRE) got behind early on and evidently wasn't on a going day. Official explanation: jockey said that the gelding was never travelling (op 11-2)

3879 BURTON LAZARS NOVICES' CLAIMING HURDLE (8 hdls) 2m
3:00 (3:00) (Class 5) 4-Y-0+ **£1,951** (£573; £286; £143)

Form RPR
2331 **1** **Lady Willa (IRE)**15 3613 4-9-11 115 TommyPhelan(3) 105+
(Mark Gillard) *led tl 2nd: trckd ldr: led 4 out: rdn clr appr 2 out: eased fnl 100yds* **11/8**1
6 **2** *25* **Starburst**23 3477 6-10-10 0 JimmyMcCarthy 80
(Brendan Powell) *trckd ldrs: rdn after 4 out and sn wknd: wnt remote 2nd run-in* **12/1**
5 **3** *3½* **Royal Holiday (IRE)**9 3711 4-10-7 0 FearghalDavis 74
(Brian Ellison) *hld up: racd keenly: rdn after 4 out: sn wknd: wnt poor 3rd run-in* **6/1**3
4 **4** *2¾* **Golden Prospect**79 2426 7-11-9 0 JamesDavies 94+
(Paul Fitzsimons) *hld up: racd keenly: hdwy to trck ldrs 4 out: wnt 2nd appr 3 out: nt fluent 3 out: sn rdn: wknd after 2 out: blnd last: lost 2 pls run-in* **9/1**
0F/ **5** *4½* **Jenny Soba**64 56 8-10-13 0 DaveCrosse 72
(Lucinda Featherstone) *hld up: reminder after 3rd: rdn after 4 out: sn wknd* **16/1**
006B **6** *14* **Stir On The Sea (IRE)**69 2633 5-10-10 92 HaddenFrost 62
(James Frost) *hld up: rdn and wknd after 4 out* **8/1**
2 **P** **Rash Call (IRE)**112 1819 7-11-6 0 PaulMoloney —
(Evan Williams) *racd keenly on outer: led 2nd: clr 3rd tl 4th: hdd 4 out: stopped qckly and p.u and dismntd bef next* **7/2**2

4m 6.30s (5.30) **Going Correction** +0.075s/f (Yiel)
WFA 4 from 5yo+ 9lb **7** Ran SP% **113.3**
Speed ratings (Par 103): **89,76,74,73,71 64**,—
toteswingers: 1&2 £3.60, 1&3 £2.80, 2&3 £9.00 CSF £18.52 TOTE £2.10: £1.10, £5.60; EX 12.40.The winner was subject to a friendly claim.
Owner T J C Seegar **Bred** Simon Keswick **Trained** Holwell, Dorset

FOCUS
A weak novice claimer and a very easy winner.

NOTEBOOK
Lady Willa(IRE) followed up her maiden win at Folkestone with an easy success on this drop in grade. She was the clear pick at the weights and with her main rival failing to complete, she was left with a simple task in the home straight. She ought to be full of confidence after this. (op 13-8 tchd 5-4)
Starburst, well beaten in a better claimer on her hurdling debut, plugged on for a remote second and will be better served by quicker ground in due course. (op 16-1)
Royal Holiday(IRE) didn't appear the most willing on his hurdling debut at Wetherby nine days earlier, and failed to raise his game for the drop in grade. (op 9-1)
Golden Prospect was the only danger to the winner in the home straight, but he again pulled too hard early on and ultimately paid the price. (op 7-1)

Rash Call(IRE) looked a big player down to this class after an encouraging debut second in October, but his absence since and being uneasy in the betting was cause for alarm. After pulling his way into a clear lead he had come back to the field, but was still in with a chance prior to going wrong on the home turn. (op 9-4 tchd 4-1)

3880 SILVER BELL MAIDEN CHASE (18 fncs) 2m 7f 110y
3:30 (3:30) (Class 5) 5-Y-0+ £2,602 (£764; £382; £190)

Form				RPR
4-P2	1		**Tafika**[29] 3391 7-11-0 110 DominicElsworth (Paul Webber) *w ldr on outer: led 11th: pushed clr run-in: comf* **4/6**[1]	120+
F-P0	2	9	**No Tears (IRE)**[21] 3505 8-11-0 93 RobertThornton (Alan King) *led narrowly: hit 2nd: hdd 11th: remained cl 2nd: rdn after 2 out: hit last: no match wnr run-in* **8/1**[3]	106+
400P	3	9	**Woodmore (IRE)**[32] 3299 7-11-0 106 (p) AndrewTinkler (Charlie Longsdon) *trckd ldrs: rdn after 3 out: sn one pce* **5/1**[2]	96
0P	4	18	**Bohemian Rock**[90] 2172 7-11-0 92 (t) AndrewThornton (Caroline Bailey) *hld up: mstke 1st: n.m.r next: brief hdwy 4 out: wknd after 3 out* **33/1**	83
	5	20	**Forever Man (IRE)**[98] 2042 8-11-0 0 (t) JohnnyFarrelly (Paul W Flynn, Ire) *trckd ldrs: mstke 11th: wknd after 4 out* **10/1**	65
-P63	F		**Jolly Boys Outing (IRE)**[10] 3702 8-10-7 0 MrBJPoste(7) (Rosemary Gasson) *hld up: j.rt 3rd and 11th: nt fluent 5 out: 6th whn n.m.r and fell sn after 4 out* **16/1**	—
0U-U	U		**Theballyedmondchap (IRE)**[17] 3586 7-10-11 0 WayneKavanagh(3) (Evan Williams) *in tch whn blnd and uns rdr 5th* **28/1**	—

6m 2.20s (-1.80) **Going Correction** +0.075s/f (Yiel) **7 Ran SP% 109.1**
Speed ratings: **106,103,100,94,87** —,—
toteswingers: 1&2 £2.80, 1&3 £1.70, 2&3 £2.10 CSF £6.16 TOTE £2.00: £1.30, £2.20; EX 4.60.
Owner The Tafika Partnership **Bred** Mrs J Webber **Trained** Mollington, Oxon

FOCUS
A weak maiden chase.

NOTEBOOK
Tafika showed his true colours when second to subsequent winner Three Chords in a novice handicap over C&D last month, and had an excellent chance to get off the mark if able to reproduce that effort. He took some time to master the runner-up, but looks an out-and-out galloper. He was easily on top at the finish and it's not hard to see why he holds an entry in the National Hunt Chase over 4m at the Cheltenham Festival. Trainer Paul Webber was later of the opinion he will probably skip that, though, and hopes he might win a big staying chase in time. (op 4-7)
No Tears(IRE) had previously disappointed for his leading connections, but did win a point before joining them and this debut over regulation fences duly brought about a more encouraging display. He should fare better as he gains experience as he still looks somewhat headstrong. (op 9-1)
Woodmore(IRE) was well backed in first-time cheekpieces despite having failed to convince on his previous outing over fences, but it was clear some way out that he going to be beaten. (op 7-1)
Bohemian Rock never threatened, but should benefit for this added experience.
Forever Man(IRE) was still going with plenty of enthusiasm prior to nearly coming down at the sixth-last fence. That cost him any chance, but this is a run he can build on. (op 8-1)

3881 GOLDEN MILLER H'CAP HURDLE (10 hdls) 2m 4f 110y
4:00 (4:00) (Class 3) (0-120,121) 4-Y-0+ £3,903 (£1,146; £573; £286)

Form				RPR
-424	1		**Daring Origyn (FR)**[23] 3490 6-11-8 115 (t) RobertThornton (Richard Lee) *hld up on outer: hdwy 4 out: rdn after 3 out: chsd ldrs last: drvn and styd on strly to ld towards fin* **8/1**[3]	123
300	2	2	**Valento**[11] 3688 6-11-8 115 SeanQuinlan (Kim Bailey) *midfield on outer: hdwy after 4 out: rdn and ev ch 2 out: led last: kpt on but hdd towards fin* **33/1**	121
0-00	3	3 ½	**Manele Bay**[74] 2514 8-11-2 109 AndrewThornton (Richard Rowe) *midfield on outer: gd hdwy on outer appr 4 out: ev ch 3 out: sn rdn: hit last: no ex run-in* **16/1**	113+
-U14	4	1	**Educated Evans (IRE)**[70] 2607 6-11-6 113 PaddyBrennan (Nigel Twiston-Davies) *led: mstke 4 out: rdn after 3 out: hdd last: wknd run-in* **25/1**	116+
4321	5	11	**Mannlichen**[3] 3840 5-12-0 121 7ex AidanColeman (Venetia Williams) *in tch on inner: hdwy 4 out: wnt 2nd 3 out: sn rdn and one pce: wknd appr last* **10/11**[1]	114+
3230	6	1 ½	**Devon Native (IRE)**[11] 3688 8-10-13 113 DannyBurton(7) (Chris Down) *trckd ldrs: rdn 3 out: wknd appr 2 out* **20/1**	102
445-	7	½	**Extreme Impact**[285] 5358 5-11-12 119 PaulMoloney (Evan Williams) *trckd ldrs: rdn and wknd after 3 out* **40/1**	107
-002	8	2 ½	**Snake Charmer**[16] 3598 8-11-3 110 (v) DaveCrosse (Milton Harris) *midfield: rdn and wknd after 3 out* **33/1**	96
0041	9	2 ½	**Apache Chant (USA)**[10] 3693 7-9-11 95 LeeEdwards(5) (Tony Carroll) *midfield: rdn appr 3 out: wknd 2 out* **12/1**	78
01-0	10	15	**Beamazed**[49] 2955 7-11-6 113 DenisO'Regan (Malcolm Jefferson) *midfield: hdwy to trck ldrs 4 out: wknd qckly after 3 out: eased* **40/1**	81
520/	11	37	**Rich Lord**[739] 3531 7-11-5 112 LeightonAspell (Ferdy Murphy) *racd keenly: hld up on outer: a towards rr* **50/1**	43
1113	12	36	**Amuse Me**[32] 3306 5-11-8 115 APMcCoy (Jonjo O'Neill) *trckd ldrs: rdn and wknd qckly after 4 out* **9/1**	10
602-	U		**Ostland (GER)**[299] 5119 6-11-4 118 KielanWoods(7) (Charlie Longsdon) *racd keenly in midfield: trckd ldrs 4 out: hdwy to chal appr 2 out: sn rdn: wkng in 5th whn uns rdr last* **6/1**[2]	118
0506	P		**Drussell (IRE)**[32] 3299 5-11-5 112 WarrenMarston (Richard Phillips) *hld up on inner: a towards rr: p.u bef last* **28/1**	—

5m 21.6s (-3.10) **Going Correction** +0.075s/f (Yiel) **14 Ran SP% 126.1**
Speed ratings (Par 107): **108,107,105,105,101 100,100,99,98,92 78,65,**—,—
toteswingers: 1&2 £12.80, 1&3 £15.20, 2&3 £66.90 CSF £245.51 CT £4122.96 TOTE £11.00: £1.90, £10.20, £6.30; EX 273.20.
Owner Gavin Macechern & Lord Daresbury **Bred** Bruno Matt **Trained** Byton, H'fords

FOCUS
This modest handicap looked more competitive than the betting suggested and so it played out. There was an uneven gallop on.

NOTEBOOK
Daring Origyn(FR) hit top gear late in the day to mow down the runner-up and register a first success over hurdles at the eighth attempt. He made smooth headway from off the pace, but looked held in between the final two flights. However, as those in front of him began to wilt, he picked up again and was going away at the finish. He may not be all that straightforward, but more positive handling over this trip could see him improve further now he has got his head in front. (op 9-1)
Valento ◆ ran a big race on ground almost certainly too taxing for his liking. He looked held by the handicapper coming into this, but it was by some way his best run since winning last summer, and reverting to a sounder surface should see him defying this sort of mark.
Manele Bay was another to come from off the pace and turned in a much-improved effort in defeat. She handles this ground well, but really looked to find the trip too demanding.
Educated Evans(IRE) set out to make all and posted a gutsy effort, despite not always being fluent. He can win one of these back up in trip, but chasing will ultimately be his game. (tchd 28-1)
Mannlichen was the clear pick here from a handicapping point of view under his penalty after bolting up at Hereford. That came just three days earlier on similarly bad ground, however, and clearly the run came too soon for him. (op 11-10 tchd 6-5 and 5-4 in places)
Amuse Me dropped out tamely from four out and, while he is happier on better ground, now has something to prove. Official explanation: jockey said that the gelding was unsuited by the heavy, soft in places ground (op 8-1)
Ostland(GER) attracted support on his belated seasonal debut and looked a big threat in the home straight. He refused to settle through the race, though, and paid the price prior to unseating at the last. (op 15-2)

3882 COALVILLE H'CAP HURDLE (8 hdls) 2m
4:30 (4:31) (Class 5) (0-95,95) 4-Y-0+ £1,951 (£573; £286; £143)

Form				RPR
0642	1		**Mayolynn (USA)**[18] 3563 5-11-12 95 AndrewThornton (Caroline Bailey) *hld up on outer: hit 4th: hdwy 4 out: 3rd whn stmbld on landing 3 out: nt fluent 2 out: styd on to ld last: sn clr* **4/1**[1]	108+
-030	2	8	**Easton Clump**[25] 3448 8-11-12 95 MarkGrant (Dominic Ffrench Davis) *trckd ldr: led after 4 out: mstke whn hdd 3 out: mstke 2 out: 3rd whn nt fluent last: wnt 2nd run-in* **8/1**	98+
3-30	3	1 ¼	**Imperial Royale (IRE)**[33] 3255 10-10-1 75 LeeEdwards(5) (Patrick Clinton) *rel to r and reminders early: prom after 2nd: led bef 4 out: sn hdd: led again 3 out: edgd rt 2 out: hdd last: wknd and lost 2nd run-in* **4/1**[1]	77
366	4	22	**Mut'Ab (USA)**[30] 3376 6-11-9 92 (b) JamieMoore (Gary Moore) *hld up in rr: hdwy appr 4 out: wnt 4th 3 out: rdn and wknd after 2 out* **15/2**[3]	70
-00P	5	23	**Pezula**[15] 3622 5-10-0 69 oh5 (b[1]) TomSiddall (Richard Phillips) *hld up: a towards rr* **20/1**	24
P50-	6	7	**Colinette**[298] 5133 8-10-0 69 oh7 CharliePoste (Robin Dickin) *hld up: a bhd* **6/1**[2]	17
0060	7	6	**Mauritino (GER)**[33] 3261 7-11-11 94 (t) APMcCoy (Jonjo O'Neill) *led: hdd bef 4 out: wknd appr 3 out* **6/1**[2]	36
P0P0	8	36	**Aboukir Bay (IRE)**[10] 3697 7-9-8 70 (bt) JoeCornwall(7) (John Cornwall) *chsd ldrs: rdn appr 4 out: wknd bef next: t.o* **28/1**	—
0-00	9	21	**Mandalay Prince**[22] 3491 7-10-10 79 TimmyMurphy (Willie Musson) *hld up: a in rr* **16/1**	—
0065	10	17	**Me Fein**[18] 3563 7-11-2 85 PaulMoloney (Barney Curley) *in tch: wknd after 4th: sn bhd: t.o* **16/1**	—
000/	P		**Young Valentino**[1223] 1525 9-9-7 69 oh10 MrTGarner(7) (Michael Appleby) *in tch: wknd qckly after 4th: t.o whn p.u bef 3 out* **33/1**	—

4m 1.40s (0.40) **Going Correction** +0.075s/f (Yiel) **11 Ran SP% 114.4**
Speed ratings (Par 103): **102,98,97,86,74 71,68,50,39,31** —
toteswingers: 1&2 £3.60, 1&3 £4.30, 2&3 £6.00 CSF £34.20 CT £135.09 TOTE £2.90: £1.10, £2.60, £2.20; EX 34.50.
Owner Mr & Mrs R Scott **Bred** Anlyn Farms **Trained** Brixworth, Northants
■ Stewards' Enquiry : Mark Grant four-day ban: disobeyed starter (16, 17, 18, 20 Feb)

FOCUS
A weak handicap.

NOTEBOOK
Mayolynn(USA) went one better than her well-held second at Warwick 18 days earlier with a ready effort off the same mark. She nearly fell after a bad mistake on the far side and wasn't great on that front in the home straight. However, as the placed horses began to tire she found her stride and was a clear-cut winner. This was a personal-best effort, but she couldn't be put up as one that will win again off a higher mark. (op 10-3 tchd 3-1)
Easton Clump looked one of the more likely winners on this switch to a handicap, but proved very easy to back. Positively ridden, he appeared the one to be on three out, but hit a flat spot on the deep surface when asked for his effort. He kept on again late to grab second and probably needs a slightly stiffer test on better ground to shine. (op 15-2)
Imperial Royale(IRE) was having just his ninth outing since winning over C&D in 2006, but he met strong support. He put in a moody effort right from the start, however, and his rider emerges with top marks for producing him to have every chance. (op 11-2 tchd 7-2)
Mut'Ab(USA) unsurprisingly found the ground against him on his handicap debut as a hurdler. (op 6-1 tchd 11-2)
Mauritino(GER) was another totally unsuited by the going. (op 9-2 tchd 7-1)
T/Plt: £238.30 to a £1 stake. Pool: £77,057.10. 235.98 winning tickets. T/Qpdt: £59.30 to a £1 stake. Pool: £5,890.83. 73.40 winning tickets. AS

3631 NEWCASTLE (L-H)
Wednesday, February 2

OFFICIAL GOING: Soft (good to soft in places; chs 5.8, hdl 5.9)
Common bends the same as last meeting.
Wind: Strong, across Weather: Cloudy

3883 BETFAIR RACING EXCELLENCE CONDITIONAL JOCKEYS' TRAINING SERIES H'CAP HURDLE (13 hdls) 3m
1:20 (1:20) (Class 5) (0-95,95) 4-Y-0+ £1,561 (£458; £229; £114)

Form				RPR
1035	1		**Wor Rom (IRE)**[15] 3621 7-11-4 90 (p) MattGriffiths(3) (Elliott Cooper) *prom on outside: chalng whn hit 8th: led next: drew clr bef 2 out: pushed out* **11/2**[2]	101+
4P4P	2	8	**Charming Knight (IRE)**[122] 1701 10-10-10 84 TrevorWhelan(5) (Jane Walton) *nt fluent early in rr: hdwy u.p 9th: styd on to go 2nd last 50yds: no ch w wnr* **33/1**	85
4/33	3	1 ¾	**Talesofriverbank**[28] 3396 8-10-0 72 ow3 AlexanderVoy(3) (Alistair Whillans) *a cl up: effrt bef 3 out: one pce after next: no imp and lost 2nd last 50yds* **8/1**	72
0-P0	4	4 ½	**Archdale Lady (IRE)**[14] 3635 7-9-11 74 EdmondLinehan(8) (Ferdy Murphy) *hld up: hdwy u.p bef 3 out: no imp bef next* **40/1**	69
00-P	5	1	**Shadow Boxer**[30] 3363 6-10-2 79 CallumWhillans(8) (Donald Whillans) *in tch: rdn bef 3 out: wknd bef next* **25/1**	73
0453	6	8	**Manoubi**[22] 3501 12-10-9 83 JakeGreenall(5) (Martin Todhunter) *cl up: led 8th to next: styd prom tl wknd after 3 out* **15/2**[3]	69
-P00	7	3 ½	**Stagecoach Opal**[50] 2941 10-11-2 95 NathanCook(10) (Sue Smith) *bhd: rdn 8th: nvr able to chal* **9/1**	77
4305	8	2 ¼	**Mrs Eff**[22] 3498 5-11-5 91 AodhaganConlon(3) (Kate Walton) *in tch: effrt bef 3 out: wknd bef next* **11/1**	71
3600	9	6	**Pickworth (IRE)**[20] 3521 6-11-2 91 KyleJames(6) (Philip Kirby) *hld up: stdy hdwy 1/2-way: wknd fr 3 out* **14/1**	67
5503	10	21	**Teenando (IRE)**[14] 3636 11-9-4 69 BenjaminStephens(10) (Sue Smith) *t.k.h in midfield: outpcd 8th: sn struggling* **9/2**[1]	22
000-	11	dist	**Soneva Gili (IRE)**[286] 5333 7-10-3 77 TonyKelly(5) (Shelley Johnstone) *racd wd: hld up: struggling 1/2-way: t.o* **40/1**	—

0505 **P** **Just Dan**16 3603 5-10-0 **69** oh5 (v) BrianToomey —
(David Thompson) *nt fluent in rr: struggling 1/2-way: t.o whn p.u bef 9th* **28/1**

52U- **P** **The Brig At Ayr**282 24 7-9-11 **73** SeveBrumpton(7) —
(John Weymes) *plld hrd: cl up tl lost pl 8th: t.o whn p.u bef 3 out* **12/1**

P-PP **P** **Bombie Boy**31 3336 6-9-7 **69** oh5 (b) StephenMulqueen(7) —
(Brian Storey) *prom: lost pl after 6th: t.o whn p.u 4 out* **80/1**

050P **P** **Rumballina**19 3540 4-9-9 **81** oh1 (b1) GaryRutherford(5) —
(Amy Weaver) *trckd ldrs: lost pl 1/2-way: t.o whn p.u bef 9th* **40/1**

00-5 **U** **Bubbly Breeze (IRE)**22 3502 6-10-13 **87** NathanMoscrop(5) —
(Pauline Robson) *in tch: stdy hdwy gng wl to trck ldrs whn blnd and uns rdr 3 out* **9/1**

000 **P** **Mind Shower (IRE)**21 3506 5-9-11 **69** oh5 RobertKirk(3) —
(Robert Wylie) *t.k.h: led to 8th: wknd next: p.u after 4 out* **18/1**

6m 30.2s (16.20) **Going Correction** +0.625s/f (Soft)
WFA 4 from 5yo+ 11lb 17 Ran SP% **123.2**
Speed ratings (Par 103): **98,95,94,93,92 90,89,88,86,79** —,—,—,—,— —,—
toteswingers: 1&2 £44.20, 1&3 £5.90, 2&3 £46.70 CSF £182.58 CT £1471.43 TOTE £5.80: £1.80, £7.80, £2.20, £11.70; EX 205.90.
Owner Campbell Cooper & Halley **Bred** Jerry Halley **Trained** Brigham, Cumbria
■ Stewards' Enquiry : Kyle James two-day ban: used whip when out of contention (Feb 16-17)

FOCUS
A low grade 69-95 conditional jockeys handicap hurdle run at a sound pace in the conditions, and in the end an emphatic winner

NOTEBOOK
Wor Rom(IRE), who scored twice over this sort of trip in April, had to race from a 10lb higher mark. Kept wide, he travelled strongly and had this in the bag two out. He can turn out without a penalty until Friday week. (op 5-1 tchd 9-2)
Charming Knight(IRE), a winner of four points in the past, was making his hurdling debut on his first start since October. He stayed on to take second spot on the run-in and this should set him up for a return to fences.
Talesofriverbank went in pursuit of the winner but tired on the run-in and may appreciate a slightly easier test. (op 7-1)
Archdale Lady(IRE), down a stone in two outings, has shown little so far but clearly appreciated this searching test of stamina. (op 50-1)
Shadow Boxer, pulled up on his return four weeks earlier, became very leg weary over the last two flights and he may appreciate a drop back in distance. (op 33-1)
Manoubi, back over hurdles, is hard to predict and called it a day three from home. (op 7-1 tchd 8-1 in a place)
Teenando(IRE) has struggled of late. He has slipped to a lenient mark but never threatened to enter the argument. Official explanation: the trainer was unable to offer any explanation for the poor performance shown (op 6-1)
Rumballina Official explanation: trainer said filly lost her right fore shoe (op 10-1)
Bubbly Breeze(IRE), having his second start for this yard, was poised to challenge when he parted company with his rider at the third last. He would have troubled the placed horses but the winner already looked in command (op 10-1)

3884 LA TAXIS H'CAP CHASE (16 fncs) 2m 4f
1:50 (1:50) (Class 5) (0-90,89) 5-Y-O+ **£1,593** (£467; £233; £116)

Form RPR
1010 **1** **Janal (IRE)**14 3631 8-10-7 **77** GaryRutherford(7) 83+
(Stuart Coltherd) *w ldrs: led 4th to 8th: led 4 out: drvn rt out: fin tired* **11/1**

04-3 **2** 1 1/4 **Soul Angel**89 2194 7-11-5 **82** (p) PaddyAspell 86
(Sandy Forster) *in rr: drvn and modest 4th 11th: kpt on fr 4 out: tk 2nd appr last: nt quite rch wnr* **7/1**3

-6FF **3** 9 **Native Coll**14 3636 11-11-6 **83** PeterBuchanan 80
(N W Alexander) *chsd ldrs: wknd 2 out* **9/1**

4P3P **4** 1 1/2 **The Green Hat (IRE)**77 2449 11-10-2 **72** MissGAndrews(7) 71
(Theresa Gibson) *w ldrs: led 8th: blnd and hdd 4 out: 3rd and hld whn blnd 2 out: sn wknd* **8/1**

5261 **5** 25 **Dark Gentleman**14 3636 8-11-2 **82** RyanMania(3) 62
(Evelyn Slack) *mde most to 4th: lost pl after 8th: wknd 11th: sn bhd: t.o 4 out* **3/1**2

0-P3 **P** **Byron Bay**14 3632 9-11-0 **77** (p) KennyJohnson —
(Robert Johnson) *hld up detached in last: t.o 8th: p.u bef 3 out* **40/1**

0PP- **P** **Adare Prince (IRE)**311 4911 10-11-12 **89** JanFaltejsek —
(Peter Salmon) *in rr: t.o 8th: p.u bef 10th* **20/1**

0P44 **P** **Apache Brave (IRE)**9 3712 8-10-0 **63** oh3 (b) RobertWalford —
(Henry Hogarth) *in rr: drvn 7th: sn bhd: t.o 9th: p.u after 12th* **8/1**

4362 **F** **Mighty Magnus (IRE)**14 3636 8-11-10 **87** JamesReveley —
(Martin Todhunter) *hld up towards rr: travelling strly whn fell 8th* **11/4**1

000P **F** **Soldiers Tree (IRE)**19 3548 6-11-0 **77** TomMessenger —
(Sue Bradburne) *in rr: fell 8th* **25/1**

5m 43.2s (16.00) **Going Correction** +0.75s/f (Soft) 10 Ran SP% **115.8**
Speed ratings: **98,97,93,93,83** —,—,—,—,—
toteswingers: 1&2 £8.20, 1&3 £15.70, 2&3 £9.80 CSF £82.84 CT £728.32 TOTE £14.40: £4.00, £1.70, £2.60; EX 110.50.
Owner S Coltherd **Bred** Niall McGrady **Trained** Selkirk, Borders

FOCUS
A low grade handicap chase that proved a real test in the conditions.

NOTEBOOK
Janal(IRE), 6lb higher than her success at Hexham in November, put a poor run behind her. She set sail for home four out, taking a useful lead, and did just enough. (op 9-1)
Soul Angel, who had shown little in two previous tries over fences, stayed on in pursuit of the three leaders. He was closing the gap all the way to the line but was never going to get there in time. (tchd 11-2)
Native Coll, without a win for almost three years, was shaping better until hitting the deck here on his previous start. Upsides four out, he was third and out on his feet jumping the last. (op 8-1)
The Green Hat(IRE) had just been headed when he blundered four out. He repeated the error two fences later and, this long-standing maiden is a very weak finisher. (op 14-1)
Dark Gentleman, 5lb higher than when opening his account over fences here, couldn't dominate and seemed to sulk. He seems incapable of running two races alike. Official explanation: trainer said, regarding the poor performance shown, tthat the race may have come too soon for the gelding having ran 14 days earlier (op 7-2 tchd 4-1 in a place)
Mighty Magnus(IRE) had not been asked a question when crashing out at the halfway mark. (op 3-1)

3885 NORTH SEA LOGISTICS NOVICES' HURDLE (9 hdls) 2m
2:20 (2:20) (Class 4) 4-Y-O+ **£2,016** (£592; £296; £147)

Form RPR
31-1 **1** **Storm Brig**82 2349 6-11-10 0 BrianHarding 129+
(Alistair Whillans) *mde all: nt fluent 5th: hit 2 out: sn pushed clr: readily* **5/4**1

4250 **2** 9 **Bunclody**18 3572 6-10-7 0 SamuelWelton(10) 108
(George Moore) *trckd ldrs: outpcd 4 out: rallied 2 out: chsd (clr) wnr run-in: no imp* **33/1**

50 **3** 1 1/2 **Bollin Felix**21 3506 7-11-3 0 RichieMcGrath 107
(Tim Easterby) *hld up: hdwy bef 3 out: shkn up and styd on fr next: nvr able to chal* **8/1**

505- **4** 3 1/2 **Hobsons Bay (IRE)**297 5138 6-11-3 0 BrianHughes 103
(Howard Johnson) *hld up in tch: stdy hdwy 4 out: effrt and pressed wnr 3 out: no ex after next: lost 2nd run-in* **33/1**

0 **5** 18 **Sweet Sugar (FR)**9 3715 5-10-7 0 TonyKelly(10) 85
(Ferdy Murphy) *hld up: pushed along bef 4 out: nvr able to chal* **50/1**

2 **6** 10 **Shadows Lengthen**20 3521 5-10-10 0 JakeGreenall(7) 75
(Michael Easterby) *cl up: disp ld fr 3rd to bef 3 out: wknd bef next* **7/2**3

00- **7** 18 **Roslin Moss**297 5144 5-10-7 0 CallumWhillans(10) 57
(Donald Whillans) *towards rr: rdn along 1/2-way: sn struggling* **150/1**

-0U0 **8** 3/4 **Aitch Factor**9 3715 5-11-3 0 PhilKinsella 56
(Henry Hogarth) *hld up: rdn bef 4 out: nvr on terms* **200/1**

9 15 **Cool Star (IRE)**115 5-10-10 0 MrJARichardson(7) 41
(David Carr) *nt fluent: hld up: pushed along after 5th: nvr on terms* **80/1**

6- **10** nk **Young Alfie**371 3693 7-11-3 0 JasonMaguire 41
(Keith Reveley) *nt fluent in rr: struggling 1/2-way: nvr on terms* **50/1**

P **P** **Daredevil Dan**20 3521 5-10-10 0 KyleJames(7) —
(Tina Jackson) *midfield: struggling 5th: sn btn: t.o whn p.u bef 3 out* **200/1**

0 **P** **Willowthewizard**73 2553 7-10-10 0 NathanMoscrop(7) —
(Shelley Johnstone) *in tch tl hit and wknd 5th: t.o whn p.u bef 3 out* **200/1**

6/00 **P** **Fairlea Bob (IRE)**73 2553 7-11-3 0 WilsonRenwick —
(Rose Dobbin) *in tch: hit and wknd 5th: t.o whn p.u bef 3 out* **100/1**

P **Nolecce**109 4-10-7 0 PaddyAspell —
(Richard Guest) *bhd: struggling 1/2-way: t.o whn p.u bef 3 out* **66/1**

1 **P** **Music Of The Moor (IRE)**25 3443 4-11-0 0 JamesReveley —
(Tom Tate) *t.k.h: hld up in tch: sddle slipped and hdwy after 2nd: p.u bef next* **3/1**2

U **Falcun**144 4-10-7 0 GrahamLee —
(Micky Hammond) *chsng ldrs whn uns rdr 5th* **50/1**

4m 20.0s (10.00) **Going Correction** +0.625s/f (Soft)
WFA 4 from 5yo+ 9lb 16 Ran SP% **120.4**
Speed ratings (Par 105): **100,95,94,93,84 79,70,69,62,61** —,—,—,—,— —
toteswingers: 1&2 £12.00, 1&3 £3.80, 2&3 £26.10 CSF £50.11 TOTE £2.90: £1.20, £5.20, £2.30; EX 46.70.
Owner W J E Scott & Mrs M A Scott **Bred** Mrs D H Mathias **Trained** Newmill-On-Slitrig, Borders

FOCUS
Plenty of dead wood and Sandown winner Music Of The Moor was soon on the sidelines

NOTEBOOK
Storm Brig saw off his challenger and kept up the gallop in relentless fashion to draw clear despite a mistake two out. He will find things tougher under a double penalty but looks a fine long-term prospect. He may now head for a Grade 2 event at Kelso next month. (op 11-8 tchd 6-4)
Bunclody, who made his hurdling debut over 2m4f, stayed on in good style, after getting outpaced, to secure second spot on the run-in. A return to further should enable him to find a race. (op 100-1)
Bollin Felix was let down by his jumping on his second start, but shaped much better here and stayed on to take third on the run-in. He too will appreciate a return to 2m4f. (tchd 15-2)
Hobsons Bay(IRE) looked a danger after three out but tired between the last two. Hopefully he will come on for this outing his first since April.
Sweet Sugar(FR), who showed form over fences in France, did better than on his first outing here but needs another run to qualify for a handicap mark. (op 66-1)
Shadows Lengthen stopped to nothing after three out and this multiple AW winner doesn't want conditions as testing as he encountered here. (op 4-1)
Music Of The Moor(IRE), dropped in at the start, took a keen hold and his saddle soon slipped. Official explanation: jockey said the geldings saddle slipped (op 5-2)
Falcun, who showed little in three outings on the Flat, was in the process of making a satisfactory hurdling debut when he lost his rider at the halfway mark. (op 5-2)

3886 WEATHERBYS PRINTING NOVICES' H'CAP CHASE (14 fncs 2 omitted) 2m 4f
2:50 (2:50) (Class 4) (0-115,114) 5-Y-O+ **£3,938**

Form RPR
3424 **1** **Lockstown**19 3552 8-11-4 **106** GrahamLee 112
(Ann Hamilton) *trckd ldrs: lft 2nd 7th: outpcd bef 4 out: rallied and 3 l down disputing 3rd whn lft alone next* **7/4**1

0440 **U** **Monsieur Jourdain (IRE)**20 3524 5-11-4 **109** (p) RichieMcGrath —
(Tim Easterby) *in tch: mstkes 8th and 5 out: hdwy to chse ldr bef next: 2 l down and styng on whn bdly hmpd and uns rdr 3 out* **10/1**

02F6 **F** **Baltic Pathfinder (IRE)**18 3574 7-11-0 **107** ShaneByrne(5) —
(Sue Smith) *cl up: led 2nd: fell 7th* **6/1**2

2-20 **F** **Mr Syntax (IRE)**50 2938 7-11-12 **114** BrianHughes —
(Tim Fitzgerald) *led to 2nd: w ldr: lft in ld 7th: 2 l in front and styng on whn fell 3 out* **15/2**3

P401 **B** **Allanard (IRE)**9 3712 7-10-3 **91** 7ex (p) JamesReveley —
(Martin Todhunter) *prom: lft 3rd 7th: chsd wnr after 5 out to bef next: sn rdn: 3 l down disputing 3rd and one pce whn b.d 3 out* **7/4**1

5m 48.8s (21.60) **Going Correction** +0.75s/f (Soft)
WFA 5 from 7yo+ 2lb 5 Ran SP% **107.9**
Speed ratings: **86**,—,—,—,—
TOTE £2.70: £2.90; EX 2.20.
Owner Hedley Walton & Ian Hamilton **Bred** Mrs Brenda Turley **Trained** Great Bavington, Northumbland

FOCUS
A dramatic handicap chase for novices, in which the picture changed completely at the third-last fence.

NOTEBOOK
Lockstown struggled to keep up on the run round to four out but was bang in contention when left alone three out. His one win over hurdles, almost two years ago now, was over 3m and stamina is clearly his forte. (op 11-4 tchd 3-1 in a place)
Monsieur Jourdain(IRE), who lacks size and scope, survived one blunder but was still in contention when unseating his rider. (op 6-5 tchd 15-8)
Baltic Pathfinder(IRE), who prefers better ground, was taking them along when hitting the deck at the halfway mark. (op 6-5 tchd 15-8)
Mr Syntax(IRE) was putting a poor effort at Catterick behind him when crashing out while in command. However, it is impossible to say how he would have fared. (op 6-5 tchd 15-8)

Allanard(IRE) was put up 12lb for his last win but carried just a 7lb penalty here. Given a patient ride, he was bang there seemingly full of running when brought down. His trainer had voiced concerns about how his horse would go in the testing conditions beforehand but he seemed to handle the ground all right. He will obviously have more on his plate when he seeks compensation. (op 6-5 tchd 15-8)

3887 MEYERTIMBER.COM NOVICES' HURDLE (11 hdls) 2m 4f
3:20 (3:21) (Class 4) 5-Y-0+ **£2,016** (£592; £296; £147)

Form RPR

223 **1** **Railway Dillon (IRE)**[20] 3528 6-10-12 109 JasonMaguire 119+
(Donald McCain) *trckd ldrs: led 4 out: rdn bef 2 out: 3l clr last: hung lft and idled run-in: drvn out nr fin* **11/4**[1]

222 **2** ½ **Fourjacks**[21] 3511 6-10-12 0 GrahamLee 117+
(Tim Easterby) *t.k.h: hld up: smooth hdwy and ev ch 4 out: rdn after next: 3 l down last: renewed chal run-in: jst hld* **3/1**[2]

60 **3** 22 **Tinseltown**[9] 3715 5-10-12 0 PaddyAspell 94
(Brian Rothwell) *hld up: hdwy bef 4 out: plugged on fr 2 out: no ch w first two* **40/1**

10-3 **4** 4 **Seren Rouge**[94] 2102 6-10-12 0 JamesReveley 90
(Keith Reveley) *hld up in midfield: stdy hdwy to trck ldrs 4 out: rdn and outpcd next: no imp fnl 2* **11/4**[1]

0/0- **5** ½ **Katapult (GER)**[641] 120 8-10-12 0 RichieMcGrath 90
(Kate Walton) *midfield: hdwy and prom 4 out: rdn and no ex fr next* **16/1**

6-5 **6** 2½ **Comeththehour (IRE)**[73] 2552 8-10-9 0 RyanMania(3) 87
(James Moffatt) *prom: drvn after 4 out: wknd next* **33/1**

00 **7** 1 **North Brook (IRE)**[28] 3399 6-10-9 0 EwanWhillans(3) 86
(Alistair Whillans) *cl up: led 6th to 4 out: rdn and wknd bef next* **100/1**

53 **8** 39 **Brave Spartacus (IRE)**[20] 3525 5-10-12 0 CampbellGillies 47
(Chris Grant) *in tch: drvn and outpcd after 7th: wknd bef 3 out* **16/1**

40 **9** 22 **Danehillsundance (IRE)**[9] 3715 7-10-12 0 (t) BarryKeniry 25
(Philip Kirby) *bhd: pushed along bef 7th: nvr on terms* **100/1**

0005 **10** 6 **Velvet Vic (IRE)**[8] 3725 5-10-12 0 PeterBuchanan 19
(Richard Guest) *bhd: struggling 7th: nvr on terms* **100/1**

0P **11** dist **Plutonium (IRE)**[20] 3521 5-10-5 0 (p) StevenGagan(7) —
(Elliott Cooper) *sn bhd: early reminders and lost tch fr 4th: continued: t.o* **100/1**

63/ **F** **Stop On**[850] 1591 6-10-12 0 BrianHarding —
(Chris Grant) *in tch: fell 3rd* **40/1**

60F- **P** **Power Flow (IRE)**[280] 42 6-10-12 0 PhilKinsella —
(Peter Atkinson) *a bhd: struggling fr 7th: t.o whn p.u bef 3 out* **100/1**

5-04 **F** **Mannered**[14] 3633 6-10-5 0 MrJohnDawson(7) —
(John Wade) *hld up towards rr: effrt bef 4 out: sn wknd: no ch whn fell next* **8/1**[3]

0- **P** **Djarouda (FR)**[297] 5144 5-10-12 0 BrianHughes —
(Howard Johnson) *in tch untl wknd appr 4 out: t.o whn p.u bef next* **40/1**

P **Why Are You Asking (IRE)**[276] 6-10-12 0 WilsonRenwick —
(Rose Dobbin) *led and sn clr: hdd 6th: wknd next: t.o whn p.u bef 3 out* **40/1**

5m 30.7s (9.60) **Going Correction** +0.625s/f (Soft) **16** Ran SP% **118.9**
Speed ratings: **105,104,96,94,94 93,92,77,68,66** —,—,—,—,—
toteswingers: 1&2 £2.80, 1&3 £22.70, 2&3 £21.80 CSF £10.56 TOTE £4.40: £1.30, £1.20, £9.00; EX 14.00.
Owner Johnson, Maxwell & Purcell **Bred** Miss Laura Duggan **Trained** Cholmondeley, Cheshire
■ Stewards' Enquiry : Jason Maguire caution: careless riding

FOCUS
Plenty of deadwood, but it was run at a strong pace in the conditions, and proved to be a match from three out.

NOTEBOOK
Railway Dillon(IRE) went on four out and to dig deep to repel the determined challenge of the runner-up. He clearly stays well and this tough type will be suited by a step up to 3m. (op 5-2)
Fourjacks, who showed a good level of form when runner-up three times in bumpers, was on the heels of the winner when hitting three out. He really knuckled down thereafter and got almost upsides on the run-in, but at the line he just missed out. He is a sure-fire future winner. (op 11-4 tchd 5-2)
Tinseltown is going the right way and though he finished a distant third, he showed enough to suggest he can pay his way in modest handicap company.
Seren Rouge shaped well and there will be better to come. (tchd 3-1)
Katapult(GER) showed that he retains some ability and hopefully he will build on this return. (tchd 20-1)
Comeththehour(IRE), runner-up four times in Irish maiden points, was having his third start over hurdles and will do better in modest handicaps. (op 40-1)
North Brook(IRE), well beaten in two bumpers, showed a glimmer of ability on his hurdling bow. (tchd 80-1)

3888 WEATHERBYS BLOODSTOCK INSURANCE H'CAP CHASE (18 fncs) 3m
3:50 (3:51) (Class 4) (0-110,110) 5-Y-0+ **£2,602** (£764; £382; £190)

Form RPR

-331 **1** **Star Player (IRE)**[22] 3501 9-11-11 109 (t) PhilKinsella 131+
(Chris Grant) *trckd ldrs: hdwy to ld 6th: styd on strly fr 4 out: drew clr between last 2: eased nr fin* **9/4**[1]

-P22 **2** 22 **Jeringa**[22] 3503 12-10-1 92 (b) MrJohnDawson(7) 89+
(John Wade) *w ldrs: jnd wnr 5th: hit 12th: rdn whn jinked lft and hit rail after 4 out: wknd 2 out: fin tired* **9/2**[2]

25-4 **3** 4½ **Its Teescomponents (IRE)**[22] 3498 9-11-12 110 JamesReveley 102
(Keith Reveley) *led to 6th: dropped bk to modest 3rd 8th: drvn and lost tch appr 4 out: kpt on in own time* **5/1**[3]

1/U- **4** 24 **Skenfrith**[439] 2412 12-10-2 86 (p) PaddyAspell 51
(Sandy Forster) *chsd ldrs to 6th: wnt poor 4th appr 11th: eventually completed* **20/1**

13-P **P** **Panama At Once**[242] 626 11-11-1 99 TomMessenger —
(Philip Kirby) *prom: reminders: mstke and lost pl 11th: sn t.o: p.u bef 11th* **9/1**

F6/5 **P** **Raining Horse (FR)**[30] 3361 9-11-3 104 HarryHaynes(3) —
(James Ewart) *hld up in rr: sme hdwy 10th: wknd and distant 5th whn p.u bef 3 out* **5/1**[3]

P-05 **P** **Sammy Spiderman**[22] 3501 8-10-10 94 (p) BrianHarding —
(Alistair Whillans) *in rr: reminders 10th: sn bhd: t.o whn p.u bef 11th* **6/1**

6m 37.4s (14.90) **Going Correction** +0.75s/f (Soft) **7** Ran SP% **111.3**
Speed ratings: **105,97,96,88**,— —,—
toteswingers: 1&2 £1.90, 1&3 £2.80, 2&3 £3.80 CSF £12.38 CT £42.71 TOTE £3.20: £1.80, £3.10; EX 12.00.
Owner Steve Wilson **Bred** Mrs Hugh Baird **Trained** Newton Bewley, Co Durham

FOCUS
A depleted field and just two in serious contention throughout the final circuit.

NOTEBOOK
Star Player(IRE) was getting the upper hand when the runner-up hit the running rail after four out and was out on his own jumping the final fence. He will go up again after this, but is sure to continue being competitive. (op 5-2)
Jeringa hit five out and looked to have little more to give when jinking left and colliding with the running rail after the next. He was out on his feet two out and may need time to recover from this. (op 11-2)
Its Teescomponents(IRE), a possible for the Eider over 4m here next month, was having her second outing in three weeks after ten months on the sidelines. After jumping off in front she could not match the first two setting out on to the second circuit, and her rider nursed her home over the final half mile. Now 8lb higher than her last success here a year ago, she is better than she has shown on her two starts. (op 7-2)
Skenfrith, having his first race for 15 months, was left well behind on the final circuit. (op 16-1 tchd 22-1)
Raining Horse(FR), whose three wins over fences were all here, didn't improve on his comeback effort and was struggling soon after halfway. He has plenty to prove now. (tchd 9-2)

3889 SENDRIG CONSTRUCTION STANDARD OPEN NATIONAL HUNT FLAT RACE 2m
4:20 (4:20) (Class 6) 4-6-Y-0 **£1,301** (£382; £191; £95)

Form RPR

1 shd **Triptico (FR)** 5-11-4 0 TomO'Brien 114+
(Ronald O'Leary, Ire) *prom: effrt 3f out: chal: carried lft and blkd ins fnl f: kpt on wl: fin 2nd: btn a short hd: awrdd r* **5/1**[3]

1 **2** **Dark Glacier (IRE)**[73] 2553 6-11-11 0 BrianHarding 121+
(Chris Grant) *racd wd: disp ld: led 1/2-way: rdn over 2f out: drifted lft ins fnl f: kpt on wl: disqualified and plcd 2nd* **3/1**[1]

3 10 **Special Catch (IRE)** 4-10-8 0 GrahamLee 94
(Rose Dobbin) *midfield: hdwy to trck ldrs over 5f out: effrt 3f out: kpt on same pce fr 2f out* **8/1**

5 **4** nk **Capital Venture (IRE)**[20] 3525 5-11-1 0 HarryHaynes(3) 104
(James Ewart) *prom: drvn along and outpcd over 3f out: plugged on fr 2f out: no imp* **16/1**

0 **5** 15 **Rojo Vivo**[81] 2368 5-11-4 0 CampbellGillies 89
(Karen McLintock) *led to 1/2-way: cl up: rdn over 5f out: wknd fr 3f out* **16/1**

6 shd **Hyde Place** 4-10-8 0 WilsonRenwick 79
(Michael Dods) *in tch: drvn and outpcd 6f out: n.d after* **50/1**

7 1¾ **Rear Admiral (IRE)** 5-10-11 0 JakeGreenall(7) 92+
(Michael Easterby) *racd wd in midfield: struggling over 3f out: sn btn* **28/1**

5 **8** 9 **Sam D'Oc (FR)**[73] 2553 5-10-11 0 MrColmMcCormack(7) 78
(Keith Reveley) *bhd: outpcd 1/2-way: shortlived effrt over 5f out: nvr on terms* **25/1**

9 20 **In The Tuns (IRE)** 5-11-4 0 RichieMcGrath 58
(Kate Walton) *hld up: drvn over 5f out: sn btn* **9/2**[2]

10 13 **Kings Canyon (IRE)** 5-11-4 0 BrianHughes 45
(Howard Johnson) *cl up tl lost pl over 6f out: n.d after* **11/1**

1 **11** 4 **Opera North**[94] 2108 4-11-1 0 JamesReveley 38
(Tom Tate) *hld up: effrt over 4f out: sn struggling* **8/1**

12 2 **Rupert Bear** 5-10-11 0 MissCWalton(7) 39
(James Walton) *bhd: struggling 1/2-way: sn btn* **200/1**

13 21 **Barseventytwo (IRE)** 6-11-4 0 BarryKeniry 18
(Alan Swinbank) *midfield: struggling after 6f: t.o* **14/1**

14 dist **Big Geordie** 6-10-11 0 CoreyJones(7) —
(Alan Kirtley) *rdr lost irons s: sn rcvrd and hld up: lost tch fr 1/2-way* **100/1**

15 1 **Not Now Later** 5-10-11 0 StephenMulqueen(7) —
(Barry Murtagh) *bhd: lost tch fr 1/2-way* **100/1**

0 **16** 9 **Khalashan (FR)**[210] 935 5-11-4 0 JasonMaguire —
(Peter Niven) *towards rr: struggling over 6f out: virtually p.u fnl 2f* **22/1**

4m 8.90s (4.50) **Going Correction** +0.625s/f (Soft)
WFA 4 from 5yo 9lb 5 from 6yo 1lb **16** Ran SP% **124.9**
Speed ratings: **112,113,107,107,100 100,99,94,84,78 76,75,64**,—,— —
toteswingers: 1&2 £8.70, 1&3 £17.90, 2&3 £12.10 CSF £19.92 TOTE £9.20: £4.30, £1.10, £4.60; EX 35.60.
Owner Mrs Ronald O'Leary **Bred** Olivier Tricot **Trained** Killaloe, Co. Clare
■ Stewards' Enquiry : Brian Harding four-day ban: careless riding (Feb 16-18 & 20)

FOCUS
The first two finished some way clear and they both look decent prospects.

NOTEBOOK
Triptico(FR), from an Irish stable that knows the time of day, moved up on the leader's inside once in line for home. Carried across the track and crowded, he never gave up battling and was rightly awarded the prize. (op 6-1)
Dark Glacier(IRE) ◆ came wide turning for home but his rider persisted in using his whip in his right hand. As a result, Dark Glacier carried his nearest challenger across the width of the course and there was a whisker in it at the post. The Stewards had no option but to reverse the first two. There will be another day for him and he is sure to make an above-average novice hurdler next term. (op 7-2 tchd 4-1)
Special Catch(IRE) made a satisfactory debut but he hung right and was left well behind by the first two in the home straight. (op 10-1 tchd 15-2)
Capital Venture(IRE) stayed on in his own time when it was all over, as he did on his debut, and will need a test of stamina when he goes hurdling.
Rear Admiral(IRE) is bred to make a chaser and may need more time. (tchd 25-1)
In The Tuns(IRE) was major mover on the morning line but he showed little on this racecourse debut. (op 13-2)
Opera North, who took a weak juvenile bumper at Carlisle on his debut, was disappointing, struggling to keep up soon after halfway and eased when behind. (op 6-1)
T/Jkpt: £176.40 to a £1 stake. Pool: £70,382.79. 291.19 winning tickets. T/Plt: £176.40 to a £1 stake. Pool £70,382.79. 291.19 winning tickets. T/Qpdt: £11.10 to a £1 stake. Pool: £6,280.21. 417.28 winning tickets. RY

3890 - 3896a (Foreign Racing) - See Raceform Interactive

3698 TOWCESTER (R-H)
Thursday, February 3

OFFICIAL GOING: Soft (7.6)
Chase course bends dolled out wide and hurdle course on inside line.
Wind: virtually nil Weather: mild with very bright sun

3897 LADBROKES GOT THE FEELING, GET THE APP "NATIONAL HUNT" NOVICES' HURDLE (8 hdls) 2m
1:40 (1:40) (Class 4) 4-Y-0+ **£2,276** (£668; £334; £166)

Form RPR

22/ **1** **Jimmy The Saint (IRE)**[1064] 4304 8-11-3 0 JasonMaguire 118+
(Donald McCain) *pressed ldr: blnd bdly 2nd: led 3rd: jnd 5th tl next: hdd briefly: battled on fr 2 out: all out* **11/2**[2]

423 **2** 2 1/4 **The Chazer (IRE)**[24] 3481 6-10-12 115 GilesHawkins(5) 116+
(Richard Lee) *kpt hanging lft: pressed ldng pair: wnt 2nd at 4th: jnd wnr 5th tl led after 3 out: hdd and outpcd and hit 2 out: drvn and kpt on but hanging bdly lft flat* **4/9**[1]

1004 **3** 19 **Ben Cee Pee M (IRE)**[14] 3645 6-11-3 102 LeightonAspell 98+
(Oliver Sherwood) *midfield: rdn to go 6 l 3rd 3 out: no ch w ldrs: tired and losing grnd fr 2 out* **15/2**

0-00 **4** 3 1/2 **Crackerjac Boy (USA)**[8] 3740 6-11-3 0 WarrenMarston 91
(Richard Phillips) *midfield: reminders 3rd: nvr gng wl after: struggling in rr 5th: plodded on past faders after next* **100/1**

-403 **5** hd **Newton Tonic**[11] 3701 6-11-3 0 FelixDeGiles 91
(Alex Hales) *hld up and keen: outpcd 5th: wl btn after next* **16/1**

00 **6** 10 **North Stack**[20] 3546 5-11-3 0 TomScudamore 81
(Michael Scudamore) *towards rr: effrt 5th: 4th but outpcd bef 3 out: eased bef next* **100/1**

003 **7** 24 **Bit Of A Clown (IRE)**[23] 3491 5-11-3 0 AndrewThornton 57
(Caroline Bailey) *t.k.h in ld: hdd 3rd: lost 2nd next and sn stopped to nil: bdly t.o 3 out* **6/1**[3]

6/P **P** **Wheretheres A Will**[82] 2365 9-11-0 0 CharlieStudd(3) —
(Michael Mullineaux) *chsd ldrs tl tired bdly after 5th: t.o and p.u 2 out* **100/1**

50 **P** **Automaticman (IRE)**[28] 3403 5-11-3 0 AndrewTinkler —
(Henry Daly) *hld up and bhd: struggling after 4th: t.o and p.u 2 out* **50/1**

00- **P** **Winnetka Dancer**[318] 4792 6-11-3 0 RodiGreene —
(David Bridgwater) *bhd: hit 1st: mstke 4th: t.o next: blnd next and p.u* **150/1**

4m 6.60s (-1.30) **Going Correction** +0.10s/f (Yiel) **10** Ran SP% **122.2**
Speed ratings (Par 105): **107,105,96,94,94 89,77,—,—,—**
toteswingers:1&2:£2.10, 1&3:£3.70, 2&3:£2.10 CSF £19.26 TOTE £4.60: £1.60, £1.10, £2.40; EX 12.50.

Owner Jon Glews & Peter Knight **Bred** R McCarthy **Trained** Cholmondeley, Cheshire

FOCUS
A weak novices' hurdle dominated by the two market leaders, and run in a fair time for the grade and ground. A big step up from the winner.

NOTEBOOK
Jimmy The Saint(IRE) defied an absence since March 2008 and outstayed The Chazer after the last for a successful hurdling debut. He survived a serious error at the second and to his credit his jumping improved thereafter. He should appreciate further in time as he's related to useful staying chaser Twelve Paces. His connections reported he could go chasing now. (op 5-1 tchd 9-2)

The Chazer(IRE) was well-backed, had race fitness on his side and set the standard after placing off 112 in a handicap hurdle at Taunton last month, but he was no match for the winner, hanging left on the run-in. The pair pulled clear, though, and he can pick up a novice race. Official explanation: jockey said gelding hung left (op 8-13 after early 4-6 and 8-11 in places)

Ben Cee Pee M(IRE) won a bumper here last year on better ground but looked just as happy in softer conditions. He plugged on up the hill best of the remainder but looks in need of a step up in trip. (tchd 8-1)

Crackerjac Boy(USA) showed his first piece of worthwhile form, shaping more encouragingly on this testing course.

Bit Of A Clown(IRE) proved disappointing after weakening tamely halfway round. Official explanation: jockey said gelding ran flat

Automaticman(IRE) Official explanation: jockey said gelding stopped quickly

3898 LADBROKES ROULETTE CONDITIONAL JOCKEYS' H'CAP CHASE (12 fncs) 2m 110y

2:10 (2:10) (Class 5) (0-95,95) 5-Y-O+ **£1,626** (£477; £238; £119)

Form RPR

30P2 **1** **Karasakal (IRE)**[16] 3612 8-11-4 95 JosephAkehurst(8) 101+
(Gary Moore) *shkn up 3rd: trckd ldrs: rdn bef 2 out: led last: edging clr whn sltly hmpd by loose horse flat: all out* **5/1**[3]

5031 **2** 1 1/4 **Kinkeel (IRE)**[11] 3699 12-10-11 83 7ex LeeEdwards(3) 87
(Tony Carroll) *pressed ldr: pckd 5th: rdn 8th: dropped bk 4th and outpcd after 3 out: kpt plugging on gamely fr next: wnt 2nd flat but nt rch wnr* **5/1**[3]

-5PP **3** 3/4 **Devils River (IRE)**[49] 2986 9-11-11 94 (p) RichieMcLernon 97
(Anna Brooks) *narrow ldr: rdn bef 2 out: hdd last: tiring fnl 100yds* **9/1**

6P5/ **4** 1 1/4 **Ilongue (FR)**[270] 10-9-11 69 oh14 RobertKirk(3) 73
(Laura Hurley) *in rr but wl in tch: sltly hmpd 4th: nt fluent 5th and 7th: rdn bef 9th: kpt on wout looking a real threat fr 2 out* **28/1**

4243 **5** 11 **Rince Donn (IRE)**[2] 3875 9-10-11 80 DavidBass 72
(Roger Curtis) *wnt 2nd and j. slowly 7th: slow again next: ev ch 3 out: rdn and fdd tamely next* **9/2**[2]

/001 **U** **Molly Round (IRE)**[11] 3703 7-10-2 71 DonalDevereux —
(Grant Cann) *jnd ldr and blnd and uns rdr 4th* **11/10**[1]

4m 29.0s (12.90) **Going Correction** +0.325s/f (Yiel) **6** Ran SP% **112.6**
Speed ratings: **82,81,81,80,75** —
toteswingers:1&2:£2.70, 1&3:£5.30, 2&3:£3.20 CSF £29.13 TOTE £6.60: £4.00, £4.20; EX 14.00.

Owner G L Moore **Bred** His Highness The Aga Khan's Studs S C **Trained** Lower Beeding, W Sussex

■ Stewards' Enquiry : Joseph Akehurst three-day ban: used whip with excessive frequency without giving gelding time to respond (Feb 17,18,20)

FOCUS
An interesting handicap chase featuring four previous course winners. The race was run at a decent gallop but the complexion changed after the favourite departed at the fourth. A chase personal best from the winner.

NOTEBOOK
Karasakal(IRE) built on his recent second over fences at Folkestone with a likeable display. He has been awkward to win with in the past but a loose horse who threatened to seriously hamper him on the run-in actually seemed to help him, as he was possibly idling in front. He could be competitive under a similarly patient ride off a higher mark. (op 9-2)

Kinkeel(IRE), effectively a stone higher than for his recent C&D success, was outpaced a fair way out but rallied well under pressure to grab second. He continues to be competitive over fences and is a credit to connections.

Devils River(IRE) appreciated dictating matters, and still held every chance at the last. If he's allowed a soft lead here under similar conditions he can register a third course win. (op 8-1)

Ilongue(FR) was 14lb out of the handicap so this was encouraging. She rallied well after coming under pressure over the final two fences. This was her seasonal reappearance and she could well come on for it. (op 22-1 tchd 33-1)

Rince Donn(IRE) has been consistent over fences but his better runs have come on flat tracks and he didn't seem to appreciate the stiff finish. (op 8-1)

Molly Round(IRE) unseated relatively early on her chasing debut here, and looked unlucky to do so as she just stumbled on landing. She can be given another chance to shine over fences in due course. (op 11-10 after early 11-8, 6-4, 13-8 and 7-4 in places)

3899 LADBROKESPOKER.COM H'CAP HURDLE (8 hdls) 2m

2:40 (2:40) (Class 4) (0-110,103) 4-Y-O+ **£2,276** (£668; £334; £166)

Form RPR

2P0/ **1** **Orang Outan (FR)**[668] 4889 9-10-10 92 DavidBass(5) 92
(Laura Hurley) *racd keenly: wnt 2nd at 3rd: led bef next: rdn and r.o gamely flat* **5/1**

-012 **2** 1 1/4 **Marlborough Sound**[237] 717 12-11-2 93 GrahamLee 93
(James Turner) *settled trcking ldrs: rdn to go 2nd bef 2 out: 2 l down last: plugged on but nvr looked as determined as wnr* **11/4**[1]

F50/ **3** 15 **Andy Gin (FR)**[697] 4373 12-10-6 83 CharliePoste 68
(Evelyn England) *chsd ldrs: blnd 4th: rdn next: outpcd after 3 out: 9 l 3rd whn hit next and fdd* **10/1**

-000 **4** 18 **Red Lancer**[102] 1997 10-11-5 96 FelixDeGiles 64
(Jonathen de Giles) *mounted outside paddock: bhd: rdn 3 out: sn struggling: hit next* **12/1**

52-4 **5** 1/2 **Yossi (IRE)**[7] 1660 7-11-12 103 (b) PaddyAspell 69
(Richard Guest) *led and 8 l clr early: hdd bef 4th: downed tools and last 3 out: mstke next* **4/1**[3]

50-0 **6** 1 3/4 **Gulf Of Aqaba (USA)**[33] 3296 5-11-3 94 DaveCrosse 58
(Ian Williams) *trckd ldrs: drvn after 3 out: fnd nthing: eased and remote whn blnd 2 out* **8/1**

12-4 **7** 18 **Nous Voila (FR)**[70] 2643 10-11-1 92 JimmyMcCarthy 38
(Alan Coogan) *in tch tl 3 out: stopped rapidly and sn t.o* **7/2**[2]

4m 10.7s (2.80) **Going Correction** +0.10s/f (Yiel) **7** Ran SP% **113.4**
Speed ratings (Par 105): **97,96,88,79,79 78,69**
toteswingers:1&2:£5.00, 1&3:£10.40, 2&3:£6.30 CSF £19.26 TOTE £6.30: £3.80, £1.10; EX 28.60.

Owner Mrs R Hurley **Bred** Pierre De Maleissye Melun **Trained** Kineton, Warwicks

■ Laura Hurley's first winner as a licensed trainer.

FOCUS
A modest 0-110 handicap hurdle with the top weight 7lb below the ceiling.

NOTEBOOK
Orang Outan(FR) was another on the card to overcome a lengthy absence (668 days). He had won from a 8lb higher mark over hurdles when last successful (for his previous trainer James Ewart) so was entitled to be competitive here, and he along with Marlborough Sound pulled a long way clear. (op 7-1)

Marlborough Sound is now two from three at the course and, like the winner, had an absence to overcome so this was a pleasing effort. He is a lightly raced gelding who could improve for the outing. (tchd 5-2 and 3-1)

Andy Gin(FR), like the front two, could improve for the run, but he was well beaten into third. (op 12-1)

Red Lancer looks in need of some help from the handicapper at present. (op 10-1 tchd 8-1)

Yossi(IRE), although poaching a useful lead, proved disappointing after being well backed. He downed tools quickly and is one to be wary of. (op 9-2 tchd 6-1)

Gulf Of Aqaba(USA) looks in need of some help from the handicapper at present. (op 7-1)

3900 BET IN PLAY AT LADBROKES H'CAP CHASE (18 fncs) 3m 110y

3:10 (3:10) (Class 4) (0-110,107) 5-Y-O+ **£2,602** (£764; £382; £190)

Form RPR

64-P **1** **Victory Gunner (IRE)**[246] 579 13-11-1 101 GilesHawkins(5) 120+
(Richard Lee) *j.w: led 5th tl 6th and fr 7th: clr w one rival fr 3 out: kpt finding more whn drvn next: wnt rt last: all out* **9/1**

0/21 **2** 2 **Atherstone Hill (IRE)**[11] 3700 9-10-1 85 7ex (v) WayneKavanagh(3) 100
(Robin Dickin) *led tl 5th and 6th tl 7th: pressed wnr after: urged along but no imp fr 2 out where 3 l down: kpt trying* **15/8**[1]

563F **3** 45 **Glebehall Bay (IRE)**[14] 3646 8-11-1 96 AidanColeman 66
(Venetia Williams) *nvr really looked happy: rdn 4th: hit 11th: j. slowly 12th and rdn: dropped out tamely and struggling bef 15th* **11/4**[2]

4P43 **4** 16 **Lavenoak Lad**[14] 3646 11-11-6 101 (t) ColinBolger 55
(Simon Burrough) *nt jump wl: rdn and lost tch 10th: plodded on: t.o whn mstke 2 out* **22/1**

2211 **5** 15 **Hobb's Dream (IRE)**[21] 3527 7-11-4 106 (p) MarkQuinlan(7) 45
(Neil Mulholland) *settled trcking ldrs: effrt 14th: rdn and wknd bef 3 out: t.o next: eased* **15/2**[3]

33-P **P** **Woodlands Genpower (IRE)**[74] 2557 13-10-6 87 (b) PaddyBrennan —
(Peter Pritchard) *dropped to rr after clambering over 2nd: sn tailed himself off and barely scraping over fences: p.u 6th* **14/1**

U-44 **P** **Ayemdee (IRE)**[50] 2953 8-11-6 104 RichieMcLernon(3) —
(Jonjo O'Neill) *sn rdn and nvr gng wl: struggling whn j. slowly 8th: continued t.o tl p.u 3 out* **11/1**

2022 **U** **Ballyegan (IRE)**[24] 3488 6-11-5 107 MrJSherwood(7) —
(Bob Buckler) *racd keenly and cl up: 3rd whn blnd bdly and uns rdr 11th* **8/1**

6m 41.6s (4.70) **Going Correction** +0.325s/f (Yiel) **8** Ran SP% **113.7**
Speed ratings: **105,104,89,84,80** —,—,—
toteswingers:1&2:£6.80, 1&3:£4.50, 2&3:£1.90 CSF £27.22 CT £59.58 TOTE £14.90: £4.70, £1.10, £2.50; EX 47.50.

Owner Ron Bartlett & F J Ayres **Bred** Exors Of The Late J Neville **Trained** Byton, H'fords

FOCUS
A competitive handicap chase which turned into a real war of attrition. The winner is rated back to his 2009 mark.

NOTEBOOK
Victory Gunner(IRE) rolled back the years with a determined front-running success off his lowest mark in a long while. His enthusiasm seems to have been rekindled by the change of stable, and after jumping fluently, he fought off his rivals one by one. Despite running right when tiring at the last, he stayed on strongly to land his tenth career success. Stamina is his forte and he could win again here judged on this first try at the course. (op 8-1 tchd 15-2)

Atherstone Hill(IRE) was well in despite a 7lb penalty for a recent C&D success, and put in a brave performance to be the only threat to the winner at the finish. He is clearly in good heart and laden with stamina but should appreciate better ground, being by Presenting. The front two pulled well clear of the remainder. (op 9-4 tchd 5-2)

Glebehall Bay(IRE), unlucky to fall after jumping well in the main at Taunton, was outpaced on the final circuit and rallied gamely, but ultimately could never live with the front pair. His jumping looked much slicker than previously but like many he was found out by the stiff finish. (op 4-1)

Lavenoak Lad ran his race but usually finds a couple too good, and is always vulnerable to improving staying chasers. (op 18-1 tchd 14-1 and 25-1)

Hobb's Dream(IRE) now could be held by the handicapper after her recent victories. (op 7-1 tchd 9-1)

Woodlands Genpower(IRE) raced without any of his old enthusiasm for the jumping game. (op 12-1 tchd 16-1)

Ayemdee(IRE) never got into contention, racing lazily in rear. (op 12-1 tchd 16-1)

3901 BEST ODDS GUARANTEED AT LADBROKES.COM MARES' MAIDEN HURDLE (10 hdls) 2m 3f 110y

3:40 (3:40) (Class 4) 4-Y-0+ **£1,951** (£573; £286; £143)

Form				RPR
34	1		**Bunglasha Lady (IRE)**[52] 2925 6-11-1 111 JasonMaguire (Warren Greatrex) *settled trcking ldrs: effrt 6th: gng 6 l clr whn wnt bdly lft 2 out: wnt lft last: unchal and eased* **5/4**[1]	115+
45	2	15	**Playful Rose (IRE)**[102] 1993 5-11-1 0 AndrewTinkler (Henry Daly) *trckd ldrs: j. slowly 6th: 6 l 3rd and wkng 3 out: plodded on and tk 16 l 2nd at last: wnr easing after* **12/1**	96
430U	3	1 ¼	**Sapphire Rouge (IRE)**[24] 3480 5-10-12 100 WayneKavanagh(3) (Seamus Mullins) *hld up in rr: wnt 4th but outpcd 3 out: 15 l 4th next: plugged on but no ch* **20/1**	96
552	4	1 ½	**Overnight Fame (IRE)**[24] 3485 7-11-1 106 PaddyBrennan (Tom George) *chsd clr ldr tl clsd to ld after 5th: rdn and hdd 2 out: tiring bdly up hill and lost two pls fr jst bef last* **7/4**[2]	95
00	5	1 ¾	**M'Lady Rousseur (IRE)**[30] 3389 5-11-1 0 TomMessenger (Chris Bealby) *midfield: rdn 5th: struggling whn hit 7th: drvn and plugging on but no hope after* **40/1**	92
-3U5	6	21	**Good Faloue (FR)**[17] 3599 6-10-12 105 AlexMerriam(3) (Neil King) *midfield: hit 5th: rdn 6th: no rspnse and struggling next: hit 3 out* **7/1**[3]	71
00-5	7	52	**Jack Rio (IRE)**[11] 3703 6-11-1 73 LiamHeard (Laura Young) *last pair: t.o 7th: fin a hurdle bhd* **50/1**	19
00	P		**Royal Crystal**[21] 3521 8-11-1 0 (t) PaddyAspell (James Turner) *t.k.h early: bhd: hit 4th: lost tch after 6th: bdly t.o whn p.u 2 out* **100/1**	—
5660	P		**St Enoder**[16] 3620 6-11-1 0 SamThomas (Brendan Powell) *prom: jnd ldr and hit 6th: stopped to nil bef 3 out and bdly t.o whn p.u 2 out* **28/1**	—
P4	P		**Colleens Pride (IRE)**[4] 3830 8-10-5 0 (b¹) GeraldQuinn(10) (Jonjo O'Neill) *taken down early: led: 8 l clr 3rd: rdn and giving up after 4th: hdd after next and sn tailed herself off: scaped over 7th and sn p.u* **66/1**	—

5m 12.0s (2.40) **Going Correction** +0.10s/f (Yiel) **10** Ran SP% **116.1**
Speed ratings (Par 105): **99,93,92,91,91 82,62,—,—,—**
toteswingers:1&2:£4.30, 1&3:£6.70, 2&3:£13.60 CSF £15.57 TOTE £2.20: £1.10, £2.10, £3.10; EX 15.60.

Owner Mrs T Brown **Bred** Desmond Devereux **Trained** Upper Lambourn, Berks

FOCUS

A weak mares' hurdle that produced an easy victory for the favourite. She was the form pick but this rates another step up.

NOTEBOOK

Bunglasha Lady(IRE) confirmed the promise shown in two previous hurdling efforts, staying on powerfully to beat inferior opposition, despite jumping left over the final two hurdles. Clearly relishing conditions, she could be one to note over further as she's an Irish point winner. Connections are keen to aim her at the valuable mares' race at Newbury on March 26. (op 11-10)

Playful Rose(IRE) kept on too late to play a hand but stayed on encouragingly up the hill. (op 14-1)

Sapphire Rouge(IRE) looks to need more of a stamina test than this after staying on well from an unpromising position. (op 25-1)

Overnight Fame(IRE) was one-paced once headed by the winner but to her credit plugged on and could be seen to better effect over further in due course. (op 2-1)

M'Lady Rousseur(IRE) never threatened but now qualifies for handicaps. (op 33-1)

Good Faloue(FR) floundered up the stiff finish. (op 13-2)

3902 LADBROKES.COM BEGINNERS' CHASE (16 fncs) 2m 6f

4:10 (4:10) (Class 4) 5-Y-0+ **£2,332** (£724; £389)

Form				RPR
2222	1		**Fredo (IRE)**[19] 3571 7-11-0 130 TomScudamore (Ian Williams) *trckd ldrs: wnt 2nd at 9th: rdn and nt finding much after: 10 l down whn presented w r at last* **11/10**[1]	130
1634	2	6	**Cool Mission (IRE)**[18] 3586 7-11-0 0 JasonMaguire (Donald McCain) *prom tl blnd 8th: j. slowly next: dropped bk last at 13th: plugged on fr 2 out and lft 2nd at last: drvn and nvr rchd wnr* **8/1**	124
122/	3	6	**Neil Harvey (IRE)**[696] 4381 8-11-0 0 LiamTreadwell (Nick Gifford) *racd on outer: t.k.h early: chsd ldrs: 10 l 3rd whn j. slowly 11th: no threat after* **13/2**[3]	117
0-43	F		**Mortimers Cross**[18] 3586 10-10-11 112 TommyPhelan(3) (John Needham) *pressed ldrs tl fell heavily 8th* **14/1**	—
/1-3	F		**A French Horse (FR)**[37] 3156 8-11-0 0 AidanColeman (Venetia Williams) *led and often j.w: hit 2nd: blnd 8th: drew clr effrtlessly 2 out: in n.d whn clipped top of last and fell: fatally injured* **11/4**[2]	138
41-4	P		**Only The Best**[90] 2191 8-11-0 120 GrahamLee (Ferdy Murphy) *j. slowly and wout fluency in detached last: rdn 12th: no rspnse: t.o and p.u 2 out* **16/1**	—

6m 4.00s (11.00) **Going Correction** +0.325s/f (Yiel) **6** Ran SP% **111.3**
Speed ratings: **93,90,88,—,— —**
toteswingers:1&2:£3.40, 1&3:£2.50, 2&3:£3.80 CSF £10.20 TOTE £2.30: £1.80, £4.80; EX 9.50.

Owner Mrs Jacky Allen & Mark Dennis **Bred** Gestut Hof Ittlingen **Trained** Portway, Worcs

FOCUS

An intriguing beginners' chase run at a steady gallop in the testing conditions. The ill-fated A French Horse is rated the 8l winner over Fredo who was a few pounds off his best.

NOTEBOOK

Fredo(IRE) stayed on moderately up the hill and was held coming to the last before being gifted the race. He deserved to get his head in front after meeting talented rivals on his previous four chasing starts. Connections are keen to go down the handicap route with a view to either a 3m or 4m race at Cheltenham. (op 13-8 tchd Evens)

Cool Mission(IRE) is now two from four here. He was officially rated 130 over hurdles so is not short of ability, and he ran well considering he'd been absent for 696 days. He could build on this if avoiding the bounce factor. (op 9-1 tchd 10-1)

Neil Harvey(IRE) found for pressure when outpaced down the back straight on the final circuit, but he needs to brush up his jumping (went left over the final two fences). He had ability over hurdles and has time on his side. (op 4-1)

Mortimers Cross took an x-rated fall when coming under pressure. (op 3-1 tchd 10-3)

A French Horse(FR) jumped boldly in the main and appeared to have the race sewn up when he fell at the the last. He got up and galloped loose briefly, but then sadly collapsed and died. (op 3-1 tchd 10-3)

Only The Best, who was switched off in rear, looked to sulk when asked for maximum effort from his jockey. (op 3-1 tchd 10-3)

3903 LADBROKESCASINO.COM INTERMEDIATE OPEN NATIONAL HUNT FLAT RACE 2m

4:40 (4:40) (Class 6) 4-6-Y-0 **£1,301** (£382; £191; £95)

Form				RPR
	1		**Destroyer Deployed**[117] 5-11-4 0 APMcCoy (Tim Vaughan) *led fr 1/2-way and gng wl: rdn and jnd over 1f out: urged along and tk command ins fnl f* **11/4**[2]	112+
4	2	2 ¾	**Howard's Legacy (IRE)**[20] 3546 5-11-4 0 AidanColeman (Venetia Williams) *trckd ldrs: rdn and wnt 2nd wl over 1f out: jnd wnr 300yds out: outpcd ins fnl f* **15/2**	107+
0-3	3	8	**Vincentian (IRE)**[14] 3651 6-11-4 0 JasonMaguire (David Arbuthnot) *slt ld at v mod pce tl 1/2-way: rdn and lost 2nd wl over 1f out: sn btn and fin tired* **16/1**	99
	4	6	**Hollow Blue Sky (FR)** 4-10-8 0 PaddyBrennan (Nigel Twiston-Davies) *cl up: pushed along 5f out: green and nvr gng wl enough after: struggling wl over 2f out* **2/1**[1]	84
P0-4	5	9	**How's My Friend**[14] 3651 6-11-4 0 TomO'Brien (Grant Cann) *pushed along after 5f: wl in tch tl racing awkwardly and wkng 3f out: t.o* **16/1**	84
2	6	8	**Monbeg Dude (IRE)**[34] 3259 6-11-4 0 TomScudamore (Michael Scudamore) *pushed along in rr after 5f: lost tch 5f out: t.o* **9/2**[3]	76
22	7	14	**Hackpenbay**[37] 3166 5-10-13 0 DavidBass(5) (Lawney Hill) *n.m.r whn losing pl after 5f and sn detached last: floundering bdly after: t.o fnl 6f* **9/1**	62
	8	7	**Silver Sophfire** 5-10-11 0 LiamTreadwell (Nick Gifford) *prom tl rdn and wknd bdly 3f out: wl t.o* **33/1**	48

4m 2.00s (-0.30) **Going Correction** +0.10s/f (Yiel)
WFA 4 from 5yo+ 9lb **8** Ran SP% **114.7**
Speed ratings: **104,102,98,95,91 87,80,76**
toteswingers:1&2:£4.20, 1&3:£4.30, 2&3:£5.80 CSF £23.74 TOTE £4.20: £1.80, £2.00, £2.90; EX 24.60.

Owner The Craftsmen **Bred** A W Buller **Trained** Aberthin, Vale of Glamorgan

FOCUS

An average bumper which was run at a sensible pace. The winner looks a fair recruit and the type to rate higher.

NOTEBOOK

Destroyer Deployed was a ready winner on his rules debut. He was a little keen early and, although headed 1f out, when asked to win the race he found plenty. He was a promising third in an Irish point and will appreciate further in time. (op 7-2 tchd 9-4)

Howard's Legacy(IRE) looked a danger to the winner 1f out and, although narrowly heading the former, was outbattled by a determined rival. The pair pulled clear of the remainder, indicating that the form is solid. (op 13-2 tchd 8-1)

Vincentian(IRE) appreciated the stamina test, staying on steadily up the hill, and looks certain to progress over further. (op 9-1)

Hollow Blue Sky(FR) looked awkward around the bends and didn't seem to appreciate the soft conditions. He is a half-brother to Baby Run, who won last season's Christie's Foxhunter Chase, and is clearly blessed with a stamina-laden pedigree. He will be effective over further. (op 5-2 tchd 3-1 and 15-8)

Monbeg Dude(IRE) didn't appreciate the uphill climb and might be seen in a better light on good ground. (op 5-1)

Hackpenbay is likely to do better on a sounder surface. (op 14-1)

T/Jkpt: Not won. T/Plt: £23.30 to a £1 stake. Pool:£75,733.34 - 2,372.00 winning tickets T/Qpdt: £6.10 to a £1 stake. Pool:£5,084.38 - 616.43 winning tickets IM

3686 WINCANTON (R-H)

Thursday, February 3

OFFICIAL GOING: Good to soft (good in places; chs 7.2; hdl 7.5)

Wind: strong breeze across Weather: cloudy with sunny periods

3904 EUROPEAN BREEDERS' FUND MARES' "NATIONAL HUNT" NOVICES' HURDLE (11 hdls) 2m 6f

2:20 (2:20) (Class 4) 4-Y-0+ **£2,602** (£764; £382; £190)

Form				RPR
2242	1		**Way Back When**[34] 3264 6-10-9 108 MrSWaley-Cohen(5) (Alan King) *mid-div: hdwy to trck ldrs 5th: rdn to chal sn after 3 out: led next: hrd pressed: kpt on wl fr last: rdn out* **6/4**[1]	112+
33	2	3 ½	**Dream Function (IRE)**[18] 3590 6-11-0 0 (t) RichardJohnson (Philip Hobbs) *prom: led 4th: hdd 2 out: sn rdn: stl upsides whn landed awkwardly last: kpt on but hld after* **15/8**[2]	111+
5043	3	6	**Genny Wren**[34] 3264 5-11-0 105 SamJones (Renee Robeson) *in tch: rdn to chse ldrs after 3 out: styd on same pce* **12/1**[3]	103
4-04	4	1	**Lost Two Stars (IRE)**[35] 3227 6-11-0 0 JoeTizzard (Colin Tizzard) *trckd ldrs: rdn after 3 out: styd on same pce* **28/1**	102
2-50	5	12	**Tsarinova**[49] 2974 6-11-0 0 RobertThornton (Alan King) *hld up towards rr: hdwy 6th: rdn in cl 3rd after 3 out: fdd fr next* **12/1**[3]	91
1066	6	4 ½	**Spe Salvi (IRE)**[24] 3480 7-11-0 0 DarylJacob (David Arbuthnot) *hld up towards rr: stdy hdwy fr 6th: rdn to chse ldrs after 3 out: wknd next* **20/1**	88
4P00	7	26	**Big Knickers**[14] 3647 6-11-0 0 DougieCostello (Neil Mulholland) *mid-div tl dropped to rr 6th: nvr bk on terms: t.o* **66/1**	64
346	8	5	**Tech Zinne**[74] 2560 5-10-7 0 TrevorWhelan(7) (George Baker) *hmpd 3 out: a towards rr: t.o* **50/1**	59
-4P3	9	1	**Some Secret**[24] 3480 6-11-0 0 JamesDavies (Chris Down) *mid-div: rdn after 6th: sn bhd: t.o* **66/1**	58
1/30	10	20	**Didbrook**[130] 1623 9-11-0 0 WayneHutchinson (Mary Hambro) *hld up towards rr: hdwy 8th: sn rdn: wknd after next: t.o* **50/1**	40
0-	11	16	**Apalachicola (IRE)**[70] 2651 5-11-0 0 PaulMoloney (Eugene M O'Sullivan, Ire) *led tl 3rd: trckd ldrs: rdn bef 3 out: wknd sn after: t.o* **18/1**	26
	12	10	**Arctic Fashion (IRE)** 6-10-7 0 MrKevinJones(7) (Seamus Mullins) *mid-div tl wknd after 6th: t.o* **150/1**	17
0-0	F		**Lady Exe**[77] 2472 6-10-9 0 (tp) KeiranBurke(5) (Chris Down) *mid-div: rdn 7th: no imp whn fell 3 out* **200/1**	—
	P		**Poshki**[298] 6-11-0 0 DavidDennis (Nigel Hawke) *mid-div tl wknd qckly after 6th: t.o whn p.u after 3 out* **150/1**	—

04 P **China Sky (IRE)**[24] 3480 6-11-0 0 .... BarryGeraghty —
(Nicky Henderson) *trckd ldrs led 3rd tl next: trckd ldrs: rdn after 3 out: wknd qckly: p.u bef next* **14/1**

00 P **Menepresents (IRE)**[36] 3200 6-11-0 0 .... HaddenFrost —
(Henrietta Knight) *in tch: stmbld bdly 6th: sn bhd: t.o whn p.u after 3 out* **100/1**

5m 16.9s (-9.60) **Going Correction** -0.375s/f (Good) **16** Ran SP% **120.0**
Speed ratings (Par 105): **102,100,98,98,93 92,82,80,80,73 67,63,—,—,— —**
toteswingers:1&2:£1.70, 1&3:£4.30, 2&3:£13.50 CSF £4.12 TOTE £2.60: £1.20, £1.50, £3.20; EX 5.50.
Owner Pall Mall Partners (NH) **Bred** Upton Viva Stud **Trained** Barbury Castle, Wilts

FOCUS
Most of these were unproven at the distance, so the form, which looks ordinary, may not be reliable.

NOTEBOOK
Way Back When, slightly up in trip again, proved that she stays well by grinding out a hard-fought victory. She may have been handed victory at the last hurdle, but there is no doubting her attitude. The final of this series is the objective. (tchd 5-4 and 13-8 in plalces)
Dream Function(IRE), up 6f in distance, looks a nice big, robust sort who should have plenty of improvement in her. She made a perfectly satisfactory start to her hurdling career, and may have won but for an awkward jump at the last. One would imagine that dropping back again in distance shouldn't pose too many problems. (op 9-4 tchd 5-2 in places)
Genny Wren finished well behind Way Back When last time when they met at Warwick, so this was a little better. No doubt she will win something in time, but she is starting to look a bit exposed. (op 14-1)
Lost Two Stars(IRE) once again shaped like a horse who promises to stay extreme distances in due course. (tchd 33-1)
Tsarinova, up 3f in distance, travelled strongly in behind but didn't get home.
Spe Salvi(IRE) moved into contention but failed to see out the trip. (op 16-1)
Apalachicola(IRE) Official explanation: jockey said mare ran too free
Poshki Official explanation: jockey said mare hung left-handed

3905 WEATHERBYS BANK NOVICES' H'CAP CHASE (13 fncs) 2m
2:50 (2:50) (Class 2) 5-Y-0+ **£9,090** (£2,839; £1,528)

Form RPR
-103 1 **Mister Stickler (IRE)**[12] 3672 7-11-3 **124** .... RobertThornton 131+
(Alan King) *trckd ldr: tk narrow advantage 3 out: 2 l clr next: rdn after last: hld on: all out* **4/1**[2]

212 2 *nk* **Betabob (IRE)**[37] 3154 8-10-0 **114** .... MrRGHenderson(7) 121
(Nick Mitchell) *hld up bhd ldng trio: wnt 3rd after 4 out: rdn after 2 out: str chal after last: jst hld off* **6/1**

121P 3 *30* **Chain Of Command (IRE)**[19] 3555 8-11-6 **127** .... WayneHutchinson 112
(Warren Greatrex) *trckd ldrs: nt fluent 5 out: mstke 4 out: sn rdn: wknd bef next: lft modest 3rd last* **5/1**[3]

1212 F **Osric (IRE)**[12] 3672 8-11-12 **133** .... BarryGeraghty 135
(Nicky Henderson) *led: nt fluent 5th (water): narrowly hdd 3 out: sn rdn: 3 l 3rd and hld whn fell last* **8/11**[1]

3m 57.6s (-2.30) **Going Correction** +0.10s/f (Yiel) **4** Ran SP% **108.9**
Speed ratings: **109,108,93,—**
CSF £21.83 TOTE £4.60; EX 17.40.
Owner Trevor Hemmings **Bred** Thomas Meagher **Trained** Barbury Castle, Wilts
■ Stewards' Enquiry : Mr R G Henderson one-day ban: used whip with excessive frequency (Feb 17)

FOCUS
Quite a range of abilities on show when considering official ratings, despite the small turnout. The first two are rated to their marks and the faller was heading for a mark about 10lb below his latest.

NOTEBOOK
Mister Stickler(IRE), 19l behind Osric at Ascot last time, had that one's measure when the Nicky Henderson-trained horse departed at the final fence. The winner possibly benefited from the drop back down in distance (he also blundered four out at the Berkshire track), as he moved up nicely and kept finding for pressure to hold off the fast-finishing runner-up. There is a chance that he may head to the Cheltenham Fesitval. (op 5-1 tchd 10-3)
Betabob(IRE), having his first start for this trainer, sat at the tail of the field before producing a good finish down the home straight. It looked for a moment like he might get past Mister Stickler, but he was never able to force his head to the front. (tchd 5-1)
Chain Of Command(IRE) ran disappointingly in a decent race at Kempton last time and failed to make any impact here. Official explanation: trainer said gelding lost both hind shoes (op 13-2 tchd 9-2)
Osric(IRE) was given a positive ride from the off but was in trouble at the third-last fence. His jumping wasn't always fluent, and he jumped to the left on occasions, before coming down at the last. (op 4-6 tchd 5-6, 10-11 in places and 8-13 in places)

3906 CARLING NOVICES' HURDLE (8 hdls) 2m
3:20 (3:20) (Class 3) 4-Y-0+ **£4,119** (£1,216; £608; £304; £152)

Form RPR
11 1 **Gibb River (IRE)**[32] 3344 5-11-12 139 .... BarryGeraghty 135+
(Nicky Henderson) *mid-div: trckd ldrs 5th: led appr 2 out: sn clr: unextended* **1/9**[1]

P 2 *12* **Sunley Peace**[15] 3626 7-11-2 0 .... JamieMoore 107+
(Gary Moore) *mid-div: hdwy 5th: rdn to chse wnr 2 out but no ch: mstke last: kpt on same pce* **14/1**[3]

3 *¾* **Leitzu (IRE)**[105] 4-10-0 0 .... HaddenFrost 88
(Mick Channon) *chsd ldrs: rdn to chse wnr briefly bef 2 out: kpt chalng for 2nd but no ch w wnr: no ex nr fin* **12/1**[2]

P 4 *¾* **Lang Shining (IRE)**[19] 2960 7-11-2 0 .... RobertThornton 103
(Jamie Osborne) *hld up towards rr: hdwy fr 4th: rdn to chse ldrs after 3 out: chal for 2nd run-in: no ex nr fin* **14/1**[3]

0 5 *12* **Benozzo Gozzoli**[32] 3344 5-10-13 0 .... JimmyDerham(3) 92
(Seamus Mullins) *in tch tl wknd after 3 out* **100/1**

050 6 *¾* **Direct Flo (IRE)**[12] 3691 4-10-0 0 .... SeanQuinlan 74
(Kim Bailey) *hld up towards rr: sme late prog: nvr a threat* **40/1**

400 7 *3 ¼* **E Street Boy**[12] 3691 5-11-2 0 .... JohnnyFarrelly 89
(David Pipe) *led tl rdn appr 2 out: sn wknd* **33/1**

200 8 *2 ¼* **Charles**[29] 3398 5-11-2 .... TomSiddall 85
(Kim Bailey) *mid-div: hit 2nd: wknd after 3 out* **66/1**

00/0 9 *1 ¾* **Honest**[12] 3691 8-10-13 0 .... EamonDehdashti(3) 83
(Karen George) *trckd ldrs: rdn after 3 out: sn wknd* **100/1**

05 10 *12* **Admission**[21] 3519 4-10-6 0 ....(t) PaulMoloney 61
(Sophie Leech) *mid-div: nt fluent 1st: hdwy 3 out: sn rdn: wknd bef next* **20/1**

600 11 *2 ¼* **Wosayu**[12] 3691 5-11-2 0 .... JoeTizzard 69
(Colin Tizzard) *chsd ldr tl rdn after 5th: wknd bef 2 out* **66/1**

60 12 *8* **Matrow's Lady (IRE)**[31] 3365 4-10-0 0 .... DougieCostello 45
(Neil Mulholland) *a towards rr* **25/1**

000 13 *50* **Turf Legends (IRE)**[24] 3478 5-11-2 0 .... RichardJohnson —
(Philip Hobbs) *lost tch fr 4th: t.o* **33/1**

3m 45.0s (-3.90) **Going Correction** -0.375s/f (Good)
WFA 4 from 5yo+ 9lb **13** Ran SP% **132.9**
Speed ratings (Par 107): **94,88,87,87,81 80,79,78,77,71 70,66,41**
toteswingers:1&2:£4.50, 1&3:£2.10, 2&3:£16.20 CSF £4.10 TOTE £1.10: £1.02, £2.70, £2.80; EX 5.50.
Owner Corbett Stud **Bred** Scuderia Pieffegi Sas **Trained** Upper Lambourn, Berks

FOCUS
This was far from a strong contest and the winner, who was value for further, is rated nowhere near his best.

NOTEBOOK
Gibb River(IRE) completed the hat-trick with the minimum off fuss to remain a smart prospect. We learnt little that we didn't know already about him, but he is clearly a serious candidate for Cheltenham Festival success, and the Supreme Novices' Hurdle appears to be the most likely target. (op 1-6 tchd 2-11in places)
Sunley Peace gave chase to the winner from two out but looked certain to lose the runner-up spot when he hit the last. Too his credit, he rallied and showed a commendable attitude after that mistake to regain second place.
Leitzu(IRE), a rare runner for the Mick Channon stable over jumps, looked to have possible stamina issues on her best Flat form, so this wasn't a bad start over hurdles, albeit she was easily held. (op 14-1)
Lang Shining(IRE) showed more than enough on this outing to suggest he can win an ordinary novice or low-grade handicap later on in the season.
Benozzo Gozzoli never really got involved but doesn't seem devoid of ability. (op 66-1)
Direct Flo(IRE) completely straightforward but looks in dire need of much further or a stiffer test. Official explanation: jockey said filly hung left-handed
E Street Boy once again suggested he has enough talent to be of interest in handicaps.

3907 GROLSCH CONDITIONAL JOCKEYS' H'CAP CHASE (21 fncs) 3m 1f 110y
3:50 (3:52) (Class 4) (0-115,115) 5-Y-0+ **£3,740** (£1,098; £549; £274)

Form RPR
-P62 1 **Sea Saffron**[33] 3300 10-10-10 **102** .... MattGriffiths(3) 114+
(Susan Gardner) *hld up towards rr: hdwy fr 12th: led after 17th: clr appr 3 out: comf* **12/1**

-0FP 2 *1 ¾* **Drybrook Bedouin**[19] 3558 9-11-7 **115** .... SClements(5) 121+
(Nick Mitchell) *chsd ldrs early: midfield 7th: nudged along after 14th: rdn and stdy prog after 4 out: wnt 2nd whn mstke 2 out: wnt rt last: styd on* **25/1**

2253 3 *6* **Sir Winston (IRE)**[21] 3527 9-9-11 **94** ....(p) EdGlassonbury(8) 96
(Victor Dartnall) *mid-div: trckd ldrs 8th: rdn 14th: disp 2nd after 4 out tl 2 out: no ex* **11/4**[1]

-263 4 *6* **Reblis (FR)**[26] 3450 6-11-0 **109** ....(p) JoshuaMoore(6) 103
(Gary Moore) *mid-div: reminders after 11th: rdn after 16th: styd on same pce fr 4 out: nvr threatened ldrs* **8/1**

2P2 5 *6* **Top Benefit (IRE)**[18] 3585 9-11-12 **115** .... CharlieHuxley 106
(Keith Goldsworthy) *stmbld bdly 1st: towards rr: hdwy to trck ldrs 12th: rdn to dispute 2nd after 4 out: fdd fr after next* **7/1**[3]

2124 6 *1* **Rebel Melody (IRE)**[32] 3347 10-11-6 **112** ....(bt) PeterToole(3) 103
(Charlie Mann) *trckd ldrs: led 6th: briefly hdd 15th: rdn whn hdd after 17th: fdd fr 3 out* **9/2**[2]

3-P0 7 *6* **Wizard Of Edge**[14] 3646 11-10-2 **91** .... CO'Farrell 76
(Ron Hodges) *led tl 2nd: chsd ldrs: struggling in rr fr 9th* **28/1**

44P/ 8 *5* **Wild Ground (IRE)**[661] 4982 10-10-4 **93** .... MichaelMurphy 71
(Kevin Bishop) *hld up bhd: hdwy fr 14th: rdn to chse ldrs after 17th: hit next: wknd* **16/1**

4-40 9 *49* **Shacklesborough (IRE)**[35] 3230 7-10-10 **102** ....(bt[1]) IanPopham(3) 36
(Paul Nicholls) *led 3rd tl 7th: trckd ldrs: rdn after 16th: wknd 4 out: t.o* **15/2**

26UP U **Picture In The Sky (IRE)**[19] 3568 10-11-4 **112** ....(p) KielanWoods(5) —
(Susan Nock) *hld up towards rr: rdn and hdwy 13th: jst taken ld whn blnd and uns rdr 15th* **20/1**

3400 P **Skipper's Lad (IRE)**[12] 3687 9-10-12 **101** ....(b) KeiranBurke —
(Colin Tizzard) *led 2nd tl 3rd: chsd ldrs: rdn after 16th: sn wknd: t.o whn p.u bef 2 out* **20/1**

50P0 P **Ginolad (AUS)**[15] 3629 11-11-6 **112** .... RTDunne(3) —
(Venetia Williams) *mid-div: trckd ldrs 8th: rdn after 12th: sn bhd: t.o whn p.u bef 4 out* **8/1**

6m 38.7s (-0.80) **Going Correction** +0.10s/f (Yiel) **12** Ran SP% **121.7**
Speed ratings: **105,104,102,100,98 98,96,95,80,— —,—**
toteswingers:1&2:£51.90, 1&3:£7.10, 2&3:£24.20 CSF £273.28 CT £1070.05 TOTE £13.90: £4.30, £8.10, £1.60; EX 382.70.
Owner G N Noye & P A Tylor **Bred** G Blight **Trained** Longdown, Devon

FOCUS
The early pace was strong so it wasn't surprising that those who raced prominently didn't feature in the finish. Ordinary form, with a step up from the cosy winner.

NOTEBOOK
Sea Saffron, back over fences after a fair effort over hurdles last time, could be seen travelling strongly throughout and bounded clear when asked to quicken. He won with a bit in hand and is evidently versatile with regards to trip. (op 14-1 tchd 11-1)
Drybrook Bedouin, back up to a more suitable trip, had been dropped 4lb since his last outing and came home strongly after having a bit of ground to make up. He looks more than capable of winning soon and will get further. (op 22-1)
Sir Winston(IRE), wearing cheekpieces for the first time, is consistent but never threatened to win. (op 4-1)
Reblis(FR) shaped respectably over the C&D last time but never featured with a serious chance here after taking plenty of kidding along from an early stage. (tchd 15-2 and 10-1)
Top Benefit(IRE), making his chase debut under rules, raced prominently and showed enough to suggest he will be winning over fences. (tchd 11-2)
Picture In The Sky(IRE) had just got into the fronk rank when unseating his jockey. He was going well at the time but it was too far out to know what would have happened at the business end of the contest. (op 16-1)

3908 STEWART TORY MEMORIAL HUNTERS' CHASE (21 fncs) 3m 1f 110y
4:20 (4:20) (Class 6) 5-Y-0+ **£936** (£290; £145; £72)

Form RPR
2-24 1 **Turthen (FR)**[250] 525 10-12-6 126 .... MissCTizzard 135
(C St V Fox) *hld up towards rr: hdwy after 17th: wnt 2nd 2 out: rdn to ld sn after last: edgd rt: all out* **13/2**[3]

21F- 2 *1* **Whizzaar**[249] 11-12-3 123 .... MrRWoollacott(3) 134
(R M Woollacott) *trckd ldr: led after 17th: rdn after 2 out: narrowly hdd sn after last: edgd lft: hld nring fin* **22/1**

40P- 3 *¾* **Halcon Genelardais (FR)**[292] 5223 11-11-5 141 .... MrJarrett(7) 127+
(Alan King) *in tch: rdn to hold pl after 15th: styd on fr 3 out: keeping on and abt to chal whn squeezed out fnl 75yds* **85/40**[1]

44-6 **4** *6* **Gentle George**[274] 151 8-12-1 124 MrPJTolman(5) 130+
(S Flook) *led tl 1st: chsd ldrs: stmbld 10th: rdn after 17th: ev ch appr 3 out: styd on same pce* **11/1**

51P/ **5** *2 3/4* **Ornais (FR)**[790] 2620 9-11-12 143 (t) MrMRMahon 118
(Paul Nicholls) *hld up towards rr: sme stdy prog fr 14th: rdn after 4 out: styd on same pce: nvr trbld ldrs* **11/4**[2]

/12- **6** *10* **Moncadou (FR)**[301] 5096 11-12-2 122 (t) MrAJBerry 114
(Jonjo O'Neill) *hld up towards rr: hdwy 12th into midfield: rdn after 16th: wknd 2 out* **7/1**

P3P- **7** *1/2* **Jayne's Crusader**[26] 8-11-12 108 MrMGMiller 111+
(Mrs S Alner) *hld up towards rr: stdy hdwy after 9th: cl up whn rdn appr 3 out: wknd 2 out* **12/1**

2P/- **8** *1/2* **Scrappie (IRE)**[277] 11-11-5 92 (t) MrDCollins(7) 108
(C R Whittaker) *a towards rr* **66/1**

13P/ **9** *9* **Kiama**[26] 9-11-5 102 MrWBiddick 97
(Mrs R Vickery) *hld up towards rr: hdwy after 17th: rdn in cl 5th appr 3 out: wknd bef 2 out* **33/1**

2-21 **10** *9* **Distant Thunder (IRE)**[268] 268 13-11-9 108 (t) MrPPrince(7) 99
(Mrs A S Hodges) *hld up towards rr: gd hdwy to trck ldr after 8th: rdn after 4 out: wknd next* **28/1**

P-35 **11** *1 3/4* **Pastek (FR)**[11] 8-11-5 78 MrMPeaty(7) 90
(Martin Peaty) *mid-div: rdn after 11th: wknd 15th* **150/1**

0-10 **12** *10* **Apollo Blaze (IRE)**[18] 10-11-9 95 MissVShaw(7) 85
(Mrs P J Shaw) *chsd ldrs tl wknd after 17th: t.o* **100/1**

F2-3 **13** *23* **Cloud Nine (IRE)**[26] 8-11-9 109 (b[1]) MissLGardner(3) 60
(Miss Jane Western) *led 1st tl after 17th: wknd after 4 out: t.o* **22/1**

1/0- **P** **Shardakhan (IRE)**[433] 2552 9-11-5 131 (b) MrRMGreen(7) —
(R M Green) *nvr fluent: a in rr: mstke 8th: p.u after 12th* **25/1**

00- **P** **Hunt Ball (IRE)**[236] 6-11-5 0 MrJHuxham(7) —
(Miss Olivia R H Brookshaw) *mid-div: rdn appr 13th: sn wknd: t.o whn p.u bef 16th* **80/1**

6m 41.7s (2.20) **Going Correction** +0.10s/f (Yiel) **15** Ran SP% **123.8**
Speed ratings: **100,99,99,97,96 93,93,93,90,87 87,84,77,—,—**
toteswingers:1&2:£41.00, 1&3:£4.70, 2&3:£23.10 CSF £136.21 TOTE £8.90: £1.90, £5.90, £2.30; EX 69.80.
Owner C St V Fox **Bred** Michel Langot **Trained** Gillingham, Dorset
■ Stewards' Enquiry : Miss C Tizzard one-day ban: careless riding (Feb 17)
Mr R Woollacott one-day ban: careless riding (Feb 17)

FOCUS
The first hunter chase of the 2010-11 season to be run in England looked a terrific affair, with many well-known horses taking part, and it produced a thrilling finish. The winner is rated 5lb off his best.

NOTEBOOK
Turthen(FR), off since finishing fourth in the Champion Hunters' Chase at Stratford, sat towards the rear early on before being produced with a well-timed effort at a course he often runs well at. He only narrowly won but was fully entitled to do so, and may head to Cheltenham for the Foxhunter Chase again, although that is far from set in stone. (op 7-1 tchd 8-1)
Whizzaar, absent since being beaten at 4-9 in a point last May, had some stamina issues to answer (he had won 3m points but his wins under rules came over shorter) but showed he stays well with a battling performance. (op 18-1 tchd 16-1)
Halcon Genelardais(FR) was being given a chance in this sphere to see if he could be rejuvenated, and he showed more than enough, even after hitting a flat spot, to make one think he will be winning something similar. Indeed, he may well have taken this had he not been squeezed out close to the line by the first two. (op 5-1 tchd 2-1)
Gentle George's form tailed off towards the end of last season, so this was better, even though his jumping left a lot to be desired at times. If he becomes more fluent, he can win more hunter chases. (op 10-1)
Ornais(FR), returning from a 790-day break, made some late ground but shaped as though this effort was needed. He pleased his trainer and the horse apparently heads to the Grand National, where he is likely to be raced more prominently. (op 2-1)
Moncadou(FR) travelled nicely towards the rear but his jumping let him down as the tempo increased. (op 13-2 tchd 6-1)
Jayne's Crusader was one of the last off the bridle and shaped with considerable promise. He had won a point recently, but should still come on for this and can win his share of points and hunter chases.
Distant Thunder(IRE) pulled much too hard and didn't see out the trip. (op 33-1 tchd 25-1)
Cloud Nine(IRE) went off at a rapid rate in the first-time blinkers and predictably weakened. (op 25-1 tchd 20-1)

3909 WORTHINGTONS STANDARD OPEN NATIONAL HUNT FLAT RACE 2m
4:50 (4:50) (Class 6) 4-6-Y-0 **£1,301** (£382; £191; £95)

Form RPR

1 **1** **Shuil Royale (IRE)**[34] 3266 6-11-10 0 TimmyMurphy 118+
(David Arbuthnot) *mid-div: smooth hdwy 3f out: led 2f out: kpt on wl: pushed out* **6/1**[3]

1 **2** *2 1/4* **Daymar Bay (IRE)**[86] 2295 5-11-5 0 JoshuaMoore(5) 114+
(Emma Lavelle) *hld up towards rr: making hdwy whn sltly hmpd on bnd 3f out: sn swtchd lft and rdn: styd on to go 2nd over 1f out: hld fnl f* **7/1**

30 **3** *2 1/2* **Revani**[33] 3294 4-10-4 0 DannyCook(3) 94
(Nick Mitchell) *hld up towards rr: hdwy over 3f out: rdn and styd on fnl 2f* **40/1**

4 *2 1/2* **Fergall (IRE)** 4-10-4 0 JimmyDerham(3) 92
(Seamus Mullins) *hld up towards rr: hdwy on inner 3f out: sn rdn: styd on* **80/1**

5 *1/2* **Greywell Boy** 4-10-7 0 DarylJacob 91
(Nick Williams) *chsd ldrs: rdn over 2f out: styd on same pce fr over 1f out* **50/1**

6 *1 3/4* **Mousenikov** 5-10-12 0 (t) MrRMahon(5) 100
(Paul Nicholls) *mid-div: hdwy 5f out: led wl over 2f out: rdn and hdd sn after: sn one pce* **50/1**

7 *7* **Sleepy (FR)** 5-11-3 0 BarryGeraghty 96+
(Nicky Henderson) *in tch: jnd ldr travelling wl 4f out: rdn over 2f out: wknd over 1f out* **11/10**[1]

8 *5* **Zagova (IRE)** 5-11-3 0 RichardJohnson 92+
(Philip Hobbs) *mid-div: hmpd on bnd 3f out: sn wknd* **33/1**

0 **9** *1 1/2* **Gypsy Moth (IRE)**[33] 3301 5-10-7 0 IanPopham(3) 83
(Caroline Keevil) *mid-div: hmpd on bnd 3f out: wknd 2f out* **100/1**

10 *3/4* **Tiagra** 4-10-7 0 DominicElsworth 77
(Paul Webber) *mid-div tl wknd 2f out* **12/1**

11 *16* **St Blazey (IRE)** 6-11-3 0 NickScholfield 73
(Paul Nicholls) *trckd ldr: led over 3f out: rdn and hdd over 2f out: sn wknd* **9/2**[2]

5 **12** *10* **Champagne Rosie**[33] 3301 5-10-10 0 WillKennedy 57
(Bob Buckler) *mid-div tl wknd over 2f out* **80/1**

0 **13** *10* **Colonial Harry**[33] 3301 4-10-7 0 DougieCostello 45
(Neil Mulholland) *chsd ldrs: rdn 4f out: wknd 3f out* **150/1**

14 *5* **Praefectus (IRE)**[304] 5-11-3 0 JohnnyFarrelly 50
(David Pipe) *led tl 3f out: sn wknd* **33/1**

30 **15** *10* **Quix**[29] 3399 5-11-3 0 RobertThornton 41
(Bob Buckler) *in tch: struggling 1/2-way: sn wl bhd* **50/1**

2 **B** **Traditional Bob (IRE)**[263] 362 6-11-3 0 JodieMogford —
(Graeme McPherson) *racd keenly: mid-div: travelling ok whn b.d on bnd 3f out* **33/1**

S **Flyit Flora** 6-10-3 0 EdGlassonbury(7) —
(Victor Dartnall) *mid-div: hdwy to trck ldrs whn stmbld and slipped up bnd 3f out* **22/1**

3m 37.8s (-5.50) **Going Correction** -0.375s/f (Good)
WFA 4 from 5yo 9lb 5 from 6yo 1lb **17** Ran SP% **125.9**
Speed ratings: **98,96,95,94,94 93,89,87,86,86 78,73,68,65,60 —,—**
toteswingers:1&2:£4.80, 1&3:£39.10, 2&3:£39.10 CSF £45.32 TOTE £6.80: £1.50, £2.70, £9.00; EX 26.00.
Owner Phil Fry & Geoff Thompson **Bred** Greenville House Stud And M Morgan **Trained** Compton, Berks

FOCUS
This had the look of a decent contest and it was won in the style of a talented performer. The only slight negative to be drawn, if there is one, was that the first three home had already seen the racecourse.

NOTEBOOK
Shuil Royale(IRE) gave every indication that he is a horse with a big future with a comfortable victory. Keen as he had been on his debut when also successful, he showed a great attitude off the bridle to come home a clear winner, pricking his ears close to the line and suggesting he had more to give if needed. There was talk that he may head to the Champion Bumper at Cheltenham afterwards, and he will be far from out of place in that race should be make the trip to Prestbury Park. (op 17-2)
Daymar Bay(IRE), the only other penalised runner in the field, was ridden with restraint but couldn't get to the winner no matter how hard he tried. He still looked a bit green and can come on again for this. (op 6-1)
Revani had two good performances behind him, albeit without winning, and gives the race some structure because he appeared to run up to his best. (op 33-1)
Fergall(IRE) hardly looked the most likely candidate on breeding, and he showed signs of greenness on the final bend, but he stayed on resolutely to make an eyecatching debut.
Greywell Boy, who cost £14,000 last May, must have pleased connections with his first run and he looks to have a future. (op 40-1)
Mousenikov threatened at the top of the home straight but could only find the one pace. (op 33-1)
Sleepy(FR) was the subject of some encouraging reports during the morning and was sent off at skinny odds. His backers must have felt confident as he started to ease his way into contention in the latter stages, but he found little off the bridle and wasn't given a hard time thereafter. (op 5-4)
Champagne Rosie Official explanation: jockey said mare hung left-handed
Traditional Bob(IRE) was brought down by Flyit Flora about 3f out. (op 16-1)
Flyit Flora looked to be starting to weaken heading into the home straight when she stumbled and hit the ground. (op 16-1)
T/Plt: £141.70 to a £1 stake. Pool:£69,270.84 - 356.77 winning tickets T/Qpdt: £14.80 to a £1 stake. Pool:£4,207.54 - 209.74 winning tickets TM

3910 - 3916a (Foreign Racing) - See Raceform Interactive

2951 BANGOR-ON-DEE (L-H)
Friday, February 4

OFFICIAL GOING: Good to soft (soft in places on chase course; hdl 7.1 chs 6.2)
Inner hurdle course used.
Wind: very strong across Weather: overcast, dry and very windy

3917 BANGORONDEERACES.CO.UK NOVICES' HURDLE (10 hdls) 2m 1f
1:25 (1:25) (Class 4) 4-Y-0+ **£2,602** (£764; £382; £190)

Form RPR

2P **1** **Harry Hunt**[25] 3484 4-10-4 118 TomMolloy(3) 109
(Graeme McPherson) *t.k.h: chsd ldrs: pushed along to chal bef 2 out: led bef last: styd on wl* **10/1**[2]

12 **2** *1 1/4* **Credit Swap**[15] 3645 6-11-10 121 AidanColeman 126+
(Venetia Williams) *hld up in tch: trckd ldng pair bef 2 out: chal between horses bef 2 out: unable qck and swtchd rt bef last: kpt on u.p flat* **11/10**[1]

-213 **3** *1/2* **Palace Jester**[21] 3542 6-11-10 122 APMcCoy 125
(Jonjo O'Neill) *w ldr tl led 6th: rdn and hdd between last 2: kpt on same pce u.p flat* **11/10**[1]

0430 **4** *10* **Kayfton Pete**[25] 3481 5-10-10 110 PeterHatton(7) 107
(Reg Hollinshead) *hld up wl in tch: chsd ldrs bef 7th: ev ch and rdn bef next: wknd between last 2* **25/1**

00 **5** *40* **Tait's Clock (IRE)**[5] 3831 5-11-0 0 MrAJBerry(3) 67
(Jonjo O'Neill) *chsd ldrs tl wknd qckly 6th: t.o after 3 out* **150/1**

6 *22* **Royal Patriot (IRE)**[83] 4-10-7 0 AlanO'Keeffe 35
(Paul Green) *bhd: j.lft 3rd: sme hdwy after 5th: struggling next: 5th and wl btn whn blnd 3 out: t.o* **100/1**

00U **7** *6* **Stays All Night (FR)**[8] 3760 5-10-12 0 MrTomDavid(5) 39
(Tim Vaughan) *plld hrd: mde most tl mstke and hdd 6th: sn wknd: t.o 2 out* **100/1**

0/ **8** *1/2* **Past Gambles (IRE)**[1031] 4943 9-10-10 0 MrBJPoste(7) 39
(Bill Moore) *a bhd: toiling after 4th: t.o after next* **100/1**

P **Timber Treasure (USA)**[144] 7-11-3 0 SeanQuinlan —
(Paul Green) *j.lft: a bhd: hmpd 5th: sn lost tch: t.o whn p.u 7th* **80/1**

0/U **F** **Backstreet Billy (IRE)**[25] 3489 7-11-3 0 RobertThornton —
(Richard Lee) *hld up in tch towards rr tl fell 5th* **20/1**[3]

4m 8.20s (-2.70) **Going Correction** +0.025s/f (Yiel)
WFA 4 from 5yo+ 9lb **10** Ran SP% **117.8**
Speed ratings (Par 105): **107,106,106,101,82 72,69,69,—,—**
Tote Swingers: 1&2 £4.70, 1&3 £2.40, 2&3 £1.10 CSF £22.42 TOTE £11.60: £2.40, £1.10, £1.10; EX 38.30.
Owner Arion Racing **Bred** Darley **Trained** Upper Oddington, Gloucs
■ Stewards' Enquiry : Tom Molloy one-day ban: used whip with excessive force (Feb 23); Fine: £290, Rule (D) 47.5, failed to attend enquiry.

FOCUS
A blustery day. There was 2mm of rain overnight and the going was good to soft on the hurdles course. There was an upset in this novice hurdle as the two clear market leaders were just outgunned by a revived rival, but the first three had official ratings of 118, 121 and 122, so the form stacks up well. The race was steadily run.

NOTEBOOK
Harry Hunt had claims on his nose defeat by a 100-1 newcomer at Hereford in November. There were mixed messages about the strength of that form and he was keen when pulled up in a visor at Towcester last time, but this 118-rated 4-y-o bounced back with a gritty effort with the headgear removed to get off the mark on the eighth attempt over hurdles. (op 11-1)

Credit Swap, who won the Cambridgeshire off 87 last October, made an immediate impact over hurdles when decisively beating a 118-rated rival at Leicester before suffering a reverse when odds-on at Taunton last time, but that form had been boosted. He looked the likely winner approaching the second last, but hit a bit of a flat spot before rallying close home. It was slightly disappointing that this useful Flat performer couldn't find a decisive burst of speed but it was still a respectable effort and he seems to have a fair amount of staying power at this discipline. (op 6-5 tchd Evens)

Palace Jester scored at Wetherby in November before a third behind a Nicky Henderson-trained hot favourite at Huntingdon. He had decent form claims and ran a creditable race under a prominent ride, but couldn't quite match the finishing kick of the winner. (op 6-5 tchd 5-4)

Kayfton Pete did well to hang in there with the front three for a long way before fading. This 110-rated hurdler is 0-8 but this run was somewhere near his best form.

Tait's Clock(IRE) went in snatches before weakening quickly and has now been well beaten at big prices in all three of his hurdle runs.

3918 DARLANDS NOVICES' HURDLE (11 hdls) 2m 4f

1:55 (1:55) (Class 4) 4-Y-0+ **£2,602** (£764; £382; £190)

Form RPR

1-21 **1** **Whoops A Daisy**[32] 3365 5-11-4 0 APMcCoy 114+
(Nicky Henderson) *a gng wl: trckd ldrs: nt fluent 6th: led bef next: clr w runner-up wl bef 2 out: rdn clr between last 2: eased flat: comf* **1/4**[1]

4-6 **2** *3 ½* **Credit Crunched (IRE)**[20] 3556 6-11-4 0 RobertThornton 106
(Alan King) *chsd ldrs: wnt 2nd 7th: clr w wnr and ev ch after 3 out: rdn and one pce fr next* **11/2**[2]

4 **3** *10* **Just Benny (IRE)**[71] 2646 6-11-4 0 SeanQuinlan 97
(Richard Phillips) *hld up wl in tch: mstke 4th: rdn and outpcd after 7th: 5th and wl hld 3 out: plugged on to go 3rd between last 2: no threat to ldrs* **100/1**

50 **4** *5* **Mickytaker (IRE)**[27] 3439 6-11-4 0 WayneHutchinson 92
(Alan King) *hld up wl in tch: 4th and outpcd 8th: styd on same pce and n.d after* **33/1**

205 **5** *nk* **Fill The Power (IRE)**[20] 3572 5-11-4 0 HenryOliver 93
(Sue Smith) *led tl outj. and hdd 1st: styd handy tl lost pl and dropped to rr 7th: mstke and lost tch next: rallied 2 out: styd on flat* **22/1**

6 *6* **Luck'N'Thanks (IRE)**[300] 8-10-8 0 KillianMoore(10) 86
(Graeme McPherson) *hld up in tch in rr: hmpd bnd after 5th: hdwy to chse ldng pair and drew clr of field 8th: swtchd rt bef next: wknd qckly bef 2 out* **100/1**

60 **7** *shd* **Lariat Sam (IRE)**[34] 3295 6-11-4 0 GerardTumelty 88
(Alan King) *wl in tch towards rr: mstke 6th: wknd after next* **125/1**

00-6 **8** *35* **Kauto Cyreo (FR)**[10] 3718 6-11-1 0 IanPopham(3) 50
(Claire Dyson) *chsd ldr tl bttr jump to ld 1st: hdd bef 7th: wknd after next: t.o 2 out* **125/1**

-F00 **9** *shd* **Twice Lucky**[25] 3489 7-11-4 0 TjadeCollier 50
(Sue Smith) *in tch: mstke 2nd: reminders after 4th: wknd 7th: t.o bef 2 out* **150/1**

-FP5 **10** *39* **Seymour Eric**[27] 3439 6-11-4 0 JohnnyFarrelly 11
(Michael Scudamore) *a in rr: j. slowly 1st: lost tch 7th: t.o 3 out* **20/1**[3]

5m 0.40s (3.00) **Going Correction** +0.025s/f (Yiel) **10** Ran SP% **111.7**
Speed ratings (Par 105): **95,93,89,87,87 85,85,71,71,55**
Tote Swingers: 1&2 £2.40, 1&3 £2.80, 2&3 £8.40 CSF £1.62 TOTE £1.30: £1.02, £1.40, £15.10; EX 2.30.
Owner Let's Live Racing **Bred** N J Henderson And Mrs S A Aston **Trained** Upper Lambourn, Berks

FOCUS

There was little strength in depth in this novices' hurdle but the potentially useful odds-on favourite put in a professional display to fight off the her main market rival and maintain an unbeaten record of 2-2 over hurdles. She was value for further but rated 5lb off her best, with the fifth setting the level.

NOTEBOOK

Whoops A Daisy was a convincing winner of a bumper and did the job in good style when overhauling a rival with stronger form claims at Hereford last month on her hurdle debut. She set a clear standard but was more workmanlike than flashy in improving her strike-rate to 3-4. However, the clear second is a fair type, so the form has some solidity and this £20,000 mare looks another promising type for a yard with a huge amount of talent in the novice ranks. She does not hold any entries at Cheltenham at this stage and the mares' final at Newbury looks a feasible target for this half-sister to prolific point/2m6f-3m chase winner Chorizo. (tchd 2-9)

Credit Crunched(IRE) showed ability before weakening behind potentially smart Chablais on his recent return from 430 days off. This former maiden point winner had a tricky task against another Nicky Henderson-trained hotpot but showed a good attitude to keep battling and shaped like a step up in trip will suit. (tchd 13-2 in a place)

Just Benny(IRE) showed little in an Irish maiden point and a bumper but there was some promise on this hurdle debut.

Mickytaker(IRE) didn't do much on his first hurdle run last month, but this stablemate of the runner-up showed a bit of ability here and could benefit from a stiffer test. (op 40-1)

Fill The Power(IRE) lost his place some way out before plugging on again for a remote fifth. This half-brother to 2m4f-2m6f chase winner Benalma still has a bit to learn, but should do better when sent handicapping over a bit further. (op 28-1 tchd 20-1)

Luck'N'Thanks(IRE) failed to complete in four point starts but he moved well for a long way and was just behind the breakaway leaders turning in before weakening on this hurdle debut.

3919 WEDDINGS IN THE PADDOCK NOVICES' H'CAP HURDLE (13 hdls) 3m

2:25 (2:26) (Class 4) (0-115,115) 4-Y-0+ **£3,252** (£955; £477; £238)

Form RPR

4050 **1** **Pie At Midnight**[23] 3509 5-11-0 103 JasonMaguire 110+
(Donald McCain) *mde all: mstke 5th: hit next: jnd 10th: drvn bef 2 out: forged ahd between last 2: idled bdly and rejnd flat: hrd drvn and fnd ex fnl 75yds* **20/1**

44 **2** *shd* **Kingsmere**[29] 3405 6-11-5 108 AndrewTinkler 111
(Henry Daly) *hld up in tch in rr: gd hdwy to trck ldrs after 8th: jnd ldrs next: drew clr w wnr after 3 out: rdn bef next: unable qck and btn last: lft w ev ch flat: hld nr fin* **5/1**[3]

6340 **3** *6* **Gunna Be A Devil (IRE)**[13] 3688 7-11-6 112 (t) IanPopham(3) 110
(Jeremy Scott) *chsd ldrs: wnt 2nd after 8th tl 10th: stl pressing ldng pair 3 out: sn wknd u.p* **4/1**[2]

3/40 **4** *2 ½* **Okafranca (IRE)**[10] 3724 6-10-13 102 WayneHutchinson 98
(Jim Old) *in tch: pushed along 8th: rdn and outpcd next: wl btn bef 3 out: plugged on steadily but no threat to ldrs* **18/1**

1043 **5** *½* **Rebel Swing**[83] 2372 5-10-9 98 HenryOliver 93
(Sue Smith) *chsd ldr tl after 8th: sn rdn and dropped himself out: 6th and wl btn bef 3 out: styd on again fr 2 out* **10/3**[1]

4U **6** *8* **Stonethrower (IRE)**[12] 3693 6-11-7 115 (t) MrTomDavid(5) 103
(Tim Vaughan) *chsd ldrs: 4th and btn bef 3 out: lost 2 pls flat* **7/1**

1046 **7** *38* **Musical Wedge**[34] 3297 7-10-5 97 TommyPhelan(3) 51
(Claire Dyson) *hld up in tch in last trio: rdn and wknd bef 9th: sn wl bhd: t.o* **18/1**

-603 **8** *12* **Morcambe**[25] 3487 6-11-5 113 DavidBass(5) 56
(Nicky Henderson) *in tch in last trio: pushed along after 7th: dropped to last after next: sn struggling and bhd: t.o* **13/2**

-323 **9** *50* **Money Finder**[249] 553 8-9-11 93 MrNSlatter(7) —
(Trevor Wall) *chsd ldrs on outer: rdn and lost pl after 8th: sn t.o* **16/1**

430- **P** **Quizwork (FR)**[301] 5119 7-11-7 110 (t) SamThomas —
(Graeme McPherson) *chsd ldrs: rdn and wknd bef 9th: t.o bef 2 out tl p.u bef last* **10/1**

5m 54.2s (3.20) **Going Correction** +0.025s/f (Yiel) **10** Ran SP% **115.8**
Speed ratings (Par 105): **95,94,92,92,91 89,76,72,55,—**
Tote Swingers: 1&2 £27.50, 1&3 £1.60, 2&3 £9.80 CSF £117.76 CT £491.45 TOTE £19.10: £4.80, £2.50, £2.60; EX 107.70.
Owner No More Excuses **Bred** Mr And Mrs K Walby **Trained** Cholmondeley, Cheshire

FOCUS

A fair novices' handicap hurdle. The pace was not very strong and they were tightly grouped for a long way before the front two forged clear and had a dramatic duel in the closing stages. The idling winner was value for further and looks on the upgrade. The form looks solid and the race should throw up future winners.

NOTEBOOK

Pie At Midnight has taken a keen hold at times and had stamina to prove on his first try beyond 2m4f. Always prominent, it looked like he might have to settle for second when the runner-up travelled well alongside him turning in, but he put in a tremendously feisty display to keep rallying and snatch the lead close home. He will get hit with a rise for this first win at the ninth attempt, but should have more to offer reinvented as a front-running staying hurdler. (tchd 22-1)

Kingsmere, a good ground point winner, travelled smoothly for a long way and was just denied in a thrilling finish stepped up in trip on handicap debut. This lightly raced type is out of a half-sister to the same connections' top-class staying hurdler Mighty Man and looks set to make a major impact in a staying handicap. (op 9-2 tchd 4-1)

Gunna Be A Devil(IRE), a dual point winner on slow ground, showed improvement with a tongue-tie applied upped in trip on just his second try in a handicap. (op 11-2)

Okafranca(IRE) was in trouble some way out but did well to plug on for fourth. He missed 2010 and has been hard to predict on the Flat and over hurdles, but the step up to 3m seems to have sparked a move back in the right direction and this could be a springboard to better things. (op 20-1 tchd 25-1)

Rebel Swing was caught flat-footed at a crucial stage before staying on again. He is consistent but his habit of hitting a flat spot can often hold him back and he has found life tough off this sort of mark since swooping late at Uttoxeter in September. (op 7-2 tchd 3-1)

Stonethrower(IRE) went a bit in snatches and couldn't hang on to the leading group when things got serious. (tchd 9-1 in a place)

Morcambe was very laboured on handicap debut and couldn't confirm the form of a promising third in a 2m4f Towcester novice last time. (tchd 8-1)

Quizwork(FR) was a huge market mover in the morning but didn't show much back from 301 days off. (op 8-1)

3920 PRIVATE PARTIES IN THE PADDOCK MAIDEN OPEN NATIONAL HUNT FLAT RACE 2m 1f

2:55 (2:57) (Class 6) 4-6-Y-0 **£1,370** (£399; £199)

Form RPR

2 **1** **Tarn Hows (IRE)**[86] 2309 5-11-4 0 AlanO'Keeffe 104
(Jennie Candlish) *hld up wl bhd: stdy prog 1/2-way: jnd ldrs 4f out: led 2f out: kpt on wl u.p* **11/2**[3]

2 *¾* **Vintage Star (IRE)** 5-11-4 0 TjadeCollier 103
(Sue Smith) *chsd ldrs: lft 2nd 12f out tl 10f out: chsd ldr again 8f out: rdn and rn green jst over 2f out: swtchd rt and rallied ins fnl f: kpt on* **14/1**

3 *2 ½* **Vision Of Lights (IRE)** 6-10-13 0 DavidBass(5) 101
(Graeme McPherson) *chsd ldrs tl lft in ld 12f out tl 10f out: led again 8f out tl hdd 2f out: styd on same pce fnl f* **11/1**

2 **4** *5* **Koultas King (IRE)**[32] 3364 4-10-3 0 MrTomDavid(5) 87
(Tim Vaughan) *chsd ldrs: rdn and outpcd over 3f out: kpt on same pce fnl 2f* **11/4**[2]

-03 **5** *4* **Wychwoods Kaddy**[101] 2025 5-10-8 0 (t) KillianMoore(10) 93
(Graeme McPherson) *t.k.h: hld up in tch in rr: hdwy 7f out: wknd over 3f out* **18/1**

00 **6** *9* **Next Man In (IRE)**[35] 3266 5-11-4 0 RobertThornton 87
(Alan King) *t.k.h: hld up in tch in midfield: rdn and wknd over 4f out: wl btn fnl 2f* **18/1**

7 *7* **Arctic Actress** 4-10-1 0 AndrewTinkler 62
(Nicky Henderson) *chsd ldrs tl rdn and wknd 4f out: wl btn over 2f out* **15/8**[1]

8 *5* **Naranga** 5-11-4 0 SeanQuinlan 76+
(Richard Phillips) *hld up in tch in rr: hdwy to chse ldrs 7f out: wknd over 3f out* **28/1**

0 **9** *3* **Money Tree**[267] 311 5-10-11 0 MrJHamer(7) 77+
(Donald McCain) *led tl hung bdly rt and hdd bnd12f out: rallied to ld again 10f out tl 8f out: sn hung rt again and lost pl: lost tch over 4f out* **25/1**

0- **10** *6* **Ruze (FR)**[546] 1166 6-11-4 0 HaddenFrost 66
(John Mackie) *hld up in tch in midfield: rdn and lost tch over 4f out* **50/1**

11 *1 ¼* **Sky Artist (IRE)** 6-11-1 0 TommyPhelan(3) 65
(Claire Dyson) *reluctant to line up: in tch in rr tl lost tch 5f out* **40/1**

0 **12** *57* **Royal Daffodil**[92] 2167 5-10-4 0 MrNSlatter(7) 7
(Donald McCain) *chsd ldr tl carried wd and lost pl bnd 12f out: rallied to chse ldr again 10f out tl 8f out: sn wknd: t.o fnl 5f* **40/1**

4m 2.90s (-2.40) **Going Correction** +0.025s/f (Yiel)
WFA 4 from 5yo+ 9lb **12** Ran SP% **116.5**
Speed ratings: **106,105,104,102,100 96,92,90,88,86 85,58**
Tote Swingers: 1&2 £25.90, 1&3 £29.90, 2&3 £80.90 CSF £73.42 TOTE £10.30: £3.00, £4.30, £5.00; EX 61.20.
Owner P and Mrs G A Clarke **Bred** James Purcell **Trained** Basford Green, Staffs

FOCUS

This looked a reasonable bumper but the two market leaders were disappointing and there was not much separating the first three. The form looks a bit suspect, but the winner deserves credit for a solid display and rates a small step up. The sixth helps set the level.

NOTEBOOK

Tarn Hows(IRE) split a couple of fellow newcomers when 12-1 second in a steadily run C&D bumper in November. It was hard to get a handle on the form, but this half-brother to decent staying chaser Kings Orchid confirmed his initial promise with a battling win under another hold-up ride. (op 7-1)

Vintage Star(IRE) travelled enthusiastically for a long way and kept grinding away, despite looking inexperienced on debut. This was a promising start in a bumper by this imposing type, particularly as he has a stack of winning pointers on his dam's side. (tchd 12-1)

Vision Of Lights(IRE), who is closely related to 2m hurdle/very smart chase winner Kadarann and useful 2m hurdle winner Kadar, put in a very encouraging performance on debut. He ran green in the home straight but was still not beaten far and is open to plenty of improvement next time. (tchd 10-1 and 14-1)

Koultas King(IRE) bustled up an odds-on winner over 1m6f at Ayr last month. That form gave him leading claims in this chosen target from seven entries in the next four days, but he was in serious trouble before the home turn and could only plug on. (tchd 7-2)

Wychwoods Kaddy couldn't land a blow from off the pace but he seems to be quietly improving and could be suited by a stiffer test over hurdles. (op 22-1 tchd 16-1)
Arctic Actress is closely related to bumper/2m-2m5f hurdle/useful chase winner Isn't That Lucky and was sent off favourite for the powerful Nicky Henderson yard on debut, but she cut out quite quickly some way out. Official explanation: trainer's rep said filly had a breathing problem (tchd 9-4 in a place)
Money Tree Official explanation: jockey said gelding hung right-handed

3921 £20 PUNTERS PACKAGE 11TH FEBRUARY NOVICES' CHASE (15 fncs) 2m 4f 110y

3:30 (3:30) (Class 3) 5-Y-O+ **£6,337** (£1,872; £936)

Form RPR
1-11 **1** **Wymott (IRE)**[50] 2979 7-11-8 142 JasonMaguire 155+
(Donald McCain) *mde all: dived 5th: rdn after 3 out: 2 l ahd: drvn and in command between last 2: eased towards fin* **8/13**[1]
6-12 **2** *10* **Bouggler**[27] 3451 6-11-4 SamThomas 143
(Emma Lavelle) *chsd wnr: wnt upsides 9th: rdn bef 2 out: 2 l down 2 out: btn between last two fences: burst blood vessel* **10/3**[2]
1-31 **3** *81* **Rackham Lerouge (FR)**[25] 3486 6-11-4 132 APMcCoy 108
(Nicky Henderson) *t.k.h: hld up in 3rd: shkn up after 12th: sn btn and eased: t.o bef next* **7/2**[3]

5m 31.4s (22.30) **Going Correction** +0.825s/f (Soft) **3** Ran SP% **107.2**
Speed ratings: **90,86,55**
CSF £2.89 TOTE £1.50; EX 2.60.
Owner Trevor Hemmings **Bred** Mrs Mary Fennell **Trained** Cholmondeley, Cheshire

FOCUS
Three useful and relatively lightly raced types lined up for this fascinating novices' chase. Wymott is a potential 160+ horse over further and the second is rated in line with his good Wincanton run.

NOTEBOOK
Wymott(IRE) had to work hard to make it 2-2 over fences when odds-on in a 3m Exeter novice chase in December. He faced stiffer opposition in this small field and was asked some serious questions by the runner-up at one point, but he jumped well for most of the way and stayed on strongly to eventually score with some authority, despite conceding 4lb to his two rivals. The highlight of his smart novice hurdle career was his defeat of subsequent Grade 1 winner Wayward Prince at Haydock and the early signs are that he is going prove at least as good as a chaser. This lightly raced 7-y-o is not very flashy in his work and would have something to find against Time For Rupert in his likely target the RSA Chase at Cheltenham. Quotes of around 14-1 are probably a fair reflection of his chance, but he is an accurate jumper and resolute galloper who should be suited by going back up in trip. (op 4-6)
Bouggler, a useful staying hurdler (rated 148), reeled in a fair sort to win a Plumpton novice on chase debut before chasing home the promising The Minack under a penalty at Wincanton. He had fair form claims and served it up to the winner some way out before failing to sustain his effort. It transpired that he had burst a blood vessel, so this was a decent run by a likeable Grade 2 winning hurdler, who should have a profitable career as a chaser provided there is no reoccurrence. (op 3-1 tchd 7-2)
Rackham Lerouge(FR), a half-brother to Punchestowns, comfortably justified odds-on favouritism in a four-runner novice chase at Towcester last month to add to his three bumper wins in France and a success in a C&D novice hurdle in February. He was an interesting contender upped in grade, despite having a bit to find, but was left behind some way out before trailing home. Official explanation: trainer's rep said, regarding running, gelding finished distressed. (op 4-1)

3922 CHELTENHAM PREVIEW EVENING 3RD MARCH H'CAP CHASE (18 fncs) 3m 110y

4:05 (4:06) (Class 3) (0-130,129) 5-Y-O+ **£6,337** (£1,872; £936; £468; £234)

Form RPR
-2U5 **1** **Far More Serious (IRE)**[13] 3687 11-11-12 129 (p) FelixDeGiles 140+
(Charlie Longsdon) *hld up in tch: hdwy to trck ldrs 12th: j. ahd next: clr 3 out: nt fluent next: sn drvn: kpt on* **11/1**
0000 **2** *7* **Dashing George (IRE)**[27] 3437 9-11-1 118 (b) LiamTreadwell 124+
(Dr Richard Newland) *hld up in rr: stdy prog fr 1/2-way: wnt 3rd bef 15th: no hdwy and looked wl hld after 3 out: plugged on again flat to go 2nd nr fin: no threat to wnr* **11/2**[3]
6P-6 **3** *1* **Ma Yahab**[27] 3444 10-11-4 121 (b) AidanColeman 123
(Venetia Williams) *chsd ldrs tl led 12th tl next: chsd wnr after tl rdn nt qckn w wnr bef 3 out: plugged on same pce and no imp after: lost 2nd nr fin* **14/1**
-524 **4** *14* **Youngstown (IRE)**[27] 3444 8-11-1 118 JasonMaguire 112+
(Donald McCain) *in tch tl lost pl and rdn bef 8th: last and u.p 1/2-way: plugged on past btn horses to go poor 4th after 3 out: no real imp after* **7/2**[1]
-PF0 **5** *12* **Leac An Scail (IRE)**[25] 3488 10-11-3 120 TjadeCollier 98
(Sue Smith) *chsd ldrs: u.p 1/2-way: outpcd after 12th: n.d fr 14th* **40/1**
3134 **6** *8* **Mohi Rahrere (IRE)**[20] 3562 8-10-8 114 (p) PeterToole[(3)] 89
(Barry Leavy) *in tch tl lost pl and mstke 11th: wl bhd 14th: kpt on again between last 2: t.o* **10/1**
1-P6 **7** *nk* **Afistfullofpebbles**[25] 3488 7-11-3 120 APMcCoy 91
(Jonjo O'Neill) *mde most tl 12th: wknd qckly 15th: wl btn after next: t.o* **8/1**
4F2P **8** *22* **Our Jim**[229] 804 9-10-6 112 AdrianLane[(3)] 63
(Donald McCain) *w ldr tl 7th: dived 4th: lost pl after 12th: wl btn 14th: t.o and eased flat* **16/1**
344- **9** *29* **Justwhateverulike (IRE)**[283] 33 10-10-8 111 (p) PaddyAspell 36
(Sandy Forster) *a in rr: struggling after 12th: lost tch after next: t.o after 3 out* **14/1**
-203 **P** **Tarateeno**[27] 3435 8-10-13 119 MichaelMurphy[(3)] —
(Pat Murphy) *in tch towards rr: mstke 1st: sn nudged along: blnd and drvn 8th: p.u after next: dismntd* **7/1**
-223 **P** **Vamizi (IRE)**[16] 3629 8-11-5 122 RobertThornton —
(Mark Bradstock) *chsd ldrs: mstke and rdn along 10th: wknd qckly 13th: wl btn whn p.u 15th* **9/2**[2]

6m 35.6s (15.80) **Going Correction** +0.825s/f (Soft) **11** Ran SP% **118.5**
Speed ratings: **107,104,104,99,96 93,93,86,77,—** —
Tote Swingers: 1&2 £13.50, 1&3 £15.00, 2&3 £25.00 CSF £72.30 CT £866.64 TOTE £16.50: £4.20, £4.00, £3.80; EX 93.70.
Owner Neysauteur Partnership **Bred** Mrs Marie Byrne **Trained** Over Norton, Oxon

FOCUS
A decent handicap chase. The pace was fair and they were well strung out before the final turn. The winner is rated back to the level of his Newbury in, and the next two were both well handicapped.

NOTEBOOK
Far More Serious(IRE) was a progressive dual chase winner last season. There was a suspicion that he might be close to a dead-lock with the handicapper off 10lb higher than his last win but he proved that theory wrong with a fairly decisive success in first-time cheekpieces. He is still not completely exposed at staying trips and could progress again with his newly acquired headgear. A possible next assignment is the Kim Muir at Cheltenham. (op 12-1)
Dashing George(IRE) showed his first competitive form since joining his new yard. He had a close call off 11lb higher in the Munster National in 2009 and could continue to work his way back. (op 5-1 tchd 6-1)
Ma Yahab ran a big race with blinkers applied on his second run back from eight months off. He has a few lengthy interruptions in his career in recent times but is well handicapped on his best form in 2010, including a fourth behind Ballabriggs in the Kim Muir at Cheltenham last spring. Another crack at that handicap is possible but he may struggle to get a run off his current rating of 121. (tchd 12-1)
Youngstown(IRE) is a generally reliable chaser but he ran a strange race this time. It looked like the game was up when he was scrubbed a along and going nowhere some way out but to his credit he kept fighting and did well to finish fourth. (tchd 10-3)
Leac An Scail(IRE) ended a long losing run at Hexham last spring but has run well below that form in three runs back from a break.
Afistfullofpebbles was up there for a long way before fading quite tamely. (tchd 15-2)
Tarateeno made several hesitant and clumsy jumps before being pulled up as if something was amiss. Official explanation: jockey said gelding lost its action (op 6-1)
Vamizi(IRE) was well backed but emtied quickly before failing to complete. (op 6-1)
T/Plt: £109.80 to a £1 stake. Pool:£55,098.46 - 366.13 winning tickets T/Qpdt: £127.40 to a £1 stake. Pool:£3,264.41 - 18.95 winning tickets SP

3519 CATTERICK (L-H)

Friday, February 4

3923 Meeting Abandoned - High winds

3435 CHEPSTOW (L-H)

Friday, February 4

OFFICIAL GOING: Soft (hdl 4.8, chs 4.7)
First flight of hurdles in back straight omitted in all hurdle races due to bad ground.
Wind: Very strong across Weather: Overcast

3930 E B F "NATIONAL HUNT" NOVICES' HURDLE (QUALIFIER) (10 hdls 1 omitted) 2m 4f

1:30 (1:31) (Class 4) 4-7-Y-O **£2,016** (£592; £296; £147)

Form RPR
1 **Listenlook (FR)**[292] 5-11-2 0 PaddyBrennan 127+
(Nigel Twiston-Davies) *mde virtually all and slt advantage thrght: strly pressed fr 3 out and u.p whn jnd last: styd on gamely to assert fnl 50yds* **25/1**
1 **2** *1* **Our Father (IRE)**[27] 3439 5-11-8 0 TimmyMurphy 131
(David Pipe) *hmpd appr 1st: hld up towards rr: impr 5th: hdwy to trck ldrs 4 out: wnt 2nd next: str chal fr 2 out: upsides last tl no ex u.p fnl 50yds* **4/9**[1]
35 **3** *10* **Roalco De Farges (FR)**[19] 3584 6-11-2 0 RichardJohnson 117+
(Philip Hobbs) *chsd ldrs: chal 4 out tl appr 3 out: outstyd by ldng duo sn after* **8/1**[3]
22-3 **4** *12* **Thomas Wild**[271] 237 6-11-2 0 RhysFlint 105+
(Philip Hobbs) *chsd ldrs: hit 4 out: btn whn wnt bdly lft next* **40/1**
41 **5** *4 ½* **Upthemsteps (IRE)**[50] 2985 6-11-8 0 DougieCostello 105
(Ian Williams) *chsd ldrs: rdn and hit 4 out: sn btn* **5/1**[2]
4- **6** *4 ½* **Thehillofuisneach (IRE)**[438] 2464 7-10-13 0 RichieMcLernon[(3)] 94
(Jonjo O'Neill) *in tch: no ch w ldrs fr 4 out* **20/1**
7 *1* **Sandy's Double** 5-10-11 0 MrRMahon[(5)] 93
(Jamie Snowden) *chsd ldrs: chal fr 5th to 6th: wknd 4 out* **100/1**
1-5 **8** *43* **Gorgehous Lliege (FR)**[32] 3374 5-10-11 0 RTDunne[(5)] 50
(Venetia Williams) *t.k.h: chsd ldrs tl wknd 4 out* **16/1**
5 **9** *19* **Beat All Out**[27] 3441 6-11-2 0 TomO'Brien 31
(Dai Burchell) *in rr: hdwy 6th: wknd 4 out: wl bhd whn hit 2 out* **100/1**
60 **10** *2 ¾* **Ledbury Star (IRE)**[5] 3836 5-11-2 0 DavidDennis 28
(Matt Sheppard) *w wnr fr 4th to 6th: wknd 4 out* **125/1**
00 **11** *9* **Fresher Fishing (IRE)**[34] 3295 7-11-2 0 (p) AndrewGlassonbury 19
(Victor Dartnall) *in tch: j. slowly 5th: wknd fr next* **100/1**
0- **12** *1 ¼* **Manics Man**[530] 1295 6-11-2 0 JamieMoore 18
(Helen Nelmes) *hit 3rd a bhd* **100/1**
0 **P** **Semelay (FR)**[20] 3569 5-11-2 0 LiamHeard —
(Laura Young) *in rr fr 4th: t.o whn p.u bef 6th* **100/1**
P **Kaygeekay (IRE)** 5-10-9 0 JamesDavies —
(Chris Down) *a bhd: t.o whn p.u bef 6th* **100/1**
R **Dont Worry** 5-10-9 0 SClements[(7)] —
(Richard Mitchell) *sn struggling in rr and wl bhd: t.o whn ref 5th* **100/1**

5m 5.20s (3.40) **Going Correction** +0.35s/f (Yiel) **15** Ran SP% **121.7**
Speed ratings: **107,106,102,97,96 94,93,76,69,67 64,63,—,—,—**
Tote Swingers: 1&2 £6.90, 1&3 £7.20, 2&3 £2.00 CSF £38.24 TOTE £34.50: £3.80, £1.10, £1.90; EX 58.60.
Owner Allan Stennett **Bred** Serpentine Bloodstock Ltd **Trained** Naunton, Gloucs

FOCUS
This fair novice hurdle was run in a time around 32 seconds over the standard. The first two are above avergae, and it was a good effort from the winner on his rules debut.

NOTEBOOK
Listenlook(FR) made just about all on this hurdles debut and battled on well to outgun the favourite. His hurdling was not that fluent and he wandered a little under pressure, but there is improvement in him over further. He handles better ground.
Our Father(IRE) ran out an impressive winner over C&D at the Welsh National meeting. There was an anxious moment going to the first, where it looked as if he might be forced through the wing, but he soon travelled nicely in touch. He looked the one to beat after moving through to challenge going best, but he did not find as much as the winner when let down on this bad ground. This scopey grey still looks weak but will be a smart prospect when he strengthens up. (op 1-2 tchd 4-7 and 8-13 in a place)
Roalco De Farges(FR), taking a small drop back in trip, was a little keen early on. He had every chance early in the straight but the first two left him trailing from the third-last. A little race should come his way. (op 12-1 tchd 7-1)
Thomas Wild was placed in each of his four bumpers, the most recent of them last May. Although well held on this hurdles bow, he did make the frame again and he appeared to see out this longer trip well enough. (op 33-1)
Upthemsteps(IRE)'s Towcester win has been boosted by the placed horses and the switch to a left-handed track promised to suit, but he faded early in the home straight over this longer trip. (tchd 4-1)
Thehillofuisneach(IRE), who has left Paul Nicholls since his last start back in November 2009, did not shape badly but needs to start catching up on lost time. (op 14-1)
Sandy's Double is out of a decent winning jumper and he ran a pleasing first race.

Semelay(FR) Official explanation: jockey said gelding was unsuited by the soft ground

3931 LINDLEY CATERING NOVICES' HURDLE (11 hdls 1 omitted) 3m
2:05 (2:05) (Class 4) 5-Y-0+ **£2,016** (£592; £296; £147)

Form				RPR
32	1		**Join Together (IRE)**[55] 2888 6-10-12 136 .... NickScholfield (Paul Nicholls) *trckd ldr: chal fr 6th tl led wl bef 4 out: pushed clr sn after: eased run-in* **5/4**[1]	139+
-422	2	20	**Super Villan**[52] 2946 6-10-12 120 .... TomScudamore (Mark Bradstock) *led: jnd by wnr fr 6th: hdd wl bef 4 out and sn no ch: jnd for poor 2nd 3 out: kpt on all out to hold that position run-in* **4/1**[3]	114
2FP0	3	1	**Russian Song (IRE)**[13] 3686 7-10-12 106 ....(p) JoeTizzard (Colin Tizzard) *in tch: nt lunt 5th and sn bhd: virtually t.o fr 4 out: kpt on fr 3 out and styd on wl to cl on mod 2nd cl home but nvr any ch w wnr* **25/1**	114
000	4	3 ¾	**Otter Mist**[34] 3295 6-10-12 0 .... AndrewGlassonbury (Victor Dartnall) *chsd ldrs: disputing poor 2nd whn mstke 4 out: styd pressing for mod 2nd tl 2 out: no ex last and dropped to 4th run-in* **50/1**	111+
1	5	57	**State Benefit (IRE)**[38] 3153 6-11-5 0 .... BarryGeraghty (Nicky Henderson) *chse ldrs tl wknd rapidly appr 4 out: t.o* **2/1**[2]	59
/601	6	42	**King Of Dubai**[19] 3585 6-11-5 120 .... RhysFlint (John Flint) *in tch tl wknd 6th: t.o* **14/1**	17
4PP-	P		**Ruttan Lake (IRE)**[306] 5016 8-10-9 75 .... RichieMcLernon(3) (Violet M Jordan) *a bhd: blnd 2nd: t.o whn p.u bef 3 out* **200/1**	—
00	P		**Rathconrath (FR)**[22] 3528 6-10-12 0 .... DavidEngland (Althea Barclay) *in rr: rdn 5th: t.o whn p.u bef 3 out* **200/1**	—
53	P		**Power Lord (IRE)**[25] 3485 6-10-12 0 .... WillKennedy (Bob Buckler) *sn bhd: t.o whn p.u bef 3 out* **33/1**	—
00	P		**Oscar The Myth (IRE)**[7] 3789 5-10-7 0 .... MrRMahon(5) (Jamie Snowden) *sn bhd: t.o whn p.u bef 4 out* **100/1**	—

6m 22.26s (2.46) **Going Correction** +0.35s/f (Yiel) **10** Ran SP% **115.2**
Speed ratings: **109,102,102,100,81 67,—,—,—,—**
Tote Swingers: 1&2 £1.60, 1&3 £7.60, 2&3 £9.80 CSF £6.66 TOTE £2.20: £1.10, £1.20, £5.40; EX 4.30.

Owner Ian J Fogg & Paul K Barber **Bred** J D Flood **Trained** Ditcheat, Somerset

FOCUS
A reasonable novice hurdle. They took things pretty steady and the time was slow. Join Together ran to a similar level as his Cheltenham second.

NOTEBOOK
Join Together(IRE) was the only one who truly saw out the trip in the conditions. Third to Court In Motion at Exeter before finishing runner-up to Mossley in a Cheltenham Grade 2, he had a lot in hand on official figures and duly ran out a wide-margin winner, pulling clear in the long home straight. He gets 3m well and the Albert Bartlett over that trip at the Cheltenham festival could come into consideration, where soft ground would enhance his prospects. (op Evens tchd 10-11 and 11-8 in places)

Super Villan had finished second in a couple of novice hurdles over an extended 2m6f and promised to stay. After making the running, he was left behind by the winner but plugged on to hold second. He is still without a win, but has been placed in six of his eight starts now. (op 5-1 tchd 11-2)

Russian Song(IRE) was in trouble early on the second circuit but stayed on past tired rivals to snatch a well beaten third. (op 20-1)

Otter Mist ◆ had not shown much in two previous tries over hurdles but his bumper debut had not been devoid of promise. He ran well for a long way and was still battling for second when making a mistake at the final flight.

State Benefit(IRE) was penalised for his win at Ffos Las. After tracking the pace he stopped quickly on the long run round to the straight and was allowed to come home in his own time. The ground is an obvious excuse. (op 9-4 tchd 15-8)

King Of Dubai, under a penalty, was in trouble a good mile out. (tchd 12-1)

3932 LINDLEY CATERING NOVICES' CHASE (12 fncs) 2m 110y
2:35 (2:36) (Class 4) 5-Y-0+ **£2,439** (£716; £358; £178)

Form				RPR
1-0F	1		**Tail Of The Bank (IRE)**[16] 3625 8-11-0 0 .... LiamHeard (Laura Young) *in rr but in tch w main gp bhd clr ldr: hdwy 8th: wnt 3rd 3 out: styd on wl to chal last: led fnl 50yds: r.o strly* **4/1**[2]	119+
3	2	1 ½	**Surfing (FR)**[37] 3193 5-11-5 150 .... BarryGeraghty (Nicky Henderson) *j. slowly 2nd: prom in main gp bhd clr ldr 5th: wnt 2nd 7th: gd prog 8th: chal 3 out: led next: jnd last: rdn run-in: hdd and no ex fnl 50yds* **4/11**[1]	122+
-406	3	3 ¼	**Dinarius**[12] 3696 6-11-0 112 ....(p) JimmyMcCarthy (Alex Hales) *kpt wd of other runners and poached 20 l s: c bk to field 8th: jnd 3 out: hdd next: one pce and hld whn hit last* **20/1**	115
0-04	4	20	**Gus Macrae (IRE)**[20] 3555 7-11-0 0 ....(t) TomScudamore (Rebecca Curtis) *t.k.h: trckd ldrs in main gp bhd clr ldr tl nt fluent and dropped to rr 4th: hdwy 8th: blnd 4 out and sn wknd* **9/1**[3]	102+
3356	5	6	**Catholic Hill (USA)**[17] 3611 6-10-7 0 .... MrPJTolman(7) (Mark Gillard) *chsd clr ldr tl 7th: wknd next* **66/1**	88

4m 27.49s (10.39) **Going Correction** +0.725s/f (Soft) **5** Ran SP% **109.6**
Speed ratings: **104,103,101,92,89**
CSF £6.24 TOTE £3.40: £1.60, £1.30; EX 6.00.

Owner Total Plumbing Supporters Club **Bred** Robert McCarthy **Trained** Broomfield, Somerset
■ Laura Young's first winner since she served a six-month ban.

FOCUS
A decent little novice chase run over 28 seconds outside the standard. The third home was well clear for a time, largely ignored by the other four, who closed right up on the home turn. The first two were well below their best with the third and fifth probably the best guide to the form.

NOTEBOOK
Tail Of The Bank(IRE) was in the process of running a big race when crashing out on his chase debut behind Surfing's stablemate Finian's Rainbow at Newbury. He crept into the race, jumping soundly, and showed a bright turn of foot in the context of this slowly run event to forge to the front after the last. This tall, imposing gelding holds an entry in the Jewson (Golden Miller) Novice Chase at Cheltenham, and the step up to 2m4f should suit. He is a really nice prospect who seems sure to go on to better things. He would not want the ground any softer. (op 11-4)

Surfing(FR) was the one to beat after the abundant promise of his British debut at Newbury. After coming through to show ahead two from home, he could not hold off the winner on the run-in. His jumping was good and he did little wrong, but this trip is perhaps on the short side for him. He is in both the Arkle and the Jewson. (op 1-2 tchd 8-15 and 4-7 in places)

Dinarius, who went early to post, got a flyer as the tapes went up. He was reeled in before the home straight, but to his credit he hung in there and was rewarded with third. A faller on his one previous chase start a year ago, he looks worth carrying on with over fences. (tchd 16-1)

Gus Macrae(IRE) closed up again in the straight and was right there when he made a mess of the final ditch, after which he was held together. The ability is there but he has something to prove now. (op 8-1)

Catholic Hill(USA) was not disgraced on this chasing debut but the nature of the race means that he may have been flattered.

3933 LINDLEY CATERING H'CAP CHASE (18 fncs) 3m
3:05 (3:07) (Class 5) (0-95,95) 5-Y-0+ **£1,593** (£467; £233; £116)

Form				RPR
6-53	1		**Lady De La Vega (FR)**[85] 2332 7-11-10 93 ....(vt) RichardJohnson (Tim Vaughan) *in rr but in tch: hdwy fr 8th: j. slowly 10th: chsd ldr after 13th: led next: c clr fr 3 out: in command whn blnd last: sn rcvrd: kpt on strly* **8/1**	108+
4-06	2	11	**Mr Chippy (IRE)**[246] 596 7-11-7 90 .... DougieCostello (Ian Williams) *in rr: hit 7th: hdwy 9th: chal 11th: led next: hdd after 13th: styd on chsng wnr but no ch fr 4 out: hit 2 out* **14/1**	92
/324	3	6	**Billy Murphy**[32] 3377 8-11-5 88 .... RhysFlint (Paul Cowley) *in rr: hit 8th: hdwy to chse ldrs 12th: styd on same pce fr 4 out* **4/1**[2]	85
-515	4	13	**Cold Harbour**[22] 3527 7-11-5 95 .... MrJEngland(7) (Evan Williams) *in rr: hdwy after 13th: nvr rchd ldrs and no imp whn j. slowly 4 out* **12/1**	81
200P	5	5	**Kiltimoney (IRE)**[18] 3609 11-10-0 69 oh8 .... TomScudamore (Richard Mitchell) *in tch: rdn 12th: wknd after next* **16/1**	46
P513	6	½	**Wasntme (IRE)**[17] 3614 8-10-2 71 ....(tp) HarrySkelton (Colin Tizzard) *in tch tl wknd 13th* **5/1**[3]	51
3323	7	15	**Dromore Hill (IRE)**[50] 2982 7-11-5 88 ....(b[1]) JimmyMcCarthy (Charlie Morlock) *nvr travelling: sn rdn along: a in rr* **3/1**[1]	50
5/P3	P		**Randolph O'Brien (IRE)**[21] 3541 11-11-7 90 .... PaddyBrennan (Nigel Twiston-Davies) *led after 2nd: hdd8th: led again 10th: hdd 12th: sn wknd: t.o whn p.u bef 14th* **16/1**	—
60-4	P		**Zimbabwe (FR)**[18] 3609 11-9-11 71 oh1 ow2 ....(p) MattGriffiths(5) (Nigel Hawke) *led tl after 2nd: wknd 10th: t.o whn p.u bef 3 out* **7/1**	—
055-	P		**Macmar (FR)**[291] 5281 11-11-3 91 ....(p) KeiranBurke(5) (John Coombe) *led to 2nd: prssed ldr: led 8th to 10th: wknd 12th: t.o whn p.u bef 3 out* **25/1**	—
P-63	P		**Daring Approach (IRE)**[82] 2392 10-11-5 88 .... JamieMoore (Helen Nelmes) *chsd ldrs to 10th: t.o whn p.u bef 14th* **16/1**	—

6m 38.6s (16.60) **Going Correction** +0.725s/f (Soft) **11** Ran SP% **121.1**
Speed ratings: **101,97,95,91,89 89,84,—,—,— —**
Tote Swingers: 1&2 £14.30, 1&3 £2.90, 2&3 £21.70 CSF £113.18 CT £521.97 TOTE £9.60: £2.00, £2.80, £1.30; EX 95.10.

Owner Mrs L D Edwards **Bred** Gerard E Sabathier & P J Sabathier **Trained** Aberthin, Vale of Glamorgan

FOCUS
A modest handicap chase which became a real slog. A step up from the easy winner with the second setting the level.

NOTEBOOK
Lady De La Vega(FR) drew clear from the last ditch for a comfortable win, although she stepped into the final fence. Running in only her second chase, she has reportedly had a wind operation since her last start and wore a tongue-tie for the first time. There is more to come from her over this sort of trip (op 15-2 tchd 9-1)

Mr Chippy(IRE) is a winning pointer but this was his chasing debut under rules, as well as his first appearance in a handicap. After travelling well into the lead, he was no match for the mare over the final four fences, but is fully entitled to come on for this first start for eight months.

Billy Murphy is a one-paced maiden but he is in good heart this winter and this was another solid effort. (tchd 9-2)

Cold Harbour closed under pressure on the home turn but was soon making no further inroads. He has yet to prove he stays this far. (op 16-1)

Dromore Hill(IRE) didn't fancy this one jot and looked quirky. Official explanation: jockey said gelding never travelled (op 4-1)

Randolph O'Brien(IRE) has a poor record going left-handed. (op 12-1)

3934 BRISTOL EVENING POST H'CAP HURDLE (10 hdls 1 omitted) 2m 4f
3:40 (3:44) (Class 4) (0-115,114) 4-Y-0+ **£2,016** (£592; £296; £147)

Form				RPR
53-6	1		**Sherwani Wolf (IRE)**[52] 2946 7-11-12 114 .... PaddyBrennan (Nigel Twiston-Davies) *chsd ldrs: slt ld 4 out: drvn clr fr 2 out: drvn out run-in* **9/2**[2]	126+
-0F0	2	6	**Timetoring**[19] 3589 9-10-9 102 ....(p) MissIsabelTompsett(5) (Bernard Llewellyn) *chsd ldrs: chal fr 5th tl appr 4 out: kpt on u.p to chse wnr fr 2 out but no imp* **12/1**	106
-434	3	4 ½	**The Boss (IRE)**[16] 3628 6-11-5 107 ....(t) NickScholfield (Jeremy Scott) *chsd ldrs: lost position 5th: gd prog after next and ev ch 4 out: chsd wnr next but no imp: one pce into 3rd 2 out* **8/1**	106
6445	4	shd	**Graduation Night**[32] 3370 5-11-5 107 .... RichardJohnson (Jamie Snowden) *chsd ldrs: drvn to chal 4 out: hit 3 out and lost pl: blnd last but kpt on again run-in* **10/1**	107+
30	5	5	**Oscar Close (IRE)**[94] 2141 6-11-3 112 .... TrevorWhelan(7) (George Baker) *chsd ldrs: led after 6th: hdd 4 out: wknd 2 out* **16/1**	105
P/6-	6	hd	**Round The Horn (IRE)**[317] 4826 11-10-7 95 ....(t) TimmyMurphy (Jim Old) *hld up in rr and racd on outer: hdwy appr 4 out: pushed along to cl on ldrs next but on terms: one pce fr 2 out* **40/1**	88
2-50	7	15	**Mae Cigan (FR)**[19] 3587 8-11-7 109 .... JimmyMcCarthy (Michael Blanshard) *chsd ldrs tl wknd 4 out* **25/1**	87
2400	8	6	**Watch Out**[25] 3481 7-10-9 97 ....(p) TomO'Brien (Dai Burchell) *nvr bttr than mid-div: wknd 4 out* **66/1**	69
-004	9	48	**Yetholm (USA)**[19] 3587 6-11-8 110 ....(p) RhysFlint (John Flint) *chsd ldrs tl wknd qckly 4 out* **6/1**	34
3505	10	22	**The Clyda Rover (IRE)**[7] 3791 7-10-5 98 .... JoshuaMoore(5) (Helen Nelmes) *j. slowly 4th and 5th: a bhd* **11/2**[3]	—
505-	11	2 ¾	**Gouranga**[334] 4469 8-9-12 88 ow1 .... EamonDehdashti(3) (Tony Carroll) *a towards rr* **40/1**	—
214P	12	6	**Be Ashored**[22] 3529 6-11-0 105 .... RichardKilloran(3) (Tim Vaughan) *bhd fr 1/2-way* **25/1**	—
5151	R		**Najca De Thaix (FR)**[10] 3724 10-11-10 112 7ex .... JamieMoore (John Spearing) *ref to r* **4/1**[1]	—
F040	P		**Giovanna**[25] 3483 10-11-11 113 ....(t) WarrenMarston (Richard Phillips) *rdn and bhd appr 5th: t.o whn p.u bef 4 out* **33/1**	—
0P1-	P		**Flowonlovelyriver (IRE)**[328] 4584 10-10-4 92 .... HarrySkelton (Rachel Hobbs) *led tl hdd after 6th: sn wknd: t.o whn p.u bef 3 out* **28/1**	—

5m 10.79s (8.99) **Going Correction** +0.35s/f (Yiel) **15** Ran SP% **122.1**
Speed ratings (Par 105): **96,93,91,91,89 89,83,81,62,53 52,49,—,—,—**
Tote Swingers: 1&2 £32.50, 1&3 £8.40, 2&3 £20.20 CSF £53.67 CT £430.80 TOTE £4.30: £1.50, £3.70, £2.30; EX 69.50.

Owner Charles Davies **Bred** Cecil Ashe **Trained** Naunton, Gloucs

FOCUS
An ordinary handicap hurdle, but one with drama at the start. A big hurdles best from the winner with the next three setting the level.

NOTEBOOK
Sherwani Wolf(IRE) was always prominent, in common with the other principals, and he stayed on well once striking the front. Taking a small drop in trip, this dual bumper winner was running in his first handicap, and was sharper for his outing at Folkestone before Christmas. He did it well, but his main market rival's refusal to race smoothed his path. (op 4-1 tchd 5-1)
Timetoring, dropped 3lb, stays further than this and stuck on for second. He likes Chepstow and this was his best effort of the season so far. (op 16-1)
The Boss(IRE), tongue tied for the first time and back over hurdles, raced wide most of the way and lacked a change of pace up the straight. He is worth stepping up to 3m. (op 15-2)
Graduation Night is gradually getting things together, but his hurdling let him down in the straight. (op 8-1)
Oscar Close(IRE) ran respectably but his best form in Ireland came over shorter. (tchd 18-1)
Round The Horn(IRE) made steady headway from off the pace before his effort flattened out.
Najca De Thaix(FR) looked to have strong claims, being 11lb well in under his penalty, but despite his rider's efforts he declined to jump off with the others. There had been a false start and it is very likely that the resultant delay unsettled him. (op 9-2 tchd 7-2)

3935 WESTERN DAILY PRESS H'CAP CHASE (16 fncs) 2m 3f 110y
4:15 (4:15) (Class 4) (0-115,115) 5-Y-0+ **£2,439** (£716; £358; £178)

Form					RPR
6-50	1		**Plein Pouvoir (FR)**[56] 2869 8-11-7 **115** ... RTDunne(5)	134+
			(Venetia Williams) *trckd ldrs: led after 12th: clr fr 3 out: v easily* **3/1**[2]	
/022	2	28	**Rateable Value**[17] 3615 7-10-7 **96** ... JoeTizzard	87
			(Colin Tizzard) *chsd ldrs: chal 7th tl led after 11th: hdd after 12th and sn no ch w wnr but styd wl clr of 3rd* **7/4**[1]	
-F0P	3	25	**Master Somerville**[74] 2587 9-11-8 **111** ... (b) RichardJohnson	77
			(Henry Daly) *led: jnd fr 7th: blnd 11th: hdd sn after: wknd qckly 12th: lft poor 3rd 3 out* **12/1**	
0011	4	33	**Massini Sunset (IRE)**[18] 3608 11-11-2 **112** ... (b) SClements(7)	45
			(Richard Mitchell) *chsd ldrs: chal 7th to 11th: rdn and wknd sn after: t.o* **4/1**[3]	
06P5	5	55	**Factotum**[20] 3562 7-10-12 **111** ... GeraldQuinn(10)	—
			(Jonjo O'Neill) *rdn along after 5th: a wl bhd: t.o* **40/1**	
0P46	6	nk	**Adajal (IRE)**[22] 3531 8-11-9 **115** ... (t) RichieMcLernon(3)	—
			(Jonjo O'Neill) *in rr: sme hdwy 6th: blnd 8th and sn wl bhd: t.o* **40/1**	
2/4-	7	9	**Poseidon's Secret (IRE)**[635] 248 8-10-13 **105** ... DannyCook(3)	—
			(John Panvert) *blnd 1st and 2nd: in rr: sme hdwy 6th: blnd 8th: t.o whn mstke 10th* **14/1**	
F-35	F		**Quintero (FR)**[16] 3628 7-11-2 **105** ... PaulMoloney	—
			(Evan Williams) *in tch: hdwy 10th: rdn after 11th: nvr quite on terms: wknd 12th: distant 3rd whn fell 3 out* **11/2**	

5m 23.05s (11.75) **Going Correction** +0.725s/f (Soft) **8** Ran SP% **116.0**
Speed ratings: **105,93,83,70,48 48,44,—**
Tote Swingers: 1&2 £1.90, 1&3 £7.90, 2&3 £3.40 CSF £9.28 CT £51.24 TOTE £5.50: £1.10, £1.80, £3.40; EX 12.70.
Owner Dr Moira Hamlin **Bred** Mme Jean-Marc & Jean-Marc Baudrelle **Trained** Kings Caple, H'fords

FOCUS
No more than a fair handicap chase. They went a reasonable pace considering the ground and came home at wide intervals. The easy winner could be flattered as nothing else got home.

NOTEBOOK
Plein Pouvoir(FR) tracked the leaders before easing to the front four from home and quickly drawing a long way clear. Lightly raced since his last win 13 months ago, he gets further and is clearly in fine heart, but he will be faced with a stiff rise in the handicap for this. His trainer thinks he is most effective giving weight to inferior rivals, as he did here. (tchd 4-1)
Rateable Value has found one too good in each of his three chase starts and was soundly beaten here, but his turn should come. This trip is on the short side for him. (op 5-2)
Master Somerville ran a better race after a winter break but was a spent force in the home straight. (op 14-1 tchd 16-1)
Massini Sunset(IRE), seeking a hat-trick, went up 8lb for his latest victory but was still officially 3lb ahead of the handicapper. He dropped away early in the straight and may struggle from his imminent career-high mark. (op 9-2 tchd 3-1)
Quintero(FR), who has dropped 5lb since switching to fences, latched onto the leading group down the far side but was a toiling third when coming down three from home. (op 5-1 tchd 6-1)

3936 DIGIBET.COM STANDARD OPEN NATIONAL HUNT FLAT RACE 2m 110y
4:50 (4:50) (Class 6) 4-6-Y-0 **£1,301** (£382; £191; £95)

Form					RPR
121	1		**Saint Luke (IRE)**[27] 3441 6-11-13 0 ... RichardJohnson	115+
			(Peter Bowen) *mde virtually all: strly chal fr over 3f out: styd on gamely u.p to assert fnl f: drvn out* **7/2**[3]	
3	2	1 3/4	**Flemi Two Toes (IRE)**[86] 2309 5-11-3 0 ... BarryGeraghty	102
			(Rebecca Curtis) *trckd ldrs and t.k.h early: chal over 3f out: stl upsides but u.p fr 2f out: no ex and one pce fnl f* **7/4**[1]	
1	3	3 1/4	**Kawa (FR)**[74] 2590 5-11-10 0 ... CharliePoste	106
			(Robin Dickin) *t.k.h early: chsd ldrs: drvn to chal fr over 3f out tl ins fnl 2f: outpcd by ldng duo whn hung lft ins fnl f* **9/4**[2]	
6	4	8	**Rowlestone Lad**[20] 3569 4-10-7 0 ... RhysFlint	81
			(Richard Price) *in rr but in tch: hdwy to chse ldrs 6f out: rdn over 3f out and sn btn* **50/1**	
	5	2 1/4	**Twin Barrels** 4-10-7 0 ... JamesDavies	79
			(Andrew Haynes) *in tch: rdn and outpcd 5f out: mod prog fnl 2f* **33/1**	
	6	18	**Bravo Riquet (FR)**[132] 5-11-3 0 ... WarrenMarston	71
			(Robin Mathew) *chsd ldrs tl wknd over 4f out* **16/1**	
054-	7	45	**My Legal Lady**[295] 5199 6-10-10 0 ... TimmyMurphy	19
			(Stuart Howe) *racd towards outside: in tch 1/2-way: wknd 6f out: t.o* **12/1**	
	8	82	**Tranquil River (IRE)** 6-10-10 0 ... MrCGreene(7)	—
			(John Upson) *a bhd: t.o and virtually p.u fnl 4f* **66/1**	
	S		**Wild Tango** 5-11-3 0 ... AndrewGlassonbury	—
			(Bob Buckler) *chsd ldrs tl wknd quickly over 6f out: virtually p.u whn collapsed 3f out* **40/1**	

4m 12.98s (7.98) **Going Correction** +0.35s/f (Yiel)
WFA 4 from 5yo 9lb 5 from 6yo 1lb **9** Ran SP% **111.8**
Speed ratings: **95,94,92,88,87 79,58,19,—**
Tote Swingers: 1&2 £2.90, 1&3 £2.60, 2&3 £2.30. Totesuper7: Win: £5,832.20 - 6 winning units. Place: £14.10 - 723 winning units.. CSF £9.48 TOTE £3.20: £1.02, £1.90, £2.20; EX 12.60.
Owner Saith O Ni & Ednyfed & Elizabeth Morgan **Bred** Joseph O'Dwyer **Trained** Little Newcastle, Pembrokes

FOCUS
Probably a decent bumper, although there was no strength in depth and the first three pulled clear. They are rated pretty much to their marks.

NOTEBOOK
Saint Luke(IRE) had already won two of these, one of them over C&D, and he produced a brave performance from the front under his double penalty. He has won a point-to-point over 3m and will surely make a useful staying novice over hurdles. (tchd 3-1)
Flemi Two Toes(IRE) was third on his debut at Bangor - runner-up has won since - and probably ran to a similar level. He could not get past a very tough opponent, but there seems no reason why he cannot win a bumper before he switches to hurdling. (op 2-1)
Kawa(FR), another who had not been seen since November, was penalised for his Ludlow victory over a subsequent winning hurdler. He did not settle as well as he might have and was the first of the three principals to feel the pinch, but he remains a useful hurdling prospect. (op 5-2 tchd 11-4)
Rowlestone Lad was left behind by the principals in the straight but this was still a big step up on what he showed first time.
Twin Barrels was staying on and can be expected to improve. (op 20-1)
Bravo Riquet(FR), an Irish point winner, weakened early in the straight.
T/Plt: £22.80 to a £1 stake. Pool:£74,376.01 - 2,371.97 winning tickets T/Qpdt: £9.80 to a £1 stake. Pool:£5,595.35 - 419.85 winning tickets ST

3760 FFOS LAS (L-H)
Saturday, February 5

OFFICIAL GOING: Good to soft (soft in places)
Fresh ground for hurdles and chase track at full width.
Wind: Strong, half against Weather: Dull, some drizzle

3937 WILLIAMHILL.COM NOVICES' HURDLE (8 hdls) 2m
1:30 (1:30) (Class 4) 4-Y-0+ **£2,602** (£764; £382; £190)

Form					RPR
11-2	1		**Sprinter Sacre (FR)**[78] 2493 5-11-3 ... BarryGeraghty	122+
			(Nicky Henderson) *trckd ldr: led 3 out: drew clr last: easily* **2/9**[1]	
30	2	10	**Sorcillera**[39] 3158 5-10-10 ... RhysFlint	99
			(John Flint) *hdwy and in tch 3rd: effrt and disputed cl 2nd 2 out: nt gng pce of wnr last* **20/1**	
1	3	1 1/4	**Kazzene (USA)**[21] 3554 4-11-0 ... TomScudamore	106+
			(David Pipe) *chsd ldng pair after 2nd: clsd up and hit 3 out: disputing 2nd and hld whn mstke last* **7/2**[2]	
30P	4	20	**Journeyman (IRE)**[20] 3584 5-11-0 ... RichardKilloran(3)	88
			(Nicky Henderson) *led tl 3 out: wknd next* **16/1**	
14-6	5	9	**Fishoutofwater (IRE)**[20] 3585 7-11-3 ... DenisO'Regan	79
			(Rebecca Curtis) *in tch tl outpcd fr 5th* **15/2**[3]	
0	6	3 3/4	**Sanctuary**[18] 3620 5-11-3 ... AlanO'Keeffe	76
			(Michael Scudamore) *chsd ldrs early: mid-div and struggling fr 4th* **33/1**	
00	7	21	**Special Cuvee**[9] 3760 5-10-10 ... OliverDayman(7)	57
			(Alison Thorpe) *a bhd: no ch 5th* **33/1**	
00	8	16	**Lady From Ige (IRE)**[16] 3645 7-10-10 ... RodiGreene	35
			(Neil Mulholland) *nt jump wl: a trailing in last: no ch 1/2-way* **50/1**	

3m 49.8s (0.80) **Going Correction** +0.025s/f (Yiel)
WFA 4 from 5yo+ 9lb **8** Ran SP% **134.3**
Speed ratings (Par 105): **99,94,93,83,78 77,66,58**
toteswingers:1&2 £1.80, 2&3 £13.40, 1&3 £1.10 CSF £12.94 TOTE £1.20: £1.02, £4.10, £1.30; EX 20.00.
Owner Mrs Caroline Mould **Bred** Christophe Masle **Trained** Upper Lambourn, Berks

FOCUS
An interesting race on paper, in what looked testing conditions but won easily by a top prospect. He was value for further but didn't need to be at his best.

NOTEBOOK
Sprinter Sacre(FR) ◆, who showed plenty of ability on his hurdling debut at Ascot (2m3f), never looked like letting his supporters down. A horse with a high cruising speed, who reportedly returned with a very dirty nose after his run at the Berkshire course, he surely has plenty more improvement to come and seems sure to develop into a Grade 1 performer. The Supreme Novices' Hurdle at Cheltenham next month is the target, but connections didn't seem fully committal afterwards, so punters may want to hold their bets for a while. (op 1-3, tchd 4-11 in places)
Sorcillera ◆ is nicely bred for jump racing and returned to something close to the performance she put up on her British debut with a brave effort. She ought to win an ordinary contest if running up to her best.
Kazzene(USA) represented the 4-y-o generation and was undone by his jumping over the last three hurdles. He stumbled after clearing the last, which probably cost him second place. (op 4-1)
Journeyman(IRE) made a lot of the running but was beaten heading to two out.
Fishoutofwater(IRE), dropping 6f in distance, disappointed once again over hurdles. (op 8-1)
Sanctuary Official explanation: jockey said gelding hung left

3938 WILLIAM HILL - HOME OF BETTING NOVICES' CHASE (18 fncs) 3m
2:05 (2:05) (Class 3) 5-Y-0+ **£5,204** (£1,528; £764; £381)

Form					RPR
-P21	1		**Massini Man (IRE)**[179] 1227 10-10-11 115 ... MissCLWills(7)	121+
			(Brendan Powell) *mde all: blnd 3rd: styd on gamely whn chal in st: rdn out* **11/1**	
1P-4	2	3 3/4	**Lord Ragnar (IRE)**[28] 3451 8-10-12 0 ... BarryGeraghty	114+
			(Nicky Henderson) *hld up: lft 3rd at 9th: hdwy to press wnr 4 out: hrd rdn 2 out: one pce* **6/5**[1]	
-21P	3	4 1/2	**Acrai Rua (IRE)**[29] 3428 8-11-4 120 ... (p) PaulMoloney	115
			(Evan Williams) *chsd wnr fr 6th tl 13th: sn outpcd* **7/1**[3]	
4P6	4	89	**Sunsalve (IRE)**[20] 3586 7-10-5 0 ... (t) AodhaganConlon(7)	53
			(Rebecca Curtis) *cl up: handy 3rd whn blnd and nrly fell 9th: nt rcvr: bhd after: no ch 14th* **40/1**	
12/0	F		**Jokers Legacy (IRE)**[28] 3440 9-10-12 0 ... (t) TomO'Brien	—
			(Tim Vaughan) *4th whn fell 1st* **6/4**[2]	

6m 24.9s (1.90) **Going Correction** -0.075s/f (Good) **5** Ran SP% **108.7**
Speed ratings: **93,91,90,60,—**
CSF £25.35 TOTE £13.10: £1.50, £1.50; EX 32.80.
Owner Steven Astaire **Bred** Patrick O'Donnell **Trained** Upper Lambourn, Berks

FOCUS
An ordinary contest but a fantastic riding performance on Massini Man by Clare Wills, who fired her mount into every fence. The form is rated around the first two.

NOTEBOOK
Massini Man(IRE) put in some fine leaps, which certainly helped him hold off a better-fancied rival. Having his first start in 179 days, he is entitled to be straighter for this, and should be of some interest if returned to handicap company next time. (op 9-1 tchd 12-1)
Lord Ragnar(IRE) loomed up to look a big danger down the home straight but he was never able to get his head to the front. He may not stay 3m well enough in a competitive race to get past proven stayers. (op 10-11)
Acrai Rua(IRE), in first-time cheekpieces, was held a long way out. (tchd 15-2)
Sunsalve(IRE) wasn't far away when making a dreadful blunder at the ninth, which effectively ended his chance. (op 25-1 tchd 50-1)

Jokers Legacy(IRE) got no further than the first on his chasing debut after being supported in the betting. (op 5-2)

3939 WILLIAM HILL WELSH CHAMPION HURDLE (8 hdls) 2m

2:40 (2:41) (Class 2) 4-Y-0+ **£28,179** (£8,325; £4,162; £2,083; £1,039)

Form				RPR
14-1	1		**Oscar Whisky (IRE)**[35] 3289 6-11-7 165 BarryGeraghty (Nicky Henderson) *trckd ldng pair: nt fluent 3rd: wnt cl 2nd at 5th: led on bit 2 out: clr whn hit last: easily* **2/7**[1]	159+
P106	2	8	**Black Jack Blues (IRE)**[77] 2516 8-11-3 147 (t) AodhaganConlon (Rebecca Curtis) *led: hit 2nd: hdd 2 out: no ch w wnr* **10/1**[3]	141
0-2F	3	3 ¾	**Tarkari (IRE)**[83] 2386 6-11-3 132 PaulMoloney (Evan Williams) *hld up in last: hdwy into 3rd after 3 out: outpcd next: disputing 2nd and btn whn blnd last* **18/1**	141+
0-55	4	7	**Won In The Dark (IRE)**[38] 3205 7-11-7 151 TomO'Brien (Sabrina J Harty, Ire) *t.k.h in 4th: wnt 3rd after 5th: wknd 3 out* **9/1**[2]	135
3036	5	16	**Barizan (IRE)**[35] 3289 5-11-7 140 DenisO'Regan (Evan Williams) *chsd ldr: j. slowly and qckly lost pl 5th: bhd whn blnd 3 out* **12/1**	122

3m 43.1s (-5.90) **Going Correction** +0.025s/f (Yiel) **5** Ran SP% **109.8**
Speed ratings (Par 109): **115,111,109,105,97**
CSF £4.03 TOTE £1.10: £1.02, £3.90; EX 2.90.

Owner Walters Plant Hire Ltd **Bred** Stephanie Hanly **Trained** Upper Lambourn, Berks

■ The Welsh Champion Hurdle was last run at Chepstow at Easter 2002, where it had been downgraded to a class B handicap.

FOCUS

This was a sadly uncompetitive contest for a decent prize. Easy winner Oscar Whisky was value for further and should run well in the Champion Hurdle. He is rated 4lb off his best.

NOTEBOOK

Oscar Whisky(IRE) travelled powerfully and, once upsides the long-time leader, moved effortlessly clear, winning with the minimum of fuss. His target will be the Champion Hurdle rather than the World Hurdle, all being well. (op 1-4)

Black Jack Blues(IRE) enjoyed himself out in front and was the only one heading into the home straight to look a danger to the winner. He rallied to good effect, but was readily held. (op 11-1)

Tarkari(IRE) ♦, held up early, made some encouraging late progress and ran a blinder despite hitting the final hurdle. One could easily see him run well in the Totesport Trophy if he heads there. (op 20-1)

Won In The Dark(IRE) was beaten just over 15l by Hurricane Fly last time, so gives those looking for a line into the best 2m Irish form something to work with. (op 11-1)

Barizan(IRE) lost his place down the back straight and has yet to rediscover his best form.

3940 WILLIAMHILL.COM H'CAP CHASE (22 fncs) 3m 4f

3:10 (3:14) (Class 2) 5-Y-0+ **£19,011** (£5,616; £2,808; £1,404; £702)

Form				RPR
3-61	1		**Blazing Bailey**[35] 3290 9-11-10 146 WayneHutchinson (Alan King) *chsd ldrs: wnt 2nd 4 out: led last: styd on wl* **9/2**[2]	156+
2F-4	2	2	**Minella Four Star (IRE)**[223] 844 8-10-3 125 TomScudamore (David Pipe) *t.k.h: led: nt fluent 10th: hld on gamely tl hdd last: kpt on* **9/1**	133
01FF	3	3	**Triggerman**[14] 3687 9-10-10 132 TomO'Brien (Philip Hobbs) *towards rr: hdwy 18th: 3rd whn mstke 2 out: styd on same pce* **12/1**	139+
24U3	4	3 ½	**I'moncloudnine (IRE)**[28] 3437 8-10-11 133 (p) BarryGeraghty (Neil Mulholland) *mid-div: hdwy 16th: no imp fr 3 out* **7/1**	135
-044	5	¾	**Ballyfitz**[28] 3437 11-10-11 133 (p) DavidEngland (Nigel Twiston-Davies) *in tch: pshd along when blnd and lost pl 17th: styd on again fr 2 out* **11/1**	137+
-305	6	11	**Character Building (IRE)**[35] 3290 11-11-2 138 DenisO'Regan (John Quinn) *in rr: modest effrt 18th: no imp* **11/1**	131
-053	7	8	**Theatre Dance (IRE)**[14] 3687 10-10-4 126 TimmyMurphy (David Arbuthnot) *racd wd: j. lft: bhd most of way* **11/1**	111
1-25	8	1 ½	**Maktu**[28] 3437 9-10-11 136 MichaelMurphy(3) (Pat Murphy) *towards rr: mstke 11th: hdwy 16th: wknd 4 out* **6/1**[3]	124+
2131	9	62	**Adams Island (IRE)**[24] 3508 7-10-7 136 (p) AodhaganConlon(7) (Rebecca Curtis) *prom: j. slowly 6th: mstke 16th: blnd 18th: sn wknd* **4/1**[1]	62
25-0	P		**Dom D'Orgeval (FR)**[119] 1777 11-10-2 124 PaulMoloney (Nick Williams) *chsd ldrs: wknd 15th: wl bhd whn p.u bef 3 out* **16/1**	—
FP10	P		**Grand Slam Hero (IRE)**[133] 1611 10-11-12 148 RhysFlint (Nigel Twiston-Davies) *nt a fluent: in tch: lost pl 9th: in rr and rdn 11th: wl bhd whn p.u bef 14th* **20/1**	—

7m 15.9s (-10.90) **Going Correction** -0.075s/f (Good) **11** Ran SP% **118.3**
Speed ratings: **112,111,110,109,109 106,103,103,85,— —**
CSF £45.13 CT £460.09 TOTE £5.90: £2.70, £2.60, £5.00; EX 65.40.

Owner Three Line Whip **Bred** A M Tombs **Trained** Barbury Castle, Wilts

FOCUS

All of these could be given a chance and the form ought to be sound. Blazing Bailey is on the upgrade over fences and is rated within 7lb of his best old hurdles form.

NOTEBOOK

Blazing Bailey, 13lb higher than when winning at Cheltenham, has suddenly rediscovered something resembling his best hurdling form over fences and took this stamina test in good style. He travelled well during the race and was never likely to stop when in with a chance, so once in front after the last, he did enough to win. One would imagine that the Festival Handicap Chase (what was the William Hill Trophy in 2010) will be on his agenda. (op 13-2)

Minella Four Star(IRE), off since finishing fourth in the Summer National, and a former stablemate of the winner, ran a stormer after such a lengthy absence, leading from the start until the final fence. The worry with him is whether he'll be able to repeat this effort next time. (op 10-1 tchd 17-2)

Triggerman hadn't completed on his previous two starts, but proved what he is capable of when staying upright. His entry in the National Hunt Chase next month would look an interesting one if he can handle the big-field quick pace they are likely to go. (op 11-1)

I'moncloudnine(IRE), with cheekpieces on for the first time, appeared to get a little outpaced at one point but stayed on resolutely in the final stages. (op 8-1)

Ballyfitz lost his place down the back straight on their final circuit (he made one shocking mistake at the 17th) but finished nicely, albeit without holding any chance of winning. (op 14-1)

Character Building(IRE) showed some promise on what would be unsuitably testing ground. (op 12-1)

Maktu looked to be making a promising forward move off the final bend but started to become one-paced heading to four out, and had little left in reserve from that point. Official explanation: trainer said gelding scoped dirty (op 11-2)

Adams Island(IRE), a novice running in a handicap for the first time, shaped really nicely for a long way but his jumping became less fluent as the tempo started to increase, and he steadily dropped away. (op 7-2)

3941 LAND ROVER H'CAP HURDLE (10 hdls) 2m 4f

3:45 (3:48) (Class 2) (0-145,137) 4-Y-0+ **£6,505** (£1,910; £955; £477)

Form				RPR
2-03	1		**Shoegazer (IRE)**[14] 3688 6-11-3 128 (t) TomScudamore (David Pipe) *trckd ldng pair: hit 3rd: wnt 2nd and hit 3 out: led last: rdn clr* **10/11**[1]	132+
4404	2	3 ¼	**Benfleet Boy**[16] 3649 7-11-8 133 BarryGeraghty (Brendan Powell) *led: racd lazily and str reminders 6th: hdd last: nt qckn* **7/1**	133+
26-0	3	1 ¼	**Rollwiththepunches**[28] 3447 6-11-5 130 (t) PaulMoloney (Philip McBride) *chsd ldr tl 3 out: one pce* **5/1**[2]	126
12UP	4	3 ½	**Oursininlaw (IRE)**[132] 1625 7-10-7 118 RhysFlint (Evan Williams) *in tch in 5th most of way: no hdwy fr 3 out* **16/1**	111
-246	5	2 ½	**Je Ne Sais Plus (FR)**[26] 3490 7-10-4 115 (t) DenisO'Regan (Tom George) *t.k.h in last: mstke 6th: outpcd 3 out* **13/2**[3]	107
4120	6	11	**Salontyre (GER)**[35] 3298 5-10-9 125 (p) MissIsabelTompsett(5) (Bernard Llewellyn) *in tch in 4th: dropped to last at 7th: sn rdn and struggling: bhd whn mstke 2 out* **9/1**	109

4m 50.6s (1.60) **Going Correction** +0.025s/f (Yiel) **6** Ran SP% **110.8**
Speed ratings (Par 109): **97,95,95,93,92 88**
CSF £7.69 CT £19.35 TOTE £1.90: £1.60, £2.30; EX 9.10.

Owner Wayne Clifford **Bred** Michael Walton **Trained** Nicholashayne, Devon

FOCUS

The pace was sound thanks to Benfleet Boy. Ordinary form, with the winner on the upgrade.

NOTEBOOK

Shoegazer(IRE) pounced on the leader clearing the final hurdle. He had run perfectly respectably on his previous start under top weight in a decent contest, so was entitled to take this. One got the impression that he is capable of defying a higher mark, and won't have a problem staying a bit further. (tchd Evens)

Benfleet Boy ran a fine race despite appearing to get distracted at about the halfway point. He soon got his equilibrium back and had every chance until Shoegazer pounced on him clearing the final hurdle. (op 8-1)

Rollwiththepunches didn't seem to have a problem with the distance, which should give his connections more options. He looks capable of winning a handicap. (op 9-2)

Oursininlaw(IRE) made nothing more than an satisfactory return to action after a layoff. (op 20-1)

Je Ne Sais Plus(FR), wearing a tongue-tie for the first time, didn't make much impression after travelling strongly, and is probably too high in the weights. (tchd 6-1)

Salontyre(GER), up in trip, soon got behind and was never dangerous. (op 12-1 tchd 8-1)

3942 PROFESSIONAL SECURITY MANAGEMENT MAIDEN HURDLE (12 hdls) 3m

4:15 (4:18) (Class 4) 5-Y-0+ **£2,602** (£764; £382; £190)

Form				RPR
	1		**Our Island (IRE)**[76] 6-11-0 TomScudamore (Tim Vaughan) *chsd ldrs: led 9th tl jst after last: rallied gamely to get bk up fnl stride* **12/1**	119+
32	2	hd	**Iron Chancellor (IRE)**[39] 3153 6-11-0 124 WayneHutchinson (Alan King) *in tch: drvn to chal 2 out: slt ld run-in: kpt on: hdd last stride* **11/8**[1]	118
	3	hd	**Swingkeel (IRE)**[112] 6-11-0 DavidEngland (Nigel Twiston-Davies) *travelled wl in 5th: wnt 3rd at 9th: chal gng strly whn hit 2 out: nt qckn run-in: kpt on wl nr fin* **9/2**[3]	120+
2	4	18	**Loose Preformer (IRE)**[24] 3505 5-11-0 BarryGeraghty (Nicky Henderson) *hld up in rr gp: gd hdwy 9th: wknd 2 out* **15/8**[2]	102
	5	17	**Giveabobback (IRE)**[33] 3385 6-11-0 PaulMoloney (Eugene M O'Sullivan, Ire) *bhd: sme hdwy appr 3 out: sn rdn and wknd* **33/1**	86
5423	6	23	**Definite Dawn (IRE)**[29] 3428 7-10-9 120 MrTomDavid(5) (Tim Vaughan) *disp ld: led 8th tl wknd next* **16/1**	66
000	7	32	**Little Frano (IRE)**[9] 3762 7-10-7 MichaelByrne(7) (Peter Bowen) *t.k.h: prom tl rdn and wknd appr 3 out* **66/1**	37
P	8	37	**Fair Rome**[9] 3761 7-10-4 DonalDevereux(3) (Peter Bowen) *disp ld tl 8th: wknd rapidly appr next: sn wl bhd* **100/1**	—
	9	¾	**Florence May** 7-10-7 LiamHeard (Lucy Jones) *plld hrd in rr: sme hdwy 7th: wknd 9th* **100/1**	—
0	P		**Lady Dixton**[20] 3590 5-10-4 RichardKilloran(3) (Tim Vaughan) *towards rr: mstke and lost tch 7th: p.u bef next* **100/1**	—

6m 4.30s (17.30) **Going Correction** +0.025s/f (Yiel) **10** Ran SP% **116.0**
Speed ratings: **72,71,71,65,60 52,41,29,29,—**
toteswingers:1&2 £11.00, 2&3 £2.20, 1&3 £15.00 CSF £30.02 TOTE £14.60: £1.40, £1.40, £1.60; EX 42.70.

Owner D W Fox **Bred** Michael F Condon **Trained** Aberthin, Vale of Glamorgan

FOCUS

It is best to presume this was a decent contest until proven otherwise, as the runners appeared to go a good pace, and the fancied runners drew well clear. The form is rated through the runner-up.

NOTEBOOK

Our Island(IRE) ♦ made a great start to his career under rules with a battling display. A winner and runner-up in three Irish point starts, he travelled strongly and showed a pleasing attitude to get to the front again after losing the lead after the final hurdle. (op 16-1)

Iron Chancellor(IRE) ♦, up in trip, came with what looked a winning run heading to the last, but wasn't able to lengthen away and got caught, after hitting the front, close to the line. He can probably win a handicap, but is fully entitled to land a similar maiden. (op 6-4)

Swingkeel(IRE) ♦, absent since mid-October, was very useful at up to 2m on the Flat and showed more than enough to suggest he'll make a decent hurdler, considering most of his best Flat form came on a much quicker surface. He looks a surefire future winner. (op 11-2)

Loose Preformer(IRE), taking a big step up in distance, moved into the race nicely but didn't appear to get home. He possibly doesn't stay this trip, as his point success came over 2m4f, or failed to handle what looked to be tacky conditions. (op 6-4)

Lady Dixton Official explanation: jockey said mare lost its action

3943 LINCWEAR STANDARD OPEN NATIONAL HUNT FLAT RACE 2m

4:50 (4:53) (Class 5) 4-6-Y-0 **£1,626** (£477; £238; £119)

Form				RPR
5	1		**Sharlene's Quest (IRE)**[18] 3623 5-10-4 MrMatthewBarber(7) (V J Hughes) *mde all: hld on gamely whn chal fnl 2f* **20/1**	103
	2	nk	**Sertao (FR)** 5-11-4 TomScudamore (Tim Vaughan) *trckd ldrs gng wl: chal on bit 2f out: shkn up and level 1f out: kpt on: nvr able to get past* **5/2**[2]	110
	3	10	**Henok (FR)** 5-11-4 DavidEngland (Nigel Twiston-Davies) *t.k.h: chsd wnr tl wknd over 1f out* **5/2**[2]	101

1 **4** 2 ½ **Valley Lad (IRE)**[75] 2576 5-11-11 .... BarryGeraghty 105
(Tim Vaughan) *towards rr: sme hdwy 4f out: no imp fnl 3f* **7/4**[1]
5 1 ½ **Call Me Frankie (IRE)** 5-11-4 .... TimmyMurphy 97
(Lucy Jones) *towards rr: sme hdwy 3f out: rdn and no imp* **33/1**
6-0 **6** 20 **Yorkshire Knight (IRE)**[23] 3525 6-11-1 .... DonalDevereux(3) 79
(Peter Bowen) *chsd ldrs: rdn over 4f out: wknd over 3f out* **8/1**[3]
0 **7** 27 **Countess Susy**[79] 2472 6-10-4 .... MrDGPrichard(7) 48
(Phillip Dando) *a in rr gp: no ch fnl 4f* **40/1**
8 77 **Dante's Lady (IRE)** 6-10-4 .... MarkQuinlan(7) —
(Neil Mulholland) *chsd ldrs 5f: bhd and drvn along 1/2-way: sn t.o* **40/1**

3m 47.2s (3.80) **Going Correction** +0.025s/f (Yiel) **8** Ran SP% **117.2**
Speed ratings: **91,90,85,84,83 73,60,21**
toteswingers:1&2 £10.80, 2&3 £2.30, 1&3 £9.80 CSF £69.96 TOTE £30.30: £5.00, £1.10, £1.50; EX 138.00.
Owner V J Hughes **Bred** Miss Aileen Gallagher **Trained** Bridgend, Bridgend

FOCUS
Probably just an ordinary contest, but it appeared to be run at a respectable gallop. The winner was just about the form pick but rates a step up.

NOTEBOOK
Sharlene's Quest(IRE) shaped nicely in a mares' bumper late last month, and got off the mark in determined style under a tidy ride from her claiming jockey. She looked sure to finish runner-up at best when two big dangers came to her, but she responded to pressure and plugged on in game fashion, proving she has the heart for a battle. (op 16-1)
Sertao(FR), who was purchased privately for £19,000 in 2009, travelled up to the winner going much the best but failed to quicken past. A big sort, he looks a nice prospect. (op 9-4 tchd 3-1)
Henok(FR), a half-brother to a French cross-country chase winner, took a good grip early, which may have attributed to his weak finish. That said, he should be capable of running even better next time with this experience under his belt. (op 10-3 tchd 9-4)
Valley Lad(IRE), penalised for his win over 1m6f here, lost his place on the home bend before plugging on. He may want staying distances when he goes over hurdles. (tchd 2-1)
Call Me Frankie(IRE) is a nice, big sort, who made a pleasing debut. (op 25-1)
T/Plt: £14.10 to a £1 stake. Pool of £68,129.27 - 3,517.94 winning tickets. T/Qpdt: £8.70 to a £1 stake. Pool of £4,182.55 - 354.58 winning tickets. LM

3442 SANDOWN (R-H)
Saturday, February 5

OFFICIAL GOING: Good (good to soft in places on both courses; good to firm in places on chase course)
Wind: Strong, half against Weather: Overcast

3944 BET ON TOTEPLACEPOT AT TOTESPORT.COM JUVENILE HURDLE (8 hdls) 2m 110y
1:25 (1:29) (Class 4) 4-Y-O **£2,602** (£764; £382; £190)

Form RPR
1 **Kumbeshwar**[46] 4-10-12 0 .... RobertThornton 120+
(Alan King) *lw: settled midfield: mstke 4th: drvn in 7th pl after 3 out: relentless prog after: wnt 2nd between last 2: styd on to ld fnl 100yds* **15/2**[3]
6643 **2** 3 ½ **Professeur Emery (FR)**[28] 3443 4-10-12 114 .... JasonMaguire 115+
(Warren Greatrex) *led and sn clr: at least 12l ahd 3 out: stl 9l up 2 out but tiring: hdd last 100yds* **5/2**[2]
3 6 **Not In The Clock (USA)**[101] 4-10-12 0 .... DarylJacob 109
(Charlie Mann) *settled midfield: effrt after 3 out: rdn and kpt on one pce bef 2 out: mstke last: tk 3rd last 100yds* **28/1**
4 2 **Moose Moran (USA)**[128] 4-10-12 0 .... APMcCoy 110+
(Nicky Henderson) *nt fluent: chsd clr ldng pair: chsd clr ldr 3 out: tried to cl bef 2 out: no imp and lost 2nd between last 2: fdd* **1/1**[1]
5 **5** 29 **Magic Prospect (FR)**[14] 3673 4-10-9 0 .... PeterToole(3) 81
(Charlie Mann) *prom in chsng gp: wnt 3rd sn after 3 out tl bef 2 out: wknd rapidly* **18/1**
6 ½ **Iron Condor**[17] 4-10-12 0 .... FelixDeGiles 82
(James Eustace) *hld up in last pair: mstke 1st: drvn to stay in tch at bk of main gp 3 out: sn no ch* **9/1**
3 **7** 42 **Miss Wendy**[76] 2556 4-10-5 0 .... ColinBolger 35
(Mark H Tompkins) *prom in chsng gp tl wknd u.p after 3 out: t.o* **40/1**
00 **8** nk **Megagrace**[52] 2965 4-10-5 0 .... JamieMoore 35
(Gary Moore) *lw: mstkes: towards rr: drvn to try to stay in tch after 3 out: sn no ch: t.o* **50/1**
00 **9** 11 **Terra Bleu (IRE)**[9] 3767 4-10-12 0 .... WarrenMarston 32
(Milton Harris) *lw: nt jump wl: a bhd: t.o fr 5th* **150/1**
10 38 **Novillero**[16] 4-10-9 0 .... JimmyDerham(3) —
(Jimmy Fox) *a in last trio: t.o fr 5th* **66/1**
P **Youm Jamil (USA)**[143] 4-10-12 0 .... RichardJohnson —
(Henry Daly) *chsd clr ldr and clr of rest: wknd and lost 2nd 3 out: poor 9th whn p.u bef next* **22/1**
R **Mountrath**[15] 4-10-9 0 .... TommyPhelan(3) —
(Brett Johnson) *chsd clr ldrs tl ducked out 3rd* **66/1**

4m 7.25s (0.05) **Going Correction** -0.075s/f (Good) **12** Ran SP% **121.4**
Speed ratings: **96,94,91,90,76 76,56,56,51,33 —,—**
toteswingers:1&2 £2.80, 2&3 £10.00, 1&3 £18.20 CSF £27.10 TOTE £6.20: £1.70, £1.50, £4.60; EX 27.40.
Owner McNeill Family & Nigel Bunter **Bred** G E Amey **Trained** Barbury Castle, Wilts

FOCUS
An informative juvenile hurdle that has produced a subsequent Triumph Hurdle winner in Detroit City, while Ashkazar, the 2008 winner, finished runner-up in the Fred Winter. This year's line-up featured several interesting hurdling debutants and three of them filled the first four places. The pace set by the runner-up was decent throughout, although the time was modest, with the wind a contributor to that. The winner has the potential to rate a lot higher on his Flat form.

NOTEBOOK
Kumbeshwar, a winner at up to 1m4f on fast and soft ground and Fibresand, who was rated 89 on sand and 82 on turf, was held up early before making relentless headway up the straight and stayed on to catch the runner-up after the last. He had been toughened up by winning three races at Southwell in a week before Christmas, and that helped him get home here. He looks a decent prospect but whether he takes his chance in the Triumph Hurdle remains to be seen, as he probably needs more jumping experience. (op 7-1 tchd 5-1)
Professeur Emery(FR) has improved with experience over hurdles, especially since making the running including over C&D on heavy ground. He went off at a rate of knots and had most of his rivals in trouble turning in. He got very tired but kept on well, only to be worn down on the run-in. He set the standard here off 114 and can surely win a similar race on an easier track, although he also has the option of handicaps. (op 3-1 tchd 9-4)
Not In The Clock(USA), who was placed at up to 1m4f on Polytrack and easy ground on the Flat, stayed on best of the rest for third on this hurdling debut. He looks capable of building on this. (op 33-1 tchd 25-1)
Moose Moran(USA), a 1m2f winner on fast ground on the Flat (rated 97), was sent off at evens, having drifted from odds-on for this hurdling debut. However, warm and on toes beforehand, his jumping was far from fluent and, despite chasing the runner-up into the straight, he weakened from the penultimate flight. He may have had excuses on account of the ground, but will need to improve his jumping if he is to be a success at this game. (op 10-11, tchd 11-10 in a place)
Magic Prospect(FR) ◆, placed on the Flat in France on heavy ground, had shown some promise on his hurdling debut behind Grandouet at Ascot. He did the same again, looking as if he might play a part on the home turn, but could make no impression thereafter. He should be of interest once qualified for handicaps. (op 16-1 tchd 14-1)
Iron Condor, a dual 1m4f Polytrack winner who appeared to stay 2m on the Flat, was held up on this hurdling debut and never got competitive. (op 12-1)

3945 TOTESPORT 0800 221 221 CONTENDERS HURDLE (LISTED RACE) (8 hdls) 2m 110y
1:55 (1:59) (Class 1) 4-Y-O+ **£9,121** (£3,422; £1,713; £854)

Form RPR
1-31 **1** **Binocular (FR)**[21] 3559 7-11-8 171 .... APMcCoy 150+
(Nicky Henderson) *hld up last: prog to trck ldr 2 out: lft in ld last: nt extended after* **1/10**[1]
/5P5 **2** 1 ¾ **Ruthenoise (FR)**[37] 3228 6-10-7 116 .... AndrewTinkler 128+
(Nicky Henderson) *led: shkn up 2 out: stl hld narrow ld whn blnd last: hdd and no ch w wnr after* **50/1**
342- **3** 10 **Siberian Tiger (IRE)**[119] 5392 6-11-0 135 .... DarylJacob 125
(Evan Williams) *lw: mostly chsd ldr tl pckd and lost 2nd 2 out: wl btn fr last* **20/1**[3]
1P11 **4** 65 **Dorabelle (IRE)**[74] 2598 6-10-7 122 .... JasonMaguire 99
(Donald McCain) *cl up: mstke 5th and next: wknd 2 out: no ch whn blnd last: virtually p.u* **14/1**[2]

4m 2.70s (-4.50) **Going Correction** -0.075s/f (Good) **4** Ran SP% **104.3**
Speed ratings (Par 111): **107,106,101,70**
CSF £5.33 TOTE £1.10; EX 7.70.
Owner John P McManus **Bred** Elie Lellouche **Trained** Upper Lambourn, Berks

FOCUS
This long-established contest has had relevance regarding the Champion Hurdle, despite featuring small fields and short-priced favourites in recent years. Binocular was value for further but still a stone off his figure in this race last year. The form could be 7lb or so out either way.

NOTEBOOK
Binocular(FR), last year's winner, was held up before making steady headway to challenge between the last two, but briefly looked as if he would struggle before the runner-up blundered at the last and conceded him the advantage. McCoy hardly moved on the run-in and, in the end, it was an easy preparation for his defence of the crown. Strictly on form he ran stones below his best, but was unimpressive here last year before bolting up at Cheltenham, and the time was 4.55secs faster than the opening juvenile hurdle. (tchd 1-12)
Ruthenoise(FR), a stable companion of the winner but rated 55lb lower, set off in front and was still leading when a bad mistake at the last presented Binocular with the advantage. She stuck on well up the run-in, and will have earned some valuable black type for breeding purposes, which apparently was the aim.
Siberian Tiger(IRE), who finished runner-up to Ashkazar over C&D last spring, had not run over hurdles since but had placed form in good company on the Flat. Having his first start since October, he was asked for an effort off the home turn but was soon beaten. (op 18-1 tchd 16-1)
Dorabelle(IRE), the winner of a bumper and three hurdle races on varying ground from six starts, was keen early but spoilt her chance with a bad mistake at the last on the far side, three out, and finished tailed off. (op 16-1)

3946 TOTEPOOL CHALLENGERS NOVICES' CHASE (REGISTERED AS THE SCILLY ISLES NOVICES' STEEPLE CHASE) GRADE 1 (17 fncs) 2m 4f 110y
2:25 (2:29) (Class 1) 5-Y-O+
£21,093 (£7,914; £3,962; £1,975; £991; £495)

Form RPR
1R12 **1** **Medermit (FR)**[35] 3291 7-11-4 155 .... RobertThornton 155+
(Alan King) *w.w in rr: prog 7th: trckd ldng pair 12th: led 3 out: drew 3l clr last: drvn and pressed nr fin: hld on wl* **5/2**[1]
-222 **2** ½ **Captain Chris (IRE)**[38] 3193 7-11-4 141 .... (t) RichardJohnson 156+
(Philip Hobbs) *lw: w.w in rr: mstke 6th: prog to trck ldrs 11th: cl up whn mstke 3 out: rdn to chse wnr last: clsd flat: jst hld* **4/1**[2]
01/1 **3** 7 **Mr Gardner (IRE)**[22] 3543 8-11-4 140 .... FelixDeGiles 150
(Nicky Henderson) *led to 7th: styd w ldr: chal and upsides 3 out: cl 2nd whn stmbld 2 out: btn after: fdd* **7/1**
2131 **4** hd **Rock Noir (FR)**[36] 3262 6-11-4 150 .... (t) APMcCoy 150
(Jonjo O'Neill) *wl plcd: cl up whn mstkes 12th: 13th and 14th: stl on terms: dropped to last of ldng gp: outpcd after 3 out: kpt on flat* **15/2**
-113 **5** 25 **Rebel Du Maquis (FR)**[57] 2867 6-11-4 146 .... NickScholfield 126
(Paul Nicholls) *wl plcd: w ldrs 12th: stl cl up 3 out: wknd and mstke 2 out: fin tired* **12/1**
11 **6** 5 **Nadiya De La Vega (FR)**[21] 3555 5-10-8 139 .... AndrewTinkler 112
(Nicky Henderson) *lw: chsd ldrs: lost pl 8th: struggling to stay in tch w ldrs fr 10th: wl bhd after 14th* **5/1**[3]
-413 **7** 9 **Reve De Sivola (FR)**[35] 3291 6-11-4 141 .... DarylJacob 114
(Nick Williams) *nt a fluent in rr: mstke 7th: nt on terms w ldrs fr next: wl bhd after 14th* **10/1**
-310 **8** 9 **Cois Farraig**[35] 3291 6-11-4 134 .... DominicElsworth 104
(Paul Webber) *lw: w ldr to 4th: lost pl rapidly and last after 6th: sn struggling: t.o* **28/1**
1421 **9** 3 ¾ **Hidden Keel**[32] 3390 6-11-4 145 .... PaddyBrennan 126
(Charlie Longsdon) *trckd ldr 4th: led 7th: hdd & wknd rapidly 3 out: virtually p.u flat* **12/1**

5m 9.20s (-9.20) **Going Correction** 0.0s/f (Good)
WFA 5 from 6yo+ 2lb **9** Ran SP% **117.4**
Speed ratings: **117,116,114,114,104 102,99,95,94**
toteswingers:1&2 £2.00, 2&3 £11.30, 1&3 £3.30 CSF £13.30 TOTE £3.90: £1.60, £1.70, £2.60; EX 10.30 Trifecta £91.50 Pool of £4037.63 - 32.62 winning units..
Owner The Dunkley & Reilly Partnership **Bred** Philippe Gasdoue **Trained** Barbury Castle, Wilts

FOCUS
This high-class novice chase has not been won by a future Cheltenham winner since Best Mate scored in 2001, en-route to Arkle success. It looked a strong line-up, although the pace did not appear that fast. Medermit was the form pick and is rated in line with his recent second. He will need to find upwards of 7lb to win a typical Arkle. Solid Grade 1 novice form.

NOTEBOOK
Medermit(FR) ◆, a high-class hurdler and winner of two of his four starts over fences plus runner-up to Hell's Bay in a Grade 2 at Cheltenham, was the highest rated runner in the contest. He jumped and travelled pretty well and had the race in safe keeping at the last, although he had to be driven out to hold off the runner-up. The impression is that he only just gets this trip and his likely target at the festival is the Arkle, in which he will be suited by the likely strong gallop. (op 10-3 tchd 7-2)

Captain Chris(IRE) was another not totally proven at this trip, but he finished well to make the winner pull out all the stops. He has now finished runner-up on all three starts over fences, admittedly to two of the market leaders for the Arkle, but still has to improve his jumping. He made errors here, the worst at the ditch in front of the stands, but still ran on well. The jockey was keen to go for the Arkle but the new Grade 2 Jewson looks his best option at the festival. (op 9-2 tchd 7-2)

Mr Gardner(IRE) ◆, a runaway winner on his third hurdles start in March 2009, was then not seen again until making all to win a 2m4f novice chase at Huntingdon in mid-January. Stepping up in grade, he was always towards the front, if tending to jump slightly right. He was still right there until stumbling on landing at the penultimate fence, from which point he weakened. This was a creditable effort just over three weeks after his reappearance, and he looks sure to win good races if keeping sound. (op 15-2)

Rock Noir(FR), who had earplugs fitted, travelled well into contention, but then hit all three of the Railway Fences on the second circuit. He still appeared to be going well approaching three out, but could not find a change of gear when required. (op 8-1)

Rebel Du Maquis(FR) won his first two starts over fences before finding Reve De Sivola too good at Cheltenham in December, but was 8lb better off. He showed up for a long way but was left behind over the last three. (op 11-1 tchd 10-1)

Nadiya De La Vega(FR) won a 4-y-o chase on her British debut and beat the useful Pepe Simo at Kempton next time, despite a blunder two out. However, she was in trouble a long way from home here. This was disappointing as she looked potentially better than this. Official explanation: jockey said mare ran flat (op 6-1)

Reve De Sivola(FR) beat the useful Wishfull Thinking and Rebel Du Maquis over 2m5f at Cheltenham in December but finished 22l behind Medermit at Cheltenham last month. Again his jumping was less than fluent and he might be best trying 3m to give him more time to get organised. (op 9-1 tchd 11-1)

Cois Farraig, winner of a Grade 2 chase over 2m4f at Newbury from three starts over fences, was in trouble around the halfway mark and is not up to this level. (op 33-1)

Hidden Keel, who jumped well in front when taking a 2m4f chase at Leicester, was up in class and, although he helped make the running, was left behind from the Pond Fence. He was allowed to come home in his own time afterwards, and the new Golden Miller Novices' Handicap (formerly Jewson) might be his best option if sent to Cheltenham. (op 9-1 tchd 17-2)

3947 TOTESCOOP6 HEROES H'CAP HURDLE GRADE 3 (11 hdls) 2m 6f

3:00 (3:08) (Class 1) 4-Y-O+

£18,813 (£7,058; £3,534; £1,762; £884; £442)

Form RPR

1115 **1** **Kilcrea Kim (IRE)**[35] 3293 6-10-12 **132**.......................... RichardJohnson 143+
(Philip Hobbs) *trckd ldng pair: wnt 2nd 8th: clsd to ld bef 2 out: hrd rdn bef last: pressed flat: plld out more nr fin* **11/2**[2]

5-42 **2** *1 ¼* **Alfie Spinner (IRE)**[21] 3566 6-10-10 **130**.............................. DarylJacob 137
(Nick Williams) *lw: trckd clr ldr to 8th: styd prom: rdn to go 2nd again bef last: clsd on ldr flat: no ex nr fin* **7/1**[3]

0255 **3** *9* **Dantari (IRE)**[21] 3561 6-10-1 **128**.. MrJEngland(7) 129+
(Evan Williams) *lw: led at str pce and spreadeagled field: clr fr 3rd: terrible blunder 7th: stl 10l ahd 3 out: tired and hdd bef 2 out: kpt on for 3rd* **20/1**

5305 **4** *½* **County Zen (FR)**[21] 3566 8-10-1 **126**.............................. GilesHawkins(5) 124
(Philip Hobbs) *hld up in midfield: prog fr 6th: rdn and hdwy after 3 out to chse ldrs bef next: one pce after* **25/1**

2441 **5** *8* **Prince Tom**[72] 2637 7-10-4 **127**.. IanPopham(3) 120
(Paul Nicholls) *wl plcd bhd ldrs: wl in tch whn hit 3 out: n.m.r sn after and lost grnd: drvn and plugged on fr 2 out* **16/1**

-106 **6** *2 ¾* **Quartz De Thaix (FR)**[21] 3561 7-11-12 **146**........................ AidanColeman 135
(Venetia Williams) *lw: chsd ldrs: rdn in 5th after 3 out: no prog and wl btn in 8th bef 2 out: plugged on* **14/1**

2061 **7** *2 ½* **Numide (FR)**[20] 3587 8-10-5 **125**.. JohnnyFarrelly 111
(Rod Millman) *hld up wl in rr: prog fr 6th: in tch w ldrs after 3 out and gng strly: rdn and no imp bef next: wknd* **33/1**

2161 **8** *8* **Mister Hyde (IRE)**[34] 3346 6-10-8 **128**.................................... APMcCoy 107
(Jonjo O'Neill) *wl plcd in midfield: chsng ldrs 3 out: drvn and no prog bef next: wknd* **7/2**[1]

41/1 **9** *9* **Supreme De Paille (IRE)**[36] 3256 9-10-5 **125**................ PaddyBrennan 96
(Nigel Twiston-Davies) *chsd ldrs: last of ldng gp in 10th 3 out: wknd u.p bef next* **20/1**

/65P **10** *1 ¾* **Altilhar (USA)**[38] 3198 8-10-2 **122**...............................(b) JamieMoore 91
(Gary Moore) *lw: hld up wl in rr: nvr on terms: t.o bef 3 out: sme late prog* **33/1**

1-01 **11** *11* **Lush Life (IRE)**[57] 2870 6-11-3 **142**...................................... DavidBass(5) 107
(Nicky Henderson) *replated bef s: out of line and last away: nvr able to get involved: t.o bef 3 out: modest late prog* **8/1**

-066 **12** *13* **Arkose (IRE)**[81] 2441 7-10-5 **125**.. LeightonAspell 73
(Oliver Sherwood) *a towards rr: lost tch ldrs 8th: t.o fr next* **40/1**

4U24 **13** *5* **Miss Overdrive**[28] 3440 7-10-2 **122**................................... NickScholfield 65
(Andy Turnell) *pushed along in rr after 5th: sn struggling: t.o bef 3 out* **25/1**

2440 **14** *1* **Pause And Clause (IRE)**[53] 2945 7-11-11 **145**................... SamThomas 87
(Emma Lavelle) *a wl in rr: already lost tch whn mstke 6th: t.o bef 3 out* **28/1**

2436 **15** *10* **Gee Dee Nen**[26] 3479 8-10-2 **122**..........................(v) AndrewGlassonbury 55
(Gary Moore) *lw: prom in chsng gp: 5th whn shocking blunder 3 out: wknd rapidly* **50/1**

1144 **16** *16* **National Trust**[35] 3303 9-10-0 **120** oh1................................(t) DaveCrosse 39
(Edward Creighton) *prom to 6th: sn wknd: t.o bef 3 out* **100/1**

5123 **17** *nk* **Mr Jay Dee (IRE)**[19] 3601 6-10-3 **123**.......................... DominicElsworth 42
(Lucy Wadham) *a in rr: wl off the pce whn hmpd 6th: t.o bef 3 out* **40/1**

/54- **P** **Roll Along (IRE)**[403] 3149 11-11-6 **140**................................ WillKennedy —
(Nigel Twiston-Davies) *swtg: sn detached in last: continued wl t.o fnl circ tl p.u bef 2 out* **50/1**

-FU4 **P** **Dansimar**[28] 3452 7-10-4 **129**.. RTDunne(5) —
(Venetia Williams) *prom tl p.u after 5th: fatally injured* **14/1**

-231 **P** **Like A Hurricane (IRE)**[98] 2081 8-10-2 **122**................. RobertThornton —
(Alan King) *nvr beyond midfield: wkng and disputing t.o 11th pl 3 out: p.u bef next* **9/1**

5m 21.0s (-9.00) **Going Correction** -0.075s/f (Good) **20** Ran SP% **126.8**
Speed ratings (Par 113): **113,112,109,109,106 105,104,101,98,97 93,88,86,86,82 77,76,—,—,—**
toteswingers:1&2 £9.10, 2&3 £74.20, 1&3 £51.90 CSF £38.47 CT £745.80 TOTE £6.80: £1.90, £2.10, £5.70, £4.10; EX 40.70 Trifecta £1088.40 Pool of £38460.37 - 26.14 winning units..
Owner James and Jean Potter **Bred** Francis O'Brien **Trained** Withycombe, Somerset

FOCUS

A good, competitive handicap hurdle whose best-known recent winner was the dual champion staying hurdler Baracouda. It is often won by an unexposed or progressive type, and that was the case again. Kilcrea Kim is still 10lb+ off what will be required in the Albert Bartlett.

NOTEBOOK

Kilcrea Kim(IRE) ◆ travelled well and stayed on resolutely up the straight to hold off the runner-up. An Irish point winner and successful on his first three starts over hurdles at up to 2m6f, he was beaten off this mark over 3m at Cheltenham last time. Dropping back in trip, he travelled well and, after going on two out, found more when challenged after the last. He continues on the way up, and he is likely to take his chance in the Albert Bartlett, although the Coral Cup looks a feasible alternative. (op 15-2 tchd 5-1)

Alfie Spinner(IRE) ◆, who stays 3m1f and acts well on testing ground, was always in the front rank and his stamina came into play after the last, but he could not get past the winner. He deserves to win a decent race soon, is qualified for the Pertemps Final at the festival and that looks a credible target for him. (op 15-2 tchd 13-2)

Dantari(IRE), a winner at up to 2m4f on good ground, set off in front, soon opened up a clear lead, and his rider kicked again down the hill on the second circuit. He was reeled in by the principals at the second-last and looked sure to drop away, but to his credit he responded to pressure and kept on to claim a deserved third place. (tchd 22-1)

County Zen(FR) finished behind Alfie Spinner at Warwick last time and was 5lb better off for 16l. He ran pretty close to that form on the revised terms, suggesting the form is sound. (op 20-1)

Prince Tom ◆, a novice who won a handicap at Taunton over 3m, was 13lb higher but representing a trainer with a terrific recent record in this race. He got to the heels of the leading group turning for home but could not make any further inroads. He seems best on a sound surface and could well pick up a decent contest this spring.

Quartz De Thaix(FR) had put up a fair effort in the Lanzarote Hurdle last time before fading, and this staying-on effort was another indication that he is running back into form. (op 16-1)

Numide(FR) scored his first success for over two years when getting home narrowly over 2m4f at Ffos Las last time. Despite being 5lb higher in a better grade, he moved up looking as if he was going to deliver a challenge early in the straight before his effort petered out.

Mister Hyde(IRE), a dual hurdles winner at 2m5f on easy ground, was raised 5lb for his last success and back up in grade, but was sent off a well-backed favourite. He had to be pushed along to get into contention leaving the back straight but had no more to offer once in line for home. (op 5-1 tchd 11-2, 6-1 in a place)

Supreme De Paille(IRE) came back from 21 months off to win over an extended 2m4f on heavy ground in December. However, he was 19lb higher here and unable to land a blow, despite keeping on. (op 14-1)

Lush Life(IRE), a bumper and three-time hurdles winner from seven starts, had successfully stepped up to 3m when scoring at Cheltenham. Re-plated before the start, he was trotting in at the rear when the starter released the tape and, after a slow jump at the first, was at the back until keeping on late. There were complaints from punters and the stewards reviewed the evidence, then forwarded the details to the BHA. Official explanation: jockey said gelding missed the break (op 9-1 tchd 10-1)

Gee Dee Nen had been racing over fences since the summer but returned to hurdles on a fair mark. He was still in contention when a bad mistake three out knocked the stuffing out of him.

Like A Hurricane(IRE) Official explanation: jockey said gelding never travelled

3948 TOTESPORT MASTERS H'CAP CHASE (22 fncs) 3m 110y

3:35 (3:40) (Class 2) 5-Y-O+

£15,655 (£4,625; £2,312; £1,157; £577; £290)

Form RPR

S0OP **1** **Eric's Charm (FR)**[28] 3444 13-10-11 **136**......................... LeightonAspell 147+
(Oliver Sherwood) *lw: trckd ldrs: blnd 2nd: nt fluent 13rd: outpcd in 6th after 4 out: rallied bef 2 out: led bef last: sn clr* **20/1**

P-50 **2** *6* **Beat The Boys (IRE)**[57] 2871 10-11-0 **139**...................... PaddyBrennan 145
(Nigel Twiston-Davies) *w ldr: led 15th: drvn and hdd 2 out: kpt on same pce after* **12/1**

-UPP **3** *nse* **Burren Legend (IRE)**[91] 2221 10-10-5 **130**.................. AndrewThornton 135
(Richard Rowe) *patiently rdn in last pair: stl only 9th jumping 17th: prog fr 4 out: clsd on ldrs: next: effrt 2 out: kpt on same pce* **8/1**

03-2 **4** *3* **Take The Breeze (FR)**[98] 2084 8-11-7 **151**...................... MrRMahon(5) 153
(Paul Nicholls) *lw: trckd ldrs: effrt after 4 out: led 2 out tl bef last: wknd* **7/2**[1]

0650 **5** *6* **Chief Yeoman**[21] 3561 11-10-0 **125**................................... AidanColeman 124
(Venetia Williams) *in tch: mstke 12th: prog and prom 14th: rdn and steadily wknd 3 out* **14/1**

-650 **6** *6* **Soulard (USA)**[14] 3677 8-10-2 **130**.. PeterToole(3) 123
(Tom George) *prom: mstke 10th: steadily wknd bef 3 out* **20/1**

3014 **7** *27* **Free World (IRE)**[21] 3558 9-10-0 **125** oh5............................ JamieMoore 92
(Warren Greatrex) *sn gng bdly in last and frequent reminders: bhd fr 14th: t.o* **14/1**

6P-0 **8** *nk* **Theatrical Moment (USA)**[85] 2343 8-10-10 **135**..................(t) APMcCoy 105
(Jonjo O'Neill) *trckd ldrs: blnd 7th: nvr really gng wl after: mstke 15th and lost tch: t.o* **8/1**

2/U3 **U** **Leading Contender (IRE)**[28] 3444 10-10-3 **128**........... RichardJohnson —
(Philip Hobbs) *lw: trckd ldrs: mstke 14th: cl 5th whn mstke and uns rdr 19th (4 out)* **9/2**[2]

F-03 **F** **Khachaturian (IRE)**[45] 3092 8-10-7 **132**............................ JasonMaguire —
(Donald McCain) *chsd ldrs on outer: pushed along in 8th but in tch whn fell 17th (6 out)* **5/1**[3]

/42- **P** **Aimigayle**[462] 2000 8-10-9 **134**... ColinBolger —
(Suzy Smith) *mstke 6th: mde most to 16th: w ldr whn mstke 18th: wknd rapidly bef 3 out: poor 7th whn p.u bef last* **8/1**

6m 21.9s (-5.90) **Going Correction** 0.0s/f (Good) **11** Ran SP% **121.0**
Speed ratings: **109,107,107,106,104 102,93,93,—,— —**
toteswingers:1&2 £34.60, 2&3 £26.50, 1&3 £40.10 CSF £239.55 CT £2083.44 TOTE £21.30: £4.60, £3.70, £3.80; EX 272.10 Trifecta £1731.10 Part won. Pool of £2339.39 - 0.10 winning units..
Owner M St Quinton & P Deal **Bred** Dominique Faugeras **Trained** Upper Lambourn, Berks

FOCUS

A decent handicap chase featuring mainly exposed and battle-hardened performers, but some returning from breaks and others with a bit to prove. It resulted in a heartwarming success for an old stager. Eric's Charm is rated a few pounds off the best of last season's form.

NOTEBOOK

Eric's Charm(FR) is a veteran now but has a good record at this track, including finishing second in this race in 2009 off 4lb higher. He had struggled in recent starts but he was given a chance by not being asked to make the running here. After being outpaced, he swept down the outside to take the lead approaching the last, and came away for a decisive success. No doubt connections will try to find another race for him back here before the end of the season. Official explanation: trainer had no explanation regarding apparent improvement in form. (op 18-1 tchd 16-1)

Beat The Boys(IRE) had lost his form since his last win in November 2009 but was only 1lb lower than for that success. He was always in the leading group and stuck to his task, showing a return to some sort of form. (tchd 11-1 and 14-1)

Burren Legend(IRE) was 10lb above his last winning mark and had failed to finish on his last three outings. Returning from a 13-week break, he moved up to challenge at the Pond Fence but, despite staying on, found the winner too strong. At least this was a step back in the right direction. (op 16-1)

Take The Breeze(FR) ◆, a four-time chase winner at up to 2m6f, appears to stay this trip. Returning from a 14-week break, he came to have every chance at the second-last before giving way. This should put him right for his targets in the spring. (tchd 9-2)

Chief Yeoman won the big hurdle at this meeting in 2009 but had not scored since, although he had posted several good efforts including finishing third in the same race last year. Having just his second run over fences since March 2008, he ran a creditable race without being able to land a blow in the straight. The impression is that he is most effective at trips short of 3m. (op 16-1)
Soulard(USA), a four-time winner over fences on a sound surface at up to 2m5f, was trying a new trip. He showed up for a long way until tiring up the hill, and looks ready to make his mark once he encounters his favoured fast ground. (op 18-1)
Theatrical Moment(USA), another well suited by good ground, has struggled in all three runs since his last success in December 2009 and did so again, being in trouble at halfway. (op 6-1)
Aimigayle, a game and versatile mare but not seen since October 2009, was resuming off a 7lb higher mark than for her last success. She made the running for a long way but dropped away before three out and was eventually pulled up. The outing should bring her on.

3949 BET TOTEPOOL AT TOTESPORT.COM H'CAP CHASE (13 fncs) 2m

4:05 (4:13) (Class 2) (0-145,143) 5-Y-0+

£8,140 (£2,405; £1,202; £601; £300; £150)

Form				RPR
2241	**1**		**Anquetta (IRE)**[25] 3494 7-10-3 **125** DavidBass(5) (Nicky Henderson) *trckd ldng pair: gd jump to ld 6th: mde rest: jnd after 3 out: forged clr again next: veered lft after last: rdn out* **6/1**[3]	135+
30-0	**2**	*2*	**Nomecheki (FR)**[7] 3808 9-11-7 **138** LiamTreadwell (Nick Gifford) *trckd ldrs: effrt to go 2nd 3 out and sn upsides: btn off 2 out: kpt on one pce* **40/1**	144
-105	**3**	*1¾*	**Edgbriar (FR)**[14] 3677 9-11-10 **141** (p) DominicElsworth (Paul Webber) *lw: pressed ldr to 6th: styd prom: outpcd in 6th after 4 out: rallied 3 out: kpt on one pce after* **10/1**	145
10P2	**4**	*nse*	**Moon Over Miami (GER)**[21] 3565 10-11-3 **134** (t) DarylJacob (Charlie Mann) *settled midfield: stdy prog fr 8th: chsd ldrs and cl up 3 out: styd on same pce after: nrly snatched 3rd* **16/1**	138
-33U	**5**	*3*	**Wessex King (IRE)**[105] 1961 7-10-5 **122** RichardJohnson (Henry Daly) *hld up: mstke 2nd: last next: stdy prog fr 7th: stl only 8th and nt on terms bef 3 out: shkn up and kpt on: nvr nr ldrs* **12/1**	124
1-40	**6**	*1½*	**King Edmund**[77] 2517 8-11-9 **140** LeightonAspell (Chris Gordon) *trckd ldrs: cl up fr 5th: nt fluent 6th and 9th: wnt 2nd next to 3 out: wkng whn mstke last* **12/1**	143
313F	**7**	*13*	**Noble Alan (GER)**[56] 2886 8-11-12 **143** BrianHarding (Nicky Richards) *settled wl in rr: prog fr 6th: chsd ldrs in 5th after 4 out: wknd after 3 out* **9/2**[2]	131
-56F	**8**	*1¾*	**My Moment (IRE)**[77] 2520 8-10-13 **130** AndrewTinkler (Henry Daly) *lw: nvr bttr than midfield: mstke 3rd: lost tch w ldrs fr 8th: poor 9th bef 3 out* **33/1**	117
1-41	**9**	*15*	**Call Me A Legend**[21] 3565 7-11-4 **135** RobertThornton (Alan King) *lw: chsd ldrs: j.v.slowly 3rd and dropped to last trio: nvr really gng after: t.o* **7/2**[1]	113
3124	**10**	*¾*	**Riguez Dancer**[28] 3446 7-11-0 **131** SamThomas (Ferdy Murphy) *lw: a in rr: struggling fr 6th: t.o after 4 out* **8/1**	104
F34U	**11**	*7*	**Blacktoft (USA)**[31] 3393 8-10-6 **123** JamieMoore (Evan Williams) *mde most to 6th: blnd 8th: stl in tch 10th: wknd rapidly 3 out* **33/1**	91
4353	**12**	*22*	**Sambulando (FR)**[21] 3555 8-10-5 **122** (t) PaddyBrennan (Tom George) *in tch whn blnd 4th: dropped to rr and j. modly after: t.o* **14/1**	68
3-P6	**R**		**Zacharova (IRE)**[52] 2962 8-10-2 **119** (b) AidanColeman (Venetia Williams) *showed no inclination to line up: ref to r* **12/1**	—

4m 1.05s (-0.75) **Going Correction** 0.0s/f (Good) **13** Ran SP% **118.8**
Speed ratings: **101,100,99,99,97 96,90,89,81,81 78,67,—**
toteswingers:1&2 £42.70, 2&3 £34.50, 1&3 £14.80 CSF £211.94 CT £2360.40 TOTE £6.70: £1.60, £10.00, £3.50; EX 263.00.
Owner The Ten From Seven **Bred** Gerry Martin **Trained** Upper Lambourn, Berks

FOCUS
A good competitive 2m event with several inexperienced chasers taking on more established rivals, and one of the former group prevailed. Solid form, with arguably another step forward from the winner.

NOTEBOOK
Anquetta(IRE), a novice who won on easy ground last time, beating a subsequent winner, was 10lb higher and taking on more experienced rivals. Given a good ride by David Bass, he went on approaching the Railway Fences but kept a bit up his sleeve and kicked again after two out. Although the gelding hung under pressure and again did not look totally straightforward, he kept on well enough to hold off his rivals. He will go up again but may have more to offer, and is a possible for the Grand Annual. (op 11-2 tchd 13-2)
Nomecheki(FR), a dual chase winner on very soft ground last season, had finished well beaten on his reappearance over hurdles. Still relatively unexposed but 13lb above his last winning mark, he came to challenge two out but the winner found more and he could not find another gear. This lightly raced 9-y-o gives the impression he has more to offer. (op 33-1)
Edgbriar(FR), all of whose wins have been at around 2m4f, had not run over a trip this short over fences. Racing off 4lb above his last winning mark, he was ridden positively and stayed on again after looking held. (op 16-1)
Moon Over Miami(GER), benefiting from being 9lb better off with the favourite for an 8l beating at Warwick last time, ran his race and seems in pretty good heart at present.
Wessex King(IRE) ◆, who is best suited by a sound surface, was returning from a 15-week absence, but got into contention from the rear before fading. The run should bring him on and he will be of interest this spring. (op 16-1)
King Edmund, a decent novice last season, winning three times at around this trip, was without the tongue tie he wore in two previous starts this season. Back from an 11-week break, he looked likely to play a major part at the last on the far side, but faded up the hill. He is another who should be better for the race. (op 11-1)
Noble Alan(GER) was another to make up ground to join the leaders leaving the back straight but failed to sustain his effort. He will presumably be aimed at a race at the Ayr Scottish National meeting, as he goes well on that track. (tchd 5-1)
Call Me A Legend was sent off favourite having won two of her three starts over fences on soft ground. Raised 9lb for beating today's fourth on her second run back from an absence due to injury last month, she jumped left and lost her place at the third and never got back into the race. She is due to take in the Grand Annual before retiring to stud, but maybe plans will be reviewed after this. Official explanation: jockey said mare was outpaced (tchd 10-3 and 4-1)
Riguez Dancer Official explanation: jockey said gelding never travelled

3950 BET TOTEPOOL ON 0800 221 221 NOVICES' H'CAP HURDLE (9 hdls) 2m 4f

4:40 (4:47) (Class 3) (0-120,125) 4-Y-0+ **£3,252** (£955; £477; £238)

Form				RPR
1154	**1**		**Firm Order (IRE)**[21] 3556 6-11-8 **116** WillKennedy (Paul Webber) *a in ldng trio: chal and upsides after 3 out: rdn bef next: led last: hld on wl* **14/1**	123
/4-1	**2**	*nk*	**Legion D'Honneur (UAE)**[276] 157 6-11-2 **110** RichardJohnson (Chris Down) *hld up wl in rr: stdy prog fr 4th: jnd ldng gp 3 out: rdn bef 2 out: wnt 2nd after last and chal: jst hld nr fin* **20/1**	117
-422	**3**	*4*	**Royale's Charter**[28] 3449 5-11-2 **110** DarylJacob (Nick Williams) *a w ldrs: chal and hit 3 out: rdn sn after: cl enough in 4th 2 out: one pce after* **4/1**[1]	113
2100	**4**	*½*	**Henry Hook (IRE)**[14] 3686 7-11-0 **115** (b1) EdGlassonbury(7) (Victor Dartnall) *led and clr to 1/2-way: hrd pressed fr 3 out: brought to nr side and stl led 2 out: hdd and no ex last* **16/1**	119
3514	**5**	*3½*	**Marleno (GER)**[26] 3481 5-11-5 **113** (t) WarrenMarston (Milton Harris) *hld up last: stdy prog fr 4th: jnd ldrs 3 out: cl enough in 5th 2 out: fdd last* **20/1**	114+
2130	**6**	*3¼*	**Regal Approach (IRE)**[38] 3198 8-11-7 **115** (p) JasonMaguire (Kim Bailey) *lw: chsd ldrs: pushed along 5th: last of ten in w a ch after 3 out but u.p: plugged on fr 2 out* **15/2**[3]	111
-100	**7**	*1½*	**Amirico (IRE)**[30] 3405 6-11-4 **112** AidanColeman (Venetia Williams) *settled towards rr: effrt and w ldng gp 3 out: sn rdn: btn bef 2 out: plugged on* **16/1**	107
/223	**8**	*17*	**Representingceltic (IRE)**[77] 2512 6-11-6 **114** ColinBolger (Pat Phelan) *prom bhd ldr: nt fluent 3 out: u.p in 6th and hld whn blnd bdly 2 out: wknd* **16/1**	102+
-344	**9**	*3*	**Wyck Hill (IRE)**[77] 2512 7-10-7 **108** MrSWDrinkwater(7) (David Bridgwater) *uns rdr in false s: prom: losing pl whn hit 6th hrd: sn bhd: t.o in 11th after 3 out: plugged on bef next* **14/1**	85
2-20	**10**	*2*	**Souter Point (USA)**[21] 3557 5-11-4 **117** DavidBass(5) (Nicky Henderson) *hld up in rr: effrt 5th: in tch in ldng gp after 3 out but u.p: wknd wl bef 2 out* **20/1**	92
1001	**11**	*nse*	**Heez A Cracker (FR)**[10] 3744 5-11-12 **125** JoshuaMoore(5) (Emma Lavelle) *lw: trckd ldrs: mstke 4th: nt fluent next: in tch but rdn after 3 out: wknd bef next: t.o* **9/2**[2]	102
-1U0	**12**	*28*	**Pro Pell (IRE)**[85] 2347 6-11-4 **112** JamieMoore (Gary Moore) *towards rr: pushed along bef 4th: nvr gng wl after: t.o fr 3 out: eased* **12/1**	62
06	**13**	*15*	**Peqeno Diablo (IRE)**[25] 3491 6-11-1 **112** IanPopham(3) (Claire Dyson) *nvr on terms: lost tch w ldng gp fr 6th: t.o after next* **100/1**	49
0-22	**14**	*20*	**Call It On (IRE)**[26] 3490 5-10-7 **108** KyleJames(7) (Philip Kirby) *prom to 3rd: wknd next: t.o bef 3 out* **20/1**	27
2355	**P**		**Smooth Classic (IRE)**[28] 3454 7-11-7 **115** PaddyBrennan (Warren Greatrex) *hld up in last pair: a in rr: t.o 3 out: p.u bef next* **28/1**	—
F6-2	**P**		**Hong Kong Harry**[77] 2512 7-11-7 **115** RobertThornton (Alan King) *nvr on terms w ldrs: lost tch whn mstke 3 out: t.o in 12th after: p.u bef 2 out* **8/1**	—
-002	**P**		**Dusky Bob (IRE)**[19] 3604 6-11-1 **109** LiamTreadwell (Nick Gifford) *pushed along after 3rd: sn dropped to last and t.o: p.u bef 2 out* **33/1**	—

5m 8.30s (2.60) **Going Correction** -0.075s/f (Good) **17** Ran SP% **126.2**
Speed ratings (Par 107): **91,90,89,89,87 86,85,78,77,76 76,65,59,51,— —,—**
toteswingers:1&2 £49.20, 2&3 £13.60, 1&3 £13.60 CSF £271.70 CT £1347.97 TOTE £15.90: £3.00, £4.60, £1.80, £4.40; EX 197.70.
Owner The Syndicators **Bred** Edmund Arthur **Trained** Mollington, Oxon

FOCUS
A big field for this fair novices' handicap hurdle which was not run in 2010, but fell to Silk Affair on her way to Cheltenham success in 2009. A small personal best from the winner.

NOTEBOOK
Firm Order(IRE), a dual hurdles winner at up to 3m1½f on a sound surface, handled this ground and put his proven stamina to good use. He went on before the last and stuck to his task resolutely. He could go for the Albert Bartlett at Cheltenham, but novice chasing next season is the plan. (op 16-1)
Legion D'Honneur(UAE) ◆, a winner over 2m5f who handles easy ground, was having his first start since May. He ran on to challenge the winner after the last but could not get past. This should put him right for the remainder of the season.
Royale's Charter had finished runner-up in a bumper and two hurdles from four starts. Having his first try beyond 2m and raised 8lb from his handicap debut, he stayed on really well having looked held and will probably appreciate even further in time. He can be found a suitable opportunity before long. (op 11-4, tchd 9-2 in a place)
Henry Hook(IRE), whose only win was at 2m5f on soft ground at Towcester, was 10lb above his last winning mark but had blinkers on for the first time. The headgear lit him up and he set off in front, only giving way near the last flight. (op 20-1)
Marleno(GER), another stepping up in trip, moved in to contention early in the straight but did not appear to get home. (op 25-1)
Regal Approach(IRE) has been running well over fences this season, winning at 2m6½f on easy ground, but is rated 6lb lower over hurdles. He looked held turning for home but kept plugging away up the hill. (op 8-1 tchd 7-1)
Amirico(IRE), a winner on heavy ground but well beaten on two starts since, was making his handicap debut. He closed on the leaders at the end of the back straight before his effort petered out.
Representingceltic(IRE), a lightly raced maiden making his handicap debut and returning from an 11-week break, ran well and was still in contention when blundering badly at the penultimate flight. He could be of interest given time to get over this.
Souter Point(USA) made a brief effort around three out but soon backed out of things. He was well beaten on his only previous try over this trip and appears not to stay. (op 25-1)
Heez A Cracker(FR), whose best form has been on right-handed tracks, was raised 10lb for his last success and weakened after coming under pressure at the last on the far side. He seems best on flat courses. (op 15-2)
Hong Kong Harry Official explanation: jockey said gelding stopped quickly
Dusky Bob(IRE) Official explanation: jockey said gelding never travelled
T/Jkpt: Not won. T/Plt: £1,485.50 to a £1 stake. Pool of £144,991.95 - 71.25 winning tickets. T/Qpdt: £729.90 to a £1 stake. Pool of £13,218.27 - 13.40 winning tickets. JN

3711 WETHERBY (L-H)

Saturday, February 5

OFFICIAL GOING: Good to soft (chs 6.1, hdl 6.2)

Wind: fresh 1/2 behind, becoming light last 2 Weather: overcast, breezy and damp, rain last 2

3951 BET ON TODAY'S TOTESCOOP6 AT TOTESPORT.COM H'CAP HURDLE (9 hdls) 2m 110y

1:10 (1:10) (Class 4) (0-100,100) 4-Y-0+ **£2,055** (£599; £299)

Form				RPR
/00-	**1**		**Lady Anne Nevill**[453] 2197 7-10-0 **74** oh4 PhilKinsella (Chris Fairhurst) *trckd ldrs: wnt 2nd appr 3 out: led appr last: drvn out* **50/1**	86+

426P **2** *4* **Ouest Eclair (FR)**[35] 3308 6-11-5 **93** .... GrahamLee 99
(Ferdy Murphy) *chsd ldrs: reminders 3rd: outpcd appr 3 out: styd on appr last: tk 2nd run-in* **14/1**

2-40 **3** *3 ½* **Sharadiyn**[247] 604 8-11-0 **93** .... JamesHalliday(5) 96
(Clive Mulhall) *trckd ldrs: led appr 3 out: j.lft 2 out: hdd appr last wknd run-in* **8/1**

4/32 **4** *6* **Sundae Best (IRE)**[17] 3631 7-11-12 **100** .... BrianHughes 99
(Howard Johnson) *chsd ldrs: drvn appr 3 out: wknd appr last* **3/1**[1]

3-05 **5** *5* **King Mak**[23] 3523 9-11-8 **99** .... RichieMcLernon(3) 91
(Marjorie Fife) *led: hdd appr 3 out: wknd between last 2* **8/1**

4400 **6** *2 ½* **Hoar Frost**[53] 2937 6-11-1 **96** .... MissPhillipaTutty(7) 86
(Karen Tutty) *chsd ldrs: reminders 2nd: outpcd 6th: kpt on fr 2 out* **25/1**

7 *3 ¾* **A Stones Throw (NZ)**[87] 2319 6-11-7 **95** ....(t) BarryKeniry 81
(Ben Haslam) *hld up towards rr: hdwy 6th: nvr nr ldrs* **20/1**

3F25 **8** *1 ¼* **Baraathen (USA)**[125] 1699 4-10-11 **95** .... AdrianLane 72
(Donald McCain) *w ldrs: lost pl appr 3 out: hmpd last* **15/2**[3]

-056 **9** *22* **South Stack**[30] 3403 6-11-9 **100** .... JamesO'Farrell(3) 66
(Michael Scudamore) *t.k.h in rr: hdwy 4th: wknd appr 3 out: sn bhd* **20/1**

2303 **10** *8* **Treason Trial**[92] 2188 10-11-7 **95** .... FearghalDavis 53
(Andrew Crook) *in rr: bhd and drvn 3rd: t.o 3 out* **33/1**

-660 **11** *1* **Bold Indian (IRE)**[102] 837 7-9-8 **74** oh7 ow1 .... PaulGallagher(7) 32
(Mike Sowersby) *in rr: sme hdwy 6th: sn wknd: bhd whn eased between last 2* **100/1**

532P **12** *8* **Mister Fizzbomb (IRE)**[11] 3727 8-10-8 **85** ....(v) HarryHaynes(3) 35
(John Wainwright) *chsd ldrs: drvn 4th: lost pl next: sn bhd: t.o 3 out* **25/1**

-423 **F** **Vin Rose**[22] 3545 6-10-11 **85** .... CampbellGillies —
(Mark Rimell) *in rr: hdwy appr 3 out: 5th and one pce whn fell last* **13/2**[2]

-4P0 **P** **Eagle Owl (IRE)**[73] 2612 5-11-9 **97** ....(t) RichieMcGrath —
(Tim Easterby) *lost pl 3rd: sn bhd: t.o whn p.u bef 3 out* **13/2**[2]

4m 18.6s (22.80) **Going Correction** +1.475s/f (Heav)
WFA 4 from 5yo+ 9lb **14 Ran SP% 115.4**
Speed ratings (Par 105): **105,103,101,98,96 95,93,92,82,78 78,74,—,—**
Tote Swingers: 1&2 £67.70, 1&3 £67.70, 2&3 £31.60 CSF £574.47 CT £6080.02 TOTE £66.30: £10.00, £5.60, £3.00; EX 636.40.
Owner Mrs C A Arnold **Bred** C W Fairhurst **Trained** Middleham Moor, N Yorks

FOCUS
After 10mm of rain overnight the ground was described as good to soft. A run-of-the-mill 0-100 handicap in which the early pace was sound. The first two produced big steps up but the next pair give the form a solid look.

NOTEBOOK
Lady Anne Nevill, who was having her first run in 15 months, was never far off the pace and recorded a shock success. This was only her sixth start over hurdles and she is at the right end of the handicap. Official explanation: trainer said, regarding apparent improvement in form, that the mare ran well last time and strengthened up having had a break. (op 40-1)
Ouest Eclair(FR), a maiden after 12 starts, never travelled early in the race but came home well. He has tried a number of different trips and it is still debatable which is his best, but he can go one place better at some point. (op 16-1)
Sharadiyn, also coming back from a break, ran well and should improve for this outing. (op 12-1)
Sundae Best(IRE) might be worth a try over further.
A Stones Throw(NZ), having his first start for connections, wasn't knocked about and will improve for this outing. He's one to keep on the right side in similar company. (op 28-1)
Vin Rose was held in fifth when coming down at the last. She appears consistent but the handicapper might just have her measure. (op 11-2)
Eagle Owl(IRE) Official explanation: trainer had no explanation for the poor form shown (op 11-2)

3952 BET TOTEPOOL AT TOTESPORT.COM NOVICES' HURDLE (12 hdls) 2m 6f
1:40 (1:40) (Class 3) 5-Y-O+ **£1,951** (£573; £286; £143)

Form RPR

1 **Moonlight Drive (IRE)**[104] 5-10-12 0 .... DougieCostello 126+
(John Quinn) *hld up: hdwy to trck ldrs 6th: wnt 2nd 9th: led next: blnd 2 out: styd on strly run-in* **9/2**[3]

1 **2** *6* **Trustan Times (IRE)**[21] 3572 5-11-5 0 .... AdrianLane 130+
(Tim Easterby) *trckd ldrs: hmpd 2nd: t.k.h and led next: hdd 3 out: 2 l down whn nt fluent last: fdd* **5/4**[1]

005 **3** *17* **Crafti Bookie (IRE)**[11] 3719 5-10-12 0 .... HenryOliver 106+
(Sue Smith) *w ldrs: led 2nd: hdd next: outpcd 9th: styd on to take modest 3rd between last 2* **100/1**

/22- **4** *12* **Scriptwriter (IRE)**[350] 4166 9-10-12 130 .... BrianHughes 93
(Howard Johnson) *chsd ldrs: outpcd appr 3 out: wknd between last 2* **7/2**[2]

3425 **5** *2 ¾* **River Dragon (IRE)**[23] 3521 6-10-12 0 .... BarryKeniry 90
(Neville Bycroft) *hld up in rr: hdwy 9th: modest 5th whn mstke next* **20/1**

2-40 **6** *16* **Shrewd Investment**[46] 3056 5-10-9 0 .... CharlieHuxley(3) 79
(Alan King) *prom whn bdly hmpd and lost pl 2nd: reminders and hdwy 7th: lost pl 9th* **20/1**

0-0 **7** *11* **Saddlers' Secret (IRE)**[85] 2355 6-10-0 0 .... JamesHalliday(5) 59
(Mark Campion) *prom: lost pl 4th: in rr fr 6th* **200/1**

03 **8** *1 ½* **Eliades Run (IRE)**[88] 2297 5-10-12 0 .... GrahamLee 65
(Ferdy Murphy) *in rr: reminders 6th: nvr on terms* **40/1**

2/0 **9** *45* **China House (IRE)**[39] 3171 8-10-12 0 .... RyanMania 24
(Lisa Williamson) *prom: hmpd and lost pl 2nd: hdwy 6th: mstke 8th: sn wknd: t.o* **100/1**

00P0 **10** *25* **Cloudy Joe (IRE)**[8] 3787 5-10-9 0 .... AdamPogson(3) 2
(Charles Pogson) *led to 2nd: lost pl 9th: sn bhd: t.o 2 out* **200/1**

-4 **B** **Wild Rhubarb**[35] 3296 6-10-2 0 .... RichieMcLernon(3) —
(Jonjo O'Neill) *chsd ldrs: b.d 2nd* **14/1**

-P00 **F** **Sheepclose (IRE)**[30] 3403 6-10-5 0 .... JakeGreenall(7) —
(Michael Easterby) *t.k.h: trckd ldrs: wknd 8th: 8th whn fell heavily last* **125/1**

6 **P** **Bravello (IRE)**[88] 2297 6-10-12 0 .... WilsonRenwick —
(Howard Johnson) *trckd ldrs 3rd: lost pl 6th: sn bhd: t.o whn p.u bef 9th* **50/1**

0-P **F** **Lady Chorister**[25] 3498 6-9-12 0 .... KyleJames(7) —
(Simon West) *w ldrs: fell 2nd* **200/1**

00 **P** **Master Conor (IRE)**[24] 3505 5-10-12 0 .... PhilKinsella —
(Henry Hogarth) *hmpd 2nd: bhd fr 4th: t.o whn p.u bef 9th* **200/1**

6 **P** **Mizen Station (IRE)**[24] 3506 6-10-12 0 .... JamesReveley —
(Oliver Sherwood) *hld up in rr: hdwy to trck ldrs7th: lost pl and 6th whn p.u bef 3 out* **9/1**

60 **P** **Alpha One (IRE)**[23] 3525 5-10-12 0 .... CampbellGillies —
(Chris Grant) *mstkes: lost pl 3rd: bhd whn blundererd 6th: t.o whn p.u bef next* **150/1**

5m 54.1s (27.30) **Going Correction** +1.475s/f (Heav) **17 Ran SP% 120.9**
Speed ratings: **109,106,100,96,95 89,85,84,68,59 —,—,—,—,— —,—**
Tote Swingers: 1&2 £2.00, 2&3 £61.00 CSF £10.24 TOTE £6.80: £2.20, £1.50, £13.90; EX 16.20.
Owner Maxilead Limited **Bred** Michael O'Donovan **Trained** Settrington, N Yorks

FOCUS
An interesting novice hurdle run at a sound pace, and the first two home, who pulled well clear, look well above average northern novices. There is a case for rating the race a lot higher.

NOTEBOOK
Moonlight Drive(IRE), a winner of an Irish point last October, travelled and jumped well throughout. Held in high regard by connections, the 5-y-o will head straight to Cheltenham for the Albert Bartlett (ground permitting), for which Totesport make him a 40-1 shot. Longer term, he has the size and scope to jump fences and is an exciting prospect. (op 5-1)
Trustan Times(IRE), a winner here over 2m4f last time out, was a little keen early (not helped by a loose horse) but still ran with credit. Time might prove that this was a smart run, and he can defy his penalty before too long. He also has the size and scope to jump fences in due course. (op 13-8)
Crafti Bookie(IRE) appears to be going the right way and will certainly win races. He will stay 3m. (op 125-1)
Scriptwriter(IRE), coming back from almost a year off, looked in need of the run. Rated 130, if he stays sound he can win a novice event at some point soon. (op 10-3)
Mizen Station(IRE), also winner of an Irish point, had travelled well early in the race but was pulled up quickly and can only be watched next time. Official explanation: trainer's rep said gelding had a breathing problem (op 8-1)

3953 BET ON LIVE FOOTBALL AT TOTESPORT.COM H'CAP CHASE (16 fncs) 2m 4f 110y
2:10 (2:11) (Class 2) (0-150,140) 5-Y-O+
£7,827 (£2,312; £1,156; £578; £288; £145)

Form RPR

23P/ **1** **Crescent Island (IRE)**[672] 4847 8-11-3 **134** .... TomMolloy(3) 148+
(Nigel Twiston-Davies) *trckd ldrs: hit 7th: hmpd and dropped bk next: hdwy to trck ldrs 12th: led on bit next: clr 2 out: 10 l ahd whn idled bdly run-in: drvn rt out* **11/1**

-P23 **2** *3 ½* **Regal Heights (IRE)**[28] 3453 10-10-8 **123** ....(p) DougieCostello 129
(Tom George) *chsd ldrs: lft in ld 8th: hdd 4 out: kpt on run-in* **7/2**[1]

F3-P **3** *15* **Isn't That Lucky**[125] 1690 8-10-10 **127** .... RichieMcLernon(3) 119
(Jonjo O'Neill) *in rr: outpcd 12th: styd on fr 3 out: tk modest 3rd towards fin* **9/1**

2614 **4** *1 ¾* **Sheriff Hutton (IRE)**[39] 3171 8-11-4 **132** .... RobertWalford 123
(Tim Walford) *w ldrs: clr 3rd 3 out: wknd run-in* **8/1**

6-01 **5** *11* **Lease Lend**[21] 3573 8-11-12 **140** ....(tp) RichieMcGrath 121
(Tim Easterby) *hld up: hdwy 9th: wknd after 4 out* **4/1**[2]

6-F0 **6** *2 ¾* **I'm Delilah**[56] 2881 9-11-8 **136** .... JamesReveley 117
(Ferdy Murphy) *chsd ldrs: j. bdly lft 4 out: sn wknd* **14/1**

-1U4 **7** *25* **Big Burrows (IRE)**[78] 2507 9-10-3 **127** .... TonyKelly(10) 86
(Ferdy Murphy) *stdd s: blnd 5th: mstke 10th: bhd fr 12th* **28/1**

10-F **8** *12* **Gansey (IRE)**[83] 2400 9-11-7 **135** .... PeterBuchanan 90
(Sue Smith) *prom: jnd ldrs 9th: blnd 12th: lost pl appr next: bhd whn blnd 2 out: eased run-in* **5/1**[3]

U-P1 **U** **Frankie Figg (IRE)**[76] 2541 9-11-8 **136** .... BrianHughes —
(Howard Johnson) *led: hmpd by loose horse bnd appr 8th: jnd whn blnd and uns rdr 8th* **13/2**

40P **U** **Charingworth (IRE)**[35] 3306 8-10-9 **123** .... GrahamLee —
(Ferdy Murphy) *stdd s: in rr: blnd and uns rdr 3rd* **17/2**

5m 24.3s (16.50) **Going Correction** +1.025s/f (Soft) **10 Ran SP% 122.3**
Speed ratings: **109,107,101,101,97 96,86,81,—,—**
Tote Swingers: 1&2 £7.50, 1&3 £19.80, 2&3 £9.70 CSF £53.49 CT £376.91 TOTE £13.70: £3.50, £1.60, £2.40; EX 51.20.
Owner Sarah Bays Jill Scott Sarah MacEchern **Bred** Mrs Jane Lane and Mrs Cecily Purcell **Trained** Naunton, Gloucs

FOCUS
A 0-150 chase in which the top weight was rated 10lb below the ceiling. The early pace was sound. The idling winner was value for furtehr and is rated to the level of his Cheltenham third.

NOTEBOOK
Crescent Island(IRE) ran out a decisive winner despite idling close home. Having his first start since April 2009 and running without his normal blinkers, his yard has been in better form over the last few days and this was a polished display. (op 17-2)
Regal Heights(IRE), 17lb below his last winning mark, ran with credit and deserves to go one better at some point soon. (op 9-2)
Isn't That Lucky, having his first start in four months, ran okay without striking as a winner waiting to happen. Plagued with breathing problems, his next run should prove informative. (op 11-1)
Sheriff Hutton(IRE), a good servant to connections over the last few seasons, is more effective on better ground. (tchd 9-1)
Lease Lend, a winner over 2m last time out, travelled well enough into the race but weakened at the business end. (op 9-2)
I'm Delilah, who tended to jump left on occasions, appears to be in the grip of the handicapper. (op 16-1 tchd 20-1)

3954 200% DEPOSIT BONUS AT TSPOKER.COM H'CAP HURDLE (12 hdls 1 omitted) 3m 1f
2:45 (2:45) (Class 3) (0-135,129) 4-Y-O+ **£2,602** (£764; £382; £190)

Form RPR

-FPU **1** **Palypso De Creek (FR)**[6] 3832 8-11-10 **127** .... TomSiddall 134+
(Charlie Longsdon) *chsd ldrs: nt fluent 3rd: mstke and reminders 5 out: wnt 2nd appr 3 out: styd on to ld appr last: drvn rt out* **7/2**[2]

0054 **2** *1 ¾* **Chester Lad**[21] 3575 6-11-2 **119** .... JanFaltejsek 124+
(George Charlton) *t.k.h racing wd: hit 4 out: wnt 3rd appr next: styd on and chal last: no ex* **7/2**[2]

P-U2 **3** *8* **Double Expresso**[21] 3575 7-11-12 **129** .... BrianHughes 128+
(Howard Johnson) *trckd ldr: upsides 5 out: led appr 3 out: rdn 2 out: hdd & wknd appr last* **7/4**[1]

3554 **4** *28* **Always Bold (IRE)**[45] 3092 6-11-5 **122** ....(b) AdrianLane 93
(Donald McCain) *led: hit 2nd: qcknd after 7th: hdd appr 3 out: wknd and mstke 3 out: sn bhd* **5/1**[3]

4600 **5** *24* **Ravati (IRE)**[20] 3587 5-9-9 **105** oh1 ....(t) MissLHorner(5) 52
(Liam Corcoran) *hld up in last: lost pl 4 out: sn bhd: t.o 2 out* **5/1**[3]

7m 6.50s (50.00) **Going Correction** +1.475s/f (Heav) **5 Ran SP% 114.1**
Speed ratings (Par 107): **79,78,75,66,59**
CSF £16.30 TOTE £6.40: £2.20, £1.80; EX 22.00.
Owner Alan Halsall **Bred** Suc Yves Chopin & Mme Francoise Roux **Trained** Over Norton, Oxon

FOCUS
There was a disappointing turnout for this 0-135 handicap hurdle, in which the top weight weighed in 6lb below the ceiling. It was run at a steady pace and what the form is worth is questionable. The winner is a 144 chaser at best and could build on this over hurdles.

NOTEBOOK
Palypso De Creek(FR), who hadn't completed in his last four chases (the first one being the Grand National), was nicely treated back over hurdles. He still looked hesitant over some of his jumps, though, and probably isn't one to take a short price about next time out. (op 9-2)
Chester Lad, a winner of two novice hurdles at Hexham last year, stayed on late in the day. This was a solid enough run but he doesn't strike as being well handicapped. (tchd 4-1)

Double Expresso looked the most likely winner when taking up the running with three to jump, but he folded tamely soon after. A drop in trip might help but he doesn't look well handicapped. (op 15-8)

Always Bold(IRE) didn't impress with his head carriage once headed. (op 6-1 tchd 9-2)

Ravati(IRE) showed very little on his first start for new connections. Official explanation: jockey said gelding lost its action (tchd 11-2)

3955 TOTESPORT.COM TOWTON NOVICES' CHASE GRADE 2 (18 fncs) 3m 1f

3:15 (3:20) (Class 1) 5-Y-0+ **£13,397** (£5,026; £2,516; £1,254; £629)

Form RPR

1-11 **1** **Wayward Prince**[84] 2357 7-11-7 144... DougieCostello 151+
(Ian Williams) *chsd ldr: nt fluent and pushed along 11th: led appr 4 out: drvn rt out* **5/6**[1]

0-1P **2** *2* **Cape Tribulation**[97] 2105 7-11-4 0... JamesReveley 144+
(Malcolm Jefferson) *t.k.h: trckd ldrs 2nd: stmbld landing 14th: chsd wnr appr next: styd on run-in* **6/1**[3]

-101 **3** *9* **Captain Americo (IRE)**[25] 3499 9-11-0 127... HarryHaynes 131
(James Ewart) *led: hdd appr 4 out: kpt on to take modest 3rd 2 out: hit last* **9/1**

0-41 **4** *18* **On His Own (IRE)**[22] 3548 7-11-0 116... BrianHughes 116
(Howard Johnson) *chsd ldrs 6th: mstke next: outpcd 9th: chsd ldrs 11th: outpcd and lost pl 4 out: mstke next: tk modest 4th towards fin* **8/1**

2241 **5** *1 ½* **Hollo Ladies (IRE)**[31] 3394 6-11-0 140... GrahamLee 114
(Ferdy Murphy) *hld up: chsd ldrs 14th: wnt handy 3rd 3 out: wknd next: tired run-in and lost 4th nr line* **5/1**[2]

6m 37.0s (27.60) **Going Correction** +1.025s/f (Soft) **5** Ran SP% **106.6**
Speed ratings: **96,95,92,86,86**
CSF £5.80 TOTE £1.90: £1.10, £2.90; EX 7.20.

Owner T J & Mrs H Parrott **Bred** M G Kilroe **Trained** Portway, Worcs

FOCUS
All five runners had already been successful over fences this season. It was run at an even pace and they all finished tired in the ground. The winner produced another step forward but may need to improve a stone+ in the RSA Chase.

NOTEBOOK
Wayward Prince brought some solid form to the table. Rated 144, jumped soundly throughout and appears to only do enough to keep the others at bay. He will head straight for the RSA at Cheltenham, and his trainer and jockey feel the better ground and stronger gallop he's likely to get there will suit him. (op 10-11)
Cape Tribulation was travelling sweetly when making a bad mistake five from home. It was creditable he got back into it and there are plenty more races to be won with him. (op 13-2 tchd 11-2)
Captain Americo(IRE), rated 127, probably ran bang up to form. He holds an entry in the 4m National Hunt Chase at Cheltenham, and the trip there should be well within his range. (op 8-1)
On His Own(IRE), rated 28lb inferior to the winner, was well held over the last few fences and will need to have his sights lowered next time. (op 15-2 tchd 7-1)
Hollo Ladies(IRE) crept nicely into the race with four to jump but weakened very quickly at the penultimate fence. The race he won at Southwell hasn't worked out that well and he can only be watched after this effort. (op 11-2)

3956 WILMOT-SMITH MEMORIAL CUP (HUNTERS' CHASE) (18 fncs) 3m 1f

3:50 (3:50) (Class 6) 6-Y-0+ **£988** (£304; £152)

Form RPR

11U- **1** **Baby Run (FR)**[303] 5096 11-11-11 136... MrWTwiston-Davies(7) 146+
(Nigel Twiston-Davies) *mde all: j. soundly: drew wl clr after 3 out: drvn out* **11/8**[1]

10-P **2** *37* **Breaking Silence (IRE)**[276] 149 10-12-4 118...(t) MrAJBerry 112
(Jonjo O'Neill) *hld up: hdwy to chse ldrs 7th: chsd wnr after 14th: 20 l 2nd last: tired run-in* **20/1**

400- **3** *2 ¼* **Offshore Account (IRE)**[20] 11-11-4 135 ow2...(t) MrNSutton(7) 106
(Mrs T L Bailey) *chsd ldrs: blnd 9th: outpcd and lost pl 14th: distant 4th whn blnd next: tk modest 3rd whn j.rt and hit last: kpt on* **7/2**[2]

365- **4** *13* **Rimsky (IRE)**[13] 10-11-7 114...(p) MissTJackson(3) 88
(Tina Jackson) *prom: lost pl 11th: sn bhd: blnd 14th: t.o next: tk distant 4th nr fin* **28/1**

242- **5** *1 ¾* **Viking Rebel (IRE)**[33] 9-11-10 127... MrOGreenall 86
(W T Reed) *trckd ldrs: clr 3rd whn mstke 12th: wknd rapidly between last 2* **8/1**

53/1 **P** **Moment Of Madness (IRE)**[262] 398 13-11-11 106... MrMWalford(3) —
(Mrs M Stirk) *trckd ldrs: t.k.h: wnt 2nd 7th: wknd qckly after 14th: sn wl bhd: t.o whn p.u bef next* **16/1**

500- **P** **Potts Of Magic**[238] 12-11-11 105... MissJCoward(3) —
(Mrs C A Coward) *in rr: hit 8th: bhd fr 10th: t.o 13th: p.u bef 4 out* **66/1**

F2P- **U** **Cleni Boy (FR)**[13] 9-11-7 122... MrCDawson(3) —
(P Grindrod) *in rr whn mstke and uns rdr 5th* **12/1**

3154 **P** **The Artful Fox**[197] 1081 10-11-11 88... MrGBrewer(3) —
(Mike Sowersby) *in rr: wnt prom 10th: lost pl 12th: sn bhd: t.o whn p.u bef 4 out* **100/1**

20P- **P** **Gypsy George**[322] 4740 10-11-3 129... MrCGreene(7) —
(Mrs S M McPherson) *nt jump wl: in tch: lost pl 6th: bhd whn blnd 12th: sn t.o: p.u bef 4 out* **6/1**[3]

U **Philasonic**[300] 8-11-3 0... MrMGarnett(7) —
(Miss S R Robertson) *towards rr whn mstke and uns rdr 6th* **50/1**

6m 49.0s (39.60) **Going Correction** +1.025s/f (Soft) **11** Ran SP% **116.0**
Speed ratings: **77,65,64,60,59** —,—,—,—,— —
Tote Swingers: 1&2 £34.00, 1&3 £1.02, 2&3 £42.90 CSF £32.50 TOTE £2.20: £1.10, £4.10, £2.50; EX 20.40.

Owner N A Twiston-Davies **Bred** Haras De Preaux **Trained** Naunton, Gloucs

■ The first winner under rules for 16-y-o rider Willie Twiston-Davies, son of Nigel and brother of Sam.

■ Stewards' Enquiry : Mr N Sutton three-day ban: weighed in 2lb heavy (Feb 22-24)

FOCUS
This proved a straightforward task for the top hunter chaser of the last couple of seasons, Baby Run. He will be tough to beat in this grade and is rated in line with his reappearance last season.

NOTEBOOK
Baby Run(FR), last season's Cheltenham Foxhunters' winner, won easily enough. He will be an ideal schoolmaster for the trainer's son Willie Twiston-Davies, who looked very polished in the saddle. (op 11-10)
Breaking Silence(IRE), a former useful chaser in Ireland, got very tired on his first run back from a nine-month absence. He will improve for this and will find easier races in the coming weeks.
Offshore Account(IRE), also a very useful chaser in Ireland, had been successful, in a point nearly three weeks earlier. He will also find easier tasks than this during the season but there is room for improvement in the jumping department. (op 10-3)
Rimsky(IRE), a former stablemate to the winner, ran okay in the first-time cheekpieces without really threatening. (op 33-1)

Moment Of Madness(IRE), despite pulling up, showed up well for a long time on his first start for almost nine months, and he should do better next time out.

3957 WETHERBYRACING.CO.UK STANDARD OPEN NATIONAL HUNT FLAT RACE 2m 110y

4:20 (4:26) (Class 6) 4-6-Y-0 **£1,267** (£369; £184)

Form RPR

3 **1** **Distime (IRE)**[10] 3752 5-11-4 0... DougieCostello 110+
(John Quinn) *hld up in mid-div: smooth hdwy to trck ldrs 6f out: led on bit over 3f out: rdn appr fnl f: styd on* **11/4**[1]

2 *1* **Medinas (FR)** 4-10-8 0... GerardTumelty 99+
(Alan King) *trckd ldrs: styd on to chse wnr over 1f out: kpt on same pce fnl 150yds* **13/2**[3]

04 **3** *7* **Red Rocco (IRE)**[24] 3511 4-9-12 0... SamuelWelton(10) 92
(George Moore) *led: hdd 4f out: one pce fnl 2f* **11/2**[2]

4 *½* **Brokethegate** 6-11-4 0... JamesReveley 102
(Chris Grant) *hld up in mid-div: hdwy 6f out: sn chsng ldrs: led 4f out: sn hdd: styd on same pce fnl 2f* **25/1**

5 *1 ½* **Sinfield (IRE)** 5-11-4 0... BarryKeniry 100
(Micky Hammond) *t.k.h in rr: hdwy 6f out: one pce fnl 3f* **20/1**

6 **6** *8* **Monashee (IRE)**[258] 448 6-11-4 0... JanFaltejsek 92
(George Charlton) *in rr: hdwy on outside 6f out: chsng ldrs over 3f out: wknd 2f out* **25/1**

7 *shd* **Think** 4-10-5 0... MrOGreenall(3) 82
(Clive Mulhall) *chsd ldrs: wknd over 2f out* **12/1**

0 **8** *12* **Mootabar (IRE)**[31] 3399 4-10-8 0... WilsonRenwick 72
(Chris Fairhurst) *trckd ldrs: wknd over 2f out* **20/1**

6 **9** *19* **Cool Steel (IRE)**[31] 3399 5-11-1 0... CharlieHuxley(3) 61
(Alan King) *hld up in mid-div: hdwy 6f out: wknd 3f out* **12/1**

10 *shd* **Pinerolo** 5-11-4 0... TjadeCollier 61
(Sue Smith) *w ldrs: drvn after 6f: lost pl 7f out* **18/1**

11 *½* **Grey Bobby** 4-10-8 0... SamJones 50
(Renee Robeson) *mid-div: lost pl 6f out* **28/1**

12 *4 ½* **Struanmore** 4-10-5 0... DannyCook(3) 46
(Paul Webber) *w ldrs: lost pl over 3f out* **17/2**

13 *nk* **Across The Tweed (IRE)** 5-11-4 0... HenryOliver 56
(Sue Smith) *trckd ldrs: reminders after 6f: lost pl 7f out* **33/1**

14 *8* **Cobbler's Rest (IRE)** 5-11-1 0... RichieMcLernon(3) 48
(Jonjo O'Neill) *trckd ldrs: lost pl 6f out: sn bhd* **18/1**

4 **15** *39* **Perfect Ending (IRE)**[23] 3525 4-10-8 0... BrianHughes —
(Richard Fahey) *mid-div: lost pl 6f out: sn bhd: t.o 3f out* **11/1**

16 *8* **Rocky Bear (IRE)** 6-11-4 0... PhilKinsella 1
(Marjorie Fife) *a in rr: t.o 3f out* **50/1**

17 *¾* **Golden King (IRE)** 6-11-4 0... RichieMcGrath —
(Lisa Williamson) *t.k.h in midfield: reminders after 6f: sn lost pl and bhd: t.o 3f out* **40/1**

0 **18** *6* **In Vigo (IRE)**[30] 3406 4-10-5 0... TomMolloy(3) —
(William Jarvis) *in rr: bhd fnl 6f: t.o 3f out* **28/1**

4m 12.6s (22.40) **Going Correction** +1.475s/f (Heav)
WFA 4 from 5yo 9lb 5 from 6yo 1lb **18** Ran SP% **131.6**
Speed ratings: **106,105,102,102,101 97,97,91,82,82 82,80,80,76,58 54,54,51**
Tote Swingers: 1&2 £5.60, 1&3 £2.40, 2&3 £19.20 CSF £18.05 TOTE £3.30: £1.10, £3.90, £1.80.

Owner Maxilead Limited **Bred** Ms Marisa & Michael Bourke **Trained** Settrington, N Yorks

FOCUS
Probably just a fair bumper. It was run at a sound pace and produced a taking winner, who was the form pick and can rate higher.

NOTEBOOK
Distime(IRE), winner of an Irish point last October, ran well when placed at Musselburgh last time out, but the stiffer nature of this track suited him perfectly. He will get an entry in the Cheltenham bumper but might well be saved for Aintree, and will have little trouble making his mark over timber in due course. (op 5-2)
Medinas(FR) a half-brother to the yard's Sweet Irony, showed up well on his debut and can go one better in similar company shortly. (op 14-1)
Red Rocco(IRE), fourth last time out at Doncaster, puts the form in some context. Certainly not devoid of ability, he can also make his mark over hurdles in due course. (op 8-1)
Brokethegate, who doesn't lack size or scope, stayed on well late in the day and has clearly got a future.
Sinfield(IRE) has a nice pedigree and will have learned from this experience. He can also win races in due course. (op 14-1)
Cool Steel(IRE), representing a yard going well, was the disappointment of the race. That said, he doesn't lack for size, and can bounce back. (op 11-1)

T/Plt: £329.90 to a £1 stake. Pool of £63,335.64 - 140.12 winning tickets. T/Qpdt: £13.70 to a £1 stake. Pool of £5,484.01 - 294.20 winning tickets. WG

3788 FONTWELL (L-H)

Sunday, February 6

OFFICIAL GOING: Good to soft (soft in places) changing to soft after race 1 (1.20)

Rail movement added 50yds per circuit to chase and 70yds per circuit to hurdles.
Wind: Strong, across Weather: light rain

3958 TIANA HONEY WATSON FUND JUVENILE HURDLE (9 hdls) 2m 2f 110y

1:20 (1:20) (Class 4) 4-Y-0 **£2,016** (£592; £296; £147)

Form RPR

P0 **1** **Whitby Jack**[15] 3673 4-10-12 0... JamieMoore 120+
(Gary Moore) *racd wd: hld up in tch and a gng wl: hdwy to trck ldrs 5th: led on bit bef 2 out: clr and wl in command whn mstke last 2: easily* **4/1**[3]

202 **2** *14* **Kuilsriver (IRE)**[22] 3554 4-10-12 0...(t) DarylJacob 107+
(Alison Thorpe) *nt a fluent: mde most: hit 6th: rdn and hdd whn slipped bnd bef next: sn no ch w wnr: plugged on flat* **13/8**[1]

0234 **3** *1* **Omaruru (IRE)**[31] 3401 4-10-12 118... SamJones 106+
(Renee Robeson) *prom: chsd ldr after 1st tl 3rd: drvn bef 2 out: sn outpcd by wnr and wl btn: plugged on u.p: mstke last* **11/4**[2]

4250 **4** *43* **Freckle Face**[34] 3366 4-10-5 108... MarkQuinlan(7) 77+
(Bill Turner) *j.big 1st: t.k.h: in tch: hdwy to chse ldr 5th tl after 3 out: sn wknd u.p: 4th and wl hld whn mstke and nrly uns rdr next: hung rt after last: t.o* **8/1**

5 *7* **Promised Wings (GER)**[14] 4-10-12 0... LeightonAspell 58
(Chris Gordon) *t.k.h: hld up in tch in rr: hdwy to chse ldng quartet: no hdwy and wl btn after 3 out: t.o between last 2* **50/1**

05 **6** *11* **Blinka Me**[10] 3767 4-10-12 0 SamThomas 48
(Alex Hales) *in tch in midfield: dropped to rr and rdn after 5th: sn struggling: losing tch whn j. slowly next: t.o after 3 out* **25/1**

U4 **7** *15* **Claimant (IRE)**[95] 2151 4-10-12 0 JamesDavies 35
(Paul Fitzsimons) *in tch in rr: j.rt 1st: rdn and struggling after 5th: t.o fr 3 out* **25/1**

5 **8** *1* **Astrovenus**[88] 1818 4-10-5 0 ColinBolger 27
(Mark H Tompkins) *racd wd: hld up in tch in rr: nt fluent 2nd: rdn and toiling after 5th: t.o fr 3 out* **40/1**

00 **9** *¾* **Brave Enough (USA)**[35] 3344 4-10-12 0 HaddenFrost 33
(Roger Curtis) *in tch tl rdn and toiling bdly after 5th: wl t.o fr 3 out* **100/1**

0500 **10** *24* **Brambley**[20] 3607 4-10-2 0 WayneKavanagh(3) —
(Seamus Mullins) *chsd ldrs: wnt 2nd 3rd tl 5th: sn lost pl: wl bhd next: t.o 3 out: virtually p.u flat* **100/1**

6 **11** *30* **Cuckoo Rock (IRE)**[22] 3554 4-10-9 0 RichieMcLernon(3) —
(Jonathan Portman) *mstkes: chsd ldr tl after 1st: chsd ldrs after tl rdn and lost tch after 5th: wl t.o bef 3 out* **16/1**

4m 45.0s (10.70) **Going Correction** +0.80s/f (Soft) **11** Ran SP% **115.8**
Speed ratings: **109,103,102,84,81 77,70,70,69,59 47**
toteswingers:1&2:£2.30, 1&3:£3.30, 2&3:£1.90 CSF £10.65 TOTE £4.90: £1.40, £1.20, £1.30; EX 12.90.
Owner C E Stedman **Bred** C E Stedman **Trained** Lower Beeding, W Sussex

FOCUS
Rail movement added 50yds per circuit to Chase and 70yds per circuit to Hurdles. After drizzle for most of the previous day the going was changed to good to soft, soft in places before this first race. The time confirmed the going as soft and the official description was soon changed to reflect that. \n\x\x This juvenile hurdle has thrown up some decent sorts in recent years, such as Blazing Bailey and Mobaasher. All but one of these had previous experience but very few were involved on the last circuit. Whitby Jack produced a massive step up but is entitled to be this good on Flat form. The next two ran to their marks.

NOTEBOOK
Whitby Jack had shown minor promise in a better race at Ascot, and his trainer had reported he had struggled to get the gelding fit. Ridden wide throughout, he asserted going to the second-last and came home at his leisure. He looks capable of winning better races with this under his belt, and he might take his chance in the Fred Winter if rated high enough. (op 5-1, tchd 6-1 in places)
Kuilsriver(IRE) had run well against a decent sort on his hurdling debut. He made much of the running but slipped slightly on the home turn and could not respond when the winner went for home. He battled back to get the runner-up spot though. (op 15-8)
Omaruru(IRE) was never far away and had his chance turning in but could not quicken. His official rating of 118 possibly flatters him. (op 9-4)
Freckle Face went with the leaders until dropping away after three out. He may be better off in moderate handicaps now. (op 9-1)
Promised Wings(GER), a German import, was making his hurdling debut having had a run on Polytrack recently. He showed a measure of promise despite being beaten a fair way.
Brambley was reported to be in season after the race. Official explanation: trainer said filly was in season

3959 KEITH WILLIAMS 50TH BIRTHDAY H'CAP CHASE (SUPPORTING THE TIANA HONEY WATSON FUND) (13 fncs) 2m 2f
1:50 (1:51) (Class 5) (0-90,85) 5-Y-0+ **£1,593** (£467; £233; £116)

Form RPR

-25F **1** **Bertenbar**[10] 3772 7-11-3 **76** AndrewThornton 97+
(Henrietta Knight) *chsd ldrs: j.rt 3rd: chsd ldr after next: led after 7th: mde rest: drvn and kpt on flat* **9/4**[1]

0501 **2** *4* **Ilewin Tom**[5] 3867 8-10-7 **66** 7ex JamesDavies 84+
(Gary Brown) *hld up in tch: hdwy to chse ldng pair after 8th: mstke 10th: chsd wnr bef next: drvn and styd on same pce bef last* **3/1**[2]

P-14 **3** *27* **Jack's Lad (IRE)**[35] 3337 12-11-8 **81** RichardJohnson 73
(Tim Vaughan) *in tch: chsd ldrs 5th: j.rt 7th: wnt 2nd 9th tl bef 3 out: wknd u.p 3 out: wl btn whn j.rt last* **3/1**[2]

5502 **4** *8* **Keyneema**[9] 3792 9-11-7 **85** (b) CO'Farrell(5) 71
(Cathy Hamilton) *chsd ldr: mstke 4th: sn dropped to last and nt gng wl: detached and u.p fr next: lost tch after 7th: t.o bef 3 out: wnt poor 4th flat* **9/2**[3]

6555 **5** *5* **Littleton Aldor (IRE)**[9] 3792 11-10-7 **73** (b) AodhaganConlon(7) 49
(Mark Gillard) *j.rt: led: rdn 5th: hdd after 7th: lost pl 9th: 4th and wl btn after next: t.o* **7/1**

4m 58.0s (23.30) **Going Correction** +1.225s/f (Heav) **5** Ran SP% **111.5**
Speed ratings: **97,95,83,79,77**
CSF £9.62 TOTE £3.00: £1.40, £2.30; EX 11.00.
Owner T J Wyatt **Bred** T J Wyatt **Trained** West Lockinge, Oxon

FOCUS
A very moderate handicap chase and it worked out as the market suggested. The winner is rated up 7lb.

NOTEBOOK
Bertenbar, who was always going well, was unaffected by a mistake at the eighth and stayed on well up the hill. This was his first success over fences and he can win more at a moderate level. (op 11-4)
Ilewin Tom had won a 3m1f chase at Folkestone the previous week from out of the handicap. Only 2lb higher under his penalty, he chased the winner home but is ideally suited by better ground. (op 11-4 tchd 100-30, 7-2 in places)
Jack's Lad(IRE) was held up but, after being close enough turning in, was soon struggling. (op 5-2)
Littleton Aldor(IRE), who did not go off at his usual fast pace, was struggling as soon as the winner went past. (op 6-1)

3960 E.B.F./SAM MATHERS 888SPORT.COM COMPETITION WINNER "NATIONAL HUNT" NOVICES' HURDLE (QUALIFIER) (9 hdls) 2m 2f 110y
2:20 (2:20) (Class 4) 4-7-Y-0 **£2,016** (£592; £296; £147)

Form RPR

21 **1** **Captain Kirkton (IRE)**[34] 3374 5-11-8 0 JamieMoore 130+
(Gary Moore) *in tch: chsd ldrs and nudged along after 5th: pushed into ld jst bef 2 out: clr whn dived last: rdn out* **4/7**[1]

2110 **2** *9* **Get It On (IRE)**[29] 3452 6-11-12 125 PaulMoloney 127+
(Evan Williams) *hld up in tch towards rr: hdwy to chse ldrs after 5th: chsd wnr and edgd rt between last 2: sn rdn and kpt on same pce: wl hld after last* **5/1**[2]

-351 **3** *6* **Featherbed Lane (IRE)**[26] 3495 6-11-8 120 TomO'Brien 115
(Anabel L M King) *chsd ldrs: led after 3 out: hdd and rdn jst bef 2 out: btn between last 2: plugged on to hold 3rd flat* **5/1**[2]

4 *hd* **Cantlow (IRE)**[77] 6-11-2 0 DominicElsworth 107
(Paul Webber) *chsd ldrs: hdwy on inner to press ldrs bef 2 out: rdn and btn after 2 out: plugged on and pressing for 3rd flat* **12/1**[3]

5 *1½* **Allerford Jack**[279] 7-10-13 0 IanPopham(3) 105
(Caroline Keevil) *t.k.h: chsd ldrs: mstke 6th: rdn bef 2 out: wknd wl bef last* **33/1**

55 **6** *35* **Airdrie (IRE)**[23] 3542 5-11-2 0 AndrewThornton 70
(Henrietta Knight) *led tl after 3rd: chsd ldr tl led again 6th: hdd after 3 out: sn wknd and wl btn: t.o flat* **18/1**

604 **7** *1¾* **Two Cloudy (IRE)**[20] 3604 5-10-13 0 (t) MichaelMurphy(3) 69
(Pat Murphy) *bhd: pushed along and dropped to last after 1st: sme modest hdwy 5th: no prog fr next: nvr trbld ldrs: t.o after 3 out* **33/1**

00-6 **8** *3½* **Finger Spin**[116] 1819 5-10-9 0 ColinBolger 58
(Mark H Tompkins) *a bhd: mstke 3rd: struggling and rdn after 5th: lost tch next: mstke 3 out: t.o* **100/1**

00-3 **9** *12* **World Watch (IRE)**[27] 3489 6-11-2 0 LeightonAspell 53
(Tom Gretton) *hld up in rr: prog into midfield after 5th: sn rdn and no hdwy: t.o bef 2 out* **33/1**

20-0 **10** *24* **Royal Mile (IRE)**[90] 2281 7-11-2 0 WayneHutchinson 29
(Warren Greatrex) *t.k.h: chsd ldr tl led after 3rd: hdd 6th: fdd rapidly after next: t.o between last 2* **50/1**

0000 **11** *35* **Kidajo**[9] 3789 5-11-2 0 HaddenFrost —
(Roger Curtis) *in tch in midfield: rdn and dropped to rr 5th: wl t.o fr next* **100/1**

60-0 **P** **Solar Express**[47] 3056 6-10-9 0 MrJackSalmon(7) —
(John Bridger) *midfield whn j. slowly 2nd: sn rdn along: dropped to rr 4th: tailing off whn p.u after next* **100/1**

600 **P** **Upper Deck (IRE)**[23] 3542 6-11-2 0 WarrenMarston —
(Richard Phillips) *a in rr: mstke 1st and 4th: rdn and lost tch after next: tailing off whn p.u 6th* **100/1**

4m 43.9s (9.60) **Going Correction** +0.80s/f (Soft) **13** Ran SP% **124.7**
Speed ratings: **111,107,104,104,103 89,88,87,81,71 57,—,—**
toteswingers:1&2:£3.00, 1&3:£2.80, 2&3:£3.40 CSF £4.05 TOTE £1.80: £1.30, £1.60, £1.20; EX 4.50.
Owner Miss Gill Arthur **Bred** Hugh O'Connor **Trained** Lower Beeding, W Sussex

FOCUS
A decent novice hurdle for the track featuring two horses already rated in the 120s taken on by a number of unexposed types. The market went 20-1 bar four and five drew clear of the rest from three out.

NOTEBOOK
Captain Kirkton(IRE) had built on his bumper debut when winning a hurdle on soft ground last month. Sent off at odds-on, he picked up well in the straight to win in good style, and this well-bred sort (from the family of high-class jumpers Celestial Gold and Fiveforthree), is progressing and looks worth running in the final of this race next month, his next target. (op 8-11)
Get It On(IRE), a dual winner in the autumn, carried his double penalty with credit, although he was unable to make any impression on the winner up the hill. Rated 125, he probably sets the standard. (op 6-1)
Featherbed Lane(IRE), rated 120 following his Leicester win, went on after three out but was soon headed by Captain Kirkton and could not respond. (op 4-1 tchd 11-2)
Cantlow(IRE), from the family of Darkness, had finished runner-up in a point on his only start. He ran pretty well here and will appreciate longer trips in future. (op 11-1)
Allerford Jack, another former pointer, put up a bold show until weakening from the second-last. He might be better on a sounder surface.

3961 WARD-THOMAS MASTER REMOVERS H'CAP CHASE (19 fncs) 3m 2f 110y
2:50 (2:50) (Class 5) (0-95,93) 5-Y-0+ **£1,951** (£573; £286; £143)

Form RPR

P03P **1** **Wide Receiver (IRE)**[34] 3377 8-10-5 **72** (vt) JimmyMcCarthy 85+
(Charlie Morlock) *mde virtually all: nt a fluent: mstke 9th: hdd 16th: sn led again: drvn after 2 out: mstke last: styd on wl u.p flat* **13/2**

0661 **2** *3* **Stop The Show (IRE)**[20] 3609 10-11-5 **86** RichardJohnson 94
(Richard Phillips) *hld up in tch in rr: mstke 3rd: hdwy to chse ldrs 10th: chsd wnr after 13th: led briefly 16th: ev ch after: rdn after 2 out: no ex and btn fnl 150yds* **7/2**[1]

0-44 **3** *½* **Guydus (IRE)**[24] 3527 7-11-8 **89** AidanColeman 97
(Venetia Williams) *in tch: j. slowly and lost pl 4th: rdn and hdwy after 13th: chsd ldng pair after 14th: clsd u.p and ch last: kpt on same pce u.p flat* **6/1**[3]

2163 **4** *25* **Portrait Royale (IRE)**[19] 3615 9-11-12 **93** FelixDeGiles 75
(Anna Newton-Smith) *in tch in last pair: hdwy to chse ldrs after 7th: lost pl 11th: rdn after 13th: wnt modest 4th wl bef 3 out: no prog and wl btn whn j.rt 2 out* **6/1**[3]

1254 **5** *2* **Heezagrey (IRE)**[24] 3530 8-10-3 **77** MarkQuinlan(7) 57
(James Evans) *mostly chsd wnr: mstke 8th: lost 2nd and u.p after 13th: 5th and wl btn after 16th* **7/1**

2-0P **P** **Quelclasse (FR)**[12] 3720 7-11-7 **88** (b[1]) DarylJacob —
(Jamie Snowden) *a in rr: pushed along 10th: rdn and no rspnse after next: losing tch whn p.u after 13th* **33/1**

6-3P **P** **Caspar Of Tarsus (IRE)**[77] 2557 8-11-2 **83** AndrewThornton —
(Gerald Ham) *chsd ldrs: struggling after 13th: mstke next: blnd 15th: sn wl btn: t.o whn p.u 2 out* **11/1**

P033 **P** **Brushford (IRE)**[9] 3792 7-10-10 **77** (t) LeightonAspell —
(Chris Gordon) *in tch: mstke 7th: struggling 12th: rdn and no rspnse after next: t.o whn p.u 3 out* **4/1**[2]

F4P4 **P** **No More Whispers (IRE)**[32] 3396 6-10-13 **80** (p) PaulMoloney —
(Evan Williams) *chsd ldrs tl lost pl and rdn 11th: losing tch whn p.u after 13th* **16/1**

7m 31.8s (30.70) **Going Correction** +1.225s/f (Heav) **9** Ran SP% **113.8**
Speed ratings: **103,102,101,94,93 —,—,—,—**
toteswingers:1&2:£8.80, 1&3:£10.10, 2&3:£4.60 CSF £30.00 CT £143.33 TOTE £7.10: £2.90, £2.30, £1.90; EX 61.50.
Owner Girls Allowed **Bred** Miss Irene Hatton **Trained** Upper Lambourn, Berks

FOCUS
A very moderate staying handicap chase but the first two were well in on the best of last season's form.

NOTEBOOK
Wide Receiver(IRE), who looked well treated on last season's form, was well backed earlier in the day and justified that support with a game effort from the front, despite making several minor jumping errors. With the tongue tie back on, he looked set to be beaten for most of the last half-mile but rallied under pressure and was drawing away at the end. (op 15-2 tchd 6-1)
Stop The Show(IRE), 6lb higher for his recent success, had no problems with the trip or the ground. His jumping was a bit slow early but was much better once he joined the leaders at about halfway. He looked the winner for most of the straight but the winner proved too resilient. (op 9-2)
Guydus(IRE) ran her best race over fences so far on this third attempt. She gradually worked her way into contention but could not find another gear in the straight. (op 9-2 tchd 4-1 and 13-2)
Portrait Royale(IRE) was held up but did not jump fluently and could never get into contention. (op 11-2 tchd 5-1)
Heezagrey(IRE) raced up with the pace until fading from four out. He seemed to handle the ground but this trip appears to stretch his stamina. (op 6-1 tchd 8-1)

Brushford(IRE) was another that was well backed, having won at this meeting last year. However, he was already struggling when making a mistake with over a circuit to go, which ended his chance. (op 6-1 tchd 13-2)

3962 ELIZABETH ARMSTRONG CONTEMPORARY EQUINE ART H'CAP HURDLE (9 hdls) 2m 2f 110y

3:25 (3:25) (Class 4) (0-115,114) 4-Y-0+ **£2,016** (£592; £296; £147)

Form				RPR
5554	1		**Marodima (FR)**27 3477 8-11-12 **114**......(p) DarylJacob (Jamie Snowden) *taken down early: mde all: clr thrght: pushed along and wl in command 2 out: styd on wl: easily* **6/1**3	126+
234P	2	18	**Murcar**36 3299 6-11-3 **112**...... OliverDayman(7) (Alison Thorpe) *hld up in last trio: rdn along and hdwy after 5th: chsd clr wnr and hld hd awkwardly u.p bef 2 out: no imp whn hit 2 out: wl btn after* **14/1**	108
-330	3	3 ¾	**Just One Thing (IRE)**38 3228 6-11-2 **104**...... PaulMoloney (Evan Williams) *chsd ldr: j.lft 4th: lost pl and mstke 6th: 4th and wl btn bef 2 out: plugged on to regain modest 3rd flat* **28/1**	96
11UP	4	6	**Rimini (FR)**22 3563 6-11-0 **109**...... MrJFMathias(7) (David Rees) *in tch in main gp: hdwy 3rd: rdn to chse clr wnr briefly bef 2 out: 3rd and wl btn whn mstke next: tired flat* **5/1**2	94
40F3	5	1	**Dot's Delight**23 2442 7-11-0 **105**...... PeterToole(3) (Mark Rimell) *in rr: rdn and outpcd after 5th: wnt poor 6th bef 2 out: plugged on fr 2 out: n.d* **6/1**3	88
000P	6	1	**Amore Mio (GER)**12 3724 6-11-3 **105**...... WarrenMarston (Richard Phillips) *chsd ldrs early: steadily lost pl and last whn rdn after 4th: lost tch 6th: styd on past btn horses fr 2 out: no ch w wnr* **8/1**	87
	7	3 ¼	**Sawago (FR)**79 5-11-4 **106**......(p) JamieMoore (Gary Moore) *t.k.h: prom in main gp: wnt 2nd 6th tl after next: sn wknd and wl btn: eased after last* **4/1**1	85
-U24	8	12	**Erdeli (IRE)**170 988 7-11-2 **104**......(tp) RichardJohnson (Tim Vaughan) *prom in main gp: chsd ldrs 3rd: j.lft 4th: wknd after 6th: wl btn and eased after 3 out: nt fluent last 2: t.o* **6/1**3	71
356U	9	22	**Whipperway (IRE)**9 3793 4-10-5 **104**...... JamieGoldstein (Sheena West) *racd off the pce in midfield: rdn and struggling after 5th: 6th and no ch whn blnd 3 out: t.o fr next* **11/1**	38
50P5	10	1	**Award Winner**17 3648 8-11-5 **110**...... RichieMcLernon(3) (Brendan Powell) *racd in midfield: dropped to rr after 5th: lost tch next: t.o after 3 out* **25/1**	54
200	11	15	**Killusty Fancy (IRE)**22 3554 4-10-6 **105**...... MarkGrant (Dominic Ffrench Davis) *a in rr: lost tch after 5th: t.o 3 out* **20/1**	23

4m 56.5s (22.20) **Going Correction** +0.80s/f (Soft)
WFA 4 from 5yo+ 9lb **11** Ran SP% **117.7**
Speed ratings (Par 105): **85,77,75,73,72 72,71,66,56,56 50**
toteswingers:1&2:£18.00, 1&3:£18.90, 2&3:£38.20 CSF £81.74 CT £2176.76 TOTE £6.20: £2.50, £3.50, £7.10; EX 67.50.
Owner Coles & Garbett Families Partnership **Bred** Earl La Vastine Et Al **Trained** Ebbesbourne Wake, Wilts

FOCUS

A modest but pretty competitive handicap hurdle. The winner, who dictated the pace, is rated a stone off last season's best.

NOTEBOOK

Marodima(FR) did not go off quite as fast as he has done in the past, but, settled in front, it was clear turning for home that all his rivals were struggling. He looked well handicapped on his old form, as he was officially rated 145 when winning a claiming hurdle last April and, racing off 114 here, he came right away up the hill for a confidence-boosting success. (op 11-2)

Murcar, having his second run back following a break, was held up before running on to chase the winner from the home turn. He carried his head awkwardly under pressure, possibly because he was racing on soft ground for the first time, and is one to bear in mind for when the ground dries up. (tchd 16-1)

Just One Thing(IRE) showed up early but was a bit keen. He looked set to drop away at the end of the back straight but stayed on again up the hill. The soft ground seemed to suit and he might get further. (tchd 25-1)

Rimini(FR), who has been racing mostly over fences of late, moved up to threaten the winner from three out but got very tired between the last two and struggled to get this far on soft ground. (op 11-2)

Dot's Delight, fit from a couple of runs on the all-weather, was held up and only ran on when the race was over. (op 5-1)

Sawago(FR), the winner of a soft-ground claiming hurdle in France, was making his debut for the yard and had his chance. However, he was another to get tired in the straight. (op 9-2)

3963 WELLPOOL BUILDING AND MAINTENANCE SERVICES H'CAP CHASE (SUPPORTING THE TIANA HONEY WATSON FUND) (16 fncs) 2m 6f

4:00 (4:00) (Class 4) (0-115,115) 5-Y-0+ **£3,252** (£955; £477; £238)

Form				RPR
02-6	1		**Royal Wedding**53 2961 9-11-9 **112**...... LiamTreadwell (Nick Gifford) *led tl after 4th: chsd ldr after: clr w ldr bef 3 out: led 2 out: clr last: styd on wl flat: rdn out* **10/1**	125+
3P-1	2	6	**Extra Bold**73 2638 9-10-12 **101**...... SamThomas (Emma Lavelle) *j.w and travelled wl: trckd ldrs: wnt 2nd 6th tl led after 10th: clr w wnr bef 3 out: hdd 2 out: sn rdn and fnd nil: btn whn j.lft and slt mstke last* **13/8**1	109+
-P13	3	36	**Sordid Secret (IRE)**30 3433 8-10-11 **100**...... PaulMoloney (Evan Williams) *w ldr tl led after 4th tl after 10th: blnd and dropped to rr next: rdn and struggling next: 4th and wl btn 3 out: wnt poor 3rd last: t.o* **4/1**2	82
3F41	4	9	**Folie A Deux (IRE)**10 3769 9-11-11 **114**......(t) RichardJohnson (Dr Richard Newland) *nt a fluent: blnd bdly 1st: nvr gng wl: reminders after 2nd: rdn and lost tch 13th: t.o after next* **7/1**	78
6406	5	20	**Alldunnandusted (IRE)**29 3450 7-10-9 **101**...... JimmyDerham(3) (Seamus Mullins) *in tch: rdn after 10th: lost tch u.p 13th: t.o fr next* **4/1**2	42
2235	6	22	**Lepido (ITY)**17 3650 7-11-1 **104**......(v) JamieMoore (Gary Moore) *hld up in tch: chsd ldng pair after 11th: cl 3rd 13th: wknd bef next: lost 3rd last: stopped to nil and dropped to last flat: t.o* **6/1**3	23

6m 14.0s (31.00) **Going Correction** +1.225s/f (Heav) **6** Ran SP% **114.0**
Speed ratings: **92,89,76,73,66 58**
toteswingers:1&2:£3.00, 1&3:£3.60, 2&3:£2.30 CSF £28.53 TOTE £10.30: £3.80, £1.50; EX 27.60.
Owner D G Trangmar **Bred** Brinkley Stud S R L **Trained** Findon, W Sussex

FOCUS

A modest but tightly knit handicap chase, but in the end they finished well strung out. The winner was a 127-rated hurdler at best and can match that over fences.

NOTEBOOK

Royal Wedding, having just his second run since last March, had previously looked best on good ground over fences, but won on soft over hurdles. After leading early he settled just off the pace, before coming there travelling well four out. He managed to get the better of the runner-up at the second-last and drew away on the flat. He might be able to build on this. (op 15-2 tchd 11-1)

Extra Bold, a winner at Taunton when last seen in November, is another who has done his winning on a sound surface. He travelled well for a long way, though, and only got found out on the climb to the line. (op 6-4 tchd 7-4 and 15-8)

Sordid Secret(IRE), relatively inexperienced over fences, showed up until the second of two major mistakes six out put her out of contention. She did run on again in the straight but was a long way behind the principals. (tchd 9-2)

Folie A Deux(IRE), who gained an unlikely victory last time, made a bad mistake at the first and was struggling thereafter. (op 8-1 tchd 17-2 and 6-1)

Alldunnandusted(IRE) tracked the pace for a fair way before being left behind on the last lap. (op 5-1 tchd 8-1 in a place)

Lepido(ITY), having just his second run over fences, was facing the longest trip and softest ground he has encountered. He was still there on the home turn but soon became legless and lost three places up the hill. (op 9-1)

3964 WORK AND LEISUREWEAR CORPORATE CLOTHING INTERMEDIATE NH FLAT RACE (CONDITIONALS & AMATEURS) 1m 6f

4:30 (4:30) (Class 6) 4-6-Y-0 **£1,370** (£399; £199)

Form				RPR
34	1		**Queen's Bay**21 3590 5-10-8 0...... RichieMcLernon(3) (Colin Tizzard) *led for 1f: chsd ldr after: jnd ldr 8f out: led 5f out: edgd lft bnd 4f out: pushed clr 2f out: in command after: pushed out: easily* **4/1**2	96+
-	2	8	**Spirit D'Armor (FR)**572 5-11-6 0...... RTDunne(5) (Venetia Williams) *t.k.h: hld up in midfield: hdwy to chse ldrs 6f out: sltly hmpd bnd 4f out: rdn and nt pce of wnr 2f out: wnt 2nd and edgd rt ins fnl f: no threat to wnr* **11/4**1	97
	3	3	**Sircharleswatford** 4-10-3 0...... JoshuaMoore(5) (Pat Phelan) *chsd ldng pair: clsd 6f out: ev ch 3f out: rdn: wandered and nt pce of wnr 2f out: btn over 1f out: lost 2nd and sltly hmpd ins fnl f* **9/1**	77
	4	1 ¾	**Dealing River** 4-10-1 0...... MrRichardCollinson(7) (Neil King) *hld up in rr: hdwy 7f out: effrt on inner and rdn to chse ldng trio jst over 2f out: nt pce of wnr and kpt on same pce after* **9/1**	75
	5	7	**Trevis** 4-10-5 0...... IanPopham(3) (Peter Bull) *t.k.h: hld up towards rr: hdwy into midfield 7f out: wnt 5th and rdn ent fnl 2f: sn outpcd and no threat to ldrs after* **11/2**3	66
	6	5	**Homer Run (IRE)** 4-9-12 0...... DarrenO'Keeffe(10) (Seamus Mullins) *hld up in last trio: hdwy into midfield and wl in tch 8f out: rdn and wknd over 3f out* **12/1**	60
	7	2 ½	**Zava River (IRE)** 4-10-3 0...... MrRMahon(5) (Jamie Snowden) *t.k.h: hld up in midfield: in tch: rdn and wknd wl over 3f out* **15/2**	57
0	8	¾	**Seventh Hussar**31 3406 5-10-11 0...... JakeGreenall(7) (Henrietta Knight) *t.k.h: chsd ldrs: clsd over 7f out: wknd qckly 3f out: tired fnl f* **20/1**	66
0	9	19	**Lord Richie (IRE)**30 3434 5-11-1 0...... MichaelMurphy(3) (Pat Murphy) *plld hrd: led after 1f: jnd 8f out: hdd 5f out: squeezed for room and hmpd bnd 4f out: sn rdn and wknd* **25/1**	44
	10	55	**Alflorabunda** 5-10-8 0...... RichardKilloran(3) (Michael Roberts) *bhd: rdn and lost tch 7f out: t.o fnl 5f* **40/1**	—
	11	7	**War Kitty** 4-9-12 0...... DonalDevereux(3) (Roger Curtis) *a towards rr: rdn and lost tch 7f out: t.o fnl 5f* **18/1**	—
	12	dist	**Major Bob** 5-10-11 0...... SClements(7) (Richard Mitchell) *bhd: lost tch 7f out: wl t.o fnl 6f* **50/1**	—

3m 39.2s (8.10) **12** Ran SP% **119.8**
toteswingers:1&2:£2.00, 1&3:£7.00, 2&3:£7.10 CSF £14.94 TOTE £5.50: £1.60, £1.80, £2.90; EX 13.60.
Owner R M Fear & Mrs R R Dickinson **Bred** Mrs P Stocker **Trained** Milborne Port, Dorset

FOCUS

Very few with experience in this bumper and those with previous runs filled the first two places. The winner is rated in line with her Ffos Las run.

NOTEBOOK

Queen's Bay is out of a staying chaser and had given the impression in previous starts that she would prefer a longer, not shorter, trip. However, she was ridden positively and, when asked to pick up off the home turn, soon had all her rivals in trouble. Her future is over hurdles and fences, so this success can be considered a bonus. (tchd 9-2)

Spirit D'Armor(FR), the winner of a bumper in France 18 months ago, was sent off favourite on this debut for connections. He had every chance, but could not respond when the winner committed. (op 100-30 tchd 5-2)

Sircharleswatford is related to minor winners on the Flat and over hurdles and ran well on this debut, being prominent throughout. He should benefit from the experience. (op 8-1)

Dealing River has a Flat pedigree but showed promise on this debut, despite taking the inside route, something most riders had been careful to avoid. He too can be expected to come on for the outing. (op 8-1)

Trevis, a half-brother to a Flat and hurdles winner, was supported in the market and, despite never getting into serious contention, hinted at promise on this racecourse debut. (op 6-1)

Homer Run(IRE), related to hurdles winners over further than 2m, was another who showed promise, only fading in the straight. (op 16-1)

T/Jkpt: £15,694.40 to a £1 stake. Pool: £44,209.61 - 2.00 winning tickets. T/Plt: £47.40 to a £1 stake. Pool: £107,418.47 - 1,653.69 winning tickets. T/Qpdt: £17.40 to a £1 stake. Pool:£7,126.96 - 301.94 winning tickets. SP

3746 MUSSELBURGH (R-H)

Sunday, February 6

OFFICIAL GOING: Good to soft (soft in places) changing to soft (good to soft in places) after race 1 (1.30)

Stands' bend moved in 6m, both bottom bends moved out 3m. Fences in back straight moved onto fresh ground and fresh ground for most of hurdles course.
Wind: Almost nil Weather: Overcast, raining

3965 SCOTTISH RACING NOVICES' HURDLE (12 hdls) 2m 4f

1:30 (1:30) (Class 3) 4-Y-0+ **£4,228** (£1,241; £620; £310)

Form				RPR
51-3	1		**Wyse Hill Teabags**23 3547 6-11-2 0...... RichieMcGrath (Jim Goldie) *w ldr: led bef 3 out: rdn and styd on strly fr next* **14/1**	126+
2124	2	3 ½	**Moon Indigo**22 3567 5-11-8 130...... BrianHughes (Howard Johnson) *trckd ldrs: effrt and ev ch bef 3 out: sn rdn: edgd rt and kpt on same pce fr next* **5/2**2	127
-122	3	15	**Skint**22 3557 5-11-7 128...... DavidBass(5) (Nicky Henderson) *trckd ldrs: drvn and outpcd bef 3 out: sn no imp* **4/7**1	116

35-2 **4** *3* **Bridlingtonbygones (IRE)**[89] 2296 6-11-2 0 .... GrahamLee 103
(Karen McLintock) *nt fluent: hld up: drvn bef 3 out: sn outpcd: n.d after* **12/1**[3]

4 **5** *7* **Gentleman Jeff (USA)**[24] 3521 7-11-12 117 .... DenisO'Regan 109
(Chris Grant) *t.k.h: led to bef 3 out: sn rdn and wknd* **22/1**

6 *16* **Gearbox (IRE)**[30] 5-10-11 0 .... MissLHorner(5) 80
(Liam Corcoran) *t.k.h: in tch tl rdn and wknd bef 3 out: t.o* **100/1**

4m 56.5s (5.00) **Going Correction** +0.05s/f (Yiel) **6** Ran SP% **111.9**
Speed ratings (Par 107): **92,90,84,83,80 74**
toteswingers:1&2:£3.10, 1&3:£2.50, 2&3:£1.10 CSF £49.35 TOTE £20.40: £4.50, £1.60; EX 66.10.

Owner P C & J W Smith **Bred** Gail And Stuart Smales **Trained** Uplawmoor, E Renfrews

FOCUS
An open race, in which most could be given a chance, but the contest didn't get interesting until the pace quickened heading to six out. The form is rated through the second, with a big step up from the winner and the third a stone+ off.

NOTEBOOK
Wyse Hill Teabags, who ran with promise in a useful maiden at this course (2m) on his hurdling debut, was given a positive ride and responded well to pressure to hold off the challengers. There was a lot to like about his performance, but whether this is reliable form is debateable. That said, he looks a nice prospect with plenty of scope.
Moon Indigo, the highest rated of these on official figures, gave some indication that he was not enjoying himself at a relatively early stage, but he did have his chance after needing some pushing. He probably won't be easy to place. (op 11-4 tchd 3-1)
Skint, back up in trip, was still open to improvement and strongly fancied to take this but, although jumping nicely, he was outpaced when the tempo quickened and was unable to get back on terms. It's probably best to ignore this run, as this was nowhere near what he has looked capable of. Nicky Henderson took all of his remaining runners on the card out of their contests later in the afternoon after this race due to the ground. (op 4-6)
Bridlingtonbygones(IRE), absent since the start of November, was held up going nicely but looked awkward/green on the final bend. He failed to make up the ground when asked to get closer, but didn't seem to be given a hard time when his chance was gone. (op 14-1)
Gentleman Jeff(USA) failed to get home as well as some of his rivals but it couldn't be said that he didn't stay, as he plugged on once joined. (op 20-1)
Gearbox(IRE) Official explanation: trainer said gelding was unsuited by the good to soft (soft in places) ground

3966 RACING UK H'CAP HURDLE (12 hdls) 2m 4f
2:00 (2:05) (Class 3) (0-120,120) 4-Y-0+ **£4,553** (£1,337; £668; £333)

Form RPR

2000 **1** **Santa's Son (IRE)**[151] 1508 11-11-12 **120** ....(t) BrianHughes 130
(Howard Johnson) *cl up: led 5th: mde rest: rdn and styd on strly fr 2 out* **16/1**

-001 **2** *3* **Pokfulham (IRE)**[23] 3551 5-11-1 **109** ....(v) JamesReveley 116
(Jim Goldie) *trckd ldrs: wnt 2nd 1/2-way: effrt after 3 out: kpt on same pce fr next* **10/1**

-124 **3** *7* **Amir Pasha (UAE)**[85] 2373 6-10-7 **111** ....(v) JoeCollier(10) 112
(Micky Hammond) *hld up in midfield: stdy hdwy bef 3 out: rdn and kpt on fr next: no imp* **11/2**[2]

5064 **4** *8* **Master Fong (IRE)**[46] 3091 5-11-5 **113** ....(b) JasonMaguire 105
(Donald McCain) *midfield: drvn 1/2-way: rallied and chsd ldrs bef 3 out: edgd rt and no ex bef next* **12/1**

-400 **5** *2 ½* **Grandad Bill (IRE)**[14] 3709 8-11-10 **118** .... RichieMcGrath 108
(Jim Goldie) *in tch tl rdn and wknd after 3 out* **6/1**[3]

0012 **6** *1 ½* **Viva Colonia (IRE)**[85] 2373 6-11-12 **120** .... DenisO'Regan 110
(David O'Meara) *hld up: smooth hdwy to trck ldrs bef 3 out: rdn and wknd bef next* **13/2**

2-1F **7** *6* **Arisea (IRE)**[218] 745 8-11-0 **108** .... PaddyAspell 90
(James Moffatt) *hld up: effrt bef 3 out: wknd bef next* **33/1**

01-4 **8** *9* **Hazeldene**[269] 309 9-11-5 **113** .... JanFaltejsek 86
(George Charlton) *t.k.h: led tl hdd 5th: cl up tl rdn and wknd after 4 out* **20/1**

-231 **9** *2 ¼* **Altan Khan**[79] 2508 6-10-9 **108** .... JamesHalliday(5) 79
(Malcolm Jefferson) *hld up: rdn after 4 out: nvr on terms* **10/3**[1]

4-36 **10** *1 ¼* **Lawgiver (IRE)**[152] 1501 10-11-4 **112** .... PhilKinsella 82
(Marjorie Fife) *towards rr: struggling 1/2-way: nvr on terms* **40/1**

-123 **11** *13* **Sunarri (IRE)**[35] 3330 7-11-5 **120** .... AlistairFindlay(7) 77
(Jane Walton) *prom tl rdn and wknd bef 3 out* **8/1**

3PUP **P** **Quatro Pierji (FR)**[81] 2447 7-11-4 **112** ....(p) RyanMania —
(James Moffatt) *towards rr: struggling 1/2-way: t.o whn p.u 4 out* **40/1**

-654 **P** **Mister Wall Street (FR)**[11] 3749 6-11-2 **110** .... GrahamLee —
(Ferdy Murphy) *midfield: struggling 7th: t.o whn p.u bef 3 out* **8/1**

4m 49.9s (-1.60) **Going Correction** +0.05s/f (Yiel) **13** Ran SP% **123.6**
Speed ratings (Par 107): **105,103,101,97,96 96,93,90,89,88 83,—,—**
toteswingers:1&2:£31.80, 1&3:£27.90, 2&3:£13.70 CSF £165.75 CT £1008.85 TOTE £17.40: £6.10, £4.10, £2.20; EX 257.10.

Owner Douglas Pryde Jim Beaumont **Bred** John Mulvaney **Trained** Billy Row, Co Durham

FOCUS
Just a modest handicap hurdle but the time compared well with the earlier novice race. The winner is rated back to his 2010 level.

NOTEBOOK
Santa's Son(IRE), off since early September, was back with Howard Johnson after four runs for another stable and thoroughly enjoyed bossing his rivals from an early stage. It's impossible to know whether he can reproduce this sort of performance next time, but he'd be difficult to beat if he did.
Pokfulham(IRE), the narrow winner of a seller last time at this course over 2m from Lennon, a stablemate of the winner, looks a fair marker to the form and didn't appear to have any problem with the trip. (op 9-1)
Amir Pasha(UAE), off since mid-November, travelled strongly under his 10lb claimer but appeared to meet traffic problems heading into the final bend, before getting in the clear and running on well. (op 9-1)
Master Fong(IRE), with blinkers back on after a couple of starts without them, took a lot of pushing, so the jockey did well to get his mount to have some sort of chance turning into the home straight.
Grandad Bill(IRE) usually runs well at this course and wasn't disgraced.
Viva Colonia(IRE), now 18lb higher than his Wetherby success in October, was back up in trip on his return to action after an 85-day layoff and was given a sensible ride under top weight until, but couldn't quicken when in with a chance. It was a good run but the handicapper seems to have him, especially in this sort of ground. (op 11-2)
Altan Khan won on his handicap debut at this course over 2m, but stopped quickly here rounding the final bend. He was reportedly unsuited by the going. Official explanation: trainer said gelding was unsuited by the soft (good to soft in places) ground (op 3-1)
Mister Wall Street(FR) Official explanation: trainer's rep said that gelding bled from the nose

3967 JOHN SMITH'S SCOTTISH TRIUMPH HURDLE (JUVENILE HURDLE) (9 hdls) 2m
2:30 (2:35) (Class 2) 4-Y-0 **£12,570** (£3,746; £1,896; £972; £508)

Form RPR

421 **1** **Vosges (FR)**[23] 3550 4-11-5 116 .... HarryHaynes 113
(James Ewart) *led tl after 4 out: sn rdn: rallied next: regained ld last: edgd rt u.p: hld on wl towards fin* **7/1**

16 **2** *hd* **The Starboard Bow**[34] 3358 4-11-5 0 .... PeterBuchanan 113
(Lucinda Russell) *trckd ldrs: hdwy to ld appr 3 out: sn hrd pressed: hdd last: rallied: kpt on wl towards fin: jst hld* **10/1**

F11 **3** *6* **Danceintothelight**[24] 3521 4-11-8 128 .... JasonMaguire 110
(Micky Hammond) *cl up: hdwy to ld after 4 out: hdd appr next: kpt on same pce fr 2 out* **11/4**[1]

315 **4** *2 ½* **Jolly Roger (IRE)**[22] 3554 4-11-5 120 .... RhysFlint 105
(John Flint) *prom: hdwy to chal 3 out: rdn and no ex bef last* **9/2**

5 *60* **Ananda Kanda (USA)**[270] 4-10-7 0 .... FearghalDavis 33
(Brian Ellison) *plld hrd: hld up: struggling 4 out: t.o* **16/1**

3 **F** **Eltheeb**[25] 3507 4-11-0 0 .... BarryKeniry 96
(George Moore) *in tch: effrt bef 3 out: no imp fr next: 8 l 5th and hld whn fell last* **4/1**[3]

P **Truly Magic**[117] 4-10-7 0 .... MissLHorner —
(Liam Corcoran) *bhd: lost tch 3rd: t.o whn mstke 4 out: p.u bef next* **100/1**

1022 **U** **Meetings Man (IRE)**[72] 2655 4-11-8 122 .... GrahamLee —
(Micky Hammond) *hld up: sprawled bdly and uns rdr 5th* **10/3**[2]

3m 54.5s (6.10) **Going Correction** +0.05s/f (Yiel) **8** Ran SP% **116.4**
Speed ratings: **86,85,82,81,51 —,—,—**
toteswingers:1&2:£6.80, 1&3:£4.60, 2&3:£5.70 CSF £72.28 TOTE £9.10: £2.50, £2.40, £1.70; EX 46.90.

Owner A Humbert N A Sperling & Mrs L Drew **Bred** Mme Henri Devin **Trained** Langholm, Dumfries & G'way

FOCUS
This race has produced some nice types in the past but with the withdrawal of both Titan De Sarti (the likely favourite) and Music Of The Moor (had good form in easy ground), along with testing conditions, one would imagine that the form of the 2011 renewal may not be reliable during the spring unless the rain continues to fall. The form is rated around the tird and fourth and looks only ordinary.

NOTEBOOK
Vosges(FR), a winner over C&D last time, confirmed the Ayr form in early January with the runner-up, but things didn't look good for him when he lost the lead heading to the final bend. However, he clearly has plenty of heart and stays well, because he rallied and was soon back in the picture before putting his head down late on to claim a tough success. He'll get an entry for the Fred Winter at Cheltenham next month. (tchd 5-1)
The Starboard Bow, who was a bit disappointing at Ayr, got right back to his best but wasn't able to force his way past an opponent in no mood to give up. He'll no doubt find his level in handicaps. (op 9-1 tchd 17-2)
Danceintothelight was unlucky not to be unbeaten coming into this and seemed sure to continue his winning run off the final bend when he surged clear going well, but his stride shortened quickly once in the home straight and he was soon passed. He looked well above average when he was going clear, so is worth another chance. (op 9-4, tchd 3-1 in a place)
Jolly Roger(IRE) didn't get home after holding every chance. (op 13-2)
Eltheeb shaped with plenty of promise on his hurdling debut behind a subsequent Grade 2 winner, but looked tired when crashing out at the last hurdle here. Everything about his profile suggested he didn't want ground this soft, so he is another that can be given another chance on a sounder surface. (op 5-1)
Truly Magic Official explanation: jockey said filly lost its action but returned sound (op 5-1)
Meetings Man(IRE) had some good form but unseated Graham Lee at the fifth when travelling well. (op 5-1)

3968 JOHN SMITH'S NOVICES' CHASE (16 fncs) 2m 4f
3:00 (3:05) (Class 3) 5-Y-0+ **£7,806** (£2,292; £1,146)

Form RPR

3150 **1** **Divers (FR)**[40] 3169 7-11-4 131 .... GrahamLee 136+
(Ferdy Murphy) *trckd ldrs: hdwy 4 out: led 2 out: rdn and kpt on wl fr last* **5/2**[2]

10-2 **2** *¾* **Nafaath (IRE)**[34] 3359 5-10-9 0 .... BrianHughes 127+
(Howard Johnson) *cl up: hit 3rd: disp ld 4 out to 2 out: kpt on u.p fr last: hld towards fin* **4/5**[1]

2140 **3** *2 ¼* **Film Festival (USA)**[40] 3170 8-11-4 127 .... FearghalDavis 132
(Brian Ellison) *set modest pce tl rdn and hdd 2 out: kpt on same pce run-in* **10/3**[3]

5m 18.2s (17.00) **Going Correction** +0.85s/f (Soft)
WFA 5 from 6yo+ 2lb **3** Ran SP% **107.2**
Speed ratings: **100,99,98**
CSF £4.97 TOTE £3.30; EX 5.90.

Owner The DPRP Divers Partnership **Bred** Alec Head And Mme Ghislaine Head **Trained** West Witton, N Yorks

FOCUS
This race had been won by Fiendish Flame and Kalahari King on its only two previous renewals. It was slowly run this yaer and the form is rated around the first two.

NOTEBOOK
Divers(FR) produced a decent performance, and it was a plan well executed - his connections walked the course before racing and felt the inside rail was better ground. He heads to the Cheltenham Festival for the Centenary Novices' Handicap Chase. (op 11-4 tchd 3-1)
Nafaath(IRE) travelled strongly throughout and may well have won had he jumped more fluently over the fences down the home straight. He has a decent engine and is worth giving another chance to on better ground. (op 8-13 tchd 8-15)
Film Festival(USA) held a slight lead for much of the race and kept on well when the race started properly from four out. (op 11-2 tchd 3-1)

3969 JOHN SMITH'S SCOTTISH COUNTY H'CAP HURDLE (9 hdls) 2m
3:35 (3:40) (Class 2) (0-145,139) 4-Y-0+
£15,655 (£4,625; £2,312; £1,157; £577; £290)

Form RPR

-003 **1** **Hunterview**[36] 3298 5-11-3 **130** ....(b) TomScudamore 142+
(David Pipe) *cl up: led bef 3 out: rdn whn j.lft next: kpt on strly run-in* **11/4**[1]

0P-5 **2** *5* **European Dream (IRE)**[22] 2373 8-10-10 **123** ....(p) PaddyAspell 129
(Richard Fahey) *hld up: hdwy after 4 out: effrt next: chsd (clr) wnr run-in: no imp* **10/1**

5550 **3** *2 ¼* **Ultimate**[29] 3447 5-10-13 **129** .... DannyCook(3) 135+
(Brian Ellison) *led: hdd whn hit 3 out: one pce fr next: lost 2nd run-in* **13/2**[3]

-600 **4** 8 **Leslingtaylor (IRE)**[40] 3170 9-11-4 **131** DougieCostello 127
(John Quinn) *hld up: rdn 4 out: sn outpcd: kpt on fr 2 out: nvr rchd ldrs* **20/1**

30-6 **5** 2 1/4 **Bureaucrat**[36] 3306 9-10-4 **117** (p) RichieMcGrath 111
(Kate Walton) *in tch: drvn and outpcd 1/2-way: sme late hdwy: nvr rchd ldrs* **40/1**

5-35 **6** 1/2 **Los Nadis (GER)**[223] 627 7-10-13 **126** RyanMania 120
(Jim Goldie) *hld up: rdn and outpcd whn nt fluent 4 out: kpt on fr last: n.d* **25/1**

0P-B **7** 3/4 **Caravel (IRE)**[106] 1956 7-11-4 **131** BrianHughes 126+
(Howard Johnson) *trckd ldrs: effrt bef 3 out: outpcd next: wkng whn hit last* **16/1**

P-10 **8** 4 1/2 **Cunning Clarets (IRE)**[8] 3808 6-10-4 **117** (b[1]) WilsonRenwick 1061
(Richard Fahey) *hld up: hit 4th: hdwy and in tch after 4 out: wknd next* **7/1**

1340 **9** 17 **Beidh Tine Anseo (IRE)**[85] 2361 5-10-4 **117** CampbellGillies 88
(Lucinda Russell) *prom tl rdn and wknd bef 3 out* **12/1**

10 29 **Premier Grand Cru (FR)**[421] 5-11-1 **131** HarryHaynes(3) 73
(James Ewart) *midfield: pushed along whn blnd 5th: sn outpcd: n.d after* **12/1**

F-00 **P** **Toshi (USA)**[35] 3334 9-10-12 **125** GrahamLee —
(Jim Goldie) *t.k.h: hld up: struggling after 4 out: t.o whn p.u bef 2 out* **20/1**

60-4 **P** **Kudu Country (IRE)**[29] 3447 5-10-11 **124** JamesReveley —
(Tom Tate) *w ldrs: blnd 4th: wknd 4 out: p.u next* **4/1**[2]

-025 **P** **Bocamix (FR)**[22] 3559 5-11-3 **130** FearghalDavis —
(Andrew Crook) *in tch tl lost pl bef 4th: sn struggling: t.o whn p.u bef 3 out* **33/1**

3m 45.6s (-2.80) **Going Correction** +0.05s/f (Yiel) **13** Ran SP% **121.6**
Speed ratings (Par 109): **109,106,105,101,100 100,99,97,88,74 —,—,—**
toteswingers:1&2:£10.40, 1&3:£4.30, 2&3:£17.00 CSF £28.90 CT £170.41 TOTE £3.70: £1.80, £4.20, £2.80; EX 42.10 Trifecta £265.20 Pool £916.33 - 2.55 winning units..
Owner Mrs Jo Tracey **Bred** Darley **Trained** Nicholashayne, Devon
■ David Pipe has now trained a winner at every jumps course in Britain.

FOCUS
A good-quality field lined up for decent prize money, and the pace appeared strong from the outset. A big step up from the winner but he's entitled to rat this high on his Flat form, and the race should work out.

NOTEBOOK
Hunterview, one of three runners who kicked on, showed plenty of courage to keep finding under pressure, even though his jumping wasn't exactly fluent in the latter stages. He'll probably get a couple of entries for the Cheltenham Festival, and gave those who have backed Totesport Trophy fancy Salden Licht next weekend a nice lift, considering how easily the Alan King-trained horse disposed of him at Exeter. (op 5-2 tchd 3-1)
European Dream(IRE), the winner of this race off a 2lb higher mark in 2009, and seventh last year, was ridden patiently but couldn't get to Hunterview despite getting weight. He was clear second best, however. (op 14-1)
Ultimate, who finished second in the Scottish Triumph Hurdle on this card last season, helped to share the pace and was still with the winner when hitting three out. That mistake was enough to hand a clear advantage to Hunterview, although you could hardly fault his attitude thereafter, as he kept on well to still claim third. (op 8-1 tchd 6-1)
Leslingtaylor(IRE), who won on his only previous run at this track, kept on fairly well without ever looking likely to get involved. (op 16-1)
Bureaucrat kept on to go past some weakening rivals.
Caravel(IRE), absent since being brought down at Aintree in October, had a 111 record at this course and looked to have a good chance of gaining another win rounding the final bend, but he weakened quickly in the home straight, most probably because of the ground - his best form is on a much quicker surface. He is one to keep an eye on. (op 14-1)
Cunning Clarets(IRE), with blinkers tried for the first time, travelled strongly but offered little off the bridle. (tchd 13-2)
Premier Grand Cru(FR), the winner of his only start over hurdles in France, where he beat Maxdelas, who won on his first outing in Britain, attracted market support during the morning but needed pushing along early, and made no impression. (op 10-1 tchd 14-1)
Kudu Country(IRE) was the third of those who set the gallop and appeared to being well until something possibly went amiss, as his jockey eased off in a matter of strides. Official explanation: vet said gelding finished lame right-fore (op 5-1 tchd 7-2 and 11-2 in a place)

3970 RACING UK ON SKY 432 H'CAP CHASE (12 fncs) 2m
4:10 (4:15) (Class 3) (0-120,117) 5-Y-0+ **£5,204** (£1,528; £764; £381)

Form RPR
1444 **1** **Elite Land**[35] 2613 8-11-9 **117** DannyCook(3) 130+
(Brian Ellison) *hld up: hdwy to chse ldrs whn hit 7th: led 4 out: rdn and r.o strly* **10/3**[2]

-436 **2** 3 1/4 **Folk Tune (IRE)**[22] 3573 8-11-8 **113** DougieCostello 120
(John Quinn) *in tch: effrt bef 4 out: chsd wnr 2 out: kpt on run-in: no imp* **7/1**

-123 **3** 6 **Seeyaaj**[204] 1023 11-11-7 **112** (t) PeterBuchanan 116+
(Lucinda Russell) *led to 4 out: blnd next: sn rdn and outpcd* **9/1**

5632 **4** 1 3/4 **Earl Grez (FR)**[10] 3769 6-10-6 **104** KyleJames(7) 103
(Philip Kirby) *t.k.h: cl up: chal 5th to 8th: rdn and outpcd fr 3 out* **5/1**[3]

3-03 **5** 8 **Or D'Oudairies (FR)**[11] 3751 9-11-2 **107** (t) GrahamLee 102
(Ferdy Murphy) *nt fluent: sn towards rr: struggling 1/2-way: btn fnl 4* **9/4**[1]

P431 **6** 7 **Follow The Sun (IRE)**[19] 3618 7-10-3 **94** BrianHughes 85
(Peter Niven) *nt fluent in rr: struggling 5 out: nvr on terms* **7/1**

6/62 **P** **Kit Carson (IRE)**[72] 2659 11-9-7 **91** oh1 GaryRutherford(7) —
(R MacDonald) *cl up: lost pl whn mstke 7th: sn struggling: t.o whn p.u bef 4 out* **14/1**

4m 2.10s (9.70) **Going Correction** +0.85s/f (Soft) **7** Ran SP% **112.2**
Speed ratings: **109,107,104,103,99 96,—**
toteswingers:1&2:£4.60, 1&3:£4.50, 2&3:£6.10 CSF £25.00 TOTE £4.10: £2.00, £2.90; EX 29.80.
Owner Dan Gilbert **Bred** T Umpleby **Trained** Norton, N Yorks

FOCUS
Not many runners but a contest that was not easy to work out before the off, despite there being 27lb between the top and bottom weights on official figures. Not form to get carried away with.

NOTEBOOK
Elite Land, who had finished runner-up on the Flat since his last try over fences, was well above his highest-winning mark, but that didn't stop him winning convincingly. Everything fell right for him and he is a good sort when a race works out for him. (op 11-4)
Folk Tune(IRE), with the tongue-tie taken off, hasn't collected a win over fences since taking a Towcester beginners chase in the autumn of 2009, but his turn shouldn't be far away after this performance. (op 8-1)
Seeyaaj, having his first run since July, took the field along and was still thereabout when clouting three out. (op 8-1)
Earl Grez(FR) had shown enough over fences to be of interest but appeared to hang a bit under pressure in the home straight. (tchd 11-2)
Or D'Oudairies(FR), with the tongue-tie back on, and down in trip, made little impression. Official explanation: jockey said gelding did not jump fluently (op 11-4 tchd 3-1)

3971 RACING UK INTERMEDIATE OPEN NATIONAL HUNT FLAT RACE 2m
4:40 (4:45) (Class 5) 4-6-Y-0 **£1,626** (£477; £238; £119)

Form RPR
0 **1** **The Tracey Shuffle**[47] 3054 5-11-3 0 TomScudamore 109+
(David Pipe) *led: hdd after 2f: led again 1/2-way: drew clr fr 3f out: unchal* **6/4**[1]

0-6 **2** 13 **Shannagarry (IRE)**[23] 3553 5-11-3 0 JanFaltejsek 93
(George Charlton) *t.k.h: in tch: effrt u.p over 4f out: sn outpcd: chsd (clr) wnr over 1f out: no imp* **11/1**

5 **3** 4 1/2 **Think Green**[23] 3553 5-10-7 0 HarryHaynes(3) 82
(James Ewart) *t.k.h: led after 2f to 1/2-way: chsd wnr tl outpcd 3f out: btn whn lost 2nd over 1f out* **3/1**[2]

3 **4** 37 **Serenader**[98] 2108 4-10-7 0 DenisO'Regan 42
(David O'Meara) *trckd ldrs tl rdn and wknd over 3f out: t.o* **7/2**[3]

0 **5** 29 **Bello Regalo (IRE)**[79] 2511 5-11-3 0 GrahamLee 23
(Malcolm Jefferson) *plld hrd: in tch tl rdn and wknd over 5f out: t.o* **5/1**

3m 47.5s (4.70) **Going Correction** +0.05s/f (Yiel)
WFA 4 from 5yo 9lb **5** Ran SP% **112.2**
Speed ratings: **90,83,81,62,48**
toteswingers:; totesuper7: Win: Not won. Place: £140.70 - 5 winning units.. CSF £18.01 TOTE £2.10: £1.10, £5.70; EX 9.60.
Owner Mrs Jo Tracey **Bred** Cotley Hill Stud **Trained** Nicholashayne, Devon

FOCUS
The absence of the likely favourite Dark Shadow robbed the race of some interest, but we surely saw a potential future star in The Tracey Shuffle. The opposition was probably modest, though.

NOTEBOOK
The Tracey Shuffle left his first run on Kempton's AW surface behind him to come home a very easy winner. Bred to make the grade over jumps, he still looked green at times so should have more to come, but it remains to be seen whether he needs easy ground to be at his best. One would imagine that Noel Chance is particularly pleased with this result, as his Mintiverdi won the aforementioned bumper at Kempton, and has seen that form boosted by a couple of talented performers now. (op 5-4)
Shannagarry(IRE) was one place behind Think Green last time but reversed that form on different ground. He shapes like a stayer. (op 9-1)
Think Green shows an exuberant nature and will surely prove better than this performance. (op 11-2)
Serenader settled nicely in behind but was beaten rounding the home bend. (op 3-1)
Bello Regalo(IRE), who appeared to disappoint on his debut considering he was sent off at 7-2, pulled much too hard and probably got bogged down in the ground. He is worth one more chance when faced with quicker ground because of his sire. (op 11-2 tchd 6-1)
T/Plt: £1,348.00 to a £1 stake. Pool: £80,420.70 - 43.55 winning tickets T/Qpdt: £32.40 to a £1 stake. Pool: £8,747.73 - 199.33 winning tickets RY

3850 AYR (L-H)
Monday, February 7
3972 Meeting Abandoned - Waterlogged

3373 LINGFIELD (L-H)
Monday, February 7
OFFICIAL GOING: Turf course - soft (heavy in places) ; all-weather - standard
Wind: Very strong, behind, Races 1-4, across remainder Weather: Overcast

3979 RAKEBACKMYPOKER.COM MARES' STANDARD OPEN NATIONAL HUNT FLAT RACE 2m
1:30 (1:30) (Class 6) 4-6-Y-0 **£1,267** (£369; £184)

Form RPR
30 **1** **Jaya Bella (IRE)**[78] 2546 6-11-2 0 WarrenMarston 89
(Milton Harris) *hld up last: prog over 3f out: wnt 4th over 2f out: drvn and styd on wl ins fnl f to ld nr fin: hld on* **15/2**[3]

0 **2** hd **Willow The Rose**[54] 2965 4-10-6 0 TimmyMurphy 79
(J R Jenkins) *hld up in last trio: plenty to do whn prog 3f out: wnt 5th 2f out: nt clr run and swtchd lft over 1f out: rn green: r.o to press wnr last strides* **22/1**

3 3/4 **Rye Park** 5-11-2 0 RichardJohnson 88
(Noel Chance) *trckd ldrs: prog 4f out: wnt 3rd over 2f out: rdn to ld over 1f out: wknd and hdd nr fin* **9/2**[1]

4 hd **Exeptional Girl** 5-10-13 0 JamesO'Farrell(3) 88
(Peter Brookshaw) *hld up in last trio: prog on outer 3f out: styd on wl fnl f: nvr quite able to chal* **14/1**

52 **5** 1 1/4 **Painted Tail (IRE)**[76] 2597 4-10-6 0 HaddenFrost 77
(James Frost) *prom: wnt 2nd 6f out: led 4f out and kicked on: hdd over 1f out: wknd last 100yds* **9/2**[1]

6 3 **Sea Fury (IRE)** 4-10-6 0 ColinBolger 74
(Suzy Smith) *prom: chsd ldr over 3f out: chal and upsides 2f out: wknd over 1f out* **14/1**

7 9 **Hopatina (IRE)** 5-11-2 0 TomScudamore 75
(Neil Mulholland) *fractious preliminaries: cl up: led 1/2-way to 4f out: wknd over 2f out* **10/1**

0 **8** 3 3/4 **Mew Gull**[53] 2987 6-11-2 0 WillKennedy 71
(Henrietta Knight) *in tch: pushed along over 4f out: wl outpcd fr 3f out* **40/1**

9 2 3/4 **Cherry On Top** 5-10-11 0 RachaelGreen(5) 68
(Anthony Honeyball) *in tch: rdn 4f out: wknd wl over 2f out* **9/2**[1]

6 **10** 24 **Cailin Maghnailbhe (IRE)**[54] 2965 4-10-6 0 DarylJacob 34
(Seamus Mullins) *t.k.h: led after 4f at slow pce: hdd 1/2-way: wknd over 4f out: t.o* **5/1**[2]

00- **11** 19 **Fortunelini**[500] 1534 6-10-11 0 (tp) KeiranBurke(5) 25
(Peter Brookshaw) *led at funereal pce for 4f: sn lost pl: last shortly after 1/2-way: t.o* **100/1**

3m 46.1s (8.10)
WFA 4 from 5yo+ 9lb **11** Ran SP% **113.2**
toteswingers:1&2: £23.20, 2&3: £19.20, 1&3: £5.40 CSF £154.73 TOTE £5.90: £2.80, £9.10, £2.70; EX 161.00.
Owner J Zambuni **Bred** Jim McDonald **Trained** Herridge, Wiltshire

FOCUS
A modest mares' bumper run on the AW. They went no pace early on but really started to quicken it up with 5f to run, and there was a bunch finish. The form is pretty meaningless.

NOTEBOOK
Jaya Bella(IRE) apparently came back with a muscle problem after failing to build on a promising debut effort when tailed off at Aintree last November. Keen in rear, she made her move round the outside of the field with over 4f to run before being switched in between runners to hit the front late on. She seems to appreciate a sound surface and could well go for the valuable mares' bumper at Aintree, although she has apparently schooled well over hurdles. (op 17-2)
Willow The Rose stepped up on a pretty inauspicious debut to only narrowly be denied. Her sire does well with his progeny on the AW, therefore she is not certain to translate this form to turf. (op 33-1 tchd 20-1)
Rye Park, who attracted plenty of support in the market, raced closer to the pace than the first two. She was only headed late on and can make amends in a similarly modest contest. (op 4-1)
Exeptional Girl, related to several winners on the Flat, put up a promising display on her debut. In rear early, she made her move fast and late, a tactic that is often successful here, but just found the line coming too soon.
Painted Tail(IRE), weak in the market, didn't seem to see out the trip on this step up from 1m5f. Official explanation: jockey said filly hung right (op 4-1)
Cailin Maghnailbhe(IRE) Official explanation: trainer said filly ran too free

3980 UP TO 70%RAKEBACK AT RAKEBACKMYPOKER.COM BEGINNERS' CHASE (14 fncs) 2m 4f 110y
2:05 (2:05) (Class 5) 5-Y-0+ **£2,740** (£798; £399)

Form RPR
-54U **1** **General Kutuzov (IRE)**[30] 3435 7-11-0 117 LiamTreadwell 120
(Nick Gifford) *disp ld: rdn on long run after 11th: narrowly hdd bef next (3 out): led again 2 out: styd on wl* **5/1**[2]
P-10 **2** *5* **Spear Thistle**[16] 3676 9-11-0 0 (p) DarylJacob 116
(Charlie Mann) *disp ld: nt fluent 11th: gng best and narrow ld bef 3 out: hdd 2 out: no ex* **8/1**[3]
5632 **3** *9* **Vino Griego (FR)**[9] 3803 6-11-0 133 JamieMoore 112+
(Gary Moore) *terrible blunder 2nd: rdr nrly off and dropped to last: prog to go 3rd at 6th: on terms w ldng pair 11th: drvn and no rspnse sn after: wl btn 3rd after 3 out* **2/5**[1]
20-P **4** *8* **Upham Atom**[28] 3485 8-11-0 0 TomSiddall 104+
(Kate Buckett) *nt a fluent and tended to jump sltly rt: in tch to 8th: poor 4th fr 11th: blnd 2 out: lost no more grnd on ldrs* **33/1**
P-5P **5** *23* **Fillyofthevalley**[19] 3627 8-10-7 0 MarkGrant 68
(Peter Jones) *in tch to 8th: wknd and poor 5th fr 11th* **100/1**
P31P **6** *11* **Sweet Seville (FR)**[9] 3807 7-10-7 0 LeightonAspell 57
(Terry Clement) *hld up in last: in tch to 8th: wknd and poor 6th fr 11th* **20/1**
5 **7** *45* **Medellin (IRE)**[8] 3838 7-10-7 0 SClements(7) 19
(Liam Corcoran) *in tch to 8th: wknd rapidly after next: t.o last after 11th* **100/1**

5m 16.4s (-1.80) **Going Correction** +0.075s/f (Yiel) **7 Ran SP% 108.9**
Speed ratings: **106,104,100,97,88 84,67**
toteswingers:1&2: £2.10, 2&3: £1.80, 1&3: £2.00 CSF £33.23 TOTE £4.30: £1.80, £1.80; EX 16.10.
Owner Barkfold Manor Stud **Bred** Jerry Murphy **Trained** Findon, W Sussex

FOCUS
The first turf race of the meeting and the ground was reported to be testing. This was a fair beginners' chase featuring several horses with reasonable form over hurdles. The form could be rated up to 10lb higher.

NOTEBOOK
General Kutuzov(IRE) displayed a good attitude to gain a battling success. A confirmed mudlark, he disputed the lead until taking it up at the last fence and drew clear on the run-in. His trainer reported he will not be risked on quick ground, and the gelding should make up into a nice staying chaser given time. (tchd 11-2)
Spear Thistle, 2-2 over hurdles at this course, led until the last and was probably just outstayed by the winner. Another who appreciates these conditions, he can soon make amends. (op 15-2)
Vino Griego(FR), sent off a short price to gain compensation for his recent Cheltenham second, clouted the second fence and tended to run in snatches thereafter. He is an untidy jumper with a high head carriage but has plenty of ability.

3981 RAKEBACKMYPOKER.COM NOVICES' HURDLE (10 hdls) 2m 3f 110y
2:35 (2:40) (Class 4) 4-Y-0+ **£2,329** (£678; £339)

Form RPR
21 **1** **Not Til Monday (IRE)**[21] 3604 5-11-11 124 TimmyMurphy 121+
(J R Jenkins) *led: narrowly hdd and rdn 3 out: rallied to join ldr 2 out: led bef last: styd on wl* **2/1**[2]
41-2 **2** *3* **Cresswell Crusader**[38] 3266 7-10-13 0 RachaelGreen(5) 114+
(Anthony Honeyball) *trckd wnr after 2nd: mstke 4th: upsides fr next: mstke 7th: led 3 out and gng much bttr: hdd bef last: rdn and nt qckn flat* **1/1**[1]
06-4 **3** *49* **Taylors Secret**[88] 2335 5-11-4 0 DavidEngland 62
(Shaun Lycett) *chsd ldrs: reminder after 4th: chsd ldng pair at 6th: lft wl bhd after next: v tired and jst hld on for 3rd* **50/1**
/26- **4** *hd* **Cuckoo Pen**[418] 2922 7-11-4 0 TomScudamore 62
(Mark Bradstock) *chsd wnr tl after 2nd: dropped to 4th at 6th and sn lost tch: eased after 3 out: shkn up and nrly snatched poor 3rd nr fin* **4/1**[3]
05/ **P** **Justalittlebitmore (IRE)**[712] 4138 8-11-1 0 AlexMerriam(3) —
(Diana Grissell) *mstkes: in tch to 5th: t.o after next: p.u after 3 out* **80/1**
P **Spiritual Art**[142] 5-10-6 0 JoshuaMoore(5) —
(Luke Dace) *a in last pair: t.o after 6th: p.u after 3 out* **33/1**
00- **P** **Easter Lad**[309] 5019 7-11-4 0 JamieMoore —
(Luke Dace) *a in fnl pair: t.o last whn p.u bef 7th* **100/1**

5m 14.7s (8.00) **Going Correction** +0.075s/f (Yiel) **7 Ran SP% 110.5**
Speed ratings (Par 105): **87,85,66,66,— —,—**
toteswingers:1&2: £1.50, 2&3: £4.40, 1&3: £6.70 CSF £4.22 TOTE £2.30: £1.40, £1.10; EX 5.00.

Owner The Three Honest Men **Bred** G J King **Trained** Royston, Herts

FOCUS
A modest novice hurdle which turned into a duel from some way out. The winner is rated to his Plumpton mark.

NOTEBOOK
Not Til Monday(IRE), claimed for £6,000 out of a Hexham seller last October, made virtually all to follow up last month's Plumpton success under his penalty. A frustrating performer on the Flat, he has really taken to jumping and is the type who his shrewd yard do well with. He displayed a high knee action and is suited to testing conditions. (tchd 9-4)
Cresswell Crusader chased home a decent sort when second in a Warwick bumper on his last start in December. Making his hurdling debut, he seemed to be going well enough when brought with his challenge three out, and having responded to pressure when briefly off the bridle after the second-last, he looked to be travelling better than the winner approaching the last. However, a slow jump there saw him concede a few lengths to Not Til Monday and he was immediately one-paced. It can be argued he should have been committed before the final flight, but it's questionable whether he would have found much. (tchd 10-11)
Taylors Secret achieved little in a remote third on this hurdles debut.
Cuckoo Pen, a half-brother to Carruthers, ran poorly after an absence of 418 days and perhaps this run was badly needed. Official explanation: jockey said gelding never travelled; vet said gelding lost a near-fore shoe (tchd 9-2)
Justalittlebitmore(IRE) Official explanation: jockey said gelding hung right

3982 GET ONLINE POKER RAKEBACK AT RAKEBACKMYPOKER.COM H'CAP CHASE (18 fncs) 3m
3:10 (3:15) (Class 4) (0-105,103) 5-Y-0+ **£2,808** (£818; £409)

Form RPR
-054 **1** **Tuskar Rock (FR)**[11] 3768 8-11-2 93 AidanColeman 101
(Venetia Williams) *trckd ldng pair: led 13th but immediately jnd: rdn after 15th: duelled w runner-up after: hld on nr fin: all out* **11/4**[1]
1F-5 **2** *nk* **Inthejungle (IRE)**[84] 2429 8-11-11 102 AndrewGlassonbury 110
(Daniel O'Brien) *pressed ldr tl w wnr after 13th: clr of rest after 15th and gng bttr: rdn 3 out: upsides after: nt qckn nr fin* **12/1**
P-21 **3** *hd* **Master D'Or (FR)**[9] 3821 11-11-11 102 PaulMoloney 111
(Sophie Leech) *nt gng that wl in last: mstke 12th: lft bhd next: no prog tl bef 3 out: wnt 3rd bef next: 5 l bhd ldng pair last: styd on: needed a few more strides* **7/2**[2]
222 **4** *12* **Topless (IRE)**[31] 3431 10-11-5 103 (b) MarkQuinlan(7) 101
(Neil Mulholland) *mde most to 13th: sn u.p: outpcd whn blnd 15th: lost 3rd and btn after 3 out* **7/2**[2]
5520 **5** *hd* **Kitley Hassle**[11] 3768 9-11-11 102 (b) HaddenFrost 98
(James Frost) *chsd ldng trio: rdn 11th: outpcd fr 14th: no prog after next: plodded on flat* **7/1**
2/43 **6** *45* **Kasimali (IRE)**[21] 3608 8-11-9 100 (b) JamieMoore 66
(Gary Moore) *in tch in 5th: rdn 13th: sn struggling: wknd 3 out: mstke 2 out: t.o* **5/1**[3]
33PP **P** **Allterrain (IRE)**[196] 1093 8-11-7 98 TimmyMurphy —
(Murty McGrath) *in tch in last pair tl wknd rapidly 10th: p.u bef 12th* **14/1**

6m 22.5s (-1.20) **Going Correction** +0.075s/f (Yiel) **7 Ran SP% 114.6**
Speed ratings: **105,104,104,100,100 85,—**
toteswingers:1&2: £6.40, 2&3: £2.90, 1&3: £2.90 CSF £32.17 CT £117.85 TOTE £3.30: £2.10, £7.30; EX 36.90.
Owner Anthony Pye-Jeary And Mel Smith **Bred** Mme Henri Devin **Trained** Kings Caple, H'fords

FOCUS
A handicap chase which took little winning. The winner took advantage of a very poor mark, with the next two setting the level.

NOTEBOOK
Tuskar Rock(FR) got off the mark at the 22nd time of asking under a strong ride from Aidan Coleman. He is not ungenuine but needs a real stamina test as he is not blessed with much speed. (op 7-2)
Inthejungle(IRE), returning from an 84-day break, seemed to be travelling best three out but is another who doesn't do anything quickly and just found the line coming too soon. (op 10-1)
Master D'Or(FR) didn't jump as well as the front two but may still have won had he got going sooner. He has been rejuvenated by his new stable and is the one to take from the race. (op 4-1 tchd 9-2)
Topless(IRE) broke her run of seconds but not quite in the way connections would have hoped. (tchd 4-1)

3983 RAKEBACKMYPOKER.COM H'CAP HURDLE (8 hdls) 2m 110y
3:40 (3:45) (Class 5) (0-95,94) 4-Y-0+ **£2,055** (£599; £299)

Form RPR
0455 **1** **Swiss Guard**[27] 3497 5-11-11 93 (t) RichardJohnson 115+
(Tim Vaughan) *prom on outer: trckd ldr 5th: led bef 2 out: pushed along and drew rt away* **5/2**[1]
-6U3 **2** *17* **Snow Patrol**[20] 3611 10-9-12 73 (v[1]) CharlieWallis(7) 73
(Nigel Dunger) *mde most: drvn after 3 out: hdd bef next: no ch w wnr after* **5/2**[1]
135- **3** *4 ½* **Canshebemine**[290] 5367 7-10-12 80 (t) HaddenFrost 74
(James Frost) *prom: chsd ldr 4th to 5th: rdn 3 out: steadily fdd in 3rd bef 2 out* **5/1**[2]
2545 **4** *12* **Just Beware**[21] 3610 9-11-5 94 (p) MrHGMiller(7) 76
(Zoe Davison) *cl up: rdn after 4th: struggling whn mstke next: wl btn in 4th fr 3 out* **6/1**[3]
55/P **P** **Hungry For More**[20] 3611 7-11-3 85 WillKennedy —
(Mark Hoad) *chsd ldr to 4th: sn wknd: t.o in 6th whn p.u bef 2 out* **20/1**
UUPO **P** **Rossmill Lad (IRE)**[76] 2594 7-10-3 76 ow2 JoshuaMoore(5) —
(Luke Dace) *stmbld 1st: mostly last: rdn and wknd 4th: t.o 3 out: p.u bef next* **6/1**[3]
FP **F** **Sonus Weld (IRE)**[21] 3607 6-11-3 85 (p) AndrewGlassonbury —
(Paddy Butler) *a in last pair: mstke 2nd: rdn and struggling after 4th: t.o after 3 out: fell last: winded* **40/1**

4m 14.1s **Going Correction** +0.075s/f (Yiel) **7 Ran SP% 109.6**
Speed ratings (Par 103): **103,95,92,87,— —,—**
toteswingers:1&2: £1.70, 2&3: £2.00, 1&3: £3.10 CSF £8.63 TOTE £2.90: £1.40, £1.80; EX 10.60.
Owner Middleham Park Racing LII & J McCarthy **Bred** Meon Valley Stud **Trained** Aberthin, Vale of Glamorgan

FOCUS
A desperately weak handicap hurdle run at a sound pace in the conditions. The facile winner improved by 20lb+ and the second ran pretty much to his mark.

NOTEBOOK
Swiss Guard, an expensive yearling purchase, proved a big let down for Ballydoyle. Dropped 8lb after two tries in handicap company and fitted with a tongue-tie for the first time, he was kept wide. He was galloping all over the leader some way out and sprinted clear from the second last for an easy success. He will shoot up in the ratings as a result and connections will be keen to turn him out under a penalty, but he will be lucky to encounter another race as weak. (op 11-4 tchd 3-1)
Snow Patrol, whose sole success was four years ago, has plummeted in the ratings and has looked ungenuine at times. In a first-time visor, he took them along but it was clear some way from home that he was going to prove no match. (tchd 9-4)
Canshebemine, 10lb higher than her sole success in selling company in bad ground at Newton Abbot a year ago, was having her first start since April and it may well have been needed. (op 4-1)
Just Beware, 8lb higher than her last success, prefers much better ground and came here out of form. She struggled to keep up three out. (tchd 13-2)

3984 DORMANSLAND H'CAP CHASE (14 fncs) 2m 4f 110y
4:15 (4:20) (Class 5) (0-95,95) 5-Y-0+ **£2,123** (£619; £309)

Form RPR
U-P0 **1** **Prince Louis (FR)**[56] 2929 8-11-12 95 (t) DarylJacob 111+
(Charlie Mann) *j.lft: led after 2nd: blnd 7th: gng strly whn blnd 3 out: drew away fr next: comf* **8/1**
4PF4 **2** *11* **Mr Bond (IRE)**[13] 3720 8-11-1 84 NickScholfield 86
(Andy Turnell) *hld up in last pair: nt fluent 5th: prog to chse wnr and mstke 8th: no imp 3 out: wl hld after* **11/4**[1]

U42U **3** *3 1/4* **Killfinnan Castle (IRE)**[10] 3790 8-10-7 **76**.......................(p) WillKennedy 73
(Violet M Jordan) *hld up last: prog 8th: in tch 11th: sn pushed along: wl hld in 3rd fr 3 out: one pce* **11/4**[1]
U53 **4** *14* **Russellstown Boy (IRE)**[36] 3337 11-11-3 **86**.................. PaulMoloney 70
(Evan Williams) *trckd ldrs: nt fluent 3rd: in tch 11th: urged along sn after: no imp 3 out: wknd last* **3/1**[2]
3053 **5** *8* **Sieglinde (FR)**[21] 3606 5-10-10 **82**................................(p) LeightonAspell 53
(Alison Batchelor) *led tl after 2nd: chsd wnr tl wknd u.p 8th: t.o in last pair 10th* **14/1**
635P **6** *73* **Maximix**[10] 3792 8-11-4 **87**.. AndrewGlassonbury —
(Gary Moore) *trckd ldrs: mstke 6th: lost interest and t.o in last pair fr 10th: virtually p.u after last* **11/2**[3]

5m 22.1s (3.90) **Going Correction** +0.075s/f (Yiel)
WFA 5 from 8yo+ 2lb **6** Ran SP% **111.5**
Speed ratings: **95,90,89,84,81 53**
toteswingers:1&2: £4.30, 2&3: £1.90, 1&3: £3.30 CSF £30.31 TOTE £9.30: £3.70, £1.80; EX 26.10.
Owner Alan Le Herissier **Bred** Alain Couetil **Trained** Upper Lambourn, Berks

FOCUS
A woefully weak handicap chase with some slip-shod jumping. The winner produced a big step up but this isn't form to be confident about.

NOTEBOOK
Prince Louis(FR), as is his wont, continually jumped left-handed in front. Back over fences, he made two serious jumping errors yet was still able to come right away for a clear-cut success. He will be lucky to find another race as poor in the shorter term. (op 15-2 tchd 9-1)
Mr Bond(IRE), a long-standing maiden with a history of breathing problems, is not a natural jumper. He went in pursuit of the winner but his jumping was never convincing and in the end he proved no match. (tchd 5-2)
Killfinnan Castle(IRE), whose two career wins have been at Fontwell, was given a patient ride. He moved up looking likely to enter the argument but was flat out and going nowhere three from the finish. (op 7-2)
Russellstown Boy(IRE), hammered a stone after his sole success at Uttoxeter in October, has come down 7lb since but he was safely held going to three out. (op 11-4 tchd 10-3)

3985 HORSERACEBASE.COM POWERFUL HORSE RACING TOOLS H'CAP HURDLE (10 hdls) 2m 3f 110y
4:45 (4:50) (Class 4) (0-115,110) 4-Y-O+ **£2,329** (£678; £339)

Form RPR
-442 **1** **Top Smart**[83] 2440 5-11-1 **101**.. JimmyDerham(3) 112+
(Seamus Mullins) *cl up: hit 6th and 7th: jnd ldr next: led bef 2 out: shkn up and styd on wl flat* **7/4**[1]
260 **2** *2 1/2* **Kalamill (IRE)**[30] 3436 4-11-2 **110**...................................(t) AidanColeman 106+
(Shaun Lycett) *hld up last: prog 5th: chsd wnr after 3 out: rdn and cl enough last: no imp flat* **2/1**[2]
6P40 **3** *15* **Grey Cruzene (USA)**[21] 3604 5-10-9 **92**.............................. ColinBolger 85
(Chris Gordon) *led: hrd rdn and hdd after 3 out: grad wknd fr next* **8/1**
0P44 **4** *87* **Chase Gate**[27] 3495 6-11-3 **100**... HaddenFrost 4
(James Frost) *cl up tl wknd rapidly bef 3 out: sn wl t.o: stl appr last as wnr fin* **6/1**[3]
-060 **5** *8* **Airedale Lad (IRE)**[167] 1361 10-9-12 **86** oh17 ow3.......... KeiranBurke(5) —
(Zoe Davison) *wnt prom 4th: wknd after next: wl t.o after 7th* **33/1**
-P44 **P** **Cosavita (FR)**[21] 3610 6-10-13 **96**....................................(t) PaulMoloney —
(David Rees) *in tch tl wknd rapidly 5th: t.o whn p.u bef 7th* **8/1**

5m 16.3s (9.60) **Going Correction** +0.075s/f (Yiel)
WFA 4 from 5yo+ 9lb **6** Ran SP% **109.1**
Speed ratings (Par 105): **83,82,76,41,38** —
Swingers:1&2: £1.70, 2&3: £2.20, 1&3: £3.10 CSF £5.50 TOTE £3.90: £2.50, £1.10; EX 6.30.
Owner The Calvera Partnership No 2 **Bred** A Price **Trained** Wilsford-Cum-Lake, Wilts

FOCUS
A modest handicap hurdle. The pace was steady until four out and the first three pulled well clear. The winner improved by 5lb and the second ran to form.

NOTEBOOK
Top Smart, a well-made type who will make a chaser in time, was taking a step up in trip on his handicap bow. He took charge on the run round to two out and went going away in the end. He can make further progress now he has broken his duck. (op 9-4 tchd 5-2)
Kalamill(IRE), runner-up first time at Fontwell, was highly tried on his next two starts. Another up in trip on his handicap bow, he tried hard to get on level terms from two out but the winner always looked to have his measure. Connections will have been encouraged by the gap he opened up back to the third. (op 11-4 tchd 15-8)
Grey Cruzene(USA), 200-1 when a well-beaten fourth here two outings ago, was another having his first try in handicap company. He took them along but was swept aside by the first two from the penultimate flight.
Chase Gate Official explanation: jockey said gelding never travelled
Cosavita(FR) Official explanation: jockey said mare lost its action
T/Plt: £255.80 to a £1 stake.Pool of £87,401.51- 249.41 winning tickets. T/Qpdt: £20.10 to a £1 stake. Pool of £10,396.46 - 381.02 winning tickets. JN

3692 MARKET RASEN (R-H)
Tuesday, February 8
OFFICIAL GOING: Good (good to soft in places; chs 6.4, hdl 7.2)
Wind: light across Weather: fine and sunny, mild

3986 CAFFREY'S IRISH ALE JUVENILE HURDLE (7 hdls 1 omitted) 2m 1f
1:35 (1:35) (Class 4) 4-Y-O **£2,276** (£668; £334; £166)

Form RPR
1 **Higgy's Ragazzo (FR)**[120] 4-10-12 .... APMcCoy 110+
(Nicky Henderson) *3rd whn lft in ld 1st: nt fluent 2nd and 3rd: jnd 4th: j.lft last 2: shkn up and qcknd clr run-in: comf* **8/15**[1]
0 **2** *2 3/4* **Kayaan**[13] 3739 4-10-12 .... WarrenMarston 97
(Pam Sly) *t.k.h: trckd ldrs: upsides 4th: crowded 2 out: styd on same pce run-in* **9/1**[3]
6 **3** *13* **Verluga (IRE)**[11] 2614 4-10-12 .... DominicElsworth 85
(Tim Easterby) *hmpd 1st: hdwy to trck ldrs 5th: wknd 2 out* **12/1**
4 *9* **Always De One**[38] 4-10-5 ....(p) ColinBolger 70
(Julia Feilden) *t.k.h: trckd ldrs: drvn omitted 3 out: wknd next* **100/1**
4 **U** **Sir Pitt**[12] 3767 4-10-12 .... DarylJacob —
(Alison Thorpe) *led: swvd lft and uns rdr 1st* **7/2**[2]
B **Brink**[95] 4-10-5 .... PhilKinsella —
(Tim Pitt) *trckd ldr: b.d first* **80/1**

4m 8.80s (2.10) **Going Correction** -0.35s/f (Good) **6** Ran SP% **107.4**
Speed ratings: **81,79,73,69,**— —
toteswingers:1&2 £1.80, 2&3 £3.30, 1&3 £1.50 CSF £5.67 TOTE £1.60: £1.10, £3.00; EX 4.00.
Owner I Higginson **Bred** Thierry Grandsir & Patrick Bruneau **Trained** Upper Lambourn, Berks
■ Higgy's Ragazzo handed trainer Nicky Henderson his fastest ever century of winners in a season.

FOCUS
A moderate novice event which proved eventful. The third-last flight was bypassed. Guessy form, but the winner was value for further and can rate higher.

NOTEBOOK
Higgy's Ragazzo(FR) was the best of these on the Flat and what already looked a straightforward task for him with a clear round was made even easier after the drama at the very first flight. That saw him left in front which wasn't ideal by any means as he ran freely and took time to warm to his jumping. Indeed he momentarily appeared in trouble after a messy leap two out which saw the runner-up nose to the front, but Tony McCoy always looked confident he would do the business and he was well on top at the finish. He is entitled to improve a deal for the experience and the ground is now starting to turn in his favour, as his two wins on the level came on a sound surface. This form is an awful a long way off justifying a trip to the Cheltenham Festival, however, and he remains around 40/1 for the Triumph Hurdle. (tchd 4-7 in a place)
Kayaan showed much-improved form on this second outing as a hurdler and clearly enjoyed the better ground. He should be winning when able to race off a stronger pace. (op 14-1)
Verluga(IRE) found this too hot yet still performed with more encouragement than he did on his hurdling debut at Wetherby. (op 9-1)
Sir Pitt had set out to make all prior to getting the first all wrong and causing the early mayhem.

3987 EUROPEAN BREEDERS' FUND "NATIONAL HUNT" NOVICES' HURDLE (QUALIFIER) (10 hdls) 2m 3f
2:05 (2:07) (Class 3) 4-7-Y-O **£4,618** (£1,356; £678; £338)

Form RPR
-212 **1** **Risaala**[14] 3721 5-10-12 120.. MissGAndrews(7) 125+
(Pam Sly) *trckd ldrs: hdwy on inner to ld and mstke last: drvn out* **7/2**[3]
4-13 **2** *1 1/2* **Thanks For Coming**[27] 3506 5-11-2 0.................................... APMcCoy 119
(Nicky Henderson) *t.k.h: trckd ldr: led and j.lft 2 out: hdd last: styd on same pce* **5/2**[1]
3 *7* **Soir D'Estruval (FR)**[162] 5-11-12 0......................... RobertThornton 123
(Alan King) *trckd ldrs: chal and crowded 2 out: kpt on same pce appr last* **15/2**
03UU **4** *4* **High Hoylander**[13] 3739 5-10-13 0 ow2............................ ShaneByrne(5) 110
(Sue Smith) *hld up in mid-div: hdwy to trck ldrs whn hit 3 out: crowded next: wknd between last 2* **40/1**
31 **5** *2* **Bottman (IRE)**[29] 3487 6-11-8 0...................................... RichardJohnson 112
(Tim Vaughan) *chsd ldrs: t.k.h: outpcd 7th: one pce appr 2 out* **3/1**[2]
5-0 **6** *1* **Mytara**[15] 3715 6-10-9 0... DavidEngland 98
(Pam Sly) *mid-div: wnt prom 5th: rdn and outpcd 3 out: no threat after* **25/1**
302 **7** *2 3/4* **Shan Blue (IRE)**[14] 3725 6-11-2 0.. RhysFlint 103
(Steve Gollings) *j.lft: led tl hdd & wknd appr 2 out* **20/1**
5 **8** *1* **Moscow Chancer (IRE)**[27] 3505 5-11-2 0...................... PaddyBrennan 104
(Tom George) *chsd ldrs: hmpd bnd bef 2 out: wknd and 7th whn j. bdly lft 2 out* **10/1**
0 **9** *3 1/4* **Foot The Bill**[270] 319 6-11-2 0... TomSiddall 98
(Patrick Holmes) *chsd ldrs: hit 6th: lost pl next* **150/1**
/1-3 **10** *2 1/4* **Flaygray**[80] 2525 7-11-2 0.. DenisO'Regan 96
(Chris Grant) *in rr: reminders 3rd: bhd fr 6th* **16/1**
U6-1 **11** *1 1/4* **Lombardy Boy (IRE)**[48] 3088 6-10-13 0............................ TomMolloy(3) 94
(Michael Banks) *in rr: bhd fr 6th* **25/1**
0-06 **12** *15* **Atared**[83] 2456 5-10-9 0.. WarrenMarston 72
(Pam Sly) *towards rr: bhd fr 3 out* **100/1**
006P **13** *75* **Sir Clad**[28] 3493 5-10-13 0..(t) TommyPhelan(3) 4
(Claire Dyson) *nt fluent in rr: bhd fr 6th: t.o 2 out: virtually p.u appr last* **250/1**
0-0 **P** **Semah George**[29] 3489 5-11-2 0.. TomMessenger —
(John Holt) *towards rr: bhd fr 6th: t.o 2 out: p.u bef last* **250/1**

4m 29.3s (-10.10) **Going Correction** -0.35s/f (Good) **14** Ran SP% **119.9**
Speed ratings: **107,106,103,101,100 100,99,98,97,96 96,89,58,**—
toteswingers:1&2 £4.50, 2&3 £4.20, 1&3 £5.40 CSF £12.32 TOTE £3.90: £1.40, £1.50, £2.10; EX 17.10.
Owner David L Bayliss **Bred** Shadwell Estate Co Ltd **Trained** Thorney, Cambs

FOCUS
A fair novice hurdle, run at a fair gallop, and the form hsould work out. A personal best from the winner.

NOTEBOOK
Risaala resumed winning ways with a gutsy effort under her regular pilot, who is decent value for her 7lb claim. She bided her time off the pace before being delivered two out on the inner and would've won by further with a better leap at the last. Returning to further was much to this consistent 5-y-o's liking and the Mares' Final at Newbury next month looks a most viable target. (op 4-1 tchd 3-1)
Thanks For Coming, whose top yard won the race last season, held every chance and finished a clear second-best. This was a nice improvement on his hurdling debut last month on ground that evidently suits, but he again looked less than straightforward under maximum pressure. (op 11-4 tchd 3-1)
Soir D'Estruval(FR) was having his first outing since winning on his hurdling debut at Vichy in France 162 days earlier and the market suggested the run may be needed. He posted a promising effort under his big penalty and appears sure to come on for the run. Chasing will ultimately be his game, but it wouldn't surprise to see him make the Final at Sandown next month. (op 6-1)
High Hoylander had unseated the last twice, but he showed up a lot better here. Dropping back to 2m may suit best, though. (op 50-1)
Bottman(IRE) ♦ looked most progressive when winning on soft ground at Towcester last month, but he found things happening too quickly for him around here. One could see him going close if going for Final next month, where the stiffer track would be much more suitable. (op 11-4 tchd 5-2)

3988 MOLSON COORS ONE STOP SHOP NOVICES' CHASE (14 fncs) 2m 6f 110y
2:35 (2:36) (Class 3) 5-Y-O+ **£5,691** (£1,671; £835)

Form RPR
0-01 **1** **Quantitativeeasing (IRE)**[32] 3429 6-11-4 0......................... APMcCoy 131+
(Nicky Henderson) *narow ld: narrowly hdd and hit 2 out: rdn to ld last: styd on wl fnl 150yds* **2/11**[1]
046F **2** *1 1/4* **Fin Vin De Leu (GER)**[22] 3598 5-10-5 0.........................(p) PeterToole(3) 117
(Charlie Mann) *j.lft: w wnr: hit 3 out: hung rt and narrow ld next: hdd last: kpt on same pce* **11/2**[2]
-344 **3** *3* **Springfield Raki**[242] 714 7-10-12 0.. RhysFlint 118
(Steve Gollings) *racd in handy 3rd: drvn and outpcd after 4 out: kpt on run-in* **18/1**[3]

5m 54.3s (8.30) **Going Correction** -0.35s/f (Good)
WFA 5 from 6yo+ 2lb **3** Ran SP% **105.3**
Speed ratings: **71,70,69**
CSF £1.61 TOTE £1.10; EX 1.40.
Owner John P McManus **Bred** Mrs C A Moore **Trained** Upper Lambourn, Berks

FOCUS
Quantitativeeasing won again despite running below his best on this quicker ground. A slow time and fairly meaningless form.

NOTEBOOK

Quantitativeeasing(IRE) followed up his easy Fontwell success last month, but was anything but impressive on this quicker surface and was given a real fright by the runner-up. Having to make a lot of the running probably wasn't that much to his liking, but he wasn't so fluent over his fences on this ground and it was surprising that he hadn't shaken off his main rival prior to making an error at the penultimate fence. To his credit he responded positively after that and, despite being bred to enjoy a sound surface, perhaps he is at his best when the mud is flying. One of the handicaps at Cheltenham looks most likely for him now. (tchd 1-6)

Fin Vin De Leu(GER) fell on his chase debut at Fakenham last month and is officially rated 19lb the winner's inferior over hurdles. He jumped too deliberately at times, perhaps remembering his previous fall, but his substitute rider kept him interested and he briefly looked as though he was going to score two out. He hung fire when in front, though, and that allowed the winner to get back on top. No doubt he can win one of these as he becomes more experienced. (op 7-1)

Springfield Raki knows all about this track, but was faced with a stiff task on his return from a 242-day absence. He only lost touch with the first pair nearing three out, however, and this rates by far his best effort over fences. (op 14-1 tchd 20-1)

3989 BBC LINCOLNSHIRE MIKE MOLLOY MEMORIAL NOVICES' H'CAP HURDLE (10 hdls) 2m 5f
3:05 (3:05) (Class 4) (0-110,107) 4-Y-0+ **£2,397** (£698; £349)

Form RPR

3061 **1** **The Magic Bishop**[28] 3500 6-11-7 **107**........................ JamesHalliday(5) 117+
(Malcolm Jefferson) *stdd s: hld up in rr: stdy hdwy after 7th: led 2 out: drew clr: readily* **8/1**

0533 **2** *8* **Silver Roque (FR)**[31] 3449 5-11-9 **104**........................ AndrewThornton 106+
(Henrietta Knight) *trckd ldrs: led 3 out: hdd next: kpt on same pce* **4/1**[1]

500P **3** *1 3/4* **Bobbisox (IRE)**[13] 3745 6-10-9 **90**........................ TomO'Brien 89
(Alex Hales) *prom: outpcd 3 out: 6th last: styd on to take 3rd towards fin* **10/1**

4055 **4** *2 1/4* **Dipity Doo Dah**[16] 3696 7-10-10 **98**........................ MichaelByrne(7) 98+
(Peter Bowen) *hdwy to chse ldrs 3rd: one pce appr 2 out: clr 3rd whn mstke last* **5/1**[2]

2-3P **5** *1 1/4* **Quetzal (IRE)**[37] 3348 6-11-5 **103**........................ CharlieHuxley(3) 98
(Alan King) *mid-div: outpcd after 7th: kpt on fr 2 out* **13/2**

2P54 **6** *1/2* **Galley Slave (IRE)**[16] 3697 6-10-0 **88**........................ MrOGarner(7) 83
(Michael Chapman) *led: hdd 3 out: grad wknd appr next* **16/1**

636 **7** *3/4* **Burnthill (IRE)**[226] 847 6-10-6 **90**........................ TommyPhelan(3) 85
(Claire Dyson) *t.k.h: w ldr: lost pl after 7th: no threat after* **11/1**

0665 **8** *nk* **Tippering (IRE)**[14] 3718 6-11-5 **105**........................ ShaneByrne(5) 101
(Sue Smith) *nt fluent in rr: reminders after 5th: sme hdwy whn mstke 3 out: no ch after* **6/1**[3]

-060 **9** *3 1/4* **Everdon Brook (IRE)**[39] 3252 6-10-7 **88**........................ CharliePoste 82
(Ben Case) *nt jump wl: wnt prom 4th: reminders after next: lost pl after 7th* **25/1**

0005 **10** *33* **Chadwell Spring (IRE)**[86] 2398 5-10-0 **81** oh4........................ CampbellGillies 38
(Mike Sowersby) *hld up towards rr: bhd fr 6th: t.o 3 out* **25/1**

33 **11** *41* **Leopard Hills (IRE)**[139] 1576 4-10-8 **100**........................ RichardJohnson 5
(Alison Thorpe) *chsd ldrs: wknd qckly 3 out: t.o next: virtually p.u* **8/1**

5m 9.20s (0.40) **Going Correction** -0.35s/f (Good)
WFA 4 from 5yo+ 10lb **11** Ran SP% **117.5**
Speed ratings (Par 105): **85,81,81,80,79 79,79,79,78,65 49**
toteswingers:1&2 £3.90, 2&3 £9.00, 1&3 £17.70 CSF £40.76 CT £323.98 TOTE £5.90: £2.30, £1.20, £3.80; EX 18.10.

Owner P Nelson **Bred** Peter Nelson **Trained** Norton, N Yorks

FOCUS

An open-looking novice handicap and fair form for the class. The first two are progressive.

NOTEBOOK

The Magic Bishop, whose trainer/rider won this last season, was 9lb higher for getting off the mark at Newcastle last month and proved easy to back. He got a very well-judged ride, however, and ultimately won with plenty left in the tank. This quicker surface helped him stay the longer trip and further improvement cannot be ruled out, but the handicapper will again have his say. With that in mind connections might do well to look for something under a penalty. (op 5-1)

Silver Roque(FR) was never far away and raced enthusiastically. He was booted for home when fellow pacesetter Galley Slave began to wilt around three out and, although that move came too soon for him, he wouldn't have beaten the winner under more patient handling. A slight drop back in trip may well work the oracle. (op 9-2)

Bobbisox(IRE), pulled up again on her previous outing, hit a flat spot before staying on dourly late in the day. She is yet to win, but this ground helped and stepping back up in trip on a similar surface is probably what she needs. (op 18-1)

Dipity Doo Dah raced on the outside through the race and failed to really raise her game for the longer distance. (op 4-1)

Quetzal(IRE) proved too keen for his own good, but this was a step back in the right direction. (op 6-1)

Tippering(IRE) proved most unwilling. (op 15-2)

3990 ERIC AND LUCY PAPWORTH H'CAP CHASE (14 fncs) 2m 6f 110y
3:35 (3:38) (Class 4) (0-105,105) 5-Y-0+ **£2,927** (£859; £429; £214)

Form RPR

2201 **1** **Mister Wiseman**[10] 3819 9-11-8 **101**........................(p) DavidDennis 114+
(Nigel Hawke) *mde all: j. soundly: drew clr fr 3 out: 12 l ahd last: eased fnl 150yds* **5/1**[3]

3516 **2** *6* **Persian Gates (IRE)**[35] 3391 7-11-7 **100**........................ TomMessenger 100
(Chris Bealby) *chsd ldrs: wnt 3rd 9th: kpt on to take 2nd run-in* **7/1**

20U **3** *nk* **Sun Tzu (IRE)**[10] 3822 7-11-12 **105**........................(b) AndrewThornton 106
(Dr Richard Newland) *chsd ldrs: wnt 2nd 9th: one pce fr 2 out* **12/1**

5P34 **4** *2 1/2* **Sycho Fred (IRE)**[86] 2402 10-10-0 **79** oh4........................(t) CampbellGillies 77
(Mike Sowersby) *in rr: hdwy 7th: one pce fr 4 out: tk modest 4th last* **7/1**

4-P2 **5** *3 1/4* **Porta Vogie (IRE)**[21] 3617 9-11-9 **105**........................ TomMolloy(3) 101
(Graeme McPherson) *hld up in rr: hdwy and handy 5th whn hit 9th: 4th and one pce whn mstke 3 out* **3/1**[1]

52P0 **6** *24* **Oranger (FR)**[12] 3772 9-10-12 **98**........................(b) MrSWDrinkwater(7) 68
(Andrew J Martin) *chsd ldrs: drvn and outpcd whn hit 10th: sn wknd* **12/1**

45UP **7** *12* **Panama Canal (IRE)**[16] 3695 6-11-6 **102**........................ AdamPogson(3) 60
(Charles Pogson) *rn wout declared tongue-tie: in rr: sme hdwy whn blnd and lost pl 10th: sn bhd* **28/1**

0333 **8** *24* **Feeling Peckish (USA)**[33] 3402 7-9-7 **79** oh2........................(t) MrTGarner(7) 13
(Michael Chapman) *prom: lost pl 5th: in rr whn blnd 7th: bhd fr 10th: t.o 3 out* **15/2**

0006 **9** *32* **Gaora Lane (IRE)**[34] 3395 10-11-7 **103**........................(b[1]) PeterToole(3) 5
(Charlie Mann) *chsd ldrs: drvn 9th: sn lost pl and bhd: t.o 3 out* **9/2**[2]

/P0P **P** **Dareios (GER)**[39] 3261 6-10-1 **80**........................(p) DavidEngland —
(John Mackie) *mstkes in rr: reminders 4th: bhd whn blnd 9th: t.o whn p.u bef 4 out* **66/1**

5m 41.1s (-4.90) **Going Correction** -0.35s/f (Good) **10** Ran SP% **116.9**
Speed ratings: **94,91,91,90,89 81,77,68,57,—**
toteswingers:1&2 £4.00, 2&3 £9.70, 1&3 £6.20 CSF £40.37 CT £400.96 TOTE £3.50: £2.10, £2.70, £3.70; EX 31.10.

Owner D R Mead **Bred** Mrs D Thomson **Trained** Woolminstone, Somerset

FOCUS

A moderate handicap, run at a sound gallop. The easy winner is rated back to his 2009 form.

NOTEBOOK

Mister Wiseman got off the mark as a chaser on heavy ground at Uttoxeter ten days earlier and has won at this venue over hurdles, but was a real market drifter here. That didn't stop him from following up with another decisive display from the front off his 5lb higher mark on the contrasting surface, however, and he is clearly a horse full of confidence at present. A bold bid for the hat-trick is now expected. (op 9-2 tchd 4-1)

Persian Gates(IRE) showed up better again for the return to this venue and it's not hard to see why he was upped to nearly 3m last time out as he did his best work at the finish. (op 8-1 tchd 13-2)

Sun Tzu(IRE) having his first outing over fences in Britain, was a clear second-best two out but he was done with from the last and remains hard to predict. (op 9-1)

Sycho Fred(IRE) met support despite racing from 4lb out of the handicap and wasn't disgraced on his return from an 86-day break.

Porta Vogie(IRE) crept into contention on the far side, but his jumping thereafter let him down and consistency is not his strong suit. (tchd 7-2)

Gaora Lane(IRE) attracted money in first-time blinkers, but he dropped out tamely and this continues his decline. (tchd 5-1)

3991 BEAUMONTCOTE MAIDEN HUNTERS' CHASE (13 fncs 4 omitted) 3m 1f
4:05 (4:08) (Class 6) 5-Y-0+ **£936** (£290; £145; £72)

Form RPR

0/ **1** **Keeverfield (IRE)**[9] 10-11-7 0........................ MissSamanthaDrake(7) 112+
(Miss S A Drake) *t.k.h early: led 2nd: mstke 2 out: 5 l ahd whn blnd last: kpt on: all out* **8/1**

2 **2** *1 1/2* **Poppy Day**[16] 8-11-0 0........................ MissJoannaMason(7) 101+
(I M Mason) *chsd ldrs: pushed along and outpcd circ to go: wnt modest 3rd appr 2 out: chsd wnr sn after last: styd on wl: nt rch wnr* **15/8**[1]

P/2- **3** *2 3/4* **Just Talking (IRE)**[36] 9-12-0 99........................ MrDMansell 105
(Miss J Houldey) *hld up: hdwy w circ to go: chsd wnr appr normal 3 out: one pce fr between last 2* **7/2**[3]

P/4- **4** *28* **Ask Bobby**[9] 12-11-11 77........................(t) MrGBrewer(3) 82
(Mrs M Sowersby) *prom to 3rd: lost pl 8th: struggling fnl circ* **16/1**

5 *12* **Indian Print (IRE)**[16] 7-11-11 0........................ MrTDavidson(3) 65
(V Thompson) *sn chsng ldrs: wknd appr 2 out: sn bhd* **3/1**[2]

00-P **6** *23* **Coppingers Court (IRE)**[16] 10-11-7 0........................ MrRHodges(7) 42
(S Rea) *in rr: drvn circ to go: wknd bef normal 4 out: sn bhd: t.o* **20/1**

6/0- **P** **Rustic John**[276] 11-11-9 0........................ MrMWall(5) —
(Michael Hawker) *prom: drvn and lost pl jst over circ to go: t.o whn p.u after 1st fence fnl circ* **50/1**

4U-P **P** **Ben Ryan (IRE)**[16] 12-11-7 74........................(v[1]) MrJHodson(7)
(S Rea) *chsd ldr: drvn circ to go: sn lost pl: t.o whn p.u after normal 4 out* **40/1**

400/ **F** **Exit To Luck (GER)**[16] 10-11-11 0........................(v[1]) MrRArmson(3) —
(S Robinson) *in rr whn fell 1st* **25/1**

6m 20.4s (-10.90) **Going Correction** -0.35s/f (Good) **9** Ran SP% **112.0**
Speed ratings: **103,102,101,92,88 81,—,—,—**
toteswingers:1&2 £4.80, 2&3 £1.90, 1&3 £5.50 CSF £22.96 TOTE £12.70: £3.00, £1.30, £1.10; EX 27.80.

Owner Miss S A Drake **Bred** John K Millar **Trained** Guiseley, West Yorks

FOCUS

A modest maiden hunter chase but pretty solid form. The fourth-last fence was omitted as it was damaged, and the third-last fence was bypassed on the last two circuits.

NOTEBOOK

Keeverfield(IRE) pulled his way to the front early on and wasn't always fluent. Indeed he hit both of the final two fences, but kept going for his rider's urgings and was always just doing enough to hold on after the last. This was his debut over regulation fences and he is rarely out of the frame in points, but his form is ordinary in that sphere so the fact he scored sums up the standard of this event. (op 15-2)

Poppy Day, a five-time Open winner between the flags, looked well held four out but rallied strongly in the home straight and was eating into the winner's advantage on the run-in. She has won over 4m1f and this was clearly too sharp for her. (op 2-1)

Just Talking(IRE) got into the race on the final circuit and looked a threat coming to the second-last, but his response when it mattered was laboured. (tchd 10-3)

Ask Bobby plugged on to reproduce his fourth in the race last season. (op 22-1)

Indian Print(IRE) dropped out disappointingly from the third-last fence and wasn't on a going day. Official explanation: jockey said gelding never trravelled (op 11-4)

3992 CORONA EXTRA STANDARD NATIONAL HUNT FLAT RACE (CONDITIONAL JOCKEYS' AND AMATEUR RIDERS' RACE) 2m 1f
4:35 (4:37) (Class 6) 4-6-Y-0 **£1,267** (£369; £184)

Form RPR

1 **1** **All That Remains (IRE)**[9] 3835 6-11-6 0........................ DavidBass(5) 112+
(Steve Gollings) *trckd ldrs: led 3f out: sn rdn and styd on wl* **2/1**[2]

2 *1 1/2* **Otterburn (IRE)** 5-10-11 0........................ JeremiahMcGrath(7) 104+
(Alan Swinbank) *trckd ldrs: hdwy to chal over 2f out: sn rdn and hung rt: styd on same pce ins fnl f* **11/10**[1]

03 **3** *10* **Sunny Ledgend**[25] 3546 6-10-11 0........................ MrSWDrinkwater(7) 94
(Andrew J Martin) *w ldr: led 7f out: sn qcknd pce: hdd 3f out: crowded over 2f out: wknd wl over 1f out* **4/1**[3]

4 *3 1/2* **Sleeping Du Granit (FR)** 5-10-11 0........................(t) PeterHatton(7) 90
(Claire Dyson) *hld up wl in tch: chal over 4f out: wkng whn sltly hmpd over 2f out* **33/1**

5 **5** *2* **Panashka (IRE)**[79] 2546 6-10-6 0........................ JamesHalliday(5) 81
(Mark Campion) *led: hdd 7f out: lost pl over 4f out* **50/1**

6 *2 1/4* **Robougg (IRE)** 5-10-11 0........................ MrJHodson(7) 86
(Claire Dyson) *hld up: sn trcking ldrs: drvn 5f out: sn lost pl and bhd* **33/1**

00 **U** **Grey Assassin**[27] 3511 4-10-1 0........................ MissCarlyFrater(7) —
(Simon West) *stdd s: t.k.h detached in last: hung bdly lft and uns rdr bnd after 3f* **100/1**

4m 7.80s (6.70) **Going Correction** -0.35s/f (Good)
WFA 4 from 5yo 9lb 5 from 6yo 1lb **7** Ran SP% **109.8**
Speed ratings: **70,69,64,62,62 60,—**
toteswingers:1&2 £1.20, 2&3 £1.60, 1&3 £1.40. totesuper7: Win: Not won. Place: £37.10 CSF £4.15 TOTE £2.70: £2.10, £1.70; EX 5.00.

Owner P J Martin **Bred** Eoin, Patrick And Cian O'Connor **Trained** Scamblesby, Lincs

FOCUS

This turned into something of a sprint and the first pair came well clear. The form is rated around the winner and third.

NOTEBOOK

All That Remains(IRE) made it 2-2 since joining current connections and completed the task gamely under a penalty. His talented conditional helped negate the extra weight and this confirms his versatility as regards underfoot conditions. He should make a fair novice hurdler when sent over further in that sphere. (op 13-8 tchd 9-4)

Otterburn(IRE) ◆ hails from a yard that must always be respected in the bumper division and, bred to win one, met solid support for his racecourse debut. His sire's progeny have a real liking for soft ground, however, and it appeared to be this surface that found him out when it mattered. He has scope and shouldn't be long in winning. (op 7-4 tchd Evens)
Sunny Ledgend has shaped as though in need of a stiffer test in his two outings to date. It therefore wasn't surprising to see him left behind by the first pair on this switch to quicker ground and due to the way the race was run. He helps to set the level. (op 7-2)
Sleeping Du Granit(FR), equipped with a tongue tie, fared best of the two from his yard and showed ability. He is more one for hurdling in due course. (op 22-1)
T/Plt: £10.60 to a £1 stake. Pool of £65,589.12 - 4,507.59 winning tickets. T/Qpdt: £7.70 to a £1 stake. Pool of £3,769.56 - 360.72 winning tickets. WG

3725 SEDGEFIELD (L-H)

Tuesday, February 8

OFFICIAL GOING: Soft (5.0)
Wind: fresh, across Weather: bright and sunny

3993 WEATHERBYS PRINTING NOVICES' H'CAP HURDLE (8 hdls) 2m 1f
1:55 (1:55) (Class 5) (0-90,90) 4-Y-0+ £1,691 (£496; £248; £124)

Form RPR
50P0 **1** **Pagan Lightning (USA)**[13] 3749 6-10-11 **82** MissECSayer(7) 88
(Dianne Sayer) *hld up: hdwy after 3 out to chse ldng pair 2 out: wnt 2nd bef last: led run-in: hld on wl drvn out* **50/1**
0552 **2** ¾ **King's Chorister**[14] 3727 5-10-3 **67** (t) BrianHarding 76+
(Barry Murtagh) *hld up: gd hdwy after 5th to trck ldrs 3 out: led on bit after 3 out: mstke 2 out: sn rdn: blnd last: sn hdd: kpt on: a jst hld* **5/1**[2]
60P- **3** 5 **Donny Briggs**[38] 5318 6-11-7 **85** (b[1]) RichieMcGrath 87
(Tim Easterby) *w ldr: led after 3 out: sn hdd: drvn bef 2 out: kpt on tl no ex run-in* **9/1**
P601 **4** 7 **Transact (IRE)**[20] 3631 6-10-12 **76** (p) GrahamLee 69
(Martin Todhunter) *midfield: wnt in snatches: rdn after 5th: kpt on to take mod 4th last* **5/1**[2]
P004 **5** 1½ **Sam Patch**[14] 3728 8-10-6 **80** (tp) CallumWhillans(10) 72
(Donald Whillans) *hld up: reminders after 3rd: kpt on after 2 out: n.d* **7/1**
5P64 **6** 6 **Railway Park (IRE)**[14] 3727 7-11-2 **80** (tp) PaddyAspell 66
(John Wainwright) *midfield: reminders after 3rd: drvn after 5th: no imp* **9/1**
6205 **7** ¾ **Bubses Boy**[16] 3697 5-11-6 **84** KennyJohnson 69
(Robert Johnson) *trckd ldrs on outer: wknd after 3 out* **28/1**
1P03 **8** 2¾ **Mycenean Prince (USA)**[14] 3727 8-11-5 **90** MissPhillipaTutty(7) 72
(Karen Tutty) *hld up: rdn bef 4th: lost tch after 5th* **16/1**
9 13 **Glad Lion (GER)**[40] 3233 10-11-1 **84** (t) EJO'Connell(5) 55
(J J Lambe, Ire) *trckd ldrs: mstke 3rd: rdn 3 out: wknd appr 2 out* **13/2**[3]
-U3P **10** 3½ **Cosmetic**[28] 3502 6-10-13 **77** BrianHughes 43
(Howard Johnson) *led: racd keenly: hdd after 3 out and wknd qckly* **9/2**[1]
-P00 **11** 8 **Autumn Harvest**[8] 3855 7-11-5 **83** (p) RyanMania 41
(William Young) *trckd ldrs: wknd after 3 out* **66/1**
54P/ **P** **Showtime Annie**[1209] 1738 10-10-6 **70** AlanO'Keeffe —
(Jennie Candlish) *hld up: wknd appr 3 out: t.o whn p.u bef 2 out* **25/1**
4m 24.4s (17.50) **Going Correction** +1.25s/f (Heav) 12 Ran SP% **114.0**
Speed ratings (Par 103): **108,107,105,102,101 98,98,96,90,89 85,—**
toteswingers:1&2 £24.30, 2&3 £11.00, 1&3 £52.00 CSF £275.73 CT £2489.14 TOTE £103.90: £20.80, £1.60, £4.20; EX 479.30.
Owner Mrs Dianne Sayer **Bred** Mr And Mrs G D Shashura And Darley **Trained** Hackthorpe, Cumbria

FOCUS
A low-grade novice handicap hurdle run at a good pace which produced a shock. The shock winner recorded bigger figures in Irish bumpers.

NOTEBOOK
Pagan Lightning(USA) was 0-5 in novice/maiden hurdles but showed a marked improvement in form on his handicap debut. He jumped well and was kept wide for better ground throughout. Although helped by the second horse stumbling at the last, he stayed on best of a strung out field to secure the upset. This was his first piece of worthwhile form since winning a bumper at Downpatrick in 2009, but what he achieved is questionable. Official explanation: trainer's rep said, regarding apparent improvement in form, that the gelding was better suited by the soft ground, had been working well at home and had stripped fitter. (op 80-1)
King's Chorister travelled like the winner from a fair way out before making crucial errors at the final two flights. He edged left at the second last and clouted the final hurdle. He was still in front after the last but idled on the run-in, and although responding for pressure he was out-fought. He is now 0-12 over hurdles, but may get his head in front if delaying his challenge as late as possible next time. (tchd 11-2)
Donny Briggs ran an encouraging race in the first-time blinkers. A 2008 bumper winner, he was pulled up on his hurdling debut but a recent run on the Flat seemed to put him right on this occasion. Obviously a customer who struggles with concentration, it will be interesting to see if he can build on this. (op 17-2 tchd 7-1)
Transact(IRE) looked to struggle with a 7lb hike in the weights after his Newcastle victory, coming under pressure early, but to his credit he stayed on better than most. Official explanation: jockey said gelding never travelled (op 4-1)
Glad Lion(GER) proved disappointing after never travelling with much enthusiasm. (op 9-2)
Cosmetic, far too keen in front, was never going to get home in the conditions. She needs to learn to settle better. (op 8-1)

3994 JOHN WADE NOVICES' HURDLE (QUALIFIER) (10 hdls) 2m 4f
2:25 (2:25) (Class 4) 4-Y-0+ £2,341 (£687; £343; £171)

Form RPR
0-14 **1** **Warrior One**[88] 2349 5-11-11 117 BrianHughes 122+
(Howard Johnson) *trckd ldrs: led 3 out: c clr after next: comf* **13/8**[1]
/5-3 **2** 14 **Vivaldi (IRE)**[8] 3850 6-11-13 124 (p) EJO'Connell(5) 116+
(J J Lambe, Ire) *midfield: hdwy to trck ldrs 3 out: wnt 2nd bef 2 out: kpt on: no match wnr* **9/4**[2]
P **3** 5 **Cloudy Too (IRE)**[102] 2075 5-11-4 0 TjadeCollier 93
(Sue Smith) *trckd ldrs: rdn appr 3 out: kpt on same pce* **16/1**
0 **4** nk **Sir Tamburlane (IRE)**[201] 1071 6-11-4 0 HenryOliver 95
(Sue Smith) *w ldr: rdn after 3 out: sn one pce: hld in 3rd whn blnd last* **28/1**
0 **5** 13 **Any Given Moment (IRE)**[28] 3491 5-11-4 0 JasonMaguire 88
(Donald McCain) *led narrowly: hdd after blunder 3 out: sn rdn: wknd after 2 out* **9/2**[3]
0 **6** 7 **Napoletano (ITY)**[26] 3521 5-11-4 0 KennyJohnson 75
(Robert Johnson) *hld up in rr: hit 6th: hdwy on outer after 4 out: rdn after 3 out and sn wknd: hld whn mstke 2 out* **100/1**
P **7** 8 **Young Firth**[26] 3519 4-10-7 0 FearghalDavis 54
(John Norton) *hld up in midfield: reminder after 5th: rdn after 4 out: no imp* **100/1**
P/60 **8** 2½ **Borderhopper**[42] 3171 7-10-8 0 TonyKelly(10) 62
(Ferdy Murphy) *hld up in midfield: rdn after 4 out: no imp* **50/1**
110F **9** 2 **Turf Trivia**[24] 3570 4-11-7 105 BarryKeniry 63
(George Moore) *trckd ldrs: rdn and wknd appr 3 out* **8/1**
6 **10** 6 **Chichina (USA)**[20] 3637 4-10-0 0 (p) PaddyAspell 36
(Tracy Waggott) *hld up: a towards rr* **40/1**
00 **11** 8 **Farmer Henry**[8] 3850 7-10-11 0 PaulGallagher(7) 46
(Sandy Forster) *midfield: rdn and wknd appr 3 out* **125/1**
050/ **12** 9 **Westwire Toby (IRE)**[674] 4876 9-11-4 0 BrianHarding 37
(Lynn Siddall) *hld up: reminders after 5th: wknd after 6th* **150/1**
5m 14.8s (22.10) **Going Correction** +1.25s/f (Heav)
WFA 4 from 5yo+ 10lb 12 Ran SP% **115.3**
Speed ratings (Par 105): **105,99,97,97,92 89,86,85,84,81 78,75**
toteswingers:1&2 £1.70, 2&3 £8.90, 1&3 £4.50 CSF £5.22 TOTE £1.70: £1.02, £1.60, £4.30; EX 6.30.
Owner Mrs B Halman & J H Johnson **Bred** Ermyn Lodge Stud Limited **Trained** Billy Row, Co Durham

FOCUS
A weak novice hurdle which didn't take much winning. Warrior One produced a step up.

NOTEBOOK
Warrior One raced wide to get the fresher ground and put in a likeable performance to run out a ready winner. He was held under a penalty at Newcastle in November and had stamina doubts up in trip, but answered them in good fashion. He is unexposed at this trip so could follow up in similar conditions. Connections said he will appreciate better ground and will jump fences next season. (op 2-1)
Vivaldi(IRE) was always going to be vulnerable under a double penalty to an improving sort and although running his race, was no match for the easy winner. He is officially rated 124 and provides the benchmark. (op 15-8 tchd 5-2)
Cloudy Too(IRE) was keen but travelled well before tiring late. He was having his first start for 102 days and it may have been needed. (op 22-1)
Sir Tamburlane(IRE) was a never-nearer fourth after making a mistake at the last flight, but stayed on steadily on the run-in, indicating he may need further. (op 25-1)
Any Given Moment(IRE), who got stuck in the mud on his hurdling debut at Leicester last month, was given a positive front-running ride but proved too free and a bad mistake three out ended his chance. He needs to jump more fluently. (op 4-1)
Turf Trivia didn't convince with his jumping, with slow leaps at some of the hurdles. (op 11-1)

3995 COLLINS SEAFOODS BEGINNERS' CHASE (QUALIFIER) (PART OF COLLINS YOUNG CHASERS SERIES) (16 fncs) 2m 4f
2:55 (2:55) (Class 4) 5-Y-0+ £3,295 (£973; £486; £243; £121)

Form RPR
5-FF **1** **The Knoxs (IRE)**[37] 3332 8-11-0 130 BrianHughes 140+
(Howard Johnson) *trckd ldr: led narrowly 3 out: mstke 2 out: 2 l up whn mstke last: sn hdd: rallied run-in: led again fnl 75yds* **1/1**[1]
0-63 **2** 2¼ **Sir Tantallus Hawk**[15] 3714 7-11-0 0 JamesReveley 133+
(Alan Swinbank) *hld up: hdwy after 9th: wnt 2nd 3 out: upsides whn mstke 2 out: lft in ld sn after last: hdd fnl 75yds: no ex* **20/1**
63U3 **3** 22 **Lord Villez (FR)**[26] 3520 7-11-0 120 GrahamLee 115
(Ferdy Murphy) *hld up: blnd 2nd: kpt on after 4 out: lft remote 3rd and blnd last* **7/1**
2624 **4** 1¾ **Mini Beck**[74] 2657 12-11-0 0 PeterBuchanan 109
(Sandy Thomson) *prom: wknd after 4 out: lft remote 4th and blnd last* **25/1**
0500 **5** 12 **Robertewenutter**[15] 3713 7-11-0 0 HenryOliver 96
(Sue Smith) *midfield: racd keenly: wknd after 6 out* **80/1**
2152 **6** 12 **Pyracantha**[26] 3520 6-11-0 0 BarryKeniry 88
(Alan Swinbank) *in tch: hit 5 out: blnd 4 out: wknd after 3 out: wl btn whn anther mstke last* **7/2**[2]
0-05 **7** 22 **Qbuster (IRE)**[15] 3712 10-11-0 95 (t) BrianHarding 61
(Sharon Watt) *hld up: reminders after 8th: a towards rr* **100/1**
000P **8** 10 **Mind Shower (IRE)**[6] 3883 5-10-11 0 (p) PaddyAspell 48
(Robert Wylie) *midfield: wknd after 9th* **200/1**
0/PF **P** **Riskier**[14] 3726 6-10-7 0 MrJohnDawson(7) —
(John Wade) *led: hdd 3 out: wknd qckly: p.u bef 2 out: lost action* **16/1**
3-P1 **F** **Lightening Rod**[42] 3171 6-10-7 0 JakeGreenall(7) 131
(Michael Easterby) *hld up: hdwy after 9th: trckd ldrs 3 out: 2 l down in 3rd whn fell last* **6/1**[3]
5m 6.40s (3.40) **Going Correction** +0.40s/f (Soft)
WFA 5 from 6yo+ 2lb 10 Ran SP% **116.2**
Speed ratings: **109,108,99,98,93 89,80,76,—,—**
toteswingers:1&2 £10.20, 2&3 £12.10, 1&3 £2.90 CSF £24.27 TOTE £2.30: £1.40, £2.80, £1.50; EX 28.70.
Owner Andrea & Graham Wylie **Bred** Miss Margaret Flynn **Trained** Billy Row, Co Durham

FOCUS
An average beginners' chase which had drama at the final fence. The winner was better than the bare result and is potentially smnart.

NOTEBOOK
The Knoxs(IRE) gave favourite backers an almighty scare at the last when blundering badly and surrendering the lead, but once back on an even keel he rallied well to win going away. A faller on his previous two chase starts, he jumped more fluently in the main, but continues to put in one novicey jump on the way round. Clearly a talented individual who beat RSA hope Wymott over hurdles last season, he is held in high regard by his trainer and has an entry in the Jewson Novices' Chase at Cheltenham. (op 5-4)
Sir Tantallus Hawk jumped stickily on his chasing debut at Wetherby last month, but put in a better round of jumping overall and was a threat to the winner after jumping the last in the lead, but he was outstayed by a better rival on the run-in. When jumping the second last the left rein went over the horse's nose which wouldn't have helped, but this was more encouraging. Connections will also be pleased with the gap the front two opened up from the rest. (op 18-1)
Lord Villez(FR) could never get into contention with the front two and is now 0-22 over fences. (op 11-2)
Mini Beck shaped encouragingly on his chasing debut against superior rivals. (op 33-1 tchd 20-1)
Pyracantha ran below the form of his chase debut second and made numerous errors over his fences. He got in too close at the fourth last which ended any hope of getting involved. (op 5-1)
Riskier Official explanation: jockey said gelding lost its action (op 11-2 tchd 13-2)
Lightening Rod, rated 126 over hurdles, was an interesting chase debutant who threatened to take a strong hand at the finish before departing at the last. He can be forgiven this blip after jumping well in the main. (op 11-2 tchd 13-2)

3996 WEATHERBYS BLOODSTOCK INSURANCE H'CAP HURDLE (13 hdls) 3m 3f 110y
3:25 (3:26) (Class 4) (0-110,110) 4-Y-0+ £2,602 (£764; £382; £190)

Form RPR
-002 **1** **Ontrack (IRE)**[14] 3729 7-10-1 **85** WilsonRenwick 90
(Rose Dobbin) *w ldr: led narrowly after 4 out: rdn bef 2 out: hld on wl u.p run-in* **4/1**[2]

2034 **2** *2 3/4* **Oniz Tiptoes (IRE)**[14] 3729 10-10-1 85..............................(v) PaddyAspell 87
(John Wainwright) *trckd ldrs on outer: ev ch 3 out: sn rdn: kpt on: wnt 2nd nr fin* 11/2[3]

P-00 **3** *3/4* **French Ties (IRE)**[14] 3729 9-10-6 90...............................(p) AlanO'Keeffe 91
(Jennie Candlish) *hld up in rr: hdwy to trck ldrs 4 out: upsides on bridle 2 out: sn drvn run-in: fnd little: lost 2nd nr fin* 11/4[1]

0134 **4** *9* **Matmata De Tendron (FR)**[77] 2602 11-10-2 93.......(p) PaulGallagher(7) 85
(Andrew Crook) *trckd ldrs: ev ch 3 out: sn rdn: wknd bef next* 12/1

2430 **5** *11* **Political Pendant**[14] 3728 10-10-0 84 oh8............................ RyanMania 67
(Rayson Nixon) *w ldr: led narrowly 6th: hdd after 4 out: wknd after 3 out* 18/1

-P14 **R** **Celian (FR)**[36] 3369 8-11-1 102... AlexMerriam(3) —
(Neil King) *led narrowly: hdd after mstke 6th: lost pl qckly and reminders after next: bhd whn mstke 9th: ref and uns rdr 4 out* 6/1

153/ **P** **Overlady**[674] 4863 9-11-4 105... HarryHaynes(3) —
(James Ewart) *trckd ldrs: wknd after 4 out: t.o whn p.u bef 2 out* 8/1

620F **P** **Ceasar's Return**[20] 3633 6-11-12 110.................................. BarryKeniry —
(George Moore) *hld up: qckly lost pl and rel to r after 9th: p.u bef 3 out* 8/1

0000 **P** **Why So Serious**[21] 3620 5-10-0 84 oh4............................... JanFaltejsek —
(Peter Salmon) *hld up: rdn and wknd after 4 out: t.o whn p.u bef 2 out* 66/1

7m 23.4s (31.40) **Going Correction** +1.25s/f (Heavy) 9 Ran SP% **113.0**
Speed ratings (Par 105): **105,104,104,101,98** —,—,—,—
toteswingers:1&2 £1.20, 2&3 £4.30, 1&3 £8.20 CSF £25.97 CT £68.89 TOTE £8.10: £2.70, £2.20, £1.40; EX 21.70.
Owner William McKeown & Malcolm Joyce **Bred** Seamus And Jan Kennedy **Trained** South Hazelrigg, Northumbria
■ Stewards' Enquiry : Wilson Renwick three-day ban: used whip with excessive frequency (Feb 22-24)

FOCUS
The runners finished extremely tired over this marathon trip. The first two both produced big steps up on their C&D form behind Midnight Diamond.

NOTEBOOK
Ontrack(IRE), second (albeit beaten 40l) in a C&D handicap off this mark last month, was headed at the second-last but fought back gamely after the last showing tremendous battling qualities to thwart the strong-travelling favourite French Ties on the run-in. The winner relishes a stamina test (won a point in heavy conditions) and his trainer thinks he is still improving with racing. He will go up in the weights for this, but could still be competitive on a soft surface. (op 7-1)
Oniz Tiptoes(IRE), 10lb below his last winning mark, raced wide in search of better ground and stayed on well to a be a closing second at the finish. He looks to be running into some form now. (tchd 5-1)
French Ties(IRE), clearly a quirky individual (ran out last time), again showed awkward tendancies in the cheekpieces when travelling all over the winner from three out, but found nothing for pressure. The jockey did everything right, delaying his challenge as late as possible, but he ran into determined rivals. He is one to be wary of backing at short prices. (tchd 3-1)
Matmata De Tendron(FR), who mixes hurdling with chasing and is a confirmed mudlark, was outpaced on the final circuit and stuck on only moderately rounding the home run. He is 3lb higher than his last winning hurdles mark, so may need some help from the assessor in this sphere. (op 10-1 tchd 9-1)
Political Pendant ran with credit from 8lb out of the handicap, but was ultimately well beaten in the home straight. (op 14-1)
Celian(FR), 7lb higher than when winning well in the mud at Uttoxeter in on New Year's Eve, refused at the tenth and looks held off this mark. (op 8-1)
Overlady had been absent for 674 days and looked in need of the run. (op 8-1)

3997 SEAN MAGEE FULL SET H'CAP CHASE (13 fncs) 2m 110y
3:55 (3:55) (Class 5) (0-90,89) 5-Y-0+ **£2,341** (£687; £343; £171)

Form RPR

536U **1** **Ice Image (IRE)**[28] 3503 9-11-3 87..............................(t) AlistairFindlay(7) 101+
(George Charlton) *w ldr: led narrowly appr last: hdd after mstke last: rallied to regain ld fnl 100yds* 5/1[2]

0P12 **2** *1 1/2* **Lerida**[21] 3618 9-11-6 83...(p) BrianHarding 92
(Sharon Watt) *mde most tl led narrowly appr last: sn regained ld: hdd fnl 100yds: no ex* 4/1[1]

333P **3** *15* **Ginger's Lad**[200] 1080 7-10-9 79..................................(p) JakeGreenall(7) 74
(Michael Easterby) *midfield: racd keenly: rdn after 3 out: sn no imp: wnt modest 3rd run-in* 13/2[3]

0261 **4** *3 1/2* **Authentic Act (IRE)**[14] 3727 7-11-6 83............................ JamesReveley 76
(Martin Todhunter) *hld up in rr: hdwy on outer to chse ldrs after 4 out: rdn after 3 out: wknd bef last: wnt 4th run-in* 13/2[3]

5P05 **5** *1 3/4* **Troodos Jet**[21] 3618 10-11-1 78... RyanMania 70
(Dianne Sayer) *trckd ldrs: rdn after 3 out: hld in dispute of 3rd whn bdly hmpd last* 14/1

-006 **6** *3* **Glengap (IRE)**[20] 3636 8-9-12 64...................................... HarryHaynes(3) 52
(Elliott Cooper) *hld up: rdn after 3 out: sn wknd* 8/1

5326 **P** **Pinewood Legend (IRE)**[14] 3727 9-11-12 89............(bt) WilsonRenwick —
(Peter Niven) *in tch on outer: nt fluent 9th: wknd after 4 out: t.o whn p.u bef last* 11/1

P/00 **U** **Flighty Mist**[79] 2547 9-10-8 78.. PaulGallagher(7) —
(Sandy Forster) *hld up: mstke and uns rdr 4th* 40/1

FFF3 **F** **Gavroche Gaugain (FR)**[14] 3730 7-11-12 89....................... GrahamLee 92
(Ferdy Murphy) *trckd ldrs on inner: hit 2nd: rdn bef 2 out: 4 l down in 3rd whn fell last* 4/1[1]

4m 27.0s (18.40) **Going Correction** +0.40s/f (Soft) 9 Ran SP% **111.9**
Speed ratings: **72,71,64,62,61 60**,—,—,—
toteswingers:1&2 £11.30, 2&3 £5.40, 1&3 £6.80 CSF £24.94 CT £128.28 TOTE £9.50: £2.90, £2.10, £2.90; EX 36.50.
Owner Sydney Ramsey & Partners **Bred** Patrick Hayes **Trained** Stocksfield, Northumberland

FOCUS
A competitive low-grade handicap chase which turned into a dual from two out. The winner was nicely in on his best form and was value for a bit further.

NOTEBOOK
Ice Image(IRE) survived a blunder at the last to register his first chase victory in 13 starts. His form had been moderate at best, but he seemed to appreciate the soft surface underfoot. This looks his grade. (op 8-1)
Lerida is a consistent sort and reliable jumper. He wasn't allowed to dominate from the front which he likes to do, but still put in a good performance, only being denied by a better handicapped rival who had a valuable 7lb conditional on board too. He will continue to pay his way for connections. (op 5-1)
Ginger's Lad was too keen to do himself justice. He did, however, find for pressure in the closing stages but needs to settle better. (op 7-1 tchd 6-1)
Authentic Act(IRE) fared well on his chasing debut considering he needs better ground to be seen at his best. (op 7-1 tchd 11-2)
Troodos Jet has been a little out of form lately and needs a stronger pace to feature than he got here. He is back on a winning mark though. (op 12-1)
Glengap(IRE), well backed in the morning, made headway three out but couldn't sustain his run over the final two fences. He has now been unplaced in all six chases and looks limited. (op 11-2)
Gavroche Gaugain(FR) has now fallen four out of five times over fences. He was booked for third at least before coming to grief at the last and it's back to jumping school for him. (op 10-3)

3998 DIGIBET.COM MAIDEN OPEN NATIONAL HUNT FLAT RACE 2m 1f
4:25 (4:25) (Class 6) 4-6-Y-O **£1,431** (£420; £210; £104)

Form RPR

1 **Turbolinas (FR)** 4-10-8 0.. RichieMcGrath 90+
(Kate Walton) *in tch on outer: trckd ldr over 3f out: led on bit over 1f out: rdn and rn green ins fnl f: hld on wl nr fin* 13/2

0 **2** *1 1/4* **Angel Sun (FR)**[14] 3731 5-11-4 0.. GrahamLee 98+
(Ferdy Murphy) *hld up: hdwy on outer over 6f out: chsd ldrs over 3f out: kpt on to go 2nd fnl 100yds* 14/1

3 *2 1/2* **Dome Run** 5-11-4 0.. BarryKeniry 94
(Alan Swinbank) *trckd ldrs: led 4f out: drvn whn hdd over 1f out: no ex and lost 2nd fnl 100yds* 11/4[1]

4 *4 1/2* **Whistle Me (IRE)** 5-11-4 0.. JamesReveley 90
(Chris Grant) *hld up: rdn and outpcd over 5f out: styd on wl fnl 2f: nrst fin* 7/2[3]

2 **5** *4 1/2* **Armedanddangerous (IRE)**[84] 2445 6-11-4 0............. DougieCostello 85
(Tom Gretton) *led: hdd 4f out: wknd over 2f out* 3/1[2]

6 *13* **No Way Hozay** 5-11-4 0...(t) BrianHughes 72
(Brian Storey) *hld up: rdn over 5f out: sn no imp* 40/1

0 **7** *4 1/2* **Pekan Two**[14] 3731 5-11-4 0... BrianHarding 68
(John Hellens) *hld up in tch: rdn over 3f out: wknd fnl 2f* 66/1

8 *1* **Viscount Victor (IRE)** 5-11-4 0...................................... TomScudamore 67
(Steve Gollings) *prom: rdn over 3f out: wknd qckly over 1f out* 5/1

0 **9** *55* **Port View (IRE)**[14] 3731 5-10-11 0............................ MrJohnDawson(7) 12
(John Wade) *trckd ldrs: rdn and wknd over 6f out: t.o* 100/1

4m 27.2s (25.90) **Going Correction** +1.25s/f (Heavy)
WFA 4 from 5yo+ 9lb 9 Ran SP% **115.5**
Speed ratings: **89,88,87,85,83 76,74,74,48**
toteswingers:1&2 £23.70, 2&3 £16.20, 1&3 £4.90 CSF £89.67 TOTE £15.20: £3.80, £4.90, £1.40; EX 118.80.
Owner Yarm Racing Partnership **Bred** Jean-Andre Quesny **Trained** Middleham Moor, N Yorks

FOCUS
A moderate bumper on paper. It was run in a slow time and was given a token rating through the fifth.

NOTEBOOK
Turbolinas(FR) travelled smoothly through the race and headed for the rail in the closing stages ,and although running about and jinking once in the lead, he was still a worthy winner. The age allowance for 4-y-os (10lb) looked to have made the difference. His trainer is now 2-2 with newcomers at this track over the past five seasons and he is related to the smart staying hurdler Mighty Man, so would be of obvious interest when sent hurdling over further in time. (tchd 15-2)
Angel Sun(FR) was a shade unlucky to be denied a passage up the rail on the run-in when staying on well, but this was much more promising than on his debut over C&D. He can win a bumper judged on this. (op 12-1 tchd 16-1)
Dome Run, from a yard who does well in this sphere, moved well into the lead at the halfway stage but was unable to stay on as strongly as the front two. He should improve for the experience. (op 3-1 tchd 9-4)
Whistle Me(IRE) stayed on again after being outpaced and should stay further over hurdles. (op 6-1)
Armedanddangerous(IRE) set the standard after his debut second at Folkestone but failed to improve sufficiently here, being a tad keen in the early stages. (op 4-1)
Viscount Victor(IRE) proved disappointing after being well-backed during the morning. (op 3-1)
T/Jkpt: Not won. T/Plt: £78.10 to a £1 stake. Pool of £84,238.32 - 787.20 winning tickets. T/Qpdt: £21.80 to a £1 stake. Pool of £6,960.25 - 235.46 winning tickets. AS

2269 CARLISLE (R-H)
Wednesday, February 9

OFFICIAL GOING: Heavy (4.5)
The first fence after the stands and the fifth-last were omitted.
Wind: moderate 1/2 against Weather: showers, damp

3999 LESLIE'S GARDEN CENTRE NOVICES' HURDLE (9 hdls) 2m 1f
1:35 (1:35) (Class 4) 4-Y-0+ **£2,226** (£649; £324)

Form RPR

2 **1** **High Ransom**[16] 3711 4-10-0 0.. BarryKeniry 99+
(Micky Hammond) *trckd ldrs: wnt 2nd 3 out: crowded run-in: styd on to ld last 75yds: gamely* 11/8[1]

-13P **2** *nk* **Bow Badger**[25] 3572 5-11-10 118.................................. WilsonRenwick 124+
(Howard Johnson) *led: t.k.h: wnt 5 l clr after 6th: hit 2 out: 1 l ahd whn blnd last: edgd rt and rdr lost whip: hdd and no ex last 75yds* 15/2[3]

3U41 **3** *20* **Si Bien (FR)**[21] 3632 6-11-0 112...................................... HarryHaynes(3) 96
(James Ewart) *chsd ldrs: wknd 3 out* 85/40[2]

/F-0 **4** *21* **Canal Cottage (IRE)**[89] 2349 7-11-3 0.......................... PeterBuchanan 73
(Lucinda Russell) *stdd s: hld up: hdwy into midfield 3rd: lost pl appr 3 out* 25/1

20U **5** *6* **Molon Labe (IRE)**[13] 3767 4-10-7 0.................................. JamesReveley 61
(Tom Tate) *hld up in rr: stdy hdwy 5th: trcking ldrs next: 4th and wkng whn mstke 3 out: bhd whn j. slowly last* 8/1

0 **6** *6* **Silent Snow (IRE)**[28] 3511 6-10-12 0.......................... JamesHalliday(5) 61
(Malcolm Jefferson) *mid-div: drvn along 3rd: lost pl and hit 6th: sn bhd* 100/1

4-P0 **7** *15* **Northern Flame (IRE)**[38] 3331 6-11-3 0............................ PaddyAspell 46
(N W Alexander) *in rr: drvn 3rd: bhd fr next: t.o 3 out* 40/1

0 **8** *9* **Cool Star (IRE)**[7] 3885 5-10-10 0............................ MrJARichardson(7) 37
(David Carr) *nt fluent and j.rt: chsd ldrs: hit 5th: lost pl and blnd next: sn bhd* 150/1

9 *5* **Odin's Raven (IRE)**[29] 6-11-3 0..................................... FearghalDavis 32
(Brian Ellison) *t.k.h: trckd ldrs: wknd 6th: sn bhd* 12/1

00 **10** *38* **Generals Love (IRE)**[40] 3259 5-11-3 0................................. AdrianLane —
(Donald McCain) *in rr: j.rt 2nd: drvn next: sn bhd: t.o 6th: virtually p.u* 100/1

0PP **11** *11* **Fred Grass**[77] 2612 5-11-0 0... JamesO'Farrell(3) —
(Jonathan Haynes) *in rr: bhd fr 5th: t.o 3 out: virtually p.u* 250/1

4m 41.9s (12.10) **Going Correction** +0.425s/f (Soft)
WFA 4 from 5yo+ 9lb 11 Ran SP% **114.0**
Speed ratings (Par 105): **88,87,78,68,65 62,55,51,49,31 26**
toteswingers:1&2:£3.10, 1&3:£1.80, 2&3:£4.80 CSF £12.07 TOTE £2.50: £1.10, £2.00, £1.10; EX 8.30.
Owner Mike And Eileen Newbould **Bred** Whatton Manor Stud **Trained** Middleham Moor, N Yorks

FOCUS
An uncompetitive contest, unlikely to provide many winners in the short-term. The pace looked fair for the conditions. The form could be 7lb out either way.
NOTEBOOK
High Ransom showed plenty of ability on her hurdling debut at Wetherby but was made to work very hard to land her first win under either code, despite getting 24lb from Bow Badger. She seemed to have ample opportunity to get past the runner-up earlier than she did, but it wasn't until the final stages that she forced her head in front. Still lightly raced, she should have more to come and may grow in confidence for the victory. (op 6-4 tchd 5-4)
Bow Badger, a C&D winner last October, was probably unlucky not to collect another success, as he had everything except for High Ransom beaten off coming to 2f out. However, he hit the last two before Wilson Renwick's whip came out of his hand after the final hurdle. That may have made the difference, considering how narrowly he was held off. (op 13-2 tchd 6-1)
Si Bien(FR) raced up with the leaders early but found nothing when he needed to quicken. (op 5-2 tchd 11-4)
Canal Cottage(IRE) kept on steadily and looks in need of much further. (op 18-1)
Molon Labe(IRE) made some ground up from the rear but looked very tired up the incline. (op 9-1)

4000 EUROPEAN BREEDERS' FUND MARES' "NATIONAL HUNT" NOVICES' HURDLE (11 hdls) 2m 4f
2:05 (2:05) (Class 4) 4-Y-0+ **£2,602** (£764; £382; £190)

Form RPR
034 **1** **Alexander Road (IRE)**[15] 3721 6-11-0 0 JasonMaguire 99+
(Donald McCain) *mde virtually all: hit 5th: styd on wl fr 3 out: drvn out: eased cl home* **11/4**[2]
50 **2** *7* **Lua De Itapoan**[55] 2987 6-11-0 0 GrahamLee 89
(Malcolm Jefferson) *hld up in rr: gd hdwy to chse ldrs 8th: wnt 2nd between last 2: styd on same pce* **18/1**
0 **3** *1 1/4* **Etoile Ardente**[29] 3498 7-10-7 0 NathanMoscrop(7) 88
(James Ewart) *hld up in rr: mstke 1st: hdwy 7th: wnt modest 3rd between last 2: one pce* **50/1**
0-06 **4** *13* **Hole In One (IRE)**[38] 3331 5-11-0 0 CampbellGillies 78
(Lucinda Russell) *trckd ldrs 4th: chsd wnr 3 out: wknd between last 2* **10/1**
6133 **5** *13* **Along Came Rosie**[29] 3498 7-10-13 107 PaulGallagher(7) 68
(Andrew Crook) *chsd ldrs: wknd between last 2* **6/4**[1]
0-66 **6** *1/2* **Lady Ida**[77] 2616 6-11-0 0 SamThomas 61
(Jennie Candlish) *hld up in rr: hdwy 6th: chsng ldrs appr 3 out: grad wknd* **10/1**
-03P **7** *11* **Allbarkanobite**[29] 3498 6-11-0 0 BrianHarding 50
(Kate Walton) *nt fluent in rr: sme hdwy appr 3 out: sn wknd: blnd 2 out* **16/1**
8 *12* **Swinside Silver**[633] 7-10-4 0 CallumWhillans(10) 38
(Donald Whillans) *w ldrs: wknd after 8th: bhd whn j.rt 2 out* **100/1**
9 *8* **Maid In Moscow (IRE)**[7] 3891 7-11-0 0 TomScudamore 30
(S R B Crawford, Ire) *trckd ldrs: wknd qckly appr 3 out* **7/1**[3]
P **10** *44* **Miss Galross (IRE)**[202] 1071 7-11-0 0 FearghalDavis —
(Nicky Richards) *in rr: bhd fr 8th: t.o next: virtually p.u* **50/1**
00 **P** **Mordetta Road**[29] 3504 6-11-0 0 PaddyAspell —
(James Turner) *mid-div: lost pl 7th: t.o 3 out: p.u bef next* **100/1**
P **Tipsy Nipper** 6-11-0 0 JamesReveley —
(William Amos) *racd wd: w ldrs 3rd: wknd rapidly 8th: t.o whn p.u bef next* **50/1**

5m 42.1s (19.30) **Going Correction** +0.425s/f (Soft) **12** Ran SP% **116.4**
Speed ratings (Par 105): **78,75,74,69,64 64,59,54,51,34** —,—
toteswingers:1&2:£6.20, 1&3:£14.60, 2&3:£34.90 CSF £46.74 TOTE £2.00: £1.10, £5.10, £22.90; EX 38.00.
Owner Brendan Richardson **Bred** J F C Maxwell **Trained** Cholmondeley, Cheshire
FOCUS
Hardly any of these made appeal on anything they had shown on the racecourse, so this is very weak form, although there could be more to come from the winner. The tempo didn't significantly rise until the 4f marker.
NOTEBOOK
Alexander Road(IRE), up in trip on her second try over hurdles, raced prominently and showed plenty of determination to gain victory. Lightly raced, she is open to more improvement. (op 2-1 tchd 3-1 in a place)
Lua De Itapoan was beaten quite a long way in two bumpers, so this looked better without being a really eyecatching performance. (op 22-1)
Etoile Ardente kept going reasonably well and shaped like she'll get further.
Hole In One(IRE), back over this distance, doesn't look totally devoid of ability, and can certainly do better with more time. (op 11-1 tchd 9-1)
Along Came Rosie set the standard off an official mark of 107 but was easily held and didn't seem to get home. (op 7-4)
Maid In Moscow(IRE) attracted significant market support but faded tamely once under pressure. (op 20-1)

4001 TEXAS LIVE IN CONCERT HERE 2ND JULY H'CAP CHASE (10 fncs 2 omitted) 2m
2:40 (2:40) (Class 4) (0-105,102) 5-Y-0+ **£2,602** (£764; £382; £190)

Form RPR
0-F2 **1** **Tartan Snow**[9] 3854 11-11-5 102 GaryRutherford(7) 121+
(Stuart Coltherd) *hld up in tch: jnd ldrs 5th: led 4 out: kpt on wl run-in* **13/2**
-004 **2** *3 1/2* **Euro American (GER)**[21] 3635 11-11-4 94 WilsonRenwick 107
(Rose Dobbin) *hld up: hdwy to chse ldrs 4 out: wnt 2nd appr last: kpt on same pce run-in* **7/1**
5-00 **3** *11* **Overbranch**[27] 3524 8-11-2 97 (b) JamesHalliday(5) 100
(Malcolm Jefferson) *prom: led 6th: hdd next: wknd run-in* **11/1**
00P6 **4** *7* **Norminster**[96] 2194 10-10-0 76 oh2 (p) RyanMania 71
(Rayson Nixon) *chsd ldrs: wknd appr 3 out* **14/1**
26P2 **5** *10* **Duke Of Malfi**[17] 3699 8-11-5 95 (p) PeterBuchanan 80
(Lucinda Russell) *led 3rd: hdd 6th: wknd 3 out* **9/2**[2]
6005 **6** *6* **Lindseyfield Lodge (IRE)**[15] 3728 10-11-3 93 (p) KennyJohnson 72
(Robert Johnson) *led to 3rd: lost pl after 6th: bhd whn hmpd 3 out* **40/1**
23-P **7** *18* **Shelomoh (IRE)**[29] 3501 10-11-11 101 PaddyAspell 62
(James Turner) *prom: lost pl after 6th: bhd whn hmpd 3 out* **13/2**
3-15 **8** *29* **Storm Surge (IRE)**[256] 516 8-11-10 100 JamesReveley 32
(Martin Todhunter) *stdd s: hld up in rr: wnt prom 5th: wknd next: hmpd 3 out: t.o whn blnd last* **6/1**[3]
3P25 **P** **Emotive**[26] 3549 8-11-9 99 CampbellGillies —
(Barry Murtagh) *prom: lost pl 4th: sn bhd: t.o whn p.u bef 4 out* **20/1**
/6P6 **F** **Banoge (IRE)**[37] 3361 9-11-7 97 GrahamLee —
(Rose Dobbin) *prom: drvn appr 4 out: 5th and wkng whn fell next* **4/1**[1]

4m 27.5s (11.40) **Going Correction** +0.85s/f (Soft) **10** Ran SP% **113.8**
Speed ratings: **105,103,97,94,89 86,77,62**,—,—
toteswingers:1&2:£8.70, 1&3:£15.20, 2&3:£21.80 CSF £50.51 CT £490.45 TOTE £8.70: £2.40, £3.10, £3.10; EX 45.50.
Owner Whitemoss Golf Syndicate **Bred** R V Westwood **Trained** Selkirk, Borders
FOCUS
The conditions thinned out the horses quite quickly as they came up the hill. The winner was very well in on his best hurdles form and the third sets the level.
NOTEBOOK
Tartan Snow, who had gone without a victory since May 2008, looked on a fair mark and, after jumping in a less-than-fluent style, finally got another win under his belt. He kept on well once in with every chance and did enough to hang on. (op 9-2)
Euro American(GER), back over fences after a few runs over hurdles, and with no win since 2007, moved nicely into contention but was unable to get on terms with Tartan Snow. All of his wins have come over 2m4f. (op 8-1)
Overbranch shaped well for a long time and looks like one to be interested next time, even though she has yet to win over fences. (tchd 10-1)
Norminster, off since early November, got outpaced before staying on again.
Duke Of Malfi looked to be in good heart but hadn't run well at this course in the past and didn't again. Official explanation: trainer had no explanation for the poor form shown (op 5-1)
Emotive Official explanation: jockey said gelding never travelled (op 11-2)
Banoge(IRE), a C&D winner in 2009 for another stable, was starting to weaken when falling three out. (op 11-2)

4002 WEATHERBYS BLOODSTOCK INSURANCE NOVICES' CHASE (10 fncs 2 omitted) 2m
3:10 (3:10) (Class 3) 5-Y-0+ **£5,204** (£1,528; £764; £381)

Form RPR
-011 **1** **Cadoudalas (FR)**[27] 3531 8-11-8 128 TomScudamore 140+
(Richard Lee) *led to 2nd: chsd ldr: hit 5th: led 3 out: drvn rt out: hld on towards fin* **10/11**[1]
2B-U **2** *nk* **Indian Groom (IRE)**[123] 1779 6-10-12 0 WilsonRenwick 130
(Howard Johnson) *trckd ldrs: mstke 1st: t.k.h: dropped bk 4th: hdwy to chse ldrs 3 out: wnt 2nd between last 2: styd on wl run-in: jst hld* **6/1**
1211 **3** *13* **Wind Shuffle (GER)**[37] 3359 8-11-4 136 GrahamLee 126
(Jim Goldie) *led 2nd: j.lft: hdd 3 out: wknd last* **9/2**[3]
2 **4** *52* **Cloonawillin Lady (IRE)**[21] 3632 8-9-12 0 StevenGagan(7) 73
(Elliott Cooper) *sn detached in last: t.o 3 out* **28/1**
12-1 **U** **King O'The Gypsies (IRE)**[92] 2300 6-10-12 0 RyanMania 120+
(Howard Johnson) *chsd ldrs: upsides whn blnd and uns rdr 3 out* **4/1**[2]

4m 27.3s (11.20) **Going Correction** +0.85s/f (Soft) **5** Ran SP% **108.3**
Speed ratings: **106,105,99,73**,—
CSF £6.53 TOTE £2.30: £1.40, £2.30; EX 8.10.
Owner Six To Five Against G D Thorp, R L Baker **Bred** Mme Evelyne Van Haaren **Trained** Byton, H'fords
■ Stewards' Enquiry : Wilson Renwick one-day ban: used whip in incorrect place (Feb 25)
FOCUS
A good race and a thrilling finish, and another step up from the progressive winner.
NOTEBOOK
Cadoudalas(FR) was heavily backed but made his supporters sweat before gaining victory. His jumping was less fluent than it had been at Hereford and he just held on from a staying-on rival. It is best to presume that he is far better than he showed here under top weight, and he may not have finished winning yet. The Arkle at Cheltenham next month is under consideration, but he'll need soft ground. (op 13-8)
Indian Groom(IRE) was dropped by the three that went clear but started to stay on when his stablemate departed three out. One couldn't be sure he was trying his best after the last, although it is also fair to say he may have been tired. (op 4-1)
Wind Shuffle(GER), the winner of his only other run over fences, went straight into the lead and took a bit of a grip. He led for quite a long time but started to jump left over the fences, giving away valuable ground. (op 3-1 tchd 5-1)
King O'The Gypsies(IRE), a 130-rated hurdler making his chasing debut, looked about to get to the front three out, seemingly going well, when taking off too early and unseating his rider. (op 9-2)

4003 PERTEMPS H'CAP HURDLE (SERIES QUALIFIER) (12 hdls) 3m 1f
3:45 (3:45) (Class 2) 5-Y-0+
£8,140 (£2,405; £1,202; £601; £300; £150)

Form RPR
P402 **1** **Knockara Beau (IRE)**[11] 3807 8-11-12 148 JanFaltejsek 153+
(George Charlton) *mde all: j.lft: hit last: edgd rt and styd on gamely run-in* **10/3**[1]
U630 **2** *1 1/4* **Heathcliff (IRE)**[25] 3566 9-10-5 127 (b) TomScudamore 129
(Richard Lee) *chsd wnr: wnt 2nd appr 3 out: 3 l down last: styd on and almost upsides 100yds out: no ex* **7/1**
4F-0 **3** *22* **Political Paddy**[102] 2094 9-10-0 122 oh6 (p) RyanMania 102
(Rayson Nixon) *prom: chsng ldrs 3 out: kpt on to take modest 3rd after next* **40/1**
11P- **4** *12* **Sa Suffit (FR)**[305] 5126 8-11-2 141 HarryHaynes(3) 111
(James Ewart) *trckd ldrs 6th: 5th and rdn whn hit 3 out: sn wknd* **13/2**
66-1 **5** *2* **Diklers Oscar (IRE)**[38] 3334 8-10-2 124 JamesReveley 90
(Keith Reveley) *hld up in rr: hdwy to trck ldrs 9th: effrt appr 2 out: sn wknd* **9/2**[2]
/2-P **6** *22* **Companero (IRE)**[25] 3568 11-11-1 137 WilsonRenwick 81
(Howard Johnson) *chsd ldrs: hit 6th and given reminders: lost pl next: sn bhd: t.o 3 out* **11/2**[3]
1001 **7** *13* **Thelobstercatcher**[13] 3771 7-10-5 130 (v) DonalDevereux(3) 61
(Peter Bowen) *chsd ldrs: lost pl 9th: sn bhd: eased run-in* **7/1**
-UF6 **P** **Mr Woods**[80] 2549 9-9-7 122 GaryRutherford(7) —
(Harriet Graham) *t.k.h in rr: drvn and lost pl after 8th: sn bhd: t.o whn p.u bef 2 out* **14/1**
634P **P** **Soft Spoken Guy (IRE)**[78] 2599 8-10-6 128 (t) MichaelMcAlister —
(Maurice Barnes) *prom: hit 2nd: drvn and in rr 6th: bhd 8th: sn t.o: p.u bef 2 out* **14/1**

6m 40.2s (2.00) **Going Correction** +0.425s/f (Soft) **9** Ran SP% **110.8**
Speed ratings: **113,112,105,101,101 94,89**,—,—
toteswingers:1&2:£3.10, 1&3:£29.30, 2&3:£25.60 CSF £25.31 CT £736.41 TOTE £5.20: £1.90, £2.70, £12.20; EX 20.60.
Owner W F Trueman **Bred** George Durrheim & Mrs Maria Mulcahy Durr **Trained** Stocksfield, Northumberland
■ Stewards' Enquiry : Jan Faltejsek three-day ban: used whip with excessive frequency without giving gelding time to respond (Feb 23-25)
Donal Devereux two-day ban: failed to ride gelding out for 6th (Feb 23-24)
FOCUS
This was by a really good race, which produced a quality weight-carrying performance from Knockara Beau. He produced a hurdles best, with the second to his mark and the pair clear.
NOTEBOOK
Knockara Beau(IRE) had a long rear view of Grands Crus at Cheltenham last time, but enhanced that horse's festival chances with a tough display. Allowed to lead, he showed plenty of guts under pressure to hold off the determined late challenge of the runner-up, giving away 21lb. He is being aimed at the final of this series. (op 7-2 tchd 3-1)

Heathcliff(IRE) ran a moody race at Warwick on his previous outing (visor on that day) but looked happier here, and kept on well up the hill. The return of blinkers may have brought about this better effort, as all his four wins have come when wearing them. (op 9-1)
Political Paddy, who had been off since October, but had cheekpieces back on, was beaten a long way. He is entitled to be straighter next time, however. (op 33-1)
Sa Suffit(FR), off since April last year, and having his first start over hurdles in Britain after running over fences since his move from France, only made a satisfactory return to action and will need to improve quite a lot to make a bigger impression next time. (op 6-1 tchd 7-1)
Diklers Oscar(IRE), raised 9lb for her win over hurdles last time, made good progress from the rear into a challenging position but faltered the second she came under pressure. (op 5-1)
Companero(IRE) needed pushing along early and was beaten before the race got serious. (op 6-1)
Thelobstercatcher, raised 9lb for winning easily at Warwick, didn't find the visor work for a second time, but hardly has the most consistent profile. (op 15-2 tchd 13-2)

4004 LLOYD MOTORS LAWN SUITES OPEN TODAY NOVICES' H'CAP CHASE (14 fncs 4 omitted) 3m 110y

4:20 (4:20) (Class 4) (0-115,115) 5-Y-O+ **£2,602** (£764; £382; £190)

Form RPR
1-00 **1** **Beamazed**[7] 3881 7-11-10 **113** .... BrianHarding 118+
(Malcolm Jefferson) *t.k.h: j. soundly: trckd ldrs: wnt 2nd 6th: upsides 2 out: led after 2 out: drvn out* **12/1**
01-4 **2** *2 ¾* **Master Eddy**[22] 3621 11-11-7 **110** .... DavidEngland 111
(Shaun Lycett) *in rr: drvn to chse ldrs 7th: chsd wnr appr last: kpt on same pce* **9/1**
0FP2 **3** *22* **Double Default (IRE)**[21] 3635 10-11-3 **106** .... (p) JamesReveley 86
(Martin Todhunter) *led: hdd after 2 out: sn wknd* **6/1**[3]
-021 **4** *½* **Aghill (IRE)**[14] 3748 7-10-10 **106** .... MarkQuinlan(7) 87
(Rose Dobbin) *chsd ldrs: hit 6th: wknd appr 3 out* **8/1**
-31P **P** **Do It For Dalkey**[21] 3636 9-10-3 **92** .... PeterBuchanan —
(Lucinda Russell) *in rr: reminders 4th: lost pl after 10th: wl bhd whn p.u bef 3 out* **7/2**[1]
4-3P **P** **On Gossamer Wings (IRE)**[27] 3522 7-10-0 **89** .... GrahamLee —
(Ferdy Murphy) *hld up in rr: swtchd outside and hdwy 9th: sn wknd: 5th whn blnd 3 out: p.u bef next* **9/2**[2]
P1-4 **P** **Whats Up Woody (IRE)**[32] 3435 6-11-12 **115** .... RyanMania —
(Howard Johnson) *chsd ldrs: 4th whn mstke 8th: wknd appr 4 out: t.o whn p.u bef 3 out* **9/2**[2]
5166 **P** **Bled (FR)**[21] 3633 6-11-2 **105** .... (b) JasonMaguire —
(Donald McCain) *chsd ldrs: hit 1st: lost pl 5th: prom 9th: wknd qckly: sn t.o: p.u bef 4 out* **11/1**

7m 0.90s (18.30) **Going Correction** +0.85s/f (Soft) **8 Ran SP% 110.0**
Speed ratings: **104,103,96,95,—** —,—,—
toteswingers:1&2:£26.00, 1&3:£8.20, 2&3:£8.00 CSF £101.24 CT £671.23 TOTE £12.40: £3.80, £4.00, £5.00; EX 106.40.
Owner T Pearcy **Bred** D L Pearcy **Trained** Norton, N Yorks

FOCUS
This was always going to be a war of attrition in these conditions, but plenty of credit has to go to Beamazed on his chasing debut. Weak form.

NOTEBOOK
Beamazed, the winner of a moderate 3m3f handicap hurdle at Sedgefield in 2009 for another trainer, travelled strongly throughout and still had enough left in had to keep going in the testing ground. This was a great start to his chasing career. (op 11-1 tchd 14-1)
Master Eddy needed a lot of pushing but stayed on well to get quite close to Beamazed. He does seem to reserve his best runs for Newbury in March, however. (op 15-2)
Double Default(IRE), with cheekpieces back on for his return to fences, set off to make all but was readily outpaced once joined. (op 8-1)
Aghill(IRE), raised 8lb for winning on his chasing debut at Musselburgh, got completely outpaced after four out and could never get back on terms. (op 11-2)
Do It For Dalkey, given a break after a disappointing effort at Newcastle, never got involved and was pulled up before three out. Official explanation: jockey said gelding had a breathing problem (op 6-1 tchd 13-2)
On Gossamer Wings(IRE), without any cheekpieces this time, was making his debut for Ferdy Murphy and moved ominously well until emptying quickly under pressure. (op 6-1 tchd 13-2)
Whats Up Woody(IRE) chased the leader, going well, but was hampered by some modest leaps when the pace increased. (op 6-1 tchd 13-2)

4005 ALEXANDRA BURKE LIVE 1ST AUGUST "JUNIOR" STANDARD OPEN NATIONAL HUNT FLAT RACE 1m 6f

4:50 (4:50) (Class 6) 4-Y-O **£1,267** (£369; £184)

Form RPR
1 **Julia Too** 4-10-5 0 .... CampbellGillies 87+
(William Amos) *swvd lft s: repeatedly bucked and rn green: hdwy to join ldrs after 4f: swtchd rt and led over 1f out: kpt on wl towards fin* **5/1**[3]
2 *½* **Irish Chaperone (IRE)** 4-10-12 0 .... JamesReveley 90
(Keith Reveley) *hld up wl in tch: drvn to chse ldrs over 2f out: nt clr run over 1f out: upsides jst ins fnl f: no ex* **2/1**[2]
3 *5* **Gogeo (IRE)** 4-10-12 0 .... BarryKeniry 84
(Alan Swinbank) *chsd ldr: led 3f out: hung lft: hdd over 1f out: wknd last 150yds* **15/8**[1]
3 **4** *2 ½* **Porridge**[37] 3364 4-10-5 0 .... MrGJCockburn(7) 81
(Lucinda Russell) *led: hdd 3f out: wknd over 1f out* **12/1**
0 **5** *36* **High Expectation**[29] 3504 4-10-0 0 .... JamesHalliday(5) 31
(James Ewart) *hld up: drvn 6f out: lost pl over 4f out: sn bhd: t.o* **20/1**
6 *½* **College Green** 4-10-12 0 .... WilsonRenwick 47
(Howard Johnson) *in rr: sn pushed along: hdwy 6f out: lost pl over 3f out: sn bhd: t.o* **8/1**
7 *52* **My Kinda Guy** 4-10-9 0 .... JamesO'Farrell(3) —
(Andrew Crook) *trckd ldrs: lost pl over 5f out: sn bhd: wl t.o* **50/1**
8 *6* **Thetasteofparadise** 4-10-5 0 .... TomScudamore —
(Bruce Hellier) *trckd ldrs: t.k.h: lost pl over 4f out: sn bhd: wl t.o* **33/1**

3m 59.2s (239.20) **8 Ran SP% 113.2**
toteswingers:1&2:£4.70, 1&3:£1.70, 2&3:£3.80 CSF £15.03 TOTE £5.50: £1.10, £1.30, £1.50; EX 14.00.
Owner J L Gledson **Bred** R D And Mrs J S Chugg **Trained** Broadhaugh, Scottish Borders

FOCUS
This didn't look a strong contest but it did produce a good battle between the front two. The fourth is the best guide to the level.

NOTEBOOK
Julia Too, a £6,000 purchase in 2010, emulated her dam by winning on her debut. She was slow to go and looked green at the start, but one couldn't fault her attitude when she was challenged in the final stages, running out a game winner. Hopefully, this run will settle her down and she can progress. (op 11-2)
Irish Chaperone(IRE), who was well backed, has plenty of size about her and kept on well to produce a pleasing debut, even after finding a bit of trouble in running. She seems sure to improve. (op 9-2)
Gogeo(IRE) looked to have possible stamina issues on breeding at this trip over a course as stiff as this, but he wasn't beaten far and can do better. (op 5-4 tchd 6-5)
Porridge, one of only two with previous experience, led for most of the contest but could only plug on at the one pace when joined and passed. (op 11-1)
T/Plt: £152.00 to a £1 stake. Pool:£59,147.47 - 283.95 winning tickets T/Qpdt: £41.40 to a £1 stake. Pool:£4,584.42 - 81.90 winning tickets WG

[2584] LUDLOW (R-H)

Wednesday, February 9

OFFICIAL GOING: Good (good to soft on golf club bend; chs 7.9, hdl 7.8)
Wind: Almost nil Weather: Overcast

4006 BROMFIELD "NATIONAL HUNT" MAIDEN HURDLE (9 hdls) 2m

1:45 (1:45) (Class 4) 4-Y-O+ **£2,602** (£764; £382; £190)

Form RPR
12 **1** **Kells Belle (IRE)**[37] 3366 5-10-10 0 .... APMcCoy 111+
(Nicky Henderson) *a.p: led narrowly appr 3 out: shkn up after last: drew away fnl 100yds: comf* **6/5**[1]
12 **2** *3* **The Cockney Mackem (IRE)**[29] 3495 5-11-3 0 .... PaddyBrennan 112+
(Nigel Twiston-Davies) *a.p: chalng and upsides fr 3 out: rdn after last: no ex fnl 100yds* **13/8**[2]
0-0P **3** *15* **Medicine Man (IRE)**[34] 3403 7-11-3 0 .... AidanColeman 96
(Ben De Haan) *led: hdd appr 3 out: styng on same pce whn j.rt 2 out: no dager to front pair after* **50/1**
4 **4** *¾* **Flowerdew (IRE)**[76] 2632 6-11-3 0 .... AndrewTinkler 96+
(Nicky Henderson) *plld hrd: midfield: hdwy 6th: trckd ldrs appr 3 out whn stl pulling: btn bef last* **12/1**
55 **5** *2 ½* **Lobby Ludd**[66] 2791 6-11-3 0 .... RichardJohnson 94
(Philip Hobbs) *prom: ev ch on outer appr 3 out: no ex fr 2 out* **15/2**[3]
000 **6** *10* **High Kite (IRE)**[37] 3365 5-11-3 0 .... HaddenFrost 84
(Henrietta Knight) *in tch: outpcd whn stmbld 3 out: plugged on at one pce but n.d after* **50/1**
3600 **7** *½* **Naughtyatiz (IRE)**[13] 3762 5-10-10 0 .... OliverDayman(7) 83
(Debra Hamer) *midfield: outpcd appr 3 out: styd on fr bef last: no imp on ldrs* **150/1**
005 **8** *1* **Practice Round (IRE)**[10] 3831 5-11-0 0 .... RichieMcLernon(3) 82
(Jonjo O'Neill) *midfield: outpcd 3 out: hung rt whn no imp 2 out* **100/1**
0/0 **9** *12* **Past Gambles (IRE)**[5] 3917 9-10-10 0 .... MrBJPoste(7) 70
(Bill Moore) *hld up in midfield: outpcd appr 3 out: nvr on terms w ldrs* **150/1**
600 **10** *2* **Tild'Or Du Granit (FR)**[13] 3767 4-9-7 0 .... RobertKirk(7) 51
(James Evans) *nt fluent a few times: a bhd* **150/1**
5300 **11** *¾* **Robello**[90] 2328 7-10-10 0 .... CharlieWallis(7) 67
(John O'Shea) *a bhd* **100/1**
0 **12** *5* **Singapore Storm (FR)**[18] 3673 4-10-7 0 .... DenisO'Regan 52
(Tom George) *a bhd* **100/1**
006- **13** *½* **Marvelous**[292] 5376 6-10-10 0 .... PaulMoloney 54
(Evan Williams) *hld up: hdwy into midfield after 6th: wknd 3 out* **66/1**
0 **14** *19* **Dennis Doyle (IRE)**[12] 3783 5-11-0 0 .... PeterToole(3) 42
(Tom George) *midfield: outpcd appr 3 out: wl btn after* **100/1**
05 **15** *23* **Onthelips (IRE)**[23] 3601 7-11-3 0 .... DaveCrosse 19
(Amy Weaver) *in tch: rdn and wknd after 6th* **150/1**

3m 48.5s (-1.00) **Going Correction** -0.375s/f (Good)
WFA 4 from 5yo+ 9lb **15 Ran SP% 115.0**
Speed ratings (Par 105): **87,85,78,77,76 71,71,70,64,63 63,60,60,51,39**
toteswingers:1&2:£1.20, 1&3:£13.60, 2&3:£23.40 CSF £3.14 TOTE £2.40: £1.10, £1.10, £7.20; EX 2.70.
Owner Brian,Gwen,Terri & Kelly Griffiths **Bred** Brian And Gwen Griffiths **Trained** Upper Lambourn, Berks

FOCUS
Rail movements meant that the hurdles track was at its shortest for some months, but the time was still over nine seconds outside the standard. The riders in the first described the ground as 'good'. This looked just an ordinary maiden hurdle, but it went to the useful Black Jack Blues a year ago and to smart pair Impek and Isio in the not too distant past. The first two drew well clear up the straight and are rated pretty much to their marks.

NOTEBOOK
Kells Belle(IRE) finally asserted, ultimately getting home in comfortable fashion. She jumped better than at Hereford, where she found one too strong on her hurdles debut, and has more to offer given a stiffer test at this trip or at a little further. (op 5-6 tchd 5-4)
The Cockney Mackem(IRE), also runner-up at Leicester, ran well on this much better ground and was alongside the winner over the last three flights before she pulled away from him in the final 100 yards. He'll appreciate further and his turn should come sooner rather than later. (op 2-1)
Medicine Man(IRE) again made the running and stuck on quite well to hold third. He looks the part and should progress from this. (op 40-1)
Flowerdew(IRE) took quite a hold on this hurdling debut and was still going well on the home turn, but could not quicken up when let down. This was a step up on what he showed in his bumper and he is well capable of winning a novice hurdle. (op 16-1)
Lobby Ludd ran a creditable race down in trip and is likely to strip fitter for this first start in two months. He is eligible for handicaps now and promises to do better in that sphere. (op 10-1 tchd 7-1)
High Kite(IRE) showed a little more than he had first time over obstacles.
Naughtyatiz(IRE) was staying on quite well past struggling rivals.
Onthelips(IRE) Official explanation: trainer said gelding bled from the nose

4007 DOWNTON BEGINNERS' CHASE (19 fncs) 3m

2:20 (2:20) (Class 4) 5-Y-O+ **£3,252** (£955; £477; £238)

Form RPR
4600 **1** **Maraafeq (USA)**[18] 3688 7-11-0 0 .... AidanColeman 123+
(Venetia Williams) *hld up: blnd 12th: hdwy 13th: pressed ldr 4 out: rdn to ld after 2 out: styd on and in command fnl 75yds* **9/4**[1]
336 **2** *2 ½* **Mexican Pete**[12] 3784 11-11-0 118 .... DaveCrosse 117
(Ian Williams) *chsd ldrs: wnt 2nd appr 12th: led bef 4 out: rdn and hdd after 2 out: no ex fnl 75yds* **5/2**[2]
0P/P **3** *17* **Platin Grounds (GER)**[26] 3543 9-11-0 0 .... PaddyBrennan 101
(Nigel Twiston-Davies) *prom: rdn appr 4 out and nt qckn: hung rt fr 2 out: one pce and lost tch w front pair after* **4/1**[3]
F630 **4** *1 ¼* **Gentleman Anshan (IRE)**[13] 3772 7-10-7 100 .... MissHannahWatson(7) 101
(Rosemary Gasson) *hld up: blnd 13th: cl up trcking ldrs appr 4 out: btn fr 2 out* **9/1**
0250 **5** *49* **Brimley**[10] 3837 8-10-11 80 .... (p) LeeStephens(3) 60
(Ann Price) *led: hdd 6th: wknd 12th: lost tch bef 15th: t.o* **22/1**
F **6** *44* **The Humbel Monk (IRE)**[13] 3761 9-10-11 0 .... PeterToole(3) 6
(Lucy Jones) *j.lft and mstkes: hld up: toiling after 11th (water): t.o* **33/1**

-000 **U** **Stripe Me Blue**[24] 3587 9-11-0 0 (b[1]) MarkGrant —
(Peter Jones) *prom: mstke 1st: led 6th: clr briefly bef 7th: clr again fr 11th (water) tl 12th: hdd and 2 l 3rd whn blnd and uns rdr 4 out* **6/1**

6m 1.60s (-6.70) **Going Correction** 0.0s/f (Good) **7** Ran SP% **110.9**
Speed ratings: **111,110,104,104,87 73,—**
toteswingers:1&2:£1.20, 1&3:£2.30, 2&3:£3.00 CSF £8.05 TOTE £3.10: £1.70, £1.60; EX 7.90.
Owner Taylor, Burrows, Johnstone, Brooks **Bred** Shadwell Farm LLC **Trained** Kings Caple, H'fords

FOCUS
The chase track was also tighter than usual, but not to the same extent as the hurdles course. A modest beginners' chase and not form to be confident about, but it makes sense on time.

NOTEBOOK
Maraafeq(USA) is a fair hurdler but had been a well beaten second on his one previous try over fences, at Towcester the best part of two years ago. He jumped poorly that day and was sketchy again here, jumping low at times and making a particularly bad blunder at the first in the back straight. Asserting between the final two fences, he had too much for the runner-up from there. This track suited him well. (tchd 11-4)
Mexican Pete had been running respectably and he had every chance on this drop in grade, but could not match the winner from the final fence. He saw out the 3m well enough. (op 85-40 tchd 11-4)
Platin Grounds(GER) ran reasonably well to a point on this second run back from a long absence, but came under pressure on the home turn and was held by the principals from there. He still has something to prove. (op 9-2 tchd 10-3)
Gentleman Anshan(IRE) recovered from a very bad mistake to turn for home on the heels of the leaders, but was unable to race on. He had a fair bit to find at these weights. (tchd 8-1 and 10-1)
Brimley, a course regular, was well held in the first-time cheekpieces. (op 40-1 tchd 20-1)
Stripe Me Blue, an early faller on his chasing debut over two years ago, raced prominently for a long way, but looked to be on the retreat when unshipping his rider at the first in the home straight. He had put in a couple of slow jumps in the early stages. (op 13-2)

4008 STANTON LACY (S) HURDLE (9 hdls) 2m
2:50 (2:50) (Class 5) 4-Y-O+ **£1,691** (£496; £248; £124)

Form				RPR
2500	**1**		**Mickmacmagoole (IRE)**[89] 2347 9-11-3 116 (p) PaulMoloney (Evan Williams) *sn prom: wnt 2nd appr 3 out where j.rt: rdn and wnt rt again 2 out: styd on to ld fnl 100yds* **3/1**[1]	111
415	**2**	2	**If I Had Him (IRE)**[18] 3686 7-11-7 109 (v) AndrewTinkler (George Baker) *led: rdn appr 2 out: wandered bef last: hdd fnl 100yds: hld cl home* **7/2**[2]	113
/1-0	**3**	12	**Cursum Perficio**[30] 3477 9-11-3 102 (tp) RichardJohnson (Richard Lee) *trckd ldrs: rdn appr 2 out: j.rt whn no ex last* **11/1**	98
5134	**4**	½	**I'm In The Pink (FR)**[11] 3818 7-11-10 114 (v) APMcCoy (David Evans) *in tch: effrt appr 3 out: kpt on same pce fr bef 2 out* **3/1**[1]	104
3P3P	**5**	5	**Smack That (IRE)**[32] 3438 9-11-3 0 (vt) WarrenMarston (Milton Harris) *hld up: hdwy after 6th: chsd ldrs 3 out: one pce fr 2 out* **12/1**	93
03-6	**6**	1 ¼	**Diddley Dee**[88] 2367 7-11-3 70 CharliePoste (Bill Moore) *in rr: kpt on fr 3 out: nt fluent 2 out: rdn after last: nvr nrr* **150/1**	90
1/6-	**7**	1 ¼	**Melvino**[331] 4648 9-10-12 106 MissIsabelTompsett(5) (John Price) *trckd ldrs tl rdn and wknd appr 3 out* **20/1**	89
	8	½	**Lord Deevert**[12] 6-10-12 0 TomO'Connor(5) (Bill Turner) *midfield: lost pl 6th: no imp after* **100/1**	89
0340	**9**	7	**Nicky Nutjob (GER)**[11] 3818 5-11-3 100 (p) DPFahy (John O'Shea) *midfield: hdwy 6th: no imp: wknd appr 3 out* **28/1**	84
0	**10**	24	**Warren Bank**[22] 3620 6-11-3 0 PaddyBrennan (Mary Hambro) *plld hrd: prom tl rdn and wknd appr 3 out* **66/1**	58
3P/P	**P**		**Wyeth**[5] 2169 7-10-12 115 (p) JoshuaMoore(5) (Gary Moore) *hld up: wnt wrong 6th: sn p.u: dismntd* **9/2**[3]	—
	P		**Jack Jicaro**[37] 5-10-10 0 MrBFurnival(7) (Nicky Vaughan) *plld hrd in midfield: wnt prom after 3rd: mstke 4th: lost pl after 5th: t.o whn p.u bef 3 out* **200/1**	—

3m 49.2s (-0.30) **Going Correction** -0.375s/f (Good)
WFA 4 from 5yo+ 9lb **12** Ran SP% **118.3**
Speed ratings (Par 103): **85,84,78,77,75 74,74,73,70,58 —,—**
toteswingers:1&2:£7.90, 1&3:£4.20, 2&3:£16.10 CSF £13.53 TOTE £6.40: £2.20, £2.20, £2.00; EX 18.40.There was no bid for the winner. If I Had Him was subject to a friendly claim.
Owner A Turton & P Langford **Bred** Tower Bloodstock **Trained** Llancarfan, Vale Of Glamorgan

FOCUS
A reasonable race of its type. The time was less than a second slower than the earlier maiden. The winner is rated 10lb off his best, with the second to his mark.

NOTEBOOK
Mickmacmagoole(IRE) is a useful sort in selling company and he was running in this grade for the first time since winning at Leicester in December 2009. Down in trip after contesting handicaps over further, he found sufficient for pressure to cut down the leader on the run-in. He no doubt has his problems, but could win again. (op 4-1)
If I Had Him(IRE) had many of his pursuers in trouble when kicking away on the home turn, but he wandered going into the last and could not hold off the winner on the flat. (op 10-3 tchd 4-1)
Cursum Perficio, on his second run back after an absence, ran well for a long way in the reapplied cheekpieces but the first two pulled away from him over the final two flights. (op 12-1 tchd 10-1)
I'm In The Pink(FR) performed respectably back in trip but lacked a change of pace. Easier ground may suit. (op 5-1)
Smack That(IRE) was 11lb clear on official figures on this big drop in class, having a rare outing over hurdles, but although he was keeping on he was never a serious threat. (op 11-1 tchd 10-1)
Diddley Dee made late progress and might be one for selling handicaps. (op 200-1)
Melvino ran a pleasing race on this first start since March. He is capable of winning a seller, but does need to settle better. (op 14-1 tchd 12-1)
Wyeth, a winner on the Flat at Lingfield recently, broke down in the back straight, sadly with fatal consequences. A similar fate befell his half-brother George Washington. (op 4-1 tchd 5-1)

4009 HENLEY HALL GOLD CUP (MARES' H'CAP HURDLE) (11 hdls) 2m 5f
3:25 (3:26) (Class 3) (0-125,123) 4-Y-0+ **£4,553** (£1,337; £668; £333)

Form				RPR
2630	**1**		**Ocean Transit (IRE)**[8] 3874 6-10-10 112 DavidBass(5) (Richard Price) *t.k.h: chsd ldrs: wnt 3rd and rdn 3 out: 2nd next: j. ahd last w ears pricked: sn forged clr* **16/1**	120+
5P52	**2**	3 ¾	**Ruthenoise (FR)**[4] 3945 6-11-5 116 AndrewTinkler (Nicky Henderson) *plld hrd: last tl 5th: smooth prog after 8th: led 3 out: rdn and hdd last: outstyd flat* **7/2**[1]	120+
2-F0	**3**	2	**Sawpit Solitaire**[40] 3260 6-10-7 104 AidanColeman (Venetia Williams) *chsd ldr 2nd tl lft in ld 3rd: hdd 5th: lost 2nd at 8th: last of four gng clr bef 3 out: sn outpcd: wnt rt last* **16/1**	107
6013	**4**	½	**Cloudy Spirit**[43] 3168 6-11-4 115 PaulMoloney (Reg Hollinshead) *trckd ldrs: wnt cl up 8th: led gng wl bef 3 out but sn hdd: lost 2nd 2 out: plugged on same pce* **15/2**[3]	117
-350	**5**	4 ½	**Laureate Des Loges (FR)**[43] 3155 7-10-11 108 RichardJohnson (Henry Daly) *hld up and bhd towards outer: pushed along and sme prog bef 3 out: nvr plcd to chal* **22/1**	106
-651	**6**	6	**Gilwen Glory (IRE)**[24] 3589 8-10-4 106 GilesHawkins(5) (Evan Williams) *bhd: rdn 7th: btn bef 3 out: plugged on past faders* **11/1**	99
3-10	**7**	nk	**Real Treasure**[24] 3587 7-11-9 120 SeanQuinlan (Kim Bailey) *midfield: effrt to press ldrs 8th: rdn and wknd wl bef 3 out* **11/1**	112
140-	**8**	¾	**Blue Nymph**[34] 4710 5-11-6 117 DougieCostello (John Quinn) *t.k.h: towards rr tl rdn and sme prog after 8th: 5th and btn bef 3 out* **18/1**	110
40-2	**9**	1 ¾	**Lady Bling Bling**[18] 3690 10-10-12 109 MarkGrant (Peter Jones) *midfield: wknd after 8th: wl btn 3 out* **10/1**	99
5314	**10**	8	**Princess Rainbow (FR)**[85] 2442 6-11-6 117 AlanO'Keeffe (Jennie Candlish) *led tl mstke and lost hind legs 3rd: led again after 5th: rdn and hdd bef 3 out: lost pl rapidly* **14/1**	108+
0204	**11**	4 ½	**Madame Jasmine**[17] 3693 6-10-0 97 ColinBolger (Suzy Smith) *pressed ldrs tl 5th: in rr after 7th: t.o 3 out* **10/1**	78
01F5	**12**	½	**Petit Fleur**[56] 2956 9-10-1 98 GerardTumelty (Julian Smith) *bhd: hdwy 5th: 2nd briefly at 8th: sn drvn and lost pl: t.o* **50/1**	76
31PP	**13**	4 ½	**Prescelli (IRE)**[18] 3690 7-10-13 115 (b) JoshuaMoore(5) (Keith Goldsworthy) *j. slowly: drvn along fr 2nd: last by 5th and nvr keen after: t.o* **50/1**	89
1-53	**14**	2 ½	**Bringewood Belle**[103] 2072 8-9-13 99 TommyPhelan(3) (John Needham) *prom tl rdn and fdd rapidly 8th: t.o next* **13/2**[2]	71
4P-1	**15**	17	**Gan On**[125] 1746 7-11-7 123 RachaelGreen(5) (Anthony Honeyball) *nvr bttr than midfield: wknd after 8th: mstkes 3 out and next: eased last: t.o* **8/1**	100

5m 3.20s (-11.60) **Going Correction** -0.375s/f (Good) **15** Ran SP% **125.2**
Speed ratings (Par 107): **107,105,104,104,102 100,100,100,99,96 94,94,92,91,85**
toteswingers:1&2:£9.10, 1&3:£33.80, 2&3:£14.50 CSF £74.08 CT £952.06 TOTE £22.10: £5.30, £1.90, £6.60; EX 179.90.
Owner Ocean's Five **Bred** Mike Channon Bloodstock Ltd **Trained** Ullingswick, H'fords

FOCUS
A competitive handicap confined to mares. It was run at a solid pace and in a decent time, and the form should stand up. A hurdles bsert from the winner, with the second 8lb off her Sandown run and the next pair to their marks.

NOTEBOOK
Ocean Transit(IRE) was taking a sizeable step up in trip and the cheekpieces were dispensed with. Staying on well to jump to the front at the last, she has reportedly undergone an operation on her vulva recently which helped her here. It will be interesting to see what the handicapper does with her now.
Ruthenoise(FR) was beaten only 13/4l by her stablemate Bincocular at Sandown on Saturday, and was put up 13lb for that. Racing off her old mark, she adopted very different tactics and was held up at the back, taking a keen hold, before scything through the field. She took a slight lead, but jumped out to her left up the straight and couldn't hold off the winner. The combination of a rise in trip and quick reappearance did for her here, and on this evidence she will struggle if she runs off her new rating. It may be that she is retired to the paddocks. (op 9-2 tchd 5-1)
Sawpit Solitaire was up with the pace throughout and stuck on well for third for her in-form yard. She remains a maiden and this effort is not going to earn her any respite from the handicapper (op 25-1)
Cloudy Spirit ran well back over hurdles after contesting a couple of jumpers' bumpers, looking a big threat on the home turn but unable to repel the challengers. (op 12-1 tchd 7-1)
Laureate Des Loges(FR) had ground and trip to suit and ran on well for fifth.
Gilwen Glory(IRE) gained last month's Ffos Las win over 3m in soft ground and she will be well suited by a return to those conditions judged on the way she was staying on. (op 14-1)

4010 ATTWOOD MEMORIAL TROPHY H'CAP CHASE (17 fncs) 2m 4f
4:00 (4:00) (Class 3) (0-130,127) 5-Y-O+ **£5,703** (£1,684; £842; £421; £210)

Form				RPR
/UP1	**1**		**Peplum (FR)**[21] 3628 8-11-8 123 JamieMoore (Gary Moore) *in tch: pushed along and nt qckn after 13th: clsd for press 3 out: r.o after last: got up to ld post* **8/1**	134
0430	**2**	hd	**Bible Lord (IRE)**[25] 3558 10-11-7 122 NickScholfield (Andy Turnell) *a.p: led 11th: rdn whn bmpd after 3 out: r.o for press run-in: hdd post* **4/1**[1]	133
4V-0	**3**	3	**Hector's Choice (FR)**[109] 1956 7-11-9 124 RichardJohnson (Richard Lee) *hld up: mstke 1st: hdwy 11th: sn chsd ldrs: chalng fr 4 out: stl ev ch last: nt qckn fnl 100yds* **9/1**	134+
-546	**4**	½	**Max Bygraves**[22] 3621 8-11-7 122 SeanQuinlan (Kim Bailey) *hld up: mstke 4 out: effrt and hdwy 3 out: hung rt fr 2 out: styd on towards fin: nt pce to get to ldrs* **12/1**	130
22F0	**5**	2 ¼	**Restezen D'Armor (FR)**[57] 2948 6-10-7 108 (b) FelixDeGiles (Charlie Longsdon) *hld up: hdwy to chse ldrs appr 4 out: rdn and styd on same pce fr 2 out* **9/2**[2]	113
P0-P	**6**	4 ½	**Qrackers (FR)**[18] 3689 7-11-12 127 (t) AidanColeman (Venetia Williams) *in tch: hit 2nd: outpcd briefly after 13th: chsd ldrs 4 out: one pce fr 2 out* **14/1**	129
-316	**7**	½	**Flemish Invader (IRE)**[76] 2629 8-11-1 116 PaddyBrennan (Nigel Twiston-Davies) *in tch: effrt whn chsng ldrs 4 out: outpcd 2 out: kpt on again towards fin* **15/2**[3]	116
6-5R	**8**	5	**The Snail**[25] 3558 8-11-9 124 PaulMoloney (Evan Williams) *led: hdd 11th: remained w ldr: rdn whn bmpd after 3 out: stl ev ch 2 out: wknd last* **14/1**	121+
0P65	**9**	35	**Tyup Pompey (IRE)**[10] 3841 10-10-3 107 LeeStephens(3) (Ann Price) *trckd ldrs: lost pl 11th: bhd bef 13th: t.o* **28/1**	82
2645	**P**		**Shadow Dancer (IRE)**[27] 3531 6-11-2 117 APMcCoy (Jonjo O'Neill) *hld up: nt fluent 8th: mstke 11th: t.o 13th: p.u bef 4 out* **4/1**[1]	—

5m 0.60s (-3.80) **Going Correction** 0.0s/f (Good) **10** Ran SP% **115.5**
Speed ratings: **107,106,105,105,104 102,102,100,86,—**
toteswingers:1&2:£12.40, 1&3:£22.30, 2&3:£9.80 CSF £40.83 CT £296.87 TOTE £11.50: £5.10, £1.90, £2.90; EX 32.90.
Owner Patrick Wilmott **Bred** Dr Vet Hubert Favre & Laurent Favre **Trained** Lower Beeding, W Sussex
■ Stewards' Enquiry : Jamie Moore two-day ban: used whip with excessive frequency (Feb 23-24)

FOCUS
An ordinary but competitive handicap chase in which no fewer than eight were in contention up the home straight. The form should prove solid, with the first two rated to their marks.

NOTEBOOK
Peplum(FR) was 9lb higher than when a surprise winner at Newbury recently. He was under pressure some way out, but stayed on well after the last to snatch it on the line, and could appreciate a return to a bit further. (op 7-1)
Bible Lord(IRE) was up with the pace throughout and fought off several challengers, only to be denied on the post. He jumped better than is often the case and has come down 21lb over the last 12 months. (op 13-2)

Hector's Choice(FR), off since the autumn, ran a big race on his chasing debut and went down fighting. The step up to 2m4f posed him no problems. (op 11-1)
Max Bygraves made a winning chase debut in September 2009 and was a stone higher for this first run over fences since. After a mistake at the first in the home straight, he was staying on without quite reaching the leaders. (op 11-1 tchd 14-1)
Restezen D'Armor(FR) ran creditably and is gradually building experience over fences. (op 5-1 tchd 7-2)
Qrackers(FR), with the tongue-tie back on, didn't run badly, although has yet to convince he wants this far. (op 10-1)
The Snail cut out some of the running and faded after taking a bump from the runner-up shortly after the third-last. (tchd 12-1)
Shadow Dancer(IRE), upped in trip, was never really going and eventually pulled up. Official explanation: jockey said gelding hung left-handed

4011 POINTTOPOINT.CO.UK HUNTERS' CHASE (19 fncs) 3m
4:30 (4:30) (Class 5) 6-Y-0+ **£1,873** (£581; £290; £145)

Form				RPR
/5-3	**1**		**Oca De Thaix (FR)**[249] 9-11-3 79 MissCharlotteEvans(7) (Keith Goldsworthy) *racd keenly: midfield: hdwy 16th: chal 2 out: stl 3rd at last: qcknd ahd flat w rdr doing little: on top fnl 50yds* **20/1**	114
33/1	**2**	*nse*	**The Cool Guy (IRE)**[280] 151 11-11-7 124 MrNPhillips(7) (Elliot Newman) *racd keenly: pressed ldr fr 2nd: rdn and ev ch 2 out tl nt qckn fr last: sltly impeded flat: fin 3rd: plcd 2nd* **3/1**[2]	119+
64-4	**3**	*¾*	**Ice Bucket (IRE)**[37] 11-11-7 108 (p) MrTWeston(3) (A Phillips) *j.w: led: rdn 2 out: kpt on gamely tl edgd sltly rt and hdd and nt qckn fnl 100yds: fin 2nd: disqualfied and plcd 3rd* **10/1**	113
5P/4	**4**	*17*	**The General Lee (IRE)**[3] 9-11-3 0 MissLBrooke(7) (Phillip Rowley) *detached in last pair tl 12th: kpt on past strugglers fr 3 out: nvr nr ldrs but tk poor 4th flat* **11/1**	96
U-	**5**	*1½*	**No Virtue**[17] 8-10-10 0 MrRJarrett(7) (S Flook) *settled towards rr: gd prog 12th: wnt prom 15th: disp 2nd 3 out: sn wknd fr next: modest 4th at last* **33/1**	88
13-2	**6**	*11*	**Herons Well**[256] 524 8-11-11 138 MrJoshHalley(7) (Rebecca Curtis) *prom: 5th whn nt fluent 16th: lost pl tamely next* **7/4**[1]	95
05-	**7**	*30*	**Orphelin Collonges (FR)**[292] 5361 9-11-5 81 MrMPrice(5) (Richard Price) *pressed ldrs tl 15th: sn dropped out: t.o* **50/1**	64
U/0-	**8**	*18*	**New Team (FR)**[341] 4424 10-11-3 97 MrJPark(7) (Mrs T Porter) *nvr bttr than midfield: flapped along and struggling fr 14th: t.o 16th* **50/1**	36
1-2F	**P**		**Lisadell King (IRE)**[257] 502 11-12-1 114 MrGMaundrell(3) (G C Maundrell) *t.k.h: nvr bttr than midfield: dropped bk last after 15th: t.o and p.u next* **9/2**[3]	—
006/	**P**		**Overbury Pearl**[282] 8-10-10 0 MrJHooper(7) (I J Hooper) *last pair and nvr gng wl: u.p 5th: mstke 8th: sn t.o: p.u 11th* **100/1**	—
0P06	**U**		**Gunnadoit (USA)**[126] 1727 6-11-3 0 (p) MrRHodges(7) (Ann Price) *midfield: dropped to rr 11th: rdn next: bmpd along and nt keen: 20 l 8th whn mstke and uns rdr 2 out* **80/1**	64
P3-P	**P**		**Dust In Time**[32] 6-11-10 0 (b1) MrBMoorcroft (Bill Turner) *chsd ldrs: mstke 6th: wnt prom 8th: rdn whn mstke 12th: blnd 13th: fading whn mstke 15th: nt keen: tailing off whn p.u 3 out* **20/1**	—

6m 6.30s (-2.00) **Going Correction** 0.0s/f (Good) **12** Ran SP% **115.6**
Speed ratings: **103,102,102,97,96 92,82,76,—,— —,—**
toteswingers:1&2:£12.40, 1&3:£22.30, 2&3:£9.80 CSF £77.64 TOTE £26.90: £3.70, £1.10, £2.20; EX 79.10.
Owner K Goldsworthy **Bred** Michel Bourgneuf **Trained** Yerbeston, Pembrokes
■ The first winner under rules for Charlotte Evans.
■ Stewards' Enquiry : Mr T Weston caution: careless riding.

FOCUS
An ordinary hunters' chase and a surprise result with several of the fancied contenders below par. The winner produced a massive step up.

NOTEBOOK
Oca De Thaix(FR) showed modest placed form in points and hunter chases back in the spring but this was his first run for the Goldsworthy yard. He had a bit to do turning into the straight, but quickened up well down the outer to show ahead after the last. He would not want the ground much softer than this. (tchd 18-1)
The Cool Guy(IRE), a winner at Cheltenham for another yard when last seen back in May, lost his pitch turning into the straight but rallied to have every chance. He was carried right by the second to cross the line on the run-in, though, and the placings were reversed by the stewards. Official explanation: vet said gelding finished lame right-fore (op 5-2 tchd 7-2)
Ice Bucket(IRE), formerly with Henrietta Knight, was well held on his pointing debut last month, but was sharper here and made a lot of the running. He only gave best on the flat and was demoted a place after drifting right on the run-in. (op 18-1)
The General Lee(IRE), who unseated this rider in a point on Sunday, was never really in it but made late headway for fourth. (op 9-1)
No Virtue is a decent pointer and is well capable of winning a minor hunter chase. This was only her second run under rules.
Herons Well was formerly a useful handicapper and he was 10lb clear on adjusted official figures. After racing keenly not far from the leaders, he faded up the home straight on this first start since the end of May. (op 85-40 tchd 9-4)
Lisadell King(IRE) was never a serious factor on this first start of the campaign and was out of touch when pulling up. (op 4-1)

4012 ONIBURY MAIDEN HURDLE (11 hdls) 2m 5f
5:00 (5:01) (Class 4) 4-Y-0+ **£2,602** (£764; £382; £190)

Form				RPR
3	**1**		**Sinbad The Sailor**[62] 1900 6-11-4 0 AndrewTinkler (George Baker) *midfield: hdwy bef 7th: led appr 3 out: mstke 2 out: drvn out and styd on run-in* **14/1**	121+
6	**2**	*5*	**Baan (USA)**[15] 3719 8-11-1 0 MichaelMurphy(3) (James Eustace) *hld up in rr: hdwy 8th: chsd ldrs appr 3 out: hit last: tk 2nd run-in: kpt on u.p but no imp on wnr* **50/1**	115
2233	**3**	*hd*	**Zakatal**[13] 3762 5-11-4 118 (bt) TomO'Brien (Philip Hobbs) *trckd ldrs: mstke 1st and 2nd: lost pl 8th: rallied to chal wnr 3 out: lost 2nd run-in: kpt on u.p but a hld after* **9/2**[2]	115
2-6	**4**	*11*	**Ardkilly Rebel (IRE)**[43] 3153 7-11-4 0 RichardJohnson (Philip Hobbs) *in tch: hmpd 2nd: prom 4th: led 7th: hdd appr 3 out: no ex fr 2 out* **13/2**	105
-122	**5**	*2½*	**Kasbadali (FR)**[93] 2281 6-11-4 0 LeightonAspell (Oliver Sherwood) *hld up in midfield: hmpd 3rd: rdn and outpcd after 8th: styd on steadily fr 3 out: no imp on ldrs* **5/1**[3]	102
	6	*16*	**Glendue** 6-11-4 0 FelixDeGiles (Nicky Henderson) *hld up: hdwy appr 8th: chsd ldrs bef 3 out: looked green whn wknd 2 out* **10/1**	91
30	**7**	*5*	**Living Proof (IRE)**[98] 2156 6-10-11 0 SamJones (Norma Twomey) *plld hrd: cl up early: midfield after: j. slowly 8th: sn wknd* **100/1**	79
0-53	**8**	*10*	**William Percival (IRE)**[79] 2590 5-10-11 0 JakeGreenall(7) (Henry Daly) *in tch: lost pl after 8th: struggling and n.d after* **40/1**	74
5	**9**	*3½*	**Viking Visitor (IRE)**[43] 3153 6-11-4 0 APMcCoy (Jonjo O'Neill) *led: hdd after 2nd: remained prom: rdn and wknd appr 3 out: wl btn whn blnd last* **5/2**[1]	83+
0204	**10**	*1*	**Tenby Jewel (IRE)**[18] 3691 6-11-4 0 JamieMoore (Keith Goldsworthy) *plld hrd: w ldr after 1st: led after 2nd: hdd 7th: wknd appr 3 out* **33/1**	70
1-	**11**	*30*	**Royal Riviera**[124] 2716 5-11-4 0 PaddyBrennan (Nigel Twiston-Davies) *trckd ldrs: j. bdly rt 3rd: lost pl bef 4th: j. slowly 7th: j. slowly 8th and lost tch: t.o* **10/1**	43
0	**12**	*22*	**Midnight Charmer**[90] 2328 5-11-4 0 NickScholfield (Emma Baker) *in rr: struggling 6th: sn t.o* **200/1**	23
0/P0	**P**		**Su Bleu (IRE)**[27] 3526 9-11-1 0 WarrenMarston(3) (Milton Harris) *bhd: t.o 6th: p.u bef 7th* **200/1**	—
3363	**U**		**Lexicon Lad (IRE)**[24] 3584 6-11-4 0 DenisO'Regan (Tom George) *midfield: bdly hmpd and uns rdr 3rd* **7/1**	—

5m 14.7s (-0.10) **Going Correction** -0.375s/f (Good) **14** Ran SP% **123.4**
Speed ratings (Par 105): **85,83,83,78,77 71,69,66,64,64 52,44,—,—**
toteswingers:1&2:£20.00, 1&3:£5.30, 2&3:£20.00. totesuper7: Win: Not won. Place: £482.30 CSF £552.19 TOTE £12.50: £2.80, £12.50, £2.40; EX 581.20.
Owner Sir Alex Ferguson **Bred** Sir Eric Parker **Trained** Whitsbury, Hants

FOCUS
Just a fair maiden hurdle. It was getting pretty dark by this stage of the afternoon and they took things quite steadily. The form is suspect but the first two were entitled to be as good as this on their Flat form.

NOTEBOOK
Sinbad The Sailor is a fair stayer on the Flat, and regularly visored on the level. Third at Plumpton on his hurdles debut in October, he appreciated the longer trip and saw it out well after moving to the front turning in. (op 9-1 tchd 16-1)
Baan(USA), Group-placed on the Flat in his younger days but only modest in that sphere now, showed a lot more than he had on his hurdles debut and is capable of winning an ordinary novice event. (op 40-1)
Zakatal is not straightforward and his jumping was untidy at times. He had his chance and has now been placed on all seven starts over hurdles without getting his head in front. (tchd 4-1)
Ardkilly Rebel(IRE) faded in the straight and has disappointed a couple of times since his second to Cannington Brook here a year ago. (op 8-1)
Kasbadali(FR), runner-up in two previous hurdles runs, was staying on without quite getting to grips with the leaders. (op 8-1)
Glendue, a half-brother to Champion Hurdle runner-up Marble Arch, shaped with a bit of promise and will come on for the experience. (op 17-2)
Living Proof(IRE), who has returned to her original trainer, might not be straightforward but does have ability.
Viking Visitor(IRE) was a useful bumper horse in Ireland but things have not gone according to plan in two starts over hurdles for these connections. Official explanation: vet said gelding finished lame left-hind (op 4-1 tchd 9-2)
T/Jkpt: Not won. T/Plt: £37.80 to a £1 stake. Pool:£61,493.10 - 1,185.91 winning tickets T/Qpdt: £16.70 to a £1 stake. Pool:£3,811.35 - 168.05 winning tickets DO

4013 - 4020a (Foreign Racing) - See Raceform Interactive

3739 HUNTINGDON (R-H)
Thursday, February 10

OFFICIAL GOING: Good changing to good to soft after race 3 (2.40)
Wind: light, across Weather: raining

4021 CAFFREYS AND CORBY H'CAP HURDLE (12 hdls) 3m 2f
1:40 (1:40) (Class 4) (0-110,110) 4-Y-0+ **£2,276** (£668; £334; £166)

Form				RPR
25-5	**1**		**Premier Des Marais (FR)**[15] 3744 8-11-9 **107** JamieMoore (Gary Moore) *hld up off the pce in rr: stdy prog 7th: mstke next: trckd ldr gng wl bef 3 out: led between last 2: clr whn mstke and wnt rt last: drvn and kpt on flat* **11/2**[2]	117+
P-F0	**2**	*8*	**Divy (FR)**[77] 2630 6-11-12 **110** AndrewTinkler (George Baker) *chsd ldrs tl led after 9th: rdn and jnd 2 out: hdd between last 2: swtchd lft last: kpt on same pce u.p flat* **8/1**[3]	114
-062	**3**	*7*	**Empire Builder (IRE)**[16] 3719 5-11-12 **110** AndrewThornton (Caroline Bailey) *mstkes: chsd ldrs: disp 2nd and rdn after 9th: wknd after next: hmpd and pushed rt last: wnt 3rd flat* **8/1**[3]	110+
1P40	**4**	*nse*	**Mtpockets (IRE)**[17] 3713 6-11-10 **108** (p) DougieCostello (Neil Mulholland) *racd wl off the pce in rr gp: reminders after 7th: modset 7th 8th: kpt on u.p fr 3 out: 5th whn hmpd and pushed rt last: pressing for 3rd nr fin: nvr trbld ldrs* **12/1**	107
305	**5**	*1¼*	**Bishophill Jack (IRE)**[33] 3448 5-11-7 **105** (t) JasonMaguire (Kim Bailey) *racd off the pce in midfield: rdn along after 7th: chsng ldrs 9th: wnt 3rd after 3 out: no imp and wl hld whn blnd bdly and wnt rt last: lost 2 pls flat* **3/1**[1]	104+
P400	**6**	*28*	**Knight Woodsman**[15] 3745 7-10-5 **92** AlexMerriam(3) (Neil King) *wl off the pce in rr: rdn and sme prog 8th: mstke next: nvr trbld ldrs: t.o* **14/1**	67
P306	**7**	*6*	**Petroupetrov (FR)**[17] 3713 8-10-13 **97** (v) TomSiddall (Richard Phillips) *racd off the pce in midfield: rdn along after 7th: no real hdwy: plugged on: nvr trbld ldrs: t.o* **25/1**	67
PPP4	**8**	*28*	**Raki Rose**[35] 3400 9-10-0 **84** oh20 (v) SamJones (Michael Scudamore) *chsd ldr: j.rt 2nd: clsd and upsides ldr 8th: rdn after 9th: wknd qckly u.p next: t.o* **100/1**	31
-4PU	**9**	*1½*	**Herald Angel (FR)**[15] 3741 8-10-13 **104** (t) MrTGarner(7) (Barry Brennan) *a in rr: rdn and lost tch 8th: t.o* **33/1**	50
	10	*26*	**Fairhaven (IRE)**[42] 3247 7-11-2 **100** (b1) FelixDeGiles (Charlie Longsdon) *racd keenly: led tl after 3 out: sn wknd: wl bhd 2 out: t.o* **12/1**	25
512-	**11**	*6*	**Sprosser (IRE)**[475] 1876 11-11-12 **110** LeightonAspell (Oliver Sherwood) *a towards rr: toiling after 7th: wl bhd fr 9th: t.o bef 3 out* **11/1**	31
/P-0	**12**	*28*	**Doctor Kilbride (IRE)**[81] 2558 8-10-6 **90** TomMessenger (Chris Bealby) *a bhd: lost tch 8th: wl t.o whn blnd 3 out* **17/2**	—
5P5-	**13**	*21*	**Toni Alcala**[468] 1997 12-10-6 **97** MrRichardCollinson(7) (Neil King) *a in rr: lost tch 8th: wl t.o after next* **100/1**	—
01/3	**P**		**Nabouko (FR)**[270] 359 10-11-4 **102** (b) SamThomas (Susan Nock) *racd off the pce in midfield: mstke 5th: struggling 8th: wl t.o whn p.u 3 out* **16/1**	—

6m 17.5s (-5.40) **Going Correction** -0.075s/f (Good) **14** Ran SP% **118.2**
Speed ratings (Par 105): **105,102,100,100,99 91,89,80,80,72 70,61,55,—**

CSF £47.57 CT £353.46 TOTE £5.90: £2.90, £2.50, £2.90; EX 69.40.
Owner Marais Racing **Bred** Jerome Geneve **Trained** Lower Beeding, W Sussex

FOCUS
The steady rain had started to get into the ground and it was reckoned to be 'on the dead side'. A modest stayers' handicap hurdle. The pace was quite strong and it proved quite a test in the deteriorating ground, and just four were in serious contention turning for home. The first two are rated close to their 2009 best.

NOTEBOOK
Premier Des Marais(FR) had shaped encouragingly on his comeback effort here two weeks earlier after 18 months on the sidelines. He travelled strongly off the pace until making stealthy headway setting out on to the final circuit. He quickly mastered the leader and ran out a convincing winner in the end, notching his first success for over three years. He is clearly right back to his best. (tchd 6-1)
Divy(FR), who looked a useful prospect when a dual bumper winner a couple of years ago, was running from a 5lb lower mark on his first start from his trainer's new base. He took it up before three out but it was soon very clear that the winner was merely waiting to strike. (op 9-1)
Empire Builder(IRE), a tall individual, was taking a step up in trip on his handicap bow. He couldn't match the first two once in line for home but showed a good attitude to snatch third spot. He will make a chaser in time. (op 13-2 tchd 6-1)
Mtpockets(IRE), a remote fifth on the run round to two out, was wearing first-time cheekpieces. All she looks to do is stay. (op 11-1)
Bishophill Jack(IRE), a winning pointer, was stepping up in trip on his handicap bow. Driven to keep in touch with a circuit to go, he was clinging on to third when he made a hash of the final flight. Some sort of headgear might help him travel better. (op 4-1)

4022 CLACTON COMRADES CARLING H'CAP CHASE (16 fncs) 2m 4f 110y
2:10 (2:10) (Class 4) (0-110,110) 5-Y-0+ **£2,602** (£764; £382; £190)

Form				RPR
00-0	1		**Midnight Appeal**[84] 2469 6-11-0 **98** RobertThornton (Alan King) *in tch and a gng wl: trckd ldr after 3 out: led last: edgd rt flat: kpt on: eased towards fin* **6/1**[2]	113+
5F2P	2	1 ¼	**Quel Bruere (FR)**[18] 3695 7-11-5 **106** (tp) TomMolloy(3) (Graeme McPherson) *chsd ldrs tl led 7th: rdn bef 2 out: hdd last: sn swtchd lft and edgd lft u.p flat: kpt on: a hld* **9/1**	117
3-00	3	4	**Mister Matt (IRE)**[57] 2961 8-11-9 **107** AndrewThornton (Bob Buckler) *t.k.h: in tch: chsd ldng pair and stl gng wl after 3 out: rdn and no ex between last 2: btn whn j.lft last* **20/1**	116
-500	4	16	**Willandrich (IRE)**[18] 3693 9-11-5 **106** MichaelMurphy(3) (Ian Williams) *in tch in midfield: outpcd 13th: 6th and u.p after 3 out: no ch w ldrs: plugged on to go modest 4th last* **8/1**[3]	101
034F	5	3 ¾	**Not So Sure Dick (IRE)**[16] 3723 6-11-1 **99** AndrewTinkler (George Baker) *t.k.h: hld up in rr: mstke 6th: hdwy into midfield after 9th: reminders after 13th: struggling 3 out: wl btn 2 out* **5/1**[1]	91
0311	6	5	**Silver Dollars (FR)**[27] 3541 10-11-3 **101** DarylJacob (David Arbuthnot) *in tch in rr of main gp: pushed along and losing tch 11th: no ch w ldrs after 3 out* **5/1**[1]	89
1-03	7	½	**Bennynthejets (IRE)**[82] 2529 9-11-5 **103** TomMessenger (Chris Bealby) *chsd ldr tl bttr jump to ld 3rd: hdd 7th: mstke 11th: 5th and wkng whn hit 13th: wknd next* **8/1**[3]	91
101F	8	18	**Manmoon (FR)**[24] 3608 8-10-12 **101** (t) MattGriffiths(5) (Nigel Hawke) *led tl j. slowly and hdd 3rd: chsd ldrs: wnt 2nd 7th: ev ch and hit 3 out: wknd u.p bef next: t.o* **11/1**	74
5-P0	9	4 ½	**Chaim (IRE)**[15] 3744 9-11-7 **105** LeightonAspell (Lucy Wadham) *hld up in tch: rdr lost iron briefly 4th: struggling 13th: wknd 3 out: wl bhd next* **10/1**	75
5-0P	10	10	**Cesium (FR)**[18] 3695 6-11-12 **110** (tp) DenisO'Regan (Tom George) *j.rt: dropped to last 3rd: pushed along and no rspnse after 8th: lost tch 13th: t.o whn blnd 2 out* **16/1**	72
/4FP	F		**Investment Affair (IRE)**[24] 3608 11-10-0 **87** CharlieHuxley(3) (Sarah Humphrey) *t.k.h: hld up in tch towards rr: rdn and struggling whn blnd and rdr lost iron briefly 13th: wl bhd whn fell 2 out* **25/1**	—
U216	P		**Carrig An Uisce (IRE)**[14] 3769 10-10-13 **100** (p) RichieMcLernon(3) (Anna Brooks) *in tch in midfield: j. slowly 2nd: slipped on landing and lost pl 11th: sn u.p and toiling: t.o whn p.u 2 out* **28/1**	—

5m 3.70s (-1.60) **Going Correction** +0.10s/f (Yiel) 12 Ran SP% **115.2**
Speed ratings: **107,106,105,98,97 95,95,88,86,83 —,—**
toteswingers:1&2 £13.70, 2&3 £31.90, 1&3 £23.60 CSF £55.83 CT £1011.83 TOTE £7.60: £2.40, £3.50, £5.80; EX 74.30.
Owner David Sewell **Bred** William Wilkinson **Trained** Barbury Castle, Wilts

FOCUS
Again the pace was sound and there were just three in serious contention turning for home. The winner should go on to rate higher still.

NOTEBOOK
Midnight Appeal from a family this trainer knows so well, made his chasing debut from his hurdle-race mark. He jumped soundly on the whole and, after taking command at the final fence, tended to idle on the run-in. Clearly fences have been the making of him and there should be a bit better to come. (op 17-2)
Quel Bruere(FR), running over his bare minimum, wore cheekpieces rather than a visor. Jumping better than on some occasions in the past, he was switched left after the last and to his credit kept going all the way to the line. He is by no means reliable. (op 14-1)
Mister Matt(IRE), from a stable struggling for winners, is a maiden under Rules after a dozen previous outings. He travelled really well but was held when jumping left-handed at the final fence. (op 16-1)
Willandrich(IRE), winner of six of his previous ten starts, five over hurdles, had won his only previous start in a chase four years earlier from a 24lb lower mark. He kept on without ever threatening to enter the argument. (op 10-1)
Not So Sure Dick(IRE), unexposed over fences, was another who never entered the argument, although he plodded on all the way to the line. Official explanation: jockey said the gelding has lost confidence since his fall last time (tchd 9-2)
Silver Dollars(FR), seeking a hat-trick from a 6lb higher mark in a more competitive event, struggled to keep up early on the final circuit. Official explanation: jockey said that the gelding was never travelling (op 4-1)

4023 RACING UK NOVICES' H'CAP CHASE (19 fncs) 3m
2:40 (2:40) (Class 3) (0-125,122) 5-Y-0+ **£4,553** (£1,337; £668; £333)

Form				RPR
-423	1		**Squadron**[31] 3479 7-11-12 **122** RobertThornton (Alan King) *chsd ldrs: wnt 2nd after 3 out: led bef last: racd idly: kpt on flat* **4/1**[2]	133+
-331	2	3 ¼	**Rear Gunner (IRE)**[26] 3562 9-11-11 **121** (p) AndrewThornton (Diana Grissell) *led: pckd 1st: j. slowly 2nd and 3rd: mstke 10th: rdn bef 2 out: hdd bef last: styd on same pce flat* **5/2**[1]	129
P6FP	3	¾	**Marc Of Brilliance (USA)**[31] 3482 8-10-11 **107** JamieMoore (Gary Moore) *hld up in tch in rr: stdy hdwy to chse ldrs 3 out: urged along and pressing ldrs last: chsd wnr: fnd little and styd on same pce flat: lost 2nd nr fin* **20/1**	111
2162	4	24	**The Ferbane Man (IRE)**[14] 3764 7-11-6 **116** (p) DougieCostello (Tim Vaughan) *pckd 2nd: chsd ldr tl after 3 out: wknd bef next: wl btn whn mstke 2 out* **5/1**[3]	105
P-24	5	18	**Sandynow (IRE)**[30] 3496 6-11-3 **113** SamThomas (Henry Daly) *in tch: j. slowly 4th: struggling and rdn whn blnd 13th: rallied briefly bef 3 out: wknd wl bef 2 out: wl btn whn j.lft 2 out: t.o* **16/1**	90
132	6	13	**Dunkelly Castle (IRE)**[33] 3450 7-11-6 **116** HaddenFrost (Roger Curtis) *in tch: mstke 7th: struggling after 9th: wl bhd whn mstke 3 out: t.o* **5/1**[3]	76
0-01	U		**Topsham Belle (IRE)**[30] 3496 7-11-8 **118** AndrewTinkler (Nicky Henderson) *in tch: pushed along after 2nd and nvr looked happy after: rdn 7th: in rr: stl in tch whn blnd bdly and uns rdr 9th* **7/1**	—
6030	P		**Ceepeegee (IRE)**[19] 3688 6-11-0 **110** (b[1]) JoeTizzard (Colin Tizzard) *in tch in last pair tl mstke and lost irons 8th: sn eased and p.u: tack problems* **10/1**	—

6m 8.50s (-1.80) **Going Correction** +0.10s/f (Yiel) 8 Ran SP% **114.1**
Speed ratings: **107,105,105,97,91 87,—,—**
toteswingers:1&2 £1.30, 2&3 £8.00, 1&3 £8.60 CSF £15.00 CT £174.03 TOTE £4.40: £2.10, £1.90, £3.60; EX 8.50.
Owner Tony Fisher & Mrs Jeni Fisher **Bred** Barry Root **Trained** Barbury Castle, Wilts

FOCUS
The rain continued to fall and the ground was belatedly changed to good to soft ahead of this novices' chase. Ordinary form, the first two in line with their previous best.

NOTEBOOK
Squadron, who had his setbacks last season, was having just his fourth start over fences and just his third after his summer break, from a mark of 122, 3lb below his hurdle-race mark. His jumping was better and, sent to the front at the last, he was always doing more than enough. The ground had come right for him and he should be capable of making further progress. (op 7-2)
Rear Gunner(IRE), 6lb higher than for his Kempton success, is a not a natural jumper but he had the right man aboard. Sticky early on and surviving a blunder at the final ditch four out, to his credit he came again on the run-in to snatch second spot. (op 3-1 tchd 10-3)
Marc Of Brilliance(USA), who has slipped to a lenient mark, crept his way into the race. He looked a real threat two out but in the end was worried out of second. The rain did not help his cause but he is clearly not easy to win with. (op 22-1)
The Ferbane Man(IRE), back over fences, was having just his second start in handicap company. His chance had long gone when he ploughed through the second-last. (op 9-2)
Sandynow(IRE), having his third start over fences from a mark 7lb below his hurdle-race mark, made far too many jumping errors. (op 14-1)
Topsham Belle(IRE), who did not have to be at her best to open her account over fences at Leicester at the second attempt, was soon being given some stern reminders and looked to be out of love with the game when giving her rider no chance at the second-last with a full circuit to go. It is back to the drawing board with her. (op 6-1 tchd 11-2)

4024 CORONA AND THREE JOLLY BUTCHERS CHATTERIS FEN JUVENILE HURDLE (8 hdls) 2m 110y
3:10 (3:11) (Class 2) 4-Y-O **£6,505** (£1,910; £955; £477)

Form				RPR
02F	1		**A Media Luz (FR)**[26] 3554 4-10-5 119 BarryGeraghty (Nicky Henderson) *a travelling wl: chsd ldr tl led sn after 3 out: sn clr and in command: hit last: eased flat* **8/15**[1]	133+
15	2	18	**Pantxoa (FR)**[61] 2882 4-11-6 129 RobertThornton (Alan King) *chsd ldng pair after 1st: rdn to chse wnr after 3 out: sn no prog and wl hld next* **9/2**[2]	122
2302	3	4 ½	**Two Kisses (IRE)**[19] 3673 4-10-13 123 SamThomas (Brendan Powell) *led: rdn along bef 3 out: hdd sn after 3 out: sn no ch w wnr: 3rd and wl hld fr next* **9/2**[2]	111
P	4	39	**Thundering Home**[7] 1135 4-10-12 0 JamieMoore (Michael Attwater) *sn bhd in last pair: dived 4th: lost tch next: wl t.o whn mstke 3 out* **66/1**	80
	5	32	**Seven Summits (IRE)**[110] 4-10-12 0 DenisO'Regan (Barney Curley) *a bhd: last and lost tch after 4th: sn wl t.o* **16/1**[3]	46

3m 51.3s (-3.60) **Going Correction** -0.075s/f (Good) 5 Ran SP% **109.0**
Speed ratings: **105,96,94,76,61**
CSF £3.39 TOTE £1.80: £1.10, £1.70; EX 2.90.
Owner Mr & Mrs R Kelvin Hughes **Bred** Dr Roger-Yves Simon & Dr Nathalie Simon **Trained** Upper Lambourn, Berks

FOCUS
This juvenile hurdle has thrown up the Triumph Hurdle winner in the past. Facile winner A Media Luz has place claims in that race now.

NOTEBOOK
A Media Luz(FR), a high-class Flat performer in France, has taken time to learn to settle but, with the help of ear plugs, had the race at her mercy when coming to grief two out at Kempton. She travelled strongly in pursuit of the leader here and, after taking charge, cruised clear. Her jumping was sound despite a minor error at the final flight and she handed out wide-margin defeats to the placed horses who, respectively on official ratings, had just 5lb and 4lb to find with her at the weights. With the benefit of the 7lb fillies' allowance she would clearly a big player in the Triumph, but she was no match for Grandouet at Newbury in December on her second try and, provided the handicapper does not go wild, the Fred Winter may be her preferred option. (tchd 1-2 and 4-7, 8-13 in places)
Pantxoa(FR), winner of his first two starts, wouldn't settle when well beaten behind Sam Winner at Cheltenham. He was much calmer this time with earplugs fitted, but attempting to concede the winner 15lb proved too much. The Fred Winter looks his best option at Cheltenham. (op 5-1)
Two Kisses(IRE), rated just 57 on the Flat, is a dual and experienced winner over hurdles. She was runner-up to Grandouet at Ascot, beaten six lengths, but she was much further behind A Media Luz here. That could prove misleading, though. (tchd 4-1 and 5-1)
Thundering Home, another rated 57 on the level, had been pulled up on his first try over hurdles and this will at least have done his confidence some good. (op 80-1)
Seven Summits(IRE), rated 90 on the Flat, has a lot to learn about jumping and was soon out of touch with the first three. (tchd 14-1 and 18-1)

4025 TURFTV H'CAP HURDLE (10 hdls) 2m 4f 110y
3:40 (3:40) (Class 4) (0-115,115) 4-Y-0+ **£2,602** (£764; £382; £190)

Form				RPR
-435	1		**Tricky Tree (IRE)**[18] 3693 5-10-13 **105** CPGeoghegan(3) (Pam Sly) *chsd ldrs: wnt 3rd after 6th: led gng wl after 3 out: clr and in command next: easily* **8/1**	118+
00-0	2	10	**Chilli Rose**[42] 3227 6-11-9 **112** RobertThornton (Alan King) *in tch: chsd ldrs and pushed along bef 3 out: chsd clr wnr 2 out: no imp* **17/2**	113
4026	3	8	**Knight Legend (IRE)**[30] 3493 12-11-0 **110** (t) MrMEnnis(7) (Sarah Humphrey) *in tch: hdwy to chse ldrs after 6th: outpcd bef 3 out: no ch w wnr: rallied fr 2 out: 3rd last: kpt on* **50/1**	104
2/03	4	3	**Burnt Oak (UAE)**[29] 3509 9-11-12 **115** BarryKeniry (Chris Fairhurst) *in tch towards rr: reminder and effrt 7th: chsd ldrs and mstke next: rdn and btn bef 2 out* **4/1**[1]	108

414 **5** *8* **Lastroseofsummer (IRE)**[40] 3308 5-10-9 **105**.............. MrJMQuinlan(7) 89
(Rae Guest) *hld up in tch in rr: hdwy after 5th: chsd ldrs 7th: rdn and wknd next: 6th and wl btn 2 out* **5/1**[2]

1P66 **6** *nse* **Just The Job (IRE)**[13] 3793 7-10-7 **103**.......................... MarkQuinlan(7) 87
(Neil Mulholland) *hld up in midfield: n.m.r and dropped in rr bnd after 5th: mstke and struggling next: styd on steadily past btn horses fr 3 out: nvr trbld ldrs* **14/1**

0-50 **7** *shd* **Haarth Sovereign (IRE)**[19] 3686 7-11-0 **108**..................(t) DavidBass(5) 94
(Lawney Hill) *led: hdd after 3 out: sn outpcd by wnr: lost 2nd and blnd 2 out: wknd qckly between last 2* **16/1**

1304 **8** *3 1/4* **Ban Uisce (IRE)**[13] 3791 6-11-1 **104**................................ DougieCostello 85
(Neil Mulholland) *hld up in tch in rr: pushed along and lost tch 6th: sme prog 3 out: nvr trbld ldrs* **13/2**[3]

20-U **9** *1* **Daraz Rose (IRE)**[31] 3483 10-10-13 **105**..................(t) MichaelMurphy(3) 85
(Barry Brennan) *in tch towards rr: rdn along after 5th: struggling next: wl btn bef 3 out* **50/1**

0330 **10** *3* **Superius (IRE)**[42] 3228 6-11-2 **105**................................(tp) SamThomas 82
(Emma Lavelle) *w ldr: ev ch and rdn after 7th: wknd rapidly sn after 3 out* **16/1**

2240 **11** *11* **Talenti (IRE)**[15] 3744 8-11-2 **105**...(t) FelixDeGiles 72
(Charlie Longsdon) *mstkes: towards rr: hdwy to chse ldrs 5th: u.p next: drvn and wknd wl bef 3 out: t.o* **9/1**

-100 **12** *22* **Crazy Bold (GER)**[22] 2626 8-10-6 **100**............................ LeeEdwards(5) 48
(Tony Carroll) *t.k.h: hld up wl in tch: wknd qckly after 7th: wl bhd after next: t.o* **11/1**

F00/ **13** *38* **Kavaloti (IRE)**[13] 4019 7-10-5 **94**......................................(b) JamieMoore 7
(Gary Moore) *nt fluent: a in rr: pushed along and no rspnse after 5th: lost tch next: wl t.o bef 3 out* **33/1**

63/P **14** *9* **Special Day (FR)**[88] 2393 7-11-4 **107**............................. LeightonAspell 12
(Lucy Wadham) *t.k.h: w ldrs tl 6th: losing pl qckly whn mstke next: blnd 3 out: wl t.o bef next* **16/1**

4m 55.8s (-3.20) **Going Correction** -0.075s/f (Good) **14** Ran SP% **121.1**
Speed ratings (Par 105): **103,99,96,95,91 91,91,90,90,89 84,76,62,58**
toteswingers:1&2 £18.30, 2&3 £61.10, 1&3 £61.10 CSF £74.63 CT £3186.88 TOTE £9.30: £2.90, £2.40, £11.50; EX 114.50.
Owner Mrs V M Edmonson **Bred** Murry Rose Bloodstock **Trained** Thorney, Cambs

FOCUS
There were half a dozen still in with a shout turning for home but in the end there was an easy winner and the first two finished clear. The form looks believable, rated through the second.

NOTEBOOK
Tricky Tree(IRE), seemingly an exposed maiden over hurdles after six previous attempts, went round in cruise control and, under his excellent claiming rider, came clear to score with plenty in hand. The soft ground presumably accounted for this vastly improved effort. (op 17-2)
Chilli Rose, a useful bumper mare, had yet to show her true colours over hurdles. She went in pursuit of the winner and, although no match, proved easily second best. With her stable in top form she should soon go one better. (op 9-1 tchd 10-1)
Knight Legend(IRE), once rated two stone higher, had been well beaten in two sellers for this yard last month. This marked something of a revival. (op 40-1)
Burnt Oak(UAE), back to form when third at Doncaster, was struggling to keep up when making a mistake two out. The rain did not aid his cause. (op 7-2)
Lastroseofsummer(IRE), a remarkable winner on her second start at Musselburgh, is another who was not suited by the fast easing ground. (op 13-2)
Haarth Sovereign(IRE) jumped boldly in front but was clinging on to third when getting the second-last all wrong. Two miles on better ground should see this 76-rated Flat performer in a more favourable light.

4026 HUNTINGDON AUDI A7 OPEN HUNTERS' CHASE (19 fncs) 3m
4:10 (4:13) (Class 6) 5-Y-0+ **£749** (£232; £116; £58)

Form RPR

0U2/ **1** **Cork All Star (IRE)**[11] 9-11-9 0...................................... MrJMQuinlan(3) 121+
(Mrs J Quinlan) *a travelling wl: trckd ldrs fr 4th: jnd ldr and drew clr 15th: led on bit after 3 out: gng clr whn slt mstke next: v easily* **8/11**[1]

30P- **2** *3 1/2* **Mount Benger**[18] 11-11-13 0.. MrSKeating(7) 116
(H Whittington) *racd in midfield: rdn along fr 10th: chsd clr wnr jst bef 2 out: no imp whn edgd rt between last 2: kpt on* **12/1**

PP4/ **3** *19* **Aztec Warrior (IRE)**[25] 10-11-5 0..................... MrGeorgeHenderson(7) 91
(Mrs Antonia Bealby) *chsd ldrs: mstke 2nd: lost pl and dropped to last next: detached fr 4th: nvr trbld ldrs after: lft 4th last: sn wnt modest 3rd* **15/2**

33-P **4** *22* **Star Double (ITY)**[11] 11-11-9 0................................ MrMatthewSmith(3) 71
(Mrs Fleur Hawes) *racd keenly: led: clr w wnr 15th: hdd after 3 out: 4th and wkng whn mstke 2 out: lft 3rd last: sn dropped to 4th again: tired flat* **16/1**

5P5- **P** **Mandingo Chief (IRE)**[33] 12-11-13 95........................(v) MissCLWills(7) —
(Miss C L Wills) *w ldr tl mstke and dropped to 4th 12th: struggling next: wl bhd whn mstke 16th: t.o whn p.u 2 out* **66/1**

PPP- **R** **Preacher Boy**[18] 12-11-5 0.. MrPPrince(7) 97
(Mrs A S Hodges) *dropped in rr after 3rd: mstke 7th: rallied 12th: wnt 3rd 2 out: keeping on but no ch w wnr whn rn out and uns rdr last* **7/1**[3]

055- **P** **Gripit N Tipit (IRE)**[377] 3731 10-11-5 123.............................(b[1]) MrMEnnis(7) —
(Sarah Humphrey) *t.k.h: chsd ldrs: wnt 2nd 12th tl 13th: 3rd and struggling next: 5th and wl btn whn eased and p.u after 3 out* **9/2**[2]

6m 18.2s (7.90) **Going Correction** +0.10s/f (Yiel) **7** Ran SP% **115.4**
Speed ratings: **90,88,82,75,— —,—**
toteswingers:1&2 £2.70, 2&3 £13.80, 1&3 £1.40 CSF £10.98 TOTE £1.90: £1.10, £2.80; EX 4.60.
Owner Cillian S Ryan **Bred** Cathal M Ryan **Trained** Newmarket, Suffolk

FOCUS
All eyes were on the favourite Cork All Star, who was value for further and should go on to rate a lot higher in this sphere.

NOTEBOOK
Cork All Star(IRE), winner of the 2007 Champion Bumper and runner-up the following year in a Grade 1 Hurdle, was back in action after a two-year break and came here on the back of two easy victories in points. He jumped accurately on the whole and made this look very simple. He is not that big but very athletic and connections have their eye on the hunter chase at Punchestown. The opposition will be much tougher but he is sure to take plenty of beating. (op 8-13 tchd 10-11)
Mount Benger, who last won under Rules two years ago, came into this on the back of three placed efforts in points. He stuck on to finish clear second-best but was no match for the winner. Nevertheless, he deserves credit for this gritty effort. (op 9-1 tchd 8-1)
Aztec Warrior(IRE), a moody individual, sulked and was soon well in arrears before being handed a distant third at the last. (op 11-1 tchd 12-1)
Star Double(ITY), leading the pack when carried out by a loose horse in the point won by Cork All Star at Higham, again set the pace but was fourth and legless when blundering two out. (op 25-1 tchd 28-1)
Preacher Boy, third in the 2006 Hennessy Gold Cup, struggled to keep up but had worked his way into a modest third when taking it into his head to run out through the wing at the final fence, giving his rider an ugly looking fall. (op 10-1)

4027 EBF/DBS MARES' STANDARD OPEN NATIONAL HUNT FLAT RACE (QUALIFIER) 2m 110y
4:40 (4:43) (Class 5) 4-7-Y-0 **£1,794** (£523; £261)

Form RPR

1 **1** **Baby Shine (IRE)**[23] 3623 5-11-9 0................................. LeightonAspell 113+
(Lucy Wadham) *led main gp: clsd and led 1/2-way: rdn and asserted 2f out: edgd lft ins fnl f: r.o wl* **3/1**[2]

62 **2** *2 1/4* **Miss Milborne**[23] 3616 5-11-2 0.. JoeTizzard 103
(Colin Tizzard) *t.k.h: prom in main gp: clsd to chse ldrs 1/2-way: rdn and outpcd over 3f out: rallied over 1f out: chsd wnr and edgd lft ins fnl f: no imp after* **12/1**

3 **3** *3/4* **Tempest River (IRE)**[41] 3266 5-11-2 0................................. DarylJacob 102
(Ben Case) *in tch in main gp: clsd to chse ldrs 1/2-way: rdn and unable qck wl over 3f out: rallied and swtchd rt ins fnl f: kpt on* **10/1**[3]

2 **4** *2 1/2* **Zahirah Moon**[105] 2052 4-10-6 0................................... AndrewThornton 91
(Lady Herries) *got flying s and sn clr: c bk to field and hdd 1/2-way: styd w wnr tl unable qck 2f out: kpt on same pce and lost 2 pls whn sltly hmpd ins fnl f* **16/1**

5 *1/2* **Ballyquin Queen (IRE)** 5-10-11 0................................. MattGriffiths(5) 100+
(Philip Hobbs) *in tch in main gp: pushed along and dropped to rr 9f out: rallied 3f out: stl modest 8th over 2f out: wnt 5th 1f out and styd on strly ins fnl f* **16/1**

1 **6** *10* **Heather Royal**[271] 332 5-11-9 0.. BarryGeraghty 106+
(Nicky Henderson) *t.k.h early: hld up towards rr of main gp: clsd and in tch 1/2-way: chsd ldrs 6f out: btn wl over 2f out* **5/4**[1]

16 **7** *5* **Dream Performance (IRE)**[56] 2987 6-11-6 0................... PeterToole(3) 93
(G C Maundrell) *in tch in main gp on outer: clsd and chsd ldrs 1/2-way: wknd qckly over 2f out* **66/1**

8 *4 1/2* **Double Silver** 4-10-6 0.. JamesReveley 72
(Keith Reveley) *hld up in last trio: clsd 9f out: struggling and losing tch 7f out: modest late hdwy: n.d* **25/1**

9 *1 1/4* **Well Sprung (IRE)** 5-11-2 0... SamThomas 81
(Peter Winkworth) *handy in main gp: clsd and chsd ldrs 1/2-way: rdn and btn 4f out: wknd qckly wl over 2f out* **100/1**

1 **10** *1/2* **Genstone Trail**[44] 3159 5-11-9 0..................................... RobertThornton 87
(Alan King) *in tch in main gp: clsd to chse ldrs 1/2-way: rdn and btn over 3f out: wknd qckly 3f out: eased ins fnl f: t.o* **12/1**

11 *26* **I'm So Special (IRE)** 5-11-2 0.. WillKennedy 57
(Noel Chance) *a in rr: pushed along after 2f: lost tch 7f out: t.o* **50/1**

12 *2* **Finmerello** 5-11-2 0.. JasonMaguire 55
(Kim Bailey) *racd in midfield of main gp: awkward bnd 10f out: rdn and struggling 7f out: wl bhd fnl 4f* **28/1**

36 **13** *1 1/2* **Reveal The Light**[26] 3576 4-10-6 0................................... PaddyAspell 44
(Garry Woodward) *racd in last trio: struggling 7f out: no ch after: t.o* **100/1**

14 *5* **Persian Forest** 5-11-2 0.. GerardTumelty 49
(Alan King) *hld up towards rr: rdn and struggling 7f out: sn lost tch: t.o* **16/1**

3 **15** *1 1/4* **Looby Magoodle**[30] 3504 5-11-2 0....................................... BrianHughes 48
(Richard Fahey) *t.k.h: prom in main gp tl lost pl qckly 7f out: wl bhd fnl 5f: t.o* **80/1**

0 **16** *25* **Bushlark**[41] 3266 5-11-2 0... SamJones 26
(Renee Robeson) *chsd ldrs tl lost pl rapidly 1/2-way: t.o fnl 6f* **150/1**

3m 54.5s (5.40) **Going Correction** -0.075s/f (Good)
WFA 4 from 5yo+ 9lb **16** Ran SP% **126.2**
Speed ratings: **84,82,82,81,81 76,74,72,71,71 58,58,57,54,54 42**
toteswingers:1&2 £3.70, 2&3 £20.70, 1&3 £5.90 CSF £39.47 TOTE £3.30: £1.60, £3.80, £2.50; EX 48.40.
Owner P A Philipps,T S Redman & Mrs L Redman **Bred** Kevin Francis O'Donnell **Trained** Newmarket, Suffolk

FOCUS
A good class mares' bumper run at a sound pace, and half a dozen came clear on the final turn. Solid form for the grade.

NOTEBOOK
Baby Shine(IRE), winner of an Irish point and a Southwell bumper, completed the hat-trick in decisive fashion. No doubt she will put her unbeaten record on the line in the final of this series at Sandown next month. (tchd 11-4)
Miss Milborne, runner-up on her second start at Folkestone after her saddle slipped, improved on that effort and deserves to make it third time lucky. (op 11-1)
Tempest River(IRE), third in an open bumper at Warwick which has stood up well, is another to have seemingly turned in an improved effort. She too should be able to find a similar event. (op 20-1)
Zahirah Moon, who gave a minor problem at the start, got off to a flyer. She stuck to her guns when headed by the winner at the halfway mark and this was a big improvement on her second place first time up in a very ordinary event at Fontwell.
Ballyquin Queen(IRE), a modest seventh on the turn in, came home to real effect and will improve a good deal for this initial effort. (op 14-1)
Heather Royal, a half-sister by Medicean to Barbers Shop, had created a good impression when scoring on her debut at Bangor in May. Very keen to post, her trainer had voiced doubts about the rain-softened ground beforehand and she was under pressure and going nowhere before the final turn. She must be given another chance. (op 13-8)
Dream Performance(IRE), who took the bypass route, is another who was probably unsuited by the changed ground.
Double Silver, from a family that has done this yard proud over the years, showed ability on her debut, staying on in her own time after being given a very patient ride. (op 20-1)
T/Jkpt: Not won. T/Plt: £294.20 to a £1 stake. Pool of £72,243.99 - 179.24 winning tickets.
T/Qpdt: £16.30 to a £1 stake. Pool of £5,562.09 - 251.10 winning tickets. SP

3870 TAUNTON (R-H)
Thursday, February 10

OFFICIAL GOING: Good (good to soft in places) changing to soft after race 3 (3.00)
Wind: light across Weather: Overcast with steady rain until 3.00.

4028 ALPHA COMPANY 40 COMMANDO ROYAL MARINES CLAIMING HURDLE (9 hdls) 2m 1f
2:00 (2:00) (Class 5) 4-Y-0+ **£2,055** (£599; £299)

Form RPR

3P1 **1** **Chrysander**[31] 3477 9-11-6 116..(vt) PaulMoloney 115+
(Evan Williams) *led 2nd: sn clr: unchal after: rdn out* **11/10**[1]

0405 **2** *11* **Sweet World**[31] 3477 7-11-7 105 DPFahy 106
(Bernard Llewellyn) *hld up in last pair: hdwy fr 6th: wnt 3rd after 3 out: sn rdn: styd on same pce: wnt 2nd bef last: no ch w wnr* **15/2**[3]
2621 **3** *3 1/4* **Olivino (GER)**[6] 1569 10-11-1 115 MissIsabelTompsett(5) 103
(Bernard Llewellyn) *prom in chsng gp: clsd on ldrs 5th: rdn to chse wnr after 3 out: a being comf hld: lost 2nd bef last* **4/1**[2]
/3-0 **4** *19* **Reymysterio (IRE)**[9] 3871 10-11-0 0 KeiranBurke(5) 84
(Patrick Rodford) *chsd ldrs: rdn after 3rd: wknd 3 out* **50/1**
006 **5** *4 1/2* **Abulharith**[20] 1798 5-10-13 80 (p) ChrisDavies(7) 83
(Ronald Harris) *lft in ld after 1st tl 2nd: chsd wnr tl 3 out: wknd bef next* **66/1**
62 **6** *7* **Starburst**[8] 3879 6-10-12 0 JimmyMcCarthy 67
(Brendan Powell) *hld up in chsng gp: wknd 6th: t.o* **20/1**
U **7** *80* **Aldorable**[26] 3554 4-9-9 0 MrTJCannon(7) —
(Roger Teal) *hld up: struggling 5th: sn wl t.o* **50/1**
30P2 **U** **Abstract Art (USA)**[30] 3493 8-11-6 106 (p) AidanColeman —
(Rachel Hobbs) *led tl propped and uns rdr sn after 1st* **4/1**[2]
U0 **F** **Yourgolftravel Com**[21] 3645 6-11-12 0 (t) TomScudamore —
(David Pipe) *hld up last: fell 5th* **22/1**

4m 5.70s (-2.30) **Going Correction** 0.0s/f (Good)
WFA 4 from 5yo+ 9lb **9** Ran SP% **113.9**
Speed ratings (Par 103): **105,99,98,89,87 83,46,—,—**
toteswingers:1&2 £5.70, 2&3 £4.40, 1&3 £1.80 CSF £9.41 TOTE £2.40: £1.10, £2.00, £1.40; EX 9.50.
Owner R E R Williams **Bred** Darley **Trained** Llancarfan, Vale Of Glamorgan

FOCUS
Most of these had run in this grade before and found it difficult to win in handicap company under either code. The easy winner is rated to the level of his recent win.

NOTEBOOK
Chrysander, who comfortably landed a similar race here last month, was handed an easy, clear lead shortly after the second hurdle and never looked like being caught. (op 11-8, tchd 6-4 in places)
Sweet World, well behind Chrysander over C&D last time, had little chance on the figures with the winner. (op 6-1)
Olivino(GER) is better on quicker ground. (op 7-2 tchd 9-2)
Reymysterio(IRE), trying hurdles for the first time, was on the ropes a long way out before keeping on.
Abulharith has been racing on the AW this winter and was comfortably held.
Abstract Art(USA), runner-up in a seller on his previous outing, launched his rider into the air after the first hurdle. (op 9-2 tchd 5-1)

4029 BRAVO COMPANY 40 COMMANDO ROYAL MARINES MAIDEN HURDLE (9 hdls) 2m 1f
2:30 (2:30) (Class 4) 4-Y-0+ **£3,425** (£998; £499)

Form RPR
3 **1** **Brampour (IRE)**[26] 3554 4-10-7 0 HarrySkelton 115+
(Paul Nicholls) *in tch: wnt 2nd whn nt fluent 5th: rdn after 3 out: led sn after 2 out: styng on wl whn lft wl clr last* **2/1**[2]
02 **2** *13* **Clowance House**[30] 3491 5-11-3 0 AidanColeman 111
(Venetia Williams) *in tch: wnt 4th after 3 out: sn rdn: styng on same pce whn lft 2nd at the last: nt gng pce to get involved* **13/2**
3 *1 3/4* **Bold Identity (IRE)**[220] 5-11-3 0 SeanQuinlan 109
(Richard Phillips) *mid-div: rdn after 6th: styng on same pce whn lft 3rd at the last: nvr trbld ldrs* **100/1**
4 **4** *1/2* **Qalinas (FR)**[9] 3872 4-10-2 0 CO'Farrell(5) 99
(David Pipe) *hld up towards rr: rdn after 6th: stdy prog but no ch w ldrs fr after 3 out: lft 4th at the last* **33/1**
-234 **5** *7* **Management (IRE)**[36] 3398 5-11-3 0 WayneHutchinson 103
(Alan King) *mid-div: rdn after 3 out: no imp: lft 5th at the last* **25/1**
4-02 **6** *5* **His Lordship**[21] 3647 7-11-3 0 NickScholfield 98
(Grant Cann) *in tch: rdn after 3 out: sn wknd* **33/1**
0-03 **7** *1 1/2* **Briefcase (IRE)**[24] 3604 6-11-3 0 PaddyBrennan 97
(Nigel Twiston-Davies) *mid-div: pckd 3rd: rdn after 6th: wknd 3 out* **22/1**
8 *11* **Vitruvian Man**[139] 5-11-3 0 JohnnyFarrelly 87
(Sophie Leech) *a towards rr* **50/1**
9 *18* **Noble Ruler**[274] 5-11-3 0 DavidEngland 71
(George Baker) *t.k.h: trckd ldrs: hit 1st: wknd after 5th: blnd 3 out: t.o* **100/1**
10 *37* **Eurhythmic (IRE)**[117] 4-10-7 0 RhysFlint 27
(Jim Old) *trckd ldrs tl wknd after 6th: t.o* **40/1**
11 *48* **Artic Journey (IRE)** 7-11-0 0 DannyCook(3) —
(Linda Blackford) *mstke 5th: a bhd: t.o* **200/1**
50 **12** *16* **Johnny Owen (IRE)**[9] 3872 5-11-3 0 PaulMoloney —
(David Brace) *plld hrd: hld up towards rr: wknd 6th: t.o* **200/1**
B **First In The Queue (IRE)**[113] 4-10-7 0 APMcCoy 111+
(Nicky Henderson) *mid-div: hdwy 5th: wnt 3rd 3 out: sn rdn: nt gng pce to get on terms: styng on whn mstke, bdly hmpd and b.d last* **6/1**[3]
F **Trop Fort (FR)**[73] 4-10-7 0 TomScudamore 112+
(David Pipe) *led: pckd whn nt fluent 2 out: sn rdn and hdd: styng on in 2 l 2nd whn fell last* **15/8**[1]

4m 3.50s (-4.50) **Going Correction** 0.0s/f (Good)
WFA 4 from 5yo+ 9lb **14** Ran SP% **117.2**
Speed ratings (Par 105): **110,103,103,102,99 97,96,91,82,65 42,35,—,—**
toteswingers:1&2 £3.20, 2&3 £28.80, 1&3 £28.80 CSF £14.10 TOTE £2.80: £1.80, £2.20, £12.10; EX 15.80.
Owner Banks, Blackshaw & Gannon **Bred** Haras De Son Altesse L'Aga Khan S C E A **Trained** Ditcheat, Somerset

FOCUS
A fascinating contest containing a few interesting runners with pretensions to being above-average performers. The three most fancied in the market pulled clear, and were the only ones left with a realistic chance heading to the final hurdle. A big step up from the winner on his debut form but he is still a long way off being a Triumph Hurdle candidate.

NOTEBOOK
Brampour(IRE) appeared to have taken control when left in the lead at the last, and bounded clear once his rivals disappeared behind him. He had taken a while to get on top, but did find plenty for pressure when asked to lengthen, and stayed on well all the way to the line. Connections have options for him at Cheltenham next month, but he is likely to be seen again before taking up any engagement at the festival. (tchd 7-4)
Clowance House was to finish second. He had needed a strong ride quite early in the contest, and didn't look like placing until handed the runner-up spot on a plate. (op 6-1 tchd 7-1)
Bold Identity(IRE), runner-up twice in three Irish Flat runs, stayed on from the rear and shaped with some promise.
First In The Queue(IRE), a triple winner on the Flat for Sylvester Kirk, was in the process of making a pleasing debut when given nowhere to go at the last. As long as his confidence hasn't been badly affected, he has the profile to make into a nice prospect. (tchd 7-4 and 2-1)
Trop Fort(FR), winner of two French bumpers, looked interesting for these connections and attracted market support during the morning. He got to the lead going well, but had been passed after two out before crashing out at the final hurdle. His jumping had been novicey at times, which it was entitled to be, and he will no doubt prove better than he showed here once that has been sorted out. (tchd 7-4 and 2-1)

4030 CHARLIE COMPANY 40 COMMANDO ROYAL MARINES NOVICES' CHASE (17 fncs) 2m 7f 110y
3:00 (3:00) (Class 4) 5-Y-0+ **£4,453** (£1,298; £649)

Form RPR
0-33 **1** **Lake Legend**[29] 3508 7-11-0 0 WayneHutchinson 123+
(Alan King) *trckd ldrs: nudged along fr 12th: chal 3 out: sn hrd rdn: hit last: led sn after: styd on* **5/6**[1]
053P **2** *3/4* **Persian Run (IRE)**[33] 3451 7-11-0 115 AidanColeman 119
(Colin Tizzard) *led: rdn whn hrd pressed 3 out: kpt on gamely to hold narrow advantage: hdd sn after last: no ex* **16/1**
2P25 **3** *11* **Top Benefit (IRE)**[7] 3907 9-10-9 115 JoshuaMoore(5) 111
(Keith Goldsworthy) *w ldr: rdn along fr 11th: ev ch 3 out: styd on same pce fr next* **15/2**[3]
6-F1 **4** *21* **Sheshali (IRE)**[94] 2278 7-11-7 127 PaulMoloney 103
(Evan Williams) *hld up in last pair but cl up: stmbld bdly 13th: sn rdn: wknd after 4 out: lft 4th 3 out* **9/1**
-204 **U** **Earth Planet (IRE)**[31] 3479 9-10-9 121 (bt) MrRMahon(5) 124+
(Paul Nicholls) *trckd ldrs: nudged along to chal whn slipped and uns rdr 3 out* **4/1**[2]
-43F **P** **Mortimers Cross**[7] 3902 10-11-0 112 RodiGreene —
(John Needham) *hld up in last pair but cl up: rdn after 11th: wknd qckly 4 out: sn p.u* **14/1**

6m 9.30s (-5.30) **Going Correction** 0.0s/f (Good) **6** Ran SP% **108.9**
Speed ratings: **108,107,104,97,— —**
toteswingers:1&2 £16.40, 2&3 £11.80, 1&3 £1.30 CSF £12.82 TOTE £1.70: £1.30, £6.60; EX 14.40.
Owner J Wright,P Wilson,F J Allen & R Preston **Bred** William Wilkinson **Trained** Barbury Castle, Wilts

FOCUS
An ordinary race that probably didn't take a lot of winning, and Lake Legend is rated below his best. Nothing of any significance happened until some pace was injected at the start of the final circuit.

NOTEBOOK
Lake Legend was the best of these over hurdles and gained a deserved success after a couple of good performances in decent novice events. One could easily see him going close in a nice staying handicap if given a realistic mark. (op 8-11 tchd 10-11)
Persian Run(IRE) held a slight lead for much of the race and found plenty for pressure. He had the run of things, though, so may be slightly flattered. (op 18-1)
Top Benefit(IRE) raced prominently before staying on at the one pace. His jumping wasn't always fluent, so that is something he can improve upon. (op 8-1 tchd 7-1)
Earth Planet(IRE) looked to be going best of the four going to three out, but lost his jockey at that point. He hasn't always looked the most straightforward of characters, so it's debateable what he would have found had he stayed upright. (tchd 7-2 and 9-2)

4031 ROYAL MARINES CHARITABLE TRUST FUND NOVICES' H'CAP HURDLE (9 hdls) 2m 1f
3:30 (3:30) (Class 3) (0-130,123) 4-Y-0+ **£6,851** (£1,997; £999)

Form RPR
-F2F **1** **Highway Code (USA)**[26] 3563 5-11-3 **119** (t) GilesHawkins(5) 126+
(Richard Lee) *in tch: rdn after 3 out: styng on in 2nd whn sprawled on landing 2 out: 8 l down and hld whn lft in ld after last* **15/2**[3]
-3P0 **2** *3 1/2* **Lidar (FR)**[83] 2493 6-11-9 **120** WayneHutchinson 121
(Alan King) *chsd ldrs: rdn after 3 out: styd on same pce fr next: lft 3rd after last: wnt 2nd nring fin* **9/2**[2]
30-4 **3** *1/2* **Up To The Mark**[102] 2109 6-10-1 **105** JakeGreenall(7) 105
(Henry Daly) *t.k.h: w ldr early: trckd ldr fr 4th: rdn after 3 out: hld fr next: lft 2nd after last tl no ex nr fin* **16/1**
3P **4** *3 1/4* **First Smash (GER)**[15] 3491 6-10-5 **105** (t) JimmyDerham(3) 101
(Milton Harris) *hld up towards rr: rdn after 3 out: styd on same pce fr after 2 out: lft 4th after last: nvr trbld ldrs* **33/1**
122 **5** *8* **Credit Swap**[6] 3917 6-11-10 **121** AidanColeman 112
(Venetia Williams) *in tch: rdn to dispute 2nd after 3 out: fdd fr after next* **9/4**[1]
00-3 **6** *2 1/2* **James Pollard (IRE)**[14] 3760 6-10-8 **105** (t) DPFahy 90
(Bernard Llewellyn) *hld up towards rr: rdn after 6th: nvr any imp* **33/1**
040 **7** *24* **Decoy (FR)**[12] 3808 5-11-12 **123** TomScudamore 84
(David Pipe) *mid-div: pushed along after 5th: wknd after next: t.o* **22/1**
-210 **8** *5* **Shinrock Hill (IRE)**[25] 3587 7-11-6 **117** TomO'Brien 73
(Philip Hobbs) *chsd ldrs: stmbld 3rd: lost pl after next: rdn after 6th: wknd after 3 out* **15/2**[3]
U353 **9** *3 3/4* **Ajman (IRE)**[87] 2423 6-10-8 **105** (t) PaulMoloney 58
(Evan Williams) *a towards rr: t.o* **10/1**
0211 **U** **Arrayan**[28] 3532 6-11-3 **119** CO'Farrell(5) 134+
(David Pipe) *led: pushed clr after 3: 8 l clr and wl in command whn rdr's foot slipped out of iron and uns rdr sn after last* **9/2**[2]

4m 7.50s (-0.50) **Going Correction** 0.0s/f (Good) **10** Ran SP% **115.9**
Speed ratings (Par 107): **101,99,99,97,93 92,81,79,77,—**
toteswingers:1&2 £6.60, 2&3 £11.90, 1&3 £22.90 CSF £40.73 CT £522.10 TOTE £12.20: £3.80, £2.40, £5.00; EX 43.90.
Owner D E Edwards **Bred** T Leung **Trained** Byton, H'fords

FOCUS
The going was changed to soft before this race and there was a dramatic twist at the end. Another step forward from the winner, but the unfortunate Arrayan was heading for another big step up.

NOTEBOOK
Highway Code(USA) appears to have a few jumping problems looking at his profile this season, and he made a pretty bad mistake here at the second-last, but he was handed success after being left in front at the final flight. He had looked all set to score last time at Warwick when falling at the last, so he was a deserved recipient of the leader's mishap. (op 8-1)
Lidar(FR) has always been well regarded so looked of obvious interest on his handicap debut. However, the ground had probably turned against him and he was one-paced under pressure. He can be given another chance on quicker ground. (op 6-1)
Up To The Mark, absent since the end of October, made a satisfactory return to action and was only run out of second place in the final stages.
First Smash(GER), sixth on the Flat since his last effort over hurdles, kept on from the rear but never looked dangerous.
Credit Swap, having his first start in handicap company, came under strong pressure rounding the home bend and offered little off the bridle down the home straight. (op 5-2 tchd 11-4 in places)

Arrayan, 19lb higher than for his last win, was chasing a hat-trick and had gone well clear when his jockey's foot came out of the right stirrup, sending him to the ground well after jumping the final hurdle. Over £10,000 was matched at 1.01 on Betfair, and those who backed him were undoubtedly incredibly unlucky not to collect. (op 7-2 tchd 10-3)

4032 DELTA COMPANY 40 COMMANDO ROYAL MARINES MARES' H'CAP HURDLE (12 hdls) 3m 110y

4:00 (4:00) (Class 5) (0-95,95) 4-Y-O+ **£2,397** (£698; £349)

Form RPR

001U **1** **Molly Round (IRE)**[7] 3898 7-10-7 **81**........................ MrSWaley-Cohen(5) 98+
(Grant Cann) *trckd ldrs: led 7th: rdn clr appr 2 out: styd on strly: eased nr fin* **3/1**[1]

36-2 **2** *18* **Saulty Max (IRE)**[28] 3530 7-11-7 **90**..............................(p) PaddyBrennan 91+
(Nigel Twiston-Davies) *in tch: tk clsr order 8th: disputing 2nd whn hit 3 out: sn rdn: no ch w wnr fr next* **7/2**[2]

-305 **3** *1 ¾* **Aeronautica (IRE)**[11] 3837 8-11-0 **83**........................ WayneHutchinson 78
(Tor Sturgis) *racd wd: hld up towards rr: hdwy after 7th: wnt 2nd 9th: rdn after 3 out: no ch w wnr fr next* **14/1**

05-0 **4** *9* **Gouranga**[6] 3934 8-10-12 **88**..(b) RobertKirk(7) 74
(Tony Carroll) *chsd ldrs tl wknd after 3 out* **12/1**

PF0- **5** *nk* **Midnight Ocean**[324] 4811 10-11-6 **89**.............................. TimmyMurphy 75
(Julian Smith) *a in rr: struggling 7th: nvr a factor* **22/1**

-400 **6** *44* **Forty Knights**[15] 3745 6-11-3 **93**.................................... MrRHawkins(7) 35
(Chris Down) *mid-div tl wknd after 8th: sn t.o* **33/1**

-012 **7** *2* **Arctic Flow**[18] 3703 7-10-4 **76**.................................... WayneKavanagh(3) 16
(Caroline Keevil) *disp ld tl 7th: wknd 9th: t.o* **11/2**

50-6 **8** *13* **Colinette**[8] 3882 8-10-0 **69** oh7..(v[1]) CharliePoste —
(Robin Dickin) *disp ld tl 7th: rdn bef next: wknd bef 9th: t.o* **14/1**

6P0/ **P** **Galandora**[989] 497 11-10-0 **69** oh3........................(t) AndrewGlassonbury —
(Dr Jeremy Naylor) *rdn after 7th: a in rr: t.o whn p.u bef 2 out* **40/1**

036/ **P** **Zuleta**[858] 1587 10-10-2 **71**.. JohnnyFarrelly —
(Laura Young) *rdn after 5th: a in rr: t.o whn p.u bef 2 out* **25/1**

030 **P** **Attainable**[57] 2960 5-11-9 **92**...(t) RhysFlint —
(Jim Old) *nvr fluent in rr: stmbld bdly 1st: j.lft progively worse: t.o whn p.u bef 7th* **28/1**

0-61 **P** **Time To Think**[39] 3338 6-11-9 **95**.................................. JimmyDerham(3) —
(Seamus Mullins) *disp ld tl blnd 7th: wknd qckly 9th: t.o whn p.u bef 2 out* **4/1**[3]

6m 3.60s (-3.50) **Going Correction** 0.0s/f (Good) **12** Ran SP% **120.7**
Speed ratings (Par 103): **105,99,98,95,95 81,80,76,—,— —,—**
toteswingers:1&2 £2.00, 2&3 £9.20, 1&3 £15.40 CSF £13.55 CT £130.22 TOTE £3.20: £2.20, £1.80, £4.10; EX 16.10.
Owner Andrew Kavanagh **Bred** Andrew Kavanagh **Trained** Cullompton, Devon.

FOCUS
A moderate race of its type. Another big step up from the winner, with the next two to their marks.

NOTEBOOK
Molly Round(IRE) was one of only a few that could be described as being in form, but the trip was a complete unknown. Racing from 10lb higher than for her Towcester success, she was given a good, positive ride, her jockey never seemingly worrying about her stamina, and rarely looked like being caught once in command. She doesn't look the biggest and would be opposable under a big weight. (op 7-2 tchd 4-1)
Saulty Max(IRE), with cheekpieces back on, made stealthy ground into a challenging position from off the pace but wasn't able to bridge the gap to the leader. (op 4-1 tchd 10-3)
Aeronautica(IRE) travelled strongly off the pace out wide, and looked a big threat as she got involved. However, she didn't find a great deal off the bridle and didn't seem to get home in these testing conditions. (op 11-1)
Gouranga, with blinkers back on, looked to be on a fair mark but made no meaningful impact. (op 20-1)
Midnight Ocean gets a mention because she was extremely slow to get into her stride but made good ground while others faltered. Her earlier exertions to get into the race told late on, but there was promise in the effort.

4033 COMMAND & LOGISTICS COMPANY 40 COMMANDO ROYAL MARINES H'CAP CHASE (12 fncs) 2m 110y

4:30 (4:30) (Class 4) (0-115,121) 5-Y-O+ **£4,453** (£1,298; £649)

Form RPR

-515 **1** **Jeczmien (POL)**[14] 3769 8-10-11 **99**..............................(t) LiamTreadwell 111+
(Nick Gifford) *chsd ldrs: led 4 out: rdn and kpt on wl fr after 2 out* **11/2**

0152 **2** *11* **The Darling Boy**[103] 2093 6-11-0 **102**..............................(t) PaddyBrennan 104+
(Tom George) *chsd ldr: jnd ldr 6th: ev ch 4 out: sn rdn: kpt on same pce fr next* **7/2**[2]

FP53 **3** *nk* **Playing With Fire (IRE)**[14] 3769 7-11-2 **104**....................... CharliePoste 106
(Robin Dickin) *hld up: hdwy into 4th after 4 out: rdn bef next: kpt on same pce* **10/3**[1]

2FP1 **4** *7* **Lord Singer (FR)**[11] 3834 6-12-0 **121** 7ex...................... JoshuaMoore(5) 116
(Gary Moore) *racd keenly: led: rchd for 7th: hdd 4 out: sn rdn: one pce fr next* **4/1**[3]

4020 **5** *4 ½* **Holyrood**[32] 3297 5-10-4 **99**..(tp) MrTomDavid(5) 89
(Tim Vaughan) *hld up bhd ldrs: pckd 4th: rdn whn hit 3 out: fdd fr next* **16/1**

30P3 **6** *13* **Akarshan (IRE)**[24] 3598 6-11-9 **111**....................................... PaulMoloney 89
(Evan Williams) *hld up but in tch: blnd 6th: sn struggling: no ch fr 4 out* **10/3**[1]

4m 14.7s (4.70) **Going Correction** 0.0s/f (Good)
WFA 5 from 6yo+ 1lb **6** Ran SP% **109.6**
Speed ratings: **88,82,82,79,77 71**
toteswingers:1&2 £5.00, 2&3 £3.60, 1&3 £4.70 CSF £23.87 TOTE £5.00: £2.20, £2.90; EX 30.50.
Owner Mrs R Gifford **Bred** Sk Golejewko Sp Z O O **Trained** Findon, W Sussex

FOCUS
The pace was always going to be strong considering a couple of these were known for their prominent-racing style. Ordinary form with a step up from the winner and the next two close to their marks.

NOTEBOOK
Jeczmien(POL), who was behind Playing With Fire last time, sat in behind while the leader got on with it. Having settled nicely, he moved into the lead travelling strongly leaving the back straight and came right away after two out to record an easy success. (op 9-2 tchd 6-1)
The Darling Boy, off since the end of October, wasn't far away and responded well to strong pressure. He shaped like he'd be worth a try over further again. (op 9-2)
Playing With Fire(IRE) ran well on her chasing debut at Warwick, and had the beating of the winner on that performance, but she got caught flat-footed as the field quickened and wasn't able to get on terms. (op 7-2)
Lord Singer(FR), penalised 7lb for his Fakenham success, was able to lead but never got away from his rivals and had little left when joined. It was probably still a fair effort giving a lot of weight away, especially as he tended to jump to his left at some of the fences. (op 10-3)
Holyrood, with cheekpieces back on, wasn't disgraced on his chasing debut but a slight mistake at the third-last effectively finished any chance he had of getting involved. (tchd 12-1)
Akarshan(IRE), taking a sharp drop in trip, attracted market support but didn't jump fluently enough to get out of last place. (op 9-2 tchd 3-1)

4034 GO COMMANDO RACING EXCELLENCE "HANDS AND HEELS" H'CAP HURDLE (CONDITIONALS/AMATEURS) (10 hdls) 2m 3f 110y

5:00 (5:00) (Class 4) (0-110,110) 4-Y-O+ **£3,768** (£1,098; £549)

Form RPR

-600 **1** **Calico Rose**[19] 3691 7-10-11 **95**.......................................(p) EdGlassonbury 99
(Victor Dartnall) *mde all: hrd pressed after 3 out: styd on wl to assert run-in* **8/1**

5625 **2** *1* **Prince Of Denial (IRE)**[56] 2977 7-11-8 **109**........ MrWTwiston-Davies(3) 113+
(Nigel Twiston-Davies) *hld up towards rr: hdwy after 5th: jnd ldrs 7th: nt fluent next: str chal sn after: no ex fr last* **5/1**[2]

R260 **3** *9* **Posh Emily**[19] 3688 8-11-9 **107**..(b) JakeGreenall 101
(Ron Hodges) *mid-div: hdwy 6th: rdn to chse ldrs after 3 out: styd on same pce* **16/1**

003 **4** *shd* **That'lldoboy (FR)**[40] 3296 5-11-6 **109**................................ MrDCollins(5) 106+
(Paul Nicholls) *trckd ldrs tl dropped in rr after 5th: hdwy after 3 out: short of room to chal for 3rd appr last: styd on run-in* **14/1**

3564 **5** *hd* **Decision**[40] 3306 5-10-13 **97**..(t) MrJFMathias 91
(Lawney Hill) *racd wd: hld up towards rr: hdwy fr 6th: rdn after 3 out: styd on same pce fr next* **11/1**

-600 **6** *1* **Come Out Firing (IRE)**[214] 962 9-11-9 **110**..................... MrCGreene(3) 104
(Michael Blake) *in tch: jnd ldrs 7th: rdn and ev ch after 3 out: one pce fr next* **50/1**

2023 **7** *3 ½* **Beside The Fire**[25] 3589 6-11-9 **110**.................................. SClements(3) 99
(Colin Tizzard) *chsd ldrs: rdn after 3 out: sn one pce* **4/1**[1]

4221 **8** *2 ¾* **Be My Light (IRE)**[15] 3745 5-11-1 **102**...........................(p) KielanWoods(3) 88
(Charlie Longsdon) *chsd ldrs tl lost pl 6th: nvr bk on terms* **11/2**[3]

2203 **9** *14* **Jump Up**[14] 3761 5-10-11 **100**.................................. MissCharlotteEvans(5) 72
(Keith Goldsworthy) *mid-div: trckd ldrs 5th tl after next: wknd 3 out* **28/1**

0112 **10** *½* **Smokey George**[36] 3396 6-11-6 **104**...................................... EdCookson 76
(Kim Bailey) *hld up towards rr: sme prog 6th: rdn after 3 out: wknd next* **7/1**

5060 **11** *2 ½* **Takamaru (FR)**[25] 3589 5-10-10 **99**....................................(b[1]) MrKEdgar(5) 68
(David Pipe) *a towards rr* **16/1**

5-02 **12** *28* **Star Galaxy (IRE)**[249] 646 11-10-1 **90**.........................(b) ThomasFlint(5) 31
(John Flint) *chsd ldrs tl wknd 3 out: t.o* **20/1**

U5/ **P** **Carrigeen King (IRE)**[207] 1041 10-11-11 **109**.................. TrevorWhelan —
(George Baker) *chsd ldrs tl 5th sn rdn: bhd fr after next: p.u after 3 out* **33/1**

5560 **U** **Mayberry**[91] 2329 6-11-7 **108**....................................... JeremiahMcGrath(3) —
(Emma Lavelle) *hld up towards rr: sprawled bdly on landing whn uns rdr 5th* **12/1**

4m 47.9s (1.90) **Going Correction** 0.0s/f (Good) **14** Ran SP% **123.2**
Speed ratings (Par 105): **96,95,92,91,91 90,89,83,83,83 82,71,—,—**
toteswingers:1&2 £16.50, 2&3 £13.70, 1&3 £20.90. totesuper7: Win: Not won. Place: Not won. CSF £47.90 CT £645.09 TOTE £9.40: £2.30, £2.10, £4.00; EX 49.20.
Owner D G Staddon **Bred** Richard Mathias **Trained** Brayford, Devon

FOCUS
Jockeyship was always going to be a factor in this sort of race, and two promising riders fought out the finish. Improved form from the winner in this ordinary handicap.

NOTEBOOK
Calico Rose, in first-time cheekpieces, had shown a glimmer of ability on her previous outing and, on her handicap debut, was soon put into the lead and responded in game fashion to gain success. It's not easy to know what to expect next time, but she does at least look to have plenty of heart. Official explanation: trainer said, regarding the apparent improvement in form, that the mare benefited from the fitting of cheek pieces and a change in riding tactics
Prince Of Denial(IRE) travelled strongly off the pace, as he has done before, and stayed on powerfully against a much lower weighted rival without ever quite getting to the front. (op 9-2)
Posh Emily, who had the blinkers back on, moved into contention going strongly but couldn't go on when required. (op 18-1)
That'lldoboy(FR), making his handicap debut, is better than the bare result, as his rider didn't get urgent on him until quite late, and then met some trouble when staying on heading to the final hurdle. (tchd 12-1)
Decision, with a tongue-tie back on, had his chance and kept on along the stands' rail. (op 10-1)
Come Out Firing(IRE), off since July and undoubtedly better on quicker ground, made a pleasing return to action. (op 66-1)
Beside The Fire, down in distance, was hard ridden rounding the final bend and looks in need of a stiffer test. (op 5-1)
Be My Light(IRE), raised 8lb for winning under this rider at Huntingdon, lost his place down the back straight and couldn't get back into contention thereafter. (op 6-1)
T/Plt: £78.80 to a £1 stake. Pool of £66,766.34 - 618.28 winning tickets. T/Qpdt: £16.70 to a £1 stake. Pool of £5,054.72 - 223.05 winning tickets. TM

4035 - 4041a (Foreign Racing) - See Raceform Interactive

3917 BANGOR-ON-DEE (L-H)

Friday, February 11

4042 Meeting Abandoned - Waterlogged

3554 KEMPTON (R-H)

Friday, February 11

OFFICIAL GOING: Chase course - good (good to soft in places); hurdle course - good to soft (good in places) changing to good to soft (good in places) all round after race 2 (2.05)
Wind: Moderate, half behind Weather: Overcast

4049 TIMEFORM BETFAIR RACING CLUB CONDITIONAL JOCKEYS' H'CAP HURDLE (8 hdls) 2m

1:30 (1:32) (Class 4) (0-115,121) 4-Y-O+ **£2,602** (£764; £382; £190)

Form RPR

566 **1** **Balerina (FR)**[36] 3401 4-10-2 **109**.....................................(p) PeterHatton(8) 109+
(Alan King) *hld up in rr: stdy prog fr 5th to trck ldrs 3 out gng wl: narrow ld 2 out: awkward last and narrowly hdd: urged along and responded to ld again nr fin* **10/1**

4-2U **2** *¾* **Screaming Brave**[12] 2636 5-11-12 **115**...................................(t) IanPopham 124+
(Sheena West) *lw: hld up in rr: stdy prog after 5th: trckd ldrs gng easily after 3 out: chal and mstke 2 out: narrow ld last: hdd nr fin* **16/1**

00-0 **3** *14* **Kings Troop**[43] 3228 5-10-11 **103**...................................... CharlieHuxley(3) 100
(Alan King) *trckd ldrs: effrt to chal after 3 out: drvn to ld bef 2 out: hdd and nt fluent 2 out: no ch ldng pair after* **12/1**

3-13 **4** *4* **Domino Dancer (IRE)**[157] 1236 7-10-10 **99** CPGeoghegan 93
(Lucy Jones) *blnd 1st: chsd ldr to 3rd: dropped to midfield after 5th: drvn and struggling after 3 out: kpt on again fr 2 out* **80/1**

15-6 **5** *shd* **Zafranagar (IRE)**[9] 2596 6-11-4 **110** LeeEdwards(3) 102
(Tony Carroll) *in tch: rdn to chse ldrs after 3 out: grad wknd bef 2 out* **15/2**

1460 **6** *½* **Niceonefrankie**[32] 3490 5-11-8 **114** RTDunne(3) 105
(Venetia Williams) *wl in tch: trckd ldrs 3 out: sn rdn: grad wknd bef 2 out* **20/1**

3-PP **7** *hd* **King Brex (DEN)**[108] 2022 8-11-6 **112** (tp) PeterToole(3) 104
(Charlie Mann) *trckd ldrs: led after 3 out gng wl: hdd bef 2 out: wknd* **66/1**

5004 **8** *10* **Salybia Bay**[40] 3338 5-10-3 **97** EdCookson(5) 81
(Andy Turnell) *trckd ldr 3rd: led briefly 3 out: wknd u.p bef 2 out* **66/1**

0-61 **9** *2 ¼* **Park Lane**[100] 2150 5-11-12 **115** RichardKilloran 95
(Paul Fitzsimons) *lw: in tch: struggling and outpcd fr 3 out: rn wd bnd bef next: no ch after* **25/1**

5541 **10** *¾* **Marodima (FR)**[5] 3962 8-11-13 **121** 7ex (p) JeremiahMcGrath(5) 100
(Jamie Snowden) *mde most to 3 out: sn wknd u.p* **9/2**[2]

P021 **11** *19* **Zelos Diktator**[18] 3343 5-10-3 **95** (p) JoshuaMoore(3) 57
(Gary Moore) *already struggling in rr whn mstke 4th: nvr a factor: t.o* **11/1**

6-40 **12** *1 ½* **According**[58] 2960 5-10-13 **105** DavidBass(3) 66
(Nicky Henderson) *lw: j. bdly early: str reminders in last after 4th: rapid prog to join ldrs 3 out: wknd as rapidly bef 2 out: t.o* **2/1**

555/ **13** *25* **Cnoc Moy (IRE)**[668] 5025 7-10-13 **102** MattGriffiths 40
(Helen Rees) *racd wd in rr: struggling bef 3 out: wl t.o* **50/1**

3-10 **14** *16* **Robain (FR)**[90] 2361 6-11-5 **111** GilesHawkins(3) 35
(Philip Hobbs) *in tch whn blnd 4th: sn dropped to last: struggling fr next: wl t.o* **7/1**[3]

3m 59.2s (-0.80) **Going Correction** +0.075s/f (Yiel)
WFA 4 from 5yo+ 9lb **14** Ran SP% **121.6**
Speed ratings (Par 105): **105,104,97,95,95 95,95,90,89,88 79,78,65,57**
toteswingers:1&2:£17.90, 1&3:£24.60, 2&3:£24.30 CSF £146.56 CT £1953.13 TOTE £12.10: £3.00, £3.70, £4.10; EX 202.80.
Owner Tim & Sarah Ingram Hill **Bred** Mathieu Lalanne **Trained** Barbury Castle, Wilts

FOCUS
An ordinary handicap, confined to conditional riders. The first two are on the upgrade and the winner is entitled to rate a lot higher on Flat form.

NOTEBOOK
Balerina(FR) shed her maiden tag over jumps at the fourth time of asking on this switch to a handicap and got a strong ride. She didn't help her rider that much through the race and it's not hard to see why connections reached for cheekpieces, but she has no doubt begun life in this sphere at the right end of the weights. If found another race before her new mark kicks in, she would escape a penalty for this. Official explanation: trainer said, regarding apparent improvement in form, this was the filly's first run in a handicap and had ran well last time. (op 12-1 tchd 16-1)
Screaming Brave travelled smoothly into contention and, despite hitting two out, looked likely to get up on the run-in. The concession of over a stone to the winner took its toll near the finish, though. He likes a sound surface so his proximity suggests the ground had not deteriorated all that much.
Kings Troop was another that travelled kindly and, while he lacked the pace of the first pair, this rates his most encouraging effort as a hurdler. His Flat form indicates a stiffer test would be more suitable and his turn could be nearing. (op 16-1 tchd 20-1)
Domino Dancer(IRE), last seen on the Flat for another yard in September, looked like finishing out the back on the far side. However, he rallied strongly for pressure turning in and should come on a bundle for the run.
Zafranagar(IRE) lacked a change of gear on his return to hurdling. (op 6-1)
Niceonefrankie shaped with more encouragement again and will be better served by returning to stiffer circuit. (op 16-1 tchd 25-1)
Park Lane Official explanation: vet said gelding was lame left-hind
Marodima(FR) was 6lb ahead of the handicapper under his penalty for bouncing back to his best at Fontwell on Sunday. He folded tamely once taken on for the lead, though, and will likely be back in claimers after this. (op 6-1)
According, making his handicap debut, went in snatches and while he may need genuinely good ground, he doesn't look in love with jumping. (op 5-2)
Robain(FR) was later reported to have stopped quickly. Official explanation: jockey said gelding stopped quickly (op 8-1)

4050 BETFAIR.COM/PAULNICHOLLS BEGINNERS' CHASE (16 fncs) 2m 4f 110y
2:05 (2:05) (Class 4) 5-Y-0+ **£3,252** (£955; £477; £238)

Form RPR
/FF5 **1** **American Trilogy (IRE)**[52] 3059 7-11-0 0 (b) NickScholfield 132+
(Paul Nicholls) *cl up on outer gng wl: j.lft fr 10th: jnd ldr 13th: led next: in command last: rdn and drew away flat* **4/1**[3]

11/2 **2** *6* **Patsy Finnegan**[28] 3543 9-11-0 122 RobertThornton 127+
(Alan King) *lw: cl up: mstke 13th: trckd ldng pair after: trying to chal whn mstke 2 out: nt qckn after: kpt on to take 2nd last strides* **6/4**[1]

0P-3 **3** *nk* **Zazamix (FR)**[34] 3447 6-11-0 0 BarryGeraghty 123
(Nicky Henderson) *j. slowly 1st and 3rd: w ldr: led 8th: rdn and hdd 3 out: one pce after next: lost 2nd last strides* **15/8**[2]

-153 **4** *28* **Sergeant Pink (IRE)**[19] 3694 5-10-11 120 (t) TomScudamore 94
(Steve Gollings) *in tch: j.lft 9th and dropped to last: lost tch fr next: tk poor 4th after 3 out: t.o* **14/1**

2202 **5** *11* **Ballinteni**[15] 3760 9-11-0 110 JoeTizzard 92
(Colin Tizzard) *pckd bdly 3rd: mde most to 8th: w ldr tl wknd qckly sn after 13th: t.o* **9/1**

5m 21.0s (1.50) **Going Correction** +0.175s/f (Yiel)
WFA 5 from 6yo+ 2lb **5** Ran SP% **111.4**
Speed ratings: **104,101,101,90,86**
CSF £11.03 TOTE £3.50: £2.10, £1.10; EX 7.60.
Owner Fulton,Donlon,Kilduff & Scott-MacDonald **Bred** F Teboul And E Lellouche **Trained** Ditcheat, Somerset

FOCUS
A good-quality beginners' chase. A step forward from the winner but he is still a long way off his best hurdles form.

NOTEBOOK
American Trilogy(IRE) had fallen on his previous two outings since resuming from his layoff, including on his chase debut two runs back, but he finished fifth in a "jumpers bumper" last time and that had clearly helped restore his confidence. A little on his toes beforehand, the longer trip here helped his jumping and his rider emerges with credit for keeping him together over the final three fences. It was his first success since winning the County Hurdle in 2009, but he has never managed to put together back-to-back wins in the past. Paul Nicholls later remarked his 7-y-o is more effective on a left-handed track and will now look for something going that way around. (op 7-2 tchd 9-2)
Patsy Finnegan was solid in the market on this second run back from injury. He was awash with sweat through the race and again didn't look a total natural over his fences. The added experience will be of benefit to him, though, and this was no disgrace considering the winner is rated 19lb his superior over hurdles. (op 13-8 tchd 7-4 and 15-8 in places)
Zazamix(FR) was a distant third to Mille Chief on his comeback last month and was back up in distance for this switch to chasing. He proved free and deliberate early on, which cost him at the business end, but this was a performance he should build on. (op 2-1 tchd 9-4 and 5-2 in places)
Sergeant Pink(IRE) remains out of form. (op 12-1)
Ballinteni, switched to fences, ran better than the bare form. His jumping was neat in the main, but he clearly failed to see out the longer trip and will be of interest back at 2m. (op 10-1 tchd 12-1)

4051 BETFAIR IPHONE & ANDROID APP NOVICES' HURDLE (10 hdls) 2m 5f
2:35 (2:35) (Class 4) 4-Y-0+ **£2,602** (£764; £382; £190)

Form RPR
10-0 **1** **Rebel Rebellion (IRE)**[83] 2512 6-11-4 0 DarylJacob 131+
(Paul Nicholls) *lw: hld up in last trio: prog to go prom 4th: jnd ldr 6th: led 2 out: rdn clr after last* **5/2**[2]

-200 **2** *6* **Oscar Papa**[34] 3439 6-11-4 125 LiamTreadwell 123
(Nick Gifford) *lw: crossed sing line 6 2nds after tapes wnt up: mde most: set stdy pce to 1/2-way: jnd after 6th: drvn and hdd 2 out: one pce and hld whn nt fluent last* **4/1**[3]

-233 **3** *4* **Sweet Irony (FR)**[79] 2612 5-11-4 118 RobertThornton 119
(Alan King) *hld up in last trio: prog to trck ldng pair after 3 out: rdn whn mstke 2 out: fnd nil* **7/4**[1]

0-50 **4** *8* **Ballyfoy (IRE)**[34] 3437 10-11-4 0 RodiGreene 113
(Jamie Poulton) *pressed ldr to 5th: sn pushed along and dropped to last after next: stl last and wl btn after 3 out: rallied to take 4th 2 out: styd on* **7/1**

5 **5** *20* **Cousin Maggie (IRE)**[14] 3789 7-10-11 0 JimmyMcCarthy 86
(Brendan Powell) *cl up: pushed along 7th: wknd after 3 out* **66/1**

33-6 **6** *3 ½* **Yukon Quest (IRE)**[78] 2634 6-11-4 0 WayneHutchinson 90
(Alan King) *trckd ldrs: wl there 3 out: rdn and wknd long bef 2 out: fin tired* **25/1**

6-05 **7** *4* **Another Dimension (IRE)**[22] 3651 5-10-11 0 CharlieWallis(7) 86
(Nigel Dunger) *cl up: mstke 3 out: sn rdn and wknd qckly bef next* **100/1**

8 *5* **Abayaan**[111] 5-11-4 0 TomScudamore 82
(Charlie Mann) *hld up in last trio: in tch 3 out: rdn and effrt sn after but sn outpcd: wknd qckly bef 2 out* **33/1**

0-54 **9** *63* **The Laodicean**[30] 3506 5-11-4 0 GerardTumelty 25
(Alan King) *in tch: nt fluent 5th and pushed along: stl jst in tch 3 out: wknd v rapidly: t.o* **20/1**

5m 35.1s (11.10) **Going Correction** +0.075s/f (Yiel) **9** Ran SP% **111.5**
Speed ratings (Par 105): **81,78,77,74,66 65,63,61,37**
toteswingers:1&2:£1.30, 1&3:£4.20, 2&3:£3.70 CSF £11.85 TOTE £2.70: £1.10, £1.40, £1.50; EX 17.40.
Owner Jared Sullivan **Bred** Frances Galloway **Trained** Ditcheat, Somerset

FOCUS
An average novice hurdle. There was a steady gallop on, after the runners stood still for around six seconds when the tape went up, and the principals had it to themselves in the home straight. A massive step up from the easy winner with the second 6lb off.

NOTEBOOK
Rebel Rebellion(IRE) ◆ choked on his hurdling debut at Ascot in November when well fancied, and he showed the benefit of a subsequent breathing operation here with a ready success. This was just his second outing for Paul Nicholls and he still looks a raw horse, but no doubt he can show more when faced with a stronger gallop in this sphere. He could well end up at Aintree's Grand National meeting in April, and he'll make a chaser in time. (op 7-2)
Oscar Papa returned to something like his best in defeat. He was kept wide throughout and shaped as though a stiffer test on better ground should see him winning over hurdles. He was later reported to have lost his front right shoe. Official explanation: vet said gelding lost right front shoe (op 7-2)
Sweet Irony(FR) travelled sweetly into contention three out, but came under pressure before hitting the penultimate flight and rates a non-stayer. He helps to set the level. (op 6-4)
Ballyfoy(IRE), last seen finishing eighth in the Welsh National, is a dour stayer and therefore it was not at all surprising to see him get done for speed on the back straight. That was down to the steady gallop and he shouldn't be discounted if reverting to fences in the Grand National Trial at Haydock next weekend. He also has the option of the Eider Chase at Newcastle later this month as well, though. (op 15-2 tchd 13-2)

4052 FOLLOW PAUL NICHOLLS ON FACEBOOK AND TWITTER NOVICES' H'CAP HURDLE (10 hdls) 2m 5f
3:10 (3:10) (Class 4) (0-105,105) 4-Y-0+ **£2,602** (£764; £382; £190)

Form RPR
-000 **1** **Pere Blanc (IRE)**[36] 3403 6-11-2 **95** DarylJacob 121+
(David Arbuthnot) *a gng easily: prom: led sn after 3 out: cruised clr bef next* **10/3**[1]

/600 **2** *15* **Russian Epic**[20] 3686 7-11-10 **103** (t) RichardJohnson 106
(Philip Hobbs) *trckd ldrs: gng bttr than nrly all of rivals whn clsd to chse wnr after 3 out: no imp: lost 2nd briefly bef 2 out: plugged on* **8/1**

3 *9* **Life Of A Luso (IRE)**[142] 1584 7-11-7 **100** TomO'Brien 96
(Paul Henderson) *hld up in rr: stdy prog to trck ldrs 7th: rdn in 5th after 3 out: no real hdwy after* **66/1**

2654 **4** *4 ½* **Nobby Kivambo (IRE)**[26] 3589 6-11-8 **101** (p) JimmyMcCarthy 91
(Brendan Powell) *led at decent pce: hdd sn after 3 out: grad wknd* **13/2**[2]

1040 **5** *26* **Royal Kicks (FR)**[32] 3483 10-11-0 **100** MrTJCannon(7) 66
(Suzy Smith) *chsd ldrs: lost pl 4th: sn drvn in rr: wl bhd fr 7th: plugged on past toiling rivals bef 2 out* **25/1**

-056 **6** *3* **Peveril Pandora**[34] 3449 8-10-12 **91** (t) BarryKeniry 55
(Jimmy Fox) *mstkes in rr: struggling and bhd 7th: sme modest hdwy after 3 out: sn wknd* **7/1**[3]

4602 **7** *6* **Cloudy Wager**[25] 3607 6-11-2 **95** FelixDeGiles 53
(Anna Newton-Smith) *hld up in rr: prog after 6th: chsd ldrs next: lost tch u.p in 6th after 3 out* **16/1**

U-0P **8** *42* **Princely Hero (IRE)**[106] 2049 7-11-12 **105** (p) LeightonAspell 26
(Chris Gordon) *t.k.h: w ldrs to 7th: wknd rapidly sn after: wl t.o* **40/1**

64-0 **9** *52* **Mossini (IRE)**[14] 3789 6-11-12 **105** JamieMoore —
(Gary Moore) *lw: a in last trio: lost tch bef 6th: wl t.o next: continued as others in front p.u* **28/1**

0000 **10** *25* **Smoking (FR)**[34] 3454 5-11-6 **99** GerardTumelty —
(Jonathen de Giles) *chsd ldrs: wknd qckly after 6th: t.o after next: continued as others in front p.u* **25/1**

0556 **P** **El Diego (IRE)**[26] 3589 7-11-8 **101** AidanColeman —
(Jamie Snowden) *lw: in tch: chsd ldrs 7th: wl btn in 7th after 3 out: wknd rapidly and p.u bef next* **18/1**

004 **P** **The Old Buccaneer (IRE)**[25] 3601 8-10-12 **94** RichieMcLernon(3) —
(Jonjo O'Neill) *in tch: rdn and jst in tch at bk of main gp bef 3 out: sn wknd: p.u bef 2 out* **9/1**

6/5P **P** **Pikasso (FR)**[86] 2452 8-10-13 **92** WarrenMarston —
(Pam Sly) *racd wd: prom: trckd ldr 5th to 7th: wknd rapidly bef 3 out: p.u bef next* **16/1**

0-40 **P** **Across The Straits (FR)**[34] 3449 7-10-11 **93**............ JimmyDerham(3) —
(Jonathan Geake) *hld up in rr: prog after 6th: in tch next: outpcd in 8th sn after 3 out: p.u bef next* **33/1**
05-0 **P** **Star King (IRE)**[36] 3403 6-11-2 **95**.. HaddenFrost —
(Henrietta Knight) *in tch tl wknd rapidly after 4th: t.o last whn p.u bef 7th* **40/1**
0400 **F** **Original Prankster (IRE)**[28] 3542 6-11-7 **100**................ PaddyBrennan 103
(Nigel Twiston-Davies) *hld up towards rr: prog fr 5th: trckd ldrs 7th: effrt after 3 out: rdn to go 7 l 2nd but no ch w wnr whn fell heavily 2 out* **10/1**
-304 **P** **Chervonet (IRE)**[25] 3599 5-10-11 **90**..........................(bt[1]) LiamTreadwell —
(Nick Gifford) *mostly chsd ldr to 5th: wknd rapidly next: t.o after 7th: p.u bef 3 out* **18/1**
-000 **P** **Beau Colonel (FR)**[39] 3366 5-10-11 **90**........................ AndrewThornton —
(Henrietta Knight) *a in rr: lost tch 6th: t.o in last pair whn p.u bef 7th* **33/1**

5m 28.1s (4.10) **Going Correction** +0.075s/f (Yiel) **18** Ran SP% **124.8**
Speed ratings (Par 105): **95,89,85,84,74 73,70,54,35,25** —,—,—,—,— —,—,—
toteswingers:1&2:£7.10, 1&3:£95.40, 2&3:£67.10 CSF £27.41 CT £1535.77 TOTE £3.60: £1.10, £2.50, £15.40, £1.90; EX 32.80.
Owner George Ward **Bred** George Ward **Trained** Compton, Berks

FOCUS
A moderate handicap with plenty of potential improvers lurking. There was an easy winner, who was value for further and should score again. The next two are rated to form.

NOTEBOOK
Pere Blanc(IRE) ◆ showed his true colours with an easy success on this handicap debut. He travelled best throughout and could have been called the winner turning for home. The longer trip made all the difference to this son of King's Theatre, who also won his bumper at this venue, and no doubt connections will now be looking for something under a penalty as he faces a hike in the handicap. Official explanation: trainer said, regarding apparent improvement in form, that the gelding was suited by a step up in trip and a change of tactics. (op 4-1)
Russian Epic, up in trip, was another that travelled kindly but he got firmly put in his place when the winner asserted for home. This was his best effort for some time and a drop back in distance may well see him off the mark.
Life Of A Luso(IRE) hit a flat spot before creeping back into contention nearing the final turn. He failed to see it out that well in the home straight, but this was more encouraging from him returning from a 142-day break on his debut for the yard. (op 50-1)
Nobby Kivambo(IRE) ran an honest race from the front back down in trip, but remains a maiden. (tchd 11-2)
Pikasso(FR) Official explanation: jockey said gelding had a breathing problem (op 8-1)
Original Prankster(IRE), another stepping up in trip, made his way to the leaders going well on the back straight but wasn't clever three out. He was still in there fighting for second place prior to coming down at the next and was in the process of running his best race to date. (op 8-1)
Chervonet(IRE) Official explanation: jockey said gelding had a breathing problem (op 8-1)

4053 40% BETTER OFF ON BETFAIR SP GRADUATION CHASE (16 fncs) 2m 4f 110y
3:45 (3:45) (Class 2) 5-Y-0+ **£13,912** (£5,088)

Form RPR
5-23 **1** **Punchestowns (FR)**[13] 3805 8-11-7 158......................... BarryGeraghty 156+
(Nicky Henderson) *lw: nt fluent 2nd and 4th: mostly chsd ldr: pushed along and no imp fr 11th: hrd rdn and clsd after 3 out: led last: sn clr* **4/6**[1]
2P-2 **2** *11* **Pasco (SWI)**[76] 2674 8-11-7 147...(t) APMcCoy 148+
(Paul Nicholls) *lw: led and j. boldly: drew away fr 10th: 12 l up bef 3 out: tired bef 2 out: hdd and btn last* **5/2**[2]
-331 **P** **Bugsy's Boy**[20] 3689 7-11-4 120....................................(p) AndrewTinkler —
(George Baker) *last fr 4th: lost tch 8th: t.o whn p.u bef 12th* **40/1**
24-0 **P** **Crack Away Jack**[20] 3675 7-11-4 149....................... WayneHutchinson —
(Emma Lavelle) *t.k.h: hld up tl disp 2nd pl fr 4th to 9th: wknd v qckly bef next: t.o whn clambered over 13th: p.u bef next* **5/1**[3]

5m 18.1s (-1.40) **Going Correction** +0.175s/f (Yiel) **4** Ran SP% **107.7**
Speed ratings: **109,104**,—,—
CSF £2.78 TOTE £1.60; EX 2.80.
Owner Mrs Judy Wilson **Bred** Gerard Ferte **Trained** Upper Lambourn, Berks
■ A 2,000th career winner over jumps in Britain for Nicky Henderson. The first was in October 1978.

FOCUS
A true-run race and the winner is rated as being 8lb off his previous best chase figure. Pasco was 4lb off his best.

NOTEBOOK
Punchestowns(FR) for most of the race looked sure to play second fiddle to the front-running Pasco. Indeed Geraghty had a look behind to check the proximity of the other pair after jumping four out. However, the leader began to badly tire from the next and this former high-class staying hurdler's stamina kicked in just at the right time. He ultimately won going away, handing his brilliant trainer a 2,000th career success in the process. It was considered that stamina may have been an issue of late and he was down in trip here, but this was significant drop on such a speedy track. Looking at the way he finished off, the test was really too sharp for him and therefore it wouldn't be surprising to see him back up to around 3m next time. His jumping in the main once more failed to really convince, however, and he just does not look as happy in this sphere as he did over hurdles. He remained at a best-priced 40/1 for the Gold Cup, while he can be backed as big as 20/1 for the Ryanair and is as short as 12/1 for another crack at the World Hurdle. Nicky Henderson later added it may be that his 8-y-o misses Cheltenham altogether, though, and waits for Aintree's Grand National meeting instead. (op 8-11)
Pasco(SWI) was returning from a 76-day break in a first-time tongue tie and ensured this was a proper test out in front. He looked all over the winner three from home, but he wilted badly from two out and was a sitting duck at the last. He did go off plenty fast enough, but it must be remembered he is officially rated 11lb lower than Punchestowns. He was later reported to have choked afterwards and is now due a breathing operation. Official explanation: trainer's rep said gelding had a breathing problem (tchd 11-4)
Crack Away Jack, well beaten on his return at Ascot last month, raced with more enthusiasm early over this longer trip. It was clear soon after turning onto the back straight something was amiss, however, and he was pulled up soon after. He will have a wind operation now and will miss the rest of the season. (tchd 4-1 and 11-2)

4054 READ PAUL NICHOLLS EXCLUSIVELY ON BETFAIR H'CAP CHASE (18 fncs) 3m
4:20 (4:20) (Class 3) (0-135,135) 5-Y-0+
£6,262 (£1,850; £925; £463; £231; £116)

Form RPR
P3F6 **1** **Carrickmines (IRE)**[19] 3693 9-10-10 **119**...........................(b) DarylJacob 135+
(Dr Richard Newland) *mde all: stdy pce to 1/2-way: clr fr 12th: pressed briefly bef 3 out: sn drew away again: easily* **5/1**[2]
142F **2** *15* **Ravethebrave (IRE)**[13] 3803 7-11-6 **129**....................... RobertThornton 131
(Alan King) *lw: nt a fluent: hld up: prog to chse wnr 14th: rdn to cl and ch bef 3 out: sn brushed aside: tired jump last* **2/1**[1]
P-1U **3** *8* **Alderburn**[83] 2531 12-11-12 **135**..................................... TomScudamore 127
(Henry Daly) *chsd wnr to 14th: sn lft bhd: dropped to wl btn 4th after next: wnt poor 3rd again last* **11/1**
-501 **4** *2 3/4* **Plein Pouvoir (FR)**[7] 3935 8-10-13 **122** 7ex..................... AidanColeman 112
(Venetia Williams) *lw: hld up: outpcd fr 12th: chsd clr ldng pair after 15th: sn rdn and no imp: wknd and lost 3rd last* **2/1**[1]
2-65 **5** *28* **Rory Boy (USA)**[83] 2522 6-11-4 **127**..............................(p) PaddyBrennan 92
(Nigel Twiston-Davies) *in tch: effrt 10th: pushed along in 5th after next: sn dropped away: t.o* **7/1**[3]
P-4P **6** *59* **Fortification (USA)**[34] 3444 8-11-3 **126**.....................(p) DominicElsworth 38
(Michael Blake) *last after mstke 3rd: lost tch 10th: wl t.o fr 12th* **14/1**

6m 22.0s (7.00) **Going Correction** +0.175s/f (Yiel) **6** Ran SP% **110.8**
Speed ratings: **95,90,87,86,77 57**
toteswingers:1&2:£4.00, 1&3:£4.50, 2&3:£1.90 CSF £15.62 TOTE £4.10: £1.20, £1.50; EX 21.40.
Owner Dr R D P And Mrs L J Newland **Bred** Joseph Murphy **Trained** Claines, Worcs

FOCUS
A modest handicap and the easy winner is value for further. The form is rated around the first two.

NOTEBOOK
Carrickmines(IRE) ◆, back over fences, pulled his way to the front early and made all with plenty left up his sleeve. He wasn't always that fluent, but it was apparent three out he was the one to be on and he rates value for further. The switch to such tactics clearly rejuvenated him and he is capable of holding his form well, as was highlighted by him landing a hat-trick last spring. It was his highest winning mark to date, though, so turning out under a penalty looks a good move. (op 13-2)
Ravethebrave(IRE) was a faller at Cheltenham last time and he was having his first outing at the track since winning his novice hurdle here last term. He emerged as the only danger to the winner four out, but his effort in chasing him proved short lived and this trip does appear to tax his stamina. (op 9-4 tchd 11-4)
Alderburn, now a 12-y-o, hit a flat spot before plugging on for third and ought to come on for the run. (op 10-1)
Plein Pouvoir(FR) was 5lb ahead of the handicapper after bolting up at Chepstow a week earlier. It was clear he wasn't going so well nearing five out and he was beaten before stamina for the longer trip really came into play. That would suggest the run came soon enough. (op 15-8 tchd 7-4)

4055 BETFAIR MOBILE MAIDEN OPEN NATIONAL HUNT FLAT RACE 2m
4:55 (4:55) (Class 5) 4-6-Y-0 **£1,712** (£499; £249)

Form RPR
1 **Cheltenian (FR)**[108] 2032 5-11-4 0................................ RichardJohnson 107+
(Philip Hobbs) *lw: trckd ldrs: smooth prog to ld over 2f out: veered lft sn after: pushed out and a holding on* **8/15**[1]
2 *1* **Montbazon (FR)** 4-10-8 0.. RobertThornton 96+
(Alan King) *lw: str: trckd ldrs: prog to chal whn bmpd 2f out: swtchd rt over 1f out: styd on wl but a hld* **3/1**[2]
0- **3** *7* **Real Tempo (FR)**[442] 2522 6-11-4 0........................... StefaanFrancois 99+
(J-M Plasschaert, Belgium) *racd wd: w ldr to 1/2 way: lost pl completely: prog again 3f out: trying to chal whn bmpd 2f out: outpcd after* **20/1**
4 *10* **Simply Ben (IRE)** 5-10-11 0.................................... MrRGHenderson(7) 88
(Colin Tizzard) *hld up wl in rr: outpcd whn pce lifted 4f out: wl in rr stl 2f out: styd on stoutly after: snatched 4th nr fin* **16/1**[3]
4 **5** *nk* **Raifteiri (IRE)**[36] 3406 4-10-5 0................................... AlexMerriam(3) 78
(Neil King) *prom: effrt to ld 4f out to over 2f out: sn wknd* **25/1**
6 *1/2* **Orsm** 4-10-8 0.. LeightonAspell 77
(Laura Mongan) *leggy: in tch: shkn up to chse ldrs 3f out: in tch over 2f out: sn outpcd* **66/1**
6 **7** *2 1/4* **Bach To Front (IRE)**[24] 3616 6-10-4 0............................ MrTJCannon(7) 78
(Sarah Wall) *mde most at stdy pce to 4f out: easily outpcd fnl 2f* **100/1**
6 **8** *1 1/2* **Gleann Eagas (IRE)**[23] 3630 4-10-8 0................................... JackDoyle 73
(Emma Lavelle) *lw: hld up in last trio: prog 4f out: chsd ldrs over 2f out: sn outpcd* **33/1**
9 *7* **Fifi L'Amour (IRE)** 5-10-11 0.. JimmyMcCarthy 69
(Linda Jewell) *lengthy: hld up in rr: wl outpcd fr 4f out: modest late hdwy* **100/1**
5 **10** *16* **Tickle Me (IRE)**[39] 3372 5-11-4 0.. HaddenFrost 60
(Henrietta Knight) *in tch: wl outpcd over 3f out: no ch after* **50/1**
11 *1 1/2* **Kindlelight Soleil (FR)** 4-10-8 0...................................... PaulMoloney 49
(Nick Littmoden) *racd wd in rr: in tch to 4f out: sn wl outpcd and btn* **20/1**
4 **12** *4* **Malibu Sun**[67] 2824 4-10-8 0.. SamJones 45
(Oliver Sherwood) *w ldrs: disp ld 4f out to over 3f out: wknd qckly fnl 2f* **33/1**
0 **13** *9* **Willard**[15] 3773 5-10-11 0... MrMWall(7) 46
(Tony Carroll) *hld up in last trio: outpcd fr 4f out: no ch after* **100/1**
0 **14** *9* **Lord Aldervale (IRE)**[80] 2597 4-10-8 0.......................... AndrewThornton 27
(Richard Rowe) *a in rr: rn green and lost tch 4f out* **33/1**
5-0 **15** *1 1/4* **Call Me Friday**[272] 332 5-10-11 0.................................. GerardTumelty 29
(Matthew Salaman) *leggy: trckd ldrs: outpcd 4f out: sn wl btn* **66/1**
16 *44* **Everkingly** 5-11-4 0... AndrewTinkler —
(Anna Brooks) *str: bit bkwd: in tch tl wknd rapidly once pce lifted 4f out: t.o* **100/1**

4m 5.00s (10.60) **Going Correction** +0.075s/f (Yiel)
WFA 4 from 5yo+ 9lb **16** Ran SP% **127.2**
Speed ratings: **76,75,72,67,66 66,65,64,61,53 52,50,45,41,40 18**
toteswingers:1&2:£1.20, 1&3:£7.00, 2&3:£15.20 CSF £1.97 TOTE £1.90: £1.10, £1.10, £5.10; EX 3.50.
Owner R S Brookhouse **Bred** Jean-Charles Haimet & J-Pascal Liberge **Trained** Withycombe, Somerset

FOCUS
Probably not a strong bumper for the track. It was slowly run and there was a messy finish. The form is suspect but the first pair can rate higher.

NOTEBOOK
Cheltenian(FR), who is a nice type, would've likely made a winning debut at Punchestown in October but for veering badly left in the home straight, and he again went out that way under maximum pressure here. That didn't do the placed horses any good, especially the runner-up, but he did look to be just in command at that stage. No doubt he has some class about him and should come on again for the experience, but it won't be surprising to see him on a left-handed circuit in future. (op 8-11 tchd 5-6 in a place)
Montbazon(FR) ◆ was backed into clear second favourite for this racecourse debut and shaped promisingly in second. He wasn't done any favours by the winner and was closing on that one at the finish, but it didn't quite look enough to make the difference between winning and losing. He ought to learn plenty and take some stopping on his next outing, which may well come in a valuable event at Doncaster next month. He'll make a hurdler in due course. (op 10-3 tchd 7-2)
Real Tempo(FR) was having his first outing since finishing eighth to Oscar Whisky on his debut in 2009. He raced awkwardly and didn't help his rider, but there was a fair bit to like about the way he got back into contention in the home straight. He too got hampered by the winner, but was feeling the pinch at that stage. (tchd 16-1 and 40-1 in places)
Simply Ben(IRE) ◆ is a half-brother to Bensalem and Grade 2-winning novice hurdler Court In Motion. On his toes beforehand, the betting suggested he would need the initial experience, but he really caught the eye motoring home from off the pace and would've likely been placed at least under more prominent handling. He looks a sure-fire winner on a stiffer track. (tchd 20-1)
Raifteiri(IRE), on his toes beforehand, ran below his debut form.

Bach To Front(IRE) Official explanation: jockey said mare hung left
Tickle Me(IRE) looks a chaser in the making.
T/Jkpt: Part won. £25,691.10 to a £1 stake. Pool: £36,184.68 - 0.50 winning tickets. T/Plt: £74.90 to a £1 stake. Pool:£86,961.47 - 847.52 winning tickets T/Qpdt: £4.60 to a £1 stake. Pool:£7,749.60 - 1,230.90 winning tickets JN

3965 MUSSELBURGH (R-H)

Friday, February 11

OFFICIAL GOING: Soft (good to soft in places; 5.1)
Wind: Almost nil Weather: Cold, overcast

4056 TURFTV BETTING SHOP SERVICE JUVENILE MAIDEN HURDLE (9 hdls) 2m
1:55 (1:55) (Class 5) 4-Y-O **£2,276** (£668; £334; £166)

Form RPR
1 **Patterning**141 4-11-0 0 DenisO'Regan 102+
(Chris Grant) *cl up: chal 4 out: led next: edgd lft bef last and run-in: kpt on strly* **4/1**3
03 2 5 **Kingdom Of Munster (IRE)**29 3519 4-11-0 0 BrianHughes 98+
(Richard Fahey) *hld up: hdwy 4 out: effrt bef 2 out: ev ch and rdn whn hit last: one pce run-in* **3/1**2
0 3 1 **Battle Honour**16 3749 4-11-0 0 PaddyAspell 95
(Sue Bradburne) *led to 3 out: sn rdn: kpt on same pce after next* **9/1**
U 4 1 1/4 **Falcun**9 3885 4-11-0 0 GrahamLee 95
(Micky Hammond) *nt fluent: in tch tl lost pl and reminders 2nd: rallied 4 out: outpcd next: mstke last: kpt on* **10/1**
5 4 **Tamanaco (IRE)**128 4-11-0 0 RobertWalford 93+
(Tim Walford) *t.k.h: chsd ldr tl mstke 5th: rdn and outpcd fr 3 out* **5/4**1
6 9 **Thescottishsoldier**214 4-10-11 0 EwanWhillans(3) 80
(Alistair Whillans) *hld up: outpcd bef 4 out: sn n.d* **80/1**
7 59 **Sixties Rock**220 4-10-9 0 JamesHalliday(5) 21
(William Young) *t.k.h: in tch tl wknd 1/2-way: t.o* **100/1**
3m 56.1s (7.70) **Going Correction** +0.425s/f (Soft) **7** Ran SP% **110.8**
Speed ratings: **97,94,94,93,91 86,57**
toteswingers:1&2:£4.60, 1&3:£12.90, 2&3:£3.30 CSF £15.68 TOTE £3.60: £2.20, £1.60; EX 16.70.
Owner Elliott Brothers And Peacock **Bred** Darley **Trained** Newton Bewley, Co Durham

FOCUS
An ordinary juvenile hurdle but the winner can rate higher.

NOTEBOOK
Patterning, a winner on the Flat in France, cost 20,000gns at the sales last October and ran out a ready winner in the end, coming right away after the last. This was a pleasing start, although more will be needed if he's to defy a penalty. (op 7-2 tchd 9-2)
Kingdom Of Munster(IRE) had an experience edge on the winner, but having moved up nicely to challenge he made a right mess of the last and was unable to recover. (op 11-4 tchd 7-2)
Battle Honour improved markedly on his debut effort at the course and seemed better suited by this slower surface. (op 11-1 tchd 7-1)
Falcun, who unseated on debut, made mistakes and was never travelling particularly well, but did run on towards the finish. (op 13-2 tchd 11-1)
Tamanaco(IRE), a 1m2f soft-ground winner on the Flat, was well fancied to make a winning debut over hurdles, but didn't find as much as expected for pressure and was ultimately well held. (op 7-4)

4057 TURFTV THE BEST OF BRITISH RACING BEGINNERS' CHASE (18 fncs) 3m
2:25 (2:25) (Class 4) 5-Y-O+ **£3,197** (£965; £497; £263)

Form RPR
2622 1 **Alderley Rover (IRE)**19 3694 7-11-0 132 (p) JasonMaguire 122+
(Donald McCain) *led to 3rd: chsd ldr: nt fluent 10th: led after 5 out: j.lft next: styd on wl* **4/6**1
133P 2 4 1/2 **Ballymacduff (IRE)**16 3750 7-11-0 108 (t) JanFaltejsek 110
(George Charlton) *cl up: led 3rd: blnd 5 out: sn hdd: kpt on fr 3 out: nt pce of wnr* **9/2**3
4305 3 17 **Political Pendant**3 3996 10-10-7 0 RyanMania 89
(Rayson Nixon) *hld up: outpcd 1/2-way: sme hdwy bef 4 out: nvr rchd ldrs* **66/1**
60U0 4 16 **Devil Water**28 3549 8-10-7 95 NathanMoscrop(7) 79
(James Ewart) *hld up: outpcd 1/2-way: n.d after* **50/1**
5-P0 U **I Witness (IRE)**97 2202 9-10-7 0 AlistairFindlay(7) —
(Jane Walton) *in tch: dropped to rr 5th: 5th and no ch whn j. awkwardly and uns rdr 11th* **100/1**
/21- F **Sitting Tennant**446 2435 8-11-0 0 BrianHughes —
(Howard Johnson) *trckd ldrs: fell heavily 6th* **3/1**2
6m 16.9s (13.50) **Going Correction** +0.70s/f (Soft) **6** Ran SP% **107.6**
Speed ratings: **105,103,97,92,— —**
toteswingers:1&2:£1.10, 1&3:£6.50, 2&3:£6.50 CSF £3.84 TOTE £1.90: £1.10, £1.90; EX 3.30.
Owner Alec Craig & Andrew Dick **Bred** Miss Kitty O'Connor **Trained** Cholmondeley, Cheshire
■ Stewards' Enquiry : Nathan Moscrop caution: used whip when clearly fourth.

FOCUS
An uncompetitive beginners' chase. The cosy winner was value for further but rated 10lb off his best.

NOTEBOOK
Alderley Rover(IRE), who took over and started to draw away from the end of the back straight, was kept up to his work down the straight for a comfortable first success over fences. It had taken him enough attempts, but the first-time cheekpieces clearly helped and he may progress returned to handicaps. (op 5-6)
Ballymacduff(IRE), pulled up with a slipping saddle when also without the usual tongue-tie over hurdles latest, took a few chances at his fences on this chasing debut, but stuck to his task well once the winner took over and can pick up something similar. (op 5-1 tchd 11-2)
Sitting Tennant, returning from a 446-day absence, took a heavy fall down the back. It's hoped he can bounce back from this. (op 9-4 tchd 7-2)

4058 TURFTV SHOWING NEWBURY LIVE TOMORROW H'CAP HURDLE (12 hdls) 2m 4f
3:00 (3:00) (Class 3) (0-135,123) 4-Y-O+ **£4,796** (£1,447; £745; £394)

Form RPR
4230 1 **Devotion To Duty (IRE)**39 3362 5-11-3 114 PeterBuchanan 122+
(Lucinda Russell) *cl up: led bef 3 out: clr next: kpt on strly* **6/1**
1243 2 10 **Amir Pasha (UAE)**5 3966 6-10-9 111 (v) JamesHalliday(5) 110
(Micky Hammond) *hld up in tch: hdwy to chse (clr) wnr bef 2 out: no imp whn mstke last* **3/1**2
2100 3 6 **Quito Du Tresor (FR)**41 3292 7-11-11 122 CampbellGillies 116
(Lucinda Russell) *led to bef 3 out: sn rdn and outpcd fr next* **9/2**
410P 4 21 **Bucephalus (IRE)**94 2300 7-11-4 115 (t) MichaelMcAlister 86
(Maurice Barnes) *in tch: hdwy 1/2-way: rdn after 4 out: wknd bef next: lft poor 4th last* **40/1**
P012 U **Rolecarr (IRE)**31 3500 8-10-5 102 AdrianLane —
(Ann Hamilton) *cl up: nt fluent 5th: mstke and uns rdr next* **7/2**3
15-0 F **Stormy Weather (FR)**76 2671 5-11-12 123 (t) BrianHughes 113
(Howard Johnson) *trckd ldrs: effrt and rdn bef 3 out: wknd next: 13 l 4th whn fell last* **11/4**1
4m 56.3s (4.80) **Going Correction** +0.425s/f (Soft) **6** Ran SP% **108.8**
Speed ratings (Par 107): **107,103,100,92,— —**
toteswingers:1&2:£2.00, 1&3:£4.90, 2&3:£3.20 CSF £22.97 TOTE £9.10: £4.90, £1.10; EX 28.10.
Owner Racing Management & Training Ltd **Bred** Sorento Farm **Trained** Arlary, Perth & Kinross

FOCUS
Just an ordinary handicap hurdle. A step up from the winner, who could be rated higher on his old Flat form.

NOTEBOOK
Devotion To Duty(IRE), below par latest, returned to his earlier form to run out a relatively easy winner, staying on strongly having gone to the front. This was his first success over hurdles and, although a rise will follow, he's the type to go in again. Official explanation: trainer had no explanation for the apparent improvement in form (tchd 13-2)
Amir Pasha(UAE), reappearing only five days after finishing third over C&D, again ran his race without troubling the winner. (op 7-2)
Quito Du Tresor(FR), back over hurdles, ended up well held but should be up to winning off this mark. (op 4-1 tchd 5-1)
Rolecarr(IRE) departed at a relatively early stage. (tchd 3-1)
Stormy Weather(FR) was well held when falling at the last. This was disappointing. (tchd 3-1)

4059 WATCH RACING UK LIVE ON SKY 432 NOVICES' HURDLE (9 hdls) 2m
3:35 (3:35) (Class 4) 4-Y-O+ **£2,602** (£764; £382; £190)

Form RPR
12 1 **Little Hercules (IRE)**29 3525 5-11-2 0 BrianHughes 106+
(Howard Johnson) *trckd ldrs: effrt and led after last: pushed out: comf* **11/4**2
4-40 2 2 **Master Beau**41 3288 7-11-2 0 JanFaltejsek 103+
(George Charlton) *prom: nt fluent 5th: effrt bef last: chsd wnr run-in: kpt on* **4/5**1
000- 3 4 **Toledo Gold (IRE)**112 4072 5-11-2 102 (t) MichaelMcAlister 99+
(Maurice Barnes) *t.k.h: led bef 3rd and sn clr: rdn whn nt fluent 2 out: mstke last: sn hdd and no ex* **66/1**
44-0 4 1 3/4 **Nelson's Chief**254 576 5-10-9 0 NathanMoscrop(7) 95
(James Ewart) *prom: outpcd 3 out: kpt on fr last: nvr rchd ldrs* **20/1**
0-10 5 shd **Cheatingsideoftown (IRE)**11 3851 5-11-2 0 TomMessenger 95
(Sue Bradburne) *led to 3rd: chsd clr ldr tl 2 out: kpt on same pce fr last* **28/1**
-005 6 2 **Erin Dancer (IRE)**41 3304 6-10-9 0 EdmondLinehan(7) 93
(Ferdy Murphy) *hld up in midfield: outpcd 4 out: styd on fr 2 out: nrst fin* **40/1**
7 1 3/4 **Sendiym (FR)**115 4-10-6 0 GrahamLee 81
(Ferdy Murphy) *t.k.h in midfield: stdy hdwy after 4 out: effrt bef 2 out: sn no ex* **13/2**3
0 8 10 **Northern Acres**16 3746 5-11-2 0 WilsonRenwick 81
(Sue Bradburne) *hld up: outpcd 1/2-way: shortlived effrt bef 2 out: sn no imp* **80/1**
000 9 7 **Dirleton (IRE)**16 3746 5-11-2 0 RichieMcGrath 74
(George Charlton) *hld up: struggling 1/2-way: nvr on terms* **66/1**
10 2 **Ravi River (IRE)**18 7-11-2 0 FearghalDavis 72
(Brian Ellison) *hld up: outpcd bef 4 out: sn btn* **16/1**
0 11 4 **Lyrical Intent**99 2162 5-11-2 0 (t) RyanMania 68
(Maurice Barnes) *mstkes in rr: no ch fr 1/2-way* **80/1**
0-54 12 3 **Cool Water**31 3504 6-10-9 0 BrianHarding 58
(John Wade) *plld hrd towards rr: struggling fr 1/2-way* **50/1**
3m 55.9s (7.50) **Going Correction** +0.425s/f (Soft)
WFA 4 from 5yo+ 9lb **12** Ran SP% **119.5**
Speed ratings (Par 105): **98,97,95,94,94 93,92,87,83,82 80,79**
toteswingers:1&2:£1.40, 1&3:£15.20, 2&3:£9.50 CSF £5.27 TOTE £2.50: £1.10, £1.30, £22.40; EX 8.40.
Owner Andrea & Graham Wylie **Bred** Frank McKevitt **Trained** Billy Row, Co Durham

FOCUS
The principals came to the fore late on in what was a modest novice hurdle. The winner can rate higher but the second was below his best bumper level.

NOTEBOOK
Little Hercules(IRE), a Catterick bumper winner who was beaten under a penalty back there next time, shaped very much as though in need of a longer trip, only really getting going inside the final furlong. On this evidence he should improve a ton for an extra 4f and can probably defy a penalty up north. (op 2-1 tchd 3-1 in places)
Master Beau, twice well held at Cheltenham this season behind smart types, was expected to find this easier and he had his chance, but was unable to stay on as strongly as the winner. He too wants further. (op 13-8 tchd 15-8 in a place)
Toledo Gold(IRE) showed much-improved form on this debut for Maurice Barnes. Sent off at 66-1, he kept finding for pressure in the first-time tongue-tie and only gave way after the last. He could be of some interest in handicaps.
Nelson's Chief looks to want further and will be of interest in handicaps. (op 16-1)
Cheatingsideoftown(IRE) stepped up on his initial effort over hurdles and is another future handicap prospect. (tchd 25-1)
Erin Dancer(IRE) will be of interest for low-grade handicaps in future. (op 25-1)
Sendiym(FR), a Flat winner in France, made no impact but should improve for the experience.

4060 WATCH RACING UK LIVE ON VIRGIN MEDIA 536 H'CAP CHASE (18 fncs) 3m
4:10 (4:10) (Class 3) (0-125,125) 5-Y-O+ **£4,119** (£1,216; £608; £304; £152)

Form RPR
P2-4 1 **Dark Ben (FR)**99 2163 11-10-11 110 DougieCostello 120+
(Simon West) *mde all: rdn 4 out: styd on wl fr next* **7/2**1
465 2 4 1/2 **Go Silver Bullet (FR)**16 3751 10-11-4 117 PeterBuchanan 124
(Lucinda Russell) *hld up in tch: stdy hdwy bef 13th: effrt and ev ch briefly bef 4 out: kpt on fr next: nt rch wnr* **16/1**
5620 3 13 **Zitenka (IRE)**29 3522 9-11-1 119 (b) JamesHalliday(5) 116
(Tim Easterby) *trckd ldrs: effrt after 4 out: wknd fr next* **9/2**2
0631 4 6 **Nelliedonethat (IRE)**28 3549 11-10-6 105 CampbellGillies 100+
(Lucinda Russell) *cl up: effrt rdn and outpcd after 5 out: wkng whn nt fluent 3 out: btn whn blnd bdly next* **5/1**3
22-1 5 7 **Logans Run (IRE)**286 91 8-11-11 124 BrianHughes 106
(Howard Johnson) *hld up in tch: hit 12th: effrt after 5 out: wknd fr next* **9/2**2

2-0P **6** *25* **Fiftyfive Degrees (IRE)**[23] 3634 10-10-10 109............... RichieMcGrath 64
(Pauline Robson) *hld up: blnd bdly 11th: sn struggling: t.o* **15/2**
50-0 **P** **Mill Side**[76] 2669 11-11-12 125.. JasonMaguire —
(Donald McCain) *prom: reminders 4th: rdn 11th: wknd fr 13th: t.o whn p.u bef 4 out* **7/1**
215P **P** **Elzahann (IRE)**[14] 3784 9-10-13 112..................................... GrahamLee —
(Ferdy Murphy) *nt fluent: a bhd: lost tch fnl circ: t.o whn p.u bef 4 out* **12/1**

6m 15.9s (12.50) **Going Correction** +0.70s/f (Soft) **8** Ran SP% **113.1**
Speed ratings: **107,105,101,99,96 88,—,—**
toteswingers:1&2:£5.70, 1&3:£4.80, 2&3:£13.90 CSF £50.35 CT £253.84 TOTE £6.00: £2.70, £4.90, £2.60; EX 59.60.
Owner J D Gordon **Bred** Naji Pharaon **Trained** Middleham Moor, N Yorks

FOCUS
The front two pulled clear in the end.

NOTEBOOK
Dark Ben(FR)'s quick and fluent jumping made the difference. Soon in front, he was bold at his fences throughout the contest and was clever at the last when getting in too close. This was a return to his very best form. (op 9-2)
Go Silver Bullet(FR) emerged as a big danger rounding for home, but he could never quite get on terms with the winner. It's coming up for two years since he last won a race. (op 20-1)
Zitenka(IRE) had trip and ground to suit but faded from the third-last. (op 6-1)
Nelliedonethat(IRE) made mistakes at a critical stage and ended up well held.
Logans Run(IRE), off since winning a novice chase at Hexham last spring, made a couple of mistakes and was quickly beaten. (op 4-1 tchd 7-2)

4061 WATCH RACING UK LIVE AT RACINGUK.COM MAIDEN HURDLE (12 hdls) 2m 4f
4:45 (4:45) (Class 5) 4-Y-0+ **£2,276** (£668; £334; £166)

Form RPR
1F2 **1** **Aikman (IRE)**[16] 3749 7-11-1 0... HarryHaynes(3) 107+
(James Ewart) *mde all: rdn 2 out: styd on strly: readily* **4/6**[1]
-022 **2** *8* **Rupert Lamb**[40] 3331 5-11-4 119.. BrianHughes 96+
(Howard Johnson) *nt fluent on occasions: in tch: hdwy bef 3 out: chsd wnr and effrt next: kpt on same pce run-in* **2/1**[2]
2 **3** *5* **Ubi Ace**[18] 3715 5-11-4 0.. RobertWalford 92+
(Tim Walford) *plld hrd: cl up tl rdn and no ex fr 2 out* **7/1**[3]
-00F **4** *3 ½* **Scotswell**[40] 3330 5-10-11 0.. GaryRutherford(7) 88
(Harriet Graham) *hld up in tch: outpcd after 4 out: struggling fr next: no imp whn hung rt fr last* **100/1**
0/0- **5** *3* **Andreo Bambaleo**[339] 4508 7-11-4 0.............................. FearghalDavis 83
(Simon West) *in tch: hdwy 4 out: rdn and wknd fr next* **150/1**
0000 **P** **Over The Clyde**[11] 3856 6-10-13 0................................ JamesHalliday(5) —
(William Young) *cl up tl lost pl after 4th: t.o whn p.u after 4 out* **200/1**

4m 56.8s (5.30) **Going Correction** +0.425s/f (Soft) **6** Ran SP% **108.0**
Speed ratings (Par 103): **106,102,100,99,98 —**
toteswingers:1&2:£1.10, 1&3:£2.20, 2&3:£1.10 CSF £2.15 TOTE £2.10: £1.20, £1.70; EX 2.60.
Owner J D Gordon **Bred** Gerry Carroll **Trained** Langholm, Dumfries & G'way

FOCUS
A weak maiden hurdle. The easy winner was the form pick and there is a case for rating the race a stone higher through the first three.

NOTEBOOK
Aikman(IRE) clearly relished this step up in trip. He drew right away from the last and looks a nice chasing prospect for next season. Firstly, though, he can probably defy a penalty. (op 5-6)
Rupert Lamb again found one too good, but may pick up a race once switched to handicaps. (op 13-8)
Ubi Ace emptied late on and deserves another chance to build on his debut promise. (op 13-2 tchd 15-2)
Scotswell should have a future in moderate handicaps. (op 150-1)
T/Plt: £13.60 to a £1 stake. Pool:£58,962.69 - 3,142.28 winning tickets T/Qpdt: £5.40 to a £1 stake. Pool:£4,870.79 - 665.62 winning tickets RY

3850 AYR (L-H)
Saturday, February 12

OFFICIAL GOING: Heavy (soft in places; chs 6.6; hdl 6.8)
Last two fences in back straight omitted all chases due to false ground.
Wind: Almost nil Weather: Cloudy

4062 IRVINE ANDERSON MEMORIAL NOVICES' HURDLE (12 hdls) 3m 110y
1:50 (1:50) (Class 4) 5-Y-0+ **£2,602** (£764; £382; £190)

Form RPR
2-32 **1** **Yes Tom (IRE)**[12] 3851 6-10-5 119............................ JeremiahMcGrath(7) 126+
(R T J Wilson, Ire) *trckd ldrs: led gng wl bef 3 out: sn clr: easily* **8/13**[1]
201P **2** *14* **Arctic Court (IRE)**[17] 3742 7-11-5 117......................... RichieMcGrath 116
(Jim Goldie) *hld up: hdwy and prom 3rd: wnt 2nd 8th tl outpcd bef 3 out: rallied to chse (clr) wnr next: no imp* **11/2**[3]
2-16 **3** *11* **Sunnyside**[104] 2102 6-11-0 0.. AlexanderVoy(5) 110
(Lucy Normile) *led tl hdd bef 3 out: lost 2nd and wknd next* **9/2**[2]
60-5 **4** *40* **Easter Vic**[18] 3729 10-10-5 81.............................(p) MichaelMcAlister 51
(Robert Goldie) *bhd and sn rdn along: outpcd whn mstke 7th: nvr on terms* **66/1**
0-05 **5** *53* **Frontier Boy (IRE)**[24] 3633 7-10-9 0.............................. HarryHaynes(3) 5
(James Ewart) *nt fluent: in tch tl wknd fr 8th: t.o* **14/1**
40 **P** **Via Archimede (USA)**[17] 3746 6-10-12 0........................ PeterBuchanan —
(Lucinda Russell) *bhd: struggling 7th: sn btn: t.o whn p.u bef last* **33/1**
P-PP **P** **Arc Warrior (FR)**[12] 3854 7-10-12 105..........................(t) JamesReveley —
(Andrew Parker) *nt fluent in rr: lost tch 7th: t.o whn p.u bef 4 out* **66/1**
02F **P** **Kalulushi (IRE)**[18] 3726 6-10-12 0.................................. AdrianLane —
(Donald McCain) *trckd ldr to 8th: wknd bef next: wl btn whn hit 3 out: sn p.u* **20/1**
0P0 **P** **Plutonium (IRE)**[10] 3887 5-10-5 0.............................. StevenGagan(7) —
(Elliott Cooper) *prom: lost pl after 3rd: lost tch fr next: t.o whn p.u bef 4 out* **150/1**

6m 29.7s (-2.10) **Going Correction** +0.15s/f (Yiel) **9** Ran SP% **113.5**
Speed ratings: **109,104,101,88,71 —,—,—,—**
toteswingers:1&2:£1.10, 1&3:£1.10, 2&3:£3.00 CSF £4.24 TOTE £1.80: £1.02, £2.30, £1.60; EX 3.90.
Owner T J Topping **Bred** B A Hamilton **Trained** Larne, Co Antrim

FOCUS
The course had lost its previous meeting five days earlier owing to waterlogging but survived a 7am inspection this time, despite a further 13mm of rain in the preceding 24 hours. Conditions were inevitably very testing, described as "hard work" by Brian Harding after race two. This didn't look much of an opener on paper, and only three were still meaningfully involved with five to jump despite them going just a steady pace early on. The easy winner was the form pick and rates a small personal best.

NOTEBOOK
Yes Tom(IRE) looked in very good order in the preliminaries and travelled effortlessly throughout the race, coasting to the front turning in and requiring minimal assistance to assert. Second to Grand National aspirant Ballabriggs over here 2m4f last time, the ordinary fractions fudged the issue to an extent over whether he stays 3m, but he deserves to remain of interest in a truer run event at this trip. (op 4-6)
Arctic Court(IRE), outclassed in a Pertemps qualifier at Huntingdon last time, looked vulnerable to the favourite under a penalty for his C&D handicap win off 110 before that. He merely boxed on past one flagging rival late on for second place, and a return to both handicap company and drier surfaces would see him more competitive again. (op 6-1)
Sunnyside raced enthusiastically in front but could offer virtually nothing once headed. He has proven effectiveness over 3m and also on soft going, but not the two together. (tchd 5-1)
Easter Vic, a winning pointer, raced no less indolently than previously in first-time cheekpieces, and her completion owes much to her rider's perseverance. (op 50-1)
Kalulushi(IRE) didn't jump as if confidence was an issue after his chasing fall last time, but still faded out of things rapidly on this deepest surface ever encountered.

4063 BET LIVE AT VICTORCHANDLER.COM NOVICES' CHASE (13 fncs 4 omitted) 2m 4f
2:20 (2:20) (Class 3) 5-Y-0+ **£5,204** (£1,528; £764; £381)

Form RPR
00-0 **1** **Alexander Oats**[280] 214 8-10-9 86.................................. HarryHaynes(3) 119+
(Robert Goldie) *hld up: hdwy bef 4 out: effrt and led bef last: kpt on strly run-in* **20/1**
-U1P **2** *3* **Sibenek (IRE)**[28] 3571 7-11-4 122...................................(p) JamesReveley 122
(Martin Todhunter) *led: rdn bef 3 out: hdd bef last: kpt on same pce run-in* **11/8**[1]
4/P5 **3** *3* **Steady Tiger (IRE)**[12] 3852 9-10-12 0................................ BrianHarding 113
(Nicky Richards) *trckd ldr: effrt bef 3 out: disputed ld after 2 out: outpcd fr last* **6/4**[2]
/P-P **4** *14* **Woody Waller**[35] 3440 6-10-12 0.. BrianHughes 102
(Howard Johnson) *nt fluent on occasions: chsd ldrs: outpcd whn hit 9th: rallied and cl up whn mstke 4 out: wknd fr next* **4/1**[3]

5m 37.8s (14.90) **Going Correction** +0.15s/f (Yiel) **4** Ran SP% **106.9**
Speed ratings: **76,74,73,68**
CSF £47.45 TOTE £23.60; EX 37.70.
Owner Robert H Goldie **Bred** Robert H Goldie **Trained** Dundonald, S Ayrshire
■ Permit holder Robert Goldie's first winner under rules for nearly 15 years.

FOCUS
There was an extended run out of the back straight in all chase races, as the last two fences in the back straight (both portables) were not in situ. This was just a modest novice chase, in which three of the four-strong field took the second last in a line. The time was very slow and the form is suspect.

NOTEBOOK
Alexander Oats, on his chasing debutant, was the most patiently ridden, and despite having been the first to receive a ride late in the back straight produced plenty from the last to scoot home. This represented a clear career best having been beaten 29l or more in all bumper and hurdles starts previously, though the repeat bid under a penalty will be far tougher. (op 22-1)
Sibenek(IRE), sporting first-time cheekpieces, tried to inject a couple of increments of pace down the back straight but could never slip the field by more than 3l. His current mark of 122 doesn't look too unreasonable judged on what he achieved in winning a Carlisle handicap last November, and a return to that sphere can see him improve on this effort. (op 6-4 tchd 6-5)
Steady Tiger(IRE) is still working his way back into form after a 21-month absence, and as he did in an identical C&D race on good last time just struggled to find sufficient gears when it mattered. His jumping held up better this time, however, and he could have something to offer in races placing greater emphasis on stamina if that improvement can be sustained. (tchd 7-4, 15-8 in places)
Woody Waller's cause on this chasing debut wouldn't have been helped by a blunder five out and a guessy leap at the next, and he was the first one beaten. This was at least his first completion in his last three jumps starts. (tchd 9-2)

4064 PLAY CASINO AT VICTORCHANDLER.COM H'CAP CHASE (13 fncs 4 omitted) 2m 4f
2:50 (2:51) (Class 5) (0-95,95) 5-Y-0+ **£1,951** (£573; £286; £143)

Form RPR
6-64 **1** **Locked Inthepocket (IRE)**[87] 2450 7-11-12 95............. RichieMcGrath 116+
(Pauline Robson) *trckd ldrs: led gng wl after 4 out: drew clr fr next: v easily* **11/4**[1]
/245 **2** *22* **Innominate (IRE)**[14] 3819 9-11-3 86.............................(t) CampbellGillies 85+
(Lucinda Russell) *led to 2nd: led 7th: qcknd 9th: hit 4 out and sn hdd: plugged on: no ch w wnr* **15/2**
4403 **3** *2 ¼* **Go On Be A Lady**[19] 3712 8-10-12 81..............................(p) BarryKeniry 74
(Alan Swinbank) *chsd ldrs: drvn and outpcd passing omitted 5 out: styd on fr 2 out: no imp* **8/1**
-05P **4** *1* **Sammy Spiderman**[10] 3888 8-11-4 87................................ BrianHarding 81+
(Alistair Whillans) *in tch: drvn and outpcd passing omitted 5 out: rallied bef 2 out: keeping on but no imp whn hmpd by faller last* **11/2**[3]
4-32 **5** *6* **Soul Angel**[10] 3884 7-11-2 85..(p) PaddyAspell 69
(Sandy Forster) *in tch: outpcd 9th: n.d after* **7/2**[2]
355P **6** *2 ½* **Master Sebastian**[32] 3501 12-11-10 93.......................... PeterBuchanan 74
(Lucinda Russell) *nt fluent in rr: struggling 7th: sme late hdwy: nvr on terms* **9/1**
P-40 **7** *¾* **Nifty Roy**[81] 2601 11-11-4 87.. BrianHughes 68
(Brian Storey) *cl up: led 2nd to 7th: cl up tl rdn and wknd bef 4 out* **28/1**
6FF3 **P** **Native Coll**[10] 3884 11-10-7 83.................................... MissLAlexander(7) —
(N W Alexander) *in tch: outpcd passing omitted 6 out: t.o whn p.u 4 out* **8/1**
/0-0 **F** **Robbie Dye**[24] 3635 9-11-3 86.. AdrianLane 79
(Donald Whillans) *hld up: hdwy to trck ldrs passing omitted 5 out: ev ch briefly after next: one pce fr 3 out: 25 l 3rd and hld whn fell last* **25/1**
00PF **P** **Soldiers Tree (IRE)**[10] 3884 6-10-3 77.......................... AlexanderVoy(5) —
(Sue Bradburne) *bhd and sn detached: t.o whn p.u bef 7th* **20/1**

5m 30.0s (7.10) **Going Correction** +0.15s/f (Yiel) **10** Ran SP% **120.3**
Speed ratings: **91,82,81,80,78 77,77,—,—,—**
toteswingers: 1&2 £4.00, 1&3 £6.80, 2&3 £4.60. CSF £24.16 CT £151.89 TOTE £4.20: £1.40, £2.20, £3.30; EX 24.00.
Owner Mr & Mrs Raymond Anderson Green **Bred** Declan Winters **Trained** Kirkharle, Northumberland

FOCUS
They seemed to go off at a better early pace in this low-grade handicap than the novice event which preceded it, and the winner duly recorded a time over six seconds faster. A big step up from the winner and the form could be rated up to 3lb higher.

NOTEBOOK
Locked Inthepocket(IRE), still available at 11-2 in places in the morning, comfortably allayed connections' pre-race fears that the going may be softer than he'd like. Looking to be going the best from early down the back straight, the issue was very quickly put beyond doubt soon after turning for home. Dropped 6lb since his last start, it will be interesting to see if he's asked to defy a penalty at Musselburgh on Wednesday before the assessor gets chance to exact retribution for this rout. (op 3-1 tchd 10-3 in a place)
Innominate(IRE) came in for a little late support and did well to remain involved for as long as he did, given he helped set decent fractions and also got far too close to four out. He has sunk 22lb in the weights since first sent handicap chasing without winning in this sphere, though once again here he showed the raw material is certainly there to win a poor heat. (op 10-1)
Go On Be A Lady lost her position halfway down the back straight and never really recovered, merely inheriting a poor third at the last. Cheekpieces have failed to elicit any significant improvement in the last two runs.
Sammy Spiderman is now 8lb lower than when a C&D win completed an Ayr hat-trick almost exactly two years ago, and it was disappointing he could do no better than this with course, trip, mark and going all in his favour for the first time this season. (op 6-1 tchd 9-2)
Soul Angel was never travelling with much purpose, and maybe this came a bit too soon after his slog around Newcastle 10 days earlier. (op 9-2)
Robbie Dye was a poor third when coming down at the last. (tchd 28-1)

4065 BEST ODDS GUARANTEED AT VICTOR CHANDLER H'CAP CHASE (10 fncs 2 omitted) 2m
3:20 (3:20) (Class 3) (0-135,132) 5-Y-0+ **£5,529** (£1,623; £811; £405)

Form RPR
1F-0 **1** **Reindeer Dippin**[33] 3490 9-11-12 **132** BrianHarding 148+
(Donald McCain) *disp ld: mstke 1st: led passing omitted 5 out: rdn next: kpt on wl* **9/1**
-020 **2** 7 **Raysrock (IRE)**[41] 3333 9-10-13 **119** (t) CampbellGillies 125
(Lucinda Russell) *in tch: rdn and outpcd after 6th: rallied 4 out: chsd wnr next: no imp* **7/2**[2]
0255 **3** 2 **Et Maintenant (FR)**[28] 3573 9-11-0 **120** PeterBuchanan 124
(Lucinda Russell) *prom: effrt bef 4 out: no imp fr 2 out* **8/1**[3]
1-43 **4** 3 ¾ **Diamond Frontier (IRE)**[80] 2613 8-11-4 **124** BrianHughes 124
(Howard Johnson) *slt ld tl hdd passing omitted 5 out: wknd fr 3 out* **7/2**[2]
P001 **5** 37 **Quicuyo (GER)**[12] 3854 8-11-0 **120** (t) RyanMania 100
(James Ewart) *chsd ldng pair: outpcd after 6th: wknd fr 4 out* **5/2**[1]
1P40 **P** **Sotovik (IRE)**[20] 3695 10-10-1 **110** EwanWhillans(3) —
(Alistair Whillans) *nt jump wl: sn bhd: struggling 5th: t.o whn p.u bef 6th* **8/1**[3]
-564 **P** **Ockey De Neulliac (FR)**[28] 3573 9-11-1 **121** GrahamLee —
(Ferdy Murphy) *bhd: reminders 4th: lost tch 6th: t.o whn p.u bef 4 out* **12/1**

4m 10.0s (-0.70) **Going Correction** +0.15s/f (Yiel) 7 Ran SP% **112.9**
Speed ratings: **107,103,102,100,82** —,—
toteswingers: 1&2 £16.90, 1&3 £14.50, 2&3 £6.50. CSF £40.06 TOTE £9.40: £4.70, £2.30; EX 52.00.
Owner Sandgrounders **Bred** D McCain **Trained** Cholmondeley, Cheshire

FOCUS
The highlight of the afternoon's card but maybe not too strong for the grade, with only the top three in the weights within a stone of the handicap ceiling and others not obviously well treated at present. The impressive winner is a decent chaser, and the next two ran to their marks.

NOTEBOOK
Reindeer Dippin had clearly benefited from his belated seasonal reappearance in a Towcester hurdle and found willingly when asked to go on up the straight. Still only four runs into his chasing career, and evidently suited by assertive tactics over galloping 2m courses, the Grand Annual wouldn't rate too fanciful a future target (already rated 3lb higher than last year's winner). (op 7-1)
Raysrock(IRE) hadn't seen it out over 2m4f last time, but got closer dropped back in trip and with a tongue-tie without looking likely to get up. Still 4lb above his highest winning mark over fences, he could remain tricky to win with in the immediate term. (op 7-1)
Et Maintenant(FR) was still thereabouts turning in and ran his race, but he has a similar profile to his stablemate Raysrock in being a bit too far above his best winning mark to recommend confidently as a winner in waiting, even following a 2lb drop for a below-par latest effort. (op 15-2)
Diamond Frontier(IRE) is still to win a handicap over jumps of any description but remains on a feasible mark judged on his best novice chase form last term. The winner's attentions won't have helped him this time, and he may still be up to winning one of these if granted an uncontested lead. (op 9-4)
Quicuyo(GER) was inspired by a first-time tongue-tie to a C&D win off 110 last time, but he's been compromised off marks as high as today's over hurdles and fences previously and was again here. (op 3-1)
Sotovik(IRE) Official explanation: jockey said gelding never travelled

4066 JIM SMITH QFSM, 57, RETIREMENT H'CAP CHASE (15 fncs 4 omitted) 3m 1f
3:55 (3:55) (Class 4) (0-105,101) 5-Y-0+ **£3,252** (£955; £477; £238)

Form RPR
-630 **1** **Garleton (IRE)**[12] 3853 10-11-4 **98** AlexanderVoy(5) 120+
(Maurice Barnes) *j.w: mde all: drew clr fr 4 out: easily* **10/3**[1]
-32P **2** 42 **Bear Dancing (IRE)**[43] 3260 7-11-11 **100** PeterBuchanan 80
(Lucinda Russell) *prom: wnt 2nd 1/2-way: rdn bef 4 out: sn no ch w wnr* **5/1**
05P **3** 1 ¾ **Blazing Diva (IRE)**[19] 3716 8-11-12 **101** CampbellGillies 79
(Sandy Thomson) *chsd wnr to 1/2-way: cl up: drvn bef 4 out: sn outpcd* **8/1**
/U-4 **4** 23 **Skenfrith**[10] 3888 12-10-8 **83** (p) PaddyAspell 38
(Sandy Forster) *prom: rdn bef 9th: wknd fr next* **13/2**
-PP6 **5** 15 **Waterski**[25] 3617 10-10-9 **84** RyanMania 24
(Jean McGregor) *hld up in tch: struggling 11th: nvr on terms* **14/1**
F1-P **P** **Seven Is Lucky (IRE)**[12] 3853 9-11-9 **98** GrahamLee —
(Jim Goldie) *hld up in tch: rdn and struggling bef 10th: t.o whn p.u bef 4 out* **7/2**[2]
P-24 **P** **Seeking Power (IRE)**[32] 3501 10-10-12 **94** (v[1]) MissLAlexander(7) —
(N W Alexander) *bhd and sn pushed along: struggling 7th: t.o whn p.u 10th* **9/2**[3]

6m 53.2s (3.30) **Going Correction** +0.15s/f (Yiel) 7 Ran SP% **111.3**
Speed ratings: **100,86,86,78,73** —,—
toteswingers: 1&2 £7.80, 1&3 £4.80, 2&3 £9.30. CSF £19.26 TOTE £3.70: £1.80, £2.90; EX 24.10.
Owner East-West Partnership **Bred** Thomas And Mrs Bridget Buckley **Trained** Farlam, Cumbria

FOCUS
A reasonably well-run race given the conditions, and many of the runners were already toiling with over a circuit to go. The winner is rated back to his best but this is not form to be confident about.

NOTEBOOK
Garleton(IRE) was neither headed nor under particularly strong pressure at any point in proceedings, and was simply being given a breather when rivals closed him down to a length leaving the final back straight. He has tended to record his victories in twos previously and is therefore entitled to remain of interest granted a similar assignment next time, even if returned to somewhere close to his highest winning mark of 106 for this. (op 7-2)
Bear Dancing(IRE) acquitted himself pleasingly on this first try over regulation fences and travelled better than all bar the winner. The impression given in his pointing starts last term that he could be suited by even longer distances in time was borne out again here by a one-paced effort up the straight, and maybe a race such as the four-miler at Hexham in March would be just the ticket. (tchd 9-2)
Blazing Diva(IRE) lacked fluency early on and was flattered to get briefly within hailing distance of the winner before the turn for home. She is back down to her highest winning mark and did come into her own this time last year (scoring twice), though, so she could find another small contest in the coming weeks. (op 10-1)
Skenfrith has dropped back to the mark off which he won a 3m5f handicap here in March 2009, but he has stood little racing since and didn't inspire much hope of a revival this time. (tchd 7-1)
Seeking Power(IRE) barely went a yard from flagfall, and it's quite possible he resented the first-time visor. (op 4-1 tchd 5-1)

4067 VICTOR CHANDLER H'CAP HURDLE (12 hdls) 2m 5f 110y
4:30 (4:30) (Class 4) (0-115,112) 4-Y-0+ **£2,602** (£764; £382; £190)

Form RPR
-602 **1** **Last Of The Bunch**[28] 3570 6-11-9 **109** BarryKeniry 111+
(Alan Swinbank) *trckd ldrs gng wl: chal appr 3 out: rdn next: led run-in: styd on wl* **14/1**
-626 **2** nk **Charlie Bucket**[32] 3502 8-10-9 **105** CallumWhillans(10) 106
(Donald Whillans) *hld up: hdwy on outside to ld bef 3 out: hdd run-in: kpt on towards fin* **25/1**
U-63 **3** 15 **Currahee**[263] 458 7-11-12 **112** (t) MichaelMcAlister 99
(Maurice Barnes) *in tch: rdn and outpcd 3 out: kpt on to take 3rd run-in: no ch w first two* **33/1**
-001 **4** 1 ¾ **Kempski**[87] 2448 11-11-0 **100** RyanMania 85
(Rayson Nixon) *led: rdn and hdd bef 3 out: kpt on same pce next* **12/1**
-420 **5** nk **What A Dream**[40] 3362 5-11-1 **101** JamesReveley 86
(William Amos) *hld up: stdy hdwy 4 out: rdn and no imp fr next* **14/1**
443 **6** 3 ½ **What A Steel (IRE)**[20] 3693 7-10-5 **94** EwanWhillans(3) 74
(Alistair Whillans) *prom: effrt appr 3 out: wknd fr next* **9/4**[1]
P265 **7** 12 **Delightfully (FR)**[40] 3362 7-10-7 **100** (b) MrGJCockburn(7) 68
(Lucinda Russell) *hld up: drvn along after 4 out: wknd bef next* **8/1**
500 **8** 14 **King Sandor (IRE)**[20] 3692 6-10-5 **101** StephenMulqueen(10) 55
(Nicky Richards) *bhd: struggling 7th: nvr on terms* **66/1**
0013 **9** 11 **Bene Lad (IRE)**[24] 3635 9-10-7 **93** RichieMcGrath 36
(Jim Goldie) *trckd ldrs tl rdn and wknd qckly bef 3 out* **7/2**[2]
/01- **10** 17 **Mr Preacher Man**[359] 4125 9-11-5 **105** PeterBuchanan 31
(Lucinda Russell) *bhd: struggling 7th: nvr on terms* **25/1**
-P4P **P** **Oscar Honey (IRE)**[108] 2036 10-11-7 **107** GrahamLee —
(Rose Dobbin) *midfield: lost pl 1/2-way: struggling fr 7th: t.o whn p.u bef 3 out* **20/1**
000 **P** **Davy Boy Legend (IRE)**[17] 3746 8-10-0 **93** GaryRutherford(7) —
(Josie Ross) *t.k.h: cl up: lost pl qckly 1/2-way: sn struggling: t.o whn p.u bef 3 out* **40/1**
5-23 **U** **Malin Bay (IRE)**[32] 3500 6-11-11 **111** BrianHarding —
(Nicky Richards) *hld up: blnd bdly and uns rdr 5th* **4/1**[3]

5m 45.2s (4.90) **Going Correction** +0.15s/f (Yiel) 13 Ran SP% **124.5**
Speed ratings (Par 105): **97,96,91,90,90 89,85,79,75,69** —,—,—
toteswingers: 1&2 £26.50, 1&3 £26.50, 2&3 £24.50. CSF £320.41 CT £10800.87 TOTE £13.10: £3.90, £6.20, £10.20; EX 421.50.
Owner E Briggs **Bred** E Briggs **Trained** Melsonby, N Yorks

FOCUS
An ordinary looking contest beforehand, and probably not the strongest form the grade, either, with none of the market leaders meaningfully involved at the end. The race has been given a downbeat rating, even though the first two came clear.

NOTEBOOK
Last Of The Bunch had to set her own pace over an inadequate 2m at Wetherby last time, but was happier sitting behind the pacesetters before being asked to take on the leader from two out. This was a game effort, but she hadn't looked up to defying this sort of mark previously and more will be required to follow up accordingly. (op 11-1)
Charlie Bucket looked to have pinched an advantage over the winner with the quicker leap at the last, but couldn't quite find any extra once headed up the run-in. His profile remains a little too inconsistent to offer unbridled optimism of his reproducing this effort next time. (op 20-1)
Currahee's record fresh previously hadn't made for inspiring reading, so this staying-on effort after 263 days away rates a very sound effort. Still 8lb above his highest winning hurdles mark, presumably a return to fences, over which he made his debut when last seen, is not far off. (op 28-1)
Kempski broke the habit of a lifetime with a win at Hexham on his latest start, having previously recorded all five victories over 2m4f here. His effort petered out over this longer trip up the straight, but he is still 12lb below his highest winning mark and may have another contest in him at this venue dropped back in distance.
What A Steel(IRE), who was well supported, had been in fair form without seeing out his races especially well before today, and it was a similar story here. He remains untried back down at 2m in handicap company. (op 11-4 tchd 3-1 in a place)
Bene Lad(IRE) may have preferred at least a share of the early lead, but posted a disappointing effort even so. (op 13-2)

4068 RONNIE CLARK RETIREMENT H'CAP HURDLE (9 hdls) 2m
5:05 (5:05) (Class 5) (0-95,95) 4-Y-0+ **£1,951** (£573; £286; £143)

Form RPR
005- **1** **Circus Clown (IRE)**[297] 5305 6-11-8 **91** GrahamLee 102+
(Jim Goldie) *hld up in tch: stdy hdwy and cl up 4 out: led bef next: kpt on strly fnl 2* **8/1**
/041 **2** 3 ½ **Kings Guard (IRE)**[24] 3635 8-11-8 **94** EwanWhillans(3) 97
(Alistair Whillans) *in tch: effrt and chsd wnr 3 out: hit next: kpt on same pce run-in* **2/1**[1]
60-0 **3** 2 **See The Legend**[83] 2547 6-11-0 **83** PaddyAspell 83
(Sandy Forster) *hld up in tch: hdwy bef 3 out: rdn bef next: kpt on same pce last* **12/1**
/5-0 **4** 10 **Crackerjack Lad (IRE)**[40] 3363 8-11-3 **86** PeterBuchanan 78+
(Lucinda Russell) *hld up: mstke and outpcd 4th: hdwy bef 3 out: rdn and wknd bef last* **9/2**[3]
4/00 **5** 7 **Miss Champagne (IRE)**[24] 3631 8-10-0 **69** oh4 BarryKeniry 52
(Andrew Wilson) *hld up in tch: effrt bef 3 out: wknd after next* **25/1**
3P00 **6** 16 **Also Jo**[24] 3631 8-11-8 **91** JamesReveley 58
(William Amos) *hld up in tch: rdn after 4 out: wknd fr next* **20/1**
0066 **7** 5 **Glengap (IRE)**[4] 3997 8-9-7 **69** oh1 (b[1]) CallumWhillans(7) 31
(Elliott Cooper) *t.k.h: led tl hdd bef 3 out: wknd fr next* **16/1**

-600 **8** *13* **Fightstar (FR)**[41] 3331 7-11-12 **95** .... CampbellGillies 44
(Lucinda Russell) *hld up: rdn along bef 4 out: nvr on terms* **25/1**

600- **9** *1* **Parson's Punch**[327] 4781 6-11-1 **89** .... AlexanderVoy(5) 37
(Lucy Normile) *hld up: drvn along bef 4 out: nvr on terms* **40/1**

5065 **10** *27* **Daniel's Dream**[12] 3855 11-10-5 **74** .... (tp) BrianHarding —
(John Dixon) *mstkes: cl up tl hit and wknd 4 out* **16/1**

6063 **11** *15* **Rhyton (IRE)**[19] 3717 4-10-10 **89** .... AdrianLane —
(Donald McCain) *chsd ldrs tl rdn and wknd 4 out* **4/1**[2]

-15P **F** **Emirate Isle**[12] 3855 7-11-12 **95** .... (p) BrianHughes —
(Brian Storey) *trckd ldrs to 4 out: sn wknd: wl btn whn fell next* **20/1**

4m 6.50s (3.40) **Going Correction** +0.15s/f (Yiel)
WFA 4 from 6yo+ 9lb 12 Ran SP% **121.7**
Speed ratings (Par 103): **97,95,94,89,85 77,75,68,68,54 47,—**
toteswingers: 1&2 £3.90, 1&3 £15.50, 2&3 £9.90. CSF £23.99 CT £202.37 TOTE £12.20: £3.00, £2.00, £3.40; EX 40.20.
Owner David McKenzie **Bred** Floors Farming & The Duke Of Devonshire **Trained** Uplawmoor, E Renfrews

FOCUS
A low-grade handicap and a massive step up from the easy winner.

NOTEBOOK
Circus Clown(IRE) put up a career-best effort on his debut for Jim Goldie. Fitness evidently wasn't considered an issue despite a 297-day absence as the Vettori gelding was sent on before the turn in, and that confidence was vindicated with a strong-staying effort. His initial handicap mark of 91 hadn't seemed conspicuously generous beforehand, but he looks an improver now and is the sort that these connections can place to advantage in modest northern handicaps from here on. Longer term, a low Flat mark looks exploitable, too. Official explanation: trainer said, regarding apparent improvement in form, that this was the gelding's first run for the yard and believed its previous trainer felt it would be better suited by soft ground. (tchd 9-1)
Kings Guard(IRE), victorious over 2m4f at Newcastle last time, was already under some pressure before a mistake in the straight and he cannot be classed as unlucky. This was nevertheless another fair effort off a 6lb higher mark, and he can continue to give a decent account, especially stepped back up in trip. (op 9-4)
See The Legend improved on this handicap debut without looking a serious threat, and a step up to 2m4f wouldn't go amiss on this evidence. (op 16-1)
Crackerjack Lad(IRE) shaped with more promise on his second run back from a lengthy absence. The better form before his setback had been recorded on good and good to soft, so he could be found a small contest granted drier conditions later in the season. (op 11-2 tchd 6-1)
Rhyton(IRE) faded out of contention before the turn for home, and is another who'd probably need a sounder surface to be seen in a better light. Official explanation: trainer's rep said gelding was unsuited by the heavy (soft in places) ground (op 10-3 tchd 5-2)
T/Plt: £8,370.40 to a £1 stake. Pool:£46,438.96 - 4.05 winning tickets. T/Qpdt: £339.30 to a £1 stake. Pool:£4,814.72 - 10.50 winning tickets RY

3624 NEWBURY (L-H)
Saturday, February 12

OFFICIAL GOING: Good to soft (hdl 6.1, chs 6.7)
Wind: Moderate ahead Weather: Sunny intervals

4069 BET TOTEPOOL ON 0800 221 221 NOVICES' HURDLE (8 hdls) 2m 110y
1:20 (1:43) (Class 3) 4-Y-0+ **£5,204** (£1,528; £764; £381)

Form RPR

-F31 **1** **Al Ferof (FR)**[23] 3647 6-11-8 137 .... HarrySkelton 142+
(Paul Nicholls) *nt fluent 1st: mde all: c readily clr fr 3 out: nt fluent last: unchal* **1/4**[1]

2 *15* **Oasis Knight (IRE)**[274] 5-11-2 0 .... BarryGeraghty 118
(Nicky Henderson) *chsd wnr to 4 out: styd cl up: drvn to go 2nd again 2 out and kpt on but nvr any ch* **5/1**[2]

5 **3** *11* **Yorgunnabelucky (USA)**[15] 3781 5-11-2 0 .... RobertThornton 108
(Alan King) *chsd ldrs: wnt 2nd 4 out but nvr nr clr ldr and subsequent unchal wnr: lost 2nd 2 out and sn wknd* **9/1**[3]

4 *14* **Archie Rice (USA)**[16] 5-11-2 0 .... PaulMoloney 95+
(Tom Keddy) *nt fluent 1st: in rr: sme hdwy appr 3 out but nvr anywhere nr ldrs: wl bhd whn nt fluent 2 out and last* **40/1**

P6 **5** *14* **Guarino (GER)**[11] 3872 7-11-2 0 .... AndrewGlassonbury 85
(Gary Moore) *chsd ldrs: hit 4th: disp 2nd 4 out: nvr nr clr ldr and subsequent wnr: wknd after 3 out* **66/1**

10 **6** *42* **The Merry Giant (IRE)**[35] 3439 5-11-2 0 .... DominicElsworth 45
(Rebecca Curtis) *in rr but in tch whn mstke and slipped bdly 4 out: no ch after* **40/1**

000 **7** *17* **Senses (USA)**[23] 3645 5-11-2 0 .... TomScudamore 30
(David Pipe) *a wl bhd: j. slowly 13th: blnd 2 out* **50/1**

4m 0.37s (-9.53) **Going Correction** -0.325s/f (Good) 7 Ran SP% **115.0**
Speed ratings (Par 107): **109,101,96,90,83 63,55**
toteswingers:1&2:£1.02, 1&3:£2.30, 2&3:£1.90 CSF £2.14 TOTE £1.30: £1.10, £1.80; EX 2.40.
Owner J Hales **Bred** J Rauch & G Chenu **Trained** Ditcheat, Somerset

FOCUS
There was a near 25-minute delay to this novice hurdle, tragedy striking in the paddock as both Fenix Two and Marching Song collapsed and sadly died after appearing to have been electrocuted by a live cable under the turf. The race was dealt a further blow when Kid Cassidy, who had briefly fallen to his knees in the paddock, was wisely withdrawn having been checked over by both his trainer Nicky Henderson and a vet down at the start. Al Ferof was value for further and is rated to his mark.

NOTEBOOK
Al Ferof(FR) was left with a relatively straightforward task following the withdrawal at the start of Kid Cassidy, who had survived what appeared to have been an electric shock in the parade ring but was plainly disturbed by it. His jumping could have been slicker, but this strong, galloping type powered clear for a comfortable success. Last year's Champion Bumper runner-up, who was expected to take very high rank over hurdles this season, he is well on his way to recapturing peak form, having fallen on his first start over hurdles, and will be an exciting prospect once faced with a longer trip. He has multiple options at the festival, with the Neptune looking favourite ahead of the Albert Bartlett at this stage. (old market op 10-11 new market op 2-7 tchd 1-1 in places)
Oasis Knight(IRE), a smart Flat performer up to 2m, started to chase the winner from two out, but never got within challenging distance. Clear of the third, this was a very pleasing start and he should have no trouble going one better upped in distance. (old market op 7-1 new market op 4-1)
Yorgunnabelucky(USA), a 92-rated Flat performer who was beaten just under 10l having been hampered on his hurdles debut, again showed enough to suggest he'll be winning once faced with an easier task. (new market op 7-1)
Archie Rice(USA), rated 68 on the Flat, was keen and never got involved on this debut over hurdles, but this was a stiff enough introduction. (new market)
The Merry Giant(IRE) appeared to be another sufferer in the incident which claimed the lives of two rivals in the parade ring, but he was allowed to take part. He finished tailed off and was later reported to be in a very traumatised state in the stables. (old market op 66-1 new market)
T/Jkpt: £1.40 to a £1 stake. Pool:£47,294.58 - 23,003.80 winning tickets T/Plt: £1.10 to a £1 stake. Pool:£18,3128.69 - 17,701.50 winning tickets ST

3767 WARWICK (L-H)
Saturday, February 12

OFFICIAL GOING: Good to soft (6.2)
Wind: Almost nil Weather: Bright and sunny

4076 WARWICK SUPPORTS THE RACING LOTTERY NOVICES' H'CAP HURDLE (8 hdls) 2m
1:40 (1:41) (Class 4) (0-110,110) 4-Y-0+ **£2,927** (£859; £429; £214)

Form RPR

-001 **1** **Shalambar (IRE)**[15] 3782 5-10-13 **102** .... LeeEdwards(5) 110+
(Tony Carroll) *pressed ldr tl led 4th: drvn 2 l clr bef 2 out: hanging lft after: nt fluent last: styd on gamely* **4/1**[1]

2125 **2** *3/4* **Switched Off**[33] 3481 6-11-9 **107** .... (v[1]) DaveCrosse 113+
(Ian Williams) *hld up: pushed along to improve whn mstke 5th: stl 6th 3 out: styd on to go 2nd 2 out: no real imp on wnr and racd w an awkward hd carriage flat* **9/2**[2]

630- **3** *7* **Peace Corps**[17] 5245 5-11-3 **101** .... (vt) DavidEngland 101
(Michael Gates) *prom: chsd wnr and drvn 2 out: one pce after* **16/1**

05F **4** *4* **Cruise Control**[30] 3526 5-10-9 **93** .... GerardTumelty 90+
(Richard Price) *last tl 3rd: stdy prog 5th: 12 l 5th and no ch w ldrs whn blnd last* **33/1**

4304 **5** *3 3/4* **Kayfton Pete**[8] 3917 5-11-5 **110** .... PeterHatton(7) 102
(Reg Hollinshead) *chsd ldrs: rdn 5th: wknd bef 2 out: lost 4th after last* **20/1**

503 **6** *1* **Art Broker (IRE)**[32] 3495 5-11-3 **108** .... JakeGreenall(7) 99
(Henry Daly) *midfield: effrt after 5th: chsd wnr bef 2 out: sn drvn and wknd* **6/1**[3]

0510 **7** *3* **Nosecond Chance (IRE)**[21] 3691 5-11-9 **110** .... PeterToole(3) 98
(Charlie Mann) *chsd ldrs fr 4th: 4th and rdn after 3 out: fdd bef next* **25/1**

5006 **8** *5* **Superior Knight**[40] 3365 7-10-12 **96** .... DavidDennis 80
(James Evans) *a bhd: no ch fr 5th* **40/1**

3P00 **9** *3 1/2* **Mega Watt (IRE)**[17] 3744 6-11-2 **100** .... (b) SamThomas 80
(Venetia Williams) *midfield: struggling after blunder 5th* **13/2**

P-0F **10** *1/2* **Irish Symphony (IRE)**[20] 3696 7-11-4 **105** .... CharlieHuxley(3) 85
(John Mackie) *nvr bttr than midfield and nt fluent: mstke 5th and drvn: sn struggling* **25/1**

24 **11** *7* **Tara Warrior (IRE)**[171] 1369 5-11-11 **109** .... JoeTizzard 83
(Tim Vaughan) *prom tl rdn and lost pl 5th* **12/1**

0 **12** *7* **Hail Caesar (IRE)**[33] 3481 5-11-9 **110** .... WayneKavanagh(3) 77
(Evan Williams) *towards rr: rdn bef 4th: sn btn* **20/1**

0000 **13** *10* **Jomade (IRE)**[23] 3645 5-10-13 **97** .... JasonMaguire 55
(Kim Bailey) *last at 3rd: sn lost tch: t.o 3 out* **20/1**

40-5 **F** **The Quantum Kid**[25] 3620 7-11-0 **98** .... CharliePoste —
(Robin Dickin) *racd wd: led tl 4th: wknd 3 out: fell next* **9/1**

3m 50.2s (-6.30) **Going Correction** -0.325s/f (Good) 14 Ran SP% **116.7**
Speed ratings (Par 105): **102,101,98,96,94 93,92,89,88,87 84,80,75,—**
toteswingers: 1&2 £5.70, 1&3 £5.30, 2&3 £9.70. CSF £19.27 CT £260.44 TOTE £6.10: £2.10, £1.10, £6.10; EX 21.90.
Owner B J Millen **Bred** His Highness The Aga Khan's Studs S C **Trained** Cropthorne, Worcs

FOCUS
An open-looking novice handicap. There was a sound enough gallop on. The winner looked nicely in and there should be more to come.

NOTEBOOK
Shalambar(IRE) came out best in a tight finish on his handicap debut over hurdles at Doncaster 15 days previously and he again showed a decent attitude to follow up off his 5lb higher mark. A sound surface looks important to his cause, which implies this ground was riding near good, and further improvement cannot be ruled out as he remains fairly unexposed. (tchd 9-2 in places)
Switched Off is a talented but quirky performer and he met solid support with a first-time visor replacing cheekpieces. He hit a flat spot after hitting four out, but rallied strongly off the home turn and was only just held. He rates the benchmark. (tchd 4-1)
Peace Corps was making his debut for the stable after winning an AW claimer 17 days earlier and he posted just about his most encouraging effort over hurdles. A step up in trip could see him get off the mark.
Cruise Control caught the eye from off the pace around three out and this was a lot more encouraging on his handicap debut over hurdles. This long-standing maiden has clearly begun on a workable mark and deserves to be ridden more positively. (op 28-1)
Art Broker(IRE) was well backed for his handicap debut as a hurdler and held every chance, but he fell in a hole from two out on this switch to better ground. (op 9-2)

4077 BET ON TOTESCOOP6 ON 0800 221 221 AT TOTESPORT.COM H'CAP CHASE (17 fncs) 2m 4f 110y
2:10 (2:11) (Class 2) 5-Y-0+
£12,524 (£3,700; £1,850; £926; £462; £232)

Form RPR

-1F0 **1** **Hey Big Spender (IRE)**[42] 3292 8-11-12 **150** .... JoeTizzard 160+
(Colin Tizzard) *settled trcking ldrs and racd keenly: effrt 11th: led 13th: rdn and kpt on stoutly fr 2 out: all out but a in control* **17/2**

1210 **2** *4* **Fine Parchment (IRE)**[35] 3438 8-10-3 **130** .... (t) PeterToole(3) 136
(Charlie Mann) *nt a fluent: cl up: hit 12th: rdn next: hit 3 out: sn drvn to chse wnr: no imp* **9/1**

-031 **3** *5* **Chance Du Roy (FR)**[35] 3438 7-11-0 **138** .... TomO'Brien 139
(Philip Hobbs) *racd keenly: led 5th tl 11th: rdn and lost 2nd after 3 out: plugged on same pce* **5/1**[3]

-030 **4** *13* **Panjo Bere (FR)**[21] 3677 8-11-0 **143** .... (b) JoshuaMoore(5) 131
(Gary Moore) *chsd ldr 2nd tl lft in ld 4th: hdd 5th: 2nd tl narrow ld 11th tl 13th: rdn and wknd after 3 out* **12/1**

2342 **5** *1* **Balzaccio (FR)**[16] 3770 6-10-11 **135** .... SamThomas 125+
(Alan King) *chsd ldrs: nt fluent 10th: rdn bef next: wknd 14th: mstke last* **4/1**[1]

1420 **6** *1/2* **Working Title (IRE)**[35] 3453 9-10-12 **136** .... AndrewTinkler 124
(Nicky Henderson) *in rr but wl in tch 11th: lost grnd tamely: wl bhd 14th: plugged on fr 2 out* **15/2**

133- **7** *88* **Latanier (FR)**[297] 5307 8-10-5 **136** .... HarryChalloner(7) 44
(Venetia Williams) *chsd ldrs: rdn 11th: kpt jumping rt after and qckly dropped to rr: t.o 14th* **9/1**

43PP **F** **Magic Sky (FR)**[28] 3568 11-9-12 **129** .... JakeGreenall(7) —
(Milton Harris) *last whn fell 2nd* **10/1**

2136 **P** **Fiendish Flame (IRE)**[35] 3446 7-11-5 **143** .... JasonMaguire —
(Donald McCain) *j. violently rt: led tl 4th: last after 7th: p.u after next* **9/2**[2]

5m 2.00s (-19.00) **Going Correction** -0.625s/f (Firm) 9 Ran SP% **113.9**
Speed ratings: **111,109,107,102,102 102,68,—,—**
toteswingers: 1&2 £14.00, 1&3 £7.00, 2&3 £8.60. CSF £79.14 CT £423.43 TOTE £13.20: £4.40, £3.60, £1.40; EX 108.70 Trifecta £259.70 Part won. Pool: £350.99 - 0.38 winning units..

Owner Brocade Racing **Bred** Oliver Brennan **Trained** Milborne Port, Dorset
■ Stewards' Enquiry : Joshua Moore one-day ban: used whip with excessive frequency (Feb 26)

FOCUS
This decent handicap was run at a solid tempo and the first three finished clear of the remainder. The form looks solid and Hey Big Spender is a top-class handicapper.

NOTEBOOK
Hey Big Spender(IRE) had previously shown his best form on stiffer tracks and therefore it wasn't surprising to see him get somewhat tapped for toe through the early parts. He made headway going strongly from halfway, however, and never looked in that much danger of being caught after taking it up from the fourth-last. This was a decent weight carrying performance off a mark of 150, and a crack at the Racing Post Chase at Kempton later this month is now possible. He was cut into as short as 10-1 for that in the ante-post betting, but picks up a 5lb penalty. (op 8-1 tchd 9-1)
Fine Parchment(IRE) rallied gamely rounding the home turn, but was never going to reel in the winner. This was much more like it from him again back on a sounder surface, although the handicapper looks to have him where he wants him. (tchd 10-1)
Chance Du Roy(FR) was 8lb higher than when opening his account for the season on testing ground at Chepstow last month, when well in front of Fine Parchment. He posted a solid effort in defeat considering the race probably didn't play out to his strengths. (op 9-2)
Panjo Bere(FR) had been struggling for form previously this term. Equipped with blinkers for the first time since winning in them over hurdles in France in 2007, he showed up a little more encouragingly, but an end to his losing run does not look immanent. (tchd 11-1)
Balzaccio(FR), a close second in novice company over course and distance 16 days earlier, felt the pinch on the back straight and never threatened. (op 9-2)
Working Title(IRE) was never going that well. (op 7-1 tchd 6-1)
Latanier(FR) clearly needed this seasonal debut. (op 8-1)
Fiendish Flame(IRE) jumped badly out to his right from the off and presumably something went amiss. Official explanation: jockey said gelding jumped badly right (op 5-1)

4078 TOTESPORT.COM KINGMAKER NOVICES' CHASE GRADE 2 (12 fncs) 2m
2:40 (2:40) (Class 1) 5-Y-O+ **£17,637** (£6,951; £3,747)

Form RPR
5-11 **1** **Finian's Rainbow (IRE)**[24] 3625 8-11-4 156 ...... AndrewTinkler 152+
(Nicky Henderson) *t.k.h: j. erratically early: wnt 2nd at 4th: qcknd and lft in ld 8th: flew over next two: unconvincing jump 2 out and again whn lft wl clr at last: heavily eased* **2/5**[1]
1311 **2** *11* **Stagecoach Pearl**[84] 2520 7-11-7 147 ...... ShaneByrne 136
(Sue Smith) *led tl 7th: nt fluent 9th: sn outpcd: 15 l 3rd 2 out: lft 2nd at last and all out to hold it* **6/1**[2]
-0F1 **3** *nk* **Tail Of The Bank (IRE)**[8] 3932 8-11-0 0 ...... LiamHeard 130+
(Laura Young) *t.k.h early: mstke 2nd: last fr 4th: wl bhd 7th: drvn and tried vainly to catch runner-up flat* **12/1**
14 **P** **Kilmurry (IRE)**[90] 2384 6-11-7 143 ...... JoeTizzard 152
(Colin Tizzard) *chsd ldr: led 7th tl blnd 8th: ev ch 3 out: trying to rally u.p but hld whn p.u sharply between last two: fatally injured* **13/2**[3]

3m 56.4s (-9.20) **Going Correction** -0.625s/f (Firm) 4 Ran SP% **106.7**
Speed ratings: **98,92,92,—**
CSF £3.21 TOTE £1.40; EX 3.50.
Owner Michael Buckley **Bred** J O'Keeffe **Trained** Upper Lambourn, Berks

FOCUS
An uncompetitive Grade 2 once Kilmurry went wrong before the last. Finian's Rainbow was value for further but a few pounds off his season's best, with the second over a stone off after a break.

NOTEBOOK
Finian's Rainbow(IRE) handed his trainer successive wins in this race, following Long Run a year ago, despite not impressing with his fencing. He was allowed to coast home after his only rival at the time went wrong when still throwing down a challenge in between the final two fences, and he must rate as flattered by the winning margin. This Grade 2 event does represent a proper jumping test with the five fences on the back straight coming up quickly, but he had jumped deliberately before arriving at that point. Indeed he hit the second-last when looking in control and Kilmurry was still in with a fighting chance. It must be remembered that rival was also conceding him 3lb, so he cannot be considered impressive here. His jockey Andrew Tinkler, however, was pleased with the manner in which he jumped when put under some pressure and expects him to learn from the experience. His odds remained largely unchanged at the top of the ante-post betting for the Arkle and, in an uninspiring year for the 2m novice division, any horse that goes there 3-3 over fences will no doubt prove popular. However, while the stiffer track there may help his cause, his jumping will be put under real scrutiny and he will need to brush it up if he is to extend his winning sequence. (tchd 4-11 and 4-9 in places)
Stagecoach Pearl, with Kilmurry breaking down, just held on to a distant second place. He has had a cracking time of it since going chasing, but after setting a decent gallop he was done with after being headed at the seventh. (op 15-2)
Tail Of The Bank(IRE) never looked that happy after taking a keen grip and probably found the ground lively enough. (op 17-2 tchd 8-1)
Kilmurry(IRE) sadly went wrong when still throwing down a challenge in between the final two fences. (op 8-1)

4079 TOM GRANT 18TH BIRTHDAY H'CAP HURDLE (12 hdls) 3m 1f
3:10 (3:10) (Class 3) (0-120,116) 4-Y-O+ **£3,903** (£1,146; £573; £286)

Form RPR
0020 **1** **Snake Charmer**[10] 3881 8-11-1 105 ......(v) DaveCrosse 109+
(Milton Harris) *bhd: nt fluent 1st and 3rd: drvn and stdy prog 8th: stl 6th bef 2 out: swtchd lft to chal between last two: led 100yds out: all out* **33/1**
-062 **2** *nk* **Crazy Eyes (IRE)**[17] 3744 6-11-8 115 ......(t) PeterToole(3) 119+
(Charlie Mann) *t.k.h in rr: hdwy 8th: nt fluent 3 out: hrd rdn 4th and looked outpcd bef 2 out where mstke: forced along to chal and ev ch flat: no ex cl home* **5/1**[1]
5063 **3** *nk* **Vin De Roy (FR)**[25] 3621 6-10-12 107 ...... RTDunne(5) 110
(Rachel Hobbs) *settled trcking ldrs: nt fluent 6th: hdwy 9th: mstke next: led 2 out tl rdn and hdd 100yds out* **9/1**
-530 **4** *4* **Red Mile (FR)**[21] 3688 6-11-8 112 ...... JackDoyle 112
(Emma Lavelle) *nt fluent 3rd: last tl 7th: rdn and mstke 8th: prog next: 4th and chsng ldrs bef 2 out: no imp after* **8/1**[3]
PPP0 **5** *6* **Tisfreetdream (IRE)**[16] 3771 10-11-8 112 ......(p) TomSiddall 107+
(Peter Pritchard) *cl up: led after 3 out: drvn and hdd next: wkng whn bmpd last* **50/1**
B-5P **6** *5* **Thedeboftheyear**[98] 2218 7-11-4 115 ...... MrRHawkins(7) 103
(Chris Down) *hld up in midfield: stdy prog 8th: led 3 out: sn hdd & wknd* **33/1**
-560 **7** *6* **Munlochy Bay**[59] 2955 7-10-8 103 ......(p) GilesHawkins(5) 86
(Matt Sheppard) *prom: led 8th: hdd and j. awkwardly 3 out: sn fdd* **14/1**
-P02 **8** *7* **Arctic Echo**[19] 3713 12-11-6 110 ......(t) AndrewThornton 87
(Rob Summers) *led 3rd tl 8th: sn drvn: wknd after next* **22/1**
4244 **9** *¾* **Father Probus**[16] 3771 5-11-8 112 ...... DavidEngland 88
(Nigel Twiston-Davies) *handy: wnt prom after 7th tl drvn bef 3 out: no rspnse and sn btn* **12/1**
6121 **10** *10* **Big Talk**[14] 3818 4-10-3 112 ......(v) MrSWDrinkwater(7) 67
(David Bridgwater) *bhd: rdn after 7th: nvr nr ldrs* **25/1**
-025 **11** *1* **Point West (IRE)**[42] 3299 7-11-4 115 ...... SClements(7) 81
(Nick Mitchell) *mstke 5th: in rr and struggling u.p bef 8th* **10/1**
3U22 **12** *10* **Deep Pockets (IRE)**[16] 3771 12-11-8 115 ...... IanPopham(3) 72
(Caroline Keevil) *led tl 3rd: rdn and lost 2nd bef 8th: sn dropped out* **8/1**[3]
2132 **13** *5* **Calypso Bay (IRE)**[27] 3589 5-11-3 110 ...... RichieMcLernon(3) 62
(Jonjo O'Neill) *midfield: rdn bef 7th: mstke and nvr gng wl after: struggling next* **7/1**[2]
12-0 **14** *½* **Broughton Green (IRE)**[16] 3771 10-11-5 116 ...... AodhaganConlon(7) 68
(Jim Old) *chsd ldrs: rdn and outpcd whn mstke 3 out* **25/1**
6030 **15** *31* **Worth A King'S**[41] 3334 5-11-10 114 ......(b) JasonMaguire 38
(Donald McCain) *mstke 2nd: cl up tl 6th: dropped bk to last bef 8th: sn t.o* **14/1**
5-05 **P** **Mr Bennett (IRE)**[16] 3771 8-11-11 115 ......(p) JohnnyFarrelly —
(David Pipe) *pressed ldrs: rdn bef 8th where terrible mstke whn looking hld: p.u after next* **14/1**
222F **P** **Vivarini**[16] 3771 7-11-4 115 ...... CharlieWallis(7) —
(John O'Shea) *bhd: last and rdn and nt gng wl 7th: t.o and p.u 3 out* **22/1**

6m 14.4s (-13.10) **Going Correction** -0.325s/f (Good)
WFA 4 from 5yo+ 11lb 17 Ran SP% **122.4**
Speed ratings (Par 107): **107,106,106,105,103 102,100,97,97,94 94,90,89,89,79 —,—**
toteswingers: 1&3 £38.60, 1&3 £91.20. 2&3 £11.30. CSF £183.30 CT £1659.17 TOTE £41.60: £7.50, £1.60, £2.40, £2.20; EX 295.00 TRIFECTA Not won..
Owner Racing Roses Partnership **Bred** The National Stud **Trained** Herridge, Wiltshire

FOCUS
A modest staying handicap, run at a proper gallop, and it produced a cracking finish. The form is solid and the winner may still be capable of a bit better than this.

NOTEBOOK
Snake Charmer hit top gear around the second-last flight and got on top where it mattered under a strong ride. He found plenty when taken to the stands' rail after the last and, back up to a suitably longer trip, had clearly benefited from a 5lb drop in the weights. It was his first success since 2009, which came off a 10lb higher mark. (op 28-1)
Crazy Eyes(IRE) returned to form when second at Huntingdon 17 days earlier and was 3lb higher for this step up in trip. He travelled sweetly into contention, but hit the third-last and that probably cost him. Clearly back at the top of his game, his turn shouldn't be far off. (op 8-1)
Vin De Roy(FR) was 3lb lower than when third at Southwell last month and posted a career-best effort with a bold run here. A slight drop back in trip could well see him open his account. (op 10-1)
Red Mile(FR) came from way off the pace and, like the runner-up, made a crucial error at three from home. It was his best effort so far, on just his second outing in a handicap, and he looks capable of further improvement over this trip. (tchd 9-1)
Tisfreetdream(IRE) came into this looking badly out of sorts, but he produced a rejuvenated effort and would've been closer at the finish had he been held onto for longer.
Calypso Bay(IRE) was beaten a long way out and ran nowhere near his previous level. (op 11-2)
Mr Bennett(IRE) Official explanation: jockey said gelding made a serious error and pulled up
Vivarini Official explanation: jockey said gelding hung left

4080 BET TOTEPOOL AT TOTESPORT.COM NOVICES' CHASE (20 fncs) 3m 2f
3:45 (3:45) (Class 3) 5-Y-O+ **£4,998** (£1,551; £835)

Form RPR
0-51 **1** **Silver Kate (IRE)**[35] 3435 8-10-11 136 ...... SamThomas 137+
(David Richards) *several slow jumps: 2nd tl led bef 14th: hdd next: led and j. slowly 17th: hdd briefly 3 out and again home turn: rdn to ld nring 2 out and readily forged clr* **3/1**[3]
-362 **2** *3¾* **Cannington Brook (IRE)**[41] 3342 7-10-12 128 ...... JoeTizzard 133
(Colin Tizzard) *trckd ldrs: mstke 12th: led 15th tl slow jump 17th: led 3 out tl rdn and hdd bef 2 out: one pce after but regained 2nd sn after last* **11/8**[1]
0-41 **3** *14* **Alfie Sherrin**[19] 3714 8-11-4 0 ...... APMcCoy 135+
(Jonjo O'Neill) *sme tentative jumps: settled trcking ldrs: j. slowly 16th: looked to be gng wl whn led bef 2 out where hdd and blnd and qckly gave up: lost 2nd after last* **2/1**[2]
5-4 **P** **Crack At Dawn (IRE)**[31] 3510 10-10-12 91 ......(b) DavidEngland —
(Michael Gates) *in tch tl mstke 10th: nt fluent 11th: bdly t.o after 13th: p.u next* **66/1**
042- **U** **My Friend Sandy**[336] 4585 10-10-12 118 ...... JasonMaguire —
(Jim Old) *led: 6 l clr briefly 6th: rdn and hdd bef 14th: sn last: 12 l adrift whn blnd and uns rdr 15th* **12/1**

6m 35.7s (-17.00) **Going Correction** -0.625s/f (Firm) 5 Ran SP% **109.6**
Speed ratings: **101,99,95,—,—**
CSF £7.85 TOTE £4.10: £1.50, £1.50; EX 7.70.
Owner David M Richards **Bred** Patrick J Hannon **Trained** Llantilio Crossenny,Monmouths

FOCUS
A decent little staying novice chase. The first three are all rated pretty much to their marks and are capable of rating higher.

NOTEBOOK
Silver Kate(IRE) was a most game winner when off the mark over fences at her beloved Chepstow last month and she followed up with another dogged display under a penalty. She put in a much-improved round of jumping on her previous outing, but wasn't so good on that front through the early parts here, and tended to go in snatches as a result. The further she went the better she got, however, and she knuckled down superbly in the home straight. This likeable mare stays all day and now deserves a crack at something more valuable. It may also prove that she develops into a Welsh National candidate next season. (op 9-4 tchd 2-1)
Cannington Brook(IRE) again found one too good. This track probably didn't play to his strengths, however, and there is little doubt he can go one better when getting back on a more galloping track. (op 7-4 tchd 15-8)
Alfie Sherrin impressed in getting off the mark over fences in what turned out to be an uncompetitive novice chase at Wetherby 19 days earlier. Tony McCoy made the journey from the abandoned Newbury to take the ride and it appeared turning for home as though he was the one to be on. However, he hit the penultimate fence and was done with soon after over this extra distance. While some may deem this as disappointing, he did need one more outing in this sphere in order to qualify for a handicap at the Cheltenham Festival next month. It should also be remembered he has been reported in the past to have benefited from time between his races, and this came plenty soon enough after his success. With that in mind, it will be fascinating to see what official mark he is now allotted over fences and, while he still has something to learn in the jumping department, the best of him has very likely still to be seen. (op 9-4 tchd 7-4)
My Friend Sandy was in the process of running a pleasing race from the front before unseating and is entitled to come on a bundle for the run so rates one to keep an eye on. (tchd 10-1)

4081 BET ON LIVE FOOTBALL AT TOTESPORT.COM NOVICES' HURDLE (11 hdls) 2m 5f
4:20 (4:21) (Class 4) 4-Y-O+ **£2,927** (£859; £429; £214)

Form RPR
6F12 **1** **Radetsky March (IRE)**[24] 3626 8-11-11 126 ...... JasonMaguire 129+
(Mark Bradstock) *rcd keenly: j. slowly 2nd: sn 2nd: led 5th: rdn and hrd pressed by one rival fr 2 out w rest wl btn: nt fluent last: hld on most tenaciously nr fin* **7/2**[2]

23-0 **2** *shd* **Romulus D'Artaix (FR)**[98] 2222 5-11-4 0 RobertThornton 121
(Alan King) *t.k.h towards rr: hdwy 7th: 4th bef 2 out where wnt 2nd: sustained effrt and rdn after: ev ch 100yds out: kpt on wl* **12/1**

4 **3** *15* **Sum Laff (IRE)**[35] 3448 7-11-1 0 PeterToole(3) 109+
(Charlie Mann) *midfield: stdy prog 7th: 5th and no ch w ldrs after 3 out: plugged on to go mod 3rd and mstke last* **8/1**

13 **4** *11* **Penny Max (IRE)**[24] 3626 5-11-4 0 SamThomas 99+
(Emma Lavelle) *hld up and bhd: clsd fr 7th: chal 3 out tl tired qckly bef next: wl btn whn wnt lft bef last and blnd* **3/1**[1]

4- **5** *4 1/2* **Solaise Express**[329] 4742 6-11-4 0 TomO'Brien 93
(Philip Hobbs) *pressed ldrs: rdn bef 6th: 5th and outpcd 3 out* **16/1**

4 **6** *12* **Reginaldinho (UAE)**[44] 3225 5-10-11 0 HarryChalloner(7) 82
(Venetia Williams) *plld hrd and chsd ldrs: rdn and fdd 3 out: mstke last: t.o* **13/2**[3]

13 **7** *1 1/2* **Max Laurie (FR)**[68] 2826 6-11-1 0 TomMolloy(3) 81
(Michael Banks) *bhd: no ch fr 6th: t.o* **28/1**

/25- **8** *shd* **Squinch**[441] 2579 7-11-4 0 PaddyBrennan 81
(Nigel Twiston-Davies) *t.k.h: chsd ldrs tl rdn and wknd 7th: t.o* **33/1**

/P-P **9** *9* **Anyauldiron (IRE)**[20] 3698 8-11-4 0 AndrewTinkler 73
(Charlie Longsdon) *nt fluent 1st: bhd: struggling bef 6th: t.o whn mstke last* **100/1**

14 **10** *1 1/2* **Court By Surprise (IRE)**[59] 2963 6-11-11 126 JackDoyle 78
(Emma Lavelle) *t.k.h on wd outside: led 2nd tl 5th: wknd after awkward jump 3 out: sn looking v tired: wl btn next: virtually p.u* **7/2**[2]

1-30 **11** *11* **Inga Bird**[46] 3153 6-10-11 0 JakeGreenall(7) 61
(Henry Daly) *plld hrd and prom: wknd after 7th: t.o* **28/1**

0540 **12** *13* **Radmores Oscar**[13] 3836 5-11-4 0 DPFahy 50
(John O'Shea) *a bhd: t.o fr 7th* **200/1**

5 **13** *nse* **Brass Tax (IRE)**[36] 3434 5-11-4 0 JimmyMcCarthy 50
(Charlie Morlock) *racd wd: bhd fr 6th: t.o 8th* **100/1**

000 **14** *35* **Ben Trovato (IRE)**[20] 3698 5-10-11 0 MrCGreene(7) 18
(John Upson) *a bhd: rdn and hopelessly t.o bef 7th* **250/1**

000 **15** *1/2* **Filimoss**[58] 2985 6-10-11 0 GerardTumelty 11
(Charlie Morlock) *sn wl bhd: hopelessly t.o after 6th* **250/1**

0 **P** **Sendefaa (IRE)**[31] 3506 6-10-8 0 CPGeoghegan(3) —
(Michael Gates) *j. slowly 3rd: last whn mstke 5th: t.o whn p.u bef next* **250/1**

40 **F** **Full Ov Beans**[43] 3266 7-11-4 0 SeanQuinlan —
(Michael Gates) *a bhd: t.o after 6th: continued in pointless pursuit: fs bhd in last whn crashing fall last* **125/1**

00 **P** **Dapple Prince (IRE)**[23] 3647 6-11-4 0 HaddenFrost —
(Tom Gretton) *plld hrd briefly: led tl 2nd: wknd qckly 5th: p.u next* **250/1**

5m 9.30s (-5.70) **Going Correction** -0.325s/f (Good) **18** Ran SP% **122.2**
Speed ratings (Par 105): **97,96,91,87,85 80,80,80,76,76 71,67,67,53,53 —,—,—**
toteswingers: 1&3 £4.70, 1&3 £14.00. 2&3 £32.90. CSF £43.69 TOTE £4.80: £2.00, £3.40, £2.80; EX 54.60.
Owner P J D Pottinger **Bred** Ms J Finn **Trained** Letcombe Bassett, Oxon

FOCUS
A decent novice hurdle that was certainly competitive. The principals came to the fore approaching the fourth-last. The winner rates a small step up, with the third helping to set the level.

NOTEBOOK
Radetsky March(IRE), who has thrived since returning to hurdles, came out on top. Although getting warm beforehand, it certainly didn't affect his performance and he pulled out plenty in a tight finish to fend off a determined challenge from the runner-up. Beaten by a useful sort under a penalty at Newbury the time before, this stiffer test clearly suited him well and he may well be capable of landing a nice handicap. First, however, it would be no surprise to see him take his chance in either the Neptune or Albert Bartlett at next month's Festival. (op 4-1)
Romulus D'Artaix(FR) failed to progress in the manner expected in three bumpers, but the longer trip on this hurdles debut was clearly in his favour and he challenged strongly in the straight. The line just came too soon, but he pulled clear of the remainder and looks well up to winning something similar. (op 11-1)
Sum Laff(IRE) looked all about stamina when fourth on his hurdles debut, and he was just getting going as he passed the line in third. He'll be of interest upped to 3m and more. (op 12-1)
Penny Max(IRE), one place behind the winner at Newbury, was fancied to reverse form over this slightly longer trip and he made headway from the rear to reach a challenging position, but didn't find for pressure and stopped quickly in the straight. (op 7-2 tchd 4-1 in places)
Solaise Express, back from 329 days off, ran well until the end of the back straight, at which point he became tired. (op 14-1)
Court By Surprise(IRE) was never far away, but like his stablemate, couldn't respond for pressure and finished very tired. Official explanation: jockey said gelding stopped very quickly; vet said gelding suffered a wound to its leg (op 4-1 tchd 9-2)
Dapple Prince(IRE) Official explanation: vet said gelding bled from the nose

4082 BET ON LIVE RUGBY AT TOTESPORT.COM STANDARD OPEN NATIONAL HUNT FLAT RACE 1m 6f
4:55 (4:56) (Class 5) 4-5-Y-O **£1,712** (£499; £249)

Form RPR

30 **1** **What A Warrior (IRE)**[42] 3294 4-10-7 0 PaddyBrennan 93+
(Nigel Twiston-Davies) *mde all: rdn over 2f out: lft in command by errnt rival ins fnl f* **50/1**

0 **2** *1 1/4* **Jojabean (IRE)**[42] 3294 4-10-7 0 RobertThornton 91+
(Alan King) *midfield: effrt to chse wnr 3f out: chal and hung bdly lft fnl f: nt rcvr* **14/1**

3 *5* **General Melchett (IRE)** 4-10-4 0 TomMolloy(3) 85
(Giles Smyly) *cl up in tight bunch: lost pl 4f out: styd on wout threatening ins fnl f: wnt 3rd fnl 100yds* **33/1**

4 *nk* **Theatre Guide (IRE)** 4-10-7 0 JoeTizzard 85
(Colin Tizzard) *pressed ldrs: rdn and nt qckn 2f out: rn green and btn 3rd over 1f out: will improve* **4/1**[2]

3 **5** *6* **Go Set Go**[107] 2052 4-10-7 0 LeightonAspell 78
(James Eustace) *outpcd 4f out: nt trble ldrs after: plugged on* **20/1**

26-0 **6** *1/2* **Cody Wyoming**[16] 3766 5-11-3 0 DominicElsworth 87
(Heather Main) *cl in bunch tl 3rd and rdn and fdd over 2f out* **66/1**

7 *hd* **Slightly Hot** 5-11-3 0 DaveCrosse 87
(Joanna Davis) *in bunch tl no ex over 2f out* **50/1**

1 **8** *2 1/4* **Elegant Touch (IRE)**[100] 2167 5-11-3 0 JackDoyle 84
(Emma Lavelle) *effrt on outer 1/2-way: no imp fnl 2f and wl btn* **5/1**[3]

0- **9** *3* **Night Rose**[303] 5199 5-10-7 0 CharlieHuxley(3) 73
(Alan King) *nvr trbld ldrs* **20/1**

10 *2 1/4* **Dark Shadow** 4-10-7 0 AndrewTinkler 68
(Nicky Henderson) *effrt to chal 3f out: fdd 2f out* **6/4**[1]

11 *8* **Skarloey** 5-10-10 0 MrMWall(7) 68
(Tony Carroll) *in rr of bunch: wknd 3f out: v tired 2f out: t.o* **100/1**

12 *15* **Smart Ruler (IRE)** 5-11-3 0 JasonMaguire 50
(David Arbuthnot) *outpcd fnl 4f: t.o* **22/1**

0 **13** *4* **Sharinga**[28] 3569 4-9-7 0 PeterHatton(7) 28
(Reg Hollinshead) *in rr of bunch: wknd and eased 2f out: t.o* **100/1**

14 *7* **Fasolo (GER)**[40] 3385 5-11-8 0 ow1 MrJPMagnier(3) 45
(C F Swan, Ire) *2nd tl 1/2-way in crawl: dropped bk to 8 l 15th 5f out: t.o* **8/1**

0 **15** *3 1/4* **Ellis**[87] 2458 4-10-7 0 TomMessenger 23
(Christopher Kellett) *8 l last 1/2-way and only one losing tch: t.o* **100/1**

16 *1 1/4* **Dawn Auction (IRE)** 4-10-7 0 CharliePoste 22
(Anthony Middleton) *t.k.h: lost tch 4f out: t.o* **100/1**

3m 24.0s (4.90) **16** Ran SP% **120.6**
toteswingers: 1&2 £7.10, 1&3 not won, 2&3 £46.70. CSF £599.20 TOTE £46.60: £6.60, £3.50, £8.20; EX 418.90.
Owner Mr & Mrs Gordon Pink **Bred** James F Barry **Trained** Naunton, Gloucs

FOCUS
Probably no more than an ordinary bumper, although it should produce winners. The sixth sets the level.

NOTEBOOK
What A Warrior(IRE) ◆, who had the experience of two previous runs, prospered under a positive ride and ran straight and true under pressure for a workmanlike success. By top class Flat-stayer Westerner, he's going to benefit from a greater test of stamina over hurdles and has a definite future.
Jojabean(IRE) ◆, behind the winner on debut, had clearly improved on that and would have gone even closer to winning had he not hung notably left. He is bred to stay well and looks a ready-made winner once switching to hurdles. (op 25-1)
General Melchett(IRE), related to numerous jumps winners, kept on nicely into third and should improve for the experience. This was a bright start.
Theatre Guide(IRE) ◆, representing the connections of last season's Champion Bumper winner Cue Card, is by the same sire, and he certainly looked the part beforehand. However, he proved too inexperienced to play a hand and ended up well held. This experience will have done him good and he'll be of interest next time. (op 9-2)
Go Set Go was going on towards the finish and will appreciate further over hurdles. (op 16-1)
Dark Shadow, whose yard has been farming winners in such events this season, has plenty of good horses in his family (Flat and jumps), but his sprinting sire is hardly renowned for his success with jumpers, and he proved disappointing. (op 11-8)
Fasolo(GER) Official explanation: trainer had no explanation for the poor form shown
T/Plt: £101.60 to a £1 stake. Pool:£65,217.00 - 468.22 winning tickets. T/Qpdt: £21.60 to a £1 stake. Pool:£4,307.69 - 147.00 winning tickets. IM

3704 LEOPARDSTOWN (L-H)
Saturday, February 12

OFFICIAL GOING: Heavy (soft to heavy in places)
Metting rescheduled after being lost to waterlogging on Sunday 6th.

4083a TOTE JACKPOT RACES 3-6 SPRING JUVENILE HURDLE (GRADE 1) (8 hdls) 2m
1:10 (1:10) 4-Y-0 **£39,224** (£11,465; £5,431; £1,810)

RPR

1 **Unaccompanied (IRE)**[43] 3272 4-10-9 PTownend 132+
(D K Weld, Ire) *trckd ldrs in 5th: impr into 3rd 2 out: led travelling best appr last: rdn and r.o wl* **5/2**[1]

2 *3* **Sailors Warn (IRE)**[44] 3239 4-11-0 AndrewJMcNamara 132
(E J O'Grady, Ire) *mid-div: 6th appr 2 out: hdwy early st: 2nd and rdn last: no imp last 100yds: kpt on* **9/2**[3]

3 *3* **Fearless Falcon (IRE)**[35] 3457 4-11-0 (b) AELynch 129
(Adrian McGuinness, Ire) *a.p: 3rd 1/2-way: cl 2nd 2 out: led ent st: rdn and hdd appr last: kpt on same pce* **20/1**

4 *1 1/2* **Chaperoned (IRE)**[35] 3457 4-10-9 RMPower 123+
(Mrs John Harrington, Ire) *hld up: 9th after 3 out: prog next: 6th early st: kpt on fr last* **20/1**

5 *hd* **Indian Daudaie (FR)**[14] 3802 4-11-0 NPMadden 127
(Paul Nicholls) *racd in 2nd: led bef 2 out: sn rdn and strly pressed: hdd ent st: no ex fr bef last* **10/3**[2]

6 *7* **Toner D'Oudairies (FR)**[44] 3239 4-11-0 (t) DNRussell 120
(Gordon Elliott, Ire) *trckd ldrs in 4th: cl up appr 2 out: sn rdn and no imp* **7/1**

7 *6* **Tillahow (IRE)**[35] 3457 4-11-0 APHeskin 114
(M F Morris, Ire) *mid-div on outer: 7th bef 2 out: sn rdn and no imp* **20/1**

8 *1 3/4* **Kalann (IRE)**[44] 3239 4-11-0 (t) MDarcy 113
(Sabrina J Harty, Ire) *hld up towards rr: 8th bef 2 out: sn rdn and no imp* **33/1**

9 *3 1/2* **Pena Dorada (IRE)**[91] 2356 4-11-0 (p) DenisO'Regan 109
(Mrs K Burke) *led: clr early: hdd & wknd qckly bef 2 out* **66/1**

10 *3* **Maxim Gorky (IRE)**[16] 3775 4-11-0 PCarberry 106
(Noel Meade, Ire) *a bhd: trailing fr 2 out* **16/1**

11 *2* **Louisville Lip (IRE)**[16] 3775 4-11-0 DJCasey 104
(Patrick J Flynn, Ire) *hld up towards rr: 10th and rdn appr 2 out: no imp: bhd whn mstke last* **11/2**

4m 3.20s (-4.30) **Going Correction** -0.175s/f (Good) **11** Ran SP% **122.3**
Speed ratings: **103,101,100,99,99 95,92,91,90,88 87**
CSF £13.78 TOTE £3.00: £1.70, £2.30, £2.80; DF 16.20.
Owner Moyglare Stud Farm **Bred** Moyglare Stud Farm Ltd **Trained** The Curragh, Co Kildare

FOCUS
Moyglare Stud and Dermot Weld have had a long association with Group 1 performers on the Flat and now, for the first time in the trainer's career, his principal patron has a Grade 1 jumper running in the famous colours. The form of the placed horses tied in but the winner surpassed them and might have even more to offer.

NOTEBOOK
Unaccompanied(IRE) won this in very taking fashion, endorsing the good impression she made when beating modest opposition on her hurdling debut at Punchestown, and putting herself firmly in the picture for the Triumph Hurdle which Weld won with Rare Holiday 21 years ago. Unaccompanied looked at home in the conditions here, and is almost certainly best suited by plenty of cut, even though she handled quickish going when opening her account at Galway last July. (op 5/2 tchd 11/4)
Sailors Warn(IRE) supplied a good standard of form having won the Grade 2 event at the same venue after Christmas. He was beaten on merit and may now go for the Fred Winter at Cheltenham to avoid bumping into the winner again. (op 11/2)
Fearless Falcon(IRE) took third place and it is difficult to see him reversing the form with the winner, but at least connections have the option of the Fred Winter as an alternative to the juvenile championship. (op 25/1)
Chaperoned(IRE) ◆ looks like a filly who will have no difficulty winning a maiden, with this effort coming in the wake of a third-placing behind two of these rivals in a Grade 3.

Indian Daudaie(FR) made a solid start in Britain when taking third place behind Local Hero when that one stretched his unbeaten sequence over hurdles to three in last month's Grade 2 at Cheltenham. The Nicholls runner could not be dismissed as a bad yardstick, helping to make this a worthy stepping-stone to the Triumph. (op 10/3 tchd 3/1)

Toner D'Oudairies(FR), detached from the first five at the finish, has not progressed since winning races at Down Royal and Fairyhouse. Official explanation: jockey said gelding whinnied in running (op 8/1)

Tillahow(IRE) could make no impression but again finished close behind Fearless Factor, providing another aspect of the likely reliability of this form.

Louisville Lip(IRE), sold to JP McManus and well fancied on the strength of a maiden win at Thurles, was a major disappointment. He has not been ruled out of the Triumph Hurdle. (op 5/1 tchd 6/1)

4084a DR. P.J. MORIARTY NOVICE CHASE (GRADE 1) (14 fncs) 2m 5f

1:45 (1:45) 5-Y-0+ £44,827 (£13,103; £6,206; £2,068)

RPR

1 **Bostons Angel (IRE)**[46] 3174 7-11-10 146 RMPower 155
(Mrs John Harrington, Ire) *trckd ldrs in 4th: impr to dispute ld fr bef 1/2-way: narrowly hdd 5 out: disp ld again fr 3 out: rdn 2 out: styd on wl u.p fr last: led cl home* **8/1**

2 *hd* **Magnanimity (IRE)**[34] 3472 7-11-10 141 DNRussell 155
(D T Hughes, Ire) *cl up and disp ld: led narrowly 5 out: jnd 3 out: rdn next: kpt on wl u.p: hdd cl home* **6/1**[3]

3 *5 ½* **Mikael D'Haguenet (FR)**[44] 3241 7-11-10 PTownend 153+
(W P Mullins, Ire) *hld up in tch: t.k.h early: prog into 4th fr 1/2-way: cl up travelling wl whn lft 3rd and hmpd 2 out: rdn st: no imp whn nt fluent last: no ex* **11/10**[1]

4 *26* **Western Charmer (IRE)**[28] 3579 9-11-10 142 PWFlood 123
(D T Hughes, Ire) *led early: hdd 4th: dropped to 5th 1/2-way: rdn 4 out: sn lost tch: lft remote 4th fr 2 out* **16/1**

P **Sam Adams (IRE)**[27] 3595 8-11-10 132 (t) PCarberry —
(Paul Nolan, Ire) *hld up in tch: dropped to rr and rdn 7th: trailing after mstke 6 out: p.u bef 3 out* **25/1**

F **Quel Esprit (FR)**[87] 2465 7-11-10 145 EMullins —
(W P Mullins, Ire) *sn disp ld: cl 3rd and rdn after 3 out: stl cl up whn fell 2 out* **2/1**[2]

5m 36.3s (-8.70) **Going Correction** +0.025s/f (Yiel) **6** Ran SP% **116.1**
Speed ratings: **117,116,114,104,— —**
CSF £53.00 TOTE £8.30: £2.50, £2.40; DF 24.80.

Owner E A P Sculler **Bred** P A D Sculler **Trained** Moone, Co Kildare

FOCUS

A race dominated in the market by the two Willie Mullins representatives, but the first two didn't read the script. That said Mikael D'Haguenet was hampered and lost momentum when Quel Esprit fell. The first two, both sons of Winged Love, each produced steps up.

NOTEBOOK

Bostons Angel(IRE) was given a fine ride by Robert Power, who injected pace into the race when it was needed, and the gelding cannot be underestimated anymore. He jumps, he travels, he's tough and gallops to the line, and probably has more gears than it appears. In short, he possesses plenty of the attributes one would like to see in a Cheltenham horse. (op 7/1)

Magnanimity(IRE) is in the same mould as the winner, producing his best run to date over fences. Jumping and travelling from the front the whole way, he went stride for stride with the winner more or less throughout and lost nothing in the jumping stakes. Most of the comments about the winner apply equally to him, though he is an old-fashioned three-mile chasing type and is probably still improving. He has as much right to go to Cheltenham as the winner. (op 11/2 tchd 13/2)

Mikael D'Haguenet(FR) was badly hampered by his stablemate at the second last, although he may not have won anyway as he struggled to close in on the two leaders afterwards. It wouldn't be a surprise if he reverted to hurdles for the time being. He jumped safely but without the fluency of the leaders and he left the impression that his fall at Fairyhouse, when overall he jumped much better, looks like it may have left its mark. (op 5/4)

Quel Esprit(FR) was the better backed of the two Willie Mullins horses and looked by far the most natural jumper of fences. He attacked most of them with relish and fiddled those he didn't meet on a proper stride. In the end he may have ended up going too quickly as he seemed to be flagging when he took off half a stride too early at the second-last and paid the penalty. (op 5/2)

4086a DELOITTE NOVICE HURDLE (GRADE 1) (9 hdls) 2m 2f

2:45 (2:47) 5-Y-0+ £44,827 (£13,103; £6,206; £2,068)

RPR

1 **Oscars Well (IRE)**[56] 3029 6-11-10 137 RMPower 153+
(Mrs John Harrington, Ire) *hld up early: 5th 1/2-way: 6th after 3 out: 4th travelling wl after 2 out: impr to ld bef last: rdn clr: easily* **7/1**

2 *5 ½* **Zaidpour (FR)**[45] 3203 5-11-9 146 PTownend 146+
(W P Mullins, Ire) *hld up: prog into 5th after 3 out: 6th and rdn after 2 out: 4th u.p st: mod 2nd and kpt on fr last* **1/1**[1]

3 *3 ½* **Shot From The Hip (GER)**[44] 3243 7-11-10 135 AndrewJMcNamara 144
(E J O'Grady, Ire) *trckd ldrs: prog into 4th after 3 out: cl 3rd 2 out: rdn to dispute ld ent st: hdd bef last: sn no ex* **6/1**[3]

4 *1 ¾* **Hidden Universe (IRE)**[44] 3238 5-11-9 MrRPMcNamara 140
(D K Weld, Ire) *mod 3rd: tk clsr order 4 out: cl 2nd and chal 2 out: disp ld ent st: hdd and one pce fr bef last* **9/2**[2]

5 *7* **Cottrelsbooley (IRE)**[45] 3201 7-11-10 131 EMullins 135
(W P Mullins, Ire) *led: rdn and strly pressed fr bef 2 out: hdd ent st: sn no ex* **11/1**

6 *5 ½* **Old McDonald**[28] 3577 6-11-10 128 PCarberry 129
(N F Glynn, Ire) *hld up towards rr: mod 7th appr 2 out: rdn and no imp* **16/1**

7 *5* **Si C'Etait Vrai (FR)**[20] 3708 5-11-9 130 DNRussell 123
(D T Hughes, Ire) *hld up: last 4 out: rdn and no imp fr next* **25/1**

8 *5 ½* **Far Away So Close (IRE)**[92] 2344 6-11-10 125 APCawley 118
(Paul Nolan, Ire) *cl 2nd: chal appr 2 out: dropped to 6th ent st: wknd* **66/1**

9 *½* **Endless Intrigue (IRE)**[44] 3243 7-11-10 DJCasey 118
(D K Weld, Ire) *towards rr: sme prog appr 2 out: no ex st* **33/1**

10 *dist* **The Bull Hayes (IRE)**[34] 3470 5-11-9 128 ADLeigh —
(Mrs John Harrington, Ire) *trckd ldrs in mod 4th: wknd 3 out: bhd whn bad mstke last: t.o* **20/1**

4m 28.4s (-12.40) **Going Correction** -0.175s/f (Good) **10** Ran SP% **122.2**
Speed ratings: **120,117,116,115,112 109,107,105,104,—**
CSF £15.24 TOTE £7.10: £2.10, £1.02, £2.10; DF 22.80.

Owner Molley Malone Syndicate **Bred** Eugene O' Leary **Trained** Moone, Co Kildare

FOCUS

Impressive in a sub-standard Grade 1 at Navan before Christmas, it was easy to underestimate Oscars Well in this race but his quality isn't in question after this performance. This is one of the strongest novice hurdles in the calendar and the first four are all smart. The time was good.

NOTEBOOK

Oscars Well(IRE) ◆ travelled and jumped in a similar fashion to the way he did at Navan. Also similar was the decisive turn of foot he showed to go to the front after the second last and he settled the issue quite quickly. This was a high-class performance against proper novices, and the quality of this performance dropping back in trip showed he possesses good speed. We already know that he's equally effective at 2m4f, and if able to handle better ground, he will go to the Neptune Investments with a big chance. (op 7/1 tchd 8/1)

Zaidpour(FR) had some questions to answer following his defeat at Leopardstown over Christmas and mostly failed to answer them. Held up just off the pace, he didn't jump with a lot of fluency and his rider was just starting to niggle before the second last. At that point he just appeared to meet a bit of trouble in running and then failed to pick up under pressure. However, he did stay on quite well from the final flight, although he made no impression on the winner. He showed nothing to suggest that he has the potential to be a Supreme Novices' winner here but showed some signs that the Neptune Investments would be more suitable, although his jumping isn't good enough on this evidence. (op 11/8)

Shot From The Hip(GER) travelled well throughout and was still going well after the second last. However, he just seemed to get a bit tired after the last and perhaps 2m in this sort of grade may just suit him better. He's likely to progress further. (op 7/1)

Hidden Universe(IRE) had the experience of just one run over hurdles. It didn't affect his jumping and, as expected, he travelled as well as anything but he faded from the final flight. Two miles on good ground is what he seems to want and one could easily see him winning a decent novice hurdle in the Spring. (op 7/2)

Cottrelsbooley(IRE) went off in front but he arguably went off too quickly. (op 10/1)

Old McDonald could be a different proposition on better ground later in the Spring. He never really got into this contest and just kept on a bit after the last.

4087a HENNESSY GOLD CUP (GRADE 1) (17 fncs) 3m

3:15 (3:20) 5-Y-0+

£89,224 (£29,482; £13,965; £4,655; £3,103; £775)

RPR

1 **Kempes (IRE)**[46] 3176 8-11-10 154 DJCasey 167
(W P Mullins, Ire) *hld up: 6th 4 out: 5th after next: smooth hdwy into 2nd after 2 out: led early st: rdn bef last: styd on wl run-in* **5/1**

2 *4 ½* **Glencove Marina (IRE)**[16] 3778 9-11-10 155 RMPower 162
(Eoin Griffin, Ire) *hld up in rr: nt fluent early: prog travelling wl 2 out: 4th into st: 2nd after last: kpt on u.p* **25/1**

3 *4 ½* **Joncol (IRE)**[46] 3176 8-11-10 157 APCawley 160
(Paul Nolan, Ire) *trckd ldrs: 4th 1/2-way: rdn bef 2 out: impr into 2nd early st: 3rd after last: one pce run-in* **13/8**[1]

4 *7* **China Rock (IRE)**[98] 2226 8-11-10 158 PCarberry 152
(M F Morris, Ire) *prom: 2nd fr 8th: disp ld fr 6 out: led bef 3 out: clr 2 out: sn rdn: hdd early st: sn no ex* **4/1**[3]

5 *5* **Made In Taipan (IRE)**[28] 3578 9-11-10 151 PTownend 146
(Thomas Mullins, Ire) *trckd ldrs: 3rd 1/2-way: 5th whn slt mstke 3 out: no imp fr next* **66/1**

6 *10* **Trafford Lad**[16] 3778 9-11-10 145 AELynch 136
(Laurence James Butler, Ire) *hld up early: prog into 5th 1/2-way: 3rd 5 out: rdn 2 out: dropped to 5th whn bad mstke last: no ex* **25/1**

7 *29* **The Listener (IRE)**[46] 3176 12-11-10 156 AndrewJMcNamara 107
(Nick Mitchell) *cl up: led fr 7th: hdd bef 3 out: rdn and wknd 2 out: eased st: t.o* **9/1**

P **Money Trix (IRE)**[46] 3176 11-11-10 158 DNRussell —
(Nicky Richards) *trckd ldrs tl mstke 5th: p.u bdly injured after 6th* **10/3**[2]

P **Let Yourself Go (IRE)**[27] 3594 9-11-10 147 SJHassett —
(Adrian Maguire, Ire) *led: hdd 7th: wknd qckly after next: p.u after 9th* **33/1**

6m 26.7s (-7.30) **Going Correction** +0.025s/f (Yiel) **9** Ran SP% **120.0**
Speed ratings: **113,111,110,107,106 102,93,—,—**
CSF £104.18 TOTE £2.90: £1.10, £5.00, £1.40; DF 88.90.

Owner John P McManus **Bred** Mick McGinn **Trained** Muine Beag, Co Carlow

FOCUS

A race marred by the death of two particpants, while The Listener was retired afterwards. Kempes is improving and this was another personal best, but there were no other solid Grade 1 types in opposition. Lines through the placed horsse suggest that Pandorama is still the number one 3m chaser in Ireland.

NOTEBOOK

Kempes(IRE) won impressively and he could make a lively Gold Cup outsider in a more open year than most. Held up off the pace, jockey David Casey made his challenge at the right time, although he was left in front to a good extent well before the final fence. However, he really found plenty and didn't stop galloping to the line on ground one would have thought was significantly softer than ideal. Indeed, he seemed to roll around a fair bit on the surface. A pleasant surprise for all concerned. (op 6/1)

Glencove Marina(IRE) tragically collapsed from a heart attack after running the race of his life. (op 20/1)

Joncol(IRE) ran flat and below his best in conditions that should have suited him. Racing handily in the group that chased the clear early leaders, he was under pressure and not making much impression after the second-last. Although he picked up for a few strides in the straight, it was short-lived and he faded on the run-in. (op 7/4 tchd 6/4)

China Rock(IRE) helped set the pace and jumped superbly in front, but he's more of a good-ground horse and it wasn't a huge surprise to see him fade badly before the final fence. However, he has a good engine and jumps brilliantly. It wouldn't be a surprise to see him being a factor in a race like the Ryanair Chase. (op 6/1)

Made In Taipan(IRE) raced handily in the leading group and was certainly close enough before the third last. In the end, he wasn't good enough but kept on reasonably well at one pace.

Trafford Lad looked more like his old self. He was travelling well enough up to the second last before tiring. He would have finished a bit closer but for a bad mistake at the last which almost stopped him completely.

The Listener(IRE) matched China Rock jump for jump, but it would seem the years took their toll and he faded badly after the second last. Winner of nine of his 29 starts, four of which were Grade 1 chases in Ireland including this race in 2008, he was subsequently retired. (op 7/1)

Money Trix(IRE) suffered a fatal leg injury having been pulled up after the sixth. (op 7/2 tchd 3/1)

Let Yourself Go(IRE) led early but dropped away and was pulled up with slightly less than a circuit to race. He was later found to have burst a blood vessel. Official explanation: jockey said gelding burst a blood vessel in running and was therefore pulled up (op 7/2 tchd 3/1)

4088 - 4090a (Foreign Racing) - See Raceform Interactive

[3295]EXETER (R-H)

Sunday, February 13

OFFICIAL GOING: Heavy (soft in places)

Hurdle on bend after winning post moved to back straight.

Wind: Quite strong, across Weather: Heavy rain all morning, light rain from start of racing.

4091 MOLSON COORS "NATIONAL HUNT" NOVICES' HURDLE (DIV I) (10 hdls) 2m 3f

2:10 (2:11) (Class 4) 4-Y-O+ **£2,276** (£668; £334; £166)

Form				RPR
1-14	1		**Highland Valley (IRE)**[64] 2888 6-11-11 133 .... JackDoyle (Emma Lavelle) *a.p: led appr 3 out: sn hrd pressed: styd on dourly: drvn out* **1/1**[1]	133+
/522	2	2	**Araldur (FR)**[18] 3739 7-11-4 125 .... RobertThornton (Alan King) *trckd ldrs: str chal fr 3 out: rdn bef 2 out: styd chalng tl no ex fnl 75yds* **11/8**[2]	125+
310-	3	20	**Lundy Sky**[309] 5129 6-11-4 0 .... AndrewThornton (Tony Newcombe) *mid-div: hdwy after 7th: wnt 3rd next: sn rdn: wknd 2 out* **20/1**	106
05	4	2½	**Inca Cave (IRE)**[21] 3698 6-10-13 0 .... KeiranBurke(5) (Patrick Rodford) *led tl 3rd: chsd ldrs: rdn after 7th: wknd after next* **80/1**	102
4/10	5	21	**Just Cloudy**[17] 3762 7-10-13 0 .... RachaelGreen(5) (Anthony Honeyball) *hld up towards rr: stdy prog fr 5th: rdn appr 3 out: sn wknd: t.o* **33/1**	81
0	6	2¾	**Numbercruncher (IRE)**[46] 3200 5-11-4 0 .... JimmyMcCarthy (Brendan Powell) *mid-div: rdn appr 3 out: wknd bef 2 out: t.o* **100/1**	78
33-0	7	1¾	**Well Refreshed**[22] 3678 7-11-4 0 .... DominicElsworth (Peter Winkworth) *mstke 1st: a towards rr: t.o* **66/1**	76
5	8	31	**Hard Tackle (IRE)**[85] 2518 5-11-1 0 .... RichieMcLernon(3) (Jonjo O'Neill) *mid-div tl wknd after 5th: t.o* **20/1**	45
	9	7	**Ruby Bay (IRE)**[330] 6-11-4 0 .... DarylJacob (Tim Vaughan) *led 3rd tl appr 3 out: wknd qckly: t.o* **12/1**[3]	38
406	10	21	**Cap Elorn (FR)**[22] 3691 5-11-4 0 .... NickScholfield (Paul Nicholls) *trckd ldrs tl wknd after 5th: t.o* **14/1**	17
0-	P		**Alfie Brown**[411] 3154 8-11-1 0 .... ChrisHonour(3) (Jacqueline Retter) *pushed along after 3rd: a towards rr: t.o whn p.u after 6th* **100/1**	—
	U		**Cruise In Luxury (IRE)** 6-10-6 0 .... GilesHawkins(5) (Kevin Bishop) *blnd and uns rdr 1st* **100/1**	—
0	P		**Spirit Of Barbadoo (IRE)**[60] 2957 5-11-4 0 .... TomScudamore (David Pipe) *mid-div: pushed along to chse ldrs 7th: sn rdn: wknd bef next: p.u bef 2 out* **33/1**	—
0	P		**Racey Lacey**[88] 2458 4-10-0 0 .... JamesDavies (Chris Down) *mid-div: hdwy 4th: nt fluent 6th: wknd next: t.o whn p.u bef 3 out* **100/1**	—

5m 0.20s (17.50) **Going Correction** +1.10s/f (Heav)

WFA 4 from 5yo+ 9lb **14** Ran SP% **128.6**

Speed ratings (Par 105): **107,106,97,96,87 86,85,72,69,61** —,—,—,—

toteswingers: 1&2 £1.10, 1&3 £8.50, 2&3 £10.00 CSF £2.69 TOTE £2.00: £1.10, £1.20, £4.50; EX 3.10.

Owner M E Thompson **Bred** Patrick Myers **Trained** Wildhern, Hants

FOCUS

The front two in the market pulled clear in this novice hurdle, after which winning rider Jack Doyle described the ground as "Close to bottomless".

NOTEBOOK

Highland Valley(IRE), off since finishing fourth in a 3m Grade 2 at Cheltenham in December, found the drop in grade and the shorter trip to his liking, although as it turned out plenty of stamina was needed. This was a fair effort considering he was conceding 7lb to the runner-up and he has numerous options at the festival, although it's highly unlikely he'd be good enough to feature. (op 5-4, tchd 11-8 in places)

Araldur(FR) has been running well since returned to hurdles this season, finishing runner-up at Leicester and Huntingdon, and although again finding one too good, he was clear of the remainder. He's not easy to place over fences, being rated 150, but it won't be long before he picks up something similar to this. (op 6-4 tchd 13-8)

Lundy Sky, back from 309 days off, shaped well considering the difficult conditions and is entitled to improve.

Inca Cave(IRE) should fare better in handicaps down the line.

Hard Tackle(IRE) should fare better in handicaps down the line.

Ruby Bay(IRE) stopped quickly in the end.

4092 BETFAIR PHONE AND ANDROID APP NOVICES' HURDLE (LISTED RACE) (8 hdls) 2m 1f

2:40 (2:41) (Class 1) 4-Y-O+ **£7,512** (£2,819; £1,411; £704; £352)

Form				RPR
1	1		**Spirit Son (FR)**[30] 3542 5-11-11 0 .... BarryGeraghty (Nicky Henderson) *trckd ldrs: jnd ldr 3 out: led next: drew clr: v easily* **4/9**[1]	154+
1	2	21	**Cedre Bleu (FR)**[25] 3624 4-10-13 0 .... SamThomas (Paul Nicholls) *trckd ldr: led appr 3 out: rdn and hdd 2 out: sn no ch w easy wnr* **10/3**[2]	122+
3311	3	41	**Lady Willa (IRE)**[11] 3879 4-10-6 115 .... AndrewThornton (Mark Gillard) *led tl appr 3 out: sn no ch w front pair: t.o* **33/1**	78
1234	4	19	**Battle Group**[121] 1855 6-11-11 137 .... TomScudamore (David Pipe) *v reluctant and hung lft thrght: detached: t.o fr 3rd: wnt poor 4th 3 out: t.o* **13/2**[3]	73
0B-0	5	27	**Monopole (IRE)**[24] 3645 7-11-3 0 .... FrancisHayes (David Pipe) *racd keenly: lost tch fr 4th: t.o* **80/1**	38
5	6	22	**Street Entertainer (IRE)**[17] 3760 4-10-7 0 .... JohnnyFarrelly (David Pipe) *lost tch fr 4th: t.o* **33/1**	6

4m 28.2s (12.70) **Going Correction** +1.10s/f (Heav)

WFA 4 from 5yo+ 9lb **6** Ran SP% **112.8**

Speed ratings (Par 111): **114,104,84,75,63 52**

toteswingers: 1&2 £1.02, 1&3 £3.70, 2&3 £8.20 CSF £2.40 TOTE £1.50: £1.10, £1.70; EX 2.50.

Owner Michael Buckley **Bred** Anne Baudrelle & Jean-Marc Baudrelle **Trained** Upper Lambourn, Berks

FOCUS

This had looked a potentially interesting duel, but Spirit Son ultimate won in some style.

NOTEBOOK

Spirit Son(FR) ◆ emerged much the best, doing it in some fashion considering the conditions. Held in the highest of regard by connections, this ex-French winner made a taking British debut at Huntingdon last month and surely booked his ticket to the Supreme Novices' with this display - for which he's now a best-priced 10-1. The better ground next month ought to be to his liking and he rates one of the likelier winners at this stage. Regardless of what he does this season, though, he should make a smashing chaser. (op 1-2, tchd 4-7 in a place)

Cedre Bleu(FR) created a very nice impression when beating a subsequent winner (same connections as Spirit Son) on his debut at Newbury, but he met his match in a major way here, the 12lb he was receiving from the winner being nowhere near enough to be able to make a race of things. He's got plenty of size about him and chasing will be his game. (op 3-1 tchd 11-4 and 7-2)

Lady Willa(IRE), winner of a claiming hurdle at Leicester, was readily dropped by the front pair, but will have done her breeding value no harm with this placing.

Battle Group didn't want to know, Tom Scudamore having to work just to get him over the early hurdles. (op 9-1 tchd 6-1)

4093 BETFAIR GRADUATION CHASE (18 fncs) 3m

3:10 (3:10) (Class 2) 5-Y-O+ **£12,674** (£3,744; £1,872; £936; £468)

Form				RPR
1-53	1		**Bakbenscher**[15] 3804 8-11-7 139 .... RobertThornton (Alan King) *hld up bhd ldrs: tk clsr order after 10th: jnd ldr 4 out: led 2 out: sn in command: pushed out* **10/3**[2]	153+
2/41	2	4	**Definity (IRE)**[16] 3788 8-11-0 140 .... NickScholfield (Paul Nicholls) *disp fr 4th: outrt ldr 10th: hit next: nt fluent whn briefly hdd 12th: rdn after 4 out: hdd 2 out: sn hld by wnr* **11/8**[1]	141
-FF2	3	24	**Bench Warrent (IRE)**[14] 3832 8-11-4 129 .... (p) PeterToole (Charlie Mann) *led: jnd 4th: hdd 10th: led briefly after 12th: rdn and ev ch after 14th: wknd fr next* **13/2**	123
0-15	4	34	**Dover's Hill**[106] 2084 9-11-0 132 .... (tp) SamTwiston-Davies (Mary Hambro) *cl up: rdr lost iron briefly whn mstke 2nd: struggling 11th: wknd after 14th: t.o* **5/1**[3]	83
5-P3	5	29	**Thunder Child**[21] 3700 11-11-0 74 .... (t) AndrewGlassonbury (Simon Burrough) *trckd ldrs: rdn in cl 4th after 14th: wknd bef next: t.o* **100/1**	54
12-P	P		**The Sliotar (IRE)**[43] 3290 10-11-0 137 .... RichardJohnson (Philip Hobbs) *trckd ldrs: struggling whn nt fluent 14th: sn wknd: t.o whn p.u bef next* **6/1**	—

6m 30.1s (20.80) **Going Correction** +0.80s/f (Soft) **6** Ran SP% **110.5**

Speed ratings: **97,95,87,76,66** —

toteswingers: 1&2 £1.70, 1&3 £3.20, 2&3 £2.10 CSF £8.50 TOTE £4.20: £2.40, £1.20; EX 7.80.

Owner Three Line Whip **Bred** Sandicroft Stud **Trained** Barbury Castle, Wilts

FOCUS

The big two drew clear in this graduation chase.

NOTEBOOK

Bakbenscher, who has long looked in need of 3m, won with plenty to spare. Sloppy jumping has hampered his progress over fences, but he finished third behind a well-handicapped sort at Cheltenham last month and, not for the first time, looked more than at home in these conditions (now 3-3 on heavy). It remains to be seen whether his jumping would be up to it in a strongly run race at the festival, but he's perfectly entitled to take his chance in something like the William Hill. He could be one for either a Scottish or Welsh Grand National this year. (op 5-1)

Definity(IRE), having only his third start over fences, jumped well when making all at Fontwell latest, but he threw in a couple of blunders on this occasion and couldn't stay on as well as the winner in the ground. This was only his sixth start in total and he will be of interest switched to handicaps. (op 11-10)

Bench Warrent(IRE) was left trailing by two classier types. He'll stand more of a chance back in handicaps. (op 9-2)

Dover's Hill was always struggling after an early blunder, which his rider did well to recover from. (op 6-1 tchd 13-2)

The Sliotar(IRE) has now pulled up on both starts for this yard, but may come good on better ground later in the year. (op 8-1)

4094 MOLSON COORS "NATIONAL HUNT" NOVICES' HURDLE (DIV II) (10 hdls) 2m 3f

3:40 (3:40) (Class 4) 4-Y-O+ **£2,276** (£668; £334; £166)

Form				RPR
2100	1		**Golden Chieftain (IRE)**[43] 3288 6-11-11 125 .... JoeTizzard (Colin Tizzard) *travelled wl: trckd ldrs: disp fr after 3rd: outrt ldr approachng 3 out: clr after 2 out: edgd lft run-in: easily* **2/1**[1]	136+
01-0	2	6	**Kind Of Easy (IRE)**[62] 2925 5-11-4 0 .... JackDoyle (Emma Lavelle) *prom: sltly hmpd 2nd: dispued fr after next tl rdn appr 3 out: sn hld by wnr: styd on same pce* **8/1**	120+
4	3	12	**Ravastree (IRE)**[25] 3626 5-11-4 0 .... RobertThornton (Alan King) *mid-div: hdwy after 5th to trck ldrs: rdn appr 3 out: sn no ch w ldng pair: styd on same pce* **5/2**[2]	108
25	4	19	**Water Garden (FR)**[42] 3346 5-11-4 0 .... TimmyMurphy (Paul Nicholls) *in tch: effrt appr 3 out: sn wknd* **11/2**[3]	88
60	5	nse	**Rockabilly (FR)**[36] 3439 6-11-1 0 .... SamTwiston-Davies(3) (Nigel Twiston-Davies) *led tl after 3rd: chsd ldrs tl after 6th: sn wknd* **12/1**	88
0-30	6	4½	**Joker Choker (IRE)**[22] 3691 6-11-4 0 .... BarryGeraghty (Nicky Henderson) *mid-div: hdwy to trck ldrs after 3rd: rdn appr 3 out: sn wknd* **8/1**	83
406P	7	1¼	**Qualitee**[15] 3816 6-10-11 0 .... DaveCrosse (Claire Dyson) *mid-div: rdn after 7th: wknd next* **100/1**	75
000	8	2½	**Flying Award (IRE)**[17] 3762 7-10-11 0 .... MarkQuinlan(7) (Susan Gardner) *trckd ldrs: rdn appr 3 out: sn wknd* **100/1**	80
00	9	10	**Jupiter Rex (FR)**[17] 3767 4-10-7 0 .... SamThomas (Venetia Williams) *a towards rr: t.o* **100/1**	59
0S-	10	24	**Deed Poll**[349] 4358 5-11-4 0 .... JamesDavies (Chris Down) *a towards rr: t.o* **100/1**	46
	P		**Maxi's Dream** 6-11-1 0 .... IanPopham(3) (Stuart Howe) *struggling 4th: a in rr: t.o whn p.u after 7th* **100/1**	—
0-0	P		**Manics Man**[9] 3930 6-11-4 0 .... DenisO'Regan (Helen Nelmes) *a towards rr: lost tch fr 4th: t.o whn p.u bef 3 out* **100/1**	—
3-03	R		**Don't Hang About**[36] 3441 6-11-4 0 .... JohnnyFarrelly (Richard Mitchell) *prom whn rn out 2nd* **28/1**	—
	P		**Surf And Turf (IRE)** 5-11-1 0 .... RichieMcLernon(3) (Jonjo O'Neill) *a towards rr: t.o whn p.u bef last* **20/1**	—

5m 2.70s (20.00) **Going Correction** +1.10s/f (Heav)

WFA 4 from 5yo+ 9lb **14** Ran SP% **121.4**

Speed ratings (Par 105): **101,98,93,85,85 83,82,81,77,67** —,—,—,—

toteswingers: 1&2 £4.70, 1&3 £2.50, 2&3 £6.30 CSF £18.83 TOTE £3.10: £1.20, £2.40, £1.60; EX 18.10.

Owner Brocade Racing **Bred** Robert Donaldson **Trained** Milborne Port, Dorset

FOCUS

Just an ordinary novice hurdle.

NOTEBOOK

Golden Chieftain(IRE) had struggled in better company since winning at Chepstow in November and although conceding weight all round on this drop in grade, he proved a different proposition faced with more testing ground, travelling like the best horse throughout. He won't be at his best until faced with 3m and fences, but can make his mark in handicap hurdles first. (op 9-4 tchd 15-8 and 5-2 in places)

Kind Of Easy(IRE) ran considerably better than on his hurdles debut, and this former bumper winner can go one better in something similar. (op 13-2)

Ravastree(IRE), fourth in a decent race on his hurdles debut at Newbury, was unable to build on that, but it's possible the ground would have been too testing. His point win came on good, so give him another chance back on a faster surface. (op 3-1 tchd 10-3)

Water Garden(FR) was again well held, but should do better in handicaps. Official explanation: jockey said gelding got tired in the heavy (soft in places) ground (op 6-1)

Rockabilly(FR) may do better in handicaps. (op 11-1)

Joker Choker(IRE) should find life easier in handicaps. (op 15-2)

4095 MOLSON COORS H'CAP CHASE (15 fncs) 2m 3f 110y

4:10 (4:10) (Class 3) (0-135,130) 5-Y-0+ **£4,553** (£1,337; £668; £333)

Form				RPR
001	1		**As De Fer (FR)**[17] [3765] 5-11-1 **122** ... SamThomas (Anthony Honeyball) *chsd ldrs: chal after 11th: narrow advantage 3 out: styd on to assert fr last: rdn out* **6/1**	140+
1-10	2	4 ½	**Requin (FR)**[22] [3688] 6-11-2 **120** ... DenisO'Regan (Victor Dartnall) *mid-div: hdwy after 11th: led 4 out tl next: sn rdn: ev ch tl no ex jst bef last* **9/2**[2]	134+
3P52	3	8	**Or Bleu (FR)**[36] [3438] 9-11-12 **130** ... RichardJohnson (Philip Hobbs) *chsd ldrs: rdn whn lost pl after 11th: styd on same pce fr 4 out: wnt 3rd bef last* **11/2**[3]	135
1212	4	6	**Inside Dealer (IRE)**[34] [3479] 7-11-8 **126** ... JoeTizzard (Colin Tizzard) *chsd ldr: led 11th: rdn and hdd bef next: styd on same pce: lost 3rd bef last* **3/1**[1]	125
1F5	5	9	**Mud Monkey**[22] [3690] 7-11-2 **120** ... (t) NickScholfield (Claire Dyson) *led: sn clr: hdd 11th: sn regained ld: rdn and hdd bef mstke 4 out: fdd* **16/1**	112
3/P-	6	36	**Down The Stretch**[300] [5281] 11-10-11 **115** ... LiamTreadwell (James Payne) *hld up: wknd after 11th: fin tired: t.o* **40/1**	69
5302	7	10	**Qulinton (FR)**[107] [2077] 7-11-10 **128** ... TomScudamore (David Pipe) *mid-div: awkward 5th (water) and struggling in rr whn hit 8th: n.d after: mstke last: fin tired* **13/2**	72
-35F	P		**Wheels Up (IRE)**[34] [3488] 10-10-11 **118** ... (t) RichieMcLernon(3) (Jonjo O'Neill) *hld up: in tch whn blnd 9th: wknd 11th: t.o whn p.u bef 4 out* **33/1**	—
1-P0	P		**Bertie May**[25] [3629] 9-10-7 **111** ... (t) WayneHutchinson (Kevin Bishop) *hld up: lost tch fr 11th: p.u bef next* **9/2**[2]	—

5m 9.80s (12.50) **Going Correction** +0.80s/f (Soft)
WFA 5 from 6yo+ 1lb **9** Ran SP% **115.6**
Speed ratings: **107,105,102,99,96 81,77,—,—**
toteswingers: 1&2 £7.60, 1&3 £3.20, 2&3 £5.30 CSF £33.94 CT £157.66 TOTE £7.60: £3.00, £1.60, £1.90; EX 41.30.
Owner Midd Shire Racing **Bred** Didier Leviel **Trained** Seaborough, Dorset

FOCUS

Two unexposed types dominated the finish of this handicap chase.

NOTEBOOK

As De Fer(FR), a rampant winner off 12lb lower on last month's British debut over fences, took a while to assert on this more testing surface, but his stamina eventually kicked in and he came clear from after the last. This progressive five-year-old clearly has more improvement in him and may well be up to completing a hat-trick. (tchd 7-1)

Requin(FR), a course winner over hurdles in December, was a stone higher for this debut over fences and he made the winner work for it. He should improve for the experience. (op 4-1 tchd 7-2)

Or Bleu(FR) was unable to match two less exposed types. (op 9-2 tchd 4-1)

Inside Dealer(IRE) has been in good form, winning here two starts back, but this was the first time he's encountered heavy ground over fences and he failed to cope. (op 10-3)

Mud Monkey ended up well held having made a lot of the running.

Qulinton(FR), off since finishing second in October, floundered late on in the heavy ground. (tchd 15-2)

4096 MOLSON COORS NOVICES' CHASE (15 fncs) 2m 3f 110y

4:40 (4:41) (Class 3) 5-Y-0+ **£4,553** (£1,337; £668; £333)

Form				RPR
4063	1		**Dinarius**[9] [3932] 6-10-12 114 ... (p) JimmyMcCarthy (Alex Hales) *mde all: rdn whn hit 3 out: styd on strly to assert appr last: pushed out* **14/1**	132+
5-30	2	8	**Ace High**[36] [3448] 7-10-12 0 ... DenisO'Regan (Victor Dartnall) *trckd ldrs: hit 11th: chal 3 out: u.p whn mstke 2 out: no ex* **11/2**[3]	125+
00-1	3	19	**Mamlook (IRE)**[27] [3600] 7-11-4 0 ... TomScudamore (David Pipe) *hld up: lft 4th at the 7th: wnt cl 3rd after 11th: rdn appr 4 out: fnd nil and sn wknd* **5/4**[1]	111
2-21	4	11	**Cool Friend (IRE)**[112] [1985] 8-10-11 125 ... NickScholfield (Jeremy Scott) *hld up: mstke and stmbld bdly 3rd: nvr on terms: wnt poor 4th 4 out* **2/1**[2]	98
	5	59	**Iheardu**[36] [3455] 5-10-9 0 ... AndrewThornton (Neil Mulholland) *awkward 1st: a last: t.o fr 10th* **22/1**	31
2/0F	U		**Jokers Legacy (IRE)**[8] [3938] 9-10-12 0 ... (tp) RichardJohnson (Tim Vaughan) *trcking ldrs whn blnd: stmbld bdly and uns rdr 7th* **11/1**	—
-336	P		**John's Gift**[59] [2979] 7-10-12 101 ... (t) AndrewGlassonbury (Bob Buckler) *trckd ldrs: rdn after 11th: sn wknd: poor 5th whn p.u bef 2 out* **33/1**	—

5m 10.0s (12.70) **Going Correction** +0.80s/f (Soft)
WFA 5 from 6yo+ 1lb **7** Ran SP% **115.5**
Speed ratings: **106,102,95,90,67 —,—**
toteswingers: 1&2 £6.80, 1&3 £3.80, 2&3 £1.40 CSF £87.64 TOTE £14.90: £4.20, £3.20; EX 85.30.
Owner A S Helaissi **Bred** Howard Barton Stud **Trained** Wardington, Oxon

FOCUS

This novice chase turned into a thorough test of stamina.

NOTEBOOK

Dinarius, who was taken to post very early, saw it out best. Third behind a couple of well-regarded types at Chepstow latest, he kept finding more off the front end and jumped more fluently than the runner-up down the stretch. This was only his third start over fences and there could be more to come in handicaps, as defying a penalty won't be easy. (op 16-1)

Ace High didn't hang around long over hurdles, but he's very much has the look of a chaser and, although unable to match the winner late on, he should find something similar on better ground. (op 15-2)

Mamlook(IRE), who picked up a penalty for winning on his chase debut at Fakenham (heavy), didn't prove as effective in the conditions this time. He's ideally suited by a sounder surface and it would not surprise to see him leave this form behind switched to handicaps. (tchd 6-4 in a place and 11-8 in places)

Cool Friend(IRE), runner-up on her first five starts over fences prior to winning at Aintree in October, was never going after a bad early blunder. (tchd 9-4)

Jokers Legacy(IRE), who had been due to run at Newbury 24 hours earlier, failed to complete for the second straight occasion. (op 10-1)

John's Gift is one to look out for once switched to handicaps on better ground. Official explanation: jockey said gelding had a breathing problem (op 10-1)

4097 MOLSON COORS INTERMEDIATE OPEN NATIONAL HUNT FLAT RACE 2m 1f

5:10 (5:10) (Class 5) 4-6-Y-0 **£1,301** (£382; £191; £95)

Form				RPR
	1		**Fingal Bay (IRE)** 5-11-4 0 ... RichardJohnson (Philip Hobbs) *in tch: led over 3f out: drew wl clr: v easily: impressive* **9/2**[2]	122+
	2	22	**Great Gusto (IRE)** 5-11-4 0 ... DenisO'Regan (Victor Dartnall) *in tch: rdn into 3rd over 3f out: styd on to go 2nd over 1f out: nvr any ch w v easy wnr* **15/2**	97
	3	1 ¾	**Queen's Grove** 5-10-6 0 ... GilesHawkins(5) (Kevin Bishop) *hld up towards rr: stdy hdwy fr 1/2-way: rdn to chse wnr over 2f out but no ch: lost 2nd over 1f out: styd on same pce* **40/1**	88
	4	18	**Alivad (IRE)** 4-10-1 0 ... LiamTreadwell (Peter Hedger) *hld up towards rr: styd on past btn horses fnl 2f: nvr trbld ldrs* **40/1**	60
	5	12	**Bob Emmet (IRE)** 6-11-4 0 ... TomO'Brien (Philip Hobbs) *mid-div tl 5f out: t.o* **9/1**	65
5	6	3 ¾	**Trade On**[95] [2315] 4-10-8 0 ... RobertThornton (Alan King) *in tch: rdn in cl 4th over 3f out: wknd over 2f out: t.o* **7/1**[3]	51
5-	7	nk	**Swains Meadow**[599] [812] 6-10-11 0 ... HaddenFrost (Kevin Bishop) *nvr bttr than mid-div: wknd over 2f out: t.o* **66/1**	54
3	8	8	**Ballabrace (IRE)**[90] [2432] 6-11-4 0 ... SamThomas (Venetia Williams) *mid-div: trcking ldrs whn rdn over 3f out: sn wknd: t.o* **11/8**[1]	53
0	9	1 ¼	**Bestwood Lodge**[100] [2186] 5-10-11 0 ... JoeTizzard (Helen Nelmes) *a towards rr: t.o* **100/1**	45
	10	31	**Spring Bay** 6-10-11 0 ... (p) WayneHutchinson (John Ryall) *slowly away and pushed along: sn t.o* **40/1**	14
0	11	4	**Atlantic Pearl**[29] [3569] 5-11-4 0 ... TomScudamore (David Pipe) *disp ld tl rdn over 3f out: sn wknd: t.o* **16/1**	17
	12	2	**The Tatkin (IRE)** 5-10-11 0 ... JohnnyFarrelly (David Pipe) *disp ld most of way: rdn over 4f out: wknd over 3f out: t.o* **14/1**	8
52/	13	28	**Miles Of Sunshine**[687] [4760] 6-10-11 0 ... MarkQuinlan(7) (Ron Hodges) *prom tl rdn over 7f out: t.o* **22/1**	—
0	14	19	**Little Ms Piggie**[24] [3651] 5-10-11 0 ... AndrewGlassonbury (Simon Burrough) *chsd ldrs: wnt prom 1/2-way: rdn over 6f out: sn wknd: t.o* **100/1**	—

4m 28.3s (19.50) **Going Correction** +1.10s/f (Heav)
WFA 4 from 5yo+ 9lb **14** Ran SP% **122.2**
Speed ratings: **98,87,86,78,72 70,70,67,66,51 49,49,35,26**
toteswingers: 1&2 £9.00, 1&3 £18.20, 2&3 £70.30. totesuper7: Win: Not won. Place: Not won. CSF £37.46 TOTE £5.10: £1.90, £2.50, £11.30; EX 39.00.
Owner Mrs R J Skan **Bred** James Kinsella **Trained** Withycombe, Somerset

FOCUS

Although not going a crawl, they wisely didn't over do it in the conditions, as runners would have finished even more tired than they did

NOTEBOOK

Fingal Bay(IRE), a half-brother to useful 3m hurdle/chase winner Oodachee, ran out an easy winner. Always travelling strongly, he powered clear down the straight and looks a bright prospect. On this evidence he'll have no trouble staying further over hurdles, but first he may be up to defying a penalty. (tchd 3-1)

Great Gusto(IRE), whose dam is a useful half-sister to 3m hurdle/chase winner Tarablaze, stayed on into second without getting anywhere near the winner, but should improve. (op 6-1)

Queen's Grove made a relatively pleasing debut and should stand more of a chance in races restricted to her own sex.

Alivad(IRE) was going on close home, having been in rear early.

Bob Emmet(IRE), a stablemate to the winner, was worn down by the ground. (op 7-1)

Trade On, who was bang there turning in, deserves another chance on better ground. (op 5-1)

Ballabrace(IRE), third at Plumpton on debut, made a swift forward move down the back, but he couldn't go through with his effort and finished tailed off. (op 9-4 tchd 5-2 and 5-4)

Atlantic Pearlwent well for a long way and was still narrowly ahead turning in, but he stopped to a virtual walk from over 2f out and this race looks sure to leave its mark. (op 14-1)

T/Plt: £61.70 to a £12 stake. Pool: £97,515.55. 1,152.73 winning tickets. T/Qpdt: £57.70 to a £1 stake. Pool: £5,857.44. 75.00 winning tickets. TM

3836 HEREFORD (R-H)

Sunday, February 13

OFFICIAL GOING: Good to soft (soft in places) changing to soft after race 1 (2.00)

Last fence omitted in all chases due to rebuilding.

Wind: Almost nil Weather: Wet

4098 LINDLEY CATERING CONDITIONAL JOCKEYS' H'CAP HURDLE (11 hdls) 2m 6f 110y

2:00 (2:00) (Class 5) (0-90,90) 4-Y-0+ **£1,951** (£573; £286; £143)

Form				RPR
0043	1		**Royal Chatelier (FR)**[15] [3822] 6-11-10 **88** ... RichardKilloran (Michael Blake) *taken wd thrght: a.p: led 4th: mde rest: rdn appr last: styd on wl and in command run-in* **11/2**[3]	94+
P5-2	2	4 ½	**Supreme Team (IRE)**[129] [1745] 8-10-8 **77** ... PeterHatton(5) (Louise Davis) *mstke 3rd: sn bhd: niggled along after 6th: hdwy 7th: chsd ldrs 3 out: outpcd after 2 out: kpt on to take 2nd run-in: no imp on wnr* **4/1**[1]	79
6062	3	7	**No Woman No Cry**[12] [3870] 6-11-2 **85** ... (p) SClements(5) (Colin Tizzard) *a.p: effrt 2 out: lft 2nd last: lost 2nd run-in: no ex fnl 150yds* **4/1**[1]	82
PP-P	4	87	**Photogenique (FR)**[31] [3530] 8-11-2 **80** ... MichaelMurphy (Rob Summers) *prom: rdn and lost pl after 4th: bhd after 5th: t.o bef 8th: plugged on for press but n.d after* **40/1**	—

103- **5** *3 ¼* **Laughing Game**358 4172 7-11-7 **85** DavidBass —
(Laura Hurley) *hld up: hdwy after 5th: rdn and wknd appr 3 out* **5/1**2

0-00 **6** *8* **Kielder Rise**31 3532 7-11-1 **79** (v1) AodhaganConlon —
(Evan Williams) *prom: lost pl bef 5th: bhd 6th: t.o bef 8th* **25/1**

656 **7** *4* **Shoudhavenownbettr (IRE)**31 3526 7-11-7 **85** (bt1) TomMolloy —
(Matt Sheppard) *led: hdd 4th: remained prom: rdn appr 7th: wknd bef 3 out* **20/1**

51/P **P** **Lescer's Lad**14 3837 14-10-12 **81** (t) JeremiahMcGrath(5) —
(Mrs A M Woodrow) *hld up: mstke 1st: struggling and bhd 3rd: t.o whn p.u bef 5th* **40/1**

/36- **P** **King Kasyapa (IRE)**627 495 9-11-7 **85** DonalDevereux —
(Peter Bowen) *trckd ldrs: wknd after 7th: t.o whn p.u bef 2 out* **10/1**

4P-P **P** **Speedy Directa (GER)**98 2244 8-11-7 **85** (t) MrMMO'Connor —
(Milton Harris) *midfield: nt fluent 2nd: wknd 7th: bhd 8th: t.o whn p.u bef last* **11/1**

U46P **P** **Stafford Charlie**17 3764 5-11-12 **90** CharlieWallis —
(John O'Shea) *hld up: hdwy 7th: rdn and wknd sn after: t.o bef 3 out: p.u bef 2 out* **33/1**

6062 **U** **Brunette'Sonly (IRE)**43 3297 6-11-5 **90** DarrenO'Keeffe(7) 92
(Seamus Mullins) *in tch: prom: effrt 2 out: jst over 2 l 2nd whn uns rdr last* **15/2**

5m 58.4s (20.40) **Going Correction** +0.975s/f (Soft)
WFA 4 from 5yo+ 10lb **12** Ran SP% **117.7**
Speed ratings (Par 103): **103,101,99,68,67 64,63,—,—,— —,—**
toteswingers: 1&2 £6.10, 1&3 £5.60, 2&3 £3.80 CSF £26.42 CT £97.54 TOTE £5.30: £3.00, £1.50, £1.90; EX 37.70.

Owner Mrs Val Butcher **Bred** Marc Trinquet And Olivier Trinquet **Trained** Trowbridge, Wilts

FOCUS
Persistent rain through the morning left the ground considerably more testing than the official version, which was amended to soft all round after the opener. A weak handicap, although the right horses came to the fore, this concerned only four from a long way out. The time was no less than 55 seconds outside the standard.

NOTEBOOK
Royal Chatelier(FR), in front at an early stage, was kept to the wide outside throughout, where the ground was considerably quicker. After coming under pressure two out, he just about looked in command when his closest pursuer exited at the last. Back up in trip here, he has plenty of stamina. He escapes a penalty for this. (op 5-1 tchd 6-1)

Supreme Team(IRE), off the track since October, ran in snatches. He came under pressure down the far side and looked set to finish fourth going to the final flight, but plugged on from there. (op 6-1)

No Woman No Cry was dropped slightly in trip after his improved run in the cheekpieces last time. Never far away, he weakened going to the last. He was reported to have finished distressed. Official explanation: vet said gelding finished distressed (op 9-2 tchd 7-2)

Photogenique(FR) was being rousted along from a very early stage, appearing a candidate to be pulled up, but she was running on past beaten opponents at the finish to claim a distant fourth. (op 50-1)

Laughing Game Official explanation: jockey said mare had no more to give

Brunette'Sonly(IRE) showed considerable improvement at Exeter, where she had today's winner back in fourth. She ran well for a long way again here but looked just held in second when her inexperienced rider was unshipped at the last. It has to go down as a soft unseat. (op 8-1)

4099 MATTHEW CLARK H'CAP CHASE (14 fncs 2 omitted) 2m 5f 110y
2:30 (2:30) (Class 5) (0-95,94) 5-Y-0+ **£2,081** (£611; £305; £152)

Form RPR

2435 **1** **Havenstone (IRE)**110 2024 10-10-11 **86** AodhaganConlon(7) 95+
(Evan Williams) *led: hdd appr 4th: remained prom: mstke 8th: rdn and outpcd 9th: lft in ld 11th: styd on u.p after last: a doing enough* **4/1**2

0005 **2** *3* **Bless My Soul**12 3873 8-10-10 **83** (t) MattGriffiths(5) 87
(Ron Hodges) *in tch: trckd ldrs after 6th: rdn bef 2 out: sn chsd wnr: kpt on u.p after last: hld cl home* **14/1**

0312 **3** *35* **Kinkeel (IRE)**10 3898 12-10-12 **83** EamonDehdashti(3) 56
(Tony Carroll) *hld up: rdn after 5th: lost tch w ldrs bef 11th: n.d after: tk poor 3rd run-in* **8/1**

P0P **4** *36* **Sourchamp (FR)**70 2795 5-9-13 **77** (t) CharlieWallis(7) 6
(Arthur Whiting) *plld hrd: hdwy to ld appr 4th: j.lft 5th and 6th: hdd 10th: wknd after 2 out* **20/1**

-346 **P** **Paradise Expected**16 3790 8-10-13 **84** (t) RichardKilloran(3) —
(Tim Vaughan) *handy: lost pl and struggling 7th: t.o whn p.u bef 9th* **7/1**3

P4/0 **P** **Quicolai (FR)**96 2286 7-11-12 **94** (t) PaddyBrennan —
(Tom George) *prom: led 10th: blnd 11th: sn hdd: wknd qckly after 2 out: tired in 3rd and losing tch w ldrs whn p.u bef last* **4/1**2

-435 **P** **Fleur De Vassy**21 3700 7-11-1 **90** HarryChalloner(7) —
(Venetia Williams) *hld up: mstke 1st: nt fluent 3rd: struggling 10th: t.o whn p.u bef 2 out* **15/8**1

5m 56.5s (36.50) **Going Correction** +1.175s/f (Heav)
WFA 5 from 7yo+ 2lb **7** Ran SP% **109.8**
Speed ratings: **80,78,66,53,— —,—**
toteswingers: 1&2 £8.50, 1&3 £3.50, 2&3 £7.90 CSF £46.27 TOTE £6.50: £3.10, £6.00; EX 54.20.

Owner Tywi Syndicate **Bred** John Meagher **Trained** Llancarfan, Vale Of Glamorgan

■ Stewards' Enquiry : Matt Griffiths two-day ban: used whip with excessive frequency (Feb 27 & tbn, remedial training)

FOCUS
The ground looked equally as bad on the chase course and the time was a minute outside the standard. Most of these were struggling a long way out and the form is worth little.

NOTEBOOK
Havenstone(IRE) was being shoved along a fair way out, but found himself in front halfway down the back straight and stayed on doggedly. Dropped another 3lb since his last run in October, he handles faster ground too and this was his first win over fences. (op 3-1)

Bless My Soul, eased 3lb since his recent chasing debut, kept trying in second and ran his best race to date so far under rules, but that is not saying much. He was reported to have finished distressed. Official explanation: vet said gelding finished distressed (op 18-1)

Kinkeel(IRE) ran a rare below-par race and was beaten by halfway, but this iron customer kept going for a remote third. (op 6-1)

Sourchamp(FR), tried in a tongue-tie, showed up for a long way on this chase debut and is young enough to improve. (op 22-1 tchd 25-1)

Paradise Expected Official explanation: jockey said mare was unsuited by the soft ground (op 11-2)

Quicolai(FR) lost his lead after a bad blunder, which rather knocked the stuffing out of him. He was tired in third when his rider pulled him up before the final fence (the usual second-last), but there was a bit of promise in this performance. (op 11-2)

Fleur De Vassy didn't fancy this from an early stage in the bad ground and was eventually pulled up. Official explanation: jockey said mare never travelled (op 11-2)

4100 MATTHEW CLARK "NATIONAL HUNT" MAIDEN HURDLE (8 hdls) 2m 1f
3:00 (3:00) (Class 4) 4-Y-0+ **£2,146** (£630; £315; £157)

Form RPR

-223 **1** **Our Mick**29 3572 5-11-3 0 JasonMaguire 120+
(Donald McCain) *racd keenly: a.p: chalng 2 out: led between last 2: j.lft and nt fluent last: styd on to draw clr run-in* **4/6**1

0-45 **2** *11* **Don't Turn Bach (IRE)**17 3762 7-11-3 0 HarrySkelton 108
(Paul Nicholls) *led: rdn and hdd between last 2: one pce run-in* **9/2**2

6-2 **3** *3* **Milo Milan (IRE)**31 3526 6-11-3 0 CharliePoste 105
(Richard Lee) *hld up: hdwy into midfield 4th: rdn to chse clr ldrs appr 2 out: styd on but nvr able to get to ldrs* **10/1**

4 *1 ½* **Storm Survivor (IRE)** 5-11-3 0 APMcCoy 104
(Jonjo O'Neill) *trckd ldrs: j. slowly 4th: outpcd fr 3 out: kpt on but n.d fr 2 out* **12/1**

0- **5** *19* **Boo Boo Booyakasha**634 403 7-11-0 0 WayneKavanagh(3) 84
(Arthur Whiting) *midfield: effrt to chse ldrs after 3 out: no imp: plugged on at one pce after* **80/1**

004 **6** *2 ½* **Bennys Mist (IRE)**14 3836 5-10-12 0 RTDunne(5) 81
(Venetia Williams) *midfield: struggling 3 out: btn after* **14/1**

0 **7** *14* **Roses Legend**14 3842 6-11-3 0 DPFahy 67
(Reginald Brown) *hld up: struggling 3 out: nvr on terms* **50/1**

26 **8** *51* **Morgan's Bay**43 3301 6-11-3 0 PaddyBrennan 16
(Tom George) *chsd ldrs tl wknd qckly appr 2 out* **7/1**3

000 **9** *11* **Jam Tomorrow (FR)**41 3365 6-11-3 0 DougieCostello 5
(Ian Williams) *midfield: dropped to rr 3rd: struggling appr 3 out* **100/1**

-0F0 **10** *4* **Fifth Sea Lord (IRE)**33 3495 6-10-10 0 ChristopherWard(7) 1
(Tom Gretton) *in tch: rdn and wknd appr 3 out* **100/1**

00 **11** *3 ¼* **Dani (IRE)**24 3651 5-10-7 0 DannyCook(3) —
(Mark Rimell) *midfield: lost pl bef 5th: bhd after* **80/1**

0200 **12** *shd* **Thomas Bell (IRE)**17 3761 7-10-10 0 CharlieWallis(7) —
(John O'Shea) *rel to r and s.v.s: a bhd* **66/1**

00/ **13** *71* **Termon Boy**820 2215 7-11-0 0 MichaelMurphy(3) —
(Rob Summers) *a bhd: t.o* **100/1**

4m 17.8s (18.40) **Going Correction** +1.175s/f (Heav) **13** Ran SP% **123.0**
Speed ratings (Par 105): **103,97,96,95,86 85,79,55,49,47 46,46,12**
toteswingers: 1&2 £2.60, 1&3 £3.20, 2&3 £6.10 CSF £4.18 TOTE £2.10: £1.10, £1.30, £2.20; EX 4.80.

Owner K Benson **Bred** K Benson & Mrs E Benson **Trained** Cholmondeley, Cheshire

FOCUS
A fair maiden hurdle. The market leaders had this between them from a long way out.

NOTEBOOK
Our Mick's Bangor second to subsequent Challow Hurdle winner Backspin was the best form on offer, but he disappointed next time. Back down in trip, he had to work to get to the front turning for home before staying on strongly after jumping out to his left over the last. He is likely to carry a penalty in another ordinary race before being asked to step up in grade. (op 4-5)

Don't Turn Bach(IRE) made a lot of the running but was held once the winner went by. He did not find much last time but, while that accusation could not really be levelled at him here, he is failing to live up to expectations over hurdles so far. (op 7-2)

Milo Milan(IRE), a remote second to stablemate Grey Gold over C&D last time, is going the right way and will be suited by a step up in trip. (op 12-1)

Storm Survivor(IRE) made a promising debut, staying on quite nicely at the end. From the family of Midlands National winner Another Excuse, he will benefit from further in time.

Boo Boo Booyakasha had not run since finishing down the field on his bumper debut in May 2009, so this was moderately encouraging. (op 100-1)

Bennys Mist(IRE) is now qualified for handicaps and will be of interest back over further in that sphere. (op 12-1)

Morgan's Bay chased the leading pair, but stopped quickly and walked across the line. He has something to prove now, but the ground was a plausible excuse here. The rider also reported that the gelding ran too free. Official explanation: jockey said gelding ran too free (op 8-1)

4101 EUROPEAN BREEDERS' FUND MARES' "NATIONAL HUNT" NOVICES' HURDLE (10 hdls) 2m 4f
3:30 (3:30) (Class 4) 4-Y-0+ **£2,341** (£687; £343; £171)

Form RPR

-425 **1** **Mizzurka**36 3442 7-11-0 115 APMcCoy 120+
(Bob Buckler) *a.p: led 7th: wandered appr last: styd on to draw clr run-in* **5/6**1

-102 **2** *4 ½* **Violin Davis (FR)**34 3480 5-11-0 0 HarrySkelton 112+
(Paul Nicholls) *hld up: hdwy 6th: chsd wnr after 3 out: ev ch 2 out: rdn appr last: one pce run-in* **7/2**2

5 **3** *13* **Kings Queen (IRE)**40 3389 5-11-0 0 PaddyBrennan 98
(Tom George) *prom to 4th: prom again 6th: ev ch 3 out: rdn and wknd 2 out* **7/2**2

F640 **4** *1 ¼* **My Viking Bay (IRE)**15 3820 7-10-7 102 CharlieWallis(7) 96
(John O'Shea) *hld up: hdwy 6th: chsd ldrs 3 out: btn bef 3 out: kpt on modly towards fin* **16/1**

63P- **P** **Chief Lady Olwyn**336 4604 12-11-0 52 TomSiddall —
(Lynn Siddall) *prom tl wknd appr 7th: t.o whn p.u bef 3 out* **100/1**

20-1 **P** **Osmosia (FR)**221 935 6-11-0 0 (t) WillKennedy —
(Paul Webber) *prom: led 6th: hdd 7th: wknd 3 out: t.o whn p.u bef 2 out* **12/1**3

PP-P **P** **Basford Lady (IRE)**93 2353 7-11-0 0 AlanO'Keeffe —
(Jennie Candlish) *led: hdd 6th: stopped qckly: t.o whn p.u bef 7th* **33/1**

06 **P** **Perjury**16 3783 7-11-0 0 TomMessenger —
(Robin Mathew) *bhd: pushed along 6th: j. slowly 7th: t.o whn p.u bef 3 out* **100/1**

5m 26.0s (30.50) **Going Correction** +1.175s/f (Heav) **8** Ran SP% **117.5**
Speed ratings (Par 105): **86,84,79,78,— —,—,—**
toteswingers: 1&2 £1.30, 1&3 £2.40, 2&3 £2.70 CSF £4.41 TOTE £2.00: £1.10, £1.10, £1.20; EX 3.60.

Owner Golden Cap **Bred** J R Weston **Trained** Henley, Somerset

FOCUS
Not a bad race of its type, but it lacked strength in depth.

NOTEBOOK
Mizzurka reportedly pulled muscles when behind Banjaxed Girl at Sandown last time, which accounted for her less than fluent hurdling that day. After picking her way around the inside where the ground was less poached, she wandered going into the last before winning a shade comfortably. Well at home in soft ground, she is set to step back up in grade in the David Nicholson Mares Hurdle at Cheltenham. In the long term she has the build and pedigree to make a nice chaser. (op 11-10 tchd 4-5)

Violin Davis(FR) finished in front of Mizzurka when they were both unplaced in the Listed mares' bumper at the Aintree Grand National meeting, but her hurdles form has not been so good and she had 7lb to find with the favourite on BHA figures. After traveling nicely she improved to look a threat after the second-last, but her rival was well in command on the run-in. An ordinary mares' race should soon come her way. (op 11-4)
Kings Queen(IRE), a winning Irish pointer, was not as keen as she had been at Leicester. She was upsides the big two jumping the last in the back straight but soon began to flag. (op 11-2)
My Viking Bay(IRE), exposed as no more than a fair performer, is perhaps flattered not to have been beaten further.
Osmosia(FR)'s bumper win back in July came on very different underfoot conditions. (op 9-1)

4102 LINDLEY GROUP H'CAP CHASE (16 fncs 3 omitted) 3m 1f 110y
4:00 (4:01) (Class 4) (0-115,115) 5-Y-0+ **£2,471** (£725; £362; £181)

Form				RPR
005U	1		**Ratify**[18] 3741 7-10-8 **97** ... LeightonAspell (Brendan Powell) *mde all: clr after 11th: stmbld whn wl in command 2 out: rdn and styd on wl after last* **9/2**[3]	116+
42-1	2	12	**Brenin Cwmtudu**[41] 3371 8-11-6 **109** ... PaulMoloney (Evan Williams) *chsd ldrs: rdn and outpcd 11th: tk 2nd appr 3 out: kpt on u.p after last: no imp* **6/1**	113
4/5	3	18	**El Jo (IRE)**[27] 3602 10-11-8 **111** ...(p) WillKennedy (Martin Bosley) *nt fluent 1st: hld up: struggling 13th: kpt on to take poor 3rd run-in: nvr a danger* **33/1**	97
0P-1	4	1 ¾	**Crank Hill**[43] 3297 9-10-3 **99** ... NathanSweeney(7) (Bob Buckler) *prom: lost pl after 3rd: nvr travelling after and n.d* **9/2**[3]	83
3/5-	5	3 ¼	**Derawar (IRE)**[314] 12-10-4 **100** ...(p) MsLucyJones(7) (Lucy Jones) *chsd ldrs tl lost pl 7th: struggling fnl circ* **33/1**	81
-214	6	3 ¾	**Runshan (IRE)**[91] 2395 11-11-3 **106** ... JasonMaguire (David Bridgwater) *w ldr tl after 8th: outpcd by wnr bef 12th: lost 2nd appr 3 out: wknd bef 2 out* **7/1**	83
3P-0	P		**Magnifico (FR)**[36] 3440 10-11-1 **111** ...(p) MrMatthewBarber(7) (Nikki Evans) *j. slowly 2nd: a bhd: t.o whn p.u bef 13th* **28/1**	—
6F3P	F		**Whataboutya (IRE)**[42] 3347 10-11-2 **115** ...(p) GeraldQuinn(10) (Jonjo O'Neill) *chsd ldrs: lost pl 7th: struggling to keep up whn fell 11th* **20/1**	—
P161	P		**Foxesbow (IRE)**[21] 3695 7-11-3 **106** ... APMcCoy (Jonjo O'Neill) *chsd ldrs: lost pl 9th: struggling after: t.o whn p.u bef 13th* **7/2**[1]	—
00U4	P		**Health Is Wealth (IRE)**[24] 3650 6-10-6 **95** ... HarrySkelton (Colin Tizzard) *hld up: hdwy to chse ldrs 6th: losing grnd whn mstke 12th: t.o whn p.u bef 2 out* **4/1**[2]	—

6m 58.8s (27.00) **Going Correction** +1.175s/f (Heav) **10** Ran SP% **119.5**
Speed ratings: **105,101,95,95,94 93,—,—,—,—**
toteswingers: 1&2 £7.40, 1&3 £18.20, 2&3 £26.00 CSF £31.13 CT £794.36 TOTE £6.90: £2.50, £1.40, £7.70; EX 37.40 TRIFECTA Not won..
Owner J J King **Bred** Mrs R Lyon **Trained** Upper Lambourn, Berks

FOCUS
An ordinary handicap chase, and quite a test in the conditions.

NOTEBOOK
Ratify was running over fences for only the second time after unseating on his recent chase debut. Setting off in front again, he was clear entering the back straight but was tiring going to the second-last, where he stumbled on landing. However, he kept going well enough for a fully deserved victory. Better ground will suit him and he has more to offer as he gains experience. (op 5-1 tchd 11-2 and 4-1)
Brenin Cwmtudu, raised 7lb after his win over shorter here, plugged on dourly after moving into second place, but he never really threatened to reel in the winner. (op 5-1)
El Jo(IRE) plugged on to grab a well-beaten third on the extended run-in. He is not badly handicapped on his old form in Ireland. (op 25-1)
Crank Hill had today's earlier winner Royal Chatelier back in fourth when winning off this mark over hurdles last time, but was never a serious factor here. (op 11-2)
Runshan(IRE) was not helped the rain-eased ground on this first start for three months, but he showed up prominently for a long way and was still in third place starting out on the extended run-in. (tchd 13-2)
Foxesbow(IRE), raised 7lb after his Market Rasen win, was in trouble by halfway. He is not the most consistent. (op 9-2)

4103 BBC HEREFORD & WORCESTER H'CAP CHASE (10 fncs 2 omitted) 2m
4:30 (4:30) (Class 5) (0-95,97) 5-Y-0+ **£2,081** (£611; £305; £152)

Form				RPR
-PP2	1		**Ours (FR)**[19] 3720 9-11-9 **92** ... JasonMaguire (Mark Rimell) *chsd ldr: led last: looked to be holding runner-up 200yds out: pressed cl home: jst hld on u.str driving* **7/2**[2]	105
-343	2	shd	**Rileyev (FR)**[18] 3741 6-10-13 **89** ... HarryChalloner(7) (Venetia Williams) *hld up in tch: mstke 4th: niggled along after 8th: str chal last: nt qckn 200yds out: styd on u.str driving cl home: jst denied* **7/2**[2]	103
0P42	3	10	**Mujamead**[12] 3875 7-10-10 **84** ...(p) LeeEdwards(5) (Sally-Anne Wheelwright) *led: hdd last: sn rdn: no ex and no ch w front pair fnl 200yds* **9/2**	87
P	4	¾	**Piment D'Estruval (FR)**[44] 3256 8-11-12 **95** ... DougieCostello (Tim Vaughan) *hld up: tk clsr order to chse ldrs 5th: wknd qckly after last* **14/1**	98
652	5	55	**Yes Man (IRE)**[12] 3873 6-11-11 **97** ...(v) DonalDevereux(3) (Peter Bowen) *chsd ldrs: j.lft 3rd: pushed along and wknd appr 2 out* **10/3**[1]	44
U0F5	P		**Goodtimetoby (IRE)**[33] 3491 8-11-6 **89** ... CharliePoste (Richard Lee) *hld up: nt fluent 5th and 7th: lost tch 2 out: t.o whn p.u bef last* **4/1**[3]	—

4m 21.1s (17.50) **Going Correction** +1.175s/f (Heav) **6** Ran SP% **112.4**
Speed ratings: **103,102,97,97,70** —
toteswingers: 1&2 £2.80, 1&3 £2.60, 2&3 £2.60 CSF £16.31 TOTE £4.70: £2.10, £2.00; EX 14.50.
Owner D J Pratt **Bred** Francois Cottin **Trained** Leafield, Oxon

FOCUS
A low-grade handicap chase.

NOTEBOOK
Ours(FR) showed a return to form when second at Leicester latest and the drop back in trip was not a problem in these conditions. Jumping to the front at the final fence and just holding off the persistent runner-up on the lengthy run-in, he had dropped to a mark 7lb lower than when gaining his last win in December 2008. (op 9-2)
Rileyev(FR) has been edging down the weights. He had previously shown a tendency to finish weakly, but that was not the case here over this shorter trip and he would have got up in a couple more strides. (op 10-3 tchd 4-1)
Mujamead ran another solid race but the game was up once he was headed at the final fence.
Piment D'Estruval(FR), dropping in trip, was well held in the end on this chasing debut, although this was an improvement on what he showed in Ireland and he should be capable of building on it. (op 12-1)
Yes Man(IRE) was unable to lead this time and faded going to the second-last. (op 7-2)
Goodtimetoby(IRE) was unsuited by the soft ground on this chasing debut. Official explanation: jockey said gelding was unsuited by the soft ground (tchd 7-2)

4104 LINDLEY CATERING H'CAP HURDLE (8 hdls) 2m 1f
5:00 (5:00) (Class 5) (0-95,100) 4-Y-0+ **£1,951** (£573; £286; £143)

Form				RPR
0-FP	1		**Decent Lord (IRE)**[262] 490 7-10-0 **68** oh2 ... SeanQuinlan (Jennie Candlish) *in tch: prom 5th: led 3 out: clr appr last: eased down run-in* **17/2**	89+
0022	2	17	**Man Of Leisure**[31] 3532 7-11-6 **91** ... CPGeoghegan(3) (Nerys Dutfield) *led: nt fluent 1st: hdd 5th: stl ev ch 3 out: rdn and chsng wnr whn hit 2 out: hld whn blnd last: no ch w wnr* **3/1**[2]	96+
0356	3	6	**Reg's Ruby**[90] 2425 5-11-5 **94** ... MrSWDrinkwater(7) (David Bridgwater) *prom: led 5th: hdd 3 out: rdn and outpcd by front 2 after 2 out: no imp after* **33/1**	90
1334	4	1 ½	**Monsieur (FR)**[16] 3782 11-11-3 **85** ... HarrySkelton (Carroll Gray) *chsd ldrs: lost pl after 3rd: clsd again 4th: hit 3 out: outpcd after: plugged on at one pce but no ch bef last* **6/1**	81
0452	5	1 ½	**Form And Beauty (IRE)**[14] 3839 9-9-12 **69** ow2 ... MrBMoorcroft(5) (Bernard Llewellyn) *in tch: hdwy appr 5th where mstke: sn outpcd: n.d after* **9/2**[3]	65
4551	6	2 ½	**Swiss Guard**[6] 3983 5-11-13 **100** 7ex ...(t) MrTomDavid(5) (Tim Vaughan) *hld up: hdwy 5th: chsd ldrs 3 out: sn rdn and outpcd: no imp after: wknd bef last* **9/4**[1]	91
0U00	7	91	**Major Potential (USA)**[18] 3740 5-11-2 **89** ... RTDunne(5) (Venetia Williams) *hld up: hdwy into midfield after 3rd: chsd ldrs 3 out: wknd bef 2 out: t.o* **20/1**	—
P-P0	8	4 ½	**Cybergenic (FR)**[87] 2467 13-10-13 **88** ... TrevorWhelan(7) (Tracey Watkins) *hld up: nt fluent 3rd: niggled along whn mstke 3 out: sn dropped away: t.o* **50/1**	—
-405	9	2 ¼	**Born To Be Wilde (IRE)**[41] 3367 6-11-10 **92** ... PaulMoloney (Evan Williams) *hld up: struggling appr 5th: t.o* **22/1**	—
45-P	P		**King Diamond (FR)**[277] 283 10-10-0 **68** oh6 ... WillKennedy (Violet M Jordan) *prom: pushed along and lost pl 5th: sn dropped away: t.o whn p.u bef 2 out* **33/1**	—

4m 22.0s (22.60) **Going Correction** +1.175s/f (Heav) **10** Ran SP% **115.7**
Speed ratings (Par 103): **93,85,82,81,80 79,36,34,33,—**
toteswingers: 1&2 £6.30, 1&3 £32.00, 2&3 £8.30 CSF £32.69 CT £811.34 TOTE £12.00: £3.70, £1.40, £4.80; EX 57.80.
Owner Mrs Judith Ratcliff **Bred** Lar O'Toole **Trained** Basford Green, Staffs

FOCUS
A very modest handicap hurdle.

NOTEBOOK
Decent Lord(IRE) ran out a wide-margin winner, value for further as he was eased on the run-in with the race in the bag. Never previously placed over hurdles, he was 2lb out of the weights and had been off since pulling up in May, but he had shown ability on his previous two starts and was well supported here. He might have prospects under a penalty. Official explanation: trainer said, regarding apparent improvement in form, that the gelding had its confidence restored having had time off. (op 8-1 tchd 10-1)
Man Of Leisure did not hurdle too well and was no match for the easy winner from the second-last. He has now finished second three times in a row over C&D. (op 7-2 tchd 4-1)
Reg's Ruby, given a three-month break, showed a lot more than she had on her handicap debut, sticking on after racing prominently. (tchd 40-1)
Monsieur(FR) is running consistently at the moment and looks a reasonable guide to the form. (op 7-1 tchd 8-1)
Form And Beauty(IRE) was found wanting off a 5lb higher mark than when finishing second over C&D latest. (op 5-1 tchd 7-2)
Swiss Guard, an easy Lingfield winner six days earlier, was held under his penalty in this slightly better race. (op 2-1 tchd 15-8 and 11-4)
T/Jkpt: Not won. T/Plt: £68.20 to a £1 stake. Pool: £101,311.79. 1,083.64 winning tickets.
T/Qpdt: £8.80 to a £1 stake. Pool: £6,798.47. 567.05 winning tickets. DO

4105 - 4106a (Foreign Racing) - See Raceform Interactive

3732 NAVAN (L-H)
Sunday, February 13

OFFICIAL GOING: Heavy

4107a LADBROKES.COM BOYNE HURDLE (GRADE 2) (12 hdls) 2m 5f
2:50 (2:50) 5-Y-0+ **£23,254** (£6,797; £3,219; £1,073)

			RPR
1		**Voler La Vedette (IRE)**[21] 3707 7-11-3 153 ... AELynch (C A Murphy, Ire) *settled bhd ldrs: 6th 1/2-way: hdwy in 5th 3 out: 3rd travelling wl 2 out: rdn to ld last: kpt on wl run-in: comf* **9/4**[1]	154+
2	2	**Rigour Back Bob (IRE)**[47] 3175 6-11-8 147 ... AndrewJMcNamara (E J O'Grady, Ire) *chsd ldrs: 3rd 1/2-way: impr to ld after 4 out: rdn and hdd 2 out: u.p in 3rd last: kpt on again run-in to go 2nd* **4/1**[3]	152
3	¾	**Oscar Dan Dan (IRE)**[16] 3796 9-11-10 146 ... PTownend (Thomas Mullins, Ire) *cl 2nd early: led 3rd: disp bef 4 out: rdn in 2nd ent st: no ex in 4th 2 out: kpt on same pce fr bef last* **10/1**	153
4	shd	**Stonemaster (IRE)**[29] 3578 6-11-3 140 ... DNRussell (D T Hughes, Ire) *chsd ldrs: 4th 1/2-way: hdwy in 3rd 3 out: rdn to ld 2 out: hdd last: no ex and kpt on same pce run-in* **7/1**	146
5	2 ½	**Shinrock Paddy (IRE)**[29] 3578 7-11-10 150 ...(t) APCawley (Paul Nolan, Ire) *settled bhd ldrs: 7th 1/2-way: rdn in 6th ent st: kpt on same pce in 5th last: no imp on ldrs* **7/2**[2]	151
6	7	**Berties Dream (IRE)**[60] 2971 8-11-10 147 ... PCarberry (Paul John Gilligan, Ire) *led: hdd 3rd: disp again bef 4 out: rdn in 3rd after 4 out: no ex in 4th 3 out: kpt on one pce* **16/1**	144
7	1 ¼	**Venalmar**[35] 3473 9-11-3 131 ... MJFerris (M F Morris, Ire) *settled bhd ldrs: 5th 1/2-way: rdn in 6th 3 out: no ex in 5th next: kpt on one pce* **33/1**	135
8	dist	**Moskova (IRE)**[16] 3796 8-10-12 135 ... RMPower (Paul Nolan, Ire) *a bhd: pushed along 1/2-way: no imp and t.o* **12/1**	—
F		**Footy Facts (IRE)**[16] 3796 11-11-3 139 ... PTEnright (Robert Tyner, Ire) *hld up towards rr: rdn and no imp ent st: fell 2 out* **25/1**	132

5m 37.6s (21.60) **9** Ran SP% **114.9**
CSF £11.48 TOTE £2.70: £1.02, £1.70, £3.00; DF 13.60.
Owner Mrs M Brophy **Bred** Mrs Margaret Brophy **Trained** Gorey, Co Wexford

FOCUS
Not many of these are on the upgrade and the easy winner did not need to repeat her best.

NOTEBOOK

Voler La Vedette(IRE) settled really well for Andrew Lynch, took a slightly greater grip on the second circuit but arrived hard on the steel to throw down her challenge between the final two flights before quickening well on the run-in to put the result beyond doubt fairly quickly. She did seem to idle a bit up the hill and left one with the slight wonder about what she would have found had something been good enough to challenge, but that might be slightly harsh. Now that she settles far better in her races she should be a far more potent threat to Quevega at Cheltenham than she ultimately was a year ago. (op 2/1)

Rigour Back Bob(IRE) certainly raced a good bit more keenly than the mare. Racing handily on the inside, he led on the approach to the straight but as soon as the winner came to him he didn't have the speed to match. He kept on best up the hill and would relish a longer trip. (op 13/2)

Oscar Dan Dan(IRE) just stayed on. Racing in the first two most of the way, he was just caught a bit for tactical speed when the pace quickened up but stamina is more his forte than the eventual fourth and he caught him on the line for third place money. (op 10/1 tchd 12/1)

Stonemaster(IRE) raced quite close to the pace and was in a perfectly good position to challenge early in the straight but he was readily outpaced by the winner and didn't seem to get up the hill from the last. One would expect 2m4f to be more of his trip on better ground. (op 7/1 tchd 6/1)

Shinrock Paddy(IRE) was a bit disappointing but he needed a more positive ride, more in keeping with the ride he got when winning the Grade 1 novice hurdle here last season. His rider was content to sit off the pace but when he hit his flat spot before the turn into the straight there was no way back and he just stayed on at one pace. (op 3/1)

Berties Dream(IRE) is a confirmed stayer of course and he needed to make this more of a test of stamina to have any chance. He dropped away in the straight. (op 14/1)

4109a TEN UP NOVICE CHASE (GRADE 2) (17 fncs) 3m

3:50 (3:52) 5-Y-O+ **£21,012** (£6,142; £2,909; £969)

			RPR
1		**Quito De La Roque (FR)**[29] 3579 7-11-8 ... DNRussell (C A Murphy, Ire) *trckd ldrs: 4th 1/2-way: j. into 2nd 4 out: rdn to ld after 3 out: clr bef last: idled cl home and reduced advantage* **1/1**[1]	154+
2	*4*	**Royal De La Thinte (FR)**[29] 3579 6-11-3 ... (t) AELynch (J T R Dreaper, Ire) *hld up in last: 4th 3 out: rdn into 2nd bef 2 out: no imp on ldr bef last: kpt on same pce run-in* **5/2**[2]	142+
3	*13*	**Slippers Percy (IRE)**[29] 3579 9-11-3 ... DGHogan (Denis Gerard Hogan, Ire) *led: hdd appr 7th: regained ld 7 out: hdd after 5 out: dropped to 4th 4 out: rdn and no imp in last 3 out: kpt on to go mod 3rd last: no imp on ldrs* **25/1**	129
4	*1 3/4*	**Bronte Bay (IRE)**[84] 2565 8-11-3 122 ... (p) DJCondon (Paul W Flynn, Ire) *chsd ldr in 2nd: 3rd appr 7th: rdn and no ex 3 out: kpt on one pce* **20/1**	127
5	*12*	**The Hurl (IRE)**[16] 3799 8-11-3 ... NPMadden (M F Morris, Ire) *chsd ldrs in 3rd: impr to ld appr 7th and mstke: hdd 7 out: led again after 5 out: rdn and hdd after 3 out: no ex and kpt on one pce* **7/2**[3]	115

6m 54.0s (24.70) **5** Ran SP% **109.4**

CSF £3.99 TOTE £1.90: £1.02, £1.70; DF 2.70.

Owner Gigginstown House Stud **Bred** Robert Mongin **Trained** Gorey, Co Wexford

FOCUS

The third and fourth are the markers to the form.

NOTEBOOK

Quito De La Roque(FR) could even afford the luxury of idling on the run-in. They went a steady pace, he jumped and travelled the whole way, took it up after the third-last and when he was asked for his effort he galloped clear. There was no flat spot, he wasn't being hard ridden from some way out, it was just very straightforward. His participation at Cheltenham seems to be very much dependant on his getting soft or heavy ground, and that would have to be deemed unlikely. (op 1/1 tchd 5/6)

Royal De La Thinte(FR) settled quite well and in stark comparison to his run at Naas last time when he fell at the last when out on his feet. He was able to run to the line on this occasion, although he may have been somewhat flattered by his proximity to the winner. (op 9/4 tchd 2/1)

Slippers Percy(IRE) helped set the steady pace but had no response when the winner went about his business and faded. (op 33/1)

Bronte Bay(IRE) did a bit of the donkey work and despite his being an undoubted stayer he doesn't have much else in his armoury and he also faded away before the second last. (op 25/1)

The Hurl(IRE) was disappointing in the sense that he completely failed to get home, but this was a performance well below his best. He tried to inject some pace into it coming out of the back straight and was still in front after the third-last but as soon as the winner went on he emptied completely. (op 4/1)

4108 - 4111a (Foreign Racing) - See Raceform Interactive

3519 CATTERICK (L-H)

Monday, February 14

OFFICIAL GOING: Good to soft (soft in places; hdl: 7.1, chs: 6.6)

Wind: moderate 1/2 behind Weather: overcast, heavy shower after race 3

4112 VALENTINE'S DAY NOVICES' HURDLE (12 hdls) 3m 1f 110y

2:20 (2:21) (Class 4) 5-Y-O+ **£2,055** (£599; £299)

Form				RPR
-2P4	**1**		**Mac Aeda**[33] 3509 7-10-12 114 ... GrahamLee (Malcolm Jefferson) *trckd ldrs: wnt cl 2nd after 7th: hrd drvn appr 2 out: led between last 2: clr last: drvn out* **11/10**[1]	123+
2-61	**2**	*18*	**Eighteen Carat (IRE)**[85] 2545 7-11-5 117 ... JasonMaguire (Donald McCain) *led: j.rt fr 4 out: hrd drvn after 3 out: nt fluent 2 out: hdd between last 2: 6 l down and wkng whn blnd last* **7/2**[2]	119+
4	**3**	*1 1/4*	**Streamtown (IRE)**[19] 3747 7-10-5 0 ... CampbellGillies (S R B Crawford, Ire) *hld up in rr: hdwy after 7th: wnt modest 3rd 4 out: 5 l 3rd and one pce whn blnd last* **15/2**[3]	101+
50-3	**4**	*29*	**Foxes Delight (IRE)**[26] 3633 7-10-5 101 ... (t) AlistairFindlay(7) (Jane Walton) *chsd ldrs: wnt distant 4th appr 2 out* **16/1**	83
/203	**5**	*8*	**Be My Deputy (IRE)**[99] 2246 6-10-12 0 ... PaddyAspell (Richard Guest) *chsd ldrs: modest 3rd whn hit 8th: wknd next* **8/1**	72
/65-	**6**	*3 3/4*	**Dollar Mick (IRE)**[297] 5354 6-10-12 97 ... RyanMania (James Moffatt) *mid-div: drvn along 7th: sme hdwy 9th: sn wknd* **50/1**	68
50	**7**	*22*	**Sam D'Oc (FR)**[12] 3889 5-10-12 0 ... JamesReveley (Keith Reveley) *in rr: bhd fr 8th: t.o 3 out* **50/1**	49
50	**8**	*42*	**Wait No More (IRE)**[30] 3572 6-10-12 0 ... JackDoyle (Sarah Humphrey) *hld up in rr: hdwy 7th: wknd 4 out: t.o next* **16/1**	11
	B		**Andy Vic (IRE)**[354] 4271 8-10-5 0 ... KyleJames(7) (Ian Brown) *in rr whn b.d 2nd* **80/1**	—
-3B6	**P**		**Greenandredparson (IRE)**[20] 3729 8-10-9 92 ... (p) JamesO'Farrell(3) (Patrick Griffin, Ire) *chsd ldrs: lost pl 7th: t.o next: p.u bef 2 out* **50/1**	—
0P-P	**P**		**Simhal**[254] 624 7-10-12 0 ... RichieMcGrath (Clive Mulhall) *t.k.h: trckd ldrs: wknd 7th: sn bhd: t.o whn p.u bef next* **200/1**	—
05P0	**P**		**Betty's Run**[21] 3717 9-10-5 59 ... TomSiddall (Lynn Siddall) *mid-div: lost pl 8th: t.o whn p.u bef 2 out* **200/1**	—
26-0	**P**		**Kensix Star (IRE)**[40] 3398 5-10-12 0 ... BrianHughes (Howard Johnson) *wnt prom 3rd: reminders 7th: sn lost pl and bhd: t.o next: p.u bef 2 out* **33/1**	—
0-PF	**F**		**Lady Chorister**[9] 3952 6-10-5 0 ... FearghalDavis (Simon West) *prom: fell 2nd* **200/1**	—
0600	**P**		**Are Olive**[48] 3167 8-10-5 78 ... RobertWalford (Tim Walford) *in rr: bhd fr 8th: t.o whn p.u bef 2 out* **125/1**	—
	P		**Twigg Echoes (IRE)** 5-10-12 0 ... WilsonRenwick (Howard Johnson) *prom: drvn 5th: sn lost pl and bhd: t.o whn p.u after 7th* **66/1**	—

6m 25.8s (-1.80) **Going Correction** +0.15s/f (Yiel) **16** Ran SP% **118.3**

Speed ratings: **108,102,102,93,90 89,82,69,—,— —,—,—,—,— —**

toteswingers:1&2 £1.70, 2&3 £5.50, 1&3 £2.90 CSF £4.48 TOTE £2.20: £1.10, £1.40, £2.30; EX 7.60.

Owner Mr & Mrs J M Davenport **Bred** J M Jefferson **Trained** Norton, N Yorks

FOCUS

A modest novice hurdle run at an even gallop, with the first three pulling well clear. The winner is on the upgrade and the placed horses are the best guides to the form.

NOTEBOOK

Mac Aeda relished this step up in trip to break his duck at the sixth attempt over hurdles. He stayed on strongly and looks a progressive sort over this distance, so should be competitive under a penalty. He has plenty of size and scope, so should make a useful chaser. (op 2-1)

Eighteen Carat(IRE), a winner at Aintree in November, ran a solid race under his penalty. He set an even gallop but was simply unable to go with the winner once turning into the straight. This was a fair effort and he will remain of interest in similar contests. (op 5-2)

Streamtown(IRE) appreciated racing over further and was running on in third. She was given a lot to do, but made eye-catching late progress and should go close in this grade, especially if ridden a little closer to the pace. (op 7-1)

Foxes Delight(IRE) probably ran his race without ever threatening.

Be My Deputy(IRE) was a little disappointing upped in trip on this second start over hurdles. He may prove better than this. (op 7-1 tchd 6-1)

Wait No More(IRE) was well supported, but never featured and should prefer better ground. (op 12-1 tchd 18-1)

4113 CATTERICKBRIDGE.CO.UK H'CAP HURDLE (8 hdls) 2m

2:50 (2:51) (Class 4) (0-115,114) 4-Y-O+ **£2,329** (£678; £339)

Form				RPR
0/33	**1**		**Fujin Dancer (FR)**[22] 3696 6-10-9 **104** ... MissHBethell(7) (Brian Ellison) *hld up towards rr: hmpd bnd after 3rd: hdwy 3 out: edgd lft appr last: j.lft: styd on strly to ld run-in: drvn out* **11/2**[2]	110+
0064	**2**	*2 3/4*	**Waterloo Corner**[32] 3523 9-10-8 **96** ... KennyJohnson (Ray Craggs) *trckd ldrs: led appr 2 out: hdd sn after last: kpt on same pce* **9/1**	99
0050	**3**	*1 3/4*	**Crosby Jemma**[87] 2508 7-11-5 **107** ... BrianHughes (Mike Sowersby) *hld up in midfield: hdwy to trck ldrs 5th: upsides last: no ex* **20/1**	108
0003	**4**	*nk*	**Jaques Vert (FR)**[14] 3855 5-11-0 **102** ... TomO'Brien (Robert Wylie) *trckd ldrs: hdwy to chal 2 out: bmpd last: styd on same pce run-in* **13/2**	104
130-	**5**	*1 1/2*	**King's Counsel (IRE)**[11] 5320 5-11-6 **108** ... (v) DenisO'Regan (David O'Meara) *wiith ldrs: led 4th: hdd appr 2 out: one pce run-in* **6/1**[3]	107
650F	**6**	*12*	**Veronicas Boy**[33] 3509 5-10-13 **101** ... BarryKeniry (George Moore) *chsd ldrs: wknd 5th: 7th whn hit and hmpd 2 out* **11/1**	90
0653	**7**	*3/4*	**Pete**[17] 3782 8-10-2 **93** ... EwanWhillans(3) (Barry Murtagh) *hld up in rr: smooth hdwy to trck ldrs 5th: shkn up appr 2 out: wknd appr last* **5/1**[1]	83
P46	**8**	*hd*	**Petrocelli**[21] 3711 4-9-7 **98** oh11 ... HenryBrooke(7) (Wilf Storey) *in rr: hit 3rd: hmpd 2 out: nvr a factor* **40/1**	76
6004	**9**	*1*	**Takaatuf (IRE)**[19] 3746 5-11-3 **105** ... GrahamLee (John Hellens) *mid-div: hdwy to chse ldrs 5th: wknd appr 2 out* **22/1**	92
-100	**10**	*31*	**Hi Dancer**[34] 3500 8-10-12 **110** ... SeveBrumpton(10) (Ben Haslam) *w.r.s: detached in last: a bhd: hmpd 2 out: t.o* **28/1**	69
00P0	**11**	*nk*	**Front Rank (IRE)**[32] 3523 11-10-8 **103** ... (p) MissECSayer(7) (Dianne Sayer) *chsd ldrs: reminders and lost pl 3rd: t.o 5th* **50/1**	62
-050	**12**	*2 1/2*	**Knock Three Times (IRE)**[107] 2094 5-10-0 **95** ... (t) MissLAlexander(7) (Wilf Storey) *in rr: bhd whn blnd 5th: sn t.o* **33/1**	51
6040	**13**	*25*	**My Brother Sylvest**[81] 2634 5-11-9 **111** ... (b[1]) RhysFlint (David Brace) *led to 4th: wknd qckly next: t.o 2 out: virtually p.u* **8/1**	45
2460	**F**		**TwentyninEblack (FR)**[54] 3090 7-11-10 **112** ... JasonMaguire (Donald McCain) *hld up: hdwy 5th: 6th and no imp whn fell 2 out* **10/1**	101

3m 52.8s (0.30) **Going Correction** +0.15s/f (Yiel)

WFA 4 from 5yo+ 9lb **14** Ran SP% **118.1**

Speed ratings (Par 105): **105,103,102,102,101 95,95,95,94,79 79,77,65,—**

toteswingers:1&2 £5.20, 2&3 £42.90, 1&3 £15.90 CSF £48.61 CT £928.22 TOTE £5.50: £1.40, £3.00, £8.10; EX 54.60.

Owner W A Bethell **Bred** Loughtown Stud Ltd **Trained** Norton, N Yorks

■ Stewards' Enquiry : Miss E C Sayer one-day ban: careless riding (tbn)

FOCUS

A competitive handicap hurdle, despite the defection of likely favourite Kaolak. The form looks solid with the four immediately behind the winner pretty much to their marks.

NOTEBOOK

Fujin Dancer(FR) gave Miss Harriet Bethell her first winner under rules, showing a game attitude to outstay his rivals. He can continue to run well and connections believe he will appreciate better ground. He may also return to the Flat in the summer.

Waterloo Corner ran a fine race in defeat, having travelled up with the pace throughout. He appreciated the drop in distance and handled the soft conditions well. A winner off this mark, he remains of interest in this grade. (op 10-1)

Crosby Jemma bounced back to something like her best on this return from nearly three months off. She travelled nicely but failed to match the winner after the last. (op 18-1)

Jaques Vert(FR), third off this mark at Ayr last month, again ran his race. This was just his second handicap start and there should be improvement to come. (op 8-1)

King's Counsel(IRE), winner of this race last year, was well supported to repeat the feat off this 6lb higher mark. He led turning in and had every chance, but couldn't hold on. He should continue to run well in this type of race. (op 5-1 tchd 7-1)

Veronicas Boy fell at Doncaster last time and was a never-nearer sixth here. (op 12-1)

Pete travelled strongly but failed to quicken when asked for his effort.

4114 WEATHERBYS BLOODSTOCK INSURANCE NOVICES' CHASE (19 fncs) 3m 1f 110y

3:20 (3:20) (Class 3) 5-Y-O+ **£5,054** (£1,838)

Form				RPR
301P	**1**		**You Know Yourself (IRE)**[22] 3695 8-10-13 109 ... ShaneByrne(5) (Sue Smith) *chsd ldr: upsides 7th and 11th: oecked 12th: lft in ld 5 out: drvn after next: hdd appr 3 out: lft fence clr: nt fluent 2 out: heavily eased run-in* **6/1**[2]	116+

4P43 **2** *66* **Almond Court (IRE)**[20] 3726 8-10-5 74.......................... KennyJohnson 45
(Robert Johnson) *racd in last: reminders and lost tch after 11th: lft distant 3rd 5 out: lft t.o 2nd 3 out: 73 l down jumping last* **100/1**

P-31 **U** **Chamirey (FR)**[22] 3702 8-11-4 0......................................(b) JasonMaguire 123+
(Donald McCain) *led: j.rt: blnd and hdd 5 out: drvn to ld appr 3 out: 3 l ahd whn blnd bdly and uns rdr 3 out* **2/9**[1]

1-4P **F** **Only The Best**[11] 3902 8-10-12 112.. GrahamLee —
(Ferdy Murphy) *racd in 3rd: reminders and lost tch appr 12th: modest 3rd whn tk heavy fall 5 out* **10/1**[3]

6m 52.1s (10.10) **Going Correction** +0.35s/f (Yiel) 4 Ran SP% **106.2**
Speed ratings: **98,77,—,—**
CSF £66.74 TOTE £5.00; EX 29.20.

Owner Mrs S Smith **Bred** Patrick O'Connell **Trained** High Eldwick, W Yorks

FOCUS
This had looked an ideal opportunity for Chamirey to land his second chase success, but that was not to be the case. The winner is ratred to his mark.

NOTEBOOK
You Know Yourself(IRE), a winner on his chasing debut at Wetherby (2m4f), pulled up early after the tack went wrong latest but had luck on his side this time, being left to cruise home in an eventful race. He handled the step up in trip and, although he would probably have finished second had the favourite not departed, he jumped nicely and may have more to offer, especially back in handicaps. (op 13-2)
Almond Court(IRE) plugged on to finish a distant second, having never got involved. (tchd 125-1)
Chamirey(FR) failed to build on his easy Towcester win, unseating his rider at the third-last fence. He travelled best turning into the straight, but a bad mistake ended his chances. He didn't exactly jump fluently, but has the ability to win a similar event under a penalty. (op 1-4)
Only The Best jumped poorly when pulled up at Towcester latest and he fell at the 15th. He needs to improve in that department to become competitive. (op 1-4)

4115 TURFTV H'CAP HURDLE (10 hdls) 2m 3f
3:50 (3:52) (Class 4) (0-115,114) 4-Y-0+ **£2,211** (£649; £324; £162)

Form RPR

0353 **1** **Bocciani (GER)**[32] 3523 6-10-7 98..............................(p) JamesO'Farrell(3) 100+
(Dianne Sayer) *hld up: stdy hdwy 6th: led on bit between last 2: carried hd high and drvn out run-in* **17/2**

P313 **2** *1 1/4* **Moon Melody (GER)**[160] 1503 8-10-0 88 oh6............... CampbellGillies 89
(Mike Sowersby) *chsd ldrs: upsides 2 out: kpt on same pce fnl 75yds* **33/1**

646- **3** *4* **Patavium (IRE)**[180] 4438 8-10-12 100................................. BrianHarding 97
(Edwin Tuer) *trckd ldrs: chal appr last: kpt on same pce* **20/1**

520 **4** *1/2* **Latin Connection (IRE)**[19] 3750 5-10-11 106............ MrBGCrawford(7) 104
(S R B Crawford, Ire) *hld up in rr: hdwy 3 out: styd on same pce appr last* **16/1**

2P-6 **5** *1 1/4* **Descaro (USA)**[88] 2477 5-11-5 107.................................. DenisO'Regan 104
(David O'Meara) *hld up in rr: stdy hdwy 7th: chsng ldrs 2 out: one pce appr last* **8/1**

41P0 **6** *9* **Mini Minster**[85] 2549 9-11-8 110.. GrahamLee 98
(Peter Atkinson) *chsd ldrs: outpcd and lost pl 6th: hdwy 3 out: wknd appr next* **33/1**

P-00 **7** *1 1/4* **Gwyre (IRE)**[32] 3523 5-10-8 96... RichieMcGrath 86
(Tim Easterby) *w ldrs: led 7th: hdd between last 2: 4th and hld whn blnd last: wknd* **25/1**

63PF **8** *1 1/2* **Greenbelt**[13] 2350 10-9-9 93.. SamuelWelton(10) 78
(George Moore) *in rr: pushed along 5th: styd on appr 2 out: nvr nr ldrs* **25/1**

5006 **9** *3/4* **Barron Watlass (IRE)**[34] 3500 7-11-2 104........................(p) BarryKeniry 89
(George Moore) *mid-div: chsng ldrs 3 out: fdd next* **11/2**[2]

323- **10** *21* **Sam Lord**[356] 4211 7-11-12 114... PaddyAspell 80
(James Moffatt) *in rr div: hdwy to chse ldrs 3 out: wknd appr next* **14/1**

0415 **11** *6* **King Benny (IRE)**[17] 3782 7-10-5 96............................. HarryHaynes(3) 56
(Elliott Cooper) *trckd ldrs: lost pl after 7th: sn bhd* **9/2**[1]

004/ **12** *2 1/2* **Dan's Heir**[111] 9-10-13 108.. MissLAlexander(7) 66
(Wilf Storey) *in rr: drvn after 5th: sn bhd* **50/1**

6-00 **13** *21* **Red Tanber (IRE)**[80] 2658 8-10-0 88 oh8.......................... AdrianLane 27
(Bruce Mactaggart) *in rr: drvn 6th: bhd fr 3 out* **33/1**

1-P5 **14** *2* **Chief Bucaneer (IRE)**[21] 3715 8-11-5 107.......................... JanFaltejsek 44
(George Charlton) *chsd ldrs: mstke 4th: wknd after 3 out* **11/2**[2]

0P-2 **15** *11* **Lennon (IRE)**[31] 3551 11-11-6 108....................................... BrianHughes 35
(Howard Johnson) *mde most: hit 5th: hdd 7th: lost pl after 3 out: sn bhd and eased* **7/1**[3]

13-F **16** *28* **Hector's House**[114] 1956 5-11-11 113...................................... RhysFlint 15
(David Brace) *in rr div: hdwy 6th: rdn and wknd after 3 out: sn bhd: t.o* **25/1**

4m 50.6s (3.80) **Going Correction** +0.15s/f (Yiel) 16 Ran SP% **122.7**
Speed ratings (Par 105): **98,97,95,95,95 91,90,90,89,80 78,77,68,67,63 51**
toteswingers:1&2 £11.90, 2&3 £47.00, 1&3 £42.10 CSF £265.37 CT £5365.91 TOTE £11.00: £2.40, £4.10, £4.20, £4.60; EX 356.30.

Owner Anthony White **Bred** Saturn Stable **Trained** Hackthorpe, Cumbria

FOCUS
A big field for this wide-open handicap hurdle and, although the form looks ordinary, the third, fourth and fifth are rated close to their form.

NOTEBOOK
Bocciani(GER), 4lb higher than when third over C&D latest, ran out a gallant winner to record his first career victory. He travelled supremely well and showed a good attitude to knuckle down after the last. He likes it round here and seemed to enjoy having the cheekpieces back on. (op 12-1)
Moon Melody(GER) ran a cracking race racing from 6lb out of the handicap. He was returning for a stable that won with him earlier in his career and will improve for the run, having been off the track for 160 days.
Patavium(IRE), returning from a 345-day absence, also travelled nicely but again found a couple too good. This was a useful effort and he should improve for the outing, having won off a higher mark. (op 28-1)
Latin Connection(IRE) appreciated the drop in distance and ran well.
Descaro(USA), off since disappointing back over hurdles in November, failed to go with the leaders once the pace lifted. (op 17-2 tchd 13-2)
Barron Watlass(IRE) raced very keenly and weakened badly. He will need to settle better if he's to improve. (tchd 5-1 and 13-2)
King Benny(IRE) was sent off favourite on this return to further, but dropped away very disappointingly. Official explanation: jockey said gelding was unsuited by the good to soft (soft in places) ground (op 7-1)
Chief Bucaneer(IRE) was well backed, but was never going after a mistake at the fourth. Official explanation: jockey said gelding made a mistake and never travelled after (op 5-1)
Lennon(IRE) took the field along early before fading badly. He no longer appears to race with enthusiasm. (op 6-1)

4116 WEATHERBYS CHELTENHAM FESTIVAL BETTING GUIDE H'CAP CHASE (15 fncs) 2m 3f
4:20 (4:20) (Class 3) (0-135,134) 5-Y-0+ **£3,252** (£955; £477; £238)

Form RPR

1431 **1** **Pret A Thou (FR)**[22] 3701 8-11-3 132........................... HarryChalloner(7) 140+
(John Bryan Groucott) *t.k.h: trckd ldr: led after 4 out: styd on wl run-in* **17/2**

13-0 **2** *2 1/4* **De Boitron (FR)**[94] 2345 7-11-12 134...................................... GrahamLee 140
(Ferdy Murphy) *hld up in rr: hdwy 11th: chsd wnr between last 2: no imp* **17/2**

0211 **3** *4* **Heavenly Chorus**[32] 3524 9-10-3 111................................ JamesReveley 115+
(Keith Reveley) *trckd ldrs: 3rd whn blnd 11th: 4th and outpcd whn hit 2 out: 5th last: styd on to take 3rd run-in* **7/1**[3]

P310 **4** *1* **Columbus Secret (IRE)**[43] 3333 6-10-2 110....................... PaddyAspell 115+
(Keith Reveley) *nt fluent in rr: hit 2nd and next: hdwy and prom 7th: effrt 11th: one pce fr 2 out: 4th whn blnd last* **15/2**

5-02 **5** *5* **Double Vodka (IRE)**[17] 3786 10-11-1 123......................... DenisO'Regan 120
(Chris Grant) *prom: hit 10th: wl outpcd 4 out: no ch after: kpt on fr 2 out* **3/1**[1]

-100 **6** *2 1/4* **Storymaker**[228] 874 10-11-5 127... BrianHarding 124
(Sandy Forster) *in rr div: reminders 7th: chsng ldrs 4 out: 2nd 2 out: 3rd last: wknd run-in* **12/1**

-130 **7** *21* **Carrietau**[82] 2613 8-10-12 120...(bt) RyanMania 102
(Barry Murtagh) *led: hdd after 4 out: wknd qckly appr 2 out: sn bhd* **16/1**

4-40 **8** *46* **Fortysecond Street (IRE)**[43] 3333 7-10-13 121............... BrianHughes 55
(Howard Johnson) *nt jump wl in rr: j. slowly and detached 3rd: t.o 4 out* **4/1**[2]

U544 **9** *dist* **Calatagan (IRE)**[43] 2423 12-10-12 123......................... JamesHalliday(3) —
(Malcolm Jefferson) *chsd ldrs: blnd 8th: pckd on landing next: lost pl bef 4 out: wl bhd whn blnd last 2: eased run-in: wl t.o: virtually p.u* **8/1**

4m 52.1s (3.30) **Going Correction** +0.35s/f (Yiel) 9 Ran SP% **115.0**
Speed ratings: **107,106,104,103,101 100,92,72,—**
toteswingers:1&2 £18.60, 2&3 £12.70, 1&3 £12.20 CSF £76.45 CT £534.68 TOTE £6.40: £2.30, £4.00, £2.70; EX 52.90.

Owner C J Tipton **Bred** Mme Robert Jeannin **Trained** Bourton, Shropshire

FOCUS
A decent handicap chase run at a good clip. The form looks solid, rated around the first four.

NOTEBOOK
Pret A Thou(FR) outjumped his rivals to land a game victory. A winner of a novice hurdle latest, he built on that display back over fences. Despite racing keenly, he relished the soft conditions and remains in good heart. (op 8-1 tchd 10-1)
De Boitron(FR), third in this last year, improved on his comeback outing to run a solid race. He jumped and travelled well but was unable to get to the winner. This rates as a good effort with his stable struggling for form. (tchd 10-1)
Heavenly Chorus made a few jumping errors, but stayed on nicely for pressure. She has been in good form of late, but this career-high mark seems beyond her. She prefers a better surface. (op 11-2 tchd 9-2)
Columbus Secret(IRE) ran a fair race, but will need to improve his jumping to compete at this level. (op 18-1)
Double Vodka(IRE), second at Doncaster last month, struggled to land a blow and may appreciate quicker ground. He can remain competitive off this sort of mark. (op 11-4)
Storymaker, returning from a 228-day layoff, finished second in this last season. He looks held off this mark but should improve for the run.
Carrietau paid the price for setting a good gallop early and faded tamely. (tchd 14-1)
Fortysecond Street(IRE) was never jumping or travelling with any promise. Official explanation: jockey said gelding lacked confidence in its jumping (op 5-1)

4117 YORKSHIRE4X4.COM ADVENTURE ACTIVITIES STANDARD OPEN NATIONAL HUNT FLAT RACE 2m
4:50 (4:50) (Class 6) 4-6-Y-0 **£1,370** (£399; £199)

Form RPR

1 **Tricksofthetrade (IRE)** 5-11-3 0.. BarryKeniry 108+
(Alan Swinbank) *trckd ldrs: led over 2f out: rn green: drvn out* **7/2**[1]

4 **2** *2 3/4* **Crowning Jewel**[62] 2943 5-11-3 0................................... JamesReveley 105
(Keith Reveley) *stdd s: hld up and bhd: gd hdwy 6f out: chsng wnr over 2f out: styd on same pce* **7/2**[1]

3 *1/2* **Jackson Cage (IRE)** 6-11-3 0... JasonMaguire 104
(Donald McCain) *hld up in midfield: hdwy over 4f out: chsng ldrs over 2f out: styd on same pce* **7/1**[2]

4 *22* **Grand Vintage (IRE)** 5-11-3 0... BrianHughes 84
(Howard Johnson) *w ldrs: t.k.h: ld 7f out: hdd 4f out: sn wknd* **12/1**

5 **5** *1/2* **Sous Mix (FR)**[48] 3166 5-10-10 0.................................... JakeGreenall(7) 84
(Michael Easterby) *w ldrs: led 4f out tl over 2f out: sn wknd* **9/1**

62 **6** *1 3/4* **Helena Of Troy**[206] 1086 5-10-0 0................................. NathanCook(10) 75
(Sue Smith) *led: t.k.h: hdd 7f out: wknd over 3f out* **14/1**

4 **7** *10* **Lure of The Night (IRE)**[106] 2108 4-10-7 0........................ TomO'Brien 63
(Brian Rothwell) *chsd ldrs: wknd 4f out* **33/1**

3 **8** *8* **Trucking Along (IRE)**[85] 2553 5-10-10 0.................. MrBGCrawford(7) 66
(S R B Crawford, Ire) *hld up in mid-div: sme hdwy 6f out: lost pl over 3f out: eased clsng stages* **7/1**[2]

9 *1/2* **Tuilan** 5-10-7 0.. DonalDevereux(3) 59
(Peter Bowen) *mid-div: forced wd bnd after 5f: wknd over 4f out* **8/1**[3]

0 **10** *7* **Go Teescomponents**[32] 3525 4-10-0 0.............. MrColmMcCormack(7) 49
(Keith Reveley) *chsd ldrs: rn wd bnd after 5f: wknd over 4f out* **66/1**

11 *3 1/4* **Cauldron** 4-10-7 0.. RichieMcGrath 47
(Tim Easterby) *in rr-div whn carried wd bnd after 5f: bhd fnl 6f* **25/1**

12 *14* **Long Range** 5-11-3 0... RyanMania 44
(Dianne Sayer) *in rr: bhd fnl 5f* **33/1**

0 **13** *dist* **Big Geordie**[12] 3889 6-10-10 0... CoreyJones(7) —
(Alan Kirtley) *t.k.h: w ldrs lost pl after 5f: sn bhd: t.o 7f out: virtually p.u* **100/1**

P- **P** **Crosstek (IRE)**[470] 2025 5-11-3 0.................................... DougieCostello —
(Alistair Whillans) *in rr: bhd and drvn 5f out: t.o whn p.u over 3f out* **40/1**

3m 51.2s (4.30) **Going Correction** +0.15s/f (Yiel)
WFA 4 from 5yo 9lb 5 from 6yo 1lb 14 Ran SP% **119.6**
Speed ratings: **95,93,93,82,82 81,76,72,72,68 66,59,—,—**
toteswingers:1&2 £3.80, 2&3 £6.90, 1&3 £10.00 CSF £13.28 TOTE £5.00: £2.60, £1.80, £4.30; EX 21.20.

Owner Adrian Butler **Bred** Glencarrig Stud **Trained** Melsonby, N Yorks

FOCUS
An ordinary bumper with the first three pulling well clear. The form is best rated around the runner-up and fifth.

NOTEBOOK

Tricksofthetrade(IRE) knuckled down well to make a winning debut. Connections expect him to improve for the outing, so he must rate a promising prospect. His yard is now 9-21 in Catterick bumpers over the last five seasons. (op 4-1 tchd 9-2)

Crowning Jewel, fourth over C&D in December, improved on that effort but could not match the winner. He may land a similar contest with more improvement to come. (op 11-4 tchd 5-2)

Jackson Cage(IRE) made an encouraging debut, pulling well clear of the remainder. He is sure to build on this experience and is bred to stay further. (op 9-1)

Grand Vintage(IRE) raced keenly early on and finished best of the rest. He is a brother to the stable's useful Santa's Son, so should improve on this debut and go on to better things. (op 16-1)

Sous Mix(FR), fifth in a Southwell Fibresand bumper in December, showed up with the pace for a long way but didn't get home. (op 17-2 tchd 10-1)

Trucking Along(IRE) failed to build on his Kelso third and was easily held. Better was obviously expected so this must rate as a poor effort. (op 10-1 tchd 13-2)

Crosstek(IRE) Official explanation: jockey said gelding lost its action and pulled up

T/Jkpt: Not won. T/Plt: £786.70 to a £1 stake. Pool of £69,254.24 - 64.26 winning tickets. T/Qpdt: £146.90 to a £1 stake. Pool of £4,983.47 - 25.10 winning tickets. WG

3604 PLUMPTON (L-H)

Monday, February 14

OFFICIAL GOING: Heavy

Hurdle course still on wide outer winter line.

Wind: Fresh, against Weather: Fine

4118 CREATE YOUR WEDDING AT PLUMPTON PAVILION MARES' NOVICES' HURDLE (9 hdls) 2m

2:00 (2:00) (Class 4) 4-Y-0+ **£2,055** (£599; £299)

Form RPR

3S4 **1** **Hazy Dawn**[27] 3623 6-10-12 0 TomScudamore 97
(Michael Scudamore) *w ldr: led 3rd: hdd and mstke 3 out: sn rdn and outpcd: rallied fr last to ld nr fin* **11/4**[1]

562 **2** ¾ **Lindsay's Dream**[18] 1971 5-10-7 99 GemmaGracey-Davison(5) 96
(Zoe Davison) *t.k.h: hld up in cl tch: effrt to ld 3 out: sn clr: 5 l ahd last: flagged and hdd nr fin* **12/1**

5 **3** 6 **Mekong Miss**[16] 3818 5-10-8 0 ow1 MrPYork(5) 90
(Raymond York) *nt a fluent: hld up last: wl in tch: effrt 3 out: disp 2nd bef next but outpcd: no ex* **40/1**

0-05 **4** 12 **Argentia**[20] 3721 6-10-12 0 AndrewThornton 77
(Lucy Wadham) *led to 3rd: w ldr tl mstke 6th: sn dropped to last and first one btn: wnt remote 4th 2 out* **7/2**[3]

5 22 **Stan's Cool Cat (IRE)**[143] 5-10-12 0 RobertThornton 62
(Alan King) *nt fluent: cl up: rdn after 6th: dropped to 5th bef 3 out and btn: t.o whn eased flat* **3/1**[2]

0 **6** 6 **Mavalenta (IRE)**[30] 3554 4-10-2 0 PaddyBrennan 49
(Nigel Twiston-Davies) *nt jump wl: cl up tl wknd rapidly 3 out: t.o whn eased flat* **11/4**[1]

4m 20.6s (19.80) **Going Correction** +1.10s/f (Heav)
WFA 4 from 5yo+ 9lb **6** Ran SP% **110.7**
Speed ratings (Par 105): **94,93,90,84,73 70**
toteswingers:1&2 £3.30, 2&3 £10.40, 1&3 £8.80 CSF £30.52 TOTE £3.50: £1.60, £3.60; EX 33.20.
Owner The King's Men **Bred** Mrs P M King **Trained** Bromsash, Herefordshire
■ Stewards' Enquiry : Gemma Gracey-Davison one-day ban: used whip in incorrect place (Feb 28)

FOCUS

An ordinary mares' novice hurdle, rated through the second.

NOTEBOOK

Hazy Dawn showed ability in two bumpers either side of slipping up at Towcester on her second outing and she made a winning debut over hurdles with a gutsy effort. She made a mistake three out and got markedly outpaced when the runner-up set sail for home, but her stamina kicked into play up the rising finish. No doubt a stiffer test will prove more to her liking as she matures, and her yard has now scored with its last three runners. (tchd 3-1)

Lindsay's Dream, tailed off on the all-weather 18 days earlier, showed the clear benefit of that outing and made a bold bid. This was a return to the form that saw her finish second in a seller on her previous outing in this sphere on just her second outing for the yard, and slightly more patient tactics could well pay off next time out. (tchd 14-1)

Mekong Miss was beaten a long way in a seller over further on her hurdling debut 16 days earlier and this was much more encouraging. Her stamina enabled her to finish where she did and a drop back down in grade could see her off the mark before long.

Argentia was beaten soon after three out and probably ran close to her previous level. (op 4-1 tchd 10-3)

Stan's Cool Cat(IRE) was useful at best on the Flat and handled soft ground well in that sphere. She proved laboured on this hurdling debut after a 143-day absence and a sounder surface is probably required. (op 11-4)

Mavalenta(IRE) met support, but was done with a good way out and looks to need more practice. (op 3-1)

4119 TIMEFORM JURY NOVICES' CHASE (18 fncs) 3m 2f

2:30 (2:30) (Class 3) 5-Y-0+ **£6,262** (£1,850; £925; £463; £231)

Form RPR

PF52 **1** **Alderluck (IRE)**[19] 3743 8-10-12 132 LiamTreadwell 135+
(Nick Gifford) *alternated ld thrght: mstke 13th: clr w runner-up fr next and great battle after: mstke 2 out and forfeited advantage: rallied to ld sn after last: styd on wl* **5/4**[1]

1022 **2** 2¼ **Fruity O'Rooney**[30] 3564 8-11-4 130 JamieMoore 136+
(Gary Moore) *alternated ld thrght: clr w wnr fr 14th: tremendous battle after: lft w advantage 2 out: hdd sn after last: one pce* **5/4**[1]

022U **3** 33 **Ballyegan (IRE)**[11] 3900 6-10-5 107 NathanSweeney(7) 99
(Bob Buckler) *jumping lacked conviction: cl up in 4th: pckd 11th: chsd ldng pair 14th but sn brushed aside: no ch whn mstke next* **5/1**[2]

005P **4** 30 **Domoly (FR)**[39] 3402 8-10-12 95 LeightonAspell 66
(Alison Batchelor) *j.rt: hld up last: mstke 10th: wnt poor 4th after 14th but stl gng wl enough: blnd next: no hdwy after* **66/1**[3]

005 **5** 41 **Ballinhassig (IRE)**[13] 3865 6-10-5 57 (p) MrTJCannon(7) 25
(Sarah Wall) *pressed ldng pair: u.p after 12th: lost 3rd and wknd fr 14th: t.o* **100/1**

7m 11.5s (20.80) **Going Correction** +0.925s/f (Soft) **5** Ran SP% **108.0**
Speed ratings: **105,104,94,84,72**
CSF £3.16 TOTE £2.40: £1.20, £1.10; EX 3.10.
Owner Mrs Celia Rayner **Bred** Jerry Cunningham **Trained** Findon, W Sussex

FOCUS

A thrilling finish between the two market leaders and straightforward novice form, with the first two to their marks.

NOTEBOOK

Alderluck(IRE) gamely got on top of old rival Fruity O'Rooney after the last to open his account over fences at the third attempt, making it 3-3 at this venue in the process. He was stepping up markedly in trip, but it looked a good move as his dam is a half-sister to Irish/Midlands National winner The Bunny Boiler, and he duly relished the stiffer test. He still has a bit to learn in the jumping department, but is entitled to do that and is open to improvement now his sort of trip has been fully established. (tchd 11-8)

Fruity O'Rooney wasn't allowed to dominate as he seems to enjoy, but he too was having his first run over this far and he ran a gallant race in defeat. He was conceding 6lb to the winner, so emerges as the best horse at the weights, and richly deserves to go one better again, but he does lack the same scope for improvement as the winner. (op 11-8 tchd 6-4 in places)

Ballyegan(IRE) had plenty to find with the front pair on official ratings. He looks a dour stayer and can be placed to get his head in front under rules when reverting to handicaps, but does still have a little to learn about jumping fences. (tchd 9-2)

Domoly(FR) ran with a little more encouragement.

4120 CREATE FOOD AND PARTY DESIGN NOVICES' H'CAP HURDLE (9 hdls) 2m

3:00 (3:00) (Class 4) (0-115,114) 4-Y-0+ **£2,055** (£599; £299)

Form RPR

5005 **1** **Beau Lake (IRE)**[19] 3745 7-10-5 **93** PaddyBrennan 103+
(Suzy Smith) *mde all: nt fluent 1st: mstke 6th: kicked clr 3 out: drvn and kpt on fr next* **11/4**[3]

23/5 **2** 4½ **Super Directa (GER)**[44] 3306 7-11-12 **114** DominicElsworth 120+
(Lucy Wadham) *trckd wnr in 2nd: mstke 6th: lost 2nd and outpcd 3 out: sn chsng again: no imp fr 2 out* **13/8**[2]

2521 **3** 28 **The Bishops Baby (IRE)**[13] 3868 8-10-12 **107** MrTJCannon(7) 92
(Richard Rowe) *hld up last: moved up to chse wnr 3 out: sn shkn up and dropped to last again: wknd 2 out: eased* **6/4**[1]

4m 15.7s (14.90) **Going Correction** +1.10s/f (Heav) **3** Ran SP% **104.8**
Speed ratings (Par 105): **106,103,89**
CSF £6.90 TOTE £3.60; EX 4.60.
Owner Bernard & Jan Wolford **Bred** Larry Murphy **Trained** Lewes, E Sussex

FOCUS

Two non-runners took a lot of interest out of this novice handicap. There was a fair pace on considering just three took part. the second is the best guide to the level.

NOTEBOOK

Beau Lake(IRE), who came in for support, had a lot to prove coming here but was 10lb lower than when finishing second at Newbury last March and finally put his best foot forward. This was his first success at the 12th time of asking, but he did get pretty much the run of the race and wouldn't be certain to build on it. (tchd 9-4 and 3-1 in a place)

Super Directa(GER) was back down in trip and got outpaced from the third-last. It was his second run back from a layoff and he is talented enough to defy this sort of mark, although his ideal trip remains open to debate. (op 7-4 tchd 15-8)

The Bishops Baby(IRE) got a peach of a ride from Cannon when getting off the mark at Folkestone 13 days earlier and, after the withdrawals, appeared to have a solid chance of following up off her 4lb higher mark. She made her move nearing three out and appeared full of running, but found nothing once push came to shove. This leaves her with a bit to prove. (op 5-4)

4121 RACE PASSES @ TIMEFORM.COM H'CAP HURDLE (12 hdls) 2m 5f

3:30 (3:30) (Class 3) (0-125,121) 4-Y-0+ **£2,927** (£859; £429; £214)

Form RPR

3315 **1** **Prince Du Seuil (FR)**[29] 3587 8-11-8 **117** RobertThornton 133+
(Alan King) *hld up in cl tch: trckd ldng pair after 8th and only one in the r stl gng easily: nt fluent 3 out: led next: cruised clr* **9/4**[1]

03P0 **2** 10 **Latin America (IRE)**[19] 3744 6-11-1 **110** (v[1]) LiamTreadwell 107
(Nick Gifford) *mde most: set stdy pce to 7th: urged along fr 9th: narrowly hdd 3 out: rdn and upsides 2 out: no ch w wnr whn mstke last* **6/1**

1235 **3** 13 **Frontier Spirit (IRE)**[23] 3678 7-11-5 **117** SamTwiston-Davies(3) 101
(Nigel Twiston-Davies) *pressed ldr fr 3rd: rdn after 9th: narrow ld next (3 out): hdd 2 out: fin v slowly* **11/4**[2]

-322 **4** 1¼ **Lupanar (IRE)**[23] 3688 7-11-7 **121** (p) JoshuaMoore(5) 104
(Gary Moore) *cl up: nt fluent 8th: rdn next: steadily wknd bef 3 out* **3/1**[3]

6410 **5** 2¾ **Wheres Johnny**[17] 3793 10-10-5 **100** (t) RodiGreene 79
(Jamie Poulton) *chsd ldr to 3rd: styd cl up but rdn fr 6th: steadily wknd bef 3 out* **10/1**

P-14 **P** **Lomitaar**[90] 2440 6-10-12 **107** AndrewTinkler —
(Tony Newcombe) *hld up in last but cl up: mstke 3rd: rushed up to chal after 8th: wknd rapidly after next: t.o whn p.u bef 2 out* **16/1**

5m 41.7s (19.40) **Going Correction** +1.10s/f (Heav) **6** Ran SP% **111.7**
Speed ratings (Par 107): **107,103,98,97,96** —
toteswingers:1&2 £1.70, 2&3 £4.70, 1&3 £3.40 CSF £15.54 TOTE £4.00: £2.60, £3.60; EX 18.00.
Owner Mrs Peter Prowting **Bred** Paul-Louis Ravier **Trained** Barbury Castle, Wilts

FOCUS

A modest handicap which produced an effortless winner. He is rated an improver with the second to the best of this season's form.

NOTEBOOK

Prince Du Seuil(FR) rates value for a good deal further. He was held off a 1lb higher mark last time, but had scored under a similarly confident ride from Thornton at Folkestone the time before and this has to rate as a clear personal-best. He enjoyed the way the race was run and would be a warm order if found an opportunity under a penalty, as the handicapper will likely take a dim view of this. (op 11-4 tchd 3-1)

Latin America(IRE) had lost his form coming here, but the former dual bumper winner was equipped with a first-time visor and comes from a stable in top form. He posted a vastly improved effort under a positive ride and is well up to winning off this sort of mark, although he clearly has temperament issues. (op 13-2 tchd 9-2)

Frontier Spirit(IRE) appeared fairly treated for his handicap debut and held every chance, posting a more encouraging display again despite running well below his mark. He doesn't look the most straightforward, though. (op 3-1 tchd 10-3)

Lupanar(IRE) had been placed on all three outings this term and benefited from the application of cheekpieces. Up 3lb for his near miss at Wincanton last month, he came under pressure nearing four out and ran well below his recent level. Perhaps the ground was to blame. (op 5-2 tchd 9-4)

Wheres Johnny, a triple course winner, tended to go in snatches and found things too hot. (tchd 11-1)

Lomitaar found the ground totally against him on this return from a 90-day absence. (op 14-1)

4122 TYSERS BEGINNERS' CHASE (11 fncs 1 omitted) 2m 1f

4:00 (4:00) (Class 4) 5-Y-0+ **£3,165** (£982; £529)

Form RPR

-153 **1** **Pascha Bere (FR)**[107] 2085 8-11-0 0 (v[1]) LiamTreadwell 137+
(Nick Gifford) *mde virtually all: slow jumps 3rd and 4th: jnd after 8th: shkn up and drew away bef 2 out* **11/4**[2]

5P-2 **2** 18 **Norman The Great**[43] 3345 7-11-0 0 RobertThornton 119+
(Alan King) *trckd ldrs: wnt 2nd and mstke 5th: chal on long run fr 8th and upsides: pushed along and fnd nil bef 2 out: wl btn after* **11/2**[3]

4 3 24 **Paddy The Yank (IRE)**[17] 3788 8-10-11 0 DannyCook(3) 85
(Richard Mitchell) *j.rt 3rd: pressed wnr to 5th: wknd after next: wl t.o* **100/1**

1522 **F** **Keki Buku (FR)**[13] 3871 8-11-0 0 (t) RichardJohnson —
(Philip Hobbs) *trckd ldrs: hmpd and fell 3rd* **4/7**[1]

0P-3 **U** **L'Homme De Nuit (GER)**[17] 3788 7-11-0 0 (t) AndrewThornton —
(Jim Best) *detached in last tl hmpd and uns rdr 3rd* **40/1**

4m 37.8s (11.90) **Going Correction** +0.925s/f (Soft) 5 Ran SP% **109.1**
Speed ratings: **109,100,89,—,—**
CSF £16.42 TOTE £3.50: £1.50, £1.90; EX 9.80.

Owner Mr and Mrs Mark Tracey **Bred** S N C Regnier Et Al **Trained** Findon, W Sussex

FOCUS
Keki Buki falling early took a lot away from this beginners' chase, but the debutant winner still impressed. The form is limited by the proximity of the third.

NOTEBOOK
Pascha Bere(FR) made a winning start to his chasing career and maintained his trainer's decent run of form, handing him a double on the card. He was equipped with a first-time visor on this first run since finishing second in a Listed handicap over hurdles at Ascot in October, and proved lit up early on. It looked as though his early exertions were taking a toll after three out, but he found plenty for maximum pressure and was fully in command coming to the next. The ground would have been soft enough for him and, entitled to come on for the run, he shouldn't be discounted under a penalty as there was plenty to like about his jumping. (op 5-2 tchd 3-1)
Norman The Great ◆, second over C&D on his chasing debut last time, was going better than the winner after jumping three from home. The more taxing ground was a worry for him beforehand, however, and once asked for an effort the surface blunted him. He looks a sure-fire winner of one of these on a sounder surface. (op 5-1 tchd 9-2 and 7-1)
Keki Buku(FR), heavily backed, appeared to jump into Paddy The Yank prior to falling in what was a most unfortunate mishap. (op 8-11 tchd 1-2)

4123 CREATE YOUR PARTY AT PLUMPTON PAVILION CONDITIONAL JOCKEYS' H'CAP HURDLE (9 hdls) 2m
4:30 (4:30) (Class 5) (0-90,90) 4-Y-0+ **£1,815** (£529; £264)

Form RPR
0503 **1** **Little Roxy (IRE)**[25] 3350 6-10-0 **64** SamTwiston-Davies 71+
(Anna Newton-Smith) *led to 3rd: led again after 5th: shkn up after 3 out: pressed next: rdn and styd on wl* **2/1**[2]

-344 **2** 2 ¾ **Stravita**[115] 1949 7-10-7 **79** (b[1]) AshleyBird(8) 81
(Jim Best) *hld up in last pair but cl up: prog to chse wnr sn after 3 out: chal next: rdn and nt qckn* **8/1**

6414 **3** 2 ¾ **Whitcombe Spirit**[13] 3868 6-11-8 **86** (b) DavidBass 86
(Jamie Poulton) *hld up in last pair but cl up: effrt 3 out: sn rdn and nt qckn: kpt on to take 3rd last: nvr able to chal* **5/4**[1]

043 **4** 6 **Storm Command (IRE)**[177] 1330 4-10-11 **88** MrTomDavid(3) 75+
(Tim Vaughan) *t.k.h: mstke 1st: led 3rd tl after 5th: w wnr whn blnd next and rdr nrly off: cl up after 3 out: nt qckn next: wknd and mstke last* **15/2**[3]

-P0P **5** 3 ¼ **Red Perfection**[22] 3703 8-10-8 **78** (p) RobertKirk(6) 68
(Tony Carroll) *w ldr to 3rd: dropped to last and pushed along after 6th: steadily outpcd fr 3 out* **8/1**

4m 22.4s (21.60) **Going Correction** +1.10s/f (Heav)
WFA 4 from 6yo+ 9lb 5 Ran SP% **111.8**
Speed ratings (Par 103): **90,88,87,84,82**
CSF £16.40 TOTE £2.60: £1.80, £2.50; EX 15.50.

Owner The Ash Tree Inn Racing Club **Bred** Ms Alyson Flower And Christ Simpson **Trained** Jevington, E Sussex

FOCUS
A weak handicap rated around the placed horses.

NOTEBOOK
Little Roxy(IRE) had been well beaten in 11 previous career outings and was hard to fancy, but was getting upwards of a stone from her rivals from the foot of the handicap on this return to hurdling. Her attitude was spot on under pressure and she has evidently found her level, but wouldn't be sure to build on this. (op 10-3 tchd 7-2)
Stravita ◆ was a market drifter on this return from a 115-day break, largely on account of underfoot conditions. However, she went through it well enough and held every chance, so shouldn't be long in scoring once reverting to a sounder surface. (op 5-1)
Whitcombe Spirit resumed winning ways, but he wasn't particularly fluent and threw his chance away by hitting a flat-spot just as the race became serious. He is still weighted to find another opening and the course may not have been to his liking, but it's not hard to see why he sports blinkers. (op 6-5 tchd 11-10 and 6-4 in a place)
Storm Command(IRE) all but came down four out and his rider performed wonders to stay aboard. He recovered to have every chance, but ultimately paid for refusing to settle early on. The run should bring him on and returning to better ground will suit. (op 6-1 tchd 11-2)

4124 TIMEFORM TV FOCUS MAIDEN OPEN NATIONAL HUNT FLAT RACE 2m 2f
5:00 (5:01) (Class 6) 4-6-Y-0 **£1,507** (£439; £219)

Form RPR
3 **1** **Cresswell Melody (IRE)**[48] 3159 4-9-10 0 RachaelGreen(5) 83+
(Anthony Honeyball) *t.k.h: a in ldng trio: led over 3f out: pushed along and styd on wl fnl 2f* **8/1**

2 2 ½ **Fitobust (IRE)** 5-11-1 0 JimmyDerham(3) 98+
(Seamus Mullins) *hld up last: prog 7f out but sn outpcd: pushed along and hdwy 4f out: rn green but chsd wnr over 2f out: styd on but readily hld* **20/1**

3 8 **Emperor's Choice (IRE)** 4-10-8 0 SamThomas 80+
(Venetia Williams) *in tch: rdn sn after 1/2-way: dropped to rr u.p over 4f out: 10th 3f out: rallied fnl 2f: snatched 3rd last strides* **5/2**[1]

5- **4** ¾ **Miss Bolte**[345] 4445 6-10-11 0 JamieGoldstein 82
(Sheena West) *wl in tch: chsd ldrs over 4f out: outpcd fnl 2f* **14/1**

0 **5** 1 **Generous Spender**[55] 3054 5-11-4 0 LiamTreadwell 88
(Mrs H J Cobb) *bucking to post: in tch: outpcd in rr 5f out: rallied over 2f out: styd on same pce ins fnl f* **100/1**

6 8 **Gilzean (IRE)** 5-11-4 0 PaddyBrennan 80
(Nigel Twiston-Davies) *mde most to over 3f out: steadily fdd* **10/3**[2]

4 **7** 1 ¼ **Blue Lovell (FR)**[117] 1920 5-10-8 0 IanPopham(3) 72
(Caroline Keevil) *in tch: outpcd over 4f out: plugged on fnl 2f: no ch* **16/1**

3 **8** 3 ¾ **Perazzi George (IRE)**[30] 3569 5-11-4 0 LeightonAspell 78
(Chris Gordon) *in tch: outpcd fr over 4f out: nvr on terms after* **7/1**

0 **9** 7 **Queen's Pawn (IRE)**[26] 3630 4-10-1 0 MissEmily-JaneHarbour(7) 58
(Raymond York) *t.k.h: w ldrs tl fdd fr 4f out* **100/1**

3 **10** 1 ¾ **Midnight King**[280] 254 5-11-4 0 AndrewTinkler 66
(George Baker) *trckd ldrs: smooth prog to go 2nd over 5f out: chal over 3f out: wknd rapidly over 2f out* **4/1**[3]

11 11 **Lisscow Lad (IRE)** 6-11-4 0 AndrewThornton 55
(Alison Batchelor) *hld up in rr: lost tch in last 6f out: no ch after* **20/1**

4m 45.6s (18.60) **Going Correction** +1.10s/f (Heav)
WFA 4 from 5yo+ 9lb 11 Ran SP% **119.3**
Speed ratings: **102,100,97,97,96 93,92,90,87,86 82**
toteswingers:1&2 £28.90, 2&3 £21.00, 1&3 £4.60. totesuper7: Win: Not won. Place: Not won. CSF £158.61 TOTE £10.40: £3.20, £10.80, £1.10; EX 164.30.

Owner Bruce McKay **Bred** Bryan Gerard Maguire **Trained** Seaborough, Dorset

FOCUS
A modest bumper that is not easy to rate.

NOTEBOOK
Cresswell Melody(IRE), third on her debut in December, ran out a ready winner despite having refused to settle through the first half of the race. Therefore, she rates better than the bare form and looks certain to come on again for the experience. (op 13-2)
Fitobust(IRE) came under pressure down the back straight, but responded gamely and was the only one to give the winner a hard time in the home straight. He was conceding over a stone to that rival, so this rates a very pleasing debut effort. (op 22-1 tchd 25-1 and 16-1)
Emperor's Choice(IRE) was heavily backed for his racecourse debut and, being by Flemensfirth, this surface wasn't expected to pose many problems. He ran in snatches going out onto the final circuit and went backwards, but made strong late headway when the race was effectively over. The experience was obviously needed and better can be expected next time. (op 5-1)
Miss Bolte posted a sound effort on her return from a 345-day absence and will appreciate getting back on better ground. (op 16-1)
Generous Spender looked like finishing out the back on the far side, but he was another that got going late on and this was a step in the right direction.
Gilzean(IRE) was another newcomer by Flemensfirth to meet support and he set out to make all. It was clear turning for home he was in trouble, though. (op 7-2 tchd 4-1 and 3-1)
Perazzi George(IRE) proved laboured from off the pace and ran some way below his debut form. (op 9-2 tchd 15-2)
Midnight King made smooth headway to get his head in front turning for home, but the ground and his lack of a recent run eventually told. He can do better. (op 7-2 tchd 11-2)
T/Plt: £212.80 to a £1 stake. Pool of £75,514.77 - 259.03 winning tickets. T/Qpdt: £48.40 to a £1 stake. Pool of £4,407.39 - 67.30 winning tickets. JN

3864 FOLKESTONE (R-H)
Tuesday, February 15

OFFICIAL GOING: Soft (good to soft in places; chs 5.8, hdl 5.3)
All hurdle track on fresh ground and running on chase bend into the home straight. Chase bends on fresh ground.
Wind: fresh, against Weather: light rain, chilly wind

4125 LADBROKES.COM CONDITIONAL JOCKEYS' H'CAP HURDLE (9 hdls) 2m 1f 110y
2:00 (2:00) (Class 5) (0-90,90) 4-Y-0+ **£1,918** (£559; £279)

Form RPR
4622 **1** **Spider Boy**[14] 3868 14-11-4 **85** (b) GemmaGracey-Davison(3) 88
(Zoe Davison) *mde all: qcknd 6th: rdn and kpt on wl bef last: gamely* **5/1**[3]

3664 **2** 1 **Mut'Ab (USA)**[13] 3882 6-11-9 **90** (b) JoshuaMoore(3) 92
(Gary Moore) *t.k.h: hld up wl in tch in last pair: hdwy to dispute 2nd 2 out: rdn to chse wnr bef last: nt qckn and a hld flat* **7/1**

6U32 **3** 4 ½ **Snow Patrol**[8] 3983 10-10-6 **73** CharlieWallis(3) 72
(Nigel Dunger) *chsd wnr tl mstke 4th: dropped to rr but stl in tch next: rallied 2 out and pressed wnr briefly ent st: sn btn* **7/2**[2]

3256 **4** 8 **Earl Of Thomond (IRE)**[42] 3392 6-11-2 **85** JakeGreenall(5) 75
(Caroline Bailey) *mstkes: chsd ldr 4th tl sn after 2 out: sn drvn: wknd ent st* **11/4**[1]

0050 **5** 1 ¾ **The Snatcher (IRE)**[64] 2927 8-11-4 **88** (b[1]) PeterCarberry(6) 76
(Richard Phillips) *t.k.h: chsd ldrs: disp 2nd bef 3 out: chsd wnr after 2 out tl wl bef last: wknd u.p ent st* **14/1**

55-P **6** 35 **Birthday Star (IRE)**[29] 3604 9-10-4 **73** PeterHatton(5) 26
(Linda Jewell) *t.k.h: hld up wl in tch: hdwy to chse ldrs 3 out: wknd u.p between last 2: t.o last* **33/1**

3424 **7** 11 **Quam Celerrime**[28] 3611 6-10-13 **77** DonalDevereux 19
(Roger Curtis) *in tch: chsd ldrs after 4th: dropped in rr and rdn bef 3 out: wknd after next: t.o bef last* **7/2**[2]

4m 34.5s (-1.10) **Going Correction** +0.025s/f (Yiel) 7 Ran SP% **109.9**
Speed ratings (Par 103): **103,102,100,97,96 80,75**
toteswingers:1&2 £9.30, 2&3 £9.30, 1&3 £3.60 CSF £35.35 CT £127.07 TOTE £4.50: £2.50, £2.30; EX 17.80.

Owner Shovelstrode Racing Club **Bred** D A Ash And Dr P Ash **Trained** Hammerwood, E Sussex

FOCUS
This was a moderate handicap hurdle with the first three rated pretty much to their marks.

NOTEBOOK
Spider Boy, runner-up when just denied here latest, made all to record his first success for nearly two years. This was a game performance and he showed he retains his ability at the grand old age of 14. (op 9-2)
Mut'Ab(USA) had achieved little over hurdles, but showed improved form on this second handicap start despite racing far too keenly. Fairly useful on the Flat, he will need to settle better and may appreciate quicker ground. (op 6-1 tchd 15-2)
Snow Patrol didn't jump or travel with much enthusiasm, but responded well for pressure without matching the front two in the straight. (op 5-1)
Earl Of Thomond(IRE) raced up with the pace, but failed to capitalise on this drop in both class and trip. He struggled to quicken once the pace lifted. (op 3-1)
The Snatcher(IRE), wearing first-time blinkers, again struggled to get home in these soft conditions. He needs a better surface to help him see out his races. (op 12-1)
Birthday Star(IRE) took a keen hold and failed to land a blow on this handicap debut. (op 25-1)
Quam Celerrime ran no sort of race, coming under pressure a long way from home. This was not his true running and he may need a drop in the weights. (tchd 3-1)

4126 LADBROKESPOKER.COM H'CAP CHASE (FOR THE NUMBER ENGAGED CHALLENGE BOWL) (18 fncs) 3m 1f
2:30 (2:30) (Class 5) (0-90,87) 5-Y-0+ **£2,397** (£698; £349)

Form RPR
5P43 **1** **Delgany Gunner**[17] 3819 7-9-10 **61** oh4 ow1 (vt) GilesHawkins(5) 87+
(Ben Pollock) *racd keenly: chsd ldrs tl j. to ld 5th: hdd 8th: 3rd whn j.lft next: lft cl 2nd after 11th: sn led: drew wl clr after next: easily* **2/1**[2]

000 **2** 32 **Run To Fly (IRE)**[19] 3762 6-11-8 **86** (p) DonalDevereux(3) 74
(Peter Bowen) *led tl outj. and hdd 5th: lft in led after 11th: sn hdd: blnd 13th: lost 3rd w wnr 3 out: no ch bef next: plugged on* **8/1**

0P4 **3** 2 ½ **Bohemian Rock**[13] 3880 7-11-12 **87** AndrewThornton 75
(Caroline Bailey) *hld up in rr: mstke 2nd: lft cl 4th after 11th: sn chsng ldng pair: mstke 13th: 3rd and wkng whn blnd 3 out: wl btn bef next* **9/2**[3]

0P52 **4** *55* **Quartz Du Monteau (FR)**[14] 3867 7-11-8 **86**..............(p) PeterToole(3) 67
(Anna Newton-Smith) *chsd ldr tl 4th: lft cl 3rd after 11th: sn dropped to last: lost tch 14th: no ch w wnr but pressing for 2nd 2 out tl bef last: virtually p.u flat: t.o* **15/8**[1]

2420 **P** **Romney Marsh**[23] 3700 10-11-7 **82**.................................... HaddenFrost —
(Roger Curtis) *chsd ldrs tl led 8th: drew clr after next: rdn along bef 10th: rdr mistk circs p.u after 11th: dropped to last and sn rdn to try and rcvr: no rspnse: wl bhd whn p.u 13th* **8/1**

6m 45.8s (10.00) **Going Correction** +0.475s/f (Soft) **5** Ran SP% **108.5**
Speed ratings: **103,92,91,74,—**
CSF £15.47 TOTE £3.20: £2.90, £5.30; EX 22.40.
Owner Charles Wilson & Charles Garside **Bred** C M Wilson **Trained** Medbourne, Leics
■ Stewards' Enquiry : Hadden Frost twelve day ban: mistook race distance (Mar 1-12)

FOCUS
A modest staying handicap chase which produced high drama. The second is the best guide to the level.

NOTEBOOK
Delgany Gunner took full advantage to run out an emphatic winner and record his first chase success. Running from 5lb out of the handicap, this was a fair effort but he will need to settle better to progress. (op 11-4 tchd 3-1)
Run To Fly(IRE), sporting first-time cheekpieces, stayed on strongly on this handicap/chase debut. He showed a willing attitude and should improve for this experience, albeit he was a distant second in this weak contest. (op 6-1 tchd 9-1)
Bohemian Rock did not jump fluently and will need to improve in that department to get competitive. (tchd 10-3)
Quartz Du Montceau(FR) never raced with any zest and, having looked like taking second up the straight, finished tamely. A winner off this mark, this may not have been his true running but he is not one to rely on. Official explanation: trainer said gelding bled from the nose (op 2-1 tchd 13-8, 9-4 in a place)
Romney Marsh was soon pulled up after her rider inexplicably rode the finish a circuit too soon. Hadden Frost, realising his mistake, tried to start riding his mount again, but she had nothing left. Following a steward's enquiry, he was given a 12-day ban. Official explanation: jockey said, regarding running and riding, that he mistook the race distance and rode a finish a circuit too early. (op 6-1 tchd 9-1)

4127 LADBROKESBINGO.COM BEGINNERS' CHASE (15 fncs) 2m 5f
3:00 (3:01) (Class 5) 5-Y-0+ **£2,397** (£698; £349)

Form RPR

3302 **1** **Asturienne**[27] 3627 7-10-7 0.. RobertThornton 124+
(Alan King) *nt jump fluently: in tch: chsd ldr 7th tl after next: rdn bef 11th: chsd ldr and mstke 12th: 2 l down and swtchd lft 2 out: finding little but chalng whn hit last: looked hld flat tl forced ahd nr fin* **4/11**[1]

026P **2** *hd* **Canni Thinkaar (IRE)**[27] 3628 10-10-9 110(b) GemmaGracey-Davison(5) 126
(Zoe Davison) *led: pushed along and qcknd after 9th: clr next: u.p and almost jnd last: edgd rt u.p flat: hdd nr fin* **12/1**

0-P4 **3** *27* **Upham Atom**[8] 3980 8-11-0 0.. TomSiddall 104+
(Kate Buckett) *chsd ldr tl 2nd: in tch: mstke and rdn 9th: hit next: sn struggling: losing tch whn blnd 12th: wnt poor 3rd after next* **8/1**[3]

155- **P** **Mrs Fawlty (IRE)**[338] 4609 8-10-7 104..................................(t) RhysFlint —
(Jim Old) *t.k.h early: chsd ldr 2nd tl 7th: wnt 2nd again after next tl 12th: 3rd and wkng whn j.lft 3 out: t.o last whn virtually ref 2 out: sn p.u* **11/2**[2]

5m 38.4s (16.20) **Going Correction** +0.475s/f (Soft) **4** Ran SP% **107.5**
Speed ratings: **88,87,77,—**
CSF £4.86 TOTE £1.40; EX 3.00.
Owner Let's Live Racing **Bred** Wood Farm Stud **Trained** Barbury Castle, Wilts

FOCUS
A fair beginners' chase run at a steady gallop and ratd around the principals.

NOTEBOOK
Asturienne built on her second to a subsequent winner at Newbury latest to grind down the leader and gain her first chase success. She showed a game attitude and will have one more run before heading for the valuable mares' novice handicap at Newbury next month. She will improve for better ground, as her jockey reported she hated the conditions. (op 2-5 tchd 1-3)
Canni Thinkaar(IRE) ran a cracking race to just be denied on the line. He enjoyed himself out in front, jumped nicely, and should go one better in similar company. (op 9-1)
Upham Atom made a few jumping errors and could not match the front two when the pace increased. (op 9-1)
Mrs Fawlty(IRE), tongue-tied on this return from 338 days off the track, jumped left and poorly throughout and was eventually pulled up on this chase debut. (op 5-1 tchd 7-1)

4128 LADBROKESGAMES.COM MAIDEN HURDLE (10 hdls) 2m 4f 110y
3:30 (3:30) (Class 4) 4-Y-0+ **£1,918** (£559; £279)

Form RPR

54U **1** **Renard D'Irlande (FR)**[62] 2954 6-11-3 0........................ AidanColeman 125+
(Venetia Williams) *a travelling wl: trckd ldrs tl wnt 2nd bef 3 out: led after 2 out: cruised clr on bit ent st: v easily* **7/4**[2]

6004 **2** *7* **Get Ready To Go (IRE)**[16] 3833 7-11-3 0...................(t) DougieCostello 108
(Neil King) *j.w: led: rdn and hdd after 2 out: brushed aside by wnr ent st: kpt on same pce after* **11/1**

0P **3** *3 ¾* **Airmen's Friend (IRE)**[24] 3678 5-11-0 0........................... PeterToole(3) 104
(Charlie Mann) *in tch in midfield on outer: hdwy to chse ldng pair sn after 2 out: u.p and btn ent st: plugged on* **40/1**

2-4 **4** *2 ¼* **O Malley's Oscar (IRE)**[14] 3866 6-11-3 0........................ DenisO'Regan 103
(Suzy Smith) *chsd ldrs: wnt 2nd 4th tl bef 3 out: mstke 2 out: sn u.p and struggling: 4th and btn ent st* **11/8**[1]

-656 **5** *18* **Venetian Lad**[14] 3866 6-11-3 0.. MarkBradburne 84
(Lydia Richards) *in tch towards rr: hdwy into midfield 5th: chsd ldrs and rdn after 2 out: sn struggling: 5th and wl btn ent st* **12/1**

6 *20* **In Good Hands** 7-10-10 0.. MrTJCannon(7) 69
(Alan Fleming) *in tch towards rr: nt fluent 1st: hdwy 7th: chsd ldrs after next: wknd qckly after 2 out: t.o last* **20/1**

7 *10* **Giant O Murchu (IRE)**[100] 7-11-3 0.............................. RobertThornton 66
(Lawney Hill) *t.k.h: hld up in tch in rr: hdwy on outer after 6th: 6th and shkn up after 2 out: sn btn: 6th and no ch ent st: virtually p.u flat: t.o* **8/1**[3]

0-54 **8** *9* **Dundry**[273] 380 10-10-10 94...............................(p) MrJackSalmon(7) 45
(Philip Sharp) *in tch: chsd ldrs after 5th: lost pl bef 3 out: wknd qckly u.p next: t.o bef last* **50/1**

005 **9** *17* **Tait's Clock (IRE)**[11] 3917 5-11-0 0................................. MrAJBerry(3) 28
(Jonjo O'Neill) *a in rr: mstke 3rd: mstke and rdn 7th: sn struggling and losing tch: t.o after 2 out* **33/1**

00 **10** *7* **Lucius Fabeo (IRE)**[21] 3719 7-11-3 0.............................. NickScholfield 21
(Anna Newton-Smith) *prom tl lost pl 4th: in rr and rdn 7th: sn struggling and lost tch after next: t.o between last 2* **100/1**

0-00 **11** *25* **Slip Duty (IRE)**[36] 3489 9-10-10 0.........................(t) AodhaganConlon(7) —
(Kate Buckett) *t.k.h: chsd ldr on outer tl 4th: losing pl whn mstke 6th: bhd and mstke 2 out: sn lost tch: t.o bef last* **100/1**

5m 26.9s (-3.10) **Going Correction** +0.025s/f (Yiel) **11** Ran SP% **119.7**
Speed ratings (Par 105): **106,103,101,101,94 86,82,79,72,70 60**
toteswingers:1&2 £3.80, 2&3 £15.20, 1&3 £15.20 CSF £19.97 TOTE £2.60: £1.10, £2.30, £4.70; EX 18.50.
Owner Hills Of Ledbury (Aga) **Bred** Mlle Marie Drion At Al **Trained** Kings Caple, H'fords

FOCUS
An ordinary maiden hurdle run at just a steady pace with the first four finishing well clear. The winner should rate higher with the fourth the best guide, rated to his bumper form.

NOTEBOOK
Renard D'Irlande(FR) ◆ relished the step up in trip to produce a taking performance and coasted home in impressive fashion. Always travelling strongly, he should be able to defy a penalty before going handicapping. (op 15-8 tchd 9-4)
Get Ready To Go(IRE) raced up with the pace throughout and had every chance, but proved no match for the winner. He enjoys a soft surface and this was an improved effort in a first-time tongue-tie. (op 9-1 tchd 17-2)
Airmen's Friend(IRE) showed improved form, staying on for pressure on this drop in grade. He seemed to handle the conditions and can remain of interest in this sort of race with more improvement to come. (op 66-1)
O Malley's Oscar(IRE), fourth on his hurdling debut here last time, plugged on at the one pace. His fancy entries look ambitious but he may build on this effort. (op 2-1)
Venetian Lad was held up but could never strike a blow.
In Good Hands did make some headway before fading tamely on this racecourse debut. He should improve for the experience.
Giant O Murchu(IRE) raced far too keenly and struggled to get home in the ground. He can improve if he learns to settle better. (op 5-1)

4129 LADBROKES.COM ON YOUR MOBILE NOVICES' HURDLE (9 hdls) 2m 1f 110y
4:00 (4:00) (Class 4) 4-Y-0+ **£1,918** (£559; £279)

Form RPR

222 **1** **Mr Muddle**[28] 3613 4-10-7 119.. JamieGoldstein 101+
(Sheena West) *led tl 4th: styd w ldr tl led again 3 out: rdn and drew clr ent st: in command whn mstke last: eased towards fin* **13/8**[1]

5 **2** *5* **Promised Wings (GER)**[9] 3958 4-10-7 0.............................. ColinBolger 91
(Chris Gordon) *hld up in last trio: stl last 3 out: pushed along and hdwy next: rdn and chsd ldrs bef last: wnt 2nd last: kpt on: no threat to wnr* **66/1**

0/0 **3** *4* **Peintre Du Roi (USA)**[12] 1812 7-11-2 0.............................. JamesDavies 98
(Natalie Lloyd-Beavis) *chsd ldrs: clsd 4th: rdn and chsd wnr bef last: no imp and lost 2nd last: plugged on* **100/1**

U0 **4** *20* **Dulce Domum**[14] 3866 5-10-2 0... MrTGarner(7) 69
(Roger Curtis) *in tch in last trio: nt fluent and pushed along after 4th: struggling bef 3 out: plugged on to pass btn horses bef last: n.d* **150/1**

-42F **5** *1 ¾* **Alwaysonthemove**[14] 3864 7-11-2 107........................... LeightonAspell 80
(Laura Mongan) *nt jump wl: racd in midfield: clsd 4th: rdn to chse wnr between last 2: flashed tail u.p and no imp ent st: 4th and wl btn whn mstke last: tired flat* **11/1**

31 **6** *22* **Union Island (IRE)**[92] 2426 5-11-9 119........................... RobertThornton 69
(Alan King) *chsd ldng pair: rdn and effrt after 2 out: wknd wl bef last: 5th and wl btn last: eased flat: t.o* **3/1**[3]

7 *33* **Lucky Dance (BRZ)**[108] 9-11-2 0................................... AndrewThornton 19
(Mark Rimmer) *t.k.h: hld up in last trio: struggling bef 3 out: t.o between last 2* **25/1**

P-1 **P** **Nobunaga**[20] 3739 6-11-9 0.. AidanColeman —
(Venetia Williams) *racd keenly: w ldr tl led 4th: hdd 3 out: wknd u.p between last 2: wl btn whn p.u last* **2/1**[2]

0 **P** **Cils Blancs (IRE)**[62] 2960 5-10-9 0..(t) SamJones —
(Michael Scudamore) *t.k.h: hld up in midfield: clsd on ldrs 4th: wknd 2 out: t.o whn p.u last* **100/1**

4m 33.2s (-2.40) **Going Correction** +0.025s/f (Yiel)
WFA 4 from 5yo+ 9lb **9** Ran SP% **112.7**
Speed ratings (Par 105): **106,103,102,93,92 82,67,—,—**
toteswingers:1&2 £23.00, 2&3 £34.30, 1&3 £34.30 CSF £92.92 TOTE £1.80: £1.10, £12.20, £23.00; EX 89.50.
Owner Saloop **Bred** Saloop Ltd **Trained** Falmer, E Sussex

FOCUS
A fair novice hurdle. The leaders set off very fast in the conditions and the winner must take credit for staying on when others folded. The winner is rated to recent course form.

NOTEBOOK
Mr Muddle ◆, runner-up on his previous three starts, made virtually all the running to land an easy victory. He jumped professionally and looks a smart prospect who seems to handle soft conditions well. He should win more races. (op 9-4)
Promised Wings(GER) had showed little on his debut at Fontwell, but built on that to run a huge race at the odds. Despite racing keenly enough, he stayed on strongly for pressure up the straight, benefiting from the quick gallop up front.
Peintre Du Roi(USA) improved on his debut, running on nicely to finish well clear of the remainder. He handled the conditions well and will be more competitive when going handicapping.
Dulce Domum never threatened but plugged on and now qualifies for handicaps. (op 100-1)
Alwaysonthemove raced keenly and stayed on turning in, but flashed his tail when asked for an effort and doesn't look straightforward. (op 16-1)
Union Island(IRE), a winner at Huntingdon on his last start, failed to go on having tracked the early pace. A fair Flat horse, he may be better than this on better ground. (op 9-4)
Nobunaga sprung a surprise to beat the useful Araldur latest, but paid the price for racing too keenly and contesting the early lead here. He was pulled up and must learn to settle to be competitive under a penalty. Official explanation: trainer had no explanation for the poor form shown (op 7-4 tchd 13-8)

4130 HOBBS PARKER TELECOM H'CAP HURDLE (11 hdls) 2m 6f 110y
4:30 (4:30) (Class 5) (0-95,92) 4-Y-0+ **£1,918** (£559; £279)

Form RPR

-423 **1** **Jordan**[18] 3791 8-11-2 **89**... MrTJCannon(7) 94+
(Suzy Smith) *in tch in midfield: pushed along and hdwy to chse ldrs 7th: led sn after 3 out: clr and rdn along between last 2: styd on wl: comf* **4/1**[1]

-044 **2** *13* **Blazing Empress**[29] 3607 6-11-8 **88**.................................. AidanColeman 81
(Sarah Humphrey) *hld up in rr: stdy prog on outer 7th: rdn to chse clr wnr wl bef last: no imp* **13/2**

0040 **3** *16* **Downe Payment (IRE)**[20] 3745 6-11-3 **90**.................... MissHGrissell(7) 65
(Diana Grissell) *led: mstke 6th: hdd sn after 3 out: sn outpcd by wnr and dived next: 3rd and wl btn ent st* **9/1**

0000 **4** *11* **Champs De Bleu (FR)**[18] 3789 8-11-10 **90**........................ JamieMoore 56
(Gary Moore) *hld up in rr: rdn and effrt bef 3 out: drvn bef 2 out: wnt modest 7th and mstke 2 out: no ch and tk poor 4th ent st: blnd last: t.o* **20/1**

5525 **5** *4 ½* **Vacario (GER)**[33] 3530 7-11-2 **85**..............................(t) TommyPhelan(3) 45
(Mark Gillard) *in tch in midfield: j. slowly 2nd and 3rd: rdn along and no rspnse after 6th: 8th and wl btn whn mstke 2 out: plugged on: t.o* **6/1**[3]

0-4P **6** *2 ¼* **Thompson**[255] 630 7-11-7 **87**.. TomSiddall 44
(Richard Phillips) *in tch: hdwy to chse ldrs after 5th: 6th and wkng 2 out: t.o bef last* **9/1**

/62- **7** *3* **Hereditary**[485] 1812 9-11-12 **92**....................................(t) AndrewThornton 46
(Linda Jewell) *hld up in last quartet: rdn and struggling after 7th: t.o after 2 out* **16/1**

646/ **8** *¾* **Star Time (IRE)**[1476] 3638 12-10-4 **70**.................................(v) SamJones 24
(Michael Scudamore) *chsd ldrs: mstke and losing pl 4th: reminders bef next: dropped to last and rdn 6th: lost tch after next: t.o 2 out* **33/1**

0-50 **9** *11* **Jack Rio (IRE)**[12] 3901 6-9-11 **66** oh1.......................(b) DonalDevereux(3) 9
(Laura Young) *hld up in rr: sme hdwy on inner 6th: no prog 3 out and wl btn whn hit next: t.o bef last* **20/1**

00-5 **10** *4 ½* **Goring Two (IRE)**[282] 215 6-10-1 **70**......................... JimmyDerham(3) 8
(Anna Newton-Smith) *in tch: hdwy to chse ldrs after 6th: rdn and struggling after 3 out: wl btn between last 2: virtually p.u bef last: t.o* **20/1**

0/PP **11** *52* **Idris (GER)**[63] 2949 10-11-3 **90**....................................(t) MrJackSalmon(7) —
(Philip Sharp) *chsd ldrs: rdn and losing pl after 6th: t.o whn blnd 3 out* **66/1**

-3PF **P** **Captain Smoothy**[45] 3305 11-11-5 **88**............................ AlexMerriam(3) —
(Neil King) *chsd ldr tl 5th: rdn and losing pl whn mstke 7th: t.o after 2 out tl p.u last* **5/1**[2]

610/ **P** **Pepito Collonges (FR)**[694] 4685 8-11-9 **89**.................(p) LeightonAspell —
(Laura Mongan) *t.k.h: chsd ldrs on outer tl wnt 2nd 5th: led after next: hdd sn after 3 out: wknd qckly after 2 out: eased ent st: p.u last* **9/1**

6m 10.0s (-1.30) **Going Correction** +0.025s/f (Yiel) **13** Ran SP% **118.9**
Speed ratings (Par 103): **103,98,92,89,87 86,85,85,81,80 61,—,—**
toteswingers:1&2 £5.40, 2&3 £25.40, 1&3 £6.80 CSF £27.95 CT £224.27 TOTE £5.70: £1.90, £1.90, £4.90; EX 35.70.
Owner D Forster Mrs SJ Somner & EW Dale **Bred** J And Mrs S Somner **Trained** Lewes, E Sussex

FOCUS
A competitive and open-looking handicap hurdle with the field finishing well strung out in the testing conditions. The second is rated to her mark and sets the standard.

NOTEBOOK
Jordan ran out a cosy winner to secure her first career success at the ninth attempt over hurdles. A most consistent type, she quickened clear before the last and this rates an improved effort. She will be reassessed but always runs her race. (op 7-2)
Blazing Empress ran with credit on this handicap debut. Travelling well, she chased the winner without looking dangerous, but this was better and she can continue to run well off this mark. (op 8-1)
Downe Payment(IRE) raced keenly towards the head of affairs and just plugged on at the one pace. (op 8-1)
Champs De Bleu(FR) was ridden patiently on this handicap debut and never looked like getting involved at the business end. (op 22-1)
Vacario(GER) ran poorly. (op 15-2)
Captain Smoothy was well supported and expected to relish the conditions, but disappointed. (op 9-2)

4131 R. E. SASSOON MEMORIAL HUNTERS' CHASE (FOR THE R. E. SASSOON MEMORIAL TROPHY) (18 fncs) 3m 1f

5:00 (5:00) (Class 6) 5-Y-0+ **£758** (£233; £116)

Form RPR

12/ **1** **Dante's Storm**[31] 9-12-4 129... MrPYork 134+
(Alan Hill) *racd wd: mde virtually all: hit 5th and 7th: clr after 10th: wl clr whn hit 2 out: v easily* **4/6**[1]

/F0- **2** *38* **Mount Sandel (IRE)**[31] 10-12-1 126............................. MrWHickman(7) 98
(Mrs Alison Hickman) *w wnr: mstke 5th and 7th: outpcd by wnr 10th: lost 2nd 12th tl chsd wnr again 16th: no imp and wl btn after: tired and all out to hold 2nd flat: t.o* **12/1**

4- **3** *1* **Jack's Present (IRE)**[31] 9-11-2 0..................................(p) MrNPearce(5) 80
(N Pearce) *nt jump wl: bhd: rdn along and short-lived effrt 11th: lost tch after next: lft poor 3rd and hmpd 3 out: clsng on tired 2nd flat: t.o* **8/1**[3]

4F4- **F** **Song Of Songs**[305] 5213 9-12-8 138.................................(b1) MrAJBerry —
(Jonjo O'Neill) *hld up in last pair: stdy hdwy 9th: chsd wnr 12th: 3 l down whn dived 14th: btn and lost 2nd next: 3rd and wkng qckly whn fell heavily 3 out* **9/2**[2]

PPP- **P** **Snakebite (IRE)**[339] 4586 11-12-0 112............................... MissPGundry —
(Miss Grace Muir) *chsd ldrs tl 3rd: bhd next: mstke 9th: lost tch 12th: wl t.o whn p.u 16th* **8/1**[3]

P **In The System (IRE)**[16] 9-11-9 0...............................(p) MrTJCannon(5) —
(David Phelan) *in tch: rdn and struggling after 12th: 5th and wl bhd whn p.u 16th* **40/1**

U **U** **Flowersoftherarest (IRE)**[2] 8-11-11 0.......................(p) MrJMQuinlan(3) —
(David Phelan) *chsd ldrs but sn pushed along: lost pl 8th: in last pair and lost tch 12th: t.o whn lft 4th: bdly hmpd and uns rdr 3 out* **66/1**

6m 44.4s (8.60) **Going Correction** +0.475s/f (Soft) **7** Ran SP% **112.0**
Speed ratings: **105,92,92,—,— —,—**
toteswingers:1&2 £3.00, 2&3 £3.20, 1&3 £2.40. totesuper7: Win: £10,500.00 Place: £290.00 CSF £9.44 TOTE £1.60: £1.10, £8.40; EX 13.90.
Owner I M Cobbold **Bred** John Plackett **Trained** Aston Rowant, Oxfordshire

FOCUS
An interesting hunter chase featuring a couple of useful types but the winner scored easily and looks smart for the grade.

NOTEBOOK
Dante's Storm ◆, an easy winner of a club members' last month, destroyed his rivals to land a bloodless success. A keen travelling sort, he jumped boldly, making the odd error, and came home in splendid isolation with his rider motionless. His odds range between 10-1 and 14-1 for the Foxhunters Chase at the Cheltenham Festival, and he looks a very smart performer. (op 8-11 tchd 4-7)
Mount Sandel(IRE), behind the winner latest, finished a remote second. He had some useful novice chase form for Oliver Sherwood and jumped well enough without getting near the winner. (op 14-1 tchd 20-1)
Jack's Present(IRE) just failed in his quest to gain second. (op 11-1)
Song Of Songs was running a good race when falling in the Byrne Group Plate at last year's Festival and fell at the third last on this hunter chase debut. Wearing first-time blinkers on his debut for this yard, he was ridden patiently but looked held when suffering a heavy fall. He will need to prove his confidence remains intact, but still rates a smart recruit in this code. (op 10-1 tchd 7-1)
Snakebite(IRE) was a fair chaser at his best, but showed little on this first start for connections. (op 10-1 tchd 7-1)
T/Plt: £173.30 to a £1 stake. Pool of £63,584.74 - 267.70 winning tickets. T/Qpdt: £10.50 to a £1 stake. Pool of £6,248.80 - 438.44 winning tickets. SP

3883 NEWCASTLE (L-H)

Tuesday, February 15

OFFICIAL GOING: Heavy (4.0)
All bends moved in 2yds to and hurdles sited in fresh places. First and last hurdle in the back straight was omitted on all circuits of all hurdle races.
Wind: Fresh, half against Weather: Overcast

4132 PARKLANDS GOLF COURSE MAIDEN HURDLE (7 hdls 2 omitted) 2m

1:40 (1:40) (Class 5) 4-Y-0+ **£1,723** (£506; £253; £126)

Form RPR

2502 **1** **Bunclody**[13] 3885 6-10-6 0.. SamuelWelton(10) 111+
(George Moore) *trckd ldrs: shkn up to ld between last 2: edgd lft and styd on strly to go clr run-in* **13/8**[1]

-404 **2** *6* **Lucky Sunny (IRE)**[21] 3718 8-11-2 0.............................. SeanQuinlan 106+
(Richard Phillips) *hld up: stdy hdwy to trck ldrs whn nt fluent 3 out: effrt and chsd wnr after next: one pce run-in* **13/8**[1]

-P **3** *3 ½* **Diamond D'Amour (IRE)**[86] 2552 5-11-2 0....................... BrianHughes 101
(Howard Johnson) *led: rdn and hdd between last 2: kpt on same pce* **8/1**[2]

000 **4** *9* **North Brook (IRE)**[13] 3887 6-10-13 0.......................... EwanWhillans(3) 91
(Alistair Whillans) *in tch: rdn and outpcd 3 out: no imp fr next* **16/1**[3]

0 **5** *14* **Stanley Bridge**[43] 3358 4-10-7 0.. BrianHarding 68
(Barry Murtagh) *hld up: rdn bef 3 out: plugged on fr next: nvr able to chal* **100/1**

0 **6** *½* **Udaya Klum**[18] 3781 8-11-2 0... TjadeCollier 77
(Sue Smith) *t.k.h: in tch tl rdn and wknd bef 3 out* **40/1**

0F-P **7** *¾* **Power Flow (IRE)**[13] 3887 6-11-2 0.................................... PaddyAspell 76
(Peter Atkinson) *midfield: drvn and outpcd bef 3 out: n.d after* **40/1**

5 **8** *4 ½* **Maddoxtown (IRE)**[45] 3322 5-11-2 0.. AELynch 71
(Robert Alan Hennessy, Ire) *hld up: effrt and pushed along bef 3 out: nvr on terms* **8/1**[2]

06U0 **9** *nk* **Matilda's Folly (IRE)**[22] 3715 6-9-13 0...................... SeveBrumpton(10) 64
(Ben Haslam) *plld hrd: prom tl rdn and wknd after 3 out* **100/1**

60 **10** *25* **Chichina (USA)**[7] 3994 4-10-0 0..................................(p) CampbellGillies 30
(Tracy Waggott) *cl up tl rdn and wknd fr 3 out* **100/1**

-0P0 **11** *81* **Politelysed**[94] 2370 5-10-9 0... KennyJohnson —
(Robert Johnson) *hld up on outside: struggling 4th: sn lost tch: t.o* **100/1**

P/0 **F** **Princess Aliuska**[27] 3637 6-10-6 0...................................... JohnKington(3) —
(Charles Smith) *hld up towards rr: tenth and wkng whn fell 3 out* **100/1**

P **Lofthouse**[138] 4-10-7 0.. PeterBuchanan —
(Alistair Whillans) *a bhd: lost tch passing omitted 4 out: t.o whn p.u after next* **80/1**

4m 34.1s (24.10) **Going Correction** +1.475s/f (Heav)
WFA 4 from 5yo+ 9lb **13** Ran SP% **115.4**
Speed ratings (Par 103): **98,95,93,88,81 81,81,78,78,66 25,—,—**
toteswingers:1&2 £1.60, 2&3 £5.00, 1&3 £3.90 CSF £3.85 TOTE £2.70: £1.10, £1.20, £2.30; EX 5.10.
Owner Mrs Alurie O'Sullivan **Bred** Mrs A M O'Sullivan **Trained** Middleham Moor, N Yorks

FOCUS
There was no strength in depth to this maiden hurdle and most were in trouble turning for home, with the principals dominating from three out. The winner is rated to recent course form backed up by the fourth and sixth.

NOTEBOOK
Bunclody turned in a career-best effort when second over C&D 13 days earlier and went one better with a ready effort to open his account. His stamina proved a vital weapon on the taxing surface and there was plenty to like about the way he went about his business. He will look vulnerable under a penalty, though. (tchd 6-4 and 7-4)
Lucky Sunny(IRE), whose previous fourth at Leicester caught the attention of the stewards, scythed through the pack to get handy on the home bend. He held every chance thereafter, but failed to see it out like the winner and reverting to a sharper track ought to suit ideally. (op 15-8 tchd 2-1)
Diamond D'Amour(IRE) ◆ was pulled up on his debut at Kelso in November. He turned in a pleasing effort from the front over this sharper test and ought to come on nicely for the experience. His half-brother Diamond Frontier, who races for the same connections, loves soft ground and was also placed in this race back in 2008. (tchd 15-2)
North Brook(IRE), down in trip, showed his most worthwhile form to date and ought to find his feet when switching to low-grade handicaps. (tchd 18-1)
Maddoxtown(IRE) looked to find the ground against him on this switch to hurdling and probably wants a longer trip. (op 13-2)

4133 NEWCASTLE FLOORING H'CAP CHASE (12 fncs 1 omitted) 2m 110y

2:10 (2:10) (Class 5) (0-90,90) 5-Y-0+ **£2,276** (£668; £334; £166)

Form RPR

0455 **1** **Prince Tam**[27] 3636 7-10-12 **76**...................................(p) CampbellGillies 94+
(Lucinda Russell) *led to 5th: cl up: led 5 out: drew clr fr next: rdn out* **7/1**

P3P4 **2** *4 ½* **The Green Hat (IRE)**[13] 3884 11-10-0 **71**................... MissGAndrews(7) 80
(Theresa Gibson) *cl up: led 5th: hdd whn hmpd next: rallied 5 out: chsd wnr and j.rt fr next: kpt on run-in: no imp* **11/2**[3]

362F **3** *13* **Mighty Magnus (IRE)**[13] 3884 8-11-9 **87**........................ JamesReveley 81
(Martin Todhunter) *in tch: hdwy to ld 7th: hdd 5 out: outpcd fr next* **5/2**[1]

3565 **4** *2 ½* **Catholic Hill (USA)**[11] 3932 6-10-8 **79**........................ MrPJTolman(7) 74+
(Mark Gillard) *mstke and nrly uns rdr 1st: hld up: pushed along whn hmpd by faller and outpcd 6th: shortlived effrt bef 4 out: sn outpcd* **12/1**

0101 **U** **Janal (IRE)**[13] 3884 8-10-12 **83**................................... GaryRutherford(7) —
(Stuart Coltherd) *trckd ldrs: hit and uns rdr 2nd* **9/1**

P32/ **F** **Wee George**[702] 4489 9-11-0 **78**.. TjadeCollier —
(Sue Smith) *prom: fell 6th* **9/1**

3603 **P** **Copper Sound**[23] 3699 7-10-7 **71**...............................(vt) TomScudamore —
(Michael Scudamore) *in tch: hdwy to ld 6th: hdd next: wknd after 5 out: p.u bef next* **3/1**[2]

0-00 **F** **Monsoon Music (IRE)**[15] 3850 7-10-5 **69**.....................(t) PeterBuchanan —
(Lucinda Russell) *fell 1st* **16/1**

4m 42.3s (21.20) **Going Correction** +1.325s/f (Heav) **8** Ran SP% **115.0**
Speed ratings: **103,100,94,93,— —,—,—**
toteswingers:1&2 £9.90, 2&3 £4.80, 1&3 £4.90 CSF £45.44 CT £122.85 TOTE £11.10: £3.70, £3.70, £2.20; EX 62.70.
Owner Mrs L R Joughin **Bred** Miss Gail Joughin **Trained** Arlary, Perth & Kinross

FOCUS
A weak handicap that proved a very eventful race and the form should be treated with some caution. The penultimate fence on the back straight was omitted. The winner is rated to the best of last year's form.

NOTEBOOK

Prince Tam relished this surface and the drop back in trip en-route to a first career success at the 18th time of asking. This ought to boost his confidence no end, but the handicapper will have his say and it's hard to recommend him as one for a follow-up. Official explanation: trainer's rep said he no explanation for the apparent improvement in form,

The Green Hat(IRE), bumped into by the winner on the far side, was niggled some way out and looked woefully one paced when his rival went for home. He kept responding to pressure in the home straight, though, and this was too sharp for him so it rates this longstanding maiden's best effort for a while. (op 6-1 tchd 5-1)

Mighty Magnus(IRE) went close over 2m4f two runs back and came down too far out to tell how he would have fared back here 13 days earlier. He was ridden more positively over the shorter trip, but was left for dead when the winner went on and he is another who remains winless. (op 3-1 tchd 10-3)

Catholic Hill(USA) is probably best forgiven this run as he got the first all wrong and was badly hampered on the back straight. (op 10-1)

Copper Sound came in for support, but he lacked fluency over his fences and ran poorly. (tchd 11-4 and 10-3)

4134 GOSFORTH DECORATING AND BUILDING SERVICES MARES' MAIDEN HURDLE (9 hdls 4 omitted) 2m 6f

2:40 (2:40) (Class 5) 4-Y-0+ **£1,723** (£506; £253; £126)

Form				RPR
2402	1		**Thornton Alice**[27] 3637 6-11-2 0 .... SeanQuinlan (Richard Phillips) *t.k.h: hld up in tch: hdwy after 6th: effrt bef 2 out: led run-in: styd on wl* **7/4**[1]	87+
	2	3 ½	**Niki Royal (FR)**[87] 6-10-11 0 .... EJO'Connell(5) (Barry Potts, Ire) *prom: hdwy to ld 3 out: rdn and 1 l in front whn blnd last: hdd run-in: kpt on same pce* **4/1**[3]	84+
21-0	3	5	**Tanzanite Bay**[44] 3330 6-11-2 0 .... PeterBuchanan (Lucinda Russell) *cl up: led after 5th: j. slowly and hdd briefly next: j. slowly and hdd 3 out: rallied: kpt on same pce fr last* **3/1**[2]	80
-666	4	15	**Lady Ida**[6] 4000 6-11-2 0 .... AlanO'Keeffe (Jennie Candlish) *led to 2nd: w ldr to 5th: trcking ldrs whn blnd next: outpcd passing omitted 4 out: n.d after* **6/1**	63
00/P	5	½	**Frosty Spring**[29] 3599 8-10-9 0 .... MrGRSmith(7) (David Thompson) *t.k.h: led 2nd to 5th: cl up tl rdn and wknd 3 out* **100/1**	61
0/P-	P		**Rock Port**[318] 4979 9-10-9 0 .... MissCWalton(7) (James Walton) *t.k.h: in tch: struggling passing omitted 4 out: t.o whn p.u after 2 out* **100/1**	—
	F		**Dallas Doll (IRE)**[17] 3829 6-11-2 0 .... AELynch (J T R Dreaper, Ire) *hld up last: stdy hdwy 6th: outpcd whn hit 3 out: sn btn: no ch whn fell next* **7/1**	—

6m 38.7s (62.70) **Going Correction** +1.475s/f (Heav) **7** Ran SP% **110.1**
Speed ratings (Par 103): **45,43,41,36,36** —,—
toteswingers:1&2 £3.00, 2&3 £3.90, 1&3 £2.30 CSF £8.59 TOTE £3.70: £1.50, £1.70; EX 8.50.
Owner The Listeners **Bred** S P Hudson **Trained** Adlestrop, Gloucs

FOCUS

An ordinary mares' novice hurdle run at a steady gallop and given a token rating through the winner.

NOTEBOOK

Thornton Alice finished second at this venue 27 days earlier and stepping up in trip saw her readily go one better. She was messed about somewhat in the home straight, but looked to be on the best ground towards the nearside and is open to further improvement over this sort of distance. (op 5-2 tchd 11-4)

Niki Royal(FR) ◆ scraped home on her point debut against her own sex 87 days earlier and posted a solid debut over hurdles. She is a sister to Renee Robeson's modest chaser Kikos, who needs a sound surface, and reverting to better ground should see her win one of these. (op 7-2)

Tanzanite Bay, well beaten on her hurdling debut last month, was ridden as though the longer trip wouldn't be a problem and posted an improved effort back against her own sex. She didn't look that straightforward in her two bumpers and again showed temperament here, but she is given the benefit of doubt until showing what she can do back on a quicker surface. (op 11-4 tchd 5-2)

Lady Ida got badly outpaced turning for home. (op 5-1 tchd 9-2)

Frosty Spring showed more and will be of greater interest once switching to fences on better ground.

4135 STRAIGHTLINE CONSTRUCTION H'CAP CHASE (14 fncs 2 omitted) 2m 4f

3:10 (3:10) (Class 4) (0-115,110) 5-Y-0+ **£2,888** (£1,050)

Form				RPR
112-	1		**Teerie Express**[318] 4983 10-10-6 97 .... MrJBewley(7) (George Bewley) *prom: stdy hdwy to press ldr 9th: clr of rest after 5 out: effrt bef 2 out: 1 l down and styng on whn mstke last: rcvrd and styd on wl to ld nr fin* **9/4**[2]	106+
P222	2	½	**Jeringa**[13] 3888 12-10-8 92 .... (b) BrianHughes (John Wade) *trckd ldr: led 7th: rdn bef 2 out: styd on run-in: hdd nr fin* **15/8**[1]	96
4000	U		**Toulouse Express (IRE)**[23] 3695 12-10-8 92 .... (v) KennyJohnson (Robert Johnson) *racd wd: led to 7th: lost 2nd next: 5 l down and disputing 3rd whn blnd and uns rdr 5 out* **14/1**	—
2F6F	P		**Baltic Pathfinder (IRE)**[13] 3886 7-11-4 107 .... ShaneByrne(5) (Sue Smith) *trckd ldrs: lost pl 7th: sn drvn along: rallied and prom whn mstke 5 out: sn btn: t.o whn p.u bef 3 out* **7/2**[3]	—
P	P		**Tooman Lane (IRE)**[28] 3617 7-11-12 110 .... PaddyAspell (Patrick Holmes) *mstkes: in tch: rdn and wknd bef 5 out: t.o whn p.u bef next* **13/2**	—

5m 52.8s (25.60) **Going Correction** +1.325s/f (Heav) **5** Ran SP% **107.8**
Speed ratings: **101,100**,—,—,—
CSF £6.83 TOTE £2.80: £1.40, £1.40; EX 7.10.
Owner G T Bewley **Bred** F A Dickinson **Trained** Bonchester Bridge, Borders

FOCUS

Not a strong race for the class. They went an average gallop and once more underfoot conditions played a big part in proceedings. The second is rated to recent course form.

NOTEBOOK

Teerie Express made light of his 318-day layoff with a last-gasp success. He kept responding to pressure in the home straight, but looked held after meeting the last fence wrong. His capable amateur was taking off 7lb, though, and that looked to make the difference as he rallied gamely on the run-in. This was a decent training performance and he is a likeable 10-y-o. (op 2-1)

Jeringa was worn down right on the wire and has now finished runner-up on his last four outings. He gave his all under his usual positive ride, however, and certainly deserves to go one better again. (tchd 2-1)

Toulouse Express(IRE) was held but still in the process of running a better race prior to departing. (op 7-1 tchd 11-2)

Baltic Pathfinder(IRE) needs better ground. (op 7-1 tchd 11-2)

Tooman Lane(IRE) has now been pulled up in two outings for the yard. (op 7-1 tchd 11-2)

4136 DIGIBET.COM H'CAP HURDLE (7 hdls 2 omitted) 2m

3:40 (3:40) (Class 5) (0-95,92) 4-Y-0+ **£1,723** (£506; £253; £126)

Form				RPR
-FP1	1		**Decent Lord (IRE)**[2] 4104 7-10-7 73 7ex .... AlanO'Keeffe (Jennie Candlish) *hld up: stdy hdwy 1/2-way: led 3 out: edgd lft last: hrd rdn and edgd lft run-in: hld on wl* **11/10**[1]	81+
6014	2	½	**Transact (IRE)**[7] 3993 6-10-10 76 .... (p) GrahamLee (Martin Todhunter) *led to 3 out: rallied u.p: ev ch run-in: hld towards fin* **11/2**[3]	81
5522	3	10	**King's Chorister**[7] 3993 5-10-1 67 .... (t) BrianHarding (Barry Murtagh) *t.k.h: hld up in tch: stdy hdwy to trck ldrs bef 3 out: rdn next: sn outpcd* **3/1**[2]	63
4443	4	42	**Devils Delight (IRE)**[27] 3631 9-10-0 76 .... JamesSmith(10) (James Moffatt) *prom: hdwy to trck ldr 3rd: rdn and wknd after omitted 4 out: t.o whn mstke last* **10/1**	29
040-	5	21	**Frith (IRE)**[427] 2895 9-10-3 74 .... AlexanderVoy(5) (Lucy Normile) *trckd ldr to 3rd: cl up: rdn and wknd passing omitted 4 out: t.o* **25/1**	6
0-00	6	28	**Sydney Cove (IRE)**[15] 3855 5-11-12 92 .... FearghalDavis (William Amos) *racd wd: hld up: struggling 4th: sn lost tch* **18/1**	—
-00P	P		**Whatevertheweather**[107] 2103 7-10-0 66 oh8 .... TomMessenger (Sandy Forster) *racd wd: cl up tl wknd passing omitted 4 out: t.o whn p.u bef 2 out* **33/1**	—

4m 32.2s (22.20) **Going Correction** +1.475s/f (Heav) **7** Ran SP% **109.1**
Speed ratings (Par 103): **103,102,97,76,66 52**,—
toteswingers:1&2 £2.20, 2&3 £2.20, 1&3 £1.60 CSF £7.09 TOTE £2.40: £1.80, £1.40; EX 6.50.
Owner Mrs Judith Ratcliff **Bred** Lar O'Toole **Trained** Basford Green, Staffs
■ Stewards' Enquiry : Alan O'Keeffe caution: careless riding; two-day ban: used whip with excessive frequency (Mar 1-2)

FOCUS

A moderate handicap in which the three market leaders pulled a long way clear. The winner is rated 11lb below his recent success.

NOTEBOOK

Decent Lord(IRE) was well ahead of the handicapper under his penalty for hacking up at Hereford two days earlier and he followed up, but made very hard work of it. He was cantering over his two main rivals coming to the penultimate flight, but hung markedly when in front and in the end had very little to spare at the finish. This was a decent advertisement of his rider's skills and he holds two future entries at this stage, one back at Hereford. He now has a touch to prove with his attitude, but should not be discounted if turned out quickly as he would still be well treated under a double penalty. (op Evens)

Transact(IRE) bounced back to form for the return to the C&D he scored over two runs back, and he gamely pushed the winner all the way to the line. He is somewhat flattered by his proximity to that rival, but still rates a sound enough benchmark. (op 6-1)

King's Chorister travelled nicely into contention, but was really done with from three out and remains a maiden. (op 7-2 tchd 4-1)

Devils Delight(IRE) proved too keen for her own good. (op 6-1)

4137 SWARLANDSELFSTORAGE.CO.UK H'CAP CHASE (16 fncs 2 omitted) 3m

4:10 (4:10) (Class 4) (0-115,115) 5-Y-0+ **£2,888** (£1,050)

Form				RPR
5-66	1		**Wild Cane Ridge (IRE)**[43] 3362 12-11-12 115 .... (b) WilsonRenwick (Rose Dobbin) *cl up: led 11th to next: 3 l down and keeping on one pce whn lft wl clr 3 out* **9/2**[3]	121
5065	2	52	**Top Dressing (IRE)**[32] 3552 10-11-8 111 .... (p) BrianHughes (Howard Johnson) *prom: outpcd bef 10th: struggling fr next: rallied to take distant 3rd after 3 out: no imp whn lft poor 2nd 3 out* **8/1**	65
/P-P	P		**King Killone (IRE)**[34] 3509 11-11-6 109 .... (p) RobertWalford (Henry Hogarth) *chsd ldr tl rdn and lost pl after 7th: lost tch next: t.o whn p.u bef 10th* **14/1**	—
/032	P		**See You There (IRE)**[27] 3634 12-11-11 114 .... (t) PeterBuchanan (Lucinda Russell) *hld up in tch: hdwy after 7th: outpcd 10th: struggling fr next: t.o whn p.u bef 4 out* **3/1**[2]	—
5-43	P		**Its Teescomponents (IRE)**[13] 3888 9-11-3 106 .... JamesReveley (Keith Reveley) *led to 11th: wknd qckly bef 5 out: t.o whn p.u bef next* **3/1**[2]	—
-0P0	U		**Mister Marker (IRE)**[15] 3852 7-11-12 115 .... FearghalDavis (Nicky Richards) *hld up: nt fluent and reminders 5th: hdwy after 7th: led 5 out: 3 l in front and keeping on wl whn hit and uns rdr 3 out* **5/2**[1]	124

6m 58.4s (35.90) **Going Correction** +1.325s/f (Heav) **6** Ran SP% **114.5**
Speed ratings: **93,75**,—,—,—,—
toteswingers:1&2:£18.60 CSF £36.81 TOTE £5.60: £4.50, £4.30; EX 36.50.
Owner Ashleybank Investments Limited **Bred** Greenville House Stud And M Morgan **Trained** South Hazelrigg, Northumbria

FOCUS

What looked a fairly competitive little handicap proved a real war of attrition and the joint top weights pulled clear coming out of the back straight. The winner is rated to the best of last year's form.

NOTEBOOK

Wild Cane Ridge(IRE) was left in front three out and came home alone to register his first success since winning over hurdles in January 2008. He had looked out of sorts in his last three outings in that sphere, but was 12lb lower than his last run over fences and therefore very well handicapped if bouncing back. This is his ground and he is obviously some way from retirement, but it's hard to envisage him following up. (op 5-1 tchd 11-2 and 4-1)

Top Dressing(IRE) was easily beaten. (op 17-2 tchd 9-1)

See You There(IRE) found things all too demanding. (op 10-3 tchd 7-2)

Its Teescomponents(IRE) stopped quickly from six out. She needs a sounder surface, but has a little to prove now. Official explanation: trainer said mare was unsuited by the heavy ground (op 10-3 tchd 7-2)

Mister Marker(IRE), a course winner over hurdles here, was making his handicap debut over fences and was well backed. He went in snatches early, but had responded to pressure and was holding the upper hand before unseating three out. That looked a tired error and it isn't a forgone conclusion that he would have scored with a clear round. (op 10-3 tchd 7-2)

4138 LA TAXIS H'CAP HURDLE (8 hdls 3 omitted) 2m 4f

4:40 (4:40) (Class 4) (0-100,100) 4-Y-0+ **£2,602** (£764; £382; £190)

Form				RPR
0613	1		**Night In Milan (IRE)**[21] 3728 5-11-12 100 .... JamesReveley (Keith Reveley) *racd wd: hld up: hdwy and cl up 1/2-way: led gng wl bef 2 out: rdn bef last: edgd lft and carried hd high run-in: hld on towards fin* **6/4**[1]	112+
PP05	2	½	**Overyou**[28] 3619 6-10-1 82 .... StevenGagan(7) (Elliott Cooper) *trckd ldrs: effrt and chsd wnr bef 2 out: sn rdn: kpt on u.p fr last* **16/1**	89

603 **3** *33* **Tinseltown**[13] 3887 5-11-11 **99** PaddyAspell 76
(Brian Rothwell) *hld up: hdwy to trck ldrs after 5th: effrt bef 2 out: sn wknd: no ch whn hit last* **11/2**[3]

-P65 **4** *33* **Ravensbill (IRE)**[27] 3635 9-10-3 **77** CampbellGillies 18
(William Amos) *cl up: wnt 2nd 1/2-way: led bef 3 out to bef next: sn wknd: t.o* **10/1**

0-0P **5** *28* **Lochore (IRE)**[99] 2271 5-10-1 **80** AlexanderVoy(5) —
(Lucy Normile) *led tl hdd bef 3 out: sn rdn and wknd bef next: t.o* **20/1**

034- **P** **Lady Sambury**[302] 5275 9-10-13 **87** MichaelMcAlister —
(Maurice Barnes) *hld up: rdn and lost tch 5th: t.o whn p.u bef next* **15/2**

500 **P** **Seminal Moment**[27] 3637 5-10-5 **82** EwanWhillans(3) —
(William Amos) *chsd ldrs: hit 2nd: lost pl after 4th: lost tch next: sn p.u* **16/1**

0650 **P** **Bob Will (IRE)**[43] 3363 6-10-9 **83** RichieMcGrath —
(Chris Grant) *trckd ldr to 1/2-way: rdn and lost pl passing omitted 4 out: sn struggling: t.o whn p.u bef last* **9/2**[2]

5m 50.0s (28.90) **Going Correction** +1.475s/f (Heav) **8** Ran SP% **110.9**
Speed ratings (Par 105): **101,100,87,74,63** —,—,—
toteswingers:1&2:£8.80, 2&3:£15.10, 1&3:£3.40 CSF £23.13 CT £100.68 TOTE £2.00: £1.50, £5.10, £1.60; EX 28.90.
Owner Richard Collins **Bred** Commandant Brendan Healy **Trained** Lingdale, Redcar & Cleveland

FOCUS
This ordinary handicap was run at an average gallop and the first pair dominated from two out. The second is back to the best of his 2010 form.

NOTEBOOK
Night In Milan(IRE) got going far too late under a conditional rider at Sedgefield on his previous outing, but was reunited with James Reveley and the pair resumed winning ways. He was produced at the right time here towards the stands' side, but this was his first outing on such ground and he hung over to the far rail under pressure on the run-in. That meant he wasn't so impressive, but he remains progressive and can defy a likely higher mark when getting back on a sounder surface. (op 5-4 tchd 7-4)
Overyou ◆, with the cheekpieces left off, took a similar course through the race as the winner, racing just off the pace and keeping wide from the back straight. She was going as well as that rival after two out and made him pull out all the stops, but was never going to reel him in. This was by far her best effort to date and she too will be better served by returning to a sounder surface. She can get off the mark in the coming weeks.
Tinseltown crept into the race turning for home, but was left behind shortly after three out and got bogged down by this taxing surface. He can score off this mark when reverting to better ground. (op 8-1)
Ravensbill(IRE) ran with more encouragement on ground that was against him. (op 11-1 tchd 12-1)
Bob Will(IRE) found the testing conditions against him. (op 4-1)
T/Jkpt: £4,512.90 to a £1 stake. Pool of £31,781.10 - 5.00 winning tickets. T/Plt: 74.90 to a £1 stake. Pool of £66,582.61 - 648.30 winning tickets. T/Qpdt: £38.20 to a £1 stake. Pool of £4,157.18 - 80.50 winning tickets. RY

3877 LEICESTER (R-H)

Wednesday, February 16

OFFICIAL GOING: Good (good to soft in places; soft on the flat course crossings; 8.1)
Wind: almost nil Weather: overcast but mild

4139 WREN H'CAP CHASE (15 fncs) 2m 4f 110y
2:10 (2:10) (Class 4) (0-105,105) 5-Y-0+ **£2,602** (£764; £382; £190)

Form RPR

2124 **1** **Handtheprizeover**[18] 3819 6-11-2 **98** PeterToole(3) 110+
(Ben Case) *dropped in rr and rdn after 5th: drvn at bk of gp and stl 4 l to find at 12th: styd on dourly for press after to get up cl home* **5/1**[3]

U311 **2** *hd* **Phar Again (IRE)**[22] 3720 8-10-12 **94** (vt) TommyPhelan(3) 104
(Claire Dyson) *t.k.h: mde most tl 12th: remained contesting ld tl drvn and hdd bef last: rallied to ld again 100yds out: battled on: jst ct* **4/1**[2]

4-U2 **3** *2 3/4* **Mylord Collonges (FR)**[91] 2453 11-11-4 **100** (p) SamTwiston-Davies(3) 108
(Susan Nock) *prom: j. slowly 6th (water): led 12th: sn rdn: disp ld tl led and j.rt last: hdd and nt qckn fnl 100yds* **8/1**

P364 **4** *1/2* **Phoenix Des Mottes (FR)**[14] 3878 8-9-12 **84** JoeCornwall(7) 91
(John Cornwall) *t.k.h: rn in snatches: disp ld 8th tl hit 10th: rdn 12th: rallied on ins 2 out: ch last: wknd flat* **9/1**

U242 **5** *shd* **Pacha D'Oudairies (FR)**[18] 3819 8-11-7 **100** DominicElsworth 109+
(Michael Blake) *in rr mostly: rdn bef 12th: tried to get on terms between last two: no imp whn mstke last: plodded on but racd awkwardly flat* **3/1**[1]

4-1P **6** *21* **Beware Chalk Pit (IRE)**[39] 3450 7-11-0 **96** JimmyDerham(3) 94
(Jonathan Geake) *cl up: blnd 9th: rdn and ev ch bef 12th: wkng whn blnd 3 out* **16/1**

-432 **P** **Lahib The Fifth (IRE)**[16] 3853 11-11-7 **100** DenisO'Regan —
(Nicky Richards) *reminder after 1st: kpt hanging bdly lft: last and rdn 7th: lost tch next: mstke 11th: sn t.o: p.u 3 out* **8/1**

0320 **U** **Shinnecock Bay**[122] 1888 7-11-12 **105** (b) LeightonAspell —
(Oliver Sherwood) *towards rr: pushed along after 5th: stmbld and uns rdr after next (water)* **14/1**

164 **P** **Roc De Guye (FR)**[20] 3769 6-10-6 **92** RobertKirk(7) —
(James Evans) *plld hrd and nt fluent: sn cl up: led briefly 11th: wkng whn mstke 3 out and p.u* **25/1**

5m 23.9s (5.00) **Going Correction** +0.20s/f (Yiel) **9** Ran SP% **110.3**
Speed ratings: **98,97,96,96,96 88**,—,—,—
toteswingers:1&2 £6.20, 2&3 £5.10, 1&3 £5.20 CSF £24.20 CT £146.00 TOTE £7.70: £2.10, £2.30, £1.80; EX 28.50.
Owner D Allen **Bred** A Buller **Trained** Edgcote, Northants

FOCUS
A wide-open handicap chase that should work out and the form is rated around the first two.

NOTEBOOK
Handtheprizeover, below par on heavy ground latest, had been running well and the return to a sounder surface enabled him to post a career-best performance, staying on in the manner of a horse who may ultimately require 3m. (op 7-1)
Phar Again(IRE), who saves his best for this course, moved nicely for much of the race and had every chance, but his 7lb higher mark ultimately made the difference. (op 7-2 tchd 10-3)
Mylord Collonges(FR), already a dual C&D winner, got to front after two out and looked the winner jumping the last, but not for the first time he jumped left, and could find no extra on the run-in. (op 5-1)
Phoenix Des Mottes(FR) looked capable of a good run off this mark, but winning once again proved beyond him. (op 10-1 tchd 11-1 and 17-2)
Pacha D'Oudairies(FR) was under pressure and beaten before the straight. This wasn't his true form, but he is still a maiden over fences, having finished runner-up six times, and is left with a bit to prove now. (op 10-3 tchd 7-2 and 11-4)
Beware Chalk Pit(IRE) deserves another chance when stepping back up in trip. (op 25-1 tchd 28-1)
Lahib The Fifth(IRE) never went a yard and something may well have been amiss. Official explanation: jockey said gelding made a mistake at water and never travelled (op 15-2)
Roc De Guye(FR) travelled well up to a point and we've still to see the best of him. Official explanation: jockey said gelding lost its action (op 15-2)

4140 WEATHERBYS CHELTENHAM FESTIVAL BETTING GUIDE NOVICES' CHASE (12 fncs) 2m
2:40 (2:40) (Class 4) 5-Y-0+ **£2,602** (£764; £382; £190)

Form RPR

122 **1** **Betabob (IRE)**[13] 3905 8-10-5 115 MrRGHenderson(7) 121+
(Nick Mitchell) *mstke 1st: taken steadily off pce: tk 4th after 4th: effrt gng wl 9th: led 2 out: sn in command: comf* **15/8**[2]

3234 **2** *8* **Lordsbridge (USA)**[25] 3672 9-10-12 113 NickScholfield 115
(Andy Turnell) *j.lft 2nd: chsd clr ldng pair: blnd 8th: wnt 2nd bef next: drvn and outpcd by wnr after 2 out* **9/2**[3]

4203 **3** *3/4* **Bathwick Quest (IRE)**[15] 3871 7-10-5 114 TomScudamore 106
(Brendan Powell) *j.rt early: chsd clr ldr tl clsd to ld bef 9th: hdd 2 out: rdn and v one pce after* **7/4**[1]

P-3U **4** *17* **L'Homme De Nuit (GER)**[2] 4122 7-10-12 112 (t) DenisO'Regan 98
(Jim Best) *sn last: t.o 5th: plodded past two stragglers in st: nvr nr ldrs* **25/1**

6-04 **5** *21* **Uncle Ant (IRE)**[46] 3304 6-10-12 102 DominicElsworth 85+
(Paul Webber) *mounted outside paddock: v hdstr to post and virtually bolted in r: led and spreadeagled field early: hdd bef 9th: wknd qckly: t.o 2 out* **14/1**

/150 **6** *55* **Washango (IRE)**[91] 2452 9-10-2 95 SamTwiston-Davies(3) 21
(Shaun Lycett) *j. v modly towards rr: struggling whn j.lft 4th: t.o after 8th* **16/1**

4m 9.10s (0.90) **Going Correction** +0.20s/f (Yiel) **6** Ran SP% **105.7**
Speed ratings: **105,101,100,92,81 54**
toteswingers:1&2 £1.10, 2&3 £2.10, 1&3 £1.40 CSF £9.49 TOTE £2.80: £1.10, £1.70; EX 8.40.
Owner Guy Henderson **Bred** Miss Carmel Salley **Trained** Piddletrenthide, Dorset

FOCUS
There was plenty of pace on here but the winner was rated to the level of his upgraded run under this rider.

NOTEBOOK
Betabob(IRE) was ridden with restraint and only made his move approaching the third-last. Once in front, he was never going to be caught and this consistent 8-y-o, who had escaped a penalty for this contest, should continue to give a good account. (tchd 7-4 and 2-1)
Lordsbridge(USA), still a maiden over fences, made a couple of jumping errors while chasing the leaders. That wasn't why he didn't win, though, as he simply wasn't good enough. (op 7-2 tchd 10-3)
Bathwick Quest(IRE) paid for chasing too strong a pace and, in hindsight, Tom Scudamore would surely have pulled in the reins a bit once it was clear she wasn't going to be able to adopt her usual front-running tactics. (op 2-1 tchd 13-8)
L'Homme De Nuit(GER) was soon in trouble, but did plug on late and could prove a different proposition in handicaps. (op 22-1)
Uncle Ant(IRE), who was very free to post, charged off in the race itself. (op 11-1)

4141 MALLARD PAWNBROKERS HUNTERS' CHASE (18 fncs) 2m 7f 110y
3:10 (3:10) (Class 2) 6-Y-0+ **£7,596** (£2,372; £1,186; £592; £296)

Form RPR

21-2 **1** **William Somers**[287] 150 10-12-0 0 MrMWall 128+
(T F Sage) *led 5th: rdn 5 l clr bef 15th: hdd 3 out: battled bk most tenaciously to ld again last: drifted rt: drvn rt out* **4/1**[3]

POP/ **2** *1 1/2* **Turko (FR)**[44] 9-11-10 131 (t) MissAliceMills 123
(Mrs L Borradaile) *midfield: hit 11th: sustained effrt fr 3 out: wnt 2nd and tried to chal and ch last: no imp flat* **14/1**

U-PP **3** *5* **Battlecry**[24] 10-11-10 130 MrWTwiston-Davies 118
(Nigel Twiston-Davies) *led briefly 1st: lost pl briefly 6th: 2nd again after 8th: led 3 out: rdn and hdd: mstke last: sn wnt rt: fading fnl 100yds* **11/4**[2]

-241 **4** *6* **Turthen (FR)**[13] 3908 10-12-4 134 MissCTizzard 121
(C St V Fox) *bhd and given plenty to do: tk 4th bef 15th: plugged on after: nvr looked like landing a blow* **11/8**[1]

FP-5 **5** *74* **Little Rocker (IRE)**[263] 10-12-0 99 MrBFurnival 49
(R Smart) *prom under flailing elbows: nt fluent 4th: drvn and wknd and mstke 12th: t.o bef 15th* **66/1**

303/ **6** *15* **Maletton (FR)**[24] 11-11-10 106 MrDJGriffiths 32
(P R M Philips) *towards rr and nvr looked dangerous: reminders 10th: 15 l 7th after 14th: t.o next* **33/1**

P-3P **P** **Turbulance (IRE)**[244] 769 9-11-10 100 (p) MrRJWilliams —
(Jason Parfitt) *bhd: rdn 5th: lost tch after 8th: t.o whn mstke 11th: p.u 15th* **66/1**

-412 **P** **Farmer Frank**[265] 493 8-12-4 0 MrCGreene —
(Nick Kent) *plld hrd and sn led: hdd 5th: wknd 8th: t.o bef 15th: p.u 2 out* **8/1**

5m 59.5s (-4.50) **Going Correction** +0.20s/f (Yiel) **8** Ran SP% **112.5**
Speed ratings: **115,114,112,110,86 81**,—,—
toteswingers: 1&2 £6.80, 1&3 £3.60, 2&3 £8.80 CSF £48.53 TOTE £6.30: £1.80, £2.80, £1.60; EX 68.20.
Owner Mr & Mrs T F Sage **Bred** Mr & Mrs T F Sage **Trained** Tetbury, Gloucestershire

FOCUS
A valuable hunter chase that attracted a good field and could be rated a lot higher on the old form of those in the frame behind the winner.

NOTEBOOK
William Somers was always likely to take some passing once allowed to lead, having shown stamina in abundance when winning over 3m5f in heavy ground at Chepstow last March, and it was no surprise to see him get the better of a duel with Battlecry when that one challenged in the straight. A highly consistent sort, on this evidence he's improved and the Cheltenham Foxhunters' looks the natural target. (op 6-1)
Turko(FR) is clearly nowhere near the horse he was, but this was a promising first run in a hunter chase, and a similar performance should see him going one better. (tchd 18-1)
Battlecry, another once smart sort, had readily won a point last month and travelled strongly for the second half of the race here (jumped slowly early on), but as was often the case over the past couple of years, his finishing effort was rather tame. Perhaps a shorter trip and/or tighter track will help. (op 2-1)
Turthen(FR) proved most disappointing. A winner at Wincanton on his recent reappearance, his trainer had expressed concerns beforehand about the race coming too soon, and the horse never looked like challenging having been restrained in rear. This clearly wasn't his best form. (tchd 5-4)

Farmer Frank may well have needed this first run back from 265 days off. (tchd 15-2)

4142 FERNIE H'CAP CHASE (12 fncs) 2m
3:40 (3:40) (Class 4) (0-110,107) 5-Y-O+ **£2,602** (£764; £382; £190)

Form RPR

-133 **1** **Baseball Ted (IRE)**[27] 3648 9-11-10 **105**............................(p) TomO'Brien 123+
(Charlie Longsdon) *t.k.h: settled 3rd: wnt 2nd at 7th: effrt gng wl to ld 9th: 8 l clr last: readily* **3/1**[2]

14P1 **2** *8* **Randjo (FR)**[19] 3792 6-11-8 **103**............................ DenisO'Regan 114+
(Victor Dartnall) *hanging lft and making mstkes: nvr looked to be gng wl: 4th and rdn after 8th: wnt 2nd between last two: nvr looked like catching wnr* **9/4**[1]

1421 **3** *7* **Guns Of Love (IRE)**[15] 3875 9-10-6 **87**............................ CharliePoste 91
(Robin Dickin) *led at str gallop: hdd 9th: sn outpcd by wnr: lost 2nd bef last and fdd* **6/1**

5PP3 **4** *25* **Devils River (IRE)**[13] 3898 9-10-12 **93**............................(p) AndrewTinkler 75
(Anna Brooks) *pressed ldr in strly run r: lost 2nd at 7th: sn rdn: fdd bef 9th: sn t.o* **9/1**

02P4 **5** *10* **Coach Lane**[27] 3648 10-11-12 **107**............................ HarrySkelton 80
(Nick Mitchell) *bhd: rdn and lost tch bef 9th: sn t.o* **10/1**

P000 **6** *15* **Orpen Wide (IRE)**[31] 3092 9-11-3 **98**............................(bt) AndrewGlassonbury 57
(Michael Chapman) *wnt cl up at 5th tl bad mstke 7th: sn downed tools and rdn and dropped bk last: t.o 9th* **40/1**

2-4P **7** *28* **Quick Fix (IRE)**[88] 2529 9-11-5 **103**............................ SamTwiston-Davies[(3)] 37
(Susan Nock) *taken down early: hld up: hdwy after 8th: 3rd but rdn bef next: sn dropped out v tamely: mstke 3 out: hopelessly t.o* **9/2**[3]

4m 9.90s (1.70) **Going Correction** +0.20s/f (Yiel) **7** Ran SP% **109.8**
Speed ratings: **103,99,95,83,78 70,56**
toteswingers:1&2 £2.50, 2&3 £2.70, 1&3 £3.00 CSF £9.75 TOTE £4.10: £1.60, £1.70; EX 11.30.

Owner Alan Peterson **Bred** Donal Fennessy **Trained** Over Norton, Oxon

■ Stewards' Enquiry : Charlie Poste three-day ban: weighed in 2lb heavy (Mar 2-4)

FOCUS
Just a modest handicap chase, though the early pace was good. The winner is on a decent mark and the third is rated to form.

NOTEBOOK
Baseball Ted(IRE) needed to have improved on his last-time-out Taunton third, and he duly did, the first-time cheekpieces making all the difference. Quickly clear after three out, he won in the style of a horse that could go in again if the headgear continues to have the same effect. (tchd 11-4 and 10-3)

Randjo(FR), 13lb higher than when winning at Fontwell, wasn't really jumping early (he was also hanging), but finally started to run on down the straight and may want a bit further now. (op 2-1 tchd 15-8)

Guns Of Love(IRE) probably paid for forcing too fast a gallop, and was swiftly brushed aside by the winner. This new 7lb higher mark may also have proved beyond him. (op 9-2)

Devils River(IRE) failed to back up his recent Towcester third. (op 17-2 tchd 8-1)

Orpen Wide(IRE) Official explanation: trainer said gelding had a breathing problem

Quick Fix(IRE), having only his second start for the yard, briefly took third turning in, but not for the first time, he found nothing for pressure, stopping quickly. He looks one to avoid. (op 8-1)

4143 DICK SAUNDERS NOVICES' HUNTERS' CHASE (15 fncs) 2m 4f 110y
4:10 (4:11) (Class 5) 6-Y-O+ **£1,561** (£484; £242; £121)

Form RPR

26-2 **1** **What Of It (IRE)**[17] 8-11-7 104............................ MrTWCEdwards[(7)] 107+
(Mrs S P George) *prom but lacked fluency: 2nd 5th tl dropped bk to 3rd and looked outpcd 8th: lft 2nd after 11th: 4 l down bef next: flapped along to ld bef last: responded gamely and a jst holding rival fnl 100yds: all out* **5/6**[1]

63-4 **2** *nk* **Louis Pasteur (IRE)**[283] 232 6-11-9 0............................ MrRGHenderson[(5)] 115+
(Nick Mitchell) *racd keenly: blnd 1st: rcvrd steadily to go 2nd at 8th: upsides and terrible mstke and nrly fell 11th: given time to rcvr and wnt 2nd bef last: sustained chal and rdn flat: no imp fnl 100yds: most unlucky* **9/4**[2]

5-25 **3** *18* **Battlefield Bob (IRE)**[24] 7-11-7 87............................ MrGGreenock[(7)] 93
(G T H Bailey) *led: hit 2nd: mstke 8th: rdn and wobbling in both directions fr 12th: mstke 2 out: hdd bef last and floundered up run-in* **15/2**[3]

P-05 **4** *29* **Cluthe Boy (IRE)**[10] 8-11-9 0............................(t) MissSSharratt[(5)] 63
(Miss S Sharratt) *immediately lost tch: t.o fr 5th* **33/1**

U- **5** *53* **Joe Soap (IRE)**[17] 10-11-9 0............................(p) MrTJCannon[(5)] 15
(Mrs C L Dennis) *rdn and reluctant and trying to r sideways: midfield: lost tch 8th: hopelessly t.o after 11th* **20/1**

4-4P **P** **Cash In Hand (IRE)**[277] 335 11-11-7 80............................ MrTEllis[(7)] —
(R Harvey) *chsd ldr tl 4th: 4th and outpcd 8th: t.o 11th: p.u 2 out* **25/1**

PP **P** **Mrsilverlining (IRE)**[10] 9-11-7 0............................ MrJFlook[(7)] —
(Miss I H Pickard) *mstke 1st: bhd: j. slowly 6th: struggling 8th: hopelessly t.o whn nrly ref and lunged over 3 out and p.u* **80/1**

0/ **P** **Cousin John (IRE)**[24] 8-11-11 0............................ MrRWoollacott[(3)] —
(R Mitford-Slade) *prom tl lost pl rapidly and p.u after 5th* **14/1**

5m 25.5s (6.60) **Going Correction** +0.20s/f (Yiel) **8** Ran SP% **116.5**
Speed ratings: **95,94,88,76,56** —,—,—
toteswingers:1&2 £1.20, 2&3 £2.30, 1&3 £2.90 CSF £3.08 TOTE £1.90: £1.10, £1.50, £1.10; EX 3.70.

Owner T W C Edwards **Bred** Mrs Margaret Norris **Trained** Stroud, Gloucestershire

FOCUS
The front pair drew clear in this novice hunter chase. The third sets the level of the form.

NOTEBOOK
What Of It(IRE) just got the better of Louis Pasteur, although that almost certainly wouldn't have been the case had the runner-up not sprawled badly on landing at the 11th. He came here in form, having picked up a point recently, and should continue to give a good account in similar contests. (op 6-5 tchd 5-4 and 11-8 in a place)

Louis Pasteur(IRE), a point winner in 2009 who ran well enough without winning in four starts over hurdles last year, looked potentially interesting on his hunter chase debut and was travelling powerfully when appearing to lose any winning chance at the 11th. It was to his credit that he recovered to challenge again, just getting outstayed late on. He should have no trouble gaining compensation. (op 3-1 tchd 2-1)

Battlefield Bob(IRE), left clear when winning a point last month, ran well for a long way on this hunter chase debut, but this often weak finisher was again found wanting late on. (op 6-1 tchd 8-1)

Cousin John(IRE) Official explanation: vet said gelding was found to have bled post race

4144 VICARAGE H'CAP CHASE (18 fncs) 2m 7f 110y
4:40 (4:40) (Class 5) (0-85,85) 5-Y-O+ **£2,276** (£668; £334; £166)

Form RPR

U2U4 **1** **One More Dinar**[15] 3873 8-11-8 **81**............................ RodiGreene 92+
(John Bryan Groucott) *hld up: stdy prog 12th: led bef 3 out: 5 l clr last rdn and hung rt flat: styd on wl* **11/1**

0623 **2** *11* **Donald Will Do (IRE)**[22] 3720 11-11-3 **76**............................ AndrewThornton 77
(Caroline Bailey) *prom: led 13th tl after 14th: 3rd and rdn bef 15th: outpcd and finding nthing next: plodded into 2nd after last* **13/2**[2]

4325 **3** *1 ¾* **Jacarado (IRE)**[22] 3720 13-10-5 **74**............................(v) ChristopherWard[(10)] 74
(Robin Dickin) *prom: led after 14th: rdn and hdd bef 3 out: j. awkwardly next: no ch w wnr after: lost 2nd after last* **8/1**[3]

/P3P **4** *5* **Randolph O'Brien (IRE)**[12] 3933 11-11-7 **83**...... SamTwiston-Davies[(3)] 79+
(Nigel Twiston-Davies) *prom: last of four w any ch but rdn bef 15th: btn next: plodded on: nt fluent last* **8/1**[3]

24/0 **5** *18* **Ballyman (IRE)**[83] 2638 10-11-1 **77**............................ JimmyDerham[(3)] 58
(Jonathan Geake) *bhd: sme prog whn mstke 14th: sn wl btn* **8/1**[3]

0005 **6** *10* **Glenfly (IRE)**[22] 3723 6-11-9 **82**............................ TomO'Brien 51
(Philip Hobbs) *trckd ldrs: upsides ldr 6th tl 7th:5th and rdn and losing tch tamely bef 15th* **6/1**[1]

25-P **7** *½* **Well Mick (IRE)**[282] 251 10-11-3 **76**............................(p) FelixDeGiles 44
(Jonathen de Giles) *wl bhd and racing idly: t.o 14th: passed stragglers* **22/1**

3330 **8** *1* **Feeling Peckish (USA)**[8] 3990 7-10-11 **77**............................(t) MrTGarner[(7)] 44
(Michael Chapman) *midfield: rdn and lost tch 14th* **14/1**

04P0 **9** *9* **Just Unique**[22] 3719 7-11-2 **78**............................ PeterToole[(3)] 37
(Mark Rimell) *nvr nr ldrs: struggling 13th* **66/1**

1430 **10** *19* **Reelwill (FR)**[43] 3388 6-11-0 **73**............................ TomMessenger 15
(Chris Bealby) *mstke 2nd: nvr trbld ldrs: lost tch 13th: t.o* **10/1**

-340 **11** *7* **Ballymorn (IRE)**[34] 3527 7-11-9 **82**............................(p) HaddenFrost 18
(Henrietta Knight) *led tl after 4th: w ldr tl 8th: struggling 13th: t.o whn blnd last* **14/1**

0460 **12** *nse* **Play The Rock (FR)**[64] 2937 8-11-3 **76**............................(b[1]) AndrewGlassonbury 12
(Philip Kirby) *j.rt 1st and nrly uns rdr: j.rt 2nd: mstke 5th: lost pl 7th: 6th and rdn and bef 15th: t.o* **20/1**

10/5 **13** *nk* **Bringewood Fox**[91] 2457 9-11-5 **85**............................(t) PeterCarberry[(7)] 21
(John Needham) *midfield: lost tch 14th: wl bhd bef next* **28/1**

0036 **14** *30* **Red Law (IRE)**[15] 3873 7-11-11 **84**............................ DenisO'Regan —
(Mark Gillard) *t.o fr 5th* **11/1**

1BP0 **P** **Lansdowne Princess**[15] 3870 6-11-3 **76**............................ JohnnyFarrelly —
(Gerald Ham) *nvr bttr than midfield: mstke 12th: struggling after: t.o and p.u 2 out* **22/1**

P0PP **P** **Dareios (GER)**[8] 3990 6-11-7 **80**............................(b[1]) DavidEngland —
(John Mackie) *midfield: wknd 12th: t.o and p.u 15th* **80/1**

6m 7.00s (3.00) **Going Correction** +0.20s/f (Yiel) **16** Ran SP% **119.7**
Speed ratings: **103,99,98,97,91 87,87,87,84,77 75,75,75,65,— —**
toteswingers:1&2 £15.50, 2&3 £6.70, 1&3 £19.80 CSF £74.66 CT £615.51 TOTE £13.70: £3.00, £1.20, £2.00, £2.80; EX 86.50.

Owner Mrs M R Winwood **Bred** Mrs A Winwood **Trained** Bourton, Shropshire

FOCUS
A competitive handicap chase and it could be rated a few pounds higher.

NOTEBOOK
One More Dinar has been threatening to win a race and his often suspect jumping, which has cost him on a few occasions, was good enough here for him to get the job done. The return to a longer trip clearly suited. (op 12-1)

Donald Will Do(IRE) boxed on best he could, but he's likely to remain vulnerable. (op 11-2 tchd 5-1)

Jacarado(IRE) again ran creditably and still appears to have it in him to win races. (op 11-1)

Randolph O'Brien(IRE) is on a very good mark these days and showed a bit more than of late. (op 13-2)

Ballyman(IRE) showed some promise as this was only his second run back from an absence, so he should come on again and can win something similar. (op 14-1)

Glenfly(IRE) fared better than he had done at the course on his recent chase/handicap debut, although he was still well held. (op 7-1)

Well Mick(IRE) should come on for this and was the only other to note. (op 20-1)

Ballymorn(IRE) Official explanation: trainer's rep said gelding finished distressed

T/Plt: £20.90 to a £1 stake. Pool of £66,577.05 - 2,319.85 winning tickets. T/Qpdt: £7.00 to a £1 stake. Pool of £4,714.25 - 497.40 winning tickets. IM

4056 MUSSELBURGH (R-H)
Wednesday, February 16

OFFICIAL GOING: Soft (good to soft in places; 6.4)
Stands bend moved back to innermost position. Bottom bend moved out 2m.
Weather: steady rain

4145 EUROPEAN BREEDERS' FUND "NATIONAL HUNT" NOVICES' HURDLE (QUALIFIER) (12 hdls) 2m 4f
1:50 (1:50) (Class 4) 4-7-Y-O **£1,951** (£573; £286; £143)

Form RPR

5122 **1** **Blenheim Brook (IRE)**[18] 3820 6-11-8 123............................ PeterBuchanan 129+
(Lucinda Russell) *trckd ldrs: hdwy to ld after 4 out: clr after next: easily* **30/100**[1]

50-0 **2** *16* **Smithy The Horse (IRE)**[123] 1867 5-11-2 0............................ JasonMaguire 97
(Donald McCain) *w ldr: reminders after 7th: rdn and outpcd after 4 out: rallied to go modest 2nd bef last* **25/1**

0045 **3** *4 ½* **Blazing Bay (IRE)**[16] 3856 6-10-9 0............................ PaddyAspell 85
(James Moffatt) *hld up in rr: hit 6th: rdn after 7th: kpt on after 2 out: n.d* **40/1**

12 **4** *3 ¼* **Khorun (GER)**[173] 1392 6-11-3 114............................ MrTomDavid[(5)] 96
(Tim Vaughan) *led: nt fluent: hdd after 4 out: stl 2nd 2 out: wknd appr last* **11/2**[2]

40/0 **5** *13* **Northern Cross (IRE)**[23] 3715 7-11-2 0............................ BrianHughes 82
(Howard Johnson) *trckd ldrs: racd keenly: nt fluent 6th and 8th: rdn after 4 out: wknd after 2 out* **33/1**

22- **6** *34* **Classical Mist**[343] 4515 7-10-9 0............................ GrahamLee 35
(David O'Meara) *hld up: racd keenly: hdwy to trck ldrs after 4 out: nt fluent 3 out: wknd qckly after* **11/1**[3]

5000 **7** *1 ¼* **Darkan Road**[16] 3851 6-11-2 0............................ JanFaltejsek 41
(George Charlton) *hld up: a towards rr: bled* **100/1**

5m 2.50s (11.00) **Going Correction** +0.475s/f (Soft) **7** Ran SP% **110.9**
Speed ratings: **97,90,88,87,82 68,68**
toteswingers:1&2 £5.30, 2&3 £8.60, 1&3 £6.00 CSF £11.13 TOTE £1.40: £1.10, £8.20; EX 11.80.

Owner The County Set Three **Bred** Richard Frisby **Trained** Arlary, Perth & Kinross

FOCUS

After persistent heavy rain, conditions were very testing, 'as soft as it ever gets here' according to winning jockey Peter Buchanan. The third and fifth set the level of the form.

NOTEBOOK

Blenheim Brook(IRE) came clear once in line for home and enjoyed an easy success - as he was entitled to. Rated 123, the aim now is the EBF Final at Sandown next month. (op 2-5)

Smithy The Horse(IRE) struggled to keep up on his second start over hurdles throughout the final circuit. After getting outpaced, he kept on to take a distant second after the final flight. He looks to stay well and will be suited by a step up to 3m. (op 20-1)

Blazing Bay(IRE), who showed poor form in four starts in bumpers, has something to learn about jumping hurdles. She kept on to finish a never dangerous third and is another who will be suited by an even stiffer test. (op 66-1)

Khorun(GER), absent since August, made several mistakes and was tired when clouting the last. The ground had turned against him. (op 5-1)

Northern Cross(IRE), having his second start after an absence of 21 months, was much too keen on just his second start over hurdles.

Classical Mist, runner-up in both of the bumpers she contested, was having her first start for 11 months. Very keen, she stopped to nothing three out and was allowed to coast home. (op 10-1)

Darkan Road Official explanation: trainer said gelding bled from the nose

4146 WEATHERBYS PRIVATE BANKING H'CAP HURDLE (13 hdls 1 omitted) 3m 110y

2:20 (2:20) (Class 4) (0-100,100) 4-Y-0+ **£2,602** (£764; £382; £190)

Form				RPR
5552	**1**		**Vallani (IRE)**[21] 3750 6-10-11 **85** ... PeterBuchanan (Lucinda Russell) *midfield on inner: chsd ldr bef 3 out: rdn 2 out: chal last: sn led: kpt on wl* **9/2**[1]	91
4321	**2**	*1 ¾*	**Festival King (IRE)**[16] 3853 9-11-12 **100** ... TimmyMurphy (Pauline Robson) *led: nt fluent 2 out: drvn and hdd after last: no ex nr fin* **11/2**[2]	105
-050	**3**	*2 ½*	**Fairynuff**[41] 3403 7-11-10 **98** ...(t) RichieMcGrath (Kate Walton) *trckd ldr: rdn after 2 out: kpt on* **9/2**[1]	101
3P06	**4**	*1 ¾*	**Proficiency**[21] 3747 6-11-3 **91** ...(v) MarkBradburne (Sue Bradburne) *prom: rdn and stl ev ch 2 out: no ex run-in* **28/1**	91
F0-2	**5**	*6*	**Wotchalike (IRE)**[273] 405 9-10-4 **85** ...(p) NathanMoscrop[(7)] (Shelley Johnstone) *hld up: hdwy to chse ldrs after 9th: one pce after 3 out* **16/1**	79
-0P3	**6**	*3*	**Soprano (GER)**[21] 3750 9-11-9 **97** ...(p) GrahamLee (Jim Goldie) *hld up towards inner: hdwy 4 out: no further imp after next* **13/2**[3]	90
0-00	**7**	*19*	**Waltham Abbey**[87] 2549 10-10-9 **90** ... MrRUtley[(7)] (Lynsey Kendall) *hld up on outer: rdn after 4 out: sn no imp* **50/1**	62
505P	**8**	*16*	**Papa Drew (IRE)**[21] 3748 7-9-11 **74** oh2 ... JamesHalliday[(3)] (Andrew Parker) *midfield: wknd after 8th* **8/1**	30
2460	**9**	*hd*	**Almutaham (USA)**[23] 3711 4-10-8 **93** ... PaddyAspell (James Moffatt) *hld up: brief hdwy 4 out: wknd bef next* **14/1**	38
P306	**10**	*nk*	**Miss Tarantella**[95] 2372 8-10-13 **87** ...(t) MichaelMcAlister (Maurice Barnes) *midfield: chsd ldr 8th: wknd after 9th* **16/1**	42
P-36	**11**	*28*	**Norwest (IRE)**[203] 1119 8-11-5 **98** ...(t) MrTomDavid[(5)] (Tim Vaughan) *midfield: wknd after 4 out* **9/1**	25
00-0	**P**		**Soneva Gili (IRE)**[14] 3883 7-10-0 **74** oh4 ... CampbellGillies (Shelley Johnstone) *trckd ldr on outer: wknd after 9th: t.o whn p.u bef 3 out* **50/1**	—
0-05	**P**		**Just Posh**[102] 2208 9-10-8 **82** ... RyanMania (Rayson Nixon) *midfield: lost pl after 7th: sn bhd: p.u bef 3 out* **16/1**	—

6m 1.80s (5.10) **Going Correction** +0.35s/f (Yiel)
WFA 4 from 6yo+ 11lb **13** Ran SP% **117.9**
Speed ratings (Par 105): **105,104,103,103,101 100,94,89,88,88 79,—,—**
toteswingers:1&2 £1.30, 2&3 £4.00, 1&3 £42.20 CSF £28.92 CT £117.73 TOTE £6.00: £2.10, £1.50, £2.50; EX 35.80.

Owner A Barclay **Bred** Owenstown Stud **Trained** Arlary, Perth & Kinross

FOCUS

A severe test of stamina in the deteriorating ground, and just half a dozen still in with a shout turning for home. The second is rated to the level of his recent improved chasing form.

NOTEBOOK

Vallani(IRE), a maiden after 19 previous attempts over hurdles, was racing from a 3lb higher mark than her second here three weeks earlier. Despite fears about how she would handle the ground, she really put her head down and battled gamely to win going away in the end. Stamina is her strong suit.

Festival King(IRE), 6lb higher than his emphatic win over fences at Ayr, attacked the hurdles but got the second last wrong and in the end found Vallani too strong. He seemed to handle the ground all right. (op 5-1)

Fairynuff, 12-1 on the morning line, was stepping up in trip on his handicap bow. A bumper winner in 2009, this was a big step up on his three previous efforts over hurdles.

Proficiency, proven on soft ground, put three moderate efforts behind her. (op 25-1 tchd 33-1)

Wotchalike(IRE), absent since May, jumped better than on some occasions in the past and prefers less testing ground.

Soprano(GER), 3lb better off with the winner, finished roughly the same distance behind Vallani last time. (op 7-1)

4147 EILDON HILL STABLES HUNTERS' CHASE (16 fncs) 2m 4f

2:50 (2:51) (Class 6) 5-Y-0+ **£1,249** (£387; £193; £96)

Form				RPR
44-2	**1**		**Zemsky (IRE)**[88] 8-11-12 126 ...(p) MrDerekO'Connor (I R Ferguson, Ire) *midfield: hdwy to trck ldr after 6 out: led on bit 4 out: pushed clr after last: comf* **4/6**[1]	107+
2P1-	**2**	*7*	**Spellchecker (IRE)**[24] 7-11-13 113 ... MrMWalford[(3)] (Mrs S J Stilgoe) *trckd ldr: racd keenly: hit but led 5 out: hdd 4 out: kpt on: no match wnr* **6/1**[2]	105+
P3P4	**3**	*2*	**Thunder Hawk (IRE)**[174] 1376 11-11-13 86 ... MrTDavidson[(3)] (Mrs L A Coltherd) *led: hdd 9th: lost pl after 6 out: rallied after 3 out: wnt 3rd last* **16/1**	101
2P30	**4**	*5*	**Bow School (IRE)**[110] 2080 10-12-1 117 ... MrWKinsey[(5)] (Mrs A C Hamilton) *chsd ldrs: nt fluent: rdn 4 out: no ex after 2 out* **9/1**[3]	100
PP/0	**5**	*6*	**Nirvana Du Bourg (FR)**[265] 493 10-11-5 0 ...(tp) MissEStead[(7)] (R A Wilson) *bdly hmpd s and slowly away: hld up: n.d* **80/1**	84
0/P-	**6**	*5*	**Quechua Des Obeaux (FR)**[17] 7-11-2 0 ...(tp) MrCDawson[(3)] (R D E Woodhouse) *trckd ldrs: hit 4th: rdn 4 out: wknd after 3 out* **16/1**	74
/4U-	**P**		**Pendle Forest (IRE)**[17] 11-10-12 71 ...(p) MissEYoung[(7)] (Miss E Young) *hld up: a bhd: p.u bef 3 out* **100/1**	—
2P6-	**P**		**Kinfayre Boy**[310] 5171 9-11-9 90 ... MrSBowden[(7)] (S Bowden) *v rel to r and bhd: p.u after 1st* **33/1**	—
P-30	**P**		**Barry The Cracker**[261] 551 8-11-5 0 ... MrMEnnis[(7)] (Stephen Melrose) *racd keenly: midfield: hdwy 10th: hit 5 out: wknd appr 4 out: p.u bef 3 out* **80/1**	—
3200	**P**		**Athoss**[231] 860 9-11-5 98 ... MrAdamNicol[(7)] (Robert Smith) *hld up: a towards rr: bhd whn p.u bef 3 out* **40/1**	—
PP-0	**P**		**Markadam**[24] 5-11-5 0 ... MrJohnDawson[(5)] (Ms Jackie Williamson) *w ldr on outer: led 9th: hdd and bmpd 5 out: wknd qckly: p.u bef 3 out* **20/1**	—
0-16	**F**		**Scotch Warrior**[256] 628 7-11-9 0 ... MrGJCockburn[(7)] (Robert Smith) *midfield: reminders after 9th: hld in 5th whn fell 3 out* **20/1**	—

5m 27.0s (25.80) **Going Correction** +1.20s/f (Heav)
WFA 5 from 7yo+ 2lb **12** Ran SP% **114.4**
Speed ratings: **96,93,92,90,88 86,—,—,—,— —,—**
toteswingers:1&2 £1.20, 2&3 £17.40, 1&3 £6.00 CSF £4.30 TOTE £1.70: £1.10, £1.50, £5.80; EX 5.60.

Owner R A Bartlett **Bred** J R Weston **Trained** Ballymena, Co Antrim

■ Stewards' Enquiry : Mr W Kinsey two-day ban: careless riding (Mar 2-3)

FOCUS

Plenty of dead wood in this truly run 2m4f contest, which produced a winner of real potential and a runner-up sure to go one better. The third sets the level in an ordinary hunter chase.

NOTEBOOK

Zemsky(IRE) ◆, a two-time winner and runner-up from four starts in Irish points during 2010, had the benefit of the record breaking four-times Irish point champion rider Derek O'Connor. The pair moved up on to the heels of the leader on the final turn and, running lazily when in front, Zemsky only needed to be pushed out for victory. He heads to Ayr next week all being well. (op 4-5 tchd 5-6, 10-11 in places)

Spellchecker(IRE), off the mark over fences on his fourth attempt at Sedgefield in March, stepped up considerably on his first start in points just three weeks earlier. Despite a blunder, he took charge five out but it was soon clear the winner was merely waiting to strike. At just seven, he has time on his side. (op 13-2)

Thunder Hawk(IRE), a winner over 3m2f at Cartmel in June, took them along for a circuit before getting badly outpaced. Only seventh four out, he took a remote third at the last fence before finishing strongly. He needs a much stiffer test. (op 18-1 tchd 14-1)

Bow School(IRE), absent since October, doesn't want the ground as soft as this. (tchd 10-1)

4148 NAIRN'S OATCAKES JUVENILE H'CAP HURDLE (9 hdls) 2m

3:20 (3:20) (Class 4) (0-115,104) 4-Y-0 **£3,252** (£955; £477; £238)

Form				RPR
635	**1**		**Antoella (IRE)**[20] 2556 4-11-0 **92** ... RichieMcGrath (Philip Kirby) *trckd ldr: led 4 out: rdn 3 out: clr next: eased towards fin* **7/1**[3]	94+
4626	**2**	*5*	**Miereveld**[19] 3782 4-11-5 **97** ...(b) FearghalDavis (Brian Ellison) *chsd ldr: wnt in snatches: hit 2nd: ev ch appr 3 out: rdn and one pce whn hit 2 out: again nt fluent last* **2/1**[1]	90
5454	**3**	*1*	**Capricornus (USA)**[33] 3550 4-11-9 **101** ...(p) GrahamLee (Ferdy Murphy) *hld up: hit 4th: hdwy on outer appr 5th: rdn 3 out: kpt on to take 3rd run-in* **9/1**	91
F250	**4**	*2 ¼*	**Baraathen (USA)**[11] 3951 4-11-3 **95** ... JasonMaguire (Donald McCain) *in tch: chsd ldr in 3rd whn mstke 3 out: sn rdn: wknd and lost 3rd run-in* **4/1**[2]	83
043	**5**	*6*	**I Got Music**[18] 3818 4-11-12 **104** ... JamesReveley (Keith Reveley) *hld up: outpcd after 4th: rdn bef 3 out and no imp: nt fluent 2 out and last* **10/1**	88
0135	**6**	*8*	**Lady Pacha**[5] 3545 4-10-11 **94** ...(b) BrianToomey[(5)] (Tim Pitt) *sn led: j. bdly lft 5th: hdd next: wknd after 3 out* **12/1**	71
P03	**7**	*43*	**Kai Broon (IRE)**[19] 3785 4-10-9 **87** ... CampbellGillies (Lucinda Russell) *midfield: pckd 4 out: rdn and sn wknd* **4/1**[2]	18

3m 57.1s (8.70) **Going Correction** +0.475s/f (Soft) **7** Ran SP% **112.6**
Speed ratings: **97,94,94,92,89 85,64**
toteswingers: 1&2 £3.80, 1&3 £13.70, 2&3 £2.80 CSF £21.39 TOTE £6.30: £3.40, £2.50; EX 27.30.

Owner Mark Wilson & John Maguire **Bred** Kildare Racing Syndicate **Trained** Castleton, N Yorks

FOCUS

A very modest juvenile handicap hurdle which went to subsequent Aintree Grade 1 winner Orsippus a year ago. The form looks sound with the four immediately behind the winner close to their marks.

NOTEBOOK

Antoella(IRE) didn't get home up the Towcester hill last time. Rated 92 on her handicap bow, she travelled strongly, impressing with her sound jumping, and after coming clear won easing right down. (tchd 15-2)

Miereveld has his quirks and had to be given reminders at various stages. He is flattered by his proximity to the winner and is one to have reservations about. (tchd 9-4)

Capricornus(USA), who finished behind I Got Music at Ayr two runs previously, made his effort wide in the back straight. He jumped better this time and is the type to step up on this when getting much better ground in the spring. (op 8-1)

Baraathen(USA), having his second start in handicap company, looks very limited and was making hard work of it in third when hitting three out. (op 7-1)

I Got Music, third in a Uttoxeter seller last time, looked on a stiff mark and never got competitive. (op 13-2 tchd 11-2)

Lady Pacha, who has struggled both over hurdles and on the Flat since her Wetherby seller success, was tried in blinkers for the first time over hurdles. She jumped violently left at some flights and looks to be going the wrong way. (op 9-1)

Kai Broon(IRE) Official explanation: jockey said gelding was unsuited by the soft (good to soft places) ground

4149 WEATHERBYS WEALTH PLANNING H'CAP HURDLE (9 hdls) 2m

3:50 (3:50) (Class 3) (0-135,130) 4-Y-0+ **£6,505** (£1,910; £955; £477)

Form				RPR
0343	**1**		**Dontpaytheferryman (USA)**[38] 2399 6-10-2 **113** ... PaulGallagher[(7)] (Brian Ellison) *mde all: qcknd clr bef 3 out: rdn 2 out: kpt on wl* **13/8**[1]	121+
0012	**2**	*3 ¼*	**Pokfulham (IRE)**[10] 3966 5-10-5 **109** ...(v) GrahamLee (Jim Goldie) *trckd wnr: rdn bef 3 out: kpt on: a hld* **3/1**[2]	114
2103	**3**	*14*	**Grand Diamond (IRE)**[89] 2508 7-10-4 **115** ... PaulNorton[(7)] (Jim Goldie) *hld up towards inner: hdwy bef 3 out: wnt 3rd bef last: n.d* **16/1**	107
0126	**4**	*4*	**Viva Colonia (IRE)**[10] 3966 6-11-2 **120** ... JasonMaguire (David O'Meara) *in tch: hdwy to chse wnr after 4 out: rdn 3 out: wknd bef next* **5/1**[3]	108
1-25	**5**	*3 ½*	**Gringo**[88] 2520 9-11-12 **130** ... BrianHughes (Howard Johnson) *hld up towards rr: rdn 3 out: n.d* **33/1**	115
514	**6**	*¾*	**King Fingal (IRE)**[19] 3781 6-11-2 **120** ... DougieCostello (John Quinn) *trckd ldr: racd keenly: rdn and wknd bef 2 out* **17/2**	103
51-	**7**	*¾*	**Kilbrannish Hill (IRE)**[19] 3797 7-11-0 **118** ...(p) TimmyMurphy (I R Ferguson, Ire) *hld up in rr on outer: hit 5th: rdn bef 3 out: sn no imp* **7/1**	100

3m 52.9s (4.50) **Going Correction** +0.475s/f (Soft) **7** Ran SP% **111.6**
Speed ratings (Par 107): **107,105,98,96,94 94,93**
toteswingers:1&2 £1.90, 2&3 £9.20, 1&3 £5.20 CSF £6.82 CT £50.57 TOTE £2.90: £1.80, £1.80; EX 6.90.

Owner Koo's Racing Club **Bred** Rojan Farms **Trained** Norton, N Yorks

The Form Book, Raceform Ltd, Compton, RG20 6NL

FOCUS
The rain had abated ahead of quite a valuable 109-130 handicap hurdle, and the first two home finished some way clear. The form is rated around the third and fourth in line with their previous form.

NOTEBOOK
Dontpaytheferryman(USA), winner of four of his last five starts on the all-weather, showing a stone and a half of improvement, returned to hurdling on a possibly lenient mark, 2lb lower than when third at Market Rasen in November. Given a positive ride, he stole a march on his rivals going to three out and, kept up to his work, never looked like being overhauled. He loves soft ground and will take plenty of beating under a penalty at Carlisle next Monday. (op 6-4 tchd 7-4, 2-1 in a place)
Pokfulham(IRE), due to race from a 4lb higher mark in future, kept on in gritty fashion. He finished well clear of the remainder and his rating is likely to shoot up again. (op 7-2)
Grand Diamond(IRE), 3lb higher than when third here in November, would have preferred better ground, but his record over hurdles now is just 1-13. (op 14-1)
Viva Colonia(IRE), 18lb higher than when winning on his first outing for this yard at Wetherby in November three starts previously, is a strong traveller but the ground almost certainly counted against him. (op 7-1)
Gringo, back over hurdles, never figured. (op 20-1)
King Fingal(IRE), keen on his handicap bow, was disappointing even though he looks to have started life in handicaps from quite a stiff mark. (op 9-1 tchd 11-1)

4150 NSPCC SCHOOL SERVICES NOVICES' H'CAP CHASE (16 fncs) 2m 4f
4:20 (4:20) (Class 4) (0-110,110) 5-Y-0+ **£3,903** (£1,146; £573; £286)

Form RPR
2623 **1** **Rossini's Dancer**[33] 3548 6-10-11 **95** .... MarkBradburne 109+
(Sue Bradburne) *hld up in tch: reminders after 9th: hdwy after 5 out: chal 3 out: led 2 out: hit last: sn hdd: rallied to regain ld nr fin* **8/1**[3]
1145 **2** *nk* **Quinder Spring (FR)**[34] 3522 7-11-8 **106** .... PeterBuchanan 119
(Lucinda Russell) *led 2nd to 7th: led again 9th: hdd 10th: lft in front 5 out: rdn whn hdd 2 out: regained ld run-in: kpt on: hdd again nr fin* **7/2**[2]
5-44 **3** *27* **Posh Bird (IRE)**[14] 3894 8-11-12 **110** .... JasonMaguire 96
(I R Ferguson, Ire) *led 1st: sn midfield: lost pl after 8th and sn bhd: wnt poor 3rd nr fin* **9/1**
-042 **4** *1* **Guns And Butter (IRE)**[33] 3549 9-11-2 **100** ....(t) GrahamLee 85
(Rose Dobbin) *in tch: racd keenly: lft 2nd 6 out: j. bdly lft 4 out: wknd after 3 out* **8/1**[3]
60-P **5** *19* **Nonotreally**[99] 2302 10-10-1 **92** .... MrRUtley(7) 58
(Lynsey Kendall) *hld up: a bhd* **66/1**
-641 **F** **Locked Inthepocket (IRE)**[4] 4064 7-11-4 **102** 7ex .... TimmyMurphy —
(Pauline Robson) *trckd ldr: led 7th: hdd 9th: led again 10th: 3 l up and gng wl whn fell 6 out* **8/11**[1]

5m 22.7s (21.50) **Going Correction** +1.20s/f (Heav) **6** Ran SP% **113.8**
Speed ratings: **105,104,94,93,86** —
toteswingers:1&2 £1.80, 2&3 £4.50, 1&3 £2.90 CSF £36.58 TOTE £9.60: £4.80, £2.10; EX 29.90.
Owner Turcan Barber Fletcher Dunning **Bred** Heather Raw **Trained** Cunnoquhie, Fife

FOCUS
The odds-on favourite departed six out, at which point the winner had plenty to do. The runner-up is rated to the level of his Market Rasen form.

NOTEBOOK
Rossini's Dancer, having just his sixth start over fences, was a modest third when he clouted the fifth-last but, making up a lot of ground going to the next, he was upsides three out. Less than fluent at the last, he dug deep to put his head in front near the line. (tchd 15-2)
Quinder Spring(FR), down in trip, made the best of his way home after being left in front. He went down fighting and should continue to give a good account of himself at this level, especially on a stiffer track going right-handed. (op 10-3 tchd 3-1)
Posh Bird(IRE), having just her third start over fences under rules, had finished behind the winner when they were third and fourth respectively here two outings ago, yet met him on 22lb worse terms. She struggled to keep up setting out on the final circuit, and was well behind before five out. She was handed a distant third on the run-in. (op 11-1)
Guns And Butter(IRE), with a tongue-tie back on, travelled strongly in the wake of the winner but stopped to nothing three out, and proceeded to jump violently left. He is a very weak finisher and was reported to have a breathing problem after the race. Official explanation: trainer's rep said gelding had a breathing problem (op 9-1 tchd 10-1)
Locked Inthepocket(IRE) was hoisted 15lb after his Ayr success and looked to have a good opportunity to follow up here under just a 7lb penalty. However, his jumping was not as good this time and, although in front, there was still plenty of work to be done when he crashed to the ground six out. (op 5-6)

4151 CMYK DIGITAL SOLUTIONS STANDARD OPEN NATIONAL HUNT FLAT RACE 2m
4:50 (4:51) (Class 5) 4-6-Y-0 **£1,626** (£477; £238; £119)

Form RPR
1 **Grandioso (IRE)** 4-10-0 0 .... PaulGallagher(7) 96+
(Howard Johnson) *trckd ldr: racd keenly: rdn over 2f out: led wl over 1f out: kpt on wl: comf* **4/1**[2]
2 **2** *5* **Pyjama Game (IRE)**[33] 3553 5-11-2 0 .... GrahamLee 99+
(Rose Dobbin) *in tch and t.k.h: rdn and outpcd 4f out: styd on wl fr over 1f out: wnt 2nd fnl 50yds* **8/11**[1]
040 **3** *2* **Dizzy River (IRE)**[21] 3752 6-11-2 0 .... TimmyMurphy 97
(George Charlton) *prom on inner: rdn over 3f out: kpt on same pce: lost 2nd fnl 50yds* **15/2**[3]
53 **4** *3/4* **Think Green**[10] 3971 5-10-6 0 .... HarryHaynes(3) 89
(James Ewart) *led: rdn whn hdd wl over 1f out: no ex ins fnl f* **12/1**
5 *3 1/2* **Danny Mags (IRE)** 4-10-2 0 .... MrTomDavid(5) 85
(Tim Vaughan) *trckd ldrs: rdn over 3f out: wknd fnl 2f* **14/1**
6 *16* **Big Red Cat (IRE)** 5-10-2 0 .... GMalone(7) 70
(John Daniel Moore, Ire) *hld up: rdn over 3f out: n.d* **25/1**
0 **7** *7* **Dancing Gizmo**[136] 1702 6-10-13 0 .... EwanWhillans(3) 70
(Alistair Whillans) *in tch on outer: chsd ldr over 4f out: rdn and wknd fnl 2f* **40/1**
8 *1/2* **Mr Mansson (IRE)** 4-10-2 0 .... AlexanderVoy(5) 60
(Lucy Normile) *hld up: a towards rr* **22/1**

3m 52.7s (9.90) **Going Correction** +0.35s/f (Yiel)
WFA 4 from 5yo+ 9lb **8** Ran SP% **114.7**
Speed ratings: **89,86,85,85,83 75,71,71**
toteswingers:1&2 £1.30, 2&3 £2.90, 1&3 £2.50. totesuper7: Win: Not won. Place: £64.00. CSF £7.14 TOTE £4.30: £1.10, £1.02, £2.30; EX 8.50.
Owner Andrea & Graham Wylie **Bred** Frank Barry **Trained** Billy Row, Co Durham

FOCUS
Probably just an ordinary bumper, run at a steady pace until the runners were in line for home. The three in the frame behind the winner are rated close to their marks.

NOTEBOOK
Grandioso(IRE) ◆, quite an imposing, deep-girthed son of Westerner, cost 30,000euros. He showed a willing attitude and came clear in the end for a most decisive success. He looks a fine long term hurdling prospect. (op 9-2)
Pyjama Game(IRE), who had Dizzy River and Think Green behind when runner-up first time out here a month previously, was being nudged along at halfway. Completely outpaced turning in and only sixth 3f out, he stayed on strongly to snatch second spot late on. He may need better ground, but basically looks one paced. (tchd 4-5)
Dizzy River(IRE), who had 5l to find with Pyjama Game, stuck to the inner in the home straight and still looks inexperienced. (op 7-1)
Think Green again travelled strongly in front and went for home coming off the final turn. She still looks on the weak side and should make a better hurdler in time. (op 16-1)
Danny Mags(IRE), who has a jumping pedigree, showed a glimmer of ability on his racecourse debut. (op 10-1)
T/Jkpt: £4,733.30 to a £1 stake. Pool of £10,000.00 - 1.50 winning tickets. T/Plt: £27.30 to a £1 stake. Pool of £51,717.60 - 1,381.39 winning tickets. T/Qpdt: £18.40 to a £1 stake. Pool of £3,399.66 - 136.20 winning tickets. AS

4156 - 4158a (Foreign Racing) - See Raceform Interactive

3937 FFOS LAS (L-H)
Thursday, February 17

OFFICIAL GOING: Soft (good to soft in places; 7.1)
Wind: Fresh across Weather: Fine

4159 E.B.F./SUN TRADE WINDOWS "NATIONAL HUNT" NOVICES' HURDLE (QUALIFIER) (10 hdls) 2m 4f
2:00 (2:00) (Class 4) 4-7-Y-0 **£3,252** (£955; £477; £238)

Form RPR
03 **1** **Maringo Bay (IRE)**[31] 3600 6-10-13 0 .... PeterToole(3) 138+
(Charlie Mann) *in tch: hdwy 6th: sn trcking ldrs: led 3 out: drew clr fr next: pushed out* **33/1**
4213 **2** *9* **Teaforthree (IRE)**[68] 2888 7-11-8 138 .... APMcCoy 136+
(Rebecca Curtis) *trckd ldrs: led after 7th: sn hdd: drvn 2 out: kpt on same pce* **2/1**[1]
4U **3** *11* **Invictus (IRE)**[23] 3719 5-11-2 0 .... RobertThornton 120+
(Alan King) *chsd ldrs: drvn bef 3 out where hmpd: one pce after* **2/1**[1]
4U31 **4** *4* **Grey Gold (IRE)**[35] 3526 6-11-8 127 .... JodieMogford 119
(Richard Lee) *t.k.h early: mid-div: hdwy 6th: one pce fr 3 out* **9/1**[3]
22U0 **5** *5* **Alesandro Mantegna (IRE)**[26] 3686 6-11-2 115 ....(p) JamieMoore 109
(Keith Goldsworthy) *trckd ldr: led 4th tl after 7th: u.p whn hmpd next: no ch after* **40/1**
0125 **6** *16* **Tullyraine (IRE)**[50] 3197 7-11-8 132 .... PaddyBrennan 98
(Nigel Twiston-Davies) *led to 4th: remained prom: hrd drvn after 7th: sn wknd* **9/2**[2]
24-1 **7** *17* **Silver Token**[130] 1795 6-11-8 118 .... TomScudamore 81
(David Brace) *mid-div: dropped to rr after 4th: struggling next: sn lost tch: t.o* **50/1**
0060 **8** *7* **Bridge Street Boy**[18] 3836 6-10-11 0 .... GilesHawkins(5) 68
(Richard Lee) *a in rr: struggling 5th: wl bhd fr next: t.o* **200/1**
62 **9** *27* **Fireitfromye (IRE)**[16] 3864 6-11-2 0 .... DarylJacob 41
(Alan Fleming) *mid-div: hit 6th: sn wknd: t.o* **33/1**
6 **F** **Croan Rock (IRE)**[100] 2291 6-11-2 0 .... DaveCrosse 117
(Ian Williams) *towards rr: hdwy 6th: outpcd by ldng pair 3 out: disputing 3rd whn fell next* **150/1**
02 **F** **Saint Are (FR)**[25] 3692 5-11-12 122 .... RichardJohnson 130
(Tim Vaughan) *trckd ldrs: cl 3rd and pushed along whn fell 3 out* **11/1**
52F **U** **Roper (IRE)**[69] 2873 6-10-13 117 .... RichieMcLernon(3) —
(Jonjo O'Neill) *towards rr: shkn up appr 6th: lost tch after next: no ch whn hmpd by loose horse 3 out and uns rdr* **50/1**
0 **B** **Shootin The Breeze (IRE)**[64] 2960 6-11-2 0 .... HaddenFrost 109
(David Pipe) *hld up: hdwy 7th: in tch in 7th and rdn whn b.d 3 out* **33/1**
P0 **P** **Fair Rome**[12] 3942 7-10-6 0 .... DonalDevereux(3) —
(Peter Bowen) *a in rr: struggling 5th: t.o whn p.u bef 3 out* **250/1**

4m 50.9s (1.90) **Going Correction** +0.425s/f (Soft) **14** Ran SP% **119.9**
Speed ratings: **113,109,105,103,101 95,88,85,74,— —,—,—,—**
toteswingers: 1&2 £14.70, 1&3 £43.40, 2&3 £1.50. CSF £100.54 TOTE £51.30: £8.60, £1.30, £1.10; EX 155.60.
Owner John & Peter Heron **Bred** J R McAleese **Trained** Upper Lambourn, Berks

FOCUS
A really strong contest judged on the form shown by those at the head of the market, so this is a race that should produce plenty of winners. Maringo Bay is rated up 10lb on his recent chase run and the two fallers were heading for personal bests.

NOTEBOOK
Maringo Bay(IRE) ◆ showed plenty of ability over fences on his previous start behind Mamlook, so it was a bit of a surprise to see him over hurdles. Keen in rear, he moved up going really well and lengthened nicely when asked to quicken. This was an impressive performance and he looks a horse with a big future. (op 20-1)
Teaforthree(IRE) ◆, returning from an absence after finishing a fine third in a 3m Grade 2 which has worked out well, settled in just behind the leaders and was the only one to make the winner work for victory. He undoubtedly bumped into a potentially smart sort, but will be helped by going up in trip again. (op 9-4)
Invictus(IRE) would have almost certainly won at Leicester last time had his rider not come off after the second-last hurdle, but he struggled to make any impact in this the moment he came off the bridle rounding the final bend. Saint Are's departure three out did hamper him, but it made no difference to his finishing position. His victory in a point came on good to firm ground, so he might be one for handicaps on better ground. (op 9-4 tchd 5-2 in places)
Grey Gold(IRE) ◆ is well regarded and won easily at Hereford in January. Up 3f in distance, he took a strong hold under restraint and was travelling with menace turning in. However, his effort was short-lived and the step up in class at this trip was a bit too much for him at this stage of his career. (op 17-2 tchd 8-1)
Tullyraine(IRE) was pitched in at the deep end on his previous start when trying his luck in the Grade 1 Challow Hurdle, and didn't run too badly, despite being well held. Sent straight into a prominent position, he came under pressure before four out and was most disappointing. (op 11-2)
Croan Rock(IRE) ◆, another chaser in the making, showed more than enough before falling two out to suggest he'll be winning races. (op 10-1 tchd 12-1)
Saint Are(FR) ◆ was still bang there when falling three out. He is a lovely looking sort, every inch a chaser in stature, and is one for the future. (op 10-1 tchd 12-1)
Shootin The Breeze(IRE) was staying on when brought down three out. (op 10-1 tchd 12-1)

4160 BRACEYS FRIENDLY BUILDERS MERCHANT NOVICES' H'CAP CHASE (16 fncs 2 omitted) 3m
2:30 (2:30) (Class 4) (0-110,109) 5-Y-0+ **£4,228** (£1,241; £620; £310)

Form RPR
-645 **1** **Winterwood (IRE)**[32] 3586 8-11-12 **109** ....(v) APMcCoy 127+
(Tim Vaughan) *trckd ldr to 4th: styd prom: wnt 2nd again 7th: hit 11th: sn rdn: led 4 out tl narrowly hdd 2 out: led again last: drvn out* **13/8**[1]

6-FP **2** *1 3/4* **Arturo Uno (IRE)**[33] 3562 8-11-4 **104**.................. SamTwiston-Davies(3) 120
(Nigel Twiston-Davies) *racd in cl tch: rdn to chal 4 out: slt ld 2 out: hdd and pckd last: no ex flat* **9/2**[3]
5154 **3** *16* **Cold Harbour**[13] 3933 7-10-12 **95**.. JamieMoore 98
(Evan Williams) *led: tended to jump lft: rdn and hdd 4 out: wknd after next* **8/1**
2634 **4** *60* **Reblis (FR)**[14] 3907 6-11-4 **106**....................................(v1) JoshuaMoore(5) 46
(Gary Moore) *prom: trckd ldr 4th to 7th: sn drvn along: dropped to rr 11th: lost tch after next: t.o* **3/1**[2]
10FP **P** **Buailteoir (IRE)**[38] 3482 9-10-13 **96**.....................................(tp) RhysFlint —
(Evan Williams) *towards rr: mstke 5th: rdn and lost tch 8th: p.u bef next* **40/1**
P133 **P** **Sordid Secret (IRE)**[11] 3963 8-11-3 **100**............................ PaulMoloney —
(Evan Williams) *in rr: reminders 6th: sn drvn and lost tch: t.o whn p.u bef 9th* **10/1**
32F4 **P** **Moorlands Teri**[21] 3763 8-10-13 **101**.............................(t) MrTomDavid(5) —
(Tim Vaughan) *towards rr: mstke 5th: drvn 9th: lost tch 11th: t.o whn blnd 3 out: p.u bef next* **16/1**

6m 15.7s (-7.30) **Going Correction** -0.175s/f (Good) **7** Ran SP% **109.8**
Speed ratings: **105,104,99,79,—,—,—**
toteswingers: 1&2 £4.00, 1&3 £5.00, 2&3 £5.80. CSF £8.89 TOTE £3.80: £3.00, £1.20; EX 13.90.
Owner Mrs L D Edwards **Bred** E Tynan **Trained** Aberthin, Vale of Glamorgan

FOCUS
A modest but competitive race in which trainer Evan Williams provided three of the seven runners. A massive step up from the winner on his modest chase form.

NOTEBOOK
Winterwood(IRE), with a visor back on after running in cheekpieces, raced prominently but made hard work of victory. However, one certainly could not fault his courage, as he kept finding for pressure, and a good jump at the last sealed it. (op 6-4)
Arturo Uno(IRE) had failed to complete in his previous two outings but seemed to be going best on the final bend, and got into a share of the lead four out. He was only one-paced from that point, and an untidy leap at the final fence just about ended his challenge. That said, this was much better and he should have a low-grade handicap in him. (op 4-1 tchd 5-1)
Cold Harbour, a winner at this course over 2m3.5f in November, set off in front and attacked his fences until his stamina appeared to give way when joined. He tended to jump to his left and there is no strong evidence yet to suggest he stays 3m. (op 9-1 tchd 11-1)
Reblis(FR), wearing a visor for the first time, enjoyed himself while the pressure wasn't on but showed less enthusiasm when his jockey asked for some effort. (op 7-2)
Buailteoir(IRE) Official explanation: jockey said gelding lost its action

4161 SUN TRADE WINDOWS MARES' H'CAP HURDLE (11 hdls) 2m 6f
3:05 (3:05) (Class 4) (0-115,109) 4-Y-0+ **£3,252** (£955; £477; £238)

Form RPR
030F **1** **Copsehill Girl (IRE)**[38] 3487 6-11-4 **101**..................... WayneHutchinson 108+
(Ian Williams) *trckd ldrs: lft in 2nd at 5th: r.o to take slt ld appr 2 out: rdn clr flat* **14/1**
33P1 **2** *6* **Rith Bob (IRE)**[31] 3607 8-11-12 **109**.................................... PaulMoloney 113+
(David Rees) *led: rdn and jnd 3 out: hdd appr 2 out: kpt on same pce tl eased whn hld by wnr fnl 50yds* **5/2**[2]
0523 **3** *15* **Illysantachristina**[18] 3839 8-9-13 **89**............................... MarkQuinlan(7) 76
(Bernard Llewellyn) *chsd ldrs: hit 7th: ev ch 3 out: sn drvn: wknd fr next* **7/1**
-531 **4** *1 3/4* **Lady De La Vega (FR)**[13] 3933 7-11-4 **101**...........................(vt) APMcCoy 89+
(Tim Vaughan) *trckd ldr tl blnd bdly and lost pl 5th: clsd again 8th: sn drvn: 4th and wkng whn mstke 3 out* **2/1**[1]
31P6 **5** *3* **Sweet Seville (FR)**[10] 3980 7-11-1 **105**........................... MattCrawley(7) 86
(Terry Clement) *in rr: rdn after 8th: sn lost tch* **25/1**
5-P0 **6** *12* **Pearl (IRE)**[35] 3529 7-11-1 **98**..(bt) DPFahy 67
(Alison Thorpe) *t.k.h in rr: hdwy bef 3rd: drvn and wknd after 8th: t.o* **28/1**
6516 **7** *9* **Gilwen Glory (IRE)**[8] 4009 8-11-2 **106**........................... AodhaganConlon(7) 66
(Evan Williams) *towards rr: nt fluent 5th: drvn fr next: lost tch 8th: t.o* **3/1**[3]

5m 34.2s (16.20) **Going Correction** +0.425s/f (Soft) **7** Ran SP% **113.4**
Speed ratings (Par 105): **87,84,79,78,77 73,70**
toteswingers: 1&2 £5.50, 1&3 £16.80, 2&3 £2.90. CSF £49.30 CT £272.18 TOTE £39.10: £11.50, £2.80; EX 71.50.
Owner Denis Gallagher **Bred** Hans-Juergen Kuehnle **Trained** Portway, Worcs

FOCUS
Not a strong contest. A massive step up from the winner with the second to form.

NOTEBOOK
Copsehill Girl(IRE), who fell at the final hurdle last time when in a poor fourth, was given a patient ride before coming through to have every chance down the home straight. She took a few strides to assert when upsides Rith Bob but found enough to collect victory. A point winner before racing under rules, she clearly stays well and handles easy ground. (op 11-1 tchd 16-1)
Rith Bob(IRE) bolted up in a novice hurdle on her previous start (officially rated 107 for that contest) and was sent straight into the lead here. She had most of her rivals beaten off coming to three out but was unable to concede 8lb to the winner in the final stages. (op 3-1)
Illysantachristina, up 5f in trip, travelled strongly throughout but weakened quickly after two out. (op 13-2)
Lady De La Vega(FR), an 11l winner of a low-grade Chepstow handicap chase on her previous start, settled nicely in second place but made a bad blunder at the fifth and dropped back through the field. She didn't jump that fluently thereafter and, although making a brief effort nearing the final bend, was readily held. (op 5-2)
Gilwen Glory(IRE), who won at this course over 3m in mid-January, didn't look to be going well early and ran dreadfully. Something may well have been amiss, as she showed little interest under pressure. (tchd 5-2)

4162 DUNRAVEN WINDOWS NOVICES' CHASE (15 fncs 2 omitted) 2m 5f
3:40 (3:40) (Class 3) 5-Y-0+ **£5,204** (£1,528; £764; £381)

Form RPR
-411 **1** **Kerada (FR)**[21] 3763 7-11-1 136.. BarryGeraghty 141+
(Nicky Henderson) *trckd ldr: hit 4th: chal 7th: led 9th and sn increased pce: drew clr fr 4 out: v easily* **2/5**[1]
552- **2** *12* **Princeful (FR)**[432] 2847 8-10-12 0.. RhysFlint 121
(Evan Williams) *t.k.h: racd in 3rd pl: lost tch w ldng pair after 11th: blnd 2 out: wnt mod 2nd flat: no ch w wnr* **14/1**[3]
P41 **3** *4* **Quo Video (FR)**[25] 3694 7-11-4 138.......................................(t) APMcCoy 124
(Tim Vaughan) *led: jnd 7th: hdd 9th: pushed along and lft bhd by wnr fr 4 out: 15 l adrift and wkng whn blnd bdly 2 out: blnd last and sn lost 2nd* **7/2**[2]
21P0 **4** *41* **Simarian (IRE)**[32] 3587 6-11-4 128.................................... PaulMoloney 80
(Evan Williams) *racd keenly in last pl: blnd 5th: mstke 9th: wknd and lost tch 11th: t.o* **14/1**[3]

5m 43.9s (13.90) **Going Correction** -0.175s/f (Good) **4** Ran SP% **107.0**
Speed ratings: **66,61,59,44**
CSF £5.63 TOTE £1.70; EX 5.50.
Owner Turf Club 2010 **Bred** E A R L La Croix Sonnet **Trained** Upper Lambourn, Berks

FOCUS
The early pace was virtually non-existent, but the winner was in a different league to her rivals. There is probably more to come from her.

NOTEBOOK
Kerada(FR) ◆ has taken really well to chasing, so although she was down in distance after winning here over 3m last time, she looked the one to beat. Settled in second until matching strides with Quo Video at halfway, she went on heading into the final bend and came readily clear. One can easily see her winning a decent handicap if connections decide to take on a better calibre of rival, but it seems likely that she'll head for the final of the mares' novice chase series at Newbury. (op 1-3)
Princeful(FR) ◆, making his debut for this trainer, took a really keen hold and was never likely to get home as a result. A strong-looking type, he will be better than he showed here with this start under his belt following a short break, especially when there is a better gallop to chase. (op 16-1)
Quo Video(FR) won by 5l last time at Market Rasen when a tongue-tie was tried for the first time and was sent straight into the lead here. He had no response to the winner when she went on, though, and he hit the final two fences, the second-last especially hard. (op 4-1)
Simarian(IRE), back over fences, was ridden with restraint and made a couple of errors on the way round. He was beaten on the home bend and his jockey quickly accepted the situation. (op 22-1 tchd 12-1)

4163 DUNRAVEN WELSH FOXHUNTERS HUNTERS' CHASE (16 fncs 2 omitted) 3m
4:15 (4:15) (Class 4) 5-Y-0+ **£4,372** (£1,355; £677; £338)

Form RPR
1F3- **1** **Sericina (FR)**[40] 8-11-0 117.. MissCRoddick(7) 132+
(Miss C Roddick) *hld up in mid-div: hdwy 10th: trckd ldr 12th: chal next: tk slt ld 2 out: r.o wl to assert flat* **15/8**[2]
3-26 **2** *2 3/4* **Herons Well**[8] 4011 8-11-11 138...................................(p) MrJoshHalley(7) 138
(Rebecca Curtis) *led: clr 9th to 11th: jnd 4 out: narrowly hdd 2 out: unable qck flat* **7/1**
4-64 **3** *17* **Gentle George**[14] 3908 8-12-4 124.. MrRBurton 122
(S Flook) *trckd ldrs: pushed along 11th: outpcd by ldng pair fr 4 out: plugged on one pce* **7/4**[1]
12-6 **4** *12* **Moncadou (FR)**[14] 3908 11-12-0 120....................................(t) MrAJBerry 109
(Jonjo O'Neill) *racd wd: in rr: hdwy 6th: lft chsng ldr 8th: lost 2nd 12th: rdn 4 out: sn wknd* **4/1**[3]
3564 **5** *44* **Classic Clover**[114] 2024 11-11-11 93.................................(t) MrMLegg(7) 65
(Colin Tizzard) *mid-div: mstke 2nd: sn pushed along: hrd rdn 9th: t.o fr 11th* **33/1**
165- **6** *20* **Holly Walk**[32] 10-11-4 103.. MrJCole(7) 38
(J Cole) *a in rr: lost tch 10th: t.o* **50/1**
13P- **P** **Celtic Boy (IRE)**[484] 1852 13-11-13 0.........................(t) MrDGPrichard(5) —
(Miss R Dando) *a in rr div: mstkes 3rd: 5th and 10th: wl bhd whn p.u bef 11th* **16/1**
-100 **P** **Apollo Blaze (IRE)**[14] 3908 10-11-7 95............................ MissVShaw(7) —
(Mrs P J Shaw) *trckd ldr tl blnd bdly and lost pl 8th: struggling 10th: t.o whn p.u bef 4 out* **50/1**

6m 17.4s (-5.60) **Going Correction** -0.175s/f (Good) **8** Ran SP% **116.4**
Speed ratings: **102,101,95,91,76 70,—,—**
toteswingers: 1&2 £3.80, 1&3 £1.10, 2&3 £1.70. CSF £15.59 TOTE £4.40: £1.20, £1.10, £1.80; EX 17.80.
Owner M T Sheppard **Bred** S T E Sogir **Trained** Shoscombe, Somerset

FOCUS
Those at the top of the market looked above-average performers for this type of event, so this is likely to be decent form, although it did look a sprint over the final three fences. Sericina is a high-class hunter and can probably rate higher.

NOTEBOOK
Sericina(FR) returned to her best in points (three from three, including two this winter) after a fall in the Cheltenham Foxhunter and a modest third at Taunton, albeit with an excuse. Chloe Roddick said before the race that her mount was in great heart, and so it proved, as the combination travelled strongly in behind before showing lots of pace to get on top after the final fence. It should be noted that she was getting plenty of weight from the runner-up, but her jockey/trainer reported afterwards that she will now go straight to Cheltenham for another try at the Foxhunters'. (tchd 7-4)
Herons Well, with cheekpieces back on, was quickly sent on and was allowed a sizable advantage at one stage. Closed down heading into the final bend, he responded to pressure and went down fighting after a prolonged battle with the winner. He will be difficult to catch under a similar ride around a sharper course. (op 13-2)
Gentle George, reunited with Richard Burton for the first time since the pair finished fourth in the 2010 Cheltenham Foxhunter, didn't run particularly well, as he should have handled the ground. He doesn't look the quickest, and may well be best off making the running if his jumping holds out. (op 2-1)
Moncadou(FR), who finished well behind Gentle George at Wincanton on their seasonal debuts, raced in rear and wide of his rivals early but cruised up as the first four broke clear, only to quickly fold under pressure. He is a two-time winner in heavy ground, so the easy going here couldn't be given as an excuse, and he has been disappointing this season after a good performance in last year's Fox Hunters' at Aintree. (tchd 9-2)

4164 BRACEYS FRIENDLY BUILDERS MERCHANT STANDARD OPEN NATIONAL HUNT FLAT RACE 2m
4:50 (4:50) (Class 5) 4-6-Y-0 **£1,626** (£477; £238; £119)

Form RPR
1 **Special Mate** 5-11-1 0.. SamTwiston-Davies(3) 106+
(Richard Lee) *trckd ldrs: wnt 2nd over 3f out: led over 2f out: sn hung lft: styd on wl* **8/1**
32 **2** *1 1/2* **Flemi Two Toes (IRE)**[13] 3936 5-11-4 0.................................... APMcCoy 102
(Rebecca Curtis) *led: rdn over 3f out: hdd over 2f out: kpt on same pce* **2/1**[1]
0 **3** *1 1/4* **All For Cash**[21] 3773 6-10-11 0.. MrCGreene(7) 101
(Kim Bailey) *prom: pushed along and reminders after 6f: lost pl 6f out: rallied u.p 2f out: styng on wl towards fin* **50/1**
2 **4** *6* **Roll The Dice (IRE)**[33] 3569 5-11-4 0.. RhysFlint 95
(Philip Hobbs) *trckd ldrs: rdn over 3f out: one pce fnl 2f* **5/1**
5 *1/2* **Pollystone (IRE)** 5-10-11 0... JoeTizzard 87
(Colin Tizzard) *in tch: hdwy 6f out: 5th and pushed along over 3f out: kpt on same pce* **11/4**[2]
6 *4 1/2* **Act Of Kindness (IRE)** 6-11-4 0.. DarylJacob 90
(Ben De Haan) *in rr: hdwy into 6th 6f out: rdn over 3f out: one pce* **25/1**
6-4 **7** *2 1/4* **Presenting Ace (IRE)**[50] 3200 5-11-4 0.......................(t) TomScudamore 88
(David Pipe) *trckd ldr: rdn 4f out: sn lost 2nd: wknd over 2f out* **9/2**[3]
8 *6* **Blue Bell House (IRE)**[109] 5-11-4 0.. RodiGreene 82
(Tracey Watkins) *in tch: t.k.h: rdn 4f out: wknd 3f out* **125/1**
9 *9* **Belle De Fontenay (FR)** 6-10-11 0................................. AndrewTinkler 66
(George Baker) *in rr of mid-div: t.k.h: wknd over 5f out* **40/1**
0 **10** *45* **Knight Blaze**[121] 1913 4-9-13 0...................................... DonalDevereux(3) 12
(David Brace) *a in rr: rdn 6f out: sn lost tch: t.o* **150/1**

11 14 **Moon Stream** 4-10-9 0 JamieMoore 5
(David Brace) *hld up in rr: rdn over 5f out: sn wknd: t.o* **66/1**

3m 49.6s (6.20) **Going Correction** +0.425s/f (Soft)
WFA 4 from 5yo+ 9lb **11** Ran SP% **117.2**
Speed ratings: **101,100,99,96,96 94,93,90,85,63 56**
toteswingers: 1&2 £9.00, 1&3 £14.10, 2&3 £14.10. CSF £23.95 TOTE £8.50: £1.90, £1.10, £19.50; EX 31.00.
Owner Walters Plant Hire Ltd **Bred** Jethro Bloodstock **Trained** Byton, H'fords

FOCUS
A fair bumper with mixed messages from the form. The second sets the level and the winner should go on to rate higher.

NOTEBOOK
Special Mate, whose dam is an unraced sister to Best Mate, Inca Trail and Cornish Rebel, fetched £38,000 at the sales as a 3-y-o and looks a fair prospect as he won despite being green and hanging under pressure. His connections can rightly dream considering his pedigree, especially as he seems sure to improve for the run. (op 12-1 tchd 14-1)
Flemi Two Toes(IRE) was sensibly given a positive ride considering his previous experience, but he found the winner too strong in the latter stages. He is an ideal marker for the form. (op 7-4)
All For Cash was hard ridden for a few strides at about halfway and lost ground. However, his rider never gave up and forced his mount to keep going into a staying-on third.
Roll The Dice(IRE) tracked the leader on the inside of the course but found only the one pace inside the final 2f. (op 10-3)
Pollystone(IRE) ◆, a half-sister to the multiple Irish graded hurdle winner Sweet Kiln, looked a little green at the business end of the race, and hung under pressure. That said, it was still a promising debut and any success she can gain will make her valuable as a broodmare. (op 4-1)
Act Of Kindness(IRE) ◆, nicely bred for jumping and related to plenty of winners, including Indian Scout, made eyecatching ground from the rear before his effort flattened out. He is one to watch for on better ground. (op 22-1)
Presenting Ace(IRE), with a tongue-tie on for the first time, raced up with the leader but didn't get home. His sire makes him worth another chance on a much quicker surface. (op 5-1 tchd 4-1)
Blue Bell House(IRE), pulled up in both of his starts in points, deserves a mention, as he ran a bit better than his final position suggests. (op 150-1 tchd 100-1)
T/Jkpt: Not won. T/Plt: £33.30 to a £1 stake. Pool: £62,272.23 - 1,361.51 winning tickets. T/Qpdt: £8.10 to a £1 stake. Pool: £4,728.75 - 427.10 winning tickets. RL

2547 KELSO (L-H)
Thursday, February 17

OFFICIAL GOING: Soft (heavy in places; 5.1)
Rails in innermost position providing fresh ground the whole way round on both courses.
Wind: Virtually Weather: dry and overcast

4165 KELSO MEMBERS NOVICES' HURDLE (8 hdls) 2m 110y
1:40 (1:42) (Class 4) 4-Y-0+ **£2,276** (£668; £334; £166)

Form				RPR
3/63	1		**Bogside (IRE)**[22] 3749 7-11-2 0 JanFaltejsek (George Charlton) *racd keenly: trckd ldrs: led 4th: hdd 3 out: rdn and led again sn after last: kpt on wl* **8/1**	111+
1P	2	2	**Music Of The Moor (IRE)**[15] 3885 4-11-0 0 JamesReveley (Tom Tate) *hld up: hdwy on inner bef 3 out: trckd ldrs after 2 out: nt rdn tl run-in: kpt on wl: wnt 2nd fnl 50yds* **11/4**[2]	107+
2111	3	nk	**Priceless Art (IRE)**[51] 3167 6-11-2 0 BarryKeniry (Alan Swinbank) *racd keenly: prom: lft in front after 3rd: hdd 4th: led again 3 out: rdn whn hdd run-in: kpt on but lost 2nd fnl 50yds* **11/8**[1]	109+
0	4	3 ½	**The Galloping Shoe**[34] 3547 6-10-13 0 EwanWhillans(3) (Alistair Whillans) *midfield and t.k.h: hdwy to trck ldrs whn nt fluent 3 out: rdn 2 out: kpt on* **33/1**	105
P3	5	3 ¼	**Rumble Of Thunder (IRE)**[24] 3715 5-11-2 0 RichieMcGrath (Kate Walton) *midfield: hmpd 2nd: hdwy to chse ldrs 2 out: rdn bef last: one pce run-in* **25/1**	102
	6	hd	**Quel Elite (FR)** 7-11-2 0 PaddyAspell (James Moffatt) *hld up: kpt on after 2 out: nrst fin* **100/1**	102
0	7	¾	**Gin Cobbler**[90] 2511 5-11-2 0 BrianHughes (Howard Johnson) *racd keenly: trckd ldrs: j.rt 2nd: ev ch last: wknd run-in* **66/1**	101
	8	12	**Nisaal (IRE)**[85] 6-11-2 0 FearghalDavis (Sandy Forster) *hld up in midfield: rdn whn swtchd rt appr last: wknd run-in* **80/1**	89
00	9	1 ¼	**Northern Acres**[6] 4059 5-11-2 0 MarkBradburne (Sue Bradburne) *midfield: wknd after 2 out* **100/1**	88
0	10	17	**Saga Surprise (FR)**[17] 3850 6-11-2 0 (t) MichaelMcAlister (Maurice Barnes) *hld up in midfield: wknd after 2 out: wl hld whn mstke last* **200/1**	71
P	11	12	**Cigalas**[97] 2349 6-11-2 0 RobertWalford (Jean McGregor) *trckd ldrs: hit 4th: wknd after 2 out* **200/1**	59
PP	12	1	**Daredevil Dan**[15] 3885 5-11-2 0 DenisO'Regan (Tina Jackson) *hld up: hit 3 out: a towards rr* **200/1**	58
50	13	3 ¾	**Barello Road**[34] 3547 5-10-9 0 CampbellGillies (Lucinda Russell) *prom: wknd after 3 out* **100/1**	47
P	14	10	**Why Are You Asking (IRE)**[15] 3887 6-11-2 0 WilsonRenwick (Rose Dobbin) *hld up in midfield: wknd after 2 out* **100/1**	44
0	15	26	**Arikinui**[17] 3850 6-10-2 0 GaryRutherford(7) (Stuart Coltherd) *midfield: wknd after 3 out: t.o* **200/1**	11
411	P		**Jukebox Melody (IRE)**[34] 3553 5-11-2 0 GrahamLee (Malcolm Jefferson) *plld hrd: led 1st: rn wd on bnd after 3rd and sn p.u* **4/1**[3]	—

4m 18.3s (16.50) **Going Correction** +0.875s/f (Soft)
WFA 4 from 5yo+ 9lb **16** Ran SP% **115.3**
Speed ratings (Par 105): **96,95,94,93,91 91,91,85,85,77 71,70,69,64,52** —
toteswingers: 1&2 £4.20, 1&3 £3.20, 2&3 £1.40. CSF £29.11 TOTE £7.60: £1.80, £1.40, £1.20; EX 30.60.
Owner Mrs A R Wood **Bred** Pat O'Donovan **Trained** Stocksfield, Northumberland

FOCUS
A modest novice hurdle. The pace was slow and some of these could be flattered. The first two are rated below their previous marks.

NOTEBOOK
Bogside(IRE) was never far behind the pace and, although pulling for his head, was always travelling powerfully, and he displayed a good turn of foot to move past a pair of useful rivals on the run-in. He jumped fluently on his hurdling debut at Musselburgh last month behind a subsequent winner and built on that promise here. He had fair form in bumpers but looks better suited to the hurdling game. (op 15-2 tchd 7-1)
Music Of The Moor(IRE), a fair sort at up to 1m4f on the Flat, made a successful switch to hurdles in a heavy-ground juvenile at Sandown last month and was unlucky last time when his saddle slipped. Well backed to make amends, he caught the eye making smooth progress from the rear but was given plenty to do on the long run-in. However, he was reported to have sustained a fracture during the race and will now face a long period on the sidelines. (op 3-1 tchd 10-3)
Priceless Art(IRE) ◆ was heavily supported to make a winning hurdling debut. Held in high regard by his trainer, and a four-time bumper winner, he was keen up with the pace and was left in front when Jukebox Melody took himself out of the race. Although one-paced on the run-in, he ran encouragingly considering his trainer didn't think he would act on the testing surface, and ultimately better ground will suit. (op 15-8 tchd 5-4)
The Galloping Shoe went as well as anything approaching the last before a slow jump halted his momentum. He might have needed the run when well beaten in a maiden hurdle at Musselburgh and shaped well on his second start over hurdles. He stayed on for pressure after the last and obviously retains a deal of ability from the Flat (officially rated 83 in that sphere). He can build on this.
Rumble Of Thunder(IRE) was too keen and needs to settle better. Official explanation: jockey said, regarding running and riding, that his orders were to get the gelding to relax, get it into a nice rhythm and jumping and to do his best, he made his effort in the home straight, pushing with hands and heels all the way to the line; vet said gelding finished lame. (op 22-1 tchd 20-1)
Quel Elite(FR) travelled well on his hurdling debut before tiring in the ground and has a future.
Jukebox Melody(IRE) caused drama when, after pulling hard, he ran extremely wide on the bend after the third and had to be pulled up. A dual bumper winner, he deserves another chance over hurdles but a watching brief is required after this errant performance. (op 3-1)

4166 OSWALD HUGHES H'CAP HURDLE (10 hdls) 2m 2f
2:10 (2:10) (Class 4) (0-110,110) 4-Y-0+ **£2,602** (£764; £382; £190)

Form				RPR
05-1	1		**Circus Clown (IRE)**[5] 4068 6-11-0 **98** 7ex GrahamLee (Jim Goldie) *trckd ldr on inner: led last: kpt on wl* **13/8**[1]	105+
-002	2	3 ¼	**Willie Hall**[29] 3633 7-11-4 **102** CampbellGillies (William Amos) *trckd ldr: led after 2 out: hdd last: kpt on run-in but no match for wnr* **9/2**[3]	106
-254	3	½	**Texas Holdem (IRE)**[25] 3696 12-11-5 **110** PeterCarberry(7) (Michael Smith) *midfield: hdwy on outer to trck ldrs 3 out: rdn 2 out: kpt on run-in* **4/1**[2]	113
10-0	4	3 ½	**Well Disguised (IRE)**[279] 316 9-11-0 **108** CallumWhillans(10) (Donald Whillans) *midfield: hdwy on outer after 3 out: ev ch last: one pce run-in* **33/1**	107
1000	5	nk	**No Supper (IRE)**[17] 3855 7-10-13 **97** BarryKeniry (George Bewley) *hld up in midfield: hdwy on inner after 3 out: kpt on one pce run-in* **50/1**	95
4530	6	¾	**Rain Stops Play (IRE)**[35] 3523 9-11-10 **108** FearghalDavis (Nicky Richards) *hld up in rr: styd on after 2 out: n.d* **50/1**	105
-3P0	7	5	**Super Baby (FR)**[35] 3523 9-10-11 **98** (p) HarryHaynes(3) (James Ewart) *led: hdd after 3 out: wknd run-in* **16/1**	91
502	8	15	**Quacity (FR)**[17] 3855 7-11-7 **105** PeterBuchanan (Lucinda Russell) *trckd ldr in 2nd: led after 3 out: hdd after 2 out: wknd run-in* **10/1**	87
0-21	9	3 ½	**Scrum V**[25] 3697 7-10-13 **97** PaddyAspell (John Davies) *trckd ldr on outer: wknd after 3 out* **16/1**	73
5-	10	13	**Suprise Vendor (IRE)**[130] 1269 5-11-3 **108** GaryRutherford(7) (Stuart Coltherd) *hld up on outer: nt fluent 6th: a towards rr* **40/1**	69
1265	11	9	**Dream Risk (FR)**[111] 2076 5-11-8 **106** (t) RichieMcGrath (Kate Walton) *midfield on inner: wknd after 4 out* **14/1**	58
-650	12	11	**Melange (USA)**[36] 3509 5-11-4 **102** (t) JanFaltejsek (George Charlton) *trckd ldrs: lost pl after 5th: bhd fr 7th* **16/1**	43

4m 44.7s (17.70) **Going Correction** +0.875s/f (Soft) **12** Ran SP% **119.0**
Speed ratings (Par 105): **95,93,93,91,91 91,89,82,80,75 71,66**
toteswingers: 1&2 £5.20, 1&3 £2.50, 2&3 £5.60. CSF £9.42 CT £25.27 TOTE £2.50: £1.20, £2.50, £2.10; EX 12.40.
Owner David McKenzie **Bred** Floors Farming & The Duke Of Devonshire **Trained** Uplawmoor, E Renfrews

FOCUS
A moderate handicap. A step up from the winner with the second improving to his bumper mark.

NOTEBOOK
Circus Clown(IRE) has looked a different proposition in handicaps since running for his new yard. He won a competitive handicap hurdle at Ayr readily last time, and defied the handicapper's 7lb rise with authority, staying on strongly after saving ground on the inside throughout. He will go up for this but in his current form must be followed under another penalty. (op 11-4, tchd 3-1 in a place)
Willie Hall, well backed for his handicap debut, looked fairly treated on his best hurdles form, and showed a likeable attitude to run on right to the line for second. This looks a workable mark for this lightly raced 7-y-o. (op 7-2)
Texas Holdem(IRE) had gone close over this C&D in the past and again showed a liking for the course with a staying-on third. He looks set for 2m4f in due course. (op 9-2 tchd 7-2)
Well Disguised(IRE) performed admirably after a 279-day absence, just tiring in the closing stages. He will strip fitter next time.
No Supper(IRE) is inconsistent but ran better than of late, looking to handle testing conditions better than some.
Rain Stops Play(IRE) travelled strongly before floundering on the surface after the last. He would like better ground. (op 33-1)

4167 LLOYD VADERSTAD H'CAP CHASE (17 fncs) 2m 6f 110y
2:40 (2:40) (Class 3) (0-130,126) 5-Y-0+ **£3,903** (£1,146; £573; £286)

Form				RPR
/1-2	1		**Always Right (IRE)**[124] 1871 9-11-4 **118** BrianHughes (John Wade) *trckd ldr on outer: led on bridle last: pushed clr run-in: comf* **7/4**[1]	137+
5252	2	8	**Camden George (IRE)**[25] 3695 10-10-12 **112** TjadeCollier (Sue Smith) *in tch: reminder 6th: rdn and outpcd after 4 out: styd on appr last: wnt 2nd nr fin* **11/2**[3]	120
2U-5	3	1	**Hockenheim (FR)**[101] 2272 10-10-10 **117** MrJBewley(7) (George Bewley) *led: rdn whn hdd last: wknd and lost 2nd nr fin* **16/1**	123
4241	4	11	**Lockstown**[15] 3886 8-10-6 **106** (p) GrahamLee (Ann Hamilton) *hld up in tch: rdn after 4 out: wknd bef last* **7/1**	101
136P	5	1	**Or De Grugy (FR)**[29] 3634 9-11-4 **123** AlexanderVoy(5) (Sue Bradburne) *prom: rdn after 4 out: wknd bef last* **16/1**	117
5F22	6	7	**Dawn Ride (IRE)**[33] 3574 10-11-3 **117** (p) BarryKeniry (Micky Hammond) *hld up: rdn after 12th: a in rr* **14/1**	107
11/2	F		**Phardessa**[32] 3587 10-11-5 **119** SeanQuinlan (Richard Phillips) *hld up: mstke and fell 1st* **8/1**	—
3-24	U		**Heez A Steel (IRE)**[35] 3522 10-11-5 **126** AlistairFindlay(7) (George Charlton) *prom: reminder and lost pl after 7th: 6th whn blnd and uns rdr 12th* **4/1**[2]	—

6m 0.25s (15.75) **Going Correction** +0.875s/f (Soft) **8** Ran SP% **113.8**
Speed ratings: **107,104,103,100,99 97,—,—**
toteswingers: 1&2 £3.90, 1&3 £20.30, 2&3 £10.80. CSF £12.15 CT £112.70 TOTE £3.50: £1.20, £2.60, £5.80; EX 14.10.

Owner John Wade **Bred** John Kelleher **Trained** Mordon, Co Durham

FOCUS

A modest handicap won easily by an unexposed chaser, who can rate higher. The second and third set the level.

NOTEBOOK

Always Right(IRE) ◆, heavily supported throughout the morning, made short work of his rivals under a confident ride. He was kept widest of all in search of better ground and jumped enthusiastically throughout. He's a prolific winning pointer and a C&D winner in a hunter chase last March, and showed he is in good heart with a comfortable success. No doubt he will be raised in the weights, but if turned out again here he will be hard to beat as he's unexposed. (op 5-2)

Camden George(IRE) is too consistent for his own good and is often raised in the weights for being beaten. He responded well to pressure from some way out, but was beaten by an unexposed sort, and he's now 1-21 over fences. (op 6-1 tchd 7-1)

Hockenheim(FR) put in a bold display of jumping out in front but couldn't sustain the decent gallop at the business end. This may have been needed after a break. (op 18-1 tchd 14-1)

Lockstown, tried in cheekpieces, saved ground on the inside but when push came to shove he didn't find as much as had looked likely. He was fortunate to land a chase at Newcastle recently when left to coast home after there were multiple fallers, and his overall profile looks patchy. (op 15-2 tchd 8-1 and 6-1)

4168 TIMEFORM FESTIVAL TRIAL NOVICES' CHASE (12 fncs) 2m 1f

3:15 (3:15) (Class 2) 5-Y-0+ **£8,066** (£2,368; £1,184; £591)

Form RPR

3421 **1** **Premier Sagas (FR)**[17] 3852 7-11-5 129 DougieCostello 144+
(Nicky Richards) *w ldr: led 5th: pushed clr after last: easily* **9/4**[2]

/154 **2** *22* **Alfie Flits**[33] 3571 9-11-5 127 BarryKeniry 120
(Alan Swinbank) *led: hdd 5th: mstke 4 out: nt fluent and lost pl 2 out: plugged on again run-in: wnt 2nd nr fin* **7/1**

2-1U **3** *½* **King O'The Gypsies (IRE)**[8] 4002 6-11-0 0 BrianHughes 118+
(Howard Johnson) *in tch in 3rd: blnd 7th and lost pl: hdwy after 4 out: wnt 2nd last: no ex towards fin* **11/8**[1]

0-12 **4** *3 ¾* **Thumbs Up**[23] 3722 6-11-5 0 JasonMaguire 115
(Donald McCain) *hld up in 4th: tk clsr order after 8th: hit next: wnt 2nd 2 out: wknd after last* **7/2**[3]

204 **P** **Soul Magic (IRE)**[17] 3853 9-11-0 83 GaryRutherford —
(Harriet Graham) *hld up in rr: t.o after 5th: p.u bef last* **100/1**

4m 32.4s (14.40) **Going Correction** +0.875s/f (Soft) 5 Ran SP% **108.6**

Speed ratings: **101,90,90,88,—**

CSF £15.80 TOTE £3.90: £2.00, £3.10; EX 16.10.

Owner David Wesley Yates **Bred** Edgar Van Haaren **Trained** Greystoke, Cumbria

FOCUS

A fair little novice chase and an easy winner who was the form pick. The form is rated through the second.

NOTEBOOK

Premier Sagas(FR), down in trip after winning a novice event over 2m4f at Ayr recently, he was given a positive ride by Dougie Costello and was able to use his proven stamina after taking up the running going onto the final circuit. He jumped best of the bunch and the further he went the better he looked. He looks one to follow when back up in trip and connections are keen to go for the 2m4f handicap chase at Cheltenham. (op 15-8)

Alfie Flits put a couple of disappointing performances behind him with a better showing. He scoped badly after a no-show at Wetherby last month but stayed on adequately on the run-in to fend off King O'The Gypsies for second. (op 13-2 tchd 5-1)

King O'The Gypsies(IRE) looks to have had his confidence dented after unseating his jockey at Carlisle, jumping sketchily at many of his fences on this occasion. To his credit he plugged on and found plenty for pressure to almost grab second. (op 7-4 after 2-1 in a place)

Thumbs Up ran down the final fence when tiring and may have been found out by the testing conditions. (op 4-1 tchd 10-3)

4169 VICTOR CHANDLER MOREBATTLE HURDLE (10 hdls) 2m 2f

3:50 (3:50) (Class 2) 4-Y-0+ **£9,757** (£2,865; £1,432; £715)

Form RPR

11-1 **1** **Peddlers Cross (IRE)**[82] 2668 6-11-10 162 JasonMaguire 161+
(Donald McCain) *in tch in 3rd: hdwy on inner to go 2nd 4 out: led on bridle bef last: drvn clr run-in* **1/6**[1]

46U0 **2** *11* **Bygones Of Brid (IRE)**[26] 3676 8-11-6 138 GrahamLee 148+
(Karen McLintock) *nt fluent: trckd ldr in 2nd: led 4 out: rdn whn hdd bef last: kpt on but no match for wnr* **10/1**[2]

305- **3** *16* **Hollins**[174] 5194 7-11-2 134 BarryKeniry 125
(Micky Hammond) *midfield: hit 6th: rdn and outpcd after 4 out: styd on after 2 out: wnt 3rd run-in* **33/1**

4-60 **4** *6* **Orsippus (USA)**[95] 2386 5-11-6 139 SamThomas 125
(Michael Smith) *hld up: hdwy on inner after 6th: chsd ldng pair 3 out: sn rdn: wknd and lost 3rd run-in* **16/1**[3]

22-4 **5** *13* **Scriptwriter (IRE)**[12] 3952 9-11-2 126 BrianHughes 105
(Howard Johnson) *hld up: rdn after 4 out: n.d* **33/1**

4/P6 **6** *22* **Bywell Beau (IRE)**[46] 3334 12-11-2 118 (t) AlistairFindlay 83
(George Charlton) *led: hdd 4 out: rdn and wknd after 3 out* **40/1**

-006 **7** *23* **Cassius (IRE)**[88] 2551 9-11-2 113 AdrianLane 60
(Bruce Mactaggart) *hld up: lost tch after 5th: t.o* **100/1**

0014 **8** *3 ¾* **Kempski**[5] 4067 11-11-2 100 RyanMania 56
(Rayson Nixon) *midfield: lost pl after 5th: bhd after next* **100/1**

10P4 **P** **Bucephalus (IRE)**[6] 4058 7-11-2 115 (t) MichaelMcAlister —
(Maurice Barnes) *hld up: lost tch after 5th: t.o whn p.u bef 3 out* **100/1**

4m 36.9s (9.90) **Going Correction** +0.875s/f (Soft) 9 Ran SP% **112.0**

Speed ratings (Par 109): **113,108,101,98,92 82,72,70,—**

toteswingers: 1&2 £1.20, 1&3 £4.20, 2&3 £8.20. CSF £2.19 TOTE £1.10: £1.02, £1.60, £2.70; EX 3.30.

Owner T G Leslie **Bred** Mrs A Delaney **Trained** Cholmondeley, Cheshire

FOCUS

A straightforward task for Peddlers Cross, who was fully entitled to win as he did. The first two reproduced their Newbury marks with the next pair below the level of last season's form.

NOTEBOOK

Peddlers Cross(IRE) returned to the track to put his Cheltenham aspirations on the line. He had 19lb in hand of his nearest rival on official ratings and registered a straightforward success, as he was entitled to. Settling well behind the leaders, getting a good tow into the race, he jumped economically throughout. He cruised to the lead after two out before staying on powerfully thereafter, but did need a reminder. Impressive in winning the Fighting Fifth Hurdle at Newbury (rearranged from Newcastle) on his comeback in November, when he defeated reigning champion hurdler Binocular, he remains a horse of tremendous potential and has a rare blend of speed and stamina which will stand him in good stead for Cheltenham. Crucially, we now know he is fit and well, and he'll go to the Champion Hurdle with a serious chance. (opened 1-6 after early 2-9 in places)

Bygones Of Brid(IRE) put in an improved display over hurdles but had no answer to the winner's turn of foot between the final two hurdles. He took up the running four out and ran creditably, running right to the line once headed by the easy winner. He was 4lb better off with Peddlers Cross on their Fighting Fifth running, but that was never going to be enough to lower the colours of a potential champion hurdler (op 14-1)

Hollins had been off the track for 174 days but has gone well fresh in the past. He was outpaced a fair way out but responded for pressure to stay on for third.

Orsippus(USA) was a remote fourth, weakening on the run-in after looking like being booked for third. He is a Grade 1 Aintree winner who appreciates spring ground so these conditions were never going to benefit him. (op 22-1)

4170 CONNOLLY'S RED MILLS HORSE FEEDS OPEN HUNTERS' CHASE (19 fncs) 3m 1f

4:25 (4:25) (Class 6) 5-Y-0+ **£1,249** (£387; £193; £96)

Form RPR

1-F **1** **Quotica De Poyans (FR)**[18] 7-11-13 120 MrCDawson(3) 93+
(Simon Shirley-Beavan) *mde all: nt fluent 5th and 11th: pressed after last: drvn and hld on wl* **8/15**[1]

1P-U **2** *1 ¾* **Optimistic Harry**[18] 12-11-9 80 MissSamanthaDrake(7) 89
(Miss S A Drake) *hld up: hdwy to go 2nd after 10th: chal after last: kpt on but hld towards fin* **15/2**[3]

23/ **3** *18* **General Striker**[25] 11-11-5 0 MissCWalton(7) 67
(Mrs L A Coltherd) *hld up in tch: chsd ldng pair after 5 out: wknd after 2 out* **9/1**

65-4 **4** *22* **Rimsky (IRE)**[12] 3956 10-11-9 109 (p) MissTJackson(3) 50
(Tina Jackson) *trckd ldr: lost pl after 12th: wknd after 5 out* **3/1**[2]

1/P- **5** *27* **Luksar (IRE)**[25] 11-11-11 97 MissCarolineHurley(5) 37
(Rose Dobbin) *trckd ldr: lost pl after 12th: wknd after 5 out* **16/1**

6m 55.9s (24.40) **Going Correction** +0.875s/f (Soft) 5 Ran SP% **117.9**

Speed ratings: **95,94,88,81,73**

CSF £5.96 TOTE £2.10: £1.10, £3.40; EX 6.40.

Owner Mrs P M Shirley-Beavan **Bred** Gilles Leblanc & Jacqueline Leblanc **Trained** Abbotrule, Borders

FOCUS

The first pair dominated this hunter chase, which was very slow compared with the earlier handicap. The winner is rated two stone off his best.

NOTEBOOK

Quotica De Poyans(FR) sauntered clear in a C&D hunter chase last March and again showed his love of the course, but this time he was made to work for it. He battled on gamely after the last to edge out Optimistic Harry in a titanic tussle. He will be back here for another hunter chase at the beginning of March. (op 4-7)

Optimistic Harry was officially rated 40lb inferior to the winner but put in a great effort to go down in a stamina-sapping finish on the run-in. He returned back to this grade after winning a point last month, and should be competitive in these events on the northern circuit. (op 7-1 tchd 8-1)

General Striker tried to go with the front two from four out but his effort was short-lived. (tchd 17-2 and 10-1)

Rimsky(IRE) was well backed but doesn't look to retain any enthusiasm at this stage of his career, and was toiling some way out. (op 7-1)

Luksar(IRE) wasn't up to winning a minor point last month, and in this grade he was out of his depth. (op 12-1)

4171 EBF/DBS MARES' STANDARD OPEN NATIONAL HUNT FLAT RACE (QUALIFIER) 2m 110y

5:00 (5:00) (Class 5) 4-7-Y-O **£1,626** (£477; £238; £119)

Form RPR

1 **Toubeera** 5-11-1 0 SamThomas 111+
(Michael Smith) *trckd ldrs: led on bridle wl over 1f out: pushed clr ins fnl f: readily* **40/1**

2 *8* **Lucia Bay** 6-11-1 0 CampbellGillies 99+
(Lucinda Russell) *hld up: gd hdwy on inner fr over 3f out: wnt 2nd over 1f out: kpt on but no match for wnr* **8/1**[3]

3 *7* **Molannarch** 5-11-1 0 JamesReveley 92
(Keith Reveley) *midfield on inner: hdwy to trck ldrs over 3f out: rdn over 2f out: kpt on one pce* **6/1**[2]

3/ **4** *nk* **Thirty Days Out (IRE)**[668] 5117 6-10-5 0 CallumWhillans(10) 92
(Donald Whillans) *in tch: hdwy on outer over 4f out: rdn and ev ch over 1f out: no ex ins fnl f* **12/1**

42 **5** *½* **Serenitatis (IRE)**[37] 3504 5-11-1 0 RichieMcGrath 92
(Tim Easterby) *trckd ldr on inner: led over 3f out: rdn whn hdd wl over 1f out: wknd ins fnl f* **16/1**

12 **6** *12* **Doynosaur**[33] 3576 4-10-13 0 DenisO'Regan 80
(Mrs K Burke) *hld up: smooth hdwy to trck ldrs over 2f out: sn rdn: wknd over 1f out* **15/8**[1]

7 *9* **Lucky Decision** 6-11-1 0 JasonMaguire 71
(Chris Grant) *led 2f: remained prom: pushed along over 6f out: wknd over 2f out* **14/1**

8 *2* **Annie's Pride** 4-10-6 0 BarryKeniry 60
(George Moore) *hld up in midfield: rdn over 4f out: n.d* **6/1**[2]

9 *4 ½* **Riverside Poppet** 5-10-12 0 (t) HarryHaynes(3) 64
(James Ewart) *hld up: brief hdwy on outer over 5f out: wknd fnl 3f* **33/1**

10 *17* **Supreme Dawn** 6-11-1 0 PaddyAspell 47
(Shelley Johnstone) *hld up: n.d* **50/1**

5 **11** *4* **Shan Valley (IRE)**[280] 311 5-10-10 0 AlexanderVoy(5) 43
(Lucy Normile) *racd keenly: trckd ldrs: wknd over 2f out* **10/1**

6 **12** *1 ½* **Miss Fernietickles**[45] 3364 4-9-13 0 GaryRutherford(7) 33
(Harriet Graham) *trckd ldrs on outer: led over 5f out: hdd over 3f out: wknd* **200/1**

4 **13** *21* **Skiddaw Secret**[33] 3576 4-10-6 0 GrahamLee 12
(John Weymes) *prom and t.k.h: led over 6f out: hdd over 5f out: wknd qckly: t.o* **28/1**

14 *25* **Mini Melody** 5-11-1 0 RyanMania —
(Stuart Coltherd) *racd keenly: led after 2f: hdd over 6f out: wknd qckly: t.o* **33/1**

4m 11.2s (15.00) **Going Correction** +0.875s/f (Soft)

WFA 4 from 5yo+ 9lb 14 Ran SP% **118.0**

Speed ratings: **99,95,91,91,91 85,81,80,78,70 68,68,58,46**

toteswingers: 1&2 £33.50, 1&3 £28.30, 2&3 £16.00. CSF £321.17 TOTE £58.60: £13.70, £2.30, £1.70; EX 483.00.

Owner Mrs H I S Calzini **Bred** Mrs H I S Calzini **Trained** Kirkheaton, Northumberland

■ Stewards' Enquiry : Harry Haynes four-day ban: used whip with excessive frequency (Mar 3-6)

FOCUS

A modest mares' bumper but the winner looks well above average.

NOTEBOOK

Toubeera ran out a ready winner on her debut under rules. She was always travelling well in behind runners, gained valuable cover which helped her settle, and once asked for her effort she powered away from her rivals. She was a big-priced winner and relished conditions, looking like she can stay further in due course. She will go hurdling straight away according to connections. (op 33-1)

Lucia Bay ◆ was the eyecatcher of the race. She was woefully outpaced a long way out but really responded well for pressure, staying on strongly for second. She will learn plenty from this introduction. (op 17-2)

Molannarch was another to stay on well on her rules debut. She was well backed and ran encouragingly from an unpromising position. (op 8-1 tchd 11-2)
Thirty Days Out(IRE) was a creditable third on her debut and looked in need of this run after travelling well for a long way. She will improve for the outing. (op 16-1)
Serenitatis(IRE) hugged the rail throughout, saving ground, and held every chance 2f out before tiring in the home straight. (op 14-1)
Doynosaur had the best form of those who had run, having won a Towcester bumper on her debut. In light of having shaped as though she'd appreciate further when second next time, though, this was a shade disappointing. She loomed up entering the home straight but didn't find a great deal, and it's possible she needs better ground. (tchd 2-1)
Annie's Pride responded to her jockey's urgings a fair way out. She needs further. (op 11-2 tchd 9-2)
T/Plt: £9.90 to a £1 stake. Pool: £63,105.56 - 4,644.46 winning tickets. T/Qpdt: £6.20 to a £1 stake. Pool: £3,501.02 - 411.82 winning tickets. AS

4172 - 4177a (Foreign Racing) - See Raceform Interactive

[3830]FAKENHAM (L-H)
Friday, February 18

OFFICIAL GOING: Good to soft (good in places; 7.2)
Course configuration same as at last meeting.
Wind: Light, swirling. Weather: overcast and very chilly

4178 WEST NORFOLK SPORTING TRUST (S) H'CAP HURDLE (9 hdls) 2m
1:30 (1:32) (Class 5) (0-90,90) 4-Y-O+ **£2,055** (£599; £299)

Form RPR
/P10 **1** **Brilliant (GER)**[109] [2135] 8-9-12 **69**.........................(v) AodhaganConlon(7) 76+
(Debra Hamer) *sn pushed along: chsd ldrs: 10 l 3rd and u.p 3 out: clsd between last two: 3rd and squeezed for room home turn: rallied and sn led after last and coaxed home: nvr looked to be gng sweetly: gd ride* **3/1**[2]
0660 **2** *hd* **Mad Professor (IRE)**[24] [3720] 8-9-7 **64** oh2.................(p) JoeCornwall(7) 69
(John Cornwall) *bhd: 12 l 4th and effrt 2 out: sneaked through on inner home turn and jnd wnr sn after last: rdn and no ex fnl strides* **10/1**
5-50 **3** *3 ¼* **Brigadore (USA)**[109] [2135] 8-11-0 **85**.........................(p) PeterCarberry(7) 89
(Alan Jones) *chsd clr ldr: clsd u.p after 3 out: hit next: led bef last and hit it: hdd after last and slowed markedly flat* **2/1**[1]
066P **4** *3 ¼* **A P Ling**[26] [3703] 4-9-7 **73** oh3..(b¹) MrTGarner(7) 65
(Christopher Kellett) *t.k.h: led 2nd and sn 6 l clr: rdn 2 out: awkward home turn: hdd bef the last and gave up* **33/1**
2-40 **5** *15* **Nous Voila (FR)**[15] [3899] 10-11-10 **88**.............................. MarkBradburne 75
(Alan Coogan) *midfield: rdn and struggling 3 out* **9/2**[3]
04F0 **6** *7* **Art Man**[41] [3449] 8-11-7 **85**.......................................(b) HaddenFrost 64
(James Frost) *chsd ldrs: hrd rdn and giving up bef 3 out* **7/1**
6000 **7** *1 ½* **Simplified**[119] [1949] 8-9-7 **64** oh5.......................................(t) MrOGarner(7) 42
(Michael Chapman) *reluctant and s.s: mstkes: in tch 3rd tl after 5th: t.o and nt keen 3 out* **50/1**
0-P6 **8** *5* **True Blue Saga (IRE)**[38] [3497] 6-11-7 **90**...................(vt) MrTomDavid(5) 63
(Tim Vaughan) *reluctant to s: slowly away and would nt try a yard: a bhd: mstke 5th: t.o 3 out* **9/1**
P40P **P** **Cherokee Story**[44] [3397] 5-11-12 **90**...........................(b) TomMessenger —
(Chris Bealby) *led tl 2nd: downed tools after 5th and tailed himself off: p.u 3 out* **40/1**

4m 12.5s (7.10) **Going Correction** +0.45s/f (Soft)
WFA 4 from 5yo+ 9lb **9** Ran SP% **115.4**
Speed ratings (Par 103): **100,99,98,96,89 85,84,82,—**
toteswingers: 1&2 £7.00, 1&3 £2.80, 2&3 £ 6.30. CSF £31.66 CT £72.86 TOTE £3.80: £1.30, £3.30, £1.30; EX 43.80.There was no bid for the winner.
Owner John Cole **Bred** Horst-D Beyer **Trained** Nantycaws, Carmarthens

FOCUS
There was 11mm of rain in the last seven days, but it was dry for the last 24 hours and the going was good to soft, good in places. A weak selling handicap, involving mostly inconsistent sorts. It was run at a good pace and there was an exciting finish. The form is straightforward with the first four pretty much bang on their marks.

NOTEBOOK
Brilliant(GER) is very hit and miss, but he whizzed round here when scoring off this mark in a C&D selling handicap two runs back. He was under pressure some way out in his attempt to repeat the trick and got involved in some scrimmaging around the final bend, but showed a gritty attitude to fight his way into the lead close home. (op 7-2)
Mad Professor(IRE) went in snatches with regular cheekpieces reapplied and was matched at 899-1 in-running, but he stayed on well from miles back and was just denied. He was a market mover for this best run for some time and would have to be of some interest in a similar race next time, but he has managed just two wins in 47 hurdle/chase starts and has more bad runs than good ones in his record in the last 12 months. (op 15-2 tchd 13-2)
Brigadore(USA) showed a good attitude to grind his way into the lead late on, but two other closers quickly loomed up and ran by him. However, this was a solid effort with cheekpieces refitted on his debut for a new yard, particularly as he flattened the second last and used up quite a bit of energy being the closest pursuer to the freewheeling leader for a long way. (op 7-2)
A P Ling had most of her rivals in trouble some way out before tiring and being reeled in approaching the last. This was a much improved effort dropped in trip and switched to trailblazing tactics with first-time blinkers applied. (op 25-1 tchd 40-1)
Nous Voila(FR) was a runaway winner off 7lb lower in this race last year, but he was disappointing in his bid for a repeat success. (tchd 7-2)

4179 ANDY DON MEMORIAL BEGINNERS' CHASE (17 fncs 1 omitted) 3m 110y
2:00 (2:00) (Class 4) 5-Y-O+ **£3,577** (£1,050; £525; £262)

Form RPR
4242 **1** **Promising Anshan (IRE)**[27] [3687] 6-10-11 129............... IanPopham(3) 134+
(Paul Nicholls) *sn led and j.w: gng bttr than only danger 3 out: rdn clr fr omitted next: unchal* **2/11**[1]
3443 **2** *21* **Springfield Raki**[10] [3988] 7-11-0 0........................... AndrewGlassonbury 118+
(Steve Gollings) *chsd wnr tl j. slowly 3rd: regained 2nd at 12th: ev ch tl rdn and j.rt 3 out: easily outpcd fr omitted 2 out and fin tired* **8/1**[2]
3 *48* **Hommage A Bach (IRE)**[176] [1385] 6-11-0 0.................... JohnnyFarrelly 72
(Paul John Gilligan, Ire) *cl up: hit 9th: sn pushed along: lost tch u.p 13th: 30 l 3rd at 15th: continued wl t.o* **33/1**
-65P **4** *14* **Rester Vrai (FR)**[43] [3402] 6-10-7 77.................................. JoeCornwall(7) 59
(John Cornwall) *lft 2nd fr 3rd tl 12th: lost tch and mstke 14th: tailing off whn hit next: extremely remote after* **150/1**
5205 **F** **Kitley Hassle**[11] [3982] 9-11-0 102.......................................(b) HaddenFrost —
(James Frost) *rdn 7th: lft last at 10th but only 3 l fr ldr whn fell 12th* **16/1**
1/6U **U** **Nodforms Paula (IRE)**[83] [2670] 8-11-0 117............... WarrenMarston —
(Milton Harris) *nt fluent in last: blnd bdly and uns rdr 9th: fatally injured* **14/1**[3]

6m 30.3s (-5.40) **Going Correction** -0.125s/f (Good) **6** Ran SP% **111.9**
Speed ratings: **103,96,80,76,— —**
toteswingers: 1&2 £1.10, 1&3 £5.10, 2&3 £9.40. CSF £2.67 TOTE £1.20: £1.10, £2.60; EX 2.30.
Owner Jared Sullivan & Simon Brown **Bred** M F Finneran **Trained** Ditcheat, Somerset

FOCUS
The hot favourite took advantage of a golden opportunity in this beginners' chase in which they finished well strung out. The first two are rated to their marks. The second-last fence was bypassed.

NOTEBOOK
Promising Anshan(IRE) set a clear standard on his close second off 126 in a 3m1f Wincanton handicap last time and had no trouble delivering in this company. He showed a tendency to jump right for most of the way and hung at times around the sharp bends but overall he did the job in good style. There should be more to come from this lightly raced sort who has improved since sent chasing for Paul Nicholls after a breathing operation, and the the Fulke Walwyn Kim Muir at Cheltenham could be his next target. (op 2-7)
Springfield Raki gave the favourite something to think about three fences from home before his effort petered out on his second run back from 242 days off. He still has a bit to learn at this discipline but his form is closely matched with his best hurdle efforts and he could be a force when switched to handicaps. (op 9-1 tchd 10-1)
Hommage A Bach(IRE) showed some promise in Irish maiden points but was well beaten in a bumper and maiden hurdle and it was a similar story on chase debut back from 176 days off.
Kitley Hassle finished second in the Devon Marathon in December but he faced a tough task against the favourite over this much sharper test and took a heavy fall at the twelfth fence. (op 10-1)

4180 EUROPEAN BREEDERS' FUND "NATIONAL HUNT" NOVICES' HURDLE (QUALIFIER) (11 hdls) 2m 4f
2:35 (2:35) (Class 3) 4-7-Y-O **£5,204** (£1,528; £764; £381)

Form RPR
425 **1** **Brunswick Gold (IRE)**[20] [3806] 6-11-2 0............................ SamThomas 118+
(Steve Gollings) *led after 1st: set modest pce: hit 6th: rdn between last two: pressed at last: hung on gamely flat* **7/4**[1]
4 **2** *1 ¼* **San Remo Bello (FR)**[113] [2056] 5-11-9 127...................... IanPopham(3) 126
(Paul Nicholls) *trckd ldrs: rdn to go 2nd bef 2 out: tried to chal bef last: no imp* **9/2**[3]
101 **3** *3* **Camden (IRE)**[32] [3599] 5-11-8 0....................................... LeightonAspell 121+
(Oliver Sherwood) *settled pressing ldrs: nt fluent 5th: rdn and outpcd after slt mstke 3 out: 4th next: rallied on ins to go 3rd bef last: no ex fnl 100yds* **4/1**[2]
6133 **4** *1 ¾* **Occasionally Yours (IRE)**[96] [2393] 7-11-5 119........ MissECrossman(7) 121
(Alan Blackmore) *chsd wnr in 2nd tl rn sltly wd bef 2 out: nt qckn after and lost 3rd bef last but nvr stopped trying* **25/1**
5 **5** *6* **Amaury De Lusignan (IRE)**[30] [3626] 5-11-2 0....... AndrewGlassonbury 106
(Gary Moore) *chsd ldrs tl hrd drvn and outpcd 3 out* **28/1**
0000 **6** *14* **Barnack**[21] [3787] 5-11-2 0.. DavidEngland 94
(Pam Sly) *bhd: rdn and outpcd after 7th: t.o whn mstke 2 out* **100/1**
4201 **7** *nk* **Caught By Witness (IRE)**[19] [3833] 6-11-8 125...........(t) WarrenMarston 99
(Milton Harris) *midfield: nt fluent 8th and rdn: struggling after* **9/2**[3]
/3-5 **8** *3* **Hudibras (IRE)**[26] [3692] 7-10-13 0.................................. PeterToole(3) 93
(Charlie Mann) *towards rr but in tch tl blnd 7th: nt rcvr: mstke next: t.o whn mstke 2 out* **10/1**
35 **9** *64* **Stanley's Choice**[89] [2560] 5-11-2 0..................................... PaulMoloney 33
(John Ferguson) *a last and nt a fluent: lost tch after 7th: sn bdly t.o* **40/1**

5m 16.3s (3.70) **Going Correction** +0.45s/f (Soft) **9** Ran SP% **112.5**
Speed ratings: **110,109,108,107,105 99,99,98,72**
toteswingers: 1&2 £1.60, 1&3 £3.50, 2&3 £4.30. CSF £9.40 TOTE £3.00: £1.30, £1.40, £1.70; EX 9.20.
Owner P J Martin **Bred** J P Murphy **Trained** Scamblesby, Lincs

FOCUS
A decent novice hurdle for the track, run at a fair pace. The form looks very solid with the three market leaders filling the first three positions.

NOTEBOOK
Brunswick Gold(IRE) had decent claims on his creditable fifth behind smart Bobs Worth in a Grade 2 novice event at Cheltenham last month and was receiving weight from his main rivals. Always prominent, he put in a solid jumping display and knuckled down well to fight off a few threats. Described by his trainer in his Stable Tour as "a big, old-fashioned chasing type", this highly regarded former point winner looks a strong galloping type who should go on to better things. His nest assignment could be in the EBF Final. (op 6-4 tchd 11-8 and 15-8)
San Remo Bello(FR) was snapped up by leading connections after a debut success over hurdles in France last May before a solid effort behind an odds-on rival at Stratford in October. He had another absence to shrug off, but ran a very creditable race to give the form pick a scare. A scopey type with plenty of potential, he looks sure to win races and should stay 3m in time. (op 5-1 tchd 6-1)
Camden(IRE) was a bit keen and displayed a low head carriage early on. He looked in serious trouble two out, but to his credit he rallied bravely to finish a close third under a penalty. This point/bumper winner looks a real fighter and remains capable of better. (op 5-1)
Occasionally Yours(IRE) ran a big race under a double penalty on ground probably slower than ideal back from 96 days off. (tchd 20-1)
Amaury De Lusignan(IRE) was a bit keen but showed some promise on his second hurdle run. He should continue to improve as he learns to settle and a switch to quicker ground could suit this gelding who was runner-up in a good-ground point. (op 33-1)
Caught By Witness(IRE) comfortably cashed in on a straightforward opportunity in a C&D maiden hurdle last time, but this 125-rated performer ran well below his best here, adding another blip to an up-and-down hurdle profile. Official explanation: vet said gelding finished distressed (tchd 4-1)
Stanley's Choice Official explanation: jockey said, regarding running and riding, that his orders were to get the gelding settled and jumping and creep into the race but it pulled very hard, didn't settle and tired turn into back straight final circuit.

4181 COUNTRYSIDE ALLIANCE H'CAP CHASE (FOR THE PRINCE CARLTON CHALLENGE CUP) (18 fncs) 3m 110y
3:10 (3:10) (Class 3) (0-130,126) 5-Y-O+ **£6,407** (£1,881; £940; £469)

Form RPR
660- **1** **Wellforth (IRE)**[64] [2993] 7-10-5 **105**...............................(b¹) JohnnyFarrelly 123+
(Paul John Gilligan, Ire) *hld up: wnt 2nd after 12th: jnd ldr and mstke 15th: drvn along: upsides tl rousted to go clr fr 2 out: 7 l ahd whn mstke last: eased fnl 100yds* **14/1**
3213 **2** *8* **Rey Nacarado (IRE)**[34] [3562] 6-10-12 **112**......................... SamThomas 120
(Charlie Longsdon) *2nd at str pce: lft in ld 7th: jnd 15th: hdd 2 out: rdn and nt qckn after* **7/4**[1]
5306 **3** *4* **Circus Of Dreams**[27] [3689] 8-11-4 **118**..........................(v) LeightonAspell 122
(Oliver Sherwood) *racd idly and nt v fluent in last: plugged on into 3rd at 15th but 8 l fr ldrs next: no imp after* **12/1**
2511 **4** *1 ¼* **Three Chords (IRE)**[19] [3832] 7-11-12 **126**..................... AndrewThornton 128
(Caroline Bailey) *chsd ldrs: outpcd by ldng pair 14th and n.d after: plugged on after 2 out but no threat* **2/1**[2]
P0F6 **5** *55* **Victorias Groom (GER)**[30] [3629] 9-11-7 **121**............... DominicElsworth 74
(Lucy Wadham) *cl up: j.rt 10th: mstke 12th: fading whn mstke 14th: t.o and eased betwen last two* **9/2**[3]

-21P **P** **Ray Mond**[19] 3832 10-11-9 **126** AlexMerriam(3) —
(Neil King) *led at str gallop tl j. j.rt and blnd 7th: blnd 10th: lost 2nd after 12th and dropped out rapidly: t.o and p.u 15th* **10/1**

6m 28.0s (-7.70) **Going Correction** -0.125s/f (Good) **6** Ran SP% **111.3**
Speed ratings: **107,104,103,102,85** —
toteswingers: 1&2 £8.50, 1&3 £6.90, 2&3 £3.50. CSF £39.84 TOTE £24.40: £11.70, £1.10; EX 50.30.
Owner Mrs N B watts **Bred** Mrs N B Watts **Trained** Athenry, Co Galway

FOCUS
There was a surprise winner in this fair handicap. A chase best from the winner, with the next two pretty close to their marks.

NOTEBOOK
Wellforth(IRE) has a very mixed record since back-to-back hurdle wins in Ireland in 2009 and was pulled up at Clonmel last time, but first-time blinkers and a step up in trip reignited him and he swept into the lead approaching the second last before forging ahead for a decisive win. He should remain well treated on his old form despite an impending rise for this victory and could go in again if the headgear continues to work.
Rey Nacarado(IRE), a heavily backed favourite, ran a very solid race and was probably a bit unlucky to run into a well-treated and revived rival. He is a young and unexposed chaser who should be able to add to his 3m2f Plumpton win off 7lb lower in December. (op 9-4)
Circus Of Dreams shaped with some promise stepped up in trip. He is not easy to predict, but has form at 2m-3m and is well treated on his best efforts last spring. (op 14-1 tchd 11-1)
Three Chords(IRE) was caught out when the front two quickened and could only plug on. This has to rate as a disappointing hat-trick bid from a horse who won over C&D last time. Official explanation: jockey said gelding ran flat (op 13-8)
Victorias Groom(GER) is potentially well treated, but he was toiling some way out and couldn't recapture form in an attempt to land a repeat success in this race. (tchd 5-1)
Ray Mond is an admirable and versatile chaser who has won seven handicaps in his last 13 runs, but his mark has shot up 57lb as a result and he has made several mistakes and now been pulled up on his last two starts. (op 9-1 tchd 12-1)

4182 WEST NORFOLK FOXHOUNDS & NORTH NORFOLK HARRIERS NOVICES' H'CAP HURDLE (13 hdls) 2m 7f 110y

3:45 (3:45) (Class 4) (0-115,115) 4-Y-0+ **£3,252** (£955; £477; £238)

Form				RPR
4P/3	**1**		**Wistow**[26] 3692 7-11-4 **107** DavidEngland (Pam Sly) *settled in rr: mstke 5th: effrt 9th: rdn after 10th: led after 3 out: gng 5 l clr whn hit 2 out: 20 l ahd last: v easily* **10/3**[1]	125+
424	**2**	*19*	**Charming Lad (IRE)**[22] 3761 6-11-9 **115** PeterToole(3) (Charlie Mann) *prom: wnt 2nd after 3 out: sn rdn: lost tch w wnr next: fin rather tired* **6/1**[3]	115
505	**3**	*2 3/4*	**Uncle Keef (IRE)**[19] 3833 5-10-8 **97** (b) PaulMoloney (Nicky Henderson) *disp ld: mstke 7th: led 10th tl hit 3 out: sn 3rd and gave up v tamely* **7/1**	95
34	**4**	*24*	**Duneen Point (IRE)**[33] 3584 7-11-7 **115** MrTomDavid(5) (Tim Vaughan) *bhd: j. deliberately 4th and rdn: passing btn horses in 15 l 4th 3 out but no further prog and nvr remotely nr ldrs* **8/1**	91
2F56	**5**	*12*	**See You Jack**[23] 3744 6-11-7 **110** AndrewThornton (Caroline Bailey) *cl up: rdn 9th: struggling next: t.o 3 out* **11/2**[2]	75
41P0	**6**	*6*	**Little Carmela**[43] 3405 7-11-2 **105** (v) MarkBradburne (Neil King) *w ldr: hit 8th: rdn and lost pl after next: 4th whn mstke 10th: sn t.o* **28/1**	65
206P	**P**		**Ultimate Quest (IRE)**[32] 3599 6-10-11 **100** AndrewGlassonbury (Michael Chapman) *midfield: hit 3rd and reminder: mstke 6th: dropped bk last bef 7th and reluctant: mstke 8th: t.o and p.u 10th* **40/1**	—
113P	**P**		**Flying Squad (UAE)**[27] 3687 7-11-7 **110** (t) WarrenMarston (Milton Harris) *last away: bhd and nvr gng wl: rdn and struggling 9th: t.o and p.u 3 out* **11/1**	—
1U00	**P**		**Pro Pell (IRE)**[13] 3950 6-11-2 **110** JoshuaMoore(5) (Gary Moore) *midfield: pushed along after 5th: rdn and no rspnse after 9th: t.o and p.u 2 out* **7/1**	—
50F1	**P**		**Balustrade (IRE)**[21] 3791 5-11-4 **107** ColinBolger (Chris Gordon) *midfield: mstke 6th: rdn and fading whn mstke 10th: t.o and p.u 3 out* **9/1**	—

6m 15.4s (9.00) **Going Correction** +0.45s/f (Soft) **10** Ran SP% **113.1**
Speed ratings (Par 105): **103,96,95,87,83 81,—,—,—,—**
toteswingers: 1&2 £2.30, 1&3 £5.30, 2&3 £10.30. CSF £23.22 CT £129.27 TOTE £2.60: £1.10, £2.80, £1.50; EX 23.40.
Owner Mrs P M Sly **Bred** D R Stoddart **Trained** Thorney, Cambs

FOCUS
This looked a competitive novice hurdle, but the favourite powered clear for an emphatic win, producing a big step up for this longer trip.

NOTEBOOK
Wistow has a bit of a mixed record, but she had decent claims on her career-best 2l third at 50-1 on her recent comeback from 23 months off at Market Rasen, and backed that up with a runaway win stepped up to this trip for the first time on her handicap debut. She will face a sharp rise in her mark after this, but is out of 3m3f winner and could be capable of further improvement over staying trips. (tchd 3-1 and 7-2)
Charming Lad(IRE) made the frame in all three outings in novice hurdles, and this good-ground Irish point winner continued that trend with a fair effort behind a progressive type up in trip on his handicap debut. (tchd 7-1)
Uncle Keef(IRE) faded late on, but this was a more encouraging effort switched to forcing tactics with first-time blinkers applied on his handicap debut, and his style suggests a return to around 2m4f could work in his favour. (tchd 8-1)
Duneen Point(IRE) went a bit in snatches and couldn't get near the leaders off a stiff looking mark on his first try in a handicap.
See You Jack was a bit keen and cut out quickly some way out on this step up in trip, which was a bit disappointing from a former point winner who attracted support. (op 13-2 tchd 5-1)

4183 WALTER WALES FOX HUNTERS' CHASE (FOR THE WALTER WALES CUP) (18 fncs) 3m 110y

4:15 (4:15) (Class 6) 5-Y-0+ **£1,021** (£314; £157)

Form				RPR
P211	**1**		**Massini Man (IRE)**[13] 3938 10-12-1 129 MissCLWills(7) (Brendan Powell) *led and j. boldly tl got too cl to 13th: rdn and lost 2nd bef 3 out and looked bdly outpcd: 6 l 3rd and rallying last: styd on v strly to ld cl home* **11/10**[1]	121+
P15-	**2**	*1 1/2*	**Rash Move (IRE)**[34] 10-11-11 0 MrTEllis(7) (F A Hutsby) *j. deliberately 3rd: settled in tch: hit 6th and 10th: wnt 2nd bef 3 out and w ldr after: rdn to ld last and 3 l clr briefly flat: tied up and cl home* **3/1**[2]	117
566-	**3**	*2 3/4*	**Jump Jet (IRE)**[332] 4807 9-11-13 117 MrMWall(5) (Miss O Curl) *racd keenly and prom: led 13th: jnd and rdn after 3 out: remained w ldr tl hit last and wknd* **11/2**[3]	115
4F4/	**4**	*25*	**Caged Tiger**[12] 12-11-7 97 (b) MrsHKemp(7) (Mrs H M Kemp) *dropped bk last at 9th: stl last and outpcd 14th: plodded on in hopeless pursuit* **66/1**	86
2P2/	**5**	*5*	**Parrain (FR)**[279] 8-11-7 0 MrRStearn(7) (J M Turner) *towards rr: outpcd and nt fluent 14th: struggling after* **17/2**	82
241/	**6**	*5*	**Leo McGarry (IRE)**[26] 8-11-7 0 (b1) MrRichardCollinson(7) (Miss Caroline Fryer) *bhd: hit 5th: nt fluent 9th: hdwy 10th: rdn bef 14th: sn dropped out and swishing tail: t.o 3 out* **22/1**	77
0PU-	**P**		**Which Pocket (IRE)**[19] 13-11-7 104 MissSSherwood(7) (D Laverty) *prom: blnd 9th: sn lost pl: t.o after 13th: p.u 15th* **33/1**	—
/24-	**P**		**Va Vavoom (IRE)**[341] 4613 13-11-11 103 MrJMQuinlan(3) (Mrs Fleur Hawes) *t.k.h in rr: nt fluent 7th and 10th: effrt 12th and pressed ldrs briefly: wknd 14th: t.o after mstke 3 out: p.u between last two* **14/1**	—

6m 39.9s (4.20) **Going Correction** -0.125s/f (Good) **8** Ran SP% **114.0**
Speed ratings: **88,87,86,78,77 75,—,—**
toteswingers: 1&2 £1.10, 1&3 £3.10, 2&3 £3.50. CSF £4.77 TOTE £3.00: £1.90, £1.10, £1.20; EX 4.10.
Owner Steven Astaire **Bred** Patrick O'Donnell **Trained** Upper Lambourn, Berks

FOCUS
A decent hunters' chase, in which there was an incredible performance by the favourite who snatched victory after looking beaten some way out. He is rated to the level og his recent win.

NOTEBOOK
Massini Man(IRE) got off the mark over regulation fences off 108 at Newton Abbot last August and shrugged off an absence when winning a 3m Ffos Las novice chase this month. He had leading claims back in a hunters' chase, but was a bit hesitant at some of the fences and it looked like the game was up when the placed horses went clear. However, he kept grinding away under a tremendous ride and produced a surging run to get up close home. (op 5-4 tchd 11-8)
Rash Move(IRE) recorded a fifth point win when scoring easily in that sphere last month. He was prominent in the betting back in a decent hunter chase and put in a feisty display to get the better of a tremendous tussle with the third horse before being mugged by a fast finisher. (op 9-4 tchd 10-3)
Jump Jet(IRE) travelled smoothly into the lead and battled bravely, but was just outgunned in the closing stages on his return from 332 days off. This was a highly creditable comeback from a horse who looks feasibly treated off a current mark of 117. (op 8-1)
Caged Tiger had plenty to find and was well beaten on his first run under rules since April 2008.
Parrain(FR) was a Grade 3 hurdle winner in France in his pomp, but he was turned over at short prices in his last two point starts and couldn't get involved on this return from 279 days off. (op 9-1 tchd 8-1)

4184 EBF/DBS MARES' INTERMEDIATE OPEN NATIONAL HUNT FLAT RACE (QUALIFIER) 2m

4:50 (4:50) (Class 4) 4-7-Y-0 **£2,055** (£599; £299)

Form				RPR
3	**1**		**Tante Sissi (FR)**[65] 2965 4-10-7 0 SamThomas (Alan King) *confidently rdn: last tl 1/2-way: smooth prog after: led on bit over 2f out: sn pushed clr: readily* **3/1**[1]	100+
	2	*7*	**Milly Malone (IRE)** 5-11-2 0 LeightonAspell (Oliver Sherwood) *hld up and bhd: effrt 4f out: wnt 2nd over 2f out and flattered briefly: rdn and sn no ch w wnr but wl clr of rest fnl f* **7/2**[2]	101+
352	**3**	*8*	**Miss Hippy (IRE)**[33] 3590 6-11-2 0 WarrenMarston (Milton Harris) *prom: rdn and outpcd 4f out: 12 l 5th 2f out: plugged on to snatch poor 3rd cl home* **4/1**[3]	93
	4	*1*	**Honeycreeper** 4-10-7 0 MarkBradburne (Renee Robeson) *cl 2nd tl led 6f out: rdn and hdd over 3 out: outpcd over 2f out: plugged on to snatch 4th* **50/1**	83
	5	*hd*	**Famagusta** 4-10-0 0 (v1) MrJMQuinlan(7) (Peter Charalambous) *prom: led over 3f out: sn rdn: hdd over 2f out: wknd ins fnl f to lose two pls nr fin* **28/1**	82
0-1	**6**	*3 3/4*	**Madame Allsorts**[31] 3616 6-11-9 0 TimmyMurphy (Willie Musson) *hld up on outside in rr: effrt 5f out: wknd tamely wl over 2f out* **11/2**	95
	7	*13*	**Silver Wren** 4-10-7 0 SamJones (Renee Robeson) *slt ld tl hdd 6f out: lost pl qckly* **33/1**	67
	8	*1/2*	**Dopen Diva** 4-10-4 0 AlexMerriam(3) (Peter Chapple-Hyam) *midfield: lost tch v tamely 4f out* **18/1**	67
3	**9**	*41*	**Rye Park**[11] 3979 5-11-2 0 TomSiddall (Noel Chance) *midfield: drvn and wknd 6f out: t.o fnl 4f* **14/1**	39
	10	*nk*	**Calcot Rose** 5-11-2 0 GerardTumelty (Alan King) *dropped bk last and drvn 1/2-way: t.o fnl 6f* **10/1**	39
0	**11**	*17*	**County Hotel (IRE)**[65] 2965 4-10-7 0 JohnnyFarrelly (Barry Brennan) *midfield: dropped out qckly 6f out: t.o 4f out: sn eased* **20/1**	14

4m 14.7s (14.90) **Going Correction** +0.45s/f (Soft)
WFA 4 from 5yo 9lb 5 from 6yo 1lb **11** Ran SP% **116.7**
Speed ratings: **80,76,72,72,71 70,63,63,42,42 34**
toteswingers:1&2:£2.30, 2&3:£2.90, 1&3:£3.40; toteSuper7: Win: £10,500. Place: £304.50. CSF £12.75 TOTE £4.30: £1.50, £2.30, £1.60; EX 18.80.
Owner Thurloe 51 **Bred** F Lefeuvre, A Lefeuvre & D Lefeuvre **Trained** Barbury Castle, Wilts
■ Stewards' Enquiry : Mark Bradburne three-day ban: weighed in 2lb heavy (Mar 5-6)

FOCUS
The favourite put in an impressive display to forge clear of her two main market rivals in this interesting bumper. The time was slow and the form is ordinary.

NOTEBOOK
Tante Sissi(FR) finished runner-up in two French bumpers before a close third behind a longer-priced stablemate in a 1m4f Newbury bumper on her British debut, a race where the jockey felt he should have held on to her a little longer. She had solid form claims and put in a smooth performance to power clear under a confident ride. A compact type with a good cruising speed and turn of foot, she looks a nice prospect. (op 2-1)
Milly Malone(IRE) attracted support and showed plenty of promise to chase home the leading form contender on debut. She is out of a 2m chase winner from a good jumping family. (op 17-2)
Miss Hippy(IRE) found dramatic improvement on her two previous bumper runs when beaten only 1l at 50-1 at Ffos Las last month with a subsequent winner over 7l back in fourth. She had claims on that effort, but got tapped for speed at a crucial stage before staying on late. (tchd 7-2)
Honeycreeper has a lower profile pedigree than some of her rivals, but was in the firing line for a long way on this encouraging debut.
Famagusta had a visor applied for her debut, but travelled well for a long way before getting tired turning in. (op 22-1)
Madame Allsorts left her debut form well behind when a convincing winner of a 2m1f heavy-ground mares' bumper at Folkestone last month, but this stoutly bred type found things happening too quickly under a penalty over this sharper test. (op 5-1 tchd 9-2 and 6-1)
T/Plt: £6.90 to a £1 stake. Pool: £51,939.33. 5,487.65 winning tickets. T/Qpdt: £3.90 to a £1 stake. Pool: £3,648.18. 685.63 winning tickets. IM

[4069]NEWBURY (L-H)

Friday, February 18

OFFICIAL GOING: Hurdle course - soft (good to soft in places; 5.6); chase course - good to soft (soft in places; 6.6)

Rearranged meeting after the card was abandoned the previous Saturday. Rails moved in on both courses with 8m of fresh ground on the hurdles track.

Wind: Moderate, behind. Weather: Overcast

4185 TOTESPORT.COM H'CAP HURDLE (12 hdls) 3m 110y

12:10 (12:10) (Class 3) (0-135,135)
4-Y-0+

£5,009 (£1,480; £740; £370; £184; £92)

Form				RPR
0120 **1**		**Stow**[23] 3742 6-10-8 117 .... AidanColeman	127+
(Venetia Williams) *trckd ldrs: wnt 2nd 8th: chal 4 out: led sn after: drvn along after 2 out: styd on strly run-in* **12/1**

-10F **2** *2 ¾* **Go Amwell**[23] 3742 8-10-5 114 .... (v) TimmyMurphy 119
(J R Jenkins) *hld up in rr: hdwy after 4 out: rdn and styd on fr 2 out chsd wnr after last but no imp* **25/1**

-441 **3** *5* **Awesome Freddie**[39] 3483 6-11-0 123 .... RobertThornton 123+
(Alan King) *chsd ldrs: wnt 2nd 3 out: sn rdn: no imp on wnr fr next: one pce whn nt fluent last: lost 2nd sn after* **15/2**

400 **4** *2 ¾* **William Hogarth**[27] 3688 6-10-13 122 .... RichardJohnson 120
(Keith Goldsworthy) *chsd ldrs: rdn after 3 out and sn outpcd by ldng trio* **16/1**

1115 **5** *8* **Cappagh (IRE)**[96] 2387 6-10-7 116 .... APMcCoy 106
(Philip Hobbs) *chsd ldrs: rdn after 3 out: wknd fr 2 out* **7/4**[1]

U240 **6** *shd* **Miss Overdrive**[13] 3947 7-10-4 120 .... MrBJPoste(7) 109
(Andy Turnell) *chsd ldrs: rdn 6th to 8th: lost pl appr 3 out: kpt on again run-in but nvr any threat* **14/1**

1-P0 **7** *shd* **Don't Push It (IRE)**[48] 3293 11-11-9 135 .... MrAJBerry(3) 125+
(Jonjo O'Neill) *swtg: hld up in rr: hdwy 2 out: styd on wl run-in but nvr any threat* **40/1**

0400 **8** *13* **Hills Of Aran**[20] 3807 9-11-12 135 .... (p) RhysFlint 111
(Keith Goldsworthy) *chsd ldrs: rdn after 5th and again appr 3 out: wknd sn after* **25/1**

26F- **9** *34* **Larks Lad (IRE)**[308] 5201 7-11-1 124 .... BarryGeraghty 66
(Nicky Henderson) *nt a fluent: in tch: hdwy after 4 out: wknd bef next* **14/1**

1010 **10** *19* **Warne's Way (IRE)**[27] 3676 8-11-4 130 .... (t) RichieMcLernon(3) 53
(Brendan Powell) *slt ld to 3rd: wknd qckly 4 out* **22/1**

5F43 **11** *4 ½* **Sangfroid**[34] 3566 7-11-7 130 .... DarylJacob 49
(Nick Williams) *rdn fr 5th: a in rr* **13/2**[3]

313- **F** **Valentine Vic (IRE)**[381] 3811 7-11-2 125 .... NickScholfield —
(Paul Nicholls) *pressed ldr tl led 3rd: hdd after 4 out: wknd bef next: wl bhd whn fell 2 out* **11/2**[2]

5m 53.71s (-14.59) **Going Correction** -0.65s/f (Firm) **12** Ran SP% **118.2**
Speed ratings (Par 107): **97,96,94,93,91 91,91,86,75,69 68,—**
Tote Swingers:1&2:£11.90, 2&3:£14.20, 1&3:£18.10 CSF £271.96 CT £2396.37 TOTE £13.80: £4.30, £6.60, £2.40; EX 229.20.

Owner GSM Properties Ltd **Bred** Plantation Stud **Trained** Kings Caple, H'fords

FOCUS

Due to a largely wet week, the ground was considered more testing than was the case last Saturday, though it was expected to ride better on the chase course and was officially described as good to soft, soft in places. The rails were moved in on both courses with 8m of fresh ground all the way around the hurdles track. This opening staying handicap was originally due to be the second place on the original card last weekend and it looked competitive, with the field only having been reduced to 12 from an initial 14 runners. They went a sound gallop, but few landed a blow in the home straight and it no doubt paid to race handily. Robert Thornton described the ground afterwards as being like "glue", but it was still a creditable winning time. A personal best from the winenr with the second back to the leevl of his old best.

NOTEBOOK

Stow, who loves soft ground, relished returning to a more galloping circuit and produced his best effort since his juvenile campaign to score decisively. He had fallen in the handicap prior to returning to form this season and should remain competitive after a likely rise. (op 16-1)

Go Amwell ◆ showed his true colours with a strong late challenge from off the pace and should be rated better than the bare form. He is an improved hurdler this season and, while a rise in the handicap is forthcoming, should be able to go one better again in the coming weeks.

Awesome Freddie was 8lb higher than when opening his account on his handicap debut last month. He looked a likely winner three out, but his new mark took its toll after the second-last. He has the scope to do better when sent chasing. (op 7-1)

William Hogarth, up in trip with the cheekpieces abandoned, was suited by racing close to the pace and probably ran close to his previous level. (tchd 18-1)

Cappagh(IRE) caught the eye on his previous outing behind the rapidly improving Grands Crus at Cheltenham's Open meeting back in November. He has missed engagements due to bad weather since, but had been left alone by the handicapper and was gambled on back up in trip. The softer ground was not really in his favour and that seemed to find him out under pressure, but the run did look needed all the same. (op 9-4 tchd 5-2 in places)

Miss Overdrive hit a flat spot before plugging on again and, although this was a step back in the right direction, she is not easy to place at present. (op 16-1)

Don't Push It(IRE) was never seriously in the race, but finished his race well and this will encourage those supporting him to become the first back-to-back winner of the Grand National since Red Rum in 1974. He will likely have one more run before then.

Hills Of Aran Official explanation: trainer said gelding bled from the nose

Larks Lad(IRE), a chaser in the making, shouldn't be fully judged on this display. Despite not always fluent, he travelled nicely before appearing to blow up and significant improvement may be around the corner.

Valentine Vic(IRE), who has the build of a chaser, was solid in the market and ran enthusiastically on the front end. He was very tired before taking a heavy fall, though, and lay winded for some time before getting to his feet. (op 9-2)

4186 AON CHASE GRADE 2 (18 fncs) 3m

12:45 (12:46) (Class 1) 5-Y-0+ **£17,103** (£6,417; £3,213; £1,602; £804)

Form RPR

1/2P **1** **Noland**[20] 3804 10-11-0 152 .... (t) APMcCoy 150
(Paul Nicholls) *lw: slt ld to 4th: styd chalng tl led 9th: blnd and hdd 14th: rcvrd to ld 3 out: edgd lft u.p run-in: hld on: all out: dismntd after line* **13/2**[3]

11-5 **2** *hd* **What A Friend**[90] 2524 8-11-10 159 .... HarrySkelton 161+
(Paul Nicholls) *lw: in tch: blnd 12th: hdwy to trck ldrs 14th: mstke 4 out: styd on again fr next: edgd lft appr last: swtchd rt run-in: rallied u.p and fin wl: jst failed* **4/5**[1]

0-10 **3** *¾* **Fair Along (GER)**[20] 3807 9-11-0 147 .... (p) RhysFlint 151
(Philip Hobbs) *w wnr: led 4th: j. slowly and hdd 9th: styd wl there and led 14th: hdd and screwed 3 out: sn one pce: rallied u.p run-in: fin wl but nt quite get up* **11/4**[2]

4 *15* **Carronhills (IRE)**[733] 3957 9-11-0 130 .... JasonMaguire 138
(Rebecca Curtis) *chsd ldrs: chal 5th to 6th: blnd 11th: dropped to rr 13th and n.d after but kpt on to take wl hld 3rd 3 out* **20/1**

-02P **5** *56* **Dance Island (IRE)**[41] 3437 8-11-2 137 .... DarylJacob 125
(Ben Case) *lw: in rr but in tch: wknd appr 4 out: lost wl hld 3rd 3 out* **16/1**

(-11.00) **Going Correction** -0.25s/f (Good) **5** Ran SP% **106.2**
Speed ratings: **108,107,107,102,84**
CSF £12.09 TOTE £5.70: £1.90, £1.30; EX 10.50.

Owner J Hales **Bred** The Niarchos Family **Trained** Ditcheat, Somerset

■ Stewards' Enquiry : Harry Skelton two-day ban: excessive use of the whip (Mar 4-5)
Rhys Flint two-day ban: excessive use of the whip (Mar 4-5)

FOCUS

The postponement of this Grade 2 event saw King George runner-up Riverside Theatre defect to the Grade 1 Ascot Chase on Saturday and he would've been a warm order here. That meant it was just an average renewal, but still a very interesting one and Paul Nicholls's domination of the race continued as he landed a sixth win since 2001.

NOTEBOOK

Noland, the second string, gamely fended off the reluctant-looking What A Friend at the business end. The winner's connections had mooted retirement after he was pulled up on his return to chasing at Cheltenham last month, but Tony McCoy persuaded them into one more run over this longer trip and his judgement proved spot on. With the tongue tie back on, he jumped best of all through the race under positive handling, the longer trip proved much to his liking and getting 10lb from his stablemate made the difference on the run-in. It was his first success since injury struck after he landed the John Durkan Memorial Chase at Punchestown in 2008 and it was great to see him back near the top of his game. He was dismounted after the line and led into the winner's enclosure after becoming distressed, but was later fine. He is most likely to skip Cheltenham and head to Aintree, all being well. Official explanation: trainer's rep said, regarding apparent improvement in form, that the gelding had benefited from the re-fitting of a tongue strap. (tchd 7-1)

What A Friend conceded upwards of 8lb to his rivals. The ground being better on the chase course was expected to suit him, but he lacked conviction at times with his jumping and again showed his customary high head carriage. He recovered from an error four out to have every chance, but didn't appear to fully go through with his effort after the last. This was the first time he had raced in a noseband since he finished second to Denman in the 2009 Hennessy, where he also wandered under maximum pressure, and it wouldn't be surprising to now see that discarded again. On the evidence of his two runs this term, though, his attitude is holding him back and it wasn't surprising to see him pushed out for the Gold Cup next month. Paul Nicholls later said his 8-y-o hated the ground, but was definitely thinking about it and he didn't rule out first-time blinkers if he runs at Cheltenham. The race he believes will really suit him is the Grand National, however, though added that may come a year too soon. (op 8-11 tchd 4-6 and 5-6 in a place)

Fair Along(GER), who returned to near his best when winning again at Wetherby on his seasonal return in October, dropped right out in the Cleeve Hurdle on his previous outing and was having his first run over fences since 2007. He was a classy novice over fences, but lost his way in this sphere and it was hard to know what to expect on his debut over the trip as a chaser. It was a decent effort from him, though, and looking at the way he rallied late on, going off quicker early on may have suited. He is well worth another go.

Carronhills(IRE) developed into a smart hunter chaser in Ireland in 2009. He had been absent the last two years, however, and this was his British debut for a new yard. A mark of 130 probably didn't do him justice beforehand, but it was still a very stiff task and he posted a very pleasing effort. He blew up before rallying down the home straight and should come on plenty. (op 22-1 tchd 25-1)

Dance Island(IRE), pulled up in the Welsh National last month, was another facing a tall order in this higher grade. He never seriously threatened, but it should restore his confidence for a crack at another valuable handicap. (op 25-1)

4187 TOTEPOOL GAME SPIRIT CHASE GRADE 2 (13 fncs) 2m 1f

1:15 (1:17) (Class 1) 5-Y-0+

£17,103 (£6,417; £3,213; £1,602; £804; £402)

Form RPR

21-0 **1** **French Opera**[41] 3446 8-11-5 156 .... BarryGeraghty 162+
(Nicky Henderson) *led to 6th: styd trcking ldr: led again 9th: rdn after 2 out: styd on strly run-in* **7/2**[2]

1F20 **2** *6* **Tchico Polos (FR)**[27] 3675 7-11-6 158 .... (t) APMcCoy 158
(Paul Nicholls) *lw: chsd ldrs: wnt 2nd appr 4 out: rdn next: nvr quite on terms w wnr and hit 2 out: one pce run-in* **5/2**[1]

U640 **3** *7* **Oiseau De Nuit (FR)**[69] 2885 9-11-4 143 .... (t) JoeTizzard 155+
(Colin Tizzard) *in rr: blnd 6th: lost tch 8th and stl last 4 out: str run fr 3 out: kpt on wl to take 3rd last but nt trble ldng duo* **33/1**

3-24 **4** *13* **Take The Breeze (FR)**[13] 3948 8-11-3 149 .... HarrySkelton 138
(Paul Nicholls) *trckd wnr: led 6th: mstke and hdd 9th: lost pl bef 4 out: tk 4th appr last* **7/1**[3]

03-4 **5** *2* **Sports Line (IRE)**[64] 2976 8-11-4 147 .... JasonMaguire 137
(Donald McCain) *t.k.h: trckd ldrs: hit 4th and 7th: styd in tch: hdwy 9th: wnt 3rd 4 out but nvr nr ldng duo: wknd and hit 2 out* **7/2**[2]

2040 **6** *1* **I'msingingtheblues (IRE)**[41] 3446 9-11-0 145 .... (t) TomScudamore 131
(David Pipe) *lw: in rr: sme prog 9th: sn wknd* **9/1**

1641 **7** *10* **Cornas (NZ)**[41] 3446 9-11-10 153 .... DarylJacob 135
(Nick Williams) *hit 2nd: in rr 6th: hdwy to chse ldrs 9th: sn wknd and mstke 4 out* **7/1**[3]

4m 3.20s (-9.80) **Going Correction** -0.25s/f (Good) **7** Ran SP% **111.0**
Speed ratings: **113,110,106,100,99 99,94**
Tote Swingers:1&2:£2.30, 2&3:£23.70, 1&3:£12.40 CSF £12.39 TOTE £3.50: £3.00, £1.20; EX 9.20.

Owner Mrs Judy Wilson & Martin Landau **Bred** N P Bloodstock Ltd **Trained** Upper Lambourn, Berks

FOCUS

Since 1990 three winners of the Game Spirit have gone on to win the Queen Mother Champion Chase at the Festival - Viking Flagship (1994), Azertyuiop (2004) and Master Minded (2008), but although there was no established stars in this year's field, the winner could be an interesting candidate for the Cheltenham feature if turning up. French Opera ran to his mark with the second close to his best.

NOTEBOOK

French Opera has won on soft ground before, but despite having a wonderful record fresh he flopped in testing ground when last of nine behind Cornas at Sandown on his return to action last month. However, despite the gluey conditions here his performance couldn't have been more different. Always up with the pace, he gradually turned the screw after leading for a second time jumping the cross fence and kept on finding enough to keep his only real danger at bay over the last four fences. His Festival target remains unclear, with the Queen Mother Champion Chase and the Grand Annual the options. He was still available at 33-1 for the former immediately after this race, but although he was only just beaten under top weight in the latter contest last season, he will be rated several pounds higher this time. (op 11-4)

Tchico Polos(FR) was beaten a long way behind Master Minded in the Victor Chandler last time, but this performance was much better. He didn't help himself by taking a keen grip in the early stages, but despite that he was right there alongside the winner turning for home. He tried hard, but his rival kept on pulling out more and he could make no impression on him from the final fence. He is likely to be aimed at the bet365.com Celebration Chase at Sandown on the final day of the season. (op 7-2)

Oiseau De Nuit(FR) was the lowest-rated runner in the field and has been well below form so far this season, but he emerges with plenty of credit from this. He looked to be tailing off after a jolting error at the sixth and was still well behind at the cross fence, but he got his second wind over the final couple of fences and was still gaining on the front pair at the line.

Take The Breeze(FR) relishes testing ground, but this was the first time he had tackled this sort of trip in a year. He was always up there, but he lost the advantage when hitting the cross fence and gradually faded out of contention. He will appreciate a return to further and still holds an entry in the Racing Post Chase in eight days' time. (tchd 15-2 in a place)

Sports Line(IRE) can be headstrong just as he was on his debut for the yard following a break at Exeter in December, but although well backed and ridden with more restraint this time, he was again inclined to over-race and also got right into the bottom of some of his fences. The game was up coming to four out, but his trainer had warned that this race would bring him on so it wouldn't be a surprise to see him fare much better in due course. (op 9-2 tchd 3-1)

I'msingingtheblues(IRE) was the only horse in the field not carrying a penalty, but he hasn't won a race in over two years and all his best form has come on a sounder surface. He never offered a threat from the back of the field and although he has been given 10st 11lb in the Grand National, he is still yet to race beyond 2m5f. (op 8-1)

Cornas(NZ) had three of today's rivals behind him when winning a decent Sandown handicap on testing ground last month, but he was badly in with each of them on these terms and proved uneasy in the market. He had been seen off with four fences still to jump. (op 6-1 tchd 9-1)

4188 TOTESPORT TROPHY HURDLE (H'CAP) GRADE 3 (8 hdls) 2m 110y

1:50 (1:50) (Class 1) 4-Y-0+

£34,206 (£12,834; £6,426; £3,204; £1,608; £804)

Form				RPR
1211	**1**		**Recession Proof (FR)**[52] 3169 5-10-8 **134** .... DougieCostello (John Quinn) *lw: gd sort: chsd ldrs: chal fr 2 out tl slt ld after last: styd on gamely u.p: all out* **12/1**	141+
0-25	**2**	*shd*	**Bothy**[52] 3169 5-10-7 **136** .... DannyCook(3) (Brian Ellison) *chsd ldr: hrd rdn appr 2 out and responded gamely to ld last: hdd sn after but styd chalng tl no ex last strides* **8/1**[3]	142
20-4	**3**	*1 ¼*	**Notus De La Tour (FR)**[27] 3676 5-11-1 **141** .... TomScudamore (David Pipe) *led: rdn appr 2 out: hdd last: rallied gamely sn after: no ex fnl 50yds* **10/1**	146
P-40	**4**	*shd*	**The Betchworth Kid**[34] 3561 6-10-12 **138** .... JimmyMcCarthy (Alan King) *in rr tl gd hdwy 2 out: swtchd lft last and r.o strly run-in: gng on cl home but nt quite rch ldng trio* **16/1**	143
11-6	**5**	*¾*	**Soldatino (FR)**[27] 3676 5-11-8 **148** .... BarryGeraghty (Nicky Henderson) *lw: in rr and j. slowly 2nd: hdwy after 4 out: drvn to chse ldrs 2 out: no ex u.p run-in* **6/1**[2]	153
-124	**6**	*1*	**Eradicate (IRE)**[20] 3808 7-11-0 **143** .... RichardKilloran(3) (Nicky Henderson) *lw: in rr: hdwy fr 3 out: styd on u.p fr 2 out: no ex u.p run-in* **33/1**	146
	7	*8*	**Solix (FR)**[96] 2418 5-11-7 **152** .... DavidBass(5) (Nicky Henderson) *chsd ldrs: rdn 3 out: wknd fr 2 out* **16/1**	148
2-06	**8**	*3 ¼*	**Get Me Out Of Here (IRE)**[96] 2386 7-11-10 **150** .... APMcCoy (Jonjo O'Neill) *trckd ldrs to 2 out: wknd sn after* **14/1**	144+
-113	**9**	*9*	**Palomar (USA)**[34] 3561 9-10-10 **136** .... FearghalDavis (Brian Ellison) *swtg: in tch tl wknd 3 out: no ch whn bdly hmpd 2 out* **33/1**	119
1115	**10**	*1 ½*	**Nearby**[83] 2668 7-11-3 **150** .... ChrisDavies(7) (Philip Hobbs) *hld up in rr: hdwy 3 out: sn rdn and wknd* **40/1**	134
21/2	**11**	*2 ¾*	**Walkon (FR)**[27] 3676 6-11-8 **148** .... RobertThornton (Alan King) *swtg:chsd ldrs: rdn and wknd appr 3 out: no ch whn bdly hmpd 2 out* **3/1**[1]	127
F-	**12**	*¾*	**Sweet My Lord (FR)**[50] 3246 5-10-6 **132** .... PTownend (W P Mullins, Ire) *chsd ldrs: n.m.r on ins after 4 out: wknd 3 out: no ch whn bdly hmpd 2 out* **8/1**[3]	113
32-1	**B**		**Salden Licht**[48] 3298 7-11-12 **152** .... WayneHutchinson (Alan King) *in rr: hdwy and hit 3 out: styng on to cl on ldng gp whn bdly hmpd and b.d 2 out* **9/1**	155
40-4	**F**		**Zanir (FR)**[34] 3557 7-10-8 **134** .... PaddyBrennan (Tom George) *chsd ldrs: rdn and styng on to dispute 4 l 4th whn fell 2 out* **20/1**	137
13F2	**F**		**Rebel Dancer (FR)**[83] 2671 6-9-12 **127** ....(t) MichaelMurphy(3) (Ian Williams) *lw: hld up in rr: hmpd on ins after 4 out: hdwy fr 3 out and clsng on ldng gp whn fell 2 out* **14/1**	130

3m 52.96s (-16.94) **Going Correction** -0.65s/f (Firm) **15** Ran SP% **126.5**

Speed ratings (Par 113): **113,112,112,112,111 111,107,106,101,101 99,99,—,—,—**

Tote Swingers:1&2:£9.40, 2&3:£24.10, 1&3:£31.80 CSF £106.33 CT £1023.82 TOTE £14.50: £3.50, £2.80, £4.10; EX 89.90.

Owner Mrs Vanessa J Stone **Bred** N P Bloodstock Ltd & Morton Bloodstock **Trained** Settrington, N Yorks

FOCUS

Considering the prize money was slashed to half its original amount it wasn't surprising the Totesport Trophy was the worst affected race numbers-wise on this rescheduled card, with the field size down from 23 to just 15 and thus leaving just the first three as each-way places. Another step forward from Recession Proof, but he is still 10lb+ off what will be required in the Supreme Novices'. Steps up from the next two.

NOTEBOOK

Recession Proof(FR) came out best in a photo finish, becoming the second successive novice to prevail. John Quinn's 5-y-o had previously won two of his three previous outings over hurdles and landed a "jumpers' bumper" at Southwell on his latest run in December. He was well in front of Bothy that day and it has to rate as a very unusual prep for this. He proved free just off the early pace here, but travelled smoothly off the home turn and found plenty for his rider's urgings when it mattered. No doubt the winner had begun life in handicaps on a decent mark, especially when looking at his four-length defeat to Dunraven Storm at Ascot in November, as that one is now rated 147. This former decent Flat handicapper has also proven his versatility regarding underfoot conditions in the past, so that isn't expected to be an issue when he turns up at next month's Cheltenham Festival. A likely reaction from the handicapper will make his life plenty tougher, but the best of him has yet to be seen and he is now due to follow the same path as last season's winner Get Me Out Of Here and head for the Supreme Novices', who finished a close second there. His odds were cut to as short as 8-1 for the Supreme and his trainer expects him to come on again for this, but that will be present a stiffer test taking on Cue Card at level weights. (tchd 14-1)

Bothy turned in a moody looking effort behind the winner on Southwell's Fibresand when last seen, but had previously made Menorah pull out all the stops in the Greatwood Hurdle at Cheltenham in November. He was 9lb higher for this return to hurdling, but had the ground in his favour and he once more posted a gallant effort only to find one that bit too strong again. He will go up again for this, but richly deserves to get his head back in front and his trainer later said the Coral Cup could be next for him. That is over further, but the likely better ground should help his stamina. (op 17-2)

Notus De La Tour(FR) was sent out from the front this time and he too ran a very brave race equipped with ear plugs. Reverting to a left-handed track looked better for him and he is now due to head for the Coral Cup next month over further. It's well worth remembering he finished second in the Fred Winter in 2010 on his only previous visit to Cheltenham.

The Betchworth Kid ran a stinker when gambled on at Kempton last month, but he has always been best in a big field on soft ground and this was a return to his very best over hurdles. He fared best of those coming from out the back and the Coral Cup looks the race for him at Cheltenham next month. However, he was pulled up on his sole outing at the Festival there last year and is a tricky character, so wouldn't be certain to put his best foot forward.

Soldatino(FR) was a real market mover for this last weekend and again proved solid here. He had his chance and posted an improved effort to emerge best of Nicky Henderson's three runners, but did rather flatten out late on. Perhaps stepping up in trip is what he needs, but his trainer later indicated the County Hurdle is his next intended port of call. (op 7-1)

Eradicate(IRE) came from a long way back and ran a very pleasing race on ground almost certainly too soft for him, even though he has placed on heavy on the Flat. An even stronger pace would have suited and he is now due to swerve Cheltenham and wait for Aintree in April. A crack at the Scottish Champion Hurdle could also figure later that month. (tchd 40-1)

Solix(FR), a Grade 3 winner over hurdles in France, was very well backed ante-post for this British debut with his leading conditional taking off 5lb. He proved very easy to back nearer the race, though, and despite having his chance it was clear two out he was in trouble. This still wasn't a bad effort under top weight and it will be interesting to see how he is now campaigned, with the Coral Cup also a possible target for him. He has the build to make a chaser.

Get Me Out Of Here(IRE) was 15lb higher than when scoring last year had run poorly in his two runs back this term. He too was well backed ante-post, but the postponement of the race saw the ground turn against him and he drifted right out before the off. It was a more encouraging display all considered and he could be a market mover in the County Hurdle next month considering he will probably be dropped a pound or two. (tchd 16-1)

Walkon(FR) was heavily backed with the extra six days expected to play right into his hands on this second run back from injury. It was apparent he was done with before three out, however, and the bounce factor very likely came into play. His trainer later said he too was of that opinion. Official explanation: trainer said gelding ran flat (op 4-1 tchd 9-2 in a place)

Sweet My Lord(FR) was the sole Irish runner this year and he met support. His inexperience found him out, however, and he was well beaten before being hampered. The best of this 5-y-o has very likely still to be seen, though, and stepping back up in trip looks on the cards. Official explanation: jockey said gelding was hampered at second last (op 9-1)

Salden Licht was staying on and in with a big chance of placing when brought down. (tchd 25-1)

Zanir(FR) was still thereabouts when falling. (tchd 25-1)

Rebel Dancer(FR) came down independently two out when keeping on from well off the pace. He remains capable of further success this term when reverting to better ground. (tchd 25-1)

4189 TOTESPORT 0800 221 221 NOVICES' HURDLE (12 hdls) 3m 110y

2:25 (2:25) (Class 4) 5-Y-0+ **£2,602** (£764; £382; £190)

Form				RPR
1	**1**		**Our Island (IRE)**[13] 3942 6-11-5 0 .... RichardJohnson (Tim Vaughan) *chsd ldrs: wnt cl 2nd 3 out: chal 2 out tl slt ld after last: hrd rdn: styd on gamely to go clr fnl 120yds* **5/1**[3]	126+
2231	**2**	*3 ¾*	**Railway Dillon (IRE)**[16] 3887 6-11-5 115 .... JasonMaguire (Donald McCain) *w ldr: led after 5th: styd chalng: led 4 out: jnd fr 2 out and hrd rdn: hdd after last: no ex fnl 120yds: all out to hold 2nd on line* **13/2**	122
1	**3**	*nse*	**Minella Stars (IRE)**[36] 3528 6-11-5 0 .... HarrySkelton (Paul Nicholls) *mde most tl after 5th: styd chalng: led again 7th: hdd 4 out: rdn next: ev ch 2 out: one pce last but kpt on u.p run-in and only jst missed taking 2nd on line* **7/4**[1]	121
FP03	**4**	*shd*	**Russian Song (IRE)**[14] 3931 7-10-12 107 ....(p) JoeTizzard (Colin Tizzard) *chsd ldrs: chal 7th to 8th: rdn and outpcd after 3 out: rallied and styd on again run-in: clsng for 2nd on line* **25/1**	114
00-P	**5**	*17*	**Tricky Trickster (IRE)**[97] 2358 8-10-12 0 .... NickScholfield (Paul Nicholls) *chsd ldrs: rdn 4 out: wknd next* **11/4**[2]	97
4-24	**6**	*½*	**Bless The Wings (IRE)**[16] 3877 6-10-12 112 .... RobertThornton (Alan King) *in rr tl hdwy 4 out: chsd ldrs appr next: sn wknd* **6/1**	97
00U/	**P**		**Bitta Dash**[1034] 5096 11-10-9 0 .... TommyPhelan(3) (Jim Wilson) *hld up bhd in tch: wknd 8th: t.o 4 out: sn p.u* **200/1**	—

6m 4.08s (-4.22) **Going Correction** -0.65s/f (Firm) **7** Ran SP% **111.7**

Speed ratings: **80,78,78,78,73 73,—**

Tote Swingers:1&2:£5.90, 2&3:£4.20, 1&3:£3.70 CSF £34.55 TOTE £6.80: £2.70, £2.80; EX 28.60.

Owner D W Fox **Bred** Michael F Condon **Trained** Aberthin, Vale of Glamorgan

FOCUS

This competitive staying novice hurdle was the one race added to the original card. It was run at a steady gallop which saw plenty in with a chance and there was a blanket finish for the places. The winner is on the upgrade but the form is nothing special.

NOTEBOOK

Our Island(IRE) followed up his debut success for connections at Ffos Las 13 days earlier and extended his winning sequence to three, having won an Irish point before joining them. He was better than the bare form that day and confirmed himself a fast-improver with a taking display under his penalty. There was plenty to like about the manner in which he travelled before knuckling down in the home straight, and plenty of cut underfoot is evidently right up his street. His point success came on quicker ground, though, and his trainer now intends to send him for the Albert Bartlett over this trip at the Cheltenham Festival. Bet365 cut him into 16-1 for that. Next year he should make a lovely novice chaser. (tchd 13-2)

Railway Dillon(IRE) posted a gutsy effort under a positive ride and just held on for second, just reversing his Hereford form with Minella Stars over the longer trip. He goes well on this sort of ground and has another novice event in him on one of the smaller tracks before going chasing next term. (tchd 6-1)

Minella Stars(IRE) comfortably held the runner-up on his hurdling debut last month and was a popular choice to follow up. He was hassled for the lead by that rival and showed his inexperience when coming under pressure from three out. He kept on having had every chance, but hit a flat spot after two out before running on again near the finish. This embryonic chaser remains a horse of potential and could well prove happier on a sounder surface. (op 6-4 tchd 5-4 and 2-1 in a place)

Russian Song(IRE) appeared well held three from home, but he motored after the last to very nearly grab second place and would've surely been bang there off a stronger gallop. His turn cannot be far off. (op 20-1)

Tricky Trickster(IRE)'s last success came in an eventful Aon Chase on this card last year. He met support back over hurdles on this return from a 97-day break, but never really looked that happy and was shaken off when things got serious from three out. He needs more of a test and it was at least a step back in the right direction. (op 4-1 tchd 9-2)

Bless The Wings(IRE) travelled sweetly, but found very little when push came to shove and needs better ground. (tchd 5-1)

4190 BET TOTEPOOL AT TOTESPORT.COM NOVICES' CHASE (18 fncs) 3m
3:00 (3:00) (Class 4) 5-Y-0+ **£3,332** (£1,034; £557)

Form RPR

2-11 **1** **Aiteen Thirtythree (IRE)**^{85} 2631 7-11-7 150.................. NickScholfield 158+
(Paul Nicholls) *lw: mde all: lft clr 10th: hit 13th: in n.d after and clr whn nt fluent 3 out: unchal* **10/11**^{1}

1/31 **2** *50* **Tarablaze**^{75} 2793 8-11-7 138.. RichardJohnson 138+
(Philip Hobbs) *lw: hit 2nd: blnd 3rd: hit 6th: lft 10 l 2nd and sltly hmpd 10th: effrt to cl on wnr whn mstke 13th: hld whn blnd 4 out: no ch and j.lft fr 3 out* **7/4**^{2}

P002 **3** *31* **Flight Leader (IRE)**^{33} 3586 11-11-0 122............................... JoeTizzard 86
(Colin Tizzard) *chsd wnr to 4th: sn no ch fr 7th: t.o* **22/1**

-21F **F** **Glenwood Knight (IRE)**^{25} 3714 8-11-7 135.................. JasonMaguire —
(Donald McCain) *trckd wnr fr 4th: 3 l 2nd and travelling okay wl whn fell 10th* **7/1**^{3}

6m 0.63s (-10.37) **Going Correction** -0.25s/f (Good) **4** Ran SP% **105.6**
Speed ratings: **107,90,80,—**
CSF £2.81 TOTE £1.50; EX 2.40.
Owner Paul K Barber & The Stewart Family **Bred** Mrs Rosemary Ross **Trained** Ditcheat, Somerset

FOCUS
This has been won by the likes of Denman and Diamond Harry in recent years. The winner was left with little to beat with the second not jumping well, but does look a high-class novice and would be worth his place in the RSA Chase field.

NOTEBOOK
Aiteen Thirtythree(IRE) was last seen leaving his previous form well behind when scoring decisively on his chasing debut over C&D in November and he followed up with another clear-cut display, jumping with aplomb in the main. He was helped by his main rival making mistakes, but there can be little doubting he would've prevailed even if that one had jumped better. Nicholls hinted after his previous success that he wasn't a likely runner in the RSA Chase, and that next season would likely be his big year with a crack at the Hennessy very much on his agenda. That could well still play out in November, but this will surely persuade connections into a trip to the Festival next month. In past years the RSA very often went to a performer that had stepped up greatly on previous hurdling form, and Aiteen Thirtythree certainly fits that profile. He has a fair bit to find with the impressive Time For Rupert, but his odds were cut across the board into around 10-1 in the ante-post betting. (op 11-10 tchd 5-6)
Tarablaze, off the mark at Exeter in December, was expected to relish stepping back up in trip and was a better hurdler than the winner. However, he hardly had a cut at his fences and really did well to finish so close in the end. These fences were evidently too daunting for him. (op 6-4 tchd 2-1)
Flight Leader(IRE) lost touch in the back straight and is now 0-9 over fences. (op 16-1 tchd 25-1)
Glenwood Knight(IRE) again paid for being too bold with his fencing and has now fallen the last twice, so is going to need his confidence building up. (tchd 6-1 and 8-1)

4191 BET TOTEPOOL ON 0800 221 221 WINTER BUMPER (STANDARD OPEN NATIONAL HUNT FLAT RACE) GRADE 2 2m 110y
3:35 (3:35) (Class 1) 4-6-Y-0
£5,701 (£2,139; £1,071; £534; £268; £134)

Form RPR

21 **1** **Ericht (IRE)**^{43} 3406 5-11-3 0.. BarryGeraghty 125+
(Nicky Henderson) *hld up in rr: hdwy 5f out: trckd ldr 4f out: shkn up to ld appr fnl 2f: c readily clr ins fnl f* **11/10**^{1}

1 **2** *4* **Bygones In Brid (IRE)**^{91} 2511 5-11-3 0...................... RobertThornton 120+
(Alan King) *w'like: hld up in rr and t.k.h: smooth hdwy fr 4f out: trckd ldng duo 3f out: chsd wnr ins fnl f and kpt on but no imp on wnr* **11/2**^{3}

1 **3** *8* **Peckhamecho (IRE)**^{104} 2222 5-11-3 0.................................. APMcCoy 113
(Rebecca Curtis) *leggy: trckd ldr: led 1/2-way: rdn 3f out: hdd appr fnl 2f: outpcd by ldng duo wl over 1f out* **7/1**

321 **4** *6* **Divine Folly (IRE)**^{29} 3651 6-10-12 0................................ DavidBass$^{(5)}$ 106
(Lawney Hill) *tall: chsd ldrs: rdn and wknd fr 3f out* **28/1**

3 **5** *19* **Street Dance (IRE)**^{24} 3731 5-11-3 0.. RhysFlint 87
(Keith Goldsworthy) *t.k.h: chsd ldrs: rdn 4f out: wknd 3f out* **40/1**

3 **6** *1 ½* **Oscar Flyer (IRE)**^{30} 3630 4-10-8 0............................. RichardJohnson 77
(Tim Vaughan) *in tch: rdn 4f out: sn wknd* **20/1**

21 **7** *9* **Balding Banker (IRE)**^{85} 2632 5-11-3 0................................ DarylJacob 77
(Paul Nicholls) *chsd ldrs tl wknd 6f out* **10/3**^{2}

2 **8** *1 ¼* **Jumps Road**^{21} 3794 4-10-8 0.. JoeTizzard 66
(Colin Tizzard) *chsd ldrs 11f: sn wknd* **20/1**

033 **9** *11* **Sunny Ledgend**^{10} 3992 6-10-10 0............................ MrSWDrinkwater$^{(7)}$ 64
(Andrew J Martin) *led tl hdd 1/2-way: wknd 5f out* **100/1**

3m 50.68s (-13.62) **Going Correction** -0.65s/f (Firm)
WFA 4 from 5yo+ 9lb **9** Ran SP% **115.0**
Speed ratings: **106,104,100,97,88 87,83,83,77**
Tote Swingers:1&2:£2.80, 2&3:£6.20, 1&3:£2.70 CSF £6.98 TOTE £2.20: £1.10, £1.80, £2.10; EX 8.50.
Owner Mrs Christopher Hanbury **Bred** Mrs M McDonagh **Trained** Upper Lambourn, Berks

FOCUS
This Grade 2 bumper was weakened by the withdrawal of the three previous winners that were originally entered last weekend. It was run at a decent gallop, though, and the form looks strong with the first four, all last-time-out winners, pulling clear. Ericht rates one of the better British-trained bumper horses this season.

NOTEBOOK
Ericht(IRE), an athletic type, came good on his second outing when winning readily at Huntingdon last month and showed himself to be fast improving with another impressive success. The return to further proved to his liking and he travelled like a smart horse before putting the race to bed under pressure. He was slashed into as short as 10-1 for the Champion Bumper at Cheltenham next month and, while this race has not produced a winner there in the past decade, Al Ferof went onto finish second there. Nicky Henderson later said he is not a fan of the Champion Bumper, but will most probably send his 5-y-o after this display. (op 5-4 tchd 6-4 in places)
Bygones In Brid(IRE) ◆ was snapped up by connections for £100,000 after making a winning debut in great style at Musselburgh three months earlier. He was settled right out the back here and emerged going strongly around 3f out. It appeared he was still somewhat green when put under pressure, though, and the winner always had his measure. He rates a very nice prospect for novice hurdling next term, may benefit for a return to better ground, and should have little trouble defying a penalty back on one of the smaller tracks. (tchd 5-1)
Peckhamecho(IRE), an athletic type, was a good-ground debut winner at Wincanton in November. He turned in a solid effort, but ultimately paid for his early exertions on the more testing surface. He should relish stepping up in trip in due course. (op 11-2 tchd 8-1)
Divine Folly(IRE), off the mark at the third attempt last month, was put in his place from 3f out but was far from disgraced. He helps to set the level. (op 20-1 tchd 33-1)
Street Dance(IRE) proved too keen on his debut for the yard in this much better race. (op 50-1 tchd 33-1)
Balding Banker(IRE) was having his first outing since winning here in November, but he weakened dramatically nearing the home turn and something presumably went amiss. (op 4-1)

T/Jkpt: £10,785.50 to a £1 stake. Pool: £15,190.89. 1.00 winning ticket. T/Plt: £281.10 to a £1 stake. Pool: £102,296.87. 265.59 winning tickets. T/Qpdt: £47.20 to a £1 stake. Pool: £9,391.64. 147.00 winning tickets. S

3944 SANDOWN (R-H)
Friday, February 18

OFFICIAL GOING: Chase course - good to soft (soft in places; good places in back straight; 7.2); hurdle course - good to soft (soft in places; 7.0)
Home bend shared by hurdlers and chasers reducing hurdle races by 25yds per circuit.
Wind: Moderate, behind. Weather: overcast

4192 RIPLEY JUVENILE HURDLE (8 hdls) 2m 110y
2:10 (2:10) (Class 4) 4-Y-O **£2,602** (£764; £382; £190)

Form RPR

04 **1** **Kayef (GER)**^{41} 3443 4-10-12 0.. AlanO'Keeffe 112+
(Michael Scudamore) *trckd ldrs: chal 3 out: led appr 2 out: styd on wl: rdn out* **9/1**

0 **2** *12* **Lucky Breeze (IRE)**^{43} 3401 4-10-5 0................................. FelixDeGiles 94
(Ed de Giles) *trckd ldrs: hit 3rd: rdn to chse wnr appr 2 out: styd on same pce* **33/1**

6 **3** *10* **Ostentation**^{27} 3673 4-10-12 0.. JamieMoore 91
(Roger Teal) *trckd ldrs: lost pl but in tch whn nt fluent 3rd: hdwy 3 out: effrt bef next: sn one pce* **8/1**

2 **4** *24* **Head Hunted**^{22} 3767 4-10-12 0.. DenisO'Regan 71
(Charlie Mann) *led: nt fluent 3rd and 4th: rdn whn hdd appr 2 out: sn wknd: t.o* **5/4**^{1}

02 **5** *2 ¼* **Kayaan**^{10} 3986 4-10-9 0.. CPGeoghegan$^{(3)}$ 67
(Pam Sly) *hld up bhd ldrs: tk clsr order 3 out: sn rdn: wknd bef next: t.o* **7/1**^{3}

0 **P** **Mountrath**^{13} 3944 4-10-12 0.. JamesDavies —
(Brett Johnson) *in last pair: t.o 4th: p.u bef 3 out* **50/1**

P **Massena (IRE)**^{111} 4-10-12 0... AidanColeman —
(Venetia Williams) *sn pressing ldr: hit 5th: lost pl qckly after 3 out: sn p.u: dismntd* **5/2**^{2}

000 **P** **Terra Bleu (IRE)**^{13} 0944 4-10-7 0.................................. MrMMO'Connor$^{(5)}$ —
(Milton Harris) *sn nudged along in last pair: t.o 5th: p.u bef 2 out* **100/1**

4m 7.00s (-0.20) **Going Correction** +0.275s/f (Yiel) **8** Ran SP% **112.5**
Speed ratings: **111,105,100,89,88 —,—,—**
toteswingers: 1&2 not won, 1&3 £7.40, 2&3 £6.40. CSF £180.34 TOTE £11.70: £2.70, £3.80, £1.50; EX 294.60.
Owner Chua, Hunter, Ong & Curtis **Bred** Gestut Brummerhof **Trained** Bromsash, Herefordshire

FOCUS
This had the look of just an ordinary juvenile hurdle for the track, but the race has thrown up two Cheltenham festival winners in recent seasons with Made In Japan going on to take the Triumph Hurdle after being successful here in 2004, and Crack Away Jack landing this and the Fred Winter three years ago. Big steps up from the first two but the form looks believable.

NOTEBOOK
Kayef(GER) showed a glimpse of potential here last month and there was support for him this time. After racing a little wide of the others, he cut down the leader on the approach to the second-last and stayed on well, drawing clear between the last two flights for a decisive win. He is progressing nicely and looks a tough individual, but while he is entered in the Triumph Hurdle, he looks more of a Fred Winter type. (op 14-1)
Lucky Breeze(IRE) jumped badly on her hurdles debut at Huntingdon but has reportedly done plenty of schooling since, although she still blundered at the first in the back straight. Chasing the winner in vain from the second-last, she is up to winning a small race for her rookie trainer.
Ostentation, well behind leading Triumph fancy Grandouet at Ascot, showed more here. He was outpaced by the leaders from the home turn but stayed on quite well for third. (op 15-2)
Head Hunted set the pace but put in successive poor jumps down the back. He weakened rapidly on the approach to the second-last and appeared to finish tired. (op 6-4 tchd 7-4)
Kayaan was keen when runner-up on his second hurdles start and was held up here. He came under pressure at the third-last and was soon out of contention. (op 8-1 tchd 13-2)
Mountrath Official explanation: jockey said gelding had a breathing problem (op 15-8 tchd 13-8)
Massena(IRE), runner-up at Auteuil in October on his one hurdles start, and sold to current connections for 150,000 euros, travelled well until stopping very quickly three from home. Pulled up, it turned out that he had banged a knee and he was sound again not long after. A lean sort, he should be worth another chance. Official explanation: jockey said gelding lost its action (op 15-8 tchd 13-8)

4193 CHEMRING GROUP H'CAP CHASE (FOR THE ALANBROOKE CHALLENGE CUP) (22 fncs) 3m 110y
2:40 (2:41) (Class 3) (0-135,132) 5-Y-0+ **£6,505** (£1,910; £955; £477)

Form RPR

0-5P **1** **Qhilimar (FR)**^{48} 3290 7-11-2 **122**.. TomO'Brien 133+
(Charlie Longsdon) *chsd ldrs: rdn after 19th: 4 l down 3 out tl str run u.p fr last: drifted lft fnl 100yds: led fnl strides* **4/1**^{1}

1432 **2** *shd* **The Rainbow Hunter**^{30} 3629 7-11-1 **128**.......................... EdCookson$^{(7)}$ 138+
(Andy Turnell) *hld up: hit 4th: tk clsr order 11th: led 3 out: rdn after next: hrd pressed run-in: drifted sltly rt u.p fnl 100yds: hdd fnl strides* **11/2**^{2}

6P-R **3** *1* **Craiglands (IRE)**^{89} 2541 9-10-7 **113**..............................(bt^{1}) DaveCrosse 122
(Ian Williams) *travelled wl in tch: tk clsr order fr 16th: wnt 2nd 19th: rdn and ev ch after 3 out: swtchd rt bef last: chalng whn short of room fnl 75yds: squeezed out nr fin* **10/1**

4U34 **4** *16* **I'moncloudnine (IRE)**^{13} 3940 8-11-11 **131**.....................(p) WillKennedy 127
(Neil Mulholland) *led 2nd: hit 7th: rdn and hdd 3 out: sn hld: wknd last* **13/2**

2146 **5** *41* **Buffalo Bob (IRE)**^{20} 3804 8-11-12 **132**............................(t) SeanQuinlan 88
(Kim Bailey) *led tl 2nd: prom: rdn after 19th: wknd bef 3 out: t.o* **6/1**^{3}

01P- **6** *6* **Temoin**^{389} 3660 11-11-5 **125**..(b) JamieMoore 75
(Richard Phillips) *slowly away: detached tl latched on to main gp 11th: struggling after 12th: lost tch again fr 14th: t.o* **33/1**

221/ **P** **Its A Dream (IRE)**^{794} 2824 11-11-11 **131**............................ FelixDeGiles —
(Nicky Henderson) *hld up: rdn whn hit 13th: grad lost tch fr 16th: t.o whn p.u bef 3 out* **11/1**

2054 **P** **Noun De La Thinte (FR)**^{19} 3832 10-11-0 **120**............... AidanColeman —
(Venetia Williams) *trckd ldrs tl 13th: sn rdn: wknd 15th: t.o whn p.u bef 3 out* **12/1**

0002 **P** **Dashing George (IRE)**^{14} 3922 9-10-13 **119**................(b) LiamTreadwell —
(Dr Richard Newland) *hld up: struggling 13th: sn wknd: p.u bef 16th* **11/2**^{2}

415 **P** **Fit To Drive**[27] 3674 9-11-6 **129**........(t) RichieMcLernon(3) —
(Brendan Powell) *prom: disp fr 9th tl rdn 18th: wknd after next: p.u bef last* **14/1**

6m 30.0s (2.20) **Going Correction** +0.275s/f (Yiel) **10** Ran SP% **113.1**
Speed ratings: **107,106,106,101,88 86,—,—,—,—**
toteswingers: 1&2 £10.10, 1&3 £54.70, 2&3 £54.70. CSF £26.04 CT £202.09 TOTE £4.70: £1.80, £2.30, £3.40; EX 31.80.
Owner Whites Of Coventry & Stephen Dunn **Bred** Michel Contignon & Mme Andree Contignon **Trained** Over Norton, Oxon
■ Stewards' Enquiry : Tom O'Brien caution: careless riding.

FOCUS
A decent handicap chase run at a fair pace. The first two ran personal bests and the form should work out.

NOTEBOOK
Qhilimar(FR), formerly trained by Alan Jones, made a successful debut for his new yard. Without headgear and ridden slightly more prominently than usual, he was still only third jumping the last but stayed on well up the hill to snatch victory on the line. He made mistakes last time but jumped soundly here. (op 5-1)
The Rainbow Hunter was unfortunate to bump into the well handicapped Sona Sasta on his last start and went up 4lb for that. Well ridden by his young jockey, he nipped through on the inside to lead on the home turn, but after fighting off the third home, was pipped right on the line. (op 9-2)
Craiglands(IRE), who was previously with Jim Goldie, travelled well in the first-time headgear. He came through to have every chance, but could not quite force his head in front and was held when he was squeezed between the first two close home. He has yet to win a handicap but is now 8lb lower than when placed four times in 2009, including in the Grand Sefton. (op 16-1 tchd 9-1)
I'moncloudnine(IRE) was 2lb lower than when finishing third in the rearranged Welsh National. Down in trip, he made much of the running until weakening from the second-last. (op 6-1 tchd 7-1)
Buffalo Bob(IRE), fitted with a first-time tongue tie, was unable to get his way in front and he weakened out of things going to the third-last. Despite a recent drop, he is still 6lb above his Newbury mark. (op 13-2 tchd 11-2)
Its A Dream(IRE) had been off since December 2008 (said to look fit enough) and was making his handicap debut at the age of eleven. He travelled quite well until a blunder had him on the back foot and was adrift when pulling up, but may be worth another chance. Official explanation: trainer's rep said gelding had a breathing problem (op 8-1)
Dashing George(IRE) Official explanation: jockey said gelding lost its action and a near hind shoe (op 8-1)
Fit To Drive, who was 10lb higher than when winning over C&D two starts back, dropped away after racing prominently. (op 8-1)

4194 ROYAL ARTILLERY GOLD CUP CHASE (FOR AMATEUR RIDERS) (SUPPORTED BY NP AEROSPACE) (22 fncs) 3m 110y
3:20 (3:27) (Class 3) 6-Y-O+ **£4,996** (£1,549; £774; £387)

Form RPR
13U- **1** **Surenaga (IRE)**[33] 9-11-7 117........(p) L-BdrSallyRandell(7) 133+
(Miss Sally Randell) *hld up in tch: hit 18th: hdwy after next: wnt 3rd 3 out: shkn up and r.o strly to ld run-in: wl rdn* **14/1**
13-2 **2** *2* **Blu Teen (FR)**[283] 268 11-11-7 118........(t) L-BdrJSole(7) 129
(D J Staddon) *in tch: trckd ldrs 9th: led 19th: rdn after last: no ex whn hdd fnl 120yds* **11/4**[2]
23-3 **3** *1 ¼* **Knighton Combe**[17] 3866 11-12-5 126........ MissLHorner 133
(Jamie Snowden) *trckd ldrs: wnt 2nd 19th: rdn and ev ch after 3 out: styd on same pce fr next* **15/8**[1]
FUF0 **4** *10* **Scots Dragoon**[27] 3688 9-12-0 119........ MajAMichael(5) 125
(Nicky Henderson) *racd wd: hld up: plenty to do 16th: hdwy after 19th: rdn after next: wnt 4th whn pckd 2 out: no further imp* **7/1**
5212 **5** *15* **Mr Big (IRE)**[32] 3602 10-12-2 116........(p) LtColOEllwood(3) 116
(Charlie Mann) *led: nt fluent 3rd: hdd 19th: sn rdn: wknd 2 out* **3/1**[3]
3/6- **6** *1 ¾* **Jamadiel (IRE)**[17] 10-11-11 109........ MissLGardner(3) 104
(S Slevin, Ire) *hld up: struggling 13th: wknd 3 out* **33/1**
030/ **7** *1 ¼* **Back Is Back (IRE)**[41] 7-11-7 102........(t) MrRGRSpencer(7) 105
(Miss Jane Western) *prom tl 18th: rdn after next: wkng whn hit 3 out* **66/1**
634/ **R** **Goldfinger (IRE)**[314] 9-11-7 100........(p) CaptMaxChenery(7) —
(Seamus Mullins) *pckd 1st: in tch: struggling fr 14th: wknd 19th: t.o whn ref last* **66/1**
/0-6 **P** **Even Homer Nods (IRE)**[264] 10-11-7 75........(t) SgtMartinDennis(7) —
(A F Gorman) *trckd ldrs tl 9th: dropped to last after 11th: lost tch fr 13th: t.o whn p.u bef 2 out* **100/1**

6m 50.4s (22.60) **Going Correction** +0.275s/f (Yiel) **9** Ran SP% **112.5**
Speed ratings: **74,73,72,69,64 64,64,—,—**
toteswingers: 1&2 £7.40, 1&3 £5.10, 2&3 £2.50. CSF £52.49 TOTE £16.10: £3.40, £1.10, £1.10; EX 61.60.
Owner 100 Regiment Royal Artillery Volunteers **Bred** Mrs Teresa Bergin **Trained** Bridgend

FOCUS
A decent renewal of this historic event. They appeared to go a strong initial gallop, but the time was 20 seconds slower than the preceding handicap. A step up from the winner and the beaten horses give the form a solid look.

NOTEBOOK
Surenaga(IRE) swept through to lead on the run-in and win going away. Ex-Irish, he has been a modest performer under rules but came here off the back of two good runs in point-to-points at Black Forest Lodge this winter. He jumped well bar a mistake at the last ditch. (op 11-1)
Blu Teen(FR) was hampered at the start but soon raced in touch. Jumping to the front four out, he could not hold off the winner after the last. Lack of a recent run may just have told on this useful hunter chaser, who was third over the Aintree fences last April. (op 3-1 tchd 7-2)
Knighton Combe, whose trainer won this race four times as a jockey, made mistakes at the first fence down the back on both circuits. Always up with the pace, he had his chance but could not quicken up. The Scottish Grand National is his reported target. (op 7-4 tchd 13-8)
Scots Dragoon, last year's Grand Military Gold Cup winner, put in a clear round and was keeping on at the end, but was never seen with a chance. (tchd 11-2 and 15-2)
Mr Big(IRE), who won this contest under a different rider a year ago and was third in 2009, jumped soundly in front but faded after he was passed at the last down the back straight. (op 4-1)
Jamadiel(IRE), a regular in these military races, might have finished closer had he not proved reluctant to start. He also lost ground with a mistake down the back when attempting to close.

4195 FINMECCANICA UK BATTLESPACE SOLUTIONS NOVICES' HURDLE (8 hdls) 2m 110y
3:55 (3:57) (Class 4) 4-Y-O+ **£3,252** (£955; £477; £238)

Form RPR
1 **Topolski (IRE)**[139] 5-11-2 0........ AidanColeman 119+
(David Arbuthnot) *travelled and j.w: in last but in tch: smooth hdwy after 3 out to ld sn after next: readily qckned clr* **14/1**[3]
0-61 **2** *7* **Lifestyle**[24] 3721 5-11-2 0........ FelixDeGiles 110+
(Nicky Henderson) *travelled wl: trckd ldrs: rdn to chal for 2nd after 2 out but nt pce of wnr* **3/1**[2]
-122 **3** *shd* **Megastar**[41] 3445 6-11-9 141........ JamieMoore 117+
(Gary Moore) *travelled strly: trckd ldr: gd jump to ld 3rd: kpt stdy pce tl rdn and hdd sn after 2 out: nt pce of wnr* **4/11**[1]
05 **4** *18* **Benozzo Gozzoli**[15] 3906 5-10-13 0........ JimmyDerham(3) 92
(Seamus Mullins) *led at stdy pce tl 3rd: w ldr tl after 3 out: outpcd appr 2 out: wknd last* **66/1**
000 **5** *7* **Mighty Monty**[21] 3789 6-11-2 0........ DenisO'Regan 86
(Victor Dartnall) *trckd ldrs: rdn after 3 out: outpcd bef next: wknd bef last* **66/1**

4m 10.4s (3.20) **Going Correction** +0.275s/f (Yiel) **5** Ran SP% **108.0**
Speed ratings (Par 105): **103,99,99,91,87**
toteswinger: 1&2 £4.60. CSF £52.14 TOTE £9.00: £4.00, £1.10; EX 31.80.
Owner P M Claydon **Bred** C H Wacker Iii **Trained** Compton, Berks

FOCUS
This novice hurdle has been won by Punchestowns and Oscar Whisky in its short history, but this year's edition was run at a crawl and the time was over 23 seconds outside the standard. The form is unlikely to prove too solid, with the two market leaders contributing to their own downfall by taking a keen hold. The winner can surely rate a lot higher in time.

NOTEBOOK
Topolski(IRE) won in nice style and is clearly going to prove a useful recruit to hurdling. Effective at 1m4f-2m on the Flat with a current BHA rating of 90 on turf, he settled far better than his principal rivals and picked up much the best in the sprint to the line to come right away. He is not entered at Cheltenham, but may go to Aintree. He should win more races in this sphere and will probably stay further. (op 16-1 tchd 10-1)
Lifestyle was bidding to give her trainer a third win in this event in four years. She had been keen when winning at Leicester and she was still taking a hold as they faced up to the final two flights here. She stayed on at just the one pace from there, just getting the better of the tussle for second but never looking like matching the winner's turn of foot. The European Breeders' Fund 'National Hunt' Novices' Hurdle at Newbury looks a suitable target, and that race should be run at a much more suitable pace. (op 9-4)
Megastar, runner-up to Minella Class in the Tolworth here last time and currently rated 141, was conceding 7lb to the winner. The early leader was going nothing like quickly enough for this rangy gelding so his jockey took him to the front at the third, but he still wanted to go faster. He made a couple of minor mistakes and when it boiled down to a sprint from the home turn he failed to pick up anything like as well as the winner. He is not quite living up to expectations over hurdles, but this race was no good for him and he remains a bright prospect, with genuine spring ground likely to suit. He holds entries at Cheltenham in both the Supreme Novices' and the longer Neptune Hurdle. He has the build of a chaser. (op 4-9)
Benozzo Gozzoli was well beaten but is now qualified for handicaps. (op 80-1)
Mighty Monty was a long way adrift when he blundered two out.

4196 EMU TECHNOLOGIES NOVICES' H'CAP HURDLE (9 hdls) 2m 4f
4:30 (4:30) (Class 4) (0-120,119) 4-Y-O+ **£3,252** (£955; £477; £238)

Form RPR
0001 **1** **Pere Blanc (IRE)**[7] 4052 6-10-9 **102** 7ex........ AidanColeman 124+
(David Arbuthnot) *travelled wl: trckd ldrs: led on bit bef 2 out: sn clr: unextended* **4/11**[1]
44U **2** *11* **Baile Anrai (IRE)**[21] 3789 7-11-6 **113**........ DougieCostello 122+
(Ian Williams) *hld up bhd ldrs: hdwy into 2nd whn swtchd lft bef 2 out: sn rdn: styd on but no ch w easy wnr* **33/1**
-631 **3** *7* **Doctor Foxtrot (IRE)**[22] 3761 6-11-6 **118**........(b) GilesHawkins(5) 117
(Philip Hobbs) *trckd ldrs: rdn after 3 out: styd on same pce fr next* **9/1**[2]
4413 **4** *1* **Ultravox (USA)**[30] 3624 4-10-8 **118**........ NathanSweeney(7) 108
(Jeremy Scott) *hld up bhd ldrs: blnd 3 out: sn rdn: styd on same pce fr next* **12/1**[3]
-452 **5** *3 ¼* **Grey Wulff (IRE)**[36] 3528 6-11-3 **110**........ JackDoyle 106
(Emma Lavelle) *led tl rdn appr 2 out: sn hld: fdd whn lost 2 pls fr last* **9/1**[2]
1202 **6** *21* **Kahfre**[23] 2439 4-10-11 **114**........(v) JamieMoore 80
(Gary Moore) *hld up bhd ldrs: rdn after 3 out: wknd bef next* **28/1**
F414 **7** *¾* **Folie A Deux (IRE)**[12] 3963 9-10-12 **108**........(tp) SamTwiston-Davies(3) 84
(Dr Richard Newland) *w ldr tl rdn after 3 out: sn wknd* **33/1**

5m 12.1s (6.40) **Going Correction** +0.275s/f (Yiel)
WFA 4 from 5yo+ 10lb **7** Ran SP% **110.3**
Speed ratings (Par 105): **98,93,90,90,89 80,80**
toteswingers: 1&2 £4.20, 1&3 £1.70, 2&3 £7.70. CSF £15.06 CT £45.95 TOTE £1.40: £1.10, £6.20; EX 16.80.
Owner George Ward **Bred** George Ward **Trained** Compton, Berks

FOCUS
An ordinary novices' handicap, this has been won in recent years by Silk Affair, who went on to land the Fred Winter at Cheltenham, and by subsequent Imperial Cup winner Qaspal. The easy winner should out and should be competitive off his new mark.

NOTEBOOK
Pere Blanc(IRE) was no less than 18lb well in under the penalty for his easy win at Kempton. He won as a horse with so much in hand ought to, travelling strongly all the way and sauntering home, but while he has improved considerably for a step up in trip, he will obviously face a sterner test off his new mark. He will go chasing next season. (op 4-9 tchd 1-2 in a place)
Baile Anrai(IRE) ◆ came through for second and was not given a hard time when it was apparent he would not be troubling the easy winner. This winning pointer is finding his feet all the time and looks one to follow. (op 20-1)
Doctor Foxtrot(IRE) was 4lb higher than when last in a handicap. He was one-paced up the straight, but plugged on for third and might be worth a try at 3m. (op 8-1 tchd 15-2)
Ultravox(USA) was in trouble after a mistake three out but did keep on for fourth, staying the longer trip well enough. (op 14-1 tchd 9-1)
Grey Wulff(IRE) had no answers at all when headed by the winner and faded out of the places after the last. (tchd 17-2)
Folie A Deux(IRE), with the cheekpieces back on for this return to hurdles, weakened after disputing the lead. (op 25-1)

4197 "UBIQUE" HUNTERS' CHASE (17 fncs) 2m 4f 110y
5:00 (5:00) (Class 5) 6-Y-O+ **£1,561** (£484; £242; £121)

Form RPR
616- **1** **Just Amazing (IRE)**[300] 5395 8-12-4 145........(t) MrRMahon 123+
(Paul Nicholls) *prom: led 4th: clr whn mstke 3 out: styd on strly* **1/1**[1]
4-0P **2** *9* **Launde (IRE)**[5] 12-11-13 93........ MrTJCannon(5) 114
(Mrs Jenny Gordon) *mid-div of chsng gp: hdwy fr 9th: rdn to chal for 2nd whn hit 3 out: sn no ch w wnr: wnt clr 2nd run-in* **100/1**
33-3 **3** *3 ½* **Almaydan**[295] 57 13-11-13 127........(b) MrWKinsey(5) 109
(Mrs K M Diggle) *led chsng gp in 5th: clsd on ldrs after 6th: wnt 2nd 12th: rdn bef 3 out: sn no ch w wnr: lost 2nd run-in* **16/1**
-210 **4** *30* **Distant Thunder (IRE)**[6] 13-11-7 108........(t) MrPPrince(7) 90+
(Mrs A S Hodges) *awkward 1st: in rr wl off str pce: stdy prog fr 12th: wnt 4th after 3 out: nvr trbld ldrs* **14/1**
000- **5** *57* **Jaamid**[33] 9-11-11 0........ MrJSHorton(7) 31
(William Hayes, Ire) *a in rr: nvr a factor: t.o* **14/1**

P1-1 **P** **Bob Hall (IRE)**[289] 153 10-12-4 129......................................(t) MrAJBerry —
(Jonjo O'Neill) *nvr travelling off str pce: hit 2nd: nvr a factor: p.u bef last* **10/3**[2]

FU-F **U** **Soleil Fix (FR)**[34] 10-11-10 125......................................(v) MrDHDunsdon —
(Nick Gifford) *chsd clr ldrs in 4th: clsd on ldrs after 6th: nt fluent 11th (water): uns rdr sn after* **14/1**

P1/ **P** **Bravery Scotch (IRE)**[292] 9-11-7 114................................ MrBJPoste(7) —
(Miss S M Taylor) *mid-div tl wknd 14th: bhd whn p.u bef last* **28/1**

/2U- **P** **Bolachoir (IRE)**[20] 9-11-3 108.. MrMTSlevin(7) —
(S Slevin, Ire) *prom in chsng gp tl after 6th: sn in rr: t.o whn p.u after 14th* **17/2**[3]

0P/P **P** **Latalanta (FR)**[281] 297 8-11-3 91...................................... MrBBentley(7) —
(Mrs P A Tetley) *pckd 1st: led at str pce tl 4th: chsd ldr tl after 6th: sn bhd: p.u bef 10th* **80/1**

2-30 **R** **Cloud Nine (IRE)**[15] 3908 8-11-5 109..............................(b) MrJHamer(5) —
(Miss Jane Western) *chsd ldr tl wknd 14th: bhd whn ref last* **33/1**

0/ **P** **Phiroza**[26] 8-10-12 0.. MrRGHenderson(5) —
(Mrs C Hobbs) *a in rr: t.o fr 11th: p.u after 14th* **100/1**

5m 34.7s (16.30) **Going Correction** +0.275s/f (Yiel) **12** Ran SP% **119.1**
Speed ratings: **79,75,74,62,41** —,—,—,—,— —,—
toteswingers: 1&2 £38.80. 1&3 £5.40, 2&3 £42.50. CSF £156.53 TOTE £1.90: £1.10, £18.80, £4.20; EX 161.70.
Owner Mrs Catherine Penny **Bred** R J Powell **Trained** Ditcheat, Somerset

FOCUS
A fair hunters' chase. The winner can rate higher on better ground, with the second limiting the rating.

NOTEBOOK
Just Amazing(IRE), not seen since finishing sixth in the Bet365 Gold Cup at the end of last season, was the pick at the weights on this hunter chase debut. Always up with the pace and generally jumping well, he survived a mistake at the Pond Fence to win easily. The aim is to qualify him for the Cheltenham Foxhunters' and he will need to finish first or second at either Taunton or Huntingdon next week if he is to get in. Also entered in the Grand National, he handled this ground well but has done most of his winning on a sound surface. (op 10-11 tchd 5-4)
Launde(IRE) had not been in much form between the flags but he ran well, staying on to grab second on the run-in.
Almaydan ran a pleasing race on this debut in the hunter ranks, but could never threaten the winner and weakened out of second place on the run-in. A very safe conveyance, he showed much of his best form for Richard Lee over 2m. (tchd 18-1)
Distant Thunder(IRE) won a point as recently as six days earlier and showed enough to suggest that he can still be competitive in ordinary hunter chases. (op 16-1 tchd 12-1)
Bob Hall(IRE) won three hunter chases last spring, his only defeat coming in the Cheltenham Foxhunters'. Racing well off the pace and putting in some sketchy jumps, he did pass struggling rivals on the second circuit but was a remote fifth when he was pulled up before the final fence. His rider reported that he was never travelling. Official explanation: jockey said gelding never travelled (op 4-1 tchd 3-1)
T/Plt: £621.00 to a £1 stake. Pool: £60,831.92. 71.50 winning tickets. T/Qpdt: £17.80 to a £1 stake. Pool: £6,494.60. 269.45 winning tickets. TM

3672 ASCOT (R-H)
Saturday, February 19

OFFICIAL GOING: Soft
Wind: Virtually nil Weather: Heavy drizzle

4198 ESPIRITO SANTO INVESTMENT BANK NOVICES' HURDLE (11 hdls) 2m 3f 110y
1:20 (1:21) (Class 2) 5-Y-0+
£6,888 (£2,035; £1,017; £509; £254; £127)

Form RPR

1 **1** **Sonofvic (IRE)**[108] 2143 6-11-5 0.. NickScholfield 141+
(Paul Nicholls) *hld up in rr: stdy hdwy 4 out: trckd ldrs next: wnt 2nd after 3 out: chal next and upsides last: led sn after: drvn out* **3/1**[3]

211 **2** *2* **Tornado Bob (IRE)**[25] 3718 6-11-8 143.............................. JasonMaguire 143+
(Donald McCain) *trckd ldr: chal 4 out: led next: rdn appr 2 out and jnd: stl slt advantage whn mstke stmbld and hdd last: rallied u.p but a jst hld* **13/8**[1]

2114 **3** *27* **Synthe Davis (FR)**[42] 3442 6-11-1 130.......................... RichardJohnson 107
(Laura Mongan) *led tl hdd 3 out: wknd wl bef last* **8/1**

-111 **4** *3 ½* **Problema Tic (FR)**[27] 3692 5-11-8 0................................ BarryGeraghty 112
(Nicky Henderson) *chsd ldrs: j. slowly 4 out: sn rdn and btn bef next: wknd qckly* **5/2**[2]

-642 **5** *9* **Smart Freddy**[45] 3398 5-11-0 115.................................... TomScudamore 94
(Lawney Hill) *chsd ldrs untl rdn and wknd 4 out* **20/1**

0-6 **6** *1* **Carabinier (FR)**[105] 2215 5-11-0 0................................... AndrewTinkler 93
(Nicky Henderson) *in rr but in tch: rdn and wknd 4 out* **66/1**

53-0 **7** *shd* **The White Admiral (IRE)**[49] 3288 6-11-0 0......................... DavidBass 92
(Nicky Henderson) *in rr: nt fluent 2nd: hit 6th and 7th: wknd 4 out* **50/1**

1/P **8** *27* **Suburban Bay**[28] 3678 6-11-0 0.. JimmyMcCarthy 65
(Alan King) *hld up off pce early: no ch whn j. slowly 4 out* **40/1**

4m 51.21s (3.21) **Going Correction** +0.40s/f (Soft) **8** Ran SP% **113.4**
Speed ratings: **109,108,97,96,92 92,91,81**
Tote Swingers: 1&2 £1.60, 1&3 £4.50, 2&3 £3.00 CSF £8.31 TOTE £4.10: £1.30, £1.20, £1.90; EX 8.10 Trifecta £72.20 Pool £1,063.21 - 10.89 winning units..
Owner Mrs Angela Hart **Bred** Mrs Rosemary Ross **Trained** Ditcheat, Somerset

FOCUS
A race won last year by exciting novice chaser Finian's Rainbow, and Nicky Henderson provided three of the eight runners, but none of his trio got involved at the end. The pace looked sound in ground described as soft, hard work and unlikely to suit plenty of horses. The winner is on the upgrade and the second, to his mark, sets the level with the third and fourth well below their previous ratings.

NOTEBOOK
Sonofvic(IRE) ◆, absent since winning on his debut under rules in early November, a race that has worked out nicely, ground out a hard-fought victory receiving 3lb from the runner-up. Both horses came clear from the home bend and gave their all until the Paul Nicholls' challenger got on top after the final hurdle. Sonofvic clearly has stamina but doesn't look short of speed either considering the way he travelled, and is an exciting prospect. He is likely to be put away until the autumn for a chasing campaign. (tchd 11-4 and 10-3 in a place)
Tornado Bob(IRE) ◆, had looked a stout stayer in his previous starts over hurdles, and conditions appeared to have come right for him after rain fell. He didn't disappoint, showing his usual good attitude, but a mistake at the last, as well as the 3lb he gave away, handed the advantage to the winner. However, he remains a horse of serious potential and will make a chaser. (tchd 6-4 and 7-4)
Synthe Davis(FR) has enjoyed a good season and quickly got to the head of affairs. She set a fair gallop and was one of three to come clear after the third last, but was treading water coming to two out and posed no threat. (op 10-1)
Problema Tic(FR) came into this with an unblemished record but ran poorly, as he was beaten a long way from home. Nicky Henderson reported afterwards that the ground had gone against his horse. (tchd 11-4 and 3-1 in places)
The White Admiral(IRE) should make a chaser.
Suburban Bay has the build to jump fences.

4199 SODEXO PRESTIGE REYNOLDSTOWN NOVICES' CHASE GRADE 2 (20 fncs) 3m
1:50 (1:50) (Class 1) 5-Y-0+ **£14,082** (£5,305; £2,655; £1,327)

Form RPR

-151 **1** **Master Of The Hall (IRE)**[24] 3743 7-11-4 144................. BarryGeraghty 148+
(Nicky Henderson) *trckd ldrs: chal fr 15th tl led 3 out: c clr on bit wl bef 2 out: v easily* **6/5**[1]

1350 **2** *6* **Billie Magern**[49] 3291 7-11-7 133... PaddyBrennan 143+
(Nigel Twiston-Davies) *mde must tl hdd and j. slowly 3 out: no ch w wnr whn blnd and dropped bk 3rd sn after 2 out: rallied to retake 2nd cl home but no ch w v easy wnr* **12/1**[2]

0-11 **3** *nk* **The Minack (IRE)**[23] 3770 7-11-4 143.................................. NickScholfield 141+
(Paul Nicholls) *trckd ldrs tl blnd bdly 14th and lost 5 l: rcvrd fr 3 out to chse wnr sn after 2 out but nvr any ch: no ex and lost 2nd cl home* **6/5**[1]

2-12 **4** *25* **Teddy's Reflection (IRE)**[39] 3496 8-11-4 129.................(p) HaddenFrost 117
(Henrietta Knight) *pressed ldr to 14th: rdn 15th: wknd 4 out* **12/1**[2]

6m 28.48s (19.48) **Going Correction** +0.40s/f (Soft) **4** Ran SP% **106.3**
Speed ratings: **83,81,80,72**
CSF £11.08 TOTE £2.20; EX 13.80.
Owner Martin Landau & Jonathan Duffy **Bred** Sweetmans Bloodstock **Trained** Upper Lambourn, Berks

FOCUS
This is a contest that is always won by a good chaser, but the lack of runners this year meant the field only went a slow gallop throughout the early stages and didn't really increase until they reached Swinley Bottom for the final time. The runner-up is the best guide to the form.

NOTEBOOK
Master Of The Hall(IRE) was just the highest rated of these on official figures and had more-or-less proved he stayed 3m at Huntingdon, where he beat a subsequent winner. Representing a trainer who had produced Burton Port and Bacchanal to take this in the past, he made a move soon after his main market rival made a crucial mistake, and never looked like being caught once he moved up stylishly to the leader and eased past. He is likely to run in the RSA Chase. (op 5-4 tchd 11-8 in a place)
Billie Magern won on four of his first five tries over fences during the summer/autumn, but had been a little disappointing on his last two starts, albeit at a decent level. Connections were hoping to find some good ground, but the rain got in and the going went against him, so it has to be said that he put up a highly commendable performance despite almost coming down after hitting two out. (op 14-1)
The Minack(IRE) came into this unbeaten in two starts over fences and was upped in trip for his step up in grade. Held up in the back pair, he was going every bit as well as his rivals when blundering at the 14th. The jockey did well to keep the partnership intact, but that was his winning opportunity gone and, although he rallied back into second place at one point after two out, he was comfortably held. Official explanation: vet said gelding sustained a cut to left-fore (op 11-10 tchd 5-4)
Teddy's Reflection(IRE), a C&D winner over fences, had plenty on at the weights and had cheekpieces fitted for the first time. Quickly into stride, he jumped nicely while sharing the pace but was readily dropped when the tempo properly increased.

4200 WEATHERBYS BLOODSTOCK INSURANCE CHASE LIMITED H'CAP (LISTED RACE) (20 fncs) 3m
2:25 (2:25) (Class 1) 5-Y-0+
£22,804 (£8,556; £4,284; £2,136; £1,072; £536)

Form RPR

P3-1 **1** **Iconoclast (IRE)**[109] 2140 10-10-4 **130** oh3......................... PaulMoloney 141+
(Alex Hales) *hld up in rr: in tch whn blnd and wl bhd 9th: j. slowly 15th: hdwy fr next: str run appr 2 out: chsd ldr last: styd on u.p to ld fnl 30yds* **7/1**

5064 **2** *nk* **The Sawyer (BEL)**[21] 3804 11-10-1 **134**...................... NathanSweeney(7) 140
(Bob Buckler) *chsd ldr tl rdn and dropped to rr appr 15th: styd on again u.p appr 3 out: chsd ldr next and j. slowly: led last: hdd and no ex fnl 30yds* **11/2**[3]

1 **3** *4* **Royal Tune (FR)**[53] 3157 6-11-0 **140**................................... JacquesRicou 143+
(G Macaire, France) *trckd ldrs: chal fr 15th tl led 4 out: travelling wl 3 out: rdn 2 out: hdd last: outpcd fnl 100yds* **5/2**[1]

3F61 **4** *15* **Carrickmines (IRE)**[8] 4054 9-10-4 **130** oh2...................(b) LiamTreadwell 117
(Dr Richard Newland) *led: blnd 12th: jnd 15th: hdd 4 out: no ch w ldr after 3 out: btn into 4th whn j. slowly 2 out* **9/1**

UPP3 **5** *6* **Burren Legend (IRE)**[14] 3948 10-10-4 **130**....................... AndrewThornton 113
(Richard Rowe) *in rr: hdwy 14th: rdn and wknd 15th: no ch whn hit 2 out* **12/1**

54-P **6** *3* **Roll Along (IRE)**[14] 3947 11-11-3 **143**..............................(p) PaddyBrennan 121
(Nigel Twiston-Davies) *chsd ldrs: disp 2nd 10th tl wknd 15th* **20/1**

F/23 **7** *10* **Breedsbreeze (IRE)**[28] 3677 9-11-10 **150**............................ DarylJacob 118
(Paul Nicholls) *in tch: hdwy 13th: blnd 14th: drvn to chse ldrs 4 out: nvr on terms and sn wknd* **7/2**[2]

-430 **U** **Exmoor Ranger (IRE)**[42] 3437 9-11-4 **144**......................... DenisO'Regan —
(Victor Dartnall) *trckd ldrs tl blnd and uns rdr 11th* **13/2**

6m 14.8s (5.80) **Going Correction** +0.40s/f (Soft) **8** Ran SP% **114.5**
Speed ratings: **106,105,104,99,97 96,93,—**
Tote Swingers: 1&2 £11.90, 1&3 £3.70, 2&3 £8.20 CSF £45.23 CT £122.59 TOTE £7.20: £1.70, £2.30, £1.60; EX 46.80 Trifecta £682.70 Part won..
Owner John & Lorraine Barlow **Bred** Andrew Kavanagh And Mary Cunnion **Trained** Wardington, Oxon
■ The first running of this event.

FOCUS
A strong contest with plenty of horses that could be fancied to run well, but it produced a most unlikely winner considering an early mishap. The first and second home were last and second last, seemingly in big trouble, before six out. The winner should be competitive when reassessed while the second is rated to his season's best.

NOTEBOOK
Iconoclast(IRE), up 6lb for his Exeter success and 3lb out of the handicap, hit the ninth hard and his task looked so hopeless that Paul Moloney considered pulling up. However, he somehow worked his way back into contention and got up in the final strides under a fantastic ride. (tchd 8-1)
The Sawyer(BEL) had been well beaten on all starts this season, so this was a lot better even though he needed a lot of pushing along to get competitive. It was a good effort by Nathan Sweeney to get him to have any chance at all. (op 15-2 tchd 8-1)

Royal Tune(FR) ◆ fairly bolted up at Ffos Las over 2m5f (nothing special about that form) on his British debut and had been suitably punished by the handicapper. He travelled strongly in behind here and eased into what looked an unassailable position rounding the final bend, however, he started to weaken after two out and was steadily worn down. Had he been held up for a little bit longer, he would have surely won and can easily be given another chance. (op 2-1 tchd 11-4 in places)

Carrickmines(IRE), raised 9lb for his victory at Kempton earlier this month, raced freely in the lead and was never likely to keep up the gallop. (op 10-1)

Burren Legend(IRE) ran really well at Sandown two weeks previously but wasn't quite up to this level. (tchd 11-1)

Roll Along(IRE) showed absolutely nothing on his return to action over hurdles at Sandown (first run for over 400-days) and didn't always look keen to get on with things on his return to fences. He was made to keep going and does at least have something to build on now. (op 25-1)

Breedsbreeze(IRE), back up to 3m, lost his chance on his previous start when making early errors and didn't always convince over the fences here. His rider was pushing him along with a circuit to go. Official explanation: jockey said gelding never travelled (op 10-3 tchd 3-1)

Exmoor Ranger(IRE) was travelling strongly until unseating. (op 8-1 tchd 9-1 in a place)

4201 BETFAIR ASCOT CHASE GRADE 1 (17 fncs) 2m 5f 110y

3:00 (3:00) (Class 1) 5-Y-O+

£84,660 (£31,995; £16,095; £8,130; £4,155; £2,160)

Form RPR

F-12 **1** **Riverside Theatre**[35] 3560 7-11-7 165 BarryGeraghty 172+
(Nicky Henderson) *trckd ldrs: chal fr 4 out: qcknd into sld ld appr 2 out: c clr last: shkn up run-in: easily* **11/10**[1]

/155 **2** *10* **Gauvain (GER)**[28] 3675 9-11-7 158 DarylJacob 166+
(Nick Williams) *trckd ldr: led 7th: hdd 11th: led again 13th: jnd fr 4 out: hdd appr last: no ch w wnr bef last but styd on wl for clr 2nd* **14/1**

6-3U **3** *11* **Deep Purple**[66] 2964 10-11-7 160 PaulMoloney 150
(Evan Williams) *led to 7th: drvn to ld again 11th: hdd 13th: one pce fr 3 out: styd on and mstke last: tk wl hld 3rd run-in* **10/1**

4-2F **4** *1 ½* **Big Fella Thanks**[84] 2673 9-11-7 151 DominicElsworth 153+
(Ferdy Murphy) *in rr tl hdwy fr 12th: hit 3 out: kpt on again to take wl hld 3rd 2 out: wknd* **14/1**

-311 **5** *2* **Tartak (FR)**[49] 3292 8-11-7 156 (t) PaddyBrennan 149
(Tom George) *chsd ldrs: blnd 7th: ht 13th: drvn to chal 13th: wknd fr 3 out* **9/2**[3]

2500 **6** *49* **Racing Demon (IRE)**[35] 3561 11-11-7 144 HaddenFrost 98
(Henrietta Knight) *in rr: lost tch 10th: blnd 11th and wl bhd after* **33/1**

/1-1 **F** **Pride Of Dulcote (FR)**[52] 3195 8-11-7 156 NickScholfield —
(Paul Nicholls) *trckd ldrs tl fell 8th: fatally injured* **10/3**[2]

5m 23.31s (-2.69) **Going Correction** +0.40s/f (Soft) **7** Ran SP% **114.2**

Speed ratings: **120,116,112,111,111 93,—**

Tote Swingers: 1&2 £5.10, 1&3 £4.70, 2&3 £16.40 CSF £16.98 TOTE £1.70: £1.40, £4.60; EX 17.50.

Owner Jimmy Nesbitt Partnership **Bred** Goldford Stud **Trained** Upper Lambourn, Berks

FOCUS

This looked a really interesting clash between two young and up-and-coming chasers, but the race was dealt a sad blow at the eighth, where the lightly-raced Pride Of Dulcote made a mistake and was fatally injured. The winner is rated close to his King George mark with the second and fourth close to their best form.

NOTEBOOK

Riverside Theatre was the clear form pick on his second to stablemate Long Run in the King George. His task was made a lot easier by the fall of his main rival, but one has to be impressed by his attitude. Barry Geraghty appeared to make him jump at plenty of the fences, but always got an excellent response. This was his eighth success, and first at Grade 1 level, and while plans remain fluid the form would give him a big chance in the Ryanair Chase at Cheltenham or the Totesport Bowl at Aintree. (op 6-4 tchd 13-8 in places and 7-4 in a place)

Gauvain(GER) ◆, up in trip after a running-on effort behind Master Minded in the Victor Chandler Chase at this course, ran a huge race and pleased his connections. He will now head to the Ryanair Chase at Cheltenham next month, and one would have to give him a chance there.

Deep Purple, well beaten when unseating behind Tartak in the Peterborough Chase, did his usual job of supplying the pace but was easily swept aside under pressure. He wants better ground. (op 9-1)

Big Fella Thanks ◆ hadn't been seen on the racecourse since his early fall in the Hennessy at Newbury, but he shaped really well here after racing keenly. He has been aimed all season at the Grand National and he returns there via Newbury, where he will bid for a repeat win in the Greatwood Gold Cup. (op 16-1 tchd 12-1)

Tartak(FR) had bounced back to his best since a tongue-tie had been fitted, and was chasing a hat-trick. He travelled nicely in the early stages but didn't find a great deal off the bridle after diving over the fifth-last, and was disappointing. (tchd 4-1 and 5-1 in places)

Racing Demon(IRE) has been doing most of his racing over hurdles recently, and it had been 14 months since his last run over fences. Third in this race behind Kauto Star and Monets Garden in 2008, and needing to go right-handed, he was struggling from an early stage.

Pride Of Dulcote(FR) had won both of his previous races this season and was highly regarded. He was going every bit as well as his rivals when he fell and suffered a fatal injury. (op 11-4 tchd 7-2 in places)

4202 BETFAIR MOBILE H'CAP HURDLE (11 hdls) 2m 3f 110y

3:35 (3:35) (Class 2) 4-Y-O+

£24,784 (£7,360; £3,680; £1,836; £920; £464)

Form RPR

104 **1** **Act Of Kalanisi (IRE)**[42] 3445 5-10-0 130 DavidBass[(5)] 134+
(Dr Richard Newland) *trckd ldrs: chal fr 6th: slt ld fr 4 out: nt fluent next: rdn and blnd 2 out: sn jnd: rallied to assert last: hld on gamely: all out* **10/1**

-124 **2** *hd* **On Borrowed Wings (IRE)**[38] 3508 8-10-8 133 DarylJacob 134
(Alan Fleming) *in tch tl lost position 4 out: styng on but plenty to do appr 2 out: str run appr last but stl only 4th: styd on strly to chse wnr fnl 25yds and swtchd rt: nt quite get up* **11/1**

-444 **3** *2* **Busker Royal**[28] 3688 8-9-13 127 RichardKilloran[(3)] 126
(Nicky Henderson) *in tch: hdwy to chse ldrs 7th: chsd wnr after 3 out: drvn to chal after 2 out: no imp after last: one pce and lost 2nd fnl 25yds* **7/1**

12-0 **4** *3 ¼* **Like Minded**[35] 3561 7-10-6 131 (t) NickScholfield 127
(Paul Nicholls) *in rr: hmpd 6th: hdwy 7th: chsd ldrs after 3 out: no imp next and outpcd appr last* **11/2**[3]

/3-5 **5** *nse* **Shalone**[28] 3676 7-11-0 139 JimmyMcCarthy 135
(Alan King) *in tch: hmpd 6th: chsd ldrs fr 4 out: wl there but u.p: one pce appr last* **15/2**

0023 **6** *14* **Lough Derg (FR)**[28] 3676 11-11-12 151 (v) TomScudamore 133
(David Pipe) *led: jnd 6th: rdn and narrowly hdd 4 out: wknd after 3 out* **7/2**[1]

10-0 **7** *12* **Open Day (IRE)**[49] 3298 5-10-4 129 DominicElsworth 99
(Jonjo O'Neill) *hit 3rd: j. slowly 4th: hit 4 out: a bhd* **20/1**

11P- **8** *63* **Copper Bleu (IRE)**[302] 5379 9-11-8 147 (t) RichardJohnson 54
(Philip Hobbs) *in rr: rdn 4th: wl bhd fr 7th* **10/1**

-3P6 **9** *15* **Tasheba**[18] 3871 6-11-6 145 BarryGeraghty 37
(Nicky Henderson) *a in rr: pushed along 5th: lsot tch fr 7th* **14/1**

2120 **B** **Drill Sergeant**[35] 3561 6-9-10 128 (t) HenryBrooke[(7)] —
(Donald McCain) *trcking ldrs whn b.d 6th* **5/1**[2]

-F40 **F** **Bogside Theatre (IRE)**[53] 3169 7-10-1 126 ow1 HaddenFrost —
(George Moore) *disputing cl 2nd whn fell 6th* **33/1**

4m 50.21s (2.21) **Going Correction** +0.40s/f (Soft) **11** Ran SP% **119.4**

Speed ratings (Par 109): **111,110,110,108,108 103,98,73,67,— —**

Tote Swingers: 1&2 £21.40, 1&3 £17.30, 2&3 £10.40 CSF £115.27 CT £830.17 TOTE £14.10: £3.70, £3.00, £2.60; EX 157.40 Trifecta £1510.80 Part won..

Owner C E Stedman & Dr R D P Newland **Bred** Mrs Joan Keaney **Trained** Claines, Worcs

■ Stewards' Enquiry : Richard Killoran five-day ban: used whip with excessive frequency (Mar 5-9)

FOCUS

Five non-runners made this a little less competitive than it had looked in the morning, but it still produced a thrilling finish. The first two are both rated as having recorded slight personal bests with the third and fifth helping to set the level.

NOTEBOOK

Act Of Kalanisi(IRE), back up in distance, looked of some interest on his handicap debut over hurdles (he'd reportedly been aimed at this race for a while), and took this despite his trainer being on the point of pulling his horse out due to the ground. He travelled really strongly throughout and hung on with grim determination after looking likely to be swallowed up on a couple of occasions, especially after blundering two out. The trainer isn't quite sure yet which race he'll aim Act Of Kalanisi for at Cheltenham next month, as there should be plenty of options. (op 9-1 tchd 11-1 in places)

On Borrowed Wings(IRE) ◆ had shown plenty of decent form in novice chases and almost caught Act of Kalanisi back over hurdles after coming from a long way off the gallop. He looks one to be interested in back over fences, especially in handicaps at Cheltenham next month. (op 10-1 tchd 12-1 in places)

Busker Royal, down in trip, made good progress through runners but has shown his best form on quicker ground, and unsurprisingly couldn't sustain his promising effort in the final stages. (op 8-1 tchd 10-1)

Like Minded had been off the course for quite a while before disappointing at Sandown, although fully entitled to need that run, and was fitted with a tongue-tie for this. He made some eyecatching ground, looking a danger on the final bend, but became one paced under pressure. (op 6-1)

Shalone ◆ has obviously been a bit fragile over the past couple of years but has a decent engine. He loomed up to be a big threat but didn't get home in the testing conditions, and can easily be given another chance on better ground. (op 8-1 tchd 7-1)

Lough Derg(FR) has a love affair with this track, running numerous good races, but didn't perform to his best here. (op 4-1)

Copper Bleu(IRE) was an interesting contender on the best of his form over hurdles and fences, and had been given a breathing operation since Punchestown. Always in rear, he would not have liked the going and made no impression. (tchd 11-1)

Drill Sergeant had nowhere to go when Bogside Theatre fell and was brought down. (tchd 28-1)

Bogside Theatre(IRE) was close up when coming down. (tchd 28-1)

4203 TRISOFT "NATIONAL HUNT" NOVICES' HURDLE (9 hdls) 2m

4:05 (4:06) (Class 2) 4-Y-O+

£6,262 (£1,850; £925; £463; £231; £116)

Form RPR

1-21 **1** **Sprinter Sacre (FR)**[14] 3937 5-11-7 137 BarryGeraghty 131+
(Nicky Henderson) *plld hrd of poor pce: trckd ldr and stl keen whn led approachng 4 out: c clr on bit fr 3 out: fin on bridle* **30/100**[1]

2 *7* **Polisky (FR)**[157] 4-10-7 0 NickScholfield 100
(Paul Nicholls) *trckd ldrs off poor pce to 1/2-way: chsd v easy wnr appr 2 out and kpt on but nvr any ch* **7/2**[2]

31-0 **3** *2 ¾* **Di Kaprio (FR)**[23] 3760 5-11-2 0 PaulMoloney 106
(Evan Williams) *led after 2nd and set poor pce after: hdd appr 4 out: sn no ch w wnr: lost 2nd and one pce approachng 2 out* **14/1**

044 **4** *5* **L'Eminence Grise (IRE)**[28] 3673 4-10-7 116 DarylJacob 92
(Nick Williams) *chsd ldrs off poor pce: hit 3rd: wknd 3 out: bhd whn hit last* **8/1**[3]

50P **5** *1 ¾* **Eldred (IRE)**[28] 3678 5-11-2 0 AndrewTinkler 99
(Nicky Henderson) *in rr off poor pce to 1/2-way: sme hdwy 3 out: nvr any ch and wknd after 3 out* **50/1**

5 **6** *10* **Faith Keeper (IRE)**[48] 3340 6-11-2 0 PaddyBrennan 89
(Nigel Twiston-Davies) *led at mod pce tl after 2nd: bhd fr 5th* **25/1**

6-46 **7** *6* **Soleil D'Avril (FR)**[52] 3196 5-11-2 0 CharlieHuxley 83
(Alan King) *a towards rr* **16/1**

05 **8** *½* **Smart Catch (IRE)**[95] 2445 5-11-2 0 LeeEdwards 83
(Tony Carroll) *a in rr* **100/1**

4m 4.58s (15.58) **Going Correction** +0.40s/f (Soft)

WFA 4 from 5yo+ 9lb **8** Ran SP% **129.6**

Speed ratings (Par 109): **77,73,72,69,68 63,60,60**

Tote Swingers: 1&2 £1.20, 1&3 £3.40, 2&3 £2.90 CSF £2.48 TOTE £1.40: £1.10, £1.30, £3.00; EX 2.10 Trifecta £10.80 Pool £1,321.49 - 90.23 winning units..

Owner Mrs Caroline Mould **Bred** Christophe Masle **Trained** Upper Lambourn, Berks

FOCUS

There was no pace on but it produced a exciting performance. The winner is value for further with the third and fifth rated to their bumper marks and seting the standard.

NOTEBOOK

Sprinter Sacre(FR) ◆ pulled like fury towards the head of affairs, so it's amazing that he found as much as he did in the final stages after being sent on. He is one of the most exciting novice hurdlers about and he'll head to Cheltenham for the Supreme Novices' Hurdle, all being well. Barry Geraghty is going to have a seriously hard task picking his mount for that contest, but if he chooses Sprinter Sacre, he knows that he'll travel strongly (a bigger field of better horses will no doubt help him settle) and can utilise a searing turn of foot if it can be harnessed. A chaser in stature, Nicky Henderson can't wait to send him over fences next season. (op 2-5 tchd 4-9 in places)

Polisky(FR) made a pleasing British debut. He had finished a place in front of Cedre Bleu on his sole start in France, who won on his debut for Paul Nicholls and then ran respectably behind Spirit Son at Exeter, another of the Henderson fancies for the Supreme at Cheltenham. (tchd 10-3 and 4-1 in places)

Di Kaprio(FR) finished well beaten on his hurdling debut for Evan Williams (ran in bumpers for Chris Bealby) but shaped with more promise this time, albeit he was one paced in the home straight.

L'Eminence Grise(IRE) has been progressing over hurdles and kept on in the tacky ground, suggesting he'll get further.

Eldred(IRE) didn't look likely to get involved on previous evidence but ran better in this, and can hopefully progress from this performance.

4204 GARDINER & THEOBALD STANDARD OPEN NATIONAL HUNT FLAT RACE 2m

4:40 (4:40) (Class 3) 4-6-Y-O **£5,204** (£1,528; £764; £381)

Form				RPR
1	1		**Mono Man (IRE)**[20] 3842 5-11-6 0 ..... BarryGeraghty *(Nicky Henderson) trckd ldr: chal over 3 out: drvn to ld over 2f out: styd on on strly fnl f: readily* **6/4**[2]	124
1	2	1 3/4	**Oscara Dara (IRE)**[53] 3166 6-10-13 0 ..... MrTJCannon(7) *(Alan Fleming) led: rdn and jnd over 3f out: hdd over 2f out: styd on wl to hold 2nd fr wl over 1f put but no imp on wnr* **12/1**[3]	122
1	3	3/4	**Persian Snow (IRE)**[112] 2087 5-11-6 0 ..... (t) RichardJohnson *(Philip Hobbs) trckd ldrs: pushed along and hdwy ins fnl 3f: swtchd lft to stands' rail and rdn 2f out: chal for 2nd over 1f out but no imp on wnr: one pce into 3rd fnl f* **10/11**[1]	122
	4	6	**Kusadiki (IRE)** 5-11-2 0 ..... AndrewThornton *(Emma Lavelle) chsd ldrs in 3rd tl wknd wl over 2f out* **33/1**	112
	5	3 3/4	**Special Vintage** 5-11-2 0 ..... AndrewTinkler *(Nicky Henderson) hld up in rr but in tch tl wknd 3f out* **25/1**	108
	6	5	**Ransson (FR)** 6-10-9 0 ..... PeterHatton(7) *(Alan King) in rr but in tch tl wknd over 3f out* **14/1**	103

3m 59.62s (16.62) **Going Correction** +0.40s/f (Soft) **6** Ran SP% **113.5**
Speed ratings: **74,73,72,69,67 65**
toteswingers: CSF £19.41 TOTE £2.50: £1.40, £3.30; EX 9.20 Trifecta £20.80 Pool £726.36 - 25.78 winning units..
Owner Mrs Christopher Hanbury **Bred** Mrs E Costelloe **Trained** Upper Lambourn, Berks

FOCUS
With every runner that had raced before having won their only outing under rules, this bumper should prove to be strong form, although confidence is tempered by the fact that the pace was very slow. The third is rated a few pounds below his previous winning mark but looks the best guide.

NOTEBOOK
Mono Man(IRE) won by a wide margin in easy ground at Hereford on his debut, and followed that success up with a comfortable victory. Always well placed, he struck for home at the right time and held on nicely. The trainer plans to give him three weeks off and see how he is after that. Aintree may be in his plans if given another run this season. (op 13-8 tchd 11-8 and 7-4 in places)
Oscara Dara(IRE) easily took a Fibresand bumper on his debut, and acquitted himself well in this better contest. It was good to see him run on again once headed, and he looks sure to win more races. (tchd 20-1 in a place)
Persian Snow(IRE), wearing a tongue-tie for the first time, was arguably a shade disappointing, although he was sat in third of the three that broke clear, and had the most ground to make up as a result. Clearly well regarded, it might pay to give him another chance on better ground. He should make a hurdler. (tchd Evens)
Kusadiki(IRE) was far from knocked about in the final stages and gave indications that he is capable of winning a lesser event.
Special Vintage, a half-brother to Flat/bumper/hurdle winners, including dual-purpose performer Gee Dee Nen, is regarded as a chaser in the longer term and looks to have plenty of size about him.
Ransson(FR), a half-brother to French Flat/hurdle/chase winner Ommega and bumper winner/fair staying maiden hurdler Qroktou, ought to be better for the experience. (op 25-1)
T/Plt: £56.00 to a £1 stake. Pool £138,440.58 - 1,801.82 winning units. T/Qpdt: £47.80 to a £1 stake. Pool £7,730.52 - 119.50 winning units. ST

2519 HAYDOCK (L-H)

Saturday, February 19

OFFICIAL GOING: Heavy (chs 3.0; hdl 3.6)
Rails on both bends moved out 3m from innermost position increasing distances by 18m per circuit. First fence in back straight omitted all chases.
Wind: Light 1/2 behind Weather: Overcast, light rain

4205 TOTEPLACEPOT VICTOR LUDORUM JUVENILE HURDLE (9 hdls) 2m

1:40 (1:40) (Class 2) 4-Y-O **£6,895** (£2,024; £1,012; £505)

Form				RPR
2	1		**Houblon Des Obeaux (FR)**[42] 3436 4-11-6 148 ..... AidanColeman *(Venetia Williams) trckd ldrs: led appr 3 out: hdd between last 2: rallied last 150yds: led nr fin* **5/4**[1]	135
12	2	3/4	**Third Intention (IRE)**[21] 3802 4-11-3 138 ..... JoeTizzard *(Colin Tizzard) lw: t.k.h: trckd ldrs: led between last 2: wnt 3 l clr sn after last: hdd and no ex towards fin* **7/2**[3]	131
1	3	5	**Kumbeshwar**[14] 3944 4-11-3 0 ..... WayneHutchinson *(Alan King) lw: hld up: hdwy to trck ldrs 6th: drvn appr next: wnt modest 3rd 2 out: kpt on one pce* **13/2**	126
111	4	9	**Local Hero (GER)**[21] 3802 4-11-6 141 ..... GrahamLee *(Steve Gollings) hld up: j.rt: trckd ldrs 3rd: drvn appr 3 out: wknd 2 out* **3/1**[2]	122
4211	5	10	**Vosges (FR)**[13] 3967 4-11-6 128 ..... HarryHaynes *(James Ewart) str: led: hdd appr 3 out: sn lost pl* **14/1**	113

4m 5.50s (1.30) **Going Correction** +0.40s/f (Soft) **5** Ran SP% **111.7**
Speed ratings: **112,111,109,104,99**
CSF £6.18 TOTE £2.40: £1.40, £1.80; EX 8.10.
Owner Mrs Julian Blackwell **Bred** Mme Marie Devilder & Benjamin Devilder **Trained** Kings Caple, H'fords

FOCUS
A competitive-looking juvenile hurdle, despite the small field. The winner is rated just below his Chepstow mark, with steps up from the placed horses and the fifth to his mark.

NOTEBOOK
Houblon Des Obeaux(FR), who is still a bit on the leg, had finished runner-up faced with similar conditions in the Grade 1 Finale Hurdle at Chepstow on his previous start, and got up in the final strides for his first win in Britain. Testing ground appears to be a must, as he's very much a galloper, so he'll go for the Triumph only if conditions are suitable. Regardless of where he heads next, though, he rates a bright chasing prospect. (op 15-8 tchd 2-1 in places)
Third Intention(IRE), worn down late on by Local Hero at Cheltenham, again travelled best and seemed quite at home in the conditions. He looked all over the winner when going on and opening up an advantage, but started to tire after the last and was eventually worn down. Clearly talented, he's entitled to take his chance in the Triumph, and it would be no surprise to see him ridden under more restraint there, where a stronger early gallop will help. (tchd 100-30)
Kumbeshwar created a good impression when making a winning debut at Sandown earlier this month and ran with credit on this step up in grade, keeping on again having been dropped by the front pair. Better ground will suit and he could be one for the Fred Winter. (op 6-1)
Local Hero(GER) clearly didn't show his true form. Previously unbeaten over hurdles and tipped by many to run a big race in next month's Triumph, having shown such a good attitude at Cheltenham last time, he was clearly unsuited by the heavy surface and was beaten early in the straight. He could bounce back, but this was hardly an ideal preparation for the festival. Official explanation: trainer said gelding was unsuited by the heavy ground (op 5-2 tchd 7-2)
Vosges(FR), a dual winner at Musselburgh, looks every inch a chaser and, having made the early running, was quickly brushed aside by the principals.

4206 ALBERT BARTLETT NOVICES' HURDLE (REGISTERED AS THE PRESTIGE NOVICES' HURDLE RACE) GRADE 2 (12 hdls) 3m

2:10 (2:11) (Class 1) 4-Y-O+
£13,226 (£4,962; £2,484; £1,238; £621; £310)

Form				RPR
	1		**Back In Focus (IRE)**[34] 6-11-4 0 ..... BrianHughes *(Howard Johnson) lw: trckd ldrs: t.k.h: wnt cl 2nd appr 3 out: led between last 2: nt fluent last: drvn and styd on strly* **16/1**	142+
-121	2	6	**Court In Motion (IRE)**[35] 3567 6-11-11 149 ..... JackDoyle *(Emma Lavelle) lw: hld up towards rr: smooth hdwy 9th: led appr next: hdd between last 2: kpt on same pce* **8/13**[1]	143
1F42	3	2 1/2	**Neptune Equester**[35] 3567 8-11-4 123 ..... FearghalDavis *(Brian Ellison) in rr: pushed along 6th: outpcd appr 3 out: kpt on to take modest 3rd last: styd on wl* **20/1**	133
-151	4	11	**Carpincho (FR)**[18] 3866 7-11-8 137 ..... AidanColeman *(Sarah Humphrey) lw: hld up in rr: hdwy to trck ldrs 8th: drvn after next: outpcd appr 3 out: modest 3rd 2 out: wknd appr last* **6/1**[2]	126
420	5	1 1/2	**Rose Of The Moon (IRE)**[21] 3806 6-11-4 0 ..... JakeGreenall *(Milton Harris) chsd ldrs: drvn after 6th: reminders after next: outpcd and lost pl appr 3 out: 7th whn mstke 2 out: kpt on run-in* **13/2**[3]	121
-F6U	6	5	**Atouchbetweenacara (IRE)**[21] 3804 10-11-4 125 .... WayneHutchinson *(Venetia Williams) led tl hdd appr 3 out: wknd appr 2 out* **25/1**	116
0111	7	7	**Lively Baron (IRE)**[48] 3330 6-11-8 123 ..... GrahamLee *(Donald McCain) trckd ldrs: t.k.h: upsides 5th: wknd appr 2 out* **9/1**	118+
1134	8	dist	**Rudanphast (IRE)**[22] 3787 6-11-8 118 ..... SamTwiston-Davies *(Peter Bowen) trckd ldrs: nt fluent 5th: blnd and lost pl next: hdwy to chse ldrs 7th: sn lost pl and bhd: t.o 3 out* **33/1**	—

6m 4.70s (4.70) **Going Correction** +0.40s/f (Soft) **8** Ran SP% **117.0**
Speed ratings (Par 115): **108,106,105,101,101 99,97,—**
Tote Swingers: 1&2:£4.50, 1&3:£110.20, 2&3:£5.40 CSF £27.91 TOTE £22.30: £3.00, £1.10, £4.10; EX 41.00 Trifecta £605.40 Pool £850.84 - 1.04 winning units..
Owner Andrea & Graham Wylie **Bred** Mrs A Connolly **Trained** Billy Row, Co Durham

FOCUS
A race lacking strength in depth that produced a shock result. The winner looks a smart prospect but the third is rated below his Warwick form.

NOTEBOOK
Back In Focus(IRE) made a successful hurdles debut, and in some style. He had shown ground such as this holds no fears when winning his point and, having travelled strongly throughout, edged ahead after two out and forged clear for pressure. Although there are doubts as to whether the favourite was at his best, this was a thoroughly likeable performance from a horse who's not expected to come into his own until sent chasing. He'll presumably head to the festival now, although he'd probably need a cut in the ground to be as effective there. (op 20-1)
Court In Motion(IRE) had been favourite for the Albert Bartlett at the festival following his easy win at this level at Warwick but this was his first try at 3m and, having travelled strongly into the straight, he failed to pick up as expected. In the end he only just finished ahead of Neptune Equester, who was some 21l behind when they met at Warwick, so it's probably safe to say he wasn't at his best, with connections feeling he ran a little flat. He's still entitled to take his chance at Cheltenham, where the better ground should suit and also enable him to see the trip out a little better. (op 4-6 tchd 4-5)
Neptune Equester ◆ is biding his time over hurdles before returning to fences and ran another fine race. A strong stayer, he was edging nearer to his old rival with every stride as they crossed the line and, returned to better ground and fences, he'll be a chaser to keep on-side. He looks ideal for the Scottish Grand National. (op 25-1)
Carpincho(FR), who will make a chaser, is already a dual winner over hurdles, but found the step up in grade/trip too much in the testing conditions. (op 7-1)
Rose Of The Moon(IRE) was never really travelling and could only plod on. (op 7-1 tchd 15-2 and 8-1 in a place)
Atouchbetweenacara(IRE) showed up well before tiring. (tchd 28-1)
Lively Baron(IRE) stopped quickly and was later reported to have a breathing problem. He had earlier been progressive and deserves another chance back on a sounder surface. Official explanation: trainer's rep said gelding had a breathing problem (tchd 17-2)

4207 TOTESCOOP6 HURDLE (REGISTERED AS THE RENDLESHAM HURDLE RACE) GRADE 2 (12 hdls) 3m

2:45 (2:45) (Class 1) 4-Y-O+
£18,528 (£6,951; £3,480; £1,735; £871; £435)

Form				RPR
61B2	1		**Cross Kennon (IRE)**[24] 3742 7-11-8 139 ..... AlanO'Keeffe *(Jennie Candlish) hld up: shkn up and trckd ldrs 7th: led 9th: hdd next: led after 2 out: j.rt last: drvn clr* **8/1**	160+
F2-5	2	6	**Bensalem (IRE)**[21] 3807 8-11-4 153 ..... WayneHutchinson *(Alan King) lw: hld up in rr: stdy hdwy 7th: led on bit 3 out: hit next: sn hdd: 3 l down last: fdd run-in* **7/4**[1]	151+
5640	3	1 3/4	**Kayf Aramis**[21] 3807 9-11-4 142 ..... SamTwiston-Davies *(Nigel Twiston-Davies) chsd ldr: drvn along 7th: outpcd appr 3 out: styd on run-in* **14/1**	148
1422	4	27	**Any Given Day (IRE)**[49] 3289 6-11-8 159 ..... GrahamLee *(Donald McCain) hld up off pce: stdy hdwy 8th: trcking ldrs whn hit next: rdn appr 3 out: 4th and wkng whn blnd 3 out: bhd and eased between last 2* **2/1**[2]	125
11-0	5	7	**Chief Dan George (IRE)**[91] 2524 11-11-4 150 ..... PaddyAspell *(James Moffatt) chsd ldrs: drvn 7th: lost pl 9th: sn bhd* **12/1**	114
6321	6	57	**Mr Moonshine (IRE)**[24] 3742 7-11-4 139 ..... HenryOliver *(Sue Smith) led: hit 3rd and 7th and next: hdd 9th: sn lost pl and bhd: t.o next* **13/2**[3]	57

6m 0.60s (0.60) **Going Correction** +0.40s/f (Soft) **6** Ran SP% **108.5**
Speed ratings (Par 115): **115,113,112,103,101 82**
Tote Swingers: 1&2:£12.70, 1&3:£14.50, 2&3:£5.30 CSF £21.60 TOTE £9.40: £3.60, £1.60; EX 23.30.
Owner P and Mrs G A Clarke **Bred** Mrs Cora Cronin **Trained** Basford Green, Staffs

FOCUS
This turned into a dour test, which wouldn't necessarily have been to the liking of the 'big two' in the market. The winner is rated a big improver with the third back to form.

NOTEBOOK
Cross Kennon(IRE), a hardened stayer, came to the fore in the conditions, recording a career-best. Back to form when second to Mr Moonshine off 138 at Huntingdon last time, he had plenty to find with the principals at the weights but handles this ground well and was always going to win, having got back to the front after two out. Fourth in the Pertemps Final at last year's festival, he may well head back to Cheltenham next month (won there earlier this season), but regardless of how he fares it will be chasing for him next term.
Bensalem(IRE) made a pleasing reappearance when fifth behind Grands Crus on his reappearance at Cheltenham and this looked an excellent opportunity. However, having travelled strongly and looking all over the winner, he began to appear in trouble having been untidy two out and was ultimately outstayed. Alan King felt he still needed it, and he now looks set to return to fences for the William Hill at Cheltenham, a race he fell in when fancied on his most recent chasing start. (op 9-4)
Kayf Aramis has been a bit below his best this season but stays forever and shaped more encouragingly, possibly appreciating the removal of his regular cheekpieces. (op 10-1)
Any Given Day(IRE), reportedly edgy and reluctant-looking before the start, found the ground against him. Highly progressive this season, twice finishing runner-up in good company over shorter at Cheltenham, he had been talked of a possible World Hurdle outsider, but it's hard to imagine him getting involved on the back of this effort. (tchd 9-4 and 85-40 in places)
Chief Dan George(IRE) never looked like winning but this may have helped to sharpen him up for the festival, where he was a winner last year. (op 11-1 tchd 10-1)
Mr Moonshine(IRE) had beaten the winner comfortably at Huntingdon last time, for which he received a 19lb hike. There was a suspicion he was flattered a touch that day, though, and he was quickly dropped by the rest on this sharp rise in grade. (op 5-1)

4208 TOTESPORT.COM GRAND NATIONAL TRIAL (HANDICAP CHASE) GRADE 3 (20 fncs 2 omitted) 3m 4f
3:20 (3:20) (Class 1) 5-Y-O+ **£43,511** (£16,796; £8,786; £4,758)

Form				RPR
1-00	**1**		**Silver By Nature**[42] 3437 9-11-12 **149** PeterBuchanan (Lucinda Russell) *trckd ldrs: wnt handy 2nd 5 out: led next: drew clr between last 2: styd on strly* **10/1**	168+
0445	**2**	*15*	**Ballyfitz**[14] 3940 11-10-10 **133** (b[1]) DavidEngland (Nigel Twiston-Davies) *chsd ldrs: drvn and outpcd 12th: styd on to take modest 3rd 4 out: tk 12 l 2nd last* **14/1**	137
0204	**3**	*6*	**Le Beau Bai (FR)**[35] 3568 8-10-7 **137** JakeGreenall(7) (Richard Lee) *in rr: lost pl 13th: hdwy appr 4 out: 5th 3 out: styd on to take 3rd clsng stages* **15/2**[2]	134
2-66	**4**	*1 ½*	**Carruthers**[84] 2673 8-11-6 **148** MrMMO'Connor(5) (Mark Bradstock) *mde most: hdd 4 out: wknd last* **7/2**[1]	145
2F65	**P**		**Madison Du Berlais (FR)**[21] 3805 10-11-9 **149** (b) DannyCook(3) (David Pipe) *hld up in rr: sme hdwy 10th: lost pl 14th: sn bhd: t.o last whn p.u bef 3 out* **28/1**	—
-614	**P**		**Mobaasher (USA)**[21] 3807 8-11-2 **139** (t) AidanColeman (Venetia Williams) *lw: mid-div: lost pl and reminders 7th: bhd fr 10th: t.o whn p.u after 14th* **8/1**[3]	—
/06-	**P**		**Sound Accord (IRE)**[461] 2304 10-10-4 **127** FelixDeGiles (Alex Hales) *in rr: hdwy to chse ldrs 8th: reminders 10th: sn lost pl: t.o 4 out: sn p.u* **40/1**	—
-140	**P**		**Etxalar (FR)**[49] 3290 8-10-3 **126** CampbellGillies (Lucinda Russell) *chsd ldrs: lost pl 12th: sn bhd: t.o whn p.u bef 4 out* **22/1**	—
0-11	**P**		**West End Rocker (IRE)**[35] 3568 9-11-4 **141** WayneHutchinson (Alan King) *lw: hld up in rr: gd hdwy 13th: sn chsng ldrs: lost pl appr 4 out: t.o 6th whn blnd 2 out: sn p.u* **8/1**[3]	—
F-40	**F**		**Jaunty Journey**[42] 3440 8-10-2 **125** (p) BrianHughes (Nigel Twiston-Davies) *chsd ldrs: wkng whn hit 4 out: 5th whn fell heavily next* **33/1**	—
4-11	**P**		**Sarde (FR)**[84] 2669 7-10-4 **127** (t) SeanQuinlan (Kim Bailey) *lw: in rr: reminders 12th: sn bhd: t.o whn p.u after 14th* **10/1**	—
/131	**P**		**Major Malarkey (IRE)**[66] 2959 8-10-5 **131** SamTwiston-Davies(3) (Nigel Twiston-Davies) *lw: chsd ldrs: hit 9th: wknd 4 out: poor 6th whn bdly hmpd next: sn p.u* **8/1**[3]	—
-P31	**P**		**Nicto De Beauchene (FR)**[42] 3444 10-11-2 **139**... AndrewGlassonbury (Victor Dartnall) *lw: mstkes: w ldr: wknd 5 out: 7th and bhd whn hmpd 3 out: t.o 5th whn p.u bef last* **16/1**	—
1-11	**P**		**King Fontaine (IRE)**[91] 2522 8-11-5 **142** GrahamLee (Malcolm Jefferson) *hld up in rr: reminders after 12th: hdwy on wd outside 14th: blnd and wknd next: bhd whn p.u bef 5 out* **10/1**	—

7m 42.3s (1.30) **Going Correction** +0.40s/f (Soft) **14** Ran SP% **120.3**
Speed ratings: **114,109,108,107,—** —,—,—,—,— —,—,—,—
Tote Swingers: 1&2:£57.10, 1&3:£27.90, 2&3:£38.50 CSF £133.64 CT £1120.87 TOTE £10.60: £3.00, £4.80, £3.00; EX 129.40 Trifecta £1110.90 Pool £50,504.02 - 33.63 winning units..
Owner G S Brown **Bred** G Brown **Trained** Arlary, Perth & Kinross
■ Another new title for this event, run previously as the Blue Square Gold Cup.
■ Stewards' Enquiry : Andrew Glassonbury two-day ban: used whip when mount was showing no response (Mar 5-6)

FOCUS
A gruelling test in the conditions, with just four of the 14 runners completing, and it was no surprise to see the hardened stayers come to the fore in the straight. The winner followed up last year's success off 5lb higher and the runner-up recorded a season's best mark.

NOTEBOOK
Silver By Nature ◆ led them home for a second year - this time off 5lb higher. He had been given a chance by the handicapper, having come down 7lb since finishing well held in the Welsh National and, just as had been the case a year ago, he took over at the fourth-last and galloped on strongly for a 15l success. The Grand National will presumably be his next stop and it's not hard to see him going well as long as there's some ease in the ground. (op 9-1 tchd 8-1)
Ballyfitz jumped better than he has done on occasions and briefly looked to be coming with a serious challenge in the first-time blinkers, but for all that he stayed on well for second it was nowhere good enough to match the winner. He, too, will presumably head for the National (fell last year). (op 16-1 tchd 12-1 and 18-1 in a place)
Le Beau Bai(FR) is very slow and even this seemed to prove an inadequate test for him as he plodded into third late on. (op 8-1 tchd 7-1)
Carruthers proved popular and adopted his usual front-running tactics. He became vulnerable from the turn in, though, and despite keeping on as best as he could it wasn't enough to hold on for a place. This is as much of a test as he wants. (op 5-1 tchd 11-2 in a place)
Mobaasher(USA), a good fourth behind Grands Crus back over hurdles when wearing cheekpieces latest, didn't want to know on this occasion, although it is worth noting he was without the headgear. He's as quirky as he is talented but would be interesting next time if the pieces return. (op 7-1)
West End Rocker(IRE), prominent in the betting for the Grand National following his Classic Chase win at Warwick, was up 8lb and failed to reproduce that form, being quickly beaten turning in. (op 7-1)
Jaunty Journey had run well for a long way and it's hoped this heavy fall doesn't leave its mark. (op 7-1)
Sarde(FR) had been on a roll when last seen but was in trouble a long way from home on this rise in grade. (op 7-1)
Major Malarkey(IRE) was 10lb higher than when winning at Newbury and was already beaten when badly hampered. (op 7-1)
Nicto De Beauchene(FR) had gone up 14lb for his easy Sandown win, but his jumping wasn't the sharpest on this step up in grade and he was beaten when hampered three out. (op 7-1)
King Fontaine(IRE), a dual course winner this season who was racing off a career-high mark, briefly moved up on the outside but a blunder threw him off his stride and he was unable to recover. (op 7-1)

4209 PERTEMPS H'CAP HURDLE (QUALIFIER) (12 hdls) 3m
3:55 (3:57) (Class 2) 5-Y-O+ **£9,107** (£2,674; £1,337; £667)

Form				RPR
13-0	**1**		**Skippers Brig (IRE)**[52] 3206 10-11-11 **134** BrianHarding (Nicky Richards) *lw: hld up in rr: stdy hdwy 8th: handy 3rd whn hit 3 out: narrow ld between last 2: styd on run-in: all out* **12/1**	140
4002	**2**	*hd*	**According To Pete**[37] 3522 10-11-6 **129** (p) GrahamLee (Malcolm Jefferson) *trckd ldrs: led and hit 3 out: hdd between last 2: upsides whn blnd last: no ex towards fin* **9/2**[2]	135
-403	**3**	*19*	**Saphire Night**[23] 3771 10-10-3 **119** (t) JakeGreenall(7) (Tom George) *chsd ldrs: drvn 7th: one pce fr 3 out: tk modest 3rd run-in* **20/1**	105
F-03	**4**	*2 ¾*	**Political Paddy**[10] 4003 9-10-7 **116** (p) RyanMania (Rayson Nixon) *chsd ldrs: led 2nd to next: outpcd 3 out: modest 5th whn hit last: kpt on* **16/1**	99
-03F	**5**	*½*	**Khachaturian (IRE)**[14] 3948 8-11-9 **132** AdrianLane (Donald McCain) *led: mstke and hdd 2nd: led next: hdd 3 out: modest 3rd last: wknd* **20/1**	116
FPU1	**6**	*9*	**Palypso De Creek (FR)**[14] 3954 8-11-9 **132** TomSiddall (Charlie Longsdon) *lw: prom: lost pl 5th: chsng ldrs 7th: lost pl next* **10/1**[3]	106
31P/	**7**	*12*	**Lightning Strike (GER)**[710] 4417 8-11-6 **129** AidanColeman (Venetia Williams) *chsd ldrs: wknd 3 out: poor 6th whn eased run-in* **16/1**	91
6013	**8**	*2 ¾*	**Stopped Out**[48] 3334 6-11-2 **125** RichieMcGrath (Kate Walton) *lw: hld up in rr: hdwy and prom 7th: wknd 3 out* **10/1**[3]	84
5/P-	**9**	*½*	**Merrydown (IRE)**[378] 3892 8-11-12 **135** FearghalDavis (Nicky Richards) *in rr: hmpd bnd after 6th: bhd whn mstke 3 out* **50/1**	94
5-23	**10**	*nse*	**Sir Kezbaah (IRE)**[34] 3587 7-10-9 **125** EdGlassonbury(7) (Jeremy Scott) *prom: drvn 6th: lost pl 8th: t.o 2 out* **7/2**[1]	83
3411	**11**	*2 ½*	**Lackamon**[32] 3621 6-11-2 **130** ShaneByrne(5) (Sue Smith) *chsd ldrs: mstke 7th: lost pl 9th: sn bhd: t.o 2 out* **9/2**[2]	86
-160	**12**	*33*	**The Shy Man (IRE)**[35] 3566 8-11-2 **125** BarryKeniry (George Moore) *a in rr: t.o 3 out: virtually p.u* **12/1**	48
00-1	**P**		**No Principles**[93] 2477 8-11-2 **125** WayneHutchinson (Julian Smith) *hld up: hdwy to chse ldrs 7th: sn drvn: wknd next: t.o whn p.u bef 3 out* **25/1**	—

6m 9.80s (9.80) **Going Correction** +0.65s/f (Soft) **13** Ran SP% **119.2**
Speed ratings: **109,108,102,101,101 98,94,93,93,93 92,81,—**
Tote Swingers: 1&2:£9.90, 1&3:£42.20, 2&3:£11.00 CSF £63.28 CT £1094.53 TOTE £15.10: £4.20, £1.90, £7.80; EX 68.30.
Owner Ashleybank Investments Limited **Bred** Kevin B Lynch **Trained** Greystoke, Cumbria

FOCUS
A thrilling finish to this staying handicap hurdle. The winner is rated as having recorded a personal best over hurdles with the second in line with recent chase figures.

NOTEBOOK
Skippers Brig(IRE), who was well beaten in a valuable handicap chase at Leopardstown over Christmas, just edged out According To Pete, although that may not have been the case had the latter not hit the last. The winner, who was clearly fitter this time, is well at home in these conditions and travelled like one with more to offer, despite being a 10-y-o. He's set to return to fences, with the Kelso Champion Chase on March 5th the target. (op 11-1 tchd 10-1, 14-1 in a place)
According To Pete, back to form when runner-up over fences at Catterick last time, still gave it a good go despite a blunder at the last, although a more fluent jump would probably have made the difference. Some 19l clear of the remainder, he deserves to go one better, although he is set to be handed a rise. (op 7-1)
Saphire Night has now put together two creditable efforts in a row, although she hardly looks a winner waiting to happen. (op 25-1)
Political Paddy is capable off this mark and will find easier opportunities.
Khachaturian(IRE) should have had some confidence restored, having fallen over fences last time. (op 16-1)
Palypso De Creek(FR) failed to build on his Wetherby win off 5lb higher. (tchd 9-1 and 11-1)
Lightning Strike(GER) ran extremely well before getting tired on this return from a 710-day absence. (op 10-1)
Sir Kezbaah(IRE) proved most disappointing, failing to pick up and finishing well beaten. Official explanation: jockey said gelding never travelled (op 4-1 tchd 10-3)
Lackamon, up 19lb for his last victory, should have fared better. (op 7-2)

4210 TOTESPORT 0800 221 221 NOVICES' H'CAP CHASE (14 fncs 1 omitted) 2m 4f
4:30 (4:30) (Class 2) 5-Y-O+ **£8,781** (£2,578; £1,289; £643)

Form				RPR
111U	**1**		**Douglas Julian**[22] 3784 9-10-2 **104** HenryOliver (Sue Smith) *trckd ldrs: led after 10th: drew clr appr 2 out: 10 l ahd last: eased* **7/2**[2]	119+
01P1	**2**	*4 ½*	**You Know Yourself (IRE)**[5] 4114 8-10-13 **115** 6ex GrahamLee (Sue Smith) *chsd ldr: blnd 1st: reminders 10th: 7 l 2nd whn blnd 2 out: kpt on same pce* **13/2**	120
-612	**3**	*hd*	**Benny Be Good**[19] 3852 8-11-11 **127** JamesReveley (Keith Reveley) *trckd ldrs: hit 4 out: kpt on same pce fr 2 out* **6/4**[1]	132
6001	**4**	*19*	**Maraafeq (USA)**[10] 4007 7-11-7 **123** AidanColeman (Venetia Williams) *nt fluent in rr: hdwy to chse ldrs 8th: lost pl appr 4 out: bhd and eased 2 out* **6/1**	114
5214	**U**		**Misstree Dancer**[21] 3803 7-11-9 **128** DannyCook(3) (Nick Mitchell) *lw: led: hdd after 10th: 4th and one pce whn blnd and uns rdr last* **4/1**[3]	128

5m 26.6s (16.60) **Going Correction** +0.65s/f (Soft) **5** Ran SP% **109.8**
Speed ratings: **92,90,90,82,—**
CSF £22.98 TOTE £4.10: £2.40, £2.10; EX 13.70.
Owner Mrs S Smith **Bred** A M Armitage **Trained** High Eldwick, W Yorks

FOCUS
A decent little handicap chase with the easy winner value for further.

NOTEBOOK
Douglas Julian seemed well suited by the drop in trip/return to testing conditions, and stayed on strongly under a positive ride for a ready victory. seemed well suited by the drop in trip/return to testing conditions, and stayed on strongly under a positive ride for a ready victory. (tchd 3-1 tchd 9-2 in a place)
You Know Yourself(IRE), gifted a race at Catterick earlier in the week, performed well under a penalty, keeping on to take second despite reportedly finding the ground too soft. He's a fine, big sort who can win more races. (tchd 7-1)

Benny Be Good didn't appear to have enough use made of him, and not for the first time. He simply couldn't quicken for pressure and either needs 3m or a more aggressive ride. (op 7-4)
Maraafeq(USA) found this considerably tougher than the minor Ludlow event he won last week. (op 5-1)
Misstree Dancer had been progressing well and finished a good fourth at Cheltenham last time, so it was disappointing to see her being well held when unseating at the last. (op 9-2)

4211 BET TOTEPOOL AT TOTESPORT.COM WALRUS HUNTERS' CHASE (16 fncs 2 omitted) 3m
5:05 (5:05) (Class 3) 5-Y-O+ £4,684 (£1,452; £726; £363)

Form				RPR
1U-1	1		**Baby Run (FR)**[14] 3956 11-11-13 136 MrWTwiston-Davies(7) (Nigel Twiston-Davies) *lw: mde all: shkn up between last 2: pushed out* 8/13[1]	148+
0P-3	2	3 ½	**Halcon Genelardais (FR)**[16] 3908 11-11-5 139 MrRJarrett(7) (Alan King) *chsd wnr fr 5th: drvn 5 out: kpt on: no imp* 2/1[2]	136
630-	3	55	**Idle Talk (IRE)**[308] 5223 12-11-7 124 (p) MrJHamer(5) (Mrs S K McCain) *chsd wnr to 5th: outpcd 8th: modest 3rd whn blnd 4 out: sn t.o* 10/1[3]	81
25-3	4	10	**Oopsmylord (IRE)**[285] 253 9-11-11 115 MrPJTolman(5) (S Flook) *outpcd and reminders 4th: last and struggling fr 6th: t.o 12th* 50/1	75
4511	F		**Ardnaclancy (IRE)**[259] 628 8-12-1 119 MrJARichardson(5) (Andrew Richardson) *outpcd 4th: last and struggling whn fell 7th* 28/1	—

6m 41.7s (27.70) **Going Correction** +0.65s/f (Soft) 5 Ran SP% **109.8**
Speed ratings: **79,77,59,56,—**
CSF £2.30 TOTE £1.70: £1.10, £1.20; EX 2.30.
Owner N A Twiston-Davies **Bred** Haras De Preaux **Trained** Naunton, Gloucs

FOCUS
This was only ever going to concern two and the winner ran to his best in giving weight to the runner-up.

NOTEBOOK
Baby Run(FR) completed his Cheltenham preparation with a ready success, idling late on as he began to tire a little. A fine jumper, he coped with the ground, rather than relished it, and the 4-1 for him to defend his Foxhunters' crown next month seems fair. (op 4-6 tchd 4-5)
Halcon Genelardais(FR), who made a pleasing debut in this sphere at Wincanton earlier in the month, was suited by the conditions and stuck to his task doggedly but always looked to be coming off second best. He should go one better at some stage. (op 9-4 tchd 7-4)
Idle Talk(IRE) has nothing like his former ability and was comfortably left behind by the front pair. (op 11-1 tchd 9-1)
T/Jkpt: Not won. T/Plt: £224.20 to a £1 stake. Pool £115,478.56 - 375.88 winning units. T/Qpdt: £111.90 to a £1 stake. Pool £5,712.32 - 37.75 winning units. WG

3816 UTTOXETER (L-H)
Saturday, February 19
4212 Meeting Abandoned - Waterlogged.

3904 WINCANTON (R-H)
Saturday, February 19

OFFICIAL GOING: Good to soft (soft in places; chs 6.3 hdl 6.4)
Hurdle course on fresh ground. Chase track out as far as possible increasing distances by about 60yds per circuit.
Wind: fresh behind in relation to straight Weather: cloudy with sunny periods

4219 BATHWICK TYRES BRIDGWATER H'CAP CHASE (21 fncs) 3m 1f 110y
2:00 (2:00) (Class 4) (0-110,110) 5-Y-O+ £4,878 (£1,432; £716; £357)

Form				RPR
0045	1		**Double Dizzy**[28] 3689 10-11-7 110 (bt) JoshuaMoore(5) (Bob Buckler) *hld up in tch: clsd on ldrs fr 15th: rdn after 17th: led 3 out: styd on gamely fr last: all out* 7/1[3]	122
-012	2	1	**Cashel Blue (USA)**[123] 1908 9-11-1 104 (b) KeiranBurke(5) (Patrick Rodford) *led: rdn after 16th: hdd 3 out: rallied to have ev ch fr last: no ex fnl 50yds: b.b.v* 8/1	114
0/12	3	14	**Sultan Fontenaille (FR)**[30] 3650 9-11-12 110 (tp) APMcCoy (David Pipe) *in tch: nt fluent 13th (water): hdwy to dispute 2nd whn nt fluent 4 out: sn rdn: unable to mount chal: wknd last* 6/5[1]	112
0541	4	22	**Tuskar Rock (FR)**[12] 3982 8-10-13 97 SamThomas (Venetia Williams) *trckd ldr: rdn after 17th: wknd after 3 out* 5/1[2]	86
2115	5	62	**Hobb's Dream (IRE)**[16] 3900 7-10-10 101 (p) MarkQuinlan(7) (Neil Mulholland) *in tch tl wknd 15th: sn t.o* 22/1	22
0343	P		**Lorum Leader (IRE)**[21] 3821 10-11-8 106 (b) TomO'Brien (Dr Richard Newland) *trckd ldrs: rdn after 16th: sn wknd: t.o whn p.u bef 3 out* 9/1	—
430-	P		**Little Eaglet (IRE)**[311] 5184 7-11-6 104 LiamHeard (Colin Heard) *awkward 2nd: struggling 9th: sn lost tch: p.u after 13th* 33/1	—
-530	U		**Aconitum (GER)**[30] 3646 6-10-12 96 (v) DougieCostello (Neil Mulholland) *nvr fluent in rr: t.o 9th: blnd whn uns rdr next* 14/1	—
00P4	P		**Theophrastus (IRE)**[32] 3615 9-11-4 102 (v[1]) RhysFlint (Nick Gifford) *in tch: rdn after 15th: wknd after 17th: bhd whn p.u bef 3 out* 7/1[3]	—

6m 50.5s (11.00) **Going Correction** +0.025s/f (Yiel) 9 Ran SP% **122.2**
Speed ratings: **84,83,79,72,53 —,—,—,—**
Tote Swingers: 1&2 £4.60, 1&3 £6.90, 2&3 £5.10 CSF £64.18 CT £114.68 TOTE £11.10: £2.50, £2.00, £1.30; EX 68.20.
Owner Martyn Forrester **Bred** Martyn Forrester **Trained** Henley, Somerset

FOCUS
After 9mm of rain overnight, the ground was officially good to soft, soft in places, although Robert Thornton, who walked the course before the first, called it soft. Racing began in grey and damp conditions. This opener, with the top weight rated 110, was a modest affair. The winner had slipped to a good mark and the second was 4lb off his hurdles figure.

NOTEBOOK
Double Dizzy lined up without a win for two years, but posted a game effort to break the sequence. Held up in the early stages, after a mistake at the first, he started to make progress at halfway and was second in the back straight last time round. He led two out and, despite being challenged by the rallying runner-up, battled on bravely. The refitting of blinkers may have helped him. (op 8-1)
Cashel Blue(USA), a distant second in a beginners' event last time, made a bold bid to lead throughout and, although he was clearly getting tired in the home straight, refused to go down without a fight. Courage and stamina are his strong suits. Official explanation: vet said gelding bled from the nose (op 11-1 tchd 12-1)
Sultan Fontenaille(FR), successful over 3m in December and backed beforehand, did not jump fluently and was a little disappointing. Patiently ridden and eased into the race turning towards home, he never looked likely to overhaul the first two in the closing stages. (tchd 11-10 and 5-4 and 6-4 in places)
Tuskar Rock(FR) was 4lb higher than when scoring at Lingfield 12 days earlier and the rise proved too much for him here. He chased the leader from the start, disputing second for much of the journey, but faded late on. (op 7-1)
Hobb's Dream(IRE), 19lb higher than when scoring at Hereford in January, could never get to grips with the principals. Her new rating looks too high. (op 16-1)

4220 BATHWICK TYRES YEOVIL H'CAP HURDLE (11 hdls) 2m 6f
2:35 (2:35) (Class 3) (0-135,132) 4-Y-O+ £5,069 (£1,497; £748; £374; £187)

Form				RPR
6116	1		**Jetnova (IRE)**[35] 3567 6-11-8 128 RobertThornton (Alan King) *hld up towards rr but in tch: trck ldrs 3 out: rdn to chal 2 out: led bef last: styd on: drvn out* 4/1[2]	132+
4305	2	3 ½	**Boomtown Kat**[28] 3688 7-10-4 113 ow1 EamonDehdashti(3) (Karen George) *trckd ldr: led appr 2 out: sn rdn: hdd appr last: styd on but no ex* 13/2[3]	114
-604	3	1 ¾	**Simply Blue**[18] 3874 7-10-10 119 PeterToole(3) (Simon Burrough) *in tch: travelling strly whn chalng 2 out: sn rdn: styd on same pce: b.b.v* 17/2	118
22PP	4	4	**Pavillon Bleu (FR)**[42] 3453 8-11-1 121 TomO'Brien (Philip Hobbs) *trckd ldrs: rdn after 7th: dropped to 7th but in tch 3 out: rallying whn stmbld last: no ex* 8/1	121+
/2PP	5	3	**Vagrant Emperor (IRE)**[24] 3742 8-11-4 124 SamThomas (Emma Lavelle) *in tch: trckd ldrs 3 out: rdn and ev ch 2 out: drifted rt and fdd last* 17/2	117
050P	6	37	**Pepporoni Pete (IRE)**[40] 3477 10-10-9 115 (tp) CharliePoste (Milton Harris) *racd keenly: cl up: rdn after 3 out: wknd bef next: t.o* 33/1	75
30P6	P		**Westlin' Winds (IRE)**[42] 3447 5-11-12 132 (b[1]) TimmyMurphy (Charles Egerton) *hld up last: rdn after 7th: wknd after 3 out: p.u bef next* 14/1	—
21	P		**Carlicue (IRE)**[34] 3584 6-11-6 126 (t) APMcCoy (Paul Nicholls) *led: blnd 8th: rdn and hdd appr 2 out: wknd qckly: p.u bef last* 13/8[1]	—

5m 23.6s (-2.90) **Going Correction** +0.025s/f (Yiel) 8 Ran SP% **113.2**
Speed ratings (Par 107): **106,104,104,102,101 88,—,—**
Tote Swingers: 1&2 £7.10, 1&3 £2.60, 2&3 £9.60 CSF £29.36 CT £206.79 TOTE £5.20: £2.30, £1.80, £2.90; EX 31.30.
Owner David Sewell **Bred** Paddy Kennedy **Trained** Barbury Castle, Wilts
■ Stewards' Enquiry : Timmy Murphy caution: used whip with excessive frequency.

FOCUS
On paper, a competitive contest, but it produced a comprehensive winner. He can probably rate higher, and the next three all ran pretty much to their marks.

NOTEBOOK
Jetnova(IRE) was taking a drop in class, having contested a Grade 2 event last time, and found this company a great deal easier to deal with. Held up in rear early on, he went fourth four out and was second with two to jump. He quickened impressively approaching the last and took a decisive advantage. A marked rise in his rating now looks likely. (op 9-2 tchd 5-1)
Boomtown Kat, a C&D winner last season and rated 112, looks the obvious yardstick. Never far off the pace, which was quite steady in the early stages, he got to the front two from home and stayed on gamely. This was a solid effort. (op 11-2)
Simply Blue, twice successful previously at this venue, again showed his liking for the course. Always in the leading group, he too appeared to run close to his best. The second of his two wins was registered from 1lb lower. Official explanation: vet said gelding bled from the nose (op 9-1 tchd 10-1)
Pavillon Bleu(FR), reverting to hurdles after two failures over fences, should have regained some confidence from this performance. He never looked likely to collect, but plugged on gamely. (op 11-1)
Vagrant Emperor(IRE), twice disappointing since his encouraging seasonal reappearance, was again below par. He was second three out, but faded in the closing stages. (op 8-1 tchd 9-1)
Carlicue(IRE), having only his third run over hurdles and a last-time-out winner, was a bitter disappointment. He led for the first 2m, racing out wide of the rest, was clearly in trouble turning into the home straight. (tchd 6-4 and 7-4)

4221 COUNTRY GENTLEMEN'S ASSOCIATION VETERANS' H'CAP CHASE (17 fncs) 2m 5f
3:10 (3:10) (Class 2) (0-145,130) 10-Y-O+ £15,713 (£4,683; £2,370; £1,215; £635)

Form				RPR
2525	1		**Swing Bill (FR)**[52] 3198 10-11-7 125 TimmyMurphy (David Pipe) *j.w: mde virtually all at gd pce: clr ldr fr 5th: unchal after: comf* 7/2[1]	141+
P232	2	8	**Regal Heights (IRE)**[14] 3953 10-11-6 124 (p) DougieCostello (Tom George) *disp 1st tl 5th: chsd wnr: rdn after 4 out: styd on but no imp on wnr* 4/1[2]	133
P-63	3	16	**Ma Yahab**[15] 3922 10-10-10 121 (b) HarryChalloner(7) (Venetia Williams) *rn in snatches: towards rr: t.o 10th: styd on fr 3 out to go modest 3rd bef last: nvr any danger* 10/1	115
3PPF	4	6	**Magic Sky (FR)**[7] 4077 11-11-11 129 CharliePoste (Milton Harris) *hld up: rdn after 10th: nvr any imp on ldrs: wnt modest 3rd briefly after 2 out: nvr trbld ldrs* 14/1	117
6-32	5	27	**Straw Bear (USA)**[22] 3788 10-11-12 130 APMcCoy (Nick Gifford) *hld up: wnt 4th 12th: rdn whn lft 3rd 4 out: nvr on terms w ldng pair: wknd 2 out* 5/1	114
3615	P		**Ursis (FR)**[35] 3558 10-11-2 120 RhysFlint (Steve Gollings) *led tl 1st: chsd clr ldrs tl 8th: sn in rr: t.o whn p.u bef 12th* 20/1	—
5152	F		**Holmwood Legend**[28] 3689 10-11-2 125 KeiranBurke(5) (Patrick Rodford) *chsd ldrs: rdn after 13th: styng on at same pce in 9 l 3rd whn mstke: stmbld and fell 4 out* 9/2[3]	—
202P	P		**Nikola (FR)**[42] 3438 10-11-7 128 (p) TomMolloy(3) (Nigel Twiston-Davies) *chsd ldrs: nt fluent 5th: rdn after 11th: sn wknd: p.u after 4 out* 20/1	—
F0-3	P		**Picts Hill**[139] 1690 11-11-4 122 SamThomas (Anthony Honeyball) *in tch: pushed along fr 6th: sn in last trio: t.o whn p.u bef 10th* 13/2	—

5m 20.8s (-4.40) **Going Correction** +0.025s/f (Yiel) 9 Ran SP% **115.7**
Speed ratings: **109,105,99,97,87 —,—,—,—**
Tote Swingers: 1&2 £4.10, 1&3 £17.10, 2&3 £25.50 CSF £18.57 CT £123.56 TOTE £4.70: £1.80, £2.10, £4.20; EX 20.40.
Owner D A Johnson **Bred** Maurice Veron **Trained** Nicholashayne, Devon

FOCUS
An interesting event, packed with old favourites. A personal best from the winner, with the second to his season's best.

NOTEBOOK

Swing Bill(FR), twice second off this mark at Cheltenham this term, gave his rivals a lesson in jumping. Headed briefly at the start, he grabbed the lead quickly and was never overtaken. Given a fine front-running ride, he was handed a couple of gentle breathers on the way round and had more than enough left up the home straight to notch a comfortable win. There should be more to come in this sort of race. (op 9-2)

Regal Heights(IRE) lined up without a win for more than three years, but suggested here that he is still capable of collecting from his current mark. The early leader, he raced in second after the winner took over and held his position thereafter. (op 9-2)

Ma Yahab, refitted with blinkers in a bid to rekindle his old spark, was not disgraced. He took third by running past toiling rivals late on, though, and never seemed likely to end a losing sequence dating back three years. (op 17-2)

Magic Sky(FR) had failed to complete in his last three races, but got round in his own time, without threatening to make a major impression.

Straw Bear(USA), who had run two decent races over fences this term, got very tired in the closing stages and was rather disappointing. (op 11-2)

Picts Hill Official explanation: jockey said gelding never travelled

4222 BATHWICK TYRES KINGWELL HURDLE GRADE 2 (8 hdls) 2m

3:45 (3:45) (Class 1) 4-Y-0+ **£39,907** (£14,973; £7,497; £3,738; £1,876)

Form				RPR
-521	1		**Mille Chief (FR)**[42] 3447 5-11-2 158 ... RobertThornton (Alan King) *disp cl 3rd: chal 2 out: sn hrd rdn: tk narrow advantage sn after last: hld on: all out* **15/8**[2]	161+
F333	2	*nse*	**Celestial Halo (IRE)**[49] 3289 7-11-6 158 ...(bt) HarrySkelton (Paul Nicholls) *chsd ldr: pressed ldr fr 3rd: rdn to ld appr 2 out: sn hrd pressed: mstke last: sn narrowly hdd: rallied fnl 100yds: jst hld* **8/1**	165+
120-	3	*18*	**Ronaldo Des Mottes (FR)**[302] 5380 6-11-2 151 ... TimmyMurphy (David Pipe) *hld up bhd front 4: stmbld 3rd: gd run on inner to hold ch appr 2 out: sn rdn: nt pce of front pair: wnt rt last* **12/1**	148
1113	4	*6*	**Silviniaco Conti (FR)**[70] 2887 5-11-10 162 ... APMcCoy (Paul Nicholls) *disp cl 3rd most of way: rdn after 3 out: outpcd appr 2 out* **7/4**[1]	146
-212	5	*23*	**Overturn (IRE)**[35] 3559 7-11-6 163 ... JasonMaguire (Donald McCain) *led tl rdn appr 2 out: wknd bef last* **4/1**[3]	135

3m 43.2s (-5.70) **Going Correction** +0.025s/f (Yiel) **5** Ran SP% **109.9**

Speed ratings (Par 115): **115,114,105,102,91**

toteswingers: CSF £15.22 TOTE £3.40: £2.00, £2.20; EX 11.60.

Owner McNeill Family **Bred** Earl Ecurie Delbart & Classic Breeding **Trained** Barbury Castle, Wilts

■ Stewards' Enquiry : Harry Skelton seven-day ban: used whip with excessive frequency without giving gelding time to respond (Mar 6-12)

FOCUS

Some classy performers have taken this event in the past decade, including Azertyiuop, Rhinestone Cowboy, Inglis Drever and Katchit. This renewal promised to throw significant light on the Champion Hurdle, as Mille Chief, Overturn and Silviniaco Conti were all among the top ten in the Festival betting before the off. They went a decent gallop, given the conditions. Another step forward from Mille Chief. He needs to find a few pounds' improvement to win the Champion Hurdle but is on a par with the other British challenghers to Binocular. Celestial Halo is rated back to the level of last season's impressive C&D win.

NOTEBOOK

Mille Chief(FR), impressive when landing a Sandown handicap by 6l from a mark of 145 on his latest outing, overcame a step up in grade to put himself on target for the Cheltenham Festival. He was arguably lucky to collect, however, as he looked booked for second until the runner-up made a hash of the final flight. That rival was also conceding 4lb so, although taking this was a commendable effort, the winner still has a fair bit to prove in order to mark himself out a potential Champion Hurdle victor. Connections are hoping for better ground on March 15. (tchd 7-4 and 2-1)

Celestial Halo(IRE), whose best form gave him a serious chance, had been below par in the early part of this season. He ran a great deal better here, though, probably close to his best, and he clearly retains plenty of ability. Not in the Champion, he holds a World Hurdle entry. (op 10-1)

Ronaldo Des Mottes(FR) had a fair bit to find on official ratings and, after making a mistake at the third flight, always seemed likely to struggle. It is to his credit that he managed to mount a challenge after the second-last, but he was comprehensively outpointed in the closing stages. (op 9-1)

Silviniaco Conti(FR), third behind Menorah in a Cheltenham Grade 2 event in December, was well below that standard here. He raced in third for much of the race, but became outpaced turning into the home straight and dropped away tamely late on. Longer trips may be better for him. (op 5-2)

Overturn(IRE), runner-up to reigning champion Binocular in Kempton's delayed Christmas Hurdle last time, was disappointing. He set off in front, as he often does, but offered little resistance once overhauled. (op 3-1)

4223 BATHWICK TYRES TAUNTON H'CAP CHASE (17 fncs) 2m 5f

4:15 (4:15) (Class 3) (0-130,126) 5-Y-0+ **£6,505** (£1,910; £955; £477)

Form				RPR
	1		**Aerial (FR)**[83] 2702 5-11-11 126 ... APMcCoy (Paul Nicholls) *travelled wl trcking ldrs: disp ld 10th tl clr ldr after 4 out: shkn up whn hit 2 out: sn wl in command: comf* **10/3**[1]	148+
14/P	2	*9*	**Tamadot (IRE)**[34] 3588 9-11-6 119 ... TomO'Brien (Philip Hobbs) *in tch: disp cl 3rd after 13th: rdn after 4 out: chsd wnr but hld fr 2 out: styd on same pce* **8/1**	130+
U562	3	*nk*	**Double The Trouble**[23] 3772 10-10-2 108 ... MrBJPoste[(7)] (Andy Turnell) *chsd ldr: disp ld 10th tl after 4 out: sn rdn: lost 2nd 2 out: styd on same pce* **12/1**	116
122	4	*16*	**I'm A Legend**[28] 3677 9-11-5 125 ...(p) MarkQuinlan[(7)] (Neil Mulholland) *in tch: rdn to dispute cl 3rd after 13th: wknd after 3 out* **4/1**[2]	118
324-	5	*½*	**Shake The Barley (IRE)**[379] 3869 8-11-1 114 ... DougieCostello (Tom George) *hld up but in tch: rdn after 13th: no ch fr 13th* **14/1**	107
5-22	6	*4½*	**Double Dash**[100] 2330 7-11-4 117 ... MarkBradburne (George Baker) *trckd ldrs: mstke 4th: rdn after 12th: wknd 4 out* **9/2**[3]	108
-343	7	*9*	**Emergency Exit (IRE)**[28] 3689 8-11-4 117 ... RhysFlint (Philip Hobbs) *hld up: hit 3rd: struggling after 11th: wknd after 4 out* **13/2**	98
2011	8	*9*	**Mister Wiseman**[11] 3990 9-11-1 114 ...(p) DavidDennis (Nigel Hawke) *led : jnd 10th: hdd 4 out: sn rdn: wknd next* **15/2**	87
-226	P		**Its Crucial (IRE)**[35] 3558 11-11-2 115 ... JasonMaguire (Nigel Twiston-Davies) *chsng ldrs whn slow jump 1st: in rr: nvr bk on terms: t.o whn p.u bef 12th* **20/1**	—

5m 27.6s (2.40) **Going Correction** +0.025s/f (Yiel)

WFA 5 from 6yo+ 2lb **9** Ran SP% **116.6**

Speed ratings: **96,92,92,86,86 84,81,77,—**

Tote Swingers: 1&2 £7.60, 1&3 £11.10, 2&3 £19.60 CSF £30.42 CT £287.10 TOTE £4.70: £1.80, £2.70, £4.20; EX 48.70.

Owner Tony Hayward And Barry Fulton **Bred** Olivier Tricot **Trained** Ditcheat, Somerset

FOCUS

A seemingly competitive handicap turned into a procession by Aerial, who should win again. The third sets the level.

NOTEBOOK

Aerial(FR) was making his first appearance for these connections since arriving from France and, judged on this, had been let in very lightly. He was always travelling smoothly, racing in third from the start, and won virtually as he liked. He did make a mistake a second-last – and then drifted right negotiating the final fence – but the ease of his victory ensures a considerable rise in his rating. His future therefore depends on the official handicapper's reaction. (op 4-1)

Tamadot(IRE), having only his second outing since a long layoff, did enough to indicate he can find a race of his current mark. In the first half-dozen from the outset, he stayed on gamely in the closing stages and cannot be faulted for effort. (op 17-2 tchd 9-1)

Double The Trouble, second at Warwick 23 days previously and carrying bottom-weight, looks a feasible marker for the form. Always chasing the pace and second for most of the race, he seemed to run right up to his best. (op 14-1 tchd 16-1)

I'm A Legend, already a three-time course winner with a fine record this season, was another to post a creditable performance, although his cause was not assisted by a mistake at the third. He will win again, when everything breaks in his favour. (op 3-1)

Shake The Barley(IRE), having his first run for 379 days, ought to improve for the outing. This run suggests he still retains enough ability to win, even if a slight easing of his rating would help him. (tchd 16-1)

Double Dash, second on each of his two previous runs this term, failed to live up to those efforts. A mistake at the fourth will not have helped. (op 5-1)

4224 BATHWICK TYRES H'CAP HURDLE (11 hdls) 2m 6f

4:50 (4:50) (Class 4) (0-105,105) 4-Y-0+ **£3,089** (£907; £453; £226)

Form				RPR
01U1	1		**Molly Round (IRE)**[9] 4032 7-11-2 100 ... MrSWaley-Cohen[(5)] (Grant Cann) *chsd ldrs: rdn after 3 out: clsd on clr ldr next: led bef last: styd on wl* **3/1**[1]	109+
0006	2	*1½*	**Whispering Jack**[23] 3762 6-11-7 103 ... PeterToole[(3)] (Charlie Mann) *mid-div: rdn and hdwy after 3 out: chsd wnr after next: styd on fr last* **16/1**	110
00-0	3	*½*	**Perkin Warbeck**[94] 2452 9-10-13 95 ... TomMolloy[(3)] (Mark Rimell) *t.k.h: hld up towards rr: c wd and hdwy ent st: styd on fr next: wnt 3rd last: kpt on* **14/1**	101
0043	4	*11*	**Ben Cee Pee M (IRE)**[16] 3897 6-11-9 102 ... LeightonAspell (Oliver Sherwood) *mid-div tl lost pl u.p 3 out: styd on again fr 2 out: wnt 4th sn after last* **8/1**[3]	98
55-P	5	*1*	**Macmar (FR)**[15] 3933 11-9-11 83 ... MrsMRoberts[(7)] (John Coombe) *nt fluent 1st: sn led: clr after 3rd: rdn and hdd after 2 out: no ex* **33/1**	79
6502	6	*12*	**Sansili**[27] 3697 4-10-4 96 ...(p) DonalDevereux[(3)] (Peter Bowen) *mid-div: rdn after 3 out: wknd next* **9/1**	70
0-00	7	*7*	**Just Tootsie**[22] 3791 7-10-9 95 ... SClements[(7)] (Nick Mitchell) *chsd clr ldr tl after 3rd: rdn appr 2 out: wknd bef last* **33/1**	73
3550	8	*2*	**Captain Becket**[22] 3791 8-10-7 91 ow1 ... TomO'Connor[(5)] (James Frost) *mid-div: rdn after 3 out: wknd next* **25/1**	67
2060	9	*nse*	**Life Long (IRE)**[27] 3693 7-11-3 96 ...(p) HarrySkelton (Anabel L M King) *chsd clr ldr fr after 3rd: rdn after 3 out: wknd bef next* **10/1**	72
P-0P	10	*70*	**Bally Conn (IRE)**[24] 3744 9-11-4 100 ... IanPopham[(3)] (Martin Hill) *a bhd: t.o 8th* **16/1**	13
10-0	11	*16*	**Stance**[289] 172 12-11-6 99 ...(p) RhysFlint (Peter Hedger) *a towards rr: t.o 3 out* **66/1**	—
P233	P		**Pocket Too**[25] 3724 8-11-12 105 ...(p) TomO'Brien (Matthew Salaman) *chsd ldrs tl 7th: sn bhd: t.o whn p.u bef 2 out* **12/1**	—
-564	P		**Sagunt (GER)**[24] 1196 8-11-8 101 ... TimmyMurphy (Joanna Davis) *in tch: nt fluent 7th: rdn after next: wknd after 3 out: t.o whn p.u bef 2 out* **12/1**	—
4-03	P		**King Of Leon (FR)**[24] 3745 7-11-7 100 ... SamThomas (Emma Lavelle) *mid-div: rdn after 8th: wknd after 3 out: t.o whn p.u bef last* **4/1**[2]	—

5m 27.0s (0.50) **Going Correction** +0.025s/f (Yiel)

WFA 4 from 6yo+ 10lb **14** Ran SP% **120.2**

Speed ratings (Par 105): **100,99,99,95,94 90,88,87,87,61 55,—,—,—**

Tote Swingers: 1&2 £15.00, 1&3 £33.50, 2&3 £26.00 CSF £49.13 CT £598.93 TOTE £5.30: £2.00, £4.10, £5.50; EX 71.60.

Owner Andrew Kavanagh **Bred** Andrew Kavanagh **Trained** Cullompton, Devon.

FOCUS

A modest event, with the top weight rated just 105, but it was strongly run. The progressive winner stepped up again, and there was a big step up from the second.

NOTEBOOK

Molly Round(IRE), raised a massive 19lb since scoring at Taunton nine days previously, defied the handicapper with a game success. Always near the head of a group chasing the front-running Macmar, she went into second two flights from home and quickly drew clear when the leader began to fade. She seemed to tire late on, not surprisingly given the ground, but held on well when the second and third came after her. Another step up in her rating appears inevitable. (op 7-2)

Whispering Jack, making his handicap debut after just four runs over hurdles, did enough to indicate he is on a reasonable mark. He was bit free early on, but this was probably his best effort to date. (tchd 18-1)

Perkin Warbeck is still lightly raced, so may have some scope for improvement. Held up in rear early on, he was doing his best work in the closing stages and may well stay longer trips. (op 20-1 tchd 22-1)

Ben Cee Pee M(IRE) was stepping up in distance after a fair third over 2m last time out and appeared to see out the extra well enough. His best form, including his bumper victory, though, has come on faster ground. (tchd 7-1)

Macmar(FR), pulled up over fences on his only previous outing this term, made a bold bid from the front. He was still at the head of affairs at the final flight and, although he tired quickly from that point, he kept battling away resolutely. (tchd 40-1)

Sansili, still a maiden but runner-up on his most recent start, was never closer than at the finish. Not for the first time, he looked short of pace. (op 8-1)

King Of Leon(FR) Official explanation: vet said gelding lost its right-fore shoe

4225 BATHWICK TYRES SALISBURY NOVICES' HURDLE (8 hdls) 2m

5:20 (5:21) (Class 4) 4-Y-0+ **£2,439** (£716; £358; £178)

Form				RPR
13	1		**Smad Place (FR)**[42] 3436 4-11-0 147 ... RobertThornton (Alan King) *w ldr: led 3rd: mstke last: nudged clr: readily* **1/4**[1]	130+
	2	*2¼*	**Jump City (FR)**[618] 5-10-13 0 ... IanPopham[(3)] (Paul Nicholls) *trckd ldrs: wnt 2nd appr 2 out: sn rdn: ev ch whn wnr hit last: kpt on but sn hld* **6/1**[2]	128
00	3	*33*	**Aragall (GER)**[122] 1914 6-11-2 0 ... MarkBradburne (George Baker) *mid-div: rdn and styd on fr 2 out but nvr any ch: wnt 3rd at the last* **66/1**	96
6064	4	*2*	**Hawkaller**[28] 3691 6-10-11 110 ... RachaelGreen[(5)] (Anthony Honeyball) *led tl 3rd: chsd wnr: rdn after 3 out: outpcd bef next: lost 3rd at the last* **9/1**[3]	93

00 **5** *10* **Rare Symphony (IRE)**[44] 3401 4-9-11 0....................(t) CPGeoghegan(3) 68
(Philip Hobbs) *mid-div: rdn after 3 out: wkng whn hit 2 out* **20/1**

06 **6** *8* **Sanctuary**[14] 3937 5-10-11 0.................................... CO'Farrell(5) 76
(Michael Scudamore) *mid-div: rdn after 3 out: wknd next* **28/1**

050 **7** *23* **Admission**[16] 3906 4-10-7 103..(t) JohnnyFarrelly 43
(Sophie Leech) *a towards rr: t.o* **50/1**

8 *2 1/4* **Rajeeva (IRE)**[266] 5-11-2 0.. SamThomas 50
(Venetia Williams) *trckd ldrs: wnt 2nd 5th: rdn after 3 out: wknd bef next: t.o* **12/1**

0000 **9** *7* **Haydens Mount**[17] 3877 6-10-11 0.................................. TomO'Connor(5) 43
(James Frost) *trckd ldrs tl wknd 3 out: t.o* **100/1**

0-00 **10** *10* **Tenitemsplustoast**[30] 3651 5-11-2 0...................................... LiamHeard 33
(Patrick Rodford) *t.k.h: a towards rr: t.o* **100/1**

0 **11** *8* **Fran's Folly**[18] 3872 5-10-2 0... MarkQuinlan(7) 18
(Neil Mulholland) *mid-div tl wknd after 3 out: t.o* **80/1**

-000 **12** *11* **Victory Bay**[18] 3872 6-10-9 0......................................(t) NathanSweeney(7) 14
(Simon Burrough) *mid-div: hdwy 5th: rdn after 3 out: sn wknd: t.o* **100/1**

0 **13** *7* **Salto Des Mottes (FR)**[26] 3715 5-11-2 0........................ DougieCostello 7
(Neil Mulholland) *a towards rr: t.o* **100/1**

P0-U **P** **History Lesson**[102] 2283 5-11-2 0...................................(p) JamesDavies —
(Alan Jones) *a bhd: t.o 4th: p.u bef 3 out* **66/1**

P **P** **Rageon (IRE)**[104] 2238 8-11-2 0... CharliePoste —
(Milton Harris) *mid-div tl wknd 3 out: t.o whn p.u bef 2 out* **100/1**

3m 48.7s (-0.20) **Going Correction** +0.025s/f (Yiel)
WFA 4 from 5yo+ 9lb **15** Ran SP% **131.3**
Speed ratings (Par 105): **101,99,83,82,77 73,61,60,57,52 48,42,39,—,—**
Tote Swingers: 1&2 £2.60, 1&3 £18.30, 2&3 £38.10 CSF £2.78 TOTE £1.40: £1.02, £1.90, £18.40; EX 3.60.
Owner Mrs Peter Andrews **Bred** Eric Aubree & Mme Maryse Aubree **Trained** Barbury Castle, Wilts

FOCUS
Little obvious strength in depth here and the red-hot favourite stood out on form. This was a decent prep for the Triumph and the second looks a certain future novice winner.

NOTEBOOK
Smad Place(FR), third in a Grade 1 event last time and among the leading half-dozen in the Triumph Hurdle betting beforehand, landed the odds without too much fuss. Always on the pace, either leading outright or disputing first place, he needed just to be nudged along to score. His jumping was not always fluent, but he beat these comfortably enough and set himself up for tougher future assignments, one of which is likely to be the Triumph, provided the ground is not too quick.
Jump City(FR), a Flat winner in France representing a trainer with a fine record in this event, posted a highly encouraging first hurdles run. Held up just off the speed until the final turn for home, he mounted a brief challenge approaching the final flight before the winner asserted his superiority. An ordinary novice event would appear to be his for the taking.
Aragall(GER), well beaten on his two previous starts over hurdles, took third on sufferance. Something had to fill that spot and, with the first two miles clear, the honour fell to him. His future is almost certainly in modest handicaps.
Hawkaller tried hard, racing in second for much of the journey, but dropped away quickly once the winner and second engaged a higher gear.
Rare Symphony(IRE), wearing a first-time tongue-tie, never held a better position than at the finish. She has possibilities in modest company now she qualifies for a mark.
Sanctuary was another to show a little promise. He too now has three runs under his belt, thus qualifying for handicaps.
T/Plt: £159.90 to a £1 stake. Pool £89,090.17 - 406.55 winning units. T/Qpdt: £76.50 to a £1 stake. Pool £4,479.93 - 43.30 winning units. TM

4226 - (Foreign Racing) - See Raceform Interactive

3795 GOWRAN PARK (R-H)
Saturday, February 19

OFFICIAL GOING: Hurdle course - soft to heavy; chase course - heavy

4227a RED MILLS CHASE (GRADE 2) (14 fncs) 2m 4f
2:30 (2:30) 5-Y-0+ **£22,413** (£6,551; £3,103; £1,034)

RPR

1 **Rubi Light (FR)**[34] 3594 6-11-6 148.. AELynch 154+
(Robert Alan Hennessy, Ire) *chsd ldr in 2nd: led 1/2-way: chal 3 out: rdn to assert bef last: kpt on wl* **7/1**

2 *10* **Roberto Goldback (IRE)**[23] 3778 9-11-8 155......................... RMPower 147
(Mrs John Harrington, Ire) *settled bhd ldrs: mainly 4th: 3rd 5 out: impr to chal 3 out: rdn bef next: no ex bef last: kpt on same pce* **5/4**[1]

3 *10* **Anothercoppercoast (IRE)**[20] 3845 11-11-3 128.................(tp) JRBarry 133
(Paul A Roche, Ire) *chsd ldrs: 3rd 1/2-way: 2nd 5 out: rdn and no ex bef st: 3rd 3 out: kpt on same pce* **50/1**

4 *9* **Scotsirish (IRE)**[20] 3844 10-11-8 152....................................... PTownend 134+
(W P Mullins, Ire) *hld up towards rr: hdwy into 4th 4 out: rdn and no imp bef st: kpt on one pce* **5/2**[2]

5 *4* **Follow The Plan (IRE)**[23] 3778 8-11-8 152............................ PFMangan 130+
(Oliver McKiernan, Ire) *hld up towards rr: rdn in 5th and no imp bef st: kpt on one pce* **5/1**[3]

6 *dist* **Chasing Cars (IRE)**[302] 5379 9-11-3 135.................................. PCarberry —
(Mrs John Harrington, Ire) *led: hdd 1/2-way: dropped to 4th 5 out: rdn in rr and wknd after 4 out: t.o* **9/1**

5m 23.0s (11.70) **6** Ran SP% **114.1**
CSF £17.55 TOTE £9.10: £3.40, £1.30; DF 31.60.
Owner W Hennessy **Bred** Patrice Vagne & Mme Valerie Vagne **Trained** Ratoath, Co Meath

FOCUS
The winner recorded a personal best after showing progressive form all season. The time doesn't support the rating.

NOTEBOOK
Rubi Light(FR) confirmed himself a good horse here with a dominating performance from the front. Jumping brilliantly from the front after taking it up at halfway, Andrew Lynch kept a nice bit in reserve and he extended again after a brilliant jump at the third-last. From there everything else was in serious trouble and he kept up that gallop to the line. He's a brilliant jumper and a horse with a real engine, but deep ground does seem to be essential to his chances. (op 5/1)
Roberto Goldback(IRE) continues to knock on the door in this type of race, although the knock was somewhat fainter on this occasion. Patiently ridden and jumping well enough, he closed to within three lengths entering the straight, but once the winner opened up again he was in trouble and could make no further impression. The ground was probably soft enough for him, but the way everything else was strung out behind him it probably wasn't that short of his best. (op 6/4 tchd 6/5)
Anothercoppercoast(IRE) had a fair bit to find on official ratings and ran very well. He laid up as close to the pace as he could, but considering he was under strong pressure to hold his place after the fourth-last, to keep going as well as he did wasn't a bad achievement at all. (op 33/1)
Scotsirish(IRE) was held up at the back, jumped one or two stickily early on and never was a real factor. (op 11/4)
Follow The Plan(IRE) ran no race and he was labouring from a long way out. (op 5/1 tchd 6/1)
Chasing Cars(IRE) dropped out at halfway and finished tailed off on his seasonal bow. (op 10/1)

4229a RED MILLS TRIAL HURDLE (GRADE 2) (9 hdls) 2m
3:40 (3:41) 4-Y-0+ **£22,413** (£6,551; £3,103)

RPR

1 **Dunguib (IRE)**[302] 5380 8-11-12 149.................................... BTO'Connell 159+
(Philip Fenton, Ire) *settled in 3rd early: slt mstke 2nd: t.k.h into 2nd after 3rd: mstke 4th: impr to chal 2 out: sn led: pushed out bef last: rdn run-in and kpt on wl* **8/11**[1]

2 *3 1/2* **Luska Lad (IRE)**[50] 3271 7-11-10 159...................................... DNRussell 153
(John Joseph Hanlon, Ire) *led: chal 2 out where mstke: sn hdd and rdn: no ex and kpt on same pce fr bef last* **6/4**[2]

3 *7* **Gimli's Rock (IRE)**[106] 2197 5-11-9 139................................(b) TPTreacy 145
(Mrs John Harrington, Ire) *chsd ldr in 2nd early: 3rd after 3rd: rdn and no ex ent st: kpt on same pce* **7/1**[3]

4m 17.6s (16.70) **3** Ran SP% **110.4**
CSF £2.29 TOTE £1.50; DF 1.80.
Owner Daniel Harnett **Bred** Liam Meade **Trained** Carrick-On-Suir, Co Tipperary

FOCUS
Dunguib was always entitled to rate higher than his novice best and should come on for the run. The second is rated a little below his recent level and the third ran a slight personal best.

NOTEBOOK
Dunguib(IRE) settled better than on some occasions during last season's ultimately anti-climactic novice campaign, and his jumping became more proficient as the tempo increased. With Brian O'Connell taking him towards the middle of the track in search of the best of the ground in the straight he jumped the last two flights quickly and accurately. It was hardly unexpected that he got a little weary in the closing stages.\n \n\x\x On the whole this was a satisfactory effort which should have the desired effect of bringing him towards a peak of condition for a test of a wholly different magnitude at Cheltenham (op 1/1)
Luska Lad(IRE)'s 159 rating (up 9lb for finishing close up in third behind Hurricane Fly and Solwhit at Leopardstown in December) probably flatters him, but he still represents a fair enough yardstick. He never looked like establishing any sort of cushion when Davy Russell tried to supply an injection of pace, and when he was awkward at the second-last the race was as good as over. Though he managed the rare feat of winning four bumpers, he was never in the same league as Dunguib in that department, and the status quo remains. (op 5/4 tchd 13/8)
Gimli's Rock(IRE), who caught Luska Lad on an off-day when winning at Down Royal in November, picked up his share of the prize-money and should emerge with his handicap mark unscathed.

4230 - 4232a (Foreign Racing) - See Raceform Interactive

3986 MARKET RASEN (R-H)
Sunday, February 20

OFFICIAL GOING: Chase course - soft (good to soft in places; 5.3); hurdle course - good to soft (soft in places; 6.0)
Rail moved out 5yds reducing circuit distance by about 13yds.
Wind: Light, half behind Weather: Overcast, misty and cold

4233 TURFTV NOVICES' HURDLE (10 hdls) 2m 5f
2:00 (2:00) (Class 4) 4-Y-0+ **£2,276** (£668; £334; £166)

Form RPR

33-1 **1** **Spirit Of Adjisa (IRE)**[257] 679 7-11-10 130................. RichardJohnson 128+
(Tim Vaughan) *lft in ld 1st: hit 2 out: pushed clr between last 2: heavily eased fnl 50yds* **10/11**[1]

-033 **2** *10* **Tiptoeaway (IRE)**[26] 3725 6-11-3 111.............................. GrahamLee 107
(Tim Easterby) *trckd ldrs: styd on to take 2nd and nt fluent last: no ch w wnr* **7/2**[2]

3-5P **3** *1 3/4* **Mister Chancer (IRE)**[45] 3405 6-11-3 0......................... RobertThornton 104
(Alan King) *chsd ldrs: kpt on same pce fr 2 out* **7/1**[3]

0 **4** *1 1/2* **Maxford Lass**[23] 3787 6-10-7 0....................................... JamesHalliday(3) 97
(John Quinn) *trckd ldrs: t.k.h: one pce fr 2 out* **33/1**

P **5** *1 1/2* **Areuwitmenow (IRE)**[26] 3719 6-11-3 0.............................. AndrewTinkler 101
(Charlie Longsdon) *chsd ldrs: outpcd appr 2 out: kpt on run-in* **66/1**

04 **6** *1/2* **Cool Strike (UAE)**[28] 3692 5-11-3 0................................. DenisO'Regan 101
(Alex Hales) *in rr: styd on appr 2 out: modest 6th last: kpt on wl* **8/1**

7 *13* **Macarthur**[95] 2461 7-11-3 0..(t) TomO'Brien 97+
(James McAuley, Ire) *led: j. slowly: blnd and hdd 1st: mid-div: hdwy 3 out: 7th whn mstke last: wknd* **33/1**

P-00 **8** *13* **Beat In Time**[112] 2109 5-10-10 0...(t) DaveCrosse 70
(John Mackie) *in rr: sme hdwy and drvn after 5th: chsng ldrs after 7th: wknd after next* **200/1**

006 **9** *15* **Drink Up**[28] 3701 7-11-3 0.. WillKennedy 64
(John O'Neill) *chsd ldrs: hit 4th: drvn next: lost pl 6th* **125/1**

50/0 **10** *20* **Westwire Toby (IRE)**[12] 3994 9-11-3 78................................. TomSiddall 46
(Lynn Siddall) *in rr: bhd fr 6th: t.o whn hmpd by loose horse 3 out* **200/1**

5-46 **11** *17* **Candleford**[23] 3787 6-11-3 0.. AndrewThornton 31
(Sally Hall) *in rr and drvn after 5th: sn bhd: t.o whn hmpd by loose horse 3 out* **18/1**

6/ **12** *2 3/4* **Danny Cool**[680] 4937 8-11-3 0... JamesReveley 28
(Keith Reveley) *stdd s: in rr: sme hdwy 7th: wknd next: sn bhd: t.o* **50/1**

U0P **13** *10* **Owls FC (IRE)**[68] 1628 5-10-7 79.. CharlieStudd(3) 12
(Michael Chapman) *in rr: bhd fr 6th: t.o 3 out* **200/1**

05 **U** **Any Given Moment (IRE)**[12] 3994 5-11-3 0........................ AdrianLane —
(Donald McCain) *chsd ldrs: 6th whn mstke and uns rdr 6th* **33/1**

00 **P** **Malenfant**[37] 3542 4-10-0 0.. JakeGreenall(7) —
(Michael Easterby) *trckd ldrs: t.k.h: wknd 7th: sn bhd: p.u bef 2 out* **150/1**

5m 10.2s (1.40) **Going Correction** +0.125s/f (Yiel)
WFA 4 from 5yo+ 10lb **15** Ran SP% **118.7**
Speed ratings (Par 105): **102,98,97,96,96 96,91,86,80,72 66,65,61,—,—**
toteswingers: 1&2 £2.90, 1&3 £2.30, 2&3 £3.00 CSF £3.87 TOTE £2.30: £1.40, £2.10, £1.40; EX 5.00.
Owner Darr, Johnson, Weston & Whitaker **Bred** C J Haughey J Flynn And E Mulhern **Trained** Aberthin, Vale of Glamorgan

FOCUS
Straightforward novice form with the winner to his mark and the second and sixth helping to set the level.

NOTEBOOK
Spirit Of Adjisa(IRE), the only previous winner over hurdles, was conceding weight all round on this first start since last summer, but that didn't prove a problem and he readily drew clear down the straight. Clearly on the up, he'll have more on under a double penalty, but should be capable of going well in decent handicaps. (op 8-11 tchd Evens)
Tiptoeaway(IRE) didn't improve as much as expected for the longer trip, readily being dropped by the winner, although it may be a different story in handicaps. He'll ultimately make a chaser. (op 9-2)
Mister Chancer(IRE) left behind a poor effort at Huntingdon and he, too, will be of interest switched to handicaps. (op 11-1)

Maxford Lass again showed ability and will have more of a chance against her own sex. (op 28-1)
Areuwitmenow(IRE), a former point winner, shaped with more promise this time. (op 50-1)
Cool Strike(UAE) got going too late, shaping like a 3m performer, and will be more interesting in handicaps. (op 10-1)

4234 RCJ ASSOCIATES LTD H'CAP HURDLE (8 hdls) 2m 1f
2:30 (2:30) (Class 4) (0-115,113) 4-Y-0+ **£2,276** (£668; £334; £166)

Form				RPR
5-50	1		**L'Eldorado (FR)**[105] 2247 6-11-7 **108** TomMessenger (Chris Bealby) *mde all: styd on wl fr 2 out: hld on wl run-in* **14/1**	117+
0-31	2	1 3/4	**Quite The Man (IRE)**[28] 3696 6-11-9 **110** GrahamLee (Malcolm Jefferson) *trckd ldrs: t.k.h: rdn and outpcd appr 2 out: styd on to take 3 l 2nd last: kpt on: unable chal* **11/4**[1]	116
102	3	8	**Break The Chain**[21] 3831 5-11-7 **108** AndrewThornton (Caroline Bailey) *chsd ldrs: kpt on same pce fr 2 out: lost 2nd and hit last* **5/1**[3]	110+
-140	4	4	**Viscount Rossini**[28] 3696 9-11-3 **111** (b) PeterCarberry[(7)] (Steve Gollings) *chsd ldrs: rdn 3 out: outpcd appr next* **7/1**	106
-200	5	11	**Souter Point (USA)**[15] 3950 5-11-12 **113** (b) BarryGeraghty (Nicky Henderson) *trckd ldrs: wknd appr 2 out* **7/2**[2]	99
604	6	2 3/4	**Ezdiyaad (IRE)**[25] 3740 7-11-10 **111** (t) PaulMoloney (Kevin Morgan) *hld up in rr: sme hdwy 3 out: sn wknd* **13/2**	94
5B6-	7	6	**Semi Detached (IRE)**[466] 2229 8-10-5 **97** LeeEdwards[(5)] (James Unett) *hld up in rr: hit 3rd and 3 out: hdwy after 3 out: lost pl appr next* **28/1**	75
4P3-	8	16	**Kempley Green (IRE)**[454] 2465 8-11-12 **113** TomScudamore (Michael Scudamore) *chsd ldrs: lost pl after 3 out: sn bhd* **14/1**	76
16-0	9	3 1/2	**Shilpa (IRE)**[280] 350 6-11-2 **103** GerardTumelty (Anabel L M King) *in rr: hit 2nd: lost pl 3 out: sn bhd* **22/1**	63

4m 9.90s (3.20) **Going Correction** +0.125s/f (Yiel) **9** Ran SP% **112.5**
Speed ratings (Par 105): **97,96,92,90,85 84,81,73,72**
toteswingers: 1&2 £8.30, 1&3 £13.80, 2&3 £2.40 CSF £52.26 CT £223.29 TOTE £22.60: £3.10, £1.30, £1.70; EX 75.00.
Owner Mrs T P Radford **Bred** Earl Haras Du Camp Benard **Trained** Barrowby, Lincs

FOCUS
Nothing more than a modest handicap hurdle with a step up from the winner and the fourth setting the level.

NOTEBOOK
L'Eldorado(FR) looked promising early last season and, despite disappointing on his handicap debut at the course in November, he had come down 7lb and received a fine ride off the front, keeping on well for pressure and always looking to be holding the favourite. He'll go back up the handicap, but is lightly raced and has more to offer. (op 16-1 tchd 20-1)
Quite The Man(IRE), 5lb higher than when scoring over C&D on his handicap debut, was closing on the winner with every stride as they reached the line, but never looked like getting to him. Clear of the third, he shapes as though a slightly stiffer test will suit. (op 5-2)
Break The Chain couldn't make an impression on the front pair on this first run in a handicap. (op 8-1)
Viscount Rossini, 6lb higher than when winning over slightly further at the course in November, was found wanting for pace. (op 15-2 tchd 8-1)
Souter Point(USA) should have run better off his lowest mark yet over hurdles. He's still a maiden and the return of blinkers failed to help. (tchd 11-4)

4235 LEGSBY ROAD H'CAP HURDLE (10 hdls) 2m 3f
3:00 (3:00) (Class 3) (0-135,133) 4-Y-0+ **£4,228** (£1,241; £620; £310)

Form				RPR
-301	1		**Pegasus Prince (USA)**[22] 3820 7-10-9 **116** JamesReveley (Keith Reveley) *in rr: hit 4th: gd hdwy appr 2 out: 4th at last: styd on strly to ld last 75yds* **15/2**[3]	122+
350	2	1	**Kauto Relko (FR)**[85] 2671 7-10-8 **122** PeterCarberry[(7)] (Rachel Hobbs) *mid-div: nt fluent 7th: hdwy to trck ldrs next: led appr 2 out: hdd and no ex clsng stages* **14/1**	127+
136P	3	4 1/2	**Fiendish Flame (IRE)**[8] 4077 7-11-9 **130** (b[1]) AdrianLane (Donald McCain) *t.k.h: led and set str pce: hdd 4th: hit 7th: led next: hdd appr 2 out: one pce* **10/1**	131
-136	4	1	**Ballybriggan (IRE)**[54] 3168 7-11-4 **125** TomO'Brien (John Quinn) *trckd ldrs: mstke 6th: one pce appr 2 out* **5/2**[1]	124
3P3-	5	16	**Bedizen**[338] 4721 8-11-1 **122** WarrenMarston (Pam Sly) *in rr: sme hdwy 7th: lost pl after next* **33/1**	108
-000	6	2	**Baccalaureate (FR)**[119] 1986 5-10-8 **115** PaddyBrennan (Nigel Twiston-Davies) *chsd ldrs: hit 3 out: lost pl appr next* **11/1**	98
3F10	7	5	**Celticello (IRE)**[22] 3808 9-10-11 **118** SamThomas (Noel Quinlan) *in rr: bhd fr 7th* **11/1**	96
1-50	8	nk	**Conquisto**[218] 1017 6-11-7 **133** DavidBass[(5)] (Steve Gollings) *t.k.h: w ldr: led 4th tl 3 out: sn wknd* **9/1**	111
0611	9	23	**The Magic Bishop**[12] 3989 6-10-10 **120** JamesHalliday[(3)] (Malcolm Jefferson) *t.k.h: trckd ldrs: wknd 3 out: bhd whn hit next: t.o* **13/2**[2]	77
/5F-	10	7	**Ruff Diamond (USA)**[512] 1539 6-10-9 **116** (t) DaveCrosse (Milton Harris) *mid-div: lost pl 7th: t.o next* **50/1**	67
6-00	11	13	**Laredo Sound (IRE)**[87] 2626 9-10-7 **117** (p) PeterToole[(3)] (Alex Hales) *chsd ldrs: wknd 3 out: t.o* **22/1**	56
0302	P		**Puerto Azul (IRE)**[87] 2636 7-10-8 **115** LeightonAspell (Oliver Sherwood) *in rr: hdwy 7th: chsng ldrs appr 2 out: 6th and wl hld whn p.u between last 2* **8/1**	—

4m 38.3s (-1.10) **Going Correction** +0.125s/f (Yiel) **12** Ran SP% **116.5**
Speed ratings (Par 107): **107,106,104,104,97 96,94,94,84,81 76,—**
toteswingers: 1&2 £27.40, 1&3 £7.90, 2&3 £28.10 CSF £101.56 CT £1056.28 TOTE £8.70: £2.20, £3.90, £3.40; EX 113.10.
Owner John Wade **Bred** Liberty Road Stables **Trained** Lingdale, Redcar & Cleveland

FOCUS
A competitive handicap and a decent pace on. The winner recorded a slight personal best with the second and fourth setting the level.

NOTEBOOK
Pegasus Prince(USA) came from well back to get up in the final half-furlong. Off the mark over hurdles at Uttoxeter latest, he needed to have improved to defy an 8lb higher mark, but duly did, and may progress again for a return to further. (tchd 7-1 and 8-1)
Kauto Relko(FR) ◆ had contested some decent handicaps this season, and looked set to capitalise on the drop in grade when going to the front. However, it soon became clear the winner was going to give him something to think about, and ultimately he couldn't hold on. There's definitely a race in him off this sort of mark, with a bare 2m perhaps suiting best. (tchd 16-1)
Fiendish Flame(IRE), back over hurdles, was responsible for setting a strong pace in the first-time blinkers and he kept it up better than expected, holding on well for third. (op 11-1 tchd 12-1)
Ballybriggan(IRE) was a tad keen early and probably paid for tracking too strong a pace. (op 7-2)
The Magic Bishop didn't settle and was found out off his new mark. (op 6-1)

Puerto Azul(IRE) Official explanation: jockey said gelding lost its action

4236 RALPH LARDER 65TH BIRTHDAY NOVICES' CHASE (14 fncs) 2m 6f 110y
3:30 (3:30) (Class 3) 5-Y-0+ **£4,664** (£1,448; £779)

Form				RPR
-15B	1		**Radium (FR)**[72] 2867 6-11-4 147 BarryGeraghty (Nicky Henderson) *sn trcking ldr: chal 3 out: narrow ld 2 out: hdd last: styd on strly to ld clsng stages* **11/8**[2]	148+
-1P2	2	nk	**Cape Tribulation**[15] 3955 7-11-4 140 DenisO'Regan (Malcolm Jefferson) *led: nt fluent 7th: j.lft 8th and next 2: pushed along appr 3 out: narrowly hdd 2 out: led last: edgd rt: hdd and no ex fnl 50yds* **4/6**[1]	147+
65P4	3	91	**Muntami (IRE)**[28] 3694 10-10-5 92 MattCrawley[(7)] (John Harris) *j. slowly 1st: chsd ldrs: nt fluent 10th: wl outpcd and lost tch appr 3 out: eventually completed* **40/1**[3]	61
640/	P		**Cottam Grange**[786] 2948 11-10-9 81 HarryHaynes[(3)] (John Wainwright) *in tch: outpcd 7th: sn bhd: t.o last10th: p.u bef 3 out* **66/1**	—
0	F		**Pipes A'Calling**[19] 3865 10-10-5 0 JackDoyle (Sarah Humphrey) *j. slowly 2nd: in rr fr 6th: wnt poor 4th 10th: blnd 3 out: fell next* **100/1**	—

5m 59.2s (13.20) **Going Correction** -0.05s/f (Good) **5** Ran SP% **107.0**
Speed ratings: **75,74,43,—,—**
toteswingers: 1&2 £2.50 CSF £2.60 TOTE £1.80: £1.60, £1.02; EX 2.50.
Owner Simon Munir **Bred** Mme Michele Juhen Cypres **Trained** Upper Lambourn, Berks

FOCUS
This novice chase played out as expected and the first two are rated to their marks in a slowly run contest.

NOTEBOOK
Radium(FR) got in too close to the last and lost momentum, but he picked up best coming towards the line and fully deserves to take his chance at the Festival, where he was second in the Martin Pipe a year ago. The Centenary would be the ideal race, although his rating may force him into the new Jewson. (op 5-4)
Cape Tribulation is a useful performer who ran Wayward Prince close last time, but for the second time over fences he jumped as though needing to go left-handed. Further suits him ideally and it would be no surprise to see him take his chance in the William Hill Handicap at the Festival. (op 8-11, tchd 5-6 in places)
Muntami(IRE) hung in there best he could, but was left behind following a blunder down the back. (op 50-1)

4237 MARKET RASEN RACECOURSE CARAVAN SITE H'CAP CHASE (12 fncs) 2m 2f
4:05 (4:05) (Class 4) (0-115,115) 5-Y-0+ **£2,927** (£859; £429; £214)

Form				RPR
S0U3	1		**Nomadic Warrior**[19] 3869 6-10-6 **95** DavidEngland (John Holt) *hld up wl in tch: effrt and chsng ldrs 8th: chal 3 out: narrow ld 2 out: hit last: drvn out* **7/2**[1]	109+
11P3	2	3 1/2	**Irish Guard**[18] 3878 10-11-5 **108** AndrewThornton (John O'Neill) *led to 3rd: w ldr: led 6th to 2 out: upsides last: no ex* **5/1**[3]	116
-0U0	3	9	**Karingreason**[28] 3695 8-10-8 **97** JamesReveley (Keith Reveley) *in rr: hdwy 9th: one pce fr next: tk modest 3rd last* **7/1**	96
-030	4	6	**Bennynthejets (IRE)**[10] 4022 9-10-10 **99** TomMessenger (Chris Bealby) *w ldrs: upsides 3 out: one pce: wkng whn hit last* **4/1**[2]	94
06/0	5	2 1/4	**Park's Prodigy**[140] 1695 7-10-11 **105** MissLHorner[(5)] (Chris Grant) *sn trcking ldrs: wknd appr 3 out* **16/1**	96
U-P2	6	22	**Polar Gunner**[100] 2352 14-11-9 **115** JamesHalliday[(3)] (Malcolm Jefferson) *w ldrs: led 3rd: hdd 6th: lost pl 9th: sn bhd* **4/1**[2]	84
-005	7	19	**Carters Rest**[20] 3854 8-10-8 **97** DenisO'Regan (Chris Grant) *t.k.h: sn trcking ldrs: drvn 7th: lost pl next: t.o 3 out* **4/1**[2]	47

4m 31.8s (-3.20) **Going Correction** -0.05s/f (Good) **7** Ran SP% **117.3**
Speed ratings: **105,103,99,96,95 86,77**
toteswingers: 1&2 £2.50, 1&3 £6.00, 2&3 £6.70 CSF £22.21 TOTE £3.70: £2.30, £2.10; EX 24.50.
Owner Ms Carol Lacey **Bred** C Lacey **Trained** Peckleton, Leics

FOCUS
A fairly moderate handicap chase with the placed horses setting the level in a soundly run handicap.

NOTEBOOK
Nomadic Warrior, still a maiden coming into this, had run a career-best when finishing third off this mark at Folkestone earlier this month and, despite hitting the last, he was always doing enough late on. Only a 6-y-o, he's heading the right way and looks capable of going in again. (tchd 10-3)
Irish Guard ran another sound race, but shall remain vulnerable to less exposed sorts off this sort of mark. (op 6-1, tchd 7-1 in a place)
Karingreason plugged on to record her best effort yet over fences. (op 15-2 tchd 8-1)
Bennynthejets(IRE) is on a good mark now and there was a bit more promise in this effort.
Park's Prodigy Official explanation: jockey said gelding had a breathing problem
Polar Gunner was below par. (op 9-2 tchd 5-1)
Carters Rest failed to settle and disappointed.

4238 WATCH RACING UK ON SKY CHANNEL 432 H'CAP CHASE (17 fncs) 3m 1f
4:35 (4:35) (Class 4) (0-100,98) 5-Y-0+ **£2,927** (£859; £429; £214)

Form				RPR
3PP6	1		**Duke Of Ormond (IRE)**[22] 3822 8-11-4 **90** (p) CharliePoste (Anna Brooks) *chsd ldrs: led 13th: styd on to draw clr appr last: eased towards fin* **33/1**	105+
0160	2	7	**Bardolet (IRE)**[49] 3336 8-11-1 **87** JamesReveley (Keith Reveley) *trckd ldrs: wnt cl 2nd 4 out: kpt on same pce between last 2* **5/1**[2]	94+
4-03	3	14	**Home She Goes (IRE)**[22] 3817 9-11-3 **92** AdamPogson[(3)] (Charles Pogson) *mstkes in rr: hdwy 4 out: styd on to take modest 3rd sn after last* **14/1**	88+
P344	4	2 1/4	**Sycho Fred (IRE)**[12] 3990 10-10-3 **75** (tp) CampbellGillies (Mike Sowersby) *hld up in rr: hdwy and clr 3rd 13th: one pce appr 3 out* **5/1**[2]	65
2533	5	1/2	**Arnold Layne (IRE)**[24] 3768 12-11-11 **97** AndrewThornton (Caroline Bailey) *w ldrs: reminders after 11th: outpcd 4 out: sn lost pl* **9/2**[1]	85
0350	6	15	**Peak Seasons (IRE)**[33] 3618 8-9-11 **72** oh6 CharlieStudd[(3)] (Michael Chapman) *in rr: hdwy and modest 4th 4 out: wknd appr next* **50/1**	50
05P4	7	28	**Kercabellec (FR)**[37] 3541 13-9-7 **72** oh14 JoeCornwall[(7)] (John Cornwall) *in rr: bhd fr 13th: t.o* **66/1**	32
50-2	8	13	**Huckleberry (IRE)**[38] 3527 9-9-9 **72** oh5 (p) LeeEdwards[(5)] (James Unett) *chsd ldrs: lost pl 11th: sn bhd: t.o 3 out* **6/1**[3]	4

PP40 **9** 7 **Raki Rose**[10] 4021 9-9-9 **72** oh8 (v) CO'Farrell(5) —
(Michael Scudamore) *led: drvn and hdd 11th: blnd next: sn lost pl and bhd: t.o 3 out* **9/1**

F005 **P** **Mister Watzisname (IRE)**[34] 3608 9-11-12 **98** (tp) FelixDeGiles —
(Charlie Longsdon) *w ldr: hit 8th: led 11th: hdd 13th: wknd rapidly next: sn t.o: p.u bef 3 out* **12/1**

0003 **F** **Artic Pride (IRE)**[21] 3837 7-10-11 **83** LeightonAspell —
(Oliver Sherwood) *towards rr: blnd 1st: fell heavily 2nd* **9/2**[1]

6m 40.0s (8.70) **Going Correction** -0.05s/f (Good) **11** Ran SP% **114.7**
Speed ratings: **84,81,77,76,76 71,62,58,56,— —**
toteswingers: 1&2 £42.70, 1&3 £50.10, 2&3 £8.30 CSF £190.02 CT £2445.29 TOTE £24.40: £5.40, £1.90, £3.60; EX 286.80.

Owner Woz 5 Now 4 **Bred** Sean Prendergast **Trained** Alderton, Northants

FOCUS
An moderate handicap and a shock winner, who rates value for further. The second is rated to his hurdles mark.

NOTEBOOK
Duke Of Ormond(IRE) was tranformed for the switch to fences and won easing down. A former point winner, he had done little over hurdles, but this is clearly his game and it will be interesting to see how the handicapper reacts.

Bardolet(IRE), disappointing previously over fences, was on the same mark as when winning over hurdles in October, and he jumped more fluently on the way to finishing a clear second. (op 11-2)

Home She Goes(IRE), well beaten on last month's debut over fences, made mistakes and never really got into it, but was keeping on down the straight and should learn from the experience. (op 10-1)

Sycho Fred(IRE) couldn't quicken under pressure. (op 9-2 tchd 4-1)

Arnold Layne(IRE) remains below a winning level despite being well handicapped.

Artic Pride(IRE) hit the very first fence before coming down at the next. (tchd 4-1)

4239 RACING UK STANDARD OPEN NATIONAL HUNT FLAT RACE 2m 1f
5:05 (5:06) (Class 6) 4-6-Y-O **£1,203** (£353; £176; £88)

Form RPR

31 **1** **Anychancedave (IRE)**[20] 3856 4-10-9 0 JeremiahMcGrath(7) 109
(Alan Swinbank) *trckd ldrs: led over 2f out: sn hdd: rallied fnl f: styd on to ld nr fin* **2/1**[1]

2 *hd* **Swinging Sultan** 4-10-9 0 JamesReveley 103+
(Keith Reveley) *hld up in rr: stdy hdwy on wd outside 6f out: led 2f out: jst ct* **20/1**

1 **3** *1 1/4* **Matthew Riley (IRE)**[26] 3731 4-11-2 0 RichieMcGrath 108
(Kate Walton) *prom: effrt 3f out: kpt on wl ins fnl f* **4/1**[3]

30- **4** *3* **Sizing Ireland (IRE)**[306] 5301 5-11-4 0 BarryGeraghty 107
(Nicky Henderson) *trckd ldrs: drvn 3f out: one pce over 1f out* **11/4**[2]

-135 **5** *8* **Batonnier (FR)**[23] 3794 5-11-11 0 RobertThornton 106
(Alan King) *hld up in mid-div: hdwy 7f out: sn trcking ldrs: wknd 2f out* **16/1**

6 *2 1/4* **Preferred Lies (IRE)** 6-11-4 0 TomScudamore 97
(Anabel L M King) *hld up in rr: hdwy 6f out: chsng ldrs and rdn 3f out: one pce* **50/1**

7 *1 3/4* **Hang Up My Boots (IRE)**[127] 1880 5-10-11 0 (t) PeterCarberry(7) 95
(James McAuley, Ire) *led: hdd 3f out: wknd over 1f out* **28/1**

8 *7* **Failed The Test (IRE)**[98] 5-10-11 0 (t) TomO'Brien 81
(James McAuley, Ire) *w ldr: wknd 2f out* **50/1**

9 *12* **Hey Nineteen (IRE)** 5-11-4 0 FelixDeGiles 76
(Charlie Longsdon) *mid-div: hdwy 6f out: sn chsng ldrs: wknd over 3f out* **25/1**

10 *2* **Nalim (IRE)** 5-11-4 0 GrahamLee 74
(Malcolm Jefferson) *in rr and sn drvn along: sme hdwy 5f out: lost pl over 3f out* **10/1**

0 **11** *7* **Handford Henry (IRE)**[24] 3773 5-11-4 0 TomMessenger 67
(John Holt) *chsd ldrs: wknd 6f out* **125/1**

0 **12** *shd* **Everkingly**[9] 4055 5-11-4 0 CharliePoste 67
(Anna Brooks) *towards rr: sme hdwy over 4f out: sn wknd* **150/1**

0 **13** *30* **Midnight Maisie**[89] 2597 4-10-2 0 AndrewTinkler 21
(Anna Brooks) *in rr: bhd and hung lft 6f out: t.o 3f out* **150/1**

14 *30* **Azebra** 6-10-11 0 TomSiddall —
(Lynn Siddall) *in rr: t.o 5f out* **150/1**

00 **15** *3 1/2* **Lemon Queen (IRE)**[86] 2660 5-10-8 0 JamesHalliday(3) —
(John Quinn) *t.k.h: sn trcking ldrs: lost pl after 7f: sn bhd: t.o 3f out* **100/1**

P **Marjac (IRE)** 4-10-9 0 DavidEngland —
(Nigel Twiston-Davies) *in rr: drvn 6f out: t.o 3f out: p.u over 1f out: fatally injured* **25/1**

4m 8.30s (7.20) **Going Correction** +0.125s/f (Yiel)
WFA 4 from 5yo+ 9lb **16** Ran SP% **118.6**
Speed ratings: **88,87,87,85,82 81,80,76,71,70 67,67,52,38,37 —**
toteswingers: 1&2 £12.50, 1&3 £3.20, 2&3 £7.10 CSF £49.17 TOTE £2.50: £1.20, £6.10, £2.00; EX 50.80.

Owner DavidManasseh,TitusBramble,LeeCattermole **Bred** Lowland Enterprises **Trained** Melsonby, N Yorks

FOCUS
A bumper that should produce winners with the third, fourth and fifth all close to pre-race marks.

NOTEBOOK
Anychancedave(IRE), a ready winner at Ayr who was well fancied to defy a penalty, looked booked for second when Swing Sultan took over from him, but this strong, galloping type stuck to it well and his experience made the difference late on. He's going to require further over hurdles and rates a decent prospect.

Swinging Sultan ◆ would have won but for displaying signs of greenness once in front. He still very nearly hung on, but even so connections will no doubt be delighted by the promise he showed. He should go one better.

Matthew Riley(IRE) performed well under a penalty and is another nice prospect with hurdles in mind.

Sizing Ireland(IRE) was found wanting for pace and probably won't be winning until sent hurdling.

Batonnier(FR) was again found out by the penalty.

Midnight Maisie Official explanation: jockey said filly hung left throughout

T/Jkpt: Not won. T/Plt: £117.40 to a £1 stake. Pool: £71,271.88. 442.99 winning tickets. T/Qpdt: £45.30 to a £1 stake. Pool: £4,263.28. 69.60 winning tickets. WG

[3993]SEDGEFIELD (L-H)
Sunday, February 20

OFFICIAL GOING: Heavy (soft in places; hdl 5.8, chs 5.5)
Divided bends, bends on fresh ground with hurdles on inside.
Wind: Virtually nil Weather: Cold and overcast

4240 PAXTONS SERVING FARMERS SINCE 1853 JUVENILE HURDLE (JOHN WADE SERIES QUALIFIER) (8 hdls) 2m 1f
2:10 (2:10) (Class 4) 4-Y-O **£3,252** (£955; £477; £238)

Form RPR

102 **1** **Palawi (IRE)**[23] 3785 4-11-5 120 DougieCostello 130+
(John Quinn) *nt fluent: racd keenly: mde all: clr after 3rd: unchal: v easily* **10/11**[1]

052 **2** *16* **Lamps**[43] 3443 4-10-12 120 DominicElsworth 107+
(Michael Blake) *in tch: wnt 2nd bef 4th: rdn after 4 out: sn no imp on wnr* **5/4**[2]

5 **3** *67* **Ananda Kanda (USA)**[14] 3967 4-10-5 0 FearghalDavis 33
(Brian Ellison) *hld up: wnt 3rd 4 out: rdn and wknd after 3 out: t.o* **33/1**

6 **4** *2 3/4* **Thescottishsoldier**[9] 4056 4-10-9 0 EwanWhillans(3) 37
(Alistair Whillans) *racd keenly: trckd ldrs: hit 1st: lost pl after 3rd: sn btn: t.o* **66/1**

63 **5** *7* **Verluga (IRE)**[12] 3986 4-10-12 0 RichieMcGrath 30
(Tim Easterby) *hld up: a bhd: t.o* **20/1**[3]

0 **P** **Brisbane (IRE)**[140] 1699 4-10-12 0 (p) RyanMania —
(Dianne Sayer) *midfield: mstke 4th: sn wknd: t.o whn p.u bef 3 out* **150/1**

P **Flyjack (USA)**[37] 4-10-12 0 BrianHughes —
(Lisa Williamson) *racd keenly: trckd clr ldr in 2nd tl 3rd: wknd qckly after 4th: t.o whn p.u bef 3 out* **125/1**

P **P** **Presidium Galaxy**[38] 3519 4-9-9 0 SamuelWelton(10) —
(George Moore) *sn detached in rr: p.u bef 4th* **66/1**

4m 21.5s (14.60) **Going Correction** +1.00s/f (Soft) **8** Ran SP% **109.0**
Speed ratings: **105,97,65,64,61 —,—,—**
toteswingers: 1&2 £1.02, 1&3 £2.80, 2&3 £4.30 CSF £2.10 TOTE £1.50: £1.10, £1.10, £3.80; EX 2.60.

Owner Bob McMillan **Bred** Jim McCormack **Trained** Settrington, N Yorks

FOCUS
Conditions were testing with the going officially described as heavy, soft in places. There was little strength in depth in this juvenile hurdle and the favourite absolutely hammered his rivals under a forcing ride. The form is rated around the first two.

NOTEBOOK
Palawi(IRE) made a bright start as a hurdler for this yard when easing clear in a minor event at Haydock and bettered that on his third hurdle run when beating all bar an exciting prospect at Doncaster last month. This 120-rated performer had a penalty to defy but quickly opened up a clear lead and that is the way it stayed en route to making it 2-4 over hurdles. He hit a few hurdles along the way and still has some room for improvement in his jumping, but his versatility regarding ground is a useful asset and this likeable, freewheeling type could make a big impact in handicaps. (op 4-5 tchd Evens)

Lamps had strong claims on his much improved fast-finishing 66-1 second from a remote position in a heavy-ground Sandown juvenile hurdle last month but he could never get anywhere near the all-the-way winner. He failed to live up to his smart pedigree on the Flat, and has a bit to prove over hurdles after this. (op 13-8)

Ananda Kanda(USA) was never involved and finished a long way back. She was a fair 6f maiden winner on the Flat but needs to settle better to get competitive over hurdles. (op 28-1 tchd 25-1)

Thescottishsoldier showed modest form at up to 1m on the Flat and it has been a similar story in two hurdle runs. (op 40-1)

Verluga(IRE) showed some ability when a tiring third of four behind a promising winner on good ground at Market Rasen, but he was toiling a long way out this time and may not have handled the testing ground. (op 16-1)

4241 DIGIBET.COM H'CAP CHASE (16 fncs) 2m 5f
2:40 (2:40) (Class 5) (0-95,97) 5-Y-0+ **£2,471** (£725; £362; £181)

Form RPR

0042 **1** **Euro American (GER)**[11] 4001 11-12-0 **97** WilsonRenwick 110+
(Rose Dobbin) *hld up in tch: hdwy to trck ldrs 5 out: led after 2 out: pushed clr bef last: rdn out run-in* **5/2**[1]

33P2 **2** *7* **Panthers Run**[27] 3712 11-10-0 **69** oh5 (t) DougieCostello 75
(Jonathan Haynes) *hld up: hdwy to trck ldr on outer after 2nd: ev ch 2 out: sn rdn: kpt on one pce* **9/1**

5030 **3** *4* **Teenando (IRE)**[18] 3883 11-10-10 **79** HenryOliver 81
(Sue Smith) *trckd ldr on inner: hit 5 out: rdn after next: kpt on same pce* **9/2**[3]

0056 **4** *9* **Lindseyfield Lodge (IRE)**[11] 4001 10-11-8 **91** (p) KennyJohnson 85
(Robert Johnson) *led: hdd after 2 out: sn wknd* **22/1**

22U5 **P** **Hasper**[20] 3853 13-11-3 **86** RyanMania —
(Sandy Forster) *trckd ldr: lost pl and reminder 9th: mstke 11th: sn wknd: t.o whn p.u bef 3 out* **5/1**

-600 **F** **Solo Choice**[12] 3619 5-10-6 **77** PeterBuchanan —
(Ian McInnes) *hld up: fell 4th* **25/1**

U233 **P** **Archie's Wish**[25] 3748 7-10-12 **81** BarryKeniry —
(Micky Hammond) *hld up in tch: hit 5 out: rdn and wknd after 4 out: p.u after next* **3/1**[2]

5m 41.66s (23.66) **Going Correction** +1.00s/f (Soft)
WFA 5 from 7yo+ 2lb **7** Ran SP% **106.6**
Speed ratings: **94,91,89,86,— —,—**
toteswingers: 1&2 £5.30, 1&3 £3.60, 2&3 £5.60 CSF £20.70 CT £77.56 TOTE £3.80: £1.60, £3.30; EX 18.90.

Owner Mrs Rose Dobbin **Bred** Euro-American Bet Verm Gmbh **Trained** South Hazelrigg, Northumbria

FOCUS
A modest handicap chase run at a fairly steady pace in the sapping ground. The placed horses set the level of the form.

NOTEBOOK
Euro American(GER) put in a revived effort switched back to fences when second over 2m at Carlisle last time. The step back up in trip was a positive for this 11-y-o, who has dropped to 29lb lower than his peak chase mark, and he knuckled down well to forge clear under a welter burden and record his first win since March 2007. (op 11-4)

Panthers Run, a front-running 13l second at Wetherby last time, ran a similar sort of race from out of the weights here. He is in fair form and could continue to run well, but the downside is that this veteran has a career record of 2-53 and has not won in 16 months. (tchd 17-2 and 10-1)

Teenando(IRE) was on and off the bridle for a long way before plugging on for some minor money. He is 14lb lower than his last win but that was almost two years ago and he has struggled to find a convincing finishing effort since then. (op 5-1)

Lindseyfield Lodge(IRE) set the pace but was a spent force approaching the second-last on ground slower than ideal. (op 16-1 tchd 25-1)

Hasper is on a fair mark and shaped with some promise on his recent return, but he was in trouble some way out and failed to complete on this second run back. (op 9-2 tchd 4-1 and 11-2)

Archie's Wish impressively made it 2-2 over fences at this track in September and had generally competed well off similar marks since, but he made a mistake when the pace quickened in this contest and was left behind before being pulled up. Official explanation: trainer said gelding was unsuited by the heavy (soft in places) ground (op 9-2 tchd 4-1 and 11-2)

4242 S G PETCH NISSAN DURHAM NOVICES' HURDLE (QUALIFIER) (8 hdls) 2m 1f

3:10 (3:12) (Class 4) 4-Y-O+ **£3,252** (£955; £477; £238)

Form | | | | RPR
52 **1** **Desert Cry (IRE)**[20] [3850] 5-11-2 0 .... JasonMaguire 140+
(Donald McCain) *trckd ldr in 2nd: led on bridle bef 2 out: rdn clr bef last: comf* **85/40**[2]

2235 **2** *13* **Maggio (FR)**[64] [3030] 6-10-13 130 .... (p) JamesO'Farrell(3) 125+
(Patrick Griffin, Ire) *trckd ldr: wnt 2nd and brought wd bef 2 out: sn rdn: kpt on but no ch w wnr* **5/2**[3]

6213 **3** *26* **Jack The Gent (IRE)**[23] [3787] 7-11-9 125 .... BarryKeniry 106+
(George Moore) *led tl appr 2 out: sn rdn: wknd bef last* **7/4**[1]

-460 **4** *24* **Harris Hawk**[27] [3715] 6-10-9 0 .... MrJohnDawson(7) 75
(John Wade) *in tch: rdn after 4 out: wknd after 3 out* **33/1**

1-03 **5** *15* **Lesanda**[32] [3637] 5-10-9 0 .... BrianHughes 53
(Richard Fahey) *midfield: rdn after 3 out: sn no imp: wknd between last 2* **12/1**

05 **6** *32* **Cool Baranca (GER)**[25] [3746] 5-10-9 0 .... RyanMania 21
(Dianne Sayer) *hld up: a in rr: t.o after 4th* **50/1**

0 **P** **Lambrini Lace (IRE)**[25] [3746] 6-10-2 0 .... HarryChalloner(7) —
(Lisa Williamson) *racd keenly: trckd ldrs: lost pl after 3rd: sn bhd: t.o whn p.u bef 2 out* **250/1**

S **Ursus**[117] 6-11-2 0 .... PaddyAspell —
(Christopher Wilson) *hld up: brief hdwy after 4 out: rdn after 3 out: wkng whn slipped up on flat bef next* **200/1**

P **Cayo**[282] 4-10-8 0 ow1 .... KennyJohnson —
(Robert Johnson) *sn detached in rr: j. bdly lft: p.u bef 4th* **250/1**

630 **P** **Alta Rock (IRE)**[39] [3511] 6-10-11 0 .... ShaneByrne(5) —
(Sue Smith) *hld up: hit 3rd: bhd after 4th: t.o whn p.u bef 2 out* **100/1**

4m 18.6s (11.70) **Going Correction** +1.00s/f (Soft)
WFA 4 from 5yo+ 9lb **10** Ran SP% **111.8**
Speed ratings (Par 105): **112,105,93,82,75 60,—,—,—,—**
toteswingers: 1&2 £1.10, 1&3 £1.10, 2&3 £1.20 CSF £7.67 TOTE £2.80: £1.50, £1.10, £1.40; EX 8.20.

Owner N.Y.P.D Racing **Bred** Fin A Co S R L **Trained** Cholmondeley, Cheshire

FOCUS

A fair novice hurdle. The three market leaders were in a breakaway group some way out before the winner made an impressive dash for glory. This was a massive step up from the winner who looks a smart novice.

NOTEBOOK

Desert Cry(IRE) ◆ was useful at best on the Flat in France and Italy and showed plenty of promise when second behind a rival making it 2-2 over hurdles last month. Plenty of money arrived for him in the morning and he travelled smoothly, then showed a decisive turn of speed to kick clear and make it third time lucky over hurdles. The key to his progress seems to be that he is learning to settle with experience, and this useful type still has plenty of potential for further improvement. (op 2-1 tchd 15-8)

Maggio(FR) had not looked out of place in graded events at Navan this winter, and set the standard on his best recent form. He travelled well into contention but couldn't respond when the winner opened up and had to settle for a remote second. There is a plenty of ability there, but he looks on a tough current mark and could continue to be difficult to place after 11 unsuccessful hurdle runs. (op 3-1, tchd 10-3 in a place)

Jack The Gent(IRE) is an imposing type who caused an upset in a 2m4f Doncaster novice hurdle before finishing placed under a penalty over the same C&D last time. This 125-rated performer had decent claims and got an easy time up front, but he was comfortably brushed aside. However, he ran into a potentially smart rival and the drop in trip, heavy ground and sharp track may have been against him. It is possible he could resume his progress next time and he remains an interesting future chase prospect. (op 2-1 tchd 9-4)

Harris Hawk was never a factor and was ultimately well beaten, but he shaped with a hint of promise. He is a half-brother to useful six-time staying chase winner Harris Bay, and should do better with time and distance. (tchd 28-1)

Lesanda was never involved faced with plenty to find on form. (op 9-1)

4243 RACECOURSE BOOKMAKERS H'CAP HURDLE (9 hdls) 2m 2f 110y

3:45 (3:58) (Class 4) (0-105,105) 4-Y-O+ **£3,252** (£955; £477; £238)

Form | | | | RPR
3531 **1** **Bocciani (GER)**[6] [4115] 6-11-9 **105** 7ex .... (p) JamesO'Farrell(3) 111
(Dianne Sayer) *trckd ldr: wnt 2nd 2 out: upsides last: drvn to ld run-in: hld on all out* **11/4**[2]

2112 **2** *½* **Rawaaj**[23] [3782] 5-11-5 **98** .... JasonMaguire 103
(Donald McCain) *led: rdn bef 2 out: hdd run-in: kpt on but a jst hld towards fin* **1/1**[1]

-220 **3** *7* **Call It On (IRE)**[15] [3950] 5-11-5 **105** .... KyleJames(7) 103
(Philip Kirby) *hld up in tch: chsd along after 4th: rdn bef 4 out: kpt on to go 3rd bef last: no threat ldng pair* **5/1**

-0P0 **4** *7* **Claude Carter**[207] [1115] 7-10-10 **92** .... EwanWhillans(3) 83
(Alistair Whillans) *hld up in tch: rdn bef 2 out: sn wknd* **20/1**

-006 **5** *5* **Jersey Boys**[25] [3746] 5-10-10 **96** .... PaulGallagher(7) 85
(Howard Johnson) *trckd ldr in 2nd: rdn bef 2 out: wknd bef last* **4/1**[3]

4m 54.4s (25.70) **5** Ran SP% **118.1**
toteswingers: 1&2 £4.40 CSF £6.71 TOTE £3.90: £1.40, £1.40; EX 7.10.

Owner Anthony White **Bred** Saturn Stable **Trained** Hackthorpe, Cumbria

FOCUS

A number of jockeys and officials inspected a patch of ground that caused a runner to slip up in the previous race, and it was decided that racing could go ahead. This was a minor handicap hurdle in which the two in-form market leaders fought out a tight finish. the winner is on the upgrade and the second still looks fairly treated.

NOTEBOOK

Bocciani(GER) capped a consistent spell with an overdue first win in a more competitive Catterick handicap the previous Monday. He had to fight hard to overhaul the long-time leader but gradually got on top to defy a penalty and make it 2-2 since cheekpieces have been applied. He can carry his head a bit high but showed a good attitude here and could continue to progress. (oldw market op 7-2 tchd 4-1 and 10-3 and 9-2)

Rawaaj was just denied by a subsequent winner in a strongly run Doncaster handicap last time, and he went down fighting off 4lb higher against another improver. He should be able to gain compensation for the two close calls, and is versatile regarding ground and trip. (old market op 11-8 tchd 5-4 and 6-4 in places)

Call It On(IRE) did quite well to keep battling for third after being driven along at an early stage, but it is a bit disappointing that this generally progressive 85-rated Flat performer hasn't been able to make more of an impact off hurdle marks in the 100s in his last three starts. (old market op 11-2 tchd 6-1)

Claude Carter couldn't hang in there when the first two quickened. He is dropping down the weights, but has not finished closer than 14l to a winner over hurdles. (old market op 28-1 tchd 33-1 and 22-1, new market op 22-1)

Jersey Boys was keen and couldn't sustain his effort on ground possibly more testing than ideal on this handicap debut. (old market op 6-1 tchd 9-2, new market op 9-2)

4244 COLLINS SEAFOODS NOVICES' CHASE (QUALIFIER) (16 fncs) 2m 4f

4:15 (4:18) (Class 4) 5-Y-O+ **£3,928** (£1,160; £580)

Form | | | | RPR
-632 **1** **Sir Tantallus Hawk**[12] [3995] 7-11-0 0 .... BarryKeniry 132+
(Alan Swinbank) *trckd ldr: rdn after nt fluent 3 out: rdr dropped whip bef 2 out: led between last 2: kpt on wl run-in* **5/4**[2]

-5U1 **2** *4* **Predictive (FR)**[87] [2641] 8-11-7 130 .... JasonMaguire 135
(Donald McCain) *led: rdn bef 2 out: hdd between last 2: one pce run-in* **4/6**[1]

/00U **3** *22* **Flighty Mist**[12] [3997] 9-10-0 78 .... PaulGallagher(7) 100
(Sandy Forster) *trckd ldr: rdn after 5 out: wknd after next* **40/1**[3]

5m 18.6s (15.60) **Going Correction** +1.00s/f (Soft) **3** Ran SP% **106.9**
Speed ratings: **108,106,97**
CSF £2.52 TOTE £3.00.

Owner Highland Racing 4 & Mrs E Melrose **Bred** S I Pittendrigh **Trained** Melsonby, N Yorks

FOCUS

There were not many runners but this was an interesting novice chase, involving a couple of decent types. The first two are rated pretty much to their marks.

NOTEBOOK

Sir Tantallus Hawk ran close to the form of his hurdle win off 129 last spring when chasing home a useful rival in a beginners' chase over C&D recently. He had leading claims on that form and jumped efficiently for most of the way before wearing down the leader. He seems to have found a bit more staying power since switched to fences, and this quadruple 2m-2m3f hurdle winner could go on to better things at this discipline.

Predictive(FR), a dual winning hurdler who was placed in a Grade 2, got off the mark on the second attempt over fences when slamming a fair dual subsequent handicap winner at Uttoxeter in November. This likeable and uncomplicated staying type was strongly supported back from a short break, but couldn't run the finishing kick out of a decent rival and was overhauled. However, this was a very respectable return from almost three months off and he should still have more to offer as a chaser. (op 8-11, tchd 4-5 in places)

Flighty Mist had masses to find and couldn't live with the first two when things got serious. (op 33-1)

4245 HAPPY 38TH ANNIVERSARY RON & PAT CRAKE MARES' NOVICES' HURDLE (JOHN WADE SERIES QUALIFIER) (10 hdls) 2m 4f

4:45 (4:45) (Class 4) 4-Y-O+ **£3,252** (£955; £477; £238)

Form | | | | RPR
0341 **1** **Alexander Road (IRE)**[11] [4000] 6-11-6 109 .... JasonMaguire 113+
(Donald McCain) *w ldr: led after 3rd tl 5th: rdn bef 3 out: led appr 2 out: drvn and kpt on wl run-in* **11/10**[1]

55- **2** *5* **Kykate**[300] [27] 5-10-11 0 .... (t) CharlieHuxley(3) 101
(Thomas Kinsey) *hld up: hdwy to trck ldrs after 6th: upsides gng wl after 3 out: rdn 2 out: kpt on same pce* **50/1**

/2-3 **3** *5* **Lady Bluesky**[91] [2547] 8-10-11 0 .... EwanWhillans(3) 96
(Alistair Whillans) *racd keenly: sn led: hdd after 3rd: led again 5th: rdn whn hdd bef 2 out: one pce* **2/1**[2]

1 **4** *18* **Newdane Dancer (IRE)**[36] [3576] 4-10-4 0 .... BrianHughes 68
(Howard Johnson) *in tch towards outer: hdwy after 4 out: ev ch 3 out: sn rdn and wknd: hld whn nt fluent 2 out* **13/2**[3]

0P00 **5** *15* **Politelysed**[5] [4132] 5-11-0 0 .... KennyJohnson 63
(Robert Johnson) *hld up: nvr a factor: blnd 2 out* **150/1**

05 **6** *¾* **Heather Glen (IRE)**[40] [3504] 5-11-0 0 .... HenryOliver 62
(Sue Smith) *hld up: nt fluent 4th: bhd fr 4 out* **50/1**

0P-P **7** *25* **Beau Peak**[26] [3729] 12-10-4 64 .... CallumWhillans(10) 37
(Donald Whillans) *prom: lost pl qckly after 5th: bhd fr next: t.o* **100/1**

P **P** **Beat The Band**[93] [2505] 6-11-0 0 .... PeterBuchanan —
(Lucinda Russell) *trckd ldrs: mstke 6th: wknd qckly after 4 out: t.o whn p.u bef 2 out* **8/1**

5m 25.3s (32.60) **Going Correction** +1.00s/f (Soft)
WFA 4 from 5yo+ 10lb **8** Ran SP% **111.0**
Speed ratings (Par 105): **74,72,70,62,56 56,46,—**
toteswingers: 1&2 £6.60, 1&3 £1.10, 2&3 £6.50 CSF £43.83 TOTE £2.20: £1.10, £8.20, £1.10; EX 46.40.

Owner Brendan Richardson **Bred** J F C Maxwell **Trained** Cholmondeley, Cheshire

FOCUS

Not a particularly strong mares' novice hurdle but the improving favourite put in a tremendously feisty display. She might however, be flattered by her current mark.

NOTEBOOK

Alexander Road(IRE) produced a dominant performance when easing 7l clear in a mares' novice hurdle at Carlisle last time. There were severe warning signs three out this time, but in defying a penalty she showed tenacity and a relentless galloping style to fight off some rivals who were travelling better than her on the way. This lightly raced sort is still learning but her form is upwardly mobile and her unflinching attitude is a very useful asset. (op 6-4, tchd evens in places)

Kykate ran a very promising race at a big price on hurdle debut back from ten months off. She is out of a bumper winning sister to a 2m-2m6f hurdle winner and should improve for the run.

Lady Bluesky achieved useful form in bumpers early on and thrived in minor staying Flat handicaps last year. Her hurdle career started with an odds-on defeat in November, and she was keen out in front before being held again. However, this was still a respectable effort behind a fair type, and she shaped like she will be more potent back at 2m. (op 15-8)

Newdane Dancer(IRE) showed a decent attitude to wear down an experienced rival when making a winning debut in a 1m5f bumper at Wetherby last month. She was getting the age allowance and moved well for a long way before fading on this hurdling debut. She should improve for the experience and a drop in trip could work in her favour. (op 11-2 tchd 7-1)

Beat The Band was at the back of the breakaway group approaching four out but she weakened very quickly before being pulled up on this return from three months off. (op 7-1 tchd 13-2)

T/Plt: £7.10 to a £1 stake. Pool: £76,842.18. 7,843.81 winning tickets. T/Qpdt: £3.40 to a £1 stake. Pool: £4,453.06. 963.94 winning tickets. AS

4246 - 4247a (Foreign Racing) - See Raceform Interactive

3577 NAAS (L-H)

Sunday, February 20

OFFICIAL GOING: Soft to heavy

4248a PADDYPOWER.COM CHASE (GRADE 2) (10 fncs) 2m

3:05 (3:05) 5-Y-O+ **£26,056** (£7,616; £3,607)

RPR

1 **Golden Silver (FR)**[21] 3844 9-11-12 168 .... PTownend 167+
(W P Mullins, Ire) *settled cl up in 3rd: smooth hdwy to chal 2 out: led early run-in and effrtlessly stretched clr: v easily* **2/13**[1]

2 *7* **Made In Taipan (IRE)**[8] 4087 9-11-10 149 .... DNRussell 153
(Thomas Mullins, Ire) *led or disp ld: strly pressed fr 2 out: hdd early run-in and no ch w easy wnr* **6/1**[2]

3 *19* **Mansony (FR)**[17] 3915 12-11-10 133 .... PWFlood 134
(A L T Moore, Ire) *disp ld and kpt to wd outside thrght: slow 4 out and lost pl: disp again briefly appr st: no ex and wknd after 2 out* **20/1**[3]

4m 28.5s (5.20) **3** Ran SP% **105.7**
CSF £1.57 TOTE £1.10; DF 1.40.

Owner Mrs Violet O'Leary **Bred** Noel Pelat **Trained** Muine Beag, Co Carlow

FOCUS
A schooling round for the winner, and it's unlikely that the other two bounced back to their best here.

NOTEBOOK
Golden Silver(FR) duly accounted for his two rivals with the minimum of fuss. Settled in a close third, he jumped and travelled throughout before he asserted his authority away from the last with his rider hardly moving a muscle. After his fourth win from six starts this season, trainer Willie Mullins is edging towards the Sportingbet.com Queen Mother Champion Chase and renewing rivalry with Big Zeb. The ground could well be the deciding factor with his trainer suggesting afterwards that if the ground came up lively he may well head for the Ryanair, but he summed up by saying: "The more I think about it I'm edging towards the shorter race." (op 1/7)

Made In Taipan(IRE) ran as well as could be expected considering he's rated 19lb lower than the winner, he probably needs further these days.

Mansony(FR), a previous C&D winner, is not the force of old and the 12-year-old dropped away tamely from before the second last to trail home last of the trio. (op 22/1)

4249a PADDYPOWER.COM NOVICE HURDLE (GRADE 2) (8 hdls) 2m

3:35 (3:35) 4-Y-O+ **£23,254** (£6,797; £3,219; £1,073)

RPR

1 **Dare To Doubt**[25] 3754 7-11-0 .... PTownend 131+
(W P Mullins, Ire) *mde all: extended advantage to 4 l travelling wl 2 out: kpt on wl fr bef last: easily* **7/2**[2]

2 *5* **Prima Vista**[42] 3474 6-11-5 124 .... PCarberry 131
(Noel Meade, Ire) *hld up towards rr: clsr early st: rdn to go 3rd whn mstke last: kpt on u.p run-in but no ch w wnr* **7/2**[2]

3 *2 ½* **Jim Will Fix It (IRE)**[36] 3577 6-11-5 .... (t) MrSRByrne 129
(Seamus Roche, Ire) *chsd ldr in 3rd: reminders 4 out: drvn along to go 2nd bef 2 out: no imp on wnr fr bef last: dropped to 3rd run-in* **14/1**

4 *1* **Aughaloor (IRE)**[25] 3753 8-11-5 .... MrPWMullins 128
(W P Mullins, Ire) *trckd ldrs: 4th 1/2-way: tk clsr order early in st: no imp appr last: kpt on one pce run-in* **9/1**

5 *1 ¼* **Four Commanders (IRE)**[10] 4037 5-11-4 .... DNRussell 125
(M F Morris, Ire) *trckd ldr in 2nd: rdn and dropped to 3rd bef 2 out: 4th and no imp whn slt mstke last: kpt on one pce* **16/1**

6 *shd* **Tornedo Shay (IRE)**[21] 3846 6-11-5 .... PTEnright 126
(T J O'Mara, Ire) *hld up towards rr: sme hdwy appr 2 out: sn no imp u.p* **9/1**

7 *2 ½* **White Star Line (IRE)**[26] 3733 7-11-5 .... PWFlood 125
(D T Hughes, Ire) *mid-div on inner: 5th 1/2-way: pushed along in tch whn nt fluent 2 out: sn no ex* **6/1**[3]

8 *6* **Darwins Fox (FR)**[36] 3580 5-11-4 .... AELynch 119
(Henry De Bromhead, Ire) *trckd ldrs whn mstke 2nd: 6th 1/2-way: sme hdwy appr 2 out: sn no ex* **5/2**[1]

3m 53.9s (-9.60) **8** Ran SP% **119.9**
CSF £17.48 TOTE £4.80: £1.50, £1.60, £3.70; DF 18.50.

Owner J T Ennis **Bred** Mrs J F Maitland-Jones **Trained** Muine Beag, Co Carlow

FOCUS
The sixth looks a solid guide to this form.

NOTEBOOK
Dare To Doubt has been improved by front-running tactics and they worked even better here. Dictating the pace and mostly jumping very fluently, she was given a fine tactical ride and kept a nice bit in reserve for the straight. When she kicked again before the second-last she had everything else in trouble and none of her rivals could make any impression. Cheltenham doesn't look to be on the agenda but she should be capable of winning a good mares' contest before the season is out, and she may well be equally suited by better ground. (op 4/1)

Prima Vista was held up but met some slight traffic problems early in the straight, including when he seemed to be slightly squeezed out jumping the second last. By the time he got going the winner had gone, but as he was unable to make any impression up the hill one couldn't call him an unlucky loser. (op 10/3)

Jim Will Fix It(IRE) fared much better here than in his maiden hurdle here the previous month. Ridden positively and tracking the winner much of the way although not jumping quite as well as her, he was being hard ridden and looked like dropping away entering the straight. He does stay well, however, and stuck at it quite well. He's improving over hurdles and will have no difficulty getting a bit further.

Aughaloor(IRE) was covered up on the inside and did close up to an extent entering the straight but didn't have the pace to get involved. He stayed on to reasonable effect. (op 8/1 tchd 10/1)

Four Commanders(IRE) raced prominently and jumped with the winner for most of the way. He just lacked a gear when she quickened again off the home bend and came home at the same pace. He's likely to improve for better ground and will end up being a better long-term prospect than many of these.

Tornedo Shay(IRE) was held up and travelled well turning into the straight. He briefly looked dangerous at the second last but couldn't close once coming under pressure. (op 9/1 tchd 10/1)

White Star Line(IRE) looked dangerous briefly when closing on the inside early in the straight but didn't find a huge amount off the bridle. (op 7/1)

Darwins Fox(FR) was very keen early on and missed a couple of early flights, but even given that he seemed to travel well enough to the home bend. As soon as he was asked to improve his position he emptied. It was a very disappointing effort, which gave no reflection of his true ability. He was subsequently found to be suffering from a respiratory tract infection. Official explanation: jockey said that gelding never travelled after making a bad mistake at 2nd hurdle; vet said that gelding was found to have a respiratory tract infection following a post-race endoscopic examination (op 11/4)

4250a WOODLANDS PARK 100 CLUB NAS NA RIOGH NOVICE CHASE (GRADE 2) (13 fncs) 2m 4f

4:10 (4:10) 5-Y-O+ **£22,413** (£6,551; £3,103; £1,034)

RPR

1 **Roi Du Mee (FR)**[11] 4014 6-11-5 .... DNRussell 149+
(Gordon Elliott, Ire) *trckd ldr in 2nd: led fr 6th: strly pressed early st: rdn and drifted rt after 2 out: j.lft at last: edgd lft u.p run-in: kpt on wl* **6/4**[1]

2 *2* **Ad Idem**[26] 3736 7-11-5 .... AndrewJMcNamara 147
(Mrs Pauline Gavin, Ire) *trckd ldrs in 3rd: wnt 2nd after 8th: chal appr 2 out: sn rdn: j.lft and slt mstke last: short of room u.p and swtchd rt ins fnl 100yds: kpt on* **7/4**[2]

3 *dist* **Alpha Ridge (IRE)**[23] 3798 9-11-5 135 .... (t) APCawley —
(Paul Nolan, Ire) *led: slt mstke and hdd 6th: bad mstke 8th and dropped to 3rd: no ex fr 3 out: btn whn awkward at last and sprawled bdly on landing* **2/1**[3]

4 *¾* **Saddler's Native (IRE)**[3] 4175 9-11-5 102 .... MWBowes —
(Patrick O Brady, Ire) *a in rr: j.rt thrght: trailing bef 5 out* **50/1**

5m 31.9s (2.90) **4** Ran SP% **111.7**
CSF £4.81 TOTE £1.90; DF 4.30.

Owner Gigginstown House Stud **Bred** Jacques Hersent & Mrs Jacqueline Hersent **Trained** Trim, Co Meath

■ Stewards' Enquiry : D N Russell caution: careless riding

FOCUS
The winner had to do this is in a different style, gutsing it out, and the form is rated through the runner-up.

NOTEBOOK
Roi Du Mee(FR) completed the hat-trick and continued his upward progression. Taking it up after a good jump early on the final circuit, he jumped and travelled from there. The runner-up did throw down a serious challenge in the straight but the winner's jumping was just better over the last two and despite wandering and then tightening up his main market rival after the final fence, he was the winner on merit. He's probably still improving and stays further. Official explanation: ssevere caution: careless riding (op 6/4 tchd 13/8)
Ad Idem didn't get the run of things in the straight but didn't do himself too many favours either. Happy to sit just off the winner, he travelled well to make his challenge in the straight. While he did have to switch to the inside of the winner he proceeded to make a mess of the final fence, and also while he did get slightly squeezed by the winner after the last he never really looked like going past. It was still a decent effort and he'll win a decent race, especially with improved jumping. (op 15/8)
Alpha Ridge(IRE) ran desperately. He was happy to bowl along but as soon as he made one mistake he was gone. That came early on the final circuit, several other mistakes followed and he eventually came home in his own time after a horrible blunder at the last.
Saddler's Native(IRE) was able to pick up some fortunate prize-money.

4251 - 4252a (Foreign Racing) - See Raceform Interactive

3999 CARLISLE (R-H)

Monday, February 21

OFFICIAL GOING: Heavy (5.3)

First flight of hurdles in back straight omitted all hurdle races.Stable bend rail on outer line. Old stable bend inner hurdle rail moved out; shared bends.
Wind: Fresh, half against Weather: Dull

4253 SUMMER FUN WITH TEXAS 2ND JULY NOVICES' HURDLE (9 hdls 2 omitted) 2m 4f

2:10 (2:10) (Class 4) 4-Y-O+ **£2,226** (£649; £324)

Form RPR

1 **Jammia (IRE)**[19] 3896 6-10-10 0 .... MrDRFox[(7)] 132+
(Noel C Kelly, Ire) *trckd ldrs: led 2nd: drew clr fr 3 out: readily* **20/1**

4255 2 *29* **River Dragon (IRE)**[16] 3952 6-11-3 105 .... GrahamLee 103
(Neville Bycroft) *trckd ldrs: rdn bef 3 out: outpcd bef next: lft 17 l 2nd last: no imp* **16/1**[3]

32-3 3 *9* **Senor Alco (FR)**[107] 2202 5-11-3 0 .... BrianHughes 101+
(Howard Johnson) *cl up: rdn and ev ch bef 3 out: outpcd fr next: lft mod 3rd whn hmpd last* **7/2**[2]

0000 4 *2 ½* **Knockando**[21] 3851 6-11-3 0 .... PeterBuchanan 92
(Lucinda Russell) *hld up: rdn after 4 out: sn outpcd: no imp fr next* **80/1**

20U5 5 *9* **Molon Labe (IRE)**[12] 3999 4-10-7 114 .... JamesReveley 82+
(Tom Tate) *hld up: hdwy to trck ldrs bef 3 out: sn rdn and outpcd whn blnd next: 4th and btn whn bdly hmpd last* **22/1**

06 6 *31* **Silent Snow (IRE)**[12] 3999 6-11-0 0 .... JamesHalliday[(3)] 52
(Malcolm Jefferson) *nt fluent on occasions: in tch: lost pl bef 4 out: n.d after* **150/1**

1-64 7 *32* **Arrow Barrow (IRE)**[27] 3725 6-10-10 0 .... MrJohnDawson[(7)] 20
(John Wade) *nt fluent on occasions: t.k.h: hld up: hdwy and prom after 3rd: wknd after 4 out* **40/1**

6 8 *17* **Gris Lord (IRE)**[21] 3856 6-11-3 0 .... DougieCostello —
(R T J Wilson, Ire) *led to 2nd: cl up tl rdn and wknd after 4 out* **20/1**

P0 P **Young Firth**[13] 3994 4-10-7 0 .... PaddyAspell —
(John Norton) *bhd: drvn and outpcd bef 5th: t.o whn p.u bef 4 out* **200/1**

1 F **Storming Gale (IRE)**[25] 3762 5-11-10 0 .... JasonMaguire 110
(Donald McCain) *t.k.h: in tch: hdwy to chse wnr 3 out: outpcd bef next: 16 l 2nd and no imp whn fell last* **4/9**[1]

P0 P **Shoal Bay Dreamer**[21] 3851 5-10-10 0 .... RyanMania —
(Dianne Sayer) *prom tl wknd bef 4 out: t.o whn p.u bef next* **200/1**

5m 30.5s (7.70) **Going Correction** +0.60s/f (Soft)
WFA 4 from 5yo+ 10lb **11** Ran SP% **116.6**
Speed ratings (Par 105): **108,96,92,91,88 75,63,56,—,— —**
Tote Swingers: 1&2 £23.40, 1&3 £10.10, 2&3 £3.10. CSF £246.94 TOTE £43.00: £3.90, £3.10, £1.40; EX 513.80.

Owner Mrs C Kelly **Bred** Mrs Catherine McCarthy **Trained** Draperstown, Co. Derry

■ Noel Kelly's first winner in Britain.

■ Stewards' Enquiry : Mr D R Fox one-day ban: used whip when clearly winning (Mar 7)

FOCUS
The opening novices' hurdle was a two-horse race according to the market but it turned out otherwise. The gallop in the very testing conditions was just steady until the final three-quarters of a mile. The impressive winner looks a decent prospect but the favourite was around a stone off.

NOTEBOOK

Jammia(IRE), runner-up in a Clonmel bumper on his debut, was well beaten at Down Royal next time. A big, relentless galloper, he went on with over a circuit to go and was out on his own when the favourite fell at the final flight. It may have been a surprise but it looked no fluke and he looks a useful recruit who clearly stays very well and is sure to make a chaser in time. (op 28-1 tchd 18-1)

River Dragon(IRE) already looks fully exposed. Rated 105, he was in third and wide when he avoided trouble and was handed a clear second at the final flight.

Senor Alco(FR), third over nearly 2m7f at Kelso on his first try over hurdles, was a tired fourth when he was hampered by the faller at the last. He might not want conditions as testing as this. (op 4-1)

Knockando, a detached sixth three out, was handed fourth when the two ahead of him were hampered at the final flight. He looks a real stayer.

Molon Labe(IRE), stepping up in trip, moved comfortably into contention at the foot of the final hill but, as here last time, emptied badly and was a tired fifth when almost brought to a standstill at the final flight. (op 20-1 tchd 25-1)

Storming Gale(IRE), an impressive looking half-brother to four winners, was a very warm order to follow up his impressive Flos Lass success. This winning Irish pointer travelled supremely well but found little under pressure and was a tired and distant second, just ahead of the exposed River Dragon, when crashing out at the final flight. This was not his true running and he must be given another chance. (op 2-5)

4254 EUROPEAN BREEDERS' FUND/THOROUGHBRED BREEDERS' ASSOCIATION MARES' NOVICES' CHASE (16 fncs) 2m 4f

2:40 (2:40) (Class 4) 5-Y-0+

£3,444 (£1,017; £508; £254; £127; £63)

Form				RPR
P363	1		**Identity Parade (IRE)**[25] 3763 7-10-12 107...................... JasonMaguire	110+
			(Donald McCain) *cl up: led 10th to next: styd upsides: drvn bef 2 out: led run-in: styd on wl* **3/1**[2]
-003	2	15	**Overbranch**[12] 4001 8-10-9 97....................................(b) JamesHalliday(3)	100+
			(Malcolm Jefferson) *led to 10th: regained ld next: rdn and hdd run-in: wknd* **9/4**[1]
24	3	10	**Cloonawillin Lady (IRE)**[12] 4002 8-10-5 89................. StevenGagan(7)	84
			(Elliott Cooper) *prom: hit 8th: pushed along fr 11th: wnt 3rd after 4 out: outpcd next: no imp bef 2 out* **7/1**
-511	4	15	**Primrose Time**[101] 2352 8-11-5 107............................... AlexanderVoy(5)	86+
			(Lucy Normile) *trckd ldrs: outpcd 5 out: lost 3rd next: btn fnl 2* **7/2**[3]
P432	5	8	**Almond Court (IRE)**[7] 4114 8-10-12 74........................(t) KennyJohnson	61
			(Robert Johnson) *s.i.s: nt fluent in rr: hdwy to join pack after 7th: struggling fr next: n.d after* **100/1**
0/P-	6	46	**Amulree**[29] 8-10-5 0.. MissLAlexander(7)	15
			(N W Alexander) *bhd: outpcd 8th: hit 10th: sn wknd* **28/1**
3053	F		**Political Pendant**[10] 4057 10-10-5 80............................ PaulGallagher(7)	—
			(Rayson Nixon) *nt fluent in rr: rdn 1/2-way: 5th and outpcd whn fell heavily 11th: fatally injured* **17/2**
P	P		**A Special Lady (IRE)**[94] 2505 6-10-12 0.......................(t) PeterBuchanan	—
			(I A Duncan, Ire) *trckd ldrs: hit 3rd: outpcd whn blnd 8th: sn lost tch: t.o whn p.u after 5 out* **33/1**

5m 31.9s (4.50) **Going Correction** +0.30s/f (Yiel) **8** Ran SP% **108.4**

Speed ratings: **103,97,93,87,83 65,—,—**

Tote Swingers: 1&2 £2.10, 1&3 £6.20, 2&3 £7.90 CSF £9.44 TOTE £3.40: £1.40, £1.10, £2.50; EX 10.20.

Owner Racegoers Club Owners Group **Bred** Mrs M Doran **Trained** Cholmondeley, Cheshire

FOCUS

An ordinary mares' novices' chase and in the end a wide-margin winner. She stepped up a lot on her chase efforts but this was believable on her hurdles form.

NOTEBOOK

Identity Parade(IRE), rated 107 over fences, was 5lb below her hurdles mark, and had finished runner-up to a smart prospect at Flos Lass on her second start over fences. She went head to head with the runner-up but was the first to come under serious pressure. Level all the way up the final hill, she came right away on the run-in. Though not very big she has a very willing attitude and should win another one of these. (tchd 5-2)

Overbranch, rated 97 after eight previous starts over fences, looked to be travelling just the better but she tired badly on the run-in and in the end it was accepted. This trip on this ground round such a stiff track as this stretched her to breaking point. She can surely find a similar event with less emphasis on stamina. (op 11-4 tchd 3-1)

Cloonawillin Lady(IRE), who looked a fair prospect when taking her Irish point, had looked very limited in two starts over fences here. Rated just 89, she showed in a clear but distant third three out. Keeping on from the last, a modest novices' handicap over 3m might be a better option. (op 15-2 tchd 8-1)

Primrose Time, having her first start since mid-November, had a stiff task under her double penalty. Struggling to keep up six out, she tired badly over the last three and may well have needed this. She would have much less on her plate returned to handicap company. (op 9-4)

4255 ALEXANDRA BURKE HERE 1ST AUGUST H'CAP HURDLE (7 hdls 2 omitted) 2m 1f

3:10 (3:11) (Class 3) (0-120,120) 4-Y-0+ **£3,252** (£955; £477; £238)

Form				RPR
5-52	1		**Cool Operator**[94] 2506 8-11-5 120................................ PaulGallagher(7)	132+
			(Howard Johnson) *cl up: led after 4 out: rdn and drew clr fr 2 out* **8/1**
5541	2	10	**Teenage Idol (IRE)**[21] 3855 7-11-12 120.............................. RyanMania	121
			(Evelyn Slack) *trckd ldrs: rdn and outpcd after 3 out: rallied to chse (clr) wnr run-in: no imp* **6/1**
3140	3	1 3/4	**Princess Rainbow (FR)**[12] 4009 6-11-7 115..................... AlanO'Keeffe	115
			(Jennie Candlish) *led tl hdd after 4 out: outpcd bef next: rallied run-in: no imp* **9/2**[2]
012U	4	5	**Rolecarr (IRE)**[10] 4058 8-10-8 102... AdrianLane	99+
			(Ann Hamilton) *cl up: ev ch and rdn bef 3 out: one pce after next: wknd and lost two pls run-in* **3/1**[1]
4005	5	16	**Grandad Bill (IRE)**[15] 3966 8-11-7 115.......................... RichieMcGrath	97
			(Jim Goldie) *hld up: mstke 3rd: rdn and outpcd after 4 out: no imp fr next* **11/2**[3]
04U5	6	20	**Shooting Times**[96] 2446 6-10-2 99................................ JamesHalliday(3)	57
			(Andrew Parker) *in tch: lost pl and outpcd bef 4th: sn detached: no ch after* **12/1**
0-65	7	21	**Bureaucrat**[15] 3969 9-11-7 115..(p) BrianHarding	52
			(Kate Walton) *in tch on outside: struggling after 4th: sn wknd: t.o* **14/1**
154-	P		**Bishops Heir**[316] 5138 6-11-4 119............................... NathanMoscrop(7)	—
			(James Ewart) *in tch tl rdn and wknd after 4 out: t.o whn p.u bef next* **11/2**[3]

4m 36.8s (7.00) **Going Correction** +0.60s/f (Soft) **8** Ran SP% **113.7**

Speed ratings (Par 107): **107,102,101,99,91 82,72,—**

Tote Swingers: 1&2 £5.40, 1&3 £7.10, 2&3 £4.10 CSF £54.20 CT £242.60 TOTE £11.40: £1.80, £2.50, £2.70; EX 29.10.

Owner T Alderson & J H Johnson **Bred** R D And Mrs J S Chugg **Trained** Billy Row, Co Durham

■ Stewards' Enquiry : Nathan Moscrop two-day ban: careless riding (Mar 7-8)

FOCUS

A competitive handicap hurdle and the gallop was relentless in the testing conditions. The first three home were in the first four throughout. There is a case for rating the form a little higher.

NOTEBOOK

Cool Operator, back to his best when runner-up from a 5lb lower mark at Musselburgh in November, was unproven on bad ground. He battled hard to take charge three out and was out on his own when he jumped the final flight like a fresh horse. He won easing down in the end under his young rider, who looks excellent value for his 7lb claim. (op 9-1)

Teenage Idol(IRE), raised a harsh 15lb for his wide-margin win in a weaker race at Ayr, worked hard to secure second spot soon after the last. He will struggle to add another win to his record from this sort of mark. (op 8-1 tchd 11-2)

Princess Rainbow(FR), 10lb higher than for her last success at Herford in November, set a good pace. She looked booked for fourth when well off the pace going to two out, but to her credit she knuckled down and stayed on all the way to the finish. She is all heart. (tchd 5-1)

Rolecarr(IRE), 20lb higher than for his win at Hexham in November, tended to run in snatches. He chased the winner three out until tiring badly soon after the final flight. (op 9-2)

Grandad Bill(IRE), having his first outing here, never looked happy and lost touch going to three out. He is slipping down the ratings and a speed track and much less testing conditions suit him a lot better. (op 9-2)

4256 CUMBERLAND SHOW 16TH JULY H'CAP CHASE (21 fncs) 3m 4f

3:40 (3:40) (Class 3) (0-125,124) 5-Y-0+ **£3,252** (£955; £477; £238)

Form			RPR
4-P1	V	**Victory Gunner (IRE)**[18] 3900 13-10-4 107.................... GilesHawkins(5)	—
	(Richard Lee) *trcking ldrs whn p.u after 11th: r voided*
1344	V	**Matmata De Tendron (FR)**[13] 3996 11-9-7 98 oh6..(p) PaulGallagher(7)	—
	(Andrew Crook) *prom: lost pl 5th: rallied to chse ldrs 9th: p.u after 11th: r voided*
PP-0	V	**Royal Mackintosh**[101] 2354 10-10-3 101.......................... BrianHarding	—
	(Alan Mactaggart) *led tl p.u after 11th: r voided*
3311	V	**Star Player (IRE)**[19] 3888 9-11-12 124..........................(t) DenisO'Regan	—
	(Chris Grant) *hld up: broke down bef 4th: fatally injured: r voided*
-003	V	**Money Order (IRE)**[36] 3588 9-11-2 117..................... RichieMcLernon(3)	—
	(Brendan Powell) *last whn mstke and uns rdr 1st: r voided*
UF6P	V	**Mr Woods**[12] 4003 9-10-12 117............................... GaryRutherford(7)	—
	(Harriet Graham) *hld up: p.u after 11th: r voided*
05P3	V	**Blazing Diva (IRE)**[9] 4066 8-10-0 98 oh1........................ CampbellGillies	—
	(Sandy Thomson) *chsd ldr tl p.u after 11th: r voided*
0-36	V	**Pennek (FR)**[68] 2953 8-11-1 113.. JamesReveley	—
	(Philip Kirby) *hld up in tch: p.u after 11th: r voided*
53/P	V	**Overlady**[13] 3996 9-10-4 105.. HarryHaynes(3)	—
	(James Ewart) *in tch whn p.u after 11th: r voided*

FOCUS

This stayers' handicap chase had to be stopped and declared void when the remaining runners were approaching the final fence with a full circuit to go. Star Player, who suffered a serious and sadly fatal leg injury on the first circuit turning away from the stands approaching the fourth fence, was stricken at a point on the track where it is very narrow and the decision was made on welfare grounds to halt the remaining runners.

NOTEBOOK

Royal Mackintosh, seeking his fifth course win, had taken them along, jumping boldly and racing with real enthusiasm. He was certainly giving every indication of being back on song under his favourite rider on his first start for 101 days.

Overlady, who took this from a 3lb lower mark two years ago, was back over fences after injury put her on the sidelines soon after. In great nick and full of beans beforehand, she travelled as sweet as a nut on the wide outside until the stoppage.

4257 SPORTING CHAMPIONS RACEDAY 20TH MARCH H'CAP HURDLE (9 hdls 2 omitted) 2m 4f

4:10 (4:11) (Class 3) (0-130,125) 4-Y-0+ **£3,252** (£955; £477; £238)

Form				RPR
-035	1		**Double Eagle**[28] 3713 9-10-11 110..................................(p) JasonMaguire	121+
			(Donald McCain) *mde all: jst in front whn rdn whn hit but lft 3 l clr 3 out: styd on strly fr next* **13/8**[1]
0032	2	8	**Mister Pete (IRE)**[41] 3502 8-10-1 105......................(p) AlexanderVoy(5)	105
			(Chris Grant) *trckd wnr: jst lost 2nd and 3 l down whn lft 2nd 3 out: one pce next: 8 l down whn blnd last* **5/2**[2]
1-P0	3	1 1/2	**Bollin Fiona**[96] 2448 7-9-9 104................................. CallumWhillans(10)	103
			(Donald Whillans) *trckd ldrs: rdn and outpcd after 4 out: lft 4th next: plugged on fnl 2: no imp* **6/1**[3]
-42F	4	22	**Degas Art (IRE)**[33] 3632 8-11-2 122............................... PaulGallagher(7)	106
			(Howard Johnson) *trckd ldrs: outpcd whn lft 3rd and checked 3 out: wknd bef next* **13/2**
/000	F		**Livvy Inn (USA)**[50] 3334 6-11-5 118................................ CampbellGillies	—
			(Lucinda Russell) *racd wd: hld up: smooth hdwy after 4 out: effrt and 1 l 2nd whn fell* **11/1**
025P	P		**Bocamix (FR)**[15] 3969 5-11-12 125.................................(t) FearghalDavis	—
			(Andrew Crook) *hld up: rdn and struggling after 4 out: t.o whn p.u next* **16/1**

5m 33.1s (10.30) **Going Correction** +0.60s/f (Soft) **6** Ran SP% **108.5**

Speed ratings (Par 107): **103,99,99,90,— —**

Tote Swingers: 1&2 £1.10, 1&3 £4.20, 2&3 £7.40 CSF £5.84 TOTE £3.10: £1.60, £1.60; EX 6.20.

Owner Dr G M Thelwall Jones **Bred** Dr G M Thelwall Jones **Trained** Cholmondeley, Cheshire

FOCUS

A weak handicap hurdle. The easy winner may still be capable of raing a bit higher, and the next two help with the level.

NOTEBOOK

Double Eagle, running from a career-low mark, recorded his first success for three years. He must have a right-handed track and, once the threat departed three out, it was plain sailing and he was eased down in the end. He is unlikely to find another race as uncompetitive in the near future. (op 15-8 tchd 6-4)

Mister Pete(IRE), 15lb higher than for his last win at Newcastle a year ago, was raised 5lb after finishing runner-up at Newcastle on his previous start. Left in second spot three out, he had been left well behind when he fell through the final flight. (op 11-4 tchd 3-1)

Bollin Fiona, who won from a 6lb lower mark here in March, was having only her second start since. Consistency does not figure on her CV. (op 7-1 tchd 11-2)

Degas Art(IRE), without a win for four years, was back over hurdles after a fall over fences last time. He prefers much better ground but it was disconcerting the way he carried his head very high and he seemed to down tools altogether three out. (op 11-2 tchd 5-1)

Livvy Inn(USA), whose sole success came two years ago on his debut, then took his chance in the Grade 1 juvenile hurdle at Aintree. Absent last term through injury, he has been dropped 11lb after three previous outings this year. He was a length down and looking a real threat to the winner when he slid on landing three out and came down. (op 8-1 tchd 12-1)

Bocamix(FR), raised 16lb after finishing runner-up behind Carlito Brigante in a weak Class 2 event at Haydock, has come down 5lb since being pulled up afterwards. He looks to have lost interest, and he stopped to nothing after four out before being pulled up. (op 8-1 tchd 12-1)

4258 CHELTENHAM FESTIVAL PREVIEW HERE 8TH MARCH H'CAP CHASE (16 fncs) 2m 4f

4:40 (4:40) (Class 4) (0-115,110) 5-Y-0+ **£2,602** (£764; £382; £190)

Form				RPR
3031	**1**		**Work Boy**[28] 3716 10-11-6 **109** ShaneByrne(5)	117
			(Sue Smith) *trckd ldrs: chal 5 out: rdn 3 out: 2 l down last: styd on to ld last 125yds: edgd lft and pushed out towards fin* **11/2**	
FP23	**2**	*3 ½*	**Double Default (IRE)**[12] 4004 10-11-6 **104** (p) JamesReveley	108
			(Martin Todhunter) *led: jnd 5 out: rdn 3 out: 2 l in front last: hdd and no ex last 125yds* **3/1**[2]	
0-42	**3**	*4 ½*	**Finlay**[27] 3723 8-11-4 **102** (t) JasonMaguire	104+
			(Donald McCain) *nt fluent: bhd: hdwy and prom 5 out: outpcd after next: no imp whn j.lft 2 out: styd on wl run-in: nt rch first two* **15/8**[1]	
P40P	**4**	*10*	**Sotovik (IRE)**[9] 4065 10-11-9 **110** EwanWhillans(3)	101
			(Alistair Whillans) *cl up: hit and outpcd 11th: no imp whn blnd 3 out* **14/1**	
/P-2	**5**	*5*	**Stoway (FR)**[32] 3648 9-11-12 **110** DougieCostello	96
			(Richard Lee) *t.k.h: prom: rdn and outpcd after 4 out: wknd next: btn whn blnd 2 out* **7/2**[3]	
0P64	**P**		**Norminster**[12] 4001 10-10-0 **84** oh10 (p) RyanMania	—
			(Rayson Nixon) *in tch: outpcd 8th: blnd and struggling 10th: sn btn: t.o whn p.u bef 4 out* **12/1**	

5m 38.0s (10.60) **Going Correction** +0.30s/f (Yiel) **6** Ran SP% **111.7**

Speed ratings: **90,88,86,82,80** —

Tote Swingers: 1&2 £1.90, 1&3 £3.10, 2&3 £2.30 CSF £22.41 TOTE £6.00: £2.20, £1.20; EX 12.20.

Owner Mrs S Smith **Bred** Mrs M Parker **Trained** High Eldwick, W Yorks

FOCUS

A modest event run at a sound pace and just the first two in serious contention up the final hill. The winner is rated to his mark.

NOTEBOOK

Work Boy, proven in bad ground, was 3lb higher than for his win over an extended 3m at Wetherby. He looked to be playing second fiddle from four out but his stamina carried the day on the run-in and he made up a couple of lengths to win going away despite wandering in front. (op 5-1 tchd 6-1)

Double Default(IRE), down in trip on just his sixth start over fences, took them along at a brisk pace. He looked to hold the upper hand until the needle hit empty on the run-in. A slightly less stiff test will be in his favour. (op 9-2)

Finlay, having just his third start over fences, didn't jump fluently. He worked his way onto the heels of the first two four out but, tending to hang, was soon left behind. He made serious inroads from the final fence suggesting the first two were stopping, and less testing ground will aid his cause. (op 2-1 tchd 7-4)

Sotovik(IRE), three times a course winner, has been off the boil since his success from a 3lb lower mark here in October. (op 12-1 tchd 16-1)

Stoway(FR), who has clearly had his problems in other yards, last tasted success almost four years ago. He ran with the choke out and was never going to get home. He was a very tired fourth when falling through the final fence. (op 10-3)

4259 X-FACTOR CARLISLE LIVE 24TH JULY MAIDEN NATIONAL HUNT FLAT RACE (CONDITIONALS' AND AMATEURS') 2m 1f

5:10 (5:10) (Class 6) 4-6-Y-0 **£1,267** (£369; £184)

Form				RPR
2	**1**		**Richie Rob**[61] 3088 5-11-0 0 BrianToomey(5)	116+
			(Neville Bycroft) *hld up: hdwy over 5f out: led over 2f out: edgd rt and drew clr over 1f out* **7/1**[3]	
05	**2**	*22*	**Rojo Vivo**[19] 3889 5-10-12 0 HenryBrooke(7)	94
			(Karen McLintock) *cl up: led over 6f out: rdn and hdd over 2f out: plugged on same pce* **14/1**	
2	**3**	*1*	**Vintage Star (IRE)**[17] 3920 5-11-0 0 ShaneByrne(5)	93
			(Sue Smith) *trckd ldrs: rdn over 5f out: ev ch over 3f out: drvn: edgd rt and kpt on same pce fnl 2f* **7/4**[1]	
2	**4**	*6*	**Edmund (IRE)**[27] 3731 4-10-3 0 PaulGallagher(7)	79
			(Howard Johnson) *in tch: effrt on outside over 5f out: outpcd 4f out: no imp fnl 2f* **4/1**[2]	
	5	*29*	**Seriatim (IRE)**[19] 3896 6-10-12 0 JeremiahMcGrath(7)	58
			(R T J Wilson, Ire) *hld up in tch: rdn over 5f out: wknd 4f out* **9/1**	
0	**6**	*12*	**Soul Bid (IRE)**[27] 3731 5-11-5 0 CampbellGillies	46
			(Chris Grant) *in tch: drvn and outpcd 1/2-way: sn struggling: no ch after: t.o* **40/1**	
6	**7**	*18*	**Hyde Place**[19] 3889 4-10-10 0 FearghalDavis	19
			(Michael Dods) *led tl hdd over 6f out: wknd wl over 3f out: t.o* **18/1**	
0	**8**	*8*	**Bunratty (IRE)**[92] 2553 5-10-12 0 MrTSpeke(7)	20
			(Robert Johnson) *in tch on outside: lost tch after 7f: t.o* **100/1**	
	9	*42*	**Cometotheboardroom (IRE)** 5-10-12 0 JakeGreenall(7)	—
			(Alan Swinbank) *plld hrd: cl up tl wknd qckly over 5f out: virtually p.u fnl 3f* **4/1**[2]	

4m 36.4s (12.20) **Going Correction** +0.60s/f (Soft)

WFA 4 from 5yo+ 9lb **9** Ran SP% **114.2**

Speed ratings: **95,84,84,81,67 62,53,49,30**

Tote Swingers: 1&2 £11.20, 2&3 £4.60 CSF £97.39 TOTE £11.50: £2.50, £2.00, £1.80; EX 71.90.

Owner C E Whiteley **Bred** D J And Mrs Deer **Trained** Brandsby, N Yorks

FOCUS

Probably a very ordinary bumper. It was run at a steady pace and there were three upsides once in line for home. The easy winner is rated up a stone and the form could be assessed higher.

NOTEBOOK

Richie Rob, runner-up in a weak bumper on the AW at Southwell first time, pulled clear with his rider leaving nothing to chance. He still looked very inexperienced but it may have been a case of him handling the testing conditions better than the placed horses. (op 9-2 tchd 4-1)

Rojo Vivo, who showed little on his first two starts, ran a lot better, going on soon after halfway and keeping the third at bay in the closing stages.

Vintage Star(IRE), runner-up first time at Bangor, was made to look very one-paced. A well-made son of Presenting, he might not have appreciated conditions as testing as this. (op 5-2)

Edmund(IRE), only a 4-y-o, was left behind from the foot of the hill and is another who was probably not seen at his best in the bad ground. (op 5-1 tchd 7-2)

T/Jkpt: Part won. £24,619.10 to a £1 stake. Pool of £34,674.92 - 0.50 winning tickets. T/Plt: £39.50 to a £1 stake. Pool of £68,905.21 - 1,272.42 winning tickets. T/Qpdt: £6.20 to a £1 stake. Pool of £6,237.73 - 735 winning tickets. RY

4098 HEREFORD (R-H)

Monday, February 21

OFFICIAL GOING: Heavy (chs 4.8 hdl 5.0)

Second flight of hurdles after winning post and final fence omitted in all races due to reconstruction.

Wind: almost nil Weather: very dull and murky, light rain later

4260 LINDLEY CATERING MAIDEN HURDLE (7 hdls 1 omitted) 2m 1f

2:20 (2:20) (Class 4) 4-Y-0+ **£2,276** (£668; £334; £166)

Form				RPR
52	**1**		**Old Way (IRE)**[29] 3701 5-11-2 0 AidanColeman	127+
			(Venetia Williams) *prom: last of three gng clr after 2 out: cl 3rd at last: drvn and outbattled rivals to ld fnl 50yds* **6/4**[1]	
02U	**2**	*1 ¼*	**Cotillion**[20] 3866 5-10-13 119 MichaelMurphy(3)	126
			(Ian Williams) *cl up: led 3 out: rdn between last two: hdd and no ex fnl 50yds* **7/4**[2]	
4U	**3**	*1 ½*	**Sir Pitt**[13] 3986 4-10-7 0 DPFahy	116
			(Alison Thorpe) *hld up: effrt 3 out: sn w ldr: drvn and pushed rt and looked awkward bef last: ev ch tl fnd little fnl 100yds* **22/1**	
6-2	**4**	*17*	**Cottage Acre (IRE)**[24] 3789 8-11-2 0 PaddyBrennan	110
			(Tom George) *hld up: effrt 3 out: cl up briefly next: rdn and lost tch w ldng trio between last two* **8/1**	
4-65	**5**	*18*	**Fishoutofwater (IRE)**[16] 3937 7-11-2 0 APMcCoy	94
			(Rebecca Curtis) *prom: led bef 3 out: hdd bef next and lost pl rapidly: poor 5th after 2 out: t.o* **7/1**[3]	
0/UF	**6**	*17*	**Backstreet Billy (IRE)**[17] 3917 7-11-2 0 AndrewThornton	73
			(Richard Lee) *last after 2nd: t.o 3 out* **50/1**	
	7	*1 ¼*	**Rye Rocket**[873] 6-11-2 0 JodieMogford	71
			(Richard Lee) *midfield: fdd 3 out: t.o bef next* **100/1**	
46	**8**	*7*	**Prince Of King**[32] 3651 6-11-2 0 JamieMoore	64
			(Helen Nelmes) *bhd: mstke 3rd: t.o after 3 out* **100/1**	
0/00	**9**	*2 ¾*	**Starlet Mandy (IRE)**[25] 3762 8-10-6 0 SamTwiston-Davies(3)	55
			(Nigel Twiston-Davies) *a bhd: struggling 4th: t.o after 3 out* **80/1**	
-030	**10**	*1 ½*	**Don't Hang About**[8] 4094 6-11-2 0 JohnnyFarrelly	60
			(Richard Mitchell) *t.k.h in rr: lost tch 3 out: sn t.o* **50/1**	
20/	**11**	*½*	**Aperitif**[1152] 3031 10-11-2 0 TomScudamore	60
			(Michael Scudamore) *plld v hrd: led bef 2nd tl after 3rd: fdd bdly: t.o 3 out* **66/1**	
60	**12**	*7*	**Onetokeep (IRE)**[92] 2560 6-11-2 0 TomO'Brien	53
			(Anabel L M King) *midfield: struggling after 3 out: t.o next* **100/1**	
5P-0	**13**	*45*	**Bay Central (IRE)**[39] 3526 7-11-2 0 (t) PaulMoloney	8
			(Evan Williams) *prom: led briefly after 3rd: stopped to nil after next and sn t.o* **66/1**	

4m 15.2s (15.80) **Going Correction** +1.05s/f (Soft)

WFA 4 from 5yo+ 9lb **13** Ran SP% **115.4**

Speed ratings (Par 105): **104,103,102,94,86 78,77,74,73,72 72,68,47**

Tote Swingers: 1&2 £1.50, 1&3 £12.60, 2&3 £11.40 CSF £4.07 TOTE £2.50: £1.50, £1.10, £4.70; EX 5.10.

Owner B C Dice **Bred** Wertheimer Et Frere **Trained** Kings Caple, H'fords

FOCUS

The principals came right away from their rivals in this average maiden. The ground took its toll on the majority and the opinion of the riders afterwards was that it rode tacky and testing. The winner was the form pick and is on the upgrade.

NOTEBOOK

Old Way(IRE) got outstayed by Pret A Thou (won over fences since) on his second outing for connections at Towcester last month and went one better with a ready effort on this much sharper track. He took time to settle, but it was clear he was going best three out. The placed horses got first run on him off the home turn and that is often the best way to ride this track, but Aidan Coleman didn't panic and he was always going to get up after the last. His future lies in handicaps and there should be more to come in that sphere. (op 2-1)

Cotillion was a tired horse prior to unseating over an extended 2m6f on similar ground at Folkestone on his previous outing. His rider did everything right on him on this drop back in trip and he ran a solid race, but did just find it that bit too sharp. (tchd 13-8)

Sir Pitt, who got no further than the first last time, showed his true colours with a gutsy effort and was only picked off on the run-in. His turn appears to be nearing. (op 25-1 tchd 20-1)

Cottage Acre(IRE) couldn't go with the first three when things got really serious and his trainer's runners continue to go through a quiet spell. This former point winner can now enter handicaps and should enjoy stepping back up in trip. (tchd 7-1)

Fishoutofwater(IRE) was kept widest of all to find the better ground and his fate was apparent around four out. He is one to keep an eye on with a view to going handicapping on a suitably sounder surface. (op 6-1)

Bay Central(IRE) Official explanation: jockey said gelding had a breathing problem

4261 WEATHERBYS BLOODSTOCK INSURANCE BEGINNERS' CHASE (14 fncs 2 omitted) 2m 5f 110y

2:50 (2:50) (Class 4) 5-Y-0+ **£2,602** (£764; £382; £190)

Form				RPR
1066	**1**		**Quartz De Thaix (FR)**[16] 3947 7-11-0 0 AidanColeman	129+
			(Venetia Williams) *cl up and gng wl: wnt 2nd after 3 out: sustained run fnl 3f: wl timed chal to get up cl home* **4/7**[1]	
0-45	**2**	*1*	**Swansbrook (IRE)**[20] 3871 8-11-0 119 RobertThornton	128
			(Alan King) *lft in ld 3rd: 2 l clr last (normal 2 out): sn rdn: hdd cl home* **11/4**[2]	
F6	**3**	*36*	**The Humbel Monk (IRE)**[12] 4007 9-10-11 0 PeterToole(3)	92
			(Lucy Jones) *hit 9th: sn wnt 2nd: ev ch tl ouj. 11th and next: wkng whn hit 2 out: t.o* **50/1**	
-400	**4**	*16*	**South O'The Border**[37] 3566 9-11-0 124 (p) PaddyBrennan	76
			(Nigel Twiston-Davies) *j. v ponderously and reluctantly: led tl climbed 3rd: reminders 5th: drvn fr 7th: no rspnse: last and struggling after 9th: t.o bef 2 out* **11/2**[3]	
PP	**P**		**Real Dandy**[96] 2454 5-10-5 0 MattCrawley(7)	—
			(Lucinda Featherstone) *detached last and nt travelling wl tl blnd 6th and p.u* **50/1**	

5m 47.7s (27.70) **Going Correction** +1.25s/f (Heav)

WFA 5 from 7yo+ 2lb **5** Ran SP% **109.6**

Speed ratings: **99,98,85,79,—**

CSF £2.65 TOTE £1.70: £1.20, £1.60; EX 2.40.

Owner Roa Arkle Partnership **Bred** Michel Bourgneuf **Trained** Kings Caple, H'fords

FOCUS

With the final fence still being rebuilt there was no fence in the home straight in each of the three races over fences on the card and therefore a very long run-in. The first two came a long way clear in this fair beginners' chase. The winner can rate higher than this over fences and the second is rated to his hurdles mark.

NOTEBOOK

Quartz De Thaix(FR) provided his trainer/rider with a quick-fire double. This was his first outing over fences since last season, when his jumping let him down, but he has improved back over hurdles since then. Indeed, he was the clear form pick here and he did just enough to land the odds under another good ride by his jockey. He had to dig deep to reel in the runner-up, but his class came to the fore inside the final furlong and this was probably too sharp for him over fences. With that in mind he could be an interesting runner in one of the handicaps at Cheltenham next month, a track where he has won over hurdles, and the Byrne Group Plate looks his most viable target - a race the stable has won twice since 2007. The Centenary Novices' Handicap is the other option. (tchd 4-6 in places)

Swansbrook(IRE), who won his bumper here, stepped up big time on his two previous efforts over fences and was only just held. He raced awkwardly at times and probably isn't one for maximum faith, but this ground was plenty deep enough for him. His trainer can place him to go one better before long. (op 7-2 tchd 4-1)

The Humbel Monk(IRE) was outclassed, but he needs better ground and should be placed to strike when switching to low-grade handicaps in due course. (tchd 40-1)

South O'The Border put in a moody effort and he now looks one to avoid at all costs. (op 4-1 tchd 6-1)

Real Dandy Official explanation: jockey said saddle slipped

4262 WEATHERBYS CHELTENHAM FESTIVAL BETTING GUIDE NOVICES' HURDLE (9 hdls 2 omitted) 2m 6f 110y

3:20 (3:20) (Class 4) 4-Y-0+ **£2,276** (£668; £334; £166)

Form RPR

3432 **1** **Simply Wings (IRE)**[39] 3529 7-11-4 118 RobertThornton 120+
(Richard Lee) *settled cl up: 2nd and gng wl clr w ldr 2 out: a lookingly sltly superior after: rdn ahd last: styd on gamely* **13/8**[1]

1 **2** 2¼ **Listenlook (FR)**[17] 3930 5-11-11 0 PaddyBrennan 127+
(Nigel Twiston-Davies) *w ldr til led 3 out: stmbld next: hrd drvn after: hdd last: one pce* **7/4**[2]

0-2 **3** 25 **Cocacobana (IRE)**[22] 3842 6-11-4 0 JodieMogford 93
(Graeme McPherson) *t.k.h: chsd ldrs: lost tch 6th: wnt remote 3rd at last* **16/1**

415 **4** 2¼ **Old Wigmore (IRE)**[72] 2888 6-11-11 0 APMcCoy 98
(Rebecca Curtis) *slt ld at really slow pce tl 3 out: wknd bdly next: lost remote 3rd at last* **11/4**[3]

0-0F **P** **Lady Exe**[18] 3904 6-10-4 0 (tp) DannyBurton(7) —
(Chris Down) *blnd 2nd and rdr lost iron: nt fluent 3rd: in last pair: rdn after 4th: bdly t.o whn p.u 2 out* **100/1**

00 **P** **Midnight Charmer**[12] 4012 5-11-4 0 NickScholfield —
(Emma Baker) *last and struggling bef 6th: sn hopelessly t.o: p.u 2 out* **200/1**

6m 1.70s (23.70) **Going Correction** +1.05s/f (Soft) **6** Ran SP% **108.5**

Speed ratings (Par 105): **100,99,90,89,—** —

Tote Swingers: 1&2 £1.30, 1&3 £2.20, 2&3 £2.50 CSF £4.62 TOTE £2.40: £1.90, £2.40; EX 4.90.

Owner G D Thorp Bevan Bros Edmonds & Sampson **Bred** G T Morrow **Trained** Byton, H'fords

FOCUS

This staying novice hurdle was another race that saw two come well clear in a decent tussle, and the form is straightforward with the first two pretty much rated to their marks.

NOTEBOOK

Simply Wings(IRE), whose stable does well here, deservedly got his head in front at the 11th time of asking. He was raised 4lb to a mark of 118 after finishing second in a C&D handicap last month and a reproduction of that effort proved good enough. His ability to go on this ground was a big factor in him winning and he should remain competitive back in handicaps, but he'll probably go up in the weights again for this. (op 15-8)

Listenlook(FR) scored from the front on his hurdling debut at Chepstow 17 days earlier and he posted a brave effort in trying to follow up. He got the longer trip without much fuss, but a combination of a bad error two out and conceding 7lb to the more experienced winner found him out. He has scope and remains a horse of potential. (op 2-1 tchd 9-4)

Cocacobana(IRE) finished a distant second to subsequent Ascot winner Mono Man on his debut for the yard 22 days previously. He kept on steadily on this switch to hurdling and looks one for handicaps in due course. (op 20-1)

Old Wigmore(IRE) set the standard, but he dropped out quickly from three out and this ground was not for him. (op 15-8)

4263 LINDLEYS FIRST FOR CONFERENCE BANQUETING H'CAP HURDLE (9 hdls 2 omitted) 2m 6f 110y

3:50 (3:50) (Class 5) (0-95,95) 4-Y-0+ **£1,723** (£506; £253; £126)

Form RPR

0-P0 **1** **Border Lad**[20] 3870 7-9-9 71 oh5 ow2 OliverDayman(7) 83+
(Alison Thorpe) *trckd ldrs: led 6th: 8 l clr and looking in full command 3 out: hit 2 out: rdn bef last: kpt on steadily* **11/1**

5P-P **2** 3 **Septos**[29] 3703 7-9-12 70 PeterToole(3) 75
(Richard Price) *cl up tl rdn and lost pl bef 6th: lft 4th 3 out: rdn and rallied to go 2nd next: tried hrd to get on terms bef last where 4 l down and drvn: no imp after* **40/1**

0060 **3** 52 **Superior Knight**[9] 4076 7-11-3 93 MarkQuinlan(7) 46
(James Evans) *chsd ldrs: disp 2nd bef 3 out: fdd bdly sn after: hit 2 out: t.o* **33/1**

2503 **4** 28 **Himayna**[29] 3697 7-11-12 95 RichardJohnson 20
(Tim Vaughan) *led at slow pce: hdd 6th: fdd qckly 3 out: plugged on into remote 4th after last* **12/1**

6013 **5** 2 **Queenstown Lad**[29] 3703 6-10-7 76 JamesDavies —
(Gary Brown) *reminder 3rd: midfield: wavered bef 4th: struggling 6th: sn hopelessly t.o: lft 5th cl home* **11/2**[3]

-003 **6** 2¾ **French Ties (IRE)**[13] 3996 9-11-7 90 (p) SamThomas 10
(Jennie Candlish) *hld up in rr: effrt travelling wl bef 6th: disp 2nd 3 out: downed tools after next: hung lft bef last: virtually plld himself up flat and lost two pls* **5/2**[2]

600 **7** 10 **Matrow's Lady (IRE)**[18] 3906 4-11-1 95 TomScudamore —
(Neil Mulholland) *racd wd: lost tch after 5th: hopelessly t.o 3 out* **16/1**

P-PP **P** **Suprendre Espere**[20] 3875 11-10-0 69 oh5 (b) RodiGreene —
(Christopher Kellett) *sn hrd drvn and reluctant in last: t.o whn mstke 3rd: p.u after next* **100/1**

0F/5 **P** **Jenny Soba**[19] 3879 8-10-10 86 MattCrawley(7) —
(Lucinda Featherstone) *immediately drvn furiously in rr and nvr fluent: lost tch after 5th: t.o whn blnd 7th: p.u 2 out* **66/1**

-040 **P** **Royaume Bleu (FR)**[24] 3791 6-11-0 83 WillKennedy —
(Alex Hales) *cl up: pushed along after 4th: wknd after next: bdly t.o whn p.u 2 out* **15/2**

0431 **F** **Royal Chatelier (FR)**[8] 4098 6-11-2 88 RichardKilloran(3) —
(Michael Blake) *chsd ldr tl rdn bef 6th: 4th and plugging on whn fell 3 out* **2/1**[1]

5m 59.9s (21.90) **Going Correction** +1.05s/f (Soft)

WFA 4 from 6yo+ 10lb **11** Ran SP% **118.8**

Speed ratings (Par 103): **103,101,83,74,73 72,69,—,—,— —**

Tote Swingers: 1&2 £30.20, 1&3 £24.70, 2&3 £62.00 CSF £340.44 CT £13165.95 TOTE £16.20: £5.40, £10.10, £5.30; EX 279.50.

Owner The Almost Hopeful Partnership **Bred** Whitegate Stud **Trained** Bronwydd Arms, Carmarthens

FOCUS

A weak handicap and the taxing surface played a massive part in proceedings. The first two came well clear and the winner was value for a bit further.

NOTEBOOK

Border Lad was probably idling in the home straight as he allowed the runner-up another chance, but his rider's decision to kick on down the back straight proved to be a winning one. He was racing from 7lb wrong and it's hard to see where this great improvement came from, but it was just his third outing for the yard and he obviously handed the ground best of all. Official explanation: trainer said, regarding apparent improvement in form, that the gelding was ridden in a handier position and was suited by the heavy ground. (op 12-1 tchd 14-1)

Septos had been pulled up in two previous outings this season and so this was obviously a lot more encouraging. His best efforts between the flags came on better ground.

Superior Knight was never a serious factor.

French Ties(IRE) found nothing off the bridle at Sedgefield last time and it was the same story here. Official explanation: jockey said gelding had a breathing problem was exhausted and pulled itself up (op 10-3)

Royal Chatelier(FR) escaped a penalty for scoring over C&D eight days earlier, but he was beaten before he came down three from home. (tchd 9-4)

4264 LINDLEY CATERING NOVICES' H'CAP CHASE (10 fncs 2 omitted) 2m

4:20 (4:20) (Class 5) (0-95,92) 5-Y-0+ **£2,276** (£668; £334; £166)

Form RPR

3432 **1** **Rileyev (FR)**[8] 4103 6-11-9 89 AidanColeman 105+
(Venetia Williams) *3rd tl wnt 2nd bef 6th tl blnd 7th: sn regained 2nd: led bef last (normal 2 out): rdn and a holding chalr on extended run-in* **11/10**[1]

5654 **2** 2 **Catholic Hill (USA)**[6] 4133 6-10-10 79 TommyPhelan(3) 91+
(Mark Gillard) *nt fluent 3rd: last tl bef 3 out: rdn to go 2nd 2f out: no imp after* **4/1**[2]

-006 **3** 12 **Betty Browneyes**[20] 3875 6-11-3 83 (t) PaddyBrennan 83
(Tom George) *led: 5 l clr briefly 3 out: rdn and hdd bef last: wknd and racd awkwardly home turn: lost 2nd 2f out* **12/1**

0- **4** 18 **Fitzgutentyte (IRE)**[9] 4085 6-11-12 92 AELynch 77
(C W J Farrell, Ire) *pressed ldrs: rdn 3 out: btn next* **11/2**

P423 **5** 27 **Mujamead**[8] 4103 7-10-13 84 (p) LeeEdwards(5) 37
(Sally-Anne Wheelwright) *chsd ldr tl bef 6th: 10 l last and fading 2 out: sn t.o* **9/2**[3]

4m 22.3s (18.70) **Going Correction** +1.25s/f (Heav) **5** Ran SP% **108.9**

Speed ratings: **103,102,96,87,73**

CSF £5.89 TOTE £1.90: £1.10, £1.30; EX 6.50.

Owner John Mayne **Bred** Mme Laurence Barreaud & Claude Barreaud **Trained** Kings Caple, H'fords

■ Stewards' Enquiry : Tommy Phelan two-day ban: used whip with excessive frequency (Mar 7-8)

FOCUS

A weak novice handicap in which none of the runners had previously scored over fences. The cosy winner is rated to his mark.

NOTEBOOK

Rileyev(FR) was only just denied over C&D off this mark eight days earlier and he gamely went one better, handing his trainer/rider a treble from as many runners on the card. He looked in trouble after hitting the seventh and wasn't great at the next, but to his credit kept responding. The extended run-in no doubt played into his hands after he kicked for home, and he finally opened his account since switching from France in 2009. He isn't the biggest so is likely to keep making the odd error over fences, but one cannot fault his attitude. (op 5-6, tchd 6-5 in places)

Catholic Hill(USA) was better than the bare form of his Newcastle fourth last week and met support. He again jumped somewhat deliberately, but stayed on gamely to finish a clear second-best. (op 9-2 tchd 7-2)

Betty Browneyes eventually paid for running somewhat with the choke out, but this was no doubt her most encouraging effort to date and she ought to be winning when her stable is back in better form. (tchd 14-1)

Fitzgutentyte(IRE), an Irish challenger, unsurprisingly found this too sharp, but still jumped well on this debut over regulation fences and is worth keeping an eye on. (op 8-1)

Mujamead was well held by the winner when third over C&D last week, but he came under pressure a long way out here and ran well below par. (op 11-2 tchd 7-2)

4265 LINDLEY CATERING H'CAP CHASE (12 fncs 2 omitted) 2m 3f

4:50 (4:50) (Class 4) (0-115,115) 5-Y-0+ **£2,927** (£859; £429; £214)

Form RPR

-13P **1** **Take It There**[42] 3482 9-11-11 114 (tp) FelixDeGiles 122+
(Alastair Lidderdale) *prom: led 7th: 4 l clr and gng best whn lft w big ld last (normal 2 out): heavily eased ins fnl f* **14/1**

6006 **2** 11 **Come Out Firing (IRE)**[11] 4034 9-11-2 105 DominicElsworth 101+
(Michael Blake) *chsd ldr tl 6th: blnd 9th: 5th and rdn and outpcd 10th: plodding on in poor 4th whn lft 2nd last: nvr remotely nr wnr* **8/1**

-35F **3** 18 **Quintero (FR)**[17] 3935 7-11-1 104 PaulMoloney 83
(Evan Williams) *chsd ldrs: 3rd and rdn at 10th: sn wknd to 5th: lft remote 3rd at last: fin tired* **6/1**[2]

0114 **4** 4 **Massini Sunset (IRE)**[17] 3935 11-11-5 115 (b) SClements(7) 84
(Richard Mitchell) *nt fluent 4th: bhd: t.o and drvn 9th: nt keen after but snatched 4th* **16/1**

0000 **5** ½ **American World (FR)**[33] 3628 7-11-10 113 APMcCoy 87
(Brendan Powell) *led tl 7th: losing pl whn terrible blunder 9th: t.o 2 out* **20/1**

-020 **U** **Star Galaxy (IRE)**[11] 4034 11-11-3 106 (b) RhysFlint 103
(John Flint) *prom: wnt 9th tl 2 out: rdn and outpcd in 7 l 3rd whn cannoned into by faller and rdr fired fr sddle last* **12/1**

-UUU **U** **King Caine (IRE)**[216] 1045 9-11-6 109 WillKennedy —
(Alan Jones) *mstkes 2nd and 3rd: rr whn blnd and uns rdr 4th* **7/1**[3]

2-24 **P** **Quilver Tatou (FR)**[34] 3612 7-10-4 96 (bt[1]) PeterToole(3) —
(Charlie Mann) *mstkes 1st and 3rd: rdn 6th: blnd 8th and no ch after: t.o and p.u 2 out* **15/2**

003- **P** **Buffalo Stampede (IRE)**[304] 5354 8-11-3 106 AidanColeman —
(Venetia Williams) *chsd ldrs: rdn and struggling 9th: wl t.o whn p.u between last two* **6/1**[2]

34U4 **F** **Abey M'Boy**[20] 3869 8-10-13 **102**.................................... LeightonAspell 105
(Oliver Sherwood) *bhd: hdwy 9th: 4th at next: chsd wnr 2 out: 4 l down and no imp whn j. bdly rt and crashing fall last: winded but rcvrd* **11/4**[1]

5m 13.0s (26.30) **Going Correction** +1.25s/f (Heavy) **10** Ran SP% **115.6**
Speed ratings: **94,89,81,80,79** —,—,—,—,—
Tote Swingers: 1&2 £22.20, 1&3 £18.20, 2&3 £9.40 CSF £119.44 CT £751.22 TOTE £13.80: £3.00, £3.20, £2.50; EX 162.00.
Owner Entertainments Committee **Bred** The Queen **Trained** Eastbury, Berks

FOCUS
A tricky looking and ordinary handicap in which the majority floundered on the ground. A small step up from the winner.

NOTEBOOK
Take It There was in pole position prior to her two only serious rivals coming to grief in a horrid incident at the final fence. She was pulled up last time out, but was in fair form beforehand and her ability to handle such ground ultimately won her the day. The first-time cheekpieces also brought about improvement. Official explanation: Trainer said, regarding apparent improvement in form, that the mare was more handily ridden and benefited from the first-time cheek pieces. (op 12-1)
Come Out Firing(IRE)was feeling the pinch prior to hitting two out and is flattered by his finishing position. He needs better ground than this, though, and it was a step back in the right direction.\n (op 15-2)
Quintero(FR) was another that got found out by the deep surface, but this outing should help to restore his confidence. (op 11-2)
Star Galaxy(IRE) was put out of the race at the last, but wasn't done with at the time and could be nearing the winner's enclosure once again. (op 10-1)
Abey M'Boy had closed up and was in second when taking a purler of a fall at the last. (op 10-1)

4266 LINDLEY CATERING H'CAP HURDLE (7 hdls 1 omitted) 2m 1f
5:20 (5:20) (Class 5) (0-95,95) 4-Y-O+ **£1,723** (£506; £253; £126)

Form RPR
FP11 **1** **Decent Lord (IRE)**[6] 4136 7-10-4 **80** 14ex.................... PeterCarberry(7) 91+
(Jennie Candlish) *blnd 2nd: trckd ldrs gng easily: wnt 2nd 2 out: led wl bef last: 6 l clr whn hit last: pushed out* **4/5**[1]
4525 **2** *9* **Form And Beauty (IRE)**[8] 4104 9-9-11 **69**........................ IanPopham(3) 70+
(Bernard Llewellyn) *led tl after 3rd: rdn bef 4th: led again 3 out: 7 l clr next: rdn and hdd wl bef last where 6 l down and blnd bdly* **5/1**[3]
P301 **3** *14* **Galantos (GER)**[22] 3839 10-11-2 **90**.............................. JoshuaMoore(5) 75
(Helen Nelmes) *chsd ldrs: rdn 4th: wknd bef 2 out* **11/2**
2006 **4** *28* **Carbon Print (USA)**[14] 3563 6-11-4 **94**........................... MarkQuinlan(7) 51
(James Evans) *hld up: effrt 3 out: rdn and btn next: sn wl bhd* **20/1**
-P00 **5** *33* **Cybergenic (FR)**[8] 4104 13-10-12 **88**................................. MrBJPoste(7) 12
(Tracey Watkins) *last pair: u.p 3 out: t.o next: sn eased* **50/1**
42-F **6** *12* **Seasonselite**[27] 3724 6-11-12 **95**.. AidanColeman 7
(Venetia Williams) *plld hrd: 2nd tl led after 3rd: hdd 3 out: tired bdly next: eased and t.o between last two* **4/1**[2]

4m 25.9s (26.50) **Going Correction** +1.05s/f (Soft) **6** Ran SP% **114.3**
Speed ratings (Par 103): **79,74,68,55,39 33**
Tote Swingers: 1&2 £1.10, 1&3 £2.50, 2&3 £2.70 CSF £5.78 TOTE £1.70: £1.10, £3.60; EX 5.20.
Owner Mrs Judith Ratcliff **Bred** Lar O'Toole **Trained** Basford Green, Staffs

FOCUS
Not a bad little handicap for the class. There was a fair enough gallop on and the form makes sense. The easy winner was well in and there is more to come.

NOTEBOOK
Decent Lord(IRE) landed a quick-fire hat-trick with a clear-cut display on his return to this venue. He initially scored easily here eight days earlier, then had to work hard when following up at Newcastle just two days later, and this was clever placing by his trainer to get the talented Peter Carberry aboard, thereby offsetting half of a double penalty. He will find things much tougher once his new mark kicks in, but he is clearly in rude health and holds two entries later this week so it wouldn't be that surprising to see him turn up again. (op Evens tchd 6-5)
Form And Beauty(IRE) disappointed here last time, but this was much better and he ran a brave race. He has one of these in him on less testing ground. (op 15-2 tchd 9-2)
Galantos(GER) was 8lb higher than when winning over C&D 22 days earlier and failed to reverse that form with the runner-up, but still posted a fair effort. (op 9-2 tchd 4-1 and 6-1)
Seasonselite put in a tame effort. She had fallen on her last outing, however, and this was her second run back from injury so she probably shouldn't be fully judged on this. (op 7-2)
T/Plt: £282.20 to a £1 stake. Pool of £71,449.21 - 184.77 winning tickets. T/Qpdt: £137.20 to a £1 stake. Pool of £3,876.50 - 20.90 winning tickets. IM

4028 TAUNTON (R-H)
Tuesday, February 22
OFFICIAL GOING: Soft (good to soft in places; 7.1)
Rails on bends moved to provide the best ground reducing each circuit by 28 metres.
Wind: virtually nil Weather: overcast

4267 WEATHERBYS BLOODSTOCK INSURANCE NOVICES' CHASE (14 fncs) 2m 3f
2:00 (2:00) (Class 4) 5-Y-O+ **£4,110** (£1,198; £599)

Form RPR
33F- **1** **Shoreacres (IRE)**[372] 4082 8-11-0 133.................................... APMcCoy 145+
(Brendan Powell) *trckd ldr: led after 7th: drew clr after 4 out: easily* **7/4**[2]
-331 **2** *28* **Qozak (FR)**[21] 3871 7-11-7 0...(t) NickScholfield 117+
(Paul Nicholls) *trckd ldrs: w wnr fr 7th: hit 9th: sn rdn: wknd after 4 out* **8/15**[1]
-040 **3** *60* **Hopeful Start (IRE)**[21] 3871 7-10-11 0...................... RichieMcLernon(3) 45
(Jonjo O'Neill) *nvr travelling: t.o fr after 4th: lft poor 3rd 10th* **25/1**[3]
0 **4** *105* **Secret Shared (IRE)**[279] 407 7-10-11 0........................... DannyCook(3) —
(Richard Mitchell) *t.o after 4th: lft remote 4th 10th* **150/1**
0F **U** **Kap West (FR)**[34] 3628 6-11-0 97.. JohnnyFarrelly —
(Laura Young) *led tl after 7th: clr 3rd but no ch w ldng pair whn blnd and uns rdr 10th* **40/1**

4m 53.2s (-3.30) **Going Correction** +0.075s/f (Yiel) **5** Ran SP% **108.5**
Speed ratings: **109,97,71**,—,—
CSF £3.12 TOTE £1.90: £1.10, £1.10; EX 2.90.
Owner David Nash **Bred** R P Walshe **Trained** Upper Lambourn, Berks

FOCUS
The ground was described by Tony McCoy after the first as "dead and sticky". This novice chase had the look of a two-horse race, but with the favourite below par the winner enjoyed a fairly bloodless success, and the form may not prove all that robust. They went a decent enough pace but the time was around 12 seconds outside the standard. Shoreacres is rated up 7lb on his best hurdles figure but Qozak was two stone off.

NOTEBOOK
Shoreacres(IRE), jumping soundly after an error at the first, drew clear of a toiling Qozak at the end of the back straight to score eased down by a wide margin. With his market rival not firing he was left with nothing to beat, but he did what he had to do well and is likely to come on for this first run since falling at Plumpton a year ago. He has twice run creditably at the Festival in the past and the Johnny Henderson Grand Annual could come into consideration. (op 15-8)
Qozak(FR) was conceding a 7lb penalty for his C&D victory three weeks earlier. He raced close up until whacking the ditch on the far side, from which point he quickly began throwing out distress signals. Previously unbeaten in four visits to Taunton, he was clearly below his best here, and the sticky ground may have been against him. He was reported by his rider to have a breathing problem. Official explanation: jockey said the gelding had a breathing problem (tchd 4-7, 8-13 in places)
Hopeful Start(IRE) was a progressive hurdler this time last year, but he has shown precious little in four runs over fences now and was immediately trailing here. This trip was too short for him, though.
Kap West(FR) led the principals until they eased past him with a circuit left, and was becoming increasingly remote when losing his rider down the back. He jumped well enough until he began to get tired.

4268 ASPEN WAITE CHARTERED ACCOUNTANTS "NATIONAL HUNT" NOVICES' HURDLE (9 hdls) 2m 1f
2:30 (2:30) (Class 4) 4-Y-O+ **£3,425** (£998; £499)

Form RPR
-212 **1** **Dark Lover (GER)**[63] 3055 6-11-4 0.................................. MrRMahon(5) 115+
(Paul Nicholls) *trckd ldrs: pressing ldr whn nt fluent 3 out: rdn into narrow advantage next: hdd last: kpt on u.str.p: led fnl 50yds* **4/9**[1]
323 **2** *nk* **Dineur (FR)**[23] 3835 5-11-2 0... RobertThornton 107+
(Alan King) *led: rdn and hdd 2 out: regained narrow advantage last: hung lft u.str.p: hdd fnl 50yds* **11/2**[2]
04 **3** *2 ½* **Glassawine**[34] 3630 4-10-4 0..(t) DannyCook(3) 94
(David Pipe) *trckd ldrs: rdn appr 2 out: styd on same pce* **12/1**[3]
5 **4** *½* **Allerford Jack**[16] 3960 7-10-13 0.. IanPopham(3) 103
(Caroline Keevil) *hld up towards rr: hdwy after 5th: rdn to chal for 3rd appr 2 out: styd on same pce* **11/2**[2]
0-00 **5** *12* **Red Rock (FR)**[33] 3645 6-11-2 0................................. WayneHutchinson 91
(Tor Sturgis) *mid-div: rdn after 3 out: no imp* **50/1**
0P **6** *3 ¼* **Spirit Of Barbados (IRE)**[9] 4091 5-11-2 0.................(t) TomScudamore 87
(David Pipe) *hld up towards rr: sme hdwy into midfield after 3 out: sn rdn: no further imp* **66/1**
00P **7** *4* **Oscar The Myth (IRE)**[18] 3931 5-11-2 0.................................. DarylJacob 83
(Jamie Snowden) *mid-div: rdn after 3 out: sn wknd* **200/1**
00 **8** *12* **Singapore Storm (FR)**[13] 4006 4-10-7 0............................ PaddyBrennan 62
(Tom George) *in tch tl wknd after 3 out* **100/1**
0000 **9** *1 ¾* **Victory Bay**[3] 4225 6-10-9 0...(t) NathanSweeney(7) 70
(Simon Burrough) *a towards rr* **200/1**
50 **10** *13* **Hard Tackle (IRE)**[9] 4091 5-11-2 0.. APMcCoy 57
(Jonjo O'Neill) *in tch: pushed along briefly after 4th: rdn after 6th: wknd after next* **20/1**
150- **11** *21* **Wallace Monument**[342] 4678 7-11-2 0.................................. JamesDavies 36
(Gary Brown) *hit 1st: chsd ldrs tl wknd qckly after 5th: t.o* **40/1**
00 **F** **Hunting Red**[265] 589 6-10-9 0... FelixDeGiles —
(Jonathen de Giles) *bhd: nt fluent 1st: bdly hmpd 2nd: t.o whn fell 5th* **100/1**
U **U** **Cruise In Luxury (IRE)**[9] 4091 6-10-4 0........................ GilesHawkins(5) —
(Kevin Bishop) *in rr: mstke 1st: blnd and uns rdr 2nd* **100/1**

4m 5.20s (-2.80) **Going Correction** -0.225s/f (Good)
WFA 4 from 5yo+ 9lb **13** Ran SP% **122.3**
Speed ratings (Par 105): **97,96,95,95,89 88,86,80,79,73 63**,—,—
Tote Swingers: 1&2 £1.90, 1&3 £1.70, 2&3 £3.20 CSF £3.53 TOTE £1.70: £1.10, £1.50, £2.10; EX 4.20.
Owner Des Nichols & Peter Hart **Bred** W Lohmann Jr **Trained** Ditcheat, Somerset

FOCUS
Paul Nicholls has now run all three runnings of this event. An ordinary novice hurdle which lacked strength in depth, this was run around 13 seconds outside the standard. Easy form to rate, with the winner to his mark.

NOTEBOOK
Dark Lover(GER) won over C&D on his hurdling debut prior to finishing second in a jumpers' bumper two months ago. He was never far from the pace but needed to work hard to land the odds, rallying to get back up after the runner-up had carried him towards the stands' rail. He has reportedly taken time to get over a schooling fall and he may only run once more this season, before switching to chasing in the autumn. Quicker ground probably suits him better. (op 8-11 tchd 4-6 in places and 8-13 in places)
Dineur(FR), placed in each of his bumpers, went to post early ahead of this hurdles debut. After making the running he fought back after the winner narrowly headed him two out, but hung left on the run-in and was just caught. He has his share of ability but does not look straightforward.
Glassawine, fitted with a first-time tongue tie for this hurdles debut, ran a pleasing race for third and is likely to appreciate a stiffer test over this trip. (op 10-1)
Allerford Jack, a former pointer, kept on willingly but lacked the pace of the principals and will benefit from a return to further. (op 9-2 tchd 4-1)
Red Rock(FR) ◆ had shown little previously but there were positives to be gleaned from this performance and handicaps are open to him now. (op 66-1 tchd 40-1)
Spirit Of Barbados(IRE) showed a little more in the tongue-tie. (tchd 50-1)
Singapore Storm(FR) is another who can now run in handicaps.

4269 SOUTHWEST-RACING.CO.UK H'CAP CHASE (14 fncs) 2m 3f
3:05 (3:05) (Class 5) (0-90,90) 5-Y-O+ **£2,740** (£798; £399)

Form RPR
-435 **1** **Kirbys Glen (IRE)**[21] 3875 9-10-11 **80**............................. KeiranBurke(5) 91+
(Patrick Rodford) *hld up last: hdwy after 10th: led sn after 3 out: in command after: rdn out* **7/1**[3]
2430 **2** *3 ¾* **Vic's World (IRE)**[20] 3878 9-11-9 **87**................................. JohnnyFarrelly 94
(James Frost) *hld up but in tch on outer: rdn after 4 out: styd on same pce to chse wnr late: a being readily hld* **5/1**[2]
P5/4 **3** *nk* **Ilongue (FR)**[19] 3898 10-9-12 **67**... DavidBass(5) 73
(Laura Hurley) *in tch: rdn to chse ldrs 10th: styd on same pce fr 3 out: wnt 3rd at the last* **10/1**
2435 **4** *3* **Rince Donn (IRE)**[19] 3898 9-11-1 **79**.................................(t) HaddenFrost 82
(Roger Curtis) *prom: led 6th: rdn and hdd sn after 3 out: no ex and lost 2 pls last* **9/1**
00PP **5** *¾* **Lidjo De Rouge (FR)**[25] 3790 12-11-0 **85**................ MrRGHenderson(7) 87
(Paul Henderson) *in tch: trckd ldrs after 7th: rdn after 4 out: sn one pce* **11/1**
3123 **6** *2 ¾* **Kinkeel (IRE)**[9] 4099 12-11-2 **83**............................... EamonDehdashti(3) 83
(Tony Carroll) *trckd ldrs: rdn after 9th: outpcd after 4 out: nvr bk on terms* **10/1**

5136 **7** *6* **Wasntme (IRE)**[18] 3933 8-10-2 **71**............................(p) MrMMO'Connor(5) 64
(Colin Tizzard) *led tl 6th: styd prom: rdn after 10th: fdd fr after 4 out* **9/2**[1]

-PP6 **8** *2* **Laneguy (FR)**[117] 2053 6-11-12 **90**.................................(t) PaddyBrennan 93+
(Tom George) *hld up but in tch: bdly hmpd 10th: nvr rcvrd* **14/1**

-0PP **F** **Quelclasse (FR)**[16] 3961 7-11-2 **80**.................................(b) RodiGreene —
(Jamie Snowden) *prom tl 6th: sn rdn: slow jump and dropped to last 8th: wknd after 10th: t.o whn fell 3 out* **40/1**

0/00 **F** **Honest**[19] 3906 8-11-11 **89**.. AndrewThornton —
(Karen George) *hld up: fell 2nd* **28/1**

P035 **F** **Celtic Ballad (IRE)**[23] 3839 5-11-4 **84**................................. JoeTizzard —
(Colin Tizzard) *trckd ldrs: hit 5th: fell 10th* **9/2**[1]

5m 1.80s (5.30) **Going Correction** +0.075s/f (Yiel)
WFA 5 from 6yo+ 1lb **11** Ran SP% **114.6**
Speed ratings: **91,89,89,88,87 86,84,83,—,— —**
Tote Swingers: 1&2 £14.00, 1&3 £11.70, 2&3 £31.10 CSF £41.82 CT £350.22 TOTE £11.80: £3.90, £2.90, £2.80; EX 54.70.
Owner P R Rodford **Bred** Mario Gentile **Trained** Ash, Somerset

FOCUS
A low-grade handicap chase, run at a fairly steady pace and in a time over eight seconds slower than the earlier novice chase. Weak form and they finished in a bit of a heap. The first two were both on good marks.

NOTEBOOK
Kirbys Glen(IRE) picked up ground under a patient ride before clearing away from the third-last. This was his first win under rules, but he has made the frame plenty of times and he was racing from a career-low mark here. From the yard successful in this race 12 months ago, he was suited by the return to slightly further. (op 13-2)
Vic's World(IRE), another to come from the rear, clouted the final fence as she moved into second and never threatened the winner. She is still awaiting her first win but, similarly to Kirbys Glen, she has a number of placed efforts to her name and has been given a chance by the handicapper. (op 9-2)
Ilongue(FR) did not run badly at Towcester and, effectively 2lb lower here, produced another creditable effort. A return to further will suit this 3m winner. (op 11-1 tchd 12-1)
Rince Donn(IRE), back in a tongue-tie, made a good chunk of the running but did not put up much resistance when he was headed.
Lidjo De Rouge(FR) is well handicapped at the moment but not running well enough to take advantage. (op 12-1 tchd 10-1)
Kinkeel(IRE) is incredibly tough and has completed the course in more than 70 chases, but he has run back-to-back lacklustre races now. (op 8-1)
Wasntme(IRE) was well held over too short a trip. (tchd 5-1)
Celtic Ballad(IRE) was with the leaders when coming down in the back straight. (op 13-2)

4270 WEATHERBYS CHELTENHAM FESTIVAL BETTING GUIDE H'CAP HURDLE (9 hdls) 2m 1f
3:40 (3:40) (Class 2) 4-Y-0+ **£13,702** (£3,994; £1,998)

Form RPR

0541 **1** **Ciceron (IRE)**[33] 3649 5-10-3 **135**...................................... AidanColeman 133+
(Venetia Williams) *cl up in last pair: smooth hdwy to chal 2 out: sn led: nt fluent last: r.o: rdn out* **11/4**[2]

0610 **2** *2* **Numide (FR)**[17] 3947 8-10-0 **132** oh7................................ JohnnyFarrelly 127
(Rod Millman) *hld up: hdwy after 3 out: rdn to chse ldrs after next: kpt on run-in: wnt 2nd nr fin* **15/2**

-102 **3** *hd* **Spear Thistle**[15] 3980 9-9-11 **132** oh4..............................(p) PeterToole(3) 127
(Charlie Mann) *led: rdn after 3 out: hdd next: kpt on gamely: no ex fr last* **12/1**

3-0F **4** *hd* **Pistolet Noir (FR)**[101] 2360 5-10-5 **137**................................. DarylJacob 132
(Paul Nicholls) *trckd ldr: jnd ldr 6th: rdn and ev ch sn after 2 out: kpt on but no ex fr last* **7/2**[3]

0-11 **5** *nse* **Iolith (GER)**[54] 3225 6-10-0 **132** oh2............................ WayneHutchinson 127
(Alan King) *trckd ldrs: led 2 out: sn rdn and hdd: kpt on but no ex fr last: lost 2nd nr fin* **5/2**[1]

1220 **6** *4 ½* **Organisateur (IRE)**[24] 3807 6-11-2 **158**...................... JamesCowley(10) 149
(Paul Nicholls) *trckd ldr: ev ch 3 out: rdn whn outpcd bef next* **5/1**

U214 **7** *3 ¾* **All For Free (IRE)**[23] 3831 5-9-7 **132** oh10......................... MrTGarner(7) 119
(Milton Harris) *trckd ldrs: rdn after 3 out: sn outpcd* **66/1**

4m 0.10s (-7.90) **Going Correction** -0.225s/f (Good) **7** Ran SP% **115.1**
Speed ratings (Par 109): **109,108,107,107,107 105,103**
Tote Swingers: 1&2 £3.60, 1&3 £9.90, 2&3 £12.50 CSF £23.34 TOTE £4.30: £2.30, £3.20; EX 25.50.
Owner Tony Verrier **Bred** Haras Du Mezeray And Skymarc Farms **Trained** Kings Caple, H'fords

FOCUS
A valuable and competitive handicap hurdle, but the race did not really develop until the turn into the straight and they finished in a bunch. The runner-up sets the level. Four of the field were out of the weights.

NOTEBOOK
Ciceron(IRE) went up 9lb for his C&D win last month but was still reasonably treated on last year's form and he is a more mature horse now. He quickened up well to lead, and although he was perhaps in front a little sooner than was desirable he was never in much danger. He could get an entry in the County Hurdle, but while the likely better ground at Cheltenham would suit, the track may not. (op 5-2 tchd 9-4)
Numide(FR), stepping down in trip, came here in decent form but was 7lb out of the handicap. Held up in last place, he ran on well after the last to get the best of a bunch finish for second. (op 9-1)
Spear Thistle, who ran over fences last time, was 4lb wrong here. He made the running and stuck on well when tackled, but ideally could have done with even softer ground. (op 14-1)
Pistolet Noir(FR), off since taking a bad fall at Cheltenham's Open meeting, has reportedly had a breathing operation since. Without the blinkers for his return to action, he ran a pleasing race and could go for the Coral Cup, where the longer trip and potentially better ground should suit. (op 13-2)
Iolith(GER) nipped through on the inside to lead off the home turn but was immediately tackled and could not quicken from there. This was a creditable effort from 2lb wrong by the novice, who bypassed the Totesport Trophy to wait for this, but he does look high enough in the weights. (op 2-1)
Organisateur(IRE) is likely to prove hard to place from his current mark, and ground and trip were against him here. He was outpaced by the principals on the home turn, where he ran a little wide under his young jockey, who was having his first ride under rules. (op 9-2)
All For Free(IRE), another novice, faced a stiff task from 10lb out of the handicap and was the first in trouble.

4271 PONTISPOOL EQUINE SPORTS CENTRE HUNTERS' CHASE (FOR THE MITFORD-SLADE CHALLENGE TROPHY) (17 fncs) 2m 7f 110y
4:15 (4:15) (Class 5) 6-Y-0+ **£1,977** (£608; £304)

Form RPR

16-1 **1** **Just Amazing (IRE)**[4] 4197 8-12-8 145..............................(t) MrRMahon 120+
(Paul Nicholls) *mde virtually all: j.lft at times: mstke 6th: rdn whn idled after 2 out: a holding on: drvn out* **1/2**[1]

464/ **2** *¾* **Come What Augustus**[16] 9-11-11 0.......................(tp) MrRWoollacott(3) 113+
(R M Woollacott) *trckd ldrs: mstke 5th: bdly hmpd 10th and lost pl: hdwy 11th: rdn after 4 out to chse ldng pair: wnt 2nd after 2 out: swtchd lft flat: styd on* **10/1**

3P/0 **3** *1 ½* **Kiama**[19] 3908 9-11-7 102.. MrJoshuaGuerriero 100
(Mrs R Vickery) *mid-div: hdwy after 10th: trckd wnr after 4 out: rdn after 3 out: hld fr 2 out: lost 2nd last* **20/1**

0/- **4** *1 ¾* **Bishy Barnaby (IRE)**[30] 10-11-7 0...................................... MrWWhite(7) 105
(G Chambers) *mid-div: hit 3rd: rdn after 11th: styd on same pce fr after 4 out* **20/1**

U402 **5** *2 ¼* **Gershwinner (IRE)**[236] 872 8-11-11 90..................... MrMWoodward(7) 107
(Ms Emma Oliver) *mid-div: hdwy after 10th: rdn after 10th: styd on same pce fr after 4 out* **50/1**

-350 **6** *9* **Pastek (FR)**[19] 3908 8-11-7 78.. MissCLBrown(7) 98
(Martin Peaty) *mid-div: hmpd 13th: sn rdn: wknd bef 3 out* **100/1**

12-P **7** *3 ¼* **Accumulus**[268] 11-11-11 115... MrRBandey(7) 95
(Miss Sally Duckett) *a towards rr* **33/1**

8 *63* **Topofdemornintou (IRE)**[9] 9-12-1 109............................. MrDDrake(7) 36
(Mrs C Cuff) *sn t.o* **66/1**

PP-0 **F** **Preacher Boy**[12] 4026 12-11-7 111.. MrPPrince(7) —
(Mrs A S Hodges) *trcking ldrs whn fell 12th* **50/1**

4-42 **F** **Ice Bucket (IRE)**[13] 4011 11-11-11 104.........................(p) MrTWeston(3) —
(A Phillips) *trcking wnr whn fell heavily 10th* **8/1**[2]

U/4- **P** **Earth Moving (IRE)**[663] 74 11-11-7 0.................... MrRobertHawker(7) —
(G E Burton) *t.o whn p.u after 10th* **100/1**

156- **P** **Zanzibar Boy**[37] 12-12-1 108................................ MrCharlieDuckworth(7) —
(Mrs K Fanshawe) *in tch: reminders after 7th: wknd 10th: hmpd 12th: t.o whn p.u bef 4 out* **50/1**

U/2- **F** **Sheriff Roscoe**[45] 11-12-0 113...(t) MrMGMiller —
(R M Woollacott) *trckd ldrs: disputing cl 2nd travelling wl whn fell heavily 13th* **9/1**[3]

66P/ **U** **Pimbury (IRE)**[323] 9-11-9 0.. MrSAllwood(5) 79
(Peter Shaw) *mid-div: rdn to chse ldrs after 13th: wknd after next: bhd whn virtually fell and uns rdr last* **20/1**

6m 11.9s (-2.70) **Going Correction** +0.075s/f (Yiel) **14** Ran SP% **123.5**
Speed ratings: **107,106,106,105,104 101,100,79,—,— —,—,—,—**
Tote Swingers: 1&2 £2.50, 1&3 £7.90, 2&3 £8.50 CSF £5.87 TOTE £1.40: £1.10, £1.70, £5.70; EX 8.20.
Owner Mrs Catherine Penny **Bred** R J Powell **Trained** Ditcheat, Somerset

FOCUS
A decent hunter chase, which was won last year by the smart Sericina. Just Amazing is rated a couple of stone off his best with the next pair close to their marks.

NOTEBOOK
Just Amazing(IRE) made pretty much all the running to follow up Friday's Sandown win and book himself a place in the Cheltenham Foxhunters' field. He did not jump as well as he can on ground that was much softer than he would ideally care for, and he idled with his race won allowing the second and third to come back at him on the run-in. The return to a left-handed track will suit. (tchd 8-13 in places)
Come What Augustus, a prolific winner between the flags, was making his chase debut under rules. Hampered by a faller a circuit left, he never stopped trying and can win a similar race on slightly better ground. (op 9-1)
Kiama was sharper for her second run back after a lengthy absence and she ran a solid race, just lacking the pace of the winner from the second-last. She is another who will not mind the ground drying up. (op 16-1)
Bishy Barnaby(IRE) picked up a string of point-to-points last year and was fitter for his recent return, but lacked the pace to land an effective blow at the leaders on this hunter chase debut. He was reported to have lost his off-hind shoe. Official explanation: vet said the gelding lost an off-hind shoe (op 18-1)
Gershwinner(IRE), formerly with Donald McCain and not an easy ride, plugged on for a creditable fifth on his debut in this sphere.
Earth Moving(IRE) Official explanation: jockey said that the gelding had bled from the nose (op 8-1 tchd 10-1)
Sheriff Roscoe, the runner-up's stablemate, was second over C&D when last in action under rules nearly a year ago. He was travelling well in a close second when he took a heavy fall five from the finish. (op 8-1 tchd 10-1)

4272 FRIENDS OF TAUNTON'S MUSGROVE PARK HOSPITAL H'CAP HURDLE (10 hdls) 2m 3f 110y
4:45 (4:46) (Class 5) (0-95,95) 4-Y-0+ **£2,055** (£599; £299)

Form RPR

0000 **1** **Body Gold (ARG)**[49] 3386 8-10-10 **79**.............................. PaddyBrennan 86+
(Nigel Twiston-Davies) *mid-div: hdwy after 5th: led 2 out: sn rdn: styd on: rdn out* **16/1**

0503 **2** *3 ¼* **Bright Decision**[50] 3367 5-11-3 **86**...................................(v[1]) DaveCrosse 88
(Joanna Davis) *trckd ldrs: led whn nt fluent 7th: hdd 3 out: sn rdn: kpt on same pce fr next: regained 2nd last* **10/1**

5-63 **3** *1 ¼* **The Composer**[90] 2609 9-10-3 **72**.................................... GerardTumelty 73
(Michael Blanshard) *mid-div: rdn after 7th: styd on fr 2 out: wnt 3rd fnl strides* **9/1**

-0 **4** *nk* **Gilt Free (IRE)**[25] 3782 9-11-9 **92**..................................(p) AndrewTinkler 92
(George Baker) *in tch: tk clsr order 5th: slt ld whn hit 3 out: rdn and hdd next: kpt on same pce: no ex whn lost 3rd fnl strides* **22/1**

4000 **5** *hd* **Jewellery (IRE)**[21] 3870 4-9-13 **85**................................ OliverDayman(7) 74
(Alison Thorpe) *mid-div: hdwy after 5th: rdn whn outpcd after 3 out: styd on again appr last: jst failed to snatch 4th* **8/1**

P062 **6** *8* **Chilbury Hill (IRE)**[23] 3840 8-11-2 **90**............................ GilesHawkins(5) 82
(Kevin Bishop) *mid-div: hdwy after 5th: rdn after next: wknd after 3 out* **3/1**[1]

0-00 **7** *1 ¾* **Kaycee (IRE)**[104] 2314 6-10-13 **82**... MarkGrant 71
(Roger Curtis) *mid-div tl rdn after 6th* **33/1**

0066 **8** *25* **Mr Bachster (IRE)**[25] 3789 6-11-12 **95**................................... JackDoyle 59
(Victor Dartnall) *hld up bhd: hdwy appr 6th: rdn bef 7th: wknd 3 out* **10/1**

2064 **9** *1* **Casual Garcia**[105] 2284 6-11-9 **95**..............................(t) TommyPhelan(3) 58
(Mark Gillard) *mid-div tl after 5th: t.o* **16/1**

4000 **10** *nk* **E Street Boy**[19] 3906 5-11-9 **92**................................... TomScudamore 55
(David Pipe) *prom tl rdn after 7th: sn wknd: t.o* **6/1**[2]

-500 **11** *hd* **Jack Rio (IRE)**[7] 4130 6-10-0 **69** oh4.............................(t) JohnnyFarrelly 32
(Laura Young) *a bhd: t.o* **40/1**

0004 **12** *11* **Red Lancer**[19] 3899 10-11-10 **93**.. FelixDeGiles 45
(Jonathen de Giles) *a bhd: t.o* **33/1**

P44P **13** *50* **Cosavita (FR)**[15] 3985 6-11-4 **94**................................(v[1]) MrJFMathias(7) —
(David Rees) *prom: led 5th tl rdn after next: sn wknd: t.o* **16/1**

4240 **P** **Lady Of Ashcott**[23] 3839 5-10-0 **69** oh3........................(p) DougieCostello —
(Neil Mulholland) *led tl 3rd: chsd ldrs tl 5th: sn in rr: t.o whn p.u bef 3 out* **7/1**[3]

4m 44.2s (-1.80) **Going Correction** -0.225s/f (Good)
WFA 4 from 5yo+ 9lb **14** Ran SP% **121.4**
Speed ratings (Par 103): **94,92,92,92,92 88,88,78,77,77 77,73,53,—**
Tote Swingers: 1&2 £20.30, 1&3 £13.80, 2&3 £12.30 CSF £162.82 CT £1548.27 TOTE £30.00: £7.30, £5.00, £4.40; EX 313.20.
Owner Alexander Harper **Bred** Don Yayo **Trained** Naunton, Gloucs

FOCUS
No more than a moderate handicap hurdle. The winner produced a big step up but there may be a bit more to come.

NOTEBOOK
Body Gold(ARG) ◆ was a decent Flat perfomer in his native Argentina but had not shown much in this country and was going handicapping off a lowly mark. Staying on strongly once striking the front, he gave the impression he can win again now that he has found his feet and that he is settling better. Official explanation: trainer's representative said, regarding the apparent improvment of form, that the gelding had learnt to settle and had benefited from the drop in class.
Bright Decision had a first-time visor in place of the cheekpieces he wore last time. Never far from the pace, he rallied for second after the last and is worth keeping to this sort of trip. (op 11-1 tchd 9-1)
The Composer is still a maiden over hurdles and he was a well-beaten third latest, but this was better as he stayed on well after a last-flight mistake. He acts on most types of ground. It was reported that he lost his off-fore shoe. Official explanation: vet said the gelding lost a right-fore shoe (op 10-1 tchd 11-1)
Gilt Free(IRE) ran respectably upped in trip in first-time cheekpieces, but more may be needed if she is to get off the mark. (op 16-1)
Jewellery(IRE) ran her best race so far over hurdles, but the drop in trip was perhaps not what she wanted. (op 9-1 tchd 15-2)
Chilbury Hill(IRE) was running off the same mark as when second at Hereford, but could never get involved. (op 10-3)
Mr Bachster(IRE) made just a short-lived forward move on this handicap debut. (op 8-1)
E Street Boy, a lightly raced novice, played up in the paddock and dropped back before the third-last. (op 13-2 tchd 8-1)

4273 TAUNTONRACECOURSE.CO.UK H'CAP HURDLE (12 hdls) 3m 110y
5:20 (5:20) (Class 5) (0-90,96) 4-Y-O+ **£2,055** (£599; £299)

Form RPR
6235 **1** **Acosta**[40] 3530 7-10-5 **72**..(b) EamonDehdashti(3) 78
(Dr Jeremy Naylor) *a.p: pushed along whn lft in narrow ld 2 out: rdn clr last: styd on* **15/2**
0P/U **2** *3 ½* **L'Apprenti Sorcier (FR)**[35] 3622 8-10-8 **72**.....................(t) DaveCrosse 74
(Joanna Davis) *hld up towards rr: gd hdwy after 7th: rdn and ev ch 2 out: sn hld: styd on same pce* **66/1**
0561 **3** *11* **Inkberrow Rose (IRE)**[24] 3822 7-11-4 **85**.................(p) TommyPhelan(3) 76
(Tom Gretton) *mid-div: hdwy 7th: ev ch 3 out: sn rdn: hld in 4th whn lft 3rd next* **13/2**[3]
-64P **4** *1 ½* **Killing Me Softly**[252] 757 10-10-13 **80**..................(v) WayneKavanagh(3) 70
(Brian Forsey) *prom tl rdn after 8th: plugged on fr after 3 out: lft 6th 2 out: wnt 4th run-in* **28/1**
2-P0 **5** *3 ½* **Lonesome Boatman (IRE)**[107] 2239 11-9-12 **69**............(p) JoshWall(7) 56
(Arthur Whitehead) *hld up bhd: stdy hdwy fr 8th: rdn after 3 out: nvr trbld ldrs: fdd last* **14/1**
06-U **6** *4 ½* **Drumbeater (IRE)**[21] 3873 11-10-4 **75**............................ MarkQuinlan(7) 57
(Bernard Scriven) *mid-div: hdwy u.p to chse ldrs after 8th: one pce after 3 out: fdd last* **40/1**
5255 **7** *9* **Vacario (GER)**[7] 4130 7-11-7 **85**...(t) SamThomas 58
(Mark Gillard) *a towards rr* **16/1**
5-04 **8** *3 ¼* **Gouranga**[12] 4032 8-11-0 **85**..(b) RobertKirk(7) 54
(Tony Carroll) *mid-div tl 3rd: sn drvn in rr: nvr a danger after* **9/1**
50-3 **9** *7* **Normally**[21] 3870 7-11-12 **90**..(p) RhysFlint 52
(John Flint) *in tch tl dropped to rr qckly after 7th* **2/1**[1]
060 **10** *33* **Lions In Law**[21] 3870 7-11-0 **85**............................(p) MrRobertHawker(7) 14
(Richard Hawker) *trckd ldrs: rdn after 7th: sn bhd: t.o* **20/1**
11 *53* **Finnbennach (IRE)**[332] 4902 6-11-5 **90**............................. SClements(7) —
(Liam Corcoran) *mid-div tl wknd after 8th: t.o* **33/1**
0-06 **F** **Insignia (IRE)**[278] 424 9-11-0 **78**..(p) JackDoyle 80
(William Reed) *racd wd: led: pushed along in narrow advantage whn fell 2 out* **4/1**[2]
4002 **P** **Murphys Appeal (IRE)**[147] 1647 7-10-13 **80**..........(b[1]) DonalDevereux(3) —
(Peter Bowen) *trckd ldrs: rdn after 7th: wknd after next: t.o whn p.u bef 2 out: dismntd* **14/1**

6m 3.60s (-3.50) **Going Correction** -0.225s/f (Good) **13** Ran SP% **122.7**
Speed ratings (Par 103): **96,94,91,90,89 88,85,84,82,71 54,—,—**
Tote Swingers: 1&2 £35.10, 1&3 £9.30, toteSuper7: Win: not won. Place: £74.20. CSF £436.17 CT £3388.55 TOTE £10.60: £3.20, £29.10, £2.30; EX 499.50.
Owner The Acosta Partnership **Bred** P T Tellwright **Trained** Shrewton, Wilts

FOCUS
A weak staying handicap where the first two finished clear. The winner is rated in line with his Huntingdon run in the autumn, and faller Insignia to his mark.

NOTEBOOK
Acosta has fallen down the weights from a peak of 100 last winter and was placed off 5lb higher earlier in the season. Always prominent, he was in with every chance when he was left with a decisive advantage two from home, ending a long lean spell for his trainer. (op 8-1 tchd 7-1)
L'Apprenti Sorcier(FR) showed little for the Sean Curran yard two seasons ago and unseated at the first on his recent debut for this stable, so this was much more encouraging. He made signficant headway down the far side and stuck on at the same pace from the second-last. (op 50-1)
Inkberrow Rose(IRE), who went up only 2lb for winning at Uttoxeter, made smooth headway down the back, but was in trouble before the home turn. (op 6-1 tchd 7-1)
Killing Me Softly was under a shove for a lot of the final circuit but plugged on for a well beaten fourth. (tchd 25-1)
Normally ran in snatches and was in trouble after he was hampered against the rail heading out on the last lap. (tchd 15-8 and 9-4, 5-2 in places)
Finnbennach(IRE) Official explanation: vet said that the gelding finished lame
Insignia(IRE) was well supported on this debut for this stable after an absence of nine months. He made most of the running and covered more ground than his rivals as he raced on the wide outside. Just about in front, but being pushed along, when he stepped into the second-last and came down, he would have gone close had he stood up. (op 8-1)
Murphys Appeal(IRE) Official explanation: jockey said that the mare finished lame (op 8-1)
T/Jkpt: £12,138.60 to a £1 stake. Pool of £42,741.90 - 2.50 winning tickets. T/Plt: £38.20 to a £1 stake. Pool of £76,923.36 - 1,469.50 winning tickets. T/Qpdt: £36.40 to a £1 stake. Pool of £5,602.29 - 113.80 winning tickets. TM

3951 WETHERBY (L-H)
Tuesday, February 22

OFFICIAL GOING: Soft (heavy in places; 5.9)
Final fence in back straight omitted in all chases due to unstable ground.
Wind: almost nil Weather: overcast, dull and very cool

4274 WETHERBY RACECOURSE SUNDAY CAR-BOOT-SALE CONDITIONAL JOCKEYS' H'CAP HURDLE (9 hdls) 2m 110y
1:40 (1:40) (Class 5) (0-95,89) 4-Y-O+ **£1,541** (£449; £224)

Form RPR
-303 **1** **Imperial Royale (IRE)**[20] 3882 10-10-12 **75**........................ LeeEdwards 83
(Patrick Clinton) *drvn along after s: sn w ldr: led after 3rd: drvn clr appr 3 out: styd on* **5/6**[1]
6600 **2** *16* **Bold Indian (IRE)**[17] 3951 7-10-1 **67**.............................. PaulGallagher(3) 59
(Mike Sowersby) *trckd ldrs 4th: wnt 2nd 6th: one pce appr next* **13/2**
0050 **3** *13* **Chadwell Spring (IRE)**[14] 3989 5-10-9 **72**................(b[1]) CampbellGillies 53
(Mike Sowersby) *hit 2nd: trckd ldrs: modest 3rd whn hit 3 out* **11/2**[3]
6PP- **4** *22* **Toby Mac**[349] 4510 9-10-7 **73**.. KyleJames(3) 30
(Lee James) *nt fluent and reminders 4th: chsd ldrs 6th: lost pl appr next: sn bhd* **16/1**
10/5 **P** **Dancing Partner (USA)**[180] 1375 10-10-0 **71**................... JoeCollier(8) —
(Micky Hammond) *led tl after 3rd: drvn 5th: wknd rapidly next: sn t.o and p.u* **9/2**[2]
600P **P** **Bunacurry**[22] 3855 6-11-12 **89**.. RyanMania —
(Barry Murtagh) *chsd ldrs 5th: wknd qckly and t.o whn p.u bef 3 out* **22/1**

4m 24.1s (28.30) **Going Correction** +1.425s/f (Heav) **6** Ran SP% **111.7**
Speed ratings (Par 103): **90,82,76,66,—** —
Tote Swingers: 1&2 £2.30, 1&3 £1.50, 2&3 £4.00 CSF £6.90 TOTE £1.70: £1.10, £3.10; EX 7.90.
Owner In The Clear Racing **Bred** Andrew Bradley **Trained** Doveridge, Derbys

FOCUS
Following 4mm of overnight rain, the going remained testing on both courses. A poor race to open the card.

NOTEBOOK
Imperial Royale(IRE) took advantage of this easy opportunity to win only his second race, and first since 2006. Lightly raced, he was a creditable third last time out and ran here off the same mark. Despite being less than keen to start, he managed to get to the front early, setting his own pace, before pulling clear in the home straight. He will have to improve to win again, but the comfortable margin suggests that he may have a little in hand if able to find a race as weak as this again. (op Evens tchd 11-10 in place)
Bold Indian(IRE) is modest on the Flat and travelled well for a while, but found nothing when asked to go with the winner. He remains well held on all hurdle starts. (op 15-2 tchd 8-1)
Chadwell Spring(IRE), once rated 76 on the Flat, was in first-time blinkers but again showed little. Sellers may be the way to go with her. (op 6-1)
Toby Mac was unsuited by the testing ground and was having his first run in 349 days, so may come on a little for the run. (op 11-1)
Dancing Partner(USA) has not had much recent racing, but on this show is one to avoid. Official explanation: rider said, regarding the running and riding, that his instructions were to jump off in the first two and coming into the home straight and go for his finish. He added that jumping the last in the back straight the gelding felt lame. The trainer confirmed the instructions. (op 6-1 tchd 7-1)

4275 WETHERBYRACING.CO.UK NOVICES' CHASE (14 fncs 2 omitted) 2m 4f 110y
2:10 (2:11) (Class 4) 5-Y-O+ **£1,951** (£573; £286; £143)

Form RPR
-20F **1** **Mr Syntax (IRE)**[20] 3886 7-11-0 114...................................... BrianHughes 114+
(Tim Fitzgerald) *trckd ldrs: lft cl 2nd 7th: led 4 out: nt fluent 2 out: drvn out* **3/1**[2]
1-66 **2** *3 ¾* **Humbie (IRE)**[40] 3520 7-11-0 115...................................... RichieMcGrath 111+
(Pauline Robson) *hld up wl in tch: dived rt and blnd 9th: sltlyt hmpd next: hit 3 out: chsd wnr next: kpt on same pce run-in* **2/1**[1]
5-00 **3** *2 ¾* **Collyns Avenue**[22] 3851 8-10-7 107......................... NathanMoscrop(7) 110+
(James Ewart) *chsd ldrs: chsd ldr 4 out: 3rd and one pce whn blnd 2 out: kpt on run-in* **33/1**
6244 **4** *22* **Mini Beck**[14] 3995 12-11-0 113.. PeterBuchanan 99
(Sandy Thomson) *chsd ldr: lft in ld 5th: hdd and stmbld bdly landing 4 out: sn lost pl and bhd* **7/2**[3]
P22- **F** **King In Waiting (IRE)**[7] 4602 8-11-0 113........................(t) DenisO'Regan —
(David O'Meara) *led: clr 4th: fell next* **7/1**
60-2 **F** **Quapriland (FR)**[105] 2287 7-10-4 93.................... SamTwiston-Davies(3) —
(Althea Barclay) *nt fluent: chsd ldrs: outpcd whn fell 10th* **5/1**

5m 38.3s (30.50) **Going Correction** +1.60s/f (Heav) **6** Ran SP% **112.7**
Speed ratings: **105,103,102,94,—** —
Tote Swingers: 1&2 £2.30, 1&3 £9.40, 2&3 £6.50 CSF £9.93 TOTE £4.50: £2.00, £1.10; EX 13.10.
Owner Regalmist Associates Ltd **Bred** M J Foley **Trained** Norton, N Yorks

FOCUS
The last fence down the far side, an open ditch, was omitted for all chases. They went a steady pace in this modest novice chase.

NOTEBOOK
Mr Syntax(IRE) finally got off the mark on his 12th start. A consistent sort, he was in front when falling three out at Newcastle on his previous start and showed himself none the worse. Now off the mark, he can find races at this level and connections believe him to be better on better ground. (op 4-1)
Humbie(IRE) ran a decent race on only his second start over fences, but is also likely to be seen to better effect on a sounder surface. He was hampered by the fall of Quapriland down the back straight, but this had only a minimal impact on the race. (op 7-4 tchd 5-2)
Collyns Avenue made a bad mistake two out that put paid to his chances on his chase debut. He has shown some ability and if able to brush up his jumping, may find an opportunity. (op 25-1)
Mini Beck was under pressure a long way from home and, despite showing some promise on his chase debut at Sedgefield last time out, it seems he may find himself unable to compete with younger, more progressive types. (op 9-2)

4276 FOLLOW WETHERBY RACECOURSE ON FACEBOOK H'CAP HURDLE (12 hdls) 2m 6f
2:40 (2:40) (Class 4) (0-115,111) 4-Y-O+ **£2,055** (£599; £299)

Form RPR
/6-6 **1** **Round The Horn (IRE)**[18] 3934 11-10-8 **93**...................(t) JasonMaguire 103+
(Jim Old) *hld up in rr: mstke 2nd: gd hdwy 9th: wnt 3rd bef next: led appr 2 out: clr between last 2: v readily* **13/2**[3]
0342 **2** *8* **Oniz Tiptoes (IRE)**[14] 3996 10-10-0 **85**............................(v) PaddyAspell 87
(John Wainwright) *chsd ldrs: outpcd after 9th: kpt on and lft 3rd 2 out: chsd wnr between last 2* **8/1**

30-4 **3** *21* **Playing The Field (IRE)**[101] 2364 6-11-9 **108**.................. DenisO'Regan 89
(David O'Meara) *trckd ldr: led appr 9th: hdd appr 2 out: wknd between last 2* **10/1**

P530 **4** *1 1/4* **Terenzium (IRE)**[29] 3713 9-10-12 **107**............................(p) JoeCollliver(10) 87
(Micky Hammond) *prom: lost pl 6th: sme hdwy and modest 5th 3 out: lft 4th next* **14/1**

0-51 **5** *19* **Wheyaye**[116] 2080 9-10-10 **95**.. BrianHughes 56
(Valerie Jackson) *prom: outpcd 7th: sme hdwy 9th: sn btn* **15/2**

3/-U **6** *hd* **Crop Walker (IRE)**[41] 3509 9-11-3 **102**.......................... RichieMcGrath 63
(Kate Walton) *nt jump wl in rr: blnd 2nd: bhd fr 9th* **33/1**

2334 **7** *2 1/4* **Auberge (IRE)**[88] 2654 7-10-7 **92**.. RyanMania 50
(Dianne Sayer) *prom: lost pl appr 3 out* **10/1**

20FP **R** **Ceasar's Return**[14] 3996 6-11-11 **110**.................................. BarryKeniry —
(George Moore) *reluctant and s.s: ref to r and stopped bef 1st* **25/1**

3132 **P** **Moon Melody (GER)**[8] 4115 8-10-0 **85** oh3.................. CampbellGillies —
(Mike Sowersby) *chsd ldrs: pushed along 4th: reminders and lost pl 7th: bhd whn p.u bef 8th* **5/1**[1]

5-PP **P** **Prideus (IRE)**[50] 3362 7-11-12 **111**...............................(t) GrahamLee —
(Brian Storey) *led: j.lft: hdd appr 9th: wknd qckly: t.o whn p.u bef next* **50/1**

P1-5 **F** **Grand Union (IRE)**[27] 3750 7-10-8 **100**...................... MrJohnDawson(7) 82
(John Wade) *trckd ldrs: upsides 9th: 3rd and keeping on same pce whn fell 2 out* **15/2**

10-4 **P** **Good For Blue (IRE)**[27] 3744 8-11-12 **111**.................. RichardJohnson —
(Richard Phillips) *hld up: hdwy 7th: sn chsng ldrs: wkng whn blnd 9th: t.o whn p.u bef next* **6/1**[2]

-P03 **P** **Sunday Sharpner (IRE)**[28] 3719 5-11-11 **110**............. JimmyMcCarthy —
(Renee Robeson) *in rr: bhd fr 9th: t.o whn p.u bef next* **12/1**

5m 55.2s (28.40) **Going Correction** +1.425s/f (Heav) **13** Ran SP% **120.2**
Speed ratings (Par 105): **105,102,94,94,87 87,86,—,—,— —,—,—**
Tote Swingers: 1&2 £8.60, 1&3 £15.00, 2&3 £15.40 CSF £57.57 CT £524.72 TOTE £9.10: £2.20, £3.20, £3.60; EX 86.10.
Owner Old Fools Partnership **Bred** N D Cronin **Trained** Barbury Castle, Wilts

FOCUS
A fair handicap hurdle run at a decent clip.

NOTEBOOK
Round The Horn(IRE) repaid connections for their perseverance to record only his second win as an 11-year-old on only his eighth start. He has presumably had his problems, but has retained the early ability he showed in bumpers, travelling well here before cruising through the field to take it up two out. Lightly raced, he may have further improvement in him and, if kept sound, seems likely to win again. Official explanation: trainer said, regarding the apparent improvement of form, that the gelding struggled with training problems in the past but ran well last time at Chepstow having had a ten month break (op 10-1)
Oniz Tiptoes(IRE) stayed on well in the closing stages and seems sure to be suited by a return to further, as he needs a real stamina test. He is 10lb lower than his last win and his next success probably isn't too far away. (tchd 7-1)
Playing The Field(IRE) failed to see out the trip in the conditions, having helped set the early pace, before emptying after the second last. This was an improved performance, but he is not the most consistent and can't be relied upon to reproduce this effort. (op 9-1)
Terenzium(IRE) has a good record here, but disappointed on his last two visits, so this was a better effort. However, he never looked like getting involved in the finish and was only able to stay on at the one pace.
Wheyaye can be expected to come on for this effort after a 116-day absence. (op 8-1)
Crop Walker(IRE) is still finding his way back after a long absence and this was only his sixth career start, so remains unexposed.
Moon Melody(GER) Official explanation: jockey said that the gelding was never travelling (op 11-2)
Grand Union(IRE) stumbled after seemingly jumping the second-last cleanly. He was in the process of running a good race, and if undaunted by this fall, can run well again, possibly over further. (op 11-2)
Good For Blue(IRE) was disappointing and it may be that he needs longer between his races. (op 11-2)

4277 YORKSHIRE POST LADIES DAY - 19TH MAY H'CAP CHASE (16 fncs 2 omitted) 3m 1f
3:15 (3:15) (Class 3) (0-135,121) 5-Y-0+ **£3,252** (£955; £477; £238)

Form RPR
-6F2 **1** **Pak Jack (FR)**[37] 3588 11-11-12 **121**............................ RichardJohnson 133
(Richard Phillips) *mde all: j.rt 3 out: kpt on wl run-in* **13/2**

U51F **2** *2 3/4* **La Pantera Rosa (IRE)**[29] 3716 8-10-11 **106**...................(p) BarryKeniry 114
(Micky Hammond) *w ldrs: upsides 3 out to last: styd on same pce* **5/1**

1P-4 **3** *6* **Kildonnan**[37] 3588 12-11-2 **111**.. JasonMaguire 115
(Jim Old) *chsd ldrs: blnd 9th: outpcd and hit 12th: kpt on to take 3rd 2 out: hit last: one pce* **9/2**[3]

6161 **4** *3/4* **Pacco (FR)**[35] 3615 8-11-7 **116**......................................(b) LeightonAspell 120+
(Oliver Sherwood) *hld up wl in tch: blnd 12th: hdwy appr 4 out: outpcd 3 out: kpt on run-in* **10/3**[1]

432P **5** *nse* **Cast Iron Casey (IRE)**[40] 3522 9-11-2 **118**.................. PaulGallagher(7) 119
(Howard Johnson) *chsd ldrs: outpcd 3 out: kpt on run-in* **11/2**

6P20 **6** *20* **Quattrocento (FR)**[34] 3629 7-11-4 **118**.......................(v) MrMPFogarty(5) 104
(Peter Bowen) *chsd ldrs: blnd 12th: wknd 3 out: sn bhd* **4/1**[2]

PP-P **P** **Adare Prince (IRE)**[20] 3884 10-10-0 **95** oh10...................... GrahamLee —
(Peter Salmon) *hld up: wnt prom 6th: rdn 12th: sn wknd: t.o whn p.u bef next* **40/1**

6m 59.8s (50.40) **Going Correction** +1.875s/f (Heav) **7** Ran SP% **109.1**
Speed ratings: **94,93,91,90,90 84,—**
Tote Swingers: 1&2 £3.40, 1&3 £4.80, 2&3 £3.10 CSF £35.02 CT £145.44 TOTE £6.50: £1.60, £3.70; EX 29.30.
Owner The Pak Jack Partnership **Bred** Mme Georges Vuillard **Trained** Adlestrop, Gloucs

FOCUS
A tight looking handicap where it paid to race prominently.

NOTEBOOK
Pak Jack(FR) ran out a game winner, battling back after the last having been headed, after attempting to make all. Rated 135 only a year ago, he looked on a fair mark, especially after his creditable second last time out, but has tended not to be one to side with in a tight finish. This was only his second win in 33 runs and Richard Johnson deserves great credit for persuading him to find enough. His mark still has some margin in it, but he is likely to need a similarly strong ride to win again. (tchd 7-1)
La Pantera Rosa(IRE) won a race at Doncaster in January that has worked out quite well, but is inconsistent and not one to back with any confidence. He ran well here, and has ability, but is not sure to repeat the effort next time. (op 6-1)
Kildonnan had plenty to find with the winner, but was 8lb better off for their last meeting and ran well, enjoying the testing conditions. (tchd 4-1)
Pacco(FR) stayed on well from the rear, and at one point looked like getting involved, but never got close enough to the leaders. He loves his racing and may appreciate being ridden more prominently next time. (op 3-1 tchd 7-2)
Cast Iron Casey(IRE) failed to see out the trip in the conditions. (op 13-2 tchd 5-1)
Quattrocento(FR) is too inconsistent to be a sound betting proposition. (op 7-2)

4278 BRAMHAM HALL FOR CONFERENCES & BANQUETS NOVICES' HURDLE (11 hdls) 2m 4f
3:50 (3:50) (Class 4) 4-Y-0+ **£1,951** (£573; £286; £143)

Form RPR
2552 **1** **River Dragon (IRE)**[1] 4253 6-11-3 105........................ RichardJohnson 99+
(Neville Bycroft) *w ldr: led after 2nd: wnt clr after 3 out: hung lft: 17 l ahd whn j.lft and nt fluent last: eased* **2/1**[2]

05-4 **2** *17* **Hobsons Bay (IRE)**[20] 3885 6-11-3 0.............................(t) BrianHughes 78
(Howard Johnson) *trckd ldrs: nt fluent: chsd wnr after 8th: rdn appr next: sn struggling: stmbld landing last* **10/11**[1]

0 **3** *nk* **Old Style (IRE)**[26] 3773 6-11-3 0.. AlanO'Keeffe 78
(Jennie Candlish) *hld up: blnd 4th: hdwy 8th: modest 3rd whn blnd 3 out: kpt on one pce* **7/1**[3]

00 **4** *2* **Drop The Hammer**[25] 3783 5-10-10 0............................. FearghalDavis 67
(David O'Meara) *chsd ldrs: reminders 3rd: outpcd 8th: kpt on fr 2 out* **25/1**

2/00 **5** *1 1/4* **China House (IRE)**[17] 3952 8-11-3 0.................................. GrahamLee 73
(Lisa Williamson) *hld up: drvn 5th: w ldrs next: rdn 8th: sn lost pl: kpt on fr 2 out* **22/1**

04-P **6** *1 1/2* **Direct Approach (IRE)**[97] 2454 7-11-3 83........................ TomSiddall 72
(Lynn Siddall) *trckd ldrs: lost pl 8th: kpt on fr 2 out* **80/1**

0-20 **7** *58* **Murrell (IRE)**[22] 3851 6-11-3 0.. RobertWalford 13
(Henry Hogarth) *led tl after 2nd: w ldrs: rdn 8th: wknd qckly and sn bhd: wl t.o* **11/1**

P-0P **8** *dist* **Newgatehopeful**[20] 3877 7-10-10 59............................(t) MrJohnWilley(7) —
(Mark Campion) *hdwy to chse ldrs 5th: mstke and lost pl 7th: t.o 3 out: eventually completed* **150/1**

006 **P** **Another Mystery**[28] 3725 6-10-10 0.................................... RyanMania —
(Evelyn Slack) *in rr: bhd fr 7th: t.o next: p.u bef 3 out* **50/1**

5m 40.8s (41.30) **Going Correction** +2.20s/f (Heav) **9** Ran SP% **118.6**
Speed ratings (Par 105): **105,98,98,97,96 96,72,—,—**
Tote Swingers: 1&2 £1.50, 1&3 £3.70, 2&3 £4.50 CSF £4.36 TOTE £2.00: £1.10, £1.10, £3.30; EX 4.90.
Owner Brian Kerr & Tony Coyle **Bred** Barronstown Stud And Cobra Bloodstock **Trained** Brandsby, N Yorks

FOCUS
An ordinary novice hurdle.

NOTEBOOK
River Dragon(IRE) ran out a comfortable winner. Kicking clear upon entering the home turn, he kept pulling away, despite making a mistake at the last. This was his second run in two days, having been a creditable runner-up 24 hours earlier in a better race at Carlisle. This was another good performance, but he is fairly exposed and is perhaps flattered by the result, as the rest are nothing special. (op 9-4 tchd 11-4)
Hobsons Bay(IRE) was below par and it may be that he wasn't suited to the step up in trip. He has previously shaped better than this and should not yet be written off. (op Evens)
Old Style(IRE) ran creditably enough, and looks to be heading in the right direction. He should come on for the experience and may be able to find a weak race to get off the mark. (op 15-2)
Drop The Hammer was a winner on soft ground on the Flat, but had been well held on her first two starts over hurdles. This was probably a similar performance.
China House(IRE) was keen early on, but travelled well for a time when settling and can improve from this. (tchd 25-1)
Direct Approach(IRE) has shown nothing over hurdles, but at least he completed.

4279 PARTY IN THE PADDOCK - 2ND JUNE H'CAP CHASE (12 fncs 1 omitted) 2m
4:25 (4:25) (Class 4) (0-115,114) 5-Y-0+ **£1,951** (£573; £286; £143)

Form RPR
6U56 **1** **Pamak D'Airy (FR)**[22] 3854 8-11-5 **107**............................... BrianHughes 113+
(Henry Hogarth) *trckd ldrs: led 7th: hdd next: upsides 3 out: led next: sn drvn clr* **7/2**[3]

20U3 **2** *6* **Sun Tzu (IRE)**[14] 3990 7-11-0 **105**.....................(b) SamTwiston-Davies(3) 106
(Dr Richard Newland) *trckd ldrs: led 8th: sn drvn: hdd and nt fluent 2 out: sn btn* **13/8**[2]

000U **3** *16* **Toulouse Express (IRE)**[7] 4135 12-10-4 **92**...............(v) KennyJohnson 77
(Robert Johnson) *racd wd: led: hdd 7th: nt fluent and reminders next: sn bhd: kpt on fr 2 out to take modest 3rd last* **14/1**

4551 **4** *16* **Prince Tam**[7] 4133 7-10-0 **83** 7ex..................................(p) CampbellGillies 65
(Lucinda Russell) *trckd ldrs: drvn appr 4 out: 3rd and btn whn mstke 3 out: eased and lost poor 3rd last: virtually p.u run-in* **6/4**[1]

4m 23.5s (27.70) **Going Correction** +1.875s/f (Heav) **4** Ran SP% **107.0**
Speed ratings: **105,102,94,86**
CSF £9.55 TOTE £4.10; EX 13.40.
Owner Hogarth Racing **Bred** Claude Yves Pelsy **Trained** Stillington, N Yorks

FOCUS
A weak handicap chase.

NOTEBOOK
Pamak D'Airy(FR) was able to take advantage of his handy mark to give his trainer his first winner since May 2010. Clearly enjoying the testing conditions, this was a much improved effort and the comfort of his victory suggests that he would not be unduly hampered by a step back up in trip, especially as his three previous wins had come at 2m4f. He will be of interest if turned out quickly under a penalty in a similar contest. (op 4-1)
Sun Tzu(IRE) has been in decent enough form, but was unable to get away from the winner entering the home straight. He probably needs more of a stamina test and would be suited by stepping back up to at least 2m4f. (op 6-4)
Toulouse Express(IRE) has badly lost his form and is not quick enough for 2m anyway. (op 12-1)
Prince Tam was running under a penalty and faded disappointingly, having travelled well for some way. He is best when able to get an easy lead, but his future will depend on how the handicapper reacts. (tchd 11-8 and 13-8)

4280 WETHERBY RACECOURSE FAMILY SUNDAY - 17TH APRIL "NEWCOMERS" STANDARD OPEN NATIONAL HUNT FLAT RACE 2m 110y
5:00 (5:00) (Class 6) 4-5-Y-O **£1,267** (£369; £184)

Form RPR
1 **Ebanour (IRE)** 4-10-9 0.. JasonMaguire 105+
(Donald McCain) *trckd ldrs: wnt cl 2nd over 5f out: led over 3f out: shkn up to go clr over 1f out: eased clsng stages* **2/5**[1]

2 *8* **Arizona River** 5-10-4 0... MrMGarnett(7) 92
(George Moore) *mid-div: hdwy and modest 4th over 3f out: styd on to take 2nd last 75yds* **33/1**

3 *2 1/4* **Count Vettori (IRE)** 5-11-4 0.. CampbellGillies 97
(David Thompson) *trckd ldrs: wnt handy 3rd over 4f out: wnt 2nd 2f out: wknd fnl 100yds* **40/1**

4 *7* **Cool Doctor (IRE)** 5-11-4 0.. RichieMcGrath 91
(Kate Walton) *mid-div: hdwy to chse ldrs 7f out: drvn over 4f out: one pce* **8/1**[2]

5 6 **Colliers Castle (IRE)** 5-10-11 0 RyanMania 77
(Lisa Williamson) *led: hdd over 3f out: wknd over 1f out* **40/1**
6 6 **Skirlaw (IRE)** 4-10-9 0 BrianHughes 69
(Howard Johnson) *w ldr: drvn over 5f out: sn lost pl* **8/1**[2]
7 10 **Starbird** 4-10-2 0 HenryBrooke(7) 59
(Mike Sowersby) *in rr: drvn 6f out: sn lost pl* **40/1**
8 3 3/4 **Here's Hockey** 5-11-4 0 BarryKeniry 64
(Mrs K Burke) *trckd ldrs: stmbld after 4f: drvn over 4f out: sn lost pl* **14/1**
9 11 **American Lover (FR)** 4-10-2 0 PaddyAspell 37
(John Wainwright) *hld up in rr: sme hdwy 6f out: lost pl over 4f out: sn bhd* **17/2**[3]
10 23 **Sunblest** 5-10-11 0 BrianHarding 23
(Lisa Williamson) *in rr: drvn 7f out: sn t.o* **80/1**

4m 26.9s (36.70) **Going Correction** +2.20s/f (Heav)
WFA 4 from 5yo 9lb **10** Ran SP% **122.3**
Speed ratings: **101,97,96,92,90 87,82,80,75,64**
Tote Swingers: 1&2 £11.00, 1&3 £10.00, 2&3 £71.00 CSF £30.17 TOTE £1.50: £1.10, £6.10, £10.40; EX 26.40.
Owner T G Leslie **Bred** His Highness The Aga Khan's Studs S C **Trained** Cholmondeley, Cheshire

FOCUS
An interesting bumper with all ten runners making their racecourse debut. Quite how good a race it turns out to be, only time will tell.

NOTEBOOK
Ebanour(IRE) was sent off a well supported favourite and won in the manner clearly expected by connections. This was a decent performance from this nicely bred gelding who cost £120,000 and pulled well clear of the rest of the field. He will face tougher challenges in the future, but based on the visual impression, he looks a nice recruit to the McCain yard who has no shortage of promising sorts. He is as short as 10-1 for the Champion bumper and may head there or to Aintree. (op 4-9)
Arizona River was unsold at 900gns in 2009, but shaped well, enjoying the trip the further she went. Her yard has a good record in bumpers and she looks a nice sort. Although she received a good ride, it may be that a professional will get the best out of her. (op 25-1)
Count Vettori(IRE) seemed a little green down the home straight but the penny seemed to be dropping near the end, and he performed better in the conditions than his breeding suggested. He would be of some interest on a sounder surface. (op 33-1)
Cool Doctor(IRE) made a pleasing debut for a yard that does well with newcomers. (op 12-1)
Colliers Castle(IRE) ran fairly green and was slightly hampered by Count Vettori, but should come on for the experience. (op 33-1)
Skirlaw(IRE) failed to settle early on and in the circumstances did well to finish where he did. He should have further improvement to come. (op 9-1 tchd 10-1)
T/Plt: £163.10 to a £1 stake. Pool of £54,019.25 - 241.73 winning tickets. T/Qpdt: £65.90 to a £1 stake. Pool of £4,124.04 - 46.30 winning tickets. WG

3781 DONCASTER (L-H)
Wednesday, February 23

OFFICIAL GOING: Good to soft changing to good to soft (soft in places) after race 1 (2:00)
Wind: light 1/2 against Weather: rain 1st 2, becoming fine

4281 WESTFIELD HEALTH "NATIONAL HUNT" NOVICES' HURDLE (8 hdls) 2m 110y
2:00 (2:00) (Class 4) 4-Y-O+ **£2,055** (£599; £299)

Form				RPR
1-2F	1		**Raya Star (IRE)**[26] 3789 5-11-2 0 RobertThornton (Alan King) *hld up in midfield: hdwy 5th: chal 3 out: sn rdn: styd on wl run-in: led last 50yds* **13/8**[1]	116+
-523	2	1 1/2	**Kings Grey (IRE)**[23] 3851 7-11-2 114 JamesReveley (Keith Reveley) *w ldrs: led after 3 out: edgd lft run-in: hdd and no ex clsng stages* **7/2**[3]	113
1-26	3	1/2	**Master Fiddle**[32] 3678 6-11-2 0 (t) AndrewTinkler (Nicky Henderson) *w ldrs: led 5th: hdd after next: rallied and upsides last: no ex last 100yds* **5/2**[2]	114+
-002	4	10	**Exotic Man (FR)**[26] 3781 6-10-9 0 MrJohnDawson(7) (John Wade) *mid-div: hdwy 5th: chsng ldrs 3 out: wknd between last 2* **14/1**	104
4-05	5	8	**Mudita Moment (IRE)**[24] 3836 6-11-2 0 CharliePoste (Anna Brooks) *chsd ldrs: drvn 5th: outpcd fr next* **28/1**	95
61P	6	2 1/2	**Lamb's Cross**[39] 3567 5-11-9 0 PaddyBrennan (Nigel Twiston-Davies) *chsd ldrs: drvn appr 3 out: wknd between last 2* **12/1**	100
-056	7	19	**Lisdonagh House (IRE)**[98] 2452 9-11-2 76 AndrewThornton (Lynn Siddall) *in rr: reminders 3rd: bhd fr 5th* **250/1**	73
0	8	1/2	**Steeldrivinman**[70] 2957 5-11-2 0 JasonMaguire (Donald McCain) *t.k.h and nt fluent in rr: bhd fr 5th* **50/1**	73
-F50	9	1 1/2	**Luso's Lad (IRE)**[43] 3500 7-11-2 109 BrianHughes (Howard Johnson) *led to 5th: lost pl bef next* **50/1**	71
P00F	10	4 1/2	**Sheepclose (IRE)**[18] 3952 6-10-13 0 MrOGreenall(3) (Michael Easterby) *in rr: bhd fr 5th* **200/1**	67
0-P0	11	16	**Nothing Ventured**[39] 3572 6-11-2 0 (t) PaddyAspell (John Norton) *in rr: bhd fr 3 out* **200/1**	51
/0-P	12	15	**Pericam**[23] 3852 6-11-2 0 RyanMania (Simon Waugh) *chsd ldrs: lost pl after 5th: sn bhd: t.o 2 out* **100/1**	36
6/PP	13	17	**Wheretheres A Will**[20] 3897 9-10-13 0 CharlieStudd(3) (Michael Mullineaux) *w ldrs: wknd 5th: sn bhd: t.o 2 out* **200/1**	19
P	P		**Speakers Corner**[21] 3877 5-11-2 0 DenisO'Regan (Barney Curley) *chsd ldrs: wknd rapidly 5th: t.o next: p.u bef last* **100/1**	—

4m 7.30s (2.60) **Going Correction** -0.225s/f (Good) **14** Ran SP% **114.5**
Speed ratings (Par 105): **84,83,83,78,74 73,64,64,63,61 53,46,38,—**
toteswingers:1&2:£2.00, 1&3:£2.00, 2&3:£2.20 CSF £7.21 TOTE £2.40: £1.50, £1.60, £1.80; EX 9.50.
Owner Simon Munir **Bred** Patrick Fennessy **Trained** Barbury Castle, Wilts

FOCUS
Officially the going was described as good to soft, but after persistent rain before racing the ground threatened to ride more testing. A decent novice hurdle on paper and the front three pulled clear.

NOTEBOOK
Raya Star(IRE) had good bumper form and was coming with what looked a winning move before falling two out on his hurdling debut at Fontwell. He made amends here with a likeable display, settling in midfield and jumping well throughout. His rider had to switch before the last and he stayed on powerfully, going away at the finish. He looks sure to improve with further experience. (tchd 2-1)
Kings Grey(IRE), well backed beforehand, stepped back in distance after finishing second behind current Grand National favourite Ballabriggs at Ayr, and again put in a good effort. He was just caught for speed by the winner late on and shapes as though a stiffer test will suit. (op 4-1 tchd 10-3)
Master Fiddle has proved a little disappointing over hurdles to date. He showed promise on his initial try, but hasn't progressed as much as one would have thought subsequently. Travelling strongly up with the pace, he wasn't fluent at the final two hurdles, and although responding to pressure, was unable to stay on as strongly as the front pair. He needs to brush up on his jumping, but has his share of ability and may yet improve. (op 9-4)
Exotic Man(FR), a half-brother to the top-class chaser Exotic Dancer, travelled well behind runners before emptying approaching the last. This was only his third hurdles start and he can continue to improve with racing, with a switch to handicaps likely to help. (tchd 11-1)
Mudita Moment(IRE) showed his first piece of worthwhile form over hurdles and this offers encouragement for handicaps. (op 33-1)
Lamb's Cross probably ran his race but could never muster a serious challenge carrying a penalty for winning a weak race at Worcester. (op 16-1)
Steeldrivinman needs to settle better after pulling fiercely for his head. (op 40-1 tchd 33-1)
Luso's Lad(IRE) tried to make all but couldn't sustain the gallop in the straight. (op 66-1)

4282 SOLUTIONS4CLEANING.CO.UK BEGINNERS' CHASE (18 fncs) 3m
2:35 (2:35) (Class 4) 5-Y-O+ **£3,425** (£998; £499)

Form				RPR
11-B	1		**Beshabar (IRE)**[102] 2357 9-11-0 138 RichardJohnson (Tim Vaughan) *chsd ldr: rdn 4 out: swtchd ins appr 2 out: led last: styd on wl towards fin* **30/100**[1]	132+
6342	2	2	**Cool Mission (IRE)**[20] 3902 7-11-0 124 (p) JasonMaguire (Donald McCain) *led: drvn 14th: jnd 3 out: hdd last: styd on same pce* **9/2**[2]	131+
P1-P	3	103	**Flowonlovelyriver (IRE)**[19] 3934 10-11-0 0 SeanQuinlan (Rachel Hobbs) *dropped to last 5th: bhd fr 8th: hit 14th: tk distant 3rd between last 2* **50/1**	—
20-P	P		**Benartic (IRE)**[130] 1864 7-11-0 0 AndrewTinkler (Nicky Henderson) *trckd 2 ldrs: j.rt 10th: wnt prom 11th: effrt next: mstke 14th: sn wknd: t.o 3rd whn nt fluent 2 out and sn p.u* **10/1**[3]	—

6m 3.60s (-8.40) **Going Correction** +0.025s/f (Yiel) **4** Ran SP% **106.2**
Speed ratings: **116,115,—,—**
CSF £2.08 TOTE £1.30; EX 1.90.
Owner Mrs M Findlay **Bred** John Cotter **Trained** Aberthin, Vale of Glamorgan
■ Stewards' Enquiry : Richard Johnson one-day ban: excessive use of the whip (Mar 9)
Jason Maguire six-day ban (reduced from seven on appeal): used whip with excessive frequency, and also wealed gelding (Mar 9-14)

FOCUS
After the opener the going was changed to good to soft, soft in places. A small field for this interesting beginners' chase, which turned into a duel between the front pair in the market from a long way out.

NOTEBOOK
Beshabar(IRE), given a short break since unluckily being brought down in a good race at Cheltenham, won his first chase, but was made to work extremely hard for it. He was given a bold sight of the fences, jumping enthusiastically in the main, but like at Cheltenham, was outpaced coming into the straight. He responded for pressure and finally got on top after jumping the last level. Connections believe he will appreciate better ground and are leaning towards running in the 4m National Hunt chase at Cheltenham. He is a brute of a horse who could be just the type for a Scottish National. (tchd 1-3)
Cool Mission(IRE) performed admirably on his fourth chase start. He had to be encouraged to go on his final circuit and was ridden along a fair way from home, but responded willingly to maximum pressure from his jockey. He held every chance after the last and was only worn down in the final strides. He deserves to go one better in an average novice chase, unless connections want to go handicapping. Jason Maguire was given a seven-day suspension for marking the horse and excessive use of the whip. (tchd 5-1)
Flowonlovelyriver(IRE) had only modest form under rules to date and was never a threat to the front two, but at least he completed. (op 40-1)
Benartic(IRE) travelled well in behind, but found nothing off the bridle when asked to go with the front pair, and was pulled up extremely tired before the last. He is entitled to learn from this chasing debut and will come on for his first run for 130 days, but may need a drop in trip. Official explanation: jockey said that the gelding had a breathing problem

4283 PENTAGON TOYOTA JUVENILE HURDLE (8 hdls) 2m 110y
3:10 (3:10) (Class 4) 4-Y-O **£2,740** (£798; £399)

Form				RPR
4	1		**Moose Moran (USA)**[18] 3944 4-10-12 0 AndrewTinkler (Nicky Henderson) *mde all: forged clr and hit 2 out: j.lft last: styd on* **3/1**[1]	115+
603	2	6	**Looks Like Slim**[32] 3673 4-10-12 117 WayneHutchinson (Ben De Haan) *trckd ldrs: t.k.h: wnt 3rd after 3 out: styd on same pce* **11/2**	110+
2P1	3	3/4	**Harry Hunt**[19] 3917 4-11-5 118 JodieMogford (Graeme McPherson) *chsd ldrs: outpcd appr 3 out: styd on to take 3rd between last 2: kpt on wl run-in* **16/1**	114
314	4	8	**Jubail (IRE)**[117] 2078 4-11-5 121 RobertThornton (Alan King) *chsd ldrs: drvn appr 3 out: wknd appr last* **9/2**[3]	109
16	5	17	**Comedy Act**[46] 3443 4-11-5 0 RichardJohnson (Philip Hobbs) *nt fluent: chsd wnr to 3 out: wknd next* **4/1**[2]	97+
4	6	3 3/4	**White Diamond**[30] 3711 4-10-2 0 JamesHalliday(3) (Malcolm Jefferson) *in rr: sme hdwy 3 out: nvr on terms* **33/1**	74
0	7	1 1/2	**Second Brook (IRE)**[48] 3401 4-10-5 0 PeterHatton(7) (Reg Hollinshead) *hld up in rr: hdwy 4th: wknd after 3 out: 6th whn blnd last* **66/1**	80
0	8	1	**Layla's Boy**[108] 2245 4-10-12 0 (t) BrianHughes (John Mackie) *hld up: hdwy 4th: modest 6th whn hit 3 out: sn wknd* **100/1**	79
	9	3/4	**City Ground (USA)**[155] 4-10-9 0 MrOGreenall(3) (Michael Easterby) *chsd ldrs 4th: outpcd next: styd on appr 3 out: hit 3 out and sn wknd* **28/1**	78
4	10	35	**Aim'Ees Star**[42] 3507 4-10-1 0 ow3 MattCrawley(7) (John Harris) *t.k.h in rr: bhd fr 5th: t.o* **200/1**	43
3	11	1 1/4	**Hades (IRE)**[92] 2600 4-10-12 0 (t) RichieMcGrath (Tim Easterby) *t.k.h towards rr: bhd fr 5th: t.o* **20/1**	46
5	12	39	**Seven Summits (IRE)**[13] 4024 4-10-12 0 DenisO'Regan (Barney Curley) *hld up: sme hdwy 4th: lost pl after next: sn bhd: wl t.o* **40/1**	11
	13	10	**Emrani (USA)**[166] 4-10-12 0 JasonMaguire (Donald McCain) *chsd ldrs: j.big and lost pl 2nd: bhd whn j.big next: t.o 4th: eventually completed* **5/1**	2
	P		**Cross The Boss (IRE)**[130] 4-10-12 0 (t) BarryKeniry (Ben Haslam) *t.k.h in rr: nt fluent 1st: bhd fr 5th: t.o whn p.u bef next* **66/1**	—
6	P		**Cabal**[26] 3785 4-10-2 0 JamesO'Farrell(3) (Andrew Crook) *mid-div: sme hdwy 5th: sn wknd: p.u bef 2 out* **100/1**	—

4m 6.70s (2.00) **Going Correction** -0.225s/f (Good) **15** Ran SP% **120.2**
Speed ratings: **86,83,82,79,71 69,68,68,67,51 50,32,27,—,—**
toteswingers:1&2:£5.60, 1&3:£10.90, 2&3:£15.30 CSF £18.67 TOTE £5.50: £1.80, £2.10, £4.30; EX 23.90.
Owner Raymond Tooth **Bred** Liberty Road Stables **Trained** Upper Lambourn, Berks

FOCUS
A decent juvenile hurdle with the field well spread out at the finish.

NOTEBOOK
Moose Moran(USA) didn't jump with any fluency on his hurdling debut at Sandown, but improvement in that department led to an easy success. He did flatten the second-last but jumped well in the main and looks a good recruit from the Flat (rated 97 in that sphere). Clearly he's got a good future ahead of him (entered in the Triumph Hurdle) and he looks one of many exciting young hurdlers from the stable. (op 7-2 tchd 9-2)
Looks Like Slim, well backed, showed that his recent third to Triumph hurdle favourite Grandouet was no fluke, staying on best of the remainder behind the easy winner. He was doing his best work at the finish and should relish a faster surface. (op 7-1 tchd 15-2)
Harry Hunt is another who stayed on well from an unpromising position, shaping like a step up in trip will suit. (op 12-1)
Jubail(IRE) had a break after finishing fourth in a decent juvenile latest and this was noted by connections to be a prep run for a tilt at the Fred Winter at Cheltenham. He needs spring ground, but will need to improve considerably to play a part at the festival, if indeed he gets in. (op 6-1)
Comedy Act didn't appreciate the testing conditions at Sandown and again looked to struggle on the rain-softened ground. He has plenty of ability and is one to keep an eye on once encountering a better surface. (op 7-2 tchd 9-2)
White Diamond was swept off her feet chasing the pace. (op 40-1)
Emrani(USA) was well supported, but after putting in a slow jump at the second, was allowed to coast home. A watching brief is best advised following this suspect start. (op 9-2 tchd 4-1)

4284 LOOK OUT FOR THE CORAL.CO.UK GREEN TICK VETERANS' H'CAP CHASE (18 fncs) 3m
3:40 (3:41) (Class 2) (0-145,135) 10-Y-O+ **£9,757** (£2,865; £1,432; £715)

Form RPR
2-20 **1** **Rambling Minster**[41] 3522 13-10-13 **122**......(b) JamesReveley 139+
(Keith Reveley) *hld up: hdwy 13th: wnt cl 2nd after 4 out: led next: clr 2 out: styd on strly: eased towards fin* **6/1**
-2P6 **2** *17* **Brooklyn Brownie (IRE)**[53] 3290 12-11-9 **135**...... JamesHalliday(3) 140+
(Malcolm Jefferson) *trckd ldrs: wnt 2nd 13th: led 4 out: hdd appr next: one pce* **8/1**
2-41 **3** *6* **Dark Ben (FR)**[12] 4060 11-10-9 **118**...... DougieCostello 114+
(Simon West) *j.rt: led: hdd 4 out: wknd next* **11/4**[2]
1-26 **4** *3 3/4* **Briery Fox (IRE)**[32] 3687 13-11-6 **129**...... MarkBradburne 122
(Henry Daly) *in rr: hdwy 11th: outpcd 4 out: mod 4th whn blnd next* **11/1**
P-0P **5** *6* **Lothian Falcon**[241] 844 12-10-10 **119**...... RobertWalford 107
(Peter Maddison) *sn pushed along: hdwy and prom 7th: outpcd appr 4 out: sn wknd* **16/1**
14-3 **6** *1 1/4* **Wogan**[95] 2522 11-11-11 **134**...... AndrewTinkler 120
(Nicky Henderson) *wnt prom 6th: lost pl and hit 4 out: sn bhd* **5/2**[1]
-03P **P** **Il Duce (IRE)**[53] 3290 11-10-12 **121**......(b) RobertThornton —
(Alan King) *chsd ldrs: 5th and outpcd whn blnd bdly 13th: sn bhd: t.o whn p.u bef 3 out* **11/2**[3]
P-20 **P** **Lennon (IRE)**[9] 4115 11-11-10 **133**...... RyanMania —
(Howard Johnson) *chsd ldrs: hit 7th: outpcd whn blnd 12th: sn bhd: t.o whn p.u bef 3 out* **40/1**

6m 7.90s (-4.10) **Going Correction** +0.025s/f (Yiel) **8** Ran SP% **112.7**
Speed ratings: **109,103,101,100,98 97,—,—**
toteswingers:1&2:£6.90, 1&3:£4.00, 2&3:£6.20 CSF £49.95 CT £159.72 TOTE £5.60: £1.50, £2.90, £1.10; EX 61.10.
Owner The Lingdale Optimists **Bred** J K M Oliver **Trained** Lingdale, Redcar & Cleveland

FOCUS
A veterans' handicap chase which was settled some way out.

NOTEBOOK
Rambling Minster had gone over two years since winning, but had some classy form to his name before that and was joint-second favourite for the Grand National in 2009. He'd dropped down the weights since and was some 21lb below his last winning mark over fences. He got a good tow into the race and cruised to the lead three out, winning with ease. This was to be his final race,and after being a grand servant for connections, he deserves a happy retirement. (op 7-1 tchd 15-2)
Brooklyn Brownie(IRE), third in this race last year, ran encouragingly at Cheltenham recently, and again put in a good display of jumping, but was beaten by a much better handicapped horse. (op 7-1)
Dark Ben(FR) put in a bold display out in front but jumped to his right at many fences which cost him ground. He plugged on when headed and is holding his form well. (op 3-1)
Briery Fox(IRE) was given a patient ride, but a mistake three out ended all realistic chance of victory. (op 16-1)
Lothian Falcon needs better ground to figure these days. (tchd 14-1)
Wogan was well backed to keep his perfect record at the course. He was a shade disappointing and had no apparent excuses. (op 2-1)
Il Duce(IRE) has come right down the weights, but this effort suggests his best days are probably over. (op 15-2)
Lennon(IRE), now an 11-y-o, doesn't look in love with the jumping game anymore. (op 15-2)

4285 LOOK OUT FOR THE CORAL.CO.UK GREEN TICK H'CAP HURDLE (11 hdls) 3m 110y
4:10 (4:12) (Class 3) (0-130,130) 4-Y-O+ **£4,553** (£1,337; £668; £333)

Form RPR
-40P **1** **Al Co (FR)**[39] 3561 6-11-12 **130**...... DougieCostello 134
(Jonjo O'Neill) *t.k.h: hdwy to trck ldrs 2nd: styd on fr 3 out: tk 3rd 2 out: led sn after last: drvn out* **28/1**
15B0 **2** *1 1/4* **Ackertac (IRE)**[39] 3561 6-11-9 **127**...... PaddyBrennan 130
(Nigel Twiston-Davies) *trckd ldrs: taken v wd bnd after 4th: led after 8th: hdd sn after last: rallied and no ex* **11/2**[3]
0-34 **3** *shd* **Seren Rouge**[21] 3887 6-10-5 **109**...... JamesReveley 113+
(Keith Reveley) *hld up in rr: stdy hdwy 7th: chal 3 out: styd on and upsides last: styd on same pce* **9/2**[2]
-633 **4** *18* **Currahee**[11] 4067 7-10-8 **112**......(t) MichaelMcAlister 100
(Maurice Barnes) *chsd ldrs: drvn 8th: wknd between last 2* **18/1**
061P **5** *3* **Phare Isle (IRE)**[39] 3566 6-11-2 **120**...... WayneHutchinson 104
(Ben Case) *hld up in rr: hdwy to chse ldrs 6th: wknd between last 2* **12/1**
-440 **6** *7* **Made In Japan (JPN)**[46] 3440 11-11-8 **126**...... DavidEngland 104
(Nigel Twiston-Davies) *in rr: sme hdwy 6th: hit 8th: sn lost pl* **40/1**
-006 **7** *22* **Always Waining (IRE)**[94] 2541 10-11-5 **123**......(p) TomO'Brien 81
(Peter Bowen) *hdwy and prom 5th: lost pl 7th: sn bhd* **20/1**
332P **8** *8* **Night Orbit**[37] 3598 7-11-4 **122**...... ColinBolger 73
(Julia Feilden) *chsd ldrs: sn drvn along: reminders 3rd: lost pl 5th: sn bhd* **50/1**
5115 **9** *25* **I'Ve Been Framed (IRE)**[28] 3742 7-11-7 **125**......(t) MarkBradburne 53
(Neil King) *chsd ldrs: wknd appr 3 out: sn bhd: t.o* **11/1**
0 **10** *shd* **Premier Grand Cru (FR)**[17] 3969 5-11-4 **125**...... HarryHaynes(3) 53
(James Ewart) *hld up in rr: hdwy 7th: wknd next: sn bhd: t.o* **33/1**
-065 **11** *nse* **Quickbeam (IRE)**[75] 2870 9-11-11 **129**...... SamThomas 57
(Venetia Williams) *chsd ldrs: lost pl after 7th: sn bhd: t.o 2 out* **7/1**
6F4- **12** *4 1/2* **Sphinx (FR)**[116] 4884 13-11-2 **120**......(b) BrianHarding 44
(Edwin Tuer) *in rr: bhd fr 7th: t.o 3 out* **20/1**
0424 **13** *12* **Flying Doctor**[125] 1932 8-10-9 **120**...... StevenGagan(7) 33
(Elliott Cooper) *in rr: bhd fr 5th: t.o 3 out* **40/1**
36-6 **P** **Pipe Banner**[119] 2035 7-11-0 **118**......(b1) AndrewTinkler —
(Nicky Henderson) *in rr: hdwy to chse ldrs 6th: lost pl after 7th: sn bhd: t.o whn p.u bef 3 out* **12/1**
4501 **P** **Wild Desert (FR)**[42] 3509 6-10-11 **115**...... RobertThornton —
(Alan King) *led: nt fluent: hdd after 8th: sn lost pl: t.o whn p.u bef 3 out* **4/1**[1]

6m 3.50s (-11.50) **Going Correction** -0.225s/f (Good) **15** Ran SP% **117.8**
Speed ratings (Par 107): **109,108,108,102,101 99,92,90,82,81 81,80,76,—,—**
toteswingers:1&2:£43.00, 1&3:£48.10, 2&3:£7.40 CSF £164.93 CT £842.63 TOTE £36.10: £11.00, £3.00, £1.20; EX 223.80.
Owner F Lloyd **Bred** Jacky Rauch & Mme Colette Rauch **Trained** Cheltenham, Gloucs

FOCUS
A fiercely competitive handicap hurdle run at a sound pace. The first three were clear of the remainder.

NOTEBOOK
Al Co(FR) put a moody display last time behind him to cause an upset. He stayed on well down the centre of the track to wear down his tiring rivals in the closing stages. He'll almost certainly need to pull out more if he's to defy a rise. Official explanation: trainer said, regarding the apparent improvement of form, that the trainer that he could not offer any explanation, other than that the yard had been out of form (op 40-1)
Ackertac(IRE), heavily backed, was kept wide throughout to get a good look at his hurdles and looked in command approaching the second-last. He ran down the final two hurdles and, although headed after the last, he rallied well to just be denied. He can win off this mark. (op 5-1 tchd 9-2)
Seren Rouge has shaped with promise in 2m4f novice hurdles this term. He was another who looked like holding all the aces before the last, only to be outbattled on the run-in. He looks to have a good future in handicaps. (op 5-1 tchd 4-1)
Currahee, usually consistent, was ultimately well held on this rise in grade. (op 16-1 tchd 20-1)
Phare Isle(IRE) didn't handle testing conditions in a good race at Warwick last month and it was deja vu on this occasion, bombing out after travelling well for so long. (op 25-1)
Made In Japan(JPN) didn't appreciate the reapplication of cheekpieces last time, and produced a better display here. However, he's thoroughly exposed and often saves his best for Cheltenham.
Always Waining(IRE) enjoyed a decent blow-out and is likely to aim to repeat last year's Topham win at Aintree. He loves the National fences and must be feared there once again. (op 16-1)
I'Ve Been Framed(IRE) held every chance four out before floundering on the surface. (op 16-1)
Quickbeam(IRE) looked to sulk once asked for maximum pressure a long way out. (op 6-1)
Pipe Banner, fitted with first-time blinkers, was far too keen and looked to badly need the run. (tchd 9-2 and 5-1 in a place)
Wild Desert(FR) was too keen in front and unable to show his true colours. He can be forgiven this run, having looked a progressive type last time. Official explanation: jockey said, regarding the poor performance shown, that the gelding was unsuited by the good to soft, soft in places going (tchd 9-2 and 5-1 in a place)

4286 CHELTENHAM PREVIEW AT DONCASTER GLASSHOUSE 9TH MARCH HUNTERS' CHASE (19 fncs) 3m 2f
4:40 (4:40) (Class 6) 5-Y-O+ **£988** (£304; £152)

Form RPR
1-16 **1** **Ice Tea (IRE)**[270] 525 11-11-13 130......(b) MrJHamer(5) 128+
(Mrs S K McCain) *w ldrs: led 7th to 10th: led 12th to 14th: led after next: hit 2 out: kpt on u.p: all out* **15/8**[1]
313- **2** *1/2* **Mister Apple's (FR)**[467] 2253 11-11-11 0......(p) MrJHodson(7) 127
(Ian Williams) *chsd ldrs: wnt clr 3rd 14th: chsd wnr appr 2 out: upsides last: no ex towards fin* **6/1**
00-3 **3** *18* **Offshore Account (IRE)**[18] 3956 11-11-7 127......(t) MrMWall(3) 107
(Mrs T L Bailey) *trckd ldrs: led 14th: hdd after next: wknd appr 2 out* **5/2**[2]
0-P2 **4** *11* **Breaking Silence (IRE)**[18] 3956 10-12-4 117......MrAJBerry 101
(Jonjo O'Neill) *hld up: nt fluent: dropped bk 11th: bhd fr 13th: tk remote 4th 2 out* **3/1**[3]
5/3- **5** *52* **Nocatee (IRE)**[347] 10-11-7 0...... MrMSeston(3) 46
(C Rae) *hld up in rr: blnd 5th: drvn 10th: lost pl next: bhd fr 12th: t.o 4 out: virtually p.u* **50/1**
22-0 **P** **Dix Villez (FR)**[31] 12-11-3 100......(p) MrAWaugh(7) —
(Miss A Waugh) *chsd ldrs: reminders 11th: sn wknd and bhd: t.o whn p.u bef 3 out* **33/1**
P **P** **Zaffman (IRE)**[3] 10-11-5 99...... MrJohnDawson(5) —
(David Pritchard) *led to 7th: led 10th: hdd and reminders 12th: sn wknd: t.o whn p.u bef 3 out* **100/1**

6m 42.7s (15.70) **Going Correction** +0.025s/f (Yiel) **7** Ran SP% **108.5**
Speed ratings: **96,95,90,86,70 —,—**
toteswingers:1&2:£2.70, 1&3:£2.00, 2&3:£2.80 CSF £11.97 TOTE £2.60: £1.10, £1.40; EX 11.70.
Owner D A Malam **Bred** Eugene McDermott **Trained** Cholmondeley, Cheshire
■ Stewards' Enquiry : Mr J Hamer caution: use of whip

FOCUS
A competitive hunters' chase. All five finishers seemed extremely tired and the race produced a thrilling, yet slow-motion finish.

NOTEBOOK
Ice Tea(IRE) enjoyed a renaissance after being switched to this sphere last spring, and showed a most willing attitude to gamely battle back when headed a few times, most importantly on the run-in to just last home. Connections are keen to aim him for the Chamionship hunters' chase at Bangor-On-Dee, which he won last year. (tchd 13-8)
Mister Apple's(FR), having his first start in this sphere, shaped well after being off the track for 467 days. He jumped sketchily early but warmed to the task during the race and went down fighting. He could be a useful recruit to this division. (tchd 13-2)
Offshore Account(IRE), a former Grade 1 winner at his best when trained in Ireland, held every chance five out but his effort was short-lived. He will be competitive in similar races if he gives his fences more respect. (tchd 9-4)
Breaking Silence(IRE) put in a moody display. He found little when coming under strong riding after the first circuit, and could improve for a more positive ride. (op 7-2)
Nocatee(IRE) was the remaining finisher, but never in serious contention.
Dix Villez(FR) doesn't seem to hold much enthusiasm any more. (op 20-1)
Zaffman(IRE) couldn't sustain his early zest when push came to shove. (op 20-1)

4287 LOOK OUT FOR THE CORAL.CO.UK GREEN TICK STANDARD OPEN NATIONAL HUNT FLAT RACE 2m 110y
5:15 (5:15) (Class 5) 4-6-Y-O **£1,541** (£449; £224)

Form RPR
1 **Malt Master (IRE)** 4-10-7 0...... AndrewTinkler 100+
(Nicky Henderson) *chsd ldrs: led over 2f out: edgd rt: styd on strly fnl f: readily* **10/3**[1]
2 *3 1/2* **Victor Hewgo** 6-11-2 0...... JamesReveley 102
(Keith Reveley) *hld up in rr: hdwy 4f out: swtchd lft over 1f out: chsd wnr last 150yds: no imp* **4/1**[2]

4-25 **3** *5* **Forever Waining (IRE)**[27] [3766] 5-11-2 0............................ TomO'Brien 99
(Peter Bowen) *trckd ldrs: led over 3f out: hdd over 2f out: fdd fnl f* **16/1**

14- **4** *2* **Theredballoon**[318] [5158] 5-11-2 0.................................. OliverWilliams(7) 102
(Chris Bealby) *led into s: in rr: hdwy 6f out: sn chsng ldrs: swtchd lft over 3f out: one pce* **25/1**

5 *4 ½* **Just Blue** 5-11-2 0.. JasonMaguire 91
(Mark Rimell) *in rr: hdwy to trck ldrs after 6f: wknd over 2f out* **16/1**

6 *½* **Amtired** 5-10-9 0... PaulGallagher(7) 90
(Brian Ellison) *mid-div: hdwy to chse ldrs after 6f: wknd over 2f out* **33/1**

3 **7** *½* **Vision Of Lights (IRE)**[19] [3920] 6-11-2 0.......................... JodieMogford 90
(Graeme McPherson) *sn prom: lost pl over 2f out* **14/1**

220 **8** *2 ¾* **Hackpenbay**[20] [3903] 5-11-2 0.. SamThomas 87
(Lawney Hill) *mid-div: jnd ldrs after 6f: wknd over 2f out* **33/1**

4 **9** *1 ¼* **Allerton (IRE)**[27] [3766] 4-10-7 0... PaddyBrennan 77
(Nigel Twiston-Davies) *hld up in rr: hdwy on outside to join ldrs after 6f: led 6f out: hdd over 3f out: wknd over 2f out* **8/1**

0 **10** *hd* **Civil Unrest (IRE)**[28] [3752] 5-10-13 0.............................. HarryHaynes(3) 85
(James Ewart) *led 1f: chsd ldrs: wknd 3f out* **50/1**

11 *½* **Bond Kathleen** 5-11-2 0.. DougieCostello 85
(Ian Williams) *sn prom: wknd 3f out* **25/1**

3 **12** *10* **Blue Blooded**[96] [2511] 5-10-9 0................................ JeremiahMcGrath(7) 75
(Alan Swinbank) *trckd ldrs: lost pl 3f out* **6/1**[3]

4 **13** *5* **Brokethegate**[18] [3957] 6-11-2 0.. DenisO'Regan 70
(Chris Grant) *led after 1f: hdd after 6f: lost pl 6f out* **7/1**

14 *7* **Jamaddji** 4-9-7 0... PeterHatton(7) 47
(Elliott Cooper) *t.k.h in rr: stmbld sn after s: drvn along after 6f: sn bhd* **33/1**

15 *36* **Tekthelot (IRE)** 5-10-9 0.. StevenGagan(7) 27
(Elliott Cooper) *w ldrs: led after 6f: hdd 6f out: sn lost pl and bhd: t.o* **40/1**

16 *6* **Fairy Mist (IRE)** 4-10-7 0... PaddyAspell 12
(Brian Rothwell) *mid-div: lost pl 7f out: sn bhd: t.o* **100/1**

0 **17** *85* **In The Tuns (IRE)**[21] [3889] 5-11-2 0................................. RichieMcGrath —
(Kate Walton) *in rr: drvn 7f out: sn bhd: t.o 4f out: virtually p.u* **33/1**

4m 1.80s (2.70) **Going Correction** -0.225s/f (Good)
WFA 4 from 5yo 9lb 5 from 6yo 1lb **17** Ran SP% **124.3**
Speed ratings: **84,82,80,79,76 76,76,75,74,74 74,69,67,63,46 44,4**
toteswingers:1&2:£5.10, 1&3:£16.90, 2&3:£17.60 CSF £14.64 TOTE £5.40: £2.50, £2.10, £3.20; EX 18.60.
Owner Distillery Stud **Bred** Michael Moakley **Trained** Upper Lambourn, Berks

FOCUS
Just an average bumper on paper.

NOTEBOOK
Malt Master(IRE) looks to be another Nicky Henderson youngster to keep an eye on in the future. He always travelled strongly in amongst horses and put the race to bed with a good turn of foot 2f out. Despite running around in the final furlong he was well on top and is worthy for more than the official winning margin suggests. (op 4-1)
Victor Hewgo couldn't justify heavy market support but ran an encouraging race. He was briefly outpaced 2f out, but responded well to be a closing second. He looks sure to win a bumper. (op 7-1)
Forever Waining(IRE) had experience on his side and held every chance 2f out. He was one-paced in the closing stages, though, and this big sort will need further in time. (tchd 14-1)
Theredballoon ran well from an unpromising position. He will strip fitter for this seasonal debut. (op 20-1)
Just Blue performed creditably on his racecourse debut and will no doubt improve for the initial experience. (op 14-1)
Vision Of Lights(IRE) Official explanation: jockey said that the gelding had a breathing problem
Allerton(IRE) was kept wide and may be better suited to a sounder surface. (op 15-2 tchd 7-1)
Blue Blooded might also want better ground, and can be given another chance in a similar race. (op 4-1)
Brokethegate didn't go on from his encouraging debut. However, being by Presenting, he will appreciate better ground. (op 9-1)
T/Jkpt: Not won. T/Plt: £38.70 to a £1 stake. Pool:£92,152.54 - 1,734.09 winning tickets T/Qpdt: £34.50 to a £1 stake. Pool:£4,553.16 - 97.50 winning tickets WG

4006 LUDLOW (R-H)

Wednesday, February 23

OFFICIAL GOING: Good to soft (soft in places on hurdle course; chs 7.4, hdl 7.2)

False wings removed proving 6yds of fresh ground on inside. All hurdle bends moved to fresh ground.
Wind: Light, across Weather: Overcast

4288 STOUR MAIDEN HURDLE (9 hdls) 2m
2:10 (2:10) (Class 5) 4-Y-0+ **£2,276** (£668; £334; £166)

Form RPR

26 **1** **Paintball (IRE)**[27] [3767] 4-10-7 0... TomSiddall 119+
(Charlie Longsdon) *trckd ldrs: mstke 3rd: nt fluent 5th: led and hit 3 out: j.rt 2 out: clr last: r.o wl: eased cl home* **7/2**[3]

03 **2** *12* **King's Realm (IRE)**[44] [3484] 4-10-0 0............................ OliverDayman(7) 106
(Alison Thorpe) *racd keenly: prom: rdn and nt qckn appr 3 out: hung rt u.p fr bef 2 out: styd on to take 2nd towards fin: no ch w wnr* **28/1**

4 **3** *1 ¼* **Brunston**[26] [3783] 5-11-2 0...(b[1]) APMcCoy 115
(Nicky Henderson) *led: hdd 3 out: btn and no ch w wnr fr last: lost 2nd towards fin* **9/4**[1]

46 **4** *9* **Reginaldinho (UAE)**[11] [4081] 5-11-2 0.............................. AidanColeman 107
(Venetia Williams) *racd keenly: j.lft 1st: prom: rdn and outpcd appr 3 out: no imp after* **5/1**

3 **5** *15* **Not In The Clock (USA)**[18] [3944] 4-10-7 0............................ DarylJacob 83
(Charlie Mann) *in tch: hmpd 1st: mstke 2nd: rdn and wknd appr 3 out* **5/2**[2]

P4 **6** *11* **Lang Shining (IRE)**[20] [3906] 7-11-2 0............................ JimmyMcCarthy 83
(Jamie Osborne) *hld up: pushed along after 6th: nvr bttr than midfield: nvr on terms w ldrs* **20/1**

0003 **7** *1 ¾* **Misstaysia (IRE)**[25] [3816] 6-10-2 0..................................... JakeGreenall(7) 74
(Henry Daly) *hld up: hdwy into midfield appr 6th: chsd ldng bunch bef 3 out: no imp whn blnd 2 out* **22/1**

505 **8** *3* **Midnight Molly**[49] [3398] 4-9-11 0.......................... SamTwiston-Davies(3) 63
(John Spearing) *midfield: struggling and n.d whn j.lft 3 out: nvr on terms* **100/1**

3000 **9** *7* **Robello**[14] [4006] 7-10-9 0... CharlieWallis(7) 72
(John O'Shea) *trckd ldrs tl mstke and wknd 6th* **150/1**

10 *6* **Dane Cottage**[44] 4-9-11 0.. LeeStephens(3) 51
(Katie Stephens) *mstke 4th: a bhd* **125/1**

50 **11** *3 ½* **Beat All Out**[19] [3930] 6-11-2 0.. WillKennedy 63
(Dai Burchell) *midfield: mstke 5th: struggling after 6th: bhd after* **100/1**

12 *2 ¾* **Querido (GER)**[26] 7-11-2 0...(t) JamesDavies 61
(Gary Brown) *cl up tl rdn and wknd appr 3 out* **80/1**

00 **13** *31* **Summer De Baune (FR)**[24] [3842] 6-10-9 0...............(t) HarryChalloner(7) 33
(John Bryan Groucott) *a bhd: t.o* **150/1**

06-0 **14** *10* **Marvelous**[14] [4006] 6-10-9 0... PaulMoloney 17
(Evan Williams) *a bhd: nt fluent 6th: nvr on terms: t.o* **100/1**

3m 59.9s (10.40) **Going Correction** +0.45s/f (Soft)
WFA 4 from 5yo+ 9lb **14** Ran SP% **117.1**
Speed ratings (Par 103): **92,86,85,80,73 67,67,65,62,59 57,55,40,35**
toteswingers:1&2:£33.50, 1&3:£2.50, 2&3:£28.20 CSF £88.79 TOTE £3.70: £1.80, £7.70, £1.10; EX 91.70.
Owner Alan Halsall **Bred** James Waldron **Trained** Over Norton, Oxon

FOCUS
The first two jockeys in this opener described the ground as 'soft', 'dead and tacky'. A couple of decent horses won this at the turn of the millennium (Impek and Isio), and Nicky Henderson had a great record in this.

NOTEBOOK
Paintball(IRE) ◆ returned to the promise he displayed on his first try over hurdles, and won in the manner most expected to see last time after settling better here. He is clearly a decent performer and holds a Triumph Hurdle entry, but one would imagine that connections will see how the handicapper rates him, and possibly the Fred Winter will end up being his race at Cheltenham next month. (tchd 3-1)
King's Realm(IRE) wasn't far away throughout and plugged on to claim second. A winner on the Flat for Sir Mark Prescott, he still has scope for some more improvement and is one for a decent ground handicap.
Brunston, beaten at 4/6 on his hurdling debut, and fitted with blinkers for the first time, was understandably well fancied. However, after enjoying an easy lead, he offered little resistance to the winner as he sailed past and also lost out on second place late on. (op 7-4 tchd 6-4)
Reginaldinho(UAE), back down in trip after running over 2m5f on his previous outing, looked to have sweated up and tended to jump to his left at some of the hurdles. He stopped fairly quickly once his effort petered out. (op 6-1 tchd 13-2)
Not In The Clock(USA) shaped nicely in a juvenile contest recently, but lost his place here at a relatively early stage and never got into contention. (op 4-1 tchd 5-1)
Querido(GER) ◆ didn't run as badly as his final position suggests, as is one to look out for on better ground during the spring on a similarly sharp track.

4289 CORVE (S) HURDLE (11 hdls) 2m 5f
2:45 (2:45) (Class 5) 4-8-Y-O **£1,691** (£496; £248; £124)

Form RPR

0P2U **1** **Abstract Art (USA)**[13] [4028] 8-11-3 106......................(p) PeterCarberry(7) 112+
(Rachel Hobbs) *mde all: hit 3 out: nt fluent last: drew clr run-in: styd on wl* **5/2**[2]

0305 **2** *11* **Diktalina**[29] [3724] 5-11-3 107... APMcCoy 95+
(Alison Thorpe) *hld up: hit 3rd: effrt to chal bef nt fluent 3 out: nt qckn appr 2 out: kpt on u.p to take 2nd cl home: no ch w wnr* **8/11**[1]

2-06 **3** *½* **Font**[26] [3786] 8-11-0 0...(t) JamesCowley(10) 101
(Paul Nicholls) *chsd ldrs: wnt 2nd 4th: w ldr: stl ev ch 2 out: rdn bef last: tired run-in: ct for 2nd cl home* **4/1**[3]

000 **4** *14* **Steely Bird**[44] [3477] 4-10-7 79...(p) NickScholfield 70
(Richard Hawker) *chsd ldr tl 4th: dropped to rr 6th: effrt appr 3 out: sn outpcd: n.d whn mstke 2 out* **50/1**

5m 30.8s (16.00) **Going Correction** +0.45s/f (Soft)
WFA 4 from 5yo+ 10lb **4** Ran SP% **108.4**
Speed ratings: **87,82,82,77**
CSF £4.94 TOTE £4.90; EX 5.20.There was no bid for the winner.
Owner Hills Of Ledbury (Aga) **Bred** Jenny L Mills **Trained** Hanley Swan, Worcs

FOCUS
An ordinary seller, in which nothing happened until heading round the final bend. The form is very questionable.

NOTEBOOK
Abstract Art(USA), who came down at the first hurdle last time, was allowed an easy lead and quickened nicely in the home straight, never looking likely to be caught once bounding clear. (op 11-4 tchd 3-1)
Diktalina, dropping into this grade for the first time, was held up and never got into it, but managed to get past Font late on. (op 11-10)
Font, who was taking a significant drop in grade back over hurdles, weakened in the latter stages. The Paul Nicholls'-trained runner didn't shape too badly but is a long way below his best. (op 5-2)
Steely Bird, up in trip, was readily outpaced the moment the pace increased significantly. (tchd 25-1)

4290 ARROW H'CAP CHASE (13 fncs) 2m
3:20 (3:20) (Class 4) (0-110,110) 5-Y-0+ **£4,163** (£1,222; £611; £305)

Form RPR

3/13 **1** **Golden Duck (IRE)**[34] [3650] 11-11-9 **107**.................................. DarylJacob 118+
(Nick Williams) *a.p: wnt 2nd after 5th (water): j.lft 3 out: rdn and hung rt bef 2 out: led appr last: styd on wl* **10/3**[2]

6532 **2** *2 ½* **Papradon**[125] [1940] 7-10-9 **96**................................ SamTwiston-Davies(3) 106+
(Nigel Twiston-Davies) *led to 3rd: led again 4th: rdn whn mstke 2 out: hdd appr last: kpt on u.p run-in but hld: nt qckn cl home* **5/1**

4321 **3** *2* **Rileyev (FR)**[2] [4264] 6-10-12 **96** 7ex.................................... AidanColeman 103
(Venetia Williams) *in tch: effrt to chse ldrs 4 out: j.lft 3 out: styd on same pce run-in* **11/4**[1]

44 **4** *2* **Trooper Clarence**[57] [3154] 7-11-5 **103**................................. PaulMoloney 108
(Evan Williams) *plld hrd: hld up in rr: nt fluent 3rd: hdwy 7th: cl up appr 4 out: carried lft 3 out: drifted rt bef next and nt qckn: kpt on same pce after* **11/2**

P650 **5** *36* **Tyup Pompey (IRE)**[14] [4010] 10-11-3 **104**........................ LeeStephens(3) 77
(Ann Price) *hld up: struggling 6th: bhd 7th: nt fluent 8th: t.o* **20/1**

/4-0 **6** *14* **Poseidon's Secret (IRE)**[19] [3935] 8-11-2 **103**...............(t) DannyCook(3) 62
(John Panvert) *prom: led 3rd to 4th: lost pl after 5th (water): sn struggling: bhd and lost tch bef 8th: t.o* **20/1**

5151 **7** *6* **Jeczmien (POL)**[13] [4033] 8-11-12 **110**............................(t) LiamTreadwell 84
(Nick Gifford) *in tch: rdn appr 7th: hit 8th: wknd bef 4 out: eased after last: t.o* **9/2**[3]

0006 **P** **Orpen Wide (IRE)**[7] [4142] 9-10-7 **98**........................(bt) OliverDayman(7) —
(Michael Chapman) *in rr: pushed along after 5th (water): lost tch bef 8th: t.o whn p.u bef 4 out* **66/1**

4m 7.40s (8.90) **Going Correction** +0.575s/f (Soft) **8** Ran SP% **111.0**
Speed ratings: **100,98,97,96,78 71,68,—**
toteswingers:1&2:£4.50, 1&3:£2.70, 2&3:£2.50 CSF £19.08 CT £48.24 TOTE £6.30: £2.30, £1.10, £1.10; EX 16.30.
Owner Mrs Sally & Miss Isobel Noott **Bred** Miss C Hayes **Trained** George Nympton, Devon

FOCUS
A modest chase.

NOTEBOOK

Golden Duck(IRE), down in distance, proved that the stable are heading in the right direction with a hard-fought success. Always close up, he took his time to assert, but found for pressure and just did enough for success. (op 3-1 tchd 7-2)

Papradon, off since being beaten narrowly over C&D last October, set off to make all and looked like being swallowed up even before making a mistake two out. However, he responded quite well when asked to go after Golden Duck again and wasn't beaten far. (op 7-1 tchd 9-2)

Rileyev(FR), making a quick reappearance after winning in testing ground at Hereford, ran well under a 7lb penalty, and shapes as a stayer at this trip rather than a horse with a turn of foot. (op 3-1 tchd 10-3)

Trooper Clarence ◆, given a break since his last outing, travelled strongly in rear and looked a big danger as he moved with menace in behind. It seemed as though it would be a matter of time before he got involved in the battle for first but possibly because of the absence, he didn't get on terms. He can go closer next time. (op 9-2 tchd 6-1)

Jeczmien(POL), up 1lb for his Taunton victory, settled in behind but received reminders early down the back straight. The handicapper appears to have his measure. (tchd 5-1)

4291 SEVERN H'CAP HURDLE (9 hdls) 2m

3:50 (3:50) (Class 3) (0-125,123) 4-Y-0+ **£4,878** (£1,432; £716; £357)

Form RPR

0230 **1** **Bally Legend**[32] 3688 6-11-4 **118** IanPopham(3) 127+
(Caroline Keevil) *prom: led appr 5th: rdn bef 2 out whn in command: styd on wl to draw clr run-in: comf* **6/1**

3250 **2** *13* **Tom O'Tara**[44] 3490 7-10-6 **106** WayneKavanagh(3) 102
(Robin Dickin) *trckd ldrs: wnt 2nd 6th: j.rt whn no imp on wnr and carried hd awkwardly 2 out: one pce fr last and no ch* **10/1**

0 **3** *16* **Big Robert**[39] 3557 7-11-1 **112** (tp) AidanColeman 94
(Matt Sheppard) *chsd ldrs: pushed along and outpcd appr 3 out: plugged on at one pce to take 3rd bef last: no ch w front 2* **16/1**

3206 **4** *3 ¼* **Scoter Fontaine (FR)**[38] 3587 5-11-4 **115** APMcCoy 94
(Rebecca Curtis) *hld up: pushed along after 6th: no imp on ldrs: wl hld after* **5/1**[2]

33 **5** *2 ½* **Rock Of Deauville (IRE)**[22] 3872 4-10-9 **115** HarrySkelton 84
(Paul Nicholls) *midfield: hdwy 6th: sn trckd ldrs: outpcd after 3 out: lost tch w ldrs 2 out: lost 3rd appr last: wknd* **3/1**[1]

-53P **6** *5* **Super Kenny (IRE)**[55] 3228 5-11-0 **114** DavidBass(3) 86
(Nicky Henderson) *hld up: hdwy after 6th: chsd ldrs appr 3 out: sn outpcd and btn* **11/2**[3]

F2F1 **7** *¾* **Highway Code (USA)**[13] 4031 5-11-7 **123** (t) GilesHawkins(5) 99+
(Richard Lee) *bhd: nvr looked happy: nt fluent 5th: sme hdwy after 6th but no imp on ldrs: wl btn 3 out* **13/2**

3304 **8** *50* **Heron Bay**[36] 3620 7-11-11 **122** (p) TomScudamore 49
(Peter Bowen) *midfield to 3rd: bhd fr 5th: toiling after 6th: t.o* **16/1**

124- **9** *14* **Robert The Brave**[515] 1539 7-11-5 **116** WillKennedy 30
(Dai Burchell) *led: nt fluent 1st: j.lft 4th: hdd appr 5th: wknd after 6th: t.o* **28/1**

3P11 **P** **Chrysander**[13] 4028 9-11-5 **116** (bt[1]) PaulMoloney —
(Evan Williams) *prom: rdn and lost pl bef 5th: bhd after 6th: p.u bef 3 out* **10/1**

3m 53.7s (4.20) **Going Correction** +0.45s/f (Soft)
WFA 4 from 5yo+ 9lb **10** Ran SP% **118.1**
Speed ratings (Par 107): **107,100,92,90,89 87,86,61,54,—**
toteswingers:1&2:£21.20, 1&3:£31.60, 2&3:£35.80 CSF £64.58 CT £919.03 TOTE £11.40: £2.90, £4.00, £7.50; EX 86.80.
Owner Brian Derrick **Bred** V Thorne, B Derrick And P R Rodford **Trained** Motcombe, Dorset

FOCUS

A competitive-looking contest, but not many got involved.

NOTEBOOK

Bally Legend, down 6f in distance, had scope for improvement and was given a positive ride. His stamina always looked assured in this type of ground, and he eased clear of his rivals the further he went. The trainer was of the view that bringing him back in distance but racing him prominently (he got bumped a bit last time at Wincanton in behind) was the best way of riding him, and she was proved correct. (op 8-1 tchd 17-2)

Tom O'Tara didn't run too badly off a mark well above his highest-winning one, but doesn't look straightforward under pressure. (op 11-1 tchd 12-1)

Big Robert, with a tongue-tie back on, travelled nicely for quite a long time and kept on steadily after being caught one-paced. (op 18-1 tchd 20-1)

Scoter Fontaine(FR) had been a shade disappointing since going into handicaps, and didn't show much more down in trip. (op 11-2 tchd 6-1)

Rock Of Deauville(IRE), making his handicap debut for respected connections, looked a huge danger as he moved up stylishly to sit on the heels of the leader, but found disappointingly little when asked to quicken. (op 10-3 tchd 7-2 in places)

Super Kenny(IRE), given a break since a moderate Taunton performance, is becoming disappointing, although he can be given another chance on better ground. (op 5-1)

Highway Code(USA), raised 4lb for a lucky Taunton success, was out the back and failed to make any impact. (op 15-2 tchd 8-1)

4292 TEME CONDITIONAL JOCKEYS' H'CAP CHASE (19 fncs) 3m

4:20 (4:20) (Class 4) (0-105,105) 5-Y-0+ **£3,252** (£955; £477; £238)

Form RPR

-416 **1** **Ere Alfie (IRE)**[52] 3349 7-11-5 **98** (p) IanPopham 111+
(Nick Williams) *mde all: drew clr fr 10th: rdn on paddock bnd after 11th (water): drew clr appr last: styd on wl* **14/1**

6222 **2** *10* **Timpo (FR)**[28] 3741 8-10-11 **98** JakeGreenall(8) 102
(Henry Daly) *chsd ldrs: j.rt 3rd: wnt 2nd 14th: rdn and no imp on wnr bef last: kpt on same pce* **6/1**[2]

-062 **3** *5* **Mr Chippy (IRE)**[19] 3933 7-10-12 **91** MichaelMurphy 92
(Ian Williams) *midfield: hdwy to chse ldrs 12th: effrt to try and chal 4 out: nt qckn 2 out: kpt on same pce fr bef last* **5/2**[1]

0-02 **4** *12* **Tora Bora (GER)**[36] 3621 9-10-6 **85** (p) MrMMO'Connor 74
(Brendan Powell) *w ldr to 9th: lost 2nd 14th: u.p after: btn 4 out: plugged on at one pce after* **13/2**[3]

-P25 **5** *7* **Porta Vogie (IRE)**[15] 3990 9-11-2 **105** KillianMoore(10) 91
(Graeme McPherson) *hld up: hdwy appr 12th: rdn whn chsng ldrs bef 4 out: sn one pce* **9/1**

4U56 **6** *6* **Ethiopia**[41] 3527 8-10-6 **91** NathanSweeney(6) 72
(Bob Buckler) *chsd ldrs: niggled along and steadily lost pl fr 8th: struggling fnl circ: no imp after* **9/1**

-161 **7** *6* **Gerrard (IRE)**[107] 2277 13-10-12 **91** CharlieHuxley 63
(Althea Barclay) *midfield: rdn and wl outpcd fr 12th: n.d after* **20/1**

P-20 **8** *hd* **Our Columbus (IRE)**[70] 2963 7-11-5 **101** SamTwiston-Davies(3) 72
(Nigel Twiston-Davies) *midfield: hdwy 5th: mstke 8th: pushed along 12th: clsd to chse ldrs 5 out: wknd 4 out* **14/1**

6230 **9** *11* **Ballabrook (IRE)**[40] 3552 9-11-0 **101** (p) HenryBrooke(8) 63
(Donald McCain) *j.lft a few times: hld uip: hdwy into midfield 6th: chsd ldrs 12th: mstke 13th: wknd after 5 out* **8/1**

-10F **10** *¾* **Killowenabbey (IRE)**[22] 3873 7-10-13 **95** (tp) AodhaganConlon(3) 56
(Debra Hamer) *bhd: sme hdwy 15th: chsd ldng bunch after 5 out: wknd 4 out* **28/1**

0P23 **11** *70* **Earcomesthedream (IRE)**[94] 2558 8-11-8 **101** (b) RTDunne —
(Peter Pritchard) *nt fluent: midfield: reminders appr 6th: bhd fr 7th: struggling fnl circ: t.o* **12/1**

3300 **P** **Feeling Peckish (USA)**[7] 4144 7-9-11 **79** oh2 (t) HarryChalloner(3) —
(Michael Chapman) *midfield: lost pl after 6th: struggling and bhd after 11th (water): t.o whn p.u bef 4 out* **50/1**

6m 19.1s (10.80) **Going Correction** +0.575s/f (Soft) **12** Ran SP% **118.5**
Speed ratings: **105,101,100,96,93 91,89,89,85,85 62,—**
toteswingers:1&2:£25.80, 1&3:£8.90, 2&3:£4.10 CSF £95.43 CT £285.22 TOTE £11.30: £2.40, £2.20, £1.60; EX 77.10.
Owner Mrs Sally & Miss Isobel Noott **Bred** R S Bennett **Trained** George Nympton, Devon

FOCUS

Not many of the runners played a significant part in this moderate contest.

NOTEBOOK

Ere Alfie(IRE) ran well below his best last time, but returned to really aggressive front-running tactics, he steadily dropped his rivals and won in convincing style. He's reportedly at his best when able to dominate. (op 12-1)

Timpo(FR) finished second for the fourth time in a row and just looks a little one-paced. That said, he should be good enough to win something similar over fences. (op 7-1)

Mr Chippy(IRE) looked of interest on his second start after an absence but was unable to force his way to the front after moving well in behind. (op 11-4)

Tora Bora(GER) helped to share the work with the winner throughout the early stages but was readily brushed aside when Ere Alfie went on. However, he kept on going and still beat plenty of rivals. (tchd 6-1 and 7-1)

Ballabrook(IRE), tried in cheekpieces for the first time, made some ground at about halfway but soon went (op 6-1 tchd 11-2)

4293 MAGNUS-ALLCROFT MEMORIAL TROPHY HUNTERS' CHASE (17 fncs) 2m 4f

4:55 (4:57) (Class 6) 5-Y-0+ **£936** (£290; £145; £72)

Form RPR

3041 **1** **Good Company (IRE)**[190] 1277 11-11-11 122 MrPJTolman(5) 128+
(S Flook) *hld up: hdwy appr 10th: c wd after 13th: rdn bef 2 out: led jst bef last: styd on wl: in command towards fin* **8/1**[3]

-PP3 **2** *6* **Battlecry**[7] 4141 10-11-5 130 MrWTwiston-Davies(7) 119+
(Nigel Twiston-Davies) *led to 4th: chsd ldr to 10th: outpcd 12th: rallied 3 out: ch after: wnt 2nd after last: rdr sn lost whip: no imp on wnr* **15/8**[2]

35-2 **3** *½* **Fresh Air And Fun (IRE)**[17] 8-11-13 113 MrARalph(7) 128+
(A G Hobbs) *chsd ldrs: blnd 4th: wnt 2nd 10th: led 12th: rdn appr 2 out: hdd jst bef last: no ex run-in* **9/1**

034- **4** *12* **Takeroc (FR)**[73] 8-11-5 149 (t) MrHDerham(7) 111
(R Barber) *trckd ldrs: wnt 2nd 13th: chalng 4 out: btn appr last* **13/8**[1]

P-05 **5** *dist* **Calgary Jock**[52] 10-11-5 0 MrHKinchin(7) 62
(Mrs J Marles) *mstkes: chsd ldrs: blnd 8th: wknd bef 13th: t.o* **66/1**

PP0/ **6** *1 ½* **Glenary (IRE)**[38] 9-11-5 0 MrRobertHawker(7) 61
(Mrs Sarah Hawker) *midfield: struggling 10th: wl outpcd 13th: t.o* **100/1**

/00- **7** *25* **Hollow Ranger (IRE)**[11] 10-11-13 0 L-BdrSallyRandell(7) 46
(Miss Sally Randell) *mstkes: a bhd: struggling fnl circ: t.o* **28/1**

R **Johnny Kilawee (IRE)**[204] 1186 7-11-9 0 MrTWeston(3) —
(M H Weston) *ref to r: tk no part no part* **20/1**

FPF/ **P** **Made In Montot (FR)**[699] 4725 11-11-12 0 MrDMansell —
(B J Clarke) *racd keenly in midfield: lost pl bef 9th (water): t.o whn p.u bef 10th* **50/1**

P- **P** **Classic Chance**[31] 11-11-12 0 (b) MrBMoorcroft —
(Miss A Ray) *chsd ldr: led 4th: clr bef 5th tl j.lft 7th: hdd 12th: wknd 13th: t.o whn p.u bef 3 out* **25/1**

/5U- **P** **Oscar D'Angron (FR)**[276] 9-11-5 0 MrAWadlow(7) —
(Mrs C J Robinson) *a bhd: wl outpcd 12th: t.o whn p.u bef 4 out* **20/1**

P06U **P** **Gunnadoit (USA)**[14] 4011 6-11-5 72 (p) MrRHodges(7) —
(Ann Price) *nvr gng wl: a bhd: mstke 4th: t.o 9th (water): p.u bef 10th* **150/1**

0-P **P** **Willie Ever**[271] 75 7-11-7 0 MrRMcCarthy(5) —
(D C Gannon) *sweating: s.v.s: a t.o: p.u bef 6th* **100/1**

5m 15.3s (10.90) **Going Correction** +0.575s/f (Soft) **13** Ran SP% **116.9**
Speed ratings: **101,98,98,93,73 73,63,—,—,— —,—,—**
toteswingers:1&2:£5.50, 1&3:£5.10, 2&3:£5.60 CSF £22.31 TOTE £8.00: £2.40, £1.60, £1.40; EX 26.50.
Owner Foxhunters In Mind **Bred** County Down Bloodstock **Trained** Leominster, Herefordshire

FOCUS

A race won by Baby Run in 2009, and not many made any serious appeal on recent starts. The early pace looked strong and helped the winner thread his way into contention.

NOTEBOOK

Good Company(IRE), having his first start for this stable after leaving Jonjo O'Neill for £5,000, sat well off those setting a good gallop, and was produced to work his way to the front before the last fence. He was entitled to need this run after a 190-day break, and handles decent ground, so is one that can win more races in the spring. (op 17-2)

Battlecry seemed a little disappointing on his debut in hunter chase company (2m7.5f), and was in danger of being left behind at one point here after helping to make the pace, but his rider kept his mount motivated and the pair briefly threatened again over the final few fences. It made no difference to the final outcome that the jockey lost his whip after the last. (op 11-8 tchd 2-1)

Fresh Air And Fun(IRE), who won over C&D when trained by Jonjo O'Neill, took it up with five to go and fought on well. He will probably be a good purchase for this type of contest. (op 6-1)

Takeroc(FR), officially rated 149, had won his only race for Paul Nicholls at 2m and fell on his pointing debut (over 3m) in December under this jockey. He moved into contention going really well but failed to get home, suggesting he really needs the minimum trip over fences in this sort of ground. (op 11-4)

4294 LUGG MAIDEN HURDLE (12 hdls) 3m

5:25 (5:25) (Class 5) 4-Y-0+ **£2,276** (£668; £334; £166)

Form RPR

4 **1** **Cantlow (IRE)**[17] 3960 6-11-4 0 DominicElsworth 127+
(Paul Webber) *hld up: hdwy appr 9th: trckd ldrs gng wl sn after: upsides fr 3 out: hit 2 out and last: sn hung rt: r.o to ld narrowly fnl 110yds: a holding on cl home* **7/2**[2]

3 **2** *nk* **Swingkeel (IRE)**[18] 3942 6-11-1 0 SamTwiston-Davies(3) 126+
(Nigel Twiston-Davies) *trckd ldrs: led after 9th: pressed 3 out: rdn appr last: hdd fnl 110yds: r.o u.p but hld cl home* **4/9**[1]

3 *7* **Hawkes Point**[298] 6-11-4 0 NickScholfield 119+
(Paul Nicholls) *hld up in tch: clsd to go prom 8th: ev ch appr 3 out: rdn and nt qckn 2 out: no ch w front pair after: one pce run-in* **5/1**[3]

54 **4** *20* **Rooftop Rainbow (IRE)**[38] 3585 7-11-1 0 DannyCook(3) 101
(Linda Blackford) *prom: led 4th tl after 6th: led again 8th: hdd after 9th: rdn and wknd appr 3 out* **33/1**

00P **5** *22* **Rathconrath (FR)**[19] 3931 6-11-4 0 WarrenMarston 81
(Althea Barclay) *prom: led after 6th: hdd 8th: rdn and wknd appr 3 out* **200/1**

0 **6** *28* **Rascella Bay**[70] 2957 5-11-1 0 PeterToole(3) 76
(Charlie Mann) *j.lft thrght: hld up: sme hdwy to chse ldrs appr 3 out: sn no further imp: dropped away bef 2 out* **40/1**

0-00 **7** *68* **Mister Concussion**[41] 3528 7-11-4 0 (t) MarkGrant —
(Peter Jones) *hld up: hdwy to chse ldrs appr 8th: wknd bef 3 out: t.o* **200/1**

3-UP **P** **Roman Landing**[24] 3836 7-11-4 72 JackDoyle —
(Peter Pritchard) *led: hdd 4th: mstke 5th: mstke 7th: sn lost pl: bhd 8th: t.o whn p.u bef 3 out* **200/1**

6m 8.20s (15.90) **Going Correction** +0.45s/f (Soft) **8** Ran SP% **115.0**
Speed ratings: **91,90,88,81,74 65,42,—**
toteswingers:1&2:£1.50, 1&3:£1.10, 2&3:£2.10. totesuper7: Win: Not won. Place: Not won. CSF £5.83 TOTE £2.60: £1.10, £1.10, £1.40; EX 7.70.
Owner R V Shaw **Bred** Mrs Ann Jenkins **Trained** Mollington, Oxon

FOCUS
Only three looked to have a realistic chance, but only two mattered at the end.

NOTEBOOK
Cantlow(IRE) was produced down the home straight to challenge the favourite. Despite wandering, he showed a decent attitude and narrowly prevailed on this big step up in trip. (op 4-1)
Swingkeel(IRE) was heavily supported in the market but proved to be disappointing. He moved up to be in the right position but either couldn't or wouldn't lengthen under pressure. His Flat victories suggest he wants quick ground, which it wasn't here, but it wouldn't be a surprise to see headgear (he wore cheekpieces on a few occasions for John Dunlop) tried again. (op 4-6 tchd 8-11)
Hawkes Point ◆, a brother to Alfie Sherrin, was a comfortable winner of a 3m Irish point last May but had been absent since. He got towards the head of affairs going well, but still looked a little green under pressure and was beaten off after two out. It was still a promising effort, however, and he will no doubt do better in time. (op 7-2)
Rooftop Rainbow(IRE) plugged on for fourth after racing prominently. (op 40-1)
Rascella Bay looks in need of more time.
T/Plt: £186.60 to a £1 stake. Pool:£50,819.55 - 198.75 winning tickets T/Qpdt: £39.80 to a £1 stake. Pool:£4,893.43 - 90.90 winning tickets DO

3823 FAIRYHOUSE (R-H)
Wednesday, February 23

OFFICIAL GOING: Heavy

4295a WINNING FAIR JUVENILE HURDLE (GRADE 2) (10 hdls) 2m
2:05 (2:06) 4-Y-O **£21,012** (£6,142; £2,909; £969)

RPR

1 **Little Green (IRE)**[27] 3774 4-10-9 PTownend 125
(E McNamara, Ire) *settled bhd ldrs: 7th 1/2-way: hdwy into 4th 2 out: rdn to chal last: sn led: kpt on wl run-in* **13/2**

2 *2* **Chaperoned (IRE)**[11] 4083 4-10-9 RMPower 123
(Mrs John Harrington, Ire) *chsd ldrs: 4th 1/2-way: 3rd 3 out: rdn bef 2 out where chal: led bef last where strly pressed: slt mstke and sn hdd: no ex and kpt on same pce run-in* **4/1**[2]

3 *¾* **Rocky Wednesday (IRE)**[26] 3795 4-11-0 PCarberry 128+
(Gordon Elliott, Ire) *settled bhd ldrs: 5th 1/2-way: hdwy in 4th 3 out: chal ent st: rdn after 2 out: no ex in 4th last: kpt on same pce run-in* **20/1**

4 *2½* **Fearless Falcon (IRE)**[11] 4083 4-11-0 (b) AELynch 125
(Adrian McGuinness, Ire) *chsd ldr in 2nd: led 3 out: rdn and chal ent st: hdd bef last: no ex and kpt on one pce* **2/1**[1]

5 *5½* **Silver Shuffle (IRE)**[26] 3795 4-11-0 BarryGeraghty 119
(J G Coogan, Ire) *settled bhd ldrs: 6th 1/2-way: clsr in 5th 3 out: rdn ent st: no ex in 5th 2 out: kpt on one pce* **14/1**

6 *3* **Accidental Outlaw (IRE)**[55] 3239 4-11-0 MPWalsh 116
(Charles O'Brien, Ire) *chsd ldrs: 3rd 1/2-way: rdn and no ex 3 out* **4/1**[2]

7 *3½* **What A Charm (IRE)**[31] 3704 4-10-9 DNRussell 108
(A L T Moore, Ire) *led: rdn and hdd 3 out: wknd ent st* **9/2**[3]

8 *dist* **Peccatorum (IRE)**[27] 3774 4-11-0 111 AndrewJMcNamara —
(A J McNamara, Ire) *a towards rr: t.o* **33/1**

4m 13.9s (1.90) **Going Correction** -0.075s/f (Good) **8** Ran SP% **119.2**
Speed ratings: **92,91,90,89,86 85,83,—**
CSF £34.57 TOTE £8.30: £2.10, £1.50, £3.00; DF 42.40.
Owner Bannermen Syndicate **Bred** Keene Bloodstock Ltd & P Brady **Trained** Rathkeale, Co. Limerick
■ Stewards' Enquiry : A E Lynch severe caution; used whip with excessive frequency

FOCUS
A Grade 2 race contested by a bunch of juveniles that didn't have a huge amount to choose between them.

NOTEBOOK
Little Green(IRE) got a patient ride in a race run at a reasonable clip and, despite displaying a head carriage that wouldn't inspire confidence, she found for pressure and seemed to tough it out. She's probably improving. (op 6/1)
Chaperoned(IRE) looks more than good enough to win at least a maiden hurdle with improved jumping. Content to track the pace here, she came through to challenge and lead at the last. A slight mistake at that flight didn't help her cause it wasn't the difference. She does miss the odd hurdle but she looks capable of winning a nice race. (op 10/3)
Rocky Wednesday(IRE) should improve on better ground. For his first completed run, though, this was a good effort, making smooth headway to dispute the lead at the second-last before the two fillies took over. He could well turn the tables should their paths cross again. (op 16/1)
Fearless Falcon(IRE) had a perfect position the whole way and had every chance when in front turning in. However, he was quite one-paced when push came to shove despite looking like fighting back coming to the last. (op 5/2)
Silver Shuffle(IRE) kept on at one pace on the inner having never really made any impression. (op 14/1 tchd 12/1)
Accidental Outlaw(IRE) was well positioned most of the way but didn't find much for pressure in the straight. (op 9/2)
What A Charm(IRE) had different tactics employed here as she bounced out and tried to make all. She jumped pretty well but emptied once challenged three out. (op 5/1 tchd 11/2)

4298a AT THE RACES BOBBYJO CHASE (GRADE 2) (20 fncs) 3m 1f
3:45 (3:45) 5-Y-O+ **£22,413** (£6,551; £3,103; £1,034)

RPR

1 **The Midnight Club (IRE)**[26] 3798 10-11-3 145 PTownend 156+
(W P Mullins, Ire) *trckd ldrs: 2nd 1/2-way: impr to ld bef 2 out: rdn bef last: chal run-in: kpt on wl u.p* **11/10**[1]

2 *1* **Arbor Supreme (IRE)**[46] 3437 9-11-3 143 DJCasey 154
(W P Mullins, Ire) *hld up towards rr: hdwy into 5th 2 out: rdn into 3rd bef last: chal run-in: jst hld* **20/1**

3 *4* **Oscar Time (IRE)**[56] 3207 10-11-3 146 MrSWaley-Cohen 151+
(M M Lynch, Ire) *chsd ldrs: 6th 1/2-way: travelled wl into 3rd 2 out: 2nd bef last: rdn and slt mstke last: no ex run-in: kpt on same pce* **9/2**[2]

4 *7* **Vic Venturi (IRE)**[39] 3578 11-11-8 155 (p) PWFlood 151
(D T Hughes, Ire) *chsd ldrs: 4th 1/2-way: 2nd 6 out: disp 3 out: rdn and hdd bef 2 out: no ex in 4th bef last: kpt on same pce* **15/2**[3]

5 *9* **Siegemaster (IRE)**[26] 3798 10-11-8 151 (b) DNRussell 142
(D T Hughes, Ire) *led: mstke 3 out: strly pressed and disp: hdd ent st: no ex in 4th 2 out: kpt on one pce* **9/2**[2]

6 *11* **Bluesea Cracker (IRE)**[102] 2358 9-11-3 141 MPWalsh 123
(J Motherway, Ire) *mid-div: 7th 1/2-way: hdwy into 5th 3 out: rdn ent st: no ex in 6th 2 out: kpt on one pce* **14/1**

P **Wheresben (IRE)**[788] 3022 12-11-3 135 MrJAFahey —
(Seamus Fahey, Ire) *sn towards rr: reminders 1/2-way: mstke 5 out: wknd and p.u bef 3 out* **50/1**

P **Mossbank (IRE)**[20] 3915 11-11-3 140 (b[1]) APHeskin —
(Michael Hourigan, Ire) *chsd ldrs: 5th 1/2-way: rdn in 6th 3 out: no ex and wknd: p.u bef 2 out* **33/1**

P **Coolcashin (IRE)**[24] 3845 10-11-6 138 TJDoyle —
(Michael J Bowe, Ire) *disp early: sn chsd ldr: 3rd 1/2-way: wknd 4 out: p.u bef 2 out* **16/1**

6m 47.4s (-14.60) **Going Correction** -0.25s/f (Good) **9** Ran SP% **118.0**
Speed ratings: **113,112,111,109,106 102,—,—,—**
CSF £25.71 TOTE £1.70: £1.50, £4.30, £1.20; DF 19.00.
Owner Mrs S Ricci **Bred** Gareth Metcalfe **Trained** Muine Beag, Co Carlow

FOCUS
This was a decent-looking race with plenty of potential Grand National clues and it saw good performances from each of the first three.

NOTEBOOK
The Midnight Club(IRE) ◆ did the job well in the end. Racing prominently the whole way, he took it up early in the straight and was there to be shot at. However, he produced good jumps at the second-last and particularly at the final fence. He gives the impression he idles in front as he finds extra when he is challenged. One would think that being in front too long at Aintree might not be the best of ideas, but he's a good horse with a gear or two for an out-and-out stayer. (op 11/8)
Arbor Supreme(IRE) is never the easiest to work out and this was very much one of his going days. Given a patient ride by David Casey, who crept him into it, he was the last horse to throw down a challenge to the winner but was a bit outclassed in the end. He does stay very well, though. (op 16/1)
Oscar Time(IRE) ◆ is very much building towards Aintree as well and there was no sounder a jumper in this race. Sitting off the pace, he was still travelling while tracking the winner turning in but just got between the final two fences. He's an interesting one for the National, not least because he jumps so well.
Vic Venturi(IRE) had some more demanding opposition against him this time but still ran well. He raced reasonably prominently and was being hard ridden to sustain a challenge early in the straight. That was beyond him and he kept on at the same pace. (op 7/1)
Siegemaster(IRE) was meeting the winner on the same terms as when beating him in the Thyestes but ran a good bit below his best. Sitting in the first two throughout, he was still in front when making a bad mistake three out and, once headed early in the straight, he emptied fairly quickly. (op 7/2)
Bluesea Cracker(IRE) didn't run a bad race on her first start since November. She was in touch with the leaders and got tired in the straight, but one would imagine that effort will bring her on a good deal. Official explanation: trainer said mare scoped badly post-race (op 12/1)

4299 - 4301a (Foreign Racing) - See Raceform Interactive

4062 AYR (L-H)
Thursday, February 24

OFFICIAL GOING: Soft (chs 6.2; hdl 7.0)
Chase course rails 14m and hurdles course 7m from innermost position.
Wind: Breezy, half against Weather: Cloudy, bright

4302 VICTORCHANDLER.COM CONDITIONAL JOCKEYS' H'CAP HURDLE (11 hdls) 2m 4f
2:20 (2:20) (Class 5) (0-90,90) 4-Y-O+ **£1,951** (£573; £286; £143)

Form RPR

-U40 **1** **Sundown Trail (IRE)**[53] 3336 6-11-3 84 FearghalDavis(3) 92+
(Nicky Richards) *in tch: stdy hdwy 1/2-way: ev ch whn nt fluent 3 out: sn led: rdn and r.o wl last* **3/1**[1]

4/32 **2** *1¼* **Classic Henri**[30] 3728 7-11-0 78 RyanMania 84
(Barry Murtagh) *trckd ldrs: led after 4 out: rdn and hdd bef 2 out: rallied: kpt on run-in* **8/1**

5-04 **3** *¾* **Crackerjack Lad (IRE)**[12] 4068 8-11-2 83 CampbellGillies(3) 87
(Lucinda Russell) *hld up: hdwy and in tch 4 out: effrt and drvn next: one pce fr last* **5/1**[3]

0003 **4** *10* **Daasij (IRE)**[184] 1361 6-10-2 69 PaulGallagher(3) 63
(N W Alexander) *hld up: hdwy to trck ldrs 4 out: outpcd next: no imp fr 2 out* **14/1**

204P **5** *2¼* **Soul Magic (IRE)**[7] 4168 9-10-13 85 GaryRutherford(8) 78
(Harriet Graham) *hld up: hdwy 1/2-way: effrt after 4 out: outpcd fr next* **20/1**

0-P5 **6** *14* **Shadow Boxer**[22] 3883 6-10-5 77 CallumWhillans(8) 55
(Donald Whillans) *hld up: reminders after 6th: drvn and outpcd next: n.d after* **10/1**

6000 **7** *4* **Pickworth (IRE)**[22] 3883 6-11-6 90 (p) KyleJames(6) 64
(Philip Kirby) *prom: lost pl 5th: n.d after* **33/1**

P052 **8** *6* **Overyou**[9] 4138 6-10-13 82 PeterHatton(5) 50
(Elliott Cooper) *hld up: stdy hdwy and in tch 1/2-way: wknd after 4 out* **7/2**[2]

-00F **9** *6* **Monsoon Music (IRE)**[9] 4133 7-10-5 69 EwanWhillans 31
(Lucinda Russell) *cl up: rdn after 4 out: wknd bef next* **40/1**

3200 **10** *10* **Barbarian**[30] 3728 5-11-9 87 JamesHalliday 39
(Alan Brown) *led to 5th: cl up tl wknd after 4 out* **50/1**

6P00 **11** *43* **Beano Boy**[24] 3850 6-9-9 64 HenryBrooke(5) —
(Brian Storey) *w ldrs: led 5th to 4 out: wknd qckly bef next* **66/1**

0142 **P** **Transact (IRE)**[9] 4136 6-10-11 75 (p) AlexanderVoy —
(Martin Todhunter) *trckd ldrs tl lost pl after 6th: struggling fr next: t.o whn p.u bef 3 out* **7/1**

5m 20.3s (8.30) **Going Correction** +0.25s/f (Yiel) **12** Ran SP% **116.9**
Speed ratings (Par 103): **93,92,92,88,87 81,80,77,75,71 54,—**
Tote Swingers: 1&2 £5.00, 1&3 £5.60, 2&3 £7.40 CSF £25.64 CT £117.27 TOTE £3.40: £1.90, £1.50, £2.80; EX 29.10.
Owner John P McManus **Bred** Mrs Catherine Ryan **Trained** Greystoke, Cumbria

FOCUS
A modest handicap with just one previous hurdle winner in the field. The form is best rated around the placed horses.

NOTEBOOK

Sundown Trail(IRE) justified heavy market support to run out a game winner, sealing the race with a big jump at the last. He relished the drop in trip and won with a bit in hand to record his first career success. Described by his trainer as big and backward, he is improving with racing. Official explanation: trainer said, regarding apparent improvement in form, that the gelding had been steadily improving and appreciated the drop back in trip. (tchd 5-2 and 7-2)

Classic Henri, 4lb higher than when second at Sedgefield last month, ran his race, but just failed to match the winner on the run-in. He travelled kindly but again found one too good. (op 9-1 tchd 7-1)

Crackerjack Lad(IRE), 3lb lower than when fourth here over 2m latest, had every chance going to the final flight but stayed on at the one pace. (op 11-2 tchd 6-1)

Daasij(IRE) was making his debut for this yard on his return from 184 days off the track and ran well for a long way. He was useful on the Flat and should strip fitter next time out. (op 12-1 tchd 16-1)

Soul Magic(IRE) was held up and plugged on at the one pace. (op 16-1)

Overyou, runner up off this mark on her last start, was disappointing. Having travelled strongly, she made good headway before flattening out quickly. She will be racing off an 8lb higher mark in future and looks set to struggle. (op 5-1)

Transact(IRE), the only previous winning hurdler in the field, raced up with the pace before being pulled up. Official explanation: jockey said gelding ran flat (op 6-1)

4303 BET NOW AT VICTORCHANDLER.COM NOVICES' HURDLE (9 hdls) 2m

2:50 (2:50) (Class 4) 4-Y-0+ **£2,602** (£764; £382; £190)

Form RPR

3232 **1** **Flinty Bay (IRE)**[32] 3696 6-11-2 118 .... DougieCostello 120+
(Nicky Richards) *hld up in tch: hdwy 4 out: ev ch whn hit next: sn drvn: rallied: led run-in: styd on wl* **2/5**[1]

4 **2** *nk* **Proud Times (USA)**[24] 3850 5-11-2 0 .... BarryKeniry 120+
(Alan Swinbank) *prom: chsd clr ldr fr 4th: led bef 3 out: shkn up after next: edgd rt: hdd and rdn run-in: kpt on fin* **4/1**[2]

5- **3** *23* **Next To Nowhere (IRE)**[350] 4536 6-11-2 0 .... BrianHarding 100+
(Nicky Richards) *hld up: hit 4th: hdwy and in tch bef 3 out: outpcd by ldng pair bef next* **33/1**

30 **4** *15* **Trucking Along (IRE)**[10] 4117 5-11-2 0 .... TimmyMurphy 82
(S R B Crawford, Ire) *hld up and bhd: stdy hdwy after 4 out: nvr nr to chal* **33/1**

-400 **5** *18* **Forcefield**[24] 3851 5-10-9 0 .... MissLAlexander(7) 64
(N W Alexander) *midfield: drvn and outpcd after 3rd: n.d after* **33/1**

/40- **6** *23* **Arran Law (IRE)**[474] 2114 7-11-2 0 .... PeterBuchanan 41
(Lucinda Russell) *chsd clr ldr to 4th: rdn and wknd after 4 out* **50/1**

00-3 **7** *3* **Toledo Gold (IRE)**[13] 4059 5-11-2 102 .... (t) MichaelMcAlister 38
(Maurice Barnes) *nt fluent on occasions: led and clr tl hdd bef 3 out: sn wknd* **16/1**

P0 **8** *13* **Cigalas**[7] 4165 6-11-2 0 .... RyanMania 25
(Jean McGregor) *hld up: shortlived effrt after 4 out: sn wknd* **100/1**

04 **P** **The Galloping Shoe**[7] 4165 6-10-13 0 .... EwanWhillans(3) —
(Alistair Whillans) *hld up toward rr: hdwy after 4 out: 4th and no imp whn blnd next: sn p.u* **7/1**[3]

P **Scottish Affair**[53] 3356 5-11-2 105 .... BrianHughes —
(J J Lambe, Ire) *prom tl wknd bef 4 out: t.o whn p.u bef next* **66/1**

0-0 **P** **Oh Landino (GER)**[235] 576 6-11-2 0 .... GrahamLee —
(Jim Goldie) *bhd: struggling 1/2-way: t.o whn p.u bef 3 out* **33/1**

/00- **P** **Sweetaboutme**[337] 4819 6-10-9 0 .... FearghalDavis —
(Nicky Richards) *a bhd: t.o whn p.u bef 3 out* **66/1**

0-P **P** **Legbeforewicket**[155] 1573 5-10-9 0 .... CampbellGillies —
(Lucinda Russell) *hld up: struggling bef 4th: t.o whn p.u bef next* **100/1**

0 **P** **Lucky Belle (IRE)**[24] 3850 4-9-7 0 .... (t) PaulGallagher(7) —
(William Young) *t.k.h: sn towards rr: struggling 1/2-way: t.o whn p.u bef 3 out* **100/1**

4m 2.00s (-1.10) **Going Correction** +0.25s/f (Yiel)
WFA 4 from 5yo+ 9lb 14 Ran SP% 129.5
Speed ratings (Par 105): **112,111,100,92,83 72,70,64,—,— —,—,—,—**
Tote Swingers: 1&2 £1.40, 1&3 £5.80, 2&3 £9.60 CSF £2.60 TOTE £1.90: £1.10, £1.10, £7.50; EX 3.40.
Owner Miss A Condon,Mrs J Magnier & M Tabor **Bred** Thomas Foy **Trained** Greystoke, Cumbria

FOCUS

A moderate novice hurdle run at a good clip, and the first two pulled well clear. The winner sets the standard and the third can rate higher.

NOTEBOOK

Flinty Bay(IRE), placed in all five starts to date, went one better here, outbattling the runner-up in the straight. Having chased home some useful sorts, this was a deserved first success. He looks a fair prospect, although the handicapper will have his say. (op 8-13 tchd 8-11)

Proud Times(USA) travelled like the winner turning into the straight before just failing. This was an improved effort on just his second run over hurdles, and he should land a similar contest. (op 7-2 tchd 3-1)

Next To Nowhere(IRE), returning from a 350-day absence, ran a fair race on this hurdles debut. He can be expected to improve for the experience.

Trucking Along(IRE), a maiden point winner, hinted at some ability on this hurdles debut. He may prefer better ground. (op 40-1)

Toledo Gold(IRE) set a good clip before tiring badly. He will need to settle better to build on his previous Musselburgh third. (op 20-1)

The Galloping Shoe, a good fourth at Kelso last time, raced off the pace before a mistake at the third-last ended his chances. He was pulled up and will need to bounce back from this.

4304 PLAY LIVE CASINO AT VICTORCHANDLER.COM MAIDEN HURDLE (11 hdls) 2m 4f

3:25 (3:25) (Class 4) 4-Y-0+ **£2,602** (£764; £382; £190)

Form RPR

06 **1** **And The Man**[53] 3330 5-11-3 0 .... DougieCostello 120+
(Nicky Richards) *in tch: hdwy to chse ldr after 7th: chal 3 out: rdn to ld bef last: styd on strly to draw clr run-in* **9/4**[2]

-523 **2** *18* **Rival D'Estruval (FR)**[72] 2939 6-11-3 121 .... TimmyMurphy 108+
(Pauline Robson) *led to after 2nd: cl up: led 7th: jnd 3 out: hdd whn nt fluent last: tired bdly but hld on for 2nd run-in* **4/6**[1]

5-2 **3** *4* **Inoogoo (IRE)**[24] 3856 6-11-3 0 .... RyanMania 98
(George Bewley) *hld up in midfield: hdwy to trck ldrs 4 out: outpcd appr next: kpt on run-in* **13/2**[3]

F-0 **4** *11* **Lewlaur Supreme (IRE)**[24] 3851 8-11-3 0 .... GrahamLee 87
(Jim Goldie) *hld up: hdwy and prom 1/2-way: outpcd after 4 out: n.d after* **66/1**

5 *½* **Ballycarron Lad (IRE)**[11] 4108 9-11-0 0 .... JamesHalliday(3) 86
(S R B Crawford, Ire) *hld up: drvn and outpcd 1/2-way: plugged on fr 3 out: nvr on terms* **40/1**

0 **6** *10* **Maid In Moscow (IRE)**[15] 4000 7-10-3 96 .... MrRJohnson(7) 69
(S R B Crawford, Ire) *in tch tl rdn and wknd fr 4 out* **66/1**

0 **7** *17* **Indian Snow (IRE)**[40] 3572 6-11-3 0 .... CampbellGillies 59
(William Amos) *blnd bdly 1st: towards rr: drvn bef 4 out: wknd bef next: t.o* **100/1**

/0-5 **8** *nse* **Katapult (GER)**[22] 3887 8-11-3 0 .... RichieMcGrath 59
(Kate Walton) *trckd ldrs tl rdn and wknd after 4 out: t.o* **20/1**

9 *36* **Watch Closely Now (IRE)**[103] 7-10-10 0 .... PeterBuchanan 16
(I A Duncan, Ire) *t.k.h: led after 2nd to 7th: wknd next: t.o* **80/1**

4-25 **P** **Still Calm**[258] 714 7-11-3 80 .... (t) MichaelMcAlister —
(Maurice Barnes) *hld up: struggling after 4 out: t.o whn p.u next* **100/1**

0- **P** **Forestside (IRE)**[22] 3892 6-11-3 112 .... BrianHughes —
(J J Lambe, Ire) *prom tl rdn and wknd after 4 out: t.o whn p.u after next* **14/1**

P **Lay De Brook** 6-10-10 0 .... JamesReveley —
(Jim Goldie) *did nt jump wl: bhd: detached and p.u after 6th* **66/1**

5m 16.8s (4.80) **Going Correction** +0.25s/f (Yiel) 12 Ran SP% 125.7
Speed ratings (Par 105): **100,92,91,86,86 82,75,75,61,— —,—**
Tote Swingers: 1&2 £3.40, 1&3 £3.00, 2&3 £1.50 CSF £4.44 TOTE £3.20: £1.20, £1.10, £2.00; EX 5.80.
Owner Little Green Syndicate **Bred** A Buller **Trained** Greystoke, Cumbria

FOCUS

A weak maiden hurdle with the form rated around the first two.

NOTEBOOK

And The Man, well backed, travelled strongly before outstaying the odds-on favourite to run out an easy winner. A big chasing type, he knuckled down well and will go over fences next season. (op 2-1)

Rival D'Estruval(FR) had shown ability in all three previous starts, but again found one too good. He pulled clear with the winner approaching three out, but was outfought and finished extremely tired. He has shown enough abiltiy to win a minor race, but was a tad disappointing. (op 11-10)

Inoogoo(IRE), runner-up in a bumper here last month, made a fair start to hurdling but could not match the front two. He may improve for the experience. (tchd 15-2)

Lewlaur Supreme(IRE) has shown little over hurdles but ran a respectable race without threatening.

Forestside(IRE), beaten on his handicap debut in Ireland earlier this month, raced too keenly in the early stages and was pulled up. (tchd 12-1)

4305 PLAY POKER AT VICTORCHANDLER.COM NOVICES' H'CAP CHASE (12 fncs) 2m

3:55 (3:56) (Class 4) (0-110,110) 5-Y-0+ **£3,252** (£955; £477; £238)

Form RPR

0/3- **1** **Prosecco (IRE)**[461] 2409 9-11-10 **108** .... PeterBuchanan 116
(Lucinda Russell) *hld up: hdwy to chse ldr after 5 out: effrt and slt ld after 2 out: lft 3 l clr last: styd on wl* **7/1**

0014 **2** *13* **Sheriff Hall (IRE)**[53] 3335 6-10-6 **90** .... (t) TimmyMurphy 90+
(George Charlton) *t.k.h: led 1st: clr 1/2-way: hdd after 2 out: 3 l down and one pce whn lft 2nd and hmpd last: no imp* **13/8**[1]

6324 **3** *21* **Earl Grez (FR)**[18] 3970 6-10-12 **103** .... KyleJames(7) 77
(Philip Kirby) *prom: reminders 1/2-way: drvn and outpcd bef 5 out: sn btn: lft poor 4th last* **10/1**

0 **4** *1¾* **Glad Lion (GER)**[16] 3993 10-10-0 **84** oh3 .... (t) BrianHughes 56
(J J Lambe, Ire) *led to 1st: chsd ldr to after 5 out: rdn and wknd bef next: no ch whn lft 30 l 3rd last* **16/1**

0300 **P** **Daytime Dreamer (IRE)**[42] 3523 7-11-1 **99** .... GrahamLee —
(Martin Todhunter) *nt fluent: hld up in tch: nt fluent and wknd 5 out: no ch whn hit 3 out: sn p.u* **11/2**[3]

00-P **P** **Oleolat (FR)**[52] 3360 9-10-6 **90** .... (t) CampbellGillies —
(William Amos) *prom: rdn and wknd 5 out: t.o whn p.u bef next* **20/1**

-F21 **F** **Tartan Snow**[15] 4001 11-11-5 **110** .... GaryRutherford(7) 118+
(Stuart Coltherd) *hld up: nt fluent 5th: smooth hdwy 5 out: effrt and disp ld after 2 out: upsides whn fell last* **3/1**[2]

4m 12.7s (2.00) **Going Correction** +0.25s/f (Yiel) 7 Ran SP% 110.7
Speed ratings: **105,98,88,87,— —,—**
Tote Swingers: 1&2 £2.90, 1&3 £5.70, 2&3 £1.90 CSF £18.51 TOTE £5.80: £2.50, £1.30; EX 21.70.
Owner Tay Valley Chasers Racing Club **Bred** W Sheldon **Trained** Arlary, Perth & Kinross

FOCUS

A mediocre novices' handicap chase run at a good gallop. The winner is rated in line with his best hurdles form, while the second can rate higher.

NOTEBOOK

Prosecco(IRE), returning from a 461-day absence, ran out a comfortable winner on just his second chase start. Having travelled nicely, he jumped neatly and was left clear by the fall of Tartan Snow at the last. A winner off this mark over hurdles, he may progress further and remains of interest in this grade. (op 6-1 tchd 8-1)

Sheriff Hall(IRE) raced keenly on this chase debut and jumped boldly out in front before tiring in the straight. He will need to settle better, but should continue to be competitive in this sort of race. (op 2-1)

Earl Grez(FR) struggled to land a blow and may need a slight drop in the weights to get more competitive. (tchd 8-1)

Glad Lion(GER) chased the leader but could never get involved at the business end. (op 20-1)

Daytime Dreamer(IRE), well backed, didn't jump fluently and was pulled up before four out. (tchd 5-1)

Oleolat(FR) Official explanation: trainer said gelding had a breathing problem (tchd 5-1)

Tartan Snow, up 8lb for his Carlisle win last time, was just making his challenge when he fell at the final flight. It is difficult to know whether he would have won, but he was sure to have given the winner a proper race. He looks capable of defying this mark if brushing up his jumping. (tchd 5-1)

4306 PLAY CASINO AT VICTORCHANDLER.COM H'CAP CHASE (19 fncs) 3m 1f

4:30 (4:30) (Class 4) (0-110,109) 5-Y-0+ **£3,252** (£955; £477; £238)

Form RPR

/056 **1** **Lampion Du Bost (FR)**[24] 3853 12-11-4 **101** .... GrahamLee 120+
(Jim Goldie) *j.w: led to 5th: pressed ldr: led 9th: given breather after next: qcknd clr after 5 out: unchal* **7/2**[2]

0214 **2** *9* **Aghill (IRE)**[15] 4004 7-11-2 **106** .... HenryBrooke(7) 109
(Rose Dobbin) *mstkes: bhd: hdwy and in tch bef 11th: trcking ldrs whn blnd 5 out: effrt after next: chsd (clr) wnr last: no imp* **6/1**[3]

05P4 **3** *2* **Sammy Spiderman**[12] 4064 8-10-2 **85** .... BrianHarding 85
(Alistair Whillans) *hld up: reminders 1/2-way: rallied 13th: outpcd 15th: plugged on fr 3 out to briefly dispute modest 2nd appr last: no imp* **3/1**[1]

44-0 **4** *4* **Justwhateverulike (IRE)**[20] 3922 10-11-7 **104** .... (p) PaddyAspell 99
(Sandy Forster) *hld up: hdwy and prom bef 11th: hit 12th: chsd (clr) wnr 4 out to bef last: sn btn* **16/1**

24P **5** *18* **Seeking Power (IRE)**[12] 4066 10-9-12 **88** .... MissLAlexander(7) 64
(N W Alexander) *bhd: lost tch fnl circ: plodded rnd* **6/1**[3]

3-PP **P** **Panama At Once**[22] 3888 11-10-9 **92** .... (p) JamesReveley —
(Philip Kirby) *chsd clr ldrs: blnd bdly 6th: nt fluent and lost pl 11th: hit next: p.u bef 13th* **13/2**

-0P6 **P** **Fiftyfive Degrees (IRE)**[13] 4060 10-11-10 107............... TimmyMurphy —
(Pauline Robson) *t.k.h: in tch: outpcd 11th: sn wknd: p.u bef 13th* **8/1**
P-P0 **P** **Quws Law (IRE)**[24] 3854 9-11-12 109............................(t) PeterBuchanan —
(Lucinda Russell) *cl up: led 5th to 9th: chsd wnr tl wknd 4 out: p.u bef 2 out* **12/1**

6m 56.8s (6.90) **Going Correction** +0.25s/f (Yiel) **8** Ran SP% **113.8**
Speed ratings: **98,95,94,93,87** —,—,—
Tote Swingers: 1&2 £4.50, 1&3 £2.30, 2&3 £2.70 CSF £24.64 CT £68.86 TOTE £3.30: £1.10, £2.50, £1.50; EX 20.90.
Owner The Dodoz Partnership **Bred** Hubert Morgat **Trained** Uplawmoor, E Renfrews
■ Stewards' Enquiry : Peter Buchanan caution: careless riding

FOCUS
An open-looking handicap chase run at a sound pace. The form is rated around the placed horses.
NOTEBOOK
Lampion Du Bost(FR) put in an exhibition of jumping to run out an emphatic winner. Making most of the running, he eased clear to record his first success since December 2007. (op 3-1 tchd 4-1)
Aghill(IRE) was held up and made steady progress before a terrible blunder at the fifth-last ended his chance. To his credit he did run on without reaching the winner. (op 8-1)
Sammy Spiderman's three career victories have come round here. He ran his race, plugging on at the one pace, and might appreciate further. (op 4-1)
Justwhateverulike(IRE) raced off the pace and could never land a blow. (op 12-1)
Seeking Power(IRE) looked well handicapped on his close second at Hexham, but struggled to get seriously involved. (op 8-1)
Panama At Once, well supported, never jumped fluently and has now been pulled up in his last three starts. (op 9-1 tchd 8-1)
Fiftyfive Degrees(IRE) raced up with the pace before fading badly. (op 9-1 tchd 8-1)
Quws Law(IRE) disputed the lead early but made mistakes and was pulled up before two out. (op 9-1 tchd 8-1)

4307 WATCH LIVE RACING AT VICTORCHANDLER.COM HUNTERS' CHASE (19 fncs) 3m 1f
5:00 (5:00) (Class 6) 6-Y-O+ **£758** (£233; £116)

Form				RPR
5-1	**1**		**Special Portrait (IRE)**[11] 7-11-13 0................................(t) MrWKinsey(5)	111+
			(Mark Hughes) *trckd ldrs: wnt 2nd 12th: effrt and led 4 out: drew clr fr last* **10/11**[1]	
340/	**2**	*9*	**Noir Et Vert (FR)**[11] 10-11-7 0.............................. MrJamieAlexander(7)	100
			(N W Alexander) *t.k.h: led to 4 out: rallied and ev ch next: one pce between last 2* **9/4**[2]	
530-	**3**	*14*	**Polobury**[11] 9-11-0 69.. MrJHamilton(7)	77
			(Harriet Graham) *in tch: outpcd bef 13th: rallied and lft mod 3rd 2 out: no imp* **20/1**	
04P/	**4**	*hd*	**Silver Breese**[32] 9-11-11 0..(t) MrCDawson(3)	84
			(R Robinson) *prom tl wknd 4 out: lft mod 4th 2 out* **33/1**	
	U		**Desertmore Star (IRE)**[11] 10-11-7 81.......................... MrAdamNicol(7)	84
			(J Smith) *trckd ldrs: hit 5 out: 10 l 3rd and no imp whn blnd and uns rdr 2 out* **11/2**[3]	
000/	**F**		**Miss Teeny Bash (IRE)**[4] 7-11-2 0.......................(p) MrJohnDawson(5)	—
			(Miss Katie Scott) *in tch: fell 10th* **25/1**	

7m 10.5s (20.60) **Going Correction** +0.25s/f (Yiel) **6** Ran SP% **110.1**
Speed ratings: **77,74,69,69**,— —
Tote Swingers: 1&2 £1.10, 1&3 £3.20, 2&3 £4.70 CSF £3.24 TOTE £2.00: £1.10, £4.30; EX 4.30.
Owner Mark Hughes **Bred Trained** Wigton, Cumbria

FOCUS
A low-grade hunter chase but the winner can rate higher and the form is rated through the second to his mark.
NOTEBOOK
Special Portrait(IRE) built on his Overton point victory 11 days earlier to run out an impressive winner. He jumped well throughout and will now head to the Foxhunter Chase at the Cheltenham Festival. He will need to improve significantly to figure there. (op Evens)
Noir Et Vert(FR), behind the winner at Overton last time, jumped bravely out in front but could not go with the winner in the straight. His losing run stretches back to April 2007, but he remains in good heart in this grade. (tchd 2-1)
Polobury did not jump with any zest but rallied to win the race for third. (op 16-1)
Silver Breese raced a little keenly just off the pace and failed to pick up having come under pressure down the back.
Desertmore Star(IRE) finished behind the winner at Overton latest, and failed to reverse the form with a 4lb pull in the weights. (op 6-1)
Miss Teeny Bash(IRE) was held up when she fell at the tenth fence. (op 6-1)

4308 BEST ODDS GUARANTEED AT VICTOR CHANDLER STANDARD OPEN NATIONAL HUNT FLAT RACE 2m
5:30 (5:30) (Class 6) 4-6-Y-O **£1,370** (£399; £199)

Form				RPR
11	**1**		**Dark Glacier (IRE)**[22] 3889 6-11-9 0.................................. BrianHarding	121+
			(Chris Grant) *mde all: rdn and hung lft briefly 3f out: kpt on strly to go clr fnl f* **15/8**[2]	
4	**2**	*4*	**Bygones Sovereign (IRE)**[30] 3731 5-11-2 0....................... GrahamLee	109
			(Karen McLintock) *in tch: outpcd and dropped to rr 1/2-way: rallied but plenty to do 3f out: styd on strly fnl f to take 2nd cl home: no ch w wnr* **7/1**[3]	
2	**3**	*nk*	**Otterburn (IRE)**[16] 3992 5-10-9 0............................ JeremiahMcGrath(7)	109
			(Alan Swinbank) *trckd ldrs gng wl: effrt and ev ch briefly 3f out: edgd lft: kpt on same pce fnl f: lost 2nd cl home* **5/4**[1]	
0-43	**4**	*19*	**Four Fiddlers (IRE)**[24] 3856 6-10-9 0........................ MissLAlexander(7)	90
			(N W Alexander) *prom: drvn and outpcd over 5f out: rallied over 3f out: sn no imp* **18/1**	
	5	*1 ½*	**Master Act (IRE)** 6-10-13 0... EwanWhillans(3)	88
			(Alistair Whillans) *trckd wnr to over 3f out: rdn and wknd over 2f out* **18/1**	
	6	*18*	**Marlee Mourinho (IRE)** 5-10-11 0................................. AlexanderVoy(5)	70
			(Lucy Normile) *bhd: drvn over 6f out: nvr on terms: t.o* **33/1**	
0	**7**	*¾*	**Al Gregg (IRE)**[24] 3856 5-10-9 0.. MrJCreswell(7)	69
			(I A Duncan, Ire) *hld up: hdwy and prom 1/2-way: wknd over 3f out: t.o* **80/1**	
	8	*nk*	**Golden Sparkle (IRE)** 5-10-2 0.................................... PaulGallagher(7)	62
			(I A Duncan, Ire) *t.k.h: trckd ldrs tl rdn and wknd fr 4f out: t.o* **50/1**	
	9	*hd*	**Edinburgh Gin Time** 5-10-9 0....................................... NathanMoscrop(7)	69
			(Lucy Normile) *bhd: struggling 1/2-way: nvr on terms: t.o* **80/1**	
05	**10**	*20*	**Playing Truant (IRE)**[52] 3364 4-10-0 0.............................. HenryBrooke(7)	40
			(James Ewart) *trckd ldrs tl rdn and wknd fr 5f out: t.o* **66/1**	

4m 1.30s (0.60) **Going Correction** +0.25s/f (Yiel)
WFA 4 from 5yo 9lb 5 from 6yo 1lb **10** Ran SP% **111.1**
Speed ratings: **108,106,105,96,95 86,86,86,85,75**
CSF £14.18 TOTE £1.90: £1.30, £1.10, £1.20; EX 13.10.
Owner Trevor Hemmings **Bred** C Kenneally **Trained** Newton Bewley, Co Durham

FOCUS
This bumper was dominated by the front three in the market.
NOTEBOOK
Dark Glacier(IRE) ◆ made all to land a gutsy success under a penalty. He showed a likeable attitude to land his second bumper and make amends for being relegated to runner-up on his last start. A £100,000 purchase, he should make a useful novice hurdler. (op 6-4 tchd 2-1)
Bygones Sovereign(IRE) ◆, fourth at Sedgefield on his debut, was outpaced running down the back but made eyecatching headway up the straight to nick second. This was a very promising run and he should go one better in similar company. (tchd 15-2)
Otterburn(IRE), well supported, travelled powerfully but failed to quicken with the winner in the last furlong. He should improve for this experience and could also land a race of this nature. (op 13-8)
Four Fiddlers(IRE) finished best of the rest and may appreciate a stiffer test once hurdling. He has now been well held in all his bumper starts. (op 14-1)
Master Act(IRE), a half brother to the smart Rainbow Peak, out of a half sister to Celtic Swing, raced too keenly and faded having been up with the pace. He should improve for this first racecourse appearance. (op 14-1 tchd 20-1)
T/Jkpt: £1,838.70 to a £1 stake. Pool:£19,423.36 - 7.50 winning tickets T/Plt: £7.60 to a £1 stake. Pool:£58,262.22 - 5,563.84 winning tickets T/Qpdt: £3.80 to a £1 stake. Pool:£3,546.88 - 685.02 winning tickets RY

4021 HUNTINGDON (R-H)
Thursday, February 24

OFFICIAL GOING: Soft (chs 6.5; hdl 6.2)
Hurdles track at widest configuration adding 70yds per circuit to distances.
Wind: light across Weather: sunny and very mild

4309 HUNTINGDON AUDI A1 MARES' NOVICES' HURDLE (10 hdls) 2m 5f 110y
2:00 (2:00) (Class 4) 4-Y-O+ **£2,602** (£764; £382; £190)

Form				RPR
12F3	**1**		**Naughty Naughty**[70] 2974 6-11-5 119....................................... APMcCoy	124+
			(Brendan Powell) *settled towards rr: smooth prog on outer after 6th: chal 3 out: led next: clr bef last: easily* **4/1**[3]	
-1FU	**2**	*4*	**Line Freedom (FR)**[25] 3830 6-11-5 0.............................. BarryGeraghty	116+
			(Nicky Henderson) *prom: lft in ld 6th: hit 3 out: drvn and hdd and nt fluent next: no match for wnr after* **2/1**[2]	
3	**3**	*7*	**Yvonne Evelyn (USA)**[29] 3740 6-10-12 0........................ RobertThornton	101
			(Alan King) *chsd ldrs: hmpd 6th: rallied after next: ev ch 3 out: drvn and outpcd by ldng pair whn mstke 2 out* **10/1**	
-505	**4**	*¾*	**Tsarinova**[21] 3904 6-10-12 0... WayneHutchinson	101
			(Alan King) *chsd ldrs: cl 4th whn mstke 3 out: sn drvn: btn next* **33/1**	
-UF5	**5**	*32*	**Lady Karabaya**[45] 3480 6-10-12 110.................................... WillKennedy	67
			(Henrietta Knight) *chsd ldrs tl wknd 6th: t.o after next* **100/1**	
26	**6**	*25*	**Glorybe (GER)**[54] 3302 5-10-12 0.................................. TomMessenger	42
			(Chris Bealby) *j.v.slowly 1st and 2nd: in tch tl wknd and mstke 7th: sn bdly t.o* **80/1**	
6-2	**7**	*16*	**Saoma (FR)**[26] 3816 5-10-12 0... LeightonAspell	26
			(Lucy Wadham) *chsd ldrs: rdn and wknd 7th: poor 5th whn j. slowly 3 out: t.o* **14/1**	
02	**8**	*3*	**Mater Mater**[25] 3830 4-9-9 0.. JakeGreenall(7)	13
			(Caroline Bailey) *led and t.k.h: clr tl 5th: hdd bef next: lost pl qckly: t.o 3 out* **40/1**	
0-00	**9**	*8*	**Top Bob (IRE)**[75] 2896 6-10-7 0.............................. MrGBarfoot-Saunt(5)	15
			(Tracey Barfoot-Saunt) *mstke 2nd: chsd ldr tl bef 4th where mstke: t.o after next* **250/1**	
332	**10**	*22*	**Dream Function (IRE)**[21] 3904 6-10-12 0.................(t) RichardJohnson	—
			(Philip Hobbs) *racd keenly: wnt 2nd bef 4th: led and landed v bdly and lost all momentum 6th: hdd and nt rcvr: hacked on: wl t.o bef 3 out* **15/8**[1]	
P0PP	**P**		**Baltrap (FR)**[95] 2554 6-10-12 72.................................... AndrewThornton	—
			(Clarissa Caroe) *mounted outside paddock: in last pair: hopelessly t.o fr 3rd tl p.u at 6th* **300/1**	
	P		**Desert Fairy**[21] 5-10-7 0.. LeeEdwards(5)	—
			(James Unett) *bhd: t.o and virtually stopping to a walk bef 6th: p.u 7th* **250/1**	
005	**P**		**Go Ruby Go**[26] 3816 7-10-12 0... PaulMoloney	—
			(Kevin Morgan) *25 l last at 1st: t.o 3rd: p.u 5th* **250/1**	
300	**P**		**Living Proof (IRE)**[15] 4012 6-10-12 0.. SamJones	—
			(Norma Twomey) *chsd ldrs tl rdn and fdd after 5th: hopelessly t.o whn p.u 3 out* **150/1**	

5m 24.8s (14.20) **Going Correction** +0.725s/f (Soft)
WFA 4 from 5yo+ 10lb **14** Ran SP% **113.7**
Speed ratings (Par 105): **103,101,99,98,87 78,72,71,68,60** —,—,—,—
Tote Swingers: 1&2 £2.10, 1&3 £4.80, 2&3 £6.70 CSF £12.08 TOTE £3.40: £1.10, £1.40, £2.30; EX 16.10.
Owner Mrs A Ellis **Bred** E R Hanbury **Trained** Upper Lambourn, Berks

FOCUS
The track was believed to be at its widest configuration, which adds around 80 yards. The ground looked soft and the runners came home well strung out. Quite a competitive contest of its type and the pace looked decent for the conditions. The winner is value for further, while the third sets the level.
NOTEBOOK
Naughty Naughty won a similar contest at Towcester over 2m in October, and hadn't been completely disgraced since, but this looked an improved performance considering the way she travelled into contention and stretched away. She is one to always have on your side in these types of events, but can't go for the valuable mares-only novice hurdle next month at Newbury because she raced on the Flat. Connections thinks she'll make a nice chaser next season.
Line Freedom(FR) hadn't managed to complete on her last two outings, and was a particularly expensive first-hurdle departure at Fakenham, where Mater Mater finished second. She looked to have been handed a golden opportunity here when her market rival lost her position, but she was never able to quicken away once in a commanding position, and her jumping remains a cause for concern. (op 9-4 tchd 5-2 in places)
Yvonne Evelyn(USA), upped in trip, proved one-paced after the first two quickened away. (op 12-1 tchd 17-2)
Tsarinova, like her stablemate in third, proved to be one-paced after the first two quickened away.
Saoma(FR), a chasing type, didn't run too badly at Uttoxeter on her return from a lengthy absence but was beaten before the race got serious here. Presumably something was amiss. (op 12-1)
Dream Function(IRE) landed badly after the sixth, losing all momentum, and was allowed to come home in her own time. It's best to forget this effort. Official explanation: jockey said mare was unsuited by the soft ground (tchd 7-4 and 2-1 in places)

Desert Fairy Official explanation: jockey said mare had a breathing problem

4310 RACING UK NOVICES' H'CAP HURDLE (8 hdls) 2m 110y

2:30 (2:30) (Class 4) (0-105,105) 4-Y-0+ **£2,276** (£668; £334; £166)

Form RPR

24/U **1** **Laterly (IRE)**[25] 3831 6-11-10 **103** RhysFlint 118+
(Steve Gollings) *led and sn clr: 20 l ahd 1/2-way: a looked uncatchable after: heavily eased fr last* **7/1**

0302 **2** *7* **Easton Clump**[22] 3882 8-11-2 **95** MarkGrant 98
(Dominic Ffrench Davis) *prom in gp bhd long ldr: mstke 4th: wnt poor 2nd and hit 3 out: plugged on: hit last: v flattered by proximity to heavily eased rival* **11/2**[3]

6421 **3** *2 1/4* **Mayolynn (USA)**[22] 3882 5-11-12 **105** AndrewThornton 104
(Caroline Bailey) *hld up early: wnt 20 l 2nd at 5th tl 3rd and rdn 3 out: plugged on same pce* **7/2**[2]

-050 **4** *20* **Thunderstorm (IRE)**[28] 3760 6-11-8 **101** APMcCoy 80
(Philip Hobbs) *chsd clr ldr tl lost pl bdly after mstke 4th: plugged on in forlorn pursuit of ldrs fr 3 out: wnt remote 4th after last* **13/8**[1]

44 **5** *6* **Golden Prospect**[22] 3879 7-11-7 **100** JamesDavies 74
(Paul Fitzsimons) *chsd ldrs: rdn and wknd 5th: mod 4th whn hit next: fin t.o and v tired* **33/1**

P004 **6** *26* **Fidelor (FR)**[30] 3724 5-11-5 **105** JakeGreenall(7) 52
(Henry Daly) *rdn and lost pl after 3rd: t.o 3 out* **8/1**

0P0 **7** *5* **Graylyn Amber**[29] 3740 6-10-9 **88** CharliePoste 30
(Robin Dickin) *t.k.h early: 12 l 2nd after 3rd: struggling fr 5th: bdly t.o next* **40/1**

260 **8** *8* **Coeur De Lionne (IRE)**[186] 1344 7-11-2 **102** (t) MrWTelfer(7) 36
(Mrs Pauline Harkin) *a wl bhd: hopelessly t.o 3 out* **33/1**

00/0 **P** **Kavaloti (IRE)**[14] 4025 7-10-10 **94** (b) JoshuaMoore(5) —
(Gary Moore) *last and reminders after 3rd: reluctant: t.o next: p.u 3 out* **40/1**

-060 **P** **Atared**[16] 3987 5-11-5 **98** WarrenMarston —
(Pam Sly) *prom in chsng gp bhd long ldr fr 3rd tl wknd bef 3 out: t.o and p.u next* **20/1**

4m 4.70s (9.80) **Going Correction** +0.725s/f (Soft) **10** Ran SP% **114.8**
Speed ratings (Par 105): **105,101,100,91,88 76,73,70,—,—**
Tote Swingers: 1&2 £7.10, 1&3 £4.60, 2&3 £1.10 CSF £41.70 CT £156.30 TOTE £11.20: £3.00, £2.10, £2.60; EX 28.10.

Owner P J Martin **Bred** Gestut Fahrhof Stiftung **Trained** Scamblesby, Lincs

FOCUS

A competitive-looking race for the level, as it contained a few interesting types, but it was blown apart by the front-running Laterly. The winner can rate higher with the second on a decent mark and to form.

NOTEBOOK

Laterly(IRE) ◆, having his first start in a handicap over hurdles, was quickly into stride and established a long lead, one that always appeared big enough to hold any challenge from behind. A winner on the Flat at Ripon over 1m4f off an official mark of 92 in 2008, and still rated close to that mark on the level, he looked potentially well treated here if retaining all of his ability, so it wasn't a big surprise to see him win with plenty in hand. Quicker ground will suit him even better considering his Flat victories, and he will be very difficult to beat around a similarly sharp track, even after going up the weights. (op 7-2)

Easton Clump managed to reverse Leicester form with Mayolynn on better terms, but never looked capable of catching the winner. (op 7-1)

Mayolynn(USA) was never a threat to the runaway winner, and could not reverse confirm Leicester form with Easton Clump on these revised terms. (op 4-1 tchd 9-2)

Thunderstorm(IRE), who won a bumper over C&D, had caught the eye a couple of times in novice events and was heavily backed on his handicap debut. He led the chasing bunch until making a mistake at the fourth and soon lost ground. It seemed sure that he was about to pull up after that, but Tony McCoy kept his mount going and the pair finished quite well, albeit slowly, past some tired rivals. (op 3-1)

Golden Prospect travelled strongly but faded quickly. (op 25-1)

4311 WEATHERBYS CHELTENHAM FESTIVAL BETTING GUIDE NOVICES' CHASE (12 fncs) 2m 110y

3:05 (3:05) (Class 3) 5-Y-0+ **£4,553** (£1,337; £668; £333)

Form RPR

5-23 **1** **Starluck (IRE)**[40] 3559 6-10-12 0 APMcCoy 142+
(Alan Fleming) *j. deliberately 1st: settled trcking ldrs: wnt 2nd after 3 out: cruised ahd next: sn clr: hrd hld* **4/9**[1]

1531 **2** *6* **Pascha Bere (FR)**[10] 4122 8-11-4 0 (v) LiamTreadwell 134+
(Nick Gifford) *t.k.h: led tl 4th: last after slow jump 6th: remained cl up: mstke 3 out and rdn: 3rd and btn 2 out: wnt 2nd fnl 100yds but no match for cantering wnr* **7/2**[2]

1031 **3** *3 1/4* **Mister Stickler (IRE)**[21] 3905 7-11-8 127 RobertThornton 131
(Alan King) *pressed ldr: led 3 out: rdn and hdd and mstke 2 out: btn last: racd awkwardly after and fdd to lose 2nd fnl 100yds* **7/1**[3]

F463 **4** *39* **Hi Tide (IRE)**[106] 2313 7-10-12 109 DarylJacob 106+
(J R Jenkins) *plld hrd: led 4th tl hdd 3 out: sn dropped bk last: lost tch bef 2 out: eased flat* **100/1**

4m 16.5s (6.30) **Going Correction** +0.725s/f (Soft) **4** Ran SP% **105.0**
Speed ratings: **114,111,109,91**
CSF £2.29 TOTE £1.50; EX 2.20.

Owner A T A Wates **Bred** Castlemartin Stud And Skymarc Farm **Trained** Beare Green, Surrey

FOCUS

With due respect to the other runners, this race was all about the chasing debut of Starluck. The winner is value for further while the third sets the standard.

NOTEBOOK

Starluck(IRE) ◆, making his chase debut, is officially rated 160 over hurdles, but this going looked far from suitable on his winning performances. However, he jumped soundly, although a bit to his left at some of the fences, and won in the manner one would have expected against these rivals. His trainer was non-committal after the event as to where the gelding would go, but it would be a shame if he didn't head for the Arkle now, for which he's a best price 12-1. He would go there the highest-rated hurdler in the line-up, and Well Chief won his first chase in February before winning at Cheltenham the following month. That said, connections will do what's best for the horse and it could be that he heads to Aintree and Punchestown if they feel he needs more time. (op 1-2 tchd 8-15)

Pascha Bere(FR) had lots to find with Starluck on hurdling form but had started well over fences, winning on his chase debut at Plumpton when a visor was applied for the first time. With that aid retained, he seemed happy when in front but less so when passed. His rider kept his mount going and was rewarded with second. (op 10-3 tchd 3-1)

Mister Stickler(IRE) set the standard of those who had run over fences, having gained a couple of victories, but faced a tough task giving weight away and wasn't up to it. There are more races to be won with him, however, and he will obviously find easier tasks than this. He's entered in a couple of handicaps at Cheltenham. (op 6-1 tchd 11-2)

Hi Tide(IRE) had no obvious chance against this calibre of rival and, despite getting to the lead for a while, was left behind. (op 80-1)

4312 NEPTUNE INVESTMENT MANAGEMENT SIDNEY BANKS MEMORIAL NOVICES' HURDLE (10 hdls) 2m 4f 110y

3:35 (3:35) (Class 2) 4-Y-0+ **£9,757** (£2,865; £1,432; £715)

Form RPR

1F21 **1** **Aikman (IRE)**[13] 4061 7-11-3 130 HarryHaynes 137+
(James Ewart) *allowed easy ld and 25 l clr early: shkn up bef 4th and a had chalrs after: hit 2 out: stl battling on gamely whn hit last: increased advantage flat: v gd ride* **16/1**

11 **2** *3* **Minella Class (IRE)**[47] 3445 6-11-11 148 BarryGeraghty 141+
(Nicky Henderson) *wnt 2nd at 3rd: clsd on wnr next: nt fluent 6th: rdn to chal and hit 2 out: drvn and nt fluent last: outbattled flat and wkng fnl 100yds* **8/11**[1]

-411 **3** *1/2* **Pride In Battle (IRE)**[36] 3626 6-11-3 133 RobertThornton 132
(Alan King) *cl up fr 4th: 4th whn mstke 7th: wnt cl 2nd and drvn next: one pce 3rd and no imp 2 out: btn last* **11/2**[3]

211 **4** *1/2* **Captain Kirkton (IRE)**[18] 3960 5-11-3 133 JoshuaMoore 131
(Gary Moore) *cl up fr 4th: wnt 2nd briefly at 7th: drvn and kpt on same pce fr 2 out* **11/4**[2]

131 **5** *9* **Extremely So**[30] 3719 5-10-10 117 PaulMoloney 115
(Philip McBride) *a last: 6 l down and rdn 3 out: sn btn and hanging lft after* **40/1**

5m 8.20s (9.20) **Going Correction** +0.725s/f (Soft) **5** Ran SP% **108.3**
Speed ratings (Par 109): **111,109,109,109,106**
CSF £29.00 TOTE £17.80: £3.50, £1.50; EX 29.10.

Owner J D Gordon **Bred** Gerry Carroll **Trained** Langholm, Dumfries & G'way

FOCUS

Even though the favourite was sent off at odds-on, this was far from a one-sided contest on paper, but it was slightly controversial as the winner was allowed a running 10l start. The winner took a big step forward while the other four ran close to previous marks.

NOTEBOOK

Aikman(IRE), who has looked a talented performer in the north, was handed a running 10l start while the riders of his rivals all sat behind waiting to hold their mounts up. James Ewart's horse was afforded a decent advantage for most of the race, for which Harry Haynes deserves credit, but was forced to work hard to win when the field closed up. Mistakes at the last couple of hurdles didn't help, but he is a resilient type and found more to win nicely. He has numerous entries at Cheltenham, but which route connections take has yet to be decided. (op 12-1)

Minella Class(IRE) had been impressive since joining these connections and took the Grade 1 Tolworth Hurdle on his previous outing. He moved well during the race and, having made the ground up on the winner, looked to hold every chance. However, possibly that move took its toll as well as the penalty he carried, and Aikman kicked on again. It was far from being a bad performance in the circumstances, but whether he'll be the number one runner for this stable in the Neptune Hurdle, if he goes for that, is debatable, as Bobs Worth arguably now looks a stronger contender. (tchd 4-6 and 4-5 in places)

Pride In Battle(IRE) won two Newbury races that have produced winners, so his form looked solid. He travelled strongly in the chasing group but didn't have a turn of pace, and could only keep on at the one pace. A step up in trip will not be against him. (tchd 5-1 and 6-1)

Captain Kirkton(IRE), who raced towards the inside of the course away from his other chasing rivals, has made rapid progress since his bumper run and has developed into a talented hurdler, but he didn't look to be going as well as his rivals for much of the race here, and shapes like a horse in need of further in this sort of company. It's also worth remembering that his rider couldn't claim his usual 5lb. (op 7-2)

Extremely So had made a good start to her career as a hurdler but was in against some smarts sorts, and predictably fell a bit short. (op 28-1)

4313 JOHN BIGG OXO H'CAP CHASE (19 fncs) 3m

4:10 (4:11) (Class 4) (0-115,113) 5-Y-0+ **£2,602** (£764; £382; £190)

Form RPR

0411 **1** **Honourable Arthur (IRE)**[29] 3741 8-11-12 **113** (p) DenisO'Regan 125+
(Victor Dartnall) *bhd tl qckly wnt prom at 5th: led 7th tl bef 13th: rdn to ld again 3 out: gng easily after: 3 l clr last: idled bdly and jnd 150yds out: rdn clr w ears pricked cl home* **11/4**[1]

-P61 **2** *2* **Backfromthecongo (IRE)**[101] 2420 10-11-5 **106** (bt) RichardJohnson 112
(Richard Lee) *trckd ldrs: clsd to ld bef 13th: hdd 3 out: sn drvn: wnt 2nd at last where v untidy jump: hung lft u.p but drew upsides ins fnl f: racd awkwardly and no ex cl home* **10/1**

4U-4 **3** *6* **King Jack**[37] 3617 9-11-9 **110** (p) WarrenMarston 113
(Richard Phillips) *led 2nd tl 4th: remained prom: mstke 13th: rdn to go 2nd bef 2 out tl last where 3 l down: sn lost 2nd and fnd v little flat* **12/1**

0P0P **4** *2* **Ginolad (AUS)**[21] 3907 11-11-0 **101** AidanColeman 99
(Venetia Williams) *handy early: lost interest and drvn and lost tch 13th: 15 l 6th 2 out: styd on after but gave himself an impossible task* **11/2**[3]

6UPU **5** *1* **Picture In The Sky (IRE)**[21] 3907 10-11-6 **110**... SamTwiston-Davies(3) 107
(Susan Nock) *midfield: drvn bef 15th: tried to get on terms after 3 out: no imp next: hung lft flat* **10/1**

P621 **6** *7* **Sea Saffron**[21] 3907 10-11-5 **111** MattGriffiths(5) 102
(Susan Gardner) *settled in rr: hdwy 12th: tried to get on terms 3 out: sn drvn: no ex bef next* **9/2**[2]

2410 **7** *21* **Ovthenight (IRE)**[27] 3784 6-11-3 **111** MissGAndrews(7) 80
(Pam Sly) *led tl 2nd: sn sulking in rr: last whn j. slowly 7th: wl bhd 10th: t.o fr 13th* **15/2**

PP05 **8** *8* **Tisfreetdream (IRE)**[12] 4079 10-11-11 **112** (p) JackDoyle 88
(Peter Pritchard) *sn prom: led 4th tl 7th: prom tl wknd and bad mstke 15th: t.o and eased after slow jump 3 out* **9/1**

P14R **P** **Celian (FR)**[16] 3996 8-10-12 **102** (b1) AlexMerriam(3) —
(Neil King) *u.p fr 2nd: v reluctant in rr: blnd 8th and p.u* **28/1**

6m 29.2s (18.90) **Going Correction** +0.725s/f (Soft) **9** Ran SP% **111.3**
Speed ratings: **97,96,94,93,93 91,84,81,—**
Tote Swingers: 1&2 £3.90, 1&3 £7.50, 2&3 £6.70 CSF £28.36 CT £271.54 TOTE £3.80: £1.10, £3.10, £3.30; EX 14.90.

Owner Miss A Woolley **Bred** Mrs Neta O Connor **Trained** Brayford, Devon

FOCUS

The conditions made this a real slog but the winner is on the upgrade and the placed horses give the form a solid look.

NOTEBOOK

Honourable Arthur(IRE) ◆ was chasing a hat-trick since cheekpieces were fitted, and was 20lb higher than for the first of his previous two victories. Held up early, he quickly moved into a prominent position and jumped beautifully until idling after the final fence, before running on. He is a likeable character as he always gave the impression that he was going to win despite being closed down a couple of times, as all he does is gallop on strongly. There is every chance he could win again, although quicker ground would be a concern for him. (tchd 3-1 and 10-3 in places)

Backfromthecongo(IRE), raised 4lb for a comfortable Leicester victory, is a reliable sort at this level but was very one-paced after the final fence. After looking the most likely winner, he was outstayed in the final strides by Honourable Arthur. (op 8-1 tchd 13-2)

The Form Book, Raceform Ltd, Compton, RG20 6NL

King Jack was back down to his last winning mark (2m41/2f at this course) after a few moderate efforts and ran a fair race. Up with the pace early, he lost his place at one point and dropped back, but arrived back on the scene looking a potential winner coming to the second-last, before weakening coming to the final fence. (op 17-2)

Ginolad(AUS), a market springer who was 11lb lower than for his last run, never made a serious challenge after getting himself behind. (op 13-2)

Sea Saffron, up 9lb for a comfortable Wincanton success, was held up to make a challenge but couldn't get on terms after making up some ground. (tchd 4-1)

Ovthenight(IRE), a C&D winner in November, was another to drop himself out. (op 9-1 tchd 10-1)

Tisfreetdream(IRE), back over hurdles after a few starts over hurdles, showed enthusiasm while in front rank but made a couple of costly jumping mistakes down the back straight and was soon beaten. (tchd 17-2 and 10-1)

Celian(FR) Official explanation: jockey said gelding did not face the first time blinkers

4314 RACING UK H'CAP HURDLE (10 hdls) 2m 4f 110y
4:40 (4:41) (Class 4) (0-100,100) 4-Y-0+ **£2,397** (£698; £349)

Form RPR

220P **1** **Rossbrin (IRE)**[48] 3432 6-10-7 **81**...(t) AndrewTinkler 88
(Anna Brooks) *taken wd: led tl 1st: prom tl rdn and outpcd after 7th: rallying in 4 l 3rd last: styd on dourly to ld nr fin* **9/1**

P666 **2** *nk* **Just The Job (IRE)**[14] 4025 7-11-5 **100**... MarkQuinlan(7) 108+
(Neil Mulholland) *settled towards rr: hdwy bef 7th: led gng wl bef 2 out: hit last: drvn and hdd cl home* **10/3**[2]

P111 **3** *1 1/4* **Decent Lord (IRE)**[3] 4266 7-10-6 **87** 21ex... PeterCarberry(7) 93+
(Jennie Candlish) *nt fluent 2nd: dropped out last tl 1/2-way: effrt 7th: chal and hit 2 out: ev ch tl nt qckn under heavy press fr last* **6/4**[1]

14 **4** *3 3/4* **Torran Sound**[8] 1018 4-11-0 **98**... MarkBradburne 91
(James Eustace) *t.k.h: led after 1st tl rdn and hdd bef 2 out: one pce after* **6/1**[3]

3560 **5** *16* **Float My Boat**[29] 3740 5-11-0 **91**... AlexMerriam(3) 77
(Sean Regan) *chsd ldrs: rdn bef 6th: outpcd 3 out: plugged on flat* **25/1**

605 **6** *12* **Drummers Drumming (USA)**[38] 3604 5-11-9 **97**...(t) JimmyMcCarthy 71
(Charlie Morlock) *rn in snatches: j. slowly 1st: bhd and pushed along bef 6th: brief effrt next: struggling after 3 out* **16/1**

-450 **7** *5* **Pollen Jock (IRE)**[118] 2080 7-11-1 **89**... TomMessenger 58
(Chris Bealby) *t.k.h early: nvr bttr than midfield: rdn and btn bef 3 out* **16/1**

05FP **8** *3* **Kilbready Star (IRE)**[25] 3837 11-10-6 **80**... JackDoyle 46
(Peter Pritchard) *bhd: lost tch 7th: t.o last whn mstke 3 out* **50/1**

9 *3 1/2* **Silver Lily (IRE)**[281] 413 9-11-5 **100**... MrMEnnis(7) 62
(Sarah Humphrey) *prom: 2nd whn mstke 5th: wkng qckly whn mstke 3 out: t.o* **50/1**

-000 **10** *2 1/4* **Benny The Swinger (IRE)**[52] 3365 6-11-0 **88**... AndrewThornton 48
(Henrietta Knight) *bhd: effrt bef 7th: sn floundering: t.o 3 out* **33/1**

0650 **11** *39* **Me Fein**[22] 3882 7-10-6 **80**... PaulMoloney —
(Barney Curley) *t.k.h on wd outside: cl up tl lost pl 6th: t.o and eased 2 out* **18/1**

-004 **P** **Crackerjac Boy (USA)**[21] 3897 6-11-11 **99**... WarrenMarston —
(Richard Phillips) *t.k.h early: mstke 3rd: prom tl wknd and nt fluent 6th: t.o next: p.u 3 out* **33/1**

5m 13.5s (14.50) **Going Correction** +0.725s/f (Soft)
WFA 4 from 5yo+ 10lb **12 Ran SP% 118.0**
Speed ratings (Par 105): **101,100,100,98,92 88,86,85,83,83 68,—**
Tote Swingers: 1&2 £6.50, 1&3 £5.60, 2&3 £2.80 CSF £38.23 CT £70.78 TOTE £16.70: £4.20, £1.30, £1.10; EX 43.20.
Owner John Moorhouse **Bred** Patrick J Slattery **Trained** Alderton, Northants
■ Stewards' Enquiry : Peter Carberry two-day ban: used whip with excessive force (Mar 10-11)

FOCUS
The early pace wasn't strong and the race turned into a sprint. The first four finished well clear and the first trio are rated pretty much to form.

NOTEBOOK
Rossbrin(IRE), tried in a tongue-tie for the first time, sat close up but got hard ridden down the back straight and looked to be losing ground. However, Andrew Tinkler persevered and the pair stayed on dourly to collect the prize. This was the horse's first victory, but he still has some scope for improvement considering this was only his ninth start over hurdles. Whether he would have won had the runner-up not hit the last hurdle is debatable. Official explanation: trainer said, regarding apparent improvement in form, that the gelding has had a soft palate operation since its last run and had benefited from wearing a tongue tie for the first time. (op 11-1 tchd 12-1)
Just The Job(IRE) had lost his way this year off marks in the 100s after gaining three wins from four in a short space of time last November. After travelling strongly and looking in command heading into the home straight, he hit the final flight and weakened in the final stages. He can gain compensation. (op 5-1)
Decent Lord(IRE) has been well placed by Jennie Candlish to win three times in quick succession but was carrying a massive 21lb penalty for this race. Trying 2m4f for the first time since his winning spree started, he came through to have every chance until his stamina gave way. (op 11-8 tchd 6-5)
Torran Sound didn't run particularly well on his last two starts on the Flat after a break (although he's never run particularly well on the AW) but was nicely supported here, and ran respectably under a positive ride. (op 8-1)

4315 POINTTOPOINT.CO.UK HUNTERS' CHASE (19 fncs) 3m
5:10 (5:12) (Class 6) 5-Y-0+ **£749** (£232; £116; £58)

Form RPR

0P-2 **1** **Mount Benger**[14] 4026 11-11-13 126... MrSKeating(7) 128+
(H Whittington) *scrubbed along fr 3rd: outpcd after 4th: nvr on bridle and forced along thrght: stl last whn hit 11th: hdwy 15th: led u.p 2 out: racd w hd on one side after: jst hld on under a grimly determined ride* **13/2**[3]

5224 **2** *hd* **Templer (IRE)**[123] 1999 10-11-13 130... MrNSutton(7) 129+
(Philip Hobbs) *cl up: blnd 14th: 4 l 3rd 2 out: lost 2nd bef 2 out: bmpd along to rally after last: level 50yds out: jst hld nr fin* **3/1**[2]

110- **3** *3 1/4* **Noakarad De Verzee (FR)**[11] 10-11-13 129... MrDMaxwell(7) 124
(Mrs Kim Smyly) *led: nt fluent 3rd: hdd 6th: led after 8th: pushed along after 3 out: hdd 2 out: ev ch last: wknd fnl 100yds* **5/6**[1]

133/ **4** *87* **Prince Of Persia**[11] 11-11-7 112... MissCLWills(5) 28
(C W Loggin) *led 6th tl 7th: str reminders bef 13th: wknd bdly 16th and awkward hd carriage: sn the best part of a fence bhd* **12/1**

200/ **P** **Basic Fact (IRE)**[25] 9-11-5 106...(b) MrRStearn(7) —
(J M Turner) *prom: led 7th tl after next: rdn and no resolve fr 9th: mstke 11th: lft 4th briefly 13th: wl t.o 15th tl p.u 2 out* **20/1**

-0 **U** **Mr Redwood**[5] 9-11-9 0... MissLGardner(3) —
(Miss L Gardner) *hld up towards rr: j. slowly 7th: wnt abt 8 l 4th and uns rdr 13th* **28/1**

U **P** **O Ellie (IRE)**[11] 7-11-9 0... MrMatthewSmith(3) —
(Miss Katie Thory) *j. slowly 5th: cl up tl lost pl 12th: hopelessly t.o 14th: p.u 2 out* **80/1**

6m 30.1s (19.80) **Going Correction** +0.725s/f (Soft) **7 Ran SP% 110.0**
Speed ratings: **96,95,94,65,—** **—,—**
Tote Swingers: 1&2 £2.50, 1&3 £2.90, 2&3 £1.02 CSF £24.59 TOTE £6.80: £2.00, £1.80; EX 11.00.
Owner Mr and Mrs R H F Fuller **Bred** London Thoroughbred Services Ltd & John **Trained** Sparsholt, Oxfordshire

FOCUS
The field quickly thinned out the further they went, and only three had any chance from quite some way out. The third is the best guide but rated below last season's course best.

NOTEBOOK
Mount Benger shaped well in an almost identical race over C&D behind Cork All Star last time, but his cause looked hopeless early as he got behind. However, this is a ride that Sean Keating can rightly be proud of, as he galvanised his mount back into contention before producing a strong ride to hold on. (op 7-2)
Templer(IRE) appeared to be the least likely to win as the first three swept into the home straight, but Nicholas Sutton is another jockey who deserves praise for getting his mount back into a position to have a chance of victory. (op 11-4 tchd 10-3 in places)
Noakarad De Verzee(FR), a dual C&D winner in the past, which included the 3m handicap chase on this card, made most of the running and kept on bravely in the final stages, narrowly missing out on the runner's-up spot. (op 5-4 tchd 6-4 in places)
Prince Of Persia was the only other to complete, but he has a bizarre head carriage, which sees him carry it almost sideways. (op 16-1)
T/Plt: £15.50 to a £1 stake. Pool:£54,161.39 - 2,546.13 winning tickets T/Qpdt: £5.40 to a £1 stake. Pool:£3,459.72 - 468.38 winning tickets IM

4316 - 4318a (Foreign Racing) - See Raceform Interactive

4035 THURLES (R-H)
Thursday, February 24

OFFICIAL GOING: Hurdle course - soft (heavy in places); chase course - heavy

4319a MICHAEL PURCELL MEMORIAL NOVICE HURDLE (GRADE 2) (12 hdls) 2m 4f
3:30 (3:30) 5-Y-0+ **£21,012** (£6,142; £2,909; £969)

RPR

1 **Hidden Cyclone (IRE)**[32] 3708 6-11-8... AndrewJMcNamara 148+
(John Joseph Hanlon, Ire) *trckd ldrs in cl 3rd: led 3 out: jnd briefly and rdn next: kpt on wl and fr bef last: hung lft cl home* **13/8**[2]

2 *2 1/2* **Pineau De Re (FR)**[53] 3353 8-11-3... BTO'Connell 139
(Philip Fenton, Ire) *racd 2nd: rdn in cl 3rd 3 out: disp ld briefly next: sn hdd and kpt on same pce fr last* **12/1**

3 *6* **Skorcher (IRE)**[21] 3913 7-11-3...(t) EMullins 133
(W P Mullins, Ire) *hld up in tch: rdn in 6th bef 3 out: kpt on same pce st: wnt mod 3rd cl home* **12/1**

4 *1/2* **Bishopsfurze (IRE)**[21] 3913 6-11-6... PTownend 136
(W P Mullins, Ire) *trckd ldrs on outer: nt fluent 6th and mstke 5 out: rdn along in 4th after 3 out: no imp in 3rd next: dropped to 4th cl home* **6/4**[1]

5 *4* **Crash (IRE)**[14] 4038 6-11-3... DNRussell 129
(Michael Hourigan, Ire) *trckd ldrs: rdn along in 5th bef 3 out: no imp* **10/1**[3]

6 *1/2* **Down In Neworleans (IRE)**[21] 3911 6-11-3 121... DEMullins 128
(Ms Margaret Mullins, Ire) *led: hdd 3 out: sn rdn and wknd* **12/1**

7 *dist* **The Pier (IRE)**[15] 4016 5-11-1 118...(t) PCarberry —
(Joseph G Murphy, Ire) *hld up in last: no imp fr 4 out: t.o* **50/1**

P **Smokey Joe Joe (IRE)**[29] 3753 5-11-1 116... PWFlood —
(Kieran Purcell, Ire) *hld up in tch: p.u qckly bef 5th* **33/1**

5m 11.5s (311.50) **8 Ran SP% 115.2**
CSF £21.40 TOTE £2.10: £1.40, £2.00, £3.00; DF 18.00.
Owner Mrs A F Mee **Bred** Ronald O'Neill **Trained** Bagenalstown, Co Carlow

NOTEBOOK
Hidden Cyclone(IRE) is clearly a horse with plenty of ability as he continues to win races of this nature in spite of his jumping. Always tanking along under Andrew McNamara, he was novicey jumping the hurdles, although he performed a little better at a quicker tempo and there was not much wrong with his two jumps in the straight. Travelling to the front three out, he didn't do a huge amount and just about did enough on the run to the line to score. He left the impression that he had any amount in reserve. (op 6/4 tchd 11/8)
Pineau De Re(FR) came back to the sort of form he had shown before Christmas. Racing prominently, he was hard-ridden for a few strides to keep his place but he responded and kept throwing down a persistent challenge to the winner, who only beat him off after the final flight, albeit with some comfort. He should be able to find a winning opportunity in a novice hurdle in due course. (op 12/1 tchd 14/1)
Skorcher(IRE) exhibited that all he does is stay and he'll be well suited by 3m plus. Racing towards the back, he made a mistake four out and started to struggle with the pace. He kept staying on at the one pace and it was enough to get him past beaten horses. (op 12/1 tchd 14/1)
Bishopsfurze(IRE) paid his hurdles the usual disrespect and wasn't able to get away with it in this company. Even so, he was some way below his best. He didn't look like getting to the leaders three out and, though he started to run on early in the straight, it was a fairly short-lived effort. (op 13/8)
Crash(IRE) raced handily but when the pace began to quicken across the top of the track, he started to struggle and kept on at one pace. (op 9/1)
Smokey Joe Joe(IRE) Official explanation: jockey said gelding never travelled and was therefore pulled up

4320 - 4322a (Foreign Racing) - See Raceform Interactive

4192 SANDOWN (R-H)
Friday, February 25

OFFICIAL GOING: Soft (good to soft in places on chase course; heavy in places on hurdle course)
Wind: Virtually nil Weather: Overcast

4323 CLARICE BEAN CONDITIONAL JOCKEYS' H'CAP HURDLE (8 hdls) 2m 110y
1:45 (1:45) (Class 4) (0-115,115) 4-Y-0+ **£2,602** (£764; £382; £190)

Form RPR

4-05 **1** **Kadouchski (FR)**[54] 3343 7-10-3 **97**... PeterHatton(5) 99
(John Berry) *in rr: drvn and hdwy appr 2 out: kpt on to chse ldr sn after and j. slowly last: styd on dourly to ld fnl 30yds* **12/1**

44 **2** *3/4* **Qalinas (FR)**[15] 4029 4-10-13 **114**... CO'Farrell(3) 106+
(David Pipe) *slt ld tl hdd bef 2nd: styd trcking ldr: slt advantage again 3 out: travelling wl appr next: rdn: hung rt and hit rails after 2 out: tired run-in: hdd and no ex fnl 30yds* **5/2**[1]

2603 **3** 2½ **Posh Emily**[15] 4034 8-11-2 **105**................................(b) MattGriffiths 104
(Ron Hodges) *towards rr fr 3rd: rdn: hdwy and j. slowly 2 out: styd on and j. slowly last: kpt on wl clsng stages: nt rch ldng duo* **11/1**

3/52 **4** hd **Super Directa (GER)**[11] 4120 7-11-5 **114**.................. MattCrawley(6) 113
(Lucy Wadham) *chsd ldrs: wnt 2nd wl bef 2 out: sn rdn: lost 2nd sn after: outpcd and j. slowly last: styd on again fnl 50yds to press fr 3rd: nt quite rch ldng duo* **11/2**[3]

3-00 **5** 15 **First Avenue**[27] 3808 6-11-9 **115**.........................(p) JoshuaMoore(3) 101
(Gary Moore) *in rr: rdn and hdwy to chse ldrs appr 2 out: no further prog u.p and wknd sn after: no ch whn hit last* **20/1**

0011 **6** 14 **Shalambar (IRE)**[13] 4076 5-11-3 **109**........................ LeeEdwards(3) 78
(Tony Carroll) *chsd ldrs: rdn after 3 out: sn wknd* **15/2**

3UU4 **7** 4½ **High Hoylander**[17] 3987 5-11-4 **110**........................ ShaneByrne(3) 75
(Sue Smith) *pressed ldr tl led wl bef 3rd: mstke 4 out: narrowly hdd 3 out: wknd sn after* **11/1**

-5FF **8** 13 **Rajamand (FR)**[92] 2630 5-11-9 **112**...................... SamTwiston-Davies 63
(Warren Greatrex) *in rr: hdwy to chse ldrs hit 4 out: styd prom tl wknd qckly after 3 out* **11/4**[2]

6226 **U** **Perfect Reward**[27] 3818 7-11-2 **113**........................ JosephAkehurst(8) —
(Gary Moore) *in rr tl uns rdr 3rd* **33/1**

4m 14.45s (7.25) **Going Correction** +0.575s/f (Soft)
WFA 4 from 5yo+ 9lb **9** Ran SP% **114.4**
Speed ratings (Par 105): **105,104,103,103,96 89,87,81,—**
toteswingers:1&2 £52.30, 2&3 £4.40, 1&3 £31.60 CSF £42.95 CT £347.51 TOTE £16.90: £4.60, £1.20, £2.10; EX 72.80.
Owner John Berry **Bred** Henrietta Charlet & Danny Charlesworth **Trained** Newmarket, Suffolk

FOCUS
A modest conditionals handicap but fairly competitive according to official ratings. The ground was testing and sticky, and the runners finished very tired despite a steady gallop. The third is the best guide to the form.

NOTEBOOK
Kadouchski(FR), whose last success was over C&D back in December 2008, has not had much racing since but was 7lb lower than for that last win and the return to this track suited him, as he stayed on from the back to wear down the favourite after the last. He is well suited by soft ground and a right-handed track with an uphill finish, as his other success was at Leicester. Official explanation: trainer said regarding apparent improvement in form, gelding is physically small and was suited by the low weight. (op 16-1)
Qalinas(FR) ◆, was backed in to favourite and also supported at long prices for the Fred Winter earlier in the day. Making his handicap debut, he was always in the first two and looked sure to win turning for home. However, he got tired between the last two and could not respond when the winner challenged. He should have no difficulty winning races on better ground. (op 3-1 tchd 7-2)
Posh Emily, who had won her only previous start here, was another held up, then stayed on to grab third and was closing down the first two at the line. She gets further than this but really prefers good or easy ground. (op 12-1 tchd 10-1)
Super Directa(GER), who ran well in a three-horse race last time on his second start after a long absence, again did well and only just missed out on a place. He has races in him and still qualifies for novice handicaps. (op 13-2)
First Avenue, dropping in grade, looked a threat when making headway entering the home straight but was beaten before the last. (op 16-1)
Shalambar(IRE), bidding for a hat-trick, was another who looked unsuited by this ground as he was struggling from a long way out. Official explanation: trainers representative said gelding was unsuited by ground (soft - heavy in places) (op 6-1)
High Hoylander helped to make the running but was beaten turning for home. (op 14-1)
Rajamand(FR), the deposed favourite, was being ridden at the last on the far side and probably found the ground against him. He might also be better going the other way around. Official explanation: trainers said gelding was unsuited by ground (soft - heavy in places) (op 9-4 tchd 3-1)

4324 CHARLIE & LOLA H'CAP CHASE (13 fncs) 2m
2:20 (2:20) (Class 3) (0-130,129) 5-Y-0+ **£5,204** (£1,528; £764; £381)

Form RPR
5345 **1** **Russian Flag (FR)**[28] 3786 8-11-5 **125**........................ AlexMerriam(3) 135+
(Neil King) *in tch: hit 9th: j. slowly 4 out: gd hdwy sn after and chsd ldr fr 3 out: led after 2 out: drvn out run-in* **7/1**

0631 **2** 3¼ **Dinarius**[12] 4096 6-11-4 **121** 7ex........................(p) JimmyMcCarthy 130+
(Alex Hales) *kpt alone and led in s: in rr: hit 9th: hdwy and hit 3 out: styd on to chse wnr appr last: no imp run-in* **11/4**[2]

FP14 **3** 12 **Lord Singer (FR)**[15] 4033 6-11-5 **122**........................(b[1]) JamieMoore 118+
(Gary Moore) *slt ld tl wnt clr 3rd: rchd for 8th: rdn appr 3 out: hdd after 2 out: wknd and lost 2nd appr last: hld on for 3rd* **11/2**[3]

0-13 **4** 4½ **Clouseau (NZ)**[43] 3531 7-11-0 **117**........................ DarylJacob 106
(Nick Williams) *j. slowly 2nd: in rr: hdwy to cl on ldrs 5th: chsd ldr after 4 out: no imp: wknd after 3 out* **5/2**[1]

0420 **5** 1¼ **Viable**[41] 3573 9-10-10 **120**........................ MissGAndrews(7) 108
(Pam Sly) *in rr drvn along fr 4 out: sme prog fr 3 out: styd on u.p run-in but nvr anywhere nr ldrs* **16/1**

304- **6** 20 **Lorient Express (FR)**[370] 4157 12-11-12 **129**................ SamThomas 97
(Venetia Williams) *chsd ldrs: hit 6th: sn btn* **16/1**

311F **7** 2 **Kilkenny All Star (IRE)**[41] 3573 10-11-0 **122**.............. ShaneByrne(5) 88
(Sue Smith) *blnd 1st: virtually t.o 4 out: mod prog fr 2 out* **7/1**

2-00 **8** 1¼ **Top Mark**[41] 3557 9-11-7 **124**........................(b[1]) WayneHutchinson 89
(Alan King) *w ldr tl after 2nd: styd 2nd tl after 4 out: wknd wl bef next* **22/1**

4m 7.11s (5.31) **Going Correction** +0.45s/f (Soft) **8** Ran SP% **111.7**
Speed ratings: **104,102,96,94,93 83,82,81**
toteswingers:1&2 £4.20, 2&3 £3.20, 1&3 £10.30 CSF £26.31 CT £111.65 TOTE £9.90: £2.60, £1.30, £1.80; EX 30.70.
Owner The Drovers & Drifters **Bred** Bernard Le Roux **Trained** Newmarket, Suffolk

FOCUS
A good, competitive handicap chase, and the two horses wearing blinkers for the first time set off at a rate of knots. The going was faster on the chase course and they finished nowhere near as tired as they had in the opening hurdle. The winner is rated to last season's course success with the second close to his previous mark.

NOTEBOOK
Russian Flag(FR), who goes well on soft ground and won on his only previous visit here, had not scored in the year since and had dropped back to 3lb below his last winning mark. He looked to be struggling at the last on the far side but began to run on once meeting the rising ground, and stayed on all the way to the line for a comfortable success. He gets further than this so has plenty of options. (op 8-1)
Dinarius is a little bit quirky but has taken well to fences when making the running. However, with several other front-runners in opposition, connections reverted to hold-up tactics and he stayed on well up the hill without making much impression on the winner. He is clearly in good heart and will face easier tasks. (tchd 5-2, 3-1 in a place)
Lord Singer(FR), wearing blinkers for the first time, set off at a good gallop and soon established a clear lead. He was still in front after the Pond Fence but was then brushed aside, although he did keep on fairly well for third. (op 10-1)
Clouseau(NZ), who won on his chasing debut on good ground, went in pursuit of the clear leader at the end of the back straight and looked set to figure in the finish, but the combination of the rising ground and soft going appeared to find him out. He should be suited by better ground and a sharper tracks this spring. (op 9-4 tchd 11-4 in a place)
Viable is another whose best form has been on flat tracks and good ground, although he did keep on from the back.

4325 RICHARD O'SULLIVAN 40TH BIRTHDAY "NATIONAL HUNT" NOVICES' HURDLE (8 hdls) 2m 110y
2:50 (2:51) (Class 4) 4-Y-0+ **£2,602** (£764; £382; £190)

Form RPR
1 **1** **Hildisvini (IRE)**[29] 3773 5-11-2 0........................ FelixDeGiles 121+
(Charlie Longsdon) *in tch: hdwy to take 3rd after 3 out: slt ld 2 out: sn rdn: styd on to assert over hand-rdn 2nd run-in* **17/2**[3]

3-13 **2** 2½ **Kid Cassidy (IRE)**[58] 3196 5-11-9 139........................ APMcCoy 126+
(Nicky Henderson) *ear plugs: ponied to s: led: narrowly hdd 2 out: stl upsides last: coaxed along under hand-riding run-in: fnd no ex and readily hld fnl 100yds* **8/11**[1]

11 **3** 12 **Shuil Royale (IRE)**[22] 3909 6-11-2 0........................ DarylJacob 108+
(David Arbuthnot) *chsd ldrs: wnt 2nd and hit 4 out: lost 3rd after 3 out: wknd 2 out* **7/4**[2]

45 **4** 37 **Brannoc (IRE)**[112] 2186 6-11-2 0........................ AndrewThornton 89
(Tony Newcombe) *trckd ldr: hit 2nd: blnd and lost 2nd 4th: wknd after 3 out: blnd 2 out* **66/1**

0-00 **5** 16 **Royal Mile (IRE)**[19] 3960 7-11-2 0........................ WayneHutchinson 53
(Warren Greatrex) *t.k.h early: a in rr* **66/1**

06 **6** 21 **Ronnie Ronalde (IRE)**[36] 3647 6-11-2 0........................ HarrySkelton 41
(Nick Mitchell) *j. slowly 1st and 2nd: nvr jumping w much fluency after and a wl bhd* **66/1**

4m 13.14s (5.94) **Going Correction** +0.575s/f (Soft) **6** Ran SP% **109.3**
Speed ratings (Par 105): **109,107,102,84,77 67**
toteswingers:1&2 £1.70, 2&3 £1.02, 1&3 £1.30 CSF £15.23 TOTE £8.50: £2.40, £1.10; EX 20.60.
Owner J H & S M Wall **Bred** Sean Wickham **Trained** Over Norton, Oxon

FOCUS
An interesting novices' hurdle with half the field making their hurdling debuts, but only three counted. The time was only slightly faster than the opening contest with the race producing something of an upset. The winner is rated an improver with the second and third below previous marks.

NOTEBOOK
Hildisvini(IRE) ◆ had progressed in bumpers, winning on his debut for new connections last time. Held up early, he came to take the advantage from the favourite going to the second last and stayed on well for pressure. He jumped well on this debut, has a decent attitude and looks quite useful, especially as he will stay further. (op 10-1 tchd 11-1)
Kid Cassidy(IRE), who was caught up in the incident at Newbury when two horses were electrocuted in the paddock, being distressed when withdrawn at the start, was reluctant to go out this time and was ponied quietly to the post. Fitted with earplugs, he made the running and still appeared to be going well when headed by the winner two out, but failed to pick up when eventually asked, carrying himself awkwardly. His rider was not hard on him in the closing stages, and we will hopefully see better from him on faster ground. Official explanation: jockey said gelding hung left (op 4-5 tchd 10-11 in a place and 5-6 in a place)
Shuil Royale(IRE), an older half-brother of the favourite, came here off the back of two bumper successes and tracked the leaders throughout. However, he failed to pick up under pressure from the home turn. (op 13-8 tchd 15-8)
Royal Mile(IRE) Official explanation: jockey said gelding was unsuited by ground (soft - heavy in places)

4326 CARLING "MADE WITH 100% BRITISH BARLEY" NOVICES' CHASE (13 fncs) 2m
3:25 (3:25) (Class 2) 5-Y-0+ **£7,827** (£2,312; £1,156)

Form RPR
/1F1 **1** **Giorgio Quercus (FR)**[31] 3722 6-11-3 0........................ BarryGeraghty 148+
(Nicky Henderson) *racd in 2nd: hit 4 out: rdn after 3 out: styd on u.p to chal fnl 120yds: carried persistently rt: jst failed: fin 2nd: plcd 1st* **11/4**[3]

-021 **2** shd **Dan Breen (IRE)**[72] 2951 6-11-3 0........................ TomScudamore 148+
(David Pipe) *mde virtually all: hit 4 out: hrd rdn and hung rt fnl 120yds: hld on all out: fin 1st: plcd 2nd* **15/8**[2]

P112 **3** 16 **Pepe Simo (IRE)**[41] 3555 7-11-3 143........................ SamThomas 135
(Paul Nicholls) *racd in 3rd: rdn along 7th: hit 4 out and wl there: rdn appr 3 out: wknd sn after* **5/4**[1]

4m 3.87s (2.07) **Going Correction** +0.45s/f (Soft) **3** Ran SP% **105.9**
Speed ratings: **111,112,103**
CSF £7.39 TOTE £2.90; EX 6.60.
Owner Sir Robert Ogden **Bred** Daniel Chassagneux Et Al **Trained** Upper Lambourn, Berks
■ Stewards' Enquiry : Barry Geraghty one-day ban; excessive use of whip (11th March)
Tom Scudamore three-day ban; careless riding (11th-13th March)

FOCUS
A good novices' chase, despite the small field, and it produced a desperate finish, and the result was amended by the stewards. The first two look smart novices.

NOTEBOOK
Giorgio Quercus(FR), all of whose four previous successes had been on right-handed tracks (the only occasions he had raced that way around) tracked the leader throughout, although he raced wide of the other pair down the back straight. He came to challenge after the last and got closer and closer, despite being carried right across the track. The Stewards had little choice but to amend the result, allowing him to maintain his record. In view of that preference, it would be no surprise if he returned here for the Imperial Cup meeting rather than go to Cheltenham. (tchd 3-1)
Dan Breen(IRE) made the running and jumped well. He looked to be in charge until tiring after the last. He went left away from the whip, but when his jockey switched the stick he went right, carrying his rival right across to the inside rail. He just held on in the photo but unsurprisingly lost the race in the Stewards' room, earning his rider a three-day ban. His best form has been on flat tracks, so Aintree or Ayr might offer him better opportunities than Cheltenham, where he is entered in both the Arkle and Grand Annual. (tchd 7-4)
Pepe Simo(IRE) was held up but it was clear at the end of the back straight that he was struggling, and he was soon beaten after being rather cut off going to the Pond Fence. He probably needs better ground than this. (op 11-8 tchd 6-5, 13-8 in a place)

4327 DAVID LINDON & CO H'CAP HURDLE (9 hdls) 2m 4f
4:00 (4:00) (Class 3) (0-120,124) 4-Y-0+ **£3,903** (£1,146; £573; £286)

Form RPR
3520 **1** **Aviador (GER)**[33] 3696 5-11-3 **108**........................ RichardJohnson 116+
(Lucy Wadham) *trckd ldrs: chal fr 5th tl led 3 out: rdn next: styd on wl u.p to go clr run-in* **14/1**

/5-2 **2** 7 **China Gold**[44] 3509 8-11-10 **115**........................ WayneHutchinson 117
(Alan King) *in tch: trckd ldrs fr 4 out: hit 2 out and hung rt whn chsng wnr sn after: hit last: one pce run-in* **13/2**[3]

3151 **3** ½ **Prince Du Seuil (FR)**[11] 4121 8-11-12 **124** 7ex................ PeterHatton(7) 126
(Alan King) *hld up in rr: gd hdwy appr 2 out: rdn and styng on whn hit last: kpt on again run-in and tk 3rd cl home: no ch w wnr* **5/1**[2]

4223 **4** ¾ **Royale's Charter**[20] 3950 5-11-6 **111**.................................... DarylJacob 112
(Nick Williams) *trckd ldrs: chsd wnr travelling wl whn hit 2 out: sn lost 2nd: one pce whn hit last: lost 3rd cl home* **9/2**[1]

-003 **5** 14 **Manele Bay**[23] 3881 8-11-5 **110**.................................... AndrewThornton 96
(Richard Rowe) *led tl appr 4th: wknd appr 2 out* **15/2**

0F35 **6** 2¾ **Dot's Delight**[7] 3962 7-11-0 **105**.................................... JasonMaguire 88
(Mark Rimell) *in tch: chsd ldrs 3 out: wknd fr 2 out* **25/1**

1230 **7** 2¼ **Lemon Silk (IRE)**[33] 3693 7-10-11 **102**................................. TomO'Brien 83
(Alex Hales) *in rr: rdn and hdwy appr 2 out: nvr on terms and wknd sn after* **7/1**

-321 **8** 2 **Laborec (IRE)**[45] 3493 8-11-9 **114**.................................(p) MarkBradburne 94
(Neil King) *in tch: rdn 5th: wknd fr 2 out* **16/1**

4231 **9** 34 **Jordan**[10] 4130 8-9-12 **96** 7ex.................................... MrTJCannon(7) 41
(Suzy Smith) *in tch: hdwy fr 4th: wknd u.p appr 2 out* **7/1**

4U4P **10** 4 **Festival Dreams**[27] 3819 6-10-4 **95**.................................(p) DaveCrosse 36
(Joanna Davis) *chsd ldrs: led appr 4th: jnd fr 5th tl hdd 3 out: wknd bef next* **33/1**

12F3 **11** 10 **Red Rouble (IRE)**[45] 3494 6-11-6 **111**............................. PaddyBrennan 42
(Nigel Twiston-Davies) *chsd ldrs to 3 out* **12/1**

040P **P** **Giovanna**[21] 3934 10-11-5 **110**.................................(t) WarrenMarston —
(Richard Phillips) *hit 3rd: rdn in rr and nvr gng after: t.o whn p.u bef 2 out* **66/1**

400 **P** **Alhaque (USA)**[41] 3557 5-11-7 **112**.................................(v[1]) JamieMoore —
(Gary Moore) *in rr: sme hdwy 4th: sn wknd: t.o whn p.u bef last* **50/1**

5m 18.66s (12.96) **Going Correction** +0.575s/f (Soft) **13** Ran SP% **115.4**
Speed ratings (Par 107): **97,94,94,93,88 87,86,85,71,70 66,—,—**
toteswingers:1&2 £21.80, 2&3 £5.80, 1&3 £41.40 CSF £97.36 CT £524.73 TOTE £19.40: £5.60, £2.30, £1.50; EX 112.80.
Owner Richard S Keeley **Bred** Gestut Am Schlossgarten **Trained** Newmarket, Suffolk

FOCUS
Plenty in this good-sized field looked to have chances in this handicap hurdle, but in the end four came clear. The runner-up and fourth help set the level.

NOTEBOOK
Aviador(GER) ◆ goes well on soft ground and appreciated the step up in trip to get off the mark over hurdles. Always in the first three, he went on going to the last on the far side, but looked under severe threat from three apparently travelling better turning in. However, he kept up the gallop in fine style and, by the last flight, had the race in the bag. He looks sure to stay further and should win more races given a suitable stamina test on soft ground. Official explanation: trainer said regarding apparent improvement in form gelding was suited by a step up in trip (op 16-1 tchd 12-1)
China Gold, the stable-preferred judged on jockey bookings, was held up before creeping into contention on the home turn. He had his chance, but the winner galloped on too strongly and he was always being held. He probably needs better ground at this trip. (op 11-2 tchd 5-1)
Prince Du Seuil(FR), carrying a penalty for his recent success, followed his stable companion into contention, seemingly going just as well. However, once in line for home he could only keep on at the one pace. (op 4-1)
Royale's Charter tracked the leaders throughout and appeared to be going as well as any turning in. However, once hitting the rising ground he soon came under pressure and had nothing in reserve. A return to 2m, better ground and cheekpieces might help him get off the mark. (op 4-1 tchd 5-1)
Manele Bay made the running but looked well beaten at the end of the back straight. However, on ground that suits, she rallied over the last two and might be worth another try over further. (op 9-1)
Dot's Delight closed on the leaders looking likely to take a hand turning in, but was in trouble before the penultimate flight.
Lemon Silk(IRE), another to close on the leaders looking likely to take a hand turning in, was also in trouble before the penultimate flight. (op 8-1)

4328 FARM FRITES H'CAP CHASE (22 fncs) 3m 110y
4:35 (4:35) (Class 3) (0-125,124) 5-Y-O+ **£4,553** (£1,337; £668; £333)

Form RPR

002P **1** **Dashing George (IRE)**[7] 4193 9-11-7 **119**.......................(b) JamieMoore 132+
(Dr Richard Newland) *chsd ldrs: chal fr 9th tl led 11th: jnd 3 out: rdn and styd on strly fr next* **10/1**

PF05 **2** 4½ **Leac An Scail (IRE)**[21] 3922 10-10-11 **114**...................... ShaneByrne(5) 122
(Sue Smith) *chsd ldrs: hit 12th: chsd wnr 4 out: chal 3 out: sn outpcd u.p* **33/1**

0530 **3** 10 **Theatre Dance (IRE)**[20] 3940 10-11-7 **119**...................... JasonMaguire 117
(David Arbuthnot) *in rr: reminders after 4th: hit 12th: styd on fr 4 out: kpt on run-in to take 3rd clsng stages but no ch w ldng duo* **9/2**[1]

0FP2 **4** nk **Drybrook Bedouin**[22] 3907 9-10-12 **117**...................... SClements(7) 113
(Nick Mitchell) *in rr: drvn and styd on fr 4 out: tk 4th cl home: nvr any ch w ldng duo* **12/1**

3001 **5** ¾ **Antonius Caesar (FR)**[31] 3723 8-10-1 **106**.................... PeterCarberry(7) 102
(Alex Hales) *led: jnd 9th: hdd 11th: styd chsng wnr to 4 out: wknd 3 out but kpt 3rd tl lost 2 pls cl home* **9/2**[1]

2P02 **6** 10 **River Indus**[36] 3646 11-10-1 **104** ow1.............................. JoshuaMoore(5) 91
(Bob Buckler) *chsd ldrs to 15th* **9/1**

-115 **7** 22 **Diamond Brook (IRE)**[27] 3803 6-11-9 **121**.......................... DarylJacob 94
(Nick Williams) *hit 4th: in tch to 16th* **13/2**[2]

001 **P** **Only Vintage (USA)**[73] 2948 11-11-12 **124**...................... RichardJohnson —
(Paul Henderson) *j. slowly 1st and 5th: in rr: hit 10th: hdwy 13th: hit 18th: sn wknd: t.o whn p.u bef 2 out* **15/2**[3]

2-61 **P** **Royal Wedding**[19] 3963 9-11-7 **119**.............................. LiamTreadwell —
(Nick Gifford) *in rr: hdwy 12th: wknd 17th: t.o whn p.u bef 3 out* **12/1**

-602 **P** **Moleskin (IRE)**[41] 3562 8-11-5 **117**.................................(p) DenisO'Regan —
(Victor Dartnall) *in tch tl rdn and dropped in rr after 11th: t.o whn p.u bef 16th* **9/2**[1]

6m 34.48s (6.68) **Going Correction** +0.45s/f (Soft) **10** Ran SP% **117.1**
Speed ratings: **107,105,102,102,102 98,91,—,—,—**
toteswingers:1&2 £19.90, 2&3 £13.60, 1&3 £3.40 CSF £242.82 CT £1689.75 TOTE £14.10: £3.40, £8.80, £1.30; EX 227.80.
Owner D & D Coatings Ltd **Bred** Miss Irene Hatton **Trained** Claines, Worcs
■ Stewards' Enquiry : Shane Byrne one-day ban; used whip with excessive frequency (11th March)

FOCUS
Another race in which plenty looked to have chances judged on official ratings, but they appeared to go a good gallop and the first two had the rest in trouble leaving the back straight. The runner-up to his mark is the best guide to the form.

NOTEBOOK
Dashing George(IRE), who disappointed over C&D the week before, was ridden much more positively and responded with a battling performance. Well suited by the ground, he jumped well and came away from his main rival from two out. He could run in either the Topham or the Bet365 Gold Cup back here if he gets a reasonable weight. (op 14-1)
Leac An Scail(IRE) has gained all his wins on a sound surface but handles soft and ran well. Racing off 4lb below his last winning mark, he kept responding to pressure but the winner proved too strong. He looks handicapped to win again before long.
Theatre Dance(IRE) was slightly slowly away and did not help his chance with a couple of moderate early jumps. His rider was chasing him along going out on the second circuit, but he kept responding and stayed on for the minor placing. (op 5-1 tchd 4-1)
Drybrook Bedouin, an ex-hunter chaser, was another who was out the back and struggling at halfway before staying on. His form suggests better ground in the spring will be in his favour. (op 11-1 tchd 14-1)
Antonius Caesar(FR) who won under a positive ride last time, adopted the tactics again but was taken on by the winner and gave best after a lap. He remained in contention until fading up the hill. (op 6-1)
River Indus usually goes well here but prefers better ground. (op 10-1)
Diamond Brook(IRE) has been in decent form but appeared not to get home over this longer trip in the ground. (op 11-2)
Only Vintage(USA) was held up early before making ground down the far side second time. However, the effort petered out crossing the Railway Fences. (tchd 5-1)
Moleskin(IRE) ran well in first-time cheekpieces last time and travelled reasonably for a circuit. However, he appeared to down tools going out on the second lap. Official explanation: vets said gelding was found to be distressed post race (tchd 5-1)

4329 HAMPTON COURT STANDARD OPEN NATIONAL HUNT FLAT RACE 2m 110y
5:05 (5:08) (Class 5) 4-6-Y-O **£1,626** (£477; £238; £119)

Form RPR

1 **Make A Track (IRE)** 5-11-2 0.. DarylJacob 109+
(David Arbuthnot) *trckd ldrs: led ins fnl 2f: drvn clr 1f out: styd on strly* **7/2**[2]

2 6 **Ambion Wood (IRE)** 5-11-2 0.. DenisO'Regan 102
(Victor Dartnall) *in rr but in tch: hdwy over 2f out: styd on to chse wnr ins fnl f: nvr any ch* **8/1**

3 2¼ **Willow's Saviour** 4-10-7 0.. FelixDeGiles 91
(Charlie Longsdon) *hld up in rr but in tch: hdwy over 3f out: chsng ldrs whn n.m.r and swtchd lft over 2f out: styd on same pce* **33/1**

1 **4** 4½ **Ballytober**[29] 3766 5-11-9 0.. RichardJohnson 104
(Philip Hobbs) *chsd ldr tl led over 3f out: rdn and hdd ins fnl 2f: sn no ch w wnr: wknd into 4th fnl f* **2/1**[1]

4P **5** 11 **Ice 'N' Easy (IRE)**[49] 3434 5-11-2 0.............................. AndrewThornton 84
(Richard Rowe) *t.k.h: chsd ldrs over 10f* **50/1**

6 shd **Univoque (FR)** 4-10-7 0.. WayneHutchinson 75
(Alan King) *chsd ldrs tl wknd qckly over 3f out* **7/2**[2]

7 97 **Clever Dick (IRE)** 5-11-2 0.. JasonMaguire —
(Warren Greatrex) *led tl hdd & wknd qckly over 3f out* **9/2**[3]

4m 14.34s (8.24) **Going Correction** +0.575s/f (Soft)
WFA 4 from 5yo 9lb **7** Ran SP% **112.0**
Speed ratings: **103,100,99,97,91 91,46**
toteswingers:1&2 £10.10, 2&3 £18.20, 1&3 £18.20. totesuper7: Win: Not won. Place: £706.30. CSF £29.49 TOTE £6.10: £2.30, £3.50; EX 20.30.
Owner George Ward **Bred** Limetree Stud Ltd **Trained** Compton, Berks

FOCUS
This bumper has thrown up some decent performers, including Lord Sam, Royal Paradise and Cockney Trucker, but in the end was dominated by newcomers. The fourth and fifth help to set the level.

NOTEBOOK
Make A Track(IRE) ◆, a half-brother to a bumper and hurdles winner from the family of Make A Stand, was well backed and duly rewarded that support with an emphatic success. He made headway in the second half of the race and, when he went on from the favourite 2f out, soon had matters under control. He looks quite useful. (op 7-1)
Ambion Wood(IRE) ◆, the son of a bumper winner and half-brother to a hurdles and chase winner, showed signs of inexperience but also plenty of promise, staying on from the back in the straight. He can win a similar race, but should make a hurdler in time. (op 7-1)
Willow's Saviour is related to a couple of point winners but ran better than expected on this debut, getting involved in the straight. He ran green under pressure and should be wiser for the experience.
Ballytober, the winner of an Irish point before taking a bumper on his debut for connections, was never far away and kicked on early in the straight to make use of his stamina. However, he could only find the one pace when challenged and might have found this ground softer than ideal. Presumably he will switch to hurdles sooner rather than later. (op 7-4 tchd 9-4, 5-2 in a place)
Univoque(FR) was supported on this debuts but was left behind in the straight. (tchd 3-1)
Clever Dick(IRE), another supported on this debuts was keen early and dropped right away from the home turn. (op 4-1 tchd 5-1)
T/Jkpt: Not won. T/Plt: £466.10 to a £1 stake. Pool of £77,673.10 - 121.65 winning tickets. T/Qpdt: £57.40 to a £1 stake. Pool of £5,298.02 - 68.20 winning tickets. ST

4076 WARWICK (L-H)
Friday, February 25

OFFICIAL GOING: Heavy (soft in places)
Wind: Almost nil Weather: Mild, cloudy

4330 STAR SPORTS THE GENTLEMAN'S BOOKMAKER "HANDS AND HEELS" H'CAP HURDLE (CONDITIONALS/AMATEURS) (8 hdls) 2m
2:10 (2:10) (Class 4) (0-105,105) 4-Y-O+ **£2,602** (£764; £382; £190)

Form RPR

3310 **1** **Dormouse**[33] 3696 6-11-9 **105**...(p) MrOJMurphy(3) 107+
(Anabel L M King) *hld up in rr: hdwy 3 out: led last: wnt 3 l clr: pushed out: jst hld on* **13/2**[3]

3344 **2** nk **Monsieur (FR)**[12] 4104 11-10-6 **85**.................................. NathanSweeney 85
(Carroll Gray) *t.k.h: chsd ldrs: outpcd and lost pl 4th: rallied and r.o wl run-in: clsng fast at fin: jst hld* **10/1**

0-33 **3** 2 **Chicklemix**[39] 3599 5-11-1 **99**... MrTBellamy(5) 97
(Pam Sly) *mid-div: hdwy 5th: rdn to chal on inner after 3 out: one pce appr last* **10/1**

4000 **4** 3¼ **Watch Out**[21] 3934 7-10-12 **94**.......................................(tp) MrMGNolan(3) 91+
(Dai Burchell) *chsd ldrs: led 5th tl last: no ex* **28/1**

0-00 **5** 4½ **Gainsborough's Art (IRE)**[255] 757 6-9-9 **79** oh3.......... KillianMoore(5) 69
(Harry Chisman) *t.k.h: in tch: stdd towards rr 3rd: rdn after 4th: sme late hdwy* **50/1**

400F **6** ¾ **Original Prankster (IRE)**[14] 4052 6-11-4 **100**.... MrWTwiston-Davies(3) 91
(Nigel Twiston-Davies) *sn towards rr: rdn along appr 3rd: hdwy next: wknd appr 2 out* **5/1**[2]

-405 **7** 5 **Nous Voila (FR)**[7] 4178 10-10-9 **88**................................... TrevorWhelan 73
(Alan Coogan) *led 2nd tl 5th: wknd 2 out* **18/1**

P003 **8** 3¼ **Like Ice**[39] 3610 6-11-3 **99**.. MrCGreene(3) 80
(Philip Middleton) *mid-div: effrt 3 out: rdn and no imp next* **14/1**

3563 **9** *1 1/2* **Reg's Ruby**[12] 4104 5-10-12 **94** MrSWDrinkwater(3) 74
(David Bridgwater) *prom tl nt fluent and wknd 3 out* **12/1**

4-20 **10** *nk* **Mossmann Gorge**[194] 1261 9-11-0 **96** MrTGarner(3) 75
(Anthony Middleton) *bhd on outer: mstke and rdn 5th: struggling after* **33/1**

-462 **11** *5* **Azione**[27] 3822 8-10-5 **84** AodhaganConlon 58
(Pat Murphy) *led: blnd 1st: hdd next: blnd and lost pl 5th* **9/2**[1]

0-36 **12** *8* **James Pollard (IRE)**[15] 4031 6-11-7 **103** (t) MrRJWilliams(3) 69
(Bernard Llewellyn) *t.k.h towards rr: hdwy and prom 1/2-way: wknd 3 out* **11/1**

000 **13** *32* **Saute**[24] 3866 5-11-0 **96** AshleyBird(3) 30
(Jim Best) *in tch tl 4th: sn wknd* **14/1**

056 **14** *11* **First Spirit**[38] 3620 5-10-8 **90** ChristopherWard(3) 13
(Robin Dickin) *prom on outer: rdn 1/2-way: sn wknd* **20/1**

0P-P **P** **Firedog (IRE)**[271] 539 7-10-5 **89** MrGHMBartlett(5) —
(Venetia Williams) *mid-div: wknd 4th: t.o whn p.u bef 3 out* **16/1**

4m 1.60s (5.10) **Going Correction** +0.25s/f (Yiel) **15** Ran SP% **120.0**
Speed ratings (Par 105): **97,96,95,94,91 91,89,87,86,86 84,80,64,58,—**
toteswingers:1&2 £9.60, 2&3 £4.20, 1&3 £22.50 CSF £66.81 CT £653.99 TOTE £5.60: £2.10, £3.40, £3.80; EX 73.20.
Owner Aiden Murphy **Bred** Deerfield Farm **Trained** Wilmcote, Warwicks

FOCUS
The ground was very testing and they went a good pace in this modest hands and heels handicap. The placed horses were rated to their marks.

NOTEBOOK
Dormouse, 5lb higher than for his Leicester success two outings previously, is only small but is proven in bad ground. Improved since being fitted with cheekpieces, he came from almost last to show ahead at the final flight. About four lengths clear on the run-in, this moody individual put the brakes on near the line and the post came just in time. Official explanation: trainer said regarding apparent improvement gelding was unsuited by making the running last time out (op 17-2 tchd 6-1)
Monsieur(FR), 6lb higher than for his fortuitous success at Bangor in November, has finished in the frame in all four starts since. He flew up the run-in and almost mugged the idling winner. (op 12-1)
Chicklemix, a soft-ground bumper winner, was making her handicap bow on just her third start over hurdles and turned in easily her best effort so far. (op 8-1)
Watch Out, who has been tried over fences since his last success at Huntingdon a year ago, came there full of running but emptied badly on the run-in. (op 33-1)
Gainsborough's Art(IRE), whose sole success was two years ago, was having his first start for this yard on his first outing since June. Out of the weights, he appeared very late on the scene. (op 66-1)
Original Prankster(IRE), who might well have finished second but for falling two out on his handicap bow at Kempton, was down in trip and was being driven along at an early stage. (op 4-1)
Azione, having her first start for a yard on the cold list, was in front when she almost lost her rider at the very first flight. She soon lost the advantage and seemed to give up. (op 11-2 tchd 7-2)
Firedog(IRE) Official explanation: vet said gelding had an irregular heart beat

4331 WHITSON BLOODSTOCK LTD JUVENILE HURDLE (8 hdls) 2m
2:40 (2:41) (Class 4) 4-Y-O **£2,602** (£764; £382; £190)

Form RPR

133 **1** **Pepite Rose (FR)**[28] 3789 4-10-12 118 AidanColeman 109
(Venetia Williams) *trckd ldrs: led on bit 2 out: drvn along run-in: a jst holding runner-up* **85/40**[2]

5251 **2** *shd* **Dhaafer**[29] 3767 4-11-5 119 RobertThornton 116
(Alan King) *w ldrs: led 4th: rdn and hdd 2 out: rallied wl run-in: a jst hld* **5/6**[1]

1100 **3** *26* **Zakeeta (IRE)**[53] 3374 4-11-5 116 (p) LeightonAspell 90
(Oliver Sherwood) *led tl 4th: hrd rdn and wknd appr 2 out* **20/1**

00 **4** *6* **Zambuka (FR)**[14] 3443 4-10-2 0 (t) MichaelMurphy(3) 70
(Pat Murphy) *plld hrd and bhd: promising hdwy and in tch 5th: rdn and wknd appr 2 out* **66/1**

5 *4 1/2* **Rock The Stars (IRE)**[114] 4-10-12 0 JoeTizzard 72
(Colin Tizzard) *plld hrd: in tch tl nt fluent and wknd 5th: 5th and btn whn j. slowly 3 out* **5/1**[3]

6 **6** *61* **Royal Patriot (IRE)**[21] 3917 4-10-12 0 AlanO'Keeffe 11
(Paul Green) *plld hrd and bhd: blnd 3rd: mstke 4th: no ch after* **250/1**

00 **P** **The De Thaix (FR)**[37] 3630 4-10-12 0 CharliePoste —
(Robin Dickin) *in tch: hdwy to join ldrs 3rd: rdn and wknd next: t.o whn p.u bef 2 out* **100/1**

3m 57.6s (1.10) **Going Correction** +0.25s/f (Yiel) **7** Ran SP% **110.9**
Speed ratings: **107,106,93,90,88 58,—**
toteswingers:1&2 £1.10, 2&3 £3.70, 1&3 £3.10 CSF £4.16 TOTE £3.50: £1.80, £1.10; EX 5.00.
Owner Potensis Limited **Bred** Pegasus Breeding Ltd **Trained** Kings Caple, H'fords

FOCUS
An interesting juvenile hurdle, but the pace was very steady to halfway. The first two are rated pretty much to their marks.

NOTEBOOK
Pepite Rose(FR), who had four outings over hurdles in France, had finished a length ahead of Dhaafer on her second start here (after a comfortable Folkestone success) when they were third and fifth respectively at Huntingdon. She then finished a respectable third against older novices at Fontwell next time. Meeting Dhaafer on 7lb better terms, she travelled best and it looked plain sailing when she jumped the last a couple of lengths ahead without having been asked a question. At the line, though, it was a close-run thing. She clearly handles testing conditions extremely well. (op 15-8 tchd 5-2)
Dhaafer, a ready winner over this C&D since Huntingdon, lacks scope. He is on the up, however, and after going on and stepping up the pace he rallied on the run-in and was just denied. He will go up about 6lb as a result of this and connections will no doubt be viewing the Fred Winter. (op 10-11 tchd 8-11)
Zakeeta(IRE), who misbehaved before running poorly at Lingfield, was led around at the start in first-time cheekpieces. Under a double penalty after two victories at Fontwell in October, she was nowhere near good enough to match the first two from three out. Her rating of 116 flatters her. (op 16-1 tchd 22-1)
Zambuka(FR), rated just 57 on the Flat, was having her third start. She was very keen in the early stages. Official explanation: vet said filly lost near fore shoe (op 100-1)
Rock The Stars(IRE), twice a winner over a mile on the Flat at three, was another who wouldn't settle in the early stages due to the very steady pace. He stopped to nothing three out and has stamina to prove now. (op 7-1)

4332 EBF STARSPORTSBET.CO.UK "NATIONAL HUNT" NOVICES' HURDLE (QUALIFIER) (9 hdls) 2m 3f
3:15 (3:15) (Class 4) 4-7-Y-O **£2,927** (£859; £429; £214)

Form RPR

415 **1** **Upthemsteps (IRE)**[21] 3930 6-11-8 0 DougieCostello 119
(Ian Williams) *prom: led 3rd tl next: led 5th tl sltly outpcd appr 2 out: rallied to ld nr fin* **11/2**[3]

4351 **2** *1/2* **Tricky Tree (IRE)**[15] 4025 5-11-5 122 CPGeoghegan(3) 118
(Pam Sly) *prom: led appr 2 out: hrd rdn and kpt on run-in: hdd nr fin* **11/4**[2]

-422 **3** *3 1/4* **Basford Bob (IRE)**[28] 3787 6-11-2 118 AlanO'Keeffe 110+
(Jennie Candlish) *t.k.h in rr: smooth hdwy 6th: chal 3 out: rdn and one pce fr next* **11/8**[1]

024 **4** *3* **Bardolf (IRE)**[55] 3301 5-11-2 0 RobertThornton 107
(Alan King) *hld up in handy 4th: chal on bit 3 out: rdn appr next: wknd appr last* **10/1**

025 **5** *26* **Saint Denis (FR)**[24] 3866 5-11-2 0 WillKennedy 80
(Alex Hales) *towards rr: rdn 5th: sn struggling* **14/1**

3-00 **6** *31* **Well Refreshed**[12] 4091 7-11-2 0 LeightonAspell 65
(Peter Winkworth) *led tl 3rd: led 4th tl next: wknd 3 out* **40/1**

106 **7** *62* **The Merry Giant (IRE)**[13] 4069 5-10-13 0 RichieMcLernon(3) —
(Rebecca Curtis) *towards rr: rdn and losing tch whn mstke 5th: sn t.o* **40/1**

0 **P** **Opera Og (IRE)**[56] 3252 5-11-2 0 AidanColeman —
(Venetia Williams) *in tch: wknd 6th: t.o whn p.u after 2 out* **8/1**

4m 50.0s (7.30) **Going Correction** +0.25s/f (Yiel) **8** Ran SP% **115.9**
Speed ratings: **94,93,92,91,80 67,41,—**
toteswingers:1&2 £3.40, 2&3 £2.40, 1&3 £2.80 CSF £21.88 TOTE £5.80: £1.40, £1.10, £1.40; EX 21.20.
Owner The Ferandlin Peaches **Bred** Pat Coffey **Trained** Portway, Worcs

FOCUS
A decent novices' hurdle, but the pace was very steady to past halfway and four were in a line two out. The runner-up is rated to his mark with the fourth close to his bumper form.

NOTEBOOK
Upthemsteps(IRE), winner of an Irish maiden point, took a maiden hurdle at Towcester in December on his hurdling bow. He didn't reproduce that effort at Chepstow next time, but bounced back here with a very plucky effort. He will make a chaser in time. (op 7-1)
Tricky Tree(IRE), hoisted 17lb after his facile win in handicap company at Huntingdon, looked to be travelling marginally best when going on two out, but after a real set-to he came off second best at the line. He deserves plenty of credit for this. (op 3-1 tchd 7-2)
Basford Bob(IRE), keen to post, proved difficult to settle. Caught flat-footed between the last two, he stuck on in his own time on the run-in. A more truly-run race and less testing conditions should see this long-term chasing prospect find a race. (op Evens tchd 10-11)
Bardolf(IRE), a slow learner in three starts in bumpers, was up in trip on his hurdling bow. He looked a real threat turning in, but faded on the run-in. He is sure to find a maiden hurdle in due course. Official explanation: vet said gelding lost near fore shoe (tchd 12-1)

4333 CALL STAR SPORTS ON 0800 0521321 H'CAP CHASE (22 fncs) 3m 5f
3:50 (3:51) (Class 3) (0-135,130) 5-Y-O+ **£4,553** (£1,337; £668; £333)

Form RPR

003V **1** **Money Order (IRE)**[4] 4256 9-10-10 **117** RichieMcLernon(3) 128+
(Brendan Powell) *hld up in rr: mstke 11th: hmpd 16th: mstke 4 out: styd on wl fr next: rdn to ld nr fin* **4/1**[2]

5113 **2** *1/2* **Incentivise (IRE)**[41] 3568 8-11-4 **122** RobertThornton 129
(Richard Lee) *hld up in 4th: drvn to ld after 2 out: kpt on u.p: hdd nr fin* **2/1**[1]

FF23 **3** *3/4* **Bench Warrent (IRE)**[12] 4093 8-11-8 **129** (p) PeterToole(3) 136
(Charlie Mann) *hld up towards rr: hdwy to trck ldr 15th: mstke 17th: chalng whn hit 2 out: kpt on* **6/1**[3]

P434 **4** *7* **Lavenoak Lad**[22] 3900 11-10-0 **104** oh5 (t) ColinBolger 105+
(Simon Burrough) *led tl 2nd: mde most fr 5th tl wknd last* **10/1**

P-1P **5** *49* **Andrew Nick (IRE)**[46] 3488 9-10-11 **118** DavidBass(3) 66
(Matt Hazell) *nt fluent: led 2nd tl blnd 5th: rdn 12th: wknd after 15th: sn wl bhd* **50/1**

331P **6** *31* **C'Monthehammers (IRE)**[41] 3568 8-11-7 **125** (b[1]) DavidEngland 42
(Nigel Twiston-Davies) *prom tl lost pl 14th: bhd after next* **13/2**

4 **F** **Carronhills (IRE)**[7] 4186 9-11-5 **130** AodhaganConlon(7) —
(Rebecca Curtis) *hld up in tch: hdwy and handy 3rd whn fell 16th* **4/1**[2]

7m 47.0s (6.00) **Going Correction** +0.40s/f (Soft) **7** Ran SP% **112.0**
Speed ratings: **107,106,106,104,91 82,—**
toteswingers:1&2 £2.30, 2&3 £2.70, 1&3 £3.30 CSF £12.46 TOTE £4.90: £3.20, £1.50; EX 13.70.
Owner John P McManus **Bred** Mrs Anne Kerr **Trained** Upper Lambourn, Berks

FOCUS
A steady pace until setting out on to the final circuit in this stamina test and there were four in a line soon after jumping the final fence. The second ran to recent course form with the third and fourth close to their marks.

NOTEBOOK
Money Order(IRE), who lost his rider at the first fence in the void race at Carlisle four days earlier, raced with his head low to the ground held up in the rear. His jumping was much better than on some occasions in the past and, working his way back upsides at the last, came out just the best in a tight three-way finish. He ran here off 117, 10lb below his hurdle mark and his stamina is clearly bottomless, but his jumping is always a worry. (op 7-1)
Incentivise(IRE), winner of four of his previous seven starts, would have finished closer behind West End Rocker and Minella Boys here in a stronger race over this C&D last time but for a final-fence blunder. Not that big, he battled back to jump the last upsides and just missed out. He deserves plenty of credit for this. (op 85-40 tchd 9-4 and 5-2 in a place)
Bench Warrent(IRE), who has yet to prove his stamina, saw his race out much better than on some occasions in the past, but came up a fraction short in the end. (op 5-1)
Lavenoak Lad, who took a weaker version of this a year ago, was in effect running from a 5lb higher mark. He stepped up the pace going out on to the final circuit, but had no more to give soon after jumping the last. (op 8-1)
Andrew Nick(IRE) Official explanation: vet said gelding lost both front shoes
C'Monthehammers(IRE), who took the 4m Devon National from an 8lb lower mark in December, wore blinkers after a poor effort when pulled up next time. He looks a moody individual and lost interest early on the final circuit. (op 17-2 tchd 6-1)
Carronhills(IRE), a smart hunter in Ireland, recorded an RPR of 138 when a not disgraced fourth in the Aon Chase just one week earlier, his first start for a year. Running under top-weight from a mark of 130, he was bang in contention when crashing out. However, connections risk a possibly lenient handicap mark by intending to run him in the Gold Cup now. (op 3-1)

4334 STAR SPORTS LAY A DECENT BET NOVICES' CHASE (FOR THE ROSCOE HARVEY TROPHY) (18 fncs) 3m 110y
4:25 (4:25) (Class 4) 5-Y-O+ **£3,252** (£955; £477; £238)

Form RPR

-343 **1** **Stoney's Treasure**[37] 3628 7-10-12 112 RobertThornton 129+
(Alan King) *hld up in last: blnd 3rd: hdwy to join ldr 12th: led 2 out: rdn clr run-in: styd on wl* **6/4**[1]

1624 **2** *7* **The Ferbane Man (IRE)**[15] 4023 7-10-12 114 (p) DougieCostello 120+
(Tim Vaughan) *t.k.h: sn cl up: outpcd in 4th whn mstke 3 out: styd on to take 2nd fnl 50yds* **11/2**

PF63 **3** *1* **Federstar (GER)**[26] 3832 9-10-9 115 JimmyDerham(3) 119
(Milton Harris) *cl up: blnd 12th: one pce fr 3 out* **10/1**

-P21 **4** *nk* **Tafika**[23] 3880 7-10-12 113 DominicElsworth 117
(Paul Webber) *j.big 5th: mde most tl 2 out: btn last: wknd bdly run-in* **3/1**[2]
233P **5** *11* **Supreme Plan (IRE)**[27] 3821 8-10-12 112 (tp) SeanQuinlan 110
(Kim Bailey) *cl up tl outpcd 14th* **9/2**[3]
6m 45.9s (18.90) **Going Correction** +0.40s/f (Soft) **5** Ran SP% **107.7**
Speed ratings: **85,82,82,82,78**
CSF £9.33 TOTE £2.50: £2.00, £1.10; EX 7.50.
Owner Mrs S C Welch **Bred** Mrs S C Welch **Trained** Barbury Castle, Wilts
FOCUS
The rain had arrived ahead of this novices' chase. On official ratings 3lb covered the five runners. The pace was very steady until the five fences in quick succession down the back straight for the final time. The form looks a little suspect as a a result.
NOTEBOOK
Stoney's Treasure, a progressive hurdler rated 113, had finished in the frame in his three previous starts over fences this time, all in handicap company. He survived a scare at the third fence, the first ditch. He moved upsides the leader travelling strongly and made it look very plain sailing in the end. He has a very willing attitude and can build on this. (op 11-8 tchd 13-8 in a place)
The Ferbane Man(IRE), keen due to the lack of pace, was left with a lot to do after a blunder three out. He stayed on strongly on the run-in to snatch second spot and no distance is likely to prove beyond him. (op 5-1 tchd 6-1)
Federstar(GER), who won three handicap hurdles in just 20 days in the spring, has been let down by his jumping over fences so far. After a bad stumble seven out, he was always playing catch-up but deserves credit for the way he stuck to his task. (tchd 12-1)
Tafika, off the mark over fences at the third attempt at Leicester, was encountering much more testing ground. His jumping was indifferent in front, but after pulling clear with the winner he was demoted two places on the run-in. He still looks something of a baby and will show further improvement in time. (op 5-2 tchd 10-3)
Supreme Plan(IRE), winner of an Irish point on his debut, is now 0-14 under rules and he was readily outpaced and left behind on his fifth start over fences. (op 13-2 tchd 4-1)

4335 EBF/DBS MARES' STANDARD OPEN NATIONAL HUNT FLAT RACE (QUALIFIER) 2m
4:55 (4:55) (Class 5) 4-7-Y-0 **£2,055** (£599; £299)

Form RPR
1 **Swincombe Flame** 5-11-0 0 WillKennedy 115+
(Nick Williams) *chsd ldrs: rdn 5f out: led over 3f out: styd alone towards inner st: drvn clr over 1f out: styd on wl* **12/1**
2 **2** *11* **Florafern**[38] 3623 6-11-0 0 LeightonAspell 104
(Oliver Sherwood) *hld up in rr: smooth hdwy 1/2-way: chal over 3f out: one pce appr fnl f* **9/2**[3]
12 **3** *3 ½* **Young Victoria**[29] 3773 5-11-0 0 JakeGreenall(7) 108
(Richard Lee) *hld up in tch on outer: hdwy 6f out: led over 4f out tl over 3f out: no ex fnl 2f* **4/1**[2]
51 **4** *8* **Sharlene's Quest (IRE)**[20] 3943 5-11-0 0 MrMatthewBarber(7) 100
(V J Hughes) *led tl over 4f out: btn over 3f out* **12/1**
0-0 **5** *3 ¼* **Night Rose**[13] 4082 5-10-11 0 CharlieHuxley(3) 89
(Alan King) *hld up in last: hdwy 6f out: sn in tch: wknd over 2f out* **25/1**
23 **6** *25* **Young Mags (IRE)**[41] 3576 4-10-2 0 SamTwiston-Davies(3) 55
(Nigel Twiston-Davies) *plld hrd: prom tl wknd qckly 4f out* **11/1**
7 *3 ¼* **Sor Brook** 5-10-11 0 TomMolloy(3) 61
(Nigel Twiston-Davies) *hld up towards rr: outpcd 7f out: n.d after* **33/1**
00 **8** *4 ½* **Hopes Up**[50] 3406 4-10-5 0 DougieCostello 48
(Ian Williams) *plld hrd: pressed ldr tl wknd 7f out* **66/1**
9 *1 ½* **Look Who's Talking** 4-10-5 0 RobertThornton 46
(Alan King) *a in rr gp: no ch fnl 6f* **5/1**
2 **10** *1* **Definite Artist (IRE)**[24] 3876 5-11-0 0 AidanColeman 54
(Venetia Williams) *in tch tl wknd 5f out* **7/2**[1]
11 *1 ½* **Iconic Rose** 4-10-2 0 CPGeoghegan(3) 44
(Pam Sly) *mid-div: sn pushed along: bhd fr 1/2-way* **25/1**
12 *6* **Russian Romance (IRE)** 6-10-4 0 ChristopherWard(10) 47
(Robin Dickin) *a towards rr: no ch fnl 6f* **50/1**
13 *12* **Sevivon** 4-10-5 0 JoeTizzard 26
(Colin Tizzard) *mid-div: hrd rdn and wknd 7f out: sn bhd* **20/1**
P **Harinya (GER)** 4-10-5 0 RodiGreene —
(David Bridgwater) *chsd ldrs: drvn along after 5f: wknd appr 1/2-way: sn bhd: t.o and p.u fr 6f out: dismntd 2f out* **80/1**
3m 53.9s (3.00) **Going Correction** +0.25s/f (Yiel)
WFA 4 from 5yo+ 9lb **14** Ran SP% **120.9**
Speed ratings: **102,96,94,90,89 76,75,72,72,71 70,67,61,—**
toteswingers:1&2 £14.30, 2&3 £5.90, 1&3 £22.40 CSF £61.86 TOTE £17.60: £6.70, £2.60, £1.02; EX 149.40.
Owner Yeo Racing Partnership **Bred** M C And Mrs Yeo **Trained** George Nympton, Devon
FOCUS
The rain continued to fall. A mares-only bumper with plenty of dead wood, but in the end a most decisive winner of some potential. Unusually for a bumper, the pace was generous and the four in behind the winner give the form a solid look.
NOTEBOOK
Swincombe Flame, quite a big newcomer, is out of a fair hurdler. After taking charge, she stuck to the inner once in line for home and powered her way clear. She will not be out of place in the mares' bumper final at Sandown next month.
Florafern, runner-up to a good prospect on her debut at Southwell, moved up looking a real threat but, brought wide in the home straight, in the end she proved no match. She will be unlucky to come up against such a good one for a third time. (op 7-2)
Young Victoria, a winner at Towcester on her debut and still green when runner-up to Hildisvini (a winner over hurdles on his debut at Sandown earlier in the afternoon), was kept wide. She moved comfortably into contention, but could only keep on in her own time once in line for home. She should stay well when she goes hurdling next term. (op 9-2)
Sharlene's Quest(IRE) clearly stays well and she made this a true test. To her credit, she kept going all the way to the line when headed, and she will appreciate 2m4f plus when she embarks on her hurdling career. (op 16-1)
Night Rose, having her third start, ran better than on her return after a wind operation here two weeks earlier, but she still looks on the weak side and tired in the home straight. (op 22-1 tchd 20-1)
Look Who's Talking came in for market support, but after being anchored towards the rear she was behind and struggling soon after halfway. (op 7-1)
Definite Artist(IRE), runner-up first time at Taunton, was hard at work at halfway and was most disappointing. (tchd 10-3 and 4-1)
T/Plt: £27.60 to a £1 stake. Pool of £59,172.68 - 1,562.73 winning tickets. T/Qpdt: £8.50 to a £1 stake. Pool of £4,519.16 - 391.99 winning tickets. LM

4336 - 4342a (Foreign Racing) - See Raceform Interactive

3930 CHEPSTOW (L-H)
Saturday, February 26
4343 Meeting Abandoned - waterlogged

4049 KEMPTON (R-H)
Saturday, February 26
OFFICIAL GOING: Good to soft (soft on bend adjacent to lake; chase 6.5, hurdle 6.2)
Wind: Fresh, half against Weather: Overcast, rain after race 3; becoming fine

4350 THEBETTINGSITE.COM ADONIS JUVENILE HURDLE (GRADE 2) (8 hdls) 2m
1:55 (1:55) (Class 1) 4-Y-0
£12,086 (£4,534; £2,270; £1,132; £568; £284)

Form RPR
1 **Zarkandar (IRE)**[180] 4-10-12 0 DarylJacob 141+
(Paul Nicholls) *w.w in 6th: clsng whn nt fluent 3 out: sn pushed along to chse ldng trio: hdwy to ld bef 2 out: hrd pressed last: drvn and styd on wl* **8/1**
2 *2 ¼* **Molotof (FR)**[53] 4-10-12 126 BarryGeraghty 137
(Nicky Henderson) *trckd ldng trio: wnt 3rd 3 out: moved up to chal 2 out: pressed wnr last: styd on same pce flat* **3/1**[2]
13 **3** *15* **Kumbeshwar**[7] 4205 4-11-2 133 RobertThornton 128
(Alan King) *t.k.h: mde most: mstke 3 out: hdd jst bef 2 out: readily outpcd* **4/1**[3]
4 *2 ¾* **Tonic Mellysse (FR)**[77] 4-11-5 0 APMcCoy 128
(Paul Nicholls) *trckd ldng pair: wnt 2nd 5th: pushed along to chal on long run after 3 out: wknd bef 2 out* **11/4**[1]
5 *10* **Lava Lamp (GER)**[131] 4-10-12 0 PaulMoloney 112
(Evan Williams) *chsd ldng quartet: lost pl 4th and wl in rr bef next: sme prog after 3 out but nvr on terms: tk remote 5th after last* **50/1**
6 *6* **Aikideau (FR)**[77] 4-10-12 0 LeightonAspell 114+
(Richard Rowe) *hld up in last trio: effrt after 5th: chsd ldng quartet after 3 out but nt on terms: wl btn whn blnd bdly last* **8/1**
2221 **7** *26* **Mr Muddle**[11] 4129 4-11-2 119 JamieGoldstein 89
(Sheena West) *pressed ldr: blnd 2nd: nt fluent 4th: lost 2nd next: wknd 3 out: t.o* **12/1**
16 **8** *19* **Maoi Chinn Tire (IRE)**[28] 3802 4-11-5 0 AlanO'Keeffe 73
(Jennie Candlish) *hld up last: nt fluent 1st: gd prog fr 5th to chse ldrs whn nt fluent 3 out: sn wknd: t.o* **25/1**
13 **9** *6* **Kazzene (USA)**[21] 3937 4-11-2 123 (t) JohnnyFarrelly 64
(David Pipe) *in tch in rr: drvn after 4th: sn struggling: wknd 3 out: wl t.o* **10/1**
3m 56.5s (-3.50) **Going Correction** +0.125s/f (Yiel) **9** Ran SP% **116.5**
Speed ratings: **113,111,104,103,98 95,82,72,69**
toteswingers:1&2 £5.80, 1&3 £6.30, 2&3 £3.60 CSF £33.32 TOTE £9.70: £3.20, £1.60, £2.10; EX 37.70 Trifecta £216.50 Pool: £2,583.40 - 8.82 winning units..
Owner Potensis Limited & Chris Giles **Bred** His Highness The Aga Khan's Studs S C **Trained** Ditcheat, Somerset
FOCUS
This Grade 2 has been a decent trial for the Triumph Hurdle, with Snow Drop, Penzance and last year Soldatino winning this before following up at Cheltenham. It has also thrown up some really top-class performers, with the likes of Well Chief and subsequent Champion Hurdlers Punjabi and Binocular taking it in their juvenile season. This year's line-up looked interesting with several having displayed useful form here, plus a number of imports and debutants with Flat form.
NOTEBOOK
Zarkandar(IRE) ◆, a half-brother to Zarkava who won over 1m4f on the Flat for the Aga Khan, jumped pretty well and, after moving up around the home turn, proved strongest over the last two flights. He handled the track and ground and, as he stayed around 2m on the Flat, he should have no difficulty with the stiffer track at Cheltenham in the Triumph Hurdle, which is his intended target now. He had looked to be the stable second string here, but he proved much the best and looks to have a decent chance in that festival contest, for which he is quoted at between 10-1 and 14-1. (op 15-2 tchd 9-1)
Molotof(FR), who had finished runner-up in both starts over hurdles in France, was making his debut for new connections who won this with a similar type in Soldatino last season. He ran pretty well and came some way clear of the rest, but as connections have Grandouet in the Triumph, this gelding might be given more time with a view to going chasing next season. (op 7-2 tchd 4-1)
Kumbeshwar, a soft-ground winner on the Flat and well suited by Fibresand, had run like a stayer on both starts over hurdles, winning on good and finishing third on heavy. He made the running this time and, although he kept galloping, was left behind by the principals in the straight. He is qualified for the Fred Winter now and that looks the likely target if he goes to the festival. (op 9-2 tchd 5-1 in a place)
Tonic Mellysse(FR), the winner of a bumper and a hurdle in France who acts well on soft ground, looked the stable first string on paper, ahead of the winner. He travelled well in behind the pace and had every chance turning in, but he could not change gear under pressure and was left behind. He gave the impression he needs a longer trip or a stiffer test of stamina. (op 10-3)
Lava Lamp(GER), a dual winner on the Flat on fast ground, had been well beaten on his only try on soft. Making his hurdling debut, he ran on late and could be one to bear in mind for when the ground dries up in the spring. (op 66-1)
Aikideau(FR) related to several French jumping winners, had shown promise on his sole start in France when today's fourth was ahead. He made a brief effort towards the end of the back straight but finished up further behind his old rival than he was in France. (op 10-1 tchd 11-1)
Mr Muddle, a progressive hurdler at a lower level, was unable to make an impact in this grade. (op 14-1)
Maoi Chinn Tire(IRE), an impressive winner of a Listed hurdle on his debut, has now been well beaten in two Grade 2s. He now qualifies for a mark and might be seen to better effect in handicaps on faster ground. (op 16-1)
Kazzene(USA), an ex-French Flat performer who won over C&D on his hurdling debut before being beaten by an older subsequent winner next time, was wearing a tongue-tie for the first time. He was another to move up going to three out but soon dropped away and was eased down. He now qualifies for the Fred Winter but will need to improve considerably on this effort to figure. (op 8-1)

4351 RACING POST WEEKENDER PENDIL NOVICES' CHASE (GRADE 2) (16 fncs) 2m 4f 110y
2:25 (2:25) (Class 1) 5-Y-0+ **£13,340** (£5,005; £2,506)

Form RPR
2222 **1** **Captain Chris (IRE)**[21] 3946 7-11-0 153 (t) RichardJohnson 147+
(Philip Hobbs) *trckd ldr: led 7th: nt fluent 11th but j. w plenty of zest apart: drew clr fr 3 out: eased flat* **2/5**[1]
1310 **2** *13* **Adams Island (IRE)**[21] 3940 7-11-4 133 (p) APMcCoy 142
(Rebecca Curtis) *led: j. slowly 3rd and nt fluent next: hdd 7th: chsd wnr after: in tch and rdn bef 3 out: sn lft bhd: eased whn no ch flat* **11/2**[3]

FF51 **3** *39* **American Trilogy (IRE)**[15] 4050 7-11-0 0....................(b) NickScholfield 119
(Paul Nicholls) *j.lft most of the fences and smetimes markedly so: a in last: lost tch fr 11th: t.o* **9/2**[2]

5m 18.8s (-0.70) **Going Correction** +0.20s/f (Yiel) **3** Ran SP% **105.0**
Speed ratings: **109,104,89**
CSF £2.68 TOTE £1.30; EX 2.70.
Owner Mrs Diana L Whateley **Bred** Mrs Noreen Walsh **Trained** Withycombe, Somerset

FOCUS
A disappointing turnout for this Grade 2, with the field cutting up from an entry of 14. Won by the Paul Nicholls yard for the last five years, the race has not had much of a bearing on the Cheltenham Festival for some time, but that could change this year. The pace was sound considering the small line-up and the time was 11 seconds outside the standard.

NOTEBOOK
Captain Chris(IRE) took advantage of a fine opportunity to get off the mark over fences, following three successive seconds behind leading Arkle fancies Ghizao (twice) and Medermit. He had shown smart form in defeat, notably in the Scilly Isles over this trip last time, but his jumping had let him down at times. Richard Johnson was keen to teach him something here and rode him positively, taking him to the front at the last with a circuit to run and kicking him into his fences. Bar one mistake, the gelding jumped really well, putting in more than one spectacular leap, and he drew clear between the last two obstacles for a comprehensive victory. His connections remain undecided about his festival target, having the choice between the new Jewson Chase at around this trip, in which they also have Wishfull Thinking, or dropping him back to 2m in the Arkle. The former race is looking the more likely race for him at this stage, as he has something to find with Ghizao and Medermit in the Arkle, but on the other hand horses with proven stamina over further do have a decent record in the 2m event. Either way he is a very likeable young chaser of whom the best has yet to be seen. Official explanation: jockey said gelding jumped left throughout (tchd 4-11)
Adams Island(IRE) ran well in the face of a very stiff task attempting to concede 4lb to Captain Chris, who is officially rated 20lb his superior. A winner twice over 3m, he was well beaten in a handicap over 3m4f last time, but his trainer was keen to give him the chance to bowl along in front back over this trip. He did make the early running, getting away with a mistake at the first ditch, but had lost his lead to the favourite with a circuit to run. Remaining in touch until the winner eased right away from him after the second-last, the Stewart Family Spinal Research Handicap Chase over 3m looks his most suitable target if he is to run at Cheltenham. (op 13-2)
American Trilogy(IRE) had won over C&D on his second chase start, but he did not prove up to the task in this much better race, jumping badly out to his left a lot of the way and losing touch with the other pair not long after halfway. He will be seen to better effect back on a left-handed track, but his confidence over fences is still not what it ought to be and he could revert to hurdling in the Coral Cup. Official explanation: jockey said that the gelding jumped left throughout (op 4-1)

4352 RACING POST CHASE H'CAP GRADE 3 (18 fncs) 3m
3:00 (3:04) (Class 1) 5-Y-0+

£57,010 (£21,390; £10,710; £5,340; £2,680; £1,340)

Form RPR

-113 **1** **Quinz (FR)**[77] 2883 7-11-0 **144**.. RichardJohnson 158+
(Philip Hobbs) *chsd ldr to 8th and fr 11th: led next: rdn 2 out: jnd last: battled on gamely to assert flat* **8/1**

-316 **2** *1 1/4* **Mount Oscar (IRE)**[49] 3453 12-10-10 **140**.....................(t) AidanColeman 152+
(Colin Tizzard) *w.w in midfield: effrt 12th: 6th and stl enough to do whn colossal blunder 4 out and rdr nrly off: gd prog after: wnt 3rd bef 3 out and 2nd 2 out: jnd wnr last: styd on but hld last 100yds* **50/1**

-144 **3** *18* **Nacarat (FR)**[42] 3560 10-11-12 **156**.................................(t) PaddyBrennan 154
(Tom George) *mstke 1st: chsd ldng pair: trckd ldr 8th to 11th: wnt 2nd again 13th: nt fluent 15th: rdn and cl enough 3 out: lost 2nd and wknd 2 out* **5/1**[2]

1F01 **4** *13* **Hey Big Spender (IRE)**[14] 4077 8-11-11 **155** 5ex................ JoeTizzard 141
(Colin Tizzard) *wl in rr whn mstke and bdly hmpd 1st: stl there whn nt fluent 11th: nvr on terms fr next: poor 8th after 4 out: mstke next: kpt on fr next* **12/1**

3P/1 **5** *15* **Crescent Island (IRE)**[21] 3953 8-10-10 **143**..................(b) TomMolloy[(3)] 117
(Nigel Twiston-Davies) *blnd 1st: wl in rr: mstke 6th: losing tch whn sltly hmpd 12th: wl bhd in 9th after 4 out: plodded on* **25/1**

4-0P **6** *1* **Razor Royale (IRE)**[91] 2673 9-10-9 **142**.............. SamTwiston-Davies[(3)] 110
(Nigel Twiston-Davies) *chsd clr ldrs: u.p fr 13th: grad wknd fr next* **10/1**

3631 **7** *7* **Tatenen (FR)**[35] 3677 7-11-6 **150**.................................... AndrewThornton 116
(Richard Rowe) *led in s: racd wd away fr rest in midfield: prog 12th: chsd clr ldng pair after 4 out to bef next: wl btn in 4th whn blnd 2 out: wknd* **16/1**

6232 **P** **Safari Adventures (IRE)**[42] 3558 9-10-0 **130**................ CampbellGillies —
(Lucinda Russell) *led at gd pce: hdd 12th: wknd and lost 3rd 4 out: poor 8th whn p.u bef last* **28/1**

-234 **P** **Piraya (FR)**[35] 3677 8-10-10 **140**....................................(vt) JohnnyFarrelly —
(David Pipe) *mstke 1st: chsd ldrs: wknd rapidly after 13th: wl t.o after 4 out: p.u bef 2 out* **20/1**

-3P0 **P** **Door Boy (IRE)**[56] 3292 8-10-2 **132**..................................... BrianHughes —
(Howard Johnson) *a wl in rr: losing tch whn sltly hmpd 12th: t.o whn p.u bef 14th* **22/1**

-1P1 **P** **Polyfast (FR)**[42] 3558 8-10-4 **134**....................................... AndrewTinkler —
(Nicky Henderson) *wl in tch in chsng gp: lost pl rapidly 11th: tailing off in last next: p.u bef 13th* **16/1**

PP11 **P** **Sagalyrique (FR)**[29] 3786 7-10-5 **135**...........................(tp) JasonMaguire —
(Donald McCain) *mostly chsd clr ldng trio: wknd qckly bef 15th: t.o whn p.u bef 3 out* **16/1**

-531 **U** **Bakbenscher**[13] 4093 8-11-0 **144** 5ex............................. RobertThornton —
(Alan King) *series of errors and wl in rr: effrt and in tch whn blnd and uns rdr 12th* **13/2**[3]

0-20 **P** **Free World (FR)**[49] 3446 7-11-5 **149**...................................... DarylJacob —
(Paul Nicholls) *last away: a wl in rr: lost tch fr 13th: wl t.o whn p.u after 15th* **33/1**

U5-1 **P** **Fistral Beach (IRE)**[49] 3453 8-10-10 **140**................................ APMcCoy —
(Paul Nicholls) *mstke 1st and collided w rival: trckd ldrs: nt fluent 10th: wknd fr 14th: poor 8th whn p.u bef 3 out* **9/2**[1]

3F21 **F** **Mostly Bob (IRE)**[29] 3784 8-10-6 **136**...............................(t) TomO'Brien —
(Philip Hobbs) *mstke 1st and collided w rival: in tch whn fell 3rd* **11/1**

6m 12.0s (-3.00) **Going Correction** +0.20s/f (Yiel) **16** Ran SP% **123.4**
Speed ratings: **113,112,106,102,97 96,94,—,—,— —,—,—,—,—,—**
toteswingers:1&2:£94.00, 2&3:£49.10, 1&3:£11.60 CSF £372.65 CT £2217.16 TOTE £8.90: £2.30, £10.60, £2.20, £2.90; EX 437.90 Trifecta £4077.10 Pool: £23,954.15 - 4.34 winning units..
Owner Andrew L Cohen **Bred** Michael Blond **Trained** Withycombe, Somerset

FOCUS
This high-class competitive handicap chase that has seen Desert Orchid and subsequent Grand National heroes Rhyme 'N Reason and Rough Quest among its former winners. It is often won by a progressive or in-form sort, and several recent winners have been lightly campaigned leading up to the race. This year's line-up looked pretty much up to standard, with the last two winners taking part again. The pace was good but only the runner-up got involved from off the pace.

NOTEBOOK
Quinz(FR) ◆, well suited by 3m on good or easy ground, has got his act together over fences this season. Although racing off a stone higher than for his last success, he was ridden positively on a track where he had won his only previous start (over hurdles). He took the lead halfway down the back second time, but looked sure to be caught when challenged by the runner-up between the last two. However, he found more for pressure and was drawing away at the finish. He has plenty of options now, but the Grand National appears the most likely target at this stage, although there are other suitable races on the Mildmay track, especially as he still qualifies for novice chases. He was as short as 16-1 in one place for the Aintree race. (tchd 17-2 and 9-1 in places)
Mount Oscar(IRE)'s best form has been at around 2m4f, but he was placed over C&D as a novice. Racing off 7lb above his last winning mark, he crept into contention on the second circuit and overcame a bad mistake at the fourth-last to close down on the winner after the penultimate fence. He looked sure to score - he went 1.1 on the exchanges - but the winner found extra and held him off. This was highly creditable effort from the veteran and, as next week's Greatwood Gold Cup will probably come too soon, connections might look for a veterans' chase for him.
Nacarat(FR), who won this in 2009 (now 9lb higher) and was narrowly beaten last year, ran another brave race under top weight. Wearing a tongue-tie for the first time, he was always in the first three, and was only seen off at the second-last, probably finding the ground too soft for him. Well suited by a flat track, he looks set for another crack at the Melling Chase at the Aintree Grand National meeting. (op 6-1)
Hey Big Spender(IRE) is well suited by soft ground but spoilt his chance here with a mistake at the first fence. He was 5lb higher than for his last success but did stay on in the closing stages, and connections have the option of the Ryanair Chase or the Byrne Group Plate at Cheltenham, with the latter offering him the best chance.
Crescent Island(IRE), who made a successful return from 22 months off at Wetherby earlier in the month, was raised 9lb for that. He was struggling early and being ridden along with over a circuit left, but kept plugging away to get into the prize-money, at the same time proving he stays this far. He is another with a couple of options at Cheltenham, but he might have to re-oppose horses that finished in front of him here. (tchd 22-1)
Razor Royale(IRE), who won this in game style 12 months ago but had finished well beaten off higher marks on four outings since, had dropped to 1lb above last year's winning mark. However, he was never travelling that comfortably, and it is to his credit that he kept going when others cried enough. (tchd 9-1)
Tatenen(FR), for whom a drop in the weights had enabled him to end a long losing run last time, was raised a whopping 13lb for that. With the ground no problem, he travelled well and looked a threat until getting very tired in the straight. (op 14-1 tchd 12-1)
Safari Adventures(IRE), closely matched with Polyfast on previous form here over shorter, made the running for a long way on ground softer than he prefers but was last when pulled up late on. (op 25-1 tchd 33-1)
Piraya(FR), whose most recent wins have been at 2m4f, had yet to prove he stays this far and, after closing up on the leaders on the second circuit, dropped right away. (op 25-1 tchd 33-1)
Sagalyrique(FR), a winner at 3m on good but most of whose form was at shorter; handles soft and is well suited by a flat track. He showed up for a long way but stopped quickly on the second lap as if something was amiss. (op 25-1 tchd 33-1)
Bakbenscher is well suited by testing ground, and had proved he stayed 3m when winning on his first attempt at the trip last time. Raised 5lb for that, his jumping was not slick enough in the early stages, although he was making a little headway when overjumping and coming down at the 12th. (op 25-1 tchd 33-1)
Free World(FR)'s rider reported that the gelding did not appear to stay in the good to soft ground. Official explanation: jockey said gelding did not appear to stay in the good to soft ground (op 25-1 tchd 33-1)
Fistral Beach(IRE), who unseated early when favourite for this last year, had been a winner on his belated seasonal debut last month but was raised 9lb for that. He again did not jump that fluently after an error at the first and was well beaten when pulled up. His rider reported that he did not appear to stay in the good to soft ground. Official explanation: jockey said gelding did not appear to stay in the good to soft ground (op 25-1 tchd 33-1)

4353 WILLIAMHILL.COM DOVECOTE NOVICES' HURDLE (GRADE 2) (8 hdls) 2m
3:35 (3:36) (Class 1) 4-Y-0+

£12,086 (£4,534; £2,270; £1,132; £568; £284)

Form RPR

2411 **1** **Sire De Grugy (FR)**[25] 3864 5-11-6 131.............................. JamieMoore 141+
(Gary Moore) *t.k.h: trckd ldrs: clsd to ld 2 out: shkn up and sn clr: pushed out* **11/4**[2]

31 **2** *11* **Empire Levant (USA)**[29] 3785 4-11-0 0............................. HarrySkelton 123
(Paul Nicholls) *hld up in tch: cl up whn nt fluent 3 out: effrt bef next: kpt on one pce to take 2nd last: no ch w wnr* **5/1**

3 *4* **Celtus (FR)**[39] 4-11-0 132... BarryGeraghty 120
(Nicky Henderson) *pressed ldr: led 3rd: mstke 5th: hdd 2 out: wknd and lost 2nd last* **2/1**[1]

-413 **4** *22* **Toubab (FR)**[49] 3445 5-11-9 141... SamThomas 107
(Paul Nicholls) *trckd ldng pair: mstkes 3rd and 4th and dropped to 5th pl: effrt whn mstke again 3 out: sn btn: t.o* **9/2**[3]

1125 **5** *15* **Pullyourfingerout (IRE)**[59] 3194 4-10-11 130......................(t) APMcCoy 82
(Brendan Powell) *led to 3rd: chsd ldr tl blnd 3 out: sn wknd: t.o* **14/1**

53 **6** *8* **Yorgunnabelucky (USA)**[14] 4069 5-11-2 0.................. RobertThornton 80
(Alan King) *nt fluent: hld up in rr: in tch 3 out: sn wknd: t.o whn blnd last* **25/1**

1160 **7** *12* **Points Of View**[139] 1797 6-11-9 130....................................(t) EdCookson 76
(Kim Bailey) *a in last pair: jst in tch bef 3 out: sn wknd: t.o* **33/1**

4m 4.90s (4.90) **Going Correction** +0.375s/f (Yiel)
WFA 4 from 5yo+ 9lb **7** Ran SP% **108.3**
Speed ratings (Par 115): **102,96,94,83,76 72,66**
toteswingers:1&2:£1.90, 1&3:£1.60, 2&3:£2.90 CSF £15.10 TOTE £3.90: £2.40, £3.90; EX 18.30.
Owner The Preston Family & Friends **Bred** La Grugerie **Trained** Lower Beeding, W Sussex

FOCUS
This looked a fair renewal of this Grade 2, but the time was more than eight seconds slower than the juveniles took in the Adonis.

NOTEBOOK
Sire De Grugy(FR) had been beaten only by leading Cheltenham fancy Bobs Worth in his three hurdles so far, landing the odds at Fakenham and Folkestone since that defeat. Keen once again, he travelled strongly and, once jumping to the front two out, eased right away for an impressive win. Well suited by flat tracks, he is not entered at Cheltenham but could go to Aintree, presumably for the Top Novices' Hurdle over this trip. A real chasing type who jumps hurdles well, all his wins have come in soft conditions. (op 3-1 tchd 10-3)
Empire Levant(USA) ◆, whose trainer won this with Escort'men a year ago, beat subsequent scorer Palawi on good ground at Doncaster. He improved before the home turn but could not prevent the winner from pulling away from him up the straight, although he did stay on to take second at the final flight. Another who is not entered at the festival, Aintree's Anniversary Hurdle against his own age group looks his target, and better ground there would suit. (tchd 9-2)
Celtus(FR) is another French import for connections, in a similar mould to Adonis runner-up Molotof, and he held an entry in that race too. Successful in three of his four starts in France, each on testing ground, he made a lot of the running, but had no answers when tackled by the winner and faded into a well-beaten third in the end. His jumping can improve and he is probably worth another chance. (op 9-4 tchd 5-2 and 11-4 in a place)

Toubab(FR), who had 7lb in hand on BHA figures,t had reportedly not been pleasing the trainer in his work. He lost his pitch with successive errors in the back straight and was no threat to the principals afterwards. Third in the 32Red Tolworth Hurdle in bad ground, he let down the form as have the pair who finished in front of him, Minella Class and Megastar. (op 7-2)

Pullyourfingerout(IRE), another who held an alternative entry in the Adonis, had finished behind Triumph Hurdle contenders Sam Winner, Grandouet and A Media Luz on his last two starts. In second place when blundering three out, he weakened soon after turning for home. The Fred Winter looks the race for him if he is to take his chance at Cheltenham. (op 10-1)

Yorgunnabelucky(USA) has faced stiff tasks since a promising hurdles debut at Doncaster and was never a factor here. He usually ran in headgear on the Flat and showed a preference for better ground. (tchd 28- 1 in a place)

Points Of View suddenly found his form when equipped with a tongue-tie last summer, but faced a very stiff task at these weights on his first start since October. Ridden by a jockey unable to claim his usual 7lb allowance, he trailed throughout, but he should do better with the run behind him back on a sound surface. (op 40-1 tchd 25-1)

4354 RACING & FOOTBALL OUTLOOK H'CAP HURDLE (10 hdls) 2m 5f

4:10 (4:10) (Class 3) (0-135,133) 4-Y-O+ **£5,204** (£1,528; £764; £381)

Form RPR

6301 **1** **Ocean Transit (IRE)**^{17} 4009 6-10-8 **118** DavidBass(3) 127
(Richard Price) *settled in last pair: rdn fr 5th and struggling: sustained prog fr 3 out: clsd to ld 2 out: drvn and hld on wl* **12/1**

-140 **2** *3* **Paint The Clouds**^{49} 3452 6-10-8 **115** WayneHutchinson 121
(Warren Greatrex) *trckd ldrs: prog fr 3 out looking dangerous: chal bef 2 out: chsd wnr after: kpt on but a hld* **16/1**

4360 **3** *nk* **Gee Dee Nen**^{21} 3947 8-11-1 **122** (v) JamieMoore 129
(Gary Moore) *led: drvn and pressed sn after 3 out: hdd 2 out: cl enough last: one pce* **16/1**

02-U **4** *10* **Ostland (GER)**^{24} 3881 6-10-4 **118** KielanWoods(7) 115
(Charlie Longsdon) *hld up in last pair: only 11th bef 3 out where nt asked serious questions but carrying hd at awkward angle: coaxed along and kpt on bef next: tk 4th nr fin* **11/2**^{2}

6-03 **5** *1* **Rollwiththepunches**^{21} 3941 6-11-5 **129** (t) SamTwiston-Davies(3) 126
(Philip McBride) *trckd ldr fr 2nd: nt fluent 3 out: drvn to chal after: wknd 2 out* **8/1**^{3}

1410 **6** *22* **Nicene Creed**^{77} 2887 6-11-2 **123** TomO'Brien 99
(Philip Hobbs) *chsd ldr to 2nd: styd prom: drvn 3 out: wknd bef next: t.o* **5/1**^{1}

4042 **7** *½* **Benfleet Boy**^{21} 3941 7-11-12 **133** APMcCoy 109
(Brendan Powell) *pressed ldrs: drvn and stl cl up 3 out: wknd bef next: t.o* **10/1**

3054 **8** *6* **County Zen (FR)**^{21} 3947 8-11-5 **126** RichardJohnson 96
(Philip Hobbs) *cl up: mstke 5th: sn rdn: struggling fr 7th: wknd and eased 3 out: t.o* **5/1**^{1}

643- **P** **Georgian King**^{466} 2345 8-10-13 **120** ColinBolger —
(Suzy Smith) *racd wd: in tch: mstke 6th: no prog next: wl bhd 3 out: p.u bef 2 out* **40/1**

-20P **P** **First Stream (GER)**^{42} 3566 7-11-4 **125** (b) BrianHughes —
(Howard Johnson) *nt fluent: in tch to 6th: wknd bef next: t.o whn p.u bef 3 out* **20/1**

U-0 **P** **Be Definite (IRE)**^{34} 3693 7-10-8 **115** PaddyBrennan —
(Tom George) *mstkes: in tch: stl chsng ldrs whn mstke 3 out: wknd: p.u bef next* **40/1**

-200 **P** **Causeway King (USA)**^{25} 3874 5-11-7 **128** (t) RobertThornton —
(Alan King) *hld up in rr: blnd bdly 6th: nt rcvr: t.o whn p.u bef 3 out* **33/1**

1-00 **P** **Puzzlemaster**^{72} 2977 5-10-13 **120** (t) DominicElsworth —
(Hughie Morrison) *settled midfield: mstkes 2nd and 3rd: in tch towards rr 7th: wknd 3 out: p.u bef next* **33/1**

113 **F** **Mr Hudson (IRE)**^{56} 3295 6-11-4 **128** (t) IanPopham(3) —
(Paul Nicholls) *wl in tch: chsd ldrs 6th: nt fluent next: wknd after 3 out: 8th whn fell next: winded* **11/2**^{2}

5m 27.7s (3.70) **Going Correction** +0.375s/f (Yiel) **14** Ran SP% **117.9**
Speed ratings (Par 107): **107,105,105,101,101 93,92,90,—,— —,—,—,—**
toteswingers:1&2:£24.90, 1&3:£40.10, 2&3:£48.60 CSF £171.23 CT £3049.06 TOTE £14.30: £3.70, £5.30, £3.90; EX 110.80.

Owner Ocean's Five **Bred** Mike Channon Bloodstock Ltd **Trained** Ullingswick, H'fords

FOCUS

A good, competitive handicap hurdle.

NOTEBOOK

Ocean Transit(IRE), proven at this trip, handles soft ground, while all her hurdles wins had come on flat, right-handed tracks. Racing 6lb above her recent winning mark, she looked in trouble early on the second circuit but picked up well and outstayed her rivals from the home turn. The mare has developed a tendency to win her races in pairs, and it remains to be seen if she can complete the hat-trick. The Martin Pipe Conditionals' Hurdle at Cheltenham is a possibility, although she may not get in and that track may not be ideal for her. (op 10-1)

Paint The Clouds ◆, whose wins had come on good and fast ground, had been held over this sort of trip recently but had dropped a little in the weights. He travelled well into contention but could not pick up when the winner ranged alongside. A return to good ground should be in his favour. (tchd 20-1)

Gee Dee Nen ◆ put up a brave show from the front, sticking on after being headed at the second-last. He has been running mostly over fences lately, and had run well until a bad mistake stopped him when returned to hurdles at Ascot last time. He is getting back to form and better ground will not hurt his cause. (op 14-1)

Ostland(GER), whose best run over hurdles was over C&D, handles soft ground but has yet to win. Nevertheless, he showed enough on this second start back to suggest he can find an opportunity before too long. (op 15-2)

Rollwiththepunches, a 2m winner on soft who appears to stay 2m4f, had eased in the weights a little and was down in grade. He ran well for a long way but did not appear to get home.

Nicene Creed, who gained both his wins on good ground and stays an extended 2m3f, had been well beaten in both tries on softer and again found the ground against him. He ran with credit in the circumstances and a return to a sound surface will help. (op 11-2)

Benfleet Boy is suited by a flat track but, racing off 7lb above his last winning mark, he was another who seemed not to get home in the conditions.

County Zen(FR), who is well suited by soft ground, didn't take to fences and has been running over longer trips of late. He was sent off favourite, but a mistake early on the second circuit put him on the back foot, and he could never get involved afterwards. He can do better. The vet reported that the gelding had lost his left-fore shoe. Official explanation: vet said gelding lost left fore shoe (op 9-2 tchd 11-2 and 6-1 in a place)

Mr Hudson(IRE), a former pointer, had won at around this trip on soft ground. Making his handicap debut off 128 and wearing a first-time tongue-tie, he was struggling when taking a tired-looking fall at the penultimate flight, after which he lay winded for several minutes. (op 6-1 tchd 5-1)

4355 DOWNLOAD RACING POST IPHONE AND ANDROID APPS H'CAP CHASE (16 fncs) 2m 4f 110y

4:45 (4:45) (Class 3) (0-130,130) 5-Y-O+ **£5,854** (£1,719; £859; £429)

Form RPR

1-24 **1** **Coup Royale (FR)**^{92} 2662 7-10-10 **114** (t) JoeTizzard 135+
(Colin Tizzard) *mstkes 1st and 2nd: settled wl in rr: poor 9th at 10th and stl making fiddly mstkes: scythed through field fr 4 out: led 2 out: cruised clr: impressive* **7/2**^{1}

14-5 **2** *8* **Soixante (IRE)**^{49} 3444 8-11-5 **123** (p) HaddenFrost 129
(Henrietta Knight) *blnd 1st and rdr nrly off: disp ld: gained upper hand 10th: hdd 2 out: no ch w wnr but kpt on* **13/2**

611 **3** *shd* **Forget It**^{35} 3690 6-11-7 **125** AndrewGlassonbury 130
(Gary Moore) *settled in midfield: prog after 9th: wnt 2nd 4 out: rdn to chal and mstke 3 out: no ch as wnr sauntered by next: continued to battle placings w runner-up* **6/1**^{3}

0-20 **4** *7* **Lady Bling Bling**^{17} 4009 10-10-4 **108** MarkGrant 112
(Peter Jones) *mstkes: in tch: rdn after 9th: prog hmpd by errors after but kpt on fr 3 out* **16/1**

10F3 **5** *16* **Cruchain (IRE)**^{42} 3558 8-10-12 **116** TomO'Brien 103
(Dai Burchell) *settled midfield: chsng ldrs in 5th whn mstkes 10th and next: no imp in 4th 3 out: wknd qckly next* **9/2**^{2}

-655 **6** *¾* **Rory Boy (USA)**^{15} 4054 6-11-2 **123** (p) SamTwiston-Davies(3) 108
(Nigel Twiston-Davies) *chsd ldrs: rdn fr 11th: wknd after 4 out* **14/1**

6506 **7** *23* **Soulard (USA)**^{21} 3948 8-11-10 **128** PaddyBrennan 90
(Tom George) *prom: lost pl after 9th: struggling in rr next: nvr on terms after* **14/1**

4-3P **8** *47* **Our Bob (IRE)**^{60} 3157 9-11-7 **125** (t) RichardJohnson 45
(Philip Hobbs) *blnd 2nd: in rr whn blnd 6th: no prog after: wl t.o fr 11th* **25/1**

U532 **F** **Outside The Box**^{27} 3838 7-10-9 **113** WillKennedy —
(Noel Chance) *disp ld to 10th: stl disputing cl enough 2nd whn fell 4 out* **12/1**

3462 **P** **Yabora (FR)**^{55} 3340 6-11-12 **130** (tp) TomSiddall —
(Charlie Longsdon) *pressed ldng pair: mstke 7th: lost pl after 11th: wknd after 4 out: poor 8th whn p.u bef last* **10/1**

P **Sprint De Ferbet (FR)**^{90} 5-11-1 **121** BarryGeraghty —
(Nicky Henderson) *mstke 1st: a in last pair: lost tch 9th: t.o whn p.u bef 12th* **17/2**

5m 24.9s (5.40) **Going Correction** +0.45s/f (Soft)
WFA 5 from 6yo+ 2lb **11** Ran SP% **118.4**
Speed ratings: **107,103,103,101,95 94,86,68,—,— —**
toteswingers:1&2:£6.20, 1&3:£3.60, 2&3:£8.00 CSF £27.40 CT £134.21 TOTE £5.00: £1.80, £2.50, £1.90; EX 31.70.

Owner Mrs Jean R Bishop **Bred** Dora Bloodstock Ltd **Trained** Milborne Port, Dorset

FOCUS

Just a fair handicap chase, contested by largely out-of-form sorts. It turned into quite a test in the ground and the time was six seconds slower than the Pendil earlier in the day.

NOTEBOOK

Coup Royale(FR) sat a long way off the pace and was still only seventh as they went into the final turn, but he cruised through to lead two from home and cleared right away for a very easy win. This intermediate trip suited and he was helped by the first-time tongue-tie, as he has reportedly choked in the past. While this was impressive, he is only going to be hit by the handicapper for it. (op 5-1)

Soixante(IRE), last year's winner, was able to race off the same mark and was sharper for his reappearance over further at Sandown. Always up in the van after a first-fence blunder, he was left in the winner's wake two from home but kept going for second. (op 7-1)

Forget It was 15lb higher than when making a winning chasing debut over C&D in November. He made a couple of errors in rear but improved to look a threat in the straight, only for the winner to ease past him. He did stick on and nearly salvaged second on the run-in. (op 5-1)

Lady Bling Bling, back over fences, was unable to reverse Wincanton novice form with Forget It. She gave herself plenty to do with some sketchy jumping and merely stayed on for pressure past toiling rivals.

Cruchain(IRE), third off 3lb lower over C&D latest, travelled quite well until his progress was checked by a blunder seven from home. (op 5-1 tchd 11-2 in a place)

Rory Boy(USA) continues to fall in the weights but was beaten before they exited the back straight. (op 12-1)

Outside The Box, upped in trip on this handicap debut, was just feeling the pinch when parting company at the last down the back. (op 10-1 tchd 15-2)

Yabora(FR), who had been kept to hurdling this season, showed up for a long way off top weight but weakened going to the home turn and was pulled up before the last. (op 10-1 tchd 15-2)

Sprint De Ferbet(FR) was in the last trio until pulling up. Running in only his third chase, his win came in heavy ground. (op 10-1 tchd 15-2)

4356 SHANGRI-LA HOTEL, DUBAI STANDARD OPEN NATIONAL HUNT FLAT RACE 2m

5:15 (5:18) (Class 5) 4-6-Y-O **£2,055** (£599; £299)

Form RPR

1 **Oscar Magic (IRE)** 4-10-4 0 SamTwiston-Davies(3) 107+
(Nigel Twiston-Davies) *w ldr: led 4f out: rdn and pressed wl over 2f out: styd on stoutly over 1f out* **5/1**^{3}

1 **2** *3 ¼* **Tour D'Argent (FR)**^{38} 3630 4-11-0 0 BarryGeraghty 111
(Nicky Henderson) *trckd ldrs: smooth prog to go 2nd over 3f out: sn chalng rdn and kpt on same pce fnl 2f* **9/4**^{1}

3 *1 ½* **Grab The Glory (IRE)** 5-11-2 0 JamieMoore 111
(Gary Moore) *hld up in midfield: effrt over 4f out: chsd clr ldng pair wl over 2f out: styd on: nrst fin* **7/1**

4 *7* **Ivor's King (IRE)** 4-10-7 0 JoeTizzard 95
(Colin Tizzard) *hld up towards rr: smooth prog fr 5f out: cl up over 3f out: outpcd over 2f out: kpt on* **16/1**

2 **5** *12* **Diamond Sweeper (IRE)**^{43} 3546 5-11-2 0 RobertThornton 92
(Alan King) *t.k.h: prom: rdn whn hmpd bhd wkng rival over 3f out: steadily fdd* **7/2**^{2}

30 **6** *nk* **Deciding Moment (IRE)**^{73} 2957 5-11-2 0 DarylJacob 92
(Ben De Haan) *fractious s and v.s.a: sn in tch in rr: stdy prog fr 5f out: clsng on ldrs in 8th over 3f out: no ex and wknd fnl 2f* **33/1**

7 *4* **Rachael's Ruby** 4-9-7 0 MrTJCannon(7) 72
(Roger Teal) *prom: wl in tch and rdn over 3f out: sn wknd* **66/1**

8 *nk* **Soutine (IRE)** 5-11-2 0 TomO'Brien 88
(Alex Hales) *hld up in rr: outpcd fr 4f out: effrt 3f out: plugged on but no ch* **50/1**

9 *6* **Irene Kennet** 4-10-0 0 .... HaddenFrost 66
(Martin Bosley) *racd wd and rn green in rr: sme prog 5f out: wl outpcd over 3f out: no ch after* **66/1**

10 *2 1/4* **War Of The World (FR)** 5-11-2 0 .... NickScholfield 79
(Paul Nicholls) *green at s: hld up in last trio: nvr a factor: plodded on past wkng rivals fnl 3f* **5/1**[3]

11 *5* **Proper Villan (IRE)** 6-10-11 0 .... MrMMO'Connor[(5)] 74
(Mark Bradstock) *hld up towards rr: effrt 5f out: no prog over 3f out: wknd* **50/1**

4 12 *6* **Hoare Abbey (IRE)**[54] 3372 5-11-2 0 .... PaddyBrennan 68
(Tom George) *led at modest pce: hdd 4f out: wknd qckly sn after* **28/1**

13 *14* **Midnight Choice** 6-11-2 0 .... LiamTreadwell 54
(Mrs H Parrott) *t.k.h: hld up in midfield: wknd 4f out: sn wl bhd* **66/1**

0 14 *41* **Thank The Groom**[30] 3773 5-11-2 0 .... AndrewThornton 13
(Martin Bosley) *hld up in midfield: effrt and in tch over 4f out: wknd rapidly over 3f out: t.o* **100/1**

0 15 *4 1/2* **Dawn Auction (IRE)**[14] 4082 4-10-7 0 .... CharliePoste —
(Anthony Middleton) *a wl in rr: struggling 6f out: t.o* **150/1**

16 *23* **Sleeping Tree (FR)** 6-11-2 0 .... HarrySkelton —
(Paul Nicholls) *a in last trio: struggling sn after 1/2-way: wl t.o and rdn rt out to fin* **16/1**

17 *79* **Master Dane (IRE)** 5-11-2 0 .... MarkBradburne —
(Martin Bosley) *prom tl wknd v rapidly over 6f out: wl t.o and walked across the line* **100/1**

4m 7.70s (13.30) **Going Correction** +0.625s/f (Soft)
WFA 4 from 5yo 9lb 5 from 6yo 1lb 17 Ran SP% **128.0**
Speed ratings: **91,89,88,85,79 78,76,76,73,72 70,67,60,39,37 25,—**
toteswingers:1&2:£5.60, 1&3:£12.70, 2&3:£8.90 CSF £16.81 TOTE £6.60: £2.30, £1.50, £2.90; EX 33.60.
Owner Mrs Lorna Berryman **Bred** NIALL RADFORD **Trained** Naunton, Gloucs

FOCUS
A decent bumper run at a fairly steady pace.

NOTEBOOK
Oscar Magic(IRE), for whom there was plenty of support, stayed on well after striking the front in the straight. It emerged that he had worked well with Imperial Commander in a racecourse gallop recently. His dam won over 2m on the Flat, as well as over hurdles, and he should get further when he goes jumping. He has been introduced to the Weatherbys Champion Bumper betting at 14-1 but doesn't make much appeal at that price in a race that is usually dominated by Irish stables. (op 8-1)
Tour D'Argent(FR), from the yard which won this with Riverside Theatre three years ago, was an uneasy favourite. Upped in trip, he ran well under the penalty he picked up for beating fellow 4-y-os at Newbury but lacked the pace of the winner up the straight. (op 5-4 tchd 5-2 and 11-4 in places)
Grab The Glory(IRE) ◆, another for whom there was plenty of support, ran a promising race, staying on after being slightly outpaced by the leaders as they turned for home. This half-brother to the decent bumper/hurdles winner Gus Macrae looks a nice sort for next season. (op 16-1)
Ivor's King(IRE) is out of a modest Flat maiden from the family of an Irish Oaks winner, but is by the same sire as the Tizzards' star Cue Card. He showed ability on this debut and a lesser bumper should be found for him. (op 20-1)
Diamond Sweeper(IRE), the Huntingdon runner-up, probably ran to a similar level. He was slightly caught on heels turning for home but the outcome was not affected. (op 4-1)
Deciding Moment(IRE) ran remarkably well to finish as close as he did after blowing the start badly. The most experienced member of the field, he is a decent prospect for staying novice hurdles. (op 50-1)
Rachael's Ruby is out of a sprinter but ran well for a long way on this debut. (op 100-1)
War Of The World(FR) is a half-brother to amongst others, useful chaser Sagalyrique, who was pulled up in the Racing Post Chase. After playing up in the preliminaries, he was slowly away and in the rear division until running on a bit late in the day. (op 8-1)
Hoare Abbey(IRE), whose dam won the Supreme Novices' Hurdle, faded after making the running. [RL] (op 25-1)
T/Jkpt: Not won. T/Plt: £274.10 to a £1 stake. Pool:£162,742.52 - 433.38 winning tickets T/Qpdt: £134.10 to a £1 stake. Pool:£9,556.43 - 52.70 winning tickets JN

4132 NEWCASTLE (L-H)
Saturday, February 26

OFFICIAL GOING: Heavy (3.4)
All bends moved to provide fresh ground; 3m bend and bend into home straight divided. First flight in back straight and fifth last fence omitted.
Wind: light 1/2 behind Weather: overcast becoming fine and sunny

4357 BET ON TOTEPLACEPOT AT TOTESPORT.COM H'CAP CHASE (14 fncs 2 omitted) 2m 4f
1:40 (1:45) (Class 3) (0-135,134) 5-Y-O+
£5,134 (£1,517; £758; £379; £189; £95)

Form RPR

0-F0 1 **Gansey (IRE)**[21] 3953 9-11-7 **129** .... BrianHarding 140
(Sue Smith) *trckd ldrs: led 2 out: drvn rt out: all out* **8/1**[3]

P-33 2 *1 3/4* **Categorical**[97] 2544 8-11-0 **122** .... JamesReveley 131
(Keith Reveley) *t.k.h in rr: hdwy appr 4 out: wnt 2nd last: styd on same pce* **7/2**[2]

P1/6 3 *5* **Nevada Royale (FR)**[98] 2522 10-11-12 **134** .... DenisO'Regan 140
(Tim Pitt) *w ldrs: led 4th: hdd briefly appr 4 out: hdd 2 out: one pce run-in* **8/1**[3]

614 4 *1 3/4* **Roi De Rose (FR)**[35] 3689 7-10-12 **120** ....(p) TomScudamore 122
(David Pipe) *w ldrs: led briefly appr 4 out: fdd run-in* **3/1**[1]

/0-P 5 *14* **New Alco (FR)**[105] 2358 10-11-12 **134** .... GrahamLee 126+
(Ferdy Murphy) *hld up in rr: hit 4 out: sn bhd: eased run-in* **10/1**

-030 6 *17* **Le Roi Rouge (FR)**[29] 3786 9-10-4 **122** .... TonyKelly[(10)] 93
(Ferdy Murphy) *wnt prom and mstke 8th: drvn 10th: sn lost pl and bhd* **14/1**

U-53 P **Hockenheim (FR)**[9] 4167 10-10-1 **116** .... MrJBewley[(7)] —
(George Bewley) *led to 4th: lost pl rapidly after 10th: bhd whn p.u bef next* **3/1**[1]

5m 49.1s (21.90) **Going Correction** +1.025s/f (Soft) 7 Ran SP% **110.2**
Speed ratings: **97,96,94,93,88 81,—**
Tote Swingers: 1&2 £3.60, 1&3 £6.30, 2&3 £5.20 CSF £34.05 TOTE £7.10: £3.10, £1.80; EX 25.50.
Owner Trevor Hemmings **Bred** Kenilworth House Stud **Trained** High Eldwick, W Yorks

FOCUS
The course survived a morning inspection and, this being the fourth meeting here in the last six weeks, the ground was expected to be just about as testing as it has ever been at Newcastle. However, the rain was thought to have helped open up the surface somewhat. The first flight in the back straight was omitted in all hurdle races. This modest handicap was run at an ordinary gallop and the first four came clear in something of a slow-motion finish. The form looks sound enough rated around the first three.

NOTEBOOK
Gansey(IRE) had never previously run here and arrived with something to prove. However, he loves going left-handed and was unbeaten in two previous outings on heavy ground. He bounced back to near his best with a cracking effort, under strong handling, and was always doing enough after hitting the front. His yard appears to be hitting form and this was actually his first win in handicap company. He is in the Martin Pipe Conditional Jockeys' Handicap over hurdles at Cheltenham next month, but surely the Byrne Group Plate is the logical option there. His liking for that track is in doubt, however, after he blundered his way round in last year's Jewson. Official explanation: trainer was unable to offer any explination as to apparent improvement (op 6-1)
Categorical emerged as the only danger to the winner from two out, but ultimately paid for running freely early on and this ground isn't really for him. He certainly deserves to go one better and rates the benchmark. (op 10-3 tchd 3-1)
Nevada Royale(FR) was having his second run back from injury and first for 98 days with the tongue-tie left off. He enjoyed himself out in front and only tired out of it late on. This was another step back in the right direction and getting back over further should help. (op 9-1 tchd 10-1)
Roi De Rose(FR) got a positive ride and held every chance. He has won on this sort of ground and probably found the grade that bit too hot. (op 10-3 tchd 7-2 and 11-4)
New Alco(FR) Official explanation: jockey said gelding made a mistake at the 4th and finished tired
Hockenheim(FR) dropped out tamely when things got serious and something presumably went amiss. Official explanation: jockey said gelding lost action but returned sound (op 7-2)

4358 BET ON TOTESCOOP6 AT TOTESPORT.COM H'CAP HURDLE (8 hdls 1 omitted) 2m
2:15 (2:20) (Class 3) (0-135,130) 4-Y-O+ **£4,435** (£1,310; £655; £327; £163)

Form RPR

F-01 1 **Reindeer Dippin**[14] 4065 9-11-1 **126** .... HenryBrooke[(7)] 131
(Donald McCain) *led 1st: hit next: styd on fr 3 out: hld on towards fin* **9/2**[1]

1/30 2 *nk* **Best Prospect (IRE)**[60] 3169 9-11-7 **125** ....(tp) BarryKeniry 130
(Michael Dods) *hld up in rr: stdy hdwy 5th: handy 3rd whn nt fluent 2 out: swtchd rt after last: styd on to chal last 50yds: nt go past* **16/1**

0-4P 3 *3* **Kudu Country (IRE)**[20] 3969 5-11-3 **121** .... GrahamLee 122
(Tom Tate) *trckd ldrs: wnt 2nd 4th: rdn appr 2 out: kpt on same pce run-in* **8/1**[3]

0400 4 *12* **Decoy (FR)**[16] 4031 5-11-1 **119** .... TomScudamore 109
(David Pipe) *mid-div: kpt on fr 3 out: tk n.d 4th appr last* **17/2**

6131 5 *3 1/4* **Night In Milan (IRE)**[11] 4138 5-10-8 **112** .... JamesReveley 98
(Keith Reveley) *hld up in rr and racd v wd: bhd fr 4th: sme hdwy 3 out: nvr on terms* **9/2**[1]

B200 6 *1 3/4* **Gifted Leader (USA)**[28] 3808 6-11-3 **121** .... DougieCostello 107
(Ian Williams) *chsd ldrs: 4th 2 out: 5th and wkng whn mstke last* **9/1**

032 7 *7* **Kingdom Of Munster (IRE)**[15] 4056 4-10-0 **113** oh1 .... PaddyAspell 81
(Richard Fahey) *mid-div: chsd ldrs 3rd: drvn after 5th: wknd appr 2 out* **25/1**

0-3P 8 *40* **Open De L'Isle (FR)**[28] 3821 9-11-2 **123** .... HarryHaynes[(3)] 60
(James Ewart) *led to 1st: drvn after next: in rr and reminders 3rd: hung rt and t.o 5th* **33/1**

3431 9 *3 1/2* **Dontpaytheferryman (USA)**[10] 4149 6-10-12 **123** .... KyleJames[(7)] 57
(Brian Ellison) *chsd ldrs: hung rt and lost pl bef 5th: sn bhd: t.o next* **11/2**[2]

2432 10 *7* **Amir Pasha (UAE)**[15] 4058 6-9-10 **110** ....(v) JoeCollivier[(10)] 37
(Micky Hammond) *trckd ldrs: t.k.h: lost pl after 4th: bhd fr next: t.o 3 out* **12/1**

40-6 R **Washington Irving (IRE)**[97] 2542 6-11-5 **130** .... PaulGallagher[(7)] —
(Howard Johnson) *hld up: hdwy on ins to trck ldrs whn rn out 4th* **8/1**[3]

P **Gorge (AUS)**[409] 9-11-7 **130** ....(t) AlexanderVoy[(5)] —
(Anthony Cosgriff) *in rr: mstke 2nd: bhd fr 4th: t.o whn p.u bef 3 out* **66/1**

4m 20.1s (10.10) **Going Correction** +0.875s/f (Soft)
WFA 4 from 5yo+ 9lb 12 Ran SP% **116.4**
Speed ratings (Par 107): **109,108,107,101,99 98,95,75,73,70 —,—**
Tote Swingers: 1&2 £18.60, 1&3 £4.80, 2&3 £21.10 CSF £70.49 CT £561.87 TOTE £6.00: £2.40, £4.60, £3.30; EX 75.00.
Owner Sandgrounders **Bred** D McCain **Trained** Cholmondeley, Cheshire

FOCUS
A wide-open handicap. It was run at a fair gallop considering the ground, but the majority were toiling before three out and it was hard work in the home straight. The placed horses set the standard.

NOTEBOOK
Reindeer Dippin ran poorly on his previous outing in this sphere, but resumed winning ways back over fences off a 6lb higher mark on his last start and followed up with a very gutsy effort. He took the race by the scruff of the neck after the second hurdle and repeatedly fought off challenges after straightening for home. It was his third success on heavy ground, he has now won 50% of his races going left-handed and he could turn up next in the Grand Annual back over fences at Cheltenham next month. The likely quicker ground there is no big concern, but a mark of 140 for that would look tough. (op 4-1 tchd 11-2)
Best Prospect(IRE), who ran in the "jumpers bumper" behind Recession Proof and Bothy on his previous outing, was 5lb higher than when winning this event cheekily in 2009. He travelled sweetly into things from out the back and he so nearly repeated the feat, but the winner was just too resolute. (op 10-1)
Kudu Country(IRE) bounced back to the sort of form that saw him finish fourth to Champion Hurdle hopeful Mille Chief two runs back, and looks worth a go over a bit further now. (op 7-1 tchd 17-2 and 13-2 in a place)
Decoy(FR) ◆ came in for support having been eased 8lb since his handicap debut last month. He got badly outpaced on the back straight and is crying out for a longer trip. (op 16-1)
Night In Milan(IRE), well backed, was progressive coming here, but made hard work of landing a moderate handicap off 12lb lower at this venue latest. He looked to hate this ground and will be better off back over further on a better surface. (op 7-1)
Gifted Leader(USA) was treading water from two out but this was more encouraging again. (tchd 7-1)
Kingdom Of Munster(IRE) found it too demanding. (op 20-1)
Open De L'Isle(FR) Official explanation: jockey said gelding hung right throughout
Dontpaytheferryman(USA) Official explanation: jockey said gelding hung right throughout
Gorge(AUS) Official explanation: jockey said gelding was never travelling

4359 BET ON LIVE FOOTBALL AT TOTESPORT.COM NOVICES' HURDLE (11 hdls 2 omitted) 2m 6f
2:45 (2:50) (Class 3) 5-Y-O+ **£4,475** (£1,351; £696; £368)

Form RPR

2344 1 **Battle Group**[13] 4092 6-11-8 137 .... TomScudamore 133
(David Pipe) *trckd ldrs: upsides 2 out: kpt on to ld last strides* **5/1**[3]

4-12 2 *shd* **Yurok (IRE)**[42] 3572 7-11-4 0 .... BrianHarding 130+
(Sue Smith) *trckd ldrs: led appr 3 out: jnd whn blnd 2 out: styd on run-in: hdd post* **8/11**[1]

60-U 3 *32* **Hawaii Klass**[38] 3633 6-10-12 0 .... WilsonRenwick 91
(Donald Whillans) *chsd ldrs: taken wd after 5th: modest 3rd appr 3 out: lft trailing bef next* **66/1**

-163 4 8 **Sunnyside**[14] 4062 6-10-13 120 AlexanderVoy(5) 93
(Lucy Normile) *led: clr 2nd to 7th: hdd appr 3 out: sn wknd* **10/3**[2]
P **Coulter Lass** 7-10-5 0 JamesReveley —
(William Amos) *last whn j. slowly 1st: in rr: sme hdwy 7th: wknd next: sn bhd: tailed off whn p.u bef 2 out* **50/1**
0B4 P **Be True (IRE)**[49] 3439 7-10-12 0 AdrianLane —
(Donald McCain) *trckd ldr: hit 3rd: rdn 8th: wknd next: bhd whn mstke 2 out: t.o whn p.u bef last* **10/1**
0 P **Swinside Silver**[17] 4000 7-9-9 0 CallumWhillans(10) —
(Donald Whillans) *pushed along 5th: lost pl and bhd after next: t.o whn p.u 8th* **125/1**

6m 7.00s (31.00) **Going Correction** +0.875s/f (Soft) 7 Ran SP% **111.0**
Speed ratings: **78,77,66,63,—,—,—**
Tote Swingers: 1&2 £1.10, 1&3 £13.20, 2&3 £10.90 CSF £8.93 TOTE £6.40: £2.20, £1.10; EX 10.30.
Owner Jolly Boys Outing **Bred** Juddmonte Farms Ltd **Trained** Nicholashayne, Devon

FOCUS
From early in the straight this developed into a duel. The form is rated around the second and third.

NOTEBOOK
Battle Group was given a fine ride by Tom Scudamore, who cajoled the quirky gelding to edge ahead close home. He held onto him for as long as possible before asking for his effort, and even then he was keen not to be too hard on him. The 6-y-o had disgraced himself at Exeter last time but showed what he is capable of on a going day here. (tchd 9-2)
Yurok(IRE) got in close at the second-last and blundered. That didn't help his cause, but he had plenty of time to put this race to bed and couldn't shake off the winner. He'll be better when he goes over fences next year. (tchd 5-6 and 10-11 in places)
Hawaii Klass plugged on up the straight to take third, but was never a danger to the first two.
Sunnyside stays 3m but doesn't want the ground this bad and, having set a decent gallop for the conditions early on, he was never going to see out the trip. (op 9-2)

4360 TOTESPORT.COM EIDER H'CAP CHASE (21 fncs 4 omitted) 4m 1f
3:15 (3:21) (Class 2) (0-150,144) 5-Y-0+ **£19,530** (£6,387; £3,624)

Form RPR
2-P6 1 **Companero (IRE)**[17] 4003 11-11-0 **132** (b[1]) PeterBuchanan 148
(Howard Johnson) *mde virtually all: j.rt 6th: 8 l ahd whn j.v.slowly 2 out: clambered over last: fin v tired* **16/1**
3-P2 2 30 **Giles Cross (IRE)**[49] 3437 9-11-4 **136** DenisO'Regan 140+
(Victor Dartnall) *sn trcking wnr: led briefly 11th: 4 l down 3 out: 10 l down and v tired whn clambered over last: eased run-in* **9/2**[1]
P0-3 3 dist **Morgan Be**[38] 3634 11-10-0 **118** oh3 RichieMcGrath —
(Kate Walton) *hld up in rr: hdwy 13th: 3rd and rdn 4 out: wknd next: poor 3rd whn p.u between last 2: eventually wnt on to complete* **13/2**[3]
0-06 P **Comply Or Die (IRE)**[42] 3568 12-11-12 **144** (b) TimmyMurphy
(David Pipe) *chsd ldrs: j. v big 8th: lost pl 5 out: remote 4th next: tired whn p.u 2 out* **12/1**
-P04 P **Flintoff (USA)**[44] 3529 10-10-12 **130** (b) TomScudamore —
(Venetia Williams) *chsd ldrs: pushed along 3rd: lost pl 8th: bhd and j. slowly 10th: sn t.o: p.u bef 5 out* **14/1**
/P2P P **Negus De Beaumont (FR)**[38] 3634 10-10-5 **123** GrahamLee —
(Ferdy Murphy) *in rr and humoured along: drvn 9th: bhd fr 15th: t.o whn p.u after 5 out* **28/1**
-504 P **Ballyfoy (IRE)**[15] 4051 10-10-11 **129** MattieBatchelor —
(Jamie Poulton) *prom: lost pl 8th: bhd fr 15th: distant 5th whn p.u bef 2 out* **7/1**
-1FP P **Newman Des Plages (FR)**[44] 3522 10-10-7 **125** JamesReveley —
(Martin Todhunter) *hld up: hdwy and in tch 9th: wknd 15th: t.o whn p.u after 5 out* **40/1**
F226 P **Dawn Ride (IRE)**[9] 4167 10-10-0 **118** oh1 (p) BarryKeniry —
(Micky Hammond) *in rr: bhd fr 13th: t.o 15th: p.u bef 5 out* **40/1**
4312 P **Minella Boys (IRE)**[42] 3568 9-10-13 **131** (tp) FelixDeGiles —
(Charlie Longsdon) *trckd ldrs: upsides 12th: 3rd and rdn whn stmbld bnd appr 3 out: sn wknd: t.o 6th whn p.u bef 3 out* **9/2**[1]
21F6 P **Overquest**[44] 3522 9-10-0 **118** oh8 DougieCostello —
(Elliott Cooper) *mid-div: hdwy to trck ldrs 7th: lost pl 11th: bhd whn p.u bef 14th: lame* **9/1**
22-1 P **Belon Gale (IRE)**[101] 2449 8-11-5 **137** WilsonRenwick —
(Howard Johnson) *chsd ldrs: lost pl 12th: sn bhd: t.o whn p.u bef next* **6/1**[2]

9m 30.9s (23.10) **Going Correction** +1.025s/f (Soft) 12 Ran SP% **115.1**
Speed ratings: **113,105,—,—,—,—,—,—,—,—,—,—**
Tote Swingers: 1&2 £15.60, 1&3 £10.50, 2&3 £7.40 CSF £85.23 CT £521.57 TOTE £19.20: £6.70, £2.50, £3.10; EX 118.70 Trifecta £1530.30 Pool: £2,088.70 - 1.01 winning units..
Owner Exors of the Late W M G Black **Bred** John Sullivan **Trained** Billy Row, Co Durham
■ Stewards' Enquiry : Denis O'Regan caution; used whip without giving mount time to respond

FOCUS
This long-standing staying handicap is always a war of attrition, but this year it was an almighty slog on the horrible ground and only three of the 12-strong field managed to complete. It certainly didn't look good and the overall form, best rated through the second, should really be taken with a pinch of salt.

NOTEBOOK
Companero(IRE) was pretty much out on his feet nearing two out and basically stepped over both of the last fences. He still had something left in reserve to sustain enough momentum to score, however, and he made just about every yard of the running. His connections had mooted retirement for him after two lacklustre efforts since returning this season, but the application of first-time blinkers worked the oracle, as he showed an awful lot more enthusiasm. He had shown in his pomp that testing ground holds no fears and that he is a dour stayer, but even this was too much for him. He comes out of the race with any amount of credit. (op 14-1)
Giles Cross(IRE) was 4lb higher than when runner-up to Synchronised in the Welsh National last month and proved popular. He was always close to the winner and rallied most gamely after hitting a flat spot turning for home. However, he stopped to a walk after two out and, although connections previously said he cannot have it testing enough, this ground did for him. He fully deserves to go one better again and could well be the sort for the Irish National in late April. (tchd 5-1)
Morgan Be finished third in this back in 2009 and, having travelled comfortably into contention, looked to have finally called it a day when stopping in the home straight. His rider later reported he initially believed he had knocked himself prior to stopping, but he was shortly afterwards satisfied he was okay and, when it became apparent nothing else was finishing, popped him over the last to claim a very remote third once more. Official explanation: jockey said, regarding finishing the race after apparently pulling up before the final fence, he thought gelding had knocked himself on landing after the second last and therefore considered pulling up, however gelding was sound to continue. (tchd 6-1)
Comply Or Die(IRE) won this off 5lb lower in his prime before going onto success in the 2008 Grand National. He showed more enthusiasm behind Minella Boys at Warwick last time, for which he was dropped 4lb, and did so again, but this ground certainly wasn't for him. While it was hardly the ideal prep for Aintree next month, don't be surprised if he runs another decent race there. (op 14-1)
Minella Boys(IRE) was 5lb higher than when just missing out in the Classic Chase at Warwick last month. He moved up looking a threat nearing the home turn, but was feeling the pinch prior to hitting a false patch of ground and losing his action. Official explanation: jockey said gelding slipped on bend turning into the home straight (op 14-1)
Belon Gale(IRE) weakened alarmingly and really before conditions became a serious issue, so something clearly went wrong with him. (op 14-1)

4361 PLAY ROULETTE & BLACKJACK AT TOTESPORT.COM NOVICES' HURDLE (8 hdls 1 omitted) 2m
3:50 (4:00) (Class 4) 4-Y-0+ **£2,374** (£697; £348; £174)

Form RPR
503 1 **Bollin Felix**[24] 3885 7-11-2 114 RichieMcGrath 114+
(Tim Easterby) *trckd ldrs: rdn and upsides 2 out: styd on to ld run-in: drvn rt out* **8/15**[1]
1 2 3 **Paddy Partridge**[227] 983 5-11-9 0 TomScudamore 118
(Tim Vaughan) *trckd ldr: led appr 3 out: hdd and no ex run-in* **5/1**[3]
4-33 3 28 **Flicka's Witness (IRE)**[263] 679 6-11-2 110 AdrianLane 86
(Donald McCain) *led: hdd appr 3 out: sn wknd* **9/2**[2]
06 4 20 **Napoletano (ITY)**[18] 3994 5-11-2 0 KennyJohnson 63
(Robert Johnson) *hld up in rr: sme hdwy 5th: lost pl appr next: tk distant 4th run-in* **40/1**
05 5 hd **Stanley Bridge**[11] 4132 4-10-7 0 BrianHarding 54
(Barry Murtagh) *trckd ldrs: modest 4th after 5th: sn wl outpcd: lost 4th run-in* **40/1**
53 6 12 **Ananda Kanda (USA)**[6] 4240 4-9-9 0 (t) BrianToomey(5) 35
(Brian Ellison) *hld up in rr: sme hdwy 5th: sn wknd* **10/1**
00-0 7 17 **Roslin Moss**[24] 3885 5-10-6 0 CallumWhillans(10) 34
(Donald Whillans) *hld up in rr: hdwy whn hit 5th: sn lost pl and bhd* **33/1**
/P-P P **Rock Port**[11] 4134 9-10-2 0 (t) MissCWalton(7) —
(James Walton) *trckd ldrs: lost pl after 5th: t.o whn p.u bef 2 out* **100/1**

4m 33.3s (23.30) **Going Correction** +0.875s/f (Soft)
WFA 4 from 5yo+ 9lb 8 Ran SP% **118.0**
Speed ratings (Par 105): **76,74,60,50,50 44,35,—**
Tote Swingers: 1&2 £2.40, 1&3 £1.80, 2&3 £2.00 CSF £3.99 TOTE £1.60: £1.10, £1.20, £1.40; EX 4.50.
Owner T D Easterby **Bred** Sir Neil & Exors Of Late Lady Westbrook **Trained** Great Habton, N Yorks

FOCUS
They went pretty steady early on here, and the first three put a gap between themselves and the rest of the field down the back straight. The winner is rated to his mark.

NOTEBOOK
Bollin Felix eventually made the most of the 7lb he was receiving from Paddy Partridge. A dual scorer in heavy ground on the Flat, he coped well with conditions and will probably get further in time. (tchd 4-7 and 8-13 in a place)
Paddy Partridge ran a decent race considering this sort of ground was all new to him and he was having to concede weight to the winner, who is proven in the mud. (op 9-2 tchd 11-2)
Flicka's Witness(IRE) didn't make things easy for himself by failing to settle early on, but his third place was never in any real danger all the way up the straight. (tchd 11-2)
Napoletano(ITY) can at least now have his attentions switched to very ordinary handicap company. (tchd 50-1)

4362 PLAY POKER AT TSPOKER.COM NOVICES' CHASE (16 fncs 2 omitted) 3m
4:25 (4:30) (Class 2) 5-Y-0+ **£10,086** (£3,688)

Form RPR
-31U 1 **Chamirey (FR)**[12] 4114 8-11-4 127 (b) TimmyMurphy 128+
(Donald McCain) *led 3rd: nt fluent 10th: wnt clr 4 out: heavily eased fnl 100yds* **1/1**[1]
1-4P 2 37 **Whats Up Woody (IRE)**[17] 4004 6-10-13 110 WilsonRenwick 86
(Howard Johnson) *j.rt: wnt prom 9th: rdn after 12th: sn wl outpcd: 3 l down whn lft distant 2nd last* **10/1**
-611 R **Tyrone House (IRE)**[31] 3751 7-11-7 119 JamesReveley 94
(John Wade) *led to 3rd: trckd wnr: upsides 11th: drvn and wknd 4 out: 20 l 2nd whn swvd bdly rt: ref and uns rdr last* **9/4**[2]
33P2 F **Ballymacduff (IRE)**[15] 4057 7-10-13 108 (t) JanFaltejsek —
(George Charlton) *t.k.h: trckd ldrs: 3rd whn fell 8th* **4/1**[3]

6m 54.3s (31.80) **Going Correction** +1.025s/f (Soft) 4 Ran SP% **109.9**
Speed ratings: **88,75,—,—**
CSF £9.12 TOTE £1.70; EX 8.90.
Owner Sir Robert Ogden **Bred** Mme Marie-France Graffard **Trained** Cholmondeley, Cheshire

FOCUS
This wasn't a strong race for the class, otherwise it could be rated higher.

NOTEBOOK
Chamirey(FR) made amends for unseating with the race at his mercy at Catterick 12 days earlier, doing the job easily. He again lacked fluency at his fences, jumping too deliberately at times, which allowed his rivals a chance on the final circuit. However, Timmy Murphy judged things to perfection and sent him confidently for home nearing the final turn. He soon had matters in control and, on ground holding no fears, he was afforded the luxury of stopping to a walk nearing the finish. He has been well handled by his present trainer and his confidence should be sky high again now. However, he still needs practice in this sphere, and may be better off going for something under a double penalty before tacking a competitive handicap. (tchd 10-11)
Whats Up Woody(IRE), who was left trailing when the winner asserted, plugged on after climbing over the final fence for a remote second. It was this former point winner's most encouraging effort yet over regulation fences, and he should find a race on better ground when this division becomes weaker towards the end of the season. (op 12-1)
Tyrone House(IRE) had won two moderate handicaps over 2m4f the last twice and was conceding 3lb to the winner, who is officially rated 8lb his superior. He jumped better in the main than that rival, but was easily left behind from the home turn and refused when out on his feet at the last. (op 11-2 tchd 7-2)
Ballymacduff(IRE), a quick-ground winner over hurdles, was well backed but didn't look particularly happy before falling on the far side. (op 11-2 tchd 7-2)

4363 200% DEPOSIT BONUS AT TSPOKER.COM STANDARD OPEN NATIONAL HUNT FLAT RACE 2m
5:00 (5:05) (Class 6) 4-6-Y-O **£1,431** (£420; £210; £104)

Form RPR
01 1 **The Tracey Shuffle**[20] 3971 5-11-10 0 TomScudamore 114+
(David Pipe) *mde all: rdn over 2f out: styd on to forge clr fnl f* **6/5**[1]
1-5 2 3 1/2 **Rocks Rule (IRE)**[104] 2403 6-11-3 0 JeremiahMcGrath(7) 111
(Alan Swinbank) *trckd wnr: rdn over 1f out: kpt on same pce* **5/2**[2]
3 11 **Dancing Art (IRE)** 5-11-3 0 JamesReveley 93
(Keith Reveley) *hld up in rr: hdwy 8f out: drvn over 4f out: tk modest 3rd over 3f out: one pce* **7/2**[3]
0 4 6 **Rear Admiral (IRE)**[24] 3889 5-10-10 0 JakeGreenall(7) 87
(Michael Easterby) *t.k.h: hdwy 8f out: drvn 4f out: sn wl outpcd* **14/1**
5 8 **First Gunner** 6-11-3 0 RobertWalford 79
(Tim Walford) *chsd ldrs: drvn 4f out: wknd over 3f out* **50/1**

6 *21* **Max My Boy (IRE)** 4-10-8 0 .... PaddyAspell 49
(Geoffrey Harker) *hld up in last: drvn 6f out: sn lost pl and bhd: t.o 3f out* **22/1**

6 **7** *20* **Little Fifi**[92] 2660 6-10-10 0 .... PeterBuchanan 31
(Sandy Thomson) *chsd ldrs: drvn 7f out: lost pl over 4f out: sn bhd: t.o 3f out* **66/1**

4m 15.6s (11.20) **Going Correction** +0.875s/f (Soft)
WFA 4 from 5yo+ 9lb **7** Ran SP% **110.7**
Speed ratings: **107,105,99,96,92 82,72**
Tote Swingers: 1&2 £1.10, 1&3 £1.60, 2&3 £2.00 CSF £4.04 TOTE £2.30: £1.60, £1.60; EX 5.40.
Owner Mrs Jo Tracey **Bred** Cotley Hill Stud **Trained** Nicholashayne, Devon

FOCUS
This bumper proved to be a lively betting heat. It was run at a sound tempo considering underfoot conditions and the form looks good with the two penalised runners dominating. They are both rated as improvers.

NOTEBOOK
The Tracey Shuffle showed a liking for soft ground when off the mark at Musselburgh 20 days previously and ran out a taking winner from the front. He proved free early on, but ensured it was a good test and really did very well to see it out in such fashion from 2f out. This half-brother to his yard's smart performer Mr Thriller is clearly above average. (op 11-8 tchd 7-4)
Rocks Rule(IRE) won on his debut over C&D last March and ran as though something was amiss on his comeback in November. This was a lot more like it again from him and he was a clear second-best, so could well win another one of these on a sounder surface. (op 13-8)
Dancing Art(IRE) came under heavy pressure off the home turn and that saw the first two get away from him. His sire's progeny often prefer quicker ground and he looks sure to come on for the experience. Therefore improvement should be expected when he encounters a sounder surface and he has a future. (op 13-2)
Rear Admiral(IRE), seventh on his debut over C&D 24 days earlier, was a market mover earlier in the day yet the support was not forthcoming on the track. He shaped better, but was another for whom the ground was too much. (op 11-1 tchd 9-1)
First Gunner, bred to be a staying chaser, was going as well as any turning for home. He got badly outpaced when the first two asserted, but should come on plenty and is one to keep an eye on with a view to jumping in due course. (op 33-1)
T/Plt: £32.20 to a £1 stake. Pool: £113,785.63 - 2,576.45 winning tickets T/Qpdt: £4.70 to a £1 stake. Pool: £6,359.91 - 990.16 winning tickets WG

4364 - 4369a (Foreign Racing) - See Raceform Interactive

3958 FONTWELL (L-H)
Sunday, February 27

OFFICIAL GOING: Good to soft (soft in places) changing to soft after race 1 (2:10)
Fresh ground on all hurdles track and on chase bends. Rail realignment added 25yds per circuit to both courses.
Wind: Light, half against Weather: Rain races 1-5, cloudy after

4370 TOTESPORT.COM SUPPORTING RACEHORSE SANCTUARY NOVICES' HURDLE (11 hdls) 2m 6f 110y
2:10 (2:11) (Class 4) 5-Y-0+ **£2,276** (£668; £334; £166)

Form RPR
341 **1** **Bunglasha Lady (IRE)**[24] 3901 6-10-12 119 .... WayneHutchinson 121+
(Warren Greatrex) *trckd ldrs: led on bit after 3 out: rdn clr run-in: styd on wl* **3/1**[2]

6-2P **2** *4 ½* **Hong Kong Harry**[22] 3950 7-10-12 113 .... RobertThornton 115
(Alan King) *chsd ldrs: rdn to chal 2 out: nt qckn run-in* **5/1**[3]

-044 **3** *17* **Lost Two Stars (IRE)**[24] 3904 6-10-5 102 .... JoeTizzard 94
(Colin Tizzard) *mstkes: w ldrs tl wknd appr 2 out* **9/1**

2-2 **4** *10* **Vico (IRE)**[101] 2482 7-10-7 120 .... MrMRMahon(5) 94
(Paul Nicholls) *prom: led briefly 3 out: wknd appr next: 4th and btn whn hung rt run-in* **5/4**[1]

3 **5** *6* **Arctic Gunner**[67] 3088 7-10-12 .... JimmyMcCarthy 85
(Geoffrey Deacon) *t.k.h towards rr: hdwy to chse ldrs 8th: wknd after 3 out* **20/1**

6565 **6** *16* **Venetian Lad**[12] 4128 6-10-12 96 .... MarkBradburne 71
(Lydia Richards) *slt ld tl wknd 3 out* **50/1**

0-66 **7** *6* **Troy Tempest (IRE)**[50] 3448 6-10-12 .... JackDoyle 66
(Emma Lavelle) *t.k.h in rr: mstke 4th: n.d fr 8th* **10/1**

6 **8** *5* **Luck'N'Thanks (IRE)**[23] 3918 8-10-12 .... JodieMogford 61
(Graeme McPherson) *mid-div on outer: outpcd 7th: sn bhd* **80/1**

0-0P **9** *4 ½* **Manics Man**[14] 4094 6-10-12 .... JamieMoore 57
(Helen Nelmes) *in tch on inner tl wknd 3 out* **125/1**

0000 **10** *46* **Kidajo**[21] 3960 5-10-12 .... DaveCrosse 16
(Roger Curtis) *mid-div: mstke 4th: wknd 7th: sn wl bhd* **125/1**

P **P** **Spiritual Art**[20] 3981 5-10-2 ow2 .... JoshuaMoore(5) —
(Luke Dace) *a bhd: mstke 8th: t.o whn p.u bef 2 out* **100/1**

4P **P** **Toomyvara (IRE)**[58] 3266 7-10-12 .... LiamTreadwell —
(Nick Gifford) *chsd ldrs: nt fluent 5th: mstke next: wkng whn mstke 8th: t.o whn p.u bef 2 out* **100/1**

6m 11.2s (28.70) **Going Correction** +1.55s/f (Heav) **12** Ran SP% **116.7**
Speed ratings: **112,110,103,99,97 91,88,86,84,67 —,—**
toteswingers:1&2:£4.30, 1&3:£5.90, 2&3:£6.60 CSF £18.02 TOTE £4.00: £1.60, £1.80, £2.00; EX 18.80.
Owner Mrs T Brown **Bred** Desmond Devereux **Trained** Upper Lambourn, Berks

FOCUS
There was 6.5mm of rain on Friday night, resulting in the ground being described as good to soft, soft in places, but conditions looked a lot more testing than that, and jockeys returning after the first race described it as very soft or heavy. The official description was changed to soft (GoingStick 4.0). With the rail having been moved, adding 25 yards to both courses per circuit, it meant that they were racing on a fresh strip of ground on the hurdles track, and on the bends on the chase course. A fair novice hurdle, and a real test in the conditions, with the second setting the level.

NOTEBOOK
Bunglasha Lady(IRE) showed that stamina is her strong suit when winning at Towcester last time. She'll get 3m without any problem, and should make a nice novice staying chaser next season. She'll now go to the valuable mares' hurdle at Newbury next month. (op 11-4)
Hong Kong Harry left a poor effort at Sandown behind and showed himself to be another for whom a real stamina test is ideal. This softer ground seemed to be in his favour. (op 6-1)
Lost Two Stars(IRE) is improving with racing and ran her best race so far, but she could do with brushing up her jumping a touch. (op 10-1 tchd 8-1)
Vico(IRE) looked the one to beat on the ratings but this was the softest ground he had encountered, and he just didn't see out his race on it. A return to a better surface should be in his favour. (tchd 6-4 and 7-4 in a place)
Arctic Gunner, debuting over hurdles, was a little keen early on, which didn't help him get home. (op 16-1)
Luck'N'Thanks(IRE) Official explanation: jockey said gelding ran to free

4371 PLAY POKER AT TSPOKER.COM NOVICES' CHASE (16 fncs) 2m 6f
2:40 (2:40) (Class 2) 5-Y-0+ **£9,624** (£3,006; £1,619)

Form RPR
0222 **1** **Fruity O'Rooney**[13] 4119 8-11-3 130 .... JamieMoore 136
(Gary Moore) *mde all: pressed by runner-up fnl circ: rdn appr 4 out: hrd drvn run-in: hld on gamely* **5/4**[1]

-601 **2** *nk* **Sarando**[41] 3605 6-11-3 130 .... (t) WillKennedy 137
(Paul Webber) *cl up: j. deliberately 2nd and 5th: rdn next: pressed wnr fr 11th: mstke 4 out: kpt on wl u.p run-in: jst hld* **15/8**[2]

4-12 **3** *36* **Pouvoir (FR)**[141] 1770 8-11-3 122 .... RobertThornton 110
(Alan King) *cl up tl slt mstke and wknd 3 out* **11/4**[3]

P **Rockoboy (IRE)**[1813] 10-10-12 0 .... DaveCrosse —
(Zoe Davison) *cl up tl wknd qckly appr 11th: sn bhd: t.o whn p.u bef 3 out* **100/1**

6m 15.2s (32.20) **Going Correction** +1.55s/f (Heav) **4** Ran SP% **106.9**
Speed ratings: **103,102,89,—**
CSF £4.00 TOTE £2.20; EX 2.80.
Owner Heart Of The South Racing **Bred** R W Russell **Trained** Lower Beeding, W Sussex

FOCUS
Just the four runners for a decent prize, but a good battle over the last few fences and up the run-in. The principals are rated to their marks.

NOTEBOOK
Fruity O'Rooney saw off the persistent challenge of Sarando and broke a run of second-place finishes. He doesn't mind testing ground, but acts on quicker too, although the handicapper probably has a fair idea of his level now, so success in handicaps might not be too easy to find. Apparently he'll go for a conditions hurdle at Auteuil next. (op 11-8 tchd 6-4 in places)
Sarando lost ground when careful at a few fences but he kept coming back for more, and he was closing the winner down as the line approached. Twice a winner in heavy ground, conditions can't be too testing for him. (op 13-8 tchd 2-1)
Pouvoir(FR) has gone well fresh in the past, so the fact that he was returning from a 141-day absence wasn't as great a concern as the going. His best form is undoubtedly on good ground, so this testing surface was far from ideal. (op 3-1 tchd 9-4)

4372 200% DEPOSIT BONUS AT TSPOKER.COM H'CAP CHASE (FOR THE CERTAIN JUSTICE CHALLENGE TROPHY) (16 fncs) 2m 6f
3:10 (3:11) (Class 4) (0-115,115) 5-Y-0+ **£2,871** (£843; £421; £210)

Form RPR
0222 **1** **Rateable Value**[23] 3935 7-10-7 96 .... JoeTizzard 107
(Colin Tizzard) *hld up in rr: hdwy and in tch 8th: effrt 3 out: rdn to ld last: styd on wl* **2/1**[1]

1144 **2** *3 ¼* **Massini Sunset (IRE)**[6] 4265 11-11-5 115 .... (b) SClements(7) 123
(Richard Mitchell) *mde most and gng wl most of way tl hdd and no ex last* **20/1**

0U65 **3** *22* **Oncle Kid (FR)**[40] 3614 9-10-3 92 .... JamieMoore 83
(Paul Henderson) *prom: wnt 2nd at 6th: hit next: mstke 12th: wknd 2 out* **16/1**

400P **4** *8* **Skipper's Lad (IRE)**[24] 3907 9-10-1 93 .... (bt) SamTwiston-Davies(3) 71
(Colin Tizzard) *chsd ldrs tl wknd 3 out* **13/2**

-0P0 **5** *12* **Princely Hero (IRE)**[16] 4052 7-10-11 100 .... LeightonAspell 66
(Chris Gordon) *t.k.h in midfield: dropped towards rr 9th: struggling fr 11th* **33/1**

1131 **6** *26* **Pete The Feat (IRE)**[40] 3614 7-10-10 99 .... FelixDeGiles 59
(Anna Newton-Smith) *towards rr: sme hdwy 10th: rdn and pckd next: struggling to hold pl whn mstke 12th: wknd 4 out* **4/1**[2]

3206 **7** *20* **Corredor Sun (USA)**[31] 3768 5-10-3 94 .... (p) DavidEngland 12
(Nigel Twiston-Davies) *w ldr tl mstke 6th: rdn 10th: wknd 12th* **16/1**

04U1 **P** **Swainson (USA)**[30] 3790 10-10-1 95 .... JoshuaMoore(5) —
(Helen Nelmes) *hld up in rr: hdwy 8th: outpcd after 10th: mstke 12th: brief rally 4 out: sn btn: bhd whn p.u bef 2 out* **9/1**

F2P2 **P** **Quel Bruere (FR)**[17] 4022 7-11-0 106 .... (tp) TomMolloy(3) —
(Graeme McPherson) *in tch: mstke 2nd: dropped to last at 6th: bhd whn blnd 11th: t.o whn p.u bef 2 out* **9/2**[3]

6m 14.0s (31.00) **Going Correction** +1.55s/f (Heav)
WFA 5 from 7yo+ 2lb **9** Ran SP% **114.3**
Speed ratings: **105,103,95,92,88 79,71,—,—**
.\n\x\x
Owner R G Tizzard **Bred** R G & Mrs S L Tizzard **Trained** Milborne Port, Dorset

FOCUS
A moderate handicap chase with the winner back to his best, and the race could be rated slightly higher.

NOTEBOOK
Rateable Value, runner-up in his previous three starts over fences, finally got off the mark under a well-judged ride from Joe Tizzard, who drew alongside Massini Sunset at the last fence and then pulled clear on the run-in. He was fully entitled to go close off this mark and, with further improvement quite possible, could well be capable of defying a rise. (op 3-1)
Massini Sunset(IRE) made most of the running and ran a brave race under top weight. Despite now being an 11-y-o, he has never been better, running here off a career-high mark, and presumably he can expect another little rise on the back of this. (op 16-1)
Oncle Kid(FR), another who was always in the van, ran well for a long way, but he's a longstanding maiden and remains one to take on. (op 10-1)
Skipper's Lad(IRE) didn't get home in the ground and is better on a sounder surface. (op 7-1 tchd 11-2)
Princely Hero(IRE), debuting over fences, is a keen-going sort, and in this ground that was always going to hurt his chances. (op 25-1)
Pete The Feat(IRE), another 4lb higher, was let down by his jumping. (tchd 7-2 and 9-2 in a place)
Corredor Sun(USA) Official explanation: jockey said gelding was unsuited by going (soft)

4373 TOTESPORT.COM NATIONAL SPIRIT HURDLE (GRADE 2) (10 hdls) 2m 4f
3:45 (3:45) (Class 1) 4-Y-0+ **£18,528** (£6,951; £3,480; £1,735; £871)

Form RPR
3332 **1** **Celestial Halo (IRE)**[8] 4222 7-11-7 162 .... (bt) HarrySkelton 153+
(Paul Nicholls) *t.k.h: pressed ldr: led 5th: comf drew clr appr 2 out: rdn and styd on wl run-in* **6/4**[2]

010- **2** *6* **Trenchant**[346] 4699 6-11-11 149 .... (b) RobertThornton 151
(Alan King) *hld up in tch: rdn to chse wnr 2 out: a wl hld* **15/2**[3]

30B5 **3** *8* **Afsoun (FR)**[60] 3199 9-11-3 140 .... AlexMerriam 135
(Neil King) *led tl 5th: rdn and btn appr 2 out* **25/1**

-214 **4** *9* **Karabak (FR)**[57] 3289 8-11-11 161 .... APMcCoy 141+
(Alan King) *handy 3rd tl blnd and slithered on landing 5th: dropped to last: rallied 3 out: hrd rdn and wknd appr next* **11/8**[1]

-2F3 5 17 **Tarkari (IRE)**[22] 3939 6-11-3 136 PaulMoloney 113
(Evan Williams) *hld up in rr: promising effrt and cl 5th whn mstke 3 out: wknd appr next: 5th and no ch whn mstke last* 10/1

5m 23.3s (23.90) **Going Correction** +1.55s/f (Heavy) **5** Ran SP% **106.8**
Speed ratings (Par 115): **114,111,108,104,98**
CSF £11.29 TOTE £2.60: £1.80, £1.10; EX 10.90.
Owner The Stewart Family **Bred** Roncon Churchtown Bloodstock & Lane Ltd **Trained** Ditcheat, Somerset

FOCUS
They went quite steady early on here. The winner is rated a stone below recent form with the second to last year's winning mark.

NOTEBOOK
Celestial Halo(IRE), who was prominent throughout, confirmed the return to form he showed in the Kingwell at Wincanton eight days earlier with a smooth success. His ability to follow up that effort so soon afterwards was a concern, but he was best in at the weights, and his cause was helped by the serious mistake made by his main market rival Karabak. He'll be left in the World Hurdle at the five-day stage in case anything goes wrong with Big Buck's, but the plan is to go straight to Liverpool for the Aintree Hurdle next, a race in which he was still going well when coming down two out last year. He should be a leading contender there, as most of his main rivals will be arriving there on the back of a hard race at Cheltenham. (tchd 6-4 early in a place)
Trenchant, who won this race last year, was expected by his trainer to need this run, having been off the track for the best part of a year. He ran well in the circumstances, especially as he was giving 4lb to the winner, and should come on for the outing. (op 8-1 tchd 17-2)
Afsoun(FR), third in this race last year, filled the same position again, which is about as good as he could have hoped for in this company. (tchd 28-1)
Karabak(FR) made a bad mistake at the fifth and slithered on landing. Although he made up the lost ground, the effort expended cost him in the latter stages. (tchd 5-4 and 6-4 in places)
Tarkari(IRE) has plenty of form in bad ground so these conditions ought not to have been a problem for him, but he was the lowest rated of these and a couple of mistakes late on didn't help. (op 12-1 tchd 9-1)

4374 FULLER'S LONDON PRIDE FOXHUNTERS TRIAL HUNTERS' CHASE (FOR THE WHITELAW CHALLENGE CUP) (17 fncs 2 omitted) 3m 2f 110y
4:15 (4:16) (Class 6) 5-Y-O+ **£1,673** (£639)

Form RPR
-262 1 **Herons Well**[10] 4163 8-11-13 138 (p) MrJoshHalley(7) 123+
(Rebecca Curtis) *mde virtually all: easily wnt 7 l clr ent st: rdn after 2 out: tiring but hld on run-in: all out* 5/6[1]
22-6 2 1 1/4 **Honour's Dream (FR)**[7] 8-11-7 90 (v) MissCLWills(5) 113
(Mrs Jenny Gordon) *pressed wnr: hrd rdn and hit 4 out: 7 l down ent st: rallied and ch fnl 100yds: jst hld* 20/1
3-5U P **Sesame Rambler (IRE)**[14] 12-12-3 101 MrJMQuinlan(3) —
(Mrs S Alner) *nvr gng wl in rr: pckd 10th: no ch 13th: t.o whn p.u after 4 out* 13/2[3]
55-P P **Gripit N Tipit (IRE)**[17] 4026 10-11-5 117 (b) MrMEnnis(7) —
(Sarah Humphrey) *in tch: wknd 13th: wl bhd whn blnd and p.u 15th* 10/1
30/- U **Super Sensation (GER)**[8] 10-11-5 89 (p) MrLOswin(7) —
(K Kukk) *bhd tl rn st into 5th (ditch) and uns rdr* 66/1
20/1 P **Horsham Lad (IRE)**[21] 7-11-9 0 MrSWDrinkwater(7) —
(F M O'Brien) *in tch: pckd 10th: outpcd by ldng pair fr 13th: 3rd and no ch whn p.u and dismntd on home turn* 11/4[2]

7m 43.0s (41.90) **Going Correction** +1.55s/f (Heavy) **6** Ran SP% **109.9**
Speed ratings: **99,98,—,—,—,—**
toteswinger:1&2:£15.46 CSF £15.46 TOTE £1.70: £1.10, £6.40; EX 17.30.
Owner Miss Rebecca Curtis **Bred** T F Mathias **Trained** Newport, Dyfed
■ A first winner in Britain for Irish-based Josh Halley.

FOCUS
Only two finishers in this fair hunter chase with the winner rated a stone below his best, although the runner-up is getting back to his 2009 form.

NOTEBOOK
Herons Well had run well behind Sericina at Ffos Las on his previous start and was fully entitled to take this. He travelled like the best horse in the race and, although things got a bit desperate close home, he can be rated as a more comfortable winner than the margin suggests. He'll go to Cheltenham next. (op 11-10 tchd 6-5 in a place)
Honour's Dream(FR), second but quite well beaten in a point last time out, faced a stiff task on paper, but he was the only one to keep tabs on the winner, kept plugging away, and in the end had his chance of glory. He clearly stays very well. (op 25-1)
Horsham Lad(IRE), a beaten favourite in both starts in points this year, again disappointed, although these were extreme conditions. (op 6-4)

4375 WILDWOOD GOLF CLUB SUPPORTS THE RACEHORSE SANCTUARY H'CAP HURDLE (9 hdls) 2m 2f 110y
4:45 (4:45) (Class 4) (0-115,110) 4-Y-O+ **£2,602** (£764; £382; £190)

Form RPR
-556 1 **Quincy Des Pictons (FR)**[172] 1509 7-11-5 **103** JodieMogford 109
(Graeme McPherson) *hld up in rr: disputing last whn blnd 6th: gd hdwy 2 out: styd on wl to ld fnl 50yds* 25/1
6662 2 1 1/2 **Just The Job (IRE)**[3] 4314 7-10-9 **100** MarkQuinlan(7) 106+
(Neil Mulholland) *hld up in tch: smooth hdwy to ld on bit after 3 out: 5 l clr whn blnd next: wknd run-in: hdd fnl 50yds* 13/8[1]
0201 3 9 **Dune Shine**[30] 3793 6-11-12 **110** LeightonAspell 106
(Oliver Sherwood) *towards rr: hdwy 6th: chsd ldrs 2 out: no ex last* 6/1[2]
-134 4 6 **Domino Dancer (IRE)**[16] 4049 7-10-10 **97** CPGeoghegan(3) 87
(Lucy Jones) *prom: hrd rdn appr 2 out: sn btn* 14/1
-500 5 3 3/4 **Haarth Sovereign (IRE)**[17] 4025 7-11-4 **105** (t) DavidBass(3) 91
(Lawney Hill) *led tl after 3 out: sn wknd* 11/1
2404 6 8 **Sun Quest**[30] 3793 7-10-13 **104** RobertKirk(7) 82
(Steven Dixon) *prom: pressed ldr 3 out: wknd appr next* 6/1[2]
0 7 27 **Sawago (FR)**[21] 3962 5-11-7 **105** JamieMoore 56
(Gary Moore) *in tch: lost pl 5th: struggling fr next* 16/1
F3P/ 8 14 **Flow Gently Along (IRE)**[674] 5194 8-10-11 **95** TomScudamore 32
(Michael Scudamore) *hld up in rr: lost tch 6th: sn wl bhd* 10/1[3]
0230 9 21 **Beside The Fire**[17] 4034 6-11-11 **109** JoeTizzard 25
(Colin Tizzard) *w ldr: mstkes 1st and 2nd: wknd qckly appr 6th* 6/1[2]

5m 10.1s (35.80) **Going Correction** +1.55s/f (Heavy) **9** Ran SP% **114.8**
Speed ratings (Par 105): **86,85,81,79,77 74,62,56,48**
toteswingers:1&2:£18.80, 1&3:£34.30, 2&3:£2.90 CSF £67.84 CT £292.75 TOTE £25.40: £4.20, £1.50, £1.80; EX 197.60.
Owner BPD Ltd **Bred** S C E A Du Marais Des Pictons **Trained** Upper Oddington, Gloucs

FOCUS
An ordinary handicap with the winner rated to his 2009 best and the second close to his mark.

NOTEBOOK
Quincy Des Pictons(FR) was making his debut for a new stable and returning to hurdles for the first time in over a year. His only previous win had come in a maiden hurdle on good ground in April 2009, but clearly the change of scenery has been a plus, and he relished this test in the conditions to outstay the runner-up. Perhaps he can now go on from this. (op 22-1)
Just The Job(IRE) cruised through the race and looked set for a comfortable success, but he didn't meet the second-last well, and then he began to paddle. The winner simply stayed on better than him in the conditions, and a return to better ground will suit him. (op 9-4 tchd 5-2 in places)
Dune Shine, 5lb higher than when successful over this C&D last time, kept plugging on but couldn't match the first two from the last. (op 5-1)
Domino Dancer(IRE) is far more effective on a sounder surface. (op 12-1)
Haarth Sovereign(IRE), who made much of the running, is better over shorter, and on quicker ground, too. (tchd 10-1)
Beside The Fire Official explanation: jockey said gelding was never travelling

4376 TRANSLLOYD GROUP SUPPORTS THE RACEHORSE SANCTUARY STANDARD OPEN NATIONAL HUNT FLAT RACE 2m 2f 110y
5:15 (5:15) (Class 6) 4-6-Y-O **£1,626** (£477; £238; £119)

Form RPR
1 1 **Destroyer Deployed**[24] 3903 5-11-10 0 RichardJohnson 113+
(Tim Vaughan) *t.k.h: trckd ldrs: disp ld 5f out: led 3f out: drvn out* 5/2[2]
0-33 2 2 3/4 **Vincentian (IRE)**[24] 3903 6-11-3 0 DarylJacob 103
(David Arbuthnot) *hld up in tch: disp ld 5f out tl 3f out: pressed wnr after: kpt on u.p* 11/2[3]
5 3 7 **Jimmy The Hat (IRE)**[120] 2087 5-11-0 0 TomMolloy(3) 96
(Giles Smyly) *prom: hrd rdn 4f out: one pce fnl 2f* 8/1
4 11 **Camas Bridge**[147] 5-11-3 0 JackDoyle 86
(Emma Lavelle) *hld up in rr: smooth hdwy 6f out: trckd ldrs gng wl 4f out: rdn 2f out: sn wknd* 85/40[1]
2B 5 44 **Traditional Bob (IRE)**[24] 3909 6-11-3 0 JodieMogford 41
(Graeme McPherson) *towards rr: effrt and in tch 7f out: struggling fnl 5f* 13/2
6 28 **Camelloe** 5-10-10 0 JoeTizzard 6
(Colin Tizzard) *hld up towards rr: effrt and in tch 7f out: wknd over 5f out* 16/1
60 7 23 **Bach To Front (IRE)**[16] 4055 6-10-10 0 GerardTumelty —
(Sarah Wall) *sn led: hdd & wknd 5f out* 50/1
4 8 19 **Alivad (IRE)**[14] 4097 4-10-0 0 LiamTreadwell —
(Peter Hedger) *chsd ldrs: rdn and lost pl 1/2-way: sn wl bhd* 33/1
0 9 33 **It's A Killer**[52] 3406 6-11-3 0 LeightonAspell —
(Richard Rowe) *w ldr: wknd qckly 1m out: sn wl bhd* 66/1
0 10 16 **West Bay Hoolie**[270] 589 5-11-3 0 JamieMoore —
(Helen Nelmes) *plld hrd towards rr: hrd rdn and lost tch 1m out: sn wl bhd* 80/1

5m 2.10s (33.40) **Going Correction** +1.55s/f (Heavy)
WFA 4 from 5yo+ 9lb **10** Ran SP% **113.9**
Speed ratings: **91,89,86,82,63 51,42,34,20,13**
toteswingers:1&2:£3.60, 1&3:£5.40, 2&3:£7.30 CSF £16.03 TOTE £3.30: £1.40, £1.60, £2.80; EX 17.50.
Owner The Craftsmen **Bred** A W Buller **Trained** Aberthin, Vale of Glamorgan

FOCUS
The key form guide to this race was a 2m Towcester bumper run earlier this month. The winner stepped up on that and the third sets the level.

NOTEBOOK
Destroyer Deployed beat Vincentian into third on his final start at Towcester and, although that rival was 7lb better off at the weights for a 10l beating, he confirmed the form. He looks a useful sort and will likely stay well when sent over hurdles. (tchd 2-1)
Vincentian(IRE) ran well but the turnaround in the weights with the winner compared with their last meeting proved insufficient for him to reverse the form. Nevertheless, he should be capable of finding a minor bumper if his connections decide to persevere with him in this sphere. (tchd 9-2)
Jimmy The Hat(IRE), fifth in a decent bumper at Ascot on his debut, is bred to stay well and he kept going for pressure. He should do better when he's sent over hurdles. (op 10-1 tchd 12-1)
Camas Bridge ◆, runner-up in a point last October to Trustan Times, who has since won a hurdle race for Tim Easterby, shaped well on his debut under rules, travelling strongly to the turn in before emptying under pressure. He ran as though in need of the outing, and should take a bit of beating in similar company next time. (op 9-4 tchd 11-4)
Traditional Bob(IRE), a half-brother to Beat The Boys, may have found conditions too testing. (op 7-1)
T/Jkpt: £3,849.00 to a £1 stake. Pool:£43,369.59 - 8.00 winning tickets T/Plt: £45.00 to a £1 stake. Pool:£110,601.65 - 1,792.68 winning tickets T/Qpdt: £9.20 to a £1 stake. Pool:£7,069.79 - 566.23 winning tickets LM

3897 TOWCESTER (R-H)
Sunday, February 27

OFFICIAL GOING: Heavy (6.5)
Wind: Fresh across Weather: Overcast

4377 GG.COM NORTHAMPTON NOVICES' HURDLE (7 hdls 1 omitted) 2m
2:30 (2:31) (Class 3) 4-Y-O+ **£3,252** (£955; £477; £238)

Form RPR
-211 1 **Whoops A Daisy**[23] 3918 5-11-0 130 RichardKilloran(3) 131+
(Nicky Henderson) *chsd ldr to 3rd: remained handy: led appr 2 out: styd on wl* 15/8[1]
2352 2 4 **Maggio (FR)**[7] 4242 6-10-13 130 (p) JamesO'Farrell(3) 126
(Patrick Griffin, Ire) *reluctant to line up: sn prom: led after 3rd: rdn and hdd appr 2 out: styd on same pce last* 5/2[2]
251 3 9 **Buddy Holly**[23] 3489 6-11-2 120 GilesHawkins(5) 123
(Violet M Jordan) *chsd ldrs: pushed along 5th: rdn to go 3rd appr 2 out: mstke and wknd last* 9/2[3]
4134 4 26 **Ultravox (USA)**[9] 4196 4-10-12 116 NickScholfield 87
(Jeremy Scott) *prom: rdn and wknd after 3 out: t.o* 5/1
050- 5 2 1/4 **Jat Punjabi**[317] 5214 7-11-2 0 RodiGreene 89
(Trevor Wall) *hld up: wknd 5th: t.o* 250/1
0 6 5 **Sustainability (IRE)**[61] 3158 6-11-2 0 AidanColeman 84
(Venetia Williams) *prom: rdn after 4th: hit next: sn wknd t.o* 33/1
P00 7 1/2 **Ostaadi**[31] 3761 5-11-2 0 (p) DPFahy 83
(Bernard Llewellyn) *hld up: hdwy 5th: wknd bef next: t.o* 150/1
10 8 2 1/2 **Lucky Landing (IRE)**[31] 3761 5-11-2 0 JasonMaguire 81
(Donald McCain) *led tl after 3rd: chsd ldr: rdn and wknd appr 2 out: t.o* 12/1
U 9 15 **Jackson (BRZ)**[18] 2540 9-11-2 0 PaddyAspell 66
(Richard Guest) *prom: pushed along 4th: wknd appr 3 out: t.o* 150/1
4/3 10 6 **Keepthebooton (IRE)**[26] 3864 8-11-2 0 TomSiddall 60
(Noel Chance) *hld up: rdn after 4th: sn wknd: t.o* 33/1

Form	Pos	Dist	Horse	RPR
0-30	11	5	**World Watch (IRE)**[21] 3960 6-10-13 0.......................... TommyPhelan(3) (Tom Gretton) *hld up: sme hdwy 5th: wknd bef next: t.o* **80/1**	55

4m 19.6s (11.70) **Going Correction** +0.975s/f (Soft)
WFA 4 from 5yo+ 9lb **11** Ran SP% **114.7**
Speed ratings (Par 107): **109,107,102,89,88 85,85,84,76,73 71**
toteswingers:1&2:£1.10, 1&3:£2.60, 2&3:£4.20 CSF £6.65 TOTE £2.70: £1.20, £1.50, £1.70; EX 7.10.
Owner Let's Live Racing **Bred** N J Henderson And Mrs S A Aston **Trained** Upper Lambourn, Berks

FOCUS
A decent novices' hurdle for the track that has thrown up some fair sorts in the past, and it panned out much as the market suggested. The winner is on the upgrade with the placed horses setting the level.

NOTEBOOK
Whoops A Daisy, a dual hurdles winner on soft ground, was facing the most testing going she had yet encountered but seemed to relish it. She was keen early on but, after settling in behind the leaders, took the lead early in the straight and bounded up the hill. The EBF Mares' Hurdle at Newbury is apparently on the agenda, although she might go up the weights again for this. (op 2-1 tchd 7-4)
Maggio(FR), rated the same as the winner following a couple of decent efforts in graded contests in Ireland, was reluctant to line up but, once jumping off, was never far away and ran his race, although proving no match for the winner. He looks a little flattered by that official mark. (tchd 9-4 and 3-1)
Buddy Holly, giving weight to two rivals rated higher, ran as well as could be expected but was very tired when hitting the last. (op 7-2 tchd 11-4 and 5-1)
Ultravox(USA), a C&D winner here last month, had a fair bit to find with the principals and was in trouble turning for home. (op 9-1)

4378 TIPZONE AT GG.COM (S) H'CAP HURDLE (7 hdls 1 omitted) 2m
3:00 (3:00) (Class 5) (0-90,90) 4-Y-O+ **£1,463** (£429; £214; £107)

Form	Pos	Dist	Horse	RPR
406-	1		**Tavalu (USA)**[401] 2528 9-10-12 **79**..............................(p) DonalDevereux(3) (Gerald Ham) *hld up: hdwy after 5th: led 2 out: rdn out* **40/1**	82
5434	2	3 3/4	**Low Delta (IRE)**[35] 3703 11-11-4 **82**.............................. DominicElsworth (Michael Blake) *hld up and bhd: hdwy appr 3 out: ev ch next: sn rdn: styd on same pce last* **4/1**[1]	81
BP4P	3	4	**Humbel Times (IRE)**[28] 3833 7-9-7 **64** oh4.................. TrevorWhelan(7) (Neil King) *chsd ldrs tl led 5th: rdn and hdd 2 out: mstke last: no ex* **17/2**	62
50/3	4	15	**Andy Gin (FR)**[24] 3899 12-11-5 **83**.............................. CharliePoste (Evelyn England) *prom: chsd ldr 5th: ev ch 2 out: sn rdn and wknd* **15/2**[3]	68
-503	5	13	**Brigadore (USA)**[9] 4178 8-11-0 **85**..............................(p) DannyBurton(7) (Alan Jones) *led 2nd to appr 4th: rdn and wknd after 3 out: t.o* **4/1**[1]	52
-300	6	3 1/2	**Lightening Fire (IRE)**[34] 3717 9-10-11 **78**..............................(b) IanPopham(3) (Bernard Llewellyn) *drvn along in rr early: hdwy after 2nd: led appr 4th: hdd next: rdn and wknd 3 out: t.o* **9/2**[2]	42
30-0	P		**Ravenscar**[40] 3618 13-10-4 **71**.............................. AdamPogson(3) (Charles Pogson) *prom: rdn after 5th: wknd after 3 out: t.o whn p.u bef next* **16/1**	—
0-00	P		**Fantastic Morning**[33] 3727 7-10-0 **64**..............................(p) TomMessenger (Violet M Jordan) *led to 2nd: chsd ldrs: rdn after 4th: sn wknd: t.o whn p.u bef 3 out* **25/1**	—
6-	P		**Grand Fella (IRE)**[73] 2990 6-11-7 **90**.............................. CO'Farrell(5) (Patrick Morris) *hld up: bhd fr 5th: t.o whn p.u bef 2 out* **9/2**[2]	—

4m 30.2s (22.30) **Going Correction** +1.40s/f (Heav) **9** Ran SP% **110.8**
Speed ratings (Par 103): **100,98,96,88,82 80,—,—,—**
toteswingers:1&2:£20.70, 1&3:£6.00, 2&3:£5.40 CSF £186.05 CT £1463.10 TOTE £27.30: £3.70, £2.20, £3.40; EX 260.20.There was no bid for the winner.
Owner G A Ham **Bred** Gainsborough Farm Llc **Trained** Rooks Bridge, Somerset
■ Stewards' Enquiry : Trevor Whelan two-day ban; excessive use of whip (13-14 March)

FOCUS
This moderate seller, run 10.4sec slower than the opening novices' hurdle, produced a surprise result. The runner-up and fourth are rated in line with recent form.

NOTEBOOK
Tavalu(USA), who had been absent for 13 months and had not run over jumps since November 2009, was better known as a fast-ground performer then but had handled soft on the rare occasions he had encountered it. He travelled well and, unaffected by a mistake four out, came through to lead at the penultimate flight for a cosy success. This was a fine piece of training to have him fit to handle these conditions, although his trainer reported he was a travelling companion for his other runner, who took the fifth race. (tchd 50-1)
Low Delta(IRE) had the ground to suit but was keen early, although his rider managed to settle him out the back. He made steady headway up the hill with his rider not resorting to the whip until after the last, but could never land a blow at the winner. (op 9-2 tchd 7-2)
Humbel Times(IRE) was well supported despite racing from out of the handicap. He responded to reminders after the third to hit the front at the end of the back straight, but looked held by the winner when a last-flight mistake ended his chance. The drop in trip helped him produce his best effort so far. (op 16-1)
Andy Gin(FR) has had a lot of time off the track since scoring his last win over C&D nearly five years ago, but showed he retains ability and might have a similar contest in him around here, given soft ground. (op 7-1 tchd 11-2)
Brigadore(USA) faded after being up there early and ran well below par. (op 7-2 tchd 9-2)
Lightening Fire(IRE) was never going that well. (tchd 4-1)
Fantastic Morning Official explanation: jockey said gelding bled from nose (op 5-1)
Grand Fella(IRE) always at the rear on his first start for new connections. (op 5-1)

4379 HAYGAIN HAY STEAMERS H'CAP CHASE (14 fncs) 2m 3f 110y
3:30 (3:31) (Class 4) (0-115,107) 5-Y-O+ **£2,602** (£764; £382; £190)

Form	Pos	Dist	Horse	RPR
3234	1		**Prophete De Guye (FR)**[31] 3772 8-11-8 **106**.................. IanPopham(3) (James Evans) *hld up: tk clsr order 11th: chsd ldr appr 2 out: led on bit flat: readily* **10/3**[2]	115+
4PF1	2	4	**Sawpit Supreme**[31] 3772 9-11-2 **97**.............................. AidanColeman (Venetia Williams) *chsd ldrs: led appr 2 out: nt fluent last: hdd and unable qck flat* **85/40**[1]	100
3-P0	3	39	**Shelomoh (IRE)**[18] 4001 10-11-5 **100**..............................(tp) PaddyAspell (James Turner) *led tl after 2nd: led again 4th: hdd 3 out: sn rdn: wknd bef next: t.o* **11/2**	63
-3U4	4	62	**L'Homme De Nuit (GER)**[11] 4140 7-11-12 **107**............(t) DenisO'Regan (Jim Best) *hld up and a bhd: t.o: j.v.slowly last* **9/2**[3]	8
1236	P		**Kinkeel (IRE)**[5] 4269 12-10-0 **84** ow1.............. EamonDehdashti(3) (Tony Carroll) *chsd ldr tl led after 2nd: hdd 4th: chsd ldr again tl led 3 out: sn hdd & wknd: p.u bef next* **9/2**[3]	—

5m 43.4s (25.20) **Going Correction** +1.40s/f (Heav) **5** Ran SP% **106.8**
Speed ratings: **105,103,87,63,—**
CSF £10.43 TOTE £3.20: £1.40, £2.00; EX 10.60.
Owner Elegant Clutter Ltd **Bred** G A E C Delorme Gerard & Vincent **Trained** Broadwas, Worcs

FOCUS
A small field for this handicap chase, but an emphatic success. The first two are rated pretty much to their marks.

NOTEBOOK
Prophete De Guye(FR), who had gained all his previous successes on good or easy ground and sharper tracks, seemed to relish conditions, was always travelling strongly, pinged the last and picked up well to reverse recent placings with the runner-up. (op 7-2)
Sawpit Supreme, who beat the winner at Warwick last month when that rival was returning from a break, was 6lb worse off but travelled well and went on turning for home. However, she had no response when the winner was produced after the last. (op 7-4 tchd 5-2)
Shelomoh(IRE) had the ground to suit and was wearing a tongue-tie and cheekpieces for the first time. He made much of the running but was done with after the third-last. Official explanation: jockey said gelding had a breathing problem (op 6-1 tchd 13-2)
L'Homme De Nuit(GER) was always at the back and was detached before halfway. He won on this ground over hurdles, but in three starts under similar conditions since has seemed not to handle it. (op 4-1)
Kinkeel(IRE), who made a couple of mistakes on the second circuit, stopped quickly from the third-last and declined to jump the next. (op 6-1 tchd 4-1)

4380 SCOTTS HEAVY HAULAGE (IRELAND) LTD H'CAP HURDLE (11 hdls 1 omitted) 3m
4:05 (4:05) (Class 4) (0-105,105) 4-Y-O+ **£1,951** (£573; £286; £143)

Form	Pos	Dist	Horse	RPR
6-61	1		**Round The Horn (IRE)**[5] 4276 11-11-7 **100** 7ex............(t) JasonMaguire (Jim Old) *hld up: hdwy 6th: led on bit appr 2 out: sn clr: eased to a walk flat* **7/4**[1]	116+
30U3	2	20	**Sapphire Rouge (IRE)**[24] 3901 5-11-4 **100**.............. WayneKavanagh(3) (Seamus Mullins) *prom: chsd ldr after 3rd: led appr 8th: hdd and wkng whn mstke 2 out* **9/1**	90
-232	3	12	**Wood Yer (IRE)**[33] 3724 5-11-10 **103**.............................. PaddyBrennan (Nigel Twiston-Davies) *hld up: hdwy 6th: rdn 8th: wknd after 3 out: t.o* **9/2**[2]	79
0240	4	5	**Hippodrome (IRE)**[35] 3693 9-10-10 **96**..........................(p) MattCrawley(7) (John Harris) *hld up: hdwy appr 4th: rdn and wknd 3 out: t.o* **16/1**	67
530U	5	2 1/4	**Aconitum (GER)**[8] 4219 6-11-6 **99**..............................(p) DougieCostello (Neil Mulholland) *led: reminders after 4th: hdd bef 8th: wknd 3 out: t.o* **5/1**[3]	68
46/0	P		**Star Time (IRE)**[12] 4130 12-9-9 **79** oh15..........................(v) CO'Farrell(5) (Michael Scudamore) *hld up: bhd fr 4th: t.o whn p.u bef last* **28/1**	—
-054	P		**Argentia**[13] 4118 6-11-4 **97**.............................. AndrewThornton (Lucy Wadham) *prom: rdn and wknd after 3 out: t.o whn p.u bef next* **14/1**	—
3040	P		**Ban Uisce (IRE)**[17] 4025 6-11-10 **103**..............................(p) RodiGreene (Neil Mulholland) *chsd ldrs to 6th: t.o whn p.u bef 2 out* **9/1**	—
166P	P		**Bled (FR)**[18] 4004 6-11-9 **105**.............................. JohnKington(3) (Donald McCain) *chsd ldr tl after 3rd: sn pushed along: wknd 6th: t.o whn p.u bef 8th* **14/1**	—

6m 52.2s (37.20) **Going Correction** +1.40s/f (Heav) **9** Ran SP% **113.9**
Speed ratings (Par 105): **94,87,83,81,80 —,—,—,—**
toteswingers:1&2:£5.20, 1&3:£2.40, 2&3:£5.60 CSF £17.97 CT £61.03 TOTE £2.10: £1.50, £3.30, £1.50; EX 23.20.
Owner Old Fools Partnership **Bred** N D Cronin **Trained** Barbury Castle, Wilts

FOCUS
A competitive staying hurdle on paper, but it was turned into a procession by the penalised winner. The winner is value for further and rated to the best of his bumper form.

NOTEBOOK
Round The Horn(IRE), having bolted up at Wetherby the previous week on his second start following the latest of several long absences, made light of his penalty and cruised into the lead off the home turn before coming right away. He literally trotted past the line and was value for considerably more than the official margin. The handicapper is sure to react after this. (op 2-1 tchd 6-4)
Sapphire Rouge(IRE) likes soft ground and finished third to a subsequent winner here on her previous start. Stepping up in trip, she led on the climb to the straight but had no answer to the winner's effort. She was clear of the rest, though. (op 8-1)
Wood Yer(IRE), placed in all three hurdles starts on soft ground, made headway in the second half of the race but was left behind by the first two from three out. (op 4-1)
Hippodrome(IRE), a course winner having his first try at the trip, ran reasonably on this second start after a break but did not appear to get home. (tchd 14-1)
Aconitum(GER), whose best previous effort was on heavy ground, was wearing cheekpieces instead of a visor. He made the running but was brushed aside after the last on the far side. (op 8-1)

4381 RACING FORUM @ GG.COM NOVICES' H'CAP CHASE (16 fncs) 2m 6f
4:35 (4:37) (Class 4) (0-115,115) 5-Y-O+ **£2,276** (£668; £334; £166)

Form	Pos	Dist	Horse	RPR
0P00	1		**Tarabela**[26] 3871 8-10-2 **94**.............................. DonalDevereux(3) (Gerald Ham) *a.p: chsd ldr 10th: lft in ld after 3 out: clr whn slipped on landing next: eased nr fin* **28/1**	97+
55-P	2	9	**Mrs Fawlty (IRE)**[12] 4127 8-11-1 **104**..............................(t) RhysFlint (Jim Old) *hld up: hdwy 8th: chsd wnr appr 2 out: styd on same pce* **7/1**[3]	92
-6FU	3	1/2	**Or Sing About (FR)**[43] 3562 9-10-12 **101**.................(v[1]) AndrewThornton (Seamus Mullins) *chsd ldr to 10th: rdn appr 3 out: sn outpcd: rallied and swtchd rt flat: styd on* **7/1**[3]	89
-042	4	9	**Preuty Boy (FR)**[35] 3702 6-11-7 **115**.............................. CO'Farrell(5) (Alan Fleming) *hld up: nt fluent 4 out: rdn after next: nvr on terms* **3/1**[2]	95
3112	F		**Panzer (GER)**[114] 2183 10-10-12 **101**.............................. JasonMaguire (Donald McCain) *hld up: hdwy 13th: rdn after 3 out: 4th and btn whn fell last* **3/1**[2]	81
1362	U		**Miss Fleur**[41] 3609 8-10-0 **89**.............................. DougieCostello (Nick Mitchell) *led: nt fluent 5th: slt ld whn mstke and uns rdr 3 out* **9/4**[1]	—

6m 21.1s (28.10) **Going Correction** +1.40s/f (Heav) **6** Ran SP% **109.2**
Speed ratings: **104,100,100,97,— —**
toteswingers:1&2:£12.70, 1&3:£7.30, 2&3:£4.70 CSF £179.53 TOTE £32.90: £14.50, £3.40; EX 120.80.
Owner G2 Recruitment Solutions Ltd **Bred** Mrs S M Reeks **Trained** Rooks Bridge, Somerset

FOCUS
A fairly wide range of abilities in this novices' handicap chase, and another surprise result. The winner is rated to the best of his hurdling form, although the race could be rated considerably higher.

NOTEBOOK
Tarabela, whose best form had been on a sound surface, had finished well beaten in two starts on heavy but completed a long-priced double for her trainer and jockey. She travelled well in the conditions and, once left in front at the last ditch, came away to win as she liked, despite pecking badly at the second-last. Apparently a nervous traveller, she looked capable of better as this was just her second chase. Official explanation: trainer said regarding apparent improvement in form, mare was suited a longer trip and a stiff track. (op 25-1 tchd 40-1)
Mrs Fawlty(IRE), another making her second start over fences, was not completely fluent but stayed on for second at a course where she gained her only previous success. (op 15-2 tchd 8-1 and 13-2)

The Form Book, Raceform Ltd, Compton, RG20 6NL

Or Sing About(FR) raced wide of the rest in second place but looked beaten at the bottom of the hill. However, he ran on again past beaten rivals in the straight. (op 9-1 tchd 6-1)
Preuty Boy(FR) was held up but was never really going, and the conditions may just have been too testing. (op 11-4 tchd 10-3)
Panzer(GER) was well beaten off prior to his last-fence tumble. (tchd 5-2)
Miss Fleur made the running and jumped pretty well until a bad error at the last ditch gave her rider no chance. She would probably have been second but for that. (tchd 5-2)

4382 FREE TIPS AT GG.COM "NEWCOMERS" STANDARD OPEN NATIONAL HUNT FLAT RACE 2m
5:05 (5:06) (Class 6) 4-5-Y-O **£1,301** (£382; £191; £95)

Form RPR
1 **Syndication (IRE)** 4-10-9 0 AidanColeman 95+
(Venetia Williams) *hld up in tch: led wl over 1f out: pushed out* **9/4**[1]
2 2 **Sing Sing Sing (FR)** 5-10-11 0 RhysFlint 95
(Barry Brennan) *chsd ldrs: led over 2f out: rdn and hdd wl over 1f out: styd on same pce ins fnl f* **15/2**
3 nk **Jackstown (IRE)** 4-10-6 0 JimmyDerham(3) 93
(Seamus Mullins) *w ldr tl led 4f out: hdd over 2f out: sn rdn: styd on same pce ins fnl f* **4/1**[2]
4 7 **Thomas Crapper** 4-10-9 0 CharliePoste 87
(Robin Dickin) *prom: rdn over 2f out: hung rt and wknd over 1f out* **9/4**[1]
5 42 **Adrenalin Flight (IRE)** 5-11-4 0 AndrewThornton 53
(Seamus Mullins) *set stdy pce tl qcknd over 5f out: hdd 4f out: wknd sn after: t.o* **5/1**[3]

4m 37.1s (34.80) **Going Correction** +1.40s/f (Heav)
WFA 4 from 5yo 9lb 5 Ran SP% **110.0**
Speed ratings: **69,68,67,64,43**
totesuper7: Win: Not won. Place: £449.20. CSF £18.61 TOTE £2.90: £1.70, £3.20; EX 16.90.
Owner Brooks, Dimsey, James & Keyes **Bred** J F C Maxwell **Trained** Kings Caple, H'fords

FOCUS
A newcomers' bumper with a very steady pace until the last half-mile. It is hard to know what the form is worth.

NOTEBOOK
Syndication(IRE), out of a French chase winner, was an uneasy favourite but proved strongest in a race that was hard work for these youngsters. He did the job nicely. (op 6-5)
Sing Sing Sing(FR), a cheaply bought relative of several French Flat winners, was close up most of the way and did not go down without a fight. There might be a mares' bumper in her. (op 8-1)
Jackstown(IRE), another cheap purchase but related to winners under all disciplines, ran well but struggled in the ground and looks to need more time. (tchd 7-2)
Thomas Crapper, a very cheap first foal of a point winner, was backed beforehand and had his chance but weakened in the straight. (op 6-1)
Adrenalin Flight(IRE) helped make the running but was done with before the home turn. (tchd 9-2 and 6-1)
T/Plt: £352.40 to a £1 stake. Pool:£93,032.32 - 192.67 winning tickets T/Qpdt: £42.90 to a £1 stake. Pool:£5,187.38 - 89.35 winning tickets CR

4383 - 4389a (Foreign Racing) - See Raceform Interactive

4112 CATTERICK (L-H)
Monday, February 28

OFFICIAL GOING: Good to soft (chs 6.9; hdl 7.5)
Wind: light 1/2 against Weather: overcast, very cool

4390 RACINGUK.COM LADY AMATEUR RIDERS' H'CAP HURDLE (10 hdls) 2m 3f
2:10 (2:11) (Class 5) (0-95,95) 4-Y-O+ **£1,714** (£527; £263)

Form RPR
3032 1 **Knight Valliant**[115] 2190 8-10-8 **84** MissEButterworth(7) 92+
(Barbara Butterworth) *hld up in rr: gd hdwy to trck ldrs 7th: led after 2 out: styd on wl: pushed out* **11/2**[1]
P05- 2 2¼ **Bright Sparky (GER)**[7] 48 8-11-5 **88** (t) MissJCoward 93+
(Michael Easterby) *mid-div: hdwy appr 2 out: chsd wnr last: no imp* **13/2**[2]
-044 3 2¾ **Winter Alchemy (IRE)**[56] 3363 6-10-13 **87** MissJRRichards(5) 90
(Nicky Richards) *chsd ldrs: styng on same pce whn j.lft last* **11/2**[1]
0 4 4½ **A Stones Throw (NZ)**[23] 3951 6-11-7 **95** (t) MissJennyCarr(5) 95
(Ben Haslam) *w ldrs: led appr 6th: hdd 7th: wknd between last 2* **16/1**
-003 5 1 **Dance Sauvage**[112] 2280 8-10-7 **81** (b) MissHBethell(5) 79
(Mike Sowersby) *t.k.h: trckd ldrs: led 7th tl after next: upsides 2 out: wknd appr last* **8/1**[3]
P030 6 shd **Mycenean Prince (USA)**[20] 3993 8-11-0 **88** MissPhillipaTutty(5) 86
(Karen Tutty) *led tl appr 6th: one pce fr 2 out: 7th whn hit last and hung rt run-in* **28/1**
300P 7 ½ **Mardood**[40] 3635 6-10-12 **86** (p) MissADawson(5) 84
(Chris Grant) *in tch: drvn 3 out: one pce* **14/1**
0PU0 8 ½ **Still Royal**[106] 2398 5-10-6 **78** MissCarolineHurley(3) 75
(John Davies) *t.k.h towards rr: styd on fr 2 out: nvr a factor* **100/1**
0000 9 2½ **Ardesia (IRE)**[31] 3782 7-11-3 **86** MissTJackson 82
(Tina Jackson) *chsd ldrs: one pce fr 2 out* **28/1**
00P/ 10 ½ **Nick The Silver**[15] 10-10-4 **80** (p) MissEYoung(7) 74
(Robert Johnson) *in rr: wnt prom 5th: one pce fr 3 out* **100/1**
4006 11 2¼ **Hoar Frost**[23] 3951 6-11-4 **94** MissGTutty(7) 86
(Karen Tutty) *mid-div: lost pl after 3 out: kpt on between last 2* **25/1**
-526 12 nk **I'm Your Man**[34] 3730 12-11-2 **92** (p) MissNSayer(7) 84
(Evelyn Slack) *chsd ldrs: wknd appr 2 out* **20/1**
3050 13 1½ **Mrs Eff**[26] 3883 5-11-2 **90** MissEStead(5) 81
(Kate Walton) *in rr: last appr 2 out: kpt on run-in* **10/1**
0500 14 1¾ **Knock Three Times (IRE)**[14] 4113 5-11-0 **90** (t) MissSMDoolan(7) 79
(Wilf Storey) *in rr: bhd whn nt fluent 7th: nvr on terms* **28/1**
P00- 15 5 **Ballamusic (IRE)**[326] 5107 9-11-12 **95** MissPGundry 83
(Andrew Parker) *in rr: stmbld bdly sn after 1st: mstke 5th: nvr on terms* **20/1**
4-1P 16 26 **Optimum (IRE)**[75] 2952 9-11-9 **95** MissPernillaHermansson(3) 56
(Richard Ford) *s.s: a bhd: t.o 5th* **22/1**
00-P U **Final Veto**[34] 3724 8-11-2 **90** MissSamanthaDrake(5) —
(Sue Smith) *mid-div: nt fluent 7th: sme hdwy whn mstke and uns rdr next* **8/1**[3]

4m 50.2s (3.40) **Going Correction** +0.125s/f (Yiel) 17 Ran SP% **118.0**
Speed ratings (Par 103): **97,96,94,93,92 92,92,92,91,90 89,89,89,88,86 75,—**
Tote Swingers: 1&2 £7.80, 1&3 £4.40, 2&3 £4.80 CSF £34.04 CT £207.52 TOTE £4.60: £1.50, £1.70, £1.40, £3.00; EX 51.20.
Owner Mrs Barbara Butterworth **Bred** P E Clinton **Trained** Bolton, Cumbria

FOCUS
The ground was expected to be riding slightly more testing than the official description of good to soft and the runners were kicking up the turf in the opener. The winning time suggested it was more like soft. This was a wide-open handicap for lady amateur riders and they went a fair gallop. The third and fourth set the level.

NOTEBOOK
Knight Valliant was coming back off a 115-day break, but has scored after a similar absence in the past and was well backed. He took it up around two out and soon had matters in control, rating value for further. This was a fully deserved success. (op 6-1)
Bright Sparky(GER), a previous C&D winner, arrived having been in good heart on the AW, and posted his best effort over hurdles for some time with the headgear abandoned. (op 6-1)
Winter Alchemy(IRE) had his chance on his return from a 56-day and helps to set the standard of the form.
A Stones Throw(NZ) turned in his best effort to date on this second outing for his present trainer and looks well worth a try over further. (op 10-1)
Dance Sauvage held every chance from the home turn, but it was his first outing since November and he was 8lb higher. (tchd 13-2)

4391 XTREMEADVENTURESUK.COM H'CAP HURDLE (12 hdls) 3m 1f 110y
2:40 (2:40) (Class 4) (0-105,105) 4-Y-O+ **£2,406** (£706; £353; £176)

Form RPR
P000 1 **Stagecoach Opal**[26] 3883 10-11-0 **93** HenryOliver 101+
(Sue Smith) *trckd ldrs: led appr 8th: hdd after 3 out: led appr next: styd on strly* **16/1**
0351 2 4½ **Wor Rom (IRE)**[26] 3883 7-11-4 **104** (p) MrNHalley(7) 107
(Elliott Cooper) *chsd ldrs: outpcd after 3 out: wnt 2nd between last 2: no imp* **8/1**
601 3 3¾ **San Deng**[46] 3523 9-10-10 **99** JoeColliver(10) 100
(Micky Hammond) *in rr: hdwy appr 2 out: kpt on to take 3rd appr last* **12/1**
-314 4 ½ **The Red Laird**[36] 3698 8-11-4 **102** GilesHawkins(5) 101
(Neil King) *led tl after 2nd: chsd ldrs: drvn 7th: outpcd after 3 out: kpt on to take modest 4th last* **11/2**[2]
0-51 5 12 **Whatdoidowiththat**[142] 1782 8-11-0 **98** ShaneByrne(5) 89+
(Sue Smith) *chsd ldrs: drvn 8th: led after 3 out: hdd appr next and nt fluent: wknd appr last* **6/1**[3]
6-56 6 nk **Comeththehour (IRE)**[26] 3887 8-11-0 **93** PaddyAspell 81
(James Moffatt) *in rr: bhd fr 9th: kpt on fr 2 out: nvr on terms* **14/1**
0124 7 ¾ **Not Talking (IRE)**[33] 3748 8-10-0 **79** oh2 DougieCostello 68
(John Quinn) *nt fluent in rr: sme hdwy appr 2 out: nvr a factor* **5/1**[1]
50F6 8 3 **Veronicas Boy**[14] 4113 5-11-6 **99** BarryKeniry 84
(George Moore) *prom: lost pl after 3 out: bhd fr next* **20/1**
-614 9 2¼ **Fentara**[30] 3822 6-11-12 **105** RobertWalford 89
(Tim Walford) *sn in rr: hdwy 9th: sn chsng ldrs: wknd appr 2 out* **11/2**[2]
-000 10 ½ **Waltham Abbey**[12] 4146 10-9-13 **85** MrRUtley(7) 67
(Lynsey Kendall) *trckd ldrs: wknd appr 2 out* **40/1**
P-25 11 17 **Flaming Breeze (IRE)**[54] 3396 6-10-6 **85** BrianHughes 52
(Henry Hogarth) *t.k.h: w ldr: led after 2nd: hdd appr 8th: lost pl 9th: sn bhd* **7/1**

6m 27.0s (-0.60) **Going Correction** +0.125s/f (Yiel) 11 Ran SP% **112.8**
Speed ratings (Par 105): **105,103,102,102,98 98,98,97,96,96 91**
Tote Swingers: 1&2 £7.80, 1&3 £4.40, 2&3 £4.80 CSF £132.99 CT £1589.96 TOTE £25.90: £6.80, £3.50, £3.90; EX 140.40.
Owner John Conroy Jaqueline Conroy **Bred** R A Hughes **Trained** High Eldwick, W Yorks

FOCUS
A moderate staying handicap and another open-looking race. There was a sound enough gallop on and again it looked fairly hard work in the home straight. The third and fourth give the form a fairly solid look.

NOTEBOOK
Stagecoach Opal, whose stable is in top form again, ran out a clear-cut winner. He previously looked out of sorts this season and hadn't scored over hurdles since 2006 (last win over fences in 2008), but is obviously now back at the top of his game. The ground also clearly held no fears for him. Official explanation: trainer's rep said, regarding apparent improvement in form, that the gelding was better suited by the good to soft ground (tchd 14-1)
Wor Rom(IRE) was a stone higher than when winning easily at Newcastle 26 days earlier and he kept on well after hitting a flat spot here, rating the benchmark. (op 7-1)
San Deng was raised 9lb for his success over 2m3f here last month. He was ridden to get the longer trip and was getting there too late in the home straight.
The Red Laird was another that hit a flat spot before plugging on again and perhaps the handicapper now has his measure.
Whatdoidowiththat, who was last seen defying a 7lb higher mark at Hexham in October and has won over C&D, was the eye-catcher. He responded to pressure off the final bend to look the biggest threat to his winning stablemate, but fitness told coming to the last. He should come on plenty. (op 5-1)
Not Talking(IRE) wasn't fluent and never seriously threatened. (op 11-2)
Fentara, up in trip, looked a possible player around four out but proved laboured under pressure. Her yard is under something of a cloud at present, though. (op 6-1 tchd 5-1)

4392 BOOK TICKETS ON-LINE AT CATTERICKBRIDGE.CO.UK H'CAP CHASE (12 fncs) 2m
3:10 (3:10) (Class 4) (0-115,114) 5-Y-O+ **£3,057** (£897; £448; £224)

Form RPR
3004 1 **Saddlers Deal (IRE)**[45] 3549 6-10-11 **99** CampbellGillies 108
(Chris Grant) *racd wd: trckd ldrs: effrt appr 3 out: styd on to take 3rd last: chsd ldr and edgd lft last 100yds: styd on to ld fnl strides* **10/3**[2]
4362 2 hd **Folk Tune (IRE)**[22] 3970 8-11-12 **114** DougieCostello 123
(John Quinn) *trckd ldrs: led 2 out: 2 l ahd run-in: drvn and jst ct* **2/1**[1]
36U1 3 1 **Ice Image (IRE)**[20] 3997 9-10-1 **96** ow1 (t) AlistairFindlay(7) 106+
(George Charlton) *led to 6th: led appr 3 out: hdd 2 out: keeping on same pce whn n.m.r nr fin* **15/2**
PP 4 13 **Tooman Lane (IRE)**[13] 4135 7-11-2 **104** (t) PaddyAspell 100
(Patrick Holmes) *trckd ldrs: nt fluent: reminders after 3rd: led 8th tl appr 3 out: wknd appr last* **22/1**
3614 5 1¼ **Border Reiver**[33] 3751 7-11-1 **103** (t) RichieMcGrath 98
(Tim Easterby) *w ldrs: led 6th: hdd 8th: reminders next: wknd after 2 out* **5/1**[3]
U561 6 ¾ **Pamak D'Airy (FR)**[6] 4279 8-11-12 **114** 7ex BrianHughes 109
(Henry Hogarth) *w ldrs: drvn 8th: lost pl appr 2 out* **6/1**
4316 U **Follow The Sun (IRE)**[22] 3970 7-10-6 **94** WilsonRenwick 84
(Peter Niven) *in rr: hdwy to chse ldrs 3 out: 7 l down overall and wl outpcd in last whn blnd and uns rdr 2 out* **12/1**

4m 1.00s (0.90) **Going Correction** -0.05s/f (Good) 7 Ran SP% **111.2**
Speed ratings: **95,94,94,87,87 86,—**
Tote Swingers: 1&2 £2.60, 1&3 £4.90, 2&3 £4.00 CSF £10.30 TOTE £3.90: £3.20, £1.10; EX 9.40.
Owner Richard Collins **Bred** Patrick Hegarty **Trained** Newton Bewley, Co Durham
■ Stewards' Enquiry : Campbell Gillies three-day ban: careless riding (Mar 14,19-20)

FOCUS
There was an average gallop on in this ordinary handicap and it saw plenty of chances in the home straight. There was a cracking finish on the run-in and the first two are rated to form.

NOTEBOOK

Saddlers Deal(IRE) finally put his best foot forward with a last-gasp success. He was dropping back from 2m4f so it wasn't surprising he needed every yard of the trip to prevail. There may be a little more to come now he has got his head in front, especially when getting on a sounder surface. (op 7-2)

Folk Tune(IRE) has never been easy to win with, but he was down in class and gambled on. He looked to have done enough when hitting the front late on, but ultimately got there that bit too soon and was mugged at the finish. (op 5-2 tchd 7-4)

Ice Image(IRE) posted a solid effort under a positive ride off his 8lb rise for getting off the mark at Sedgefield 20 days earlier, and doesn't look weighted out of winning again just yet. (op 9-1)

Tooman Lane(IRE) had been pulled up in two previous outings this term, but he went with an awful lot more enthusiasm this time and only gave way late on. The first-time tongue tie clearly helped. (op 18-1)

4393 SUPPORT RACING WELFARE'S RACING LOTTERY NOVICES' HURDLE (10 hdls) 2m 3f

3:40 (3:42) (Class 4) 4-Y-0+ **£2,406** (£706; £353; £176)

Form RPR

26 **1** **Shadows Lengthen**[26] 3885 5-10-10 0 JakeGreenall(7) 120+
(Michael Easterby) *trckd ldrs: smooth hdwy to trck 2 ldrs appr 2 out: led on bit between last 2: shkn up and pushed clr run-in* **11/2**[3]

21 **2** *8* **A Bridge Too Far (IRE)**[35] 3715 5-11-10 0 JasonMaguire 121+
(Donald McCain) *trckd ldrs: chal appr 2 out: styd on same pce appr last* **5/4**[1]

5400 **3** *3* **Total Submission**[58] 3288 6-11-10 120 WarrenMarston 119+
(Martin Keighley) *led to 2nd: w ldrs: led appr 6th: rdn appr 2 out: hdd appr last: kpt on one pce* **2/1**[2]

2364 **4** *8* **Dr Flynn (IRE)**[45] 3547 6-11-3 0 WilsonRenwick 102
(Howard Johnson) *chsd ldrs: rdn 3 out: outpcd appr next* **14/1**

6 **5** *shd* **Quel Elite (FR)**[11] 4165 7-11-3 0 PaddyAspell 103
(James Moffatt) *in rr: hdwy 3 out: kpt on between last 2* **25/1**

P **6** *19* **Moonlight Blaze**[125] 1135 4-10-7 0 BarryKeniry 75
(Chris Fairhurst) *led 2nd tl appr 6th: wknd 3 out* **100/1**

0006 **7** *½* **The Tiddly Tadpole**[33] 3749 6-10-10 0 HenryBrooke(7) 84
(Simon West) *chsd ldrs 5th: rdn 3 out: sn lost pl* **66/1**

4-04 **8** *3 ¾* **Nelson's Chief**[17] 4059 5-10-10 0 NathanMoscrop(7) 81
(James Ewart) *in tch: drvn after 5th: lost pl after 7th* **33/1**

0 **9** *5* **Quelle Chance (IRE)**[34] 3725 5-11-3 0 BrianHughes 77
(Howard Johnson) *towards rr: hit 3 out: sn bhd* **100/1**

B **10** *9* **Andy Vic (IRE)**[14] 4112 8-10-10 0 KyleJames(7) 68
(Ian Brown) *in rr: bhd fr 6th* **150/1**

530 **11** *1 ¼* **Brave Spartacus (IRE)**[26] 3887 5-11-3 0 CampbellGillies 67
(Chris Grant) *t.k.h: sn trcking ldrs: hung rt: and reminders bnd after 5th: lost pl after 7th* **66/1**

12 *nk* **Umverti**[133] 6-10-7 0 JamesHalliday(3) 60
(Joanne Foster) *chsd ldrs: drvn 3 out: sn lost pl* **66/1**

0 **13** *3 ¾* **Royal Willy (IRE)**[45] 3547 5-10-12 0 MissLHorner(5) 64
(Chris Grant) *t.k.h in rr: nt fluent: reminders after 1st: bhd fr 7th* **150/1**

-035 **14** *23* **Wychwoods Kaddy**[24] 3920 5-11-3 0 (t) JodieMogford 43
(Graeme McPherson) *in rr: bhd fr 7th* **80/1**

0-0 **P** **Lucky Lukey**[54] 3398 5-11-3 0 RichieMcGrath —
(Richard Ford) *in rr: lost pl and t.o whn p.u bef 7th* **250/1**

P0 **P** **Miss Galross (IRE)**[19] 4000 7-10-10 0 FearghalDavis —
(Nicky Richards) *in rr: reminders and wknd after 5th: t.o whn p.u bef next* **250/1**

4m 45.4s (-1.40) **Going Correction** +0.125s/f (Yiel)
WFA 4 from 5yo+ 9lb **16** Ran SP% **116.4**
Speed ratings (Par 105): **107,103,102,99,98 90,90,89,87,83 82,82,81,71,—** —
Tote Swingers: 1&2 £2.90, 1&3 £3.30, 2&3 £1.80 CSF £12.36 TOTE £7.10: £2.10, £1.10, £1.50; EX 14.80.

Owner T A F Frost **Bred** London Thoroughbred Services Ltd **Trained** Sheriff Hutton, N Yorks

FOCUS

The market leaders dominated this modest novice hurdle and the form looks fair, wih the fifth the best guide.

NOTEBOOK

Shadows Lengthen made it third time lucky over hurdles with a ready success. He got bogged down at Newcastle last time and this ground still looked soft enough for him up in trip. He handled it without fuss, however, and got a lovely ride from his conditional jockey. It will be interesting to see what handicap mark he is now given. Official explanation: trainer's rep said, regarding apparent improvement in form, on the gelding's last run, the yard was under a cloud but, it seems to be in better form recently. (op 9-2)

A Bridge Too Far(IRE) was snapped up for £65,000 after winning on his hurdling debut at Wetherby last month, when trained by Paul Webber. He attracted plenty of support under his penalty and looked the most likely winner turning for home. His jumping over the last two let him down, however, and he failed to see out the extra distance that well as a result. (op 6-4 tchd Evens and 13-8 in a place)

Total Submission's stable has been under a cloud this year and it was his first run back from a 58-day break. He has shown a liking for better ground and this would've been sharp enough for him, so it wasn't that surprising to see him feel the pinch after three out. He still ran well, though, and rates the benchmark with a mark of 120. (op 9-4 tchd 3-1)

Dr Flynn(IRE) travelled nicely into contention but flattened from the home turn and will look better off once handicapping. (op 12-1)

Quel Elite(FR) was never seriously in the race from off the pace, yet was doing his best work towards the finish over this longer trip. (tchd 22-1)

Brave Spartacus(IRE) was keen and later reported by his jockey to have hung right throughout. Official explanation: jockey said gelding hung right throughout (op 50-1)

4394 RACINGUK.COM BEGINNERS' CHASE (19 fncs) 3m 1f 110y

4:10 (4:10) (Class 4) 5-Y-0+ **£3,057** (£897; £448; £224)

Form RPR

36P5 **1** **Wolf Moon (IRE)**[31] 3784 8-11-0 116 WarrenMarston 131+
(Martin Keighley) *trckd ldrs: led 4th to 7th: led 12th: drew clr appr 3 out: 6 l ahd whn hit last: eased clsng stages* **15/8**[2]

-36V **2** *3* **Pennek (FR)**[7] 4256 8-11-0 113 RichieMcGrath 121
(Philip Kirby) *racd wd: led tl appr 3rd: chsd ldrs: wnt 2nd appr 3 out: kpt on same pce: flattered* **11/2**[3]

323F **3** *20* **Silent Cliche (IRE)**[34] 3726 7-11-0 124 BrianHughes 106
(Howard Johnson) *trckd ldrs: reminders after 2nd: led 7th to 12th: wknd appr 3 out: nt fluent 2 out* **7/4**[1]

34PP **4** *16* **Soft Spoken Guy (IRE)**[19] 4003 8-11-0 0 MichaelMcAlister 92
(Maurice Barnes) *t.k.h: trckd ldrs: j. slowly 7th: dropped bk next: hdwy to chse ldrs 12th: wknd 14th* **15/2**

25 **F** **Chapolimoss (FR)**[99] 2545 7-11-0 0 JamesReveley —
(Martin Todhunter) *hld up: hdwy and handy 4th whn fell 11th* **12/1**

3 **P** **Hommage A Bach (IRE)**[10] 4179 6-11-0 0 (b[1]) JohnnyFarrelly —
(Paul John Gilligan, Ire) *w ldrs: led appr 3rd: hdd next: reminders 11th: sn lost pl and bhd: t.o 13th: p.u bef 4 out* **20/1**

4P4 **P** **Ramborob (IRE)**[96] 2615 6-11-0 84 PeterBuchanan —
(Mike Sowersby) *lost pl 8th: bhd fr 11th: t.o whn mstke next: p.u bef 4 out* **150/1**

6m 37.4s (-4.60) **Going Correction** -0.05s/f (Good) **7** Ran SP% **111.4**
Speed ratings: **105,104,97,93,—** —,—
Tote Swingers: 1&2 £2.80, 1&3 £1.70, 2&3 £2.10 CSF £12.15 TOTE £2.30: £1.70, £1.90; EX 14.70.

Owner Mrs Louise Jones **Bred** Alistair Corrigan **Trained** Condicote, Gloucs

FOCUS

A modest beginners' chase but run at a sound -enough gallop. The winner is value for further with the second rated to his mark.

NOTEBOOK

Wolf Moon(IRE) opened his account over fences at the fifth time of asking and rates value for a deal better than the bare margin. He was a useful hurdler last term, but has had excuses this year as a chaser due to his yard being under a cloud. That has seen his rating in this sphere drop to a mark 10lb lower than his hurdle rating of 126, but he showed here he has a definite future in staying handicaps over fences. It is hoped that a rise in the weights for this will see him sneak into one of the handicaps at the festival next month. He is a dual winner at Cheltenham, should have little trouble with the likely quicker ground, and the Kim Muir could be just the race for him. (op 2-1)

Pennek(FR), whose latest outing at Carlisle was a voided race, was taken wide under a positive ride for most of the way. He rallied gamely to keep the winner up to his work and, although flattered by his proximity, this dour stayer can surely be found an opening over fences. (op 6-1 tchd 5-1)

Silent Cliche(IRE) fell at Sedgefield on his previous outing and wasn't that clever over the first here, after which he was handed a reminder. He had his chance, but it was clear around six out the winner held his measure and his previous experience may have affected him here. He has become expensive to follow, but could be the sort to improve for better ground in due course. (tchd 2-1)

Soft Spoken Guy(IRE) lost touch from six out, but at least got home this time and could win a weaker contest before the end of term. (op 8-1 tchd 7-1)

4395 TURFTV MARES' NOVICES' H'CAP HURDLE (8 hdls) 2m

4:40 (4:40) (Class 5) (0-95,95) 4-Y-0+ **£1,781** (£519; £259)

Form RPR

-06P **1** **Just Maddie**[34] 3727 7-10-6 **82** (p) PaulGallagher(7) 88+
(Rayson Nixon) *w ldrs: led after 3 out: styd on fr next: eased towards fin* **18/1**

P005 **2** *1* **Politelysed**[8] 4245 5-9-7 **69** oh5 HenryBrooke(7) 70
(Robert Johnson) *stdd s: hld up detached in last: nt fluent 3rd: shkn up and hdwy next: chsng ldrs appr 2 out: kpt on to take 2nd last* **8/1**

/005 **3** *9* **Miss Champagne (IRE)**[16] 4068 8-10-0 **69** oh5 PaddyAspell 62
(Andrew Wilson) *trckd ldrs to 3rd: hdwy 3 out: chsng wnr next: wknd after last* **15/2**[3]

4P/P **4** *4* **Showtime Annie**[20] 3993 10-9-7 **69** oh1 PeterCarberry(7) 58
(Jennie Candlish) *hld up: hdwy 3 out: wnt modest 4th 2 out: one pce* **12/1**

645P **5** *15* **Knockaveen (IRE)**[97] 2598 6-10-11 **80** (p) BrianHughes 56
(Andrew Crook) *mid-div: outpcd 4th: tk poor 5th sn after last* **11/1**

PP-0 **6** *2 ¾* **Hazy Oaks**[34] 3728 8-10-7 **81** (v[1]) BrianToomey(5) 59
(Kevin M Prendergast) *trckd ldrs: led 4th tl after 3 out: hmpd and lost pl appr next* **5/2**[1]

66P4 **7** *13* **A P Ling**[10] 4178 4-9-7 **78** oh8 (b) MrTGarner(7) 31
(Christopher Kellett) *led: hit 2nd: hdd 4th: wknd next: sn bhd* **14/1**

6404 **8** *12* **Scarvagh Rose**[40] 3631 6-11-9 **92** WilsonRenwick 43
(Rose Dobbin) *t.k.h in mid-div: sme hdwy 5th wknd next: eased 2 out* **7/2**[2]

-060 **P** **Tchikita (FR)**[40] 3637 8-10-12 **88** NathanMoscrop(7) —
(James Ewart) *chsd ldrs: lost pl 4th: sn bhd: t.o whn p.u bef 2 out* **10/1**

3m 58.8s (6.30) **Going Correction** +0.125s/f (Yiel)
WFA 4 from 5yo+ 9lb **9** Ran SP% **110.7**
Speed ratings (Par 103): **89,88,84,82,74 73,66,60,—**
Tote Swingers: 1&2 £17.30, 1&3 £21.10, 2&3 £5.10 CSF £143.38 CT £1134.15 TOTE £17.60: £8.90, £2.20, £2.00; EX 105.70.

Owner Rayson & Susan Nixon **Bred** G R S And Mrs Nixon **Trained** Ettrickbridge, Borders

FOCUS

This weak mares' handicap was run at a sound tempo and the first pair came clear late on. The form is rated around the placed horses.

NOTEBOOK

Just Maddie came under pressure on the back straight, but kept responding to her rider's urgings and ran out a game winner. She was hard to fancy for this and had yet to win a race, but some of her best previous form made her look feasibly treated off 82. The return of cheekpieces also helped and she deserves extra credit as she chased the early pace. Official explanation: trainer said, regarding apparent improvement in form, that the mare was better suited by being able to dominate. (op 14-1 tchd 20-1)

Politelysed was well backed but was another very hard to fancy, as she raced from 5lb out of the handicap. Things didn't look good for supporters when she got taken off her feet early on, but she got better the further she went and was the only danger to the winner from two out. She can be found an opening on better ground in this sort of class. (op 12-1 tchd 14-1 and 16-1 in a place)

Miss Champagne(IRE), another racing from 5lb out of the handicap, stayed on to look a danger in the home straight, but flattened out in between the final two flights. (op 7-1 tchd 8-1)

Showtime Annie shaped a lot better on this second outing for her yard. (tchd 10-1 and 14-1)

Hazy Oaks was well beat in a first-time visor and is one to tread carefully with. (op 3-1 tchd 9-4)

Scarvagh Rose ran a lifeless race. Official explanation: jockey said mare ran too free (tchd 10-3)

4396 WE RACE AGAIN ON MARCH 9TH MAIDEN NATIONAL HUNT FLAT RACE (CONDITIONAL/AMATEUR RIDERS) 2m

5:10 (5:11) (Class 6) 4-6-Y-0 **£1,370** (£399; £199)

Form RPR

5 **1** **Sinfield (IRE)**[23] 3957 5-10-8 0 JoeColliver(10) 108+
(Micky Hammond) *trckd ldrs: wnt cl 2nd over 3f out: led over 2f out: hung lft and drvn clr fnl f* **7/2**[2]

2 *7* **Valsesia (IRE)** 4-9-10 0 ow1 PaulGallagher(7) 87
(Howard Johnson) *sn chsng ldrs: drvn over 3f out: wnt 3rd 150yds out: styd on to take 2nd towards fin* **4/1**[3]

3 *¾* **Sir Charlie Hutch (GER)** 6-10-11 0 JeremiahMcGrath(7) 103+
(Alan Swinbank) *w ldrs: led after 5f: hung bdly lft and hdd over 2f out: wknd fnl 150yds* **4/1**[3]

4 *1* **Oscar Baby (IRE)** 5-10-4 0 (p) MrNHalley(7) 94
(Elliott Cooper) *hld up in mid-div: outpcd 4f out: styd on fnl 2f: tk 4th and hmpd clsng stages* **16/1**

3 **5** *1 ½* **Evans Wood**[53] 3406 4-10-2 0 (t) JakeGreenall(7) 90
(Michael Easterby) *stdd s: t.k.h and sddle sn briefly slip: hdwy to chse ldrs over 3f out: wknd fnl f* **11/4**[1]

The Form Book, Raceform Ltd, Compton, RG20 6NL

0 **6** *16* **Think**[23] 3957 4-10-9 0 .... CampbellGillies 75
(Clive Mulhall) *t.k.h: trckd ldrs: outpcd 6f out: hung lft 3f out: grad wknd* **11/1**

0 **7** *9* **Beyond The Tweed**[45] 3553 5-11-1 0 .... HarryHaynes(3) 76
(James Ewart) *hld up in rr: hdwy 7f out: sn chsng ldrs: rn wd and lost pl 3f out* **14/1**

00U **8** *5* **Grey Assassin**[20] 3992 4-10-9 0 .... FearghalDavis 63
(Simon West) *s.i.s: in rr: dropped bk bnd after 6f: bhd fnl 6f* **150/1**

00 **9** *7* **Khalashan (FR)**[26] 3889 5-10-11 0 .... HenryBrooke(7) 65
(Peter Niven) *led 5f: sn drvn: lost pl 5f out: sn bhd* **33/1**

00 **10** *6* **Go Teescomponents**[14] 4117 4-10-2 0 .... MrRLindsay(7) 51
(Keith Reveley) *lost pl after 6f: t.o 6f out* **66/1**

11 *1* **Perfect Deal** 4-10-2 0 .... EdmondLinehan(7) 50
(Michael Easterby) *sn chsng ldrs: lost pl 6f out: sn bhd* **40/1**

3m 56.8s (9.90) **Going Correction** +0.125s/f (Yiel)
WFA 4 from 5yo+ 9lb **11** Ran SP% **117.3**
Speed ratings: **80,76,76,75,74 66,62,59,56,53 52**
CSF £17.67 TOTE £4.10: £1.10, £1.90, £2.40; EX 18.50.
Owner Mike And Eileen Newbould **Bred** Mrs G Galvin **Trained** Middleham Moor, N Yorks

FOCUS
This bumper for conditional/amateur riders was run at a steady gallop and most took a keen hold. The fifth to tenth help set the level.

NOTEBOOK
Sinfield(IRE) stepped up plenty on his debut fifth at Wetherby 23 days earlier and ran out a convincing winner. He travelled kindly into contention and soon put the race to bed when asked for maximum effort around 2f out. Bred to make his mark over jumps, he clearly appreciates some cut and looks a fair prospect for novice hurdling. His trainer reported he has already schooled nicely and that could be it now until next term. (op 3-1 tchd 11-4)
Valsesia(IRE) ◆ is out of an unraced mare that is half-sister to three winners in this division. She lost out by hitting a flat spot on the home turn, but was eating up the ground late on and should go close next time out. (op 7-1)
Sir Charlie Hutch(GER), bred for the Flat, hails from a yard that must always be respected in bumpers and posted a pleasing debut effort. He looks sure to come on for it. (tchd 9-2)
Oscar Baby(IRE) is a half-sister to Wor Rom, who finished runner-up in the staying handicap hurdle earlier on this card. She showed her inexperience, but was doing decent late work and is another sure to benefit for the initial outing. (tchd 14-1)
Evans Wood failed to settle on his debut behind the subsequently impressive Ericht at Huntingdon last month and that was again his undoing here. Official explanation: jockey said gelding ran too free (op 3-1 tchd 7-2)
T/Jkpt: Not won. T/Plt: £678.00 to a £1 stake. Pool: £77,487.77 - 83.42 winning tickets T/Qpdt: £23.30 to a £1 stake. Pool:£5,423.99 - 225.40 winning tickets WG

4118 PLUMPTON (L-H)
Monday, February 28

OFFICIAL GOING: Soft (chs 5.9, hdl 5.7)
Wind: virtually nil Weather: showers, cold

4397 WHATS ON BRIGHTON AND HOVE MAIDEN HURDLE (9 hdls) 2m
2:20 (2:21) (Class 5) 4-Y-0+ **£1,815** (£529; £264)

Form RPR

0 **1** **The Hague**[32] 3760 5-10-11 0 .... MrTomDavid(5) 106+
(Tim Vaughan) *chsd clr ldr: mstke 4th: clsd and led bef 3 out: drew clr and in command whn mstke 2 out: eased flat: comf* **14/1**

4 **2** *15* **Alystar (IRE)**[33] 3739 5-10-9 0 .... APMcCoy 82
(Nicky Henderson) *prom in main gp: clsd after 6th: chsd wnr next: wknd bef 2 out: wl hld whn blnd last: hld on for 2nd cl home* **3/1**[3]

0 **3** *shd* **Lucky Dance (BRZ)**[13] 4129 9-11-2 0 .... AndrewThornton 88
(Mark Rimmer) *prom in main gp: clsd on ldrs and cl 3rd 3 out: wknd bef next: mstke 2 out: plugged on flat and pressing for 2nd nr fin* **66/1**

52 **4** *1* **Promised Wings (GER)**[13] 4129 4-10-7 0 .... ColinBolger 78
(Chris Gordon) *hld up off the pce in midfield: clsd on ldrs after 6th: rdn and wknd bef 2 out: 4th and wl hld whn mstke last* **11/4**[2]

453- **5** *½* **Golden Games (IRE)**[314] 5051 5-10-9 0 .... MattieBatchelor 78
(Daniel O'Brien) *hld up wl bhd in rr: rdn and hdwy 6th: wnt modest 5th after 3 out: kpt on but nvr any ch w wnr* **50/1**

256 **6** *17* **Koup De Kanon (FR)**[42] 3604 5-11-2 0 .... JackDoyle 70
(Emma Lavelle) *mstkes: hld up in rr: hdwy 6th: 6th and no prog after 3 out: wl btn bef next* **2/1**[1]

00U0 **7** *10* **Stays All Night (FR)**[24] 3917 5-10-13 0 .... RichardKilloran(3) 58
(Tim Vaughan) *led and sn wl clr: j.rt 5th: hdd bef 3 out: wknd qckly wl bef 2 out: wl btn whn j.rt 2 out: t.o* **125/1**

8 *½* **Craicajack (IRE)**[26] 4-10-7 0 .... DaveCrosse 49
(Edward Creighton) *racd off the pce in midfield: rdn and effrt 5th: no real hdwy and mstke next: wl btn fr 3 out: t.o* **80/1**

050 **9** *½* **Onthelips (IRE)**[19] 4006 7-10-13 0 .... AlexMerriam(3) 57
(Amy Weaver) *a wl off the pce towards rr: rdn and no hdwy after 6th: nvr on terms: t.o: b.b.v* **100/1**

000P **10** *½* **Sulpius (GER)**[44] 3556 6-10-9 0 .... NathanSweeney(7) 57
(Bob Buckler) *racd wl off the pce in midfield: no prog whn mstke 6th: nvr on terms: t.o* **10/1**

0- **11** *10* **Fleetstone**[429] 3027 6-10-9 0 .... SeanQuinlan 40
(Richard Phillips) *racd wl off the pce in midfield: wknd after 6th: t.o bef 2 out* **66/1**

0-60 **12** *16* **Castle Myth (USA)**[27] 607 5-10-6 0 ....(p) AshleyBird(10) 31
(Jim Best) *t.k.h: prom in main gp tl after 5th: wl t.o after 3 out* **16/1**

00-0 **P** **Padys Arkle (IRE)**[149] 1680 7-11-2 0 .... JamieMoore —
(Brett Johnson) *plld hrd early: hld up wl bhd in last pair: lost tch bef 6th: t.o whn p.u after 3 out* **66/1**

4m 10.6s (9.80) **Going Correction** +0.55s/f (Soft)
WFA 4 from 5yo+ 9lb **13** Ran SP% **116.1**
Speed ratings (Par 103): **97,89,89,88,88 80,75,74,74,74 69,61,—**
Tote Swingers: 1&2 £6.10, 1&3 £70.60, 2&3 £26.00 CSF £55.58 TOTE £24.70: £4.40, £1.30, £9.80; EX 78.70.
Owner Diamond Racing Ltd **Bred** Darley **Trained** Aberthin, Vale of Glamorgan

FOCUS
Nothing more than a modest maiden hurdle. The form is probably modest and best rated through the fourth.

NOTEBOOK
The Hague, never involved and well held when 25-1 for his hurdles debut at Ffos Las, prospered under a more positive ride and coped with the ground much better than expected, galloping on strongly for an easy success. He'll find life tougher under a penalty, though. (op 16-1)
Alystar(IRE) improved on her initial effort, just holding on for second following a blunder at the last. She'll be capable of winning on better ground in the coming months. (op 9-4)
Lucky Dance(BRZ) has embarked on a hurdles career rather late in life, but he showed considerably more than he had done on his hurdles debut, keeping on again to just miss second.
Promised Wings(GER) was disappointing considering he had finished second to a fair type at Folkestone previously. (tchd 5-2)
Golden Games(IRE) was going on late and could do better in low-grade handicaps. (op 40-1)
Koup De Kanon(FR) made mistakes and never got close enough to challenge. This was his third run over hurdles, though, so it would be no surprise to see him leave this form well behind switched to handicaps. (op 11-4)
Stays All Night(FR) was never going to last having made the running. (op 100-1)
Onthelips(IRE) Official explanation: vet said gelding had bled from the nose

4398 EUROPEAN BREEDERS' FUND/THOROUGHBRED BREEDERS' ASSOCIATION MARES' NOVICES' CHASE (14 fncs) 2m 4f
2:50 (2:50) (Class 4) 5-Y-0+ **£3,429** (£1,247)

Form RPR

3021 **1** **Asturienne**[13] 4127 7-11-4 120 ....(p) RobertThornton 134+
(Alan King) *a gng wl: trckd ldrs tl wnt 2nd after 8th: led on bit after 3 out: clr whn stmbld on landing next: stdd and j.rt last: eased flat: v easily* **2/1**[2]

PP11 **2** *25* **Evella (IRE)**[30] 3817 7-11-7 130 .... AlexMerriam(3) 110
(Neil King) *led: blnd and rdn lost iron briefly 11th: rdn and hdd after next: sn btn: wl btn between last 2* **10/11**[1]

P **Present Gem (IRE)**[16] 4085 8-10-12 0 ....(t) TomO'Brien —
(Paul John Gilligan, Ire) *hld up in tch: mstke 1st: cl 4th whn p.u qckly bef 9th: dismntd* **20/1**

P-10 **P** **Gan On**[19] 4009 7-10-7 0 .... RachaelGreen(5) —
(Anthony Honeyball) *in tch in last pair: rdn and struggling after 6th: losing tch whn j. slowly next: p.u bef 9th* **5/1**[3]

4P06 **U** **Karingabay Queen**[27] 3865 6-10-5 0 ....(b) MrBJPoste(7) —
(Kevin Tork) *j.rt 3rd: chsd ldr tl after 8th: rdn and lost tch after next: tailing off whn blnd bdly and uns rdr 11th* **66/1**

5m 28.1s (20.80) **Going Correction** +0.625s/f (Soft) **5** Ran SP% **108.6**
Speed ratings: **83,73,—,—,—**
CSF £4.31 TOTE £2.70: £1.10, £1.60; EX 5.30.
Owner Let's Live Racing **Bred** Wood Farm Stud **Trained** Barbury Castle, Wilts

FOCUS
An uncompetitive mares' chase and not form to be confident about.

NOTEBOOK
Asturienne, wearing first-time cheekpices, came out much the best. She was unimpressive when winning at Folkestone the time before, but travelled strongly in the headgear, and won the style of a horse with more to come. (op 7-4)
Evella(IRE), made favourite to complete the hat-trick, following ready wins at Fakenham and Uttoxeter, was quickly brushed aside and the double penalty is probably going to continue to make life tough. (tchd 5-6 and Evens)
Present Gem(IRE) Official explanation: jockey said mare was lame (op 15-2)
Gan On was quickly in trouble on this first run over fences, offering little encouragement for the immediate future. (op 15-2)

4399 MCR PRINT H'CAP HURDLE (9 hdls) 2m
3:20 (3:20) (Class 4) (0-115,111) 4-Y-0+ **£2,055** (£599; £299)

Form RPR

0051 **1** **Beau Lake (IRE)**[14] 4120 7-11-0 99 .... PaddyBrennan 109+
(Suzy Smith) *mde virtually all: j.rt: mstke 2nd: pushed clr after 3 out: mstke next: j.rt again last: drvn and in command flat: eased fnl 50yds* **7/2**[2]

0PP0 **2** *5* **Olympian (FR)**[49] 3490 9-11-10 109 ....(b) AndrewGlassonbury 112
(Philip Middleton) *hld up in tch in rr: mstke 6th: hdwy to chse ldng pair after 3 out: drvn and chsd wnr bef next: styd on same pce flat* **9/1**

305 **3** *11* **Oscar Close (IRE)**[24] 3934 6-11-3 109 .... TrevorWhelan(7) 100
(George Baker) *in tch in midfield: chsd ldrs bef 3 out: rdn and btn bef 2 out: wnt modest 3rd between last 2: plugged on flat* **9/4**[1]

-P60 **4** *4½* **Chocolat (IRE)**[236] 933 6-10-9 94 ....(t) AidanColeman 81
(Susan Nock) *racd wd: w wnr tl after 3 out: btn bef next: 4th and wl btn between last 2* **16/1**

0333 **5** *14* **Sebastiano (FR)**[27] 3868 8-11-10 109 ....(p) JamieMoore 84
(Gary Moore) *racd wd: hld up in tch towards rr: rdn and effrt bef 3 out: little rspnse and wl btn bef 2 out* **9/2**[3]

-U16 **6** *5* **Rushwee (IRE)**[30] 3820 9-11-5 111 .... MattCrawley(7) 79
(Lucy Wadham) *t.k.h: chsd ldrs: rdn and struggling after 6th: wknd and wl btn after 3 out* **8/1**

4105 **7** *6* **Wheres Johnny**[14] 4121 10-11-0 99 ....(t) MattieBatchelor 61
(Jamie Poulton) *dropped to last 2nd: rdn and struggling after 4th: lost tch 6th: t.o* **12/1**

0605 **8** *13* **Airedale Lad (IRE)**[21] 3985 10-9-10 88 oh19 ow3 .... MrJBanks(7) 37
(Zoe Davison) *in tch in rr: rdn and lost tch after 6th: t.o bef 2 out* **66/1**

-000 **9** *6* **Prince Pippin (IRE)**[37] 3686 5-11-5 107 .... IanPopham(3) 65
(Michael Madgwick) *chsd ldrs tl wknd qckly sn after 3 out: wl btn and blnd last: virtually p.u flat: t.o* **14/1**

4m 7.60s (6.80) **Going Correction** +0.55s/f (Soft) **9** Ran SP% **114.0**
Speed ratings (Par 105): **105,102,97,94,87 85,82,75,72**
Tote Swingers: 1&2 £7.50, 1&3 £2.80, 2&3 £7.10 CSF £34.20 TOTE £4.40: £1.90, £2.60, £1.10; EX 43.10.
Owner Bernard & Jan Wolford **Bred** Larry Murphy **Trained** Lewes, E Sussex

FOCUS
Few got into this handicap hurdle. The winner stepped up and the second was back to the best of last season's form.

NOTEBOOK
Beau Lake(IRE), raised 6lb for his recent C&D victory in heavy ground, leading throughout and finding plenty under strong pressure in the straight, despite idling a little late on. Clearly progressive, 2m on this sort of ground suits him well, but another step forward is required for him to complete a hat-trick.
Olympian(FR) is currently 6lb lower than when winning over C&D last April, and this run very much suggested he's ready to strike again. (tchd 17-2 and 10-1)
Oscar Close(IRE) looked a potential improver dropping in trip, but he became readily outpaced before plodding on again. (tchd 5-2)
Chocolat(IRE) has yet to make an impact since arriving from France, although her recent efforts have been more encouraging. (op 14-1)
Sebastiano(FR) often needs things to fall right and he found little here under pressure.
Prince Pippin(IRE) Official explanation: trainer said gelding had a breathing problem

4400 WHIPPERS DELIGHT H'CAP CHASE (FOR THE HIGHFIELDS FARM CHALLENGE TROPHY) (12 fncs) 2m 1f
3:50 (3:50) (Class 4) (0-115,109) 5-Y-0+ **£3,089** (£907; £453; £226)

Form RPR

2F05 **1** **Restezen D'Armor (FR)**[19] 4010 6-11-10 107 ....(p) AndrewTinkler 127+
(Charlie Longsdon) *hld up in last pair: hdwy and hmpd 5th: chsd ldr next: lft in clr ld and sltly hmpd 7th: in n.d after: mstke 2 out: eased flat* **5/2**[1]

0610 **2** *26* **She's Humble (IRE)**[27] 3869 9-10-13 96 .... AndrewThornton 89
(Linda Jewell) *chsd ldr: struggling whn barging match w rival after 6th: lft 4th and hmpd next: t.o bef next: plugged on to go poor 2nd 2 out* **7/1**

2F42 **3** *8* **Owner Occupier**[27] 3869 6-10-10 **100**............................ MrTJCannon(7) 86
(Chris Gordon) *in tch: mstke and hmpd 5th: mstke next: lft 2nd and hmpd 7th: rdn and no imp on wnr whn mstke 9th: wl btn next: lost 2nd 2 out* **11/4**[2]

444P **4** *30* **Sumdancer (NZ)**[42] 3608 9-10-11 **97**................................ IanPopham(3) 61
(Michael Madgwick) *chsd ldr: mstke 3rd: j. slowly and lost pl 6th: barging match w rival bef next: lft 5th and hmpd 7th: sn t.o* **13/2**

0344 **F** **The Hardy Boy**[31] 3792 11-10-4 **87**................................(t) NickScholfield —
(Anna Newton-Smith) *led tl fell 7th* **9/1**

-P01 **P** **Prince Louis (FR)**[21] 3984 8-11-12 **109**..............................(t) DarylJacob —
(Charlie Mann) *mstkes: t.k.h: in tch: lft 3rd and hmpd 7th: sn lost tch w ldng pair: 4th and wl btn whn blnd bdly 9th: t.o whn p.u next* **9/2**[3]

4m 34.1s (8.20) **Going Correction** +0.625s/f (Soft) **6** Ran SP% **109.3**
Speed ratings: **105,92,89,74,**— —
Tote Swingers: 1&2 £3.80, 1&3 £1.30, 2&3 £4.90 CSF £18.11 TOTE £3.30: £1.10, £3.30; EX 23.50.
Owner The Hopeful Seven **Bred** L Hervo, Miss C Hervo & Miss R Hervo **Trained** Over Norton, Oxon

FOCUS
Things were beginning to heat up when The Hardy Boy fell and caused interference to the majority of the field. The form could be a few pounds out either way, although this did appear a step up from the winner.

NOTEBOOK
Restezen D'Armor(FR), who was travelling best at the time when left in front, went on to gain a first career victory. He hasn't looked the easiest in the past, but clearly appreciated the fitting of cheekpieces (instead of blinkers) for the first time in this country, and should have gained plenty of confidence from this. (tchd 11-4)
She's Humble(IRE) had quite a rough run through the race, but she did at least keep going. (op 15-2)
Owner Occupier finished tired, losing out on second. (op 5-2)
Sumdancer(NZ) is back on a good mark, but remains some way below his best. (op 7-1)
The Hardy Boy was running a nice race in the first-time tongue-tie, so it's hoped his confidence isn't jolted too badly by this incident. (op 5-1)
Prince Louis(FR) had gone up a harsh-looking 14lb for winning at Lingfield and he was never going this time, jumping sloppily. (op 5-1)

4401 EUROPEAN OFFICE PRODUCTS MARES' H'CAP HURDLE (12 hdls) 2m 5f
4:20 (4:20) (Class 4) (0-105,104) 4-Y-0+ **£2,055** (£599; £299)

Form RPR
0120 **1** **Arctic Flow**[18] 4032 7-9-11 **78** oh2.............................. WayneKavanagh(3) 82
(Caroline Keevil) *chsd ldr tl nt fluent 4th: chsd ldr again 7th tl after next: 4th and drvn after 3 out: wnt 2nd and 2 l down last: led fnl 100yds: styd on wl* **7/2**[1]

F234 **2** *1 1/4* **Here's The Key (FR)**[30] 3817 7-11-3 **95**.....................(bt[1]) DenisO'Regan 99
(Paul Webber) *j.lft at times: rdn and kpt finding ex after 3 out: 2 l up whn mstke last: hdd and no ex fnl 100yds* **7/1**

51F4 **3** *2 1/4* **Kaituna (IRE)**[31] 3789 5-11-12 **104**................................... LeightonAspell 107
(Oliver Sherwood) *hld up in tch: hdwy after 7th: chsng ldrs and rdn after 3 out: keeping on same pce whn mstke last: no imp flat* **9/2**[2]

4521 **4** *12* **Can't Remember**[52] 3432 6-10-12 **95**............................ OliverDayman(5) 85
(Alison Thorpe) *taken down early: hld up in tch: hdwy to chse ldr after 7th tl bef 3 out: wknd u.p bef 2 out* **9/2**[2]

-04 **5** *1/2* **Gilt Free (IRE)**[6] 4272 9-11-0 **92**...................................(v[1]) AndrewTinkler 81
(George Baker) *in tch: chsd ldr bef 2 out: rdn and nt qckn after 3 out: struggling whn wnt lft and blnd 2 out: tired whn wnt bdly lft again last* **7/1**

0535 **P** **Sieglinde (FR)**[21] 3984 5-10-3 **81**..................................(b) TimmyMurphy —
(Alison Batchelor) *chsd ldr 4th tl 7th: wknd rapidly after next: wl t.o whn p.u 2 out* **22/1**

005- **P** **Hi Ho Silvia**[360] 4414 6-10-0 **81**.. AlexMerriam(3) —
(Neil King) *chsd ldrs on outer: lost pl and rdn along after 8th: mstke next: sn lost tch and t.o whn p.u 3 out* **10/1**

36B2 **P** **Twin Bud**[31] 3791 6-11-4 **99**..(p) JimmyDerham(3) —
(Anna Newton-Smith) *in tch in rr: pushed along after 6th: lost tch w ldrs after 9th: t.o whn p.u last* **5/1**[3]

5m 34.8s (12.50) **Going Correction** +0.55s/f (Soft) **8** Ran SP% **113.7**
Speed ratings (Par 105): **98,97,96,92,91** —,—,—
Tote Swingers: 1&2 £5.30, 1&3 £3.80, 2&3 £7.20 CSF £27.65 CT £110.61 TOTE £3.50: £1.50, £4.00, £1.90; EX 27.40.
Owner Mrs C J Dunn **Bred** Mrs H R Dunn **Trained** Motcombe, Dorset

FOCUS
A moderate but competitive handicap hurdle in which the placed horses set the level.

NOTEBOOK
Arctic Flow's low weight kicked in late on and she flew up the hill for a second C&D success. She failed to stay 3m at Taunton last time, but had earlier been progressing well and can continue to give a good account. (op 5-1)
Here's The Key(FR), reverting to hurdles, did a lot of hard work out in front in the first-time blinkers, and was unable to match the winner on the climb to the line. (op 13-2)
Kaituna(IRE) ran creditably under top weight on this first start in a handicap. Better ground will suit. (tchd 4-1 and 5-1 in a place)
Can't Remember was below form, finishing tired. (op 4-1 tchd 5-1)
Gilt Free(IRE) came home tired, having travelled well for a long way. (op 8-1)

4402 WINDSOR PARTNERS AMATEUR RIDERS' H'CAP CHASE (FOR THE GAY KINDERSLEY SALVER) (18 fncs) 3m 2f
4:50 (4:50) (Class 4) (0-115,114) 5-Y-0+ **£2,966** (£920; £459; £229)

Form RPR
U220 **1** **Deep Pockets (IRE)**[16] 4079 12-11-4 **111**................ MrRGHenderson(5) 121+
(Caroline Keevil) *prom: mstke 4th: outpcd in 4th and rdn 13th: lft 10 l 2nd whn blnd and nrly uns rdr 15th: 15 l down next: clsd u.p to ld last: styd on wl* **6/1**

5-F3 **2** *1 3/4* **Western Whisky (FR)**[56] 3371 9-11-1 **106**.................(p) MrJFMathias(3) 112+
(Richard Lee) *hld up in tch: hdwy to join ldr after 12th: drew clr w ldr after next: lft 10 l clr 15th: 15 l clr next: reduced advantage bef next: rdn and hdd last: kpt on same pce flat* **13/2**

1246 **3** *9* **Rebel Melody (IRE)**[25] 3907 10-11-2 **111**.......(bt) MrCharlieDuckworth(7) 107
(Charlie Mann) *taken down early: chsd ldrs on outer: mstke 10th: outpcd by ldng pair and pushed along 13th: lft 3rd 13th: plugged on but nvr a threat to ldrs after* **8/1**

-130 **4** *19* **Gentleman Jimmy**[43] 3589 11-10-8 **96**................................ MrRMahon 72
(Hughie Morrison) *led tl 6th: styd prom tl dropped to last and lost tch after next: lft poor 4th 15th* **9/2**[3]

5U-P **U** **Ya I Know (IRE)**[46] 3522 10-10-3 **98**...............................(tp) MrMEnnis(7) —
(Sarah Humphrey) *hld up in tch in last pair: blnd 2nd: mstke and uns rdr 4th* **12/1**

-34P **U** **Double Pride**[31] 3784 7-11-5 **114**.....................................(b) MrRJarrett(7) —
(Alan King) *hld up in tch tl blnd and uns rdr 4th* **7/2**[2]

2023 **F** **Strongbows Legend**[31] 3784 6-10-13 **108**..................... MissCVHart(7) —
(Charlie Longsdon) *j.w: w ldrs tl led 6th: gng clr w rival whn nt fluent 13th: stl gng wl whn fell 15th* **9/4**[1]

7m 15.8s (25.10) **Going Correction** +0.625s/f (Soft) **7** Ran SP% **117.6**
Speed ratings: **86,85,82,76,**— —,—
Tote Swingers: 1&2 £4.40, 1&3 £5.90, 2&3 £9.40 CSF £44.55 CT £317.21 TOTE £7.50: £3.00, £3.70; EX 26.00.
Owner The Deep Pockets Partnership **Bred** L N Sloan **Trained** Motcombe, Dorset

FOCUS
Quite a dramatic race with Strongbows Legend leaving Western Whisky clear, and that one then idling in front and being claimed after the last. The form is rated around the first two, with the winner to his mark.

NOTEBOOK
Deep Pockets(IRE) had looked set for third at best at one stage, but stuck to his task and saw it out best. He had been in good form over hurdles until last time, and did well to recover from a blunder down the back, now having three C&D wins to his name. This was the highest mark he has ever won off. (op 9-2 tchd 13-2)
Western Whisky(FR) travelled best throughout the race and was still tanking when being left clear. In hindsight he'd have been better off had Strongbows Legend stayed on his feet, though, as he began to tire out on his own and had nothing left when joined. There's clearly a race in him off this sort of mark. (op 7-1)
Rebel Melody(IRE) was readily held and remains below his best. (op 13-2)
Gentleman Jimmy didn't put up much of a fight having come under pressure. (op 6-1)
Strongbows Legend was still right there and in with every chance when getting four out all wrong. It's hoped this doesn't affect his confidence too severely. (op 3-1)

4403 AMERICAN EXPRESS PROUD SPONSORS OF AITC H'CAP HURDLE (14 hdls) 3m 1f 110y
5:20 (5:20) (Class 5) (0-95,92) 4-Y-0+ **£1,815** (£529; £264)

Form RPR
0-46 **1** **Hazy Bay**[31] 3791 6-11-3 **83**.. TomO'Brien 86+
(Michael Roberts) *chsd ldrs: clr in ldng quartet after 10th: lft w ev ch and hmpd 3 out: sn led: rdn clr bef 2 out: styd on wl* **14/1**

0004 **2** *14* **Champs De Bleu (FR)**[13] 4130 8-11-5 **85**.......................... JamieMoore 74
(Gary Moore) *t.k.h early: hld up towards rr: stdy prog 7th: clr in ldng quartet 10th: rdn to chse ldr after 11th: lft in ld next: sn hdd: btn after 2 out: mstke last* **12/1**

6036 **3** *15* **Chouromanesco (FR)**[35] 3717 8-11-6 **86**................(b[1]) MattieBatchelor 58
(Mark Bradstock) *mde most tl 10th: mstke and struggling next: lft 3rd 3 out: sn wl btn* **10/1**

P403 **4** *18* **Grey Cruzene (USA)**[21] 3985 5-11-9 **89**.............................. ColinBolger 43
(Chris Gordon) *nt a fluent: towards rr: j. slowly 6th: rdn and struggling after 8th: t.o fr 11th* **14/1**

F-30 **5** *6* **Doctored**[41] 3611 10-10-8 **77**.. DavidBass(3) 25
(Daniel O'Brien) *chsd ldrs: mstke 2nd: rdn and lost tch w ldng quartet 10th: t.o whn lft 5th 3 out* **8/1**[3]

660P **P** **Patrick Dee**[29] 3833 6-9-7 **66** oh6..............................(b[1]) TrevorWhelan(7) —
(Christine Dunnett) *racd keenly: w ldr tl dropped out qckly u.p after 9th: wl t.o whn p.u 11th* **66/1**

6-22 **F** **Saulty Max (IRE)**[18] 4032 7-11-10 **90**............................(p) PaddyBrennan 93+
(Nigel Twiston-Davies) *mstkes: chsd ldrs: wnt 2nd and hit 9th: led next: 3 l clr and stl gng okay whn fell 3 out* **15/8**[1]

062U **P** **Brunette'Sonly (IRE)**[15] 4098 6-11-10 **90**.................... AndrewThornton —
(Seamus Mullins) *a towards rr: lost tch qckly u.p 10th: wl t.o whn p.u bef 3 out* **6/1**[2]

05P4 **P** **Domoly (FR)**[14] 4119 8-11-12 **92**...................................(p) LeightonAspell —
(Alison Batchelor) *hld up in rr: mstke 8th: rdn and lost tch after next: t.o whn p.u 11th* **20/1**

6m 51.4s (22.60) **Going Correction** +0.55s/f (Soft) **9** Ran SP% **96.6**
Speed ratings (Par 103): **87,82,78,72,70** —,—,—,—
CSF £110.61 CT £912.47 TOTE £10.30: £3.30, £2.10, £2.50.
Owner Mike Roberts **Bred** M J Roberts **Trained** Bodle Street Green, E Sussex

FOCUS
A weak handicap hurdle in which the runners finished tired, and a race that did not take much winning.

NOTEBOOK
Hazy Bay picked up the pieces for a first career victory. He had shaped with promise off 3lb higher at Fontwell last time and this stiffer test was clearly in his favour. Although only moderate, this was just his eighth start, so there could be more to come over a staying trip. (op 16-1)
Champs De Bleu(FR), dropped 5lb from his handicap debut, is another lightly raced sort open to improvement. He's not had much racing for an 8-y-o, but looks to have the ability to win a small race. (op 10-1)
Chouromanesco(FR), although ending up well held, showed a bit more zest in the first-time blinkers. (op 8-1)
Saulty Max(IRE) looked all over the winner, being in front and travelling well, until she crashed out at the third from home (tchd 9-4 in a place)
Brunette'Sonly(IRE) was struggling with a circuit to run and clearly failed to run her race. (tchd 9-4 in a place)
T/Plt: £64.30 to a £1 stake. Pool:£78,868.34 - 895.26 winning tickets T/Qpdt: £23.30 to a £1 stake. Pool:£7,117.09 - 225.40 winning tickets SP

4159 FFOS LAS (L-H)
Tuesday, March 1

OFFICIAL GOING: Soft
Wind: Light - Moderate, behind Weather: Fine

4404 DESIGN OFFICE MAIDEN HURDLE (8 hdls) 2m
2:20 (2:20) (Class 5) 4-Y-0+ **£1,951** (£573; £286; £143)

Form RPR
2-33 **1** **Timesawastin (IRE)**[55] 3398 5-11-1 0................................ PaulMoloney 118+
(Evan Williams) *mde all: j.lft and hung lft fr 3 out: clr 2 out: readily* **1/1**[1]

2040 **2** *6* **Tenby Jewel (IRE)**[20] 4012 6-11-1 0.................................. SamThomas 105
(Keith Goldsworthy) *midfield: hdwy to trck ldrs 4th: chsd wnr appr 3 out: sn no imp: no ch fr 2 out* **14/1**

3 *9* **Sing Of Run**[138] 4-10-4 0..(t) JamesO'Farrell(3) 89
(Peter Brookshaw) *chsd ldrs: rdn 3 out: kpt on same pce fr 2 out* **200/1**

02 **4** *nk* **Alonso De Guzman (IRE)**[30] 3833 7-11-1 0..............(t) RichardJohnson 97
(Tim Vaughan) *racd in 2nd pl: pressed wnr whn nt fluent 4th: rdn and lost 2nd appr 3 out: sn outpcd: plugged on at one pce after* **7/2**[2]

0 **5** *3 1/2* **Maadraa (IRE)**[33] 3760 6-11-1 0...(t) DPFahy 93
(Bernard Llewellyn) *hld up: pckd 1st: hdwy to chse ldrs appr 3 out: one pce fr next* **11/1**

6 *5* **Starry Mount**[17] 4-10-7 0.. JamesDavies 80
(Andrew Haynes) *midfield: rdn and wknd 3 out* **66/1**

4 **7** *1 ¾* **Storm Survivor (IRE)**[16] 4100 5-10-12 0.................. RichieMcLernon(3) 86
(Jonjo O'Neill) *midfield: pushed along after 5th: outpcd and btn appr 3 out* **11/2**[3]

0- **8** *3 ¾* **Domos Boy (IRE)**[496] 1849 8-10-12 0................................ MrAJBerry(3) 85
(Jonjo O'Neill) *midfield: j. slowly 3rd: bhd fr next: nvr on terms after* **40/1**

006 **9** *¾* **North Stack**[26] 3897 5-11-1 0.. TomScudamore 81
(Michael Scudamore) *bhd: niggled along appr 3 out: no hdwy* **33/1**

0- **10** *11* **Going Nowhere Fast (IRE)**[19] 4039 6-10-10 100........ OliverDayman(5) 70
(Alison Thorpe) *midfield: hdwy 4th: pushed along and wknd appr 3 out: n.d whn mstke 2 out* **33/1**

F **Small Fly (IRE)**[150] 1687 7-10-8 0.............................. NathanSweeney(7) 99
(Bob Buckler) *hld up: hdwy to chse ldrs appr 3 out: 3rd abt 8 l off pce and styng on whn fell 2 out* **66/1**

3m 55.8s (6.80) **Going Correction** +0.50s/f (Soft)
WFA 4 from 5yo+ 7lb 11 Ran SP% **114.4**
Speed ratings (Par 103): **103,100,95,95,93 91,90,88,87,82** —
toteswingers:1&2 £12.90, 2&3 £101.70, 1&3 £101.70 CSF £15.86 TOTE £1.70: £1.10, £2.20, £33.60; EX 15.10.
Owner Mrs C A Waters **Bred** Walter Connors **Trained** Llancarfan, Vale Of Glamorgan
■ Stewards' Enquiry : James O'Farrell six-day ban: weighed in 2lb heavy (Mar 15-20)

FOCUS
A weak maiden hurdle with the winner value for further and the fourth and fifth helping to set the level.

NOTEBOOK
Timesawastin(IRE) had shown more than enough in two previous starts over hurdles to suggest a race such as this would come his way, and it's possible he'll be up to defying a penalty in another modest contest. (tchd 6-4 in places)
Tenby Jewel(IRE) was no match for the winner, but did keep on and should do better in handicaps. (op 20-1)
Sing Of Run, who failed to beat a rival home in two starts on the Flat for another yard, shaped surprisingly well given his long odds.
Alonso De Guzman(IRE), runner-up over 2m4f at Fakenham latest, kept on in a manner to suggest a return to further is required. (op 11-4)
Maadraa(IRE) improved a little for the fitting of a tongue-tie. (tchd 10-1)
Storm Survivor(IRE) failed to build on his initial effort, but is probably one for handicaps anyway. (op 4-1)
Small Fly(IRE), beaten 18l in a bumper in Ireland last October, was in the process of making a satisfactory hurdles debut when coming down two out.

4405 DIGIBET CONDITIONAL JOCKEYS' H'CAP HURDLE (11 hdls) 2m 6f
2:50 (2:50) (Class 5) (0-90,90) 4-Y-O+ **£1,951** (£573; £286; £143)

Form RPR

-P01 **1** **Border Lad**[8] 4263 7-10-4 71 7ex............................... AodhaganConlon(3) 83+
(Alison Thorpe) *chsd ldr: led appr 4 out: clr 3 out: 10 l ahd and wl in command whn blnd last: eased down run-in* **11/8**[1]

-5P6 **2** *6* **Zi Missile (IRE)**[194] 1293 7-9-11 66................................ MichaelByrne(5) 63
(Mary Evans) *chsd ldrs: wnt 2nd 4 out: rdn and no imp 3 out: no ch w wnr* **8/1**

0001 **3** *28* **Body Gold (ARG)**[7] 4272 8-11-5 86 7ex.............. SamTwiston-Davies(3) 65+
(Nigel Twiston-Davies) *hld up in rr: niggled along 4 out: effrt sn after: u.p whn blnd 3 out: sn wl btn* **6/4**[2]

0000 **4** *5* **Little Frano (IRE)**[24] 3942 7-11-9 90.......................... DonalDevereux(3) 54
(Peter Bowen) *led: hdd appr 4 out: sn wknd and lost tch* **13/2**[3]

5m 53.5s (35.50) **Going Correction** +0.50s/f (Soft)
WFA 4 from 6yo+ 8lb 4 Ran SP% **106.5**
Speed ratings (Par 103): **55,52,42,40**
CSF £10.02 TOTE £2.10; EX 7.40.
Owner The Almost Hopeful Partnership **Bred** Whitegate Stud **Trained** Bronwydd Arms, Carmarthens

FOCUS
A race that looked to concern only two, but with one of those, Body Gold, failing to reproduce his best, it was left to Border Lad to collect. The winner is value for further and rated to the level of his recent win.

NOTEBOOK
Border Lad was penalised for his Hereford success, but actually got to race off the same mark (out of the handicap at Hereford), and always looked in control having gone on four out. He'll face stiffer tasks in future, but is clearly progressive. (op 11-10 tchd 6-4)
Zi Missile(IRE), returning to hurdles without the cheekpieces she wore on her latest start, showed improved form on this debut for a new yard. (op 9-1)
Body Gold(ARG), who improved dramatically for the switch to handicaps at Taunton last week, was expected to go close under a penalty, but he didn't travel with the same fluency and was beaten before the straight. It's possible the race came too soon. (op 15-8)
Little Frano(IRE) failed to improve for the switch to handicaps. (op 11-2)

4406 CELTIC LAGER - WALES' PREMIUM LAGER NOVICES' CHASE (12 fncs 1 omitted) 2m
3:20 (3:20) (Class 3) 5-Y-O+ **£5,204** (£1,528; £764; £381)

Form RPR

2-4F **1** **Fahrisee (IRE)**[63] 3156 8-10-12 0....................................... PaulMoloney 129+
(Evan Williams) *chsd clr ldr: clsd and abt 5 l down 4 out: nt fluent whn chalng 2 out: led appr last: edgd lft and r.o wl run-in: clr towards fin* **8/1**

P522 **2** *3 ½* **Ruthenoise (FR)**[20] 4009 6-10-2 0.............................. DavidBass(3) 117+
(Nicky Henderson) *racd keenly: led: sn clr: dragged hind-legs across 5th whn at least 16 l ahd: advantage reduced to abt 5 l 4 out: pressed 2 out: hdd appr last: no ex fnl 100yds* **8/11**[1]

-124 **3** *12* **Thumbs Up**[12] 4168 6-11-4 0.. JasonMaguire 120
(Donald McCain) *chsd ldrs: dropped to last 8th: rdn whn mstke 3 out: sn no imp: kpt on u.p to take mod 3rd towards fin* **11/4**[2]

31P **4** *1 ¼* **Holoko Heights**[163] 1558 6-11-4 0.............................(v) RichardJohnson 117
(Tim Vaughan) *mstke 1st: racd in last pl: wnt 3rd 8th: clsd a little 3 out: one pce fr 2 out: nt fluent last: lost 3rd towards fin* **15/2**[3]

4m 3.10s (-1.90) **Going Correction** +0.125s/f (Yiel) 4 Ran SP% **107.4**
Speed ratings: **109,107,101,100**
CSF £15.06 TOTE £8.30; EX 15.40.
Owner Hugh Williams **Bred** I Williams **Trained** Llancarfan, Vale Of Glamorgan

FOCUS
Probably not form to put much trust in, Ruthenoise charging into a clear lead and having nothing left in the tank. The winner is rated to his hurdles form but could be rated higher.

NOTEBOOK
Fahrisee(IRE), who caused a 100-1 surprise when scoring over hurdles at Hereford a year ago, hadn't achieved anything in two previous starts over fences, falling latest, but he jumped better on the whole and the race fell into his lap. He'll have more on under a penalty now, so could struggle. (op 5-1 tchd 9-1)
Ruthenoise(FR), a free-going sort over hurdles, again refused to settle and soon found herself clear. She jumped low at her fences, making a couple of mistakes, and it always looked inevitable she would be claimed late on by something. She's got the ability to win races and will probably get away with these tactics one day. (op 5-6 tchd 4-6)
Thumbs Up isn't really progressing from a promising start as a chaser, but could do better handicapping. (op 3-1 tchd 10-3)
Holoko Heights needs better ground and should improve on this first outing since breaking a blood-vessel in September. (tchd 9-1)

4407 FELINFOEL BREWERS' DRAGON STOUT H'CAP HURDLE (12 hdls) 3m
3:55 (3:55) (Class 4) (0-115,111) 4-Y-O+ **£2,602** (£764; £382; £190)

Form RPR

2030 **1** **Jump Up**[19] 4034 5-10-13 98... TomO'Brien 100
(Keith Goldsworthy) *chsd ldrs: mstke 8th: pushed along after 4 out: rdn appr 2 out: led jst after last: styd on towards fin* **11/1**

6146 **2** *1 ½* **Monsieur Cadou (FR)**[34] 3745 6-11-3 102...................... PaddyBrennan 104
(Tom George) *chsd ldrs: wnt 2nd appr 3 out: rdn and ev ch whn mstke 2 out: nt qckn and lost 2nd bef last: hung lft run-in: styd on fnl 75yds to regain 2nd but hld* **7/1**[3]

6544 **3** *¾* **Nobby Kivambo (IRE)**[18] 4052 6-10-10 100..........(p) MrMMO'Connor(5) 101
(Brendan Powell) *j.lft a few times: sn led: rdn between last 2: hit last sn hdd: no ex fnl 50yds* **5/1**[2]

34P- **4** *½* **Heraldry (IRE)**[339] 4895 11-11-9 111............................. JamesO'Farrell(3) 111
(Peter Brookshaw) *hld up towards rr: hdwy after 4 out: chsd ldrs 3 out: rdn and edgd lft appr last: styd on towards fin: nt quite gng pce to mount serious chal* **33/1**

2-30 **5** *32* **Bring On The Judge (IRE)**[42] 3621 8-11-8 110. SamTwiston-Davies(3) 78
(Nigel Twiston-Davies) *hld up: hdwy into midfield 6th: rdn and in tch but no real imp on ldrs 3 out: wknd bef 2 out* **8/1**

22U3 **6** *1 ¼* **Ballyegan (IRE)**[15] 4119 6-10-13 105......................... NathanSweeney(7) 71
(Bob Buckler) *prom: rdn and outpcd after 4 out: wknd bef 2 out* **9/2**[1]

0554 **7** *19* **Dipity Doo Dah**[21] 3989 7-10-12 97............................... RichardJohnson 44
(Peter Bowen) *in tch: wnt 2nd 8th: rdn and lost 2nd appr 3 out: wknd bef 2 out: sn eased* **9/2**[1]

02P0 **8** *86* **Tin Pot Man (IRE)**[33] 3764 5-11-6 105.............................(t) PaulMoloney —
(Evan Williams) *midfield: lost pl bef 7th: t.o fr 4 out* **20/1**

-2P0 **P** **Winchester Red**[30] 3840 9-10-12 104............................(t) MrJEngland(7) —
(Evan Williams) *midfield: lost pl after 6th: t.o whn p.u bef 3 out* **25/1**

101- **F** **Crannaghmore Boy (IRE)**[367] 4295 6-11-11 110................. RhysFlint —
(Keith Goldsworthy) *prom: stl 5th and handy whn fell 8th* **7/1**[3]

344 **P** **Duneen Point (IRE)**[11] 4182 7-11-4 108......................... MrTomDavid(5) —
(Tim Vaughan) *hld up: reminders appr 8th: t.o whn p.u bef 4 out: fin lame* **10/1**

6m 18.0s (31.00) **Going Correction** +0.50s/f (Soft) 11 Ran SP% **118.1**
Speed ratings (Par 105): **68,67,67,67,56 56,49,21**,—,— —
toteswingers:1&2 £16.00, 2&3 £2.80, 1&3 £9.50 CSF £84.45 CT £440.15 TOTE £8.40: £2.10, £1.80, £2.00; EX 113.50.
Owner Ashley Hart **Bred** D J And Mrs Deer **Trained** Yerbeston, Pembrokes

FOCUS
A competitive handicap hurdle with the first three pretty much to their marks in an ordinary contest.

NOTEBOOK
Jump Up, well held on two previous handicap runs, including at Taunton latest, was up to 3m for the first time and showed much-improved form, getting on top after the last. He's unexposed at this trip, so could improve again. (op 9-1)
Monsieur Cadou(FR), 7lb above his last winning mark, bounced back from a poor effort at Huntingdon, just not being able to fend off the winner, having hung on the flat.
Nobby Kivambo(IRE) finally looked like he was going to break his duck coming to the last, but met it completely wrong and lost all his momentum. (op 6-1 tchd 9-2)
Heraldry(IRE) should have been a length or two closer, his rider seeming to over-do the waiting tactics. Making his debut for the yard, he was noted travelling best turning in but never quite got close enough to challenge. This was a promising start.
Bring On The Judge(IRE) ended up well held having been bang there leaving the back straight. He's only lightly raced and not one to give up on just yet. (op 9-1)
Ballyegan(IRE), reverting to hurdles, jumped big and was quickly left trailing. (op 5-1 tchd 4-1)
Dipity Doo Dah was another who could make no further impression in the straight, having moved well up with the pace down the back. (op 5-1)
Crannaghmore Boy(IRE), having his first start in 367 days, was still chasing the pace when coming down. It's hoped his confidence isn't too badly dented. (op 17-2)
Duneen Point(IRE) Official explanation: vet said gelding was lame right-hind (op 17-2)

4408 DOUBLE DRAGON NATIONAL ALE OF WALES H'CAP CHASE (15 fncs 2 omitted) 2m 5f
4:30 (4:30) (Class 3) (0-125,123) 5-Y-O+ **£5,204** (£1,528; £764; £381)

Form RPR

5001 **1** **Patman Du Charmil (FR)**[42] 3617 9-11-8 122.(b) SamTwiston-Davies(3) 132
(Nigel Twiston-Davies) *led: rdn and hdd appr 4 out: 1 l down 3 out: sn lft in front: clr bef last: styd on wl whn in command run-in* **7/2**[3]

-024 **2** *12* **Horsford (IRE)**[38] 3690 7-11-6 117..............................(t) TomScudamore 122+
(David Pipe) *chsd ldr: mstke 2nd: led appr 4 out: 1 l ahd and gng nicely whn blnd 3 out: sn hdd: wl hld bef last* **9/4**[2]

5244 **3** *5* **Youngstown (IRE)**[25] 3922 8-11-5 116............................. JasonMaguire 108
(Donald McCain) *chsd ldrs: outpcd appr 4 out: nvr a threat to ldrs* **7/4**[1]

P253 **4** *6* **Top Benefit (IRE)**[19] 4030 9-10-13 110............................... SamThomas 99
(Keith Goldsworthy) *nt fluent: a bhd: struggling to keep up after 11th: nvr a threat* **9/2**

5m 28.8s (-1.20) **Going Correction** +0.125s/f (Yiel) 4 Ran SP% **107.5**
Speed ratings: **107,102,100,98**
CSF £11.35 TOTE £4.60; EX 9.10.
Owner H R Mould **Bred** Mme Guilhaine Le Borgne **Trained** Naunton, Gloucs

FOCUS
The outcome of this novice chase took a dramatic turn when Horsford, in front and looking the like winner, made a bad blunder three out which he was unable to recover from. The winner is rated to the best of his 2009 form.

NOTEBOOK
Patman Du Charmil(FR), 8lb higher than when scoring at Southwell in January, had luck on his side and, although finishing second would have been no disgrace, more is required if he's to complete a hat-trick. (op 3-1)
Horsford(IRE), switching to handicaps on only his second start over fences, jumped well in the main and went on before four out. He looked in control when making his race-ending blunder, but should gain compensation at some stage. (tchd 15-8)
Youngstown(IRE) was comfortably held back in third and doesn't yet look capable of capitalising on his declining mark. Official explanation: jockey said gelding never travelled (op 5-2)

Top Benefit(IRE) jumped slowly throughout and never looked like winning. (op 7-2)

4409 CELTIC PRIDE - PREMIUM SUMMER ALE H'CAP CHASE (17 fncs 2 omitted) 3m 1f 110y

5:05 (5:05) (Class 4) (0-105,102) 5-Y-0+ **£3,122** (£916; £458; £228)

Form				RPR
4/14	**1**		**Marias Rock**[32] 3790 9-10-9 **85** .... NickScholfield *(Jeremy Scott) prom: str chal fr 4 out: r.o for press to ld narrowly fnl 50yds: gamley prevailed in driving fin* **10/3**[2]	92
/5-5	**2**	*shd*	**Derawar (IRE)**[16] 4102 12-10-4 **87** ....(p) MsLucyJones(7) (Lucy Jones) *hld up: clsd 12th: led 13th: pressed rest of way: rdn appr last: hdd narrowly fnl 50yds: r.o u.p* **10/1**	95
141F	**3**	*1 ¼*	**Canal Bank (IRE)**[36] 3716 7-11-9 **102** ....(tp) RichieMcLernon(3) (Jonjo O'Neill) *hld up: clsd 4 out: effrt to chal 2 out: rdn and tried to qckn appr last: styd on run-in: nt quite gng pce of front pair* **4/1**[3]	109
3230	**4**	*6*	**Dromore Hill (IRE)**[25] 3933 7-10-10 **86** ....(v) JimmyMcCarthy (Charlie Morlock) *led: rdn along appr 5th: hdd 13th: sn lost pl: rallied and j.rt 4 out: 4th and jst over 2 l off pce whn mstke 2 out: one pce bef last* **4/1**[3]	89
515-	**5**	*11*	**Quiet Bob (IRE)**[332] 4989 8-10-11 **87** .... RichardJohnson (Philip Hobbs) *nt fluent: hld up: hit 9th: effrt bhd ldrs but unable to chal appr 3 out: wknd bef 2 out: eased whn wl btn bef last* **9/4**[1]	79
0002	**6**	*hd*	**Run To Fly (IRE)**[14] 4126 6-9-12 **77** ....(p) DonalDevereux(3) (Peter Bowen) *prom: rdn after 13th: losing pl whn bmpd 4 out: wknd bef 2 out* **8/1**	68

6m 50.8s (3.80) **Going Correction** +0.125s/f (Yiel) **6** Ran SP% **114.0**
Speed ratings: **99,98,98,96,93 93**
toteswingers:1&2 £9.10, 2&3 £12.10, 1&3 £4.10 CSF £32.20 TOTE £3.70: £1.70, £3.20; EX 36.20.

Owner G T Lever **Bred** Mrs V M Withers **Trained** Brompton Regis, Somerset

FOCUS
An open handicap chase in which all of the runners were still in with a chance turning in. The placed horses are rated close to their marks.

NOTEBOOK
Marias Rock just edged it in a tight finish. This is her second win since returning from a lengthy absence, and she showed here that this longer trip is within range. She shouldn't go up much and can probably continue to give a good account. (op 7-2 tchd 11-4)

Derawar(IRE), well beaten on his recent return to rules, had received a big drop in the weights and very nearly capitalised on it, pulling out plenty for pressure down the straight and just losing out. (op 12-1)

Canal Bank(IRE), a dual winner late last year who fell when off this mark on his latest outing, was gradually gaining on the front two, but could never quite get there. (op 3-1 tchd 11-2)

Dromore Hill(IRE) tried to rally once headed, but was one paced. (op 9-2 tchd 5-1)

Quiet Bob(IRE) was returning from 332 days off and made mistakes. (op 3-1)

Run To Fly(IRE) was unable to build on his Folkestone second, quickly being beaten off. (tchd 15-2)

4410 MELLUSION STANDARD OPEN NATIONAL HUNT FLAT RACE 2m

5:35 (5:36) (Class 5) 4-6-Y-0 **£1,431** (£420; £210; £104)

Form				RPR
2	**1**		**Sertao (FR)**[24] 3943 5-11-4 0 .... RichardJohnson (Tim Vaughan) *in tch: chalng fr over 3f out: rdn over 2f out: hung lft whn upsides ins fnl f: led narrowly post* **6/4**[1]	103
0-	**2**	*nse*	**Mike Towey (IRE)**[351] 4649 6-11-4 0 .... TomO'Brien (Peter Bowen) *a.p: led narrowly over 3f out: rdn 2f out: hrd pressed: hdd post* **25/1**	103
2	**3**	*1 ¾*	**Bathwick Brave (IRE)**[40] 3651 4-10-10 0 .... TomScudamore (David Pipe) *led: hdd over 3f out: sn rdn: stl ev ch over 2f out: clsd 3rd but hld whn checked abt 100yds out: one pce cl home* **9/4**[2]	93
	4	*11*	**Canopy Of Stars** 5-11-4 0 .... PaddyBrennan (Tom George) *hld up: cl bhd ldng bunch 6f out: pushed along over 4f out: rdn and outpcd by ldrs over 3f out: no imp after* **13/2**[3]	90
	5	*7*	**Toreador (FR)** 4-10-7 0 .... SamTwiston-Davies(3) (Nigel Twiston-Davies) *in tch: pushed along over 4f out: wknd over 3f out* **12/1**	75
5	**6**	*3 ¾*	**Twin Barrels**[25] 3936 4-10-10 0 .... JamesDavies (Andrew Haynes) *prom: lost pl 9f out: bhd and u.p 6f out: lost tch over 4f out* **33/1**	71
35	**7**	*6*	**Street Dance (IRE)**[11] 4191 5-11-4 0 .... RhysFlint (Keith Goldsworthy) *plld hrd: hld up: hdwy to go prom 10f out: rdn and wknd over 4f out* **7/1**	73
0-	**8**	*nk*	**Seffier**[590] 1000 6-10-8 0 .... JamesO'Farrell(3) (Peter Brookshaw) *a bhd: struggling 6f out: lost tch* **100/1**	66

3m 56.8s (13.40) **Going Correction** +0.50s/f (Soft)
WFA 4 from 5yo+ 7lb **8** Ran SP% **112.1**
Speed ratings: **86,85,85,79,76 74,71,71**
toteswingers:1&2 £2.50, 2&3 £4.00, 1&3 £1.80. totesuper7: Win: Not won. Place: £1344.00 CSF £41.27 TOTE £2.60: £1.10, £4.80, £1.10; EX 36.60.

Owner West Coast Haulage Limited **Bred** Yvon Alcan **Trained** Aberthin, Vale of Glamorgan

FOCUS
Three drew clear in what was an ordinary bumper and the form is rated around the first two.

NOTEBOOK
Sertao(FR), not beaten far at the course on debut, found plenty for strong pressure to get up close home. He had a hard enough race and may take a while to get over it, but clearly has a future, with further likely to suit over hurdles. (op 11-10 tchd 13-8 in places)

Mike Towey(IRE), a former point winner who was well held on his bumper debut, showed much-improved form. He battled well without quite doing enough, but is another with a future over jumps. (op 20-1)

Bathwick Brave(IRE) kept on right the way to the line, looking like a horse in need of a stiffer test. (op 11-4)

Canopy Of Stars is going to need further, so showed some promise. (op 8-1)

Toreador(FR) is related to some useful winners, so could have been expected to show more. (op 14-1)

Street Dance(IRE) was disappointing considering he had contested a decent event at Newbury latest. (op 10-1)

T/Jkpt: Not won. T/Plt: £1,886.00 to a £1 stake. Pool of £74,666.47 - 28.90 winning tickets. T/Qpdt: £469.00 to a £1 stake. Pool of £4,817.12 - 7.60 winning tickets. DO

4139 LEICESTER (R-H)

Tuesday, March 1

OFFICIAL GOING: Heavy (soft in places)
Wind: almost nil Weather: dull and cold

4411 LADBROKES.COM CAPTAIN MACHELL NOVICES' H'CAP CHASE (12 fncs) 2m

2:30 (2:30) (Class 4) (0-110,107) 5-Y-0+ **£2,602** (£764; £382; £190)

Form				RPR
P533	**1**		**Playing With Fire (IRE)**[19] 4033 7-11-9 **104** .... CharliePoste (Robin Dickin) *mde all: gng best whn mstke 3 out: rdn clr next: eased flat* **5/2**[2]	113+
4050	**2**	*6*	**Nous Voila (FR)**[4] 4330 10-10-11 **92** .... MarkBradburne (Alan Coogan) *racd in last: 7 l down 3 out: plugged on gamely after: wnt 2nd clhome but nvr nr wnr* **15/2**	89
0P21	**3**	*1*	**Karasakal (IRE)**[26] 3898 8-11-3 **98** .... JamieMoore (Gary Moore) *taken wd: shkn up 5th: drvn and nt keen after 8th: nvr making any imp fr next: snatched 3rd* **9/4**[1]	95
0/-	**4**	*nse*	**Foretto (GER)**[12] 4176 9-11-12 **107** ....(t) JohnnyFarrelly (D J Ryan, Ire) *chsd wnr: hit 3 out: wknd last: lost two pls fnl 50yds* **5/1**	103
1522	**5**	*1*	**The Darling Boy**[19] 4033 6-11-4 **102** ....(t) PeterToole(3) (Tom George) *nt fluent 1st: mstkes 6th and 8th and dropped to rr: tried to rally next: plodded on but nvr gng wl enough fr 3 out* **3/1**[3]	100+

4m 23.0s (14.80) **Going Correction** +0.925s/f (Soft) **5** Ran SP% **112.8**
Speed ratings: **100,97,96,96,95**
CSF £19.03 TOTE £4.10: £2.10, £2.20; EX 21.00.

Owner Mrs A L Merry **Bred** Mrs D A Merry **Trained** Atherstone on Stour, Warwicks

FOCUS
The going was described as "tacky" for this all-chase card. A wide open novice handicap run at a decent gallop in the conditions. The winner made a step up and the race can be rated a few pounds higher.

NOTEBOOK
Playing With Fire(IRE) ran out a comfortable winner of her first chase on only her third start over fences. Despite making a slight mistake at the second last, she jumped well in the main to make all and draw well clear. She is improving over fences and should be competitive if turned out quickly under a penalty, potentially at Kempton on Saturday. (op 11-4 tchd 9-4)

Nous Voila(FR) stayed on from the rear to take second, his best run for some time. A Grade 2 winner in his hurdling days, he is 0-15 over fences but this was his first chase start since May 2009 and he should have the ability to be competitive at this level. (op 10-1 tchd 11-2)

Karasakal(IRE) disappointed and was under pressure a long way from home. Only 3lb higher than his win last time out, he is suited by a patient ride and is worth another chance as this was probably not his true running. (op 5-2 tchd 3-1)

Foretto(GER) looked to have a difficult task off top-weight and will need a drop in mark to get involved. (op 7-1)

The Darling Boy needs to jump better to give himself any chance. (op 9-4)

4412 LADBROKES.COM SQUIRE OSBALDESTON H'CAP CHASE (18 fncs) 2m 7f 110y

3:00 (3:00) (Class 4) (0-105,103) 5-Y-0+ **£2,927** (£859; £429; £214)

Form				RPR
-666	**1**		**Tim The Chair (IRE)**[47] 3528 6-11-11 **102** .... JackDoyle (Emma Lavelle) *lft 2nd at 3rd: rdn to join ldr 15th: blnd next: given time to rcvr: 2 l down last: rousted ahd fnl 100yds* **4/1**[3]	118+
-1P6	**2**	*1 ½*	**Beware Chalk Pit (IRE)**[13] 4139 7-11-0 **94** .... JimmyDerham(3) (Jonathan Geake) *trckd ldrs: effrt bef 15th: led gng wl bef 3 out: lft w 4 l advantage next: 2 l ahd last: wknd and ct cl home* **14/1**	103
PP61	**3**	*10*	**Duke Of Ormond (IRE)**[9] 4238 8-11-6 **97** 7ex ....(p) CharliePoste (Anna Brooks) *continually j.lft: led at v slow pce tl 2nd: lft in ld 3rd: done no favours by loose horse down bk st: hdd 15th: sn btn and plodded on* **10/3**[1]	99
3644	**4**	*3*	**Phoenix Des Mottes (FR)**[13] 4139 8-10-0 **84** .... JoeCornwall(7) (John Cornwall) *nt bttr than midfield: blnd 11th: outpcd bef 15th: plugging on after last: wnt 4th flat* **9/1**	81
P0OP	**5**	*1 ¾*	**Osolomio (IRE)**[42] 3621 8-11-12 **103** ....[1] SeanQuinlan (Jennie Candlish) *hit 1st: racd keenly: hld up: mstke 13th: clsd after 14th and j. ahd briefly 15th: shkn up and immediately downed tools and wl btn* **8/1**	99
-213	**6**	*9*	**Master D'Or (FR)**[22] 3982 11-11-11 **102** .... JohnnyFarrelly (Sophie Leech) *bhd: hdwy 10th: nt fluent 14th and lost pl: fdd qckly bef 2 out* **5/1**	90
154P	**U**		**The Artful Fox**[24] 3956 10-10-4 **88** .... PaulGallagher(7) (Mike Sowersby) *t.k.h: led 2nd tl uns rdr 3rd* **20/1**	—
3243	**R**		**Billy Murphy**[25] 3933 8-10-9 **86** .... MarkBradburne (Paul Cowley) *t.k.h early: rn in snatches: dropped bk last at 12th: stl jst in tch whn n.m.r and rn out 15th* **7/2**[2]	—

6m 24.0s (20.00) **Going Correction** +0.925s/f (Soft) **8** Ran SP% **114.5**
Speed ratings: **103,102,99,98,97 94,—,—**
CSF £52.97 CT £205.63 TOTE £3.90: £1.80, £3.90, £1.40; EX 78.30.

Owner Frisky Fillies 5 **Bred** Ms E Busher **Trained** Wildhern, Hants

FOCUS
An interesting handicap with a few improving types. The winner stepped up on his hurdles form with the placed horses setting the standard.

NOTEBOOK
Tim The Chair(IRE) survived a bad mistake two out to win on his chasing debut, having previously shown little over hurdles. A former point winner, chasing was always going to be his game and he looked to be on a fair enough mark to start with. He was good value for more than the winning distance and can only improve from this over staying trips. Official explanation: trainer said, regarding apparent improvement in form, that the gelding appeared to benefit from racing over fences for the first time and the longer trip. (op 11-2)

Beware Chalk Pit(IRE) won a weaker race over 3m2f in November, but was unlucky here to run into a good horse who was well handicapped. Stamina is his forte and he is sure to be suited by a return to further. The front two drew well clear. (tchd 16-1)

Duke Of Ormond(IRE) made the early running and did well to plug on, but was undone by his penalty. He should do well when running off his true mark (7lb lower) and can win again. (op 3-1)

Phoenix Des Mottes(FR) has done all his winning on a sounder surface, and looks as though he remains on a fair enough mark when the ground improves. (op 10-1 tchd 8-1)

Osolomio(IRE) travelled well but found nothing, and is too inconsistent to be a sound betting proposition. (op 7-1 tchd 13-2)

The Form Book, Raceform Ltd, Compton, RG20 6NL

Master D'Or(FR) was keen early, giving him no chance of getting home in the conditions. (op 9-2 tchd 6-1)

4413 LADBROKES.COM SILEBY NOVICES' H'CAP CHASE (15 fncs) 2m 4f 110y
3:35 (3:35) (Class 5) (0-90,90) 5-Y-O+ **£1,951** (£573; £286; £143)

Form RPR
0036 **1** **French Ties (IRE)**[8] 4263 9-11-8 **85**................................(p) SeanQuinlan 93+
(Jennie Candlish) *hdwy 5th: led 9th: 4 l clr 2 out: hung lft and idling flat: urged along and all out to hold a rival who would nt go past* **11/2**[3]

0360 **2** *1 ¾* **Red Law (IRE)**[13] 4144 7-10-11 **77**..........................(b[1]) TommyPhelan[(3)] 83
(Mark Gillard) *set slow pce: hdd after 5th: pressed wnr fr 9th: outpcd and 4 l down 2 out: rallied last: n.g.t fnl 100yds and fin weakly* **8/1**

4/05 **3** *18* **Ballyman (IRE)**[13] 4144 10-10-2 **68**.............................. JimmyDerham[(3)] 55
(Jonathan Geake) *towards rr: 5th and outpcd bef 12th: wnt 15 l 3rd 3 out: rdn and nvr able to cl* **9/4**[1]

-0P1 **4** *3* **Chord**[134] 1901 7-11-10 **87**.. AndrewThornton 71
(Simon Earle) *tubed: taken wd: clsd to ld after 5th tl 9th: lost pl after 11th: poor 4th 2 out* **8/1**

P63F **5** *3 ¾* **Jolly Boys Outing (IRE)**[27] 3880 8-11-5 **89**..................... MrBJPoste[(7)] 70
(Rosemary Gasson) *plld hrd in rr: getting outpcd whn mstke 11th: wl btn after* **20/1**

03P- **6** *3 ½* **Chamacco (FR)**[484] 2042 11-10-10 **73**............................ JohnnyFarrelly 50
(Sophie Leech) *midfield: effrt 11th: losing tch w ldng pair in 6 l 3rd at 12th: fading after* **12/1**

232P **7** *13* **Monty's Moon (IRE)**[32] 3790 9-10-5 **75**.....................(b) PeterCarberry[(7)] 39
(Rachel Hobbs) *nt jump wl and rn in snatches: lost tch after mstke 10th: rdn and fnd nthing: t.o* **4/1**[2]

-P06 **P** **Roi De Garde (FR)**[103] 2473 5-11-12 **90**........................ TomMessenger —
(Chris Bealby) *racd keenly: cl up: j.v.slowly 1st: nt fluent 7th: blnd 9th: rdn next: sn lost pl: wl bhd whn p.u last* **8/1**

5m 46.3s (27.40) **Going Correction** +0.925s/f (Soft) **8** Ran SP% **111.9**
Speed ratings: **84,83,76,75,73 72,67,—**
CSF £45.39 CT £124.94 TOTE £5.40: £1.50, £3.50, £2.10; EX 59.40.
Owner Alan Baxter **Bred** T F Lacy **Trained** Basford Green, Staffs

FOCUS
A moderate race run at no early pace. The winner is rated to his mark in a poor contest.

NOTEBOOK
French Ties(IRE) hasn't always been the gamest, but was able to dictate things from halfway down the back and Sean Quinlan did well to ensure he never got into a battle with the runner-up. He seems to have been suited by the drop back in trip, as this helped him get into a nice jumping rhythm, and he found plenty after the last to record his first win over fences. He clearly has ability, but is not the most consistent and can't be relied upon to repeat this performance. (op 5-1 tchd 13-2)
Red Law(IRE) put in a much improved effort and was clearly rejuvenated by first-time blinkers. Third here off 13lb higher in January, he had shown little in two subsequent runs but, if able to repeat this effort, is on a winnable mark. The front two pulled well clear. (op 7-1)
Ballyman(IRE) was having only his third run since a lengthy lay-off, but despite appearing on a feasible mark, is now 0-16 under rules and will need to find a very weak race to win. (op 7-2)
Chord took up the running with a circuit to go, but was unsuited by the testing conditions. Once rated 127 over hurdles, this run should put him right for a spring campaign. (op 11-2 tchd 5-1)
Jolly Boys Outing(IRE) was held up, but never looked like getting involved on his handicap debut and has struggled under rules. (op 18-1)
Chamacco(FR) was returning from a 484-day absence and is entitled to come on for the run. (tchd 16-1)
Monty's Moon(IRE) Official explanation: jockey said gelding hung left in straight

4414 LADBROKES.COM RUTLAND WATER NOVICES' CHASE (18 fncs) 2m 7f 110y
4:10 (4:10) (Class 3) 5-Y-O+ **£5,054** (£1,838)

Form RPR
45U1 **1** **Galaxy Rock (IRE)**[44] 3586 7-11-4 0................................(b) APMcCoy 123+
(Jonjo O'Neill) *led fr 5th: hacked clr after 14th: 15 l ahd whn j. bdly lft 3 out* **30/100**[1]

3P **2** *42* **Hommage A Bach (IRE)**[1] 4394 6-10-12 0.................(b) JohnnyFarrelly 72
(Paul John Gilligan, Ire) *a in last: blnd 6th: lft 3rd at 10th: lft 8 l in 2nd at 11th: soldiering on in hopeless pursuit whn poor jumps at fnl four fences* **20/1**[3]

0/2P **U** **Not So Prudent (IRE)**[37] 3702 7-10-12 0.......................... DavidEngland —
(Nigel Twiston-Davies) *led tl 5th: j. bdly lft and blnd next: j.lft after: 2 l down whn j.lft: blnd and uns rdr 11th* **4/1**[2]

65P4 **U** **Rester Vrai (FR)**[11] 4179 6-10-5 66................................ JoeCornwall[(7)] —
(John Cornwall) *a in 3rd: 7 l down and looked to be struggling whn blnd and uns rdr 10th* **25/1**

6m 29.2s (25.20) **Going Correction** +0.925s/f (Soft) **4** Ran SP% **105.5**
Speed ratings: **95,81,—,—**
CSF £5.56 TOTE £1.30; EX 4.10.
Owner Michael & John O'Flynn **Bred** Arctic Tack Stud **Trained** Cheltenham, Gloucs

FOCUS
An uncompetitive novices' chase with the second the best guide to the form.

NOTEBOOK
Galaxy Rock(IRE) had an easy task made even more so by two fallers down the back straight, which left him in splendid isolation. His second consecutive chase win, he cruised home and jumped safely as we learnt little that we didn't already know. If able to continue to find races as poor as this, he is sure to continue his winning run, but connections may be rewarded by stepping him up in grade, at least to find out just how good he is. (tchd 1-3)
Hommage A Bach(IRE), pulled up the day before at Catterick, completed in his own time to pick up some decent prizemoney for connections. Nothing else can be read into this performance, as he has shown little previously. (op 16-1)
Not So Prudent(IRE) looked the only danger to the winner beforehand, but his fall handed the race to the winner. If able to recover his confidence, he seems a likely sort to win races at this level. (op 7-2)
Rester Vrai(FR) is rated only 66 and had an impossible task. (op 7-2)

4415 LADBROKES.COM COTTESMORE MAIDEN HUNTERS' CHASE (18 fncs) 2m 7f 110y
4:45 (4:45) (Class 6) 6-Y-O+ **£1,249** (£387; £193; £96)

Form RPR
1 **Over The Phone (IRE)**[23] 6-12-0 0................................... MrTWeston[(3)] 120+
(A G Hobbs) *confidently rdn: settled in 3rd pl tl wnt 2nd after 14th: rdn 2 out: led last: sn asserted* **1/1**[1]

2 *6* **Drom**[23] 8-11-10 0... MrDJGriffiths[(7)] 115+
(P S Davies) *led 2nd and set decent gallop in abt 6 l ld: smetimes j.lft: blnd 12th: nt fluent 3 out where gng clr w wnr: rdn and hdd and hit last: sn outstyd* **8/1**

42-3 **3** *19* **Thirtytwo Red (IRE)**[299] 173 10-12-3 98................ MrJoshuaGuerriero 94
(R J Alford) *chsd ldrs: wnt 3rd bef 15th: 6 l down next: wknd to 15 l 3rd at last* **3/1**[2]

-054 **4** *4* **Cluthe Boy (IRE)**[13] 4143 8-11-12 86..........................(t) MissSSharratt[(5)] 90
(Miss S Sharratt) *bhd: hit 10th: bounced along enthusiastically and outpcd after 14th: no ch fr next* **14/1**

0-P6 **5** *6* **Coppingers Court (IRE)**[21] 3991 10-11-10 63................ MrJHodson[(7)] 84
(S Rea) *last whn mstke 3rd: lost tch after 14th* **40/1**

00P/ **6** *2* **French Bey (IRE)**[16] 11-11-5 0.................................. MissSPhizacklea[(5)] 75
(Mrs L Pomfret) *nt fluent: midfield: mstke 12th: bmpd along and lost tch bef 15th* **50/1**

-4PP **7** *7* **Cash In Hand (IRE)**[13] 4143 11-11-10 80..........................(b) MrTEllis[(7)] 77
(R Harvey) *blnd 6th: chsd ldr tl after 14th: rdn and dropped out qckly next* **28/1**

8 *51* **Quick Bay**[276] 7-11-12 0.. MrJHamer[(5)] 24
(G C Evans) *mstkes in last: rdn and struggling after 8th: t.o fr 15th* **40/1**

0/ **F** **Rugged Jem (IRE)**[273] 574 10-12-0 0.......................... MrJFMathias[(3)] —
(Richard Mathias) *led tl hdd and fell 2nd* **13/2**[3]

6m 23.7s (19.70) **Going Correction** +0.925s/f (Soft) **9** Ran SP% **116.4**
Speed ratings: **104,102,95,94,92 91,89,72,—**
toteswingers:1&2 £3.00, 2&3 £4.20, 1&3 £1.70 CSF £9.86 TOTE £2.20: £1.10, £2.90, £1.50; EX 12.20.
Owner Mrs J Hitchings **Bred** Damien Fitzhenry & Paddy Fitzhenry **Trained** Hanley Swan, Worcs

FOCUS
A maiden hunter chase with a number of newcomers that make it difficult to get a grip on the form. The third to last year's for looks the best guide.

NOTEBOOK
Over The Phone(IRE), a well-backed favourite, ran out a ready winner, drawing clear after the last to convert his progressive point form to rules racing on his hunter chase debut. Coming into this race on the back of three consecutive wins, he looks an improving sort and likely to win his fair share of hunter chases if kept to this sphere. The intermediate final at Cheltenham's hunter-chase meeting is the long-term target. (op 10-11 tchd 11-10)
Drom put in a good front-running display and had a chance jumping the last, but was unable to match the turn of foot of the winner on what was also his rules debut. He remains progressive and can win races. (op 9-1 tchd 10-1)
Thirtytwo Red(IRE) is a five-time point winner and was having his first run in 299 days. He travelled well before emptying after the second last, and can be expected to come on plenty for the run. (op 7-2 tchd 11-4)
Cluthe Boy(IRE), dropping down in class, was unsuited by the testing ground and tends to run best on a sound surface. (op 16-1)
Coppingers Court(IRE) was a point winner in January but has struggled since in both his racecourse starts. (op 28-1)
French Bey(IRE) has been running respectably in points after a decent lay-off, but had plenty to find with the market leaders and was never on terms. (op 40-1)

4416 LADBROKES.COM JOHN O'GAUNT H'CAP CHASE (15 fncs) 2m 4f 110y
5:15 (5:15) (Class 4) (0-110,109) 5-Y-O+ **£2,602** (£764)

Form RPR
PP21 **1** **Ours (FR)**[16] 4103 9-10-12 **98**.. PeterToole[(3)] 102
(Mark Rimell) *pressed rival: mstke 9th: hit 10th: drvn bef 12th and looked outpcd tl clsd as opponent fr 2 out: led last: sn in command* **10/11**[1]

5162 **2** *4 ½* **Persian Gates (IRE)**[21] 3990 7-11-3 **100**..................(b[1]) TomMessenger 100
(Chris Bealby) *plld hrd in slt ld: nt fluent 4th: looked likely to assert fr 12th tl rdn and threw in the towel after 2 out: hdd last: nt run on* **10/11**[1]

5m 35.6s (16.70) **Going Correction** +0.925s/f (Soft) **2** Ran SP% **104.8**
Speed ratings: **105,103**
TOTE £1.40.
Owner D J Pratt **Bred** Francois Cottin **Trained** Leafield, Oxon

FOCUS
A match that looked a coin toss on paper. The winner is rated to his mark.

NOTEBOOK
Ours(FR), despite making consecutive mistakes down the back, battled back in the home straight before pulling clear after the second-last to run out a ready winner. Racing off 1lb lower than for his C&D win in 2008, he looked to be on a fair mark and has recently found his form, beating subsequent winner Rileyev last time out. He is equally adept at 2m or 2m4f and remains in good enough heart to manage a rise in the weights, especially round here. (tchd 5-6)
Persian Gates(IRE) looked to have jumped his rival into submission, but found nothing off the bridle. He tends to be best at Market Rasen, and despite being lightly raced over fences, looks well held off a mark of 100. The first-time blinkers appeared to have had no effect. (tchd Evens)
T/Plt: £51.30 to a £1 stake. Pool of £67,022.79 - 952.41 winning tickets. T/Qpdt: £6.40 to a £1 stake. Pool of £5,465.14 - 625.57 winning tickets. IM

3917 BANGOR-ON-DEE (L-H)
Wednesday, March 2

OFFICIAL GOING: Soft (5.0)
Wind: Light, across Weather: Fine

4417 CLWYD SPECIAL RIDING CENTRE MARES' "NATIONAL HUNT" NOVICES' HURDLE (9 hdls) 2m 1f
2:20 (2:20) (Class 4) 4-Y-O+ **£2,081** (£611; £305; £152)

Form RPR
20 **1** **Bellaboosh (IRE)**[29] 3876 5-10-12 0.. APMcCoy 104+
(Nicky Henderson) *chsd ldr: upsides 4 out: nt fluent and lost a little grnd 3 out: rallied to chal 2 out: led appr last: styd on wl to draw clr run-in* **5/1**[3]

2411 **2** *4 ½* **Empress Orchid**[32] 3816 6-11-12 113................................ JasonMaguire 112+
(Donald McCain) *led: hit 3rd: rdn whn nt fluent and pressed 2 out: hdd appr last: no ex run-in* **11/8**[1]

06P0 **3** *11* **Qualitee**[17] 4094 6-10-12 0.. DaveCrosse 87
(Claire Dyson) *hld up: pushed along 4 out: outpcd by ldrs fr next: lft mod 3rd last: no ch* **25/1**

1-03 **4** *11* **Tanzanite Bay**[15] 4134 6-10-12 0..................................... PeterBuchanan 75
(Lucinda Russell) *trckd ldrs tl wknd appr 3 out* **13/2**

6000 **5** *3 ¾* **Tild'Or Du Granit (FR)**[21] 4006 4-9-11 0............................ RobertKirk[(7)] 63
(James Evans) *prom tl rdn and wknd after 3 out* **150/1**

0666 **F** **Spe Salvi (IRE)**[27] 3904 7-10-12 0.. DarylJacob 92
(David Arbuthnot) *in tch: trckd ldrs gng ok 4 out: rdn and outpcd by ldrs after 3 out: mstke 2 out: 3rd and abt 9 l off the pce whn fell last* **7/2**[2]

25 **P** **Inthesettlement**[70] 3088 6-10-12 0.. AdrianLane —
(Donald McCain) *plld hrd: a bhd: j.rt and nt fluent: lost tch 4th: t.o whn p.u sn after* **10/1**

4m 14.6s (3.70) **Going Correction** +0.475s/f (Soft)
WFA 4 from 5yo+ 7lb **7** Ran SP% **107.9**
Speed ratings (Par 105): **110,107,102,97,95 —,—**
toteswingers:1&2 £1.10, 2&3 £6.90, 1&3 £17.30 CSF £11.30 TOTE £3.50: £2.20, £1.50; EX 7.50.

Owner D Minton **Bred** Ardobrien Stud Ltd **Trained** Upper Lambourn, Berks

FOCUS

The going remained soft after a dry night. A mares' novice event which had some potential improvers, and the front two came clear. The first two were stepping up and the third is rated to her bumper mark.

NOTEBOOK

Bellaboosh(IRE) showed a glimmer of promise in two bumper runs and the switch to hurdling brought about significant improvement. She responded well to pressure after being outpaced following a couple of slow jumps, and put in her best leap at the last to win going away. She's stoutly-bred and could defy a penalty up in trip. (op 7-2)

Empress Orchid, penalised for two novice victories, was allowed to dictate matters and was only outstayed between the final two hurdles when the 14lb concession to the winner told. She may have done her winning for now. (op 6-5 tchd 6-4)

Qualitee never got into a challenging position. (op 28-1)

Tanzanite Bay hasn't built on her decent Cheltenham bumper form. (op 6-1 tchd 11-2)

Tild'Or Du Granit(FR) hugged the rail throughout but had no response to her rider's urgings. She looks set for modest handicaps.

Spe Salvi(IRE), well backed, was booked for third before taking a heavy fall. She was keeping on before coming to grief, suggesting further is required, and can be given another chance. (op 13-2)

Inthesettlement failed to settle again on hurdling debut and never gave herself the chance to show her potential. (op 13-2)

4418 ARKLE FINANCE MARES' H'CAP HURDLE (12 hdls) 3m

2:50 (2:50) (Class 4) (0-110,110) 4-Y-0+ **£2,927** (£859; £429; £214)

Form / RPR

5613 **1** **Inkberrow Rose (IRE)**[8] 4273 7-9-12 85 ....(p) TommyPhelan(3) 95+
(Tom Gretton) *w ldr: led 4 out: rdn whn strly pressed and jnd 2 out: styd on and plld away fnl 110yds* **7/2**[3]

5524 **2** *5* **Overnight Fame (IRE)**[27] 3901 7-11-7 105 .... PaddyBrennan 112+
(Tom George) *hld up bhd ldrs: wnt 2nd appr 3 out: rdn and upsides wnr fr 2 out: nt fluent last: wknd qckly fnl 110yds: eased whn wl hld cl home* **9/2**

522 **3** *12* **Bounds And Leaps**[38] 3698 6-11-0 98 .... TomScudamore 90
(Michael Scudamore) *led: hdd 4 out: rdn appr 3 out: outpcd by front pair sn after: wl btn 2 out* **9/4**[2]

30F1 **4** *29* **Copsehill Girl (IRE)**[13] 4161 6-11-7 105 .... WayneHutchinson 72
(Ian Williams) *hld up bhd ldrs: fiddled 6th: shkn up after 7th: rdn and outpcd appr 4 out: lost tch bef 2 out: eased sn after* **15/8**[1]

6m 3.00s (12.00) **Going Correction** +0.475s/f (Soft) 4 Ran SP% **106.0**
Speed ratings (Par 105): **99,97,93,83**
CSF £16.23 TOTE £5.30; EX 20.30.

Owner Alan S Clarke **Bred** R R Clarke **Trained** Inkberrow, Worcestershire

FOCUS

A small field for this moderate handicap hurdle, which was run at a crawl until an injection of pace approaching five out. The winner is rated to her bumper form with a step up from the second.

NOTEBOOK

Inkberrow Rose(IRE) has been much improved in cheekpieces lately and produced a gutsy display to fend off the runner-up. She had the rail to run against and her rider's 3lb claim clearly helped. She is still unexposed over staying trips and could improve again. (op 9-2)

Overnight Fame(IRE) cruised through the race with sound jumping and looked set to collect over the last, but wasn't fluent and got outbattled by a tougher horse. She could be seen in better light either dropped in trip or on a flatter track. (op 5-1 tchd 11-2)

Bounds And Leaps got worked up in the paddock which may have dented her chances. She was one paced when the tempo increased down the back straight, but seems to have begun tackling handicaps off a fair mark, so can be given another chance. (op 15-8)

Copsehill Girl(IRE) was expected to go close after winning over 2m6f at Ffos Las, but that may have taken its toll and she struggled from a fair way out. Official explanation: jockey said that the mare was unsuited by the soft ground (tchd 7-4, 2-1 in a place)

4419 WEATHERBYS BLOODSTOCK INSURANCE JUVENILE H'CAP HURDLE (9 hdls) 2m 1f

3:20 (3:20) (Class 4) (0-115,105) 4-Y-0 **£3,168** (£936; £468; £234; £117)

Form / RPR

6262 **1** **Miereveld**[14] 4148 4-10-11 **97** ....(v) PaulGallagher(7) 97+
(Brian Ellison) *mde all: kicked abt 5 l clr after 4 out: rdn appr 2 out: styd on wl bef last: wl in command after* **9/4**[1]

6351 **2** *6* **Antoella (IRE)**[14] 4148 4-11-8 **101** .... RichieMcGrath 94
(Philip Kirby) *racd in 2nd pl: racing keenly w wnr 3rd: nt qckn after 4 out: unable to chal wnr after: no imp bef last* **9/2**[3]

U264 **3** *3 ¾* **Tom Wade (IRE)**[46] 3563 4-11-12 **105** .... RichardJohnson 94
(John Harris) *chsd ldrs: rdn and outpcd after 3 out: one pce and n.d after* **7/1**

2504 **4** *1* **Baraathen (USA)**[14] 4148 4-10-7 **93** .... HenryBrooke(7) 82
(Donald McCain) *hld up: nt fluent 3rd: rdn and outpcd 3 out: nvr a threat to ldrs: wl btn whn nt fluent last* **7/2**[2]

464 **5** *22* **Plus Ultra (IRE)**[98] 2614 4-10-2 **88** .... KyleJames(7) 64
(Philip Kirby) *a bhd: niggled along and lost tch 4 out: t.o whn nt fluent last* **7/2**[2]

4m 19.5s (8.60) **Going Correction** +0.475s/f (Soft) 5 Ran SP% **105.9**
Speed ratings: **98,95,93,92,82**
CSF £11.32 TOTE £2.70: £2.90, £2.10; EX 7.20.

Owner J D Cotterill **Bred** St Clare Hall Stud **Trained** Norton, N Yorks

FOCUS

A moderate handicap hurdle with those in the frame behind the winner close to their marks.

NOTEBOOK

Miereveld reversed form with Antoella (16lb better off with rider's allowance) under a good front-running ride from in-form Paul Gallagher. The jockey was allowed to set his own fractions up front and, despite the horse idling two from home, kept the partnership going to win handsomely. Miereveld could be competitive after being reassessed if allowed to dictate. (op 2-1)

Antoella(IRE) failed to confirm her Musselburgh victory with the winner. She raced freely throughout, which didn't help, but had plenty to do anyway with an 9lb rise for that success. She plugged on for second and at least continues in form. (op 3-1)

Tom Wade(IRE) was easily held on heavy ground for his handicap debut at Warwick and travelled better on this quicker surface. He is an improving sort and may be of interest in a similar event. (op 13-2 tchd 11-2)

Baraathen(USA) reached for many of the hurdles and needs to brush up in the jumping department. (op 4-1 tchd 3-1)

Plus Ultra(IRE) seemed to be on a fair mark for his handicap debut but put in a moody show. He was sluggish at several hurdles and is best watched until looking more enthusiastic. (op 5-1)

4420 WEATHERBYS CHELTENHAM FESTIVAL BETTING GUIDE H'CAP HURDLE (11 hdls) 2m 4f

3:50 (3:51) (Class 3) (0-135,131) 4-Y-0+ **£5,204** (£1,528; £764; £381)

Form / RPR

6102 **1** **Numide (FR)**[8] 4270 8-11-6 125 .... JohnnyFarrelly 127+
(Rod Millman) *hld up in rr: hdwy after 3 out: chsd ldr appr last: r.o to ld towards fin* **4/1**[2]

2301 **2** *1 ¼* **Devotion To Duty (IRE)**[19] 4058 5-11-3 122 .... PeterBuchanan 122
(Lucinda Russell) *led: hdd after 3rd: led again after 5th: rdn appr last: hdd and hld towards fin* **7/1**[3]

120B **3** *3 ¼* **Drill Sergeant**[11] 4202 6-11-9 128 ....(t) JasonMaguire 126
(Donald McCain) *chsd ldr: led after 3rd: hdd after 5th: lost pl whn possibly tried to pull himself up on paddock bnd sn after: racd in rr: nt fluent 3 out: rallied to chse ldrs 2 out: kpt on u.p bef last: one pce run-in* **4/1**[2]

-030 **4** *2* **Briefcase (IRE)**[20] 4029 6-10-1 106 .... PaddyBrennan 102
(Nigel Twiston-Davies) *chsd ldrs: wnt 2nd and chalng 3 out: rdn and ev ch whn mstke 2 out: nt qckning whn swtchd lft appr last: no ex run-in* **4/1**[2]

05-1 **5** *¾* **Nortonthorpe Lad (IRE)**[300] 170 9-11-7 131 ....(p) OliverDayman(5) 127+
(Alison Thorpe) *hld up: hdwy appr 6th: trcking ldrs whn mstke 3 out: short of room jst after and outpcd: u.p and keeping on same pce whn nt fluent last: no imp after* **28/1**

0-00 **6** *27* **Open Day (IRE)**[11] 4202 5-11-6 125 .... APMcCoy 99
(Jonjo O'Neill) *hld up: effrt to chse ldrs 3 out: wkng whn nt fluent 2 out* **5/2**[1]

7 *22* **La Bombonera (FR)**[256] 5-11-9 128 .... AidanColeman 73
(Venetia Williams) *chsd ldrs: wnt 2nd after 5th: stl ev ch after 4 out: lost 2nd 3 out: sn wknd: t.o* **14/1**

5m 3.40s (6.00) **Going Correction** +0.475s/f (Soft) 7 Ran SP% **111.2**
Speed ratings (Par 107): **107,106,105,104,104 93,84**
toteswingers:1&2 £3.70, 2&3 £2.50, 1&3 £2.80 CSF £29.28 TOTE £3.40: £1.30, £3.50; EX 20.50.

Owner Midd Shire Racing **Bred** S C E A Haras De Manneville **Trained** Kentisbeare, Devon

FOCUS

The feature race on the card which was a tight betting contest. The first two are rated to recent form with the fourth to his mark.

NOTEBOOK

Numide(FR), keen in the early stages, settled much better once the pace quickened on the final circuit, and ran on strongly to mug the runner up. Already due to go up 5lb from the weekend, Johnny Farrelly reported the horse only has one burst of speed and he has to be delivered as late as possible. He has an entry in the Coral Cup but would need plenty to drop out one would think. (op 7-2)

Devotion To Duty(IRE) was the first to quicken for home and was only narrowly denied by an in-form rival. He continues on an upward curve and will win more races. (op 11-2)

Drill Sergeant has plenty of ability but is a quirky individual. He showed awkward tendencies when running lazily during the middle part of the race. He stayed on well but remains a risky betting propersition. (op 3-1)

Briefcase(IRE) ran a decent race on his handicap debut. He came with a promising challenge two out but had no answer to the front pair's change of gears. He is lightly raced, unexposed over this distance and can improve. (op 11-2)

Nortonthorpe Lad(IRE) was reported to need the run after 300 days off the track so this was a pleasing effort. The drawback is he's now racing off a high enough mark. (op 18-1)

Open Day(IRE), well backed in the market, has shown nothing this term. (op 9-2)

La Bombonera(FR) was a dual winner in France so may be better than he showed here. (tchd 16-1)

4421 ARKLE FINANCE H'CAP HURDLE (12 hdls) 3m

4:20 (4:22) (Class 3) (0-130,124) 4-Y-O+ **£3,612** (£1,067; £533; £266; £133)

Form / RPR

0501 **1** **Pie At Midnight**[26] 3919 5-11-0 **112** .... JasonMaguire 117+
(Donald McCain) *mde all: hung sltly rt thrght: rdn appr 2 out: styd on wl run-in* **5/2**[1]

11F6 **2** *2* **Kauto The Roc (FR)**[35] 3742 7-10-12 **120** .... CiaranMckee(10) 120
(Alan King) *in tch: rdn to chse wnr appr 2 out: kpt on u.p run-in: no real imp* **11/4**[2]

4004 **3** *2 ½* **South O'The Border**[9] 4261 9-11-9 **124** .... SamTwiston-Davies(3) 122
(Nigel Twiston-Davies) *hld up: outpcd appr 3 out: styd on to take 3rd run-in: nt gng pce to rch front 2* **12/1**

-660 **4** *1 ¼* **Sullumo (GER)**[35] 3742 8-11-5 **120** ....(p) PeterToole(3) 118
(Charlie Mann) *chsd ldrs: wnt 2nd appr 7th: lost 2nd bef 2 out where j.rt: 3rd and u.p whn mstke last: lost 3rd and one pce run-in* **9/2**[3]

0020 **5** *3 ¾* **Barrie Burn (IRE)**[60] 3296 5-11-0 **112** .... APMcCoy 106
(Jonjo O'Neill) *hld up: hdwy to chse ldrs after 3 out: sltly carried rt 2 out: wknd bef last* **5/1**

F2P0 **6** *3 ¾* **Our Jim**[26] 3922 9-10-8 **106** .... AdrianLane 95
(Donald McCain) *sn chsd ldr: lost 2nd appr 7th: rdn and wknd bef 2 out* **17/2**

6m 14.6s (23.60) **Going Correction** +0.475s/f (Soft) 6 Ran SP% **108.3**
Speed ratings (Par 107): **79,78,77,77,75 74**
toteswingers:1&2 £1.80, 2&3 £4.80, 1&3 £3.10 CSF £9.27 TOTE £3.30: £1.30, £1.80; EX 8.80.

Owner No More Excuses **Bred** Mr And Mrs K Walby **Trained** Cholmondeley, Cheshire

FOCUS

Just a steady gallop for this handicap hurdle with those in the frame behind the winner setting the level.

NOTEBOOK

Pie At Midnight defied a hefty rise (9lb) for winning here last month with a determined front-running display. He set a sedate pace early but gradually quickened it up on the final circuit, and despite hanging into the whip on the run-in, he was a worthy winner. His jumping was slick and stamina is clearly his forte. He looks able to pick up similar staying races, as he won with something up his sleeve. (op 11-4 tchd 3-1)

Kauto The Roc(FR) has run with credit this season and was expected to go close, but a crucial error three out seemed to stop his momentum. He stayed on strongly after that mistake in the manner of an improving horse, who can win off this sort of mark. (tchd 5-2)

South O'The Border looked rejuvenated by a return to hurdles. He had been out of sorts over fences and is fairly handicapped on his best hurdling form. He could be found a moderate race now he seems to have his mind on the job. (op 8-1)

Sullumo(GER) was well behind the runner-up last time but got closer to him this time. He is down to a competitive mark. (op 13-2 tchd 4-1)

Barrie Burn(IRE) was far too keen to do himself justice on this handicap debut. His pedigree suggests this trip will be the making of him but he needs to learn to relax during his races. (op 9-2 tchd 11-2)

Our Jim raced freely but wasn't beaten far. This was more encouraging than of late, as it was his first hurdles start since 2008. This gives connections more options. (op 9-1 tchd 10-1)

4422 EXCEL SIGNS LTD. NOVICES' HURDLE (11 hdls) 2m 4f
4:50 (4:50) (Class 4) 4-Y-O+ **£2,927** (£859; £429; £214)

Form RPR

041 **1** **Non Dom (IRE)**[50] 3491 5-11-9 120 TomScudamore 123+
(Hughie Morrison) *a.p: led appr last: sn clr: styd on wl and in command run-in* **9/4**[2]

22/1 **2** *4 ½* **Jimmy The Saint (IRE)**[27] 3897 8-11-9 0 JasonMaguire 118+
(Donald McCain) *led: mstke 4 out: rdn and hdd appr last: no ex run-in and no ch w wnr: jst hld on for 2nd* **6/5**[1]

60- **3** *nse* **Romantic Lead**[17] 4105 6-11-2 110 (t) JohnnyFarrelly 109
(Paul John Gilligan, Ire) *hld up in rr: hdwy 4 out: rdn and chsd ldrs 2 out: styd on after last: clsd on runner-up cl home: jst failed to get up for 2nd* **20/1**

4-6 **4** *13* **Thehillofuisneach (IRE)**[26] 3930 7-11-2 0 APMcCoy 98
(Jonjo O'Neill) *prom tl pushed along and wknd after 3 out* **11/2**[3]

45 **5** *6* **Tribal Dance (IRE)**[147] 1729 5-11-2 0 DarylJacob 93+
(Ben Case) *hld up: hdwy appr 7th: rdn to chse ldrs bef 3 out: wknd 2 out* **50/1**

05U **6** *16* **Any Given Moment (IRE)**[10] 4233 5-10-13 0 JohnKington(3) 74
(Donald McCain) *prom tl rdn and wknd appr 4 out* **40/1**

02FP **7** *2 ½* **Kalulushi (IRE)**[18] 4062 6-11-2 0 AdrianLane 72
(Donald McCain) *trckd ldrs tl wknd after 4 out* **66/1**

8 *56* **Alone They Stand (IRE)**[374] 6-10-13 0 MrAJBerry(3) 16
(Jonjo O'Neill) *hld up: struggling appr 4 out: sn wl btn* **28/1**

30 **9** *nk* **Ballabrace (IRE)**[17] 4097 6-11-2 0 AidanColeman 15
(Venetia Williams) *midfield: lost pl 6th: wl bhd 4 out* **12/1**

00 **10** *28* **Ellis**[18] 4082 4-10-7 0 RodiGreene —
(Christopher Kellett) *bhd: struggling after 5th: t.o fr 7th* **200/1**

400 **U** **Danehillsundance (IRE)**[28] 3887 7-11-2 0 (t) BarryKeniry —
(Philip Kirby) *trckd ldrs: lost pl 7th: struggling and bhd whn blnd and uns rdr 2 out* **150/1**

5m 7.20s (9.80) **Going Correction** +0.475s/f (Soft)
WFA 4 from 5yo+ 8lb **11** Ran SP% **114.6**
Speed ratings (Par 105): **99,97,97,91,89 83,82,59,59,48** —
toteswingers:1&2 £1.60, 2&3 £6.70, 1&3 £7.40 CSF £5.10 TOTE £3.30: £1.10, £2.30, £2.90; EX 6.10.
Owner Raymond Tooth **Bred** Mrs Ann Kennedy **Trained** East Ilsley, Berks

FOCUS
A novice hurdle with just a few promising types, and the front three pulled clear. The placed horses are rated to their marks.

NOTEBOOK
Non Dom(IRE), carrying a 7lb penalty for winning at Leicester, maintained his upward curve with a decisive victory. Once he had mastered the front running Jimmy The Saint between the final two hurdles, he held his head slightly high but stayed on powerfully. Connections may send him to the Aintree for a handicap. (tchd 2-1)
Jimmy The Saint(IRE) was fancied to confirm the impression shown at Towcester last month but was just run down by a more progressive horse. He's now eight and connections may go chasing to make up for lost time. (op 6-4)
Romantic Lead ran an encouraging race. He was outpaced on the final circuit but responded well for pressure and was narrowly denied in the photo for second. He looks like making into a nice staying sort. (op 16-1)
Thehillofuisneach(IRE), a maiden point winner in 2009, was nicely backed during the day. He travelled well before fading approaching three out, and could be better suited to a sounder surface. (tchd 6-1)
Tribal Dance(IRE) ran on for pressure after being badly outpaced. This was a promising hurdles debut for a horse that didn't show much in bumpers.
Ballabrace(IRE) was slightly disappointing, although he wasn't given a hard time when beaten. This was his hurdles debut so he may be able to improve on this in time. (op 14-1)

4423 ERDDIG WORKING SHIRES MAIDEN NATIONAL HUNT FLAT RACE (CONDITIONAL JOCKEYS' AND AMATEUR RIDERS' RACE) 2m 1f
5:20 (5:20) (Class 5) 4-6-Y-O **£1,541** (£449; £224)

Form RPR

3 **1** **Jackson Cage (IRE)**[16] 4117 6-10-12 0 HenryBrooke(7) 99+
(Donald McCain) *mde all: shkn up over 1f out: plld out more ins fnl f: pushed out* **5/4**[1]

0 **2** *2* **Sole Survivor (FR)**[60] 3294 4-10-4 0 JakeGreenall(7) 89+
(Paul Webber) *in tch: effrt over 2f out: chsd wnr over 1f out: sn ev ch: green and nt qckn ins fnl f* **3/1**[2]

3 *3* **Western High** 6-10-9 0 AshleyBird(10) 94
(Jim Best) *hld up: pushed along and outpcd over 5f out: effrt on outer over 3f out: styd on to take 3rd ent fnl f: nt gng pce to trble front 2* **10/1**

4 **4** *1 ¼* **Whistle Me (IRE)**[22] 3998 5-11-2 0 JohnKington(3) 93
(Chris Grant) *prom: rdn and ev ch over 2f out: no ex ins fnl f* **6/1**[3]

5 *1 ½* **Warren Chase (IRE)** 6-10-12 0 MrOJMurphy(7) 92
(Anabel L M King) *hld up in tch: rdn over 2f out: one pce fr over 1f out* **7/1**

0 **6** *9* **Waywood Princess**[31] 3842 6-10-5 0 HarryChalloner(7) 76
(John Bryan Groucott) *prom tl lost pl 3f out: pushed along and btn 2f out* **40/1**

7 *82* **Marina Bay** 6-10-5 0 KyleJames(7) —
(Christopher Kellett) *in rr: niggled along over 6f out: lost tch 4f out: t.o* **50/1**

4m 23.0s (17.70) **Going Correction** +0.475s/f (Soft)
WFA 4 from 5yo+ 7lb **7** Ran SP% **109.7**
Speed ratings: **77,76,74,74,73 69,30**
toteswingers:1&2 £2.10, 2&3 £5.50, 1&3 £2.10. totesuper7: Win: Not won. Place: £26.90. CSF £4.61 TOTE £2.40: £1.20, £1.80; EX 5.70.
Owner Penketh And Sankey Jech Racing Club **Bred** Edmond Coleman **Trained** Cholmondeley, Cheshire

FOCUS
Just an average bumper on paper with six still in with a chance 3f out. The winner is rated below his bumper form with the fourth helping to set the level.

NOTEBOOK
Jackson Cage(IRE) had the best form of those who had run, and made all to win with something to spare. He looks a nice hurdles prospect for a yard who continue to churn out promising youngsters. (op Evens tchd 11-8)
Sole Survivor(FR), who was well backed, loomed up to the winner 1f out but never looked like going through with his effort. He wandered in the closing stages and still looks a big baby. He was reported to have worked well with RSA Chase hope Time For Rupert, and will be interesting over further, but could pick up a bumper on the way to better things. (tchd 11-4 and 7-2)
Western High was keen to post and, although outpaced by the front two, kept on right the way to the line, looking like a horse who needs a stiffer test. (tchd 14-1 in a place)
Whistle Me(IRE) was respected after a promising debut and wasn't beaten far here. (op 7-1 tchd 11-2)
Warren Chase(IRE) travelled well for a long way and could be competitive in a similarly modest event. (op 12-1 tchd 13-2)
Waywood Princess raced wide throughout and didn't build on her debut.
Marina Bay was the first off the bridle and was extremely green. (op 40-1)
T/Plt: £65.10 to a £1 stake. Pool of £56,655.72 - 634.40 winning tickets. T/Qpdt: £3.60 to a £1 stake. Pool of £4,194.32 - 847.57 winning tickets. DO

4125 FOLKESTONE (R-H)
Wednesday, March 2

OFFICIAL GOING: Soft (heavy in places; 5.1)
Hurdles and chase course on same bend entering home straight.
Wind: fresh, across Weather: hazy, sunshine

4424 WOOD-MIZER BAND SAWMILL MAIDEN HURDLE (9 hdls) 2m 1f 110y
2:10 (2:10) (Class 5) 4-Y-O+ **£1,918** (£559; £279)

Form RPR

/524 **1** **Super Directa (GER)**[5] 4323 7-11-1 114 DominicElsworth 120+
(Lucy Wadham) *mde all: rdn and forged clr ent st: styd on wl: comf* **11/8**[1]

314 **2** *12* **Avoca Promise (IRE)**[56] 3399 6-11-1 0 JimmyMcCarthy 108
(Charles Egerton) *in tch in mid: mstke 1st: hdwy 4th: chsd ldr next: pressed wnr 2 out: rdn and btn ent st* **2/1**[2]

2 **3** *20* **Cozy Tiger (USA)**[35] 3740 6-11-1 0 LeightonAspell 92
(Willie Musson) *hld up in last trio: hdwy 4th: chsd ldng pair 6th: mstke 2 out: rdn and btn wl bef last* **5/2**[3]

0 **4** *19* **Mission Complete (IRE)**[29] 3872 5-10-12 0 RichieMcLernon(3) 68
(Jonjo O'Neill) *in tch in rr: mstke 4th: rdn and struggling bef next: lost tch 3 out: wnt poor 4th ent st: t.o* **50/1**

5 *5* **Cunning Plan (IRE)**[127] 4-10-0 0 MissEmily-JaneHarbour(7) 55
(Raymond York) *racd wd: chsd ldrs: rdn and blnd 6th: sn wknd: t.o 2 out* **100/1**

0 **6** *4* **Classic Port (FR)**[78] 2011 7-11-1 0 ColinBolger 59
(Suzy Smith) *hld up wl bhd: lost tch 5th: t.o whn mstke 2 out* **66/1**

7 *10* **New Den**[32] 4-10-7 0 (p) SamThomas 41
(Jim Boyle) *nt jump wl: chsd ldr tl 5th: blnd and lost pl next: sn losing tch: 4th and wl btn whn blnd 2 out: t.o* **22/1**

4m 35.1s (-0.50) **Going Correction** +0.025s/f (Yiel)
WFA 4 from 5yo+ 7lb **7** Ran SP% **112.8**
Speed ratings (Par 103): **102,96,87,79,77 75,70**
toteswingers:1&2 £1.30, 2&3 £1.70, 1&3 £1.10 CSF £4.46 TOTE £2.70: £1.50, £1.30; EX 6.30.
Owner Richard S Keeley **Bred** Mrs I Bodewein **Trained** Newmarket, Suffolk

FOCUS
The betting strongly suggested the three clear market leaders would dominate this ordinary maiden and so it played out. The ground unsurprisingly looked hard work and winning rider Dominic Elsworth confirmed that to be the case. The form is rated around the first two.

NOTEBOOK
Super Directa(GER) shed his maiden tag over jumps at the seventh time of asking on this return from handicap company. He only tired in the latter stages off a mark of 114 on bad ground at Sandown last week, and set the standard here. Being allowed a flyer at the start no doubt helped him nearing the business end and he was comfortably on top coming to the last. A slightly stiffer test as the ground dries up should be more to his liking in the spring. (op 15-8, tchd 2-1 in a place)
Avoca Promise(IRE) won one of his three outings in bumpers and was unsurprisingly popular for this hurdling debut. He wasn't always fluent and again showed his inexperience. This ground was probably more testing than he cares for, though. (tchd 15-8)
Cozy Tiger(USA), runner-up on his hurdling debut in January, moved up going well nearing two out but wasn't clever over that flight and was soon in trouble. He likes some cut, but he probably found this ground too much. (op 9-4)
Mission Complete(IRE) was beaten a long way out, but is bred to come into his own over further and is one to keep an eye on with a view to going handicapping in due course.
New Den Official explanation: trainer said gelding suffered a breathing problem

4425 WOOD-MIZER SMALL MILL MARES' NOVICES' HURDLE (10 hdls) 2m 4f 110y
2:40 (2:40) (Class 4) 4-Y-O+ **£2,058** (£699)

Form RPR

26 **1** **Victrix Gale (IRE)**[43] 3623 5-10-13 0 AndrewTinkler 120+
(Nicky Henderson) *t.k.h: a gng wl: chsd ldr: clsd to press ldr after 5th: lft in ld 7th: readily drew clr bef last: eased flat* **4/1**[2]

6404 **2** *49* **My Viking Bay (IRE)**[17] 4101 7-10-6 102 CharlieWallis(7) 80
(John O'Shea) *j.lft: led tl stmbld on landing and hdd 7th: sn struggling: 3rd and wl btn 2 out: wnt poor 2nd ent st: blnd last: eased flat: t.o* **7/1**[3]

53 **F** **Mekong Miss**[16] 4118 5-10-8 0 MrPYork(5) 73
(Raymond York) *t.k.h early: hld up in rr: clsd 5th: lft 2nd 7th: clr w wnr next: wknd qckly u.p after 2 out: dropped to last ent st: t.o and v tired whn fell last* **10/1**

42 **P** **Addiction**[76] 2987 6-10-13 0 LeightonAspell —
(Oliver Sherwood) *hung rt thrght: racd wd: nt jump wl: hld up in last pair: clsd 5th: niggled along and nt gng wl whn mstke next: last whn blnd and lost tch 3 out: mstke 2 out and p.u* **1/2**[1]

5m 31.4s (1.40) **Going Correction** +0.025s/f (Yiel) **4** Ran SP% **108.3**
Speed ratings (Par 105): **98,79,—,—**
CSF £23.83 TOTE £2.60; EX 12.90.
Owner Mr & Mrs R Kelvin Hughes **Bred** Mrs Elizabeth Grant **Trained** Upper Lambourn, Berks

FOCUS
With Addiction running a shocker the door was left wide open for the winner. The winner stepped up a fair amount on his bumper form.

NOTEBOOK
Victrix Gale(IRE), with the favourite running a shocker, ran out an effortless winner. This ground was of definite concern beforehand, but she went through it well and hurdled by far the best of these. Her pedigree suggests she will relish getting on quicker ground in this sphere. Her confidence should be high after this and there ought to be plenty more to come as she matures physically. This was also another indication that her powerful yard remains in top form. (op 3-1)
My Viking Bay(IRE), an exposed maiden, plugged on for a remote second and goes some way to helping put the form into perspective. (op 8-1)
Mekong Miss moved up as the biggest danger to the winner three out, but she had dropped right away before taking a tired fall at the last. Dropping back in trip is clearly what she wants. (op 17-2 tchd 8-1)

Addiction was just held in deep ground on her second outing in a bumper at Towcester when last seen in December, and she proved all the rage here. Her trainer said beforehand that she had recovered sufficiently from an infection which caused her break, but looking at her lifeless effort it probably took a lot more out of her than connections realised. Official explanation: jockey said that the mare was never travelling (op 17-2 tchd 8-1)

4426 WOOD-MIZER THIN KERF H'CAP CHASE (FOR THE "GAY RECORD" CHALLENGE TROPHY) (12 fncs) 2m

3:10 (3:11) (Class 5) (0-90,90) 5-Y-0+ **£2,332** (£724; £389)

Form				RPR
4354	1		**Rince Donn (IRE)**[8] 4269 9-10-12 **79**.....(t) DavidBass(3) (Roger Curtis) *hld up in tch: 4th and rdn after 3 out: 3rd and looked wl hld between last 2: lft 2nd and hmpd last: sn lft in ld: rdn out* **3/1**[1]	82
0-03	2	3/4	**Big Bertie (IRE)**[29] 3865 7-11-1 **79**..... AndrewThornton (Anna Newton-Smith) *led: bmpd 3rd: hdd and rdn bef 2 out: 3 l down and looked hld whn lft in ld: bdly hmpd and brought to a stand stl last: sn hdd: tried to rally flat: no imp fnl 50yds* **3/1**[1]	86+
0P45	3	13	**Bearneen Boy (IRE)**[5] 3611 8-10-3 **67**..... DougieCostello (Neil King) *chsd ldr: rdn after 3 out: sn lost pl and wl btn bef 2 out: lft 3rd last* **3/1**[1]	58
F52P	P		**Wishes Or Watches (IRE)**[33] 3792 11-9-11 **66**..... AnthonyFreeman(5) (John Upson) *chsd ldrs: j.rt and bmpd rival 3rd: mstke and dropped to last 5th: rdn and struggling next: lost tch 8th: wl bhd whn p.u 3 out* **11/2**[3]	—
0P42	F		**Watergate (IRE)**[78] 2947 5-11-12 **90**..... LeightonAspell (Richard Rowe) *racd wd: t.k.h: chsd ldrs on outer: dived 5th: j.lft next: mstke 8th: hdwy to chse ldr after 3 out: led next: 3 l clr and looked wnr whn fell last* **4/1**[2]	102

4m 18.4s (11.20) **Going Correction** +0.775s/f (Soft) **5** Ran SP% **110.4**

Speed ratings: **103,102,96,—,—**

CSF £12.41 TOTE £3.70: £2.90, £1.10; EX 11.30.

Owner R P Behan **Bred** Arrow Field Syndicate **Trained** Lambourn, Berks

FOCUS

A wide-open little handicap in which all had questions to answer. There was drama at the last fence when Watergate fell with the race at his mercy. The clear second at that stage, Big Bertie, then got stopped in his run after jumping it, as jockey Andrew Thornton had steered a similar course into the fence, and that cost him. The winner was lucky and he is rated as finishign third to the fall, who is rated to his hurdles form.

NOTEBOOK

Rince Donn(IRE) was well held in third prior to the final-fence incident, but he avoided the melee as a result and landed running. He was able to hold off the rallying runner-up near the finish and has now landed his two wins in Britain over C&D, but was a very lucky winner. (tchd 11-4 and 10-3 in a place)

Big Bertie(IRE) jumped a lot better than was the case on his chase debut over further here last time, but was done for speed by Watergate off the home turn. He rallied gamely and has to rate as somewhat unfortunate. There will be other days for this imposing 7-y-o. (op 7-2)

Bearneen Boy(IRE) was down to the same mark as when last successful in this event in 2009. He hasn't been in the same sort of form this term, however, and was beaten three out. (op 10-3 tchd 5-2)

Wishes Or Watches(IRE) made early errors and remains out of sorts. (op 4-1 tchd 13-2)

Watergate(IRE) drifted on account of this deep surface and things didn't look good for him as he came under pressure five out. He found a second wind, though, and the race was his to lose at the last. There is surely a contest for him on decent ground, providing he comes out of this okay. (op 4-1 tchd 13-2)

4427 LASTEC ARTICULATOR H'CAP HURDLE (11 hdls) 2m 6f 110y

3:40 (3:40) (Class 4) (0-110,109) 4-Y-0+ **£2,397** (£698; £349)

Form				RPR
4-00	1		**Mossini (IRE)**[19] 4052 6-11-3 **100**..... JamieMoore (Gary Moore) *chsd ldrs: led and hit 2 out: rdn ent st: clr and in command whn followed rail and veered bdly lft flat: pushed out after: eased towards fin* **25/1**	109+
-400	2	2 1/4	**Current Climate (IRE)**[59] 3346 7-10-11 **94**..... AndrewThornton (Richard Rowe) *hld up in tch towards rr: hdwy to trck ldrs 3 out: 3rd and unable qck u.p ent st: rallied u.p flat: r.o* **25/1**	96
00P6	3	shd	**Amore Mio (GER)**[24] 3962 6-11-4 **101**..... WarrenMarston (Richard Phillips) *in tch in midfield: chsd ldr 3 out tl bef last: outpcd u.p ent st: rallied flat: r.o* **5/1**[3]	103
1000	4	1 1/4	**Amirico (IRE)**[25] 3950 6-11-7 **109**..... MrWBiddick(5) (Venetia Williams) *hld up in tch in rr: stdy hdwy bef 3 out: upsides wnr and travelling wl after 2 out: chal ent st: rdn and btn whn hit last: lost 2 pls fnl 100yds* **4/1**[2]	110
0042	5	41	**Get Ready To Go (IRE)**[15] 4128 7-11-7 **104**.....(t) DougieCostello (Neil King) *chsd ldr tl 2nd: styd chsng ldrs tl led 8th: hdd 2 out: rdn and wknd wl bef last: t.o* **7/2**[1]	64
045P	6	51	**Whatever Next (IRE)**[28] 3878 9-10-12 **98**.....(b[1]) AlanCreighton(3) (Edward Creighton) *t.k.h: chsd ldr in 2nd tl led 4th tl 7th: sn lost pl and bhd: t.o bef 2 out* **28/1**	7
002P	7	31	**Dusky Bob (IRE)**[25] 3950 6-11-7 **104**.....(b[1]) SamThomas (Nick Gifford) *led tl 4th: chsd ldr tl led again 7th: hdd 8th: wknd qckly whn mstke 3 out: wl t.o between last 2* **10/1**	—
PP34	P		**Little Al**[101] 2558 8-11-0 **97**.....(b) LeightonAspell (Oliver Sherwood) *racd wd: a in last and nvr gng wl: lost tch and p.u after 6th* **8/1**	—
4454	P		**Graduation Night**[26] 3934 5-11-8 **105**..... TomO'Brien (Jamie Snowden) *in tch in midfield: rdn and wknd qckly 2 out: 6th and wl btn whn eased and p.u bef last* **4/1**[2]	—
0403	P		**Downe Payment (IRE)**[15] 4130 6-9-11 **87**..... MissHGrissell(7) (Diana Grissell) *in tch in midfield: rdn and lost pl 7th: losing tch whn mstke 3 out: t.o whn p.u last* **8/1**	—

6m 8.70s (-2.60) **Going Correction** +0.025s/f (Yiel) **10** Ran SP% **121.3**

Speed ratings (Par 105): **105,104,104,103,89 71,60,—,—,—**

toteswingers:1&2 £25.00, 2&3 £33.80, 1&3 £27.60 CSF £486.44 CT £3614.00 TOTE £36.30: £8.20, £12.00, £2.70; EX 419.80.

Owner J A Gent **Bred** Pat Hickey **Trained** Lower Beeding, W Sussex

■ Stewards' Enquiry : Jamie Moore trainer said, regarding the apparent improvement of form, that horse was better suited by being ridden more prominently

FOCUS

This ordinary handicap was run at a fair gallop and it saw changing fortunes in the home straight. Not form to be confident about.

NOTEBOOK

Mossini(IRE), up again in trip, produced vastly improved form to score a first success at the sixth time of asking. It was just his second outing in a handicap and the ground clearly held no fears. He should be rated value for a bit further as he tried to duck out where the rail cuts away on the run-in, but wouldn't be the first horse to have attempted such antics here. Chasing will be his game next term, but there should be more to come over this sort of trip over hurdles in the meantime. (tchd 33-1)

Current Climate(IRE) was another to show much-improved form on this handicap debut. He rallied gamely from the last, looking in need of even further, and should be winning when reverting to a sounder surface.

Amore Mio(GER) had stamina to prove, but he rallied gamely along with the runner-up and this was a definite step back in the right direction. He is certainly very well handicapped at present if able to build on this. (op 6-1 tchd 13-2)

Amirico(IRE) was patiently ridden and came there cantering over his rivals leaving the back straight. His rider began to get animated nearing the last, however, and he didn't even place in the end. It may be unwise to think the longer trip was to blame, as he also failed to really see it out over 2m4f at Sandown on his previous outing. (tchd 7-2)

Get Ready To Go(IRE) looks to want dropping back in trip. (op 4-1 tchd 9-2)

4428 WOOD-MIZER KENT NATIONAL (HANDICAP CHASE) (22 fncs) 3m 7f

4:10 (4:10) (Class 3) (0-130,118) 5-Y-0+ **£5,204** (£1,528; £764; £381)

Form				RPR
-P1V	1		**Victory Gunner (IRE)**[9] 4256 13-10-10 **107**..... GilesHawkins(5) (Richard Lee) *chsd ldr tl led 5th: hdd 13th: chsd ldr after: rdn after 3 out: upsides last: hung lft: kpt on wl u.p to ld fnl 100yds* **5/2**[1]	120
U-5P	2	1/2	**Noble Bily (FR)**[59] 3347 10-10-8 **103**..... AlexMerriam(3) (Neil King) *t.k.h: chsd ldrs tl wnt 2nd 9th: led 13th: hit 18th: rdn bef 2 out: kpt on gamely tl hdd and no ex fnl 100yds* **5/1**	115
-632	3	2 1/2	**Rate Of Knots (IRE)**[61] 3263 8-11-7 **116**..... RichieMcLernon(3) (Jonjo O'Neill) *hld up in tch in last pair: hdwy 15th: chsd ldng pair 17th: mstke 18th: rdn and outpcd after 3 out: swtchd rt and rallied between last 2: no imp fnl 100yds* **7/1**	126
1251	4	39	**Rudinero (IRE)**[41] 3646 9-9-11 **92** oh1.....(t) MichaelMurphy(3) (Barry Brennan) *led tl 5th: chsd ldr tl 9th: styd wl in tch tl mstke 17th: sn struggling: 4th and wkng whn mstke 3 out: t.o 2 out* **4/1**[2]	62
1326	5	44	**Dunkelly Castle (IRE)**[20] 4023 7-11-9 **115**..... LeightonAspell (Roger Curtis) *racd wd: in tch tl dropped to last and rdn 16th: lost tch bef 18th: t.o fr 3 out* **8/1**	41
P-0P	P		**Old Benny**[53] 3437 10-11-12 **118**.....(b) RobertThornton (Alan King) *in tch: mstke 4th: rdn along 16th: 5th and wkng whn hit 19th: wl btn after next: t.o whn p.u 2 out* **9/2**[3]	—
33-4	U		**No More Prisoners (IRE)**[29] 3865 11-9-9 **92** oh2.....(tp) MissLHorner(5) (Liam Corcoran) *in tch in last pair tl uns rdr 4th* **22/1**	—

8m 29.6s (36.70) **Going Correction** +0.775s/f (Soft) **7** Ran SP% **111.4**

Speed ratings: **83,82,82,72,60 —,—**

toteswingers:1&2 £3.70, 2&3 £12.20, 1&3 £2.10 CSF £14.75 TOTE £3.80: £2.90, £3.20; EX 20.80.

Owner Ron Bartlett & F J Ayres **Bred** Exors Of The Late J Neville **Trained** Byton, H'fords

FOCUS

There was a cracking finish to this marathon handicap. The first three were to their marks and the form looks solid.

NOTEBOOK

Victory Gunner(IRE), whose latest Carlisle outing came in a voided race, is now 2-2 since joining Richard Lee, who has clearly found the key to him again. He looked held by the runner-up turning for home, but stays all day and jumped the last better when rallying. He nearly threw it away when hanging left near the finish, but his superior stamina won him the day. (op 7-2)

Noble Bily(FR), last year's winner, had failed to complete in two of his four outings since, but met support for this repeat bid and very nearly pulled it off. He just paid late on for running freely through the race and this rates a career-best in defeat. (op 9-2 tchd 11-2)

Rate Of Knots(IRE) was very easy to back. She made her move on the final circuit, but started to toil on the home turn. She rallied nearing the last and clearly got the trip, but isn't a simple ride. (op 9-2 tchd 4-1)

Rudinero(IRE) was racing off a 9lb higher mark than when winning at Taunton over 3m3f 41 days earlier, where he was left in the lead three out. He ran his race, but was beat from three out. (op 5-1 tchd 11-2)

Old Benny had been given a right chance by the handicapper after a 12lb drop since pulling up in the Welsh National on his previous outing. He tried to rally around five out, but it proved short-lived and his decline continues. (tchd 7-2)

4429 LASTEC MAIDEN HUNTERS' CHASE (15 fncs) 2m 5f

4:40 (4:40) (Class 6) 5-Y-0+ **£758** (£233; £116)

Form				RPR
3-PP	1		**Dust In Time**[21] 4011 6-11-11 90.....(b) MissAGoschen(3) (Bill Turner) *bhd and nvr jumping fluently: reminders and no rspnse after 9th: passed btn rivals and 12 l 4th 2 out: stl 10 l down last: clsd rapidly and swtchd lft as ldrs expired to ld towards fin* **11/2**	94
25/4	2	1 3/4	**Supa Tramp**[46] 8-11-11 88..... MrPBull(3) (Mrs Suzy Bull) *t.k.h: hld up wl off the pce in rr: hdwy after 6th: mstke 9th: chsd ldr 3 out: rdn and chal next: led bef last: clr and edgd rt flat: pricked ears and faltered bdly fnl 75yds: sn hdd and btn* **11/4**[1]	93
	3	1 3/4	**Captain Knock (IRE)**[10] 8-11-9 101..... MrTJCannon(5) (David Phelan) *led and clr w rival tl wnt on 5th: reduced ld after 8th: rdn and hdd after 2 out: stl ev ch but tired last: plugged on same pce fnl 100yds* **4/1**[2]	91
5/U-	4	4	**Jazz Attack (IRE)**[10] 12-11-11 0..... MrRHFowler(3) (Miss M Tomlinson) *racd off the pce in midfield: lost pl and reminder 8th: rallied and mstke 10th: 3rd and rdn after 3 out: plugged on same pce and no real imp after* **15/2**	87
0	5	10	**Man From Moscow**[17] 8-11-7 0.....(v[1]) MrWHickman(7) (Mrs Alison Hickman) *chsd clr ldng pair tl 8th: styd chsng ldrs tl struggling 11th: wl btn bef 2 out* **8/1**	77
F5-5	6	18	**High Toby**[10] 12-12-0 79..... MrPYork (Raymond York) *prom in main gp: chsd ldr after 8th tl bef 3 out: wknd wl bef 2 out* **12/1**	65
55P-	P		**Blue Dark (FR)**[31] 7-11-7 0..... MissCDouglas(7) (Edward Creighton) *prom in main gp: 6th and wkng whn blnd bdly 10th: p.u bef next* **5/1**[3]	—
U-5	F		**Joe Soap (IRE)**[14] 4143 10-11-9 82.....(b[1]) MrRGHenderson(5) (Mrs C L Dennis) *clr w ldr tl 5th: chsd ldr after and clr of field tl racd awkwardly and lost pl rapidly u.p after 8th: wl bhd whn fell 12th* **20/1**	—

5m 47.7s (25.50) **Going Correction** +0.775s/f (Soft) **8** Ran SP% **114.0**

Speed ratings: **82,81,80,79,75 68,—,—**

toteswingers:1&2 £6.80, 2&3 £3.60, 1&3 £4.10 CSF £21.70 TOTE £7.30: £2.70, £1.10, £1.20; EX 32.20.

Owner T.O.C.S. Ltd **Bred** T O C S Ltd And W G M Turner **Trained** Sigwells, Somerset

FOCUS

There was a decent gallop on in this moderate maiden hunter chase and the winner came from an awful long way back, which saw in-running carnage on the exchanges. The winner is rated to the best of his bumper and hurdles form with the second close to his mark.

NOTEBOOK

Dust In Time was off the mark in a point on quick ground in December, but had failed to complete the last twice, including when making mistakes on his debut in this sphere last month. He looked like tailing off on the final circuit, but found a second wind just as those in front were toiling, and ran out a very unlikely winner. (op 9-1)

Supa Tramp was the form pick here and he looked to have made a winning challenge at the final fence despite not looking to get that much assistance from the saddle. He emptied near the finish, however, and was mugged where it mattered. (op 5-2 tchd 3-1)
Captain Knock(IRE) had unseated in all bar one of his point outings for current connections and was tailed off on the other occasion, but came in for significant support. His jumping was a lot more assured, but he was taken on out in front early, and ultimately paid the price. (tchd 10-3)
Jazz Attack(IRE) probably needs a stiffer test. (op 7-1 tchd 13-2)
Blue Dark(FR) was quickly pulled up after hitting six out, but looked done with at that stage. (op 9-2 tchd 4-1)

4430 WOOD-MIZER INTERMEDIATE OPEN NATIONAL HUNT FLAT RACE — 2m 1f 110y

5:10 (5:11) (Class 5) 4-6-Y-O **£1,370** (£399; £199)

Form RPR

1 **1** **Arbeo (IRE)**[54] 3434 5-11-9 0 .... SamThomas 110+
(Diana Grissell) *hld up in tch: trckd ldrs 12f out: ev ch and shkn up ent st: rdn to ld ent fnl f: styd on* **4/9**[1]

2 *2 ½* **Getaway Driver (IRE)** 4-10-1 0 .... MrTGarner(7) 93+
(Warren Greatrex) *hld up in tch: gd hdwy on inner to ld 3f out: rdn and clr w wnr over 1f out: hdd ent fnl f: one pce* **7/1**[3]

3 *7* **Millksheikh** 4-10-1 0 .... MissEmily-JaneHarbour(7) 86
(Raymond York) *chsd ldr: ev ch 5f out tl unable qck over 2f out: kpt on same pce fr over 1f out* **20/1**

6 **4** *7* **Motou (FR)**[34] 3773 6-11-2 0 .... WarrenMarston 89
(Richard Phillips) *hld up in tch in last pair: clsd 7f out: rdn and btn wl over 2f out* **11/2**[2]

0 **5** *2 ½* **War Kitty**[24] 3964 4-9-12 0 .... DavidBass(3) 69
(Roger Curtis) *led: hung to paddock bnd over 9f out: hdd 3f out: wknd ent st* **50/1**

0 **6** *11* **Great Kicker (IRE)**[58] 3372 6-11-2 0 .... JoeTizzard 73
(Colin Tizzard) *t.k.h: hld up wl in tch: rdn and dropped to last ent fnl 3f: sn wknd* **8/1**

4m 53.4s (28.20) **Going Correction** +0.025s/f (Yiel)
WFA 4 from 5yo+ 7lb **6** Ran SP% **115.0**
Speed ratings: **38,36,33,30,29 24**
toteswingers:1&2 £1.30, 2&3 £8.50, 1&3 £3.00 CSF £4.60 TOTE £1.30: £1.10, £2.20; EX 4.50.
Owner Nigel & Barbara Collison **Bred** William J O'Doherty **Trained** Brightling, E Sussex

FOCUS
With no market confidence in the two newcomers it was no surprise the winner was well backed. The winner is rated to his mark.

NOTEBOOK
Arbeo(IRE) proved all the rage under his penalty, and he made it 2-2, but had to work harder than the odds suggested. He was impressive on bad ground when last seen on his debut at Fontwell in January and he moved up going nicely as the dash for home developed leaving the back straight. He had to dig deep to fend off the runner-up, however, and was another advertisement of how difficult it can be to defy a penalty in bumpers. This son of Brian Boru is clearly at home on soft ground and looks a nice prospect for novice hurdling. (op 5-6)
Getaway Driver(IRE)'s trainer boasted a 55% strike-rate here before this event and houses the current favourite for the Champion Bumper next month, but his runner was still very weak in the betting. He got a lovely split up the inside turning for home which saw him put it up to Arbeo, but ultimately got found out by a lack of experience. A clear second-best, he should improve sufficiently to win one of these. (op 13-2 tchd 9-1)
Millksheikh, whose dam was a 2m5f hurdle winner, posted a pleasing effort and ought to come on plenty for the experience. (op 22-1 tchd 33-1)
Motou(FR) probably ran to a similar level as when sixth on his debut at Warwick. (op 5-1 tchd 15-2)
T/Plt: £247.80 to a £1 stake. Pool to £65,165.09 - 191.95 winning tickets. T/Qpdt: £54.00 to a £1 stake. Pool of £4,552.18 - 62.30 winning tickets SP

4431 - 4436a (Foreign Racing) - See Raceform Interactive

4288 LUDLOW (R-H)

Thursday, March 3

OFFICIAL GOING: Good (good to soft in places; chs 7.8, hdl 7.7)
False wings removed from fences giving 6yds of fresh ground on inside. All bends on both tracks moved out course near maximum configuration.
Wind: light across Weather: cold but bright

4437 BET LIVE AT CORBETTSPORTS.COM "NATIONAL HUNT" NOVICES' HURDLE (9 hdls) — 2m

2:30 (2:30) (Class 4) 4-Y-0+ **£2,602** (£764; £382; £190)

Form RPR

2230 **1** **Arthur's Pass**[47] 3556 7-11-1 0 .... RhysFlint 114+
(Tom George) *prom in 2nd or 3rd bhd clr ldr: effrt in 3rd and rdn bef 3 out: led and hit last: kpt on stoutly and sn in command* **12/1**

051 **2** *4 ½* **Furrows**[40] 3691 6-11-7 0 .... LeightonAspell 115+
(Oliver Sherwood) *towards rr: hdwy 6th: last of 6 w ch bef 3 out: hit next: tried to chal whn rdn between last two: kpt on and wnt 2nd cl home but nt rch wnr* **14/1**

122 **3** *½* **The Cockney Mackem (IRE)**[22] 4006 5-11-1 117 .... PaddyBrennan 109
(Nigel Twiston-Davies) *2nd or 3rd bhd clr ldr: hit 5th: clsd on long run to st to ld bef 3 out where mstke: drvn and hdd flat: nt qckn and lost 2nd nr fin* **4/6**[1]

2-P4 **4** *15* **Ballagio (IRE)**[59] 3365 6-11-1 0 .... SeanQuinlan 100+
(Kim Bailey) *nt a fluent: prom in chsng gp: mstke 5th: rdn and brief effrt bef 3 out: 8 l 4th and wkng whn mstke next* **14/1**

5P0F **5** *4 ½* **Bahr Nothing (IRE)**[36] 3739 5-10-8 0 .... JakeGreenall(7) 90
(Henry Daly) *hld up and bhd: mstke 5th: prog fr 3 out: kpt on wl after last but nvr gng pce to chal* **150/1**

2320 **6** *8* **Flichity (IRE)**[71] 3089 6-11-1 118 .... AdrianLane 83
(Donald McCain) *chsd ldrs and plld hrd: 5th and effrt bef 3 out: coaxed along and sn fnd nil: wl btn bef next* **9/1**[3]

-060 **7** *11* **Lilac Belle**[37] 3721 5-10-8 0 .... (t) WillKennedy 66
(Alex Hales) *bhd: effrt 6th: 7th but detached fr ldrs bef 3 out: no imp* **100/1**

P **8** *¾* **Surf And Turf (IRE)**[18] 4094 5-11-1 0 .... APMcCoy 72
(Jonjo O'Neill) *midfield but wl off pce: no ch fr 6th* **33/1**

50P **9** *5* **Automaticman (IRE)**[28] 3897 5-11-1 0 .... AndrewTinkler 68
(Henry Daly) *set fast pce and sn 12 l clr: had all but five others in trble fr 6th: hdd bef 3 out and dropped out rapidly: t.o* **100/1**

00 **10** *2 ¾* **Roses Legend**[18] 4100 6-11-1 0 .... DPFahy 65
(Reginald Brown) *a wl off pce: no ch fr 6th: t.o whn j.rt last* **100/1**

000 **11** *14* **Summer De Baune (FR)**[8] 4288 6-10-8 0 .... (t) HarryChalloner(7) 53
(John Bryan Groucott) *hit 3rd: a wl off pce: no ch fr 6th: t.o next* **200/1**

12 *½* **Thorney Rose (IRE)**[347] 7-10-8 0 .... TomMessenger 45
(Robin Dickin) *hld up and t.k.h: in last whn j. slowly 4th: t.o whn mstke next* **200/1**

6 **13** *shd* **Glendue**[22] 4012 6-11-1 0 .... (t) BarryGeraghty 52
(Nicky Henderson) *nvr gng pce of ldrs: struggling 6th: t.o 3 out* **9/2**[2]

60 **14** *15* **Otis Tarda (IRE)**[40] 3691 5-11-1 0 .... RichardJohnson 39
(Philip Hobbs) *towards rr: struggling 6th: bdly t.o* **66/1**

00 **15** *27* **Dennis Doyle (IRE)**[22] 4006 5-10-12 0 .... PeterToole(3) 14
(Tom George) *nvr gng pce of ldrs: struggling 6th: hopelessly t.o next* **200/1**

3m 51.5s (2.00) **Going Correction** +0.325s/f (Yiel) **15** Ran SP% **118.8**
Speed ratings (Par 105): **108,105,105,98,95 91,86,85,83,82 75,74,74,67,53**
toteswingers:1&2:£5.70, 1&3:£4.30, 2&3:£5.40 CSF £157.06 TOTE £17.90: £3.50, £3.80, £1.10; EX 98.10.
Owner Vicki Robinson & James Williams **Bred** A E Smith And Co **Trained** Slad, Gloucs

FOCUS
A fairly ordinary novice hurdle. The winner improved to his bumper mark.

NOTEBOOK
Arthur's Pass, well beaten on his hurdles debut at Kempton earlier in the year, had shown promise in bumpers and he posted a much-improved effort, leading before the last and staying on well. This ended a losing run for the yard and it will be interesting to see how he fares under a penalty. Official explanation: trainer said, regarding apparent improvement in form, that the gelding was better suited by the drop in trip and faster ground. (op 14-1)
Furrows made good headway leaving the back and stayed on without being able to match the winner. This was a fair effort under a penalty. (op 11-1 tchd 10-1)
The Cockney Mackem(IRE) was disappointing considering he looked all over the winner when kicked into the lead turning for home. Not for he first time, he was found wanting for pace and surely now he'll be upped in distance. (op 8-11 tchd 10-11)
Ballagio(IRE) is now qualified for a mark and should fare better in handicaps. (op 11-1)
Bahr Nothing(IRE), who had fallen early last time, kept on late, for the first time showing ability, and is another potentially interesting handicap prospect.
Flichity(IRE) failed to settle and didn't get home. (tchd 8-1)
Glendue never threatened, ultimately being pulled up, and looks one of his leading stable's lesser lights, albeit he'll probably do better once handicapped. (op 13-2)

4438 HORSE WEIGH NOVICES' CHASE (17 fncs) — 2m 4f

3:00 (3:00) (Class 3) 5-Y-0+ **£5,596** (£1,689; £870; £460)

Form RPR

V-03 **1** **Hector's Choice (FR)**[22] 4010 7-10-12 125 .... RichardJohnson 138+
(Richard Lee) *j.w and mde all at decent pce: forged clr after 2 out: kpt gng strly* **15/8**[2]

-213 **2** *10* **Philippides (IRE)**[51] 3496 7-11-4 140 .... PaulMoloney 139+
(Evan Williams) *2nd or 3rd and t.k.h: pckd and mstke 10th: chsd wnr fr 12th: rdn 14th: pressed wnr but looking hld tl mstke 2 out: outpcd after* **1/1**[1]

0014 **3** *21* **Maraafeq (USA)**[12] 4210 7-11-4 121 .... AidanColeman 122
(Venetia Williams) *disp 2nd tl rdn and hit 12th: nt fluent 13th and outpcd: no ch and jumping modly after* **9/2**[3]

F63 **4** *28* **The Humbel Monk (IRE)**[10] 4261 9-10-9 0 .... PeterToole(3) 92
(Lucy Jones) *w ldr tl mstke 1st: jumping lft in 4th after: lost tch 6th: t.o after mstke 11th* **80/1**

P0 **P** **Norwich Well (IRE)**[56] 3405 6-10-12 0 .... LeightonAspell —
(Oliver Sherwood) *last and several awful jumps: lost tch 6th: blnd 8th and 9th (water): hopelessly t.o whn p.u 11th* **25/1**

5m 7.30s (2.90) **Going Correction** +0.10s/f (Yiel) **5** Ran SP% **108.0**
Speed ratings: **98,94,85,74,—**
CSF £4.18 TOTE £4.00: £1.30, £1.30; EX 4.20.
Owner James and Jean Potter **Bred** Mme Marie Prod'Homme **Trained** Byton, H'fords

FOCUS
A decent novice chase that concerned only two in the straight. A step up from the winenr and the second is rated to his chase mark.

NOTEBOOK
Hector's Choice(FR), who made a pleasing chase debut in a handicap off 124 at the course last month, found himself able to dominate in this small field and he galloped on too strongly for the favourite down the straight, ultimately winning with a bit in hand. Clearly progressive, he can win again. (tchd 13-8)
Philippides(IRE), off since disappointing over almost 3m at Leicester in January, is already a dual course winner (once over fences) and the decent ground looked in his favour. He travelled well enough, but having held every chance turning in, didn't jump as well as the winner and couldn't race on after two out. This was disappointing for a horse who had promised much earlier in the season. (tchd 10-11 and 5-4)
Maraafeq(USA) looked vulnerable under a penalty and was readily dropped by the front two. (op 5-1 tchd 11-2)
The Humbel Monk(IRE) wasn't without promise and should do better in handicaps. (op 100-1)

4439 BET AT CORBETTSPORTS.COM "NATIONAL HUNT" NOVICES' H'CAP HURDLE (11 hdls) — 2m 5f

3:30 (3:39) (Class 3) (0-120,116) 4-Y-0+ **£4,435** (£1,310; £655; £327; £163)

Form RPR

143 **1** **Havingotascoobydo (IRE)**[39] 3698 6-11-0 **104** .... WarrenMarston 120+
(Martin Keighley) *plld hrd and dropped out last: racd on outside: effrt whn nt fluent 8th: rdr lost iron for abt 200yds: qcknd to ld bef 3 out but kpt wandering in both directions after: in command whn j.rt last: rather impressive* **9/4**[1]

-4P0 **2** *2* **Gortenbuie (IRE)**[61] 3295 6-10-13 **103** .... DominicElsworth 113+
(Henrietta Knight) *t.k.h in rr: j. slowly 1st: effrt after 8th: wnt 2nd bef 2 out and hit it: rdn and kpt on but a hld* **25/1**

363U **3** *13* **Lexicon Lad (IRE)**[22] 4012 6-11-10 **114** .... PaddyBrennan 110
(Tom George) *taken down early: t.k.h and hld up in rr: stmbld bdly after 1st: last briefly bef 7th: rdn and effrt on inner bef 3 out: nt trble ldng pair fr next* **11/2**[3]

6030 **4** *½* **Morcambe**[27] 3919 6-11-9 **113** .... (b[1]) BarryGeraghty 109
(Nicky Henderson) *2nd or 3rd tl rdn bef 3 out: sn lost pl: plodded on to repass strugglers* **16/1**

4606 **5** *hd* **Niceonefrankie**[20] 4049 5-11-7 **111** .... AidanColeman 107
(Venetia Williams) *prom: nt fluent 7th: lost pl and rdn next: nt trble ldrs fr 3 out* **7/1**

2U05 **6** *5* **Alesandro Mantegna (IRE)**[14] 4159 6-11-9 **113** .... (p) TomO'Brien 105
(Keith Goldsworthy) *led and often j.lft: did nt set a str pce: rdn and hdd bef 3 out: sn lost pl* **7/1**

5100 **7** *61* **Nosecond Chance (IRE)**[19] 4076 5-11-0 **107** .... (t) PeterToole(3) 83
(Charlie Mann) *trckd ldrs: nt fluent 7th: wnt 2nd bef 3 out and chal briefly and hit it: drvn and wknd v tamely bef next: virtually p.u after last* **14/1**

5215 **8** *14* **Jay J**[101] 2584 7-11-12 **116** .... TimmyMurphy 40
(Andrew Price) *plld hrd: midfield: pressed ldrs 5th tl 6th: dropped bk last and rdn bef 8th: sn t.o* **9/1**

555 **P** **Lobby Ludd**[22] 4006 6-10-10 **100** RichardJohnson —
(Philip Hobbs) *chsd ldrs: tended to make sme deliberate jumps: lost pl qckly 8th: sn p.u and appeared to go wrong* **9/2**[2]
5m 17.9s (3.10) **Going Correction** +0.325s/f (Yiel) **9** Ran SP% **115.7**
Speed ratings (Par 107): **107,106,101,101,101 99,75,70,—**
toteswingers:1&2:£9.80, 1&3:£3.50, 2&3:£20.60 CSF £51.88 CT £282.35 TOTE £3.20: £1.20, £5.60, £2.40; EX 57.60.Peqeno Diablo was withdrawn. Price at time of withdrawal 66-1. Rule 4 does not apply.
Owner D Bishop C Bowkley M Parker M Thornton **Bred** Daniel Kenneally **Trained** Condicote, Gloucs

FOCUS
Two handicap debutants drew clear and both produced big steps up, with the next two setting the level.

NOTEBOOK
Havingotascoobydo(IRE) stayed on best, although things would have been much closer had the runner-up not lost momentum when in the process of joining him two out. An ex-Irish point scorer switched to handicaps following just two runs over hurdles, he travelled strongly in rear (pulled a bit early) and, despite a very slow jump four out, at which his rider lost an iron, he still arrived going best rounding for home. He was certainly made to work for it, but kept finding and promises to be suited by 3m. There's probably more to come. (op 11-4 tchd 7-2)
Gortenbuie(IRE) hadn't shown much previously, but the switch to handicaps on decent going enabled him to show dramatically improved form. He tracked the winner into the straight and was about to join him when getting the second-last all wrong. He was unable to recover the momentum following this, but finished clear of the remainder and should go one better, despite an inevitable rise. (tchd 20-1)
Lexicon Lad(IRE), another moving into handicaps, stumbled quite badly at the path early in the race, but had plenty of time to recover and he just about came out third best. Going up to 3m should help in future. (tchd 7-1)
Morcambe plugged on again in the first-time blinkers, although he still doesn't look much of a betting proposition. (tchd 14-1)
Niceonefrankie still appears to be in the grip of the handicapper. (op 17-2 tchd 9-1 in a place)
Jay J, off since reportedly breaking a blood vessel in November, was quickly beaten off down the back. (op 10-1 tchd 11-1)
Lobby Ludd was quickly pulled up, suggesting something was amiss. Official explanation: jockey said gelding pulled up lame (op 4-1 tchd 7-2)

4440 FORBRA GOLD CHALLENGE CUP (HANDICAP CHASE) (19 fncs) 3m
4:00 (4:05) (Class 3) (0-135,134) 5-Y-0+ **£7,604** (£2,246; £1,123; £561; £280)

Form RPR
3-P3 **1** **Isn't That Lucky**[26] 3953 8-11-1 **123** APMcCoy 134+
(Jonjo O'Neill) *midfield and declined pce of two tearaways: wnt 4th at 10th: effrt 13th: led after 3 out: drvn whn j.lft last: urged home* **7/2**[1]
5464 **2** *1 1/4* **Max Bygraves**[22] 4010 8-11-0 **122** SeanQuinlan 130
(Kim Bailey) *bhd: pushed along 6th: clsd in 5th after 15th: tk 2nd bef last and tried hrd to get on terms: a jst hld* **4/1**[2]
-300 **3** *2 1/4* **Pigeon Island**[82] 2886 8-11-11 **133** (b) PaddyBrennan 140+
(Nigel Twiston-Davies) *last and rdn 2nd: j. slowly 4th: mstke 7th and nt travelling or jumping wl for long way: modest 6th bef 16th: consented to run on stoutly after and wnt 3rd flat but gave himself too much to do* **9/1**
/UP- **4** *1 1/2* **Oakfield Legend**[323] 5181 10-11-2 **124** (t) RhysFlint 130+
(John Flint) *pckd 3rd but led after and wnt a great gallop w one serious pursuer: mstke 14th: rdn bef 16th: hdd after 3 out: hit next: one pce but kpt trying* **7/1**
-5R0 **5** *17* **The Snail**[22] 4010 8-11-0 **122** PaulMoloney 114
(Evan Williams) *chsd ldrs: wnt 8 l 3rd at 10th: lost pl 12th: struggling 16th* **14/1**
05F0 **6** *23* **Pickamus (FR)**[40] 3677 8-11-12 **134** AndrewTinkler 105
(Henry Daly) *led tl 3rd: sn 12 l clr w ldr: nt fluent 5th: hit 9th: lost 2nd bef 16th: dropped out qckly and fin v tired* **14/1**
1P3P **7** *54* **No Panic (IRE)**[113] 2305 8-11-5 **127** (p) TomO'Brien 46
(Peter Bowen) *prom bhd clr ldng pair tl 10th: nt a fluent: drvn bef 12th: no rspnse: t.o fr 14th: fence bhd 16th* **20/1**
15-2 **8** *8* **Calusa Caldera (IRE)**[101] 2582 9-10-11 **119** RichardJohnson 31
(Philip Hobbs) *bhd: last and rdn 11th: t.o fr 13th: fence bhd 16th* **9/2**[3]
4136 **U** **Just Smudge**[96] 2674 9-11-6 **128** AidanColeman 128
(Venetia Williams) *chsng gp but off the pce of two ldrs: mstke 12th: hit 14th: effrt 15th: 2nd briefly bef next: 8 l 4th and wkng whn mstke and uns rdr 2 out* **8/1**
6m 6.10s (-2.20) **Going Correction** +0.10s/f (Yiel) **9** Ran SP% **112.1**
Speed ratings: **107,106,105,105,99 92,74,71,—**
toteswingers:1&2:£4.10, 1&3:£7.50, 2&3:£6.60 CSF £17.77 CT £112.42 TOTE £4.00: £1.60, £1.90, £1.60; EX 20.00.
Owner Mrs Valda Burke **Bred** R Aston **Trained** Cheltenham, Gloucs

FOCUS
Plenty of pace on here, courtesy of confirmed front-runners Oakfield Legend and Pickamus. The form looks solid and the winner should still be on a fair mark after being reassessed.

NOTEBOOK
Isn't That Lucky, united with McCoy for the first time, travelled strongly throughout and stayed on well enough having taken over after two out. A horse who has suffered with breathing difficulties throughout his career, the return to this sort of trip clearly suited him well and he may well take his chance once again in the Fulke Walwyn Kim Muir, a race in which he was still up there, albeit beaten, when falling last year. (op 9-2)
Max Bygraves, ridden patiently, emerged as a big threat in the straight and seemed to appreciate the step up to 3m. (op 9-2)
Pigeon Island, on a reasonable mark, had no trouble with this longer trip and ran well, despite appearing to struggle for much of the way. He's presumably festival-bound once again. (op 11-1 tchd 12-1)
Oakfield Legend, making his debut for John Flint, often goes best fresh but it was clear after 2f that his chance had been reduced as a result of Pickamus taking him on. Considering the pair went quick early, he did well to last as long as he did. (op 9-2)
Pickamus(FR) is back on a competitive mark and certainly seems to like it here, but the step up to 3m looked a bit of a shot in the dark and having been forced to go quickly early, he was never going to last home. He's best going this way round and don't write him off returned to 2m4f. (op 20-1)
Calusa Caldera(IRE) was in trouble with a circuit to run and clearly failed to run his race. (op 4-1 tchd 7-2)
Just Smudge has gone well fresh in the past, but was held when unshipping his rider late on. (op 11-2)

4441 FREE £10 BET AT CORBETTSPORTS.COM CONDITIONAL JOCKEYS' H'CAP HURDLE (12 hdls) 3m
4:30 (4:33) (Class 4) (0-110,110) 4-Y-0+ **£2,602** (£764; £382; £190)

Form RPR
0062 **1** **Whispering Jack**[12] 4224 6-11-7 **108** PeterToole(3) 121+
(Charlie Mann) *trckd ldrs: wnt 2nd after 9th: sn rdn: led bef last: a holding only real danger after* **9/2**[2]
2400 **2** *2 1/4* **Talenti (IRE)**[21] 4025 8-10-10 **102** (tp) KielanWoods(8) 113
(Charlie Longsdon) *j.w: cl 2nd tl led 6th: stl gng wl bef 3 out w only one serious pursuer: rdn and hdd bef last: nt qckn* **15/2**
-603 **3** *15* **Calusa Shadow**[61] 3297 7-10-13 **100** (p) GilesHawkins(3) 97
(Philip Hobbs) *t.k.h: rn in snatches: jnd ldrs 6th: drvn and lost pl next: 4th and rdn and btn bef 3 out* **9/2**[2]
360 **4** *hd* **Burnthill (IRE)**[23] 3989 6-10-1 **88** (t) KyleJames(3) 87
(Claire Dyson) *several positions: nt fluent 2nd: mstke 5th: 6th and outpcd after slow jump 9th: sn drvn and btn: j.rt 2 out* **15/2**
5600 **5** *6* **Munlochy Bay**[19] 4079 7-11-3 **101** (p) DavidBass 92
(Matt Sheppard) *bhd: sn rdn and nvr looked to be gng wl: reminders bef 7th: n.d after short lived effrt after 9th* **11/2**[3]
-F03 **6** *9* **Sawpit Solitaire**[22] 4009 6-11-0 **104** HarryChalloner(6) 93
(Venetia Williams) *racd keenly and pressed ldrs: effrt in 3rd but rdn after 9th: 10 l 4th and btn bef next: j. fnl three flights modly* **4/1**[1]
-0P0 **7** *45* **Bally Conn (IRE)**[12] 4224 9-10-11 **95** (p) IanPopham 38
(Martin Hill) *nt a fluent: slt ld tl 6th: j. slowly next: chsd ldr tl 3rd and fading bef 3 out* **18/1**
-4P6 **8** *30* **Fortification (USA)**[20] 4054 8-11-1 **99** (p) RichardKilloran 15
(Michael Blake) *reluctant in last: sn rdn: tailed himself off after 9th* **10/1**
P/0P **9** *22* **King Gabriel (IRE)**[228] 1025 9-11-9 **110** (t) MattCrawley(3) 6
(Tracey Watkins) *t.k.h in rr: rdn 8th: sn struggling: hopelessly t.o bef 3 out* **66/1**
6m 2.30s (10.00) **Going Correction** +0.325s/f (Yiel) **9** Ran SP% **111.1**
Speed ratings (Par 105): **96,95,90,90,88 85,70,60,52**
toteswingers:1&2:£11.90, 1&3:£9.00, 2&3:£6.40 CSF £35.89 CT £153.37 TOTE £4.90: £2.00, £2.00, £1.70; EX 34.40.
Owner Roger Bender & Mrs Sarah Bender **Bred** Miss Kerry Lane **Trained** Upper Lambourn, Berks

FOCUS
The front pair came clear in what was a modest handicap hurdle. The winner probably has more to offer and the second is rated back to something like his best.

NOTEBOOK
Whispering Jack was always the likely winner once getting Talenti off the bridle, his superior stamina kicking in late on. Unexposed, having recorded a career-best when second at Wincanton last time, the 5lb rise wasn't enough to stop him, but he will need to progress again if he's to defy much of a rise. A step up to 3m should help. (op 4-1 tchd 7-2)
Talenti(IRE) is certainly talented, but he's yet to win a handicap under either code and, despite having travelled strongly throughout under a good ride, he was always likely to be found wanting once strongly pressed late on. (op 12-1)
Calusa Shadow was close enough to challenge leaving the back, but couldn't race on in the straight. (op 5-1 tchd 4-1)
Burnthill(IRE) promises to be suited by 3m, so isn't one to give up on just yet. (op 8-1 tchd 17-2)
Munlochy Bay failed to pick up for pressure. (op 5-1 tchd 6-1)
Sawpit Solitaire failed to build on her good last-time-out effort at the course. (tchd 7-2 and 9-2)
Bally Conn(IRE) Official explanation: jockey said gelding finished lame

4442 CHASE MEREDITH MEMORIAL TROPHY (HUNTERS' CHASE) (19 fncs) 3m
5:00 (5:00) (Class 6) 6-Y-0+ **£936** (£290; £145; £72)

Form RPR
P/44 **1** **The General Lee (IRE)**[22] 4011 9-11-3 93 MissLBrooke(7) 109
(Phillip Rowley) *led 4th: j. boldly: nt fluent 11th (water): kpt galloping strly fr 3 out: in command last: pushed out* **8/1**
1-U5 **2** *3 1/4* **Mad Victor (IRE)**[25] 10-11-7 102 MrBJPoste(7) 110
(Miss S M Taylor) *settled towards rr: 3rd and effrt 10th: wnt 2nd at 14th: drvn 3 out: unable to make any imp after* **11/2**[3]
4-1P **3** *24* **Martha's Kinsman (IRE)**[278] 525 12-12-0 120 MrOGreenall 87
(Henry Daly) *chsd ldrs: wnt 2nd 9th tl 14th: sn rdn: struggling to keep up w ldng pair fr 3 out* **3/1**[2]
U-5 **4** *1 3/4* **No Virtue**[22] 4011 8-10-10 0 MrRJarrett(7) 75
(S Flook) *last pair: sme hdwy 11th: 4th next: rdn and lost tch after 15th* **15/2**
305- **5** *20* **Give Me Love (FR)**[312] 6 11-11-3 82 MrSWDrinkwater(7) 64
(Miss Louise Danton) *trckd ldrs: rdn and outpcd 12th: 20 l 4th bef 16th: t.o but kpt plugging on* **33/1**
0/6- **6** *6* **Posh Dude (IRE)**[60] 10-11-3 0 (p) MrJSherwood(7) 59
(Simon Sherwood) *hit 5th: rdn 7th: sn lost tch: t.o after 15th* **9/1**
0113 **P** **Sea Wall**[190] 1373 9-12-4 125 MrAJBerry —
(Jonjo O'Neill) *chsd ldrs: nt fluent 11th (water): sn lft bhd: bdly t.o whn p.u 16th* **5/2**[1]
P-21 **P** **Blaze Ahead (IRE)**[95] 11-11-11 104 (p) MrBJPowell(7) —
(Brendan Powell) *led tl 4th: rdn and lost pl 7th: sn downed tools: mstke 10th: t.o 12th: nrly two fences bhd whn p.u 3 out* **8/1**
6m 16.8s (8.50) **Going Correction** +0.10s/f (Yiel) **8** Ran SP% **115.9**
Speed ratings: **89,87,79,79,72 70,—,—**
toteswingers:1&2:£11.90, 1&3:£9.00, 2&3:£6.40 CSF £52.05 TOTE £10.40: £2.20, £2.00, £2.00; EX 89.50.
Owner A Squires **Bred** Joseph Murphy **Trained** Bridgnorth, Shorpshire

FOCUS
A competitive-looking hunter chase but the time was slow compared with the handicap. The form is rated around the first two and could be up to 7lb out either way.

NOTEBOOK
The General Lee(IRE) gained a deserved success. Allowed to stride on down the back with over a circuit to race, he jumped enthusiastically and found plenty when urged to do so by his rider. He had finished ahead of the runner-up at Stratford last May and will presumably head back to the big meeting there this time round. (op 12-1 tchd 15-2)
Mad Victor(IRE), runner-up in a point last month, travelled nicely into contention and ran well without being able to get past his old rival. (op 7-2)
Martha's Kinsman(IRE), third in this a year ago, was found wanting for speed towards the end of the back straight and ended up well held. His main aim will presumably once again be the 4m1f event he won at Cheltenham last May. (op 4-1)
No Virtue ran about as well as expected. (op 14-1 tchd 7-1)
Sea Wall was struggling a long way from the finish and clearly failed to put his best foot forward. Making his debut in this sphere, he looked the one to beat on rules form and probably warrants another chance. (op 2-1 tchd 11-4 and 3-1 in places)

4443 CORBETT ON BESTBETTING.COM STANDARD OPEN NATIONAL HUNT FLAT RACE 2m
5:30 (5:30) (Class 5) 4-5-Y-0 **£1,431** (£420; £210; £104)

Form RPR
1 **Parsnip Pete** 5-11-2 0 PaddyBrennan 96+
(Tom George) *t.k.h trcking ldrs: effrt 3f out: pushed along to ld 300yds out: a gng best after* **10/1**
2 *2 1/2* **Little Fritz (FR)** 4-10-8 0 BarryGeraghty 86
(Nicky Henderson) *midfield: rdn to chal in last of five gng clr 3f out: sn given a bump: no imp on wnr over 1f out: snatched 2nd* **4/6**[1]

64 **3** *hd* **Rowlestone Lad**27 3936 4-10-8 0 RhysFlint 86
(John Flint) *led and t.k.h: rdn and hdd over 1f out: kpt on steadily but lost 2nd cl home* **8/1**3

4 *9* **Milaneen** 5-10-9 0 TomO'Brien 79
(Keith Goldsworthy) *prom: drvn 3f out: sn wknd* **11/2**2

00 **5** *11* **Seventh Hussar**25 3964 5-11-2 0 DominicElsworth 76
(Henrietta Knight) *hld up in last pair: passed sme struggling rivals in fnl half m: no ch* **40/1**

0 **6** *5* **Blue Bell House (IRE)**14 4164 5-10-9 0 MrBJPoste(7) 72
(Tracey Watkins) *w ldrs tl rdn and wknd tamely 3f out* **66/1**

30 **7** *1 1/4* **Midnight King**17 4124 5-11-2 0 AndrewTinkler 70
(George Baker) *midfield: lost tch 5f out* **10/1**

4 **8** *10* **Sleeping Du Granit (FR)**23 3992 5-11-2 0 (t) WayneHutchinson 61
(Claire Dyson) *lost tch qckly 5f out* **20/1**

0 **9** *1* **Edieskaia (IRE)**37 3731 5-11-2 0 RichardJohnson 60
(Tim Vaughan) *bhd: rdn and brief effrt but nt look keen 5f out: sn labouring: mod 6th st* **33/1**

0 **10** *24* **Skarloey**19 4082 5-10-9 0 MrMWall(7) 39
(Tony Carroll) *t.k.h: lost tch 5f out: t.o fnl 3f* **80/1**

0 **11** *43* **John The Glass**106 2458 4-10-8 0 LiamTreadwell —
(Mark Wellings) *plld hrd and cl up tl stopped to nil 6f out: sn hopelessly t.o* **200/1**

3m 51.0s (7.10) **Going Correction** +0.325s/f (Yiel)
WFA 4 from 5yo 7lb **11** Ran SP% **118.0**
Speed ratings: **95,93,93,89,83 81,80,75,75,63 41**
toteswingers:1&2:£3.70, 1&3:£12.20, 2&3:£3.10 CSF £16.81 TOTE £12.10: £2.80, £1.10, £2.20; EX 21.10.
Owner The Parsnips **Bred** A E Smith And Co **Trained** Slad, Gloucs

FOCUS
A weak bumper and the form could be out by up to 10lb either way.

NOTEBOOK
Parsnip Pete took over travelling well and always looked to be doing enough, capping a fine day for the previously out-of-form Tom George stable, who had trained this one's half-brother Arthur's Pass to victory earlier on the card. He's a good-looking sort with promise of more to come, but it's always hard to defy a penalty in bumpers. (tchd 9-1)
Little Fritz(FR) is nicely bred and kept finding for pressure down the straight, but his lack of experience was there was all to see. He should improve and can go one better. (tchd 4-7 and 8-11)
Rowlestone Lad, making his debut for John Flint, ran his best race yet and remains steadily progressive. (op 12-1)
Milaneen, closely related to bumper winner Fassaroe, shaped promisingly and should be up to winning against her own sex. (op 7-1)
Seventh Hussar wasn't without promise, running his best race yet. (tchd 50-1)
Midnight King was again a little disappointing, considering he's well regarded by his trainer. (op 11-1 tchd 12-1)
T/Plt: £39.70 to a £1 stake. Pool:£61,021.35 - 1,121.25 winning tickets T/Qpdt: £21.90 to a £1 stake. Pool:£4,156.86 - 140.30 winning tickets IM

4267 TAUNTON (R-H)

Thursday, March 3

OFFICIAL GOING: Good to soft (good in places; 7.8)
Rail realignment increased distances by 20m per circuit.
Wind: mild across Weather: overcast with sunny periods

4444 EXMOUTH COMMUNITY COLLEGE NOVICES' HURDLE (10 hdls) 2m 3f 110y
2:20 (2:21) (Class 4) 4-Y-O+ **£3,425** (£998; £499)

Form RPR

-P15 **1** **Henry King (IRE)**30 3874 7-11-9 122 (t) DenisO'Regan 126+
(Victor Dartnall) *mde all: set stdy pce tl qcknd after 7th: styd on strly fr 2 out: pushed out* **4/1**3

-343 **2** *9* **Merehead (FR)**54 3439 5-11-2 0 DarylJacob 112+
(Paul Nicholls) *trckd wnr: rdn after 3 out: styd on but nt pce to chal* **11/4**2

3-02 **3** *10* **Romulus D'Artaix (FR)**19 4081 5-11-2 0 RobertThornton 102+
(Alan King) *in tch: wnt cl 3rd 5th: rdn after 3 out: nvr gng pce to chal front pair: mstke last* **6/5**1

0P6 **4** *6* **Spirit Of Barbados (IRE)**9 4268 5-11-2 0 (t) TomScudamore 93+
(David Pipe) *hld up towards rr: hdwy after 6th: rdn after 3 out: styd on fr 2 out: nvr trbld ldrs* **25/1**

04P **5** *5* **Generous Bob**32 3836 4-10-4 0 WayneKavanagh(3) 79
(Seamus Mullins) *mid-div: rdn after 7th: styd on same pce fr after 3 out: nvr trbld ldrs* **100/1**

1-0 **6** *nk* **Royal Riviera**22 4012 5-10-13 0 SamTwiston-Davies(3) 91
(Nigel Twiston-Davies) *trckd ldrs: slow 2nd: rdn after 7th: one pce fr next* **12/1**

/0-4 **7** *3 1/4* **Barton Cliche**42 3647 6-11-2 0 DougieCostello 84
(Neil Mulholland) *trckd ldrs: pushed along after 6th: rdn after 3 out: sn one pce* **33/1**

0-45 **8** *21* **How's My Friend**28 3903 6-11-2 0 NickScholfield 63
(Grant Cann) *in tch tl 6th: no ch fr after 7th: t.o* **50/1**

9 *8* **Dolores Ortiz (IRE)**574 5-10-4 0 MattGriffiths(5) 48
(Philip Hobbs) *rdn after 7th: nvr bttr than mid-div: wknd 3 out: t.o* **50/1**

6 **10** *1/2* **Homer Run (IRE)**25 3964 4-10-4 0 JimmyDerham(3) 46
(Seamus Mullins) *a towards rr: t.o* **100/1**

0 **11** *23* **Nik Nak Too**35 3773 5-11-2 0 AndrewThornton 32
(Seamus Mullins) *nt fluent 1st: wnt lft 3rd: a in rr: t.o* **100/1**

0 **12** *22* **Golden King (IRE)**26 3957 6-11-2 0 RodiGreene 10
(Lisa Williamson) *t.k.h early: mid-div: slow whn wnt lft 5th: sn in rr: t.o* **200/1**

0P **13** *15* **Semelay (FR)**27 3930 5-11-2 0 LiamHeard —
(Laura Young) *mid-div: hdwy 5th: mstke next: dropped to rr qckly: t.o fr next* **200/1**

0-5 **P** **Boo Boo Booyakasha**18 4100 7-10-13 0 MichaelMurphy(3) —
(Arthur Whiting) *hld up towards rr: p.u on bnd after 5th: dismntd* **100/1**

4m 35.8s (-10.20) **Going Correction** -0.55s/f (Firm)
WFA 4 from 5yo+ 7lb **14** Ran SP% **115.5**
Speed ratings (Par 105): **98,94,90,88,86 85,84,76,72,72 63,54,48,—**
toteswingers:1&2:£2.40, 1&3:£1.90, 2&3:£1.30 CSF £14.75 TOTE £4.10: £1.50, £1.30, £1.20; EX 17.70.
Owner Mrs C Barber **Bred** M Conaghan **Trained** Brayford, Devon

FOCUS
The rails were moved to fresh ground on the bends, adding approximately 20m per circuit. The ground was described by some jockeys after the opener as dead in places. The betting suggested that only three could be seriously considered in this ordinary novice hurdle. The winner produced a small step up but the third was a stone+ off.

NOTEBOOK
Henry King(IRE), the only runner with a penalty, was stepped up in trip and won under a fine front-running ride by Denis O'Regan, who controlled the fractions and increased them to suit his horse. He is clearly a useful type when at his best (rated 122 before this victory) and now seems to enjoy dominating. (tchd 9-2)
Merehead(FR) had performed well in a couple of maidens and once again shaped respectably. A chaser in stature, one would imagine he'll win something similar before going chasing. (op 3-1 tchd 5-2)
Romulus D'Artaix(FR) ran nicely on his hurdling debut after a break, but failed to reproduce that promise here. He was niggled along down the back straight and never threatened to cause the leader too many problems. A more galloping track may suit him at this sort of distance. (op 11-10 tchd 5-4)
Spirit Of Barbados(IRE) ◆, up in trip, caught the eye with his staying-on effort and is definitely one to keep an eye on for handicaps. (op 33-1)
Generous Bob ran much better than he had done on his hurdling debut, but needs to build on this.
Royal Riviera was well beaten on his first outing for this trainer and did no better in this (op 14-1)
Barton Cliche wasn't disgraced after racing quite prominently.
Dolores Ortiz(IRE), absent since August 2009, is related to winners but didn't manage a success for Stuart Williams on the Flat. She'll need to settle much better in the future to have any chance of getting home over hurdles, as she pulled very hard.
Boo Boo Booyakasha Official explanation: jockey said gelding lost its action

4445 ROYAL BATH & WEST BEGINNERS' CHASE (17 fncs) 2m 7f 110y
2:50 (2:50) (Class 4) 5-Y-O+ **£3,768** (£1,098; £549)

Form RPR

46F2 **1** **Fin Vin De Leu (GER)**23 3988 5-10-12 0 (p) DarylJacob 136+
(Charlie Mann) *j.lft at times: mde all: in command after 4 out: stmbld bdly sn after last: rdn out: comf* **7/1**

1/22 **2** *11* **Patsy Finnegan**20 4050 9-11-0 122 RobertThornton 127+
(Alan King) *trckd ldrs: wnt 2nd 10th: mstke 12th: rdn and ev ch after 4 out: hld fr next: mstke 2 out* **9/4**1

204U **3** *6* **Earth Planet (IRE)**21 4030 9-10-9 121 (bt) MrRMahon(5) 119
(Paul Nicholls) *cl up: wnt 3rd 11th: pushed along after 12th: rdn after 4 out: sn hld: styd on same pce* **4/1**2

4 *12* **Gotoyourplay (IRE)**63 7-11-0 0 NickScholfield 108
(Andy Turnell) *cl up: struggling to hold pl whn hit 11th: sn btn* **16/1**

5 *12* **Ballydonagh (IRE)**1054 8-11-0 0 JackDoyle 97
(Emma Baker) *hld up bhd ldrs tl outpcd 11th: no ch after* **100/1**

5 **6** *36* **Iheardu**18 4096 5-10-12 0 AndrewThornton 63
(Neil Mulholland) *bdly hmpd 1st: continued but a wl detached* **50/1**

P-04 **U** **Erzen (IRE)**97 2664 6-11-0 127 SamThomas —
(Venetia Williams) *bkng off fence bef blundering and uns rdr 1st* **9/2**3

53P2 **P** **Persian Run (IRE)**21 4030 7-11-0 121 JoeTizzard —
(Colin Tizzard) *w wnr tl after 7th: rdn and lost pl rapidly after 10th: p.u bef next* **4/1**2

5m 58.9s (-15.70) **Going Correction** -0.55s/f (Firm) **8** Ran SP% **110.3**
Speed ratings: **104,100,98,94,90 78,—,—**
toteswingers:1&2:£2.70, 1&3:£5.50, 2&3:£3.10 CSF £22.43 TOTE £4.30: £1.50, £1.10, £2.30; EX 25.80.
Owner R Curry, Cathy Leuchars & R P Michaelson **Bred** Newsells Park Stud Ltd **Trained** Upper Lambourn, Berks

FOCUS
A decent contest full of promising types, but won in convincing style by Fin Vin De Leu, who seemingly produced a big step up. The form is suspect though.

NOTEBOOK
Fin Vin De Leu(GER) was far from disgraced against Quantitativeeasing - on many people's shortlists for Cheltenham in whichever race he runs in - at Market Rasen. Daryl Jacob's mount had a tendency to jump left here, but was always going well up front and moved away from his rivals the further he went. An error at last fence, which saw him stumble after it, probably caused his supporters' hearts to skip a beat, but he never really looked like coming down. His immediate future will depend on how the handicapper assesses him. (op 6-1)
Patsy Finnegan, up in distance, had two solid performances over fences behind him already but was unable to get upsides the winner as the tempo increased, and a mistake two out didn't make any difference to the final outcome. That jumping error aside, he probably ran a bit below his official mark. (tchd 5-2)
Earth Planet(IRE) was going well over C&D last time when unseating his rider at the third-last here earlier in the month, but went from travelling to needing pushing along quite quickly, and never made his presence felt. (op 9-2)
Iheardu was badly hampered by Erzen's departure and was soon trailing. Official explanation: jockey said gelding was badly hampered at first
Erzen(IRE) shaped with some promise in a decent-looking chase at Newbury last November, his first start for this trainer, but had been absent since. However, he got no further than the first here when appearing to jump the fence at a strange angle. (tchd 4-1)
Persian Run(IRE) dropped out alarmingly with a circuit to go, so presumably something was amiss with him as he had looked to be going well until losing his position rapdily. Official explanation: jockey said gelding stopped quickly but he had no explanation for the poor run (tchd 4-1)

4446 TONY DAVIS HALF CENTURY NOVICES' H'CAP HURDLE (12 hdls) 3m 110y
3:20 (3:20) (Class 4) (0-115,115) 4-Y-O+ **£3,425** (£998; £499)

Form RPR

1004 **1** **Henry Hook (IRE)**26 3950 7-11-5 **115** (b) EdGlassonbury(7) 123+
(Victor Dartnall) *mde all: styd on strly fr after 3 out: mstke last: pushed out: comf* **6/1**3

1U11 **2** *7* **Molly Round (IRE)**12 4224 7-11-1 **109** MrSWaley-Cohen(5) 109
(Grant Cann) *hld up towards rr: pushed along in last after 7th: stdy prog fr next: disp 2nd u.p after 3 out: styd on but no ch w wnr fr next* **9/2**2

5304 **3** *hd* **Red Mile (FR)**19 4079 6-11-9 **112** JackDoyle 115+
(Emma Lavelle) *hld up: tk clsr order after 7th: pushed along 9th: rdn in 4th after 3 out: styd on to chal for 2nd run-in: no ch w wnr* **9/2**2

0-32 **4** *9* **Round Tom (FR)**54 3448 6-11-7 **115** MrRMahon(5) 110
(Paul Nicholls) *trckd wnr: pushed along 9th: rdn after 3 out: lost 2nd next: fdd fr last* **15/2**

0/00 **5** *18* **Cypress Grove (IRE)**59 3370 8-10-11 **100** DarylJacob 78
(John Ryall) *trckd ldrs: nt fluent 6th: reminders bef 8th: sn rdn: wknd after 3 out* **9/1**

-0F1 **6** *6* **Kaybeew**35 3764 6-11-7 **113** SamTwiston-Davies(3) 83
(Nigel Twiston-Davies) *in tch: rdn bef 9th: wknd after 3 out: t.o* **14/1**

0553 **7** *6* **Wise Hawk**44 3619 6-10-0 **89** oh2 (t) JamesDavies 54
(Chris Down) *mid-div: rdn after 3 out: sn wknd: t.o* **33/1**

00/0 **P** **Aureate**13 2021 7-10-13 **105** WayneKavanagh(3) —
(Brian Forsey) *hld up: hdwy to trck ldrs 4th: wknd after 7th: sn t.o: p.u bef 9th* **66/1**

2120 **P** **Kylenoe Fairy (IRE)**54 3452 7-11-0 **110** (t) TrevorWhelan(7) —
(Paul Henderson) *trckd ldrs: struggling after 7th: outpcd next: t.o after 3 out: p.u bef last* **22/1**

4343 **P** **The Boss (IRE)**27 3934 6-11-2 **105**................(t) NickScholfield —
(Jeremy Scott) *chsd ldrs: hit 6th: outpcd 8th: t.o whn p.u after 3 out* **11/4**1
5m 49.7s (-17.40) **Going Correction** -0.55s/f (Firm) **10** Ran SP% **114.5**
Speed ratings (Par 105): **105,102,102,99,94 92,90,—,—,—**
toteswingers:1&2:£6.40, 1&3:£4.70, 2&3:£4.50 CSF £32.51 CT £132.74 TOTE £6.90: £2.10, £1.70, £1.80; EX 41.50.
Owner Under The Radar **Bred** P J Hassett **Trained** Brayford, Devon

FOCUS
Modest stuff at best, but it had looked competitive for the level before the off. However, and for the third race in a row at this meeting, front-running tactics proved key. The form looks solid.

NOTEBOOK
Henry Hook(IRE), who had the blinkers retained after a good run at Sandown (2m4f) in them, gained a healthy advantage on his rivals from the start and rarely looked like being caught. It's debateable whether he can reproduce this performance again unless allowed an easy lead as he'd been well beaten off this mark, albeit over shorter distances, three times previously and will go up to a career-high after this victory. Connections felt he settled better here, which is a positive for the future. (op 9-1)
Molly Round(IRE) has really hit form this year, winning three times from four starts, but had been raised 38lb in the process. She lost her place with a circuit to go and briefly looked in danger of being dropped, but her jockey got her back to have a small chance before she couldn't go on again. (tchd 4-1)
Red Mile(FR) attracted some market support, but ran much the same as he had done at Warwick last time, being held up before keeping on at the one pace. (op 6-1 tchd 7-1)
Round Tom(FR), back up in trip for his first try in handicap company, is a fine, big sort who had his chance before fading. He will no doubt do better over fences in time. (op 5-1)
The Boss(IRE) was running over a distance that looked sure to suit him but, after being well supported in the betting, he came under heavy pressure after five out and soon had no chance. Official explanation: trainer said gelding was distressed (op 7-2)

4447 SOUTHWEST-RACING.CO.UK NOVICES' H'CAP CHASE (12 fncs) 2m 110y
3:50 (3:50) (Class 4) (0-105,102) 5-Y-0+ **£3,425** (£998; £499)

Form RPR
PP60 **1** **Laneguy (FR)**9 4269 6-11-0 **90**................(t) DenisO'Regan 105+
(Tom George) *hld up: smooth hdwy fr 6th: led on bit sn after 3 out: easily* **9/2**3
65-P **2** *9* **Floradora Do**61 3300 9-9-13 **78** oh2 ow2................ JimmyDerham(3) 80
(Ron Hodges) *hld up: hdwy after 4 out: rdn after 3 out: styng on to chal for 2nd whn mstke last: kpt on but no ch w easy wnr* **16/1**
6542 **3** *hd* **Catholic Hill (USA)**10 4264 6-9-12 **77**................ TommyPhelan(3) 83+
(Mark Gillard) *trckd ldr: pckd 3rd: ev ch whn blnd 4 out and lost pl: rdn whn hmpd 3 out: styd on fr last* **9/4**1
4351 **4** *hd* **Kirbys Glen (IRE)**9 4269 9-10-8 **87** 7ex................ KeiranBurke(3) 90
(Patrick Rodford) *hld up: hdwy fr 6th: led sn after 4 out: sn rdn: hdd after 3 out: sn no ch w wnr: mstke last: lost 2 pls fnl strides* **10/3**2
/0P- **5** *6* **Coda Agency**29 4869 8-11-12 **102**................ DarylJacob 100
(David Arbuthnot) *hld up: hdwy after 5th: rdn after 4 out: sn one pce* **6/1**
P/0- **6** *33* **Arthurs Dream (IRE)**353 4656 9-10-10 **86**................ RodiGreene 51
(Nick Ayliffe) *trckd ldrs: wkng whn hit 6th: sn in rr: t.o* **33/1**
10F0 **F** **Killowenabbey (IRE)**8 4292 7-10-12 **95**................(tp) AodhaganConlon(7) —
(Debra Hamer) *trckd ldrs: cl 4th travelling wl whn fell 4 out* **10/1**
P0P4 **F** **Sourchamp (FR)**18 4099 5-9-11 **76** oh7................(t) WayneKavanagh(3) 77
(Arthur Whiting) *sn led: wnt lft and stmbld 3rd: hdd and rdn sn after 4 out: ev ch whn fell next* **9/1**
4m 11.1s (1.10) **Going Correction** -0.55s/f (Firm) **8** Ran SP% **114.2**
Speed ratings: **75,70,70,70,67 52,—,—**
toteswingers:1&2:£20.30, 1&3:£4.50, 2&3:£5.80 CSF £64.60 CT £201.56 TOTE £6.00: £1.70, £4.40, £1.30; EX 69.60.
Owner Mrs Laura Day **Bred** Loic Malivet And Mme Martine Malivet **Trained** Slad, Gloucs

FOCUS
It was difficult to get too enthusiastic about the chances of plenty of these, so the form is unlikely to be strong. it makes sense though and there should be more to come from the winner.

NOTEBOOK
Laneguy(FR) had finished a long way behind Kirbys Glen last time at this course (2m3f) after being badly hampered when still going well, but reversed that form with ease after moving strongly throughout. He hasn't had a lot of racing and really should be capable of winning next time with a clear round at this level. (op 5-1 tchd 4-1)
Floradora Do, making her chasing debut under rules from out of the handicap (plus her jockey carried 2lb overweight), was given a patient ride and never quite got into contention. It was a nice start over fences, however, and she can do better. (op 25-1)
Catholic Hill(USA), due to go up 5lb from Saturday, was never far way and rallied after a mistake four out to keep on again. (tchd 2-1 and 5-2)
Kirbys Glen(IRE), raised 7lb for winning here over 2m 3½f last time, made good ground throughout the final circuit and hit the front after four out before being swamped shortly after the next. (op 3-1)
Coda Agency has run well on the Flat since running over hurdles last March, winning three times at 2m, but needed niggling quite a way out and failed to get competitive. (op 9-2 tchd 4-1)
Killowenabbey(IRE) looked far from beaten when taking off a bit too early at the fourth-last. (op 11-1 tchd 12-1)
Sourchamp(FR), a well-backed outsider who was running from out of the handicap, showed plenty out in front until falling at the third-last. He'd been quite free but was not completely done with when coming to grief. (op 11-1 tchd 12-1)

4448 CARLSBERG LAGER H'CAP HURDLE (10 hdls) 2m 3f 110y
4:20 (4:20) (Class 4) (0-115,115) 4-Y-0+ **£3,425** (£998; £499)

Form RPR
3036 **1** **Fountains Flypast**59 3366 7-11-3 **111**................ RachaelGreen(5) 121+
(Anthony Honeyball) *mid-div: hdwy 3 out: led next: tended to edge rt: hit last: styd on wl fnl 100yds: rdn out* **6/1**
2405 **2** *1¾* **Laustra Bad (FR)**34 3793 8-11-3 **111**................(bt) COFarrell(5) 118
(David Pipe) *trckd ldrs: chal 3 out: sn rdn: ev ch whn nt fluent last: no ex fnl 100yds* **9/2**2
6252 **3** *7* **Prince Of Denial (IRE)**21 4034 7-11-9 **115**........ SamTwiston-Davies(3) 115
(Nigel Twiston-Davies) *trckd ldrs: ev ch 3 out: sn rdn: styd on same pce fr next* **7/2**1
6033 **4** *¾* **Posh Emily**6 4323 8-10-11 **105**................(b) MattGriffiths(5) 104
(Ron Hodges) *racd keenly: prom: led after 6th: rdn and hdd after 3 out: styd on same pce fr next* **5/1**3
0 **5** *14* **Falcon Island**39 3709 6-11-12 **115**................(t) JoeTizzard 104
(Colin Tizzard) *mid-div: nt fluent 4th: tk clsr order 6th: rdn after next: nt gng pce to threaten: fdd fr next: egded lft run-in* **17/2**
3P4 **6** *2½* **First Smash (GER)**21 4031 6-10-11 **103**................(t) JimmyDerham(3) 87
(Milton Harris) *rdn after 5th: a towards rr* **16/1**
212- **7** *2¼* **She's On The Case (IRE)**347 4767 6-10-10 **104**.... MrSWaley-Cohen(5) 88
(Grant Cann) *mid-div: hit 6th: struggling after next: wknd after 3 out* **7/1**
4031 **8** *17* **Lucy's Perfect**63 3227 5-11-10 **113**................(b) TomScudamore 87
(David Pipe) *led tl after 6th: sn rdn: wknd after 3 out: t.o* **17/2**
B-05 **9** *26* **Monopole (IRE)**18 4092 7-10-2 **101**................ FrancisHayes(10) 44
(David Pipe) *mid-div tl 5th: sn pushed along: t.o* **33/1**
-560 **P** **Johnny Mullen (IRE)**47 3557 8-11-9 **112**................ DarylJacob —
(Paul Henderson) *rdn after 5th: a towards rr: bhd whn p.u bef 3 out* **20/1**
4m 32.2s (-13.80) **Going Correction** -0.55s/f (Firm) **10** Ran SP% **118.5**
Speed ratings (Par 105): **105,104,101,101,95 94,93,86,76,—**
toteswingers:1&2:£7.30, 1&3:£5.00, 2&3:£5.00 CSF £34.32 CT £110.58 TOTE £7.70: £3.20, £1.70, £2.20; EX 43.50.
Owner The Fountains Partnership **Bred** Mrs M H Bowden **Trained** Seaborough, Dorset

FOCUS
Most of the runners could be given some sort of chance if reproducing something resembling their best performances. The early pace didn't seem strong. The winner improved to the level of his decent bumper form and the next three are rated pretty much to their marks.

NOTEBOOK
Fountains Flypast, up in trip on his handicap debut, settled beautifully in behind but needed a strong ride from Rachael Green to win. It's quite possible that his stamina started to ebb away late on considering how well he travelled earlier, but he still had enough to prove successful. A drop in distance won't be against him and connections reported afterwards that they felt the better ground he got here suited their horse. He has a couple of forthcoming entries and would be of interest under a penalty. (op 5-1)
Laustra Bad(FR), with a tongue-tie and blinkers on this time, is really well handicapped on his last win, but that had come back in 2007. He gained plenty of support in the betting and his jockey tried to pinch it going into the home bend, but he couldn't shake off the winner and lost out in the tussle to the line. (op 15-2)
Prince Of Denial(IRE) didn't run too badly off a 6lb higher mark than last time (op 4-1 tchd 5-1 in places)
Posh Emily kept on well but is still above her highest winning mark. (op 6-1)
Falcon Island, fitted with a tongue-tie on his first run for this trainer after leaving Ireland, looked to have one or two fair pieces of form but was made to look one paced after coming under pressure. (tchd 10-1)

4449 RICHARD WILLIAMS MEMORIAL HUNTERS' CHASE (17 fncs) 2m 7f 110y
4:50 (4:51) (Class 5) 6-Y-0+ **£1,977** (£608; £304)

Form RPR
1F-2 **1** **Whizzaar**28 3908 11-12-5 **131**................ MrRWoollacott(3) 128+
(R M Woollacott) *a.p: led 12th: in command fr 4 out: hit last: comf* **6/5**1
41B- **2** *7* **Chesnut Annie (IRE)**25 10-11-11 0................ MissIsabelTompsett 106+
(Miss H E Roberts) *led most of way tl 12th: sn rdn: styd chsng wnr but comf hld fr after 4 out* **7/4**2
4025 **3** *2* **Gershwinner (IRE)**9 4271 8-11-11 90................ MrMWoodward(7) 110
(Ms Emma Oliver) *hld up last but in tch: rdn after 12th: disp 3rd after 4 out: styd on same pce: nvr threatened ldrs* **12/1**
F- **4** *¾* **Different Trades (IRE)**11 7-11-7 0................ MrJBarber(7) 107
(Bob Buckler) *trckd ldrs tl lost pl 4th: in tch whn hit 7th: rdn to dispute 3rd after 4 out: mstke 3 out: styd on same pce* **20/1**
3-31 **5** *24* **Mustangsallyrally (IRE)**18 10-12-3 117................(tp) MrDGPrichard(5) 98+
(R Barber) *hld up in tch: rdn in 3rd after 11th tl 13th: looked hld whn hmpd 4 out* **8/1**3
0- **U** **Liberty Rock (FR)**19 12-11-7 0................ MrEDavid(7) —
(Miss S Butler) *trckd ldrs: reminders after 8th: rdn after 10th: disputing 3rd whn blnd bdly and uns rdr 4 out* **40/1**
6m 3.00s (-11.60) **Going Correction** -0.55s/f (Firm) **6** Ran SP% **107.8**
Speed ratings: **97,94,94,93,85** —
toteswingers:1&2:£1.60, 1&3:£2.00, 2&3:£2.70 CSF £3.46 TOTE £2.40: £1.70, £1.10; EX 3.80.
Owner J F Symes **Bred** Mrs J A Gawthorpe **Trained** South Molton, Exmoor

FOCUS
The two market leaders dominated this hunter chase from the start. Whizzaar is rated better than the bare result but still below his recent Wincanton second.

NOTEBOOK
Whizzaar comfortably came out on top despite a few hairy moments over the final three fences, which was surprising considering his jumping had looked so assured earlier in the contest. A prolific winner in points and hunter chases, he will be hard to beat in races of this type around tight tracks. He has an entry in the Foxhunter at Cheltenham but isn't guaranteed to take up that engagement until connections discuss their options. (op 11-8 tchd Evens)
Chesnut Annie(IRE) quickly gained the upper hand and looked to enjoy herself while in front, but the winner breezed past her after six out and she couldn't get back to him. That said, she is a resilient sort, as she didn't give up and plugged on for an honourable, albeit well beaten, second. (op 6-4 tchd 11-8)
Gershwinner(IRE) was one-paced down the home straight. (op 14-1 tchd 16-1 and 11-1)
Different Trades(IRE) ran almost identical race to the third being one paced down the home straight. (op 18-1 tchd 16-1)
Mustangsallyrally(IRE) wasn't going anywhere quickly in rear when hampered by the fall of Liberty Rock. (op 9-1)
Liberty Rock(FR) was looking held when coming down four from home. (op 25-1)

4450 TAUNTON FOR LIFE H'CAP HURDLE (9 hdls) 2m 1f
5:20 (5:20) (Class 5) (0-95,95) 4-Y-0+ **£2,055** (£599; £299)

Form RPR
050/ **1** **Webbswood Lad (IRE)**715 4576 10-10-11 **83**................(t) TomMolloy(3) 93+
(Martin Bosley) *hld up towards rr: stdy prog fr 5th: wnt 2nd 2 out: rdn to ld bef last: r.o wl* **22/1**
3442 **2** *2½* **Monsieur (FR)**6 4330 11-10-9 **85**................ NathanSweeney(7) 92
(Carroll Gray) *hld up towards rr: hdwy after 4th to join ldrs next: led 3 out: rdn whn hdd bef last: styd on but no ex* **7/2**2
6642 **3** *6* **Mut'Ab (USA)**16 4125 6-11-7 **90**................(b) JamieMoore 92
(Gary Moore) *racd keenly: mid-div: rdn after 3 out: styd on same pce fr next: wnt 3rd at the last* **11/4**1
0000 **4** *6* **E Street Boy**9 4272 5-11-9 **92**................ TomScudamore 89
(David Pipe) *hld up towards rr: rdn and hdwy after 3 out: no further imp fr next* **16/1**
0P/P **5** *3* **Sunset Boulevard (IRE)**15 1489 8-11-1 **84**................(b) SamThomas 79
(Jim Best) *mid-div: hdwy 5th: rdn to chse ldr after 3 out tl next: fdd* **8/1**
6000 **6** *2* **Naughtyatiz (IRE)**22 4006 5-11-5 **95**................ AodhaganConlon(7) 87
(Debra Hamer) *mid-div: hit 3rd: hdwy after 5th: rdn after 3 out: sn hld* **20/1**
0434 **7** *1½* **Storm Command (IRE)**17 4123 4-10-2 **84**................ MrTomDavid(5) 68
(Tim Vaughan) *led tl 4th: styd prom: rdn whn squeezed up after 3 out: sn wknd* **7/1**3
/00F **8** *1¾* **Honest**9 4269 8-11-6 **89**................ AndrewThornton 78
(Karen George) *rdn after 6th: nvr bttr than mid-div: wknd after 3 out* **22/1**
-050 **9** *3½* **Tiger Dream**22 2452 6-11-2 **92**................ MrRHawkins(7) 78
(Chris Down) *prom tl drvn 5th: sn in rr* **16/1**
4243 **10** *1* **Sparkling Brook (IRE)**220 1095 8-11-1 **84**................ FelixDeGiles 70
(Jennifer Mason) *trckd ldrs: led after 5th tl hdd 3 out: sn rdn: wknd* **12/1**

000 11 *80* **Lady From Ige (IRE)**[26] 3937 7-10-6 **75**............ RodiGreene —
(Neil Mulholland) *racd keenly: prom: led 4th tl rdn whn nt fluent next: sn wknd: t.o* **8/1**

3m 58.9s (-9.10) **Going Correction** -0.55s/f (Firm)
WFA 4 from 5yo+ 7lb 11 Ran SP% **116.5**
Speed ratings (Par 103): **99,97,95,92,90 89,89,88,86,86 48**
toteswingers:1&2:£9.90, 1&3:£8.50, 2&3:£3.90 CSF £96.57 CT £284.48 TOTE £32.50: £6.30, £2.00, £1.80; EX 174.50.
Owner H J M Webb **Bred** Frank Dunne **Trained** Chalfont St Giles, Bucks

FOCUS
A moderate handicap hurdle and the early pace wasn't strong, but the time was fair for the grade. The winner got back towards his 2009 mark.

NOTEBOOK
Webbswood Lad(IRE), who'd been off since March 2009, and came into this a long-standing maiden under both codes. He put up an encouraging performance to break his duck but, pleasing though the performance was, there is no way of telling whether this 10-y-o can do this again next time.
Monsieur(FR) is an infrequent winner but is consistent all the same. His jockey made a bid for victory rounding the home bend but was unable to hold off Webbswood Lad. He is an excellent marker to the strength of this race. (op 4-1)
Mut'Ab(USA) didn't run too badly on his previous outing at Folkestone, and was well backed on this better ground, but he couldn't get into a strong challenging position after being in rear early. He won his only race on the Flat, a maiden for Clive Brittain, in July 2008, so is not the sort to be taking short prices about too often. (op 3-1)
E Street Boy disappointed slightly on his handicap debut at the course just over a week previously (2m3½f), and was ridden differently here, but it didn't make a great deal of difference to his chance of winning. (op 14-1)
Sunset Boulevard(IRE) hadn't run over hurdles since September, but had been racing on the AW in the interim. He threaded his way into a challenging position here, and looked dangerous going to two out, but soon backed out of it and weakened quickly. (op 7-1)
Storm Command(IRE) almost certainly burnt himself out by racing too freely. (op 15-2 tchd 8-1)
Lady From Ige(IRE), making her handicap debut, didn't always jump fluently and was another to take a strong hold early. She dropped out rapidly after being headed. (op 11-1 tchd 7-1)
T/Jkpt: Not won. T/Plt: £14.60 to a £1 stake. Pool:£84,443.63 - 4,203.36 winning tickets T/Qpdt: £8.30 to a £1 stake. Pool:£4,814.77 - 424.80 winning tickets TM

4281 DONCASTER (L-H)
Friday, March 4

OFFICIAL GOING: Good (chs 7.5, hdl 7.7)
Rails moved where possible to provide fresh ground.
Wind: almost nil Weather: dull and overcast

4451 CORAL.CO.UK GREEN TICK WIN MORE EVERY RACE CONDITIONAL JOCKEYS' NOVICES' HURDLE (8 hdls) 2m 110y
2:10 (2:10) (Class 4) 4-Y-0+ **£2,740** (£798; £399)

Form RPR
250 **1** **Red Merlin (IRE)**[37] 3749 6-10-7 0............ HenryBrooke(8) 116+
(Donald McCain) *hld up: wnt prom 3rd: carried rt 5th: led next: edgd rt and hld on run-in* **6/1**[2]
322 **2** *1 ¼* **Kaolak (USA)**[37] 3746 5-11-1 114............ JamesHalliday 112
(Keith Reveley) *w ldrs: led 3rd to 5th: crowded and styd on same pce run-in* **7/1**[3]
222 **3** *nk* **American Ladie**[53] 3481 5-10-5 120............ CharlieHuxley(3) 105
(Alan King) *chsd ldrs: drvn appr 2 out: crowded and styd on same pce run-in* **6/5**[1]
/3-2 **4** *2 ¼* **Swift Lord (IRE)**[31] 3865 6-10-12 0............ JoshuaMoore(3) 109
(Gary Moore) *mid-div: chsd ldrs 5th: sn drvn along: one pce fr 2 out* **6/1**[2]
5 *1 ¾* **Dubai Crest**[79] 5-10-12 0............ DavidBass(3) 107
(Nicky Henderson) *t.k.h: trckd ldrs: swtchd rt between last 2: kpt on one pce* **17/2**
-401 **6** *hd* **Solis**[35] 3781 5-10-13 112............ JoeColliver(8) 115+
(Micky Hammond) *chsd ldrs: j.lft 3 out: one pce fr next* **20/1**
7 *6* **Masterful Act (USA)**[98] 4-9-13 0............ EdmondLinehan(8) 94
(Ferdy Murphy) *towards rr: hdwy appr 3 out: outpcd fr next* **16/1**
0/ **8** *1* **Stronghaven (IRE)**[720] 4474 7-10-9 0............ PaulGallagher(6) 102
(Howard Johnson) *nt jump wl: led to 3rd: led 5th to next: 7th and fading whn blnd last* **100/1**
56 **9** *27* **Faith Keeper (IRE)**[13] 4203 6-10-12 0............ SamTwiston-Davies(3) 73
(Nigel Twiston-Davies) *in rr: drvn 4th: bhd fr 3 out* **66/1**
S **10** *1* **Ursus**[12] 4242 6-11-1 0............ CampbellGillies 87
(Christopher Wilson) *t.k.h in rr: reminders and sme hdwy 5th: wkng whn hit next: j.rt 2 out: sn bhd and eased* **150/1**
0 **11** *12* **Vitruvian Man**[22] 4029 5-11-1 0............ RichieMcLernon 60
(Sophie Leech) *chsd ldrs: j.rt 5th: lost pl appr next: sn bhd: blnd 2 out* **50/1**
P **Grey Garth (IRE)**[615] 4-10-7 0............ FearghalDavis —
(James Bethell) *in rr: blnd 1st and 4th: sn t.o: p.u bef next* **100/1**

3m 56.7s (-8.00) **Going Correction** -0.35s/f (Good)
WFA 4 from 5yo+ 7lb 12 Ran SP% **113.8**
Speed ratings (Par 105): **104,103,103,102,101 101,98,98,85,84 79,—**
Tote Swingers: 1&2 £6.80, 1&3 £2.80, 2&3 £2.90 CSF £43.96 TOTE £6.90: £2.00, £1.90, £1.30; EX 41.30.
Owner Timeform Betfair Racing Club & M Taylor **Bred** Keatly Overseas Ltd **Trained** Cholmondeley, Cheshire

FOCUS
An ordinary novice hurdle and the bulk of the field remained tightly grouped until jumping the third-last. The third was a stone off her Taunton run.

NOTEBOOK
Red Merlin(IRE), rated 96 on the Flat, had twice been disappointing since a decent first effort over hurdles but it transpired that he had been suffering from a back problem. Racing out wide for much of the way before taking it up two out, he got a bit close to the last flight but still had his ears pricked at that point and won with a bit more in hand than the margin would suggest. There should be more to come from him if his problems have been ironed out and he holds an entry in the Supreme Novices', though the Swinton at Haydock may be a more likely target. (op 11-2 tchd 5-1)
Kaolak(USA) appeared to be travelling better than the winner between the last two flights, but failed to take advantage of his rival getting close to the last. He barely seems to stay the trip, but should be able to win a hurdle on a sharp track. (tchd 15-2)
American Ladie, runner-up in her first three starts over hurdles, including behind the previous day's Taunton winner Henry King at the same track last time, had every chance with few excuses and is becoming expensive to follow. (tchd 5-4 and 11-8 in places)
Swift Lord(IRE), having his first start in a year when runner-up in a Folkestone maiden chase a month ago, tried to get into it after three out but he was under pressure to do so and lacked a turn of foot. A return to further looks needed. (op 8-1)
Dubai Crest, a four-time winner at up to 1m3f on the Flat, was never far away on this hurdling debut and showed enough to suggest a race like this can be found. (op 10-1 tchd 8-1)
Solis, penalised for winning under today's rider over C&D in January, had every chance between the last two flights and wasn't knocked about on the run-in once his chance had gone. (op 14-1)
Masterful Act(USA), last seen easily winning a 1m6f Wolverhampton maiden in November for Ed Vaughan, hinted at some ability on this hurdles debut and better can be expected.
Grey Garth(IRE) Official explanation: vet said gelding pulled up distressed

4452 CORAL.CO.UK GREEN TICK WIN MORE EVERY RACE CLAIMING HURDLE (8 hdls) 2m 110y
2:45 (2:45) (Class 5) 4-6-Y-0 **£2,055** (£599; £299)

Form RPR
435F **1** **Hypnotic Gaze (IRE)**[106] 2477 5-11-4 106............ TomSiddall 109+
(Martin Keighley) *hld up in rr: effrt 5th: hdwy appr next: hit 3 out: chal last: sn led: drvn out* **7/1**
30-5 **2** *1 ¾* **King's Counsel (IRE)**[18] 4113 5-11-6 107............(v) DenisO'Regan 107
(David O'Meara) *led tl appr 2 out: narrow ld appr last: sn hdd and no ex* **11/4**[2]
5215 **3** *10* **Tri Nations (UAE)**[127] 2054 6-11-2 113............(vt[1]) WarrenMarston 99+
(Milton Harris) *t.k.h: trckd ldrs: wnt 2nd 5th: led appr 2 out: hdd and 1 1/2 l down in 3rd whn blnd last: wknd* **11/2**[3]
0435 **4** *2 ¾* **I Got Music**[16] 4148 4-10-5 100............(b[1]) JamesReveley 79
(Keith Reveley) *trckd ldrs: wknd 2 out* **9/1**
-005 **5** *15* **First Avenue**[7] 4323 6-11-3 115............(p) JoshuaMoore(5) 84
(Gary Moore) *blnd 1st: sn drvn along off pce: nt fluent: sme hdwy 5th: nt keen and lost pl next* **5/2**[1]
-311 **6** *4 ½* **Tayarat (IRE)**[102] 2586 6-11-4 123............(b) KyleJames(7) 80
(Michael Chapman) *hld up in rr: drvn 5th: sn bhd* **11/2**[3]
P624 **P** **Moonbalej**[90] 2369 4-10-8 93............(vt) DaveCrosse —
(Milton Harris) *sn w ldr: wknd 5th: sn bhd: t.o whn p.u bef next* **40/1**

3m 58.1s (-6.60) **Going Correction** -0.35s/f (Good)
WFA 4 from 5yo+ 7lb 7 Ran SP% **110.9**
Speed ratings: **101,100,95,94,87 85,—**
Tote Swingers: 1&2 £2.40, 1&3 £6.60, 2&3 £4.30 CSF £25.50 TOTE £9.00: £4.40, £1.70; EX 31.00.
Owner Mrs Belinda Keighley **Bred** Tally-Ho Stud **Trained** Condicote, Gloucs

FOCUS
A moderate claiming hurdle. They went a decent early pace, but it eventually told and the winning time was 1.4 seconds slower than the opener. The runner-up sets the level.

NOTEBOOK
Hypnotic Gaze(IRE) couldn't lay up early and trailed the field for the first half of the contest, but he started to pick a few off a few as the early pace began to tell and took full advantage when the leaders wilted coming to the last. The form is modest, but he remains comparatively unexposed over hurdles. (op 17-2)
King's Counsel(IRE), dropping in class, set a decent pace and battled back well after being headed two out, but the winner saw his race out much the better. (op 3-1 tchd 10-3)
Tri Nations(UAE), reportedly suffering from a breathing problem when last seen at Stratford in October, was tried in a visor alongside the usual tongue tie, but he was far too keen early and that cost him. He looked the likely winner when leading two from home, but his earlier exertions then took their toll and he was already booked for third when his rider performed miracles to stay aboard following a major blunder at the last. (op 7-1 tchd 5-1)
I Got Music had blinkers on for the first time, but didn't seem to improve much for them. (op 8-1 tchd 11-1)
First Avenue, taking another drop in class, didn't help his jockey at all and was on and off the bridle throughout. (op 11-4)
Tayarat(IRE) was bidding for a hat-trick on this return from three months off after winning twice at Ludlow for Evan Williams, but he never looked happy at any stage. He was reported to have a breathing problem. Official explanation: jockey said gelding had a breathing problem (op 7-2)

4453 GREEN TICK FOR BETTER ODDS AT CORAL.CO.UK NOVICES' CHASE (15 fncs) 2m 3f
3:20 (3:20) (Class 3) 5-Y-0+ **£5,204** (£1,528; £764; £381)

Form RPR
1403 **1** **Film Festival (USA)**[26] 3968 8-11-4 127............ FearghalDavis 132+
(Brian Ellison) *t.k.h: w ldrs: led 7th: narrowly hdd run-in: edgd lft: styd on to ld towards fin: all out* **8/1**
6321 **2** *nk* **Sir Tantallus Hawk**[12] 4244 7-11-4 0............ BarryKeniry 133+
(Alan Swinbank) *nt fluent: in tch: chsd ldrs 11th: wnt cl 2nd 3 out: nt fluent next: narrow ld 100yds out: crowded: hdd towards fin* **9/2**
21/1 **3** *5* **Glencree (IRE)**[50] 3520 7-11-4 125............ BrianHughes 128+
(Howard Johnson) *t.k.h: jnd ldrs 5th: effrt and hung lft 2 out: fdd last 100yds* **4/1**[3]
/4-0 **4** *12* **Our Bomber Harris**[111] 2360 7-10-12 0............ NickScholfield 114+
(Paul Nicholls) *led 1st: t.k.h: blnd 2nd: hdd 7th: hit 11th: 4th and wkng whn mstke 3 out* **7/2**[2]
0F-P **5** *20* **Master Alfredo**[115] 2283 7-10-9 0............ SamTwiston-Davies(3) 89
(Susan Nock) *nt fluent in last: bhd fr 11th: t.o* **100/1**
0-UP **U** **Halla San**[48] 3566 9-10-12 0............ GrahamLee —
(Richard Fahey) *trckd ldrs: 3rd and effrt whn blnd and uns rdr 4 out* **14/1**
6123 **U** **Benny Be Good**[13] 4210 8-11-4 127............ JamesReveley —
(Keith Reveley) *led: nt fluent and hdd 1st: blnd and uns rdr 4th* **2/1**[1]

4m 46.7s (-2.30) **Going Correction** +0.025s/f (Yiel) course record 7 Ran SP% **112.5**
Speed ratings: **105,104,102,97,89 —,—**
Tote Swingers: 1&2 £6.20, 1&3 £8.50, 2&3 £4.40 CSF £42.21 TOTE £8.70: £4.00, £3.80; EX 31.10.
Owner Koo's Racing Club **Bred** Jim Ryan And Geraldine Ryan **Trained** Norton, N Yorks
■ Stewards' Enquiry : Barry Keniry caution: used whip down shoulder in the forehand.

FOCUS
This fair novice chase was littered with jumping errors. The first three are rated pretty much to their marks.

NOTEBOOK
Film Festival(USA) had his favoured ground and returned to winning form under a positive ride. Despite battling on gamely to keep his rivals at bay over the last four fences, he seemed likely to be beaten when headed halfway up the run-in, but then rallied to force his head back in front where it mattered. He and the runner-up did make contact after the last, but it didn't affect the result and he was allowed to keep the race. He may take his chance in the Grand Annual. (op 11-2)
Sir Tantallus Hawk was ridden with more patience and appeared to have timed his effort just right halfway up the run-in, but he was just outbattled. He seems to handle all sorts of ground and there will be another day. (tchd 5-1 and 11-2 in places)
Glencree(IRE), given a short break since making a successful return from 633 days off at Catterick in January, did his chances no good by taking a fierce hold early and though still in with every chance coming to the last, then found little off the bridle. He can win more races when settling better. (op 10-3)
Our Bomber Harris's last few starts had been well spread out and this 132-rated hurdler was returning from another break for this chasing debut. Unfortunately, his jumping wasn't fluent from early on and deteriorated as the race progressed. (op 9-2)
Halla San, rated 98 on the Flat and 125 over hurdles, was keen enough on this chasing debut but wasn't out of it when jettisoning his rider at the fourth-last. (op 16-1 tchd 18-1)

Benny Be Good, for whom there was a plunge beforehand, ballooned the first and a terrible blunder at the fourth sent his rider into orbit. (op 16-1 tchd 18-1)

4454 GREEN TICK FOR BETTER ODDS AT CORAL.CO.UK E B F MARES' "NATIONAL HUNT" NOVICES' HURDLE (10 hdls) 2m 3f 110y

3:55 (3:55) (Class 4) 4-Y-0+ **£2,732** (£802; £401; £200)

Form RPR

6040 **1** **Definitley Lovely**[53] 3480 6-10-9 0 SamTwiston-Davies(3) 105+
(Nigel Twiston-Davies) *led 1st: mde rest: styd on wl fr 3 out: drvn out* **10/1**

2403 **2** 3 ½ **Sara's Smile**[37] 3747 5-10-12 104 AdrianLane 101
(Donald McCain) *mid-div: trckd ldrs 6th: wnt 2nd between last 2: kpt on: no imp* **4/1**[3]

2221 **3** 5 **Aneyeforaneye (IRE)**[37] 3747 5-11-2 108 JamesHalliday(3) 104
(Malcolm Jefferson) *trckd ldrs: wnt 2nd 3rd: wknd and j.lft last* **3/1**[2]

-1F0 **4** 7 **High Benefit (IRE)**[57] 3403 6-11-5 106 RobertThornton 97
(Alan King) *hld up: trckd ldrs 6th: effrt 3 out: wknd next* **2/1**[1]

53 **5** 10 **Kings Queen (IRE)**[19] 4101 5-10-12 0 DougieCostello 79
(Tom George) *chsd ldrs: wknd appr 3 out* **5/1**

22-6 **6** 14 **Classical Mist**[16] 4145 7-10-12 0 DenisO'Regan 69
(David O'Meara) *hld up in rr: sme hdwy 7th: lost pl appr next* **14/1**

30-0 **7** 32 **Alfie's Pearl**[38] 3721 6-10-9 0 (b[1]) AdamPogson(3) 33
(Charles Pogson) *t.k.h: led tl j. slowly and hdd 1st: lost pl 7th: t.o next* **66/1**

0 **8** 13 **Persian Forest**[22] 4027 5-10-12 0 JimmyMcCarthy 20
(Alan King) *hld up in rr: sme hdwy 7th: sn wknd: t.o next* **100/1**

06P **9** 33 **Perjury**[19] 4101 7-10-12 0 TomMessenger —
(Robin Mathew) *nt jump wl: lost pl 3rd: reminders 6th: sn bhd: t.o 3 out: eventually completed* **200/1**

4m 39.5s (-11.80) **Going Correction** -0.35s/f (Good) course record **9** Ran SP% **113.7**
Speed ratings (Par 105): **109,107,105,102,98 93,80,75,62**
Tote Swingers: 1&2 £7.30, 1&3 £8.20, 2&3 £1.80 CSF £49.80 TOTE £4.60: £1.20, £1.70, £1.70; EX 43.90.
Owner C B Brookes **Bred** Mrs J A Jones **Trained** Naunton, Gloucs

FOCUS
An ordinary mares' novices' hurdle and they finished well spread out. The third and fourth set the level.

NOTEBOOK
Definitley Lovely was disappointing when well backed at Taunton last time, but she got it right here. Soon in front, her jumping was assured and a flying leap at the final flight removed any doubts over her getting caught. A strongly built mare, she looks a potential chaser in the making. Official explanation: trainer's rep said, regarding apparent improvement in form, that he was unable to explain the poor run last time but, the mare appeared suited by the better ground. (op 8-1 tchd 7-1)
Sara's Smile, closely matched with Aneyeforaneye on their Musselburgh meeting in January, moved threateningly into contention on the long run to three out and had her chance, but she lacked the speed to get to the winner. (tchd 7-2)
Aneyeforaneye(IRE) has been a free-going sort in the past, but she seemed to get the run of the race here and had every chance before failing to quicken. (op 5-2)
High Benefit(IRE) may have been remembering her heavy Bangor fall when running poorly at Huntingdon last time, but that didn't put punters off here. However, her efforts to get into the race over the last three flights were laboured and it may be best to just watch her for the time being. (op 3-1)
Kings Queen(IRE), an Irish point winner, hadn't got home in her first two starts over hurdles on softer ground but, despite these quicker conditions, she dropped out tamely here also. (tchd 13-2)

4455 WIN MORE WITH THE CORAL.CO.UK GREEN TICK MARES' H'CAP HURDLE (8 hdls) 2m 110y

4:30 (4:30) (Class 3) (0-125,122) 4-Y-0+ **£4,228** (£1,241; £620; £310)

Form RPR

40-0 **1** **Blue Nymph**[23] 4009 5-11-5 115 DougieCostello 126+
(John Quinn) *trckd ldrs: effrt appr 3 out: qcknd to ld between last 2: r.o strly: eased towards fin* **8/1**

-320 **2** 8 **Dream Esteem**[34] 3808 6-11-12 122 TomScudamore 123
(David Pipe) *trckd ldrs: hung lft fr 3 out: wnt 2nd between last 2: no imp* **3/1**[2]

5661 **3** 1 ½ **Balerina (FR)**[21] 4049 4-11-1 119 (p) RobertThornton 111
(Alan King) *chsd ldrs: narrow ld 3 out: hdd next: kpt on to take 3rd run-in* **5/1**[3]

560U **4** 6 **Mayberry**[22] 4034 6-10-10 106 JackDoyle 101
(Emma Lavelle) *hld up in rr: hdwy appr 3 out: led 2 out: sn hdd: 3rd and wkng whn hit last* **22/1**

0503 **5** 2 **Crosby Jemma**[18] 4113 7-10-11 107 BrianHughes 99
(Mike Sowersby) *hld up: hdwy 4th: one pce fr 3 out* **14/1**

14- **6** ¾ **Veiled**[167] 2917 5-11-1 111 AndrewTinkler 102
(Nicky Henderson) *trckd ldrs: led on bit appr 3 out: sn hdd: wknd qckly between last 2* **9/4**[1]

2113 **7** 13 **Heavenly Chorus**[18] 4116 9-10-10 106 JamesReveley 86
(Keith Reveley) *chsd ldrs: lost pl appr 3 out* **8/1**

1335 **8** 5 **Along Came Rosie**[23] 4000 7-10-11 107 FearghalDavis 80
(Andrew Crook) *in rr: drvn along 4th: outpcd 3 out: lost pl appr 2 out: hung rt between last 2* **28/1**

2650 **9** 2 ¾ **Dream Risk (FR)**[15] 4166 5-10-9 105 (t) RichieMcGrath 75
(Kate Walton) *led: hdd appr 3 out: sn lost pl* **16/1**

3m 56.8s (-7.90) **Going Correction** -0.35s/f (Good)
WFA 4 from 5yo+ 7lb **9** Ran SP% **115.0**
Speed ratings (Par 107): **104,100,99,96,95 95,89,86,85**
Tote Swingers: 1&2 £8.40, 1&3 £7.20, 2&3 £7.10 CSF £32.88 CT £133.80 TOTE £8.00: £2.90, £1.20, £2.10; EX 40.70.
Owner Maxilead Limited **Bred** Lawn Stud **Trained** Settrington, N Yorks

FOCUS
They didn't go much of a pace early in this mares' handicap hurdle and all nine runners were still within a couple of lengths of each other approaching the third-last. the winner is rated up a stone, with the second to her mark.

NOTEBOOK
Blue Nymph had been disappointing on the Flat and over hurdles since winning over C&D 14 months ago, though the extra 5f proved too much for her at Ludlow last time and this return to 2m suited her much better. She quickened up quite impressively between the last two flights to put the race to bed, and the way she acted on this good ground bodes well for a spring campaign. (op 10-1)
Dream Esteem, not disgraced in a hot race at Cheltenham last time, had her chance starting up the home straight but couldn't match the winner's finishing pace. She has been edging up the weights, despite not winning, so will need to find improvement from somewhere. (op 4-1)
Balerina(FR) also had her chance, but was outpaced by the front pair over the last two flights. She was put up 10lb for last month's Kempton win and that looks an overreaction. (op 6-1 tchd 4-1)
Mayberry has found life tough since going handicapping, but was travelling better than anything after three from home. However, once asked for her effort she found nothing like as much as had seemed likely. (op 14-1 tchd 25-1)
Crosby Jemma never looked like winning and still looks a few pounds too high in the weights. (op 9-1)
Veiled was making her debut for the yard on this first start since September. She swept into the lead around the outside looking the likely winner coming to three out, but found little on reaching that flight and dropped tamely away. This was disappointing. (op 2-1 tchd 15-8)

4456 WIN MORE WITH THE CORAL.CO.UK GREEN TICK H'CAP CHASE (15 fncs) 2m 3f

5:05 (5:05) (Class 3) (0-125,119) 5-Y-0+ **£5,204** (£1,528; £764; £381)

Form RPR

-041 **1** **Qianshan Leader (IRE)**[129] 2022 7-11-12 119 JackDoyle 131+
(Emma Lavelle) *led to 2nd: chsd ldr: nt fluent: led 11th: hdd next: led 2 out: kpt on wl run-in* **3/1**[1]

160- **2** 1 ½ **Kealshore Boy**[356] 4578 8-11-11 118 BrianHughes 126+
(Howard Johnson) *hld up: hdwy 4 out: chsng ldrs 2 out: 4th last: styd on to take 2nd last 50yds* **7/1**

4642 **3** 1 **Prince Des Marais (FR)**[33] 3834 8-11-11 118 (t) AndrewThornton 124
(Caroline Bailey) *trckd ldrs: slt ld 4 out: hdd 2 out: styd on same pce run-in* **6/1**

4623 **4** 1 **Enfant De Lune (FR)**[33] 3834 7-11-8 115 RobertThornton 120
(Alan King) *hld up: trckd ldrs 9th: chalng whn nt fluent last: one pce* **6/1**

3104 **5** 2 ¼ **Columbus Secret (IRE)**[18] 4116 6-11-3 110 JamesReveley 115+
(Keith Reveley) *nt fluent: pushed along in rr 8th: outpcd 11th: kpt on and modest 5th whn mstke last: styd on* **5/1**[3]

1300 **6** 8 **Carrietau**[18] 4116 8-11-5 119 (t) HenryBrooke(7) 115
(Barry Murtagh) *led 2nd: hdd 11th: wknd after next* **18/1**

0601 **7** 6 **Cranky Corner**[38] 3730 7-11-4 116 ShaneByrne(5) 104
(Sue Smith) *chsd ldrs: pushed along 10th: wknd 3 out* **4/1**[2]

0040 **8** 32 **Yetholm (USA)**[28] 3934 6-11-1 108 (p) JohnnyFarrelly 64
(John Flint) *j.rt in rr: wnt prom 7th: sn lost pl: bhd fr 11th: t.o* **16/1**

4m 45.9s (-3.10) **Going Correction** +0.025s/f (Yiel) course record **8** Ran SP% **113.9**
Speed ratings: **107,106,105,105,104 101,98,85**
Tote Swingers: 1&2 £1.50, 1&3 £18.10, 2&3 £12.30 CSF £24.00 CT £117.22 TOTE £4.40: £2.30, £1.80, £1.60; EX 31.50.
Owner The Pick 'N' Mix Partnership **Bred** Robin Harold-Barry **Trained** Wildhern, Hants

FOCUS
A decent and competitive handicap chase. A big step forward from the winner and there should be more to come.

NOTEBOOK
Qianshan Leader(IRE) was 7lb higher than when last seen winning at Taunton in October, but neither the higher mark nor the absence did him any harm at all. Always up there, his jumping wasn't that fluent at times, but he produced a good one at the last just when he needed it and ran on strongly up the run-in. A big, strong type, the hat-trick must be a possibility on his favoured sound surface. (op 7-2 tchd 4-1)
Kealshore Boy, lightly raced in the last couple of seasons and returning from another long absence, stayed on well over the last four fences and was still closing at the line, but his last two wins have come after lengthy layoffs so he won't necessarily improve from this. (tchd 15-2)
Prince Des Marais(FR) had the ground he likes and had every chance turning for home, but couldn't quicken where it mattered. His two wins have come over 2m, but he does stay this sort of trip. (op 11-2)
Enfant De Lune(FR), closely matched with Prince Des Marais on January's Fakenham running, rather flattered to deceive as he was the nearest challenger to the winner jumping the last, but faded on the run-in. (op 7-1)
Columbus Secret(IRE), held in handicaps since winning at Catterick maiden chase, not for the first time didn't jump too well, including a blunder at the last, but the way he stayed on suggests he may be worth stepping back up to 3m. (op 9-2)
Cranky Corner, 9lb higher than when making a successful chasing debut at Sedgefield last time, dropped out disappointingly from the fourth-last.

4457 WIN MORE WITH THE CORAL.CO.UK GREEN TICK STANDARD OPEN NATIONAL HUNT FLAT RACE 2m 110y

5:35 (5:36) (Class 6) 4-6-Y-0 **£1,541** (£449; £224)

Form RPR

1 **Fourth Estate (IRE)** 5-10-13 0 DavidBass(3) 113+
(Nicky Henderson) *trckd ldrs: led over 2f out: styd on wl fnl f* **11/2**[3]

2 2 ¾ **Harvey's Hope** 5-11-2 0 JamesReveley 108+
(Keith Reveley) *trckd ldrs: chsd wnr over 1f out: styd on same pce* **14/1**

1- **3** hd **Nuts N Bolts**[348] 4757 5-11-9 0 BarryKeniry 115
(Alan Swinbank) *hld up in rr: effrt 4f out: sn chsng ldrs: rdn over 2f out: 4th over 1f out: styd on wl fnl 150yds* **3/1**[1]

3 **4** 2 ¾ **Karinga Dancer**[36] 3766 5-11-2 0 (t) NickScholfield 106
(Paul Nicholls) *w ldr: led after 4f out: hdd over 2f out: wknd fnl 150yds* **14/1**

11 **5** 4 **All That Remains (IRE)**[24] 3992 6-11-5 0 JeremiahMcGrath(7) 112
(Steve Gollings) *hld up in rr: hdwy to trck ldrs after 5f: effrt 3f out: hung lft: wknd over 1f out* **11/1**

6 **6** 3 **Tartan Tiger (IRE)**[38] 3731 5-11-2 0 DougieCostello 98
(John Quinn) *in rr: drvn 6f out: kpt on fnl 3f* **28/1**

31 **7** 2 ¼ **Distime (IRE)**[27] 3957 5-11-4 0 GilesHawkins(5) 103
(John Quinn) *trckd ldrs: drvn over 4f out: outpcd over 2f out: sn wknd* **7/2**[2]

8 2 **Murphy's Choice** 4-10-8 0 BrianHughes 86
(Paul Webber) *hld up in rr: effrt over 4f out: kpt on: nvr on terms* **9/1**

9 32 **Dorlesh Way (IRE)** 4-10-8 0 PaddyAspell 54
(Patrick Holmes) *in rr: hdwy to chse ldrs after 5f: lost pl over 4f out: t.o 3f out* **66/1**

10 nk **Busby Berkeley (IRE)** 5-11-2 0 RobertThornton 61
(Martin Keighley) *prom: drvn along 6f out: lost pl over 3f out: t.o* **11/2**[3]

34 **11** 5 **Serenader**[26] 3971 4-10-8 0 DenisO'Regan 48
(David O'Meara) *led 4f: chsd ldrs: lost pl over 3f out: eased over 1f out: t.o* **33/1**

12 7 **My Island Rose (IRE)** 5-10-6 0 JamesHalliday(3) 42
(Julie Camacho) *hld up in rr: t.k.h: sme hdwy on outside 6f out: sn lost pl: t.o 3f out* **80/1**

0 **13** 6 **Sleeping Policeman (FR)**[135] 1927 5-11-2 0 AndrewTinkler 43
(Anna Bramall) *chsd ldrs: lost pl over 4f out: sn bhd: t.o* **150/1**

3m 54.4s (-4.70) **Going Correction** -0.35s/f (Good)
WFA 4 from 5yo+ 7lb **13** Ran SP% **119.4**
Speed ratings: **97,95,95,94,92 91,89,89,73,73 71,68,65**
Tote Swingers: 1&2 £20.50, 1&3 £7.80, 2&3 £12.00. Tote Super7: win fund: Not won. place fund: £169.10. CSF £77.62 TOTE £6.00: £2.10, £5.00, £1.50; EX 74.40.
Owner Out The Box Racing **Bred** Darley **Trained** Upper Lambourn, Berks

FOCUS
As with most bumpers, there was no pace on early but this race should produce winners and the winner looks a nice type. The fourth and fifth give the form a solid look.

NOTEBOOK
Fourth Estate(IRE), a half-brother to the useful hurdler Prima Vista and a Listed winner on the Flat, was travelling best of all when taking it up around 3f from home and ran on strongly to score. He has a bright future and is bred to be useful. (op 5-1 tchd 9-2 and 6-1)
Harvey's Hope moved into contention on the inside turning for home and battled on well to just hold on to second. A half-brother to the useful hurdler/chaser Monolith and a couple of middle-distance winners on the Flat, he should also make his mark over obstacles. (tchd 12-1)
Nuts N Bolts, not seen since making a successful debut in a Carlisle bumper just under a year ago, had every chance and was still going forward at the line. This was a decent effort under his penalty and it will be interesting to see how he is campaigned. (op 5-1)
Karinga Dancer, a fair third on his Ffos Las debut, was keen enough in front but managed to hang in there until a furlong from home. He isn't one of the stable's stars, but has race in him. (op 11-1)
All That Remains(IRE) had a 10lb penalty to carry after winning a couple of seven-runner bumpers at Fakenham and Market Rasen and the task proved beyond him, though he was there with every chance 3f from home so wasn't disgraced under the circumstances. (op 12-1)
Tartan Tiger(IRE), well beaten on his Sedgefield debut, looked the stable's second string but he was noted making up a lot of late ground so obviously has some ability. (op 33-1 tchd 25-1)
Distime(IRE) was impressive when winning at Wetherby in February, but he was being ridden along turning into the home straight and could make little impression from then on. (op 11-4)
Busby Berkeley(IRE), a half-brother to the winning hurdler/chaser Rindoon, attracted plenty of market support earlier in the day, but he was one of the first beaten. (tchd 6-1)
Serenader was reported to have a breathing problem. Official explanation: jockey said gelding had a breathing problem
T/Plt: £76.80 to a £1 stake. Pool:£89,519.95 - 850.25 winning tickets T/Qpdt: £17.90 to a £1 stake. Pool:£6,876.57 - 284.25 winning tickets WG

4185 NEWBURY (L-H)

Friday, March 4

OFFICIAL GOING: Hurdle course - soft (good to soft in places; 5.3); chase course - good to soft (soft in places; 6.6)
Rails on hurdles track moved out 4m.
Wind: Virtually nil Weather: Sunny

4458 EMMA LAVELLE RACING JUVENILE HURDLE (8 hdls) 2m 110y
2:20 (2:20) (Class 4) 4-Y-O **£2,927** (£859; £429; £214)

Form RPR
2343 **1** **Omaruru (IRE)**[26] 3958 4-10-12 118 SamJones 106
(Renee Robeson) *chsd ldrs: rdn along 4th and outpcd 4 out: rallied to chse ldrs next: led appr 2 out: rdn run in: hld on all out* **7/1**[3]
3023 **2** *nk* **Two Kisses (IRE)**[22] 4024 4-11-5 123 APMcCoy 113
(Brendan Powell) *trckd ldr: blnd and lost pl 3 out: rallied to chse wnr after 2 out: edgd lft appr last: styd on gamely u.p run-in: fin wl: nt quite get up* **5/1**[2]
55 **3** *12* **Magic Prospect (FR)**[27] 3944 4-10-9 0 PeterToole(3) 93
(Charlie Mann) *in tch: rdn and one pce appr 3 out: styd on fr next and chsd ldng duo appr last but nvr any ch* **20/1**
4 *14* **Battleoftrafalgar**[87] 4-10-12 0 JamieMoore 79
(Michael Attwater) *chsd ldrs: j. slowly 3rd: wknd 3 out* **20/1**
41 **5** *2 ¾* **Moose Moran (USA)**[9] 4283 4-11-5 0 BarryGeraghty 85
(Nicky Henderson) *led tl hdd appr 2 out: wknd qckly* **4/11**[1]
6 **6** *13* **Prince Of Dreams**[37] 3739 4-10-12 0 FelixDeGiles 66
(Ed de Giles) *chsd ldrs tl wknd qckly 3 out* **16/1**
4P **7** *3 ½* **Missionaire (USA)**[55] 3443 4-10-12 0 WayneHutchinson 60
(Tony Carroll) *plld hrd: chsd ldrs tl wknd qckly appr 3 out* **33/1**
5000 **8** *5* **Brambley**[26] 3958 4-10-2 0 JimmyDerham(3) 48
(Seamus Mullins) *a in rr: lost tch fr 4 out* **100/1**
0 **9** *29* **Eurhythmic (IRE)**[22] 4029 4-10-12 0 (t) JasonMaguire 26
(Jim Old) *a in rr: lost tch fr 4 out* **40/1**
4m 5.00s (-4.90) **Going Correction** -0.225s/f (Good) **9** Ran SP% **124.3**
Speed ratings: **102,101,96,89,88 82,80,78,64**
Tote Swingers: 1&2 £2.00, 1&3 £6.30, 2&3 £8.00 CSF £41.43 TOTE £7.60: £1.20, £1.60, £5.20; EX 33.60.
Owner Nick Brown Racing **Bred** Highbury Stud Ltd **Trained** Tyringham, Bucks

FOCUS
This opening juvenile hurdle didn't go the way the market suggested it would. Ordinary form, with a small step up from the winner.

NOTEBOOK
Omaruru(IRE), who had been performing to a similar level in defeat of late, looked a beaten horse down the back, but he rallied well for pressure and, having got the front two out, stayed on well to fend off a determined challenge from McCoy aboard Two Kisses. A horse with plenty of size about him, hurdling is his game (didn't live up to expectations for Mark Johnston on the Flat), and he may well improve a bit now he's got his head in front.
Two Kisses(IRE) has been running well behind Triumph Hurdle-bound horses of late and this was another good effort conceding 7lb to the winner. She may well have won had she not lost her place following a blunder at the first in the straight, and deserves to find another race. (op 9-2)
Magic Prospect(FR), down the field behind fair types on his first two starts, made good ground to reach a challenging position turning in and, although unable to make an impression on the front pair, he very much looks a horse to be interested in once switched to handicaps.
Battleoftrafalgar, rated 83 on the Flat, should improve on this initial experience.
Moose Moran(USA) appeared to have this at his mercy, following last month's ready Doncaster success, but having again set out to make all, he started to look vulnerable on straightening and was a beaten horse when untidy two out. The Triumph Hurdle will certainly be out now, and it's doubtful whether he'll even participate at Aintree following such a lacklustre display. Official explanation: trainer was unable to offer any explanation as to poor run (tchd 2-5)
Prince Of Dreams moved well for a long way and will be one to watch out for in low-grade handicaps later in the year.

4459 BERRY BROS & RUDD "NATIONAL HUNT" NOVICES' HURDLE (10 hdls) 2m 5f
2:55 (2:55) (Class 4) 5-Y-0+ **£2,602** (£764; £382; £190)

Form RPR
1 **Handy Andy (IRE)**[40] 5-10-12 0 JoeTizzard 130+
(Colin Tizzard) *hld up towards rr but in tch: stdy hdwy appr 3 out: trckd ldr 2 out: slt ld last: drvn and styd on strly run-in: won gng away* **11/1**
12 **2** *3 ¾* **Our Father (IRE)**[28] 3930 5-11-4 0 TimmyMurphy 131+
(David Pipe) *trckd ldrs: trckd ldr after 4 out: chal next: led appr 2 out: rdn and narrowly hdd last: no ex and outpcd by wnr fnl 110yds* **11/10**[1]
-023 **3** *6* **Victoria Rose (IRE)**[41] 3678 6-9-12 111 NathanSweeney(7) 110
(Simon Burrough) *trckd ldrs: led 5th: jnd 3 out: hdd appr next: outpcd by ldng duo whn lft clr 3rd last* **11/1**
3-00 **4** *16* **The White Admiral (IRE)**[13] 4198 6-10-12 0 BarryGeraghty 102
(Nicky Henderson) *chsd ldrs to 3 out: mod prog again whn lft poor 4th last* **33/1**
5 *3 ¼* **Good Order** 6-10-12 0 PaddyBrennan 98
(Tom George) *nt fluent in rr tl sme hdwy after 4 out: mod prog fr 2 out* **33/1**
600 **6** *½* **Lariat Sam (IRE)**[28] 3918 6-10-12 0 SamThomas 97
(Alan King) *nt fluent: a towards rr* **100/1**
6 **7** *11* **Forlovenormoney (IRE)**[117] 2238 7-10-12 0 DarylJacob 89
(Paul Nicholls) *chsd ldrs: rdn 3 out: wknd qckly and j. slowly 2 out* **10/1**
00/0 **8** *1 ¼* **Abitofargybargy (IRE)**[40] 3698 9-10-12 0 LiamTreadwell 85
(Richard Price) *led to 5th: styd chsng ldrs tl wknd and bmpd 3 out* **250/1**
46 **9** *½* **Our Golden Boy (IRE)**[33] 3842 5-10-12 0 JamesDavies 85
(Mark Usher) *in tch: j. slowly 4th: wnt rt and wknd 3 out* **100/1**
10 *24* **Prominent Hill (IRE)**[307] 6-10-12 0 (t) RichardJohnson 61
(Philip Hobbs) *chsd ldrs to 4th: wknd and hit 6th* **33/1**
2-F **P** **Dixie Bull (IRE)**[98] 2666 6-10-12 0 APMcCoy —
(Charles Egerton) *chsd ldrs: chal 6th tl blnd bdly 4 out: nt rcvr: in rr and p.u bef next* **4/1**[2]
-406 **U** **Shrewd Investment**[27] 3952 5-10-12 0 GerardTumelty 88
(Alan King) *in tch: hit 2nd: hmpd 4 out: wknd next: no ch whn mstke and uns rdr 2 out* **50/1**
3 **F** **Soir D'Estruval (FR)**[24] 3987 5-11-8 122 WayneHutchinson 122
(Alan King) *in tch tl rdden and one pce appr 3 out: styd on again fr 2 out: 12 l 4th and one pce whn fell last* **13/2**[3]
5m 13.49s (-5.51) **Going Correction** -0.225s/f (Good) **13** Ran SP% **119.9**
Speed ratings: **101,99,97,91,89 89,85,85,84,75 —,—,—**
Tote Swingers: 1&2 £3.50, 1&3 £7.50, 2&3 £4.00 CSF £23.97 TOTE £8.10: £2.10, £1.10, £2.50; EX 30.10.
Owner Brocade Racing **Bred** John Connolly **Trained** Milborne Port, Dorset

FOCUS
Quite a decent novice hurdle, the winner setting a good standard. The winner looks a smart recruit.

NOTEBOOK
Handy Andy(IRE) ◆, a heavy-ground point winner in January who was subsequently purchased for £115,000, was noted travelling particularly well down the back and, having come to challenge, he eventually got the better of the penalised runner-up, drawing away close home. A fine-looking sort, he has a bit of class about him and, although it will all be about chasing with him, he can win again over hurdles first. A trip to Aintree isn't being ruled out. (op 7-1)
Our Father(IRE), beaten at odds of 4-9 under a penalty at Chepstow latest, having earlier made a winning debut over that same C&D, was faced with drier ground this time and showed improved form, going on after three out and keeping on right the way to the line. He too is a future chaser. (op 6-4 tchd 7-4 in places and 13-8 in a place)
Victoria Rose(IRE) ◆ again ran well in defeat and is almost certain to win a race against her own sex. (op 12-1)
The White Admiral(IRE) ◆ wasn't given a hard time once his chance had gone. He'll be of particular interest switched to handicaps, especially on a sound surface, and should make a nice chaser next season. (op 25-1)
Good Order, related to several winners, showed a little promise and should improve for the experience.
Forlovenormoney(IRE) ended up well held, but does look more of a long-term prospect. (op 16-1)
Dixie Bull(IRE), a last-time-out faller, was pulled up soon after a bad blunder down the back. Official explanation: jockey said gelding pulled up after making a bad mistake (tchd 7-2, 9-2 in a place)
Soir D'Estruval(FR) looked vulnerable giving weight all round, but was actually in the process of running a fair race when coming down. (tchd 7-2, 9-2 in a place)

4460 SECURON H'CAP CHASE (IN AID OF WEST BERKSHIRE MENCAP) (FOR THE GEOFFREY GILBEY TROPHY) (13 fncs) 2m 1f
3:30 (3:32) (Class 3) (0-130,127) 5-Y-0+ **£3,903** (£1,146; £573; £286)

Form RPR
1331 **1** **Baseball Ted (IRE)**[16] 4142 9-10-13 **114** (p) TomO'Brien 123+
(Charlie Longsdon) *sn chsng ldrs: wnt 2nd 4 out: chal fr 3 out tl led after 2 out: drvn out run-in* **5/1**[3]
0B2P **2** *1 ¼* **Fiftyonefiftyone (IRE)**[41] 3690 7-11-5 **120** LeightonAspell 127
(Oliver Sherwood) *trckd ldrs: chal fr 6th tl led appr 4 out: jnd 3 out: hit 2 out and hdd sn after: styd on u.p run-in but no imp run-in* **12/1**
3020 **3** *4 ½* **Qulinton (FR)**[19] 4095 7-11-9 **127** DannyCook(3) 130
(David Pipe) *chsd ldrs: ev ch and rdn 3 out: wknd next* **5/1**[3]
50-1 **4** *¾* **Noble Crusader (USA)**[115] 2293 8-11-12 **127** (b) SamThomas 129
(Richard Lee) *in rr but in tch: hdwy and j. slowly 9th: hit 4 out and dropped to rr: stl 6th after 3 out: styd on strly appr last: fin wl to cl on 3rd nr fin and gaining on ldng duo cl home* **12/1**
226P **5** *15* **Its Crucial (IRE)**[13] 4223 11-10-8 **109** PaddyBrennan 99
(Nigel Twiston-Davies) *chsd ldrs: chal 6th to 7th: wknd after 9th* **11/2**
-613 **6** *9* **Babe Heffron (IRE)**[48] 3574 10-11-2 **117** SamJones 102
(Tom George) *led: mstke 2nd: blnd 5th: jnd fr 6th tl hdd appr 4 out: sn wknd* **9/2**[2]
-P6R **R** **Zacharova (IRE)**[27] 3949 8-11-4 **119** (bt) AidanColeman —
(Venetia Williams) *ref to r* **11/1**
33U5 **P** **Wessex King (IRE)**[27] 3949 7-11-6 **121** RichardJohnson —
(Henry Daly) *in rr but in tch whn blnd 4th: hit 5th: rcvrd to chse ldrs whn blnd 9th: stl in tch whn mstke 4 out: wknd qckly and p.u next* **10/3**[1]
4m 8.52s (-4.48) **Going Correction** -0.075s/f (Good) **8** Ran SP% **113.7**
Speed ratings: **107,106,104,103,96 92,—,—**
Tote Swingers: 1&2 £5.40, 1&3 £4.30, 2&3 £7.00 CSF £57.60 CT £313.47 TOTE £4.10: £1.30, £3.30, £1.70; EX 40.70.
Owner Alan Peterson **Bred** Donal Fennessy **Trained** Over Norton, Oxon

FOCUS
The front pair drew clear in what was a fair handicap chase. The winner was well in on his recent form and the second ran a small personal best.

NOTEBOOK
Baseball Ted(IRE) came out on top, despite idling on the long run-in, following up last month's Leicester win off this new career-high mark. Clearly progressive since having the cheekpieces applied, he'll have to do more again to complete a hat-trick, but it's possible. (op 9-2)
Fiftyonefiftyone(IRE) moved best for much of the race and looked the likeliest winner turning in. He rallied well once headed, but was always coming out second best on the run-in. Previously inconsistent, he's still to win a race, but can put that right if kept to these conditions. Official explanation: jockey said gelding lost right fore shoe (op 11-1 tchd 10-1)
Qulinton(FR) was a bit below his best and remains vulnerable off this mark. (op 7-1 tchd 9-2)
Noble Crusader(USA), off since winning at Lingfield in November, was 7lb higher and looked to be struggling a long way out, but he responded well to pressure and would have got up for third in another 100 yards. He should be sharper next time. (op 9-1)
Its Crucial(IRE) should have been more competitive off this mark. He remains below his best. (op 6-1 tchd 5-1)
Babe Heffron(IRE), whose yard returned to form with a bang the previous day, made a couple of early blunders and was quickly beaten off. (op 4-1)
Zacharova(IRE) has now refused to race on consecutive occasions. (op 14-1 tchd 10-1)

Wessex King(IRE)'s jumping let him down in a major way, making several notable errors, including one at the first in the straight which effectively ended his race. (op 7-2)

4461 ARKELL'S BREWERY NOVICES' H'CAP CHASE (17 fncs) 2m 6f 110y

4:05 (4:05) (Class 3) (0-125,125) 5-Y-0+ **£3,903** (£1,146; £573; £286)

Form RPR

2-04 **1** **Meet The Critics (IRE)**[161] 1603 8-10-11 **110**................ AidanColeman 119+
(Brendan Powell) *tendency to jump rt: in rr but in tch: hdwy 13th: wnt 3rd 3 out: drvn to chal next: led sn after: styd on wl run-in* **16/1**

54U1 **2** *1 ½* **General Kutuzov (IRE)**[25] 3980 7-11-12 **125**................. LiamTreadwell 130
(Nick Gifford) *pressed ldr tl slt ld 3 out: jnd next: hdd sn after: styd on u.p run-in but no imp on wnr* **8/1**

1241 **3** *9* **Handtheprizeover**[16] 4139 6-10-0 **102**................................ PeterToole(3) 102+
(Ben Case) *mde most tl narrowly hdd 3 out: stl upsides u.p next: wknd bef last* **6/1**[3]

2455 **4** *10* **Frontier Dancer (IRE)**[41] 3672 7-11-12 **125**.................. PaddyBrennan 114
(Nigel Twiston-Davies) *chsd ldrs: hit 9th: rdn 12th: lost tch after 13th: no ch after but tk mod 4th run-in* **11/1**

0023 **5** *1 ¾* **Babysitter (IRE)**[33] 3838 8-10-13 **112**...................................... APMcCoy 101
(Jonjo O'Neill) *in rr but in tch: hmpd 10th: rdn 13th and nvr rchd ldrs: blnd and wknd 4 out: j.big 3 out and next* **9/2**[2]

000- **6** *4* **River D'Or (FR)**[370] 4303 6-11-6 **119**....................................... DarylJacob 104
(Paul Nicholls) *in tch: chsd ldrs 13th: nvr on terms and wknd 4 out* **9/2**[2]

P-33 **7** *57* **Zazamix (FR)**[21] 4050 6-11-9 **122**...................................... BarryGeraghty 53
(Nicky Henderson) *chsd ldrs: rdn 9th: wknd qckly appr 4 out* **6/1**[3]

442 **P** **Kingsmere**[28] 3919 6-11-0 **113**.. RichardJohnson —
(Henry Daly) *blnd and rr 1st: mstke 2nd: styd in rr tl hmpd 10th: t.o whn p.u bef 13th* **7/2**[1]

F633 **F** **Federstar (GER)**[7] 4334 9-10-13 **115**.........................(p) JimmyDerham(3) —
(Milton Harris) *chsd ldrs: blnd 8th: stl rt there whn fell 10th* **20/1**

5m 45.47s (-4.83) **Going Correction** -0.075s/f (Good) **9** Ran SP% **117.2**
Speed ratings: **105,104,101,97,97 95,76,—,—**
Tote Swingers: 1&2 £29.30, 1&3 £19.20, 2&3 £5.20 CSF £136.63 CT £866.59 TOTE £16.20: £4.30, £2.50, £1.50; EX 170.40.
Owner The Roysun Syndicate **Bred** W Carroll **Trained** Upper Lambourn, Berks

FOCUS
A fairly competitive novice handicap chase. The winner should go on to rate higher and the second is on the upgrade.

NOTEBOOK
Meet The Critics(IRE), who was the complete outsider on this first start over fences, had shown a couple of pieces of form over hurdles and was previously a dual point winner, so perhaps this win wasn't a total surprise, especially with the Brendan Powell yard gong well. He jumped soundly in the main and found plenty when re-pressed after the last, suggesting there's more to come. (op 14-1)
General Kutuzov(IRE) is built to carry weight and he ran a fine race off 125 on this handicap debut, staying on right the way to the line once headed. There should be further improvement to come, especially over 3m. (op 15-2 tchd 9-1)
Handtheprizeover, raised 4lb for his narrow Leicester victory, ran well to a point, but simply wasn't good enough in this better race. (op 7-1)
Frontier Dancer(IRE) is likely to remain vulnerable off this mark. (op 12-1 tchd 9-1)
Babysitter(IRE) was unable to improve for the switch to handicaps on better ground, being left behind in the straight. (op 15-2 tchd 8-1 in a place)
River D'Or(FR) travelled well for a long way on this first start in a year, but he got tired late on and ended up well held. (op 5-1)
Zazamix(FR) was disappointing and doesn't look to be progressing. (tchd 13-2)
Kingsmere, whose dam is a half-sister to the stable's former star hurdler Mighty Man, was well fancied on this first start over fences, but made a notable blunder at the first and was then later hampered. Nothing went right, so he can be given another chance. (op 12-1)
Federstar(GER) was still travelling well when coming down, but he's not a frequent winner. (op 12-1)

4462 ELLE SECURITY NOVICES' H'CAP HURDLE (8 hdls) 2m 110y

4:40 (4:40) (Class 3) (0-120,116) 4-Y-0+ **£3,903** (£1,146; £573; £286)

Form RPR

4232 **1** **The Chazer (IRE)**[29] 3897 6-11-11 **115**.............................. SamThomas 123+
(Richard Lee) *trckd ldrs: rdn and styd on fr 2 out: rdn to ld fnl 120yds: r.o strly* **7/1**

501 **2** *1* **Alcalde**[33] 3831 5-11-6 **110**... WillKennedy 115
(John Berry) *chsd ldrs: ev ch fr 3 out: chal next and slt ld u.p sn after last: hdd and no ex fnl 120yds* **5/1**[2]

1122 **3** *nk* **Rawaaj**[12] 4243 5-10-8 **98**.. JasonMaguire 103
(Donald McCain) *chsd ldrs: chal fr 4 out tl led after 3 out: nt fluent and narrowly hdd sn after last: styd on same pce* **8/1**

0054 **4** *5* **Great Hero**[33] 3840 6-11-6 **110**.. SeanQuinlan 110
(Richard Phillips) *chsd ldrs: j. slowly 4th: rdn and styd on fr 2 out to take 4th last but no imp on ldng trio* **40/1**

5026 **5** *6* **Gentle Bob (IRE)**[40] 3698 6-11-9 **113**.............................. PaddyBrennan 109
(Tom George) *in tch: hdwy to trck ldrs 3 out and nt fluent outpcd fr next* **25/1**

2-44 **6** *2 ½* **O Malley's Oscar (IRE)**[17] 4128 6-11-1 **105**.............. DominicElsworth 97
(Suzy Smith) *chsd ldrs to 3 out: sn rdn and btn* **13/2**[3]

36F5 **7** *1 ¼* **Royal And Ancient (IRE)**[34] 3820 4-10-7 **108**........(tp) JimmyDerham(3) 90
(Milton Harris) *in rr: sme hdwy appr 3 out: sn rdn: nvr rchd ldrs* **28/1**

36-0 **8** *8* **Group Leader (IRE)**[38] 3718 5-11-6 **110**........................ TimmyMurphy 92
(J R Jenkins) *in rr: pushed along and lost position 4 out: sme hdwy next: sn wknd: mstke last* **50/1**

-014 **9** *2 ¾* **Lively Fling (USA)**[34] 3820 5-11-12 **116**........................ AidanColeman 96
(Venetia Williams) *chsd ldrs: rdn and wknd 3 out* **11/1**

2-64 **10** *1* **Ardkilly Rebel (IRE)**[23] 4012 7-11-4 **108**.................. RichardJohnson 95
(Philip Hobbs) *led: blnd 4 out but retained slt advantage tl hdd after 3 out: wknd qckly* **9/1**

-452 **11** *8* **Don't Turn Bach (IRE)**[19] 4100 7-11-2 **106**................................ RWalsh 77
(Paul Nicholls) *hld up in rr: pushed along 3 out: no imp on ldrs and sn wknd* **2/1**[1]

F0F- **12** *10* **Right Stuff (FR)**[342] 3574 8-11-9 **113**................................ JamieMoore 74
(Gary Moore) *hld up in rr: hdwy to trck ldrs appr 3 out: sn wknd* **16/1**

4m 2.91s (-6.99) **Going Correction** -0.225s/f (Good)
WFA 4 from 5yo+ 7lb **12** Ran SP% **122.9**
Speed ratings (Par 107): **107,106,106,104,101 100,99,95,94,93 90,85**
Tote Swingers: 1&2 £7.20, 1&3 £6.40, 2&3 £5.10 CSF £42.85 CT £295.56 TOTE £8.40: £2.30, £2.40, £1.40; EX 47.10.
Owner Mr & Mrs C R Elliott **Bred** Frank Tobin **Trained** Byton, H'fords

FOCUS
A fairly open novice handicap hurdle and the form has a solid look.

NOTEBOOK
The Chazer(IRE), surprisingly beaten at 4-9 in a novice hurdle at Towcester latest, came out on top. The return to a sounder surface was clearly in his favour and it's possible returning to a longer trip will help coax further improvement.
Alcalde, off the mark in good style at Fakenham, looked potentially interesting off a decent mark switched to handicaps, but found one too strong. He could stay a bit further and has more to offer. Official explanation: jockey said gelding lost left fore shoe (op 7-1)
Rawaaj was up there throughout and again ran his race.
Great Hero ran his best race yet and should find a small contest at a lower level.
Gentle Bob(IRE) ran his best race yet and should find a small contest at a lower level. (op 22-1 tchd 20-1)
O Malley's Oscar(IRE) failed to last home. (op 15-2 tchd 6-1)
Ardkilly Rebel(IRE) didn't get home. (op 12-1)
Don't Turn Bach(IRE) provided Ruby Walsh with his comeback ride, but having travelled well for most of the race, he found little for pressure in the straight and was allowed to coast home in his own time. This wasn't the first time he's found little for pressure and the formerly useful bumper performer (for Willie Mullins) now has more to prove than ever. Official explanation: trainer was unable to offer any explanation as to poor run (op 9-4)

4463 RICKETY BRIDGE HUNTERS' CHASE (IN AID OF WEST BERKSHIRE MENCAP) (17 fncs) 2m 6f 110y

5:15 (5:15) (Class 6) 6-Y-0+ **£988** (£304; £152)

Form RPR

1 **1** **Fort View (IRE)**[33] 7-11-11 0...................................(p) MrRGHenderson(5) 121+
(Polly Gundry) *in rr: hdwy fr 9th: styng on whn lft in ld 13th: pushed along and styd on wl fr 2 out: readily* **16/1**

1P/5 **2** *1* **Ornais (FR)**[29] 3908 9-11-12 140..(t) MrRMahon 118+
(Paul Nicholls) *chsd ldrs: j. slowly 8th: rdn 12th: chsd wnr fr 13th: styd on u.p but a hld* **1/1**[1]

P10/ **3** *12* **Darkness**[699] 4848 12-11-13 135.................................... MrJSherwood(7) 113+
(Simon Sherwood) *chsd ldrs tl rdn and lost pl 13th: styd on again fr 3 out to take 4th after 2 out but nvr a threat: tk 3rd run-in* **7/2**[2]

/P2- **4** *2 ¼* **Back To Bid (IRE)**[13] 11-11-7 121...................................(p) MrJMahot(5) 102
(James Danahar) *in rr: hit 10th and 11th: hdwy fr 13th: styd on to take 3rd fr 3 out but no imp on ldng duo: lost 3rd run-in* **40/1**

0-21 **5** *29* **It's Like That (IRE)**[289] 406 11-12-6 114................................ MrAJBerry 88
(Jonjo O'Neill) *towards rr: hdwy 8th: chsd ldrs 13th: wknd and j. slowly 3 out* **10/1**

-2FP **6** *3* **Lisadell King (IRE)**[23] 4011 11-11-13 114.......................... MrJBanks(7) 82
(G C Maundrell) *j. poorly in rr thrght* **9/1**[3]

450- **P** **Sovereign King**[364] 4417 9-11-9 0...................................... MrMWall(3) —
(Miss C Herrington) *in tch: chsd ldrs 13th: sn wknd: t.o whn p.u bef 3 out* **14/1**

P5-P **U** **Mandingo Chief (IRE)**[22] 4026 12-12-1 92..................(p) MissCLWills(5) —
(Miss C L Wills) *racd in 2nd ntil leff in ld 3rd: stl narrow ldr whn uns rdr 13th* **100/1**

/14- **U** **Overlut (FR)**[305] 9-11-11 0.. MrPJTolman(5) —
(R Scrine) *led tl uns rdr 3rd* **14/1**

/4-P **U** **Earth Moving (IRE)**[10] 4271 11-11-5 76................. MrRobertHawker(7) —
(G E Burton) *chsd ldrs tl uns rdr 9th* **200/1**

1FP- **P** **Joaaci (IRE)**[12] 11-11-9 0... MrRHawkins(7) —
(Mrs P J Shaw) *in rr fr 7th: blnd 10th: t.o whn p.u bef 13th* **33/1**

5m 47.14s (-3.16) **Going Correction** -0.075s/f (Good) **11** Ran SP% **117.4**
Speed ratings: **102,101,97,96,86 85,—,—,—,— —**
Tote Swingers: 1&2 £4.40, 1&3 £13.70, 2&3 £2.40 CSF £34.15 TOTE £26.00: £3.60, £1.10, £1.70; EX 43.40.
Owner Guy Henderson **Bred** Noel Delahunty **Trained** Axminster, East Devon

FOCUS
A big step up from the winner in this hunter chase but the runner-up was again well below his best.

NOTEBOOK
Fort View(IRE), although below his best in points of late, was a winner on his sole previous outing in hunter chase company. Having made headway to take it up turning in, he showed too much pace for Ornais and then held on well after the last. This was a likeable effort. (op 12-1)
Ornais(FR) had been pinpointed by Nicholls as one of his leading National hopes after the weights were announced, so ought to have been up to winning this at a course where he was impressive as a novice. He stays forever and was trying his best to get back at the winner after the last, but the line was always coming too soon. The stamina demands of the National would suit, as would potentially good ground, but there's an obvious doubt as to whether he's got the class these days. (tchd 4-5)
Darkness, off since finishing 13th in the 2009 Grand National, having sustained a hairline fracture, has winning form at this course to his name and he made a satisfactory return, staying on again in third. He should be sharper next time. (op 5-1)
T/Jkpt: Not won. T/Plt: £183.80 to a £1 stake. Pool:£93,752.85 - 372.25 winning tickets. T/Qpdt: £22.40 to a £1 stake. Pool:£8,861.31 - 292 winning tickets ST

4451 DONCASTER (L-H)

Saturday, March 5

OFFICIAL GOING: Good (7.7)
Wind: light 1/2 behind Weather: overcast

4464 CORAL.CO.UK GREEN TICK WIN MORE EVERY RACE H'CAP HURDLE (11 hdls) 3m 110y

2:10 (2:10) (Class 2) (0-140,130) 4-Y-0+ **£9,757** (£2,865; £1,432; £715)

Form RPR

2236 **1** **Five Star Wilsham (IRE)**[42] 3688 7-10-13 **117**........... DominicElsworth 125+
(Jeremy Scott) *trckd ldrs gng wl: wnt cl 2nd 3 out: led appr next: drvn out run-in* **9/2**[1]

6313 **2** *2 ¼* **Doctor Foxtrot (IRE)**[15] 4196 6-10-8 **117**..................(b) GilesHawkins(5) 123
(Philip Hobbs) *prom: effrt appr 3 out: styd on to chse wnr between last 2: kpt on same pce* **12/1**

4111 **3** *9* **Bellflower Boy (IRE)**[80] 2955 8-11-10 **128**................(tp) TomScudamore 126
(Dr Richard Newland) *w ldr: led 5th: hdd appr 2 out: one pce* **14/1**

4413 **4** *2 ¾* **Awesome Freddie**[15] 4185 6-11-5 **123**.......................... RobertThornton 119+
(Alan King) *trckd ldrs: effrt 3 out: fdd run-in* **13/2**

2P41 **5** *1 ¾* **Mac Aeda**[19] 4112 7-11-10 **128**.. DougieCostello 121
(Malcolm Jefferson) *chsd ldrs: one pce fr 3 out* **6/1**[3]

1541 **6** *7* **Firm Order (IRE)**[28] 3950 6-11-4 **122**.................................. WillKennedy 109
(Paul Webber) *chsd ldrs: rdn after 8th: wknd appr 2 out* **7/1**

0201 **7** *nk* **Snake Charmer**[21] 4079 8-10-6 **110**...................................(v) DaveCrosse 103+
(Milton Harris) *in rr: hdwy 6th: chsng ldrs whn mstke: 3 out: wknd and eased appr next* **14/1**

5-51 **8** *3 ¼* **Premier Des Marais (FR)**[23] 4021 8-10-8 **117**............. JoshuaMoore(5) 99
(Gary Moore) *hld up towards rr: drvn and hdwy 8th: wknd appr 2 out* **5/1**[2]

1100 **9** *12* **Solway Sam**[85] 2870 8-11-12 **130**.. TomSiddall 100
(Lisa Harrison) *hld up in rr: hdwy 6th: lost pl appr 3 out: sn bhd* **28/1**

-100 **10** *3¾* **Moghaayer**[38] 3742 6-11-0 **118**.. AndrewTinkler 84
(Nicky Henderson) *mid-div: rdn 8th: sn wknd* **14/1**

0060 **11** *6* **Always Waining (IRE)**[10] 4285 10-11-2 **120**..................(p) BrianHughes 80
(Peter Bowen) *led to 5th: outpcd after 7th: lost pl appr 3 out: sn bhd* **40/1**

10F2 **12** *9* **Go Amwell**[15] 4185 8-11-1 **119**..(v) DenisO'Regan 70
(J R Jenkins) *in rr: detached in last: nt fluent 4th: t.o 8th* **14/1**

5m 53.0s (-22.00) **Going Correction** -0.60s/f (Firm) **12** Ran SP% **115.2**
Speed ratings (Par 109): **111,110,107,106,105 103,103,102,98,97 95,92**
Tote Swingers: 1&2 £12.40, 1&3 £25.10, 2&3 £16.50 CSF £55.83 CT £698.38 TOTE £4.90: £1.80, £5.20, £2.90; EX 60.70 Trifecta £531.20 Part won. Pool: £717.92- 0.10 winning units..
Owner Mr & Mrs Richard Organ **Bred** P O'Gorman **Trained** Brompton Regis, Somerset

FOCUS
The going remained good after a dry night, although some riders felt it was riding slower than the previous day. A fair handicap hurdle. The first two are on the upgrade and the next three were all fairly close to their marks.

NOTEBOOK
Five Star Wilsham(IRE) had been running well in defeat off this mark, but the switch to better ground enabled him to improve, as did the return to 3m. It's possible there's more to come, and the fact he was clear with the runner-up bodes well. (op 6-1)
Doctor Foxtrot(IRE), well held off 1lb higher latest, was another to improve for the return to 3m. These conditions suit him well.
Bellflower Boy(IRE), 26lb higher than when his winning run began in November, was weak in the market but actually ran well, just not being able to race on with two lower-weighted rivals. (op 10-1)
Awesome Freddie needed to have improved to win off this mark and was unable to do so. (op 6-1)
Mac Aeda is very one-paced indeed. He was going on again close home and is going to benefit from marathon trips once chasing. (op 7-1 tchd 15-2)
Firm Order(IRE) couldn't handle the 6lb rise for his Sandown win. (op 13-2 tchd 15-2)
Premier Des Marais(FR), the Huntingdon winner, was disappointing despite having to race off 10lb higher. (op 6-1)

4465 CROWN HOTEL BAWTRY NOVICES' H'CAP HURDLE (8 hdls) 2m 110y
2:40 (2:42) (Class 4) (0-105,105) 4-Y-0+ **£2,740** (£798; £399)

Form RPR

336- **1** **Coeur De Fou (FR)**[364] 4446 6-11-10 **103**...................(t) DougieCostello 109+
(Tom George) *mid-div: hdwy 5th: styd on fr 3 out: led last: drvn out* **7/1**[3]

625F **2** *1½* **J'Adhere (FR)**[34] 3834 6-11-7 **105**.................................... MrTomDavid(5) 109
(Tim Vaughan) *hld up in rr: gd hdwy 5th: led between last 2: hdd last: no ex* **10/1**

0034 **3** *3½* **Jaques Vert (FR)**[13] 4113 5-11-9 **102**.................................. BrianHughes 103
(Robert Wylie) *trckd ldrs: led appr 3 out: hdd between last 2: kpt on same pce* **7/2**[1]

4543 **4** *1¼* **Capricornus (USA)**[17] 4148 4-10-6 **100**.................(p) EdmondLinehan(7) 92
(Ferdy Murphy) *trckd ldrs: chal 3 out: one pce between last 2* **10/1**

0P-3 **5** *5* **Donny Briggs**[25] 3993 6-10-6 **85**.......................................(b) JamesReveley 80
(Tim Easterby) *chsd ldrs: one pce fr 2 out* **6/1**[2]

6231 **6** *12* **Nouailhas**[80] 2956 5-10-13 **99**.. PeterHatton(7) 83
(Reg Hollinshead) *hld up in rr: mstke 1st: sme hdwy appr 3 out: sn wknd* **9/1**

4140 **7** *3* **Folie A Deux (IRE)**[15] 4196 9-11-9 **105**..........(bt[1]) SamTwiston-Davies(3) 84
(Dr Richard Newland) *chsd ldrs: hung lft and wknd between last 2: 7th whn blnd last* **16/1**

650 **8** *hd* **Gtaab**[60] 3386 5-11-12 **105**... DominicElsworth 84
(Paul Webber) *mid-div: effrt 5th: lost pl appr next* **20/1**

60 **9** *¾* **Lil Ella (IRE)**[40] 3711 4-10-8 **95**... TomSiddall 65
(Patrick Holmes) *in rr: sme hdwy 5th: wknd appr next* **16/1**

2403 **10** *2¾* **Meridiem**[34] 3831 7-10-6 **85**... DenisO'Regan 60
(Sean Regan) *in rr: sme hdwy 5th: hung lft and wknd appr next* **22/1**

0560 **11** *40* **South Stack**[28] 3951 6-11-4 **97**... TomScudamore 32
(Michael Scudamore) *in rr: blnd 1st: t.o 3 out: eventually completed* **25/1**

660/ **P** **Pumboo (FR)**[847] 2066 8-10-8 **87**...(t) WillKennedy —
(Geoffrey Harker) *in rr: bhd fr 5th: t.o whn p.u bef next* **50/1**

000 **P** **Lindoro**[36] 3781 6-10-1 **85**..(p) BrianToomey(5) —
(Kevin M Prendergast) *led and sn wl clr: wknd 5th: hdd appr next: sn bhd: t.o whn p.u bef last* **33/1**

0-00 **F** **Steptoe**[42] 3691 6-10-6 **85**... AndrewTinkler —
(Nicky Henderson) *mid-div: drvn 5th: bhd whn fell 2 out* **10/1**

240 **P** **Tara Warrior (IRE)**[21] 4076 5-11-12 **105**................................. JoeTizzard —
(Tim Vaughan) *a in rr: drvn after 4th: t.o whn p.u bef next* **16/1**

3m 54.9s (-9.80) **Going Correction** -0.60s/f (Firm)
WFA 4 from 5yo+ 7lb **15** Ran SP% **121.8**
Speed ratings (Par 105): **99,98,96,96,93 88,86,86,86,84 66,—,—,—,—**
Tote Swingers: 1&2 £12.60, 1&3 £7.00, 2&3 £9.10 CSF £70.69 CT £292.02 TOTE £7.40: £2.50, £3.40, £2.10; EX 74.70.
Owner Lady Clarke **Bred** S C E A De La Fontaine **Trained** Slad, Gloucs

FOCUS
A moderate but competitive handicap hurdle. The winner is rated back to his 2009 form.

NOTEBOOK
Coeur De Fou(FR), whose trainer has suddenly struck form, hadn't run since Newbury on this day a year ago, but showed improved form in the refitted tongue-tie to make a winning return. He's open to further improvement and should jump a fence next season. (op 6-1)
J'Adhere(FR), a faller over fences latest, looked the winner when going on after two out, but he was unable to stay on as strongly after the last. (op 9-1)
Jaques Vert(FR), who was well backed, went on straightening for home and had his chance. (op 7-1)
Capricornus(USA) couldn't quicken on having come there going well.
Donny Briggs prefers softer ground than this and could not find and extra gear in the straight. (op 13-2 tchd 7-1)

4466 WIN MORE WITH THE CORAL.CO.UK GREEN TICK GRIMTHORPE CHASE H'CAP CHASE (19 fncs) 3m 2f
3:15 (3:16) (Class 2) 5-Y-0+ **£29,272** (£8,595; £4,297; £2,146)

Form RPR

1-21 **1** **Always Right (IRE)**[16] 4167 9-10-10 **130**.......................... JamesReveley 145+
(John Wade) *in rr: blnd 2nd: hdwy 13th: sn chsng ldrs: led 3 out: 3 l ahd last: all out* **9/2**[1]

-0P5 **2** *hd* **Lothian Falcon**[10] 4284 12-10-0 **120** oh9...............(p) RobertWalford 131
(Peter Maddison) *in rr: hdwy to chse ldrs 8th: pushed along 13th: chsd wnr 3 out: styd on run-in and almost level last 50yds: jst hld* **33/1**

3056 **3** *14* **Character Building (IRE)**[28] 3940 11-11-1 **135**.............. DougieCostello 132
(John Quinn) *prom: outpcd 12th: styd on fr 4 out: wnt modest 3rd sn after last* **9/1**

30-0 **4** *2¼* **Ogee**[112] 2358 8-11-5 **139**.. JimmyMcCarthy 137+
(Renee Robeson) *trckd ldrs: hit 5 out: sn outpcd: kpt on fr 2 out* **11/2**[3]

-502 **5** *hd* **Beat The Boys (IRE)**[28] 3948 10-11-3 **140**.......... SamTwiston-Davies(3) 134
(Nigel Twiston-Davies) *w ldrs: kpt on same pce fr 3 out* **16/1**

2P-5 **6** *16* **Killyglen (IRE)**[64] 3271 9-11-12 **146**................................... DenisO'Regan 132+
(S R B Crawford, Ire) *mde most: hdd 3 out: 4th and wkng whn mstke next* **17/2**

-41U **7** *9* **Meanus Dandy (IRE)**[104] 2543 8-11-1 **138**...................(b) IanPopham(3) 110
(Paul Nicholls) *chsd ldrs: hit 11th: drvn 13th: wknd 4 out* **7/1**

1-0F **8** *27* **Merigo (FR)**[104] 2543 10-11-3 **137**.. TomSiddall 79
(Andrew Parker) *in rr: drvn 8th: outpcd 12th: hit 14th: sn bhd: t.o* **33/1**

11-0 **P** **Ringaroses**[63] 3293 10-10-12 **132**................................(t) DominicElsworth —
(Jonjo O'Neill) *in rr: blnd 1st: j.lft: bhd fr 14th: t.o whn p.u bef 4 out* **12/1**

F-42 **P** **Minella Four Star (IRE)**[28] 3940 8-10-8 **128**................. TomScudamore —
(David Pipe) *chsd ldrs: 6th and sing to struggle whn bdly hmpd 5 out: immediately p.u* **5/1**[2]

2-12 **F** **Presenting Forever (IRE)**[85] 2871 7-11-11 **145**................. BrianHughes —
(Howard Johnson) *trckd ldrs: cl 3rd whn fell 5 out* **7/1**

6m 11.8s (-15.20) **Going Correction** -0.30s/f (Good) course record **11** Ran SP% **115.2**
Speed ratings: **111,110,106,105,105 100,98,89,—,— —**
Tote Swingers: 1&2 £26.40, 1&3 £10.20, 2&3 £64.60 CSF £120.36 CT £1265.80 TOTE £5.00: £1.90, £8.30, £2.80; EX 184.60 Trifecta £1337.20 Part won. Pool: £1807.12 - 0.20 winning units..
Owner John Wade **Bred** John Kelleher **Trained** Mordon, Co Durham
■ Stewards' Enquiry : Robert Walford two-day ban: used whip in incorrect place (19th-20th March)

FOCUS
There was no hiding place for what was a decent handicap chase, Killyglen, spurred on by Beat The Boys and Minella Four Star, ensuring it was a proper test, so it was no surprise to see the finish fought out by two horses who were ridden with restraint.

NOTEBOOK
Always Right(IRE) ◆, who won the hunter chase at Kelso on this day last year, scored in the style of a potentially very useful handicapper at that course last month and, although up 12lb, he was a well backed favourite. His jumping may have been a bit sticky through the early stages, but he'd probably never been asked to go so fast so early in a race before, and once Presenting Forever came down at the fifth-last, impeding Ogee and Minella Four Star in the process, the race looked at his mercy, with the leaders suddenly stopping. In hindsight James Reveley would probably have held on to him for a bit longer as, having jumped to the front three out, he idled late on and was very nearly caught. He can be rated better than the bare form and looks a likely candidate for the Scottish Grand National, providing the ground isn't too quick. (op 6-1)
Lothian Falcon, a veteran racing from 9lb out of the handicap, has struggled for form this season, albeit he showed a bit more over C&D latest. His excellent showing can, in large, be put down to the fact he was held up early off the strong pace, although in fairness he did join in the competition a lot sooner than the winner and was clearly aided by the cheekpieces. Clear of the remainder, this was a spirited effort. (tchd 40-1)
Character Building(IRE) is well weighted but never got close enough to challenge. A creditable seventh in last year's National, it'll presumably be straight to Aintree for him now. (op 12-1)
Ogee, kept fresh for this, had conditions to suit and held a nice early position off the pace. He was going well when making a mistake and then getting slighted impeded at five from home, being unable to make any impression in the straight thereafter. He could be another Scottish National type. (op 6-1 tchd 13-2)
Beat The Boys(IRE) sat too close to the pace and was unable to build on his last-time-out Sandown second. (op 14-1 tchd 12-1)
Killyglen(IRE) ◆, runner-up in the race off 2lb higher a year ago when with Howard Johnson, had everything in his favour for another big run, but it was clear after 2f that he was going too fast and he was out on his feet from two out. Talked of as a possible Grand National horse beforehand, there were positives to be taken from this with Aintree in mind, namely his jumping at the open ditches, and it's not hard to see him running well for a long way, as he's very much a good-ground horse who can be hard to pass if getting into his rhythm. (op 7-1 tchd 13-2)
Meanus Dandy(IRE), another slightly impeded five out, was already being ridden at that point and could make no impression in the straight. (op 8-1 tchd 13-2)
Merigo(FR) was never travelling, completing in his own time. (op 40-1)
Ringaroses Official explanation: jockey said gelding made mistakes throughout (op 6-1)
Minella Four Star(IRE) was beginning to struggle, having been up on the pace, when badly hampered by Presenting Forever at the fifth-last. (op 6-1)
Presenting Forever(IRE), 7lb higher than when runner-up to Gold Cup-bound Midnight Chase at Cheltenham in December, held a perfect sit chasing the pace on the inside, and he was still seemingly going well when getting five out all wrong and coming down. It's hoped this doesn't affect his confidence too badly. (op 6-1)

4467 GREEN TICK FOR BETTER ODDS AT CORAL.CO.UK NOVICES' HURDLE (10 hdls) 2m 3f 110y
3:50 (3:51) (Class 3) 4-Y-0+ **£4,228** (£1,241; £620; £310)

Form RPR

1P **1** **Drive Time (USA)**[35] 3806 6-11-8 0...................................... BrianHughes 125
(Howard Johnson) *trckd ldrs: effrt appr 3 out: led appr 2 out: j.lft: j.lft and hit last: styd on wl* **4/1**[3]

3P02 **2** *1½* **Lidar (FR)**[23] 4031 6-11-8 120... RobertThornton 122
(Alan King) *chsd ldr: reminders after 7th: kpt on same pce run-in* **7/2**[2]

1200 **3** *nk* **Pena Dorada (IRE)**[21] 4083 4-10-13 120........................... DenisO'Regan 114
(Mrs K Burke) *nt fluent: in rr: hdwy 7th: sn chsng ldrs: kpt on same pce appr last* **9/1**

113 **4** *7* **Vertige Dore (FR)**[74] 3056 6-11-8 0...................................... DarylJacob 115
(Paul Nicholls) *trckd ldrs: drvn appr 3 out: wknd between last 2* **10/3**[1]

1-66 **5** *1¾* **Comeragh King**[49] 3572 7-11-2 0.. JamesReveley 107
(Tim Fitzgerald) *hld up in rr: hdwy appr 3 out: sn chsng ldrs: kpt on one pce fr 2 out* **33/1**

6 **6** *nk* **Akbabend**[36] 3781 5-10-13 0..............................(t) SamTwiston-Davies(3) 109+
(Charlie Mann) *chsd ldrs: upsides 3 out: hung lft and wknd between last 2* **28/1**

2313 **7** *7* **Rio Gael (IRE)**[112] 2373 5-11-12 126..........................(p) TomScudamore 112
(Peter Bowen) *led: hdd appr 2 out: wknd appr last* **15/2**

04 **8** *14* **Sir Tamburlane (IRE)**[25] 3994 6-11-2 0................................ HenryOliver 86
(Sue Smith) *outpcd and dropped to rr 4th: bhd fr 7th: t.o 3 out* **40/1**

-322 **9** *27* **Brother Bob (IRE)**[104] 2540 5-11-2 115................................. TomSiddall 59
(Charlie Longsdon) *in rr: wnt prom 6th: drvn next: sn lost pl: t.o whn blnd 2 out* **5/1**

0-00 **10** *27* **Lureyno**[38] 3740 5-11-2 0..(tp) JimmyMcCarthy 32
(Renee Robeson) *towards rr: hdwy to chse ldrs 6th: wknd next: t.o 3 out* **100/1**

4m 37.2s (-14.10) **Going Correction** -0.60s/f (Firm) course record
WFA 4 from 5yo+ 7lb **10** Ran SP% **113.6**
Speed ratings (Par 107): **104,103,103,100,99 99,96,91,80,69**
Tote Swingers: 1&2 £3.60, 1&3 £6.90, 2&3 £5.70 CSF £17.83 TOTE £5.00: £1.70, £1.70, £2.20; EX 12.70.
Owner Andrea & Graham Wylie **Bred** Centennial Farms Mgmt Co , Inc **Trained** Billy Row, Co Durham

FOCUS
Nothing more than an ordinary novice hurdle. The first three are rated to their marks.

NOTEBOOK
Drive Time(USA) ◆, a C&D winner on debut who stopped quickly upped to Grade 2 company at Cheltenham in January, found this level much more to his liking and, despite walking through the last, won with a bit in hand. It'll be all about chasing with him next season and he looks a horse with a bright future. (tchd 7-2 and 9-2)
Lidar(FR) hasn't developed into the horse connections had hoped, but his last two efforts have been better now and it's possible he'll be a different proposition once sent chasing. (tchd 10-3 and 4-1)
Pena Dorada(IRE), receiving weight all round, had struggled in graded company the last twice, and found this easier assignment and the step up in trip to his liking. He'll be one for handicaps. (op 14-1)
Vertige Dore(FR), a winner on his only previous hurdles start, was found wanting under a penalty over this longer trip. (op 4-1 tchd 9-2)
Comeragh King will be of interest once eligible for handicaps after another run. (op 25-1)
Brother Bob(IRE) was well below par, never getting into it, and it wouldn't be a surprise to learn that something was amiss. Official explanation: trainer was unable to offer any explanation as to poor run (op 4-1)

4468 DBS SPRING SALES BUMPER (A STANDARD OPEN NATIONAL HUNT FLAT RACE) 2m 110y
4:25 (4:25) (Class 2) 4-5-Y-0
£34,585 (£11,534; £5,767; £2,880; £1,733; £1,153)

Form				RPR
2	**1**		**Montbazon (FR)**[22] 4055 4-10-8 0 ... RobertThornton (Alan King) *hld up in tch: smooth hdwy to trck ldr over 4f out: shkn up to ld over 1f out: drvn and styd on wl last 150yds* **13/8**[1]	118+
21	**2**	3 ½	**Close House**[61] 3364 4-10-12 0 ... TomScudamore (David Pipe) *w ldrs: led after 7f: hdd over 1f out: kpt on same pce* **4/1**[2]	119+
	3	1 ¼	**Captain Sunshine** 5-11-2 0 ... JackDoyle (Emma Lavelle) *in rr: reminders bnd after 2f: hdwy 6f out: chsd ldng pair 3f out: styd on fnl f* **25/1**	120+
3	**4**	11	**Magnifique Etoile**[36] 3794 4-10-1 0 ... KielanWoods(7) (Charlie Longsdon) *mid-div: hdwy 6f out: one pce fnl 3f* **66/1**	101
44	**5**	2 ¼	**Kings Lodge**[34] 3835 5-10-13 0 ... DavidBass(3) (Nicky Henderson) *chsd ldrs: one pce fnl 3f* **16/1**	107
63	**6**	3	**Theatrical Star**[61] 3372 5-11-2 0 ... JoeTizzard (Colin Tizzard) *t.k.h in mid-div: hdwy 6f out: wknd fnl 3f* **14/1**	104
2	**7**	7	**Majorica King (FR)**[58] 3406 5-11-2 0 ... DominicElsworth (Oliver Sherwood) *in rr: hdwy 6f out: nvr nr ldrs* **22/1**	97
	8	6	**Mystic Appeal (IRE)** 5-11-2 0 ... WillKennedy (Jeremy Scott) *trckd ldrs: wknd 3f out* **100/1**	91
	9	½	**Oscar Nominee (IRE)** 4-10-8 0 ... AndrewTinkler (Nicky Henderson) *in rr: hdwy and in tch 7f out: fdd fnl 4f* **7/1**[3]	83
13	**10**	9	**Kawa (FR)**[29] 3936 5-11-6 0 ... CharliePoste (Robin Dickin) *hld up in rr: hdwy 6f out: wknd 3f out* **25/1**	86
00	**11**	3 ¼	**Atlantic Pearl**[20] 4097 5-10-13 0 ... (t) DannyCook(3) (David Pipe) *in rr: bhd fnl 6f* **100/1**	78
5	**12**	4 ½	**Greywell Boy**[30] 3909 4-10-8 0 ... DarylJacob (Nick Williams) *trckd ldrs: wknd over 3f out: eased over 1f out* **14/1**	70
306	**13**	10	**Deciding Moment (IRE)**[7] 4356 5-11-2 0 ... DenisO'Regan (Ben De Haan) *hld up in rr: hdwy 6f out: lost pl over 4f out* **66/1**	64
31	**14**	½	**Hes Our Lad (IRE)**[114] 2335 5-11-1 0 ... RachaelGreen(5) (Anthony Honeyball) *hld up in rr: hdwy 6f out: hung lft and wknd over 3f out* **16/1**	67
006	**15**	18	**Next Man In (IRE)**[29] 3920 5-10-13 0 ... CharlieHuxley(3) (Alan King) *in rr: bhd and reminders 6f out: sn t.o* **100/1**	45
22	**16**	9	**D'Gigi**[38] 3752 5-10-9 0 ... JamesReveley (Keith Reveley) *in rr: sme hdwy 7f out: sn hmpd and lost pl: sn bhd and eased: t.o* **20/1**	29
2-	**17**	1 ¾	**Holme Rose**[323] 5218 5-10-2 0 ... HenryBrooke(7) (Donald McCain) *mid-div: drvn after 6f: lost pl 7f out: t.o 4f out* **14/1**	28
0	**18**	74	**Wonmorenomore (IRE)**[144] 1817 5-10-13 0 ... IanPopham(3) (Anthony Middleton) *led 7f: wknd qckly: t.o 5f out: eventually completed* **100/1**	—

3m 47.8s (-11.30) **Going Correction** -0.60s/f (Firm)
WFA 4 from 5yo 7lb **18** Ran SP% **126.1**
Speed ratings: **102,100,99,94,93 92,88,86,85,81 80,77,73,72,64 60,59,24**
Tote Swingers: 1&2 £3.10, 1&3 £21.80, 2&3 £29.10 CSF £6.78 TOTE £2.50: £1.40, £2.20, £6.40; EX 10.60.
Owner David Sewell **Bred** Pierre Julienne **Trained** Barbury Castle, Wilts

FOCUS
A valuable bumper but it was nowhere near as competitive as the field size suggested, and for the second time in three years, Alan King was responsible for the winner. The first three are all decent bumper horses.

NOTEBOOK
Montbazon(FR) travelled strongly throughout and only did what was required once in front, looking green and being value for more than the official winning margin. Unlucky not to make a winning debut at Kempton, he looks a very useful prospect and could be one for the Aintree bumper. (op 2-1)
Close House, bought for £100,000 after winning a junior bumper at Ayr in January, kicked on turning in and had everything beaten off bar the winner. This was his first try at 2m and he looks to have the scope to make a nice hurdler. (op 9-2)
Captain Sunshine ◆, one of only three newcomers in the race, is related to winners and he won't be long in getting his head in front either judging by this effort. He was keeping on right the way to the line and should have learned plenty. (op 28-1)
Magnifique Etoile proved one-paced in the straight, but again showed promise. (op 80-1)
Kings Lodge kept on again and is going to benefit from a stiffer test once sent hurdling. (op 22-1)
Theatrical Star may not win a bumper, but should improve once switched to hurdles. (tchd 16-1)
Oscar Nominee(IRE) cost £100,000 and, although lacking in the experience department, it would have been nice to see him show a bit more. (op 8-1 tchd 13-2)
D'Gigi Official explanation: jockey said mare suffered interference in running

4469 CHANTELLE LINDLEY 21ST BIRTHDAY NOVICES' CHASE (18 fncs) 3m
5:00 (5:01) (Class 4) 5-Y-0+ **£2,927** (£859; £429)

Form				RPR
656P	**1**		**Indian Pipe Dream (IRE)**[11] 1923 9-10-7 90 ... KyleJames(7) (Aytach Sadik) *wl away: mde all: pushed along 13th: styd on wl fr 2 out: 7 l ahd last: drew further clr* **16/1**[3]	117+
-331	**2**	11	**Lake Legend**[23] 4030 7-11-7 130 ... RobertThornton (Alan King) *trckd wnr: effrt 4 out: sn rdn: 3 l down whn mstke 2 out: no ch after* **4/11**[1]	116+
4432	**3**	17	**Springfield Raki**[15] 4179 7-11-0 117 ... TomScudamore (Steve Gollings) *hld up: cl up 9th: pushed along 14th: wknd 3 out* **11/4**[2]	92

6m 23.6s (11.60) **Going Correction** -0.30s/f (Good) **3** Ran SP% **105.9**
Speed ratings: **68,64,58**
CSF £23.44 TOTE £7.50; EX 17.70.
Owner A Sadik **Bred** Roger A Ryan **Trained** Wolverley, Worcs

FOCUS
A three-horse race but not the result many were expecting. The time was very slow and the winner set his own pace. He has been rated to his previous chase best with the other two below par.

NOTEBOOK
Indian Pipe Dream(IRE), the disregarded outsider of three, made all and sprinted right away to win with plenty in hand. As they went very steady, this was always going to turn into a sprint and, being a former Flat racer, he was always likely to be at an advantage. His jumping was also the most fluent of the trio, but it's highly doubtful whether a race will fall as kindly for him again. (op 14-1 tchd 11-1)
Lake Legend hadn't achieved much in winning at Taunton and his jumping was hesitant when the pace lifted. He briefly looked like getting to the winner coming to two out, but was untidy there, and soon got left behind. This was disappointing. (op 3-10 tchd 2-5)
Springfield Raki was readily dropped by the front pair and also proved rather disappointing. Perhaps a switch to handicaps will give him more of a chance. (op 7-2)

4470 CORAL.CO.UK GREEN TICK WIN MORE EVERY RACE H'CAP CHASE (12 fncs) 2m 110y
5:35 (5:35) (Class 2) (0-145,139) 5-Y-0+ **£11,709** (£3,438; £1,719; £858)

Form				RPR
4441	**1**		**Elite Land**[27] 3970 8-10-9 **124** ... DannyCook(3) (Brian Ellison) *trckd ldrs: led 7th: jnd 2 out: hld on towards fin* **15/2**	134
-F06	**2**	nk	**I'm Delilah**[28] 3953 9-11-7 **133** ... JamesReveley (Ferdy Murphy) *led to 5th: chsd wnr fr 8th: upsides 2 out: no ex nr fin* **11/2**[1]	144+
-3F0	**3**	14	**Rivaliste (FR)**[56] 3438 6-11-9 **135** ... DarylJacob (Paul Nicholls) *t.k.h: w ldr: led and blnd 5th: hdd 7th: 3rd and one pce whn mstke 3 out: hit next* **6/1**[2]	132
-406	**4**	4 ½	**King Edmund**[28] 3949 8-11-12 **138** ... DominicElsworth (Chris Gordon) *chsd ldrs: outpcd appr 4 out: blnd 2 out: kpt on* **7/1**[3]	130
12-U	**5**	1 ¼	**Silk Drum (IRE)**[49] 3565 6-11-6 **132** ... BrianHughes (Howard Johnson) *chsd ldrs: drvn 4 out: wknd last* **11/2**[1]	122
-015	**6**	1 ½	**Lease Lend**[28] 3953 8-11-12 **138** ... (tp) DougieCostello (Tim Easterby) *t.k.h in rr: mstke 2nd: sme hdwy 6th: outpcd 4 out: one pce whn hit next* **11/2**[1]	129
00P-	**7**	nk	**Beggars Cap (IRE)**[351] 4716 9-11-1 **130** ... SamTwiston-Davies(3) (Ferdy Murphy) *t.k.h in rr: hdwy 6th: sn chsng ldrs: wknd last* **25/1**	118
2-20	**8**	2 ¼	**Fred Bojangals (IRE)**[112] 2373 9-10-13 **125** ... (p) AdrianLane (Ann Hamilton) *in tch: lost pl 8th: sn bhd* **16/1**	111
0P24	**9**	3 ½	**Moon Over Miami (GER)**[28] 3949 10-11-8 **134** ... (t) TomScudamore (Charlie Mann) *prom: hit 5th: lost pl 8th: sn bhd* **12/1**	117
11F0	**P**		**Kilkenny All Star (IRE)**[8] 4324 10-10-8 **120** ... DenisO'Regan (Sue Smith) *in rr: detached last whn blnd 4th: t.o 6th: p.u bef 4 out* **12/1**	—
-2P0	**P**		**Awesome George**[74] 3060 7-11-6 **135** ... CharlieHuxley(3) (Alan King) *in rr: bhd fr 7th: t.o whn p.u bef 3 out* **16/1**	—

3m 55.8s (-9.20) **Going Correction** -0.30s/f (Good) **11** Ran SP% **115.7**
Speed ratings: **109,108,102,100,99 98,98,97,96,— —**
Tote Swingers: 1&2 £11.30, 1&3 £14.20, 2&3 £10.50 CSF £48.64 CT £265.64 TOTE £9.80: £2.30, £2.70, £2.60; EX 72.20.
Owner Dan Gilbert **Bred** T Umpleby **Trained** Norton, N Yorks

FOCUS
Two drew clear in what was a fair handicap chase. The progressive winner stepped up again and the second is rated back to his best.

NOTEBOOK
Elite Land, 7lb higher than when winning at Musselburgh, took the race by the scruff of the neck coming to five out and just did enough to hold on. Clearly progressive, he's the type who could run well at Aintree next month. (op 7-1)
I'm Delilah signalled a return to form. A previous C&D winner, she raced clear with the favourite and would probably have won had James Reveley been a bit bolder with her over the last couple of fences, slowing on her coming into the last when a big leap would probably have handed her the momentum to go on and win. (op 13-2 tchd 5-1)
Rivaliste(FR) was readily dropped by the front pair, but did keep on again.
King Edmund ◆ wasn't ridden as aggressively as usual. He certainly has more to offer and will be of interest returned to a right-handed track.
Silk Drum(IRE) is probably too high in the handicap. (op 6-1)
Lease Lend never got into it having been keen under restraint early on. (op 5-1 tchd 6-1)
T/Plt: £4,271.90 to a £1 stake. Pool:£122,307.03 - 20.90 winning tickets. T/Qpdt: £528.00 to a £1 stake. Pool:£6,779.52 - 9.50 winning tickets. WG

4165 KELSO (L-H)
Saturday, March 5

OFFICIAL GOING: Good to soft (soft in places; 6.0)
Rail on hurdles course moved out 4metres.
Wind: Slight, half behind Weather: Overcast, dry

4471 BEDMAX H'CAP CHASE (FOR THE HAMILTON MEMORIAL TROPHY) (12 fncs) 2m 1f
2:00 (2:00) (Class 4) (0-115,115) 5-Y-0+ **£3,903** (£1,146; £573; £286)

Form				RPR
-P26	**1**		**Polar Gunner**[13] 4237 14-11-6 **112** ... JamesHalliday(3) (Malcolm Jefferson) *trckd ldrs: ev ch fr 1/2-way: rdr lost briefly after 2 out: led run-in: drvn out* **18/1**	119
0130	**2**	1	**Bene Lad (IRE)**[21] 4067 9-10-6 **95** ... RichieMcGrath (Jim Goldie) *trckd ldrs: nt fluent 7th: swtchd rt appr 4 out: effrt after 2 out: styd on to take 2nd towards fin* **5/2**[1]	102+
6P25	**3**	½	**Duke Of Malfi**[24] 4001 8-10-8 **97** ... (p) PeterBuchanan (Lucinda Russell) *led: rdn 2 out: hdd run-in: one pce and lost 2nd nr fin* **7/1**	101
1233	**4**	6	**Seeyaaj**[27] 3970 11-11-9 **112** ... (t) CampbellGillies (Lucinda Russell) *bhd: nt fluent and outpcd 8th: rallied bef 2 out: one pce fr last* **5/1**[3]	111
0424	**5**	58	**Guns And Butter (IRE)**[17] 4150 9-10-11 **100** ... WilsonRenwick (Rose Dobbin) *in tch: reminders after 3rd: rallied: wknd fr 4 out: t.o* **7/1**	46
3P00	**U**		**Super Baby (FR)**[16] 4166 9-10-6 **102** ... (p) NathanMoscrop(7) (James Ewart) *pressed ldr: hit and uns rdr 2nd* **15/2**	—

F21F U Tartan Snow[9] 4305 11-11-5 115 GaryRutherford(7) —
(Stuart Coltherd) *hld up in tch: stl gng wl whn clipped heels and uns rdr bef 4 out* 7/2[2]

4m 22.0s (4.00) **Going Correction** +0.425s/f (Soft) 7 Ran SP% **109.5**
Speed ratings: **107,106,106,103,76** —,—
Tote Swingers: 1&2 £1.80, 1&3 £27.90, 2&3 £4.00 CSF £59.59 TOTE £23.80: £7.20, £1.80; EX 95.50.
Owner Mrs M E Dixon **Bred** Mrs P Nicholson **Trained** Norton, N Yorks

FOCUS
A modest contest to open with, but competitive all the same. The pace seemed respectable and the ground was described by one of the jockeys afterwards as being a bit sticky. The first two are rated pretty much to their marks.

NOTEBOOK
Polar Gunner is on a fair mark in his advancing years and put everything into the finish after getting to the front - his jockey lost a stirrup for a few strides after jumping two out. This is proof if any was needed that age does not need to be a barrier to victory if you are willing to try hard. Official explanation: trainer said regarding apparent improvement in form, gelding was suited by a stronger pace (op 14-1 tchd 20-1)
Bene Lad(IRE), back over fences after a spell hurdling this season, was close up but was outpaced before staying on well again in the final 100 yards. (op 3-1 tchd 10-3)
Duke Of Malfi, third is this race last year, deserves lots of credit for a determined performance from the front, and was battling all the way to the line. (op 13-2)
Seeyaaj was entitled to have come on for his last run, his first after a lengthy break, but got a little behind here after brushing through a few fences, and wasn't able to get into a winning position. (op 7-2)
Tartan Snow is having his fair share of bad luck recently, as he fell at the last fence on his previous start when in with every chance of winning, and was tripped up here on the flat when clipping the heels of Bene Lad. (tchd 10-3)

4472 CYRIL ALEXANDER MEMORIAL NOVICES' CHASE (12 fncs) 2m 1f
2:30 (2:30) (Class 3) 5-Y-0+ **£4,553** (£1,337; £668; £333)

Form				RPR
/3-1	**1**		**Nine Stories (IRE)**[112] 2373 6-10-12 0 WilsonRenwick (Howard Johnson) *in tch: j. bdly rt 3rd: j.rt next two: hdwy 6th: ev ch 2 out: led last: rdn and edgd lft: kpt on wl* **6/4**[1]	123+
0/5-	**2**	*2*	**Signalman**[654] 389 7-10-5 0 NathanMoscrop(7) (James Ewart) *hld up last: hit and outpcd 2nd: gd hdwy to trck ldrs 4 out: led next: blkd 2 out: hdd last: kpt on u.p* **12/1**	120+
1542	**3**	*17*	**Alfie Flits**[16] 4168 9-11-4 124 BarryKeniry (Alan Swinbank) *chsd ldrs: reminders after 6th: rallied: rdn and outpcd 3 out: no imp fr next* **11/2**[3]	109
1-40	**4**	*6*	**Hazeldene**[27] 3966 9-10-12 0 JanFaltejsek (George Charlton) *t.k.h: led 1st: j.rt and mstke 4th: hdd next: hit 6th: ev ch next: upsides whn j.rt and blkd 2 out: sn wknd* **15/2**	104
2113	**5**	*5*	**Wind Shuffle (GER)**[24] 4002 8-11-4 135 RichieMcGrath (Jim Goldie) *led to 1st: led 5th: hit 7th: hdd 3 out: rdn and wknd fr next* **2/1**[2]	101

4m 23.6s (5.60) **Going Correction** +0.425s/f (Soft) 5 Ran SP% **108.2**
Speed ratings: **103,102,94,91,88**
CSF £15.58 TOTE £2.40: £1.40, £3.70; EX 19.00.
Owner Andrea & Graham Wylie **Bred** Stefano Stivali **Trained** Billy Row, Co Durham

FOCUS
This was a race of changing fortunes, as those who raced prominently dropped out while two of the three in behind stayed on to fight out the finish. The form is rated around the first pair's hurdles form.

NOTEBOOK
Nine Stories(IRE), off since a hurdling success in mid-November, jumped out to the right at some of the fences early in the contest while travelling well, but got straighter over them the further he went. It was a nice start to his chasing career and he gave the impression he'll have plenty more improvement to come. Howard Johnson had used this race in the past for some decent horses, but this was the first one to win for him after Silk Drum (second), Degas Art (unseated), Circassian (fell) and Percussionist (second) were all beaten. (op 2-1)
Signalman hadn't been seen since running at this course in May 2009 and ran a strange race. There was a point where it looked like he was going to play no part at all in the finish, but by halfway he was cruising in behind the leaders. He understandably got tired late on but this was a thoroughly likable start over fences. (op 11-1)
Alfie Flits got well beaten by a decent sort over this C&D last time (soft ground) and failed to make any impression this time. (op 9-2)
Hazeldene, making his chasing debut, had a win at this course to his credit over hurdles (2m2f) but made too many bad errors at the fences while racing keenly to give himself any chance of winning. (op 17-2)
Wind Shuffle(GER) helped to set a good tempo but was beaten shortly after two out. He had been well beaten on his only previous try at this course over hurdles. (op 15-8 tchd 7-4)

4473 TERRY FRAME JOINERS NOVICES' HURDLE (8 hdls) 2m 110y
3:05 (3:05) (Class 4) 4-Y-0+ **£2,602** (£764; £382; £190)

Form				RPR
0122	**1**		**Pokfulham (IRE)**[17] 4149 5-11-8 115 (v) RichieMcGrath (Jim Goldie) *hld up in midfield: stdy hdwy 1/2-way: effrt bef 2 out: led run-in: drvn out* **4/1**[2]	116+
42	**2**	*1*	**Proud Times (USA)**[9] 4303 5-11-1 121 BarryKeniry (Alan Swinbank) *prom: nt fluent 4 out: effrt bef 2 out: chsd wnr run-in: kpt on u.p: hld nr fin* **5/6**[1]	109+
1	**3**	*6*	**Patterning**[22] 4056 4-11-0 0 CampbellGillies (Chris Grant) *t.k.h: cl up: led bef 3 out: hdd run-in: sn outpcd* **11/2**[3]	102
4-15	**4**	*12*	**Freddie Brown**[33] 3850 7-11-1 0 JanFaltejsek (George Charlton) *plld hrd in midfield: nt fluent 2nd: sn prom: effrt bef 2 out: flashed tail and no ex run-in* **6/1**	93
64	**5**	*1 1/2*	**Thescottishsoldier**[13] 4240 4-10-4 0 EwanWhillans(3) (Alistair Whillans) *trckd ldrs: rdn 3 out: wknd fr next* **50/1**	82
03	**6**	*5*	**Battle Honour**[22] 4056 4-10-7 0 PaddyAspell (Sue Bradburne) *led to 3 out: wknd after next* **16/1**	77
	7	*18*	**Hotgrove Boy**[223] 4-10-0 0 MrMEnnis(7) (George Foster) *midfield: outpcd 3 out: sn btn* **200/1**	61
06	**8**	*1/2*	**Udaya Klum**[18] 4132 8-10-10 0 ShaneByrne(5) (Sue Smith) *t.k.h: hld up: outpcd after 4 out: btn fnl 2* **66/1**	69
00	**9**	*21*	**Isla Patriot**[50] 3553 5-11-1 0 PeterBuchanan (N W Alexander) *hld up on outside: struggling 1/2-way: sn btn: t.o* **200/1**	50
0	**10**	*35*	**Sixties Rock**[22] 4056 4-10-4 0 JamesHalliday(3) (William Young) *in tch tl hit and wknd 3 out: t.o* **125/1**	10
00-P	**11**	*20*	**Tommy Gun**[116] 2296 5-11-1 0 (t) MichaelMcAlister (Maurice Barnes) *mstkes: t.k.h: sn bhd: struggling fr 1/2-way: t.o* **150/1**	—
0	**12**	*3 1/2*	**Long Range**[19] 4117 5-10-12 0 JamesO'Farrell(3) (Dianne Sayer) *a bhd: lost tch fr 4th: t.o* **200/1**	—
00	**P**		**Arikinui**[16] 4165 6-10-3 0 AlexanderVoy(5) (Stuart Coltherd) *prom: lost pl appr 4th: sn struggling: t.o whn p.u bef 2 out* **200/1**	—
P0	**P**		**Why Are You Asking (IRE)**[16] 4165 6-11-1 0 WilsonRenwick (Rose Dobbin) *hld up: struggling 4th: sn btn: t.o whn p.u bef 2 out* **80/1**	—
0	**P**		**Mini Melody**[16] 4171 5-10-1 0 GaryRutherford(7) (Stuart Coltherd) *a bhd: struggling 1/2-way: t.o whn p.u bef last* **200/1**	—

4m 7.50s (5.70) **Going Correction** +0.425s/f (Soft)
WFA 4 from 5yo+ 7lb 15 Ran SP% **118.7**
Speed ratings (Par 105): **103,102,99,94,93 91,82,82,72,55 46,44**,—,—,—
Tote Swingers: 1&2 £1.90, 1&3 £2.00, 2&3 £1.10 CSF £7.90 TOTE £4.40: £1.70, £1.10, £2.40; EX 8.80.
Owner Ambrose Turnbull **Bred** Killian Farm **Trained** Uplawmoor, E Renfrews

FOCUS
Nothing appeared to want to make the running so, as a result,, lots of horses took a good grip while the pace was slow. This was a fair novice hurdle for the track and the form looks sound.

NOTEBOOK
Pokfulham(IRE), back in novice company, won carrying a penalty. His experience possibly told in the final stages as he battled with the odds-on favourite to the line.
Proud Times(USA), who should have beaten the winner on BHA ratings, especially as he got weight, lost his place for a few strides and shaped like a horse that will get further. (op 10-11 tched evens in places)
Patterning won a juvenile maiden in February and looked like collecting again when he hit the front. The uphill finish may have caught him out though, and he is worth another chance on a flatter track.
Freddie Brown is a fine, big chasing type but needs to learn to settle and respect hurdles.
Thescottishsoldier reversed form with Battle Honour, on their run behind Patterning at Musselburgh, and is one to look for in handicaps.

4474 TOTESPORT.COM PREMIER CHASE (17 fncs) 2m 6f 110y
3:40 (3:40) (Class 2) 5-Y-0+ **£9,393** (£2,775; £1,387; £694; £346)

Form				RPR
3-01	**1**		**Skippers Brig (IRE)**[14] 4209 10-10-12 138 BrianHarding (Nicky Richards) *trckd ldrs: smooth hdwy bef 3 out: effrt after last: led fnl 150yds: r.o wl* **3/1**[2]	148+
1-11	**2**	*1 3/4*	**Ballabriggs (IRE)**[33] 3851 10-11-2 150 JasonMaguire (Donald McCain) *j.w: cl up: chal 7th: led 3 out: nt fluent next: rdn and hdd last 150yds: r.o* **8/13**[1]	149
1-05	**3**	*8*	**Chief Dan George (IRE)**[14] 4207 11-11-4 148 (p) PaddyAspell (James Moffatt) *led: jnd 7th: hdd 3 out: outpcd after next: plugged on run-in: nt rch first two* **9/2**[3]	144
0U-5	**4**	*9*	**Watch My Back**[133] 1958 10-10-12 142 RichieMcGrath (Ferdy Murphy) *hld up in tch: stdy hdwy 3 out: effrt whn hit last: sn wknd* **18/1**	131
PP65	**5**	*97*	**Waterski**[21] 4066 10-10-12 69 (p) AlexanderVoy (Jean McGregor) *cl up: hit and dropped to rr 12th: lost tch fr next: t.o* **200/1**	43

5m 56.3s (11.80) **Going Correction** +0.425s/f (Soft) 5 Ran SP% **110.9**
Speed ratings: **96,95,92,89,55**
CSF £5.64 TOTE £3.80: £1.80, £1.10; EX 8.80.
Owner Ashleybank Investments Limited **Bred** Kevin B Lynch **Trained** Greystoke, Cumbria

FOCUS
The two previous renewals of this race didn't have many runners, so it wasn't a surprise to see a small field. Virtually nothing happened for the first 2m, if not a bit further, so the result is unlikely to be reliable. The winner is rated to his chase mark with Ballabriggs 5lb off last season's best. He is going to need a pesonal best in the Grand National.

NOTEBOOK
Skippers Brig(IRE) ◆, a winner over hurdles last month, thrives in heavy ground, which it wasn't here, and travelled noticeably well throughout. There was a moment when it seemed as though the jockey may have waited a shade too long after the final fence to deliver his effort but, under a strong ride, he got on terms and won going away, in the manner of a horse with plenty of speed. He has an entry in the Stewart Family Spinal Research Handicap (formerly the William Hill Trophy) and the Grand National, but won't run in either unless the ground is in his favour. He also needs quite a few to come out if he is to run at Aintree, for which he is top-priced 40-1. (op 10-3 tchd 7-2)
Ballabriggs(IRE) ◆, whose trainer/owner/jockey had Cloudy Lane fall at the first in this two years previously when odds-on, ran a fine race with his ultimate aim this season in mind. Back over fences after a couple of pleasing successes in novice hurdles, he moved with menace throughout, got to the front at what looked the right time but couldn't get away from the winner. Those who have backed him for the Grand National need not worry that he was denied here and, all things considered, this was a pleasing performance. (op 8-11)
Chief Dan George(IRE) had been well beaten on his two outings this season but had cheekpieces back on, presumably in an attempt to spark a revival in form. He has a decent record at this course but was giving weight away to his rivals, so didn't run too badly in a modestly run event. Connections feel there is more to come and he certainly doesn't lack for guts under pressure. (tchd 5-1)
Watch My Back, absent since disappointing in the Old Roan Chase behind Monet's Garden, shaped with promise until being outpaced after clipping the final fence. His problem is that he is well above his last winning mark, so needs to find extra to be competitive in decent handicaps. (op 14-1 tchd 12-1)

4475 TOTEPOOL PREMIER KELSO HURDLE (NOVICES' HURDLE) (GRADE 2) (10 hdls) 2m 2f
4:15 (4:15) (Class 1) 4-Y-0+
£17,103 (£6,417; £3,213; £1,602; £804; £402)

Form				RPR
12-4	**1**		**Bold Sir Brian (IRE)**[101] 2612 5-11-1 0 PeterBuchanan (Lucinda Russell) *hld up: hdwy and in tch 4 out: effrt and led after last: rdn and styd on strly* **20/1**	131+
521	**2**	*3 3/4*	**Desert Cry (IRE)**[13] 4242 5-11-5 135 JasonMaguire (Donald McCain) *t.k.h: hld up: smooth hdwy and prom whn nt fluent 3 out: led briefly and shkn up last: kpt on same pce run-in* **9/4**[2]	133+
1-31	**3**	*4 1/2*	**Wyse Hill Teabags**[27] 3965 6-11-8 125 RichieMcGrath (Jim Goldie) *cl up: led 3 out: rdn and hdd last: sn outpcd by first two* **16/1**	130
1242	**4**	*9*	**Moon Indigo**[27] 3965 5-11-5 128 WilsonRenwick (Howard Johnson) *hld up in midfield: hit 4 out: rdn next: no imp fnl 2* **10/1**	119
/631	**5**	*6*	**Bogside (IRE)**[16] 4165 7-11-5 118 JanFaltejsek (George Charlton) *hld up in midfield: hdwy and ev ch 3 out: rdn and wknd fr last* **18/1**	113
1113	**6**	*1 1/2*	**Priceless Art (IRE)**[16] 4165 6-11-1 0 BarryKeniry (Alan Swinbank) *hld up in midfield: hit 3rd: effrt after 3 out: no ex fr next* **8/1**[3]	109
1-11	**7**	*10*	**Storm Brig**[31] 3885 6-11-5 132 BrianHarding (Alistair Whillans) *nt fluent in rr: reminders after 5th: drvn and outpcd after 4 out: nvr on terms* **6/4**[1]	106

2115 **8** *16* **Vosges (FR)**[14] 4205 4-11-0 127....................................(p) CampbellGillies 84
(James Ewart) *cl up: drvn and outpcd bef 3 out: sn n.d* **33/1**

F113 **9** *1 1/4* **Danceintothelight**[27] 3967 4-10-11 123.............................. FearghalDavis 79
(Micky Hammond) *in tch: drvn and outpcd after 6th: struggling fr next* **33/1**

1230 **10** *51* **Sunarri (IRE)**[27] 3966 7-11-5 119....................................... AlistairFindlay 42
(Jane Walton) *t.k.h: led to 3 out: sn rdn and lost pl: t.o* **50/1**

4m 32.7s (5.70) **Going Correction** +0.425s/f (Soft)
WFA 4 from 5yo+ 7lb **10** Ran SP% **114.7**
Speed ratings (Par 115): **104,102,100,96,93 93,88,81,80,58**
Tote Swingers: 1&2 £9.30, 1&3 £7.90, 2&3 £47.70 CSF £64.23 TOTE £18.10: £2.70, £1.20, £3.30; EX 64.00.
Owner A R Trotter **Bred** Heinz Pollmeier **Trained** Arlary, Perth & Kinross
■ Stewards' Enquiry : Wilson Renwick two-day ban; careless riding (19th-20th March)

FOCUS
Some smart horses have taken this contest in the past, and this year's running looked particularly competitive. The winner produced a huge step up but it looks believable. The second was 7lb off his facile Sedgefield win.

NOTEBOOK
Bold Sir Brian(IRE) ◆ beat some horses with solid form comfortably. The horse is seemingly been well regarded by connections and is a lovely, big sort, but this was a huge step up on his hurdling debut back in November. He can only get better and rates an exciting prospect. Now that he has claimed a Grade 2 success, it wouldn't be surprising to see him given a chance in the John Smith's Mersey Novices' Hurdle, the race that last year's winner Bygones Of Brid ran in behind Champion Hurdle fancy Peddlers Cross. (op 22-1)
Desert Cry(IRE) ◆, officially the highest-rated of these, was a wide-margin winner at Sedgefield on his last start after a couple of fair efforts and moved into contention here in effortless style after travelling strongly. The uphill finish may have caught him out and can easily be given another chance on a flatter course. He looks the sort for the John Smith's Top Novices' Hurdle considering the speed he shows, if connections went to Aintree. (tchd 2-1 and 12-5)
Wyse Hill Teabags was giving weight away to everything and is clearly an above-average sort. Considering he cost only 500gns as a yearling, he seemingly has surpassed all expectations considering his price tag, and should have a good future. (op 14-1)
Moon Indigo, 9lb better off with Wyse Hill Teabags on their recent Musselburgh clash, couldn't reverse the form and never looked likely to either despite keeping on. (op 14-1)
Bogside(IRE) won a novice at the course (2m) and finished in front of Priceless Art then as well, although the latter was better off at the weights this time. Fifth place doesn't really do justice to George Charlton's runner and he remains a progressive sort with a decent engine. (op 16-1)
Storm Brig, whose only defeat was when trying to give 7lb to Wyse Hill Teabags in an Ayr bumper, has looked a classy individual and his previous win had worked out really well. Up 2f in distance, he put in a lifeless performance and something must have been wrong with him. Official explanation: jockey said gelding was never travelling (op 11-8 tchd 5-4 in places)

4476 ROYAL CALEDONIAN HUNT HUNTERS' CHASE (17 fncs) 2m 6f 110y
4:50 (4:50) (Class 6) 5-Y-0+ **£1,249** (£387; £193; £96)

Form RPR

1-F1 **1** **Quotica De Poyans (FR)**[16] 4170 7-12-1 117................ MrCDawson(3) 125+
(Simon Shirley-Beavan) *mde all: hit 7th: styd on strly fr 2 out: readily* **11/8**[1]

-16F **2** *7* **Scotch Warrior**[17] 4147 7-11-7 0.................................... MrAdamNicol(7) 111
(Robert Smith) *chsd wnr thrght: effrt bef 2 out: kpt on run-in: no imp* **66/1**

511F **3** *8* **Ardnaclancy (IRE)**[14] 4211 8-11-13 119.................. MrJARichardson(5) 111
(Andrew Richardson) *midfield on outside: outpcd 4 out: hmpd 2 out: plugged on last: no ch w first two* **7/1**[3]

42-5 **4** *2* **Viking Rebel (IRE)**[28] 3956 9-11-10 122.............................. MrOGreenall 100
(W T Reed) *midfield: hdwy and prom whn hit 9th: nt fluent 4 out* **3/1**[2]

P1-2 **5** *33* **Spellchecker (IRE)**[17] 4147 7-11-7 113............... MrRichardCollinson(7) 72
(Mrs S J Stilgoe) *hld up in tch: pushed along bef 12th: outpcd next: n.d after* **9/1**

650/ **6** *1 1/2* **Joueur D'Estruval (FR)**[20] 14-11-3 0......................... MissSMDoolan(7) 67
(Wilf Storey) *hld up: hdwy and prom after 11th: blnd and outpcd 4 out: struggling fr next* **28/1**

0-34 **7** *5* **Think Lucky**[20] 8-11-11 99.................................. MrColmMcCormack(3) 66
(Mrs N Naughton) *midfield: outpcd after 11th: no imp whn hmpd 2 out* **50/1**

1200 **8** *1 1/4* **Twelve Paces**[129] 2036 10-11-7 101........................... MissLAlexander(7) 65
(N W Alexander) *bhd: outpcd fnl circ: nvr on terms* **20/1**

6540 **9** *22* **Ellandshe (IRE)**[20] 11-11-3 50...(b) MrRWilson(7) 41
(William Young) *midfield: lost pl whn blnd 10th: sn struggling: fin 10th: plcd 9th* **200/1**

0-PS **D** *1* **I See A Star**[7] 8-11-7 0..(t) MissEStead(7) —
(Miss E Stead) *in tch: outpcd 12th: sn n.d: fin 9th: disqualified and plcd last: rdr weighed in light* **50/1**

2-P3 **F** **Doc Row (IRE)**[20] 11-11-3 114..................................... MrGJCockburn(7) 85
(Miss V Renwick) *chsd ldrs: blnd 13th: 10 l 5th and outpcd whn fell 2 out* **10/1**

U- **P** **Laura's Light (IRE)**[295] 323 9-11-11 0.........................(b) MrRLindsay(7) —
(Alan J Brown) *bhd: struggling 1/2-way: t.o whn p.u bef last* **33/1**

5m 57.5s (13.00) **Going Correction** +0.425s/f (Soft) **12** Ran SP% **115.8**
Speed ratings: **94,91,88,88,76 76,74,73,65,73 —,—**
Tote Swingers: 1&2 £5.00, 1&3 £2.30, 2&3 £24.80 CSF £115.26 TOTE £1.90: £1.10, £7.30, £3.10; EX 67.30.
Owner Mrs P M Shirley-Beavan **Bred** Gilles Leblanc & Jacqueline Leblanc **Trained** Abbotrule, Borders
■ Stewards' Enquiry : Miss E Stead three-day ban; weighted in light (20th-22th March)

FOCUS
A race won by Always Right last year, who won the featured Grimthorpe Chase earlier in the afternoon at Doncaster. This year's winner is an above average hunter who can probably rate higher.

NOTEBOOK
Quotica De Poyans(FR), who was still engaged in the Premier Chase earlier on the card at the overnight stage, will surely win more of these types of races but must be worth a try in a handicap soon off what will be an attractive mark if his jumping holds out. (tchd 11-10 and 13-8 in a place)
Scotch Warrior reversed form with Ardnaclancy on their meeting at Hexham last June and looks up to winning a race of this nature. (op 50-1)
Ardnaclancy(IRE) got behind and had little chance of getting involved with a winning chance. (op 10-1)
Viking Rebel(IRE) hasn't won over fences since coming under rules after landing a couple of hurdles for Nicky Richards, and could only find one pace for pressure. (op 4-1 tchd 9-2)

4477 VOICE OF RUGBY H'CAP HURDLE (11 hdls) 2m 6f 110y
5:25 (5:26) (Class 4) (0-110,109) 4-Y-0+ **£2,602** (£764; £382; £190)

Form RPR

6F4 **1** **Golfer's Crossing (IRE)**[33] 3851 8-11-12 109............... CampbellGillies 123+
(Lucinda Russell) *mde virtually all: rdn and styd on strly fr 2 out* **10/1**

5F20 **2** *9* **Leith Walk (IRE)**[53] 3500 8-10-2 95........................... CallumWhillans(10) 98
(Donald Whillans) *hld up: gd hdwy to chse wnr bef 2 out: rdn and no imp run-in* **10/1**

0412 **3** *11* **Kings Guard (IRE)**[21] 4068 8-10-10 96.......................... EwanWhillans(3) 91+
(Alistair Whillans) *hld up: hdwy and prom 1/2-way: effrt and rdn bef 2 out: one pce fr last* **5/2**[1]

201 **4** *4* **Everaard (USA)**[38] 3750 5-11-9 106...............................(p) JasonMaguire 97
(Kate Walton) *hld up: hdwy and in tch 3 out: rdn whn nt fluent next: sn no imp* **6/1**[2]

6656 **5** *1/2* **Bertie Milan (IRE)**[33] 3852 6-11-8 105................................. PaddyAspell 94
(Sue Bradburne) *towards rr: drvn along 1/2-way: effrt bef 2 out: nvr able to chal* **14/1**

/PP6 **6** *2* **Role On (IRE)**[38] 3751 9-11-10 107...............................(t) WilsonRenwick 97
(Rose Dobbin) *prom: rdn and outpcd whn hmpd 2 out: sn wknd* **16/1**

/-U6 **7** *hd* **Crop Walker (IRE)**[11] 4276 9-11-5 102........................... RichieMcGrath 89
(Kate Walton) *midfield: outpcd 4 out: n.d after* **16/1**

-200 **8** *9* **Tahiti Pearl (IRE)**[41] 3693 7-11-0 102.............................. ShaneByrne(5) 81
(Sue Smith) *t.k.h: w ldr tl wknd fr 2 out* **10/1**

4205 **9** *13* **What A Dream**[21] 4067 5-11-3 100....................................... JanFaltejsek 67
(William Amos) *plld hrd: prom tl rdn and wknd appr 2 out* **7/1**[3]

-P00 **10** *2* **Northern Flame (IRE)**[24] 3999 6-10-12 95..................... PeterBuchanan 60
(N W Alexander) *in tch: outpcd and dropped to rr 1/2-way: n.d after* **40/1**

5-0 **11** *1 3/4* **Suprise Vendor (IRE)**[16] 4166 5-11-0 104................. GaryRutherford(7) 68
(Stuart Coltherd) *hld up: effrt whn nt fluent 3 out: sn rdn and btn* **33/1**

-P6P **12** *2 1/4* **Witness Run (IRE)**[247] 875 11-10-0 83 oh3..............(t) TomMessenger 45
(Sandy Thomson) *in tch on outside: struggling after 4 out: btn after next* **66/1**

650P **13** *25* **Goffa Crag**[53] 3502 7-11-3 100.. FearghalDavis 39
(Nicky Richards) *trckd ldrs: blnd bdly 4 out: sn struggling: t.o* **33/1**

3600 **F** **Moufatango (FR)**[33] 3851 5-11-3 100................................ BrianHarding 89
(Nicky Richards) *hld up in midfield: stdy hdwy bef 3 out: disputing 4th and 4 l down whn fell next* **11/1**

5m 47.8s (6.80) **Going Correction** +0.425s/f (Soft) **14** Ran SP% **119.2**
Speed ratings (Par 105): **105,101,98,96,96 95,95,92,88,87 86,85,77,—**
Tote Swingers: 1&2 £29.40, 1&3 £4.00, 2&3 £31.10 CSF £102.69 CT £331.14 TOTE £7.90: £2.90, £2.90, £1.40; EX 107.20.
Owner Lord Leigh **Bred** Damien Crowe **Trained** Arlary, Perth & Kinross

FOCUS
This didn't look the easiest race to work out but it was won in good style by Golfer's Crossing, who produced a big step up.

NOTEBOOK
Golfer's Crossing(IRE) ◆ hadn't been completely disgraced on his return to hurdling last time behind Ballabriggs and won easily. Judged on this effort, he is one to have on side next time, whether it's over hurdles or fences. (op 9-1)
Leith Walk(IRE), who travelled really strongly, was only 1lb above her last winning mark, and ran well. She clearly bumped into a horse in front of the handicapper and had no chance of winning despite getting loads of weight. (op 9-1)
Kings Guard(IRE), who was checked over by the vet at the start after appearing to get kicked, was at least a proven winner, albeit at a low level, and plugged on after being held up. (tchd 9-4)
Everaard(USA), raised 13lb for winning a 3m contest at Musselburgh, made an early mistake and always looked to be struggling to make up ground when his jockey worked his way through runners. (op 11-2 tchd 5-1)
Bertie Milan(IRE), swiftly returned to hurdles after one try over fences under rules, was hard ridden some way out and only made progress past horses when some were tiring. (op 16-1)
What A Dream had nothing left after pulling hard. (op 15-2 tchd 8-1)
Moufatango(FR) was making his handicap debut at a lowly level, and may have made a challenge for a place had he not come down after jumping two out. (op 16-1)
T/Plt: £58.00 to a £1 stake. Pool:£60,267.97 - 758.47 winning tickets. T/Qpdt: £4.50 to a £1 stake. Pool:£5,2114.49 - 847.68 winning tickets. RY

4350 KEMPTON (R-H)
Saturday, March 5

OFFICIAL GOING: Good (good to soft in places)
All bends moved out 4m to provide fresh ground and all distances as advertised.
Wind: Fresh, across Weather: Mostly cloudy, cold

4478 BETFRED "WHEN BOTH TEAMS SCORE..." NOVICES' HURDLE (8 hdls) 2m
1:45 (1:45) (Class 4) 4-Y-0+ **£2,602** (£764; £382; £190)

Form RPR

050 **1** **Smart Catch (IRE)**[14] 4203 5-11-1 0............................ WayneHutchinson 107+
(Tony Carroll) *trckd ldrs: pushed along and effrt 2 out: led bef last: styd on wl* **66/1**

50 **2** *3 1/2* **Cleaver**[49] 3556 10-11-1 0... LiamTreadwell 105+
(Lady Herries) *t.k.h: led to 3 out: nt qckn w hd at awkward angle bef next: styd on again fr last to take 2nd nr fin* **33/1**

2 **3** *2* **Silicium (FR)**[47] 3599 5-11-1 0... BarryGeraghty 102
(Nicky Henderson) *pressed ldr: led 3 out: shkn up and pressed bef next: hdd bef last: wknd flat* **4/9**[1]

-U06 **4** *2 1/2* **Somewhatinevitable (IRE)**[38] 3740 6-11-1 0....................... SamJones 100
(Paul Webber) *t.k.h: hld up in rr: swift move fr 5th to press ldr 3 out: pushed along and upsides 2 out: wknd last* **11/1**[3]

- **5** *4* **King Supreme (IRE)**[13] 6-10-12 0.................................. JimmyDerham(3) 97
(Richard Hannon) *patiently rdn in rr: hit 4th hrd: sltly outpcd after 3 out: shkn up and kpt on same pce fr next: nt disgracd* **25/1**

-2 **6** *1 1/4* **Spirit D'Armor (FR)**[27] 3964 5-10-10 0.................................. RTDunne(5) 95
(Venetia Williams) *several fiddly mstkes: hld up: moved up to threaten on long run to 2 out: sn outpcd: shufed along and one pce after* **8/1**[2]

7 *14* **Laudatory**[158] 5-11-1 0.. GerardTumelty 83
(Charlie Morlock) *in tch tl wknd on long run after 3 out: no ch next* **11/1**[3]

00P **8** *28* **Track Star (IRE)**[102] 2594 6-11-1 0....................................(t) RodiGreene 57
(Luke Dace) *hld up last: lost tch 5th: sn t.o* **100/1**

9 *15* **The Wonga Coup (IRE)**[34] 4-10-7 0.................................... ColinBolger 36
(Pat Phelan) *t.k.h: j. erractically: in tch to 3 out: wknd: t.o* **80/1**

F **Akinndi (IRE)**[500] 4-10-7 0.. PaulMoloney 75
(Evan Williams) *t.k.h: trckd ldrs: lost grnd bef 2 out: 12 l 7th and wkng qckly last: fell 75yds out* **8/1**[2]

4m 0.50s (0.50) **Going Correction** -0.375s/f (Good)
WFA 4 from 5yo+ 7lb **10** Ran SP% **118.6**
Speed ratings (Par 105): **83,81,80,79,77 76,69,55,47,—**
toteswingers:1&2 £30.30, 2&3 £6.30, 1&3 £13.20 CSF £1257.12 TOTE £100.70: £11.70, £6.40, £1.10; EX 1611.00.
Owner Cover Point Racing **Bred** His Highness The Aga Khan's Studs S C **Trained** Cropthorne, Worcs

FOCUS
The bends had been moved out on to fresh ground since last week's meeting, but the distances reportedly remained the same and jockeys reported the going to be 'dead'. Two horses fought for the initial lead but the pace was not too strong and they remained there at the finish, though both had to give way to an unconsidered 66-1 shot. The time was slow and this is weak form for the track, rated around the second and fourth.

NOTEBOOK
Smart Catch(IRE) left all previous form behind to spring something of a shock for connections, although the manner of his victory suggested he won on merit. Just fractionally outpaced leaving the back straight, he was soon in the mix of challengers and stayed on in determined fashion for a convincing success. Whether he will scale the same heights as last year's winner, the recent Pendil Novice Chase victor Captain Chris, is debatable, but he has enough speed and stamina to pay his way over hurdles. (tchd 100-1)
Cleaver was keen to lead and a bit too free during the race, and he began to pay the price when swamped entering the straight, but he got a second wind and stayed on again. His attitude is a little wayward, though at ten years old he is unlikely to change now, but his jumping was better here and he showed enough ability to be able to score over a longer trip.
Silicium(FR) was all the rage, with the market expecting him to come on for his debut run in the mud over at Fakenham over 2m4f. He was too free disputing the lead and has an awkward head carriage, but he still held a chance at the last before those earlier efforts looked to take their toll. (op 4-7, tchd 4-6 in a place and 8-13 in places)
Somewhatinevitable(IRE) travelled best of all to the home turn but faded in the straight. He might do better now he is qualified for handicaps, but might need faster ground to help him see out the minimum trip. (op 9-1)
King Supreme(IRE) put up a fair performance for his hurdling debut but he jumped a little too carefully. (tchd 33-1)
Spirit D'Armor(FR) was not fluent enough on his hurdling debut, but does have some ability if he can improve his jumping.

4479 BETFRED "...IT'S GOALS GALORE" NOVICES' HURDLE (10 hdls) 2m 5f
2:15 (2:16) (Class 4) 4-Y-0+ **£2,602** (£764; £382; £190)

Form RPR
5222 **1** **Araldur (FR)**[20] 4091 7-11-2 125 WayneHutchinson 127+
(Alan King) *t.k.h: hld up in rr: prog to trck ldrs after 7th: effrt bef 2 out: led bef last where mstke: hrd pressed and rdr dropped whip 150yds out: styd on wl* **5/2**[2]
2002 **2** *1 ¼* **Oscar Papa**[22] 4051 6-11-2 125 LiamTreadwell 123
(Nick Gifford) *led 4th to next: w ldr tl led again sn after 3 out: narrowly hdd bef 2 out: stl chalng whn mstke last: upsides briefly flat: hld whn rdr dropped whip 75yds out* **9/2**
21-1 **3** *3 ¼* **Buck Mulligan**[56] 3448 6-11-8 124 PaulMoloney 126
(Evan Williams) *t.k.h: hld up in last pair: gd prog bef 3 out to join ldrs: narrow ld bef 2 out: hdd between bef last: nt qckn* **3/1**[3]
2 **4** *25* **Oasis Knight (IRE)**[21] 4069 5-11-2 0 BarryGeraghty 98
(Nicky Henderson) *trckd ldrs: cl 3rd whn mstke 3 out and lost pl: sn pushed along and steadily lost tch w ldrs* **2/1**[1]
5 *½* **Only Witness (IRE)**[104] 6-11-2 0 SamJones 97
(Brendan Powell) *hld up: prog to trck ldrs 6th: rdn and cl enough after 3 out: sn wknd* **33/1**
50P5 **6** *19* **Eldred (IRE)**[14] 4203 5-11-2 0 FelixDeGiles 80
(Nicky Henderson) *t.k.h: in tch to 7th: sn struggling: t.o* **33/1**
P **7** *16* **Rebel High (IRE)**[136] 1922 7-11-2 0 DavidDennis 66
(Derek Frankland) *pressed ldrs: led 5th: mstke 7th: hdd & wknd sn after 3 out: t.o* **100/1**
8 *26* **Campden Society (IRE)**[306] 8-10-9 0 JodieMogford 35
(Peter Hiatt) *led to 4th: lost pl qckly next: t.o* **150/1**
0 **9** *63* **Rock And Ska (FR)**[34] 3842 6-11-2 0 (t) GerardTumelty —
(James Evans) *a in last: lost tch after 6th: wl t.o* **100/1**

5m 12.3s (-11.70) **Going Correction** -0.375s/f (Good) **9** Ran SP% **113.6**
Speed ratings (Par 105): **107,106,105,95,95 88,82,72,48**
toteswingers:1&2 £1.90, 2&3 £2.60, 1&3 £1.50 CSF £13.71 TOTE £3.50: £1.20, £1.10, £2.20; EX 13.90.
Owner David Sewell **Bred** Baudouin De La Motte Saint Pierre Et Al **Trained** Barbury Castle, Wilts

FOCUS
A decent renewal of this contest. The pace was just fair, and the three horses rated in the 120s battled out the finish as they came clear of the field. The fortm is sound enough.

NOTEBOOK
Araldur(FR) has been lightly raced since winning three chases at the end of 2008, and although he had not won over hurdles since his return from a layoff after fracturing his pelvis he had been running well. He jumped slowly six out and got outpaced briefly, but was soon up there challenging and, despite jumping right at the last, he dug deep to get the better of a game front-runner. He looks like he is getting back to his best and this tough campaigner should continue to do well over hurdles this season. (op 9-4 tchd 11-4)
Oscar Papa had run a couple of good races in defeat over this trip. Disputing the early lead, he came under pressure on the home turn but showed a gutsy attitude in a battle from there, just giving way near the line. He should be gaining his first hurdling success before too long. (op 7-2)
Buck Mulligan, held up early, was the third of the trio to draw clear of the rest, but he was the first to crack. Already a winner over chases and hurdles, he ran close to his mark in giving weight to higher rated horses. (op 4-1)
Oasis Knight(IRE) looked to need a step up in trip when well beaten into second on his hurdling debut behind Al Ferof at Newbury last month, but after a mistake at the last in the back straight he was readily outpaced. He might need a bit more time to get the hang of things. (op 5-2 tchd 15-8)
Only Witness(IRE), a former pointer, made some progress in the back straight before getting outpaced, but this was still an encouraging debut and he could improve on this for his in-form stable.
Rock And Ska(FR) Official explanation: jockey said gelding had a breathing problem

4480 BETFRED NOVICES' CHASE (18 fncs) 3m
2:50 (2:50) (Class 3) 5-Y-0+ **£5,204** (£1,528; £764)

Form RPR
-325 **1** **Be There In Five (IRE)**[41] 3694 7-10-12 138 FelixDeGiles 132+
(Nicky Henderson) *mostly j.w: cl up: led 15th and immediately 4 l clr: rdn and pressed briefly 2 out: styd on wl and clr again last* **9/2**[3]
4231 **2** *7* **Squadron**[23] 4023 7-11-4 129 WayneHutchinson 133
(Alan King) *often nt as fluent as rivals: cl up: mstke 15th and outpcd: tried to cl on wnr after 3 out: wl hld after 2 out: fdd* **11/8**[2]
F521 **3** *¾* **Alderluck (IRE)**[19] 4119 8-11-4 132 LiamTreadwell 135+
(Nick Gifford) *led: blnd 13th: hdd and nt fluent 15th: struggling to keep on terms after: btn whn mstke 2 out* **11/10**[1]

6m 14.8s (-0.20) **Going Correction** +0.075s/f (Yiel) **3** Ran SP% **107.9**
Speed ratings: **103,100,100**
CSF £10.37 TOTE £4.10; EX 8.00.
Owner Simon Munir **Bred** Anthony Hanahoe **Trained** Upper Lambourn, Berks

FOCUS
An interesting contest despite the paucity of runners. The winner can rate higher on hurdles form and the other two made errors.

NOTEBOOK
Be There In Five(IRE) was a smart hurdler, including a defeat of Cheltenham-bound Aiteen Thirtythree a year ago, but overall has yet to match that level as a chaser, putting in a poor round of jumping when going right-handed at Market Rasen in January, and consequently he was the outsider of the field. However, he jumped straight in the main here and was the most fluent of the trio. He did hang left a little on the bend going out for the final circuit, but otherwise had no problems, and put in a flying leap that took him to the lead at the last in the back straight. He may still need to prove he can cope jumping in bigger fields, but on this evidence this big and rangy sort looks back on track. (op 4-1)
Squadron appreciated the better ground to gain his first chasing success at Huntingdon last time, but his jumping was sticky at times on softer ground here. Although he possesses Flat speed, he jumps quite low and needs faster ground to show his best. (op 6-4 tchd 5-4)
Alderluck(IRE) set a moderate pace but after a mistake in the back straight his jumping never fully recovered. He got the better of a protracted duel with Fruity O'Rooney at Plumpton last month and is a decent performer but is just lagging behind his official mark over fences. (op 5-4 tchd 11-8)

4481 BETFRED H'CAP HURDLE (12 hdls) 3m 110y
3:25 (3:25) (Class 4) (0-115,115) 4-Y-0+ **£3,252** (£955; £477; £238)

Form RPR
004 **1** **Kasban**[103] 2581 7-10-9 105 (t) TrevorWhelan[(7)] 111+
(Luke Dace) *pressed ldr to 8th: sn pushed along: responded wl to ld after 3 out: styd on stoutly fr next* **7/1**[3]
/23- **2** *5* **Nemetan (FR)**[467] 2474 10-10-8 97 PaulMoloney 98
(Victor Dartnall) *mde most: jnd 8th: hdd after 3 out: clr w wnr bef next: kpt on but readily hld* **7/2**[2]
3440 **3** *2 ½* **Wyck Hill (IRE)**[28] 3950 7-11-3 106 RodiGreene 106
(David Bridgwater) *hld up last: mstke 9th: prog 3 out but sn rdn and outpcd: styd on fr 2 out to take 3rd nr fin* **8/1**
4242 **4** *1 ¼* **Charming Lad (IRE)**[15] 4182 6-11-12 115 JamesDavies 115
(Charlie Mann) *trckd ldrs: mstke 6th: rdn and nt qckn on long run after 3 out: wnt 3rd and mstke 2 out: no imp: one pce after* **8/1**
-5P6 **5** *1 ¼* **Thedeboftheyear**[21] 4079 7-11-3 113 DannyBurton[(7)] 110
(Chris Down) *pressed ldng pair: jnd ldr 8th: upsides and rdn 3 out: grad fdd bef next* **9/1**
0460 **6** *9* **Musical Wedge**[29] 3919 7-10-3 95 TommyPhelan[(3)] 85
(Claire Dyson) *racd wd: in tch: prog 8th: cl up and rdn 3 out: wknd bef next* **40/1**
6651 **7** *½* **Kristoffersen**[130] 2023 11-11-0 103 OwynNelmes 91
(Helen Nelmes) *settled in last pair: rdn and struggling in last after 8th: sn no ch: plugged on* **16/1**
2421 **8** *1* **Way Back When**[30] 3904 6-11-7 110 WayneHutchinson 97
(Alan King) *trckd ldrs: cl up whn mstke 3 out: sn rdn and wknd bef next* **10/3**[1]
00P3 **9** *dist* **Bobbisox (IRE)**[25] 3989 6-10-1 90 FelixDeGiles —
(Alex Hales) *trckd ldrs: lost pl 8th: wknd after next: t.o and virtually p.u bef 2 out* **15/2**

6m 14.55s (-12.95) **Going Correction** -0.375s/f (Good) **9** Ran SP% **110.1**
Speed ratings (Par 105): **105,103,102,102,101 98,98,98,—**
toteswingers:1&2 £3.00, 2&3 £6.60, 1&3 £7.30 CSF £30.02 CT £186.73 TOTE £9.40: £2.90, £2.10, £2.20; EX 29.00.
Owner J D Sells **Bred** Ardenode Stud **Trained** Five Oaks, W Sussex
■ Stewards' Enquiry : Trevor Whelan one-day ban; used whip in the wrong place (19th March)

FOCUS
Last week's Racing Post Chase hero Quinz won this race last year, but the race has been downgraded since then, although it was still a fair contest. A step up from the winner but this is not a race to get carried away with.

NOTEBOOK
Kasban, who had previously been held up in his hurdles last autumn, raced much more prominently on his return from a winter break. He began to feel the pressure in the back straight but rallied to deliver a strong and decisive run to the line. He got hampered when staying on in his last race here, causing him to require stitches afterwards, and had been raised 5lb since. He needed faster ground on the Flat and thus could be progressive over hurdles, where connections intend to keep him for a further season. (op 13-2, tchd 8-1 in places)
Nemetan(FR) ◆ had not raced since November 2009 but has since switched to a stable in grand form. He looked best suited by the stiff tests of Exeter and Towcester over fences two seasons ago, but performed with credit here, staying up with the lead until the last. He looks on an exploitable mark over hurdles. (op 11-4)
Wyck Hill(IRE) stayed on steadily in the home straight but could not get to the winner. He disappointed at Sandown last time but looks set to do better on faster ground this spring.
Charming Lad(IRE) was right there on the home turn but once again could not quite see out the trip. He won an Irish point on good ground and might need fences to bring out the best in him.
Thedeboftheyear looked well handicapped if able to come on for last month's reappearance. Racing prominently, she travelled well to the home turn but was soon struggling for pace. She might be best just watched at present. (op 11-1)
Way Back When had been admirably consistent in mares' events, but this step up to handicaps proved too much as she began to struggle down the back straight. (op 7-2 tchd 3-1 and 4-1 in places)

4482 BETFRED CASINO NOVICES' H'CAP CHASE (12 fncs) 2m
4:00 (4:01) (Class 4) (0-130,122) 5-Y-0+ **£3,998** (£1,241; £668)

Form RPR
444 **1** **Trooper Clarence**[10] 4290 7-10-6 102 PaulMoloney 112+
(Evan Williams) *sn settled bhd clr ldng pair: clsd 7th: chalng whn only one of four ldrs to jump 4 out properly and led: drew clr after 3 out: eased flat* **11/4**[1]
5331 **2** *13* **Playing With Fire (IRE)**[4] 4411 7-11-1 111 7ex FelixDeGiles 111+
(Robin Dickin) *hld up in 4th: clsd on ldrs 7th: chalng whn mstke 4 out: chsd wnr after: mstke 3 out: sn btn after: eased flat* **11/4**[1]
P143 **3** *10* **Lord Singer (FR)**[8] 4324 6-11-2 122 (b) JosephAkehurst[(10)] 110
(Gary Moore) *led in s: t.k.h: led 2nd: clr after next: mstke 4th: blnd 7th and rdr nrly off: hdd and mstke 4 out: sn wl btn in 3rd* **3/1**[2]
-024 **F** **Arctic Ben (IRE)**[37] 3765 7-11-1 111 AndrewThornton —
(Henry Daly) *led to 2nd: chsd clr ldr: clsd 7th: tk narrow ld and fell 4 out* **7/2**[3]
/50U **P** **Quinola Des Obeaux (FR)**[45] 3632 7-10-13 112 (t) TomMolloy[(3)] —
(Frank Sheridan) *hld up last: lost tch 5th: t.o next: p.u bef 8th* **12/1**

3m 58.9s (0.90) **Going Correction** +0.075s/f (Yiel) **5** Ran SP% **108.2**
Speed ratings: **100,93,88,—,—**
CSF £10.44 TOTE £3.30: £2.10, £2.70; EX 6.60.
Owner Exors of the Late P M De Wilde **Bred** E A Moorey **Trained** Llancarfan, Vale Of Glamorgan

FOCUS
With Lord Singer in the field the pace was inevitably strong but unsustainable. This was quite a weak race but the winner might be capable of better.

NOTEBOOK

Trooper Clarence appreciated the fast pace, enabling him to creep along quietly, always in touch, and he jumped adequately before eventually staying on for a comfortable success. A dual winner over hurdles in the French provinces, he broke a blood-vessel on his British chasing debut on soft ground, but showed improved form on better ground at Ludlow last time. Connections are hoping the handicapper does not overreact as the race fell apart, but he could withstand being raised a bit. (op 5-2 tchd 3-1)

Playing With Fire(IRE) put up a good performance to gain her first chasing success earlier in the week, but the combination of the penalty and proximity of that run led to her running a bit flat here, and her jumping was low at times. She ran with credit nevertheless. (op 3-1 tchd 10-3)

Lord Singer(FR) was edgy at the start and had to be led in, but then took his jockey into the lead to set a strong pace. His jumping became somewhat ragged as he got tired, and his jockey did well to remain on board after an error in the back straight, but he kept going although well beaten. His style of running and his record suggest that tight tracks are more suitable. (op 10-3 tchd 5-2)

Arctic Ben(IRE) was still going well and looked sure to play a part in the finish but knuckled on landing and somersaulted when vying for position at the fourth-last.\n\x\x \n\x\x \b Quinola Des Obeaux\p was always labouring in rear and was eventually pulled up. Official explanation: was still going well and looked sure to play a part in the finish but knuckled on landing and somersaulted when vying for position at the fourth-last.\n\x\x \n\x\x \b Quinola Des Obeaux\p was always labouring in rear and was eventually pulled up.

Quinola Des Obeaux(FR) was always labouring in rear and was eventually pulled up. Official explanation: was always labouring in rear and was eventually pulled up.

4483 BETFRED H'CAP CHASE (18 fncs) 3m

4:35 (4:35) (Class 4) (0-100,96) 5-Y-0+ **£3,252** (£955; £477; £238)

Form RPR

5414 **1** **Tuskar Rock (FR)**[14] 4219 8-11-7 **96**.......... RTDunne(5) 106+
(Venetia Williams) *pressed ldrs: wnt 2nd 12th: led and lft clr 3 out: drvn and pressed after last: hld on wl* **7/1**[3]

1610 **2** *½* **Gerrard (IRE)**[10] 4292 13-11-4 **91**.......... TomMolloy(3) 100
(Althea Barclay) *j. awkwardly 1st: settled in midfield: effrt fr 12th: rchd 5th 4 out: styd on to chse wnr 2 out: clsd last: jst hld fnl 75yds* **16/1**

-000 **3** *9* **Lambro River (IRE)**[58] 3405 6-10-12 **89**.......... EdGlassonbury(7) 90
(Alison Batchelor) *j.lft: chsd ldrs: wl in tch in 4th 4 out: trying to mount a chal whn j.lft 3 out: one pce after* **50/1**

40PP **4** *4 ½* **Silver Bay**[52] 3510 10-11-9 **93**.......... SamJones 92+
(Oliver Sherwood) *smetimes j.rt: prog fr midfield to go prom 9th: chsd ldr 10th to next: rdn in 3rd whn bmpd 3 out: steadily fdd fr next* **14/1**

-P02 **5** *6* **No Tears (IRE)**[31] 3880 8-11-9 **93**.......... WayneHutchinson 85
(Alan King) *w ldrs: led 6th: rdn whn hdd: mstke and bmpd rival 3 out: wknd* **9/2**[1]

2U41 **6** *3 ¾* **One More Dinar**[17] 4144 8-11-9 **93**.......... RodiGreene 83
(John Bryan Groucott) *many sloppy jumps in rr: effrt fr 12th: rchd 6th after 4 out but nt on terms: blnd next: no ch after* **8/1**

2430 **7** *2 ½* **Billy Murphy**[4] 4412 8-11-2 **86**.......... AndrewThornton 71
(Paul Cowley) *j.v.slowly 2nd: nvr looked happy in rr: rchd 7th 4 out but nowhere nr ldrs: no prog after* **9/1**

2545 **8** *7* **Heezagrey (IRE)**[27] 3961 8-9-13 **76**.......... MarkQuinlan(7) 55
(James Evans) *mstke 4th: a in rr: rdn 11th: no prog and struggling fr next* **12/1**

0 **9** *43* **Fairhaven (IRE)**[23] 4021 7-11-12 **96**..........(b) FelixDeGiles 36
(Charlie Longsdon) *pressed ldrs: hmpd 6th: disputing cl 3rd whn blnd 13th: wknd rapidly: t.o* **12/1**

/6F2 **F** **One And All (IRE)**[37] 3765 8-11-0 **89**.......... MattGriffiths(5) —
(Nigel Hawke) *prom: narrow ld 5th tl crashing fall next* **14/1**

03P1 **P** **Wide Receiver (IRE)**[27] 3961 8-10-8 **78**..........(vt) PaulMoloney —
(Charlie Morlock) *led to 5th: chsd ldr to 10th: wknd rapidly after next: t.o whn p.u bef 14th* **8/1**

03P2 **P** **Bob Casey (IRE)**[36] 3790 9-11-4 **88**.......... LiamTreadwell —
(Keith Goldsworthy) *wl in rr: mstke 4th: blnd 6th and then bdly hmpd: nvr really in the r after: t.o in last whn p.u bef 2 out* **11/2**[2]

6m 13.35s (-1.65) **Going Correction** +0.075s/f (Yiel) **12 Ran SP% 114.8**
Speed ratings: **105,104,101,100,98 97,96,93,79,—,—,—**
toteswingers:1&2 £26.80, 2&3 £51.00, 1&3 not won. CSF £106.28 CT £5067.46 TOTE £10.50: £2.50, £4.50, £12.00; EX 89.40.

Owner Anthony Pye-Jeary & Mel Smith **Bred** Mme Henri Devin **Trained** Kings Caple, H'fords

FOCUS

A moderate handicap but the time was good for the grade. The winner took advantage of a good mark.

NOTEBOOK

Tuskar Rock(FR) has not always seemed the strongest finisher but was able to capitalise on a falling handicap mark when clinging on at Lingfield last month. He flopped next time, although that may have come too soon, and he was just 3lb higher this time round. Racing up with the pace throughout, he repelled several challengers and had to call on all his reserves to gamely fight off the strong-finishing second. This was only his second win, but he showed some tenacity in a finish, which suggests he could win again this season. (op 13-2)

Gerrard(IRE) made steady progress but lost some momentum with a slowish jump at the last in the back straight, but came with a strong late run and very nearly got up. He is on a career-high mark, which does not give the 13-y-o much room for manoeuvre, but he does go well at this time of year. (op 14-1 tchd 12-1)

Lambro River(IRE) was up against it on this chasing debut, but he moved up to challenge around the home turn before his run flattened out. (tchd 40-1)

Silver Bay was rated 10lb higher a year ago but has struggled to last home in his subsequent 3m chases. His jumping was more assured than last time, but it fell apart as he tired up the straight. This was a step in the right direction and a drop in trip might help.

No Tears(IRE), a former winning Irish pointer had only poor form in hurdles but improved for the switch to fences and looked on a fair mark for his handicap debut. He jumped well at the head of affairs but weakened badly from the home turn. (op 7-2)

One More Dinar had been raised 12lb for winning a moderate race at Leicester last month but jumped poorly and was always struggling to get on terms with the leaders. (op 15-2)

Wide Receiver(IRE) Official explanation: jockey said gelding stopped quickly

Bob Casey(IRE) Official explanation: jockey said gelding was hampered by faller

4484 BETFRED 850 SHOPS NATIONWIDE MAIDEN OPEN NATIONAL HUNT FLAT RACE 2m

5:10 (5:10) (Class 6) 4-6-Y-0 **£1,370** (£399; £199)

Form RPR

1 **Be My Present** 4-10-1 0.......... FelixDeGiles 98+
(Charlie Longsdon) *t.k.h: hld up in tch: smooth prog 4f out: led over 2f out: rdn over 1f out: styd on wl* **15/2**[3]

2 *4* **Cape Breton** 5-11-2 0.......... PaulMoloney 107
(Patrick Chamings) *t.k.h: hld up in rr: stdy prog fr 5f out: effrt on inner to chal over 2f out: chsd wnr after: styd on but readily hld* **14/1**

35 **3** *1 ¼* **Go Set Go**[21] 4082 4-10-5 0.......... MichaelMurphy(3) 98
(James Eustace) *settled towards rr: prog on outer 4f out: rdn to chal over 2f out: kpt on same pce after* **8/1**

0 **4** *14* **Tiagra**[30] 3909 4-10-5 0.......... TomMolloy(3) 84
(Paul Webber) *sn pressed ldr: led wl over 3f out tl over 2f out: wknd* **16/1**

4 **5** *1* **Cold Knight**[49] 3569 5-11-2 0.......... WayneHutchinson 91
(Alan King) *hld up in rr: pushed along in 9th over 3f out: sn lft bhd by ldrs but plugged on* **10/3**[2]

6 **6** *5* **Robougg (IRE)**[25] 3992 5-10-13 0.......... TommyPhelan(3) 86
(Claire Dyson) *led to wl over 3f out: rdn and steadily wknd* **66/1**

6 **7** *½* **Nomansland (IRE)**[100] 2632 5-11-2 0.......... APMcCoy 86
(Nicky Henderson) *hld up in midfield: prog to threaten 4f out: wknd qckly over 2f out* **5/4**[1]

0 **8** *7* **Struanmore**[28] 3957 4-10-8 0.......... SamJones 71
(Paul Webber) *tk fierce hold early: prom tl wknd 4f out* **50/1**

5 **9** *8* **Trevis**[27] 3964 4-10-8 0.......... LiamTreadwell 63
(Peter Bull) *t.k.h: cl up tl wknd wl over 3f out* **33/1**

10 *7* **Key To Milan** 5-11-2 0.......... JamesDavies 64
(Chris Down) *in tch to 6f out: sn wknd and bhd* **40/1**

11 *66* **My Lucky Lady (IRE)** 5-10-9 0.......... DaveCrosse —
(Roger Curtis) *in tch to 6f out: wknd: wll t.o* **40/1**

3 **P** **Sircharleswatford**[27] 3964 4-10-1 0.......... GarethThomas(7) —
(Pat Phelan) *plld hrd: prom: veered bdly lft bnd after 4f: wknd rapidly 6f out: t.o whn p.u 3f out: fatally injured* **25/1**

3m 59.5s (5.10) **Going Correction** -0.375s/f (Good)
WFA 4 from 5yo 7lb **12 Ran SP% 118.1**
Speed ratings: **72,70,69,62,61 59,59,55,51,48 15,—**
CSF £98.27 TOTE £13.60: £4.00, £5.70, £1.10; EX 87.00.

Owner Mrs L Suenson-Taylor **Bred** Mrs L Suenson-Taylor **Trained** Over Norton, Oxon

FOCUS

The first three came clear of the field in this ordinary bumper. The form is rated around the third and the sixth.

NOTEBOOK

Be My Present loomed up on the home turn travelling notably well, and she quickened clear for a decisive success. She is bred for chasing but looks to have enough speed for hurdles too. This was a rare first-time-out bumper success for the stable, but it has been in good form of late. (op 8-1)

Cape Breton is well bred for the Flat and cost 150,000gns as a foal, but never made it to the track and was resold for just £9,500. He showed enough speed and stamina to offer connections encouragement for a future career over jumps. (op 12-1)

Go Set Go had enough pace to go clear of the field, but just lacked a bit of strength against older rivals. He might just need a bit of time. (op 15-2)

Tiagra led narrowly around the home turn but could not sustain it, in the process making only a small improvement on his bumper debut. (op 12-1)

Cold Knight of whom more improvement was expected after his encouraging debut at Warwick in January, but he could never get competitive. (op 11-4)

Nomansland(IRE) was once again a well-backed favourite but after making good progress in the back straight he could not go through with the effort and is becoming expensive to follow. (op 15-8)

T/Plt: £235.30 to a £1 stake. Pool of £58,582.32 - 181.73 winning tickets. T/Qpdt: £199.80 to a £1 stake. Pool of £2,592.42 - 9.60 winning tickets. JN

4458 NEWBURY (L-H)

Saturday, March 5

OFFICIAL GOING: Hurdle course - soft (good to soft in places); chase course - good to soft (soft in places)

Rail on hurdles track moved out 4m.

Wind: Moderate behind Weather: Overcast

4485 BETFAIR SUPPORTING GREATWOOD H'CAP HURDLE (10 hdls) 2m 5f

1:55 (1:55) (Class 3) (0-130,130) 4-Y-0+ **£6,505** (£1,910; £955; £477)

Form RPR

00B0 **1** **Tobago Bay**[17] 3557 6-11-4 **122**..........(b) JamieMoore 128
(Gary Moore) *w ldr tl slt ld fr 4th: wnt 5 l clr after 3 out: drvn appr last: rdn out* **12/1**

1P-4 **2** *½* **Arctic Wings (IRE)**[51] 3520 7-10-11 **120**.......... LeeEdwards(5) 126
(Tony Carroll) *t.k.h: hmpd 1st: hdwy 4 out: pushed along 3 out to dispute 2nd: chsd wnr appr 2 out: styd on u.p run-in and clsng nr fin: a jst hld* **16/1**

02F **3** *½* **Saint Are (FR)**[16] 4159 5-11-7 **125**.......... RichardJohnson 130
(Tim Vaughan) *hit 1st: in rr but in tch: mstke 6th: rdn and plenty to do 3 out: styd on after 2 out and kpt on wl run-in: gng on cl home* **5/1**[2]

3-61 **4** *13* **Sherwani Wolf (IRE)**[29] 3934 7-11-3 **121**.......... PaddyBrennan 113
(Nigel Twiston-Davies) *chsd ldrs: rdn and hit 3 out: styd on same pce u.p fr 2 out* **4/1**[1]

1-0F **5** *2* **Benbane Head (USA)**[49] 3575 7-11-7 **125**.......... WarrenMarston 117
(Martin Keighley) *in rr: hit 6th and 4 out: styd on fr 2 out: nt rch ldrs* **11/2**[3]

4-62 **6** *22* **Credit Crunched (IRE)**[29] 3918 6-10-13 **117**.......... SamThomas 88
(Alan King) *in tch: rdn 4 out: n.m.r on ins whn blnd 3 out: sn btn* **9/1**

0100 **7** *10* **Warne's Way (IRE)**[15] 4185 8-11-12 **130**..........(b) LeightonAspell 92
(Brendan Powell) *in rr but in tch: rdn 5th: sme hdwy appr 3 out: sn wknd* **25/1**

0P6P **8** *7* **Westlin' Winds (IRE)**[14] 4220 5-11-12 **130**..........(tp) MrTGreenall 81
(Charles Egerton) *chsd ldrs: rdn 4 out: wknd sn after* **50/1**

5-0F **9** *14* **Stormy Weather (FR)**[22] 4058 5-10-12 **123**..........(bt[1]) PaulGallagher(7) 60
(Howard Johnson) *chsd ldrs: disp 2nd and rdn 3 out: hung bdly lft and wknd sn after* **20/1**

211 **10** *1 ½* **Not Til Monday (IRE)**[26] 3981 5-11-1 **119**.......... TimmyMurphy 55
(J R Jenkins) *slt ld to 4th: styd pressing wnr and upsides appr 3 out: wknd sn after: eased whn no ch* **10/1**

4241 **11** *5* **Daring Origyn (FR)**[31] 3881 6-10-10 **121**..........(t) JakeGreenall(7) 52
(Richard Lee) *rdn 4 out: a in rr* **7/1**

6043 **U** **Simply Blue**[14] 4220 7-10-12 **119**.......... PeterToole(3) —
(Simon Burrough) *stmbld and uns rdr 1st* **14/1**

2PP5 **F** **Vagrant Emperor (IRE)**[14] 4220 8-11-4 **122**..........(b[1]) AidanColeman 100
(Emma Lavelle) *blnd 1st: ij tch: hit 5th: trckd ldrs 3 out: wknd next: 6th and no ch whn fell last* **11/1**

5m 2.32s (-16.68) **Going Correction** -0.725s/f (Firm) **13 Ran SP% 122.8**
Speed ratings (Par 107): **102,101,101,96,95 87,83,81,75,75 73,—,—**
toteswingers:1&2 £38.90, 2&3 £31.10, 1&3 £18.40 CSF £186.43 CT £1099.89 TOTE £16.70: £5.90, £5.50, £2.20; EX 397.40 Trifecta £569.60 Part won. Pool of £769.78 - 0.10 winning units..

Owner Heart Of The South Racing **Bred** J James **Trained** Lower Beeding, W Sussex

■ Stewards' Enquiry : Jamie Moore eight-day ban; excessive use of whip (19th-26th March)

FOCUS

The ground on the hurdles course was described as soft, good to soft in places, but the jockeys reported it as on the easy side of good. A fair handicap hurdle in which the pace was sound and the time suggested the ground was much drier than the official description.

NOTEBOOK

Tobago Bay had not won for the best part of two years but ran better than of late on Polytrack last time with the blinkers refitted. Never far away, he kicked on turning in and kept going under pressure to hold the persistent challenge of the runner-up. His form suggests he is a spring horse and he should not go up too much for this. There was a sting in the tail for his rider, as he marked the winner with his whip and picked up an eight-day ban. (op 20-1)

Arctic Wings(IRE) won the 2m hurdle on this card last season and was 2-3 at the track coming into this. Racing off 4lb higher than a year ago, he went in pursuit of the winner from the third-last and gradually ate into that rival's advantage, despite carrying his head rather high. He clearly likes it here and will be interesting if returning later in the month.

Saint Are(FR) ◆, a hurdles winner in France in June, was still in with a chance when falling last time and was making his handicap debut here. He was struggling to go the pace from an early stage but stayed on well up the straight and was overhauling the first two at the line. He should be winning before long. (op 15-2)

Sherwani Wolf(IRE), a dual bumper winner and 2m4f hurdles winner on soft, was raised 7lb by the handicapper from the mark he had then for this handicap debut. He was never far away but could keep going at only the one pace, and possibly the drying ground did not suit. (op 5-1)

Benbane Head(USA), a bumper winner on heavy and 3m1f hurdles winner on fast, was held up and could only stay on at one pace in the straight. However, he reportedly made a noise and will now have a wind operation. (op 9-2)

Credit Crunched(IRE) finished runner-up to a subsequent winner at Bangor last time and was making his handicap debut. He was kept to the inside, despite the fact that the fourth jumped across him on several occasions, and was still towards the inner when hampered three out. He ran on but the principals had gone beyond recall. (op 8-1)

Not Til Monday(IRE) had been running well and won both his hurdles starts for the yard since joining in the autumn. He made the running but was already on the retreat when hampered three out. (tchd 9-1 and 12-1 in a plave)

Vagrant Emperor(IRE), whose best effort was on his return from 18 months off over C&D in November, had disappointed since but a return here in first-time blinkers produced a better performance, despite some sketchy jumping which eventually saw him fall at the final flight. (op 12-1)

4486 BLUE SQUARE SUPPORTING GREATWOOD VETERANS' H'CAP CHASE (21 fncs) 3m 2f 110y

2:25 (2:27) (Class 2) (0-145,143)
10-Y-0+

£10,019 (£2,960; £1,480; £740; £369; £185)

Form				RPR
2322	**1**		**Regal Heights (IRE)**[14] 4221 10-10-7 **124**....................(p) PaddyBrennan (Tom George) *in rr: hit 7th: hdwy 16th and chsd ldrs next: rdn and lost pl 4 out: rdn and plenty to do 2 out: str run appr last: fin strly: led fnl 30yds* **5/1**[2]	133
-1U3	**2**	*1*	**Alderburn**[22] 4054 12-11-1 **132**........................ RichardJohnson (Henry Daly) *led: sn clr: stdd 10th: jnd 3 out: narrowly hdd 2 out: chal last: led sn after: hdd and nt qckn fnl 30yds* **12/1**	139
2U51	**3**	*3*	**Far More Serious (IRE)**[29] 3922 11-11-2 **138**.....(p) MrSWaley-Cohen[(5)] (Charlie Longsdon) *in tch: hit 4th: chsd ldr 17th: chal 3 out: slt ld next: sn rdn: hdd after last: wknd fnl 75yds* **7/1**[3]	143
-633	**4**	*2 ½*	**Ma Yahab**[14] 4221 10-10-3 **120**..(b) AidanColeman (Venetia Williams) *chsd ldrs: rdn 4 out: fnd no ex fr 2 out and styd on one pce* **9/1**	122
40U4	**5**	*20*	**Appleaday (IRE)**[45] 3629 10-10-2 **119**................................(p) TomO'Brien (Paul Webber) *chsd ldrs: rdn 17th: wknd 3 out* **15/2**	106
0642	**6**	*2 ¼*	**The Sawyer (BEL)**[14] 4200 11-11-0 **138**.................... NathanSweeney[(7)] (Bob Buckler) *chsd ldr to 17th: wknd fr 4 out* **15/2**	120
0U21	**7**	*10*	**Cornish Sett (IRE)**[42] 3687 12-11-0 **131**.......................... NickScholfield (Caroline Keevil) *j. slowly 9th: hit 12th: a in rr* **10/3**[1]	104
PPF4	**8**	*6*	**Magic Sky (FR)**[14] 4221 11-10-7 **124**................................... SeanQuinlan (Milton Harris) *hit 2nd: 3rd and 5th: hit 17th and 4 out: a in rr* **20/1**	91
00P1	**U**		**Eric's Charm (FR)**[28] 3948 13-11-12 **143**........................ LeightonAspell (Oliver Sherwood) *in rr: hdwy 9th: chsng ldrs whn stmbld and uns rdr 16th: fatally injured* **10/1**	—
/P-P	**P**		**Cane Brake (IRE)**[36] 3798 12-11-3 **134**............................(p) SamThomas (Conor O'Dwyer, Ire) *in rr: lost tch fr 10th: t.o whn p.u bef 15th* **33/1**	—
0451	**P**		**Double Dizzy**[14] 4219 10-9-12 **118**.................................... KeiranBurke[(3)] (Bob Buckler) *rdn along 13th: sn towards rr: t.o whn p.u bef last: sddle slipped* **20/1**	—

6m 33.33s (-22.67) **Going Correction** -0.60s/f (Firm) 11 Ran SP% **115.0**

Speed ratings: **109,108,107,107,101 100,97,95,—,— —**

toteswingers:1&2 £7.40, 2&3 £15.60, 1&3 £6.00 CSF £58.65 CT £419.89 TOTE £5.90: £1.80, £3.50, £2.90; EX 74.40 Trifecta £812.70 Pool: £1230.04 - 1.12 winning units..

Owner Mrs Janet Heler **Bred** Mrs R Deane **Trained** Slad, Gloucs

FOCUS

A good veterans' chase, although many of these were on long losing runs. The winner is rated to his season's best with the runner-up to his mark.

NOTEBOOK

Regal Heights(IRE) was on a long losing run but had been more consistent since cheekpieces were fitted. He had been well beaten in all five previous starts at this track and looked set to suffer the same fate again, as he was under pressure a fair way from home. However, he stayed on well in the closing stages and got to the front near the line. He is in the Grand National but is a 100-1 chance for that and may struggle to get in. (op 6-1)

Alderburn, a 3m winner around here and well suited by a flat track and good or easy going, had not won since March 2007 but was suited by the drying ground. He set off at a good pace and established a clear lead, but was given a breather around halfway. He was challenged all the way up the straight by the third but got the better of that rival at the last only to be run down by the late surge of the winner. He deserves to gain compensation and could well do so if repeating this effort. (op 9-1 tchd 8-1)

Far More Serious(IRE) likes this track (winner and second on only two previous starts here) and looked set to win when challenging the runner-up early in the straight. However, he could never get the better of that rival and faded from the last fence. This extended trip seemed to find him out. (tchd 8-1)

Ma Yahab ◆, without a win for more than three years, is well suited by good and easy ground and blinkers have helped him return to form. He had a good bit to find with today's winner on Wincanton form and finished a good deal closer, so his turn might not be far away. (op 8-1)

Appleaday(IRE) had not won for over two years and had been struggling for form but had gradually dropped in the weights, and the first-time cheekpieces helped him produce a better effort. (op 10-1)

The Sawyer(BEL) bounced back to form when staying on to finish second over 3m at Ascot last time but the combination of a 4lb higher mark and the longer trip seemed to find him out. (tchd 7-1)

Cornish Sett(IRE) dead-heated for the feature race on this card back in 2006 and his new trainer has reinvigorated him of late. However, he was struggling some way from home and never got involved. (op 9-2)

Eric's Charm(FR), last year's winner, was bidding to repeat that success off the same mark. Sadly this durable character stumbled badly on landing on the second circuit and broke a leg. He was the winner of 12 races in nine seasons racing, including two bumpers and three hurdles. (op 8-1)

Cane Brake(IRE) Official explanation: jockey said gelding was never travelling (op 8-1)

4487 WILTSHIRE COUNTY SHOW SUPPORTING GREATWOOD GOLD CUP H'CAP CHASE (GRADE 3) (16 fncs) 2m 4f

3:00 (3:00) (Class 1) 5-Y-0+

£25,654 (£9,625; £4,819; £2,403; £1,206; £603)

Form				RPR
2102	**1**		**Fine Parchment (IRE)**[21] 4077 8-10-4 **130**......................(t) PeterToole[(3)] (Charlie Mann) *chsd ldrs: wnt 2nd 4 out: led 2 out: sn rdn: hld on wl run-in* **12/1**	137
0F13	**2**	*½*	**Tail Of The Bank (IRE)**[21] 4078 8-10-10 **133**........................ LiamHeard (Laura Young) *in rr: hdwy 11th: chsd ldrs fr 12th: rdn 3 out: rallied and styd on strly run-in to chse wnr nr fin: gng on last strides* **8/1**[2]	139
5251	**3**	*1 ¾*	**Swing Bill (FR)**[14] 4221 10-10-13 **136**.............................. TimmyMurphy (David Pipe) *pressed ldr: upsides fr 9th to 12th: one pce 2 out: rallied run-in: fin wl: gng on cl home* **7/1**[1]	141
-2F4	**4**	*shd*	**Big Fella Thanks**[14] 4201 9-11-12 **149**.................................. GrahamLee (Ferdy Murphy) *in rr tl stdy hdwy fr 12th: styd on wl fr 3 out: chsd wnr last: no imp but styd on wl run-in* **8/1**[2]	153
-U53	**5**	*1*	**Prince De Beauchene (FR)**[56] 3438 8-11-1 **138**.............. SamThomas (Howard Johnson) *chsd ldrs: pushed along appr 4 out: one pce 2 out: styd on wl run-in: kpt on cl home* **16/1**	141
-120	**6**	*¾*	**Matuhi**[84] 2886 8-10-7 **135**..(t) CO'Farrell[(5)] (David Pipe) *mde most tl hdd 2 out: styd pressing ldrs tl no ex run-in* **17/2**[3]	138
-250	**7**	*6*	**Maktu**[28] 3940 9-10-10 **136**.. MichaelMurphy[(3)] (Pat Murphy) *in rr: nt fluent 10th: styd on fr 3 out: nt rch ldrs* **12/1**	133
P-F5	**8**	*1 ¾*	**Niche Market (IRE)**[98] 2673 10-11-12 **149**................................ RWalsh (Paul Nicholls) *in tch tl pushed along and dropped towards rr 11th: no ch w ldrs whn j.big 3 out* **10/1**	144
5014	**9**	*17*	**Plein Pouvoir (FR)**[22] 4054 8-10-4 **127**............................ AidanColeman (Venetia Williams) *in tch to 7th: hit 9th: wknd bef 4 out* **14/1**	110
P-P2	**10**	*56*	**Saphir Des Bois (FR)**[34] 3841 7-10-12 **135**................. RichardJohnson (Peter Bowen) *nvr jumpng w much fluency: a in rr: blnd 4 out: t.o* **12/1**	65
-244	**F**		**Take The Breeze (FR)**[15] 4187 8-11-7 **149**........................ MrRMahon[(5)] (Paul Nicholls) *in rr and hit 7th: hit 10th: no ch whn fell last* **11/1**	133
3451	**P**		**Russian Flag (FR)**[8] 4324 8-10-8 **134**............................ AlexMerriam[(3)] (Neil King) *in tch 6th: j. slowly and rr 11th: btn whn blnd 4 out: t.o whn p.u bef last* **33/1**	—
0313	**P**		**Chance Du Roy (FR)**[21] 4077 7-11-0 **137**............................ TomO'Brien (Philip Hobbs) *blnd 1st: in rr tl p.u bef 5th* **11/1**	—
4311	**P**		**Pret A Thou (FR)**[19] 4116 8-10-9 **139**.......................... HarryChalloner[(7)] (John Bryan Groucott) *chsd ldrs: hit 5th and 8th: t.o whn blnd 3 out: p.u bef next* **25/1**	—
U23U	**F**		**Ikorodu Road**[66] 3198 8-10-12 **135**................................... JohnnyFarrelly (Martin Keighley) *fell 1st* **7/1**[1]	—

4m 54.27s (-17.73) **Going Correction** -0.60s/f (Firm) 15 Ran SP% **125.9**

Speed ratings: **111,110,110,110,109 109,106,106,99,77 —,—,—,—,—**

toteswingers:1&2 £19.90, 2&3 £19.60, 1&3 £19.70 CSF £110.20 CT £744.95 TOTE £11.70: £2.70, £3.20, £3.50; EX 115.00 Trifecta £1346.40 Pool: £30768.34 - 16.91 winning units..

Owner N W A Bannister **Bred** Timothy Considine **Trained** Upper Lambourn, Berks

FOCUS

A typically competitive renewal of this quality handicap chase, although not many appeared well handicapped. The winner was close to his Warwick run, with a step forward from the second. Big Fella Thanks was only 3lb off last season's winning mark.

NOTEBOOK

Fine Parchment(IRE) ◆ has won over 3m2f but his last two successes were over this sort of trip. Although 12lb above his last winning mark, he was never far away and jumped fluently. After kicking on at the second-last, he ran on gamely once challenged on the flat. He is in the Byrne Group Plate at Cheltenham, for which he was quoted at 16-1, and, with C&D form there this season, he could be interesting, although he might struggle to get in. The Topham is his likely target now, and his good jumping should be an important factor there.

Tail Of The Bank(IRE) ◆, a lightly raced novice over fences but running against useful types such as Finian's Rainbow, was up in trip for handicap debut off 133. He ran really well, staying on strongly on the flat to make the winner pull out all the stops. He is in the Jewson but that might prove too hot for him, and a handicap at Aintree might offer better prospects. (op 9-1 tchd 10-1)

Swing Bill(FR) ◆ won a veterans' chase over slightly further last time, beating the winner of the previous race. Raised 11lb, he made the running but looked beaten early in the straight before stay on strongly in the closing stages. He is clearly in good heart and can win again before long. (op 9-1)

Big Fella Thanks ◆, who won this last year, has since moved trainers and was back seeking the double from a 2lb lower mark. He ran a fine race and looked a big danger until fading from the last. The run should set him up for another tilt at the Grand National, for which he is a best-priced 16-1. (tchd 15-2)

Prince De Beauchene(FR) stays this trip and ran well despite being 6lb above his last winning mark. He looks one to bear in mind if we get any rain. (op 14-1)

Matuhi, well suited by this sort of trip and fast ground, ran well up with the pace for a long way and was still disputing third at the last before weakening. (op 9-1 tchd 10-1)

Maktu, a dual 3m winner who handles most ground, was 13lb above his last winning mark and had been well beaten over marathon trips on his last two starts. Trying his shortest trip over fences to date, he could be aimed at the bet365 Gold Cup next month. (op 16-1)

Niche Market(IRE) had not won since taking Irish Grand National in 2009 and joined Paul Nicholls after last season's Grand National. He ran well in the Hennessy from 8lb out of the handicap when last seen but had never run over a trip this short. This should help put him right for the National. (op 14-1)

Chance Du Roy(FR) Official explanation: jockey said gelding lost his action (tchd 13-2)

Ikorodu Road came down at the first and his jumping is beginning to become a cause for concern. (tchd 13-2)

4488 LADBROKES SUPPORTING GREATWOOD H'CAP HURDLE (8 hdls) 2m 110y

3:35 (3:35) (Class 3) (0-135,135) 4-Y-0+

£7,514 (£2,220; £1,110; £555; £277; £139)

Form				RPR
-102	**1**		**Via Galilei (IRE)**[32] 3874 6-10-12 **121**................................... JamieMoore (Gary Moore) *hmpd 3rd and in rr: stdy hdwy after 4 out: trckd ldr 2 out: qcknd to ld last: drvn and styd on strly run-in* **8/1**	133

3321 **2** 2 ¼ **Pateese (FR)**[37] 3760 6-10-11 **120**................................ RichardJohnson 130
(Philip Hobbs) *chsd ldrs: lft pressing for ld 3rd tl def advantage sn after 3 out: rdn 2 out: hdd last: kpt on but no ch w wnr* **8/1**

0 **3** 6 **Sire Collonges (FR)**[42] 3676 5-11-2 **125**.................................... RWalsh 129
(Paul Nicholls) *hld up towards rr: pushed along and styd on fr 2 out: chsd ldng duo last but nvr any imp* **7/1**[3]

032 **4** 7 **King's Realm (IRE)**[10] 4288 4-9-9 **117** oh7.................... OliverDayman(5) 106
(Alison Thorpe) *chsd ldrs: rdn 3 out: styd on same pce fr next* **50/1**

P-52 **5** ½ **European Dream (IRE)**[27] 3969 8-11-2 **125**....................(p) GrahamLee 121
(Richard Fahey) *j. slowly 1st: in rr: hdwy 3 out: styd on fr 2 out but nvr rchd ldrs* **17/2**

5-65 **6** 3 ½ **Zafranagar (IRE)**[22] 4049 6-9-9 **109** oh1.......................... LeeEdwards(5) 104
(Tony Carroll) *chsd ldrs to 3 out: wknd fr 2 out* **14/1**

-155 **7** ½ **Made In Time (IRE)**[49] 3556 6-10-13 **122**............................(t) APMcCoy 114
(Rebecca Curtis) *hld up in rr: pushed along and sme prog after 3 out: nvr gng pce to rch ldrs* **5/2**[1]

2020 **8** 10 **King's Revenge**[32] 3874 8-10-1 **117**............................(b) PeterCarberry(7) 101
(Shaun Lycett) *hmpd 3rd: chsd ldrs tl wknd u.p fr 3 out* **16/1**

2301 **9** 6 **Bally Legend**[10] 4291 6-11-4 **130**.. KeiranBurke(3) 106
(Caroline Keevil) *front rnk tl lft in slt ld fr 3rd: rdn after 4 out: hdd sn after 3 out: wknd qckly* **13/2**[2]

60-P **10** 13 **Puyol (IRE)**[104] 2542 9-11-5 **135**.................................... HarryChalloner(7) 98
(Lisa Williamson) *in rr: hdwy to chse ldrs 4 out: wknd next* **33/1**

2140 **11** 17 **All For Free (IRE)**[11] 4270 5-10-13 **122**......................... WarrenMarston 68
(Milton Harris) *rdn 4th: a in rr* **40/1**

02P- **12** 7 **Meridian City (IRE)**[345] 4833 7-10-9 **125**...................... PaulGallagher(7) 64
(Howard Johnson) *chsd ldrs: rdn appr 3 out and sn btn* **33/1**

5-20 **13** 11 **Ned Ludd (IRE)**[17] 2868 8-10-8 **120**.......................(p) RichieMcLernon(3) 48
(Jonathan Portman) *chsd ldrs tl wknd qckly fr 4 out* **50/1**

0-01 **14** 2 ½ **Ellerslie Tom**[283] 469 9-11-10 **133**... DPFahy 59
(Alison Thorpe) *pressed ldr tl bdly hmpd 3rd: dropped to rr and nt rcvr: hit next* **50/1**

0631 **F** **Karky Schultz (GER)**[32] 3874 6-11-3 **126**....................... PaddyBrennan —
(James Eustace) *led tl fell 3rd: fatally injured* **10/1**

3m 54.53s (-15.37) **Going Correction** -0.725s/f (Firm)
WFA 4 from 5yo+ 7lb **15** Ran SP% **123.0**
Speed ratings (Par 107): **107,105,103,99,99 97,97,93,90,84 76,72,67,66,—**
toteswingers:1&2 £5.30, 2&3 £15.30, 1&3 £11.00 CSF £68.91 CT £476.93 TOTE £7.80: £2.30, £2.30, £3.10; EX 45.40 Trifecta £350.70 Pool: £1246.42 - 2.63 winning units..
Owner C E Stedman **Bred** J S Bolger **Trained** Lower Beeding, W Sussex

FOCUS
A decent handicap hurdle including several unexposed sorts and they dominated the finish. A step up from the winner but there may be more to come.

NOTEBOOK
Via Galilei(IRE) ◆, a winner on his handicap debut over C&D in November, was now off 13lb higher. He had run well on his previous start and was always travelling smoothly, looking the likely winner from early in the straight. He found enough to score this time, after a good jump at the last, and could be on course for the County Hurdle. (op 7-1 tchd 13-2)
Pateese(FR), placed three times over hurdles (including here) before winning ordinary maiden hurdle at Ffos Las in January, was making his handicap debut and ran with credit, although the winner always looked to have his measure. He can find a similar contest before long. (tchd 9-1 in a place)
Sire Collonges(FR), a French hurdles winner but well beaten on his British debut in January, was down in class but also in trip, and ran as if he needs a return to further, staying on steadily in the straight. Connections are looking to the future and expect him to make a staying chaser in time. (op 8-1)
King's Realm(IRE), a 2m winner on Polytrack, had finished placed in ordinary novices' hurdles and was 7lb wrong on this handicap debut. He ran with credit and should have a race in him at a modest level. (op 40-1)
European Dream(IRE) had not won for over two years but is a capable sort on flat tracks and looks to be running back into form. (op 9-1)
Zafranagar(IRE) had been running and winning mainly on the all-weather this winter and was back to 1lb above his last winning mark. He showed up well until tiring from the penultimate flight. (op 16-1 tchd 18-1)
Made In Time(IRE) winner of a bumper and runner-up to Al Ferof in a Grade 2 bumper here, had been a winner over 2m6f over hurdles but was dropped in trip for this handicap debut off 122. He looked to find this trip on drying ground too short for him. (op 3-1 tchd 10-3 and 7-2 in a place)
King's Revenge had not won for nearly four years but is capable of decent efforts at around this trip, particularly on good ground, and ran with credit. (op 18-1)
Karky Schultz(GER), who gamely beat today's winner at Taunton last time, made the running but sadly took a fatal fall at the third flight.

4489 BARRATT DAVID WILSON GREATWOOD NOVICES' HURDLE (12 hdls) 3m 110y
4:10 (4:10) (Class 4) 4-Y-0+ **£3,903** (£1,146; £573; £286)

Form RPR

P034 **1** **Russian Song (IRE)**[15] 4189 7-11-3 115........................(p) AidanColeman 122+
(Colin Tizzard) *chsd ldrs: drvn along fr 4 out: styd on u.p to ld appr last: drvn out* **10/1**

1013 **2** 3 ¼ **Camden (IRE)**[15] 4180 5-11-10 120.................................... LeightonAspell 126
(Oliver Sherwood) *w ld: led 3rd: jnd and rdn 3 out: kpt slt advantage next: hdd appr last and kpt on same pce* **8/1**[3]

2 **3** 1 ½ **Rangitoto (IRE)**[37] 3761 6-11-3 0.. RWalsh 116
(Paul Nicholls) *trckd ldrs: pushed along to chal over 3 out: stl upsides and rdn next: styd on run-in but no imp on ldng duo* **1/1**[1]

15 **4** 7 **State Benefit (IRE)**[29] 3931 6-11-10 0.............................. BarryGeraghty 117
(Nicky Henderson) *trckd ldrs: pushed along 3 out: sn no ex: btn bef next* **6/1**[2]

432 **5** 8 **Double Whammy**[32] 3866 5-11-3 119.............................. MattieBatchelor 101
(Jamie Poulton) *j. slowly 1st: in rr but in tch: rdn and dropped wl bhd 3 out: styd on u.p fr 2 out and kpt on run-in but nvr any ch* **6/1**[2]

43 **6** nk **Ravastree (IRE)**[20] 4094 5-11-3 0... SamThomas 101
(Alan King) *in rr but in tch: pushed along 4 out: dropped in rr after 3 out and no ch after* **8/1**[3]

00 **7** 14 **Traffic Chaos (IRE)**[41] 3698 6-11-0 0.................................(t) PeterToole(3) 87
(Charlie Mann) *led to 3rd: wknd bef 3 out* **50/1**

60-0 **8** 17 **Keltic Crisis (IRE)**[66] 3200 7-10-10 0.................................... MrPHarty(7) 75
(Jonathan Geake) *t.k.h: chsd ldrs: blnd 4th: wknd 4 out* **80/1**

6m 8.74s (0.44) **Going Correction** -0.725s/f (Firm) **8** Ran SP% **113.1**
Speed ratings (Par 105): **70,68,68,66,63 63,59,53**
toteswingers:1&2 £8.70, 2&3 £2.90, 1&3 £3.40 CSF £82.73 TOTE £10.20: £2.20, £2.10, £1.10; EX 69.30.
Owner John and Heather Snook **Bred** Anthony Kelleher **Trained** Milborne Port, Dorset

FOCUS
A fair stayers' novice hurdle in which most had only limited experience and the pace was steady until around halfway. The first two are on the upgrade.

NOTEBOOK
Russian Song(IRE), who had gone 14 starts without success in bumpers, hurdles and over fences, ran well over C&D in a similar race at the last meeting and proved the strongest in a three-way battle up the straight. He looks to be on the upgrade but his current official rating of 115 gives an indication of the strength of the form. (op 12-1)
Camden(IRE) ◆, rated 5lb higher than the winner but giving him 7lb, made much of the running and dictated an ordinary gallop despite being keen. He fought off the favourite but could not resist the more experienced winner. The step up in trip was no disadvantage for this point winner, and he should make a fair novice chaser next season. (op 10-1)
Rangitoto(IRE), whose trainer had the best recent record in the race, was sent off favourite. He jumped in slick fashion and came to join the leader three out, but then showed signs of greenness when asked to win his race and found little for pressure. He is not one to write off yet. Official explanation: jockey said gelding has a breathing problem (tchd 11-10 and 5-4 in a place)
State Benefit(IRE), another point winner and a 2m6f hurdles winner on good ground, failed to handle soft last time but disappointed here, having appeared to move into contention on the home turn. (tchd 5-1)
Double Whammy had shown fair form on soft ground in two previous starts but looked one-paced on this better going. (op 11-2)
Ravastree(IRE), yet another point winner, had been held on softer ground but the faster surface here did not appear the answer. (tchd 9-1)

4490 TYTO CONSULTANCY SUPPORTING GREATWOOD NOVICES' H'CAP CHASE (FOR THE JACKY UPTON TROPHY) (15 fncs) 2m 2f 110y
4:45 (4:45) (Class 3) (0-125,123) 5-Y-0+ **£5,204** (£1,528; £764; £381)

Form RPR

6-24 **1** **Cottage Acre (IRE)**[12] 4260 8-10-11 **108**......................... PaddyBrennan 124+
(Tom George) *trckd ldr: chal 7th: led next: gng clr whn hit 2 out: easily* **9/2**[2]

1UP4 **2** 12 **Rimini (FR)**[27] 3962 6-11-3 **114**.. AidanColeman 116
(David Rees) *chsd ldrs: wnt 2nd and rdn 2 out: no imp on easy wnr: styd on same pce* **15/2**

2342 **3** 3 ¾ **Lordsbridge (USA)**[17] 4140 9-11-0 **111**............................ NickScholfield 109
(Andy Turnell) *in rr hdwy 11th: rdn 3 out: styd on same pce fr next and nvr any ch w easy wnr* **4/1**[1]

5034 **4** nk **Special Occasion**[32] 3871 7-11-12 **123**................................. TomO'Brien 120
(Caroline Keevil) *rdn along in rr fr 2nd and nvr travelling: hit 4th: stl last 4 out: sme hdwy and hit 2 out: styd on u.p appr last: fin wl to take 4th cl home and clsng on 3rd* **8/1**

-3P0 **5** 1 ¼ **Our Bob (IRE)**[7] 4355 9-11-5 **116**................................(t) RichardJohnson 113
(Philip Hobbs) *chsd ldrs: hit 6th and 7th: styd on to chse wnr 4 out: no ch fr next: wknd last* **16/1**

3-1P **6** 5 **Mallusk (IRE)**[49] 3562 6-11-6 **117**... SeanQuinlan 114+
(Kim Bailey) *in rr: hit 10th effrt and blnd 11th: tried to improve again and mstke 4 out: sn wknd* **9/1**

1226 **7** 8 **In The Zone (IRE)**[66] 3198 7-11-5 **119**...................... RichieMcLernon(3) 104
(Jonjo O'Neill) *in rr: hdwy 8th: chsd ldrs fr 11th but nvr on terms: wknd next* **9/1**

5123 **8** 19 **Kack Handed**[36] 3786 8-10-9 **113**...................................... JakeGreenall(7) 90
(Henry Daly) *led: jnd 7th: narrowly hdd next: blnd 9th: chsng wnr whn blnd 11th: wknd and mstke 4 out* **13/2**

-044 **9** 39 **Gus Macrae (IRE)**[29] 3932 7-11-7 **118**...........................(t) BarryGeraghty 75
(Rebecca Curtis) *trckd ldrs: hit 2nd and 6th: blnd and dropped in rr 7th: sme hdwy 9th: wknd 11th: eased whn no ch after 4 out* **6/1**[3]

4m 36.19s (-7.81) **Going Correction** -0.60s/f (Firm) **9** Ran SP% **114.6**
Speed ratings: **92,86,85,85,84 82,79,71,54**
toteswingers:1&2 £7.10, 2&3 £5.80, 1&3 £9.00 CSF £37.67 CT £145.18 TOTE £5.80: £2.40, £3.20, £2.00; EX 51.60.
Owner Thoroughbred Ladies **Bred** S J Treacy **Trained** Slad, Gloucs

FOCUS
A tightly knit novices' handicap chase on paper but a runaway winner. He was up 10lb on his best hurdles form and should rate higher.

NOTEBOOK
Cottage Acre(IRE) ◆, whose handler had trained the winner of this twice in the preceding three years with unexposed sorts, scored an impressive success. This former point winner was ridden positively and relished jumping the fences. He was left clear when Kack Handed blundered five out and made the best of his way home. He ran on strongly and looks one to keep on-side in the short term at least, although the handicapper will have his say now. (op 6-1)
Rimini(FR), a C&D winner on similar ground before Christmas, had returned to hurdles when the ground went soft. He came out of the pack to chase the winner but could make little impression, although he is probably a fair guide to the level of the form. (tchd 8-1)
Lordsbridge(USA) was 7lb better off with today's runner-up for just over a length compared with their running over C&D in December. He ran reasonably without matching that form and his losing run now extends to three years. (op 9-2)
Special Occasion had gained all his bumper/hurdle wins on soft ground and was being ridden along after just a couple of fences. His rider's persistence paid off however, as he stayed on well in the closing stages. Easier ground will suit and he might appreciate a return to farther, although the re-application of blinkers could help. (op 10-1)
Our Bob(IRE), who has had his share of problems, joined the leaders at the 7th but faded after chasing the winner into the straight. (op 14-1)
Mallusk(IRE) appeared to be making headway when a mistake at the cross-fence ended his chance. (op 8-1)
In The Zone(IRE) ran in snatches and failed to figure on this faster ground. (tchd 10-1)
Gus Macrae(IRE) Official explanation: vet said gelding bled from nose

4491 LESLEY FIELD'S 60TH BUMPER YEAR STANDARD OPEN NATIONAL HUNT FLAT RACE (SUPPORTING GREATWOOD BUMPER) 2m 110y
5:20 (5:20) (Class 5) 4-6-Y-0 **£2,055** (£599; £299)

Form RPR

2 **1** **Medinas (FR)**[28] 3957 4-10-8 0... GerardTumelty 106+
(Alan King) *in rr hdwy 6f out: pushed along to chse ldrs over 3f out: qcknd to chal between horses over 1f out: led ins fnl f: r.o strly* **17/2**[3]

2 1 **Global Fella (IRE)** 6-10-9 0.................................... JeremiahMcGrath(7) 113+
(Nicky Henderson) *towards rr: hdwy 6f out: drvn to chse ldrs and green 3f out: chal 2f out led sn after: hdd and nt qckn ins fnl f* **28/1**

3 5 **Broomfield** 4-10-8 0... RWalsh 100+
(Paul Nicholls) *t.k.h: chsd ldrs: pushed along and edgd lft over 3f out: jnd 2f out: hdd sn after: one pce ins fnl f* **5/4**[1]

3 **4** 2 ¾ **Hinton Indiana**[52] 3511 6-11-2 0.. SamThomas 106
(Nicky Henderson) *chsd ldr 9f out to 7f out: styd chsng ldrs: drvn along 3f out: outpcd 2f out: wknd ins fnl f* **16/1**

3 **5** 2 ½ **Awaywiththegreys (IRE)**[118] 2237 4-10-8 0...................... TomO'Brien 95
(Peter Bowen) *chsd ldrs: rdn and styd on same pce fnl 3f: kpt on again ins fnl f* **14/1**

1 **6** *1 ¾* **Hit The Headlines (IRE)**[50] 3546 5-11-9 0...................... BarryGeraghty 109
(Nicky Henderson) *trckd ldrs: wnt 2nd 7f out: pushed along over 3f out: no imp: wknd 2f out* **11/8**[2]

6 **7** *94* **Ammo Away**[34] 3835 5-11-2 0.. RichardJohnson 7
(Tim Vaughan) *led 3f: wknd over 5f out: t.o* **50/1**

8 *½* **The Gurner (IRE)** 4-10-8 0.. PaddyBrennan —
(Charlie Longsdon) *a towards rr: lost tch over 5f out: t.o* **18/1**

3m 57.44s (-6.86) **Going Correction** -0.725s/f (Firm)
WFA 4 from 5yo+ 7lb **8** Ran SP% **120.3**
Speed ratings: **87,86,84,82,81 80,36,36**
toteswingers:1&2:£17.60, 2&3:£11.30, 1&3:£2.00 CSF £208.09 TOTE £10.40: £1.70, £4.80, £1.30; EX 108.90.
Owner Mr & Mrs F D Bell **Bred** Mme Laurence Gagneux **Trained** Barbury Castle, Wilts

FOCUS
This bumper had fallen to the useful types Rock On Ruby and Bellvano in the last two seasons, but this year's running was probably just an ordinary race for the track. Nicky Henderson had trained two of the four previous winners and was represented by three this time. The winner is rated up 7lb on his debut run.

NOTEBOOK
Medinas(FR), comparatively diminutive but more experienced, came between his two rivals to score on his second start. He was settled off the pace and gradually crept into contention before running on too well for the runner-up. Whether he makes a jumper remains to be seen, although his trainer has done well with similar sorts in the past. (op 8-1 tchd 9-1)
Global Fella(IRE) ◆, a half-brother to Flat winners out of a Flat and hurdles scorer, has plenty of size but was the trainer's third string here, judged on jockey bookings. However, he travelled really well and was probably beaten only by his inexperience. He should not be too long in upholding the family tradition and should make a jumper next season. (op 22-1 tchd 20-1)
Broomfield ◆, a half-brother to the likes of Behrajan, was well backed on this racecourse debut. However, he took a keen hold and settled only when allowed to lead after half a mile. He still looked the likely winner early in the straight before his exertions took their toll. He remains a decent prospect and will hopefully settle better next time. (op 7-4 tchd 2-1)
Hinton Indiana, a half-brother to a hurdler/chaser, ran well but looks to lack a turn of foot. His sibling is well suited by soft ground and that might also suit him when his attention is turned to jumping. (op 20-1)
Awaywiththegreys(IRE), who is related to the useful Flat performer Shabernak and decent staying hurdler Souffleur, ran well behind the useful Keys back in November. He kept on in the straight without troubling the leaders and probably has races in him. (op 12-1)
Hit The Headlines(IRE), penalised for his success on soft ground at Huntingdon, was the stable first string and moved up to join the leader looking a big threat turning for home. However, he soon came under pressure and dropped away disappointingly before being eased. Maybe the drying ground did not suit him. (op 6-4 tchd 11-10)
T/Jkpt: Not won. T/Plt: £346.20 to a £1 stake. Pool of £186,138.32- 392.38 winning tickets. T/Qpdt: £19.50 to a £1 stake. Pool of £10,514.73 - 398.95 winning tickets. ST

4492 - 4498a (Foreign Racing) - See Raceform Interactive

[4309]HUNTINGDON (R-H)
Sunday, March 6

OFFICIAL GOING: Good to soft (chs 6.5, hdl 6.9)
Wind: Light against Weather: Overcast

4499 100% CHELTENHAM ON RACING UK MAIDEN HURDLE (8 hdls) 2m 110y
2:10 (2:13) (Class 4) 4-Y-0+ **£2,602** (£764; £382; £190)

Form RPR

B **1** **First In The Queue (IRE)**[24] 4029 4-10-7 0............................ APMcCoy 107+
(Nicky Henderson) *chsd ldrs: led appr 5th: blnd 2 out: j.lft last: rdn out* **9/4**[2]

1-40 **2** *2 ½* **Fontano (FR)**[43] 3678 5-10-12 0.. AlexMerriam(3) 110
(Emma Lavelle) *chsd ldrs: ev ch fr 3 out: mstke next: rdn appr last: styd on same pce flat* **7/2**[3]

-523 **3** *4 ½* **Robin De Creuse (FR)**[39] 3739 5-11-1 122.................. RichardJohnson 108+
(Philip Hobbs) *hld up: hdwy 5th: rdn whn j.rt 2 out: styd on same pce* **15/8**[1]

4 **4** *1* **Archie Rice (USA)**[22] 4069 5-10-8 0.................................. MattCrawley(7) 107+
(Tom Keddy) *hld up and bhd: swtchd lft and r.o appr last: nvr nr to chal* **14/1**

00 **5** *nse* **Mick's Dancer**[33] 3872 6-11-1 0.. WarrenMarston 104
(Richard Phillips) *hld up: styd on fr 2 out: nvr nrr* **100/1**

/UF6 **6** *1 ¼* **Backstreet Billy (IRE)**[13] 4260 7-11-1 0.......................... AndrewThornton 104
(Richard Lee) *hld up: hdwy 3 out: mstke next: no ex last* **80/1**

00 **7** *6* **Second Brook (IRE)**[11] 4283 4-10-0 0................................ PeterHatton(7) 89
(Reg Hollinshead) *hld up: hdwy after 3 out: nvr trbld ldrs* **25/1**

U **8** *6* **December**[37] 3783 5-11-1 0... JackDoyle 92
(Christine Dunnett) *hld up: hdwy 4th: wknd after 2 out* **150/1**

0-4 **9** *6* **Sirjosh**[11] 842 5-11-1 0.. PaulMoloney 87
(Des Donovan) *hld up in tch: plld hrd: wknd appr 2 out* **66/1**

10 *10* **That's Mine (IRE)** 5-10-12 0...................................... RichieMcLernon(3) 78
(Jonjo O'Neill) *mid-div: hdwy 5th: wknd 3 out: t.o* **50/1**

11 *8* **Two Tone**[24] 5-10-12 0... AdamPogson(3) 70
(Garry Woodward) *hld up: a in rr: t.o* **200/1**

12 *nk* **Kingaroo (IRE)**[19] 5-11-1 0.. JamieMoore 70
(Garry Woodward) *prom: nt fluent 2nd: blnd next: sn lost pl: bhd fr 4th: t.o* **50/1**

0 **13** *50* **Dancing Belle**[35] 3302 6-10-8 0... DarylJacob 18
(J R Jenkins) *hld up in tch: racd keenly: wknd after 3 out: t.o* **150/1**

F **Abbotts Mount**[28] 7-11-1 0... SamJones —
(Michael Scudamore) *trckd ldr: t.k.h: nt fluent 2nd: rdn bef 3 out: sn wknd: fell last* **100/1**

260 **P** **Morgan's Bay**[21] 4100 6-11-1 0... PaddyBrennan —
(Tom George) *led and t.k.h: hdd bef 5th: qckly wknd: p.u sn after* **9/1**

3m 55.4s (0.50) **Going Correction** -0.075s/f (Good)
WFA 4 from 5yo+ 7lb **15** Ran SP% **118.7**
Speed ratings (Par 105): **95,93,91,91,91 90,87,84,82,77 73,73,50,—,—**
Tote Swingers: 1&2 £3.40, 1&3 £2.00, 2&3 £2.80 CSF £10.42 TOTE £3.80: £1.40, £1.30, £1.20; EX 14.10.
Owner Liam Breslin **Bred** Holborn Trust Co **Trained** Upper Lambourn, Berks
■ Stewards' Enquiry : Matt Crawley ten-day ban: running and riding (Mar 20 to 29)

FOCUS
The hurdles track was back to its standard configuration, and at its tightest. There didn't seem to be a great deal of depth to this maiden hurdle and the time was modest. It has been rated around the first three.

NOTEBOOK
First In The Queue(IRE) had run an encouraging race behind Triumph Hurdle bound Brampour on debut at Taunton until being brought down at the final hurdle. Weak in the betting here, he lacked the size of most of his rivals but kept on well after hitting the front, and won nicely despite crashing through two out. His jumping will need to become more fluent but he does at least know how to win. (tchd 5-2 in places)
Fontano(FR), down in trip, had shown ability over hurdles previously and more than confirmed that impression again. A horse with plenty of scope, he is now qualified for handicaps. (op 4-1 tchd 9-2)
Robin De Creuse(FR), held up this time, was solid in the betting but offered little once coming under strong pressure. He has something to prove now but will surely do better over fences in time. (tchd 7-4)
Archie Rice(USA) ◆ shaped better than his final position suggested at Newbury last time, and was a massive eyecatcher here after being held up for far too long in rear while travelling strongly. The jockey gave his mount plenty to do (although he was instructed by Tom Keddy to hold Archie Rice up) considering the horse has been known to race prominently on the Flat, and has won over 1m4f. Punters who had backed him each way are entitled to feel aggrieved that he didn't make it into third at least. The jockey was suspended for 10 days for failing to take all reasonable and permissible measures to attain the best possible position, but the trainer wasn't fined (and horse not banned) because the stewards accepted that he issued appropriate instructions. (op 18-1)
Mick's Dancer ◆, another who was in rear early, looks capable of better when ridden closer to the lead, as a couple of his Flat victories, at about 1m2f, came when racing at the head of affairs. He can go for handicaps now and will appreciate quicker ground.
Backstreet Billy(IRE) ran well and looks a chaser in the making. (op 100-1)
Second Brook(IRE) ran much better than he had last time, his first start after a 40-day ban from racing, and is another now qualified for handicaps. (op 33-1)
Morgan's Bay dropped out as though something was amiss after the fourth. His trainer reported before the off that he feels the horse needs to grow up still. Morgan's Bay will also need to learn to settle if he is to make his mark. Official explanation: trainer said gelding finished distressed

4500 RACING UK WELCOMES BACK RUBY MAIDEN HURDLE (10 hdls) 2m 4f 110y
2:40 (2:43) (Class 4) 4-Y-0+ **£2,602** (£764; £382; £190)

Form RPR

-050 **1** **Another Dimension (IRE)**[23] 4051 5-10-9 0.................. CharlieWallis(7) 115+
(Nigel Dunger) *chsd ldrs: lft in ld after 5th: rdn clr flat* **66/1**

66 **2** *8* **Wiesentraum (GER)**[51] 3546 5-11-2 0............................ LeightonAspell 108
(Lucy Wadham) *hld up in tch: rdn and j.rt 2 out: wnt 2nd flat: styd on same pce* **16/1**

0P3 **3** *1* **Airmen's Friend (IRE)**[19] 4128 5-10-13 0.......................... PeterToole(3) 108
(Charlie Mann) *chsd ldrs: rdn after 3 out: styd on same pce appr last* **9/2**[2]

30-4 **4** *1* **Sizing Ireland (IRE)**[14] 4239 5-11-2 0.................................... APMcCoy 108+
(Nicky Henderson) *chsd ldr to 3rd: remained handy: lft 2nd again after 5th: rdn appr 2 out: mstke and no ex last* **5/2**[1]

62 **5** *2 ¾* **Baan (USA)**[25] 4012 8-11-2 0... PaddyBrennan 104
(James Eustace) *hld up: hdwy 5th: rdn whn hmpd 2 out: styd on same pce* **9/2**[2]

354 **6** *2 ½* **Loch Ba (IRE)**[55] 3487 5-11-2 0.. DenisO'Regan 101
(Henrietta Knight) *hld up: hdwy 3 out: sn rdn: styd on same pce* **6/1**[3]

500 **7** *1* **Beat All Out**[11] 4288 6-11-2 0.. TomO'Brien 100
(Dai Burchell) *hld up: hdwy 6th: wknd 2 out: b.b.v* **28/1**

556 **8** *2* **Airdrie (IRE)**[28] 3960 5-11-2 0... AndrewThornton 98
(Henrietta Knight) *prom: rdn to chse wnr briefly after 3 out: wknd last* **8/1**

0-P0 **9** *21* **Rich Live (FR)**[35] 3836 6-10-13 0..................................... AlexMerriam(3) 79
(Lady Anne Connell) *hld up: hdwy 5th: wknd after 3 out: t.o* **150/1**

6-10 **10** *2 ½* **Lombardy Boy (IRE)**[26] 3987 6-10-13 0........................... TomMolloy(3) 77
(Michael Banks) *mid-div: bhd fr 5th: t.o* **12/1**

500 **11** *18* **Wait No More (IRE)**[20] 4112 6-11-2 0.................................... JackDoyle 61
(Sarah Humphrey) *hld up: bhd fr 5th: t.o* **80/1**

5-F **12** *10* **Cruising Bye**[68] 3156 5-10-11 0................................. AnthonyFreeman(5) 52
(Jonjo O'Neill) *hld up: hdwy and mstke 5th: nt fluent and wknd next: t.o* **22/1**

6-06 **13** *13* **Yorkshire Knight (IRE)**[29] 3943 6-10-13 0................. DonalDevereux(3) 40
(Peter Bowen) *hld up: mstke 5th: sn pushed along: j. slowly and wknd next: t.o* **66/1**

00-0 **14** *55* **Bloodyburn Bay (IRE)**[40] 3719 7-11-2 0.......................(t) JodieMogford —
(Graeme McPherson) *led and sn clr: hung lft fr 5th: hdd & wknd bef next: t.o* **80/1**

00 **P** **Sharinga**[22] 4082 4-9-7 0... PeterHatton(7) —
(Reg Hollinshead) *bhd whn mstke 1st: p.u bef next* **125/1**

4m 52.5s (-6.50) **Going Correction** -0.075s/f (Good)
WFA 4 from 5yo+ 8lb **15** Ran SP% **118.6**
Speed ratings (Par 105): **109,105,105,105,104 103,102,102,94,93 86,82,77,56,—**
Tote Swingers: 1&2 £133.30, 1&3 £40.20, 2&3 £10.20 CSF £851.60 TOTE £84.10: £15.80, £3.20, £2.00; EX 473.70.
Owner N A Dunger **Bred** Gerard Murphy **Trained** Pulborough, W Sussex

FOCUS
A race that will have taken little winning judged on these horse's previous performances over hurdles, but the time was fair for the grade. The winner produced a massive step up.

NOTEBOOK
Another Dimension(IRE) was handed the lead when the wayward Bloodyburn Bay went wide at the stables' bend, and kept on in resolute style to claim a first victory. He has plenty of size and scope to improve and wants this type of ground according to connections. He is due to got the sales in April/May, which was always the plan no matter what had happened here. Official explanation: trainer's rep said regarding apparent improvement in form gelding was suited by drying ground (op 100-1)
Wiesentraum(GER) showed a modicum of ability in a Newbury bumper before being a bit disappointing next time, but made a pleasing hurdling debut, staying on well from off the pace.
Airmen's Friend(IRE) attracted plenty of money in the betting during the morning, and did well without ever looking like winning. (op 4-1 tchd 7-2)
Sizing Ireland(IRE) had shown more than enough in bumpers to be respected here, especially up in distance, but needed to be hard ridden quite early to stay in contention, and a mistake at the last ended his chance of a place. (op 11-4 tchd 3-1)
Baan(USA) ran well last time at Ludlow, although he did start at 50/1 in a modest-looking contest, but wasn't really competitive here. (op 4-1)
Loch Ba(IRE) looked worth a try over further but didn't get into a position to challenge after being held up. He stayed on well after the last and will no doubt prove good enough to win something in time. Connections feel he well make a lovely chaser, and suggested he'll be tried over fences when next seen. (tchd 11-2 and 13-2)
Beat All Out was backed at long prices during the morning but couldn't get on terms. Official explanation: trainer said gelding bled from nose (op 20-1)
Airdrie(IRE), who looked the stable's second string, but was supported in the betting, didn't appear to get home after moving up on the final bend going well. He is now qualified for handicaps and will make a chaser, so he could be one to watch for in a novices' handicap chase. (op 16-1)
Bloodyburn Bay(IRE) Official explanation: jockey said gelding hung badly left

Sharinga Official explanation: jockey said saddle slipped

4501 EVERY CHELTENHAM RACE EXCLUSIVELY ON RACING UK H'CAP HURDLE (10 hdls) 2m 5f 110y

3:10 (3:12) (Class 4) (0-115,115) 4-Y-0+ **£2,276** (£668; £334; £166)

Form RPR
0134 **1** **Cloudy Spirit**[25] 4009 6-11-12 **115** PaulMoloney 125+
(Reg Hollinshead) *hld up: hdwy 6th: led appr 3 out: nt fluent last: comf* **11/4**[1]
2210 **2** *4* **Be My Light (IRE)**[24] 4034 5-10-6 **102** (p) KielanWoods(7) 107
(Charlie Longsdon) *a.p: rdn to chse wnr appr 2 out: styng on same pce whn hung rt flat* **4/1**[2]
0410 **3** *4* **Apache Chant (USA)**[32] 3881 7-10-6 **100** (p) LeeEdwards(5) 102
(Tony Carroll) *chsd ldrs: rdn 3 out: no ex last* **9/2**[3]
-333 **4** *21* **Chicklemix**[9] 4330 5-10-13 **102** WarrenMarston 86
(Pam Sly) *hld up: mstke 6th: hdwy next: rdn and wknd appr 2 out* **13/2**
0444 **5** *1* **Emperor Charlie**[41] 3713 7-10-5 **101** EdmondLinehan(7) 83
(Ferdy Murphy) *chsd ldr tl led 7th: hdd bef next: rdn and wkng whn mstke 2 out* **9/1**
-114 **6** *10* **Lyster (IRE)**[282] 503 12-11-0 **106** LeeStephens(3) 78
(Graeme McPherson) *in rr and niggled along: pushed along 5th: wknd 7th: t.o* **16/1**
U-00 **7** *10* **Optimus Maximus (IRE)**[55] 3490 6-11-9 **115** (t) TommyPhelan(3) 78
(Claire Dyson) *led to 7th: nt fluent 3 out: sn rdn and wknd: t.o* **40/1**
06-0 **P** **Very Edgy (IRE)**[42] 3693 7-11-3 **106** (bt[1]) APMcCoy —
(Charles Egerton) *prom: reminders after 4th: wknd qckly and p.u bef 6th* **11/2**

5m 11.3s (0.70) **Going Correction** -0.075s/f (Good) **8** Ran SP% **111.9**
Speed ratings (Par 105): **95,93,92,84,84 80,76,—**
Tote Swingers: 1&2 £2.40, 1&3 £3.60, 2&3 £4.40 CSF £13.85 CT £45.64 TOTE £4.00: £1.30, £1.40, £2.00; EX 15.90.

Owner Mrs Norma Harris **Bred** Mrs Norma Harris **Trained** Upper Longdon, Staffs

FOCUS

An ordinary handicap in which the second and third set the level.

NOTEBOOK

Cloudy Spirit looked of interest after a solid effort last time and was given a good ride by Paul Moloney, who kept her to the inside of the course and made a race-winning move heading the final bend. Connections are hoping to get her into the Martin Pipe Conditionals Jockeys' Handicap at Cheltenham with the penalty for taking this, but she looks to have little chance of making the cut. (op 3-1)

Be My Light(IRE) won off a mark of 94 at this course in February, under this jockey, and did the best of those who chased down the winner. This was an improvement on her Taunton performance. (tchd 7-2)

Apache Chant(USA) had the cheekpieces swiftly put back on after a moderate effort at Leicester, in what was probably unsuitable ground, and responded well to strong pressure to keep going at the one pace. (op 6-1)

Chicklemix, up over 5f in trip after a decent effort at Warwick last time, didn't obviously appear to stay the trip. (op 5-1 tchd 9-2)

Emperor Charlie, down in trip, dropped out quickly after racing prominently. (op 10-1)

Very Edgy(IRE) had blinkers and a tongue-tie fitted for this after showing little over hurdles, and is one to completely avoid judged on this mullish effort. (op 5-1 tchd 6-1)

4502 FREE ANNUAL SUBSCRIPTION PROMOTION AT RACINGUK.COM H'CAP CHASE (19 fncs) 3m

3:40 (3:40) (Class 3) (0-120,120) 5-Y-0+ **£4,553** (£1,337; £668; £333)

Form RPR
3160 **1** **Flemish Invader (IRE)**[25] 4010 8-11-7 **115** PaddyBrennan 125+
(Nigel Twiston-Davies) *a.p: lft 2nd 3 out: led after next: styd on wl* **5/1**[3]
F55 **2** *2 3/4* **Mud Monkey**[21] 4095 7-11-10 **118** (t) NickScholfield 127+
(Claire Dyson) *led: rdn and hdd after 2 out: j.rt last: styd on same pce flat* **10/1**
6FP3 **3** *20* **Marc Of Brilliance (USA)**[24] 4023 8-10-13 **107** JamieMoore 100
(Gary Moore) *hld up: hdwy 10th: hmpd 3 out: rdn and wknd appr last* **9/2**[2]
3254 **4** *28* **Ballyvesey (IRE)**[105] 2543 6-11-12 **120** (p) TomO'Brien 82
(Peter Bowen) *hld up: hdwy 10th: rdn and wknd appr 2 out: t.o* **5/1**[3]
04-6 **5** *30* **Speed Bonnie Boat**[43] 3690 8-11-2 **110** RichardJohnson 45
(Henry Daly) *nt fluent: bhd fr 3rd: t.o* **12/1**
0F65 **U** **Victorias Groom (GER)**[16] 4181 9-11-8 **116** LeightonAspell —
(Lucy Wadham) *chsd ldr to 6th: wnt 2nd again 10th: jnd ldr 15th: cl 2nd whn blnd and uns rdr 3 out* **7/1**
1-PP **P** **Costa Courta (FR)**[49] 3588 9-11-9 **117** JimmyMcCarthy —
(Charlie Morlock) *sn prom: chsd ldr 6th tl blnd 10th: sn lost pl: bhd fr 12th: t.o whn p.u bef 2 out* **9/1**
-F32 **P** **Western Whisky (FR)**[6] 4402 9-10-12 **106** (p) JodieMogford —
(Richard Lee) *nt a fluent: chsd ldrs: mstke 8th: lost pl bef next: bhd fr 12th: t.o whn blnd 16th: j.v.slowly next: p.u bef 2 out* **4/1**[1]

6m 3.90s (-6.40) **Going Correction** -0.075s/f (Good) **8** Ran SP% **110.8**
Speed ratings: **107,106,99,90,80 —,—,—**
Tote Swingers: 1&2 £9.30, 1&3 £3.70, 2&3 £5.70 CSF £47.96 CT £228.99 TOTE £5.20: £2.00, £2.00, £2.60; EX 60.50.

Owner Mrs E M Bathurst **Bred** Robert McCarthy **Trained** Naunton, Gloucs

FOCUS

The pace set by the leader seemed an honest one. This was probably not a strong handicap but the winner is on the upgrade and the second ran to his best.

NOTEBOOK

Flemish Invader(IRE) was back up to 3m after a few runs over various distances short of this trip, and got into the winner's enclosure again under a waiting ride. He wins in his turn but will need to find something extra now after winning off a career-high mark here. (op 9-2 tchd 4-1)

Mud Monkey had fallen and been well beaten since his win at this course over 2m4f110y in late November, and his career record didn't suggest this distance was what he wanted, but he made a good fist of attempting to make every yard and got plenty in trouble when the race gathered momentum. A drop in trip can see him win again. (op 11-1 tchd 12-1)

Marc Of Brilliance(USA) hadn't won in handicap company coming into this and didn't look like bucking that trend here, especially after being slightly hampered by a fallen jockey. (tchd 5-1)

Ballyvesey(IRE), 5lb lower than when last seen back in November in the Becher Chase, only has one victory to his name and was never a factor in the final stages. (op 11-2 tchd 6-1)

Speed Bonnie Boat doesn't look overly big and showed nothing again over fences. (op 16-1)

Victorias Groom(GER) is well handicapped on his winning form and was thereabouts when unseating Leighton Aspell at the third last. It was a bit too far out to know what would have happened to him, but he was far from beaten. (op 15-2 tchd 13-2)

Costa Courta(FR) was 8lb lower than his last run, but ended his chance at the tenth when blundering while racing keenly. Official explanation: vet said gelding sustained a leg injury (op 15-2 tchd 13-2)

Western Whisky(FR) jumped moderately and gave the slight impression that he may have sulked a bit for some reason. (op 15-2 tchd 13-2)

4503 DOWNLOAD THE FREE RACING UK APP H'CAP HURDLE (8 hdls) 2m 110y

4:10 (4:11) (Class 4) (0-115,117) 4-Y-0+ **£2,276** (£668; £334; £166)

Form RPR
23 **1** **Ubi Ace**[23] 4061 5-11-12 **115** RobertWalford 125+
(Tim Walford) *hld up: plld hrd: hdwy 3rd: led appr 2 out: rdn out* **7/1**[3]
4152 **2** *5* **If I Had Him (IRE)**[25] 4008 7-10-13 **109** (v) TrevorWhelan(7) 113
(George Baker) *led: rdn and hdd appr 2 out: no ex flat* **5/1**[2]
U-50 **3** *3/4* **Double Handful (GER)**[54] 3497 5-10-11 **100** AidanColeman 103
(Venetia Williams) *hld up: hdwy 5th: sn drvn along: outpcd 3 out: styng on u.p whn lft 3rd last* **25/1**
-340 **4** *8* **Wester Ross (IRE)**[43] 3688 7-11-12 **115** (b) PaddyBrennan 114
(James Eustace) *prom: jnd ldr and blnd 4th: rdn appr 3 out: wknd sn after* **9/1**
210F **5** *4* **Babilu**[33] 3874 6-11-8 **111** (p) TomO'Brien 105
(Dai Burchell) *hld up: hdwy 4th: rdn and wknd appr 2 out: bhd whn hmpd last* **12/1**
1/4P **6** *2 1/4* **Sole Bonne Femme (IRE)**[40] 3724 9-10-9 **105** (tp) CharlieWallis(7) 96
(Gerard Butler) *prom: racd keenly: rdn and wknd appr 2 out* **50/1**
6046 **7** *11* **Ezdiyaad (IRE)**[14] 4234 7-11-6 **109** (t) DenisO'Regan 90
(Kevin Morgan) *chsd ldr to appr 4th: sn rdn and wknd: t.o* **16/1**
0/0 **8** *20* **Silent Jo (JPN)**[42] 3696 9-10-8 **100** RichieMcLernon(3) 88
(Jonjo O'Neill) *hld up: rdn 4th: bhd whn hmpd next: t.o* **33/1**
0/03 **9** *1/2* **Peintre Du Roi (USA)**[19] 4129 7-11-2 **105** JamesDavies 67
(Natalie Lloyd-Beavis) *mid-div: rdn and dropped to rr bef 4th: t.o* **33/1**
20/0 **F** **Rich Lord**[32] 3881 7-11-2 **112** EdmondLinehan(7) —
(Ferdy Murphy) *hld up: in rr whn fell 5th* **33/1**
442 **F** **Qalinas (FR)**[9] 4323 4-11-6 **117** TomScudamore 113
(David Pipe) *mid-div: hdwy 4th: rdn and ev ch after 3 out: 3 l 3rd and looked hld whn fell last* **5/6**[1]

3m 54.4s (-0.50) **Going Correction** -0.075s/f (Good)
WFA 4 from 5yo+ 7lb **11** Ran SP% **121.9**
Speed ratings (Par 105): **98,95,95,91,89 88,83,74,73,— —**
Tote Swingers: 1&2 £4.70, 1&3 £12.00, 2&3 £17.50 CSF £41.81 CT £848.88 TOTE £7.00: £2.20, £2.00, £3.40; EX 38.70.

Owner N J Maher **Bred** Steel's Thoroughbred Breeding **Trained** Sheriff Hutton, N Yorks

FOCUS

A big step up from the winner but entitled to be this good on his Flat form. Faller Qalinas was heading for a personal best without suggesting that he'd be good enough to win at Cheltenham.

NOTEBOOK

Ubi Ace had shown more than enough in a couple of novice events to be of interest here, including once behind the exciting Sidney Banks winner Aikman, but looked to have compromised his chance by pulling really hard in the early stages. However, he started to settle a bit better the further he went and showed a turn of foot to get away from his rivals when asked to make his winning bid. He appeared to doss when getting his nose in front, but did enough to collect a comfortable success under top weight. There is a chance he could head to Aintree. (op 13-2)

If I Had Him(IRE) won a seller last November and ran really well again at a higher level. He is a sound marker to the form considering his recent efforts. (op 13-2)

Double Handful(GER) could be given a small chance on bits of form and probably ran as well as could have been expected without threatening to win. He may want further. (tchd 28-1)

Wester Ross(IRE), down almost 5f in distance, is a consistent-enough sort but made a serious error five out when just about in the lead, and never figured after starting to weaken heading to the next hurdle. (op 14-1 tchd 17-2)

Babilu has been running well this season and had her chance after three out before weakening. (op 14-1)

Qalinas(FR) was the only juvenile in this handicap. Strongly supported in the betting, this flatter track looked sure to suit after he tired late on at Sandown but he was outpaced turning into the home straight before coming down at the final hurdle. He was almost certainly held when falling, and his recent effort may have taken quite a bit out of him. (op 8-11)

4504 RACING UK ON SKY432 AND VIRGIN536 H'CAP CHASE (14 fncs 2 omitted) 2m 4f 110y

4:40 (4:42) (Class 4) (0-105,104) 5-Y-0+ **£2,740** (£798; £399)

Form RPR
-F3P **1** **Douryna**[58] 3431 8-10-13 **91** DarylJacob 116+
(Colin Tizzard) *chsd ldr tl led 7th: clr whn j.rt 2 out: comf* **8/1**
25F1 **2** *13* **Bertenbar**[28] 3959 7-10-8 **86** SamThomas 97
(Henrietta Knight) *a.p: chsd wnr 11th: rdn and wknd 2 out* **8/1**
2423 **3** *2 1/2* **Crystal Prince**[37] 3790 7-10-7 **85** (tp) FelixDeGiles 93
(Charlie Longsdon) *hld up: hdwy 10th: rdn and wkng whn mstke 2 out* **13/2**
-003 **4** *1 1/2* **Mister Matt (IRE)**[24] 4022 8-11-12 **104** AndrewThornton 111
(Bob Buckler) *chsd ldrs tl rdn and wknd appr 2 out* **6/1**[3]
P-12 **5** *7* **Extra Bold**[28] 3963 9-11-9 **101** JackDoyle 102
(Emma Lavelle) *led to 7th: chsd ldr to 11th: rdn and wknd appr 2 out* **10/3**[1]
24 **6** *1 1/4* **Back Bob Back (IRE)**[101] 2642 6-11-12 **104** PaddyBrennan 104
(Tom George) *prom: rdn after 3 out: wknd bef next* **4/1**[2]
0-2F **7** *shd* **Quapriland (FR)**[12] 4275 7-10-12 **93** SamTwiston-Davies(3) 91
(Althea Barclay) *hld up: drvn along 10th: wknd after 3 out* **20/1**
2356 **8** *57* **Lepido (ITY)**[28] 3963 7-11-7 **99** (v) JamieMoore 46
(Gary Moore) *hld up: bhd fr 10th: t.o* **16/1**
1333 **U** **Turbo Shandy**[199] 1299 8-11-9 **101** TomO'Brien —
(Dai Burchell) *hld up: blnd and uns rdr 1st* **25/1**
03-P **P** **Buffalo Stampede (IRE)**[13] 4265 8-11-11 **103** AidanColeman —
(Venetia Williams) *hld up: hdwy 10th: wknd 3 out: t.o whn p.u bef next* **11/1**

5m 2.40s (-2.90) **Going Correction** -0.075s/f (Good) **10** Ran SP% **115.7**
Speed ratings: **102,97,96,95,92 92,92,70,—,—**
Tote Swingers: 1&2 £7.60, 1&3 £10.10, 2&3 £5.00 CSF £69.64 CT £442.95 TOTE £10.30: £2.60, £2.50, £2.30; EX 61.30.

Owner Chasing Gold Racing Club **Bred** R W Russell **Trained** Milborne Port, Dorset

FOCUS

The last fence down the back was omitted due to earlier damage. An open-looking contest full of interesting types. A big step up from the easy winner and the second remains on a fair mark.

NOTEBOOK

Douryna had looked to have enough ability to win a race of this nature in a couple of her three previous attempts over fences, and justified that opinion on a day where everything went right for her. The handicapper is sure to hit her hard for this, so connections will want to get her out under a penalty before any rating hike kicks in. (op 7-1)

Bertenbar, raised 10lb for winning an uncompetitive affair at Fontwell, is probably improving a little but bumped into a horse that had a lot in hand. (tchd 7-1)

Crystal Prince is a confirmed low-grade performer and plugged on after coming under pressure a long way out. (op 7-1 tchd 15-2)

Mister Matt(IRE) ran well off a 3lb higher mark over C&D last time, but pulled too hard here under restraint, and made little impact after losing his place. (op 9-2)
Extra Bold, eased in trip, likes decent ground but did himself no favours by racing keenly while in front. He dropped away after being headed before keeping on again. (op 4-1)
Back Bob Back(IRE) represented a trainer bang in form and looked of obvious interest sent over fences after only a couple of tries over hurdles. A winning pointer, he still looks a little unfurnished and should have more to come when his jumping becomes more fluent. (op 5-1 tchd 11-2)

4505 JOIN NOW AT RACINGUK.COM STANDARD NATIONAL HUNT FLAT RACE (CONDITIONALS & AMATEURS) 2m 110y

5:10 (5:11) (Class 6) 4-6-Y-0 **£1,370** (£399; £199)

Form RPR
1 **Glorious Feeling (IRE)** 5-10-8 0 DavidBass(3) 104+
(Nicky Henderson) *a.p: chsd ldr over 3f out: led over 1f out: swtchd lft ins fnl f: r.o wl* **11/8**[1]
20 2 9 **Kaylif Aramis**[64] 3294 4-10-3 0 MrWTwiston-Davies(7) 92
(Nigel Twiston-Davies) *led: rdn and hdd over 1f out: styd on same pce fnl f* **2/1**[2]
3 3 ¾ **Real Milan (IRE)** 6-11-1 0 RichieMcLernon(3) 96
(Anabel L M King) *chsd ldrs: outpcd over 4f out: rallied over 1f out: styd on* **15/2**[3]
4 2 **Newport Rose** 5-10-8 0 PeterToole(3) 87
(Ben Case) *chsd ldr tl rdn over 3f out: wknd over 1f out* **33/1**
5 5 **Murchan High (IRE)** 6-10-8 0 SamTwiston-Davies(3) 82
(Jim Best) *hld up: drvn along 1/2-way: nvr on terms* **16/1**
02 6 1 ½ **Willow The Rose**[27] 3979 4-10-0 0 TomMolloy(3) 73
(J R Jenkins) *hld up: hdwy 1/2-way: rdn and wknd over 2f out* **9/1**
7 35 **Open The Light** 4-10-0 0 CPGeoghegan(3) 38
(Giles Bravery) *hld up: rdn over 6f out: wknd 4f out: t.o* **25/1**

3m 58.1s (9.00) **Going Correction** -0.075s/f (Good)
WFA 4 from 5yo+ 7lb 7 Ran SP% **109.9**
Speed ratings: **75,70,69,68,65 65,48**
Tote Swingers: 1&2 £1.20, 1&3 £2.70, 2&3 £3.00. totesuper7: Win: Not won. Place: Not won. CSF £3.88 TOTE £2.10: £1.30, £1.70; EX 4.20.
Owner John P McManus **Bred** B Walsh **Trained** Upper Lambourn, Berks

FOCUS
As is usual in most bumpers, the early tempo was slow and not a great deal happened until the pace started to increase. Ordinary bumper form but the winner should rate higher.

NOTEBOOK
Glorious Feeling(IRE) ◆, representing respected connections, looks to have plenty of substance about her and got nicely on top down the home straight to win going away. She pricked her ears and edged towards the stands' rail in the latter stages, so should be mentally stronger next time. (op 6-4 tchd 5-4)
Kaylif Aramis, down in grade after being tried in a Listed Cheltenham bumper when last seen, was unsurprisingly asked to use his experience and take the field a long. He remained there until the winner loomed up to him, but had no response to her and came home at the one pace. (op 9-4 tchd 5-2)
Real Milan(IRE) ◆ is a good-looking sort, who ran on well after looking green. He will surely be good enough to win something with time. (op 10-1)
Newport Rose was bang there until turning in and made a fair debut. (op 28-1 tchd 25-1)
Willow The Rose appeared to be kept wide on some less-poached ground but it made little difference. She still looked a bit green despite this being her third start. (op 7-1)
T/Jkpt: Not won. T/Plt: £226.60 to a £1 stake. Pool of £101,299.70 - 326.28 winning tickets. T/Qpdt: £30.80 to a £1 stake. Pool of £6,848.85 - 164.32 winning tickets. CR

4240 SEDGEFIELD (L-H)

Sunday, March 6

OFFICIAL GOING: Good to soft (soft in places; chs 6.5, hdl 6.7)
Divided bends with hurdles on outside.
Wind: light, half behind Weather: Bright and sunny

4506 KIEL & BALDVIN NOVICES' HURDLE (QUALIFIER) (PART OF JOHN WADE NOVICE HURDLE SERIES) (10 hdls) 2m 4f

2:20 (2:20) (Class 4) 4-Y-0+ **£2,081** (£611; £305; £152)

Form RPR
P3 1 **Cloudy Too (IRE)**[26] 3994 5-10-11 0 ShaneByrne(5) 126+
(Sue Smith) *in tch: hdwy to trck ldr 4 out: led 3 out: pushed clr bef next: comf* **7/1**[3]
-612 2 14 **Eighteen Carat (IRE)**[20] 4112 7-11-9 117 JasonMaguire 119
(Donald McCain) *led: hit 3 out and sn hdd: kpt on but no match wnr* **13/8**[1]
-23U 3 13 **Malin Bay (IRE)**[22] 4067 6-11-2 111 FearghalDavis 101
(Nicky Richards) *trckd ldr: rdn after 3 out: sn one pce* **15/8**[2]
0453 4 9 **Blazing Bay (IRE)**[18] 4145 6-10-9 0 PaddyAspell 85
(James Moffatt) *trckd ldr: rdn and wknd after 3 out* **16/1**
0060 5 2 ¾ **The Tiddly Tadpole**[6] 4393 6-10-9 0 HenryBrooke(7) 90
(Simon West) *in tch: trckd ldr 4 out: lost pl appr 3 out: rdn and wknd bef next* **33/1**
06 6 12 **Soul Bid (IRE)**[13] 4259 5-11-2 0 CampbellGillies 79
(Chris Grant) *hld up in tch: hdwy into midfield 5th: rdn after 6th: sn wknd* **100/1**
7 1 **Skybull (IRE)** 5-11-2 0 BrianHughes 78
(Howard Johnson) *midfield: lost pl and reminder 5th: wknd after 4 out* **8/1**
500 8 2 ¾ **Sam D'Oc (FR)**[20] 4112 5-11-2 0 RichieMcGrath 75
(Keith Reveley) *hld up: nt fluent 6th: hdwy after 4 out: hit 3 out and sn wknd* **50/1**
P-P0 9 19 **Beau Peak**[14] 4245 12-9-13 60 CallumWhillans(10) 51
(Donald Whillans) *trckd ldr: lost pl after 4th: bhd after 6th* **250/1**
4-56 10 9 **Tears From Heaven (USA)**[268] 712 5-11-2 0 BarryKeniry 50
(Mrs S Sunter) *hld up: a towards rr* **100/1**
00 P **Bunratty (IRE)**[13] 4259 5-11-2 0 (t) KennyJohnson —
(Robert Johnson) *nt fluent: a in rr: t.o whn p.u 3 out* **200/1**

5m 10.5s (17.80) **Going Correction** +0.725s/f (Soft) 11 Ran SP% **109.0**
Speed ratings (Par 105): **93,87,82,78,77 72,72,71,63,60** —
Tote Swingers: 1&2 £3.90, 1&3 £4.40, 2&3 £2.60 CSF £17.61 TOTE £8.90: £2.30, £1.50, £1.20; EX 20.60.
Owner Formulated Polymer Products Ltd **Bred** E J O'Sullivan **Trained** High Eldwick, W Yorks

FOCUS
The ground had dried out and was described as "very dead". Plenty of deadwood, and after a sound gallop there were only five in contention early on the final circuit and just three at the third-last. The winner looks an above-average northern novice.

NOTEBOOK
Cloudy Too(IRE), a well-beaten third on heavy ground here on his previous start, seemed to appreciate the much less testing ground. He moved on to the heels of the leader five out and when sent to the front after three out he quickly put his seal on the race. He clearly stays well and should be able to defy a penalty. (op 13-2)
Eighteen Carat(IRE), runner-up over further at Catterick after a three-month break, is jumping better now. He took them along but in the end was no match conceding the winner 12lb taking into account the rider's 5lb allowance. (op 7-4 tchd 6-4)
Malin Bay(IRE), seemingly progressive before unseating his rider on his previous start, had a fractional advantage over the runner-up on official ratings so this must go down as a shade disappointing. (tchd 7-4 and 2-1)
Blazing Bay(IRE) jumped better than on his first try over hurdles but he stopped to nothing three out. (op 12-1)
The Tiddly Tadpole, who showed little on his first two tries over hurdles, travelled surprisingly well until tiring three out. A low-grade handicap over 2m would seem a better option.

4507 VESTURVON BEGINNERS' CHASE (QUALIFIER) (PART OF COLLINS SEAFOODS YOUNG CHASERS SERIES) (13 fncs) 2m 110y

2:50 (2:50) (Class 4) 5-Y-0+ **£3,197** (£965; £497; £263)

Form RPR
23-0 1 **Sam Lord**[20] 4115 7-11-0 0 PaddyAspell 129+
(James Moffatt) *led 2nd: clr after 3rd: nt fluent 3 out: pushed out run-in: unchal* **16/1**
-P1F 2 4 ½ **Lightening Rod**[26] 3995 6-10-7 0 JakeGreenall(7) 125+
(Michael Easterby) *racd keenly: hld up: hdwy to go 2nd 2 out: nt rdn tl between last 2: kpt on but too much to do w wnr* **6/4**[1]
-F23 3 29 **Catch Bob (IRE)**[34] 3852 7-11-0 122 GrahamLee 106+
(Ferdy Murphy) *led 1st: sn stdd into 2nd: rdn after 3 out: lost 2nd 2 out: sn wknd: wl hld whn blnd last* **2/1**[2]
-000 4 14 **Gwyre (IRE)**[20] 4115 5-10-7 0 RichieMcGrath 79
(Tim Easterby) *in tch: lost pl after 6th: bhd fr 4 out* **20/1**
00-P F **Fushe Jo**[36] 3808 7-11-0 0 BrianHughes —
(Howard Johnson) *in tch: blnd and fell 4th* **5/1**[3]
21P4 U **Humbel Ben (IRE)**[35] 3838 8-11-0 0 WillKennedy —
(Alan Jones) *hld up: mstke and uns rdr 1st* **11/1**
0P/6 P **Craicneasy (IRE)**[141] 1869 8-11-0 0 AdrianLane —
(Bruce Mactaggart) *hld up: nt fluent 3rd: bhd after next: j. bdly rt 6th: p.u bef next* **100/1**

4m 14.7s (6.10) **Going Correction** +0.425s/f (Soft) 7 Ran SP% **110.0**
Speed ratings: **102,99,86,79,**— —,—
Tote Swingers: 1&2 £4.30, 1&3 £3.90, 2&3 £1.50 CSF £39.41 TOTE £13.40: £4.80, £1.40; EX 50.30.
Owner Coachmans Cottagers **Bred** Wickfield Farm Partnership **Trained** Cartmel, Cumbria

FOCUS
An all-the-way and decisive winner of this beginners' chase, and he's rated up 9lb on his besrt hurdles form. The second was given too much to do.

NOTEBOOK
Sam Lord, winner just once from 19 starts over hurdles and rated 112 in that sphere, was making his chasing debut on just his second run for this yard. Soon bowling along in a clear lead, his jumping was sound apart from the third-last. His rider took no chances jumping the last and he was never threatened. He picked up the reputation of being ungenuine in his previous yard but hopefully has turned over a new leaf. (op 12-1)
Lightening Rod, booked for third when falling at the last on his first try over fences here last month, was very keen in the early stages. Sent in pursuit of the winner two out he stayed on but had given him too much rope. His turn is only delayed. (op 2-1, tchd 5-2 in places)
Catch Bob(IRE), dropping back in trip, couldn't dominate. He lost second spot two out and was a tired third when blundering at the last. He needs even better ground and should not be written off yet. (op 9-4)
Gwyre(IRE), rated 92 over hurdles, hadn't shown much in three previous starts this time and she was well beaten off some way out on her chasing bow. (op 16-1)
Fushe Jo, a hard-to-train 129 rated hurdler, came down at the fourth fence, an open ditch. (op 4-1)
Craicneasy(IRE) Official explanation: jockey said gelding had a breathing problem (op 4-1)

4508 ARCTIC WARRIOR H'CAP HURDLE (13 hdls) 3m 3f 110y

3:20 (3:20) (Class 4) (0-110,108) 4-Y-0+ **£2,081** (£611; £305; £152)

Form RPR
6653 1 **Mauricetheathlete (IRE)**[52] 3529 8-10-11 **93** JasonMaguire 103+
(Martin Keighley) *prom: led 6th: rdn after 3 out: kpt on wl* **5/1**[2]
344V 2 7 **Matmata De Tendron (FR)**[13] 4256 11-10-1 **90** (p) PaulGallagher(7) 93
(Andrew Crook) *trckd ldrs: hdwy to go 2nd after 6th: rdn after 4 out: chal 3 out: kpt on but no match wnr* **25/1**
/600 3 1 ¾ **Borderhopper**[26] 3994 7-10-3 **85** GrahamLee 85
(Ferdy Murphy) *in tch on outer: hdwy to trck ldrs after 4 out: rdn 3 out: nt fluent 2 out: kpt on one pce* **28/1**
3422 4 2 ¼ **Oniz Tiptoes (IRE)**[12] 4276 10-10-3 **85** (v) PaddyAspell 84
(John Wainwright) *trckd ldrs: nt fluent 8th: rdn after next: sn outpcd: rallied appr 2 out: styd on* **5/1**[2]
-P03 5 6 **Bollin Fiona**[13] 4257 7-10-11 **103** CallumWhillans(10) 96
(Donald Whillans) *in tch: rdn after 4 out: sn one pce* **20/1**
0-43 6 7 **Playing The Field (IRE)**[12] 4276 6-11-5 **108** HenryBrooke(7) 95
(David O'Meara) *hld up: rdn after 8th: hdwy to trck ldrs after 4 out: wknd appr 2 out* **14/1**
0021 7 18 **Ontrack (IRE)**[26] 3996 7-10-6 **88** WilsonRenwick 59
(Rose Dobbin) *hld up: reminders early: rdn after 4th: nvr on terms* **7/2**[1]
0F60 8 49 **Veronicas Boy**[6] 4391 5-11-3 **99** (v) BarryKeniry 25
(George Moore) *hld up: sltly hmpd 5th: a in rr* **28/1**
4325 9 16 **Almond Court (IRE)**[13] 4254 8-9-7 **82** oh11 (tp) MrAdamNicol(7) —
(Robert Johnson) *led narrowly: hdd 6th: remained prom: hrd rdn 4 out: wknd after next* **66/1**
-040 P **Gouranga**[12] 4273 8-10-0 **82** oh2 (b) MattieBatchelor —
(Tony Carroll) *early reminders in rr: wl bhd whn hmpd by loose horse and p.u 5th* **10/1**
0435 B **Rebel Swing**[30] 3919 5-11-2 **98** HenryOliver —
(Sue Smith) *chsd ldrs: b.d 5th* **7/1**
3512 F **Wor Rom (IRE)**[6] 4391 7-11-1 **104** MrNHalley(7) —
(Elliott Cooper) *w ldrs: fell 5th* **11/2**[3]

7m 8.50s (16.50) **Going Correction** +0.725s/f (Soft) 12 Ran SP% **116.2**
Speed ratings (Par 105): **105,103,102,101,100 98,93,79,74,**— —,—
Tote Swingers: 1&2 £17.80, 1&3 £50.30, 2&3 £52.20 CSF £123.67 CT £3144.71 TOTE £6.80: £2.60, £4.70, £8.10; EX 86.40.
Owner Geoff Slatter **Bred** Sean Naughton **Trained** Condicote, Gloucs

FOCUS
A severe test of stamina in this modest handicap and the pace was generous.

NOTEBOOK

Mauricetheathlete(IRE), dropped 10lb after being amateur ridden on his last three starts, is quite a big sort and a proven thorough stayer. Making the best of his way home, he stayed on in willing fashion and won going away at the line. After coming to a halt the stable has come into a rich vein of form over the past five days, but it remains to be seen wether the owner's grandson regains the ride. (op 11-2)

Matmata De Tendron(FR), a winner of four handicap chases over this course and distance, one from a 10lb higher mark, is getting a bit long in the tooth, but he remains as enthusiastic as ever and never gave up in pursuit of the winner. (tchd 22-1)

Borderhopper, who took the bypass route, has started life in handicaps from a very low mark. He looked a real threat three out but in the end had no excuse.

Oniz Tiptoes(IRE), who took this a year ago from a 10lb higher mark, ran respectably for the third time in a row, but his losing run is now 12 months long and seems likely to continue. (tchd 9-2)

Ontrack(IRE), 3lb higher than when accounting for Oniz Tiptoes and Matmata De Tendron over this course and distance last month, never went a yard. Soon given sharp reminders in the end, his rider gave up the lost cause. He had looked open to further improvement and this was simply too bad to be true. (tchd 4-1)

Gouranga, tumbling down the ratings, was reluctant. Soon detached in last, she was tailed off when pulled up after being cannoned into by a loose horse. She looks one to avoid. (op 7-1)

Wor Rom(IRE), raised a stone after his clear-cut Newcastle success, was bang in the firing line when falling at the fifth flight. (op 7-1)

4509 ICE FRESH H'CAP CHASE (16 fncs) 2m 4f

3:50 (3:50) (Class 5) (0-95,89) 5-Y-0+ £2,341 (£687; £343; £171)

Form RPR

00U3 **1** **Flighty Mist**[14] 4244 9-10-9 **78** .... PaulGallagher(7) 93+
(Sandy Forster) *hld up: hdwy after 9th: chsd ldrs 4 out: chal 3 out: rdn to ld between last 2: kpt on wl* **8/1**

32/F **2** *4 ½* **Wee George**[19] 4133 9-10-11 **78** .... ShaneByrne(5) 87
(Sue Smith) *trckd ldr: led after 4 out: rdn whn hdd between last 2: one pced* **13/2**[3]

P654 **3** *¾* **Ravensbill (IRE)**[19] 4138 9-10-11 **73** .... CampbellGillies 80
(William Amos) *hld up: slow 9th: hdwy 5 out: outpcd after 3 out: styd on wl after 2 out* **10/1**

3P22 **4** *2 ¼* **Panthers Run**[14] 4241 11-10-2 **64** .... (t) DougieCostello 69
(Jonathan Haynes) *hld up in tch: rdn after 4 out: kpt on same pce: nvr on terms: b.b.v* **9/2**[1]

2615 **5** *27* **Dark Gentleman**[32] 3884 8-11-3 **82** .... (b[1]) JamesO'Farrell(3) 75+
(Evelyn Slack) *led: clr 3rd to 8th: hdd after 4 out: wknd after next* **9/2**[1]

00U3 **6** *9* **Toulouse Express (IRE)**[12] 4279 12-11-12 **88** .... (v) KennyJohnson 64
(Robert Johnson) *prom on outer: rdn after 4 out: slow 3 out: sn wknd* **18/1**

0303 **P** **Teenando (IRE)**[14] 4241 11-10-11 **73** .... JasonMaguire —
(Sue Smith) *trckd ldrs: lost pl qckly after 9th: t.o whn p.u bef 3 out* **11/2**[2]

505P **P** **Just Dan**[32] 3883 5-9-8 **64** .... GaryRutherford(7) —
(David Thompson) *hld up in rr: reminders after 8th: bhd whn p.u bef11th* **20/1**

0002 **P** **Mansonien L'As (FR)**[40] 3726 5-11-12 **89** .... GrahamLee —
(Ferdy Murphy) *hld up: rdn after 10th: sn no imp: t.o whn p.u bef 3 out* **9/2**[1]

5m 9.70s (6.70) **Going Correction** +0.425s/f (Soft) **9** Ran SP% **113.5**
Speed ratings: **103,101,100,100,89 85,—,—,—**
Tote Swingers: 1&2 £10.10, 1&3 £6.10, 2&3 £14.30 CSF £58.07 CT £524.44 TOTE £11.60: £3.80, £2.70, £1.90; EX 64.50.

Owner J R Jeffreys **Bred** J R Jeffreys **Trained** Kirk Yetholm, Borders

FOCUS

A low-grade handicap chase run at a sound pace. The form is rated around the second.

NOTEBOOK

Flighty Mist seemed to show vastly improved form when third in a novice chase here two weeks ago. She recorded an RPR of 100 that day yet her official rating remained unchanged at just 78. Improving from the rear, she landed upsides two out and soon had it in the bag. It was her trainer's first win for 10 months. (op 6-1)

Wee George, who fell early on on his return after two years on the sidelines, had completed just twice from five previous starts over fences. Having taking charge, he was very much second best in the end. (op 7-1 tchd 6-1)

Ravensbill(IRE), a long-standing maiden coming late to fences, stayed on in willing fashion after struggling to keep up four out and will be suited by a stiffer test. (op 9-1)

Panthers Run's one win over fences from 29 previous attempts was 18 months ago now. He was later reported to have bled from the nose. Official explanation: trainer said gelding bled from nose (op 5-1 tchd 4-1)

Dark Gentleman, 5lb higher than his all-the-way success at Newcastle two outings ago, took them along in first-time blinkers, but his chance had long gone when he blundered two out. (op 6-1)

Teenando(IRE) continues out of form and was another some way behind when calling it a day. Official explanation: jockey said gelding never was never travelling (op 11-2 tchd 6-1)

Mansonien L'As(FR), a maiden over fences in France, made his handicap debut from a low mark, but he dropped away in a matter of strides before being pulled up. (op 11-2 tchd 6-1)

4510 FROSTI H'CAP CHASE (13 fncs) 2m 110y

4:20 (4:20) (Class 5) (0-90,89) 5-Y-0+ £2,211 (£649; £324; £162)

Form RPR

FF3F **1** **Gavroche Gaugain (FR)**[26] 3997 7-11-2 **89** .... TonyKelly(10) 97+
(Ferdy Murphy) *trckd ldrs: rdn 4 out: chal 2 out: led bef last: drvn and kpt on wl run-in* **8/1**[3]

P122 **2** *3 ¾* **Lerida**[26] 3997 9-11-3 **87** .... (p) HenryBrooke(7) 92
(Sharon Watt) *led narrowly: hdd after 6th: led again after 3 out: hdd bef last: one pce run-in* **2/1**[1]

2614 **3** *3 ¾* **Authentic Act (IRE)**[26] 3997 7-11-6 **83** .... GrahamLee 85
(Martin Todhunter) *hld up: hdwy after 6 out: rdn and outpcd after 5 out: rallied after 3 out: ev ch 2 out: drvn and one pce run-in* **15/2**[2]

/62P **4** *12* **Kit Carson (IRE)**[28] 3970 11-11-0 **84** .... PaulGallagher(7) 76
(R MacDonald) *midfield: hrd rdn after 5 out: sn no imp: lft in remote 4th last* **12/1**

P055 **5** *18* **Troodos Jet**[26] 3997 10-10-11 **77** .... (p) JamesO'Farrell(3) 51
(Dianne Sayer) *midfield: wknd after 5 out* **15/2**[2]

P646 **6** *4 ½* **Railway Park (IRE)**[26] 3993 7-11-1 **78** .... (p) PaddyAspell 48
(John Wainwright) *midfield: hit 2nd: reminders after 5th: lost pl after 7th: sn bhd* **14/1**

0-FP **7** *9* **Whatcanyasay**[159] 1647 10-10-0 **66** .... (b) JamesHalliday(3) 28
(Evelyn Slack) *trckd ldrs: led after 6th: rdn whn hdd after 3 out: wknd after next* **10/1**

/P0F **P** **Steel Man (IRE)**[105] 2548 9-10-0 **63** oh12 .... AdrianLane —
(Bruce Mactaggart) *hld up: a bhd: t.o whn p.u bef 2 out* **33/1**

P006 **F** **Also Jo**[22] 4068 8-11-10 **87** .... CampbellGillies 86
(William Amos) *mstkes: prom: rdn 4 out: outpcd after 3 out: hld in 4th whn blnd and fell last* **18/1**

101U **P** **Janal (IRE)**[19] 4133 8-10-13 **83** .... GaryRutherford(7) —
(Stuart Coltherd) *trckd ldrs: lost pl appr 7th: sn wknd: t.o whn p.u bef last* **9/1**

600F **P** **Solo Choice**[14] 4241 5-10-9 **77** .... AlexanderVoy(5) —
(Ian McInnes) *hld up in rr: j. bdly rt 4th: sn bhd: t.o whn p.u bef 7th* **33/1**

4m 21.5s (12.90) **Going Correction** +0.425s/f (Soft) **11** Ran SP% **112.6**
Speed ratings: **86,84,82,76,68 66,62,—,—,—, —**
Tote Swingers: 1&2 £5.70, 1&3 £8.00, 2&3 £3.40 CSF £24.23 CT £124.65 TOTE £10.60: £2.50, £1.40, £2.00; EX 24.60.

Owner Universal Recycling Company **Bred** Jean-Marie Huss **Trained** West Witton, N Yorks

FOCUS

Another low grade handicap chase and again the pace was sound.

NOTEBOOK

Gavroche Gaugain(FR), third here in January, the only time he had completed in five starts over fences, broke his duck at the 16th attempt. After a three-way battle he took command on the run-in to give his trainer a welcome winner. (op 9-1)

Lerida, much improved since switching to this yard, is now 12lb higher than his last win at Huntingdon in January three outings ago. After a head to head, he was tired near the line. (op 5-2)

Authentic Act(IRE), twice a winner over hurdles round here, had finished some way behind Lerida here last month on his first try over fences. He worked hard to join issue with the first two on the run down to the last but in the end came up well short. He prefers even better ground. (op 7-1)

Kit Carson(IRE), without a win for almost five years, has struggled since sitting out two years on the sidelines. He was handed a modest fourth place at the final fence. (op 10-1)

Whatcanyasay, whose four wins over fences have come here - the latest from a 22lb higher mark over two years ago, had been absent since pulling up at the track in September. After showing ahead, he seemed to fold tamely and in the end was well beaten. (op 14-1 tchd 9-1)

Also Jo, who has been out of form over hurdles, was making his chase debut. He survived several jumping mistakes and was booked for a respectable fourth when falling heavily at the final fence. (op 16-1)

4511 BARDI H'CAP HURDLE (10 hdls) 2m 4f

4:50 (4:50) (Class 5) (0-95,99) 4-Y-0+ £1,691 (£496; £248; £124)

Form RPR

-500 **1** **Amjad**[152] 1666 14-9-7 **69** .... (p) HenryBrooke(7) 73
(Simon West) *hld up in rr: hdwy into midfield after 5th: chsd ldrs 4 out: chal 3 out: led narrowly between last 2: hld on u.p run-in* **66/1**

/322 **2** *nk* **Classic Henri**[10] 4302 7-10-11 **83** .... JamesO'Farrell(3) 87
(Barry Murtagh) *midfield: hdwy to trck ldrs 4 out: upsides on bit 2 out: sn drvn: kpt on but a jst hld run-in* **4/1**[1]

0045 **3** *11* **Sam Patch**[26] 3993 8-10-1 **80** .... (tp) CallumWhillans(10) 74
(Donald Whillans) *prom: led after 6th: hdd 4 out: regained ld after 3 out: hdd between last 2: wknd run-in* **9/1**

60-0 **4** *2* **Zero Six Zoo (IRE)**[116] 2314 8-11-2 **85** .... GrahamLee 76
(Karen McLintock) *trckd ldrs on outer: rdn and outpcd after 4 out: kpt on again after 2 out* **16/1**

-05P **5** *22* **Just Posh**[18] 4146 9-9-13 **75** .... (p) PaulGallagher(7) 47
(Rayson Nixon) *midfield: rdn and outpcd 4 out: nvr on terms* **12/1**

00P4 **6** *6* **Yes Mate**[63] 3336 7-9-7 **69** oh1 .... MissECSayer(7) 35
(Dianne Sayer) *midfield: hdwy to trck ldrs 6th: led 4 out: hdd after 3 out: wknd bef next* **7/1**

04-0 **7** *4 ½* **Patrixtoo (FR)**[305] 157 10-10-2 **71** .... BrianHughes 33
(Tim Fitzgerald) *midfield: rdn bef 4 out: sn no imp* **6/1**[2]

0564 **8** *13* **Lindseyfield Lodge (IRE)**[14] 4241 10-10-11 **80** .... (p) KennyJohnson 30
(Robert Johnson) *led towards outer: hdd after 6th: wknd after next* **25/1**

-006 **9** *22* **Sydney Cove (IRE)**[19] 4136 5-11-3 **86** .... FearghalDavis 17
(William Amos) *prom tl rdn and wknd after 4 out* **28/1**

-403 **10** *18* **Sharadiyn**[29] 3951 8-11-8 **94** .... JamesHalliday(3) 8
(Clive Mulhall) *trckd ldrs: outpcd after 4 out: wknd bef next* **13/2**[3]

-000 **11** *4 ½* **Red Tanber (IRE)**[20] 4115 8-10-11 **80** .... AdrianLane —
(Bruce Mactaggart) *hld up: rdn after 4 out: a towards rr* **40/1**

3101 **12** *22* **Sea Cliff (IRE)**[19] 3728 7-11-9 **99** .... EdGlassonbury(7) —
(Andrew Crook) *prom: rdn after 6th: wknd after next: t.o* **17/2**

0-0P **P** **Soneva Gili (IRE)**[18] 4146 7-10-0 **69** oh5 .... CampbellGillies —
(Shelley Johnstone) *chsd ldrs: rdn and wknd after 6th: t.o whn p.u 3 out* **66/1**

004 **P** **Some Catch (IRE)**[41] 3717 5-10-0 **69** oh9 .... DougieCostello —
(Elliott Cooper) *hld up: a bhd: p.u 3 out* **8/1**

5m 13.2s (20.50) **Going Correction** +0.725s/f (Soft) **14** Ran SP% **118.0**
Speed ratings (Par 103): **88,87,83,82,73 71,69,64,55,48 46,37,—,—**
Tote Swingers: 1&2 £46.50, 1&3 £51.50, 2&3 £10.50 CSF £311.58 CT £2666.70 TOTE £74.10: £13.80, £1.40, £3.00; EX 533.30 TRIFECTA Not won..

Owner Miss Kate Milligan **Bred** Saeed Manana **Trained** Middleham Moor, N Yorks

FOCUS

The top-weight in this handicap hurdle was 10lb higher than the previous chase yet the prize-money was over £500 less. Again the pace was generous and there were three in a line at the penultimate flight. Modest form, the winner 5lb off last season's best.

NOTEBOOK

Amjad, now in his 15th year, recorded his first success for a year and a half. His usual run style is to stay on late in the day from an unpromising position, but here, on his first outing for five months, he was in contention throughout the final circuit and in the end the old boy did just enough.

Classic Henri, raised 5lb after his improved second at Ayr, came there cruising on the run round to two out. After a good battle he came off just second best at the line. (tchd 9-2)

Sam Patch, closely matched with Sea Cliff and Classic Henri on C&D running in January, found 2m too short next time. After regaining the lead three out he weakened between the last two. (tchd 10-1)

Zero Six Zoo(IRE), who had shown precious little in four previous starts over hurdles, had been dropped 5lb after his handicap bow. He couldn't keep up with the first three over the final three flights and is worth a try over further. (op 18-1 tchd 14-1)

Sea Cliff(IRE), runner-up in an all-weather handicap since his narrow and hard-fought success from Classic Henri here, had to race from a 10lb higher mark, and he stopped to nothing some way from home. His rider reported he was never travelling. Official explanation: jockey said gelding was never travelling (op 7-1 tchd 9-1)

T/Plt: £337.30 to a £1 stake.Pool of £97,035.12 - 210.00 winning tickets. T/Qpdt: £99.30 to a £1 stake. Pool of £6,513.88 - 48.50 winning tickets. AS

4512 - 4520a (Foreign Racing) - See Raceform Interactive

[4404]FFOS LAS (L-H)

Monday, March 7

OFFICIAL GOING: Good to soft (good in places; 7.5)

Wind: virtually nil Weather: sunny

4521 NOAH'S ARK APPEAL AND AAI CARE JOLLY NOVICES' HURDLE (8 hdls) 2m

2:20 (2:20) (Class 4) 4-Y-0+ **£2,439** (£716; £358; £178)

Form RPR

F-3 **1** **Katchmore (IRE)**[105] 2570 4-10-7 0 JimmyMcCarthy 106+
(Michael Blanshard) *mde all: set stdy gallop: wandered 1st: drew clr w runner-up 3 out: in command next: pushed out flat: comf* **14/1**

0402 **2** *9* **Tenby Jewel (IRE)**[6] 4404 6-11-1 0 SamThomas 105
(Keith Goldsworthy) *chsd wnr: wnt upsides wnr after 5th: drvn and outpcd after next: kpt on same pce and no ch w wnr between last 2* **9/4**[1]

3154 **3** *5* **Jolly Roger (IRE)**[29] 3967 4-11-0 120 (p) RhysFlint 101
(John Flint) *in tch: chsd ldng pair bef 3 out: sn u.p and outpcd: 3rd and wl hld whn mstke last* **9/4**[1]

34P2 **4** *2 1/4* **Murcar**[29] 3962 6-11-3 112 OliverDayman(5) 105
(Alison Thorpe) *chsd ldr tl after 5th: 4th and struggling u.p next: 4th and wl hld 2 out* **7/2**[2]

05 **5** *13* **Knockdolian (IRE)**[48] 3613 4-10-7 0 (t) PaddyBrennan 83
(Roger Charlton) *nt jump wl: hld up in tch: j. awkwardly and nrly uns rdr 2nd: rdn and wknd bef 3 out* **5/1**[3]

6 *3/4* **Que On Time (IRE)**[41] 3735 7-10-1 0 MichaelByrne(7) 79
(Tim Vaughan) *t.k.h: hld up in tch: rdn and wknd bef 3 out: wl btn whn mstke 2 out* **40/1**

3m 57.0s (8.00) **Going Correction** +0.75s/f (Soft)
WFA 4 from 5yo+ 7lb **6** Ran SP% **109.5**
Speed ratings (Par 105): **110,105,103,101,95 95**
toteswingers:1&2 £6.50, 2&3 £1.40, 1&3 £2.20 CSF £44.34 TOTE £16.70: £3.60, £1.40; EX 47.50.
Owner Sara Collie,Nigel Kelly & Alison Auvray **Bred** M J Lewin And D Grieve **Trained** Upper Lambourn, Berks

FOCUS
A modest novice hurdle, rated around the runner-up and third. The winner produced a big step up.

NOTEBOOK
Katchmore(IRE) made just about all to open his account over hurdles at the third attempt and land his first success of any description at the 11th time of asking. He had been absent since finishing a remote third over C&D in November, but has clearly improved since then and the better ground did the trick. He's entitled to come on for it, but a penalty will make his life more difficult. (op 12-1 tchd 16-1)
Tenby Jewel(IRE), second over C&D six days earlier, emerged as the only danger to the winner from two out. He put in his place soon after, though, and likely found the run coming soon enough. (op 10-3)
Jolly Roger(IRE)'s effort proved short-lived on this drop down in class and first-time cheekpieces failed to have the desired effect. (op 2-1)
Murcar was well beaten and continues to prove vulnerable under his penalty. (op 3-1)

4522 STENA LINE - MAKING GOOD TIME H'CAP HURDLE (11 hdls) 2m 6f

2:50 (2:50) (Class 5) (0-90,87) 4-Y-0+ **£1,788** (£525; £262; £131)

Form RPR

-633 **1** **The Composer**[13] 4272 9-10-11 **72** JimmyMcCarthy 87+
(Michael Blanshard) *hld up in tch towards rr: hdwy 6th: drew clr w runner-up 8th: led bef next: clr and in command 2 out: pushed out flat: comf* **8/1**

5P **2** *19* **Gleannacreim (IRE)**[53] 3530 8-11-5 **80** RichardJohnson 83+
(Tim Vaughan) *hld up in tch in last trio: hdwy on outer 6th: led bef 8th and sn clr w wnr: hdd bef 3 out: drvn and btn bef 2 out: no ch w wnr: plugged on for 2nd* **6/1**[2]

P011 **3** *13* **Border Lad**[6] 4405 7-10-13 **79** OliverDayman(5) 67
(Alison Thorpe) *in tch in midfield: j.rt and mstke 5th: hdwy on inner to ld and mstke 7th: sn hdd: 3rd and wknd u.p bef 3 out: no ch whn hit last* **9/4**[1]

-FPP **4** *8* **Wham Bang**[53] 3530 7-10-10 **71** (p) SeanQuinlan 50
(Robin Mathew) *in tch in midfield: 5th and wknd u.p after 8th: wl btn next: plugged on to go poor 4th last: t.o* **25/1**

64P4 **5** *1* **Killing Me Softly**[13] 4273 10-11-1 **79** (v) IanPopham(3) 57
(Brian Forsey) *mde most tl 6th: 6th and wknd u.p after 8th: wl btn next: t.o* **17/2**

P546 **6** *7* **Standing Order**[82] 2956 8-10-10 **71** (t) JamieMoore 43
(Richard Ford) *hld up in tch in rr: hdwy 6th: 4th and drvn after 8th: sn wknd: wl btn whn hit 2 out: t.o* **25/1**

P/40 **7** *11* **Kings Story (IRE)**[60] 3400 7-10-8 **69** JohnnyFarrelly 31
(Sophie Leech) *in tch: reminders after 3rd: u.p and toiling after 6th: 7th and t.o bef 3 out* **16/1**

5032 **P** **Bright Decision**[13] 4272 5-11-12 **87** (b1) DaveCrosse —
(Joanna Davis) *in tch in midfield on outer: mstke 1st: hdwy to press ldrs after 5th: j.lft and wknd qckly 8th: t.o whn p.u next* **11/1**

-P0P **P** **Tinalliat (FR)**[38] 3792 8-10-9 **70** (v1) RhysFlint —
(David Rees) *w ldrs tl lost pl u.p 7th: bhd next: t.o whn p.u 3 out* **28/1**

P3-P **P** **Castlemaine Vic (IRE)**[53] 3530 8-10-13 **81** (v) PeterHatton(7) —
(Adrian Wintle) *in tch in midfield: reminders after 4th: dropped to last and u.p after 5th: t.o 7th tl p.u 8th* **12/1**

P-00 **P** **Walls Way**[105] 2589 7-11-6 **86** LeeEdwards(5) —
(Tony Carroll) *in tch in last trio: rdn and wknd 8th: t.o whn p.u next* **15/2**[3]

5P62 **P** **Zi Missile (IRE)**[6] 4405 7-9-12 **66** MichaelByrne(7) —
(Mary Evans) *chsd ldrs: led 6th tl blnd bdly: hdd and lost pl next: nt rcvr and lost tch 8th: t.o whn p.u 3 out* **12/1**

0004 **P** **Steely Bird**[12] 4289 4-10-6 **79** (tp) PeterToole(3) —
(Richard Hawker) *chsd ldrs tl lost pl u.p 7th: bhd next: t.o whn p.u 3 out* **33/1**

5m 35.4s (17.40) **Going Correction** +0.75s/f (Soft)
WFA 4 from 5yo+ 8lb **13** Ran SP% **122.1**
Speed ratings (Par 103): **98,91,86,83,83 80,76,—,—,— —,—,—**
toteswingers:1&2 £13.20, 2&3 £5.00, 1&3 £4.10 CSF £55.04 CT £147.35 TOTE £9.20: £2.70, £2.70, £2.10; EX 70.80.
Owner A D Jones **Bred** D A And Mrs Hicks **Trained** Upper Lambourn, Berks
■ A double for Michael Blanshard, his first winners over jumps since 2009.

FOCUS
An ordinary handicap, run at a steady gallop and few landed a serious blow. The winner posted his best hurdles figure since 2009.

NOTEBOOK
The Composer came right away from the runner-up nearing the penultimate flight and was a most decisive winner, handing his jockey/trainer a quick double. He was 0-18 over hurdles coming here (only sixth in this event last season), but he had been in better form of late and this quicker surface enabled him to produce a clear career best. The handicapper will likely make his life an awful lot harder now, though, so surely looking for something under a penalty is his best option.
Gleannacreim(IRE) met support on his return from a 53-day break and was the only one to go with the winner leaving the back straight. It was clear jumping three out he was getting the worst of the argument with that rival, though, and he ultimately finished well beaten. He was still a clear second-best, however, and his turn probably isn't far off. (tchd 11-2)
Border Lad, 8lb higher, was laboured from four out and it was probably the combination of quicker ground along with the run coming soon enough that did for him. (op 2-1 tchd 5-2)
Wham Bang made up ground on the far side, but was done with from the fourth-last. He had failed to complete in three previous spins this term so it was a step back in the right direction. (op 40-1 tchd 50-1)
Bright Decision Official explanation: jockey said gelding did not face the blinkers
Walls Way Official explanation: jockey said gelding had a breathing problem

4523 HALL & ROCHE H'CAP CHASE (15 fncs) 2m 3f 110y

3:25 (3:25) (Class 4) (0-115,112) 5-Y-0+ **£3,089** (£907; £453; £226)

Form RPR

-60P **1** **Ready Or Not (IRE)**[81] 2982 8-10-7 **93** AndrewGlassonbury 102+
(Bob Buckler) *mstkes: hld up in tch: blnd 4th: hdwy to chse ldng pair 10th: rdn to chal 3 out: j. awkwardly but landed in ld 2 out: sn drvn and racd awkwardly: forged ahd fnl 100yds: rdn out* **7/1**

14P **2** *1 1/2* **Silver Story**[216] 1177 8-11-10 **110** (t) RichardJohnson 115
(Tim Vaughan) *led: rdn after 3 out: hdd next: stl ev ch u.p last: no ex and btn fnl 100yds* **11/2**

24-5 **3** *18* **Shake The Barley (IRE)**[16] 4223 8-11-11 **111** PaddyBrennan 109+
(Tom George) *in tch: hit 6th: chsd ldr 9th: ev ch whn blnd 12th: 3rd and keeping on same pce whn nt fluent 2 out: sn wknd* **15/8**[1]

020U **4** *37* **Star Galaxy (IRE)**[14] 4265 11-11-6 **106** (b) RhysFlint 61
(John Flint) *hld up in tch: hdwy on outer to chse ldrs 8th: j. slowly and lost pl next: lost tch wl bef 12th: t.o whn j.rt 2 out* **10/1**

F402 **P** **High Jack (IRE)**[33] 3878 9-11-8 **108** NickScholfield —
(Andy Turnell) *chsd ldr tl 7th: lost pl and mstke 10th: lost tch next: sn eased and t.o whn p.u 12th* **7/2**[2]

0P50 **P** **Award Winner**[29] 3962 8-11-12 **112** APMcCoy —
(Brendan Powell) *j.lft: chsd ldrs: j.lft and mstke 3rd: wnt 2nd 7th tl 9th: wknd qckly bef 11th: sn eased and t.o: p.u 12th* **5/1**[3]

5m 1.10s (-4.90) **Going Correction** -0.10s/f (Good) **6** Ran SP% **110.6**
Speed ratings: **105,104,97,82,— —**
toteswingers:1&2 £8.80, 2&3 £3.30, 1&3 £3.10 CSF £41.38 TOTE £8.10: £3.60, £4.00; EX 45.70.
Owner Christopher And Anne Collier **Bred** James T Williams **Trained** Henley, Somerset

FOCUS
A tight handicap, run at a sound enough gallop. The winner is rated to his hurdles mark with the second to form.

NOTEBOOK
Ready Or Not(IRE) made numerous errors, but still ran out a ready enough winner on his first outing since pulling up on his chase debut in December. He initially came under pressure turning for home, but responded and hit top gear from the third-last. He proved awkward under pressure, but his rider was at his strongest and he was well on top at the line. There ought to be improvement in him after this career-first win and the sounder surface was obviously to his liking, so he could defy a likely rise. (op 8-1)
Silver Story ◆ was returning from a 216-day absence and raced in a first-time tongue-tie. He proved game in attempting to make all, but found the winner that bit too quick where it mattered. There should be another race in him before long back over a stiffer test. (tchd 5-1 and 6-1)
Shake The Barley(IRE) was well backed. He held every chance, but wasn't fluent over his fences and was feeling the pinch prior to hitting four out. (op 7-4 tchd 6-4)
High Jack(IRE) fell in a hole on the far side. Official explanation: jockey said gelding lost its action (tchd 9-2)
Award Winner made mistakes and remains hard to predict. (tchd 9-2)

4524 BRIGHTWELLS THE BLOODSTOCK EQUINE AUCTIONEER H'CAP HURDLE (10 hdls) 2m 4f

4:00 (4:00) (Class 3) (0-125,124) 4-Y-0+ **£4,553** (£1,337; £668; £333)

Form RPR

5001 **1** **Mickmacmagoole (IRE)**[26] 4008 9-11-4 **116** (p) APMcCoy 119
(Evan Williams) *chsd ldr tl led bef 3 out: rdn bef 2 out: drvn and kpt on between last 2: styd on wl flat* **5/1**[2]

U411 **2** *2 3/4* **Sparrow Hills (IRE)**[44] 3688 7-11-5 **124** RobertKirk(7) 125
(Steven Dixon) *led tl bef 3 out: sn rdn: rallying u.p and disputing 2nd whn bmpd last: sn lft chsng wnr: no imp flat* **5/1**[2]

2333 **3** *2* **Zakatal**[26] 4012 5-11-4 **116** (bt) RichardJohnson 118+
(Philip Hobbs) *j.lft: hld up in tch: hdwy to press wnr 3 out: rdn and nt qckning whn j.lft and mstke 2 out: disputing 2nd and one pce whn j.lft and bmpd rival last: 3rd and one pce flat* **4/1**[1]

-11P **4** *10* **Comehomequietly (IRE)**[142] 1864 7-11-5 **124** MrJFMathias(7) 115
(David Rees) *t.k.h: hld up in tch: rdn and wknd bef 3 out: wl btn whn bdly hmpd last* **6/1**[3]

-500 **5** *58* **Mae Cigan (FR)**[31] 3934 8-10-8 **106** JimmyMcCarthy 44
(Michael Blanshard) *hld up in tch: hmpd 2nd: rdn and mstke 7th: sn wknd: t.o fr 2 out* **13/2**

P/6P **P** **Sexy Rexy (IRE)**[39] 3768 10-10-8 **106** PaddyBrennan —
(Nigel Twiston-Davies) *mstke 1st: sn pushed along and wl nt gng wl after: reminders after 2nd: bhd and rdn after 4th: lost tch next: t.o whn p.u 7th* **12/1**

F050 **F** **Troubletimestwo (FR)**[34] 3874 5-10-7 **110** LeeEdwards(5) 111
(Tony Carroll) *chsd ldrs: rdn and sltly outpcd bef 3 out: rallying u.p in 4th whn squeezed for room: bmpd and fell last* **9/1**

U056 **F** **Alesandro Mantegna (IRE)**[4] 4439 6-11-1 **113** (p) JamieMoore —
(Keith Goldsworthy) *hld up in tch tl fell 2nd* **6/1**[3]

5m 0.50s (11.50) **Going Correction** +0.75s/f (Soft) **8** Ran SP% **112.9**
Speed ratings (Par 107): **107,105,105,101,77 —,—,—**
toteswingers:1&2 £4.70, 2&3 £1.50, 1&3 £2.60 CSF £29.58 CT £108.11 TOTE £3.90: £1.10, £3.10, £1.30; EX 23.80.
Owner A Turton & P Langford **Bred** Tower Bloodstock **Trained** Llancarfan, Vale Of Glamorgan

FOCUS
An open-looking if ordinary handicap run at an average gallop, and it proved fairly eventful. The winner is rated to form.

NOTEBOOK
Mickmacmagoole(IRE) ended his losing run in a seller at Ludlow last month and followed up with a ready display on this return to a handicap. This extended his record under the champion jockey to 3-4 and although a rise will make things tougher, it wouldn't surprise to see him make a bold bid for the hat-trick. (tchd 9-2)

Sparrow Hills(IRE) was bidding for a hat-trick off 7lb higher and made a good fist of it under a positive ride. He gives the form a fair look. (op 9-2)
Zakatal, keen early on, emerged with every chance only to once more fail to fully go through with his effort when it really mattered and remains one to avoid for win-only purposes. (op 9-2)
Comehomequietly(IRE) was last seen pulling up in his quest for a hat-trick at Cheltenham in October. He shaped well enough before tiring, but does now look weighted to his best. (op 11-2)
Sexy Rexy(IRE) Official explanation: jockey said gelding was lame (op 10-1)
Troubletimestwo(FR), up in trip, was responding to pressure and running an improved race prior to departing, having been hampered at the last flight. (op 10-1)

4525 TUSKAFIVE OF FISHGUARD H'CAP CHASE (18 fncs) 3m
4:35 (4:35) (Class 5) (0-90,88) 5-Y-O+ **£2,081** (£611; £305; £152)

Form RPR

5-52 **1** **Derawar (IRE)**[6] 4409 12-11-4 **87**..........(p) MsLucyJones(7) 102+
(Lucy Jones) *chsd ldr: led 2nd tl 6th: chsd ldr after tl led again 13th: mde rest: drew clr 3 out: styd on wl* **7/2**[3]

3P2P **2** *10* **Bob Casey (IRE)**[2] 4483 9-11-12 **88**..........(p) JamieMoore 94
(Keith Goldsworthy) *chsd ldr tl led 6th: hit 8th and 9th: hdd 13th: styd w wnr tl rdn and btn 3 out: plugged on same pce after* **5/1**

6612 **3** *18* **Stop The Show (IRE)**[29] 3961 10-11-11 **87**.......... RichardJohnson 80
(Richard Phillips) *hld up in tch: hdwy to chse ldrs and blnd 12th: chsd ldng pair and drvn after 14th: no imp and wl btn next* **11/4**[2]

-024 **4** *2* **Tora Bora (GER)**[12] 4292 9-11-1 **77**..........(p) SamThomas 68
(Brendan Powell) *led tl 2nd: mstke and lost pl 5th: nvr travelling wl after: rdn and modest 4th after 14th: no prog after* **5/2**[1]

4PP0 **5** *50* **Fourpointone**[39] 3768 10-10-13 **75**..........(p) FelixDeGiles 18
(Ed de Giles) *in tch in last pair: hdwy to chse ldrs after 5th: lost pl and pushed along after 9th: lost tch 14th: eased and j.rt last: virtually p.u flat: t.o* **12/1**

0600 **6** *¾* **Lions In Law**[13] 4273 7-11-1 **80**..........(b[1]) PeterToole(3) 22
(Richard Hawker) *in tch: chsd ldrs 10th: struggling u.p whn j.rt 14th: sn wl bhd: virtually p.u flat: t.o* **9/1**

6m 20.6s (-2.40) **Going Correction** -0.10s/f (Good) **6** Ran SP% **111.8**
Speed ratings: **100,96,90,90,73 73**
CSF £20.55 TOTE £4.40: £2.00, £2.00; EX 21.10.
Owner Simon Jones **Bred** His Highness The Aga Khan's Studs S C **Trained** Kilgetty, Pembrokeshire
■ A first winner under rules as a trainer for Lucy Jones.
■ Stewards' Enquiry : Richard Johnson five-day ban: used whip in manner causing gelding to be wealed (Mar 21-25)

FOCUS
A very ordinary handicap run at a fair gallop. The winner improved on his recent C&D run.

NOTEBOOK
Derawar(IRE), well backed, finished second over slightly further at this venue six days earlier and he went one better with a most decisive display. His rider took the race by the scruff of the neck exiting the back straight for the last time and he put the runner-up firmly in his place after the penultimate fence. The quicker ground made all the difference to him. (op 5-1)
Bob Casey(IRE), equipped with first-time cheekpieces, was turning out after being badly hampered prior to pulling up at Kempton two days earlier and met support. He was the only one to give the winner a serious race off the home turn, but cried enough before the second-last. He helps to set the level. (op 9-2 tchd 4-1)
Stop The Show(IRE) arrived here near the top of his game and did his best, but this quicker surface found him out. (op 5-2)
Tora Bora(GER) was sent out to make all, but went in snatches from an early stage and is one to tread carefully with. (op 11-4)

4526 LLEWELLYN HUMPHREYS NOVICES' HUNTERS' CHASE (17 fncs) 2m 5f
5:10 (5:10) (Class 6) 5-Y-0+ **£1,374** (£426; £212; £106)

Form RPR

5-31 **1** **Oca De Thaix (FR)**[26] 4011 9-11-7 105.......... MissCharlotteEvans(7) 114+
(Keith Goldsworthy) *racd wd early: in tch: hdwy to press ldr 5th tl mstke 10th: lost pl next: j.lft 13th: 7th wl bef 3 out: urged along and clsng on ldrs on inner bef 3 out: chal 2 out: j. ahd last: r.o wl flat* **5/2**[1]

6-21 **2** *1 ¾* **What Of It (IRE)**[19] 4143 8-11-9 106.......... MrTWCEdwards(5) 111
(Tom George) *led: rdn bef 2 out: hdd last: kpt on gamely but outpcd by wnr flat* **3/1**[2]

/54- **3** *2 ¼* **Pathian Prince**[23] 8-11-7 0.......... MrJFMathias(3) 106
(E R Clough) *in tch: mstke 2nd: hdwy to chse ldrs 12th: 3rd and rdn 2 out: edgd lft and styd on same pce between last 2* **7/2**[3]

0-00 **4** *13* **Mccauley (IRE)**[22] 8-11-3 0.......... MrMatthewHampton(7) 97+
(Paul Swaffield) *in tch: mstke 8th: hdwy to chse ldrs 10th: hit 11th: 5th and struggling u.p whn mstke 3 out: mstke 2 out: sltly hmpd last: plugged on to go 4th flat* **33/1**

P- **5** *3 ¾* **Cloran Jack (IRE)**[296] 7-11-3 0.......... MrMatthewBarber(7) 91
(Marc Barber) *chsd ldrs tl wnt 2nd 10th: ev ch 14th: unable qck and hit 3 out: wknd bef next: 4th and wl hld whn mstke last* **33/1**

30/0 **6** *9* **Back Is Back (IRE)**[17] 4194 7-11-3 94..........(t) MrJBarber(7) 82
(Miss Jane Western) *chsd ldr tl 5th: styd in tch tl wknd u.p after 13th: wl btn 3 out* **10/1**

P-P **7** *1* **Classic Chance**[12] 4293 11-11-10 0.......... MrBMoorcroft 81
(Miss A Ray) *bhd: hit 5th: mstke 6th: pushed along and hdwy 10th: chsd ldng trio after 13th: struggling whn mstke 14th: sn wknd* **22/1**

00P/ **8** *5* **Backstreet Lad**[23] 9-11-3 0..........(t) MrNDeakin(7) 76
(Wyn Morris) *in tch: rdn and struggling 12th: wknd after next: t.o* **16/1**

U **Saalback (USA)**[23] 9-10-10 80.......... MissJodieHughes(7) —
(Luke Price) *mstkes: in tch in rr: sme hdwy into midfield after 8th: rdn and struggling 10th: t.o whn blnd and uns rdr 3 out* **25/1**

P/P- **U** **Gem Mill (IRE)**[16] 9-11-3 57..........(b) MrGHumfrey(7) —
(Mrs Gillian Davies) *in tch towards rr: short of room on landing and uns rdr 3rd* **100/1**

P263 **P** **Ace High Blue (IRE)**[23] 9-11-3 99..........(t) MrJEngland(7) —
(R W J Willcox) *t.k.h: in tch on outer: mstke 4th: j.rt 6th: struggling in rr 12th: t.o whn blnd bdly 14th: p.u next* **12/1**

00/ **P** **Rash Oak (IRE)**[22] 9-11-3 0..........(t) MrPJohn(7) —
(P D Thomas) *t.k.h: in tch in midfield: dropped in rr and rdn 11th: losing tch whn p.u 13th* **66/1**

/P-6 **P** **Viking Affair (IRE)**[200] 1296 7-11-5 0.......... MrPJTolman(5) —
(Rebecca Curtis) *mstkes: t.k.h: hld up in tch towards rr: sme hdwy 10th: wknd after 13th: wl bhd whn p.u last* **16/1**

5m 31.6s (1.60) **Going Correction** -0.10s/f (Good) **13** Ran SP% **120.9**
Speed ratings: **92,91,90,85,84 80,80,78,—,— —,—,—**
toteswingers:1&2 £3.50, 2&3 £2.70, 1&3 £2.20 CSF £9.92 TOTE £5.30: £1.10, £2.00, £1.40; EX 11.30.
Owner K Goldsworthy **Bred** Michel Bourgneuf **Trained** Yerbeston, Pembrokes
■ Stewards' Enquiry : Mr N Deakin one-day ban: used whip when out of contention (Mar 21)
Mr Matthew Hampton two-day ban: used whip with excessive frequency (Mar 21-22)

FOCUS
No real strength in depth to this novice hunter chase. There was a cracking finish and the form looks solid with the market leaders coming clear. The first pair are rated to their marks.

NOTEBOOK
Oca De Thaix(FR), who went early to post, was a surprise winner on his return to regulation fences at Ludlow last month and followed up in good style over this shorter trip. He looked in trouble when getting outpaced on the far side, but rallied gamely off the home turn and wasn't going to be denied once getting his head to the front. The ground had come in his favour again and he's clearly improved since joining his current stable. The Aintree Fox Hunters' next month is his big target. (tchd 9-4)
What Of It(IRE) had to work hard when a somewhat fortunate winner at Leicester 19 days earlier and he made a bold bid to back that up, but just got outstayed by the winner. He rates a decent benchmark. (tchd 10-3)
Pathian Prince wasn't particularly fluent early on, but it looked as though his talented jockey had delivered him perfectly in the home straight. He proved laboured under maximum pressure, though, and ultimately finished with something in the tank so doesn't look that straightforward. (op 4-1)
Mccauley(IRE) stepped up markedly on the level of his return in a point 22 days earlier and could build on this back over 3m. (op 25-1)
Cloran Jack(IRE) went well for a long way, but looked to pay late on for taking time to settle.

4527 LONGFORD STANDARD OPEN NATIONAL HUNT FLAT RACE 2m
5:40 (5:41) (Class 6) 4-6-Y-O **£1,561** (£458; £229; £114)

Form RPR

1 **Speed Master (IRE)** 5-11-4 0.......... APMcCoy 120+
(Nicky Henderson) *in tch: chsd ldr over 4f out: rdn to ld jst over 2f out: rdn and hdd over 1f out: kpt on ins fnl f to ld again nr fin* **13/8**[1]

2 *1* **The Rockies (IRE)** 4-10-10 0.......... WayneHutchinson 111+
(Evan Williams) *t.k.h: hld up in tch: hdwy to chse ldrs and rn green 3f out: chal and racd awkwardly 2f out: led over 1f out: hanging lft after: hdd nr fin* **10/1**

24 **3** *12* **Koultas King (IRE)**[31] 3920 4-10-10 0.......... RichardJohnson 101
(Tim Vaughan) *t.k.h: chsd ldrs: wnt 2nd 12f out tl 6f out: rdn and wknd jst over 2f out* **11/2**[3]

350 **4** *4* **Street Dance (IRE)**[6] 4410 5-11-4 0.......... SamThomas 105
(Keith Goldsworthy) *t.k.h: hld up in tch in rr: hdwy to chse ldrs 4f out: rdn and wknd jst over 2f out* **16/1**

3 **5** *2 ¾* **Henok (FR)**[30] 3943 5-11-1 0.......... SamTwiston-Davies(3) 103
(Nigel Twiston-Davies) *t.k.h: led: rdn along and qcknd over 3f out: hdd jst over 2f out: wknd over 1f out: lost 2 pls ins fnl f* **5/2**[2]

23 **6** *6* **Bathwick Junior**[48] 3616 4-10-3 0.......... RhysFlint 82
(John Flint) *t.k.h: chsd ldr tl 12f out: wnt 2nd again 6f out tl over 4f out: wknd qckly 3f out: sn bhd* **12/1**

7 *24* **Gracious Beau** 5-11-4 0.......... JamieMoore 76
(Keith Goldsworthy) *hld up in tch in last trio: hdwy to chse ldrs 5f out: wknd qckly 3f out: sn bhd: t.o* **25/1**

8 *18* **Supralunary** 5-11-4 0.......... SeanQuinlan 59
(Robin Mathew) *t.k.h: hld up in tch in last trio: rdn and lost tch over 5f out: t.o* **66/1**

3m 51.5s (8.10) **Going Correction** +0.75s/f (Soft)
WFA 4 from 5yo 7lb **8** Ran SP% **110.1**
Speed ratings: **109,108,102,100,99 96,84,75**
toteswingers:1&2 £3.30, 2&3 £6.50, 1&3 £2.20. totesuper7: Win: Not won. Place: £331.60. CSF £17.62 TOTE £2.50: £1.10, £2.40, £1.10; EX 16.00.
Owner Walters Plant Hire Ltd **Bred** J Keegan And J Hamilton **Trained** Upper Lambourn, Berks

FOCUS
Two debutants came clear in the final furlong here and both can rate higher as they mature. A fair bumper for the track.

NOTEBOOK
Speed Master(IRE) came out on top where it mattered and rewarded good support on his debut, enhancing his leading stable's decent record at the track in the process. He showed his inexperience, but Tony McCoy made his mind up late on and he may just have found the ground quick enough. There should be plenty of improvement in him and he ought to get 2m4f without much bother when sent hurdling (op 9-4 tchd 11-8)
The Rockies(IRE) ◆ was said to be backward and weak beforehand by his trainer, but he still emerged to give the favourite a real fright. His inexperience found him out nearing the finish as he hung left, however, and he actually ended up on the chase course after the line. Providing he learns for the initial experience, as he is fully entitled to do, then he ought to take a lot of beating next time out. (op 14-1)
Koultas King(IRE) got outpaced before running on again late and looks ready to go hurdling. (op 4-1)
Street Dance(IRE), equipped with ear plugs for the first time, again spoilt his chances of getting home by refusing to settle early on. (op 14-1 tchd 18-1)
Henok(FR), third on his debut over C&D last month, couldn't go with the first pair from 2f out and was another that paid for racing keenly. (op 15-8 tchd 11-4)
T/Jkpt: Not won. T/Plt: £224.80 to a £1 stake. Pool of £115,041.48 - 373.55 winning tickets. T/Qpdt: £59.20 to a £1 stake. Pool of £6,500.21 - 81.12 winning tickets. SP

[1488]NEWTON ABBOT (L-H)
Monday, March 7

OFFICIAL GOING: Good to soft (soft in places; 5.2)
Wind: mild across Weather: sunny

4528 BHE & ST RACING TO SCHOOL MAIDEN HURDLE (8 hdls) 2m 1f
2:00 (2:00) (Class 5) 4-Y-O+ **£1,849** (£539; £269)

Form RPR

22 **1** **Alla Svelta (IRE)**[39] 3762 5-11-1 121.......... PaulMoloney 115+
(Evan Williams) *mde all: drew clr after 3 out: styd on wl fr last: pushed out* **6/5**[1]

05 **2** *10* **Maadraa (IRE)**[6] 4404 6-11-1 0..........(t) DPFahy 109+
(Bernard Llewellyn) *nt a fluent: mid-div: hdwy after 4th: wnt 3rd next: wnt 2nd after 3 out: clsng on wnr whn hit 2 out: sn rdn: hld whn hit last* **11/1**[3]

043 **3** *62* **Glassawine**[13] 4268 4-10-7 0..........(t) TomScudamore 42
(David Pipe) *trckd wnr: drew clr chsng wnr 5th: lost 2nd and wknd after 3 out: t.o* **2/1**[2]

4 *25* **Murdoch**[1002] 7-11-1 0.......... JoeTizzard 28
(Colin Tizzard) *towards rr: wnt remote 4th after 3 out: nvr a threat: t.o* **16/1**

0/44 **5** *2* **Court Gamble (IRE)**[23] 7-10-5 0.......... KeiranBurke(3) 19
(Nerys Dutfield) *chsd ldrs tl after 4th: t.o fr next* **50/1**

0S-0 **6** *hd* **Deed Poll**[22] 4094 5-11-1 0.......... JamesDavies 26
(Chris Down) *in tch tl wknd after 4th: sn wl bhd: t.o* **100/1**

0 **7** *19* **Rajeeva (IRE)**[16] 4225 5-11-1 0.......... AidanColeman 9
(Venetia Williams) *mid-div: wnt 3rd after 4th tl next: sn wknd: t.o* **14/1**

4/3- **8** *2 ¼* **Cinnamon Hill**[629] 737 7-10-8 92.......... RodiGreene —
(Nick Ayliffe) *a bhd: t.o fr 5th* **20/1**

0-UP **P** **History Lesson**[16] 4225 5-11-1 0 (p) WillKennedy —
(Alan Jones) *nvr fluent: j.rt: sn t.o: p.u bef 5th* **50/1**

P **Curlew (IRE)**[124] 5-11-1 0 AndrewThornton —
(Chris Down) *in tch tl 4th: wknd qckly: t.o whn p.u bef next: b.b.v* **22/1**

P **P** **Poshki**[32] 3904 6-10-8 0 LiamHeard —
(Nigel Hawke) *trckd ldrs: pckd 1st: wknd qckly after 4th: p.u bef next* **150/1**

4m 19.7s (14.00) **Going Correction** +0.95s/f (Soft)
WFA 4 from 5yo+ 7lb **11** Ran SP% **114.4**
Speed ratings (Par 103): **105,100,71,59,58 58,49,48,—,— —**
toteswingers:1&2 £3.90, 2&3 £5.70, 1&3 £1.10 CSF £14.28 TOTE £2.20: £1.10, £3.20, £1.20; EX 14.40.
Owner P Conway & John Lee Jones **Bred** Barry Tierney **Trained** Llancarfan, Vale Of Glamorgan

FOCUS
A modest novice hurdle that was expected to concern only two runners, but Glassawine was well below par. The winner can probably go on to rate higher.

NOTEBOOK
Alla Svelta(IRE), dropping in trip, raced freely throughout and had everything in trouble mid-way down the back. Those exertions took their toll in the final 3f, as he started to tire and briefly looked vulnerable to Maadraa, but a good jump at the last sealed it for him. A fine, big sort, he should make a chaser, although one would like to see him relax more in his races first. (tchd 6-4 in places)
Maadraa(IRE) needed this for a mark. He showed improved form, being the only one able to give the winner a race, but blundered at each of the last two hurdles and could find no extra. He should have no trouble going one better. (op 12-1 tchd 10-1)
Glassawine had shaped nicely on his recent hurdles debut, but quickly began to struggle once coming under pressure down the back. He appeared to finish tired and may be more of a handicap prospect. (op 15-8)
Murdoch, off for 1002 days and making his debut over hurdles, never got involved, finishing tailed off. (tchd 20-1)
Curlew(IRE) Official explanation: jockey said gelding bled from the nose

4529 NEWTON ABBOT RACECOURSE H'CAP CHASE (13 fncs) 2m 110y
2:30 (2:30) (Class 4) (0-115,113) 5-Y-0+ **£3,084** (£905; £452; £226)

Form RPR
3213 **1** **Rileyev (FR)**[12] 4290 6-10-9 **96** AidanColeman 108+
(Venetia Williams) *trckd ldrs: rdn after 4 out: led 2 out: nt fluent last: kpt on wl* **1/1**[1]

P-5P **2** 4½ **Knapp Bridge Boy**[265] 755 11-10-0 **87** oh10 LiamTreadwell 90
(James Payne) *prom: led 5th tl 7th: led next tl rdn after 4 out: kpt on same pce fr 2 out: regained 2nd bef last* **16/1**

03P- **3** 7 **Digital Media (IRE)**[473] 2390 9-9-7 **87** oh3 (t) NathanSweeney[(7)] 86
(Simon Burrough) *trckd ldrs: hit 7th: sn rdn: kpt on fr last: nvr able to chal* **5/1**[3]

UU25 **4** hd **Jocheski (IRE)**[116] 2330 7-11-12 **113** AndrewThornton 113
(Tony Newcombe) *hld up bhd ldrs: rdn after 4 out: r.o fr last but nvr any threat* **4/1**[2]

2P45 **5** ½ **Coach Lane**[19] 4142 10-11-4 **105** DarylJacob 104
(Nick Mitchell) *led tl 5th: sn cajoled along: led 7th tl nt fluent next: rdn to ld after 4 out: nt fluent next: sn rdn whn idling: hdd bef 2 out: fdd fr last* **5/1**[3]

4m 17.1s (10.60) **Going Correction** +0.75s/f (Soft) **5** Ran SP% **109.2**
Speed ratings: **105,102,99,99,99**
CSF £13.49 TOTE £2.60: £2.10, £11.60; EX 17.30.
Owner John Mayne **Bred** Mme Laurence Barreaud & Claude Barreaud **Trained** Kings Caple, H'fords

FOCUS
Rileyev was presented with a golden opportunity to gain a second win over fences and rates a chase personal best in this weak handicap.

NOTEBOOK
Rileyev(FR) gained a fairly straightforward victory, going on two out and soon having the race in the bag, and a scrappy jump at the last was his only moment of concern. He shouldn't go up too much and can probably win again if continuing to hold his form. (op 10-11 tchd 11-10)
Knapp Bridge Boy had been in terrible form when last seen and was having to run from 10lb wrong, but this was a good effort. (tchd 18-1)
Digital Media(IRE) shaped well on this return from a 473-day absence, keeping on after the last. He should be sharper next time. (op 6-1 tchd 9-2)
Jocheski(IRE), 11lb higher than when gaining his sole previous win over hurdles, was closing at the finish and may want further. (op 9-2)
Coach Lane dropped away in the straight and remains well below his best. (tchd 11-2)

4530 NEWTON ABBOT RACECOURSE NOVICES' H'CAP HURDLE (8 hdls) 2m 1f
3:05 (3:05) (Class 4) (0-105,103) 4-Y-0+ **£2,706** (£788; £394)

Form RPR
6-23 **1** **Milo Milan (IRE)**[22] 4100 6-11-12 **103** CharliePoste 108+
(Richard Lee) *trckd ldrs: rdn bef 3 out: led 2 out: wnt lft last: styd on wl: rdn out* **3/1**[2]

6001 **2** 3¾ **Calico Rose**[25] 4034 7-11-5 **103** (p) EdGlassonbury[(7)] 103
(Victor Dartnall) *trckd ldr: pushed along after 4th: rdn after 3 out: led briefly bef next: hung lft u.p: styd on same pce* **11/4**[1]

05F4 **3** 5 **Cruise Control**[23] 4076 5-11-1 **92** DarylJacob 90
(Richard Price) *hld up: hdwy after 5th: led briefly appr 2 out: sn rdn: no ex bef last* **13/2**

035 **4** 20 **Spinning Waters**[34] 3872 5-11-2 **96** DannyCook[(3)] 79
(Dai Burchell) *in tch: hit 2nd: reminders: mstke and rdr lost iron briefly 4th: sn rdn in last but jst in tch: wknd 2 out* **4/1**[3]

P-P0 **5** 22 **Whatshallwedo**[40] 3739 6-10-7 **84** LiamHeard 42
(Chris Down) *trckd ldrs: rdn bef 3 out: wknd bef 2 out: t.o* **33/1**

2344 **P** **Navajo Nation (IRE)**[152] 1723 5-11-1 **97** (p) TomO'Connor[(5)] —
(Bill Turner) *trckd ldrs: rdn appr 5th: sn wknd: bhd whn p.u bef 3 out* **15/2**

3303 **F** **Just One Thing (IRE)**[29] 3962 6-11-11 **102** PaulMoloney 102
(Evan Williams) *led: nt fluent 5th: rdn and hdd bef short of room 2 out: disputing 3rd but hld whn fell last* **7/1**

4m 27.1s (21.40) **Going Correction** +0.95s/f (Soft) **7** Ran SP% **112.2**
Speed ratings (Par 105): **87,85,82,73,63 —,—**
toteswingers:1&2 £1.20, 2&3 £6.20, 1&3 £3.10 CSF £11.53 TOTE £3.10: £1.50, £1.40; EX 9.10.

Owner Mrs Caroline Shaw **Bred** J R Weston **Trained** Byton, H'fords

FOCUS
Just a moderate handicap hurdle, but the form is sound.

NOTEBOOK
Milo Milan(IRE), one of the first under pressure on this handicap debut, kept responding and, having come to challenge two out, he had the race sewn up at the last. There should be more to come from this son of Milan, who is clearly going to stay further. (op 7-2)
Calico Rose, a game winner over 2m3f at Taunton latest, perhaps wasn't made enough use of on this drop in trip. She kept responding and stayed on right the way to the line, suggesting there's more to come as she goes back up in trip. (op 10-3 tchd 7-2)
Cruise Control travelled well into contention, but didn't see it out as well as the front pair. (op 7-1 tchd 15-2)
Spinning Waters, well backed throughout the day, made a bad early blunder (rider lost iron) and was soon trailing. He did make some late headway, though, and probably deserves another chance. (op 7-2 tchd 10-3)
Navajo Nation(IRE) Official explanation: jockey said gelding lost its action (op 6-1)
Just One Thing(IRE) had run his race and was beaten when coming down at the last. (op 6-1)

4531 ST AUSTELL BREWERY NOVICES' CHASE (16 fncs) 2m 5f 110y
3:40 (3:40) (Class 3) 5-Y-0+ **£5,672** (£1,665; £832; £415)

Form RPR
0661 **1** **Quartz De Thaix (FR)**[14] 4261 7-11-4 132 AidanColeman 142+
(Venetia Williams) *trckd ldr: chal 12th: led 3 out: pushed 3 l clr: styd on strly fr last: comf* **3/1**[3]

-302 **2** 18 **Ace High**[22] 4096 7-10-12 0 DenisO'Regan 125+
(Victor Dartnall) *trckd ldrs: mstke 10th: reminder: wnt 2nd sn after 3 out: effrt next: sn hld* **9/2**

23UF **3** 18 **Ikorodu Road**[2] 4487 8-10-12 135 JasonMaguire 99
(Martin Keighley) *trckd ldr: hit 9th: reminders and sn pushed along: hit 11th: rdn and lost tch bef 4 out: wnt modest 3rd run-in* **7/4**[1]

1135 **4** 1½ **Rebel Du Maquis (FR)**[30] 3946 6-11-3 141 MrRMahon[(5)] 107
(Paul Nicholls) *led: rdn appr 4 out: hdd sn after 3 out: wknd next: lost 3rd nr fin* **5/2**[2]

5m 31.5s (10.10) **Going Correction** +0.75s/f (Soft) **4** Ran SP% **108.1**
Speed ratings: **111,104,97,97**
CSF £14.42 TOTE £4.40; EX 11.50.
Owner Roa Arkle Partnership **Bred** Michel Bourgneuf **Trained** Kings Caple, H'fords

FOCUS
A competitive looking novice chase. The winner was a 148 hurdler at best and is improving over fences. The third and fourth hold down the form.

NOTEBOOK
Quartz De Thaix(FR), a hard-fought winner on heavy ground at Hereford on his return to fences, appreciated the sounder surface and travelled well before asserting and drawing clear from the third-last. He holds several engagements at next week's festival, with either the Centenary or Byrne Group Plate looking the likely target. (op 11-4 tchd 5-2)
Ace High also appreciated the sounder surface, having been bogged down in heavy ground at Exeter. He travelled well for much of the way, but his inexperience was there for all to see, making several errors, and the winner just stayed on too strongly. (tchd 5-1)
Ikorodu Road, an early faller in a valuable handicap at Newbury just two days earlier, jumped hesitantly and was quickly beaten off down the back. He's talented, but seems to have lost his confidence and is one to avoid for the time being. (op 2-1)
Rebel Du Maquis(FR), dropping in grade, set off at a decent tempo, but he was in trouble by three out and the double penalty seemingly proved too much for him. (op 11-4)

4532 NEWTONABBOTRACING.COM H'CAP HURDLE (10 hdls) 2m 6f
4:15 (4:15) (Class 4) (0-115,115) 4-Y-0+ **£2,706** (£788; £394)

Form RPR
2306 **1** **Devon Native (IRE)**[33] 3881 8-11-0 **110** (t) DannyBurton[(7)] 120
(Chris Down) *hld up in last pair: hdwy after 7th: rdn to ld after 3 out: nt fluent last: styd on: rdn out* **11/2**[2]

-611 **2** 1½ **Round The Horn (IRE)**[8] 4380 11-11-7 **110** 7ex (t) JasonMaguire 120+
(Jim Old) *hld up bhd: nt fluent 2nd: slow 3rd: hdwy after 7th: rdn to chse wnr appr 2 out: styd on: a being hld: dismntd: lame* **15/8**[1]

16/P **3** 8 **Zed Candy (FR)**[37] 3821 8-11-5 **115** (p) HarryChalloner[(7)] 116
(Richard Ford) *in tch: tk clsr order 7th: sn rdn: styd on same pce fr 2 out* **16/1**

0F02 **4** 3½ **Timetoring**[31] 3934 9-10-9 **103** (p) MissIsabelTompsett[(5)] 102
(Bernard Llewellyn) *led: hit 4th: rdn and hdd after 3 out: styd on same pce fr next* **15/2**

3P12 **5** 8 **Rith Bob (IRE)**[18] 4161 8-11-7 **110** PaulMoloney 101
(David Rees) *trckd ldrs tl lost pl appr 7th: sn rdn: plugged on: nvr bk on terms* **15/2**

3052 **6** 34 **Boomtown Kat**[16] 4220 7-11-12 **115** AndrewThornton 75
(Karen George) *trckd ldr tl rdn after 7th: wknd after 3 out: t.o* **7/1**[3]

0004 **7** 21 **Watch Out**[10] 4330 7-10-2 **94** (tp) CPGeoghegan[(3)] 35
(Dai Burchell) *racd keenly: mid-div: hit 6th: rdn whn blnd 3 out: sn wknd: t.o* **10/1**

3430 **8** 10 **Emergency Exit (IRE)**[16] 4223 8-11-6 **109** TomO'Brien 41
(Philip Hobbs) *trckd ldr: wkng whn nt fluent 3 out: sn t.o* **8/1**

5m 44.7s (24.50) **Going Correction** +0.95s/f (Soft) **8** Ran SP% **112.3**
Speed ratings (Par 105): **93,92,89,88,85 73,65,61**
toteswingers:1&2 £3.60, 2&3 £6.40, 1&3 £10.70 CSF £16.13 CT £151.60 TOTE £5.10: £1.20, £1.70, £6.10; EX 22.20.
Owner P McClave **Bred** P McClave **Trained** Mutterton, Devon
■ Stewards' Enquiry : Danny Burton one-day ban: used whip with excessive frequency (Mar 21)

FOCUS
An open handicap hurdle and a personal best from the winner.

NOTEBOOK
Devon Native(IRE), unsuited by testing ground the last twice, looked potentially interesting in a first-time tongue-tie and bounced right back to her best, going on leaving the back and grinding it out. She could win again with the ground having now come in her favour. (op 8-1)
Round The Horn(IRE), bidding for a hat-trick, was 10lb higher than when winning in heavy ground at Towcester and didn't travel as well. He still closed to hold every chance, but the winner proved too determined. Official explanation: vet said gelding returned lame left-fore (op 2-1 tchd 13-8)
Zed Candy(FR) had won two of his five starts over hurdles back in 2008 and had been in good form on the AW. He plugged on into third, albeit without looking the most cooperative. (op 14-1)
Timetoring ran well for a long way off the front end. (op 17-2)
Rith Bob(IRE) plodded on having been outpaced. (op 8-1)

4533 BETFAIR RACING EXCELLENCE CONDITIONAL JOCKEYS' TRAINING SERIES STANDARD NATIONAL HUNT FLAT RACE 2m 1f
4:50 (4:50) (Class 6) 4-6-Y-0 **£1,493** (£435; £217)

Form RPR
4 **1** **Themilanhorse (IRE)**[39] 3773 5-10-11 0 JamesCowley[(7)] 111+
(Paul Nicholls) *trckd ldr: led over 6f out: styd on wl fnl 2f: pushed out* **6/4**[1]

51 **2** 5 **Hayjack**[63] 3372 6-11-11 0 HarryChalloner 113
(Venetia Williams) *trckd ldr: wnt 2nd 6f out: rdn over 2f out: styd on but a being hld by wnr* **7/2**[2]

S **3** 10 **Flyit Flora**[32] 3909 6-10-11 0 PeterCarberry 90
(Victor Dartnall) *mid-div: hdwy to chse ldng pair over 4f out: sn rdn: styd on but no further imp on ldng pair fr over 2f out* **4/1**[3]

4 20 **Fennis Ted (IRE)**[58] 3462 5-10-13 0 SClements[(5)] 79
(Liam Corcoran) *trckd ldrs: rdn 5f out: sn btn: wnt modest 4th 2f out* **11/1**

0 **5** 10 **Magical Man**[120] 2237 4-10-10 0 AodhaganConlon 62
(Debra Hamer) *led tl over 6f out: rdn over 4f out: wknd over 2f out: t.o* **12/1**

	6	*10*	**Declan Og (IRE)**[386] [4068] 6-11-4 0 ... DannyBurton (Chris Down) *a towards rr: t.o* **25/1**		61
	7	*6*	**Posh Totty** 4-10-0 0 ... EdCookson(3) (Richard Price) *mid-div tl 6f out: t.o* **20/1**		41
	8	*58*	**Star Potential** 4-10-3 0 ... MattGriffiths (Susan Gardner) *a towards rr: t.o* **16/1**		—
0	**9**	*46*	**Jovial Starry Nite**[46] [3651] 6-10-11 0 ... NathanSweeney (Carroll Gray) *t.o 1/2-way* **100/1**		—
	10	*25*	**Looselastic**[275] 6-10-11 0 ... CharlieWallis (John Panvert) *w ldr for 7tf: struggling in rr fr over 7f out: t.o* **50/1**		—

4m 17.8s (17.70) **Going Correction** +0.95s/f (Soft)
WFA 4 from 5yo+ 7lb **10** Ran SP% **115.7**
Speed ratings: **96,93,88,79,74 70,67,40,18,6**
toteswingers:1&2 £2.20, 2&3 £2.80, 1&3 £2.40 CSF £6.32 TOTE £3.60: £1.90, £1.10, £1.80; EX 7.20.
Owner Arron & Katya Banks **Bred** Michael Heskin **Trained** Ditcheat, Somerset
■ The first winner under rules for 17-y-o James Cowley, son of former jump jockey Colin Cowley.

FOCUS
A relatively weak bumper and the first two stood out on pre-race figures.

NOTEBOOK
Themilanhorse(IRE) kicked on leaving the back and saw it out well to give his rider a first success. He'll need to improve to defy a penalty, but should stay further once sent hurdling. (tchd 2-1 in a place)
Hayjack stayed on right the way to the line, just lacking the pace of the winner. This was a creditable effort and he too will want a stiffer test over hurdles. (op 3-1 tchd 4-1)
Flyit Flora, in the process of running well when slipping up on debut, confirmed that initial promise with a keeping-on third. (op 5-1 tchd 7-2)
Fennis Ted(IRE) caught the eye in fourth, staying on without being given an overly hard time. This was his first run for the yard and improvement can be expected. (op 9-1)
Magical Man is unlikely to come good until presented with a sterner test over jumps. (op 11-1)

4534 LADIES DAY 25 MAY NOVICES' HUNTERS' CHASE (16 fncs) 2m 5f 110y
5:20 (5:20) (Class 6) 5-Y-O+ **£898** (£276; £138)

Form				RPR
3-42	**1**		**Louis Pasteur (IRE)**[19] [4143] 6-11-7 105 ... MrRGHenderson(5) (Nick Mitchell) *hld up in tch: tk clsr order 9th: mstke 10th: rdn to chse ldr after 4 out: nt fluent next: styd on to take narrow advantage last: rdn clr* **4/6**[1]	106+
U-43	**2**	*5*	**Walter De Wodeland**[43] 10-11-5 0 ... MissJBuck(7) (Miss J Du Plessis) *trckd ldrs: led 11th: 4 l clr after 3 out: hdd last: no ex* **9/2**[2]	99
0P0/	**3**	*11*	**Agoodun**[721] [4526] 10-11-12 66 ... MrWBiddick (Mrs F Johnson) *trckd ldr: rdn after 4 out: styd on same pce fr next* **16/1**	90
6054	**P**		**Pearly Star**[15] 10-11-5 0 ... (tp) MissAliceMills(7) (D Bryant) *led tl 11th: sn rdn: wknd 3 out: p.u bef last* **14/1**	—
00/	**P**		**I'm Innocent**[22] 10-11-5 0 ... MrRHawkins(7) (Mrs S Watson) *in tch: rdn after 9th: blnd bdly next: qckly lost tch: p.u bef 11th* **33/1**	—
646-	**P**		**The Apprentice (IRE)**[23] 9-11-12 0 ... MrJoshuaGuerriero (M J Vanstone) *nvr fluent: j.rt: bdly at times: a in last: losing tch whn p.u bef 9th* **5/1**[3]	—

5m 44.7s (23.30) **Going Correction** +0.75s/f (Soft) **6** Ran SP% **110.3**
Speed ratings: **87,85,81,—,— —**
CSF £4.16 TOTE £1.80: £1.70, £1.60; EX 4.20.
Owner R W Humphreys **Bred** Miss Sue Berry **Trained** Piddletrenthide, Dorset

FOCUS
A weak novice hunter chase. The winner was the form pick but below his Leicester mark.

NOTEBOOK
Louis Pasteur(IRE), unlucky not to make a winning debut in this sphere at Leicester (beaten a neck following a terrible blunder), jumped hesitantly and looked beaten leaving the back, but he stays this trip stronger than the runner-up and got well on top following a good jump at the last. He can add to this success as long as his jumping improves. (tchd evens in places)
Walter De Wodeland went on travelling best and briefly looked to have the winner in trouble, but he began to tire after two out and was brushed aside from the last. Perhaps a shorter trip will help. (op 7-2 tchd 3-1)
Agoodun didn't fare too badly returning from 721 days off, closing on the front pair late on. (op 22-1 tchd 25-1)
The Apprentice(IRE) ran an absolute shocker on his debut in this sphere. (op 9-2 tchd 11-2)
T/Plt: £16.90 to a £1 stake. Pool of £63,080.97 - 2,720.07 winning tickets. T/Qpdt: £12.80 to a £1 stake. Pool of £4,183.08 - 241.37 winning tickets. TM

4091 EXETER (R-H)
Tuesday, March 8

OFFICIAL GOING: Good (good to soft in places)
The hurdle on the bend after the winning post was moved to the back straight.
Wind: mild across Weather: sunny

4535 EUROPEAN BREEDERS' FUND MARES' "NATIONAL HUNT" NOVICES' HURDLE (10 hdls) 2m 3f
2:30 (2:30) (Class 4) 4-Y-0+ **£2,602** (£764; £382; £190)

Form				RPR
-133	**1**		**Semi Colon (FR)**[39] [3781] 5-11-0 0 ... APMcCoy (Nicky Henderson) *in tch: hdwy to ld appr 3 out: sn in command: pushed out run-in* **2/1**[1]	117+
6-6	**2**	*6*	**Lucky Mix**[51] [3590] 5-11-0 0 ... RobertThornton (Alan King) *mid-div: pushed along and hdwy after 7th: rdn to dispute 2nd 3 out: styd on but no ch w wnr* **11/1**	107
452	**3**	*1*	**Playful Rose (IRE)**[33] [3901] 5-11-0 0 ... RichardJohnson (Henry Daly) *trckd ldrs: jnd ldr after 6th: rdn and ev ch appr 3 out: styd on but no ex fr last* **11/2**[3]	106
331	**4**	*8*	**Pepite Rose (FR)**[11] [4331] 4-11-3 118 ... AidanColeman (Venetia Williams) *in tch: disp 2nd 3 out: sn rdn: 4th and hld whn mstke last* **11/4**[2]	105+
3S41	**5**	*9*	**Hazy Dawn**[22] [4118] 6-11-6 0 ... TomScudamore (Michael Scudamore) *w ldr tl rdn after 7th: grad fdd fr 3 out* **25/1**	97
-61P	**6**	*2 3/4*	**Time To Think**[26] [4032] 6-11-3 94 ... JimmyDerham(3) (Seamus Mullins) *led tl rdn 3 out: grad fdd* **11/1**	94
4P30	**7**	*1/2*	**Some Secret**[33] [3904] 6-11-0 0 ... JamesDavies (Chris Down) *chsd ldr tl rdn after 6th: grad wknd fr 3 out* **50/1**	89
UU	**8**	*23*	**Cruise In Luxury (IRE)**[14] [4268] 6-11-0 0 ... JohnnyFarrelly (Kevin Bishop) *a towards rr* **200/1**	67
	9	*1*	**Pretty Penny**[318] 7-11-0 0 ... WarrenMarston (Martin Keighley) *a towards rr* **16/1**	66
-220	**10**	*2 3/4*	**Verde Goodwood**[39] [3787] 5-11-0 0 ... LeightonAspell (Oliver Sherwood) *a towards rr* **12/1**	64
000	**11**	*43*	**Dani (IRE)**[23] [4100] 5-10-11 0 ... (t) PeterToole(3) (Mark Rimell) *in tch tl rdn after 6th: sn bhd: t.o* **100/1**	25
0	**12**	*32*	**Hopatina (IRE)**[29] [3979] 5-11-0 0 ... DougieCostello (Neil Mulholland) *struggling 5th: a towards rr: t.o* **66/1**	—
0	**13**	*2 3/4*	**El Pescadero (IRE)**[150] [1778] 5-11-0 0 ... RodiGreene (Nick Ayliffe) *lost tch fr 4th: t.o* **100/1**	—

4m 43.4s (0.70) **Going Correction** -0.05s/f (Good)
WFA 4 from 5yo+ 7lb **13** Ran SP% **115.4**
Speed ratings (Par 105): **96,93,93,89,85 84,84,74,74,73 55,41,40**
toteswingers:1&2:£3.60, 1&3:£3.20, 2&3:£9.50 CSF £23.97 TOTE £3.20: £1.50, £2.40, £2.50; EX 25.70.
Owner Mrs Caroline Mould **Bred** Michel Bourgneuf **Trained** Upper Lambourn, Berks

FOCUS
A modest mares' novice hurdle. They went an average gallop and the form looks sound. Tony McCoy said after riding the winner that the surface was "good". A small step up from the winner with the second and seventh helping to set the level.

NOTEBOOK
Semi Colon(FR) ◆ gained her first win over hurdles at the third time of asking with a comfortable display. She had been a shade disappointing in two outings in this sphere since winning her bumper in November, but this quicker ground made her look a different proposition. She strongly appeals as the type to progress now her powerful stable looks to have found the key to her, and she could win a nice prize. (op 15-8 tchd 7-4)
Lucky Mix ◆ was making her hurdling debut after a 51-day break and attracted early support, but drifted out again in the betting ring. She was niggled as early as the fifth flight, but kept responding and steadily stayed on to post an encouraging effort. An even stiffer test should suit ideally. (op 10-1 tchd 12-1)
Playful Rose(IRE), another who was backed, shaped as though she needs a longer trip on this sort of ground and it was her best effort so far. (op 15-2 tchd 8-1 and 5-1)
Pepite Rose(FR) was saddled with a double penalty after gaining her second success with a little to spare at Warwick 11 days earlier. Her best form has been on testing ground, though, and she looked held before stamina became a serious issue for this longer trip. (op 9-4)
Hazy Dawn, a recent Plumpton winner, looked sure to be suited by the extra distance here, but was in better company under a penalty and had cried enough before three out. (op 20-1)

4536 WEATHERBYS BLOODSTOCK INSURANCE H'CAP HURDLE (10 hdls) 2m 3f
3:00 (3:00) (Class 4) (0-115,112) 4-Y-0+ **£3,252** (£955; £477; £238)

Form				RPR
-106	**1**		**Black Phantom (IRE)**[42] [3724] 5-10-12 **98** ... NickScholfield (Andy Turnell) *led tl 2nd: prom: led 6th: lft wl clr 2 out: easily* **12/1**	116+
50P6	**2**	*20*	**Pepporoni Pete (IRE)**[17] [4220] 10-11-12 **112** ... (tp) CharliePoste (Milton Harris) *trckd ldrs: rdn to chse wnr after 7th tl after 3 out: lft 2nd again 2 out but wl hld: wnt lft last* **25/1**	112
353	**3**	*9*	**Roalco De Farges (FR)**[32] [3930] 6-11-12 **112** ... RichardJohnson (Philip Hobbs) *led tl 2nd: trckd ldrs: rdn wl after 7th: wknd next: lft 3rd 2 out* **5/2**[1]	103
0062	**4**	*14*	**Come Out Firing (IRE)**[15] [4265] 9-11-7 **107** ... DominicElsworth (Michael Blake) *trckd ldrs: rdn after 7th: wknd next: lft 4th 2 out* **10/1**	86
5530	**5**	*4 1/2*	**Wise Hawk**[5] [4446] 6-10-1 **87** ... (t) JamesDavies (Chris Down) *mid-div: rdn after 4th: hdwy after 6th: mstke 7th: wknd bef 3 out* **12/1**	61
0644	**6**	*13*	**Hawkaller**[17] [4225] 6-11-5 **110** ... RachaelGreen(5) (Anthony Honeyball) *hld up towards rr: hdwy 7th: sn rdn: nvr rchd ldrs: wkng whn mstke 2 out: dismntd after line: lame* **11/1**	73
406	**7**	*18*	**Uncle Bunge (IRE)**[93] [2795] 5-10-8 **94** ... TimmyMurphy (Liam Corcoran) *mid-div: hdwy 7th: sn rdn: wknd next: t.o* **16/1**	40
0006	**8**	*10*	**Baccalaureate (FR)**[16] [4235] 5-11-10 **110** ... (t) PaddyBrennan (Nigel Twiston-Davies) *mid-div tl 5th: sn in rr: t.o* **8/1**[3]	47
P3P/	**P**		**Manners (IRE)**[717] 13-10-7 **100** ... MrSParish(7) (Audrey Manners) *mid-div tl 6th: t.o whn p.u bef 3 out* **66/1**	—
1252	**F**		**Switched Off**[24] [4076] 6-11-12 **112** ... (v) DougieCostello (Ian Williams) *hld up towards rr: stdy prog after 7th: wnt 3rd 3 out: travelling ok in 3 l 2nd whn fell 2 out* **11/2**[2]	116+
12-0	**P**		**She's On The Case (IRE)**[5] [4448] 6-11-4 **104** ... TomO'Brien (Grant Cann) *mid-div tl 7th sn in rr: p.u bef 3 out* **9/1**	—
-13P	**U**		**Animation (IRE)**[67] [3264] 7-11-7 **110** ... (t) JimmyDerham(3) (Seamus Mullins) *hld up towards rr: rdn and hdwy after 7th: styng on in 4th but no ch whn blnd and uns rdr 2 out* **10/1**	105

4m 39.0s (-3.70) **Going Correction** -0.05s/f (Good) **12** Ran SP% **118.2**
Speed ratings (Par 105): **105,96,92,86,85 79,71,67,—,— —,—**
toteswingers:1&2:£48.60, 1&3:£15.20, 2&3:£17.90 CSF £262.01 CT £994.15 TOTE £22.60: £3.30, £3.70, £1.50; EX 190.30.
Owner T L Morshead **Bred** R Frisby **Trained** Broad Hinton, Wilts

FOCUS
There was just an ordinary gallop on in this moderate handicap and few got seriously involved from off the pace. This was a big step up from the winner but the third was disappointing.

NOTEBOOK
Black Phantom(IRE) was given a positive ride and kicked for home off the final bend. He was still in command prior to Switched Off falling two out, but that rival was closing and he therefore rates flattered by the winning margin. This was a welcome return to form, though, and should rate a career-best effort. It also proves his versatility regards underfoot conditions, but he now has to show he can put two good runs together. (op 18-1)
Pepporoni Pete(IRE) was suited by racing handily and kept on gamely enough, but would have likely been fourth without the drama at the penultimate flight. (op 18-1)
Roalco De Farges(FR), a handicap debutant, duelled with the winner for the lead, but was made to look paceless when that rival asserted after the fourth-last flight. He too is flattered by his finishing position and the majority of his stable's runners continue to perform indifferently. (op 11-4)
Hawkaller Official explanation: vet said gelding was lame
Switched Off, 5lb higher, made his move leaving the back straight and had work to do but was eating into the winner's advantage prior to crashing out. He has found consistency in this sphere of late, so it's hoped the experience doesn't affect his confidence, as he can be tricky. (op 14-1 tchd 16-1)
Animation(IRE) was the other who made up decent ground from off the pace prior to being badly hampered and unseating two out. She looks to have benefited for her recent time off the track and the tongue-tie was having a positive effect. (op 14-1 tchd 16-1)

4537 DEVON NATIONAL H'CAP CHASE (21 fncs) 3m 6f 110y
3:30 (3:30) (Class 3) (0-125,122) 5-Y-O+ **£6,337** (£1,872; £936; £468; £234)

Form				RPR
-11F	**1**		**Ammunition (IRE)**[82] [2984] 11-11-2 **112** ... PaddyBrennan (Nigel Twiston-Davies) *mid-div: trckd ldrs 10th: rdn to chal after 4 out: led sn after last: styd on gamely drvn out* **16/1**	124+

223P **2** 1 3/4 **Vamizi (IRE)**[32] 3922 8-11-8 **118** MattieBatchelor 129+
(Mark Bradstock) *mid-div: nt fluent 13th: hdwy fr 17th: led 4 out: sn rdn and hrd pressed: nodded and hdd sn after last: no ex* **13/2**[2]

FP24 **3** 7 **Drybrook Bedouin**[11] 4328 9-10-13 **116** SClements(7) 121
(Nick Mitchell) *hld up towards rr: hdwy fr 17th: rdn bef 4 out: wnt 3rd and mstke 3 out: styd on same pce* **17/2**

P026 **4** 12 **River Indus**[11] 4328 11-9-10 **99** NathanSweeney(7) 90
(Bob Buckler) *dispued most of way tl outrt ldr 14th: rdn and hdd 4 out: styd on same pce* **11/1**

P-PP **5** 5 **Kilbeggan Blade**[57] 3488 12-11-9 **119** (v) JasonMaguire 105
(Robin Dickin) *towards rr: reminders after 9th: styd on past btn horses fr 4 out: nvr trbld ldrs* **25/1**

1614 **6** 7 **Pacco (FR)**[14] 4277 8-11-6 **116** (b) LeightonAspell 96
(Oliver Sherwood) *hld up towards rr: pushed along bef 14th: rdn bef 17th: nvr trbld ldrs* **22/1**

410- **7** 2 1/2 **Cowboyboots (IRE)**[339] 13-10-12 **115** MrSParish(7) 93
(Audrey Manners) *a towards rr: nvr a factor* **33/1**

1P30 **8** 3/4 **Peut Etre Sivola (FR)**[45] 3687 8-11-4 **114** (vt) JohnnyFarrelly 91
(David Pipe) *trckd ldrs: rdn bef 17th: wknd 4 out* **20/1**

2-F1 **9** 34 **Shaking Hands (IRE)**[40] 3768 7-11-8 **118** (bt) TomScudamore 65
(David Pipe) *trckd ldrs: nt fluent 7th: rdn after 17th: wknd bef 4 out* **6/1**[1]

P04P **10** 44 **Flintoff (USA)**[10] 4360 10-11-12 **122** (b) RodiGreene 29
(Venetia Williams) *reluctant to s: reminders: a in rr: t.o* **33/1**

0122 **B** **Cashel Blue (USA)**[17] 4219 9-10-11 **110** (b) KeiranBurke(3) —
(Patrick Rodford) *disp tl after 13th: fading towards rr whn b.d next* **10/1**

0023 **P** **Flight Leader (IRE)**[18] 4190 11-11-12 **122** (p) JoeTizzard —
(Colin Tizzard) *mid-div early: bhd and rdn 10th: t.o whn p.u bef 16th* **22/1**

-P0P **P** **Bertie May**[23] 4095 9-11-0 **110** (t) WayneHutchinson —
(Kevin Bishop) *a towards rr: struggling whn nt fluent 15th: sme prog after 17th: wknd next: p.u bef last* **12/1**

F **Ten Fires (GER)**[9] 4388 9-11-11 **121** (p) JackDoyle —
(D T Hughes, Ire) *mid-div: travelling wl in tch whn fell 14th* **7/1**[3]

1215 **F** **Abbey Dore (IRE)**[47] 3646 8-9-13 **98** JimmyDerham(3) —
(Seamus Mullins) *mid-div: rdn after 17th: styng on same pce in 6th whn fell 4 out* **12/1**

-551 **P** **Raise You Five (IRE)**[62] 3395 7-11-5 **115** APMcCoy —
(Jonjo O'Neill) *hld up early: mid-div 7th: pushed along to chse ldrs after 13th: wknd qckly next: t.o whn p.u bef 17th* **10/1**

7m 49.7s (1.10) **Going Correction** +0.05s/f (Yiel) **16** Ran SP% **121.6**
Speed ratings: **100,99,97,94,93 91,90,90,81,70** —,—,—,—,— —
toteswingers:1&2:£35.10, 1&3:£58.10, 2&3:£21.10 CSF £107.52 CT £960.68 TOTE £13.30: £4.50, £3.60, £2.70, £2.90; EX 123.90.
Owner Miss Katharine J Holland **Bred** D Morrissey **Trained** Naunton, Gloucs

FOCUS
Races don't come much more open than this year's Devon National. There were plenty of chances nearing the fourth-last, but the principals came clear thereafter. The placed horses are help set the level.

NOTEBOOK
Ammunition(IRE) ran out a gritty winner and bounced right back to his best on this return from an 81-day absence. He had pulled up on his last outing, but that was when bidding for a hat-trick and the ground came in his favour on this step back up in trip. He looked vulnerable when old rival Vamizi, whom he beat on 6lb better terms here in October, challenged in the home straight, but he was getting the same amount from him again here and that made the difference over the extra distance. His form figures at the track now read 2234411. (op 12-1)
Vamizi(IRE), also pulled up on his previous start, was well backed to show his true colours over this severe test and did just that. He too likes this venue and certainly deserves to get off the mark for the season. (tchd 7-1)
Drybrook Bedouin was another who attracted support throughout the day. He lacked fluency early on, but improved the further he went and looked a danger three out. He couldn't raise his game from then on and the trip just found him out, but there is surely another race for him now the ground is drying out. (op 9-1)
River Indus went well for a long way off his low weight. (tchd 10-1 and 12-1)
Kilbeggan Blade was more encouraging again, though he was never a serious factor. (op 22-1)
Cashel Blue(USA) Official explanation: vet said gelding bled from the nose (op 6-1 tchd 11-2)
Flight Leader(IRE) prefers softer ground and was struggling early under top weight. (op 6-1 tchd 11-2)
Ten Fires(GER), an Irish-raider, had something to prove on such ground, but has always looked to want a proper test and he was going nicely prior to falling on the final circuit, bringing down the fading Cashel Blue in the process. (op 6-1 tchd 11-2)
Raise You Five(IRE) wasn't on a going day and her stable needs to bounce back quickly before its current form becomes an issue for the festival next week. (op 6-1 tchd 11-2)

4538 WEATHERBYS CHELTENHAM FESTIVAL BETTING GUIDE 2011 NOVICES' CHASE (18 fncs) 3m

4:00 (4:00) (Class 4) 5-Y-0+ **£3,903** (£1,146; £573; £286)

Form RPR

-05P **1** **Mr Bennett (IRE)**[24] 4079 8-10-12 115 (p) TomScudamore 122+
(David Pipe) *trckd ldrs: nt fluent 14th: sn rdn: led 3 out: styng on but hrd pressed whn lft w clr advantage last: drvn out* **16/1**

-P43 **2** 1 3/4 **Upham Atom**[21] 4127 8-10-12 100 LiamTreadwell 119
(Kate Buckett) *hld up bhd: pushed along after 10th: rdn and prog after 14th: disputing 4th whn blkd 4 out: styd on fr next: lft 2nd at the last: kpt on* **25/1**

-252 **3** 22 **Cobbler's Queen (IRE)**[40] 3763 7-10-5 111 AndrewTinkler 103+
(Henry Daly) *trckd ldr: rdn to ld bef 4 out: hdd 3 out: disputing cl 2nd whn blnd 2 out: wkng whn lft 3rd at the last* **11/2**[2]

-PU4 **4** 12 **Victory Parade (IRE)**[108] 2513 8-10-7 114 (p) AodhaganConlon(5) 87
(Rebecca Curtis) *led: drvn along fr 13th: hdd bef blundering 4 out: grad fdd* **15/2**

2121 **5** 8 **Aztec Treasure (NZ)**[82] 2982 7-10-12 114 APMcCoy 80
(Jonjo O'Neill) *mid-div: rdn after 14th: nvr able to cl: wknd next* **3/1**[1]

-0F0 **6** 24 **Estates Recovery (IRE)**[102] 2663 6-10-12 115 RichardJohnson 59
(Philip Hobbs) *hld up towards rr: hmpd 8th: lost tch next: sme hdwy 14th but nvr rching ldrs: wknd bef 4 out* **8/1**

000U **7** 17 **Stripe Me Blue**[27] 4007 9-10-12 107 (b) MarkGrant 43
(Peter Jones) *mid-div: hmpd 10th: wknd 12th: t.o* **50/1**

1-42 **F** **Master Eddy**[27] 4004 11-10-12 110 DavidEngland —
(Shaun Lycett) *in tch whn fell 10th* **8/1**

P-46 **F** **Le Commencement (IRE)**[152] 1739 9-10-12 112 PaulMoloney —
(Sophie Leech) *hld up towards rr: fell 8th (water)* **40/1**

-P02 **P** **Pliny (IRE)**[62] 3395 7-10-12 111 AidanColeman —
(Venetia Williams) *mid-div tl wknd 11th: t.o whn p.u after 14th* **7/1**[3]

-125 **F** **Oscar Prairie (IRE)**[40] 3772 6-10-12 110 (t) WayneHutchinson —
(Warren Greatrex) *in tch whn fell 7th* **8/1**

1500 **U** **Rhum (FR)**[82] 2975 6-10-9 113 SamTwiston-Davies(3) 121+
(Nigel Twiston-Davies) *mid-div: hdwy after 11th: rdn to chse ldrs after 14th: styd on fr 4 out: str chal whn blnd bdly and uns rdr last* **10/1**

6m 7.50s (-1.80) **Going Correction** +0.05s/f (Yiel) **12** Ran SP% **121.2**
Speed ratings: **105,104,97,93,90 82,76,**—,—,— —,—
toteswingers:1&2:£35.40, 1&3:£10.80, 2&3:£35.40 CSF £329.44 TOTE £10.00: £3.50, £14.50, £1.50; EX 507.30.
Owner B A Kilpatrick **Bred** B A Kilpatrick **Trained** Nicholashayne, Devon

FOCUS
A competitive 0-115 novice chase which was run at a sound gallop and it proved an eventful affair. The runner-up is rated to his hurdles best.

NOTEBOOK
Mr Bennett(IRE) had looked well out of sorts in three previous outings since returning from injury this term, but was a dual point winner in 2008 and there was always a chance switching to fences would see him in a better light. He was also officially best in at the weights. This was a return to the sort of form that saw him placed in fair novice hurdles during the 2008/09 season and he can be rated value for a bit further as he idled after the last. Whether he would have held on had Rhum not departed at the last is up for debate, though, and he wouldn't be sure to build on this as he has had his problems.
Upham Atom did some decent late work and posted his best effort over fences so far. He will go up in the handicap, though. (op 50-1)
Cobbler's Queen(IRE) was in the process of running a big race on her handicap debut, but had begun to feel the pinch prior to losing all chance when hitting the penultimate fence. She is another indication her yard is coming into form again. (op 13-2 tchd 7-1)
Victory Parade(IRE) ensured this was a decent test, but paid for his early exertions from four out and a drop back in trip may be required. (op 8-1)
Aztec Treasure(NZ) was hiked up 12lb for cosily winning a weak handicap and making it 2-2 at Towcester 82 days earlier. He proved easy to back and always looked to be going that bit quicker than he ideally wanted en-route to a below-par effort. (tchd 7-2)
Rhum(FR) was last seen pulling up on his chase debut in December and had stamina to prove. Despite proving a hard ride he was doing his best work late on, but just when asked for big leap at the last he put down and unseated. He would have gone very close but for that. (op 11-1 tchd 17-2)

4539 WEATHERBYS BANK NOVICES' HURDLE (12 hdls) 2m 7f 110y

4:30 (4:30) (Class 4) 4-Y-0+ **£2,602** (£764; £382; £190)

Form RPR

10-3 **1** **Lundy Sky**[23] 4091 6-11-3 0 AndrewThornton 121+
(Tony Newcombe) *mde all: blnd bdly 2nd: drew clr fr 2 out: readily* **5/1**[3]

1-13 **2** 14 **Glitzy D'Ocala (FR)**[42] 3718 6-11-3 0 RichardJohnson 106+
(Philip Hobbs) *in tch: tk clsr order 6th: trckd wnr after 7th: rdn appr 3 out: sn wl hld* **5/6**[1]

0/0 **3** 0 **Noddies Way**[110] 2192 8-11-0 0 SamTwiston-Davies(3) 90
(John Panvert) *chsd ldrs: rdn after 8th: wnt 3rd bef 3 out but nvr any ch* **20/1**

1P3 **4** 6 **Stolen Thunder**[37] 3836 6-11-9 116 JackDoyle 97
(Emma Lavelle) *hld up bhd: pushed along after 6th: plugged on fr 3 but nvr any ch w ldng trio* **5/2**[2]

PPU- **5** 22 **Rockandahardplace (IRE)**[338] 5008 8-10-12 0 MrGBarfoot-Saunt(5) 71
(Tracey Barfoot-Saunt) *trckd ldrs: rdn after 7th: wknd bef 3 out: t.o* **66/1**

53P **6** 1 3/4 **Power Lord (IRE)**[32] 3931 6-10-10 0 NathanSweeney(7) 69
(Bob Buckler) *mid-div tl 7th: sn wknd: t.o* **11/1**

0P0 **7** 25 **Another Round (IRE)**[47] 3647 7-11-3 0 RodiGreene 47
(Laura Young) *chsd ldrs tl 6th: sn rdn: mstke 7th: sn wknd: t.o* **100/1**

0U/P **8** 67 **Bitta Dash**[18] 4189 11-11-3 0 DavidDennis —
(Jim Wilson) *mid-div tl wknd after 6th: t.o* **100/1**

6- **U** **City Well**[350] 4793 8-11-3 0 LiamHeard —
(Laura Young) *hld up towards rr: 6th whn blnd and uns rdr 8th* **66/1**

6m 2.40s (3.40) **Going Correction** -0.05s/f (Good) **9** Ran SP% **117.9**
Speed ratings (Par 105): **92,87,84,82,75 74,66,43,**—
toteswingers:1&2:£2.00, 1&3:£12.40, 2&3:£6.70 CSF £10.15 TOTE £5.60: £1.50, £1.10, £3.00; EX 13.00.
Owner Newcombe's Devonians **Bred** G And Mrs Whittaker **Trained** Yarnscombe, Devon

FOCUS
This moderate novice hurdle was run at a solid enough gallop and the first pair dominated from four out. The third is the best guide to the level, with the easy winner up a stone.

NOTEBOOK
Lundy Sky ◆ made all for a most decisive success and landed his first win over hurdles at the second attempt. This was just his third outing since winning his bumper on deep ground last March and he was thought good enough to take his chance in the decent bumper on Grand National day next time (well beaten). He nearly exited at the second, but thereafter his jumping was sound and he was given a well-judged ride from the front. Stamina is clearly his forte and there should be more to come. (op 9-2)
Glitzy D'Ocala(FR) won a bumper here on his first outing for Phillip Hobbs two runs back and shaped well on his introduction to hurdling last time. He was faced with better ground, but that was expected to help him see out the longer trip and he was the one to beat here. Richard Johnson never looked confident of reeling in the winner from four out, though, and he was ultimately no match for that rival. (op Evens tchd 11-10)
Noddies Way was returning from a 110-day break and turned in his best effort by some way over hurdles. He is a dour stayer on the Flat and so it wasn't that surprising to see him doing his best work late on, and he is one to side with now he can enter handicaps. Official explanation: vet said gelding had lost an off fore shoe (op 14-1)
Stolen Thunder, easy to back, needs dropping out but he found himself with too much to do and never threatened. He's better than this. Official explanation: jockey said the gelding was unsuited by the ground (op 11-4 tchd 3-1)
Rockandahardplace(IRE) was making his debut for a new stable and ran with more encouragement considering he had failed to get home in four of his last five outings. Dropping back in trip in a low-grade handicap could well see him off the mark as he should come on plenty. (op 50-1)
Bitta Dash Official explanation: vet said gelding had lost an off fore shoe

4540 UPTON LAKES AND LODGES AMATEUR RIDERS' H'CAP HURDLE (8 hdls) 2m 1f

5:00 (5:00) (Class 5) (0-95,94) 4-Y-0+ **£1,873** (£581; £290; £145)

Form RPR

-004 **1** **Lupita (IRE)**[104] 2609 7-9-7 **68** oh1 (t) O-CdtJessicaLodge(7) 71
(Derrick Scott) *in tch: rdn to chal 3 out: edgd lft but kpt on gamely to ld fnl 75yds* **12/1**

5/0- **2** 3/4 **Only Hope**[667] 237 7-9-13 **74** (t) MrGHMBartlett(7) 77+
(Rachel Hobbs) *hld up: hdwy appr 5th: led 3 out: hung lft after 2 out: hit last: no ex whn hdd fnl 75yds* **16/1**

2603 **3** 1/2 **The Fox's Decree**[110] 2478 7-11-4 **93** (t) MrDHiskett(7) 95
(Martin Keighley) *mid-div: rdn and hdwy appr 3 out: styd on: nrst fin* **9/2**[1]

-000 **4** 1 3/4 **Just Tootsie**[17] 4224 7-11-6 **93** MrRGHenderson(5) 93
(Nick Mitchell) *wl bhd 2nd: hdwy wl after 5th: styd on u.p fr 3 out: nrst fin* **10/1**

1-00 **5** ½ **Sovereign Spirit (IRE)**[32] 3703 9-10-8 **83**.........(tp) MissAmyAppleton[(7)] 84
(Chris Gordon) *prom: rdn after 5th: styd on same pce fr 3 out* **28/1**
0222 **6** 4½ **Man Of Leisure**[23] 4104 7-11-2 **91**.................................. MrBenClarke[(7)] 91+
(Nerys Dutfield) *trckd ldrs: led 5th tl mstke 3 out: grad fdd fr next* **9/2**[1]
0363 **7** 10 **Chouromanesco (FR)**[8] 4403 8-10-11 **86**.................(p) MrABradstock[(7)] 73
(Mark Bradstock) *mid-div: c wd in st: blnd 3 out: no imp* **16/1**
4-40 **8** 15 **Taste The Wine (IRE)**[32] 2937 5-11-5 **94**..................... MrRJWilliams[(7)] 77+
(Bernard Llewellyn) *mid-div: hdwy 5th: rdn and wknd appr 3 out* **6/1**[2]
36/P **9** ¾ **Zuleta**[26] 4032 10-9-7 **68**.. MrBJPoste[(7)] 40
(Laura Young) *a towards rr: t.o* **28/1**
0500 **10** 5 **Tiger Dream**[5] 4450 6-11-3 **92**....................................(b) MrRHawkins[(7)] 60
(Chris Down) *led tl 5th: sn wknd: t.o* **16/1**
4143 **11** 1 **Whitcombe Spirit**[22] 4123 6-10-11 **86**..................(b) MrDanielBurchell[(7)] 53
(Jamie Poulton) *lft at s: a bhd: t.o* **12/1**
06-1 **12** 27 **Tavalu (USA)**[9] 4378 9-10-11 **86** 7ex.................... MrMatthewHampton[(7)] 29
(Gerald Ham) *lost tch 2nd: t.o* **9/1**[3]
603P **P** **Copper Sound**[21] 4133 7-11-2 **84**.......................................(v) MrMMahon —
(Michael Scudamore) *chsd ldrs tl rdn 2nd: sn wknd: t.o whn p.u bef 3 out* **10/1**

4m 16.9s (1.40) **Going Correction** -0.05s/f (Good) **13** Ran SP% **118.8**
Speed ratings (Par 103): **94,93,93,92,92 90,85,78,78,75 75,62,—**
toteswingers:1&2:£29.20, 1&3:£17.70, 2&3:£28.00 CSF £185.79 CT £996.70 TOTE £14.10: £3.80, £8.40, £3.50; EX 249.90.
Owner Mrs D D Scott **Bred** Roland H Alder **Trained** Selworthy, Somerset
■ Jessica Lodge's first winner under rules.

FOCUS
A typically weak handicap for amateur riders. It was run at a solid gallop and saw changing fortunes in the home straight. The fourth is the best guide to the level.

NOTEBOOK
Lupita(IRE) was 1lb out of the weights and looked to have plenty on her plate returning from a 104-day break, but had previously shown her best jumping form at this track. She travelled sweetly throughout, though, and kept finding plenty when asked to grind down the runner-up from two out. It was her first her first win over hurdles and first success since winning on the level in 2008 for another yard, plus it was the rider's first win under rules. (op 10-1)
Only Hope crept into things turning for home and looked for most of the home straight as though she would score. It was her first outing for 667 days, however, and she was mugged near the line as fitness told. She too was debuting for a new yard and this was much more like it. (op 20-1)
The Fox's Decree met support back from a 110-day break and shaped as though the run would do him good. He helps to set the level. (op 6-1)
Just Tootsie ◆, dropped back from 2m6f, really caught the eye staying on late having got well behind at halfway. He can surely build on this over slightly further. (op 8-1)
Sovereign Spirit(IRE) was staying on late and posted a step back in the right direction. (op 40-1)
Man Of Leisure, runner-up on his last three starts, was bang there before hitting the second-last and faded from there on. (op 6-1)
Taste The Wine(IRE) Official explanation: vet said gelding lost an off fore shoe
T/Jkpt: £1,445,671.25 to a £1 stake. Pool:£2,036,156.75 - 1.00 winning ticket T/Plt: £409.10 to a £1 stake. Pool:£189,315.08 - 337.74 winning tickets T/Qpdt: £111.80 to a £1 stake. Pool:£9,503.00 - 62.90 winning tickets TM

4357 NEWCASTLE (L-H)
Tuesday, March 8

OFFICIAL GOING: Soft (heavy in places in back straight; good to soft in places last 4f; 5.5)
First hurdle in the back straight omitted in all hurdle races; damaged ground.
Wind: Fresh, half against Weather: Sunny

4541 STARSPORTSBET.CO.UK "NATIONAL HUNT" NOVICES' HURDLE (8 hdls 1 omitted) 2m
2:20 (2:21) (Class 4) 4-Y-0+ **£2,016** (£592; £296; £147)

Form RPR
411P **1** **Jukebox Melody (IRE)**[19] 4165 5-11-1 0............................ GrahamLee 98+
(Malcolm Jefferson) *plld hrd: hld up: gd hdwy to ld 3 out: shkn up and nt fluent next: pushed out run-in* **5/2**[2]
60P **2** 2½ **Alpha One (IRE)**[31] 3952 5-11-1 0.................................. CampbellGillies 91
(Chris Grant) *t.k.h early: chsd ldrs: nt fluent 1st: effrt and chsd wnr after 3 out: rdn and edgd rt next: kpt on run-in* **50/1**
/0-5 **3** 3 **Andreo Bambaleo**[25] 4061 7-11-1 0..................................... TomSiddall 88
(Simon West) *set stdy pce to after 2nd: chsd ldr to 4 out: sn drvn and outpcd: rallied bef 2 out: kpt on run-in: no imp* **14/1**
5-3 **4** 3½ **Next To Nowhere (IRE)**[12] 4303 6-11-1 0....................... FearghalDavis 85
(Nicky Richards) *t.k.h: hld up towards rr: hdwy 4 out: effrt next: no imp fr 2 out* **9/4**[1]
F-P0 **5** 3 **Power Flow (IRE)**[21] 4132 6-11-1 81.................................. PaddyAspell 82
(Peter Atkinson) *prom: led and qcknd after 2nd: hdd 3 out: outpcd fr next* **14/1**
4042 **6** 13 **Lucky Sunny (IRE)**[21] 4132 8-11-1 120.............................. SeanQuinlan 72
(Richard Phillips) *hld up in tch: hdwy to chse ldr 4 out: ev ch next: outpcd whn nt fluent 2 out: sn wknd* **7/2**[3]
00 **7** 7 **Sleep In First (FR)**[116] 2355 5-11-1 0.............................. JodieMogford 62
(Anna Bramall) *cl up: hit 4th: rdn after 4 out: wknd bef next* **100/1**
0 **8** 5 **Rocky Bear (IRE)**[31] 3957 6-10-8 0................................. KyleJames[(7)] 57
(Marjorie Fife) *t.k.h: hld up in tch: struggling 1/2-way: sn wknd* **100/1**
6 **9** 23 **Alleged Vanity (IRE)**[54] 3525 5-11-1 0............................ DenisO'Regan 34
(Chris Grant) *nt fluent on occasions: sn bhd: lost tch 1/2-way: t.o* **7/1**

4m 17.3s (7.30) **Going Correction** +0.125s/f (Yiel) **9** Ran SP% **111.3**
Speed ratings (Par 105): **86,84,83,81,80 73,70,67,56**
toteswingers:1&2:£11.10, 1&3:£5.30, 2&3:£46.70 CSF £84.13 TOTE £3.50: £1.10, £17.50, £5.10; EX 87.00.
Owner Richard Collins **Bred** Finbar Leahy **Trained** Norton, N Yorks

FOCUS
This was a weak novice event run at a sedate gallop. The race has been given a token rating through the third and the winner should rate a lot higher in time.

NOTEBOOK
Jukebox Melody(IRE), son of St Leger winner Brian Boru, is a dual bumper winner and put an errant performance on his hurdling debut behind him, taking this with plenty in hand. He pulled hard throughout but scythed through the pack in the straight and won going away. He's still green, clearly a work in progress, and should appreciate further in time. (op 9-4 tchd 11-4)
Alpha One(IRE) put in a career-best performance to chase home the winner. He was a little sketchy at some hurdles but looks to be improving with racing. (op 80-1)
Andreo Bambaleo was one-paced down the back straight but stayed on over the final two hurdles, showing more promise than he had previously. (op 12-1 tchd 16-1)
Next To Nowhere(IRE) showed a glimmer of promise on his hurdles debut at Ayr and was backed to improve for that experience, but was one-paced when under pressure two out. He looks to need further already. (op 5-2 tchd 11-4 in a place)
Power Flow(IRE) had shown little thus far but was well backed. He made a bold show from the front but couldn't sustain his effort in the straight. (op 40-1)
Lucky Sunny(IRE) was a slight disappointment. He made good headway down the back straight but an error two out stopped all momentum. Perhaps a sharper track will suit better. (op 5-2)

4542 GOSFORTH DECORATING AND BUILDING SERVICES CONDITIONAL JOCKEYS' H'CAP HURDLE (10 hdls 1 omitted) 2m 4f
2:50 (2:50) (Class 5) (0-95,90) 4-Y-0+ **£1,723** (£506; £253; £126)

Form RPR
P552 **1** **Cute N You Know It**[43] 3717 8-9-13 **66**......................(p) PaulGallagher[(3)] 71+
(Andrew Crook) *trckd ldrs: led bef 3 out: drvn bef next: hld on wl run-in* **4/1**[3]
3060 **2** 1¼ **Miss Tarantella**[20] 4146 8-11-0 **85**.........................(t) StephenMulqueen[(7)] 87
(Maurice Barnes) *hld up in tch: stdy hdwy after 4 out: effrt and chsd wnr bef 2 out: ev ch and edgd rt run-in: r.o* **13/2**
0-PU **3** 3 **Final Veto**[8] 4390 8-11-9 **90**... ShaneByrne[(3)] 91
(Sue Smith) *prom: nt fluent 6th and next: effrt 3 out: kpt on fr last: nt pce of first two* **3/1**[2]
-0P5 **4** 23 **Lochore (IRE)**[21] 4138 5-10-8 **75**.................................... AlexanderVoy[(3)] 51
(Lucy Normile) *led to bef 3 out: sn drvn: outpcd after next: wknd qckly run-in* **10/1**
5P0P **P** **Betty's Run**[22] 4112 9-9-11 **64** oh5...................................... KyleJames[(3)] —
(Lynn Siddall) *pressed ldr: hit 3rd: rdn 6th: wknd next: t.o whn p.u bef 2 out* **25/1**
0520 **P** **Overyou**[12] 4302 6-11-7 **88**... PeterCarberry[(3)] —
(Elliott Cooper) *prom: reminders after 6th: wknd after next: t.o whn p.u bef 2 out* **5/2**[1]
0U00 **P** **Aitch Factor**[34] 3885 5-11-8 **86**.. CampbellGillies —
(Henry Hogarth) *nt fluent on occasions: hld up: outpcd 6th: lost tch next: p.u bef 2 out* **8/1**

5m 22.5s (1.40) **Going Correction** +0.125s/f (Yiel) **7** Ran SP% **111.0**
Speed ratings (Par 103): **102,101,100,91,— —,—**
toteswingers:1&2:£6.50, 1&3:£3.60, 2&3:£2.00 CSF £27.59 TOTE £3.10: £2.00, £3.00; EX 18.80.
Owner J Saxby, A Gillway Partnership **Bred** Beech Tree Stud **Trained** Middleham Moor, N Yorks

FOCUS
A poor handicap hurdle and the front three pulled well clear. The idling winner is rated to her mark along with the next pair.

NOTEBOOK
Cute N You Know It was extremely well handicapped on her best form and landed a deserved victory under a good ride from promising conditional Paul Gallagher. She hugged the rail throughout and, once hitting the front, displayed a good attitude to bravely fend off the runner up. Andy Crook said she's essentially a three-miler but got away with the shorter distance under the soft conditions. She is, however, far from certain to follow up given her overall profile.
Miss Tarantella has shown nothing recently but only went down to a more determined rival on the run-in. (op 6-1 tchd 11-2)
Final Veto hit a flat spot around the final bend but responded to pressure and wasn't beaten far by the front two. This was encouraging as it was the first time he's completed this term. (op 11-4 tchd 5-2)
Lochore(IRE) took up the running going on the final circuit but was never able to keep up the pace and a drop in trip could be the answer. (tchd 12-1)
Overyou was pulled up after failing to respond to pressure a fair way out. She looks to be well held off her current handicap mark. Official explanation: vet said mare bled from the nose (op 10-3)

4543 STP CONSTRUCTION NOVICES' H'CAP CHASE (18 fncs) 3m
3:20 (3:20) (Class 4) (0-115,114) 5-Y-0+ **£2,439** (£716; £358; £178)

Form RPR
2414 **1** **Lockstown**[19] 4167 8-11-2 **104**...(p) GrahamLee 112
(Ann Hamilton) *prom: nt fluent 6th: stdy hdwy to chse ldr after 5 out: effrt and swtchd rt appr 2 out: led last: hld on wl run-in* **9/4**[1]
32P2 **2** hd **Bear Dancing (IRE)**[24] 4066 7-10-10 **98**......................... PeterBuchanan 106
(Lucinda Russell) *led to 2nd: cl up: led 10th: rdn bef 4 out: hdd last: rallied: jst hld* **3/1**[2]
242 **3** 34 **The Ferbane Man (IRE)**[11] 4334 7-11-12 **114**...............(p) SamThomas 92
(Tim Vaughan) *cl up: hit 3rd: ev ch whn hit 5 out: rdn and wknd fr next* **9/4**[1]
243 **4** 27 **Cloonawillin Lady (IRE)**[15] 4254 8-10-1 **89**......................... TomSiddall 36
(Elliott Cooper) *led 2nd to 10th: cl up tl outpcd 5 out: lost tch fr next* **4/1**[3]

6m 25.8s (3.30) **Going Correction** +0.125s/f (Yiel) **4** Ran SP% **106.5**
Speed ratings: **99,98,87,78**
CSF £8.72 TOTE £4.20; EX 10.40.
Owner Hedley Walton & Ian Hamilton **Bred** Mrs Brenda Turley **Trained** Great Bavington, Northumberland
■ Stewards' Enquiry : Graham Lee caution: careless riding

FOCUS
Only four runners, but a competitive novices' handicap chase and it produced a good finish, with the front two pulling clear. The winner is rated to his mark, with a big step up from the runner-up.

NOTEBOOK
Lockstown, patiently ridden, looked set to stay on for a convincing victory after pinging the last, but he was made to battle. He saves his best for this track and could defy a rise under a similar hold-up ride. (op 2-1)
Bear Dancing(IRE), having his second start over regulation fences, looks to be suited by a severe stamina test. The 4m race at Hexham later this month could be a possibility. (op 7-2)
The Ferbane Man(IRE) looks to need a good pace to run at but jumping errors cost him any chance. He hasn't had many chances in handicap company and could be of interest on a sounder surface. (op 2-1 tchd 15-8)
Cloonawillin Lady(IRE) couldn't cut it against her own sex last time out and struggled to get involved here. This was her handicap debut and it looks a high enough mark for her based on what she's achieved. Official explanation: vet said mare bled from the nose (op 9-2 tchd 7-2)

4544 COMPLETE FOOTBALL H'CAP HURDLE (8 hdls 1 omitted) 2m
3:50 (3:50) (Class 4) (0-110,110) 4-Y-0+ **£2,016** (£592; £296; £147)

Form RPR
0022 **1** **Willie Hall**[19] 4166 7-11-5 **103**.. CampbellGillies 110+
(William Amos) *set stdy pce: nt fluent on occasions: hdd 3 out: rallied after next: drvn to ld run-in: styd on wl* **15/8**[1]
12U4 **2** nk **Rolecarr (IRE)**[15] 4255 8-11-3 **101**...................................... AdrianLane 105
(Ann Hamilton) *prom: outpcd bef 4 out: rallied to ld next: hdd run-in: kpt on fin* **5/1**[2]
0005 **3** 3½ **No Supper (IRE)**[19] 4166 7-10-11 **95**................................... BarryKeniry 97
(George Bewley) *t.k.h: hld up last but in tch: hdwy after 3rd: effrt and ev ch 3 out to last: one pce run-in* **8/1**
-1F0 **4** 4 **Arisea (IRE)**[30] 3966 8-11-7 **105**... PaddyAspell 102
(James Moffatt) *in tch: effrt bef 3 out: rdn and one pce fr next* **14/1**
1000 **5** 3¼ **Hi Dancer**[22] 4113 8-11-7 **110**.. GilesHawkins[(5)] 103
(Ben Haslam) *chsd wnr: ev ch 3 out: rdn and wknd after next* **10/1**

0421 **6** 2 1/4 **Euro American (GER)**[16] 4241 11-11-2 **100** WilsonRenwick 91
(Rose Dobbin) *hld up in tch: drvn and outpcd after 4 out: no imp fr next* **5/1**[2]

1404 **F** **Viscount Rossini**[16] 4234 9-11-5 **110** (b) PeterCarberry(7) —
(Steve Gollings) *trcking ldrs whn fell heavily 4th: fatally injured* **6/1**[3]

4m 15.0s (5.00) **Going Correction** +0.125s/f (Yiel) **7** Ran SP% **109.3**
Speed ratings (Par 105): **92,91,90,88,86 85,—**
toteswingers:1&2:£1.20, 1&3:£8.00, 2&3:£11.40 CSF £10.76 TOTE £3.90: £2.20, £1.10; EX 7.00.
Owner R H Hall **Bred** G E Leech **Trained** Broadhaugh, Scottish Borders
■ Stewards' Enquiry : Barry Keniry two-day ban: careless riding (Mar 22-23)
Adrian Lane two-day ban: used whip with excessive frequency (Mar 23-22)

FOCUS
A fair handicap for the grade which was run at a steady gallop, and there were three in a line at the final flight. The winner can rate higher and the next two set the level.

NOTEBOOK
Willie Hall was the unexposed improver in the line-up and, although he wandered and lost the lead approaching two out, he was straightened up thereafter to stay on strongly and fend off Rolecarr. He looks to be going the right way over hurdles and can go in again off a higher mark. (op 9-4)
Rolecarr(IRE) hasn't got much margin for error off his current mark but continues in form. He's a fairly consistent performer who should be given a chance up in trip before long. (op 11-2)
No Supper(IRE) is running into form. He travelled well for a long way and held every chance two out before lacking the pace of the front two. He is on a winnable mark. (tchd 7-1)
Arisea(IRE) plugged on after being out paced in the home straight. Being by Cape Cross she will probably be seen to better effect on good ground. (op 12-1)
Hi Dancer has been in poor form under both codes this season and continues to struggle from this handicap mark. (op 8-1 tchd 15-2)
Euro American(GER) didn't respond to pressure when struggling a fair way out. (tchd 4-1)

4545 SWARLANDFENCESTORAGE.CO.UK NOVICES' HURDLE (10 hdls 1 omitted) 2m 4f

4:20 (4:20) (Class 4) 4-Y-0+ **£2,016** (£592; £296; £147)

Form RPR

0332 **1** **Tiptoeaway (IRE)**[16] 4233 6-11-2 112 GrahamLee 109+
(Tim Easterby) *t.k.h: chsd clr ldr: smooth hdwy to ld 3 out: drew clr fr next: nt fluent last: eased run-in* **4/6**[1]

502 **2** 5 **Lua De Itapoan**[27] 4000 6-10-9 0 DenisO'Regan 90
(Malcolm Jefferson) *hld up: outpcd 4 out: rallied after next: wnt 13 l 2nd last: kpt on but no ch w eased-down wnr* **9/2**[3]

-P3 **3** 8 **Diamond D'Amour (IRE)**[21] 4132 5-11-2 0 BrianHughes 98+
(Howard Johnson) *led and clr: hit 4 out: hdd next: rdn whn blnd and sprawled bdly 2 out: lost 2nd and wknd last* **3/1**[2]

00 **4** nk **Money Tree**[32] 3920 5-11-2 0 AdrianLane 88
(Donald McCain) *t.k.h: hld up in tch: outpcd 4 out: plugged on fnl 2: no imp* **25/1**

0/0 **P** **Dr Light (IRE)**[124] 2166 7-11-2 0 JodieMogford —
(Anna Bramall) *prom: outpcd 6th: sn wknd: t.o whn p.u 3 out* **66/1**

4-P6 **P** **Direct Approach (IRE)**[14] 4278 7-11-2 83 TomSiddall —
(Lynn Siddall) *in tch: outpcd bef 6th: sn struggling: t.o whn p.u 3 out* **33/1**

5m 20.6s (-0.50) **Going Correction** +0.125s/f (Yiel) **6** Ran SP% **111.4**
Speed ratings (Par 105): **106,104,100,100,— —**
toteswingers:1&2:£1.30, 1&3:£1.30, 2&3:£1.20 CSF £4.17 TOTE £1.80: £1.50, £1.80; EX 2.90.
Owner Trevor Hemmings **Bred** L Baxter And Noreen Smith **Trained** Great Habton, N Yorks

FOCUS
A modest novice hurdle on paper, but it produced a runaway winner. The eased-down winner was the form pick and is rated to his mark.

NOTEBOOK
Tiptoeaway(IRE), second to a highly regarded sort last time out, tracked the tearaway leader and powered to the lead in the straight, winning with authoritative ease. He's a big, scopey individual who should make a chaser in due course, but he can win another novice hurdle in the mean time. (op 5-6 tchd 10-11 in a place)
Lua De Itapoan stayed on late for second but was never going to trouble the easy winner. Malcolm Jefferson reported she will be a nice sort for next season and, being by Silver Patriarch, she will surely appreciate a severe stamina test in future. (op 5-1)
Diamond D'Amour(IRE) set a furious tempo and was easily reeled in by the impressive winner. He made a horrendous mistake when tiring two out but he was simply not in the winner's league. He looks up to claiming a race if allowed a similarly soft lead. (tchd 7-2)
Money Tree was badly outpaced before consenting to run on and was probably flattered to almost head the tiring third horse. This was a step in the right direction though. (op 16-1)
Direct Approach(IRE) Official explanation: jockey said the gelding had a breathing problem

4546 PARKLANDS H'CAP CHASE (16 fncs) 2m 4f

4:50 (4:51) (Class 3) (0-130,125) 5-Y-0+ **£4,553** (£1,337; £668; £333)

Form RPR

-332 **1** **Categorical**[10] 4357 8-11-12 **125** JamesReveley 131
(Keith Reveley) *hld up in tch: stdy hdwy to ld 3 out: hit and hdd 2 out: rallied and regained ld last: pushed out* **11/2**

/31- **2** nk **Quiqui De L'Isle (FR)**[92] 7-11-0 **116** HarryHaynes(3) 123+
(Anna Bramall) *hld up in tch: stdy hdwy 1/2-way: cl up whn hit 10th: ev ch 4 out: effrt whn hit 2 out: styd on u.p towards fin* **7/1**

/224 **3** nse **Blackpool Billy (IRE)**[36] 3854 9-10-13 **112** GrahamLee 118
(Ferdy Murphy) *hld up: nt fluent 2nd: hdwy 10th: led 4 out to next: and 2 out to last: kpt on u.p run-in* **9/2**[3]

2553 **4** 6 **Et Maintenant (FR)**[24] 4065 9-11-7 **120** PeterBuchanan 121
(Lucinda Russell) *prom: hit 7th: effrt 4 out: rdn and one pce fr 2 out* **10/1**

-001 **5** 27 **Beamazed**[27] 4004 7-11-5 **118** DenisO'Regan 94
(Malcolm Jefferson) *in tch: hdwy and cl up after 6th: pckd 9th: ev ch 5 out: wknd fr next* **3/1**[1]

2522 **6** 3 **Camden George (IRE)**[19] 4167 10-10-13 **112** HenryOliver 88
(Sue Smith) *cl up: hit 5th: sn pushed along: outpcd whn hit 5 out: sn btn* **7/2**[2]

-434 **7** 1 1/4 **Diamond Frontier (IRE)**[24] 4065 8-11-10 **123** WilsonRenwick 91
(Howard Johnson) *led tl hdd 4 out: wknd bef next: eased whn no ch run-in* **15/2**

5m 25.9s (-1.30) **Going Correction** +0.125s/f (Yiel) **7** Ran SP% **114.1**
Speed ratings: **107,106,106,104,93 92,91**
toteswingers:1&2:£3.70, 1&3:£2.30, 2&3:£4.60 CSF £41.43 TOTE £6.00: £2.40, £3.60; EX 51.20.
Owner Rug, Grub & Pub Partnership **Bred** Darley **Trained** Lingdale, Redcar & Cleveland

FOCUS
The feature race of the day and it produced a thrilling finish. Solid form with the winner and third to their marks.

NOTEBOOK
Categorical, given a good, patient ride, narrowly prevailed ahead of two improving types. A previous C&D winner, he is a consistent sort who could defy a small rise at this track. (op 5-1)
Quiqui De L'Isle(FR), the winner of his last three starts in France (two over hurdles, one over fences), only went down in a driving finish on his return to Britain. He had been off for three months and is entitled to come on for this. (op 8-1)
Blackpool Billy(IRE) was keeping on well again at the finish and could win off this mark on similarly soft ground. (op 7-2 tchd 5-1)
Et Maintenant(FR) blundered at a few fences which compromised his chance. Once asked for pressure, he only found the one pace and looks a tad high in the handicap currently. (op 9-1)
Beamazed made multiple jumping errors which ended his chance. Official explanation: trainer said, regarding the apparent improvement of form, that the gelding was unsuited by the two miles and four furlongs and needs stepping up to a longer trip (op 4-1)
Camden George(IRE) didn't jump well enough. (op 5-1)
Diamond Frontier(IRE) set a good pace but couldn't sustain the effort on the final circuit. (op 7-1 tchd 6-1)

4547 S.V. RUTTER LTD "NEWCOMERS" STANDARD OPEN NATIONAL HUNT FLAT RACE 2m

5:20 (5:20) (Class 6) 4-5-Y-0 **£1,431** (£420; £210; £104)

Form RPR

1 **Chapter Five** 4-10-3 0 JamesReveley 90+
(Keith Reveley) *hld up last: smooth hdwy over 3f out: led gng wl over 1f out: sn pushed along: kpt on wl fnl f* **4/1**[2]

2 4 **Pudsey House** 4-10-3 0 PaulGallagher(7) 90
(Howard Johnson) *w ldr: led 1/2-way to over 2f out: sn rdn and flashed tail: chsd wnr over 1f out: kpt on same pce fnl f* **6/1**

3 nk **Wild Child Lucy** 5-10-8 0 EwanWhillans(3) 91
(Alistair Whillans) *t.k.h: prom: hdwy to ld over 2f out: hdd over 1f out: kpt on same pce fnl f* **13/2**

4 10 **Plenmeller (IRE)** 5-10-13 0 ShaneByrne(5) 88
(Sue Smith) *set slow pce: hdd 1/2-way: outpcd 5f out: plugged on fnl 2f: no ch w first three* **9/1**

5 1/2 **Highrate (IRE)** 5-11-4 0 HenryOliver 87
(Sue Smith) *trckd ldrs: effrt and ev ch over 3f out to 2f out: edgd lft and wknd over 1f out* **7/2**[1]

6 10 **Sun Lady (FR)** 5-10-11 0 KennyJohnson 70
(Robert Johnson) *hld up: stdy hdwy and prom over 5f out: wknd over 3f out* **22/1**

7 3 1/2 **Farewell Bluebell (IRE)** 4-10-10 0 SamThomas 66
(Tim Vaughan) *hld up in tch: stdy hdwy 5f out: wknd over 3f out* **9/2**[3]

8 9 **King Kalium (IRE)** 5-11-4 0 GrahamLee 65
(Bruce Mactaggart) *t.k.h: prom tl rdn and wknd fr over 4f out* **10/1**

4m 26.1s (21.70) **Going Correction** +0.125s/f (Yiel)
WFA 4 from 5yo 7lb **8** Ran SP% **111.5**
Speed ratings: **50,48,47,42,42 37,35,31**
toteswingers:1&2:£6.10, 1&3:£4.70, 2&3:£6.90 CSF £26.60 TOTE £4.20: £1.10, £2.50, £2.10; EX 29.90.
Owner Mr & Mrs Hutton & Mrs Laing **Bred** Mrs Lesley A Hutton **Trained** Lingdale, Redcar & Cleveland

FOCUS
A very steady tempo for the bumper and there was no doubt about the winner from 2f out.

NOTEBOOK
Chapter Five, from a good Flat family, travelled smoothly through her race and won cosily in the end. She could well progress into a slick hurdler in time, being a sister to a useful 2m hurdle winner. (op 9-2 tchd 5-1)
Pudsey House led for the majority of the race at a sedate gallop, and although outpaced rounding the home turn, he stuck on once off the bridle. He can improve for this encouraging first outing. (op 4-1)
Wild Child Lucy, a sister to chaser Sammy Spiderman out of a sister to Heltornic, rates as a potential winner in the making. She was keen in the early stages but looked to get the hang of things in the closing stages and was staying on well down the straight. (op 7-1 tchd 6-1)
Plenmeller(IRE) stayed on from an unpromising position. (op 10-1 tchd 8-1)
Highrate(IRE) travelled well for a long way and should appreciate better ground in due course, being by Presenting. (op 4-1 tchd 3-1)
Farewell Bluebell(IRE), well supported, didn't find much when asked for his effort but his jockey wasn't hard on him once beaten. (tchd 5-1)
T/Plt: £246.30 to a £1 stake. Pool:£65,148.17 - 193.07 winning tickets T/Qpdt: £24.10 to a £1 stake. Pool:£5,571.02 - 170.45 winning tickets RY

4390 CATTERICK (L-H)

Wednesday, March 9

OFFICIAL GOING: Good (good to soft in places on chase course; chs 7.1, hdl 8.3)
Wind: fresh 1/2 against Weather: overcast, very breezy

4548 BODUGI.COM LAUNCHES SOCIAL BETTING (S) HURDLE (8 hdls) 2m

2:20 (2:20) (Class 5) 4-Y-0+ **£1,781** (£519; £259)

Form RPR

320- **1** **Wake Board (FR)**[558] 1318 6-10-5 115 (t) KillianMoore(10) 106+
(Graeme McPherson) *mde all: clr fr 5th: nt fluent 2 out: eased run-in: unchal* **6/4**[1]

4-P0 **2** 18 **Perfectus (IRE)**[55] 3523 7-10-12 88 JamesHalliday(3) 88
(Malcolm Jefferson) *chsd ldrs: wnt 2nd 5th: kpt on same pce appr 2 out: no imp* **5/1**[3]

6612 **3** 5 **Bromhead (USA)**[34] 3497 5-11-9 99 JamesReveley 93
(Kevin Morgan) *hld up in rr: hdwy 5th: clr 3rd next: rdn appr 2 out: kpt on same pce* **9/4**[2]

0503 **4** 19 **Chadwell Spring (IRE)**[15] 4274 5-10-1 64 (b) HenryBrooke(7) 59
(Mike Sowersby) *chsd ldrs: wknd appr 2 out* **20/1**

00 **5** 3/4 **Royal Willy (IRE)**[9] 4393 5-10-10 0 MissLHorner(5) 66
(Chris Grant) *prom: lost pl 4th: bhd fr 3 out: 5th whn hit last* **11/1**

6002 **6** 19 **Bold Indian (IRE)**[15] 4274 7-10-8 64 PaulGallagher(7) 49
(Mike Sowersby) *hld up: hdwy to chse ldrs after 5th: lost pl appr 2 out* **20/1**

P/0F **7** 1 1/4 **Princess Aliuska**[22] 4132 6-10-5 0 JohnKington(3) 41
(Charles Smith) *hld up in rr: bhd fr 5th* **66/1**

P446 **8** 1 3/4 **Daraybad (FR)**[138] 1949 9-11-1 72 (v) FearghalDavis 46
(Andrew Crook) *prom: lost pl 5th: 7th whn mstke last* **33/1**

P000 **P** **Autumn Harvest**[29] 3993 7-10-10 74 (p) AlexanderVoy(5) —
(William Young) *chsd wnr: wknd qckly and hit 5th: sn bhd: t.o whn p.u bef 2 out* **40/1**

3m 50.6s (-1.90) **Going Correction** -0.075s/f (Good) **9** Ran SP% **112.2**
Speed ratings (Par 103): **101,92,89,80,79 70,69,68,—**
toteswingers:1&2:£3.60, 1&3:£1.10, 2&3:£4.10 CSF £8.55 TOTE £3.60: £1.20, £1.70, £1.10; EX 13.00.The winner sold for 7,000gns to Dr Richard Newland
Owner T S Palin **Bred** S C E A Haras Des Monts D'Arree **Trained** Upper Oddington, Gloucs
■ Killian Moore's first winner.

FOCUS
After a shower early in the morning the ground eased to Good, Good to Soft in places on the chase course. There was a strong headwind in the straight. Very few had any recent form in this seller and two stood out on official ratings, although one was returning from a long absence. The form is rated around the second and third.

NOTEBOOK
Wake Board(FR) was having his first run for his new trainer on his first start since August 2009. Backed into favourite, he set off in front and was quite keen under his conditional rider. However, he was clear with a circuit to go and never looked like being reeled in. He was rated 123 when last seen and the handicapper will be looking to put him back up to around that sort of mark, so it will be no surprise if he is turned out again in a similar contest at Stratford next Monday. He was sold to Richard Newland at the subsequent auction. (op 2-1)
Perfectus(IRE) was dropping into a seller for the first time and was supported in the ring. He chased the winner from the third-last but could make no impression. (op 13-2 tchd 7-1)
Bromhead(USA) was the form horse, having shown decent form earlier in the year before disappointing on the Flat last time. He came through to chase the winner with the runner-up after three out, but had no more to offer from the penultimate flight. (op 13-8)
Chadwell Spring(IRE) chased the leader throughout and made little impression. (op 16-1 tchd 25-1)
Royal Willy(IRE) at least now qualifies for a handicap mark. (op 12-1 tchd 10-1)

4549 CATTERICKBRIDGE.CO.UK MAIDEN CHASE (12 fncs) 2m
2:50 (2:51) (Class 4) 5-Y-0+ **£2,927** (£859; £429; £214)

Form / RPR
5005 **1** **Robertewenutter**[29] 3995 7-11-0 92 HenryOliver 99+
(Sue Smith) *chsd ldr: mstke 2nd: led appr 3 out: drvn out* **5/2**[2]
650P **2** 1 ¾ **Bob Will (IRE)**[22] 4138 6-11-0 0 (p) CampbellGillies 96
(Chris Grant) *chsd ldng pair: wnt 2nd bef last: kpt on same pce run-in* **11/2**
P0/0 **3** 13 **Kyathos (GER)**[44] 3717 10-10-7 0 MrGRSmith(7) 88+
(David Thompson) *midfield: outpcd 8th: lft poor 3rd and hmpd last* **20/1**
2-05 **4** 29 **Conflictofinterest**[260] 822 9-11-0 0 GrahamLee 59
(Kevin Hunter) *midfield: drvn and outpcd 5th: bhd fr 8th: t.o 3 out* **3/1**[3]
0-P5 **5** 3 ¾ **Nonotreally**[21] 4150 10-10-7 89 MrRUtley(7) 55
(Lynsey Kendall) *in last: t.o 5th* **22/1**
3206 **F** **Flichity (IRE)**[6] 4437 6-11-0 0 RichieMcGrath 93
(Donald McCain) *t.k.h: led: hdd appr 3 out: 3rd and wkng whn fell last* **9/4**[1]

4m 0.40s (0.30) **Going Correction** -0.05s/f (Good) **6** Ran SP% **108.8**
Speed ratings: **97,96,89,75,73** —
toteswingers:1&2:£3.40, 1&3:£9.60, 2&3:£17.60 CSF £15.19 TOTE £2.20: £1.90, £3.80; EX 16.10.
Owner C Bradford-Nutter **Bred** Digby Laws **Trained** High Eldwick, W Yorks

FOCUS
A very moderate maiden chase with half the field making their chasing debuts. The winner is rated to his Sedgefield mark.

NOTEBOOK
Robertewenutter is another keen sort but his rider was able to get a good lead from the favourite. After jumping stickily early, he warmed to his task and went past the his market rival three out before finding enough to hold off the runner-up's late effort. He looks capable of better if continuing to settle. (tchd 9-4 and 11-4)
Bob Will(IRE) ran his best recent race over hurdles here before Christmas. Wearing cheekpieces for this chasing debut, he gradually closed on the leaders from three out but never looked like getting past the winner, although that rival went across him on the run-in. This was not a bad effort and good ground clearly suits. (op 13-2 tchd 7-1)
Kyathos(GER) was outpaced from halfway down the back, but is suited by a sound surface and might do better later in the spring and summer. (op 16-1 tchd 14-1)
Conflictofinterest, having his first run since being sold out of Paul Nicholls' yard cheaply, was beaten a long way from home.
Flichity(IRE), a half-brother to Amberleigh House, made the running and jumped well on this chasing debut. However, he did not put up much resistance when headed at the first in the straight and was beaten in third when taking a heavy fall at the final fence. (tchd 11-4 in places)

4550 XTREMEADVENTURESUK.COM H'CAP HURDLE (10 hdls) 2m 3f
3:20 (3:20) (Class 5) (0-90,91) 4-Y-0+ **£1,849** (£539; £269)

Form / RPR
U005 **1** **Samizdat (FR)**[43] 3727 8-10-5 74 MissECSayer(7) 87+
(Dianne Sayer) *chsd ldrs: led 6th: styd on wl between last 2* **11/1**
0321 **2** 1 ¾ **Knight Valliant**[9] 4390 8-11-12 91 7ex JamesO'Farrell(3) 102
(Barbara Butterworth) *hld up: hdwy 3 out: chsd wnr next: styd on same pce run-in* **9/2**[1]
5005 **3** 9 **Border Tale**[116] 2372 11-11-9 85 (v) BrianHughes 89
(James Moffatt) *midfield: hdwy 3 out: kpt on to take 3rd between last 2: no imp* **8/1**
6125 **4** 4 ½ **Sambelucky (IRE)**[44] 3717 6-11-11 87 JamesReveley 86
(Keith Reveley) *in rr: bhd fr 6th: styd on fnl 2: nrst fin* **11/2**[2]
0034 **5** shd **Daasij (IRE)**[13] 4302 6-9-13 68 PaulGallagher(7) 67
(N W Alexander) *hdwy 6th: sn chsng ldrs: one pce appr 2 out* **7/1**[3]
0000 **6** 7 **Waltham Abbey**[9] 4391 10-11-2 85 MrRUtley(7) 78
(Lynsey Kendall) *prom: outpcd appr 2 out* **20/1**
0306 **7** 9 **Mycenean Prince (USA)**[9] 4390 8-11-5 88 (p) MissPhillipaTutty(7) 73
(Karen Tutty) *prom: lost pl after 5th: sn btn* **25/1**
0035 **8** 2 **Dance Sauvage**[9] 4390 8-11-5 81 (b) CampbellGillies 71+
(Mike Sowersby) *trckd ldrs: wknd appr 2 out* **14/1**
0630 **9** 2 **Rhyton (IRE)**[25] 4068 4-11-4 89 AdrianLane 61
(Donald McCain) *nt fluent: chsd ldrs to 3 out: sn lost pl* **14/1**
00-5 **10** ½ **Waldo Winchester (IRE)**[293] 423 8-11-2 78 WilsonRenwick 62+
(Noel Wilson) *chsd ldrs: wknd appr 2 out* **16/1**
00P0 **11** 42 **Mardood**[9] 4390 6-11-10 86 (p) DenisO'Regan 29
(Chris Grant) *chsd ldrs: lost pl after 7th: t.o next* **15/2**
P-P4 **12** 14 **Photogenique (FR)**[24] 4098 8-10-11 76 MichaelMurphy(3) 6
(Rob Summers) *sn bhd: t.o 6th* **80/1**
0PP0 **13** 69 **Fred Grass**[28] 3999 5-10-4 66 TomMessenger —
(Jonathan Haynes) *led to 6th: wknd qckly: t.o 2 out* **100/1**
05P5 **P** **Just Posh**[3] 4511 9-10-13 75 (p) GrahamLee —
(Rayson Nixon) *sn bhd: t.o 6th: p.u bef 2 out* **20/1**
P-06 **P** **Hazy Oaks**[9] 4395 8-11-0 81 BrianToomey(5) —
(Kevin M Prendergast) *bhd fr 7th: t.o whn p.u bef 2 out* **20/1**

4m 42.9s (-3.90) **Going Correction** -0.075s/f (Good)
WFA 4 from 5yo+ 7lb **15** Ran SP% **116.8**
Speed ratings (Par 103): **105,104,100,98,98 95,91,90,90,89 72,66,37,—,—**
toteswingers:1&2:£13.00, 1&3:£20.10, 2&3:£8.90 CSF £53.97 CT £425.74 TOTE £10.90: £3.70, £2.40, £3.60; EX 87.20.
Owner Mrs Freda Rayson **Bred** Peter Spiller **Trained** Hackthorpe, Cumbria

FOCUS
A competitive handicap hurdle. The time was good and it can pay to be positive about the form. The winner took advantage of a good mark.

NOTEBOOK
Samizdat(FR) made a return to form having been rated 35lb higher following two successive wins last March. He took advantage of the handicapper's leniency and, always travelling well, ran on too strongly for the gallant runner-up. (op 9-1)
Knight Valliant, carrying a 7lb penalty for his C&D win the week before, put up a brave effort in defeat and was clear of the rest. He might not have finished winning yet. (op 5-1)
Border Tale, another who has dropped in the handicap, being 27lb lower than at this time last year, had the visor back on and ran better, if proving no match for the principals. (op 12-1)
Sambelucky(IRE), a C&D winner in December, needs to be held up but was left with a lot to do from three out and never got competitive.
Daasij(IRE) is nowhere near as good over hurdles as he was on the Flat, and faded here as if he might prefer dropping back to 2m. (tchd 15-2)
Mardood, last year's winner, was 2lb lower than when completing his hat-trick last spring but was beaten at the middle flight on the far side. (op 8-1)
Hazy Oaks's jockey reported the mare was never travelling. Official explanation: jockey said mare never travelled

4551 FLAT RACING STARTS ON 30TH MARCH NOVICES' H'CAP CHASE (19 fncs) 3m 1f 110y
3:50 (3:50) (Class 4) (0-100,99) 5-Y-0+ **£2,927** (£859; £429; £214)

Form / RPR
1602 **1** **Bardolet (IRE)**[17] 4238 8-11-2 89 JamesReveley 99+
(Keith Reveley) *hld up in rr: gd hdwy 14th: chsng ldrs 4 out: led 2 out: comf* **5/2**[1]
300P **2** 2 ¾ **Feeling Peckish (USA)**[14] 4292 7-9-10 76 (t) MrTGarner(7) 80
(Michael Chapman) *chsd ldrs: led 3 out: hdd next: kpt on same pce* **16/1**
F644 **3** 7 **Bobby Donald (IRE)**[51] 3606 9-10-8 81 TomSiddall 81
(Richard Phillips) *chsd ldrs: blnd 12th: sn outpcd: styd on to take 3rd appr last: no imp* **12/1**
/40- **4** 5 **Nicky Tam (IRE)**[515] 1705 9-10-4 77 RobertWalford 74+
(Henry Hogarth) *chsd ldr: led 6th: hdd 3 out: wknd between last 2* **15/2**
65-6 **5** 7 **Dollar Mick (IRE)**[23] 4112 6-11-8 95 PaddyAspell 85
(James Moffatt) *in rr: sme hdwy whn blnd 13th: kpt on fr 3 out* **5/1**[2]
4033 **6** 20 **Go On Be A Lady**[25] 4064 8-10-6 79 BarryKeniry 48
(Alan Swinbank) *in rr: bhd fr 12th: t.o 4 out* **13/2**[3]
P020 **7** 54 **Arctic Echo**[25] 4079 12-11-9 99 (bt[1]) MichaelMurphy(3) 19
(Rob Summers) *midfield: lost pl 14th: t.o 4 out* **7/1**
2U-P **P** **The Brig At Ayr**[35] 3883 7-10-0 73 RichieMcGrath —
(John Weymes) *in rr: bhd fr 12th: t.o whn p.u bef 15th* **7/1**
4P4P **P** **Ramborob (IRE)**[9] 4394 6-10-11 84 (bt[1]) PeterBuchanan —
(Mike Sowersby) *led to 6th: reminders and lost pl after 11th: bhd whn blnd next: t.o whn p.u whn p.u bef 13th* **16/1**

6m 35.5s (-6.50) **Going Correction** -0.05s/f (Good) **9** Ran SP% **114.8**
Speed ratings: **108,107,105,103,101 95,78,—,—**
toteswingers:1&2:£9.80, 1&3:£4.80, 2&3:£21.30 CSF £39.27 CT £406.01 TOTE £3.10: £1.40, £6.30, £2.70; EX 49.40.
Owner Mrs Stephanie Smith **Bred** George Durrheim & Mrs Maria Mulcahy Durr **Trained** Lingdale, Redcar & Cleveland

FOCUS
A moderate novices' handicap chase, and a repeat success for owner and trainer. The form is rated around the first two.

NOTEBOOK
Bardolet(IRE), whose form over hurdles and fences was on soft ground, handled this faster surface and won in straightforward fashion under a typical Reveley waiting ride. He jumped fluently and it was clear at the last on the far side he had his rivals covered. He appreciated the good gallop and should be able to go on from this. (op 11-4 tchd 3-1 in places)
Feeling Peckish(USA), whose sole success came on this sort of ground, made a bold bid but could not hold the winner after going on three out. (op 20-1)
Bobby Donald(IRE), back on better ground, ran well for a long way and kept on after losing his place halfway down the back on the second lap.
Nicky Tam(IRE) overcame a mistake at the first to make much of the running, but had nothing left when headed three out. This was a decent effort for new connections on his first start for 17 months. (tchd 8-1)
Dollar Mick(IRE) was held up and was making progress with the winner when making a mistake at the ditch halfway down the far side. His jumping suffered and he was struggling thereafter. (op 13-2)

4552 BOOK RACEDAY HOSPITALITY ON 01748 811478 MARES' NOVICES' HURDLE (8 hdls) 2m
4:20 (4:20) (Class 4) 4-Y-0+ **£2,276** (£668; £334; £166)

Form / RPR
55-2 **1** **Kykate**[17] 4245 5-10-9 0 (t) CharlieHuxley(3) 101+
(Thomas Kinsey) *hld up: hdwy and prom 3 out: led next: edgd lft fr last: kpt on strly* **11/2**[3]
-035 **2** 4 ½ **Lesanda**[17] 4242 5-10-12 101 BrianHughes 97
(Richard Fahey) *cl up: effrt and ev ch 2 out: kpt on fr last: nt gng pce of wnr* **7/1**
46 **3** 6 **White Diamond**[14] 4283 4-10-1 0 JamesHalliday(3) 83
(Malcolm Jefferson) *prom: effrt and pushed along 2 out: sn one pce* **5/1**[2]
06P1 **4** 8 **Just Maddie**[9] 4395 7-10-12 82 (p) PaulGallagher(7) 91
(Rayson Nixon) *mde most tl rdn and hdd 2 out: sn outpcd* **16/1**
5 1 **Thingathong (FR)**[232] 4-10-4 0 AdrianLane 74
(Donald McCain) *nt fluent: t.k.h: prom: outpcd whn mstke 3 out: plenty to do next: hung lft and styd on wl run-in: no imp* **25/1**
42-6 **6** 1 ¾ **Flora's Pride**[116] 2370 7-10-12 104 JamesReveley 82
(Keith Reveley) *hld up on outside: stdy hdwy and prom 3 out: effrt next: sn no ex* **7/2**[1]
530 **7** 6 **Sweet Caroline (IRE)**[42] 3747 4-10-4 109 FearghalDavis 67
(Nicky Richards) *trckd ldrs tl rdn and wknd bef 2 out* **5/1**[2]
8 7 **Piverina (IRE)**[29] 6-10-12 0 PaddyAspell 69
(Julie Camacho) *hld up: stdy hdwy and in tch 3 out: wknd bef next* **33/1**
6P **9** 5 **Cabal**[14] 4283 4-10-4 0 TomMessenger 57
(Andrew Crook) *hld up: hdwy and in tch 3 out: rdn and wknd bef next* **16/1**
626 **10** 10 **Helena Of Troy**[23] 4117 5-10-12 0 HenryOliver 56
(Sue Smith) *midfield on outside: hdwy and prom whn nt fluent 3 out: stmbld and lost pl bnd appr 2 out* **20/1**
0P **11** 7 **Lambrini Lace (IRE)**[17] 4242 6-10-5 0 HarryChalloner(7) 49
(Lisa Williamson) *cl up tl rdn and wknd after 4 out: no ch fnl 2* **200/1**
-540 **12** 13 **Cool Water**[26] 4059 6-10-12 0 CampbellGillies 38
(John Wade) *t.k.h: a bhd: struggling fr 1/2-way* **100/1**
060- **P** **Loch Dhu (IRE)**[503] 1860 7-10-9 0 EwanWhillans(3) —
(Alistair Whillans) *t.k.h: disp ld to 3rd: wknd after next: t.o whn p.u bef 2 out* **66/1**

PP P **Beat The Band**[17] 4245 6-10-12 0 PeterBuchanan —
(Lucinda Russell) *towards rr: drvn whn mstke 3 out: sn btn: t.o whn p.u next* **7/1**

3m 50.8s (-1.70) **Going Correction** -0.075s/f (Good)
WFA 4 from 5yo+ 7lb 14 Ran SP% **122.2**
Speed ratings (Par 105): **101,98,95,91,91 90,87,83,81,76 72,66,—,—**
toteswingers:1&2:£3.60, 1&3:£28.50, 2&3:£28.90 CSF £42.74 TOTE £7.60: £2.10, £1.80, £2.00; EX 33.10.

Owner Mrs T R Kinsey **Bred** B Baggott & H Clewlow **Trained** Ashton, Cheshire
■ A first winner under rules in more than a decade for trainer Thomas Kinsey, although from few runners.

FOCUS
This mares' novices' hurdle looked the best race on the card with a couple rated in the 100s. The winner ran to the level of her Sedgefield run.

NOTEBOOK
Kykate, runner-up on her hurdling debut on heavy ground, built on that and took this in good style. She looks capable of making her mark in mares' handicaps now. (op 9-1)

Lesanda, whose best form had been on soft, handled this faster ground and was never far away. Although unable to contain the winner, she came clear of the rest and may have a small race in her over hurdles.

White Diamond, a good-ground winner on the Flat, ran her best race over hurdles on similar going here. She now qualifies for a handicap mark and that is where her future lies. (tchd 11-2)

Just Maddie, the winner of a handicap off 82 last time, had a good deal on giving weight to higher-rated rivals, but ran with credit from the front. (op 12-1)

Thingathong(FR), making her hurdling debut on her first run for the yard, got outpaced at the end of the back straight before staying on again. Her rider reported that the filly did not jump well. Official explanation: jockey said filly jumped poorly and hung left (op 20-1)

Flora's Pride had been runner-up on the Flat and over hurdles here previously. She moved up to look a big danger turning for home, but was outpaced by the principals after the second-last. (tchd 4-1)

Sweet Caroline(IRE), with the highest official rating, was never far away but faded from the home turn. (op 6-1)

Helena Of Troy Official explanation: jockey said mare stumbled briefly and lost its action

Beat The Band Official explanation: jockey said mare lost its action but returned sound

4553 JOHN WADE SKIP HIRE NOVICES' HUNTERS' CHASE (19 fncs) 3m 1f 110y
4:50 (4:50) (Class 6) 5-Y-0+ £749 (£232; £116; £58)

Form				RPR
4166	1		**Call Me Mulligan (IRE)**[159] 1661 7-11-9 110 MrMEnnis(7) (John Hellens) *w ldr: led 4th: stmbld 13th: clr whn stmbld 3 out: styd on strly: eased towards fin* **17/2**	108+
F33-	2	9	**Stagecoach Diamond**[11] 12-11-5 0 (b[1]) MissHBethell(7) (W A Bethell) *t.k.h: trckd ldrs: chsd wnr fr 14th: kpt on same pce fr 4 out* **11/2**[2]	92
U-	3	2	**Keen Whip**[11] 9-11-9 0 MrMWalford(3) (C Brader) *chsd ldrs: outpcd and reminders after 12th: rallied 4 out: kpt on one pce* **33/1**	90
-5F3	4	1 3/4	**Braden Brook (IRE)**[31] 8-11-7 69 MrJohnDawson(5) (John Wade) *led to 4th: one pce fr 4 out* **15/2**	89
	5	66	**Lem Putt (IRE)**[24] 8-11-5 0 MrISmith(7) (Mrs N Naughton) *hld up in rr: mstke 1st: hdwy to case ldrs whn mstke 12th: wknd appr 3 out: sn bhd: t.o* **5/2**[1]	44
6P0/	6	12	**Valiant Shadow (GER)**[24] 9-11-5 95 (p) MissEStead(7) (R A Wilson) *prom: lost pl 13th: sn bhd: t.o 3 out* **40/1**	18
5P-	U		**The Viking**[24] 12-11-9 0 MrColmMcCormack(3) (Mrs Sarah L Dent) *in rr-div: blnd and uns rdr 2nd* **22/1**	—
	F		**Walter's Laddie**[24] 10-11-5 0 (b[1]) MrJonathanBailey(7) (Stuart Morris) *prom: fell 6th* **6/1**[3]	—
4B-P	F		**Oxford De Lagarde (FR)**[24] 9-11-9 90 MrGBrewer(3) (Mrs Alison Christmas) *fell 1st* **20/1**	—
3324	P		**Murphys Beau (IRE)**[17] 9-11-5 59 MrGRSmith(7) (Mrs S Foster) *in rr: bhd fr 12th: bhd whn p.u bef last* **14/1**	—
4P/4	P		**Silver Breese**[13] 4307 9-11-7 77 (t) MrJBewley(5) (R Robinson) *chsd ldrs: wknd 15th: bhd whn p.u bef last* **33/1**	—
005/	P		**Saddlers Singer (IRE)**[38] 8-11-5 67 MrECameron(7) (E N Cameron) *towards rr: reminders10th: bhd fr 12th: t.o 3 out: p.u bef last* **50/1**	—
	P		**Yes I Can (IRE)**[24] 7-11-9 0 MrCDawson(3) (Miss Maria D Myco) *hld up in rr: sme hdwy whn blnd 12th: 7th and no imp whn blnd 4 out: hit 2 out: bhd whn p.u bef last* **10/1**	—

6m 43.0s (1.00) **Going Correction** -0.05s/f (Good) 13 Ran SP% **115.7**
Speed ratings: **96,93,92,92,71 68,—,—,—,—,—,—,—**
toteswingers:1&2:£3.60, 1&3:£28.50, 2&3:£28.90 CSF £49.64 TOTE £6.00: £2.00, £2.50, £6.30; EX 48.40.

Owner J A Hellens **Bred** Chris McDonnell **Trained** Pittington, Co Durham
■ Stewards' Enquiry : Miss E Stead one-day ban: used whip when out of contention (Mar 23)

FOCUS
A weak novices' hunter chase. The form is rated through the winner to his best.

NOTEBOOK
Call Me Mulligan(IRE) had the highest mark of those with official ratings but had to give weight all round. A winner over 2m7f on good for Rebecca Curtis in the summer, he was sold for £6,500 to current connections. He landed too steeply halfway down the back second time but his rider set sail for home soon after, and was clear when making a similar error three out. It did not stop him though, and he came home to score with something in hand to give his rider a first winner under rules. (op 8-1)

Stagecoach Diamond was fitted with blinkers for the first time on this debut for new connections and ran creditably, although no match for the winner. He has failed to win in 25 starts over fences now, but has been runner-up seven times. (op 13-2)

Keen Whip reversed placings with the favourite compared with recent point form, and ran well on what was effectively his first start under rules. (op 25-1)

Braden Brook(IRE) won a point last time but had shown little under rules previously. He was always in the leading group but was one paced in the last half-mile. Official explanation: vet said gelding finished lame right-fore (op 7-1)

Lem Putt(IRE) was sent off favourite based on his pointing form but was another to make mistakes down the far side second time when trying to make headway, and tired in the straight. (tchd 11-4)

Walter's Laddie, yet another graduating from points, took a heavy fall on the first circuit. (op 17-2 tchd 8-1)

Yes I Can(IRE), whose trainer had won this twice before with unexposed sorts, came into this with a similar profile, being a point winner making his debut under rules. However, he found these fences more formidable and his jumping suffered after a mistake early on the last circuit. (op 17-2 tchd 8-1)

4554 TURFTV.CO.UK MARES' STANDARD NATIONAL HUNT FLAT RACE (CONDITIONALS & AMATEURS) 2m
5:20 (5:20) (Class 6) 4-6-Y-0 £1,370 (£399; £199)

Form				RPR
	1		**Bahira (IRE)** 4-9-13 0 HenryBrooke(7) (Donald McCain) *trckd ldrs: led over 2f out: drvn out: hld on towards fin* **9/2**[1]	93+
10	2	nk	**Sparkling Hand**[105] 2616 5-11-2 0 AlexanderVoy(5) (Peter Atkinson) *trckd ldrs: chal over 3f out: rallied to chse wnr over 1f out: no ex towards fin* **14/1**	107
	3	12	**Miss Bellatrix** 4-10-1 0 BrianToomey(5) (Neville Bycroft) *in rr: hdwy on outside 7f out: chsng ldrs over 3f out: one pce fnl 2f* **12/1**	81
534	4	hd	**Think Green**[21] 4151 5-10-11 0 HarryHaynes(3) (James Ewart) *led tl over 2f out: wknd over 1f out* **13/2**[3]	89
4-0	5	7	**Landenstown Rose (IRE)**[125] 2167 5-10-11 0 JohnKington(3) (Donald McCain) *trckd ldrs: wknd 2f out* **20/1**	84
5	6	1	**De Vine Memory**[42] 3752 4-10-6 0 CampbellGillies (Peter Niven) *mid-div: drvn 6f out: outpcd over 3f out: kpt on fnl f* **9/2**[1]	74
425	7	1 1/4	**Serenitatis (IRE)**[20] 4171 5-10-7 0 PaulGallagher(7) (Tim Easterby) *mid-div: drvn 6f out: lost pl over 3f out* **6/1**[2]	81
1-00	8	6	**Silvers Spirit**[55] 3525 5-11-0 0 MrColmMcCormack(7) (Keith Reveley) *trckd ldrs: wknd 3f out* **25/1**	82
0-	9	1/2	**Knickerbokerglory**[332] 5150 5-10-7 0 MissEButterworth(7) (Barbara Butterworth) *hld up in rr: hdwy 6f out: hung lft and lost pl over 2f out* **40/1**	75
5	10	21	**Tobetall**[53] 3576 4-10-3 0 JamesHalliday(3) (Malcolm Jefferson) *mid-div: lost pl over 3f out* **16/1**	48
5	11	10	**Colliers Castle (IRE)**[15] 4280 5-10-7 0 HarryChalloner(7) (Lisa Williamson) *trckd ldrs: lost pl 3f out* **25/1**	47
40	12	6	**Skiddaw Secret**[20] 4171 4-10-6 0 FearghalDavis (John Weymes) *in rr: drvn 7f out: nvr on termds* **40/1**	34
	13	49	**Tudor Beat** 5-10-7 0 MrJohnDawson(7) (Ron Barr) *in rr: bhd fnl 7f: t.o 3f out* **40/1**	—
	14	hd	**Wilkinson Court** 4-10-3 0 CharlieHuxley(3) (John Mackie) *mid-div: drvn after 6f: sn bhd: t.o 3f out* **7/1**	—

3m 46.6s (-0.30) **Going Correction** -0.075s/f (Good)
WFA 4 from 5yo 7lb 14 Ran SP% **116.5**
Speed ratings: **97,96,90,90,87 86,86,83,82,72 67,64,39,39**
toteswingers:1&2:£17.50, 1&3:£21.30, 2&3:£40.10 CSF £61.43 TOTE £7.10: £3.40, £2.80, £3.00; EX 67.10.

Owner William Lilley **Bred** Tom Cross **Trained** Cholmondeley, Cheshire
■ Stewards' Enquiry : Harry Haynes two-day ban: weighed in 2lb heavy (Mar 23,25)

FOCUS
An ordinary mares' bumper but a good finish. The winner can rate higher.

NOTEBOOK
Bahira(IRE), the first foal of a Flat and hurdles winner on the continent, was made joint favourite on this debut and was never far away. She was sent for home over 2f out only to run green, but found more when challenged to just hold a more experienced rival. She looks to have a future and will know more next time. (tchd 7-2)

Sparkling Hand, a surprise winner on her debut, was beaten under a penalty in a better race on soft next time. She did better back on this good ground and gave the winner a real fight, only losing out near the finish. There is nothing wrong with her attitude. (op 10-1 tchd 9-1)

Miss Bellatrix, a half-sister to a winning pointer, made eye-catching headway to join the leaders on the home turn, but then found them quickening away from her and she could not respond. This was a decent effort and she looks capable of making a hurdler. (op 16-1)

Think Green, in the fame in two of her three bumpers, made the running but was done for pace in the straight. She will now go hurdling and is another who should make a jumper. (op 5-1 tchd 7-1)

De Vine Memory, the other joint favourite, was keen early and was on the retreat leaving the back straight. (op 6-1)

Serenitatis(IRE) had plenty of experience but was under pressure and beaten some way from home. (op 13-2 tchd 7-1)

T/Jkpt: Not won. T/Plt: £197.80 to a £1 stake. Pool:£64,590.48 - 238.27 winning tickets T/Qpdt: £57.40 to a £1 stake. Pool:£3,848.73 - 49.56 winning tickets WG

[4370]FONTWELL (L-H)
Wednesday, March 9

OFFICIAL GOING: Chase course - good to soft (good in places); hurdle course - good (good to soft in places; 7.9)
All bends on inner line.
Wind: Moderate, across Weather: Sunny intervals

4555 PLATINUM LACE GENTLEMENS CLUB, BRIGHTON NOVICES' HURDLE (11 hdls) 2m 6f 110y
2:00 (2:00) (Class 4) 4-Y-0+ £2,374 (£697; £348; £174)

Form				RPR
43	1		**Sum Laff (IRE)**[25] 4081 7-11-0 109 PeterToole(3) (Charlie Mann) *mde virtually all: j. path after home turn all 3 circs: hrd rdn appr last: hld on wl* **6/4**[2]	115+
3-1F	2	1 1/4	**Vincitore (FR)**[158] 1675 5-11-3 117 KielanWoods(7) (Charlie Longsdon) *hld up in tch: wnt 2nd 3 out: kpt on u.p run-in: a hld* **11/2**[3]	115
55	3	8	**Cousin Maggie (IRE)**[26] 4051 7-10-10 0 JimmyMcCarthy (Brendan Powell) *pressed wnr tl 3 out: sn outpcd* **25/1**	94
022	4	7	**Clowance House**[27] 4029 5-11-3 115 (b[1]) AidanColeman (Venetia Williams) *hld up in tch: wnt 3rd and gng wl 3 out: j. path ent st: rdn and btn whn blnd 2 out* **5/4**[1]	97
0-23	5	5	**Cocacobana (IRE)**[16] 4262 6-11-3 0 JodieMogford (Graeme McPherson) *hld up in tch in rr: hdwy after 3 out: wknd next* **25/1**	92
1003	6	52	**Zakeeta (IRE)**[12] 4331 4-11-0 113 (p) LeightonAspell (Oliver Sherwood) *trckd ldrs: pushed along after 7th: wknd 3 out* **20/1**	40

5m 35.4s (-7.10) **Going Correction** -0.125s/f (Good)
WFA 4 from 5yo+ 8lb 6 Ran SP% **112.3**
Speed ratings (Par 105): **107,106,103,101,99 81**
toteswingers:1&2:£2.60, 1&3:£6.10, 2&3:£11.00 CSF £9.59 TOTE £2.50: £1.60, £2.80; EX 12.00.

Owner Bryan & Philippa Burrough **Bred** Thomas Deacon **Trained** Upper Lambourn, Berks

FOCUS
An ordinary but competitive novices' hurdle run at a steady gallop with the pace only quickening after the turn in. Steps up from the first two.

NOTEBOOK
Sum Laff(IRE), a staying-on third at Warwick last month, built on that display to run out a comfortable winner. Despite running wide on the bends, jumping the path three times and wandering around on the run-in, he won with a bit in hand. Clearly a talented customer and a chaser in the making, he should improve for racing as he showed many signs of greenness and doesn't look the easiest ride. (op 13-8 tchd 7-4)
Vincitore(FR) fell when going well here in October and ran a fair race under a penalty on this return from a 158-day absence, due to a bruised tendon. Racing a little keenly early, he stayed on strongly after the last. (tchd 5-1 and 6-1)
Cousin Maggie(IRE) travelled up with the pace throughout, but failed to quicken once things got serious turning for home. (op 28-1)
Clowance House, runner-up on his last two starts, had the first-time blinkers on and travelled kindly for a long way before emptying quickly in the straight. A useful type on the Flat, this was a poor effort and he looks one to treat with caution. (op 6-4)
Cocacobana(IRE), a well-beaten third at Hereford on his hurdles debut, was again well held. (tchd 20-1)
Zakeeta(IRE) was the first under pressure down the back and never threatened the leaders. (op 16-1)

4556 BETFAIR SPONSORS AT EVERY UK RACECOURSE H'CAP CHASE (13 fncs) 2m 2f
2:30 (2:30) (Class 5) (0-95,94) 5-Y-O+ **£1,951** (£573; £286; £143)

Form				RPR
P4	**1**		**Piment D'Estruval (FR)**[24] 4103 8-11-12 **94**.................. DougieCostello (Tim Vaughan) *t.k.h in rr: hdwy on bit 3 out: led after next: mstke last: sn hdd: rallied to ld fnl strides* **11/4**[1]	100+
-F05	**2**	*hd*	**Meneur (FR)**[21] 3869 9-11-9 **91**.................. JamieMoore (Gary Moore) *sn towards rr: hdwy 9th: disp 2nd 2 out: slt ld run-in: kpt on u.p: hdd fnl strides* **7/1**	96
6-4P	**3**	*2*	**Ede's**[51] 3606 11-10-6 **74**.................. ColinBolger (Pat Phelan) *chsd ldrs: rdn and outpcd 3 out: styd on run-in* **12/1**	77
43	**4**	*5*	**Paddy The Yank (IRE)**[23] 4122 8-11-2 **87**.................. DannyCook(3) (Richard Mitchell) *led tl after 7th: mstke 9th: no ex 2 out* **10/1**	89+
P-P0	**5**	*8*	**Anyauldiron (IRE)**[25] 4081 8-11-1 **83**.................. AndrewTinkler (Charlie Longsdon) *towards rr: hdwy 5th: blnd 8th: mstke next: outpcd fr 4 out* **9/2**[3]	80
4/0P	**6**	*4*	**Quicolai (FR)**[24] 4099 7-11-6 **88**..................(t) PaddyBrennan (Tom George) *chsd ldr: led after 7th tl wknd qckly after 2 out* **3/1**[2]	80
5-P2	**7**	*45*	**Floradora Do**[6] 4447 9-10-3 **74**.................. JimmyDerham(3) (Ron Hodges) *a bhd: j.lft and blnd 2nd: no ch fr 8th* **13/2**	22

4m 37.0s (2.30) **Going Correction** -0.35s/f (Good) **7** Ran SP% **112.5**
Speed ratings: **80,79,79,76,73 71,51**
toteswingers:1&2:£3.80, 1&3:£14.20, 2&3:£9.90 CSF £21.03 TOTE £4.00: £1.50, £2.40; EX 15.30.
Owner Mrs K P Brown **Bred** Mme Bernard Le Gentil **Trained** Aberthin, Vale of Glamorgan

FOCUS
A modest handicap chase. The winner is rated to his mark.

NOTEBOOK
Piment D'Estruval(FR), fourth on his chasing debut at Hereford last month, improved on that to run out a game winner, rallying once headed after the last. Having travelled smoothly, he wasn't fluent at the last but battled back on the rail. This was his first career success at the 15th attempt, but he remains unexposed over fences and his rider thinks he will be better on a more galloping track. (op 3-1)
Meneur(FR) ran a brave race, responding for pressure to lead after the last and was just denied. Having dropped 23lb in the past 12 months, he looked on a competitive mark and should continue go well in this grade. (op 9-2)
Ede's was pulled up at Plumpton in January, but bounced back to run a fair race, staying on nicely without threatening the first two. (op 10-1)
Paddy The Yank(IRE) raced towards the head of proceedings before being swamped on this handicap debut. He may need to jump better to get closer. (op 17-2 tchd 11-1)
Anyauldiron(IRE) made several errors and could never land a blow. He should improve for this experience. (op 8-1)
Quicolai(FR), pulled up at Hereford latest, ran a better race, jumping boldly in front. He just tired entering the straight. (op 4-1)
Floradora Do, runner-up on her chase debut at Taunton last time, made a blunder early on and failed to get involved. She is due to go up 4lb in the future and needs to bounce back from this. Official explanation: jockey said mare made a mistake second and never travelled (op 11-2 tchd 5-1)

4557 BETFAIR SPONSORS LAMBOURN OPEN DAY MAIDEN HURDLE (9 hdls) 2m 2f 110y
3:00 (3:00) (Class 5) 4-Y-O+ **£1,951** (£573; £286; £143)

Form				RPR
/223	**1**		**Gurtacrue (IRE)**[65] 3365 6-11-2 125.................. PaulMoloney (Evan Williams) *trckd ldrs: rdn appr 2 out: pressed ldrs last: drvn to ld nr fin* **6/5**[1]	117+
54	**2**	*nk*	**Allerford Jack**[15] 4268 7-10-13 0.................. IanPopham(3) (Caroline Keevil) *chsd ldr: led appr 2 out: hrd rdn and edgd rt run-in: kpt on: hdd nr fin* **3/1**[2]	116
6-23	**3**	*10*	**Penchesco (IRE)**[105] 2122 6-11-2 110.................. LeightonAspell (Amanda Perrett) *trckd ldrs: j.rt 1st and 5th: rdn to chal last: wknd run-in* **5/1**[3]	109
435	**4**	*18*	**Coolbeg (IRE)**[45] 3701 5-11-2 0.................. PaddyBrennan (Tom George) *led tl wknd appr 2 out* **9/1**	91
30P4	**5**	*1 1/4*	**Journeyman (IRE)**[32] 3937 5-11-2 0.................. AndrewTinkler (Nicky Henderson) *in tch: rdn 3 out: sn btn* **22/1**	89
/105	**6**	*13*	**Just Cloudy**[24] 4091 7-11-2 0.................. SamThomas (Anthony Honeyball) *hld up towards rr: shkn up 2 out: nvr trbld ldrs* **20/1**	78
	7	*9*	**Petit Ecuyer (FR)**[178] 5-11-2 0.................. JamieMoore (Gary Moore) *in tch: j.rt 4th: promising effrt 3 out: wknd qckly appr next* **25/1**	70
	8	*41*	**Sir William Orpen**[19] 4-10-7 0.................. ColinBolger (Pat Phelan) *t.k.h towards rr: no ch fr 6th* **40/1**	24
	9	*41*	**Private Patient (IRE)** 7-11-2 0.................. AndrewThornton (Anna Newton-Smith) *towards rr: j. slowly and dropped to last 2nd: wl bhd fr 5th* **80/1**	—
00/P	**10**	*1 1/2*	**Young Valentino**[35] 3882 9-10-11 59.................. GemmaGracey-Davison(5) (Michael Appleby) *towards rr: mstke 3rd: rdn and struggling after 5th: sn wl bhd* **150/1**	—

4m 28.3s (-6.00) **Going Correction** -0.125s/f (Good)
WFA 4 from 5yo+ 7lb **10** Ran SP% **114.4**
Speed ratings (Par 103): **107,106,102,95,94 89,85,68,50,50**
toteswingers:1&2:£1.50, 1&3:£1.30, 2&3:£2.30 CSF £4.46 TOTE £2.20: £1.10, £1.20, £1.80; EX 5.50.
Owner Mr & Mrs William Rucker **Bred** John Halliday **Trained** Llancarfan, Vale Of Glamorgan

FOCUS
Just an average maiden hurdle with the front two pulling well clear. The winner ran to his mark and the next two were clear.

NOTEBOOK
Gurtacrue(IRE), rated 125 and placed in three hurdle starts to date, ran out a hard-fought winner to record his first hurdle success. Having come under pressure down the back, he knuckled down and responded gallantly to collar the runner-up. This was a deserved first victory, but he was given a great ride and looks flattered by his current rating. (op 11-8 tchd 6-4 in places)
Allerford Jack, fourth at Taunton last time, ran his race but was just worn down late on. He is a consistent sort, but once again found one too good. He should continue to go close in minor contests and may go one better in time. (op 4-1)
Penchesco(IRE), disappointed on the AW when last seen, but had shown fair form when in the frame in two hurdles starts. He had every chance coming to the last but was simply not good enough. (op 4-1)
Coolbeg(IRE) raced keenly out in front but struggled once headed and stayed on at the one pace. (tchd 8-1)
Journeyman(IRE) has shown ordinary form to date and may fare better in handicap company. (op 16-1)
Just Cloudy may find handicapping easier. (op 16-1)

4558 BETFAIR SUPPORTS PRIDE OF RACING AWARD H'CAP CHASE (19 fncs) 3m 2f 110y
3:30 (3:30) (Class 4) (0-115,110) 5-Y-O+ **£2,932** (£910; £490)

Form				RPR
3-5P	**1**		**Rapid Increase (IRE)**[39] 3821 8-11-12 **110**.................. APMcCoy (Jonjo O'Neill) *chsd ldr: led 14th: pushed clr fr 2 out: comf* **6/1**	127+
224	**2**	*16*	**Topless (IRE)**[30] 3982 10-11-2 **100**..................(p) DougieCostello (Neil Mulholland) *led tl 14th: pressed wnr tl wknd 2 out* **9/2**	100
4/53	**3**	*66*	**El Jo (IRE)**[24] 4102 10-11-6 **104**..................(p) WillKennedy (Martin Bosley) *in tch: rdn 12th: sn wknd: wl bhd fr 14th: b.b.v* **11/1**	44
362U	**P**		**Miss Fleur**[10] 4381 8-10-2 **89**.................. DannyCook(3) (Nick Mitchell) *in tch: hrd rdn 6th: sn struggling: t.o 13th: p.u bef 4 out* **4/1**[3]	—
1P62	**P**		**Beware Chalk Pit (IRE)**[8] 4412 7-10-7 **94**.................. JimmyDerham(3) (Jonathan Geake) *in tch: rdn 13th: wknd 15th: lft mod 3rd after 2 out: no ch whn p.u bef last* **10/3**[2]	—
6526	**P**		**Jack The Soldier (IRE)**[43] 3720 7-9-10 **87**.................. MrTJCannon(7) (Chris Gordon) *chsd ldrs: pushed along 13th: sltly outpcd 15th: rallied 3 out: cl 3rd and hrd rdn whn p.u after 2 out: fatally injured* **3/1**[1]	87

6m 48.1s (-13.00) **Going Correction** -0.35s/f (Good) **6** Ran SP% **108.9**
Speed ratings: **105,100,80,—,— —**
toteswingers:1&2:£8.90, 1&3:£12.80, 2&3:£3.80 CSF £30.26 TOTE £4.40: £2.00, £2.10; EX 15.00.
Owner Mrs Gay Smith **Bred** B And Q Syndicate **Trained** Cheltenham, Gloucs

FOCUS
A weak and open-looking handicap chase run at a good clip, with just three finishers. The form is rated around the first two.

NOTEBOOK
Rapid Increase(IRE), pulled up in heavy ground at Uttoxeter in January, bounced back to form, out-jumping and outstaying his rivals. He travelled strongly and took the lead on the final circuit to win with authority. He raced lazily once in front and needed his jockey's urgings to keep his mind on the job. Official explanation: trainer said, regarding apparent improvement in form, that the gelding was better suited by the faster ground (op 5-1 tchd 9-2)
Topless(IRE) had the cheekpieces replacing the blinkers and once again ran a bold race, again settling for second. She remains a maiden over fences after 24 starts and has now filled the runner-up spot on ten occasions. (op 5-1)
El Jo(IRE) showed better form when third at Hereford on his latest start, but was struggling with a circuit to go and plugged on at one pace. Official explanation: trainer said gelding bled from the nose (tchd 12-1)
Miss Fleur unseated at Towcester last week and was never involved. She needs a slower surface to be seen in better light. Official explanation: jockey said mare was unsuited by the good to soft (good in places) ground (tchd 3-1)
Beware Chalk Pit(IRE), runner up off this mark at Leicester last week, could never get competitive and appreciates softer ground. He will go up 4lb in the future and may struggle off that new mark, although his trainer reported he had a breathing problem. Official explanation: trainer said gelding had a breathing problem (tchd 3-1)
Jack The Soldier(IRE) was running on in third when he sadly broke a leg between the last two fences. (tchd 3-1)

4559 BETFAIR FUNDS THE PJA DOCTOR H'CAP HURDLE (10 hdls) 2m 4f
4:00 (4:01) (Class 5) (0-95,95) 4-Y-O+ **£1,951** (£573; £286; £143)

Form				RPR
P422	**1**		**I Can Run Can You (IRE)**[42] 3745 5-11-12 **95**.................. APMcCoy (Jonjo O'Neill) *mde all: rdn and styd on wl fr 2 out: drvn out* **2/1**[1]	101+
126P	**2**	*2 1/4*	**Hurricane Electric (IRE)**[51] 3603 6-11-4 **90**.................. TomMolloy(3) (Graeme McPherson) *prom: pressed wnr 3 out: hld fr next: kpt on u.p run-in* **11/2**[2]	90
P-P2	**3**	*1/2*	**Septos**[16] 4263 7-10-3 **75**..................(p) PeterToole(3) (Richard Price) *chsd wnr tl outpcd and lost pl 7th: rallied appr last: styd on run-in* **11/2**[2]	75
6655	**4**	*12*	**Galant Star (FR)**[17] 3338 5-11-4 **87**.................. JamieMoore (Gary Moore) *mid-div: hdwy into 3rd after 3 out: btn next* **9/1**	76
62-0	**5**	*10*	**Hereditary**[22] 4130 9-11-2 **90**..................(tp) JoshuaMoore(5) (Linda Jewell) *towards rr: rdn appr 7th: nvr trbld ldrs* **14/1**	70
0-50	**6**	*5*	**Goring Two (IRE)**[22] 4130 6-9-11 **69** oh2.................. JimmyDerham(3) (Anna Newton-Smith) *in tch: rdn 7th: wknd after 3 out* **33/1**	45
3P-0	**7**	*2 1/4*	**Formedable (IRE)**[43] 3728 9-10-8 **77**..................(p) WillKennedy (Violet M Jordan) *towards rr: rdn and n.d fr 7th* **40/1**	51
1201	**8**	*8*	**Arctic Flow**[9] 4401 7-10-11 **83** 7ex.................. IanPopham(3) (Caroline Keevil) *t.k.h: chsd ldrs tl wknd 3 out* **7/1**	49
P500	**9**	*4 1/2*	**Wardington Lad**[40] 3782 9-11-7 **93**.................. SamTwiston-Davies(3) (Michael Appleby) *prom: mstke 6th: hrd rdn and wknd 3 out* **6/1**[3]	55
055P	**10**	*19*	**Keckerrockernixes (IRE)**[50] 3611 5-10-10 **79**..........(b[1]) LeightonAspell (Richard Rowe) *a in last: mstke 2nd: rdn and struggling 6th: sn wl bhd* **20/1**	24

4m 56.7s (-2.70) **Going Correction** -0.125s/f (Good) **10** Ran SP% **117.7**
Speed ratings (Par 103): **100,99,98,94,90 88,87,84,82,74**
toteswingers:1&2:£1.80, 1&3:£3.60, 2&3:£5.50 CSF £13.69 CT £53.24 TOTE £3.20: £2.30, £3.40, £1.60; EX 17.70.
Owner Mrs Gay Smith **Bred** Noel O'Brien **Trained** Cheltenham, Gloucs

FOCUS
This 0-95 handicap was won in good style by the top weight who was value for further and produced a personal best.

NOTEBOOK

I Can Run Can You(IRE), up 7lb for his clear second at Huntingdon in January, made all to record his first career success at the ninth attempt. This was a deserved victory, having run with credit throughout the season. He jumped cleanly and despite running around on the run-in, had a little left in the tank. (op 9-4 tchd 11-4)

Hurricane Electric(IRE) appreciated this return to a sound surface and was the only one to give the favourite a real race. He responded well to pressure, but could never peg him back. (tchd 5-1)

Septos, sporting first-time cheekpieces and raised 5lb for his second at Hereford latest, probably ran his race, staying on up the straight having been outpaced. (op 6-1 tchd 13-2 and 5-1)

Galant Star(FR) has failed to fire on the AW lately but ran a fair race here, plugging on under pressure on this second handicap start. (op 12-1)

Hereditary raced in the rear and ran on past beaten horses. He remains on a good mark, but doesn't appear to retain his old ability. (tchd 12-1)

Arctic Flow, 5lb higher than for her Plumpton win last month, raced up with the pace but faded. The drying ground was not to her advantage. (tchd 15-2)

Wardington Lad, showed promise at Doncaster (2m) latest, but dropped away here as if something was amiss. (op 13-2)

4560 BETFAIR SUPPORTS MOORCROFT RACEHORSE WELFARE CENTRE H'CAP CHASE (16 fncs) 2m 6f

4:30 (4:30) (Class 5) (0-90,90) 5-Y-O+ **£2,602** (£764; £382; £190)

Form				RPR
P431	1		**Delgany Gunner**[22] 4126 7-10-6 **75**........(vt) GilesHawkins(5) (Ben Pollock) *led: hit 6th: hdd 3 out: led next: drvn clr* **7/1**[3]	92+
053-	2	6	**Marigolds Way**[316] 36 9-11-7 **90**........RachaelGreen(5) (Anthony Honeyball) *mid-div: hdwy 12th: led 3 out tl next: sn outpcd* **5/1**[2]	101+
00P5	3	1 1/4	**Kiltimoney (IRE)**[33] 3933 11-9-11 **64** oh3........(b[1]) SamTwiston-Davies(3) (Richard Mitchell) *sn prom: mstke and outpcd 12th: styd on u.p fr 2 out* **12/1**	73
/053	4	1/2	**Ballyman (IRE)**[8] 4413 10-10-1 **68**........JimmyDerham(3) (Jonathan Geake) *pressed wnr tl after 4 out: one pce* **9/2**[1]	76
4FPF	5	17	**Investment Affair (IRE)**[27] 4022 11-11-0 **78**........JackDoyle (Sarah Humphrey) *in tch: wnt prom at 7th: outpcd 4 out: 4th and btn whn mstke next* **22/1**	71
0052	6	12	**Bless My Soul**[24] 4099 8-11-0 **83**........(t) MattGriffiths(5) (Ron Hodges) *chsd ldrs tl 4 out* **8/1**	65
05-0	7	2 1/2	**Orphelin Collonges (FR)**[18] 9-10-9 **80**........MrMPrice(7) (Richard Price) *bhd: mod effrt 12th: sn wknd and eased* **20/1**	60
4302	8	3/4	**Curragh Dancer (FR)**[44] 3337 8-10-10 **81**........(p) NathanSweeney(7) (Paddy Butler) *chsd ldrs tl 7th: mid-div and rdn whn mstke 10th: struggling after* **18/1**	60
0PP5	9	17	**Lidjo De Rouge (FR)**[15] 4269 12-11-5 **83**........TomO'Brien (Paul Henderson) *sn outpcd towards rr: no ch fr 11th* **15/2**	47
42U3	10	24	**Killfinnan Castle (IRE)**[30] 3984 8-10-8 **72**........(p) WillKennedy (Violet M Jordan) *bhd: rdn 11th: modest 8th whn pckd 4 out* **9/2**[1]	14
-5P5	P		**Fillyofthevalley**[30] 3980 8-10-10 **74**........MarkGrant (Peter Jones) *bhd: blnd 2nd: mstke 10th: sn no ch: t.o whn p.u bef 4 out* **18/1**	—

5m 39.2s (-3.80) **Going Correction** -0.35s/f (Good) **11** Ran SP% **115.7**

Speed ratings: **92,89,89,89,83 78,77,77,71,62** —

CSF £42.25 CT £415.65 TOTE £6.60: £2.80, £3.50, £2.80; EX 36.00.

Owner Charles Wilson & Charles Garside **Bred** C M Wilson **Trained** Medbourne, Leics

FOCUS

A poor but competitive contest run at a good gallop. A step up from the winner.

NOTEBOOK

Delgany Gunner, up 14lb for last month's Folkestone handicap chase win, followed up in good style here. Jumping boldly, he made most and despite hanging, held off the runner-up down the straight. He is clearly in good heart, but will have another hike to cope with. (op 8-1 tchd 13-2)

Marigolds Way, well supported on this return from 316 days off for new connections, made her challenge on the final bend and led briefly, but hung badly right and failed to match the winner. She can be expected to improve for the outing. (tchd 9-2)

Kiltimoney(IRE), wearing first-time blinkers, travelled towards the head of affairs and stayed on again after getting outpaced. His losing run stretches back to December 2007. (tchd 14-1)

Ballyman(IRE), well backed, struggled to sustain his effort and plugged on for a modest fourth. (op 11-2)

Killfinnan Castle(IRE) was bitterly disappointing. Having been held up he never get involved and didn't pick up for his rider's urgings. He prefers softer conditions and should do better with cut in the ground. (op 5-1)

4561 BETFAIR SUPPORTS OAKSEY HOUSE STANDARD OPEN NATIONAL HUNT FLAT RACE 2m 2f 110y

5:00 (5:00) (Class 6) 4-6-Y-O **£1,431** (£420; £210; £104)

Form				RPR
6	1		**Super Ken (IRE)**[132] 2052 4-10-7 0........TomO'Brien (Chris Gordon) *chsd ldr: lft in ld after 3f: drvn clr 1f out: styd on wl* **28/1**	96+
2	4 1/2	**Ashes House (IRE)**[130] 5-11-2 0........APMcCoy (Tim Vaughan) *chsd wnr: hrd rdn over 1f out: one pce* **11/4**[3]	101
5	3	1/2	**Rich Buddy**[53] 3569 5-11-2 0........SeanQuinlan (Richard Phillips) *prom tl bdly hmpd and dropped to last after 3f: rallied into 3rd 2f out: kpt on fnl f* **14/1**	105+
5	4	12	**Adrenalin Flight (IRE)**[10] 4382 5-11-2 0........AndrewThornton (Seamus Mullins) *bhd: pushed along 4f out: styd on to take 4th ins fnl f* **25/1**	90
5-4	5	3/4	**Miss Bolte**[23] 4124 6-10-9 0........JamieGoldstein (Sheena West) *in tch: outpcd 5f out: no imp* **25/1**	82
6	4	**Aaly** 4-10-7 0........MarkBradburne (Lydia Richards) *in tch tl outpcd 4f out* **33/1**	76
7	15	**Old Rusty Cross (IRE)** 6-11-2 0........AndrewTinkler (Nicky Henderson) *prom tl wknd 3f out* **9/4**[2]	72
00	8	hd	**Gypsy Moth (IRE)**[34] 3909 5-10-6 0........IanPopham(3) (Caroline Keevil) *in tch tl wknd 4f out* **16/1**	65
42	S		**Howard's Legacy (IRE)**[34] 3903 5-11-2 0........AidanColeman (Venetia Williams) *led tl slowed up suddenly and uns rdr on bnd into bk st after 3f* **2/1**[1]	—
P		**Flixter** 4-10-0 0........MrHGMiller(7) (Zoe Davison) *a towards rr: t.o 6f out: p.u 3f out* **100/1**	—

4m 29.8s (1.10) **Going Correction** -0.125s/f (Good)

WFA 4 from 5yo+ 7lb **10** Ran SP% **118.4**

Speed ratings: **92,90,89,84,84 82,76,76,—,—**

toteswingers:1&2:£12.00, 1&3:£4.00, 2&3:£16.10. totesuper7: Win: Not won. Place: Not won. CSF £102.47 TOTE £41.50: £4.90, £1.10, £4.10; EX 170.60.

Owner JFK Partnership **Bred** James Hennelly **Trained** Morestead, Hants

FOCUS

This low-grade bumper was run at just a fair pace and produced drama when favourite Howard's Legacy jinked and unseated his jockey early on. The fifth is the best guide to the level.

NOTEBOOK

Super Ken(IRE) improved signicantly on his debut run to make most and win a shade cosily. He showed a nice attitude, despite showing signs of greenness, to gamely hold off the constant challenge of the second and he appreciated the step up in trip.

Ashes House(IRE), an Irish point winner, was a tad keen but travelled nicely and had every chance but could not go past the winner. He may land a similar event and should stay further (tchd 3-1)

Rich Buddy, fifth at Warwick on his debut, was badly hampered by the unseating of Aidan Coleman aboard the favourite, but still ran on strongly to finish a clear third. This was a fair effort considering, and he should go close with better luck. Official explanation: jockey said gelding suffered interference in running (op 16-1 tchd 11-1)

Adrenalin Flight(IRE) plugged on having raced towards the rear. He may need a softer surface. (op 33-1)

Old Rusty Cross(IRE), representing the powerful Nicky Henderson yard, showed up for a long way before fading tamely in the straight. He may improve for the experience, but it was disappointing how he failed to finish his race. Official explanation: jockey said gelding hung badly right (op 3-1 tchd 2-1)

Howard's Legacy(IRE) jinked and unseated his jockey early on. (tchd 9-4 and 5-2 in a place)

Flixter Official explanation: jockey said gelding lost its action (tchd 9-4 and 5-2 in a place)

T/Plt: £68.20 to a £1 stake. Pool:£88,257.02 - 943.32 winning tickets T/Qpdt: £16.20 to a £1 stake. Pool:£6,085.15 - 276.72 winning tickets LM

4562 - 4567a (Foreign Racing) - See Raceform Interactive

4253 CARLISLE (R-H)

Thursday, March 10

OFFICIAL GOING: Soft (heavy in places)

First hurdle in the back straight omitted on all circuits. Middle fence in the back straight and penultimate fence in home straight omitted.

Wind: Strong, half against Weather: Cloudy, fine

4568 SPORTING CHAMPIONS RACEDAY 20TH MARCH NOVICES' HURDLE (10 hdls 2 omitted) 3m 1f

2:10 (2:10) (Class 4) 4-Y-O+ **£2,226** (£649; £324)

Form				RPR
3411	1		**Alexander Road (IRE)**[18] 4245 6-11-3 110........(t) HenryBrooke(7) (Donald McCain) *mde virtually all: rdn and edgd lft after 2 out: styd on gamely run-in* **4/1**[2]	115+
-1F1	2	1 1/2	**Eyre Square (IRE)**[66] 3061 6-11-3 0........JamesReveley (Keith Reveley) *w wnr: rdn after 3 out: kpt on u.p fr last* **4/6**[1]	108+
3	11	**Lord Rudi (IRE)**[13] 4339 7-10-12 114........RTDunne(5) (R K Watson, Ire) *nt fluent on occasions: prom: hdwy on outside and ev ch 3 out: one pce next: hld whn mstke last: wknd* **5/1**[3]	100
0-F1	4	23	**Jago River (IRE)**[104] 2657 5-11-10 0........BrianHughes (Howard Johnson) *trckd ldrs: rdn and outpcd whn hit 2 out: btn whn mstke last* **9/1**	87

6m 48.3s (10.10) **Going Correction** +0.50s/f (Soft) **4** Ran SP% **106.7**

Speed ratings (Par 105): **103,102,99,91**

CSF £7.32 TOTE £4.90; EX 7.10.

Owner Brendan Richardson **Bred** J F C Maxwell **Trained** Cholmondeley, Cheshire

FOCUS

The ground was described as 'heavy' and a strong, swirling 45mph wind made conditions even more testing. A four-runner 3m novices' hurdle. The pace was not strong and all four were in line turning for home. The winner is on the upgrade and can rate higher.

NOTEBOOK

Alexander Road(IRE), a winner here and at Sedgefield, is rated 110. Described as 'babyish', she was stepping up in trip and had her stone penalty reduced by her excellent young rider's 7lb claim. She stole a crucial advantage going to the second-last and in the end did enough. She is still on the up. (op 10-3)

Eyre Square(IRE), who showed ability in two previous starts over hurdles, has since won three times over fences and is now rated 119. Without a penalty he looked to have been found a good opportunity, but he allowed the winner to poach a two-lengths lead and, hard as he tried on the run-in, he could not quite close the gap. He certainly has the ability to open his account over hurdles given a truer test. (op 4-5)

Lord Rudi(IRE), rated 114, was stepping up in trip. He joined issue travelling just as well as the first two but had emptied out when he blundered at the last. (op 9-2)

Jago River(IRE), absent since opening his account at Musselburgh in November after a final-flight fall on his first try over hurdles when booked for second spot at Wetherby, had plenty to find. The first to come under pressure, he had dropped right away when making a mess of the penultimate flight. (op 10-1)

4569 BORDER ESK "NATIONAL HUNT" NOVICES' HURDLE (10 hdls 1 omitted) 2m 4f

2:40 (2:40) (Class 4) 4-Y-O+ **£2,226** (£649; £324)

Form				RPR
25	1		**Armedanddangerous (IRE)**[30] 3998 6-11-2 0........MarkBradburne (Tom Gretton) *towards rr: rdn after 4th: rallied bef 3 out: kpt on wl fr next to ld last 50yds: styd on* **18/1**	106
066	2	hd	**Silent Snow (IRE)**[17] 4253 6-10-13 0........JamesHalliday(3) (Malcolm Jefferson) *led to 4th: styd upsides: led bef 3 out to bef next: regained ld bef last: hdd last 50yds: rallied u.p* **100/1**	106
00	3	8	**Foot The Bill**[30] 3987 6-11-2 0........TomSiddall (Patrick Holmes) *trckd ldrs: rdn and led bef 2 out to bef last: no ex run-in* **22/1**	98
1	4	15	**Tigre D'Aron (FR)**[45] 3711 4-11-0 0........BrianHughes (Howard Johnson) *t.k.h: cl up: led 4th to bef 3 out: outpcd whn lft 4th next: wknd* **10/11**[1]	81
1-30	5	1 1/4	**Flaygray**[30] 3987 7-11-2 0........CampbellGillies (Chris Grant) *cl up: effrt and ev ch bef 3 out: lft cl 3rd next: sn wknd* **17/2**[3]	85
6	87	**The Dagda (IRE)**[341] 5005 7-10-13 0........HarryHaynes(3) (Kevin Hunter) *bhd: struggling 4th: sn lost tch: t.o* **33/1**	—
7	58	**The Bravetraveller (IRE)**[704] 8-10-13 0........JamesO'Farrell(3) (Barbara Butterworth) *a bhd: lost tch bef 4th: t.o* **40/1**	—
12/6	P		**Vivona Hill**[38] 3851 7-11-2 0........BarryKeniry (Alan Swinbank) *in tch: rdn and outpcd bef 4 out: sn btn: t.o whn p.u after next* **3/1**[2]	—
0	P		**Princess Cherry (IRE)**[140] 1934 6-10-2 0........GaryRutherford(7) (Harriet Graham) *midfield: struggling 4th: sn btn: t.o whn p.u bef 4 out* **250/1**	—
0004	F		**Knockando**[17] 4253 6-11-2 0........PeterBuchanan (Lucinda Russell) *trckd ldrs: effrt and disputing cl 2nd whn fell 2 out* **14/1**	98
6	P		**No Way Hozay**[30] 3998 5-10-9 0........(t) HenryBrooke(7) (Brian Storey) *a bhd: struggling bef 4 out: t.o whn p.u after next* **100/1**	—

5 P **First Gunner**[12] 4363 6-11-2 0 .... RobertWalford —
(Tim Walford) *a bhd: struggling 4th: t.o whn p.u bef 4 out* **40/1**

5m 29.8s (7.00) **Going Correction** +0.50s/f (Soft)
WFA 4 from 5yo+ 8lb **12** Ran SP% **114.4**
Speed ratings (Par 105): **106,105,102,96,96 61,38,—,—,— —,—**
toteswingers:1&2 £45.00, 2&3 £45.00, 1&3 £45.00 CSF £1045.24 TOTE £42.90: £6.30, £16.70, £16.70; EX 533.20.
Owner The Beats Working Partnership **Bred** Tony McKiernan **Trained** Inkberrow, Worcestershire

FOCUS
Desperate conditions made even worse by a hail storm and in the end just five managed to complete. Ordinary novice form, with improvement from the first two.

NOTEBOOK
Armedanddangerous(IRE), runner-up in a heavy-ground bumper at Folkestone in November on his debut, was having his first try over hurdles on his third start. Happy in midfield and only sixth with plenty of work to do three out, he had to sidestep a faller at the next. He made up half a dozen lengths on the run-in to snatch the prize out of the fire near the line. A big, scopey type, he runs as though 3m will suit him even better but the form must be treated with caution. (op 20-1)
Silent Snow(IRE), well beaten in two previous starts over hurdles, was sent off an unconsidered 100/1 chance. In the firing line throughout, he regained the lead between the last two only to miss out near the line. He deserves plenty of credit for this.
Foot The Bill, an Irish maiden point winner, had shown little on his first try over hurdles. In the firing line throughout, after being headed on the run down to the last he tired markedly on the run-in. (op 20-1)
Tigre D'Aron(FR) was stepping up in trip and was a shade too keen for his own good. He stopped to nothing up the final hill and looks the type to go chasing in the autumn. (op 11-10 tchd 5-4 and 11-8 in a place)
Flaygray, a fast-ground bumper winner, jumped a lot better than on his debut but still has something to learn in that department. After taking charge he was third when hampered by the faller two out and could hardly raise a gallop on the run-in. (op 11-1 tchd 8-1)
Vivona Hill, a very useful bumper horse, had shaped well on his return after injury at Ayr but here he seemed to get hopelessly bogged down in the very bad ground. (op 5-2 tchd 9-4)
Knockando, a slow learner, looked to have plenty to find but was back in the firing line when taking a fall two out. As it transpired he might well have won. (op 5-2 tchd 9-4)

4570 SHARLEEN SPITERI/TEXAS 2ND JULY BEGINNERS' CHASE (12 fncs 4 omitted) 2m 4f
3:15 (3:16) (Class 4) 5-Y-O+ **£2,602** (£764; £382; £190)

Form RPR
0P0U 1 **Mister Marker (IRE)**[23] 4137 7-11-0 115 .... FearghalDavis 123+
(Nicky Richards) *cl up: ev ch fnl circ: led 4 out (usual 5 out): styd on wl u.p fr last* **9/4**[3]
3U33 2 *2* **Lord Villez (FR)**[30] 3995 7-11-0 120 .... GrahamLee 121
(Ferdy Murphy) *led to after 5th: ev ch fr 4 out (usual 5 out): drvn and kpt on same pce run-in* **2/1**[2]
B-U2 3 *14* **Indian Groom (IRE)**[29] 4002 6-11-0 0 .... WilsonRenwick 109
(Howard Johnson) *t.k.h: in tch: hdwy to ld after 5th: hdd 4 out: ev ch whn hit 2 out (usual 3 out): wknd bef last* **6/4**[1]
/P-6 4 *38* **Amulree**[17] 4254 8-10-0 0 .... MissLAlexander[(7)] 62
(N W Alexander) *prom: cl up after 5th: rdn 4 out (usual 5 out): wknd fr next* **66/1**
0/ 5 *4* **Pan Pan (FR)**[689] 5113 8-10-11 0 .... HarryHaynes[(3)] 65
(Anna Bramall) *bhd: lost tch bef 5th: t.o* **40/1**

5m 33.5s (6.10) **Going Correction** +0.50s/f (Soft) **5** Ran SP% **108.0**
Speed ratings: **107,106,100,85,83**
CSF £7.12 TOTE £2.50: £2.10, £1.10; EX 6.90.
Owner The Market Grafter Syndicate **Bred** Mrs M M Kelly **Trained** Greystoke, Cumbria

FOCUS
The ground was less testing on the chase course. Just three to consider seriously in this ordinary beginners' chase, which was run at a sound pace. The first two are rated to their marks.

NOTEBOOK
Mister Marker(IRE), a 120-rated hurdler, had a 3m handicap chase in the bag when blundering his rider out of the saddle three out at Newcastle. He jumped to the front here and stayed on in very willing fashion on the run-in. The stable has hit a rich vein of form in the last two weeks. (op 2-1 tchd 5-2)
Lord Villez(FR), a maiden here and in France after 22 previous starts over fences, tends to run in fits and starts. He came again to land almost level at the last, but his head carriage under pressure does not inspire confidence. All the same his turn must come one day. (op 9-4)
Indian Groom(IRE), a 135-rated hurdler, had gone under by a neck here on his first completed outing over fences. That was over 2m and his stamina seemed to give out on the extended run down to the last. (op 13-8 tchd 7-4)
Amulree, placed in two points, faced an impossible task but shaped nicely until the foot of the final hill. Low-grade handicaps beckon further down the line.
Pan Pan(FR), absent for almost two years, seems to have inherited none of the ability of his half-brother Antonin, a past winner of the Racing Post Chase and successful the same season at the Cheltenham Festival. (op 28-1)

4571 STARSPORTSBET.CO.UK H'CAP CHASE (15 fncs 4 omitted) 3m 2f
3:45 (3:45) (Class 4) (0-110,103) 5-Y-O+ **£3,252** (£955; £477; £238)

Form RPR
5P3V 1 **Blazing Diva (IRE)**[17] 4256 8-11-6 97 .... WilsonRenwick 111+
(Sandy Thomson) *mde virtually all: rdn and drew clr fr 2 out (usual 3 out): eased nr fin* **12/1**
1-1 2 *15* **Billsgrey (IRE)**[107] 2602 9-10-13 90 .... CampbellGillies 88
(William Amos) *hld up: rdn after 11th: sn outpcd: rallied 3 out (usual 4 out): chsd (clr) wnr run-in: no imp* **7/2**[2]
P-0V 3 *3/4* **Royal Mackintosh**[17] 4256 10-11-10 101 .... GrahamLee 99
(Alan Mactaggart) *cl up: reminders 9th: outpcd 11th: plugged on fnl 2: nvr able to chal* **10/3**[1]
12-1 4 *2 1/4* **Teerie Express**[23] 4135 10-11-1 99 .... MrJBewley[(7)] 96
(George Bewley) *w wnr tl rdn and outpcd 2 out (usual 3 out): wknd and lost two pls run-in* **5/1**[3]
3/PV 5 *21* **Overlady**[17] 4256 9-11-5 103 .... NathanMoscrop[(7)] 77
(James Ewart) *chsd ldng pair: drvn 4 out (usual 5 out): wknd bef 2 out: t.o* **15/2**
0652 6 *36* **Top Dressing (IRE)**[23] 4137 10-11-10 101 ....(p) BrianHughes 39
(Howard Johnson) *hld up towards rr: drvn and outpcd 11th: sn btn: t.o* **22/1**
4UP2 P **Shrewd Investor (IRE)**[45] 3716 11-11-1 92 ....(b[1]) RobertWalford —
(Henry Hogarth) *in tch: rdn and outpcd bef 4 out (usual 5 out): wknd fr next: t.o whn p.u bef last* **7/1**
-43P P **Its Teescomponents (IRE)**[23] 4137 9-11-11 102 .... JamesReveley —
(Keith Reveley) *hld up: rdn 11th: sn btn: t.o whn p.u bef 2 out (usual 3 out)* **15/2**

7m 19.1s (11.90) **Going Correction** +0.50s/f (Soft) **8** Ran SP% **110.0**
Speed ratings: **101,96,96,95,89 77,—,—**
toteswingers:1&2 £11.80, 2&3 £3.30, 1&3 £7.50 CSF £51.09 CT £162.73 TOTE £12.50: £2.30, £1.80, £1.60; EX 66.90.
Owner Mr & Mrs A M Thomson **Bred** Donal Dorgan **Trained** Lambden, Berwickshire

FOCUS
A truly run stayers' handicap and the clear-cut winner was in the first two throughout. She is rated back to her best 2010 form.

NOTEBOOK
Blazing Diva(IRE), who had gone with plenty of zest in the void race here two weeks earlier, has slipped to a mark 4lb lower than her last success at Newcastle a year ago. She kicked well clear on the extended run down to the last and in the end won easing up. She tended to jump left-handed and is even better suited by going the other way round. (op 20-1)
Billsgrey(IRE), a winner over this C&D in April from a mark of 64, was raised another 13lb after following up at Sedgefield in November. Asked to race from a mark of 90 here, he was a remote fourth at the bottom of the hill but stayed on in willing fashion to claim second spot on the run-in. On this showing no trip will be too far. (op 9-2)
Royal Mackintosh, whose four career wins have been round here, was another to have hinted at a comeback in the void race. He couldn't dominate and was under pressure setting out on to the final circuit. To his credit he stayed on in willing fashion up the final hill. (op 4-1)
Teerie Express, winner of three of his previous four starts, was up just 2lb after his latest Newcastle success. He matched strides with the winner and ultimately paid a heavy penalty. (op 9-2 tchd 11-2)
Overlady, who had shaped well on just her second start back after a lengthy spell on the sidelines in the void race here, kept tabs on the first two. She tired in the final half-mile but should not be written off yet. (op 7-1 tchd 8-1)

4572 CARLISLE-RACES.CO.UK RACING EXCELLENCE "HANDS AND HEELS" H'CAP HURDLE (CONDITIONALS/AMATEURS) (9 hdls 2 omitted) 2m 4f
4:20 (4:20) (Class 4) (0-115,115) 4-Y-O+ **£2,226** (£649; £324)

Form RPR
2543 1 **Texas Holdem (IRE)**[21] 4166 12-11-7 110 .... AodhaganConlon 114+
(Michael Smith) *midfield: hdwy to ld bef 3 out: kpt on strly fr last* **9/2**[2]
4-40 2 *3 1/2* **Ascendant**[67] 3334 5-11-9 115 ....(b[1]) MrJBewley[(3)] 115
(Howard Johnson) *t.k.h: hld up: hdwy bef 3 out: chsd wnr bef last: no imp run-in* **25/1**
40 3 *nk* **Dickie Henderhoop (IRE)**[104] 2654 6-9-11 91 oh4 ow2.. MrRWilson[(5)] 91
(Lucy Normile) *bhd: nt fluent 4th: rdn bef 4 out: styd on fr 2 out: nrst fin* **16/1**
0120 4 *nk* **Rare Coincidence**[6] 2372 10-11-4 110 ....(p) CallumWhillans[(3)] 110
(Roger Fisher) *led to bef 3 out: sn rdn: rallied: kpt on run-in* **25/1**
652 5 *23* **Go Silver Bullet (FR)**[27] 4060 10-11-2 108 .... MrGJCockburn[(3)] 87
(Lucinda Russell) *trckd ldrs: rdn whn blnd 2 out: sn btn* **8/1**
0060 6 *3 1/4* **Hoar Frost**[10] 4390 6-10-0 94 .... MissGTutty[(5)] 71
(Karen Tutty) *hld up: effrt bef 3 out: no imp next: btn whn blnd last* **16/1**
0503 7 *1/2* **Fairynuff**[22] 4146 7-10-11 100 ....(t) JeremiahMcGrath 75
(Kate Walton) *prom: effrt bef 3 out: sn rdn and wknd bef last* **3/1**[1]
-540 8 *12* **Woody Valentine (USA)**[256] 846 10-10-11 105 .... MissRobynGray[(5)] 66
(Evelyn Slack) *t.k.h: in tch on outside tl rdn and wknd bef 3 out* **40/1**
0662 9 *4* **Farmers Cross (IRE)**[46] 3693 7-10-13 105 .... TonyKelly[(3)] 62
(Ferdy Murphy) *hld up: hdwy and prom after 4 out: wknd bef 2 out* **6/1**[3]
0P00 10 *5* **Front Rank (IRE)**[24] 4113 11-10-7 101 .... MissNSayer[(5)] 53
(Dianne Sayer) *cl up tl rdn and wknd fr 3 out* **40/1**
0122 11 *3* **Marlborough Sound**[35] 3899 12-10-9 98 .... HenryBrooke 47
(James Turner) *midfield: effrt after 4 out: wknd fr next* **7/1**
52-P 12 *11* **Below The Deck (IRE)**[107] 2598 8-10-8 100 .... MissEButterworth[(3)] 38
(Barbara Butterworth) *bhd: struggling 4 out: nvr on terms* **14/1**

5m 32.2s (9.40) **Going Correction** +0.50s/f (Soft) **12** Ran SP% **112.1**
Speed ratings (Par 105): **101,99,99,99,90 88,88,83,82,80 79,74**
toteswingers:1&2 £12.60, 2&3 £32.80, 1&3 £25.90 CSF £108.65 CT £1624.67 TOTE £7.10: £1.80, £10.60, £5.30; EX 94.50.
Owner Mrs Sandra Smith **Bred** Burren Racing Syndicate **Trained** Kirkheaton, Northumberland

FOCUS
A competitive 'hands and heels' handicap hurdle and all but four were still in contention three from home. The first four came clear and are rated to their marks in this ordinary race.

NOTEBOOK
Texas Holdem(IRE), 8lb below his last success over five years ago now, had finished a good third in a stronger event than this at Kelso last time. Driven clear between the last two, he enjoyed a decisive success. (tchd 4-1)
Ascendant, a 93-rated stayer on the level, won on his hurdling debut but it has been downhill since. Now rated 115, on just his seventh start over hurdles he sported blinkers for the first time and ran much better, staying on to chase the winner approaching the last. (op 18-1)
Dickie Henderhoop(IRE), out of the handicap and burdened with overweight, was having just his second start for this yard. A maiden after ten previous starts, he stayed on in good style from way off the pace and will be suited by a return to 3m. (op 20-1 tchd 22-1)
Rare Coincidence, in front when pulling up in the controversial Wolverhampton all-weather race, took them along as is his wont, and he deserves credit for the way he stuck to his task up the final hill. (op 18-1)
Go Silver Bullet(FR), back over hurdles from a 9lb lower mark, has yet to make his mark over hurdles and he weakened up the final hill. (op 13-2)
Fairynuff, third over 3m at Musselburgh from a 2lb lower mark, didn't improve for the drop in trip and is proving expensive to follow. (op 7-2)

4573 ALEXANDRA BURKE ULN 1ST AUGUST H'CAP CHASE (9 fncs 3 omitted) 2m
4:50 (4:51) (Class 4) (0-100,96) 5-Y-O+ **£2,602** (£764; £382; £190)

Form RPR
-22F 1 **Against The Wind**[113] 2450 8-11-11 95 .... PeterBuchanan 108
(Lucinda Russell) *led to 2nd: cl up: effrt 2 out (usual 3 out): led appr last: styd on strly run-in* **7/2**[2]
0142 2 *2 1/2* **Sheriff Hall (IRE)**[14] 4305 6-11-6 90 ....(t) JanFaltejsek 100
(George Charlton) *t.k.h: cl up: led 3rd: hdd appr last: sn rdn: kpt on towards fin* **5/2**[1]
6P6F 3 *3* **Banoge (IRE)**[29] 4001 9-11-12 96 ....(b[1]) WilsonRenwick 104
(Rose Dobbin) *hld up: hdwy and prom 1/2-way: effrt after 2 out: disp 2nd run-in: edgd rt and sn no ex* **9/1**
FF3P 4 *20* **Native Coll**[26] 4064 11-10-2 79 .... MissLAlexander[(7)] 66
(N W Alexander) *chsd ldrs: led 2nd to next: bmpd 4th: sn outpcd: rdn and no imp fr 3 out (usual 4 out)* **12/1**
U53P 5 *2 1/2* **More Shennanigans**[51] 3618 10-9-7 70 oh5 .... PaulGallagher[(7)] 55
(Jean McGregor) *midfield: drvn and outpcd 1/2-way: n.d after* **11/1**
0U04 6 *2 3/4* **Devil Water**[27] 4057 8-11-2 93 .... NathanMoscrop[(7)] 75
(James Ewart) *in tch gng wl: bmpd 4th: effrt bef 3 out (usual 4 out): wknd next* **12/1**
6P44 7 *22* **Solway Blue**[145] 1873 9-10-2 72 .... PaddyAspell 32
(Lisa Harrison) *bhd: j. slowly and outpcd 5th: sn struggling* **16/1**
40-5 U **Frith (IRE)**[23] 4136 9-10-3 78 .... AlexanderVoy[(5)] —
(Lucy Normile) *in tch whn blnd and uns rdr 3rd* **12/1**

62F3 **P** **Mighty Magnus (IRE)**[23] 4133 8-11-2 **86**............................ GrahamLee —
(Martin Todhunter) *bhd: hmpd 3rd: struggling after next: t.o whn p.u 3 out* **6/1**[3]

4m 21.9s (5.80) **Going Correction** +0.50s/f (Soft) **9** Ran SP% **112.4**
Speed ratings: **105,103,102,92,91 89,78,—,—**
toteswingers:1&2 £2.90, 2&3 £4.10, 1&3 £5.10 CSF £12.77 CT £69.23 TOTE £5.30: £2.60, £1.10, £4.50; EX 12.90.
Owner Mrs Wilma Wright **Bred** D J G And Mrs Wright **Trained** Arlary, Perth & Kinross

FOCUS
A low-grade 2m handicap chase and three almost in a line jumping the last. The first three finished clear, and the form is sound.

NOTEBOOK
Against The Wind, who suffered a cut having been booked for second spot when falling at the last at Hexham in November, came back fresh and well and stuck on in willing fashion to open his account over fences at the sixth time of asking. (op 3-1)
Sheriff Hall(IRE), very keen when runner-up from the same mark on his chase debut at Ayr last month, again raced with the choke out. He impressed with his sound jumping and to his credit came again on the run-in to claim second spot in the closing stages. He has a high cruising speed and likely to be suited by less-testing conditions. He looks a winner waiting to happen. (op 3-1)
Banoge(IRE), a winner twice over fences in the past for another yard, has slipped to a more realistic mark. In first-time blinkers, after showing clear in second soon after the last, he didn't find an awful lot and edging towards the far rail he was on the retreat near the line. He doesn't look a great battler. (op 11-1)
Native Coll, back on his last winning mark, was dropping back in trip and merely kept on in his own time up the final hill after being left comfortably behind. (op 10-1)

4574 RACING UK CHANNEL 432 INTERMEDIATE OPEN NATIONAL HUNT FLAT RACE 2m 1f
5:20 (5:21) (Class 6) 4-6-Y-O **£1,267** (£369; £184)

Form RPR
052 **1** **Rojo Vivo**[17] 4259 5-10-11 0............................ HenryBrooke(7) 107+
(Karen McLintock) *cl up: led 1/2-way: rdn and styd on strly fnl 2f* **13/2**
0 **2** *16* **Kings Canyon (IRE)**[36] 3889 5-10-11 0............................ PaulGallagher(7) 92
(Howard Johnson) *in tch: hdwy to chse wnr 1/2-way: effrt and ev ch 4 out: one pce fnl 2f* **18/1**
06- **3** *3/4* **Mini The Minx (IRE)**[333] 5144 5-10-1 0............................ CallumWhillans(10) 83
(Donald Whillans) *prom: drvn and outpcd over 5f out: rallied over 2f out: styd on to take 3rd towards fin* **20/1**
3-04 **4** *1 3/4* **Zaru (FR)**[38] 3856 5-11-1 0............................ HarryHaynes(3) 88
(James Ewart) *in tch: effrt over 3f out: edgd lft and outpcd 2f out* **6/1**
1 **5** *3 3/4* **Julia Too**[29] 4005 4-10-10 0............................ CampbellGillies 77
(William Amos) *hld up: hdwy and prom 6f out: rdn and no ex over 2f out* **3/1**[1]
6 *16* **Little Glenshee (IRE)** 5-10-4 0............................ MissLAlexander(7) 61
(N W Alexander) *towards rr: hdwy 1/2-way: rdn and outpcd over 4f out: n.d after* **50/1**
3 **7** *22* **Molannarch**[21] 4171 5-10-11 0............................ JamesReveley 54
(Keith Reveley) *hld up: stdy hdwy 1/2-way: rdn over 5f out: sn btn* **7/2**[2]
0 **8** *5* **Nalim (IRE)**[18] 4239 5-11-4 0............................ GrahamLee 41
(Malcolm Jefferson) *trckd ldrs to 1/2-way: sn rdn and wknd: eased whn btn fnl 2f* **12/1**
9 *14* **Gleann Na Ndochais (IRE)**[123] 5-11-1 0............................ EwanWhillans(3) 27
(Alistair Whillans) *hld up: drvn over 6f out: sn struggling* **9/2**[3]
10 *4 1/2* **Tresor De L'Isle (FR)** 4-10-10 0............................ RichieMcGrath 15
(Anna Bramall) *bhd: struggling 1/2-way: nvr on terms* **18/1**
0 **11** *dist* **Supreme Dawn**[21] 4171 6-10-11 0............................ PeterBuchanan —
(Shelley Johnstone) *led to 1/2-way: sn lost pl: virtually p.u fnl 4f* **66/1**

4m 33.0s (8.80) **Going Correction** +0.50s/f (Soft)
WFA 4 from 5yo+ 7lb **11** Ran SP% **119.5**
Speed ratings: **99,91,91,90,88 81,70,68,61,59 —**
toteswingers:1&2 £15.70, 2&3 £38.70, 1&3 £10.70. totesuper7: Win: Not won. Place: Not won. CSF £115.69 TOTE £5.60: £1.30, £14.70, £12.80; EX 67.00.
Owner David Maughan **Bred** A W Buller **Trained** Ingoe, Northumberland

FOCUS
Probably a very ordinary bumper run at a sound pace and they came home well strung out. Not form to be confident about.

NOTEBOOK
Rojo Vivo, having his fourth start and runner-up beaten 22 lengths here two weeks earlier, went on at about the halfway mark and kept up the gallop up the final hill to draw right away in the final furlong. He will need a trip when he goes hurdling. (op 8-1 tchd 9-1)
Kings Canyon(IRE), who cost £30,000 as a 3-y-o, stepped up markedly on his debut effort. (op 16-1)
Mini The Minx(IRE), well beaten in two bumpers last year, stayed on in willing fashion up the hill and is another who looks to have stamina in abundance.
Zaru(FR), another having his fourth start, was given a much more patient ride but he looks to have his limitations. (op 9-2 tchd 13-2)
Julia Too, very green when winning on her debut here last month, was up in trip and was well held at the foot of the final hill. (op 4-1)
Molannarch, from the family of Bayrouge and a half-sister to last year's winner, sat off the pace and made a brief forward move going into the home turn. Conditions were probably too testing for her. (tchd 4-1)
T/Plt: £2,836.00 to a £1 stake. Pool of £53,030.08 - 13.65 winning tickets. T/Qpdt: £16.60 to a £1 stake. Pool of £6,314.11 - 280.10 winning tickets. RY

4424 FOLKESTONE (R-H)
Thursday, March 10

OFFICIAL GOING: Good
Wind: Strong, half behind Weather: Cloudy

4665 BET ON TOTEPLACEPOT AT TOTESPORT.COM MAIDEN HURDLE (11 hdls) 2m 6f 110y
2:20 (2:20) (Class 5) 4-Y-O+ **£1,918** (£559; £279)

Form RPR
44U2 **1** **Baile Anrai (IRE)**[20] 4196 7-11-3 116............................ DougieCostello 122+
(Ian Williams) *trckd ldrs: wnt 2nd after 2 out gng easily: waited tl after last to ld: pushed out: comf* **4/7**[1]
1225 **2** *2 3/4* **Kasbadali (FR)**[29] 4012 6-11-3 115............................ LeightonAspell 113
(Oliver Sherwood) *w ldr: led 6th: hit 8th: drvn after 2 out: hdd after last: kpt on but comf hld* **5/2**[2]
0 **3** *53* **Sandy's Double**[34] 3930 5-11-3 0............................ DarylJacob 93
(Jamie Snowden) *t.k.h: cl up: chsd ldr after 6th tl after 2 out: sn btn: heavily eased flat* **8/1**[3]
06/ **4** *64* **Personal Flair**[376] 8-10-10 0............................ JackDoyle —
(Sarah Humphrey) *mde most to 6th: mstke 8th and wknd: sn t.o: lft remote 4th last* **50/1**
050P **5** *4* **Luna Lightning**[52] 3607 7-10-10 0............................(p) AndrewThornton —
(Linda Jewell) *in tch to 1/2-way: sn bhd: wl t.o* **100/1**
F **Nobody's Business (IRE)**[1040] 10-10-10 0............................ MrHGMiller(7) —
(Zoe Davison) *cl up: mstke 8th and wknd: poor 4th whn fell last: winded* **100/1**

5m 58.8s (-12.50) **Going Correction** -0.825s/f (Firm) **6** Ran SP% **107.3**
Speed ratings (Par 103): **88,87,68,46,44 —**
toteswingers:1&2 £1.02, 2&3 £2.50, 1&3 £2.30 CSF £2.09 TOTE £1.30: £1.10, £1.40; EX 2.10.
Owner Massive **Bred** Fred Williams **Trained** Portway, Worcs

FOCUS
A very ordinary race that looked like a match between the two market leaders, who drew well clear. The winner and third are much better than the bare result.

NOTEBOOK
Baile Anrai(IRE) ran out a comfortable winner, cruising upsides the runner-up in the home straight, before drawing clear after the last. Second last time out to a handicap good thing, he wasn't required to run up to that level, but seemed to appreciate the step up in trip, suggesting he may enjoy even further. He is a progressive sort and will make a chaser in the near future. (tchd 4-6 and 8-11 in a place)
Kasbadali(FR) took up the running with more than a circuit to go, but was unable to go with the winner after the last. A former bumper winner, he can pick up a race at this sort of level. (op 2-1)
Sandy's Double was the subject of a little market support (12-1 into 8-1), but had no chance with the front two, especially as he was too keen early on. A stronger pace over a shorter trip may help, but is likely to make more of an impact when sent handicapping. (op 12-1 tchd 7-1)
Nobody's Business(IRE) took a heavy fall at the last on this first run under rules, following a 1040-day absence from points. His jumping was generally slow, but he may come on for the outing if recovering from this experience.

4666 LIPSCOMB.CO.UK BEGINNERS' CHASE (15 fncs) 2m 5f
2:50 (2:50) (Class 5) 5-Y-O+ **£2,397** (£698; £349)

Form RPR
22/3 **1** **Neil Harvey (IRE)**[35] 3902 8-11-0 122............................ LiamTreadwell 131+
(Nick Gifford) *trckd ldr: rdn to ld after 3 out: hit 2 out: rdn out and in command after* **9/4**[1]
26P2 **2** *4 1/2* **Canni Thinkaar (IRE)**[23] 4127 10-10-9 113(b) GemmaGracey-Davison(5) 126
(Zoe Davison) *led: drvn and hdd after 3 out: kpt on but readily hld fr 2 out* **9/2**
-04U **3** *2 1/4* **Erzen (IRE)**[7] 4445 6-11-0 127............................ AidanColeman 126
(Venetia Williams) *j. slowly 1st: 3rd and reminders 2nd: chsd ldng pair 6th: cl enough after but nvr looked willing enough to chal* **5/2**[2]
1-02 **4** *46* **Days Of Pleasure (IRE)**[68] 3308 6-10-7 109............................ MrTJCannon(7) 90
(Chris Gordon) *sn wl off the pce in 5th: wnt remote 4th after 11th: wl t.o* **11/4**[3]
P **P** **Rockoboy (IRE)**[11] 4371 10-10-7 0............................ MrHGMiller(7) —
(Zoe Davison) *a bhd in last pair: wl t.o 10th: p.u bef 3 out* **100/1**
40/P **P** **Midsummer Legend**[69] 3264 7-10-7 0............................(t) SamJones —
(Norma Twomey) *chsd ldng pair to 6th: wknd 9th: wl t.o whn p.u bef 2 out* **22/1**
000 **P** **Lucius Fabeo (IRE)**[23] 4128 7-11-0 0............................ AndrewThornton —
(Anna Newton-Smith) *a in last: t.o 1/2-way: ms bhd whn p.u bef 3 out* **100/1**

5m 21.2s (-1.00) **Going Correction** -0.05s/f (Good) **7** Ran SP% **110.5**
Speed ratings: **99,97,96,78,— —,—**
toteswingers:1&2 £1.20, 2&3 £8.70, 1&3 £3.60 CSF £11.94 TOTE £3.60: £1.30, £1.40; EX 10.40.
Owner Neil Fairbrother & Paul Beck **Bred** C Berry **Trained** Findon, W Sussex

FOCUS
A competitive beginners' chase run at a strong gallop. Decent novice form for the track.

NOTEBOOK
Neil Harvey(IRE) has always looked like a chasing sort, and got his head in front for the first time over fences with seemingly plenty in hand. He made a pleasing enough chasing debut last time out after a significant absence, and built on that here, jumping well throughout and drawing clear after the last. Connections expect him to be better with more give in the ground and he looks a nice sort for soft-ground staying chases next season. (op 7-2 tchd 4-1)
Canni Thinkaar(IRE) attempted to make all, and battled well in the home straight, but was always held by the winner. Although a late convert to chasing, he is a sound jumper and once again seemed to run his race. His record over C&D is very good (runner-up three times) and, although he will remain vulnerable to more progressive types, his first chase win doesn't appear too far away. (op 11-4 tchd 5-1)
Erzen(IRE), rated 130 over hurdles, didn't enjoy himself at all, racing moodily. Reluctant to jump the first, he never got into any rhythm and it appears increasingly unlikely he will be as good over fences as hurdles, although a return to a softer surface may be of some assistance. (tchd 9-4)
Days Of Pleasure(IRE), the only other finisher, was well outpaced and disappointed. This was however, his chasing debut so he may come on for the experience, and should appreciate the re-application of a visor. (op 7-2 tchd 5-2)

4667 BET ON LIVE GOLF AT TOTESPORT.COM NOVICES' HURDLE (9 hdls) 2m 1f 110y
3:25 (3:25) (Class 4) 4-Y-O+ **£1,918** (£559; £279)

Form RPR
54U1 **1** **Renard D'Irlande (FR)**[23] 4128 6-11-8 120............................ AidanColeman 135+
(Venetia Williams) *trckd ldrs: wnt 2nd sn after 2 out: led on long run bef last: cruised clr* **1/2**[1]
-450 **2** *20* **Spiritual Guidance (IRE)**[43] 3740 8-11-1 104............................ WayneHutchinson 100
(Warren Greatrex) *cl up: chsd ldr after 5th tl after 2 out: outpcd on long run bef last: kpt on to take 2nd again flat* **9/1**[3]
-562 **3** *5* **Behindcloseddoors (IRE)**[47] 3691 5-11-1 114............................ SeanQuinlan 98+
(Kim Bailey) *led and gd pce early: rdn and hdd on long run bef last: sn btn: lost 2nd flat* **9/2**[2]
U166 **4** *4* **Rushwee (IRE)**[10] 4399 9-11-8 111............................ DominicElsworth 102+
(Lucy Wadham) *pressed ldr tl mstke 5th: struggling to keep in tch in 4th after next: outpcd after 2 out* **10/1**
0-35 **5** *dist* **Dark Dancer**[79] 3060 7-10-8 0............................ FelixDeGiles —
(Laura Mongan) *immediately detached in last pair: ct up by 4th: lft bhd again next and pushed along: wl t.o* **28/1**
P **Aboukir**[580] 5-11-1 0............................ LeightonAspell —
(Oliver Sherwood) *immediately detached in last pair: ct up by 4th: lft bhd again next: p.u suddenly 6th* **33/1**

4m 17.0s (-18.60) **Going Correction** -0.825s/f (Firm) **6** Ran SP% **110.3**
Speed ratings (Par 105): **108,99,96,95,— —**
toteswingers:1&2 £1.70, 2&3 £2.20, 1&3 £1.10 CSF £5.73 TOTE £1.50: £1.20, £1.70; EX 5.60.
Owner Hills Of Ledbury (Aga) **Bred** Mlle Marie Drion At Al **Trained** Kings Caple, H'fords

FOCUS
A modest novice hurdle run at a sound gallop. The easy winner stepped up again and looks a decent novice.
NOTEBOOK
Renard D'Irlande(FR) won at an absolute canter in the manner expected of a 1-2 favourite, his second consecutive comfortable victory. Jumping well, he took it up turning for home before pulling clear on the bridle to score by a wide margin. Although the form of his first win has not worked out well, he is a horse of some potential and seems equally adept at anything from 2m to 2m4f, and chasing is likely to be the long-term plan. (op 4-7 tchd 8-13)
Spiritual Guidance(IRE) had a bit to find on ratings, but run creditably enough to suggest that a race at this level is not out of reach. (tchd 13-2)
Behindcloseddoors(IRE) was not particularly fluent at his hurdles and will need to brush up on that before he wins any races. However, he has shown some signs of ability and does have scope for further improvement. (op 4-1)
Rushwee(IRE) made a mistake down the side of the track that put paid to his chances and this was his third consecutive poor run, making him one for the swerve list for now. (op 12-1)
Dark Dancer was out of her depth and has shown nothing so far. (op 33-1)

4668 STREETGRAFIX.CO.UK H'CAP CHASE (12 fncs) 2m
3:55 (3:55) (Class 5) (0-90,89) 5-Y-0+ **£2,397** (£698; £349)

Form / RPR
0063 **1** **Betty Browneyes**[17] 4264 6-11-4 **81**.....................(t) AidanColeman 95+
(Tom George) *pressed ldr: led 9th: drew clr after 3 out: in n.d after: eased flat* **8/1**
0F40 **2** *3* **Goring One (IRE)**[44] 3723 6-11-6 **83**..................... AndrewThornton 92
(Anna Newton-Smith) *mde most to 9th: chsd wnr after: outpcd after 3 out: kpt on flat but no threat* **13/2**[3]
-000 **3** *10* **Eastern Supreme (IRE)**[103] 2667 6-11-12 **89**..................(t) SeanQuinlan 92+
(Kim Bailey) *in tch: chsd ldng pair 6th: mstkes 8th and 3 out: outpcd in 4th after: plugged on to take 3rd again nr fin* **7/4**[1]
3541 **4** *½* **Rince Donn (IRE)**[8] 4426 9-11-5 **85** 7ex..................... DavidBass(3) 85
(Roger Curtis) *in tch: pushed along 7th in last pair: prog next: chsd ldng pair 3 out: nt qckn and no imp bef next: lost 3rd nr fin* **17/2**
P453 **5** *5* **Bearneen Boy (IRE)**[8] 4426 8-10-4 **67**..................(t) DougieCostello 63
(Neil King) *racd wd: hld up: in tch in rr to 8th: sn outpcd and btn* **4/1**[2]
0/6P **6** *14* **Carmond (GER)**[44] 3724 7-11-2 **79**..................(p) SamJones 65
(Oliver Sherwood) *pushed along in rr after 5th: struggling to keep in tch fr 8th: wknd 3 out* **9/1**
0P4F **P** **Sourchamp (FR)**[7] 4447 5-10-3 **69**..................(t) EamonDehdashti(3) —
(Arthur Whiting) *mstkes: chsd ldrs: lost pl 7th: wknd 9th: t.o whn p.u bef 2 out* **9/1**

4m 4.60s (-2.60) **Going Correction** -0.05s/f (Good) 7 Ran SP% **111.3**
Speed ratings: **104,102,97,97,94 87,—**
toteswingers:1&2 £8.00, 2&3 £2.40, 1&3 £8.90 CSF £53.61 TOTE £6.80: £6.70, £3.30; EX 36.20.
Owner Capt & Mrs J A George **Bred** Mrs R Hoare & Miss S Hoare **Trained** Slad, Gloucs
FOCUS
A trappy handicap run at no more than an ordinary gallop. The cosy winner is on the upgrade.
NOTEBOOK
Betty Browneyes ran out a cosy winner for the in-form Tom George yard, despite being a marked drifter throughout the day. She built on her pleasing third last time out and clearly enjoyed the return to a sounder surface. She may be turned out under a penalty at Market Rasen, where she would be competitive if replicating this effort. (op 5-1)
Goring One(IRE) was taking a big drop in trip, and that seemed his undoing as he was staying on well in the closing stages, having been outpaced turning for home. He jumped better than he has before, but has not appeared the most consistent, so is not sure to build on this, though a step up in distance is sure to assist. (tchd 11-2 and 7-1)
Eastern Supreme(IRE), who was well supported, has disappointed since his early bumper promise, but looked on a tempting mark for his chase debut. However this was another poor effort, though the way he was staying on at the end suggests that he will appreciate a return to further. (op 5-2 tchd 11-4)
Rince Donn(IRE) always looked like struggling under his penalty and will run off 5lb lower after this, which should give him a better chance. (op 15-2 tchd 9-1)
Bearneen Boy(IRE) was held up and took a long time to get going, as he laboured his way round. (tchd 7-2 and 9-2 in places)
Carmond(GER) (op 14-1 tchd 16-1)
Sourchamp(FR) made a bad mistake down the side that put him out the race. (op 6-1)

4669 HAPPY 40TH BIRTHDAY SHARON DAVEY-HOLPIN H'CAP CHASE (16 fncs 2 omitted) 3m 1f
4:30 (4:30) (Class 4) (0-100,100) 5-Y-0+ **£2,740** (£798; £399)

Form / RPR
0P4P **1** **Theophrastus (IRE)**[19] 4219 9-11-10 **98**..................... LiamTreadwell 116+
(Nick Gifford) *prom: mde most fr 6th: clr 3 out and pushed along: in n.d whn mstke last* **3/1**[1]
22F2 **2** *10* **Behind The Scenes (IRE)**[186] 1478 9-10-13 **87**.......... AndrewThornton 93
(Tim McCarthy) *mde most to 6th: chsd wnr after: outpcd 3 out: no ch after* **10/3**[2]
1634 **3** *2¼* **Portrait Royale (IRE)**[32] 3961 9-11-4 **92**..................... FelixDeGiles 97
(Anna Newton-Smith) *hld up last: pushed along and prog to chse ldng pair after 12th: chal for 2nd 2 out: one pce* **9/2**[3]
14RP **4** *23* **Celian (FR)**[14] 4313 8-11-8 **99**..................... AlexMerriam(3) 82
(Neil King) *led briefly 3rd: pushed along and lost pl next: rdn and outpcd in 4th pl after 12th: no ch after next* **8/1**
420P **5** *21* **Romney Marsh**[23] 4126 10-10-8 **82**..................... MattieBatchelor 46
(Roger Curtis) *in tch: mstke 8th: rdn and outpcd fr 12th: no ch after: t.o* **11/1**
403P **6** *10* **Alteranthela (IRE)**[62] 3431 7-11-3 **91**..................... LeightonAspell 46
(Richard Rowe) *in tch: outpcd and j. slowly in last pl 12th: sn no ch: t.o* **11/2**
U-PU **7** *2½* **Ya I Know (IRE)**[10] 4402 10-11-10 **98**..................(tp) JackDoyle 51
(Sarah Humphrey) *prom to 10th: lost pl and struggling 12th: sn last and wl bhd: t.o* **7/1**

6m 31.3s (-4.50) **Going Correction** -0.05s/f (Good) 7 Ran SP% **113.6**
Speed ratings: **105,101,101,93,87 83,83**
CSF £13.67 CT £42.88 TOTE £3.60: £1.70, £1.10; EX 18.70.
Owner Core Strength **Bred** Sunnyhill Stud **Trained** Findon, W Sussex
FOCUS
The first fence down the back straight was omitted for this open handicap chase. The winner is rated back to the level of his Chepstow run in the autumn.
NOTEBOOK
Theophrastus(IRE) put his poor recent form behind him to take advantage of his slipping mark, which has fallen from 122 to 98, and clearly enjoyed the return to good ground. Taking it up down the back straight with a circuit and a half still to go, he jumped boldly and had the race won turning for home. His recent profile suggests that he isn't assured to repeat the effort, but he is still well handicapped if this sparks a revival. (op 4-1)
Behind The Scenes(IRE) was runner-up for the fourth time in his last five runs, confirming his consistency after a 186-day absence. This run should set him up for a spring campaign, but he has failed to win in 15 attempts, which is becoming a big concern. (op 11-4 tchd 7-2)
Portrait Royale(IRE) was only 2lb higher than for her C&D win in November, but she has been disappointing since and was quickly taken off her feet here. A return to testing ground is essential. (tchd 5-1)
Celian(FR) is temperamental and completed for only the third time in his last nine runs. (op 10-1)
Romney Marsh failed to see out the stamina test. (op 15-2 tchd 12-1)
Alteranthela(IRE) has proved much less effective over fences than hurdles. (op 7-1 tchd 5-1)

4670 BET ON LIVE TENNIS AT TOTESPORT.COM H'CAP HURDLE (9 hdls) 2m 1f 110y
5:00 (5:00) (Class 4) (0-100,98) 4-Y-0+ **£2,055** (£599; £299)

Form / RPR
P42F **1** **Watergate (IRE)**[8] 4426 5-11-4 **90**..................... LeightonAspell 100+
(Richard Rowe) *w ldr: led 6th: rdn and hrd pressed last: kpt on wl flat* **5/2**[1]
0 **2** *3¼* **Giant O Murchu (IRE)**[23] 4128 7-11-4 **93**..................... DavidBass(3) 99
(Lawney Hill) *hld up in last pair: smooth prog 6th: chsd wnr 3 out: shkn up after next: chal and nrly upsides last: nt qckn flat* **10/3**[2]
5-10 **3** *14* **Musashi (IRE)**[138] 1971 6-11-2 **98**..................... NathanAdams(10) 93
(Laura Mongan) *hld up last: trckd ldrs after 6th gng easily: outpcd and pushed along after 2 out: n.d after* **14/1**
0210 **4** *10* **Zelos Diktator**[27] 4049 5-11-4 **95**..................(p) JoshuaMoore(5) 79
(Gary Moore) *chsd ldrs: reminder 4th: rdn 6th: sn outpcd and btn* **5/1**
6221 **5** *11* **Spider Boy**[23] 4125 14-10-9 **86**..................(b) GemmaGracey-Davison(5) 61
(Zoe Davison) *mde most to 6th: rdn and steadily wknd after 3 out* **9/2**[3]
5-P6 **6** *22* **Birthday Star (IRE)**[23] 4125 9-9-7 **72** oh4..................(t) PeterHatton(7) 27
(Linda Jewell) *in tch: rdn and wknd after 6th: t.o* **20/1**
-005 **P** **Red Rock (FR)**[16] 4268 6-11-12 **98**..................... WayneHutchinson —
(Tor Sturgis) *in tch: rdn and wknd 5th: t.o last whn p.u bef 2 out* **8/1**

4m 21.0s (-14.60) **Going Correction** -0.825s/f (Firm) 7 Ran SP% **109.0**
Speed ratings (Par 105): **99,97,91,86,82 72,—**
toteswingers:1&2 £5.50, 2&3 £11.40, 1&3 £4.10 CSF £10.41 TOTE £3.90: £2.50, £1.20; EX 9.80.
Owner The Stewart Family **Bred** Irish National Stud **Trained** Sullington, W Sussex
FOCUS
A modest handicap hurdle in which the front two pulled well clear. The winner was on a good mark and is rated to the best of his hurdles form.
NOTEBOOK
Watergate(IRE) finally got off the mark, having fallen at the final fence last time with the race his for the taking. Running back over hurdles off the same mark, this looked an ideal opportunity on ground to suit. In the end he had to battle it out, but the way he pulled clear in the closing stages suggests that a step up in trip would help. This win should boost his confidence, and connections are likely to keep him on the go over hurdles until they can go back novice chasing next season. (op 2-1)
Giant O Murchu(IRE), an Irish point winner in November, seemed to enjoy the better ground, settling much better this time. He looks the sort to win his fair share of races, again probably over further. The front two pulled well clear.\n (op 7-2 tchd 4-1)
Musashi(IRE), a stone higher than for his win at Plumpton in September, is surely too high in the weights and needs some help from the handicapper. (op 10-1)
Zelos Diktator won here in January, but has disappointed since and it may be that he needs further than this on good ground. (op 11-2 tchd 6-1 and 9-2)
Spider Boy has been running well recently, but would have appreciated a bit of cut. (tchd 4-1)
Birthday Star(IRE) seems to be a difficult horse to train. (op 22-1 tchd 25-1 and 18-1)
T/Plt: £18.70 to a £1 stake. Pool of £59,468.03 - 2,309.47 winning tickets. T/Qpdt: £12.60 to a £1 stake. Pool of £3,459.99 - 202.32 winning tickets. JN

4219 WINCANTON (R-H)
Thursday, March 10

OFFICIAL GOING: Good to firm (good in places)
Rail realignment increased distances by 60yds per circuit on both tracks.
Wind: strong against Weather: overcast

4671 NEW BETFAIR EACH-WAY MULTIPLES H'CAP CHASE (13 fncs) 2m
2:00 (2:00) (Class 4) (0-105,105) 5-Y-0+ **£2,699** (£792; £396; £197)

Form / RPR
4-P **1** **Roudoudou Ville (FR)**[130] 2107 6-11-9 **102**..................... DenisO'Regan 123+
(Victor Dartnall) *chsd ldrs: hit 8th: j. sightly lft last 3: led 3 out: 3 l clr next: kpt on wl: comf* **4/1**[2]
P455 **2** *9* **Coach Lane**[3] 4529 10-11-5 **105**..................(p) SClements(7) 114
(Nick Mitchell) *prom: led 6th: rdn and hdd 3 out: kpt on but hld fr next* **16/1**
P601 **3** *5* **Laneguy (FR)**[7] 4447 6-11-4 **97** 7ex..................(t) PaddyBrennan 100
(Tom George) *chsd ldrs: rdn after 4 out: wnt 3rd next: kpt on same pce* **11/8**[1]
4213 **4** *shd* **Guns Of Love (IRE)**[22] 4142 9-10-8 **87**..................... CharliePoste 91
(Robin Dickin) *led tl 6th: chsd ldr tl rdn appr 3 out: kpt on same pce* **11/2**[3]
03F4 **P** **January**[112] 2484 8-11-8 **101**..................(t) TimmyMurphy —
(Liam Corcoran) *hld up but in tch: struggling whn awkward 4 out: wknd bef next: p.u bef 2 out* **7/1**
RP-1 **P** **Marsh Court**[37] 3873 8-11-9 **102**..................... TomO'Brien —
(Jamie Snowden) *slowly away: a in last: t.o fr 5th: p.u bef 8th* **15/2**

3m 57.9s (-2.00) **Going Correction** -0.275s/f (Good) 6 Ran SP% **107.6**
Speed ratings: **94,89,87,86,—,—**
toteswingers:1&2 £18.40, 2&3 £3.50, 1&3 £1.02 CSF £46.05 TOTE £5.40: £3.10, £11.10; EX 72.00.
Owner Exors of the Late P M De Wilde **Bred** J Poumaillou **Trained** Brayford, Devon
FOCUS
A moderate handicap which was run at a decent clip. The easy winner was up a stone on his hurdles fugure.
NOTEBOOK
Roudoudou Ville(FR) ◆ relished the underfoot conditions en-route to a first success in Britain. He was a dual bumper winner in France on fairly sound surfaces and had shown a liking for good ground on his hurdling debut for the Alners last term. He was pulled up on soft ground when having his first outing for Victor Dartnall at Carlisle in October, but that yard is now in much better form and he proved a totally different proposition here. This first success over fences, at the second attempt, ought to boost his confidence plenty and he appeals strongly as the sort to hold his own in a higher grade. His trainer later put the improvement down to a wind operation since his last run, and also the quicker ground. (op 7-2 tchd 3-1)
Coach Lane is on a long losing run but shaped a little better at Newton Abbot three days earlier, and this was a lot more like it from him in first-time cheekpieces. It's hoped he can go on from this again now the ground has come more in his favour. (tchd 14-1)

Laneguy(FR) would be able to reproduce that form under his penalty, as he was officially 5lb "well in". It was clear turning for home he was in trouble, though, and the combination of quicker ground and run coming so soon was probably to blame. (tchd 6-4)
Guns Of Love(IRE) wasn't particularly fluent under his usual positive ride and wasn't helped by being taken on for the lead. He still posted another game effort, though, and rates the benchmark. (op 6-1)
January attracted support with the ground in his favour returning from a 112-day break, but disappointed. (tchd 7-1 and 8-1)
Marsh Court, 9lb higher, had to be kidded into jumping off and was taken off her feet after hitting the first two fences. Something clearly went amiss. (tchd 7-1 and 8-1)

4672 DAILY NICHOLLS FESTIVAL COLUMN ON BETFAIR H'CAP HURDLE (8 hdls) 2m

2:30 (2:30) (Class 3) (0-120,118) 4-Y-0+ **£4,293** (£1,260; £630; £314)

Form				RPR
0/-0	**1**		**The Cayterers**[40] 2128 9-10-3 **100**.................... LeeEdwards(5)	109+
			(Tony Carroll) *trckd ldrs: led appr 2 out: sn clr: r.o wl* **9/1**	
0064	**2**	4 ½	**Robin Will (FR)**[61] 3454 6-11-10 **116**.................... NickScholfield	116
			(Paul Nicholls) *cl up: rdn after 3 out: hung lft after 2 out: wnt 2nd last: styd on same pce* **15/2**	
2502	**3**	2	**Tom O'Tara**[15] 4291 7-11-0 **106**.................... CharliePoste	104
			(Robin Dickin) *led tl rdn appr 2 out: styd on same pce* **15/2**	
UFP4	**4**	5	**Forest Rhythm (IRE)**[47] 3686 7-10-12 **107**.................... JimmyDerham(3)	101
			(Seamus Mullins) *hld up but wl in tch: rdn after 3 out: styd on but nvr gng pce to get on terms* **6/1**[2]	
-421	**5**	19	**Midnight Opera**[109] 2540 5-11-5 **118**.................... MarkQuinlan(7)	96
			(Neil Mulholland) *trckd ldrs: rdn after 3 out: wknd bef next: hmpd last* **15/2**	
654	**6**	10	**Bun Oir (USA)**[58] 3491 4-10-9 **109**.................... (p) TomO'Brien	68
			(Charlie Longsdon) *prom: rdn after 3 out: wknd bef next* **7/1**[3]	
04-5	**7**	nk	**Rayon Vert (FR)**[124] 2216 6-10-10 **102**.................... (t) RichardJohnson	69
			(Philip Hobbs) *in tch: effrt after 3 out: wknd next* **10/1**	
1/F0	**U**		**No To Trident**[41] 3793 6-10-11 **103**.................... RhysFlint	92
			(John Flint) *hld up but wl in tch: effrt after 3 out: one pce fr next: 5th and wl hld whn stmbld bdly and uns rdr sn after last* **5/1**[1]	
3530	**P**		**Ajman (IRE)**[28] 4031 6-10-12 **104**.................... (t) PaulMoloney	—
			(Evan Williams) *prom tl 5th: blnd bdly 3 out: sn wknd: p.u bef next* **9/1**	
003	**P**		**Aragall (GER)**[19] 4225 6-11-6 **112**.................... AndrewTinkler	—
			(George Baker) *hld up but wl in tch: rdn after 3 out: sn wknd: p.u bef next* **20/1**	

3m 43.2s (-5.70) **Going Correction** -0.275s/f (Good)
WFA 4 from 5yo+ 7lb **10** Ran SP% **112.6**
Speed ratings (Par 107): **103,100,99,97,87 82,82,—,—,—**
toteswingers:1&2 £32.50, 2&3 £10.50, 1&3 £17.60 CSF £72.21 CT £529.97 TOTE £10.10: £3.80, £2.30, £2.20; EX 88.80.
Owner R D Willis and M C Watts **Bred** Acrum Lodge Stud **Trained** Cropthorne, Worcs

FOCUS
An open handicap. There was an uneven pace on and it paid to race handily. A big hurdles best from the winner.

NOTEBOOK
The Cayterers arrived for this first outing over hurdles since November after two solid efforts in defeat on the AW, and ran out a ready winner. He was given a well-judged ride and hit top gear nearing two out. It was clear he was doing to do the business soon after and there could well be more to come after a likely rise, as he is well treated over hurdles in comparison with his Flat form. (op 6-1)
Robin Will(FR) ◆ proved uneasy in the betting for this switch to a handicap. He still ran just about his most encouraging effort to date, though, and really should be found an opening when reverting to a slightly stiffer test. (op 9-1)
Tom O'Tara proved free out in front early on, but was able to dominate the gallop and that saw him hold every chance in the home straight. He sets the level. (op 8-1)
Forest Rhythm(IRE) did best of those coming from off the pace and rates a little better than the bare form. (op 8-1)
Midnight Opera was making his handicap debut after a 109-day break and, not that surprisingly, found this too sharp back on quicker ground. Don't give up on him. (op 13-2 tchd 8-1 in a place)
No To Trident failed to raise his game for the better ground and was going backwards prior to unseating. (op 11-2 tchd 6-1)

4673 TIMEFORM BETFAIR RACING CLUB NOVICES' CHASE (21 fncs) 3m 1f 110y

3:00 (3:00) (Class 3) 5-Y-0+ **£4,664** (£1,448; £779)

Form				RPR
-154	**1**		**Dover's Hill**[25] 4093 9-11-1 127.................... (t) SamTwiston-Davies(3)	149+
			(Mary Hambro) *led tl rdn after 17th: rallied to regain ld 3 out: styd on strly to draw clr fr next: readily* **13/8**[2]	
-511	**2**	22	**Silver Kate (IRE)**[26] 4080 8-11-1 136.................... SamThomas	128+
			(David Richards) *nt a fluent: trckd wnr: awkward 13th (water): jnd wnr 15th: led after 17th: rdn after 4 out: hdd next: sn btn* **11/8**[1]	
04U3	**3**	9	**Earth Planet (IRE)**[7] 4445 9-10-7 121.................... (bt) MrMMahon(5)	112
			(Paul Nicholls) *trckd ldng pair: rdn after 17th: outpcd after 4 out* **9/2**[3]	
-F14	**P**		**Sheshali (IRE)**[28] 4030 7-11-4 124.................... PaulMoloney	—
			(Evan Williams) *chsd ldng trio: pushed along after 12th: lost tch 15th: p.u bef 4 out* **10/1**	

6m 35.2s (-4.30) **Going Correction** -0.275s/f (Good) **4** Ran SP% **107.5**
Speed ratings: **95,88,85,—**
CSF £4.36 TOTE £2.50; EX 5.10.
Owner Mrs Richard Hambro **Bred** Cotswold Stud **Trained** Bourton-on-the-Hill, Gloucs

FOCUS
An interesting novice chase, run at a sound gallop. A small personal best from the winner and the form could be rated a stone higher through the second and third.

NOTEBOOK
Dover's Hill gamely registered a second career success over fences. He likes to dominate, but wasn't left alone in front by the bang in-form Silver Kate and he appeared in trouble as that rival went past him on the final circuit. He responded in great style for his rider's urgings, though, and got back in front nearing the penultimate fence. He was comfortably on top at the last and this return to a sounder surface proved right up his street. Connections would do well to look for a bigger prize for him again after this as he should be high on confidence. There may be something for him at Aintree next month, but he does seem happier going this way round and one could see him running a big race in one of handicaps at the Punchestown Festival in May. (op 15-8 tchd 6-4)
Silver Kate(IRE) was the one to beat again despite a double penalty and things looked good for her as she went on at the fourth-last. She didn't extend thereafter, though, and her response was a tame one when the winner renewed his challenge. That was largely down to the quicker surface, but she did also pay for trying to push that rival hard from the off. She is also arguably at her best going left-handed and she remains capable of better, with the Welsh National at her beloved next season Chepstow the big target. She was later reported to have lost a shoe. (op 5-4 tchd 6-4)
Earth Planet(IRE) went well in the slipstream of the front pair for a long way, but he had cried enough before three and remains hard to win with. (op 5-1)
Sheshali(IRE) was expected to enjoy the quicker ground, but he was outpaced from the start and has now run well below par in two outings back this year. (op 8-1)

4674 BETFAIR.COM/MOBILE NOVICES' H'CAP CHASE (17 fncs) 2m 5f

3:35 (3:35) (Class 4) (0-115,112) 5-Y-0+ **£2,927** (£859; £429; £214)

Form				RPR
0-01	**1**		**Midnight Appeal**[28] 4022 6-11-6 **106**.................... RobertThornton	121+
			(Alan King) *hld up: jnd ldrs 13th: led after 4 out: idling whn nt fluent and jnd last: fnd plenty: pushed clr* **15/8**[1]	
-32P	**2**	2 ½	**Psi (USA)**[71] 3198 6-11-8 **108**.................... (b) JamieMoore	118
			(Gary Moore) *hld up bhd ldrs: cl 4th 13th: trckd wnr bef 3 out: rdn sn after 2 out: ev ch last: no ex* **6/1**[3]	
2033	**3**	22	**Bathwick Quest (IRE)**[22] 4140 7-11-12 **112**.................... TomScudamore	104
			(David Pipe) *led: hit 7th: rdn and hdd after 4 out: wknd 2 out: wnt lft last* **13/2**	
4P12	**4**	13	**Randjo (FR)**[22] 4142 6-11-3 **103**.................... DenisO'Regan	81
			(Victor Dartnall) *prom: hit 7th: rdn after 13th: wknd after next* **10/3**[2]	
054	**5**	64	**Inca Cave (IRE)**[25] 4091 6-11-1 **104**.................... (p) KeiranBurke(3)	25
			(Patrick Rodford) *nvr travelling: a in last: t.o fr after 8th: continued* **10/1**	
-204	**P**		**Lady Bling Bling**[12] 4355 10-11-6 **106**.................... MarkGrant	—
			(Peter Jones) *chsd ldrs tl 8th: sn pushed along: lost tch fr 10th: t.o whn p.u bef 3 out* **15/2**	
4-06	**P**		**Poseidon's Secret (IRE)**[15] 4290 8-10-8 **97**.................... (p) DannyCook(3)	—
			(John Panvert) *in tch tl 7th: t.o 9th: p.u bef 11th* **33/1**	

5m 16.6s (-8.60) **Going Correction** -0.275s/f (Good) **7** Ran SP% **109.3**
Speed ratings: **105,104,95,90,66 —,—**
toteswingers:1&2 £2.80, 2&3 £2.80, 1&3 £2.90 CSF £12.40 TOTE £2.90: £1.90, £1.90; EX 16.40.
Owner David Sewell **Bred** William Wilkinson **Trained** Barbury Castle, Wilts

FOCUS
A modest novice handicap, run at a sound gallop and two came clear in the home straight. Another step up from the progressive winner.

NOTEBOOK
Midnight Appeal ◆ followed up his chase debut success at Huntingdon last month off an 8lb higher mark, and again completed the task with something left in the tank. He moved by far the best through the race and looked set to go clear after taking it up going easily turning for home. He got there far too soon, however, as he idled markedly in between the final two fences and that allowed the runner-up his chance. Once that rival came at him he picked up again, though, and he is clearly fast improving. A sound surface looks important to his cause and a bold bid for the hat-trick is expected. (op 7-4 tchd 2-1)
Psi(USA) ◆, pulled up when last seen in December, travelled nicely into contention and held every chance from two out. He found the idling winner too resolute and remains winless over jumps, but can surely find a race before the season's end. (op 13-2 tchd 11-2)
Bathwick Quest(IRE), making her debut for David Pipe, was hassled for the lead pretty much throughout and eventually her stamina gave way over this longer trip. She deserves to find an opening over fences. (op 15-2 tchd 8-1)
Randjo(FR) was ridden as though stamina for this extra distance was no problem, but lacked fluency and stopped quickly on the back straight. He plugged on thereafter and has won on quick ground before, so it's hard to know what to make of this below-par effort. (tchd 3-1 and 7-2)

4675 BETTER ODDS ANYWHERE WITH BETFAIR MOBILE H'CAP HURDLE (10 hdls) 2m 4f

4:05 (4:05) (Class 5) (0-90,90) 4-Y-0+ **£1,951** (£573; £286; £143)

Form				RPR
-4P0	**1**		**Emmaslegend**[119] 2329 6-11-10 **88**.................... (t) ColinBolger	108+
			(Suzy Smith) *mid-div: hdwy after 7th: led appr 2 out: sn drew wl clr: easily* **16/1**	
-000	**2**	20	**Rivermouth**[36] 3877 6-11-5 **83**.................... (b[1]) RobertThornton	85
			(Alan King) *mid-div: rdn 3 out: styd on fr next: wnt 2nd run-in: no ch w wnr* **25/1**	
3340	**3**	1 ¾	**Miss Miracle**[85] 2956 4-10-12 **85**.................... (p) APMcCoy	77
			(Jonjo O'Neill) *sn trcking ldrs: led 3 out: rdn and hdd appr 2 out: sn hld by wnr: lost 2nd towards fin* **9/2**[2]	
6-F0	**4**	¾	**Diamanpeg (IRE)**[216] 1199 7-10-6 **70**.................... (v) RhysFlint	70
			(David Rees) *trckd ldrs: ev ch 3 out: sn rdn: styd on same pce fr next* **12/1**	
005	**5**	nse	**Jewellery (IRE)**[16] 4272 4-10-12 **85**.................... JamieMoore	76
			(Alison Thorpe) *chsd ldrs: rdn appr 7th: lost pl after hitting 3 out: styd on again fr last* **10/1**	
3400	**6**	15	**Jan Jandura (IRE)**[42] 3761 6-11-12 **90**.................... (t) RichardJohnson	76
			(Tim Vaughan) *hld up towards rr: stdy prog fr after 6th: rdn into 4th bef 2 out: wknd bef last* **11/1**	
P-PP	**7**	9	**Speedy Directa (GER)**[25] 4098 8-11-2 **80**.................... (vt) WarrenMarston	58
			(Milton Harris) *trckd ldrs: led 3rd tl 3 out: sn rdn: wknd bef next* **33/1**	
1P2	**8**	1 ¾	**Chestnut Ben (IRE)**[51] 3611 6-11-0 **78**.................... JamesDavies	55
			(Gary Brown) *hld up towards rr: hdwy after 7th: rdn after 3 out:* **12/1**	
00P	**9**	31	**Our Flora**[59] 3480 6-11-4 **82**.................... NickScholfield	31
			(Kim Bailey) *mid-div tl 4th: sn drvn in rr: t.o* **40/1**	
423F	**10**	29	**Vin Rose**[33] 3951 6-11-4 **85**.................... (t) PeterToole(3)	8
			(Mark Rimell) *a towards rr: t.o* **12/1**	
035F	**11**	17	**Celtic Ballad (IRE)**[16] 4269 5-11-6 **84**.................... JoeTizzard	—
			(Colin Tizzard) *prom early: drvn in rr 4th: sn t.o* **12/1**	
-400	**12**	65	**Fun Guy**[64] 3398 6-11-3 **88**.................... (t) NathanSweeney(7)	—
			(Bob Buckler) *mid-div tl wknd qckly 6th: sn t.o* **20/1**	
5-P5	**F**		**Macmar (FR)**[19] 4224 11-10-10 **81**.................... MrsMRoberts(7)	—
			(John Coombe) *prom: wknd sn after 3 out: bhd whn fell last* **4/1**[1]	
1P4P	**U**		**Gunship (IRE)**[105] 2645 10-10-13 **84**.................... (b) MrRGHenderson(7)	—
			(Cathy Hamilton) *led tl 3rd: in tch whn stmbld and uns rdr 5th* **22/1**	
0565	**F**		**Ladies Best**[117] 2367 7-11-2 **85**.................... (t) MattGriffiths(5)	—
			(Gordon Edwards) *hld up towards rr: fell heavily 3rd* **17/2**[3]	

4m 48.3s (-8.50) **Going Correction** -0.275s/f (Good)
WFA 4 from 5yo+ 8lb **15** Ran SP% **121.1**
Speed ratings (Par 103): **106,98,97,97,96 90,87,86,74,62 55,29,—,—,—**
toteswingers:1&2 £54.30, 2&3 £11.90, 1&3 £22.20 CSF £370.17 CT £2106.28 TOTE £23.70: £6.30, £5.60, £1.90; EX 613.50 TRIFECTA Not won..
Owner Pete Mercer **Bred** P J Mercer **Trained** Lewes, E Sussex

FOCUS
A weak handicap, run at a fair gallop and a very easy winner.

NOTEBOOK
Emmaslegend showed vastly improved form to score a first-career success at the ninth time of asking. She had shown ability in her final bumper run, but been out of sorts since and was hard to fancy returning from a 119-day break. Her time off the track has clearly been of benefit, however, and she was equipped with a first-time tongue tie. A hike in the handicap can now be expected so turning out under a penalty could be her best option. She is bred to be better than this level, though, and should be treated as an improver. (op 25-1)
Rivermouth looked anything but a simple ride in first-time blinkers on his handicap debut, but this was still by far his most encouraging effort. A step back up in trip looks on the cards. (op 22-1)

Miss Miracle turned in her best effort by some way on this handicap debut after a break. It was the first time she had sported cheekpieces since winning on her final Flat run for Clive Cox and she unsurprisingly proved much more at home on the quicker ground. (tchd 5-1)
Diamanpeg(IRE) posted a much-improved effort back from a 216-day layoff and is entitled to build on this. (op 18-1)
Jewellery(IRE) proved game and is worth a try over even further. (op 6-1)
Macmar(FR), very supported, dropped out tamely on the back straight and was well behind prior to falling at the last. (op 7-1)

4676 BETFAIR IPHONE & ANDROID APP MAIDEN HURDLE (DIV I) (8 hdls) 2m
4:40 (4:40) (Class 4) 4-Y-0+ **£1,951** (£573; £286; £143)

Form				RPR
2345	**1**		**Management (IRE)**[28] 4029 5-11-1 0 RobertThornton (Alan King) *trckd ldrs: led 2 out: sn rdn and edgd lft: wnt sltly rt last: styd on wl to assert: rdn out* **7/4**[1]	106+
3	**2**	*2 ½*	**Leitzu (IRE)**[35] 3906 4-10-0 0 WillKennedy (Mick Channon) *mid-div: hdwy on inner appr 2 out: wnt sltly rt last 2: rdn and ev ch last: kpt on same pce* **4/1**[3]	89
20	**3**	*3 ½*	**Spirit Is Needed (IRE)**[41] 3781 5-11-1 0 WarrenMarston (Milton Harris) *disp ld fr 3rd: outrt ldr after 3 out tl next: styd on same pce* **3/1**[2]	99
PP	**4**	*nk*	**Final Flyer (IRE)**[200] 1344 7-10-10 0 OliverDayman(5) (Alison Thorpe) *disp ld tl after 3 out: rdn in cl 3rd bef next: swtchd rt bef last: styd on same pce* **100/1**	99
5/	**5**	*3*	**Kings Flagship**[712] 4760 6-11-1 0 LiamHeard (Chris Down) *hld up towards rr: in tch whn rdn after 3 out: styd on wout ever threatening* **22/1**	96
0	**6**	*5*	**Captain Cool (IRE)**[8] 2958 4-10-4 0 JimmyDerham(3) (Richard Hannon) *mid-div: rdn into cl 5th 2 out: wknd last* **7/1**	84
6	**7**	*11*	**Gearbox (IRE)**[13] 3965 5-10-10 0 MissLHorner(5) (Liam Corcoran) *trckd ldrs: hit 5th: rdn after 3 out: wknd bef 2 out* **16/1**	80
00	**8**	*9*	**Salto Des Mottes (FR)**[19] 4225 5-10-8 0 MarkQuinlan(7) (Neil Mulholland) *hld up: mstke 3 out: sn rdn: wknd bef next* **125/1**	71
50-0	**9**	*48*	**Wallace Monument**[16] 4268 7-11-1 0 (p) JamesDavies (Gary Brown) *disp tl 3rd: chsd ldrs: rdn after 3 out: sn wknd: t.o* **50/1**	23
U0F	**U**		**Yourgolftravel Com**[28] 4028 6-10-12 0 (t) DannyCook(3) (David Pipe) *hld up bhd: tried to refuse and uns rdr bef 3rd* **20/1**	—

3m 47.6s (-1.30) **Going Correction** -0.275s/f (Good)
WFA 4 from 5yo+ 7lb **10** Ran SP% **112.6**
Speed ratings (Par 105): **92,90,89,88,87 84,79,74,50,—**
toteswingers:1&2 £2.20, 2&3 £3.20, 1&3 £2.50 CSF £8.36 TOTE £3.60: £2.10, £1.10, £1.30; EX 7.80.
Owner The Nighthawkers **Bred** Bluegate Stud **Trained** Barbury Castle, Wilts

FOCUS
An ordinary maiden, run at a steady gallop and in a relatively slow time. The winner was the form pick and produced a small step up.

NOTEBOOK
Management(IRE), well backed, got off the mark and made it third time lucky over hurdles. He showed an engine in bumpers, but had been beaten a long way in two previous outings since going jumping. The sounder surface was much more to liking, however, and he was given a sensible ride considering the race wasn't run to suit. He is not one of his yard's brighter lights, but is entitled to improve for a stiffer test. (op 11-4)
Leitzu(IRE) was probably most suited by the way the race unfolded and she posted a much-improved effort on this second outing over hurdles. The better ground no doubt helped and she clearly has a future at this game. (op 7-2)
Spirit Is Needed(IRE) was always up there and got done for speed when things became serious off the home turn. He needs a stiffer test and is capable of better. (op 5-2 tchd 10-3)
Final Flyer(IRE)'s proximity does little for the form as he had never previously completed. It was his first outing for 200 days, though, and he was helped by racing up with the ordinary gallop. The better ground also suited. (op 125-1)
Kings Flagship ought to come on a bundle for this first run since his debut in March 2009 and is yet another that will want a stiffer test to shine. (op 16-1)
Captain Cool(IRE) couldn't quicken sufficiently when it mattered, but he stays well on the Flat and was unsuited by the steady gallop. This was a step in the right direction. (op 13-2 tchd 6-1)

4677 BETFAIR IPHONE & ANDROID APP MAIDEN HURDLE (DIV II) (7 hdls 1 omitted) 2m
5:10 (5:13) (Class 4) 4-Y-0+ **£1,951** (£573; £286; £143)

Form				RPR
P2	**1**		**Sunley Peace**[35] 3906 7-11-1 0 JamieMoore (Gary Moore) *mid-div: awkward 2nd: hdwy into 2nd after 3 out: rdn to ld appr last: styd on wl: drvn out* **7/4**[1]	121+
1-13	**2**	*6*	**Mawsem (IRE)**[119] 2322 5-11-1 0 AndrewTinkler (George Baker) *trckd ldrs: rdn after 3 out: styd on same pce fr next: wnt 2nd towards fin: no ch w wnr* **7/4**[1]	114
0	**3**	*¾*	**Sea Change (IRE)**[61] 3443 4-10-7 0 (b[1]) TomScudamore (David Pipe) *led 2nd: rdn and hdd after 2 out: styd on same pce: lost 2nd towards fin* **4/1**[2]	105
65-	**4**	*8*	**Peedeeque**[339] 5050 5-11-1 0 NickScholfield (Andy Turnell) *trckd ldrs: rdn after 3 out: one pce fr next* **16/1**[3]	106
-306	**5**	*8*	**Joker Choker (IRE)**[25] 4094 6-10-12 0 RichardKilloran(3) (Nicky Henderson) *mid-div: rdn after 3 out: nvr any imp* **16/1**[3]	99
5	**6**	*21*	**Stan's Cool Cat (IRE)**[24] 4118 5-10-8 0 RobertThornton (Alan King) *trckd ldrs: rdn to chse ldr briefly after 3 out: wknd next: t.o* **16/1**[3]	73
	7	*½*	**Guam (IRE)**[102] 6-10-12 0 DannyCook(3) (Nick Mitchell) *sweating: led tl 2nd: chsd ldr tl nt fluent next: sn in rr: t.o* **50/1**	80
6-06	**8**	*6*	**Cody Wyoming**[26] 4082 5-11-1 0 SamThomas (Heather Main) *a towards rr: t.o* **33/1**	74
-000	**9**	*53*	**Tenitemsplustoast**[19] 4225 5-11-1 0 LiamHeard (Patrick Rodford) *a bhd: t.o* **150/1**	27
6	**U**		**Caunay**[41] 3794 4-10-0 0 MarkQuinlan(7) (Neil Mulholland) *mid-div: struggling 3rd: wknd after 3 out: t.o whn blnd and uns rdr last* **100/1**	—

3m 42.4s (-6.50) **Going Correction** -0.275s/f (Good)
WFA 4 from 5yo+ 7lb **10** Ran SP% **116.9**
Speed ratings (Par 105): **105,102,101,97,93 83,82,79,53,—**
toteswingers:1&2 £1.40, 2&3 £2.10, 1&3 £3.10 CSF £4.82 TOTE £2.40: £1.10, £1.30, £1.60; EX 6.40.
Owner Davies, Sunley and Cox **Bred** Milton Park Stud Partnership **Trained** Lower Beeding, W Sussex

FOCUS
The flight after the winning post was omitted; low sun. This second division of the maiden was the more interesting of the pair and it was run at a much better gallop. Sound form for the class, with a big step up from the winner and the second to his mark.

NOTEBOOK
Sunley Peace improved when a well-held second to Supreme Novice hopeful Gibb River here last time out, and stepped up on that to go one better and open his account over hurdles. He travelled best of all in the race and got to the front nearing the last despite not being fluent two out. He stayed very well on the Flat and so wasn't for catching after the last, and this quicker ground was much more to his liking. It will be interesting to see what handicap mark he now gets. (tchd 13-8 and 15-8)
Mawsem(IRE) ◆, a dual bumper winner, was the form pick here on the level of his hurdling debut at Ludlow in November. He proved easy to back, though, and lost out by hitting a flat spot nearing the home turn. He's crying out for a stiffer test and should improve. (op 15-8 tchd 2-1)
Sea Change(IRE) was interesting in first-time blinkers back on better ground and he duly improved a lot on the form of his hurdling debut at Sandown in January. He too probably needs a stiffer test and has one of these within his compass. (op 7-1)
Peedeeque showed ability in two bumpers and didn't go unbacked for this switch to hurdling, despite returning from a 339-day layoff. He got outpaced when it mattered, but again showed promise and can build on this over further. (op 20-1)
T/Jkpt: Not won. T/Plt: £417.90 to a £1 stake. Pool of £69,881.87 - 122.07 winning tickets.
T/Qpdt: £26.40 to a £1 stake. Pool of £4,494.11 - 125.60 winning tickets. TM

4678 - 4683a (Foreign Racing) - See Raceform Interactive

4302 AYR (L-H)
Friday, March 11

OFFICIAL GOING: Soft (good to soft in places on hurdle course; hdl 7.4; chs 6.9)
Wind: Strong, half against Weather: Overcast

4684 BACARDI ORIGINALS MAIDEN HURDLE (11 hdls) 2m 4f
2:10 (2:10) (Class 5) 4-Y-0+ **£2,055** (£599; £299)

Form				RPR
110-	**1**		**Drumbaloo (IRE)**[12] 4383 7-11-2 0 RCColgan (J J Lambe, Ire) *prom: hdwy whn lft 3 l 2nd 3 out: led next: drvn out fr last* **2/1**[2]	111+
	2	*3 ¼*	**Rathnaroughy (IRE)**[26] 4111 7-11-2 0 CampbellGillies (S R B Crawford, Ire) *nt fluent: hld up: hdwy and lft 8 l 3rd 3 out: sn rdn: hung lft and chsd wnr run-in: r.o* **20/1**	106
-	**3**	*2 ¼*	**Bennative (IRE)**[14] 4338 6-10-13 95 SWJackson(3) (S Donohoe, Ire) *led: jst hdd whn lft 3 l in front 3 out: hdd next: one pce and lost 2nd run-in* **18/1**	103
/005	**4**	*33*	**China House (IRE)**[17] 4278 8-11-2 0 GrahamLee (Lisa Williamson) *t.k.h: in tch: drvn and outpcd after 4 out: no imp fr next* **25/1**	70
0-5P	**5**	*1 ½*	**Izzy Bella**[59] 3498 5-10-9 77 MarkBradburne (Sue Bradburne) *in tch: drvn and outpcd whn lft mod 4th 3 out: sn no imp* **80/1**	61
056	**6**	*21*	**Heather Glen (IRE)**[19] 4245 5-10-9 0 HenryOliver (Sue Smith) *nt jump wl: sn bhd: struggling fnl circ: nvr on terms* **66/1**	40
	7	*nse*	**Georgiebegood (IRE)**[339] 10-10-9 0 PeterBuchanan (S R B Crawford, Ire) *towards rr: struggling fr 7th: sn btn* **50/1**	40
P	**8**	*22*	**Lay De Brook**[15] 4304 6-10-9 0 JamesReveley (Jim Goldie) *nt fluent in rr: struggling fr 7th: t.o* **100/1**	18
	F		**Realt Mor (IRE)**[761] 6-11-2 0 DougieCostello (Nicky Richards) *t.k.h: pressed ldr: jst led gng wl and 1 l in front whn fell 3 out* **5/4**[1]	114+
00P-	**P**		**Boston Lad (IRE)**[510] 1791 7-10-11 0 AlexanderVoy(5) (Lucy Normile) *trckd ldrs tl wknd 7th: t.o whn p.u bef 4 out* **125/1**	—
0	**P**		**Emrani (USA)**[16] 4283 4-10-4 0 (p) JohnKington(3) (Donald McCain) *nt fluent: prom: lost pl after 2nd: reminders next: sn struggling: t.o whn p.u after 7th* **10/1**[3]	—
0004	**U**		**North Brook (IRE)**[24] 4132 6-10-13 0 EwanWhillans(3) (Alistair Whillans) *hld up: hdwy to chse ldrs 6th: four l 3rd and one pce whn stmbld and uns rdr 3 out* **11/1**	100

5m 21.7s (9.70) **Going Correction** +0.375s/f (Yiel)
WFA 4 from 5yo+ 8lb **12** Ran SP% **115.5**
Speed ratings (Par 103): **95,93,92,79,79 70,70,61,—,— —,—**
toteswingers:1&2:£6.00, 1&3:£9.00, 2&3:£28.70 CSF £41.47 TOTE £3.50: £1.80, £2.50, £3.90; EX 25.80.
Owner Tee Bee Racing Ltd/N Patterson/N Wilson **Bred** Stephanie Hanly **Trained** Dungannon, Co. Tyrone

FOCUS
After 6mm of rain overnight the ground was described as 'very holding'. An ordinary maiden hurdle. The picture changed dramatically at the third-last flight and in the end the result was an Irish-trained one-two-three.

NOTEBOOK
Drumbaloo(IRE), a winner three times in bumper company including a Grade 2 success, was having his fourth start over hurdles. Hard at work four out, he looked booked for second spot when the leader departed. He made very hard work of it in the end. (op 11-4)
Rathnaroughy(IRE), an Irish point winner, was making his hurdling debut. He was handed third spot three out and chased the winner going to the last. He looks to have a lot more stamina than speed. (op 14-1)
Bennative(IRE), another winning Irish pointer, has struggled to make much impact over hurdles. He took the favourite along and was left in front. He fought back when headed and this was a much more encouraging effort. (op 20-1)
Realt Mor(IRE)winner of maiden point in Ireland two years ago on his only previous start, was all the rage and travelled supremely well upsides the leader. Taking charge going to three out, he looked in total command when he came down. A grand type, he will surely make amends. (tchd 11-8 and 6-4 in a place)
Emrani(USA), a winner three times on the Flat last year in Ireland, jumped poorly and was tailed off first time. He again did not jump fluently and was soon being driven along. He lost touch early on the final circuit and is one to have severe reservations about. (tchd 11-8 and 6-4 in a place)
North Brook(IRE), steadily coming to hand, was stepping up in trip and was fourth and held when getting rid of his rider three out. (tchd 11-8 and 6-4 in a place)

4685 CORONA BEGINNERS' CHASE (19 fncs) 3m 1f
2:45 (2:45) (Class 4) 5-Y-0+ **£3,332** (£1,034; £557)

Form				RPR
3422	**1**		**Cool Mission (IRE)**[16] 4282 7-11-0 129 (p) GrahamLee (Donald McCain) *led to 2nd: cl up: led 12th: rdn and styd on wl fr 3 out* **4/6**[1]	127+
/P53	**2**	*8*	**Steady Tiger (IRE)**[27] 4063 9-11-0 113 FearghalDavis (Nicky Richards) *trckd ldrs: wnt 2nd 13th: effrt bef 4 out: no ex fr 2 out* **5/1**[2]	115
3P2F	**3**	*4 ½*	**Ballymacduff (IRE)**[13] 4362 7-11-0 108 (t) JanFaltejsek (George Charlton) *j.rt: led 2nd to 12th: outpcd bef 5 out: n.d after* **5/1**[2]	110

P **P** **The Skanky Farmer**[125] 2202 11-11-0 0........................ PeterBuchanan —
(Sandy Thomson) *hld up in tch: blnd 6th: sn struggling: t.o whn p.u 12th* **50/1**

-405 **P** **Kingsmoss (IRE)**[39] 3851 6-11-0 114........................ RCColgan —
(J J Lambe, Ire) *hld up in tch: outpcd 8th: rallied 11th: wknd next: t.o whn p.u 3 out* **8/1**[3]

7m 0.50s (10.60) **Going Correction** +0.30s/f (Yiel) **5** Ran SP% **106.4**
Speed ratings: **95,92,91,—,—**
CSF £4.19 TOTE £1.80: £1.40, £2.10; EX 4.20.
Owner T G Leslie **Bred** Mrs Eleanor Kent **Trained** Cholmondeley, Cheshire

FOCUS
This was run at just a steady pace in the testing conditions. The winner was value for further and didn't need to improve.

NOTEBOOK
Cool Mission(IRE), runner-up behind two much stronger opponents in his two previous starts, opened his account over fences at the fifth attempt. He tends to run lazily and sported cheekpieces for a second time. After regaining the lead, he had only to be kept up to his work, but it was hardly impressive. (op 8-11)
Steady Tiger(IRE) who had 16lb to find with the winner, has taken time to find his form after 21 months on the sidelines. Stepping up in trip, he stuck to his task in vain pursuit and deserves to go one better. (tchd 9-2)
Ballymacduff(IRE), a headstrong sort who had two and a half stone to find with the winner and 19lb with the runner-up, jumped better on just his third start over fences, even though he was inclined to go right-handed at times. He looked likely to drop right away starting the home turn but to his credit was sticking on at the line. He will be better going the other way round and should improve and find a novices' chase. (op 11-2)
The Skanky Farmer Official explanation: trainer said gelding bled from the nose

4686 GUINNESS NOVICES' H'CAP HURDLE (9 hdls) 2m
3:20 (3:20) (Class 4) (0-105,102) 4-Y-0+ **£2,602** (£764; £382; £190)

Form RPR

-P26 **1** **Imperial Breeze (IRE)**[57] 3523 6-11-9 **99**........................(t) RCColgan 104+
(J J Lambe, Ire) *hld up: hdwy 4 out: effrt next: rdn to chal run-in: led nr fin* **8/1**

5223 **2** *shd* **King's Chorister**[24] 4136 5-9-7 **76** oh3........................(t) HenryBrooke(7) 80+
(Barry Murtagh) *hld up: smooth hdwy and cl up whn hit 3 out: led bef last: hrd pressed run-in: hdd nr fin* **3/1**[1]

F-04 **3** *7* **Lewlaur Supreme (IRE)**[15] 4304 8-11-0 **90**........................ GrahamLee 87
(Jim Goldie) *chsd ldr to 3rd: wnt 2nd 4 out: rdn and no ex fr 2 out* **4/1**[2]

40-6 **4** *3 ½* **Arran Law (IRE)**[15] 4303 7-11-7 **97**........................ CampbellGillies 94+
(Lucinda Russell) *led and clr: rdn 3 out: hdd bef last where blnd: sn btn* **16/1**

F-04 **5** *10* **Canal Cottage (IRE)**[30] 3999 7-11-6 **96**........................ PeterBuchanan 79
(Lucinda Russell) *midfield: rdn and outpcd after 5th: plugged on fr 2 out: nvr on terms* **7/1**[3]

0-0P **6** *1 ¼* **Oh Landino (GER)**[15] 4303 6-9-7 **76**........................ PaulNorton(7) 58
(Jim Goldie) *bhd: struggling 1/2-way: sme late hdwy: nvr on terms* **10/1**

0P04 **7** *½* **Claude Carter**[19] 4243 7-10-9 **88**........................ EwanWhillans(3) 70
(Alistair Whillans) *chsd ldrs: drvn after 4 out: wknd fr next* **12/1**

00-0 **8** *9* **Agricultural**[39] 3850 5-9-11 **76**........................ JamesHalliday(3) 49
(Lucy Normile) *t.k.h: chsd wnr fr 3rd to 4 out: sn rdn: wknd bef next* **14/1**

000 **9** *16* **Parc Des Princes (USA)**[44] 3746 5-11-4 **94**........................ DougieCostello 51
(Nicky Richards) *bhd: struggling 1/2-way: nvr on terms* **16/1**

2-54 **10** *8* **Beverly Hill Billy**[39] 3855 7-11-5 **102**........................ PaulGallagher(7) 51
(Sandy Forster) *prom tl rdn and wknd after 4 out* **15/2**

4m 7.00s (3.90) **Going Correction** +0.375s/f (Yiel) **10** Ran SP% **115.6**
Speed ratings (Par 105): **105,104,101,99,94 94,93,89,81,77**
toteswingers:1&2:£6.20, 1&3:£8.40, 2&3:£3.60 CSF £32.71 CT £111.83 TOTE £9.00: £2.90, £1.40, £2.10; EX 41.60.
Owner Tee Bee Racing Limited **Bred** Thomas Norris **Trained** Dungannon, Co. Tyrone

FOCUS
A modest 2m handicap hurdle run at a sound pace, and there were just four in serious contention three from home. There is a case for rating the form a few pounds higher.

NOTEBOOK
Imperial Breeze(IRE), dropped in trip after failing to see out an extra 3f on his handicap debut at Catterick, improved from off the pace in a first-time tongue-tie. Inclined to hang when produced going to the last, in the end he did just enough. (op 9-1)
King's Chorister, a maiden after 13 attempts but placed in his last three starts, settled much better. Running from 3lb out of the handicap, after hitting the front, he battled back well and was only just denied. He deserves to get off the mark. (op 7-2 tchd 11-4 and 4-1 in a place)
Lewlaur Supreme(IRE), having his third outing for this yard, was another dropping back in trip. In pursuit of the leader four out, he kept on to snatch a well-held third soon after the final flight. (op 7-1)
Arran Law(IRE), making his handicap debut on his second start in two weeks after 16 months on the sidelines, set a brisk pace but was third and well held when blundering at the last. He is entitled to improve again. (op 12-1)
Beverly Hill Billy Official explanation: trainer said gelding bled from the nose

4687 CARLSBERG H'CAP HURDLE (12 hdls) 3m 110y
3:55 (3:56) (Class 5) (0-95,95) 4-Y-0+ **£2,055** (£599; £299)

Form RPR

0-54 **1** **Easter Vic**[27] 4062 10-10-9 **81**........................(p) JamesO'Farrell(3) 89+
(Robert Goldie) *bhd: drvn 1/2-way: plenty to do 4 out: hdwy bef next: led between last 2: styd on strly* **16/1**

P4P2 **2** *3 ½* **Charming Knight (IRE)**[37] 3883 10-10-9 **85**........................ AlistairFindlay(7) 89
(Jane Walton) *cl up: led 4 out: clr bef next: hdd between last 2: rallied: kpt on same pce run-in* **6/1**[3]

0-5U **3** *19* **Bubbly Breeze (IRE)**[37] 3883 6-11-4 **87**........................ JamesReveley 74
(Pauline Robson) *hld up: stdy hdwy 1/2-way: rdn bef 4 out: rallied to chse ldr briefly next: wknd fr 2 out* **7/2**[2]

U401 **4** *8* **Sundown Trail (IRE)**[15] 4302 6-11-8 **91**........................ FearghalDavis 71
(Nicky Richards) *trckd ldrs: rdn after 4 out: wknd bef 2 out* **5/2**[1]

5521 **5** *23* **Vallani (IRE)**[23] 4146 6-11-8 **91**........................ PeterBuchanan 45
(Lucinda Russell) *led: mstke and hdd 4 out: wknd bef next* **7/2**[2]

0P36 **P** **Soprano (GER)**[23] 4146 9-11-12 **95**........................(p) GrahamLee —
(Jim Goldie) *nt jump wl: sn towards rr: effrt u.p 8th: wknd next: t.o whn p.u 3 out* **7/1**

34-P **P** **Lady Sambury**[24] 4138 9-11-2 **85**........................(t) MichaelMcAlister —
(Maurice Barnes) *hld up: stdy hdwy 1/2-way: wknd after 7th: t.o whn p.u bef 4 out* **25/1**

P000 **P** **Beano Boy**[15] 4302 6-9-7 **69** oh9........................(v[1]) HenryBrooke(7) —
(Brian Storey) *cl up tl lost pl after 6th: sn lost tch: p.u bef next* **40/1**

6m 38.3s (6.50) **Going Correction** +0.375s/f (Yiel) **8** Ran SP% **112.0**
Speed ratings (Par 103): **104,102,96,94,86 —,—,—**
toteswingers:1&2:£8.70, 1&3:£9.30, 2&3:£4.90 CSF £103.14 CT £415.04 TOTE £15.80: £3.30, £3.20, £1.90; EX 98.90.
Owner Robert H Goldie **Bred** Robert H Goldie **Trained** Dundonald, S Ayrshire

FOCUS
They seemed to go off too fast for their own good in this modest stayers' handicap hurdle. A step up from the winner, who is lightly raced for her age.

NOTEBOOK
Easter Vic, a point winner in the distant past, has come down 12lb since her handicap debut three outings previously. She came from way off the pace to master the runner-up going to the final flight, but whether this result flatters this seemingly exposed 10-y-o remains to be seen. (op 18-1 tchd 20-1)
Charming Knight(IRE), a winner of four points, had shown improved form when runner-up at Newcastle on his previous start. He has shown he stays really well and, taking charge four out, went down fighting. (op 15-2 tchd 9-2)
Bubbly Breeze(IRE), looking a big danger when losing his rider three out in the Newcastle race in which Charming Knight was runner-up, was given an ultra-patient ride. He moved up with a circuit to go but, driven four out, could only keep on at same pace from the next. He might make a better chaser next time round. \n\x\x \bSundown Trail\p, who landed a punt here from a 7lb lower mark when dropped back to 2m4f, emptied badly in the home straight and will no doubt drop back in trip.\n (op 5-1)
Vallani(IRE), off the mark at the 22nd attempt at Musselburgh from a 6lb lower mark, set what seemed a very strong gallop and in the end he stopped to nothing. (op 3-1)
Soprano(GER) didn't jump well and was soon being cajoled along. He looks one to have severe reservations about now. (op 13-2 tchd 15-2)

4688 COCA-COLA H'CAP HURDLE (FOR THE JAMES BARCLAY CHALLENGE TROPHY) (12 hdls) 2m 5f 110y
4:30 (4:30) (Class 4) (0-105,99) 4-Y-0+ **£2,602** (£764; £382; £190)

Form RPR

4U56 **1** **Shooting Times**[18] 4255 6-11-6 **96**........................ JamesHalliday(3) 101
(Andrew Parker) *hld up bhd ldrs: smooth hdwy to chal 2 out: led last: rdn out* **10/1**

023- **2** *1 ½* **Top Brass (IRE)**[14] 4341 10-11-2 **96**........................ MrCCully(7) 98
(James H Black, Ire) *hld up in tch: rdn and outpcd bef 3 out: rallied next: styd on to take 2nd towards fin: nt rch wnr* **5/1**[3]

6000 **3** *nk* **Fightstar (FR)**[27] 4068 7-11-3 **90**........................(p) CampbellGillies 93
(Lucinda Russell) *cl up: led 2nd: rdn whn jnd 2 out: hdd last: kpt on u.p run-in* **9/1**

-P0U **4** *9* **I Witness (IRE)**[28] 4057 9-10-9 **89**........................(t) AlistairFindlay(7) 82
(Jane Walton) *cl up: effrt bef 3 out: rdn and outpcd fr next* **12/1**

0-03 **5** *3 ½* **See The Legend**[27] 4068 6-10-10 **83**........................ PaddyAspell 72
(Sandy Forster) *trckd ldrs: drvn and outpcd appr 3 out: wknd fr next* **15/8**[1]

06 **6** *3 ¾* **Maid In Moscow (IRE)**[15] 4304 7-10-11 **91**........................ MrRMJohnston(7) 76
(S R B Crawford, Ire) *stdd in tch on outside: effrt bef 3 out: sn outpcd: n.d after* **18/1**

-405 **7** *1 ¾* **Miss Abbey**[44] 3747 7-11-7 **94**........................(t) GrahamLee 78
(Jim Goldie) *t.k.h: trckd ldrs: effrt 3 out: wknd bef next* **4/1**[2]

00F0 **P** **Monsoon Music (IRE)**[15] 4302 7-9-11 **73** oh9........................ EwanWhillans(3) —
(Lucinda Russell) *led to 2nd: cl up tl lost pl 7th: struggling after next: t.o whn p.u bef 3 out* **12/1**

6m 0.80s (20.50) **Going Correction** +0.375s/f (Yiel)
WFA 4 from 6yo+ 8lb **8** Ran SP% **111.2**
Speed ratings (Par 105): **77,76,76,73,71 70,69,—**
toteswingers:1&2:£4.50, 1&3:£7.50, 2&3:£5.60 CSF £56.15 CT £454.80 TOTE £13.20: £2.80, £1.10, £2.90; EX 52.10.
Owner Mrs I C Lancaster **Bred** Mrs J M Lancaster **Trained** Ecclefechan, D'fries & G'way
■ Stewards' Enquiry : Mr C Cully five-day ban: used whip with excessive frequency without giving gelding time to respond (Mar 25,31,Apr 4,5,7)

FOCUS
Another modest handicap hurdle. They went much steadier this time and as a result all bar one were still in with a shout turning for home. The first two are rated to their marks.

NOTEBOOK
Shooting Times, stepping up in trip on just his second try in handicap company, travelled strongly and in the end did more than enough. There should be a bit better to come. Official explanation: trainer said, regarding apparent improvement in form, that the gelding appreciated the step up in trip and the flat course. (op 7-1)
Top Brass(IRE), an Irish raider, did not lack support. Having his second outing in two weeks after a ten-month break, he kept on to chase home the winner without ever really threatening him. (op 13-2 tchd 9-2)
Fightstar(FR), whose jumping was not error free, took charge and was clinging on to second spot when he made his final error at the final flight. He might appreciate much less testing ground. (op 11-1 tchd 12-1)
I Witness(IRE), who failed to get round on his chase debut, was having just his second start in handicap company. (op 16-1)
See The Legend, having her second start in four weeks after missing nine months, was stepping up up in trip from a 6lb higher mark. She never really threatened. (tchd 7-4 and 2-1 and 9-4 in a place)
Miss Abbey, making her handicap bow, travelled strongly under a patient ride but in the end dropped right away. She may need much better ground than she encountered here. Official explanation: trainer said filly suffered a breathing problem (tchd 9-2)

4689 JOHN SMITH'S H'CAP CHASE (19 fncs) 3m 1f
5:05 (5:05) (Class 3) (0-135,133) 5-Y-0+ **£5,204** (£1,528; £764; £381)

Form RPR

6301 **1** **Garleton (IRE)**[27] 4066 10-9-13 **111**........................ AlexanderVoy(5) 124+
(Maurice Barnes) *led to 3rd: cl up: led 7th: mde rest: rdn and styd on gamely fr 2 out* **10/3**[1]

-24U **2** *1 ½* **Heez A Steel (IRE)**[22] 4167 10-10-12 **126**........................ AlistairFindlay(7) 133
(George Charlton) *cl up: chal fnl circ: rdn 3 out: kpt on fr last: nt pce of wnr* **8/1**

0-01 **3** *10* **Alexander Oats**[27] 4063 8-10-9 **119**........................ HarryHaynes(3) 117
(Robert Goldie) *hld up: stdy hdwy and in tch whn mstke 14th: sn rdn: plugged on fr 2 out: no imp* **20/1**

U1P2 **4** *½* **Sibenek (IRE)**[27] 4063 7-11-1 **122**........................(p) JamesReveley 119
(Martin Todhunter) *midfield: blnd 3rd: hdwy and prom 12th: effrt bef 4 out: outpcd fr next* **12/1**

0561 **5** *14* **Lampion Du Bost (FR)**[15] 4306 12-10-8 **115**........................ GrahamLee 100
(Jim Goldie) *cl up: rdn after 5 out: wknd bef 3 out* **5/1**[3]

F052 **6** *13* **Leac An Scail (IRE)**[14] 4328 10-10-9 **116**........................ HenryOliver 86
(Sue Smith) *prom: outpcd whn blnd 12th: sn struggling* **9/2**[2]

032P **7** *18* **See You There (IRE)**[24] 4137 12-10-7 **114**........................(t) PeterBuchanan 66
(Lucinda Russell) *sn towards rr: struggling 1/2-way: nvr on terms* **11/1**

-661 **P** **Wild Cane Ridge (IRE)**[24] 4137 12-10-9 **116**........................(b) WilsonRenwick —
(Rose Dobbin) *bhd: rdn and outpcd 1/2-way: t.o whn p.u bef 5 out* **7/1**

F6PV **P** **Mr Woods**[18] 4256 9-10-3 **117**........................(p) GaryRutherford(7) —
(Harriet Graham) *a bhd: struggling 1/2-way: t.o whn p.u bef 4 out* **14/1**

1-PP **P** **Palace Merano (FR)**[57] 3522 8-10-8 **118**....................(b[1]) JohnKington(3) —
(Donald McCain) *cl up: led 3rd to 7th: blnd and lost pl 11th: bhd whn mstke 13th: p.u bef 5 out* **25/1**

6m 52.6s (2.70) **Going Correction** +0.30s/f (Yiel) **10** Ran SP% **112.8**
Speed ratings: **107,106,103,103,98 94,88,—,—,—**
toteswingers:1&2:£5.40, 1&3:£11.20, 2&3:£9.80 CSF £29.39 CT £453.34 TOTE £3.70: £1.30, £2.70, £5.40; EX 33.60.
Owner East-West Partnership **Bred** Thomas And Mrs Bridget Buckley **Trained** Farlam, Cumbria

FOCUS
A decent stayers' handicap chase in which the pace was generous. The winner seems to have improved and there may be more to come.

NOTEBOOK
Garleton(IRE), who relishes give underfoot, was racing from a 13lb higher mark after his easy C&D win a month ago. Again his jumping was a pleasure to watch and, racing with real enthusiasm, he was always holding the runner-up. He seems better than ever and is a credit to his yard. (op 9-2)
Heez A Steel(IRE), having just his sixth start over fences, is an out-and-out stayer. He renewed his effort to chase the winner from four out but hard as he tried he could not get his head in front. He is 2lb below his hurdle-race mark and deserves a second chase success. (op 10-1)
Alexander Oats, raised an incredible 33lb after accounting for Sibenek in a novices' chase here last month on his chasing debut, stuck on in his own time to claim a never dangerous third spot at the last. (op 12-1)
Sibenek(IRE), who again had the cheekpieces on, ran to his course form with the runner-up and is starting to build a more consistent profile. (op 10-1)
Lampion Du Bost(FR), raised a stone after his wide-margin C&D success last month, had to race from a career-high mark and couldn't dominate this time. (op 11-2)
Leac An Scail(IRE) was struggling to keep up early on the final circuit. (op 4-1)
Mr Woods Official explanation: trainer said gelding bled from the nose

4690 J20 CONDITIONAL JOCKEYS' H'CAP CHASE (17 fncs) 2m 4f
5:40 (5:42) (Class 5) (0-95,88) 5-Y-O+ **£1,951** (£573; £286; £143)

Form RPR

2452 **1** **Innominate (IRE)**[27] 4064 9-11-7 **86**........................(tp) CampbellGillies(3) 99+
(Lucinda Russell) *led to 3rd: cl up: led 11th: mde rest: drew clr fr 2 out: comf* **7/4**[1]

-325 **2** *5* **Soul Angel**[27] 4064 7-11-6 **85**........................(v[1]) PaulGallagher(3) 86
(Sandy Forster) *cl up: rdn along 1/2-way: ev ch bef 4 out: one pce fr 2 out* **3/1**[2]

-400 **3** *24* **Nifty Roy**[27] 4064 11-11-7 **83**........................(p) JamesHalliday 60
(Brian Storey) *cl up: led 3rd: blnd 10th: hdd next: outpcd 5 out: n.d after* **20/1**

-20P **4** *29* **King Penda (IRE)**[44] 3748 8-11-9 **88**........................ FearghalDavis(3) 36
(Nicky Richards) *t.k.h: hld up in tch: stdy hdwy 1/2-way: rdn and wknd qckly bef 4 out* **7/2**[3]

50/ **U** **Instigator**[69] 3321 8-11-9 **85**........................(bt) SWJackson —
(S Donohoe, Ire) *mstkes: in tch: struggling 9th: sn lost tch: t.o whn mstke and uns rdr last* **9/2**

5m 40.9s (18.00) **Going Correction** +0.30s/f (Yiel) **5** Ran SP% **106.5**
Speed ratings: **76,74,64,52,—**
CSF £7.01 TOTE £2.50: £1.40, £2.00; EX 7.10.
Owner Mr And Mrs T P Winnell **Bred** Michael Crean **Trained** Arlary, Perth & Kinross

FOCUS
A depleted field for this low-grade finale and just two seriously involved from five out. The winner was value for further and the second ran to his mark.

NOTEBOOK
Innominate(IRE), with all the aids fitted, opened his account over fences at the 19th time of asking, racing from a mark 20lb below what he achieved over hurdles. He is jumping better now, was in total command four out and cruised home. (op 9-4)
Soul Angel, given reminders setting out on to the final circuit, wore a visor for the first time. He was the only one to keep tabs on the winner but was always playing second fiddle. (tchd 5-2)
Nifty Roy, without a win for almost four years, was tried in cheekpieces. After a blunder early on the final circuit he was left well behind from five out. He looks a light of other days. (op 12-1)
King Penda(IRE), pulled up over 3m on his first try over fences, wouldn't settle and stopped to nothing five out. Presumably he has some sort of problem. (tchd 11-4)
Instigator Official explanation: jockey said, regarding running and riding, although the gelding became detached, it had jumped satisfactorily until the last fence.
T/Jkpt: Not won. T/Plt: £237.30 to a £1 stake. Pool:£55,791.78 - 171.61 winning tickets T/Qpdt: £71.90 to a £1 stake. Pool:£4,130.51 - 42.50 winning tickets RY

4411 LEICESTER (R-H)
Friday, March 11

OFFICIAL GOING: Good to firm (good in places; good to soft on the flat course crossings; 8.9)
Wind: Fresh across Weather: Overcast

4691 QUEENS ROYAL LANCERS NOVICES' H'CAP CHASE (12 fncs) 2m
2:30 (2:30) (Class 4) (0-110,108) 5-Y-O+ **£2,602** (£764; £382; £190)

Form RPR

4220 **1** **Autumm Spirit**[44] 3745 7-10-0 **82** oh1........................(t) CharliePoste 86+
(Robin Dickin) *a.p: led appr last: styd on wl* **6/1**

0P36 **2** *5* **Akarshan (IRE)**[29] 4033 6-11-7 **108**........................ AodhaganConlon(5) 106
(Evan Williams) *a.p: rdn to chse wnr appr last: styd on same pce flat* **5/1**[3]

0-04 **3** *6* **Golden Dream (IRE)**[44] 3741 7-10-10 **92**........................(t) TomMessenger 89
(Caroline Bailey) *hld up: mstke 2nd: hdwy 5th: reminders after 7th: blnd and outpcd 4 out: styd on appr last: wnt 3rd nr fin* **15/2**

3602 **4** *1* **Red Law (IRE)**[10] 4413 7-9-11 **82** oh5........................(b) TommyPhelan(3) 77
(Mark Gillard) *chsd ldrs: lft 2nd 4th: led 4 out: hdd appr last: wknd flat* **9/2**[2]

023 **5** *24* **Olympian Boy (IRE)**[88] 2927 7-11-3 **102**........................ RichieMcLernon(3) 76
(Anabel L M King) *led to 4 out: wknd appr last: t.o* **4/1**[1]

0040 **6** *7* **Salybia Bay**[28] 4049 5-10-4 **93**........................ MrBJPoste(7) 57
(Andy Turnell) *hld up in tch: rdn and wknd after 3 out: t.o* **28/1**

0502 **7** *14* **Nous Voila (FR)**[10] 4411 10-10-3 **92**........................ KyleJames(7) 43
(Alan Coogan) *sn wl bhd: t.o* **15/2**

-0P3 **P** **Medicine Man (IRE)**[30] 4006 7-11-6 **102**........................ JackDoyle —
(Ben De Haan) *racd keenly: trckd ldr tl blnd and lost pl 4th: p.u bef next* **9/1**

0F5P **P** **Goodtimetoby (IRE)**[26] 4103 8-10-1 **86**........................ CharlieHuxley(3) —
(Richard Lee) *hld up: hdwy 5th: wknd and p.u bef 4 out* **10/1**

4m 3.00s (-5.20) **Going Correction** -0.40s/f (Good) **9** Ran SP% **115.2**
Speed ratings: **97,94,91,91,79 75,68,—,—**
toteswingers:1&2:£4.60, 1&3:£6.80, 2&3:£7.50 CSF £36.59 CT £228.52 TOTE £8.10: £1.90, £1.40, £2.40; EX 55.70.
Owner The Lordy Racing Partnership **Bred** Mrs J Hoskins And Brian Wilson **Trained** Atherstone on Stour, Warwicks
■ Stewards' Enquiry : Tom Messenger two-day ban: used whip with excessive frequency (Mar 25-26)

FOCUS
The ground was heavy for the last meeting here ten days earlier, but with predominately dry weather since the going for this meeting was much quicker. The winning jockey in the first described it as good. This was a very moderate novices' handicap chase and the form amount to little. The winner produced a small step up on her modest hurdles form.

NOTEBOOK
Autumm Spirit was making her chasing debut after showing a little ability on soft ground over hurdles. Moving into contention on the outside of the field exiting the back straight, she took advantage when the leader faltered from the third-last and had the race in the bag after leading between the last two. The form is modest, but she has the scope to improve over fences and connections believe she will be better over further. (op 8-1)
Akarshan(IRE), who had not jumped at all well in his previous tries over fences, had his chance when making progress running to the fourth-last and did his best, but could make no impression on the mare. (op 9-2 tchd 6-1)
Golden Dream(IRE), a dual Irish point winner, was tailed off on his debut over regulation fences over 3m at Huntingdon last time, but this much shorter trip seemed too sharp as he plugged on again to snatch third after making an almighty mess of the fourth-last. He wore a tongue tie for the first time. (op 13-2 tchd 8-1)
Red Law(IRE) improved plenty for the blinkers when runner up over further on soft ground at this track ten days earlier and looked the likely winner here when hitting the front before four out, but slow jumps three out and two out lost him the advantage and he was soon on the retreat. (op 11-2 tchd 4-1)
Nous Voila(FR), 0-15 over fences, has shown his best form on soft ground and was taken off his feet from the very start. (op 9-1 tchd 7-1)

4692 KIRKBY MALLORY BEGINNERS' CHASE (15 fncs) 2m 4f 110y
3:05 (3:05) (Class 4) 5-Y-O+ **£2,602** (£764; £382)

Form RPR

-452 **1** **Swansbrook (IRE)**[18] 4261 8-11-0 124........................ WayneHutchinson 128+
(Alan King) *led: pckd 8th: sn hdd: hmpd appr 4 out: sn rdn: led 2 out: clr last: pushed out* **4/11**[1]

124 **2** *34* **Khorun (GER)**[23] 4145 6-10-9 0........................ MrTomDavid(5) 104+
(Tim Vaughan) *chsd wnr tl led after 8th: edgd rt and hmpd appr 4 out: mstke 4 out: hdd & wknd 2 out: t.o* **3/1**[2]

3 *dist* **Society Fashion** 6-10-7 0........................(t) JackDoyle —
(Noel Chance) *prom tl j. slowly 2nd and 3rd: sn t.o* **14/1**[3]

5m 20.4s (1.50) **Going Correction** -0.40s/f (Good) **3** Ran SP% **105.0**
Speed ratings: **81,68,—**
CSF £1.78 TOTE £1.30; EX 1.40.
Owner Favourites Racing & Andrew Gemmell **Bred** Alastair Pim **Trained** Barbury Castle, Wilts
■ Stewards' Enquiry : Mr Tom David two-day ban: careless riding (Mar 25,31)

FOCUS
A three-runner beginners' chase, but it only concerned two from an early stage and this doesn't look form to get excited about. The winner has been given a token rating to his mark.

NOTEBOOK
Swansbrook(IRE) had the edge in experience over his two rivals over regulation fences, but having set the early pace he put himself at a disadvantage when going down on his nose jumping the eighth and losing a length or two. However, he was back in front jumping two out and soon pulled right away from his wilting rival. It seems unlikely that he had to run up to his mark of 124 to win this the way he did, but connections believe that this ground was quick enough for him. (op 2-5 tchd 4-9)
Khorun(GER), a 113-rated hurdle and winner of an Irish point, seemed to be going better than the favourite after his mistake at halfway but he appeared to lose his hind legs when colliding with his rival on the crown of the home bend. A mistake four out halted his momentum and he got very tired after jumping the second-last. (op 11-4 tchd 5-2)
Society Fashion, whose dam was successful three times in moderate company over fences, looked very reluctant almost from flag-fall on this belated racecourse debut. (op 10-1)

4693 LEICESTERSHIRE AND DERBYSHIRE YEOMANRY H'CAP CHASE (AMATEUR RIDERS) (15 fncs) 2m 4f 110y
3:40 (3:40) (Class 5) (0-95,94) 5-Y-O+ **£2,186** (£677; £338; £169)

Form RPR

2-0P **1** **Mr Goofy (IRE)**[262] 824 10-11-4 **93**........................ MrRJarrett(7) 103+
(Michael Scudamore) *a.p: led 6th to 10th: led 11th to 2 out: rallied to ld flat: styd on wl* **16/1**

5013 **2** *4 ½* **Ponchatrain (IRE)**[109] 2575 11-11-5 **94**........................(v) MrTBellamy(7) 101+
(Martin Keighley) *racd keenly: sn prom: led 3rd tl after 5th: led 10th to next: led 2 out: rdn and hdd flat: no ex* **5/1**[3]

0P43 **3** *2 ½* **Bohemian Rock**[24] 4126 7-10-1 **76**........................(t) MrJSherwood(7) 79
(Caroline Bailey) *prom: drvn along 7th: outpcd 4 out: styd on appr last* **7/2**[1]

0400 **4** *9* **Kilvergan Boy (IRE)**[67] 3371 7-11-1 **90**.............. MrWTwiston-Davies(7) 85
(Nigel Twiston-Davies) *chsd ldrs: pushed along 4th: sn lost pl: bhd 8th: styd on flat* **4/1**[2]

0/F- **5** *2* **Top Dawn (IRE)**[342] 11-10-1 **76**........................ MrJMRidley(7) 72
(Matt Sheppard) *led to 3rd: led after 5th: hdd next: rdn appr 4 out: wknd next* **17/2**

P4P3 **6** *13* **Humbel Times (IRE)**[12] 4378 7-9-7 **68** oh8.......... MrRichardCollinson(7) 54
(Neil King) *hld up: bhd fr 7th: t.o* **17/2**

5024 **7** *30* **Keyneema**[33] 3959 9-10-8 **83**........................(p) MissKatySquires(7) 37
(Cathy Hamilton) *hld up in tch: bhd fr 7th: t.o* **16/1**

PF42 **F** **Mr Bond (IRE)**[32] 3984 8-10-8 **83**........................ MrBJPoste(7) —
(Andy Turnell) *hld up: hdwy 5th: disputing cl 3rd whn fell 8th* **7/2**[1]

5m 13.2s (-5.70) **Going Correction** -0.40s/f (Good) **8** Ran SP% **113.9**
Speed ratings: **94,92,91,87,87 82,70,—**
toteswingers:1&2:£22.70, 1&3:£36.30, 2&3:£1.60 CSF £93.31 CT £348.72 TOTE £25.10: £4.40, £1.10, £1.50; EX 90.70.
Owner Mrs Lesley Sluman **Bred** Mrs K Stamp **Trained** Bromsash, Herefordshire
■ Rob Jarrett's first winner under rules.
■ Stewards' Enquiry : Mr J M Ridley two-day ban: used whip with excessive frequency (Mar 25,31)

FOCUS
A moderate handicap chase in which recent winning form was notable by it absence, but the winning time was still 7.2 seconds faster than the three-runner beginners' chase. The winner is rated in line with last season's Towcester hunter chase run.

NOTEBOOK
Mr Goofy(IRE) wasn't running well when last seen in June, but the absence since seems to have done him the world of good. One of three to break clear starting the turn for home, the favourite seemed to be travelling much better than him all the way up the straight, but come the run-in he wanted it that much more and that made all the difference. (op 11-1)
Ponchatrain(IRE) was reappearing from 109 days off, but has gone well fresh in the past and he seemed to be running all over the winner after jumping the fourth from home. He still looked sure to win at the last, but did nothing in front up the run-in and finished very weakly. This was one that got away. (op 3-1)

Bohemian Rock hasn't shown much since winning an Irish point early last year and looked a horrible ride here, racing in snatches and hanging at various stages. The fact that he wasn't beaten far at the line shows that the ability is there, but he can't be backed with any confidence. (op 4-1 tchd 9-2)
Kilvergan Boy(IRE), well beaten over hurdles and fences since finishing runner-up over hurdles at Uttoxeter last June, was also on and off the bridle at various stages and his final position owes much to the perseverance of his rider. (op 6-1)
Top Dawn(IRE) had shown nothing under rules or in points since winning at Hereford in May 2008 and, having been up there from the off, was a beaten horse four from home. (op 12-1 tchd 8-1)
Mr Bond(IRE), 8lb better off with Ponchatrain for a length beating at Lingfield in November, isn't the best of jumpers and was still in contention when crashing out at the eighth. (op 10-3 tchd 4-1)

4694 SHERWOOD RANGERS YEOMANRY H'CAP CHASE (18 fncs) 2m 7f 110y
4:15 (4:15) (Class 4) (0-105,104) 5-Y-0+ **£2,602** (£764; £382; £190)

Form RPR
5004 **1** **Willandrich (IRE)**[29] 4022 9-11-5 **97** .... DaveCrosse 107+
(Ian Williams) *hld up: hdwy 9th: led appr 4 out: rdn bef last: styd on wl: eased nr fin* **2/1**[1]
00P3 **2** *8* **Woodmore (IRE)**[37] 3880 7-11-6 **98** .... (p) DarylJacob 104+
(Charlie Longsdon) *prom: chsd wnr 3 out: rdn and ev ch last: no ex flat* **3/1**[2]
1265 **3** *10* **Rash Moment (FR)**[123] 2277 12-11-0 **92** .... (p) AlanO'Keeffe 86
(Michael Scudamore) *hld up: hdwy to chse ldr 6th: led 12th to appr 4 out: wknd bef last* **12/1**
3112 **4** *60* **Phar Again (IRE)**[23] 4139 8-11-2 **97** .... (vt) TommyPhelan(3) 36
(Claire Dyson) *led to 2nd: led 3rd to 12th: mstke 14th: rdn and wknd 4 out: t.o* **10/3**[3]
-0P0 **P** **Cesium (FR)**[29] 4022 6-11-12 **104** .... (bt[1]) WayneHutchinson —
(Tom George) *nt fluent: led 2nd to 3rd: dropped to rr 7th: bhd fr 9th: t.o whn p.u bef 11th* **9/2**

5m 54.3s (-9.70) **Going Correction** -0.40s/f (Good) **5** Ran SP% **107.3**
Speed ratings: **100,97,94,74,—**
CSF £8.05 TOTE £1.90: £1.10, £2.20; EX 9.10.
Owner Will Tyrrell Richard Tyrrell Andrew Dick **Bred** John Halliday **Trained** Portway, Worcs

FOCUS
A weak handicap chase. A step up from both the winner and second.
NOTEBOOK
Willandrich(IRE) was having only his third start over fences and still had to convince over this far, but he has plenty of winning form on this sort of ground and a 9lb drop since his return to chasing last month brought about a return to form. He showed a good attitude after leading at the fourth last and with his stamina now proven and his liking for a sound surface established, he could be in for a good spring. (op 7-4 tchd 9-4)
Woodmore(IRE), 8lb lower than when a well-beaten third over C&D last month, like the winner was having only his third try over fences. Always handy, he tried to get on terms with the winner over the final four fences, but lacked the pace to do so and may need to drop a few more pounds if he is to break his duck over obstacles. (op 7-2 tchd 11-4)
Rash Moment(FR) made much of the running, but had little left to offer from four out. He remains 9lb above his last winning mark, but may come on for this first start since November. (op 11-1 tchd 10-1)
Phar Again(IRE), 3lb higher than when narrowly thwarted in his bid for a course hat-trick over 2m4f last month, hadn't shone in his previous attempts over this sort of trip and again ran as though his stamina gave out. (op 3-1 tchd 11-4)
Cesium(FR) was tried in blinkers having run three moderate races since returning from a break, but he never looked happy and it was little surprise to see him pulled up. Official explanation: trainer's rep said gelding had a breathing problem (op 5-1 tchd 4-1)

4695 CAVALRY H'CAP CHASE (14 fncs 1 omitted) 2m 4f 110y
4:50 (4:50) (Class 3) (0-125,123) 5-Y-0+ **£3,903** (£1,146; £573; £286)

Form RPR
5623 **1** **Double The Trouble**[20] 4223 10-10-4 **108** .... MrBJPoste(7) 126+
(Andy Turnell) *trckd ldr: a gng wl: led after 7th: clr last: easily* **9/4**[2]
1-0P **2** *31* **Bradford Boris**[48] 3689 7-11-5 **116** .... DarylJacob 108
(Nick Williams) *led: mstke 7th: sn hdd: chsd wnr: rdn and wknd after 2 out: t.o* **15/8**[1]
22F6 **3** *51* **Dead Or Alive (IRE)**[27] 8-11-7 **123** .... (tp) MrTomDavid(5) 64
(Tim Vaughan) *nt fluent: chsd ldrs: blnd and wknd 3 out: t.o* **6/1**
241 **4** *78* **Courella (IRE)**[169] 1589 7-11-2 **118** .... AodhaganConlon(5) —
(Evan Williams) *hld up and a bhd: t.o* **7/2**[3]
F **Knocknagow Leader (IRE)**[111] 2534 9-11-7 **121** .... RichieMcLernon(3) —
(Jonjo O'Neill) *fell 1st: fatally injured* **12/1**

5m 6.70s (-12.20) **Going Correction** -0.40s/f (Good) **5** Ran SP% **109.8**
Speed ratings: **107,95,75,46,—**
CSF £7.11 TOTE £2.30: £1.10, £2.00; EX 8.60.
Owner L G Kimber **Bred** L G Kimber **Trained** Broad Hinton, Wilts

FOCUS
A fair handicap chase run in a considerably faster time than the two earlier races over the same trip, but marred by the fatal fall of Knocknagow Leader at the first. The easy winner is rated back to his old best.
NOTEBOOK
Double The Trouble has been running well in defeat lately and the ground was very much in his favour. Sent to the front at halfway, he gradually turned the screw and a flying leap at the final ditch, three out, put the result beyond doubt. He can win again under similar conditions. (op 3-1 tchd 10-3)
Bradford Boris ran poorly in two starts in January, having previously been off for ten months, but this was better, although he had no answer to the winner over the final four fences. He remains 13lb above his last winning mark and needs more respite. (op 9-4)
Dead Or Alive(IRE) was having his first start under rules since August, though he did make a successful return in a point last month, but his jumping wasn't up to scratch here. He had been left behind when his rider performed a minor miracle to stay on board after a terrible blunder at the final ditch. (op 4-1)
Courella(IRE), not seen since winning off 8lb lower at Fontwell in September, was never in the race and presumably needed it.

4696 THRUSTERS HUNTERS' CHASE (12 fncs) 2m
5:25 (5:25) (Class 6) 5-Y-0+ **£1,249** (£387; £193; £96)

Form RPR
34-4 **1** **Takeroc (FR)**[16] 4293 8-11-5 0 .... (t) MrHDerham(7) 126+
(R Barber) *hld up in tch: chsd ldr 4 out: led after 2 out: sn clr: easily* **10/11**[1]
00/P **2** *30* **Basic Fact (IRE)**[15] 4315 9-11-5 95 .... (b) MrRStearn(7) 99
(J M Turner) *chsd ldrs tl wknd 3 out: lft poor 2nd last: t.o* **22/1**
-253 **3** *11* **Battlefield Bob (IRE)**[23] 4143 7-11-6 87 ow1 .... MrGGreenock(7) 93
(G T H Bailey) *led to 7th: wknd appr 2 out: lft poor 3rd last: t.o* **6/1**[2]
/PP- **4** *9* **Naxox (FR)**[33] 10-11-5 0 .... MissRachelKing(7) 83
(Ms A Hardy) *hld up: hdwy 5th: wknd appr 3 out: t.o* **33/1**
0PP- **5** *16* **Muhtenbar**[449] 2933 11-11-13 0 .... MrJonathanBailey(7) 75
(Ms A E Embiricos) *prom: lost pl appr 3rd: pushed along 6th: sn lost tch: t.o* **16/1**
00P- **6** *71* **Cheapside (IRE)**[20] 6-11-5 0 .... (t) MrOGarner(7) 3
(D C Gannon) *hld up: mstke 6th: sn wknd: t.o* **66/1**
PF/P **7** *51* **Made In Montot (FR)**[16] 4293 11-11-5 0 .... (t) MrHKinchin(7) —
(B J Clarke) *prom: mstke 4th: sn lost pl: bhd fr 6th: t.o* **66/1**
320- **P** **Mister Pous (FR)**[54] 12-11-12 0 .... MrDMansell —
(Miss J Houldey) *a bhd: t.o whn p.u bef 6th* **25/1**
4-22 **U** **Fairwood Present (IRE)**[287] 499 13-11-5 0 .... MrRJarrett(7) 111
(John Buxton) *prom: led 7th: blnd 2 out: sn hdd: wkng whn blnd and uns rdr last* **6/1**[2]
P6-P **P** **Kinfayre Boy**[6] 9-11-9 90 .... MrSBowden(7) —
(S Bowden) *a in rr: t.o whn p.u bef 8th* **25/1**
00-5 **U** **Jaamid**[21] 4197 9-12-3 113 .... MrMWall(3) —
(William Hayes, Ire) *chsd ldrs tl blnd and uns rdr 4th* **9/1**[3]

3m 58.9s (-9.30) **Going Correction** -0.40s/f (Good) **11** Ran SP% **114.8**
Speed ratings: **107,92,86,82,74 38,13,—,—,— —**
toteswingers:1&2:£24.80, 1&3:£1.80, 2&3:£27.10 CSF £27.63 TOTE £1.80: £1.02, £8.60, £3.80; EX 23.50.
Owner Chris Giles,Paul Nicholls & Julie Derham **Bred** Dr Armand Israel & Serge Becerra **Trained** Beaminster, Dorset
■ The first winner under rules for Harry Derham.

FOCUS
An unusual trip for hunter chasers. The pace was sound and very few ever got into it. Takeroc will be tough to beat over this trip in hunter chases.
NOTEBOOK
Takeroc(FR) still holds an official chase rating of 149 (had some 39lb in hand of the next best in here) and was expected to relish this return to the minimum trip. Always travelling well, his task was made easier by the shenanigans of Fairwood Present over the last two fences, but he would probably have won comfortably anyway. He will continue to take the beating in similar contests. (op 11-10)
Basic Fact(IRE) had the ground in his favour and showed up for a long way, but he wasn't in the same parish as the winner and this trip would have been much too sharp. (op 28-1)
Battlefield Bob(IRE) set the pace until rounding the home bend, but looks a short runner even over this trip. (op 7-1)
Naxox(FR), pulled up in his last four starts over fences including two points, proved reluctant to go out onto the track and obviously has his quirks. (op 28-1)
Fairwood Present(IRE) had no problem with the conditions, but was having his first start since last May. Sent to the front on the home bend, he still held a lead of a couple of lengths when he swerved right at the second-last, banked the fence and almost sent his rider out the side door. Headed soon after, he was well beaten when repeating the feat at the last, sending his rider somersaulting under the running rail and into the grass bank. He can be rated clear second-best on merit. (op 15-2)
T/Plt: £41.60 to a £1 stake. Pool:£51,010.67 - 894.88 winning tickets T/Qpdt: £10.90 to a £1 stake. Pool:£4,371.23 - 294.20 winning tickets CR

4323 SANDOWN (R-H)
Friday, March 11

OFFICIAL GOING: Good (good to soft in places on hurdle course; chs 7.8, hdl 7.6)
Wind: Moderate, half against Weather: Cloudy

4697 ANNINGTON AMATEUR RIDERS' H'CAP HURDLE (8 hdls) 2m 110y
2:20 (2:20) (Class 4) (0-115,110) 4-Y-0+ **£3,123** (£968; £484; £242)

Form RPR
-PP0 **1** **King Brex (DEN)**[28] 4049 8-12-0 **109** .... (tp) LtColOEllwood(3) 115+
(Charlie Mann) *t.k.h: j.w: trckd ldr 3rd: led 5th: pushed along and drew clr after 2 out* **11/2**
2-10 **2** *7* **Vertueux (FR)**[7] 2361 6-11-9 **108** .... L-BdrSallyRandell(7) 109
(Tony Carroll) *hld up: wl in tch fr 4th: effrt after 3 out: trying to cl whn mstke 2 out: kpt on same pce fr last to take 2nd nr fin* **9/2**[3]
0334 **3** *3/4* **Posh Emily**[8] 4448 8-11-10 **105** .... (b) MissLGardner(3) 104
(Ron Hodges) *hld up: wl in tch fr 4th: prog to press wnr 3 out: upsides bef 2 out: nt qckn and btn after: lost 2nd nr fin* **3/1**[1]
U-0P **4** *2 1/4* **Be Definite (IRE)**[13] 4354 7-11-13 **110** .... MrTWCEdwards(5) 107
(Tom George) *hld up: wl in tch fr 4th: outpcd and pushed along after 3 out: plugged on one pce after* **5/1**
PP02 **5** *8* **Olympian (FR)**[11] 4399 9-12-3 **109** .... MissLHorner 99
(Philip Middleton) *racd wd: hld up: wl in tch fr 4th: prog to chal on long run bef 2 out: sn wknd qckly* **7/2**[2]
060 **6** *7* **Peqeno Diablo (IRE)**[34] 3950 6-11-8 **107** .... O-CdtJessicaLodge(7) 90
(Claire Dyson) *mostly chsd ldr to 3rd: chal and upsides 5th: wknd on long run to 2 out* **16/1**
P266 **P** **Zhukov (IRE)**[38] 3869 9-11-8 **107** .... MajGFWheeler(7) —
(Kevin Tork) *a in last: t.o fr 4th: p.u bef 2 out* **25/1**
3U44 **P** **L'Homme De Nuit (GER)**[12] 4379 7-11-11 **110** .... (p) L-BdrJSole(7) —
(Jim Best) *mde most to 5th: wknd rapidly on long run after 3 out: p.u bef 2 out* **16/1**

4m 5.00s (-2.20) **Going Correction** +0.05s/f (Yiel) **8** Ran SP% **113.1**
Speed ratings (Par 105): **107,103,103,102,98 95,—,—**
toteswingers:1&2:£4.60, 1&3:£6.80, 2&3:£7.50 CSF £30.03 CT £86.85 TOTE £7.70: £1.70, £1.50, £1.40; EX 25.50.
Owner Nigel Kempner & Lady Hart **Bred** Ove Henriksen **Trained** Upper Lambourn, Berks

FOCUS
After a fortnight or so without rain the ground had been watered, from 3mm to 40mm being put on different parts of the track. The ground seemed to be riding on the slow side of good. The opener was a modest handicap hurdle confined to military amateurs, and is not form to take too seriously. The race was solidly run and the winner is rated back towards his best.
NOTEBOOK
King Brex(DEN) won a handicap chase on this card 12 months ago, when 8lb higher, and his veteran jockey has a fine record at this fixture. He travelled well again, taking something of a tug, and was well in command from the second-last. (op 5-1 tchd 6-1)
Vertueux(FR) had not run over hurdles since November but has been kept busy on the AW and his yard has a decent record in the race. He was never quite close enough to make his presence felt, a mistake two out not helping, but did stay on to snatch second, filling the same position as 12 months ago. (tchd 5-1)
Posh Emily last year's winner, was 6lb worse off with Vertueux this time round but had the services of a more experienced partner. The mare had her chance, but could not race on with King Brex from two out and lost second on the run-in. She is due to be dropped a pound now. (op 11-4)
Be Definite(IRE) was 5lb lower than at Kempton and jumped better, but he was outpaced by the leaders from the home turn. He did stick on, suggesting that a return to further might suit. (op 8-1 tchd 9-2)
Olympian(FR) had run well at Plumpton and was 3lb well in. After racing wide, he emerged to look a threat only to drop away tamely from the second-last. This was disappointing. (op 3-1)

L'Homme De Nuit(GER), reverting to hurdles, had the cheekpieces back. He won the tussle for the lead, but slowed into successive flights down the back and was on the retreat prior to the home turn.

4698 CHARLES STANLEY H'CAP CHASE (13 fncs) 2m

2:55 (2:55) (Class 3) (0-125,122) 5-Y-0+ **£5,204** (£1,528; £764; £381)

Form RPR

F423 **1** **Owner Occupier**[11] 4400 6-9-11 **100** .... MrTJCannon(7) 109+
(Chris Gordon) *chsd ldr: clsd to ld bef 3 out: 2 l clr 2 out: drvn out flat* **10/3**[1]

-406 **2** *3/4* **Tempting Paradise (IRE)**[40] 3841 8-10-11 **107** .... PaulMoloney 116+
(Evan Williams) *in tch: nt fluent 4th and sn lost pl: last at 9th: rallied bef 3 out: drvn and styd on to take 2nd flat: clsng on wnr fin* **11/2**

2430 **3** *2 1/2* **Cortinas (GER)**[48] 3686 9-11-1 **114** ....(t) IanPopham(3) 121
(Claire Dyson) *pckd 1st: hld up in 6th: prog to chse ldng pair 9th: cl enough 3 out: nt fluent 2 out but sn chsd wnr: nt qckn last: lost 2nd flat* **16/1**

P0F **4** *7* **Vinmix De Bessy (FR)**[40] 3834 10-11-7 **122** ....(p) JoshuaMoore(5) 123
(Gary Moore) *hld up in last: nt fluent 6th: prog fr 8th: gd hdwy after 4 out to chal and w wnr 3 out: wknd after next* **8/1**

5410 **5** *1 1/2* **Marodima (FR)**[28] 4049 8-11-5 **120** ....(p) MissLHorner(5) 119
(Jamie Snowden) *led to s early: j. boldly: led: hdd bef 3 out: fdd fr next* **11/2**

532F **6** *2* **Outside The Box**[13] 4355 7-11-3 **113** .... TomSiddall 111
(Noel Chance) *prom on ins: nt fluent 8th: mstke next and lost pl: sn last and looked like tailing off: styd on again quite stoutly fr last* **4/1**[2]

4225 **7** *45* **Classic Fly (FR)**[156] 1731 8-10-8 **104** .... FelixDeGiles 80
(Arthur Whiting) *in tch: rdn 8th: wknd after 4 out: virtually p.u flat: bled fr nose* **9/2**[3]

4m 6.80s (5.00) **Going Correction** +0.275s/f (Yiel) **7** Ran SP% **109.0**

Speed ratings: **98,97,96,92,92 91,68**

toteswingers:1&2:£3.80, 1&3:£9.90, 2&3:£14.80 CSF £19.78 TOTE £3.10: £2.80, £1.60; EX 27.00.

Owner Mrs D M Lawes **Bred** Bearstone Stud **Trained** Morestead, Hants

FOCUS

An ordinary handicap chase for the track. It was run at a decent clip but the time was around 16 seconds outside the standard. The second and third set the level.

NOTEBOOK

Owner Occupier jumped better than he did at Plumpton last time, where he was also hampered a couple of times. Showing ahead going to the Pond Fence, he did not have a great deal to spare at the line as the runner-up closed, but deserves credit for the win as he was never far from the generous pace. He had been beaten off this mark in his last five chases, but is only six and there is improvement in him on similar ground. (op 7-2 tchd 3-1 and 4-1 in a place)

Tempting Paradise(IRE) had his ground on this second run back from over six months off. He lost his pitch down the far side but rallied gamely and was clawing back the winner's lead up the hill. (op 5-1)

Cortinas(GER) was making his second appearance for the Dyson stable after being claimed from Charlie Mann. He travelled quite well and made progress from the back to go second between the last two fences, but could make no further impression on the winner. (op 14-1 tchd 12-1)

Vinmix De Bessy(FR) was third of four in this race a year ago when 2lb higher. Held up in last, he closed to jump the Pond Fence upsides the winner, only to fade after the next. This was effectively only his second run, and his first over fences, since May. (op 10-1)

Marodima(FR) jumped boldly in front but could never really get clear and he was pegged back going to the third-last. His last win over fences came in April 2008. (op 9-2 tchd 6-1)

Outside The Box was a faller at Kempton latest and the drop back in trip was expected to suit. Unable to lead with Marodima in opposition, he dropped out of contention after getting each of the three railway fences wrong, but he was running on again when it was all over and is probably worth another chance. (op 9-2 tchd 5-1)

Classic Fly(FR), 12lb higher than when last in a handicap, probably needed this first outing in five months. It was reported that he bled. Official explanation: jockey said gelding bled from the nose (op 5-1 tchd 4-1)

4699 GRAND MILITARY GOLD CUP (A CHASE FOR AMATEUR RIDERS) (SPONSORED BY THE MILITARY MUTUAL) (22 fncs) 3m 110y

3:30 (3:30) (Class 3) 6-Y-0+ **£5,621** (£1,743; £871; £435)

Form RPR

3-22 **1** **Blu Teen (FR)**[21] 4194 11-11-7 118 ....(t) L-BdrJSole(7) 131+
(D J Staddon) *hld up: last to 16th: prog bef 3 out: brought to chal and gd jump to ld last: urged clr* **4/1**[2]

-161 **2** *2 3/4* **Ice Tea (IRE)**[16] 4286 11-11-11 130 ....(b) MissLGardner(3) 129+
(Mrs S K McCain) *led: clr 16th: hrd pressed after 3 out: hdd and one pce last* **7/2**[1]

3U-1 **3** *2 1/2* **Surenaga (IRE)**[21] 4194 9-11-12 123 ....(p) L-BdrSallyRandell(7) 133
(Miss Sally Randell) *patiently rdn in last pair: prog on inner fr 4 out: chal and nrly upsides 2 out: nt qckn bef last* **8/1**

UF04 **4** *8* **Scots Dragoon**[21] 4194 9-12-0 115 .... MajAMichael(5) 127+
(Nicky Henderson) *wl in tch: jnd ldrs 13th: blnd bdly 15th: sn lost pl: struggling in 7th bef 3 out: plugged on* **15/2**

3-33 **5** *2 3/4* **Knighton Combe**[21] 4194 11-12-5 123 .... MissLHorner 121
(Jamie Snowden) *in tch: chsd ldng pair 12th tl lost pl 14th: renewed effrt 4 out: nt qckn and lost pl again after 3 out: fdd: fin lame* **9/2**[3]

3100 **6** *6* **Cois Farraig**[34] 3946 6-12-5 130 .... MrTWCEdwards(5) 123+
(Paul Webber) *cl up: chsd ldng pair 16th: wnt 2nd briefly 3 out: wknd rapidly fr next* **7/2**[1]

13PP **7** *27* **Flying Squad (UAE)**[21] 4182 7-11-12 108 ....(t) MajGFWheeler(7) 99
(Milton Harris) *chsd ldr 5th: cl enough 14th: nt qckn next: lost 2nd and wknd qckly bef 3 out* **50/1**

2125 **8** *28* **Mr Big (IRE)**[21] 4194 10-12-2 121 ....(p) LtColOEllwood(3) 66
(Charlie Mann) *chsd ldr to 5th: mstke 12th: sn lost pl: dropped to last by 17th: t.o whn blnd 3 out* **14/1**

6m 29.95s (2.15) **Going Correction** +0.275s/f (Yiel) **8** Ran SP% **114.1**

Speed ratings: **107,106,105,102,101 99,91,82**

toteswingers:1&2:£3.50, 1&3:£6.40, 2&3:£5.10 CSF £18.92 TOTE £4.90: £1.50, £1.60, £2.60; EX 23.40.

Owner Lt Col STW Bridge KRH & Maj El Bridge RA **Bred** Bertrand Compignie **Trained** Shepton Mallet, Somerset

FOCUS

An up-to-scratch edition of this historic race, which was worth the best part of £2,000 less to the winner than it had been a year ago. The pace was solid and the form should be too, the unorthodox nature of this event notwithstanding. The first five in the Royal Artillery Gold Cup over C&D three weeks earlier turned out again. The winner is rated up 2lb on that form.

NOTEBOOK

Blu Teen(FR) finished second to Surenaga in the Royal Artillery Gold Cup last month and was 5lb better off now. Given a patient and well judged ride, he improved to lead at the last and ran on strongly. He could run in the Cheltenham Foxhunters' next week, but is more likely to wait for the Aintree version, in which he was third last year. Official explanation: It's a great thrill, but without Paul Nicholls, Paul Barber and Andy Stewart, who used to own Blu Teen, we wouldn't be here today. He's a seriously classy horse, but he's had all of the problems under the sun. Legs, wind, bleeding - you name it, he's had it. We got the tactics slightly wrong in the Royal Artillery.You have to creep and creep, and Jody gave him a peach.-D J Staddon, trainer. (op 5-1)

Ice Tea(IRE), winner of three of his last four hunter chases, was 10lb clear on BHA figures. Given a bold ride, and clear at times during the contest, he was collared after a slight mistake at the final fence. (tchd 4-1 and 9-2 in a place)

Surenaga(IRE) was foiled in his bid to complete a rare Royal Artillery-Grand Military double, the 5lb penalty making things tough. His capable rider produced him to have every chance between the last two fences but he couldn't find a change of gear from there. (op 6-1)

Scots Dragoon, last year's winner, was ridden closer to the pace than he had been when fourth in the Royal Artillery. He lost his position after a bad blunder down the far side but did stay on again. (op 6-1 tchd 8-1)

Knighton Combe, third in the Royal Artillery, faded going to two out and was reported to have finished lame. Official explanation: jockey said gelding finished lame (tchd 5-1)

Cois Farraig, successful in a substandard Grade 2 novice event earlier in the season, represented owners who have had a good deal of success in this race. Giving weight away all round, he weakened from the third-last on this first try at 3m under rules. (op 9-2)

Flying Squad(UAE), another yet to conclusively prove he stays, dropped away going to the Pond Fence. He has lost his way recently, but he had a stiff task at these weights and it is too early to be writing him off.

Mr Big(IRE), fifth in the Royal Artillery Gold Cup latest, was the first in trouble. (op 16-1 tchd 12-1)

4700 CHARLES STANLEY H'CAP HURDLE (11 hdls) 2m 6f

4:05 (4:05) (Class 3) (0-120,122) 4-Y-0+ **£3,903** (£1,146; £573; £286)

Form RPR

21F0 **1** **Time For Spring (IRE)**[37] 3877 7-11-12 **120** .... FelixDeGiles 131+
(Charlie Longsdon) *settled in midfield: prog to chse ldng trio 3 out: galvanized to ld bef 2 out where mstke: drvn and hld on wl fr last* **14/1**

1431 **2** *1* **Havingotascoobydo (IRE)**[8] 4439 6-11-3 **111** 7ex....... WarrenMarston 121+
(Martin Keighley) *hld up and in last early: gd prog to join ldrs 7th: wnt 2nd 3 out: gng best bef next but surprised by wnr surging by: rdn and nt qckn after: kpt on* **15/8**[1]

U00P **3** *4* **Pro Pell (IRE)**[21] 4182 6-10-13 **107** .... JamieMoore 112
(Gary Moore) *wl in tch: drvn 3 out and outpcd: kpt on bef next: styd on u.p to take 3rd after last* **20/1**

31 **4** *1 1/2* **Sinbad The Sailor**[30] 4012 6-11-9 **117** .... AndrewTinkler 121
(George Baker) *prom in chsng gp: chsd ldr 8th to 3 out: cl enough in 3rd bef next: sn lft bhd: plugged on fr last* **9/1**

U144 **5** *1 1/2* **Educated Evans (IRE)**[37] 3881 6-11-5 **113** .... PaddyBrennan 118+
(Nigel Twiston-Davies) *pressed ldr to 3rd and clr of rest: settled bhd after tl led 6th: hdd bef 2 out where mstke: wknd and mstke last* **15/2**[3]

-00P **6** *29* **Puzzlemaster**[13] 4354 5-11-7 **115** ....(t) DominicElsworth 92
(Hughie Morrison) *hld up in rr: effrt fr 7th: rchd 7th on long run to 2 out but nowhere nr ldrs: wknd sn after: tailedoff* **33/1**

4-12 **7** *13* **Legion D'Honneur (UAE)**[34] 3950 6-11-7 **115** .... SamThomas 80
(Chris Down) *settled in rr: blnd 5th: struggling fr 7th: no ch after 3 out: t.o* **15/2**[3]

01-F **8** *12* **Crannaghmore Boy (IRE)**[10] 4407 6-10-11 **110**......... JoshuaMoore(5) 64
(Keith Goldsworthy) *chsd ldng pair to 6th: sn u.p: wknd bef 3 out: t.o* **20/1**

230 **9** *6* **Foynes Island (IRE)**[106] 2630 5-11-0 **108** .... RichardJohnson 57
(Philip Hobbs) *hld up in rr: prog fr 7th: drvn to chse ldrs in 6th after 3 out but nt on terms: wknd rapidly bef next: t.o* **11/1**

2UP4 **10** *13* **Oursininlaw (IRE)**[34] 3941 7-11-7 **115** .... PaulMoloney 52
(Evan Williams) *nt jump wl in rr: struggling fr 7th: wl btn after 3 out: t.o* **25/1**

0035 **P** **Manele Bay**[14] 4327 8-11-2 **110** .... AndrewThornton —
(Richard Rowe) *mstke 4th and sn dropped to last: struggling fr 6th: t.o in last pair whn p.u bef 2 out* **25/1**

0041 **P** **Henry Hook (IRE)**[8] 4446 7-11-7 **122** 7ex................(b) EdGlassonbury(7) —
(Victor Dartnall) *racd wd and often hanging lft: led and clr after 3rd: hdd and mstke 6th: wknd rapidly: t.o in last pair whn p.u bef 2 out* **5/1**[2]

5m 27.15s (-2.85) **Going Correction** +0.05s/f (Yiel) **12** Ran SP% **120.1**

Speed ratings (Par 107): **107,106,105,104,104 93,88,84,82,77 —,—**

toteswingers:1&2:£8.10, 1&3:£44.70, 2&3:£11.10 CSF £39.43 CT £559.09 TOTE £17.30: £5.10, £1.50, £5.50; EX 44.40 Trifecta £670.80 Part won. Pool: £906.49 - 0.90 winning units..

Owner MacEchern, Pottinger, Badcock **Bred** John Conway **Trained** Over Norton, Oxon

FOCUS

Quite a competitive handicap hurdle, and solid, decent form which should work out. The pace was sound and only the first five were still in contention turning for home.

NOTEBOOK

Time For Spring(IRE), a lightly raced novice, made a successful handicap debut, the better ground seeming to suit. Sweeping to the front going to the second-last, he hit the flight and had to work hard to hold on to his advantage from there. He should have more to offer. Official explanation: trainer said, regarding apparent improvement in form, that the gelding was better suited by the good (good to soft places) ground (op 9-1)

Havingotascoobydo(IRE) was 4lb well in under the penalty he picked up in a novice handicap at Ludlow last week. Travelling well, despite taking a tug again, he came through to look a big threat but the winner had the legs of him from the second-last. He kept on after landing flat-footed at the last and was not beaten far, suggesting he ought to be competitive even from his new mark. (op 9-4)

Pro Pell(IRE) is only a pound above his last winning mark and ran his best race for a while, staying on for third without ever threatening the leading pair. (op 16-1 tchd 22-1)

Sinbad The Sailor, another recent Ludlow winner, was contesting his first handicap on only this third run over hurdles. He looked to be on a fair mark and ran well for a long way. (op 10-1 tchd 8-1)

Educated Evans(IRE) was made plenty of use of again but could not sustain his effort, although he was still in third when making a tired mistake at the last. He should get 3m in time. (op 8-1)

Legion D'Honneur(UAE) was expected to be better for his comeback run here last month, but he made quite a bad mistake on the first circuit and was in trouble not long after that. (tchd 7-1)

Henry Hook(IRE) was a pound ahead of the handicapper under the penalty for his Taunton win, but was racing off a career-high mark. Making a lot of the running and clear for a time, he hung out to his left when headed and was eventually pulled up. He is not straightforward. Official explanation: jockey said gelding hung badly left (op 7-1)

4701 QUEEN ELIZABETH THE QUEEN MOTHER MEMORIAL HUNTERS' CHASE (SPONSORED BY AGUSTAWESTLAND) (22 fncs) 3m 110y

4:40 (4:40) (Class 4) 6-Y-0+ £2,498 (£774; £387; £193)

Form RPR

13-2 **1** **Mister Apple's (FR)**[16] 4286 11-11-13 120............(p) MrTWCEdwards(5) 125+
(Ian Williams) *trckd ldrs: nt fluent 15th whn last of three w ch: wnt 2nd and chal 3 out: narrow ld next: urged along and hld on flat* **5/2**[2]

0FP0 **2** ¾ **Seymar Lad (IRE)**[12] 11-11-11 117.................................. L-BdrJSole(7) 123
(Miss V Collins) *led: jnd and mstke 3 out: narrowly hdd next: kpt on flat: jst hld* **28/1**

2-62 **3** 6 **Honour's Dream (FR)**[12] 4374 8-11-3 90.........(v) O-CdtJessicaLodge(7) 109
(Mrs Jenny Gordon) *mostly chsd ldr tl 3 out: one pce* **16/1**

140- **4** 22 **I Hear Thunder (IRE)**[26] 13-12-1 0............................ LtColOEllwood(3) 102
(Nick Mitchell) *cl up: mstke 12th and lost tch: struggling and nvr on terms after* **7/1**

125- **P** **Ultimate Limit**[373] 4381 11-11-11 0.......................... L-BdrSallyRandell(7) —
(Alan Fleming) *hld up last: lost tch and p.u bef 13th: sddle slipped* **9/2**[3]

0P/2 **U** **Turko (FR)**[23] 4141 9-11-5 123..(t) MajAMichael(5) —
(Mrs L Borradaile) *trckd ldrs: disputing cl 3rd whn blnd bdly and uns rdr 15th* **6/4**[1]

6m 37.8s (10.00) **Going Correction** +0.275s/f (Yiel) 6 Ran SP% **108.6**
Speed ratings: **95,94,92,85,—** —
toteswingers:1&2:£6.50, 1&3:£3.60, 2&3:£6.90 CSF £41.93 TOTE £3.30: £1.60, £6.50; EX 66.00.
Owner P J Vogt **Bred** Viscount Yves De Soultrait **Trained** Portway, Worcs

FOCUS

An ordinary hunter chase, and with a couple of fancied contenders not completing the form is by no means strong. The winner is rated to his mark. The time was around eight seconds slower than the Grand Military Gold Cup.

NOTEBOOK

Mister Apple's(FR) ran well on his debut in this sphere when second at Doncaster to the Grand Military runner-up, Ice Tea. He looked to have work to do in third taking the railway fences, but took a narrow lead two out before idling in front, always holding the runner-up. This proved his effectiveness going right-handed and he should win more of these. He could run at Aintree. (op 9-4 tchd 2-1 and 11-4 in a place)

Seymar Lad(IRE), a useful handicap chaser for Emma Lavelle a couple of seasons ago, has been well held in three point-to-points this winter. Going out in front, he made his only error when getting in too close to the Pond Fence and went down fighting. (op 22-1)

Honour's Dream(FR) ran well until fading but remains without a victory over fences. He has now been placed in two hunter chases this year but has only finished in front of one horse. (op 20-1 tchd 12-1)

I Hear Thunder(IRE), winner of a members' point last month, was struggling after a blunder on the final circuit. (op 8-1 tchd 17-2)

Ultimate Limit, unraced for a year, was in last place until pulling up with a slipped saddle. Official explanation: jockey said saddle slipped (op 13-8 tchd 7-4 and 2-1 in places)

Turko(FR), a one-time smart performer for Paul Nicholls, had 11lb in hand on official figures. He was a close fourth and going well when he blundered away his rider at the final ditch. (op 13-8 tchd 7-4 and 2-1 in places)

4702 SSAFA FORCES HELP "NATIONAL HUNT" NOVICES' HURDLE (8 hdls) 2m 110y

5:15 (5:15) (Class 4) 4-Y-0+ £3,252 (£955; £477; £238)

Form RPR

0-01 **1** **Rebel Rebellion (IRE)**[28] 4051 6-11-5 0........................... IanPopham(3) 132+
(Paul Nicholls) *trckd ldr: led 2 out gng easily: sn drew clr* **15/8**[1]

2231 **2** 7 **Our Mick**[26] 4100 5-11-8 118.. RichardJohnson 126+
(Donald McCain) *led: mstke 1st: nt fluent after: kicked on after 3 out: hdd 2 out: kpt on but no ch w wnr* **11/4**[3]

3 12 **Taoiri (FR)**[54] 4-11-0 0.. RobertThornton 104
(Alan King) *hld up in 4th: nudged along and effrt on long run to 2 out: sn wknd* **2/1**[2]

50 **4** 10 **Moscow Chancer (IRE)**[31] 3987 5-11-1 0....................... PaddyBrennan 97
(Tom George) *trckd ldr: nt fluent 3rd: rdn after 3 out: wknd bef 2 out* **11/1**

44 **5** 4½ **Flowerdew (IRE)**[30] 4006 6-11-1 0................................... AndrewTinkler 96+
(Nicky Henderson) *nt fluent: hld up in last pair: rdn after 3 out: wknd bef next* **20/1**

40 **P** **Malibu Sun**[28] 4055 4-10-7 0... LeightonAspell —
(Oliver Sherwood) *a in last pair: wknd 5th: t.o whn p.u after 3 out: dismntd* **66/1**

4m 6.10s (-1.10) **Going Correction** +0.05s/f (Yiel)
WFA 4 from 5yo+ 7lb 6 Ran SP% **109.4**
Speed ratings (Par 105): **104,100,95,90,88** —
toteswingers:1&2:£1.20, 1&3:£1.50, 2&3:£1.50. totesuper7: Win: Not won. Place: £1,925.00 CSF £7.20 TOTE £2.60: £1.60, £1.40; EX 7.60.
Owner Jared Sullivan **Bred** Frances Galloway **Trained** Ditcheat, Somerset

FOCUS

An interesting novice hurdle which has been won by some decent types in the last few years, including Mighty Man and last season's winner Lush Life. They stood still for a few seconds after the tapes rose, but went a reasonable pace once under way. The winner is rated to his Kempton level and the second can rate higher.

NOTEBOOK

Rebel Rebellion(IRE) ◆ won well over 2m5f at Kempton and followed up in nice style. Settling well on this marked drop in trip, he jumped to the front two from home and soon had it in the bag. The wind operation is helping him realise his potential and more will be heard of him. He should make a nice chaser in time. (op 9-4 tchd 7-4)

Our Mick made the running but hurdled less than fluently. He stuck on when headed by the winner and this was improved form. In the longer term he has the scope to make a chaser, but he will need to jump better. (op 7-2)

Taoiri(FR) looked interesting as two starts back at Pau he beat Molotof, who was runner-up to leading Triumph Hurdle fancy Zarkandar in the Adonis at Kempton. Third over fences on his last start in France, and now in the same ownership as Molotof, he was well held by the leading pair from the second-last and may need more time to acclimatise. A longer trip could be what he needs. (op 15-8 tchd 7-4)

Moscow Chancer(IRE) was under pressure on the home turn and is not really seeing out his races, the drop in trip not helping here. He may still have some strengthening to do. (op 9-1 tchd 17-2)

Flowerdew(IRE)'s yard had won four of the last eight runnings of this. Held up at the back, he was close enough on the home turn but stopped pretty quickly from there. His hurdling lacked fluency. (op 14-1)

T/Plt: £52.10 to a £1 stake. Pool:£67,938.12 - 950.19 winning tickets T/Qpdt: £9.00 to a £1 stake. Pool:£4,756.12 - 388.43 winning tickets JN

4671 WINCANTON (R-H)

Friday, March 11

OFFICIAL GOING: Good to firm (chs 8.3, hdl 8.2)

Rail realignment increased distances by 60yds per circuit on both tracks.

Wind: mild against Weather: overcast

4703 STARSPORTSBET.CO.UK MARES' NOVICES' HURDLE (11 hdls) 2m 6f

2:00 (2:00) (Class 4) 5-Y-0+ £2,764 (£811; £405; £202)

Form RPR

1022 **1** **Violin Davis (FR)**[26] 4101 5-10-5 116................................ MrRMahon(5) 114
(Paul Nicholls) *trckd ldrs: chal 3 out: tk narrow advantage 2 out: styd on fr last: drifted rt nr fin: drvn out* **7/2**[3]

0-02 **2** 1½ **Chilli Rose**[29] 4025 6-10-10 115....................................... RobertThornton 113+
(Alan King) *racd quite keenly: led: rdn wl after 3 out: narrowly hdd next: 1 l down last: edgd lft and no ex run-in* **5/2**[2]

121 **3** ½ **Kells Belle (IRE)**[30] 4006 5-11-3 0.. APMcCoy 120
(Nicky Henderson) *trckd ldrs: wnt 3rd after 6th: nrly upsides 3 out: sn rdn: 2 l down 2 out: ch last: kpt on same pce* **11/8**[1]

0443 **4** 71 **Lost Two Stars (IRE)**[12] 4370 6-10-10 102........................... JoeTizzard 49
(Colin Tizzard) *trckd ldr tl 5th: hit next: sn rdn: lost tch fr 7th: t.o* **12/1**

44 **R** **Accordingtoeileen (IRE)**[40] 3842 6-10-7 0........ SamTwiston-Davies(3) —
(Nigel Twiston-Davies) *ref to r: tk no part* **20/1**

0/0- **U** **Carsington**[651] 324 7-10-3 0.. ChrisDavies(7) —
(Lucinda Featherstone) *stmbld bdly: sddle slipped and uns rdr 1st* **150/1**

601 **F** **Farewellatmidnight**[40] 3830 5-11-3 0............................ JimmyMcCarthy —
(Alex Hales) *trckd ldrs: rdn and wknd sn after 3 out: disputing modest 4th whn fell next* **33/1**

5m 17.0s (-9.50) **Going Correction** -0.30s/f (Good) 7 Ran SP% **109.0**
Speed ratings: **105,104,104,78,—** —,—
toteswingers:1&2:£2.60, 1&3:£1.20, 2&3:£1.40 CSF £11.66 TOTE £5.00: £2.50, £1.50; EX 14.70.
Owner Andrew Polson **Bred** Claude Quellier **Trained** Ditcheat, Somerset

FOCUS

Rail realignment increased distances by 60yds per circuit on both tracks. The ground was again good to firm, leading to a plethora of non-runners throughout the afternoon. The front three in the market pulled miles clear and the runner-up sets the level.

NOTEBOOK

Violin Davis(FR), who travelled the best of the trio into the straight, saw it out well for her first win over hurdles. She should have no trouble defying a penalty and will now head to Newbury for a mares' race next month. (op 5-1)

Chilli Rose soon held a clear advantage, but had been joined by the end of the back straight and, despite boxing on right the way to the line, she was again found wanting for a finishing kick. (tchd 9-4)

Kells Belle(IRE), penalised for her Ludlow success, was up markedly in trip, but didn't seem to fail through lack of stamina. She appeared not to let herself down on ground, McCoy doing well to get her to even challenge in the straight, and could find no extra after the last. (op 5-4)

Lost Two Stars(IRE) was beaten racing out on to the final circuit. (tchd 11-1)

Accordingtoeileen(IRE) was reluctant to line up and then failed to jump off when the tapes went up. (op 18-1)

Farewellatmidnight was exposed under her penalty. (op 28-1)

4704 WINCANTON GOLF COURSE H'CAP HURDLE (11 hdls) 2m 6f

2:35 (2:35) (Class 4) (0-110,108) 4-Y-0+ £2,927 (£859; £429; £214)

Form RPR

0621 **1** **Whispering Jack**[8] 4441 6-11-9 **108**.................................. PeterToole(3) 119+
(Charlie Mann) *a.p: led appr 2 out: rdn and edgd lft bef last: styd on: drvn rt out* **5/4**[1]

3 **2** 1 **Life Of A Luso (IRE)**[28] 4052 7-11-1 **100**..................(t) JimmyDerham(3) 107
(Paul Henderson) *trckd ldrs: nudged along 8th: rdn after 3 out: upsides next: swtchd rt sn after: ev ch last: kpt on* **8/1**[3]

6002 **3** 19 **Russian Epic**[28] 4052 7-11-7 **103**..(t) TomO'Brien 96
(Philip Hobbs) *trckd ldr: blnd 4th: mstke 3 out: sn rdn: ch 2 out: wknd bef last* **11/4**[2]

5214 **4** 6 **Can't Remember**[11] 4401 6-10-8 **95**................................ OliverDayman(5) 80
(Alison Thorpe) *trckd ldrs: rdn after 3 out: wknd bef next* **11/1**

4U40 **5** 13 **Skipper Robin (FR)**[47] 3693 5-11-9 **108**............ SamTwiston-Davies(3) 81
(Nigel Twiston-Davies) *led: rdn and hdd appr 2 out: wknd bef last* **9/1**

1-12 **P** **Restart (IRE)**[243] 954 10-11-12 **108**...................................... TimmyMurphy —
(Lucinda Featherstone) *trckd ldrs: rdn after 8th: wknd qckly after 3 out: p.u bef next* **9/1**

5m 16.8s (-9.70) **Going Correction** -0.30s/f (Good)
WFA 4 from 5yo+ 8lb 6 Ran SP% **110.6**
Speed ratings (Par 105): **105,104,97,95,90** —
toteswingers:1&2:£2.80, 1&3:£1.10, 2&3:£4.50 CSF £11.10 CT £21.73 TOTE £2.20: £1.40, £3.80; EX 15.40.
Owner Roger Bender & Mrs Sarah Bender **Bred** Miss Kerry Lane **Trained** Upper Lambourn, Berks

FOCUS

The front pair came clear in this modest handicap and the second is rated in line with his best form.

NOTEBOOK

Whispering Jack, successful at Ludlow last week, overcoming a blunder at the last. He looked all over the winner turning in, so actually made quite hard work of it, but can be rated better than the bare form and deserves a crack at something better. He'll probably have one more run before going chasing. (op 7-4)

Life Of A Luso(IRE) confirmed the promise shown at Kempton on his recent British debut, reversing that form with Russian Epic. (op 13-2)

Russian Epic again looked a non-stayer. (op 3-1)

Can't Remember was beaten down the back. (op 8-1)

Skipper Robin(FR) doesn't respect his hurdles, again making numerous errors, but he had all bar the winner off the bridle approaching the end of the back straight and showed enough to suggest he has a future over fences. (op 10-1 tchd 8-1)

Restart(IRE) offered little on this return from 243 days off. (op 8-1 tchd 10-1)

4705 CHILDRENS DAY 27TH MARCH H'CAP CHASE (22 fncs) 3m 3f 110y

3:10 (3:10) (Class 4) (0-105,104) 5-Y-0+ £3,903 (£1,146; £573; £286)

Form RPR

14-4 **1** **Choumakeur (FR)**[43] 3764 9-11-5 **100**..........................(bt) DannyCook(3) 120+
(David Pipe) *trckd ldrs: jnd ldr 7th: led 13th: in command fr after 4 out: wnt sltly rt last 3: pushed out* **9/2**[2]

00P4 **2** 10 **Skipper's Lad (IRE)**[12] 4372 9-11-1 **93**............................(bt) JoeTizzard 101+
(Colin Tizzard) *hld up bhd ldrs: rdn after 15th: wnt 2nd appr 3 out: styd on same pce: nvr threatened wnr* **9/2**[2]

-150 **3** *1 3/4* **De Bansha Man (IRE)**[66] 3391 6-11-9 **104**......... SamTwiston-Davies(3) 109
(Nigel Twiston-Davies) *trckd ldrs: chsd wnr after 13th: rdn appr 15th: lost 2nd 3 out: styd on same pce* **7/1**

2146 **4** *3 1/2* **Runshan (IRE)**[26] 4102 11-11-2 **101**........................ MrSWDrinkwater(7) 104
(David Bridgwater) *led tl 13th: chsd ldrs: rdn after 15th: styd on same pce fr after 4 out* **5/1**[3]

-5P2 **5** *10* **Noble Bily (FR)**[9] 4428 10-11-8 **103**.............................. AlexMerriam(3) 96
(Neil King) *trckd ldrs: rdn after 16th: 5th whn mstke 4 out: sn btn* **3/1**[1]

/664 **6** *18* **Front Street (IRE)**[63] 3428 7-10-1 **82**..................(v[1]) MichaelMurphy(3) 59
(Pat Murphy) *pushed along in last 10th: rdn after next: nvr threatened to get bk on terms: lost tch 18th* **7/1**

4P10 **P** **Autumn Red (IRE)**[45] 3723 11-11-5 **97**.......................(bt) DenisO'Regan —
(Paul Webber) *struggling in rr 5th: sn detached: t.o whn p.u bef 14th* **16/1**

6m 59.5s (-8.70) **Going Correction** -0.30s/f (Good) **7** Ran SP% **108.9**
Speed ratings: **100,97,96,95,92 87,—**
toteswingers:1&2:£2.90, 1&3:£7.00, 2&3:£4.10 CSF £22.73 CT £123.44 TOTE £2.20: £1.10, £4.70; EX 20.60.
Owner E A P Scouller **Bred** Olivier Delegue **Trained** Nicholashayne, Devon

FOCUS
A fairly modest staying handicap chase in which the third sets the level.

NOTEBOOK
Choumakeur(FR), weak in the market, had run well over hurdles on his return from a lengthy absence at Ffos Las in January and could be called the winner here midway down the back. Bouncing off the fast ground, he readily skipped clear, but given can be a bit tricky it was no surprise to see him carry his head a touch high under pressure down the straight. He had looked on a very fair mark and this consistent type may win again, with him being just as effective over hurdles. (op 3-1)
Skipper's Lad(IRE) is well weighted on old form and ran his best race for a while for his in-form stable. (op 5-1)
De Bansha Man(IRE) had previously disappointed over fences, so this must be seen as a step in the right direction.
Runshan(IRE) was headed with a circuit to run and steadily dropped away. (op 9-2)
Noble Bily(FR) had a bit to prove on the ground and failed to give his running. (op 7-2)

4706 KINGWELL RESTAURANT NOVICES' HURDLE (10 hdls) 2m 4f
3:45 (3:45) (Class 4) 4-Y-0+ **£2,439** (£716; £358; £178)

Form RPR

-440 **1** **Bold Addition (FR)**[48] 3686 6-11-2 119............................ NickScholfield 126+
(Paul Nicholls) *trckd ldrs: hit 6th: disp ld 3 out tl drew wl clr on bit bef 2 out: v easily* **8/13**[1]

1-0 **2** *35* **Sizing Santiago (IRE)**[134] 2059 5-10-13 0.......... SamTwiston-Davies(3) 89
(Nigel Twiston-Davies) *trckd ldrs: prom 4th: disp fr 6th: rdn after 3 out: sn hdd and no ch w wnr: all out to hold on for modest 2nd* **3/1**[2]

0 **3** *3/4* **Abayaan**[28] 4051 5-10-13 0... PeterToole(3) 88
(Charlie Mann) *trckd ldrs: rdn after 3 out: sn no ch: clsd on runner-up appr last: hld nr fin* **8/1**[3]

4 *36* **Taminkle (FR)**[89] 5-11-2 0.. WillKennedy 56
(Caroline Keevil) *led tl 3 out: sn rdn: wknd bef next: t.o* **14/1**

00 **5** *19* **San Salito (FR)**[70] 3266 5-10-9 0....................................... EdCookson(7) 39
(Giles Smyly) *trckd ldrs: rdn after 3 out: wknd bef next: t.o* **50/1**

3-04 **6** *62* **Reymysterio (IRE)**[29] 4028 10-10-13 83............................ KeiranBurke(3) —
(Patrick Rodford) *prom early: reminders after 3rd: sn in rr: t.o fr after 6th* **33/1**

0 **P** **Artic Journey (IRE)**[29] 4029 7-10-13 0.............................. DannyCook(3) —
(Linda Blackford) *prom tl after 5th: sn bhd: t.o whn p.u bef 3 out* **100/1**

4m 48.6s (-8.20) **Going Correction** -0.30s/f (Good) **7** Ran SP% **110.6**
Speed ratings (Par 105): **104,90,89,75,67 42,—**
toteswingers:1&2:£1.10, 1&3:£1.60, 2&3:£5.50 CSF £2.56 TOTE £1.30: £1.10, £1.90; EX 2.50.
Owner Mrs Sue Craven **Bred** Mme Jacques Thoreau **Trained** Ditcheat, Somerset

FOCUS
The withdrawal of Thanks For Coming meant that only two could be considered in what was a weak novice hurdle. The third sets the level.

NOTEBOOK
Bold Addition(FR) gained an overdue first win over hurdles. Always travelling well off what was a very steady gallop, he went on turning in and quickly sprinted clear. He isn't straightforward, but this ground suits him well and he can probably defy a penalty. (op 5-6)
Sizing Santiago(IRE), a bumper winner who was tailed off on his first start over hurdles in October, has since left Philip Hobbs. He failed to settle early and very much jumped his hurdles like a chaser, stopping quickly in the straight as the winner went on. He's left with something to prove for now, but should do better over fences. (op 11-4 tchd 7-2)
Abayaan stepped up on his initial effort, staying on to make a race of it for second, and he could pick up a small race.

4707 ROY AND STEVEN HANNEY MEMORIAL H'CAP HURDLE (8 hdls) 2m
4:20 (4:21) (Class 5) (0-95,94) 4-Y-0+ **£1,951** (£573; £286; £143)

Form RPR

06-4 **1** **Allformary**[306] 224 5-9-7 **68** oh5.....................................(t) EdCookson(7) 86+
(Kim Bailey) *hld up but wl in tch: hdwy 3 out: led appr 2 out: qcknd readily clr: pushed out* **5/1**[2]

0016 **2** *20* **Roxane Bruere (FR)**[40] 3839 6-9-12 **76**...............(t) ChristopherWard(10) 77
(Robin Dickin) *led: rdn and hdd appr 2 out: kpt on but nt pce of wnr* **8/1**

53-5 **3** *7* **Golden Games (IRE)**[11] 4397 5-11-1 **83**.......................... MattieBatchelor 78
(Daniel O'Brien) *trckd ldrs: hung lft and lost pl after 3rd: rdn to chse ldrs after 3 out: styd on same pce* **6/1**

000 **4** *1* **Special Cuvee**[34] 3937 5-11-7 **94**................................(t) OliverDayman(5) 90+
(Alison Thorpe) *trckd ldrs: struggling in tch whn hmpd 3 out: sn one pce: hung rt u.p after 2 out* **12/1**

066 **5** *16* **Sanctuary**[20] 4225 5-11-5 **92**...(p) CO'Farrell(5) 70
(Michael Scudamore) *prom: rdn and ev ch after 3 out: wknd next* **11/2**[3]

0000 **6** *4 1/2* **Victory Bay**[17] 4268 6-10-3 **78**.................................(t) NathanSweeney(7) 52
(Simon Burrough) *t.k.h in tch: effrt after 3 out: wknd bef next* **25/1**

60/P **F** **Driving Miss Suzie**[40] 3839 7-11-1 **90**.........................(p) MrPJTolman(7) —
(Debra Hamer) *trckd ldrs: travelling ok whn fell 3 out* **20/1**

-6P0 **P** **Commit To Memory**[62] 3449 6-11-3 **85**.................................. TomO'Brien —
(Paul Henderson) *hld up in tch: hit 1st: p.u after 2nd: dismntd* **5/1**[2]

0000 **P** **Senses (USA)**[27] 4069 5-11-0 **85**.....................................(v) DannyCook(3) —
(David Pipe) *trckd ldrs: hit 3 out: sn rdn and btn: p.u bef next* **10/3**[1]

3m 43.4s (-5.50) **Going Correction** -0.30s/f (Good) **9** Ran SP% **113.5**
Speed ratings (Par 103): **101,91,87,87,79 76,—,—,—**
toteswingers:1&2:£4.50, 1&3:£7.50, 2&3:£5.60 CSF £43.45 CT £243.35 TOTE £5.10: £1.60, £2.20, £2.20; EX 43.90.
Owner J Perriss **Bred** Ms R A Myatt **Trained** Andoversford, Gloucs

FOCUS
A poor handicap hurdle rated around the placed horses.

NOTEBOOK
Allformary, rated just 63 on the back of three well-beaten runs over hurdles in 2010, was 5lb out of the handicap, but proved positive in the market and fairly bolted up, cruising to the lead two out and readily drawing clear. The tongue-tie was clearly a big help and, on this evidence, it will be a surprise if she doesn't go in again. (op 7-1)
Roxane Bruere(FR) stuck on best she could once headed. (tchd 9-1)
Golden Games(IRE), who was under pressure early down the back, consented to plug on late. Official explanation: jockey said mare was lame (op 5-1)
Special Cuvee will be of some interest once his mark drops, having been hampered here. Official explanation: jockey said gelding was hampered by faller three out (op 17-2)
Sanctuary didn't get home having raced freely through the early stages. (op 6-1)
Commit To Memory Official explanation: vet said gelding pulled up lame left-hind (op 4-1)
Senses(USA), who looked on a good mark judged on his Flat form, showed little enthusiasm once coming under pressure following a bad blunder three out. Official explanation: jockey said gelding stopped quickly (op 4-1)

4708 DICK AND SUE WOODHOUSE MEMORIAL HUNTERS' CHASE (FOR THE DICK WOODHOUSE TROPHY) (17 fncs) 2m 5f
4:55 (4:57) (Class 6) 5-Y-0+ **£936** (£290; £145; £72)

Form RPR

3P-0 **1** **Jayne's Crusader**[12] 8-12-0 108.. MrMGMiller 109+
(Mrs S Alner) *hld up towards rr: stdy prog fr 12th: trckd ldrs 3 out: gd jump last to ld sn after: rdn flat: all out* **5/4**[1]

234- **2** *nk* **Oracle Des Mottes (FR)**[20] 12-11-7 117...................(t) MissAliceMills(7) 113+
(R Barber) *in tch: pushed along after 13th: chal 3 out: narrow advantage whn hmpd last: sn hdd: kpt on nr fin* **6/1**[2]

2315 **3** *1 1/4* **Ryeman**[33] 9-12-4 103..(bt[1]) MrJoshuaGuerriero 111
(Andrew Jackson) *trckd ldrs: led 2 out: sn rdn: hdd last: kpt on but no ex* **13/2**[3]

/53- **4** *9* **Light Des Mulottes (FR)**[327] 5249 12-11-7 0.................... MrSCoady(7) 104+
(S J Coady) *chsd ldrs: blnd 4th: mstke 13th: rdn after 4 out: hld whn pckd 3 out: lft 4th last* **12/1**

2/F- **5** *5* **Run For Moor (IRE)**[327] 10-11-7 0...................................... MrPMason(7) 96
(Jennifer Mason) *mid-div: hdwy 12th: led 3 out: sn hdd: wknd after next: lft 5th last* **22/1**

PF1/ **6** *7* **Master John (IRE)**[12] 10-12-4 0... MissPGundry 92
(E Walker) *chsd ldrs tl after 11th: rdn after 13th: wknd after 4 out* **14/1**

5645 **7** *34* **Classic Clover**[22] 4163 11-12-1 93..................................(t) MrMLegg(7) 66
(Colin Tizzard) *struggling in rr fr 5th: t.o* **33/1**

B-60 **F** **Eljay's Boy**[12] 13-11-9 92..(t) MrRGHenderson(5) —
(J Myerscough-Walker) *mid-div: rdn after 13th: wknd after next: bhd whn fell last* **50/1**

255/ **P** **Touch Of Flame**[6] 12-12-0 86.. MrWBiddick —
(K J Cumings) *hld up towards rr: hdwy into midfield 10th: wknd 4 out: bhd whn p.u bef 2 out* **25/1**

P5-0 **P** **The Venetian (IRE)**[19] 10-11-7 92................................(p) MissAPearn(7) —
(Miss G G Haywood) *mid-div: hit 1st: towards rr whn mstke 9th (water): nt fluent 11th: p.u bef next* **28/1**

-30R **U** **Cloud Nine (IRE)**[21] 4197 8-11-9 109..............................(b) MrJHamer(5) 105
(Miss Jane Western) *led tl rdn 3 out: kpt on: cl 4th whn stmbld bdly and uns rdr last* **12/1**

5PU- **P** **Alfatrix (IRE)**[20] 8-11-9 0... MrSAllwood(5) —
(M G Miller) *j.lft at times: trckd ldrs: rdn after 11th: wknd after 13th: bhd whn p.u bef last* **25/1**

5m 15.4s (-9.80) **Going Correction** -0.30s/f (Good) **12** Ran SP% **114.5**
Speed ratings: **106,105,105,101,100 97,84,—,—,— —,—**
toteswingers:1&2:£1.20, 1&3:£1.70, 2&3:£10.50 CSF £7.52 TOTE £2.70: £1.50, £2.40, £2.10; EX 7.50.
Owner Mr & Mrs T P Tory & Mrs D Dampney **Bred** Paul Murphy **Trained** Droop, Dorset

FOCUS
A competitive enough hunter chase in which the third and fourth are the best guides to the form.

NOTEBOOK
Jayne's Crusader gradually crept into it and a good jump at the last sealed it for him. These conditions clearly suited him well, but he'll need to improve if he's to follow up. (op 7-4 tchd Evens)
Oracle Des Mottes(FR) would probably have won had his rider not slowed on him going into the last, at which he got in too close. He rallied close home, but the line came too soon. (tchd 15-2)
Ryeman travelled well in the first-time blinkers and had his chance, but couldn't match the front pair after the last. (op 7-1 tchd 8-1)
Cloud Nine(IRE) was in the process of recording an improved effort, keeping on in fourth, when departing at the last. (op 14-1 tchd 10-1)
Alfatrix(IRE) Official explanation: vet said gelding bled from the nose (op 14-1 tchd 10-1)

4709 TURFTV MAIDEN OPEN NATIONAL HUNT FLAT RACE 2m
5:30 (5:30) (Class 6) 4-6-Y-0 **£1,370** (£399; £199)

Form RPR

3 **1** **Shinko Moon**[143] 1913 4-10-10 0.. WillKennedy 93
(Jo Crowley) *mde all: kpt on gamely: rdn out* **6/1**[3]

2 *1 1/4* **Chance Encounter (IRE)** 5-11-1 0................................ DannyCook(3) 100
(Linda Blackford) *a.p: rdn and ev ch fr over 2f out tl swtchd rt ent fnl f: kpt on* **40/1**

0 **3** *1/2* **Suspect (GER)**[72] 3200 5-10-13 0.................................(t) MrRMahon(5) 100
(Paul Nicholls) *hld up: hdwy over 3f out: rdn over 2f out: edgd rt over 1f out: styd on same pce* **9/4**[1]

50 **4** *2* **Champagne Rosie**[36] 3909 5-10-4 0........................... NathanSweeney(7) 91
(Bob Buckler) *trckd ldrs: rdn 3f out: styd on same pce fnl 2f* **25/1**

5 *2 3/4* **Titch Strider (IRE)** 6-10-8 0.............................. SamTwiston-Davies(3) 89
(John Panvert) *trckd ldrs: rdn 3f out: styd on same pce fnl 2f* **13/2**

6 *3* **Pinkneys Prince** 4-10-5 0... GilesHawkins(5) 85
(Nick Williams) *trckd ldrs: effrt 3f out: one pce fr over 1f out* **7/2**[2]

0 **7** *1* **Romany Quest**[69] 3301 4-10-10 0.................................. AndrewGlassonbury 84
(Linda Blackford) *trckd ldrs: rdn 3f out: sn one pce* **50/1**

8 *1/2* **Bob Lewis**[118] 5-11-4 0... TimmyMurphy 91
(Chris Down) *hld up: hdwy over 4f out: effrt 3f out: one pce fr over 1f out* **10/1**

9 *nk* **Uncle Johnny** 6-10-13 0.. RachaelGreen(5) 91
(Anthony Honeyball) *hld up: sme hdwy over 3f out: sn rdn: one pce fr over 1f out* **7/1**

0 **10** *dist* **Major Bob**[33] 3964 5-11-4 0... JohnnyFarrelly —
(Richard Mitchell) *prom tl 1/2-way: t.o* **100/1**

P **Weebitevil** 4-10-3 0.. GerardTumelty —
(Matthew Salaman) *a towards rr: t.o whn p.u ins fnl f: dismntd* **20/1**

3m 38.8s (-4.50) **Going Correction** -0.30s/f (Good)
WFA 4 from 5yo+ 7lb **11** Ran SP% **116.2**
Speed ratings: **99,98,98,97,95 94,93,93,93,— —**
toteswingers:1&2:£14.20, 1&3:£4.10, 2&3:£11.30 CSF £228.18 TOTE £6.40: £1.50, £11.00, £1.10; EX 323.80.

Owner Mrs Liz Nelson **Bred** Mrs R I Nelson **Trained** Whitcombe, Dorset

FOCUS

There was more pace on here than in most bumpers and it turned into a good test at the distance. The winner stepped up on his form at shorter with the fourth back to form in an ordinary contest.

NOTEBOOK

Shinko Moon, off since finishing third at Exeter on his debut in October, really saw his race out well, having been in front a long time, and looks to have a nice future, although whether he'll be up to defying a penalty remains to be seen. (tchd 11-2)

Chance Encounter(IRE), half-brother to a 3m1f hurdle winner, showed plenty on this racecourse debut, keeping on right the way to the line, and should improve. (op 33-1)

Suspect(GER) failed to meet with expectations at Newbury in December, but had clearly learned from that experience and the first-time tongue-tie enabled him to improve. He travelled strongly before staying on under pressure and should progress again. (op 7-4)

Champagne Rosie ran creditably, improving on previous efforts. (op 40-1)

Titch Strider(IRE) shaped as though a longer trip will suit once hurdling. (op 9-1)

Pinkneys Prince travelled well up to a point and should show the benefit of this experience next time. (op 9-2)

Weebitevil Official explanation: jockey said filly was lame behind

T/Plt: £31.50 to a £1 stake. Pool:£59,106.52 - 1,368.75 winning tickets T/Qpdt: £6.10 to a £1 stake. Pool:£3,232.29 - 387.98 winning tickets TM

^{4684}AYR (L-H)

Saturday, March 12

OFFICIAL GOING: Heavy (chs 6.7, hdl 6.9)

Rail on hurdles course moved out 5 metres from innermost line and chases 14m to provide fresh ground. Common bend on home turn.

Wind: Slight, half against Weather: Overcast, dull

4711 AWARD WINMNING WESTERN HOUSE HOTEL NOVICES' HURDLE (9 hdls) — 2m

2:15 (2:15) (Class 4) 4-Y-O+ **£2,602** (£764; £382; £190)

Form				RPR
304	1		**Trucking Along (IRE)**^{16} [4303] 5-11-1 0 .... CampbellGillies (S R B Crawford, Ire) *t.k.h: chsd ldrs: led 5th: j.lft 3 out: rdn and styd on strly fr next: clr whn hit last: eased run-in* **9/1**	125+
020-	2	*6*	**Sole Witness (IRE)**^{13} [4385] 7-10-10 114 .... (t) EJO'Connell$^{(5)}$ (C A McBratney, Ire) *in tch: outpcd bef 3 out: rallied to chse wnr bef next: no imp* **15/8**^{2}	113
F4	3	*20*	**Omokoroa (IRE)**^{47} [3715] 5-11-1 0 .... GrahamLee (Donald McCain) *led: hdd whn nt fluent 5th: cl up: effrt and 1 l down whn mstke 3 out: wknd bef next* **11/10**^{1}	96
	4	*5*	**Chookie Hamilton**^{73} 7-11-1 0 .... JamesReveley (Keith Dalgleish) *cl up tl rdn and wknd bef 3 out* **7/1**^{3}	90

4m 24.5s (21.40) **Going Correction** +1.00s/f (Soft) **4** Ran SP% **104.9**

Speed ratings (Par 105): **86,83,73,70**

CSF £24.33 TOTE £8.10; EX 24.70.

Owner Mrs Denise Bailey/David Bailey **Bred** Michael Doyle **Trained** Larne, Co Antrim

FOCUS

Further rain during the morning turned the ground to heavy all round, and riders in the first confirmed that it was "testing". They took things steadily in this uncompetitive novice hurdle until the pace quickened on the home turn. The time was 45 seconds outside the standard and this isn't form to treat too seriously. There was a 1-2 for Irish stables and the runner-up is the best guide to the level.

NOTEBOOK

Trucking Along(IRE), although sent off the outsider of the four, had not shaped badly over C&D on his recent hurdles debut. He quickened things up turning in and with his nearest pursuer blundering at the first in the straight, he was never seriously threatened, winning eased down. He handled the ground well enough and gets further. (op 10-1 tchd 8-1)

Sole Witness(IRE)'s two wins both came in heavy ground at Down Royal, so conditions weren't a problem. Fitted with a first-time tongue-tie, he was outpaced when the tempo lifted and merely plugged on for second. He probably needs further. (op 9-4)

Omokoroa(IRE), who led for the first half of the race, was in second when he blundered three from home, effectively ending his chance. The ground was a ready excuse here but he has not built on the promise of his hurdles debut. Official explanation: jockey said gelding was unsuited by the heavy ground (op 10-11)

Chookie Hamilton is a fairly useful performer on the Flat and there were no stamina doubts ahead of this hurdling debut. After taking a bit of a hold, he was caught out by the increase in pace approaching the third-last and very quickly beaten. His hurdling had not been particularly fluent and the ground was probably against him. (op 13-2 tchd 6-1)

4712 STARSPORTSBET.CO.UK NOVICES' H'CAP HURDLE (12 hdls) — 3m 110y

2:50 (2:50) (Class 4) (0-110,103) 4-Y-O+ **£2,602** (£764; £382; £190)

Form				RPR
435B	1		**Rebel Swing**^{6} [4508] 5-11-7 98 .... HenryOliver (Sue Smith) *chsd ldrs: rdn bef 2 out: led whn lft 3 l in front next: drvn out run-in* **7/2**^{2}	99+
00U6	2	*4 1/2*	**Artic Night (FR)**^{40} [3850] 5-11-4 95 .... FearghalDavis (Nicky Richards) *t.k.h: hld up: hdwy to chse ldrs and effrt bef 3 out: lft 3 l 2nd next: kpt on same pce run-in* **9/1**	93
5	3	*6*	**Ballycarron Lad (IRE)**^{16} [4304] 9-11-2 100 .... MrBGCrawford$^{(7)}$ (S R B Crawford, Ire) *hld up: drvn and outpcd after 4 out: styd on fr 2 out: nrst fin* **9/1**	91
1-PP	4	*5*	**Seven Is Lucky (IRE)**^{28} [4066] 9-11-4 95 .... GrahamLee (Jim Goldie) *led: jst hdd whn lft cl 3rd 2 out: sn rdn: wknd last* **9/2**^{3}	83
-566	5	*6*	**Comeththehour (IRE)**^{12} [4391] 8-10-13 90 .... PaddyAspell (James Moffatt) *trckd ldrs: nt fluent 4 out: rdn and wknd bef next* **5/1**	70
-043	P		**Crackerjack Lad (IRE)**^{16} [4302] 8-10-10 87 .... CampbellGillies (Lucinda Russell) *hld up: hdwy after 4 out: outpcd whn blnd 3 out: sn btn: t.o whn p.u bef last* **3/1**^{1}	—
	P		**Izind An Affair (IRE)**^{10} [4433] 6-10-9 91 .... (b^{1}) EJO'Connell$^{(5)}$ (C A McBratney, Ire) *prom: j. slowly and lost pl 7th: lost tch next: t.o whn p.u bef 4 out* **20/1**	—
6650	U		**Tippering (IRE)**^{32} [3989] 6-11-7 103 .... ShaneByrne$^{(5)}$ (Sue Smith) *t.k.h: trckd ldrs: effrt and disputing ld whn pckd and uns rdr 2 out* **8/1**	103

6m 53.4s (21.60) **Going Correction** +1.00s/f (Soft) **8** Ran SP% **117.9**

Speed ratings (Par 105): **105,103,101,100,98** —,—,—

toteswingers:1&2:£8.90, 1&3:£4.40, 2&3:£29.40 CSF £35.19 CT £265.17 TOTE £4.30: £1.50, £3.40, £3.10; EX 45.60.

Owner Broadway Racing Club 15 **Bred** Mrs D R Schreiber **Trained** High Eldwick, W Yorks

FOCUS

A very ordinary novice handicap, run at an understandably steady pace and the winner and the unseater at the second-last help set the level.

NOTEBOOK

Rebel Swing looked in trouble when losing his position before the home turn, but one thing he does is stay. Rallying and upsides when left clear two out, he won decisively in the end. He had been beaten off similar marks on his last five starts since scoring off 9lb lower at Uttoxeter, and probably didn't improve here, but could have more to offer in testing ground. (op 4-1)

Artic Night(FR), upped in trip for this handicap debut, improved from the rear to race on the heels of the leaders turning in. He was left in second spot two from home but was held by the winner from there. (tchd 10-1)

Ballycarron Lad(IRE), representing the Irish yard successful in the opener, was another handicap debutant who has been racing over shorter. He looked well beaten at one stage but did plug on past some tired rivals. (tchd 8-1)

Seven Is Lucky(IRE), better known as a chaser nowadays, made a lot of the running but had no answers when headed. Official explanation: jockey said gelding bled from the nose (op 6-1)

Comeththehour(IRE) was struggling before the home turn.

Crackerjack Lad(IRE), placed over 2m4f here latest, travelled fairly well at the back of the field, but his brief forward move was halted by a mistake at the first in the home straight. Eventually pulled up, he didn't stay in this ground. Official explanation: jockey said gelding ran flat (op 7-2)

Tippering(IRE) made steady headway and was just in front when he stumbled two out and unshipped his rider. He would have been involved in the shake-up and is worth another try at this sort of trip, but a cautionary note is that he did not look too enthusiastic last time and took something of a hold here. (op 7-2)

4713 BREWIN DOLPHIN H'CAP CHASE (19 fncs) — 3m 1f

3:25 (3:25) (Class 4) (0-105,105) 5-Y-O+ **£3,252** (£955; £477; £238)

Form				RPR
5P43	1		**Sammy Spiderman**^{16} [4306] 8-10-1 83 .... (v^{1}) EwanWhillans$^{(3)}$ (Alistair Whillans) *chsd ldrs: wnt 2nd and blnd 12th: effrt 4 out: sn drvn: swtchd rt bef last: styd on wl run-in: led nr fin* **5/2**^{1}	90+
P232	2	*1/2*	**Double Default (IRE)**^{19} [4258] 10-11-12 105 .... (p) JamesReveley (Martin Todhunter) *cl up: led 3rd: stmbld 11th: effrt 3 out: rdn and edgd lft after next: wnt 2 l clr run-in: no ex and hdd nr fin* **11/4**^{2}	108
U-44	3	*30*	**Skenfrith**^{28} [4066] 12-10-0 79 oh4 .... (p) PaddyAspell (Sandy Forster) *led to 3rd: chsd ldr tl mstke 12th: rdn 6 out: outpcd bef next: tk modest 3rd bef 2 out: no imp* **5/1**	51
4216	4	*90*	**Euro American (GER)**^{4} [4544] 11-11-11 104 .... WilsonRenwick (Rose Dobbin) *nt fluent: in tch: stdy hdwy 6 out: mstke and rdn 5 out: wknd fr next* **6/1**	60
112F	F		**Panzer (GER)**^{13} [4381] 10-10-13 99 .... MrJHamer$^{(7)}$ (Donald McCain) *in tch: mstke 5th: fell heavily 10th* **9/2**^{3}	—

7m 25.8s (35.90) **Going Correction** +1.45s/f (Heav) **5** Ran SP% **104.4**

Speed ratings: **100,99,90,61,**—

CSF £8.83 TOTE £2.80: £1.60, £1.80; EX 8.60.

Owner John & Liz Elliot, A Brunton, P Copeland **Bred** J J Elliot **Trained** Newmill-On-Slitrig, Borders

FOCUS

A modest handicap chase, but a stirring finish as the first two pulled well clear. Conditions looked just as testing on the chase track and the time was very slow. The second is rated to his recent mark.

NOTEBOOK

Sammy Spiderman had dropped to a mark 12lb lower than when completing an Ayr hat-trick just over two years ago. Travelling quite well in the first-time visor, and surviving a bad blunder down the far side, he looked held just after the last but responded gamely to snatch the race. He is well at home in deep ground. (op 2-1)

Double Default(IRE) stumbled at the 11th and Reveley did well to stay aboard, but the gelding jumped well otherwise. Making most of the running, he looked set for his first win in a long time but began to tire after the last and was cut down. He is lightly raced for his age and a minor chase should come his way at some point, but he has developed a habit of being caught on the run-in. (op 7-2)

Skenfrith, who was 4lb out of the weights, was never going well after losing his early lead. He plugged on for a remote third and has been well beaten on his three runs this term despite making the frame each time. (op 9-2)

Euro American(GER) is a noted mudlark, but was 7lb higher than when scoring at Sedgefield two runs back and this came too soon after his run over hurdles four days earlier. This trip stretches him. (op 11-2)

Panzer(GER), having only his fourth run over fences, has now come down the last twice. (op 4-1)

4714 AYRSHIRE POST H'CAP CHASE (FOR THE HUGH BARCLAY CHALLENGE TROPHY) (17 fncs) — 2m 4f

4:00 (4:00) (Class 3) (0-125,125) 5-Y-O+ **£6,330** (£1,965; £1,058)

Form				RPR
-F00	1		**Stormin Exit (IRE)**^{48} [3706] 8-11-12 125 .... JamesReveley (Jim Goldie) *cl up: led 3rd to 9th: regained ld bef 3 out: rdn and styd on strly fr next* **2/1**^{2}	137+
641F	2	*12*	**Locked Inthepocket (IRE)**^{24} [4150] 7-10-11 110 .... RichieMcGrath (Pauline Robson) *hld up in tch: hdwy bef 4 out: swtchd lft and chsd wnr next: rdn whn nt fluent 2 out: no imp* **15/8**^{1}	109
31-	3	*4*	**Schindlers Maze (IRE)**^{14} [4366] 9-10-11 110 .... (t) GrahamLee (James H Black, Ire) *led tl nt fluent and hdd 3rd: cl up: led 9th: hit 11th: rdn and hdd bef 3 out: sn btn* **8/1**	107+
0311	P		**Work Boy**^{19} [4258] 10-10-11 115 .... ShaneByrne$^{(5)}$ (Sue Smith) *cl up: rdn 5 out: wknd bef next: t.o whn p.u bef 2 out* **5/2**^{3}	—

5m 50.9s (28.00) **Going Correction** +1.45s/f (Heav) **4** Ran SP% **107.8**

Speed ratings: **102,97,95,**—

CSF £6.18 TOTE £2.60; EX 4.00.

Owner Fyffees & Robinson **Bred** Jamie Davidson **Trained** Uplawmoor, E Renfrews

FOCUS

An ordinary handicap chase rated around the first two but not form to be confident about.

NOTEBOOK

Stormin Exit(IRE) found this markedly less competitive than the races he had been contesting at Aintree and Leopardstown this season. Generally jumping well, he was back in front three out and ran out a comfortable winner. He has an entry in the Grand Annual at Cheltenham, but even with the penalty he picked up he might struggle to get in. (op 7-4)

Locked Inthepocket(IRE), held up in last place for most of the way, did move into second three out but could do little to prevent the winner from pulling away. He jumped better than he had at Musselburgh but was racing off 15lb higher than for his C&D win. (op 7-4 tchd 2-1)

Schindlers Maze(IRE), tried in a tongue-tie, was running for only the second time since winning at Newcastle off 10lb lower a year ago. Just headed when blundering three out, he was very weary from that point. (tchd 13-2)

Work Boy, attempting a hat-trick, was a further 6lb higher than when beating earlier runner-up Double Default at Carlisle. Relegated to a toiling last on the home turn, he was well adrift when pulling up. Official explanation: trainer's rep had no explanation for the poor form shown (op 7-2)

4715 ABBOTT RISK CONSULTING H'CAP HURDLE (FOR THE AYRSHIRE YEOMANRY CUP) (11 hdls) 2m 4f

4:30 (4:31) (Class 3) (0-125,122) 4-Y-0+ £5,529 (£1,623; £811; £405)

Form				RPR
0140	1		**Kempski**[23] 4169 11-9-11 100 ... PaulGallagher(7) (Rayson Nixon) *mde all: rdn after 4 out: styd on gamely u.p fr next* 7/1[3]	107
5-11	2	hd	**Circus Clown (IRE)**[23] 4166 6-10-11 107 ... GrahamLee (Jim Goldie) *prom: lft 2nd 4 out: effrt and rdn 2 out: hit last: chal run-in: jst hld* 2/1[1]	114
01P2	3	12	**Arctic Court (IRE)**[28] 4062 7-11-7 117 ... RichieMcGrath (Jim Goldie) *hld up: pushed along whn checked 4 out: effrt and cl up bef next: no ex fr 2 out* 10/1	115+
0351	4	4 ½	**Double Eagle**[19] 4257 9-11-8 118 ... (p) PaddyAspell (Donald McCain) *trckd ldrs: hmpd 4 out: sn outpcd: no imp fr next* 5/1[2]	108
000F	5	25	**Livvy Inn (USA)**[19] 4257 6-11-8 118 ... CampbellGillies (Lucinda Russell) *hld up: hdwy and cl up bef 3 out: rdn and wknd fr next* 7/1[3]	88
0542	6	28	**Chester Lad**[35] 3954 6-11-12 122 ... JanFaltejsek (George Charlton) *bhd: struggling 7th: t.o* 11/1	59
6334	7	2 ½	**Currahee**[17] 4285 7-11-0 110 ... (t) MichaelMcAlister (Maurice Barnes) *prom: drvn and outpcd whn hmpd 4 out: sn btn: eased whn no ch* 8/1	45
5412	F		**Teenage Idol (IRE)**[19] 4255 7-11-7 120 ... JamesO'Farrell(3) (Evelyn Slack) *cl up: chal gng wl whn fell 4 out* 7/1[3]	—

5m 28.5s (16.50) **Going Correction** +1.00s/f (Soft) 8 Ran SP% **116.0**
Speed ratings (Par 107): **107,106,102,100,90 79,78,—**
toteswingers:1&2:£2.70, 2&3:£2.60, 1&3:£7.20 CSF £22.44 CT £142.45 TOTE £9.30: £2.60, £1.40, £2.10; EX 33.60.
Owner Rayson & Susan Nixon **Bred** W T Kemp **Trained** Ettrickbridge, Borders

FOCUS
A fair and reasonably competitive handicap hurdle in which the third looks the best guide.

NOTEBOOK
Kempski won this race in 2008 and again a year later, when 12lb higher than he was here, while his trainer also won this event back in 2002. Outclassed behind Peddlers Cross at Kelso latest, the bottomweight was much more at home back over his favourite C&D and underfoot conditions were ideal. Holding on bravely after making nearly all the running, he is likely to be retired at the end of the season. (op 15-2 tchd 8-1)
Circus Clown(IRE) was up a further 9lb on this bid for a hat-trick. He came through to hold every chance but found the winner a tough horse to pass, although he nearly snatched it after his rider switched his stick late on. The step up in trip was not a problem. (op 15-8)
Arctic Court(IRE), the runner-up's stablemate, was a one-paced third dropped back in trip but may not have appreciated conditions as testing as this. (tchd 11-1)
Double Eagle had no problem with the ground but was 8lb higher than when scoring at Carlisle and is more at home on right-handed circuits. (op 6-1 tchd 13-2)
Livvy Inn(USA), who might have beaten today's fourth at Carlisle had he not come down, looked threatening at the first in the home straight but soon cried enough. (op 15-2 tchd 13-2)
Teenage Idol(IRE), still 15lb higher than when winning over 2m here in January, had just taken it up and was travelling well when he stepped into the fourth-last and came down. (op 12-1 tchd 13-2)

4716 "KILMARNOCK STANDARD" H'CAP CHASE (12 fncs) 2m

5:05 (5:05) (Class 3) (0-125,122) 5-Y-0+ £6,179 (£1,814; £907; £453)

Form				RPR
0202	1		**Raysrock (IRE)**[28] 4065 9-11-10 120 ... (t) CampbellGillies (Lucinda Russell) *mde all: hit and jnd 7th: styd on strly fr 3 out: easily* 11/10[1]	132+
5FP-	2	5	**Mighty Massini (IRE)**[14] 4367 8-11-7 122 ... EJO'Connell(5) (C A McBratney, Ire) *prom: drvn and outpcd bef 4 out: rallied to chse wnr between last 2: no imp* 13/2	123
-1P1	3	2	**Desperate Dex (IRE)**[57] 3544 11-10-6 102 ... GrahamLee (Ferdy Murphy) *t.k.h: prom: nt fluent and outpcd 6th: struggling 5 out: plugged on fnl 2: no imp* 3/1[2]	102
6010	4	17	**Cranky Corner**[8] 4456 7-11-1 116 ... ShaneByrne(5) (Sue Smith) *cl up: chal 6th: rdn and edgd lft after 4 out: wknd fr 2 out* 7/2[3]	99

4m 30.8s (20.10) **Going Correction** +1.45s/f (Heav) 4 Ran SP% **108.2**
Speed ratings: **107,104,103,95**
CSF £7.55 TOTE £2.20; EX 9.90.
Owner A Irvine **Bred** Kevin Neville **Trained** Arlary, Perth & Kinross

FOCUS
Not a strong race for the grade but a step up from the winner with the placed horses a few pounds below their best.

NOTEBOOK
Raysrock(IRE) went one better than when second to subsequent winner Reindeer Dippin over C&D latest, and the tongue tie looks to have had a beneficial effect. Mixing some spectacular leaps with untidy errors, he made all and drew clear from the second-last to win very comfortably. (op 6-4)
Mighty Massini(IRE), whose Irish stable won this race two years ago, had failed to finish on his last three starts but ran respectably when getting round earlier in the season. He was never a serious threat here but did stay on quite well for second, albeit flattered by his proximity to the winner. (op 11-2)
Desperate Dex(IRE) had won four of his last six starts but was another 5lb higher. A quirky sort, he was left behind after one or two untidy jumps but plugged on and was not beaten that far in the end. (op 11-4 tchd 9-4)
Cranky Corner challenged for the lead on the home turn but could not get past Raysrock and weakened rapidly after the second-last. The ground was an obvious excuse.

4717 IRVINE HERALD STANDARD OPEN NATIONAL HUNT FLAT RACE 2m

5:35 (5:35) (Class 6) 4-6-Y-0 £1,370 (£399; £199)

Form				RPR
	1		**Jonny Delta** 4-10-8 0 ... JamesReveley (Jim Goldie) *hld up in tch: smooth hdwy to ld over 1f out: shkn up and sn clr: easily* 5/1[3]	107+
	2	16	**Rudemeister (IRE)**[302] 5-11-2 0 ... RichieMcGrath (Andrew Parker) *prom: rdn and outpcd over 3f out: rallied over 1f out: styd on to chse wnr towards fin* 4/1[2]	95
	3	¾	**Fog Patches (IRE)**[168] 5-11-2 0 ... CampbellGillies (Lucinda Russell) *led: clr 3f out: rdn and hdd over 1f out: hung lft ins fnl f: wknd and lost 2nd cl home* 8/1	95
1	4	3 ¾	**Tricksofthetrade (IRE)**[26] 4117 5-11-2 0 ... JeremiahMcGrath(7) (Alan Swinbank) *t.k.h: trckd ldrs: effrt and hdwy over 2f out: edgd lft: wknd over 1f out* 4/6[1]	97
00-	5	12	**Santiago Boy**[329] 5227 5-10-9 0 ... PaulGallagher(7) (Linda Perratt) *trckd ldr: drvn over 3f out: wknd over 2f out* 20/1	78

4m 14.7s (14.00) **Going Correction** +1.00s/f (Soft)
WFA 4 from 5yo 7lb 5 Ran SP% **112.5**
Speed ratings: **105,97,96,94,88**
CSF £24.69 TOTE £7.40: £4.20, £4.00; EX 25.50.
Owner Johnnie Delta Racing **Bred** Miss Gill Quincey **Trained** Uplawmoor, E Renfrews

FOCUS
This was no more than an ordinary bumper, but they went a reasonable pace considering the bad ground and small field and the winner looks above average. This is not a race to be confident about.

NOTEBOOK
Jonny Delta, out of a 1m6f scorer, was Jim Goldie's first bumper runner this season, but the trainer sent out out a 20-1 winner of this race a year ago. Held up before easing into second early in the straight, the 4-y-o was soon in front and ran out a smooth winner. More should be heard of him. (op 6-1)
Rudemeister(IRE), a half-brother to staying chaser Mark The Book, joined connections for £75,000 after winning an Irish point on good ground last May. He was relegated to last place when the race began in earnest on the home turn, but stayed on stoutly in the latter stages to grab second. When he goes over hurdles a longer trip will suit him. (op 9-2 tchd 5-1)
Fog Patches(IRE) is another recruit from the Irish pointing field, finishing second of four finishers on his one start back in September. He made the running and tried to kick away early in the straight, but was soon caught by the winner and could not hold on to second as he tired. (tchd 7-1)
Tricksofthetrade(IRE), penalised for his Catterick win, was found wanting in this much softer ground, but had received favourable comments from his trainer after his debut so may be worth another chance. Official explanation: jockey said gelding was unsuited by the heavy ground (op 8-13 tchd 8-11 and 4-5 in places)
Santiago Boy, off the track for 11 months, has been well beaten in three Ayr bumpers now. (op 16-1 tchd 22-1)
T/Plt: £902.60 to a £1 stake. Pool:£60,501.66 - 48.93 winning tickets T/Qpdt: £14.80 to a £1 stake. Pool:£4,511.34 - 224.75 winning tickets RY

3930 CHEPSTOW (L-H)

Saturday, March 12

OFFICIAL GOING: Good (good to soft in places; chs 6.2; hdl 6.3)
Wind: Mild across Weather: Overcast with occasional light showers

4718 BET365.COM CONDITIONAL JOCKEYS' H'CAP CHASE (18 fncs) 3m

2:35 (2:35) (Class 4) (0-100,100) 5-Y-0+ £2,439 (£716; £358; £178)

Form				RPR
-P23	1		**Quazy De Joie (FR)**[46] 3723 7-11-0 91 ... (t) RichieMcLernon(3) (Jonjo O'Neill) *in tch: trckd ldrs 7th: rdn to chse ldr after 4 out: str run fr last: led fnl 40yds* 11/2[3]	100+
1216	2	nk	**Ukrainian Star (IRE)**[39] 3867 8-11-2 90 ... (p) PeterToole (Martin Keighley) *prom: led 5th: tendency to jump sltly rt: dived at 2 out: sn rdn: styd on gamely: drifted lft and no ex whn hdd fnl 40yds* 15/2	99+
/141	3	2	**Marias Rock**[11] 4409 9-11-0 88 ... MattGriffiths (Jeremy Scott) *trckd ldrs: rdn to chse ldr after 5 out: styd on but nvr quite able to chal: 3rd and hld whn swtchd rt towards fin* 9/2[1]	93
600P	4	10	**Jayjay Valentine**[44] 3768 8-10-11 91 ... EdGlassonbury(6) (Victor Dartnall) *hld up: trckd ldrs 10th: cl 4th whn mstke 5 out: sn rdn: styd on same pce fr 3 out* 5/1[2]	90+
-200	5	12	**Our Columbus (IRE)**[17] 4292 7-11-2 93 ... SamTwiston-Davies(3) (Nigel Twiston-Davies) *trckd ldrs: rdn 11th: disputing 4th whn blnd bdly 3 out: wknd* 9/1	81
1-P3	6	hd	**Flowonlovelyriver (IRE)**[17] 4282 10-10-8 85 ... PeterCarberry(3) (Rachel Hobbs) *in tch: rdn after 13th: wknd after 5 out: wnt lft 2 out* 8/1	69
4-FP	7	6	**Mocho (IRE)**[44] 3772 10-11-5 93 ... (t) MichaelMurphy (Mrs H Parrott) *hld up: tk clsr order 11th: rdn appr 5 out: nvr able to get on terms: wknd 4 out* 20/1	75
P-14	8	28	**Crank Hill**[27] 4102 9-11-1 95 ... NathanSweeney(6) (Bob Buckler) *led tl 5th: prom: rdn after 11th: blnd 13th: wknd bef 5 out* 10/1	48
346P	9	64	**Paradise Expected**[27] 4099 8-10-10 84 ... (t) RichardKilloran (Tim Vaughan) *in tch: pushed along after 7th: wknd after 13th: t.o: virtually p.u run-in* 14/1	—
1/3P	P		**Nabouko (FR)**[30] 4021 10-11-12 100 ... (b) GilesHawkins (Susan Nock) *hld up: reminders after 7th: lost tch bef 9th: p.u bef 12th* 33/1	—
1360	P		**Wasntme (IRE)**[18] 4269 8-9-9 74 oh4 ... (b) JakeGreenall(5) (Colin Tizzard) *hld up: pushed along after 7th: rdn after next: no ch fr 13th: t.o whn p.u bef 5 out* 11/1	—

6m 19.5s (-2.50) **Going Correction** -0.075s/f (Good) 11 Ran SP% **114.9**
Speed ratings: **101,100,100,96,92 92,90,81,60,—,—**
toteswingers: 1&2 £3.70, 1&3 £2.00, 2&3 £3.40. CSF £45.77 CT £200.86 TOTE £5.10: £1.70, £3.00, £1.60; EX 50.00.
Owner John P McManus **Bred** Jacqueline Bernadon **Trained** Cheltenham, Gloucs

FOCUS
Racing was washed out here two weeks earlier but it had dried considerably in the meantime and rode just on the slow side of good. There were just four in with a shout four from home in this modest conditional jockeys' stayers' handicap chase. The winner is rated to thisseason's best mark with the third helping set the level.

NOTEBOOK
Quazy De Joie(FR) broke his duck over fences at the 13th attempt. His sole previous success came in a novices' hurdle at Towcester over two years ago, but stamina is his forte and he stayed on in relentless fashion up the home straight to edge ahead near the line. (op 9-2 tchd 4-1)
Ukrainian Star(IRE), from a stable back in top form, has been raised 5lb since finishing a distant sixth at Folkestone last month. He continually jumped to his right and was hanging on grimly in front when he missed out the second last. In the end that proved crucial. (op 7-1 tchd 8-1)
Marias Rock, a point winner in the past, has returned in good form. Raised 3lb after his last-gasp Ffos Las success, he travelled strongly but could not match the first two on the run-in. (op 4-1 tchd 7-2)
Flowonlovelyriver(IRE), who took a handicap hurdle on this card a year ago from the same mark when Irish-trained, was having just his third start over fences. Despite having finished last in both previous races, he did not go unbacked but after racing keenly in the early stages and a blunder five out, he dropped right out going to the final fence. (op 16-1)

NOTEBOOK

Skint, who had run well when second to County Hurdle contender Ski Sunday off 3lb lower over 2m at Kempton on his penultimate start/handicap debut, proved disappointing back in novice company at Musselburgh last time, but he was the stable selected on jockey bookings and duly turned in an improved effort. It was clear leaving the back that Geraghty had plenty up his sleeve aboard the 5-y-o, and in hindsight he'd probably have delayed going on so soon, as he had little left crossing the line. He's not in at Cheltenham, but is expected to make a chaser next term.

Mic's Delight(IRE) came into this bidding for a hat-trick. Some 18lb higher than when winning a handicap on his penultimate start, he's clearly progressing fast, and was on top a few strides after the line. He confirmed last-time-out form with Global Power and is expected to improve once upped to 3m on softer ground. He'll be chasing next season. (op 11-1)

Occasionally Yours(IRE), carrying a feather weight taking his rider's claim into account, was having his 15th run over hurdles (considerably more than any of these) but he's clearly tough and managed to reverse recent Fakenham form with Brunswick Gold and Sam Remo Bello. (op 50-1)

Global Power(IRE), whose trainer had concerns over the drying ground, was held up off the pace early and was the only one to make any significant headway, staying on well up the straight without having the pace to seriously challenge. He should appreciate a stiffer test over fences next season. (tchd 14-1)

San Remo Bello(FR), the apparent Paul Nicholls second-string, was making his handicap debut following just two runs and showed much-improved form, looking a threat turning in before flattening out late on. He's another expected to make a better chaser. (tchd 16-1)

Dynaste(FR) was always going to be doing well to make all, having gone up 12lb from his narrow Taunton victory, and despite a spirited effort, he could find no extra from before the last. (op 8-1 tchd 17-2)

Lively Baron(IRE), dropping in grade having contested a Grade 2 at Haydock last time, made a mistake down the back which led to him becoming outpaced and losing his position. He stayed on again, though, and this three-time winner remains capable of better, with 3m over fences next season likely to bring improvement.

Grafite made some late headway, having got too far back, and ran to form with the runner-up and fourth. (op 40-1)

Owen Glendower(IRE) never threatened.

Invictus(IRE), having briefly made some headway, came under pressure and dropped away. (op 14-1)

The Reformer(IRE) was a no-show on this handicap debut. Official explanation: trainer had no explanation for the poor form shown (op 8-1)

Cucumber Run(IRE) saw plenty of daylight and was beaten soon after a mistake down the back.

Captain Kirkton(IRE) went wrong through the early stages and sadly suffered fatal injuries. (tchd 12-1 in places)

4726 MOBILE BETTING AT PADDYPOWER.COM H'CAP CHASE (22 fncs) 3m 110y

2:25 (2:27) (Class 3) (0-135,135) 5-Y-O+ **£6,505** (£1,910; £955; £477)

Form RPR

1 **Mon Parrain (FR)**[266] 5-11-0 **100**................................ RWalsh 102+
(Paul Nicholls) *lw: trckd ldng pair: wnt 2nd 4 out: led on bit 3 out: sn clr: unextended* **9/2**[3]

0U45 **2** *22* **Appleaday (IRE)**[7] 4486 10-10-6 **115**....................(p) DominicElsworth 117
(Paul Webber) *w ldr: led 3rd tl 8th: led again 12th: rdn whn hdd 3 out: sn no match for easy wnr* **9/2**[3]

2341 **3** *7* **Prophete De Guye (FR)**[13] 4379 8-10-4 **113**.................. TimmyMurphy 108
(James Evans) *hld up: hit 2nd: hdwy after 4 out: rdn after next: wnt modest 3rd bef 2 out* **10/1**

3063 **4** *10* **Circus Of Dreams**[22] 4181 8-10-7 **116**....................(v) LeightonAspell 104
(Oliver Sherwood) *in tch: lost pl whn nt fluent 12th: lost tch after 14th: stl in rr whn hit 3 out: styd on after next: wnt poor 4th last* **9/1**

3312 **5** *12* **Rear Gunner (IRE)**[30] 4023 9-10-13 **122**..................(p) AndrewThornton 97
(Diana Grissell) *led tl 3rd: led again after 8th: hdd after mstke 12th: hit 5 out: nt fluent 4 out: wknd appr 2 out* **7/2**[1]

6220 **6** *42* **Five Dream (FR)**[70] 3292 7-11-9 **135**....................(b) IanPopham(3) 72
(Paul Nicholls) *hld up: rdn after 4 out: sn btn* **9/1**

-11P **P** **Sarde (FR)**[21] 4208 7-11-1 **124**....................(t) SeanQuinlan —
(Kim Bailey) *t.k.h early: in tch: rdn and outpcd after 4 out: wknd qckly after next: p.u bef last* **4/1**[2]

15P **U** **Fit To Drive**[22] 4193 9-11-4 **127**....................(t) AidanColeman —
(Brendan Powell) *hld up: blnd and uns rdr 15th* **9/1**

6m 15.5s (-12.30) **Going Correction** -0.175s/f (Good)
WFA 5 from 7yo+ 1lb **8** Ran SP% **117.7**
Speed ratings: **112,104,102,99,95 82,—,—**
toteswingers:1&2:£4.50, 1&3:£3.60, 2&3:£6.90 CSF £26.30 CT £194.26 TOTE £4.90: £2.20, £1.70, £2.10; EX 23.70 Trifecta £198.60 Pool: £883.01 - 3.29 winning units..

Owner Mr And Mrs J D Cotton **Bred** Serge Dubois **Trained** Ditcheat, Somerset

FOCUS

They went a good pace throughout in this staying handicap chase, but in contrast to the opening contest, this was won in a canter by French import Mon Parrain. He looks a high-class recruit with the runner-up rated to this season's best.

NOTEBOOK

Mon Parrain(FR) ◆, a French import who had been expected to need it, proved spring-heeled at his fences and made a mockery of his opening mark of 133. Ruby Walsh, for whom this was a welcome first winner since returning from injury, barely had to flex a muscle aboard the 5-y-o, who readily drew clear having taken a narrow lead at the Pond Fence. His jumping really was impressive and it will be fascinating to see where he goes next, with Aintree presumably under consideration. Wherever he runs, though, the handicapper will have done his best to ensure there isn't a repeat of this demolition. (op 7-2 tchd 5-1 anf 11-2 in a place)

Appleaday(IRE) was soon up on the speed and saw off Rear Gunner, but it was clear from the last of the Railway fences that he was a sitting duck. He stuck on well once headed, though, and remains well weighted on old form. (op 11-2)

Prophete De Guye(FR), up 7lb, appeared to be going well under Murphy, but he couldn't quicken for pressure, keeping on in third. (op 8-1)

Circus Of Dreams plugged on again having got well back. (tchd 8-1)

Rear Gunner(IRE) was unable to maintain the good gallop he had helped set and started to struggle from the Railway fences. (op 9-2)

Sarde(FR), pulled up in heavy ground at Haydock, was again disappointing and looks to have lost his form. (op 11-2)

4727 PADDY POWER IMPERIAL CUP H'CAP HURDLE (LISTED RACE) (8 hdls) 2m 110y

3:00 (3:02) (Class 1) (0-150,149) 4-Y-O+

£34,206 (£12,834; £6,426; £3,204; £1,608; £804)

Form RPR

1322 **1** **Alarazi (IRE)**[42] 3808 7-10-3 **126**.................................. DominicElsworth 141+
(Lucy Wadham) *lw: in tch: stdy hdwy fr 3 out: trckd ldrs travelling wl 2 out: qcknd to chal last and sn led: drvn out run-in* **10/1**[3]

1021 **2** *2 ¾* **Via Galilei (IRE)**[7] 4488 6-10-6 **129**.................................. JamieMoore 139+
(Gary Moore) *lw: hld up in mid-div: stdy hdwy 3 out: travelling wl whn slt ld 2 out: rdn and jnd last: hdd sn after and nt pce of wnr run-in but kpt on wl for 2nd* **7/1**[1]

3212 **3** *2 ½* **Pateese (FR)**[7] 4488 6-10-2 **125**.................................. RichardJohnson 133
(Philip Hobbs) *chsd ldrs: wnt cl 2nd 3 out: chal 2 out: sn hrd drvn: one pce appr last* **16/1**

130F **4** *2 ¼* **Lucaindubai (IRE)**[49] 3676 5-10-0 **123**.................................. PaulMoloney 130
(Evan Williams) *chsd ldrs: rdn 2 out: styng on same pce whn nt fluent last* **25/1**

5503 **5** *8* **Ultimate**[34] 3969 5-10-3 **129**.................................. DannyCook(3) 129
(Brian Ellison) *led: hit 3 out: narrowly hdd 2 out: wknd last* **25/1**

1246 **6** *3 ¼* **Eradicate (IRE)**[22] 4188 7-11-2 **142**.................................. DavidBass(3) 139
(Nicky Henderson) *chsd ldrs: rdn and one pce whn nt fluent 2 out: no ch w ldrs whn hit last* **16/1**

1021 **7** *1* **Numide (FR)**[10] 4420 8-10-7 **130**.................................. JohnnyFarrelly 126
(Rod Millman) *j. slowly 1st: in rr: stl plenty to do appr 2 out: styd on appr last but nvr any ch* **33/1**

-2U2 **8** *½* **Screaming Brave**[29] 4049 5-9-11 **123** oh1....................(t) IanPopham(3) 119
(Sheena West) *towards rr whn hmpd 4 out: hdwy fr 3 out: nvr rchd ldrs and one pce fr next* **25/1**

P-B0 **9** *8* **Caravel (IRE)**[34] 3969 7-10-6 **129**.................................. BrianHughes 118
(Howard Johnson) *in tch: hdwy 3 out: no imp on ldrs whn j. slowly 2 out: btn whn j. slowly last* **50/1**

0-23 **10** *3 ¼* **Fiulin**[133] 2083 6-10-7 **130**.................................. PaddyBrennan 114
(Evan Williams) *chsd ldrs to 4 out: wknd after next* **8/1**[2]

-404 **11** *1 ½* **The Betchworth Kid**[22] 4188 6-11-2 **139**.................................. RobertThornton 122
(Alan King) *hit 3rd: towards rr: rdn 3 out: nvr bttr than mid-div* **12/1**

0/0 **12** *1* **Alpine Eagle (IRE)**[62] 3474 7-11-4 **141**....................(p) APMcCoy 123
(Mrs John Harrington, Ire) *in rr: rdn and sme prog on outside bnd appr 2 out: no imp whn mstke and wknd sn after* **10/1**[3]

/6-0 **13** *2 ½* **Prince Of Fire (GER)**[21] 4226 6-10-3 **126**.................................. PCarberry 106
(C F Swan, Ire) *towards rr whn hmpd 4 out: sme prog to cl on ldrs 3 out but nvr on terms: wknd bef last* **20/1**

P-42 **14** *1 ¾* **Arctic Wings (IRE)**[7] 4485 7-9-11 **125**.................................. LeeEdwards(5) 103
(Tony Carroll) *mid-div 4th: sme hdwy and rdn 3 out: nvr rchd ldrs and wknd sn after* **33/1**

1315 **15** *½* **Dona**[51] 3649 7-10-4 **134**.................................. PeterHatton(7) 112
(Alan King) *nvr bttr than mid-div: bhd most of way* **66/1**

20B3 **16** *1 ¼* **Drill Sergeant**[10] 4420 6-9-12 **128**....................(bt1) HenryBrooke(7) 105
(Donald McCain) *chsd ldrs tl wknd u.p after 3 out* **16/1**

F4-F **17** *6* **Song Of Songs**[25] 4131 9-10-5 **128**....................(v1) WillKennedy 99
(Jonjo O'Neill) *in rr: effrt into mid div 3 out: sn wknd* **10/1**

521 **18** *½* **Old Way (IRE)**[19] 4260 5-10-0 **123** oh2.................................. MattieBatchelor 94
(Venetia Williams) *lw: chsd ldrs tl wknd qckly 3 out* **16/1**

0-23 **19** *18* **Tito Bustillo (FR)**[51] 3649 6-10-13 **136**.................................. RWalsh 91
(Paul Nicholls) *rdn 3rd: nvr really travelling and a towards rr* **16/1**

0FF- **20** *2 ¼* **Kangaroo Court (IRE)**[323] 5379 7-11-3 **140**.................................. JackDoyle 93
(Emma Lavelle) *hit 3rd: hmpd and bhd 4 out* **25/1**

211U **21** *3 ¼* **Arrayan**[30] 4031 6-10-8 **131**.................................. BarryGeraghty 81
(David Pipe) *pressed ldr 3rd to 4 out: wknd qckly u.p after 3 out* **7/1**[1]

1600 **22** *36* **Points Of View**[14] 4353 6-10-5 **128**....................(t) SeanQuinlan 45
(Kim Bailey) *bhd most of way: no ch fr 4 out* **100/1**

-P61 **P** **Cheshire Prince**[126] 2213 7-10-1 **127**.................................. AlexMerriam(3) —
(Neil King) *in tch to 4 out: sn wknd: t.o whn p.u bef last* **25/1**

20-3 **F** **Ronaldo Des Mottes (FR)**[21] 4222 6-11-12 **149**.................................. TimmyMurphy —
(David Pipe) *lw: in tch whn fell 4 out* **12/1**

3m 54.63s (-12.57) **Going Correction** -0.45s/f (Good) **24** Ran SP% **135.8**
Speed ratings (Par 111): **111,109,108,107,103 102,101,101,97,96 95,95,93,93,92 92,89,89,80,79 78,61,—,—**
toteswingers:1&2:£12.40, 1&3:£24.70, 2&3:£24.20 CSF £73.37 CT £1166.61 TOTE £14.40: £3.80, £2.20, £4.10, £9.80; EX 51.00 Trifecta £967.10 Pool: £16,075.84 - 12.30 winning units..

Owner Johnny Eddis **Bred** His Highness The Aga Khan's Studs S C **Trained** Newmarket, Suffolk

FOCUS

Traditionally a competitive handicap hurdle and this year's running of the race was no different, with them betting 7-1 the field. They didn't go overly quick early (time 7.63secs slower than RP standard), but the tempo lifted from a fair way out and there weren't that many going like a winner as they straightened for home. The first two were rated towards their best Flat form with the third on the upgrade.

NOTEBOOK

Alarazi(IRE) ◆ picked up the best on the run-in, overcoming a slightly untidy jump at the last to win readily and confirm himself as fast improving. Narrowly denied off 8lb lower at Cheltenham on his recent handicap debut, the winner was formerly useful on the Flat and displayed plenty of speed in putting this race to bed, suggesting that, if he gets into the County Hurdle next Friday, he'll be a major player under a penalty in a bid to plunder a £75,000 bonus. (op 17-2)

Via Galilei(IRE), from the in-form Gary Moore stable, had won nicely at Newbury a week earlier, beating Pateese, and he briefly looked like defying the 8lb rise coming to two out. It soon became clear the winner was cantering all over him, though, and despite getting the better jump at the last, he was quickly left trailing. Jamie Moore felt he may have gone too soon, but he wouldn't have beaten the winner anyway. Clearly progressive, he's also in the County and could take his chance if getting in. (tchd 15-2 and 8-1 in places)

Pateese(FR), 3lb better off with the runner-up on Newbury form, was close enough turning in, but lacked the pace of the front two. Another progressive type, he can win a nice handicap and may be suited to Aintree. (op 20-1)

Lucaindubai(IRE) had fallen when in the process of running a really good race at Ascot last time. Down in trip, he was never far away and kept on right the way to the line, suggesting a return to further will suit. He's another likely Aintree type. (tchd 28-1)

Ultimate was always likely to prove vulnerable at the business end, but he kept battling away despite the inevitable and held on for fifth. He's still too high in the handicap.

Eradicate(IRE), fourth in the same Cheltenham race at the winner, had since run well in the Totesport Trophy, but this run again suggested he's too high in the weights at present.

Numide(FR), up 5lb for his Bangor win over further, was ridden under restraint and got going all too late.

Screaming Brave was trying to close at the finish, having been impeded by the fall of Ronaldo Des Mottes four out. (op 33-1)

Fiulin met with late support, but he was outpaced when the tempo increased down the back and, not for the first time, looks in need of further. He's still a maiden over hurdles. (op 14-1 tchd 20-1 in a place)

The Betchworth Kid failed to build on his Totesport Trophy fourth, an early blunder knocking him back. (op 14-1)

Arrayan, who had the hat-trick at his mercy when his rider lost an iron and unseated at Taunton last time, still proved popular despite a 12lb rise, but he was now a total of 38lb higher than when winning at Wincanton in January and, having been ridden forcefully, he was a beaten horse by the end of the back straight. (tchd 15-2)

4728 EBF/DBS MARES' STANDARD OPEN NATIONAL HUNT FLAT RACE FINAL (LISTED RACE) 2m 110y

3:35 (3:37) (Class 1) 4-7-Y-0

£8,551 (£3,208; £1,606; £801; £402; £201)

Form				RPR
1	1		**Swincombe Flame**[15] 4335 5-11-4 0 .... DarylJacob (Nick Williams) *str: scope: trckd ldrs: rdn 3f out: led over 1f out: drvn and kpt on wl ins fnl f* **7/1**	122+
31	2	2 ¼	**Tante Sissi (FR)**[22] 4184 4-10-10 0 .... RobertThornton (Alan King) *midfield: hdwy over 4f out: trckd ldr gng wl 3f out: rdn 2f out: kpt on ins fnl f: wnt 2nd towards fin* **6/1**	112
11	3	1 ¼	**Baby Shine (IRE)**[30] 4027 5-11-4 0 .... LeightonAspell (Lucy Wadham) *lw: trckd ldrs: led over 3f out: sn rdn: hdd over 1f out: no ex and lost 2nd towards fin* **9/2**[2]	119
33	4	¾	**Tempest River (IRE)**[30] 4027 5-11-0 0 .... WayneHutchinson (Ben Case) *midfield: hdwy to chse ldrs 5f out: rdn over 3f out: kpt on wl ins fnl f* **33/1**	114
11	5	4 ½	**Zhakiera Spirit**[60] 3504 5-11-4 0 .... BrianHughes (Howard Johnson) *str: scope: lw: in tch: hdwy over 4f out: chal over 3f out: rdn over 2f out: sn one pce: wknd ins fnl f* **7/2**[1]	115
5	6	4 ½	**Ballyquin Queen (IRE)**[30] 4027 5-11-0 0 .... RichardJohnson (Philip Hobbs) *in tch towards inner: rdn and outpcd 5f out: kpt on fr over 2f out* **14/1**	106
3523	7	hd	**Miss Hippy (IRE)**[22] 4184 6-11-0 0 .... WarrenMarston (Milton Harris) *midfield: rdn and outpcd over 5f out: kpt on fnl 3f* **66/1**	106
3	8	7	**Pyleigh Lass**[39] 3876 5-10-11 0 .... IanPopham[(3)] (Jeremy Scott) *hld up in midfield: rdn over 5f out: one pce* **40/1**	100
43	9	hd	**Golden Gael**[70] 3301 5-11-0 0 .... WillKennedy (Jeremy Scott) *trckd ldrs: rdn and lost pl 5f out: one pce fnl 3f* **100/1**	100
0-16	10	nk	**Madame Allsorts**[22] 4184 6-11-4 0 .... TimmyMurphy (Willie Musson) *hld up: rdn over 3f out: kpt on: n.d* **66/1**	103
1	11	1	**Kentford Grey Lady**[39] 3876 5-11-4 0 .... JackDoyle (Emma Lavelle) *racd keenly: hld up in rr: hdwy over 4f out: rdn over 3f out: one pce* **11/2**[3]	102
1	12	15	**Toubeera**[23] 4171 5-11-4 0 .... SamThomas (Michael Smith) *midfield on outer: rdn over 7f out: sn lost pl and wknd* **18/1**	89
1/1	13	1	**Mintiverdi**[81] 3054 7-11-4 0 .... TomSiddall (Noel Chance) *hld up: a towards rr* **11/1**	88
5	14	4 ½	**Famagusta**[22] 4184 4-9-13 0 .... (v) MrJMQuinlan[(7)] (Peter Charalambous) *in tch: lost pl over 6f out: sn wknd* **100/1**	72
254	15	¾	**Cresswell Bramble**[39] 3876 7-10-9 0 .... JoshuaMoore[(5)] (Keith Goldsworthy) *led narrowly: rdn whn hdd over 3f out: sn wknd* **40/1**	79
10	16	4 ½	**Monnow Made (IRE)**[55] 3590 6-11-4 0 .... JimmyMcCarthy (Charles Egerton) *hld up: hdwy into midfield over 4f out: rdn 3f out: wknd over 1f out* **28/1**	79
41	17	2 ¾	**Kaffie**[55] 3590 6-11-4 0 .... SeanQuinlan (Kim Bailey) *w ldr: rdn and wknd over 3f out* **25/1**	77
24	18	66	**Zahirah Moon**[30] 4027 4-10-6 0 .... MattieBatchelor (Lady Herries) *hld up: a in rr: t.o* **40/1**	—
2	19	dist	**Milly Malone (IRE)**[22] 4184 5-11-0 0 .... DominicElsworth (Oliver Sherwood) *hld up: a towards rr* **12/1**	—
0	20	35	**Doyen Diva**[22] 4184 4-10-6 0 .... JamieMoore (Peter Chapple-Hyam) *hld up: bhd fr 1/2-way: t.o* **100/1**	—

3m 54.2s (-11.90) **Going Correction** -0.45s/f (Good)
WFA 4 from 5yo+ 7lb **20** Ran SP% **134.0**
Speed ratings: **110,108,108,108,105 103,103,100,100,100 99,92,92,90,89 87,86,55,—,—**
toteswingers:1&2:£5.90, 1&3:£4.00, 2&3:£5.40 CSF £49.33 TOTE £8.10: £2.00, £2.10, £2.40; EX 47.33 Trifecta £150.90 Pool: £1,399.36 - 6.86 winning units..
Owner Yeo Racing Partnership **Bred** M C And Mrs Yeo **Trained** George Nympton, Devon

FOCUS

A strong-looking edition of this prestigious mares' bumper that should prove a useful source of winners with next season in mind. The winner and third are rated small improvers with the sixth, seventh and ninth to their marks.

NOTEBOOK

Swincombe Flame ◆, who chased the early pace, improved markedly on her heavy-ground Warwick debut success and powered to victory having taken over approaching the final furlong. Stamina really came into it inside the final 2f and this daughter of Exit To Nowhere, whose dam was a 3m hurdles winner, really came strong. She'll need a stiffer test over hurdles and looks a bright prospect. (tchd 13-2 and 15-2)

Tante Sissi(FR) had cruised to victory at Fakenham last time, her first try over 2m, and she again travelling powerfully into this contest. She was unable to stay on as powerfully as the winner, but should be seen to good effect if sent for the mares' bumper at Aintree. (op 8-1)

Baby Shine(IRE) ◆, unbeaten in a point and two bumpers, beating a few of these at Hutningdon last month, really did travel and looked all over the winner when going on over 3f out, but she began to get tired and was eventually outstayed. She should make an even better hurdler and is one to keep on-side next season. (tchd 4-1 and 5-1 in places)

Tempest River(IRE), 3l behind Baby Shine at Huntingdon, ran to form, keeping on right the way to the line, and looks sure to benefit from a stiffer test over hurdles. (op 50-1 tchd 66-1)

Zhakiera Spirit, a sister to the useful Megastar, had created a big impression in winning both her starts and she appeared to be absolutely tanking along on turning in, but she had perhaps travelled a bit too well early, and as a result had nothing left for the final 2f. A promising effort none the less, she should win her share over hurdles next season, but may take her chance in the at Aintree mares' bumper first. (tchd 4-1)

Ballyquin Queen(IRE), another from the Huntingdon contest, should appreciate a stiffer test once hurdling. (tchd 16-1)

Miss Hippy(IRE) came home well and should appreciate a stiffer test once hurdling.

Kentford Grey Lady, an easy winner at Taunton on debut, was ridden too far out of her ground and deserves another chance to build on that initial promise. (op 6-1)

4729 PADDYPOWER.COM EXTRA PLACES AT CHELTENHAM NOVICES' CHASE (FOR THE BURNT OAK AND SPECIAL CARGO CUP) (13 fncs) 2m

4:10 (4:10) (Class 3) 5-Y-0+ £4,553 (£1,337; £668; £333)

Form				RPR
0-13	1		**Mamlook (IRE)**[27] 4096 7-11-1 0 .... DannyCook[(3)] (David Pipe) *trckd ldr: drvn to ld bef last: pushed along run-in and a jst doing enough* **7/2**[2]	142+
3-4	2	nk	**Gandalfe (FR)**[117] 2427 6-10-5 0 .... (b[1]) MrTJCannon[(7)] (Alan Fleming) *led: mstke 4th: rdn 3 out: hdd bef last: rdn and rallied run-in and gng on cl home but a hld* **25/1**	135
-231	3	4	**Starluck (IRE)**[16] 4311 6-11-4 0 .... APMcCoy (Alan Fleming) *lw: j. slowly 1st: trckd ldrs in 3rd: hit 4th: blnd 8th: stdy hdwy to trck ldng duo 3 out: qcknd to chal whn hit 2 out and stmbld: shkn up and kpt on again run-in but no imp* **2/5**[1]	142+
-124	4	95	**Harry Tricker**[81] 3059 7-11-8 0 .... (p) JamieMoore (Gary Moore) *a in last pl: wl bhd fr 4th: no ch whn j. slowly 7th: t.o* **13/2**[3]	55

3m 58.79s (-3.01) **Going Correction** -0.175s/f (Good) **4** Ran SP% **110.8**
Speed ratings: **100,99,97,50**
CSF £34.43 TOTE £4.30; EX 59.20.

Owner P A Deal & G Lowe **Bred** Peter Jones And G G Jones **Trained** Nicholashayne, Devon

FOCUS

Hard to know what to make of this form, with Starluck's jumping letting him down and the pacemaker nearly pulling off a shock victory. The third would have gone close bar errors and is rated in line with his chasing debut form.

NOTEBOOK

Mamlook(IRE) was disappointing at Exeter last time, having made a successful debut at Fakenham, and this was more like his true form, travelling better on the drier ground and showing a good attitude to fend off a rallying runner-up. He could be one for a handicap at Aintree with a return to further on potentially quicker ground likely to help. (op 4-1)

Gandalfe(FR), off since finishing well beaten on his chasing debut in November (had excuses), seemed a different horse in the first-time blinkers, setting a good clip and jumping well. Although it was clear he was getting tired from the Pond Fence, he stuck at it once headed and very nearly got back up under an animated Tom Cannon, who lost his balance and nearly came off just after the line. Although disappointed by the favourite's display, this performance will have pleased connections, and now it just remains to be seen whether he can back it up in second-time headgear.

Starluck(IRE)'s performance confirms connections decision to miss the Arkle was the right one. The decision to run a pacemaker in Gandalfe, who very nearly pulled off a shock victory, probably backfired, though, as their stable star couldn't jump proficiently enough at pace, nearly falling at the first of the Railway fences and making another bad blunder and then stumbling at the second-last, from which he was unable to recover. He had jumped well enough when making a winning debut at Huntingdon and, although this experience could teach him long-term, he's left with plenty to prove if sticking over fences at Aintree. (op 4-9)

Harry Tricker, conceding weight all round having gone 2-2 over fences previously (awarded race second occasion), was last seen running in a jumpers' bumper, and the way he performed on this return to fences suggests something may have been amiss. (tchd 6-1)

4730 PADDYPOWER.COM MONEY BACK SPECIALS AT CHELTENHAM H'CAP CHASE (17 fncs) 2m 4f 110y

4:40 (4:40) (Class 3) (0-130,129) 5-Y-0+ £5,204 (£1,528; £764; £381)

Form				RPR
152F	1		**Holmwood Legend**[21] 4221 10-11-5 **125** .... KeiranBurke[(3)] (Patrick Rodford) *trckd ldrs: led 2nd tl after 3rd: styd pressing ldr: led 8th to 9th: chal 11th tl led 13th: drvn clr appr last: rdn out* **14/1**	134+
UP11	2	5	**Peplum (FR)**[31] 4010 8-11-7 **129** .... JoshuaMoore[(5)] (Gary Moore) *lw: chsd ldrs: hit 12th and lost position: hdwy to chse ldrs 3 out: kpt on to chse wnr last but no imp run-in* **5/2**[1]	134
2124	3	2	**Inside Dealer (IRE)**[27] 4095 7-11-8 **125** .... JoeTizzard (Colin Tizzard) *led to 2nd: led 3rd: hdd sn after: styd pressing ldrs: hit 13th: styd front rnk and ev ch 2 out: chsd wnr sn after but no imp: lost 2nd last and one pce* **7/2**[2]	128
P-R3	4	3 ½	**Craiglands (IRE)**[22] 4193 9-10-13 **116** .... (bt) DaveCrosse (Ian Williams) *lw: in tch: mstke 5th: j. slowly 8th: hdwy and mstke 3 out: lost pl: rallied u.p and j. slowly last: kpt on run-in to take 4th cl home* **7/2**[2]	118+
-025	5	nk	**Double Vodka (IRE)**[26] 4116 10-11-5 **122** .... PaddyBrennan (Chris Grant) *in tch: blnd 4 out: hdwy to chse ldrs 3 out: wknd and j. slowly last: lost 4th cl home* **6/1**[3]	120
/10-	6	22	**Checkerboard (IRE)**[356] 4756 8-11-4 **121** .... BrianHughes (Howard Johnson) *led after 3rd: hdd 8th: led again 9th: blnd and hdd 13th: stl ev ch 3 out: wknd qckly* **12/1**	104
056F	7	25	**Alesandro Mantegna (IRE)**[5] 4524 6-11-4 **121** .... (p) JamieMoore (Keith Goldsworthy) *in rr: hit 7th: in tch 9th: mstke and wknd 13th: hit 4 out: t.o* **14/1**	76
05P0	P		**Pocket Aces (IRE)**[88] 2948 9-11-2 **119** .... AndrewThornton (Richard Rowe) *in tch: hdwy and in tch 8th: blnd and wknd 12th: t.o whn p.u bef last* **11/1**	—

5m 17.24s (-1.16) **Going Correction** -0.175s/f (Good) **8** Ran SP% **116.7**
Speed ratings: **95,93,92,91,90 82,72,—**
toteswingers:1&2:£5.70, 1&3:£5.80, 2&3:£4.10 CSF £52.05 CT £155.39 TOTE £15.20: £3.40, £1.50, £1.70; EX 77.70.

Owner Brian Derrick **Bred** Mrs P M Underhill **Trained** Ash, Somerset

FOCUS

Just a fair handicap chase rated around the placed horses. There were several in with a chance jumping the Pond Fence.

NOTEBOOK

Holmwood Legend was up there throughout and produced good jumps at each of the last two fences, which was pleasing considering he was a faller the time before. (op 12-1)

Peplum(FR), up another 6lb, stayed on grittily in second without being able to match the winner. He needs to pull out more to win off this mark. (op 9-2)

Inside Dealer(IRE) has been doing well, but he made mistakes at the Railway fences and couldn't quicken on in the straight.

Craiglands(IRE) made a few notable blunders and did well to stay on again for fourth. (op 11-4)

Double Vodka(IRE) struggled for much of the race and, despite rallying to close up at the Pond Fence, he could soon find no extra. (op 10-1)

Checkerboard(IRE), who was returning from a year off, shaped with some promise. He tanked through much of the race, despite a blunder at the second of the Railway fences, and should come on appreciably for the outing. (tchd 11-1 and 14-1)

T/Jkpt: Not won. T/Plt: £483.00 to a £1 stake. Pool:£224,701.23 - 339.57 winning tickets T/Qpdt: £41.20 to a £1 stake. Pool:£11,021.65 - 197.96 winning tickets ST

4737 - (Foreign Racing) - See Raceform Interactive

4233 MARKET RASEN (R-H)

Sunday, March 13

OFFICIAL GOING: Good (chs 6.6, hdl 7.0)

All bends moved out increasing each circuit by 24yds.

Wind: Light, half against Weather: Fine and sunny

4738 BODUGI.COM LAUNCHES SOCIAL BETTING CONDITIONAL JOCKEYS' H'CAP HURDLE (10 hdls) 2m 3f

2:20 (2:20) (Class 4) (0-105,101) 4-Y-0+ **£2,276** (£668; £334; £166)

Form RPR

P-00 **1** **Won More Night**44 3782 9-10-4 **79**.....(t) IanPopham 84+
(Martin Keighley) *t.k.h in rr: smooth hdwy whn nt clr run sn after 2 out: chal last: sn led: drvn clr* **11/2**3

-055 **2** 3 **King Mak**36 3951 9-11-6 **98**..... KyleJames(3) 96
(Marjorie Fife) *led: qcknd 3 out: reminders appr next: hdd and no ex sn after last* **11/2**3

-210 **3** 2 **Scrum V**24 4166 7-11-6 **95**..... GilesHawkins 92
(John Davies) *trckd ldrs: 4th and one pce whn hit last* **11/2**3

6615 **4** 1/2 **Sacco D'Oro**9 3840 5-11-3 **92**..... BrianToomey 88
(Michael Mullineaux) *hld up in rr: hdwy to trck ldrs 3 out: kpt on same pce run-in* **11/1**

0 **5** 1 1/2 **Silver Lily (IRE)**17 4314 9-11-6 **95**.....(t) CharlieHuxley 89
(Sarah Humphrey) *chsd ldrs: drvn and outpcd 2 out: one pce run-in* **28/1**

-24P **6** 10 **Quilver Tatou (FR)**20 4265 7-11-1 **93**.....(p) PeterToole(3) 79
(Charlie Mann) *chsd ldrs: hung rt and wknd last* **13/2**

0060 **7** 5 **Barron Watlass (IRE)**27 4115 7-11-4 **101**..... SamuelWelton(8) 81
(George Moore) *hld up in rr: drvn and outpcd appr 2 out: sn lost pl* **5/1**2

46-3 **P** **Patavium (IRE)**27 4115 8-11-6 **100**..... NathanMoscrop(5) —
(Edwin Tuer) *trckd ldrs: t.k.h: sddle slipped and led 6th: p.u bef next* **4/1**1

4m 44.8s (5.40) **Going Correction** -0.525s/f (Firm) **8** Ran SP% **107.9**

Speed ratings (Par 105): **67,65,64,64,64 59,57,—**

toteswingers: 1&2 £5.70, 1&3 £4.30, 2&3 £5.70 CSF £31.77 CT £150.61 TOTE £6.70: £1.80, £2.30, £2.30; EX 38.40.

Owner D A Thorpe **Bred** D A Thorpe **Trained** Condicote, Gloucs

FOCUS

This proved a rather straightforward for the winner, although the time was very slow and the third is the best guide to the level.

NOTEBOOK

Won More Night was ridden confidently under restraint and readily picked up to assert after the last. From a yard that has returned to form recently, she was on her lowest mark yet over hurdles and connections will no doubt be keen to get her out before being reassessed. (op 6-1)

King Mak kept finding under pressure and just lacked the winner's acceleration. (op 5-1)

Scrum V bounced back from a below-par effort on softer at Kelso. (op 7-1)

Sacco D'Oro could only find the one pace under pressure (op 8-1)

Barron Watlass(IRE) Official explanation: jockey said gelding was unsuited by the slow early pace

Patavium(IRE) remains on a decent mark, but was unable to capitalise on it as a result of a slipping saddle. Official explanation: jockey said saddle slipped (op 10-3)

4739 BODUGI.COM £15,000 CHELTENHAM FESTIVAL GIVEAWAY NOVICES' HURDLE (10 hdls) 2m 3f

2:50 (2:50) (Class 4) 4-Y-0+ **£2,397** (£698; £349)

Form RPR

630P **1** **Alta Rock (IRE)**21 4242 6-10-11 0..... ShaneByrne(5) 108+
(Sue Smith) *hld up in rr: stdy hdwy and 9th 2 out: 6th last: str run to ld last 75yds: readily* **80/1**

3232 **2** 2 **Dineur (FR)**19 4268 5-11-2 0..... RobertThornton 107
(Alan King) *nt fluent: led to 2nd: t.k.h: trckd ldr: led appr 2 out: hung lft and hdd last 75yds* **3/1**3

6 **3** 8 **Maraased**49 3692 6-11-2 0..... RhysFlint 98
(Steve Gollings) *in tch: hdwy to chse ldrs 3 out: kpt on same pce fr next* **12/1**

00 **4** 2 **Cap Falco (IRE)**60 3511 6-11-2 0..... TomO'Brien 97
(Anabel L M King) *in rr-div: reminders 5th: hdwy 7th: styd on same pce fr 2 out* **50/1**

2133 **5** nk **Jack The Gent (IRE)**21 4242 7-11-9 125..... BarryKeniry 105
(George Moore) *w ldr: led 2nd: nt fluent 6th: hdd appr 2 out: 2nd whn blnd 2 out: wknd last 100yds* **11/4**2

-14P **6** 1 **Harvest Song (IRE)**108 2630 5-11-9 115.....(b1) WillKennedy 102
(Henrietta Knight) *chsd ldrs: rdn appr 2 out: wknd last 100yds* **25/1**

006 **7** 2 1/2 **Whiskey Ridge (IRE)**48 3715 5-11-2 0..... HenryOliver 92
(Sue Smith) *mid-div: sme hdwy appr 2 out: one pce* **25/1**

8 28 **Provost**13 7-11-2 0..... BrianHughes 64
(Michael Easterby) *in rr: t.o 3 out* **50/1**

5232 **9** 3 1/2 **Kings Grey (IRE)**18 4281 7-11-2 114..... JamesReveley 64
(Keith Reveley) *in tch: hdwy to trck ldrs 3 out: effrt next: sn wknd: 8th whn blnd last: eased: t.o* **13/8**1

0P00 **10** 16 **Cloudy Joe (IRE)**36 3952 5-10-13 0.....(p) AdamPogson(3) 45
(Charles Pogson) *in rr: bhd fr 5th: t.o 7th* **125/1**

0 **11** 37 **No Through Road**42 3842 4-10-7 0..... AlanO'Keeffe —
(Michael Scudamore) *a in rr: bhd fr 6th: t.o next* **100/1**

32-0 **12** hd **Montiyra (IRE)**275 713 7-11-2 80..... PaddyAspell 7
(Lynn Siddall) *in rr: bhd fr 6th: t.o 3 out* **125/1**

4m 35.8s (-3.60) **Going Correction** -0.525s/f (Firm)

WFA 4 from 5yo+ 7lb **12** Ran SP% **112.9**

Speed ratings (Par 105): **86,85,81,80,80 80,79,67,66,59 43,43**

toteswingers: 1&2 £24.30, 1&3 £59.00, 2&3 £9.00 CSF £298.84 TOTE £77.30: £16.40, £1.50, £3.30; EX 897.10.

Owner Mrs S Smith **Bred** M W Hickey **Trained** High Eldwick, W Yorks

FOCUS

Quite a turn-up for this novice hurdle with a big step up from the winner. The placed horses and the seventh are rated in line with their pre-race marks.

NOTEBOOK

Alta Rock(IRE) came through strongly at the finish and showed his recent heavy-ground Sedgefield running to be all wrong, causing a shock in the process. He had shown promise at this course on similar ground in bumpers and, although this was clearly unexpected, there's no reason to believe it was a fluke. It'll be interesting to see how he fares under a penalty. Official explanation: trainer said, regarding apparent improvement in form, that the gelding was better suited by the good ground (op 100-1)

Dineur(FR), who could have jumped better, prospered under a positive ride and looked the winner despite a mistake two out. He appeared vulnerable to the winner after the last, though, and was readily swept aside close home. Something similar should come his way. (op 7-2)

Maraased improved on his initial effort, keeping on in third.

Cap Falco(IRE) had shown promise on his first run in bumpers and there were plenty of positives to be taken from this first effort as a hurdler.

Jack The Gent(IRE), disappointing in heavy ground last time, tired in the straight having done plenty of early running. He remains vulnerable under the penalty.

Kings Grey(IRE) was the disappointment of the race, failing to pick up in the straight having been held up. He's better than this. (op 6-4, tchd 7-4 in places)

4740 CALVERTS CARPETS YORK H'CAP CHASE (14 fncs) 2m 6f 110y

3:20 (3:20) (Class 4) (0-110,108) 5-Y-0+ **£2,927** (£859; £429; £214)

Form RPR

2443 **1** **Maurisca (FR)**87 2975 6-11-12 **108**..... FelixDeGiles 123+
(Charlie Longsdon) *t.k.h: trckd ldrs: blnd 7th: led 9th: clr 3 out: eased towards fin* **2/1**1

4224 **2** 8 **Oniz Tiptoes (IRE)**7 4508 10-10-8 **90**.....(p) PaddyAspell 97
(John Wainwright) *chsd ldrs: outpcd 8th: chsd ldrs 11th: wnt 2nd appr next: kpt on: no imp* **9/1**

0U03 **3** 22 **Karingreason**21 4237 8-11-0 **96**..... JamesReveley 80
(Keith Reveley) *in rr: hdwy to chse ldrs 8th: rdn and wknd 3 out* **5/1**2

1622 **4** 3 **Persian Gates (IRE)**12 4416 7-11-4 **100**.....(b) TomMessenger 81
(Chris Bealby) *chsd ldrs: hit 10th: wknd 3 out* **6/1**

343P **P** **Lorum Leader (IRE)**22 4219 10-11-5 **101**..... TomO'Brien —
(Dr Richard Newland) *trckd ldrs: led 7th: hdd 9th: wknd qckly 11th: t.o whn p.u bef 2 out* **11/2**3

61P0 **P** **Ragador**137 2034 10-11-0 **101**..... ShaneByrne(5) —
(Sue Smith) *w ldr: led 4th to 7th: sn drvn: lost pl next: bhd whn p.u bef 11th* **14/1**

1453 **P** **Brimham Boy**45 3772 9-11-8 **104**.....(t) WarrenMarston —
(Martin Keighley) *led: hdd 4th: lost pl 8th: sn bhd: t.o whn p.u bef 10th* **6/1**

5m 36.6s (-9.40) **Going Correction** -0.525s/f (Firm) **7** Ran SP% **110.6**

Speed ratings: **95,92,84,83,— —,—**

toteswingers: 1&2 £3.40, 1&3 £2.40, 2&3 £6.10 CSF £18.27 TOTE £2.40: £1.50, £3.50; EX 13.70.

Owner Hamer & Hawkes **Bred** Haras De La Rousseliere & Mme K Monclin **Trained** Over Norton, Oxon

FOCUS

A modest handicap chase with the winner recording a slight personal best.

NOTEBOOK

Maurisca(FR), off since finishing third off this mark at Exeter in December, travelled well throughout and gradually pulled away for a ready success. Clearly on the up, the good ground suited him well and it's likely he'll go in again before the season is out.

Oniz Tiptoes(IRE) boxed on best for second, but never looked like reaching the winner. (op 11-1)

Karingreason failed to improve for the step back up in trip, looking tired inside the final 2f. (op 6-1, tchd 13-2 in a place)

Persian Gates(IRE) was below his best back in fourth. (op 7-1)

Lorum Leader(IRE) was another to stop quickly. (tchd 6-1)

Brimham Boy quickly lost his place and was eventually pulled up. Official explanation: trainer's rep said gelding was unsuited by the good ground (tchd 6-1)

4741 CALVERTS CARPETS YORK NOVICES' H'CAP CHASE (14 fncs) 2m 4f

3:50 (3:50) (Class 5) (0-95,93) 5-Y-0+ **£1,626** (£477; £238; £119)

Form RPR

6-63 **1** **Apache Blue (IRE)**107 2656 7-11-1 **89**..... MrJohnDawson(7) 96
(John Wade) *in rr: hdwy 10th: chsng ldrs next: led appr last: styd on u.p* **6/1**2

6602 **2** 1 3/4 **Mad Professor (IRE)**23 4178 8-9-7 **67** oh5.....(p) JoeCornwall(7) 72
(John Cornwall) *chsd ldrs: outpcd 9th: chsng ldng pair 4 out: wnt 2nd last: styd on same pce* **8/1**

-033 **3** 6 **Home She Goes (IRE)**21 4238 9-11-4 **88**..... AdamPogson(3) 91+
(Charles Pogson) *w ldrs: led 9th: hdd after 4 out: led next: hdd and blnd last: sn wknd* **7/1**3

054P **4** nk **Argentia**14 4380 6-11-9 **90**..... DenisO'Regan 90
(Lucy Wadham) *jnd ldrs 7th: wnt 2nd 9th: led after 4 out: hdd next: wknd between last 2* **9/1**

5P43 **5** 15 **Muntami (IRE)**21 4236 10-10-10 **84**..... MattCrawley(7) 71
(John Harris) *chsd ldrs: drvn 8th: sn outpcd: hdwy 4 out: sn lost pl* **8/1**

40/P **P** **Cottam Grange**21 4236 11-11-0 **81**..... PaddyAspell —
(John Wainwright) *in rr: t.o 9th: p.u bef 3 out* **50/1**

/PP0 **P** **Wheretheres A Will**18 4281 9-9-9 **67** oh3..... BrianToomey(5) —
(Michael Mullineaux) *hld up towards rr: bhd fr7th: t.o whn p.u bef 9th* **28/1**

0600 **P** **Life Long (IRE)**22 4224 7-11-9 **93**..... RichieMcLernon(3) —
(Anabel L M King) *mid-div: lost pl and blnd 10th: sn bhd: t.o whn p.u bef 3 out* **10/1**

33P3 **P** **Ginger's Lad**33 3997 7-10-12 **79**..... BrianHughes —
(Michael Easterby) *chsd ldrs: wknd rapidly appr 7th: sn t.o and p.u* **9/2**1

/U35 **P** **Quintus (FR)**66 3402 7-11-6 **87**..... TomMessenger —
(Chris Bealby) *mstkes: led to 9th: sn wknd: t.o whn p.u bef 3 out* **10/1**

6-06 **P** **Simply Strong (IRE)**47 3723 7-11-4 **88**.....(t) PeterToole(3) —
(Charlie Mann) *chsd ldrs: wknd 9th: sn bhd: t.o whn p.u bef 3 out* **15/2**

5m 1.00s (-4.70) **Going Correction** -0.525s/f (Firm) **11** Ran SP% **112.5**

Speed ratings: **88,87,84,84,78 —,—,—,—,—**

toteswingers: 1&2 £13.10, 1&3 £11.80, 2&3 £5.30 CSF £51.31 CT £340.30 TOTE £7.50: £2.20, £2.50, £2.60; EX 58.20.

Owner John Wade **Bred** John Fallon **Trained** Mordon, Co Durham

FOCUS

Less than half the field managed to complete in what was a moderate handicap chase. The placed horses set the level.

NOTEBOOK

Apache Blue(IRE), off since finishing third on his chasing debut back in November, had been dropped 3lb and showed improved form, going on before the last and winning with a bit in hand. There should be more to come at the right level. (early 8-1 in a place)

Mad Professor(IRE), just denied in a selling handicap at Fakenham, ran a good race on this return to fences from 5lb wrong. (op 9-1)

Home She Goes(IRE) stuck on best she could once headed. (op 17-2)

Argentia returned to form, albeit she was well held. (tchd 17-2)

Wheretheres A Will Official explanation: trainer said gelding has a breathing problem (op 5-1)

Ginger's Lad stopped as though something was amiss. This clearly wasn't his running. Official explanation: vet said gelding finished distressed (op 5-1)

4742 MARTIN DENT FINAL FLIGHT OF FREEDOM H'CAP HURDLE (12 hdls) 3m

4:25 (4:25) (Class 3) (0-125,123) 4-Y-0+ **£4,098** (£1,203; £601; £300)

Form RPR

0001 **1** **Stagecoach Opal**13 4391 10-10-3 **100**..... HenryOliver 114+
(Sue Smith) *trckd ldrs: led 9th: styd on wl fr 2 out: drvn out* **9/2**3

3011 **2** *8* **Pegasus Prince (USA)**[21] 4235 7-11-12 **123** JamesReveley 130+
(Keith Reveley) *in rr: hdwy after 9th: chsd wnr 2 out: no imp* **7/2**[2]

6021 **3** *9* **Last Of The Bunch**[29] 4067 6-11-7 **118** BarryKeniry 115
(Alan Swinbank) *chsd ldrs: blnd and rdr lost iron briefly 1st: outpcd 2 out: kpt on run-in* **13/2**

0622 **4** *nk* **Crazy Eyes (IRE)**[29] 4079 6-11-5 **119** (t) PeterToole(3) 116
(Charlie Mann) *hld up: hdwy 9th: chsng ldrs next: 3rd and rdn whn hit 2 out: kpt on one pce* **3/1**[1]

6203 **5** *nse* **Zitenka (IRE)**[30] 4060 9-11-2 **116** (b) JamesHalliday(3) 113
(Tim Easterby) *towards rr: outpcd 3 out: kpt on between last 2* **14/1**

66PP **6** *4* **Love Of Tara**[57] 3566 9-11-2 **120** MrPMason(7) 113
(Jennifer Mason) *jnd ldrs 5th: drvn 3 out: wknd appr next* **25/1**

1600 **7** *1 1/2* **The Shy Man (IRE)**[22] 4209 8-11-2 **123** SamuelWelton(10) 114
(George Moore) *hld up in rr: hdwy 3 out: sn drvn: wknd after next* **10/1**

32P0 **8** *10* **Night Orbit**[18] 4285 7-11-2 **120** (v) CharlieWallis(7) 104
(Julia Feilden) *chsd ldrs: drvn 7th: lost pl 9th: sn bhd* **33/1**

5544 **9** *13* **Always Bold (IRE)**[36] 3954 6-11-4 **115** (v[1]) AdrianLane 83
(Donald McCain) *led: hdd 9th: sn lost pl: wl bhd fr 2 out* **11/1**

111/ **10** *17* **Surface To Air**[987] 812 10-11-12 **123** TomMessenger 74
(Chris Bealby) *chsd ldrs: wknd and mstke 8th: sn bhd: t.o 3 out* **20/1**

5m 44.2s (-17.80) **Going Correction** -0.525s/f (Firm) **10** Ran SP% **114.4**
Speed ratings (Par 107): **108,105,102,102,102 100,100,97,92,87**
toteswingers: 1&2 £3.00, 1&3 £6.40, 2&3 £3.90 CSF £20.14 CT £100.94 TOTE £5.90: £2.00, £1.50, £2.70; EX 27.00.
Owner John Conroy Jaqueline Conroy **Bred** R A Hughes **Trained** High Eldwick, W Yorks

FOCUS
A fairly low-grade handicap hurdle but the third, fourth and fifrth help give the form a solid look.

NOTEBOOK
Stagecoach Opal, 7lb higher than when winning at Catterick, again prospered under a positive ride and stayed on strongly down the straight, winning with a good bit in hand. He had slipped to a good mark, but is likely to find things tougher in future, so will be doing well to complete a hat-trick. (op 6-1)
Pegasus Prince(USA) stayed on without looking likely to beat the winner, the further 7lb rise clearly proving too much. (op 4-1)
Last Of The Bunch, a winner at Ayr, performed well considering she was 9lb higher on much livelier ground. (op 15-2 tchd 8-1)
Crazy Eyes(IRE) had gone up 4lb for his latest defeat and proved rather one-paced in the straight. (op 7-2)

4743 STONEACRE KIA RED NOSE COMIC RELIEF "NATIONAL HUNT" NOVICES' HURDLE (8 hdls) 2m 1f
4:55 (4:57) (Class 4) 4-Y-O+ **£2,397** (£698; £349)

Form RPR

1364 **1** **Ballybriggan (IRE)**[21] 4235 7-11-8 125 DougieCostello 118+
(John Quinn) *chsd ldr: lft in ld 2 out: forged clr run-in: eased clsng stages* **4/9**[1]

1355 **2** *8* **Batonnier (FR)**[21] 4239 5-11-1 0 RobertThornton 98
(Alan King) *trckd ldrs: lft 2nd 2 out: no ch w wnr* **13/2**[3]

04 **3** *3 1/4* **Rear Admiral (IRE)**[15] 4363 5-11-1 0 BrianHughes 98+
(Michael Easterby) *hld up: hdwy to trck ldrs 3 out: hmpd and lft 3rd 2 out: kpt on same pce* **28/1**

00F0 **4** *21* **Sheepclose (IRE)**[18] 4281 6-11-1 0 PaddyAspell 74
(Michael Easterby) *hld up in last: drvn 3 out: nvr on terms* **66/1**

6/0 **5** *18* **Danny Cool**[21] 4233 8-11-1 0 JamesReveley 56
(Keith Reveley) *chsd ldrs: dropped bk 4th: bhd fr 3 out* **25/1**

3020 **F** **Shan Blue (IRE)**[33] 3987 6-11-1 0 RhysFlint 98
(Steve Gollings) *led and sn clr: j. bdly lft: 1 1/2 l ahd whn fell 2 out* **9/2**[2]

4m 5.60s (-1.10) **Going Correction** -0.525s/f (Firm)
WFA 4 from 5yo+ 7lb **6** Ran SP% **109.6**
Speed ratings (Par 105): **81,77,75,65,57** —
toteswingers: 1&2 £1.10, 1&3 £4.00, 2&3 £6.40 CSF £3.69 TOTE £1.50: £1.10, £2.00; EX 3.50.
Owner Stewart Andrew & Jim Shaw **Bred** C Kenneally **Trained** Settrington, N Yorks

FOCUS
A relatively weak novice hurdle in which the easy winner stood out and the form could be rated higher.

NOTEBOOK
Ballybriggan(IRE) set the standard, having finished fourth in a course handicap last time, and his rider was eager not to challenge on the outside of Shan Blue, who was jumping badly left. However, he quickly asserted once that one came down two out, and cruised to a comfy victory. He can continue to give a good account back in handicaps. (op 1-2)
Batonnier(FR) made mistakes on this hurdling debut, but kept on for pressure and looks sure to improve for a stiffer test. (op 11-2 tchd 5-1)
Rear Admiral(IRE) ran quite a promising race, looking better than the bare form considering he was hampered. (op 22-1)
Shan Blue(IRE) clearly has an engine, the fact he still held a narrow lead two out considering how much ground he was losing in jumping out to his left. It's hoped this fall doesn't affect his confidence, as he would be of interest in a handicap going the opposite way round. (op 13-2)

4744 TREVOR LINFOOT H'CAP CHASE (12 fncs) 2m 2f
5:25 (5:26) (Class 4) (0-105,105) 5-Y-O+ **£2,927** (£859; £429; £214)

Form RPR

00 **1** **Himrayn**[60] 3509 8-11-0 **96** RichieMcLernon(3) 118+
(Anabel L M King) *hld up: hdwy to trck ldrs 5th: led 3 out: drew clr run-in* **17/2**

1430 **2** *10* **Quipe Me Posted (FR)**[88] 2961 7-11-12 **105** DenisO'Regan 119+
(Suzy Smith) *trckd ldrs: led after 6th: hdd 3 out: 2 l down whn stmbld landing last: sn wknd* **9/2**[2]

5P40 **3** *9* **Kercabellec (FR)**[21] 4238 13-9-7 **79** oh26 JoeCornwall(7) 83
(John Cornwall) *chsd ldrs: outpcd 6th: rallied 4 out: kpt on to take modest 3rd last* **66/1**

64P **4** *4 1/2* **Roc De Guye (FR)**[25] 4139 6-10-6 **92** RobertKirk(7) 92
(James Evans) *hld up: hdwy to join ldrs 7th: wknd appr 2 out* **18/1**

3132 **5** *7* **Persian Prince (IRE)**[46] 3751 11-10-13 **99** MrJohnDawson(7) 93
(John Wade) *led 2nd: sn hdd: hit 7th: lost pl next* **4/1**[1]

F654 **6** *6* **Iona Days (IRE)**[61] 3494 6-11-11 **104** HaddenFrost 92
(Henrietta Knight) *led to 2nd: chsd ldrs: outpcd 8th: modest 4th after 9th: sn wknd* **11/2**[3]

2425 **7** *21* **Pacha D'Oudairies (FR)**[25] 4139 8-11-7 **100** (b[1]) DominicElsworth 69
(Michael Blake) *trckd ldrs: lost pl 9th: sn bhd* **11/2**[3]

0032 **8** *8* **Overbranch**[20] 4254 8-11-1 **97** (b) JamesHalliday(3) 59
(Malcolm Jefferson) *in rr: drvn and reminders after 5th: bhd fr 7th: t.o 9th* **6/1**

0U32 **P** **Sun Tzu (IRE)**[19] 4279 7-11-12 **105** (b) TomO'Brien —
(Dr Richard Newland) *drvn early: in rr: bhd fr 7th: t.o 9th: p.u bef next* **13/2**

4m 23.2s (-11.80) **Going Correction** -0.525s/f (Firm) **9** Ran SP% **113.9**
Speed ratings: **105,100,96,94,91 88,79,75,—**
toteswingers: 1&2 £9.50, 1&3 £15.20, 2&3 £19.20 CSF £46.84 CT £2352.59 TOTE £8.60: £2.60, £2.30, £8.30; EX 58.40.
Owner Touchwood Racing **Bred** R W Russell **Trained** Wilmcote, Warwicks

FOCUS
A ready success for the winner in what was a low-grade handicap chase. The winner can rate higher and the placed horses set the level.

NOTEBOOK
Himrayn, who was on his lowest mark since handicapping, came away for a ready success. He's lightly raced for his age and could be capable of further progress at the right level. (tchd 8-1)
Quipe Me Posted(FR) had won off this mark over hurdles and a small race can come his way over fences too judging by this effort. (op 5-1)
Kercabellec(FR) did exceptionally well from a whopping 26lb out of the handicap, staying on again under pressure. (op 50-1)
Roc De Guye(FR) ran a bit better this time. (op 25-1)
Persian Prince(IRE) made mistakes and slowly faded. He was disappointing. (op 7-2)
Iona Days(IRE) was also disappointing and doesn't seem to be progressing. (op 7-1)
T/Jkpt: Not won. T/Plt: £139.50 to a £1 stake. Pool: £96,429.10. 504.58 winning tickets. T/Qpdt: £9.70 to a £1 stake. Pool: £6,868.41. 523.90 winning tickets. WG

4330 WARWICK (L-H)
Sunday, March 13

OFFICIAL GOING: Good (good to firm in places on chase course; good to soft in places in back straight on hurdle course; hdl 7.0, chs 7.8)
Wind: Virtually nil Weather: Bright and sunny

4745 WHITSON BLOODSTOCK LTD H'CAP HURDLE (11 hdls) 2m 5f
2:05 (2:07) (Class 4) (0-115,110) 4-Y-O+ **£2,602** (£764; £382; £190)

Form RPR

343P **1** **The Boss (IRE)**[10] 4446 6-11-7 **105** NickScholfield 108
(Jeremy Scott) *w ldr: lft in ld 3rd tl 4th: mstke 5th: styd upsides ldr tl rdn to ld 8th tl bef 2 out: drvn to ld again last: hld on gamely u.p flat: all out* **5/1**[2]

51-5 **2** *1/2* **Equity Release (IRE)**[43] 3822 10-10-10 **101** (t) PeterHatton(7) 103
(Louise Davis) *in tch in midfield: rdn to chse ldrs bef 2 out: ev ch 2 out: swtchd rt between last 2: kpt on u.p flat: a hld by wnr* **16/1**

0623 **3** *nk* **Empire Builder (IRE)**[31] 4021 5-11-9 **107** AndrewThornton 111+
(Caroline Bailey) *t.k.h: chsd ldrs: hmpd 3rd and dropped bk into midfield: mstke 7th: rdn to chse ldrs after 3 out: mstke and stmbld bdly 2 out: rallied u.p flat: styd on to go 3rd nr fin* **5/1**[2]

-540 **4** *3/4* **The Laodicean**[30] 4051 5-11-10 **108** WayneHutchinson 109
(Alan King) *hld up wl in tch towards rr: hdwy 8th: rdn and ev ch whn mstke 2 out: styd on same pce u.p flat* **8/1**

/0P3 **5** *1* **De Welsh Wizzard**[42] 3840 8-11-6 **104** JackDoyle 106+
(Emma Lavelle) *racd keenly: led tl blnd and hdd 3rd: led again next tl hdd 8th: sn rdn along: led again travelling wl bef 2 out: rdn and hdd last: no ex and btn fnl 75yds* **6/1**[3]

40PP **6** *2 1/2* **Giovanna**[16] 4327 10-11-8 **106** (t) SeanQuinlan 104
(Richard Phillips) *in tch in last trio: mstke 5th and 6th: pushed along after 7th: hdwy and in tch bef 2 out: no imp whn j.lft last: rdn and kpt on same pce flat* **22/1**

0034 **7** *2* **Deputy Dog (IRE)**[58] 3542 5-11-11 **109** APMcCoy 105
(Jonjo O'Neill) *chsd ldrs: nt fluent 2nd: lost pl and rdn along after 6th: rallied on long run to next and jnd ldrs 7th: ev ch whn mstke 8th and 9th: drvn and unable qck bef 2 out: btn whn sltly hmpd between last 2* **4/1**[1]

114- **F** **Senor Shane (IRE)**[409] 3706 8-11-5 **106** (t) CharlieStudd(3) —
(Chris Gordon) *hld up wl in tch in midfield: hdwy 8th: 4th and stl travelling okay whn fell 3 out* **16/1**

P-0P **P** **Mr Valentino (IRE)**[55] 3599 6-10-9 **96** (t) DavidBass(3) —
(Lawney Hill) *in tch: pushed along after 3rd: rdn and lost pl after 6th: lost tch after next: t.o 3 out tl p.u next* **14/1**

-300 **P** **Inga Bird**[29] 4081 6-11-5 **110** JakeGreenall(7) —
(Henry Daly) *t.k.h: prom: mstke and pckd 2nd: rdn and struggling 7th: bhd after next: t.o whn p.u bef 2 out* **16/1**

4063 **P** **Salut Honore (FR)**[42] 3833 5-11-4 **102** SamJones —
(Alex Hales) *hld up wl in tch in last trio: rdn after 6th: struggling and losing tch after next: t.o 3 out tl p.u next* **10/1**

5m 5.00s (-10.00) **Going Correction** -0.55s/f (Firm) **11** Ran SP% **116.5**
Speed ratings (Par 105): **97,96,96,96,96 95,94,—,—,— —**
toteswingers: 1&2 £16.70, 1&3 £4.10, 2&3 £16.40 CSF £78.98 CT £422.22 TOTE £4.40: £1.10, £5.00, £2.50; EX 79.90.
Owner Mrs Messer-Bennetts,ClarkeHall & Gilbert **Bred** Mrs Kathleen Ferguson **Trained** Brompton Regis, Somerset
■ Stewards' Enquiry : Wayne Hutchinson four-day ban: used whip with excessive frequency without giving gelding time to respond (Mar 27-30)

FOCUS
There were a number of non-runners due to what was perceived as drying conditions, but the winning jockey in the first reported the ground was "dead". Not many arrived in much form for this ordinary handicap, which produced a bunch finish. The pace in the first part of the race was steady and the time was 19 seconds outside the standard, but the form should prove reliable enough with the fifth, sixth and seventh close to their marks.

NOTEBOOK
The Boss(IRE) was at the forefront all the way and, although hard driven in the final half-mile, gamely held off the challengers. He disappointed when stepped up to 3m at Taunton, but there was an excuse there and he is worth another go at that trip, as he is a winning pointer. He is likely to try chasing again next season. (op 6-1)
Equity Release(IRE) travelled well at the back of the field for a long way. Having made ground he was slightly outpaced by the leaders approaching the home straight, but ran on well nearest the rail after the last. He clearly stays this trip and another race should be found for him.
Empire Builder(IRE)'s bad mistake two out proved costly, as he was staying on well again at the line and nearly grabbed second. This was a commendable effort seeing as the drop in trip was against him. He should make a chaser next season. (op 6-1)
The Laodicean ran well on this handicap debut and was one of five still in there fighting at the last. He landed in second but could not quite quicken up. (op 17-2 tchd 15-2)
De Welsh Wizzardcame in for support, with the drying ground a plus. Overcoming an early mistake, he was among the pacesetters throughout and was going best of the principals turning for home, only to fade out of the frame on the run-in. (op 5-1)
Giovanna looked like finishing right out the back at one stage but she stayed on and wasn't beaten that far in the end. This was too sharp for her, and she's now 17lb lower than her last winning mark. (op 25-1 tchd 20-1)

Deputy Dog(IRE) was expected to be suited by the rise in trip on this handicap debut. He came under pressure from McCoy down the far side but remained in contention until between the last two flights. The ground may not have been ideal. (op 9-2 tchd 5-1)

Senor Shane(IRE) completed a handicap chase hat-trick last winter but this was his first run since January 2010. Running off his 9lb lower hurdles mark, he was by no means out of it when he came down three from home. He was without the visor he wore last term. (op 12-1)

4746 E.B.F./T.B.A. MARES' NOVICES' CHASE (17 fncs) 2m 4f 110y

2:35 (2:36) (Class 4) 5-Y-O+ **£3,742** (£1,287)

Form				RPR
P112	1		**Evella (IRE)**[13] 4398 7-11-5 125 AlexMerriam(3) (Neil King) *led tl 3rd: chsd ldr after tl led again bef 11th: sn clr and in command: easily* **4/7**[1]	134+
00P5	2	68	**Pezula**[39] 3882 5-10-9 64 TomSiddall (Richard Phillips) *nt fluent: detached last fr 3rd: t.o 9th: wnt poor 2nd and hit 3 out:* **8/1**[3]	60
	P		**Pipsacre**[294] 7-10-3 0 (t) JakeGreenall(7) (Henry Daly) *t.k.h: chsd wnr tl j. into ld 3rd: hdd bef 11th: sn in trble and btn next: t.o and gng v slowly after 12th: dropped to last 3 out: sn p.u* **2/1**[2]	—

5m 16.0s (-5.00) **Going Correction** -0.45s/f (Good) **3** Ran SP% **108.1**
Speed ratings: **91,65,—**
CSF £4.27 TOTE £1.40; EX 2.90.

Owner Mrs S M Richards **Bred** Donal Boyle **Trained** Newmarket, Suffolk

FOCUS
A weakly contested event for mares with the winner rated to her mark.

NOTEBOOK
Evella(IRE) was quickly in command once regaining the lead and won by a very wide margin. A good jumper, she has now won three of her last four starts, but her victories have been in uncompetitive races with few finishers. She seems to handle most types of ground and has earned a crack at the mares' chasing series finale at Newbury later this month. (op 8-11tched 4-5 in a place)

Pezula is a very moderate hurdler and it looks likely to prove a similar story over fences. Quickly left trailing by the other two, she did keep going and found herself in a remote second with three to jump. (op 7-1)

Pipsacre had been successful in a club members' point when last in action back in May. Making her rules debut, she was pretty keen and soon pulled her way into the lead, but once the favourite went past her on the second circuit she was immediately beaten. Weary when pulling up on the home turn, having been relegated to last, she may have needed the run and could be more at home on right-handed tracks. Official explanation: trainer said filly had a breathing problem (op 15-8 tchd 7-4)

4747 HAPPY 65TH BIRTHDAY MALCOLM WALLS NOVICES' HURDLE (12 hdls) 3m 1f

3:05 (3:06) (Class 4) 4-Y-O+ **£2,602** (£764; £382; £190)

Form				RPR
P/31	1		**Wistow**[23] 4182 7-11-2 125 SeanQuinlan (Pam Sly) *in tch: chsd ldng pair after 7th: led 9th: urged along and drew clr bef 2 out: sn in command: easily* **10/11**[1]	125+
P5	2	4	**Areuwitmenow (IRE)**[21] 4233 6-11-3 0 AndrewTinkler (Charlie Longsdon) *hld up in tch towards rr: hdwy and chsd ldrs after 7th: rdn bef 9th: chal 3 out: nt qckn w wnr and drvn bef 2 out: plugged on same pce and no threat to wnr after* **5/1**[3]	114
00P5	3	22	**Rathconrath (FR)**[18] 4294 6-11-3 0 WayneHutchinson (Althea Barclay) *chsd ldrs: ev ch 8th tl rdn and btn sn after 3 out: wl hld whn j. bdly lft last* **40/1**	96
43	4	12	**Just Benny (IRE)**[37] 3918 6-11-3 0 TomSiddall (Richard Phillips) *rn in snatches: j. slowly and pushed along 3rd: hdwy 7th: in tch next: rdn and wl outpcd by ldrs 9th: t.o bef 2 out: wnt poor 4th last* **12/1**	84
3	5	1 1/4	**Hawkes Point**[18] 4294 6-11-3 0 DarylJacob (Paul Nicholls) *hld up in tch towards rr: nt fluent 1st: hdwy to chse ldrs after 7th: ev ch 9th: wknd qckly after next: t.o between last 2* **5/2**[2]	83
50-5	P		**Jat Punjabi**[14] 4377 7-11-3 0 CharliePoste (Trevor Wall) *t.k.h early: in tch: reminders after 5th: struggling u.p bef 8th: t.o whn blnd 3 out: p.u next* **40/1**	—
5PPP	P		**Dancing Legend**[47] 3724 5-10-10 79 JodieMogford (Peter Hiatt) *led tl 9th: sn wknd: t.o whn p.u 2 out* **100/1**	—
6-43	P		**Taylors Secret**[34] 3981 5-11-0 0 (b[1]) SamTwiston-Davies(3) (Shaun Lycett) *t.k.h: chsd ldr tl after 8th: sn wknd u.p: t.o whn p.u 2 out* **20/1**	—
00-P	P		**Winnetka Dancer**[38] 3897 6-11-3 0 RodiGreene (David Bridgwater) *in tch: lost pl and rdn along 6th: mstke next: sn lost tch: wl t.o whn p.u 8th* **100/1**	—
00P	P		**Sharinga**[7] 4500 4-9-7 0 PeterHatton(7) (Reg Hollinshead) *a bhd: rdn and struggling after 7th: t.o whn blnd 9th: p.u next* **100/1**	—

6m 7.40s (-20.10) **Going Correction** -0.55s/f (Firm)
WFA 4 from 5yo+ 9lb **10** Ran SP% **117.9**
Speed ratings (Par 105): **110,108,101,97,97 —,—,—,—,—**
toteswingers: 1&2 £2.00, 1&3 £8.60, 2&3 £24.00 CSF £6.08 TOTE £2.40: £1.10, £1.30, £5.90; EX 6.70.

Owner Mrs P M Sly **Bred** D R Stoddart **Trained** Thorney, Cambs

FOCUS
An ordinary novice hurdle, lacking strength in depth and the easy winner stood out. She is value for further with steps up from the placed horses.

NOTEBOOK
Wistow was raised 18lb after winning at Fakenham so connections opted to run her under a penalty back in a non-handicap. Scooting clear off the home turn, she won with a good deal in hand and can certainly add to her tally at around this trip. (op 5-4 tched 11-8 and 6-4 in a place)

Areuwitmenow(IRE) ◆ came under pressure after a mistake down the back but rallied to pose the only threat to the winner from the home turn. He was well held by her, in truth, but finished a long way clear of the others, with the step up in trip suiting him. (tchd 11-2)

Rathconrath(FR), a winning pointer, ran his best race so far under rules, but after racing wide down the back straight he had been seen off prior to the home turn. (op 50-1)

Just Benny(IRE) looked in trouble early on the second circuit but stayed on steadily in the latter stages, albeit never a threat to the principals. Going the right way, he looks a likely type for handicaps in time. (op 11-1)

Hawkes Point, who had Rathconrath well behind when third on his hurdles debut, was clearly below form. He produced a brief challenge four out but had run his race shortly after taking the next. Official explanation: jockey said, regarding running and riding, that the gelding emptied on him in home straight and would not have responded to a more vigorous ride. (op 2-1)

4748 AIR WEDDING HUNTERS' CHASE (17 fncs) 2m 4f 110y

3:35 (3:36) (Class 6) 5-Y-O+ **£936** (£290; £145; £72)

Form				RPR
15-2	1		**Rash Move (IRE)**[23] 4183 10-11-9 120 MrTEllis(7) (F A Hutsby) *racd in midfield: clsd on ldrs 6th: wnt 2nd after 10th: hit 12th: ev ch 3 out: rdn to ld bef next: hdd between last 2: sltly hmpd by loose horse and mstke last: sn led again: kpt on gamely u.p* **11/4**[2]	119+
0411	2	1/2	**Good Company (IRE)**[18] 4293 11-11-13 122 MrBJPoste(7) (S Flook) *hld up in rr: hdwy 7th: chsd ldng pair 13th: pressing ldrs whn slipped bdly on landing 3 out: rallied and ev ch whn mstke next: led bef last: hmpd by loose horse and mstke last: sn hdd and nt qckn* **3/1**[3]	127+
14-U	3	18	**Overlut (FR)**[9] 4463 9-11-11 116 MrPJTolman(5) (R Scrine) *led: j. awkwardly 6th: hdd and rdn after 3 out: mstke next: wknd between last 2* **11/2**	102
300/	4	3 3/4	**Locksmith**[14] 11-11-5 0 MrRichardCollinson(7) (Mrs S J Stilgoe) *t.k.h: chsd ldrs: mstke 9th: hit 12th: 4th and struggling next: no prog and btn after 3 out* **12/1**	93
1-1P	5	8	**Bob Hall (IRE)**[23] 4197 10-12-6 129 (t) MrAJBerry (Jonjo O'Neill) *hld up in rr: clsd on ldrs 7th: pushed along after next and nvr looked happy after: rdn bef 11th: wnt 4th bef 3 out: no imp 2 out and wl hld whn blnd bdly last* **5/2**[1]	104+
P0P-	6	21	**Silly Wupple**[371] 4465 9-11-5 93 MrsHKemp(7) (Mrs H M Kemp) *t.k.h: hld up in rr: mstke 2nd: clsd and in tch 8th: wkng whn mstke 12th: t.o 3 out* **28/1**	67
605/	7	6	**High Rank**[673] 12-11-5 84 MissCVHart(7) (H J Franklin) *chsd ldr tl after 10th: lost pl on long run bef next: bhd and t.o 3 out* **100/1**	61
	U		**Castletown Cross (IRE)**[22] 10-10-12 91 MrOWadlow(7) (R Hirons) *chsd ldrs tl blnd and uns rdr 1st* **50/1**	—
/0P-	P		**Willing Weasel (IRE)**[28] 9-11-5 81 MrNPhillips(7) (Miss M Chesterman) *racd in midfield: clsd and in tch 7th: struggling after 10th: last and losing tch 12th: t.o 14th tl p.u 3 out* **100/1**	—
0P/P	P		**What A Cliche**[7] 8-11-5 68 (t) MrECameron(7) (E N Cameron) *j.rt: racd in midfield early: dropped to rr and racd wd 7th: lost tch 10th: wl t.o whn p.u 12th* **100/1**	—

5m 11.4s (-9.60) **Going Correction** -0.45s/f (Good) **10** Ran SP% **111.7**
Speed ratings: **100,99,92,91,88 80,78,—,—,—**
toteswingers: 1&2 £2.40, 1&3 £3.70, 2&3 £4.70 CSF £11.15 TOTE £3.60: £1.10, £1.70, £2.80; EX 10.90.

Owner K Hutsby **Bred** Mrs M M Roche **Trained** Stratford-Upon-Avon, Warwicks

FOCUS
An ordinary hunter chase. All the principals were pestered to an extent by the loose Castletown Cross, who departed at the first. The second is rated close to previous Ludlow form.

NOTEBOOK
Rash Move(IRE) made a pleasing return to action when second at Fakenham and he built on that with a determined display. He came off the bridle after hitting one down the far side and was narrowly ahead when again untidy at the last, but battled on well. Point-to-points included he has run just a dozen times in his life, but he has won seven times now. (op 3-1after early 7-2 in a place tchd 5-2)

Good Company(IRE) was arguably unlucky, as he was travelling well just off the lead when he slipped badly three out, losing momentum. He was awkward again over the last, not helped by the proximity of the loose horse, and was just outbattled up the run-in. (op 11-4)

Overlut(FR) made a lot of the running, worried all the while by the loose horse, and only gave best on the home turn. Essentially a decent jumper, he did not get far on his recent return to the track at Newbury so is entitled to have just needed this run. (op 9-1)

Locksmith, a one-time smart chaser under rules, was the best in on official figures here and had been performing respectably in points, but he was comfortably held in fourth. (op 9-1 tchd 16-1 in a place)

Bob Hall(IRE) had a fruitful time of it in 2010 but ran a lacklustre race on his return to action at Sandown and it was a similar story here. Coming under pressure on the last circuit, he did labour into a remote fourth but that was as close as he got and he lost that position with a blunder at the last. (op 85-40)

4749 D W CLARK DRAINAGE H'CAP CHASE (FOR THE CRUDWELL CUP) (22 fncs) 3m 5f

4:05 (4:06) (Class 3) (0-125,122) 5-Y-O+ **£4,553** (£1,337; £668; £333)

Form				RPR
0130	1		**Justabout**[73] 3230 8-10-1 **97** (t) DaveCrosse (Colin Tizzard) *led: rdn and mstke 18th: hdd next: nt fluent 3 out: looked hld whn mstke 2 out: stl 5 l down last: rallied as ldr idled flat: swtchd rt fnl 75yds: styd on u.p to ld on post* **9/1**	110+
-FP2	2	nse	**Arturo Uno (IRE)**[24] 4160 8-10-8 **107** SamTwiston-Davies(3) (Nigel Twiston-Davies) *in tch in last pair: hdwy to chse ldr 17th: led 19th: rdn clr after next: looked in command 2 out: 5 l clr last: idled and drvn flat: hdd on post* **7/2**[2]	120+
4344	3	2	**Lavenoak Lad**[16] 4333 11-9-10 **99** (t) NathanSweeney(7) (Simon Burrough) *chsd ldrs: hdwy to press ldrs 13th tl 17th: 3rd and outpcd next: kpt on u.p between last 2: styd on flat: nt rch ldrs* **9/2**[3]	107
0015	4	74	**Antonius Caesar (FR)**[16] 4328 8-10-3 **106** PeterCarberry(7) (Alex Hales) *w wnr tl 15th: rdn and struggling bef next: dropped to last 16th: lost tch 18th: lft poor 4th and hmpd 2 out* **9/2**[3]	47
-125	R		**Shammy Buskins**[238] 1032 9-11-0 **113** (p) DavidBass(3) (Lawney Hill) *ref to r: tk no part* **13/2**	—
1P-6	F		**Temoin**[23] 4193 11-11-12 **122** (b) JamieMoore (Richard Phillips) *reminders s: in tch in last whn fell 2nd* **20/1**	—
U151	F		**Sweden (IRE)**[56] 3588 7-11-8 **118** PaulMoloney (Evan Williams) *nt fluent: in tch in last pair: hdwy to press ldrs 6th: dropped to rr again 8th: pushed along and hdwy to press ldrs again 16th: j. slowly and struggling next: 4th and wl btn whn fell 2 out: fatally injured* **3/1**[1]	—

7m 22.3s (-18.70) **Going Correction** -0.45s/f (Good) **7** Ran SP% **111.7**
Speed ratings: **107,106,106,86,— —,—**
toteswingers: 1&2 £6.70, 1&3 £5.40, 2&3 £3.10 CSF £39.20 CT £158.88 TOTE £10.20: £4.50, £2.50; EX 54.90.

Owner Brocade Racing **Bred** H T Cole **Trained** Milborne Port, Dorset

FOCUS
The day's feature event was weakened by no fewer than five non-runners, and the field was quickly depleted further by the second fence. This is very ordinary form for the grade with the third to his C&D mark..

NOTEBOOK

Justabout made a lot of the running but his jumping began to get ragged in the latter stages and he seemed held in second after clouting the third-last. With the leader stopping on the run-in, he got up right on the line for an unlikely victory. Without the cheekpieces on this return from a break, he was only 2lb higher than when scoring at Taunton in November. He had his ground and clearly stayed the longer trip well. (op 8-1)

Arturo Uno(IRE) seemed fully in command from the home turn, but idled after the last and was nailed right on the post. He remains without a win over jumps to his name, but this effort showed he stays well. (op 4-1)

Lavenoak Lad, a C&D winner, looked well held turning in but was trying to rally when he blundered at the last. This thorough stayer would probably have preferred easier ground. (tchd 5-1)

Antonius Caesar(FR) was unable to get to the front and was in trouble with six to jump. He has twice been held from this mark since his Leicester win. (op 7-1 tchd 15-2)

Temoinwho had also proved reluctant to start, fell heavily at the second. (op 11-4 tchd 5-2)

Sweden(IRE) was well beaten when taking a fall two from home which sadly proved fatal. (op 11-4 tchd 5-2)

4750 HENRY AND RYAN HUTSBY MEMORIAL HUNTERS' CHASE (FOR THE WILLOUGHBY DE BROKE TROPHY) (20 fncs) 3m 2f

4:40 (4:41) (Class 6) 5-Y-0+ **£936** (£290; £145; £72)

Form				RPR
F45-	1		**Starburst Diamond (IRE)**[21] 9-11-5 0 .... MrDCollins(7) (C R Whittaker) *chsd ldr 4th tl 6th: wnt 2nd again 8th tl mstke and lost pl 12th: rallied after next: led bef 14th tl outj. and hdd 15th: chsd ldr after: drvn between last 2: led sn after last: kpt on: rdn out* **9/2**[3]	125+
2-64	2	2 1/4	**Moncadou (FR)**[24] 4163 11-12-2 120 .... (t) MrAJBerry (Jonjo O'Neill) *hld up in tch in rr: hdwy on outer to chse ldr 6th tl 8th: in tch towards rr after tl hdwy to chse ldr 14th: j. ahd next: rdn bef last: drvn and hdd and sn after last: fnd little and sn btn* **5/2**[2]	128+
16P-	3	18	**Shillingstone**[15] 9-11-13 0 .... MrGGreenock(7) (G T H Bailey) *in tch: stmbld on downhill run bef 4th: wnt 2nd 12th tl mstke and rdr lost reins next: chsd ldng pair and rdn 16th: no prog u.p after 3 out: wl btn between last 2* **13/8**[1]	119+
214-	4	7	**Bantry Bere (IRE)**[329] 5249 7-11-9 117 .... MrMEnnis(7) (Mrs Fleur Hawes) *mstkes: several positions: chsd ldrs and mstke 14th: struggling whn j. slowly next: disputing modest 4th and wl btn whn bmpd 2 out* **9/1**	109
430/	5	5	**Broken Reed (IRE)**[22] 12-11-5 97 .... MrOWadlow(7) (R Hirons) *t.k.h early: chsd ldr tl 4th: styd chsng ldrs tl rdn and struggling after 13th: disputing modest 4th 3 out: no prog and wl btn whn j.rt and bmpd rival next* **25/1**	99
4PP0	6	11	**Cash In Hand (IRE)**[12] 4415 11-11-5 72 .... (b) MrTEllis(7) (R Harvey) *j.rt: led tl hdd and rdn bef 14th: 4th and wkng u.p 16th: wl bhd bef 2 out: t.o* **33/1**	89
44P/	7	dist	**Up The Pub (IRE)**[14] 13-11-5 86 .... (t) MrBJPoste(7) (Mrs J Weston) *a in rr: in tch: rdn 11th: lost tch and t.o after 13th: wl t.o fr 16th* **50/1**	—
P2-4	F		**Back To Bid (IRE)**[9] 4463 11-11-5 117 .... (p) MrNdeBoinville(7) (James Danahar) *in tch in last whn fell 4th* **9/1**	—

6m 38.2s (-14.50) **Going Correction** -0.45s/f (Good) **8** Ran SP% **113.6**
Speed ratings: **104,103,97,95,94 90,—,—**
toteswingers: 1&2 £3.10, 1&3 £2.30, 2&3 £1.50 CSF £16.46 TOTE £6.40: £1.30, £1.20, £1.50; EX 18.90.
Owner C R Whittaker **Bred** M J Halligan **Trained** Radstock, Somerset

FOCUS

A fair hunter chase with the winner in line with his hurdles form.

NOTEBOOK

Starburst Diamond(IRE), a one-time useful chaser for Alan King, was a decent second on his recent pointing debut at Godstone. Never far from the pace, the grey needed shoving along after clouting one on the second circuit, but kept trying and got up on the run-in. He stays very well. (op 11-2)

Moncadou(FR) showed ahead in the back straight and looked in control two out, but he got in a little close to the last and was just worn down. This was his best effort of the year and he looks set for a bold showing again in the Aintree Fox Hunters', in which he was runner-up last year. The last fence excepted, he jumped well here. (op 7-2)

Shillingstone, a fancied contender for the Fulke Walwyn Kim Muir this time last year when trained by the Alners, made a winning pointing debut in an open at Horseheath last month. He had 9lb in hand on official ratings here, but did not jump fluently under his inexperienced rider and was never going that well. (op 11-10)

Bantry Bere(IRE) may improve for this first run in 11 months. (op 8-1 tchd 10-1)

4751 FERGUSON NASH THOROUGHBRED ENGLISH TAILORING WARWICK CONDITIONAL JOCKEYS' H'CAP HURDLE (8 hdls) 2m

5:10 (5:12) (Class 4) (0-100,100) 4-Y-0+ **£2,740** (£798; £399)

Form				RPR
26P2	1		**Ouest Eclair (FR)**[36] 3951 6-11-4 **98** .... RobertMcCarth(6) (Ferdy Murphy) *chsd ldrs: ev ch gng wl 3 out: led: rn green and mstke 2 out: wandered between last 2: nt fluent last: kpt on wl u.p flat: drvn out* **10/1**	104
005	2	1/2	**Rare Symphony (IRE)**[22] 4225 4-10-8 **93** .... (t) CPGeoghegan(3) (Philip Hobbs) *in tch: rdn and effrt after 3 out: ev ch fr next: kpt on u.p but a hld by wnr flat* **4/1**[1]	91
/0-0	3	6	**Street Devil (USA)**[89] 2426 6-11-7 **95** .... GilesHawkins (Pat Murphy) *hld up in tch in rr: hdwy and stl gng wl whn nt clr run after 3 out: rdn and effrt whn sltly impeded bef 2 out: hdwy u.p between last 2: chsd ldrs flat: no imp fnl 50yds* **33/1**	95
-200	4	2 1/4	**Mossmann Gorge**[16] 4330 9-11-5 **93** .... (p) MattGriffiths (Anthony Middleton) *hld up in tch in rr: hdwy 4th: rdn to ld after 3 out: hdd next: nt qckn w ldrs between last 2: one pce flat* **33/1**	91
5654	5	hd	**Welcome Stranger**[173] 1569 11-11-2 **95** .... (t) PeterHatton(5) (Louise Davis) *in tch in midfield: hdwy to chse ldrs 5th: rdn and nt qckn bef 2 out: edgd rt between last 2: kpt on same pce u.p flat: nvr gng pce to threaten ldrs* **10/1**	93
4645	6	3/4	**Plus Ultra (IRE)**[11] 4419 4-10-5 **87** .... SamTwiston-Davies (Philip Kirby) *mstkes: hld up in tch in rr: hdwy 5th: chsd ldrs and hanging lft bef 2 out: nt qckn between last 2: styd on same pce and no threat to ldrs u.p flat* **12/1**	76
5-36	7	5	**Feeling (IRE)**[123] 1971 7-11-8 **96** .... DonalDevereux (Dai Burchell) *led: mstke 3 out: sn rdn: hdd bef 2 out: btn whn j. slowly last: wknd flat* **20/1**	89
060	8	6	**Langley**[45] 3767 4-10-8 **93** .... MichaelMurphy(3) (Pat Murphy) *in tch: hdwy to chse ldrs 3rd: ev ch 5th tl 3 out: wknd bef next* **25/1**	72
0030	9	nk	**Misstaysia (IRE)**[18] 4288 6-10-12 **94** .... JakeGreenall(8) (Henry Daly) *stdd s: t.k.h: hld up in tch in rr: hdwy into midfield after 3rd: wknd qckly bef 2 out* **18/1**	81
-123	10	nk	**Jeanry (FR)**[116] 2452 8-11-2 **97** .... JoshWall(7) (Arthur Whitehead) *t.k.h: chsd ldrs: wnt 2nd after 3rd tl mstke and lost pl 3 out: wl btn 2 out* **11/2**[3]	87
-005	11	1 1/4	**Gainsborough's Art (IRE)**[16] 4330 6-9-11 **76** .... KillianMoore(5) (Harry Chisman) *in tch towards rr: pushed along after 3rd: hdwy next: chsd ldrs and rdn 3 out: wknd wl bef next* **6/1**	62
/40-	12	50	**Edgebury**[662] 398 8-11-1 **92** .... PeterCarberry(3) (Paul Webber) *t.k.h: hld up wl in tch in midfield: rdn 3 out: wknd bef next: wl bhd and virtually p.u flat* **20/1**	33
0PP	P		**Mr Johnson (IRE)**[91] 8-9-9 **74** oh10 .... EdCookson(5) (Michael Gates) *chsd ldr tl after 3rd: dropped to rr 5th: sn lost tch: t.o whn p.u 2 out* **66/1**	—
-503	U		**Double Handful (GER)**[7] 4503 5-11-6 **100** .... HarryChalloner(6) (Venetia Williams) *chsd ldrs tl j. bdly rt and uns rdr 1st* **9/2**[2]	—

3m 45.6s (-10.90) **Going Correction** -0.55s/f (Firm)
WFA 4 from 5yo+ 7lb **14** Ran SP% **119.7**
Speed ratings (Par 105): **105,104,101,100,100 100,97,94,94,94 93,68,—,—**
toteswingers: 1&2 £12.20, 1&3 £67.20, 2&3 £28.70 CSF £46.43 CT £1300.71 TOTE £13.30: £2.90, £1.50, £9.00; EX 57.00 TRIFECTA Not won..
Owner C W Cooper **Bred** Joel Lemarie Et Al **Trained** West Witton, N Yorks
■ A winner on his first ride in Britain for Robert McCarth.

FOCUS

A modest handicap hurdle. The first two pulled clear on the short run-in and the fourth and fifth help set the level.

NOTEBOOK

Ouest Eclair(FR), who went up 5lb for his improved second at Wetherby, held on well after striking the front despite running about a bit. He stays further than this and can run off the same mark if found an opportunity in the next 12 days. His jockey, who was having his first ride in Britain, looks promising. (op 11-1 tchd 12-1)

Rare Symphony(IRE) had been down the field in her three hurdles runs so far, albeit behind one or two useful opponents. A winner on the Flat in Ireland, she ran a better race on this handicap debut, holding every chance at the last but just held by the winner. A small race should come her way. (op 11-4)

Street Devil(USA), having his first run since leaving Barry Brennan, stayed on quite well from the rear for third on this handicap debut, having encountered a bit of trouble in running. A step up in trip may suit.

Mossmann Gorge had the cheekpieces back on and showed in front off the home turn, but his time in the lead was only brief.

Welcome Stranger, whose sole win came over C&D five years ago, ran creditably in the tongue-tie. (op 9-1)

Plus Ultra(IRE) showed more enthusiasm than he had at Bangor without looking straightforward. (op 14-1 tchd 16-1)

Feeling(IRE) ran a fair race after a winter break. (tchd 22-1)

Langley did not shape without promise on this handicap debut. (op 33-1)

T/Plt: £35.80 to a £1 stake. Pool: £70,971.36. 1,444.95 winning tickets. T/Qpdt: £7.60 to a £1 stake. Pool: £5,218.96. 503.60 winning tickets. SP

4731 LIMERICK (R-H)

Sunday, March 13

OFFICIAL GOING: Soft (soft to heavy in places)

4755a I.T.B.A FILLIES SCHEME EUROPEAN BREEDERS FUND DAWN RUN MARES NOVICE CHASE (GRADE 3) (14 fncs) 2m 6f

3:55 (3:56) 5-Y-0+ **£23,814** (£6,961; £3,297; £1,099)

			RPR
1		**Aura About You (IRE)**[17] 4317 8-10-11 .... MNDoran (Paul Nolan, Ire) *mainly 3rd: rdn in 3rd ent st: wnt 2nd after 2 out: led last: kpt on wl run-in* **6/1**[3]	137+
2	3	**For Bill (IRE)**[15] 4365 8-11-3 .... (t) DNRussell (Michael Winters, Ire) *mainly 2nd: disp ld fr 6 out: slow jump and hdd 3 out: sn rdn: cl 2nd ent st: dropped to 3rd after 2 out: kpt on and regained 2nd run-in* **4/11**[1]	140
3	7	**Gentle Alice (IRE)**[14] 4387 7-11-0 124 .... PTownend (Daniel G Murphy, Ire) *led bef 2nd: jnd fr 6 out: led travelling wl fr 3 out: rdn and strly pressed 2 out: hdd last: dropped to 3rd run-in* **11/2**[2]	130+
4	3 1/2	**Kylebeg Krystle (IRE)**[14] 4386 7-10-11 111 .... (t) APCrowe (Denis Gerard Hogan, Ire) *hld up: cl 4th 3 out: sn rdn: no ex in 4th st* **16/1**	124
5	17	**Uncommited (IRE)**[69] 3384 11-10-11 .... (b) SGMcDermott (Noel G Hynds, Ire) *hld up: no imp fr 4 out* **50/1**	107
6	7	**Castlerock Rose (IRE)**[21] 7-10-11 .... MJFerris (D Rohan, Ire) *led tl mstke 1st and hdd bef next: dropped to last fr 6th: no imp fr 4 out* **50/1**	100

6m 22.9s (382.90) **6** Ran SP% **112.8**
CSF £9.34 TOTE £5.20: £2.10, £1.02; DF 9.60.
Owner James F Mernagh **Bred** J F Mernagh **Trained** Enniscorthy, Co. Wexford

FOCUS

The form is sound with the first three all running close to their marks.

NOTEBOOK

Aura About You(IRE) came home best. In what was a slowly run contest, she came off the bridle quite early as they descended from the third-last but the further they went the stronger she went and the more momentum she had. It was a good performance in a race that probably wasn't run to suit her and she has really rediscovered her form. (op 5/1)

For Bill(IRE) was below her best, although it's unlikely the slow pace would have suited her either. Her jumping wasn't quite as fluent as it normally was and it was matched and outdone in fact by Gentle Alice, and she came off the bridle on the descent to the straight. In the end she kept going under pressure and stayed on to get second after the final fence, but it was certainly a far more laboured effort than we have become used to. Another thing to consider is that both of her runs at this venue have been below-par efforts. (op 2/5)

Gentle Alice(IRE) jumped like a buck in front while dictating a pace that only quickened relatively late, and she travelled so well before the second-last it was hard to see her beaten, but she weakened considerably from the final fence. (op 5/1 tchd 6/1)

Kylebeg Krystle(IRE) didn't jump with any great fluency compared with those in front of her and got outpaced a bit coming down the hill to the straight, but she did come home reasonably well, finishing well clear of the two outsiders. (op 12/1)

4756 - 4766a (Foreign Racing) - See Raceform Interactive

[4397] PLUMPTON (L-H)

Monday, March 14

OFFICIAL GOING: Good to soft (good in places; hdl 6.9, chs 7.0)

Wind: medium, behind Weather: overcast, dry

4767 STARSPORTSBET.CO.UK "NATIONAL HUNT" NOVICES' HURDLE (12 hdls) 2m 5f

2:00 (2:00) (Class 4) 5-Y-0+ **£2,055** (£599; £299)

Form RPR

0 **1** **Turtlethomas (IRE)**[59] 3546 5-10-12 0 HarrySkelton 122+
(Lawney Hill) *chsd ldrs: j.big 1st: chsd ldr 8th: led 3 out: rdn and drew clr bef next: styd on wl: pushed out* **33/1**

-200 **2** *18* **Inner Steel (IRE)**[116] 2482 6-10-12 104 MarkBradburne 109+
(Lydia Richards) *t.k.h: chsd ldr tl led 5th: hdd 3 out: sn rdn: btn whn mstke 2 out: wkng whn stmbld last: hld on for 2nd nr fin* **17/2**

55 **3** *½* **Amaury De Lusignan (IRE)**[24] 4180 5-10-12 0 JamieMoore 106
(Gary Moore) *in tch: j.big 2nd: hdwy to chse ldrs 6th: rdn and unable qck bef 3 out: drvn and btn wl bef 2 out: wnt 3rd 2 out: no ch w wnr but kpt on to press for 2nd nr fin* **5/4**[1]

0B **4** *3 ¼* **Shootin The Breeze (IRE)**[25] 4159 6-10-12 0 HaddenFrost 105+
(David Pipe) *taken down early: t.k.h: nt fluent: in tch: j. slowly 4th: chsd ldng pair and rdn after 9th: wknd after 3 out* **7/2**[2]

6B2P **5** *4 ½* **Twin Bud**[14] 4401 6-10-2 98 (p) SamTwiston-Davies[(3)] 93
(Anna Newton-Smith) *chsd ldrs: rdn and struggling whn mstke 3 out: wl btn bef next* **8/1**[3]

00/ **6** *76* **General Lygon**[692] 5137 8-10-12 0 LiamTreadwell 30
(Peter Hiatt) *racd keenly: led tl 5th: chsd ldr after tl 8th: sn rdn and lost pl: t.o bef 3 out* **100/1**

4 **7** *½* **Fennis Ted (IRE)**[7] 4533 5-10-12 0 TimmyMurphy 30
(Liam Corcoran) *a bhd: reminders 6th: lost tch after next: wl t.o fr 9th* **25/1**

0350 **8** *1* **Wychwoods Kaddy**[14] 4393 5-10-12 0 (t) JodieMogford 29
(Graeme McPherson) *t.k.h early: hld up in rr: rdn and struggling after 7th: lost tch 9th: sn t.o* **66/1**

6040 **P** **Two Cloudy (IRE)**[36] 3960 5-10-9 102 (t) MichaelMurphy[(3)] —
(Pat Murphy) *hld up in tch towards rr: shkn up after 7th: 6th and rdn bef 3 out: no prog 5th and wl btn whn lost action and p.u bef 2 out: fatally injured* **14/1**

6 **F** **Ransson (FR)**[20] 4204 6-10-5 0 PeterHatton[(7)] —
(Alan King) *t.k.h: hld up in tch: wl in tch in 7th and stl travelling okay whn fell 9th* **9/1**

5m 17.3s (-5.00) **Going Correction** +0.025s/f (Yiel) **10** Ran SP% **114.2**

Speed ratings: **110,103,102,101,100 71,70,70,—,—**

toteswingers:1&2:£11.20, 1&3:£12.10, 2&3:£4.60 CSF £276.51 TOTE £22.10: £3.60, £2.10, £1.40; EX 208.10.

Owner Norman Thomas **Bred** Thomas Stacey **Trained** Aston Rowant, Oxon

FOCUS

A fairly weak novice hurdle. The second to fifth were all within a few pounds of their pre-race marks and the winner looks above average.

NOTEBOOK

Turtlethomas(IRE), well beaten in a Huntingdon bumper in January, improved for the better ground/switch to hurdles and ran out a comfortable winner. This clearly wasn't expected, but he deserves a chance to show it wasn't a fluke. (op 20-1)

Inner Steel(IRE) came back to the sort of form that saw him finish second on his debut over hurdles last spring. He'll be of some interest sent handicapping. (op 12-1 tchd 8-1)

Amaury De Lusignan(IRE) needed this for a mark and should do better in handicaps. (op 11-8)

Shootin The Breeze(IRE), held when being brought down last time, was keen early and failed to jump fluently. He's from a good yard, though, so should do better in time.

Ransson(FR) was in the process of improving on his initial effort when falling. It's hoped this doesn't affect his confidence too severely.

4768 STRAIGHTFORWARD RACING NOVICES' H'CAP CHASE (14 fncs) 2m 4f

2:30 (2:30) (Class 4) (0-105,104) 5-Y-0+ **£3,089** (£907; £453; £226)

Form RPR

354P **1** **Horseshoe Reef (AUS)**[72] 3306 8-11-9 **104** SamTwiston-Davies[(3)] 113+
(Jamie Snowden) *chsd ldr: led 7th: mde rest: rdn and forged clr after 3 out: in command next: mstke last: drvn flat: a holding on* **4/1**

040P **2** *1 ¼* **Ban Uisce (IRE)**[15] 4380 6-11-3 **102** (tp) MarkQuinlan[(7)] 107
(Neil Mulholland) *chsd ldrs: mstke 5th: dived 11th: drvn and outpcd after next: mstke 2 out: rallied to chse clr wnr between last 2: kpt on u.p and clsng on wnr flat* **10/3**[2]

01F0 **3** *15* **Manmoon (FR)**[32] 4022 8-11-4 **101** (t) MattGriffiths[(5)] 96
(Nigel Hawke) *led: hdd after 6th: stmbld next: rdn and unable qck after 3 out: hit next: lost 2nd and wknd between last 2* **7/2**[3]

-3P5 **4** *3 ¼* **Quetzal (IRE)**[34] 3989 6-11-6 **101** CharlieHuxley[(3)] 89
(Alan King) *j.rt at times: hld up in tch: outpcd after 10th: rdn and no imp whn mstke 3 out: n.d after: j.rt 2 out* **5/2**[1]

3560 **P** **Lepido (ITY)**[8] 4504 7-11-7 **99** (v) JamieMoore —
(Gary Moore) *a in rr: reminders and rdn after 8th: styd on in tch but no real rspnse: drvn 10th: wknd next: mstke 3 out: eased and p.u next* **11/2**

5m 17.0s (9.70) **Going Correction** +0.15s/f (Yiel) **5** Ran SP% **109.3**

Speed ratings: **86,85,79,78,—**

CSF £17.01 TOTE £4.50: £2.50, £1.10; EX 21.30.

Owner The Horseshoe Racing Partnership **Bred** Hamilton Stud (nz) Ltd **Trained** Ebbesbourne Wake, Wilts

FOCUS

A modest handicap chase. The first two came clear and ran to their marks.

NOTEBOOK

Horseshoe Reef(AUS), pulled up over hurdles on his most recent outing, had clearly benefited from a break and showed much-improved form on this handicap debut over fences. Official explanation: trainer said, regarding apparent improvement in form, that the gelding was suited by the better ground (op 9-2)

Ban Uisce(IRE), making his chasing debut, rallied under strong pressure and showed his recent Towcester effort to be all wrong. (tchd 7-2)

Manmoon(FR) was readily brushed aside and ended up well held. (op 11-4)

Quetzal(IRE) tended to go out to his right on this first run over fences and was beaten by the end of the back straight. (op 7-2)

Lepido(ITY) was never travelling and his rider eventually accepted the situation. (tchd 5-1)

4769 WARM WELCOME TO MARK SPRATT H'CAP HURDLE (9 hdls 1 omitted) 2m 2f

3:00 (3:00) (Class 4) (0-115,107) 4-Y-0+ **£2,569** (£748; £374)

Form RPR

5233 **1** **Illysantachristina**[25] 4161 8-9-13 **87** MarkQuinlan[(7)] 94+
(Bernard Llewellyn) *t.k.h: chsd ldrs: wnt 2nd 4th: lft in ld and bdly hmpd next: mde rest: rdn after 2 out (actual last): r.o wl and asserted fnl 150yds: rdn out* **5/2**[1]

1F50 **2** *2 ¾* **Petit Fleur**[33] 4009 9-10-11 **95** SamTwiston-Davies[(3)] 98
(Julian Smith) *t.k.h: hld up in tch: lft chsng ldrs 5th: chsd wnr 7th: ev ch next: rdn wl bef 2 out (actual last): no ex u.p and one pce bypassing last* **3/1**[2]

5213 **3** *7* **The Bishops Baby (IRE)**[28] 4120 8-11-5 **107** MrTJCannon[(7)] 104
(Richard Rowe) *hld up in tch in rr: lft wl in tch and hmpd 5th: trckd ldng pair 3 out: pushed along bef 2 out: (actual last): rdn and fnd little on long run-in: wknd fnl 150yds* **13/2**[3]

1P06 **4** *½* **Little Carmela**[24] 4182 7-11-8 **103** (vt) MarkBradburne 100
(Neil King) *chsd ldr tl 4th: styd chsng ldrs: drvn and outpcd after 9th: no imp u.p after 3 out* **12/1**

5622 **5** *44* **Lindsay's Dream**[28] 4118 5-11-2 **102** GemmaGracey-Davison[(5)] 59
(Zoe Davison) *t.k.h: hld up in tch: hdwy after 3rd: chsd ldr 6th tl mstke and lost pl next: wknd qckly 3 out: t.o* **13/2**[3]

P604 **F** **Chocolat (IRE)**[14] 4399 6-10-9 **90** (t) AidanColeman —
(Susan Nock) *led tl fell 5th: fatally injured* **3/1**[2]

4m 36.0s (276.00) **6** Ran SP% **112.9**

toteswingers:1&2:£3.20, 1&3:£1.50, 2&3:£4.10 CSF £10.78 TOTE £4.20: £1.90, £2.70; EX 10.20.

Owner Marc Cohen **Bred** R And Mrs S Edwards **Trained** Fochriw, Caerphilly

FOCUS

The final flight was bypassed. A moderate handicap hurdle. The winner produced a step up and the second ran to form.

NOTEBOOK

Illysantachristina had been shaping as though a small race would come her way and she readily got off the mark, despite having been hampered early. She is only lowly weighted and can win again. (op 3-1)

Petit Fleur remains 11lb higher than when last winning and is likely to remain vulnerable. (op 4-1)

The Bishops Baby(IRE) tried to rally but never actually looked like winning. (op 9-2)

Chocolat(IRE) was sadly fatally injured when crashing out at the fifth. (op 7-2)

4770 RSA H'CAP CHASE (12 fncs) 2m 1f

3:30 (3:30) (Class 4) (0-110,110) 5-Y-0+ **£3,089** (£907; £453; £226)

Form RPR

2131 **1** **Rileyev (FR)**[7] 4529 6-11-5 **103** 7ex AidanColeman 116+
(Venetia Williams) *hld up in tch: trckd ldrs after 7th: wnt 2nd travelling wl 3 out: pushed ahd jst bef next: sn clr and in command: eased flat: v easily* **6/4**[1]

344F **2** *14* **The Hardy Boy**[14] 4400 11-10-3 **87** (t) MattieBatchelor 84
(Anna Newton-Smith) *chsd ldr tl led after 3rd: rdn and hdd jst bef 2 out: sn brushed aside by wnr: kpt on for clr 2nd* **13/2**[3]

320P **3** *13* **High Oscar**[71] 3349 10-10-4 **95** MrTJCannon[(7)] 81
(Richard Rowe) *hld up in tch: rdn and struggling 9th: no ch w ldrs after 3 out: wnt modest 3rd next* **5/1**[2]

434 **4** *11* **Paddy The Yank (IRE)**[5] 4556 8-10-0 **87** SamTwiston-Davies[(3)] 73+
(Richard Mitchell) *mstkes: chsd ldrs: wnt 2nd 6th tl 7th: wkng whn mstke 10th: 4th and wl btn whn blnd bdly next* **5/1**[2]

44P4 **5** *6* **Sumdancer (NZ)**[14] 4400 9-10-7 **94** (v[1]) MarcGoldstein[(3)] 64
(Michael Madgwick) *t.k.h: led tl after 3rd: chsd ldr tl 6th: wnt 2nd again next: ev ch and mstke 9th: wknd qckly next: t.o* **10/1**

1510 **P** **Jeczmien (POL)**[19] 4290 8-11-12 **110** (t) LiamTreadwell —
(Nick Gifford) *in tch in rr: reminders after 6th: j. slowly next and sn struggling: t.o 9th tl p.u 2 out* **13/2**[3]

4m 26.2s (0.30) **Going Correction** +0.15s/f (Yiel) **6** Ran SP% **109.1**

Speed ratings: **105,98,92,87,84 —**

toteswingers:1&2:£2.30, 1&3:£1.90, 2&3:£5.60 CSF £10.82 TOTE £2.20: £1.30, £4.50; EX 9.70.

Owner John Mayne **Bred** Mme Laurence Barreaud & Claude Barreaud **Trained** Kings Caple, H'fords

FOCUS

This was not a strong race but the winner rates another personal best.

NOTEBOOK

Rileyev(FR) looked the one to beat, having won well at Fakenham last week, and never had a moment's worry, leading before two out and gradually drawing clear. He's thriving on racing and can continue to give a good account. (op 15-8, tchd 2-1 in places)

The Hardy Boy was clearly none the worse for his last-time-out fall and remains fairly treated. (tchd 11-2)

High Oscar is edging back towards a decent mark, but never looked like capitalising on it here.

Paddy The Yank(IRE) made too many errors. (op 6-1)

Jeczmien(POL) Official explanation: trainer said gelding had a breathing problem

4771 HEPWORTH CONQUEROR STOUT AT PLUMPTON RACECOURSE H'CAP HURDLE (9 hdls) 2m

4:00 (4:00) (Class 5) (0-90,90) 4-Y-0+ **£1,815** (£529; £264)

Form RPR

5031 **1** **Little Roxy (IRE)**[28] 4123 6-10-0 **67** SamTwiston-Davies[(3)] 75+
(Anna Newton-Smith) *chsd ldr tl mstke 5th: wnt 2nd again 3 out: sn rdn to ld: clr but idling bef next: hrd pressed after last: fnd ex towards fin* **9/4**[2]

5454 **2** *½* **Just Beware**[35] 3983 9-11-7 **90** (p) GemmaGracey-Davison[(5)] 97
(Zoe Davison) *chsd ldrs: rdn and mstke 6th: chsd clr ldr u.p 2 out: clsd qckly bef last as wnr idled: ev ch flat: no ex towards fin* **13/2**[3]

6050 **3** *19* **Airedale Lad (IRE)**[14] 4399 10-9-7 **64** (p) MrJBanks[(7)] 53
(Zoe Davison) *chsd ldrs: wnt 2nd 5th: ev ch next tl 3 out: sn outpcd by wnr: 3rd and wl btn between last 2* **11/1**

566- **4** *7* **Chigorin**[391] 4093 10-10-8 **72** (t) LiamTreadwell 55
(James Sheppard) *t.k.h: hld up off the pce in last trio: hdwy 3 out: wnt modest 4th 2 out: sn no hdwy and wknd bef last* **18/1**

0-65 **5** *7* **Bella Medici**[109] 2639 6-10-12 **79** MichaelMurphy[(3)] 56
(Pat Murphy) *t.k.h: hld up in rr: rdn along and hdwy after 4th: struggling whn mstke next: no ch 3 out* **8/1**

0/62 **6** *2 ½* **Dansilver**[54] 2433 7-11-4 **82** (b) JamieMoore 57
(Jim Best) *racd freely: led: mstke 3rd: hit 6th: hdd sn after 3 out: sn wknd: 5th and wl btn whn hit 2 out* **6/4**[1]

0PPP **7** *38* **Baltrap (FR)**[18] 4309 6-10-8 **72**........................ MarkBradburne 12
(Clarissa Caroe) *a in last trio: dropped to last and toiling 5th: lost tch next: t.o fr 3 out* **50/1**

4m 5.40s (4.60) **Going Correction** +0.025s/f (Yiel) **7** Ran SP% **110.8**
Speed ratings (Par 103): **89,88,79,75,72 71,52**
toteswingers:1&2:£2.70, 1&3:£5.70, 2&3:£9.90 CSF £16.03 CT £122.96 TOTE £4.00: £3.00, £3.90; EX 10.90.
Owner The Ash Tree Inn Racing Club **Bred** Ms Alyson Flower And Chris Simpson **Trained** Jevington, E Sussex
■ Stewards' Enquiry : Gemma Gracey-Davison two-day ban: used whip in incorrect place (Mar 28-29)

FOCUS
The front pair drew clear in this modest handicap and are rated to their marks.

NOTEBOOK
Little Roxy(IRE), a course winner in heavy last time, was up only 3lb and had no trouble with the faster surface, just finding enough to hold on. She should remain competitive at a lowly level. (op 5-2 tchd 11-4)
Just Beware, who remains 4lb above her last winning mark, ran right up to her best under top weight. (op 15-2 tchd 11-2)
Airedale Lad(IRE) was unable to race on with the front pair. (op 9-1 tchd 8-1)
Dansilver, a recent claiming winner on the Flat, looked the one to beat off what was still a reasonable mark, but he refused to settle and clearly failed to give his running. (op 2-1)

4772 @PLUMPTONRACEDAY TWITTER H'CAP CHASE (18 fncs) 3m 2f
4:30 (4:30) (Class 5) (0-90,96) 5-Y-0+ **£1,853** (£544; £272; £135)

Form RPR

1 **Present A Star (IRE)**[16] 8-10-4 **67**........................ ColinBolger 89+
(Sarah Humphrey) *a gng wl: chsd ldrs: clsd 6th: hit 9th: mstke 11th: j. ahd 3 out: sn clr: j.rt next: eased flat: easily* **10/3**[1]

0-4P **2** *16* **Zimbabwe (FR)**[38] 3933 11-10-0 **63** oh1........................(p) JamieMoore 68
(Nigel Hawke) *led: hdd 12th: sn rdn: led again next but stl u.p: hdd 3 out: wl btn next: plugged on* **6/1**

U566 **3** *4 ½* **Ethiopia**[19] 4292 8-11-2 **86**........................ NathanSweeney(7) 86
(Bob Buckler) *w ldr: led 12th tl next: styd upsides ldr tl 15th: 3rd and wl btn after next* **7/2**[2]

-521 **4** *5* **Derawar (IRE)**[7] 4525 12-11-12 **96** 7ex........................(p) MsLucyJones(7) 93
(Lucy Jones) *towards rr: sltly hmpd 1st: clsd and in tch in midfield 7th: hmpd bnd after next: 5th and rdn after 13th: plugged on but no imp on ldrs after: nvr able to chal* **9/2**[3]

0000 **5** *47* **Ben Trovato (IRE)**[30] 4081 5-10-2 **67**........................ CharliePoste 18
(John Upson) *mstkes: in midfield: chsd ldrs whn reminder 6th: hit 12th: rdn and struggling bef 14th: 4th and btn whn blnd and nrly uns rdr 15th: t.o last fr next* **15/2**

4P-P **P** **Lutin Collonges (FR)**[306] 278 12-10-3 **66**........................ TomO'Brien —
(Michael Roberts) *bhd: clsd and in tch 7th: rdn and struggling after 12th: sn lost tch: t.o whn p.u 14th: burst blood vessel* **16/1**

3PUP **P** **Rapid Return (IRE)**[48] 3723 8-10-8 **71**........................(p) SeanQuinlan —
(Richard Phillips) *chsd ldrs: clsd 6th: barging match w rival after next: lost pl reminders 8th: lost tch u.p after 13th: t.o whn p.u 15th* **16/1**

2304 **P** **Dromore Hill (IRE)**[13] 4409 7-11-7 **84**........................(v) GerardTumelty —
(Charlie Morlock) *bhd and nvr gng or jumping wl: rdn along and no reponse after 2nd: lost tch 8th: t.o whn p.u 13th* **7/1**

7m 0.30s (9.60) **Going Correction** +0.15s/f (Yiel)
WFA 5 from 7yo+ 1lb **8** Ran SP% **113.8**
Speed ratings: **91,86,84,83,68** —,—,—
toteswingers:1&2:£2.50, 1&3:£4.70, 2&3:£3.40 CSF £23.53 CT £73.08 TOTE £6.20: £2.70, £2.50, £1.20; EX 27.20.
Owner Mrs S J Humphrey **Bred** Mrs J P Duffy **Trained** West Wratting, Cambs

FOCUS
A fairly straightforward win for Present A Star, who was clearly on a very good mark for his British debut.

NOTEBOOK
Present A Star(IRE) was travelling strongest from some way out and quickly asserted having taken over at the last down the back. Recently successful in an Irish point, this sort of surface is clearly important to him and he can go in again. Official explanation: trainer said, regarding apparent improvement in form, that this was the gelding's first run for her and it had always worked well at home since arriving from Ireland. (op 3-1 tchd 11-4)
Zimbabwe(FR), well handicapped on old form, was no match for the winner but boxed on well enough to suggest he can still win a race. Official explanation: vet said gelding lost a left-fore shoe (op 13-2 tchd 11-2)
Ethiopia is coming down the weights and showed a bit more zest, despite ending up well held. (op 9-2)
Derawar(IRE) endured a nightmare run, getting hampered on two separate occasions, and finishing well beaten. (tchd 4-1)
Ben Trovato(IRE) Official explanation: trainer said gelding was distressed
Lutin Collonges(FR) Official explanation: trainer said gelding bled from the nose
Dromore Hill(IRE) Official explanation: jockey said gelding never travelled

4773 DIRTY DANCING DRIVE IN MOVIE H'CAP HURDLE (14 hdls) 3m 1f 110y
5:00 (5:05) (Class 4) (0-105,99) 4-Y-0+ **£2,055** (£599; £299)

Form RPR

2040 **1** **Madame Jasmine**[33] 4009 6-11-1 **95**........................ MrTJCannon(7) 100
(Suzy Smith) *t.k.h early: hld up in rr: hdwy after 10th: chsd ldng trio bef 3 out: rdn and chsd clr ldr bef 2 out: u.p between last 2: 3 l down last: styd on wl under hands and heels to ld nr fin* **6/1**[3]

6020 **2** *nk* **Cloudy Wager**[31] 4052 6-11-0 **90**........................ SamTwiston-Davies(3) 95
(Anna Newton-Smith) *chsd ldrs: rdn to ld after 3 out: clr next: stl 2 l clr and drvn flat: hdd nr fin* **12/1**

30U5 **3** *9* **Aconitum (GER)**[15] 4380 6-11-1 **95**........................(p) MarkQuinlan(7) 93
(Neil Mulholland) *w ldr: drvn to ld bef 3 out: hdd wl bef 2 out: one pce: u.p and btn 2 out: hit last* **14/1**

3060 **4** *12* **Petroupetrov (FR)**[32] 4021 8-11-8 **95**........................ SeanQuinlan 79
(Richard Phillips) *led and drvn tl hdd wl bef 3 out: wknd u.p bef 2 out: hit last* **12/1**

F0-5 **5** *4* **Midnight Ocean**[32] 4032 10-10-12 **85**........................(p) TimmyMurphy 65
(Julian Smith) *hld up in last trio: rdn and effrt after 9th: wknd bef 3 out* **4/1**[2]

5656 **6** *16* **Venetian Lad**[15] 4370 6-11-6 **93**........................ MarkBradburne 57
(Lydia Richards) *t.k.h: in tch: rdn and struggling after 11th: wkng whn blnd next: t.o* **9/1**

1050 **7** *7* **Wheres Johnny**[14] 4399 10-11-10 **97**........................(t) MattieBatchelor 54
(Jamie Poulton) *chsd ldrs: rdn and struggling after 10th: wknd next: wl bhd and eased bef 2 out: t.o* **25/1**

0-5P **P** **Rock 'N' Roller (FR)**[54] 2983 7-11-12 **99**........................ JamieMoore —
(Gary Moore) *hld up in last trio: blnd 2nd: mstke and rdn 9th: struggling next: tailing off whn eased and p.u bef 3 out* **11/1**

4002 **P** **Current Climate (IRE)**[12] 4427 7-11-9 **96**........................ TomO'Brien —
(Richard Rowe) *in tch in midfield: dropped to last and pushed along 6th: sn eased and p.u next* **6/1**[3]

0442 **P** **Blazing Empress**[27] 4130 6-11-3 **90**........................ AidanColeman —
(Sarah Humphrey) *t.k.h: hld up in last trio: hdwy and stl gng wl whn stmbld and lost action 10th: immediately p.u: fatally injured* **7/2**[1]

6m 37.2s (8.40) **Going Correction** +0.025s/f (Yiel) **10** Ran SP% **115.0**
Speed ratings (Par 105): **88,87,85,81,80 75,73**,—,—,—
toteswingers:1&2:£16.40, 1&3:£26.60, 2&3:£9.80 CSF £72.91 CT £963.03 TOTE £7.30: £1.70, £4.90, £4.20; EX 55.30.
Owner Mrs Yvonne Allsop **Bred** Mrs Yvonne Allsop **Trained** Lewes, E Sussex

FOCUS
A low-grade staying handicap hurdle, with steps up from the first two.

NOTEBOOK
Madame Jasmine, up to this sort of trip for the first time, produced a strong late finish for her first win over hurdles. The surface was also in her favour and she shouldn't be put up too much. (op 8-1)
Cloudy Wager, well beaten on her recent handicap debut, showed improved form but couldn't quite see out the longer trip, being worn down close home. (tchd 11-1)
Aconitum(GER) is still a maiden and couldn't race on with the front two. (tchd 12-1)
Midnight Ocean never got close enough to challenge. (op 5-1)
Current Climate(IRE) Official explanation: jockey said gelding never travelled; trainer said, on return, gelding appeared distressed (op 4-1)
Blazing Empress was making ground when sadly sustaining a fatal injury. (op 4-1)
T/Plt: £82.30 to a £1 stake. Pool:£65,456.01 - 580.50 winning tickets T/Qpdt: £14.10 to a £1 stake. Pool:£5,518.08 - 288.92 winning tickets SP

2053 STRATFORD (L-H)
Monday, March 14

OFFICIAL GOING: Good (good to firm in places on hurdle course; hde 9.6, chs 9.0)
Wind: nil Weather: very warm and sunny

4774 CHELTENHAM CASHBACKS AT BETFAIR.COM/PROMOTIONS JUVENILE HURDLE (9 hdls) 2m 110y
2:10 (2:10) (Class 3) 4-Y-0 **£5,204** (£1,528; £764; £381)

Form RPR

1021 **1** **Palawi (IRE)**[22] 4240 4-11-8 127........................ DougieCostello 132+
(John Quinn) *j.w and mde all at brisk pce: clr w one rival by 6th: rdn bef last: kpt on stoutly* **1/3**[1]

2 *2 ¾* **Sidney Melbourne (USA)**[167] 4-10-9 0........................ PeterToole(3) 120+
(Charlie Mann) *chsd wnr fr 2nd and only one to keep tabs on him after 5th: rdn 2 out: 2 l down and hld whn pckd last* **5/1**[2]

03 **3** *31* **Grams And Ounces**[49] 3711 4-10-12 0........................ DominicElsworth 94+
(Amy Weaver) *chsd wnr tl 2nd: 10 l 3rd and outpcd at 6th: plugged on* **12/1**[3]

004 **4** *8* **Zambuka (FR)**[17] 4331 4-10-0 0........................(t) MissLHorner(5) 73
(Pat Murphy) *immediately lost tch and nvr looked to be gng wl: t.o whn blnd 6th: wnt hopeless 4th next* **33/1**

5050 **5** *7* **Midnight Molly**[19] 4288 4-10-5 0........................ TomSiddall 66
(John Spearing) *j. slowly: rdn and struggling bef 5th: t.o next* **66/1**

P **6** *50* **Youm Jamil (USA)**[37] 3944 4-10-12 0........................ RichardJohnson 23
(Henry Daly) *j. indifferently in rr: struggling 5th: t.o next: last whn blnd 3 out* **22/1**

3m 49.0s (-7.00) **Going Correction** -0.175s/f (Good) **6** Ran SP% **108.2**
Speed ratings: **109,107,93,89,86 62**
toteswingers:1&2:£1.40, 1&3:£1.40, 2&3:£1.60 CSF £2.15 TOTE £1.40: £1.10, £1.90; EX 2.40.
Owner Bob McMillan **Bred** Jim McCormack **Trained** Settrington, N Yorks

FOCUS
No strength in depth to this juvenile event, which was run at a solid tempo and the first pair dominated. The winner stepped up on what was already a good standard and is rated to the level of his best Flat form.

NOTEBOOK
Palawi(IRE) gamely defied his double penalty and registered a third win over hurdles from five outings. He set out to make it a test and looked vulnerable as the runner-up came at him turning for home, but his response when it mattered was taking. He was well on top at the line and this confirms his versatility regards ground. A stiffer test will be in his favour as he matures, a flat track also looks best for him and he is in the right hands to progress further. (op 2-5 tchd 1-2 in places)
Sidney Melbourne(USA) ◆ is fair at best on the level and won over 1m6f in that sphere. A sound surface is in his favour and he posted a pleasing introduction to hurdling. A stiffer track on similar ground should see him winning. (op 11-2)
Grams And Ounces was never seriously in the hunt, but again showed he has a race in him over hurdles when switching to handicap company. (op 8-1)
Zambuka(FR) ran with more encouragement despite being beaten a long way at Warwick 17 days earlier, but didn't appear comfortable on this much quicker surface. Official explanation: jockey said filly was unsuited by the good (good to firm places) ground (op 25-1)

4775 BETFAIR IPHONE & ANDROID APP NOVICES' H'CAP CHASE (12 fncs) 2m 1f 110y
2:40 (2:40) (Class 4) (0-115,115) 5-Y-0+ **£3,998** (£1,241; £668)

Form RPR

0-43 **1** **Up To The Mark**[32] 4031 6-11-2 **105**........................ RichardJohnson 117+
(Henry Daly) *led tl j. slowly 2nd: chsd ldr tl lft in front 3 out: sn rdn: drew clr after 2 out* **3/1**[2]

5225 **2** *10* **The Darling Boy**[13] 4411 6-10-12 **101**........................(t) PaddyBrennan 104
(Tom George) *trckd ldrs: pushed along 5th: lft 2nd 3 out: 2 l down and hrd drvn 2 out: hld after: 6 l 2nd at last* **10/3**[3]

1130 **3** *44* **Amuse Me**[40] 3881 5-11-9 **115**........................ RichieMcLernon(3) 78
(Jonjo O'Neill) *j. slowly 1st: hacked rnd in last pair and tended to lack fluency: shkn up but wl bhd 8th: lft remote 3rd 3 out* **6/1**

F **Pin D'Estruval (FR)**[529] 1585 8-10-9 **98**........................(t) DavidDennis —
(Matt Sheppard) *led 2nd: 5 l clr and looked wnr whn crashing fall 3 out* **8/1**

1506 **F** **Washango (IRE)**[26] 4140 9-9-13 **95**........................ PeterCarberry(7) —
(Shaun Lycett) *in last pair: struggling 5th: mstke 8th: remote last whn fell 2 out* **22/1**

6234 **U** **Enfant De Lune (FR)**[10] 4456 7-11-12 **115**........................ WayneHutchinson —
(Alan King) *pressed ldrs tl blnd 8th and uns rdr* **9/4**[1]

4m 17.2s (10.10) **Going Correction** +0.50s/f (Soft) **6** Ran SP% **108.6**
Speed ratings: **97,92,73**,—,— —
toteswingers:1&2:£1.40, 1&3:£2.30, 2&3:£3.70 CSF £12.71 TOTE £4.40: £3.40, £2.90; EX 12.80.
Owner StrachanGabbGriffithHarfordLewis&Graham **Bred** Biddestone Stud **Trained** Stanton Lacy, Shropshire

FOCUS
An eventful novice handicap. the winner is rated up the best part of a stone on his hurdles form.
NOTEBOOK
Up To The Mark picked up the pieces at the ninth and ran on strongly thereafter to gain a career-first win at the tenth attempt. Henry Daly's horses have shown signs of turning the corner of late and this chase debutant was his first winner since January 3. He has to rate as somewhat fortunate, but he was well backed and the switch to fences on quick ground clearly helped his cause. (op 7-2)
The Darling Boy crept into the race going well around the ninth, but was under the pump two fences later and found the winner far too strong. This was better than his heavy-ground fifth 13 days earlier and he sets the level, but he may just have found it lively enough. (op 7-2 tchd 3-1)
Amuse Me, easy to back, jumped deliberately on this switch to chasing and was beat a long way out. (op 11-2)
Pin D'Estruval(FR) was debuting for a new yard after a 529-day layoff and running a blinder prior to coming down. There's no doubt a race in him if he's none the worse. (op 17-2 tchd 6-1)
Enfant De Lune(FR) was not done with prior to unseating and is a frustrating performer. (op 17-2 tchd 6-1)

4776 NEW BETFAIR EACH WAY MULTIPLIER (S) HURDLE (10 hdls) 2m 3f
3:10 (3:10) (Class 5) 4-7-Y-O **£1,951** (£573; £286; £143)

Form RPR
226U **1** **Perfect Reward**[17] 4323 7-11-5 113 JoshuaMoore(5) 120+
(Gary Moore) *hld up: wnt prom 5th: chal ldrs 7th: led sn after next: drvn clr fr 2 out* **11/2**
35F1 **2** *12* **Hypnotic Gaze (IRE)**[10] 4452 5-11-7 108 TomSiddall 105
(Martin Keighley) *towards rr: rdn and outpcd 7th: mod 4th bef 2 out: 11 l 3rd and plugging on last: snatched modest 2nd cl home* **9/4**[1]
2153 **3** *1 3/4* **Tri Nations (UAE)**[10] 4452 6-11-7 111 (vt) WarrenMarston 103
(Milton Harris) *t.k.h: prom: wnt 2nd after 6th: chal next: w ldr and drvn 3 out: nt keen and btn next: lost 2nd cl home* **5/2**[2]
0400 **4** *17* **My Brother Sylvest**[28] 4113 5-11-7 108 RhysFlint 88
(David Brace) *racd keenly in 6 l ld and occasionally j.rt: hdd 3 out: fnd nil and qckly dropped out* **5/1**[3]
6005 **5** *4 1/2* **Ravati (IRE)**[37] 3954 5-10-11 100 (tp) MissLHorner(5) 77
(Liam Corcoran) *hld up in last pair: outpcd fr 6th: wl bhd next* **17/2**
6 *3/4* **Crosscannon (IRE)**[280] 7-10-6 0 ThomasFlint(10) 76
(John Flint) *midfield: rdn and struggling 6th* **14/1**
40F **7** *dist* **Full Ov Beans**[30] 4081 7-10-9 0 MrJEngland(7) —
(Michael Gates) *nt fluent 2nd: in last pair: struggling 5th: hopelessly t.o bef 3 out* **50/1**
0P **P** **Sendefaa (IRE)**[30] 4081 6-10-2 0 (v[1]) EdCookson(7) —
(Michael Gates) *chsd clr ldr: nt fluent 2nd: hit 4th: lost pl qckly and hit next: t.o and blnd 8th: sn p.u after* **50/1**

4m 27.9s (-3.60) **Going Correction** -0.175s/f (Good) **8** Ran SP% **112.5**
Speed ratings: **100,94,94,87,85 84,—,—**
toteswingers:1&2:£2.30, 1&3:£3.30, 2&3:£2.30 CSF £18.20 TOTE £5.30: £2.50, £1.10, £1.40; EX 17.00.There was no bid for the winner. Hypnotic Gaze was claimed by Mr A. B. Haynes for £7,000.
Owner G L Moore **Bred** Normandie Stud Ltd **Trained** Lower Beeding, W Sussex
FOCUS
A typically weak seller, run at an average gallop. The form is rated around the second and third's recent Doncaster run.
NOTEBOOK
Perfect Reward kept up the decent form of his yard and ran out a clear-cut winner. He made his move on the back straight and, despite needing plenty of driving to get to the front, ultimately had plenty spare at the finish. This was his first win away from easy ground. (tchd 5-1)
Hypnotic Gaze(IRE) was off the mark over hurdles on good ground in a claimer at Doncaster ten days earlier. He got markedly outpaced on this quicker ground and sharper track, despite this being a step up in trip. (op 2-1 tchd 5-2)
Tri Nations(UAE) is a tricky horse to win with, but this is his ground and he went well for a long way, finishing closer to the runner-up than was the case at Doncaster over 2m last time out. (op 3-1)
My Brother Sylvest, with the headgear left off, set out to make all yet didn't help his cause by jumping right and was beaten from four out. (op 13-2 tchd 9-2)
Ravati(IRE) Official explanation: jockey said gelding finished lame but subsequently returned sound

4777 CHELTENHAM CASHBACKS AT BETFAIR.COM/PROMOTIONS H'CAP CHASE (17 fncs) 2m 7f
3:40 (3:40) (Class 3) (0-120,119) 5-Y-O+ **£6,337** (£1,872; £936; £468; £234)

Form RPR
450P **1** **Commemoration Day (IRE)**[66] 3433 10-11-3 110 FelixDeGiles 119+
(Charlie Longsdon) *settled towards rr: 4 l 4th and effrt 3 out: styd on wl fr 2 out to ld last: rdn clr* **4/1**[3]
0405 **2** *3 1/2* **Royal Kicks (FR)**[31] 4052 10-10-13 109 JimmyDerham(3) 116
(Suzy Smith) *trckd ldrs: j. deliberately 8th: j.slowly 3 out: led next: rdn 2 l clr on home turn: hdd and hit last and hung lft: nt qckn flat* **7/1**
/123 **3** *2 3/4* **Sultan Fontenaille (FR)**[23] 4219 9-11-3 110 (bt) TomScudamore 116
(David Pipe) *blnd 4th: racd towards rr of bunch after tl effrt 13th: 2nd whn j. slowly next: one of three in line for ld 2 out: drvn and nt qckn between last two* **2/1**[1]
P104 **4** *2 3/4* **Darstardly Dick (IRE)**[51] 3687 8-11-12 119 (b) DenisO'Regan 121
(Victor Dartnall) *rn in snatches and generally looked reluctant to keep up: j. slowly 6th: rdn 11th: slow next: 6 l last bef 14th: drvn and failed to deliver a chal after* **5/2**[2]
P050 **5** *19* **Tisfreetdream (IRE)**[18] 4313 10-11-2 109 (p) JackDoyle 97
(Peter Pritchard) *lft in ld 4th tl 8th: led again 10th: hdd and outj. by two rivals 2 out: dropped out v tamely* **7/1**
-PFP **P** **Direct Flight (IRE)**[63] 3483 13-11-10 117 (t) TomSiddall —
(Jeremy Scott) *led tl j. slowly 4th: led again 8th tl 10th: nt fluent 12th: lost tch rapidly 14th: t.o and p.u after 2 out: b.b.v* **25/1**

5m 48.8s (7.20) **Going Correction** +0.50s/f (Soft) **6** Ran SP% **110.8**
Speed ratings: **107,105,104,103,97 —**
toteswingers:1&2:£4.50, 1&3:£2.60, 2&3:£2.40 CSF £28.70 TOTE £7.10: £4.40, £2.10; EX 39.30.
Owner Alan Bosley **Bred** Reg Griffin And Jim McGrath **Trained** Over Norton, Oxon
FOCUS
There was a fair gallop on in this modest handicap and it saw plenty in with a chance. The winner may have more to offer and the next two were close to their marks.
NOTEBOOK
Commemoration Day(IRE) ◆ was well supported on this debut for the in-form Charlie Longsdon and bounced right back to his best, landing a third course success in the process. He looked held turning out of the back straight for the last time, but responded most strongly to pressure and hit the final fence running, which he pinged. There was still something in the tank at the finish and he has won off a stone higher mark before, so will still look feasibly treated after a rise for this. (op 9-2)
Royal Kicks(FR) was another who responded gamely for pressure on the final circuit and made a bold bid off the final bend. He put in a brave leap at the last, but still hit it and was a sitting duck for the winner at that stage. This was his best effort for a while. Official explanation: jockey said gelding hung left (op 8-1)
Sultan Fontenaille(FR), with blinkers replacing cheekpieces, hit the fourth and wasn't clever at the fifth, after which he got a reminder. He was better on that front as the race went on, though, and had his chance. (op 7-4 tchd 9-4)
Darstardly Dick(IRE), ridden to get the trip, was never going that well and got markedly outpaced when the gallop lifted. (op 10-3)
Direct Flight(IRE) Official explanation: vet said gelding bled from the nose

4778 DAILY NICHOLLS FESTIVAL COLUMN ON BETFAIR H'CAP HURDLE (9 hdls) 2m 110y
4:10 (4:11) (Class 3) (0-125,121) 4-Y-O+ **£5,204** (£1,528; £764; £381)

Form RPR
602 **1** **Remember Now (IRE)**[70] 3376 5-11-2 111 APMcCoy 115+
(Nicky Henderson) *settled in midfield: effrt after 6th: led next: hrd drvn and strly chal fr last: hung on gamely cl home* **5/2**[1]
0303 **2** *shd* **Tatispout (FR)**[67] 3403 4-10-2 105 FelixDeGiles 100+
(Charlie Longsdon) *bhd: nt fluent 6th: clsd on ins bef 2 out: tk 2nd between last two: sustained chal but hanging lft whn cajoled along fr last: ev ch but jst hld* **5/2**[1]
2310 **3** *3 3/4* **Altan Khan**[36] 3966 6-10-10 108 JamesHalliday(3) 108
(Malcolm Jefferson) *bhd: shkn up 3rd: nt fluent 4th: rdn and styd on bef 3 out: 3rd and no imp whn mstke last* **6/1**[2]
3622 **4** *3/4* **Folk Tune (IRE)**[14] 4392 8-11-0 116 KyleJames(7) 114
(John Quinn) *t.k.h: pressed ldrs: disp 3rd bef 6th: rdn and outpcd 2 out: lost 3rd at last* **10/1**[3]
1-0F **5** *6* **Shadrack (IRE)**[138] 2037 7-11-4 113 HenryOliver 106
(Sue Smith) *pressed ldr tl led 6th: drvn and hdd 3 out: stl 2nd bef next: sn btn* **16/1**
/6-0 **6** *1 1/2* **Melvino**[33] 4008 9-10-7 102 DPFahy 93
(John Price) *pressed ldng pair tl rdn and wknd bef 3 out* **20/1**
6124 **7** *1/2* **Freedom Fire (IRE)**[141] 1998 5-11-2 116 JoshuaMoore(5) 106
(Gary Moore) *hld up: rdn and effrt 6th: fnd little and sn btn after next* **10/1**[3]
0-40 **8** *7* **Farleigh House (USA)**[53] 2076 7-11-6 118 AlexMerriam(3) 102
(Neil King) *trckd ldrs: effrt to dispute 3rd bef 6th: ev ch 3 out: wknd qckly bef next* **16/1**
3116 **9** *25* **Tayarat (IRE)**[10] 4452 6-11-5 121 (bt) MrTGarner(7) 79
(Michael Chapman) *led tl 6th: dropped out rapidly after next: t.o* **40/1**
3-F0 **10** *53* **Hector's House**[20] 4115 5-11-1 110 RhysFlint 15
(David Brace) *j. slowly in last: nvr tk any interest: t.o bef 6th* **33/1**
F30- **F** **Veiled Applause**[135] 5128 8-11-9 118 DougieCostello —
(John Quinn) *midfield: rdn and wkng whn fell 3 out* **10/1**[3]

3m 54.3s (-1.70) **Going Correction** -0.175s/f (Good)
WFA 4 from 5yo+ 7lb **11** Ran SP% **120.6**
Speed ratings (Par 107): **97,96,95,94,92 91,91,87,76,51 —**
toteswingers:1&2:£2.80, 1&3:£3.80, 2&3:£3.90 CSF £9.36 CT £34.43 TOTE £3.70: £2.30, £1.10, £2.50; EX 12.30 Trifecta £89.60 Pool: £886.48 - 7.32 winning units..
Owner John P McManus **Bred** Elie Lellouche **Trained** Upper Lambourn, Berks
FOCUS
This didn't look the strongest of races for the class, but the form looks solid with three progressive horses filling the places.
NOTEBOOK
Remember Now(IRE) ◆, a half-brother to Binocular, was making his handicap debut after a 70-day break and just did enough to open his account. He had been too free in novice company previously, and again took time to settle here, but he was going by far the best nearing the home turn. He looked set to win readily when skipping clear, but probably idled somewhat and the runner-up looked like getting on top after the last. Tony McCoy was at his strongest, however, and forced his head in front at the line. This better ground obviously helped his cause and there is likely more to come. (op 2-1 tchd 3-1)
Tatispout(FR) ◆, another handicap debutante, was well backed to hand her stable a quick-fire double and only just failed. She too ran free early, but hit something of a flat spot nearing the final turn. Her response was spot on, though, as she hit top gear in the home straight and she ought to find compensation next time. (op 4-1 tchd 9-2)
Altan Khan came unstuck over 2m4f on soft ground last time, but was off the mark over this trip on good ground on his penultimate outing and he gives this form a solid look. He just looked to find this track too sharp and is another who can be placed to score again in the coming weeks. (op 8-1)
Folk Tune(IRE), runner-up over fences the last twice, also found this track too sharp but is another who helps to set the level of the form. He is a difficult horse to win with, though. (op 11-1 tchd 12-1)
Shadrack(IRE) went well under a positive ride and should come on nicely for the run. Official explanation: vet said gelding lost its left-fore shoe (tchd 14-1)

4779 BETFAIR.COM/MOBILE NOVICES' HUNTERS' CHASE (FOR THE THE CREDIT CALL CUP) (17 fncs) 2m 7f
4:40 (4:48) (Class 5) 5-Y-O+ **£1,873** (£581; £290; £145)

Form RPR
U2/1 **1** **Cork All Star (IRE)**[32] 4026 9-12-1 134 MrJMQuinlan(3) 125+
(Mrs J Quinlan) *hld up gng wl: wnt 4th after 11th: blnd 3 out: tk cl 2nd next: led between last two: pushed clr: readily* **1/3**[1]
U/4 **2** *5* **May Be Possible (IRE)**[23] 12-11-7 0 MrTGarner(7) 112
(R Bryan) *led: hdd bef 9th: led again 11th: drvn and hdd between last two: one pce and no ch w wnr* **20/1**
00/3 **3** *18* **Openditch (FR)**[30] 9-11-7 0 MrMWilesmith(7) 95
(Mrs C Wilesmith) *mstke 2nd (water): cl up: led bef 9th tl 11th: blnd next: lost 2nd at 13th: fdd qckly after 2 out* **11/2**[2]
6PU/ **4** *5* **Moscow Court (IRE)**[9] 13-11-7 88 (p) MrWTelfer(7) 91
(Mrs David Plunkett) *j. slowly at times: prom: reminders 9th: struggling whn j. slowly 12th: wl bhd fr next* **33/1**
U-54 **5** *15* **No Virtue**[11] 4442 8-11-0 76 MrJarrett(7) 70
(S Flook) *in last pair: mstke 10th: sn rdn: struggling after: t.o 12th* **14/1**[3]
6P/0 **6** *3 1/2* **Pouilly (FR)**[29] 8-11-11 0 (t) MrMatthewSmith(3) 74
(Mrs Fleur Hawes) *pressed ldrs: 4th whn mstke 14th: wkng whn blnd next: fdd bdly after 2 out: t.o* **22/1**

5m 48.9s (7.30) **Going Correction** +0.50s/f (Soft) **6** Ran SP% **109.1**
Speed ratings: **107,105,99,97,92 90**
toteswingers:1&2:£1.40, 1&3:£1.30, 2&3:£1.50 CSF £8.58 TOTE £1.30: £1.10, £4.90; EX 6.70.
Owner Cillian S Ryan **Bred** Cathal M Ryan **Trained** Newmarket, Suffolk
FOCUS
A straightforward task for the classy winner, who has the potential to rate a lot higher.

NOTEBOOK

Cork All Star(IRE) ◆ made it 4-4 since joining current connections for a hunter chase career and booked his ticket for the Punchestown Festival in May. He was rightly sent off a warm order, but wasn't quite as impressive on this quicker surface. He still did the job with plenty left up his sleeve, though, and it will take a smart sort to lower his colours in this sphere. (op 3-10 tchd 2-7)

May Be Possible(IRE) ◆ was left clear when gaining his fourth point success 23 days earlier, but confirmed himself to be near the top of his game with a solid effort behind the classy winner. He can no doubt win one of these on a stiffer track. (op 14-1)

Openditch(FR), runner-up in both his points since joining current connections, wasn't always fluent on this return to regulation fences and cried enough nearing three out. He probably needs dropping back in trip. (op 7-1)

Moscow Court(IRE) did his best on this return to rules, but was outclassed and is now 0-18 over regulation fences. (tchd 28-1)

4780 DAILY NICHOLLS COLUMN ON BETFAIR MAIDEN OPEN NATIONAL HUNT FLAT RACE 2m 110y

5:10 (5:12) (Class 5) 4-6-Y-0 **£1,951** (£573; £286; £143)

Form				RPR
50	1		**Scales (IRE)**[42] 3856 5-11-4 0 GrahamLee (Malcolm Jefferson) *hld up and t.k.h: effrt 6f out: sustained chal on ins fnl 2f: duelled w rival ins fnl f: forged to ld on nod* **11/1**	103+
	2	*nse*	**Jawhary** 4-10-10 0 RichardJohnson (Philip Hobbs) *settled towards rr: effrt 5f out: n.m.r and swtchd to outside: led 350yds out: drvn and r.o: jst pipped* **15/8**[1]	95+
	3	*2 ¼*	**Kowloon (IRE)** 5-11-4 0 WayneHutchinson (Warren Greatrex) *bhd: effrt 1/2-way: led 5f out tl wl over 1f out: rdn and nt qckn fnl f* **8/1**[3]	101
30	4	*6*	**Victor Leudorum (IRE)**[45] 3794 4-10-7 0 PeterToole[(3)] (Charlie Mann) *midfield: effrt 4f out: rdn and no imp fnl 2f* **12/1**	87
	5	*shd*	**Stapleton (IRE)**[352] 6-10-13 0 JoshuaMoore[(5)] (Philip Middleton) *bhd: prog 5f out: rdn over 2f out: nt qckn* **18/1**	95
0	6	*6*	**Dancing Teasel**[89] 2965 4-10-3 0 JackDoyle (Emma Lavelle) *on her toes: midfield: effrt 5f out: btn 2f out* **8/1**[3]	74
0	7	*2 ¼*	**Fifi L'Amour (IRE)**[31] 4055 5-10-11 0 JimmyMcCarthy (Linda Jewell) *settled in rr: sme prog fnl 3f: nvr able to chal* **50/1**	80
	8	*hd*	**Wallbro (IRE)** 6-11-4 0 DPFahy (Lawney Hill) *pressed ldrs tl rdn and wknd over 2f out* **10/1**	86
	9	*nk*	**Before Bruce** 4-10-7 0 TommyPhelan[(3)] (Claire Dyson) *trckd ldrs: wnt prom 1/2-way: fdd fnl 3f* **50/1**	78
	10	*8*	**Mill Mick** 4-10-10 0 RhysFlint (John Mackie) *midfield: effrt 1/2-way: wknd fnl 4f* **25/1**	70
606-	11	*11*	**Tarashan**[350] 4932 6-10-11 0 BarryKeniry (Ted Haynes) *last for much of way: outpcd after 6f: t.o* **66/1**	60
30	12	*2 ¾*	**Vision Of Lights (IRE)**[19] 4287 6-11-1 0 TomMolloy[(3)] (Graeme McPherson) *rdn after 6f: labouring 1/2-way: t.o* **7/1**[2]	64
	13	*13*	**Cashwell** 4-10-10 0 DenisO'Regan (David Evans) *led 4f: prom tl 1/2-way: t.o* **12/1**	43
3	14	*37*	**Count Vettori (IRE)**[20] 4280 5-11-4 0 WillKennedy (David Thompson) *led after 4f tl hdd 6f out and stopped to nil: sn hopelessly t.o* **12/1**	14
00	15	*hd*	**Everkingly**[22] 4239 5-11-1 0 RichieMcLernon[(3)] (Anna Brooks) *prom and keen: led 6f out: hdd and stopped to nil 5f out: hopelessly t.o* **50/1**	14

3m 47.6s (-2.80) **Going Correction** -0.175s/f (Good)
WFA 4 from 5yo+ 7lb **15 Ran SP% 126.5**
Speed ratings: **99,98,97,95,95 92,91,91,90,87 81,80,74,57,57**
toteswingers:1&2:£7.40, 1&3:£19.90, 2&3:£9.10. totesuper7: Win: Not won. Place: Not won. CSF £32.36 TOTE £14.20: £2.90, £1.50, £2.60; EX 39.60.
Owner Trevor Hemmings **Bred** Michael Long **Trained** Norton, N Yorks

FOCUS

A bumper run at a fair tempo and the winner, fourth and sixth set the level.

NOTEBOOK

Scales(IRE) made it third time lucky with a last-gasp success. He had shown ability without getting home on his two previous outings, but this switch to quicker ground was right up his street as he travelled sweetly. He looked like playing second fiddle at the furlong marker, but Graham Lee got stuck into him and he also had the rail to help his cause. He should make a nice novice hurdler over a trip next term. (op 9-1)

Jawhary ◆ so nearly gave his powerful stable a welcome winner. This Flat-bred 4-y-o was confidently ridden and made his challenge off the home turn, looking the most likely winner. However, he had to switch wide on the back straight to get a run from off the pace and that move likely cost him at the business end as he narrowly failed. A sound surface clearly suits and he shouldn't be long in making amends. (op 3-1)

Kowloon(IRE) in turn came nicely clear of the remainder in third. He raced wide and showed his inexperience, but it was a promising start for this son of Flemensfirth, a sire best known for his soft-ground progeny. (op 9-1 tchd 10-1)

Victor Leudorum(IRE) returned to something like his debut form at Southwell, when well in front of the winner, and looks ready to go hurdling over a stiffer test. (op 11-1)

Stapleton(IRE), runner-up in an Irish point when last seen 352 days previously, showed ability and ought to come on a bundle. (op 20-1)

T/Plt: £39.60 to a £1 stake. Pool:£62,396.95 - 1,148.00 winning tickets T/Qpdt: £20.70 to a £1 stake. Pool:£5,184.14 - 185.20 winning tickets IM

4444 TAUNTON (R-H)

Monday, March 14

OFFICIAL GOING: Good (good to firm in places; 9.0)

Rail moved on bends reducing each circuit by 42metres. Second fence in the back straight (open ditch) omitted after the 2.50; damage.

Wind: mild across Weather: cloudy with sunny periods

4781 LADIES DAY - 29TH MARCH FILLIES' JUVENILE HURDLE (9 hdls) 2m 1f

2:20 (2:20) (Class 4) 4-Y-0 **£3,425** (£998; £499)

Form				RPR
6613	1		**Balerina (FR)**[10] 4455 4-10-10 118 (p) RobertThornton (Alan King) *prom: led 6th tl next: rdn to chal after 3 out: led narrowly last: kpt on: all out* **4/6**[1]	95+
0P	2	*½*	**Racey Lacey**[29] 4091 4-10-10 0 JamesDavies (Chris Down) *trckd ldrs: led 3 out: rdn after 2 out: narrowly hdd last: kpt on* **100/1**	94
50	3	*10*	**Clyffe Top**[55] 3616 4-10-10 0 LeightonAspell (Jonathan Portman) *hld up: rdn and hdwy after 3 out: wnt 4th whn hit next: styd on to go 3rd run-in: nvr rchd ldrs* **50/1**	84
06	4	*5*	**Mavalenta (IRE)**[28] 4118 4-10-10 0 DarylJacob (Nigel Twiston-Davies) *led tl 3rd: prom: led after 5th tl next: rdn after 3 out: wkng in 3rd whn hit last* **14/1**	81
	5	*1 ¾*	**Shianda**[147] 4-10-10 0 AndrewGlassonbury (Gary Moore) *mid-div: rdn after 6th: nvr any imp on ldrs* **16/1**	77
	6	*8*	**Shesells Seashells**[175] 4-10-10 0 AdrianLane (Donald McCain) *mid-div: hdwy after 5th: rdn after 3 out: wkng whn nt fluent 2 out* **5/1**[2]	71
	7	*7*	**Sentosa**[134] 4-10-10 0 JimmyMcCarthy (Michael Blanshard) *awkward 1st: a towards rr* **14/1**	62
0	8	*21*	**Dane Cottage**[19] 4288 4-10-7 0 LeeStephens[(3)] (Katie Stephens) *prom: led 3rd tl after 5th: sn wknd: t.o* **33/1**	41
00	9	*19*	**Knight Blaze**[25] 4164 4-10-7 0 DonalDevereux[(3)] (David Brace) *lost tch u.p fr 5th: t.o* **100/1**	22
	F		**Napoleons Mistress (IRE)**[530] 4-10-10 0 AndrewTinkler (Nicky Henderson) *racd keenly: hld up towards rr: hdwy 6th: rdn after 3 out: wknd bef next: fell last* **13/2**[3]	77

3m 53.1s (-14.90) **Going Correction** -0.875s/f (Firm) **10 Ran SP% 116.1**
Speed ratings: **100,99,95,92,91 88,84,74,66,—**
toteswingers:1&2:£12.60, 1&3:£11.40, 2&3:£38.50 CSF £109.79 TOTE £1.90: £1.10, £11.10, £8.10; EX 115.70.
Owner Tim & Sarah Ingram Hill **Bred** Mathieu Lalanne **Trained** Barbury Castle, Wilts

FOCUS

A sunny, drying day and jockeys reported the ground to be good to firm after the opener. The rail had been moved out on the bends, reducing each circuit by 42 metres. A very weak juvenile fillies' event. The winner is rated a stone off her best form.

NOTEBOOK

Balerina(FR) set a clear standard, and was backed as if defeat was out of the question. She duly obliged but her supporters were made to sweat as Racey Lacey ensured she had to pull out all the stops in the straight. She appreciated tackling better ground (trainer reported that she doesn't like winter ground) but even so, on this evidence she isn't anything out of the ordinary. (op 8-11, tchd 4-5 in places)

Racey Lacey had been tailed off in a bumper before being pulled up on her hurdles debut. This was clearly a huge turnaround and perhaps the better ground she encountered here made all the difference. If that's the case then she's an interesting filly for the spring/summer.

Clyffe Top plugged on for third and she is another who seemed to improve for the better ground (well beaten on heavy last time).

Shesells Seashells made a fairly inauspicious start to her career. (op 6-1)

4782 ENTER THE RACECARD COMPETITION BEGINNERS' CHASE (12 fncs) 2m 110y

2:50 (2:50) (Class 4) 5-Y-0+ **£3,768** (£1,098; £549)

Form				RPR
B2P2	1		**Fiftyonefiftyone (IRE)**[10] 4460 7-11-0 124 LeightonAspell (Oliver Sherwood) *tendency to jump lft at times: trckd ldr: led 4th: drew wl clr after 4 out: easily* **9/4**[3]	130+
P-00	2	*23*	**Bay Central (IRE)**[21] 4260 7-11-0 0 PaulMoloney (Evan Williams) *hld up 4th: wnt 3rd 7th: chal for 2nd fr 3 out: wnt clr 2nd bef last: nvr any ch w wnr* **20/1**	104
4022	3	*27*	**Flaming Gorge (IRE)**[54] 3628 6-11-0 117 DarylJacob (Nick Williams) *led tl 4th: chsd wnr: rdn after 8th: sn no ch w wnr: wkng whn lost 2nd after 2 out* **7/4**[1]	89
04	4	*94*	**Secret Shared (IRE)**[20] 4267 7-11-0 0 JohnnyFarrelly (Richard Mitchell) *lost tch after 5th: t.o* **100/1**	—
3140	P		**Pennellis (FR)**[74] 3229 7-11-0 0 (t) NickScholfield (Paul Nicholls) *chsd ldng pair: struggling and losing tch whn blnd 7th: sn p.u* **15/8**[2]	—

3m 57.7s (-12.30) **Going Correction** -0.875s/f (Firm) **5 Ran SP% 107.7**
Speed ratings: **93,82,69,25,—**
CSF £28.00 TOTE £4.20: £2.10, £4.00; EX 18.70.
Owner A Taylor **Bred** P O'Connell **Trained** Upper Lambourn, Berks

FOCUS

A modest beginners' chase. The easy winner was the form pick but probably only ran to a similar level to Newbury.

NOTEBOOK

Fiftyonefiftyone(IRE) had this in safe keeping from a fair way out. This was less competitive than the company he'd been keeping in recent starts and he appreciated the drop in class, and the drier ground, posting a most emphatic performance. He did display a tendency to edge to his left over the obstacles, but that didn't prevent him putting in some exuberant leaps. (tchd 5-2)

Bay Central(IRE) wasn't always foot-perfect over the obstacles and he struggled to keep tabs on the leaders through the early parts of the contest, but he stuck on past a disappointing Flaming George in the closing stages and looks capable of building on this. (op 16-1 tchd 14-1)

Flaming Gorge(IRE) began to lose touch on the leader down the far side and this ground may have been too quick for him. Official explanation: jockey said gelding would not let itself down on the good ground (tchd 15-8)

Pennellis(FR) had a big shout if translating his hurdles form to this sphere but he was pulled up pretty abruptly down the far side and something looks to have gone amiss with him. Official explanation: jockey said gelding bled from the nose (op 9-4)

4783 GREYHOUND INN AT STAPLE FITZPAINE H'CAP HURDLE (9 hdls) 2m 1f

3:20 (3:20) (Class 3) (0-130,123) 4-Y-0+ **£6,165** (£1,797; £449; £449)

Form				RPR
125/	1		**Advancement**[878] 1739 8-11-9 **120** JohnnyFarrelly (Sophie Leech) *j. sltly rt: mde all: hit 3 out: hld on gamely fr last: all out* **14/1**	122+
5036	2	*½*	**Art Broker (IRE)**[30] 4076 5-10-1 **105** JakeGreenall[(7)] (Henry Daly) *hld up in last pair but in tch: hdwy after 3 out: sn rdn: ev ch last: kpt on but no ex* **11/2**[3]	104
034P	3	*nk*	**Gilded Age**[44] 3808 5-11-12 **123** RobertThornton (Alan King) *trckd ldrs: mstke 3 out: sn rdn: styng on in v cl 4th whn short of room last: kpt on* **2/1**[1]	127+
1206	3	*dht*	**Salontyre (GER)**[37] 3941 5-11-7 **123** (p) MissIsabelTompsett[(5)] (Bernard Llewellyn) *trckd ldr: rdn after 3 out: ev ch last: kpt on bt no ex* **4/1**[2]	122
4P0	5	*2 ¾*	**Knight In Purple**[115] 2508 7-10-13 **110** (vt) AndrewTinkler (John Mackie) *trckd ldr: rdn after 3 out: kpt on same pce fr next* **4/1**[2]	106
00	6	*10*	**Hail Caesar (IRE)**[30] 4076 5-10-9 **106** PaulMoloney (Evan Williams) *hld up last but in tch: rdn after 3 out: nvr any imp* **11/2**[3]	94

3m 50.0s (-18.00) **Going Correction** -0.875s/f (Firm) **6 Ran SP% 110.8**
Speed ratings (Par 107): **107,106,106,106,105 100**
toteswingers:AD&AB:£9.50, AB&GA:£2.70, AD&S:£1.50, AD&GA:£1.40, AB&S:£3.00 CSF £81.48 TOTE £22.70: £8.90, £4.70; EX 32.20.
Owner M J Lethbridge **Bred** Raymond Cowie **Trained** Kingsbridge, Devon

FOCUS

A cracker of a race with four in with a fighting chance coming over the final flight. A good effort from the winner but the third was unlucky.

NOTEBOOK

Advancement just wouldn't be passed, despite having been off the track for 878 days, and he toughed it out in grand style. This 8-y-o had been keeping good company as a novice, and was second in the Listed Summer Handicap Hurdle at Market Rasen on his penultimate start, so is clearly useful, and this confirms he's lost none of that ability. Still relatively lightly raced for his age, there is no reason why he can't go on from this, not least because of his terrific attitude. (op 7-1)

Art Broker(IRE), tackling quick ground for the first time over hurdles, kept chipping away and finished strongly but could never get past. This was arguably his best effort so far and, his stable had a winner at Stratford earlier in the afternoon, so looks to be running into form. (op 10-3)

Salontyre(GER) didn't see out 2m4f at Exeter last time. He shaped much better and has won off a higher mark this season. (op 9-2 tchd 7-2)

Gilded Age was still bang there when losing momentum with a mistake at the final hurdle on the far side, but he worked his way back into it and finished his race well. Whilst he's not fulfilled the promise of his juvenile campaign, there are surely races in him off this sort of mark. (op 9-2 tchd 7-2)

4784 LEWIS RAVEN - 90TH BIRTHDAY CELEBRATION H'CAP CHASE (12 fncs 2 omitted) 2m 3f

3:50 (3:50) (Class 4) (0-100,97) 5-Y-O+ **£3,675** (£1,248)

Form				RPR
-P35	1		**Thunder Child**29 4093 11-10-0 **71** oh5 (t) AndrewGlassonbury (Simon Burrough) *mde all: jnd 8th: rdn whn lft in clr ld next: drew clr: comf* **11/4**1	94+
2351	2	28	**Normandy Landings**67 3402 8-11-1 **86** (p) RodiGreene (Neil Mulholland) *trckd ldrs: rdn whn lft 2nd 4 out: sn readily hld: wknd 2 out* **11/2**	77
52F3	U		**Chilla Cilla**41 3873 8-10-10 **81** (t) NickScholfield (Anthony Honeyball) *w wnr tl 8th: pushed along disputing 3rd whn blnd and uns rdr 4 out* **7/2**2	—
0FPP	P		**Buailteoir (IRE)**25 4160 9-11-8 **93** PaulMoloney (Evan Williams) *nt a fluent: trckd ldrs: dropped to last and reminders after 6th: p.u bef next* **5/1**3	—
3514	F		**Kirbys Glen (IRE)**11 4447 9-11-0 **88** KeiranBurke(3) (Patrick Rodford) *hld up in last but in tch: hdwy to dispute ld 8th: fell heavily next* **11/4**1	—

4m 39.6s (-16.90) **Going Correction** -0.875s/f (Firm) 5 Ran SP% **107.6**

Speed ratings: **100,88,—,—,—**

CSF £15.97 TOTE £2.80: £1.10, £2.80; EX 17.40.

Owner Richard Weeks **Bred** L Fuller **Trained** West Buckland, Somerset

FOCUS

The open ditch in the back straight was omitted. A modest handicap chase. The winner was well in on last season's hunter chase form and the second was a stone+ off.

NOTEBOOK

Thunder Child looked in trouble when under pressure down the far side, but the heavy fall of Kirbys Glen gifted the bottom weight with a huge lead over the struggling Normandy Landings. The grey only had to keep galloping and stay on his feet to take advantage, and he did so with little fuss to justify some fairly strong market support throughout the day. This was his first success at the 14th attempt over fences but he has run on unsuitably testing ground on both previous starts this winter and his sole previous success came on good to firm. (op 7-2)

Normandy Landings, who won at Huntingdon last time, ran a little disappointingly despite finishing second. (op 4-1)

Buailteoir(IRE) Official explanation: jockey said gelding lost its action but returned sound (op 10-3 tchd 7-2)

Kirbys Glen(IRE), who broke his duck over C&D last month, was travelling much the best when coming down and needs close attention in similar company next time. (op 10-3 tchd 7-2)

4785 LONDON INN AT WATCHET H'CAP HURDLE (10 hdls) 2m 3f 110y

4:20 (4:20) (Class 4) (0-105,105) 4-Y-O+ **£3,425** (£998; £499)

Form				RPR
5645	1		**Decision**32 4034 5-10-13 **95** (t) DannyCook(3) (Lawney Hill) *mde all: kpt on strly fr 2 out: comf* **5/1**2	105+
P0/1	2	10	**Orang Outan (FR)**39 3899 9-11-4 **100** DavidBass(3) (Laura Hurley) *in tch: rdn to chse wnr after 3 out: kpt on but a being comf hld* **10/1**3	100+
2226	3	6	**Man Of Leisure**6 4540 7-10-9 **91** KeiranBurke(3) (Nerys Dutfield) *in tch: tk clsr order after 5th: rdn in 3rd after 3 out: styd on same pce* **4/1**1	83
P040	4	5	**Tiger Breeze (USA)**63 3477 5-11-5 **98** AndrewGlassonbury (Bob Buckler) *hld up: rdn into 4th after 3 out but nvr any ch w ldrs* **18/1**	85
0006	5	31	**Naughtyatiz (IRE)**11 4450 5-10-7 **91** AodhaganConlon(5) (Debra Hamer) *w wnr tl rdn after 6th: wknd 3 out: t.o* **11/1**	47
14P0	6	22	**Be Ashored**38 3934 6-11-7 **103** RichardKilloran(3) (Tim Vaughan) *a towards rr: lost tch after 6th: t.o* **12/1**	37
4422	F		**Monsieur (FR)**11 4450 11-10-6 **90** GilesHawkins(5) (Carroll Gray) *in tch tl rdn after 6th: fell next: fatally injured* **5/1**2	—
B6-0	F		**Semi Detached (IRE)**22 4234 8-11-2 **95** DarylJacob (James Unett) *trckd ldrs: wnt 2nd after 6th tl after next: sn rdn: wknd after 3 out: fell next* **12/1**	75
/650	P		**Southway Star**224 1158 6-10-5 **84** JamesDavies (Susan Gardner) *in tch tl rdn after 5th: bhd fr next: p.u bef 7th* **25/1**	—
3022	P		**Easton Clump**18 4310 8-11-2 **95** MarkGrant (Dominic Ffrench Davis) *trckd ldrs tl after 5th: sn bhd: p.u bef 7th* **4/1**1	—

4m 26.7s (-19.30) **Going Correction** -0.875s/f (Firm) 10 Ran SP% **115.3**

Speed ratings (Par 105): **103,99,96,94,82 73,—,—,—,—**

toteswingers:1&2:£7.10, 1&3:£5.50, 2&3:£8.10 CSF £52.96 CT £219.03 TOTE £3.90: £1.40, £3.90, £2.30; EX 49.50.

Owner The Go 90 Partnership **Bred** D D And Mrs Jean P Clee **Trained** Aston Rowant, Oxon

FOCUS

Weak form for the grade and another front-running winner. He recorded a personal best.

NOTEBOOK

Decision ran his rivals ragged to finally get off the mark over hurdles. His sole Flat win came on a sound surface and, having shaped well enough on soft ground in two starts this year, he relished being able to skip off this sort of ground and proved a different animal. He could win under a penalty if connections can find a similar opening, but he looks one to keep an eye on for the summer as he could make hay on tight tracks like this. (op 4-1)

Orang Outan(FR) was clear of the remainder in second despite an 8lb rise and has run very well. He seems quite versatile with regards to trip and ground. (op 8-1 tchd 15-2)

Man Of Leisure plugged on for third but remains winless. (op 11-2 tchd 6-1)

Tiger Breeze(USA), making his handicap debut, didn't really improve for tackling better ground. (op 20-1 tchd 16-1)

Easton Clump Official explanation: jockey said gelding pulled up lame

4786 ROYAL DEVON YEOMANRY OPEN HUNTERS' CHASE (15 fncs 2 omitted) 2m 7f 110y

4:50 (4:55) (Class 5) 5-Y-O+ **£1,977** (£608; £304)

Form				RPR
/13-	1		**King Cyrus (IRE)**666 345 9-11-7 0 MrMWoodward(7) (Ms Emma Oliver) *mde all: outrt ldr after 9th: hrd pressed fr 3 out: kpt on wl to assert fr last: pushed out* **12/1**	120+
5-23	2	3 ½	**Fresh Air And Fun (IRE)**19 4293 8-11-11 0 MrARalph(7) (A G Hobbs) *hld up but in tch: hdwy 9th to trck wnr: rdn after 4 out: upsides 3 out: nt fluent 2 out or last: no ex* **9/4**1	125+
22P5	3	14	**Captain Marlon (IRE)**195 1447 10-11-10 92 MrJoshuaGuerriero (Miss C Wright) *in tch: struggling 11th: styd on fr 3 out but nvr gng to trble ldng pair* **18/1**	98
2104	4	½	**Distant Thunder (IRE)**24 4197 13-11-7 108 (t) MrPPrince(7) (Mrs A S Hodges) *cl up tl outpcd after 4 out: styd on again fr 2 out* **11/2**3	101
/2-F	5	1 ¼	**Sheriff Roscoe**20 4271 11-11-7 105 MrRWoollacott(3) (R M Woollacott) *trckd ldrs: rdn after 4 out: hld fr next* **5/2**2	96
4-32	6	19	**Nobody Tells Me (FR)**8 10-11-9 105 MrIChanin(5) (E Walker) *trckd ldrs: blnd 6th: rdn after 4 out: wknd next* **11/2**3	85
01PP	U		**City Heights (IRE)**191 1469 9-12-1 122 MrMWall(3) (Giles Smyly) *disp tl 9th: chsd ldrs: rdn after 11th: chalng for 3rd whn stmbld bdly and uns rdr 3 out* **11/1**	105

5m 49.7s (-24.90) **Going Correction** -0.875s/f (Firm) 7 Ran SP% **111.4**

Speed ratings: **106,104,100,100,99 93,—**

toteswingers:1&2:£4.50, 1&3:£21.40, 2&3:£8.10 CSF £38.68 TOTE £14.60: £5.50, £1.50; EX 63.10.

Owner R O Oliver **Bred** Mrs V Wilkinson **Trained** Lower Ashton, Devon

FOCUS

The open ditch in the back straight was omitted. An ordinary hunter chase, rated around the first two.

NOTEBOOK

King Cyrus(IRE) overcame a 666-day lay-off to land just his second win under rules. Despite having his rivals fairly well strung out down the back, the runner-up probably took over at the third last, but King Cyrus fenced with more fluency and that probably won him the race. (op 11-1)

Fresh Air And Fun(IRE) probably took over at the third last, but his jumping let him down over the final two fences. He is a reliable yardstick who came here in decent form, but he paid for those late mistakes. (op 3-1)

Captain Marlon(IRE) didn't run badly given he faced a tough task on these terms. (op 10-1)

Distant Thunder(IRE), who faced tougher opposition at Sandown last time, was ultimately disappointing back in fourth. (tchd 6-1)

4787 THE WURZELS HERE- EVENING MEETING 12TH APRIL H'CAP HURDLE (12 hdls) 3m 110y

5:20 (5:21) (Class 5) (0-90,90) 4-Y-O+ **£2,055** (£599; £299)

Form				RPR
5500	1		**Captain Becket**23 4224 8-11-2 **85** TomO'Connor(5) (James Frost) *in tch: shkn up to chse ldr after 3 out: led after next: styd on wl: pushed out* **4/1**1	92+
3253	2	3 ¼	**Jacarado (IRE)**26 4144 13-9-8 **68** (v) ChristopherWard(10) (Robin Dickin) *trckd ldrs: led after 8th: rdn appr 2 out: hdd bef last: styd on same pce* **5/1**3	70
P/U2	3	3 ¼	**L'Apprenti Sorcier (FR)**20 4273 8-10-11 **75** (t) DaveCrosse (Joanna Davis) *in tch: struggling to hold pl after 7th: styd on appr 2 out: wnt 3rd whn nt fluent last: no further imp* **11/2**	74
0P01	4	9	**Bernard**127 2239 11-10-12 **81** (p) GilesHawkins(5) (Kevin Bishop) *in tch: rdn to chse ldr after 3 out tl next: one pce whn nt fluent last: fdd flat* **8/1**	70
P0/P	5	¾	**Galandora**32 4032 11-10-2 **66** (t) AndrewGlassonbury (Dr Jeremy Naylor) *led tl after 8th: rdn after next: one pce fr next* **33/1**	55
5P2	6	10	**Gleannacreim (IRE)**7 4522 8-10-13 **80** RichardKilloran(3) (Tim Vaughan) *prom tl rdn after 7th: wkng whn hmpd 3 out* **9/2**2	58
6-U6	7	shd	**Drumbeater (IRE)**20 4273 11-10-3 **72** AodhaganConlon(5) (Bernard Scriven) *in tch: racd wd: rdn after 8th: wknd 3 out* **11/1**	50
0000	8	19	**Sheezatreasure (IRE)**60 3532 6-10-12 **79** (b1) IanPopham(3) (James Evans) *hld up: hdwy after 7th: rdn bef 3 out: wknd bef 2 out* **33/1**	38
6/0P	9	58	**Star Time (IRE)**15 4380 12-9-9 **64** (v) CO'Farrell(5) (Michael Scudamore) *prom tl 8th: sn wl in rr: t.o* **22/1**	—
0004	U		**Gallimaufry**70 3367 5-10-10 **74** RodiGreene (Neil Mulholland) *hld up: pushed along and no imp whn blnd bdly and uns rdr 3 out* **6/1**	—

5m 46.5s (-20.60) **Going Correction** -0.875s/f (Firm) 10 Ran SP% **114.2**

Speed ratings (Par 103): **97,95,94,92,91 88,88,82,63,—**

toteswingers:1&2:£5.20, 1&3:£6.20, 2&3:£4.00 CSF £23.60 CT £107.70 TOTE £5.20: £2.10, £1.20, £2.20; EX 30.20.

Owner Share My Dream **Bred** J D Frost **Trained** Scorriton, Devon

FOCUS

A moderate handicap. The winner should still be well treated when reassessed, and the next two are rated to their marks.

NOTEBOOK

Captain Becket travelled nicely before swooping past Jacarado in the straight and coming readily clear. The winner, who relished the return to a sound surface, was 10lb lower than when successful at Newton Abbot last summer and the way he got the job done here suggests he could overcome a rise. Official explanation: trainer said, regarding apparent improvement in form, that the gelding was better suited by the faster ground and longer trip. (op 6-1)

Jacarado(IRE) tanked through the early stages and took over down the back but he was a sitting duck for the winner and had no answer as he went past. To his credit he kept on well enough for second but his frustrating run in this sphere continues. (op 13-2)

L'Apprenti Sorcier(FR) came under pressure earlier than many but to his credit he kept responding and saw his race out well. This ground may have been a bit too lively for him and he'll be interesting back on a slower surface. (op 5-1 tchd 6-1)

Bernard ran okay back from a break, but wasn't quite at his best. (op 15-2)

Galandora shaped with more encouragement on this second run back from a long absence under conditions that suit.

T/Jkpt: Not won. T/Plt: £155.90 to a £1 stake. Pool:£88,495.07 - 414.28 winning tickets T/Qpdt: £53.10 to a £1 stake. Pool:£5,420.56 - 75.47 winning tickets TM

3802 CHELTENHAM (L-H)

Tuesday, March 15

OFFICIAL GOING: Chase & hurdle courses - good (good to soft in places); cross country course - good to firm (good in places; chase and hurdle 7.7, cross country 8.8)

Wind: Moderate, across Weather: Fine

4788 STAN JAMES SUPREME NOVICES' HURDLE GRADE 1 (8 hdls) 2m 110y

1:30 (1:30) (Class 1) 4-Y-0+

£57,010 (£21,390; £10,710; £5,340; £2,680; £1,340)

Form / RPR

F311 **1** **Al Ferof (FR)**[31] 4069 6-11-7 142 .... RWalsh 155+
(Paul Nicholls) *hld up in rr: prog on outer to trck ldrs 5th: sltly outpcd after 2 out and drvn: r.o bef last: led fnl 120yds: drvn out* **10/1**[3]

11 **2** *2* **Spirit Son (FR)**[30] 4092 5-11-7 149 .... BarryGeraghty 154+
(Nicky Henderson) *trckd ldrs: nt fluent 5th: prog to chal 2 out: drvn to ld immediately after last: hung rt flat: hdd and outpcd last 120yds* **5/1**[2]

-211 **3** *3 ¼* **Sprinter Sacre (FR)**[24] 4203 5-11-7 145 .... APMcCoy 151+
(Nicky Henderson) *trckd ldrs: led jst bef 3 out: jnd 2 out but stl gng strly: rdn whn hit last: immediately hdd and fdd* **11/1**

-112 **4** *1 ¼* **Cue Card**[94] 2887 5-11-7 159 .... JoeTizzard 150
(Colin Tizzard) *t.k.h: hld up in midfield: prog bef 3 out: jnd ldr 2 out: rdn sn after: hanging and nt qckn bef last: fdd* **7/4**[1]

2111 **5** *1 ½* **Recession Proof (FR)**[25] 4188 5-11-7 137 .... RobertThornton 147
(John Quinn) *settled in midfield on inner: struggling to hold pl after 5th: outpcd 3 out: rallied into 5th bef last: styd on but nvr a threat* **12/1**

6 *7* **Rathlin**[10] 4493 6-11-7 127 .... JasonMaguire 140
(P J Rothwell, Ire) *wl plcd: jnd ldrs 5th: led briefly bef 3 out: stl w ldrs bef 2 out: sn wknd* **33/1**

122 **7** *1 ½* **Zaidpour (FR)**[31] 4086 5-11-7 146 .... PTownend 139
(W P Mullins, Ire) *hld up in rr: prog after 5th: in tch in midfield whn blnd 3 out: lft bhd after* **11/1**

415 **8** *¾* **Spanish Treasure (GER)**[48] 3739 5-11-7 0 .... NickScholfield 138
(Andy Turnell) *mstkes: rdn in rr after 5th: wl bhd after 3 out: modest late prog* **66/1**

0-00 **9** *4* **Far Away So Close (IRE)**[31] 4086 6-11-7 130 .... DNRussell 134
(Paul Nolan, Ire) *hld up in last: sme prog after 5th: in midfield whn j.lft 3 out: sn outpcd and btn* **66/1**

111 **10** *3 ¾* **Gibb River (IRE)**[40] 3906 5-11-7 139 .... AndrewTinkler 131
(Nicky Henderson) *wl in rr: pushed along fr 5th: effrt on outer 3 out: sn no prog: wknd after 2 out* **22/1**

3111 **11** *7* **Marsh Warbler**[66] 3436 4-10-13 151 .... FearghalDavis 115
(Brian Ellison) *prom on inner: j. slowly 5th: wknd 3 out: wl bhd fr next* **22/1**

01-4 **12** *10* **Hidden Universe (IRE)**[31] 4086 5-11-7 135 .... MrRPMcNamara 113
(D K Weld, Ire) *led tl after 1st: styd prom: losing pl whn sltly hmpd 3 out: eased after next* **16/1**

13 *8* **Magen's Star (IRE)**[40] 3912 6-11-0 144 .... DJCondon 98
(T Stack, Ire) *t.k.h: led after 1st: jnd and mstke 2nd: hdd & wknd qckly bef 3 out* **14/1**

30- **14** *13* **Sheer Genius (IRE)**[16] 4385 6-11-7 118 .... AndrewJMcNamara 92
(John Joseph Murphy, Ire) *a in rr: rdn after 5th: struggling bef next: t.o* **150/1**

1124 **P** **Dunraven Storm (IRE)**[115] 2519 6-11-7 147 .... RichardJohnson —
(Philip Hobbs) *jnd ldr and hit 2nd: disp ld tl wknd rapidly bef 3 out: p.u bef 2 out: lame* **20/1**

3m 52.1s (-9.90) **Going Correction** -0.075s/f (Good) course record
WFA 4 from 5yo+ 7lb **15** Ran SP% **119.1**
Speed ratings (Par 117): **120,119,117,116,116 112,112,111,110,108 104,100,96,90,—**
toteswingers:1&2:£6.70, 1&3:£14.50, 2&3:£8.60 CSF £55.64 CT £571.90 TOTE £10.10: £2.60, £2.00, £3.00; EX 54.90 Trifecta £603.30 Pool: £13,189.85 - 16.17 winning units..
Owner J Hales **Bred** J Rauch & G Chenu **Trained** Ditcheat, Somerset
■ A change of race sponsors.

FOCUS

It was dry overnight and also in the morning before racing, but still the ground was officially described as good, good to soft in places. This looked an above-average Supreme Novices' and it was run at a decent gallop, resulting in a time nearly 2secs quicker than the Champion Hurdle. The first four held every chance and all rate exciting chase prospects, each rating 150 or above. The fifth helps set the level, rated in line with his Flat mark.

NOTEBOOK

Al Ferof(FR) ◆, given a ride of great precision, relished the climb from the last to run out a ready winner. He was no match for Cue Card when a clear second-best in the Champion Bumper last year, but is the stronger stayer of the two and tracked his old rival from the off. He appeared to get caught a little flat-footed when the leaders went for home, but Walsh timed his run to perfection and a fine leap at the last sealed it. He had come good over hurdles the last twice, winning the controversial opener on the original Totesport Trophy card at Newbury a month earlier, and was well backed in the lead up to the race. This was still a vast improvement, however, and it was really his stamina that won him the day. He should make up into something special when sent chasing next season and, while a longer trip ought to prove his optimum in that sphere, he will very likely be trained for the Arkle Trophy. (tchd 9-1)

Spirit Son(FR), slightly on his toes beforehand, rallied to make a bold bid and led after the last. He hung right to the stands' rail on the run-in, though, and looked to be feeling the quicker ground. He couldn't cope with the winner when it mattered, but ran a blinder in defeat and is a classy prospect for novice chasing. A return to easier ground should suit ideally. He may go to Aintree. (op 11-2 tchd 6-1)

Sprinter Sacre(FR) ◆ was going best of all turning in, but tired up the hill and was held prior to hitting the last. He bravely held on to third and this handsome, strong-travelling performer is another that is really something to look forward to for chasing. Indeed he could well turn out the best of these over fences next season. (tchd 10-1)

Cue Card had the best form on offer after three previous spins over hurdles, including when third on his previous outing behind Menorah when testing his credentials for the Champion Hurdle in the Grade 2 International Hurdle in December. He was subject of bullish reports coming into the race, but he had been absent since and only Montelado back in 1993 has managed the Champion Bumper/Supreme double. He was produced early enough, however, considering the race was run at a strong gallop and in hindsight may have been better off being held on to for longer. Once again he took time to settle, though, and he may well have paid for that up the home straight. It was still a commendable effort and, with time firmly on his side, may prove himself to be better than this in due course. A step up in trip could also now suit. He may go to Aintree. (op 9-4 tchd 5-2 in places)

Recession Proof(FR) was following the same path as last year's narrow runner-up Get Me Out Of Here, who also won the Totesport Trophy on his previous outing. That race wasn't as strong as in previous years due to it being rearranged and worth only half the original prize money, though, and Robert Thornton was also a late substitute aboard him due to the injury to his regular pilot the previous day. He ran really well, but lacked the tactical pace to stay prominent when it got serious and he too probably found the ground lively enough. He is a solid benchmark for the form. (op 10-1)

Rathlin, a chaser in the making, only got off the mark over hurdles ten days earlier when beating an exposed sort on bad ground at Gowran. His owner's retained rider Davy Russell also preferred Far Away So Close and he looked to have an awful lot on his plate. He has been waiting for some better ground, however, and he ran a bold race under a positive ride. He is another who may have fared even better under slightly more patient tactics and the best of him is likely still to be seen. (tchd 40-1 and 50-1 in a place)

Zaidpour(FR) appeared to have the world at his feet when winning the Grade 1 Royal Bond last year. He had been beaten into second at the top level since, though, and the vibes were negative for him beforehand with connections feeling he wanted easier ground. He drifted back on the far side and just as he was trying to get back into the race he whacked the third-last. He was keeping on up the home straight and it may well be that he wants to get back on a right-handed track and softer ground. However, he does now have something to prove. (op 12-1)

Spanish Treasure(GER) was facing a tough task in such company and, after making errors, got badly outpaced. He was noted staying on late in the day and should relish a stiffer test over fences in due course.

Far Away So Close(IRE) was a maiden when finishing ninth to Menorah last season and he ran a similar race this time around, so is another that helps to set the level. (tchd 150-1 in a place)

Gibb River(IRE) found things happening all too quickly on this big step up in class. He has the scope to jump a fence and looks more than ready for a longer trip. (op 20-1)

Marsh Warbler made it 3-4 as a hurdler when winning the Grade 1 Finale Juvenile Hurdle in January, a race that very much went his way. He skipped the Triumph for this in order to get easier ground, but juveniles have a poor record in this race and the decision to run backfired. (op 20-1 tchd 16-1 in places)

Hidden Universe(IRE) is slightly on the leg. (tchd 14-1)

Dunraven Storm(IRE) Official explanation: jockey said gelding lost its action; vet said gelding lost a shoe and was lame right-hind

4789 IRISH INDEPENDENT ARKLE CHALLENGE TROPHY CHASE GRADE 1 (13 fncs) 2m

2:05 (2:05) (Class 1) 5-Y-0+

£74,113 (£27,807; £13,923; £6,942; £3,484; £1,742)

Form / RPR

2221 **1** **Captain Chris (IRE)**[17] 4351 7-11-7 153 .... (t) RichardJohnson 166+
(Philip Hobbs) *trckd ldrs: pushed along and styd on wl fr 3 out: wnt 2nd bef 2 out: rdn to chal last: led sn after: styd on strly* **6/1**

-111 **2** *2 ¾* **Finian's Rainbow (IRE)**[31] 4078 8-11-7 156 .... BarryGeraghty 163+
(Nicky Henderson) *disp 2nd: slt ld 7th: rdn 2 out: jnd and hit last: hdd sn after: kpt on but no imp on wnr* **7/2**[2]

1211 **3** *6* **Realt Dubh (IRE)**[51] 3705 7-11-7 147 .... PCarberry 157
(Noel Meade, Ire) *a wl in tch: hdwy to chse ldrs fr 3 out: styd on u.p to chse ldng duo fr 2 out but no imp run-in* **17/2**

R121 **4** *¾* **Medermit (FR)**[38] 3946 7-11-7 155 .... RobertThornton 157
(Alan King) *in rr: rdn after 4 out and styd on to chse ldrs after 3 out but nvr gng pce to get into contention: wl hld whn hit last* **11/4**[1]

-211 **5** *19* **Ghizao (GER)**[76] 3193 7-11-7 157 .... TimmyMurphy 140+
(Paul Nicholls) *chsd ldrs: blnd 4 out: rallied to go 2nd after 3 out but nvr rchd ldr: wknd next: no ch whn nt fluent last* **4/1**[3]

1F12 **6** *4 ½* **Giorgio Quercus (FR)**[18] 4326 6-11-7 148 .... PaddyBrennan 132
(Nicky Henderson) *hit 2nd and 4th: in rr: hit 8th: blnd 3 out: nvr in contention* **33/1**

0211 **7** *½* **Dan Breen (IRE)**[18] 4326 6-11-7 148 .... (b[1]) TomScudamore 131
(David Pipe) *disp 2nd tl chsd ldr 8th: hit 9th: wknd after 3 out* **20/1**

1314 **8** *20* **Rock Noir (FR)**[38] 3946 6-11-7 146 .... (t) APMcCoy 121+
(Jonjo O'Neill) *j. poorly in rr: lost tch fr 8th* **14/1**

3112 **9** *hd* **Stagecoach Pearl**[31] 4078 7-11-7 147 .... ShaneByrne 111
(Sue Smith) *led to 7th: wknd qckly appr 4 out* **40/1**

2111 **P** **West With The Wind**[200] 1390 6-11-7 148 .... PaulMoloney —
(Evan Williams) *in rr: hit 3rd: 5th and 6th: sn lost tch: t.o whn p.u bef 3 out* **33/1**

3m 51.68s (-6.32) **Going Correction** +0.05s/f (Yiel) **10** Ran SP% **113.5**
Speed ratings: **117,115,112,112,102 100,100,90,90,—**
toteswingers:1&2:£3.50, 1&3:£7.80, 2&3:£6.70 CSF £26.27 CT £177.29 TOTE £7.00: £2.20, £2.00, £2.60; EX 28.90 Trifecta £149.00 Pool: £11,868.82 - 58.90 winning units..
Owner Mrs Diana L Whateley **Bred** Mrs Noreen Walsh **Trained** Withycombe, Somerset
■ Stewards' Enquiry : Robert Thornton one-day ban: used whip with excessive frequency (Mar 29)

FOCUS

This didn't appear to be one of the stronger recent runnings of the Arkle, on paper at least, as away from the front four in the market there was virtually no strength-in-depth. It was run at a solid gallop. Captain Chris looks well up to standard and will rate higher over further, while Finian's Rainbow produced a personal best and the next pair ran up to their best.

NOTEBOOK

Captain Chris(IRE) got a fine ride and ran out a taking winner. He completed his preparation for the Festival with an easy enough victory in the Grade 2 Pendil at Kempton, again over further, and the decent ground here really suited the 7-y-o son of King's Theatre, indeed he flourished on a similarly sound surface last spring. More so than ever these days, the Arkle seems to be going to a horse thought to need further and perhaps the most impressive aspect of this win was his jumping, which many had worried about beforehand as he'd shown a tendency to jump right. Kept wide early, once Johnson realised the horse had his eye in he started firing him at his fences and he came up every time, being switched inside at the top of the hill, and the result looked inevitable once he more or less drew alongside the runner-up. Punchestown may be next and, assuming all goes well there, he's likely to head into summer quarters as a leading candidate for the King George, a race which promises to suit him ideally. (op 15-2 tchd 8-1 in places)

Finian's Rainbow(IRE) had beaten a combined total of ten runners in going 3-3 in minor events at Newbury (twice) and Warwick. Fifth in last season's Neptune, he had proved hard to settle in his races this season and had not impressed with his jumping in the Kingmaker last time. However, as can often be the case, his fencing was much-improved for encountering a truly run race for the first time, and he took over tanking at the seventh. Geraghty seemed confident he had plenty left running downhill, looking over his right shoulder having pinged three out, but he had a real fight on his hands from the first in the straight and could find no extra after the last. There were many positives to take from this with next season in mind, but perhaps the key negative is that he's already eight. Aintree is a possibility. (op 9-2)

Realt Dubh(IRE), twice a Grade 1 winner from Jewson-bound Noble Prince this season, had done his winning with plenty of cut in the ground but had no trouble with these faster conditions and, having hit a brief flat spot, came back on the bridle rounding for home. He was unable to race on with the front pair, though, just being found wanting for a bit of pace, and he seems likely to prove best over further next season. His next target is likely to be the Powers Gold Cup at Fairyhouse over Easter. (op 8-1 tchd 10-1 in a place)

Medermit(FR), slightly on his toes beforehand, was the best of these over hurdles and boasted the most solid credentials, having won the Grade 1 Scilly Isles, from Captain Chris, and being proven in a championship event at the Festival, having narrowly gone down to Go Native in the 2009 Supreme. He hadn't got off to the best of starts over fences, but looked to be getting better all the time and trainer Alan King had made no secret he felt he held outstanding claims. The signs were there early in the race, though, as his jumping lacked zest and Thornton didn't look entirely happy. He tried his best to close and briefly reached a position from which he could have challenged, but just lacked the legs of these, and in hindsight he'd probably have been happier on softer going. Indeed, after the race his trainer admitted he wished he'd have run him in the Jewson. (op 3-1)

Ghizao(GER) had left his hurdles form behind with impressive wins here, on his second start, and at Newbury, both times beating today's winner, to whom he gave 10lb on the latter occasion. The ground had probably dried a bit too much for him, but he travelled powerfully until a notable blunder four out knocked him off his stride. It was to his credit he managed to recover and get back into contention, but having turned in he started to empty and ended up well held. He clearly has a big engine and should prove himself to be better than this next season. In the meantime he could run at Aintree. (op 7-2)

Giorgio Quercus(FR), awarded the race having narrowly been denied by Dan Breen at Sandown last month, probably ran up to the best of his capabilities. (op 25-1)

Dan Breen(IRE), on his toes beforehand, was up there early in the first-time blinkers and did too much. (op 16-1)

Rock Noir(FR), fourth in the Scilly Isles, jumped poorly early on and was found out in a truly run race on decent going. (op 12-1)

Stagecoach Pearl, readily brushed aside by the runner-up in the Kingmaker, had his moment of glory out in front before stopping quickly.

West With The Wind had mopped up some modest novice chases at Ffos Las last summer and found this all too much returning from 200 days off. (op 28-1)

4790 STEWART FAMILY SPINAL RESEARCH H'CAP CHASE GRADE 3 (19 fncs) 3m 110y

2:40 (2:40) (Class 1) 5-Y-0+

£42,757 (£16,042; £8,032; £4,005; £2,010; £1,005)

Form RPR

2-52 **1** **Bensalem (IRE)**[24] 4207 8-11-2 **143**................................ RobertThornton 156+
(Alan King) *patiently rdn and wl off the pce: stdy prog to join ldrs 13th: wnt 2nd and mstke 3 out: led narrowly 2 out: nt fluent last and sn jnd: gained upper hand last 75yds* **5/1**[2]

-122 **2** ½ **Carole's Legacy**[52] 3674 7-11-5 **146**................................ BarryGeraghty 158+
(Nicky Henderson) *wl plcd: clr in ldng quintet fr 4 out: rdn bef next: where disputing 2nd: upsides 2 out: persistent chal after last: jst outpcd last 75yds* **9/1**

4130 **3** 11 **Reve De Sivola (FR)**[38] 3946 6-10-13 **140**........................(p) DarylJacob 145+
(Nick Williams) *trckd ldrs: hmpd 3rd: wnt 2nd and blnd 12th: mstke 4 out: mstke 3 out and dropped to 4th: sltly hmpd 2 out: fdd* **9/1**

-103 **4** 17 **Fair Along (GER)**[25] 4186 9-11-7 **148**.................................(p) RhysFlint 130
(Philip Hobbs) *wl in rr and nvr appeared to be gng wl: t.o fr 15th: styd on fr 3 out: no ch* **25/1**

-11P **5** 3½ **King Fontaine (IRE)**[24] 4208 8-10-13 **140**............................ GrahamLee 118
(Malcolm Jefferson) *mstkes in midfield: rdn bef 11th: lost tch fr 13th: poor 9th after 4 out: kpt on* **16/1**

430U **6** 4½ **Exmoor Ranger (IRE)**[24] 4200 9-11-3 **144**....................... DenisO'Regan 118
(Victor Dartnall) *worst away in ragged s: wl bhd in last pair: hmpd 5th: sme prog fr 11th: rchd remote 6th after 4 out: no imp after* **25/1**

P3P0 **7** 2½ **No Panic (IRE)**[12] 4440 8-10-0 **127**.............................(p) AidanColeman 98
(Peter Bowen) *prom: clr in ldng quintet 4 out: sn wknd u.p* **80/1**

6426 **8** 7 **The Sawyer (BEL)**[10] 4486 11-10-4 **138**..................... NathanSweeney(7) 102
(Bob Buckler) *led: hdd and blnd 3rd: lost 2nd and blnd 9th: steadily lost tch fr 12th: poor 8th after 4 out* **40/1**

-611 **9** 4 **Blazing Bailey**[38] 3940 9-11-12 **153**............................ WayneHutchinson 113
(Alan King) *a wl in rr: struggling fr 1/2-way: wl t.o fr 14th: scooted up run-in* **16/1**

F614 **10** 19 **Carrickmines (IRE)**[24] 4200 9-10-1 **128**...........................(b) JamieMoore 69
(Dr Richard Newland) *sn wl bhd in last pair: hmpd 5th: j.rt fr 1/2-way: wl t.o after* **40/1**

6P51 **11** 2¼ **Wolf Moon (IRE)**[15] 4394 8-10-0 **122** 5ex oh1................ TomScudamore 66
(Martin Keighley) *shoddy rnd of jumping and sn lost decent pl: toiling in rr fr 1/2-way: t.o fr 15th* **10/1**

4322 **12** 7 **The Rainbow Hunter**[25] 4193 7-9-12 **132**.......................... EdCookson(7) 64
(Andy Turnell) *nt a fluent: in tch in midfield: clinging on to ldng gp 13th: sn lft bhd: poor 7th after 4 out* **20/1**

-053 **F** **Chief Dan George (IRE)**[10] 4474 11-11-7 **148**................(p) PaddyAspell —
(James Moffatt) *bustled along after 2nd: in tch in midfield whn fell 5th* **33/1**

P-01 **P** **Rare Bob (IRE)**[65] 3473 9-11-10 **151**......................................(b) PWFlood —
(D T Hughes, Ire) *led 3rd and maintained furious pce: hdd 11th: eased and p.u bef next* **20/1**

-0P6 **U** **Razor Royale (IRE)**[17] 4352 9-10-8 **138**.............. SamTwiston-Davies(3) —
(Nigel Twiston-Davies) *chsd ldrs: losing pl on inner whn jinked out and uns rdr bef 12th* **25/1**

2-03 **F** **Sunnyhillboy (IRE)**[94] 2886 8-10-12 **139**.................................. APMcCoy —
(Jonjo O'Neill) *hld up in rr: fell heavily 7th* **9/2**[1]

33 **P** **Slippers Percy (IRE)**[30] 4109 9-10-6 **136**.................... DGHogan(3) —
(Denis Gerard Hogan, Ire) *nvr on terms w ldrs: wl in rr whn blnd bdly 12th: t.o after slow jump 14th: p.u bef 3 out* **50/1**

1-62 **F** **Great Endeavour (IRE)**[94] 2886 7-11-7 **148**....................... TimmyMurphy 154+
(David Pipe) *one of the slowest away: rapid prog to join ldrs 5th: wnt 2nd 9th: led 11th: hit next: clr 15th: rdn after 3 out: narrowly hdd and fell 2 out* **13/2**[3]

3102 **U** **Adams Island (IRE)**[17] 4351 7-10-1 **133**...............(p) AodhaganConlon(5) —
(Rebecca Curtis) *cl 3rd whn blnd and rdr knocked out of sddle 3rd* **16/1**

6m 10.0s (-8.30) **Going Correction** +0.05s/f (Yiel) **19** Ran SP% **127.0**

Speed ratings: **115,114,111,105,104 103,102,100,99,92 92,89,**—,—,—,—,—,—,—

toteswingers:1&2:£8.30, 1&3:£10.10, 2&3:£9.60 CSF £45.41 CT £411.04 TOTE £6.50: £2.30, £1.90, £2.40, £4.60; EX 56.10 Trifecta £348.50 Pool: £13,749.11 - 29.18 winning units..

Owner Alan Marsh & John D Duggan **Bred** Peter O'Reilly **Trained** Barbury Castle, Wilts

■ New sponsors for this race, run in recent years as the William Hill Trophy.

■ Stewards' Enquiry : Barry Geraghty one-day ban: careless riding (Mar 29)

FOCUS

Traditionally a competitive handicap chase and it proved a thorough examination this year, with the pace really heating up a long way from home and many of the runners failing through inadequate jumping. The start was an unsatisfactory one, with a few of the runners, including Great Endeavour, appearing not to be ready. Benslaem was well in and is rated to his mark, while Carole's Legacy continues on the upgrade.

NOTEBOOK

Bensalem(IRE), who had travelled the strongest, toughed it out in an enthralling finish to make up for the last year, when he was going like the winner until getting the 'old' second-last all wrong and coming down. He had raced exclusively over hurdles since that spill, finishing an excellent second to Quevega at Punchestown and twice running creditably this season, including when bogged down on heavy ground behind a thorough stayer at Haydock last month. Off the same mark as last year for this return to fences, he avoided the fallers that could so easily have interfered with him and it became clear from a long way out that he was hacking. Nudged into the straight, he was left with a narrow lead when Great Endeavour departed two out and, despite having got in close at the last, he battled hard on the run-in and just edged out the gallant mare. The form looks solid, with 11l back to smart novice hurdler Reve De Sivola, and he probably deserves a step up in grade now, with the Grade 1 Punchestown Gold Cup looking a possible target. (op 13-2)

Carole's Legacy, runner-up to Quevega in the mares' race last year, again filled that position off 5lb lower in a graded handicap over shorter here in January and very nearly pulled it off on this step back up in trip, narrowly failing despite a typically spirited effort. She'll be a valuable broodmare, but has more wins in her yet, assuming connections decide to stick at it with her. (op 12-1)

Reve De Sivola(FR) was runner-up in last year's Neptune here and subsequently won a Grade 1 at Punchestown. He hasn't reached the same heights over fences, but won at the course in December and travelled better than expected in the first-time cheekpieces on this handicap debut. He made his share of mistakes, but did well to recover from being hampered by a faller and was still close enough turning in, but again got impeded two out and could soon find no extra. He's entitled to improve as he gains further experience. (tchd 10-1 in places)

Fair Along(GER) came from an absolute mile back to snatch a place. He was never involved, but displayed his willingness once again. (tchd 22-1)

King Fontaine(IRE) left his Haydock running in heavy ground behind, making numerous errors but boxing on admirably having been under pressure from quite an early stage. (op 25-1)

Exmoor Ranger(IRE) was the worst affected of those caught unawares at the start and also met some trouble in running. He made some late headway, but remains 9lb above his last winning mark.

No Panic(IRE) had lost his form and had a bit to prove in such a competitive field, but he had slipped back to his last successful mark and actually ran well for a long way. Official explanation: vet said gelding returned with a cut to its right-fore (op 66-1)

Blazing Bailey had won two lesser contests and found this all a bit competitive. He was going on best at the finish.

Wolf Moon(IRE), 6lb out of the handicap, was saddled with a 5lb penalty for his recent Catterick success and unsurprisingly found this all too much. (op 11-1)

Chief Dan George(IRE), last year's winner, was slightly on his toes beforehand and came down early. (op 5-1 tchd 11-2 in places)

Rare Bob(IRE) Official explanation: jockey said gelding had a breathing problem (op 5-1 tchd 11-2 in places)

Sunnyhillboy(IRE) promised to improve for the longer distance and would surely have been involved, considering how the race panned out, had he not taken a heavy tumble at the seventh. (op 5-1 tchd 11-2 in places)

Great Endeavour(IRE), last year's Plate winner, had finished runner-up to Poquelin in the December Gold Cup off 6lb lower and promised to be suited by the longer trip. He wasn't helped by getting left at the start, but was rushed up to race prominently and kicked on a long way out. He started to look vulnerable towards the bottom of the hill, though, and was in the process of being headed when taking a heavy fall two out. It's to be hoped this doesn't leave its mark. (op 5-1 tchd 11-2 in places)

4791 STAN JAMES CHAMPION HURDLE CHALLENGE TROPHY GRADE 1 (8 hdls) 2m 110y

3:20 (3:20) (Class 1) 4-Y-0+

£210,937 (£79,143; £39,627; £19,758; £9,916; £4,958)

Form RPR

-111 **1** **Hurricane Fly (IRE)**[51] 3707 7-11-10 167.. RWalsh 170+
(W P Mullins, Ire) *hld up in tch: stdy hdwy to trck ldrs 2 out and sn travelling wl: drvn to take slt ld last: rdn and edgd rt run-in: hld on all out* **11/4**[1]

1-11 **2** 1¼ **Peddlers Cross (IRE)**[26] 4169 6-11-10 162........................ JasonMaguire 169
(Donald McCain) *trckd ldrs: led 4th: narrowly hdd 2 out: drvn to ld sn after: narrowly hdd last but upsides: carried rt run-in and kpt on gamely u.p: nt pce of wnr fnl 50yds* **9/2**[3]

4-11 **3** 5 **Oscar Whisky (IRE)**[38] 3939 6-11-10 165....................... BarryGeraghty 164
(Nicky Henderson) *hit 2nd: chsd ldrs: nt fluent 3rd: chsd ldr 3 out: led next: hdd sn after: kpt on gamely for 3rd but no ch w ldng duo* **7/1**

3-43 **4** 2 **Thousand Stars (FR)**[51] 3707 7-11-10 160............................ PTownend 163
(W P Mullins, Ire) *in rr: hdwy and nt fluent 3 out: styng on whn bmpd on outer bnd after 2 out: styd on to take 4th run-in but a hld by ldng trio* **33/1**

2-11 **5** 1¼ **Menorah (IRE)**[94] 2887 6-11-10 164............................. RichardJohnson 163
(Philip Hobbs) *chsd ldrs: hit 4 out: rdn to stay rt there 2 out: one pce whn hit last: wknd run-in* **3/1**[2]

1144 **6** 2 **Clerk's Choice (IRE)**[94] 2887 5-11-10 155............................ TomMolloy 160
(Michael Banks) *in rr: hdwy fr 3 out and in tch next: nvr rchd ldng trio: no imp on ldrs whn hit last: wknd run-in* **50/1**

2125 **7** 5 **Overturn (IRE)**[24] 4222 7-11-10 162.. GrahamLee 154
(Donald McCain) *led to 4th: styd pressing ldrs: wkng on inner whn hmpd bnd after 2 out* **40/1**

36-1 **8** ¾ **Dunguib (IRE)**[24] 4229 8-11-10 165................................... BTO'Connell 155
(Philip Fenton, Ire) *in tch: rdn and bmpd 3 out: wknd next* **10/1**

21-4 **9** ½ **Khyber Kim**[59] 3559 9-11-10 164.. PaddyBrennan 153
(Nigel Twiston-Davies) *in rr: rdn and hdwy 3 out: nvr rchd ldrs: wknd after 2 out* **12/1**

6U02 **10** 10 **Bygones Of Brid (IRE)**[26] 4169 8-11-10 138..................... TimmyMurphy 145
(Karen McLintock) *chsd ldr to 3rd: wkng whn hmpd 3 out* **200/1**

5211 **11** ½ **Mille Chief (FR)**[24] 4222 5-11-10 158.............................. RobertThornton 142
(Alan King) *rdn 3 out: a towards rr* **16/1**

3m 53.71s (-8.29) **Going Correction** -0.075s/f (Good) course record **11** Ran SP% **112.9**

Speed ratings (Par 117): **116,115,113,112,111 110,108,107,107,102 102**

toteswingers:1&2:£2.80, 1&3:£4.50, 2&3:£5.10 CSF £14.69 CT £75.92 TOTE £3.40: £1.50, £1.80, £2.50; EX 16.10 Trifecta £66.50 Pool: £29,712.67 - 330.29 winning units..

Owner George Creighton & Mrs Rose Boyd **Bred** Agricola Del Parco **Trained** Muine Beag, Co Carlow

■ New sponsors for this great race, replacing Smurfit Kappa.

■ Stewards' Enquiry : Jason Maguire caution: used whip with excessive frequency.

FOCUS

Last year's champion Binocular was withdrawn after a medication failed to clear his system in time, but while his absence was hugely disappointing for the race, this was still a hot Champion Hurdle. They didn't got all that quick early, which resulted in a winning time nearly 2secs slower than the Supreme Novices', but the right two horses still came clear late on. Hurricane Fly produced a good effort in a steadily run race and can rate higher. Peddlers Cross stepped up with the next pair rated to their marks and Menorah 3lb off his best.

NOTEBOOK

Hurricane Fly(IRE) emerged on top and confirmed himself to be the best 2m hurdler around, registering an eighth Grade 1 success. He attracted heavy support, but has been known to get buzzed up before a race and, equipped with first-time earplugs to deal with the unique atmosphere, was noticeably sweating at the start. He also ran with the choke out in mid-field, but jumped superbly and as the race began to warm up from three out it was clear he was going best of all. He the hit front full of running and winged the last, but probably got there plenty soon enough as he idled and allowed the rallying Peddlers Cross a big chance. He kept responding, however, and was nicely on top at the finish. Once again this was another superb ride from Ruby Walsh, who was taking over the reins from Paul Townend (who had done nothing wrong this term) and is now 4-4 on him. This rids any previous doubts about his worth in beating the same horses all the time in Ireland, and it must be remembered that the horse so often second to him at home, Solwhit, is himself a six-time Grade 1 winner. He became the first horse since Alderbrook in 1995 to win this race without previously having run at the track, and became the first winner at the track at the 45th attempt for his sire Montjeu. All ground comes alike to him and he has that blend of speed and stamina, so there is no real negative for him. It is also the first season that he has remained sound all the way through. The 4/1 offered about next year's renewal looks too big. (op 3-1 tchd 7-2 in places)

Peddlers Cross(IRE), the pick of the paddock, was following a well-trodden path having won last year's Neptune Investment Novices' Hurdle and it was unbeaten coming here. He tracked his front-running stablemate and was asked for his effort nearing three out. However, he is more of a grinder than a speed horse and would have ideally enjoyed more of a test. That made him a sitting duck for the winner, but his attitude once headed was brave and he pushed him all the way to the finish. There is little doubt the better horse won, though, although it was another clear personal-best from this former point winner in defeat. He finished a clear second-best and deserves be rated the best domestic hurdler in the division. A stiffer test is probably ideal and therefore another trip to Aintree next month is likely to be on his agenda. He had a hard race, but if he comes out out of this sufficiently well he can resume winning ways in the Aintree Hurdle, remembering he won at both this meeting and Aintree last year. As for next season, a decision on whether he goes chasing will be made later on. (tchd 5-1 in places)

Oscar Whisky(IRE) was left his stable's main hope after the withdrawal of Binocular. He was still a sound contender, having only once tasted defeat in last year's Supreme Novices' behind Menorah and after winning here on his comeback in January over 2m4f. He ran the race of his life in third, jumping well bar the third flight, and is another that is probably at his very best over a stiffer test. With that in mind a trip to the Grand National meeting for the Aintree Hurdle now looks likely and he wouldn't be without hope of reversing form with Peddlers Cross there. (op 8-1)

Thousand Stars(FR), who landed last year's County Hurdle, also ran a big race in defeat. He pulled through the early parts and stayed on bravely late in the day, considering he didn't enjoy the best of runs from two out. He has now been beaten fives times by his winning stablemate and clearly isn't in the same league, but fully deserves to bag a graded event before the season ends. (op 22-1)

Menorah(IRE) has impressed this season and made it 3-3 at the track when winning his two previous outings. However, he was a short price on form alone (no winners have emerged from his races yet this term) and no horse since Granville Again in 1993 had won this without running since the turn of the year. Add to that the horrid record of Supreme Novices' winners following up in the big one, and he really had plenty to overcome. He ran his race without ever threatening in the home straight and this is probably as good as he is. He could run at Punchestown in May. Connections may well switch him to chasing next season and he would have to be seriously considered in the Arkle if taking to fences. (op 4-1)

Clerk's Choice(IRE)'s proximity could be used to hold the form down. However, he loves this track and, on much more suitable ground, got closer to Menorah than was the case on his previous outing here in December. (op 40-1 tchd 100-1 in a place)

Overturn(IRE) is a smart horse in his own right and has been remarkably progressive since initially winning over hurdles last year. He was always up against it, but this probably wasn't his track and he could have more to offer over a longer trip in this sphere.

Dunguib(IRE) posted a personal best when winning on his belated return at Gowran last month. He certainly didn't go unbacked, but got himself very warm beforehand and had nothing left in the tank when it mattered. Chasing will surely be on his agenda next season. (op 9-1 tchd 8-1)

Khyber Kim came back wrong after running a tame race on his comeback in the Christmas Hurdle in January. Given his usual hold-up ride, he offered very little when asked for an effort and has to now prove he is not in decline, although it is a little soon to be fully writing him off. (tchd 11-1 and 14-1 in a place)

Bygones Of Brid(IRE), well beaten by Peddlers Cross at Kelso last month, had a near-impossible task and was retreating prior to being hampered. (op 150-1)

Mille Chief(FR) confirmed his credentials for this when winning the Kingwell Hurdle at Wincanton 24 days earlier and was expected to really enjoy this much sounder surface. He endured a hard race that day, however, and may well have still been feeling the effects, as he was very disappointing. (op 14-1)

4792 GLENFARCLAS H'CAP CHASE (A CROSS COUNTRY CHASE) (32 fncs) — 3m 7f

4:00 (4:00) (Class 2) 5-Y-O+

£25,048 (£7,400; £3,700; £1,852; £924; £464)

Form				RPR
04-3	**1**		**Sizing Australia (IRE)**[30] 4110 9-10-9 **140** ..... AELynch (Henry De Bromhead, Ire) *prom: mostly trckd ldr fr 7th tl led 22nd: mstke 25th: jnd 2 out: styd on gamely to assert after last* **13/2**[3]	144+
15-2	**2**	*1 1/4*	**Garde Champetre (FR)**[34] 4013 12-11-12 **157** ..... (t) MissNCarberry (E Bolger, Ire) *patiently rdn in 5th: bmpd by rival and stmbld 5th: prog to join ldrs 26th: rdn and styd on to take 2nd flat: no imp on wnr nr fin* **5/1**[2]	160
40-0	**3**	*1*	**A New Story (IRE)**[9] 4515 13-10-5 **141** ..... APHeskin(5) (Michael Hourigan, Ire) *sweating: trckd ldrs: effrt fr 3 out: swtchd lft bef last: styd on to take 3rd last stride* **12/1**	142
F-F0	**4**	*shd*	**Maljimar (IRE)**[73] 3290 11-10-3 **134** ..... DarylJacob (Nick Williams) *hld up in last pair: stdy prog fr 21st: wnt 3rd 26th: jnd wnr gng wl 2 out: rdn and nt qckn bef last: wknd nr fin* **9/2**[1]	136
	5	*1 1/2*	**Quezac De La Roque (FR)**[21] 7-10-6 **137** ..... (t) DavidCottin (F-M Cottin, France) *trckd ldrs: cl up whn mstke 26th: one of five w ch after 2 out: no ex bef last* **20/1**	137
1P-0	**6**	*11*	**Poker De Sivola (FR)**[77] 3171 8-10-7 **138** ..... MsKWalsh (Ferdy Murphy) *hld up in detached last: effrt whn mstke 27th: trying to make prog whn blnd 3 out: tk modest 6th after 2 out: no imp* **8/1**	129+
43-1	**7**	*4 1/2*	**Another Jewel (IRE)**[24] 4228 9-10-6 **137** ow2 ..... JLCullen (Denis Paul Murphy, Ire) *in tch towards rr tl wknd fr 4 out* **12/1**	120
P-PP	**8**	*2 1/4*	**Dream Alliance**[66] 3437 10-10-10 **141** ..... (b) TomO'Brien (Philip Hobbs) *awkward jump 2nd and mstke 3rd: lost pl and pushed along: styd in tch but nt really handling the test: wknd 4 out* **40/1**	123
-41F	**9**	*7*	**Gullible Gordon (IRE)**[114] 2543 8-10-11 **142** ..... HarrySkelton (Paul Nicholls) *in tch in midfield: outpcd fr 4 out: wl btn after next* **12/1**	117
1P1/	**10**	*15*	**Lord Nellerie (FR)**[34] 4013 12-9-11 **135** ..... MissEvannaMcCutcheon(7) (David Peter Nagle, Ire) *mde most to 22nd: wknd qckly 4 out* **25/1**	95
2-04	**11**	*6*	**Freneys Well**[123] 2346 11-10-9 **140** ..... PCarberry (E Bolger, Ire) *trckd ldr to 7th: styd prom tl wknd 4 out* **16/1**	94
021-	**P**		**L'Ami (FR)**[44] 3848 12-11-11 **156** ..... MrJTMcNamara (E Bolger, Ire) *wl in tch tl p.u suddenly bef 22nd: lame* **9/1**	—
0-53	**R**		**One Cool Cookie (IRE)**[34] 4013 10-10-8 **139** ..... (tp) DNRussell (C F Swan, Ire) *in tch in rr tl rn out 16th (2nd cheese wedge)* **16/1**	—
-P10	**P**		**Oscar Bay (IRE)**[202] 1373 9-10-5 **136** ..... HaddenFrost (James Frost) *struggling in rr fr 1/2-way: t.o whn p.u bef 4 out* **28/1**	—
4/	**P**		**Quolibet (FR)**[107] 2704 7-10-10 **144** ..... (p) MrAJBerry(3) (Jonjo O'Neill) *prom tl wknd qckly 20th: p.u bef next* **50/1**	—

8m 6.22s (-31.78) **Going Correction** -0.75s/f (Firm) course record **15** Ran SP% **120.6**

Speed ratings: **111,110,110,110,110 107,106,105,103,99 98,—,—,—,—**

toteswingers:1&2:£6.70, 1&3:£17.90, 2&3:£13.80 CSF £37.47 CT £390.24 TOTE £7.70: £2.60, £2.50, £3.70; EX 41.70 Trifecta £234.80 Pool: £9,584.56 - 30.20 winning units..

Owner Ann & Alan Potts Partnership **Bred** James P Linnane Mrcvs **Trained** Knockeen, Co Waterford

■ Stewards' Enquiry : J L Cullen three-day ban: weighed-in 2lb heavy (Mar 29-31)

FOCUS

Officials had not got as much watering done on the cross country course as was hoped this year and it was a quick surface, advertised by three horses pulling up sharply. They went a sound enough gallop and there was a cracking finish with the first five pretty much upsides approaching the last fence. A typical renewal, with the winner and third pretty much rated to their C&D marks. The runner-up was 5lb off his best.

NOTEBOOK

Sizing Australia(IRE), although only 11th in this last year, had excuses that day and had been placed on his three other outings over C&D. He ran out a very deserving winner, reversing December form with old rival Garde Champetre on a stone better terms, and this removes any doubts about his heart for a battle as he was always up there. His versatility regards ground is a very useful asset and, while he will find it tougher off a higher mark if returning next season, he certainly has time still on his side being a 9-y-o (youngest winner since the race's inception in 2005). (op 15-2 tchd 8-1 in places)

Garde Champetre(FR), who was badly hampered when bidding for a hat-trick in this race last season, beat the winner on his last visit here in December and resumed winning ways at Punchestown last month. He raced off 4lb lower than last year, but did face a tough task trying to confirm form with Sizing Australia being a stone worse off. Regular pilot Nina Carberry gave him plenty to do and he was outpaced nearing the fourth-last, but he showed his class by throwing down a strong challenge in the home straight. The quicker ground really did for him here and he's clearly not done with yet. (op 11-2)

A New Story(IRE), now a 13-y-o, ran a very pleasing race over hurdles in his prep for this just nine days earlier. He won this last year and turned in another blinder to grab third on the line considering he too would have found the ground quicker than he cares for. He has now made the frame in this for the last four seasons and rates a rock-solid benchmark. (op 10-1)

Maljimar(IRE), returning from a 73-day break, had been targeted at this event and made plenty of appeal from a handicapping point of view. Very well backed, he cruised up looking all over the winner turning for home. However, he found just the same pace when asked for maximum effort and lost third near the finish. He too gives the form a good look. Official explanation: vet said gelding returned with a cut to its left-fore (op 5-1)

Quezac De La Roque(FR) won a cross-country event over 3m3f in France in November. He moved sweetly through the race and held every chance until emptying from the last fence. The ground was probably the reason for that and he is one to be interested in if coming back for one of these next winter. (tchd 22-1 in a place)

Poker De Sivola(FR), well backed, was having just his third outing since winning the 4m National Hunt Chase at last year's festival. It wasn't surprising to see him outpaced in rear early on, but he was making up ground nicely prior to a mistake three from home. He was done with thereafter, but this shows there is still something left in the tank. (op 10-1)

Another Jewel(IRE) is a specialist in this sphere, but he wants softer ground and didn't appear to let himself down when asked for an effort. (tchd 14-1)

L'Ami(FR) was sharply pulled up and surely found this ground too lively. Official explanation: vet said gelding was lame (tchd 10-1)

Oscar Bay(IRE) Official explanation: jockey said gelding never travelled (tchd 10-1)

4793 DAVID NICHOLSON MARES' HURDLE GRADE 2 (9 hdls) — 2m 4f

4:40 (4:40) (Class 1) 4-Y-O+

£39,431 (£14,854; £7,434; £3,717; £1,862; £931)

Form				RPR
311-	**1**		**Quevega (FR)**[327] 5348 7-11-5 158 ..... RWalsh (W P Mullins, Ire) *hld up towards rr: stdy hdwy 3 out: trckd ldr 2 out: led on bit wl bef last: sn clr: imprssive* **5/6**[1]	157+
1111	**2**	*10*	**Sparky May**[52] 3674 6-11-5 148 ..... KeiranBurke (Patrick Rodford) *t.k.h in rr: blnd 2nd: gd hdwy to trck ldrs 6th: wnt 2nd 3 out: led appr 2 out: rdn sn after: hdd wl bef last and no ch w wnner but styd on wl to hold 2nd run-in* **4/1**[2]	143+
3011	**3**	*1*	**Ocean Transit (IRE)**[17] 4354 6-11-0 124 ..... DavidBass (Richard Price) *in rr: drvn along fr 6th and stl u.p whn hdwy 3 out: kpt on under hrd driving run-in to take 3rd nr fin and clsng on 2nd but no ch w wnr* **50/1**	136
-523	**4**	*1/2*	**Alasi**[52] 3674 7-11-0 136 ..... DominicElsworth (Paul Webber) *t.k.h: hld up in rr: hdwy 3 out: kpt on to take 3rd after next but no imp on ldng trio: one pce and wknd into 4th cl home* **33/1**	133
0-4	**5**	*3 3/4*	**Stephanie Kate (IRE)**[20] 4296 5-11-0 128 ..... PCarberry (C F Swan, Ire) *mid-div: hdwy on ins whn hmpd on bnd after 4 out: styd on again fr 2 out: kpt on run-in but nvr any ch of rching ldrs* **50/1**	130
1116	**6**	*2 1/2*	**L'Accordioniste (IRE)**[52] 3674 6-11-0 140 ..... PaddyBrennan (Nigel Twiston-Davies) *in tch: hdwy 4 out: rdn to chse ldrs next: nvr on terms: wknd last* **8/1**[3]	127
2201	**7**	*1*	**Banjaxed Girl**[66] 3442 7-11-5 152 ..... SamTwiston-Davies (Nigel Twiston-Davies) *led tl hdd appr 2 out: wknd wl bef last* **8/1**[3]	131
2313	**8**	*1 1/2*	**Santera (IRE)**[13] 2579 7-11-0 139 ..... (p) RhysFlint (John Flint) *chsd ldrs: rdn and kpt on fr 3 out: wknd after 2 out* **40/1**	128
2406	**9**	*2 1/2*	**Miss Overdrive**[25] 4185 7-11-0 118 ..... NickScholfield (Andy Turnell) *chsd ldrs tl rdn and dropped to rr 6th: styd on again after 2 out but nvr any ch* **100/1**	122
-1F6	**10**	*6*	**Alegralil**[66] 3442 6-11-5 145 ..... JasonMaguire (Donald McCain) *chsd ldrs: wnt 3rd 3 out: rdn and wknd fr 2 out* **40/1**	121
110/	**11**	*6*	**La Vecchia Scuola (IRE)**[129] 209 7-11-0 143 ..... (p) GrahamLee (Jim Goldie) *rdn 4 out: a in rr* **20/1**	110
1403	**12**	*4 1/2*	**Princess Rainbow (FR)**[22] 4255 6-11-0 114 ..... AlanO'Keeffe (Jennie Candlish) *t.k.h: in tch: rdn and wknd 3 out* **200/1**	106
0-3	**13**	*3/4*	**Lonesome Dove (IRE)**[58] 3592 6-11-0 125 ..... DJCasey (C F Swan, Ire) *in rr: hit 4th: no ch fr 4 out* **100/1**	105
2113	**14**	*3/4*	**Silver Gypsy (IRE)**[66] 3442 6-11-0 135 ..... (t) SeanQuinlan (Kim Bailey) *chsd ldrs tl wknd fr 3 out* **25/1**	104

4m 48.08s (-1.92) **Going Correction** -0.075s/f (Good) **14** Ran SP% **119.6**

Speed ratings (Par 115): **100,96,95,95,93 92,92,91,90,88 86,84,84,83**

toteswingers:1&2:£1.50, 1&3:£21.80, 2&3:£40.30 CSF £3.79 CT £95.76 TOTE £1.80: £1.10, £1.80, £12.30; EX 4.30 Trifecta £246.80 Pool: £13,789.36 - 41.33 winning units..

Owner Hammer & Trowel Syndicate **Bred** Pierre Rives **Trained** Muine Beag, Co Carlow

FOCUS

The fourth running of this mares' race and another facile success for Quevega, who has now won the last three renewals. She was value for further and is rated to her mark, with the fourth and ninth helping set the level.

NOTEBOOK

Quevega(FR) ◆ had been faced in the past two seasons with a major market rival with proven high-class ability (United and Voler La Vedette), but there was nothing fitting that description in her way this time and, despite rumours about her wellbeing just as there had been when she made her reappearance in this race a year ago, she once again proved in a different league. Ridden confidently by Walsh, she smoothly closed up running down the hill and, despite the runner-up's rider looking around as she strode clear, that one was untidy two out and the result soon became inevitable. The only moment of concern came when she took a chance at the last. It was another fine training performance from Willie Mullins and she will now head for the Aintree Hurdle, setting up a potential clash with the likes of Peddlers Cross. As for next season, this race will be hers for the taking once more, but considering she's already got three under her belt it would be nice to see her take her chance in the World Hurdle. (op 10-11 tchd 4-5, evens in places and 11-10 in a place)

Sparky May blundered at the second, after which her rider briefly lost an iron, and then raced keenly. That had also been the case when winning at Ascot the time before and it didn't stop her, but this time she was up against a top-class mare and simply proved no match in the straight. She battled well to hold on for second and it's hoped she stays in training. (tchd 9-2 and 7-2 in places)

Ocean Transit(IRE), rated just 124, has been much-improved of late, winning handicaps at Ludlow and Kempton, and ran well above expectations, responding to pressure and finishing well to bustle up the far classier runner-up.

Alasi has good course form to her name and she briefly threatened to stay on into second, but could find no extra after two out. (tchd 28-1)

Stephanie Kate(IRE) ◆ should have finished closer, being continually hampered on the inner after four out before staying on up the straight. She should have been a few lengths closer.

L'Accordioniste(IRE) ran a shocker behind the runner-up at Ascot, but had earlier been most progressive and she took a small step back in the right direction, for all that she was still below her best. (op 9-1)

Banjaxed Girl is a very tough mare, but she suffered for playing her hand too early and was below her best. (op 11-1)

Alegralil Official explanation: vet said mare lost a left-hind shoe

La Vecchia Scuola(IRE) looked in need of the run beforehand. (op 16-1)

Princess Rainbow(FR) Official explanation: vet said mare left a left-fore shoe

Lonesome Dove(IRE) looks a chaser in the making.

Silver Gypsy(IRE) Official explanation: vet said mare returned with a cut to its right-fore

4794 CENTENARY NOVICES' H'CAP CHASE (LISTED RACE) (16 fncs) 2m 4f 110y

5:15 (5:16) (Class 1) (0-140,140) 5-Y-O+

£28,505 (£10,695; £5,355; £2,670; £1,340; £670)

Form				RPR
1501	1		**Divers (FR)**[37] 3968 7-11-4 **132** ... GrahamLee *(Ferdy Murphy) hld up wl in rr: stdy prog fr 9th gng strly: trckd ldrs after 3 out: brought w wl-timed chal after 2 out: led sn after last: rdn clr* **10/1**	145+
-011	2	2 ¾	**Quantitativeeasing (IRE)**[35] 3988 6-11-11 **139** ... APMcCoy *(Nicky Henderson) trckd ldrs: cl up on long run after 13th: rdn and effrt after 3 out: narrow ld next: hdd and one pce sn after last* **7/1**[3]	147+
1212	3	2	**Tullamore Dew (IRE)**[57] 3600 9-11-11 **139** ... LiamTreadwell *(Nick Gifford) led 3rd to 5th: styd prom: rdn in cl 5th after 3 out: outpcd fr next: styd on wl flat to take 3rd nr fin* **13/2**[2]	146+
6323	4	1 ¼	**Vino Griego (FR)**[36] 3980 6-11-5 **133** ... (b¹) JamieMoore *(Gary Moore) prom: led 10th to 12th: led again 3 out and gng v strly: narrowly hdd 2 out: shkn up and no rspnse: fdd tamely after last* **20/1**	137
/412	5	1 ½	**Definity (IRE)**[30] 4093 8-11-8 **136** ... RWalsh *(Paul Nicholls) hld up in midfield: nudged by rival 6th: wl in tch bhd ldrs bef 3 out: outpcd after: kpt on fr last* **3/1**[1]	139
F3-2	6	¾	**Tharawaat (IRE)**[17] 4368 6-11-9 **137** ... (bt) DNRussell *(Gordon Elliott, Ire) prom: mstke 9th: effrt to chse ldr 3 out: sn rdn: nt qckn 2 out: fdd* **14/1**	140
2513	7	1 ¼	**Swing Bill (FR)**[10] 4487 10-11-8 **136** ... TimmyMurphy *(David Pipe) pressed ldrs: mstke 11th and lost pl: tried to rally 3 out: kpt on one pce fr next* **14/1**	139
1242	8	hd	**On Borrowed Wings (IRE)**[24] 4202 8-11-8 **136** ... (p) DarylJacob *(Alan Fleming) j.rt 1st and 2nd: wl in rr: mstke 9th: lost tch after 12th: wl bhd bef 3 out: styd on fr 2 out: nrst fin* **12/1**	136
3110	9	1 ¾	**Shakalakaboomboom (IRE)**[45] 3803 7-11-3 **134** ... DavidBass(3) *(Nicky Henderson) wl plcd bhd ldrs: effrt and wl in tch 3 out: steadily wknd bef 2 out* **33/1**	132
/0-3	10	2 ¾	**Glenstal Abbey (IRE)**[31] 4088 7-11-7 **135** ... (t) DJCasey *(C F Swan, Ire) lost pl and mstke 8th: wl in rr next: effrt again at rr of main gp bef 3 out: no hdwy after* **40/1**	131
116	11	6	**Nadiya De La Vega (FR)**[38] 3946 5-11-10 **139** ... BarryGeraghty *(Nicky Henderson) prom: led 5th to 10th: led 12th tl hdd and mstke 3 out: wkng whn mstke 2 out: eased* **20/1**	129
	12	2	**Lastoftheleaders (IRE)**[30] 4106 8-11-5 **133** ... AndrewJMcNamara *(A L T Moore, Ire) towards rr: mstke 12th: lost tch next: tried to latch on to main gp 3 out: wknd next* **25/1**	120
1163	13	8	**Sway (FR)**[55] 3627 5-11-1 **133** ... RichieMcLernon(3) *(Jonjo O'Neill) hld up: in tch whn mstke 11th: stl in main gp whn mstke 3 out: wknd* **50/1**	111
211F	P		**Songe (FR)**[59] 3561 7-11-12 **140** ... (t) TomSiddall *(Charlie Longsdon) settled in midfield: losing pl whn mstke 8th: sn dropped to last and jumping wnt to pieces: t.o whn p.u bef 13th* **50/1**	—
F513	P		**American Trilogy (IRE)**[17] 4351 7-11-6 **134** ... (b) NickScholfield *(Paul Nicholls) settled in midfield: lost pl steadily fr 9th: bhd after 13th: t.o whn p.u bef 2 out* **14/1**	—
212F	P		**Osric (IRE)**[40] 3905 8-11-5 **133** ... AndrewTinkler *(Nicky Henderson) hld up wl in rr: stdy prog on inner 9th: in tch whn nt fluent 13th: sn dropped away: t.o whn p.u bef 2 out* **20/1**	—
4211	P		**Premier Sagas (FR)**[26] 4168 7-11-11 **139** ... JasonMaguire *(Nicky Richards) blnd and lost pl 4th: wknd rapidly: t.o whn p.u bef 8th* **20/1**	—
413	P		**Quo Video (FR)**[26] 4162 7-11-6 **137** ... (t) RichardKilloran(3) *(Tim Vaughan) nt jump wl: a wl in rr: t.o 13th: p.u bef 2 out* **100/1**	—
F231	P		**Rougham**[52] 3672 5-11-7 **136** ... RichardJohnson *(Philip Hobbs) led to 3rd: losing pl qckly whn blnd 8th: t.o fr 12th: p.u bef 2 out* **20/1**	—
-114	P		**Swincombe Rock**[110] 2631 6-11-6 **137** ... SamTwiston-Davies(3) *(Nigel Twiston-Davies) racd wd in midfield: reminders after 8th: lost tch 12th: t.o whn p.u bef 2 out* **33/1**	—

5m 7.50s (-3.50) **Going Correction** +0.05s/f (Yiel) **20** Ran SP% **128.5**

Speed ratings: **108,106,106,105,105 104,104,104,103,102 100,99,96,—,—,—,—,—,—,—**

toteswingers:1&2:£12.50, 1&3:£13.40, 2&3:£6.50. totesuper7: Win: Not won. Place: £527.10. CSF £69.10 CT £509.05 TOTE £11.30: £2.60, £1.90, £1.90, £5.50; EX 104.60 Trifecta £290.50 Pool: £10,698.19 - 27.24 winning units..

Owner The DPRP Divers Partnership **Bred** Alec Head And Mme Ghislaine Head **Trained** West Witton, N Yorks

■ A new title for this event, which was previously sponsored by Jewson.

FOCUS

The inaugural running of this chase in a slightly altered form, with it now restricted to horses rated no higher than 140, with the idea to force those rated in excess of that into the new Grade 2 race over this trip. It was a rough race, but the form still looks solid. The first two are on the upgrade, with the next half-dozen close to their previous marks.

NOTEBOOK

Divers(FR) ◆, who had won with more in hand than it looked at Musselburgh last time, was produced in top shape by Ferdy Murphy to post a career-best, overcoming some trouble in running and staying on strongly up the run-in to win with a fair bit in hand. He jumped soundly enough and is value for more than the official winning margin. He's likely to stay 3m, but like the yard's 2007 winner of the equivalent of this race L'Antartique, the Paddy Power back here in November is sure to be at the forefront of connections' mind. (op 11-1)

Quantitativeeasing(IRE) had twice won readily in minor events since the Cheltenham run in November and coped well in this more competitive race, but conceding 7lb to his old rival proved too much. It was a fine effort from a horse likely to need further in time and he could feature in some top staying handicaps next season. (op 9-1)

Tullamore Dew(IRE), runner-up in last season's Coral Cup off 4lb lower, has some decent form to his name over fences and was soon prominent, but he didn't get the cleanest of jumps three out, after which he became outpaced. To his credit, though, he did rally, and managed to take third off the tiring Vino Griego. Stepping up to 3m now looks a good move. (op 7-1 tchd 6-1 and 8-1 in places)

Vino Griego(FR) ◆ has still to win over fences, but he's a fine-looking sort with a big engine and once again travelled strongly in first-time blinkers. However, as has all too often been the case this season, his finishing effort was rather tame. He deserves to have his confidence boosted in a minor event. (tchd 22-1 and 25-1 in places)

Definity(IRE) proved most popular in the market, despite many thinking he should have lined up in the 3m handicap earlier on the card. The way he stayed on having been outpaced suggested the longer distance of that race would have suited, and this lightly raced 8-y-o remains capable of better as he goes back up in trip. (tchd 7-2 and 4-1 in places)

Tharawaat(IRE) moved through travelling strongly, but the response was limited once straightened for home.

Swing Bill(FR) has had a busy season of it, but he's a thoroughly likeable sort who tried his hardest to get back into the mix for the places after a couple of mistakes. (tchd 16-1)

On Borrowed Wings(IRE) lost ground in jumping out to his right early in the cheekpieces, so got too far back to win, but did stay on late in the day. (op 14-1)

Glenstal Abbey(IRE) Official explanation: vet said gelding lost a right-fore shoe

Nadiya De La Vega(FR) looked vulnerable off this mark and was beaten before the straight.

American Trilogy(IRE), the 2009 County Hurdle winner, was not on a going day. (tchd 16-1 in places)

Swincombe Rock Official explanation: vet said gelding lost a left-fore shoe (tchd 16-1 in places)

T/Jkpt: £142,083.50 to a £1 stake. Pool:£200,117.69 - 1.00 winning ticket T/Plt: £60.60 to a £1 stake. Pool:£970,517.56 - 11,686.68 winning tickets T/Qpdt: £9.30 to a £1 stake. Pool:£40,783.77 - 3,221.34 winning tickets JN

4506 SEDGEFIELD (L-H)

Tuesday, March 15

OFFICIAL GOING: Soft (good to soft in places in straight; chs 5.3, hdl 5.4)

Divided bends, chases dolled off inside.

Wind: Breezy, half against Weather: Overcast

4795 WELCOME TO SEDGEFIELD FROM FREEBETTING.CO.UK MARES' NOVICES' HURDLE (QUALIFIER) (10 hdls) 2m 4f

1:45 (1:45) (Class 4) 4-Y-O+ £2,081 (£611; £305; £152)

Form				RPR
43	1		**Streamtown (IRE)**[13] 4432 7-10-12 103 ... PeterBuchanan *(S R B Crawford, Ire) hld up towards rr: smooth hdwy to trck ldrs 3 out: led next: rdn and kpt on wl fr last* **2/5**[1]	98+
6664	2	1	**Lady Ida**[28] 4134 6-10-12 0 ... MarkGrant *(Jennie Candlish) led to bef 7th: led after 3 out to next: kpt on u.p run-in* **14/1**[3]	97
0-00	3	25	**Alfie's Pearl**[11] 4454 6-10-9 0 ... (p) AdamPogson(3) *(Charles Pogson) plld hrd: cl up: led bef 7th to after 3 out: outpcd fr next: tk modest 3rd run-in* **22/1**	73
P45P	4	2	**Glaced Over**[114] 2547 6-10-12 106 ... RichieMcGrath *(Raymond Shiels) nt fluent: hld up: hdwy and in tch after 3 out: wnt modest 3rd bef next: sn outpcd* **6/1**[2]	73
P0P	5	3 ¼	**Shoal Bay Dreamer**[22] 4253 5-10-12 0 ... JamesReveley *(Dianne Sayer) trckd ldrs: rdn bef 3 out: wknd bef next* **100/1**	67
564	6	¾	**Floraclock**[112] 2598 6-10-12 0 ... HenryOliver *(Sue Smith) w ldr to 1/2-way: sn rdn: wknd after 3 out* **16/1**	66
0/P5	7	19	**Frosty Spring**[28] 4134 8-10-5 0 ... MrGRSmith(7) *(David Thompson) prom tl rdn and wknd after 3 out* **50/1**	47
60	8	5	**Little Fifi**[17] 4363 6-10-7 0 ... AlexanderVoy(5) *(Sandy Thomson) hld up on outside: struggling fr 4th: lost tch after next* **66/1**	42
0052	9	35	**Politelysed**[15] 4395 5-10-12 73 ... KennyJohnson *(Robert Johnson) bhd: struggling fr 1/2-way: t.o* **14/1**[3]	7
	P		**Cherry Cake** 7-10-12 0 ... TomMessenger *(Philip Kirby) prom: lost pl 1/2-way: sn struggling: t.o whn p.u 3 out* **33/1**	—
0P	P		**Last Chorus**[126] 2297 5-10-12 0 ... AdrianLane *(Tracy Waggott) a bhd: lost tch 1/2-way: t.o whn p.u 3 out* **125/1**	—

5m 12.4s (19.70) **Going Correction** +0.65s/f (Soft) **11** Ran SP% **117.5**

Speed ratings (Par 105): **86,85,75,74,73 73,65,63,49,—,—**

toteswingers:1&2:£2.50, 1&3:£5.00, 2&3:£11.70 CSF £7.17 TOTE £1.50: £1.10, £1.90, £5.60; EX 5.80.

Owner Barry Murphy **Bred** Pat Tobin **Trained** Larne, Co Antrim

■ Stewards' Enquiry : Adam Pogson one-day ban: used whip in incorrect place (Mar 29)

FOCUS

The ground was described as soft, good to soft in places with the jockeys reporting that the ground was riding "rather tacky and dead" A weak mares' novices' hurdle ran in a time of 37 seconds outside the Racing Post standard. The winner was the clear form pick and ther's a case for rating the race up to 10lb higher.

NOTEBOOK

Streamtown(IRE) looked to have found a good opportunity to open her account now tackling her own sex after some respectable efforts in novice hurdles recently. She had to dig deep to assert from the last, but did so in a likeable manner and appreciated this step back up in distance. (tchd 9-4)

Lady Ida had shown in the past she possesses some ability and this brave effort confirms that. She made the winner dig deep after sitting at the head of affairs for most of the way and a little opportunity should fall her way in due course. (op 12-1 tchd 16-1)

Alfie's Pearl has been tried in headgear after failing to build on some promising bumper runs. This was a better effort than of late, but she will still have to build upon this to be of interest. (op 25-1)

Politelysed was disappointing as she looked well in the preliminaries, but could never get involved. (op 16-1)

4796 COLLINS SEAFOODS MAIDEN CHASE (QUALIFIER) (PART OF THE COLLINS SEAFOODS YOUNG CHASERS SERIES) (16 fncs) 2m 4f

2:20 (2:20) (Class 4) 5-Y-0+ **£2,602** (£764; £382; £190)

Form RPR

-423 **1** **Finlay**[22] 4258 8-11-0 102..............(t) AdrianLane 110+
(Donald McCain) *t.k.h: cl up: ev ch fnl circ: led 12th to 3 out: drvn next: 1 l down whn mstke last: styd on wl to ld nr fin* **85/40**[1]

-436 **2** ½ **Playing The Field (IRE)**[9] 4508 6-11-0 0.............. BrianHughes 108
(David O'Meara) *t.k.h: cl up: led 7th to 12th: styd upsides: led 3 out: hung lft after next: rdn and kpt on run-in: hdd nr fin* **5/2**[2]

F546 **3** 13 **Poseidon (GER)**[150] 1868 9-10-7 90.............. MrJohnDawson(7) 96
(John Wade) *hld up in tch: hdwy and cl up fr 6th: ev ch 4 out: outpcd bef 2 out: sn n.d* **15/2**

5F **4** 1 **Chapolimoss (FR)**[15] 4394 7-11-0 107..............(t) JamesReveley 95
(Martin Todhunter) *led to 2nd: stdd in tch: effrt and stdy hdwy whn nt fluent 11th: rdn and outpcd after 3 out: sn n.d* **7/2**[3]

6466 **U** **Railway Park (IRE)**[9] 4510 7-10-11 78..............(p) HarryHaynes(3) —
(John Wainwright) *uns rdr 1st* **40/1**

P **List Of Life (IRE)**[394] 6-11-0 0.............. RobertWalford —
(Tim Walford) *cl up: led 2nd to 7th: struggling after 9th: losing tch whn p.u next* **13/2**

5m 10.1s (7.10) **Going Correction** +0.65s/f (Soft) **6** Ran SP% **110.3**
Speed ratings: **111,110,105,105,—** —
toteswingers:1&2:£1.30, 1&3:£3.40, 2&3:£3.10 CSF £7.83 TOTE £2.40: £1.10, £1.80; EX 6.30.
Owner D Lockwood, P Edwards, J Koumas **Bred** Simon Edwards **Trained** Cholmondeley, Cheshire
■ Stewards' Enquiry : Adrian Lane one-day ban: used whip with excessive frequency (Mar 29)

FOCUS
An ordinary maiden chase, but a decent pace was set with all four of the remaining runners holding a chance three out. The winner was below his Carlisle run over further.

NOTEBOOK
Finlay looked to have blown his chances after missing the last, but to his credit he picked up well to reel in the leader nearing the finish to win going away. He had the best chasing form on offer with a fine second at Leicester behind Antonius Caesar in January. There was plenty to like about his jumping and his attitude so should continue to pay his way when handicapping. (op 2-1 tchd 15-8)

Playing The Field(IRE) looked to have the winner held at bay after drawing half a length clear at the last before getting collared towards the finish. This was a fair effort returning to fences and he can go one better before long. (op 4-1)

Poseidon(GER) was returning from a 160-day break. He had his chance turning in, but had no more to offer soon after and will be better suited when back in handicaps. (op 5-1 tchd 8-1)

Chapolimoss(FR) looked to have a decent chance of gaining some compensation after falling on chasing debut at Catterick. He jumped well on the whole, but was readily brushed aside after three out and was a little disappointing on the pick of his hurdling form. (op 3-1)

List Of Life(IRE), a winning pointer on a disqualification, dropped out tamely after taking them along for the best part of a circuit and can only be watched at present. Official explanation: jockey said gelding had a breathing problem (op 7-1 tchd 8-1)

4797 CHAMPION HURDLE FREE BETS WITH FREEBETTING.CO.UK H'CAP HURDLE (8 hdls) 2m 1f

2:55 (2:56) (Class 4) (0-115,113) 4-Y-0+ **£2,081** (£611; £305; £152)

Form RPR

53-0 **1** **Shifting Gold (IRE)**[19] 3523 5-10-9 101..............(b) BrianToomey(5) 103+
(Kevin Ryan) *t.k.h: cl up: chal 4 out: led 2 out: rdn and edgd rt: styd on wl run-in* **7/1**[3]

0-52 **2** ½ **King's Counsel (IRE)**[11] 4452 5-10-13 107.............. HenryBrooke(7) 107
(David O'Meara) *cl up: led 4 out to 2 out: styd upsides: kpt on u.p run-in: hld nr fin* **3/1**[1]

0642 **3** *nk* **Waterloo Corner**[29] 4113 9-10-11 98.............. KennyJohnson 99
(Ray Craggs) *hld up: rdn after 3 out: hdwy and ev ch next to run-in: kpt on: hld towards fin* **4/1**[2]

5-05 **4** 8 **Agglestone Rock**[63] 3500 6-11-5 113.............. KyleJames(7) 105
(Philip Kirby) *t.k.h: hld up bhd ldng gp: stdy hdwy bef 3 out: effrt bef next: sn outpcd* **3/1**[1]

0040 **5** 2¼ **Takaatuf (IRE)**[29] 4113 5-11-1 102.............. BrianHughes 91
(John Hellens) *trckd ldrs: effrt bef 2 out: wknd between last 2* **14/1**

-650 **6** 14 **Bureaucrat**[22] 4255 9-11-11 112..............(p) RichieMcGrath 87
(Kate Walton) *racd wd: led to 4 out: rdn and wknd fr next* **14/1**

0600 **7** 5 **Barron Watlass (IRE)**[2] 4738 7-11-0 101..............(p) BarryKeniry 71
(George Moore) *hld up in tch: stdy hdwy 1/2-way: rdn and wknd after 3 out* **15/2**

-33P **8** 45 **Classic Contours (USA)**[122] 2375 5-11-9 110.............. JamesReveley 35
(Tracy Waggott) *hld up: struggling fr 4 out: eased whn no ch fnl 2f* **25/1**

6500 **P** **Dream Risk (FR)**[11] 4455 5-11-2 103..............(t) WilsonRenwick —
(Kate Walton) *hld up on outside: struggling fnl circ: t.o whn p.u 2 out* **22/1**

4m 16.2s (9.30) **Going Correction** +0.65s/f (Soft) **9** Ran SP% **115.8**
Speed ratings (Par 105): **104,103,103,99,98 92,89,68,—**
toteswingers:1&2:£4.60, 1&3:£7.50, 2&3:£4.00 CSF £29.07 CT £96.48 TOTE £9.60: £2.00, £1.30, £2.10; EX 30.50.
Owner Hambleton Racing Ltd VIII **Bred** Watership Down Stud **Trained** Hambleton, N Yorks

FOCUS
A fair pace for this 0-115 handicap hurdle with the front five drawing clear on the run to two out and a cracking three-way battle from the last. The winner is rated back to the best of his juvenile form.

NOTEBOOK
Shifting Gold(IRE) is a fine servant to his connections and had been successful on the all-weather over the winter. He probably found the trip far enough at Catterick when finishing behind Waterloo Corner in January, but this drop back 2f did the trick. A very likeable individual, he had got in here off a handy looking mark of 101 so will probably have to find a little more improvement in the future, but nonetheless he should continue to pay his way under both codes. (op 15-2 tchd 8-1)

King's Counsel(IRE) was racing without usual headgear, but again gave another good account of himself. A reliable performer who usually runs his race, he probably needs a little respite from the handicapper to get his head back in front. (op 7-2)

Waterloo Corner, last year's winner, came here in good heart after a good run at Catterick last time and duly ran right up to that level again. (op 9-2)

Agglestone Rock, the gamble of the race, who had a good time of it over fences last season, wasn't disgraced over hurdles last time and coupled with the fact that his only previous visit to the course was a successful one, you could understand where the support was coming from. He travelled strongly into the race going to three out, but when asked to go about his business could only keep on at the same pace. (op 5-2 tchd 10-3)

Takaatuf(IRE) ran one of his better races, but his overall profile is rather patchy. He was a fair performer on the level and should be capable of figuring when things fall his way. (op 18-1)

4798 ENJOY THE CHELTENHAM FESTIVAL WITH FREEBETTING.CO.UK "NATIONAL HUNT" NOVICES' H'CAP HURDLE (8 hdls) 2m 1f

3:35 (3:35) (Class 4) (0-105,105) 4-Y-0+ **£2,081** (£611; £305; £152)

Form RPR

0056 **1** **Erin Dancer (IRE)**[32] 4059 6-11-5 105.............. RobertMcCarth(7) 107+
(Ferdy Murphy) *in tch: stdy hdwy 4 out: effrt after 2 out: led last: rdn and r.o wl* **4/1**

5044 **2** ½ **Baraathen (USA)**[13] 4419 4-9-11 91.............. HenryBrooke(7) 83
(Donald McCain) *cl up: drvn and outpcd 4 out: rallied next: led 2 out to last: kpt on run-in: hld nr fin* **11/4**[2]

3644 **3** 4 **Dr Flynn (IRE)**[15] 4393 6-11-5 105.............. PaulGallagher(7) 102
(Howard Johnson) *t.k.h: cl up: drvn and outpcd 3 out: rallied next: kpt on same pce run-in* **5/2**[1]

060 **4** 4½ **Udaya Klum**[10] 4473 8-10-5 84.............. HenryOliver 77
(Sue Smith) *led: rdn and hdd 2 out: wknd fr last* **3/1**[3]

-P00 **P** **Nothing Ventured**[20] 4281 6-10-0 79 oh4..............(t) BrianHughes —
(John Norton) *t.k.h: in tch: rdn 4 out: wknd next: t.o whn p.u bef 2 out* **14/1**

00PP **P** **Bunacurry**[21] 4274 6-10-1 80.............. RichieMcGrath —
(Barry Murtagh) *in tch on outside: rdn and wknd appr 3 out: t.o whn p.u bef next* **20/1**

4m 27.2s (20.30) **Going Correction** +0.65s/f (Soft)
WFA 4 from 6yo+ 7lb **6** Ran SP% **111.7**
Speed ratings (Par 105): **78,77,75,73,—** —
toteswingers:1&2:£1.40, 1&3:£1.02, 2&3:£4.80 CSF £15.48 TOTE £4.00: £4.80, £3.50; EX 17.00.
Owner J and A Millar **Bred** Tally-Ho Stud **Trained** West Witton, N Yorks

FOCUS
A low grade 0-105 handicap hurdle with four of the six runners making their handicap debuts. A big step up from the winner with the next three pretty much to their marks.

NOTEBOOK
Erin Dancer(IRE) had some fair form in bumpers, but had only performed to a modest level so far over hurdles. He did make it a winning start in handicaps off a mark of 105, but will probably have to find further improvement if he is to follow up as the runner-up had been beaten off a mark of 93 previously. Official explanation: trainer's rep said, regarding apparent improvement in form, that the gelding benefited from an uncompetitive race and first run in a handicap. (op 5-1 tchd 7-2)

Baraathen(USA) had been beaten off a mark of 93 in juvenile handicaps recently and had been dropped 2lb here. He can rate as the benchmark which can only be modest. (tchd 5-2 and 3-1)

Dr Flynn(IRE) had respectable bumper form and had shown promise on all three hurdle starts, and looked to be on a reasonable mark of 105. He had his chance, but could only keep on at the same pace and might want stepping back up in trip. (op 15-8)

Udaya Klum had been well-supported for his handicapping debut off a lowly mark of 84 and was ridden from the front to make this a test. He was still in front when coming under pressure going to two out, but had no more to offer when headed going to the last. This was disappointing considering a big run was expected in a weak affair. (op 9-2)

4799 FREE HORSE RACING BETS WITH FREEBETTING.CO.UK H'CAP CHASE (15 fncs 1 omitted) 2m 4f

4:15 (4:16) (Class 5) (0-85,83) 5-Y-0+ **£1,886** (£553; £276; £138)

Form RPR

4P36 **1** **Humbel Times (IRE)**[4] 4693 7-10-2 62..............(p) AlexMerriam(3) 73
(Neil King) *towards rr: drvn and outpcd 9th: rallied 4 out: styd on wl fr 2 out: wnt 4 l 2nd last: led towards fin* **9/1**

0P46 **2** 1¾ **Yes Mate**[9] 4511 7-9-11 61.............. HenryBrooke(7) 72+
(Dianne Sayer) *hld up: hdwy 9th: chsng ldrs after next: edgd lft and led between last 2: 4 l clr whn mstke last: kpt on: hdd and no ex towards fin* **9/2**[3]

40-4 **3** 2¾ **Nicky Tam (IRE)**[6] 4551 9-11-6 77..............(t) RobertWalford 84
(Henry Hogarth) *prom: hit 1st: rdn and outpcd 3 out: rallied bef last: kpt on run-in* **8/1**

-FP0 **4** 7 **Whatcanyasay**[9] 4510 10-10-2 66..............(p) MissECSayer(7) 69
(Evelyn Slack) *cl up: led 11th to between last 2: jst lost 2nd whn hit last: wknd* **25/1**

P250 **5** 13 **Coldwells (IRE)**[43] 3853 11-11-12 83..............(p) JamesReveley 80
(Martin Todhunter) *led: hit 8th: hdd 10th: cl up tl rdn and wknd bef 2 out* **7/1**

00P0 **6** 8 **Mind Shower (IRE)**[35] 3995 5-10-6 64..............(p) RichieMcGrath 45
(Robert Wylie) *midfield: blnd 7th: hit and outpcd 9th: sn struggling* **16/1**

3P42 **7** 2 **The Green Hat (IRE)**[28] 4133 11-10-7 71.............. MissGAndrews(7) 48
(Theresa Gibson) *bhd and detached: no ch fnl circ* **4/1**[2]

0P/0 **P** **Nick The Silver**[15] 4390 10-11-6 77..............(p) KennyJohnson —
(Robert Johnson) *bhd: hit 9th: sn struggling: t.o whn p.u bef 3 out* **50/1**

0-0P **P** **Ravenscar**[16] 4378 13-10-11 71.............. AdamPogson(3) —
(Charles Pogson) *cl up tl wknd fr 11th: t.o whn p.u bef last* **25/1**

6543 **U** **Ravensbill (IRE)**[9] 4509 9-10-13 73.............. EwanWhillans(3) —
(William Amos) *in tch: cl sixth whn blnd bdly and uns rdr 10th* **7/2**[1]

0F00 **F** **Fifth Sea Lord (IRE)**[30] 4100 6-10-0 60.............. TommyPhelan(3) —
(Tom Gretton) *fell heavily 1st* **12/1**

5m 14.1s (11.10) **Going Correction** +0.65s/f (Soft) **11** Ran SP% **117.2**
Speed ratings: **103,102,101,98,93 90,89,—,—,—** —
toteswingers:1&2:£9.10, 1&3:£16.80, 2&3:£16.10 CSF £49.48 CT £343.48 TOTE £11.70: £3.10, £2.90, £1.10; EX 50.40.
Owner The St Gatien Racing For Fun Partnership **Bred** Miss Olivia Maher And Barry Mason **Trained** Newmarket, Suffolk

FOCUS
The first fence after the winning post was bypassed on the second circuit. A low-grade handicap chase that took little winning, but run at a reasonable pace. A step up from the winner in the headgear.

NOTEBOOK
Humbel Times(IRE) got up in the dying strides to score on his second attempt over fences. He had been placed off 2lb higher over hurdles, but had been tailed off on his chasing debut when unsuited by the firmish ground. Now wearing cheekpieces, he looked anything but the winner turning out of the back straight but stuck to his rider's urging gamely and eventually reeled in the leader nearing the finish. Official explanation: trainer said, regarding apparent improvement in form, that the gelding benefited from the application of cheek pieces (op 10-1)

Yes Mate had been placed off higher marks over hurdles, but had to step up on previous efforts over fences. He moved into the race well and got to the front going to the last, looking to have the race in the bag. He got collared nearing the finish and will struggle to find an easier opportunity than this. (tchd 4-1)

Nicky Tam(IRE), wearing a tongue-tie for the first time, moved into the race travelling well enough but could only stay on at the same pace when asked for his effort. He remains a maiden but looks on a feasible mark when upped back up in trip in a similar contest. (op 7-1)

Whatcanyasay ran a better race than of late off a handy looking mark and looked to have stolen it two out before tiring going the last.

The Green Hat(IRE) was struggling in rear from an early stage and could never get involved. Official explanation: trainer had no explanation for the poor form shown (tchd 7-2)

4800 FREE BETTING WITH FREEBETTING.CO.UK H'CAP CHASE (13 fncs) 2m 110y

4:55 (4:55) (Class 5) (0-95,96) 5-Y-O+ **£1,886** (£553; £276; £138)

Form RPR

0U31 **1** **Flighty Mist**[9] 4509 9-10-12 **85** 7ex.................................. PaulGallagher[(7)] 94+
(Sandy Forster) *prom: mstke 2nd: reminders 4th: rallied 6th: rdn to ld after 3 out: styd on wl fr next* **11/4**[1]

F3F1 **2** *2 ½* **Gavroche Gaugain (FR)**[9] 4510 7-11-9 **96** 7ex.................. TonyKelly[(7)] 100
(Ferdy Murphy) *cl up: chsng clr ldr whn hit 9th: effrt and ev ch 3 out: sn rdn: kpt on fr last: nt pce of wnr* **4/1**[2]

062- **3** *2 ¾* **Braddock Island**[321] 48 8-11-12 **92**.................................. BarryKeniry 92
(Mrs S Sunter) *w ldr: led 4th: clr after next to 4 out: hdd after next: kpt on same pce fr 2 out* **17/2**[3]

1222 **4** *6* **Lerida**[9] 4510 9-11-0 **87**.. HenryBrooke[(7)] 82
(Sharon Watt) *led to 4th: cl up: rdn and outpcd bef 9th: no imp fr 2 out* **11/4**[1]

6143 **5** *30* **Authentic Act (IRE)**[9] 4510 7-11-3 **83**.............................. JamesReveley 47
(Martin Todhunter) *bhd and sn detached: nvr on terms* **4/1**[2]

15PF **P** **Emirate Isle**[31] 4068 7-11-12 **92**....................................(p) WilsonRenwick —
(Brian Storey) *nt jump wl: sn bhd and detached: blnd 9th: p.u bef next* **12/1**

4m 27.6s (19.00) **Going Correction** +0.65s/f (Soft) **6** Ran SP% **111.6**
Speed ratings: **81,79,78,75,61** —
toteswingers:1&2:£4.20, 1&3:£15.50, 2&3:£7.40 CSF £14.03 TOTE £6.40: £5.70, £4.80; EX 15.30.
Owner J R Jeffreys **Bred** J R Jeffreys **Trained** Kirk Yetholm, Borders

FOCUS
A tight little handicap on paper. The winner was well handiacpped and will still be competitive when reassessed.

NOTEBOOK
Flighty Mist continued her progress of late to run out a deserved winner and follow up her recent C&D success. She had to defy a 7lb penalty and a drop back in trip but, under her capable rider, she stayed on stoutly after taking up the running after three out. She will have to improve again to cope with any rise when reassessed, but she is shaping as though she is capable of doing so. (op 3-1)
Gavroche Gaugain(FR) has had his jumping problems but finally got off the mark over C&D last time and, like the winner was trying to defy a penalty. He put in a sound round of jumping and had his chance, but ultimately was outstayed by the winner. (tchd 7-2 and 9-2)
Braddock Island made this a fair pace and ran a respectable race on his return to action after nearly a year on the sidelines. He will be better for the outing. (op 8-1 tchd 9-1)
Lerida, a model of consistency since joining this yard, was a little disappointing after sitting prominently for much of the way but lost his place tamely in the back straight and could never get back on terms. (tchd 7-2)
Authentic Act(IRE) was well backed, but was immediately detached and never got into contention. Official explanation: jockey said gelding never travelled (op 9-2 tchd 3-1)
Emirate Isle's round of jumping was strewn with errors before his rider called it a day. (op 10-1)

4801 CHELTENHAM FESTIVAL FREE BETS WITH FREEBETTING.CO.UK STANDARD OPEN NATIONAL HUNT FLAT RACE 2m 1f

5:25 (5:30) (Class 6) 4-6-Y-O **£1,431** (£420; £210; £104)

Form RPR

1 **Keep Kicking (IRE)** 4-10-10 0.. BrianHughes 105+
(Clive Mulhall) *trckd ldrs gng wl: shkn up to chal 2f out: rdn and led 1f out: edgd lft: jst hld on* **9/4**[2]

13 **2** *nse* **Matthew Riley (IRE)**[23] 4239 4-11-3 0.............................. RichieMcGrath 112
(Kate Walton) *t.k.h: trckd ldrs: effrt and led over 2f out: hdd 1f out: edgd lft and styd on wl towards fin: jst hld* **2/1**[1]

2 **3** *17* **Valsesia (IRE)**[15] 4396 4-9-10 0...................................... PaulGallagher[(7)] 81
(Howard Johnson) *set stdy pce: led tl hdd over 2f out: sn outpcd by first two* **6/1**

02 **4** *7* **Angel Sun (FR)**[35] 3998 5-10-11 0............................ EdmondLinehan[(7)] 89
(Ferdy Murphy) *hld up: rdn and outpcd over 5f out: plugged on fr 2f out: nvr rchd ldrs* **8/1**

6 **5** *1 ¼* **Amtired**[20] 4287 5-10-13 0.. BrianToomey[(5)] 88
(Brian Ellison) *hld up: hdwy and in tch over 4f out: rdn and wknd wl over 1f out* **12/1**

6 *23* **Sine Mora** 5-11-4 0.. AdrianLane 65
(Donald McCain) *hld up: hdwy and prom over 4f out: wknd 3f out* **11/2**[3]

0 **7** *9* **Starbird**[21] 4280 4-10-3 0.. HenryBrooke[(7)] 48
(Mike Sowersby) *w ldr: rdn and wknd fr over 3f out* **80/1**

0 **8** *24* **Indicco**[99] 2824 4-10-3 0.. WilsonRenwick 17
(Ruth Carr) *in tch tl wknd over 4f out: eased whn no ch fnl 2f* **100/1**

0 **9** *10* **Azebra**[23] 4239 6-10-4 0.. KyleJames[(7)] 15
(Lynn Siddall) *bhd: rdn after 6f: lost tch 1/2-way: eased whn no ch fnl 2f* **150/1**

0 **10** *11* **Billy Teal**[154] 1817 6-11-4 0.. DaveCrosse 11
(G P Kelly) *prom: drvn 1/2-way: rallied: wknd over 5f out: eased whn btn fnl 2f* **100/1**

4m 29.5s (28.20) **Going Correction** +0.65s/f (Soft)
WFA 4 from 5yo+ 7lb **10** Ran SP% **116.5**
Speed ratings: **59,58,50,47,47 36,32,20,16,10**
toteswingers:1&2:£3.00, 1&3:£7.60, 2&3:£3.70 CSF £7.20 TOTE £4.40: £1.20, £1.10, £1.80; EX 10.40.
Owner Andrew Kitching **Bred** Sunny Days Ltd **Trained** Scarcroft, W Yorks
■ Stewards' Enquiry : Brian Hughes caution: used whip down shoulder in the forehand

FOCUS
An ordinary pace for this bumper. The winner is a promising recruit and can rate higher.

NOTEBOOK
Keep Kicking(IRE) attracted plenty of interest and was backed down from 25-1 throughout the day. He landed the punt, but was all out to do so. After travelling best turning, in the runner-up stole a length on him at the furlong marker and he had to dig deep to repel him once gaining a narrow advantage in the dying strides. From the family of dual Group 1 winner Daliapour and Queen's Vase winner Dalampour, he has the size and scope to develop into an exciting prospect over hurdles. He ought to be capable of defying a penalty, as he looked as though he would come on for the outing. (op 3-1 tchd 10-3)
Matthew Riley(IRE)an impressive winner over C&D before running with credit under a penalty at Market Rasen, lost nothing in defeat and sets a good standard.\n (op 9-4 tchd 7-4)
Valsesia(IRE) should find an opening before long after running respectably in defeat, but could not match the principals' pace when they quickened in the straight.\n (op 13-2)
Angel Sun(FR)continues to show some promise, getting outpaced over 3f out before staying on again in the latter part of the race.\n (tchd 7-1)
Amtired has shown a bit of promise on both his starts.
T/Plt: £86.90 to a £1 stake. Pool:£55,297.02 - 464.32 winning tickets T/Qpdt: £35.00 to a £1 stake. Pool:£3,217.03 - 68.00 winning tickets RY

4788 CHELTENHAM (L-H)

Wednesday, March 16

OFFICIAL GOING: Good (good to soft in places; 7.8)
An unprecedented six winners for the Irish, who also had the first four in the Queen Mother Champion Chase.
Wind: Moderate, across Weather: Grey

4802 141ST YEAR OF NATIONAL HUNT CHASE CHALLENGE CUP (AMATEUR RIDERS' NOVICES' CHASE) (25 fncs) 4m

1:30 (1:30) (Class 2) 5-Y-O+
£45,015 (£14,062; £7,027; £3,517; £1,755; £885)

Form RPR

1F25 **1** **Chicago Grey (IRE)**[78] 3174 8-11-6 151...................(t) MrDerekO'Connor 155+
(Gordon Elliott, Ire) *taken down early: v patiently rdn in rr: stdy prog fr 19th to trck ldrs 3 out: crept through on inner to chal 2 out: led last: rdn clr: readily* **5/1**[1]

1-B1 **2** *4 ½* **Beshabar (IRE)**[21] 4282 9-11-6 138..................................... MrTomDavid 149
(Tim Vaughan) *led to 3rd: trckd ldrs after: effrt to dispute ld 20th: led 3 out and kicked on: hdd last: styd on but readily outpcd* **9/1**

3251 **3** *8* **Be There In Five (IRE)**[11] 4480 7-11-6 138................ MrSWaley-Cohen 141
(Nicky Henderson) *trckd ldrs in abt 7th: effrt fr 4 out: cl up next: tried to chal bef 2 out: sn lft outpcd* **20/1**

4-1 **4** *3 ¼* **Alfa Beat (IRE)**[182] 1527 7-11-6 149..........................(p) MrRPMcNamara 139
(C Byrnes, Ire) *trckd ldrs in 5th: mstke 18th: nt fluent 4 out: effrt next: tried to chal 2 out: sn wknd* **11/2**[2]

5 *9* **Some Target (IRE)**[45] 3845 7-11-6 139............................. MrPWMullins 130
(W P Mullins, Ire) *hld up wl in rr: last 1/2-way: plenty to do whn sme prog after 4 out: bmpd along after next to take 6th but nt on terms: nvr in chalng position* **6/1**[3]

0-11 **6** *4 ½* **Sona Sasta (IRE)**[56] 3629 8-11-6 128.................................. MrJJCodd 126
(David Pipe) *disp ld fr 3rd tl hdd 3 out: hanging after: wkng whn mstke 2 out* **11/1**

2213 **7** *13* **Pearlysteps**[46] 3803 8-11-6 140...................................... MrTGreenall 114
(Henry Daly) *settled midfield: blnd 5th: rdn and no prog on long run to 3 out: wl btn after* **11/1**

0UP- **8** *1 ¾* **Carlas Dream (IRE)**[20] 4317 9-10-13 110............................ MrBO'Neill 103
(Denis Paul Murphy, Ire) *many minor mstkes in rr: lost tch after 4 out: wl bhd next: kpt on fr last* **200/1**

34PU **9** *8* **Double Pride**[16] 4402 7-11-6 114..(b) MrDMurphy 101
(Alan King) *t.k.h: hld up in rr: sme prog on outer 21st: no imp on ldrs 3 out: wknd next* **100/1**

42- **10** *½* **Arabella Boy (IRE)**[21] 4299 6-11-6 131............................ MissNCarberry 101
(E Bolger, Ire) *hld up wl in rr: mstke 12th: no prog 4 out: wl bhd bef next* **12/1**

31U1 **11** *1 ¾* **Chamirey (FR)**[18] 4362 8-11-6 135.................................(b) MrROHarding 99
(Donald McCain) *t.k.h: disp ld 3rd to 11th: styd prom: mstke 18th: wknd rapidly 3 out* **14/1**

1306 **12** *37* **Regal Approach (IRE)**[39] 3950 8-11-6 121........................(p) MrCGreene 62
(Kim Bailey) *settled midfield: mstkes 4th: 13th and 20th: wknd u.p after 4 out: t.o* **50/1**

1013 **P** **Captain Americo (IRE)**[39] 3955 9-11-6 127............................ MrATDuff —
(James Ewart) *prom: jnd ldr 11th tl wknd rapidly after 19th: sn bhd: t.o bef 3 out: p.u bef 2 out* **16/1**

131P **U** **Major Malarkey (IRE)**[25] 4208 8-11-6 128.......................... MrJTCarroll —
(Nigel Twiston-Davies) *cl up whn blnd and uns rdr 3rd* **20/1**

1321 **P** **Aberdale (IRE)**[112] 2615 7-11-6 132..(t) MrAJBerry —
(Jonjo O'Neill) *settled in midfield: wknd 18th and sn last: t.o whn p.u bef 3 out* **10/1**

-414 **P** **On His Own (IRE)**[39] 3955 7-11-6 116................................ MrOGreenall —
(Howard Johnson) *pressed ldrs: nt fluent 17th: several mstkes after and lost pl fr 19th: t.o whn p.u bef 2 out* **33/1**

8m 20.7s (-1.10) **Going Correction** +0.25s/f (Yiel) **16** Ran SP% **118.2**
Speed ratings: **111,109,107,107,104 103,100,100,98,97 97,88,—,—,—,—**
toteswingers:1&2:£7.00, 1&3:£20.50, 2&3:£39.10 CSF £45.27 CT £835.27 TOTE £5.00: £2.30, £3.60, £4.40; EX 59.00 Trifecta £1257.00 Pool: £7,502.86 - 4.41 winning units..
Owner John Earls **Bred** Mrs R H Lalor **Trained** Trim, Co Meath
■ Gordon Elliott and Derek O'Connor's first Cheltenham Festival winner. Elliott completed a double with Carlito Brigante.
■ Stewards' Enquiry : Mr Derek O'Connor two-day ban: used whip in incorrect place (Mar 31,Apr 4)

FOCUS
Clerk Of the course Simon Claisse reported in the morning that there was light rain overnight, but not appreciable enough to measure. He felt the ground might be marginally quicker but essentially much like the previous day. \n\x\x This looked a fantastically open National Hunt Chase, where it appeared as though stamina would be needed. However, the early pace was far from strong, and although you did need to get every yard, the ability to stay 4m at a brisk gallop wasn't properly tested. Seven horse rated officially 140+ since 2002 had been beaten, and no outright favourite since 1992 had won this. Chicago Grey was value for further and is rated to his mark, with a personal best from Beshabar.

NOTEBOOK
Chicago Grey(IRE) was the highest-rated horse in the field. He had shown some good form over fences, especially his effort when chasing home RSA Chase favourite Time For Rupert at this course in December - Racing Post Chase winner Quinz was one place behind that day - but had been absent since finishing down the field in the Grade 1 Fort Leney at Punchestown in late November. Given a wonderfully confident ride towards the rear before moving through runners with ease, it was a perfect performance by horse and jockey to get to the front at exactly the right time, and claim victory. The only minus with him is that he could be difficult to place now once the handicapper raises him, and Graded races will have to be his best option. He may run in the Irish or Scottish National, though. (tchd 11-2)
Beshabar(IRE) didn't look the quickest at Doncaster last time when beating a horse whose jockey was banned for excessive use of the whip, as he took an age to get on top, and the early tempo here looked against him. The jockey dropped his mount in after being in the lead, but had the intelligence to get his mount close up with a circuit to go, and then quicken at the top of the hill to get his rivals off the bridle. The pair made the best of their way home but bumped into a horse with great form over fences, given a quality ride. The handicapper will no doubt raise Beshabar for this run, but he could be the type for the Grand National at Aintree next spring if connections can preserve his mark, or get it down a little beforehand, as long as he is ridden prominently, as he was here. (op 8-1)
Be There In Five(IRE) represented a trainer/jockey to be feared in this type of event, and had bounced back to his best last time in a small field at Kempton. A horse with scope, who beat RSA fancy Aiteen Thirtythree over hurdles, he was never far away when the race took shape, and looked dangerous after three out. He started to weaken heading to two out, though, and gave the impression that the trip was a little too far.

Alfa Beat(IRE)'s form was impossible to fault since his winning spree started and it just seemed to be a case of whether he stayed this trip (trainer was confident his horse would) as to how big his chance was. Absent since winning the 3m Kerry National in September, he was ridden to keep out of trouble wide of the field and just wasn't good enough and/or didn't get home. Connections said afterwards that their horse may go to Punchestown. (op 5-1 tchd 6-1 in a place)
Some Target(IRE) came into this off a victory at Punchestown over 3m4f at the end of November, so stamina looked most unlikely to prove a problem. Relatively lightly raced for his age, he may not have been ideally suited by being ridden out the back when the race was quickening, but he stayed on well without having any serious chance of winning. (op 13-2)
Sona Sasta(IRE) was a dual winner over hurdles but really came to life since going over fences. Not seen out since trouncing a field at Newbury in January, connections had booked a leading amateur rider and he gave his mount the right sort of ride up with the pace but, ultimately, the horse wasn't good enough to hold off the challengers late on while hanging.
Pearlysteps attracted some market support but made a few little jumping errors and couldn't get involved. (op 14-1)
Arabella Boy(IRE) had been regularly ridden by Nina Carberry, so the partnership was always going to be a solid one, but it was stamina that looked a possible issue. Thought to be a cross-country horse in the making, his chance went when he jumped slowly at one in the back straight on their final circuit, which knocked him backward when he needed to make ground. (op 14-1)
Chamirey(FR) finished third in last season's Pertemps Final for Alan King, so had some good festival form behind him already, and his chasing profile wasn't too bad apart from unseating his jockey on his third start over them. However, he raced too keenly when the pace wasn't strong, and it wasn't a big surprise to see him weaken in the latter stages after a mistake. (op 16-1)
Aberdale(IRE) was the selected runner from a stable that has a good record in this contest, but hadn't been out since winning at Wetherby in late November. A tongue-tie was put back on (first time over fences), but he ran poorly, being beaten a long way from home.

4803 NEPTUNE INVESTMENT MANAGEMENT NOVICES' HURDLE (REGISTERED AS BARING BINGHAM NOVICES' HURDLE) GRADE 1 (10 hdls) 2m 5f

2:05 (2:05) (Class 1) 4-Y-O+ **£57,010** (£21,390; £10,710; £5,340; £2,680; £1,340)

1 **1** **First Lieutenant (IRE)**[77] 3203 6-11-7 142 DNRussell 151+
(M F Morris, Ire) *chsd ldrs: rdn fr 2 out: n.m.r last: 2 l down on ldr sn after: rallied gamely u.p run-in: led last stride* **7/1**

-112 **2** *shd* **Rock On Ruby (IRE)**[46] 3806 6-11-7 147 (t) DarylJacob 150
(Paul Nicholls) *in tch: gd hdwy to chse ldrs 2 out: rdn and 1 l down whn lft w 2 l ld last: styd on wl u.p: ct last stride* **13/2**[3]

3 *4 1/2* **So Young (FR)**[35] 4016 5-11-7 140 RWalsh 148+
(W P Mullins, Ire) *hld up towards rr but in tch: gd hdwy to chse ldrs 2 out: styng on to press for 2nd whn blnd last: sn outpcd by ldng duo but kpt on wl for 3rd* **2/1**[1]

11 **4** *2 1/4* **Oscars Well (IRE)**[32] 4086 6-11-7 147 RMPower 151+
(Mrs John Harrington, Ire) *t.k.h: racd in tch: hdwy to chal 2 out: led sn after: 1 l ld and styng on whn mstke and sprawled bdly last: nt rcvr* **4/1**[2]

1223 **5** *1 1/2* **Megastar**[26] 4195 6-11-7 141 JamieMoore 142
(Gary Moore) *in rr and nt fluent 2nd and 3rd: hdwy 2 out: sn rdn and nvr rchd ldrs: nt fluent last: kpt on run-in* **16/1**

112 **6** *nse* **Minella Class (IRE)**[20] 4312 6-11-7 148 BarryGeraghty 142
(Nicky Henderson) *trckd ldrs: slt ld after 3 out: rdn last and sn hdd: wknd appr last* **10/1**

F211 **7** *2 1/2* **Aikman (IRE)**[20] 4312 7-11-7 136 HarryHaynes 139
(James Ewart) *led: nt fluent 3rd: hdd after 3 out: outpcd after 2 out: styd on again run-in* **33/1**

3326 **8** *1 1/4* **Ohio Gold (IRE)**[46] 3806 5-11-7 123 JoeTizzard 138
(Colin Tizzard) *in rr: hdwy and nt fluent 3 out: wnt sharply lft to ins appr 2 out and nt fluent: no prog after* **100/1**

1133 **9** *6* **Habbie Simpson**[46] 3806 6-11-7 136 RobertThornton 134
(Alan King) *in rr: hdwy and rdn 3 out: styng on to chse ldrs whn blnd 2 out: sn wknd* **25/1**

-141 **10** *6* **Highland Valley (IRE)**[31] 4091 6-11-7 134 JackDoyle 126
(Emma Lavelle) *chsd ldr to 4th: wknd 2 out* **50/1**

2112 **P** **Tornado Bob (IRE)**[25] 4198 6-11-7 143 JasonMaguire —
(Donald McCain) *trckd ldr 4th tl appr 3 out: wknd sn after: t.o whn p.u bef 2 out* **10/1**

6161 **F** **Accordintolawrence (IRE)**[47] 3789 5-11-7 118 FelixDeGiles —
(Charlie Longsdon) *in tch: hit 6th: rdn and wknd after 4 out: bhd whn fell next* **100/1**

5m 10.5s (-2.90) **Going Correction** +0.125s/f (Yiel) **12** Ran SP% **114.0**
Speed ratings (Par 117): **110,109,108,107,106 106,105,105,103,100 —,—**
toteswingers:1&2:£6.70, 1&3:£4.20, 2&3:£3.40 CSF £48.60 CT £123.43 TOTE £8.00: £2.10, £1.60, £1.60; EX 60.10 Trifecta £221.00 Pool: £13,348.14 - 44.69 winning units..
Owner Gigginstown House Stud **Bred** Mrs Mary O'Connor **Trained** Fethard, Co Tipperary

FOCUS

The smallest field in the 40-year history of this race, but a reasonable renewal nevertheless and one with abundant drama from the final flight to the line. It's unlikely any of these have Champion Hurdle aspirations, like Istabraq, Hardy Eustace or last year's winner Peddlers Cross, but most of this field will pay to follow next term. Long-term ante-post fancy Bobs Worth was surprisingly missing from the line-up, and in his absence the three Irish contenders dominated the market. \n\x\x The pace was less than strong, only gradually winding up on the second circuit, and most of the field were still close enough coming down the hill towards the third-last. The time was nine seconds outside the standard, confirming that the ground was not riding that quick. This was a fourth winner in the last six years for the Irish. First Lieutenant is on the upgrade but is rated 3lb below the level of an average winner. The next two were close to their mark and Oscars Well has been assessed as dead-heating.

NOTEBOOK

First Lieutenant(IRE) ◆ got up with a couple of strides to go. The form of his Grade 1 win at Leopardstown over Christmas was let down by the runner-up Zaidpour on Tuesday, but the return to this longer trip looked sure to be in his favour. Never far from the pace, he looked booked for second halfway up the run-in only to produce a strong burst to snatch the race. He seems to handle all types of ground, is a winner at the top level at 2m and 2m5f and promises to get further still. A high-class chasing prospect, he could emulate his owner's Weapon's Amnesty, another son of Presenting who won the RSA Chase a year after winning one of the novice hurdles at the meeting. (op 13-2)
Rock On Ruby(IRE), runner-up to Bobs Worth in a Grade 2 here in January, his only previous defeat over hurdles, was passed over by Ruby Walsh in favour of So Young. The shortest priced of the British contenders, he was one of a host to travel well and improved to chase the leaders off the turn. Keeping on when left in front shortly after the last, he was a couple of lengths to the good and not stopping, but was unable to contain the winner's late thrust and was touched off on the line. He could go to Aintree for the Grade 2 Mersey Novices' Hurdle over 2m4f. (op 15-2)
So Young(FR), who came in for a wave of support, represented the yard successful in recent seasons with Mikael D'Haguenet and Fiveforthree. Upped in grade after two easy wins in Ireland, he was staying on and in with a chance when he blundered quite badly at the last, having become unbalanced after a coming-together with the winner on the approach to the flight. He was no threat after his error but kept on well enough for third, and is set to go to Punchestown early in May. (tchd 9-4 in places)
Oscars Well(IRE) ◆ had already been successful at this level at Navan and Leopardstown, defeating Zaidpour in the latter race. After travelling powerfully, taking something of a hold, he was in front, but with three in close pursuit, when he stumbled badly after the last. Whether he would have won remains open to conjecture, but the incident - it can't really be called a mistake as he jumped the flight well - cost him valuable momentum. He remains a very bright prospect, another chasing type, and this was a fine run on ground that might have been quicker than ideal. (op 7-2)
Megastar, the Tolworth runner-up, has not quite attained the heights expected of him over hurdles but he is another high-class chasing prospect. Now 5lb better off with Rock On Ruby for a 6l beating at Newbury earlier in the season, he was held up in rear and, although improving to reach the heels of the leaders, could never quite land a telling blow.
Minella Class(IRE) took a narrow lead three out but was outpaced by the principals on the approach to the last. The Tolworth winner reversed Huntingdon form with Aikman on these 8lb better terms and ran entirely creditably without quite being good enough. Nicky Henderson's search for a winner of this race continues. (op 12-1)
Aikman(IRE) came here with a progressive profile but was gifted a very soft lead in the Sidney Banks at Huntingdon and his rider was again unable to claim his usual 3lb. After making the running he was swamped from the second-last.
Ohio Gold(IRE) is a consistent performer but has come up short in good company and remains a maiden over hurdles. He appeared to run as well as ever, albeit never seen with a serious chance, but may have been flattered by his proximity in this fairly steadily run race.
Habbie Simpson, third to Bobs Worth here on his last two starts, was just about close enough on the inside when a mistake two out ended his lingering chances. He should make a 3m chaser next term. (op 28-1 tchd 33-1)
Highland Valley(IRE) hurdled well enough but could not hold on to his prominent position when the race really developed. Most of his form has come in testing ground. (op 40-1)
Tornado Bob(IRE), from the stable of Peddlers Cross, tracked the pace before weakening right out of it and pulling up. He has been showing very useful form in soft ground this term and these faster conditions were not expected to pose him any problems. (tchd 9-1)
Accordintolawrence(IRE) was just starting to retreat when he came down three from home. (tchd 9-1)

4804 RSA CHASE GRADE 1 (19 fncs) 3m 110y

2:40 (2:40) (Class 1) 5-Y-O+

£74,113 (£27,807; £13,923; £6,942; £3,484; £1,742)

Form RPR

-411 **1** **Bostons Angel (IRE)**[32] 4084 7-11-4 146 RMPower 158+
(Mrs John Harrington, Ire) *trckd ldrs: wnt prom 15th: clsng whn lft in ld 3 out: drvn and hdd next: kpt on u.p to ld again flat: clung on to dwindling advantage nr fin* **16/1**

0-12 **2** *nk* **Jessies Dream (IRE)**[66] 3472 8-11-4 151 TimmyMurphy 156
(Gordon Elliott, Ire) *t.k.h: hld up in rr: prog 11th: clsd on ldrs 3 out and sn lft 2nd: rdn to ld 2 out: hung rt under maximum press and hdd flat: kpt on nr fin* **10/1**

111 **3** *3/4* **Wayward Prince**[39] 3955 7-11-4 147 APMcCoy 155
(Ian Williams) *in tch: mstke 9th: nt gng as wl as most fr 12th: u.p in 8th after 4 out: styd on dourly fr 3 out: clsd on tiring ldrs flat and snatched 3rd fin* **15/2**[2]

3-12 **4** *nse* **Magnanimity (IRE)**[32] 4084 7-11-4 145 DNRussell 155
(D T Hughes, Ire) *trckd ldrs: lost pl after mstkes 12th and 13th: renewed effrt after 4 out: rdn to chse ldng pair 2 out but nt qckn: kpt on to cl nr fin but lost 3rd fnl stride* **16/1**

2-11 **5** *5* **Time For Rupert (IRE)**[95] 2883 7-11-4 161 WillKennedy 155+
(Paul Webber) *settled in rr: nvr gng w any great purpose: shoved along fr 11th: no prog and last of remaining runners after 14th: plugged on fr 2 out: nvr nrr: b.b.v* **7/4**[1]

1511 **6** *8* **Master Of The Hall (IRE)**[25] 4199 7-11-4 148 BarryGeraghty 146
(Nicky Henderson) *trckd ldrs: blnd bdly 14th: styd in contention: disputing 2nd and clsng whn sltly hmpd 3 out: wknd and lost 3rd next* **16/1**

03 **7** *53* **Elysian Rock**[66] 3472 7-11-4 126 MJFerris 110
(M F Morris, Ire) *mde most tl mstke and hdd 12th: w ldr whn blnd 4 out: wkng whn terrible blunder 3 out: t.o and clambered over last* **150/1**

-1F1 **U** **The Giant Bolster**[46] 3803 6-11-4 146 RodiGreene —
(David Bridgwater) *last whn mstke 5th and eventually uns rdr* **20/1**

-F53 **F** **Mikael D'Haguenet (FR)**[32] 4084 7-11-4 155 RWalsh —
(W P Mullins, Ire) *settled midfield: blnd 7th: no prog whn fell 14th* **15/2**[2]

F6-F **F** **Quel Esprit (FR)**[32] 4084 7-11-4 145 PTownend —
(W P Mullins, Ire) *chsd ldng pair 7th: j.rt 9th: led 12th: lft clr 4 out: gng wl enough but being clsd down whn fell 3 out* **20/1**

-111 **P** **Wymott (IRE)**[40] 3921 7-11-4 148 (p) JasonMaguire —
(Donald McCain) *mstkes and tk little interest in rr: wknd 12th: t.o whn p.u bef 15th* **11/1**

-111 **P** **Aiteen Thirtythree (IRE)**[26] 4190 7-11-4 159 DarylJacob 136
(Paul Nicholls) *pressed ldr to 11th: rdn 4 out: wkng whn hmpd 3 out: poor 7th whn p.u bef last* **8/1**[3]

6m 16.55s (-1.75) **Going Correction** +0.25s/f (Yiel) **12** Ran SP% **116.3**
Speed ratings: **112,111,111,111,110 107,90,—,—,— —,—**
toteswingers:1&2:£24.90, 1&3:£15.20, 2&3:£8.00 CSF £158.99 CT £1307.03 TOTE £22.20: £4.90, £3.30, £2.50; EX 230.50 Trifecta £840.20 Pool: £14,124.89 - 12.44 winning units..
Owner E A P Scouller **Bred** P A D Scouller **Trained** Moone, Co Kildare
■ Robbie Power's first festival winner.
■ Stewards' Enquiry : Timmy Murphy six-day ban; excessive use of whip (Mar 30-Apr 4)

FOCUS

A decent RSA Chase but maybe not form to get carried away with, as the two fallers were still travelling well and Time For Rupert was clearly not at his best. A small step up from Bostons Angel but he's rated a bit below the mark of an average winner. Jessies Dream is rated to his mark with slight improvement from the next two.

NOTEBOOK

Bostons Angel(IRE), despite winning two Grade 1 chases coming into this, and holding most of his Irish contemporaries on form, was allowed to go off a long price, presumably because punters saw his recent victories had come on easy ground (his jockey reported afterwards that his mount had been winning in Ireland in spite of the going), but he came into the picture going well and showed a great attitude under pressure to hold on in a thrilling finish. 50/1 and pulled up in last season's Albert Bartlett, he has developed into a much better chaser than hurdler, and connections will no doubt have an eye on the Gold Cup next year, although Jessica Harrington, who enjoyed many a good Wednesday at the festival with Moscow Flyer in the past, had her horse down as Midlands National type. However, he will need to keep improving significantly to be a serious challenger for the big prize run on the Friday at this meeting, as this form looks below previous recent runnings of the race. He is unlikely to run again this season.
Jessies Dream(IRE) ◆ held a verdict over the winner when they met in the Grade 1 Drinmore in December, but the trip was the concern here for Gordon Elliott's charge, and his stamina didn't quite last out as well as Bostons Angel's, probably because he took a decent grip under Timmy Murphy throughout, even though there appeared to be a fair gallop set at least. Appearing to be travelling all over the winner rounding the home bend, and still in front heading to the last, and for a few strides after it, he got worried out of it in the final 100 yards while hanging right under pressure. He was beaten on merit, at this trip, and will be a serious performer over a shorter trip. He will contest the Grade 1 Growise Novices' Chase at Punchestown later this spring. The jockey got a six-day ban for excessive use of the whip and not giving his mount time to respond. (op 9-1)

Wayward Prince had yet to finish out of the first two since racing under rules (he also landed an Irish point) and had developed into an exciting staying novice when taking the Grade 1 Sefton Novices' Hurdle at Aintree last year. Unbeaten in three attempts over fences, including once at this course, connections felt the better ground here plus a stronger gallop would suit. However, he was never going well early before staying on nicely in the latter stages. It's not easy to know what to make of the performance, but he looks a a proper stayer and the Hennessy at Newbury later in the year seems a logical starting point. (op 8-1)

Magnanimity(IRE) had form mixed in with the first two, but had finished behind Boston Angel over the winter both times he faced him, and was held again after losing his place at a crucial stage when making mistakes. He looked tired in the final stages.

Time For Rupert(IRE) was seen by many as a festival banker after making a smooth transition to chasing, which comprised of two victories at this course. Runner-up in last year's World Hurdle, his fluent jumping over fences made him look difficult to oppose, but he failed to fire and didn't look near the horse he had done earlier in the season. His trainer Paul Webber initially felt that his horse's lack of experience counted against him (Time For Rupert missed the Argento Chase in January due to bad scope, which would have no doubt helped in that regard), but later reported he had a significant bleed and felt that he showed great courage in the circumstances. Official explanation: jockey said gelding never travelled; vet said gelding was found to be coughing (tchd 11-4 in places early op 9-4)

Master Of The Hall(IRE) ◆ made solid progression over fences, sometimes under the radar, until taking Ascot's Reynoldstown Novices' Chase in good style after his market rival made a mistake at around the halfway stage. He came with a purposeful effort heading to three out but wasn't able to sustain that momentum heading to the next and weakened. The way he travelled into contention stamped him down as an above-average performer, and he looks in the mould of his stablemate Riverside Theatre, a hugely talented performer at about 3m or shorter. Aintree's Mildmay Novices' Chase could be next for him. (tchd 20-1)

Mikael D'Haguenet(FR) was the enigma of this race, as his reputation had been dented with some moderate efforts since falling on his chasing debut in Ireland after a lengthy break. Reunited with Ruby Walsh for the first time over fences, he was still travelling strongly when coming down at the 14th and looked far from beaten at the time.\n (op 8-1 tchd 7-1)

Quel Esprit(FR) The bad-luck story of the race was undoubtedly \bQuel Esprit\p, who ran twice over hurdles at the festival last season with no success. His jumping had been indifferent throughout, some were bold and some were sloppy, but he was travelling strongly when ploughing through three out, giving his jockey no chance of staying in the saddle. Undoubtedly talented, his jumping will remain a concern until he can prove otherwise.\n (op 8-1 tchd 7-1)

Aiteen Thirtythree(IRE) always had a bit of a reputation after coming under rules, but it wasn't hard to argue that he'd been a little disappointing over hurdles considering how highly he was rated until landing his last run over them at Cheltenham. However, he had proved a different proposition since going over fences this season and could not have been any more impressive in both starts over them. One got the impression here, though, that outsider Elysian Rock didn't help his cause by taking him on in front, and the pair probably ruined their chances by going that bit too quickly early. That said, one would have expected the Nicholls-trained horse to last a bit longer than he did. Official explanation: jockey said gelding did not travel (op 8-1 tchd 7-1)

4805 SPORTINGBET.COM QUEEN MOTHER CHAMPION CHASE GRADE 1 (13 fncs) 2m

3:20 (3:20) (Class 1) 5-Y-O+

£182,432 (£68,448; £34,272; £17,088; £8,576; £4,288)

Form			Horse	Jockey	RPR
-223	**1**		**Sizing Europe (IRE)**[45] 3844 9-11-10 160 (Henry De Bromhead, Ire) *trckd ldr: led 7th: drvn fr 2 out: 1/2 l ld last: rdn and styd on strly to go clr run-in* **10/1**	AELynch	176+
-112	**2**	*5*	**Big Zeb (IRE)**[45] 3844 10-11-10 174 (C A Murphy, Ire) *trckd ldrs: mstke 8th: trckd wnr after 3 out: drvn and nt fluent 2 out: rallied and 1/2 l down last: outpcd run-in but styd on wl for clr 2nd* **3/1**[2]	BarryGeraghty	171
1-14	**3**	*4*	**Captain Cee Bee (IRE)**[77] 3204 10-11-10 158 (Edward P Harty, Ire) *in tch: hit 9th: rallied fr 3 out: styd on wl fr 2 out to take 3rd at last: kpt on run-in but no imp on ldng duo* **14/1**	APMcCoy	166
2111	**4**	*1 ½*	**Golden Silver (FR)**[24] 4248 9-11-10 168 (W P Mullins, Ire) *in rr but in tch: hdwy 3 out: styd on wl fr 2 out to dispute 3rd at last: nvr nr ldng duo and one pce run-in* **11/1**	PTownend	165
-332	**5**	*1 ¾*	**Somersby (IRE)**[53] 3675 7-11-10 170 (Henrietta Knight) *chsd ldrs: wnt 2nd 4 out: blnd next: styd in tch w ldrs u.p tl wknd bef last* **8/1**	RobertThornton	165
1-01	**6**	*3 ½*	**French Opera**[26] 4187 8-11-10 164 (Nicky Henderson) *chsd ldrs: blnd 4 out: wknd and hit 3 out* **22/1**	AndrewTinkler	162
1-46	**7**	*9*	**I'm So Lucky**[53] 3675 9-11-10 153 (bt[1]) (David Pipe) *hld up in rr: hdwy to cl on ldrs appr 3 out and travelling on sn after: shkn up and wknd qckly 2 out* **66/1**	TomScudamore	152
-111	**8**	*6*	**Master Minded (FR)**[53] 3675 8-11-10 175 (Paul Nicholls) *t.k.h: hld up in tch: stdy hdwy to trck ldrs 3 out: rdn sn after: 4 l off wnr in 3rd whn blnd bdly 2 out: nt rcvr and eased* **2/1**[1]	RWalsh	166+
6410	**9**	*½*	**Cornas (NZ)**[26] 4187 9-11-10 153 (Nick Williams) *hit 2nd: a towards rr: no ch fr 4 out* **150/1**	LeightonAspell	145
1-11	**10**	*nse*	**Woolcombe Folly (IRE)**[95] 2881 8-11-10 169 (Paul Nicholls) *towards rr but wl in tch: hit 4 out: sn rdn: wknd 3 out: no ch whn blnd 2 out* **7/1**[3]	DarylJacob	159+
-463	**10**	*dht*	**Mad Max (IRE)**[53] 3675 9-11-10 155 (Nicky Henderson) *tubed: led to 7th: wknd after 4 out* **20/1**	PCarberry	148

3m 54.92s (-3.08) **Going Correction** +0.25s/f (Yiel) **11 Ran SP% 117.3**

Speed ratings: **117,114,112,111,110 109,104,101,101,101 101**

toteswingers:1&2:£7.80, 1&3:£12.80, 2&3:£10.30 CSF £40.40 CT £431.19 TOTE £10.60: £2.60, £1.60, £3.50; EX 29.70 Trifecta £379.10 Pool: £20,541.27 - 40.08 winning units..

Owner Ann & Alan Potts Partnership **Bred** Mrs Angela Bracken **Trained** Knockeen, Co Waterford

FOCUS

A decent edition of this championship event, with the defending title holder taken on by a dual previous winner and last year's Arkle hero. Run at a sound pace and in a time just under three seconds slower than the standard, it was a race dominated by Irish stables, their four runners taking the first four places. Sizing Europe is rated up 10lb on last season's Arkle level and Big Zeb just a pound off last season's win. Master Minded is rated level with the third.

NOTEBOOK

Sizing Europe(IRE), last year's Arkle winner, had not tasted victory since but he got it right on the day that mattered with a fine display. In the first two all the way, he showed ahead at the water jump but there were plenty close enough behind turning to face up to the final two fences. The runner-up had got to within half a length at the last, but Sizing Europe stayed on really strongly to forge clear He was tried over 3m earlier in the season, finishing second to Gold Cup runners China Rock and Kauto Star, before being found wanting back at 2m behind Big Zeb and Golden Silver in the Tied Cottage at Punchestown. Well suited by good ground, he is likely to head to Punchestown next month, with the Irish version of the Champion Chase the most obvious target, but connections would not run scared of stepping him back up to 3m at some stage. His success means that all the last 13 Arkle winners to have run here 12 months later have made the first three, and he is the fifth of them to win both races. (op 8-1 tchd 11-1)

Big Zeb(IRE) ran a fine race in his attempt to record back-to-back victories but found one too strong on the day. After travelling well he overcame a small error two out to jump the last just half a length down, but he could only keep on at the same pace up the hill as the winner found more. His win a year ago came on going officially described as good, but his trainer thought that this ground was a little dead for his charge. He will take on Sizing Europe again at Punchestown. (op 10-3)

Captain Cee Bee(IRE) didn't like the heavy conditions when fourth behind Big Zeb and Golden Silver at Leopardstown and was another for whom this dead ground may not have been ideal. The 2008 Supreme Novices' winner, he broke a blood vessel when favourite behind Sizing Europe in last year's Arkle. He rallied after clouting the ninth but could make no impression on his compatriots after staying on into third place. (op 12-1 tchd 11-1)

Golden Silver(FR) closed on the downhill run to the third-last and kept staying on without ever promising to win this. Again held by Big Zeb, as on four of their five previous meetings, he is ideally served by real winter ground and has enjoyed an excellent season with four Grade 2 wins. This run confirmed that he does act around Cheltenham, but while he may struggle to win a race of this nature he should enjoy plenty more success back home in Ireland. (op 10-1 tchd 12-1)

Somersby(IRE) had been placed at his two previous Festivals, running Sizing Europe to three parts of a length in the Arkle a year ago. With Robert Thornton taking over from Hadden Frost, his regular jockey this season, he ran here rather than in the 5f longer Ryanair Chase. The youngest horse in the race, he was under pressure in second when he went through the third-last and weakened between the last two fences. He is well capable of winning races at the top level but is surely going to have to go back up in trip. (tchd 9-1)

French Opera successful in a rearranged Game Spirit Chase at Newbury, was unable to lead in this better company. He made a bad mistake at the ditch at the top of the hill and could never recover, although to his credit he was keeping on again late. He is likely to run at Aintree. (op 20-1)

I'm So Lucky, who had a lot to find on official ratings, was tried in blinkers for the first time. Reverting to hold-up tactics, he looked a threat on the home turn, only for his effort to peter out shortly afterwards. The end-of-season Sandown race he won last term looks a suitable target. (op 100-1)

Master Minded(FR) failed for the second time to add to his wins in 2008 and 2009. A well-beaten fourth in a troubled campaign last year, he looked back to something like his best this season following a breathing operation, but only scrambled home as Somersby closed in the Victor Chandler at Ascot last time. Improving to track the leaders, he was in third place but under pressure when he hit the second-last halfway up, dropping right back through the field and eased up by Walsh. The error was reminiscent of the one he made in last season's Game Spirit at Newbury, and he did well to stand up. Like 12 months ago, connections were of the opinion that the ground was too quick for him. He is likely to be stepped back up in trip now, with the Melling Chase at Aintree the target, ground permitting. He was beaten by Voy Por Ustedes in that race three years ago, following his sensational 19l victory over the same horse here. (op 3-1 tchd 10-3 in a place)

Cornas(NZ) was never a factor and, likeable and talented though he is, is not up to this level. (tchd 125-1)

Mad Max(IRE), who has been tubed since his last appearance, made a mistake at the ditch in the back straight not long after he had lost his lead to Sizing Europe. He won at Aintree last spring and it would be no surprise to see him in the Melling Chase next month. (tchd 13-2)

Woolcombe Folly(IRE), well beaten in last year's Arkle, was an impressive winner in a fast time of a handicap at the December meeting here off 154, and was officially raised 15lb for that. He missed his intended prep in the Game Spirit after coughing and remained something of an unknown quantity going into this. Never close enough to mount a challenge, he was held when blundering two from home, where his stablemate Master Minded also nearly came down. (tchd 13-2)

4806 CORAL CUP (HANDICAP HURDLE) GRADE 3 (10 hdls) 2m 5f

4:00 (4:00) (Class 1) 4-Y-O+

£39,907 (£14,973; £7,497; £3,738; £1,876; £938)

Form			Horse	Jockey	RPR
2-10	**1**		**Carlito Brigante (IRE)**[46] 3823 5-11-0 142 ow2 (t) (Gordon Elliott, Ire) *mostly trckd clr ldng pair: cl up fr 5th: wnt 2nd bef 2 out gng strly: led bef last and in command whn lft clr there: easily* **16/1**	DNRussell	157+
-252	**2**	*6*	**Bothy**[26] 4188 5-10-7 138 (Brian Ellison) *prom in chsng gp: disp cl 3rd 3 out: rdn in 3rd after 2 out: lft 2nd last: no ch w wnr* **12/1**	DannyCook(3)	142
-604	**3**	*½*	**Orsippus (USA)**[27] 4169 5-10-8 136 (Michael Smith) *hld up in midfield: prog on inner after 5th: in tch whn hit 3 out: rdn and effrt 2 out: lft 3rd last: styd on to press runner-up nr fin* **33/1**	DJCondon	140
3441	**4**	*2 ¼*	**Battle Group**[18] 4359 6-10-9 137 (David Pipe) *hld up in midfield: mstke 6th and shuffled bk: effrt again 3 out: 10th and last of those w any ch after 2 out: hanging bdly lft bef last but styd on wl to take 4th flat* **33/1**	TomScudamore	138
0	**5**	*4 ½*	**Solix (FR)**[26] 4188 5-11-10 152 (Nicky Henderson) *prom bhd ldrs: mstke 5th: lost pl 3 out: effrt again 2 out: no imp bef last: fdd* **25/1**	BarryGeraghty	151
2553	**6**	*1 ¼*	**Dantari (IRE)**[39] 3947 6-10-0 128 (Evan Williams) *led and clr to 5th: hdd 3 out: fading whn hit 2 out* **25/1**	JamieMoore	124
1/20	**7**	*1 ¾*	**Walkon (FR)**[26] 4188 6-11-12 154 (Alan King) *wl plcd bhd ldrs: cl enough 3 out: rdn whn mstke 2 out: grad fdd* **16/1**	RobertThornton	149
-636	**8**	*2 ¾*	**Arcalis**[46] 3807 11-10-10 138 (Howard Johnson) *wl in tch: 10th whn blnd 5th and lost pl: struggling in rr after 7th: styd on after 2 out* **20/1**	BrianHughes	133+
-0F4	**9**	*1 ½*	**Pistolet Noir (FR)**[22] 4270 5-10-6 137 (Paul Nicholls) *hld up in rr: no prog and struggling after 7th: styd on after 2 out: nrst fin* **33/1**	IanPopham(3)	126
/P3-	**10**	*3 ¾*	**Aachen**[410] 3739 7-9-12 131 (Venetia Williams) *mostly in midfield: rdn and no prog fr 3 out: sn lost tch w ldrs* **33/1**	RTDunne(5)	117
2	**11**	*nk*	**Call The Police (IRE)**[28] 4153 8-10-12 140 (W P Mullins, Ire) *hld up in midfield: effrt 3 out: chsng ldrs whn hit 2 out: no prog after: wknd bef last* **7/2**[1]	RWalsh	127
3520	**12**	*¾*	**Mohanad (IRE)**[15] 1967 5-10-1 129 (Sheena West) *settled in midfield: lost pl 6th: effrt again 3 out: sn lost tch w ldrs* **100/1**	JamieGoldstein	113
10-2	**13**	*4 ½*	**Trenchant**[17] 4373 6-11-7 149 (b) (Alan King) *wl in rr: last at 5th: pushed along and no prog after 7th: modest late prog* **33/1**	WayneHutchinson	129
4443	**14**	*½*	**Busker Royal**[25] 4202 8-9-13 130 (Nicky Henderson) *mstke 1st: hld up wl in rr: effrt and sme prog on outer bef 3 out: wknd 2 out* **40/1**	RichardKilloran(3)	109
-325	**15**	*nk*	**Straw Bear (USA)**[25] 4221 10-10-7 135 (Nick Gifford) *mstke 1st: a wl in rr: last at 7th: no ch 3 out: modest late prog* **33/1**	LiamTreadwell	115
1-11	**16**	*nk*	**Aegean Dawn**[117] 2498 6-11-0 145 (Nicky Henderson) *hld up in rr: rdn after 6th and struggling: prog on outer on long run to 3 out: chsd ldrs 2 out: wknd qckly bef last* **5/1**[2]	DavidBass(3)	124

2 **17** 3 1/2 **Ballyhaunis**[52] 3708 6-10-7 **135**....(t) PTownend 110
(W P Mullins, Ire) *nvr bttr than midfield: no prog whn blnd 3 out: wknd* **10/1**[3]
1P/0 **18** 3 **Lightning Strike (GER)**[25] 4209 8-10-1 **129**.... AidanColeman 101
(Venetia Williams) *prom in chsng gp: rdn and wknd fr 3 out* **14/1**
4-F0 **19** 1 1/2 **Song Of Songs**[4] 4727 9-9-11 **128**....(v) RichieMcLernon(3) 99
(Jonjo O'Neill) *a wl in rr: no ch fr 3 out* **66/1**
6051 **20** 18 **Tiger O'Toole (IRE)**[53] 3676 6-10-9 **137**.... PaulMoloney 90
(Evan Williams) *hld up in last trio: no prog after 7th: no ch whn blnd 3 out: t.o* **20/1**
P-42 **21** 3 1/4 **Lord Ragnar (IRE)**[39] 3938 8-10-1 **129**.... AndrewTinkler 79
(Nicky Henderson) *nt fluent: wl in rr: rapid prog on outer after 7th to chse ldrs: wknd as rapidly bef 3 out: t.o* **50/1**
-124 **F** **For Non Stop (IRE)**[77] 3197 6-10-7 **135**.... DarylJacob 140
(Nick Williams) *chsd clr ldr and clr of rest to 5th: led 3 out: rdn and hdd bef last: 2 l down whn fell last* **5/1**[2]
5m 9.30s (-4.10) **Going Correction** +0.125s/f (Yiel) 22 Ran SP% **132.5**
Speed ratings (Par 113): **112,109,109,108,106 106,105,104,104,102 102,102,100,100,100 100,98,97,97,90 89,—**
toteswingers:1&2:£45.70, 1&3:£207.30, 2&3:£106.90 CSF £177.61 CT £6212.67 TOTE £17.80: £3.20, £2.70, £8.50, £8.70; EX 185.50 Trifecta £5309.20 Pool: £15,844.11 - 2.20 winning units..
Owner Gigginstown House Stud **Bred** Ballylinch Stud **Trained** Trim, Co Meath
■ Stewards' Enquiry : D N Russell three-day ban: weighed-in 2lb heavy (Mar 30-Apr 1)

FOCUS
Along with the County Hurdle run on Friday, this is undoubtedly one of the hottest hurdle races of the whole season. The main body of the field completely ignored Dantari's trailblazing tactics and rode their mounts conservatively. The pack descended on the leader three from home and any number of them came their cruising. The winner's time was over a second quicker than First Lieutenant's in the Neptune earlier in the card. Carlito Brigante was up a stone on his previous best and there may be more to come. The next three and faller For Non Stop are rated to their marks in a solid renewal.

NOTEBOOK
Carlito Brigante(IRE) had started his season on a high over hurdles but his form had dwindled since. Favourite for the previous year's Triumph Hurdle, he'd had an operation on his breathing during the winter and connections felt that this was the first time he'd got his ground, and he duly built on it. Today was clearly the day, the jockey more or less said that afterwards, and after cruising up to challenge he was holding his closest pursuer when he was left clear despite Davy Russell putting up 2lb overweight. Chasing next season is on the agenda.
Bothy couldn't be faulted on his two tries over hurdles this season, as he'd gone mighty close to landing a couple of big handicap prizes. Trying 4f further than he'd ever run over, this was another solid effort but he was unlikely to have finished runner-up had For Non Stop not fallen. That said, he must be a pleasure to own and is all heart. (tchd 11-1)
Orsippus(USA) ◆ showed plenty of ability as a juvenile hurdler, winning a Grade 1 at Aintree, but he had found this season quite tough as a result. Third in last year's Fred Winter and attempting this sort of trip for the first time, he kept on well reunited with David Condon and showed a lot of promise for the spring.
Battle Group has looked to have a mind of his own in the past, but is talented when putting it all in, as he proved at Newcastle last time. He came home well despite hanging, but was never going to win. (tchd 40-1 in a place)
Solix(FR) was well beaten on his first start for Nicky Henderson in the Totesport Trophy after showing a good level of ability in France, but improved on that performance again under a big weight. His connections will undoubtedly be looking forward to chasing with him. (tchd 28-1)
Dantari(IRE) is a confirmed front-runner and employed his trail-blazing style once again, but the main body of the field completely ignored his tactics and rode their mounts conservatively. As was the case at Sandown on his previous start, he showed tremendous resilience once joined and battled on for a game sixth placing.
Walkon(FR) made an encouraging return to action after a 660-day layoff at Ascot when runner-up to Tiger O'Toole, but didn't reproduce that sort of performance next time when well beaten in the Totesport Trophy. He got closer to Solix here, however, so this is a step back in the right direction. (op 20-1)
Arcalis has been a regular at this meeting for years and, of course, achieved his finest moment when taking the 2005 Supreme Novices' Hurdle. Runner-up in last year's County Hurdle, he made a crucial mistake at the wrong time but ran on in his usual good style in the closing stages. (op 16-1)
Pistolet Noir(FR) came from miles behind and kept plugging on when others were faltering. (op 28-1 tchd 40-1 in a place)
Call The Police(IRE) sprung to prominence with a fine second in the MCR Hurdle at Leopardstown (his first run for Wille Mullins after a 399-day break) and then duly bolted up in a non-handicap race next time. The trip looked of some concern in a race that was always going to be run quickly, and one got the impression that he didn't stay considering how quickly he weakened. (op 4-1)
Aegean Dawn, forced to miss the Imperial Hurdle recently after schooling badly, was so impressive earlier in the season, but was racing off a 26lb higher mark here than at Ascot. He looked to be in trouble plenty early enough, even allowing for the weight rise, and only made a token bid towards the outside of the field before fading. (op 6-1)
Ballyhaunis had some solid form in Irish novice hurdles, and there certainly wasn't any disgrace being beaten by potentially top-class Hidden Cyclone (a winner twice since) on his last performance. However, this sort of race appeared beyond him at this stage and he can be given another chance.
Lightning Strike(GER), available at 66-1 in a place the previous day, was ridden prominently but dropped right out. (tchd 25-1 early op 16-1)
For Non Stop(IRE)looked potentially well handicapped on his effort behind Grands Crus at this course in mid November despite being 10lb higher (Nick William's horse was a disappointing favourite for the Grade 1 Challow Hurdle afterwards) and appeared to have been laid out for this. Well placed under a positive ride, he looked all set to take the prize,It was bad luck on all connections of For Non Stop that he came down at the last, as he'd been given a great ride by Daryl Jacob and didn't deserve to come away with nothing.\n (op 6-1)

4807 FRED WINTER JUVENILE H'CAP HURDLE GRADE 3 (8 hdls) 2m 110y
4:40 (4:40) (Class 1) 4-Y-O
£34,206 (£12,834; £6,426; £3,204; £1,608; £804)

Form RPR
00 **1** **What A Charm (IRE)**[21] 4295 4-10-6 **115**....(p) PTownend 121+
(A L T Moore, Ire) *mid-div 3rd: hdwy to chse ldrs 3 out: styd on u.p to chse ldr appr last whn str chal and bmpd: led sn after: hld on wl u.p* **9/1**
133 **2** *nk* **Kumbeshwar**[18] 4350 4-11-7 **133**.... CharlieHuxley(3) 139
(Alan King) *t.k.h: led after 1st: rdn 2 out: edgd rt u.p whn jnd last: hdd sn after but styd chalng tl no ex cl home* **33/1**
2512 **3** 4 1/2 **Dhaafer**[19] 4331 4-10-10 **119**....(p) RobertThornton 122
(Alan King) *in tch: chsd ldrs fr 4th: rdn and ev ch 3 out: chsd ldr next: swtchd lft appr last: styd on same pce run-in* **16/1**
23 **4** 1 3/4 **Plan A (IRE)**[47] 3795 4-11-8 **131**.... PCarberry 132
(Gordon Elliott, Ire) *hld up in rr: hdwy on ins 3 out: chsd ldrs next: rdn to dispute 3rd appr last: one pce run-in* **4/1**[1]
3144 **5** 3 1/2 **Jubail (IRE)**[21] 4283 4-10-12 **121**.... WayneHutchinson 118
(Alan King) *chsd ldrs: rdn 3 out: wknd appr last* **33/1**
335 **6** 1 1/2 **Rock Of Deauville (IRE)**[21] 4291 4-10-3 **112**....(t) HarrySkelton 110
(Paul Nicholls) *in rr: hdwy 3 out: rdn and nt fluent 2 out: btn whn mstke last* **33/1**
33 **7** 2 **Tenor Nivernais (FR)**[43] 3874 4-11-1 **124**.... AidanColeman 118
(Venetia Williams) *in rr: pushed along and no prog 3 out: stl plenty to do fr next and 10th appr last: styd on run-in: gng on nr fin* **11/2**[2]
0320 **8** 3/4 **Kingdom Of Munster (IRE)**[5] 4358 4-10-0 **109**....(v) BrianHughes 103
(Richard Fahey) *in rr: hdwy 3 out: drvn to chse ldrs fr next: wknd bef last* **100/1**
261 **9** 3/4 **Paintball (IRE)**[21] 4288 4-11-0 **123**.... RichardJohnson 118+
(Charlie Longsdon) *chsd ldrs: chalng whn mstke 4 out: stl ev ch next: wknd bef last* **15/2**[3]
162 **10** 3/4 **The Starboard Bow**[38] 3967 4-11-3 **126**.... PeterBuchanan 119
(Lucinda Russell) *mid-div: rdn and outpcd 3 out: kpt on again run-in* **100/1**
2P13 **11** 1 3/4 **Harry Hunt**[21] 4283 4-11-0 **123**.... JodieMogford 114
(Graeme McPherson) *led tl after 1st: chsd ldrs to 3 out: wknd after next* **66/1**
2643 **12** 1 3/4 **Tom Wade (IRE)**[14] 4419 4-9-11 **109** oh4.... SamTwiston-Davies(3) 99
(John Harris) *in rr: hit 1st: brief effrt 3 out: nvr in contention* **100/1**
1124 **13** 2 1/4 **Beyond (IRE)**[172] 1610 4-11-0 **123**.... DNRussell 110
(Evan Williams) *in tch: rdn 3 out: wknd next* **16/1**
041 **14** 1 3/4 **Kayef (GER)**[26] 4192 4-10-11 **120**.... TomScudamore 106
(Michael Scudamore) *in rr and blnd 2nd: sme hdwy 4th: wknd 3 out* **16/1**
1234 **15** 4 **Akula (IRE)**[46] 3802 4-11-2 **125**.... ColinBolger 107
(Mark H Tompkins) *nvr bttr than mid-div: mstke and wknd 4 out* **40/1**
522 **16** 7 **Titan De Sarti (FR)**[56] 3624 4-11-6 **129**.... APMcCoy 108
(Nicky Henderson) *hit 4th: nvr beyond mid-div* **8/1**
P01 **17** 4 1/2 **Whitby Jack**[38] 3958 4-11-9 **132**.... JamieMoore 103
(Gary Moore) *chsd ldrs tl wknd qckly 2 out* **14/1**
113 **18** 3/4 **Lady Willa (IRE)**[31] 4092 4-10-3 **115**.... TommyPhelan(3) 86
(Mark Gillard) *chsd ldrs to 3 out* **100/1**
2210 **19** 4 1/2 **Mr Muddle**[18] 4350 4-10-10 **119**.... AndrewGlassonbury 88
(Sheena West) *chsd ldrs: hit 3rd and sn rdn: wknd 4 out* **100/1**
6032 **20** 14 **Looks Like Slim**[21] 4283 4-10-8 **117**.... DominicElsworth 71
(Ben De Haan) *a in rr* **33/1**
0444 **21** 6 **L'Eminence Grise (IRE)**[25] 4203 4-10-7 **116**.... DarylJacob 65
(Nick Williams) *chsd ldrs to 3 out* **20/1**
315 **22** 7 **Mark Twain (IRE)**[46] 3802 4-11-6 **129**....(t) JasonMaguire 71
(Kim Bailey) *a in rr* **100/1**
3 **P** **Celtus (FR)**[18] 4353 4-11-9 **132**.... BarryGeraghty —
(Nicky Henderson) *hld up in mid-div: hdwy 4 out: chsd ldrs fr next: stl in tch but rdn whn blnd 2 out: nt rcvr: eased and p.u bef last* **12/1**
3m 58.5s (-3.50) **Going Correction** +0.125s/f (Yiel) **23** Ran SP% **126.7**
Speed ratings: **113,112,110,109,108 107,106,106,105,105 104,103,102,102,100 96,94,94,92,85 82,79,—**
CSF £285.54 CT £4628.17 TOTE £10.80: £2.50, £7.30, £4.10, £2.20; EX 520.80 Trifecta £9156.30 Part won. Pool: £12,373.47 - 0.50 winning units..
Owner C Jones **Bred** Kenilworth House Stud **Trained** Naas, Co Kildare
■ Paul Townend's first festival winner.

FOCUS
The seventh year of this juvenile handicap, and not a strong renewal. The only one of the five-day declarations to come out was Indian Daudaie, who would have been topweight, and the weights were raised 5lb as a result. Half of the field, the winner included, wouldn't have got into recent, stronger editions of the race, and there was a much greater spread of abilities on show this year. Only five of the field had run in a handicap before. The first two are rated up 12lb, with improvement from the next pair too.

NOTEBOOK
What A Charm(IRE) followed Gaspara and Silk Affair as female winners of this race and was one of just two fillies in this line-up. She was also the only runner not to have made the frame over hurdles, having finishing unplaced in all three of her runs, although two of them were in Grade 2 company. She was a smart performer on the Flat though, successful in the Leopardstown November Handicap off 98 on her final start, and the cheekpieces she wore then were used for the first time over hurdles.\nAlways withing striking distance of the lead, she took a bump from the runner-up approaching the last then found plenty to hold him off up the hill, the pair coming clear. There should be more improvement to come from her and the David Nicholson race could be a potential target here in future, as she promises to get further. Official explanation: trainer said, regarding apparent improvement in form, that the filly appreciated the better ground and the fitting of cheek pieces. (op 8-1 tchd 10-1)
Kumbeshwar was one of just three in this field to have been declared at the five-day stage for the Triumph Hurdle. Pulling his way into the lead early, he jinked left going to the last, giving the winner a bump, and went down fighting up the hill. This was a good effort considering how free he had been, and he was facing a stiff task attempting to give away 18lb to the filly. He handled the drier ground well and there could be more improvement in him tried in headgear, which he wore on the Flat.
Dhaafer, the runner-up's stablemate, ran well for a long way but was carried slightly wide by Kumbeshwar on the home turn and could not find a change of pace from there. This was a solid run in the first-time cheekpieces and he saw out the stiffer test well, as he had been promising to do.
Plan A(IRE), well backed for this, broke his duck at Gowran on his first run since leaving the Quinlans' Newmarket yard. Another who had been declared for the Triumph, he made smooth progress coming down the hill but couldn't race on with the leaders approaching the last, where he landed flat-footed. The ground was perhaps not as soft as he would have liked. (tchd 9-2)
Jubail(IRE) ran a solid race on ground that suits and was the third Alan King runner in the first five, coming on for his return from a break at Doncaster, where he had finished behind two he beat here. Earlier this season he had a verdict over Plan A at Kempton to his name, but he could not confirm the form with that improved performer despite being 10lb better off. (tchd 40-1 in a places)
Rock Of Deauville(IRE), at the back when slightly hampered at the second, improved three out but could not sustain it. He had disappointed previously but the tongue tie contributed towards this better run.
Tenor Nivernais(FR) had taken on older horses in his two races since coming to Britain and Via Galilei, a place ahead of him at Taunton, boosted the form when second in the Imperial Cup. He was at the back and going nowhere at the top of the hill, but stayed on strongly when meeting the rising ground. (op 6-1)
Kingdom Of Munster(IRE), who was very useful for Aidan O'Brien at two, travelled well in the reapplied visor but could not quicken up from the home turn.
Paintball(IRE)'s Ludlow win had been boosted by runner-up King's Realm, and he was well supported. He had his chance, but a mistake four out didn't help and he was held from the second-last. (op 8-1)
The Starboard Bow was never a factor, but he was staying on and is worth a try over further, as he gets 2m well on the Flat.
Titan De Sarti(FR) was never in the hunt and failed to run his race. (op 10-1)
Whitby Jack travelled well for a long way only to fade two from home. He looked harshly handicapped on what he had achieved. (op 10-1)

Celtus(FR) was beginning to drop away when he blundered two out and was soon pulled up.

4808 WEATHERBYS CHAMPION BUMPER (STANDARD OPEN NATIONAL HUNT FLAT RACE) GRADE 1 — 2m 110y

5:15 (5:15) (Class 1) 4-6-Y-O

£31,355 (£11,764; £5,890; £2,937; £1,474; £737)

Form	Pos	Dist	Horse / Trainer / Comment	Jockey	SP	RPR
1	1		**Cheltenian (FR)**[33] 4055 5-11-5 122 (Philip Hobbs) *wl plcd: trckd ldrs gng easily over 3f out: clsd and shkn up to ld wl over 1f out: rdn clr*	RichardJohnson	**14/1**	138+
11	2	5	**Destroyer Deployed**[17] 4376 5-11-5 117 (Tim Vaughan) *chsd ldr after 4f: disp ld over 3f out: sn drvn: hdd wl over 1f out: styd on but readily outpcd*	AidanColeman	**66/1**	131
2	3	4 ½	**Aupcharlie (IRE)**[10] 4518 5-11-5 122 (P E Collins, Ire) *hld up wl in rr: gd prog on wd outside fr 5f out to dispute ld over 3f out: hdd and fdd wl over 1f out*	MrJPMcKeown	**33/1**	126
2-	4	4 ½	**Go All The Way (IRE)**[328] 5351 6-11-5 123 (Nigel Twiston-Davies) *hld up wl in rr: rdn and struggling over 4f out: prog u.p on inner fr 3f out: kpt on but no further hdwy over 1f out*	PaddyBrennan	**16/1**	122
112	5	1 ¾	**Cinders And Ashes**[74] 3294 4-10-12 121 (Donald McCain) *prom: prog to dispute ld over 3f out: hdd & wknd wl over 1f out*	JasonMaguire	**14/1**	114
211	6	shd	**Ericht (IRE)**[26] 4191 5-11-5 133 (Nicky Henderson) *trckd ldrs: pushed along and cl enough over 3f out: nt qckn over 2f out: wl outpcd after*	BarryGeraghty	**5/1**[1]	121
1-	7	¾	**Divine Rhapsody (IRE)**[330] 5301 5-11-5 121 (P J Rothwell, Ire) *hld up towards rr: rdn 4f out and struggling: only 12th 2f out: styd on wl after: nrst fin*	PCarberry	**13/2**[2]	120
15	8	¾	**Cousin Khee**[74] 3294 4-10-12 113 (Hughie Morrison) *hld up in midfield: chsd ldrs over 3f out: outpcd over 2f out: hanging and fdd over 1f out*	SamThomas	**33/1**	112
1	9	1	**Oscar Magic (IRE)**[18] 4356 4-10-12 117 (Nigel Twiston-Davies) *wl in rr whn hung rt bnd after 4f: stl wl in rr and drvn 5f out: late prog: nvr a threat*	SamTwiston-Davies	**12/1**	111
011	10	½	**The Tracey Shuffle**[18] 4363 5-11-5 116 (David Pipe) *led to over 3f out: steadily wknd*	(p) TomScudamore	**50/1**	118
2-	11	½	**Double Double (FR)**[290] 542 5-11-5 123 (Charles O'Brien, Ire) *set off in detached last: stl wl out the bk 4f out: bmpd along and kpt on steadily after: hopeless task*	MrPJMcMahon	**20/1**	118
1211	12	nk	**Saint Luke (IRE)**[40] 3936 6-11-5 117 (Peter Bowen) *trckd ldrs: stl wl in tch 4f out: wknd over 2f out*	TomO'Brien	**66/1**	117
	13	6	**Star Neuville (FR)**[78] 3178 5-11-5 120 (John Joseph Hanlon, Ire) *hld up in midfield on outer: prog 5f out: rdn to dispute ld over 3f out to over 2f out: wknd qckly*	APMcCoy	**14/1**	114
111	14	4 ½	**Dark Glacier (IRE)**[20] 4308 6-11-5 119 (Chris Grant) *chsd ldr 4f: lost pl bdly on inner 1/2-way and wl in rr whn hmpd sn after: no ch fnl 3f*	DenisO'Regan	**50/1**	108
	15	1 ¾	**Tusa Eire (IRE)**[46] 3829 5-11-5 113 (W P Mullins, Ire) *t.k.h: hld up in midfield: pushed along and no prog downhill over 3f out: rdn and wknd 2f out*	RWalsh	**20/1**	106
31	16	7	**Knockalongi**[63] 3511 5-11-5 118 (Oliver Sherwood) *a wl in rr: no ch fnl 4f*	LeightonAspell	**100/1**	102
	17	7	**Dynamic Approach (IRE)**[150] 1898 5-11-5 118 (Edward U Hales, Ire) *prom tl lost pl rapidly 5f out: sn wl in rr*	MrRPMcNamara	**33/1**	94
12	18	1 ¾	**Bygones In Brid (IRE)**[26] 4191 5-11-5 128 (Alan King) *hld up: a wl in rr: lost tch w ldrs over 4f out*	RobertThornton	**20/1**	95
11	19	6	**Knight Pass (IRE)**[70] 3399 5-11-5 128 (Warren Greatrex) *hld up in midfield: in tch but pushed along over 4f out: wknd 3f out*	WayneHutchinson	**7/1**[3]	92
2-1	20	12	**Master Murphy (IRE)**[124] 2355 6-11-5 115 (Jane Walton) *pressed ldrs tl wknd rapidly over 4f out*	AlistairFindlay	**100/1**	76
1	21	11	**Felix Yonger (IRE)**[49] 3752 5-11-5 113 (Howard Johnson) *hld up in midfield towards outer: wknd over 3f out*	BrianHughes	**66/1**	66
	22	21	**Raise The Beat**[150] 1898 6-11-5 129 (C A Murphy, Ire) *t.k.h: hld up in midfield: in tch 5f out: wknd rapidly sn after: t.o*	(t) MrMPFogarty	**8/1**	47
1	23	5	**Twentyfourcarat (IRE)**[116] 2518 6-11-5 119 (Ian Williams) *dropped to last bef 1/2-way and sn wl t.o*	TimmyMurphy	**25/1**	43
	P		**Lord Gale (IRE)**[31] 4111 5-11-5 120 (W P Mullins, Ire) *uns rdr gng to post: tk fierce hold: hld up in midfield: wknd over 4f out: t.o whn p.u 1f out*	MrPWMullins	**20/1**	—

3m 51.85s (-4.55) **Going Correction** +0.125s/f (Yiel)

WFA 4 from 5yo+ 7lb **24** Ran SP% **129.3**

Speed ratings: **115,112,110,108,107 107,107,106,106,106 105,105,102,100,99 96,93,92,89,84 78,69,66,—**

toteswingers:1&2:£112.30, 1&3:£244.30, 2&3:£459.70. CSF £762.55 CT £25756.10 TOTE £16.90: £5.60, £17.00, £14.20; EX 1392.00 TRIFECTA Not won..

Owner R S Brookhouse **Bred** Jean-Charles Haimet & J-Pascal Liberge **Trained** Withycombe, Somerset

FOCUS

The Irish had traditionally dominated this contest but their stranglehold was broken last year by Cue Card, and British-trained runners again proved the stronger, filling five of the first six places. It was strongly run and plenty showed improvement in what was not a vintage renewal, but it should still throw up winners.

NOTEBOOK

Cheltenian(FR) ◆, bought for £210,000 here in November after promising second to fellow newcomer at Punchestown, proved himself a decent prospect when beating subsequent impressive winner Montbazon at Kempton last month, and went someway to justifying his price tag again with a commanding performance once getting to the front. There was also a strong chance switching to a left-handed circuit would suit better and so it proved. He shapes like a horse that will be suited by further than 2m over hurdles, despite looking to have some speed when needed, and his trainer said afterwards that his horse is most likely to develop into a Neptune or Albert Bartlett Hurdle type next season, so the 12-1 on offer in places for the Supreme Hurdle makes little to no appeal at this stage. He could run again before the end of this season.

Destroyer Deployed ◆ belied his odds with a fantastic performance after running up with the leaders throughout. He is another who will surely need a trip over hurdles, because he came under strong pressure before finding more, and is an exciting prospect for his owners. It was also a nice boost for Fontwell racecourse, which had been the track Cue Card raced over before taking this. (op 50-1)

Aupcharlie(IRE) ◆, a brother to smart French hurdler La Grande Dame, has shown much better form on slower ground in Ireland since a narrow Hexham defeat last June, but came with what looked a strong move heading to the final bend. However, he still looked green under pressure, which is surprising considering he had plenty of experience, and needed to be organised to get going again. This seemed a promising effort, and he should be even better if he needs more time.

Go All The Way(IRE) ◆, who looked really well beforehand, was bought for £310,000 at Doncaster last May after producing a highly encouraging debut second to 2010 Champion Bumper seventh Bishopsfurze at Punchestown last spring. Making his debut for Nigel Twiston-Davies, he was going nowhere at one point before keeping on well up the home straight. He should benefit for the outing and also looks an exciting prospect. (op 20-1)

Cinders And Ashes ◆ is a Juddmonte cast-off (dam French 12.5f Group 2 winner) and cost just £4,500. He had already proved himself a bargain, and was only narrowly denied by Keys in Listed event here on New Year's Day, after winning two junior bumpers. Prominent throughout, he ran with plenty of credit until he stamina steadily ebbed away in the final stages. He looks well worth a try on the Flat at some stage. (tchd 16-1)

Ericht(IRE), who was given plenty to do when runner-up on debut at Ascot in November, improved on his first run when winning at Huntingdon and Newbury afterwards, comfortably beating Bygones In Brid in a Grade 2 event on the latter track. The Henderson-trained runner didn't seem to have any obvious excuses and failed to get competitive. (op 6-1)

Divine Rhapsody(IRE) had looked a smart prospect when landing the 20-runner Goffs Land Rover Bumper on good ground on debut at Punchestown last April. The form of that contest had worked out well (next four all successful since), but he was caught flat-footed here and only made late progress. (op 15-2)

Cousin Khee ran a bit better than his final position suggests and can make more progress with experience.

The Tracey Shuffle, somewhat surprisingly fitted with first-time cheekpieces after two perfectly good performances in northern bumpers, can be expected to leave this performance behind when going hurdling on softer ground.

Double Double(FR) didn't look in a great mood early for some reason, and got a long way back. He can be given another chance.

Knight Pass(IRE), representing the owner responsible for 1999 Champion Bumper winner Monsignor, showed a pleasing attitude when winning on debut at Sandown in November, and then at Southwell two months later, but he failed miserably to demonstrate anything like that sort of potential here, and was a big disappointment.

Raise The Beat showed little on testing ground on his debut but looked a different proposition on much faster ground since, and won at Down Royal and Naas. He moved strongly into contention but found little the moment he came under pressure. Maybe the five-month absence counted against him, or possibly something went amiss on the day. (op 7-1)

Twentyfourcarat(IRE) Official explanation: jockey said gelding ran flat

T/Jkpt: Not won. T/Plt: £933.20 to a £1 stake. Pool:£918,439.44 - 718.42 winning tickets T/Qpdt: £211.90 to a £1 stake. Pool:£38,065.53 - 132.92 winning tickets JN

4499 HUNTINGDON (R-H)

Wednesday, March 16

OFFICIAL GOING: Good (8.1)

Wind: modest across Weather: fog clear

4809 BET ON THE CHELTENHAM FESTIVAL TOTEPLACEPOT LADY RIDERS' H'CAP HURDLE (8 hdls) — 2m 110y

1:45 (1:46) (Class 4) (0-100,100) 4-Y-0+ **£2,397** (£698; £349)

Form	Pos	Dist	Horse / Trainer / Comment	Jockey	SP	RPR
0051	1		**Samizdat (FR)**[7] 4550 8-10-0 **81** 7ex (Dianne Sayer) *chsd clr ldrs: wnt 2nd bef 5th: clsd on ldr 3 out: led bef next: rdn between last 2: gd jump to settle issue last: r.o wl: readily*	MissECSayer(7)	**4/1**[2]	95+
060P	2	8	**Atared**[20] 4310 5-10-9 **90** (Pam Sly) *hld up wl bhd: hdwy after 4th: rdn to chse wnr bef 2 out: drvn and styd on same pce between last 2: hit last*	MissBAndrews(7)	**33/1**	97
1344	3	3 ¾	**Domino Dancer (IRE)**[17] 4375 7-11-2 **94** (Lucy Jones) *chsd ldr and clr of field: mstke 4th: lost 2nd bef 5th: 4th and in tch 3 out: rdn and btn bef next*	MissIsabelTompsett(5)	**4/1**[2]	98
-0P5	4	12	**Keep Guessing**[93] 2927 8-10-13 **94** (Warren Greatrex) *led: sn clr: mstke 5th: coming bk to field and mstke 3 out: rdn and hdd bef next: wknd 2 out*	(p) MissZoeLilly(7)	**12/1**	86
025	5	3	**Kayaan**[26] 4192 4-10-8 **96** (Pam Sly) *plld hrd: hld up in rr: pushed along and hdwy bef 5th: rdn and btn bef 2 out: mstke last*	MissGAndrews(7)	**3/1**[1]	80
0030	6	1 ¼	**Like Ice**[19] 4330 6-11-4 **97** (Philip Middleton) *racd off the pce in midfield: rdn and outpcd after 5th: plugged on same pce and wl btn after*	MissLHorner(5)	**16/1**	85
0065	7	38	**Jersey Boys**[24] 4243 5-10-11 **92** (Howard Johnson) *prom in main gp: mstke 2nd: rdn and struggling after 5th: wknd bef next: t.o*	MissLAlexander(7)	**16/1**	46
0345	8	¾	**Boo**[208] 1313 9-10-4 **85** (James Unett) *a in rr: lost tch 4th: t.o fr next*	MissJCWilliams(7)	**16/1**	39
05-2	F		**Bright Sparky (GER)**[16] 4390 8-10-9 **90** (Michael Easterby) *racd off the pce in midfield tl fell 4th*	(t) MissJCoward(7)	**5/1**[3]	—
6-00	P		**Shilpa (IRE)**[24] 4234 6-11-5 **100** (Anabel L M King) *racd off the pce in midfield: rdn and struggling after 4th: lost tch bef 3 out: t.o whn p.u 2 out*	MissJennyCarr(7)	**22/1**	—

3m 44.1s (-10.80) **Going Correction** -0.50s/f (Good)

WFA 4 from 5yo+ 7lb **10** Ran SP% **114.3**

Speed ratings (Par 105): **105,101,99,93,92 91,73,73,—,—**

toteswingers:1&2:£24.70, 1&3:£3.20, 2&3:£19.00 CSF £108.97 CT £559.39 TOTE £4.70: £1.60, £9.70, £1.30; EX 203.60.

Owner Mrs Freda Rayson **Bred** Peter Spiller **Trained** Hackthorpe, Cumbria

FOCUS

Not a strong race, but it was won in emphatic fashion by Samizdat, who stepped up on his recent win.

NOTEBOOK

Samizdat(FR) powered clear up the straight having been given a patient ride and a super leap at the last merely highlighted how much this back-to-form 8yo had left in the tank. Although penalised for his recent Catterick success, he clearly has plenty in hand of the assessor now back to form and can go in again if connections can find a suitable contest. (op 9-2)

Atared is still unexposed and this was a major step forward on anything she had achieved to date. Perhaps this better ground helped and, in finishing nicely clear of the rest, she looks more than capable of winning off this sort of mark with further improvement likely.

Domino Dancer(IRE) ran reasonably well but was pretty well beaten in the end despite looking like he's on a handy mark. (op 9-2 tchd 7-2)

Keep Guessing set a strong pace and dropped away. (op 10-1)

Kayaan needs to learn to settle as he was far too free in the early stages. (tchd 7-2, 4-1, 11-4 and 10-3 in places)

4810 BET ON THE CHELTENHAM FESTIVAL TOTEJACKPOT MAIDEN HURDLE (8 hdls) — 2m 110y

2:20 (2:20) (Class 4) 4-Y-0+ **£2,602** (£764; £382; £190)

Form	Pos	Dist	Horse / Trainer / Comment	Jockey	SP	RPR
5	1		**Dubai Crest**[12] 4451 5-10-7 0 (Nicky Henderson) *a gng wl: hld up in tch: hdwy to chse ldr 3 out: led next: sn pushed clr: mstke last: r.o wl: fdr: rdn out*	JeremiahMcGrath(7)	**6/5**[1]	109+

0 **2** *6* **Masterful Act (USA)**[12] 4451 4-10-7 0 GrahamLee 94
(Ferdy Murphy) *hld up in rr: nt fluent 3rd: hdwy 5th: chsd ldng pair bef 2 out: rdn and outpcd by wnr between last 2: wnt 2nd last: no threat to wnr but r.o* **7/2**[2]
3 *6* **Eseej (USA)**[20] 6-11-0 0 JimmyMcCarthy 96
(Peter Hiatt) *led: rdn and hdd 2 out: sn outpcd by wnr: lost 2nd last: wknd flat* **10/1**
14-4 **4** *2 3/4* **Theredballoon**[21] 4287 5-10-7 0 OliverWilliams(7) 94
(Chris Bealby) *taken down early and led arnd at s: t.k.h: hld up in rr: hdwy and mstke 3 out: chsd ldrs and j.rt next: 4th and j.rt last: hung lft u.p flat and styd on same pce flat* **9/1**
55 **5** *10* **Sous Mix (FR)**[30] 4117 5-10-7 0 JakeGreenall(7) 84
(Michael Easterby) *hld up in tch in midfield: stl in tch whn nt clr run bnd bef 2 out: slt hmpd 2 out: nudged along and kpt on same pce flat* **66/1**
03 **6** *nk* **Lucky Dance (BRZ)**[16] 4397 9-11-0 0 AndrewThornton 84
(Mark Rimmer) *chsd ldrs: nt fluent 2nd: rdn and btn after 3 out: wknd next* **20/1**
4 **7** *3* **Always De One**[13] 3986 4-9-11 0 (p) CharlieStudd(3) 67
(K F Clutterbuck) *hld up towards rr: hdwy after 5th: rdn and no hdwy bef 2 out* **100/1**
8 *1 1/4* **Valid Reason**[91] 4-10-7 0 TomMessenger 75
(Dean Ivory) *t.k.h: mstke 5th: chsd ldr tl 3 out: rdn and wknd bef next* **15/2**[3]
0 **9** *2 1/4* **Lajidaal (USA)**[69] 3401 4-10-2 0 JoshuaMoore(5) 71
(Gary Moore) *chsd ldrs: rdn after 5th: wknd after 3 out* **33/1**
10 *1* **Cast Of Stars (IRE)**[102] 4-10-7 0 RhysFlint 72
(Evan Williams) *mstkes: hld up in rr: mstke 4th: hdwy after next: chsd ldrs after 3 out: mstke next: sn fdd* **25/1**
U0 **11** *3 1/4* **December**[10] 4499 5-10-11 0 (t) AlexMerriam(3) 74
(Christine Dunnett) *hld up in tch in midfield: rdn 3 out: wknd bef next* **100/1**
00 **12** *19* **Dancing Belle**[10] 4499 6-10-4 0 MarcGoldstein(3) 50
(J R Jenkins) *hld up in rr: mstke 2nd: rdn and lost tch after 5th: t.o bef 2 out* **150/1**
13 *33* **Trepalo (FR)**[145] 4-10-7 0 TomSiddall 20
(Alison Batchelor) *midfield: j.lft 2nd: j. slowly and dropped to rr next: lost tch 4th: t.o fr next* **33/1**
0 **14** *2 3/4* **Remarkable Rocket (IRE)**[114] 2590 7-10-7 0 MrJFlook(7) 25
(Andrew Price) *j. bdly: midfield whn j. v awkwardly 1st: hdwy to chse ldrs 3rd: j.lft and lost pl rapidly 5th: t.o bef 2 out* **100/1**

3m 46.0s (-8.90) **Going Correction** -0.50s/f (Good)
WFA 4 from 5yo+ 7lb **14** Ran SP% **118.1**
Speed ratings (Par 105): **100,97,94,93,88 88,86,86,85,84 83,74,58,57**
toteswingers:1&2:£1.80, 1&3:£4.00, 2&3:£11.50 CSF £4.72 TOTE £2.20: £1.10, £2.30, £3.70; EX 6.70.
Owner A D Spence **Bred** Bearstone Stud **Trained** Upper Lambourn, Berks

FOCUS
A modest novice hurdle in which the first two ran to their marks.

NOTEBOOK
Dubai Crest, an 80-rated performer on the Flat, built on his hurdles debut at Doncaster, settling better this time, to come home a pretty easy winner. Although the form isn't anything to get excited about, he stretched clear in pretty impressive style after taking the lead over the second last and is in the right hands. (op 13-8 tchd 15-8 and 2-1 in a place)
Masterful Act(USA) was a stronger stayer than the winner on the level so this was a promising effort as he kept on well to come clear in second and he looks nailed-on to fair much better granted a stiffer test of stamina. (op 9-4)
Eseej(USA), making his hurdles debut, ran well but although this was encouraging his best Flat form has come on the AW, and he's never won on turf. (op 9-1)
Theredballoon, a bumper winner at this track, didn't run badly but hasn't really shaped like he's improved for switch to hurdles. (op 11-1 tchd 12-1)

4811 TOTETRIFECTA ON ALL CHELTENHAM FESTIVAL RACES H'CAP CHASE (19 fncs) 3m
2:55 (2:55) (Class 4) (0-100,100) 5-Y-0+ **£2,602** (£764; £382; £190)

Form RPR
P403 **1** **Kercabellec (FR)**[3] 4744 13-9-7 **74** oh21 JoeCornwall(7) 83+
(John Cornwall) *chsd ldr tl led 2nd: hdd after next: clr w ldr after: rdn to ld between last 2: clr last: styd on wl* **20/1**
-03P **2** *15* **King Of Leon (FR)**[25] 4224 7-11-5 **100** StephenO'Donovan(7) 97
(Emma Lavelle) *t.k.h: chsd ldr 2nd tl led after next: pushed along bef 2 out: hdd between last 2: sn btn: wknd flat* **4/1**[2]
6021 **3** *4 1/2* **Bardolet (IRE)**[7] 4551 8-11-8 **96** 7ex JamesReveley 87
(Keith Reveley) *nt a fluent: racd wl off the pce in last pair: wnt modest 3rd 10th: rdn 15th: stl 20 l down 3 out: plugged on but no imp: nvr trbld ldrs* **4/6**[1]
-5P4 **4** *6* **Absolute Shambles**[43] 3867 7-10-3 **84** (v[1]) MrTJCannon(7) 72
(Chris Gordon) *nvr jumping fluently or travelling wl: led tl 2nd: sn off the pce in last trio: rdn 8th: lost tch 14th* **9/2**[3]
1PP- **P** **Doc Reason (IRE)**[529] 1602 8-10-10 **91** MrMatthewSmith(7) —
(Patrick Gilligan) *mstke: a in rr: blnd 14th: t.o next: j.lft 2 out: p.u last* **25/1**

6m 5.40s (-4.90) **Going Correction** -0.075s/f (Good) **5** Ran SP% **106.8**
Speed ratings: **105,100,98,96,—**
CSF £85.76 TOTE £21.90: £4.30, £1.20; EX 81.50.
Owner J R Cornwall **Bred** Loic Malivet And Roger-Yves Simon **Trained** Long Clawson, Leics

FOCUS
A turn-up here as hotpot Bardolet put in a laboured effort. The winner is rated to the level of his recent Market Rasen second.

NOTEBOOK
Kercabellec(FR) took advantage of the favourite not running well by staying on much too resolutely for King Of Leon. The pair dominated from a long way out. He swooped past the runner-up and kept on strongly to post his first win since March 2007 despite racing from 21lb out of the weights (not taking into account Joe Cornwall's claim). (op 12-1)
King Of Leon(FR) looked to have matters under control but ran out steam before the last. (tchd 5-1)
Bardolet(IRE) appreciated the return to better ground at Catterick last week but was a different animal today. He was held up under a patient ride, but the gap between him and the front pair only grew down the back on the final circuit and it was soon clear he wasn't going to get involved. (tchd 1-2)

4812 BLACK BULL SAWSTON DEAN'S FINAL FREEDOM H'CAP HURDLE (12 hdls) 3m 2f
3:35 (3:35) (Class 4) (0-110,102) 4-Y-0+ **£2,276** (£668; £334; £166)

Form RPR
604 **1** **Burnthill (IRE)**[13] 4441 6-10-2 **85** (t) PeterHatton(7) 92
(Claire Dyson) *in tch: blnd bdly 1st: chsd ldr after 6th: rdn to ld bef 2 out: drvn and kpt on wl flat* **10/3**[2]
3046 **2** *1* **More Equity**[49] 3750 9-11-11 **101** JamesReveley 106
(Dianne Sayer) *chsd ldrs: rdn to chse wnr 2 out: clsd and ch last: styd on same pce u.p flat* **9/2**[3]
55-P **3** *4 1/2* **Willow Wren**[116] 2532 6-11-5 **95** (t) SamJones 96
(Renee Robeson) *in tch: reminders after 5th: stl in tch but rdn fr 6th: kpt on same pce u.p fr 2 out* **10/3**[2]
5443 **4** *3 3/4* **Nobby Kivambo (IRE)**[15] 4407 6-11-12 **102** (p) JimmyMcCarthy 101
(Brendan Powell) *led: mstke 7th: rdn and hdd bef 2 out: fnd little u.p: sn btn* **2/1**[1]
005 **5** *12* **M'Lady Rousseur (IRE)**[41] 3901 5-11-7 **97** TomMessenger 86
(Chris Bealby) *nt fluent: reminder after 2nd: in tch: hdwy to chse ldrs 7th: j. slowly and rdn 8th: wknd u.p bef 2 out* **16/1**
-POP **6** *dist* **Kirkum (IRE)**[58] 3599 6-9-8 **76** oh46 ow1 MissCareyWilliamson(7) —
(Diana Weeden) *a bhd: j.rt 1st: pushed along and struggling 4th: t.o fr 8th* **80/1**
P5-0 **P** **Toni Alcala**[34] 4021 12-10-13 **92** (p) AlexMerriam(3) —
(Neil King) *chsd ldr: mstke 3rd: rdn along after next: mstke and lost pl 6th: lost tch qckly after next: t.o whn p.u 9th* **33/1**
3-4U **P** **No More Prisoners (IRE)**[14] 4428 11-11-3 **98** (tp) MissLHorner(5) —
(Liam Corcoran) *many reminders: in tch towards rr: hdwy to chse ldrs and rdn after 7th: styd in tch tl eased and p.u after 9th: dismntd* **22/1**

6m 17.7s (-5.20) **Going Correction** -0.50s/f (Good) **8** Ran SP% **112.1**
Speed ratings (Par 105): **88,87,86,85,81 —,—,—**
toteswingers:1&2:£3.10, 1&3:£2.50, 2&3:£3.90 CSF £17.98 CT £51.81 TOTE £4.20: £1.10, £1.80, £1.10; EX 22.30.
Owner Miss C Dyson **Bred** Mrs Christine Kelly **Trained** Cleeve Prior, Worcs

FOCUS
A lot of these were in trouble a long way out and everything was off the bridle leaving the back. Ordinary form with the first two to their marks.

NOTEBOOK
Burnthill(IRE) managed to poach a couple of lengths on the field turning for home and, although More Equity made him work fairly hard after the last, he was always doing enough to hold on. The winner's jumping remains far from foot-perfect, but he is improving gradually and he clearly stays well. (op 7-2 tchd 4-1)
More Equity hasn't won since the summer of 2009 but his mark is creeping back down again and this was a real sign that she could be ready to strike again, now only 3lb above that last winning mark. (op 4-1 tchd 5-1)
Willow Wren was being ridden with a circuit to go but, to her credit, she kept chipping away and never let the leading group get away. (op 7-2 tchd 9-2)
Nobby Kivambo(IRE) had everything in his favour here as he tried to shed his longstanding maiden tag but the writing was on the wall some way out and he is not one to trust. (op 5-2 tchd 13-8)
No More Prisoners(IRE) Official explanation: vet said gelding pulled up distressed

4813 BOB BROWN MEMORIAL H'CAP CHASE (12 fncs) 2m 110y
4:15 (4:18) (Class 4) (0-100,97) 5-Y-0+ **£2,602** (£764; £382; £190)

Form RPR
6024 **1** **Red Law (IRE)**[5] 4691 7-9-13 **77** (b) MrTJCannon(7) 85
(Mark Gillard) *led tl outj. and hdd 1st: led again 3rd: clr fr 5th: rdn between last 2: nt fluent last: racd awkwardly u.p but in command flat: rdn out* **5/2**[1]
6022 **2** *7* **Mad Professor (IRE)**[3] 4741 8-9-7 **71** oh9 (p) JoeCornwall(7) 73
(John Cornwall) *sn bhd: j. slowly and outpcd 3rd: pushed along and hdwy 8th: chsd ldr after 3 out: 3 l down 2 out: no prog after: btn whn nt fluent last* **9/2**[2]
0555 **3** *22* **Troodos Jet**[10] 4510 10-10-6 **77** (p) JamesReveley 60
(Dianne Sayer) *chsd ldrs: wnt 2nd after 8th tl after 3 out: sn rdn and fnd little: wl btn 2 out* **11/2**[3]
0304 **4** *53* **Bennynthejets (IRE)**[24] 4237 9-11-5 **97** OliverWilliams(7) 30
(Chris Bealby) *pressed ldrs whn mstke 1st: nvr gng wl after: reminders after 4th and 5th: last and lost tch qckly 8th: lft 4th and t.o 3 out* **5/2**[1]
00 **U** **Fairhaven (IRE)**[11] 4483 7-11-0 **92** (b) KielanWoods(7) —
(Charlie Longsdon) *w ldr tl j. to ld 1st: j. bdly rt: hdd and reminders 3rd: chsd wnr after: mstke 8th: 4th and wkng whn blnd bdly and uns rdr 3 out* **9/2**[2]

4m 6.50s (-3.70) **Going Correction** -0.075s/f (Good) **5** Ran SP% **108.9**
Speed ratings: **105,101,91,66,—**
CSF £13.20 TOTE £3.00: £1.40, £2.70; EX 13.10.
Owner T J C Seegar & Mrs T Connor **Bred** Richard Cavanagh **Trained** Holwell, Dorset

FOCUS
Poor fare. The winner was on a good mark and ran close to form.

NOTEBOOK
Red Law(IRE) made most of the running and he kept rolling when Mad Professor began to close between the third- and second-last. Despite having his head cocked to one side the winner saw his race out well, something he had been failing to do on many of his previous starts, hence the winless record, but he appreciated this sharp course and was given a nice positive ride by the promising Tom Cannon. (op 3-1)
Mad Professor(IRE) was 9lb wrong at the weights but he is at least in decent heart and this was another respectable effort. (op 10-3 tchd 5-1)
Troodos Jet was just one-paced when coming under pressure and was a little disappointing given how much he appeared to have in his favour. (op 4-1)
Bennynthejets(IRE) was never a threat having raced sluggishly early and he doesn't appear to have the requisite speed for this kind of test. Official explanation: jockey said gelding never travelled (tchd 15-8)

4814 TOTEPOOL FLEXI BETTING AT THE CHELTENHAM FESTIVAL H'CAP HURDLE (10 hdls) 2m 5f 110y
4:55 (4:55) (Class 5) (0-90,95) 4-Y-0+ **£2,055** (£599; £299)

Form RPR
4P01 **1** **Emmaslegend**[6] 4675 6-11-12 **95** 7ex (t) MrTJCannon(7) 114+
(Suzy Smith) *chsd ldrs: led on bit 7th: cruised clr after next: eased flat: v easily* **1/1**[1]
1254 **2** *14* **Sambelucky (IRE)**[7] 4550 6-11-11 **87** JamesReveley 86
(Keith Reveley) *in tch towards rr: hdwy and mstke 7th: 4th and rdn bef next: no ch w wnr after 3 out: wnt modest 2nd between last 2* **7/2**[2]
0505 **3** *11* **Masterpoint**[178] 1549 11-9-13 **68** MissCLWills(7) 57
(Richard Harper) *racd wd: in tch: hdwy to chse ldrs after 5th: rdn and btn 3 out: wnt modest 2nd bef next: wknd to 3rd between last 2* **33/1**
06P0 **4** *63* **Sir Clad**[36] 3987 5-10-1 **70** (vt[1]) GeraldQuinn(7) 21
(Claire Dyson) *j.lft: led: clr tl 6th: hdd next: wknd u.p after 3 out: eased flat: t.o* **40/1**
0/P0 **P** **Young Valentino**[7] 4557 9-9-9 **62** oh3 GemmaGracey-Davison(5) —
(Michael Appleby) *v.s.a: t.k.h: hld up in detached last: dived 1st: lost tch qckly after 5th: wl t.o whn p.u 7th* **80/1**
5FP0 **P** **Kilbready Star (IRE)**[20] 4314 11-10-10 **72** TomSiddall —
(Peter Pritchard) *t.k.h: hld up in tch: lost pl 6th: sn struggling and lost tch: t.o 3 out tl p.u next* **14/1**

6003 **P** **Borderhopper**[10] 4508 7-11-9 **85** GrahamLee —
(Ferdy Murphy) *mounted on crse: t.k.h: hld up in tch in rr: hdwy to chse ldrs after 5th: mstke next: sn pushed along: wknd next: t.o whn p.u 2 out* **4/1**[3]

05-P **P** **Hi Ho Silvia**[16] 4401 6-11-2 **81** (p) AlexMerriam(3) —
(Neil King) *chsd ldr: mstke 6th: rdn and lost pl bef next: sn bhd: t.o whn p.u 2 out* **28/1**

0600 **P** **Everdon Brook (IRE)**[36] 3989 6-11-9 **85** (p) CharliePoste —
(Ben Case) *in tch towards rr: rdn after 6th: wknd next: t.o whn p.u 2 out* **20/1**

5m 6.40s (-4.20) **Going Correction** -0.50s/f (Good) **9** Ran SP% **113.7**
Speed ratings (Par 103): **87,81,77,55,— —,—,—,—**
CSF £4.66 CT £62.55 TOTE £2.00: £1.30, £1.60, £6.30; EX 3.70.
Owner Pete Mercer **Bred** P J Mercer **Trained** Lewes, E Sussex

FOCUS
A terribly weak handicap. The winner was thrown in but produced another step up under a claimer.

NOTEBOOK
Emmaslegend is a well-handicapped mare and jumped to the front at the final flight down the back before moving effortlessly clear and was in no danger in the straight. She looks a different horse this year, with the tongue-strap on, and is clearly well ahead of the handicapper. (op 11-10 tchd 6-5)
Sambelucky(IRE) has shaped like he would appreciate a return to this sort of trip, but he was no match for the winner and doesn't appeal as a winner in the near future. (op 10-3 tchd 3-1)
Masterpoint ran a little better than last time but is clearly very modest. (op 25-1)
Sir Clad dropped away and isn't improving. (op 33-1)
Young Valentino Official explanation: jockey said gelding never travelled
Borderhopper Official explanation: jockey said gelding ran too soon

4815 TOTEPOOL CHELTENHAM FESTIVAL BETTING AT TOTESPORT.COM STANDARD OPEN NATIONAL HUNT FLAT RACE 2m 110y
5:30 (5:30) (Class 6) 4-6-Y-0 **£1,370** (£399; £199)

Form RPR

1 **Keyaza (IRE)** 4-9-9 0 TrevorWhelan(7) 105+
(Tobias B P Coles) *t.k.h: chsd ldrs: jnd ldr 1/2-way tl led over 3f out: drew clr over 2f out: rn green u.p and wandered 2f out: pushed out hands and heels and kpt on wl after: easily* **5/1**[2]

2 *12* **Tiradia (FR)** 4-10-2 0 JakeGreenall(7) 97
(Michael Easterby) *hld up in tch in last: rn green bnd on 10f out: rdn over 4f out: hdwy to chse clr wnr over 2f out: no imp after* **16/1**

53 **3** *3 ¾* **Cue To Cue**[57] 3623 5-10-9 0 JamesReveley 93
(Keith Reveley) *led after 1f tl 1/2-way: styd handy tl rdn and nt qckn wl over 2f out: 3rd and wl hld fnl 2f* **2/5**[1]

40 **4** *10* **Sleeping Du Granit (FR)**[13] 4443 5-10-9 0 (t) PeterHatton(7) 90
(Claire Dyson) *t.k.h: led for 1f: pressed ldr tl led again 1/2-way: hdd and rdn wl over 2f out: sn wknd* **50/1**

5 *hd* **Sillkom** 4-10-4 0 GilesHawkins(5) 83
(Ben Pollock) *t.k.h: hld up wl in tch: rdn and chsd wnr 3f out tl over 2f out: sn wknd* **33/1**

6 *7* **Graceful Spirit** 4-10-2 0 JohnnyFarrelly 69
(Des Donovan) *plld hrd: hld up in tch: hdwy on outer to chse ldrs 6f out: hung lft and wknd qckly ent fnl 3f* **16/1**

7 *46* **Renovatio (FR)** 5-11-2 0 GerardTumelty 37
(Anabel L M King) *t.k.h: hld up wl in tch: rdn and wknd qckly 4f out: t.o and eased fnl 2f* **12/1**[3]

3m 45.5s (-3.60) **Going Correction** -0.50s/f (Good)
WFA 4 from 5yo+ 7lb **7** Ran SP% **112.5**
Speed ratings: **88,82,80,75,75 72,50**
toteswingers:1&2:£4.30, 1&3:£1.40, 2&3:£1.70 CSF £72.53 TOTE £4.00: £1.60, £5.40; EX 51.40.
Owner R S Hoskins **Bred** Newberry Stud Company **Trained** Newmarket, Suffolk

FOCUS
A fair bumper. The cosy winner can rate higher but the favourite was 10lb off.

NOTEBOOK
Keyaza(IRE) shot a few lengths clear turning for home before powering further away from her toiling rivals to score in most impressive style on debut. Nicely-bred, being out of a Yorkshire Oaks winner, she has clearly had her problems given she was sold out of Michael Halford's stable for just 7,500gns, but she could be a bargain on this evidence and looks one to keep a close eye on wherever she goes next. (op 13-2)
Tiradia(FR) is bred to want a much stiffer test of stamina in time (from same family as Innox and L'Ami) so this was quite a promising first run.
Cue To Cue was most disappointing as she was floundering as the winner quickened away and could only keep on at the one pace. She has already shown that she is much better than this, although maybe she has bumped into two above average rivals here. (op 1-2)
Sleeping Du Granit(FR) took a while to settle and doesn't seem to be progressing at the moment. (op 40-1)
T/Plt: £81.40 to a £1 stake. Pool:£51,269.41 - 459.68 winning tickets T/Qpdt: £22.00 to a £1 stake. Pool:£2,987.76 - 100.30 winning tickets SP

4802 CHELTENHAM (L-H)
Thursday, March 17

OFFICIAL GOING: Good (good to soft in places; 7.9)
The day concluded with a charity Flat race over 1m3f, not under rules. It was won by Plato, trained by Henry Cecil and ridden by Lorna Fowler.
Wind: Almost nil Weather: Fine

4816 JEWSON NOVICES' CHASE (REGISTERED AS THE GOLDEN MILLER NOVICES' CHASE) GRADE 2 (16 fncs) 2m 4f
1:30 (1:30) (Class 1) 5-Y-0+
£51,309 (£19,251; £9,639; £4,806; £2,412; £1,206)

Form RPR

4-22 **1** **Noble Prince (GER)**[53] 3705 7-11-4 146 APMcCoy 164+
(Paul Nolan, Ire) *trckd ldrs: hit 9th: chsd ldr and nt fluent 4 out: rdn and one pce appr 2 out: rallied u.p sn after to chal last: sn led: r.o wl u.p run-in: rdn out* **4/1**[2]

F121 **2** *4* **Wishfull Thinking**[47] 3804 8-11-4 155 (t) RichardJohnson 162+
(Philip Hobbs) *trckd ldr 4th: led 6th: rdn appr 2 out: jnd whn mstke last: sn hdd: one pce u.p but kpt on for clr 2nd* **7/2**[1]

-134 **3** *5* **Loosen My Load (IRE)**[77] 3241 7-11-4 143 AELynch 155+
(Henry De Bromhead, Ire) *chsd ldrs: rdn and hit 3 out: chsd ldr u.p appr 2 out: wknd u.p bef last* **11/2**[3]

15B1 **4** *2 ½* **Radium (FR)**[25] 4236 6-11-4 144 FelixDeGiles 152
(Nicky Henderson) *in tch: chsd ldrs fr 10th: riddn and hit 3 out: disp 2nd briefly appr next: wknd appr last* **33/1**

5-12 **5** *3 ¾* **Blazing Tempo (IRE)**[49] 3779 7-10-11 138 PTownend 142
(W P Mullins, Ire) *hld up in rr: stdy hdwy and hit 3 out: rdn and effrt sn after: nvr rchd ldrs and wknd fr 2 out* **11/1**

0-F0 **6** *nk* **Mr Thriller (FR)**[75] 3291 6-11-4 150 (bt[1]) TomScudamore 147
(David Pipe) *chsd ldrs: rdn and j. slowly 3 out: lost position u.p: kpt on again last: styng on cl home* **20/1**

3-13 **7** *11* **Mr Cracker (IRE)**[53] 3705 6-11-4 139 DNRussell 139
(Michael Hourigan, Ire) *trckd ldrs: dropped towards rr 10th: hdwy and hit 4 out: chsng ldrs whn hit 3 out: sn wknd* **16/1**

1346 **8** *21* **Cootehill (IRE)**[47] 3803 7-11-4 128 PaddyBrennan 120
(Nigel Twiston-Davies) *a in rr: bhd whn blnd 10th: no ch after* **80/1**

-122 **9** *15* **Bouggler**[41] 3921 6-11-4 143 SamThomas 99
(Emma Lavelle) *chsd ldr to 4th: rdn along 8th: wknd 10th: no ch whn blnd 4 out* **25/1**

1/13 **P** **Mr Gardner (IRE)**[40] 3946 8-11-4 146 BarryGeraghty —
(Nicky Henderson) *led: nt fluent 4th and 5th: blnd and hdd 6th: nvr jumping w any fluency after and wknd 8th: mstke 9th and p.u after next* **6/1**

1F10 **P** **Robinson Collonges (FR)**[96] 2886 6-11-4 148 RWalsh —
(Paul Nicholls) *a in rr and nvr really travelling: j. slowly 7th: lost tch 8th: blnd 9th: t.o whn p.u bef 12th* **6/1**

4m 49.82s (-14.38) **Going Correction** -0.30s/f (Good) **11** Ran SP% **113.2**
Speed ratings: **116,114,112,111,109 109,105,96,90,— —**
toteswingers:1&2:£2.20, 1&3:£4.10, 2&3:£3.10 CSF £17.53 CT £75.47 TOTE £4.40: £1.90, £1.80, £1.70; EX 12.10 Trifecta £42.90 Pool: £10,198.540 - 175.80 winning units..
Owner D P Sharkey **Bred** Gestut Etzean **Trained** Enniscorthy, Co. Wexford
■ Tony McCoy's 200th winner of the season.

FOCUS
The going stick read 7.9 after a little drizzle overnight, although nothing that was measurable. Tony McCoy described the going as good, while Richard Johnson said it was good, perfect all the way round. \n\x\x This was the first running of this race, registered in the name of Golden Miller, who won five consecutive Gold Cups between 1932-1936. It was also the first contest of the week on the New Course. The galloped looked at least fair, despite a couple of horse taking a grip in behind. The form is solid and well up to Grade 1 standard, with a sizeable step up from Noble Prince, who along with Wishfull Thinking is a high-class novice.

NOTEBOOK
Noble Prince(GER) ◆ was a very smart hurdler at his best, and wasn't disgraced in last year's County Hurdle, even after being hampered. However, if anything, he has looked better over fences and his form in Ireland looked out of the top drawer against Arkle third Realt Dubh in Grade 1 chases. Up in distance for this, his trainer looked to have hit form at the right time, and under a typically strong Tony McCoy ride, charged away from the runner-up after the last to win going away. A clearly delighted Paul Nolan reported that this race was always the target, as the Arkle and RSA Chase were never on the agenda, and his horse may now head to Punchestown. (tchd 7-2)
Wishfull Thinking ◆ was officially the highest-rated runner in the field after making healthy improvement since going over fences. Things didn't start too well when he came down at the first fence at Aintree on his chasing debut, but everything after had been progressive and exciting. His win last time out was particularly good, when he beat seasoned handicappers here over 2m5f in January, giving weight away and a beating to the capable Calgary Bay. Never far away here, he was given an attacking ride once in front and jumped mainly well until making a small error at the last fence. It looked as though the winner would have got him considering the momentum he had at the time, but this was still a fine performance by the Hobbs-trained horse, and he looks to have a good future. There are no firm plans for the horse but there is a chance he could run again this season at Aintree and/or Punchestown.
Loosen My Load(IRE) ◆ has a good record of getting his head in front and has looked, on occasions, capable of mixing it with the best when getting decent ground to race on. His form against Arkle winner Captain Chris at this course in November entitled him to be thereabouts, and this sort of distance had seemed about right for him. However, he raced far too keenly to get home up the hill, and looked tired coming to the final fence. A slight ease in distance or a flatter course will help him during the spring. (op 13-2)
Radium(FR), who seemingly would have been aimed at Tuesday's Centenary Handicap Chase but for what his trainer described as a ridiculous BHA rating, finished miles behind Loosen My Load back in November (2m), and was brought down when still in with every chance in a race over 2m5f in which Wishfull Thinking finished second to Reve De Sivola. He made a promising move when the race started to take shape here, but he was unable to find the necessary pace to keep tabs on the front three as they stretched clear. He doesn't look to have the stature to carry big weights. (tchd 40-1 in a place)
Blazing Tempo(IRE) had other options during the week but connections settled on this because of the 2m4f trip. The drying ground was expected to suit, and she had a 7lb sex allowance on her side, but after being held up in rear, she didn't look quite good enough for this level against geldings. (op 12-1)
Mr Thriller(FR), with a tongue-tie and blinkers fitted for the first time, didn't run badly on ground that was unlikely to suit on his best form. He's still to win over fences, so unless connections have a stab at a Grade 1 or a valuable handicap, it probably makes sense to keep him as a novice for next season. (op 16-1)
Mr Cracker(IRE) travelled strongly behind the leading bunch but weakened quite quickly once pressure was applied after a couple of jumping mistakes. About 10l behind Noble Prince when they met last time in the Irish Arkle, he was felt to have not handled the going. Official explanation: trainer said gelding was unsuited by the good (good to soft places) ground
Bouggler's jockey reported that the gelding felt lame on pulling up. Official explanation: vet said gelding appeared lame on pulling up
Mr Gardner(IRE) made a good return to action after a very lengthy absence at Huntingdon, when winning by a long way, and bettered that at Sandown in the Scilly Isles Novices' Chase (a place behind this week's Arkle winner Captain Chris) when possibly a bit unlucky not to get a bit closer due to a stumble two from home. Sure to like decent ground, he assumed the lead early but he pecked at the fourth and fifth before a more serious error at the sixth, and lost his position at the head of the field. Another a couple of minor errors followed, especially at the water jump, and he was pulled up sharply after the ninth. The jockey stated afterwards his mount was unsuited by the ground. Official explanation: trainer said gelding was unsuited by the good (good to soft places) ground (tchd 13-2)
Robinson Collonges(FR) looked a top prospect in the autumn/early winter and seemed to be going better than Wishfull Thinking when they clashed at Wincanton in November when coming down in the latter stages. He then faced a stiff task at Cheltenham over 2m4f in the Vote AP Gold Cup in December, but had excuses for that effort behind stablemate Poquelin, and hadn't been seen on the racecourse since. Settled in rear here, he showed no sparkle and wasn't a threat at any stage before pulling up. (tchd 13-2)

4817 PERTEMPS FINAL (HANDICAP HURDLE) (LISTED RACE) (12 hdls) 3m
2:05 (2:05) (Class 1) 5-Y-0+
£39,907 (£14,973; £7,497; £3,738; £1,876; £938)

Form RPR

0000 **1** **Buena Vista (IRE)**[61] 3561 10-10-3 **138** (b) CO'Farrell(5) 148
(David Pipe) *sn led: rdn clr after 2 out: abt 5 l clr last: styd on wl and a in command run-in* **20/1**

4-42 **2** *4* **Son Amix (FR)**[67] 3475 5-10-6 **136** PCarberry 142
(Thomas Cooper, Ire) *hld up: hdwy 9th: rdn to chse wnr between last 2: no imp: all out to hold on for 2nd cl home* **16/1**

/1-4 **3** *hd* **Sivota (IRE)**[67] 3475 7-10-7 **137**....(t) RWalsh 144+
(W P Mullins, Ire) *in rr: stl plenty of work to do appr 2 out: hdwy to take 3rd appr last: r.o and clsd on runner-up towards fin* **9/1**[3]
4021 **4** *10* **Knockara Beau (IRE)**[36] 4003 8-11-12 **156**.... JanFaltejsek 153
(George Charlton) *a.p: w ldr 7th: chalng for 2nd 2 out: rdn and outpcd sn after: no ex bef last* **33/1**
-020 **5** *nk* **Queiros Bleu (FR)**[25] 4247 7-10-4 **134**.... AELynch 130
(Henry De Bromhead, Ire) *hld up in rr: hdwy whn nt fluent 3 out: chsd ldrs after 2 out: styd on same pce* **33/1**
5220 **6** *2 ½* **Barwell Bridge**[61] 3561 5-10-8 **138**....(t) WayneHutchinson 131
(Warren Greatrex) *midfield: pushed along appr 2 out: styd on to chse ldng bunch between last 2: no imp* **25/1**
6230 **7** *1* **Viking Blond (FR)**[75] 3293 6-10-7 **137**.... PaddyBrennan 129
(Nigel Twiston-Davies) *chsd ldrs: niggled along after 9th: rdn bef 2 out: one pce and btn appr last* **40/1**
63/ **8** *3* **Heavenly Blues (GER)**[29] 4153 9-10-4 **134**.... MsKWalsh 123
(T M Walsh, Ire) *hld up: rdn after 2 out: styd on appr last: nt pce to get competitive* **40/1**
/312 **9** *1 ¾* **Tarablaze**[27] 4190 8-10-8 **138**.... TomO'Brien 125
(Philip Hobbs) *midfield: hdwy appr 7th: sn trckd ldrs: wnt 2nd 2 out: sn lost 2nd u.p: wkng whn nt fluent last: wl btn after* **20/1**
-P00 **10** *hd* **Don't Push It (IRE)**[27] 4185 11-10-5 **135**.... APMcCoy 122
(Jonjo O'Neill) *hld up: hdwy into midfield appr 3 out: kpt on u.p run-in: nt pce to get on terms w ldrs* **14/1**
11 *shd* **Rivage D'Or (FR)**[25] 4251 6-10-2 **137**.... BryanJCooper(5) 124
(D T Hughes, Ire) *hld up: hdwy into midfield 8th: chsd ldng bunch 2 out: wknd appr last* **10/1**
F-24 **12** *nk* **Micheal Flips (IRE)**[61] 3566 7-11-2 **146**.... NickScholfield 133
(Andy Turnell) *hld up: stdy hdwy into midfield appr 8th: rdn to chse ldrs after 2 out: wknd appr last* **20/1**
10-3 **13** *1 ½* **Chartreux (FR)**[75] 3293 6-10-3 **133**.... TomScudamore 120
(David Pipe) *in tch: pushed along whn chalng for 2nd and hit 2 out: wknd appr last* **6/1**[1]
6403 **14** *7* **Kayf Aramis**[26] 4207 9-10-9 **142**.... SamTwiston-Davies(3) 120
(Nigel Twiston-Davies) *chsd ldrs: rdn appr 8th: wknd bef 2 out* **20/1**
FF40 **15** *3 ½* **Gwanako (FR)**[47] 3807 8-10-5 **140**.... MrRMahon(5) 115
(Paul Nicholls) *in tch: pushed along and outpcd appr 2 out: sn btn* **25/1**
-221 **16** *9* **Barafundle (IRE)**[111] 2663 7-10-10 **140**.... AlanO'Keeffe 113
(Jennie Candlish) *chsd ldrs: nt fluent 3rd: rdn after 3 out: wknd 2 out* **8/1**[2]
614P **17** *14* **Mobaasher (USA)**[26] 4208 8-11-4 **148**....(vt) AidanColeman 100
(Venetia Williams) *towards rr: rdn after 7th: lost tch 3 out: nvr on terms* **33/1**
0445 **18** *9* **Duke Of Lucca (IRE)**[75] 3289 6-11-4 **148**.... RichardJohnson 91
(Philip Hobbs) *hld up: sme hdwy into midfield 7th: nt fluent 8th: u.p after: lost tch after 3 out* **25/1**
-422 **19** *6* **Alfie Spinner (IRE)**[40] 3947 6-10-8 **138**.... DarylJacob 75
(Nick Williams) *in tch: pushed along and wknd 3 out* **12/1**
/-05 **20** *7* **Essex (IRE)**[46] 3848 11-10-9 **139**....(v[1]) PTownend 69
(Denis W Cullen, Ire) *midfield: pushed along after 7th: bhd appr 3 out: toiling after* **100/1**
4400 **21** *hd* **Pause And Clause (IRE)**[40] 3947 7-10-12 **142**....(p) JackDoyle 72
(Emma Lavelle) *in tch: lost pl bef 6th: bhd whn blnd 7th: t.o fr 3 out* **33/1**
3216 **22** *nse* **Mr Moonshine (IRE)**[26] 4207 7-10-9 **139**.... HenryOliver 69
(Sue Smith) *midfield: rdn and lost pl 9th: lost tch 3 out* **40/1**
-010 **P** **Lush Life (IRE)**[40] 3947 6-10-12 **142**.... BarryGeraghty —
(Nicky Henderson) *chsd ldrs: lost pl after 6th: bhd whn p.u bef 7th: fatally injured* **10/1**

5m 40.1s (-20.90) **Going Correction** -0.525s/f (Firm) **23** Ran SP% **124.5**
Speed ratings: **113,111,111,108,108 107,107,106,105,105 105,105,104,102,101 98,93,90,88,86 86,86,—**
toteswingers:1&2:£175.50, 1&3:£152.20, 2&3:£34.70 CSF £252.70 CT £3089.47 TOTE £23.50: £4.30, £4.40, £2.60, £8.90; EX 533.90 Trifecta £6096.80 Pool: £13,182.29 - 1.60 winning units..
Owner Matt Archer & The Late Miss J Broadhurst **Bred** Lodge Park Stud **Trained** Nicholashayne, Devon
■ Conor O'Farrell's first ever ride at the festival.

FOCUS
Traditionally a competitive staying handicap hurdle and it was no different this year, with perhaps all bar one of the 23 runners given a chance of sorts. There was certainly no hanging around (winning time 0.90secs quicker than RP Standard), so stamina was required in abundance. The form looks solid and Buena Vista is rated up 5lb on last year's win.

NOTEBOOK
Buena Vista(IRE) was running at his seventh consecutive festival. Just as he had done 12 months ago off 5lb lower, he turned the screw on his rivals a long way from home and powered up the hill having flown the last. Many had expected David Pipe to take this with Chartreux, who had been laid out for the race, but so had this fellow, and he fairly whizzed around the course under a fine ride from Conor O'Farrell. Although now a 10-y-o, he clearly retains all his dash, and there's no reason why he can't return next season and put up another bold show in his bid for a hat-trick. Official explanation: trainer said, regarding apparent improvement in form, that the gelding was suited by the better ground (op 18-1)
Son Amix(FR) fared best of the Irish challenge. Fourth off 3lb lower in last season's Fred Winter, he improved for the step up to this trip when second on heavy ground at Leopardstown and took another step forward here, just being unable to get close enough to seriously challenge the winner.
Sivota(IRE), two places behind Son Amix at Leopardstown, probably should have reversed form, being held up right at the back before finishing strongly to just miss second. He remains unexposed as a stayer. \n\x\x This was a cracking effort from top weight \bKnockara Beau\p, who had finished second to Grands Crus in the Cleeve before winning a handicap off 8lb lower at Carlisle. Never far away, he kept plugging on once his winning chance had gone and deserved to hold on for a place. He could go to Punchestown if the ground is soft enough and will return to fences next season.\n (tchd 17-2)
Knockara Beau(IRE), who had finished second to Grands Crus in the Cleeve before winning a handicap off 8lb lower at Carlisle, put up a cracking effort under top weight. Never far away, he kept plugging on once his winning chance had gone and deserved to hold on for a place. He could go to Punchestown if the ground is soft enough and will return to fences next season. (op 25-1)
Queiros Bleu(FR) ◆ was noted travelling well at the top of the hill and started to edge closer, but he was never going the pace to launch a challenge. He should develop into a useful staying chaser next season.
Barwell Bridge showed his last-time-out Kempton running to be all wrong, returning to the sort of form shown when second over C&D in December. (tchd 22-1)
Viking Blond(FR), another who returned to form, was up there chasing the pace and stuck on for pressure on ground he likes.
Heavenly Blues(GER) lacked the pace to get involved on ground that would have been quick enough.
Tarablaze, back from an unsuccessful spell over fences, wouldn't have appreciated the drying ground, but travelled well none the less and fared better than his finishing position suggests.
Don't Push It(IRE) will no doubt have delighted connections. He raced with plenty of zest before sticking on under pressure and is sure to prove popular back at Aintree next month.
Rivage D'Or(FR) hasn't always convinced with his attitude under pressure and slowly drifted away having been unable to respond once ridden. (tchd 9-1, tchd 12-1 in a place)
Micheal Flips(IRE) again failed to convince he has the stamina for 3m. (op 22-1)
Chartreux(FR), who suffered for getting into a duel too soon when third at the course on New Year's Day, had been kept fresh with this in mind and just crept in at the bottom of the weights. However, having again been ridden plenty close enough to the pace, he was soon in trouble after a mistake two out and dropped away, possibly finding the ground a touch on the quick side. (op 13-2)
Barafundle(IRE) has been below his best on two visits here.
Alfie Spinner(IRE), previously progressive, was another to disappoint. (op 14-1)
Lush Life(IRE) had the beating of a few of these on his December C&D win and could be forgiven his last-time-out Sandown effort, but was never travelling here and was pulled up at halfway, sadly having broken a hind leg. The winner of four of his previous eight starts, his career highlight was when beating Menorah at Ascot last season. (op 11-1, tchd 12-1 in a place)

4818 RYANAIR CHASE (REGISTERED AS THE FESTIVAL TROPHY STEEPLE CHASE) GRADE 1 (17 fncs) 2m 5f
2:40 (2:40) (Class 1) 5-Y-0+

£154,896 (£58,116; £29,099; £14,508; £7,281; £3,640)

Form RPR
-4FP **1** **Albertas Run (IRE)**[61] 3560 10-11-10 **166**.... APMcCoy 168+
(Jonjo O'Neill) *led to 3rd: styd pressing ldr: slt ld 4th to 8th: led 9th: hdd 10th: styd chalng: hit 13th: rdn after 4 out: led 3 out: hrd drvn and styd on u.p run-in: hld on wl* **6/1**[2]
3054 **2** *1* **Kalahari King (FR)**[54] 3675 10-11-10 **162**.... GrahamLee 167+
(Ferdy Murphy) *hld up in rr: hdwy and hit 4 out: styng on whn hit next: str run appr 2 out to chse wnr sn after last: styd on strly but a hld* **7/1**[3]
21 **3** *2* **Rubi Light (FR)**[26] 4227 6-11-10 **157**.... AELynch 166+
(Robert Alan Hennessy, Ire) *w wnr: led 3rd: hdd next: styd chalng: hit 7th: led next: hdd 9th: led 10th: rdn: hdd and blnd 3 out: lost 2nd next: chsd wnr again last: no imp: one pce into 3rd run-in* **16/1**
-251 **4** *4 ½* **Poquelin (FR)**[96] 2886 8-11-10 **170**.... RWalsh 162
(Paul Nicholls) *trckd ldrs: drvn along after 4 out: one pce next: effrt u.p appr 2 out but rchd ldrs: kpt on same pce* **2/1**[1]
455- **5** *nk* **Voy Por Ustedes (FR)**[337] 5183 10-11-10 **155**.... BarryGeraghty 160
(Nicky Henderson) *trckd ldrs: rdn 3 out and one pce sn after: kpt on again whn hit last: styd on again cl home* **11/1**
-263 **6** *4* **J'y Vole (FR)**[49] 3778 8-11-3 **161**.... PTownend 150
(W P Mullins, Ire) *hld up in rr and t.k.h: hdwy 13th: wnt cl 3rd 4 out: rdn to chse wnr 2 out but no imp and wknd sn after* **8/1**
3115 **7** *10* **Tartak (FR)**[26] 4201 8-11-10 **156**....(t) PaddyBrennan 150
(Tom George) *chsd ldrs: hit 8th: blnd 12th: rdn next: hit 3 out and sn wknd* **16/1**
1552 **8** *6* **Gauvain (GER)**[26] 4201 9-11-10 **158**.... DarylJacob 142
(Nick Williams) *chsd ldrs: hit 2nd: dropped to rr 7th: mstke 10th: no ch whn blnd 4 out* **11/1**
F014 **9** *2 ¾* **Hey Big Spender (IRE)**[19] 4352 8-11-10 **154**.... JoeTizzard 138
(Colin Tizzard) *t.k.h: in rr but in tch: sme prog whn hit 13th: no ch after* **18/1**
2322 **10** *2 ½* **Roberto Goldback (IRE)**[26] 4227 9-11-10 **156**.... RMPower 136
(Mrs John Harrington, Ire) *t.k.h: mstke 2nd: blnd 5th: sn bhd: no ch whn blnd 4 out* **16/1**
/230 **P** **Breedsbreeze (IRE)**[26] 4200 9-11-10 **150**.... NickScholfield —
(Paul Nicholls) *hit 8th and 10th: nvr travelling: a in rr: t.o whn p.u bef 2 out* **40/1**

5m 7.30s (-12.10) **Going Correction** -0.30s/f (Good) **11** Ran SP% **113.2**
Speed ratings: **111,110,109,108,108 106,102,100,99,98 —**
toteswingers:1&2:£5.30, 1&3:£21.40, 2&3:£23.70 CSF £46.39 CT £633.52 TOTE £6.20: £2.20, £2.40, £2.90; EX 32.30 Trifecta £417.90 Pool: £13,425.91 - 23.76 winning units..
Owner Trevor Hemmings **Bred** Oliver And Salome Brennan **Trained** Cheltenham, Gloucs
■ A protestor against Ryanair got on to the track on the run-in, coming very close to the horses.

FOCUS
For all that this was a quality affair, it is worth noting the horses that didn't make the line-up for various reasons. Riverside Theatre missed the race due to hairline fracture to his pelvis, Tranquil Sea was withdrawn the preceding Saturday when scoping badly, while Captain Cee Bee (third) and Somersby (fifth) came out after running in the Queen Mother the previous day, and Rare Bob was also declared a non-runner after pulling up in Spinal Research Handicap on Tuesday.\n\x\x The early pace was surprisingly steady. A solid renewal, with Albertas Run rated a few pounds off last season's mark, Kalahari King rated right up up to his best and Rubi Light priducing a step up, but Poquelin 6lb off last year's mark.

NOTEBOOK
Albertas Run(IRE) took a crashing fall at Ascot earlier in the season, and finished stiff and sore after his poor effort in the King George, so this was a brave performance to collect this contest for the second time in succession, a third victory at the Festival all told. Good ground is the key to him, as he regularly shows his best when there isn't any ease underfoot, but something that is clearly evident is that he is all heart and gives everything when his rider asks for him to go on. Always close up here, his jumping wasn't perfect but he responded and responded, finding more for pressure and he came away again once in command. Trevor Hemmings was apparently keen to run in the Gold Cup too, but Jonjo O'Neill was seemingly able to twist the owner's arm and got the right result. The horse may go for the Melling Chase at Aintree, which he won last year. Official explanation: trainer said, regarding apparent improvement in form, that the gelding was suited by the better ground (tchd 13-2)
Kalahari King(FR), runner-up in the 2009 Arkle, didn't run too badly in last season's Champion Chase but hadn't sparkled after that, and had been mainly disappointing since Punchestown. It was surprising in some ways to see him so relatively short in the betting taking that into account, but he did have a decent record running at this course in March, so it didn't come as a great surprise to see the horse raise his game again at Prestbury Park, travelling strongly, and jumping with exuberance under restraint, before keeping on well up the hill. It's unfortunate for him that he is a nearly horse at this meeting, but connections have had plenty of enjoyment throughout the years with him, including a Grade 1 victory, and he runs up to his best when it counts. (op 5-1)
Rubi Light(FR) ◆ had a reputation of being a grand jumper of fences, but the ground seemed to have gone against him considering his best form in his homeland. Considering his relative lack of experience, this was a fantastic performance by the 6-y-o, who rallied under pressure and fought on again to secure third. It would be nice to see him now given a break and time to grow into his frame, as connections will surely reap a rich dividend next season. He could run at Punchestown in the meantime.
Poquelin(FR) had a clear chance considering his rivals had plenty of questions to answer, but he wasn't able to reverse last year's form with Albertas Run after having a smooth passage on the inside. Undoubtedly talented, it appears that Poquelin is not quite good enough to win a competitive Grade 1. (op 5-2, tchd 3-1 in a place)
Voy Por Ustedes(FR), a fascinating participant, was making his debut for the Nicky Henderson stable. A stalwart of this meeting in the past, he had appeared to lose his form in the latter stages of his time with Alan King, who was mainly out of form last season, but it was heart-warming to see the old campaigner shows loads of enthusiasm for the game, and even kick on again after the last. One hopes that his fire has been re-ignited and he will be seen at Aintree next. (op 12-1)

J'y Vole(FR) was unlucky in the race last season when finishing a place behind Poquelin, as she got hampered after three out. She hasn't run badly since but hadn't been able to get her head in front recently, and her trainer reported in the morning that her preparation hadn't gone well this time in the lead up to the race, which seemed a plausible excuse for this effort as she was tanking into the contention three out but didn't pick up as looked likely.

Tartak(FR) doesn't look an easy ride, as although he came under strong pressure quite a way out while others were still moving well, he kept going and wasn't beaten a long way.

Gauvain(GER) had run really well on his previous outing behind Riverside Theatre, and promised to run a decent race here on the back of that, but not for the first time he didn't repeat his previous performance, and is just a hard horse to predict. (op 10-1)

4819 LADBROKES WORLD HURDLE GRADE 1 (12 hdls) 3m

3:20 (3:20) (Class 1) 4-Y-O+

£148,226 (£55,614; £27,846; £13,884; £6,968; £3,484)

Form	Pos	Dist	Horse	Jockey	RPR
1-11	**1**		**Big Buck's (FR)**[78] 3199 8-11-10 174	RWalsh	166+
			(Paul Nicholls) *trckd ldrs: wnt 2nd 8th: rdn to ld between last 2: rdr dropped whip: j.lft last: hung lft run-in whn pressed: plld out more fnl 100yds and wl on top at fin* **10/11**[1]		
-111	**2**	1 ¾	**Grands Crus (FR)**[47] 3807 6-11-10 169	(t) TomScudamore	163+
			(David Pipe) *hld up in last early: hdwy after 3 out: gng wl trcking ldrs bef 2 out: rdn and chsd wnr appr last: chalng run-in: nt qckn and hld fnl 100yds* **7/2**[2]		
-411	**3**	2 ¾	**Mourad (IRE)**[48] 3796 6-11-10 158	PTownend	161
			(W P Mullins, Ire) *hld up: hdwy into midfield appr 7th: trckd ldrs bef 2 out: rdn in 3rd pl bef last: styd on run-in: nt pce to shake-up front 2* **8/1**[3]		
1B21	**4**	½	**Cross Kennon (IRE)**[26] 4207 7-11-10 153	AlanO'Keeffe	160
			(Jennie Candlish) *j.rt: led at stdy pce: tempo increased bef 3 out: rdn and hdd between last 2: outpcd by ldrs: styd on u.p run-in but hld* **50/1**		
-132	**5**	½	**Rigour Back Bob (IRE)**[32] 4107 6-11-10 154	AndrewJMcNamara	163+
			(E J O'Grady, Ire) *hld up in midfield: hmpd and shuffled bk on bnd after 3 out: towards rr tl styd on again appr last: clsng towards fin* **80/1**		
-456	**6**	2 ¾	**Berties Dream (IRE)**[32] 4107 8-11-10 150	(p) AELynch	160+
			(Paul John Gilligan, Ire) *prom: j. slowly 4th: tightened up on bnd after 3 out and lost pl: pushed along 2 out: rallied after last: styd on towards fin but n.d to ldrs* **50/1**		
4224	**7**	*shd*	**Any Given Day (IRE)**[26] 4207 6-11-10 159	JasonMaguire	157
			(Donald McCain) *hld up: hdwy into midfield appr 2 out: rdn appr last: styd on u.p but no real imp on ldrs: one pce fnl 100yds* **66/1**		
2/1-	**8**	¾	**Fiveforthree (IRE)**[29] 4152 9-11-10 163	DJCasey	158+
			(W P Mullins, Ire) *hld up: hdwy after 3 out: effrt to chse ldrs and abt 4 l off the pce appr last where j.lft: edgd rt whn no ex and wl btn fnl 110yds* **12/1**		
3033	**9**	½	**Restless Harry**[47] 3807 7-11-10 153	HenryOliver	156
			(Robin Dickin) *trckd ldrs: n.m.r and hmpd after 2 out: sn rdn and lost pl: no imp bef last* **40/1**		
0025	**10**	6	**Powerstation (IRE)**[48] 3796 11-11-10 157	DNRussell	151
			(Eamon O'Connell, Ire) *in tch: trcking ldrs appr 2 out: rdn bef last: sn wknd* **50/1**		
122-	**11**	15	**Souffleur**[343] 5093 8-11-10 151	TomO'Brien	134
			(Peter Bowen) *hld up: outpcd after 2 out: nvr on terms* **100/1**		
3-44	**12**	¾	**Zaynar (FR)**[96] 2884 6-11-10 158	(p) BarryGeraghty	134
			(Nicky Henderson) *nt fluent and rn in snatches: niggled along after 9th: wknd 2 out: eased whn wl btn appr last* **12/1**		
4051	**13**	30	**Ashkazar (FR)**[75] 3293 7-11-10 161	TimmyMurphy	129
			(David Pipe) *prom: lost pl but stl wl there bef 6th: n.m.r and hmpd on bnd after 9th: bhd after* **22/1**		

5m 50.8s (-10.20) **Going Correction** -0.525s/f (Firm) **13 Ran SP% 117.5**

Speed ratings (Par 117): **96,95,94,94,94 93,93,92,92,90 85,85,75**

toteswingers:1&2:£1.60, 1&3:£3.30, 2&3:£4.70 CSF £3.74 CT £15.64 TOTE £1.80: £1.10, £1.90, £2.10; EX 4.50 Trifecta £11.10 Pool: £21,221.82 - 1,413.15 winning units..

Owner The Stewart Family **Bred** Henri Poulat **Trained** Ditcheat, Somerset

■ Stewards' Enquiry : D N Russell three-day ban: careless riding (Apr 2-4)

FOCUS

This was arguably the most eagerly anticipated race of the week, certainly the biggest clash. It certainly lived up to its billing, as although run at an unsatisfactory steady pace until the tempo increased racing away from the stands on the final circuit, the 'big' four had all moved to the head of the field by the bottom of the hill, led on the turn in by outsider Cross Kennon, and any one of the quartet could have been called the winner racing inside the final 2f. Many will question the form with outsiders filling the next four spots, but that was largely due to the steady pace, and it's best just to focus on the front trio. They finished in the right order but it's not a race that lends itself to a big figure as they finished in a bit of a heap.Big Buck's was 10lb below his best with Grands Crus 8lb off.

NOTEBOOK

Big Buck's(FR), as we've seen so many times in the past, found the most, surging to the front well before the last and readily pulling out extra on the climb to the line, this despite Ruby Walsh having dropped his whip around a furlong and a half from home, which wouldn't have been at all ideal on a notoriously idle performer. Many had questioned whether he'd have the pace of Grands Crus, who probably represented the most dangerous rival he had faced since reverting to hurdles two seasons ago, but Walsh was seen at his finest, being fully aware of the lack of early pace and positioning the 8-y-o in a prominent stalking position. If ever he was going to be beaten, this was probably it, with three high-class types waiting to take their shot, but one always got the impression he would extend again and that's just what he did, having got a good jump at the last, when it momentarily looked as though the runner-up would go past. This win confirms him as a truly great staying hurdler, if indeed it needed confirming, and another ringing endorsement for the horse was that after the race Walsh said he'd have the speed to go close in a truly-run Champion Hurdle. We'll almost certainly never see him in that race, but many will be asking the whether we will see him back over fences in next season's Gold Cup, as with Kauto Star and Denman set to be veterans, the sad loss of Pride Of Dulcote, and a disappointing run from Aiteenthirtythree in Wednesday's RSA, Nicholls will be on the lookout for his next staying chasing star, so it may be that it's hard to resist the temptation, despite post-race comments that he'll "never see a fence again". If he does stay hurdling it's hard to imagine he won't set himself apart from previously top stayers, such as Inglis Drever who won three between 2005-8, and make it four in a row, for which he's a best-priced 2-1. He'll now bid to follow up at Aintree, just as he did last year. (op Evens after early 5-4 in a place)

Grands Crus(FR) has made big strides since winning a course handicap off 126 earlier in the season, and his emergence made the race. His jaw-dropping display in the Cleeve, when pulling Scudamore's arms out before storming clear, was visually one of the most impressive we've seen and his trainer had not been shy in how bullish he was over his chance. The two big questions, though, were how he would settle and whether he'd handle this quicker ground, and while he dropped his head nicely towards the rear, he never looked overly happy on the surface, which speaks volumes for his raw ability. Despite this, he effortlessly moved closer running down the hill, tracking Big Buck's into the straight, and being the last off the bridle. However, having been produced to win the race coming to the last and more or less got alongside soon after, he found himself unable to answer as the champ went again. His progress has been astounding and, being just a 6-y-o, it's hoped he can make further strides. It will be fascinating to see whether connections stick to the original plan and send him chasing, as having come so close, they may be tempted to have another crack at this, especially if Big Buck's reverts to fences. (tchd 4-1)

Mourad(IRE)'s trainer was himself talking up his chances throughout the week, the 6-y-o having twice readily won Grade 2s on testing ground since reappearing with a good fourth behind Hurricane Fly in the Hatton's Grace. Improving all the time, he was always well positioned under Townend, who moved him into a menacing stalking position running downhill, but when asked to go and win the race, he just lacked the acceleration of the front pair, and indeed, perhaps the class. This goes down as a career-best and he'll probably go to Punchestown before a possible crack at one of the valuable races at Auteuil in the summer. (tchd 9-1 in a place)

Cross Kennon(IRE) ,whose last-time-out Haydock win over this week's Spinal Research Chase winner Bensalem had been put down to the testing ground, showed himself to be anything but a plodder on this much livelier going, rallying well having been passed by the major players. He had the run of things out in front, but deserves huge credit none the less. Fences may be an option next season for this former point winner. (op 40-1)

Rigour Back Bob(IRE), having lost his position as a result of being hampered, flew up the hill and nothing was finishing better. He finished closer to Mourad than he had done at Leopardstown over Christmas, appreciating the faster surface, and could develop into a smart novice chaser next season, assuming that's the route he takes. (op 100-1)

Berties Dream(IRE), last season's shock Albert Bartlett winner, has struggled this season, including tried over fences early on, but he showed what he is capable of when right with the first-time cheekpieces applied, staying on again having been another to lose his pitch.

Any Given Day(IRE), disappointing on unsuitably heavy ground behind Cross Kennon at Haydock, left that form behind but the way he ran seemed to confirm 3m stretches him.

Fiveforthree(IRE) travelled as though retaining all his old ability. He's had little luck with injuries since winning at the 2008 Festival, but enjoyed a nice comeback win over 2m at Punchestown and looked a live threat with 2f to run. He was unable to find any extra from the last, but perhaps will come on again, and may join Mourad at Punchestown before a possible venture to France. (tchd 11-1)

Restless Harry, although admirably tough and consistent, has been chasing the shadow of most of the top performers all season and this run again confirmed he's not a Grade 1 performer, for all that the ground was probably too fast. He's set to go over fences next season.

Powerstation(IRE), third to Big Buck's for each of the past two seasons, doesn't have the legs for it now he's 11.

Zaynar(FR), third in last year's Champion Hurdle, has had a disappointing season and the return of cheekpieces failed to help, racing lazily before dropping right out. He'll go chasing next season. (op 16-1)

Ashkazar(FR), who swooped late to win a handicap off 152 at the course in January, was soon beaten after getting hampered. (op 33-1)

4820 BYRNE GROUP PLATE (HANDICAP CHASE) GRADE 3 (17 fncs) 2m 5f

4:00 (4:00) (Class 1) 5-Y-O+

£42,757 (£16,042; £8,032; £4,005; £2,010; £1,005)

Form	Pos	Dist	Horse	Jockey	RPR
52F1	**1**		**Holmwood Legend**[5] 4730 10-10-6 **130** 5ex	KieranBurke(3)	146+
			(Patrick Rodford) *trckd ldrs: chal 3 out: sn led: rdn bef 2 out: hit last: styd on strly run-in* **25/1**		
42-P	**2**	3 ½	**Aimigayle**[40] 3948 8-10-6 **127**	ColinBolger	139+
			(Suzy Smith) *mde most tl jnd 3 out and sn hdd: styd on wl to hold 2nd appr last but no imp on wnr* **25/1**		
0	**3**	1 ¾	**Beautiful Sound (IRE)**[60] 3596 9-10-6 **127**	JasonMaguire	139+
			(Gordon Elliott, Ire) *in rr: blnd 2nd: mstke 3rd: sme hdwy whn hmpd 4 out: kpt on after 3 out: chsd ldrs last: hung lft run-in but kpt on* **9/2**[1]		
-406	**4**	5	**Consigliere (FR)**[68] 3438 8-11-10 **145**	(bt) TomScudamore	149
			(David Pipe) *hld up in mid-div: hdwy 10th: chsd ldrs 4 out: wknd last* **20/1**		
-410	**5**	2	**Call Me A Legend**[40] 3949 7-11-0 **135**	RobertThornton	139
			(Alan King) *in rr: hdwy 10th: drvn to chse ldrs 3 out: one pce whn mstke 2 out: no ch after* **20/1**		
1206	**6**	½	**Matuhi**[12] 4487 8-10-9 **135**	(t) CO'Farrell(5)	137
			(David Pipe) *in rr: hdwy and hmpd 4 out: rallied next: one pce fr 2 out* **16/1**		
6611	**7**	3	**Quartz De Thaix (FR)**[10] 4531 7-11-2 **137** 5ex	AidanColeman	136
			(Venetia Williams) *in rr and rdn along fr 7th: u.p whn nt fluent 4 out: styd on u.p fr 2 out: nt rch ldrs* **7/1**[3]		
4302	**8**	3 ½	**Bible Lord (IRE)**[36] 4010 10-10-5 **126**	NickScholfield	123
			(Andy Turnell) *hit 1st: pressed ldrs: rdn and ev ch 3 out: wknd bef next* **20/1**		
1053	**9**	5	**Edgbriar (FR)**[40] 3949 9-11-6 **141**	(p) DominicElsworth	133
			(Paul Webber) *chsd ldrs tl lost pl 4 out: rallied and wl in tch 3 out: wknd 2 out* **14/1**		
1006	**10**	5	**Storymaker**[31] 4116 10-10-5 **126**	PaddyAspell	111
			(Sandy Forster) *hit 3rd: wl bhd tl styd on fr 2 out: kpt on clsng stages* **100/1**		
6310	**11**	1 ¾	**Tatenen (FR)**[19] 4352 7-11-12 **147**	AndrewThornton	130
			(Richard Rowe) *blnd 4th and 9th: a in rr* **33/1**		
-F01	**12**	2 ¾	**Gansey (IRE)**[19] 4357 9-11-0 **135**	PeterBuchanan	115
			(Sue Smith) *pressed ldrs fr 6th: chal fr 4 out to 3 out: sn wknd* **25/1**		
60-1	**13**	26	**Aigle D'Or**[111] 2665 8-11-3 **138**	APMcCoy	117
			(Nicky Henderson) *chsd ldrs tl lost pl 10th: no ch whn hmpd 4 out* **11/2**[2]		
2415	**14**	3 ½	**Hollo Ladies (IRE)**[40] 3955 6-11-4 **139**	GrahamLee	90
			(Ferdy Murphy) *mstkes 4th and 8th: a in rr* **9/1**		
224	**15**	5	**I'm A Legend**[26] 4223 9-9-11 **125**	(p) MarkQuinlan(7)	71
			(Neil Mulholland) *chsd ldrs tl blnd 10th: sn bhd* **20/1**		
136U	**F**		**Just Smudge**[14] 4440 9-10-7 **128**	SamThomas	—
			(Venetia Williams) *bhd fr 6th: no ch whn fell 4 out* **33/1**		
P112	**P**		**Peplum (FR)**[5] 4730 8-10-8 **129**	JamieMoore	—
			(Gary Moore) *blnd and bhd 6th: struggling u.p in rr fr 10th: t.o whn p.u bef 2 out* **18/1**		
234P	**P**		**Piraya (FR)**[19] 4352 8-11-3 **138**	(tp) JohnnyFarrelly	—
			(David Pipe) *in rr: t.o whn p.u bef 8th* **33/1**		
0140	**P**		**Plein Pouvoir (FR)**[12] 4487 8-10-1 **127**	RTDunne(5)	—
			(Venetia Williams) *chsd ldrs: hit 5th: wknd fr 10th: t.o whn p.u bef 3 out* **50/1**		

P-45 **F** **You're The Top (FR)**[138] 2086 7-11-2 **137**........................ BarryGeraghty —
(Nicky Henderson) *trckd ldrs: j. slowly 7th: stl in bhd ldrs but drvn and one pce whn fell 4 out* **16/1**

5m 8.17s (-11.23) **Going Correction** -0.30s/f (Good) **20** Ran SP% **122.1**
Speed ratings: **109,107,107,105,104 104,103,101,99,97 97,96,86,84,83 —,—,—,—,—**
toteswingers:1&2:£143.50, 1&3:£26.30, 2&3:£35.40 CSF £513.44 CT £3320.18 TOTE £41.00: £8.40, £6.20, £1.40, £6.70; EX 977.70 Trifecta £8967.40 Part won. Pool: £12,118.22 - 0.50 winning units..
Owner Brian Derrick **Bred** Mrs P M Underhill **Trained** Ash, Somerset
■ The first festival winner for both Pat Rodford and Keiran Burke, runner-up with Sparky May earlier in the week.

FOCUS
This didn't look the strongest renewal of this race as most recent renewals contained a runner rated at least 150 and the highest here was rated 147. Holmwood Legend showed big improvement, up 10lb on his lateset win. The second is rated 4lb off her best with the third better than the bare result.

NOTEBOOK
Holmwood Legend had run and won the previous Saturday at Sandown from Peplum. Exposed and having his eighth start of the season, the 5lb he was penalised for his Esher success may have just about got him into this race (the bottom weight here got in off 125), and a trainer/jockey combination gained their biggest success of the season in financial terms. Pat Rodford is due to retire fairly soon, so this was a perfect way to close a training career.
Aimigayle ran an exceptional race considering she was pulled up last time on her return from a 429-day break. She was given a bold ride from the front early, and kept going well all the way to the line after being headed and seemingly going nowhere turning in. It remains to be seen whether this takes a lot out of her, but she is nothing if not game.
Beautiful Sound(IRE) ◆ was being aimed for the Kim Muir, and had a top amateur rider already booked for that race, but didn't make the cut for that contest. The extra distance of that race would have helped him no end (although it's debatable as to whether he'd have beaten runaway winner Junior), as he came home strongly after being well behind, a tactic that didn't work out well on the day. Lightly raced for a 9-y-o, he is one to watch out for in the coming weeks over bit further. (op 11-2)
Consigliere(FR), third in last season's Grand Annual off the same official rating, ideally wants softer ground, so this was a good effort, although he still doesn't always look as if he's loving life under pressure, even with the tongue-tie back on.
Call Me A Legend, whose connections had toyed with going for the Grand Annual before she got taken off her legs last time at that distance, is probably off to the paddocks now after a battling performance. (op 18-1)
Matuhi came with a promising effort after racing in midfield but faltered late on.
Quartz De Thaix(FR), running under a penalty, ran on too late after getting behind. (op 13-2)
Gansey(IRE) was just about leading into the final bend but weakened dramatically thereafter. He ran better than his final position suggests.
Aigle D'Or has a decent record when kept fresh, and had been deliberately kept off the track since his win at Newbury in November - he had Matuhi and Call Me A Legend behind that day. However, his runs at the Festival previously had not been good, but he wasn't completely beaten when hampered by a faller four out, although he still had work to do after running into the back of a rival jumping the water. (op 9-2)
Hollo Ladies(IRE), down in trip and back on better ground, never featured.
Just Smudge ◆ appeared to be travelling strongly, albeit with quite a bit to do, when falling at the fourth from home. (op 40-1)
Piraya(FR) Official explanation: jockey said gelding was outpaced (op 40-1)
You're The Top(FR) ◆, who went off favourite for last year's Grand Annual, was travelling ominously well when falling four out, and would surely have been involved in the finish considering his position at the time. (op 40-1)

4821 FULKE WALWYN KIM MUIR CHALLENGE CUP (HANDICAP CHASE) (AMATEUR RIDERS) (21 fncs) 3m 1f 110y

4:40 (4:40) (Class 2) (0-140,140) 5-Y-O+

£30,010 (£9,375; £4,685; £2,345; £1,170; £590)

Form				RPR

1-32 **1** **Junior**[75] 3293 8-11-6 **134**........................(b) MrJJCodd 157+
(David Pipe) *trckd ldrs: wnt 2nd after 9th: chsng clr ldr whn mstke 17th: clsd 3 out: led sn after: clr bef 2 out: styd on strly and wl in command after* **10/3**[1]

2P-0 **2** *24* **Faasel (IRE)**[97] 2871 10-11-9 **137**........................(bt) MrRMahon 135
(David Pipe) *trckd ldrs: hit 8th: rdn to chse wnr appr 2 out: kpt on u.p* **20/1**

2P-3 **3** *3 ¼* **Deal Done (FR)**[18] 4388 7-11-8 **136**........................(v[1]) MrRPMcNamara 132+
(D T Hughes, Ire) *prom: led 3rd: clr at 15th: 5 l ld 4 out: reduced advantage 3 out: hdd sn after: lost 2nd appr 2 out: plugged on at one pce after* **20/1**

5U11 **4** *½* **Galaxy Rock (IRE)**[16] 4414 7-11-3 **131** 5ex................(b) MrJTMcNamara 126
(Jonjo O'Neill) *midfield: pckd 7th: impr to trck ldrs 15th: pushed along appr 3 out: kpt on same pce* **18/1**

4-36 **5** *8* **Pomme Tiepy (FR)**[48] 3798 8-11-3 **131**........................(b[1]) MsKWalsh 116
(W P Mullins, Ire) *hld up in midfield: hit 12th: styd on fr 2 out: prog to go 5th at last: nvr able to trble ldrs* **14/1**

2221 **6** *6* **Fredo (IRE)**[42] 3902 7-11-2 **130**........................(p) MrJDMoore 109
(Ian Williams) *hld up: hdwy into midfield appr 9th: rdn whn chsng ldrs bef 17th: outpcd bef 3 out: no imp after* **16/1**

U513 **7** *nk* **Far More Serious (IRE)**[12] 4486 11-11-10 **138**.......(p) MrSWaley-Cohen 117
(Charlie Longsdon) *midfield: hdwy and in tch w ldrs 10th: chsd ldrs in 3rd pl 4 out tl after 3 out: no imp after and btn* **16/1**

3502 **8** *1 ¼* **Billie Magern**[26] 4199 7-11-2 **137**........................ MrWTwiston-Davies[(7)] 118
(Nigel Twiston-Davies) *hld up in midfield: mstke 12th: mstke 17th: sn outpcd: n.d after* **16/1**

U210 **9** *5* **Cornish Sett (IRE)**[12] 4486 12-10-12 **131**................ MrRGHenderson[(5)] 106
(Caroline Keevil) *midfield: losing pl whn mstke 7th: nt fluent 10th: rdn after 12th: kpt on modly fr 2 out* **50/1**

03F5 **10** *7* **Khachaturian (IRE)**[26] 4209 8-11-4 **132**........................ MrCMotherway 98
(Donald McCain) *in tch: rdn and wknd after 15th* **20/1**

U0- **11** *26* **Saddlers Storm (IRE)**[18] 4384 9-11-8 **136**................ MrDerekO'Connor 76
(A J Martin, Ire) *hld up: hit 8th: rdn after 13th (water): nvr able to get on terms* **12/1**[3]

02P5 **12** *9* **Dance Island (IRE)**[27] 4186 8-11-5 **136**........................ MissGAndrews[(3)] 67
(Ben Case) *towards rr: rdn 14th: nvr on terms* **33/1**

2P10 **13** *19* **Den Of Iniquity**[75] 3293 10-11-6 **134**........................ MrMJO'Connor 46
(Warren Greatrex) *nt fluent: a in rr: struggling fnl circ: t.o* **66/1**

PU16 **14** *½* **Palypso De Creek (FR)**[26] 4209 8-11-1 **132**....................(b) MrMWall[(3)] 43
(Charlie Longsdon) *trckd ldrs: rdn appr 15th: wknd next: t.o* **50/1**

2111 **15** *21* **Massini Man (IRE)**[27] 4183 10-10-10 **129**................ MissCLWills[(5)] 19
(Brendan Powell) *led after 1st: hdd 3rd: remained handy tl lost pl 11th: bhd 15th: t.o* **33/1**

6221 **16** *3 ¼* **Alderley Rover (IRE)**[34] 4057 7-11-4 **132**....................(p) MrROHarding 19
(Donald McCain) *prom tl rdn and wknd after 15th: t.o* **25/1**

PP35 **P** **Burren Legend (IRE)**[26] 4200 10-10-13 **130**................ MrTJCannon[(3)] —
(Richard Rowe) *led: hdd after 1st: in tch: rdn and lost pl appr 13th (water): t.o whn p.u bef 4 out* **28/1**

-02P **U** **Richard's Sundance (IRE)**[61] 3568 9-11-9 **137**.... MrJoshuaGuerriero —
(Victor Dartnall) *midfield: hit 9th: disputing 6th but outpcd by ldrs whn mstke and uns rdr 4 out* **20/1**

-0P5 **P** **Can't Buy Time (IRE)**[75] 3292 9-11-12 **140**........................ MrAJBerry —
(Jonjo O'Neill) *hld up: impr into midfield 6th: rdn after 12th: wknd bef 16th: t.o whn p.u bef 2 out* **18/1**

13-P **P** **Galant Nuit (FR)**[96] 2888 7-11-6 **134**........................ MissNCarberry —
(Ferdy Murphy) *a bhd: t.o whn p.u bef 4 out* **15/2**[2]

-100 **P** **Minella Theatre (IRE)**[54] 3677 8-11-2 **130**........................ MrRBurton —
(Henrietta Knight) *a bhd: struggling after 11th: t.o whn p.u bef 17th* **25/1**

-124 **P** **Teddy's Reflection (IRE)**[26] 4199 8-11-1 **129**................ MrOGreenall —
(Henrietta Knight) *nt fluent 1st: midfield: lost pl bef 5th: t.o whn p.u bef 4 out* **66/1**

6144 **P** **Sheriff Hutton (IRE)**[40] 3953 8-10-13 **130**................ MrMWalford[(3)] —
(Tim Walford) *in tch: mstke 6th and reminders: sn lost pl: struggling whn mstke 13th (water): t.o whn p.u bef 15th* **33/1**

F21F **P** **Mostly Bob (IRE)**[19] 4352 8-11-1 **136**........................(t) MrJABest[(7)] —
(Philip Hobbs) *hld up: rdn along fnl circ: t.o whn p.u bef 2 out* **12/1**[3]

6m 20.5s (-17.70) **Going Correction** -0.30s/f (Good) **24** Ran SP% **131.0**
Speed ratings: **115,107,106,106,104 102,102,101,100,97 89,87,81,81,74 73,—,—,—,— —,—,—,E**
toteswingers:1&2:£10.90, 1&3:£12.90, 2&3:£318.90. totesuper7: Win: Not won. Place: £938.00 CSF £74.21 CT £1225.50 TOTE £3.10: £1.40, £4.90, £5.60, £4.60; EX 47.50 Trifecta £2102.20 Pool: £11,363.76 - 4.00 winning units..
Owner Middleham Park Racing LI **Bred** P C Green **Trained** Nicholashayne, Devon
■ Stewards' Enquiry : Mr R Mahon caution: used whip with excessive frequency.

FOCUS
This didn't look as competitive as the field size indicated and the searching gallop set by Deal Done ensured it was a thorough examination, with only six still being in with a shout after the fourth-last. The winning time was only 0.50secs over RP Standard. Junior is rated up a stone on his previous best with Faasel 10lb off his mark in this race last year. There is a case for rating the race a few pounds higher.

NOTEBOOK
Junior ◆, off since finishing third in a course handicap over hurdles on New Year's Day, forged his way to the front soon after three out and the result looked inevitable from then on. With this dour galloper being a particularly strong stayer, he duly drew right away, landing some tidy bets in the process. His case was there for all to see, having finished a fine third off this mark when trying to go toe for toe with Gold Cup contender Midnight Chase over 3m3f at the course in November, and the faster conditions here were only a positive for the versatile 8-y-o, who had landed the Ascot Stakes over 2m4f at the Royal meeting last summer - which is quite an accomplishment to have on his CV. Currently 25-1 for the Grand National, he would have lots in his favour if getting in (stays forever, likes good ground, gritty attitude), but it's far from guaranteed and the Scottish National, which should suit him down the ground, could be a suitable option. He'll head back to Royal Ascot in the summer. (op 7-2, tchd 4-1 in places)
Faasel(IRE), last year's runner-up and stablemate to the winner, who had been laid out for the race off only 2lb higher this time, moved well for much of the way and went into second well before two out, but could do nothing as Junior powered away. He's been called some names in his time and hasn't won as often as he should, but is clearly still capable of running well in a big handicap when conditions are right.
Deal Done(FR) produced a bold effort having expended plenty of energy in a first-time visor. Clear from before the 15th, he looked unlikely to stop at one stage, but took a chance at the fourth from home and, once the winner got within striking distance, it was a matter of when, not if, he was passed. To his credit he did keep on.
Galaxy Rock(IRE) would have found this much more competitive than when winning at either Ffos Las or Leicester (picked up a 5lb penalty for the latter win), but he acquitted himself well and kept on in the manner of a proper stayer. He could be another one for the Scottish National. (op 16-1)
Pomme Tiepy(FR) looked on a nice mark on old form and promised to improve for the return to a sounder surface in the first-time blinkers. She ran well, boxing on up the straight, but never looked like winning.
Fredo(IRE) gained a deserved, if somewhat fortunate, win at Towcester last time and looked one of the more interesting outsiders. However, he took a while to settle and, despite briefly threatening to get involved running down the hill, could make no further headway in the straight. (op 20-1)
Far More Serious(IRE) had his chance from a long way out but didn't get home. (op 20-1)
Billie Magern made early errors and could never find a rhythm.
Cornish Sett(IRE) tried to keep on again, having been niggled early on the final circuit, but was never in it.
Saddlers Storm(IRE), whose trainer isn't in the best of form at present, made a couple of mistakes and was never involved. (op 11-1)
Massini Man(IRE) found this more competitive than the races he has been winning. (op 40-1)
Richard's Sundance(IRE) was in the process of running a creditable race when unseating his rider four out. (op 14-1)
Galant Nuit(FR), third last year and seemingly laid out for the race, was the most notable disappointment. His name was barely mentioned in commentary and he's left with a bit to prove. (op 14-1)
Mostly Bob(IRE) may have been feeling the effects of his Racing Post Chase fall. (op 14-1)
T/Jkpt: Not won. T/Plt: £219.20 to a £1 stake. Pool:£902,226.06 - 3,003.34 winning tickets
T/Qpdt: £25.60 to a £1 stake. Pool:£38,127.21 - 1,101.17 winning tickets ST

2446 HEXHAM (L-H)

Thursday, March 17

OFFICIAL GOING: Heavy (4.3)
First fence in back straight omitted in all chases.
Wind: Fresh, against Weather: Overcast

4822 JOHN SPENCE COMMUNITY HIGH SCHOOL CONDITIONAL JOCKEYS' MARES' H'CAP HURDLE (8 hdls) 2m 110y

2:20 (2:20) (Class 4) (0-110,100) 4-Y-O+ **£2,740** (£798; £399)

Form				RPR

2-33 **1** **Lady Bluesky**[25] 4245 8-11-8 **99**........................ EwanWhillans[(3)] 105+
(Alistair Whillans) *cl up: led bef 4 out: mde rest: 8 l clr last: kpt on* **7/4**[1]

-515 **2** *2 ¾* **Wheyaye**[23] 4276 9-11-3 **94**........................ HenryBrooke[(3)] 96
(Valerie Jackson) *prom: drvn and outpcd after 3 out: rallied after next: chsd (clr) wnr run-in: no imp* **9/4**[2]

0620 **3** *5* **Bollin Ruth**[65] 3500 9-11-4 **100**........................ CallumWhillans[(8)] 97
(Donald Whillans) *set stdy pce: led to 4th: cl up: ev ch next to 2 out: outpcd between last 2* **11/2**

0004 **4** *6* **Gwyre (IRE)**[11] 4507 5-11-4 **92**........................ JamesHalliday 84
(Tim Easterby) *trckd ldrs: drvn after 3 out: rallied: wknd fr next* **9/1**

4434 **P** **Devils Delight (IRE)**[30] 4136 9-9-7 **75**..........................(t) JamesSmith(8) —
(James Moffatt) *t.k.h: in tch: hdwy to ld 4th: sddle sn slipped: hdd bef next: p.u bef 3 out* **9/2**[3]

4m 44.5s (27.10) **Going Correction** +1.50s/f (Heav) **5** Ran SP% **110.7**
Speed ratings (Par 105): **96,94,92,89,—**
CSF £6.31 TOTE £2.20: £2.30, £1.10; EX 7.50.
Owner Mrs S Harrow Mrs L M Whillans **Bred** C E Whiteley **Trained** Newmill-On-Slitrig, Borders

FOCUS
The first action at Yarridge Heights since November, and after a dry spell the ground was described as 'more holding, dead rather than heavy'. A very steady early pace in this conditional jockeys' mares' handicap hurdle. The winner is on the upgrade over hurdles and should rate higher.

NOTEBOOK
Lady Bluesky, a winner three times on the Flat in 2010, was making her handicap debut from a possibly lenient mark of 99 compared with her rating of 67 on the level. She settled better and a good jump two out sealed it, but in the end she had to be kept up to her work. She can surely win again at a similar level. (tchd 11-8)
Wheyaye, who took a 2m6f race at Wetherby in October from a 4lb lower mark, found herself hopelessly outpaced three out. She stayed on in good style to close the winner down on the run-in but this trip, even on a track as stiff as this, is too short for her. (op 4-1)
Bollin Ruth, who took this in 2008 - her one success in 19 starts now - was runner-up a year later. Having her second start after a six-month lay-off, she raced with plenty of enthusiasm but stopped to nothing going to the last. (op 7-2)
Gwyre(IRE), back over hurdles, was hard at work three out and was made to look very one-paced. Her sole success from a dozen starts over hurdles now was over an extra half mile at Sedgefield. (op 7-1)
Devils Delight(IRE), who has a history of wind problems, was back here after a second operation. Her saddle slipped before she landed in front at the fourth and she was pulled up after the next. Official explanation: jockey said saddle slipped (op 11-2 tchd 6-1)

4823 SWALLOW NOVICES' CHASE (11 fncs 1 omitted) 2m 110y
2:55 (2:55) (Class 4) 5-Y-0+ **£3,252** (£955; £477)

Form RPR
P-P4 **1** **Woody Waller**[33] 4063 6-10-7 0.................................... PaulGallagher(7) 124+
(Howard Johnson) *set stdy pce: mde all: rdn and 3 l clr last: styd on wl run-in* **7/1**[3]

/5-2 **2** 3 **Signalman**[12] 4472 7-10-7 0.. NathanMoscrop(7) 122+
(James Ewart) *trckd ldrs: blnd and nrly uns rdr 4 out: sn rcvrd: outpcd 2 out: rallied to chse (clr) wnr run-in: no imp* **6/4**[2]

-1U3 **3** 1 ½ **King O'The Gypsies (IRE)**[28] 4168 6-11-0 0.................... BrianHughes 118
(Howard Johnson) *trckd wnr: effrt and ev ch 2 out: no ex fr last: lost 2nd run-in* **5/6**[1]

4m 37.4s (27.60) **Going Correction** +1.50s/f (Heav) **3** Ran SP% **107.1**
Speed ratings: **96,93,92**
CSF £16.11 TOTE £7.30; EX 8.90.
Owner Mrs S Johnson & Exors of W M G Black **Bred** P M Hicks **Trained** Billy Row, Co Durham

FOCUS
A depleted field and the gallop was just fair in this novices' chase. The winner improved to the level expected from his Flat form.

NOTEBOOK
Woody Waller, rated 125 over hurdles, had won on the Flat last April. He had jumped moderately when last of four on his first try over fences but was much better this time in front. He opened up a gap of about three lengths at the last and was never in any real trouble. Quite a big type, he should go on from here. (tchd 11-2)
Signalman, rated 120 over hurdles, was a staying-on runner-up at Kelso on his first try over fences. A blunder four out cost him little ground and after struggling to keep up two out he stayed on to snatch a never dangerous second spot on the run-in. He deserves to go one better. (op 6-5 tchd 7-4)
King O'The Gypsies(IRE), a 130-rated hurdler, had unseated his rider when holding every chance and finished a well-beaten third on his two previous tries over fences. Not very big and hardly a natural jumper, he was hard at work two out and never really looked like seriously threatening his stablemate. He lost second spot on the run-in and, though he will be suited by much better ground, he looks to lack the scope to go far over fences. Official explanation: trainer had no explanation for the poor form shown (op 11-10 tchd 5-4 in a place)

4824 CHRISTINE BOYLE NOVICES' HURDLE (8 hdls) 2m 110y
3:35 (3:36) (Class 4) 4-Y-0+ **£2,740** (£798; £399)

Form RPR
0222 **1** **Rupert Lamb**[34] 4061 5-11-0 119.. BrianHughes 113+
(Howard Johnson) *t.k.h: mde most: clr after 2 out: 6 l up last: rdn run-in: jst hld on* **5/6**[1]

5031 **2** shd **Bollin Felix**[19] 4361 7-11-6 114.. RichieMcGrath 119+
(Tim Easterby) *prom: nt fluent 1st: hdwy to chse wnr bef 4 out: effrt whn hit 2 out: rallied and 6 l down last: kpt on strly: jst failed* **13/8**[2]

00F4 **3** 26 **Scotswell**[34] 4061 5-10-7 0.. GaryRutherford(7) 86
(Harriet Graham) *prom: drvn and outpcd bef 2 out: plugged on fr last: no imp* **28/1**

00P **4** 5 **Bunratty (IRE)**[11] 4506 5-11-0 0.. KennyJohnson 80
(Robert Johnson) *t.k.h: prom: mstke 4 out: rdn 2 out: sn wknd* **200/1**

0 **5** 1 ½ **Funky Munky**[116] 2552 6-10-11 0.. EwanWhillans(3) 78
(Alistair Whillans) *hld up: sme hdwy bef 4 out: wknd after next* **33/1**

5000 **6** 28 **Sam D'Oc (FR)**[11] 4506 5-11-0 0.. JamesReveley 50
(Keith Reveley) *hld up: struggling 4 out: btn after next: t.o* **16/1**

P6 **7** 30 **Moonlight Blaze**[17] 4393 4-10-7 0.. BarryKeniry 13
(Chris Fairhurst) *t.k.h: w ldr tl lost pl qckly bef 4 out: struggling fr next: t.o* **12/1**[3]

4m 39.0s (21.60) **Going Correction** +1.50s/f (Heav)
WFA 4 from 5yo+ 7lb **7** Ran SP% **113.1**
Speed ratings (Par 105): **109,108,96,94,93 80,66**
toteswingers:1&2:£1.20, 1&3:£3.90, 2&3:£4.90 CSF £2.44 TOTE £1.60: £1.10, £1.30; EX 3.10.
Owner Andrea & Graham Wylie **Bred** Miss S E Hall **Trained** Billy Row, Co Durham

FOCUS
A very steady gallop until the second-last hurdle and as the betting suggested just a two-horse race. The first pair are rated close to their marks.

NOTEBOOK
Rupert Lamb, a useful bumper horse, had finished runner-up on his last three starts. Back in trip, he jumped better setting a very steady pace in front. He looked nailed-on when taking a decisive advantage on the run up to the final flight but he idled badly on the run-in, and in the end the post came just in time. (op 5-4)
Bollin Felix had 11lb to find with the winner on official ratings. His jumping was not fault free and he looked booked for a modest second spot until making up many lengths on the idling winner on the run-in. Just denied at the line, his mark of 114 will shoot up as a result of this. (op 11-10)
Scotswell, eight lengths behind Rupert Lamb when they were runner-up and fourth respectively at Musselburgh on his second completed start over hurdles, is gradually getting the hang of things and low-grade handicaps now beckon. (op 22-1)
Bunratty(IRE), who did not jump fluently when pulled up on his first try over hurdles, showed a fair bit more if a fraction keen until he tired.
Funky Munky, a regressive plater on the Flat, again showed little on his second try over hurdles. (op 40-1 tchd 25-1)
Moonlight Blaze Official explanation: trainer said gelding was found to have bled

4825 BLACK GROUSE H'CAP CHASE (23 fncs 2 omitted) 4m
4:15 (4:15) (Class 4) (0-110,106) 5-Y-0+ **£2,927** (£859; £429; £214)

Form RPR
44V2 **1** **Matmata De Tendron (FR)**[11] 4508 11-10-5 **92**.......(p) PaulGallagher(7) 100
(Andrew Crook) *trckd ldrs: led 5 out: rdn 2 out: 3 l clr last: hld on wl u.p* **11/2**[3]

4P5 **2** ½ **Seeking Power (IRE)**[21] 4306 10-9-7 **80**.................... MissLAlexander(7) 88
(N W Alexander) *in tch: rdn fr 14th: rallied and chsng ldrs whn hit 3 out: rcvrd and chsd wnr after next: 3 l down last: styd on run-in: hld nr fin* **4/1**[1]

PPP **3** 42 **Panama At Once**[21] 4306 11-10-8 **88**..........................(p) JamesReveley 53
(Philip Kirby) *cl up: rdn and outpcd 4 out: wknd fr next* **10/1**

2136 **4** 9 **Master D'Or (FR)**[16] 4412 11-11-8 **102**.............................. PaulMoloney 58
(Sophie Leech) *hld up: stdy hdwy 16th: rdn and wknd fr 3 out* **9/1**

P3V1 **5** 11 **Blazing Diva (IRE)**[7] 4571 8-11-10 **104** 7ex.................... WilsonRenwick 49
(Sandy Thomson) *mde most to 5 out: cl up: ev ch after 2 out: wknd qckly* **11/2**[3]

1-12 **P** **Billsgrey (IRE)**[7] 4571 9-10-10 **90**.................................... CampbellGillies —
(William Amos) *in tch: mstke and lost pl 3rd: wknd fr 18th: t.o whn p.u bef last* **9/2**[2]

30-3 **P** **Polobury**[12] 9-9-7 **80** oh10.. GaryRutherford(7) —
(Harriet Graham) *bhd: pushed along and lost tch 14th: t.o whn p.u bef 5 out* **12/1**

-4PF **P** **Only The Best**[31] 4114 8-11-0 **101**.. TonyKelly(7) —
(Ferdy Murphy) *bhd: rdn 14th: struggling fr 17th: t.o whn p.u bef 5 out* **7/1**

2142 **R** **Aghill (IRE)**[21] 4306 7-11-5 **106**.. HenryBrooke(7) —
(Rose Dobbin) *mstkes: prom: wnt 2nd 17th: hit next: hit and outpcd 4 out: struggling fr next: disputing 5th and wl btn whn ref last* **17/2**

9m 39.1s (43.70) **Going Correction** +1.50s/f (Heav) **9** Ran SP% **118.8**
Speed ratings: **105,104,94,92,89 —,—,—,—**
toteswingers:1&2:£6.30, 1&3:£16.40, 2&3:£13.20 CSF £29.41 CT £218.29 TOTE £7.00: £1.80, £1.30, £4.80; EX 38.90.
Owner Lucky Catch Partnership **Bred** Gerard Mercier **Trained** Middleham Moor, N Yorks
■ Stewards' Enquiry : Paul Gallagher four-day ban: used whip with excessive frequency (Mar 31-Apr 3)

FOCUS
This modest 80-106 stayers' handicap was a severe test and just three figured three from home. The winner ran to his mark and the second produced a step back in the right direction.

NOTEBOOK
Matmata De Tendron(FR), a proven out-and-out stayer, went on four from home. He pressed home the advantage but at the line there was not one ounce to spare. This was his eighth career success on his 53rd start. (tchd 5-1, 6-1 and 13-2 in a place)
Seeking Power(IRE), 16lb better off with the winner for a head defeat here in November, has a pronounced soft-ground action. Given reminders with a circuit to go, he stuck to his task in pursuit of the winner up the final hill and was slowly but steadily closing the gap at the line. (op 6-1)
Panama At Once, pulled up on his three previous starts this time, was having his third start for this yard. After helping set the pace, he dropped away before rallying to snatch a distant third spot. At least he completed this time. (op 9-1 tchd 12-1)
Master D'Or(FR), who made the almost 400-mile trip from Devon, trailed the field until keeping on late to snatch a distant fourth spot. Stamina was clearly not an issue. (op 8-1)
Blazing Diva(IRE), raised 11lb, had just a 7lb penalty to carry. After help force the pace she stopped to nothing between the last two and this extreme trip looked beyond her. Official explanation: jockey said mare hung right-handed throughout (tchd 5-1 and 6-1)
Billsgrey(IRE), runner-up behind Blazing Diva at Carlisle, was never travelling and was out of contention at an early stage. (op 5-1)

4826 GOLDEN PLOVER H'CAP HURDLE (10 hdls 2 omitted) 3m
4:55 (4:55) (Class 5) (0-95,95) 4-Y-0+ **£2,055** (£599; £299)

Form RPR
2650 **1** **Delightfully (FR)**[33] 4067 7-11-5 **95**..........................(b) MrGJCockburn(7) 104+
(Lucinda Russell) *hld up last but in tch: stdy hdwy to chse ldr after 3 out: effrt and led bef last: styd on strly run-in* **13/8**[1]

-P00 **2** 9 **Beau Peak**[11] 4506 12-9-4 **69** oh9..........................(b) CallumWhillans(10) 70
(Donald Whillans) *t.k.h: cl up: led 4th: clr next to bef 2 out: rdn and hdd bef last: no ex* **22/1**

0000 **3** 12 **Bach Street Girl (IRE)**[65] 3498 7-10-8 **77**.............................. TomSiddall 69
(Lynn Siddall) *hld up in tch: lft 3rd 5th: rdn and outpcd after 3 out: rallied next: no ex whn lft 8 l 3rd last: no imp* **14/1**

5521 **U** **Cute N You Know It**[9] 4542 8-9-7 **69** oh3...................(p) PaulGallagher(7) —
(Andrew Crook) *hld up in tch: bdly hmpd and uns rdr 5th* **7/4**[2]

3250 **F** **Almond Court (IRE)**[11] 4508 8-10-3 **72** ow1...............(tp) KennyJohnson 67
(Robert Johnson) *cl up: lft 2nd 5th: outpcd appr 2 out: sn rallied: 6 l 3rd and outpcd whn fell last* **8/1**

00-0 **F** **Ruby Queen (IRE)**[51] 3728 9-10-2 **71** ow2.............. RichieMcGrath —
(Geoffrey Harker) *led to 4th: chsng ldr whn stmbld and fell next* **7/1**[3]

7m 3.60s (50.40) **Going Correction** +1.50s/f (Heav) **6** Ran SP% **109.1**
Speed ratings (Par 103): **76,73,69,—,— —**
CSF £27.09 TOTE £2.70: £1.10, £14.30; EX 36.50.
Owner Robert Boyd **Bred** Francis Ruel & Le Metayer Freres **Trained** Arlary, Perth & Kinross

FOCUS
A low-grade handicap hurdle and only half of the six runners completed. The first two are rated to form.

NOTEBOOK
Delightfully(FR), conceding lumps of weight away all round, was in no hurry to join issue. In pursuit of the leader soon after three out, in the end she took this weak contest by a decisive margin. (op 15-8)
Beau Peak, 11lb out of the handicap, soon pulled her way to the front. Placed just once from 17 previous starts over hurdles and like that day blinkered, she looked in command much of the way but, done no favours by a loose horse going to the last, she was soon left trailing. (op 25-1)
Bach Street Girl(IRE), an Irish point winner two years previously, was making her handicap debut. She made a brief renewed effort two out but was a distant fourth when hampered at the last. (op 11-1 tchd 16-1)
Cute N You Know It, unpenalised for her Newcastle success, was put out of the race at an early stage. (op 9-1 tchd 7-1)
Almond Court(IRE), a maiden after 25 races, was booked for a modest third when coming down at the last. (op 9-1 tchd 7-1)

4827 FALCON H'CAP CHASE (14 fncs 1 omitted) 2m 4f 110y
5:25 (5:25) (Class 5) (0-95,90) 5-Y-0+ **£2,055** (£599; £299)

Form RPR
3252 **1** **Soul Angel**[6] 4690 7-11-0 **85**..(v) PaulGallagher(7) 90
(Sandy Forster) *cl up: chal 10th: led 3 out to next: rdn and regained ld appr last: hld on gamely* **5/2**[1]

4536 **2** *1* **Manoubi**[43] 3883 12-11-3 **81** JamesReveley 85
(Martin Todhunter) *in tch: hdwy to ld 2 out: rdn and hdd appr last: kpt on run-in* **11/4**[2]
0361 **3** *1 ¾* **French Ties (IRE)**[16] 4413 9-11-12 **90** (p) SeanQuinlan 93
(Jennie Candlish) *t.k.h: hld up: stdy hdwy 4 out: effrt and cl 3rd last: one pce run-in* **7/2**[3]
4003 **4** *43* **Nifty Roy**[6] 4690 11-11-5 **83** (p) RichieMcGrath 42
(Brian Storey) *mde most to 3 out: rdn and wknd fr next* **25/1**
P224 **5** *3* **Panthers Run**[11] 4509 11-10-0 **64** (t) BrianHughes 20
(Jonathan Haynes) *trckd ldrs: rdn and outpcd whn hit 3 out: sn wknd* **5/1**
0U36 **P** **Toulouse Express (IRE)**[11] 4509 12-11-10 **88** (v) KennyJohnson —
(Robert Johnson) *bhd: struggling 9th: t.o whn p.u bef next* **20/1**
01UP **P** **Janal (IRE)**[11] 4510 8-10-12 **83** GaryRutherford[(7)] —
(Stuart Coltherd) *cl up: drvn and outpcd bef 10th: t.o whn p.u bef 3 out* **12/1**

5m 56.4s (42.90) **Going Correction** +1.50s/f (Heav) **7** Ran SP% **110.4**
Speed ratings: **78,77,76,60,59** —,—
toteswingers:1&2:£2.30, 1&3:£1.70, 2&3:£3.80 CSF £9.49 CT £20.97 TOTE £2.10: £1.60, £2.20; EX 9.50.
Owner Soul Searchers **Bred** Miss J A Challen **Trained** Kirk Yetholm, Borders

FOCUS
A low-grade handicap chase run at a very steady pace and just three in contention from two out. The first three are rated to their marks.

NOTEBOOK
Soul Angel, runner-up at Ayr just six days earlier when tried in a visor for the first time, came out just best on the run-in giving his promising claimer a three-timer on the card. (op 11-4 tchd 3-1 and 2-1)
Manoubi, who took this a year ago from the same mark under this rider, put some modest efforts behind him after a six-week break. He likes it round here but, in his 13th year, this is as good as he is capable of now. (op 7-2)
French Ties(IRE), 5lb higher than his narrow Leicester success, was dropped in. He wouldn't settle but looked a real threat going to the last, although in the end he came up short. (tchd 4-1)

[4377]TOWCESTER (R-H)
Thursday, March 17

OFFICIAL GOING: Good to soft (good in places; 8.1)
Wind: medium across Weather: bright and sunny

4828 BET ON THE CHELTENHAM FESTIVAL TOTEPLACEPOT MARES' NOVICES' HURDLE (11 hdls) 2m 5f
2:30 (2:30) (Class 4) 5-Y-0+ **£2,276** (£668; £334; £166)

Form RPR
-063 **1** **Francesa**[51] 3721 6-10-3 109 JakeGreenall[(7)] 115+
(Henry Daly) *hld up in midfield: clsd after 5th: chsd ldr after 8th: chal and nt fluent next: led wl bef 2 out: sn clr: styd on wl: comf* **13/2**[3]
0433 **2** *14* **Genny Wren**[42] 3904 5-10-10 103 SamJones 103
(Renee Robeson) *nt a fluent: chsd ldrs: wnt 2nd after 6th: led and mstke 8th: jnd and mstke next: sn rdn and hdd wl bef next: btn 2 out* **11/4**[2]
261 **3** *15* **Victrix Gale (IRE)**[15] 4425 5-11-3 0 AndrewTinkler 99
(Nicky Henderson) *t.k.h early: hld up in midfield: clsd after 5th: mstke 8th: chsd ldng trio bef 3 out: rdn and sn struggling: wl btn whn j.lft 2 out* **4/5**[1]
4042 **4** *3* **My Viking Bay (IRE)**[15] 4425 7-10-3 102 (p) CharlieWallis[(7)] 86
(John O'Shea) *hld up in last pair: rdn and effrt to chse ldng trio bef 3 out: no prog and wl btn bef 2 out* **14/1**
5-16 **5** *68* **Tazzarine (FR)**[77] 3227 5-10-10 0 JimmyMcCarthy 25
(Charles Egerton) *a in rr: rdn and struggling whn hit 8th: sn lost tch: t.o after 3 out: fin tired* **20/1**
P06U **6** *12* **Karingabay Queen**[17] 4398 6-10-3 0 (b) MrBJPoste[(7)] 14
(Kevin Tork) *led: clr tl mstke 5th: mstke and hdd next: rdn and dropped to rr after next: t.o 3 out: fin tired* **150/1**
P **Mrs Peacock (IRE)**[123] 6-10-6 0 ow3 StephenO'Donovan[(7)] —
(Norma Twomey) *t.k.h: mostly chsd ldr tl led 6th: hdd 8th: sn rdn and wknd rapidly: t.o whn p.u 2 out* **33/1**

5m 29.0s (1.80) **Going Correction** -0.20s/f (Good) **7** Ran SP% **110.6**
Speed ratings: **88,82,76,75,49 45**,—
toteswingers:1&2:£4.40, 1&3:£2.20, 2&3:£1.02 CSF £23.33 TOTE £4.50: £1.90, £1.90; EX 31.40.
Owner The Glazeley Partnership 2 **Bred** Mrs M D W Morrison **Trained** Stanton Lacy, Shropshire

FOCUS
Racing took place in warm, drying conditions, albeit with the wind starting to pick up shortly before the opener. They went a respectable early gallop in this ordinary mares' novice hurdle, and few were meaningfully involved inside the final three quarters of a mile. A big step up from the winner with the second setting the level.

NOTEBOOK
Francesa's best form efforts to date had been recorded on softer ground than this, but she travelled comfortably throughout and readily broke the resolve of each of her main rivals in turn. One of many from her yard going much better now, she can make her mark in routine mares' handicaps. (op 6-1 tchd 7-1)
Genny Wren was well backed, but didn't jump quite as fluently as the winner and proved very short of extra gears late on. Out of a mare who came into her own in 3m chases, such races may also see her in a better light eventually. (op 4-1 tchd 9-2)
Victrix Gale(IRE) settled quicker than when recording a bloodless winning hurdles debut at Folkestone, but the effort when asked to join the leaders proved most laboured. This drier surface should have presented no issues, so the likeliest conclusion to draw is that the more undulating course didn't suit. Official explanation: jockey said filly may have been in season (op 8-11 tchd 4-7)
My Viking Bay(IRE) ran Victrix Gale much closer than at Folkestone, but still looks a long way off winning one of these. A tough mark of 102 tempers expectations of better in handicaps, too. Official explanation: vet said mare lost a shoe (op 11-1 tchd 16-1)

4829 BET ON THE CHELTENHAM FESTIVAL TOTEJACKPOT H'CAP CHASE (18 fncs) 3m 110y
3:05 (3:05) (Class 5) (0-90,89) 5-Y-0+ **£1,951** (£573; £286; £143)

Form RPR
/212 **1** **Atherstone Hill (IRE)**[42] 3900 9-11-12 **89** (v) CharliePoste 108+
(Robin Dickin) *chsd ldrs: j. bdly rt and bmpd rival 1st: chsd ldr 7th: clr w ldr fr 10th: led bef 3 out: clr bef 2 out: styd on dourly: eased towards fin* **15/8**[1]
-P05 **2** *11* **Lonesome Boatman (IRE)**[23] 4273 11-10-4 **74** (p) JoshWall[(7)] 83
(Arthur Whitehead) *hld up in midfield: outpcd by ldrs: modest 4th 12th: chsd ldng pair 3 out: clsd and wnt 2nd 2 out: no imp and btn last: wknd fnl 100yds* **9/1**
3P1P **3** *9* **Wide Receiver (IRE)**[12] 4483 8-11-1 **78** (vt) JimmyMcCarthy 78
(Charlie Morlock) *chsd ldrs early: sltly hmpd and lost pl 7th: pushed and outpcd whn n.m.r bnd after 9th: 6th and virtually t.o 14th: rallied bef 2 out: styd on to go 3rd flat: no threat to wnr* **8/1**[3]
4311 **4** *6* **Delgany Gunner**[8] 4560 7-11-0 **82** 7ex (vt) GilesHawkins[(5)] 79
(Ben Pollock) *t.k.h: dashed into ld after 1st: clr w wnr fr 10th: hdd: drvn and swtchd lft 3 out: 3rd and btn 2 out: wknd after* **11/4**[2]
5450 **5** *21* **Heezagrey (IRE)**[12] 4483 8-10-7 **73** IanPopham[(3)] 49
(James Evans) *detached in last: pushed along and lost tch 10th: t.o 12th: plodded on* **8/1**[3]
0-20 **6** *11* **Huckleberry (IRE)**[25] 4238 9-10-1 **67** (p) LeeEdwards[(3)] 33
(James Unett) *led tl after 1st: chsd ldr tl 7th: 3rd and outpcd after 9th: rallied briefly 13th: no hdwy 15th: wknd next: t.o between last 2* **9/1**
5P4P **7** *dist* **Domoly (FR)**[17] 4403 8-11-1 **85** MrJackSalmon[(7)] —
(Alison Batchelor) *in tch: rdn and struggling after 9th: lost tch 12th: wl t.o fr 14th* **33/1**
5-56 **U** **High Toby**[15] 4429 12-10-1 **71** MissEmily-JaneHarbour[(7)] —
(Raymond York) *bdly bmpd and uns rdr 1st* **22/1**

6m 28.3s (-8.60) **Going Correction** -0.20s/f (Good) **8** Ran SP% **111.0**
Speed ratings: **105,101,98,96,89 86**,—,—
toteswingers:1&2:£6.60, 1&3:£4.40, 2&3:£7.20 CSF £17.86 CT £102.99 TOTE £4.00: £1.80, £2.80, £1.20; EX 14.60.
Owner Colin & Co **Bred** William Deacon **Trained** Atherstone on Stour, Warwicks

FOCUS
A low-grade contest but one run at a decent clip throughout. The winner is on the upgrade.

NOTEBOOK
Atherstone Hill(IRE) played the role of villain and hero in the race, lurching to his right and knocking Emily-Jayne Harbour off High Toby at the first fence, but travelling better than anything after that and not too hard pushed to assert from the final ditch. His C&D record now stands at 121, with a 2l second to a revitalised veteran last time no disgrace, and this big gelding can continue to pay his way at this venue with sounder surfaces evidently of no concern. (op 13-8)
Lonesome Boatman(IRE) was the only one to give meaningful chase to the winner from half a mile out. His two previous second places had been recorded here on a decent surface, too, but consistency isn't his strong suit even granted these apparently preferred conditions.
Wide Receiver(IRE) may have resented not having a closer look at the lead, and the occasional attentions of the loose horse didn't help, either. He remains on a historically workable mark and can prove better than this when more falls his way again. (op 7-1)
Delgany Gunner, seeking a hat-trick, refused to settle. He hadn't lasted home over this C&D last October and gave himself scant chance of doing so this time. Official explanation: jockey said gelding ran too free (op 7-2)

4830 TOTETRIFECTA ON ALL CHELTENHAM FESTIVAL RACES H'CAP HURDLE (8 hdls) 2m
3:45 (3:45) (Class 3) (0-120,119) 4-Y-0+ **£3,252** (£955; £477; £238)

Form RPR
5-00 **1** **Valid Point (IRE)**[72] 3386 5-10-5 **98** ow1 (t) RhysFlint 105+
(Jim Old) *chsd ldrs: chal 3 out: sn led: clr whn j.lft 2 out: drvn between last 2: wnt lft and mstke last: drvn and kpt on flat* **11/2**[3]
-051 **2** *3* **Kadouchski (FR)**[20] 4323 7-10-1 **101** PeterHatton[(7)] 102
(John Berry) *chsd ldrs: pushed along and unable qck bef 3 out: swtchd lft last: chsd wnr u.p fnl 100yds: no imp* **4/1**[1]
1303 **3** *1 ¼* **Liberty Seeker (FR)**[75] 3303 12-10-8 **108** MattCrawley[(7)] 109
(John Harris) *hld up in last trio: pushed along and hdwy bef 3 out: chsd ldrs and rdn bef 2 out: styd on same pce between last 2: j.lft and lft 2nd last: no ex flat* **12/1**
P025 **4** *4* **Olympian (FR)**[6] 4697 9-11-5 **112** (bt) AndrewGlassonbury 111+
(Philip Middleton) *hld up in midfield hdwy to chse ldrs 3 out: chsd wnr and rdn bef next: no imp and looked hld whn blnd bdly and lost 2 pls last: nt rcvr* **6/1**
2006 **5** *7* **Gifted Leader (USA)**[19] 4358 6-11-9 **119** MichaelMurphy[(3)] 109
(Ian Williams) *sn pushed along in midfield: rdn and chsng ldrs after 3 out: j.lft and btn 2 out* **9/2**[2]
2-00 **6** *12* **Anak (IRE)**[27] 3306 5-11-1 **118** (b) AshleyBird[(10)] 97
(Jim Best) *racd in last trio: mstke 3rd: struggling u.p after 5th: wl btn after next* **22/1**
00 **7** *3 ½* **Sawago (FR)**[18] 4375 5-10-2 **100** JoshuaMoore[(5)] 77
(Gary Moore) *w ldr tl led 5th: pressed and hit next: sn hdd: wknd qckly bef 2 out* **16/1**
-501 **8** *25* **L'Eldorado (FR)**[25] 4234 6-11-7 **114** TomMessenger 68
(Chris Bealby) *led tl 5th: rdn bef next: wknd qckly after 3 out: t.o* **9/2**[2]
320U **9** *10* **Shinnecock Bay**[29] 4139 7-10-11 **104** (b) LeightonAspell 49
(Oliver Sherwood) *a in rr: pushed along after 2nd: nvr gng wl after: lost tch bef 3 out: t.o* **22/1**
1615 **P** **Monkhair (IRE)**[238] 1066 6-10-4 **100** LeeEdwards[(3)] —
(Tony Carroll) *t.k.h early: hld up in tch in last trio: j.lft and struggling 5th: sn lost tch: t.o whn p.u 2 out* **11/1**

4m 1.80s (-6.10) **Going Correction** -0.20s/f (Good) **10** Ran SP% **116.6**
Speed ratings (Par 107): **107,105,104,102,99 93,91,79,74**,—
toteswingers:1&2:£6.60, 1&3:£10.70, 2&3:£7.80 CSF £28.35 CT £249.50 TOTE £7.10: £2.00, £2.20, £2.80; EX 35.50.
Owner W E Sturt **Bred** Pier House Stud **Trained** Barbury Castle, Wilts

FOCUS
The feature race of the afternoon, but they didn't appear to go off too fast early on and the tight-knit field only started to be stretched out from the third last. The winner stepped up on his hurdles efforts but is entitled to rate a lot higher on his Flat form.

NOTEBOOK
Valid Point(IRE) was a prolific handicap winner on the Flat for Sir Mark Prescott in 2009 and his mark of 97 for this handicap debut hadn't looked especially generous on the balance of his hurdling achievements to-date. He had a first-time tongue-tie at his disposal here, however, and that helped him last home despite wandering into the last two flights. Previously unplaced over hurdles, the Stewards noted trainer Jim Old's comments that the gelding was improved by the tongue-tie and the better ground, and have passed those comments on to the BHA. Official explanation: trainer said, regarding apparent improvement in form, that the gelding has had training problems, and may have been suited by the faster ground and the first-time tongue strap. (op 13-2 tchd 7-1)
Kadouchski(FR) had recorded all three hurdles wins, including at Sandown last time, around right-handed courses with uphill finishes. This probably wasn't run as enough of a test for him to get up, but he remains in fair heart and is also still 3lb below his highest winning mark. (op 9-2)
Liberty Seeker(FR) landed a C&D non-handicap seller last November and all his hurdles victories since October 2004 have come in such races. He never quite looked like bucking that trend despite making late gains up the straight. (op 9-1)
Olympian(FR), well handicapped and sporting a first-time tongue-tie, got to the winner's coat-tails but then produced less than seemed likely. A bad peck at the last wasn't the difference between winning and losing, and he's proving a touch frustrating at present. (tchd 5-1)
L'Eldorado(FR) was back up 6lb for a recent Market Rasen win but faded out of this very tamely even so. (tchd 5-1)

Monkhair(IRE) showed nothing, but she needed a few runs to get her eye in last summer and may do so again.

4831 TOTEPOOL FLEXI BETTING AT THE CHELTENHAM FESTIVAL NOVICES' CHASE (14 fncs) 2m 3f 110y

4:25 (4:25) (Class 4) 5-Y-O+ £0

Form RPR

266P **V** **Zhukov (IRE)**[6] 4697 9-10-5 97 (b[1]) MrBJPoste(7) —
(Kevin Tork) *mde most tl fell 6th*

4/P- **V** **Cengiz (IRE)**[587] 1163 9-10-9 79 LeeEdwards(3) —
(Aytach Sadik) *taken down early: sn bhd: lost tch after 4th tailing off whn swvd on landing and uns rdr 6th*

3631 **V** **Identity Parade (IRE)**[24] 4254 7-10-5 112 AdrianLane 110
(Donald McCain) *chsd ldrs: j.lft 4th: lft disputing ld and hmpd 6th: gng best and led after 3 out: in command whn distracted: tried to refuse and fell last*

1 **V** **Radharc Na Mara (IRE)**[19] 4366 7-10-2 115 PeterToole(3) 102
(J T R Dreaper, Ire) *chsd ldr tl lft disputing ld 6th: rdn after 3 out: drvn and btn bef next: hld whn lft in ld: bdly hmpd and uns rdr last*

FOCUS
A small piece of history. All four runners lost their jockeys during the course of the contest and, with remounting now banned, the race was declared void, the first time this has happened. All bets were refunded.

NOTEBOOK
Zhukov(IRE) just seemed to overjump at the second downhill fence and came to earth a long way after.
Cengiz(IRE), in a muck sweat on his first start for 587 days, had barely gone a yard and was already remote when unseating.
Identity Parade(IRE) had hung and jumped left on occasions, looking surprisingly ill at ease given that her win last time had been around another stiff right-handed course in Carlisle. However, she looked to have the matter completely settled when jinking, slowing and taking an inelegant fall at the last. Adrian Lane suggested afterwards that the mare had been distracted by spectators at the fence. Either way, this hadn't been a wholly convincing display up to that point.
Radharc Na Mara(IRE) went from moving comfortably to pushed along in relatively short order at the foot of the hill, and would have been a fortunate winner had she been able to clear both the final fence and the fallen Identity Parade successfully. A winner over 3m3f at Sedgefield two starts before, a return to longer trips will likely suit better.

4832 TOTEPOOL CHELTENHAM FESTIVAL BETTING AT TOTESPORT.COM HUNTERS' CHASE (16 fncs) 2m 6f

5:05 (5:05) (Class 6) 6-Y-O+ £936 (£290; £145; £72)

Form RPR

00-2 **1** **Double Mead**[17] 9-11-4 119 MrsAlexDunn(5) 130+
(Mrs K R Smith-Maxwell) *taken down early: confidently rdn: hld up in rr: stdy prog after 9th: lft 2nd and sltly hmpd 11th: led bef 3 out: cruised clr bef 2 out: v easily* **11/10[1]**

\- **2** *27* **Orient Legend**[25] 8-11-5 0 (p) MrTEllis(7) 103
(Miss Jennifer Pidgeon) *led tl 3rd: chsd ldr tl led again 7th: pckd bdly and hdd 9th: lft in ld 11th tl hdd bef 3 out: rdn and wl btn bef 2 out: plugged on* **12/1**

/U1- **3** *9* **Pass The Parsel (IRE)**[32] 10-11-9 0 MrJonathanBailey(7) 99
(G T H Bailey) *chsd ldrs: mstke 6th: lft 3rd 11th: rdn and struggling bef 3 out: wknd bef 2 out: 3rd and wl hld whn mstke last* **13/2[3]**

5P-P **4** *2 1/4* **Ballygalley Bob (IRE)**[19] 10-11-13 105 MrRStearn(7) 100
(Miss Caroline Fryer) *chsd ldrs: mstke 2nd: struggling whn lft 5th and hmpd 11th: wl btn 3 out: plodded on* **9/2[2]**

-21P **5** *32* **Blaze Ahead (IRE)**[14] 4442 11-11-13 104 (p) MrBJPowell(7) 71
(Brendan Powell) *led 3rd tl 6th: rdn along bef next: losing pl whn lft 4th 11th: wl btn 3 out: t.o bef next: eased flat* **8/1**

3P5- **6** *55* **Mr Parson (IRE)**[26] 11-11-12 45 MrGBarfoot-Saunt 13
(David Lewis) *chsd ldrs on outer: dropped to last and reminders after 6th: losing tch whn blnd bdly 9th: t.o whn hmpd by loose horse 11th* **66/1**

66/U **F** **Brightwell**[11] 10-11-9 0 MrJMQuinlan(3) —
(Miss P C Lownds) *in tch: hdwy to join ldrs 8th: lft in ld next tl fell 11th* **7/1**

5m 51.9s (-1.10) **Going Correction** -0.20s/f (Good) **7** Ran SP% **111.9**
Speed ratings: **94,84,80,80,68 48,—**
toteswingers:1&2:£3.70, 1&3:£3.40, 2&3:£9.30 CSF £14.24 TOTE £1.40: £1.10, £5.20; EX 7.10.
Owner Mrs K R Smith-Maxwell **Bred** Ashfield, Dawson And McGregor **Trained** Himbleton, Worcester

FOCUS
Not a hunter chase that took too much winning, but a taking performance from Double Mead, who can rate higher and win again.

NOTEBOOK
Double Mead gradually picked off the more prominently ridden rivals on the final circuit and can count an awkward leap at the final ditch as the only slight jumping blemish. Still capable enough to place in handicap chases off 120 last season, she has quickly made up into a decent ladies' pointer on a sound surface, and can continue to be placed to advantage in both that sphere and hunter chasing this spring. (op 8-11)
Orient Legend has run into some really progressive types in intermediate points the last twice, and he again gave his all here before his efforts took their toll. He deserves to go one better, although it will require a slightly weaker race than this to do so. (op 14-1 tchd 16-1)
Pass The Parsel(IRE) took a 2m3f maiden hunter here last spring, but there were jumping errors that day and again here (also fell in a point latest). He needs to raise his game in that department to take another one of these. (op 17-2 tchd 9-1)
Ballygalley Bob(IRE) disappointed a touch, given that his handler has been in terrific form in East Anglian points, and the gelding had looked right at home around Horseheath's undulating, galloping right-handed circuit a month earlier. (op 13-2)
Blaze Ahead(IRE), last year's winner, can be a hard ride, and wasn't for humouring today once headed.

4833 BEAT THE BOOKIES WITH TOTEPOOL CONDITIONAL JOCKEYS' H'CAP HURDLE (10 hdls) 2m 3f 110y

5:35 (5:35) (Class 5) (0-95,95) 4-Y-O+ £1,626 (£477; £238; £119)

Form RPR

040P **1** **Gouranga**[11] 4508 8-10-8 80 RobertKirk(3) 89+
(Tony Carroll) *mostly chsd ldr: rdn to ld after 3 out: clr next: styd on wl* **15/2**

04 **2** *9* **A Stones Throw (NZ)**[17] 4390 6-11-4 92 (t) JakeGreenall(5) 95
(Ben Haslam) *hld up in tch in last trio: reminder after 7th: chsd ldrs 3 out: rdn to chse clr wnr bef next: no imp and hld whn dived last* **7/2[1]**

2404 **3** *8* **Hippodrome (IRE)**[18] 4380 9-11-7 93 (p) MattCrawley(3) 87
(John Harris) *chsd ldrs: rdn bef 3 out: drvn and wknd 2 out* **8/1**

-005 **4** *7* **Sovereign Spirit (IRE)**[9] 4540 9-11-0 83 (tp) RichardKilloran 71
(Chris Gordon) *in tch: hdwy to ld after 6th: rdn and hdd after 3 out: wknd u.p next* **6/1[3]**

5000 **5** *1* **Wardington Lad**[8] 4559 9-11-7 93 KyleJames(3) 80
(Michael Appleby) *t.k.h: hld up in rr: effrt 3 out: rdn and no hdwy bef next: wl hld whn mstke last* **9/1**

0042 **6** *4 1/2* **Champs De Bleu (FR)**[17] 4403 8-11-2 85 JoshuaMoore 68
(Gary Moore) *hld up in tch: hdwy to chse ldrs 7th: rdn and wknd qckly bef 2 out* **5/1[2]**

P-0P **P** **Aymard Des Fieffes (FR)**[115] 2589 9-9-9 69 oh5 PeterHatton(5) —
(Nikki Evans) *chsd ldrs: rdn and wknd bef 3 out: wl bhd whn p.u 2 out* **28/1**

03-5 **F** **Laughing Game**[32] 4098 7-10-12 81 DavidBass —
(Laura Hurley) *t.k.h: in tch tl fell 6th* **5/1[2]**

0-60 **P** **Acquisitive (FR)**[46] 3837 5-11-12 95 TomMolloy —
(Nigel Twiston-Davies) *mstkes: led tl after 5th: rdn along and losing pl next: bhd and losing tch whn p.u bef 3 out* **10/1**

5m 5.50s (-4.10) **Going Correction** -0.20s/f (Good) **9** Ran SP% **115.3**
Speed ratings (Par 103): **100,96,93,90,90 88,—,—,—**
toteswingers:1&2:£7.90, 1&3:£8.70, 2&3:£8.80 CSF £34.57 CT £217.79 TOTE £10.50: £3.90, £1.50, £2.30; EX 49.40.
Owner Group 1 Racing (1994) Ltd **Bred** The Earl Cadogan **Trained** Cropthorne, Worcs

FOCUS
A weak handicap run at a pedestrian pace until halfway. There is a case for rating the form a few pounds higher.

NOTEBOOK
Gouranga, winless in 15 since completing the second half of a brace off 7lb higher exactly two years previously, seemed to enjoy the drop back in trip and made doubly sure of victory with two excellent leaps up the straight. Not especially consistent latterly, it's no sure thing that she'll replicate the effort next time. Official explanation: trainer said, regarding apparent improvement in form, that the mare benefited from the drop in trip and the removal of blinkers. (op 13-2 tchd 6-1)
A Stones Throw(NZ), dropped 3lb despite an up to scratch effort at Catterick last time, ran in snatches in a race that may not have been run to suit and could make no impression late on. Unraced beyond today's trip so far, a greater stamina test may be required. (op 5-1)
Hippodrome(IRE) is 2lb lower than his sole British winning mark now, but he could find no extra gears once the winner had flown over what had become slightly quicker ground than ideal. (op 13-2)
Sovereign Spirit(IRE) faded away as if this had come too soon after his improved Exeter effort nine days previously. (tchd 11-2)
Wardington Lad Official explanation: jockey said gelding finished lame
Champs De Bleu(FR)'s early over-keenness, rather than a stumble two flights in, contributed to his below-part effort. It's not the first time he has refused to settle, either, and maybe some form of headgear could be tried out to pacify him. (tchd 11-2)
Laughing Game back to within 1lb of her winning mark of last season, was still to play her hand when crashing out. (op 11-2)
T/Plt: £52.20 to £1 stake. Pool:£52,521.61 - 733.44 winning tickets T/Qpdt: £7.70 to a £1 stake. Pool:£3,483.45 - 330.59 winning tickets SP

4834a - 4846a (Foreign Racing) - See Raceform Interactive

4816 CHELTENHAM (L-H)

Friday, March 18

OFFICIAL GOING: Good (good to soft in places on hurdle course; 8.0)
7yds fresh ground on inside of chase course used, reducing dist by 24yds per circ c/w Thursday. Hurdle bends moved in 4yds reducing distances by 18yds.
Wind: Almost nil Weather: Fine

4847 JCB TRIUMPH HURDLE GRADE 1 (8 hdls) 2m 1f

1:30 (1:31) (Class 1) 4-Y-O

£57,010 (£21,390; £10,710; £5,340; £2,680; £1,340)

Form RPR

1 **1** **Zarkandar (IRE)**[20] 4350 4-11-0 DarylJacob 147+
(Paul Nicholls) *in tch: clsd 2 out: led appr last: r.o wl run-in: a in control* **13/2[3]**

1 **2** *2 1/4* **Unaccompanied (IRE)**[34] 4083 4-10-7 142 PTownend 136
(D K Weld, Ire) *hld up: hdwy travelling wl appr 2 out: swtchd bef last: wnt 2nd run-in: styd on but no imp on wnr* **11/2[2]**

5211 **3** *2 3/4* **Grandouet (FR)**[55] 3673 4-11-0 148 BarryGeraghty 140+
(Nicky Henderson) *trckd ldrs: chalng 2 out: led briefly appr last: nt qckn run-in: styd on same pce fnl 100yds* **13/2[3]**

114 **4** *nk* **Sam Winner (FR)**[69] 3436 4-11-0 146 RWalsh 141+
(Paul Nicholls) *bhd 3rd: hdwy after 2 out: rdn and styd on appr last: fin wl but nt quite get to ldrs* **4/1[1]**

4U3 **5** *2 1/2* **Sir Pitt**[25] 4260 4-11-0 118 DPFahy 137
(Alison Thorpe) *hld up in midfield: hdwy appr 2 out: sn chalng: rdn and edgd lft to chse ldrs bef last: kpt on run-in* **200/1**

412 **6** *1 1/2* **Sailors Warn (IRE)**[34] 4083 4-11-0 142 AndrewJMcNamara 136
(E J O'Grady, Ire) *racd keenly: led: hdd appr 2nd: remained prom: led 5th: rdn and hdd bef last: no ex run-in* **33/1**

122 **7** *1/2* **Third Intention (IRE)**[27] 4205 4-11-0 138 JoeTizzard 138+
(Colin Tizzard) *mstke 1st: hld up: hdwy appr 2 out: rdn between last 2: styd on run-in: nt pce to rch ldrs* **11/1**

1114 **8** *1/2* **Local Hero (GER)**[27] 4205 4-11-0 140 RhysFlint 135
(Steve Gollings) *midfield: mstke 3rd: nt fluent 3 out: sn rdn: kpt on u.p appr last: no imp on ldrs* **20/1**

31 **9** *1/2* **Brampour (IRE)**[36] 4029 4-11-0 132 HarrySkelton 135
(Paul Nicholls) *in tch: chalng 2 out: rdn appr last: kpt on same pce* **20/1**

131 **10** *nk* **Smad Place (FR)**[27] 4225 4-11-0 147 RobertThornton 134
(Alan King) *trckd ldrs: rdn and nt qckn after 2 out: one pce bef last* **11/1**

6 **11** *1 1/2* **Aikideau (FR)**[20] 4350 4-11-0 LeightonAspell 132
(Richard Rowe) *towards rr: hdwy whn mstke 2 out: kpt on u.p appr last: nvr able to chal ldrs* **100/1**

2022 **12** *3 1/4* **Kuilsriver (IRE)**[40] 3958 4-11-0 120 (t) JasonMaguire 129
(Alison Thorpe) *hld up: rdn and sme hdwy appr last: nvr able to trble ldrs* **125/1**

13 *3 3/4* **Walter De La Mare (IRE)**[27] 4230 4-11-0 RMPower 125
(John Joseph Murphy, Ire) *hld up: rdn and styd on after 2 out: nt pce to rch ldrs* **200/1**

2 **14** *3 1/4* **Molotof (FR)**[20] 4350 4-11-0 143 AndrewTinkler 125
(Nicky Henderson) *prom: chalng 2 out: sn rdn: wknd appr last* **16/1**

11 **15** *2 3/4* **First Fandango**[74] 3358 4-11-0 135 (vt[1]) SamThomas 119
(Tim Vaughan) *trckd ldrs: lost pl after 3 out: rdn bef next: wknd appr last* **50/1**

21 **16** *1 3/4* **Houblon Des Obeaux (FR)**[27] 4205 4-11-0 148 AidanColeman 118
(Venetia Williams) *prom: led appr 2nd: hdd 5th: pushed along after 3 out: wknd bef next* **22/1**

21 **17** *9* **High Ransom**[37] 3999 4-10-7 112 (p) BarryKeniry 102
(Micky Hammond) *nt fluent: bhd after 1st: struggling 5th: nvr on terms* **125/1**

0 **18** *10* **Tillahow (IRE)**[34] 4083 4-11-0 139 DNRussell 99
(M F Morris, Ire) *in tch: mstke 3rd: lost pl 4th: pushed along and losing grnd appr 2 out: wl btn after* **80/1**

1110 **19** *1* **Architrave**[125] 2356 4-11-0 136 RichardJohnson 98
(Tim Vaughan) *prom: pushed along appr 2 out: wknd bef last* **40/1**

F **20** *3 ¼* **Trop Fort (FR)**[36] 4029 4-11-0 TomScudamore 94
(David Pipe) *mstke 1st: a bhd* **50/1**

0 **P** **New Den**[16] 4424 4-11-0 (tp) CampbellGillies —
(Jim Boyle) *bhd: mstke 1st: p.u after 3rd* **250/1**

U **Mister Carter (IRE)**[69] 3457 4-11-0 133 WJLee 132
(T Stack, Ire) *midfield: stl gng okay whn blnd and uns rdr 2 out* **50/1**

02F1 **P** **A Media Luz (FR)**[36] 4024 4-10-7 137 APMcCoy —
(Nicky Henderson) *in tch: t.k.h: rdn and wknd after 2 out: bhd whn p.u bef last* **12/1**

3m 54.2s (-17.10) **Going Correction** -0.625s/f (Firm) **23** Ran SP% **122.6**
Speed ratings: **115,113,112,112,111 110,110,110,109,109 109,107,105,104,102 102,97,93,92,91 —,—,—**
Tote Swingers: 1&2 £6.30, 1&3 £8.10, 2&3 £6.90 CSF £37.22 CT £249.31 TOTE £6.90: £1.80, £1.50, £2.20, £1.60; EX 34.30 Trifecta £131.20 Pool: £10,174.62 - 57.35 winning units..
Owner Potensis Limited & Chris Giles **Bred** His Highness The Aga Khan's Studs S C **Trained** Ditcheat, Somerset

■ Daryl Jacob's first festival winner.

FOCUS

The riders in the opener agreed that the ground was good, Daryl Jacob describing it as "pretty similar" to Thursday's going. \n\x\x The field got a running start as they were already moving pretty quickly as they left the collecting ring to turn onto the racecourse proper. The pace was solid and they were inside the standard by nearly two seconds. An up-to-scratch and open edition of the championship event for juveniles, and with the right horses coming to the fore the form looks quite strong. Zarkandar impressed, and although he is rated only an average winner he looks sure to rate a lot higher. The next three were all close to their pre-race marks but the field finished a little more bunched than would have been expected.

NOTEBOOK

Zarkandar(IRE) ◆ lacked the experience of the vast majority of Triumph Hurdle winners, arriving with just a single run over hurdles under his belt, but that outing brought a smart victory in Kempton's Adonis Hurdle which has become the leading trial for this race. Jumping fluently, he raced in eighth or ninth before cutting through the field on the home turn to the extent that he took it up before the last. Another good jump clinched it and he stayed on strongly for pressure up the hill. A really classy recruit to hurdling, the half-brother to Zarkava is another from the Aga Khan's breeding operation which has had a big impact in this event over the years. Connections are keen to run him in the Anniversary Hurdle at Aintree. He will be aimed at the Champion Hurdle next season and although only Katchit has won both races in the last four decades, Zarkandar looks as talented a Triumph Hurdle winner as we have seen for some time and must rate a serious contender at this stage. (tchd 7-1 in places)

Unaccompanied(IRE), whose trainer won this event back in 1990, came here two from two over hurdles after taking the Grade 1 Spring Juvenile Hurdle at Leopardstown last month. She travelled well but had to be shaken up for a few strides after the third-last. Having given chase to the winner before the final flight, she ran on willingly but the gelding was just too strong for her. This was a fine effort on quicker ground than she had experienced over hurdles and she will run in the Listed Salsabil Stakes at Navan before a crack at Punchestown's Champion 4-Y.O Hurdle. (op 6-1 tchd 7-1 in places)

Grandouet(FR)'s Newbury win over stablemate A Media Luz looked the strongest form on offer. Bidding to provide Nicky Henderson with a third successive Triumph winner, and a sixth in all, he was always well placed and came there cruising on the home turn, but he was tackled by the first two on the approach to the last and weakened in the final 50 yards. He should run well if turning out in either the Punchestown race or the Anniversary Hurdle at Aintree. (op 7-1 tchd 15-2)

Sam Winner(FR), Zarkandar's stablemate, beat Grandouet when in receipt of 8lb here in December, but was only fourth to Tuesday's disappointment Marsh Warbler in the Finale at Chepstow. He ran a remarkable race, becoming outpaced in rear down the back and looking set to finish well behind, but coming home very strongly up the hill once switched, only just failing to salvage third place. The ground was faster than he'd have liked and he remains a smart prospect, with a switch to chasing scheduled for the autumn. (op 6-1 tchd 7-1 in places)

Sir Pitt, a huge-priced maiden, ran a cracking race and touched down over the final flight in fourth place. This was a much improved run from him, but his proximity does cast a slight doubt over the form.

Sailors Warn(IRE) got away to a flier and raced keenly up with the pace throughout. Sticking to the inside on the home turn, he was still just about in front as they straightened up but faded from there. He handled the quicker ground well and boosted the form of Unaccompanied's Leopardstown win.

Third Intention(IRE) settled better than he had been doing previously, the bigger field and quicker pace suiting. He came under a drive at the top of the hill and, although never really a factor, was staying on well at the end. (tchd 12-1)

Local Hero(GER), who beat Third Intention in the Grade 2 Finesse Hurdle here, lost his pitch down the back before keeping on again.

Brampour(IRE) ran well for a long way, but couldn't quicken up between the last two flights. (op 18-1)

Smad Place(FR) came off the bridle after dragging his hind legs through the fifth. He kept on at the same pace and will be suited by a step up in trip or a return to slower conditions. (op 9-1)

Aikideau(FR), a maiden who made his British debut in the Adonis Hurdle, was never nearer than at the finish.

Molotof(FR), Zarkandar's nearest pursuer in the Adonis, challenged three out but was weakening when untidy at the final flight. He is a useful individual, and at this stage his novice status remains intact for next season. (tchd 18-1)

Houblon Des Obeaux(FR) is suited by testing conditions and he weakened out of it after helping force the pace. (op 20-1)

Architrave faded between the last two flights on his first start since the autumn.

New Den Official explanation: jockey said gelding never travelled (op 10-1)

A Media Luz(FR) raced far too keenly, failing to settle at all, and although she was still on the premises at the second-last she weakened quickly from there and was pulled up. (op 10-1)

4848 VINCENT O'BRIEN COUNTY H'CAP HURDLE GRADE 3 (8 hdls) 2m 1f

2:05 (2:05) (Class 1) 5-Y-0+

£39,907 (£14,973; £7,497; £3,738; £1,876; £938)

Form RPR

3-1 **1** **Final Approach**[68] 3474 5-10-12 139 RWalsh 145+
(W P Mullins, Ire) *mstke 1st: in rr: pushed along after 3 out: stl plenty to do fr 2 out: str run appr last: styd on wl u.p run-in to ld last stride* **10/1**

-060 **2** *nse* **Get Me Out Of Here (IRE)**[28] 4188 7-11-7 148 (t) APMcCoy 153
(Jonjo O'Neill) *hld up towards rr: gd hdwy 2 out: hrd drvn to chal last: led sn after: styd on wl u.p run-in: hdd last stride* **7/1**[2]

1150 **3** *1 ½* **Nearby**[28] 4188 7-11-1 149 ChrisDavies(7) 153
(Philip Hobbs) *in tch: rdn and hdwy fr 2 out: styd on u.p run-in: tk 3rd last strides but nt pce of ldng duo* **66/1**

P663 **4** *½* **Cockney Trucker (IRE)**[48] 3808 9-10-7 134 RichardJohnson 138
(Philip Hobbs) *in tch: hdwy 3 out: rdn 2 out: rdn to take slt ld last: hdd sn after: one pce cl home and lost 3rd last strides* **33/1**

2-1B **5** *nk* **Salden Licht**[28] 4188 7-11-12 153 RobertThornton 157
(Alan King) *chsd ldrs: rdn appr 2 out: one pce appr last: styd on again u.p run-in: gng on cl home* **25/1**

213- **6** *nse* **Alaivan (IRE)**[48] 3823 5-11-3 144 AndrewJMcNamara 147
(E J O'Grady, Ire) *chsd ldrs: rdn 2 out: chal last: no ex fnl 30yds* **10/1**

21-5 **7** *1 ½* **Blackstairmountain (IRE)**[69] 3461 6-11-4 145 (t) PTownend 146
(W P Mullins, Ire) *hld up in rr: stl plenty to do whn rdn and hdwy fr 2 out: styd on run-in but no imp on ldrs* **16/1**

14-3 **8** *nk* **Dirar (IRE)**[22] 1133 6-10-11 138 PCarberry 142+
(Gordon Elliott, Ire) *in rr: stl plenty to do whn rdn and hdwy after 2 out: styd on run-in but nt rch ldrs* **8/1**[3]

20/1 **9** *½* **Ski Sunday**[62] 3557 6-11-2 143 SamThomas 145
(Lawney Hill) *chsd ldrs: rdn to chal fr 2 out: stl upsides last: wknd fnl 100yds* **11/1**

2054 **10** *¾* **Gloucester**[34] 1797 8-9-12 130 CO'Farrell(5) 130
(Michael Scudamore) *in rr: hdwy fr 2 out: kpt on u.p appr last and run-in: nt rch ldrs* **66/1**

1-65 **11** *1 ¾* **Soldatino (FR)**[28] 4188 5-11-7 148 BarryGeraghty 146
(Nicky Henderson) *towards rr: hdwy 3 out: drvn to chse ldrs 2 out: wknd appr last* **11/1**

0031 **12** *¾* **Hunterview**[40] 3969 5-10-9 139 (b) DannyCook(3) 136
(David Pipe) *pressed ldr tl slt ld fr 4th: rdn appr 2 out: narrowly hdd last: sn wknd* **33/1**

0-4F **13** *shd* **Zanir (FR)**[28] 4188 7-10-7 134 PaddyBrennan 131
(Tom George) *in tch: rdn and one pce appr 2 out: styd on again u.p appr last: no ex and wknd run-in* **25/1**

0-43 **14** *1 ¾* **Notus De La Tour (FR)**[28] 4188 5-11-1 142 TomScudamore 139
(David Pipe) *chsd ldrs: rdn appr 2 out: wknd bef last* **20/1**

3221 **15** *nk* **Alarazi (IRE)**[6] 4727 7-10-4 131 5ex DominicElsworth 126
(Lucy Wadham) *in rr: rdn and sme hdwy appr 2 out: nvr on terms: wknd bef last* **6/1**[1]

-104 **16** *¾* **Inventor (IRE)**[210] 1311 6-10-13 140 JasonMaguire 135
(Donald McCain) *in rr: sme prog appr 2 out: nvr rchd ldrs* **100/1**

03P **17** *¾* **Premier Dane (IRE)**[62] 3561 9-10-2 129 FearghalDavis 123
(Nicky Richards) *chsd ldrs: rdn 3 out: wknd after 2 out* **66/1**

-005 **18** *nse* **Secret Dancer (IRE)**[48] 3808 6-10-2 129 TomO'Brien 123
(Alan Jones) *a in rr* **16/1**

64-0 **19** *7* **Spring Jim**[47] 2498 10-10-6 133 FelixDeGiles 120
(James Fanshawe) *mid-div: rdn 3 out: bhd appr next* **40/1**

2F35 **20** *2 ¼* **Tarkari (IRE)**[19] 4373 6-10-9 136 PaulMoloney 120
(Evan Williams) *hit 4th: bhd most of way* **66/1**

PU-4 **21** *6* **Grey Soldier (IRE)**[34] 4088 6-10-11 138 (bt[1]) DNRussell 120
(Gordon Elliott, Ire) *in rr and blnd 3rd: nt fluent next: sme hdwy on ins whn hmpd after 3 out: sn btn* **14/1**

-010 **22** *42* **Ellerslie Tom**[13] 4488 9-10-6 133 DarylJacob 69
(Alison Thorpe) *led tl hdd 4th: wknd bef 2 out* **125/1**

2162 **U** **Praxiteles (IRE)**[98] 2868 7-9-13 129 (t) SamTwiston-Davies(3) 114
(Rebecca Curtis) *nvr jumping w much fluency: no ch whn hmpd and uns rdr last* **40/1**

31F5 **P** **Dee Ee Williams (IRE)**[62] 3555 8-11-6 147 (p) LiamTreadwell —
(Nick Gifford) *pressed ldrs tl wknd qckly 2 out: p.u bef last* **50/1**

5411 **F** **Ciceron (IRE)**[24] 4270 5-10-10 137 AidanColeman 134
(Venetia Williams) *in tch: chsd ldrs fr 4th: rdn and no imp on ldrs whn fell last* **33/1**

10-2 **P** **Bellvano (GER)**[72] 3393 7-10-13 140 DJCasey —
(Nicky Henderson) *in tch: sme hdwy appr 2 out: sn wknd: p.u bef last* **40/1**

3m 54.77s (-16.53) **Going Correction** -0.625s/f (Firm) **26** Ran SP% **129.5**
Speed ratings: **113,112,112,112,111 111,111,111,110,110 109,109,109,108,108 107,107,107,104,103 100,80,—,E**
Tote Swingers: 1&2 £30.70, 1&3 £198.90, 2&3 £137.30 CSF £70.09 CT £4459.58 TOTE £12.80: £3.00, £2.10, £30.50, £8.90; EX 125.00 TRIFECTA Not won..
Owner Douglas Taylor **Bred** D Taylor **Trained** Muine Beag, Co Carlow

■ Stewards' Enquiry : P Townend three-day ban: careless riding (Apr 1-3)

FOCUS

A typically highly competitive renewal of this handicap hurdle that used to be the closing race of the meeting. Subsequent Champion Hurdler Rooster Booster in 2002 was the highest profile recent winner, and not since Sporazene scored off 151 (when the weights were artificially compressed by a late withdrawal of the top weight Rigmarole), had the winner been rated above 135. Irish runners had won three of the previous four renewals and made it four from five with a last-gasp success. The winning time was just over half a second slower than the Triumph. Solid form and easy to rate, with the first five all within 2lb of their marks.

NOTEBOOK

Final Approach won a valuable and competitive handicap at Leopardstown in January from a subsequent winner. As a result he was 16lb higher and, after a mistake at the first, was well back for most of the way. He had the majority of the field still ahead of him on the home turn and around 15 in front going to the last, but he made relentless progress under an inspired Ruby Walsh and got up to score on the post. He might be aimed at a Flat handicap in the autumn. (tchd 11-1 and 12-1in places)

Get Me Out Of Here(IRE), the winner of the totesport Trophy in 2010, narrowly lost out to Menorah in the Supreme Novices' at this meeting last year and suffered the same fate. He had struggled to regain his form this season but, having had a soft palate operation and fitted with a first-time tongue tie, he was heavily backed, was always going well, and looked the winner when moving up to join the leaders on the home turn. McCoy had to get serious to get the gelding to the front, but he kept finding and was unlucky to lose out right on the line. His rider reported that the gelding choked on the run-in and, although he might go to Aintree, will be given another, more permanent, wind operation in the summer. (op 10-1 tchd 11-1 in places)

Nearby ◆, a progressive hurdler in the autumn, was rated 24lb higher than for the first of his three successes. He had found the ground too soft on his return in the totesport Trophy but ran a fine race here, staying on well up the hill to be nearest at the line. He goes well on a flat track and Aintree and the Swinton Hurdle at Haydock could be on the agenda, providing the rain stays away.

Cockney Trucker(IRE), third in this in 2009 off 4lb lower, was mostly chasing last season but had been gradually finding his form back over hurdles this term. Again showing his liking for this track and good ground, he ran really well and did best of those to race near the pace. (op 40-1)

Salden Licht looked a high-class horse when scoring at Exeter on his return to hurdles and was sent off favourite for the totesport trophy. He was making headway when brought down there, but was racing off 11lb higher here than for his previous success. He ran a terrific race off top weight, only unable to find extra after the last.

Alaivan(IRE), third to Soldatino in the Triumph Hurdle last season, had had the form of his most recent wins boosted, as the runners-up in those races finished second in the Pertemps Final and won the Coral Cup earlier in the week. He too ran well, but was a bit too keen in the race and paid for it from the final flight. (tchd 11-1)

Blackstairmountain(IRE), a Grade 1 winning hurdler last season on good ground, had run about a stone below his mark when touched off over 2m4f on heavy last time. However, he bounced back with this trip and ground more in his favour. He came through from the rear ahead of his stable companion, the winner, but lacked an extra gear from the last.

Dirar(IRE) ◆, the winner of last year's Ebor on the Flat and third in the Galway Plate on his last start over hurdles, had had a recent run on the AW to tune up for this. He was another held up out the back and tried to follow the winner through, but could not stay with that rival despite passing a number of rivals in the closing stages. Surely this stayer would have benefited from being ridden closer to the pace. (op 6-1)

Ski Sunday, runner-up in the Fred Winter in 2009, had had a lot of time off since but won on his return when beating subsequent EBF Final winner Skint at Kempton. He had been given 62 days to recover, but was 10lb higher and the tongue tie he wore then was left off. He ran pretty well up with the leaders until weakening going to the final flight.

Gloucester, tenth and sixth in the last two runnings of this and well suited by good ground, stayed on from the rear without ever being able to reach a challenging position. (tchd 80-1 in places)

Soldatino(FR) won the Triumph Hurdle at this meeting last year on only his second start in this country. He had posted a good effort when fifth in the totesport Trophy and ran well again off the same mark. (op 14-1)

Hunterview, well beaten in the Fred Winter last season but back to form at Musselburgh last time, helped make the running and only faded up the hill. He will be seen to better effect back on a flatter track.

Zanir(FR), fourth in this last year off 2lb lower, had fallen when closing in the totesport Trophy on his previous start. He was another who tracked the pace for a long way before tiring up the hill. (tchd 28-1)

Notus De La Tour(FR), runner-up in the Fred Winter last season, tracked the pace for a long way before tiring up the hill. He had finished third in the totesport Trophy last time (ahead of a number of these), but failed to run to that level and might prefer a little more cut in the ground.

Alarazi(IRE) won the Imperial Cup the previous weekend and was chasing a big bonus. He had been touched off here in January (with Cockney Trucker behind) off 13lb lower, but the combination of a 5lb penalty and seeing a lot of daylight on the outside of the field early contributed to him failing to get seriously involved. (tchd 9-1 early, op 7-1)

Premier Dane(IRE), third in this in 2007 and sixth in 2008, showed up for a fair way but is probably not quite up to this level nowadays.

Grey Soldier(IRE), wearing a tongue tie and blinkers combination for the first time, was 12lb above his last winning mark but spoilt his chance with a bad mistake early in the race and he then stumbled on the home turn, although he already looked held at that point.

Dee Ee Williams(IRE), third in this last year before winning at Aintree, had been racing over fences this season. Returning to hurdles with first-time cheekpieces replacing the usual visor or blinkers, he raced prominently before dropping away from the bottom of the hill. He reportedly finished distressed. Official explanation: jockey said gelding finished distressed

Bellvano(GER) Official explanation: vet said gelding lost left hind shoe

4849 ALBERT BARTLETT NOVICES' HURDLE (REGISTERED AS THE SPA NOVICES' HURDLE RACE) GRADE 1 (12 hdls) 3m

2:40 (2:40) (Class 1) 4-Y-O+

£57,010 (£21,390; £10,710; £5,340; £2,680; £1,340)

Form	Pos	Btn	Horse	Jockey	RPR
-111	1		**Bobs Worth (IRE)**[48] 3806 6-11-7 150 (Nicky Henderson) *midfield: hdwy appr 7th: led between last 2: j.lft and tried to assert last: edgd rt towards fin: drvn out and styd on wl* **15/8**[1]	BarryGeraghty	153+
1115	2	2 1/4	**Mossley (IRE)**[62] 3567 5-11-7 145 (Nicky Henderson) *hld up: hdwy 3 out: trckd ldrs appr 2 out: chalng bef last and wnt 2nd: nt qckn last: tried to rally fnl 100yds: sn swtchd rt: no ex and hld cl home* **12/1**	APMcCoy	149
1212	3	6	**Court In Motion (IRE)**[27] 4206 6-11-7 146 (Emma Lavelle) *racd keenly in midfield: nt fluent 7th: hdwy appr 8th: chalng 2 out: stl ev ch between last 2: one pce and no ch w front 2 run-in* **9/1**	JackDoyle	144
210	4	5	**Champion Court (IRE)**[48] 3806 6-11-7 0 (Martin Keighley) *racd keenly: hld up: hdwy appr 3 out: trckd ldrs bef 2 out: rdn between last 2: outpcd by front trio bef last: btn and no imp after* **16/1**	WarrenMarston	139
1151	5	1 1/4	**Kilcrea Kim (IRE)**[41] 3947 6-11-7 142 (Philip Hobbs) *in tch: pushed along appr 2 out: effrt to chse ldrs on bnd between last 2: outpcd bef last: no imp after* **6/1**[2]	RichardJohnson	140+
5B02	6	6	**Ackertac (IRE)**[23] 4285 6-11-7 133 (Nigel Twiston-Davies) *midfield: lost pl 7th: rdn and outpcd appr 2 out: kpt on modly u.p bef last but no threat to ldrs* **40/1**	PaddyBrennan	132
11	7	3 1/4	**Our Island (IRE)**[28] 4189 6-11-7 129 (Tim Vaughan) *in tch: nt fluent 4th: lost pl appr 6th: mstke 8th: pushed along whn hmpd 2 out: n.d after* **33/1**	TomScudamore	131+
2132	8	hd	**Teaforthree (IRE)**[29] 4159 7-11-7 138 (Rebecca Curtis) *prom: chalng whn blnd 2 out: rdn and wknd between last 2* **28/1**	AidanColeman	128
	9	1	**Allee Garde (FR)**[44] 3891 6-11-7 0 (W P Mullins, Ire) *hld up: mstke 2nd: stl towards rr of main bunch whn nt fluent and sltly hmpd 2 out: nvr a danger* **66/1**	DJCasey	131+
1322	10	4 1/2	**Sybarite (FR)**[62] 3556 5-11-7 130 (Nigel Twiston-Davies) *trckd ldrs: pushed along and wkng whn forced wd 2 out: wl btn* **25/1**	SamTwiston-Davies	123
3012	11	3 1/4	**No Secrets (IRE)**[55] 3678 7-11-7 129 (Warren Greatrex) *led: hrd pressed 2 out: rdn and hdd between last 2: wknd bef last* **50/1**	WayneHutchinson	118
F121	P		**Radetsky March (IRE)**[34] 4081 8-11-7 130 (Mark Bradstock) *prom tl rdn and wknd appr 2 out: t.o whn p.u after 2 out* **66/1**	JasonMaguire	—
-230	P		**Fiulin**[6] 4727 6-11-7 130 (Evan Williams) *prom: lost pl 7th: struggling 9th: t.o whn p.u after 2 out* **66/1**	PaulMoloney	—
6-11	P		**Gagewell Flyer (IRE)**[47] 3846 7-11-7 144 (W P Mullins, Ire) *hld up: mstke 5th: hdwy into midfield appr 3 out: wknd bef 2 out: p.u bef last* **15/2**[3]	PTownend	—
321	P		**Join Together (IRE)**[42] 3931 6-11-7 140 (Paul Nicholls) *midfield: lost pl appr 8th: bhd after: t.o whn p.u bef 2 out* **8/1**	RWalsh	—
1161	F		**Jetnova (IRE)**[27] 4220 6-11-7 136 (Alan King) *hld up: hdwy appr 7th: in tch but niggled along whn fell 2 out* **40/1**	RobertThornton	138
5P-2	P		**Start Me Up (IRE)**[43] 3913 7-11-7 131 (C F Swan, Ire) *hld up: hdwy 8th: yet to be asked for effrt and in midfield whn bdly hmpd 2 out: nt rcvr: t.o whn p.u bef last* **80/1**	DNRussell	—
1	P		**Moonlight Drive (IRE)**[41] 3952 5-11-7 0 (John Quinn) *nt fluent: hld up: outpcd appr 3 out: t.o whn p.u bef 2 out* **20/1**	GrahamLee	—

5m 42.2s (-18.80) **Going Correction** -0.625s/f (Firm) **18** Ran SP% **123.1**

Speed ratings (Par 117): **106,105,103,101,101 99,98,98,97,96 95,—,—,—,— —,—,—**

Tote Swingers: 1&2 £6.20, 1&3 £4.40, 2&3 £14.70 CSF £23.03 CT £175.47 TOTE £2.70: £1.50, £3.10, £3.00; EX 26.00 Trifecta £143.40 Pool: £11,478.91 - 59.19 winning units..

Owner The Not Afraid Partnership **Bred** Mrs L Eadie **Trained** Upper Lambourn, Berks

FOCUS

The seventh running of this event, the fourth since it attained Grade 1 status, and it looked a decent renewal. They went a sound pace which produced another quick time. Cosy winner Bobs Worth stood out on the figures and is rated to his mark, with stablemate Mossley running to his mark. The third is rated 3lb off.

NOTEBOOK

Bobs Worth(IRE) ◆, to the surprise of many taken out of Wednesday's Neptune Hurdle to run in this, had 4lb in hand on official figures and underlined his superiority with a comfortable win. Off the track since beating Neptune runner-up Rock On Ruby in a Grade 2 over an extended 2m4f here in January, he confirmed himself a very smart staying novice, the step up to 3m not troubling him at all. After whacking the third-last he moved smoothly to the front shortly after turning for home, and although he drifted into the centre of the track after the last before edging back over to the stands' rail, he was always in command. Fences surely beckon next season and it's not hard to envisage him returning in 12 months' time as a leading candidate for the RSA Chase. (op 5-2 tchd 7-4)

Mossley(IRE), like his stablemate, had Grade 2-winning form at Cheltenham to his name. Much more at home in the prevailing conditions than he had been behind Court In Motion at Warwick, he chased his stablemate going to the last and stayed on willingly up the hill, but was always just being held. He definitely goes chasing next term and his gritty demeanour should ensure him further success. (tchd 14-1)

Court In Motion(IRE) travelled strongly and was in front for a few strides on the home turn, but the winner soon eased past and he couldn't counter, weakening a little after the last. The ground was not ideal for him and this was a fine effort from a lovely individual who looks another smart chasing prospect for next term.

Champion Court(IRE) ◆ lost a shoe and sustained cuts when behind Bobs Worth last time, but earlier took the Grade 2 Hyde Novices' Hurdle here, a race that has produced four winners of this event. Anchored in rear and taking a keen hold, he was still tanking along going to the second-last but could only plug on at the same pace when let down. He has yet to reach his full potential and is another fascinating prospect. A drop back to 2m4f may suit and he could run at Aintree. (op 12-1 tchd 18-1 in places)

Kilcrea Kim(IRE), back against novices after taking a competitive Sandown handicap, was in a similar position all the way and kept on without mustering a change of gear. He just lacked the class of the principals here, but has enjoyed a successful season and should make a chaser next term. (op 8-1)

Ackertac(IRE), another chasing prospect, only ran here after getting eliminated from the Pertemps Final. He came under a shove down the far side but stayed on for sixth.

Our Island(IRE) lost his place with a circuit to go and dropped to the rear, but his rider persisted and the gelding plugged on for seventh. He is already a winning pointer and is a potential staying chaser. (op 28-1)

Teaforthree(IRE), third in Mossley's race here in December, was up with the pace for a long time but a blunder two from home had him on the back foot. (op 33-1 tchd 25-1)

Allee Garde(FR), a Down Royal maiden winner, made an early error and was never really a factor, already held when hampered two out, but this was still a promising display from one lacking in hurdling experience. (op 50-1)

Sybarite(FR), second to Champion Court here earlier in the season, was the shorter priced of the Twiston-Davies pair but was in trouble at the top of the hill. (op 20-1)

No Secrets(IRE) made the running and tried to stretch them running down to the second-last, but was caught after the flight and immediately beaten. He is probably worth another try at 3m in slightly lesser company. (op 40-1 tchd 33-1)

Gagewell Flyer(IRE) went quite well until the approach to the second-last, but was starting to weaken when he was hampered at the flight. Pulled up after, he found this stretching his stamina and his hat-trick of wins in Ireland came on a testing surface. (op 8-1 tchd 9-1 in places)

Join Together(IRE) had something to find with both Mossley and Court In Motion on earlier meetings. He failed to give his running, dropping right out down the far side before pulling up, and seems ideally suited by the mud. (op 8-1 tchd 9-1 in places)

Jetnova(IRE) has proved largely consistent this term and he ran well in the face of this stiff task. He was not far behind the leaders when he came down two from home. (op 8-1 tchd 9-1 in places)

Start Me Up(IRE) Official explanation: jockey said gelding ran too free and was hampered by a faller (op 8-1 tchd 9-1 in places)

Moonlight Drive(IRE) was reportedly unsuited by the ground. Official explanation: jockey said gelding was unsuited by the good (good to soft places) ground (op 8-1 tchd 9-1 in places)

4850 TOTESPORT CHELTENHAM GOLD CUP CHASE GRADE 1 (22 fncs) 3m 2f 110y

3:20 (3:20) (Class 1) 5-Y-O+

£285,050 (£106,950; £53,550; £26,700; £13,400; £6,700)

Form	Pos	Btn	Horse	Jockey	RPR
3-31	1		**Long Run (FR)**[62] 3560 6-11-10 179 (Nicky Henderson) *in tch: blnd 3rd: hit 10th: trcking ldrs whn blnd 12th: styd rt there: nt fluent 4 out: rdn bef next: styd on to chal 2 out: led bef last: drvn and styd on strly run-in* **7/2**[1]	MrSWaley-Cohen	183+
24-3	2	7	**Denman (IRE)**[111] 2673 11-11-10 179 (Paul Nicholls) *towards rr early: in tch 11th: hdwy to chse ldrs 16th: rdn 18th: slt ld 3 out: hdd sn after: narrow ld again next: hdd bef last: styd on gamely run-in but no ch w wnr* **8/1**	SamThomas	176
F-13	3	4	**Kauto Star (FR)**[62] 3560 11-11-10 174 (Paul Nicholls) *chsd ldrs: nt fluent 10th: led 12th: hdd 14th: led again 17th: hit 4 out: narrowly hdd next: led again sn after: upsides whn jst hdd 2 out: one pce into 3rd appr last: fading and jst hld on for that position cl home* **5/1**[3]	(t) RWalsh	174
1-52	4	nse	**What A Friend**[28] 4186 8-11-10 159 (Paul Nicholls) *in rr: hdwy fr 16th: chsd ldrs after next: nvr quite on terms and one pce whn mstke 2 out: rallied run-in to press for 3rd cl home but nvr a threat to ldng duo* **25/1**	(b[1]) DarylJacob	172
1111	5	8	**Midnight Chase**[98] 2871 9-11-10 163 (Neil Mulholland) *led: hit 10th: jnd next: hdd 12th: rdn 16th: outpcd 17th: plenty to do fr 3 out: styd on again fr 2 out: kpt on run-in but nvr any ch* **9/1**	TomScudamore	167
-322	6	3 3/4	**Tidal Bay (IRE)**[48] 3805 10-11-10 166 (Howard Johnson) *dropped to rr 10th: blnd 11th: virtually t.o after 4 out: styd on again fr 2 out: fin wl but nvr any ch* **16/1**	BrianHughes	163
1-P1	7	shd	**Pandorama (IRE)**[80] 3176 8-11-10 166 (Noel Meade, Ire) *in tch tl lost position and dropped to rr 17th: styd on again fr 2 out but nvr any ch* **14/1**	PCarberry	163
/B01	8	3 1/2	**Neptune Collonges (FR)**[48] 3805 10-11-10 168 (Paul Nicholls) *blnd 3rd: in rr: hit 6th: rdn and bhd fr 15th: mod prog again fr 2 out* **33/1**	RobertThornton	162

-664 **9** *34* **Carruthers**[27] 4208 8-11-10 146 MattieBatchelor 127
(Mark Bradstock) *in rr: blnd 4th: j. slowly 11th and no ch after: t.o whn blnd 3 out* **66/1**

1U-1 **P** **Imperial Commander (IRE)**[118] 2524 10-11-10 185 PaddyBrennan —
(Nigel Twiston-Davies) *chsd ldrs: mstke 13th: pressed ldrs 16th: blnd 4 out: sn wknd: t.o whn p.u bef last: dismntd: fin lame* **4/1**[2]

-3U1 **P** **Kempes (IRE)**[34] 4087 8-11-10 162 (t) APMcCoy —
(W P Mullins, Ire) *in rr: blnd 5th: in tch 12th: wknd 14th: blnd 17th: t.o whn p.u bef 4 out* **9/1**

1-10 **P** **Weird Al (IRE)**[111] 2673 8-11-10 152 JasonMaguire —
(Ian Williams) *prom early: bhd fr 7th: wknd 12th: t.o whn p.u bef 14th: b.b.v* **20/1**

1134 **P** **China Rock (IRE)**[34] 4087 8-11-10 159 BarryGeraghty —
(M F Morris, Ire) *trckd ldrs: chal 11th tl led 14th: hdd but upsides 17th: wknd after 4 out: p.u bef2 out: dismntd* **25/1**

6m 29.7s (-24.10) **Going Correction** -0.40s/f (Good) course record **13** Ran SP% **119.4**
Speed ratings: **119,116,115,115,113 112,112,111,101,— —,—,—**
Tote Swingers: 1&2 £4.60, 1&3 £4.20, 2&3 £6.60 CSF £29.91 CT £142.52 TOTE £4.30: £2.00, £3.00, £2.20; EX 33.00 Trifecta £175.20 Pool: £34,061.77 - 143.79 winning units..

Owner Robert Waley-Cohen **Bred** Mrs Marie-Christine Gabeur **Trained** Upper Lambourn, Berks
■ Nicky Henderson's first Gold Cup winner.

FOCUS

A strong renewal of the most prestigious chase of the jumping season, with the winners of the last four runnings all present, plus horses that made the frame in each of the last three years. In addition there were half a dozen young pretenders, headed by the King George winner Long Run, the Irish Hennessy winner Kempes and Lexus Chase winner Pandorama. The pace was relentless throughout and all the main players were there running down from the fourth-last, so there appeared no fluke about the result. Long Run continued the trend of well above average winners, up 3lb on his King George mark. Denman ran to last year's Gold Cup mark and Kauto Star ran his best race since the 2009 King George, while What A Friend was up 7lb. The time was a new record for the nominal distance of the race, but the Clerk Of The Course Simon Claisse reported the actual distance was around 80yds shorter than in the past.

NOTEBOOK

Long Run(FR) overcame several minor mistakes to outstay his older rivals up the hill, breaking the track record. He had looked a devastating performer on a flat track when winning the delayed King George VI Chase in January, but his two defeats since coming to Britain had both been at this course, suggesting he might not be as effective on an undulating track. However, he proved the doubters wrong in emphatic fashion, finding plenty up the hill and ultimately drawing away for a comfortable success. He became the first 6-y-o to score since Mill House in 1963, and his rider became the first amateur to win the race since Jim Wilson on Little Owl thirty years previously, and the combination looks set to be a major player here for several years to come, all things being equal. A tilt at the Grand Steeple-Chase de Paris is looking unlikely but the gelding could run in the Totesport Bowl at Aintree. (op 4-1)

Denman(IRE), the 2008 winner under today's rider, has now been runner-up for the last three years. He had looked as if age was just beginning to catch up with him in recent races, but he put up a mighty effort this time, having been held up in the early stages. He joined issue on the run down the hill and got the better of his stable companion and old rival at the second-last, only to be out-speeded by the younger winner soon after. He has put up some wonderful displays of steeplechasing over the years and this was yet another. He may go to Aintree and will race on next season. (op early 11-1 tchd 9-1)

Kauto Star(FR), who made history when becoming the first horse to regain the title in 2009, also ran a great race. He took over early on the second circuit and gradually stretched most of his rivals, but he was taken on by the runner-up after three out and had nothing left once headed going to the next. He is another who has been a major star in the last five years and he went down fighting again. He won't be retired just yet and could run again this season. (op 13-2)

What A Friend, who has always been talented if a little quirky, was fitted with blinkers for the first time having looked less than straightforward again at Newbury last time. He travelled well in them and ran a fine race, nearly catching Kauto Star for third and finishing well ahead of the others. Winner of the Totesport Bowl at the meeting last year, he is set to head to Aintree again and will run in the Grand National if the ground's good. He will be 15lb well in on official figures.

Midnight Chase was stepping up from handicaps having been most progressive when winning three times around this course before Christmas. He adopted his normal front-running tactics but was taken on early on the second circuit and looked sure to drop away. However, he stays really well and he kept responding to his substitute rider's urgings to keep on for fifth. He is another who could make up into a Grand National contender next season. (op 11-1 tchd 12-1 in places)

Tidal Bay(IRE) has a decent record around here, including at the Festival, and was fancied to make the frame. He was out the back as usual early and ran on in the closing stages, but prefers a little give in the ground and the sound surface meant the principals were not stopping quickly enough up the hill for him to catch them. The Grand National remains a possibility. (tchd 18-1 and 20-1 in places)

Pandorama(IRE), the Lexus Chase winner, tracked the leaders early and overcame getting hampered on the bend turning for home first time to still be there at the top of the hill. However, from that point he could not keep with the leaders and is another who would have preferred softer ground. He came home sore and won't run again this season. (tchd 16-1)

Neptune Collonges(FR), another who'd have preferred softer ground, was struggling from an early stage on this surface and did well to finish as close as he did. He could be set for another trip to Punchestown if the ground is right for him. (op 28-1)

Carruthers is not up to this level and never figured under a change of tactics. He ran well at Aintree last year and might well return there next month.

Imperial Commander(IRE), last year's winner, got involved with the leaders on the second circuit and was bang there when hitting the fourth-last fence, from which point he dropped away quickly and was pulled up. It transpired that he was slightly lame afterwards on his near fore, and broke a blood-vessel, so he can be forgiven this. He is likely to be put away for the summer now, with the Betfair Chase his next target. Official explanation: vet said gelding was lame left-fore and also distressed (tchd 25-1)

Kempes(IRE), the winner of the Irish Hennessy, handled good ground last spring but looked suited by soft earlier this season and was unable to compete at this level (tchd 25-1)

Weird Al(IRE) has had his problems, having missed this meeting last year and then been absent since the Hennessy, and after starting up with the leaders, was at the back and struggling after a circuit. He was reported to have bled from the nose. Official explanation: jockey said gelding bled from the nose (tchd 25-1)

China Rock(IRE) had beaten this week's Queen Mother winner Sizing Europe on good ground back in the autumn and the return to that surface saw him run a fine race for a long way. However, he paid for his exertions from the top of the hill and was later reported to have lost his action. Official explanation: jockey said gelding lost its action (tchd 25-1)

4851 CHRISTIE'S FOXHUNTER CHASE CHALLENGE CUP (22 fncs) 3m 2f 110y

4:00 (4:00) (Class 2) 5-Y-O+

£21,007 (£6,562; £3,279; £1,641; £819; £413)

Form RPR

4-21 **1** **Zemsky (IRE)**[30] 4147 8-12-0 125 (p) MrDerekO'Connor 150+
(I R Ferguson, Ire) *hld up in midfield: hmpd 9th: stdy hdwy fnl circ: wnt 2nd after 3 out: abt 2 l down whn lft in clr ld 2 out: pushed out and styd on wl after last: idled and drifted rt run-in whn wl in command* **33/1**

6- **2** *17* **Mid Div And Creep**[41] 11-11-7 0 MissGAndrews 125
(Alan Hill) *chsd ldrs: outpcd bef 18th: over 13 l off the pce 2 out: kpt on and wnt 2nd run-in: no ch w wnr* **100/1**

3 *2* **Oscar Delta (IRE)**[26] 8-12-0 0 MrDMurphy 131
(James Joseph Mangan, Ire) *midfield: stdy hdwy fr 4 out: styd on fr 2 out: continued to prog run-in but nvr a threat* **25/1**

1- **4** *9* **On The Fringe (IRE)**[34] 4089 6-12-0 134 MrJTMcNamara 126+
(E Bolger, Ire) *midfield: hmpd 9th: stdy hdwy bef 18th: chsd ldrs bef 3 out: wnt mod 2nd appr last: lost 2nd run-in: plugged on at one pce* **3/1**[1]

12/1 **5** *7* **Dante's Storm**[31] 4131 9-12-0 129 MrPYork 124+
(Alan Hill) *in tch: mstke 11th: wnt cl 2nd 13th: blnd 15th and gd rcvry: pushed along whn hit 18th: mstke 3 out sn lost 2nd: abt 18 l down whn mstke and lft 2nd 2 out: lost 2nd appr last: wknd run-in* **10/1**

052- **6** *2 1/4* **Gone To Lunch (IRE)**[27] 11-12-0 138 (p) MrNHarris 113
(Mrs C C Scott) *towards rr: rdn along and gng nowhere bef 13th: kpt on past btn horses fr 2 out: nvr a danger* **7/1**[3]

2242 **7** *3 3/4* **Templer (IRE)**[22] 4315 10-12-0 128 MrNSutton 112
(Philip Hobbs) *midfield: mstke and hmpd 9th: outpcd fr 13th: nvr on terms w ldrs* **40/1**

2414 **8** *nk* **Turthen (FR)**[30] 4141 10-12-0 134 MissCTizzard 110
(C St V Fox) *midfield: effrt but no imp on ldrs bef 3 out: nvr a threat* **20/1**

46P- **9** *6* **Amicelli (GER)**[27] 12-12-0 108 MrOGreenall 104
(Mrs C A Coward) *a bhd: toiling thrght fnl circ: nvr on terms* **66/1**

5-11 **10** *3* **Special Portrait (IRE)**[22] 4307 7-12-0 109 (t) MrWKinsey 102
(Mark Hughes) *towards rr: pushed along after 8th: nvr on terms* **100/1**

10-3 **11** *13* **Noakarad De Verzee (FR)**[22] 4315 10-12-0 126 MrDMaxwell 90
(Mrs Kim Smyly) *trckd ldrs: lost pl bef 11th: outpcd by ldrs after: struggling fnl circ* **150/1**

1044 **12** *3* **Distant Thunder (IRE)**[4] 4786 13-12-0 108 (t) MrPPrince 87
(Mrs A S Hodges) *a bhd: t.o fnl circ* **100/1**

P-21 **P** **Mount Benger**[22] 4315 11-12-0 129 MrSKeating —
(H Whittington) *a bhd: nvr gng wl: t.o whn p.u bef 17th* **66/1**

U-11 **U** **Baby Run (FR)**[27] 4211 11-12-0 136 MrWTwiston-Davies 148
(Nigel Twiston-Davies) *led: hit 8th: niggled but stl abt 2 l up whn blnd and uns rdr 2 out* **3/1**[1]

00/1 **P** **Oscatello (USA)**[26] 11-12-0 113 MissPGundry —
(Ross Oliver) *in tch: mstke 8th and 10th: lost pl 10th: towards rr fr 11th: t.o whn p.u bef 4 out* **40/1**

/30- **U** **Reach For The Top (IRE)**[344] 5096 10-12-0 124 MrBJTuckey 112
(M J Tuckey) *chsd ldrs: pushed along and outpcd bef 13th: 6th and n.d whn blnd and uns rdr last* **66/1**

FP-P **P** **Joaaci (IRE)**[14] 4463 11-12-0 107 MrRHawkins —
(Mrs P J Shaw) *trckd ldrs: blnd 5th: lost pl 7th: rdn after 12th: t.o whn p.u bef 15th* **150/1**

11-4 **U** **Theatre Diva (IRE)**[27] 10-11-7 120 MissJBuck —
(Miss J Du Plessis) *towards rr: mstke and uns rdr sme way after 8th* **100/1**

PF-P **P** **Jaunty Flight**[33] 9-11-7 133 (t) MrTGreenall —
(David M Easterby) *a bhd: t.o whn p.u bef 11th* **20/1**

35-6 **F** **Description (IRE)**[27] 9-12-0 119 MissCEwart —
(Mrs Jenny Gordon) *prom tl fell 9th* **66/1**

2621 **U** **Herons Well**[19] 4374 8-12-0 135 (p) MrJoshHalley —
(Rebecca Curtis) *prom: cl 3rd and stl gng wl whn blnd and uns rdr 13th* **33/1**

6-11 **P** **Just Amazing (IRE)**[24] 4271 8-12-0 136 (t) MrRMahon —
(Paul Nicholls) *chsd ldrs: lost gound bef 13th: grad wknd: t.o whn p.u bef 2 out* **13/2**[2]

F3-1 **P** **Sericina (FR)**[29] 4163 8-11-7 128 MissCRoddick —
(Miss C Roddick) *a bhd: t.o whn p.u bef 17th* **20/1**

-643 **P** **Gentle George**[29] 4163 8-12-0 124 MrRBurton —
(S Flook) *midfield: outpcd fr 13th: wl bhd whn p.u bef 3 out: dismntd* **33/1**

6m 37.2s (-16.60) **Going Correction** -0.40s/f (Good) **24** Ran SP% **128.0**
Speed ratings: **108,102,102,99,97 96,95,95,93,93 89,88,—,—,— —,—,—,—,— —,—,—,—**
Tote Swingers: 1&2 £0.00, 1&3 £157.40, 2&3 £342.60 CSF £1770.10 CT £56151.86 TOTE £68.00: £11.50, £35.40, £5.00; EX 2626.70 TRIFECTA Not won..

Owner R A Bartlett **Bred** J R Weston **Trained** Ballymena, Co Antrim

FOCUS

A competitive field for the most prestigious hunter chase of the season. The pace was fast and furious and the field was quickly well strung out with a group of five soon opening up a break on the others. Zemsky was left clear two out and recorded a massive step up on his previous rules form, looking an above-average winner. Baby Run has been rated to his mark and as finishing 2l second.

NOTEBOOK

Zemsky(IRE) was ridden very patiently by the experienced Derek O'Connor, who asked his mount to improve from the water jump on the second circuit. Easing into second place off the home turn, he was a couple of lengths down and still travelling well when he was presented with the race at the second-last. He idled when in front and there is a doubt over what he would have found, but he was certainly going better than Baby Run at the time of the latter's departure. A winner over 2m4f at Musselburgh a month ago, there were stamina doubts over this extended trip, but he clearly stays well. Connections have the choice between the big hunter chases at Punchestown and Stratford later this spring.

Mid Div And Creep was prominent in the main body of the field, but became outpaced on the second circuit. She did stay on again and moved into a remote second after the last. Winner of a dozen point-to-points, this admirable mare was running for only the second time over regulation fences. (op 80-1)

Oscar Delta(IRE) had won his last three between the flags in Ireland, beating last season's runner-up in this race, Kilty Storm, in the first of them. Another who was held up some way off the strong gallop, he stayed on over the last four fences but was never close enough to mount a challenge.

On The Fringe(IRE) came here on the back of winning Leopardstown's Raymond Smith Memorial Hunter Chase, Ireland's key trial for this event. Held up, he was hampered by a faller at the ninth and made a couple of jumping errors, never reaching a challenging position, although he did take the final fence in second place before tiring. He could be a different proposition if returning in a year's time, although connections may opt to switch him to handicaps next term. In the meantime he could bid for a second win in the Champion Hunters Chase at Punchestown. (op 10-3 tchd 7-2 in places)

Dante's Storm, the runner-up's stablemate, is another prolific winner who has run rarely in hunter chases. Lightly raced, and beaten just once in ten career starts, he was prominent for a long way but made several juddering errors which eventually took their toll. (tchd 11-1)

Gone To Lunch(IRE), a dual Scottish National runner-up, recovered from a life-threatening ailment last summer to land a couple of points this year. He stayed on but was never a factor. (op 9-1)

Turthen(FR) Official explanation: vet said gelding finished distressed

Baby Run(FR) adopted similar trailblazing tactics to last year and made a brave bid to become the first back-to-back winner since Double Silk in 1993-4. Sam Twiston-Davies had been in the saddle 12 months ago, but this time it was his 16-year-old brother Willie's turn. The combination turned the screw from the top of the hill and succeeded in burning off most of their pursuers, but Zemsky gradually closed them down. Baby Run was being niggled along, but was finding for pressure, when he put in an extra stride at the second-last and gave the talented Twiston-Davies no chance. The gelding failed to get round at Aintree last spring and his tendency to get in too close to a few may find him out again there. (tchd 7-2 in places)
Reach For The Top(IRE), third last year, ran well for a long way but was a tired sixth when he unshipped his rider at the last. He should be sharper for this first run in 11 months and could find success in the closing weeks of the season. (tchd 7-2 in places)
Jaunty Flight Official explanation: vet said mare bled from the nose (tchd 7-2 in places)
Herons Well was in the leading group and still travelling well within himself when he stumbled and lost his rider. (tchd 7-2 in places)
Just Amazing(IRE) was expected to improve for the return to a left-handed circuit, but he was the first of the breakaway five to feel the pinch and was eventually pulled up. Official explanation: vet said gelding had bled from the nose (tchd 7-2 in places)
Sericina(FR), who completed a four-timer when beating Herons Well last time, was never going here. Official explanation: vet said mare finished distressed (tchd 7-2 in places)

4852 MARTIN PIPE CONDITIONAL JOCKEYS' H'CAP HURDLE (10 hdls) 2m 4f 110y

4:40 (4:41) (Class 2) (0-140,140) 4-Y-0+

£28,179 (£8,325; £4,162; £2,083; £1,039; £522)

Form RPR

1 **Sir Des Champs (FR)**[52] 3733 5-11-3 **134** .... EMullins(3) 143+
(W P Mullins, Ire) *hld up in rr: hdwy appr 2 out: rdn and str run appr last: fin strly to ld fnl 20yds* **9/2**[1]

2532 2 ½ **Son Of Flicka**[117] 2542 7-11-6 **140** .... HenryBrooke(6) 147
(Donald McCain) *in tch: lost pl 4 out: rdn and rallied after next: rdn to ld bef last: kpt on: hdd and outpcd fnl 20yds* **28/1**

0-34 3 2 **First Point (GER)**[62] 3561 8-11-7 **138** .... DavidBass(3) 143
(Nicky Henderson) *chsd ldrs: rdn appr 2 out: str chal wl bef last and ev ch last: one pce fnl 50yds* **20/1**

35 4 4 **Indian Daudaie (FR)**[34] 4083 4-10-8 **138** .... JamesCowley(8) 131
(Paul Nicholls) *trckd ldrs: chal 2 out: led sn after: hdd bef last: wknd run-in* **25/1**

3502 5 10 **Kauto Relko (FR)**[26] 4235 7-10-10 **127** .... PeterCarberry(3) 124+
(Rachel Hobbs) *in rr: hdwy and hmpd 4 out: styd on fr 2 out: kpt on run-in but no imp on ldrs* **50/1**

05-3 6 2 **Hollins**[29] 4169 7-10-10 **132** .... JoeColliver(8) 121
(Micky Hammond) *in rr: rdn after 3 out: styd on appr last: kpt on run-in: nt rch ldrs* **10/1**

0365 7 nk **Barizan (IRE)**[41] 3939 5-11-12 **140** ....(v) AodhaganConlon 129
(Evan Williams) *led: t.k.h: hit 2nd: hdd after 2 out: wknd wl bef last* **16/1**

4205 8 ¾ **Rose Of The Moon (IRE)**[27] 4206 6-10-9 **128** ....(t) JakeGreenall(5) 118
(Milton Harris) *chsd ldrs: outpcd after 4 out: styd on again after 2 out: nt rch ldrs* **12/1**

-031 9 1 **Shoegazer (IRE)**[41] 3941 6-11-2 **133** ....(t) CO'Farrell(3) 120
(David Pipe) *mid-div: hdwy 4 out: heels clipped by faller and wknd qckly bef last* **13/2**[2]

1252 10 ½ **Karasenir (IRE)**[57] 3649 5-11-6 **137** .... GilesHawkins(3) 125
(Philip Hobbs) *blnd 5th: in rr: sme hdwy fr 2 out* **25/1**

4243 11 5 **Monetary Fund (USA)**[78] 3229 5-10-8 **130** .... JeremiahMcGrath(8) 113
(Nicky Henderson) *hit 2nd: rdn 3 out: mod prog whn hmpd wl bef last* **18/1**

0035 12 shd **Higgy's Boy (IRE)**[98] 2868 6-10-13 **130** ....(b) RichardKilloran(3) 111
(Nicky Henderson) *hit 1st: bhd tl sme late prog* **28/1**

1513 13 2¾ **Prince Du Seuil (FR)**[21] 4327 8-10-6 **128** .... PeterHatton(8) 107
(Alan King) *in rr: hdwy 4 out: wknd bef 2 out* **33/1**

1066 14 2¾ **Astracad (FR)**[76] 3288 5-11-9 **140** .... SamTwiston-Davies(3) 116
(Nigel Twiston-Davies) *chsd ldrs: rdn 3 out: wknd next* **14/1**

111- 15 3 **Qaspal (FR)**[370] 4591 7-11-6 **137** .... MattGriffiths(3) 110
(Philip Hobbs) *in rr: hit 3rd: sme prog 3 out: no prog whn hmpd wl bef last* **10/1**

1130 16 16 **Palomar (USA)**[28] 4188 9-11-8 **136** .... FearghalDavis 93
(Brian Ellison) *hit 3rd: sme prog 3 out: sn wknd* **33/1**

2-10 17 2½ **Riptide**[124] 2387 5-11-2 **133** ....(b) JohnKington(3) 87
(Donald McCain) *chsd ldrs: rdn 4th: wknd 4 out* **66/1**

1110 18 65 **Sahrati**[22] 1357 7-10-13 **127** .... DonalDevereux 16
(Michael Blake) *hit 4th: a in rr* **100/1**

42-3 B **Siberian Tiger (IRE)**[41] 3945 6-11-7 **135** .... BryanJCooper —
(Evan Williams) *towards rr: bdly hmpd and b.d 4 out* **22/1**

3-55 S **Shalone**[27] 4202 7-11-8 **139** .... CharlieHuxley(3) 122
(Alan King) *trckd ldrs: 5th and rdn whn clipped heels of Shoegazer and slipped up wl bef last* **20/1**

-151 F **King Of The Night (GER)**[49] 3787 7-11-7 **138** .... IanPopham(3) —
(Paul Nicholls) *chsd ldrs: stl rt there whn fell 4 out* **8/1**[3]

0 P **La Bombonera (FR)**[16] 4420 5-10-11 **128** .... RTDunne(3) —
(Venetia Williams) *in tch to 6th: sn wknd: t.o whn p.u after 3 out* **100/1**

1610 B **Mister Hyde (IRE)**[41] 3947 6-10-11 **128** .... RichieMcLernon(3) —
(Jonjo O'Neill) *chsng ldrs: rdn and stl wl there whn bdly hmpd and b.d 4 out* **16/1**

4m 45.22s (-19.78) **Going Correction** -0.625s/f (Firm)
WFA 4 from 5yo+ 8lb **23** Ran SP% **128.8**
Speed ratings (Par 109): **112,111,111,109,105 104,104,104,104,103 102,102,100,99,98 92,91,66,—,— —,—,—**
Tote Swingers: 1&2 £22.50, 1&3 £45.50, 2&3 £162.70 CSF £137.30 CT £2358.01 TOTE £4.70: £2.20, £7.10, £6.50, £6.20; EX 114.90 Trifecta £4182.20 Pool: £40,851.29 - 1.92 winning units..
Owner Gigginstown House Stud **Bred** Dominique Clayeux **Trained** Muine Beag, Co Carlow
■ A first festival winner for Emmet Mullins, nephew of the winning trainer.
■ Stewards' Enquiry : David Bass five-day ban: used whip causing gelding to be wealed (Apr 1-5)

FOCUS

The third running of this handicap hurdle for conditional jockeys run in honour of the former multiple champion trainer. A highly competitive event on paper with just 13lb covering the entire field and a race of changing fortunes. It was relatively the fastest of the hurdle races on the card. A step up from Sir Des Champs, who can rate higher, with a personal best from the second and the third to his best.

NOTEBOOK

Sir Des Champs(FR), a winner in France before scoring on his debut for his current yard at Navan in January, was unexposed but the good ground was a question mark. He was held up and jumped carefully early on, with the result that he was well behind running down the hill. However, he picked up strongly from the penultimate flight and was able to run down the second near the line. He looks to have plenty more to offer, especially on soft ground, and could well be back for the Coral Cup next season. (tchd 5-1 in places)
Son Of Flicka is well suited by good and soft ground but had looked best on a flat track, despite having been placed around here on his only previous try. He responded to pressure from three out to get to the front, only to be run down by the strong-finishing winner. This was a brave effort from the top weight and he might be able to gain compensation at Aintree next month, having run well there in the autumn. (op 25-1 tchd 33-1)
First Point(GER) has mixing fences and hurdles of late and his better efforts were over the former. He was in the leading group for most of the way and stuck to his task well up the hill. He could be back here for a race at the April meeting, having won there back in 2009.
Indian Daudaie(FR), another ex-French gelding, ran reasonably over the course in January and did so again. Stepping up in trip for this handicap debut, he was ridden positively and seemed to handle the good ground.
Kauto Relko(FR), a winner at 2m on heavy in Ireland and placed at 2m3f on easy ground on his first try at the trip, was held up early before making headway to chase the leaders into the straight, but was one paced up the hill after a mistake at the last.
Hollins posted a couple of fair efforts here last spring and stayed on late from the rear on just his second start since. He seems best suited by softer ground. (op 14-1)
Barizan(IRE) has a good record around here, having won once and placed in three more of five previous starts. However, his only unplaced effort was on his sole previous run over this distance, and after making the running it appeared he did not quite last the trip. (op 18-1)
Rose Of The Moon(IRE), runner-up to the earlier winner Bobs Worth on easy ground around here in January, was wearing a tongue tie for this handicap debut. He lost a good early pitch before running on again, and having done similar in his previous outing, it might be he needs some form of headgear to help him concentrate. (op 14-1)
Shoegazer(IRE), a dual winner at around this trip, had looked well suited by flat tracks and, after joining the leaders at the bottom of the hill, seemed to struggle up the climb to the line. (op 15-2 tchd 8-1)
Karasenir(IRE), a dual winner on good ground but whose best efforts have been on right-handed tracks, stayed on after making an error at around halfway. (op 20-1)
Qaspal(FR) completed a hat-trick when winning last year's Imperial Cup but failed to get a run at this meeting last year and had been absent since. He was held up but could only make modest progress, and was beaten when having to jump the faller on the run to the last.
Shalone travelled well into the race, but was hampered more than once after the second-last and appeared to be hanging to his left, possibly feeling the ground. He was still chasing the leaders when appearing to clip heels and take a heavy fall on the run to the last. He looked sore afterwards. (op 10-1)
King Of The Night(GER) had won two of his three starts over hurdles including over 2m here, finishing fifth behind Cue Card on his other start. Making his handicap debut, he was just behind the leaders when taking a heavy fall at the seventh. (op 10-1)

4853 JOHNNY HENDERSON GRAND ANNUAL CHASE CHALLENGE CUP (H'CAP) GRADE 3 (14 fncs) 2m 110y

5:15 (5:16) (Class 1) 5-Y-O+

£42,757 (£16,042; £8,032; £4,005; £2,010; £1,005)

Form RPR

6403 1 **Oiseau De Nuit (FR)**[28] 4187 9-10-13 **145** ....(t) SClements(7) 158+
(Colin Tizzard) *in tch: shkn up and clsd to chal bef 2 out and sn led: drvn out and styd on wl after last: wl in command after* **40/1**

/56- 2 3¼ **Askthemaster (IRE)**[34] 4088 11-10-8 **136** ....(t) PTEnright(3) 146
(Robert Tyner, Ire) *trckd ldrs: chalng appr 2 out: sn in 2nd: rdn and nt qckn bef last: styd on but hld by wnr run-in* **50/1**

U-25 3 2¼ **Leo's Lucky Star (USA)**[69] 3446 9-10-11 **139** ....(t) DannyCook(3) 147
(David Pipe) *hld up: hdwy appr 4 out: shkn up bef 2 out: wnt 3rd at last: styd on run-in but no imp on front 2* **20/1**

3-02 4 6 **De Boitron (FR)**[32] 4116 7-10-12 **137** .... GrahamLee 142+
(Ferdy Murphy) *hld up: hdwy appr 4 out: nt fluent 2 out: sn rdn and nt qckn: kpt on run-in: no imp on ldrs* **8/1**[3]

1003 5 1 **Quito Du Tresor (FR)**[35] 4058 7-10-5 **130** .... CampbellGillies 135+
(Lucinda Russell) *midfield: hit 2nd: hdwy appr 3 out: chsd ldrs 2 out: mstke last: kpt on same pce run-in* **40/1**

2411 6 hd **Anquetta (IRE)**[41] 3949 7-10-4 **132** .... DavidBass(3) 135
(Nicky Henderson) *trckd ldrs: hit 2nd: wnt 2nd 10th: led briefly appr 2 out: rdn and one pce bef last: no ex run-in* **9/1**

0406 7 8 **I'msingingtheblues (IRE)**[28] 4187 9-11-5 **144** ....(t) TomScudamore 141
(David Pipe) *in tch: mstke and lost pl 9th: outpcd 3 out: one pce and no imp after* **4/1**[1]

1123 8 2 **Pepe Simo (IRE)**[21] 4326 7-11-4 **143** .... RWalsh 138
(Paul Nicholls) *towards rr: hit 3rd: u.p after 3 out: kpt on but nvr able to get on terms after* **11/1**

3003 9 ½ **Pigeon Island**[15] 4440 8-10-8 **133** ....(b) PaddyBrennan 126
(Nigel Twiston-Davies) *towards rr: drvn along 10th: nvr able to get on terms w ldrs* **14/1**

522F 10 6 **Keki Buku (FR)**[32] 4122 8-10-7 **132** ....(t) RichardJohnson 124
(Philip Hobbs) *midfield: j. slowly and mstke 8th: hmpd 10th: bhd and outpcd whn mstke 4 out: nvr on terms after* **20/1**

0313 11 2 **Mister Stickler (IRE)**[22] 4311 7-10-5 **130** ....(t) WayneHutchinson 115
(Alan King) *midfield: pushed along after 10th: outpcd appr 3 out: j.lft 2 out: n.d after* **25/1**

1240 12 ½ **Riguez Dancer**[41] 3949 7-10-5 **130** .... RichieMcGrath 117
(Ferdy Murphy) *hld up: outpcd whn mstke 10th: nvr on terms* **50/1**

-663 13 1¾ **Oh Crick (FR)**[69] 3446 8-11-6 **145** .... RobertThornton 128
(Alan King) *midfield: outpcd after 4 out: nvr on terms* **8/1**[3]

3F-1 14 4 **Shoreacres (IRE)**[24] 4267 8-10-10 **135** .... APMcCoy 115
(Brendan Powell) *midfield: hit 9th: outpcd after: wl btn bef 2 out* **6/1**[2]

4031 15 3 **Film Festival (USA)**[14] 4453 8-10-7 **132** 5ex .... FearghalDavis 109
(Brian Ellison) *midfield: rdn appr 3 out: wknd bef 2 out* **33/1**

0001 16 ½ **Santa's Son (IRE)**[40] 3966 11-11-2 **141** ....(t) BrianHughes 117
(Howard Johnson) *chsd ldrs: wnt 2nd 7th to 10th: rdn and wknd appr 3 out* **100/1**

3-45 17 4½ **Sports Line (IRE)**[28] 4187 8-11-6 **145** .... TimmyMurphy 117
(Donald McCain) *hld up: outpcd 4 out: nvr able to get on terms* **28/1**

3420 18 4½ **Tanks For That (IRE)**[48] 3808 8-11-3 **142** .... BarryGeraghty 126+
(Nicky Henderson) *led: blnd 1st: sn hdd: remained prom: led 5th: rdn and hdd between 3 out and 2 out: wkng whn blnd 2 out: sn eased and allowed to coast home* **11/1**

2P04 R **Chaninbar (FR)**[118] 2515 8-11-12 **151** ....(vt) SeanQuinlan —
(Milton Harris) *ref to r: tk no part* **100/1**

0P-0 U **Beggars Cap (IRE)**[13] 4470 9-10-2 **130** .... SamTwiston-Davies(3) —
(Ferdy Murphy) *in tch: 7th whn blnd and uns rdr 10th* **28/1**

0-02 P **Nomecheki (FR)**[41] 3949 9-11-1 **140** .... LiamTreadwell —
(Nick Gifford) *midfield: mstke 1st: bhd fr 4th: t.o whn p.u bef 2 out* **25/1**

2201 F **Grand Lahou (FR)**[47] 3841 8-10-3 **133** .... MrTomDavid(5) —
(Tim Vaughan) *chsd ldrs: nt fluent 1st: stmbld 4th: wnt 2nd 8th: hit 9th: sn lost 2nd: wknd bef 3 out: n.d whn fell 2 out* **66/1**

36P3 **P** **Fiendish Flame (IRE)**[26] 4235 7-11-4 **143**.....................(b) JasonMaguire —
(Donald McCain) *j.rt: led after 1st: hdd 5th: remained prom tl wknd 9th: t.o whn p.u bef 2 out* **28/1**

3m 52.8s (-13.90) **Going Correction** -0.40s/f (Good) course record **23** Ran SP% **132.6**
Speed ratings: **116,114,113,110,110 110,106,105,105,102 101,101,100,98,96 96,94,92,—,— —,—,—**
Tote Swingers: 1&2 £215.60, 1&3 £90.80, 2&3 £575.00. totesuper7: Win: Not won. Place: Not won. CSF £1354.15 CT £33190.70 TOTE £69.40: £9.20, £9.20, £4.60, £2.80; EX 6245.40 TRIFECTA Not won..
Owner Terry Warner **Bred** Guy Cherel **Trained** Milborne Port, Dorset
■ A winner for Steven Clements on his first ride at Cheltenham. The final 'score' at the festival was GB 14 winners, Ireland 13.

FOCUS
A competitive edition of the season's most important 2m handicap chase, but perhaps not a strong renewal. The weights were raised 7lb at the overnight stage, and topweight Chaninbar, who was conceding 5lb and more, was the first out of the contest as he refused to race. Oiseau De Nuit was very well in on several pieces of form and is rated to his best, with a step up from the second and the next two to their marks. The time was good.

NOTEBOOK
Oiseau De Nuit(FR) had been pulled up off the same mark in this race last year, but had to come under consideration on the form he showed when third in the Grade 2 Game Spirit Chase at Newbury last month, when he stayed on well after a blunder. Settled not far behind the leaders, he was ridden on the home turn and soon quickened up to lead, pulling away for a comfortable success. The Red Rum Handicap Chase at Aintree and the Queen Mother Celebration Chase at Sandown look suitable April targets.
Askthemaster(IRE) the only Irish-trained runner in the field, was prominent throughout and stuck on well for second. He gets further than this, a plus in such a strongly run affair, but is most at home in soft ground. He still holds a Grand National entry. (op 66-1)
Leo's Lucky Star(USA) improved from off the pace and was running on after the last. He had been freshened up by a break and the better ground was a plus. (op 22-1)
De Boitron(FR) had been laid out for this since winning here last April and he ran well, staying on from off the gallop without ever quite getting to the leaders.
Quito Du Tresor(FR) had ground conditions to suit and belied his price with a prominent effort. He never looked like winning, but a mistake at the last possibly cost him fourth place. Aintree is more his track so he could be worth running in the Red Rum Chase. (op 50-1)
Anquetta(IRE) perhaps got there too soon in a race very close to his trainer's heart. He moved into second behind stablemate Tanks For That going nicely, but his effort fizzled out after he looked sure to be involved in the finish. He isn't straightforward but has more to offer. (op 8-1)
I'msingingtheblues(IRE) has become well handicapped and he ran respectably without really getting involved. His losing run extends back to January 2009. (tchd 5-1)
Pepe Simo(IRE), another novice, was never in the hunt with an early mistake not helping his cause. (op 18-1)
Pigeon Island picked up the pieces off a fast pace last year and ran a not dissimilar race off 4lb higher this time around, although his finishing position of ninth was as good as it got. He needs further now. (op 16-1)
Oh Crick(FR), the 2009 winner, was fifth in the Queen Mother Champion Chase 12 months ago and looked well treated off 145, but he could never get beyond midfield. (tchd 10-1 in places)
Shoreacres(IRE) had run well at a couple of previous festivals, but could never get into this after a couple of errors. (tchd 11-2)
Tanks For That(IRE) had been targeted at this since finishing second to Woolcombe Folly here before Christmas. He survived a first-fence blunder and was in front heading into the home turn, only to weaken very quickly. Something was presumably amiss. (op 10-1)
Grand Lahou(FR), who had raced in the front rank, was weakening when he took a heavy fall two out after an opponent jumped across him. (op 50-1)
T/Jkpt: Not won. T/Plt: £4,332.10. Pool: £969,985.40 - 163.45 winning units. T/Qpdt: £530.70. Pool: £45,633.74 - 63.62 winning units. ST

4178 FAKENHAM (L-H)
Friday, March 18

OFFICIAL GOING: Good (7.3)
Fresh ground all the way round on hurdle course.
Wind: virtually nil Weather: light cloud

4854 NORTH NORFOLK RADIO (S) HURDLE (9 hdls) 2m
2:20 (2:20) (Class 5) 4-Y-0+ **£2,055** (£599; £299)

Form RPR
/4P6 **1** **Sole Bonne Femme (IRE)**[12] 4503 9-10-7 105.........(tp) CharlieWallis(7) 100
(Gerard Butler) *mde all: j.rt and slowly at times: hit 3 out: rdn and asserted after 2 out: racd idly but in command bef last: rdn out flat* **7/1**[3]
F100 **2** 4 ½ **Celticello (IRE)**[26] 4235 9-11-2 116................................ MrJMQuinlan(7) 104+
(Noel Quinlan) *t.k.h: hld up wl in tch: 4th and rdn bef 2 out: unable qck bef last: sn drvn: chsd wnr flat: no imp* **5/4**[1]
30 **3** 1 ½ **Miss Wendy**[10] 3944 4-10-0 0.. ColinBolger 80
(Mark H Tompkins) *chsd wnr tl after 3 out: sn rdn and unable qck: chsd wnr again between last 2: no imp: lost 2nd flat* **10/1**
P546 **4** 10 **Galley Slave (IRE)**[38] 3989 6-11-0 87...................... AndrewGlassonbury 85
(Michael Chapman) *chsd ldng pair: rdn and lost pl bef 3 out: 5th and wl btn next: styd on flat* **10/1**
1533 **5** 4 ½ **Tri Nations (UAE)**[4] 4776 6-11-5 111...............................(vt) DaveCrosse 87
(Milton Harris) *hld up in tch in midfield: hdwy after 6th: pressed wnr after 3 out tl rdn and fnd nil after 2 out: wknd qckly ent st* **7/4**[2]
0300 **6** 11 **Renege The Joker**[147] 1953 8-10-7 87........................... MrMMarris(7) 73
(Sean Regan) *hld up in tch in last trio: rdn and struggling bef 3 out: wknd bef 2 out: wl btn whn mstke last* **50/1**
F-P **7** 27 **Abby Belle (IRE)**[149] 1921 5-10-4 0................................ PeterToole(3) 40
(Mrs H Parrott) *t.k.h: hld up in tch in last trio: rdn and lost tch qckly bef 3 out: eased flat: t.o* **33/1**
8 ½ **Silver Astralis**[232] 4-9-7 0...(p) TrevorWhelan(7) 32
(Christine Dunnett) *hld up in last: mstke 6th: sn lost tch: t.o fr 3 out* **66/1**

4m 7.00s (1.60) **Going Correction** -0.20s/f (Good)
WFA 4 from 5yo+ 7lb **8** Ran SP% **117.9**
Speed ratings (Par 103): **88,85,85,80,77 72,58,58**
Tote Swingers: 1&2 £3.50, 1&3 £7.60, 2&3 £6.00 CSF £17.33 TOTE £6.20: £2.00, £1.10, £1.20; EX 20.10.There was no bid for the winner. Celticello wasa claimed by Mr J. E. Snowden for £6,000. Galley Slave was subject to a friendly claim.
Owner Beetle N Wedge Partnership **Bred** Denis Cleary **Trained** Newmarket, Suffolk

FOCUS
An ordinary seller. The winner was close to his mark with the second below his best.

NOTEBOOK
Sole Bonne Femme(IRE)'s form since coming over here didn't make inspiring reading, but he did have some fair efforts to his name in Ireland earlier in his career and clearly appreciated the drop in grade. A rare jumps winner for his predominantly Flat yard, he wouldn't be an obvious sort to follow up, even kept to this level. (op 13-2)
Celticello(IRE) is generally a force to be reckoned with in this grade, underlining that with a win over further here in January, but he left the impression he wasn't at his best on this occasion, never looking like getting to the winner. (op 6-4 tchd 13-8)
Miss Wendy showed a level more in keeping with her hurdling debut with her sights lowered, but there's no obvious indication she's going to be any better than poor in this sphere. (op 9-1)
Galley Slave(IRE) had strong form claims and presumably found this coming a bit quick after Stratford on Monday, weakening quickly after two out.

4855 ROBERT CASE MEMORIAL BEGINNERS' CHASE (18 fncs) 3m 110y
2:55 (2:55) (Class 3) 5-Y-0+ **£6,537** (£2,029; £1,092)

Form RPR
1 **Cottage Flyer (IRE)**[5] 6-11-0 0...(p) JohnnyFarrelly 125+
(Paul John Gilligan, Ire) *j.w: mde all: looked to be gng best whn lft wl clr 15th: idling bdly and racing awkwardly bef 2 out: rdn and a holding runner-up after* **3/1**[2]
04U3 **2** 9 **Erzen (IRE)**[8] 4666 6-10-7 127.. HarryChalloner(7) 117
(Venetia Williams) *nt a fluent: nvr really travelling and pushed along at times: 3rd and rdn whn j.rt 14th: lft modest 2nd next: clsd as ldr idled bef 2 out: no imp flat: dismntd after fin: lame* **7/2**[3]
1P65 **3** 25 **Sweet Seville (FR)**[29] 4161 7-10-1 93 ow1...................... MattCrawley(7) 93
(Terry Clement) *in tch in rr: rdn along 7th: lost tch u.p after 13th: lft poor 3rd 15th* **20/1**
PP **P** **Rockoboy (IRE)**[8] 4666 10-10-9 0.................. GemmaGracey-Davison(5) —
(Zoe Davison) *in tch in last pair: j. slowly 1st: wnt 4th and rdn 11th: wknd 13th: t.o whn lft 4th 15th: p.u 2 out* **66/1**
4323 **P** **Springfield Raki**[13] 4469 7-11-0 117........................ AndrewGlassonbury —
(Steve Gollings) *lft 2nd at 2nd tl rdn and downed tools 12th: bhd and lost tch after next: t.o whn p.u 15th* **7/1**
3-50 **U** **Hudibras (IRE)**[28] 4180 7-10-11 117...............................(p) PeterToole(3) —
(Charlie Mann) *chsd ldr tl uns rdr 2nd* **9/2**
61P5 **U** **Phare Isle (IRE)**[23] 4285 6-11-0 0... CharliePoste —
(Ben Case) *in tch: chsd wnr 12th: rdn along after next: 2 l down whn j.rt and uns rdr 15th* **9/4**[1]

6m 38.5s (2.80) **Going Correction** +0.025s/f (Yiel) **7** Ran SP% **114.9**
Speed ratings: **96,93,85,—,— —,—**
Tote Swingers: 1&2 £1.60, 1&3 £24.50, 2&3 £8.00 CSF £14.50 TOTE £4.80: £3.40, £3.90; EX 16.80.
Owner E Gilligan **Bred** John Joe Shaughnessy **Trained** Athenry, Co Galway

FOCUS
A modest maiden chase and guessy form with the winner an unknown quantity. The second is rated 9lb off his chase best.

NOTEBOOK
Cottage Flyer(IRE) had only got off the mark in points at the weekend and still deserves some credit, making most and jumping well in the main. That said, things will be a lot tougher in novices', while a stiff mark could await if the handicapper takes a literal view of this defeat of a 122-rated rival. (op 4-1)
Erzen(IRE) was a useful hurdler, but it'll be a surprise if he gets close to that level over fences judged on his efforts so far. He never really convinced with his jumping and off the bridle a long way out and unable to make any real inroads despite the winner idling in front. Official explanation: vet said gelding returned lame (op 5-2 tchd 4-1)
Springfield Raki Official explanation: jockey said gelding stopped quickly (op 5-2 after 3-1 in a place)
Phare Isle(IRE), a winner over hurdles here in January, may well have made a winning start to his chasing career had he not unseated four out, going well in second at the time. His jumping was sound enough prior to that and there's no reason why he shouldn't prove as effective over fences as hurdles. (op 5-2 after 3-1 in a place)

4856 TIM BARCLAY MEMORIAL H'CAP CHASE (16 fncs) 2m 5f 110y
3:35 (3:35) (Class 3) (0-125,119) 5-Y-0+ **£6,381** (£1,873; £936; £467)

Form RPR
6423 **1** **Prince Des Marais (FR)**[14] 4456 8-11-11 **118**...........(t) AndrewThornton 127+
(Caroline Bailey) *racd keenly: chsd ldrs tl led 9th: mde rest: drew clr fr 13th: eased flat: easily* **9/4**[1]
0263 **2** 16 **Knight Legend (IRE)**[36] 4025 12-11-5 **119**.......................(t) MrMEnnis(7) 111
(Sarah Humphrey) *hld up in tch: effrt 11th: chsd clr wnr bef 3 out: kpt on but no imp* **12/1**
412P **3** 19 **Farmer Frank**[30] 4141 8-11-5 **119**.. MrCGreene(7) 94
(Nick Kent) *hld up in tch in last pair: hdwy 11th: chsd ldr bef next: rdn and struggling after 12th: 3rd and btn 2 out: wknd between last 2* **6/1**
-61P **4** 4 ½ **Royal Wedding**[21] 4328 9-11-12 **119**....................... AndrewGlassonbury 89
(Nick Gifford) *led: bmpd 4th: hdd next: rdn and dropped to rr 11th: lost tch u.p after next: t.o* **8/1**
6P22 **5** 13 **Canni Thinkaar (IRE)**[8] 4666 10-11-1 **113**.(b) GemmaGracey-Davison(5) 72
(Zoe Davison) *chsd ldr: j.rt and bmpd rival 4th: led next tl hdd 9th: wknd u.p 12th: t.o 3 out* **9/2**[3]
60-1 **F** **Wellforth (IRE)**[28] 4181 7-11-6 **113**...............................(b) JohnnyFarrelly —
(Paul John Gilligan, Ire) *in tch in last pair tl fell 2nd* **5/2**[2]

5m 38.5s (-3.30) **Going Correction** +0.025s/f (Yiel) **6** Ran SP% **110.6**
Speed ratings: **107,101,94,92,87** —
Tote Swingers: 1&2 £6.60, 1&3 £4.30, 2&3 £8.20 CSF £24.29 TOTE £3.30: £2.20, £2.80; EX 29.60.
Owner C W Booth **Bred** Gaec Lancray **Trained** Brixworth, Northants

FOCUS
A weak but open handicap and a very easy winner, rated to last season's best.

NOTEBOOK
Prince Des Marais(FR) recorded a facile success. He's got a good recent record on good going or firmer, which should continue to hold him in good stead at this time of year, and he'll take a bit of stopping under a penalty if taking up his engagement at Southwell next Thursday. (tchd 5-2 and 11-4 in places)
Knight Legend(IRE) got second on his return to chasing, but was no match for the winner and it's hard to believe he was close to the form he was showing last summer.
Farmer Frank did well in hunter chases last summer, but had been pulled up on his return in that sphere in February and didn't shape with any immediate promise on his handicap bow. (tchd 5-1)
Royal Wedding was runner-up in this last year, but has been disappointing on both starts since last month's Fontwell win and doesn't seem the easiest to catch right these days. (op 13-2)
Wellforth(IRE) didn't get the chance to show whether the blinkers would work for a second time, departing early. (op 11-4 tchd 9-4)

4857 WILLIAM BULWER-LONG MEMORIAL NOVICES' FOX HUNTERS' CHASE (16 fncs) 2m 5f 110y
4:15 (4:17) (Class 6) 5-Y-0+ **£936** (£290; £145; £72)

Form RPR
1 **Enigma Variations (IRE)**[12] 9-11-3 84.................................. MrTEllis(7) 93
(G J Tarry) *led tl 7th: chsd ldr after: drvn and pressed ldr between last 2: ev ch last: hung rt flat: kpt on to ld on post* **10/3**[2]

3 **2** *shd* **Captain Knock (IRE)**[16] 4429 8-11-7 93 MrTJCannon(3) 93
(David Phelan) *chsd ldr 3rd tl led 7th: clr 13th: rdn bef 2 out: drvn between last 2: hrd pressed and pckd last: kpt on u.p flat: edgd lft towards fin: hdd on post* **5/1**3

34/P **3** *2 1/4* **Roaringwater (IRE)**[19] 12-11-3 0 (p) MissCHaydon(7) 91
(Miss C M E Haydon) *several positions: chsd ldrs: sltly hmpd 12th: mstke and rdn next: chsd ldng pair bef 2 out: pressed ldrs last: no ex flat* **16/1**

3-P4 **4** *9* **Star Double (ITY)**[12] 11-11-3 79 (p) MrMEnnis(7) 84
(Mrs Fleur Hawes) *in tch: hdwy to chse ldrs 8th: 3rd and hit 13th: drvn and wknd bef 2 out* **33/1**

4/4- **5** *1/2* **Chef De Cour (FR)**[19] 10-11-3 0 MissCHobson(7) 83
(J P Owen) *t.k.h: hld up in tch in midfield: struggling and outpcd 13th: plugged on same pce fr next* **25/1**

5/42 **6** *hd* **Supa Tramp**[5] 8-11-7 95 (p) MrPBull(3) 84
(Mrs Suzy Bull) *t.k.h: hld up in tch towards rr: hdwy 9th: rdn and no prog after 3 out* **5/1**3

/24- **P** **Goscar Rock (IRE)**[351] 4972 10-11-3 0 MissJMcGuire(7) —
(P Hall) *racd wd: j.lft: a in last pair: mstke 10th: hit next and sn lost tch: p.u 12th* **10/1**

P03/ **F** **Lillie Lou**[12] 8-10-10 76 MrTGarner(7) —
(Ray Fielder) *in tch towards rr tl fell 5th* **28/1**

50-0 **P** **Don't Think Twice (IRE)**[26] 8-11-3 99 (vt1) MrRichardCollinson(7) —
(Miss Caroline Fryer) *t.k.h: chsd ldr tl 3rd: styd prom tl rdn and rapidly dropped out after 12th: t.o whn p.u 2 out* **25/1**

PP2/ **P** **Mr Dass (IRE)**[12] 9-11-7 94 MrMatthewSmith(3) —
(Matthew Smith) *t.k.h: in tch in rr: mstke 8th: sn struggling: t.o 11th tl p.u 2 out* **40/1**

1-0 **P** **Caulkin (IRE)**[26] 8-11-5 0 MrDKemp(5) —
(David Kemp) *hld up in rr: rdr lost iron briefly 3rd: hdwy 8th: rdr lost iron again 10th: sddle slipped next: sn eased and p.u* **11/4**1

U **Gort Na Lea (IRE)**[19] 8-11-7 0 MrJMQuinlan(3) —
(A J Kennedy, Ire) *in tch: blnd 1st: blunderd and uns rdr 12th* **14/1**

5m 45.4s (3.60) **Going Correction** +0.025s/f (Yiel) **12** Ran SP% **121.2**
Speed ratings: **94,93,93,89,89 89,—,—,—,— —,—**
Tote Swingers: 1&2 £7.80, 1&3 £13.20, 2&3 £21.40 CSF £20.17 TOTE £3.70: £1.90, £3.20, £3.30; EX 18.60.
Owner J T B Hunt **Bred** Michael Fennessy **Trained** Brackley, Northants

FOCUS
Just an ordinary novice hunter chase, though it did at least provide a thrilling finish. Modest form which makes sense on time.

NOTEBOOK
Enigma Variations(IRE) has enjoyed a good time in points since coming over from Ireland and made a winning hunter chase bow, impressing with the way he travelled and responding to nail the long-time leader on the line. He's a lightly raced 9-y-o so has the potential to do a bit better still. (op 5-2 tchd 7-2)
Captain Knock(IRE) has had some problems getting round in points, but has done nothing wrong in this sphere the last twice. Stepping up on his Folkestone form here, he all but got off the mark under Rules, being nailed on the line after being well ridden from the front. (tchd 11-2)
Roaringwater(IRE) came here on the back of a point win and ran well, but he's not the easiest of rides and it'll be a weak hunter chase he wins (tchd 14-1)
Supa Tramp had finished in front of Captain Knock at Folkestone, but didn't come close to reproducing that here. (op 7-1)
Caulkin(IRE) Official explanation: jockey said saddle slipped

4858 TOTEPOOL FAKENHAM SILVER CUP H'CAP HURDLE (9 hdls) 2m
4:55 (4:55) (Class 3) (0-125,123) 4-Y-0+ **£7,155** (£2,101; £1,050; £524)

Form RPR

/331 **1** **Fujin Dancer (FR)**[32] 4113 6-10-6 **110** MissHBethell(7) 117
(Brian Ellison) *hld up off the pce towards rr: hdwy after 5th: chsd ldng pair bef 3 out: wnt 2nd between last 2: racd awkwardly bef last: j.lft last: styd on u.p to ld fnl 50yds* **13/2**2

-002 **2** *1* **Amazing King (IRE)**[156] 1827 7-11-5 **123** KyleJames(7) 130+
(Philip Kirby) *hld up off the pce in midfield: hdwy after 5th: chsd clr ldr bef 3 out: rdn and j. ahd 2 out: hit last: idled flat: drvn and hdd fnl 50yds: no ex* **10/1**

105 **3** *19* **Dark Ranger**[125] 2375 5-10-7 **109** BrianToomey(5) 103+
(Tim Pitt) *hld up wl bhd: hdwy after 5th: chsd ldng trio 3 out: kpt on but no real imp: hld whn lft 3rd and bdly hmpd by loose horse last* **12/1**

P3-5 **4** *14* **Bedizen**[26] 4235 8-11-6 **120** CPGeoghegan(3) 96
(Pam Sly) *chsd ldrs: mstke 5th: sn rdn and lost pl: no ch w ldrs 3 out: lft poor 4th last* **8/1**

244P **5** *25* **Trumpstoo (USA)**[25] 1931 5-11-4 **115** TomSiddall 69
(Richard Fahey) *racd off the pce in midfield: rdn and struggling after 5th: no ch after next: t.o between last 2* **33/1**

11F- **6** *9* **Zorro De La Vega (FR)**[493] 2215 8-10-5 **102** (tp) ColinBolger 48
(Sarah Humphrey) *chsd ldrs tl wnt 2nd after 4th: lost 2nd after 6th: sn wknd: wl bhd 2 out: t.o* **16/1**

PP01 **7** *12* **King Brex (DEN)**[7] 4697 8-11-2 **116** 7ex (tp) PeterToole(3) 51
(Charlie Mann) *chsd ldr tl after 4th: struggling after 5th: wl bhd after next: t.o 2 out* **7/1**3

2513 **8** *14* **Buddy Holly**[19] 4377 6-11-9 **120** WillKennedy 42
(Violet M Jordan) *a in rr: nt fluent 2nd and 3rd: rdn and toiling in last after 4th: lost tch next: t.o bef 3 out* **10/1**

-400 **P** **Farleigh House (USA)**[4] 4778 7-11-4 **118** (t) AlexMerriam(3) —
(Neil King) *in rr: pushed along and sme hdwy after 5th: nvr on terms w ldrs: 5th and no ch whn blnd 2 out: wl bhd whn p.u last* **25/1**

4/U1 **F** **Laterly (IRE)**[22] 4310 6-11-3 **114** AndrewGlassonbury 116
(Steve Gollings) *led and set fast gallop: rdn after 3 out: hdd next: drvn and btn between last 2: 3rd and wl hld whn fell last* **11/10**1

3m 59.2s (-6.20) **Going Correction** -0.20s/f (Good) **10** Ran SP% **123.1**
Speed ratings (Par 107): **107,106,97,90,77 73,67,60,—,—**
Tote Swingers: 1&2 £5.80, 1&3 £6.40, 2&3 £8.60 CSF £72.64 CT £779.31 TOTE £5.30: £1.80, £3.70, £4.30; EX 55.20.
Owner W A Bethell **Bred** Loughtown Stud Ltd **Trained** Norton, N Yorks

FOCUS
A modest handicap, run at a decent gallop and in a good time for the grade. Another step up from the winner.

NOTEBOOK
Fujin Dancer(FR) has made a fine start for Brian Ellison, striking up a good partnership with this rider into the bargain, coming from off the pace as usual to snatch the spoils close home. He could go up a fair bit in the weights with the front two pulling clear, but is clearly thriving at present. (tchd 11-2)
Amazing King(IRE) had his ideal conditions on his return from a five-month break and showed he's better than ever. He looked set for victory approaching the last, but got in close, losing vital momentum in the process, and was nailed near the finish. He'll go up again in the weights for this, but is likely to continue to give a good account when the emphasis is on speed. (op 9-1 tchd 11-1)
Dark Ranger never threatened in third, but this was still a fairly satisfactory return from a break and he may build on this. He's another who's always going to be at his best over hurdles with the emphasis on speed. (op 11-1 tchd 14-1)
Bedizen had been placed in this race for the past two years, but wasn't anywhere near his best on this occasion and was beaten from early on the final circuit. (tchd 7-1)
Buddy Holly's hurdles win had come under much more testing conditions, but he had plenty of form on a firmer surface on the Flat and might have been expected to do better. (op 17-2 tchd 8-1)
Laterly(IRE) was backed as if defeat was out of the question, but his rider was probably guilty of overdoing things in front, and the gelding was weakening in third when falling at the last. The way he went through the race for a long way suggests this one-time useful Flat performer is still on a good mark, and he's one to bear in mind if none the worse. (op 7-4)

4859 MY FAIR LADY CONDITIONAL JOCKEYS' MAIDEN HURDLE (7 hdls 2 omitted) 2m
5:30 (5:30) (Class 4) 4-Y-0+ **£2,871** (£843; £421; £210)

Form RPR

004 **1** **Goodwood Starlight (IRE)**[76] 3302 6-10-9 0 (t) AshleyBird(8) 110+
(Jim Best) *t.k.h: hld up in rr: swtchd rt and hdwy bnd after 5th: nt clr run bef 3 out (actual 2 out): pushed ahd on long run to last: sn clr: whn mstke and rdr lost iron last: eased towards fin* **9/4**2

553 **2** *5* **Magic Prospect (FR)**[14] 4458 4-10-7 105 PeterToole(3) 93
(Charlie Mann) *hld up in tch: nt clr run bhd a wall of horses 3 out: fnlly in the clr and rdn after bypassing 2 out: wnt 2nd flat: plugged on but no ch w wnr* **1/1**1

0 **3** *1* **Odin's Raven (IRE)**[37] 3999 6-11-3 0 BrianToomey 101+
(Brian Ellison) *t.k.h: hld up in tch: effrt 6th: chsd clr wnr on long run to last: no imp: lost 2nd flat* **20/1**

220- **4** *2 1/4* **Sheila's Castle**[126] 2211 7-10-5 0 TrevorWhelan(5) 90
(Sean Regan) *hld up in tch in last trio: rdn along after 6th: nt clr run bef next: swtchd rt and pressing for placing bypassing 2 out: plugged on same pce after* **16/1**

5 *4* **Mister Frosty (IRE)**[24] 5-11-3 0 MarcGoldstein 94
(George Prodromou) *t.k.h: chsd ldrs: wnt 2nd after 2nd: pressed ldr and hit 5th: led next: mstke and bmpd 3 out (actual 2 out) sn hdd and outpcd by wnr: wknd on long run to last* **20/1**

4530 **6** *4 1/2* **Thoresby (IRE)**[71] 3403 5-11-3 111 CPGeoghegan 91
(Ben Case) *chsd ldrs: ev ch whn mstke 3 out: sn rdn and outpcd: wknd on long run to last* **11/2**3

1P0U **7** *11* **Bad Sir Brian (IRE)**[49] 3789 6-11-3 0 JoshuaMoore 80
(Nick Gifford) *j.rt and several slow jumps: led: hit 5th: pushed along and hdd 6th: styd pressing ldrs tl wknd u.p on long run bef last* **20/1**

/60- **8** *10* **Drawback (IRE)**[9] 830 8-10-11 100 CDTimmons(6) 71
(Barry Brennan) *chsd ldr tl after 2nd: styd chsng ldrs tl rdn and dropped to last 6th: wknd next* **28/1**

9 *7* **Northumberland**[43] 5-11-0 0 KyleJames(3) 64
(Michael Chapman) *t.k.h: chsd ldrs tl 4th: rdn and struggling whn n.m.r bnd after 6th: wknd next: t.o* **100/1**

0 **10** *7* **Marvo**[10] 2495 7-11-0 0 AshleyMorgan(3) 58
(Mark H Tompkins) *hld up in last pair: hdwy whn pushed wd bnd and lost pl after 5th: hdwy to press ldrs on outer whn mstke and stmbld 3 out (actual 2 out): sn wknd: t.o* **25/1**

4m 11.2s (5.80) **Going Correction** -0.20s/f (Good)
WFA 4 from 5yo+ 7lb **10** Ran SP% **124.6**
Speed ratings (Par 105): **77,74,74,72,70 68,63,58,54,51**
Tote Swingers: 1&2 £1.10, 1&3 £2.70, 2&3 £9.40 CSF £4.98 TOTE £4.80: £2.20, £1.10, £3.70; EX 7.40.
Owner Goodwood Starlight Partnership **Bred** Lynn Lodge Stud **Trained** Lewes, E Sussex

FOCUS
Flight of hurdles omitted on both circuits due to the low sun. A reasonable maiden hurdle for the course, the first five home all winners on the Flat. They are all entitled to rate higher. The time was slow compared with the earlier handicap.

NOTEBOOK
Goodwood Starlight(IRE) hadn't achieved a great deal on his three previous starts over hurdles, but was still capable of some pretty useful form on the Flat last year so it was no surprise to see him improve, surviving a mistake at the last to win comfortably. He should have more to offer and he'd be an interesting one for handicaps as, even after this win, he should still get a potentially fair mark compared to what he's capable of on the level. (op 5-1)
Magic Prospect(FR) couldn't justify short-priced favouritism, but was caught in a bit of a pocket when the winner made his move and would have been a bit further clear of the rest but for that. There's no obvious sign of him translating his fairly useful Flat form to hurdles at this stage, but a similar event should come his way at some stage. (op 5-4 tchd 6-4)
Odin's Raven(IRE) stepped up on last month's hurdling bow, the emphasis more on speed probably helping and is the type to do better still in this sphere, particularly once eligible for handicaps. (op 12-1)
Sheila's Castle had been well beaten on her hurdling debut back in 2009, but was placed on all four starts in Flat handicaps last year so this effort doesn't come as a surprise. She may do better still. Official explanation: vet said mare lost a shoe (op 11-1)
Thoresby(IRE) hasn't built on his initial promise over hurdles, though a blunder at what turned out to be the second-last didn't help. (op 4-1 tchd 13-2)
T/Plt: £119.30 to a £1 stake. Pool:£96,985.40 - 344.07 winning tickets. T/Qpdt: £39.20 to a £1 stake. Pool:£4,433.67 - 83.60 winning tickets. SP

4521 FFOS LAS (L-H)
Saturday, March 19

OFFICIAL GOING: Good (7.5)
Wind: Light, half-against Weather: Sunny

4860 BRIDGESTONE "NATIONAL HUNT" MAIDEN HURDLE (8 hdls) 2m
2:35 (2:36) (Class 4) 4-Y-0+ **£3,252** (£955; £477; £238)

Form RPR

3504 **1** **Street Dance (IRE)**[12] 4527 5-11-0 0 RhysFlint 114+
(Keith Goldsworthy) *hld up: hdwy to chse ldrs appr 3rd: led gng wl bef 2 out: clr last: easily* **28/1**

1-03 **2** *6* **Di Kaprio (FR)**[28] 4203 5-11-0 0 PaulMoloney 106
(Evan Williams) *led: hdd appr 2 out: rdn in 2nd and nt qckning whn hit last: one pce and no ch w wnr after* **6/5**1

400 **3** *2 3/4* **Mariinsky (GER)**[48] 3840 5-11-0 105 RichardJohnson 104
(Tim Vaughan) *prom: chalng 3 out: u.p whn blnd 2 out: edgd lft after and one pce* **7/1**

0-00 **4** *14* **Mac Beattie**[58] 3645 5-10-9 0 AodhaganConlon(5) 90
(Evan Williams) *hld up: pushed along after 5th: chsd ldng quartet appr 3 out but no imp: tk mod 4th run-in: nt pce to get competitve* **50/1**

030- **5** *3* **Midnight Tuesday (FR)**[344] 5112 6-10-11 0....... SamTwiston-Davies(3) 89
(Nigel Twiston-Davies) *prom: chalng 3 out: rdn and wknd 2 out: wl btn whn hit last* **3/1**[2]

-655 **6** *4 ½* **Fishoutofwater (IRE)**[26] 4260 7-10-11 0.......................... MrAJBerry(3) 83
(Rebecca Curtis) *chsd ldrs: outpcd fr 3 out: dropped away bef 2 out* **5/1**[3]

56 **7** *shd* **Trade On**[34] 4097 4-10-7 0.......................... WayneHutchinson 76
(Alan King) *hld up: rdn and struggling appr 3 out: nvr on terms w ldrs: wl btn* **18/1**

1060 **8** *68* **The Merry Giant (IRE)**[22] 4332 5-11-0 0.................. DominicElsworth 22
(Rebecca Curtis) *hld up bhd: lost tch appr 4th: t.o* **28/1**

5 **9** *1 ¼* **Call Me Frankie (IRE)**[42] 3943 5-11-0 0........................ TimmyMurphy 21
(Lucy Jones) *nt fluent: j.lft a few times: a bhd: lost tch bef 3 out: t.o* **33/1**

60 **10** *21* **Ammo Away**[14] 4491 5-10-11 0.................................. RichardKilloran(3) 2
(Tim Vaughan) *chsd ldrs: losing pl whn mstke 3rd: u.p and bhd bef 5th: lost tch bef 3 out: t.o* **66/1**

3m 52.3s (3.30) **Going Correction** +0.375s/f (Yiel)
WFA 4 from 5yo+ 7lb **10** Ran SP% **118.2**
Speed ratings (Par 105): **106,103,101,94,93 90,90,56,56,45**
Tote Swingers: 1&2 £3.80, 1&3 £7.70, 2&3 £4.50 CSF £64.09 TOTE £33.50: £4.90, £1.30, £1.30; EX 78.30.
Owner Racing Coast **Bred** Brenda Noone **Trained** Yerbeston, Pembrokes

FOCUS
An ordinary maiden hurdle run at a steady pace, and in a time around 12 seconds outside the Racing Post standard.\n\x\x Richard Johnson described it as "good, watered ground", while Rhys Flint thought it was "a bit dead and a bit rough in places". A step up from the winner on his bumper form with the next two setting trhe level.

NOTEBOOK
Street Dance(IRE), in the frame in two of his four bumpers, ran out a comfortable winner on his hurdles debut. Fitted with earplugs and keen once again, he moved up to track the leaders down the far side and, after showing in front two out, pulled clear for a very comfortable win. With the market leaders below par there is a doubt over what he beat, but he looks capable of winning again. (op 20-1 tchd 18-1)
Di Kaprio(FR) appeared the one to beat on the strength of his run behind Supreme Novices' third Sprinter Sacre at Ascot last month, but the suspicion is that he was flattered by that effort in a slowly run race. Again making the running, he could not offer much resistance when headed by the winner two from home. (op 5-4 tchd 6-4 and 7-4 in places)
Mariinsky(GER), well held in a couple of easy-ground handicaps and currently rated 105, was always to the fore but a mistake two from home when beginning to toil spelt the end of his challenge. (op 15-2 tchd 13-2)
Mac Beattie ◆, a stablemate of the beaten favourite, had shown little previously but there were positives in this performance. After allowing the leading four to pull away from him soon after the home turn, he kept on quite nicely without being given a hard time. His hurdling has room for improvement.
Midnight Tuesday(FR) showed ability last term, beaten only four lengths by the very useful Master Of The Hall at Newbury, but had not run since finishing last in a Grade 1 at Aintree in April. He weakened appreciably from the first flight in the straight and this may have been needed. (op 10-3 tchd 7-2)
Fishoutofwater(IRE), whose trainer won this last year, came in for support, but he was never seen with a serious chance and continues to disappoint. (op 13-2 tchd 9-2)

4861 BRIDGESTONE NOVICES' HURDLE (12 hdls) 3m
3:10 (3:11) (Class 4) 4-Y-0+ **£3,252** (£955; £477; £238)

Form RPR

32 **1** **Swingkeel (IRE)**[24] 4294 6-10-13 123.................. SamTwiston-Davies(3) 128+
(Nigel Twiston-Davies) *trckd ldrs: wnt 2nd 9th: chalng 3 out: led narrowly but niggled jst after: abt a nk in front whn lft abt 18 l clr 2 out: unchal after: eased cl home* **7/4**[1]

4003 **2** *24* **Total Submission**[19] 4393 6-11-8 119............................ WarrenMarston 113
(Martin Keighley) *hld up in tch: rdn to chse ldng duo after 9th: outpcd bef 3 out: lft abt 18 l 2nd and forced wd by faller 2 out: kpt on for press but no ch w wnr* **7/1**

1-13 **3** *1 ¼* **Buck Mulligan**[14] 4479 6-11-8 128.............................. PaulMoloney 111
(Evan Williams) *hld up in last pl: nt fluent 4th: pushed along after 9th: sme hdwy appr 3 out: lft in mod 3rd and forced wd by faller 2 out: kpt on u.p run-in and tried to chal for 2nd but hld* **10/3**[2]

4154 **4** *20* **Old Wigmore (IRE)**[26] 4262 6-11-3 124.................. AodhaganConlon(5) 91
(Rebecca Curtis) *led: hdd briefly appr 3rd: hdd bef 9th: sn u.p: wknd sn after* **14/1**

0132 **5** *9* **Camden (IRE)**[14] 4489 5-11-8 125.................................... LeightonAspell 83
(Oliver Sherwood) *hld up: nt fluent 2nd: pushed along appr 9th: nvr on terms and wl bhd after* **9/2**[3]

1340 **F** **Rudanphast (IRE)**[28] 4206 6-11-8 118.......................... RichardJohnson 124
(Peter Bowen) *w ldr but continually outj.: led briefly appr 3rd: led again bef 9th: rdn and hdd narrowly after 3 out: stl chalng for press abt a nk down whn fell 2 out* **15/2**

2540 **P** **Cresswell Bramble**[7] 4728 7-10-4 0............................. JoshuaMoore(5) —
(Keith Goldsworthy) *racd keenly: chsd ldrs: j.lft 3rd: lost pl 7th: bhd 9th: sn lost tch and t.o: p.u bef 2 out* **40/1**

6m 2.80s (15.80) **Going Correction** +0.375s/f (Yiel) **7** Ran SP% **111.0**
Speed ratings (Par 105): **88,80,79,72,69 —,—**
Tote Swingers: 1&2 £5.40, 1&3 £2.50, 2&3 £8.00 CSF £13.79 TOTE £3.00: £1.40, £3.90; EX 17.60.
Owner Mrs M E Slade **Bred** R J Cornelius **Trained** Naunton, Gloucs

FOCUS
A decent novice hurdle for the grade. It was steadily run, but there were just two still in contention turning for home and the race was decided at the second-last. A step up from the winner who is entitled to rate a lot higher on Flat form. Faller Rudanphast was heading for a personal best.

NOTEBOOK
Swingkeel(IRE) was left to come home as he liked after Rudanphast fell when upsides at the second-last flight. Narrowly beaten in his two previous runs over hurdles, both at this trip, he stays well but there is a doubt over how much he would have found had it come down to a scrap. He may go to Aintree for the Grade 1 Sefton Novices' Hurdle, where he would need to improve. (op 9-4)
Total Submission was in trouble on the home turn but found himself in an unmerited second two from home, where he had to swerve the faller. He has yet to convince that he stays this far. (op 13-2 tchd 11-2)
Buck Mulligan, runner-up in a 3m chase on this card a year ago, had run well in his two outings since reverting to hurdles. Held up in last place, he did pick up ground going into the home turn but was quickly no threat to the first pair. He had been keen going to post and is not a straightforward ride. (op 3-1 tchd 11-4 and 7-2)
Old Wigmore(IRE) disputed the lead with Rudanphast, jumping the better, before weakening disappointingly before the end of the back straight. This ground should not have posed him a problem and he was a long way below the form he showed behind Mossley in a Cheltenham Grade 2 earlier in the season. (op 11-1 tchd 16-1)
Camden(IRE) did not have much to find on his best form but was always struggling to make an impact. (tchd 4-1)
Rudanphast(IRE), back down in grade, came off the bridle after Swingkeel and was still in with every chance when he stepped into the second-last and came down. Hopefully he will be none the worse for what looked a heavy fall. (op 10-1)

4862 LAND MATTERS H'CAP HURDLE (10 hdls) 2m 4f
3:45 (3:49) (Class 3) (0-125,125) 4-Y-0+ **£5,854** (£1,719; £859; £429)

Form RPR

P-00 **1** **My Shamwari (IRE)**[46] 3874 7-11-6 **119**...................... RichardJohnson 125+
(Philip Hobbs) *hld up: hdwy 6th: chsd ldrs appr 3 out: effrt and swtchd rt to chal whn nt fluent 2 out: upsides whn hit last: str chal run-in: r.o to ld towards fin* **9/2**[3]

1061 **2** *nk* **Black Phantom (IRE)**[11] 4536 5-11-2 **115**..................... NickScholfield 119
(Andy Turnell) *chsd ldr: rdn after 7th: led appr 3 out: sn pressed: hdd narrowly bef 2 out: regained slt ld after last: a hrd pressed: hdd and hld towards fin* **7/1**

2064 **3** *1* **Scoter Fontaine (FR)**[24] 4291 5-10-10 **112**...................... MrAJBerry(3) 115
(Rebecca Curtis) *chsd ldrs: chalng 3 out: led narrowly appr 2 out: hdd after last: ev ch tl nt qckn and hld fnl 30yds* **4/1**[2]

1-F0 **4** *15* **Crannaghmore Boy (IRE)**[8] 4700 6-10-4 **106**........... DonalDevereux(3) 96
(Keith Goldsworthy) *led: rdn and hdd appr 3 out: sn wknd* **16/1**

2100 **5** *4* **Mac Halen (IRE)**[221] 1230 8-10-6 **110**..................... AodhaganConlon(5) 96
(Evan Williams) *hld up: nt fluent 1st: outpcd appr 3 out: nvr a danger* **25/1**

2353 **6** *6* **Frontier Spirit (IRE)**[33] 4121 7-10-13 **115**........... SamTwiston-Davies(3) 96
(Nigel Twiston-Davies) *in tch: rdn whn chsng ldrs appr 3 out: sn wknd* **10/1**

11P4 **7** *10* **Comehomequietly (IRE)**[12] 4524 7-11-9 **122**........................ RhysFlint 94
(David Rees) *chsd ldrs: niggled along appr 7th: wknd bef 3 out* **11/1**

2133 **8** *110* **Palace Jester**[43] 3917 6-11-9 **122**...............................(t) DominicElsworth —
(Jonjo O'Neill) *hld up: blnd bdly 2nd: bhd after: rdn appr 7th: t.o* **10/3**[1]

2210 **9** *8* **Gambo (IRE)**[62] 3587 5-10-13 **112**.. PaulMoloney —
(Evan Williams) *hld up: niggled along and lft bhd 7th: t.o* **11/2**

4m 57.7s (8.70) **Going Correction** +0.375s/f (Yiel) **9** Ran SP% **116.3**
Speed ratings (Par 107): **97,96,96,90,88 86,82,—,—**
Tote Swingers: 1&2 £131.10, 1&3 £13.80, 2&3 £17.40 CSF £36.26 CT £136.58 TOTE £6.20: £2.20, £2.70, £1.10; EX 43.90.
Owner Mrs Julie Phillips **Bred** Mrs Catherine And Michael Norris **Trained** Withycombe, Somerset

FOCUS
A fair handicap which saw the first three draw clear to contest a fine finish. The form seems sound, with the second and third to their marks, but the time was 20 seconds outside the standard.

NOTEBOOK
My Shamwari(IRE), patiently ridden, was going the best of the three principals from some way out, but came off the bridle after getting in too close to the second last. Quickly back on an even keel, he inched ahead on the flat. He had been well held in two appearances for this yard but came in for support last time and had been dropped another 3lb since. (op 5-1 tchd 11-2)
Black Phantom(IRE) was ridden along on the turn but responded well to go down fighting. This was a good effort, but the 17lb rise for his win at Exeter just told.
Scoter Fontaine(FR), his connections' only runner after the withdrawal of Made In Time, came in for support. He did little wrong and just about had his nose in front jumping the final flight, but could not quite fend off challengers either side of him up the run-in. The slightly better ground helped. (op 5-1)
Crannaghmore Boy(IRE), dropped 4lb after finishing well back at Sandown, was quickly beaten after surrendering his lead turning for home. (tchd 18-1)
Mac Halen(IRE) is entitled to come on for this first run since August but is still 8lb above his last winning mark. (op 16-1)
Palace Jester, who had the tongue tie back on, could never recover from a bad mistake at just the second flight. (op 3-1 tchd 7-2)

4863 TRUSTMARK DESIGN & PRINT H'CAP CHASE (17 fncs) 2m 5f
4:20 (4:20) (Class 4) (0-115,115) 5-Y-0+ **£3,837** (£1,158; £596; £315)

Form RPR

115 **1** **Prince Massini (IRE)**[77] 3308 10-10-8 **97**.......................... PaulMoloney 107+
(Evan Williams) *hld up: hdwy appr 9th: prom whn mstke 10th: led on bnd after 13th: hdd 3 out: mstke whn rival j. across him 2 out: sn rdn: swtchd rt and sltly outpcd by ldr bef last: rallied run-in to ld post* **5/1**

5254 **2** *nse* **Storm Of Applause (IRE)**[132] 2234 10-11-12 **115**....... RichardJohnson 124
(Philip Hobbs) *prom: pushed along and outpcd sltly whn possibly short of room on bnd after 13th: sn swtchd rt: rallied to take 2nd appr 4 out: led 3 out: j.lft 2 out: rdn and big jump last: all out run-in: hdd post* **11/4**[1]

UP42 **3** *31* **Rimini (FR)**[14] 4490 6-11-11 **114**.. RhysFlint 100
(David Rees) *trckd ldrs: prom 11th: ev ch on bnd after 13th: pushed along appr 4 out: wknd 3 out: sn lost tch w front 2* **9/2**

5322 **4** *11* **Papradon**[24] 4290 7-10-6 **98**.............................. SamTwiston-Davies(3) 71
(Nigel Twiston-Davies) *led: rdn and hdd on bnd after 13th: wkng whn mstke 4 out: lost tch: t.o* **4/1**[3]

2-12 **F** **Brenin Cwmtudu**[34] 4102 8-11-1 **109**....................... AodhaganConlon(5) —
(Evan Williams) *hld up: disputing 4th whn fell 11th: fatally injured* **10/3**[2]

400 **P** **Railway Diva (IRE)**[62] 3584 7-10-4 **93**.................................. SamJones —
(Evan Williams) *prom: mstke 3rd: lost pl 5th: bhd after 8th: t.o 13th: p.u bef 2 out* **16/1**

5m 26.6s (-3.40) **Going Correction** -0.475s/f (Good) **6** Ran SP% **110.5**
Speed ratings: **87,86,75,70,— —**
Tote Swingers: 1&2 £3.40, 1&3 £5.50, 2&3 £1.70 CSF £18.90 TOTE £7.70: £2.90, £1.60; EX 13.30.
Owner R E R Williams **Bred** Robert McCarthy **Trained** Llancarfan, Vale Of Glamorgan

FOCUS
A modest handicap chase which saw quite a tussle between the first pair, who pulled clear. Easy form to rate.

NOTEBOOK
Prince Massini(IRE), twice a winner over hurdles earlier this season, has never won off a mark this high before but was well treated on his best old form. Rallying when switched before the last, he got up on the post and might have won more easily but for a couple of errors. He goes well fresh. (tchd 11-2)
Storm Of Applause(IRE) ran a big race on this return from a winter break and looked the likely winner when showing ahead three out, but he was just touched off. He is difficult to win with but is currently on the mark off which he was last successful. (op 3-1 tchd 5-2)
Rimini(FR) dropped right away from the third-last. He has won over 3m in points but this was the longest trip he'd tackled over fences. (tchd 5-1)
Papradon is a hard ride and dropped away after making the running. (op 7-2)
Brenin Cwmtudu, a stablemate of the winner, was put down after a fall in the back straight. (tchd 3-1 and 7-2)

Railway Diva(IRE) Official explanation: jockey said mare bled from the nose (tchd 3-1 and 7-2)

4864 LAND MATTERS H'CAP CHASE (18 fncs) 3m
4:55 (4:56) (Class 3) (0-135,133) 5-Y-0+ £6,970 (£2,059; £1,029; £514; £257)

Form RPR
1113 1 **Bellflower Boy (IRE)**[14] 4464 8-10-10 116..................(tp) TimmyMurphy 125+
(Dr Richard Newland) *hld up bhd: niggled along 14th: hdwy appr 4 out: led bef 2 out where j.lft: clr whn j.lft again last: readily* 4/1[2]
02P3 2 1 3/4 **Postmaster**[48] 3841 9-11-9 132..................(t) RichardKilloran(3) 136
(Tim Vaughan) *hld up: hdwy 11th: chsd ldrs 4 out: rdn appr 3 out: styd on to take 2nd run-in: nt rch wnr* 33/1
-P31 3 3/4 **Isn't That Lucky**[16] 4440 8-11-8 133.................. DominicElsworth 135+
(Jonjo O'Neill) *trcking ldrs in tch: wnt 2nd after 3 out: mstke 2 out: rdn and swtchd rt between last 2 and nt qckn: blnd last: lost 2nd run-in but kpt on u.p* 11/4[1]
P206 4 17 **Quattrocento (FR)**[25] 4277 7-10-8 114..................(b[1]) DarylJacob 102
(Peter Bowen) *led appr 1st where blnd: hdd appr 2 out: wknd bef last* 13/2[3]
P523 5 7 **Or Bleu (FR)**[34] 4095 9-11-10 130.................. RichardJohnson 112
(Philip Hobbs) *led tl appr 1st: remained handy chsng ldrs: wnt 2nd bef 4 out: rdn 3 out: lost 2nd bef 2 out: sn wknd: eased whn btn bef last* 8/1
3312 6 2 1/2 **Lake Legend**[14] 4469 7-11-7 127.................. WayneHutchinson 106
(Alan King) *midfield: j. slowly 10th: mstke 12th: sn outpcd: hdwy to chse ldrs appr 4 out: rdn 3 out: wknd bef last* 7/1
F-PP 7 70 **Mr Robert (IRE)**[81] 3157 10-11-2 127.................. AodhaganConlon(5) 43
(Evan Williams) *hld up: outpcd fr 4 out: dropped away: t.o* 25/1
UP-4 P **Oakfield Legend**[16] 4440 10-11-3 123..................(t) RhysFlint —
(John Flint) *prom: blnd 11th: lost pl qckly and p.u bef 4 out* 13/2[3]
5PU P **Fit To Drive**[7] 4726 9-11-7 127..................(t) SamJones —
(Brendan Powell) *midfield: lost pl bef 10th: pushed along after 11th: t.o whn p.u bef 2 out* 25/1
4554 U **Frontier Dancer (IRE)**[15] 4461 7-10-13 122...(b[1]) SamTwiston-Davies(3) —
(Nigel Twiston-Davies) *in tch: mstke 5th: blnd bdly and almost fell whn uns rdr 11th* 14/1
21P3 P **Acrai Rua (IRE)**[42] 3938 8-10-12 118..................(p) PaulMoloney —
(Evan Williams) *chsd ldrs: nt fluent 1st: lost pl bef 5th: wknd 14th: t.o whn p.u bef 4 out* 20/1

6m 7.40s (-15.60) **Going Correction** -0.475s/f (Good) 11 Ran SP% 119.0
Speed ratings: **107,106,106,100,98 97,74,—,—,— —**
Tote Swingers: 1&2 £32.10, 1&3 £3.00, 2&3 £19.30 CSF £128.22 CT £427.49 TOTE £6.30: £2.40, £4.80, £2.40; EX 210.00.
Owner The Five Nations Partnership **Bred** Frank Sinnott **Trained** Claines, Worcs

FOCUS
A competitive handicap chase run at a reasonable pace, and the form looks solid. The winner was 3lb off his best hurdles form.

NOTEBOOK
Bellflower Boy(IRE) notched a hat-trick over hurdles earlier in the season and was able to race off his 12lb lower chase mark. Held up in last place, he picked his way through the field to lead two out and came away to score readily, value for a greater margin of victory. The cheekpieces and tongue-tie weren't on when he last ran over fences. (tchd 7-2)
Postmaster was staying on stoutly after the last and his new stable should find a suitable opportunity for him. (op 25-1)
Isn't That Lucky, racing off 5lb higher than when successful at Ludlow, saved ground on the inside and travelled well. He looked a big player at the third-last, but jumped out to his left at the next and was just held when blundering at the final fence. The ground might have been a little dead for him. (op 7-2)
Quattrocento(FR) had been given a chance by the handicapper and he made a lot of the running in the blinkers, only fading out of things from the second-last. (op 6-1)
Or Bleu(FR) helped force the pace but his stamina for this longer trip failed to last out. (op 15-2)
Lake Legend, despite making a couple of errors and needing reminders, looked a threat turning into the straight, but his effort petered out. He has yet to convince that this is his trip. (op 15-2 tchd 8-1)
Oakfield Legend was pulled up with something possibly having gone amiss. Official explanation: jockey said gelding pulled up lame (op 15-2)

4865 STRADEY ARMS CONDITIONAL JOCKEYS' H'CAP CHASE (18 fncs) 3m
5:30 (5:30) (Class 4) (0-100,98) 5-Y-0+ £3,577 (£1,050; £525; £262)

Form RPR
1543 1 **Cold Harbour**[30] 4160 7-11-9 95.................. AodhaganConlon 102+
(Evan Williams) *w ldr: pair clr of others fr 5th: led 11th: shook off rival 4 out: sn clr: abt 11 l clr and wl in command whn blnd last: eased down towards fin* 5/1
0026 2 1 1/2 **Run To Fly (IRE)**[18] 4409 6-9-11 72..................(p) DonalDevereux(3) 74
(Peter Bowen) *sn chsd clr ldrs: mstke 10th and 14th: stdy hdwy bef 4 out: tk 2nd appr last: styd on u.p run-in: clsd on wnr but no ch towards fin: flattered* 7/2[3]
P2P2 3 7 **Bob Casey (IRE)**[12] 4525 9-11-1 87..................(p) JoshuaMoore 84
(Keith Goldsworthy) *sn led: clr w other rival fr 5th: hdd 11th: lost grnd on wnr appr 4 out: no ch whn blnd 2 out: lost 2nd appr last: wknd run-in* 2/1[1]
F634 4 4 1/2 **The Humbel Monk (IRE)**[16] 4438 9-11-2 88.................. RichardKilloran 79
(Lucy Jones) *chsd clr ldrs: struggling and bhd after 14th: n.d* 9/1
2436 5 3/4 **Reland (FR)**[58] 3646 6-11-9 98.................. SamTwiston-Davies(3) 89
(Nigel Twiston-Davies) *nt fluent: hld up: bhd 6th: struggling 14th: hrd at work and tried to make hdwy bef 4 out: no imp* 3/1[2]
4050 F **Born To Be Wilde (IRE)**[34] 4104 6-10-11 88.................. SClements(5) —
(Evan Williams) *bhd: rdn and t.o after 14th: fell 3 out* 14/1

6m 17.5s (-5.50) **Going Correction** -0.475s/f (Good) 6 Ran SP% 113.9
Speed ratings: **90,89,87,85,85 —**
Tote Swingers: 1&2 £4.00, 1&3 £2.20, 2&3 £1.60 CSF £23.32 TOTE £4.40: £1.10, £2.40; EX 22.10.
Owner Fox And Hounds Racing **Bred** Crandon Park Stud **Trained** Llancarfan, Vale Of Glamorgan

FOCUS
A weak race for conditionals, run in a time ten seconds slower than the earlier handicap. The winner and third took each other on up front and with a circuit to run were a long way clear of the other four, none of whem was ever seen with a serious chance. A personal best from Cold Harbour, with the second to his mark.

NOTEBOOK
Cold Harbour jumped much better than Bob Casey and had seen him off at the first up the straight. He nearly threw it away at the last, but the truth is that he won much more comfortably than the margin suggests. Belying any stamina concerns and adding to his win over an extended 2m3f here earlier in the season, he doesn't get a penalty for this. (op 7-2)
Run To Fly(IRE) was a remote third for most of the final circuit but kept trying and was not beaten far in the end. He is flattered by this, and although he has finished second in two of his last three starts he has not achieved much in doing so. That said, he is lightly raced and young enough to improve. (op 15-2)
Bob Casey(IRE) matched strides with Cold Harbour for a long way, but made a string of mistakes and understandably became tired over the last four fences. He is very modest but is in decent heart at present. (op 11-4)
The Humbel Monk(IRE) showed little on his handicap debut. (op 11-1)
Reland(FR) was never travelling sweetly. (op 2-1)
Born To Be Wilde(IRE), representing the same connections as the winner, was always at the rear of the field on this switch to fences and eventually came down. (op 11-1)

4866 KSB BLOODSTOCK STANDARD OPEN NATIONAL HUNT FLAT RACE 2m
6:00 (6:01) (Class 5) 4-6-Y-0 £1,951 (£573; £286; £143)

Form RPR
1 **Hard To Swallow (IRE)**[94] 5-11-3 0.................. WarrenMarston 119+
(Martin Keighley) *hld up in midfield: hdwy 1/2-way: wnt 2nd 5f out: led over 3f out: rdn over 1f out: r.o wl to draw clr fnl f: eased cl home* 8/1
2 6 **Oscar Sunset (IRE)** 4-10-5 0.................. AodhaganConlon(5) 104+
(Evan Williams) *hld up in rr: niggled along over 6f out: hdwy 5f out: chsd front 2 2f out: styd on to take 2nd wl ins fnl f: no ch w wnr* 25/1
3 1 1/2 **Court Minstrel (IRE)** 4-10-10 0.................. PaulMoloney 102
(Evan Williams) *midfield: hdwy 5f out: wnt 2nd over 2f out: rn green: outpcd by wnr 1f out: no ch after: lost 2nd wl ins fnl f* 22/1
4 13 **Victor Echo (IRE)** 5-11-0 0.................. DavidBass(3) 98
(Nicky Henderson) *chsd ldrs: rdn and outpcd over 4f out: plugged on fnl 2f: nt pce to get on terms w front 3* 3/1[2]
5 2 1/2 **Foxbridge (IRE)**[328] 5-11-0 0.................. SamTwiston-Davies(3) 95
(Nigel Twiston-Davies) *led: hdd over 3f out: rdn and wknd 2f out* 5/1[3]
11- 6 7 **Big Time Billy (IRE)**[344] 5114 5-10-13 0.................. MichaelByrne(7) 93
(Peter Bowen) *midfield: clsed to chse ldrs 5f out: rdn and outpcd over 4f out: lost tch w ldrs over 2f out* 2/1[1]
7 1/2 **Kayfontaine** 5-10-10 0.................. DominicElsworth 82
(Jonjo O'Neill) *midfield: pushed along and outpcd 4f out: nvr a threat* 20/1
8 6 **Katys Jools** 4-10-0 0.................. RichardKilloran(3) 69
(Tim Vaughan) *chsd ldrs tl rdn and wknd 5f out* 25/1
9 2 **Hindon Road (IRE)** 4-10-10 0.................. WayneHutchinson 74
(Alan King) *midfield: rdn and wknd 5f out* 14/1
10 26 **Grindy (IRE)** 5-11-3 0.................. RhysFlint 58
(Evan Williams) *hld up: struggling over 5f out: t.o* 33/1
0 11 nk **Gracious Beau**[12] 4527 5-10-10 0.................. MrPJohn(7) 58
(Keith Goldsworthy) *chsd ldr tl rdn 5f out: sn wknd: t.o* 66/1
12 5 **Fanzee Man** 4-10-10 0.................. JamesMillman 46
(Rod Millman) *s.s: hld up: struggling 6f out: t.o* 16/1
13 8 **Montybella (IRE)** 4-10-10 0.................. SamJones 39
(Evan Williams) *hld up: struggling over 5f out: t.o* 40/1

3m 48.2s (4.80) **Going Correction** +0.375s/f (Yiel)
WFA 4 from 5yo 7lb 13 Ran SP% 122.3
Speed ratings: **103,100,99,92,91 88,87,84,83,70 70,68,64**
Tote Swingers: 1&2 £41.00 CSF £197.20 TOTE £5.90: £2.20, £7.20, £6.10; EX 335.90.
Owner Mrs Louise Jones **Bred** B Kavanagh **Trained** Condicote, Gloucs

FOCUS
This looked a decent bumper and winners should emerge from it, but there was not much previous form to go on. The winner looks a smart recruit.

NOTEBOOK
Hard To Swallow(IRE) ◆ already had a victory to his name, successful in a maiden point for four-year-olds in Ireland three months ago. He stayed on strongly to win eased down on this rules debut and looks to have a bright future, particularly on easier ground. (op 7-1 tchd 9-1)
Oscar Sunset(IRE)'s trainer was responsible for just over a quarter of all the runners on the card and was rewarded with the second and third from his four in this. The gelding, out of a winning hurdler, stayed on late to to gun down his stablemate and grab second. This was a decent race of its stype and he has plenty of ability. (op 20-1)
Court Minstrel(IRE) had looked to be going as well as the winner early in the straight but ran notably green. A half-brother to six winners, could be the brighter prospect of the Williams pair. (op 20-1)
Victor Echo(IRE) was hard at work leaving the back straight but stayed on well in the latter stages and looks to have plenty of stamina. (op 7-2 tchd 11-4)
Foxbridge(IRE), like the fourth, carried the colours of course owner Dai Walters. Winner of an Irish maiden point last spring, he faded after setting a reasonable pace and perhaps had too much use made of him. (tchd 9-2)
Big Time Billy(IRE) was unbeaten in two but had not been seen since winning the Listed bumper for mares at the Grand National meeting last April. Fit enough for this return, she was disappointing but is still eligible to contest the Aintree race again. (op 5-2)
Kayfontaine, whose dam was a prolific middle-distance winner, showed a bit of promise on this debut and should do better. (op 16-1)
Katys Jools, Bakbenscher's half-sister, is another with improvement in her.
T/Plt: £174.50. Pool: £69,905 - 284.06 winning units. T/Qpdt: £72.00. Pool: £3,760.62 - 38.60 winning units. DO

4541 NEWCASTLE (L-H)
Saturday, March 19

OFFICIAL GOING: Soft (heavy in places in back straight; good to soft in places last 4f) changing to soft (good to soft in places) after race 2 (2.45)
Rail on bend into home straight moved in 4yds for better ground, 3m bend divided. First hurdle in back straight omitted in all hurdle races.
Wind: Breezy, across Weather: Cloudy, fine

4867 BET ON TOTESCOOP6 AT TOTESPORT.COM H'CAP HURDLE (8 hdls 1 omitted) 2m
2:10 (2:10) (Class 3) (0-130,130) 4-Y-0+ £3,642 (£1,069; £534; £267)

Form RPR
/302 1 **Best Prospect (IRE)**[21] 4358 9-11-12 130..................(tp) BarryKeniry 130+
(Michael Dods) *prom: smooth hdwy to chse ldr 3 out: gng wl last: shkn up and led last 50yds: hld on* 15/8[1]
-004 2 hd **Culcabock (IRE)**[76] 3334 11-11-2 120.................. CampbellGillies 118
(Lucinda Russell) *led: rdn bef 2 out: hdd last 50yds: rallied: jst hld* 6/1
0-60 3 6 **Washington Irving (IRE)**[21] 4358 6-11-7 130.................. PaulGallagher(5) 123
(Howard Johnson) *cl up: wnt 2nd 4 out tl nt fluent next: one pce whn hit 2 out: sn outpcd* 11/4[3]
123U 4 19 **Benny Be Good**[15] 4453 8-11-9 127.................. JamesReveley 107
(Keith Reveley) *pressed ldr tl rdn and outpcd 4 out: lost tch fr next* 9/4[2]

4m 11.0s (1.00) **Going Correction** 0.0s/f (Good) 4 Ran SP% 106.5
Speed ratings (Par 107): **97,96,93,84**
CSF £11.05 TOTE £2.60; EX 8.70.
Owner D Neale **Bred** Farmers Hill Stud **Trained** Denton, Co Durham

FOCUS
With no notable front-runner in the field this was always going to be a tactical affair and the pace was steady until it quickened turning out of the back straight. The winner is rated value for further and to his mark.
NOTEBOOK
Best Prospect(IRE) was up 5lb and had the best recent form on offer but is not the most straightforward. He travelled well into the race, tracking the long-time leader but, gave his supporters a few anxious moments when he failed to pick up as quick as his rider would have liked after meeting the last wrong. It probably played into his hands, as he has to be delivered late and, won with more in hand than the finishing margin would suggest. He should not be hit too hard for this. (op 2-1 tchd 9-4, 7-4 and 5-2 in places)
Culcabock(IRE)'s connections were a little worried about the soft conditions, as most of his form is on better ground but, he ran a respectable race after having to dictate the pace. He has dropped below his last winning mark and with his stable hitting form he can gain some compensation when the ground dries. (op 9-2)
Washington Irving(IRE) is a smart performer on is day but ran out here last time after a fair effort over 2 1/2 miles at Aintree. Dropping back to the minimum in a tricky little race did not play to his strengths and he could only stay on at the same pace from three out. (tchd 5-2)
Benny Be Good is a consistent performer who handles these conditions. He was dropping back down in trip and reverting to hurdles after nearly a year and, was another who did not appreciate the lack of a strong gallop being readily outpaced. (op 5-2)

4868 GUINNESS H'CAP CHASE (13 fncs) 2m 110y
2:45 (2:45) (Class 4) (0-105,102) 5-Y-0+ **£2,439** (£716; £358)

Form RPR
5514 **1** **Prince Tam**[25] 4279 7-10-6 **82**....................(p) CampbellGillies 94+
(Lucinda Russell) *mde all: clr 4 out: rdn and kpt on wl fr 2 out* **15/8**[2]
43-0 **2** *1 1/4* **Cabbyl Doo**[47] 3850 8-11-7 **97**.................... PaddyAspell 105
(James Moffatt) *chsd wnr to 8th: regained 2nd bef next: effrt 4 out: kpt on fr last: nvr able to chal* **7/1**[3]
0041 **3** *44* **Saddlers Deal (IRE)**[19] 4392 6-11-12 **102**.................... GrahamLee 81
(Chris Grant) *nt fluent: trckd ldrs: effrt and wnt 2nd 8th: hit and wknd fr next: t.o* **4/6**[1]
4m 25.0s (3.90) **Going Correction** 0.0s/f (Good) **3** Ran SP% **107.3**
Speed ratings: **90,89,68**
CSF £9.23 TOTE £2.40; EX 8.50.
Owner Mrs L R Joughin **Bred** Miss Gail Joughin **Trained** Arlary, Perth & Kinross
FOCUS
Only three runners for this 0-105 handicap chase with just a modest pace being set. the winner is rated to his C&D mark.
NOTEBOOK
Prince Tam won a weak handicap over C&D penultimate start off a slipping mark but disappointed at Wetherby last time under a penalty. He was given an easy lead here and had to do little to return to winning ways but this was a weak affair and he does not possess the most consistent profile. (op 6-4)
Cabbyl Doo was making his chasing debut put straight into handicap company after showing some promise in hurdles but has always looked as though he would do better in this sphere. He has had his problems and if connections can keep him sound he should be capable of repaying their patience before long. (op 11-2 tchd 5-1)
Saddlers Deal(IRE) was a well-backed odds-on favourite but the writing was on the wall before hitting the last in the back straight. Probably, this run can be ignored, as he never ran any sort of race off a muddling pace on what looked a feasible 3lb higher mark than when opening his account at Catterick last time. Official explanation: jockey said gelding was unsuited by the soft (good to soft places) ground (op 10-11 tchd Evens and 11-10 in a place)

4869 WIN A FORTUNE WITH TOTEPOOL H'CAP HURDLE (11 hdls 2 omitted) 3m
3:20 (3:20) (Class 3) (0-130,120) 4-Y-0+ **£3,642** (£1,069; £534; £267)

Form RPR
6/P3 **1** **Zed Candy (FR)**[12] 4532 8-10-13 **114**....................(p) HarryChalloner(7) 120+
(Richard Ford) *t.k.h: in tch: stdy hdwy 1/2-way: led and hit 3 out: drew clr fr next* **11/1**
-U60 **2** *6* **Crop Walker (IRE)**[14] 4477 9-10-6 **100**.................... RichieMcGrath 100
(Kate Walton) *trckd ldrs: effrt and chsd (clr) wnr 2 out: no imp fr last* **11/1**
6262 **3** *7* **Charlie Bucket**[35] 4067 8-10-9 **113**.................... CallumWhillans(10) 106
(Donald Whillans) *hld up: rdn bef 3 out: plugged on fr next: no imp* **15/2**
1634 **4** *nk* **Sunnyside**[21] 4359 6-11-2 **115**.................... AlexanderVoy(5) 107
(Lucy Normile) *led 1st tl hdd 3 out: lost 2nd and outpcd next* **7/1**[3]
1315 **5** *2* **Night In Milan (IRE)**[21] 4358 5-11-2 **110**.................... JamesReveley 101
(Keith Reveley) *hld up: mstke 2nd: hdwy and prom whn hit 4 out: drvn and outpcd fr next* **11/4**[1]
2010 **6** *3* **Snake Charmer**[14] 4464 8-11-2 **110**....................(v) DaveCrosse 100
(Milton Harris) *hld up: outpcd whn nt fluent 4 out: n.d after* **13/2**[2]
-034 **7** *23* **Political Paddy**[28] 4209 9-11-2 **115**....................(p) PaulGallagher(5) 84
(Rayson Nixon) *prom: drvn fr 1/2-way: wknd after 4 out: t.o* **7/1**[3]
/5-P **8** *20* **The Whisperer (IRE)**[316] 193 10-11-12 **120**.................... GrahamLee 79
(Nicky Richards) *t.k.h: in tch: lost pl 1/2-way: wknd fr 4 out: t.o* **16/1**
-2FP **P** **Minster Shadow**[59] 3634 12-10-12 **106**....................(v) CampbellGillies —
(Chris Grant) *led to 1st: cl up tl rdn and wknd after 4 out: t.o whn p.u 2 out* **8/1**
6m 9.50s (-4.50) **Going Correction** 0.0s/f (Good) **9** Ran SP% **110.4**
Speed ratings (Par 107): **107,105,102,102,101 100,93,86,—**
toteswingers: 1&2 £69.00, 1&3 £4.90, 2&3 £27.00. CSF £113.43 CT £917.35 TOTE £11.90: £2.60, £3.40, £2.40; EX 185.20 TRIFECTA Not won..
Owner J T S (International) Ltd **Bred** Haras De Saint Pair Du Mont **Trained** Butterton, Staffs
FOCUS
The going changed to soft, good to soft in places. An ordinary pace for this reasonable staying handicap hurdle. The winner is rated back to the level of his 2008 form.
NOTEBOOK
Zed Candy(FR) stayed on strongly to run out a decisive winner. He has been in good heart on the Flat over the winter and ran respectably over 2m6f at Newton Abbot last time. He saw out this step up in trip well but will find life difficult after being reassessed for this. (op 8-1)
Crop Walker(IRE) has had his problems and has shown little since returning to action this season. Has shown some promise back in 2008 and this step up in trip brought about some improvement, although, never going to trouble the winner. This will give connections more options if they can keep him going. (op 12-1)
Charlie Bucket went close off 8lb lower mark over an extended 2m5f at Ayr last month but he saw out this step up in trip well enough without ever getting seriously competitive. He remains a maiden but does not possess the most convincing of profiles. (op 13-2)
Sunnyside dictated the steady gallop on his handicap debut but after hitting three out had little more to offer. He will have to step on recent efforts if to win off this mark, but this point-to-point winner might be of interest when his attention is switched to fences. (op 8-1)
Night In Milan(IRE) was the disappointment in the field after being a very well supported favourite. He moved through well enough on this step up to three miles but when asked to close entering the straight, failed to do so and, was soundly beaten soon after. On this evidence he might well be in the grip of the handicapper. (op 7-2)

Minster Shadow Official explanation: jockey said gelding had a breathing problem

4870 BUSHMILLS IRISH WHISKEY NOVICES' HURDLE (8 hdls 1 omitted) 2m
3:55 (3:55) (Class 4) 4-Y-0+ **£2,471** (£725; £362; £181)

Form RPR
P35 **1** **Rumble Of Thunder (IRE)**[30] 4165 5-11-0 0.................... RichieMcGrath 122+
(Kate Walton) *cl up: led 4 out: jnd briefly bef next: styd on strly fr 2 out: 12 l up whn lft wl clr last* **6/4**[2]
0-53 **2** *33* **Andreo Bambaleo**[11] 4541 7-11-0 0.................... TomSiddall 84
(Simon West) *prom: drvn and outpcd bef 3 out: lft 28 l 2nd last: no imp* **8/1**[3]
0P54 **3** *11* **Lochore (IRE)**[11] 4542 5-10-9 69.................... AlexanderVoy(5) 73
(Lucy Normile) *led to 4 out: drvn and outpcd bef next: lft poor 3rd last* **33/1**
P0P **4** *8* **Miss Galross (IRE)**[19] 4393 7-10-7 0.................... FearghalDavis 58
(Nicky Richards) *bhd: drvn and struggling 1/2-way: sme late hdwy: nvr on terms* **40/1**
5 *nk* **Enjoy Your Life (IRE)**[223] 4-10-2 0.................... PaulGallagher(5) 58
(Andrew Crook) *prom tl rdn and outpcd after 4 out: n.d after: lost action: eased and ct for 4th cl home* **12/1**
-PP0 **6** *43* **Solway Dornal**[281] 711 6-10-11 0.................... HarryHaynes(3) 22
(Lisa Harrison) *prom to 1/2-way: sn rdn and wknd: t.o* **50/1**
560 **7** *21* **Media Stars**[140] 2092 6-11-0 78.................... KennyJohnson —
(Robert Johnson) *bhd and detached: lost tch 4th: t.o* **50/1**
11P1 **F** **Jukebox Melody (IRE)**[11] 4541 5-11-6 0.................... GrahamLee 110
(Malcolm Jefferson) *t.k.h: hld up in tch: smooth hdwy to chal bef 3 out: outpcd whn rdn and edgd lft bef next: 12 l 2nd whn fell last* **1/1**[1]
4m 8.50s (-1.50) **Going Correction** 0.0s/f (Good)
WFA 4 from 5yo+ 7lb **8** Ran SP% **118.1**
Speed ratings (Par 105): **103,86,81,77,76 55,44,—**
toteswingers: 1&2 £2.40, 1&3 £6.50, 2&3 £8.00. CSF £13.79 TOTE £2.30: £1.10, £1.40, £3.40; EX 17.50.
Owner Mrs K Walton **Bred** Rathasker Stud **Trained** Middleham Moor, N Yorks
FOCUS
Only two could be seriously considered for this novice hurdle, which proved to be the case as they quickened well clear of the remainder entering the straight. The winner is entitled to rate higher on Flat form.
NOTEBOOK
Rumble Of Thunder(IRE) was useful at his best on the Flat and was steadily progressive in three runs over hurdles. He made full use of his weight concession from the winner and after turning in soon put the race to bed before being left well clear at the last. He looks capable of paying his way in the future. (op 7-4 tchd 15-8)
Andreo Bambaleo had to find a bit to get on terms with recent C&D run behind Jukebox Melody and was a well beaten third when the latter crashed out at the last. He has been progressing over hurdles and now qualifies for a mark.
Lochore(IRE) had it all to do on these terms, as he has achieved little so far over hurdles being only rated 69. (op 25-1)
Enjoy Your Life(IRE) Official explanation: jockey said, regarding riding, that the gelding hung left and lost its action on run-in.
Jukebox Melody(IRE) has a tendency to do himself no favours by pulling too hard but, had picked up three novices along the way and set the standard. Again he failed to settle but he threw down a strong challenge entering the straight before the winner asserted at the next. He was a tired second when falling at the last but still looks value for further success if his confidence is not affected. (op 5-4)

4871 GUINNESS ST PATRICKS DAY H'CAP CHASE (18 fncs) 3m
4:30 (4:30) (Class 4) (0-110,107) 5-Y-0+ **£2,439** (£716; £358; £178)

Form RPR
-662 **1** **Copper's Gold (IRE)**[52] 3748 7-11-4 **99**....................(b) CampbellGillies 108+
(Lucinda Russell) *j.rt: led to 11th: led 5 out: styd on wl fr next: eased towards fin* **6/4**[1]
01P- **2** *5* **Aitch Doubleyou (IRE)**[342] 5149 11-11-2 **102**.................... PaulGallagher(5) 100
(Henry Hogarth) *chsd wnr: led 11th to 5 out: ev ch next: one pce fr 3 out* **7/2**[3]
2000 **3** *12* **Twelve Paces**[14] 4476 10-10-7 **95**.................... MissLAlexander(7) 81
(N W Alexander) *nt fluent: prom: pushed along 11th: struggling after 5 out: plugged on fnl 2: no imp* **4/1**
3PP0 **4** *26* **Flying Squad (UAE)**[8] 4699 7-11-12 **107**....................(t) DaveCrosse 83
(Milton Harris) *t.k.h: in tch: hit 8th: effrt after 5 out: wknd fr next* **5/2**[2]
6m 33.6s (11.10) **Going Correction** 0.0s/f (Good) **4** Ran SP% **110.8**
Speed ratings: **81,79,75,66**
CSF £7.00 TOTE £1.80; EX 5.40.
Owner John R Adam **Bred** Miss E Violet Sweeney **Trained** Arlary, Perth & Kinross
FOCUS
A weak 0-110 staying chase with question marks surrounding all four of the runners. A step up from the winner.
NOTEBOOK
Copper's Gold(IRE) had the best recent form on offer with a decent effort at Musselburgh in January. He was unproven on ground such as this and did have a tendency to jump out to his left but ran out a deserved winner after making virtually all. A weak affair and he holds few secrets but is clearly on good terms with himself at the moment. (op 15-8 tchd 2-1)
Aitch Doubleyou(IRE) was returning here after another lengthy absence and ran respectably. He kept on well enough from the last after holding every chance entering the straight on this step up in trip but he is rather hit-and-miss overall. (op 11-4 tchd 5-2)
Twelve Paces was well beaten in a hunters' chase on return to action for new yard and again, here, was soundly beaten. Formerly quite useful he clearly can only be watched at present. (tchd 9-2)
Flying Squad(UAE) was a dual chase winner in January but has badly lost his way since. He kept chasing the leading pair after turning in but tired two out and was all but pulled up after the last. (op 3-1)

4872 GUINNESS NOVICES' H'CAP HURDLE (11 hdls 2 omitted) 2m 6f
5:05 (5:05) (Class 5) (0-95,92) 4-Y-0+ **£2,211** (£649; £324; £162)

Form RPR
0453 **1** **Sam Patch**[13] 4511 8-10-1 **77**....................(tp) CallumWhillans(10) 84+
(Donald Whillans) *prom: smooth hdwy to ld bef 3 out: rdn and drew clr fr last* **7/2**[2]
-541 **2** *10* **Easter Vic**[8] 4687 10-11-5 **90**....................(p) AlexanderVoy(5) 89
(Robert Goldie) *sn pushed along towards rr: hdwy and prom after 5th: outpcd 7th: styd on fr 2 out: tk 2nd run-in: no ch w wnr* **11/2**[3]
0500 **3** *1* **Mrs Eff**[19] 4390 5-11-8 **88**.................... RichieMcGrath 84
(Kate Walton) *t.k.h: mde most to bef 3 out: rdn and one pce after next* **15/2**
P0U4 **4** *nk* **I Witness (IRE)**[8] 4688 9-10-13 **86**....................(t) AlistairFindlay(7) 84
(Jane Walton) *sn w ldr: rdn bef 3 out: one pce fr next* **10/1**

333 **5** *11* **Talesofriverbank**[45] 3883 8-10-3 **72**.............................. EwanWhillans(3) 57
(Alistair Whillans) *trckd ldrs: outpcd 4 out: rallied after next: wknd fr 2 out* **3/1**[1]

45P5 **6** *20* **Knockaveen (IRE)**[19] 4395 6-10-4 **75**........................(p) PaulGallagher(5) 40
(Andrew Crook) *hld up in tch: stdy hdwy and prom 5th: ev ch 4 out: wknd bef next* **16/1**

-P05 **7** *1 ½* **Power Flow (IRE)**[11] 4541 6-11-12 **92**................................. PaddyAspell 55
(Peter Atkinson) *prom: drvn and outpcd bef 4 out: btn next* **16/1**

-000 **8** *1 ½* **Solway Silver**[161] 1783 5-10-11 **80**.. HarryHaynes(3) 42
(Lisa Harrison) *prom: outpcd and struggling 7th: sn n.d* **20/1**

064 **9** *89* **Napoletano (ITY)**[21] 4361 5-11-6 **86**................................ KennyJohnson —
(Robert Johnson) *nt fluent: plld hrd: hld up: hdwy to join ldrs after 6th: wknd after next: t.o* **18/1**

P000 **P** **Northern Flame (IRE)**[14] 4477 6-11-12 **92**.................... CampbellGillies —
(N W Alexander) *nt fluent: a bhd: t.o whn p.u 3 out* **11/1**

5m 56.4s (20.40) **Going Correction** 0.0s/f (Good) **10** Ran SP% **113.6**
Speed ratings (Par 103): **62,58,58,57,53 46,46,45,13,—**
toteswingers: 1&2 £4.20, 1&3 £8.10, 2&3 £6.50. CSF £22.84 CT £133.71 TOTE £4.70: £1.70, £2.30, £1.80; EX 21.10.
Owner Allan Gilchrist **Bred** Allan Gilchrist **Trained** Hawick, Borders

FOCUS
A low-grade handicap hurdle that was run at a fair pace. The form is rated around the second to fourth.

NOTEBOOK
Sam Patch got off the mark at the 16th attempt off a mark of 77. He had pieced together some respectable efforts in similar contests of late and made full use of his rider's 10lb allowance to draw clear from the last to run out a comfortable winner. He has been tried over varying trips before so it can only be taken on trust that he can go on from this. Official explanation: caution: used whip when clearly winning. (op 9-2)
Easter Vic came from well off the pace to get off the mark at Ayr last time and, again, looked far from being involved when struggling down the back straight with plenty to do. As is her trait, she again stayed on from two out but was never going to reel in the winner after going second on the run-in. (op 5-1 tchd 9-2)
Mrs Eff had a couple of modest efforts to overcome since switching to handicaps but this step back up in trip was expected to suit. She had her chance going to three out but was held from the second last before fading on the run-in. (op 7-1 tchd 13-2)
I Witness(IRE) ran respectably with tongue-tie kept on, but could only stay on at the same pace in the straight. (tchd 11-1)
Talesofriverbank was a shade disappointing as he had solid claims on recent efforts, receiving weight all round but, he could never quite get on terms turning in and finished soundly beaten. (tchd 10-3)

4873 FREEBETTING.CO.UK H'CAP HURDLE (10 hdls 1 omitted) 2m 4f
6:40 (6:40) (Class 4) (0-110,109) 4-Y-0+ **£2,471** (£725, £362, £181)

Form RPR

0322 **1** **Mister Pete (IRE)**[26] 4257 8-11-3 **105**.........................(p) AlexanderVoy(5) 111+
(Chris Grant) *w ldr: led 1/2-way: mde rest: hit 2 out: styd on strly* **7/4**[1]

1401 **2** *7* **Kempski**[7] 4715 11-11-5 **107**.. PaulGallagher(5) 102
(Rayson Nixon) *led to 1/2-way: w ldr: drvn fr 6th: rallied: kpt on same pce fr 2 out* **11/4**[2]

4005 **3** *5* **Forcefield**[23] 4303 5-10-13 **103**.................................... MissLAlexander(7) 96
(N W Alexander) *prom: nt fluent 5th: pushed along 4 out: effrt next: edgd lft and one pce 2 out* **15/2**

P3P5 **4** *7* **Smack That (IRE)**[38] 4008 9-11-12 **109**...........................(vt) DaveCrosse 94
(Milton Harris) *t.k.h: hld up in tch: smooth hdwy 4 out: rdn and no ex after next* **12/1**

5P40 **5** *34* **Black Apache (IRE)**[114] 2644 7-11-1 **98**.............................. AdrianLane 47
(Donald McCain) *trckd ldrs: rdn 4 out: wknd bef next* **15/2**

-266 **P** **Solway Ally**[292] 553 8-10-11 **97**...................................... HarryHaynes(3) —
(Lisa Harrison) *sn bhd and detached: t.o whn p.u after 4th* **11/2**[3]

5m 27.1s (6.00) **Going Correction** 0.0s/f (Good) **6** Ran SP% **109.6**
Speed ratings (Par 105): **88,85,83,80,66 —**
toteswingers: 1&2 £1.10, 1&3 £3.30, 2&3 £4.80. CSF £6.83 TOTE £2.50: £1.60, £1.70; EX 5.10.
Owner David Armstrong **Bred** Tom Radley **Trained** Newton Bewley, Co Durham

FOCUS
A match on paper. Argubaly a step up from the winner, but the second is better on heavy ground.

NOTEBOOK
Mister Pete(IRE) eventually came out on top, drawing clear going to the last. He was returning to a track he acts well around to record his third course success, in similar conditions and, has now posted two solid efforts off his highest mark to date of 105. He has to be respected round here again, but after being reassessed life will become testing. (op 6-4 tchd 2-1)
Kempski was being nudged along from a fair way out but stuck to his task gamely before giving way after two out. He handled his 7lb rise well enough and always commands respect whenever turning out at Ayr. (op 3-1 tchd 5-2)
Forcefield had come in for some support and had his chance going to three out but, after briefly flattering, could only stay on at the same pace. (op 12-1)
Smack That(IRE) was beaten in a seller at Ludlow last time and, after travelling well on the heels of the leaders three out, failed to see out this step up in trip. (op 10-1)
Black Apache(IRE) has been disappointing since scoring at Uttoxeter in bad ground last season and again dropped out tamely here after being absent for 114 days. (op 6-1 tchd 11-2)
Solway Ally was never travelling from an early stage. Official explanation: jockey said mare never travelled (op 13-2 tchd 5-1)
T/Plt: £406.30 to a £1 stake. Pool:£78,911.51 - 141.78 winning tickets. T/Qpdt: £32.10 to a £1 stake. Pool:£4,408.52 - 101.40 winning tickets. RY

3816 UTTOXETER (L-H)
Saturday, March 19

OFFICIAL GOING: Good to soft (soft in places) changing to good to soft after race 1 (1.55)
Divided bends, hurdles on inside and fresh ground on both courses. Middle flight in back straight omitted in all hurdle races.
Wind: lkight 1/2 against Weather: fine and sunny

4874 TOTEJACKPOT NOVICES' H'CAP HURDLE (9 hdls 1 omitted) 2m
1:55 (1:57) (Class 4) (0-115,112) 4-Y-0+ **£2,534** (£748; £374; £187; £93)

Form RPR

1260 **1** **Tharaya**[120] 2508 6-11-5 **108**.. TommyPhelan(3) 117+
(Claire Dyson) *hld up: hdwy to trck ldrs 5th: chsd ldr appr 3 out: led 2 out: drvn clr run-in* **28/1**

0511 **2** *9* **Beau Lake (IRE)**[19] 4399 7-11-6 **106**............................... PaddyBrennan 108
(Suzy Smith) *j.rt: w ldr: led appr 3 out: hdd 2 out: kpt on same pce* **11/4**[2]

3045 **3** *3* **Kayfton Pete**[35] 4076 5-11-0 **107**.................................... PeterHatton(7) 108+
(Reg Hollinshead) *blnd 1st: hmpd next: wnt prom 4th: kpt on same pce fr 2 out* **16/1**

0352 **4** *1 ¼* **Lesanda**[10] 4552 5-11-3 **103**... BrianHughes 99
(Richard Fahey) *chsd ldrs: one pce fr 3 out* **9/1**

6-00 **5** *9* **Group Leader (IRE)**[15] 4462 5-11-5 **105**...................(b[1]) AidanColeman 93
(J R Jenkins) *w ldrs: reminders 5th: sn lost pl* **25/1**

P4P0 **6** *4 ½* **Tar (IRE)**[272] 793 7-10-6 **92**..(t) CharliePoste 76
(Matt Sheppard) *chsd ldrs: wknd appr 2 out* **66/1**

060 **7** *17* **Speed Dating**[55] 3692 5-11-4 **104**...(b) APMcCoy 81
(John Quinn) *nt fluent: chsd ldrs: mstke 5th: rdn 3 out: wknd next: eased and j. bdly rt last* **6/4**[1]

543 **8** *11* **Bagutta Sun**[131] 2282 5-11-1 **101**.. LiamHeard 60
(Barry Leavy) *mid-div: bhd fr 6th* **33/1**

-P31 **9** *22* **Matako (FR)**[121] 2480 8-11-5 **108**.. IanPopham(3) 47
(Caroline Keevil) *in rr: bhd fr 6th: t.o* **8/1**[3]

/0-3 **F** **Morning Farewell**[143] 2038 7-11-9 **112**.........................(tp) DannyCook(3) —
(William Clay) *trckd ldrs: fell 2nd* **20/1**

/40U **P** **Paquet Cadeau (FR)**[58] 3648 8-11-1 **101**......................... AndrewTinkler —
(Henry Daly) *led tl appr 3 out: wknd qckly: t.o whn p.u bef 2 out* **16/1**

3m 53.2s (-2.00) **Going Correction** -0.275s/f (Good) **11** Ran SP% **116.0**
Speed ratings (Par 105): **94,89,88,87,82 80,72,66,55,— —**
toteswingers: 1&2 £17.60, 1&3 £21.40, 2&3 £8.70. CSF £101.33 CT £1321.22 TOTE £38.40: £7.10, £1.30, £4.50; EX 123.60 TRIFECTA Not won..
Owner Miss S J Turner **Bred** Barry Walters Catering **Trained** Cleeve Prior, Worcs

FOCUS
A moderate handicap, run at a fair gallop. A step up from the easy winner, with the next three setting the level.

NOTEBOOK
Tharaya came home a comfortable winner on her first outing for four months. She travelled kindly and soon had matters in control after hitting the front. This was her debut for the stable and it rates a career-best effort, so the change of scenery has clearly helped. She is due to go novice chasing in the summer. (op 22-1)
Beau Lake(IRE), 7lb higher, was again given a positive ride and ran his race in this quest for the hat-trick, setting the level of the form. The handicapper probably now has him where he wants him. (tchd 3-1)
Kayfton Pete was hampered by the faller at the second flight and got behind. He still came through to post an improved run, however, and is slowly getting the hang of hurdling. (op 22-1)
Lesanda, a handicap debutante, looked a player four out but found little for pressure. (tchd 8-1)
Speed Dating attracted heavy support for his handicap debut as a hurdler and looked on an appealing mark considering his Flat form. The blinkers were on for the first time in this sphere, but he proved free early and found nothing once put under some pressure. He now has it to prove. Official explanation: trainer had no explanation for the poor form shown (op 15-8 tchd 11-8 and 2-1 in a place)
Paquet Cadeau(FR) Official explanation: jockey said gelding hung right throughout

4875 TOTESCOOP6 H'CAP HURDLE (10 hdls 2 omitted) 2m 6f 110y
2:25 (2:25) (Class 3) (0-135,132) 4-Y-O+ **£4,182** (£1,235; £617; £308; £154)

Form RPR

1001 **1** **Golden Chieftain (IRE)**[34] 4094 6-11-9 **129**......................... JoeTizzard 138+
(Colin Tizzard) *sn trcking ldrs: drvn to ld 2 out: clr last: pushed out* **9/1**

4223 **2** *6* **Basford Bob (IRE)**[22] 4332 6-10-12 **118**.............................. AlanO'Keeffe 122+
(Jennie Candlish) *hld up in rr: mstke 6th: gd hdwy appr 2 out: chsd wnr appr last: styd on same pce* **8/1**[3]

2PP4 **3** *1* **Pavillon Bleu (FR)**[28] 4220 8-11-0 **120**................................ TomO'Brien 121
(Philip Hobbs) *chsd ldrs: one pce fr 2 out* **16/1**

-230 **4** *shd* **Sir Kezbaah (IRE)**[28] 4209 7-11-5 **125**.............................. FelixDeGiles 126
(Jeremy Scott) *chsd ldrs: drvn 7th: outpcd 2 out: 6th last: styd on wl* **10/1**

55 **5** *1 ¼* **Barbatos (FR)**[45] 3877 5-10-6 **112**.............................. TomScudamore 113
(Ian Williams) *trckd ldrs: wknd last* **5/2**[1]

5-06 **6** *2 ¼* **Red Harbour (IRE)**[70] 3452 7-11-7 **127**.. RWalsh 126
(Paul Nicholls) *hld up: stdy hdwy 3 out: chsng ldrs next: sn drvn: wknd appr last* **7/2**[2]

/034 **7** *6* **Burnt Oak (UAE)**[37] 4025 9-10-9 **115**.............................. WilsonRenwick 107
(Chris Fairhurst) *in rr: bhd whn sltly hmpd 3 out: nvr on terms* **16/1**

-011 **8** *3 ½* **Reindeer Dippin**[21] 4358 9-11-5 **132**................................ HenryBrooke(7) 122
(Donald McCain) *t.k.h: w ldrs: led appr 3rd: hdd 2 out: sn wknd* **10/1**

2F31 **9** *17* **Naughty Naughty**[23] 4309 6-11-8 **128**.. APMcCoy 102
(Brendan Powell) *in rr: hdwy 6th: pushed along next: sn lost pl: t.o last* **10/1**

3012 **10** *2* **Devotion To Duty (IRE)**[17] 4420 5-11-5 **125**................. PeterBuchanan 97
(Lucinda Russell) *led tl appr 3rd: chsd ldrs: lost pl appr 2 out: sn bhd* **12/1**

0650 **F** **Quickbeam (IRE)**[24] 4285 9-11-9 **129**.............................. AidanColeman —
(Venetia Williams) *chsd ldrs: drvn 7th: lost pl and fell 3 out* **33/1**

5m 18.6s (-12.30) **Going Correction** -0.275s/f (Good) **11** Ran SP% **121.6**
Speed ratings (Par 107): **110,107,107,107,107 106,104,103,97,96 —**
toteswingers: 1&2 £18.90, 1&3 £32.40, 2&3 £39.80. CSF £81.86 CT £1153.99 TOTE £11.50: £3.00, £2.80, £5.50; EX 117.30 TRIFECTA Not won..
Owner Brocade Racing **Bred** Robert Donaldson **Trained** Milborne Port, Dorset

FOCUS
A decent handicap, run at an average gallop. Another step from the winner and improvement from the second too, with the next pair close to their marks.

NOTEBOOK
Golden Chieftain(IRE) confirmed himself a fast-improving 6-y-o with a taking display to follow up his win at Exeter last month. He looked high enough in the weights for this handicap debut, but travelled like a decent horse throughout and powered clear when asked to win the race. Evidently this much sounder surface was to his liking and, although the handicapper will now have his say, there could well be more to come. One could see him taking high rank over fences next season. (tchd 11-1)
Basford Bob(IRE), up in trip for his handicap debut, came from well off the pace and looked a brief threat to the winner between the final two flights. He wasn't clever at the last but the bird had flown and, for all that he is consistent, he is hard to win with.
Pavillon Bleu(FR) turned in a sound enough effort, but continues to look held by the handicapper.
Sir Kezbaah(IRE) got markedly outpaced before staying on again late and needs a stiffer test on this sort of ground.
Barbatos(FR) looked to have begun life in handicaps on a potentially lenient mark. He once again paid for running too enthusiastically, though. (op 11-4 tchd 7-2)
Red Harbour(IRE) had the assistance of Ruby Walsh for the first time since just getting up in the EBF Final at Sandown as a novice in this month last year. He travelled smoothly into contention, but his response when asked for an effort was very one paced and he's become disappointing. (op 9-2)

Devotion To Duty(IRE) Official explanation: jockey said gelding had a breathing problem

4876 TOTESPORT.COM MIDLANDS GRAND NATIONAL CHASE (H'CAP) (LISTED RACE) (22 fncs 2 omitted) 4m 1f 110y
3:00 (3:02) (Class 1) 5-Y-0+ £41,770 (£16,124; £8,434; £4,568)

Form RPR

-42P **1** **Minella Four Star (IRE)**[14] 4466 8-9-9 **133** oh5 CO'Farrell(5) 149+
(David Pipe) *chsd ldrs: led bef 4 out: styd on wl* **25/1**

4452 **2** *11* **Ballyfitz**[28] 4208 11-10-0 **133** oh2 (p) DavidEngland 137
(Nigel Twiston-Davies) *dropped to rr 4th: hdwy 6 out: styd on wl fr 2 out: tk modest 3rd last: kpt on wl to take 2nd towards fin* **16/1**

-561 **3** *1* **Synchronised (IRE)**[70] 3437 8-11-12 **159** APMcCoy 162
(Jonjo O'Neill) *mid-div: dropped to rr 11th: hdwy 6 out: chsd wnr 2 out: kpt on same pce: lost 2nd towards fin* **9/2**[1]

1-PP **4** *13* **Gentle Ranger (IRE)**[126] 2358 9-10-0 **133** (tp) TomScudamore 127
(David Pipe) *chsd ldr: wknd 3 out: lft poor 4th last* **16/1**

6334 **P** **Ma Yahab**[14] 4486 10-10-0 **133** oh14 (b) RodiGreene —
(Venetia Williams) *in rr: t.o 15th: p.u bef 6 out* **40/1**

0/ **P** **Noble Concorde**[13] 4516 9-9-9 **133** oh7 (p) MrRMahon(5) —
(J H Culloty, Ire) *chsd ldrs: wknd 5 out: t.o whn p.u bef 2 out* **20/1**

P-32 **P** **Halcon Genelardais (FR)**[28] 4211 11-10-0 **133** oh5 RobertThornton —
(Alan King) *in rr: reminders after 1st: sn drvn along: bhd fr 15th: t.o whn p.u bef 15th* **7/1**[3]

-P61 **P** **Companero (IRE)**[21] 4360 11-10-8 **141** (b) PeterBuchanan —
(Howard Johnson) *chsd ldrs: lost pl 5th: mstke 9th: t.o 11th: p.u bef 16th* **25/1**

120- **P** **Toby Jug**[476] 2576 10-10-2 **135** (b) JackDoyle —
(Sarah Humphrey) *bhd fr 13th: t.o whn p.u bef 11th* **20/1**

2043 **P** **Le Beau Bai (FR)**[28] 4208 8-9-9 **135** JakeGreenall(7) —
(Richard Lee) *bhd whn blnd 3rd: t.o 15th: p.u bef next* **10/1**

1FF3 **R** **Triggerman**[42] 3940 9-10-0 **133** oh1 TomO'Brien 131
(Philip Hobbs) *hdwy to chse ldrs 11th: wnt 2nd 3 out: 4th and wkng whn ref last* **10/1**

P31P **P** **Nicto De Beauchene (FR)**[28] 4208 10-10-4 **137** (p) DenisO'Regan —
(Victor Dartnall) *led: hdd bef 4 out: wknd and bhd whn p.u bef 2 out* **16/1**

-413 **P** **Alfie Sherrin**[35] 4080 8-10-6 **139** RichieMcLernon —
(Jonjo O'Neill) *in rr: bhd fr 10th: t.o whn p.u bef 16th* **12/1**

2-1P **P** **Belon Gale (IRE)**[21] 4360 8-10-4 **137** WilsonRenwick —
(Howard Johnson) *in rr: reminders 5th: bhd whn blnd 9th: t.o whn p.u bef 11th* **28/1**

F233 **P** **Bench Warrent (IRE)**[22] 4333 8-9-11 **133** oh4 (p) PeterToole(3) —
(Charlie Mann) *in rr: bhd fr 15th: t.o whn p.u bef 2 out* **14/1**

0-P5 **F** **Tricky Trickster (IRE)**[29] 4189 8-10-13 **146** RWalsh —
(Paul Nicholls) *mid-div: fell 2nd* **13/2**[2]

-5P1 **R** **Qhilimar (FR)**[29] 4193 7-10-0 **133** oh6 (p) AndrewTinkler —
(Charlie Longsdon) *chsd ldrs: lost pl 6 out: in rr whn ref next* **10/1**

8m 39.5s (-20.50) **Going Correction** -0.275s/f (Good) **17** Ran SP% **126.4**
Speed ratings: **113,110,110,107,—,—,—,—,—,—,—,—,—,—,—,—,—**
toteswingers: 1&2 £114.70, 1&3 £67.30, 2&3 £17.60. CSF £358.67 CT £2152.55 TOTE £28.70: £6.00, £3.50, £2.00, £4.50; EX 366.40 Trifecta £6162.00 Pool: £177,367.75 - 21.30 winning units..
Owner Ashton Racing Club **Bred** Clare A Kehoe **Trained** Nicholashayne, Devon

FOCUS
The second fence in the back straight was bypassed on the last two circuits because of a stricken horse. Drying ground made this season's Midlands National a complicated affair. The participation of last year's winner also ensured that eight ran from out of the handicap and there was a strong gallop on, which dictated it was again a thorough test. Only four finished this time, compared to just three last season, and it paid to race handily. Minella Four Star is rated up 11lb on his previous best, with Ballyfitz to the level of his recent form and Synchronised 3lb off his best.

NOTEBOOK
Minella Four Star(IRE) bounced back to form and ran out a brave winner. He was going backwards prior to pulling up in the Grimthorpe Chase on his previous outing, when well fancied, and therefore had plenty to prove. A sound surface has always been to his liking, though, and he showed he stays all day when winning over 3m4f two seasons ago. He hardly put a foot wrong at his fences and, despite being 5lb out of the weights, Conor O'Farrell's claim negated that. Surprisingly it was just the jockey's second ever winner over fences. He will now take a hike up the handicap, but that will help him get into the better marathon handicaps and he could be just the type for the Grand National next season.
Ballyfitz finished a well-held second at Haydock on heavy ground last month. He went in snatches, but was staying on dourly late on and is clearly back in decent heart. This pays a compliment to Grand National hopeful Silver By Nature, who beat him easily last time out. (tchd 20-1)
Synchronised(IRE) was having just his second outing over fences since taking the race on desperate ground last term and a 9lb rise for winning the Welsh National took him to a 16lb higher mark for his repeat bid. He was very well backed earlier in the day, but the drying surface was a big concern and it no doubt cost him a follow-up success. He looked like he may pull up when getting so far behind from halfway, but he showed tremendous courage to get back into contention from five out and emerges with a lot of credit. (op 5-1)
Gentle Ranger(IRE) beat his winning stablemate over 3m4f at Cheltenham last April and was 3lb better off, but had been pulled up in two previous runs this term. The ground suited him, though, and he showed his true colours again with a solid effort in defeat. (op 14-1)
Halcon Genelardais(FR) would have preferred softer ground and was beaten from a very early stage. He may well now head off for an honourable retirement. (op 8-1 tchd 6-1)
Le Beau Bai(FR) is another mud-lover and this ground was against him. (op 8-1 tchd 6-1)
Triggerman went well for a long way, but stamina deserted him in the home straight and he cried enough at the last. (op 8-1 tchd 6-1)
Alfie Sherrin looked on a workable mark for his handicap debut as a chaser. He was easy to back and beaten way before stamina became an issue, though. (op 8-1 tchd 6-1)
Tricky Trickster(IRE) was heavily backed despite arriving for this return to chasing looking out of sorts. He got no further than the second fence, however, and took some time to get up to his feet. He was found to have suffered a hairline fracture of the neck and his future is in doubt. (op 8-1 tchd 6-1)

4877 BET ON TODAY'S FOOTBALL AT TOTESPORT.COM NOVICES' H'CAP CHASE (17 fncs 1 omitted) 3m
3:35 (3:35) (Class 3) (0-135,130) 5-Y-0+ £4,731 (£1,516; £842)

Form RPR

3431 **1** **Stoney's Treasure**[22] 4334 7-11-3 **121** RobertThornton 134+
(Alan King) *trckd ldrs: lft cl 2nd 12th: led after 14th: drew clr fr 3 out: eased towards fin* **5/1**[3]

2260 **2** *12* **In The Zone (IRE)**[14] 4490 7-10-13 **117** RichieMcLernon 118
(Jonjo O'Neill) *trckd ldrs: chsd wnr fr bef 4 out: no imp* **14/1**

214U **3** *3 3/4* **Misstree Dancer**[28] 4210 7-11-9 **127** HarrySkelton 126
(Nick Mitchell) *chsd ldrs: blnd 12th: 3rd and drvn next: one pce fr 3 out* **12/1**

0143 **P** **Maraafeq (USA)**[16] 4438 7-11-1 **119** SamThomas —
(Venetia Williams) *chsd ldrs: lost pl and reminders after 6th: t.o 9th: p.u bef 11th* **14/1**

5U12 **P** **Predictive (FR)**[27] 4244 8-11-12 **130** JasonMaguire —
(Donald McCain) *mde most tl after 14th: 4th and wkng whn p.u bef 3 out* **6/1**

-241 **U** **Cottage Acre (IRE)**[14] 4490 8-11-5 **123** PaddyBrennan —
(Tom George) *prom: blnd 1st and 7th: outpcd and in rr whn stmbld landing and uns rdr 12th* **4/1**[1]

6012 **F** **Sarando**[20] 4371 6-11-12 **130** (tp) WillKennedy —
(Paul Webber) *w ldr: stmbld landing and fell 12th* **12/1**

5-1P **P** **Zarrafakt (IRE)**[114] 2629 7-11-10 **128** JackDoyle —
(Emma Lavelle) *j.rt in rr: bhd fr 13th: distant 5th whn p.u bef 2 out* **11/2**

4111 **P** **Honourable Arthur (IRE)**[23] 4313 8-11-3 **121** (p) DenisO'Regan —
(Victor Dartnall) *towards rr: bhd fr 13th: poor distant 4th whn p.u bef 2 out* **9/2**[2]

P **P** **Sprint De Ferbet (FR)**[21] 4355 5-11-0 **119** AndrewTinkler —
(Nicky Henderson) *chsd ldrs: drvn 10th: blnd next: bhd whn p.u bef 12th* **33/1**

6m 14.8s (-0.30) **Going Correction** -0.275s/f (Good)
WFA 5 from 6yo+ 1lb **10** Ran SP% **116.2**
Speed ratings: **89,85,83,—,—,—,—,—,—,—**
toteswingers: 1&2 £131.10, 1&3 £13.80, 2&3 £17.40. CSF £69.13 CT £798.16 TOTE £6.40: £1.90, £2.90, £3.10; EX 92.50 Trifecta £685.00 Part won. Pool: £925.79 - 0.60 winning units..
Owner Mrs S C Welch **Bred** Mrs S C Welch **Trained** Barbury Castle, Wilts

FOCUS
The fourth-last fence was omitted; damaged. This looked to be a competitive novice handicap, but only three got home. The fourth-last fence was bypassed. Another step up from the easy winner with the second to his mark.

NOTEBOOK
Stoney's Treasure ◆ a peach of a ride at Warwick last month and that experience had clearly boosted his confidence as he followed up in great style on this return to handicap company. He was raised to a 9lb higher mark for this, but the better ground was right up his street and he jumped superbly at times, especially over the third and second-last fences. The step up to 3m has been the making of him and he could well bag a decent handicap down the line, perhaps even if heading to Aintree's Grand National meeting next month. (tchd 11-2)
In The Zone(IRE) ◆ travelled sweetly and looked the only real danger to the winner turning for home. He came under pressure nearing three out, however, and it looked to be a case of stamina limitations with him. He's one to look out for when reverting to a slightly sharper test.
Misstree Dancer, well held when unseating at the last on her previous outing, posted a solid effort in defeat back up in trip. She ideally seems to want easier ground and is open to a little improvement over fences. (tchd 11-1)
Maraafeq(USA) Official explanation: jockey said gelding never travelled (tchd 11-2)
Predictive(FR) knows all about this track and gave his all, but was probably found out by the livelier ground. Official explanation: jockey said gelding lost its action (tchd 11-2)
Cottage Acre(IRE) was hiked up 15lb for winning easily on his chase debut at Newbury a fortnight earlier. His jumping was decent that day, but it badly let him down on this step back up in trip. He came to grief when hampered after the 12th by Sarando. (tchd 11-2)
Sarando was still going okay prior to meeting the 12th all wrong. (tchd 11-2)
Zarrafakt(IRE), returning from a 114-day break, jumped far too deliberately early on and looked to need the run. Official explanation: jockey said gelding never travelled (tchd 11-2)
Honourable Arthur(IRE) was another 8lb higher in his quest for the hat-trick and was beaten soon after feeling the pinch around the 12th fence. (tchd 11-2)

4878 TOTEPOOL FLEXI BETTING NOVICES' H'CAP HURDLE (10 hdls 2 omitted) 2m 4f 110y
4:10 (4:10) (Class 5) (0-95,95) 4-Y-0+ £2,211 (£649; £324; £162)

Form RPR

-006 **1** **Well Refreshed**[22] 4332 7-11-9 **92** SamThomas 100+
(Peter Winkworth) *hld up in rr: blnd 7th: gd hdwy next: upsides last: sn led: drvn out* **6/1**[3]

20P1 **2** *3* **Rossbrin (IRE)**[23] 4314 6-11-4 **87** (t) AndrewTinkler 93+
(Anna Brooks) *trckd ldrs: led appr 3 out: hit 2 out: jnd last: sn hdd: styd on same pce* **9/4**[1]

0/00 **3** *18* **Westwire Toby (IRE)**[27] 4233 9-10-6 **75** WillKennedy 63
(Lynn Siddall) *in rr: styd on fr 3 out: tk modest 3rd sn after last* **33/1**

/00- **4** *4* **A Bid Too Far (IRE)**[420] 3615 7-11-8 **91** (t) AndrewThornton 77
(Lawney Hill) *chsd ldrs: led after 6th: hdd appr 3 out: wknd between last 2: lost modest 3rd run-in* **6/1**[3]

431F **5** *11* **Royal Chatelier (FR)**[26] 4263 6-11-10 **93** DenisO'Regan 68
(Michael Blake) *towards rr: reminders 5th: bhd fr 3 out* **5/1**[2]

P0P **6** *12* **Young Firth**[26] 4253 4-10-1 **78** (p) RodiGreene 34
(John Norton) *chsd ldrs: 4th whn blnd 3 out: sn wknd* **33/1**

020 **7** *14* **Mater Mater**[23] 4309 4-11-4 **95** TomMessenger 38
(Caroline Bailey) *prom: lost pl 7th: hit next: sn bhd: t.o 2 out* **20/1**

00P0 **8** *shd* **Oscar The Myth (IRE)**[25] 4268 5-11-3 **91** MrRMahon(5) 42
(Jamie Snowden) *chsd ldrs: lost pl and mstke 6th: wknd next: t.o 2 out* **14/1**

-P6P **P** **Direct Approach (IRE)**[11] 4545 7-11-0 **83** (t) JasonMaguire —
(Lynn Siddall) *chsd ldrs: wknd qckly 3 out: t.o last whn p.u bef last* **22/1**

0600 **P** **Takamaru (FR)**[37] 4034 5-11-12 **95** (b) TomScudamore —
(David Pipe) *led: reminders 5th: hdd after next: sn lost pl: t.o whn p.u bef 2 out* **6/1**[3]

001P **P** **Baggsy (IRE)**[43] 3484 4-10-13 **93** LeeEdwards(3) —
(Patrick Clinton) *in rr: drvn 5th: bhd fr 7th: t.o 2 out: sn p.u* **14/1**

4m 59.2s (-4.80) **Going Correction** -0.275s/f (Good)
WFA 4 from 5yo+ 8lb **11** Ran SP% **118.6**
Speed ratings (Par 103): **98,96,90,88,84 79,74,74,—,—,—**
toteswingers: 1&2 £2.40, 1&3 £93.00, 2&3 £58.70. CSF £19.70 CT £413.33 TOTE £7.20: £2.40, £1.40, £10.20; EX 27.70.
Owner P Winkworth **Bred** N H Bloodstock Ltd **Trained** Chiddingfold, Surrey

FOCUS
A weak novice handicap and the first two, both well backed, came clear from two out. The winner improved to the level of his bumper form, and the second stepped up too.

NOTEBOOK
Well Refreshed got a confident ride and scored readily, opening his account at the seventh time of asking. He showed ability in bumpers, but had been well beaten in three novice hurdles since resuming this year. It was his handicap debut, however, and the quicker ground was clearly more to his liking. He doesn't have many miles on the clock and could improve a bit further. Official explanation: trainer's rep said, regarding apparent improvement in form, that the gelding's jumping had improved on the better ground. (op 9-2)
Rossbrin(IRE) made a bold bid to follow up his win on soft ground at Huntingdon last month off a 6lb higher mark. He travelled sweetly under a prominent ride and made the winner work, but looked to be getting the worst of the argument prior to meeting the last wrong. He rates the benchmark. (op 11-4)
Westwire Toby(IRE) was never a threat and plugged on at his own pace from out the back, but this was more encouraging on his handicap debut.

A Bid Too Far(IRE) showed little for his previous stable and was returning from a 420-day layoff. It was his debut for a trainer known for improving horses, however, and he went really well until fitness became an issue in the home straight. He should be capable of finding a race. (op 7-1 tchd 11-2)

4879 BET TOTEPOOL AT TOTESPORT.COM STANDARD OPEN NATIONAL HUNT FLAT RACE (DIV I) 2m
4:45 (4:46) (Class 6) 4-6-Y-O **£1,821** (£534; £267; £133)

Form				RPR
2	1		**Ambion Wood (IRE)**[22] 4329 5-11-3 0 DenisO'Regan (Victor Dartnall) *hld up in mid-div: smooth hdwy 4f out: led on bit over 2f out: shkn up and styd on wl: readily* **3/1**[1]	112+
0	2	5	**Slightly Hot**[35] 4082 5-11-3 0 TomO'Brien (Joanna Davis) *hld up towards rr: hdwy 4f out: styd on to take 2nd last 150yds* **25/1**	104
301	3	6	**What A Warrior (IRE)**[35] 4082 4-11-3 0 PaddyBrennan (Nigel Twiston-Davies) *led: hdd over 2f out: kpt on one pce fnl f* **11/2**	98
42S	4	shd	**Howard's Legacy (IRE)**[10] 4561 5-11-3 0 SamThomas (Venetia Williams) *w ldrs: wnt 2nd over 1f out: kpt on same pce* **7/2**[2]	98
	5	3/4	**Fox Appeal (IRE)** 4-10-10 0 JackDoyle (Emma Lavelle) *chsd ldrs: one pce fnl 3f* **8/1**	90
	6	14	**Halucha (IRE)**[300] 6-11-3 0 WillKennedy (Paul Webber) *in rr: hdwy to chse ldrs 7f out: wknd 2f out* **25/1**	85
	7	7	**Karrical** 6-11-3 0 JasonMaguire (Donald McCain) *trckd ldrs: t.k.h: wknd over 2f out* **12/1**	78
4	8	15	**Time Do (FR)**[50] 3794 4-10-7 0 IanPopham(3) (Caroline Keevil) *prom: lost pl 6f out* **33/1**	58
	9	13	**Sedano (FR)** 5-11-3 0 RobertThornton (Alan King) *in rr: drvn and sme hdwy 6f out: lost pl over 3f out* **4/1**[3]	53
	10	1 1/4	**Empress Chang (IRE)** 4-10-0 0 PeterToole(3) (Christopher Kellett) *chsd ldrs: lost pl 5f out* **50/1**	38
3	P		**Gizzit (IRE)**[48] 3842 5-11-3 0 AndrewThornton (Karen George) *t.k.h in mid-div: lost pl 7f out: sn bhd: t.o whn p.u over 2f out* **14/1**	—
	P		**Diesel Tom** 5-10-10 0 KyleJames(7) (Michael Appleby) *in rr: drvn after 6f: sn bhd: t.o 6f out: p.u over 2f out* **25/1**	—

3m 46.1s (-3.50) **Going Correction** -0.275s/f (Good)
WFA 4 from 5yo+ 7lb 12 Ran SP% 124.5
Speed ratings: **97,94,91,91,91 84,80,73,66,65 —,—**
toteswingers: 1&2 £24.70, 1&3 £2.00, 2&3 £32.40. CSF £90.46 TOTE £4.50: £2.10, £4.90, £1.30; EX 156.00.
Owner O C R Wynne & Mrs S J Wynne **Bred** Michael O'Dwyer **Trained** Brayford, Devon

FOCUS
This has been won by decent sorts and the impressive Ambion Wood looks like being another one. He can rate higher.

NOTEBOOK
Ambion Wood(IRE) ◆ ran distinctly green on his debut at Sandown 22 days earlier and was again green to post here, but the previous experience had clearly taught him plenty as he raced more professionally. He had something to prove on the different ground, but is half-brother to a good-to-firm winner and evidently versatile on that front. There was an awful lot to like about the manner in which he completed the task and won with any amount in hand. Indeed, he looks sure to come on again for this outing and has plenty of scope, so rates an exciting prospect. The Grade 2 bumper at Aintree on Grand National day next month would look a viable target. (op 4-1 tchd 9-2)
Slightly Hot stepped up markedly on the level of his debut seventh at Warwick and enjoyed this stiffer test. He ought to come on again and will get further over hurdles. (op 20-1)
What A Warrior(IRE) had the runner-up well behind when off the mark at Warwick last month. He again set out to make all, but hit a flat spot 3f out and was well held under his penalty.
Howard's Legacy(IRE) slipped up when favourite on his third outing at Fontwell ten days earlier. He held every chance, but was firmly put in his place by the winner and may have found the ground lively enough. (op 4-1)
Fox Appeal(IRE), half-brother to a bumper winner, showed ability and should learn a good deal for the initial experience.
Sedano(FR) is related to a French bumper winner and one over hurdles. The debut outing seemed badly needed. (op 5-1)

4880 BET TOTEPOOL ON 0800 221 221 H'CAP CHASE (14 fncs 2 omitted) 2m 5f
5:20 (5:20) (Class 4) (0-105,106) 5-Y-O+ **£2,862** (£840; £420; £209)

Form				RPR
0U31	1		**Nomadic Warrior**[27] 4237 6-11-9 **102** DavidEngland (John Holt) *in tch: hdwy to trck ldrs 9th: chal 2 out: edgd lft: led last: styd on wl* **5/1**[2]	110
FPF5	2	2 3/4	**Investment Affair (IRE)**[10] 4560 11-10-2 **81** oh6 ow2 JackDoyle (Sarah Humphrey) *sn trcking ldrs: led 3 out: crowded between last 2: hdd last: kpt on same pce* **16/1**	87
5-P2	3	48	**Mrs Fawlty (IRE)**[20] 4381 8-11-10 **103** (t) JasonMaguire (Jim Old) *w ldr: led passing omitted 4 out: hdd 3 out: wknd qckly next* **7/1**[3]	65
-4P0	4	75	**Quick Fix (IRE)**[31] 4142 9-11-7 **100** (tp) AndrewThornton (Susan Nock) *led: hdd passing omitted 4 out: sn wknd: t.o 2 out* **14/1**	—
00P5	P		**Osolomio (IRE)**[18] 4412 8-11-2 **95** AlanO'Keeffe (Jennie Candlish) *in last: blnd 2nd: sltly hmpd 8th: sn bhd: t.o whn p.u bef 3 out* **8/1**	—
6641	F		**Valley View (IRE)**[46] 3869 5-11-13 **106** APMcCoy (Jonjo O'Neill) *hld up towards rr: t.k.h: hit 4th: hdwy to trck ldrs whn fell 8th* **4/6**[1]	—

5m 31.0s (7.50) **Going Correction** -0.275s/f (Good) 6 Ran SP% 112.8
Speed ratings: **74,72,54,26,— —**
toteswingers: 1&2 £11.00, 1&3 £3.50, 2&3 £19.60. CSF £61.11 TOTE £5.80: £2.20, £6.10; EX 67.90.
Owner Ms Carol Lacey **Bred** C Lacey **Trained** Peckleton, Leics
■ Stewards' Enquiry : David England caution: careless riding.

FOCUS
The fourth-last fence was omitted; damaged. A moderate little handicap, run at an average gallop. The fourth-last fence was again omitted. The winner is improving as he steps up in distance.

NOTEBOOK
Nomadic Warrior finally got off the mark at Market Rasen 27 days previously and he followed up with a gutsy effort off a 7lb higher mark. He was faced with quicker ground here and had stamina to prove, but the better surface helped him see it out. He's progressive and still only a 6-y-o, so should go close in his quest for the hat-trick despite another likely rise. (op 11-2)
Investment Affair(IRE), who was effectively 8lb 'wrong', looked for a long way in the home straight as though he was eventually going to end his long losing run. He got outstayed by the winner from the last, but this was much better from him and he is currently very well handicapped on his previous best efforts. (tchd 18-1)
Mrs Fawlty(IRE) wasn't always fluent and probably found the ground quicker than she cares for. (op 6-1 tchd 5-1)
Quick Fix(IRE) raced enthusiastically out in front and was a spent force at the top of the home straight. (op 10-1)
Valley View(IRE) had the winner back in third when landing some hefty bets on his handicap and chasing debut at Folkestone 46 days earlier and was again heavily backed despite being 10lb higher. He proved a bit free here and hadn't convinced with his jumping prior to guessing at the eighth and coming down. (op 5-6 tchd Evens in places)

4881 BET TOTEPOOL AT TOTESPORT.COM STANDARD OPEN NATIONAL HUNT FLAT RACE (DIV II) 2m
5:50 (5:50) (Class 6) 4-6-Y-O **£1,821** (£534; £267; £133)

Form				RPR
	1		**Denali Highway (IRE)** 4-10-10 0 RobertThornton (Alan King) *trckd ldrs: effrt over 2f out: styd on strly to ld last 100yds* **5/1**[3]	92+
2	2	1 1/4	**Grand Vision (IRE)**[51] 3766 5-11-3 0 JoeTizzard (Colin Tizzard) *trckd ldrs: t.k.h: led 3f out: hdd ins fnl f: no ex* **9/4**[1]	98+
	3	2	**La Belle Sauvage** 4-10-3 0 HarrySkelton (Venetia Williams) *w ldrs: kpt on to r upsides 1f out: kpt on same pce* **4/1**[2]	82+
1	4	4	**Eastlake (IRE)**[163] 1749 5-11-10 0 APMcCoy (Jonjo O'Neill) *trckd ldrs: effrt 3f out: wknd over 1f out* **4/1**[2]	99
0	5	3/4	**Pentopyn Harry**[161] 1778 5-11-3 0 AndrewTinkler (Tony Newcombe) *w ldr: wknd over 1f out* **40/1**	91
5-0	6	3 3/4	**Swains Meadow**[34] 4097 6-10-10 0 JohnnyFarrelly (Kevin Bishop) *hld up: hdwy to trck ldrs 7f out: effrt over 2f out: wknd over 1f out* **40/1**	81
0-4	7	2	**Todareistodo**[117] 2576 5-11-3 0 JasonMaguire (Jim Old) *hld up in rr: hdwy 4f out: outpcd over 2f out* **28/1**	86
	8	3/4	**Barton Felix** 4-10-10 0 PaddyBrennan (Neil Mulholland) *in rr: drvn 4f out: lost pl over 2f out* **10/1**	78
0	9	1 1/4	**Praefectus (IRE)**[44] 3909 5-11-3 0 (t) TomScudamore (David Pipe) *t.k.h in rr: drvn and lost pl over 2f out* **20/1**	84
	10	4 1/2	**Best Start** 5-11-0 0 TommyPhelan(3) (Claire Dyson) *led: drvn over 4f out: hdd 3f out: wknd 2f out* **20/1**	79
	11	2	**Lady Treacle (IRE)** 5-10-10 0 AndrewThornton (Caroline Bailey) *mid-div: outpcd over 3f out: lost pl over 2f out* **14/1**	70

4m 4.70s (15.10) **Going Correction** -0.275s/f (Good)
WFA 4 from 5yo+ 7lb 11 Ran SP% 121.0
Speed ratings: **51,50,49,47,47 45,44,43,43,40 39**
toteswingers: 1&2 £5.10, 1&3 £2.60, 2&3 £2.40 CSF £16.11 TOTE £6.80: £2.20, £1.40, £1.90; EX 19.60.
Owner Ian Payne & Kim Franklin **Bred** Desmond Amond **Trained** Barbury Castle, Wilts

FOCUS
The second division of the bumper and it was run at a steady gallop and in a slow time compared with the other division. The form still looks sound enough and the first three can rate higher.

NOTEBOOK
Denali Highway(IRE), whose stable won the second division of this race last season, dug deep under maximum pressure late on and made a winning debut. He is bred to appreciate further over jumps so it wasn't surprising to see him get outpaced due to the way the race was run. His attitude was spot on when it mattered, though, and he won with a little in hand. (op 13-2)
Grand Vision(IRE) ◆ was undone by a lack of pace on his debut on soft ground at Ffos Las 51 days earlier and has since changed hands for £75,000. He was again faced with a steady gallop here, but travelled best of all into the home straight. He probably just found himself in front too soon, however, as he was mugged late on by the winner. There is no doubt one of these in him granted more of a test. (tchd 5-2)
La Belle Sauvage, the third foal of Lady Rebecca, was well backed and held every chance. She ran green in the home straight and ought to sharpen up for the experience. (op 5-1 tchd 11-2)
Eastlake(IRE) was penalised for his debut success at Worcester in October. He got outpaced in the home straight and is sure to enjoy a stiffer test when sent hurdling. He rates the benchmark. (op 7-2)
T/Jkpt: Not won. T/Plt: £321.60 to a £1 stake. Pool:£214,994.70 - 487.97 winning tickets. T/Qpdt: £46.20 to a £1 stake. Pool:£12,298.99 - 196.84 winning tickets. WG

4882 - 4888a (Foreign Racing) - See Raceform Interactive

4568 CARLISLE (R-H)
Sunday, March 20

OFFICIAL GOING: Soft (heavy in places; 5.7)
New stable bend rail moved out 3yds; old stable bend moved in 4yds. Middle fence in back straight omitted; first flight of hurdles in back straight omitted.
Wind: Breezy, half against Weather: Dull

4889 FAMILY FESTIVAL 2ND JULY NOVICES' HURDLE (9 hdls 2 omitted) 2m 4f
2:30 (2:31) (Class 4) 4-Y-O+ **£2,226** (£649; £324)

Form				RPR
0-U3	1		**Hawaii Klass**[22] 4359 6-11-1 0 WilsonRenwick (Donald Whillans) *prom: pushed along bef 2 out: swtchd rt to avoid loose horse and led last: rdn out run-in* **14/1**	104+
040	2	2 1/4	**Sir Tamburlane (IRE)**[15] 4467 6-11-1 0 HenryOliver (Sue Smith) *chsd ldr: effrt and ev ch bef 3 out: drvn next: styd on fr last: nt rch wnr* **12/1**	103+
2/12	3	1 3/4	**Jimmy The Saint (IRE)**[18] 4422 8-11-7 119 JasonMaguire (Donald McCain) *t.k.h early: led: nt fluent 3rd: hmpd by loose horse bnd after 5th: hdd briefly 3 out: hdd last: kpt on same pce u.p* **8/13**[1]	109+
2-66	4	nse	**Classical Mist**[16] 4454 7-10-8 0 GrahamLee (David O'Meara) *hld up towards rr: hdwy and prom 4 out: effrt and carried rt bef 2 out: one pce run-in* **22/1**	92
	5	6	**Mia's Vic (IRE)**[7] 4761 6-10-8 0 MrDRFox(7) (Noel C Kelly, Ire) *hld up in midfield: hdwy on outside to ld briefly whn carried lft by loose horse after 3 out: hung rt bef next: sn one pce* **9/2**[2]	95
3	6	1 1/2	**Dancing Art (IRE)**[22] 4363 5-11-1 0 JamesReveley (Keith Reveley) *trckd ldrs: rdn bef 2 out: sn outpcd: n.d after* **8/1**[3]	93
60-P	7	34	**Loch Dhu (IRE)**[11] 4552 7-10-5 0 EwanWhillans(3) (Alistair Whillans) *t.k.h: hld up: shortlived effrt after 4 out: wknd fr next* **100/1**	50
6	8	3/4	**The Dagda (IRE)**[10] 4569 7-10-12 0 HarryHaynes(3) (Kevin Hunter) *bhd: rdn 4 out: sn struggling* **80/1**	56
	9	2 1/2	**Grey Locker** 8-10-8 0 TomSiddall (Lynn Siddall) *a bhd: struggling 1/2-way: nvr on terms* **125/1**	46
	10	17	**Monty's Brig**[1142] 10-11-1 0 PeterBuchanan (Jane Clark) *hld up: rdn after 4 out: wknd bef next* **80/1**	36
6P	11	14	**No Way Hozay**[10] 4569 5-11-1 0 (t) BrianHughes (Brian Storey) *prom: stdy hdwy after 5th: wknd after next: t.o* **100/1**	22

P U **Tipsy Nipper**[39] 4000 6-10-8 0 CampbellGillies —
(William Amos) *in tch on outside: j.lft: sddle slipped and uns rdr 2nd* **100/1**

5m 26.1s (3.30) **Going Correction** +0.35s/f (Yiel) **12** Ran SP% **116.2**
Speed ratings (Par 105): **107,106,105,105,102 102,88,88,87,80 75,—**
Tote Swingers: 1&2 £19.50, 1&3 £2.80, 2&3 £3.10 CSF £154.66 TOTE £20.50: £3.50, £3.20, £1.02; EX 220.70.

Owner Allan Gilchrist **Bred** Allan Gilchrist **Trained** Hawick, Borders

FOCUS
An ordinary novice hurdle, run at an average gallop. The loose horse pestered the leaders from four out and that caused for something of a messy finish. A step up from the winner.

NOTEBOOK
Hawaii Klass stepped up markedly on previous efforts and ran out a gutsy winner to shed his maiden tag at the sixth time of asking. He came under pressure a fair way out but kept battling under pressure and clearly stays well. (tchd 16-1)
Sir Tamburlane(IRE) was always up there and he too evidently stays well, indeed he probably wants a stiffer test. He can build on this. (op 14-1)
Jimmy The Saint(IRE) proved all the rage to resume winning ways. He set out to make all at an ordinary tempo, but it's not hard to see why he sports a crossed noseband as he took a keen hold. He also tried to run out around the paddock bend and his rider did well to hold onto him there. He jumped the last with the winner, but early exertions took a toll and he was well held under his penalty. (op 4-6 tchd 4-7)
Classical Mist proved friendless in the betting, but this was his best effort to date over hurdles and more in keeping with his bumper form. He should be winning when faced with a sounder surface and now qualifies for a mark. (op 16-1)
Mia's Vic(IRE) didn't show much on his debut at Navan a week earlier, but was representing connections that landed a touch here with their first British winner last month. Well backed, he made a bold move three out but ran green and paid late for taking time to settle. (op 8-1)
Dancing Art(IRE) was something of an eyecatcher on his debut at Newcastle last month and it was again the case on this switch to hurdling. He moved nicely just off the pace, but didn't get a good passage on the inside turning for home and it's fair to say the rider wasn't hard on him (never went for whip). He's one to keep an eye on. (op 11-2)

4890 EASTER FAMILY FUN 23RD APRIL BEGINNERS' CHASE (14 fncs 2 omitted) 2m 4f
3:00 (3:00) (Class 4) 5-Y-O+ **£2,602** (£764; £382; £190)

Form				RPR
U332	**1**		**Lord Villez (FR)**[10] 4570 7-11-0 120 GrahamLee (Ferdy Murphy) *in tch: effrt 4 out: swtchd lft bef last: led run-in: edgd rt and pushed out run-in* **5/2**[2]	116+
1321	**2**	*3 ¼*	**Victors Serenade (IRE)**[56] 3698 6-11-0 0 SamThomas (Anthony Honeyball) *cl up: nt fluent 8th: ev ch 4 out: rdn and led 2 out: hdd run-in: kpt on same pce* **7/5**[1]	114+
22-F	**3**	*8*	**King In Waiting (IRE)**[26] 4275 8-11-0 113 (t) JamesReveley (David O'Meara) *cl up: led 2nd tl hdd after 4 out: ev ch to 2 out: outpcd pce run-in* **11/1**	104
1000	**4**	*3 ½*	**Solway Sam**[15] 4464 8-11-0 125 RichieMcGrath (Lisa Harrison) *hld up: outpcd 5 out: plugged on fr 2 out: nvr rchd ldrs* **5/1**[3]	99
4P00	**5**	*4*	**Just Unique**[32] 4144 7-10-11 70 (t) PeterToole[(3)] (Mark Rimell) *prom: outpcd whn mstke 9th: no imp fr 4 out* **50/1**	96
2-35	**6**	*nk*	**Milans Man (IRE)**[74] 3394 6-11-0 0 BrianHughes (Howard Johnson) *led to 2nd: cl up: rdn to ld after 4 out: hdd 2 out: wknd fr last* **13/2**	95

5m 20.2s (-7.20) **Going Correction** -0.225s/f (Good) **6** Ran SP% **110.5**
Speed ratings: **105,103,100,99,97 97**
Tote Swingers: 1&2 £1.10, 1&3 £6.30, 2&3 £7.50 CSF £6.54 TOTE £3.50: £2.20, £1.40; EX 7.00.

Owner A G Chappell **Bred** Ange-Marie Michelosi **Trained** West Witton, N Yorks

FOCUS
The open ditch on the back straight was omitted in all chases for the second successive meeting. An ordinary beginners' chase run at a fair enough gallop. The winner is rated to his mark with the next two below the level of their hurdles form.

NOTEBOOK
Lord Villez(FR) finally opened his account and was doing all his best work at the finish. He didn't convince over his fences in the main, but saved his best jump for the last and outpaced the runner-up from there on. This should serve his confidence well. (op 9-4 tchd 11-4)
Victors Serenade(IRE) showed himself to be a proper stayer over hurdles and his previous Towcester success has worked out well. Unsurprisingly well backed, he was novicey at times on this switch to chasing and ultimately looked to find this too sharp. The holding ground also may not have been ideal as he tended to go out to his left at times, and he can find an opening before long (op 6-4 tchd 7-4)
King In Waiting(IRE) went off quickly in front and put in some bold jumps prior to coming down on his chasing debut last time out. He went out to make all again and jumped neatly considering his previous mishap. In the end stamina found him out, but it was certainly a run he can build on. (op 10-1)
Solway Sam is officially rated 5lb superior to the winner, but he hasn't been in good form over hurdles of late and jumped too deliberately out the back on this chasing debut. He ought to learn plenty. (op 7-1)
Milans Man(IRE), back from a 74-day break, responded to pressure from three out but ultimately looked in need of the run. (op 6-1 tchd 5-1)

4891 NEWS & STAR NOVICES' CHASE (16 fncs 2 omitted) 3m 110y
3:30 (3:30) (Class 3) 5-Y-O+ **£4,878** (£1,432; £716)

Form				RPR
P-11	**1**		**Alvarado (IRE)**[64] 3571 6-11-8 141 WilsonRenwick (Howard Johnson) *nt fluent: trckd ldrs: blnd 1st: hit and wnt 2nd 9th: effrt and led bef last: styd on strly run-in* **5/4**[1]	134+
36V2	**2**	*2 ¼*	**Pennek (FR)**[20] 4394 8-10-12 113 RichieMcGrath (Philip Kirby) *t.k.h early: chsd ldr: blnd and lost 2nd 9th: outpcd next: rn wd bnd bef 4 out: rallied next: ev ch last: kpt on run-in* **7/2**[3]	121
0011	**3**	*12*	**As De Fer (FR)**[35] 4095 5-11-7 135 SamThomas (Anthony Honeyball) *led: blnd 7th: rdn 3 out: hdd bef last: wknd run-in* **11/8**[2]	126+

6m 33.1s (-9.50) **Going Correction** -0.225s/f (Good)
WFA 5 from 6yo+ 1lb **3** Ran SP% **108.8**
Speed ratings: **106,105,101**
CSF £5.13 TOTE £1.70; EX 5.00.

Owner Andrea & Graham Wylie **Bred** P R Joyce **Trained** Billy Row, Co Durham

FOCUS
An interesting little novice chase and, despite all three holding every chance in the home straight, it was certainly an incident-packed race. The second sets the level, with the other pair about a stone off.

NOTEBOOK
Alvarado(IRE) emerged on top from the last to make it 3-3 as a chaser and extend his unbeaten record at this venue to four. His previous form this season has worked out nicely and he was an easy winner at Wetherby when last seen in January. He walked through the final fence that day and hit the very first fence this time, which no doubt affected his confidence as he lacked fluency pretty much throughout from that point. He also looked uneasy on the tacky ground, but jockey Wilson Renwick was seen at his best winning the opener and was again at the top of his game in getting him home here. The longer trip suited and this talented 6yo still looks capable of better providing he learns more respect for his fences. (tchd 11-8)
Pennek(FR) had plenty to find on official figures, but he used to be rated plenty higher as a hurdler and was the proven stayer. He jumped best of all, but again hit his customary flat spot on the final circuit. It appeared coming to the last as though he may hit the front, but the winner simply wanted it more. There is no doubt there's a race in him over fences, but his attitude seems to be holding him back. (op 5-1)
As De Fer(FR) has been a revelation since switching to fences for current connections and was particularly impressive when beating a subsequent winner last month. However he proved free out in front here and made one or two notable errors. Such positive tactics over this longer trip found him out from the second-last and a drop back in trip is on the cards. (op 5-4)

4892 TEXAS IN CONCERT 2ND JULY NOVICES' H'CAP HURDLE (8 hdls 1 omitted) 2m 1f
4:00 (4:00) (Class 4) (0-110,106) 4-Y-O+ **£2,226** (£649; £324)

Form				RPR
1223	**1**		**Rawaaj**[16] 4462 5-11-8 102 JasonMaguire (Donald McCain) *chsd clr ldr to 4th: regained 2nd after next: effrt and led 2 out: hld on gamely u.p* **11/4**[1]	103
1113	**2**	*hd*	**Decent Lord (IRE)**[24] 4314 7-10-11 91 AlanO'Keeffe (Jennie Candlish) *hld up: stdy hdwy and cl up 2 out: sn rdn: styd on wl run-in: jst hld* **11/4**[1]	92
P-65	**3**	*2 ¾*	**Descaro (USA)**[34] 4115 5-11-12 106 GrahamLee (David O'Meara) *hld up: effrt bef 3 out: hdwy and cl 3rd last: kpt on same pce run-in* **4/1**[2]	104
6F50	**4**	*8*	**Royal And Ancient (IRE)**[16] 4462 4-11-3 104 (t) WarrenMarston (Milton Harris) *prom: chsd clr ldr 4th to after next: outpcd 3 out: n.d after* **12/1**	87
3512	**5**	*½*	**Antoella (IRE)**[18] 4419 4-10-7 101 KyleJames[(7)] (Philip Kirby) *plld hrd: led: hit 3rd: clr to 3 out: hdd next: 4 l 4th and one pce whn blnd last: wknd* **11/2**[3]	88
2050	**P**		**What A Dream**[15] 4477 5-11-4 98 JamesReveley (William Amos) *prom: outpcd 4 out: struggling bef next: t.o whn p.u bef last* **7/1**	—

4m 37.8s (8.00) **Going Correction** +0.35s/f (Yiel)
WFA 4 from 5yo+ 7lb **6** Ran SP% **108.9**
Speed ratings (Par 105): **95,94,93,89,89 —**
Tote Swingers: 1&2 £1.40, 1&3 £3.70, 2&3 £2.30 CSF £10.28 TOTE £3.10: £1.70, £1.90; EX 7.80.

Owner Tim & Miranda Johnson Partnership **Bred** Shadwell Estate Company Limited **Trained** Cholmondeley, Cheshire

■ Stewards' Enquiry : Alan O'Keeffe three-day ban: used whip with excessive frequency (Apr 3-5)

FOCUS
This moderate novice handicap was run at a solid gallop thanks to the free-going Antoella. The first two were bang-in-form, and are rated to their marks.

NOTEBOOK
Rawaaj turned in a very brave effort and gained reward for his consistency. He tended to go somewhat in snatches, probably due to the way the race unfolded, but there could be no faulting his attitude over the final three flights. It rates a career-best effort. (tchd 3-1)
Decent Lord(IRE) was back down in trip after he got outstayed when bidding for a four-timer on his previous outing 24 days earlier. Racing off a career-high mark, he again travelled nicely into contention but couldn't quicken so well on this drying ground. He remains capable of further success off this sort of mark, but probably does need a stiffer test now the ground is changing. (op 5-2 tchd 9-4)
Descaro(USA), down in trip/class, enjoys a sound surface on the Flat and was taken wide to find the better ground in the back straight. He got outpaced before staying on to have his chance in the home straight, but the surface really did for him. (op 9-2)
Royal And Ancient(IRE) was done for speed and remains a maiden. (op 14-1 tchd 11-1)
Antoella(IRE) was taken early to post and set off too fast for her own good out in front. (op 5-1)
What A Dream knew their fate a long way out and he continues out of sorts. A longer trip is what he ideally needs, though. (op 8-1)

4893 BETTER ODDS ANYWHERE WITH BETFAIR MOBILE NOVICES' H'CAP CHASE (14 fncs 2 omitted) 2m 4f
4:30 (4:30) (Class 3) (0-130,122) 5-Y-O+ **£6,505** (£1,910; £955; £477)

Form				RPR
-4P2	**1**		**Whats Up Woody (IRE)**[22] 4362 6-10-9 110 PaulGallagher[(5)] (Howard Johnson) *prom: hdwy to ld bef 4 out: clr 2 out: styd on strly run-in* **10/1**	117+
P0U1	**2**	*2 ½*	**Mister Marker (IRE)**[10] 4570 7-11-12 122 FearghalDavis (Nicky Richards) *prom: pushed along fr 1/2-way: effrt and chsd (clr) wnr appr 2 out: no imp run-in* **3/1**[2]	124
440U	**3**	*5*	**Monsieur Jourdain (IRE)**[46] 3886 5-10-13 109 (p) RichieMcGrath (Tim Easterby) *chsd ldr: rdn and outpcd bef 4 out: plugged on fr 2 out: no imp* **12/1**	107
11U1	**4**	*7*	**Douglas Julian**[29] 4210 9-11-5 115 HenryOliver (Sue Smith) *led: nt fluent 9th: hdd bef 4 out: lost 2nd 2 out: wknd* **11/4**[1]	108
/3-1	**5**	*34*	**Prosecco (IRE)**[24] 4305 9-11-3 113 PeterBuchanan (Lucinda Russell) *hld up in tch: outpcd whn nt fluent 5 out: sn btn: t.o* **4/1**[3]	89
4141	**P**		**Lockstown**[12] 4543 8-10-10 106 (p) GrahamLee (Ann Hamilton) *trckd ldrs: rdn and outpcd bef 9th: struggling after next: t.o whn p.u 4 out* **3/1**[2]	—

5m 19.3s (-8.10) **Going Correction** -0.225s/f (Good) **6** Ran SP% **113.4**
Speed ratings: **107,106,104,101,87 —**
Tote Swingers: 1&2 £6.10, 1&3 £5.40, 2&3 £7.90 CSF £41.00 TOTE £11.20: £3.40, £1.90; EX 70.30.

Owner J Howard Johnson & Exors of W M G Black **Bred** Michael Hayes **Trained** Billy Row, Co Durham

FOCUS
Not the strongest race for the class with the top weight rated 8lb lower than the race ceiling, but the form still looks sound. The winner stepped up a lot on his previous chase form.

NOTEBOOK
Whats Up Woody(IRE) finished a distant second on horrible ground at Newcastle last month and, back in handicap company, proved a totally different proposition on this drying surface. He wasn't in serious danger after taking it up turning for home and rates value for a little further as he was idling. This was his first win short of 3m and he has few miles on the clock. (tchd 12-1)
Mister Marker(IRE)'s win over C&D ten days earlier was given a boost when the second that day Lord Villez took the earlier beginners' chase. He lost out by hitting a flat spot in the back straight, but still posted a sound effort in defeat and rates the benchmark. (op 11-4)

Monsieur Jourdain(IRE), who was easy to back, travelled nicely, but it looked a case of him finding nothing when put under some pressure around five out. However, he rallied in the home straight and it's not hard to see why he wears headgear. (tchd 11-1)
Douglas Julian has been highly progressive since going chasing this season and couldn't have won much easier at Haydock last time. His jumping wasn't quite as good on this tacky surface, however, and he was held off his new 11lb higher mark. (op 5-2 tchd 9-4 and 10-3 in a place)
Prosecco(IRE) was 5lb higher than when winning on his return from a layoff last month and had stamina to prove. An error five out didn't help his cause, but he probably needs dropping back in trip. (op 5-1)
Lockstown landed a second win from his last three outings at Newcastle 12 days earlier and was just 2lb higher. He was in trouble before going out onto the far side, though, and wasn't on a going day. It may well be that he needs to revert to a left-handed circuit. Official explanation: trainer said gelding was found to have a sore back (op 9-2)

4894 CARIBBEAN FAMILY DAY 30TH MAY INTERMEDIATE OPEN NATIONAL HUNT FLAT RACE 2m 1f
5:00 (5:00) (Class 6) 4-6-Y-O **£1,267** (£369; £184)

Form				RPR
3	1		**Dreamers Of Dreams (IRE)**[52] 3773 6-11-3 0 GrahamLee (Malcolm Jefferson) *trckd ldrs: led 1/2-way: hdd briefly over 2f out: rdn and hld on gamely fnl f* **85/40**[1]	106+
23	2	1 ¼	**Vintage Star (IRE)**[27] 4259 5-10-12 0 ShaneByrne(5) (Sue Smith) *t.k.h in midfield: stdy hdwy and prom 1/2-way: outpcd 3f out: rallied: edgd rt and chsd wnr over 1f out: kpt on fnl f: hld nr fin* **4/1**[3]	105
2	3	4	**Irish Chaperone (IRE)**[39] 4005 4-10-10 0 JamesReveley (Keith Reveley) *hld up: hdwy over 5f out: rdn and outpcd whn swvd bdly lft 2f out: sn rcvrd and kpt on fnl f: nt rch first two* **5/1**	95+
	4	9	**Boruler (IRE)** 5-11-3 0 JasonMaguire (Donald McCain) *prom: drvn and outpcd over 2f out: n.d after* **3/1**[2]	92
0-0	5	3 ¼	**Bonnie Baloo**[35] 5-10-3 0 JeremiahMcGrath(7) (Alan Swinbank) *hld up: smooth hdwy on outside to ld briefly over 2f out: wandered and wknd appr fnl f* **22/1**	82
5	6	7	**Master Act (IRE)**[24] 4308 6-11-0 0 EwanWhillans(3) (Alistair Whillans) *hld up: drvn and outpcd over 4f out: hung lft and no imp fr over 2f out* **22/1**	82
0	7	15	**Rupert Bear**[46] 3889 5-10-10 0 MissCWalton(7) (James Walton) *bhd: outpcd over 5f out: nvr on terms* **200/1**	67
4	8	8	**Grand Vintage (IRE)**[34] 4117 5-11-3 0 BrianHughes (Howard Johnson) *t.k.h: cl up: hung lft bnd after 5f: hung lft over 4f out: sn wknd: eased whn no ch fnl 2f* **12/1**	69
5-0	9	4 ½	**The Giggler (IRE)**[66] 3525 5-11-3 0 BarryKeniry (Alan Swinbank) *hld up: struggling 5f out: sn wknd* **16/1**	54
0	10	14	**Not Now Later**[46] 3889 5-11-3 0 CampbellGillies (Barry Murtagh) *t.k.h: led: hung bdly lft and hdd 1/2-way: sn lost pl: eased fnl 4f* **200/1**	40

4m 29.8s (5.60) **Going Correction** +0.35s/f (Yiel)
WFA 4 from 5yo+ 7lb 10 Ran SP% **116.9**
Speed ratings: **100,99,97,93,91 88,81,77,75,68**
Tote Swingers: 1&2 £2.50, 1&3 £2.10, 2&3 £1.80 CSF £10.65 TOTE £3.20: £1.40, £1.80, £1.40; EX 10.70.
Owner Dean Bostock And Raymond Bostock **Bred** Con Troy **Trained** Norton, N Yorks

FOCUS
The first three came nicely clear in this fair bumper for the track. the winner is rated to his mark.

NOTEBOOK
Dreamers Of Dreams(IRE) ran with promise on his debut at Warwick in January and, on his debut for a new stable, got off the mark with a dogged display. He was never far away and knuckled down bravely to repel challenges in the home straight. He is going to want further once sent hurdling and clearly has a future. (op 3-1)
Vintage Star(IRE) showed his previous effort over C&D to be all wrong and returned to the sort of form that saw him finish runner-up on his debut. He too will appreciate racing over further in due course. (op 9-2 tchd 5-1)
Irish Chaperone(IRE) was just held over 1m6f on his debut at this course last month, but that form had been let down and he proved easy to back. He showed his inexperience more than once, most notably when jinking at the wing of the missing flight two furlongs out, but this was still another promising effort and he evidently stays well. (op 7-2)
Boruler(IRE) had his chance, but he just left the impression this initial outing would do him good. (op 10-3 tchd 7-2)
Bonnie Baloo looked the one to be on turning for home, but she fell in a hole once put under pressure and failed to see it out. This was an encouraging debut for her new yard. (op 14-1)
Master Act(IRE) has some scope and is one to keep an eye on with a view to going hurdling in due course. (op 28-1)
Grand Vintage(IRE) Official explanation: jockey said gelding hung left
Not Now Later Official explanation: jockey said gelding hung left
T/Plt: £15.40 to a £1 stake. Pool of £63,742.91 - 3,012.90 winning tickets. T/Qpdt: £10.70 to a £1 stake. Pool of £3,687.71 - 252.85 winning tickets. RY

4528 NEWTON ABBOT (L-H)
Sunday, March 20

OFFICIAL GOING: Good to soft (soft in places; 5.6)
All bends moved out 2 -3 metres since last meeting.
Wind: virtually nil Weather: sunny

4895 RNLI NOVICES' HURDLE (8 hdls) 2m 1f
2:15 (2:16) (Class 4) 4-Y-0+ **£2,706** (£788; £394)

Form				RPR
1	1		**Topolski (IRE)**[30] 4195 5-11-6 0 DarylJacob (David Arbuthnot) *mid-div: smooth hdwy after 5th: trckd ldrs after next: led appr last: easily* **15/8**[2]	130+
05	2	4	**Falcon Island**[17] 4448 6-11-0 112 (t) JoeTizzard (Colin Tizzard) *prom: led 3rd tl 5th: rdn to ld appr 2 out: hdd appr last: kpt on but no ch w wnr* **15/2**	113
0011	3	5	**Shammick Boy (IRE)**[47] 3872 6-11-12 137 DenisO'Regan (Victor Dartnall) *led tl 3rd: led 5th: rdn and hdd appr 2 out: kpt on same pce* **7/4**[1]	121
40	4	5	**Fennis Ted (IRE)**[6] 4767 5-10-7 0 SClements(7) (Liam Corcoran) *in tch: rdn in 4th after 3 out: one pce fr next* **50/1**	103
0-0	5	½	**Domos Boy (IRE)**[19] 4404 8-10-11 0 MrAJBerry(3) (Jonjo O'Neill) *mid-div: rdn after 3 out: styd on same pce* **50/1**	103
0-40	6	1 ¼	**Barton Cliche**[17] 4444 6-10-7 0 MarkQuinlan(7) (Neil Mulholland) *mid-div: trckd ldrs 3rd: rdn after 3 out: sn one pce* **40/1**	102
500	7	10	**Hard Tackle (IRE)**[26] 4268 5-11-0 0 RichieMcLernon (Jonjo O'Neill) *rdn after 5th: a towards rr* **40/1**	92
254	8	½	**Water Garden (FR)**[35] 4094 5-11-0 0 TimmyMurphy (Paul Nicholls) *a towards rr* **7/1**[3]	91
5	9	¾	**Only Witness (IRE)**[15] 4479 6-11-0 0 SamJones (Brendan Powell) *rdn after 5th: a towards rr* **16/1**	90
344P	10	1 ¼	**Navajo Nation (IRE)**[13] 4530 5-10-9 97 (p) TomO'Connor(5) (Bill Turner) *trckd ldrs: rdn after 3 out: sn wknd* **22/1**	89
000	11	26	**Fresher Fishing (IRE)**[44] 3930 7-11-0 0 (p) AndrewGlassonbury (Victor Dartnall) *rdn after 5th: a towards rr: t.o* **80/1**	63

4m 11.6s (5.90) **Going Correction** +0.575s/f (Soft) 11 Ran SP% **115.7**
Speed ratings (Par 105): **109,107,104,102,102 101,96,96,96,95 83**
Tote Swingers: 1&2 £3.80, 1&3 £1.70, 2&3 £3.20 CSF £15.08 TOTE £2.80: £1.40, £1.20, £1.20; EX 17.10.
Owner P M Claydon **Bred** C H Wacker Iii **Trained** Compton, Berks

FOCUS
All bends moved out 2-3 metres since last meeting. A reasonable novice hurdle for the grade, run at a fairly steady pace and in a time around 20 seconds outside the Racing Post standard. The ground was on the soft side of good, described by riders in the first as "a bit dead" and "tacky, and hard work in places".

NOTEBOOK
Topolski(IRE) had the very useful Megastar behind when making a winning hurdling debut at Sandown. He maintained his unbeaten record with a very smooth success, value for a greater margin of victory, and looks worth stepping up in class. He has a choice of Grade 2 engagements at Aintree, either in the Top Novices' Hurdle over 2m or the Mersey over 2m4f. A fluent jumper, he has plenty of pace for the shorter trip but promises to get further too. (op 7-4 tchd 13-8)
Falcon Island failed to win over hurdles in Ireland for either Gordon Elliott or Jessica Harrington. Back in novice company on his second run for this yard, he showed just about in front two out but was soon left standing by the winner. He hung between the last two flights and it may be that he's not straightforward. (op 9-1)
Shammick Boy(IRE), officially rated 137, was penalised for both his Taunton wins. Again going off in front, he was always shadowed by the runner-up and had to give way going to the second-last. He may not prove easy to place in the short term. (op 13-8 tchd 2-1)
Fennis Ted(IRE) ran well for a long way but was dropped by the leading three going to the home turn. He had caught the eye in a bumper previously and definitely has ability. (op 66-1 tchd 80-1)
Domos Boy(IRE) ◆, a winning Irish pointer, stayed on nicely and handicaps over further will see him in a better light.
Barton Cliche, a chasing type, was not knocked about and can improve. (op 50-1)

4896 SILKS COFFEE LOUNGE H'CAP CHASE (16 fncs) 2m 5f 110y
2:45 (2:45) (Class 4) (0-115,114) 5-Y-0+ **£3,057** (£897; £448; £224)

Form				RPR
-011	1		**Midnight Appeal**[10] 4674 6-11-11 113 RobertThornton (Alan King) *trckd ldrs: jnd ldrs 11th: nt fluent 4 out: sn rdn: led after 3 out: wnt lft next: styd on: drvn out* **11/8**[1]	124+
2U0-	2	1 ¼	**Man From Highworth**[29] 12-11-5 114 MrSParish(7) (Audrey Manners) *hld up: trckd ldrs 4 out: rdn after 3 out: styd on to chse wnr last: no ex* **28/1**	120
0U4P	3	2 ¾	**Health Is Wealth (IRE)**[35] 4102 6-10-0 91 SamTwiston-Davies(3) (Colin Tizzard) *hmpd 1st: in tch: led after 4 out: rdn and hdd after 3 out: cl 2nd whn hmpd next: kpt on same pce* **5/2**[2]	98+
PF12	4	16	**Sawpit Supreme**[21] 4379 9-10-9 97 AidanColeman (Venetia Williams) *trckd ldrs: ev ch 4 out: sn rdn: wknd after next* **9/2**[3]	87
402P	5	¾	**High Jack (IRE)**[13] 4523 9-11-6 108 NickScholfield (Andy Turnell) *led: rdn after 11th: hdd after 4 out: wknd after next* **12/1**	98
P-FP	6	75	**This Way (IRE)**[69] 3482 9-10-4 95 (t) JimmyDerham(3) (John Ryall) *w ldr: hit 8th: rdn appr 10th: wknd 12th: t.o* **11/1**	16
0005	7	3 ¾	**American World (FR)**[27] 4265 7-11-10 112 RichieMcLernon (Brendan Powell) *cl up: rdn appr 10th: losing tch whn hit 11th: t.o* **16/1**	30

5m 25.5s (4.10) **Going Correction** +0.325s/f (Yiel) 7 Ran SP% **114.2**
Speed ratings: **105,104,103,97,97 70,68**
Tote Swingers: 1&2 £8.50, 1&3 £2.00, 2&3 £10.70 CSF £30.91 CT £91.48 TOTE £2.80: £1.10, £18.20; EX 43.10.
Owner David Sewell **Bred** William Wilkinson **Trained** Barbury Castle, Wilts

FOCUS
An ordinary handicap chase run over 16 seconds outside the standard, suggesting that the chase course might have been riding slightly quicker than the hurdles track.

NOTEBOOK
Midnight Appeal joined the leaders down the far side and saw off a challenge from the third before staying on well to hold the runner-up. Completing a hat-trick off a 15lb higher mark than for the first leg, there is further improvement in him and he handles quicker ground too. (op 13-8 tchd 7-4)
Man From Highworth came through to look a threat at the last but was just held. Now at the veteran stage, he has been contesting point-to-points and will be suited by a return to further. This was his first ever run in a handicap chase bar the one for hunter chasers here two years ago. (op 25-1)
Health Is Wealth(IRE), who has been dropped 4lb since his last start, came in for support. He was alongside the winner, but not going as well, when he came off worse in a mid-air collision with him at the second-last. The return to a shorter trip suited. (op 7-2)
Sawpit Supreme was racing off the same mark as when runner-up at Towcester. This slightly longer trip should have been within her compass but she weakened three from home. (op 7-2)
High Jack(IRE) could not hold on to his lead exiting the back straight and is perhaps more effective on right-handed circuits. (op 9-1)
This Way(IRE) showed a tendency to jump to his right. (op 20-1)

4897 BOOK YOUR CONFERENCE NOW MARES' NOVICES' HURDLE (10 hdls) 2m 6f
3:15 (3:15) (Class 4) 4-Y-0+ **£2,569** (£754; £377; £188)

Form				RPR
P125	1		**Rith Bob (IRE)**[13] 4532 8-11-5 109 PaulMoloney (David Rees) *disp ld tl clr ldr after 7th: drew clr fr 2 out: easily* **5/2**[1]	113+
44R	2	7	**Accordingtoeileen (IRE)**[9] 4703 6-10-9 0 SamTwiston-Davies(3) (Nigel Twiston-Davies) *trckd ldrs: rdn to chse wnr after 3 out: kpt on but hld fr next* **10/1**[3]	97
F036	3	3 ½	**Sawpit Solitaire**[17] 4441 6-10-12 104 AidanColeman (Venetia Williams) *trckd ldrs: rdn to chal briefly after 3 out: styd on same pce fr next* **5/2**[1]	95
2440	4	24	**Hill Forts Gloria (IRE)**[80] 3227 6-10-9 95 JimmyDerham(3) (Seamus Mullins) *trckd ldrs: rdn after 3 out: wknd bef next* **8/1**[2]	76
33	5	28	**Yvonne Evelyn (USA)**[24] 4309 6-10-12 103 RobertThornton (Alan King) *racd keenly: trckd ldrs: rdn after 3 out: wknd qckly: t.o* **5/2**[1]	47
0	6	44	**Poetic Beat**[61] 3623 6-10-12 0 SeamusDurack (Seamus Durack) *in tch tl rdn after 5th: sn lost tch: t.o* **25/1**	7
00	7	7	**Fran's Folly**[29] 4225 5-10-5 0 MarkQuinlan(7) (Neil Mulholland) *disp ld tl wknd appr 7th: sn bhd: t.o whn blnd last* **66/1**	1

00 **P** **El Pescadero (IRE)**[12] 4535 5-10-12 0 .... RodiGreene —
(Nick Ayliffe) *slowly away: pushed along after 4th: bhd whn p.u after 6th: dismntd* **80/1**

5m 34.7s (14.50) **Going Correction** +0.575s/f (Soft)
WFA 4 from 5yo+ 8lb 8 Ran SP% **112.5**
Speed ratings (Par 105): **96,93,92,83,73 57,54,—**
Tote Swingers: 1&2 £4.20, 1&3 £2.20, 2&3 £4.70 CSF £28.21 TOTE £3.20: £1.80, £1.60, £1.80; EX 20.20.
Owner D Rees **Bred** George Ward **Trained** Clarbeston, Pembrokes

FOCUS
A modest mares' hurdle.

NOTEBOOK
Rith Bob(IRE), the only previous winner in the field, shrugged off her penalty to make most of the running. Suited by getting her way in front, she is a tough performer and her attitude should bring her further success in ordinary company. (op 11-4)
Accordingtoeileen(IRE) dug in her heels and refused to race on her hurdles debut but didn't do much wrong here. Daughter of a decent hurdler/chaser, she will suited by a further step up in trip. (op 8-1)
Sawpit Solitaire, back in novice company having found 3m too far last time, faded on the home turn. She has been placed five times now but is still awaiting her first win. (op 11-4 tchd 3-1)
Hill Forts Gloria(IRE) dropped away on the turn out of the back straight and is not progressing. (op 9-1)
Yvonne Evelyn(USA), who had been third in two novice hurdles at Huntingdon, was disappointing. Taking quite a hold, she tracked the winner until stopping quickly as soon as she came off the bridle. (tchd 9-4)
El Pescadero(IRE) Official explanation: vet said mare pulled up lame

4898 WINNING POST RESTAURANT NOVICES' CHASE (20 fncs) 3m 2f 110y
3:45 (3:45) (Class 3) 5-Y-O+ **£5,334** (£1,566; £783; £391)

Form RPR
6F21 **1** **Fin Vin De Leu (GER)**[17] 4445 5-11-3 131 .... (p) DarylJacob 140+
(Charlie Mann) *mde all: drew clr fr 2 out: comf* **7/4**[1]
2-31 **2** *14* **Aldertune (IRE)**[8] 4720 7-11-4 129 .... (b[1]) NickScholfield 126
(Paul Nicholls) *trckd wnr: rdn after 3 out: hld whn hit 2 out* **9/4**[2]
225U **3** *27* **Voramar Two**[8] 4720 8-10-12 140 .... (t) RichardJohnson 96
(Philip Hobbs) *trckd wnr: rdn appr 4 out: sn btn: t.o* **7/4**[1]
0640 **4** *20* **Casual Garcia**[26] 4272 6-10-9 0 .... (t) TommyPhelan[(3)] 78
(Mark Gillard) *chsd ldrs tl 14th: no ch fr next: t.o* **28/1**[3]

6m 51.7s (7.10) **Going Correction** +0.325s/f (Yiel)
WFA 5 from 6yo+ 1lb 4 Ran SP% **106.9**
Speed ratings: **102,97,89,83**
CSF £5.98 TOTE £2.70; EX 5.00.
Owner R Curry, Cathy Leuchars & R P Michaelson **Bred** Newsells Park Stud Ltd **Trained** Upper Lambourn, Berks

FOCUS
A decent novice chase on paper, but they took things very steadily until the final circuit. With the second and third disappointing the form does not look too solid.

NOTEBOOK
Fin Vin De Leu(GER) followed up his Taunton win, jumping soundly bar a mistake five out and making just about all. He is progressing nicely, but his two main rivals were below par and the form of this victory is not all it seems. If he gets in he could go for the Scottish Grand National, but he is only five and it would be asking a lot of him in that stamina test. No five-year-old has won the Scottish National since the 19th century. (op 15-8)
Aldertune(IRE) was fitted with blinkers for the first time after idling when winning at Chepstow. He looked to be going as well as the winner as they turned out of the back straight, but found nothing when let down. It could be that the trip stretched him, but it was not a true test of stamina and he is starting to look one to be wary of. (tchd 5-2)
Voramar Two, officially rated 140, and 15lb clear on these terms, was quickly toiling halfway down the back. Runner-up in each of his first three chases, he has not gone on from that and is starting to look regressive. Official explanation: jockey said gelding had a breathing problem (op 2-1)
Casual Garcia, a modest hurdler, faced a stiff task on this chase debut and was left behind after a blunder with a circuit left. (op 20-1)

4899 NEWTONABBOTRACING.COM H'CAP HURDLE (8 hdls) 2m 1f
4:15 (4:16) (Class 5) (0-95,95) 4-Y-O+ **£1,747** (£509; £254)

Form RPR
3122 **1** **Maizy Missile (IRE)**[122] 2467 9-11-9 89 .... PaulMoloney 96+
(Mary Evans) *trckd ldr: rdn after 3 out: led next: styd on wl: rdn out* **5/1**[1]
0660 **2** *3* **Mr Bachster (IRE)**[26] 4272 6-11-12 92 .... DenisO'Regan 95
(Victor Dartnall) *led: rdn whn hdd 2 out: styd on same pce* **10/1**
-045 **3** *nse* **Gilt Free (IRE)**[20] 4401 9-11-12 92 .... (v) AndrewTinkler 95
(George Baker) *hld up towards rr: hdwy after 4th: rdn to chse ldng pair after 3 out: styd on same pce fr next* **15/2**
4340 **4** *19* **Storm Command (IRE)**[17] 4450 4-10-7 80 .... RichardJohnson 59
(Tim Vaughan) *hld up towards rr: struggling after 5th: plugged on to take modest 4th: nvr trbld ldrs* **15/2**
50/1 **5** *1 ½* **Webbswood Lad (IRE)**[17] 4450 10-11-8 91 .... (t) TomMolloy[(3)] 76
(Martin Bosley) *hld up bhd: hdwy on outer appr 5th: rdn after 3 out: wknd next* **13/2**[3]
6 *4 ½* **Braddock (IRE)**[11] 4599 8-11-4 89 .... (t) TomO'Connor[(5)] 70
(Bill Turner) *hld up towards rr: sme prog into midfield 3 out: wknd bef next* **12/1**
-P05 **7** *4 ½* **Whatshallwedo**[13] 4530 6-10-10 76 .... LiamHeard 52
(Chris Down) *chsd ldrs: hit 4th: rdn after 3 out: wknd next* **33/1**
0000 **8** *2 ¼* **Haydens Mount**[29] 4225 6-10-4 70 .... (t) HaddenFrost 46
(James Frost) *in tch: rdn to dispute 4th after 3 out: wknd next* **9/1**
044 **9** *2 ½* **Baltic Ben (USA)**[201] 1442 4-10-10 83 .... DarylJacob 48
(Alison Thorpe) *mid-div tl wknd 3 out* **7/1**
/3-0 **10** *22* **Cinnamon Hill**[13] 4528 7-11-7 87 .... RodiGreene 39
(Nick Ayliffe) *mid-div: rdn after 4th: sn bhd: t.o* **33/1**
5F43 **P** **Cruise Control**[13] 4530 5-11-11 91 .... TimmyMurphy —
(Richard Price) *mid-div: hit 2nd: pushed along after 4th: losing pl whn p.u bef 3 out* **11/2**[2]

4m 17.5s (11.80) **Going Correction** +0.575s/f (Soft)
WFA 4 from 5yo+ 7lb 11 Ran SP% **114.1**
Speed ratings (Par 103): **95,93,93,84,83 81,79,78,77,67 —**
Tote Swingers: 1&2 £14.40, 1&3 £7.30, 2&3 £11.70 CSF £52.45 CT £367.20 TOTE £4.50: £1.70, £3.70, £2.50; EX 74.00 Trifecta £430.10 Part won. Pool: £581.31 - 0.72 winning units..
Owner Mary And Billy Evans **Bred** Mrs M Evans **Trained** Clarbeston Road, Pembrokeshire

FOCUS
A low-grade handicap hurdle. The first three came clear.

NOTEBOOK
Maizy Missile(IRE) came under pressure on the home turn but stayed on to win a shade readily. A consistent mare, she shrugged off a 4lb rise on this return from a four-month break and could have more to offer. (op 6-1)
Mr Bachster(IRE), eased 3lb since his handicap debut, was ridden very differently and went off in front. Only headed two from home, this was an improved effort and he overturned Taunton form with today's third Gilt Free. (op 15-2)
Gilt Free(IRE) again travelled quite well but this drop back in trip may not have been ideal. (op 8-1 tchd 7-1)
Storm Command(IRE) settled better and plugged on from the back for a well-beaten fourth. This was probably a step in the right direction. (op 17-2)
Webbswood Lad(IRE), 8lb higher than when winning at Taunton on his return from an absence, could never get into it. (op 6-1)
Cruise Control, 8lb higher than when winning at Taunton on his return from an absence, could never get into it. Official explanation: jockey said gelding never travelled (op 7-1)

4900 RIVER TEIGN H'CAP HURDLE (10 hdls) 2m 6f
4:45 (4:45) (Class 5) (0-90,90) 4-Y-O+ **£1,747** (£509; £254)

Form RPR
000 **1** **Flying Award (IRE)**[35] 4094 7-10-13 84 .... MissLGardner[(7)] 103+
(Susan Gardner) *mid-div: hdwy after 6th: led 3 out: styd on wl fr next: readily* **7/1**[3]
0040 **2** *6* **Boosha**[51] 3791 6-11-5 90 .... PeterCarberry[(7)] 103
(Rachel Hobbs) *mid-div: rdn and hdwy after 3 out: chsd wnr bef next: a being hld* **12/1**
PP03 **3** *17* **Petroglyph**[62] 3603 7-11-5 90 .... (p) MarkQuinlan[(7)] 88
(Noel Quinlan) *trckd ldrs: rdn after 3 out: wknd next* **3/1**[2]
35-3 **4** *3 ¾* **Canshebemine**[41] 3983 7-11-2 80 .... (t) HaddenFrost 74
(James Frost) *hld up towards rr: stdy hdwy fr 7th: rdn after 3 out: wnt modest 4th after 2 out: nvr threatened* **8/1**
P4PU **5** *4 ½* **Gunship (IRE)**[10] 4675 10-10-11 82 .... (b) MrRGHenderson[(7)] 72
(Cathy Hamilton) *led tl 3 out: sn rdn: wknd bef next* **18/1**
6P03 **6** *¾* **Qualitee**[18] 4417 6-11-11 89 .... DaveCrosse 78
(Claire Dyson) *a towards rr* **16/1**
-06F **7** *17* **Insignia (IRE)**[26] 4273 9-11-3 81 .... (p) DenisO'Regan 55
(Victor Dartnall) *chsd ldrs tl wknd after 6th: t.o* **13/8**[1]
6/P0 **8** *11* **Zuleta**[12] 4540 10-9-12 65 .... (b[1]) MarcGoldstein[(3)] 29
(Laura Young) *trckd ldrs: rdn after 6th: wknd next* **33/1**
0-00 **9** *70* **Stance**[29] 4224 12-11-12 90 .... (v[1]) LeightonAspell —
(Peter Hedger) *a towards rr: lost tch after 6th: t.o* **40/1**
P54P **P** **Wiesenfurst (GER)**[56] 3699 7-10-7 76 ow1 .... (t) TomO'Connor[(5)] —
(John Berwick) *trckd ldrs tl 4th: sn in rr: lost tch 6th: p.u after 3 out* **33/1**
00F0 **P** **Honest**[17] 4450 8-11-7 85 .... AndrewThornton —
(Karen George) *mid-div tl wknd after 6th: bhd whn p.u bef 3 out* **25/1**

5m 31.2s (11.00) **Going Correction** +0.575s/f (Soft) 11 Ran SP% **117.7**
Speed ratings (Par 103): **103,100,94,93,91 91,85,81,55,— —**
Tote Swingers: 1&2 £15.70, 1&3 £6.40, 2&3 £11.90 CSF £81.63 CT £307.70 TOTE £9.50: £2.60, £4.20, £1.40; EX 106.70.
Owner Mr & Mrs P George & Mrs B Russell **Bred** James V Neville **Trained** Longdown, Devon

FOCUS
A weak handicap hurdle run at a reasonable pace.

NOTEBOOK
Flying Award(IRE) had not shown much previously over hurdles in novice events over a little shorter, being beaten a minimum of just under 43 lengths, but was a different proposition on this handicap debut in lowly company. In front turning out of the back, he ran out a comfortable winner and there may be more to come from him over 3m as he won at that trip between the flags. It probably won't pay to get carried away with this form, though. Official explanation: trainer said, regarding apparent improvement in form, that the gelding had been wrong all winter and was just coming into itself. (op 13-2, after 14-1 in a place, tchd 6-1)
Boosha kept on to look a possible danger going to the second-last, but the winner pulled away from there. She had never been placed before in nine tries and is clearly very moderate. (op 11-1 tchd 14-1)
Petroglyph, as at Uttoxeter in heavy ground latest, was a well-beaten third. He continues to drop in the weights and is now 11lb lower than when completing a hat-trick in late 2009. (tchd 11-4 and 7-2 in a place)
Canshebemine, who won a seller on this card a year ago, was held on this step up in trip. She never landed a blow but did seem to stay. (tchd 7-1)
Gunship(IRE) was immediately in trouble after losing his lead and remains a maiden over hurdles. (op 16-1 tchd 20-1)
Insignia(IRE), in with every chance when falling at Taunton, has changed stables since. He was well supported, only to drop away rather tamely early on the final circuit. Official explanation: jockey said gelding ran flat (op 11-4)

4901 TOTNES AND BRIDGETOWN RACES COMPANY NOVICES' HUNTERS' CHASE (16 fncs) 2m 5f 110y
5:15 (5:15) (Class 6) 5-Y-O+ **£824** (£253; £126)

Form RPR
1 **1** **Over The Phone (IRE)**[19] 4415 6-11-13 0 .... MrTWeston[(3)] 114+
(A G Hobbs) *cl up: led after 3 out: kpt on wl: pushed out* **4/6**[1]
043P **2** *6* **Quaddick Lake (IRE)**[15] 8-11-12 95 .... MrWBiddick 102
(A J Farrant) *trckd ldrs tl lost pl 6th: hdwy after 10th: rdn after 3 out: styd on to go 2nd run-in: no ch w wnr* **9/1**
420/ **3** *3 ¾* **Commander Kev (IRE)**[49] 10-11-5 0 .... MrJBanks[(7)] 101
(Mrs K Hobbs) *hld up: mstke 3rd: hdwy after 10th: mstke 12th: rdn after 4 out: chsd wnr after 2 out: 5th whn awkward last: lost 2nd run-in* **6/1**[2]
-432 **4** *11* **Walter De Wodeland**[13] 4534 10-11-5 97 .... MrJABest[(7)] 90
(Miss J Du Plessis) *led: rdn and hdd after 3 out: fdd appr last* **7/1**[3]
0/ **5** *14* **Stoneraker (IRE)**[21] 10-11-5 0 .... MrRHawkins[(7)] 75
(G Chambers) *mid-div: hdwy 9th: pressed ldr 11th: rdn after 4 out: wknd after next* **33/1**
6 *10* **Minireturn (IRE)**[15] 9-11-0 78 .... MrRGHenderson[(5)] 56
(M J Vanstone) *hld up: hdwy 8th: rdn after 4 out: sn wknd* **50/1**
0/ **7** *1 ¾* **Tatsu (IRE)**[21] 8-11-5 0 .... (t) MrLRowe[(7)] 61
(L S Rowe) *prom: hit 11th: rdn and wknd after 4 out* **66/1**
P/4- **8** *18* **General Blackthorn**[35] 12-11-5 87 .... MrMGreen[(7)] 43
(Norman G Crouch) *chsd ldrs tl 10th: sn bhd: t.o* **66/1**
405- **9** *63* **Sparkbridge (IRE)**[15] 8-11-5 64 .... (p) MrJLegg[(7)] —
(J Legg) *a detached: t.o* **80/1**
3 **P** **Deloughtane (IRE)**[21] 11-11-5 0 .... (p) MissAPearn[(7)] —
(R M Woollacott) *w ldr early: in tch whn hit 5th: wknd 10th: t.o whn p.u after 3 out* **20/1**
-335 **P** **Calzaghe (IRE)**[237] 1092 7-11-5 0 .... (t) MissAliceMills[(7)] —
(D Bryant) *a towards rr: t.o whn p.u bef 11th* **25/1**
0/ **P** **Two Wheel Drive (IRE)**[8] 11-10-12 0 .... MrJCole[(7)] —
(J Cole) *a towards rr: t.o whn p.u bef 11th* **100/1**

060/ **P** **Nicholas The Spark (IRE)**[15] 9-11-5 0...................... MissJennyCarr(7) —
(Mrs Angela Davis) *in tch: reminders after 8th: rdn after next: sn wknd: p.u bef 11th* **66/1**

5m 32.7s (11.30) **Going Correction** +0.325s/f (Yiel) **13** Ran SP% **117.0**
Speed ratings: **92,89,88,84,79 75,75,68,45,— —,—,—**
Tote Swingers: 1&2 £2.50, 1&3 £1.80, 2&3 £8.90 CSF £6.58 TOTE £1.60: £1.10, £2.70, £1.50; EX 6.60.
Owner Mrs J Hitchings **Bred** Damien Fitzhenry & Paddy Fitzhenry **Trained** Hanley Swan, Worcs

FOCUS
A very modest hunter chase, but the pace was sound.\n

NOTEBOOK
Over The Phone(IRE) is a useful type in this grade and he supplemented his Leicester gains with a comfortable victory, his fifth successive win all told. His target is a race at Cheltenham's hunter chase evening early in May, and he will have one more run before then. (op 5-6)
Quaddick Lake(IRE), who never fulfilled early promise over hurdles, won a members' point recently. Staying on to go second after the last, he remains a less than straightforward ride. (op 8-1 tchd 15-2)
Commander Kev(IRE) made several mistakes on this hunter chase debut and one at the last probably cost him second. (op 5-1)
Walter De Wodeland was runner-up over C&D latest and fifth in this race 12 months ago. He made the running to the home turn and, not for the first time, finished weakly. (op 8-1)
T/Jkpt: £5,390.50 to a £1 stake. Pool of £1,360,852.28 - 179.24 winning tickets. T/Plt: £74.10 to a £1 stake. Pool of £150,237.70 - 1,479.82 winning tickets. T/Qpdt: £31.00 to a £1 stake. Pool of £6,072.24 - 144.86 winning tickets. TM

4902 - 4909a (Foreign Racing) - See Raceform Interactive

4471 KELSO (L-H)
Monday, March 21

OFFICIAL GOING: Good to soft (good in places; 6.6)
All rails moved out two metres.
Wind: Fresh, half against Weather: Cloudy, fine

4910 NSPCC SCHOOL SERVICE NOVICES' HURDLE (10 hdls) 2m 2f
2:10 (2:10) (Class 4) 4-Y-0+ **£2,602** (£764; £382; £190)

Form RPR
-313 **1** **Wyse Hill Teabags**[16] 4475 6-11-6 133.................. RichieMcGrath 124+
(Jim Goldie) *t.k.h: w ldr: led 2 out: pushed clr run-in* **8/11**[1]
65 **2** *10* **Quel Elite (FR)**[21] 4393 7-11-0 0.. PaddyAspell 106
(James Moffatt) *prom: rdn and outpcd after 4 out: rallied 2 out: styd on to chse (ch) wnr towards fin* **11/1**
-154 **3** *3/4* **Freddie Brown**[16] 4473 7-11-0 0.. JanFaltejsek 104
(George Charlton) *plld hrd: hld up on outside: stdy hdwy after 5th: pushed along after next: rallied 2 out: drifted lft and styd on run-in* **10/1**[3]
P030 **4** *3/4* **Kai Broon (IRE)**[33] 4148 4-10-7 86.............................. CampbellGillies 96
(Lucinda Russell) *mde most to 2 out: rdn and kpt on same pce fr last* **66/1**
5-23 **5** *12* **Inoogoo (IRE)**[25] 4304 6-11-0 0.. BarryKeniry 95
(George Bewley) *prom: rdn whn lft cl 3rd 3 out: outpcd next: no imp whn mstke last* **20/1**
0/05 **6** *3 3/4* **Northern Cross (IRE)**[33] 4145 7-11-0 0.............................. BrianHughes 89
(Howard Johnson) *hld up: outpcd after 4 out: plugged on fr 2 out: nvr rchd ldrs* **66/1**
2 **7** *6* **Rathnaroughy (IRE)**[10] 4684 7-11-0 0.............................. MarkBradburne 84
(S R B Crawford, Ire) *prom: lft cl 4th 3 out: rdn and no ex fr next* **18/1**
00-0 **8** *hd* **Parson's Punch**[37] 4068 6-10-9 85................................ AlexanderVoy(5) 84
(Lucy Normile) *midfield: lost pl 1/2-way: sme late hdwy: nvr on terms* **150/1**
000 **9** *17* **Isla Patriot**[16] 4473 5-11-0 0.. PeterBuchanan 68
(N W Alexander) *nt fluent: bhd: pushed along bef 4 out: nvr on terms* **200/1**
00 **10** *1/2* **Vittachi**[145] 2033 4-10-4 0.. EwanWhillans(3) 61
(Alistair Whillans) *bhd: pushed along fnl circ: nvr on terms* **100/1**
0 **11** *1 1/2* **Nisaal (IRE)**[32] 4165 6-11-0 0.. TomMessenger 66
(Sandy Forster) *towards rr: struggling bef 4 out: sn btn* **50/1**
-PP **12** *26* **Legbeforewicket**[25] 4303 5-10-0 0.............................. MrGJCockburn(7) 36
(Lucinda Russell) *midfield on outside: struggling fr 6th: btn fnl 3* **200/1**
00 **13** *22* **Saga Surprise (FR)**[32] 4165 6-11-0 0........................(t) MichaelMcAlister 23
(Maurice Barnes) *a bhd: struggling bef 4 out: t.o* **200/1**
-P0P **P** **Paul Revere (IRE)**[49] 3850 7-11-0 0.............................. WilsonRenwick —
(Nicky Richards) *a bhd: struggling fnl circ: t.o whn p.u 2 out* **150/1**
061 **P** **And The Man**[25] 4304 5-11-6 0.. FearghalDavis —
(Nicky Richards) *trckd ldrs: cl 3rd and pushed along whn p.u appr 3 out* **3/1**[2]

4m 38.3s (11.30) **Going Correction** +0.30s/f (Yiel)
WFA 4 from 5yo+ 7lb **15** Ran SP% **119.1**
Speed ratings (Par 105): **86,81,81,80,75 73,71,71,63,63 62,51,41,—,—**
CSF £10.53 TOTE £2.10: £1.40, £3.20, £3.00; EX 10.10.
Owner P C & J W Smith **Bred** Gail And Stuart Smales **Trained** Uplawmoor, E Renfrews

FOCUS
Not the most competitive novice hurdle but the placed horses set the level.

NOTEBOOK
Wyse Hill Teabags, the clear form pick, drew right away after the last for a ready success. He's the type to make an impact in decent handicap hurdles. (tchd Evens in a place)
Quel Elite(FR) ran arguably his best race to date, keeping on in the manner of a horse likely to stay further. This was only his third start and he remains capable of better. (op 12-1)
Freddie Brown wasn't made as much use of as usual and was seen putting in his best work in the final 2f. He appreciates a sound surface and can win over hurdles in the summer. (tchd 11-1)
Kai Broon(IRE) was up there throughout and ran a better race, despite ending up well held. (op 80-1)
Inoogoo(IRE) is a fine, big sort who probably won't be winning until switched to handicaps. He's very much a chaser. (op 22-1)
And The Man was still up there with every chance when suddenly pulling up before the third-last, something presumably going amiss. (tchd 4-1 in a place)

4911 D.G. PRYDE LTD NOVICES' H'CAP CHASE (17 fncs) 2m 6f 110y
2:40 (2:40) (Class 4) (0-115,113) 5-Y-0+ **£3,332** (£1,034; £557)

Form RPR
6231 **1** **Rossini's Dancer**[33] 4150 6-10-13 100.............................. MarkBradburne 115+
(Sue Bradburne) *chsd ldr to 10th: cl up: shkn up bef 2 out: led gng wl bef last: drew clr run-in* **5/1**[3]
6145 **2** *17* **Border Reiver**[21] 4392 7-11-0 101...................................(t) RichieMcGrath 102
(Tim Easterby) *led and clr to 8th: hdd 2 out: rallied and ev ch last: no ch w wnr run-in* **5/1**[3]
066 **3** *3/4* **Maid In Moscow (IRE)**[10] 4688 7-10-0 87 oh2............. CampbellGillies 86
(S R B Crawford, Ire) *bhd: hdwy and prom 8th: led 2 out: sn rdn: hdd bef last: kpt on same pce* **12/1**
2243 **R** **Blackpool Billy (IRE)**[13] 4546 9-11-12 113.............................. GrahamLee —
(Ferdy Murphy) *hld up: nt fluent 1st: j. slowly next: ref 3rd* **7/4**[1]
220- **P** **Chicago Outfit (IRE)**[334] 5305 6-11-3 111................. MrJohnDawson(7) —
(John Wade) *in tch: sddle slipped 1st: p.u next* **22/1**
0443 **U** **Winter Alchemy (IRE)**[21] 4390 6-10-0 87 oh1............... WilsonRenwick —
(Nicky Richards) *chsd clr ldrs: hdwy 8th: reminders next: 4 l 4th and pushed along whn blnd and uns rdr 11th* **5/2**[2]

5m 56.5s (12.00) **Going Correction** +0.30s/f (Yiel) **6** Ran SP% **110.3**
Speed ratings: **91,85,84,—,— —**
toteswingers:1&2 £3.30, 2&3 £7.20, 1&3 £6.60 CSF £28.00 TOTE £4.20: £1.60, £2.10; EX 31.40.
Owner Turcan Barber Fletcher Dunning **Bred** Heather Raw **Trained** Cunnoquhie, Fife

FOCUS
Quite an eventful race with the winner to the level of his upgraded Musselburgh win.

NOTEBOOK
Rossini's Dancer, a recent winner at Musselburgh, began to assert after the last, eventually drawing right away for an easy success. He's clearly in the form of his life, but the handicapper is sure to make things tougher for him in future. (tchd 11-2)
Border Reiver tried to rally having been headed, but was left trailing on the run-in. (op 13-2)
Maid In Moscow(IRE), outpaced early on this chasing debut, warmed to her task and took over seemingly travelling best two out, but she stopped rather quickly in front before keeping on again. There should be something similar in her on this ground. (op 9-1 tchd 14-1 in a place)
Blackpool Billy(IRE) decided he didn't fancy taking the third and refused. (op 14-1)
Chicago Outfit(IRE)'s saddle slipped after a blunder at the first. Official explanation: jockey said he lost an iron (op 14-1)
Winter Alchemy(IRE), a chasing debutant, wasn't out of it when unseating with a circuit to go. (op 14-1)

4912 ARPAL 120TH ANNIVERSARY H'CAP HURDLE (8 hdls) 2m 110y
3:10 (3:10) (Class 4) (0-115,115) 4-Y-0+ **£2,602** (£764; £382; £190)

Form RPR
0552 **1** **King Mak**[8] 4738 9-10-2 98.. KyleJames(7) 109+
(Marjorie Fife) *trckd ldrs: nt fluent 4 out: sn drvn: rallied bef 2 out: led bef last: kpt on strly* **15/2**[3]
5204 **2** *7* **Latin Connection (IRE)**[35] 4115 5-11-3 106.................. CampbellGillies 109
(S R B Crawford, Ire) *hld up: smooth hdwy bef 2 out: effrt and chsd wnr run-in: no imp* **10/1**
253F **3** *7* **County Colours (IRE)**[54] 3751 6-10-13 107................... PaulGallagher(5) 104
(Howard Johnson) *t.k.h: prom: ev ch 4 out: led next to bef last: kpt on same pce run-in* **8/1**
5306 **4** *1 1/2* **Rain Stops Play (IRE)**[32] 4166 9-11-3 106....................... FearghalDavis 101
(Nicky Richards) *hld up: hdwy and in tch bef 2 out: outpcd last* **14/1**
/P66 **5** *1/2* **Bywell Beau (IRE)**[32] 4169 12-11-4 114........................(t) AlistairFindlay(7) 109
(George Charlton) *led to 3 out: rallied: wknd fr last* **5/1**[2]
0053 **6** *5* **No Supper (IRE)**[13] 4544 7-10-6 95.. BarryKeniry 85
(George Bewley) *hld up: drvn after 3 out: nvr able to chal* **9/1**
1221 **7** *nk* **Pokfulham (IRE)**[16] 4473 5-11-12 115..................................(v) GrahamLee 109+
(Jim Goldie) *chsd ldr: ev ch 3 out: upsides whn blnd next: sn wknd* **5/2**[1]
4040 **8** *41* **Scarvagh Rose**[21] 4395 6-10-0 89.................................... WilsonRenwick 42
(Rose Dobbin) *hld up in midfield: drvn and outpcd after 4 out: lost tch fr next* **22/1**
04P **P** **The Galloping Shoe**[25] 4303 6-11-7 113....................(t) EwanWhillans(3) —
(Alistair Whillans) *towards rr: outpcd bef 4th: struggling next: t.o whn p.u 2 out* **15/2**[3]
056 **R** **Cool Baranca (GER)**[29] 4242 5-9-8 90........................... HenryBrooke(7) 99+
(Dianne Sayer) *prom: hdwy whn blnd bdly: rdr lost irons and dislodged bridle 4 out: rallied and cl up whn hit next: 2 l down disputing 2nd whn rn out last* **11/1**

4m 3.70s (1.90) **Going Correction** +0.30s/f (Yiel) **10** Ran SP% **118.3**
Speed ratings (Par 105): **107,103,100,99,99 97,96,77,—,—**
toteswingers:1&2 £8.40, 2&3 £13.10, 1&3 £11.80 CSF £80.09 CT £622.57 TOTE £9.40: £2.90, £2.90, £3.40; EX 72.70.
Owner Mrs Marion Turner **Bred** Mrs Gail C List **Trained** Stillington, N Yorks

FOCUS
They went a good gallop for what was a modest handicap hurdle, making it a proper test at the distance. The runner-up is rated to his mark.

NOTEBOOK
King Mak, runner-up off this mark at Market Rasen over further, looked beaten after four out, but he kept grinding away and, having hit the front before the last, stayed on strongly to draw clear on the run-in, ending a losing run for his trainer in the process. (op 8-1)
Latin Connection(IRE) was ridden confidently and stayed on to draw clear of the third, but the winner wasn't for catching. (op 11-1 tchd 12-1)
County Colours(IRE), a faller over fences last time, travelled well on this return to hurdles, but lacked the pace to accelerate from the last. (tchd 17-2)
Rain Stops Play(IRE) remains a maiden over hurdles. (op 11-1)
Bywell Beau(IRE) found the ground a bit lively. He tried to stay on again, having been headed, and probably needs a stiffer test on this kind of surface. (op 13-2 tchd 7-1)
Pokfulham(IRE), a course winner earlier in the month, was a bit keen early, but still held every chance when walking through the second-last. This effectively ended his chance. Official explanation: jockey said gelding made a bad mistake 2nd last and failed to recover (op 3-1)
Cool Baranca(GER) ◆ deserves a mention as, despite her rider Henry Brooke losing his irons and having steering problems following the mare's blunder four out, the pair kept going and were still in the mix for a place when going the wrong side of the last hurdle. This was her handicap debut and it's hard to think she's not capable of winning something similar. (op 14-1)

4913 RUTHERFORD CENTENARY - ISUZU IN THE BORDERS H'CAP CHASE (12 fncs) 2m 1f
3:40 (3:40) (Class 3) (0-130,130) 5-Y-0+ **£5,854** (£1,719; £859; £429)

Form RPR
21FU **1** **Tartan Snow**[16] 4471 11-10-4 115.............................. GaryRutherford(7) 124+
(Stuart Coltherd) *hld up: hdwy and prom 1/2-way: hit 4 out: effrt 2 out: led run-in: styd on strly* **13/2**[3]
56F0 **2** *4 1/2* **My Moment (IRE)**[44] 3949 8-11-10 128.............................. AndrewTinkler 134
(Henry Daly) *cl up: led 4 out: rdn: hung lft and hdd run-in: stened and kpt on same pce* **9/2**[2]
-255 **3** *3 1/4* **Gringo**[33] 4149 9-11-12 130.. BrianHughes 132
(Howard Johnson) *hld up: outpcd bef 4 out: rallied 2 out: effrt last: kpt on same pce run-in* **8/1**
3006 **4** *6* **Carrietau**[17] 4456 8-10-6 117..(t) HenryBrooke(7) 115
(Barry Murtagh) *led to 7th: cl up tl outpcd after 2 out: plugged on run-in: no imp* **9/1**
0015 **5** *11* **Quicuyo (GER)**[37] 4065 8-10-13 120.............................(t) HarryHaynes(3) 108
(James Ewart) *cl up: ev ch 3 out to last: wknd run-in* **9/1**

-404 **6** 1/2 **Hazeldene**[16] 4472 9-10-8 **112** JanFaltejsek 100
(George Charlton) *cl up: led 7th to 4 out: rdn and wknd fr 2 out* **10/1**

P0P0 **7** 16 **Bob's Dream (IRE)**[49] 3855 9-10-11 **115** (t) FearghalDavis 87
(William Amos) *hld up: drvn and outpcd 8th: n.d after* **12/1**

1130 **8** 9 **Heavenly Chorus**[17] 4455 9-10-7 **111** JamesReveley 75
(Keith Reveley) *nt fluent: a bhd: blnd 5th: sn n.d* **7/1**

2021 **U** **Raysrock (IRE)**[9] 4716 9-11-12 **130** (t) CampbellGillies —
(Lucinda Russell) *hld up in tch: blnd and uns rdr 6th* **7/2**[1]

4m 20.0s (2.00) **Going Correction** +0.30s/f (Yiel) **9** Ran SP% **114.1**
Speed ratings: **107,104,103,100,95 95,87,83,—**
CSF £36.18 CT £237.14 TOTE £6.60: £2.90, £2.00, £3.00; EX 25.30.
Owner Whitemoss Golf Syndicate **Bred** R V Westwood **Trained** Selkirk, Borders
■ Stewards' Enquiry : Henry Brooke one-day ban: careless riding (Apr 4)

FOCUS
A fairly ordinary handicap chase but the form looks solid rated around the placed horses to their marks.

NOTEBOOK
Tartan Snow has had problems with his jumping, but his latest course unseat came after he clipped heels (going well at time), and he more than made up for that here, pulling away having taken over after the last. He was 13lb higher than when winning last month and is clearly progressive, despite his age. (op 5-1)
My Moment(IRE) had made a long journey to race here and this signalled a return to form. His jumping was better than it has been, but he was looking around and hanging on the run-in and can't be banked on to repeat this form, as his profile suggests. (op 5-1)
Gringo rallied well but never actually looked like winning. He's still to win a handicap over fences, although in fairness he's not had many tries. (tchd 17-2)
Carrietau kept on again after leading for a long way. (op 12-1)
Quicuyo(GER) had the winner behind when scoring at Ayr in January, went well for a long way and can show himself better than this. Official explanation: jockey said gelding had a breathing problem (op 17-2 tchd 10-1)
Raysrock(IRE) made a costly early blunder and got rid of his rider. (op 4-1 tchd 9-2)

4914 P & G ALLAN H'CAP HURDLE (11 hdls) 2m 6f 110y
4:10 (4:10) (Class 4) (0-115,112) 4-Y-0+ **£2,602** (£764; £382; £190)

Form RPR

00-0 **1** **Sendali (FR)**[69] 3500 7-11-5 **105** BrianHughes 108
(Chris Grant) *in tch: hdwy after 2 out: edgd rt and led run-in: styd on wl u.p* **16/1**

6565 **2** 2 **Bertie Milan (IRE)**[16] 4477 6-11-4 **104** (p) MarkBradburne 105
(Sue Bradburne) *trckd ldrs: drvn and outpcd after 3 out: rallied bef last: styd on to take 2nd towards fin: nt rch wnr* **15/2**

F202 **3** 1/2 **Leith Walk (IRE)**[16] 4477 8-10-1 **97** CallumWhillans(10) 99+
(Donald Whillans) *prom: effrt and ev ch last: swtchd lft run-in: kpt on same pce towards fin* **4/1**[2]

-360 **4** 3/4 **Lawgiver (IRE)**[43] 3966 10-11-2 **109** (p) KyleJames(7) 109
(Marjorie Fife) *hld up: hdwy bef 3 out: led bef last to run-in: kpt on same pce* **12/1**

6503 **5** 1 1/2 **Catleen (IRE)**[33] 4157 7-10-13 **99** CampbellGillies 98
(S R B Crawford, Ire) *hld up: stdy hdwy bef 2 out: rdn after last: kpt on: nrst fin* **3/1**[1]

-640 **6** 7 **Arrow Barrow (IRE)**[28] 4253 6-10-7 **100** MrJohnDawson(7) 94
(John Wade) *t.k.h: trckd ldrs: chal after 3 out: to bef last: hung lft and hit last: wknd run-in* **20/1**

0055 **7** 2 1/2 **Grandad Bill (IRE)**[28] 4255 8-11-12 **112** RichieMcGrath 102
(Jim Goldie) *hld up: stdy hdwy 4 out: sn pushed along: effrt bef 2 out: sn no imp* **15/2**

3340 **8** 3 1/4 **Auberge (IRE)**[27] 4276 7-10-5 **91** JamesReveley 79
(Dianne Sayer) *led or disp ld to bef last: wknd run-in* **7/1**[3]

5-00 **9** 2 3/4 **Suprise Vendor (IRE)**[16] 4477 5-10-7 **100** GaryRutherford(7) 85
(Stuart Coltherd) *hld up: rdn after 3 out: wknd fr next* **50/1**

5304 **10** 1 1/2 **Terenzium (IRE)**[27] 4276 9-11-5 **105** (p) BarryKeniry 88
(Micky Hammond) *hld up: struggling bef 3 out: nvr on terms* **20/1**

2014 **11** 4 1/2 **Everaard (USA)**[16] 4477 5-11-5 **105** (p) GrahamLee 84
(Kate Walton) *hit 6th: disp ld to 3 out: wknd fr next* **9/1**

5m 48.7s (7.70) **Going Correction** +0.30s/f (Yiel) **11** Ran SP% **116.1**
Speed ratings (Par 105): **98,97,97,96,96 93,93,91,90,90 88**
toteswingers:1&2 £27.20, 2&3 £10.10, 1&3 £19.00 CSF £126.30 CT £580.30 TOTE £26.00: £5.00, £1.70, £2.10; EX 238.60.
Owner Elliott Brothers And Peacock **Bred** Sarl Haras Du Taillis Et Al **Trained** Newton Bewley, Co Durham
■ Stewards' Enquiry : Brian Hughes one-day ban: careless riding (Apr 4)

FOCUS
A competitive handicap hurdle although the form is ordinary but sound, with the first three close to their marks.

NOTEBOOK
Sendali(FR), whose last victory came on the Flat last April, was just 1lb higher than when gaining his last hurdles success and it was he who stayed on best after the last. Consistency has never been a strong point, however, so it can't be guaranteed he'll repeat this next time. (op 14-1)
Bertie Milan(IRE) kept on again to claim second, being helped by the first-time cheekpieces. A step up to 3m should suit. (op 10-1 tchd 11-1)
Leith Walk(IRE) also kept on right the way to the line, recording another fair effort in defeat. (op 9-2)
Lawgiver(IRE) remains 6lb above his last winning mark and could find no extra on the run-in. (op 9-1)
Catleen(IRE) was evidently well fancied, but failed to improve as much as expected for the better ground, keeping on too late. (op 4-1)
Arrow Barrow(IRE) ran better than his finishing position implies and remains capable of better. (op 18-1)

4915 EILDON HILL STABLES OPEN HUNTERS' CHASE (FOR THE CHARLIE BROWN TROPHY) (19 fncs) 3m 1f
4:40 (4:40) (Class 6) 5-Y-0+ **£1,249** (£387; £193; £96)

Form RPR

-F11 **1** **Quotica De Poyans (FR)**[16] 4476 7-11-13 120 MissKBryson(7) 130+
(Simon Shirley-Beavan) *mde all: blnd 12th: clr 2 out to last: pushed clr again run-in* **5/4**[1]

11F3 **2** 9 **Ardnaclancy (IRE)**[16] 4476 8-12-1 118 MrJARichardson(5) 121
(Andrew Richardson) *hld up: hdwy 1/2-way: chsd wnr 4 out: effrt and clsd last: one pce run-in* **8/1**[3]

46P- **3** 25 **Hot 'N' Holy**[334] 5318 12-11-5 0 MrGRSmith(7) 90
(David Thompson) *prom: drvn and outpcd 2 out: no imp last* **66/1**

3P43 **4** 9 **Thunder Hawk (IRE)**[33] 4147 11-11-13 92 (p) MrTDavidson(3) 85
(Mrs L A Coltherd) *chsd wnr to 7th: cl up: drvn and outpcd 13th: n.d after* **20/1**

5/ **5** 25 **Northern Revoque (IRE)**[43] 9-10-12 0 MrTMorrison(7) 67
(T Morrison) *prom: chsd wnr 7th: blnd next: hit 13th: lost 2nd 4 out: wknd fr 2 out* **33/1**

323P **6** dist **Nile Moon (IRE)**[15] 10-11-13 99 (p) MissLSutcliffe(7) —
(Mrs C Sutcliffe) *bhd: lost tch fnl circ: nvr on terms* **40/1**

/3-5 **P** **Nocatee (IRE)**[26] 4286 10-11-9 86 (p) MrMSeston(3) —
(C Rae) *a bhd: lost tch 1/2-way: t.o whn p.u bef 4 out* **100/1**

260/ **U** **Seafire Lad (IRE)**[36] 10-11-7 80 (p) MrJohnDawson(5) —
(Ms Jackie Williamson) *in tch: 6 l down whn blnd bdly and uns rdr 14th* **125/1**

/13- **P** **Abragante (IRE)**[513] 1887 10-11-13 0 MrMEnnis(7) —
(Mrs D Monteith) *bhd: stdy hdwy bef 14th: wknd 2 out: t.o whn p.u bef last* **14/1**

116- **F** **Robbers Glen (IRE)**[15] 11-12-6 0 MrsVJackson —
(Valerie Jackson) *hld up in tch: fell 6th: fatally injured* **15/8**[2]

6m 33.3s (1.80) **Going Correction** +0.30s/f (Yiel) **10** Ran SP% **110.4**
Speed ratings: **109,106,98,95,87 72,—,—,—,—**
toteswingers:1&2 £2.60, 2&3 £45.40, 1&3 £20.20 CSF £10.43 TOTE £1.80: £1.02, £2.20, £10.20; EX 8.00.
Owner Mrs P M Shirley-Beavan **Bred** Gilles Leblanc & Jacqueline Leblanc **Trained** Abbotrule, Borders
■ Stewards' Enquiry : Mr G R Smith six-day ban: used whip causing a minor weal in incorrect place (Apr 4,5,7,9-11)
Mr T Davidson two-day ban: careless riding (Apr 4-5); four-day ban: used whip with excessive frequency (Apr 10-12,15)

FOCUS
This had looked a bit of a match on paper, but it didn't develop due to the demise of the second favourite. The runner-up is rated to form and the winner can rate higher.

NOTEBOOK
Quotica De Poyans(FR) stayed on dourly for his fourth course success. Already a dual winner here this year, he took up his customary front-running role and, despite a couple of mistakes with just over a circuit to go, he galloped on relentlessly under pressure. Only seven, he'll have his sights raised next season, with either a crack at the Cheltenham Foxhunter or a switch to handicaps on the cards. (op 11-10 tchd 11-8)
Ardnaclancy(IRE) briefly looked a threat to the winner, but was left trailing once again after they touched down on the run-in. (op 10-1)
Hot 'N' Holy fared better than his 66/1 odds entitled him to. (op 50-1)
Thunder Hawk(IRE) tried to rally but could not go with the leaders. (op 28-1)
Robbers Glen(IRE) had looked a big danger to the favourite, having returned with two point-to-point victories, but he took a fatal fall at the sixth fence. A multiple point winner who had also scored five times under rules, he twice ran well at Cheltenham, finishing fifth and sixth respectively in the 2009 and 2010 Foxhunter. (op 2-1 tchd 7-4, 9-4 in a place)

4916 ROSIE'S CATERING & MICHAEL WARES CATER HIRE STANDARD OPEN NATIONAL HUNT FLAT RACE 2m 110y
5:10 (5:10) (Class 6) 4-6-Y-0 **£1,301** (£382; £191; £95)

Form RPR

1 **Nodform Richard** 5-11-3 0 GrahamLee 109
(Karen McLintock) *t.k.h: prom: hdwy over 4f out: chal over 2f out: led over 1f out: pushed out ins fnl f* **4/1**[2]

22 **2** 2 1/2 **Pyjama Game (IRE)**[33] 4151 5-11-3 0 WilsonRenwick 107
(Rose Dobbin) *hld up in tch: hdwy over 5f out: led over 2f out to 1f out: kpt on ins fnl f* **9/1**

0-54 **3** 10 **Farm Pixie (IRE)**[129] 2355 5-10-12 0 PaulGallagher(5) 98
(Ann Hamilton) *hld up: pushed along over 5f out: no imp tl styd on fr 2f out: no ch w first two* **50/1**

3 **4** 4 1/2 **Dome Run**[41] 3998 5-10-10 0 JeremiahMcGrath(7) 94
(Alan Swinbank) *hld up: rdn over 5f out: plugged on fnl 2f: nrst fin* **12/1**

66 **5** 1 **Monashee (IRE)**[44] 3957 6-10-10 0 AlistairFindlay(7) 93
(George Charlton) *t.k.h: cl up: led over 6f out to over 2f out: edgd rt over 1f out: wknd ins fnl f* **33/1**

6 3/4 **Balivernier** 5-11-3 0 JanFaltejsek 92
(George Charlton) *hld up: pushed along over 5f out: styd on fnl 2f: nvr rchd ldrs* **16/1**

7 5 **George My Friend** 5-10-10 0 KyleJames(7) 88
(Simon Waugh) *hld up: rdn over 4f out: sn no imp* **80/1**

8 7 **Runswick Relax** 5-10-10 0 MrJohnDawson(7) 82
(John Wade) *hld up: pushed along 5f out: nvr able to chal* **33/1**

2 **9** 7 **Harvey's Hope**[17] 4457 5-11-3 0 JamesReveley 87+
(Keith Reveley) *trckd ldrs: outpcd over 5f out: rallied over 3f out: wknd and eased fnl 2f* **2/1**[1]

1 **10** 2 3/4 **Turbolinas (FR)**[41] 3998 4-10-10 0 HenryBrooke(7) 73
(Kate Walton) *in tch: drvn and outpcd over 4f out: btn fnl 2f* **8/1**[3]

0- **11** 15 **Raggios Boy**[365] 4757 5-11-0 0 EwanWhillans(3) 59
(Barry Murtagh) *hld up: pushed along over 4f out: sn btn* **150/1**

12 3 **Roger Beantown (IRE)**[123] 2492 6-11-10 0 BrianHughes 64
(Howard Johnson) *led to over 6f out: rdn and wknd fr over 4f out* **4/1**[2]

13 25 **Money Dieu (IRE)** 6-10-10 0 MichaelMcAlister 27
(Stephen Marshall) *bhd: struggling over 4f out: sn btn* **80/1**

0 **14** 18 **Mr Mansson (IRE)**[33] 4151 4-10-5 0 AlexanderVoy(5) 11
(Lucy Normile) *midfield: stdy hdwy to trck ldrs 6f out: wknd fr over 3f out* **100/1**

15 57 **Playing Footsie** 5-10-3 0 MissLAlexander(7) —
(N W Alexander) *nrly uns rdr at s: a in last and detached: nvr on terms* **80/1**

4m 3.30s (7.10) **Going Correction** +0.30s/f (Yiel)
WFA 4 from 5yo+ 7lb **15** Ran SP% **121.2**
Speed ratings: **95,93,89,87,86 86,83,80,77,75 68,67,55,47,20**
toteswingers:1&2 £5.40, 2&3 £73.20, 1&3 £27.10 CSF £38.96 TOTE £4.70: £2.00, £3.10, £14.20; EX 45.60.
Owner Alan Lamont **Bred** Peter E Clinton **Trained** Ingoe, Northumberland

FOCUS
The pace was a good one, rather unusually for a bumper, and the front pair drew clear. They look above average with the fourth and fifth setting the level.

NOTEBOOK
Nodform Richard found plenty for pressure and won with a bit in hand. From a yard well respected in bumpers, he still looks to have a bit to learn, but should have a future, especially once faced with a stiffer test over jumps. There'll presumably be plenty of interest in him from more powerful yards, as like many youngsters from the stable, he is for sale. (tchd 6-1 in a place)
Pyjama Game(IRE) has now finished runner-up on all three starts. He again did nothing wrong, holding every chance, and deserves to win one before sent hurdling. (op 7-1 tchd 10-1)
Farm Pixie(IRE), off since November, ran well and should benefit from a longer trip over hurdles.
Dome Run stayed on late and managed to reverse first-time-out form with Turbolinas, the latter clearly not running his race. (op 10-1 tchd 16-1)
Harvey's Hope, a promising second at Doncaster on his debut, was well supported at the head of the market, but quickly found himself outpaced and ended up well beaten. (op 5-2 tchd 15-8)

Turbolinas(FR) failed to run his race having failed to confirm previous form with the fourth. (op 9-1 tchd 7-1)
Roger Beantown(IRE), purchased after winning a Thurles bumper in November, looked vulnerable under a penalty and, having cut out the early running, he stopped very quickly. Although this clearly wasn't his form, he's left with something to prove. Official explanation: jockey said gelding hung left-handed final mile (tchd 9-2)
T/Plt: £123.50 to a £1 stake. Pool of £78,706.09 - 465.15 winning tickets. T/Qpdt: £29.60 to a £1 stake. Pool of £6,477.65 - 161.55 winning tickets. RY

[3979]LINGFIELD (L-H)
Monday, March 21

OFFICIAL GOING: Good to soft (soft in places on hurdle course; chs 6.8, hdl 6.7); all-weather - standard
Wind: light, across Weather: sunny and bright

4917 LINGFIELDPARK.CO.UK MAIDEN HURDLE (6 hdls 2 omitted) 2m 110y
2:30 (2:30) (Class 5) 4-Y-0+ **£2,055** (£599; £299)

Form RPR
-060 **1** **Cody Wyoming**[11] 4677 5-11-0 0 .... DominicElsworth 103
(Heather Main) *hld up towards rr: hmpd 1st: prog after 4th: chsd ldrs gng wl after 3 out: pushed along to chse ldr bypassing 2 out: rdn to ld fnl 150yds: r.o wl* **100/1**
0 **2** *1 3/4* **Petit Ecuyer (FR)**[12] 4557 5-11-0 0 .... AndrewGlassonbury 101
(Gary Moore) *in tch: clsd on ldr after 5th: led sn after 3 out (actual last): rdn ent fnl 2f: drvn over 1f out: hdd and no ex fnl 150yds* **33/1**
44 **3** *7* **Archie Rice (USA)**[15] 4499 5-11-0 0 .... TimmyMurphy 99+
(Tom Keddy) *hld up in rr: hmpd 1st: stl plenty to do whn hmpd on bnd after 4th: gd hdwy to chse ldrs 3 out: (actual last): rdn bypassing 2 out: drvn to chse ldng pair over 1f out: no imp* **11/4**[1]
4 *2* **Bariolo (FR)**[47] 7-11-0 0 .... WillKennedy 93
(Noel Chance) *chsd ldrs: clsd on ldr bef 3 out (actual last): wnt 2nd ent st tl bypassing 2 out: sn wknd* **33/1**
5 **5** *nk* **Cunning Plan (IRE)**[19] 4424 4-10-0 0 .... MissHGrissell[(7)] 87
(Raymond York) *chsd ldr tl after 3rd: wnt 2nd again 5th tl ent st: wknd bypassing 2 out: plugged on* **150/1**
0 **6** *13* **Jacko's Boy**[67] 3526 8-11-0 0 .... WarrenMarston 60
(Martin Keighley) *chsd ldrs: wnt 2nd after 3rd tl 5th: rdn and struggling 3 out (actual last): 6th and wl btn ent st* **16/1**
40 **7** *4 1/2* **Storm Survivor (IRE)**[20] 4404 5-10-11 0 .... MrAJBerry[(3)] 77
(Jonjo O'Neill) *bhd: rdn and losing tch 3rd: virtually t.o bef 3 out (actual last): hdwy into midfield ent st: n.d* **14/1**
0 **8** *1 3/4* **Craicajack (IRE)**[21] 4397 4-10-7 0 .... DaveCrosse 69
(Edward Creighton) *a towards rr: j.rt 3rd: sn rdn and struggling: edgd lft after next: virtually t.o 3 out (actual last): plugged on ent st: n.d* **100/1**
9 *1 3/4* **Crazy Colours**[33] 5-10-7 0 .... MrHGMiller[(7)] 74
(Zoe Davison) *hld up in rr: rdn and losing tch 4th: virtually t.o 3 out (actual last): sme hdwy whn swtchd sharply rt to bypass 2 out: plugged on: n.d* **150/1**
04 **10** *19* **Mission Complete (IRE)**[19] 4424 5-11-0 0 .... RichieMcLernon 57
(Jonjo O'Neill) *a towards rr: hmpd 2nd: rdn and struggling after 3rd: t.o 3 out (actual last): n.d* **66/1**
11 *2 1/4* **Bute Street**[29] 6-11-0 0 .... TomScudamore 55
(Ron Hodges) *stdd s: hld up wl in rr: hmpd 2nd: rdn and no rspnse after next: t.o 3 out (actual last)* **20/1**
12 *16* **Eagle Nebula**[29] 7-11-0 0 .... MattieBatchelor 41
(Brett Johnson) *in tch: lost pl qckly after 4th: t.o after 3 out (actual last)* **25/1**
63 **13** *14* **Ostentation**[31] 4192 4-10-7 0 .... ColinBolger 21
(Roger Teal) *t.k.h: in tch: edgd lft after 4th: rdn bef 3 out(actual last): wknd qckly on downhill run to st: t.o bypassing 2 out: eased ins fnl f* **6/1**[3]
0-0P **14** *1/2* **Padys Arkle (IRE)**[21] 4397 7-10-7 0 ....(v[1]) MarkQuinlan[(7)] 28
(Brett Johnson) *led: clr after 2nd: rdn and rapidly coming bk to field whn blnd 3 out (actual last): sn hdd and fdd: t.o and virtually p.u ins fnl f* **100/1**
00 **15** *8* **Nik Nak Too**[18] 4444 5-10-11 0 .... JimmyDerham[(3)] 20
(Seamus Mullins) *t.k.h: hld up in tch in midfield: lost pl 4th: t.o after 3 out (actual last)* **200/1**
16 *dist* **Kingston Folly**[5] 4-10-7 0 .... JamesDavies —
(Andrew Haynes) *chsd ldrs tl lost pl qckly after 4th: t.o whn mstke 3 out (actual last): virtually p.u after* **100/1**
U **Diamond Twister (USA)**[12] 5-11-0 0 .... RodiGreene —
(Lisa Williamson) *taken down early: towards rr whn blnd and uns rdr 1st* **50/1**
F **Buona Sarah (IRE)**[19] 4-9-11 0 .... MarcGoldstein[(3)] —
(Sheena West) *t.k.h: in tch: mstke and bdly hmpd 1st: fell next: fatally injured* **16/1**
-26 **U** **Spirit D'Armor (FR)**[16] 4478 5-11-0 0 .... AidanColeman —
(Venetia Williams) *chsd ldrs tl veered bdly rt and uns rdr 3rd* **6/1**[3]
11-0 **F** **The Strawberry One**[90] 3055 6-10-7 0 .... DarylJacob —
(David Arbuthnot) *chsd ldrs tl fell 1st* **3/1**[2]

4m 2.50s (-11.60) **Going Correction** -0.50s/f (Good)
WFA 4 from 5yo+ 7lb **20 Ran SP% 122.4**
Speed ratings (Par 103): **107,106,102,101,101 95,93,92,91,82 81,74,67,67,63** —,—,—,—,—
toteswingers:1&2 £116.20, 2&3 £55.30, 1&3 £28.30 CSF £2016.78 TOTE £118.20: £34.10, £10.60, £1.70 TRIFECTA Exacta: Not won..
Owner Highnote Thoroughbreds **Bred** Spencer Bloodstock **Trained** Kingston Lisle, Oxon
■ Stewards' Enquiry : Colin Bolger four-day ban: careless riding (Apr 4,5,10,11)

FOCUS
This opening maiden was a weak affair and proved to be highly eventful with four coming down over the first three flights. That meant the last two hurdles were bypassed and few got seriously involved. Suspect form with the first two making big steps up.

NOTEBOOK
Cody Wyoming improved greatly on the level of his hurdling debut and shed his maiden tag at the sixth attempt. He moved smoothly into contention from off the pace and dug deep to emerge on top in the home straight. This was a clear personal-best effort and the drying ground evidently suited. Official explanation: trainer said, regarding apparent improvement in form, that the gelding jumped better and was more fluent. (op 80-1)
Petit Ecuyer(FR) showed the benefit of his hurdling debut 12 days earlier and posted a pleasing effort, just getting reeled in late on. It was only his second outing for Gary Moore and he obviously has a future. (op 66-1)
Archie Rice(USA) was a massive eye-catcher at Huntingdon on his previous outing 15 days earlier (jockey banned for ten days) when staying on all too late. With Timmy Murphy taking over the reins he was once more ridden out the back and, having found a troubled passage, again made his move late on. He was never going to get close enough to challenge, but this would suggest possible stamina limitations and moving to a sharper track looks on the cards. He also now has the option of handicaps. (op 5-2)
Bariolo(FR), a moderate 1m4f AW winner, was starting life rather late over hurdles but doesn't have many miles on the clock. He posted a respectable debut effort and ought to enjoy a stiffer test. (op 40-1)
Cunning Plan(IRE) hit a flat spot before running on again and this was better from him.
Spirit D'Armor(FR) made errors on his hurdling debut last time and clearly failed to learn from that experience. (op 9-1)
The Strawberry One, a dual bumper winner, got the first all wrong and took a heavy fall. (op 9-1)

4918 FOREST ROW NOVICES' HURDLE (8 hdls 2 omitted) 2m 3f 110y
3:00 (3:33) (Class 4) 4-Y-0+ **£2,329** (£678; £339)

Form RPR
11 **1** **Hildisvini (IRE)**[24] 4325 5-11-7 0 .... FelixDeGiles 121+
(Charlie Longsdon) *trckd ldrs: wnt 2nd after 6th: led bef 2 out: pressed and rdn between last 2: j. bdly lft last: hanging lft but kpt on wl flat* **10/11**[1]
502 **2** *1/2* **Cleaver**[16] 4478 10-11-1 110 .... LeightonAspell 114
(Lady Herries) *t.k.h: hld up in tch in midfield: hdwy to chse ldrs bypassing 7th: pressed wnr ent st: mstke 2 out: sn swtchd lft and rdn: sltly hmpd last: drvn and nt qckn flat* **12/1**
3 *26* **Sir Royal (USA)**[12] 6-11-1 0 .... SamThomas 92
(Brendan Powell) *plld hrd: hld up towards rr: hdwy after 6th: trckd ldrs and clr of field wl bef 2 out: wnt 3rd and j. slowly 2 out: sn wknd* **20/1**
2110 **4** *1 1/2* **Not Til Monday (IRE)**[16] 4485 5-11-13 119 .... TimmyMurphy 101
(J R Jenkins) *led: rdn after 6th: hdd bef 2 out: 4th and btn 2 out: wknd after* **7/1**[3]
33 **5** *48* **Junior Jack**[64] 3585 6-11-1 0 .... WarrenMarston 46
(Martin Keighley) *chsd ldr after 3rd tl after 6th: wknd u.p bypassing 3 out: t.o ent st: mstke last* **11/4**[2]
4P5 **6** *1* **Ice 'N' Easy (IRE)**[24] 4329 6-11-1 0 .... AndrewThornton 45
(Richard Rowe) *mstkes: chsd ldr tl after 3rd: styd prom: rdn and struggling after 6th: t.o ent st* **50/1**
F **7** *7* **Nobody's Business (IRE)**[11] 4665 10-10-8 0 .... MrHGMiller[(7)] 38
(Zoe Davison) *s.i.s: in tch in rr: mstke 4th: struggling and rdn 6th: wl t.o bef 2 out* **150/1**
0 **8** *3/4* **Alone They Stand (IRE)**[19] 4422 6-11-1 0 .... RichieMcLernon 38
(Jonjo O'Neill) *in tch towards rr: mstke 4th: sme hdwy bef next: struggling and lost tch after 6th: wl t.o bef 2 out* **66/1**
0-00 **9** *34* **Late Red**[132] [illegible] 9-11-1 0 .... MattieBatchelor 7
(Jamie Poulton) *t.k.h: hld up in tch in rr: wknd after 5th: wl t.o bef 3 out: blnd last* **100/1**
10 *13* **Joinedupwriting**[15] 6-10-11 0 ow1 .... MrPYork[(5)] —
(Raymond York) *racd wd: t.k.h: chsd ldrs 3rd tl 5th: wknd next: wl t.o bef 2 out* **66/1**
-355 **P** **Dark Dancer**[11] 4667 7-10-8 0 .... HarrySkelton —
(Laura Mongan) *chsd ldrs: j.rt 3rd: lost pl rapidly 5th: t.o whn p.u 2 out* **66/1**
0-0 **P** **Fleetstone**[21] 4397 6-10-8 0 .... SeanQuinlan —
(Richard Phillips) *in tch in rr: rdn and toiling after 4th: wl t.o whn p.u 2 out* **100/1**
00P **P** **Midnight Charmer**[28] 4262 5-11-1 0 ....(t) NickScholfield —
(Emma Baker) *in tch tl 5th: bhd after next: wl t.o whn p.u 2 out: distressed after r* **200/1**
00 **P** **Midnight Maisie**[29] 4239 4-9-7 0 .... MrBJPoste[(7)] —
(Anna Brooks) *t.k.h: hld up in tch: mstke and sddle slipped 4th: sn eased and p.u* **200/1**

4m 57.5s (-9.20) **Going Correction** -0.50s/f (Good)
WFA 4 from 5yo+ 7lb **14 Ran SP% 114.1**
Speed ratings (Par 105): **98,97,87,86,67 67,64,64,50,45** —,—,—,—
toteswingers:1&2 £3.70, 2&3 £6.10, 1&3 £3.80 CSF £13.10 TOTE £1.80: £1.10, £1.80, £3.10; EX 10.50.
Owner J H & S M Wall **Bred** Sean Wickham **Trained** Over Norton, Oxon

FOCUS
There was a delay of half an hour after the opener due to a lack of ambulances, as two were required to take injured jockeys to hospital. The general opinion of the riders was that the ground was riding "dead". There was no strength in depth to this novice event, which was run at an average gallop, and the first pair came right away in the home straight. Most of the runners were freely sweating due to it being delayed and the last flight in the back straight was omitted. Not form to be confident about although it could rate higher.

NOTEBOOK
Hildisvini(IRE) landed the hat-trick by following up his debut success over hurdles at Sandown last month and showed a good attitude under a penalty. He got warm beforehand and took time to settle the issue once asked for maximum effort. Looking at the way he ran about from two out this tacky ground probably wasn't to his liking, and he remains a promising young horse. Things will be tougher under a double penalty, though. (tchd 4-5 and Evens in places)
Cleaver again proved keen, but he threw down a strong challenge to the winner and wasn't done any favours when that rival jumped left at the last. He still found him too resolute, however, and his attitude comes into question after this.
Sir Royal(USA)'s sole win on the level came off a mark of 72 over 1m4f. Another awash with sweat, he made stylish headway late on before flattening out in the home straight, and this looked an encouraging introduction to jumping. However, he collapsed due to exhaustion afterwards and could be set for a spell on the sidelines. Official explanation: trainer said gelding finished distressed (tchd 22-1)
Not Til Monday(IRE), a C&D winner, set out to make all, but was in trouble before the home turn and finished well beaten off under his double penalty. (op 6-1)
Junior Jack attracted support back down in trip, but proved free and turned in a lacklustre display. (op 3-1)
Midnight Maisie Official explanation: jockey said saddle slipped

4919 ASHURST WOOD NOVICES' H'CAP CHASE (14 fncs) 2m 4f 110y
3:30 (4:17) (Class 4) (0-100,97) 5-Y-0+ **£2,808** (£818; £409)

Form RPR
F402 **1** **Goring One (IRE)**[11] 4668 6-10-12 **83** .... AndrewThornton 100+
(Anna Newton-Smith) *mde all: j. slowly 2nd: gng best bef 3 out: rdn and readily asserted after last: comf* **3/1**[2]
0534 **2** *5* **Ballyman (IRE)**[12] 4560 10-9-11 **71** oh5 .... JimmyDerham[(3)] 81
(Jonathan Geake) *in tch in midfield: rdn bef 10th: clsd and pressing ldrs 11th: chsd wnr 3 out: ev ch and rdn next: stl ev ch last: drvn and readily brushed aside flat: kpt on* **11/4**[1]
0P05 **3** *8* **Princely Hero (IRE)**[22] 4372 7-11-7 **92** ....(v[1]) LeightonAspell 95
(Chris Gordon) *chsd wnr: hmpd 2nd: sn chsd ldng pair: pressed ldrs 9th tl rdn and struggling bef 3 out: 3rd and btn 2 out* **11/1**

P20 **4** *23* **Chestnut Ben (IRE)**[11] 4675 6-10-7 **78**............................ JamesDavies 57
(Gary Brown) *racd wd: hld up in tch: gd jump and hdwy 6th: cl up whn j. awkwardly 11th: sn pushed along and struggling: 4th and wl btn next* **9/1**

/436 **5** *3/4* **Kasimali (IRE)**[42] 3982 8-11-8 **93**........................(v[1]) AndrewGlassonbury 71
(Gary Moore) *hld up in last pair: rdn and struggling 7th: no ch w ldrs fr 11th: plugged on flat* **7/1**

34P2 **6** *1/2* **Whatcanisay**[62] 3614 12-10-0 **71**....................................(bt) HaddenFrost 49
(James Frost) *in tch in midfield: dropped to last and pushed along after 5th: lost tch w ldrs 10th: no ch after: plugged on and swtchd lft flat* **6/1**[3]

P213 **7** *1/2* **Karasakal (IRE)**[20] 4411 8-11-2 **97**.......................(p) JosephAkehurst(10) 74
(Gary Moore) *a in rr: mstke 2nd: rdn and struggling 7th: lost tch 10th: no ch after: plugged on flat* **7/1**

66PV **8** *18* **Zhukov (IRE)**[4] 4831 9-11-5 **97**.......................................(t) MrBJPoste(7) 56
(Kevin Tork) *t.k.h: pressed ldr after 2nd tl bef 11th: sn rdn: wknd rapidly after 11th: dropped to last 2 out: t.o* **16/1**

5m 9.60s (-8.60) **Going Correction** -0.275s/f (Good) **8** Ran SP% **115.2**
Speed ratings: **105,103,100,91,91 90,90,83**
toteswingers:1&2 £2.50, 2&3 £6.20, 1&3 £6.60 CSF £12.32 CT £77.69 TOTE £6.10: £2.20, £1.10, £3.80; EX 14.50.
Owner George Goring **Bred** R E Daniels **Trained** Jevington, E Sussex
■ Stewards' Enquiry : Hadden Frost three-day ban: weighed-in 2lb heavy (Apr 4,5,10)

FOCUS
Another delay before this moderate novice handicap due to Sir Royal collapsing in the preceding novice hurdle. That meant that all of these runners were awash with sweat. While this is again form to be treating with some caution, the two market leaders still fought it out. The winner stepped up for the longer trip and can rate higher.

NOTEBOOK
Goring One(IRE) ◆ came home a ready winner to register a first success at the ninth attempt. He was positively ridden back up in trip, and there was a fair bit to like about the manner in which he came clear late on having been hassled for the lead throughout. Clearly improving, he would have to be of serious interest if turned out under a penalty. (op 10-3 tchd 4-1)
Ballyman(IRE), well backed altough 5lb out of the weights, responded to pressure five out and was the only one to give the winner a serious race. (op 4-1)
Princely Hero(IRE) showed improved form in a first-time visor, but again struggled to see out his race despite this being a drop back in trip. (tchd 17-2 and 12-1)
Chestnut Ben(IRE), on his chasing debut, jumped efficiently before tiring and should be more at home over fences back at around 2m with more cut underfoot. (op 10-1 tchd 17-2)

4920 MARSH GREEN (S) H'CAP HURDLE (8 hdls) 2m 110y
4:00 (4:48) (Class 5) (0-90,90) 4-Y-0+ **£2,055** (£599; £299)

Form RPR

6423 **1** **Mut'Ab (USA)**[18] 4450 6-11-7 **90**...............................(b) JoshuaMoore(5) 106+
(Gary Moore) *hld up in midfield: j.rt and bmpd rival 2nd: hdwy and mstke 5th: chsd ldrs next: led and mstke 2 out: sn drvn clr: in command last: comf* **11/4**[1]

35F0 **2** *12* **Celtic Ballad (IRE)**[11] 4675 5-10-8 **79**...........................(b[1]) SClements(7) 83
(Colin Tizzard) *chsd ldr after 2nd: clsd on ldr 3 out: led bef next: hdd 2 out: drvn and btn bef last* **9/1**

3442 **3** *9* **Stravita**[35] 4123 7-10-5 **79**..(b) AshleyBird(10) 75
(Jim Best) *hld up wl bhd: hdwy 5th: chsd ldrs and rdn 3 out: sn outpcd: 5th and wl hld next: plugged on between last 2: wnt modest 3rd flat* **7/2**[2]

P/0P **4** *3 3/4* **Barodine**[12] 3224 8-10-13 **77**... TomScudamore 73
(Ron Hodges) *j.rt: bhd: rdn 2nd: hdwy and chsd ldng trio after 3 out: no prog and btn next: wnt modest 3rd between last 2 tl flat* **10/1**

60PP **5** *9* **Patrick Dee**[21] 4403 6-9-7 **64** oh4...............................(b) TrevorWhelan(7) 49
(Christine Dunnett) *led and sn clr: j.big 3rd: pressed after 3 out: rdn and hdd bef next: wknd qckly 2 out: 5th and wl btn whn j.rt 2 out* **40/1**

5466 **6** *3 3/4* **Standing Order**[14] 4522 8-9-10 **67**..........................(tp) HarryChalloner(7) 48
(Richard Ford) *racd off the pce in midfield: bmpd 2nd: hdwy 5th: rdn and wknd after next* **8/1**

0006 **7** *1 1/4* **Ostaadi**[9] 4721 5-11-1 **79**..(b) DPFahy 59
(Bernard Llewellyn) *in tch: rdn and struggling whn mstke 5th: wl btn after next* **6/1**

4342 **8** *1 1/2* **Low Delta (IRE)**[22] 4378 11-11-5 **83**.......................... DominicElsworth 62
(Michael Blake) *a off the pce towards rr: t.o bef 2 out* **11/2**[3]

6 **9** *28* **Que On Time (IRE)**[14] 4521 7-11-0 **85**..................(t) MrMatthewBarber(7) 39
(Tim Vaughan) *chsd ldrs: losing pl whn mstke 5th: t.o bef 2 out* **33/1**

PPP0 **10** *66* **Baltrap (FR)**[7] 4771 6-10-8 **72**....................................(p) AndrewThornton —
(Clarissa Caroe) *chsd ldr tl after 2nd: sn lost pl: wl t.o last fr 5th* **100/1**

4m 4.20s (-9.90) **Going Correction** -0.50s/f (Good) **10** Ran SP% **115.1**
Speed ratings (Par 103): **103,97,93,91,87 85,84,84,70,39**
toteswingers:1&2 £15.80, 2&3 £15.80, 1&3 £1.10 CSF £27.08 CT £88.35 TOTE £3.80: £1.60, £2.10, £1.40; EX 29.90.The winner was sold to E Creighton for 7,000gns.
Owner Ms J Lambert **Bred** Darley **Trained** Lower Beeding, W Sussex

FOCUS
A typically weak selling handicap, run at a sound enough gallop. A personal-best from the winner with the runner-up rated to last season's form.

NOTEBOOK
Mut'Ab(USA) had performed more encouragingly the last twice and this was the most suitable ground he had encountered this year. It was also a drop in class for him, so it wasn't surprising to see him score comfortably as he was formerly very useful on the Flat. He showed his quirks by running around from two out, but could have more to offer, despite a likely hike in the handicap, now he has got his head back in front. (op 3-1)
Celtic Ballad(IRE) travelled kindly into contention, but was firmly put in his place by the winner. He was still a clear second-best and has now found his sort of level. (op 17-2)
Stravita should have appreciated this drying ground, but she got too far back to mount any sort of challenge and is capable of much better. (op 9-2, tchd 5-1 in places)
Barodine stayed on off the home turn, but jumping errors mounted up and he also paid for refusing to settle early on. (op 17-2 tchd 8-1)

4921 HARTFIELD H'CAP CHASE (18 fncs) 3m
4:30 (5:15) (Class 4) (0-105,99) 5-Y-0+ **£2,808** (£818; £409)

Form RPR

P3P- **1** **Sole Agent (IRE)**[65] 9-11-6 **93**...............................(b) MattieBatchelor 101
(Diana Grissell) *j.w: mde all: gng best wl bef 3 out: 2 l clr last: drvn and tiring fnl 150yds: a holding on: all out* **33/1**

P613 **2** *3/4* **Duke Of Ormond (IRE)**[20] 4412 8-11-10 **97**.................(p) CharliePoste 105
(Anna Brooks) *in tch: reminders and hdwy to chse wnr 10th: rdn after 13th: drvn and mstke 2 out: 2 l down last: no imp tl clsd as wnr tired fnl 150yds* **7/1**[2]

45P6 **3** *6* **Whatever Next (IRE)**[19] 4427 9-11-4 **91**............................ TimmyMurphy 92
(Edward Creighton) *t.k.h: chsd ldr tl 6th: rdn and struggling 15th: rallied u.p 2 out: wnt 3rd last: plugged on same pce flat* **20/1**

1316 **4** *11* **Pete The Feat (IRE)**[22] 4372 7-11-12 **99**.......................... FelixDeGiles 98+
(Anna Newton-Smith) *j.rt: in tch: j.rt and mstke 7th: bmpd 10th: chsd ldng pair u.p after 15th: no prog and btn 2 out: lost 3rd last: wknd flat* **12/1**

1 **5** *13* **Present A Star (IRE)**[7] 4772 8-10-1 **74** 7ex.......................... ColinBolger 53
(Sarah Humphrey) *in tch: mstke 8th and 13th: rdn and fnd little 15th: drvn and wl btn bef 3 out: 5th and wl btn 2 out* **8/11**[1]

P3P4 **6** *1 3/4* **Randolph O'Brien (IRE)**[33] 4144 11-10-3 **79**...... SamTwiston-Davies(3) 56
(Nigel Twiston-Davies) *in tch: chsd ldr 6th tl 10th: rdn and struggling after 13th: wknd 15th: 6th and wl bhd 3 out* **10/1**

P0P4 **7** *61* **Ginolad (AUS)**[25] 4313 11-11-12 **99**.................................... SamThomas 22
(Venetia Williams) *several positions and several slow jumps: dropped to last and v reluctant u.p after 9th: t.o fr 11th* **15/2**[3]

033P **F** **Brushford (IRE)**[43] 3961 7-10-3 **76**...........................(bt[1]) LeightonAspell —
(Chris Gordon) *hld up in tch tl bmpd and fell 10th* **14/1**

6m 13.6s (-10.10) **Going Correction** -0.275s/f (Good) **8** Ran SP% **113.3**
Speed ratings: **105,104,102,99,94 94,73,—**
toteswingers:1&2 £8.20, 2&3 £12.00, 1&3 £28.80 CSF £236.40 CT £4700.40 TOTE £35.60: £4.00, £2.00, £4.40; EX 207.20.
Owner Mrs Suzie Russell **Bred** J Costello **Trained** Brightling, E Sussex

FOCUS
There was a sound gallop on in this ordinary staying handicap. The runner-up sets the level.

NOTEBOOK
Sole Agent(IRE) produced a bold front-running display. He has never been easy to predict and lost his form under rules last year. He finished second in a point back from a break on his debut for present connections though, and has clearly enjoyed the change of scenery as he looked a rejuvenated performer here. It was his first success beyond 2m1f and, for all that he evidently now stays well, it therefore wasn't surprising to see him tire near the finish.
Duke Of Ormond(IRE) ◆ proved hard work for his rider, but kept responding and was closing on the winner near the finish. This ground was probably lively enough for him and he can still find another opening this term. (tchd 15-2)
Whatever Next(IRE), back over fences, rallied from three out and it's not hard to see why he was tried in blinkers last time. His losing run continues. (op 18-1)
Pete The Feat(IRE) gave his all, but was a spent force from two out and has had a fairly long season. (op 10-1)
Present A Star(IRE) was well ahead of the handicapper under his penalty for scoring easily on his debut for connections at Plumpton a week earlier. He stopped quickly leaving the back straight, however, and presumably found the run coming too soon. Official explanation: trainer said gelding was unsuited by the good to soft ground (op 5-6, tchd Evens in places)
Ginolad(AUS) turned in a mulish effort at Huntingdon on his previous outing, but this was even worse and he looks completely out of love with racing. Official explanation: jockey said gelding never travelled (op 8-1)

4922 EDENBRIDGE CONDITIONAL JOCKEYS' H'CAP HURDLE (10 hdls) 2m 3f 110y
5:00 (5:46) (Class 4) (0-105,104) 4-Y-0+ **£2,329** (£678; £339)

Form RPR

10/P **1** **Pepito Collonges (FR)**[34] 4130 8-9-13 **87**..............(b) NathanAdams(10) 101+
(Laura Mongan) *racd wd: chsd ldrs tl led 3rd: mde rest: gng best and drew clr after 3 out: moved ins bef 2 out: swtchd rt to outer again 2 out: wl in command after: heavily eased flat* **25/1**

-446 **2** *2 3/4* **O Malley's Oscar (IRE)**[17] 4462 6-11-11 **103**...................... KeiranBurke 103
(Suzy Smith) *chsd ldrs: chsd wnr 3 out: sn u.p and outpcd by wnr: wl hld 2 out: plugged on flat: no threat to wnr* **7/2**[1]

500/ **3** *1* **Rock Salmon**[743] 4377 8-11-8 **100**.. DavidBass 100
(Lucy Wadham) *in tch: mstke 1st and 5th: chsd ldng pair and rdn after 3 out: 3rd and no ch w wnr next: plugged on flat* **8/1**

-055 **4** *8* **Mudita Moment (IRE)**[26] 4281 6-11-8 **100**.................. RichieMcLernon 93
(Anna Brooks) *t.k.h: in tch in midfield: chsd ldrs 6th: 4th and struggling ent st: wl hld fr next* **4/1**[2]

1430 **5** *1 1/2* **Whitcombe Spirit**[13] 4540 6-10-8 **86**..................................(b) CO'Farrell 78
(Jamie Poulton) *hld up bhd: pushed along and hdwy on inner after 3 out: n.m.r bnd ent st: sn swtchd rt and mstke 2 out: plugged on same pce after: mstke and pckd last* **16/1**

40-0 **6** *hd* **Home**[34] 2049 6-11-3 **95**.. RichardKilloran 85
(Brendan Powell) *in tch in midfield: rdn and struggling after 3 out: plugged on same pce and no threat to wnr after* **16/1**

00F6 **7** *8* **Original Prankster (IRE)**[24] 4330 6-11-5 **100**..... SamTwiston-Davies(3) 83
(Nigel Twiston-Davies) *in tch: rdn and racd awkwardly after 6th: styd chsng ldrs tl wknd after 3 out: wl btn next* **8/1**

F/3- **8** *3 3/4* **Ballyveeney (IRE)**[418] 3683 7-11-3 **101**........................ HarryChalloner(6) 81
(Venetia Williams) *wl in tch: rdn and wknd qckly after 3 out: wl btn next* **8/1**

-001 **9** *7* **Won More Night**[8] 4738 9-10-8 **86** 7ex..................................(t) IanPopham 69+
(Martin Keighley) *hld up towards rr: hdwy into midfield 3 out: n.m.r on inner bnd bef 2 out: sn rdn and no hdwy after: mstke 2 out: eased flat: dismntd qckly after fin* **9/2**[3]

4034 **10** *6* **Grey Cruzene (USA)**[21] 4403 5-10-5 **83**................................ PeterToole 51
(Chris Gordon) *led tl 3rd: w wnr after tl lost pl rapidly u.p 3 out: wl bhd whn mstke next* **25/1**

5360 **11** *2 1/4* **Shropshirelass**[183] 1551 8-11-2 **97**............... GemmaGracey-Davison(3) 63
(Zoe Davison) *in tch towards rr: rdn 6th: sme hdwy into midfield after next: wknd qckly after 3 out: wl bhd between last 2* **25/1**

0/0P **12** *13* **Kavaloti (IRE)**[25] 4310 7-10-6 **87**..............................(b) JoshuaMoore(3) 41
(Gary Moore) *pressed ldrs: rdn after 7th: wknd rapidly after 3 out: wl bhd whn blnd next: eased flat: t.o* **66/1**

0000 **P** **Prince Pippin (IRE)**[21] 4399 5-11-12 **104**..................(tp) MarcGoldstein —
(Michael Madgwick) *in tch in rr: rdn after 6th: losing tch qckly whn p.u sn after 7th* **50/1**

5m 5.10s (-1.60) **Going Correction** -0.50s/f (Good) **13** Ran SP% **120.5**
Speed ratings (Par 105): **83,81,81,78,77 77,74,72,70,67 66,61,—**
toteswingers:1&2 £26.50, 2&3 £9.70, 1&3 £75.70 CSF £110.36 CT £796.20 TOTE £37.20: £9.80, £1.10, £1.80; EX 230.10.
Owner Mrs P J Sheen **Bred** G A E C Delorme Freres **Trained** Epsom, Surrey

FOCUS
An open handicap for conditional riders. They went a decent early pace, but still few got seriously involved from off the pace and the principals came clear. The placed horses set the level.

NOTEBOOK
Pepito Collonges(FR) was pulled up on his return from a lay-off last month and compromised his chance this time by refusing to settle early on. He was also taken notably wide after pulling his way to the front, but it was apparent turning for home he would take some catching and he ultimately won eased down. He therefore rates value for further and would escape a penalty if turning out quickly.
O Malley's Oscar(IRE) was well backed for this step up in trip. He has been headstrong in the past and didn't prove the most straightforward again here. To his credit he stayed on late and probably wants an even stiffer test. (op 4-1)
Rock Salmon was debuting for Lucy Wadham after a 743-day layoff and had the assistance of David Bass, so it wasn't that surprising to see money for him. He looked the biggest threat to the winner turning for home, but flattened out and the run just looked needed. (op 14-1)
Mudita Moment(IRE), another that attracted support, travelled well enough on the inside but didn't look straightforward when asked to pick up. Official explanation: jockey said gelding hung right throughout (op 5-1)

Won More Night fell in a hole under pressure and probably found the run coming soon enough. Official explanation: jockey said mare hung badly right (op 10-3)

4923 LINGFIELD PARK MARRIOTT HOTEL & COUNTRY CLUB MAIDEN OPEN NATIONAL HUNT FLAT RACE 2m
5:30 (6:13) (Class 5) 4-6-Y-O £1,370 (£399; £199)

Form				RPR
05	1		**Peintre Ster (IRE)**[50] 3835 4-10-7 0 AlexMerriam(3) (Neil King) *t.k.h: hld up in tch: chsd ldrs 3f out: rdn to chal on inner over 1f out: led ins fnl f: r.o wl* 50/1	92
0	2	1	**Smart Ruler (IRE)**[37] 4082 5-11-3 0 DarylJacob (David Arbuthnot) *hld up off the pce in last trio: hdwy over 5f out: chsd ldng quartet over 2f out: nt clr run and swtchd rt 1f out: chsd wnr fnl 100yds: no imp after* 10/1	98
	3	1 1/4	**Faraway Downs** 5-10-12 0 JoshuaMoore(5) (Gary Moore) *t.k.h: chsd ldrs: press ldr over 3f out: ev ch and rdn ent fnl 2f: led 1f out: sn hdd: no ex fnl 100yds* 11/1	97
2	4	shd	**Cape Breton**[16] 4484 5-11-3 0 PaulMoloney (Patrick Chamings) *hld up wl bhd in last pair: hdwy on outer over 5f out: pressed ldrs and shkn up ent fnl 2f: rdn and unable qck over 1f out: styd on same pce u.p fnl f* 11/10[1]	97
3	5	1	**Millksheikh**[19] 4430 4-10-3 0 MissHGrissell(7) (Raymond York) *chsd ldr tl led 4f out: rdn wl over 1f out: hdd 1f out: no ex and btn fnl 100yds* 20/1	89
	6	6	**Going Twice** 6-11-3 0 AndrewThornton (Steve Woodman) *in tch in midfield: lost pl and rr of main gp over 4f out: swtchd rt and hdwy on outer 3f out: outpcd and btn 2f out: styd on same pce after* 50/1	90
5	7	1	**Murchan High (IRE)**[15] 4505 6-10-10 0 TomScudamore (Jim Best) *t.k.h: chsd ldrs: rdn and struggling whn edgd lft over 2f out: one pce and no threat to ldrs 2f out* 25/1	82
3	8	3 1/2	**Jackstown (IRE)**[22] 4382 4-10-0 0 DarrenO'Keeffe(10) (Seamus Mullins) *hld up in tch: outpcd and reminders over 2f out: swtchd rt over 1f out: no threat to ldrs but kpt on ins fnl f* 15/2[3]	79
	9	1/2	**Inverclyde (IRE)** 4-10-6 0 ow1 TomO'Connor(5) (Bill Turner) *in tch in midfield: hdwy over 5f out: chsd ldrs and n.m.r over 2f out: wknd ent fnl 2f* 22/1	79
	10	6	**Phlorian** 5-11-0 0 (t) JamesO'Farrell(3) (John Panvert) *wl off the pce in last pair: rdn and struggling over 5f out: styd on past btn horses fr over 1f out: nvr trbld ldrs* 50/1	79
	11	hd	**Just Watch Ollie (IRE)** 5-11-3 0 DominicElsworth (John Coombe) *a towards rr: pushed along and struggling over 6f out: plugged on same pce and n.d fnl 4f* 11/1	79
6	12	nk	**Orsm**[30] 4055 4-10-10 0 LeightonAspell (Laura Mongan) *hld up in tch towards rr: pushed along and hdwy over 4f out: wknd over 2f out* 5/1[2]	72
00	13	18	**Dance Til Midnight**[62] 3616 4-9-10 0 MrTJCannon(7) (Richard Rowe) *led tl 4f out: lost pl and dropped rr 3f out: wl bhd fnl 2f* 80/1	47

3m 33.8s (-4.20)
WFA 4 from 5yo+ 7lb 13 Ran SP% **121.9**
toteswingers:1&2 £103.10, 2&3 £11.90, 1&3 £76.30. totesuper7: Win: Not won. Place: Not won. CSF £479.93 TOTE £74.40: £12.40, £2.70, £3.10; EX 207.60.
Owner Mrs J K Buckle **Bred** Old Carhue Stud **Trained** Newmarket, Suffolk

FOCUS
An ordinary Polytrack bumper. There was an uneven gallop set and it was an advantage to race handily.

NOTEBOOK
Peintre Ster(IRE) was nicely placed when the pace lifted and came home a fairly ready winner. He hadn't shown a great deal in two previous outings on turf, but has a Flat pedigree and the switch to the AW round here evidently suited. He'll struggle to defy a penalty. (op 66-1)
Smart Ruler(IRE), well beaten on his debut over 1m6f last month, looked by far the most likely winner turning for home. He didn't really help his rider by running green under pressure however, and was always being held late on. This was still a nice bit of improvement. (tchd 11-1)
Faraway Downs is bred to make his mark over further once sent jumping and he shaped nicely on his debut under a prominent ride. He ought to come on plenty. (op 12-1)
Cape Breton was a popular choice after his promising debut second at Kempton 16 days earlier. However, he was awash with sweat at the start and wasn't at all suited being held up last off the stop-start gallop. He showed his engine by making up plenty of ground on the far side, but had nothing left in the tank when it mattered. (op 6-4)
Millksheikh was suited by racing near the lead, but kept on gamely when headed and he looks the best guide for the form.
Orsm was laboured and never looked like improving on his debut effort at Kempton last month. (op 9-2)
T/Jkpt: Not won. T/Plt: £225.20 to a £1 stake. Pool of £76,147.32 - 246.73 winning tickets. T/Qpdt: £61.60 to a £1 stake. Pool of £6,204.02 - 74.42 winning tickets. SP

4535 EXETER (R-H)
Tuesday, March 22

OFFICIAL GOING: Good
Wind: mild across Weather: sunny periods

4924 FINLAKE HOLIDAY PARK NOVICES' (S) HURDLE (8 hdls) 2m 1f
2:30 (2:30) (Class 5) 4-Y-0+ £1,951 (£573; £286; £143)

Form				RPR
330	1		**Leopard Hills (IRE)**[42] 3989 4-10-7 100 DPFahy (Alison Thorpe) *mid-div: hdwy 5th: rdn and j.lft fr 3 out: led last: drvn out* 13/2	88+
06B6	2	3 1/4	**Stir On The Sea (IRE)**[48] 3879 5-10-7 85 (bt) HaddenFrost (James Frost) *mid-div: hdwy 5th: rdn after 3 out: styd on to hold ch last: kpt on but no ex* 13/2	81
565F	3	2 1/4	**Ladies Best**[12] 4675 7-10-9 85 (t) MattGriffiths(5) (Gordon Edwards) *led chsng gp: clsd on ldrs 2nd: rdn to ld appr 3 out: sn hung bdly lft: hdd last: no ex whn drifted across to nr siderails* 6/1[3]	88+
0	4	2 1/2	**Dolores Ortiz (IRE)**[19] 4444 5-10-7 0 RhysFlint (Philip Hobbs) *chsd ldr: clr of remiander tl 2nd: rdn appr 3 out: sn one pce* 16/1	77
504	5	1 1/2	**Ask The Oracle**[131] 2323 5-10-9 100 (t) MissIsabelTompsett(5) (Bernard Llewellyn) *mid-div of chsng gp: hdwy after 2nd: effrt appr 3 out: sn one pce* 11/2[2]	82
2111	6	7	**Marino Prince (FR)**[71] 2643 6-11-9 111 TomScudamore (Jim Best) *hld up bhd: clsng whn blnd bdly and virtually fell 5th: nvr rcvrd* 5/4[1]	93+
-P20	7	26	**Floradora Do**[13] 4556 9-10-4 76 JimmyDerham(3) (Ron Hodges) *j.lft: mid-div: rdn after 5th: wkng whn hit 3 out: t.o* 33/1	46
6	8	16	**Pedasus (USA)**[61] 1238 5-10-7 0 (p) ChrisDavies(7) (Ronald Harris) *hld up: hdwy 5th: effrt bef next: sn wknd: t.o* 50/1	38
0006	9	24	**Victory Bay**[11] 4707 6-10-7 74 (tp) NathanSweeney(7) (Simon Burrough) *led: rdn and hdd appr 3 out: sn wknd: t.o* 50/1	17
0-0	10	26	**Fluters House**[247] 1031 7-10-11 0 DonalDevereux(3) (Gerald Ham) *prom in chsng gp: clsd on ldrs 2nd: wknd 5th: t.o* 80/1	—
P-0	11	3 1/2	**Stellar Cause (USA)**[49] 3872 5-11-0 0 JohnnyFarrelly (Nick Ayliffe) *t.o fr 3rd* 100/1	—

4m 10.0s (-5.50) **Going Correction** -0.375s/f (Good)
WFA 4 from 5yo+ 7lb 11 Ran SP% **115.8**
Speed ratings (Par 103): **97,95,94,93,92 89,77,69,58,45 44**
toteswingers: 1&2 £4.40, 1&3 £3.90, 2&3 £9.30 CSF £46.34 TOTE £7.20: £2.10, £2.50, £2.10; EX 38.80.There was no bid for the winner. Marino Prince was claimed by P. T. Midgley for £6,000.
Owner Mrs A M Thorpe **Bred** S And S Hubbard Rodwell **Trained** Bronwydd Arms, Carmarthens

FOCUS
A moderate enough contest that was blown wide open when 5-4 favourite Marino Prince made a terrible blunder and all but fell at the fifth. The third is rated in line with this season's mark.

NOTEBOOK
Leopard Hills(IRE), well beaten in a handicap on his recent debut for the yard, appreciated the drop in trip/grade and stayed on well having taken over before the last. He's probably a bit better than this level and can win again. (op 8-1 tchd 6-1)
Stir On The Sea(IRE) is still a maiden, but had claims on some of her old form and ran well. (op 17-2 tchd 6-1)
Ladies Best didn't look straightforward under pressure, but this have helped restore confidence. (op 17-2 tchd 11-2)
Dolores Ortiz(IRE) improved on her initial effort over hurdles. (tchd 12-1)
Ask The Oracle should improve on this first outing since November. (op 8-1 tchd 9-2)
Marino Prince(FR), chasing a four-timer over jumps, was conceding 9lb all round and, having started to close down the back, he made a race-ending blunder. It's hard to tell how he'd have fared, but he deserves another chance. (op 4-5 tchd 13-8 and 7-4 in places)
Stellar Cause(USA) Official explanation: trainer said that the gelding bled from the nose

4925 THERACINGLOTTERY.COM H'CAP HURDLE (8 hdls) 2m 1f
3:00 (3:00) (Class 4) (0-115,115) 4-Y-0+ £2,732 (£802; £401; £200)

Form				RPR
4052	1		**Laustra Bad (FR)**[19] 4448 8-11-7 115 (bt) CO'Farrell(5) (David Pipe) *hld up in tch: tk clsr order 3 out: led 2 out: sn clr: comf* 11/4[1]	123+
-0P4	2	9	**Be Definite (IRE)**[11] 4697 7-11-2 108 PeterToole(3) (Tom George) *trckd ldr: led briefly appr 3 out: sn rdn: styd on but no ch w wnr fr 2 out* 8/1	104
25F2	3	3 3/4	**J'Adhere (FR)**[17] 4465 6-11-1 109 MrTomDavid(5) (Tim Vaughan) *hld up: bdly hmpd 1st: smooth hdwy to ld 3 out: narrowly hdd whn blnd next: sn rdn: 3rd and hld whn mstke last* 5/1[3]	100
0324	4	5	**King's Realm (IRE)**[17] 4488 4-11-4 114 DPFahy (Alison Thorpe) *trckd ldr: hmpd 2nd: rdn appr 3 out: kpt on same pce* 9/2[2]	97
5630	5	9	**Consulate (IRE)**[117] 2636 7-11-7 110 TomO'Brien (Gordon Edwards) *trckd ldrs: rdn appr 3 out: wknd bef 2 out* 12/1	90
422	6	12	**Call To Arms (IRE)**[68] 3519 4-10-12 111 DonalDevereux(3) (Peter Bowen) *in tch: wnt cl 3rd after 5th: sn rdn: wknd next: mstke 2 out* 10/1	76
564P	7	3/4	**Sagunt (GER)**[31] 4224 8-10-12 101 (t) SeanQuinlan (Joanna Davis) *trckd ldrs tl after 4th: sn no ch* 16/1	69
2000	8	5	**Killusty Fancy (IRE)**[44] 3962 4-10-4 100 (t) MarkGrant (Dominic Ffrench Davis) *led: rdn and hdd appr 3 out: sn wknd* 16/1	62
FP44	F		**Forest Rhythm (IRE)**[12] 4672 7-10-13 105 JimmyDerham(3) (Seamus Mullins) *fell heavily 1st* 9/2[2]	—

4m 7.20s (-8.30) **Going Correction** -0.375s/f (Good)
WFA 4 from 6yo+ 7lb 9 Ran SP% **119.4**
Speed ratings (Par 105): **104,99,98,95,91 85,85,83,—**
toteswingers: 1&2 £7.10, 1&3 £3.00, 2&3 £5.10 CSF £26.16 CT £107.45 TOTE £2.90: £1.10, £3.90, £2.00; EX 32.50.
Owner Mrs Sarah Ling **Bred** Jean Pierre Dubois **Trained** Nicholashayne, Devon

FOCUS
A low-grade handicap hurdle rated around the placed horses.

NOTEBOOK
Laustra Bad(FR) hadn't won since his novice days back in 2007, but his recent Taunton second suggested a race was due to come his way and, once J'Adhere made a race-ending blunder two out, the prize was his. He'll no doubt be out under a penalty before reassessed. (op 4-1)
Be Definite(IRE) built on the promise of his Sandown fourth, keeping on without matching the winner.
J'Adhere(FR), despite being hampered at the first, came there cantering in the straight and looked all over the winner coming to three out, but he was being challenged when he made a complete mess of two out. He could find no extra soon after.
King's Realm(IRE) could have been expected to do a touch better on this drop in grade. He's also declared to run at Warwick today. (op 5-1)

4926 ELIZABETH FINN CARE NOVICES' CHASE (15 fncs) 2m 3f 110y
3:35 (3:35) (Class 3) 5-Y-0+ £5,724 (£1,680; £840; £419)

Form				RPR
4210	1		**Hidden Keel**[45] 3946 6-11-4 139 FelixDeGiles (Charlie Longsdon) *travelled strly: led 2nd: mde rest: 14 l clr 7th: j.rt last 4 fences: lft wl clr 2 out: unchal* 11/10[1]	141+
5312	2	29	**Pascha Bere (FR)**[26] 4311 8-11-4 0 LiamTreadwell (Nick Gifford) *chsd ldrs: rdn after 11th: nvr any imp on front pair: lft 2nd 2 out* 3/1[2]	109
20/6	3	1 1/2	**Belcantista (FR)**[133] 2286 9-10-12 0 TomO'Brien (Philip Hobbs) *chsd ldrs: rdn after 11th: nvr any imp on front pair: lft 3rd 2 out* 11/2	104
0041	4	14	**Lupita (IRE)**[14] 4540 7-10-0 0 (t) GilesHawkins(5) (Derrick Scott) *chsd ldrs: pckd 3rd: struggling in last after next: nvr threatened* 50/1	83
4-04	F		**Our Bomber Harris**[18] 4453 7-10-12 0 HarrySkelton (Paul Nicholls) *led tl 2nd: chsd ldr: 14 l 2nd 7th: rdn after 11th: 4 l down next: styng on in 2 l 2nd whn sltly unsighted by wnr gng rt and fell 2 out* 9/2[3]	125

4m 46.3s (-11.00) **Going Correction** -0.375s/f (Good) 5 Ran SP% **108.1**
Speed ratings: **107,95,94,89,—**
CSF £4.74 TOTE £2.30: £1.10, £2.70; EX 4.30.
Owner Mrs Peter Matthey & John F Horn **Bred** Mrs M J Matthey **Trained** Over Norton, Oxon
■ Stewards' Enquiry : Tom O'Brien £140 fine: entered the parade ring after the signal to mount was given
Felix De Giles £140 fine: entered the parade ring after the signal to mount was given

FOCUS
Not a particularly competitive novice chase with the winner rated 9lb off.

NOTEBOOK

Hidden Keel, virtually pulled up when failing to run his race in the Grade 1 Scilly Isles at Sandown, had earlier looked a useful novice and he soon found himself in a clear lead, travelling strongly. Although Our Bomber Harris closed in the straight, he was still on the bridle and appeared to have plenty in the tank when being left clear. He's got the potential to make a smart handicap chaser and could be of interest if sent to Aintree. (op Evens tchd 6-5 in places)

Pascha Bere(FR), readily brushed aside by Starluck at Huntingdon, had earlier made a winning debut at Plumpton but he failed to reproduce his best here. (op 11-4 tchd 10-3)

Belcantista(FR) hasn't been easy to train and has now finished well beaten in both starts over fences here. He used to have plenty of ability, though, so probably isn't one to give up on yet. (tchd 6-1)

Our Bomber Harris, who made a few mistakes on his chasing debut at Doncaster, was in the process of running a much-improved race, and had jumped a lot better, until getting the second-last wrong in dramatic fashion. It's hoped this spill doesn't have a long-term effect. (op 13-2)

4927 CANADATRAVELCENTRE.CO.UK NOVICES' H'CAP CHASE (18 fncs) 3m

4:10 (4:10) (Class 4) (0-110,109) 5-Y-O+ **£3,903** (£1,146; £573; £286)

Form — RPR

P4P1 **1** **Theophrastus (IRE)**[12] 4669 9-11-12 **109** .... LiamTreadwell 120+
(Nick Gifford) *trckd ldrs: chal 4 out: rdn to take narrow advantage next: styd on: drvn out* **2/1**[1]

5314 **2** *2* **Lady De La Vega (FR)**[33] 4161 7-11-9 **106** ....(vt) TomScudamore 115
(Tim Vaughan) *trckd ldrs: hit 4th: rdn into narrow advantage 4 out: hdd next: styd on* **9/2**[2]

-024 **3** *22* **Days Of Pleasure (IRE)**[12] 4666 6-11-5 **109** ....(p) MrTJCannon(7) 98
(Chris Gordon) *disp ld most of way: rdn after 14th: hdd bef next: sn hld: wknd bef last* **9/1**

6006 **4** *10* **Lions In Law**[15] 4525 7-9-11 **83** oh15 ....(bt) PeterToole(3) 63
(Richard Hawker) *hld up: blnd 3rd: struggling 6th: nvr threatened* **16/1**

UPU5 **5** *16* **Picture In The Sky (IRE)**[26] 4313 10-11-10 **107** ....(p) SeanQuinlan 79
(Susan Nock) *disp ld most of way: rdn after 14th: hdd bef next: wknd 3 out* **8/1**

4322 **F** **Take A Mile (IRE)**[34] 2184 9-11-9 **109** .... JimmyDerham(3) —
(Seamus Mullins) *trcking ldrs whn fell 9th* **6/1**[3]

556P **P** **El Diego (IRE)**[39] 4052 7-10-13 **96** .... HarrySkelton —
(Jamie Snowden) *in tch tl bdly hmpd 9th and lost pl: hdwy 11th: bdly hmpd again 12th: sn p.u* **9/1**

P001 **F** **Tarabela**[23] 4381 8-11-3 **103** .... DonalDevereux(3) —
(Gerald Ham) *hld up but in tch: hit 1st: cl 5th whn fell 12th* **15/2**

6m 9.60s (0.30) **Going Correction** -0.375s/f (Good) **8** Ran SP% **114.6**

Speed ratings: **84,83,76,72,67** —,—,—

toteswingers: 1&2 £3.90, 1&3 £4.20, 2&3 £15.30 CSF £11.95 CT £64.37 TOTE £3.10: £1.30, £2.40, £1.10; EX 10.70.

Owner Core Strength **Bred** Sunnyhill Stud **Trained** Findon, W Sussex

■ Stewards' Enquiry : Tom Scudamore caution: used whip with excessive frequency

FOCUS

The front pair drew clear in what was a modest novice handicap chase. The winner is rated to his best with the second on the upgrade.

NOTEBOOK

Theophrastus(IRE), put up 1lb for his Folkestone victory, his first over fences, coped well under top weight and stayed on strongly to assert. He seems to have got his act together, although will need to progress again to complete a hat-trick. (op 5-2 tchd 11-4)

Lady De La Vega(FR), 13lb higher than when winning at Chepstow on her penultimate start, was a touch disappointing over hurdles last time, but appreciated the return to fences and returned to something like her best. (op 11-2)

Days Of Pleasure(IRE) ended up well held, but had run well to a point. (tchd 8-1)

El Diego(IRE) Official explanation: trainer said that the gelding suffered a cut nose after being badly hampered

4928 ROBERT WEBB TRAVEL OPEN HUNTERS' CHASE (18 fncs) 3m

4:45 (4:46) (Class 6) 5-Y-O+ **£936** (£290; £145; £72)

Form — RPR

P0-P **1** **Kornati Kid**[44] 9-11-13 134 ....(p) MrOJMurphy(7) 122+
(Anabel L M King) *trckd ldrs: chal 4 out: sn rdn: led last: styd on wl: rdn out* **7/1**

432- **2** *1 3/4* **Keenan's Future (IRE)**[485] 2438 10-12-6 0 ....(t) MrOGreenall 121
(Ian Williams) *hld up: hdwy 13th: chal 4 out: led 2 out: hdd last: styd on but no ex* **11/4**[1]

101/ **3** *3 1/4* **You Do The Math (IRE)**[31] 11-11-13 114 .... MrJSHorton(7) 117
(William Hayes, Ire) *hld up towards rr: hdwy 13th: led next: rdn whn hrd pressed fr 4 out: hdd 2 out: sn swtchd lft and hld: edgd lft fnl 75yds* **16/1**

/1-1 **4** *1/2* **Ask Again**[9] 12-11-13 111 .... MissSarahWest(7) 120+
(Miss Sarah West) *prom: reminder after 12th: outpcd next: styd on again fr 3 out: keeping on to chal for 3rd whn short of room nr fin* **9/2**[2]

5 *2* **Think On This (IRE)**[44] 8-11-5 0 .... MrJABest(7) 107
(Mrs C M Budd) *hld up: hdwy fr 12th: rdn to chse ldrs 4 out: styd on same pce* **20/1**

230- **6** *2 1/4* **Burntoakboy**[9] 13-11-5 0 .... MrDJGriffiths(7) 107
(David Griffiths) *trckd ldrs: jnd ldr 11th tl after 13th: rdn appr 4 out: styng on same pce in 6th whn blnd last* **12/1**

5-60 **7** *nk* **Over The Creek**[16] 12-11-13 117 .... MissJBuck(7) 113
(M J Coate) *chsd ldrs: rdn appr 4 out: styd on same pce* **18/1**

0253 **8** *4 1/2* **Gershwinner (IRE)**[19] 4449 8-11-9 103 .... MrMWoodward(7) 106
(Ms Emma Oliver) *in tch early: towards rr 7th: struggling after 12th: nvr bk on terms* **15/2**

/34- **9** *19* **Imperial Sun (IRE)**[23] 12-11-5 96 .... MrPPrince(7) 87
(Mrs A S Hodges) *a bhd: t.o* **40/1**

/26- **10** *3* **Crystal D'Ainay (FR)**[341] 5198 12-11-5 107 ....(t) MissHLewis(7) 81
(Miss Hannah Lewis) *a towards rr: t.o* **6/1**[3]

2-33 **11** *29* **Thirtytwo Red (IRE)**[21] 4415 10-11-12 90 .... MrRMahon 55
(R J Alford) *chsd ldrs: reminders 10th: sn in rr: t.o* **11/1**

100P **12** *12* **Apollo Blaze (IRE)**[10] 10-11-9 95 .... MissVShaw(7) 48
(Mrs P J Shaw) *led 3rd tl 14th: sn rdn: wknd bef next: t.o* **28/1**

6m 11.8s (2.50) **Going Correction** -0.375s/f (Good) **12** Ran SP% **121.2**

Speed ratings: **80,79,78,78,77 76,76,75,68,67 58,54**

toteswingers: 1&2 £6.70, 1&3 £6.90, 2&3 £10.60 CSF £27.65 TOTE £6.40: £1.90, £1.80, £12.20; EX 31.70.

Owner Aiden Murphy **Bred** S Charlton And B Mayoh **Trained** Wilmcote, Warwicks

FOCUS

Quite a competitive hunter chase in which the first three are capable of better, and the fourth and sixth set the level.

NOTEBOOK

Kornati Kid, already a dual course winner, had won a point in January and, although pulling up next time, the application of cheekpieces improved him enough to make a successful debut in this sphere. (op 15-2)

Keenan's Future(IRE), a 128-rated chaser off for 485 days, came through looking the likely winner in the straight, but met with a strong challenge and, having spent too much time in the air at the last, was run out of it on the run-in. He'll pick up something if going the right way from this. (tchd 10-3)

You Do The Math(IRE) a four-time hunter chase winner, hadn't run under rules since the spring of 2009 and was pulled up in a point last month, but had clearly come on a ton and this performance suggests he retains all his old ability. (tchd 18-1)

Ask Again kept on again having been outpaced. (op 4-1)

Burntoakboy wasn't disgraced. (op 10-1)

Crystal D'Ainay(FR) failed to make a show and is clearly a shadow of the horse he once was. (op 17-2)

4929 SHOP AT REWARDS4RACING.COM NOVICES' H'CAP HURDLE (12 hdls) 2m 7f 110y

5:20 (5:23) (Class 4) (0-105,105) 4-Y-O+ **£2,602** (£764; £382; £190)

Form — RPR

605 **1** **Rockabilly (FR)**[37] 4094 6-11-8 **101** .... DavidEngland 110
(Nigel Twiston-Davies) *chsd ldrs: rdn to hold pl after 7th: styd on to ld 2 out: kpt on fr last: drvn out* **14/1**

P300 **2** *1* **Some Secret**[14] 4535 6-10-8 **87** .... JamesDavies 95
(Chris Down) *in tch tl lost pl after 6th: hdwy u.p appr 3 out: styd on to chse wnr last: no ex* **22/1**

6531 **3** *2 1/2* **Mauricetheathlete (IRE)**[16] 4508 8-11-0 **100** .... MrNSlatter(7) 108+
(Martin Keighley) *mid-div: mstke 2nd: hdwy 6th: rdn to chse ldr after 7th: styd on same pce fr 3 out: edgd lft flat: wnt 3rd nr fin* **6/1**[3]

544 **4** *1/2* **Rooftop Rainbow (IRE)**[27] 4294 7-11-4 **100** .... PeterToole(3) 106
(Linda Blackford) *chsd ldrs: rdn whn hit 9th: styd on same pce fr 3 out: lost 4th nr fin* **10/1**

5223 **5** *15* **Bounds And Leaps**[20] 4418 6-11-5 **98** .... TomScudamore 90
(Michael Scudamore) *mid-div: rdn after 9th: no imp: wknd after 2 out* **11/2**[2]

0434 **6** *1 1/4* **Ben Cee Pee M (IRE)**[31] 4224 6-11-8 **101** ....(p) SamJones 92
(Oliver Sherwood) *trckd ldrs: rdn after 9th: wknd 2 out* **17/2**

144 **7** *18* **Torran Sound**[26] 4314 4-10-10 **98** .... MarkBradburne 76+
(James Eustace) *mid-div: hdwy after 8th: narrow advantage whn mstke 3 out: sn rdn: hdd & wknd: t.o* **9/2**[1]

30-P **8** *1 1/2* **Little Eaglet (IRE)**[31] 4219 7-11-4 **97** ....(b[1]) LiamHeard 70
(Colin Heard) *led 2nd: rdn after 9th: hdd bef next: wkng whn hit 2 out: t.o* **20/1**

454P **9** *1 3/4* **Graduation Night**[20] 4427 5-11-6 **104** .... MrRMahon(5) 76
(Jamie Snowden) *a towards rr: t.o* **9/1**

0005 **10** *10* **Mighty Monty**[32] 4195 6-11-5 **98** .... JackDoyle 61
(Victor Dartnall) *hld up towards rr: hdwy 8th: sn rdn: wknd bef 3 out: t.o* **12/1**

-14P **11** *10* **Lomitaar**[36] 4121 6-11-12 **105** .... JohnnyFarrelly 59
(Tony Newcombe) *a bhd: t.o* **20/1**

2030 **12** *5* **Whereveryougoigo (IRE)**[55] 3745 5-11-7 **100** ....(v) TomO'Brien 49
(Peter Bowen) *hld up towards rr: hdwy 8th: sn rdn: wknd bef 3 out: t.o* **12/1**

0/03 **13** *52* **Noddies Way**[14] 4539 8-11-0 **100** .... HarryChalloner(7) 2
(John Panvert) *a towards rr: struggling fr 6th: t.o* **22/1**

-U30 **P** **Spiritonthemount (USA)**[11] 2183 6-10-13 **92** ....(b) LiamTreadwell —
(Peter Hiatt) *led tl 2nd: chsd ldr: rdn whn lost 2nd after 5th: wknd 9th: t.o whn p.u bef 3 out* **33/1**

0000 **P** **Filimoss**[38] 4081 6-10-1 **80** ....(b[1]) GerardTumelty —
(Charlie Morlock) *sn wl bhd: p.u bef 8th* **100/1**

5m 46.9s (-12.10) **Going Correction** -0.375s/f (Good)

WFA 4 from 5yo+ 8lb **15** Ran SP% **121.7**

Speed ratings (Par 105): **105,104,103,103,98 98,92,91,91,87 84,82,65,**—,—

toteswingers:1&2 £38.10, 2&3 £34.00, 1&3 £2.60 CSF £294.32 CT £2055.47 TOTE £11.50: £3.20, £11.80, £2.70; EX 467.60.

Owner Mrs Caroline Mould **Bred** Bruno Vagne **Trained** Naunton, Gloucs

FOCUS

A wide-open handicap hurdle with a big step up from the winner and the third getting back to his old best, and form to be positive about.

NOTEBOOK

Rockabilly(FR), well held in three novice hurdles, looked a likely improver for the switch to handicaps and duly came good, getting to the front two out and staying on well. He's clearly all about stamina and should make a decent staying handicap chaser next season. Official explanation: trainer's representative said, regarding the apparent improvement in form, that the gelding appeared better suited by the faster ground, and longer trip

Some Secret put up a much-improved effort up in trip for this handicap debut.

Mauricetheathlete(IRE), up 7lb for his Sedgefield victory, had every chance and found the combination of a weights rise and shorter trip against him.

Rooftop Rainbow(IRE) was edging closer at the finish and already looks in need of fences. He was clear of the remainder.

Torran Sound cruised into contention and took over coming to three out, but Mark Bradburne, for whatever reason, slowed his mount dramatically coming into the hurdle and he duly belted it, ending his chance.

Filimoss Official explanation: jockey said that the mare was never travelling

T/Jkpt: Not won. T/Plt: £245.30 to a £1 stake. Pool of £86341.92 - 256.87 winning units. T/Qpdt: £21.30 to a £1 stake. Pool of £7957.41 - 275.74 winning units. TM

4478 KEMPTON (R-H)

Tuesday, March 22

OFFICIAL GOING: Good (chs 7.5, hdl 7.3)

Wind: virtually nil Weather: bright and sunny

4930 KINNELL AND CERTASS "NATIONAL HUNT" NOVICES' HURDLE (8 hdls) 2m

2:10 (2:10) (Class 4) 4-Y-O+ **£2,552** (£749; £374; £187)

Form — RPR

113 **1** **Shuil Royale (IRE)**[25] 4325 6-11-0 0 .... DarylJacob 117+
(David Arbuthnot) *t.k.h: hld up in tch: chsd ldng pair 3 out: shkn up to chal bef 2 out: led last: wanting to hang rt u.p: pushed along hands and heels and asserted fnl 75yds* **13/8**[1]

0501 **2** *1* **Smart Catch (IRE)**[17] 4478 5-11-6 0 .... WayneHutchinson 118
(Tony Carroll) *chsd ldrs: wnt 2nd after 4th: chal bef 2 out: led 2 out: sn rdn: drvn and hdd last: no ex and btn fnl 75yds* **13/2**[3]

6F **3** *6* **Croan Rock (IRE)**[33] 4159 6-11-0 0 .... JasonMaguire 106
(Ian Williams) *led at stdy gallop: qckned gallop 5th: hdd and rdn 2 out: wknd last* **7/1**

025/ **4** *6* **Toulaman (GER)**[758] 4086 6-10-9 0 .... JoshuaMoore(5) 100
(Gary Moore) *t.k.h: in tch: rdn and sltly outpcd bef 2 out: rallied between last 2: no ch w ldrs but kpt on flat* **40/1**

U064 **5** *16* **Somewhatinevitable (IRE)**[17] 4478 6-11-0 0................. DenisO'Regan 88
(Paul Webber) *hld up in last pair: hdwy bef 3 out: rdn and no hdwy 2 out: btn whn j.lft last: eased towards fin* **8/1**

1-40 **6** *11* **There And Then**[51] 3836 5-11-0 0................................ AndrewThornton 73
(Seamus Mullins) *mstke 3rd: w ldr tl after 4th: rdn and wknd after 3 out: btn whn j.rt next* **40/1**

3 **7** *5* **Monroe Park (IRE)**[80] 3324 6-11-0 0............................ MattieBatchelor 68
(Noel Quinlan) *t.k.h: hld up in rr: in tch tl rdn and wknd after 3 out: wl btn next: eased flat: t.o* **66/1**

60 **8** *7* **Homer Run (IRE)**[19] 4444 4-10-0 0.............................. MrKevinJones(7) 54
(Seamus Mullins) *t.k.h: j.big 1st: struggling 3 out: sn lost tch: t.o between last 2* **100/1**

00-5 **P** **Premier Article (IRE)**[49] 3864 6-11-0 0................. AndrewGlassonbury —
(Gary Moore) *racd in midfield: mstke 3rd: rdn and struggling after 5th: lost tch next: wl bhd whn p.u 2 out* **100/1**

-2F1 **F** **Raya Star (IRE)**[27] 4281 5-11-6 0................................... RobertThornton —
(Alan King) *t.k.h: hld up towards rr: j. awkwardly 2nd: fell 4th* **5/2**[2]

3m 54.7s (-5.30) **Going Correction** -0.90s/f (Hard)
WFA 4 from 5yo+ 7lb **10** Ran SP% **112.0**
Speed ratings (Par 105): **77,76,73,70,62 57,54,51,—,—**
toteswingers: 1&2 £2.90, 1&3 £4.70, 2&3 £7.10 CSF £12.18 TOTE £3.30: £1.90, £1.10, £2.70; EX 11.00.

Owner Phil Fry & Geoff Thompson **Bred** Greenville House Stud And M Morgan **Trained** Compton, Berks

FOCUS
An interesting novice hurdle run at a steady early gallop. The winner is rated to his bumper mark with the second on the upgrade.

NOTEBOOK
Shuil Royale(IRE) came out on top and despite receiving 6lb from the runner-up, he put in an impressive performance. Given cover in midfield, he joined the long-time leader turning for home before quickening nicely before the last and battling on well after to get his head in front. A winner of two bumpers, he had disappointed on his hurdling debut, but that was a decent race (winner won the previous day) and he confirmed his early promise here. He can handle any ground, may even get further, and looks a lovely prospect. (tchd 6-4 and 7-4, 15-8 in a place)

Smart Catch(IRE) proved his 66-1 success last time out was no fluke with this creditable second under a penalty, running into a progressive winner. A sound surface seems the key and he is sure to have a big say in similar races in the coming months. (op 6-1 tchd 7-1)

Croan Rock(IRE) attempted to use his stamina to make all, but was reeled in by the front two in the home straight. On ground that seemed unlikely to suit, this was a good run from this future chaser who is sure to appreciate further and some cut. (op 11-1 tchd 12-1)

Toulaman(GER) was under pressure some way from home, but stayed on well to pinch fourth. This was a creditable run after a 758-day absence having twice being placed in bumpers, and although he looked fit enough beforehand he's fully entitled to come on for the run, shaping as though further will suit. (op 33-1)

Somewhatinevitable(IRE) again shaped with promise having been held up in rear early on, but he looks sure to be suited by further and will make a chaser in time. (tchd 17-2)

Homer Run(IRE) Official explanation: jockey said that the gelding was keen early on

Raya Star(IRE), wh ohas the build to make a chaser, has now fallen twice over hurdles and will need to leave those experiences well behind. (op 2-1)

4931 LIQUID PLASTICS LEADERS NOVICES' H'CAP CHASE (16 fncs) 2m 4f 110y
2:40 (2:40) (Class 4) (0-115,114) 5-Y-0+ **£3,084** (£905; £452; £226)

Form RPR

3423 **1** **Lordsbridge (USA)**[17] 4490 9-11-9 **111**........................... NickScholfield 124
(Andy Turnell) *chsd ldr 5th tl 11th: rdn to chse clr ldr after 13th: swtchd lft and clsng 2 out: swtchd rt between last 2: j. ahd last: styd on wl: drvn out* **10/3**[2]

32P2 **2** *3 ½* **Psi (USA)**[12] 4674 6-11-6 **108**...............................(b) AndrewGlassonbury 118
(Gary Moore) *j.lft: hld up in last pair: mstke 2nd and 7th: gd hdwy 10th: chsd ldr next: led sn after 13th and sn clr: rdn and j.lft 2 out: outj. and hdd last: eged lft u.p and sn btn* **3/1**[1]

2P3- **3** *12* **Approved Force (USA)**[398] 4098 7-11-12 **114**............... LeightonAspell 115+
(Lucy Wadham) *t.k.h: in tch: chsd ldrs 9th: mstke 11th: struggling next: wl btn 3 out: wnt 3rd 2 out: styng on same pce and wl hld whn rdr lost iron last* **9/1**

05U1 **4** *6* **Ratify**[37] 4102 7-11-7 **109**.. SamThomas 104
(Brendan Powell) *led: mstke 12th: hdd sn after next: drvn and btn bef 3 out: wknd qckly 3 out: hld on to modest 4th towards fin* **10/3**[2]

204P **5** *nk* **Lady Bling Bling**[12] 4674 10-10-13 **101**..................... WayneHutchinson 97
(Peter Jones) *chsd ldr tl 5th: mstke 7th: 5th and struggling 11th: wl btn 13th: plugged on and pressing for modest 4th flat* **11/2**[3]

P/P3 **P** **Platin Grounds (GER)**[41] 4007 9-11-7 **112**......... SamTwiston-Davies(3) —
(Nigel Twiston-Davies) *in tch: j. slowly 1st and 2nd: j. slowly again 4th and nrly uns: rdn and lost tch rapidly after 9th: wl t.o whn p.u 12th: burst blood vessel* **7/1**

5m 15.4s (-4.10) **Going Correction** -0.05s/f (Good) **6** Ran SP% **109.0**
Speed ratings: **105,103,99,96,96** —
toteswingers: 1&2 £1.50, 1&3 £2.10, 2&3 £1.20 CSF £13.21 TOTE £3.00: £1.40, £2.10; EX 16.80.

Owner The Rakkam Wahed Consortium **Bred** Juddmonte Farms Inc **Trained** Broad Hinton, Wilts

FOCUS
A wide open novice handicap chase with the runner-up to the level of his recent Wincanton form.

NOTEBOOK
Lordsbridge(USA) won his first chase in 14 attempts, enjoying the trip the further he went to take advantage of what looked a reasonable mark. Dropped in grade and upped in distance, this was his first win since 2008 and just reward for this 9-y-o, who has been consistent in his recent runs. He may turn out again on Friday over 3m under a penalty, a trip which should pose no problems on this evidence. (op 5-1)

Psi(USA) looked to have the race won turning for home, travelling comfortably, but in truth he never jumped well enough to merit victory. Jumping slightly left at all his fences and brushing through the top of plenty, he remains winless in Britain and may not be the easiest to find a race for. (op 9-4 tchd 2-1)

Approved Force(USA) stayed on well in the closing stages and shaped well enough after a 398-day absence. Although he hasn't won since 2007, he again showed promise and can find a find a chase. (op 15-2 tchd 13-2)

Ratify set a decent early pace, but was probably undone by the step back in trip and is sure to be suited by a return to further. He remains fairly unexposed over fences. (op 3-1 tchd 4-1)

Lady Bling Bling continues to struggle over fences and may be suited by a return to hurdles. (op 8-1)

Platin Grounds(GER) Official explanation: vet said the gelding had bled form the nose

4932 YOU CAN'T LOSE - SKYLINE ROOFING NOVICES' HURDLE (10 hdls) 2m 5f
3:15 (3:15) (Class 4) 4-Y-0+ **£2,552** (£749; £374; £187)

Form RPR

2232 **1** **Basford Bob (IRE)**[3] 4875 6-11-1 118................................ AlanO'Keeffe 122+
(Jennie Candlish) *hung and j.lft: mde virtually all: mstkes: dived and blnd 6th: rdn and j.lft 2 out: wnt bdly lft again and mstke last: drvn and hld on wl flat* **15/8**[1]

32-1 **2** *nk* **Lion On The Prowl (IRE)**[325] 97 7-11-7 0.................(t) JasonMaguire 126+
(Kim Bailey) *t.k.h: chsd wnr thrght: rdn and followed wnr lft 2 out: wnt lft again last: sn lft w ev ch flat: hrd drvn and a jst hld after* **5/1**[3]

-023 **3** *4* **Romulus D'Artaix (FR)**[19] 4444 5-11-1 0........................ RobertThornton 115
(Alan King) *t.k.h: chsd ldrs: rdn bef 2 out: followed ldng pair and wnt lft 2 out: styd on same pce u.p between last 2* **3/1**[2]

020 **4** *5* **Silver Accord (IRE)**[54] 3771 8-11-7 118.......................... LeightonAspell 116
(Oliver Sherwood) *in tch in midfield: pushed along after 7th: rdn whn mstke next: btn bef 2 out: plugged on same pce between last 2* **11/1**

010- **5** *6* **Neltara**[346] 5129 7-10-12 0.. TommyPhelan(3) 104
(Claire Dyson) *hld up in midfield: hdwy to chse ldrs 3 out: rdn and unable qck bef next: wknd qckly between last 2* **12/1**

3-0 **6** *24* **Rebelious (IRE)**[137] 2186 6-11-1 0.............................. AndrewThornton 87
(Seamus Mullins) *hld up in rr: rdn and short-lived effrt after 3 out: wknd and wl btn 2 out: eased flat: t.o* **50/1**

2-FP **7** *2 ½* **Dixie Bull (IRE)**[18] 4459 6-11-1 0.................................. JimmyMcCarthy 77
(Charles Egerton) *in tch in midfield: mstke 5th: dropped in rr and struggling bef 3 out: lost tch wl bef 2 out: t.o* **15/2**

35 **8** *5* **Not In The Clock (USA)**[27] 4288 4-10-7 0.........................(t) DarylJacob 64
(Charlie Mann) *hld up in last pair: rdn and wknd bef 2 out: wl bhd and eased after last: t.o* **14/1**

5m 11.0s (-13.00) **Going Correction** -0.90s/f (Hard)
WFA 4 from 5yo+ 8lb **8** Ran SP% **112.9**
Speed ratings (Par 105): **88,87,86,84,82 73,72,70**
toteswingers: 1&2 £3.60, 1&3 £1.10, 2&3 £1.90 CSF £11.49 TOTE £3.10: £1.10, £1.40, £1.50; EX 11.90.

Owner Alan Baxter **Bred** Seamus Egan **Trained** Basford Green, Staffs

FOCUS
A fair novices' hurdle with the winner better than the result and the third and fourth a few pounds below their best.

NOTEBOOK
Basford Bob(IRE) showed his class to make almost all and run out a good winner, despite jumping left. Kept wide throughout, this was his first hurdle win in six attempts, building on his second three days previously. Game when challenged after the last, he kept finding for pressure and his attitude suggests that he can win again under a penalty. (op 2-1 tchd 9-4 in places)

Lion On The Prowl(IRE) was returning from a 325-day absence, having won his only previous hurdle start, and ran an excellent race under a penalty in defeat. The trip seemed to suit, and he should come on plenty for the run even though fitness appeared no real concern here. He is unexposed and is sure to keep improving, though like the winner he may appreciate going the other way round. (op 11-2)

Romulus D'Artaix(FR) tracked the leaders all the way round, but never looked like getting involved in the finish. He doesn't look the gamest once asked for an effort off the bridle and it may be that even further brings the best out of him, though he looks like one to avoid taking too short a price about for now. (op 11-4)

Silver Accord(IRE) was under pressure down the back straight, but stayed on well enough. He is fairly exposed and may be suited by a return to handicap company, probably over 3m. (op 12-1 tchd 9-1)

Neltara was making his hurdles debut after a 346-day absence and looked like playing his part in the finish turning for home, but tired in the home straight. Ninth in last year's Aintree Bumper, he clearly has ability and should come on plenty for the run, both in terms of experience and fitness, and looks one to keep on-side. (op 16-1)

4933 SFS INTEC NEW GENERATION H'CAP HURDLE (10 hdls) 2m 5f
3:50 (3:52) (Class 3) (0-130,129) 4-Y-0+ **£4,608** (£1,353; £676; £337)

Form RPR

0011 **1** **Pere Blanc (IRE)**[32] 4196 6-11-8 **125**.............................. JasonMaguire 139+
(David Arbuthnot) *j.rt at times: hld up towards rr: shkn up and hdwy to chse ldrs 3 out: led next: rdn bef last: clr whn hit last: rdn and readily fnd ex flat: r.o wl* **7/2**[1]

2-U4 **2** *4* **Ostland (GER)**[24] 4354 6-10-8 **118**................................... KielanWoods(7) 123
(Charlie Longsdon) *hld up wl in tch: hmpd 3rd: mstke 5th: effrt bef 2 out: chsd wnr and hung lft u.p between last 2: continued to hang lft and kpt on same pce flat* **9/2**[2]

-244 **3** *2* **Phoenix Flight (IRE)**[10] 2081 6-10-7 **113**........................ IanPopham(3) 116
(James Evans) *hld up in last trio: hdwy 3 out: chsd ldrs and rdn bef 2 out: drvn and kpt on flat: no threat to wnr* **8/1**

2234 **4** *shd* **Royale's Charter**[25] 4327 5-10-8 **111**.................................. DarylJacob 114
(Nick Williams) *hld up in tch towards rr: hmpd 3rd: hdwy to trck ldrs after 3 out: rdn and unable qck jst bef 2 out: kpt on u.p flat but no threat to wnr* **6/1**[3]

-02F **5** *14* **Sophies Trophy (IRE)**[59] 3676 6-11-12 **129**.....................(t) ColinBolger 120
(Pat Phelan) *t.k.h: wl in tch: mstke 5th: pressed ldr after 7th: led next tl hdd and hit 2 out: wknd between last 2* **16/1**

302P **6** *4* **Puerto Azul (IRE)**[30] 4235 7-10-12 **115**........................... LeightonAspell 100
(Oliver Sherwood) *hld up in tch in rr: hmpd 3rd: mstke 5th: effrt and hdwy after 3 out: rdn and no prog jst bef 2 out: one pce and wl hld between last 2* **16/1**

-200 **7** *3 ¾* **Ned Ludd (IRE)**[17] 4488 8-11-0 **117**...........................(p) RichieMcLernon 98
(Jonathan Portman) *in tch: rdn along 7th: chsd ldrs next: wknd bef 2 out* **40/1**

4056 **8** *2 ½* **Aather (IRE)**[30] 3808 6-11-7 **124**.. TimmyMurphy 103
(Alan Fleming) *hld up in last trio: hmpd 3rd: effrt on inner after 3 out: stl only midfield whn blnd bdly next: n.d after* **17/2**

4112 **9** *hd* **Sparrow Hills (IRE)**[15] 4524 7-11-1 **125**.......................... RobertKirk(7) 103
(Steven Dixon) *t.k.h: chsd ldrs: wnt 2nd after 4th: led 7th: rdn and hdd next: wknd bef 2 out* **17/2**

3603 **10** *15* **Gee Dee Nen**[24] 4354 8-11-3 **125**...............................(v) JoshuaMoore(5) 88
(Gary Moore) *chsd ldr after 2nd tl after 4th: rdn bef 7th: wknd qckly sn after 3 out: wl bhd next: t.o* **12/1**

43-P **U** **Georgian King**[24] 4354 8-10-12 **115**.................................. DenisO'Regan —
(Suzy Smith) *chsd ldr tl after 2nd: blnd bdly and uns rdr next* **14/1**

1150 **P** **I'Ve Been Framed (IRE)**[27] 4285 7-11-7 **124**..........(p) DominicElsworth —
(Neil King) *led tl 7th: sn rdn bhd and struggling sn after next: wl bhd and p.u 2 out* **20/1**

5m 1.40s (-22.60) **Going Correction** -0.90s/f (Hard) **12** Ran SP% **120.2**
Speed ratings (Par 107): **107,105,104,104,99 97,96,95,95,89** —,—
toteswingers: 1&2 £7.70, 1&3 £12.60, 2&3 £12.40 CSF £20.21 CT £120.47 TOTE £3.70: £1.10, £2.80, £3.50; EX 28.10.
Owner George Ward **Bred** George Ward **Trained** Compton, Berks

FOCUS
A competitive handicap hurdle with the winner value for further, while the placed horses are rated to their best. The form should work out.

NOTEBOOK
Pere Blanc(IRE) ◆ defied a 23lb rise in the handicap to run out an impressive winner and notch up the hat-trick. Travelling sweetly throughout, he looked to have the race in the bag after the last, but was asked to quicken away from the runner-up which he did very impressively. He is an exciting prospect and will make a nice 3m chaser in time, though there are sure to be further hurdle races in him as he still appears ahead of the handicapper. (op 3-1 tchd 4-1, 9-2 in places)
Ostland(GER) ◆ saved ground all the way round up the inside and put in another creditable C&D performance. He was unlucky to run into the progressive winner and can find a race soon. (op 6-1 tchd 13-2)
Phoenix Flight(IRE) has been running well recently on the Flat and improved here on his fourth off the same mark at Ascot in October. Travelling sweetly into the race, he should come on for this return to hurdling and is another who can find a race. (tchd 9-1 in places)
Royale's Charter has been consistent on all hurdle starts and put in another creditable performance, but for as well as he travels, it is a growing concern that he hasn't yet won. (tchd 13-2)
Sophies Trophy(IRE) led the field turning for home and looked to hold a chance two out, but may have failed to see out the trip. Second to Mille Chief in January, he is likely to be suited by a drop back to 2m. (op 14-1 tchd 12-1)
Puerto Azul(IRE) is very inconsistent. (op 20-1)
Ned Ludd(IRE) has shown nothing of late.

4934 FLAG-SOPREMA WATERPROOFING CLASSIC H'CAP CHASE (12 fncs) 2m
4:25 (4:25) (Class 3) (0-120,120) 5-Y-0+
£5,460 (£1,613; £806; £403; £201; £101)

Form RPR

1311 **1** **Rileyev (FR)**[8] 4770 6-10-13 **107** 7ex.................... SamThomas 119+
(Venetia Williams) *racd wl off the pce in midfield: clsd after 5th: wnt 3rd next: lft 2nd 8th: led bef 3 out: clr and rdn whn j.lft 2 out: kpt on wl* **3/1**[1]

4303 **2** *3* **Cortinas (GER)**[11] 4698 9-11-3 **114**..................(t) IanPopham(3) 121
(Claire Dyson) *racd wl off the pce in midfield: clsd after 5th: cl 4th after 9th: chsd wnr bef 3 out: drvn and no imp between last 2* **12/1**

4205 **3** *8* **Viable**[25] 4324 9-11-3 **118**.................... MissGAndrews(7) 122+
(Pam Sly) *j.rt: wl bhd in last trio: j. violently rt 1st: sme hdwy whn j.rt again and blnd 6th: jst in tch and rdn bef 3 out: plugged on fr 2 out: wnt 3rd flat: no threat to ldng pair* **10/1**

2-44 **4** *5* **Riddleofthesands (IRE)**[96] 2986 7-10-5 **102**...... SamTwiston-Davies(3) 100+
(Nigel Twiston-Davies) *led and sn wl clr w rival tl wnt clr after 5th: pressed whn blnd bdly and hdd 8th: stl disputing 2nd and rdn 3 out: wknd next: snatched 4th on post* **5/1**[3]

-134 **5** *shd* **Clouseau (NZ)**[25] 4324 7-11-8 **116**.................... DarylJacob 111
(Nick Williams) *hld up wl bhd in last pair: mstke 2nd: hdwy 6th: pressing for 2nd 3 out: sn rdn: wknd u.p between last 2: fdd and lost 2 pls flat* **5/1**[3]

1221 **6** *6* **Betabob (IRE)**[34] 4140 8-11-5 **120**.................... MrRGHenderson(7) 110
(Nick Mitchell) *wl bhd in last: mstke 2nd and 3rd: clsd 8th: in tch and rdn bef 3 out: wknd bef 2 out* **5/1**[3]

3U5P **7** *3 ¾* **Wessex King (IRE)**[18] 4460 7-11-11 **119**.................... AndrewTinkler 105
(Henry Daly) *chsd clr ldng pair: clsd and wnt 2nd 6th: lft in ld 8th tl hdd after next: rdn and racd awkwardly u.p bef 3 out: wknd 3 out* **9/2**[2]

-045 **P** **Uncle Ant (IRE)**[34] 4140 6-10-8 **102**.................... DominicElsworth —
(Paul Webber) *mstkes: w ldr and sn clr of field tl 5th: fdd and losing pl next: last and tailing off whn mstke 9th: sn p.u: burst blood vessel* **25/1**

4m 4.70s (6.70) **Going Correction** -0.05s/f (Good) **8** Ran SP% **113.8**
Speed ratings: **81,79,75,73,72 69,68**,—
toteswingers: 1&2 £10.20, 1&3 £10.90, 2&3 £15.70 CSF £35.97 CT £317.77 TOTE £6.70: £3.70, £5.80, £7.10; EX 43.80.
Owner John Mayne **Bred** Mme Laurence Barreaud & Claude Barreaud **Trained** Kings Caple, H'fords

FOCUS
An average handicap chase, run at a frenetic pace by the early pace-setters. Another step up from the winner with the second to his Sandown mark.

NOTEBOOK
Rileyev(FR) ◆, a handicap good thing, ran up the hat-trick and has now won four of his last five races. Due to go up 5lb in the handicap on Saturday, he took full advantage here and has numerous entries in the coming days before his new mark takes effect. The way he is running, he will have a good chance wherever he takes up his engagements. (op 11-4 tchd 5-2, 7-2 in places)
Cortinas(GER) is a consistent sort, but struggles to win and hasn't done so since November 2009. He gives the form some shape, but will need the help of the handicapper to be winning anytime soon. (tchd 11-1)
Viable was exuberant and big at his fences, but stayed on eye-catchingly. He is suited by a sound surface, and is only 2lb higher than his last wining mark. If able to brush up on his jumping, his next win doesn't seem to far away, especially if stepped up in trip. (op 12-1)
Riddleofthesands(IRE) set off at a frenetic pace, and looked like tailing off once swamped by the field, but this was an impressive effort to stay on all the way to the line. If able to get an uncontested lead, he may be off interest in a similar race. (op 6-1 tchd 13-2, 15-2 in a place)
Clouseau(NZ) crept nicely into the race, enjoying the return to a sound surface, but found nothing when asked for an effort. He remains unexposed over fences, but doesn't look the gamest. (tchd 11-2)
Betabob(IRE) was poor and never got involved. Official explanation: trainer said the gelding had bled form the nose (tchd 11-2)
Wessex King(IRE) faded quickly. (tchd 4-1 and 5-1)
Uncle Ant(IRE) Official explanation: vet said the gelding had bled form the nose

4935 SIKASPEC CONDITIONAL JOCKEYS' NOVICES' H'CAP HURDLE (8 hdls) 2m
5:00 (5:00) (Class 4) (0-115,111) 4-Y-0+ **£2,552** (£749; £374; £187)

Form RPR

0052 **1** **Rare Symphony (IRE)**[9] 4751 4-9-12 **93**..................(t) CPGeoghegan(3) 91+
(Philip Hobbs) *taken down early: chsd ldr: mstke 3rd: pushed along 3 out: rdn and ev ch 2 out: sn drvn: led last: kpt on u.p and forged ahd flat* **6/4**[1]

6451 **2** *1 ½* **Decision**[8] 4785 5-11-3 **102** 7ex..................(t) DavidBass 105
(Lawney Hill) *led: hit 3 out: hrd pressed next: rdn and hdd bef last: stl ev ch last: styd on same pce and no ex fnl 75yds* **11/4**[2]

0F-0 **3** *1 ¼* **Right Stuff (FR)**[18] 4462 8-11-7 **109**.................... JoshuaMoore(3) 111
(Gary Moore) *in tch in midfield: chsd ldng pair after 3 out: rdn and ev ch next: led between last 2: mstke and hdd last: no ex and btn fnl 100yds* **12/1**

6546 **4** *2 ½* **Bun Oir (USA)**[12] 4672 4-10-4 **104**..................(bt) GeraldQuinn(8) 95
(Charlie Longsdon) *in tch towards rr: hdwy to chse ldrs and rdn after 3 out: kpt on u.p between last 2: nvr quite gng pce to rch ldrs* **20/1**

2005 **5** *3* **Souter Point (USA)**[30] 4234 5-11-9 **111**.................... RichardKilloran(3) 106
(Nicky Henderson) *in tch in rr: rdn along after 4th: drvn 3 out: no imp next: plugged on u.p flat: nvr gng pce to trble ldrs* **8/1**

FU0 **6** *6* **Al Amaan**[54] 2294 6-10-11 **104**.................... JosephAkehurst(8) 94
(Gary Moore) *hld up in tch in rr: hdwy bef 3 out: chsd ldng quartet and rdn along bef 2 out: no hdwy 2 out* **28/1**

4103 **7** *8* **Apache Chant (USA)**[16] 4501 7-10-11 **99**..................(p) LeeEdwards(3) 81
(Tony Carroll) *in tch in midfield: pushed along after 2nd: nvr gng wl after: rdn after 4th: wknd after 3 out* **13/2**[3]

426- **8** *60* **Minder**[18] 5255 5-11-6 **105**..................(p) RichieMcLernon 26
(Jonathan Portman) *chsd ldrs: rdn and wknd qckly after 3 out: eased and lost tch jst bef next: wl t.o whn blnd last* **25/1**

3m 57.4s (-2.60) **Going Correction** -0.90s/f (Hard)
WFA 4 from 5yo+ 7lb **8** Ran SP% **110.9**
Speed ratings (Par 105): **70,69,68,67,65 62,58,28**
toteswingers: 1&2 £1.90, 1&3 £3.30, 2&3 £5.00 CSF £5.75 CT £30.11 TOTE £2.20: £1.10, £1.10, £4.70; EX 6.60.
Owner Mrs Caren Walsh **Bred** Peter Reynolds & Robert Dore **Trained** Withycombe, Somerset
■ Stewards' Enquiry : C P Geoghegan two-day ban: used whip with excessive frequency (Apr 5, 10)

FOCUS
A thrilling finish to this novice handicap hurdle, with the front three jumping the last together. The first three are rated close to their marks.

NOTEBOOK
Rare Symphony(IRE) got off the mark over hurdles with a brave performance, finding plenty for pressure under a forceful ride. Second on her handicap debut last time out, she looked to have a good chance racing off the same mark before being re-assessed. She will receive a hike in the weights and it may be that she appreciates the application of blinkers to keep her up to her work, as she has previously won in them on the Flat. (op 13-8 tchd 5-4)
Decision attempted to make all under a penalty and was just out-battled in the closing stages. Due to go up 10lb, he should be able to keep running well if putting in a similar level of performance to this. (op 3-1 tchd 10-3)
Right Stuff(FR) was a significant market drifter, but ran well on the return to a sound surface. However, he didn't look the gamest for a battle after the last and is now 0-10 over hurdles, which suggests he isn't too keen to get his head in front. (op 17-2)
Bun Oir(USA) showed more than he has before, but will need to repeat this to prove that he isn't just moderate.
Souter Point(USA) was under pressure a long way from home, but kept plugging on and looked as though a significant step up in trip is required. (tchd 17-2, 10-1 in a place and 15-2 in places)
Al Amaan was too keen early on and needs to settle to see out his races fully. (op 22-1)
Apache Chant(USA) wasn't suited by the drop in trip on such a sharp track. (op 7-1 tchd 6-1)

4936 MARLEY ETERNIT FIRED SIENNA HUNTERS' CHASE (16 fncs) 2m 4f 110y
5:30 (5:30) (Class 5) 6-Y-0+ **£2,498** (£774; £387; £193)

Form RPR

13-3 **1** **I Have Dreamed (IRE)**[143] 2086 9-11-11 134.................... MrRJarrett(7) 125+
(S Flook) *hld up in rr: stdy hdwy 9th: lft 3rd 11th: chsd ldr after 13th: led next: sn rdn clr: in n.d fr 2 out: pushed out flat* **5/1**[3]

50-P **2** *30* **Sovereign King**[18] 4463 9-11-7 108.................... MrMWall(3) 90
(Miss C Herrington) *in tch: hdwy to chse ldrs 8th: lft 2nd 11th tl after 13th: 3rd and wl btn 3 out: wnt modest 2nd last: no ch w wnr* **11/1**

312- **3** *14* **Jurado Express (IRE)**[338] 5249 15-12-4 0.................... MrAJBerry 93+
(Miss Michelle Bentham) *w ldr tl lft in ld 11th: hdd 3 out: sn btn: lost 2nd last: fin tired: dismntd sn after fin* **7/1**

-055 **4** *24* **Calgary Jock**[27] 4293 10-11-10 0.................... MrPYork 56
(Mrs J Marles) *mstkes: chsd ldrs: struggling whn lft 4th 11th: lost tch next: t.o bef 3 out* **40/1**

-P36 **U** **Silver Adonis (IRE)**[233] 1151 10-12-1 124..................(p) MrTWeston(3) —
(Dr Richard Newland) *hld up in last trio: hdwy and mstke 8th: wl in tch whn blnd and uns rdr next* **10/3**[1]

3153 **U** **Ryeman**[11] 4708 9-12-0 112..................(bt) MrWBiddick —
(Andrew Jackson) *in tch: mstke 7th: 3rd whn blnd and uns rdr 10th* **7/2**[2]

30RU **U** **Cloud Nine (IRE)**[11] 4708 8-11-5 106..................(b) MrJHamer(5) —
(Miss Jane Western) *led tl 8 blnd and uns rdr 11th* **7/1**

235- **P** **Pelennor (FR)**[17] 7-11-5 96..................(t) MrPJTolman(5) —
(R Scrine) *nt jump wl: a bhd: hmpd 10th: sn lost tch: wl t.o whn p.u 2 out* **6/1**

05 **U** **Westcoat Lad**[9] 6-11-3 0.................... MrRMcDowall(7) —
(Kevin Tork) *last whn uns rdr 1st* **66/1**

5m 18.2s (-1.30) **Going Correction** -0.05s/f (Good) **9** Ran SP% **113.5**
Speed ratings: **100,88,83,74**,— —,—,—,—
toteswingers: 1&2 £3.20, 1&3 £2.40, 2&3 £23.50 CSF £55.41 TOTE £4.50: £1.50, £4.40, £1.60; EX 62.10.
Owner Glyn Byard **Bred** Dr T A Ryan **Trained** Leominster, Herefordshire

FOCUS
A modest hunter chase that could be rated a lot higher but limited by the modest time.

NOTEBOOK
I Have Dreamed(IRE) was best in on ratings here on his hunter chase debut and he ran out a comfortable winner of this weak contest. Racing without his usual headgear, he crept dangerously into the race down the back as his rivals all made mistakes, before pulling clear in the home straight, finishing well ahead of the rest. Having raced mainly at shorter than this, the trip appeared to cause no problems and, if kept to hunter chases, can pick up his share. (op 9-2 tchd 4-1)
Sovereign King was another making his hunter-chase debut and shaped well enough, but was unable to match the turn of foot of the winner. He should find an opportunity in a similarly weak race. (op 12-1 tchd 14-1)
Jurado Express(IRE) put in a marvellous performance, belying his years, and jumping like the old pro that he is. He travelled well, but was unable to quicken at the right moment and it appears that Father Time has finally caught up. (op 9-2)
Calgary Jock has shown little and did so again here. (op 66-1)

T/Plt: £11.80 to a £1 stake.Pool of £69,369.77 - 4,276.53 winning tickets. T/Qpdt: £4.70 to a £1 stake. Pool of £5,077.37- 791.64 winning tickets. SP

4205 HAYDOCK (L-H)

Wednesday, March 23

OFFICIAL GOING: Good (good to fim in places on hurdle course; watered; chs 4.9; hdl 6.3)

Both bends moved out 6 metres from innermost rail position, increasing all distances by 38 metres per circuit.

Wind: almost nil Weather: fine and sunny, very mild

4937 HAYDOCK PARK OPEN DAY 30TH MARCH H'CAP CHASE (18 fncs) 3m

2:10 (2:11) (Class 4) (0-115,115) 5-Y-O+ **£3,252** (£955; £477; £238)

Form				RPR
4431	1		**Maurisca (FR)**[10] 4740 6-11-13 **115** 7ex FelixDeGiles (Charlie Longsdon) *trckd ldrs: t.k.h: jnd ldr sn after 14th: chaling whn hit next: led 2 out: 4 l ahd last: sn rdn: all out* **5/2**[1]	127+
4-35	2	2 ¼	**Marleybow (IRE)**[147] 2036 8-11-8 **110** TomScudamore (Richard Lee) *trckd ldrs: wnt 2nd 9th: led 14th: hdd and blnd 2 out: rallied run-in: kpt on same pce* **9/2**[2]	118
6P44	3	13	**Daldini**[63] 3634 9-10-10 **103** ShaneByrne(5) (Sue Smith) *chsd ldrs: lost pl 8th: hdwy to chse ldng pair 14th: 3rd and outpcd whn blnd next: one pce* **9/2**[2]	100
1563	4	18	**Seize**[58] 3716 9-11-6 **108** PaddyAspell (James Moffatt) *in rr: bhd fr 11th* **14/1**	86
5615	5	1 ¾	**Lampion Du Bost (FR)**[12] 4689 12-11-10 **112** GrahamLee (Jim Goldie) *led to 5th: drvn 9th: lost pl and reminders next: sn bhd* **20/1**	89
-215	6	4 ½	**It's Like That (IRE)**[19] 4463 11-11-9 **114** MrAJBerry(3) (Jonjo O'Neill) *in rr: hdwy to chse ldrs 11th: modest 3rd 3 out: wknd appr last: eased clsng stages* **17/2**	89
432P	7	19	**Lahib The Fifth (IRE)**[35] 4139 11-10-12 **100** FearghalDavis (Nicky Richards) *in rr and reminders 10th: reminders 12th: poor 5th whn blnd 14th: t.o* **16/1**	55
2443	P		**Youngstown (IRE)**[22] 4408 8-11-12 **114** (b[1]) JasonMaguire (Donald McCain) *trckd ldrs: led 5th: blnd 11th: hdd 14th: sn wknd: bhd whn p.u bef 2 out* **5/1**[3]	—

6m 13.7s (-0.30) **Going Correction** -0.175s/f (Good) **8** Ran SP% **109.4**

Speed ratings: **93,92,87,81,81 79,73,—**

toteswingers:1&2:£3.00, 1&3:£3.30, 2&3:£4.60 CSF £13.29 CT £41.80 TOTE £3.10: £1.60, £1.90, £1.80; EX 11.20.

Owner Hamer & Hawkes **Bred** Haras De La Rousseliere & Mme K Monclin **Trained** Over Norton, Oxon

FOCUS

A fair handicap chase, though the front pair had the race to themselves over the final four fences. The winning time was 23.7 seconds outside standard, suggesting that the ground still hat a bit of moisture in it. The winner is on the upgrade and the second sets the level.

NOTEBOOK

Maurisca(FR) relished the better ground when hacking up at Market Rasen ten days earlier and was put up 10lb for that, so he was well in under his 7lb penalty. Always travelling well, a mistake four from home looked as though it might prove expensive, but his main rival repaid the compliment two fences later, which was probably just as well as he didn't do much in front after that. He should continue to pay his way now that conditions have come right for him. (tchd 11-4)

Marleybow(IRE) had been given a break since disappointing on his second run for connections over this C&D in October, but he has a great record fresh and this was another solid effort. He looked to be getting the worst of it when blundering two from home, but the winner then doing little in front meant that he only went down narrowly. His profile suggests that he may not improve for the run, but he probably won't have to in order to go one better.

Daldini is normally a front-runner, but didn't lead this time. He plugged on again for a remote third after losing his place mid-race, but although he is 15lb below his last winning mark of 13 months ago, all his successes over fences have come on much softer ground than this. (tchd 5-1 in a place)

Seize had his favoured ground, but he ran poorly on his debut for the yard at Wetherby in January and was never nearer here despite finishing fourth. (tchd 12-1)

It's Like That(IRE), returning from 289 days off when beaten a long way in a Newbury hunter chase earlier this month, made a move down the back straight on the final circuit but it came to nothing. (op 9-1)

Youngstown(IRE) had blinkers on for the first time and raced freely once taking up the running, but a bad blunder at the 11th stopped him in his tracks, and he stopped to nothing after being collared by the front pair five from home.

4938 SAM'S BARS NOVICES' LIMITED H'CAP CHASE (13 fncs) 2m

2:40 (2:43) (Class 3) (0-130,127) 5-Y-O+ **£4,664** (£1,448; £779)

Form				RPR
-662	1		**Humbie (IRE)**[29] 4275 7-10-6 **114** TimmyMurphy (Pauline Robson) *nt fluent: hdwy to chse ldng pair 5th: wnt 2nd 4 out: led 2 out: 5 l ld whn j.lft last: carried hd high: drvn out* **9/2**[3]	126+
1/13	2	4	**Glencree (IRE)**[19] 4453 7-11-3 **125** BrianHughes (Howard Johnson) *chsd ldr: nt fluent 6th: lost pl 4 out: tk modest 2nd last: no imp* **6/4**[1]	128
3P05	3	1 ¼	**Our Bob (IRE)**[18] 4490 9-10-5 **113** (t) TomO'Brien (Philip Hobbs) *led: hdd 2 out: one pce run-in* **10/3**[2]	115
45	U		**Gentleman Jeff (USA)**[45] 3965 7-10-9 **117** CampbellGillies (Chris Grant) *hld up in last: sme hdwy whn blnd and uns rdr 5th* **8/1**	—

4m 10.2s (-0.80) **Going Correction** -0.175s/f (Good) **4** Ran SP% **92.4**

Speed ratings: **95,93,92,—**

CSF £8.66 TOTE £3.60; EX 6.10.

Owner Mr & Mrs Raymond Anderson Green **Bred** Colman O'Flynn **Trained** Kirkharle, Northumberland

FOCUS

This race was weakened by the late withdrawal of Thumbs Up, who proved mulish when asked to move out onto the track at the start, and then refused to line up with the others. The other four went off at a decent pace but it is not a race to be confident about, despite the winner being value for further.

NOTEBOOK

Humbie(IRE) was dropping to this trip for the first time and appeared to have a mountain to climb with Glencree on Catterick January running, even on these revised terms, but the good pace here helped him and he was given a well-judged ride by Murphy, who let the leaders get on with it before picking them off two from home. He jumped badly out to his left at the last and then idled on the run-in, suggesting he is not yet the finished article. He is likely to be aimed at the 3m novice chase at Ayr on Scottish National day. (op 5-1)

Glencree(IRE) did far too much too early when third at Doncaster over 3f further last time so this drop in trip ought to have been in his favour, but his jumping was far from fluent and he could only plug on after getting outpaced starting up the home straight. (tchd 13-8)

Our Bob(IRE) was racing over this shorter trip for the first time over obstacles and tried to make it a decent test, but he couldn't match the winner over the final two fences and probably needs a return to 2m4f. (op 4-1)

4939 HAYDOCK PARK BONUS (S) HURDLE (9 hdls) 2m

3:15 (3:15) (Class 3) 4-7-Y-O **£4,878** (£1,432; £716; £357)

Form				RPR
0644	1		**Master Fong (IRE)**[45] 3966 5-11-5 110 (b) JasonMaguire (Donald McCain) *trckd ldrs: led 2 out: styd on u.p* **3/1**[2]	110+
1033	2	2	**Grand Diamond (IRE)**[35] 4149 7-10-12 115 PaulNorton(7) (Jim Goldie) *hld up: hdwy 3 out: handy 3rd whn mstke next: stmbld on landing last: kpt on to take 2nd last 75yds* **5/2**[1]	110+
2621	3	¾	**Miereveld**[21] 4419 4-10-7 103 PaulGallagher(5) (Brian Ellison) *led: hdd appr 2 out and nt fluent: kpt on same pce run-in* **6/1**	101
31P4	4	hd	**Holoko Heights**[22] 4406 6-11-9 0 (vt) TomScudamore (Tim Vaughan) *chsd ldrs: drvn 5th: wknd between last 2* **9/2**	112
331	5	14	**Bring Sweets (IRE)**[29] 1825 4-10-5 103 MissHBethell(7) (Brian Ellison) *t.k.h: trckd ldrs: wknd appr 2 out* **4/1**[3]	90+
66	6	½	**Royal Patriot (IRE)**[26] 4331 4-10-4 0 TommyPhelan(3) (Paul Green) *t.k.h in rr: nt fluent: hdwy appr 3 out: wknd appr 2 out: modest 4th whn mstke last* **100/1**	84
22FP	7	6	**Vivarini**[39] 4079 7-11-5 113 CharlieWallis(7) (John O'Shea) *chsd ldrs: lost pl 3 out* **22/1**	96

3m 55.6s (-8.60) **Going Correction** -0.40s/f (Good)

WFA 4 from 5yo+ 7lb **7** Ran SP% **111.4**

Speed ratings: **105,104,103,103,96 96,93**

toteswingers:1&2:£2.50, 1&3:£3.20, 2&3:£2.20 CSF £10.64 TOTE £3.60: £2.10, £1.70; EX 11.80.There was no bid for the winner.

Owner Woodland Racings **Bred** Keatly Overseas Ltd **Trained** Cholmondeley, Cheshire

FOCUS

Quite a valuable prize for a seller and the front three pulled a long way clear of the rest. the fourth and fifth help set the level of the form with the winner to last season's best.

NOTEBOOK

Master Fong(IRE), down in grade, was successful the last time he tackled a sound surface. Well backed beforehand, he was always up there and did enough once taking it up after three out. Despite wearing blinkers, he does tend to look around a bit so isn't one to lump on. (op 9-2)

Grand Diamond(IRE), back on his favoured surface and marginally best in at the weights, was given a patient ride and may have finished closer had he not been untidy at the last two flights, but he looked second-best on merit. (op 2-1)

Miereveld, down to this level for the first time over hurdles after making all to win a Bangor handicap on softer ground last time, was minus his usual headgear. He tried to make all the running again and battled on well once losing the advantage after the third-last. (op 11-2)

Holoko Heights wore a tongue tie for the first time, but was receiving reminders before exiting the back straight. (tchd 4-1 and 11-2)

Bring Sweets(IRE) has been in fair form on the all-weather since winning a Wetherby maiden hurdle in October. He travelled well off the pace, if a little keen, but found nothing once asked for effort. (op 5-1)

4940 GEOFF BELLMON 80TH BIRTHDAY GEORGE CLOONEY LOOKALIKE H'CAP HURDLE (10 hdls) 2m 4f

3:50 (3:50) (Class 3) (0-135,128) 4-Y-O+ **£6,505** (£1,910; £955; £477)

Form				RPR
F253	1		**Mad Moose (IRE)**[121] 2581 7-11-1 **120** SamTwiston-Davies(3) (Nigel Twiston-Davies) *trckd ldrs: led after 7th: clr 2 out: eased towards fin* **14/1**	132+
3-00	2	12	**Glingerbank (IRE)**[80] 3334 11-11-3 **119** FearghalDavis (Nicky Richards) *chsd ldrs: hit 6th: wnt modest 2nd 2 out: styd on: no ch w wnr* **40/1**	121
4106	3	¾	**Nicene Creed**[25] 4354 6-11-7 **123** TomO'Brien (Philip Hobbs) *chsd ldrs: lost pl 7th: 7th 2 out: 6th last: styd on wl run-in* **3/1**[1]	122
6-15	4	shd	**Diklers Oscar (IRE)**[42] 4003 8-11-8 **124** JamesReveley (Keith Reveley) *chsd ldrs: lost pl 5th: hdwy and poor 5th 2 out: styd on appr last* **8/1**[3]	122
0B01	5	3 ¼	**Tobago Bay**[18] 4485 6-11-7 **128** (b) JoshuaMoore(5) (Gary Moore) *led tl after 7th: one pce fr next* **8/1**[3]	123
-356	6	3 ¼	**Los Nadis (GER)**[45] 3969 7-11-9 **125** RichieMcGrath (Jim Goldie) *chsd ldrs tl lost pl 5th: sme hdwy 3 out: no threat* **10/1**	118
1264	7	3 ¼	**Viva Colonia (IRE)**[35] 4149 6-11-2 **118** BrianHughes (David O'Meara) *hld up: hdwy to trck ldrs 7th: wnt 2nd 3 out: wknd next* **9/1**	108
20PP	8	12	**First Stream (GER)**[25] 4354 7-11-1 **122** PaulGallagher(5) (Howard Johnson) *hld up in rr: pushed along 5th: bhd fr 3 out* **10/1**	103
1116	9	3 ½	**Maska Pony (IRE)**[131] 2344 7-11-11 **127** GrahamLee (George Moore) *hld up in rr: bhd fr 7th* **11/1**	103
-132	10	27	**Thanks For Coming**[43] 3987 5-11-3 **119** AndrewTinkler (Nicky Henderson) *in rr: wnt prom 4th: lost pl appr 3 out: sn bhd: t.o last* **4/1**[2]	70
4320	11	12	**Amir Pasha (UAE)**[25] 4358 6-10-3 **108** (v) JamesHalliday(3) (Micky Hammond) *wnt prom 2nd: w ldr 5th: lost pl appr 7th: sn bhd: t.o 2 out* **18/1**	48

4m 39.6s (-33.90) **Going Correction** -1.50s/f (Hard) **11** Ran SP% **118.1**

Speed ratings (Par 107): **107,102,101,101,100 99,97,93,91,80 76**

toteswingers:1&2:£17.80, 1&3:£11.00, 2&3:£41.80 CSF £411.37 CT £2123.09 TOTE £16.30: £3.70, £7.60, £1.90; EX 531.10 TRIFECTA Not won..

Owner N A Twiston-Davies **Bred** Miss E And Miss M Murphy **Trained** Naunton, Gloucs

FOCUS

This had looked a competitive handicap hurdle, but it became a one-horse race. The form looks fairly sound with the runner-up and fourth the guides.

NOTEBOOK

Mad Moose(IRE) split a couple of subsequent winners when fourth at Kempton at November when last seen and was 18lb higher than for his last success, but he still won this in emphatic fashion. Having moved smoothly to the front four out, he just went further and further clear and in view of his liking for good ground and a tight left-handed track, he could be interesting for a race at Aintree. A step up in trip wouldn't bother him. (op 12-1)

Glingerbank(IRE) did well to plug on for a remote second considering his jumping wasn't always fluent. He had been beaten a long way in both previous starts this term, so this was more encouraging. (op 33-1)

Nicene Creed, less exposed over hurdles than most, had disappointed on easier ground the last twice and ran on again here after losing his place at halfway. (tchd 4-1 in a place)

Diklers Oscar(IRE) dropped back to almost last jumping four out before staying on again. She is still 9lb above her last winning mark. (tchd 15-2)

Tobago Bay, put up 6lb for his narrow victory at Newbury earlier this month, made the early running but could only plug on at one pace after being headed by the winner four out. (tchd 10-1 in a place)

Los Nadis(GER), back off his last winning mark, was entitled to need his return from eight months off on unsuitably soft ground at Musselburgh last month and ran an interesting race here. Another to completely lose his place before halfway, he ran on again over the last three flights but was by no means knocked about and looks capable of better.

Viva Colonia(IRE) hadn't had his ground in his previous two starts, but was 16lb higher than when beating First Stream at Wetherby in October. He was travelling every bit as well as the winner when moving into contention after jumping four out, but found nothing off the bridle and didn't get home.

Thanks For Coming, making his handicap debut after winning a bumper and placing in a couple of novice hurdles, was close enough exiting the back straight but then came under pressure and stopped to nothing. Official explanation: trainer's rep had no explanation for the poor form shown (tchd 5-1 in places)

4941 BRAVO INNS H'CAP CHASE (15 fncs) 2m 4f

4:25 (4:25) (Class 3) (0-135,135) 5-Y-0+ **£5,204** (£1,528; £764; £381)

Form — RPR

2-5F **1** **Nikos Extra (FR)**[161] 1828 7-11-2 **125** WayneHutchinson 141+
(Alan King) *hld up: stdy hdwy 6th: wnt 2nd on bit after 5 out: carried lft 2 out: led gng easily best last: drvn clr* **7/2**[2]

-113 **2** *8* **Invisible Man (FR)**[178] 1627 6-11-9 **132** (t) TomScudamore 139
(Ian Williams) *led: drvn 4 out: j.lft 2 out: hdd last: eased whn wl btn towards fin* **9/4**[1]

-P20 **3** *24* **Saphir Des Bois (FR)**[18] 4487 7-11-12 **135** TomO'Brien 118
(Peter Bowen) *chsd ldr: hrd drvn and hit 10th: wl outpcd appr 4 out: modest 4th whn hit 2 out: tk 3rd towards fin* **12/1**

200 **4** *½* **Fred Bojangals (IRE)**[18] 4470 9-11-1 **124** (p) BrianHughes 107
(Ann Hamilton) *t.k.h: trckd ldrs: clr 3rd whn j.lft 3 out: sn rdn: wknd next* **20/1**

611R **5** *10* **Tyrone House (IRE)**[25] 4362 7-10-10 **119** JamesReveley 93
(John Wade) *hld up in rr: hdwy 8th: lost pl 11th: sn bhd* **15/2**

6556 **6** *22* **Rory Boy (USA)**[25] 4355 6-10-7 **119** (p) SamTwiston-Davies(3) 73
(Nigel Twiston-Davies) *chsd ldrs: drvn 8th: sn lost pl: bhd fr 11th: t.o* **11/2**

-031 **P** **Hector's Choice (FR)**[20] 4438 7-11-9 **132** SamThomas —
(Richard Lee) *in rr: reminders 4th: last whn blnd 7th: bhd fr 8th: last whn p.u bef 3 out* **9/2**[3]

5m 3.00s (-7.00) **Going Correction** -0.175s/f (Good) **7 Ran SP% 110.8**
Speed ratings: **107,103,94,94,90 81,—**
toteswingers:1&2:£2.60, 1&3:£9.00, 2&3:£6.20 CSF £11.53 TOTE £4.30: £3.00, £1.50; EX 13.50.

Owner Mr And Mrs J D Cotton **Bred** Eurl Du Chene & Dr Vet Roger Yves Simon **Trained** Barbury Castle, Wilts

FOCUS
A fair handicap chase which was dominated by the two horses returning from lengthy absences. The form is not the most solid, although the winner is on a good mark and the second is rated to his best.

NOTEBOOK
Nikos Extra(FR) hadn't been seen since falling when still in with every chance at Wetherby in October, but he could hardly have won this more impressively. He was travelling like a dream when moving up to stalk the leader after five out, but his rider was at pains not to get after him until the last possible moment. Still on the bridle when leading at the last, he found plenty when shaken up on the run-in and looks set for a profitable spring. (op 4-1 tchd 10-3 and 9-2 in a place)

Invisible Man(FR) was returning from 178 days off and jumped boldly out in front. He had most of his rivals in trouble after four out, but the winner was the exception and he was allowed to retain the advantage on sufferance until jumping the last. With the ground now coming in his favour, he should be winning again before long. (op 5-2)

Saphir Des Bois(FR), who ran poorly in the Greatwood Gold Cup at Newbury last time, was still in touch when a mistake at the tenth seemed to knock the stuffing out of him. Most of his best form has come on soft ground. (op 14-1)

Fred Bojangals(IRE), still 12lb higher than for his last win at Ayr a year ago, took a keen hold in the early stages and that seemed to take its toll on him after jumping the fourth-last. (op 22-1 tchd 18-1)

Tyrone House(IRE) refused at the last when bidding for a hat-trick over 3m on heavy ground at Newcastle last month, but although these conditions should have suited him better he was comfortably held off an 8lb higher mark than for his last win. (op 8-1)

Rory Boy(USA) ran poorly again and has become very disappointing despite a tumbling mark. (op 6-1)

Hector's Choice(FR), having only his third start over fences after easily winning a Ludlow novice chase earlier this month, was in trouble after blunders at the seventh and eighth and this was extremely disappointing. Official explanation: jockey said gelding never travelled (op 7-2)

4942 WHIZZ-KIDZ CHARITY "FIXED BRUSH" NOVICES' HURDLE (10 hdls) 2m 4f

5:00 (5:00) (Class 4) 4-Y-0+ **£2,602** (£764; £382; £190)

Form — RPR

212 **1** **A Bridge Too Far (IRE)**[23] 4393 5-11-8 121 JasonMaguire 126+
(Donald McCain) *j.rt: mde all: sent clr appr 3 out: eased towards fin: unchal* **2/5**[1]

4016 **2** *13* **Solis**[19] 4451 5-10-12 116 JoeColliver(10) 108
(Micky Hammond) *trckd wnr: chsd wnr 2 out: no imp* **7/2**[2]

0 **3** *9* **That's Mine (IRE)**[17] 4499 5-11-1 0 RichieMcLernon 92
(Jonjo O'Neill) *trckd ldrs: t.k.h: wknd appr 3 out: tk modest 3rd run-in* **33/1**

2000 **4** *2* **Tahiti Pearl (IRE)**[18] 4477 7-10-10 100 ShaneByrne(5) 92
(Sue Smith) *hld up in tch: wnt 2nd after 7th: 3rd and wkng whn hit last* **12/1**[3]

0 **5** *1* **The Musical Guy (IRE)**[49] 3877 5-10-12 0 SamTwiston-Davies(3) 91
(Nigel Twiston-Davies) *j.rt: in rr: wnt prom 5th: outpcd and lost pl 7th: sn bhd* **12/1**[3]

4m 51.8s (-21.70) **Going Correction** -0.90s/f (Hard) **5 Ran SP% 112.0**
Speed ratings (Par 105): **107,101,98,97,97**
CSF £2.35 TOTE £1.40: £1.10, £1.40; EX 2.20.

Owner Glen's Fools **Bred** William O'Keeffe **Trained** Cholmondeley, Cheshire

FOCUS
This "fixed brush" novice hurdle suffered from three non-runners, especially the forecast favourite Cantlow, who was withdrawn on veterinary advice. They went a very steady pace early and the form could be rated a few pounds either way.

NOTEBOOK
A Bridge Too Far(IRE) had shown decent form in his first two starts over hurdles and appeared to face a penalty kick here following the withdrawal of Cantlow. Making all at his own pace, he never looked in any danger of defeat and this told us little new about him. (new market op 4-9)

Solis has gone well for this rider lately, but had stamina to prove over this longer trip. The way the race was run didn't fully test his stamina, but he was still well beaten by a far superior rival and his jockey losing his whip before two out made no difference. (new market op 3-1)

That's Mine(IRE) showed nothing on his Huntingdon debut and probably didn't improve much on that here. (new market op 20-1)

4943 TURFTV STANDARD OPEN NATIONAL HUNT FLAT RACE 2m

5:30 (5:31) (Class 5) 4-5-Y-0 **£1,626** (£477; £238; £119)

Form — RPR

1 **Ballyclough (IRE)** 4-10-4 0 AnthonyFreeman(5) 106+
(Jonjo O'Neill) *hld up in rr: shkn up 6f out: hdwy over 3f out: led over 1f out: styd on wl* **28/1**

043 **2** *4* **Red Rocco (IRE)**[46] 3957 4-9-13 0 SamuelWelton(10) 102
(George Moore) *w ldr: styd on same pce appr fnl f* **33/1**

1 **3** *¾* **Ebanour (IRE)**[29] 4280 4-11-2 0 JasonMaguire 108
(Donald McCain) *hld up towards rr: hdwy 7f out: rdn and chsng ldrs over 2f out: hung rt and styd on same pce* **13/8**[1]

4 **4** *½* **Hollow Blue Sky (FR)**[48] 3903 4-10-6 0 SamTwiston-Davies(3) 100
(Nigel Twiston-Davies) *led: hdd over 1f out: one pce* **5/1**[3]

5 *1¾* **City Press (IRE)** 5-11-2 0 AndrewTinkler 106
(Nicky Henderson) *trckd ldrs: drvn 4f out: wknd over 1f out* **11/4**[2]

42 **6** *½* **Crowning Jewel**[37] 4117 5-11-2 0 JamesReveley 105
(Keith Reveley) *hld up in rr: hdwy 6f out: outpcd over 4f out: kpt on fnl 2f: nvr a threat* **7/1**

30 **7** *¾* **Aldiva**[52] 3842 5-11-2 0 WayneHutchinson 104
(Alan King) *in rr-div: drvn and hdwy 4f out: wknd over 1f out* **33/1**

35 **8** *4* **Awaywiththegreys (IRE)**[18] 4491 4-10-9 0 TomO'Brien 93
(Peter Bowen) *chsd ldrs: wknd over 2f out* **33/1**

02 **9** *38* **Sole Survivor (FR)**[21] 4423 4-10-9 0 DominicElsworth 80
(Paul Webber) *chsd ldrs: lost pl 3f out: bhd whn heavily eased ins fnl f: t.o* **14/1**

64 **P** **Way To Finish**[56] 3752 5-11-2 0 PaddyAspell —
(James Moffatt) *tk fierce hold in last: p.u 7f out: lame* **33/1**

3m 50.7s (-7.90) **Going Correction** -0.45s/f (Good)
WFA 4 from 5yo 7lb **10 Ran SP% 115.8**
Speed ratings: **101,99,98,98,97 97,96,94,75,—**
toteswingers:1&2:£16.10, 1&3:£14.10, 2&3:£14.80 CSF £682.11 TOTE £39.50: £8.60, £9.40, £1.10; EX 394.10.

Owner John P McManus **Bred** Miss Elizabeth Kennedy **Trained** Cheltenham, Gloucs

FOCUS
This had looked an interesting bumper, but the early pace was predictably modest and a few took a keen grip. As a result the second and fourth horses may be flattered. That said, the form looks fair with the third and sixth to eighth setting the level.

NOTEBOOK
Ballyclough(IRE), a 105,000euros brother to the useful bumper/hurdle/chase winner Crocodiles Rock amongst others, was patiently ridden but he showed a good turn of foot to lead a furlong out and was well on top at the line. He has a future. (op 33-1 tchd 25-1)

Red Rocco(IRE) had been quietly progressive in three bumpers, but he was helped by being up on the pace in a steadily run race which helped him last as long as he did. He should win races over hurdles. (tchd 40-1)

Ebanour(IRE), penalised after bolting up on his debut in a Wetherby bumpers last month, found disappointingly little off the bridle inside the last 2f and was inclined to hang away to his right. He has a bit to prove now. (op 7-4 tchd 15-8)

Hollow Blue Sky(FR) didn't seem to handle Towcester on his debut last month and this was better, but he was probably also suited by being up with the pace in a slowly run race. (op 6-1 tchd 9-2)

City Press(IRE), a 65,000euros brother to the winning chaser Anseo, and a half-brother to two winners over hurdles, could only plug on after coming off the bridle half a mile out but is entitled to improve. (op 5-2 tchd 3-1)

Crowning Jewel had run well in a couple of Catterick bumpers, but found this a bit tougher. (op 9-1)

Way To Finish Official explanation: vet said gelding pulled up lame right-hind

T/Jkpt: Not won. T/Plt: £96.20 to a £1 stake. Pool:£81,348.03 - 617.00 winning tickets T/Qpdt: £9.00 to a £1 stake. Pool:£6,218.49 - 508.34 winning tickets WG

4260 HEREFORD (R-H)

Wednesday, March 23

OFFICIAL GOING: Good (good to firm in places; watered; chs 7.0; hdl 7.6)
Wind: almost nil Weather: fine and warm

4944 LINDLEY CATERING CONDITIONAL JOCKEYS' NOVICES' HURDLE (8 hdls) 2m 1f

2:00 (2:00) (Class 4) 4-Y-0+ **£2,146** (£630; £315; £157)

Form — RPR

2501 **1** **Red Merlin (IRE)**[19] 4451 6-11-0 126 HenryBrooke(6) 136+
(Donald McCain) *racd in 3rd: impr to trck ldr after 5th: chal 2 out: sn led: drew clr appr last: v easily* **2/5**[1]

12 **2** *10* **Paddy Partridge**[25] 4361 5-11-6 118 RichardKilloran 118
(Tim Vaughan) *trckd ldr tl relegated to 3rd after 5th: sn rdn along: wnt 2nd again after 2 out and drvn: sn outpcd by easy wnr* **5/1**[2]

3 *17* **Behtarini (IRE)**[208] 4-10-7 0 AodhaganConlon 88
(Evan Williams) *hld up in 4th: dropped to last 4th: pushed along after next: wknd 3 out: wnt mod 3rd jst after last* **6/1**[3]

310- **4** *3¾* **Deejan (IRE)**[43] 4592 6-10-2 0 MichaelByrne(5) 82
(Tim Vaughan) *racd keenly: led: j. path after 2nd: jnd 2 out: sn hdd: wknd steadily and lost mod 3rd jst after last* **50/1**

2F0F **U** **Cityar (FR)**[62] 2322 7-11-0 0 PeterToole 77
(John O'Shea) *hld up in last: impr a pl 4th: rdn bef 3 out: sn wknd: last and wl btn whn stmbld and uns rdr last* **66/1**

3m 58.6s (-0.80) **Going Correction** +0.15s/f (Yiel)
WFA 4 from 5yo+ 7lb **5 Ran SP% 105.8**
Speed ratings (Par 105): **107,102,94,92,—**
CSF £2.61 TOTE £1.40: £1.10, £1.70; EX 2.50.

Owner Timeform Betfair Racing Club & M Taylor **Bred** Keatly Overseas Ltd **Trained** Cholmondeley, Cheshire

FOCUS
A novice hurdle run at a good tempo thanks to pace-setting Deejan. The winner can rate higher and the second sets the level.

NOTEBOOK
Red Merlin(IRE) could be called the winner a long way from home. Rated 96 on the Flat and winner of the Old Newton Cup in 2009, confirmed his well-being with a slick round of jumping, and was far too good for his rivals. He looks to have learnt from his previous hurdling efforts and has gained confidence with each run. He can continue to improve in novice events and should be up to handling another penalty next time. (tchd 1-2 in places)

Paddy Partridge is progressing well over hurdles and was simply beaten by a superior rival. He was outpaced in the back straight but responded to pressure thereafter. He handles quick ground well and will have no trouble going one better in a similar race. Tim Vaughan thinks a step up in trip is in order. (op 4-1)

Behtarini(IRE), a maiden on the Flat for John Oxx, gave the hurdles plenty of air on his hurdling debut for new connections. He should come on for this experience. (op 13-2 tchd 7-1)

Deejan(IRE) tried to make all under a front-running ride but she couldn't sustain her pace from two out. She looks one for modest handicaps over the minimum trip. (op 40-1)

Cityar(FR) was ponderous at his hurdles in the main and unseated his rider at the final flight. He needs to improve his jumping. (tchd 50-1)

4945 LORD SCUDAMORE RACING TO SCHOOL H'CAP CHASE (14 fncs) 2m 3f

2:30 (2:30) (Class 5) (0-95,89) 5-Y-0+ **£2,265** (£703; £378)

Form RPR

4031 **1** **Kercabellec (FR)**[7] 4811 13-9-7 **60** 7ex........................ JoeCornwall(7) 80
(John Cornwall) *taken down early: j. sltly lft at times: cl up: led 3rd tl after 11th: remained prom: pushed along fr 3 out: 2 l down last: r.o to ld fnl 100yds: won gng away* **5/2**[1]

00P0 **2** *4* **Wee Ziggy**[30] 1732 8-10-3 **73**........................ MichaelByrne(7) 88
(Michael Mullineaux) *in rr tl clsd 3rd: jnd ldrs after 5th: pckd bdly 7th: trckd ldr 9th: tk narrow ld after 11th: rdn after 2 out: 2 l ld last: hdd and no ex fnl 100yds* **14/1**

005P **3** *17* **Mister Watzisname (IRE)**[31] 4238 9-11-12 **89**..............(tp) PaulMoloney 87
(Charlie Longsdon) *slt ld to 3rd: styd prom tl dropped to last 10th: rdn and wknd bef 3 out: lft poor 3rd appr last* **13/2**[3]

-143 **P** **Jack's Lad (IRE)**[45] 3959 12-10-12 **80**........................ MrTomDavid(5) 88
(Tim Vaughan) *towards rr: slt mstke 4th: hdwy into 3rd whn blnd bdly and gd rcvry 10th: sn rallied: cl up whn hit 3 out: sn rdn: 3rd and hld whn p.u bef last: lame* **4/1**[2]

0P14 **P** **Chord**[22] 4413 7-11-3 **87**........................ PeterCarberry(7) —
(Simon Earle) *in tch tl dropped in rr 4th: bhd fr next: t.o whn p.u bef 7th* **4/1**[2]

2505 **P** **Brimley**[42] 4007 8-10-4 **70**........................(p) LeeStephens(3) —
(Ann Price) *in tch to 4th: sn outpcd in rr: t.o whn p.u bef 7th* **4/1**[2]

4m 50.1s (3.40) **Going Correction** +0.15s/f (Yiel) **6** Ran SP% **108.6**
Speed ratings: **98,96,89,—,—** —
toteswingers:1&2:£11.90, 1&3:£11.90, 2&3:£3.90 CSF £28.36 TOTE £3.50: £1.40, £7.20; EX 27.80.

Owner J R Cornwall **Bred** Loic Malivet And Roger-Yves Simon **Trained** Long Clawson, Leics

FOCUS

A weak handicap chase with question marks over all the runners and best rated around the first two.

NOTEBOOK

Kercabellec(FR) ended his long losing run from way out of the handicap at Huntingdon, for which he was penalised 7lb here, and followed up despite being 3lb 'wrong'. He jumped enthusiastically throughout and, although headed after four out, he rallied thereafter and quickened away from his only serious rival on the run-in. He is far from certain to continue his winning spree but at least he's more reliable these days. (tchd 11-4)

Wee Ziggy, on his chasing debut, made one notable error (7th) but jumped well in the main. He threatened to end his 44-race losing streak when holding every chance at the final obstacle, but he was slower away from the fence than the winner and couldn't match his pace. This was far more encouraging and it's possible he could win a chase. (op 12-1)

Mister Watzisname(IRE) was outpaced before two out and currently doesn't look in love with the jumping game. Official explanation: jockey said gelding moved poorly and hung left-handed (op 8-1)

Jack's Lad(IRE) made a terrible mistake at the 10th and Tom David deserves credit for keeping the partnership intact. However, something went amiss later on, as he was pulled up before the last. Official explanation: jockey said gelding was lame (op 7-2)

Chord Official explanation: jockey said gelding had a breathing problem (op 7-2)

Brimley Official explanation: jockey said gelding lost its action (op 7-2)

4946 DIGIBET.COM NOVICES' HURDLE (10 hdls) 2m 4f

3:05 (3:05) (Class 4) 4-Y-0+ **£2,146** (£630; £315; £157)

Form RPR

-5P3 **1** **Mister Chancer (IRE)**[31] 4233 6-11-1 110........................ JimmyMcCarthy 113+
(Alan King) *racd in 3rd: clsd to trck ldr 5th: led bef 3 out: hit 2 out: sn pushed along: drew clr of only serious pursuer bef last: v comf* **1/1**[1]

5 **2** *28* **Mr Moss (IRE)**[55] 3761 6-11-1 0........................ PaulMoloney 95+
(Evan Williams) *hld up in tch: hdwy 7th: wnt 2nd after 3 out: rdn and nt qckn after next: sn lft bhd by wnr: eased whn no ch nr fin* **11/10**[2]

5400 **3** *30* **Radmores Oscar**[39] 4081 5-11-1 0........................ DPFahy 61
(John O'Shea) *towards rr: struggling fr 6th: sn lost tch: wnt poor 3rd after 2 out: t.o* **20/1**[3]

000 **4** *37* **Countess Susy**[11] 4719 6-10-3 0........................ MrTomDavid(5) 21
(Phillip Dando) *led: j.lft and reminder 5th: hdd bef 3 out: sn wknd: lost 3rd after next: t.o whn blnd last* **40/1**

PP- **5** *94* **Princess Zhukova (IRE)**[384] 4399 6-10-1 0........................ MrBJPoste(7) —
(Chris Nenadich) *towards rr: rdn along 7th: sn lost tch: wl t.o* **100/1**

/445 **P** **Court Gamble (IRE)**[16] 4528 7-10-5 0........................ KeiranBurke(3) —
(Nerys Dutfield) *t.k.h: trckd ldr to 5th: wknd after 7th: poor 5th whn p.u bef 2 out* **28/1**

00 **P** **Persian Forest**[19] 4454 5-10-5 0........................ CharlieHuxley(3) —
(Alan King) *t.k.h in rr: reminder after 4th: rdn and lost tch 6th: t.o whn p.u bef 3 out* **40/1**

4m 53.4s (-2.10) **Going Correction** +0.15s/f (Yiel) **7** Ran SP% **111.7**
Speed ratings (Par 105): **110,98,86,72,34** —,—
toteswingers:1&2:£1.02, 1&3:£4.40, 2&3:£6.50 CSF £2.33 TOTE £2.10: £1.10, £1.10; EX 2.10.

Owner Bensaranat Club **Bred** John Doyle **Trained** Barbury Castle, Wilts

FOCUS

What looked a match on paper developed into a duel from a fair way out, but the winner pulled clear from his market rival from two out. The placed horses set the level in a weak contest.

NOTEBOOK

Mister Chancer(IRE) hugged the rail throughout and saw off his only real danger with ease. He had shown a decent standard in bumpers and this was a step in the right direction over hurdles. This will boost his confidence and he looks a decent prospect for a summer-jumping campaign. (op 10-11 tchd 5-6 and 11-10)

Mr Moss(IRE) couldn't keep up with the easy winner but came away from the remainder. Although he is a winner on quick ground in a maiden point, his knee action suggests he may appreciate a bit of cut. He would also be of interest on a stiffer track. (op 11-8 tchd 6-4)

Radmores Oscar plugged on for a remote third and looks booked for modest handicaps. (tchd 25-1)

Countess Susy was keen in front before being readily brushed aside from three out. She has no form of any worthwhile note.

Princess Zhukova(IRE) completed a race after being pulled up on her previous two starts.

4947 SEVERN VALLEY CATERING H'CAP HURDLE (8 hdls) 2m 1f

3:40 (3:40) (Class 5) (0-90,85) 4-Y-0+ **£1,723** (£506; £253; £126)

Form RPR

3-66 **1** **Diddley Dee**[42] 4008 7-11-5 **85**........................ MrBJPoste(7) 91+
(Bill Moore) *hld up in rr: hdwy 4th: chsd ldr after 2 out: 5 l down whn blnd last: r.o u.p to catch hanging ldr nr fin* **7/1**

5000 **2** *1 ¼* **Tiger Dream**[15] 4540 6-11-5 **85**........................(bt) MrRHawkins(7) 91+
(Chris Down) *trckd ldr: led 5th: drew clr fr next: rdn between last 2: stl 5 l up last: drvn and hung rt flat: hdd nr fin* **5/1**[3]

6P40 **3** *6* **A P Ling**[23] 4395 4-9-11 **70**........................(b) TrevorWhelan(7) 64
(Christopher Kellett) *mstke 1st: trckd ldng pair tl mstke and dropped to last 3rd: struggling 5th: hdwy into 3rd past tiring rivals after 2 out: sn one pce and no imp on first two* **5/1**[3]

4303 **4** *25* **Sparkling Brook (IRE)**[11] 4721 8-11-8 **81**........................ NickScholfield 56
(Jennifer Mason) *led: hit 4th: hdd next: lost 2nd after 2 out: sn wknd: t.o* **3/1**[1]

P/P4 **5** *3 ¼* **Showtime Annie**[23] 4395 10-10-6 **65**........................ AlanO'Keeffe 37
(Jennie Candlish) *hld up towards rr: hit 5th: rdn next: sn wknd: t.o* **9/2**[2]

0/4 **6** *¾* **Vintage Quest**[11] 4721 9-10-9 **75**........................ MrDGPrichard(7) 47
(Dai Burchell) *in tch tl rdn and wknd 3 out: t.o* **11/2**

0-00 **U** **Wallace Monument**[13] 4676 7-11-3 **79**........................(t) LeeStephens(3) —
(Gary Brown) *jinked lft and uns rdr 1st* **16/1**

4m 5.40s (6.00) **Going Correction** +0.15s/f (Yiel)
WFA 4 from 6yo+ 7lb **7** Ran SP% **110.3**
Speed ratings (Par 103): **91,90,87,75,74 73,—**
toteswingers:1&2:£8.50, 1&3:£6.10, 2&3:£5.60 CSF £38.41 TOTE £6.00: £2.40, £2.60; EX 35.80.

Owner Mrs I M Moore **Bred** Shaun Moore **Trained** Ledsham, Cheshire

FOCUS

A poor handicap hurdle but the first three ran close to their marks.

NOTEBOOK

Diddley Dee had run in a seller last time and the switch to a handicap saw him gain his first win in ten races under rules. He made a hash of the last hurdle when coming to challenge his idling rival, but stayed on well to get up in the final strides. Consistency isn't his strong point, however, so this form isn't strong. (op 5-1)

Tiger Dream had shown nothing in handicap hurdles previously but with a first-time tongue-tie fitted he put in a better display. He looked to have the race sewn up from a fair way out but threw it away by idling in front, and hanging right from the last. He's not certain to confirm this improvement. (op 9-2 tchd 4-1)

A P Ling made numerous jumping errors but stayed on better than most. He needs to improve his hurdling. (op 15-2 tchd 8-1)

Sparkling Brook(IRE) doesn't look the most resolute of characters and, once headed, found little for pressure. (tchd 10-3)

Wallace Monument unseated the rider at the first hurdle after edging left. (tchd 14-1)

4948 SIS LIVE H'CAP CHASE (16 fncs) 2m 5f 110y

4:15 (4:15) (Class 4) (0-115,108) 5-Y-0+ **£3,332** (£1,034; £557)

Form RPR

6304 **1** **Gentleman Anshan (IRE)**[42] 4007 7-10-11 **100**. MissHannahWatson(7) 112+
(Rosemary Gasson) *racd in cl 3rd: trckd ldr 13th: sn led: drew clr appr 2 out: easily* **7/2**[3]

F0P3 **2** *11* **Master Somerville**[47] 3935 9-11-12 **108**........................(b) MarkBradburne 104
(Henry Daly) *slt ld tl hdd 12th: rdn in 3rd after next: wnt 2nd again appr 2 out: no ch w easy wnr* **15/8**[2]

6505 **3** *23* **Tyup Pompey (IRE)**[28] 4290 10-11-3 **102**........................ LeeStephens(3) 82
(Ann Price) *disp ld jumping wl: def advantage 12th: hdd after next: sn hrd rdn and wknd: j.lft last 3 and lost 2nd 2 out* **7/1**

-336 **F** **Molanna View (IRE)**[52] 3840 6-11-9 **105**........................ JackDoyle —
(Emma Lavelle) *hld up in last: sltly slow 10th and reminder: stl 4th but in tch whn fell 12th* **6/4**[1]

5m 22.1s (2.10) **Going Correction** +0.15s/f (Yiel) **4** Ran SP% **109.5**
Speed ratings: **102,98,89,—**
CSF £10.51 TOTE £5.70; EX 10.70.

Owner Mrs Rosemary Gasson **Bred** Richard J Hennessy **Trained** Banbury, Oxon

FOCUS

An uninspiring four-runner affair but not an easy race to pin down.

NOTEBOOK

Gentleman Anshan(IRE) is a big, scopey sort who jumped boldly and was always in control from a long way out. He's lightly raced and open to improvement over fences, so one can see him rising up the handicap ranks. (op 9-4 tchd 4-1)

Master Somerville jumped economically throughout but was no match for his well-handicapped rival. He is back on a winning mark. (op 9-4)

Tyup Pompey(IRE) was 7lb below his last winning mark over fences, and jumped well but got outstayed by the others. He's now ten and it may be that his best days are behind him. (op 11-2 tchd 15-2)

Molanna View(IRE) took a heavy fall at the 12th on this chasing debut. He'd been niggled along prior to that mistake but was still well in contention. (op 11-4)

4949 LINDLEY CATERING H'CAP HURDLE (10 hdls) 2m 4f

4:50 (4:50) (Class 5) (0-95,95) 4-Y-0+ **£1,723** (£506; £253; £126)

Form RPR

0050 **1** **Gainsborough's Art (IRE)**[10] 4751 6-10-0 **76**........................ KillianMoore(7) 77
(Harry Chisman) *hld up in tch: clsd to trck ldrs 6th: hrd rdn after 3 out: chal last: sn led and drvn clr* **6/1**

6545 **2** *3 ¾* **Welcome Stranger**[10] 4751 11-11-5 **95**........................(t) PeterHatton(7) 93
(Louise Davis) *led to 5th: styd prom: rdn after next: tk narrow ld after 2 out: jnd last: sn hdd and no ex* **3/1**[2]

05F0 **3** *4 ½* **Carys's Lad**[57] 3728 8-10-3 **75**........................ CharlieStudd(3) 68
(Michael Mullineaux) *in rr: awkward jump 4th: rdn after 6th: sn lost tch: stl wl bhd 2 out: r.o past 3 rivals flat* **4/1**[3]

/P6P **4** *3 ¼* **Troys Run (IRE)**[69] 3530 8-10-9 **85**........................(p) MrBJPoste(7) 75
(Bill Moore) *racd keenly: cl up: led 5th: rdn 3 out: hdd after 2 out: sn wknd: lost 3rd flat* **12/1**

-P4P **5** *¾* **Ortega (FR)**[77] 3396 9-9-9 **71**........................(p) JoeCornwall(7) 60
(John Cornwall) *racd w hd low: trckd ldrs tl lost pl 6th: outpcd fr next: lost tch 3 out: modest hdwy fr 2 out* **17/2**

-060 **6** *19* **Frankie Falco**[118] 2640 5-11-5 **88**........................ JodieMogford 72
(Giuseppe Fierro) *in rr: hdwy to trck ldr 6th: rdn after 3 out: wknd between last 2: t.o: fin lame* **25/1**

504 U **Jinksy Minx**[123] 2528 4-10-8 92 MrTJCannon(7) —
(Suzy Smith) *midfield: 4th whn blnd bdly and uns rdr 3rd* **5/2**[1]
5m 11.1s (15.60) **Going Correction** +0.15s/f (Yiel)
WFA 4 from 5yo+ 8lb **7** Ran SP% **109.9**
Speed ratings (Par 103): **74,72,70,69,69 61,—**
toteswingers:1&2:£1.50, 1&3:£2.50, 2&3:£3.50 CSF £22.84 CT £73.98 TOTE £8.40: £5.70, £1.10; EX 24.40.
Owner Cottington Wood Appleyard Foord Cooke **Bred** Tim Taylor **Trained** Moreton-In-Marsh, Gloucs

FOCUS
A weak handicap hurdle run at a sedate gallop. The first two are rated close to their marks with the third to form.

NOTEBOOK
Gainsborough's Art(IRE) had dropped down the weights since winning from a 19lb higher mark in 2009 and produced a gutsy display to fend off Welcome Stranger on the run-in. He isn't likely to find a race as weak as this next time, however, and could be one to take on if a skinny price. (tchd 11-2)
Welcome Stranger came into the contest in reasonable form and was just outbattled. He may appreciate a drop in trip. (op 11-4 tchd 7-2)
Carys's Lad finished strongly for third after initially being outpaced on the home turn. He looks to be crying out for a step up in distance and is one to note in a similarly weak event. (op 5-1 tchd 7-2)
Troys Run(IRE) was too keen in front and needs to settle better. (op 14-1 tchd 10-1)
Frankie Falco Official explanation: jockey said horse finished lame
Jinksy Minx gave her jockey no chance of staying aboard when blundering the third. (op 11-4)

4950 "MR DOW JONES" MEMORIAL HUNTERS' CHASE (14 fncs) 2m 3f
5:20 (5:20) (Class 6) 5-Y-O+ £923 (£283; £141)

Form				RPR
6P0/	1		**My Way De Solzen (FR)**[10] 11-11-12 0 MrRMahon (Gabe Mahon) *mde all: rdn between last 2: styd on wl to pull clr flat* **9/2**[3]	125+
4-41	2	9	**Takeroc (FR)**[12] 4696 8-11-9 145 (t) MrHDerham(7) (R Barber) *hld up towards rr: clsd 5th: hit 10th: chsd wnr and rdn after 2 out: 4 l down and looked hld whn hit last: no ex* **5/4**[1]	123+
4112	3	9	**Good Company (IRE)**[10] 4748 11-12-6 122 MrRBurton (S Flook) *midfield tl dropped to rr 5th: hdwy 10th: rdn next: chsd wnr after 3 out tl hit next and wknd* **11/4**[2]	114
-004	4	5	**Mccauley (IRE)**[16] 4526 8-11-5 96 MrMatthewHampton(7) (Paul Swaffield) *trckd wnr: mstkes 1st and 9th: lost 2nd whn blnd 3 out: wkng in 4th whn mstke 2 out* **33/1**	105+
PPP/	5	9	**Dreux (FR)**[10] 9-11-5 115 MrJNorman(7) (R J Rowsell) *in tch: mstke 8th and reminders: lost tch w ldrs fr next* **9/1**	92
-22U	6	2	**Fairwood Present (IRE)**[12] 4696 13-11-5 117 MrRJarrett(7) (John Buxton) *midfield: blnd 1st: rdn and wknd 10th* **14/1**	90
P-55	7	8	**Little Rocker (IRE)**[24] 10-11-9 94 MrBFurnival(7) (R Smart) *chsd ldrs: mstkes 5th and 9th: wknd 10th* **33/1**	87
P404	8	1 3/4	**No Greater Love (FR)**[10] 9-11-5 80 MissJBuck(7) (Mrs T Porter) *in rr: mstke 4th: wknd and lost tch 10th* **80/1**	80
PP-4	9	18	**Naxox (FR)**[12] 4696 10-11-5 92 MissRachelKing(7) (Ms A Hardy) *chsd ldrs: pckd 7th: wknd after 11th: t.o* **125/1**	62
6-00	P		**Ticket To Ride (FR)**[167] 1745 13-11-5 0 MrJHooper(7) (I J Hooper) *t.k.h bhd ldrs: wknd 8th: lost tch 10th: t.o whn p.u bef 3 out* **200/1**	—

4m 47.3s (0.60) **Going Correction** +0.15s/f (Yiel) **10** Ran SP% **114.4**
Speed ratings: **104,100,96,94,90 89,86,85,78,—**
toteswingers:1&2:£1.40, 1&3:£4.00, 2&3:£2.40 CSF £10.81 TOTE £3.60: £1.10, £1.10, £1.50; EX 11.80.
Owner Jerry Wright **Bred** Catherine Ricous-Guerin & Jacques Guerin **Trained** Stratford Upon Avon

FOCUS
For many, this was the most interesting contest on the card, and it produced an emphatic success for a former star. The winner can rate a fair bit higher judged on his old form with the runner-up close to his recent winning mark.

NOTEBOOK
My Way De Solzen(FR), winner of the 2006 World Hurdle and 2007 Arkle, has been rejuvenated by a successful point career, and was allowed a soft lead for his hunter chase debut. He showed some of his old sparkle, jumping with great enthusiasm, and powered clear from his rivals on the home turn. Connections may now send him for the Fox Hunters' Chase at Aintree. (op 3-1)
Takeroc(FR) travelled well into the race but could never get to grips with the winner. He pulled clear of the third and will continue to run well in these races. (op 13-8 tchd 6-5)
Good Company(IRE) held Takeroc on their Ludlow run, but was one paced when asked for maximum effort. He remains in good heart and should continue to be competitive. (op 5-2 tchd 9-4 and 3-1)
Mccauley(IRE) ran respectably but multiple jumping errors cost him any chance of making the frame.
Dreux(FR) was well-backed and kept on nicely for pressure, but the downside is that he's been inconsistent lately (op 40-1)
Fairwood Present(IRE) was outpaced from four out and may need a stiffer test.
Naxox(FR) didn't settle and needs to relax in his races. (op 100-1)
T/Plt: £83.80 to a £1 stake. Pool:£56,129.87 - 488.68 winning tickets T/Qpdt: £30.30 to a £1 stake. Pool:£4,388.34 - 107.10 winning tickets RL

4745 WARWICK (L-H)
Wednesday, March 23

OFFICIAL GOING: Good (good to firm in places; watered; 8.1)
Wind: Moderate across Weather: Sunny

4951 WARWICK FOR WEDDINGS MAIDEN HURDLE (11 hdls) 2m 5f
2:20 (2:20) (Class 4) 4-Y-0+ £2,602 (£764; £382; £190)

Form				RPR
2333	1		**Sweet Irony (FR)**[40] 4051 5-11-1 121 RobertThornton (Alan King) *hld up in rr: hdwy to trck ldrs 6th: wnt 2nd after 3 out: slt ld next: c clr run-in: easily* **5/4**[1]	119+
	2	7	**Rossmore Lad (IRE)**[73] 6-11-1 0 DarylJacob (Charlie Longsdon) *chsd ldrs: led after 3 out: narrowly hdd 2 out: sn one pce: no ch w wnr after last but kpt on wl for clr 2nd* **7/1**[3]	109+
06	3	7	**Captain Cool (IRE)**[13] 4676 4-10-4 0 JimmyDerham(3) (Richard Hannon) *in rr: hdwy and in tch fr 6th: rdn and outpcd appr 3 out: rdn and rallied sn after: wnt 3rd appr 2 out but no imp on ldng duo* **16/1**	92
P0	4	4 1/2	**Rebel High (IRE)**[18] 4479 7-11-1 0 LiamTreadwell (Derek Frankland) *led to 2nd: styd pressing ldr to 4 out: rdn and outpcd 3 out: styd on again fr 2 out to take 4th whn nt fluent last* **80/1**	96
2	5	1 1/2	**Faultless Feelings (IRE)**[76] 3405 5-11-1 0 RhysFlint (Philip Hobbs) *chsd ldrs: rdn to go 2nd briefly sn after 3 out: wknd wl bef next* **7/4**[2]	93
0-	6	11	**Touz Master (FR)**[290] 659 7-10-8 0 MrCGreene(7) (Nick Kent) *slt ld fr 2nd tl hdd & wknd after 3 out* **28/1**	85
504	7	54	**Mickytaker (IRE)**[47] 3918 6-11-1 0 GerardTumelty (Alan King) *a in rr: j. slowly 4th: hit 5th: t.o after 7th* **14/1**	28
0	8	6	**Astroleo**[50] 1829 5-11-1 0 ColinBolger (Mark H Tompkins) *a in rr: t.o after 6th* **66/1**	22
00	U		**Remarkable Rocket (IRE)**[7] 4810 7-10-8 0 MrJFlook(7) (Andrew Price) *blnd 1st: mstke 2nd: in rr: in tch whn j. slowly 6th: hit 7th: wknd 4 out: no ch whn mstke and uns rdr last* **100/1**	—
0-00	P		**Keltic Crisis (IRE)**[18] 4489 7-10-8 0 MrPHarty(7) (Jonathan Geake) *in rr: rdr lost irons 5th: p.u bef next* **80/1**	—
0	P		**Tranquil River (IRE)**[47] 3936 6-10-8 0 StephenO'Donovan(7) (John Upson) *nt fluent 1st: wknd 6th: t.o next: p.u bef 3 out* **150/1**	—

4m 49.27s (-25.73) **Going Correction** -1.30s/f (Hard)
WFA 4 from 5yo+ 8lb **11** Ran SP% **114.9**
Speed ratings (Par 105): **97,94,91,89,89 85,64,62,—,— —**
toteswingers:1&2:£3.30, 1&3:£5.30, 2&3:£10.90 CSF £10.62 TOTE £2.10: £1.10, £2.10, £2.80; EX 11.40.
Owner S M Smith **Bred** Mme Laurence Gagneux **Trained** Barbury Castle, Wilts

FOCUS
A moderate maiden, run at a sound gallop and the form should work out with the first pair coming clear. The winner is rated value for further and to his mark.

NOTEBOOK
Sweet Irony(FR) finally shed his maiden tag and completed the task with plenty left in the tank. He failed to see out 2m4f at Kempton on his previous outing, but this quicker ground made all the difference. There is still room for improvement with his hurdling, but he can defy a penalty on similar ground now he's got his head in front. (tchd 6-5 and 11-8 in places)
Rossmore Lad(IRE) ◆ made it third time lucky in an Irish point in January and has joined an in-form yard for his career under rules. He travelled sweetly and held every chance, but was put in his place by the winner from two out. A slightly easier surface may be ideal and he can score before long. (op 8-1)
Captain Cool(IRE) promised to enjoy this stiffer test on better ground, looking at his Flat form, and so it proved as he posted his best effort yet as a hurdler. He is now eligible for a mark. Official explanation: vet said gelding suffered heat stress (op 20-1)
Rebel High(IRE) proved free up with the lead early on and hit a flat spot before plugging on in the home straight. This was his most encouraging run since switching to hurdles and he too is now qualified for handicaps. Official explanation: vet said gelding suffered heat stress (op 100-1 tchd 66-1)
Faultless Feelings(IRE), whose yard has a decent record in the race, felt the pinch around three out. He was in the process of rallying prior to being hampered on the inside turning for home and, while he certainly wouldn't have troubled the winner, it no doubt cost him ground. Official explanation: vet said gelding was lame left-fore (op 13-8)

4952 WHITSON BLOODSTOCK LTD NOVICES' HURDLE (8 hdls) 2m
2:55 (2:57) (Class 4) 4-Y-0+ £2,740 (£798; £399)

Form				RPR
2F10	1		**Highway Code (USA)**[28] 4291 5-11-6 123 (t) RobertThornton (Richard Lee) *trckd ldrs: chal 4th: slt ld 3 out: nudged along appr 2 out: j. slowly and nt fluent last: hrd drvn run-in: hld on u.p* **9/4**[1]	110+
	2	1	**Astrodiva**[34] 5-10-7 0 ColinBolger (Mark H Tompkins) *t.k.h: trckd ldrs: chsd wnr after 3 out: rdn next: rallied u.p last: kpt on run-in: one pce cl home* **40/1**	93
66	3	3 3/4	**Prince Of Dreams**[19] 4458 4-10-7 0 LiamTreadwell (Ed de Giles) *t.k.h in rr: pushed along after 4 out: hdwy fr 3 out: styd on run-in but nvr gng pce to chal* **12/1**	89+
	4	2	**Cape Schanck**[640] 7-11-0 0 DaveCrosse (Alan Coogan) *in tch: hdwy fr 4 out: chsd ldrs and nt fluent 3 out: one pce u.p 2 out: styd on run-in* **40/1**	94
	5	6	**Strathcal**[186] 5-11-0 0 CharliePoste (Anna Brooks) *w ldr: led after 3rd: narrowly hdd and rdn and mstke 3 out: wknd and hit 2 out* **9/2**[2]	89
0	6	hd	**Red Whisper**[291] 637 7-10-11 0 MichaelMurphy(3) (Rob Summers) *plld v hrd and hld up wl in rr: nt fluent: hmpd 4th: pushed along and styd on appr 2 out: kpt on run-in but nvr any threat* **80/1**	90
34	7	1/2	**Anaya**[39] 3519 4-10-0 104 HarrySkelton (David Bourton) *hit 1st: in tch: rdn and hit 4 out: sn dropped in rr u.p: styd on again appr last but nvr any ch* **10/1**[3]	75
S-06	8	21	**Deed Poll**[16] 4528 5-11-0 0 (t) JamesDavies (Chris Down) *led tl hdd after 3rd: wknd fr 4 out* **100/1**	67
	9	18	**Sirdave**[26] 5-11-0 0 JodieMogford (Peter Hiatt) *in rr whn hmpd 4 out: nt rcvr* **40/1**	49
6-00	10	31	**Marvelous**[28] 4288 6-10-7 0 TomMessenger (Evan Williams) *in rr whn bdly hmpd 4 out: nt rcvr* **100/1**	11
00	F		**Layla's Boy**[28] 4283 4-10-7 0 (t) RhysFlint (John Mackie) *in rr: hit 3rd and 4th: fell 4 out* **25/1**	—

3m 39.6s (-16.90) **Going Correction** -1.30s/f (Hard)
WFA 4 from 5yo+ 7lb **11** Ran SP% **80.1**
Speed ratings (Par 105): **90,89,87,86,83 83,83,72,63,48 —**
toteswingers:1&2:£9.10, 1&3:£3.10, 2&3:£15.40 CSF £48.41 TOTE £2.00: £1.10, £4.20, £3.00; EX 51.30.
Owner D E Edwards **Bred** T Leung **Trained** Byton, H'fords
■ Stewards' Enquiry : Michael Murphy Fine £140, failed to report poor performance.

FOCUS
This was markedly weakened by the non-runner. Average novice form but the form could rate higher.

NOTEBOOK
Highway Code(USA) turned in a shocker at Ludlow last time, but was progressive beforehand and this was a notable drop in grade. The ground was probably quick enough for him and, although he would struggle to defy a double penalty in this division, he looks the sort to appreciate switching to fences in due course. (op 5-2 tchd 85-40)
Astrodiva is a longstanding maiden on the Flat and had largely been well held on the AW through the winter. She was the only one to give the winner a serious race on this switch to hurdling, however, and posted a very encouraging effort. Providing she goes forward for the experience, there really ought to be a race for her in this sphere.
Prince Of Dreams ◆, well backed, proved keen to post and took an age to settle under heavy restraint. He was staying on strongly in the home straight, however, and this was a definite step in the right direction. He can now go handicapping. Official explanation: vet said gelding finished distressed (op 25-1 tchd 10-1)
Cape Schanck, a 1m2f handicap winner in Hong Kong, travelled sweetly on this hurdling debut for new connections and looked a possible threat four out. It was his first outing for 640 days, however, and he fired off the home bend. (op 28-1)
Strathcal proved solid enough in the market ahead of this hurdling debut for his new trainer and, as a triple 1m4f winner on the level, it wasn't surprising to see him set the gallop. He was feeling the pinch prior to hitting the third-last and this first run since September was needed. (tchd 11-2)

Red Whisper, tailed off on his debut last summer, was another that proved keen out the back. He caught the eye staying on late in the day, though, and should come on plenty. Official explanation: jockey said, regarding running and riding, that his orders were to settle the gelding early, it proved difficult to settle and raced freely from the start which, in retrospect, he should have reported at scale, adding that it jumped poorly early and became detached from the field, thereafter he rode sympathetically in order to enable it to finish effectively and as the race developed was able to progress through the field. (op 66-1)
Marvelous Official explanation: jockey said mare was hampered by faller

4953 TURFTV H'CAP CHASE (22 fncs) 3m 5f
3:30 (3:31) (Class 4) (0-100,98) 5-Y-0+ **£3,252** (£955; £477; £238)

Form RPR
5335 **1** **Arnold Layne (IRE)**[31] 4238 12-11-7 **93**........................ AndrewThornton 103+
(Caroline Bailey) *w ldr to 6th: chal fr 10th tl led 15th: reminders appr 16th: styd on u.p fr 2 out: hld on wl nr fin* **3/1**[2]
4505 **2** *1 3/4* **Heezagrey (IRE)**[6] 4829 8-9-8 **73**.................................... MarkQuinlan[(7)] 79
(James Evans) *in rr but in tch: outpcd 18th: rallied fr 3 out and styd on fr next: kpt on to take 2nd fnl 100yds: gng on cl home but a hld* **13/2**
00P2 **3** *3 1/4* **Feeling Peckish (USA)**[14] 4551 7-10-4 **76**..........(t) AndrewGlassonbury 80
(Michael Chapman) *in tch: chsd ldrs fr 16th: chsd wnr u.p 3 out: no imp whn hit last: wknd into 3rd fnl 100yds* **13/2**
5-4P **4** *15* **Crack At Dawn (IRE)**[39] 4080 10-11-3 **89**......................(b) DavidEngland 82
(Michael Gates) *chsd ldrs: hit 9th: chsd wnr fr 17th to 3 out: wknd and hit 2 out* **8/1**
2514 **P** **Rudinero (IRE)**[21] 4428 9-10-10 **89**...............................(t) CDTimmons[(7)] —
(Barry Brennan) *mde most tl hdd 15th: wknd 17th: t.o whn p.u bef last* **9/2**[3]
2222 **P** **Timpo (FR)**[28] 4292 8-11-5 **98**.. JakeGreenall[(7)] —
(Henry Daly) *chsd ldrs: dropped in rr 6th: rdn and hit 9th: wknd 12th: mstke 14th: losing tch whn p.u bef 16th* **11/4**[1]

7m 12.09s (-28.91) **Going Correction** -1.30s/f (Hard) course record **6** Ran SP% **107.6**
Speed ratings: **87,86,85,81,—** —
toteswingers:1&2:£4.10, 1&3:£4.20, 2&3:£6.00 CSF £19.73 TOTE £4.10: £1.70, £2.90; EX 20.70.
Owner Mr & Mrs R Scott **Bred** Mrs Valerie Dalgetty **Trained** Brixworth, Northants

FOCUS
A tricky marathon handicap with doubts hanging over most beforehand. The runner-up is rated to his mark in a weak handicap.

NOTEBOOK
Arnold Layne(IRE) finally got his head back in front and ended a losing run that stretched back to his success here in February 2008. His will to win had come into question of late and he needed plenty of driving here, but his proven stamina won him the day. The better ground also clearly holpod. Ho roportodly now hoado off for rotiromont on a winning noto. (op 10 3)
Heezagrey(IRE) is a quirky customer and this is certainly not the first time he has stayed on all too late after going in snatches. (op 9-1)
Feeling Peckish(USA) posted one of his better efforts at Catterick a fortnight earlier and went well again before stamina for this longer trip became an issue. He is probably the best guide to the form. (op 8-1)
Crack At Dawn(IRE) was faced with a more realistic task again and posted a much more encouraging effort as a result. He didn't stay the extra distance but can be found an opening off this mark back over 3m. (op 6-1 tchd 5-1)
Rudinero(IRE) set out to make all, but was done with seven from home and eventually pulled up. (op 4-1 tchd 5-1)
Timpo(FR), a runner-up on his last four outings, looked well worth a try over this longer trip. He appeared to spit the dummy out at an early stage, but was another that pulled up and perhaps something was amiss. Official explanation: trainer said gelding finished distressed (op 4-1 tchd 5-1)

4954 HOLDSWORTH PERSONNEL 25TH ANNIVERSARY JUVENILE H'CAP HURDLE (FOR THE STEPHEN ALLDAY PERPETUAL PLATE) (8 hdls) 2m
4:05 (4:05) (Class 3) (0-130,129) 4-Y-0 **£6,505** (£1,910; £955)

Form RPR
1255 **1** **Pullyourfingerout (IRE)**[25] 4353 4-11-4 **128**........(t) JeremiahMcGrath[(7)] 126+
(Brendan Powell) *mde all: pushed clr appr last: drvn and styd on strly run-in* **11/4**[3]
152 **2** *7* **Pantxoa (FR)**[41] 4024 4-11-12 **129**.................................. RobertThornton 120
(Alan King) *t.k.h early: jnd for 1 l 2nd fr 4th: drvn and chsd wnr 3 out: no imp whn nt fluent next: no ch appr last but clr of 3rd* **11/8**[1]
24 **3** *12* **Head Hunted**[33] 4192 4-10-10 **113**... DarylJacob 97
(Charlie Mann) *j. slowly 1st and j.big 2nd: disputing 1 l 2nd whn hit 4 out: rallied to dispute 2nd again next: wknd and no ch whn j. slowly 2 out* **13/8**[2]

3m 36.51s (-19.99) **Going Correction** -1.30s/f (Hard) **3** Ran SP% **106.9**
Speed ratings: **97,93,87**
CSF £6.57 TOTE £4.80; EX 5.70.
Owner K Rhatigan **Bred** T Quayle **Trained** Upper Lambourn, Berks

FOCUS
Not a good turn out for the prize money on offer. It was run at a fair gallop and the form ought to work out.

NOTEBOOK
Pullyourfingerout(IRE) hadn't been at his best, albeit in better company, the last twice but he bounced back to form on this handicap debut and won readily. He was allowed to dictate matters out in front, which clearly suited, and he had the race in safe keeping before the final flight. The handicapper will now make his life a good deal harder. (op 9-4 tchd 7-2)
Pantxoa(FR) made a winning British debut over C&D in November and had run well in defeat since. He did finish behind the winner at Cheltenham in December and, while entitled to reverse the form on paper, the 7lb claimed by that one's jockey here played its part. (op 7-4)
Head Hunted was backed to return to the sort of form that saw him finish runner-up over C&D on his hurdling bow, but the ground was probably quicker than he really cares for and he was held after making errors at three and four from home. (tchd 11-8)

4955 BUCKLE AND HYDE HANDBAGS AND ACCESSORIES MARES' H'CAP HURDLE (11 hdls) 2m 5f
4:40 (4:40) (Class 4) (0-115,110) 4-Y-0+ **£2,602** (£764; £382; £190)

Form RPR
14-6 **1** **Veiled**[19] 4455 5-11-9 **110**.. DavidBass[(3)] 126+
(Nicky Henderson) *hld up in tch: hdwy and mstke 4 out: trckd ldrs next: narrow advantage and nt fluent 2 out: stl jnd last: rdn run-in: asserted fnl 50yds: readily* **7/2**[1]
P064 **2** *2 1/2* **Little Carmela**[9] 4769 7-11-0 **103**.................................(vt) GilesHawkins[(5)] 110
(Neil King) *chsd ldrs: drvn along 7th: chal 3 out: led sn after: narrow ld but upsides 2 out: stl chalng last: outpcd fnl 50yds* **16/1**
P655 **3** *8* **Thedeboftheyear**[11] 4722 7-11-5 **110**.............................. DannyBurton[(7)] 110
(Chris Down) *chsd ldrs: chal 7th: slt ld bef 4 out: jnd next: hdd sn after: one pce appr 2 out: wknd bef last* **9/1**
5054 **4** *5* **Tsarinova**[27] 4309 6-11-4 **102**.. RobertThornton 96
(Alan King) *chsd ldrs: drvn along after 4 out: styd on same pce after next* **9/2**[2]
3505 **5** *nk* **Laureate Des Loges (FR)**[42] 4009 7-11-1 **106**.............. JakeGreenall[(7)] 100
(Henry Daly) *in rr but in tch: hdwy 7th: chsd ldrs after 4 out: styd on same pce after next* **5/1**[3]
2144 **6** *nk* **Can't Remember**[12] 4704 6-10-4 **93**............................. OliverDayman[(5)] 87
(Alison Thorpe) *in rr but in tch: rdn and sme hdwy 4 out: nvr rchd ldrs and styd on same pce fr 2 out* **25/1**
0-U0 **7** *3 3/4* **Daraz Rose (IRE)**[41] 4025 10-10-9 **100**..........................(t) CDTimmons[(7)] 91
(Barry Brennan) *in rr: hit 5th: rdn 4 out: sme hdwy 3 out: nvr in contention* **12/1**
4213 **8** *11* **Mayolynn (USA)**[27] 4310 5-11-6 **104**............................... AndrewThornton 87
(Caroline Bailey) *hit 2nd: in rr: sme prog 4 out: wknd next* **8/1**
2342 **9** *25* **Here's The Key (FR)**[23] 4401 7-11-0 **98**.........................(bt) WillKennedy 52
(Paul Webber) *w ldr fr 4th to 4 out: wknd qckly next* **10/1**
0P30 **10** *9* **Bobbisox (IRE)**[18] 4481 6-10-5 **89**.. ColinBolger 34
(Alex Hales) *mde most tl hdd bef 4 out: wknd qckly* **16/1**
0002 **P** **Zepnove (IRE)**[81] 3307 5-10-3 **90**.................................(p) AlexMerriam[(3)] —
(Neil King) *bhd fr 5th: no ch whn blnd 3 out: t.o whn p.u bef 2 out* **16/1**

4m 47.27s (-27.73) **Going Correction** -1.30s/f (Hard) **11** Ran SP% **116.5**
Speed ratings (Par 105): **100,99,96,94,93 93,92,88,78,75** —
toteswingers:1&2:£14.50, 1&3:£8.90, 2&3:£30.00 CSF £56.87 CT £468.77 TOTE £4.30: £1.70, £7.40, £4.20; EX 78.70.
Owner Pump & Plant Services Ltd **Bred** Cheveley Park Stud Ltd **Trained** Upper Lambourn, Berks

FOCUS
An open handicap for mares, run at a fair gallop. The winner is value for further with the third to the best of this year's form.

NOTEBOOK
Veiled made amends for a lacklustre effort on her debut for Nicky Henderson 19 days earlier with a gutsy effort on this step up in trip. She travelled into the race three out looking the most likely winner, but didn't handle the home turn that well and two clumsy leaps over the last two flights ensured she was all out at the finish. She is open to improvement, especially over this sort of distance, and can defy a rise. (op 4-1)
Little Carmela responded gamely to pressure on the back straight and was only just held by the winner. This is her trip and she deserves to go in again after this. (op 28-1 tchd 33-1)
Thedeboftheyear posted one of her better efforts over a trip probably sharper than she ideally cares for. (tchd 11-1)
Tsarinova was expected to enjoy this return to quicker ground, but lacked any sort of gear change and needs more use made of her. (op 5-1 tchd 11-2)
Laureate Des Loges(FR) was well backed down in grade, but she too looks to want more positive handling. (tchd 11-2)
Can't Remember kept on without threatening from off the pace and looks held by the handicapper.

4956 TURFTV H'CAP HURDLE (8 hdls) 2m
5:10 (5:11) (Class 4) (0-100,99) 4-Y-0+ **£2,740** (£798; £399)

Form RPR
-000 **1** **Citrus Mark**[65] 3604 6-11-0 **87**... WillKennedy 92+
(Paul Webber) *hld up in rr: stdy hdwy to trck ldr after 3 out: narrow ld sn after: pushed along and in command last: rdn and styd on wl fnl 75yds* **8/1**
0 **2** *2* **Bell Harbour (IRE)**[71] 3497 9-11-12 **99**........................... LiamTreadwell 102+
(Evan Williams) *hit 1st: in rr: hdwy appr 3 out: styng on whn mstke 2 out: chsd wnr sn after last and kpt on but a readily hld* **10/1**
5464 **3** *1* **Galley Slave (IRE)**[5] 4854 6-10-7 **87**................................. KyleJames[(7)] 87
(Michael Chapman) *chsd ldrs: slt ld fr 4 out: narrowly hdd after 3 out: sn rdn: one pce appr last and lost 2nd sn after* **4/1**[2]
445 **4** *13* **Golden Prospect**[27] 4310 7-11-9 **96**.................................. JamesDavies 86
(Paul Fitzsimons) *chsd ldrs but j. modly thrght: wknd appr 2 out* **4/1**[2]
1230 **5** *9* **Ton-Chee**[259] 933 12-11-4 **98**...(t) JoshWall[(7)] 76
(Arthur Whitehead) *t.k.h: w ldr 3rd to 4th: wknd 3 out* **10/1**
0500 **6** *28* **Admission**[32] 4225 4-11-1 **95**..(tp) JohnnyFarrelly 38
(Sophie Leech) *t.k.h: led to 4 out: wknd qckly after 3 out* **5/2**[1]
06P2 **U** **Motor Home**[156] 1902 5-11-0 **87**.................................(t) JimmyMcCarthy —
(Charlie Morlock) *prom early: rdn and bhd whn blnd and uns rdr 4th* **11/2**[3]

3m 38.85s (-17.65) **Going Correction** -1.30s/f (Hard)
WFA 4 from 5yo+ 7lb **7** Ran SP% **113.2**
Speed ratings (Par 105): **92,91,90,84,79 65,—**
toteswingers:1&2:£6.70, 1&3:£3.80, 2&3:£6.60 CSF £76.08 TOTE £9.80: £4.50, £16.40; EX 114.30 Trifecta £295.00 Not won. Pool of £398.75 - 0.60 winning units..
Owner Economic Security **Bred** G R Waters **Trained** Mollington, Oxon

FOCUS
Another open-looking handicap. The first three came well clear and the placed horses help set the standard.

NOTEBOOK
Citrus Mark stepped up plenty on previous form and made a winning handicap debut. He got a lovely tow into the race and found plenty when asked for everything in the home straight. The quicker ground evidently suited and he has begun life in this sphere at the right end of the weights, so may well follow up. Official explanation: trainer's rep said, regarding apparent improvement in form, that the gelding may have been better suited by the faster ground and has been suffering from niggling back problems. (op 15-2 tchd 9-1)
Bell Harbour(IRE) responded to pressure turning into the home straight and went down fighting under top weight. He's well treated on his Irish form and can soon find an opening, but probably needs a stiffer test on this ground. (op 17-2)
Galley Slave(IRE) was well backed despite having been beaten in a seller the previous week. He got a positive ride and held every chance, rather summing up the level of the form. (op 9-2 tchd 7-2)
Golden Prospect again didn't help his chance by refusing to settle on this handicap debut and is going to prove hard to win with over hurdles. (op 11-2)
Ton-Chee proved keen early on his return from a 259-day break and was well beaten off, but ought to come on plenty. (op 8-1 tchd 12-1)
Admission, in first-time cheekpieces, could have been thrown in on this handicap debut as a hurdler considering he was running off the same mark as he is rated on the Flat (95). Going from the front isn't the way to ride him, but the manner in which he threw in the towel was most alarming. Official explanation: vet said gelding bled from the nose (op 7-2 tchd 4-1 in a place)
Motor Home was a market drifter on his first outing since October and was in trouble prior to unseating. (op 5-1 tchd 9-2)

4957 FLAT SEASON IS NEXT STANDARD OPEN NATIONAL HUNT FLAT RACE 2m
5:40 (5:41) (Class 6) 4-6-Y-0 **£1,507** (£439; £219)

Form RPR
1 **Valdez** 4-10-11 0... RobertThornton 98+
(Alan King) *trckd ldrs: wnt 2nd 4f out: pushed along to ld over 2f out: c readily clr fnl f: easily* **6/5**[1]

4 **2** *8* **Thomas Crapper**[24] 4382 4-10-11 0 CharliePoste 87
(Robin Dickin) *in rr but in tch: hdwy 4f out: rdn and styd on fnl 2f: wnt 2nd fnl 50yds but no ch w wnr* **17/2**

0 **3** *1/2* **Black Cache (IRE)**[130] 2368 5-11-4 0 DavidEngland 94
(Nigel Twiston-Davies) *t.k.h: sn led: rdn 3f out: hdd over 2f out: sn outpcd by wnr: edgd lft and green fnl f: lost 2nd fnl 50yds* **4/1**[2]

0 **4** *15* **Bond Kathleen**[28] 4287 5-11-1 0 MichaelMurphy(3) 89+
(Ian Williams) *chsd ldrs tl hung bdly rt and dropped wl bhd 4f out: styd on again fnl 2f but nt rcvr* **8/1**[3]

5 *4 1/2* **Cocoa Minnie (IRE)** 5-10-11 0 WillKennedy 67
(Paul Webber) *hld up in rr: rdn and sme hdwy fr 4f out: nvr rchd ldrs and wkng whn green and hung rt bnd 3f out* **4/1**[2]

00 **6** *1 1/4* **Skarloey**[20] 4443 5-11-1 0 LeeEdwards(3) 73
(Tony Carroll) *chsd ldrs tl wknd qckly 3f out* **50/1**

3m 34.14s (-16.76) **Going Correction** -1.30s/f (Hard)
WFA 4 from 5yo 7lb **6** Ran SP% **109.1**
Speed ratings: **89,85,84,77,75 74**
toteswingers:1&2:£2.60, 1&3:£2.90, 2&3:£2.90. totesuper7: Win: Not won. Place: Not won CSF £11.54 TOTE £1.60: £1.10, £2.30; EX 9.20.
Owner Alan King **Bred** David & Julie Andrews **Trained** Barbury Castle, Wilts

FOCUS
A modest bumper with an easy debut winner and the second setting the level.

NOTEBOOK
Valdez ◆ ran out an easy debut winner to give his yard a fourth success (double here) on the day. Alan King's 4-y-o is closely related to winners on the Flat from 7f-2m and did things professionally through the race. He came right away when asked to win and took time to pull up, so clearly has a decent future. (op 5-4 tchd 13-8)
Thomas Crapper was backed into favouritism on his debut at Towcester, but despite promising to enjoy this better ground, one couldn't give him away in the betting. He travelled nicely off the pace but, while he gifted the winner first run in the home straight, it made no difference to the result. He can take one of these back on a stiffer track. (op 5-1)
Black Cache(IRE) was very keen when tailed off on his debut in November. He was better on that front in the lead here and posted a game effort in defeat. He too probably needs a stiffer test and is going the right way. (op 9-2 tchd 7-2)
Bond Kathleen, out the back on his debut last month, would've have been plenty closer had he handled the turn into the home straight. He can build on this. (op 15-2 tchd 7-1)
Cocoa Minnie(IRE), related to four bumper winners, proved too green to do himself justice on this racecourse debut and ought to learn a good deal. (op 11-2 tchd 6-1)
T/Plt: £747.80 to a £1 stake. Pool:£51,204.81 - 49.98 winning tickets T/Qpdt: £192.40 to a £1 stake. Pool:£3,823.23 - 14.70 winning tickets ST

4889 CARLISLE (R-H)
Thursday, March 24

OFFICIAL GOING: Good to soft (good in places; 7.4)
Middle fence in back straight omitted all chases. Old Stable bend and back straight rail on inside line.
Wind: Almost nil Weather: Sunny

4958 MAXWELLTOWN HOMES LTD NOVICES' H'CAP HURDLE (9 hdls) 2m 1f
2:20 (2:20) (Class 4) (0-110,107) 4-Y-0+ **£2,123** (£619; £309)

Form RPR

-331 **1** **Lady Bluesky**[7] 4822 8-11-3 **101** EwanWhillans(3) 104
(Alistair Whillans) *chsd clr ldr: smooth hdwy to ld 2 out: rdn out fr last* **5/4**[2]

6P21 **2** *1 3/4* **Ouest Eclair (FR)**[11] 4751 6-11-3 **98** GrahamLee 99
(Ferdy Murphy) *hld up in tch: nt fluent 1st: hdwy after 4 out: effrt next: edgd rt and chsd wnr last: r.o u.p* **11/10**[1]

F000 **3** *2 1/2* **Twice Lucky**[48] 3918 7-10-0 **81** HenryOliver 80
(Sue Smith) *led clr to 3 out: rdn and hdd next: kpt on same pce last* **18/1**[3]

F0-0 **4** *14* **Lisbon Lion (IRE)**[34] 3746 6-10-10 **91** PaddyAspell 77
(James Moffatt) *hld up in tch: nt fluent 3rd: effrt appr 3 out: wknd fr next* **25/1**

00PP **5** *nk* **Whatevertheweather**[37] 4136 7-10-0 **81** oh31 TomMessenger 67
(Sandy Forster) *chsd ldrs: mstke 2nd: nt fluent 4 out: rdn and wknd fr next* **100/1**

055 **6** *7* **Stanley Bridge**[26] 4361 4-9-9 **88** oh2 PaulGallagher(5) 61
(Barry Murtagh) *t.k.h early: hld up: effrt after 4 out: wknd fr next* **22/1**

-P30 **7** *19* **Lago Verde (SWI)**[167] 1757 6-11-12 **107** (t) PeterBuchanan 69
(Lucinda Russell) *hld up in tch: hit 1st: pushed along 4th: lost tch 4 out: t.o* **33/1**

4m 22.8s (-7.00) **Going Correction** -1.025s/f (Hard)
WFA 4 from 6yo+ 7lb **7** Ran SP% **109.5**
Speed ratings (Par 105): **75,74,73,66,66 62,54**
toteswingers:1&2:£1.10, 1&3:£3.00, 2&3:£2.80 CSF £2.73 TOTE £2.00: £2.10, £1.10; EX 3.80.
Owner Mrs S Harrow Mrs L M Whillans **Bred** C E Whiteley **Trained** Newmill-On-Slitrig, Borders

FOCUS
A weak race that did not take much winning. The first two are rated close to their marks.

NOTEBOOK
Lady Bluesky, who had at least proved she is capable of getting her head in front and was only 2lb higher than when winning last time (she will go up another 3lb from the weekend), won easily after cruising to the front. She may head for a race at the Scottish National meeting next, but will have a break at sometime, and then go on the Flat again. (op 6-4 tchd 13-8)
Ouest Eclair(FR), unpenalised for winning a conditional riders' handicap last time from a subsequent winner, was a bit sluggish at his hurdles on occasions and didn't move with the same fluency as the winner when the tempo lifted. He is due to go up 9lb from the weekend. (tchd Evens)
Twice Lucky is related to plenty of winners, and this was much more like it on his handicap debut after racing a bit freely in front. A horse with plenty of size, he might be one for a novice handicap chase before too long. (op 14-1)
Lisbon Lion(IRE) hadn't shown a great deal over hurdles, and didn't fare much better here on his handicap debut in this sphere after showing some signs of promise on the AW at Wolverhampton last time. (op 22-1)

4959 FANTAILS RESTAURANT NOVICES' CHASE (11 fncs 1 omitted) 2m
2:50 (2:50) (Class 4) 5-Y-0+ **£2,602** (£764; £382)

Form RPR

-FF1 **1** **The Knoxs (IRE)**[44] 3995 8-11-5 135 BrianHughes 145+
(Howard Johnson) *nt fluent early: trckd ldrs: hdwy to ld after 5 out: j.lft fr next: drew clr fnl 2: comf* **4/7**[1]

3-01 **2** *19* **Sam Lord**[18] 4507 7-11-5 130 PaddyAspell 134+
(James Moffatt) *led to 1st: chsd ldr: ev ch whn hit 5 out: rdn 3 out: no ex fr next* **85/40**[2]

U413 **3** *29* **Si Bien (FR)**[43] 3999 6-10-12 115 NathanMoscrop(7) 102
(James Ewart) *t.k.h: led 1st: hit 5 out: sn hdd: rdn and wknd fr next* **8/1**[3]

4m 3.40s (-12.70) **Going Correction** -0.775s/f (Firm) **3** Ran SP% **106.8**
Speed ratings: **100,90,76**
CSF £2.15 TOTE £1.40; EX 2.10.
Owner Andrea & Graham Wylie **Bred** Miss Margaret Flynn **Trained** Billy Row, Co Durham

FOCUS
An interesting-looking small-field contest. The first two ran to their marks and the winner can rate higher.

NOTEBOOK
The Knoxs(IRE) found this plain sailing. From a stable that has done well in this race (provided last year's winner Diamond Frontier), he had been talked of as a possible Jewson Novices' Chase contender after winning last time, and proved a league above his closest pursuer once making his move to the front, even after jumping to his left at the fences late on. One would imagine that connections will be keen to try him in a better event next time (Brian Hughes seemingly has a high opinion of him), and he would be interesting in a handicap in the coming weeks. (op 4-6 tchd 8-11 in a place)
Sam Lord won on his chasing debut at Sedgefield, but had something to find with The Knoxs on official figures and ran like a horse who is slightly more than 5lb inferior to the winner. (op 9-4 tchd 2-1)
Si Bien(FR) won a beginners' chase but was disappointing when returned to hurdles for his last start. Back over fences, he looked to have plenty on at the weights and faded tamely the moment he was taken on. (op 6-1 tchd 17-2)

4960 RACING UK ON CHANNEL 432 H'CAP HURDLE (11 hdls) 2m 4f
3:25 (3:25) (Class 4) (0-105,103) 4-Y-0+ **£2,123** (£619; £309)

Form RPR

156 **1** **Winged Farasi**[100] 2937 7-10-11 **95** MissJFoster(7) 103+
(Joanne Foster) *prom: pushed along 3 out: effrt after next: led run-in: styd on wl* **22/1**

4600 **2** *3/4* **Almutaham (USA)**[36] 4146 4-10-5 **90** PaddyAspell 90
(James Moffatt) *hld up: outpcd 1/2-way: rallied but plenty to do 3 out: chsd wnr last 100yds: r.o* **22/1**

0006 **3** *4* **Waltham Abbey**[15] 4550 10-9-10 **80** MrRUtley(7) 83
(Lynsey Kendall) *led: clr 1/2-way to 2 out: hdd run-in: kpt on same pce* **16/1**

0511 **4** *4 1/2* **Samizdat (FR)**[8] 4809 8-10-4 **88** 7ex MissECSayer(7) 89+
(Dianne Sayer) *w ldr to 5th: chsd clr ldr: effrt and ev ch last: wknd run-in* **2/1**[1]

6-3P **5** *7* **Patavium (IRE)**[11] 4738 8-11-2 **100** NathanMoscrop(7) 93
(Edwin Tuer) *hld up: hdwy after 4 out: rdn and outpcd fr next* **6/1**[3]

3222 **6** *9* **Classic Henri**[18] 4511 7-10-8 **88** JamesO'Farrell(3) 75
(Barry Murtagh) *hld up: effrt and rdn whn hit 3 out: sn wknd* **9/2**[2]

004U **7** *3* **North Brook (IRE)**[13] 4684 6-11-9 **103** EwanWhillans(3) 85
(Alistair Whillans) *t.k.h early: prom: rdn and outpcd bef 4 out: n.d after* **25/1**

00-0 **8** *10* **Ballamusic (IRE)**[24] 4390 9-10-13 **90** RichieMcGrath 63
(Andrew Parker) *prom: outpcd bef 7th: wknd fr next* **16/1**

1FPP **P** **Newman Des Plages (FR)**[26] 4360 10-11-9 **100** GrahamLee —
(Martin Todhunter) *bhd: struggling 1/2-way: p.u after 4 out: lame* **17/2**

-035 **P** **See The Legend**[13] 4688 6-10-6 **83** TomMessenger —
(Sandy Forster) *hld up: outpcd bef 4 out: sn btn: t.o whn p.u next* **8/1**

5m 1.40s (-21.40) **Going Correction** -1.025s/f (Hard)
WFA 4 from 6yo+ 8lb **10** Ran SP% **111.7**
Speed ratings (Par 105): **101,100,99,97,94 90,89,85,—,—**
toteswingers:1&2:£39.20, 1&3:£44.30, 2&3:£23.30 CSF £373.04 CT £7622.98 TOTE £27.90: £5.60, £5.50, £4.80; EX 383.10.
Owner The Smash Block Partnership **Bred** The National Stud **Trained** Menston, W Yorks
■ Stewards' Enquiry : Miss J Foster five-day ban: used whip with excessive frequency (Apr 7,9-12)

FOCUS
A low-grade contest run at a fair gallop. A step up from the winner with the second to his mark.

NOTEBOOK
Winged Farasi, returning from a break, finished in front of Samizdat before that horse's winning spree started and confirmed his superiority here with a strong finish under his trainer/jockey. He has shown fair form when fresh, so it's not easy to predict whether he'll repeat this sort of level next time.
Almutaham(USA) hadn't won a race under any code, and only shown limited promise, but this was better, as he stayed on dourly up the hill under strong pressure. (op 25-1)
Waltham Abbey had been beaten over 22l by Samizdat last time. Enterprisingly ridden, he did manage to reverse that form after going off at a good pace, but didn't have enough left up the hill, despite his low weight, to keep going.
Samizdat(FR) was chasing a hat-trick off a 14lb higher mark than for the first of those successes, and had every chance before fading. The distance at this track (he's a dual winner over 2m1f here) probably just found him out. (tchd 9-4)
Patavium(IRE), whose saddle slipped last time, is on a fair mark but didn't get home after racing a little keenly under restraint. (op 13-2 tchd 7-1)
Classic Henri has been running really well since returning from a lengthy absence, but he got caught flat-footed here and this was disappointing. Official explanation: jockey said gelding never travelled (op 5-1)
Newman Des Plages(FR), returned to hurdles after failing to complete over fences in his previous three starts, looked well treated compared to his chase rating but was never going well and eventually pulled up lame. (op 11-1)
See The Legend attracted money during the morning but gave supporters no hope of collecting. Official explanation: jockey said mare was unsuited by the good to soft (soft in places) ground (op 11-1)

4961 TEXAS LIVE HERE 2ND JULY H'CAP CHASE (14 fncs 2 omitted) 2m 4f
4:00 (4:00) (Class 4) (0-115,115) 5-Y-0+ **£5,204** (£1,528; £764; £381)

Form RPR

1P12 **1** **You Know Yourself (IRE)**[33] 4210 8-11-7 **115** ShaneByrne(5) 123+
(Sue Smith) *t.k.h: prom: hdwy 8th: hit and rdn 4 out: rallied to ld 2 out: hld on wl fr last* **7/2**[3]

1302 **2** *3/4* **Bene Lad (IRE)**[19] 4471 9-10-7 **96** RichieMcGrath 103
(Jim Goldie) *hld up in tch: effrt and hdwy 3 out: chsd wnr last: kpt on u.p* **11/4**[1]

22F1 **3** *3/4* **Against The Wind**[14] 4573 8-10-13 **102** PeterBuchanan 108
(Lucinda Russell) *cl up: effrt and led 3 out: hdd next: kpt on u.p fr last* **3/1**[2]

113P **4** *13* **Ocarina (FR)**[68] 3574 9-11-0 **110** (p) NathanMoscrop(7) 108
(James Ewart) *nt fluent on occasions: cl up: led 8th: hdd 3 out: wknd fr next* **12/1**

5114 **5** *98* **Primrose Time**[31] 4254 8-10-13 **107** AlexanderVoy(5) 13
(Lucy Normile) *led to 8th: rdn and struggling after next: lost tch 5 out: no ch whn mstke 2 out* **9/1**

243R **R** **Blackpool Billy (IRE)**[3] 4911 9-11-10 **113**............................ GrahamLee —
(Ferdy Murphy) *ref to r* **9/2**

5m 9.30s (-18.10) **Going Correction** -0.775s/f (Firm) **6** Ran SP% **109.8**
Speed ratings: **105,104,104,99,60** —
toteswingers:1&2:£2.30, 1&3:£2.40, 2&3:£2.10 CSF £13.26 TOTE £3.70: £1.90, £1.20; EX 12.20.
Owner Mrs S Smith **Bred** Patrick O'Connell **Trained** High Eldwick, W Yorks

FOCUS
They raced in a bunch for most of the contest. Easy form to rate.

NOTEBOOK
You Know Yourself(IRE) is lightly raced for his age and is quite capable on a going day, as two victories suggest in a seven-race career. He is a tough customer and isn't the type to shirk a fight, which will help his cause as he climbs the weights. (tchd 4-1)
Bene Lad(IRE) didn't run too badly on his return to fences earlier this month but wasn't able to close down the winner, who wasn't for beating. (op 10-3)
Against The Wind, up 7lb for winning over 2m last time at this course, had his chance and wasn't disgraced as three horses fought for supremacy from two out. (op 10-3 tchd 7-2)
Ocarina(FR), returning from a break, looked high in the handicap and hit a flat spot after three out, which ruined his chance of being involved in the finish. (op 9-1)
Primrose Time failed in her bid for a hat-trick last time over C&D (novice company) and was readily brushed aside when headed here. Official explanation: jockey said mare finished distressed (op 12-1 tchd 17-2)
Blackpool Billy(IRE) blotted his copybook three days earlier when refusing at the third fence and didn't look a betting proposition as a result, but connections felt that a Grakle noseband he wore there had unsettled him, and were hopeful of a better show. However, despite schooling well since, and again on the morning of this race, he was evidently in a recalcitrant mood, and didn't even jump off this time. (op 4-1)

4962 EASTER FAMILY DAY 23RD APRIL NOVICES' H'CAP CHASE (16 fncs 2 omitted) 3m 110y
4:35 (4:35) (Class 4) (0-110,109) 5-Y-0+ **£2,740** (£798; £399)

Form RPR
53 **1** **Ballycarron Lad (IRE)**[12] 4712 9-11-0 **97**........................ CampbellGillies 110+
(S R B Crawford, Ire) *hld up in tch: outpcd fr 5th: plenty to do fnl circ: hdwy 3 out: swept past wkng rivals after next: sn clr* **5/2**[2]

F6FP **2** *11* **Baltic Pathfinder (IRE)**[37] 4135 7-11-3 **105**..................... ShaneByrne(5) 107
(Sue Smith) *j.lft: cl up: rdn and outpcd 5 out: rallied whn hit and outpcd next: rallied to chse wnr bef last: no imp* **4/1**[3]

P/6P **3** *13* **Craicneasy (IRE)**[18] 4507 8-9-9 **83** oh14........................ PaulGallagher(5) 73
(Bruce Mactaggart) *nt fluent: cl up: led 10th: wnt rt and hit 4 out: sn hdd: styd upsides: hit 2 out: wkng whn hit last* **28/1**

1452 **4** *nk* **Quinder Spring (FR)**[36] 4150 7-11-12 **109**..................(p) PeterBuchanan 100
(Lucinda Russell) *led to 10th: styd upsides: hmpd and hit 4 out: sn led: hdd after 2 out: sn wknd* **5/6**[1]

6m 29.0s (-13.60) **Going Correction** -0.775s/f (Firm) **4** Ran SP% **106.6**
Speed ratings: **90,86,82,82**
CSF £11.27 TOTE £1.90; EX 11.60.
Owner Mrs H J Bond **Bred** Mrs Tom O'Donnell **Trained** Larne, Co Antrim

FOCUS
This long-distance chase was never going to be a proper test of stamina, but it produced a quite remarkable outcome considering the winner's position at about halfway. The winner was well in on one Irish run but this is not form to be confident about.

NOTEBOOK
Ballycarron Lad(IRE), back over fences, kicked in a turbo gear and surged to the front after three out and went away to win comfortably. Matched for a few pounds between 300-370 on Betfair due to being detached in the middle part of the race, it's impossible to know what to expect next time if losing his place as he did here. He obviously has plenty of ability but may not be the easiest to keep interested. (tchd 9-4)
Baltic Pathfinder(IRE), whose trainer had a two from two record in this contest, didn't look too happy for much of the race and was going nowhere up the hill, but as the two in front of him faded he did enough to get into second place, which had seemed unlikely from some way out. (tchd 9-2)
Craicneasy(IRE), racing from 14lb out of the handicap, jumped to the lead on the final circuit. He seemed sure to be involved in the finish but some indifferent jumping eventually cost him. (op 20-1)
Quinder Spring(FR), who had cheekpieces back on, made much of the running and only faded between the last two fences. (op 10-11 tchd evens in a place)

4963 X-FACTOR STARS 24TH JULY H'CAP CHASE (11 fncs 1 omitted) 2m
5:10 (5:10) (Class 4) (0-100,98) 5-Y-0+ **£1,821** (£534; £267; £133)

Form RPR
/P0P **1** **Spirit Calling (IRE)**[69] 3549 10-11-12 **98**...................(tp) PeterBuchanan 109+
(Lucinda Russell) *in tch: hdwy 3 out: led last 100yds: kpt on wl* **17/2**

5553 **2** *2 1/4* **Troodos Jet**[8] 4813 10-9-10 **75**....................................(p) MissECSayer(7) 82
(Dianne Sayer) *prom: hdwy to ld 3 out: rdn and hdd last 100yds: kpt on same pce* **7/1**

P420 **3** *3* **The Green Hat (IRE)**[9] 4799 11-10-0 **72** oh1...................... BrianHughes 77
(Theresa Gibson) *led to 1st: cl up: led 4th to 6th: styd upsides: effrt and ev ch 2 out: one pce run-in* **17/2**

0-5U **4** *4* **Frith (IRE)**[14] 4573 9-10-1 **78**.. AlexanderVoy(5) 79
(Lucy Normile) *hld up: hdwy to trck ldrs 3 out: rdn and kpt on same pce after next* **10/1**

-054 **5** *8* **Conflictofinterest**[15] 4549 9-11-3 **92**............................ EwanWhillans(3) 86
(Kevin Hunter) *hld up: hdwy on outside bef 4 out: rdn and no imp fr next* **16/1**

2/F2 **6** *3 1/4* **Wee George**[18] 4509 9-10-7 **79**.. HenryOliver 72
(Sue Smith) *cl up led 3rd to next: led 6th: rdn and hdd 3 out: wkng whn hit last* **3/1**[1]

006F **7** *15* **Also Jo**[18] 4510 8-11-1 **87**.. CampbellGillies 70
(William Amos) *blnd and nrly uns rdr 1st: hld up: hdwy and prom after 5 out: rdn and outpcd whn hit 3 out* **22/1**

300P **8** *12* **Daytime Dreamer (IRE)**[28] 4305 7-11-10 **96**......................(t) GrahamLee 62
(Martin Todhunter) *hld up: rdn and outpcd 5 out: nvr on terms* **11/2**[3]

6U13 **9** *1 1/4* **Ice Image (IRE)**[24] 4392 9-11-4 **97**.............................(t) AlistairFindlay(7) 62
(George Charlton) *cl up: led 1st to 3rd: struggling fr 6th: btn fr 4 out* **4/1**[2]

4m 6.40s (-9.70) **Going Correction** -0.775s/f (Firm) **9** Ran SP% **113.3**
Speed ratings: **93,91,90,88,84 82,75,69,68**
toteswingers:1&2:£6.30, 1&3:£11.50, 2&3:£9.00 CSF £65.02 CT £520.67 TOTE £11.40: £3.20, £2.00, £3.00; EX 77.00.
Owner John R Adam & Sons **Bred** J Tyrrell **Trained** Arlary, Perth & Kinross

FOCUS
A low-grade chase which saw changing fortunes up the home straight. The second sets the level.

NOTEBOOK
Spirit Calling(IRE) had a tongue-tie added to his cheekpieces in a bid to rekindle his enthusiasm, and it certainly worked. It's not easy to know whether the drop in trip or fitting of the tongue-tie made the difference, maybe it was a mix of the both, but his profile doesn't suggest he's one to be backing to win next time. (op 10-1)
Troodos Jet won this race last season off a 1lb higher mark and looked all set to collect again as he moved effortlessly into the lead three out, but the winner slowly made inroads and stayed on just the stronger to get past in the latter stages. (op 17-2)
The Green Hat(IRE), 1lb out of the handicap, was always close up and kept on well for strong pressure. He can throw in the odd good performance but is still seeking a first victory under rules. (op 9-1 tchd 8-1)
Frith(IRE) moved up to the heels of the leaders moving strongly, but couldn't quicken when he needed to. (op 9-1 tchd 8-1)
Conflictofinterest had an official rating of 133 over hurdles at his peak for Paul Nicholls, but didn't show a lot after a year off and on his debut for this stable last time. This was slightly better, but one couldn't be sure he's a straightforward ride. (op 12-1)
Wee George didn't seem to help his jockey a great deal at times, and is another in the race still looking for a first win. (op 9-4 tchd 10-3)
Daytime Dreamer(IRE), with a tongue-tie put back on, failed to make any impression. (op 12-1 tchd 5-1)
Ice Image(IRE), 10lb higher than when winning two starts previously, was disappointing. Official explanation: jockey said gelding did not jump fluently throughout (op 9-2 tchd 5-1)

4718 CHEPSTOW (L-H)
Thursday, March 24

OFFICIAL GOING: Good (good to soft in places; watered; chase 6.2, hurdle 6.0)
Wind: mild across Weather: sunny

4964 EASYODDS.COM MARES' NOVICES' HURDLE (8 hdls) 2m 110y
2:10 (2:10) (Class 4) 4-Y-0+ **£2,016** (£592; £296; £147)

Form RPR
4032 **1** **Sara's Smile**[20] 4454 5-10-12 106.. JasonMaguire 103+
(Donald McCain) *mde all: nt fluent 3 out: clr advantage next: kpt on wl: rdn out* **5/1**[2]

2223 **2** *3* **American Ladie**[20] 4451 5-10-12 120................................ RobertThornton 101+
(Alan King) *w wnr: pushed along appr 4 out: ev ch whn nt fluent 3 out: sn rdn: hld fr next: kpt on same pce* **4/11**[1]

3 *17* **Bow To No One (IRE)**[116] 5-10-12 0................................. WillKennedy 87
(Alan Jarvis) *hld up in last but in tch: hdwy appr 4 out: rdn in 3rd after 3 out: mstke next: wknd last* **5/1**[2]

2200 **4** *2 1/4* **Verde Goodwood**[16] 4535 5-10-12 0................................ LeightonAspell 84
(Oliver Sherwood) *cl up: rdn whn mstke 4 out: wknd after 2 out* **50/1**[3]

0P00 **5** *4* **Rolline (IRE)**[79] 3389 6-10-9 92.................................... DonalDevereux(3) 78
(Stuart Kittow) *trckd ldrs: pushed along after 4th: rdn bef 4 out: wknd 2 out* **50/1**[3]

6-P **6** *54* **Fraam Lea**[155] 1921 5-10-5 0... MrJFlook(7) 29
(Andrew Price) *racd keenly: trckd ldrs: rdn after 4th: sn wknd: t.o* **100/1**

4m 4.80s (-5.80) **Going Correction** -0.375s/f (Good) **6** Ran SP% **111.6**
Speed ratings (Par 105): **98,96,88,87,85 60**
toteswingers:1&2:£1.02, 1&3:£1.70, 2&3:£1.10 CSF £7.60 TOTE £6.70: £2.50, £1.80; EX 8.50.
Owner T J Crehan **Bred** R D And Mrs J S Chugg **Trained** Cholmondeley, Cheshire

FOCUS
The ground was described as good, good to soft in places, with 4mm of water applied to the track on Monday and 3mm selectively the previous day. It was described by Jason Maguire as "mainly good but a bit dead in places". A modest mares' novice hurdle run at a steady gallop. A small personal best from the winner but the second was again below her best.

NOTEBOOK
Sara's Smile, dropping in trip, finished runner-up at Doncaster on her last start and went one better here to record her first career success. Making all, she raced keenly early, but travelled best and outfought the odds-on favourite in the straight, despite wandering around under pressure. Her trainer expects her to jump a fence next season. (op 9-2)
American Ladie, rated 120 and placed in all four hurdles starts, including behind a subsequent winner last time, must rate as disappointing. She tracked the pace all the way but was unable to quicken and could not match the winner. She is becoming very expensive to follow. (op 4-9)
Bow To No One(IRE), a fair sort on the Flat, was patiently ridden and, despite making some headway turning for home, was never able to strike a blow. She should benefit from this hurdles debut but needs to settle better and this was a poor contest.
Verde Goodwood hugged the inside throughout and could not make an impact, plugging on at the one pace.
Rolline(IRE) was pushed along running down the back straight and never threatened. (tchd 66-1)

4965 LINDLEY CATERING H'CAP HURDLE (8 hdls) 2m 110y
2:40 (2:40) (Class 5) (0-95,93) 4-Y-0+ **£1,723** (£506; £253; £126)

Form RPR
0354 **1** **Spinning Waters**[17] 4530 5-11-7 **93**..............................(p) OliverDayman(5) 98+
(Dai Burchell) *trckd ldr: led appr 4 out where nt fluent: rdn and hdd appr last: kpt on to ld again towards fin* **6/1**

0010 **2** *1/2* **Won More Night**[3] 4922 9-10-9 **79**....................................(t) IanPopham(3) 81+
(Martin Keighley) *travelled best for most of way: hld up: hdwy appr 4 out: sn trcking ldng pair: shkn up to ld last: rdn and hdd run-in: fnd little* **13/8**[1]

0061 **3** *nk* **Lightening Fire (IRE)**[12] 4724 9-10-7 **79**.........(p) MissIsabelTompsett(5) 81
(Bernard Llewellyn) *led: rdn and hdd appr 4 out: kpt chsng wnr: ev ch last: no ex towards fin* **10/3**[3]

/05- **4** *53* **Jessica**[521] 1833 6-10-0 **77**.. DarrenO'Keeffe(10) 31
(Seamus Mullins) *hmpd 1st: chsd ldrs: wnt wdst on bnd bef 2nd: struggling 3rd: wknd 3 out: t.o* **20/1**

2521 **5** *40* **Form And Beauty (IRE)**[12] 4721 9-10-6 **80**.................(b) MarkQuinlan(7) —
(Bernard Llewellyn) *wnt rt and nt fluent 1st: trckd ldrs: rdn after 4th: wknd bef next: t.o: b.b.v* **11/4**[2]

4m 6.50s (-4.10) **Going Correction** -0.375s/f (Good) **5** Ran SP% **106.9**
Speed ratings (Par 103): **94,93,93,68,49**
CSF £15.67 TOTE £4.10: £1.50, £3.80; EX 20.20.
Owner B M G Group **Bred** R E Crutchley **Trained** Briery Hill, Blaenau Gwent

FOCUS
A moderate handicap hurdle and there were three in contention running to the last. The time was fair for the grade and the winner is on the upgrade.

NOTEBOOK
Spinning Waters, wearing cheekpieces on this second handicap start, took it up about four out to record his first hurdles success. The headgear had the desired effect and he gamely knuckled down on the run-in. This is weak form but he showed a good attitude, responding well to his rider's urgings, and the better ground he got here may well have made all the difference considering his winning Flat form. (op 5-1)
Won More Night, down in trip, was making a quick reappearance having been hampered and dismounted at Lingfield three days earlier.The subject of strong market support, she travelled strongly and looked the winner approaching two out, but on the run to the final flight her jockey asked her to win the race and her response was minimal. Having won off this mark on her penultimate start, she is due to go up 8lb and may struggle with that hike. (op 5-2)
Lightening Fire(IRE), up 4lb for his success here 12 days earlier, marginally regained the lead over the last, but was outbattled in the closing stages. (op 3-1)

Jessica jumped poorly on this return from a 521-day absence. She was reported to have lost a shoe. Official explanation: vet said mare lost a right-fore shoe (op 16-1)
Form And Beauty(IRE) got off the mark in first-time blinkers here on his last start, and was never travelling off 11lb higher. He was reported to have bled form the nose, so may be given another chance. Official explanation: vet said gelding bled from the nose (op 2-1)

4966 LINDLEY CATERING H'CAP CHASE (18 fncs) 3m
3:15 (3:15) (Class 4) (0-115,115) 5-Y-0+ **£3,252** (£955; £477; £238)

Form				RPR
125F	**1**		**Oscar Prairie (IRE)**[16] 4538 6-11-7 **110**..................(p) WayneHutchinson (Warren Greatrex) *chsd ldrs: nt fluent 2nd: rdn after 11th: chal 5 out: led 3 out: styd on wl to assert run-in: drvn out* **10/1**	118
023F	**2**	*5*	**Strongbows Legend**[24] 4402 6-11-5 **108**........................ AndrewTinkler (Charlie Longsdon) *hld up in last pair: hdwy 10th to join ldrs: led 5 out: rdn and hdd 3 out: kpt chalng: mstke next: ev ch last: no ex* **2/1**[1]	114+
-660	**3**	*1 3/4*	**Troy Tempest (IRE)**[25] 4370 6-11-2 **105**................................ JackDoyle (Emma Lavelle) *hld up last but in tch: hdwy 12th to trck ldrs: mstke 5 out: sn rdn: styd on same pce: wnt 3rd run-in* **13/2**	109
5-53	**4**	*3 3/4*	**Priors Glen (IRE)**[168] 1739 7-11-5 **115**.................. StephenO'Donovan(7) (Emma Lavelle) *trckd ldrs: jnd ldr 8th: led 11th: hdd 5 out: sn rdn: styd on same pce: lost 3rd run-in* **8/1**	114
4P2	**5**	*14*	**Silver Story**[17] 4523 8-11-10 **113**....................................(t) TomScudamore (Tim Vaughan) *trckd ldrs: awkward on landing 12th: sn pushed along: rdn whn mstke 4 out and rdr lost iron briefly: wknd after3 out* **6/1**[3]	106+
P1V1	**6**	*40*	**Victory Gunner (IRE)**[22] 4428 13-11-4 **112**................... GilesHawkins(5) (Richard Lee) *trckd ldr tl 8th: rdn after 11th: wknd 5 out: t.o* **6/1**[3]	61
3P-0	**P**		**Freeze Up (IRE)**[83] 3263 9-11-4 **107**................................ TomO'Brien (Philip Hobbs) *led tl 11th: sn drvn: wknd bef 5 out: t.o whn p.u bef 4 out* **11/2**[2]	—

6m 17.6s (-4.40) **Going Correction** -0.225s/f (Good) **7** Ran SP% **110.8**
Speed ratings: **98,96,95,94,89 76,—**
toteswingers:1&2:£4.30, 1&3:£9.40, 2&3:£3.10 CSF £29.75 TOTE £16.80: £8.50, £1.10; EX 36.80.
Owner The Weathercocks **Bred** Noel O'Connor **Trained** Upper Lambourn, Berks

FOCUS
A tight and competitive handicap chase. Ordinary form, the winner rated to his hurdles mark.

NOTEBOOK
Oscar Prairie(IRE), sporting first-time cheekpieces, stayed on strongly for pressure to record his first chase victory. Having been one of the first under the whip, he rallied and his jumping in the straight was enough to see off his rivals. This was only his third chase start so he remains open to improvement, albeit in this modest grade. (tchd 11-1)
Strongbows Legend, who was going well when falling on his last start, ran a fair race, just finding the one too good on the run-in. He jumped better here, bar a mistake two out, and this should help build some confidence. (op 9-4)
Troy Tempest(IRE), the ride of stable jockey Jack Doyle, was held up on his chasing debut and didn't jump fluently but ran on strongly from the second last. He should improve for this experience and may be suited by further. (op 9-1)
Priors Glen(IRE), third in a beginners' chase at Exeter in October (tongue-tied), raced up with the pace and stayed on at the one pace. He is better suited to going right-handed. He was reported to have lost a shoe. Official explanation: vet said gelding lost a left-hind shoe (op 17-2 tchd 10-1)
Silver Story showed up for a long way but made several jumping errors and struggled as a result. (op 5-1 tchd 9-2)
Victory Gunner(IRE) is 4-12 around here but didn't jump well enough on this occasion. Official explanation: jockey said gelding never travelled (op 5-1)
Freeze Up(IRE) made the running early before fading tamely. (op 6-1 tchd 9-2)

4967 ONSHORE MARINE MEDICAL SERVICES LTD BRISTOL H'CAP CHASE (16 fncs) 2m 3f 110y
3:50 (3:50) (Class 4) (0-115,114) 5-Y-0+ **£3,252** (£955; £477; £238)

Form				RPR
4-P1	**1**		**Roudoudou Ville (FR)**[14] 4671 6-11-12 **114**.......................... JackDoyle (Victor Dartnall) *j.w: a.p: led 11th: drew clr fr 5 out: v easily* **11/8**[1]	138+
60P1	**2**	*15*	**Ready Or Not (IRE)**[17] 4523 8-10-11 **99**................ AndrewGlassonbury (Bob Buckler) *led tl 11th: rdn appr 5 out: sn hld* **4/1**[3]	105
0064	**3**	*24*	**Amble Forge (IRE)**[12] 4723 9-11-0 **102**...............................(p) JoeTizzard (Colin Tizzard) *t.k.h early: trckd ldrs: rdn after 11th: pressed for 3rd fr 5 out tl hit 3 out: no ch w front pair* **5/2**[2]	83
F255	**4**	*45*	**Bushwacker (IRE)**[143] 2124 7-10-11 **102**................... JimmyDerham(3) (Seamus Mullins) *hld up: chal for 3rd 5 out: rdn whn mstke 4 out: wknd next* **7/1**	63
20U4	**R**		**Star Galaxy (IRE)**[17] 4523 11-10-7 **105**.......................(b) ThomasFlint(10) (John Flint) *t.k.h early: trckd ldrs: dropped to last and drvn after 9th: lost tch after 11th: ref 2 out* **16/1**	—

5m 8.30s (-3.00) **Going Correction** -0.225s/f (Good) **5** Ran SP% **109.1**
Speed ratings: **97,91,81,63,—**
CSF £7.18 TOTE £2.40: £1.10, £3.80; EX 6.20.
Owner Exors of the Late P M De Wilde **Bred** J Poumaillou **Trained** Brayford, Devon

FOCUS
Just a small field for this handicap chase, which was run at a slow pace. The easy winner is on the upgrade and can rate higher.

NOTEBOOK
Roudoudou Ville(FR), raised 12lb for his Wincanton success, put in a slick round of jumping to run out an effortless winner. Jumping to the front down the back, he coasted home and handled the step up in distance without being challenged. He should go close under a penalty in similar contests and relishes better ground. He may now head to the Perth festival. (op 13-8 tchd 5-4)
Ready Or Not(IRE), a winner at Ffos Las on his last start, was running off a 6lb higher mark and jumped neatly out in front before being outclassed by the winner. He can continue to improve having had just the three chase starts. (op 7-2 tchd 10-3)
Amble Forge(IRE) raced keenly and could never get seriously involved. Although feasibly handicapped on old form, he has not shown enough recently to make him of any interest. (op 11-4 tchd 3-1)
Bushwacker(IRE), back from a 143-day break, was held up and made numerous mistakes. (op 15-2 tchd 8-1)
Star Galaxy(IRE) jumped poorly and unseated his rider after refusing at the second last. (op 12-1)

4968 LINDLEYS FIRST FOR BANQUETING H'CAP HURDLE (12 hdls) 3m
4:25 (4:25) (Class 4) (0-115,115) 4-Y-0+ **£2,016** (£592; £296; £147)

Form				RPR
5160	**1**		**Gilwen Glory (IRE)**[35] 4161 8-10-10 **104**................ AodhaganConlon(5) (Evan Williams) *trckd ldrs: rdn after 8th: led and hit 2 out: styd on wl to draw clr* **7/1**	111+
2523	**2**	*8*	**Prince Of Denial (IRE)**[21] 4448 7-11-9 **115**......... SamTwiston-Davies(3) (Nigel Twiston-Davies) *in tch: jnd ldrs 8th: led 4 out: nt fluent next: sn rdn: hdd 2 out: styd on same pce* **5/2**[2]	116+
3055	**3**	*4 1/2*	**Bishophill Jack (IRE)**[42] 4021 5-11-2 **105**......................(t) JasonMaguire (Kim Bailey) *trckd ldrs tl dropped to last of bunch 5th: rdn and hdwy after 8th: styd on same pce fr 3 out* **15/8**[1]	104
0600	**4**	*4 1/2*	**Always Waining (IRE)**[19] 4464 10-11-11 **114**...................(p) TomO'Brien (Peter Bowen) *trckd ldr: rdn to chal appr 4 out: styd on same pce fr 3 out* **6/1**[3]	106
1146	**5**	*12*	**Lyster (IRE)**[18] 4501 12-10-13 **105**.................................... LeeStephens(3) (Graeme McPherson) *hld up: rdn after 8th: nvr any imp* **9/1**	86
-U60	**6**	*3/4*	**Drumbeater (IRE)**[10] 4787 11-9-7 **89** oh17..................(p) MarkQuinlan(7) (Bernard Scriven) *led tl awkward 4 out: chsd ldrs tl wknd bef 2 out* **33/1**	69
P03P	**7**	*58*	**Sunday Sharpner (IRE)**[30] 4276 5-11-4 **107**.............(p) JimmyMcCarthy (Renee Robeson) *hld up: hit 4th: rdn after 8th: sn wknd: t.o* **12/1**	35
/0P0	**P**		**King Gabriel (IRE)**[21] 4441 9-10-10 **106**...................(t) MissJennyCarr(7) (Tracey Watkins) *t.k.h: hld up: effrt whn short of room on bnd after 8th: wknd bef next: t.o whn p.u bef 3 out* **50/1**	—

6m 8.10s (-11.70) **Going Correction** -0.375s/f (Good) **8** Ran SP% **112.7**
Speed ratings (Par 105): **104,101,99,98,94 94,74,—**
toteswingers:1&2:£3.90, 1&3:£4.60, 2&3:£2.60 CSF £24.81 CT £45.49 TOTE £9.50: £1.30, £1.60, £1.20; EX 24.10.
Owner Keith And Sue Lowry **Bred** R Jenks **Trained** Llancarfan, Vale Of Glamorgan

FOCUS
An ordinary handicap hurdle with question marks over most of the field. There may still be more to come from the winner, and the next two were pretty much to their marks.

NOTEBOOK
Gilwen Glory(IRE) appreciated the step back up in trip and bounced back to form in good style. A winner off 2lb lower, she had disappointed the last twice, but travelled nicely this time and put the race to bed between the last two flights. Not the most consistent, she clearly thrives over this distance. Official explanation: trainer said, regarding apparent improvement in form, that the mare appeared to be better in its coat and may be inconsistent. (op 6-1)
Prince Of Denial(IRE), up in trip, led over the third last and had every chance but was unable to go with the winner. He stayed on one-paced and remains a maiden. (tchd 11-4)
Bishophill Jack(IRE) disappointed on his handicap debut last time, and was again a beaten favourite. He raced lazily on and off the bridle and didn't jump cleanly before being unable to go with the front two in the straight. This was a moody display and he needs to jump better. (op 11-4)
Always Waining(IRE) was having his final prep for Aintree as he bids to repeat his victory in last year's Topham Chase. He showed up nicely for a long way and this should put him spot on for next month. (op 8-1)
Lyster(IRE) raced towards the back and may improve fitness-wise for this second run back from a break. (op 13-2)
Drumbeater(IRE), running from well out of the weights, took the field along before weakening after an error four from home. (tchd 25-1)

4969 SJH MACHINERY KUBOTA DEALER HUNTERS' CHASE (18 fncs) 3m
4:55 (4:55) (Class 6) 5-Y-0+ **£923** (£283; £141)

Form				RPR
-311	**1**		**Oca De Thaix (FR)**[17] 4526 9-11-10 111............. MissCharlotteEvans(7) (Keith Goldsworthy) *racd keenly: hld up: hdwy to join ldrs 4th: led 9th: in command whn hit last 2: comf* **6/4**[1]	125+
16P-	**2**	*14*	**Worship The Stars**[18] 10-11-8 103...................................... MrJMahot(5) (Miss Sarah-Jayne Davies) *in tch: jnd ldrs 8th: rdn and ev ch 5 out tl 3 out: styd on same pce: hit last: eased flat* **12/1**	110+
25-P	**3**	*11*	**Ultimate Limit**[13] 4701 11-12-0 0...................................... MrTJCannon(3) (Alan Fleming) *hld up: hdwy 11th: rdn to chse ldng pair after 5 out: no ch whn nt fluent 2 out: fdd* **7/2**[2]	104
5-34	**4**	*1 3/4*	**Oopsmylord (IRE)**[33] 4211 9-11-6 115...........................(p) MrRJarrett(7) (S Flook) *prom tl rdn after 12th: hld whn lft 4th 5 out: plugged on* **6/1**[3]	94
/P-0	**5**	*5*	**Celestial Dragon (IRE)**[12] 10-11-2 89..................... MissRachelKing(7) (James Richardson) *chsd ldrs tl 10th: sn rdn: plugged on fr 5 out but nvr bk on terms* **33/1**	86
6450	**6**	*41*	**Classic Clover**[13] 4708 11-11-10 91..................................(bt) MrMLegg(7) (Colin Tizzard) *led tl 9th: sn drvn: lost tch fr 12th: t.o* **33/1**	57
13F-	**7**	*dist*	**Black Beauty**[19] 8-11-6 0.. MrJPark(7) (Mrs T Porter) *hld up: struggling 10th: sn wl t.o* **14/1**	12
2-4F	**P**		**Back To Bid (IRE)**[11] 4750 11-11-2 117...........................(p) MissJBuck(7) (James Danahar) *struggling in last whn stmbld by winning post w circ to run: sn p.u: lame* **10/1**	—
0/06	**F**		**Back Is Back (IRE)**[17] 4526 7-11-6 89........................(tp) MrRWoollacott(3) (Miss Jane Western) *in tch: tk clsr order 10th: rdn to dispute 3rd whn fell 5 out* **12/1**	—

6m 21.3s (-0.70) **Going Correction** -0.225s/f (Good) **9** Ran SP% **113.5**
Speed ratings: **92,87,83,83,81 67,52,—,—**
toteswingers:1&2:£7.10, 1&3:£3.00, 2&3:£8.50 CSF £20.38 TOTE £1.70: £1.02, £4.00, £3.10; EX 17.80.
Owner K Goldsworthy **Bred** Michel Bourgneuf **Trained** Yerbeston, Pembrokes

FOCUS
This hunter chase was run at a steady gallop. The winner was the form pick but this was arguably a step up.

NOTEBOOK
Oca De Thaix(FR), well backed, followed up his recent victories at Ludlow and Ffos Las with a bloodless victory, simply outclassing his rivals. Racing enthusiastically throughout, he made the odd error but cruised clear approaching three out, relishing the step up in distance, and should win more races in this grade. His trainer said he will be back here for the Welsh Champion Novice Hunter Chase. (op 11-8 tchd 5-4 and 7-4 in places)
Worship The Stars responded nicely for pressure, chasing the favourite all the way to the line. He jumped well enough and stretched well clear of the remainder. He may gain compensation in a minor contest.
Ultimate Limit, pulled up with a slipped saddle on his hunter chase debut, was held up before a mistake at the fourth last ended his chance. He never jumped with any fluency and needs to improve in that department, but did show useful form in handicaps last season and may land a similar race. (tchd 10-3)
Oopsmylord(IRE), wearing first-time cheekpieces and the subject of early support, raced up with the pace before being outpaced and fading in the straight. His last win was over two years ago. (op 8-1)
Back To Bid(IRE), rated 117, was never going and was pulled up. Official explanation: jockey said gelding pulled up lame (op 9-1 tchd 11-1)

4970 DIGIBET.COM CATERING INTERMEDIATE OPEN NATIONAL HUNT FLAT RACE 2m 110y
5:30 (5:30) (Class 6) 4-6-Y-0 **£1,431** (£420; £210; £104)

Form				RPR
	1		**Mr Hooper** 5-11-3 0.. JackDoyle (Victor Dartnall) *trckd ldrs: led 5f out: styd on wl fnl 2f: readily* **8/1**	116+
20	**2**	*5*	**Gospel Preacher**[56] 3773 6-11-3 0.................................. RobertThornton (Alan King) *mid-div: hdwy over 4f out: rdn to chse wnr 3f out: kpt on but a being hld fnl 2f* **6/1**	111

0-2 **3** *7* **Mike Towey (IRE)**[23] 4410 6-11-3 0 TomO'Brien 104+
(Peter Bowen) *prom: rdn to chse wnr over 4f out tl over 3f out: styd on same pce fnl 2f* **5/1**[3]
4 *nk* **Black Thunder (FR)** 4-10-5 0 MrRMahon(5) 97+
(Paul Nicholls) *hld up towards rr: rdn over 6f out: hdwy over 4f out: wnt 4th whn hung bdly lft 2f out: no further imp* **9/2**[2]
45 **5** *3* **Five Rivers (IRE)**[83] 3266 5-11-3 0 WayneHutchinson 101
(Warren Greatrex) *t.k.h: mid-div: rdn and styd on same pce fnl 3f* **13/2**
6 *7* **Ardkilly Gunner (IRE)**[84] 6-11-3 0 TomScudamore 94
(Ian Williams) *trckd ldrs: led over 10f out: hdd 5f out: sn rdn: wknd over 2f out* **4/1**[1]
6 **7** *2* **Gilzean (IRE)**[38] 4124 5-11-0 0 SamTwiston-Davies(3) 93
(Nigel Twiston-Davies) *t.k.h: trckd ldrs: rdn over 4f out: wknd over 2f out* **16/1**
8 *16* **Kalantari (IRE)** 4-10-10 0 PaulMoloney 71
(Evan Williams) *sme prog over 6f out but mainly towards rr* **14/1**
40 **9** *3/4* **Blue Lovell (FR)**[38] 4124 5-10-7 0 IanPopham(3) 71
(Caroline Keevil) *chsd ldrs: pushed along 1/2-way: wknd 6f out* **50/1**
10 *1* **Hawk Run** 5-11-3 0 RichieMcLernon 77
(Jonjo O'Neill) *a towards rr* **33/1**
000 **11** *3 1/2* **Gypsy Moth (IRE)**[15] 4561 5-10-10 0 (t) WillKennedy 67
(Caroline Keevil) *led for 6f: styd prom: rdn and wknd over 4f out* **50/1**
12 *18* **Barrison** 4-10-10 0 GerardTumelty 50
(Simon Earle) *a in rr: t.o* **66/1**
0 **P** **Ashbourne Folly (IRE)**[63] 3651 5-10-10 0 NathanSweeney(7) —
(Bob Buckler) *mid-div tl over 6f out: sn p.u: lame* **50/1**

(-5.00) **Going Correction** -0.375s/f (Good)
WFA 4 from 5yo+ 7lb **13** Ran SP% **116.4**
Speed ratings: **96,93,90,90,88 85,84,77,76,76 74,66,—**
totesuper7: Win: Not won. Place: Not won CSF £52.63 TOTE £10.60: £2.00, £2.00, £2.20; EX 54.60.
Owner Mrs J E Purdie **Bred** Mrs J E Purdie **Trained** Brayford, Devon

FOCUS
An open-looking bumper which should produce future winners. The winner looks a decent recruit and the form has a solid look.

NOTEBOOK
Mr Hooper travelled kindly before staying on nicely to dispose of his rivals in the manner of a good horse. Related to staying chasers, he looks a fair prospect who should stay further. His stable is now 7-40 with bumper debutants here in recent seasons. (op 6-1)
Gospel Preacher, runner up on debut before a disappointing favourite last time, ran much better here, knuckling down for pressure without managing to reel in the impressive winner. He has shown some fair form and rates a good marker, who should land a similar event. (op 5-1)
Mike Towey(IRE), well backed, was touched off at Ffos Las earlier this month and again ran his race, but he was just beaten by superior horses. He could win a minor contest. (op 15-2)
Black Thunder(FR), from the family of the smart Tataniano, raced extremely green and was under pressure some way out. He hung left when asked for his effort, before running on strongly, just failing to gain third. He can build on this debut and can land a bumper in due course. His powerful stable is now 7-14 with newcomers here and he rates one to keep an eye on. (tchd 4-1)
Five Rivers(IRE), nibbled at in the market, raced a tad keenly and again bumped into a few fair sorts. (op 8-1 tchd 6-1)
Ashbourne Folly(IRE) Official explanation: vet said gelding pulled up lame right-fore
T/Plt: £12.40 to a £1 stake. Pool:£56,608.73 - 3,315.43 winning tickets T/Qpdt: £3.80 to a £1 stake. Pool:£3,646.97 - 698.21 winning tickets TM

3617 SOUTHWELL (L-H)

Thursday, March 24

OFFICIAL GOING: Good (7.8)
Golf Club bend on inside, home straight bend on outside.
Wind: almost nil Weather: fine and sunny, warm

4971 ROY BOYLES 80TH BIRTHDAY H'CAP CHASE (19 fncs) 3m 110y
2:00 (2:00) (Class 4) (0-115,113) 5-Y-0+ **£2,667** (£783; £391; £195)

Form RPR
125R **1** **Shammy Buskins**[11] 4749 9-11-12 **113** (p) AndrewThornton 125+
(Lawney Hill) *reluctant to jump off and rdr set off briefly w no irons: hdwy to trck ldrs 7th: led on bit 4 out: clr next: heavily eased run-in* **5/1**[3]
2463 **2** *17* **Rebel Melody (IRE)**[24] 4402 10-11-3 **107** (bt) PeterToole(3) 96
(Charlie Mann) *led to 2nd: chsd ldr: one pce fr 4 out* **15/8**[1]
3 *11* **Melchizedek (IRE)**[49] 3914 7-10-3 **97** PeterCarberry(7) 76
(Rachel Hobbs) *in rr: outpcd 12th: wnt poor 3rd after 4 out: one pce: b.b.v* **6/1**
P612 **4** *2 1/2* **Backfromthecongo (IRE)**[28] 4313 10-11-0 **108** (bt) JakeGreenall(7) 85
(Richard Lee) *chsd ldrs: drvn 7th: lost pl next: bhd fr 13th: t.o 3 out* **9/4**[2]
4100 **5** *3/4* **Ovthenight (IRE)**[28] 4313 6-11-1 **109** (b) MissGAndrews(7) 85
(Pam Sly) *led 2nd: mstke and hdd 13th: wknd 15th: poor 4th whn blnd 2 out* **13/2**

6m 29.3s (3.30) **Going Correction** +0.30s/f (Yiel) **5** Ran SP% **109.8**
Speed ratings: **106,100,97,96,96**
CSF £15.14 TOTE £6.80: £2.50, £1.20; EX 16.50.
Owner P J Morgan **Bred** D I Bare **Trained** Aston Rowant, Oxon

FOCUS
A modest handicap chase. The easy winner was value for further.

NOTEBOOK
Shammy Buskins held strong form claims on ground he likes, but coming into the race with a bit to prove having refused to race last time. It was again clear at the start that he wasn't keen to get on with it, but he consented to jump away this time and could be called the winner a long way out, being heavily eased late on. This is his time of year and he may well follow up, but it clearly one to be a bit wary of. (op 11-2)
Rebel Melody(IRE), down 4lb from last time, plugged on at the one pace. (op 9-4 tchd 7-4)
Melchizedek(IRE) ran with some promise, but did reportedly burst a blood vessel on this British debut. Official explanation: trainer's rep said gelding bled from the nose (op 15-2)
Backfromthecongo(IRE) ran a lifeless race, being nudged along and labouring with over a circuit to race. This clearly wasn't his form, but he's now left with a bit to prove. (op 2-1 tchd 5-2)
Ovthenight(IRE) made mistakes and was relegated to last late on. (op 11-2 tchd 7-1)

4972 WEATHERBYS BLOODSTOCK INSURANCE H'CAP CHASE (16 fncs) 2m 4f 110y
2:30 (2:30) (Class 3) (0-120,120) 5-Y-0+ **£4,943** (£1,451; £725; £362)

Form RPR
6231 **1** **Double The Trouble**[13] 4695 10-11-8 **116** NickScholfield 126+
(Andy Turnell) *trckd ldrs: wnt handy 2nd after 4 out: hit next: level last: styd on to ld run-in: drvn rt out* **13/8**[1]
552 **2** *3/4* **Mud Monkey**[18] 4502 7-11-7 **118** (t) TommyPhelan(3) 126
(Claire Dyson) *led: j.rt: drvn 4 out: jnd last: hdd and no ex run-in* **10/3**[2]
P6P0 **3** *24* **Fighting Chance (IRE)**[53] 3841 11-11-10 **118** (t) DarylJacob 104
(Richard Lee) *chsd ldr: wknd after 4 out* **11/2**
U254 **4** *7* **Jocheski (IRE)**[17] 4529 7-11-2 **110** AndrewThornton 89
(Tony Newcombe) *in rr: hdwy and in tch 9th: outpcd and lost pl 12th: sn bhd* **5/1**[3]
P-PP **5** *7* **Leamington Lad (IRE)**[172] 1690 8-11-12 **120** PaddyBrennan 93
(Nigel Twiston-Davies) *nt fluent in rr: reminders 5th: bhd and drvn 9th: t.o 12th* **6/1**

5m 18.0s (3.00) **Going Correction** +0.30s/f (Yiel) **5** Ran SP% **107.5**
Speed ratings: **106,105,96,93,91**
CSF £7.16 TOTE £1.90: £1.60, £1.60; EX 6.60.
Owner L G Kimber **Bred** L G Kimber **Trained** Broad Hinton, Wilts

FOCUS
This concerned only two from the end of the back straight. The winner is rated in line with his easy recent win, with the second pretty much to their mark.

NOTEBOOK
Double The Trouble just picked up best after the last. Although up 8lb, conditions again looked in his favour and he showed a willing attitude under pressure. Connections will try and find him one more race before the season is out. (op 2-1)
Mud Monkey ran a thoroughly game and enthusiastic race. Kicking on from quite a way out, he jumped well in the straight and made sure the winner worked for it, but was just found wanting for acceleration on the flat. (op 3-1 tchd 7-2)
Fighting Chance(IRE) took a step back in the right direction, hanging in there until the end of the back straight. This trip probably stretches him, though. (op 7-1 tchd 15-2)
Jocheski(IRE) made mistakes and ended up well held (op 11-2)
Leamington Lad(IRE) started to lose touch with over a circuit to go and remains in miserable form. (op 4-1)

4973 BETTING SECRETS REVEALED AT RACINGPROFITS.NET OPEN HUNTERS' CHASE (19 fncs) 3m 110y
3:00 (3:00) (Class 6) 5-Y-0+ **£758** (£233; £116)

Form RPR
00/4 **1** **Locksmith**[11] 4748 11-11-1 0 MrRichardCollinson(7) 106
(Mrs S J Stilgoe) *nt fluent in rr: hdwy to chse ldrs after 9th: wnt 2nd 14th: led between last 2: drvn rt out* **8/1**
/441 **2** *1 1/4* **The General Lee (IRE)**[21] 4442 9-11-5 104 MissLBrooke(7) 109
(Phillip Rowley) *trckd ldrs: led 6th: hdd between last 2: kpt on run-in: no ex* **4/1**[3]
U **3** *1* **Gort Na Lea (IRE)**[6] 4857 8-11-1 0 MrGHMBartlett(7) 104
(A J Kennedy, Ire) *in rr-div: hdwy to 9th: wnt modest 3rd appr 3 out: chsng ldng pair between last 2: styd on run-in* **28/1**
22 **4** *20* **Poppy Day**[26] 8-10-8 95 MissJoannaMason(7) 79+
(I M Mason) *in rr-div: dropped rt bk after 9th: t.o 4 out: distant 7th next: kpt on to take poor 4th run-in* **10/3**[1]
-P24 **5** *3 1/4* **Breaking Silence (IRE)**[29] 4286 10-12-2 117 (t) MrAJBerry 92
(Jonjo O'Neill) *mid-div: reminders 8th: wnt prom 13th: wknd 15th* **7/2**[2]
30/5 **6** *2 1/2* **Broken Reed (IRE)**[11] 4750 12-11-1 97 MrOWadlow(7) 81
(R Hirons) *prom: lost pl after 12th: sn bhd: t.o 3 out* **18/1**
24-P **7** *6* **Goscar Rock (IRE)**[6] 4857 10-11-8 0 MrPYork 76
(P Hall) *led to 6th: chsd ldrs: wknd 4 out* **11/1**
8 *1 1/4* **Kilcascan**[11] 7-11-1 0 MissHannahWatson(7) 74
(Rosemary Gasson) *in rr: sme hdwy 12th: sn wknd: t.o 3 out* **9/1**
PPP- **P** **Copper Bay (IRE)**[387] 4366 9-11-1 0 MrJABest(7) —
(Mrs C M James) *promy: lost pl 8th: t.o whn p.u bef 13th* **50/1**
PP06 **P** **Cash In Hand (IRE)**[11] 4750 11-11-1 72 (b) MrWTelfer(7) —
(R Harvey) *chsd ldrs: lost pl 11th: t.o 14th: p.u bef 3 out* **40/1**
P1-P **P** **Over To Joe**[18] 11-11-9 0 (p) MrGBrewer(3) —
(C C Pimlott) *in rr: drvn 12th: bhd next: t.o whn p.u bef 4 out* **20/1**
P **Cottage River (IRE)**[718] 11-11-3 0 MrPJTolman(5) —
(P Hall) *prom: reminders 5th: lost pl next: bhd fr 10th: blnd 13th: t.o whn p.u bef 15th* **33/1**
P-PF **P** **Prelude D'Estruval (FR)**[314] 317 8-11-1 74 (b) MrNSlatter(7) —
(Miss N L Elliott) *chsd ldrs: lost pl 13th: t.o whn p.u bef 15th* **80/1**

6m 33.4s (7.40) **Going Correction** +0.30s/f (Yiel) **13** Ran SP% **116.8**
Speed ratings: **100,99,99,92,91 91,89,88,—,— —,—,—**
toteswingers:1&2:£8.00, 1&3:£10.90, 2&3:£24.90 CSF £37.86 TOTE £6.90: £2.00, £2.30, £4.80; EX 70.90.
Owner Mrs S J Stilgoe **Bred** The Queen **Trained** Hutton-Le-Hole, North Yorks
■ Sarah Jane Stilgoe's first winner under rules.

FOCUS
The front three drew clear in this hunters' chase. The winner was rated 140+ in his youth and the form is rated through the second's recent win.

NOTEBOOK
Locksmith, a former useful chaser with Martin Pipe, was well held on his recent debut in this sphere and looked a suspect stayer on this step up to 3m. He moved prominent down the back, travelling strongly, and found plenty once in front to register his first win in almost four years. On this evidence he can win again, with a drop back in trip of no inconvenience. (op 9-1)
The General Lee(IRE) took over a long way from the finish and had everything bar the winner beaten off by the end of the back straight. However, despite a spirited rally once headed, he was always booked for second. (op 9-2)
Gort Na Lea(IRE), who unseated his rider at Fakenham last week, got too far back here, but did run on well down the straight and was closing as they crossed the line. (op 25-1)
Poppy Day could have done with more of a test at the distance. (op 11-4)
Breaking Silence(IRE) should have done better on this return to quicker ground and seems to have lost his form. (op 4-1)
Copper Bay(IRE) Official explanation: jockey said gelding stopped quickly

4974 SOUTHWELL-RACECOURSE.CO.UK "NATIONAL HUNT" MAIDEN HURDLE (11 hdls) 2m 4f 110y
3:35 (3:35) (Class 4) 4-Y-0+ **£2,329** (£678; £339)

Form RPR
000 **1** **Traffic Chaos (IRE)**[19] 4489 6-10-12 0 (t) PeterToole(3) 105
(Charlie Mann) *chsd ldrs: styd on fr 2 out: led appr last: drvn clr run-in* **16/1**
0006 **2** *5* **Barnack**[34] 4180 5-11-1 95 DavidEngland 103+
(Pam Sly) *chsd ldrs: led 2 out: hdd and hld whn stmbld landing last* **11/1**
24 **3** *4 1/2* **Roll The Dice (IRE)**[35] 4164 5-10-10 0 MattGriffiths(5) 96
(Philip Hobbs) *trckd ldrs: outpcd appr 2 out: kpt on one pce* **11/2**[3]
0-0P **4** *5* **Amroth Bay**[61] 3678 7-11-1 0 AlanO'Keeffe 92+
(Jennie Candlish) *hld up towards rr: hdwy 3 out: outpcd appr next: kpt on appr last* **9/1**
2536 **5** *5* **Dontupsettherhythm (IRE)**[71] 3505 6-10-12 0 AdamPogson(3) 97+
(Charles Pogson) *j.rt: led: hdd 2 out: 4th and wkng whn eased appr last* **13/2**
455 **6** *2 1/4* **Tribal Dance (IRE)**[22] 4422 5-11-1 0 DarylJacob 85
(Ben Case) *in rr-div: hdwy 6th: outpcd 3 out: kpt on fr next* **11/1**

2-4S **7** *2* **Wizard Of Odds**[39] 9-10-12 109 .... MrDHDunsdon(3) 83
(Tom Gretton) *t.k.h in mid-div: hit 8th: outpcd next: kpt on steadily fr 2 out* **9/2**[2]

-P44 **8** *5* **Ballagio (IRE)**[21] 4437 6-11-1 110 .... (t) SeanQuinlan 81
(Kim Bailey) *trckd ldrs: lost pl appr 2 out* **3/1**[1]

5P4U **9** *18* **Rester Vrai (FR)**[23] 4414 6-10-8 0 .... JoeCornwall(7) 62
(John Cornwall) *mid-div: drvn 4th: bhd fr 8th* **100/1**

0 **10** *72* **Pretty Penny**[16] 4535 7-10-8 0 .... WarrenMarston —
(Martin Keighley) *chsd ldrs: lost pl 6th: t.o 3 out: virtually p.u appr next: eventually completed* **33/1**

11 *23* **Eco Boxer (IRE)**[312] 7-10-8 0 .... HenryBrooke(7) —
(Nick Kent) *s.s: t.k.h: jnd ldrs 2nd: wknd qckly 8th: t.o 2 out: eventually completed* **20/1**

12 *15* **Homeleigh Sir** 7-10-12 0 .... JamesHalliday(3) —
(Shaun Harris) *s.s: in rr: t.o 8th: eventually completed* **100/1**

0/P **P** **Lisa's Enigma**[98] 2985 8-10-10 0 .... (bt[1]) PaulCallaghan(5) —
(Shaun Harris) *s.v.s: in last: detached 5th: t.o 7th: p.u bef next: lame* **150/1**

5m 14.1s (3.40) **Going Correction** +0.30s/f (Yiel) **13** Ran SP% **114.8**
Speed ratings (Par 105): **105,103,101,99,97 96,95,94,87,59 51,45,—**
toteswingers:1&2:£19.30, 1&3:£15.70, 2&3:£9.00 CSF £166.89 TOTE £21.10: £4.40, £4.20, £2.70; EX 253.20.

Owner C Hunter,D Batten,S Beccle,T Stapleton **Bred** Patrick Doyle **Trained** Upper Lambourn, Berks

FOCUS

A wide-open maiden hurdle. Big steps up from the first two, and the fifth is worth a lot more than the bare mark.

NOTEBOOK

Traffic Chaos(IRE), who won the last of his six starts in points, had been well held over hurdles to date, but the switch to a sounder surface saw him in a completely different light and he stayed on strongest down the straight. There should be more to come. (op 20-1)

Barnack was another to leave his previous effort behind. He looked the likely winner at one stage, but was being challenged when making a complete mess of the last, and could soon find no extra. He could be one for handicaps. (op 10-1)

Roll The Dice(IRE), weak in the market on this hurdles debut, cruised into contention down the back, but came under pressure before the straight and proved very one paced. He clearly needs a stiffer test. (op 5-1 tchd 6-1)

Amroth Bay, making his debut for the yard, made some late headway and will be of interest once handicapping. (tchd 10-1)

Dontupsettherhythm(IRE) ran well for a long way and is now eligible for handicaps. (op 15-2)

Tribal Dance(IRE) was keeping on and should do better in time. (tchd 10-1)

Wizard Of Odds couldn't quicken under pressure and ran below expectations. The Stewards enquired into his performance and were offered the explanation that he finished sore behind. Official explanation: jockey said, regarding running and riding, that his orders were to ride the race as he found it and set off in a prominent position, there was little early pace and the gelding began to run free, he decided to drop back through the field and allow it to settle, he was happy until it made a mistake at the 4th last, lost ground and was forced wide round the final bend, asked for an effort after 2nd last but when it's stride shortened, he was concerned for its welfare and held it together to the line; trainer confirmed adding that it had a recurring back problem; vet said that on 2nd examination it had become significantly stiff behind. (op 4-1)

Ballagio(IRE), who made a notable blunder at the first, held an ideal sit on the inside, but made more mistakes racing down the back and had nothing left by the time they reached the straight. This was a disappointing effort. (op 4-1)

Lisa's Enigma Official explanation: trainer said gelding had a breathing problem and pulled up lame

4975 MEMBERSHIP OF SOUTHWELL GOLF CLUB CLAIMING HURDLE (11 hdls) 2m 4f 110y

4:10 (4:10) (Class 5) 4-Y-0+ **£1,541** (£449; £224)

Form RPR

P2U1 **1** **Abstract Art (USA)**[29] 4289 8-10-13 115 .... (p) PeterCarberry(7) 109+
(Rachel Hobbs) *trckd ldrs: t.k.h: styd on to ld 2 out: 8 l ahd last: pushed out* **7/4**[1]

2P00 **2** *3 ½* **Night Orbit**[11] 4742 7-11-2 120 .... CharlieWallis(7) 106
(Julia Feilden) *chsd ldrs: sn drvn along: lost pl 3rd: hdwy 3 out: styd on to take n.d 2nd last 50yds* **13/2**

P6P0 **3** *½* **Westlin' Winds (IRE)**[19] 4485 5-11-5 125 .... (tp) JakeGreenall(7) 110
(Charles Egerton) *chsd ldrs: blnd 7th: kpt on fr 2 out: tk n.d 2nd last* **5/2**[2]

2/10 **4** *2 ¾* **Hernando's Boy**[100] 2940 10-11-5 111 .... JamesReveley 102
(Keith Reveley) *trckd ldrs: jnd ldr 4th: led appr 3 out: hdd 2 out: one pce: fdd last* **11/2**[3]

0/03 **5** *14* **Kyathos (GER)**[15] 4549 10-10-12 66 .... (p) MrGRSmith(7) 88
(David Thompson) *hld up towards rr: hdwy to trck ldrs 4th: wknd 3 out* **100/1**

P446 **6** *29* **Vasodilator (IRE)**[141] 2152 8-11-4 0 .... MichaelMurphy(3) 62
(Pat Murphy) *led: hdd appr 3 out: wknd qckly: t.o next* **33/1**

/P0- **U** **Tell Henry (IRE)**[586] 1215 11-11-2 0 .... JamesHalliday(3) —
(C I Ratcliffe) *prom: uns rdr 2nd* **16/1**

UUUU **P** **King Caine (IRE)**[31] 4265 9-11-6 117 .... PaddyBrennan —
(Alan Jones) *hld up in rr: sme hdwy 7th: sn wknd: t.o whn p.u bef 2 out* **9/1**

/P50 **P** **Frosty Spring**[9] 4795 8-10-5 0 .... (p) KyleJames(7) —
(David Thompson) *in rr: reminders 4th: sn bhd: t.o whn p.u bef 2 out* **100/1**

5m 16.1s (5.40) **Going Correction** +0.30s/f (Yiel) **9** Ran SP% **114.5**
Speed ratings (Par 103): **101,99,99,98,93 82,—,—,—**
toteswingers:1&2:£3.20, 1&3:£3.30, 2&3:£4.50 CSF £13.87 TOTE £3.70: £1.50, £2.80, £1.10; EX 15.90.Westlin' Winds was claimed Mr Dan Gilbert for £12,000.

Owner Hills Of Ledbury (Aga) **Bred** Jenny L Mills **Trained** Hanley Swan, Worcs

FOCUS

Quite a competitive claimer. The winner is rated 6lb off his Ludlow winning mark with the modest fifth plenty close enough.

NOTEBOOK

Abstract Art(USA), although unable to lead, still ran out a ready winner, taking over with a quick jump two out and racing clear. He wasn't doing a lot in front late on, so can be rated better than the bare form, and probably has it in him to win back in handicap company. (op 2-1 tchd 13-8)

Night Orbit appreciated the drop in grade and came out best in the battle for second. (op 8-1 tchd 9-1 and 6-1)

Westlin' Winds(IRE) was under pressure a long way out, but he did respond and boxed on for a place. (op 3-1)

Hernando's Boy scored at this level earlier in the season and he tried to press on down the back, but lost all momentum when James Reveley slowed him right down coming to the first in the straight, at which he was untidy, and was then quickly beaten. (op 9-2 tchd 6-1)

King Caine(IRE) Official explanation: jockey said gelding lost its action and pulled up

4976 DINE IN THE PANTRY H'CAP HURDLE (13 hdls) 3m 110y

4:45 (4:45) (Class 5) (0-90,90) 4-Y-0+ **£1,541** (£449; £224)

Form RPR

65P **1** **Reefer Beefer (IRE)**[80] 3378 6-11-12 90 .... AndrewThornton 105+
(Tony Newcombe) *hld up: stdy hdwy 9th: led after 3 out: 4 l ahd last: drvn out* **7/1**[3]

0000 **2** *8* **Pickworth (IRE)**[28] 4302 6-11-8 86 .... JamesReveley 95
(Philip Kirby) *prom: chsd ldrs 7th: wnt 2nd appr 2 out: kpt on same pce appr last* **9/1**

5-22 **3** *19* **Supreme Team (IRE)**[39] 4098 8-10-6 77 .... PeterHatton(7) 71
(Louise Davis) *chsd ldrs: drvn 6th: outpcd 3 out: kpt on to take poor 3rd last* **7/2**[2]

-4P6 **4** *6* **Thompson**[37] 4130 7-11-6 84 .... TomSiddall 70
(Richard Phillips) *w ldrs: led 4th: hit 9th: hdd 3 out: sn lost pl* **12/1**

5034 **5** *1 ½* **Chadwell Spring (IRE)**[15] 4548 5-9-7 64 .... (b) HenryBrooke(7) 48
(Mike Sowersby) *hld up in rr: hdwy 9th: led 3 out: sn hdd: fdd appr next: wknd run-in* **14/1**

0333 **6** *31* **Home She Goes (IRE)**[11] 4741 9-11-9 90 .... AdamPogson(3) 46
(Charles Pogson) *chsd ldrs: sn lost pl 3 out: bhd whn eased next: t.o* **8/1**

RPP0 **R** **Orpen Bid (IRE)**[58] 3727 6-10-0 67 .... CharlieStudd(3) —
(Michael Mullineaux) *ref to r: lft s* **20/1**

P400 **P** **Smiling Applause**[159] 1860 12-9-9 66 .... (p) KillianMoore(7) —
(Harry Chisman) *in rr: sn drvn along: t.o 6th: p.u after next* **16/1**

0/P5 **P** **Galandora**[10] 4787 11-9-13 66 .... (t) EamonDehdashti(3) —
(Dr Jeremy Naylor) *chsd ldrs: reminders 8th: sn bhd: t.o 10th: p.u bef 2 out* **12/1**

P0P6 **P** **Kirkum (IRE)**[8] 4812 6-9-8 65 oh34 ow1 .... MissCareyWilliamson(7) —
(Diana Weeden) *in rr: drvn 7th: sn bhd: t.o whn p.u bef 2 out* **100/1**

-22F **P** **Saulty Max (IRE)**[24] 4403 7-11-12 90 .... (p) PaddyBrennan —
(Nigel Twiston-Davies) *led to 4th: blnd 10th: wknd rapidly next: sn wl bhd: t.o whn p.u bef next* **10/3**[1]

0560 **P** **First Spirit**[27] 4330 5-11-9 87 .... CharliePoste —
(Robin Dickin) *hld up in rr: hdwy to chse ldrs 8th: lost pl after 10th: sn bhd: t.o whn p.u bef 2 out* **33/1**

6m 25.9s (18.40) **Going Correction** +0.30s/f (Yiel) **12** Ran SP% **115.5**
Speed ratings (Par 103): **82,79,73,71,70 61,—,—,—,— —,—**
toteswingers:1&2:£15.80, 1&3:£8.50, 2&3:£7.40 CSF £65.66 CT £258.29 TOTE £10.10: £2.90, £3.00, £1.70; EX 63.70.

Owner B G C Partnership **Bred** Miss Laura Doran **Trained** Yarnscombe, Devon

FOCUS

A moderate handicap hurdle. The easy winner is rated up the best part of a stone.

NOTEBOOK

Reefer Beefer(IRE), off since pulling up on his heavy-ground handicap debut in January, was a different proposition over this longer trip on faster ground, travelling strongly throughout and outstaying his rivals down the straight. He's got plenty of size about him and can go on to better things. Official explanation: trainer said, regarding apparent improvement in form, that the gelding appeared to be better suited by the longer trip. (op 13-2 tchd 8-1)

Pickworth(IRE) left her previous form behind, closing up to challenge turning for home, but not staying on as well as the winner.

Supreme Team(IRE) kept plugging away on ground he probably found a touch fast. (op 9-2)

Thompson ran on again having lost his position and got behind. (op 10-1)

Chadwell Spring(IRE) moved nicely into contention, but couldn't race on in the straight, her stamina appearing to run out. (op 20-1)

Home She Goes(IRE), the only other to complete, was below her best on this return to hurdles. (tchd 15-2)

Galandora Official explanation: trainer said mare had a breathing problem (op 7-2 tchd 3-1)

Saulty Max(IRE) looked the winner when falling at Plumpton last time and may have still been feeling the effects of that spill here, dropping right out before pulling up. (op 7-2 tchd 3-1)

4977 GOLF AND RACING AT SOUTHWELL H'CAP HURDLE (9 hdls) 2m

5:20 (5:20) (Class 4) (0-105,104) 4-Y-0+ **£2,329** (£678; £339)

Form RPR

0-5F **1** **The Quantum Kid**[40] 4076 7-11-3 95 .... CharliePoste 98+
(Robin Dickin) *mde all: hld on gamely run-in* **8/1**

0605 **2** *¾* **The Tiddly Tadpole**[18] 4506 6-10-9 94 .... HenryBrooke(7) 95
(Simon West) *chsd ldrs: drvn 5th: outpcd 3 out: kpt on appr next: styd on run-in: tk 2nd nr fin* **7/1**[3]

25-6 **3** *½* **Golden Button (IRE)**[80] 3367 6-11-0 92 .... (t) TomSiddall 96+
(Kim Bailey) *nt fluent in rr: bhd fr 6th: hdwy and modest 5th appr 2 out: styd on wl appr last: tk 3rd cl home* **7/2**[1]

0405 **4** *nk* **Takaatuf (IRE)**[9] 4797 5-11-10 102 .... AndrewThornton 102
(John Hellens) *trckd ldrs: chsd wnr sn after three out: edgd lft between last 2: kpt on same pce run-in* **9/2**[2]

6123 **5** *nk* **Bromhead (USA)**[15] 4548 5-11-5 97 .... JamesReveley 99
(Kevin Morgan) *hld up in rr: hdwy to trck ldrs 5th: drvn 3 out: swtchd rt between last 2: cl 3rd whn mstke last: kpt on same pce* **7/2**[1]

-000 **6** *19* **King Of The Titans (IRE)**[29] 2128 8-11-5 104 .... MrMatthewSmith(7) 87
(Patrick Gilligan) *in tch: hdwy to chse ldrs 3 out: lost pl appr next: sn bhd* **25/1**

0350 **P** **Dance Sauvage**[15] 4550 8-9-12 79 ow1 .... (b) JamesHalliday(3) —
(Mike Sowersby) *chsd ldrs 2nd: drvn 5th: lost pl appr 3 out: t.o whn p.u bef next* **9/2**[2]

2600 **P** **Coeur De Lionne (IRE)**[28] 4310 7-11-0 99 .... (t) MrWTelfer(7) —
(Mrs Pauline Harkin) *chsd ldrs: reminders 6th: sn lost pl: t.o whn p.u bef 2 out* **33/1**

4m 5.70s (8.60) **Going Correction** +0.30s/f (Yiel) **8** Ran SP% **111.2**
Speed ratings (Par 105): **90,89,89,89,89 79,—,—**
toteswingers:1&2:£14.10, 1&3:£5.00, 2&3:£7.40 CSF £58.33 CT £224.70 TOTE £12.40: £3.50, £3.10, £1.10; EX 50.50.

Owner Miss E J Wright **Bred** Brick Kiln Stud & Lariston Apartments Ltd **Trained** Atherstone on Stour, Warwicks

FOCUS

A low-grade handicap hurdle that produced a bunch finish. Ordinary but sound form.

NOTEBOOK

The Quantum Kid showed much-improved form for this quicker surface and held on well after the last. This was only his fifth attempt over hurdles and he could win again through the summer. (tchd 15-2)

The Tiddly Tadpole seemed helped by the drop in trip, having not got home at Sedgefield last time. (op 11-2)

Golden Button(IRE) would almost certainly have won had she not got so far back. For all that she jumped a bit big early, she was allowed to drift back and had too much running to do in the straight, albeit she may well have got up anyway had she not messed up the last. (tchd 3-1 and 4-1)

Takaatuf(IRE) moved well for a long way until slowly fading in the straight. (tchd 5-1)

Bromhead(USA) held every chance and was a little disappointing, finding no extra following a bad blunder at the last. (op 4-1)
T/Jkpt: Not won. T/Plt: £83.40 to a £1 stake. Pool:£63,125.98 - 552.36 winning tickets T/Qpdt: £40.70 to a £1 stake. Pool:£4,404.28 - 79.90 winning tickets WG

4978 - 4985a (Foreign Racing) - See Raceform Interactive

4485 NEWBURY (L-H)
Friday, March 25

OFFICIAL GOING: Good
Rail realignment increased hurdle races by 26metres per circuit, and chase races by 20metres per circuit.
Wind: Virtually nile Weather: Sunny

4986 EVENTS BAR MANAGEMENT MAIDEN HURDLE (10 hdls) 2m 5f
2:10 (2:11) (Class 3) 4-Y-0+ **£3,903** (£1,146; £573; £286)

Form RPR
6P **1** **Mizen Station (IRE)**[48] 3952 6-11-1 0 LeightonAspell 120
(Oliver Sherwood) *w ldr: chal 3 out: rdn appr 2 out: styd on wl to take slt ld last: hld on all out* **25/1**

-246 **2** *nk* **Bless The Wings (IRE)**[35] 4189 6-11-1 112 RobertThornton 120
(Alan King) *in tch: hdwy to trck ldrs fr 4 out: chal fr 3 out: disp cl 2nd last: prssed wnr fnl 75yds but a jst hld* **11/4**[2]

-402 **3** *4 1/2* **Easter Meteor**[54] 3836 5-11-1 119 JackDoyle 118+
(Emma Lavelle) *set mod pce: jnd and hit 3 out: stl hrd pressed whn hit next: narrowly hdd last: styd on to dispute cl 2nd run-in: wknd fnl 75yds* **11/8**[1]

0244 **4** *20* **Bardolf (IRE)**[28] 4332 5-11-1 0 WayneHutchinson 98
(Alan King) *in tch: hdwy 4 out: rdn 3 out and outpcd: styd on to take wl hld 4th nr fin* **14/1**

662 **5** *3/4* **Wiesentraum (GER)**[19] 4500 5-11-1 0 DominicElsworth 97
(Lucy Wadham) *t.k.h: chsd ldrs: ev ch and rdn 3 out: wknd and hung lft fr 2 out: no ch whn edgd rt run-in: lost mod 4th cl home* **16/1**

24 **6** *3 3/4* **Oasis Knight (IRE)**[20] 4479 5-11-1 0 (p) BarryGeraghty 94
(Nicky Henderson) *in tch: hit 6th and 4 out: sn rr: rdn and hdwy to press ldrs 3 out: wknd next* **9/2**[3]

5/5 **7** *13* **Kings Flagship**[15] 4676 6-11-1 0 JamesDavies 82
(Chris Down) *chsd ldrs: rdn 3 out: sn wknd* **33/1**

5 **8** *2 1/2* **Two Bob (IRE)**[139] 2222 6-11-1 0 TomO'Brien 82
(Philip Hobbs) *chsd ldrs: blnd 4 out: no ch after* **18/1**

60 **9** *41* **Bravo Riquet (FR)**[13] 4719 5-10-12 0 TommyPhelan(3) 43
(Robin Mathew) *hit 2nd: sn rr: hit 4 out and wl bhd: t.o whn mstke last* **100/1**

000P **P** **Running Upthathill (IRE)**[71] 3530 7-11-1 69 SamThomas —
(Venetia Williams) *rdn and bhd fr 4th: t.o whn p.u bef 2 out* **100/1**

5m 18.3s (-0.70) **Going Correction** -0.15s/f (Good) **10** Ran SP% **113.5**
Speed ratings (Par 107): **95,94,93,85,85 83,78,77,62,—**
toteswingers:1&2 £23.60, 2&3 £2.40, 1&3 £9.70 CSF £92.14 TOTE £32.80: £4.80, £1.50, £1.60; EX 60.20.
Owner Million In Mind Partnership **Bred** John Bowler **Trained** Upper Lambourn, Berks

FOCUS
Rail moved out 26m per circuit on the hurdles course and 20m per circuit on the chase track. Watered ground that was riding good as advertised. This looked a fair maiden hurdle, but there wasn't a lot of depth to it and the first three came clear. They went a steady pace for the first half of the contest and the time was 18 seconds outside the Racing Post standard, but a contributory factor was that they stood still for a few seconds after the tape was released. A big step up from the winner and the form could be rated a little higher.

NOTEBOOK
Mizen Station(IRE) was pulled up at Wetherby last time, but an excuse came to light as he was reported to have had a breathing problem. Always up with the pace, he looked held two from home but fought his way to the front on the run-in for a game victory. The ground clearly suited and he will benefit from going over 3m in time. He looks a chasing type. (op 33-1)
Bless The Wings(IRE), who appreciated the drop back in trip and better surface, had become warm in the preliminaries. He improved to hold every chance and showed the right attitude under pressure, just failing to peg back the winner.
Easter Meteor was the one to beat on his second to Cucumber Run at Hereford. Travelling well and making the running, he looked set to win two out when still on the bridle, but was worn down on the flat and faded in the last 75 yards. The ground should have suited. (op 15-8)
Bardolf(IRE) was outpaced by the leaders from the home turn but plugged on. He looks a stayer and 3m will suit him. (op 12-1)
Wiesentraum(GER) went well until coming off the bridle two out and fading. He carried his head slightly to one side. (op 14-1)
Oasis Knight(IRE) has his quirks and headgear was on for the first time over hurdles. He did not seem to get home and hasn't built on his debut second to Al Ferof here. (op 4-1)
Two Bob(IRE) was in trouble after a mistake at the last down the back on this hurdles debut, but he is out of a smart jumper and may do better next term. (tchd 16-1)

4987 WISE CATERING LTD H'CAP CHASE (17 fncs) 2m 6f 110y
2:40 (2:41) (Class 3) (0-130,128) 5-Y-0 **£4,752** (£1,404; £702; £351; £175)

Form RPR
5-20 **1** **Calusa Caldera (IRE)**[22] 4440 9-11-3 119 (p) TomO'Brien 134+
(Philip Hobbs) *tendency to jump rt: trckd ldr: slt advantage 4 out: pushed clr after 3 out: styd on wl* **11/1**

42F2 **2** *13* **Ravethebrave (IRE)**[42] 4054 7-11-12 128 RobertThornton 129
(Alan King) *blnd 1st: in tch: chsd ldrs fr 8th: tendency to jump rt fr 10th: blnd 4 out: sn u.p: styd on fr last to take wl-hld 2nd fnl 120yds* **7/2**[2]

21PP **3** *1* **Ray Mond**[35] 4181 10-11-6 125 AlexMerriam(3) 127+
(Neil King) *led and j. bdly rt thrght: hit 11th: rdn 13th: narrowly hdd 4 out: btn fr next: lost wl hld 2nd fnl 120yds* **18/1**

1601 **4** *15* **Flemish Invader (IRE)**[19] 4502 8-11-6 122 PaddyBrennan 108
(Nigel Twiston-Davies) *j. bdly rt thrght: chsd ldrs to 12th: no ch whn veered bdly rt 13th and again 3 out* **8/1**

0344 **5** *5* **Special Occasion**[20] 4490 7-11-5 121 DarylJacob 102
(Caroline Keevil) *j.rt: hit 8th and bhd: no ch fr 11th* **18/1**

3-4P **P** **Emperor Concerto**[131] 2395 8-11-4 120 LeightonAspell —
(Lucy Wadham) *tendency to jump rt: a bhd: t.o 12th: p.u bef 3 out* **15/2**[3]

4642 **P** **Max Bygraves**[22] 4440 8-11-8 124 JasonMaguire —
(Kim Bailey) *mstke 1st and nvr really travelling after: tendency to jump rt: lost tch 9th: t.o whn p.u bef 13th* **3/1**[1]

1243 **F** **Inside Dealer (IRE)**[13] 4730 7-11-8 124 JoeTizzard —
(Colin Tizzard) *j.rt: chsd ldrs: wkng into mod 5th whn fell 13th* **3/1**[1]

5m 47.0s (-3.30) **Going Correction** -0.15s/f (Good) **8** Ran SP% **114.0**
Speed ratings: **99,94,94,88,87 —,—,—**
toteswingers:1&2 £10.60, 2&3 £21.80, 1&3 £28.00 CSF £50.25 CT £694.10 TOTE £11.60: £2.60, £1.50, £2.40; EX 34.70.
Owner Peter Luff **Bred** B D Darrer **Trained** Withycombe, Somerset

FOCUS
A fair handicap chase run at a sound gallop. The long-time leader jumped badly right, prompting most of the others to imitate him. Only three remained in contention turning into the home straight and, with the two joint favourites among the disappointments, this form may not prove too strong. A step up from the winner with the first two a few pounds below their best.

NOTEBOOK
Calusa Caldera(IRE) ran no sort of race at Ludlow but bounced back in the first-time cheekpieces, leading at the first up the straight and staying on strongly. While he ran out a wide-margin winner, it was a race that rather fell apart and it remains to be seen if he can back this up. Official explanation: trainer said, regarding apparent improvement in form, that the gelding appeared better suited by first-time cheek pieces. (op 12-1)
Ravethebrave(IRE) was one-paced from the turn in but did plug on to take second on the flat. He is largely consistent and on this showing he could be worth another try over 3m. (op 4-1)
Ray Mond made a lot of the running, jumping each fence badly out to his right, and could not counter once headed at the first in the straight. This was a better effort, but he remains 8lb higher than for his last win. (tchd 20-1)
Flemish Invader(IRE) was comfortably held off this 7lb higher mark and it could be that he will prove happier back on a right-handed track.
Emperor Concerto, for whom hold-up tactics failed to have the desired effect, never figured. (op 7-2)
Max Bygraves was never going kindly and eventually pulled up. (op 7-2)
Inside Dealer(IRE) was already beaten when coming down at the cross fence. (op 7-2)

4988 RACING UK FOR YOUR PUB CALL 0870 351 8834 H'CAP HURDLE (12 hdls) 3m 110y
3:15 (3:15) (Class 4) (0-115,115) 4-Y-0+ **£2,602** (£764; £382; £190)

Form RPR
0/60 **1** **Counting House (IRE)**[120] 2636 8-11-12 115 JasonMaguire 127+
(Jim Old) *hld up in rr: hdwy 4 out: trckd ldr 2 out: led last: drvn clr run-in* **22/1**

-42F **2** *8* **Master Eddy**[17] 4538 11-11-7 110 DavidEngland 114
(Shaun Lycett) *in tch: rn in snatches and rdn along fr 6th: a rt there and kpt on u.p fr 3 out: chsd wnr run-in but no imp* **14/1**

3043 **3** *5* **Red Mile (FR)**[22] 4446 6-11-9 112 JackDoyle 113
(Emma Lavelle) *pressed ldrs: led 5th: narrowly hdd 8th: styd upsides tl slt ld again 3 out: hdd appr last: wknd and lost 2nd run-in* **15/2**[3]

2013 **4** *11* **Dune Shine**[26] 4375 6-11-7 110 LeightonAspell 100
(Oliver Sherwood) *in rr: hdwy appr 3 out: styd on u.p to take 4th run-in but nvr nr ldrs* **12/1**

041 **5** *8* **Kasban**[20] 4481 7-11-2 112 (t) TrevorWhelan(7) 94
(Luke Dace) *pressed ldrs: upsides fr 6th tl wknd appr 3 out* **9/2**[2]

040 **6** *dist* **Cool Strike (UAE)**[33] 4200 5-11-4 107 SamThomas —
(Alex Hales) *a in rr: t.o whn veered bdly lft 2 out* **8/1**

1-52 **F** **Equity Release (IRE)**[12] 4745 10-10-5 101 (t) PeterHatton(7) —
(Louise Davis) *in tch tl wknd 4 out: t.o whn fell last* **25/1**

14-F **P** **Senor Shane (IRE)**[12] 4745 8-11-0 106 (t) CharlieStudd(3) —
(Chris Gordon) *in rr: hit 4th: j. slowly 7th: t.o whn p.u after 3 out: dismntd* **25/1**

5520 **P** **Outlaw Tom (IRE)**[57] 3771 7-11-9 112 (b) PaulMoloney —
(Alex Hales) *slt ld to 5th: wknd after next: t.o 4 out: p.u bef 2 out* **25/1**

0060 **P** **Baccalaureate (FR)**[17] 4536 5-11-2 105 PaddyBrennan —
(Nigel Twiston-Davies) *a in rr: t.o whn p.u bef 2 out* **25/1**

-2P2 **P** **Hong Kong Harry**[26] 4370 7-11-12 115 RobertThornton 100+
(Alan King) *in rr: j. slowly 2nd: hdwy 7th: chsd ldrs fr 4 out: wknd 2 out: p.u and dismntd run-in* **8/1**

-216 **P** **Full Of Joy (IRE)**[57] 3771 6-11-12 115 APMcCoy 100+
(Jonjo O'Neill) *trckd ldrs: slt ld fr 8th to 3 out: stl wl there whn lost action and p.u bef 2 out* **7/2**[1]

0304 **P** **Morcambe**[22] 4439 6-11-7 110 (bt) BarryGeraghty —
(Nicky Henderson) *chsd ldrs tl wknd qckly appr 3 out: t.o whn p.u bef 2 out* **16/1**

2300 **P** **Foynes Island (IRE)**[14] 4700 5-11-1 104 (t) TomO'Brien —
(Philip Hobbs) *in tch tl j. in rr 6th and sn bhd: t.o whn p.u bef 2 out* **16/1**

6m 4.73s (-3.57) **Going Correction** -0.15s/f (Good) **14** Ran SP% **120.2**
Speed ratings (Par 105): **99,96,94,91,88 —,—,—,—,— —,—,—,—**
toteswingers:1&2 £56.70, 2&3 £13.00, 1&3 £35.70 CSF £280.36 CT £2512.97 TOTE £23.20: £5.70, £3.40, £2.70; EX 366.50.
Owner W E Sturt **Bred** Colm McEvoy **Trained** Barbury Castle, Wilts
■ Stewards' Enquiry : David England five-day ban: used whip with excessive frequency (Apr 8-12)

FOCUS
An ordinary handicap hurdle. The first two were well in on old form and there's a case for rating the race a few pounds higher.

NOTEBOOK
Counting House(IRE) had shown little in three starts (one on the Flat) since finishing seventh to Ballyfitz in the Pertemps Final three years previously, but had come down a stone in that period. Under a patient ride, he improved to lead two out before clearing away. He has come to himself this spring and may run at the Cheltenham April meeting. (op 20-1)
Master Eddy, last year's winner was unbeaten in three starts over C&D, those three victories all coming in March and representing all his career wins. Back over hurdles, he was given some sharp reminders early on the final circuit. He responded to pressure to have his chance but lacked the pace of the winner in the latter stages. (tchd 16-1)
Red Mile(FR) raced a lot more prominently than he had in previous races and proved his tactical versatility, holding every chance after racing up with the pace throughout. He handled the quicker ground well. (op 8-1 tchd 9-1)
Dune Shine stayed on steadily from the rear without ever getting to grips with the leaders. He saw the longer trip out well enough. (tchd 11-1)
Kasban was held off 7lb higher than when scoring at Kempton, fading from the third-last after racing up with the pace. (op 6-1 tchd 4-1)
Senor Shane(IRE) Official explanation: jockey said gelding pulled up lame (op 5-1 tchd 10-3)
Hong Kong Harry, fitted with earplugs for the second time and upped in trip, made headway to look a threat three out, but he dropped away from the next and was pulled up lame on the run-in. Official explanation: jockey said gelding pulled up lame (op 5-1 tchd 10-3)
Full Of Joy(IRE) improved to lead in the straight but had just been headed when he was pulled up quickly before the second-last, with something appearing amiss. Official explanation: trainer had no explanation for the poor form shown (op 5-1 tchd 10-3)

4989 OAKLEY COACHBUILDERS NOVICES' H'CAP CHASE (FOR THE BROWN CHAMBERLIN TROPHY) (18 fncs) 3m
3:50 (3:51) (Class 3) (0-130,128) 5-Y-0+ **£4,878** (£1,432; £716; £357)

Form RPR
P-15 **1** **Bai Zhu (IRE)**[118] 2670 7-11-12 128 FelixDeGiles 134
(Nicky Henderson) *mde all: hrd pressed and u.p fr 3 out: styd on wl run-in: jst hld on: all out* **11/4**[1]

6451 **2** *nse* **Winterwood (IRE)**[36] 4160 8-11-0 **116**.............................(v) SamThomas 123+
(Tim Vaughan) *in tch: j. slowly 8th and dropped in rr: hdwy to catch ldrs fr 10th: rdn 3 out and kpt on same pce: hrd drvn: outpcd and 7 l 4th after last: str run fnl 120yds: yds: fin fast: jst failed* **7/1**

00-6 **3** *3/4* **River D'Or (FR)**[21] 4461 6-10-12 **114**.................................... DarylJacob 119
(Paul Nicholls) *chsd wnr to 6th: styd disputing 2nd tl chsd wnr again 14th to 4 out: wnt 2nd after next: rallied to chal last: styd upsides u.p tl no ex fnl 25yds: lost 2nd last strides* **5/1**[3]

/222 **4** *2 3/4* **Patsy Finnegan**[22] 4445 9-11-6 **122**................................ RobertThornton 127
(Alan King) *hit 1st and 3rd: in rr: chsd ldrs 8th: j. slowly 10th: hdwy 13th: chsd ldrs next: wnt narrow 2nd 4 out: stl disputing 2nd 3 out: one pce appr last* **5/1**[3]

3P2P **5** *43* **Persian Run (IRE)**[22] 4445 7-11-5 **121**..............................(tp) JoeTizzard 85
(Colin Tizzard) *chsd ldrs: wnt 2nd 6th tl hit 14th: wknd qckly* **14/1**

1P40 **P** **Darby's Turn (IRE)**[13] 4723 9-11-6 **122**.......................... WarrenMarston —
(Richard Phillips) *in tch whn blnd 6th: hit next: sn wl bhd: t.o whn p.u bef 14th* **33/1**

3-PP **P** **Buffalo Stampede (IRE)**[19] 4504 8-9-7 **102** oh4......... HarryChalloner(7) —
(Venetia Williams) *sn towards rr: bhd whn blnd and rdr lost iron 13th: t.o whn p.u bef 4 out* **10/1**

4F12 **U** **Frankie Anson (IRE)**[56] 3784 7-11-5 **121**............................ BarryKeniry —
(Micky Hammond) *in tch fr 7th: hit 11th: nudged along and styng on in 4 l 6th whn mstke and uns rdr 14th* **4/1**[2]

6m 6.27s (-4.73) **Going Correction** -0.15s/f (Good) **8** Ran SP% **111.2**
Speed ratings: **101,100,100,99,85** —,—,—
toteswingers:1&2 £4.50, 2&3 £6.10, 1&3 £4.40 CSF £21.04 CT £86.73 TOTE £3.10: £1.50, £2.10, £1.60; EX 22.90.
Owner The Perfect Day Partnership **Bred** Coisdeel Syndicate **Trained** Upper Lambourn, Berks
■ Stewards' Enquiry : Sam Thomas two-day ban: used whip with excessive frequency (Apr 10-11)
Felix De Giles caution: used whip with excessive frequency.

FOCUS
A fair novices' handicap chase. A step up from the winner with the second a bit below his recent Ffos Las level.

NOTEBOOK
Bai Zhu(IRE) ◆ made all the running and proved game in fending off the third, but would have lost the race in another stride. He put in a fine round of jumping and, entitled to come on for this first start since the Hennessy meeting, he will be kept on the go in the spring. (op 10-3 tchd 5-2 and 7-2 in places)
Winterwood(IRE), 7lb higher than when winning at Ffos Las, is due to go up another pound. Receiving reminders with a a lap to run, he looked held in fourth taking the last but ran on strongly and very nearly snatched the race. He is perhaps not straightforward but is in good heart at present. (op 5-1)
River D'Or(FR) stepped up on what he showed on his recent chasing debut and only gave best close home after racing in the front rank the whole way. He is worth keeping to 3m. (op 7-1)
Patsy Finnegan, in a handicap for the first time over fences, ran another sound race and his consistency should be rewarded at some point, although he would not want the ground to dry up too much. A mistake at the ditch down the back didn't help his cause. (op 9-2 tchd 11-2 in places)
Persian Run(IRE), tried in cheekpieces and a tongue tie, was still going quite well when he belted the cross fence, five from home. Soon toiling, he still has something to prove. (op 12-1)
Darby's Turn(IRE) Official explanation: trainer said gelding pulled up distressed (op 7-2)
Frankie Anson(IRE) had already started to feel the pinch when unseating at the cross fence. (op 7-2)

4990 COFFEE YARD HANDS AND HEELS" NOVICES' H'CAP HURDLE (RACING EXCELLENCE) (CONDITIONALS/AMATEURS) (10 hdls) 2m 3f
4:25 (4:25) (Class 3) (0-120,120) 4-Y-0+ **£3,903** (£1,146; £573; £286)

Form RPR

-263 **1** **Master Fiddle**[30] 4281 6-11-6 **114**..............................(t) JeremiahMcGrath 123+
(Nicky Henderson) *trckd ldrs led bef 2 out: styd on strly run-in* **9/2**[1]

360P **2** *4* **What An Oscar (IRE)**[85] 3228 6-10-4 **101**........... MrWTwiston-Davies(3) 104+
(Nigel Twiston-Davies) *blnd 1st: sn in tch: pushed along and one pce 3 out: styd on wl fr 2 out: tk 2nd fnl 120yds but no imp on wnr* **16/1**

120P **3** *1* **Kylenoe Fairy (IRE)**[22] 4446 7-10-11 **105**.......................(t) TrevorWhelan 106
(Paul Henderson) *in rr: hdwy fr 3 out: styd on fr 2 out and kpt on to take 3rd fnl 100yds: nt pce of ldng duo* **33/1**

6050 **4** *3 1/4* **Teshali (IRE)**[52] 3874 5-10-8 **105**.................................(t) JamesCowley(3) 104
(Paul Nicholls) *chsd ldrs: wnt 2nd 5th: chal 3 out: sn led: hdd bef 2 out: no ch w wnr sn after: wknd and dropped to 4th fnl 120yds* **16/1**

-223 **5** *nse* **Raduis Bleu (FR)**[58] 3744 6-11-5 **116**............................ CiaranMckee(3) 114
(Alan King) *hmpd 2nd: in rr: in tch 4th: rdn and outpcd after 3 out: styd on again appr last: kpt on cl home* **8/1**

P44F **6** *24* **Forest Rhythm (IRE)**[3] 4925 7-10-8 **105**...................... MrKevinJones(3) 81
(Seamus Mullins) *wl bhd 4th: stl plenty to do whn j. slowly 3 out: mod prog after 2 out* **16/1**

-333 **7** *9* **Flicka's Witness (IRE)**[27] 4361 6-10-12 **106**.................... HenryBrooke 74
(Donald McCain) *nt fluent 1st: in tch: chsd ldrs fr 4 out: wknd and mstke 3 out* **25/1**

501P **8** *3/4* **Wild Desert (FR)**[30] 4285 6-11-4 **115**.............................. KielanWoods(3) 85
(Charlie Longsdon) *led: clr 4th: jnd 3 out: sn hdd: wknd after 2 out* **11/2**[2]

553 **9** *50* **Cousin Maggie (IRE)**[16] 4555 7-10-2 **96**..................... AodhaganConlon 19
(Brendan Powell) *rdn and bhd fr 5th: t.o* **16/1**

4-50 **10** *1* **Rayon Vert (FR)**[15] 4672 6-10-1 **100**.......................................(t) MrJABest(5) 22
(Philip Hobbs) *in tch: drvn and wknd after 4 out: no ch whn mstke next: t.o* **33/1**

22/ **11** *57* **Ommega (FR)**[503] 9-10-12 **111**........................... MrMatthewHampton(5) —
(Gerald Ham) *chsd ldrs: mstke 4th: wknd fr next: t.o* **100/1**

03 **P** **Big Robert**[30] 4291 7-11-1 **109**...(tp) PeterCarberry —
(Matt Sheppard) *blnd 2nd and rdr lost iron: hit 3rd: j. slowly 4th: a in rr: t.o whn p.u bef 2 out* **12/1**

0116 **P** **Shalambar (IRE)**[28] 4323 5-11-1 **109**...................................... RobertKirk —
(Tony Carroll) *chsd ldrs to 5th: wknd next: t.o whn p.u bef 2 out* **7/1**[3]

5012 **U** **Alcalde**[21] 4462 5-11-7 **115**.. PeterHatton 114
(John Berry) *mid-div: hdwy fr 4 out: mstke next: styng on to dispute 7th and wl in tch w chsng gp bhd str travelling wnr whn stmbld bdly and uns rdr after 2 out* **9/2**[1]

4m 43.0s (-7.60) **Going Correction** -0.15s/f (Good) **14** Ran SP% **117.3**
Speed ratings (Par 107): **110,108,107,106,106 96,92,92,71,70 46**,—,—,—
toteswingers:1&2 £17.80, 2&3 £57.60, 1&3 £26.50 CSF £70.14 CT £2114.77 TOTE £5.80: £2.20, £6.20, £11.50; EX 96.70.
Owner Mrs E Roberts **Bred** Mrs E C Roberts **Trained** Upper Lambourn, Berks

FOCUS
They went a solid pace in this ordinary 'hands and heels' handicap. The winner is on the upgrade.

NOTEBOOK
Master Fiddle travelled well into the race and won comfortably despite diving at the last. He had no problem with the better ground and if anything is likely to stay a bit further yet. Chasing will be his game next season. (tchd 4-1)
What An Oscar(IRE)'s rider did well to stay aboard after his mount took a bump at the first. The gelding was never far from the action, but lost a prominent pitch before running on again after the last. He had been dropped 3lb after a poor effort at Taunton when last seen nearly three months ago. (tchd 14-1)
Kylenoe Fairy(IRE), another given a chance by the handicapper, was staying on quite nicely from the rear over a trip on the short side for her. (op 28-1)
Teshali(IRE) chased the pace all the way and was still in second place over the last, but in the end he only just held fourth. This was just his fifth run over hurdles and it was a better effort, with the longer trip a plus. (op 20-1 tchd 25-1)
Raduis Bleu(FR) ran a solid race and clearly handled the quicker ground, but perhaps the drop in trip was not what he wanted. (op 9-1 tchd 10-1)
Forest Rhythm(IRE) ◆ was never in the hunt, but this should have helped his confidence after his first-flight fall earlier in the week. He is quite well handicapped at present and could be one to keep an eye on. (tchd 20-1)
Wild Desert(FR), making his debut for this yard, had ground conditions to suit but paid for going off rather quickly in front. (op 5-1 tchd 9-2 and 6-1 in places)
Shalambar(IRE) appeared to have underfoot conditions in his favour but dropped out disconcertingly quickly down the far side and was eventually pulled up. (op 8-1)
Alcalde, raised 5lb for his second over shorter here where he lost a shoe, was beaten when he stumbled and gave his rider no chance a stride or two after landing over the second-last. (op 8-1)

4991 CHRIS BEEK RACING HUNTERS' CHASE (18 fncs) 3m
5:00 (5:00) (Class 6) 6-Y-0+ **£988** (£304; £152)

Form RPR

P/2U **1** **Turko (FR)**[14] 4701 9-11-5 123..(t) MrJABest(7) 140+
(Mrs L Borradaile) *led 5th: c clr fr 3 out: easily* **11/8**[1]

PP32 **2** *31* **Battlecry**[30] 4293 10-11-5 117.............................. MrWTwiston-Davies(7) 112
(Nigel Twiston-Davies) *led to 5th: chsd wnr after: one pce whn hit 4 out: no ch fr next but stl clr 2nd* **5/2**[2]

-42F **3** *25* **Ice Bucket (IRE)**[31] 4271 11-11-12 104...............................(p) MrTWeston 88
(A Phillips) *chsd ldrs: in tch 14th: wknd into mod 4th sn after: styd on again fr poor 3rd appr 2 out* **8/1**

00P/ **4** *9* **Gallant Approach (IRE)**[20] 12-11-5 124..................... MrMJLinehan(7) 85
(Tim Billington) *in rr: t.o 12th: styd on in own time fr 2 out to take poor 4th last strides* **10/1**

346- **5** *shd* **Lord Ryeford (IRE)**[40] 11-11-7 130........................... MrTWCEdwards(5) 79
(Mrs S P George) *in rr but in tch whn j.big 10th: sme prog 14th: sn no ch: wknd bef next: lost poor 4th last strides* **6/1**[3]

P0-P **6** *49* **King Harald (IRE)**[12] 13-11-5 112............................... MrABradstock(7) 35
(A Bradstock) *a in rr: mstke 1st: hit 3rd and 5th: t.o fr 11th: blnd 4 out* **16/1**

6m 1.63s (-9.37) **Going Correction** -0.15s/f (Good) **6** Ran SP% **111.0**
Speed ratings: **109,98,90,87,87 70**
toteswingers:1&2 £1.02, 2&3 £3.70, 1&3 £2.50 CSF £5.26 TOTE £2.20: £1.30, £1.30; EX 4.30.
Owner Mr & Mrs D Borradaile **Bred** Bernard Forges **Trained** Beaminster, Dorset

FOCUS
There were some fine old-timers in this hunters' chasers, but most are at the veteran stage now and understandably operating well below their former levels. The form could be rated up to 7lb higher and the winner should be hard to beat in this grade.

NOTEBOOK
Turko(FR), the youngest horse in the line-up, was without a win since taking Sandown's Future Stars Chase in 2007, but had been placed in Grade 1 company since then. A smart recruit to hunter chasing, he ran out a very comfortable winner, jumping soundly and drawing well clear over the last four fences. He can add to this in the coming weeks, with the big end-of-season hunter chase at Stratford his target. (tchd 6-4 in places)
Battlecry, a notably weak finisher, was beaten a lot further by Turko than he had been at Leicester, getting steadily left behind over the final line of fences. (tchd 2-1 and 11-4 in places)
Ice Bucket(IRE), who was seen off by the home turn, last tasted victory three years ago. He has made the frame plenty of times since and is not one for win-only purposes. (op 15-2)
Gallant Approach(IRE), like the first two, has a Grand National appearance to his name. He won a Didmarton open earlier this month but was beaten a long way out on this hunter chase debut. (op 12-1 tchd 16-1)
Lord Ryeford(IRE), the pick on BHA figures, was in trouble with five to jump although he was still in a remote third place approaching the last. His useful handicap chase form when trained by Tom George came over shorter trips. (op 7-1)
King Harald(IRE) acts as a schoolmaster for his young rider these days. (op 20-1 tchd 25-1)

4992 FLOOR V DAVIS HL1979 H'CAP HURDLE (8 hdls) 2m 110y
5:35 (5:35) (Class 3) (0-135,134) 4-Y-0+ **£3,903** (£1,146; £573; £286)

Form RPR

3130 **1** **Rio Gael (IRE)**[20] 4467 5-11-2 **124**..................................(p) BarryGeraghty 129+
(Peter Bowen) *led tl after 2nd: styd trcking ldr: chal 3 out: slt ld sn after but jnd fr next and sn rdn: stl strly chal last: styd on u.p run-in: edgd rt fnl 50yds: hld on wl* **12/1**

6634 **2** *3/4* **Cockney Trucker (IRE)**[7] 4848 9-11-12 **134**........................ TomO'Brien 138+
(Philip Hobbs) *trckd ldrs: drvn to chal fr 3 out and str chal whn j.v.slowly last and lost momentum: rallied fnl 120yds: swtchd lft fnl 50yds: kpt on cl home but a hld* **7/4**[1]

R-RP **3** *13* **Sacrilege**[122] 2593 6-10-12 **120**...(b) MattieBatchelor 110
(Daniel O'Brien) *t.k.h: led after 2nd: jnd 3 out: hdd sn after and one pce: styd on u.p to hold 3rd after 2 out: hung lft run-in* **66/1**

2U20 **4** *3 1/4* **Screaming Brave**[13] 4727 5-10-11 **122**.......................(t) MarcGoldstein(3) 109
(Sheena West) *in rr but in tch: rdn 3 out: styd on u.p to take wl hld 4th nr fin* **7/1**

P21 **5** *shd* **Sunley Peace**[15] 4677 7-10-12 **120**.......................... AndrewGlassonbury 109
(Gary Moore) *chsd ldrs: hit 3rd: rdn appr 3 out: outpcd and btn whn blnd 2 out: lost wl hld 4th nr fin* **5/1**[2]

1-04 **6** *12* **General Ting (IRE)**[139] 2213 6-10-8 **116**.......................... LeightonAspell 100
(Lucy Wadham) *t.k.h in rr: hit 4th: no ch whn mstke 3 out: hung lft 2 out* **9/1**

/-01 **7** *9* **The Cayterers**[15] 4672 9-9-13 **110**.................................... LeeEdwards(3) 83
(Tony Carroll) *in rr but in tch: mstke 4 out: wknd fr next: no ch whn mstke last* **15/2**

3513 **U** **Featherbed Lane (IRE)**[47] 3960 6-10-12 **120**........................ APMcCoy —
(Anabel L M King) *blnd and uns rdr 1st* **6/1**[3]

4m 4.41s (-5.49) **Going Correction** -0.15s/f (Good) **8** Ran SP% **110.8**
Speed ratings (Par 107): **106,105,99,98,97 92,88**,—
toteswingers:1&2 £11.40, 2&3 £18.30, 1&3 £11.80. totesuper7: Win: Not won. Place: £181.80 CSF £32.39 CT £1292.95 TOTE £16.80: £3.20, £1.40, £6.90; EX 35.00.
Owner Mrs Karen Bowen **Bred** Glending Bloodstock **Trained** Little Newcastle, Pembrokes

FOCUS
A fair handicap hurdle run at a reasonable pace. A step up from the winner, and the second is rated to form.

NOTEBOOK
Rio Gael(IRE) was back in front three from home and held off the runner-up despite idling on the flat and drifting to his right. He was entitled to be sharper for his return from a break at Doncaster, where the extended 2m3f appeared to find him out. (tchd 11-1 and 14-1)

Cockney Trucker(IRE), the County Hurdle fourth, represented a yard that had won three of the last five runnings of this event. After jumping out to his right as usual, he had every chance when hitting the final flight and was unable to counter after. He was 3lb well-in so this was slightly disappointing. (op 9-4 tchd 5-2 in places)
Sacrilege consented to race this time and ran respectably, albeit finishing a well beaten third in the end. Perhaps the blinkers, replacing cheekpieces, were a help. (op 80-1 tchd 50-1)
Screaming Brave has been running creditably, including in the Imperial Cup last time, but he was never really a factor here. (tchd 6-1)
Sunley Peace, a Wincanton maiden hurdle winner, looked on a fair mark for this handicap debut but was well held, although he may have clung on to a place had he not blundered at the second-last. (op 4-1)
The Cayterers went up 10lb for his win on the same Wincanton card but still ought to have run better than he did. (op 7-1 tchd 11-2)
T/Jkpt: Not won. T/Plt: £378.50 to a £1 stake. Pool of £103,859.01 - 200.27 winning tickets. T/Qpdt: £90.50 to a £1 stake. Pool of £8,485.17 - 69.36 winning tickets. ST

4795 SEDGEFIELD (L-H)

Friday, March 25

OFFICIAL GOING: Good (chs 6.7, hdl 7.3)
Common bends with hurdles on outside.
Wind: virtually nil Weather: Bright and sunny

4993 JOHN WADE GROUP NOVICES' HURDLE (QUALIFIER) (PART OF THE JOHN WADE NOVICES' HURDLE SERIES) (10 hdls) 2m 4f

2:20 (2:20) (Class 4) 4-Y-O+ **£2,211** (£649; £324; £162)

Form			Horse	Jockey	SP	RPR
2-45	1		**Scriptwriter (IRE)**[36] 4169 9-10-10 120 (Howard Johnson) *trckd ldr: chal after 3 out: rdn appr 2 out: led last: drvn and kpt on run-in*	PaulGallagher(5)	**10/3**[2]	109
5-24	2	*1 ½*	**Bridlingtonbygones (IRE)**[47] 3965 6-11-1 0 (Karen McLintock) *led: rdn 2 out: hdd last: kpt on but a hld run-in*	GrahamLee	**5/1**[3]	108
60P2	3	*7*	**Alpha One (IRE)**[17] 4541 5-11-1 0 (Chris Grant) *trckd ldrs: rdn bef 2 out: kpt on same pce*	CampbellGillies	**33/1**	103
5400	4	*24*	**Cool Water**[16] 4552 6-10-8 0 (John Wade) *in tch: hdwy to trck ldrs after 4 out: hit 3 out: rdn and wknd after 2 out*	PeterBuchanan	**150/1**	76
00	5	*7*	**Gin Cobbler**[36] 4165 5-11-1 0 (Howard Johnson) *hld up in tch: rdn after 3 out: wknd bef next*	BrianHughes	**25/1**	74
00	6	*13*	**Glasson Lad (IRE)**[87] 3166 4-10-2 0 ow2 (Fordy Murphy) *hld up: rdn after 6th: hdwy after 4 out: wknd after 3 out*	RobertMcCarth(7)	**100/1**	56
0	7	*64*	**The Bravetraveller (IRE)**[15] 4569 8-10-12 0 (Barbara Butterworth) *hld up: rdn 6th and sn lost tch: t.o*	JamesO'Farrell(3)	**150/1**	5
03	8	*23*	**Old Style (IRE)**[31] 4278 6-11-1 0 (Jennie Candlish) *trckd ldrs: rdn and outpcd after 6th: nt fluent next and sn lost tch: t.o*	AlanO'Keeffe	**28/1**	—
261	F		**Shadows Lengthen**[25] 4393 5-11-0 123 (Michael Easterby) *midfield: fell 5th*	JakeGreenall(7)	**4/6**[1]	—

5m 2.30s (9.60) **Going Correction** +0.475s/f (Soft)
WFA 4 from 5yo+ 8lb **9** Ran SP% **112.3**
Speed ratings (Par 105): **99,98,95,86,83 78,52,43,—**
toteswingers:1&2 £1.60, 2&3 £5.20, 1&3 £15.40 CSF £17.95 TOTE £3.30: £1.30, £1.10, £4.60; EX 14.80.
Owner J Howard Johnson **Bred** Newgate Stud Co **Trained** Billy Row, Co Durham

FOCUS
The ground, which had been watered, remained good. The winner did not need to be at his best, and the second ran to his mark.

NOTEBOOK
Scriptwriter(IRE) gained a a long overdue first success as a hurdler. He had shown some very useful form over the past couple of years, most notably when sixth in the 2009 Pertemps Final and when chasing home Peddlers Cross at Haydock last season. He still made hard work of it, looking beaten after two out, but he stays well and, having taken over at the last, just did enough on the run-in. He wouldn't be one to rely on for a follow-up, however. (op 7-2 tchd 3-1)
Bridlingtonbygones(IRE) ran his best race to date over hurdles. He travelled well in front throughout, and looked all over the winner taking two out, but had been headed at the last and couldn't get back up. He's fairly modest, but can probably win a small race. (op 9-2 tchd 11-2)
Alpha One(IRE) is clearly improving and he too can pick up a small race. (op 28-1)
Old Style(IRE) Official explanation: jockey said gelding had a breathing problem
Shadows Lengthen looked the one to beat following an impressive display at Catterick and it was still the early stages of the race when he came down. It's hoped this heavy fall doesn't leave its mark. (op 5-6)

4994 BETFAIR TRAINING SERIES CONDITIONAL JOCKEYS' H'CAP HURDLE (PART OF RACING EXCELLENCE INITIATIVE) (10 hdls) 2m 4f

2:50 (2:50) (Class 5) (0-95,94) 4-Y-O+ **£1,951** (£573; £286; £143)

Form			Horse	Jockey	SP	RPR
0P00	1		**Mardood**[16] 4550 6-11-1 **83** (Chris Grant) *trckd ldr: wnt 2nd 2 out: drvn to ld run-in: kpt on*	(v[1]) AlexanderVoy	**9/1**	87
5260	2	*2 ¼*	**I'm Your Man**[25] 4390 12-11-2 **89** (Evelyn Slack) *led: rdn and hdd run-in: kpt on*	(p) CallumWhillans(5)	**15/2**[3]	91
0-04	3	*½*	**Zero Six Zoo (IRE)**[19] 4511 8-10-13 **81** (Karen McLintock) *w ldr: nt fluent 6th and briefly pushed along: rdn and outpcd after 3 out: styng on and disputing 4th whn mstke last: kpt on wl towards fin*	RobertMcCarth	**9/4**[1]	83
0602	4	*½*	**Miss Tarantella**[17] 4542 8-10-10 **85** (Maurice Barnes) *trckd ldr: hdwy to join ldr 4 out: rdn and outpcd appr 2 out: sltly hmpd last: kpt on one pce run-in*	(t) StephenMulqueen(7)	**6/1**[2]	87
044P	5	*½*	**Cornish Castle (USA)**[187] 1559 5-10-3 **76** (Andrew Crook) *hld up in tch: hdwy on inner to hold ev ch 2 out: sn rdn: no ex run-in*	JoeColliver(5)	**6/1**[2]	78
55-0	6	*27*	**Echoes Of Dawn (IRE)**[147] 2080 7-11-12 **94** (Howard Johnson) *in tch: chsd along bef 3 out: wknd bef next*	PaulGallagher	**9/1**	72
132P	7	*1 ½*	**Moon Melody (GER)**[31] 4276 8-11-5 **92** (Mike Sowersby) *trckd ldrs: wknd after 3 out*	(p) TonyKelly(5)	**8/1**	67
U1-0	F		**Rexmehead (IRE)**[321] 211 10-10-13 **81** (Andrew Wilson) *hld up on outer: rdn and wknd appr 2 out: wl hld whn fell last*	(b) MattGriffiths	**16/1**	56
500P	P		**Seminal Moment**[38] 4138 5-10-6 **77** (William Amos) *hld up: wknd after 6th: t.o whn p.u bef 2 out*	NathanMoscrop(3)	**20/1**	—

5m 5.30s (12.60) **Going Correction** +0.475s/f (Soft) **9** Ran SP% **112.9**
Speed ratings (Par 103): **93,92,91,91,91 80,80,—,—**
toteswingers:1&2 £6.50, 2&3 £4.50, 1&3 £11.20 CSF £72.27 CT £203.10 TOTE £8.70: £3.00, £3.70, £1.30; EX 91.10.
Owner W Raw **Bred** Wrottesley Limited **Trained** Newton Bewley, Co Durham

FOCUS
Quite a competitive handicap hurdle. The first two were very well in the best of last season's form.

NOTEBOOK
Mardood, wearing a first-time visor, had slipped back to a very good mark and he got on top after the last. He completed a hat-trick around this time last year and could go in again if the headgear continues to have the same effect. Official explanation: trainer said, regarding apparent improvement in form, that the gelding appreciated the first-time visor and also comes to itself at this time of year. (op 7-1)
I'm Your Man, who was in front and under pressure a long way out, kept responding and only found a horse half his age too good late on. (op 6-1)
Zero Six Zoo(IRE) stayed on again having been outpaced, but never actually looked like winning. (op 4-1)
Miss Tarantella travelled well, but was unable to quicken on. (op 13-2)
Cornish Castle(USA) could find no more after two out. (op 8-1)

4995 SPORTPOOL.CO.UK NOVICES' HURDLE (QUALIFIER) (PART OF THE JOHN WADE NOVICES' HURDLE SERIES) (8 hdls) 2m 1f

3:25 (3:26) (Class 4) 4-Y-O+ **£2,211** (£649; £324; £162)

Form			Horse	Jockey	SP	RPR
0	1		**City Ground (USA)**[30] 4283 4-10-0 0 (Michael Easterby) *racd keenly: in tch: hdwy after 3 out: led 2 out: edgd lft u.p and hdd fnl 100yds: rallied to ld again line*	JakeGreenall(7)	**8/1**	98
1136	2	*shd*	**Priceless Art (IRE)**[20] 4475 6-11-0 0 (Alan Swinbank) *trckd ldr: led on bit after 3 out: hdd narrowly 2 out: sn rdn: regained narrow ld fnl 100yds: hdd line*	TomScudamore	**8/13**[1]	106
5311	3	*1*	**Bocciani (GER)**[33] 4243 6-11-9 111 (Dianne Sayer) *trckd ldrs: hdwy to hold ev ch 2 out: sn rdn: kpt on*	JamesO'Farrell(3)	**7/1**[3]	116
	4	*16*	**Wadnaan**[237] 4-10-7 0 (Ferdy Murphy) *midfield: rdn and outpcd after 3 out: kpt on to go 4th bef last: n.d*	GrahamLee	**6/1**[2]	83
14/	5	*2 ¼*	**Hunters Belt (IRE)**[122] 4238 7-11-0 0 (Noel Wilson) *hld up: hdwy after 3 out: wnt 4th bef 2 out: no imp*	WilsonRenwick	**25/1**	88
6/05	6	*11*	**Danny Cool**[12] 4743 8-11-0 0 (Keith Reveley) *trckd ldrs: slow 4th: wknd after 3 out*	JamesReveley	**66/1**	81
0	7	*6*	**Provost**[12] 4739 7-11-0 0 (Michael Easterby) *hld up: n.d*	PaddyAspell	**50/1**	72
00	8	*41*	**Colorado Kid (IRE)**[79] 3399 5-11-0 0 (Howard Johnson) *midfield: reminders after 3rd: wknd after 4 out: t.o*	BrianHughes	**40/1**	35
0	F		**Umverti**[25] 4393 6-10-4 0 (Joanne Foster) *led: hdd after 3 out: sn wknd: hld whn fell 2 out*	(t) JamesHalliday(3)	**40/1**	62
	P		**Phantom Serenade (IRE)**[193] 6-11-0 0 (Michael Dods) *hld up: v slow 4th and sn lost tch: p.u after next*	(t) RichieMcGrath	**66/1**	—
P	P		**Pont De Nuit**[71] 3519 4-10-7 0 (Tracy Waggott) *hld up: a bhd: t.o whn p.u bef 2 out*	CampbellGillies	**125/1**	—

4m 13.0s (6.10) **Going Correction** +0.475s/f (Soft)
WFA 4 from 5yo+ 7lb **11** Ran SP% **114.3**
Speed ratings (Par 105): **104,103,103,95,94 89,86,67,—,— —**
toteswingers:1&2 £2.30, 2&3 £1.30, 1&3 £8.90 CSF £13.21 TOTE £5.80: £1.80, £1.10, £1.50; EX 17.90.
Owner Wiendiola **Bred** Mrs E Scott Jr & Mrs L Macelree **Trained** Sheriff Hutton, N Yorks
■ Stewards' Enquiry : Jake Greenall two-day ban: careless riding (Apr 10-11)

FOCUS
Just an ordinary novice hurdle, but it produced a good finish, with three horses still in with a chance after the last. A big step up from the winner, who is entitled to rate a lot higher on his Flat form.

NOTEBOOK
City Ground(USA) just came out on top, surviving a Stewards' enquiry in the process, having carried the runner-up left on the run-in. He was the best horse on the day, though, travelling strongly and perhaps not being kicked on soon enough. This was a big step up on his initial hurdling effort. (tchd 9-1)
Priceless Art(IRE) won a couple of jumpers' bumpers in December and, although well held in a Grade 2 hurdle at Kelso last time, this was expected to prove a lot easier. He was under pressure turning in, though, and despite a game rally after the last, was just edged out. It could be argued he'd have won had he not been carried left, although there's little doubt City Ground is the better long-term prospect. (op 4-5 tchd 4-7 tchd 10-11 in a place)
Bocciani(GER), chasing a hat-trick, ran really well under the double penalty, just backing out of it in the closing stages. (op 5-1 tchd 8-1)
Wadnaan, formerly with Mark Johnston on the Flat, kept on into fourth and should improve on this initial experience of hurdles. Official explanation: jockey said gelding had a breathing problem (op 8-1 tchd 17-2)
Hunters Belt(IRE) stayed on to chase the leaders turning for home, but his rider took it easy over the last couple of hurdles, the horse possibly getting tired. He had won a bumper two years ago, and also been successful on the Flat last year, so may be one to watch out for in handicaps. (op 22-1 tchd 20-1)
Umverti had run with credit, but was tired, when falling two out. (op 33-1)
Phantom Serenade(IRE) Official explanation: jockey said gelding pulled up distressed (op 33-1)

4996 COLLINS SEAFOODS BEGINNERS' CHASE (QUALIFIER) (PART OF THE COLLINS SEAFOODS YOUNG CHASERS SERIES) (16 fncs) 2m 4f

4:00 (4:00) (Class 4) 5-Y-O+ **£2,665** (£827; £445**Stalls** Far side

Form			Horse	Jockey	SP	RPR
F233	1		**Catch Bob (IRE)**[19] 4507 7-10-7 118 (Ferdy Murphy) *j.rt: trckd ldr: lft in ld 6 out: sn clr: easily*	TonyKelly(7)	**9/2**[2]	123+
553P	2	*31*	**Cloudy Dawn**[66] 3622 6-10-9 77 (Sue Smith) *hld up: nt fluent 9th: lft in 2nd 6 out: no ch w wnr*	ShaneByrne(5)	**20/1**	92
-25P	3	*33*	**Still Calm**[29] 4304 7-11-0 82 (Maurice Barnes) *trckd ldrs in 3rd: struggling fr 9th: lft in poor 3rd 6 out: n.d*	(t) MichaelMcAlister	**50/1**	75
/PFP	U		**Riskier**[45] 3995 6-10-7 0 (John Wade) *racd keenly: led: blnd and uns rdr 10th*	MrJohnDawson(7)	**10/1**[3]	—
P1F2	B		**Lightening Rod**[19] 4507 6-10-7 126 (Michael Easterby) *racd keenly: hld up: wnt 2nd after 8th: lft in ld 10th: b.d by loose horse 5 out*	JakeGreenall(7)	**4/11**[1]	—

5m 13.6s (10.60) **Going Correction** +0.55s/f (Soft) **5** Ran SP% **107.3**
Speed ratings: **100,87,74,—,—**
CSF £50.44 TOTE £3.00: £1.10, £3.90; EX 29.40.
Owner A & S Enterprises Ltd **Bred** Pat Droney **Trained** West Witton, N Yorks

FOCUS
An eventful contest. The easy winner was left with little to beat and is rated to his mark

NOTEBOOK
Catch Bob(IRE) was left with a clear advantage six from home and safely negotiated the fences for a first victory over fences. He was very fortunate, but could be the type to win again returned to handicaps. (op 7-2)
Cloudy Dawn completed in his own time for second. (op 14-1)
Riskier was still going quite well when he unseated his rider at the tenth. (op 9-1)

Lightening Rod was brought down when Riskier, who unseated his jockey at the tenth, fell riderless at the eleventh. Lightening Rod had pulled his way clear and would almost certainly have won, with it simply a case of being in the wrong place at the wrong time. He should gain compensation. (op 9-1)

4997 CLEANER AIR SOLUTIONS FREE SOLAR ELECTRICITY H'CAP CHASE (21 fncs) 3m 3f
4:35 (4:35) (Class 4) (0-110,109) 5-Y-0+ **£2,602** (£764; £382; £190)

Form				RPR
15PP	1		**Elzahann (IRE)**[42] 4060 9-11-7 **104** ... GrahamLee (Ferdy Murphy) *in tch on outer: trckd ldrs 7th: mstke 11th: led 2 out: rdn clr bef last* **5/1**[3]	114+
2222	2	9	**Jeringa**[38] 4135 12-10-9 **92** ... (b) BrianHughes (John Wade) *prom and t.k.h: led 14th: rdn whn hdd 2 out: sn no match wnr* **9/2**[2]	92
6314	3	3 ¾	**Nelliedonethat (IRE)**[42] 4060 11-11-4 **101** ... CampbellGillies (Lucinda Russell) *trckd ldrs on inner: rdn after 4 out: kpt on one pce* **6/1**	98
54PU	4	hd	**The Artful Fox**[24] 4412 10-10-0 **88** ... PaulGallagher[(5)] (Mike Sowersby) *trckd ldrs: rdn after 5 out: kpt on one pce* **12/1**	83
303P	5	3	**Teenando (IRE)**[19] 4509 11-9-4 **83** oh10 ... NathanCook[(10)] (Sue Smith) *midfield: rdn after 4 out: no imp after next* **14/1**	77
2242	6	6	**Oniz Tiptoes (IRE)**[12] 4740 10-10-7 **90** ... (p) PaddyAspell (John Wainwright) *wnt in snatches: hld up: rdn after 14th: n.d* **2/1**[1]	81
0PPP	P		**Fine By Me (IRE)**[100] 2953 12-11-12 **109** ... (p) GerardTumelty (Julian Smith) *led: hdd 14th: sn wknd: t.o whn p.u bef 4 out* **12/1**	—
-00F	U		**Froggy Lane**[58] 3748 8-10-6 **89** ... FearghalDavis (Simon West) *racd keenly: hld up: rdn and hdwy after 5 out: disputing 3rd whn blnd and uns rdr 2 out* **14/1**	86

7m 7.12s (18.12) **Going Correction** +0.55s/f (Soft) **8 Ran SP% 111.2**
Speed ratings: **95,92,91,91,90 88,—,—**
toteswingers:1&2 £4.10, 2&3 £5.30, 1&3 £16.70 CSF £26.63 CT £131.85 TOTE £5.50: £2.80, £1.40, £1.70; EX 28.50.
Owner Ian Allan Todd **Bred** Denis Cummins **Trained** West Witton, N Yorks

FOCUS
A modest handicap chase. The winner is rated to the level of her lucky Ayr win.

NOTEBOOK
Elzahann(IRE), a fortunate winner at Ayr earlier in the season, had completely lost her form subsequently, but she relished this fast surface and proved well at home over the distance, leading two out and gradually drawing clear. She's now won 7-21 races and could go in again if building on this. (op 9-2 tchd 4-1)
Jeringa has now finished second on each of his last five starts. He doesn't appear to do a lot wrong, but just lacks a finishing kick. (tchd 5-1)
Nelliedonethat(IRE) plugged on again after being ridden. (op 9-2 tchd 7-1)
The Artful Fox ran better than last time. (op 18-1 tchd 11-1)
Oniz Tiptoes(IRE) raced lazily, as he often does, but usually puts in a later rattle. That wasn't the case this time, however, and he simply looked to have one of his off days. (op 9-4)
Fine By Me(IRE) stopped quickly and looks gone at the game. (tchd 11-1 and 14-1)
Froggy Lane was in the process of running an improved race when unseating his rider two out. His jumping remains a problem. (tchd 11-1 and 14-1)

4998 CLEANERAIRSOLUTIONS.CO.UK SOLAR POWERED H'CAP HURDLE (8 hdls) 2m 1f
5:10 (5:10) (Class 4) (0-110,110) 4-Y-0+ **£2,211** (£649; £324; £162)

Form				RPR
0005	1		**Hi Dancer**[17] 4544 8-11-3 **108** ... JakeGreenall[(7)] (Ben Haslam) *prom: rdn after 2 out: led run-in: kpt on drvn out* **25/1**	113
-033	2	2 ¼	**Lap Of Honour (IRE)**[69] 3570 7-11-0 **98** ... GrahamLee (Ferdy Murphy) *trckd ldrs on inner: led on bit after 3 out: rdn between last 2: hdd run-in: one pce* **8/1**	101
6423	3	hd	**Waterloo Corner**[10] 4797 9-10-9 **98** ... (p) PaulGallagher[(5)] (Ray Craggs) *in tch: hdwy to chse ldrs after 3 out: chal 2 out: upsides last: no ex towards fin* **5/2**[1]	101
2232	4	7	**King's Chorister**[14] 4686 5-9-7 **84** oh5 ... (t) CallumWhillans[(7)] (Barry Murtagh) *midfield: smooth hdwy to trck ldrs after 3 out: rdn 2 out: sn one pce* **8/1**	80
P460	5	12	**Petrocelli**[39] 4113 4-10-0 **91** oh4 ... PaddyAspell (Wilf Storey) *hld up: hdwy on inner 3 out: sn rdn: wknd appr 2 out* **33/1**	72
UU40	6	3 ½	**High Hoylander**[28] 4323 5-11-4 **107** ... ShaneByrne[(5)] (Sue Smith) *t.k.h early: in tch on inner: hdwy to trck ldrs 3 out: sn rdn: wknd 2 out* **7/1**[3]	92
10F0	7	nk	**Turf Trivia**[45] 3994 4-10-4 **105** ... SamuelWelton[(10)] (George Moore) *hld up: n.d* **16/1**	80
2000	8	1	**Barbarian**[29] 4302 5-10-1 **85** ... RichieMcGrath (Alan Brown) *led early: remained prom: wknd appr 3 out* **16/1**	66
0024	9	12	**Exotic Man (FR)**[30] 4281 6-11-5 **110** ... MrJohnDawson[(7)] (John Wade) *hld up: rdn appr 2 out: sn no imp* **11/1**	81
5400	10	23	**Woody Valentine (USA)**[15] 4572 10-11-1 **102** ... JamesO'Farrell[(3)] (Evelyn Slack) *hld up: lost tch after 4th: t.o* **22/1**	52
5114	F		**Samizdat (FR)**[1] 4960 8-9-11 **88** 7ex ... MissECSayer[(7)] (Dianne Sayer) *sn led: mstke 3rd: hit 3 out: sn hdd: wkng in 5th whn fell last* **9/2**[2]	85
34F	F		**Groove Master**[125] 2528 4-10-2 **93** ... CampbellGillies (William Amos) *in tch: fell 2nd* **25/1**	—

4m 13.9s (7.00) **Going Correction** +0.475s/f (Soft)
WFA 4 from 5yo+ 7lb **12 Ran SP% 116.6**
Speed ratings (Par 105): **102,100,100,97,91 90,90,89,84,73 —,—**
toteswingers:1&2 £10.10, 2&3 £5.70, 1&3 £19.60 CSF £202.82 CT £688.61 TOTE £31.90: £6.30, £2.10, £1.30; EX 95.00.
Owner R Tocher **Bred** Mrs E Roberts **Trained** Middleham Moor, N Yorks

FOCUS
A fair handicap hurdle, although it was certainly open, with the front three jumping the last in a line. The winner is rated to the level of last summer's best form.

NOTEBOOK
Hi Dancer displayed the best finishing kick, appreciating the return to a sounder surface and capitalising on his declining mark. He had run as though on his way back at Newcastle last time, and will be of some interest if turned out again quickly. (op 20-1)
Lap Of Honour(IRE) went on travelling best leaving the back, but despite a flying leap at the last, was unable to fend off the winner. Perhaps he's best held on to for longer.
Waterloo Corner is proving consistent. He came to hold every chance in the straight, but just couldn't quicken. (op 11-4 tchd 3-1)
King's Chorister, either second or third on each of his last four starts, never quite got close enough to throw down a serious challenge. (op 10-1)
Woody Valentine(USA) Official explanation: jockey said, regarding running and riding, that his orders were to drop in, look for better ground by taking the gelding wide and obtain the best possible placing, adding that it never really travelled with enthusiasm and knowing that it would not respond to strong handling he felt it prudent to ride out with hands and heels; vet said gelding was sore over its right-hind lumbar region and was not walking out freely.

Samizdat(FR), reappearing just 24 hours after finishing fourth at Carlisle, had run well, but had nothing left to offer when crashing out at the last. (op 5-1 tchd 7-2)
T/Plt: £86.60 to a £1 stake. Pool of £70,174.35 - 590.94 winning tickets. T/Qpdt: £15.60 to a £1 stake. Pool of £6,189.62 - 291.90 winning tickets. AS

4417 BANGOR-ON-DEE (L-H)
Saturday, March 26

OFFICIAL GOING: Good (6.8)
The fence after the winning post and the fifth-last fence were omitted; ground damaged.
Wind: almost nil Weather: overcast

4999 UNISON WREXHAM HEALTHCARE CLAIMING HURDLE (9 hdls) 2m 1f
2:05 (2:05) (Class 4) 4-Y-0+ **£2,192** (£639; £319)

Form				RPR
P11P	1		**Chrysander**[31] 4291 9-10-9 115 ... (vt) AodhaganConlon[(5)] (Evan Williams) *mde all: clr fr 3 out: 16 l ahd last: eased towards fin* **10/11**[1]	113+
PP4	2	15	**Final Flyer (IRE)**[16] 4676 7-11-5 0 ... OliverDayman[(5)] (Alison Thorpe) *chsd 2 clr ldrs: wnt poor 3rd 3 out: one pce fr next* **25/1**	107
00P0	3	¾	**Freddy's Star (IRE)**[55] 3840 9-11-7 109 ... DannyBurton[(7)] (Alan Jones) *t.k.h: blnd 1st: trckd 2 clr ldrs: tk modest 3rd 2 out: one pce* **20/1**	112+
6213	4	2 ¼	**Miereveld**[3] 4939 4-10-8 103 ... (v) PaulGallagher[(5)] (Brian Ellison) *chsd wnr: reminders 5th: rdn next: 4 l down whn blnd 2 out: stl 2nd whn hit last: sn wknd* **3/1**[2]	97+
-160	5	3 ¾	**Le Corvee (IRE)**[36] 1972 9-11-7 116 ... LeeEdwards[(3)] (Tony Carroll) *mid-div: nvr nr ldrs* **11/1**	100
206F	6	2 ½	**Flichity (IRE)**[17] 4549 6-12-0 115 ... JasonMaguire (Donald McCain) *hld up in rr: sme hdwy 4th: wknd 3 out* **14/1**	102
0004	7	1 ¼	**Special Cuvee**[15] 4707 5-11-4 92 ... (t) DPFahy (Alison Thorpe) *mid-div: lost pl 4th: t.o 3 out* **33/1**	90
1-03	8	18	**Cursum Perficio**[45] 4008 9-11-0 100 ... (t) SamThomas (Richard Lee) *in rr: t.o 3 out* **17/2**[3]	70
3400	9	7	**Nicky Nutjob (GER)**[45] 4008 5-10-13 98 ... CharlieWallis[(7)] (John O'Shea) *stdd s: a bhd: t.o 3 out* **33/1**	70

4m 0.40s (-10.50) **Going Correction** -0.475s/f (Good)
WFA 4 from 5yo+ 7lb **9 Ran SP% 117.4**
Speed ratings (Par 105): **105,97,97,96,94 93,93,84,81**
toteswingers:1&2 £22.10, 2&3 not won, 1&3 £22.10 CSF £32.35 TOTE £2.00: £1.10, £8.30, £4.40; EX 42.60.
Owner R E R Williams **Bred** Darley **Trained** Llancarfan, Vale Of Glamorgan

FOCUS
Just one horse mattered according to the market, and indeed the race panned out exactly as anticipated. The winner is rated 2lb off his recent best.

NOTEBOOK
Chrysander readily fought off his sole challenger to gallop on strongly to the line, with the chasing pack struggling in his wake. He can sulk if unable to get to the lead, and flopped in handicap company at Ludlow last time, but in this grade he's out on his own, registering his third win this year in claiming hurdles. (op 2-1)
Final Flyer(IRE) led the chasing pack but the winner had established an insurmountable lead before he set about reducing the deficit with any seriousness, but he is gradually improving nevertheless. (op 18-1)
Freddy's Star(IRE) was the first to set about chasing down the leaders, but he jumped slowly at the fourth-last and lost valuable momentum. He has struggled this season and has since switched stables, so this effort was not too bad, especially since his best form hitherto has been at Exeter. (op 14-1)
Miereveld, a winner of a juvenile hurdle at this track earlier this month, likes to set the pace and attempted to match strides with the winner. He was struggling to keep up by the home turn, but was always going to be outclassed by that rival and as such ran respectably. (tchd 11-4 and 10-3)

5000 PUREDARTS.CO.UK "NATIONAL HUNT" NOVICES' HURDLE (9 hdls) 2m 1f
2:40 (2:40) (Class 4) 4-Y-0+ **£2,602** (£764; £382; £190)

Form				RPR
11	1		**Bear's Affair (IRE)**[67] 3620 5-11-6 0 ... FelixDeGiles (Nicky Henderson) *trckd ldrs: wnt 2nd 4th: upsides 2 out and wnt lft wl clr last* **8/15**[1]	118+
0000	2	35	**Robello**[31] 4288 7-10-7 0 ... (p) CharlieWallis[(7)] (John O'Shea) *towards rr: drvn 5th: kpt on fr 2 out: tk distant 2nd sn after last* **66/1**	76
00	3	1	**Steeldrivinman**[31] 4281 5-11-0 0 ... AdrianLane (Donald McCain) *stdd s: t.k.h in rr: j.rt: hdwy 5th: wnt modest 3rd appr 2 out: wknd and lft distant 2nd last* **33/1**[3]	77
404	4	11	**Sleeping Du Granit (FR)**[10] 4815 5-10-11 0 ... (t) TommyPhelan[(3)] (Claire Dyson) *chsd ldrs: outpcd 6th: wknd 2 out* **66/1**	64
0000	5	5	**Summer De Baune (FR)**[23] 4437 6-10-7 0 ... (t) HarryChalloner[(7)] (John Bryan Groucott) *mstkes: chsd ldrs: wknd 6th: sn bhd* **200/1**	59
2312	F		**Our Mick**[15] 4702 5-11-6 122 ... JasonMaguire (Donald McCain) *led: hit 2nd: nt fluent next: drvn 3 out: jnd next: fell heavily last* **6/4**[2]	116

4m 3.00s (-7.90) **Going Correction** -0.475s/f (Good) **6 Ran SP% 111.7**
Speed ratings (Par 105): **99,82,82,76,74 —**
toteswingers:1&2 £7.10, 2&3 not won, 1&3:£4.90 CSF £26.30 TOTE £2.00: £1.02, £30.20; EX 33.80.
Owner G B Barlow **Bred** T J Whitley **Trained** Upper Lambourn, Berks

FOCUS
With no strength in depth, the race revolved around the two previous winners. Bear's Affair and faller Our Mick are both rated around a stone off their best.

NOTEBOOK
Bear's Affair(IRE) moved up to challenge his main rival, doing everything comfortably. Though he was awkward at the second-last he lost no momentum on the charge to the final flight and was just getting the better of things when left clear. He is now unbeaten in three starts, appreciates good ground and his trainer reportedly has high hopes for him over fences next season. (op 8-13 tchd 4-6 in a place)
Robello, in first time cheekpieces, was a bit keen held up off the pace, but stayed on late to claim a never-nearer second. This was a step forward from his previous indifferent form but he will need to continue improving to make any impact in handicaps. (op 50-1)
Steeldrivinman was very keen in the rear and put in some novicey jumps, but showed a glimmer of ability to gain a few places from the home turn. He might need the summer to strengthen up. (op 25-1)

Our Mick hasn't always that fluent over the hurdles, but dug deep in a bid to fend off the challenge of the favourite. He was just coming to the end of his tether when stepping at the last and skidding to the ground under the rail. He's been consistent this season, in the frame on all his starts, with his sole hurdles win coming on much softer ground. (op 7-4 tchd 15-8)

5001 TOMMY'S DARTS NOVICES' CHASE (14 fncs 4 omitted) 3m 110y

3:15 (3:17) (Class 4) 5-Y-O+ **£3,252** (£955; £477; £238)

Form				RPR
3120	**1**		**Tarablaze**[9] 4817 8-11-7 138 .... TomO'Brien (Philip Hobbs) *trckd ldrs: t.k.h: wnt cl 2nd gng wl 4 out: led 2 out: 8 l ahd whn hit last: hung lft and rdn out* **5/4**[1]	142+
4221	**2**	*14*	**Cool Mission (IRE)**[15] 4685 7-11-7 129 .... (p) JasonMaguire (Donald McCain) *mde most: drvn 9th: hdd 2 out: no ch w wnr: eased towards fin* **7/4**[2]	131
3212	**3**	*35*	**Sir Tantallus Hawk**[22] 4453 7-11-7 130 .... BarryKeniry (Alan Swinbank) *nt fluent: in tch: drvn along 10th: sn outpcd: tk remote 3rd after 3 out: hit last* **7/2**[3]	100
04	**4**	*1 1/4*	**Tom Bach (IRE)**[14] 4720 7-11-0 0 .... GerardTumelty (Richard Price) *j.rt: w ldr to 8th: sn wl outpcd and bhd* **40/1**	89
1U40	**P**		**Big Burrows (IRE)**[49] 3953 9-11-0 119 .... TonyKelly(7) (Ferdy Murphy) *trckd ldrs: wnt 2nd 6th: led briefly 9th: 3rd and wkng whn hit 4 out: sn lost pl and bhd: t.o whn p.u bef 2 out* **12/1**	—
F-P5	**F**		**Master Alfredo**[22] 4453 7-11-0 0 .... WayneHutchinson (Susan Nock) *in rr: fell 9th* **66/1**	—

6m 12.6s (-7.20) **Going Correction** -0.275s/f (Good) **6** Ran SP% **114.7**
Speed ratings: **100,95,84,83,**— —
toteswingers:1&2 £1.02, 2&3 £1.70, 1&3 £1.30 CSF £4.17 TOTE £1.90: £1.60, £1.10; EX 4.10.
Owner Mrs Diana L Whateley **Bred** Mrs S J Brasher **Trained** Withycombe, Somerset

FOCUS
A reasonable novice chase. Straightforward form and the winner can rate higher.

NOTEBOOK
Tarablaze coped well over these relatively easier fences and took advantage of the four omitted obstacles to outclass his rivals. He had gained his first chasing success when scrambling home at Exeter, but next time his jumping went to pieces behind Aiteen Thirtythree at Newbury. However, a confidence-boosting run in the Pertemps Final at Cheltenham showed that he was in good form and he had no problems with this simpler task. He definitely has ability but might need to prove it in stiffer contests to silence his doubters. (op 6-4 tchd 13-8)
Cool Mission(IRE) was niggled throughout the final circuit and was eventually outpaced by the winner. This was still a decent effort and he ran up to form considering he is better on galloping tracks, and perhaps also softer ground nowadays. (op 2-1)
Sir Tantallus Hawk was held up, presumably to eke out his stamina, but after a slow jump at the ditch (the fourth) he could never get into it, and was tiring by the second last. He has been in good form in novice chases over 2m4f but on this evidence he did not see out the step up in trip. (op 10-3 tchd 4-1)
Tom Bach(IRE) was a bit too keen racing alongside Cool Mission, and he eventually faded out of it. (op 28-1)
Big Burrows(IRE) jumped a bit better on this better ground, but weakened tamely from the fourth-last. Official explanation: vet said gelding returned distressed (tchd 14-1)

5002 TOMMY'S DARTS H'CAP CHASE (12 fncs 3 omitted) 2m 4f 110y

3:50 (3:50) (Class 3) (0-135,133) 5-Y-O+ **£4,435** (£1,310; £655; £327; £163)

Form				RPR
-123	**1**		**Pouvoir (FR)**[27] 4371 8-11-1 122 .... WayneHutchinson (Alan King) *hld up: hdwy to chse ldrs 9th: led between last 2: 4 l ahd last: readily* **9/2**[2]	134+
1P04	**2**	*3*	**Simarian (IRE)**[37] 4162 6-10-10 122 .... (p) AodhaganConlon(5) (Evan Williams) *chsd ldrs: reminders 8th: sn outpcd: rallied appr 2 out: styd on appr next: snatched 2nd nr fin* **8/1**	127
0060	**3**	*hd*	**Storymaker**[9] 4820 10-11-4 125 .... PaddyAspell (Sandy Forster) *hdwy to chse 2 ldrs 7th: led appr 2 out: hdd between last 2: kpt on same pce* **7/1**	130
5423	**4**	*12*	**Alfie Flits**[21] 4472 9-10-11 118 .... (t) BarryKeniry (Alan Swinbank) *in rr: lost tch 8th: poor 6th 3 out: kpt on to take modest 4th between last 2* **9/1**	113
-113	**5**	*17*	**Sir Ian (IRE)**[121] 2629 8-11-6 127 .... FelixDeGiles (Charlie Longsdon) *trckd ldr: t.k.h: led 3 out: sn drvn hdd appr next: sn wknd* **2/1**[1]	110+
201F	**6**	*6*	**Grand Lahou (FR)**[8] 4853 8-11-7 133 .... CO'Farrell(5) (Tim Vaughan) *led: hit 7th: hdd 3 out: wknd appr next* **8/1**	107
2166	**P**		**Kellystown Lad (IRE)**[63] 3672 8-11-2 123 .... GrahamLee (Ferdy Murphy) *in rr: reminders 5th: bhd fr 8th: t.o 3 out: p.u bef next* **13/2**[3]	—

5m 5.10s (-4.00) **Going Correction** -0.275s/f (Good) **7** Ran SP% **109.6**
Speed ratings: **96,94,94,90,83 81,**—
toteswingers:1&2 £5.10, 2&3 £6.30, 1&3 £31.30 CSF £34.81 TOTE £5.60: £2.10, £5.50; EX 43.60.
Owner Mr & Mrs R Scott **Bred** Count Edouard Decazes **Trained** Barbury Castle, Wilts

FOCUS
A fair handicap, run at a decent gallop. The winner should have more to offer over fences and the next two were close to their marks.

NOTEBOOK
Pouvoir(FR) jumped soundly travelling well, crept into the race before the home turn and came home strongly for a comfortable success. A promising and classy juvenile hurdler, he lost his way subsequently and has been lightly raced over the past couple of years, but showed that more was to come on his reappearance run at Fontwell last month on unsuitably soft ground. That warm-up put him straight for this where he was able to capitalise on an attractive mark in his first handicap chase, and he could feasibly go in again. (op 4-1)
Simarian(IRE) chased down the leaders but was feeling the pace as they turned for home, before he stayed on again near the line. He is not as good over fences as he was over hurdles as he is not a natural jumper, but he has been given a sliver of a chance by the handicapper and there could be another tight-track chase in him. (op 7-1 tchd 17-2)
Storymaker was taken off his feet somewhat at festival pace nine days ago, but the C&D winner faced an easier task here. He improved his position on the final circuit but hit a flat spot before rallying, but could only find one pace at the end. Maybe this race came just a bit too soon. (tchd 13-2)
Alfie Flits was getting detached towards the end of the back straight but he plugged on to be gaining a little at the finish. He has been struggling a bit in novice events of late and was tried in a tongue-tie here, but he was unable to benefit from a potentially handy mark, though he is generally better on softer ground. (op 10-1)
Sir Ian(IRE) was stepping up in class and having his first run back from a winter break, so he should come on for this. (op 9-4 tchd 5-2)
Grand Lahou(FR) was a bit hesitant at several fences, perhaps remembering his fall in the Grand Annual at Cheltenham, and he does not truly stay this far. (op 9-1)
Kellystown Lad(IRE) Official explanation: vet said gelding returned distressed

5003 TOMMY SHONE H'CAP HURDLE (12 hdls) 3m

4:20 (4:20) (Class 2) (0-140,132) 4-Y-O+ **£6,337** (£1,872; £936; £468; £234)

Form				RPR
1341	**1**		**Cloudy Spirit**[20] 4501 6-11-4 124 .... HarrySkelton (Reg Hollinshead) *hld up in rr: stdy hdwy 9th: chsd ldr appr 2 out: led between last 2: drvn out* **11/1**	134+
6F-0	**2**	*2*	**Larks Lad (IRE)**[36] 4185 7-11-1 121 .... FelixDeGiles (Nicky Henderson) *trckd ldrs: led 9th: hdd between last 2: styd on same pce* **8/1**[2]	128
0011	**3**	*3 1/4*	**Stagecoach Opal**[13] 4742 10-10-4 110 .... HenryOliver (Sue Smith) *chsd ldrs: styd on same pce fr 2 out* **9/2**[1]	114
004	**4**	*1 3/4*	**William Hogarth**[36] 4185 6-11-2 122 .... RhysFlint (Keith Goldsworthy) *mid-div: hdwy 8th: chsng ldrs appr 2 out: 4th and one pce whn hit last* **11/1**	125
/P-0	**5**	*2*	**Merrydown (IRE)**[35] 4209 8-11-11 131 .... FearghalDavis (Nicky Richards) *in tch: hdwy to chse ldrs 9th: hung lft and one pce between last 2* **12/1**	132
0/6-	**6**	*10*	**Liberate**[648] 224 8-11-12 132 .... TomO'Brien (Philip Hobbs) *in rr: kpt on fr 3 out: nvr nr ldrs* **16/1**	124
3333	**7**	*6*	**Zakatal**[19] 4524 5-10-2 115 .... (bt) ChrisDavies(7) (Philip Hobbs) *in rr: sme hdwy 8th: nvr nr ldrs* **8/1**[2]	102
0130	**8**	*6*	**Ouzbeck (FR)**[140] 2221 9-11-5 132 .... StephenO'Donovan(7) (Emma Lavelle) *t.k.h: w ldrs: wknd appr 2 out* **16/1**	113
F430	**9**	*8*	**Sangfroid**[36] 4185 7-11-10 130 .... DarylJacob (Nick Williams) *chsd ldrs: reminders 4th: drvn 7th: lost pl 9th* **12/1**	104
P510	**10**	*1*	**Wolf Moon (IRE)**[11] 4790 8-11-6 126 .... WarrenMarston (Martin Keighley) *prom: reminders 6th: lost pl 8th: sn bhd* **10/1**	99
5011	**11**	*11*	**Pie At Midnight**[24] 4421 5-11-0 120 .... JasonMaguire (Donald McCain) *led: hdd 4 out: wknd and 9th whn mstke 2 out: sn eased* **9/1**[3]	93+
1F62	**12**	*1/2*	**Kauto The Roc (FR)**[24] 4421 7-10-10 123 .... MrRJarrett(7) (Alan King) *in rr: hdwy 3rd: sn chsng ldrs: hit 5th: lost pl after 3 out* **10/1**	85
1-R3	**13**	*12*	**Ernst Blofeld (IRE)**[127] 2500 7-11-10 130 .... (t) AdrianLane (Donald McCain) *in rr: bhd fr 5th: t.o 3 out* **25/1**	82
6000	**14**	*27*	**The Shy Man (IRE)**[13] 4742 8-11-0 120 .... BarryKeniry (George Moore) *in rr: dropped to last 5th: sn t.o* **16/1**	47

5m 37.9s (-13.10) **Going Correction** -0.475s/f (Good) **14** Ran SP% **122.1**
Speed ratings (Par 109): **102,101,100,99,99 95,93,91,89,88 85,84,80,71**
toteswingers:1&2 £28.80, 2&3 £6.50, 1&3 £4.20 CSF £98.42 CT £464.44 TOTE £13.60: £3.20, £3.80, £2.60; EX 156.00.
Owner Mrs Norma Harris **Bred** Mrs Norma Harris **Trained** Upper Longdon, Staffs

FOCUS
A fair handicap, run at an uneven gallop. Solid form and the winner is very progressive.

NOTEBOOK
Cloudy Spirit, stepping up in trip after a comfortable success at Huntingdon earlier this month off a 9lb lower mark, made eye-catching progress against the rail in the back straight and she stayed on well to run out a ready winner. She is versatile and possesses a bit of speed, and looks able to continue her run of form if the handicapper allows. (op 12-1)
Larks Lad(IRE) raced prominently and travelled well, but was just collared on the flat. He had his novice chase season delayed after sustaining a cut in a fall at Ayr in April that kept him out of action, so he is being kept over hurdles for the time being, where he has enough ability to win. (op 10-1)
Stagecoach Opal has been in grand form of late, notching up two wins in lesser company. He raced prominently and stuck to the task but was just undone by the latest 10lb rise. (op 6-1)
William Hogarth, on a reasonable mark in his attempt to build on a respectable performance when stepped up to this trip at Newbury last month, was covered up in mid-division but could not pick up as well as expected. He has been kept on the go this season and might just appreciate a break now. (tchd 12-1)
Merrydown(IRE) made good progress down the back but soon felt the pace and lugged to his left in the straight. He has had his problems with just two runs in the past two years, but was nibbled in the market here and indeed looks capable of rewarding connections' patience, especially on softer ground. (tchd 14-1)
Liberate, off the track since June 2009, never really got into it but should come on for this. (op 14-1)
Zakatal is consistent but could never get competitive stepping up in trip in a bid to gain his first win. (op 9-1)

5004 PUREDARTS.CO.UK H'CAP CHASE (10 fncs 2 omitted) 2m 1f 110y

4:55 (4:55) (Class 4) (0-115,110) 5-Y-O+ **£3,252** (£955; £477)

Form				RPR
0051	**1**		**Robertewenutter**[17] 4549 7-10-8 92 .... HenryOliver (Sue Smith) *t.k.h: led and clr tl after 7th: rdn between last 2: kpt on: hld on wl* **6/4**[1]	102+
0006	**2**	*1 1/4*	**Seigneur Des Bois (FR)**[123] 2601 5-11-5 103 .... GrahamLee (Ferdy Murphy) *in last and sn pushed along: reminders 5th: jnd 2nd 7th: chsd wnr next: styd on same pce run-in* **9/4**[3]	112
2334	**3**	*32*	**Seeyaaj**[21] 4471 11-11-12 110 .... (t) PeterBuchanan (Lucinda Russell) *chsd wnr to 3 out: wknd appr next: eased whn bhd run-in* **7/4**[2]	97

4m 23.7s (1.60) **Going Correction** -0.275s/f (Good) **3** Ran SP% **107.1**
Speed ratings: **85,84,70**
CSF £4.79 TOTE £2.70; EX 5.30.
Owner C Bradford-Nutter **Bred** Digby Laws **Trained** High Eldwick, W Yorks

FOCUS
An uncompetitive event. The winner ran up to his mark, with a big step up on his British form from the second and the third well below form.

NOTEBOOK
Robertewenutter raced enthusiastically in the lead, jumped adequately, and though he was perhaps coming to the end of his tether he showed a good attitude to keep going and fend off the late challenger. He gained his first win earlier this month in just a modest maiden chase at Catterick, but he put up a reasonable time there to hint at better things to come and might be a bit ahead of the handicapper at the moment. (op 13-8)
Seigneur Des Bois(FR) has been struggling on softer ground this winter, but still jumped slowly off this better ground. He was under pressure from some way out but responded to his jockey's urgings to put up a challenge to the winner. This was a reasonable return following a winter break, but he does not look to have that much progression in him. (op 3-1 tchd 2-1)

Seeyaaj was under pressure from the third-last but could find no response, and was disappointing. He looks to have a stiff task from his current mark to offset his apparent decline. (op 11-8 tchd 15-8)

5005 NORTH EAST WALES UNISON INTERMEDIATE OPEN NATIONAL HUNT FLAT RACE 2m 1f

5:25 (5:26) (Class 5) 4-6-Y-0 **£1,541** (£449; £224)

Form				RPR
	1		**Granville Island (IRE)** 4-10-10 0 AlanO'Keeffe (Jennie Candlish) *t.k.h in last: stdy hdwy 4f out: chsd ldng pair 2f out: styd on to ld fnl stride* **11/4**[2]	103+
3	**2**	*shd*	**General Melchett (IRE)**[42] 4082 4-10-7 0 TomMolloy[(3)] (Giles Smyly) *w ldr: led over 1f out: hdd post* **9/2**[3]	103
31	**3**	*2 1/2*	**Jackson Cage (IRE)**[24] 4423 6-11-10 0 JasonMaguire (Donald McCain) *led: qcknd pce 5f out: hdd over 1f out: kpt on same pce* **9/4**[1]	114
	4	*23*	**Timeforagin** 4-9-12 0 CO'Farrell[(5)] (Brian Eckley) *trckd ldrs: drvn over 5f out: outpcd over 2f out: kpt on to take poor 4th nr fin* **9/1**	70
3	**5**	*shd*	**Sir Charlie Hutch (GER)**[26] 4396 6-11-3 0 BarryKeniry (Alan Swinbank) *chsd ldrs: drvn over 3f out: hung lft and wknd 2f out* **9/2**[3]	84
0	**6**	*19*	**Best Start**[7] 4881 5-11-0 0 TommyPhelan[(3)] (Claire Dyson) *trckd ldrs: drvn 6f out: lost pl over 3f out: sn bhd* **25/1**	65
6	**7**	*12*	**Sine Mora**[11] 4801 5-11-3 0 AdrianLane (Donald McCain) *t.k.h in rr: lost pl over 3f out: sn bhd* **14/1**	53
0	**8**	*3 3/4*	**Midnight Choice**[28] 4356 6-11-3 0 SamThomas (Mrs H Parrott) *uns rdr and rn loose bef s: hld up in rr: lost pl over 4f out: t.o 2f out* **33/1**	49

4m 4.10s (-1.20) **Going Correction** -0.475s/f (Good)
WFA 4 from 5yo+ 7lb **8** Ran SP% **117.3**
Speed ratings: **83,82,81,70,70 61,56,54**
toteswingers:1&2 £5.60, 2&3 £3.40, 1&3 £2.60 CSF £16.12 TOTE £3.30: £1.80, £1.20, £1.10; EX 16.70.
Owner P and Mrs G A Clarke **Bred** Gareth Metcalfe **Trained** Basford Green, Staffs

FOCUS
A modest bumper and the principals came clear. There is a case for rating the race a lot higher but the time was slow.

NOTEBOOK
Granville Island(IRE) was quite keen on his racecourse debut, but he was held up at the back of the field until the pace lifted going to the home turn. His jockey nearly overdid the confident ride, as he had to dig deep to get on terms and only just prevailed in a photo. However, the tactics did highlight that he has a turn of foot and stays well, as you might expect from a gelding related to useful hurdles and chase winners at distances from 2m to 2m6f. (op 4-1)
General Melchett(IRE) tracked the leader throughout and fought all the way to the line, showing that he has improved on his Warwick bumper debut. (op 4-1)
Jackson Cage(IRE) set the pace and though he remained in touch with the leading pair in the closing stages, the penalty for his C&D win earlier this month just proved too much. He looks as if he might do best on softer ground. (op 5-2 tchd 11-4)
Timeforagin attracted some market support for her bumper debut, but she could not go with the leaders as the pace quickened and was well beaten, though she did win the battle for third. (op 14-1)
Sir Charlie Hutch(GER) was struggling by the final turn and hung left in the straight, suggesting this Flat-bred did not see out the trip. (op 4-1)
T/Plt: £73.30 to a £1 stake. Pool of £49,155.41 - 489.02 winning tickets. T/Qpdt: £22.10 to a £1 stake. Pool of £3,280.04 - 109.80 winning tickets. WG

4986 NEWBURY (L-H)
Saturday, March 26

OFFICIAL GOING: Good
Rail realignment increased hurdle distances by 20metres per circuit and chases by 15metres per circuit.
Wind: Nil Weather: Hazy sunshine

5006 JOHN OWEN JONES 30TH BIRTHDAY JUVENILE H'CAP HURDLE (10 hdls) 2m 3f

1:45 (1:46) (Class 3) (0-130,135) 4-Y-O **£6,505** (£1,910; £955; £477)

Form				RPR
1344	**1**		**Ultravox (USA)**[27] 4377 4-10-12 **114** NickScholfield (Jeremy Scott) *bmpd 1st: disp ld fr next and remained upsides tl led wl bef 3 out: rdn sn after and strly chal fr 2 out and thrght run-in tl asserted fnl 50yds: gamely* **11/2**	118
3024	**2**	*1 1/2*	**Franklino (FR)**[57] 3785 4-10-5 **107** RobertThornton (Alan King) *in tch: chsd ldrs fr 6th: rdn to chal fr 2 out and stl upsides run-in: fnd no ex and one pce fnl 50yds* **11/2**	110
0232	**3**	*26*	**Two Kisses (IRE)**[22] 4458 4-11-7 **123** APMcCoy (Brendan Powell) *led: bmpd 1st: narrowly hdd 6th: sn rdn: styd upsides tl wknd after 3 out: lft mod 3rd whn hit 2 out: blnd last* **11/4**[1]	106
524	**4**	*12*	**Promised Wings (GER)**[26] 4397 4-10-2 **104** ColinBolger (Chris Gordon) *in rr but in tch: rdn along fr 6th: styd on to take mod 4th after 2 out* **20/1**	76
2026	**5**	*7*	**Kahfre**[25] 4196 4-10-4 **111** (v) JoshuaMoore[(5)] (Gary Moore) *in tch: chsd ldrs and pushed along 4 out: drvn to chal next: u.p and 1 l 3rd whn blnd bdly 2 out: nt rcvr* **8/1**	98+
165	**6**	*77*	**Comedy Act**[31] 4283 4-11-6 **122** (b[1]) RichardJohnson (Philip Hobbs) *chsd ldrs: slt ld fr 6th but sn hanging lft: hdd wl bef 3 out: continued to hang bdly and sn btn: t.o whn blnd 2 out* **5/1**[3]	15
415	**P**		**Moose Moran (USA)**[22] 4458 4-11-8 **124** BarryGeraghty (Nicky Henderson) *chsd ldrs: rdn and btn after 4 out: t.o whn p.u bef 2 out* **4/1**[2]	—

4m 41.77s (-8.83) **Going Correction** -0.45s/f (Good) **7** Ran SP% **110.0**
Speed ratings: **100,99,88,83,80 48,—**
toteswingers:1&2 £6.90, 2&3 £3.80, 1&3 £2.90 CSF £32.45 CT £92.90 TOTE £7.10: £3.60, £3.30; EX 37.50.
Owner Jonathan Harvey **Bred** Hascombe Stud **Trained** Brompton Regis, Somerset

FOCUS
Due to the warm conditions on Friday afternoon, 3mm of water was put on in the home straight overnight to freshen up the ground. The jockeys were unanimous in describing the going as dead afterwards and Tony McCoy was certainly not complimentary. He said "It's good, but a little bit dead. I don't think it's particularly nice." The first two are on the upgrade.

NOTEBOOK
Ultravox(USA) didn't look the most obvious candidate against some unexposed sorts, but he showed a good attitude after making plenty of the running and put in a tough, game effort. He has become a lot more consistent since going hurdling and obviously stays well. (op 13-2 tchd 7-1)
Franklino(FR) didn't do a great deal on his handicap debut, but had been rested since that disappointing performance. Up to a trip well worth trying with him considering his previous efforts, and with Robert Thornton riding after his intended mount was pulled out, this was a lot better. However, he was still unable to get his head in front, but deserves a chance to build on this. (op 15-2)
Two Kisses(IRE) returned to her best last time here (Moose Moran behind) but was easily beaten off before the home turn and wouldn't have been third had Kahfre not ploughed through two out. (op 3-1)
Promised Wings(GER), making his handicap debut, couldn't be easily fancied and was well held. (op 16-1)
Kahfre ◆ ploughed through two out, almost sending his jockey to the floor. The Gary Moore-trained runner was far from beaten when making his mistake, although he was making hard work of it, and is one to keep an eye out for in the coming weeks if the ground stays quick. (tchd 9-1)
Comedy Act, readily beaten by Moose Moran at Doncaster, had blinkers on for the first time and travelled best of all, but he stopped alarmingly quickly once he'd had enough. (op 4-1)
Moose Moran(USA) had proved to be either hit or miss since going over hurdles, and one pleasing performance at Doncaster was flanked with two ordinary performances, including at this course. Up in trip, this was another 'miss' and he isn't a serious betting proposition until becoming more consistent. (op 7-2)

5007 E B F/THOROUGHBRED BREEDERS' ASSOCIATION MARES' NOVICES' CHASE FINALE H'CAP (LISTED RACE) (17 fncs) 2m 6f 110y

2:15 (2:15) (Class 1) 5-Y-0+ **£17,038** (£6,505; £3,325; £1,732; £937)

Form				RPR
-11F	**1**		**Easter Legend**[100] 2978 7-11-7 **136** JackDoyle (Emma Lavelle) *hit 1st: hld up in rr: hit 9th: hdwy to trck ldrs and hit 13th: chal 4 out: sn led: drvn clr run-in* **6/1**[3]	148+
2125	**2**	*5*	**Magical Legend**[140] 2214 10-10-0 **115** (t) PaddyBrennan (Sophie Leech) *in rr: hdwy 12th: rdn fr 4 out: chsd wnr after 2 out: kpt on run-in but no ch w wnr* **11/1**	120
F3P1	**3**	*6*	**Douryna**[20] 4504 8-9-7 **115** oh10 MrRGHenderson[(7)] (Colin Tizzard) *hit 2nd: chsd ldr tl led 13th: hdd after 4 out: lost 2nd after 2 out: styd on same pce* **10/1**	116
-214	**4**	*15*	**Cool Friend (IRE)**[41] 4096 8-10-10 **125** NickScholfield (Jeremy Scott) *in tch: hit 10th: chsd ldrs 13th: rdn next: one pce 3 out: wknd after 2 out* **7/1**	112
0211	**5**	*20*	**Asturienne**[26] 4398 7-10-10 **125** (p) RobertThornton (Alan King) *chsd ldrs: rdn 4 out: wknd after next* **4/1**[2]	102
2523	**U**		**Cobbler's Queen (IRE)**[18] 4538 7-10-0 **115** oh4 (p) AndrewTinkler (Henry Daly) *in rr: hit 6th and 7th: rdn after 12th: bhd and no ch whn blnd: hmpd and uns rdr 4 out* **14/1**	—
1132	**P**		**Smuglin**[56] 3817 8-11-1 **130** TimmyMurphy (Donald McCain) *chsd ldrs tl rdn and dropped in rr 7th: t.o 12th: p.u bef 4 out* **14/1**	—
4111	**F**		**Kerada (FR)**[37] 4162 7-11-10 **139** BarryGeraghty (Nicky Henderson) *trckd ldrs fr 5th: led 12th: hdd next: upsides and styng on whn fell 4 out* **3/1**[1]	—
1121	**P**		**Evella (IRE)**[13] 4746 7-10-7 **125** AlexMerriam[(3)] (Neil King) *led to 12th: sn wknd: p.u bef next* **8/1**	—

5m 37.84s (-12.46) **Going Correction** -0.25s/f (Good) **9** Ran SP% **113.7**
Speed ratings: **111,109,107,101,95 —,—,—,—**
toteswingers:1&2 £13.50, 2&3 £85.50, 1&3 £24.00 CSF £65.93 CT £645.37 TOTE £6.80: £2.20, £3.40, £3.00; EX 63.00 Trifecta £684.90 Part won. Pool: £925.57 - 0.41 winning units..
Owner Simon Willes **Bred** Simon Willes **Trained** Wildhern, Hants

FOCUS
The race conditions and title may have been slightly different this season (there are no qualifiers for this Finale), but it was another rock-solid renewal. There was quite a wide range of abilities on show when considering official ratings, but the market had an open look and many could be easily fancied. The impressive winner is up 10lb on her best hurdles form, with the next two to their marks.

NOTEBOOK
Easter Legend, off since mid-December, failed in her bid to land a hat-trick at Exeter last time when falling (possibly held at the time), but could be spotted travelling with ominous ease throughout here and won in the manner of a good horse after getting a couple of reminders to go about her business. She may now be retired to the paddocks. (tchd 11-2)
Magical Legend, returning from a long absence, crept into the race from off the pace but couldn't bridge the gap to the winner, hard though she tried. It was a decent effort and she claimed some black type. (op 12-1 tchd 10-1)
Douryna ◆ looked an interesting runner off such a low weight (she was 10lb out of the handicap), and almost certainly ran up to her best. She should be winning more races at a lower level. (op 14-1)
Cool Friend(IRE) had plenty of experience on her side over fences and some of her form was decent, but she came under pressure soon after four out and wasn't able to get to make her presence felt. The trainer had reported beforehand that a reoccurrence of an old injury had hampered his horse in its preparation for this, and had been slightly pessimistic as a result. (op 8-1)
Asturienne came into this off the back of two victories after splitting Kerada and Smuglin at this course. She ran a bit flat and maybe left her race in the paddock, where she was said to have been on her toes. (op 7-2 tchd 9-2 in a place)
Kerada(FR), third in the mares' hurdle final on this card last season, had been so impressive since going over fences and looked the one to beat, even under top weight. However, having been kept wide early, she seemed to be feeling her burden for a lot of the contest and was only staying on at the one pace when taking a nasty tumble three out. Hopefully, she won't be unduly affected by the fall. (op 11-4 tchd 7-2)

5008 E B F MARES' "NATIONAL HUNT" NOVICES' HURDLE FINALE LIMITED H'CAP (LISTED RACE) (10 hdls) 2m 5f

2:50 (2:51) (Class 1) 4-Y-0+

£20,523 (£7,700; £3,855; £1,922; £964; £482)

Form				RPR
1FU2	**1**		**Line Freedom (FR)**[30] 4309 6-10-12 **125** JeremiahMcGrath[(7)] (Nicky Henderson) *chsd ldrs: n.m.r on ins bnd after 3rd: j. slowly 5th: rdn to chse ldrs 3 out: slt ld next: drvn and hld on wl run-in* **12/1**	135+
0221	**2**	*1 1/2*	**Violin Davis (FR)**[15] 4703 5-10-11 **117** RWalsh (Paul Nicholls) *hld up in mid-div: hdwy appr 3 out: styd on u.p and nt fluent last: chsd wnr fnl 50yds but a hld* **12/1**	125
4	**3**	*1 1/2*	**Shop Dj (IRE)**[87] 3202 6-11-8 **128** (t) ADLeigh (Peter Fahey, Ire) *bdly hmpd and dropped in rr bnd after 3rd: hdwy 3 out: styd on fr next: disp 2nd run-in and kpt on but a hld by wnr* **13/2**[2]	137+
4251	**4**	*3 1/4*	**Mizzurka**[41] 4101 7-10-9 **122** NathanSweeney[(7)] (Bob Buckler) *chsd ldrs: led 4th: narrowly hdd 4 out: led again 3 out: narrowly hdd next: styd on same pce run-in* **20/1**	126
1331	**5**	*2*	**Semi Colon (FR)**[18] 4535 5-10-7 **113** APMcCoy (Nicky Henderson) *chsd ldrs: chal 4 out and stl upsides fr next to 2 out: styd on same pce u.p run-in* **6/1**[1]	117+

U112 **6** *9* **Molly Round (IRE)**[23] 4446 7-10-4 **110** oh1 NickScholfield 104
(Grant Cann) *in rr: hdwy and rdn 4 out: chsd ldrs next: wknd fr 2 out* **25/1**

/311 **7** *2 1/4* **Wistow**[13] 4747 7-11-2 **125** CPGeoghegan(3) 117
(Pam Sly) *chsd ldrs: rdn 3 out: wknd after next* **11/1**

P011 **8** *1 1/4* **Emmaslegend**[10] 4814 6-10-9 **115** (t) ColinBolger 106
(Suzy Smith) *chsd ldrs: led 4 out: hdd next: wknd after 2 out* **8/1**[3]

4112 **9** *2 1/2* **Empress Orchid**[24] 4417 6-10-0 **113** HenryBrooke(7) 102
(Donald McCain) *chsd ldrs: chal 6th to 3 out: wknd next* **22/1**

13PU **10** *1* **Animation (IRE)**[18] 4536 7-10-1 **110** JimmyDerham(3) 98
(Seamus Mullins) *in rr: hdwy 5th: wknd after 3 out* **40/1**

4210 **11** *7* **Way Back When**[21] 4481 6-10-4 **110** RobertThornton 91
(Alan King) *in rr tl hdwy to chse ldrs 4 out: wknd qckly next* **16/1**

1213 **12** *4 1/2* **Kells Belle (IRE)**[15] 4703 5-11-1 **121** AndrewTinkler 103+
(Nicky Henderson) *n.m.r bnd after 3rd: in tch tl n.m.r and dropped in rr after 4 out: no ch after* **25/1**

0631 **13** *42* **Francesa**[9] 4828 6-10-8 **114** RichardJohnson 53
(Henry Daly) *hmpd and rr bnd after 3rd: hdwy appr 3 out: wknd sn after and mstke 2 out* **22/1**

3110 **14** *3/4* **Malindi Bay**[100] 2983 6-10-9 **115** SeanQuinlan 54
(Kim Bailey) *in rr and hmpd bnd after 3rd: no ch after* **33/1**

2213 **15** *4* **Aneyeforaneye (IRE)**[22] 4454 5-10-4 **110** oh2 DominicElsworth 45
(Malcolm Jefferson) *plld hrd: chsd ldrs to 4 out* **22/1**

2111 **16** *50* **Whoops A Daisy**[27] 4377 5-11-7 **130** RichardKilloran(3) 20
(Nicky Henderson) *chsd ldrs: rdn to chal 3 out: wknd qckly: virtually p.u run-in* **9/1**

1214 **U** **Alverstone**[63] 3674 8-10-11 **120** (t) DavidBass(3) —
(Lawney Hill) *towards rr but wl in tch whn hmpd and uns rdr bnd after 3rd* **8/1**[3]

0401 **P** **Definitley Lovely**[22] 4454 6-10-1 **110** SamTwiston-Davies(3) —
(Nigel Twiston-Davies) *led: blnd 3rd: hdd 4th: wknd after next: t.o whn p.u bef 3 out* **16/1**

5m 1.98s (-17.02) **Going Correction** -0.45s/f (Good) **18** Ran SP% **125.7**
Speed ratings (Par 111): **114,113,112,111,110 107,106,106,105,104 102,100,84,84,82 63,—,—**
toteswingers:1&2 £30.10, 2&3 £23.70, 1&3 £36.90 CSF £133.82 CT £1039.04 TOTE £18.30: £4.00, £2.60, £2.30, £6.10; EX 145.20 Trifecta £1446.50 Pool: £18,452.92 - 9.44 winning units..
Owner Mr & Mrs R Kelvin Hughes **Bred** Mme Georges Vuillard **Trained** Upper Lambourn, Berks
■ Stewards' Enquiry : Jeremiah McGrath caution: used whip with excessive frequency.
A D Leigh two-day ban: used whip with excessive frequency down shoulder in the forehand (Apr 10-11)

FOCUS
As with the preceding race on the card, the name may have changed slightly but the field was bang up to scratch, with unexposed types from leading stables taking on more exposed ones with plenty of good form in the book. Solid form, with the winner rated up 7lb. The early pace didn''t look frenetic, which is probably why so many had a chance coming to three out.

NOTEBOOK
Line Freedom(FR) seemed to be beaten fair and square at Huntingdon on her previous start and was due to be ridden by Barry Geraghty before he was stood down after a fall in the previous contest. His misfortune provided the talented claimer Jeremiah McGrath with an excellent opportunity to gain a big-race success and he did everything right when in with a chance, holding his mount together in the latter stages as she kept on. She was reported to have been retired after this success.
Violin Davis(FR) ◆ has been making progress and got the job done last time when finishing in front of Kells Belle (who was well beaten in this). She had work to do with Mizzurka on a previous outing, but had the assistance of Ruby Walsh for the first time over hurdles. She doesn't lack scope and is one to watch out for over fences, should connections head in that direction. (tchd 11-1)
Shop Dj(IRE) appeared to have some good form in Ireland, especially on her last run, where she finished second to a classy sort and ahead of some decent performers. Said by her trainer to not be the biggest, but strong, she was out the back early after being hampered, but appeared to be going well. She threaded her way through runners, sometimes meeting trouble, but had every chance once in line for home and wasn't good enough under a big weight. (op 7-1 tchd 8-1)
Mizzurka is clearly capable of good form when putting her mind to it (trainer feels she is at her best with ease in the going), so this was a fine performance after being up with the pace throughout.
Semi Colon(FR) had the potential to be a good bit better than her official mark for respected connections, and looked a possible winner at one stage in the home straight when staying closer to the inside of the course than some of her rivals. However, her stamina seemed to ebb away at this level late on, and she lost fourth close home after wandering a little. (op 7-1 tchd 5-1)
Molly Round(IRE) has enjoyed a good season and ran another cracker without being quite good enough. (op 28-1)
Wistow, chasing a hat-trick, hadn't beaten anything of note and struggled in this better company when the tempo lifted. (op 12-1 tchd 14-1)
Emmaslegend gained the first of her two successes coming into this off an official rating of 88 (which looked fully justified), so this looked a tall order off a 27lb higher mark. She ran respectably up to a point, but faded late on.
Whoops A Daisy had a fantastic profile, but the weight she had to carry slightly tempered enthusiasm. She seemed to find this big field of talented mares too tough at this stage of her career (op 8-1)
Alverstone's only defeats this year had come when a long way behind Sparky May, but she was given no chance to play a part here, as she unseated her rider on the flat as the field headed out for their final circuit. Unfortunately, she picked up an injury which has ended her racing career. (op 10-1 tchd 11-1)

5009 DON & DOT ROSEFF MEMORIAL H'CAP CHASE (21 fncs) 3m 2f 110y
3:25 (3:25) (Class 2) (0-140,136) 5-Y-0+
£10,019 (£2,960; £1,480; £740; £369; £185)

Form RPR

2132 **1** **Rey Nacarado (IRE)**[36] 4181 6-10-1 **111** (p) AndrewTinkler 122
(Charlie Longsdon) *hld up in rr: hit 6th and next: stdy hdwy 16th: trckd ldr after 4 out: sddle slipped bk after 2 out: drvn to ld last: styd on wl* **7/2**[2]

2500 **2** *2* **Maktu**[21] 4487 9-11-12 **136** RWalsh 146
(Pat Murphy) *in tch: trckd ldrs 16th: wnt 2nd 17th: chalng whn lft in ld 4 out: rdn 2 out: hdd last: kpt on same pce* **13/2**

F044 **3** *14* **Scots Dragoon**[15] 4699 9-10-2 **115** DavidBass(3) 113
(Nicky Henderson) *chsd ldrs: dropped in rr 15th: styd on again to take wl hld 3rd fr 2 out* **7/1**

0-04 **4** *13* **Ogee**[21] 4466 8-11-10 **134** JimmyMcCarthy 122
(Renee Robeson) *chsd ldrs: hit 4th: blnd 15th: wknd after 17th: lost wl hld 3rd fr 2 out* **5/2**[1]

P35P **5** *18* **Burren Legend (IRE)**[9] 4821 10-10-11 **128** MrTJCannon(7) 99
(Richard Rowe) *in rr: j. slowly 12th: hdwy 16th: blnd 17th and sn wknd* **12/1**

451P **6** *2 1/2* **Double Dizzy**[21] 4486 10-10-3 **118** (bt) JoshuaMoore(5) 84
(Bob Buckler) *led to 4th: styd pressing ldr and drvn along fr 10th: hit 16th: wknd bef 4 out* **20/1**

-264 **7** *31* **Briery Fox (IRE)**[31] 4284 13-11-2 **126** MarkBradburne 64
(Henry Daly) *j. slowly 3rd: bhd most of way* **16/1**

0-14 **P** **Noble Crusader (USA)**[22] 4460 8-11-3 **127** (b) TomScudamore —
(Richard Lee) *in rr: hit 14th and bhd: t.o whn p.u bef 17th* **16/1**

5303 **F** **Theatre Dance (IRE)**[29] 4328 10-10-9 **119** (v1) APMcCoy —
(David Arbuthnot) *w ldr: led 4th: hdd 10th: led again 13th: mstke 16th: rdn and jnd whn fell 4 out* **9/2**[3]

6m 42.35s (-13.65) **Going Correction** -0.25s/f (Good) **9** Ran SP% **119.0**
Speed ratings: **110,109,105,101,96 95,86,—,—**
toteswingers:1&2 £5.90, 2&3 £8.00, 1&3 £5.20 CSF £27.72 CT £153.91 TOTE £4.80: £2.10, £2.10, £2.20; EX 35.30 Trifecta £350.50 Pool: £871.57 - 1.83 winning units..
Owner Runthatbymeagainagain **Bred** Sweet Wall **Trained** Over Norton, Oxon

FOCUS
A competitive contest with some interesting horses taking their chance on forecast ground they had been struggling to find during the winter. However, it's debatable whether the going was good considering earlier comments by some jockeys.

NOTEBOOK
Rey Nacarado(IRE) was lurking at the bottom of the weights and represented a stable in great form. His chance didn't look completely obvious judged on his previous two starts, but the return of cheekpieces may have got him concentrating, as he stayed on really strongly over the final three fences to get the runner-up at the right time despite his saddle starting to slip backwards after two out. (op 5-1)
Maktu ◆, ridden by Ruby Walsh for the first time, was only 4lb higher than when a fine second at Haydock in November (to the progressive King Fontaine), and was back over what looked a more suitable trip. Favourite for the Welsh National in late December, the jockey got him beautifully settled and did everything right before the weight the partnership had to give away to Rey Nacarado told. It was fine performance and he looks worth his chance in the Bet365 Gold Cup, especially if Pat Murphy could somehow gain the services of Ruby again, who appeared to really get on with the horse. (op 11-2)
Scots Dragoon was struggling quite early and needed to be hard ridden down the back straight on their final circuit. He looked a lost cause at one point, and likely to pull up, but he was made to keep going and ran on when it was all too late. (op 13-2 tchd 8-1)
Ogee appeared to have lots in his favour after being dropped another 5lb since his last run (his first for 112 days), and was 3lb lower than when a fine third in the 2010 William Hill Trophy at the Cheltenham Festival. The ground had looked ideal, but the watering overnight plus a rain shower before they started went against him, and he can be given one more chance before being regarded as disappointing. (op 11-4)
Burren Legend(IRE) took this off an 8lb lower mark last season and made good ground into contention before weakening. (op 14-1)
Theatre Dance(IRE) had a visor tried in an attempt to revive his fortunes off what looked a handy mark, and he ran well after showing lots of zest until falling four out when joined. He did look in trouble at that point, but probably would have posted a good performance. (op 11-2)

5010 JOHN HAINE MEMORIAL NOVICES' HURDLE (8 hdls) 2m 110y
4:00 (4:01) (Class 4) 4-Y-0+ **£3,252** (£955; £477; £238)

Form RPR

6 **1** **Current Event (FR)**[125] 2540 4-10-7 0 RWalsh 130+
(Paul Nicholls) *trckd ldr: qcknd to chal 3 out: sn led: c clr fr 2 out: v easily* **15/8**[2]

-402 **2** *18* **Fontano (FR)**[20] 4499 5-10-11 116 AlexMerriam(3) 114
(Emma Lavelle) *in rr but in tch: hdwy appr 3 out: chsd wnr fr 2 out but nvr any ch and wl btn run-in* **9/2**[3]

1 **3** *11* **Tony Star (FR)**[79] 3401 4-10-13 0 RichardJohnson 106
(Philip Hobbs) *led: jnd 3 out: sn hdd: wknd and nt fluent 2 out: j. slowly last* **13/8**[1]

50 **4** *14* **Only Witness (IRE)**[6] 4895 6-11-0 0 TomSiddall 92
(Brendan Powell) *in rr: wl behnd 3 out: styd on to take poor 4th run-in* **50/1**

3 **5** *3 1/2* **Cheney Manor**[79] 3405 6-10-7 0 MrNdeBoinville(7) 88
(Nicky Henderson) *chsd ldrs: hit 3 out: wknd qckly next* **9/1**

F-31 **6** *35* **Katchmore (IRE)**[19] 4521 4-10-13 121 JimmyMcCarthy 56
(Michael Blanshard) *chsd ldrs: rdn after 4 out: wknd and mstke 3 out: t.o* **16/1**

P0 **P** **Surf And Turf (IRE)**[23] 4437 5-11-0 0 DominicElsworth —
(Jonjo O'Neill) *a in rr: t.o fr 4 out: p.u bef 2 out* **25/1**

4m 3.56s (-6.34) **Going Correction** -0.45s/f (Good)
WFA 4 from 5yo+ 7lb **7** Ran SP% **112.7**
Speed ratings (Par 105): **96,87,82,75,74 57,—**
toteswingers:1&2 £2.10, 2&3 £2.40, 1&3 £1.10 CSF £10.69 TOTE £2.90: £1.60, £2.30; EX 12.00.
Owner Mrs Bunty Millard **Bred** M L Bloodstock Limited **Trained** Ditcheat, Somerset

FOCUS
The impressive winner fulfilled the promise of his French form and the next three were all within 5lb of their pre-race marks.

NOTEBOOK
Current Event(FR) ◆ was clearly disappointing on his opening effort for this stable at Aintree way back in November, but the trainer reported before the race that they found that his breathing wasn't right there, so the horse had an operation. Said to be going nicely at home, this was much more like it and he looks one to follow over both hurdles and fences in the coming weeks. (op 11-4)
Fontano(FR) has plenty of ability and closed up going strongly, but found the winner too classy and couldn't go on when in with every chance. (tchd 11-2)
Tony Star(FR) was the most interesting runner considering his opening effort for this stable at Huntingdon, where he had plenty of subsequent winners in behind. However, he played up a little at the start and then took a good grip under Richard Johnson when the jumped off. He probably did too much out in front and had nothing to offer when Current Event bounded past. (op 11-8 tchd 5-4)
Only Witness(IRE) kept on but never threatened. (op 40-1)
Cheney Manor probably wasn't aided by the water that had got into the ground, but still looked really one paced under pressure. (op 15-2 tchd 10-1)

5011 BROADBASE H'CAP CHASE (13 fncs) 2m 1f
4:30 (4:31) (Class 3) (0-125,125) 5-Y-0+ **£3,903** (£1,146; £573; £286)

Form RPR

4302 **1** **Quipe Me Posted (FR)**[13] 4744 7-9-13 **105** MrTJCannon(7) 124+
(Suzy Smith) *trckd ldr fr 2nd: led appr 4 out: pushed clr fr next: comf* **2/1**[1]

0411 **2** *14* **Qianshan Leader (IRE)**[22] 4456 7-11-11 **124** JackDoyle 128
(Emma Lavelle) *led tl after 1st: hit 6th and dropped towards rr: hit 9th: pushed along and styd on fr 3 out: wnt 2nd and hit lst: kpt on but nvr any ch w wnr* **9/4**[2]

0034 **3** *16* **Mister Matt (IRE)**[20] 4504 8-9-10 **102** NathanSweeney(7) 92
(Bob Buckler) *chsd ldrs: rdn appr 4 out: no imp and kpt on to hold mod 3rd fr 2 out* **7/2**[3]

1433 **4** *9* **Lord Singer (FR)**[21] 4482 6-11-7 **120** (b) AndrewGlassonbury 102
(Gary Moore) *led afer 1st: t.k.h: rdn 9th: hdd appr 4 out: sn no ch w wnr: wl btn whn mstke 2 out* **12/1**

4552 **P** **Coach Lane**[16] 4671 10-10-6 **105**....(p) LiamTreadwell —
(Nick Mitchell) *in rr: rdn and hdwy to cl on ldrs 8th: wknd and hit 4 out: mstke next: p.u bef last* **9/1**

P-22 **P** **Norman The Great**[40] 4122 7-11-12 **125**.... RobertThornton —
(Alan King) *a in rr: lost tch after 8th: t.o whn p.u bef 4 out* **9/1**

4m 9.49s (-3.51) **Going Correction** -0.25s/f (Good) **6** Ran SP% **114.0**
Speed ratings: **98,91,83,79,—** —
toteswingers:1&2 £1.10, 2&3 £2.50, 1&3 £1.50 CSF £7.45 TOTE £3.80: £1.80, £1.40; EX 9.90.
Owner Scoobyless Partnership **Bred** Gheorghe Codre **Trained** Lewes, E Sussex

FOCUS

This was never going to be a slowly run affair with habitual front-runner Lord Singer taking his place in the line-up, but most of his rivals ignored him. The winner stepped up on his Market Rasen run and there's a case for rating the race a bit higher.

NOTEBOOK

Quipe Me Posted(FR) ◆ had been mainly well beaten over fences since going over them but, on only his second start for this trainer, won this by a wide margin once taking it up. In front of a dual subsequent winner last time, connections will want to get him out fairly quickly if they can. (op 7-2 tchd 4-1)

Qianshan Leader(IRE) was chasing a hat-trick (previous wins were well spaced) off a 5lb higher mark than his previous start, but got caught one paced before running on again after the winner had gone beyond recall. (op 15-8 tchd 7-4)

Mister Matt(IRE), down in trip, raced a bit keenly while being held up and, after looking dangerous after five out, soon found less than expected and was no threat. He also started jumping to his left at the final few fences. (op 4-1 tchd 9-2)

Lord Singer(FR) ran his race from the front again but was readily held once joined. (op 10-1 tchd 14-1)

Coach Lane is well handicapped on the majority of his victories but didn't get involved here, hard though he tried, before being pulled up. (op 10-1 tchd 15-2)

Norman The Great, making his handicap debut, likes a decent surface so the ease in the ground was all against him, and this effort is best ignored. (op 10-1 tchd 15-2)

5012 WEST BERKSHIRE RACING CLUB "JUNIOR" BUMPER (STANDARD OPEN NATIONAL HUNT FLAT RACE) 1m 4f 110y

5:05 (5:05) (Class 5) 4-Y-O **£2,055** (£599; £299)

Form RPR

1 **Turbo Du Ranch (FR)** 4-10-12 0.... RobertThornton 107
(Warren Greatrex) *in rr: gd hdwy over 3f out: styd on wl to press ldrs whn green and hung lft fr 2f out: drvn and kpt on wl thrght fnl f to ld cl home* **16/1**

3 **2** *nk* **Broomfield**[21] 4491 4-10-12 0.... RWalsh 106
(Paul Nicholls) *hld up in rr: hdwy over 3f out: drvn and qcknd to chse ldrs 2f out: slt ld 1f out: styd on wl: hdd and no ex cl home* **11/10**[1]

3 *3 ¾* **Judge Davis** 4-10-9 0.... IanPopham(3) 101
(Caroline Keevil) *chsd ldrs: drvn to chal ins fnl 2f: slt ld over 1f out: sn hdd: styd on same pce ins fnl f* **33/1**

4 *1 ¼* **Ginger Fizz** 4-10-5 0.... CharliePoste 92
(Ben Case) *chsd ldrs: rdn and slt ld 2f out: hdd over 1f out: kpt on same pce u.p* **25/1**

5 *3* **Frolic Along (IRE)** 4-9-12 0.... HenryBrooke(7) 87
(J R Jenkins) *in rr: hdwy 3f out: chsd ldrs fr 2f out: kpt on same pce fr over 1f out* **40/1**

0 **6** *1 ¼* **Dark Shadow**[42] 4082 4-10-9 0.... DavidBass(3) 92
(Nicky Henderson) *in tch whn pushed along and lost position over 5f out: styd on u.p fnl 2f: gng on cl home* **8/1**[3]

20 **7** *hd* **Jumps Road**[36] 4191 4-10-12 0.... JoeTizzard 92
(Colin Tizzard) *chsd ldrs: rdn to chal 3f out: wknd ins fnl 2f* **12/1**

8 *1 ¼* **Silver Stirrup (IRE)** 4-10-12 0.... APMcCoy 90
(Jonjo O'Neill) *chsd ldrs: pushed along 3f out: wknd ins fnl 2f* **11/4**[2]

9 *3* **Lady Kathleen** 4-10-5 0.... DominicElsworth 79
(Paul Webber) *in rr: rdn along 3f out: kpt on fnl 2f: nt rch ldrs* **16/1**

10 *½* **Forgotten Promise** 4-10-5 0.... WillKennedy 78
(Jo Crowley) *chsd ldr: narrow ld over 3f out: sn rdn hdd 2f out: wknd ins fnl f* **40/1**

11 *hd* **Duke Of Monmouth (IRE)** 4-10-9 0.... PeterToole(3) 85
(Charlie Mann) *mid-div: rdn and styd on to get in bhd ldrs 3f out: sn one pce: styd on again ins fnl f* **16/1**

6 **12** *2 ½* **Conigre**[139] 2237 4-10-12 0.... AndrewThornton 82+
(Tor Sturgis) *chsd ldrs: rdn to chal whn green and hung lft over 2f out: wknd over 1f out* **40/1**

50 **13** *7* **Trevis**[21] 4484 4-10-12 0.... LiamTreadwell 71
(Peter Bull) *led: rdn 4f out: jnd over 3f out: narrowly hdd sn after: styd front rnk tl wknd over 2f out* **66/1**

60 **14** *10* **Cailin Maghnailbhe (IRE)**[47] 3979 4-10-2 0.... JimmyDerham(3) 49
(Seamus Mullins) *a towards rr* **40/1**

0 **15** *11* **Rachael's Ruby**[28] 4356 4-9-12 0.... MrTJCannon(7) 32
(Roger Teal) *chsd ldrs tl wknd over 3f out* **40/1**

3m 7.42s (1.62) **Going Correction** -0.45s/f (Good) **15** Ran SP% **131.2**
Speed ratings: **85,84,82,81,79 79,79,78,76,76 75,74,70,63,57**
toteswingers:1&2 £8.10, 2&3 £30.00, 1&3 £103.30 CSF £35.09 TOTE £19.90: £3.70, £1.10, £9.00; EX 68.60.
Owner Gdm Partnership **Bred** Yannick Berlin & Jean-Michel Peccot **Trained** Upper Lambourn, Berks

FOCUS

This race has produced several talented individuals in the past, but Oscar Whiskey and Whiteoak stood out. This was probably an ordinary bumper for the track.

NOTEBOOK

Turbo Du Ranch(FR) ◆, described as a 'funny character', stayed on in dour style after taking a little while to get organised in the home straight. The win didn't surprise the trainer, who said the horse had shown a bit at home, and the plan is to run in another bumper before going hurdling. (tchd 20-1)

Broomfield takes a strong hold just like his half-brother Beherayn, but still almost managed to win down in trip. He needs to learn to settle to get 2m eventually, even around a tight course, but he is one for the Flat possibly now his trainer is taking out a license for that code. (op 11-8)

Judge Davis looks a fine, big gelding and must have pleased connections no need. He seems sure to have plenty more improvement to come. (op 40-1)

Ginger Fizz has a nice Flat pedigree and showed plenty of ability on her first start. (op 33-1 tchd 22-1)

Frolic Along(IRE) was green and took a while to get the hang of things before keeping on.

Dark Shadow seemed to have stamina limitations when a warm favourite at Warwick (1m6f) on his debut last month, but just looked like hard work this time. (tchd 15-2)

Silver Stirrup(IRE) is closely related to smart hurdler Won In The Dark and fetched 110,000euros last year, but only made a satisfactory debut. (op 3-1 tchd 10-3)

Lady Kathleen really got caught out when the tempo lifted but stayed on nicely when it was too late. (op 20-1)

T/Jkpt: Not won. T/Plt: £1,608.10 to a £1 stake. Pool of £169,345.27 - 76.87 winning tickets. T/Qpdt: £43.00 to a £1 stake. Pool of £12,366.67 - 212.56 winning tickets. ST

4774 STRATFORD (L-H)

Saturday, March 26

OFFICIAL GOING: Good (good to firm in places; watered; 9.7)

All bends moved to provide fresh ground.

Wind: virtually nil Weather: misty, chilly

5013 JENKINSONS CATERERS NOVICES' HURDLE (10 hdls) 2m 3f

2:20 (2:21) (Class 4) 4-Y-O+ **£3,252** (£955; £477; £238)

Form RPR

310 **1** **Hes Our Lad (IRE)**[21] 4468 5-10-10 0.... RachaelGreen(5) 98+
(Anthony Honeyball) *hld up in rr: hdwy to trck ldng pair gng wl and pckd 3 out: led between last 2: nudged along and in command flat* **6/1**[2]

31 **2** *2* **Pilgreen (FR)**[88] 3158 6-11-8 118.... PaulMoloney 98
(Evan Williams) *racd keenly: mstkes and j.rt at times: led: jnd 7th: rdn and hit rail after 3 out: hdd and mstke next: stl ev ch and mstke last: styd on same pce flat* **1/2**[1]

03 **3** *2 ¼* **Abayaan**[15] 4706 5-10-12 0.... (t) PeterToole(3) 88
(Charlie Mann) *t.k.h early: chsd ldr: mstke 2nd: jnd ldr 7th: rdn after next: slt ld and mstke 2 out: sn hdd: wknd flat* **6/1**[2]

460 **4** *3* **Our Golden Boy (IRE)**[22] 4459 5-11-1 0.... DaveCrosse 85
(Mark Usher) *in tch: j.rt 1st: reminders 5th: chsng ldrs and drvn bef 7th: outpcd after 3 out: plugged on but no threat to ldrs between last 2* **18/1**[3]

60 **5** *3 ½* **Luck'N'Thanks (IRE)**[27] 4370 8-11-1 0.... JodieMogford 82
(Graeme McPherson) *t.k.h early: chsd ldrs: mstke 5th: rdn and unable qck after 7th: mstke next: wknd bef 2 out* **33/1**

-43P **6** *6* **Taylors Secret**[13] 4747 5-11-1 0.... (b) DavidEngland 76
(Shaun Lycett) *t.k.h early: in tch: reminders 5th: j.rt and rdn next: drvn 7th: wknd 3 out* **28/1**

00/0 **7** *36* **Termon Boy**[41] 4100 7-10-12 0.... (t) MichaelMurphy(3) 44
(Rob Summers) *mstkes: a in rr: last and rdn 6th: lost tch after next: t.o* **150/1**

4m 37.4s (5.90) **Going Correction** +0.425s/f (Soft) **7** Ran SP% **107.6**
Speed ratings (Par 105): **104,103,102,100,99 96,81**
toteswingers:1&2:£1.02, 1&3:£3.30, 2&3:£1.10 CSF £8.72 TOTE £5.80: £1.90, £1.10; EX 9.80.
Owner A Smith S E Wall A J Forde **Bred** Alistair Corrigan **Trained** Seaborough, Dorset

FOCUS

On an overcast afternoon, the ground was described as good, good to firm in places. Many of the jockeys thought it rode good ground the whole way around. Very little strength in depth in this novice hurdle, which was run at an even tempo. the winner can rate higher but the second was below form.

NOTEBOOK

Hes Our Lad(IRE) put up a pleasing performance. The winner of a bumper before disappointing under a penalty in the same sphere last time out, he jumped well and can win again in similar company, especially at this time of the year. (op 11-2 tchd 5-1)

Pilgreen(FR), the odds-on favourite, had been held up early on both previous career starts, but was forced to make the running and probably wasn't suited the way the race developed. He is worth another chance in novice company as the handicapper hasn't taken any chances rating him 118. (op 4-7)

Abayaan travelled and jumped nicely throughout. Rated 68 on the Flat, a maiden hurdle at this time of the year should be well within his grasp. (op 11-2 tchd 13-2)

Our Golden Boy(IRE), having his second start over hurdles, ran better here and will find life easier in modest handicaps in due course. (op 20-1 tchd 22-1)

5014 BORDEAUX-UNDISCOVERED.CO.UK WINES AT STRATFORD (S) HURDLE (9 hdls 1 omitted) 2m 3f

2:55 (2:55) (Class 5) 4-7-Y-O **£2,055** (£599; £299)

Form RPR

U32P **1** **Sun Tzu (IRE)**[13] 4744 7-10-10 105.... (b) MrTWeston(5) 97
(Dr Richard Newland) *chsd ldr tl lft w ldr 3rd tl bef 7th: rdn and looked reluctant after: fnlly responded to press to chal and hit last: sn led: rdn out* **5/2**[1]

6300 **2** *2* **Rhyton (IRE)**[17] 4550 4-10-4 87.... (p) JohnKington(3) 88
(Donald McCain) *mstkes: lft in ld 2nd: rdn after 7th: hit 2 out: hdd flat: no ex and sn btn* **14/1**

U40 **3** *6* **Claimant (IRE)**[48] 3958 4-10-7 108.... (b[1]) SamJones 84
(Paul Fitzsimons) *t.k.h: in tch: lft chsng ldrs and hmpd 3rd: jnd ldr 7th: ev ch and rdn bef 2 out: hit 2 out: nt qckn and struggling whn n.m.r and swtchd rt between last 2: wknd last* **8/1**

303 **4** *28* **Miss Wendy**[8] 4854 4-10-0 90.... MattieBatchelor 53
(Mark H Tompkins) *nvr really travelling in last pair: pushed along and hmpd 3rd: reminders and struggling after 5th: t.o bypassing 3 out* **5/1**[3]

44P0 **5** *13* **Navajo Nation (IRE)**[6] 4895 5-10-8 97.... (v[1]) MarkQuinlan(7) 53
(Bill Turner) *nvr really travelling and sn pushed along: in tch: hmpd 3rd: rdn 5th: lost tch u.p next: t.o after 7th* **7/1**

0F0F **F** **Killowenabbey (IRE)**[23] 4447 7-11-3 0.... (p) DonalDevereux(3) —
(Debra Hamer) *led tl fell 3rd: fatally injured* **22/1**

5F12 **U** **Hypnotic Gaze (IRE)**[12] 4776 5-11-6 108.... (p) JamesDavies —
(Andrew Haynes) *hld up in tch in rr untl bdly hmpd and uns rdr 3rd* **11/4**[2]

0000 **P** **Roses Legend**[14] 4719 6-10-12 78.... KeiranBurke(3) —
(Reginald Brown) *in tch: rdn and hdwy to chse ldrs after 5th: lost pl qckly next: t.o whn p.u 7th* **25/1**

4m 38.7s (7.20) **Going Correction** +0.425s/f (Soft)
WFA 4 from 5yo+ 7lb **8** Ran SP% **110.4**
Speed ratings: **101,100,97,85,80 —,—,—**
toteswingers:1&2:£10.10, 1&3:£2.90, 2&3:£8.30 CSF £33.57 TOTE £3.00: £1.40, £3.60, £2.00; EX 37.00.There was no bid for the winner
Owner Too Easy Racing & Dr R D P Newland **Bred** Paul Ryan **Trained** Claines, Worcs

FOCUS

A very ordinary seller run at a sound pace and highly unlikely to throw up many future winners. The race was weakened further when Killowenabbey fell fatally at the third, in turn hampering Hypnotic Gaze, who unseated his rider. The third-last flight was bypassed on the final circuit. The winner is rated 10lb off and this is not form to treat too seriously.

NOTEBOOK

Sun Tzu(IRE), rated 105, was well backed beforehand and in the end got the job done. Versatile regarding the ground, he isn't one to take a short price about in a follow-up bid. (op 7-2)

Rhyton(IRE), rated 87, was a winner of a maiden for Sir Michael Stoute on the Flat but has shown very little over hurdles so far. He probably will lose his maiden tag at some point over hurdles, but this is his level and is one of his, respected, yard's lesser lights. Official explanation: vet said gelding lost its near-fore shoe (op 11-1)

Claimant(IRE), rated 108, was wearing blinkers for the first time here and showed he might also have his day in the sunshine. He has had fewer chances than most, this being his fourth start over hurdles. (tchd 13-2)

Miss Wendy handles this ground but was never going, not being helped by being hampered early on. (tchd 9-2)

5015 HAPPY BIRTHDAY CHARLIE WHEELWRIGHT H'CAP CHASE (14 fncs) 2m 4f

3:30 (3:31) (Class 4) (0-110,106) 5-Y-0+ **£5,204** (£1,528; £764; £381)

Form RPR

001 **1** **Himrayn**[13] 4744 8-11-12 **106**.................................... RichieMcLernon 122+
(Anabel L M King) *in tch: wnt 2nd 10th: qcknd clr w ldr sn after 2 out: led bef last: pushed along and r.o wl flat: comf* **9/4**[1]

0- **2** *7* **The Paddy Premium (IRE)**[52] 3895 11-10-13 **100**....... PeterCarberry[(7)] 107
(M A Molloy, Ire) *in tch: mstke 7th and 9th: outpcd u.p 2 out: rallied bef last: chsd wnr flat: styd on but no threat to wnr* **11/2**

P41 **3** *2* **Piment D'Estruval (FR)**[17] 4556 8-11-3 **97**...................... JohnnyFarrelly 103
(Tim Vaughan) *hld up in rr: hdwy 9th: j. ahd 2 out: sn rdn and qcknd clr w wnr: hdd bef last: drvn and btn last: lost 2nd flat* **9/2**[3]

6444 **4** *10* **Phoenix Des Mottes (FR)**[25] 4412 8-9-11 **84**................. JoeCornwall[(7)] 79
(John Cornwall) *in tch in last pair: pushed along and outpcd after 8th: rallied 11th: j.rt and struggling 2 out: 4th and wl hld bef last* **7/2**[2]

35F3 **5** *12* **Quintero (FR)**[33] 4265 7-11-8 **102**....................................(p) PaulMoloney 86
(Evan Williams) *led tl 2 out: sn btn* **11/2**

236P **6** *10* **Kinkeel (IRE)**[27] 4379 12-9-11 **80**............................... EamonDehdashti[(3)] 55
(Tony Carroll) *chsd ldr tl 10th: sn u.p and lost pl bef next: wknd 3 out* **14/1**

5m 0.10s (5.90) **Going Correction** +0.475s/f (Soft) **6** Ran SP% **108.6**
Speed ratings: **107,104,103,99,94 90**
CSF £13.73 TOTE £3.00: £1.10, £3.50; EX 15.70.
Owner Touchwood Racing **Bred** R W Russell **Trained** Wilmcote, Warwicks

FOCUS

A 0-110 handicap chase, in which the top weight was 4lb below the ceiling rating. It was run at an even tempo. The winner is progressive and can rate higher.

NOTEBOOK

Himrayn followed up his Market Rasen win and is now 2-2 over fences. Travelling strongly throughout, he could still be well handicapped and can win again. (op 5-2)
The Paddy Premium(IRE), 3lb higher than his last winning mark, was running here without the cheeckpieces he wore last time out. He gives the impression a step up in trip would suit nowadays. Official explanation: vet said gelding lost its near-hind shoe (op 15-2)
Piment D'Estruval(FR), up 3lb for his victory, looked like taking a serious hand turning for home and possibly didn't quite see out the extra distance. Unexposed over fences, he can win again back at the minimum trip. (op 7-2)
Phoenix Des Mottes(FR) was ridden along from just after halfway and didn't strike as a winner to happen. (op 10-3 tchd 11-4)
Quintero(FR), wearing cheekpieces, weakened quickly turning for home and can only be watched at present. (tchd 5-1)
Kinkeel(IRE), who was having his 100th career start under rules (one on the AW), was struggling a fair way out. (op 12-1)

5016 HAPPY 70TH BIRTHDAY BERTIE CONDITIONAL JOCKEYS' H'CAP HURDLE (10 hdls) 2m 3f

4:05 (4:05) (Class 5) (0-95,96) 4-Y-0+ **£2,276** (£668; £334; £166)

Form RPR

4206 **1** **Sail And Return**[72] 3532 7-11-5 **93**..........................(t) JosephAkehurst[(5)] 103+
(Philip Middleton) *chsd ldrs: blnd 3rd: mstke 6th: clsd on ldrs bef 3 out: rdn and ev ch 2 out: led bef last: drvn clr flat* **11/1**

6P04 **2** *3 1/4* **Sir Clad**[10] 4814 5-9-10 **69** oh3 ow1..............................(vt) GeraldQuinn[(5)] 75
(Claire Dyson) *led: clr w rival after 3rd: wnt on and 2 l clr 2 out: rdn bef next: hdd between last 2: no ex and btn after last* **40/1**

3443 **3** *1* **Domino Dancer (IRE)**[10] 4809 7-11-11 **94**......................... KeiranBurke 98
(Lucy Jones) *w ldr: drew clr of field after 3rd: dropped to 3rd and drvn after 2 out: styd on same pce u.p between last 2* **5/1**[2]

6-41 **4** *7* **Allformary**[15] 4707 5-11-0 **91**...(t) EdCookson[(8)] 90
(Kim Bailey) *hld up in rr: hdwy after 5th: chsd ldng trio after next: rdn and no hdwy bef 2 out: wknd between last 2* **7/2**[1]

40-0 **5** *22* **Edgebury**[13] 4751 8-11-3 **89**... PeterCarberry[(3)] 67
(Paul Webber) *racd in midfield: rdn and no imp after 6th: no ch w ldrs fr next* **25/1**

0222 **6** *nk* **Mad Professor (IRE)**[10] 4813 8-9-8 **69** oh2.................(p) JoeCornwall[(6)] 47
(John Cornwall) *in tch: lost pl and rdn along after 5th: no ch w ldrs after next: plugged on fr 2 out* **7/1**[3]

0/PF **7** *19* **Driving Miss Suzie**[15] 4707 7-11-4 **90**............................(p) KyleJames[(3)] 51
(Debra Hamer) *mstkes: in rr: reminders after 3rd: struggling and losing tch after 6th: t.o 2 bef 2 out* **20/1**

231F **8** *1/2* **Ruby Valentine (FR)**[128] 2480 8-11-1 **84**........................... MattGriffiths 44
(Jim Wilson) *a in rr: rdn and no reponse after 6th: t.o bef 2 out* **8/1**

0-03 **9** *3 1/4* **Street Devil (USA)**[13] 4751 6-11-13 **96**.............................. GilesHawkins 53
(Pat Murphy) *hld up in midfield: rdn and effrt after 6th: 5th and no imp after next: wknd bef 2 out: tired between last 2* **8/1**

5053 **10** *16* **Masterpoint**[10] 4814 11-9-11 **69** oh5............................. TrevorWhelan[(3)] 12
(Richard Harper) *racd in midfield: rdn and struggling after 6th: 7th and wl btn whn mstke 2 out: virtually p.u after last: t.o* **20/1**

F432 **11** *2 1/2* **Cloonavery (IRE)**[153] 1995 9-9-11 **69**.....................(v) EdGlassonbury[(3)] 10
(Derek Frankland) *hld up in rr: sme hdwy into midfield after 5th: rdn and lost tch after next: t.o after 3 out* **10/1**

/P0P **P** **Young Valentino**[10] 4814 9-10-0 **69** oh11.......................(p) JohnKington —
(Michael Appleby) *chsd ldrs: j.rt and mstke 1st: rdn and dropped out rapidly after 5th: tailing off whn p.u next* **66/1**

0-06 **P** **Gulf Of Aqaba (USA)**[15] 3899 5-11-5 **88**....................(b) MichaelMurphy —
(Ian Williams) *t.k.h: hld up in rr: rdn and no hdwy after 6th: lost tch bef 3 out: t.o whn p.u 2 out* **14/1**

0005 **P** **Tild'Or Du Granit (FR)**[24] 4417 4-9-12 **78**.......................... RobertKirk[(3)] —
(James Evans) *prom in main gp: mstke 5th and 6th: sn struggling: wl bhd bef 3 out: t.o whn p.u 2 out* **22/1**

4m 33.8s (2.30) **Going Correction** +0.425s/f (Soft)
WFA 4 from 5yo+ 7lb **14** Ran SP% **119.4**
Speed ratings (Par 103): **112,110,110,107,98 97,89,89,88,81 80,—,—,—**
toteswingers:1&2:£0.00, 1&3:£8.80, 2&3:£30.80 CSF £394.72 CT £2469.70 TOTE £13.40: £4.80, £12.50, £2.00; EX 634.90.
Owner P W Middleton **Bred** Andrew And Mrs S R B Davis **Trained** Dorton, Bucks

FOCUS

A 0-95 handicap hurdle confined to conditional jockeys. It was run at a solid pace and very few got competitive. The first four pulled well clear. the winner improved to the level of his bumper form.

NOTEBOOK

Sail And Return lost his maiden tag at the 12th attempt here with a polished display. Below par on his last two starts, he jumped nicely throughout and it will be interesting to see how he goes next time out. (op 12-1)
Sir Clad helped force the early speed and stuck to his task close home. Rated only 69, this was only his fifth race over hurdles and can go one better at some point shortly. (op 50-1)
Domino Dancer(IRE), the other pace setter, also ran with credit and might be seen in better light back at the minimum trip. (op 13-2)
Allformary, who was racing off a 23lb higher mark than for an easy win at Wincanton last time out, was held up early but had no excuses in the latter stages. The handicapper might just be in charge of her now. (tchd 4-1)
Edgebury, having his second start after a break, stayed on a little near the end and might be worth stepping up in trip. (op 16-1)

5017 BORDEAUX-UNDISCOVERED.CO.UK WINES AT STRATFORD NOVICES' H'CAP CHASE (17 fncs) 2m 7f

4:35 (4:35) (Class 4) (0-105,102) 5-Y-0+ **£3,903** (£1,146; £573; £286)

Form RPR

3PPP **1** **Grenoli (FR)**[155] 1952 10-10-6 **89**.................................(bt) JoeCornwall[(7)] 95
(John Cornwall) *in tch: lft 3rd 12th: chsd ldr after next: j. ahd 2 out: rdn along and gd jump to go clr last: kpt on under hands and heels flat* **8/1**

0306 **2** *1* **Like Ice**[10] 4809 6-10-12 **95**..................................... JosephAkehurst[(7)] 100
(Philip Middleton) *t.k.h: j.rt: hld up in last: hdwy 12th: chsd ldrs next: j.rt 2 out: rdn to chse wnr and hanging rt bef last: ch whn j. slowly last: kpt on fnl 100yds* **9/1**

1F03 **3** *22* **Manmoon (FR)**[12] 4768 8-11-4 **99**.................................(t) MattGriffiths[(5)] 86
(Nigel Hawke) *chsd ldr tl 8th: wnt 2nd again 11th tl lft in ld next: outj. and hdd 2 out: sn rdn and wknd* **7/1**[3]

4002 **4** *3/4* **Talenti (IRE)**[23] 4441 8-11-12 **102**..............................(tp) PaddyBrennan 87
(Charlie Longsdon) *chsd ldrs: wnt 2nd 8th tl 11th: lft 2nd again next tl after 13th: rdn bef 3 out: drvn and little rspnse bef 2 out: wknd wl bef last* **13/8**[1]

5431 **5** *65* **Cold Harbour**[7] 4865 7-11-11 **101**... PaulMoloney 27
(Evan Williams) *led: reminders after 5th: dived 10th: blnd and hdd 12th: sn bhd: lost tch 14th: t.o fr 2 out* **7/4**[2]

5m 49.9s (8.30) **Going Correction** +0.475s/f (Soft) **5** Ran SP% **108.1**
Speed ratings: **104,103,96,95,73**
CSF £58.15 TOTE £11.30: £3.40, £2.40; EX 32.30.
Owner J R Cornwall **Bred** Jerome Miceli **Trained** Long Clawson, Leics

FOCUS

A staying novice handicap chase for horses rated 0-105, in which the top weight was 3lb below the ceiling rating. It didn't take much winning with a couple of the market leaders running well below par. The winner is rated 6lb off his level of form from this time last year.

NOTEBOOK

Grenoli(FR) had failed to finish in his last three starts, but bounced back here in good style. What he achieved is questionable but his small yard is in good form and we will learn more next time out. The handicapper shouldn't be too harsh for this success. (op 17-2 tchd 10-1)
Like Ice, also coming from a yard going well, was a little sluggish on his first try over fences and that told at the business end. Although he is still a maiden after 12 starts, he can go one better at some point in similar company. (op 10-1 tchd 11-1 and 8-1)
Manmoon(FR) is finding the handicapper is in charge at present. (op 6-1 tchd 11-2)
Talenti(IRE) has run well below par in his two tries over fences and can only be watched in this sphere. (op 7-4 tchd 6-4)
Cold Harbour, a winner at Ffos Las the previous week, could have done with company in front. He made a bad mistake going out on the final circuit and it is best to ignore this run. (tchd 13-8 and 15-8)

5018 SIS LIVE H'CAP CHASE (12 fncs) 2m 1f 110y

5:10 (5:11) (Class 5) (0-90,90) 5-Y-0+ **£2,602** (£764; £382; £190)

Form RPR

3506 **1** **Peak Seasons (IRE)**[34] 4238 8-9-13 **66**......................... CharlieStudd[(3)] 75
(Michael Chapman) *chsd ldrs: wnt 2nd 8th: rdn and no imp on ldr after 2 out: 3 l down and looked hld last: kpt on u.p fnl 100yds: led nr fin* **9/2**[3]

5320 **2** *nk* **Bid Art (IRE)**[184] 1591 6-11-1 **82**.........................(t) SamTwiston-Davies[(3)] 91
(Jamie Snowden) *led tl 2nd: chsd ldr tl lft in ld 7th: pushed along bef last: 3 l clr and looked in command last: drvn and fnd little flat: hdd nr fin* **5/2**[2]

-0PP **3** *13* **Ravenscar**[11] 4799 13-9-10 **67**... JoeCornwall[(7)] 64
(Charles Pogson) *in tch in rr: hmpd 6th: chsd ldng pair after 8th: rdn 3 out: j.big next: wknd bef last* **8/1**

P **4** *5* **Back To Paris (IRE)**[33] 1552 9-11-2 **87**.............................. KyleJames[(7)] 82
(Philip Kirby) *t.k.h: led 2nd: j.lft: mstke and hdd 7th: blnd next: 4th and rdn 3 out: wknd next* **18/1**

0631 **U** **Betty Browneyes**[16] 4668 6-11-12 **90**..........................(t) PaddyBrennan —
(Tom George) *j.rt: hld up in tch: j.rt and blnd 4th: mstke: stmbld bdly and uns rdr 6th* **6/5**[1]

4m 18.2s (11.10) **Going Correction** +0.475s/f (Soft) **5** Ran SP% **108.6**
Speed ratings: **94,93,88,85,—**
CSF £15.78 TOTE £4.30: £1.10, £2.30; EX 14.40.
Owner J E Reed **Bred** Peter Gleeson **Trained** Market Rasen, Lincs

FOCUS

A very modest 0-90 handicap chase which was run at a sound pace, it was weakened even further when the favourite Betty Browneyes crashed out at halfway. The winner had slipped to a very good mark and is rated 8lb off this season's best.

NOTEBOOK

Peak Seasons(IRE) got up in the shadow of the post for his first win in nearly two years. Running off 22lb below that last winning mark, he obviously is well treated but his overall profile suggests he isn't one to take a short price about next time out. (tchd 7-2)
Bid Art(IRE), well backed beforehand, looked the most likely winner before tying up close home. He might struggle to find a race as weak as this next time out, in a bid to go one better. (op 10-3 tchd 9-4)
Ravenscar has tumbled in the weights but doesn't strike as a winner waiting to happen. Official explanation: vet said gelding lost its near-fore shoe (op 10-1 tchd 12-1)
Back To Paris(IRE) was too keen on his first run over fences and can only be watched for the time being. (op 12-1)

5019 COVENTRY STANDARD OPEN NATIONAL HUNT FLAT RACE 2m 110y

5:40 (5:41) (Class 5) 4-6-Y-O **£1,951** (£573; £286)

Form RPR

1 **Penelope Pips** 4-10-2 [0].. PaulMoloney 75
(Evan Williams) *disp ld at v stdy gallop: pushed along whn gallop qcknd 4f out: rdn over 2f out: led narrowly ins fnl f: kpt on* **11/10**[2]

2 *hd* **Dazzling Rita** 5-10-9 [0].. DavidEngland 82
(Shaun Lycett) *disp ld at v stdy gallop: led narrowly and travelling best whn gallop qcknd 4f out: hung rt and rn green bnd over 2f out: rdn over 1f out: hdd ins fnl f: kpt on* **1/1**[1]

0 **3** *7* **Bollistick**[133] 2368 5-11-2 [0].. MarkBradburne 82
(Michael Mullineaux) *trckd rivals: rdn and outpcd whn gallop qcknd 4f out: one pce and hld fnl 3f* **8/1**[3]

4m 18.0s (27.60) **Going Correction** +0.425s/f (Soft)
WFA 4 from 5yo 7lb **3** Ran SP% **108.7**
Speed ratings: **52,51,48**
CSF £2.61 TOTE £1.70; EX 1.70.

Owner Mr & Mrs William Rucker **Bred** Denis, James And Daniel Crowley **Trained** Llancarfan, Vale Of Glamorgan

FOCUS

A very disappointing turnout for this bumper which was run at a crawl to halfway and it's hard to put a figure on this race or take the form seriously.

NOTEBOOK

Penelope Pips probably could have done with a stronger gallop and did well to win the way the race panned out. She will find it tougher under a penalty but can make her mark over timber in due course. (op 4-6)

Dazzling Rita, well backed, proved she isn't devoid of ability and it will be interesting to see how she goes next time out. (op 2-1)

Bollistick, well held on his debut, was again found out when the sprint for home started. He doesn't lack for size and might do better over hurdles further down the line. (op 13-2 tchd 6-1)

T/Plt: £2,002.80 to a £1 stake. Pool:£51,579.79 - 18.80 winning tickets T/Qpdt: £1,391.30 to a £1 stake. Pool:£3,008.42 - 1.60 winning tickets SP

5020 - 5024a (Foreign Racing) - See Raceform Interactive

4759 NAVAN (L-H)

Saturday, March 26

OFFICIAL GOING: Hurdle course - yielding; chase course - good to yielding (soft in back straight)

5025a WEBSTER CUP CHASE (GRADE 2) (14 fncs) 2m 4f

5:00 (5:00) 5-Y-O+ **£21,012** (£6,142; £2,909; £969)

RPR

1D **Hughies Grey (IRE)**24 4434 7-11-5 126 MDarcy 136
(Mervyn Torrens, Ire) *chsd ldrs: 2nd 1/2-way: impr to ld ent st: clr bef 2 out: rdn and reduced advantage last: strly pressed clsng stages: all out subsequently disqualified: furosemide in sample* **7/1**

1 *shd* **See U Bob (IRE)**37 4174 8-11-5 142 MPWalsh 136+
(Paul Nolan, Ire) *settled bhd ldrs: 6th 1/2-way: 4th 5 out: rdn 3 out: u.p in 3rd 2 out: clse 2nd last: kpt on run-in: jst failed: fin2nd, shd: awrdd r* **6/1**3

2 *3/4* **Whatuthink (IRE)**27 4388 9-11-5 140 TJDoyle 135+
(Oliver McKiernan, Ire) *hld up towards rr: rdn in 7th 3 out: lft 6th 2 out: styd on in 4th last: kpt on same pce: fin3rd, shd & 3/4l: subs plcd 2nd* **11/1**

3 *9* **Duers (IRE)**20 4515 9-11-8 135 (p) AELynch 131
(Paul Magnier, Ire) *hld up towards rr: hdwy into 5th 3 out: rdn and no ex in 6th bef next: lft 5th: kpt on one pce: fin 4th, subs plcd 3rd* **12/1**

4 *3 1/2* **I Hear A Symphony (IRE)**62 3706 9-11-5 127 (t) RCColgan 125
(J J Lambe, Ire) *chsd ldrs: 4th 1/2-way: rdn in 3rd 3 out: no imp in 2nd bef 2 out: 3rd last: no ex run-in: fin 5th, subs plcd 4th* **20/1**

5 *7* **Made In Taipan (IRE)**27 4384 9-11-5 147 AndrewJMcNamara 118
(Thomas Mullins, Ire) *chsd ldr: led 2nd: clr 4th: reduced advantage 6 out: rdn and hdd ent st: no ex after 3 out: lft 4th 2 out: fin 4th, subs plcd 5th* **9/4**2

P **Jayo (FR)**38 4153 8-11-5 141 PTownend —
(W P Mullins, Ire) *settled bhd ldrs: 5th 1/2-way: rdn in 6th 3 out: no ex: p.u bef last* **2/1**1

F **Oscar Looby (IRE)**87 3206 8-11-10 136 (tp) PCarberry 133
(Noel Meade, Ire) *led: hdd 2nd: mstke 5th: 4th whn mstke 6 out: dropped to rr 4 out: sn rdn: styd on into 4th whn fell 2 out* **10/1**

5m 20.6s (-19.70) **8** Ran SP% **120.8**

CSF £50.75 TOTE £7.90: £1.50, £1.60, £2.90; DF 67.90.

Owner Mrs Lucy McCallan **Bred** Michael Keane **Trained** Omagh, Co Tyrone

■ This race was previously known as the An Uaimh Chase.

FOCUS

The time was relatively slow and the form is rated around the first three. The winner is rated to his Downpatrick level over 2m4f.

NOTEBOOK

Hughies Grey(IRE) ◆, winner of the Ulster National on his previous start, was down 1m in distance here and, having raced close up throughout, went to the front before three ou. He got away with a sloppy jump at the last to win all out in a tight finish. A rise in the ratings is on the cards but trainer Mervyn Torrens immediately nominated the Irish Grand National as the target for the winner, commenting: "I think Fairyhouse will suit him as he does things much easier going right-handed." He was subsequently disqualified after testing positive for furosemide. (op 10/1)

See U Bob(IRE), rated 16lb higher than the winner whom he was meeting at level weights, was held up before getting into contention four out. Third and under pressure two out, he was a closing second at the final fence and stayed on under pressure, just failing to get up. (op 9/2)

Whatuthink(IRE), whose only chase win was achieved over 2m, had won over this trip over hurdles. He raced in rear until starting to make headway after four out. Fourth approaching the last, he stayed on quite well in the closing stages. (op 12/1)

Duers(IRE), a five-time winner over fences, appreciates good ground. Held up, he closed on the leaders approaching three out, but was soon struggling to make any impression.

I Hear A Symphony(IRE), both of whose chase wins were achieved over shorter distances, has a couple of hurdle wins to his credit at this trip. He had plenty on at the weights here and after being close up most of the way, was done with between the last two fences.

Made In Taipan(IRE) was best in at the weights, although he hasn't won since scoring here over two years ago. Runner-up over hurdles on his previous start, he led from the second fence and was soon clear until six out. A mistake five out and a lesser one at the final ditch (four out) did nothing for his cause and he was headed before three out. (op 15/8)

Jayo(FR) was reported to have never travelling at any stage. (op 3/1)

Oscar Looby(IRE), back from a break and better suited by testing ground, led to the second fence. He made mistakes at the fifth and six out and dropped behind, before making headway to be in contention for possibly a first four placing when he fell two out. (op 3/1)

5026 - (Foreign Racing) - See Raceform Interactive

4822 HEXHAM (L-H)

Sunday, March 27

OFFICIAL GOING: Good to soft (good in places; 6.7)

Rail at top of hill moved out, and rail down back straight moved to give fresh ground.

Wind: Breezy, half against Weather: Cloudy

5027 SIS NOVICES' HURDLE (DIV I) (8 hdls) 2m 110y

2:10 (2:11) (Class 4) 4-Y-0+ **£2,055** (£599; £299)

Form RPR

2321 **1** **Flinty Bay (IRE)**31 4303 6-11-6 121 FearghalDavis 109+
(Nicky Richards) *trckd ldr: led 3 out: blnd bdly next: sn rcvrd: rdn and clr whn nt fluent last: styd on wl: eased towards fin* **8/13**1

00P4 **2** *2* **Bunratty (IRE)**10 4824 5-11-0 0 KennyJohnson 96
(Robert Johnson) *led tl hit and hdd 3 out: ev ch and rdn next: kpt on fr last: no ch w eased-down wnr* **50/1**

S0 **3** *10* **Ursus**23 4451 6-11-0 0 PaddyAspell 87
(Christopher Wilson) *nt fluent on occasions: hld up: hdwy bef 2 out: kpt on fr last: no ch w first two* **100/1**

5-32 **4** *6* **Vivaldi (IRE)**28 4385 6-11-12 124 (b) RCColgan 96
(J J Lambe, Ire) *prom: pushed along after 2 out: no imp whn mstke last* **5/2**2

5 *3/4* **Tower**53 4-10-7 0 CampbellGillies 74
(Chris Grant) *nt fluent: in tch: lost pl 1/2-way: styd on fr 2 out: nvr able to chal* **11/1**3

05 **6** *3* **Funky Munky**10 4824 6-10-11 0 EwanWhillans(3) 78
(Alistair Whillans) *hld up: stdy hdwy after 2 out: nvr nr ldrs* **40/1**

0-00 **7** *nk* **Roslin Moss**29 4361 5-10-4 0 CallumWhillans(10) 78
(Donald Whillans) *nt fluent: in midfield: outpcd 3 out: rallied after next: no imp bef last* **100/1**

-560 **8** *3 1/4* **Tears From Heaven (USA)**21 4506 5-11-0 0 BarryKeniry 75
(Mrs S Sunter) *bhd: struggling bef 3 out: nvr on terms* **100/1**

PP00 **9** *2* **Fred Grass**18 4550 5-10-11 64 JamesO'Farrell(3) 73
(Jonathan Haynes) *in tch: outpcd after 3 out: btn bef next* **250/1**

000 **10** *1* **Overpriced**143 2167 5-10-0 0 (t) MissAngelaBarnes(7) 65
(Maurice Barnes) *hld up: nt fluent 3rd: hit 3 out: sn rdn and btn* **100/1**

6-0P **11** *6* **Kensix Star (IRE)**41 4112 5-11-0 0 BrianHughes 67
(Howard Johnson) *trckd ldrs tl rdn and wknd fr 2 out* **28/1**

03- **12** *1/2* **Endeavor**633 846 6-11-0 0 JamesReveley 66
(Dianne Sayer) *t.k.h in midfield: hdwy and prom 2nd: rdn bef 2 out: wknd after 2 out* **28/1**

PP0 **13** *10* **Daredevil Dan**38 4165 5-11-0 0 RichieMcGrath 57
(Tina Jackson) *t.k.h: hld up: strugging 3 out: sn btn* **125/1**

4m 25.9s (8.50) **Going Correction** 0.0s/f (Good)

WFA 4 from 5yo+ 7lb **13** Ran SP% **115.3**

Speed ratings (Par 105): **80,79,74,71,71 69,69,68,67,66 63,63,58**

toteswingers:1&2 £12.40, 2&3 £58.60, 1&3 £23.00 CSF £48.65 TOTE £1.80: £1.10, £5.60, £12.00; EX 35.40.

Owner Miss A Condon,Mrs J Magnier & M Tabor **Bred** Thomas Foy **Trained** Greystoke, Cumbria

FOCUS

Punters only wanted to know about two in this despite the fairly big field, as both the market leaders were a long way clear on Racing Post ratings. Ordinary form, with the winner rated 11lb off his best but value for further. the time was very slow.

NOTEBOOK

Flinty Bay(IRE) was the best backed and collected a second successive victory despite some indifferent jumping. There had been signs that he might make a blunder before he whacked two out, but such is his ability he was still able to win. (op 4-6)

Bunratty(IRE) is a fine, big chasing type and put up a much improved performance. He will surely make his mark over fences in time.

Ursus, a winning sprinter, stayed on from the back and can go into handicaps now.

Vivaldi(IRE), under a double penalty, was a bit keen under restraint and offered little off the bridle when asked to close. Official explanation: trainer said gelding finished lame behind (op 9-4 tchd 2-1)

Tower, a 2m Flat winner at Kempton last October, lost his place at a crucial stage on his debut for this trainer, but made late eyecatching progress. (op 14-1)

5028 SIS NOVICES' HURDLE (DIV II) (8 hdls) 2m 110y

2:40 (2:40) (Class 4) 4-Y-0+ **£2,055** (£599; £299)

Form RPR

0416 **1** **Attaglance**102 2954 5-11-3 120 JamesHalliday(3) 110+
(Malcolm Jefferson) *mde all: clr bef last: unchal* **2/1**1

2-P0 **2** *2 3/4* **Below The Deck (IRE)**17 4572 8-10-4 95 JamesO'Farrell(3) 89
(Barbara Butterworth) *chsd ldrs: rdn and chsd (clr) wnr between last 2: kpt on run-in: no imp* **22/1**

0 **3** *5* **Sendiym (FR)**44 4059 4-10-7 0 GrahamLee 87
(Ferdy Murphy) *hld up in midfield: mstke 4 out: hdwy bef 2 out: kpt on run-in nt gng pce of first two* **13/2**3

4 *12* **It's A Mans World**19 5-10-9 0 BrianToomey(5) 83
(Kevin M Prendergast) *hld up: blnd 3 out: nt fluent next: hdwy whn hit last: nrst fin* **40/1**

0-P0 **5** *2* **Loch Dhu (IRE)**7 4889 7-10-4 0 EwanWhillans(3) 72
(Alistair Whillans) *bhd: rdn and hdwy 2 out: no imp bef last* **150/1**

0-00 **6** *8* **Agricultural**16 4686 5-10-9 73 AlexanderVoy(5) 72
(Lucy Normile) *t.k.h: hld up: sme hdwy after 2 out: nvr on terms* **150/1**

50-0 **7** *10* **Smudger**68 3620 6-11-0 0 HenryOliver 63
(Sue Smith) *led tl j. slowly and hdd 1st: cl up tl rdn and wknd after 2 out* **20/1**

0 **8** *2 1/4* **Piverina (IRE)**18 4552 6-10-7 0 PaddyAspell 54
(Julie Camacho) *in tch: rdn bef 2 out: sn wknd* **40/1**

9 *9* **Talk Of Saafend (IRE)**214 6-10-7 0 JamesReveley 46
(Dianne Sayer) *hld up: rdn bef 2 out: sn struggling* **28/1**

P261 **10** *1 1/4* **Imperial Breeze (IRE)**16 4686 6-11-6 103 (t) RCColgan 58
(J J Lambe, Ire) *midfield: drvn and outpcd after 3 out: btn next* **12/5**2

0/P **11** *nk* **Some Lad (IRE)**308 442 6-11-0 0 PeterBuchanan 51
(Mrs A C Hamilton) *in tch tl rdn and wknd fr 2 out* **150/1**

5-42 **12** *1 1/2* **Hobsons Bay (IRE)**33 4278 6-11-0 108 BrianHughes 50
(Howard Johnson) *trckd ldr tl rdn and wknd between last 2* **7/1**

0403 **13** *31* **Dizzy River (IRE)**39 4151 6-11-0 0 TimmyMurphy 22
(George Charlton) *nt fluent: bhd: lost tch fr 1/2-way: t.o* **14/1**

4m 17.0s (-0.40) **Going Correction** 0.0s/f (Good)

WFA 4 from 5yo+ 7lb **13** Ran SP% **114.7**

Speed ratings (Par 105): **100,98,96,90,89 86,81,80,76,75 75,74,59**

toteswingers:1&2 £14.40, 2&3 £16.10, 1&3 £4.50 CSF £48.53 TOTE £2.60: £1.20, £7.30, £2.40; EX 55.00.

Owner H Young, G Eifert, R Snyder **Bred** H Young **Trained** Norton, N Yorks

FOCUS

Not much happened in the second division of the novice hurdle, which was much quicker than the first. Weak form but the easy winner was value for further.

NOTEBOOK

Attaglance set off in front and was hardly ever troubled to win comfortably. The lengthy absence he needed to overcome proved no barrier, and he will be difficult to catch when allowed an easy lead. (op 9-4)

Below The Deck(IRE) was never far off the pace and kept on well to claim second. She is still seeking a first win after plenty of attempts. (op 28-1)

Sendiym(FR) ran better than he had done on his British debut despite making one bad error, so possibly the better ground helped. (op 9-2 tchd 7-1)

It's A Mans World looked to have possible stamina issues judged on his winning Flat form, so connections well be encouraged by this performance. Official explanation: jockey said gelding had a breathing problem (op 28-1)

Imperial Breeze(IRE) showed improved form when a tongue-tie was tried for the first time on his previous outing, but it failed to work here on quicker ground. Official explanation: trainer said gelding was unsuited by the track (op 4-1 tchd 9-4)

Hobsons Bay(IRE) , without a tongue-tie this time, shaped well for quite a way but weakened rapidly under pressure. He still looked green on occasions, which means there ought to be more improvement. (op 11-2)

5029 NORTHERN RACING CLUB BEGINNERS' CHASE (19 fncs) 3m 1f
3:10 (3:10) (Class 4) 5-Y-O+ **£2,602** (£764; £382; £190)

Form RPR
-PU3 **1** **Final Veto**[19] 4542 8-10-9 0 ShaneByrne(5) 110+
(Sue Smith) *t.k.h early: prom: hmpd 2nd: wnt 2nd 13th: squeezed through on ins to chal briefly bef last: rdn and 2 l down last: led run-in: hld on wl* **3/1**[2]
23F3 **2** *nk* **Silent Cliche (IRE)**[27] 4394 7-11-0 121 (b[1]) BrianHughes 110+
(Howard Johnson) *led: jnd bef last: sn rdn and edgd lft: 2 l up last: hrd rdn and hdd run-in: kpt on: jst hld* **8/11**[1]
P/0P **3** *20* **Nick The Silver**[12] 4799 10-11-0 77 (p) KennyJohnson 92+
(Robert Johnson) *t.k.h: trckd ldr: mstke 3rd: mstke and lost 2nd 13th: hit 4 out: outpcd whn hit 3 out: wknd fr next* **28/1**
30- **4** *45* **City Of Doral**[14] 4764 9-11-0 110 RCColgan 44
(J J Lambe, Ire) *t.k.h: prom: hit 7th: rdn and outpcd whn mstke 4 out: sn lost tch* **7/1**[3]
-050 **5** *62* **Qbuster (IRE)**[47] 3995 10-10-7 87 (t) HenryBrooke(7) —
(Sharon Watt) *in tch: rdn and outpcd 13th: lost tch fr next* **12/1**
0/5 **P** **Pan Pan (FR)**[17] 4570 8-10-11 64 HarryHaynes(3) —
(Anna Bramall) *trckd ldrs: reminders 3rd: outpcd after 11th: t.o whn p.u bef 4 out* **40/1**

6m 50.5s (18.30) **Going Correction** -1.025s/f (Hard) **6** Ran SP% **109.0**
Speed ratings: **101,100,94,80,60** —
toteswingers:1&2 £1.02, 2&3 £5.60, 1&3 £4.00 CSF £5.54 TOTE £3.70: £1.10, £2.50; EX 5.80.
Owner The McGoldrick Partnership **Bred** G And Mrs Middlebrook **Trained** High Eldwick, W Yorks

FOCUS
A low-grade beginners' chase. The time was slow and the form was suspect.

NOTEBOOK
Final Veto was able to gain victory on his chasing debut after being a persistent challenger from two out. His jockey was made to work hard to get his mount to the front, and isn't one to be backing next time at a short price to back this up. (op 4-1)
Silent Cliche(IRE) looked as though he would gain his first win under rules with blinkers fitted for the first time, but although he jumped quite soundly out in front, he never pulled away and appeared to doss in the latter stages. (op 4-6)
Nick The Silver raced prominently until a mistake three out finally sealed his fate. (op 22-1 tchd 33-1)

5030 ROE DEER H'CAP HURDLE (10 hdls) 2m 4f 110y
3:40 (3:40) (Class 3) (0-125,122) 4-Y-O+ **£2,927** (£859; £429; £214)

Form RPR
0PU **1** **Charingworth (IRE)**[50] 3953 8-10-10 **113** EdmondLinehan(7) 115
(Ferdy Murphy) *hld up: hdwy 2 out: chsd ldr bef last: rdn to ld run-in: hld on wl* **12/1**
6203 **2** *nk* **Bollin Ruth**[10] 4822 9-9-7 **99** CallumWhillans(10) 101
(Donald Whillans) *hld up in midfield: hdwy bef 4 out: led after 2 out: rdn bef last: hung lft and hdd run-in: r.o* **7/1**[3]
5431 **3** *1 ½* **Texas Holdem (IRE)**[17] 4572 12-11-4 **114** WillKennedy 115
(Michael Smith) *in tch: effrt after 2 out: kpt on fr last: nt rch first two* **11/2**[2]
412F **4** *3 ¼* **Teenage Idol (IRE)**[15] 4715 7-11-7 **120** JamesO'Farrell(3) 118
(Evelyn Slack) *hld up: hdwy between last 2: rdn and no imp run-in* **8/1**
6300 **5** *6* **Stick Together**[63] 3695 8-10-10 **109** (b) JamesHalliday(3) 102
(Malcolm Jefferson) *prom: hdwy to chse ldr after 2 out to bef last: wknd run-in* **25/1**
6F41 **6** *15* **Golfer's Crossing (IRE)**[22] 4477 8-11-10 **120** CampbellGillies 99
(Lucinda Russell) *cl up: led 5th: hdd whn hit 3 out: led briefly after next: wknd bef last* **9/2**[1]
2U42 **7** *shd* **Rolecarr (IRE)**[19] 4544 8-10-9 **105** GrahamLee 84
(Ann Hamilton) *t.k.h: prom: rdn and wknd after 2 out* **7/1**[3]
P304 **8** *10* **Bow School (IRE)**[39] 4147 10-10-6 **102** PeterBuchanan 72
(Mrs A C Hamilton) *t.k.h: trckd ldrs tl rdn and wknd after 2 out* **14/1**
P000 **9** *47* **Front Rank (IRE)**[17] 4572 11-10-3 **99** JamesReveley 26
(Dianne Sayer) *led to 5th: cl up tl lost pl 4 out: wknd fr next: t.o* **33/1**
26/ **P** **Supreme Ruler (IRE)**[1114] 4360 8-11-10 **120** PaddyAspell —
(Patrick Holmes) *t.k.h: hld up: sddle slipped and p.u after 3rd* **40/1**
5521 **P** **River Dragon (IRE)**[33] 4278 6-10-7 **108** BrianToomey(5) —
(Neville Bycroft) *w ldrs: led 3 out to next: sn wknd: t.o whn p.u bef last* **16/1**
3/1- **U** **Whisky Magic (FR)**[521] 1856 7-11-7 **122** PaulGallagher(5) —
(Howard Johnson) *t.k.h: hld up: stmbld and uns rdr 2nd* **12/1**
6140 **P** **Fentara**[27] 4391 6-10-8 **104** RobertWalford —
(Tim Walford) *nt fluent in rr: struggling 6th: t.o whn p.u bef 2 out* **9/1**

5m 11.0s (-1.50) **Going Correction** 0.0s/f (Good) **13** Ran SP% **116.8**
Speed ratings (Par 107): **102,101,101,100,97 92,92,88,70,— —,—,—**
CSF £90.81 CT £521.25 TOTE £16.70: £5.40, £3.70, £2.40; EX 202.70 Trifecta £326.30 Part won. Pool of £440.00 - 0.10 winning units..
Owner Simon Roberts & A & S Enterprises **Bred** Mary Fanning McCormack **Trained** West Witton, N Yorks

■ Edmond Linehan's first winner over jumps, to go with six on the Flat in Ireland.
■ Stewards' Enquiry : Callum Whillans caution: careless riding.

FOCUS
A competitive contest run at a fair gallop, which resulted in a tight finish. Solid form with the winner rated to his hurdles best.

NOTEBOOK
Charingworth(IRE) was almost impossible to fancy on anything he had done since his fair reappearance effort, but he was delivered with a late challenge here and got to the front at the right moment to gain a narrow success. It's impossible to predict what he'll do next time judged on his overall profile. (op 11-1)
Bollin Ruth has consistent figures at this course, and showed that she loves it around here with another good effort. She cruised to the front at what looked the right time but wasn't able to hold on. (op 8-1)
Texas Holdem(IRE) was tucked away in midfield before staying on in the latter stages. It was a good performance by the veteran. (op 6-1)
Teenage Idol(IRE) is in good form, despite the fall on his last run, but is high in the handicap judged on his handicap victory. All his wins have come at shorter trips.
Stick Together had her chance but didn't get home as well as those in front of her. She is entitled to come on for the run. (op 33-1)
Golfer's Crossing(IRE), up 11lb for his win last time, was going nicely towards the head of affairs but soon came under pressure when challenged and found disappointingly little rounding the final bend. Official explanation: trainer had no explanation for the poor form shown (tchd 5-1)
Supreme Ruler(IRE) Official explanation: jockey said saddle slipped

5031 RED FOX "NATIONAL HUNT" NOVICES' HURDLE (12 hdls) 3m
4:10 (4:10) (Class 4) 5-Y-O+ **£2,740** (£798; £399)

Form RPR
1F12 **1** **Eyre Square (IRE)**[17] 4568 8-10-12 116 JamesReveley 119+
(Keith Reveley) *trckd ldrs: led 3 out: hdd briefly next: kpt on strly to go clr bef last: comf* **7/4**[1]
24B0 **2** *12* **Majestic Mayhem (IRE)**[148] 2090 8-11-12 123 BarryKeniry 123+
(George Moore) *cl up: ev ch 3 out: led briefly next: outpcd by wnr bef last* **16/1**
0-00 **3** *23* **Saddlers' Secret (IRE)**[50] 3952 6-10-2 0 JamesHalliday(3) 79
(Mark Campion) *hld up towards rr: drvn along and outpcd fr 1/2-way: sme late hdwy: no ch w first two* **150/1**
5022 **4** *3 ½* **Lua De Itapoan**[19] 4545 6-10-5 0 GrahamLee 76
(Malcolm Jefferson) *t.k.h: hld up: hmpd 5th: hdwy and prom 4 out: rdn and outpcd bef 2 out: btn bef last* **11/2**[3]
5P **5** *1 ½* **First Gunner**[17] 4569 6-10-12 0 RobertWalford 82
(Tim Walford) *cl up: rdn along fr 8th: reminders next: rallied: outpcd bef 2 out: btn whn hung lft last* **50/1**
2-RF **6** *¾* **Bay Cherry (IRE)**[73] 3522 9-10-12 0 WilsonRenwick 83
(Howard Johnson) *disp ld: led 6th to 3 out: rdn and sn struggling: n.d after* **11/2**[3]
03P0 **7** *27* **Allbarkanobite**[46] 4000 6-10-5 0 (t) RichieMcGrath 50
(Kate Walton) *hld up: struggling after 4 out: nvr on terms* **20/1**
0060 **8** *5* **Whiskey Ridge (IRE)**[14] 4739 5-10-12 0 HenryOliver 53
(Sue Smith) *rn in snatches: midfield: struggling 8th: n.d after* **18/1**
0 **9** *22* **Highland Cathedral**[22] 7-10-5 0 MissCWalton(7) 33
(James Walton) *nt fluent: bhd: struggling 4 out: t.o* **100/1**
04 **P** **Drum Bustible (IRE)**[14] 4759 7-10-12 111 RCColgan —
(J J Lambe, Ire) *led to 6th: cl up tl wknd bef 3 out: t.o whn p.u bef last* **14/1**
2-33 **F** **Senor Alco (FR)**[34] 4253 5-10-12 0 BrianHughes —
(Howard Johnson) *trckd ldrs: stmbld and fell 5th* **4/1**[2]
555 **U** **Sous Mix (FR)**[11] 4810 5-10-5 0 JakeGreenall(7) —
(Michael Easterby) *hld up in tch: bdly hmpd and uns rdr 5th* **33/1**

6m 9.40s (-3.80) **Going Correction** 0.0s/f (Good) **12** Ran SP% **116.3**
Speed ratings: **106,102,94,93,92 92,83,81,74,— —,—**
CSF £31.34 TOTE £3.20: £1.20, £4.60, £25.60; EX 41.50.
Owner John Wade **Bred** William Neville **Trained** Lingdale, Redcar & Cleveland

FOCUS
The first two came well clear of the remainder from some way out, so this isn't form to get carried away with. The cosy winner improved towards the level of his chase best.

NOTEBOOK
Eyre Square(IRE) had sound claims at this level and duly won with plenty in hand when getting to the front. It will have at least boosted his confidence, but there isn't a great deal more to take from the performance. (op 15-8 tchd 9-4)
Majestic Mayhem(IRE), last seen in a Grade 2 hurdle, deserves credit giving weight away to Eyre Square on his return from a lengthy break. He should have no problem winning something similar unless coming up against an unexposed sort. (tchd 18-1)
Saddlers' Secret(IRE) took third but never had a winning chance.
Lua De Itapoan, up to a trip expected to suit, definitely had her chance seriously affected when the fancied Senor Alco came down. Now qualified for handicaps, one would hope that she is raced more prominently in the future. (op 4-1)

5032 PRIMARY WEBSITES H'CAP CHASE (19 fncs) 3m 1f
4:40 (4:40) (Class 4) (0-115,115) 5-Y-O+ **£2,927** (£859; £429; £214)

Form RPR
0-33 **1** **Morgan Be**[29] 4360 11-11-12 **115** RichieMcGrath 123+
(Kate Walton) *trckd ldrs: smooth hdwy to ld bef last: rdn and hrd pressed run-in: hld on gamely* **14/1**
141P **2** *hd* **Lockstown**[7] 4893 8-11-3 **106** (p) GrahamLee 112
(Ann Hamilton) *hld up in midfield: hdwy on ins and prom whn blnd and lost pl 13th: rallied 3 out: effrt and chsd wnr run-in: kpt on u.p: jst hld* **7/1**[3]
5226 **3** *6* **Camden George (IRE)**[19] 4546 10-11-4 **112** ShaneByrne(5) 113
(Sue Smith) *hld up: nt fluent 7th: hdwy and prom 9th: outpcd after 4 out: rallied after next: chsd wnr bef last to run-in: sn outpcd* **6/1**[2]
226P **4** *13* **Dawn Ride (IRE)**[29] 4360 10-11-12 **115** (p) BarryKeniry 107+
(Micky Hammond) *hld up: stdy hdwy whn hit and outpcd 4 out: hit next: no imp fr 2 out* **33/1**
142R **5** *hd* **Aghill (IRE)**[10] 4825 7-10-9 **105** HenryBrooke(7) 94
(Rose Dobbin) *bhd: struggling 1/2-way: sme late hdwy: nvr on terms* **11/1**
/PV5 **6** *1 ¾* **Overlady**[17] 4571 9-10-8 **100** HarryHaynes(3) 89
(James Ewart) *a cl up: led 4 out: hdd whn mstke last: sn wknd* **16/1**
0P6P **7** *3 ¼* **Fiftyfive Degrees (IRE)**[31] 4306 10-10-10 **99** (b[1]) TimmyMurphy 83
(Pauline Robson) *t.k.h: cl up: led 13th to 4 out: rdn bef 2 out: wknd between last 2* **7/1**[3]
0P4 **P** **Sotovik (IRE)**[34] 4258 10-11-2 **108** EwanWhillans(3) —
(Alistair Whillans) *t.k.h: prom: blnd 10th: hit and wknd 13th: t.o whn p.u after 4 out* **20/1**
13F- **P** **Its A Classic**[391] 4363 10-11-8 **111** (p) MarkGrant —
(Pat Murphy) *midfield: reminders and outpcd 9th: struggling 13th: t.o whn p.u after 4 out* **14/1**
2-14 **P** **Teerie Express**[17] 4571 10-10-2 **98** MrJBewley(7) —
(George Bewley) *bhd: shortlived effrt 13th: struggling bef next: t.o whn p.u bef 4 out* **6/1**[2]
6621 **P** **Copper's Gold (IRE)**[8] 4871 7-11-6 **109** (b) PeterBuchanan —
(Lucinda Russell) *led to 13th: rallied and ev ch 4 out: rdn and wknd bef 2 out: t.o whn p.u bef last* **8/1**
P2F3 **P** **Ballymacduff (IRE)**[16] 4685 7-11-5 **108** (t) JanFaltejsek —
(George Charlton) *hld up: hit 4th: outpcd 12th: t.o whn p.u bef 4 out* **11/2**[1]

6m 37.5s (5.30) **Going Correction** -1.025s/f (Hard) **12** Ran SP% **115.3**
Speed ratings: **75,74,73,68,68 68,67,—,—,— —,—**
toteswingers:1&2: £17.40, 2&3: £9.80, 1&3: £16.50 CSF £107.20 CT £658.12 TOTE £11.50: £3.40, £2.80, £2.50; EX 128.40.
Owner S Breakspeare **Bred** Martin Blandford **Trained** Middleham Moor, N Yorks

FOCUS
Plenty of these looked to have a chance and the race changed complexion a few times over the final fences. The winner may still be capable of a bit better.

NOTEBOOK
Morgan Be, who eventually managed to complete in the stamina-sapping Eider Chase last month, could always be spotted travelling strongly on ground he was unproven on and, after needing to be pushed along off the final bend for a few strides, kept on resolutely to gain a narrow success. He was fairly handicapped for this, so a large rise in the weights would hamper his chances of winning next time. (op 16-1)

Lockstown was disappointing down in trip last time, but kept on well here after getting behind and almost ground out another victory. (op 10-1)
Camden George(IRE) looked like disappearing off the radar at one stage when coming off the bridle, but he stayed on again for strong pressure to gain another placing. (op 8-1)
Dawn Ride(IRE), who also ran in the Eider last time, made ground from off the pace but wasn't that fluent over the fences, which stopped him getting involved. (tchd 25-1)
Aghill(IRE) got miles behind at one point but somehow managed to keep going and finish on the heels of the fourth. (op 16-1)
Fiftyfive Degrees(IRE) was bang there for much of the contest in his first-time blinkers, but folded tamely when under pressure. (tchd 15-2)
Copper's Gold(IRE) never looked to be going with a great deal of enthusiasm out in front, and it wasn't a surprise when he seemingly dropped the lot when he'd had enough. Official explanation: trainer said gelding finished distressed (op 11-2 tchd 9-1)
Ballymacduff(IRE) made no meaningful impression on his handicap debut over fences. Official explanation: jockey said gelding was unsuited by the good to soft (soft in places) ground (op 11-2 tchd 9-1)

5033 HEXHAM FOR TOURISTS MAIDEN OPEN NATIONAL HUNT FLAT RACE (DIV I) 2m 110y

5:10 (5:12) (Class 5) 4-6-Y-O **£1,370** (£399; £199)

Form				RPR
	1		**Boston Bob (IRE)**39 [4158] 6-10-13 0 .... PaulGallagher(5) (Howard Johnson) *trckd ldrs: led 6f out: edgd lft and styd on strly fr over 1f out* **4/6**1	111+
3/4	2	7	**Thirty Days Out (IRE)**38 [4171] 6-10-1 0 .... CallumWhillans(10) (Donald Whillans) *hld up: smooth hdwy and in tch 1/2-way: effrt and chsd wnr over 1f out: kpt on ins fnl f: no imp* **9/2**2	95
	3	12	**Burgundy Beau** 5-11-4 0 .... CampbellGillies (William Amos) *hld up on outside: stdy hdwy and in tch 1/2-way: effrt and ev ch over 2f out: outpcd fr over 1f out* **16/1**	92
0	4	19	**Riverside Poppet**38 [4171] 5-10-8 0 .... HarryHaynes(3) (James Ewart) *hld up in tch: rdn and outpcd over 5f out: plugged on over 1f out: no imp* **22/1**	67
60	5	13	**My Idea**295 [637] 5-11-4 0 .... MichaelMcAlister (Maurice Barnes) *hld up: stdy hdwy and prom 1/2-way: rdn and wknd fr 4f out* **50/1**	62
4	6	8	**Plenmeller (IRE)**19 [4547] 5-10-13 0 .... ShaneByrne(5) (Sue Smith) *led to 6f out: sn drvn along: wknd over 4f out* **7/1**3	55
0-0	7	6	**Knickerbokerglory**18 [4554] 5-10-8 0 .... JamesO'Farrell(3) (Barbara Butterworth) *t.k.h: cl up: chal 6f out: wknd 4f out* **33/1**	43
0	8	nk	**Edinburgh Gin Time**31 [4308] 5-10-13 0 .... AlexanderVoy(5) (Lucy Normile) *sn w ldr: drvn 1/2-way: wknd over 5f out* **80/1**	50
0	9	35	**Thetasteofparadise**46 [4005] 4-10-4 0 .... BarryKeniry (Bruce Hellier) *bhd: rdn after 6f: stuggling over 6f out: t.o* **100/1**	4
	10	66	**Glen Rhydian** 5-11-4 0 .... PeterBuchanan (Ian McInnes) *t.k.h: midfield: struggling fr 1/2-way: t.o* **40/1**	—
	11	42	**Celtic Mystique** 4-10-4 0 .... PaddyAspell (Christopher Wilson) *prom: lost pl after 6f: lost tch 1/2-way: virtually p.u* **66/1**	—
0	12	2 1/2	**Dorlesh Way (IRE)**23 [4457] 4-10-4 0 .... HenryBrooke(7) (Patrick Holmes) *midfield: struggling 1/2-way: sn lost tch: virtually p.u* **66/1**	—

4m 12.0s (-0.70) **Going Correction** 0.0s/f (Good)
WFA 4 from 5yo+ 7lb **12** Ran SP% **113.5**
Speed ratings: **101,97,92,83,77 73,70,70,53,22 2,1**
toteswingers:1&2: £1.80, 2&3: £4.60, 1&3: £3.90 CSF £3.14 TOTE £1.70: £1.30, £1.40, £2.80; EX 4.50.
Owner Andrea & Graham Wylie **Bred** Burgage Stud **Trained** Billy Row, Co Durham

FOCUS
This didn't seem a competitive contest and so it proved. The first two are rated pretty much to their marks.

NOTEBOOK
Boston Bob(IRE) bounded clear once in the ascendancy and readily held on once asked to kick away. The winner of a Tallow maiden point, and third in a heavy-ground Punchestown bumper for previous connections, when not fancied, he is entitled to progress with experience. (op Evens)
Thirty Days Out(IRE) showed promise on her return from a long absence last time, and proved that wasn't a fluke with another good performance. She has a small contest at least in her. (op 4-1 tchd 5-1)
Burgundy Beau showed quite a bit of ability on his first start, and came miles clear of the fourth. (op 14-1 tchd 18-1)
Riverside Poppet, who was led to the start, finished well beaten on her first run and again this time, but did at least plug on. (op 18-1)
Plenmeller(IRE) shaped with some promise at Newcastle on his first start, but he failed to build on that here. (op 5-1)

5034 HEXHAM FOR TOURISTS MAIDEN OPEN NATIONAL HUNT FLAT RACE (DIV II) 2m 110y

5:40 (5:40) (Class 5) 4-6-Y-O **£1,370** (£399; £199)

Form				RPR
42	1		**Bygones Sovereign (IRE)**31 [4308] 5-11-4 0 .... GrahamLee (Karen McLintock) *mde virtually all: qcknd 1/2-way: pushed wl clr fnl 2f* **5/2**2	115+
2	2	17	**Victor Hewgo**32 [4287] 6-11-4 0 .... JamesReveley (Keith Reveley) *hld up on outside: stdy hdwy over 6f out: effrt and chsd (clr) wnr over 1f out: no imp* **13/8**1	100
	3	12	**Hidden Harmony (IRE)**148 5-11-4 0 .... WilsonRenwick (Rose Dobbin) *prom: chsd wnr over 6f out to over 1f out: sn btn* **7/1**3	91
54	4	1 1/2	**Capital Venture (IRE)**53 [3889] 5-11-1 0 .... HarryHaynes(3) (James Ewart) *trckd ldrs: drvn and outpcd over 6f out: plugged on fr 2f out: no imp* **11/1**	88
	5	2	**Ahhdehken** 6-11-1 0 .... EwanWhillans(3) (Alistair Whillans) *hld up: hdwy over 5f out: rdn and outpcd fr over 2f out* **50/1**	86
0	6	53	**Annie's Pride**38 [4171] 4-10-4 0 .... BarryKeniry (George Moore) *t.k.h: cl up to 1/2-way: wknd over 5f out: t.o* **22/1**	24
50	7	2 3/4	**Tobetall**18 [4554] 4-10-1 0 .... JamesHalliday(3) (Malcolm Jefferson) *hld up: pushed along over 5f out: sn btn: t.o* **66/1**	22
2	8	1/2	**Pudsey House**19 [4547] 4-10-6 0 .... PaulGallagher(5) (Howard Johnson) *hld up: rdn 1/2-way: sn no rspnse: lost tch fnl 5f* **10/1**	28
	9	1/2	**Tutchec (FR)** 4-10-4 0 .... NathanMoscrop(7) (James Ewart) *towards rr: struggling over 5f out: sn btn* **12/1**	28
0	10	32	**My Island Rose (IRE)**23 [4457] 5-10-11 0 .... PaddyAspell (Julie Camacho) *cl up to 1/2-way: sn rdn and struggling: virtually p.u* **100/1**	—
	11	55	**Mr Coates** 5-10-11 0 .... MrMSeston(7) (Simon Waugh) *trckd ldrs: rdn along 1/2-way: lost tch 6f out: virtually p.u* **80/1**	—

4m 11.3s (-1.40) **Going Correction** 0.0s/f (Good)
WFA 4 from 5yo+ 7lb **11** Ran SP% **114.3**
Speed ratings: **103,95,89,88,87 62,61,61,61,45 20**
toteswingers:1&2: £1.90, 2&3: £4.20, 1&3: £4.90. totesuper7: Win: £6,406.10. Place: £25.10. CSF £6.50 TOTE £3.80: £1.20, £1.10, £2.30; EX 6.40.
Owner Alan Lamont **Bred** Mrs S Brennan **Trained** Ingoe, Northumberland

FOCUS
An excellent piece of enterprise saw Graham Lee steal this race on Bygones Sovereign. The winner was the form pick but is rated up 6lb.

NOTEBOOK
Bygones Sovereign(IRE) stole this from the front. He forged clear while dominating their rivals and was never going to be caught. The winning time was marginally quicker than the first division. (op 3-1)
Victor Hewgo shaped nicely on his debut after attracting market support, but had little chance of catching the winner here after being settled in rear. His chance would have been boosted had he sat a bit closer to Bygones Sovereign in the middle part of the race. (op 2-1 tchd 9-4 and 6-4)
Hidden Harmony(IRE) was an interesting newcomer to bumpers on his maiden point form in Ireland, where on his only completed start he finished in front of Cheltenham Champion Bumper runner-up Destroyer Deployed, and showed more than enough to suggest he'll win something, sooner rather than later. (op 9-2)
Capital Venture(IRE) looked certain to finish a well-beaten fifth at best when the field came round the final bend, but he kept on stoutly and recorded another staying-on performance. (op 8-1 tchd 12-1)
Ahhdehken didn't quite get home after shaping nicely, and was mugged for fourth in the final stages. (op 40-1)
T/Jkpt: £21,511.10 to a £1 stake. Pool of £302,974.28 - 10.00 winning tickets. T/Plt: £102.60 to a £1 stake. Pool of £114,311.39 - 813.15 winning tickets. T/Qpdt: £29.80 to a £1 stake. Pool of £7,394.59 - 183.20 winning tickets. RY

4703 WINCANTON (R-H)

Sunday, March 27

OFFICIAL GOING: Good to firm (chs 8.6, hdl 8.4)
Wind: mils half behind Weather: sunny

5035 BLACKMORE BUILDING CONTRACTORS NOVICES' HURDLE (8 hdls) 2m

2:25 (2:26) (Class 4) 4-Y-0+ **£2,665** (£827; £445)

Form				RPR
4215	1		**Midnight Opera**17 [4672] 5-10-13 117 .... MarkQuinlan(7) (Neil Mulholland) *mde all: rdn after 2 out: styng on gamely whn lft clr sn after the last: rdn out* **4/1**2	121+
41	2	12	**Waldvogel (IRE)**60 [3749] 7-11-6 0 .... APMcCoy (Nicky Richards) *chsd wnr: j.lft at times: nt a fluent: pushed along to cl on wnr after 3 out: 1 l down whn stmbld sn after last: sn hld and eased* **2/9**1	120+
	3	49	**Hatchet Man**891 5-11-0 0 .... HarrySkelton (Carroll Gray) *hld up in last pair: wnt modest 3rd after 2 out: nvr any trble to ldng pair* **33/1**	60
4	B		**Murdoch**20 [4528] 7-11-0 0 .... JoeTizzard (Colin Tizzard) *chsd ldng pair: mstke 3 out: sn rdn: wknd bef next: modest 5th whn hmpd and b.d last* **14/1**3	33
6U	F		**Caunay**17 [4677] 4-10-7 0 .... TomScudamore (Neil Mulholland) *hld up in last pair: wnt modest 3rd bef 2 out: wandering in 4th whn fell last* **50/1**	36

3m 39.7s (-9.20) **Going Correction** -0.20s/f (Good)
WFA 4 from 5yo+ 7lb **5** Ran SP% **113.4**
Speed ratings (Par 105): **115,109,84,—,—**
CSF £5.78 TOTE £2.90: £1.10, £1.40; EX 7.70.
Owner D J Bridger **Bred** Avon Thoroughbreds **Trained** Burlescombe, Devon

FOCUS
Only two mattered here, but the market got it wrong.

NOTEBOOK
Midnight Opera ran out a gutsy winner from the front. Neil Mulholland's 5-y-o had shaped as though he needed the run on his return from a break here last time out and he proved a lot sharper on this switch back to novice company. His jumping won him the day in the home straight and he is obviously versatile regards going. A return to handicaps is now on the cards and he should make a nice chaser down the line. This was his trainer's first winner since January. (tchd 7-2)
Waldvogel(IRE), a rare runner here for his stable, beat a useful field when off the mark at Musselburgh two months earlier and proved all the rage under his penalty. He lacked fluency pretty much throughout and a messy leap at the last, when looking in trouble, sealed his fate. Official explanation: jockey said gelding lost its action after jumping final flight (op 1-4)
Hatchet Man was the only other finisher. This was his hurdling debut after an 891-day layoff and he should come on a bundle.

5036 CHILDREN'S TRUST NOVICES' H'CAP CHASE (13 fncs) 2m

2:55 (2:55) (Class 4) (0-110,110) 5-Y-0+ **£3,252** (£955; £477; £238)

Form				RPR
3F4P	1		**January**17 [4671] 8-10-8 **99** .... (t) SClements(7) (Liam Corcoran) *chsd ldng pair: lft 2nd 7th: led 9th: nt fluent 2 out: rdn out run-in* **9/2**3	106+
4441	2	1 1/2	**Trooper Clarence**22 [4482] 7-11-12 **110** .... PaulMoloney (Evan Williams) *trckd ldr: led 6th tl 9th: chsd wnr: rdn after 4 out: kpt on fr last but a being hld* **11/8**1	112
0406	3	7	**Salybia Bay**16 [4691] 5-10-9 **93** .... NickScholfield (Andy Turnell) *chsd ldrs: lft 3rd 7th: rdn after 4 out: styd on same pce fr next* **8/1**	90
5423	4	26	**Catholic Hill (USA)**24 [4447] 6-9-11 **84** oh2 .... TommyPhelan(3) (Mark Gillard) *chsd ldrs: lft 4th 7th: rdn after 8th: wknd after 4 out* **7/2**2	64
0P3P	P		**Medicine Man (IRE)**16 [4691] 7-11-4 **102** .... JackDoyle (Ben De Haan) *led tl 6th: w ldr whn lost hind legs on landing 7th: nt rcvr: p.u bef next* **11/2**	—

4m 1.20s (1.30) **Going Correction** -0.10s/f (Good) **5** Ran SP% **109.0**
Speed ratings: **92,91,87,74,—**
CSF £11.42 TOTE £5.20: £1.80, £1.60; EX 10.20.
Owner L Gilbert **Bred** Darley **Trained** Charlton Adam, Somerset

FOCUS
A moderate novices' handicap, run at a decent clip and the winner is value for a bit further.

NOTEBOOK
January easily went to the front down the back straight and, despite tying up on the run-in, never looked in that much danger thereafter. He had his ideal ground here and rates value for a bit further as he probably idled after the last. Consistency isn't really his strong suit, however. Official explanation: trainer said, regarding apparent improvement in form, that the gelding had returned from a four-month break and had jumped poorly on its previous run. (tchd 4-1)

Trooper Clarence came good for his connections at Kempton 22 days previously and was racing off an 8lb higher mark. He again took time to settle and wasn't always foot perfect. He was coming back at the winner late on, but is somewhat flattered by his proximity and doesn't look the most resolute. (op 5-4 tchd 11-10)
Salybia Bay never seriously threatened, but this was a step up from him on his second outing as a chaser. (op 9-1 tchd 12-1)
Catholic Hill(USA) never looked happy on this quick surface and remains winless over jumps. (op 9-2)
Medicine Man(IRE) ran with the choke out early on, but was still in a share of the lead prior to getting the seventh all wrong and was quickly pulled up. Official explanation: jockey said saddle slipped (op 5-1 tchd 7-1)

5037 ARMISHAWS REMOVALS H'CAP CHASE (21 fncs) 3m 1f 110y
3:25 (3:25) (Class 4) (0-115,114) 5-Y-0+ **£3,415** (£1,002; £501; £250)

Form RPR
P432 **1** **Upham Atom**[19] 4538 8-11-10 **112** LiamTreadwell 124+
(Kate Buckett) *hld up: hdwy 13th: mstke 17th: lft cl 2nd 3 out: narrow advantage next: styd on wl to assert run-in: rdn out* **10/1**
0P42 **2** *1 3/4* **Skipper's Lad (IRE)**[16] 4705 9-10-1 **92** (bt) SamTwiston-Davies(3) 99
(Colin Tizzard) *in tch: wnt 3rd after 9th: rdn to ld appr 3 out: hdd 2 out: ev ch last: no ex* **7/2**[1]
4-41 **3** *60* **Choumakeur (FR)**[16] 4705 9-11-10 **112** (bt) TomScudamore 65
(David Pipe) *chsd ldrs: reminders after 7th: led 9th: reminders after 12th: rdn and hdd 17th: hmpd on bnd sn after: wknd 4 out: t.o* **7/2**[1]
53-2 **4** *9* **Marigolds Way**[18] 4560 9-9-11 **90** (b[1]) RachaelGreen(5) 35
(Anthony Honeyball) *hld up: hdwy after 9th: trckd ldr 11th: rdn in cl 3rd after 17th: wknd qckly after next: t.o* **7/2**[1]
P6F5 **5** *5* **Cullahill (IRE)**[76] 3479 9-10-13 **108** NathanSweeney(7) 49
(Bob Buckler) *led tl 3rd: struggling in rr after 12th: no ch fr 17th* **7/1**[3]
P243 **P** **Drybrook Bedouin**[19] 4537 9-11-5 **114** (p) SClements(7) —
(Nick Mitchell) *chsd ldrs: short of room 1st: reminders after 8th and 10th: rdn fr 13th: no ch fr after 17th: p.u bef 2 out* **11/2**[2]
0F06 **U** **Estates Recovery (IRE)**[19] 4538 6-11-5 **107** RichardJohnson 107
(Philip Hobbs) *led 3rd tl 9th: chsd ldrs: reminders after 15th: led 17th: pckd bdly 4 out: narrowly hdd u.p whn virtually fell and uns rdr 3 out* **9/1**
6m 34.6s (-4.90) **Going Correction** -0.10s/f (Good) **7** Ran SP% **113.6**
Speed ratings: **103,102,84,81,79** —,—
toteswingers:1&2: £6.70, 2&3: £2.40, 1&3: £5.10 CSF £44.94 TOTE £17.00: £6.90, £3.70; EX 54.40.
Owner Mrs D Buckett **Bred** M J Le May **Trained** Upham, Hants
■ Kate Buckett's first winner under rules.
■ Stewards' Enquiry : Richard Johnson two-day ban: careless riding (Apr 10-11)

FOCUS
This ordinary staying handicap was run at a sound gallop and the first pair came a long way clear in a battling finish.

NOTEBOOK
Upham Atom posted his best effort so far on his third outing over fences when second at Exeter 19 days earlier and, off a 12lb higher mark, went one better with a fairly ready effort. He did well to get back into contention after hitting the fifth-last and there was plenty to like about his attitude late on. This was his first win since scoring in a bumper in 2008. (tchd 11-1)
Skipper's Lad(IRE) ◆, well backed, returned to form when second over further here last time out and was 1lb lower. He ran a bold race, finishing well clear of the remainder, and deserves to get his head back in front. (op 9-2)
Choumakeur(FR) was hiked up 12lb for beating the runner-up over 3m3f here 16 days earlier. He can be quirky and this was one of his moodier efforts. (tchd 3-1)
Marigolds Way posted a laboured effort in first-time blinkers. Official explanation: jockey said mare bled from the nose (op 9-2 tchd 5-1)
Drybrook Bedouin gave himself little chance with a sloppy round of jumping and disappointed. (op 8-1 tchd 15-2)
Estates Recovery(IRE) was in the process of running a much-improved race prior to coming to grief three out and would have been involved at the finish. (op 8-1 tchd 15-2)

5038 ELEANOR BISS NOVICES' HURDLE (11 hdls) 2m 6f
3:55 (3:55) (Class 4) 4-Y-0+ **£2,602** (£764; £382; £190)

Form RPR
1402 **1** **Paint The Clouds**[29] 4354 6-11-7 118 APMcCoy 121+
(Warren Greatrex) *j.lft at times: a.p: led 7th: drew wl clr after 3 out: v easily* **1/2**[1]
0 **2** *24* **Campden Society (IRE)**[22] 4479 8-10-8 0 JodieMogford 79
(Peter Hiatt) *led tl 5th: prom: rdn to chse wnr after 3 out: sn no ch* **66/1**
65-4 **3** *5* **Peedeeque**[17] 4677 5-11-1 0 NickScholfield 77
(Andy Turnell) *trckd ldrs: nt fluent 5th: rdn after 3 out: wknd bef 2 out* **15/2**[3]
0 **4** *8* **Guam (IRE)**[17] 4677 6-11-1 0 HarrySkelton 70
(Nick Mitchell) *trckd ldrs: rdn along fr 8th: wknd after 3 out* **28/1**
/10- **5** *15* **Fire And Rain (FR)**[576] 1320 8-11-1 124 SamThomas 56
(Emma Lavelle) *prom: led 5th tl 7th: wknd qckly: t.o* **11/4**[2]
5m 21.8s (-4.70) **Going Correction** -0.20s/f (Good) **5** Ran SP% **110.0**
Speed ratings (Par 105): **100,91,89,86,81**
CSF £20.09 TOTE £1.60: £1.10, £8.40; EX 55.50.
Owner Peter Deal & Jill & Robin Eynon **Bred** Guy Reed And Mrs A H Daniels **Trained** Upper Lambourn, Berks

NOTEBOOK
Paint The Clouds ran well in a handicap at Kempton on his previous outing and this quicker surface looked right up his street. He wasn't always foot perfect, but should be high in confidence after this and can bag a handicap before the season's end as he's open to improvement over this sort of trip. (op 8-13, tchd 4-6 and 8-11 in places)
Campden Society(IRE) plugged on to finish a clear second-best and showed a nice bit of improvement. She ought to have no trouble getting 3m. (op 50-1)
Peedeeque failed to really raise his game for the longer trip and still has something to learn about jumping. It was just his second outing over hurdles, though, and he is now eligible for a mark. (op 11-2 tchd 8-1)
Fire And Rain(FR) looked badly in need of the run on this return from a 576-day absence and lost touch on the second circuit. He ought to improve a good deal. (op 3-1 tchd 7-2)

5039 WESSEX WASTE H'CAP CHASE (17 fncs) 2m 5f
4:25 (4:25) (Class 4) (0-115,105) 5-Y-0+ **£3,498** (£1,086; £584)

Form RPR
4021 **1** **Goring One (IRE)**[6] 4919 6-10-11 **90** 7ex AndrewThornton 95
(Anna Newton-Smith) *led at gd pce: nt fluent 9th: hdd 13th: rdn after 4 out: 3 l down last: str run whn swtchd rt fnl 75yds: led fnl strides* **2/1**[1]
40P2 **2** *hd* **Ban Uisce (IRE)**[13] 4768 6-11-5 **105** (tp) MarkQuinlan(7) 112+
(Neil Mulholland) *pressed ldr: led 13th: 2 l clr last: sn rdn: no ex whn ct nring fin* **9/2**[3]
32 **3** *28* **Life Of A Luso (IRE)**[16] 4704 7-11-5 **98** (t) TomO'Brien 86+
(Paul Henderson) *chsd ldrs: clsd on ldng pair to chal for 2nd 4 out: hld fr next: stmbld bdly 2 out* **5/1**
0/51 **F** **Magic Marmalade (IRE)**[66] 3650 8-11-12 **105** RichardJohnson —
(Philip Hobbs) *chsd ldrs tl lost tch 7th: plenty to do u.p whn fell 12th* **9/4**[2]
0004 **U** **Just Tootsie**[19] 4540 7-10-7 **93** SClements(7) —
(Nick Mitchell) *chsd ldrs tl blnd bdly 4th and lost pl: awkward whn uns rdr 7th* **8/1**
5m 19.4s (-5.80) **Going Correction** -0.10s/f (Good) **5** Ran SP% **110.1**
Speed ratings: **107,106,96**,—,—
CSF £11.03 TOTE £2.30: £1.50, £2.00; EX 12.20.
Owner George Goring **Bred** R E Daniels **Trained** Jevington, E Sussex

FOCUS
A moderate handicap, run at a decent gallop.

NOTEBOOK
Goring One(IRE) was well ahead of the handicapper under a 7lb penalty for getting off the mark at Lingfield six days earlier and he followed up with a last-gasp success. He did plenty from the front early on, but was hassled for that position by the runner-up and looked like having to play second fiddle when that rival eased past him after four out. He kept battling, however, and Andrew Thornton got a great tune out of him from the final fence. He evidently stays well and the ground was probably quicker than he ideally cares for. This progressive 6-y-o emerges with a lot of credit. (op 85-40)
Ban Uisce(IRE) ◆ runner-up on his chasing debut at Plumpton last time and it looked for a long while as though he was going to resume winning ways. He paid for his early exertions from the final fence, though, and was mugged near the line. There is surely a race for him in the coming weeks, especially if he gets some more cut underfoot again. (op 6-1)
Life Of A Luso(IRE), having his first outing over fences for current connections, closed from four out but was beaten before hitting the last. (op 4-1)
Magic Marmalade(IRE) proved popular to follow up his chasing/handicap debut success off 6lb lower at Taunton 66 days earlier. He was keen under restraint, got well behind before the final circuit and had very little chance prior to departing. This leaves him with a bit to prove. (op 2-1)

5040 ALEXANDRA BURKE HERE 5TH MAY CONDITIONAL JOCKEYS' H'CAP HURDLE (10 hdls) 2m 4f
5:20 (5:20) (Class 5) (0-95,95) 4-Y-0+ **£1,951** (£573; £286; £143)

Form RPR
0004 **1** **E Street Boy**[24] 4450 5-11-2 **88** CO'Farrell(3) 105+
(David Pipe) *hld up: hdwy 5th: led on bit appr 2 out: sn wl in command: eased run-in* **11/8**[1]
2263 **2** *2 1/2* **Man Of Leisure**[13] 4785 7-11-7 **90** KeiranBurke 90
(Nerys Dutfield) *chsd ldr: reminder after 5th: upsides 3 out: sn rdn: kpt on same pce fr next: no ch w v easy wnr whn regained 2nd towards fin* **4/1**[3]
6033 **3** *1/2* **The Fox's Decree**[19] 4540 7-11-12 **95** (tp) IanPopham 96
(Martin Keighley) *led: rdn after 3 out: hdd bef next: sn wl hld by wnr: hit last: no ex whn lost 2nd towards fin* **7/2**[2]
/400 **4** *6* **Kings Story (IRE)**[20] 4522 7-10-2 **69** oh5 (b[1]) GilesHawkins 66
(Sophie Leech) *chsd ldrs: awkward 3 out: sn rdn and one pce: hit last* **13/2**
-006 **5** *14* **Kielder Rise**[42] 4098 7-10-3 **72** (tp) AodhaganConlon 56
(Evan Williams) *chsd ldrs: rdn after 5th: sn bhd* **16/1**
-000 **6** *17* **Kaycee (IRE)**[33] 4272 6-10-9 **78** PeterToole 58
(Roger Curtis) *hld up: rdn after 3 out: nvr any imp: wknd bef 2 out: t.o* **8/1**
000 **7** *1 3/4* **Salto Des Mottes (FR)**[17] 4676 5-10-9 **85** AGuerin(7) 50
(Neil Mulholland) *in tch: struggling 7th: sn btn: wknd bef 2 out: t.o* **25/1**
4m 55.6s (-1.20) **Going Correction** -0.20s/f (Good) **7** Ran SP% **118.5**
Speed ratings (Par 103): **94,93,92,90,84 78,77**
toteswingers:1&2: £3.60, 2&3: £2.80, 1&3: £2.20 CSF £8.17 TOTE £3.00: £1.20, £2.30; EX 9.80.
Owner Roger Stanley & Yvonne Reynolds **Bred** Kelanne Stud Ltd **Trained** Nicholashayne, Devon

FOCUS
A weak handicap, confined to conditional riders and it saw a very easy winner.

NOTEBOOK
E Street Boy ◆, a big market mover earlier in the day, won easily and shed his maiden tag at the seventh time of asking. He could have been called the winner a long way out and rates value for an awful lot further than the winning margin. Stepping back up in trip on quick ground was obviously much to his liking and he will escape a penalty if taking up either of his engagements later in the week. Considering the handicapper will have his say for this, he should prove very hard to stop following up. (op 6-4)
Man Of Leisure returned to something like his best, but rates greatly flattered by his proximity to the winner. He deserves to go one better, but the handicapper looks to have him where he wants him. (op 9-2)
The Fox's Decree was a sitting duck for the winner turning into the home straight. He plugged on once headed, but failed to confirm his last-time-out form with the runner-up on identical terms. (tchd 3-1)
Kings Story(IRE) despite him being 5lb out of the handicap, and he posted an improved effort in first-time blinkers. (op 10-1)
Salto Des Mottes(FR) Official explanation: trainer said gelding had a breathing problem
T/Plt: £34.70 to a £1 stake. Pool of £63,895.99 - 1,341.24 winning tickets. T/Qpdt: £20.60 to £1 Pool £4,332.24 -155.40 tckts TM 5041a-5046a (Foreign Racing) See Raceform Interactive

4909 AUTEUIL (L-H)
Sunday, March 27

OFFICIAL GOING: Turf: very soft

5047a PRIX DE MARSAN (HURDLE) (CONDITIONS) (4YO) (TURF) 2m 2f
1:30 (12:00) 4-Y-0 **£28,965** (£14,482; £8,448; £5,732; £2,715)

RPR
1 **Oklahoma Seven (FR)**[110] 4-10-3 0 SebastienLeloup —
(J-L Gay, France) **96/10**
2 *1 1/2* **Tornade Precieuse (FR)**[26] 4-10-1 0 AlbanDesvaux —
(Mme M Desvaux, France) **24/1**
3 *8* **Pokerdor (FR)**[19] 4-10-6 0 JeremyDaSilva —
(Y Fouin, France) **12/1**
4 *2* **Off By Heart (FR)**[26] 4-10-8 0 JacquesRicou —
(G Macaire, France) **13/10**[1]
5 *3* **Story Malinas (FR)** 4-10-3 0 (p) MathieuCarroux —
(A Chaille-Chaille, France) **53/10**[3]
6 *3/4* **Nisaro De Cimbre (FR)** 4-10-6 0 (b) DavidBerra —
(L Viel, France) **13/1**
7 *dist* **Horatio Caine (FR)**[106] 2882 4-10-3 0 DarylJacob —
(Nick Williams) *hdd gp chsng clr ldr: jnd for 2nd after 5th (of 11 flights): rdn: outpcd and lost grnd after 3 out: bhd fr 2 out* **45/1**

8 snk **Prince Picard (FR)**[21] 4-10-10 0 GregoryAdam —
(M Rolland, France) 3/1[2]

4m 30.58s (270.58) 8 Ran SP% 114.8
PARI-MUTUEL (all including 1 euro stakes): WIN 10.60; PLACE 2.90, 4.60, 3.30; DF 58.20; SF 155.00.
Owner Claude Guedj **Bred** C Guedj **Trained** France

5049a PRIX MITSOUKO III (CHASE) (CONDITIONS) (5YO, NON-THOROUGHBREDS) (TURF) 2m 5f 110y
3:40 (12:00) 5-Y-O **£21,517** (£10,758; £6,275; £4,258; £2,017)

RPR
1 **Septland (FR)**[19] 5-10-6 0 DavidBerra —
(P Peltier, France) 6/4[1]
2 8 **Saint Ber Song (FR)** 5-10-8 0 MathieuCarroux —
(A Chaille-Chaille, France) 12/1
3 2 1/2 **Sans Histoire (FR)**[21] 5-11-3 0 AlainDeChitray —
(A Adeline De Boisbrunet, France) 13/2[2]
4 10 **Savigny (FR)**[21] 5-11-0 0 FredericDaviault(5) —
(E Clayeux, France) 16/1
5 5 **Soprano Vallis (FR)**[110] 5-11-3 0 (p) DavidCottin —
(G Chaignon, France) 214/1
6 15 **Sacre Toi (FR)**[21] 5-11-3 0 (p) StephanePaillard —
(E Leray, France) 25/1
F **Sieur De La Prise (FR)**[19] 5-10-6 0 ow3 JonathanPlouganou —
(F-M Cottin, France) 22/1
P **Shalimar Fromentro (FR)**[71] 3564 5-10-8 0 DarylJacob —
(Nick Williams) *trckd ldrs: slt mstke 13th: outpcd 4 out: sn pushed along and no imp: p.u on fnl bnd after 3 out* 8/1[3]
F **Siam De La Roque (FR)**[285] 5-11-7 0 AnthonyThierry —
(J Follain, France) 11/1
P **Soleil Du Mou (FR)**[21] 5-10-12 0 BenoitDelo —
(T Doumen, France) 39/1
F **Salto Royal (FR)**[119] 5-10-10 0 AnthonyLecordier —
(P Peltier, France) 36/1

5m 54.08s (7.08) 11 Ran SP% 100.2
PARI-MUTUEL (all including 1 euro stakes): WIN 2.30 (coupled with Salto Royal); PLACE 1.50, 3.00, 1.80; DF 17.30; SF 23.60.
Owner J Detre & T Cypres **Bred** T Cypres **Trained** France

5048a (Foreign Racing) - See Raceform Interactive

4767 PLUMPTON (L-H)
Monday, March 28

OFFICIAL GOING: Good to firm (hdl 8.4, chs 8.6)
Wind: Almost nil Weather: Fine, warm

5050 AT THE RACES ON FACEBOOK MAIDEN HURDLE (9 hdls) 2m
2:10 (2:10) (Class 5) 4-Y-O+ **£1,815** (£529; £264)

Form RPR
1 **Galiotto (IRE)**[18] 5-11-0 0 JamieMoore 106+
(Gary Moore) *hld up in 5th and last of those in tch: clsd on ldrs 3 out and sn 3rd: chal 2 out: led last: rdn out* 20/1
24-4 2 2 1/2 **Ragdollianna**[125] 2592 7-10-7 100 TimmyMurphy 98+
(Murty McGrath) *hld up in 3rd tl trckd ldr fr 5th: clsd 3 out: led next: hdd and nt qckn last* 9/2[3]
4/3 3 11 **Highly Regal (IRE)**[9] 2495 6-10-7 103 (t) MrTJCannon(7) 95
(Roger Teal) *led at gd clip: clr fr 4th: c bk to field 3 out: hdd & wknd 2 out* 8/1
32 4 11 **Leitzu (IRE)**[18] 4676 4-10-0 103 WillKennedy 70
(Mick Channon) *chsd ldr to 5th: styd in tch: cl up 3 out: wknd bef next* 7/2[2]
00 5 2 1/4 **Lajidaal (USA)**[12] 4810 4-10-7 0 AndrewGlassonbury 77
(Gary Moore) *hld up and immediately wl bhd: wnt remote 6th at 6th: shoved along after 3 out: styd on quite takingly after* 40/1
0 6 15 **Joinedupwriting**[7] 4918 6-10-10 0 ow1 MrPYork(5) 69
(Raymond York) *hld up and immediately wl bhd: nvr bttr than remote 6th: no prog fr 3 out* 100/1
7 4 1/2 **Bedgebury Knight** 6-11-0 0 MattieBatchelor 64
(Brett Johnson) *hld up and immediately wl bhd: j. slowly 1st: mstke 4th: nvr remotely involved: hmpd 2 out* 100/1
-PP 8 12 **Soccerjackpot (USA)**[184] 590 7-11-0 0 PaddyBrennan 69+
(Nigel Twiston-Davies) *nt jump wl: chsd ldrs in 4th: clsd 3 out: sn rdn and wknd rapidly* 11/8[1]
9 29 **Edgeworth (IRE)**[10] 5-11-0 0 (t) SamThomas 27
(Brendan Powell) *hld up in last and immediately wl bhd: nvr remotely involved: wknd 2 out: clambered over last: t.o* 10/1
F F **Small Fly (IRE)**[27] 4404 7-10-7 0 NathanSweeney(7) —
(Bob Buckler) *hld up and immediately wl bhd: nvr involved: t.o in 8th whn fell 2 out* 28/1

3m 54.6s (-6.20) **Going Correction** -0.125s/f (Good)
WFA 4 from 5yo+ 7lb 10 Ran SP% 115.3
Speed ratings (Par 103): **110,108,103,97,96 89,86,80,66,—**
toteswingers:1&2:£7.70, 1&3:£14.80, 2&3:£6.20 CSF £104.72 TOTE £19.00: £4.10, £1.90, £3.10; EX 79.20.
Owner Andrew Bradmore **Bred** Ballintaggart Syndicate **Trained** Lower Beeding, W Sussex

FOCUS
An ordinary and open-looking maiden hurdle run at a good clip. The winner is rated in line with his Flat form.

NOTEBOOK
Galiotto(IRE), rated just 54 on the Flat, relished the switch to hurdling to run out a comfortable winner. Always tracking the brisk pace, he travelled nicely before kicking clear after the last. This was a nice debut, albeit in a modest contest. (op 25-1)
Ragdollianna, rated 100 over hurdles and back from a 125-day absence, raced far too freely and struggled to match the winner on the run-in. She may strip fitter for this outing, but will need to settle better to see out her races. If doing so, she may pick up a minor event. (op 4-1)
Highly Regal(IRE), third at Ascot when last seen over hurdles, made the running before tiring entering the straight. (op 10-1)
Leitzu(IRE), runner-up at Wincanton earlier this month, could not quicken and just stayed on at the one pace in the straight. (op 11-4)
Lajidaal(USA) ran on strongly from well back, but could never get seriously involved. (tchd 33-1)
Soccerjackpot(USA), well supported for this stable debut on his return from an absence, showed up for a long way, but didn't jump fluently and was beaten on the home turn. He will need to brush up his jumping. (op 7-4)

5051 ATTHERACES.COM EXCLUSIVE HUGH TAYLOR TIPPING NOVICES' H'CAP CHASE (14 fncs) 2m 4f
2:40 (2:40) (Class 4) (0-100,97) 5-Y-O+ **£2,602** (£764; £382; £190)

Form RPR
3020 1 **Curragh Dancer (FR)**[19] 4560 8-10-8 79 AndrewGlassonbury 83
(Paddy Butler) *often j.rt and frequent reminders: chsd ldr to 5th and 7th to 10th: mstke 4 out and dropped to 4th: lft 3rd and hmpd 2 out: clsd and lft in ld last: all out* 17/2
4065 2 3/4 **Alldunnandusted (IRE)**[50] 3963 7-11-9 97 JimmyDerham(3) 100
(Seamus Mullins) *nt a fluent: chsd ldr 5th to 7th and again 10th: 6 l down and looked wl hld whn lft in ld 2 out: blnd and hdd last: nt rcvr* 10/3[2]
535P 3 3 3/4 **Sieglinde (FR)**[28] 4401 5-9-7 71 MarkQuinlan(7) 67
(Alison Batchelor) *in tch to 9th: sn dropped out u.p and t.o after next: lft poor 4th 2 out: clsd on tiring rivals and tk 3rd nr fin* 7/1[3]
-506 4 3/4 **Goring Two (IRE)**[19] 4559 6-10-0 71 oh7 MattieBatchelor 66
(Anna Newton-Smith) *nt a fluent: in tch: chsd ldng pair 4 out: no imp next: lft w ch 2 out: wknd after last* 8/1
03P2 F **King Of Leon (FR)**[12] 4811 7-11-7 92 JackDoyle 103+
(Emma Lavelle) *led: only one travelling wl on fnl circ: 6 l up and seemingly in n.d whn j.rt and fell 2 out* 10/11[1]

5m 16.6s (9.30) **Going Correction** 0.0s/f (Good) 5 Ran SP% 109.6
Speed ratings: **81,80,79,78,—**
CSF £35.14 TOTE £6.60: £3.30, £1.60; EX 23.60.
Owner Miss M Bryant **Bred** Haras De Bois Carrouges & Coolmore Stud **Trained** East Chiltington, E Sussex

FOCUS
Just a small field for this modest handicap chase. The faller was set for a clear win and the first two are both better than the bare result.

NOTEBOOK
Curragh Dancer(FR) took full advantage of the favourite's mishap to run out a fortuitous winner. Having been under the whip a long way from home, he found for pressure and did well to rally having been hampered by the fall of the leader. He would not have won had the favourite stood up, but deserves credit for capitalising on jumping errors from the others. (op 7-1)
Alldunnandusted(IRE), rated higher over hurdles, chased the pace and, having led going to the last, made a terrible blunder and had to settle for second. He remains a maiden after six chase starts. (op 3-1 tchd 11-4 and 7-2)
Sieglinde(FR) had the headgear left off and, having looked well beaten, ran on up the straight to grab third after the last. (op 8-1)
Goring Two(IRE), running from 7lb out of the handicap on this chase debut, jumped markedly right on occasion and could not go with the leaders after the last. (op 9-1)
King Of Leon(FR), 8lb lower than when second behind a subsequent winner at Huntingdon last time, travelled and jumped strongly and had the race at his mercy before a taking a heavy fall at the second-last. Providing this doesn't dent his confidence too much, he should make amends in this grade. (op Evens tchd 6-5)

5052 ATTHERACES.COM FREE REPLAYS NOVICES' HURDLE (12 hdls) 2m 5f
3:10 (3:10) (Class 4) 4-Y-O+ **£2,055** (£599; £299)

Form RPR
3326 1 **Sircozy (IRE)**[67] 3649 5-11-7 122 JamieMoore 115+
(Gary Moore) *trckd ldr: mstke 3 out and briefly dropped to 3rd: pushed up to chal 2 out: led bef last: shkn up and styd on* 2/9[1]
0-2 2 2 3/4 **Blazing Bolte**[80] 3434 6-10-5 0 MarcGoldstein(3) 94
(Sheena West) *led at modest pce: urged along after 3 out: hdd and one pce bef last* 5/1[2]
0-5 3 40 **Tinabianca (FR)**[69] 3616 5-10-5 0 JimmyDerham(3) 64
(Seamus Mullins) *hld up in last: mstke 7th: wnt 2nd briefly 3 out: sn wknd: eased after 2 out: t.o* 12/1[3]

5m 26.1s (3.80) **Going Correction** -0.125s/f (Good) 3 Ran SP% 106.2
Speed ratings (Par 105): **87,85,70**
CSF £1.75 TOTE £1.10; EX 1.50.
Owner A E Dean **Bred** Allevamento Pian Di Neve Srl **Trained** Lower Beeding, W Sussex

FOCUS
An uncompetitive novice hurdle produced a comfortable success for the long odds-on favourite, who didn't need to be at her best.

NOTEBOOK
Sircozy(IRE), rated 122, had shown fair form in handicaps this term and ran out a comfortable winner under a penalty. Having tracked the leader, he needed to be pushed along entering the straight before taking command between the last two flights. He should remain of interest when upped in class as he enjoys a quick surface and stronger gallop. (op 1-4 tchd 2-7 in places)
Blazing Bolte, runner-up in a heavy ground bumper at Fontwell in January, ran a creditable race on this hurdles debut. Taking the field along, she jumped cleanly and was just outclassed in the closing stages. She should build on this display and land a novice hurdle before long. (op 6-1)
Tinabianca(FR) could not quicken when the pace lifted and was simply beaten by superior horses on this hurdles debut. She should benefit form this experience. (op 9-1 tchd 14-1)

5053 AT THE RACES SKY 415 H'CAP CHASE (18 fncs) 3m 2f
3:40 (3:40) (Class 4) (0-100,100) 5-Y-O+ **£2,602** (£764; £382; £190)

Form RPR
5P44 1 **Absolute Shambles**[12] 4811 7-10-6 80 ColinBolger 90+
(Chris Gordon) *chsd ldng pair: wnt 2nd after 4th: drvn to ld after 7th: mde most after: flat out fnl circ: mstke 2 out and jnd: battled on wl flat* 13/2
6344 2 3/4 **Reblis (FR)**[39] 4160 6-11-12 100 JamieMoore 107
(Gary Moore) *settled in rr as others vied for the ld: wnt 3rd 11th and tracked wnr after 13th: rdn 3 out: upsides after next: fnd nil flat* 11/4[2]
-4P2 3 19 **Zimbabwe (FR)**[14] 4772 11-9-11 74 oh12 (p) SamTwiston-Davies(3) 65
(Nigel Hawke) *won early battle for ld: hdd after 7th and sn u.p: dropped to 4th at 12th and struggling: nvr on terms after* 13/2
5663 4 4 1/2 **Ethiopia**[14] 4772 8-10-3 84 NathanSweeney(7) 70
(Bob Buckler) *tried to ld but unable to do so: dropped to 4th pl after 4th and sn receiving reminders: nvr gng wl after: last after 7th and sn t.o* 7/4[1]
3PPP 5 55 **Allterrain (IRE)**[49] 3982 8-11-4 92 (t) TimmyMurphy 29
(Murty McGrath) *cl up: wnt 2nd after 7th: drvn to chal after 10th: wknd rapidly 14th: t.o* 5/1[3]

6m 55.5s (4.80) **Going Correction** 0.0s/f (Good) 5 Ran SP% 106.4
Speed ratings: **92,91,85,84,67**
CSF £22.84 TOTE £9.50: £4.00, £1.70; EX 24.90.
Owner The Not Over Big Partnership **Bred** R Bowers **Trained** Morestead, Hants

FOCUS
A poor handicap chase with question marks over the whole field. The winner was some way off his best.

NOTEBOOK
Absolute Shambles had shown little this season but returned to form, making all to score in game fashion. A winner off 8lb higher in January, he looked nicely treated and jumped neatly before outbattling the runner-up on the run-in. His trainer reported that intense schooling has helped build the horse's confidence. (tchd 6-1)
Reblis(FR) had the headgear left off and was bidding to give Gary Moore a treble on the card. Held up early, he was under pressure with a circuit to go and found for his riding's urgings to join the winner at the last, before being outfought. Although this was a better effort, he remains a maiden over fences. (op 5-2)
Zimbabwe(FR), runner-up over C&D on his last start, was another under the pump very early and plodded on for a distant third. (tchd 7-1)
Ethiopia, third here on his last outing, was outpaced and hard at it with a circuit to go, before plugging on. He needs a further drop in the weights to get competitive. (op 2-1 tchd 13-8 tchd 85-40 in places)
Allterrain(IRE), wearing a first-time tongue-tie, was never travelling and could not get involved. (op 9-2)

5054 AT THE RACES VIRGIN 534 CONDITIONAL JOCKEYS' H'CAP HURDLE (12 hdls) 2m 5f
4:10 (4:10) (Class 4) (0-110,108) 4-Y-0+ **£2,055** (£599; £299)

Form				RPR
0P35	1		**De Welsh Wizzard**[15] 4745 8-11-0 **104** StephenO'Donovan(8) (Emma Lavelle) *t.k.h: led 3rd: mde rest: in command whn blnd 2 out: rdn out* **9/4**[2]	108+
406U	2	4 ½	**Shrewd Investment**[24] 4459 5-11-9 **108** CharlieHuxley(3) (Alan King) *cl up: effrt 9th: rdn to dispute 2nd fr next (3 out): clr 2nd after 2 out: no imp on wnr* **7/2**[3]	105
B2P5	3	3 ¾	**Twin Bud**[14] 4767 6-11-2 **98** (p) SamTwiston-Davies (Anna Newton-Smith) *led to 3rd: blnd 5th: rdn after 9th: no imp on wnr after 3 out: one pce fr next* **5/1**	93
2300	4	7	**Lemon Silk (IRE)**[31] 4327 7-11-1 **100** PeterCarberry(3) (Alex Hales) *cl up: nt fluent 9th: rdn to dispute 2nd sn after tl wknd 2 out* **2/1**[1]	87
4P06	5	9	**Be Ashored**[14] 4785 6-11-4 **100** RichardKilloran (Tim Vaughan) *cl up: rdn after 8th: lost tch next: bhd after* **12/1**	81

5m 18.1s (-4.20) **Going Correction** -0.125s/f (Good) **5** Ran SP% **110.7**
Speed ratings (Par 105): **103,101,99,97,93**
CSF £10.50 TOTE £2.30: £1.20, £2.30; EX 13.50.
Owner N Mustoe **Bred** Helshaw Grange Stud Ltd **Trained** Wildhern, Hants
FOCUS
A trappy handicap hurdle run at a fair gallop. Modest form with the cosy winner rated to his best.
NOTEBOOK
De Welsh Wizzard, a close fifth off this mark at Warwick on his last start, survived a blunder at the second-last to make most. Despite racing keenly enough, he quickened entering the straight and was always holding the second. He will escape a penalty and remains of interest this spring as he seems to relish the quick conditions. His trainer will find a similar contest in the near future. (tchd 5-2)
Shrewd Investment ran a fair race on this handicap debut. He appreciated the fast ground but could not peg back the winner. (op 9-2)
Twin Bud showed up for a long way but was just unable to land a serious blow and stayed on at the one pace.
Lemon Silk(IRE) came under pressure running down the back and failed to quicken entering the straight. He needs a drop in the weights to be competitive. (op 9-4 tchd 5-2)
Be Ashored raced up with the pace before fading tamely. (op 9-1)

5055 ATRVIRTUALOWNER.COM NEW SEASON H'CAP CHASE (12 fncs) 2m 1f
4:40 (4:40) (Class 5) (0-95,95) 5-Y-0+ **£1,899** (£589; £317)

Form				RPR
6102	1		**She's Humble (IRE)**[28] 4400 9-11-12 **95** RichardJohnson (Linda Jewell) *pressed ldr: led 7th: hdd after 3 out: over a l down but stl gng wl enough whn lft clr 2 out: rdn out* **7/2**[3]	102
F052	2	20	**Meneur (FR)**[19] 4556 9-11-10 **93** JamieMoore (Gary Moore) *trckd ldng pair: pushed along after 8th: no imp next: wl btn whn lft 2nd 2 out: eased flat* **6/4**[1]	90
4P45	3	29	**Sumdancer (NZ)**[14] 4770 9-11-5 **91** (v) MarcGoldstein(3) (Michael Madgwick) *cl up tl rdn and wknd after 7th: t.o fr next: lft remote 3rd 2 out* **6/1**	54
3202	F		**Bid Art (IRE)**[2] 5018 6-10-10 **82** (t) SamTwiston-Davies(3) (Jamie Snowden) *j. sltly rt: led to 7th: pushed along after next: effrt to ld again after 3 out: over a l up whn fell 2 out* **2/1**[2]	85

4m 23.3s (-2.60) **Going Correction** 0.0s/f (Good) **4** Ran SP% **109.8**
Speed ratings: **106,96,82,—**
CSF £9.44 TOTE £4.00; EX 7.80.
Owner Valence Racing Too **Bred** Pat Jones **Trained** Sutton Valence, Kent
FOCUS
A weak handicap chase run at a sound pace. The faller is rated 7lb off his good recent run. The winner looked set to score anyway and ran to her mark.
NOTEBOOK
She's Humble(IRE) benefited from the second-last fall of Bid Art to land her third chase success. In contention jumping two out, she was left clear to coast home. Her jockey felt the mare would have won anyway, but it was impossible to know for sure. (op 11-4)
Meneur(FR), narrowly beaten at Fontwell earlier this month, was well supported to go one better but never jumped or travelled with any zest and this rates a tame effort. He is a maiden over fences and looks high enough in the weights. (op 9-4)
Sumdancer(NZ) failed to strike a blow. Although 6lb lower than his last winning mark, he has been in dire form and looks a risky betting proposition. (op 11-2 tchd 13-2 in a place)
Bid Art(IRE), runner-up at Stratford just two days earlier, took the lead turning into the straight before making a hash of the second-last. He was just in front, would have had a fight on his hands and will need to bounce back from this. With confidence still intact, he should pick up a similarly modest race. (op 15-8 tchd 9-4)

5056 FOLLOW AT THE RACES ON TWITTER MAIDEN OPEN NATIONAL HUNT FLAT RACE 2m 2f
5:10 (5:10) (Class 6) 4-6-Y-0 **£1,507** (£439; £219)

Form				RPR
600	1		**Bach To Front (IRE)**[29] 4376 6-10-10 0 AndrewGlassonbury (Sarah Wall) *mde all at decent pce: drvn over 2f out: styd on wl* **12/1**	93+
50	2	12	**Murchan High (IRE)**[7] 4923 6-10-10 0 PaddyBrennan (Jim Best) *prom: chsd wnr 5f out: drvn 3f out: no imp* **5/1**[3]	82
	3	¾	**No Idea** 6-10-10 0 RichardJohnson (Tim Vaughan) *hld up: prog to trck ldrs 7f out: rdn 3f out: disp 2nd after: no imp on wnr* **7/4**[1]	81
0	4	20	**Inverclyde (IRE)**[7] 4923 4-10-3 0 MarkQuinlan(7) (Bill Turner) *chsd wnr to 5f out: steadily outpcd* **12/1**	63
	5	6	**Landenstown Lad (IRE)** 5-11-0 0 JimmyDerham(3) (Seamus Mullins) *cl up: rdn and lost tch 7f out: sn bhd* **9/1**	65
	6	30	**Chartplan (IRE)** 5-10-10 0 MrTJCannon(7) (Roger Teal) *sn struggling in last: lost tch sn after 1/2-way: wl bhd fnl 6f* **4/1**[2]	38
	7	dist	**Fools Mate** 4-10-3 0 MrJackSalmon(7) (Alison Batchelor) *prom to 1/2-way: wknd rapidly and sn wl t.o* **14/1**	—
40	8	¾	**Astralogical (IRE)**[55] 3876 6-10-10 0 GerardTumelty (Alan King) *chsd ldrs: wnt 3rd briefly 1/2-way: sn wknd: virtually p.u 3f out* **6/1**	—

4m 24.9s (-2.10) **Going Correction** -0.125s/f (Good)
WFA 4 from 5yo+ 7lb **8** Ran SP% **119.4**
Speed ratings: **99,93,93,84,81 68,—,—**
toteswingers:1&2:£8.30, 1&3:£5.50, 2&3:£3.30 CSF £73.68 TOTE £9.50: £1.50, £1.60, £1.80; EX 92.50.
Owner J P C Wall **Bred** Michael Doyle **Trained** Dallington, E Sussex
■ Stewards' Enquiry : Andrew Glassonbury caution: used whip with excessive frequency.
FOCUS
A low-grade maiden bumper. The modest second sets the level.
NOTEBOOK
Bach To Front(IRE), well beaten in three bumper starts to date, led from pillar to post to record an easy victory. She relished this quicker ground and never saw another rival. There may be improvement to come as she was a tad green and edged right at the stable exit, but this was a poor contest. Official explanation: trainer's rep said, regarding apparent improvement in form, that the mare was better suited by the quicker ground. (op 14-1)
Murchan High(IRE) raced keenly towards the head of affairs before failing to reach the winner. Although this was an improved run, this was a weak race. (op 4-1)
No Idea, related to jump winners, crept into the race but never had any chance with the winner. She can be expected to improve for this outing. (op 2-1 tchd 2-1 in places)
Inverclyde(IRE) became outpaced down the back and stayed on at the one pace. (op 14-1)
Landenstown Lad(IRE) Official explanation: trainer said gelding became upset in the preliminaries.
Chartplan(IRE) was held up and simply could not get involved. Held in high regard by his trainer, he is expected to improve for the experience. (op 17-2)
Astralogical(IRE) had shown only a hint of ability in two starts and having been up with the pace she faded quickly. (op 9-2)
T/Plt: £271.20 to a £1 stake. Pool:£56,958.12 - 153.29 winning tickets T/Qpdt: £28.90 to a £1 stake. Pool:£5,188.10 - 132.42 winning tickets JN

4828 TOWCESTER (R-H)
Monday, March 28

OFFICIAL GOING: Good (good to firm in places; watered; 8.7)
First hurdle at 3m start omitted on all circuits; unsuitable ground
Wind: virtually nil Weather: bright and sunny

5057 ODDSANYWHERE.COM H'CAP HURDLE (7 hdls 1 omitted) 2m
2:30 (2:30) (Class 5) (0-95,94) 4-Y-0+ **£1,626** (£477; £238; £119)

Form				RPR
4030	1		**Meridiem**[23] 4465 7-10-11 **82** (t) ChrisHonour(3) (Sean Regan) *in tch: chsd ldr bef 3 out: pushed ahd bef 2 out: clr whn j.lft 2 out: styd on wl* **14/1**	93+
P00	2	2 ¼	**Graylyn Amber**[32] 4310 6-11-2 **84** CharliePoste (Robin Dickin) *taken down early: led: hdd and drvn bef 2 out: kpt on but a hld after* **25/1**	91
0500	3	11	**French Leave (IRE)**[59] 3791 9-11-4 **93** (tp) EdGlassonbury(7) (Victor Dartnall) *chsd ldrs: wnt 2nd after 3rd tl bef 3 out: drvn and outpcd by ldrs wl bef 2 out: plugged on same pce after* **8/1**	90
0060	4	1 ¾	**Drink Up**[36] 4233 7-10-10 **78** MarkGrant (John O'Neill) *in tch in midfield: rdn after 5th: styd on into modest 5th bef 2 out: plugged on fr 2 out but no threat to ldrs* **20/1**	75
60P2	5	11	**Atared**[12] 4809 5-11-5 **94** MissGAndrews(7) (Pam Sly) *t.k.h early: in tch: hdwy to chse ldrs 5th: 3rd and drvn after 3 out: no prog and btn whn mstke 2 out: wknd between last 2* **5/1**[1]	82
0162	6	5	**Roxane Bruere (FR)**[17] 4707 6-9-12 **76** (t) ChristopherWard(10) (Robin Dickin) *t.k.h: chsd ldr tl after 3rd: rdn and struggling 5th: wknd next* **8/1**	57
/P45	7	2 ¾	**Showtime Annie**[5] 4947 10-9-7 **68** oh3 KillianMoore(7) (Jennie Candlish) *in tch in rr: mstke and pckd 1st: rdn 4th: wl btn 3 out: plugged on past btn horses fr 2 out* **28/1**	47
000	8	2 ¾	**Brave Enough (USA)**[50] 3958 4-10-6 **81** (b[1]) HaddenFrost (Roger Curtis) *in tch towards rr: rdn and effrt after 5th: no real hdwy and wl btn after next* **25/1**	50
66-4	9	8	**Chigorin**[14] 4771 10-10-2 **70** (t) LiamTreadwell (James Sheppard) *in tch in midfield: hmpd 4th: rdn and effrt after next: wknd 3 out: t.o* **22/1**	39
-000	10	52	**Contentwithmyluck (IRE)**[79] 3454 5-9-11 **68** oh3.(vt[1]) TommyPhelan(3) (Tom Gretton) *mstkes: chsd ldrs: mstke 5th: sn u.p and struggling: wknd bef next: wl t.o 2 out* **66/1**	—
056	11	7	**Blinka Me**[50] 3958 4-10-12 **87** JimmyMcCarthy (Alex Hales) *in tch towards rr: rdn and struggling after 5th: losing tch whn j.lft next: wl t.o bef 2 out* **12/1**	—
2004	U		**Mossmann Gorge**[15] 4751 9-11-6 **93** (p) MattGriffiths(5) (Anthony Middleton) *hld up in tch in rr tl bdly hmpd and uns rdr 4th* **12/1**	—
P65	F		**Guarino (GER)**[44] 4069 7-10-13 **86** JoshuaMoore(5) (Gary Moore) *in tch in midfield tl fell 4th* **7/1**[3]	—
0000	B		**Mid Wicket (USA)**[147] 2131 5-11-3 **92** JeremiahMcGrath(7) (Mouse Hamilton-Fairley) *hld up in tch towards rr tl b.d 4th* **25/1**	—
2564	B		**Earl Of Thomond (IRE)**[41] 4125 6-11-0 **82** AndrewThornton (Caroline Bailey) *a towards rr: nudged along after 2nd: b.d 4th* **11/2**[2]	—

3m 57.5s (-10.40) **Going Correction** -0.75s/f (Firm)
WFA 4 from 5yo+ 7lb **15** Ran SP% **114.4**
Speed ratings (Par 103): **96,94,89,88,83 80,79,77,73,47 44,—,—,—,—**
toteswingers:1&2:£47.40, 1&3:£31.70, 2&3:£37.30 CSF £311.22 CT £2960.53 TOTE £21.70: £5.00, £10.50, £3.30; EX 281.10.
Owner Matthew Hustler **Bred** Beech Tree Stud **Trained** Snetterton, Norfolk
FOCUS
The watered ground was officially described as Good, good to firm in places and clerk of the course Robert Bellamy was of the opinion it may ride slightly slower than anticipated due to lack of grass cover. This was a wide-open handicap to open proceedings and, despite there being a fair gallop on, it paid to race handily. a big step up from the cosy winner on his hurdles form.
NOTEBOOK
Meridiem flopped on his handicap debut 23 days earlier, but had placed at this venue the time before and the return here saw him in a much better light. He travelled by far the best throughout and was kept to his task when sent to the front off the home turn. The first-time tongue tie also clearly had a positive effect and it was his first success at the ninth attempt. Official explanation: trainer said, regarding apparent improvement in form, that the gelding appeared suited by the track and benefit from the first-time tongue strap. (tchd 16-1)

Graylyn Amber turned in a brave effort from the front and finished well clear of the rest. The quicker ground evidently suited. (op 20-1)

French Leave(IRE), another never far away, was equipped with first-time cheekpieces and appeared to blow up rounding the home turn on this first outing for two months. He was keeping on again towards the finish and ought to come on a good bit. (tchd 9-1)

Drink Up, who didn't go unbacked, hit a flat spot before staying on dourly from two out. He has begun life in handicaps on a workable mark.

Atared, 4lb higher, failed to see it out on this stiffer track. (op 11-2)

Guarino(GER) crashed out and caused three rivals to come to grief. (tchd 6-1)

Earl Of Thomond(IRE) was brought down in the melee in the back straight, but he looked in trouble at the time. (tchd 6-1)

5058 HAYGAIN HAY STEAMERS H'CAP CHASE (12 fncs) 2m 110y
3:00 (3:00) (Class 4) (0-110,108) 5-Y-0+ **£2,276** (£668; £334; £166)

Form				RPR
132-	**1**		**Tooka**[342] 5292 10-10-6 **93**.....(p) MattGriffiths(5)	100
			(Anthony Middleton) *mde virtually all: drvn and forged ahd bef 2 out: idling between last 2: edgd lft u.p flat: kpt on wl* **4/1**[3]	
3P-3	**2**	*1 1/4*	**Digital Media (IRE)**[21] 4529 9-10-2 **84**.....(t) NickScholfield	92+
			(Simon Burrough) *t.k.h: chsd ldrs: mstke 7th and 9th: clsd on ldrs after 3 out: chsd wnr next: drvn and pressed wnr last: keeping on same pce and hld whn swtchd rt flat* **13/2**	
2201	**3**	*12*	**Autumm Spirit**[17] 4691 7-10-7 **89**.....(t) CharliePoste	86
			(Robin Dickin) *nt a fluent: w ldr tl after 3 out: sn drvn: lost 2nd 2 out: wknd between last 2* **9/4**[1]	
4335	**4**	*1 1/2*	**Good Old Days (IRE)**[90] 3154 12-11-4 **100**..... JasonMaguire	94
			(Kim Bailey) *t.k.h: chsd ldrs: rdn and clsd after 3 out: wknd after 2 out: wl hld whn j. slowly last* **11/4**[2]	
3033	**5**	*15*	**Liberty Seeker (FR)**[11] 4830 12-11-12 **108**..... AndrewThornton	92
			(John Harris) *j.lft: last fr 4th: j. bdly lft 5th: lost tch bef 3 out* **5/1**	

4m 8.60s (-7.50) **Going Correction** -0.575s/f (Firm) 5 Ran SP% **107.4**

Speed ratings: **94,93,87,87,80**

CSF £24.93 TOTE £4.80: £4.30, £5.30; EX 30.20.

Owner A Middleton **Bred** R J Matthews **Trained** Granborough, Bucks

FOCUS

The jockeys after the opener reported the ground was patchy with some juice in it. This moderate handicap was another open-looking event and the first two came clear up the home straight. The first three are rated to their marks.

NOTEBOOK

Tooka shrugged off a 342-day absence and ran out a most game winner. He was resuming off a mark 3lb higher than for his last win in 2010 and he obviously likes this venue, with it being his third success at the course. One will have to be mindful of the potential bounce factor next time out, but this was a very pleasing comeback effort. (op 9-2 tchd 7-2)

Digital Media(IRE), third on his comeback from injury 21 days earlier, had been dropped 3lb and was the only one to give the winner a serious race from three out. He deserves to go one better again. (op 5-1)

Autumm Spirit, a recent Leicester winner, was racing off a 7lb higher mark and proved easy to back. Her rider took a confident look behind after four out, but she almost immediately came under pressure from there on and was well beaten off. (op 2-1 tchd 5-2)

Good Old Days(IRE) was returning from a three-month break and proved keen to post. He rallied turning for home, but proved very one paced and perhaps the run was needed. (op 7-2 tchd 5-2)

Liberty Seeker(FR) lost touch from an early stage on this first run over fences since 2008. (op 11-2)

5059 FREE BETS AT GG.COM NOVICES' HURDLE (7 hdls 1 omitted) 2m
3:30 (3:30) (Class 4) 4-Y-0+ **£2,276** (£668; £334; £166)

Form				RPR
2221	**1**		**Araldur (FR)**[23] 4479 7-11-6 127..... RobertThornton	127+
			(Alan King) *mde all: mstke 3rd and 3 out: readily drew clr bef 2 out: eased flat* **30/100**[1]	
-100	**2**	*15*	**Lombardy Boy (IRE)**[22] 4500 6-10-11 0..... AlexMerriam(3)	99
			(Michael Banks) *mstkes: chsd ldrs: rdn and outpcd after 3 out: rallied to press for 2nd and mstke last: kpt on u.p to snatch 2nd nr fin* **25/1**[3]	
1023	**3**	*hd*	**Break The Chain**[36] 4234 5-11-6 107..... AndrewThornton	107+
			(Caroline Bailey) *chsd wnr: rdn and btn bef 2 out: wl btn whn mstke last: lost 2nd nr fin* **5/1**[2]	
5	**4**	*3*	**Stapleton (IRE)**[14] 4780 6-10-9 0..... MattGriffiths(5)	96
			(Philip Middleton) *hld up in last quartet: mstke 3 out: sn drvn: pressing for placings but no ch w wnr 2 out: no ex last* **25/1**[3]	
0	**5**	*11*	**Mutanaker**[60] 3767 4-10-7 0..... FelixDeGiles	80
			(Ed de Giles) *hld up in last pair: mstke 2nd: rdn after 3 out: no prog and wl hld whn mstke next: wknd* **33/1**	
	6	*66*	**Overlay** 7-10-7 0..... MarkGrant	12
			(John O'Neill) *in tch in last quartet: hung lft bef 3 out: mstke 3 out: sn lost tch: t.o* **25/1**[3]	
PPP	**P**		**Rockoboy (IRE)**[10] 4855 10-10-7 0..... MrJBanks(7)	—
			(Zoe Davison) *chsd ldrs tl lost action and p.u after 4th: dismntd* **250/1**	
	P		**Patrick's Secret** 7-10-7 0..... MrHGMiller(7)	—
			(Zoe Davison) *hld up in last pair: rdn and lost tch qckly after 4th: t.o whn p.u after 3 out* **100/1**	

4m 0.50s (-7.40) **Going Correction** -0.75s/f (Firm)

WFA 4 from 5yo+ 7lb 8 Ran SP% **109.5**

Speed ratings (Par 105): **88,80,80,78,73 40,—,—**

toteswingers:1&2:£2.10, 1&3:£1.10, 2&3:£5.30 CSF £11.61 TOTE £1.20: £1.02, £3.00, £1.10; EX 10.20.

Owner David Sewell **Bred** Baudouin De La Motte Saint Pierre Et Al **Trained** Barbury Castle, Wilts

■ A milestone for Robert Thornton, who rode his 1,000th winner under rules in Britain in this race.

FOCUS

The easy winner was value for further and is rated to his mark.

NOTEBOOK

Araldur(FR) was found a golden opportunity to follow up his Kempton success 23 days earlier and he completed the task with an easy display. He raced enthusiastically at the head of affairs and wasn't always fluent. He was officially rated 20lb superior to main market rival Break The Chain, however, and once fighting off that rival's challenge from three out, came clear up the home straight. It may be he is best off looking for another one of these under a double penalty (rated 150 over fences) and this was jockey Robert Thornton's 1000th career winner. (op 4-11 after eary 2-5 and 4-9 in a place)

Lombardy Boy(IRE), despite lacking fluency, posted his best effort so far has a hurdler and it's not hard to see why he has been tried over further, as he got markedly outpaced. He is now eligible for handicaps. (op 20-1)

Break The Chain ultimately paid for trying to put it up to the winner and definitely emerges as the second best horse in the race. He can find a handicap off his mark now the ground has turned quick. (tchd 11-2)

Stapleton(IRE) showed ability on his debut a fortnight earlier and wasn't disgraced on this switch to hurdling, shaping as though he wants further. (op 20-1)

5060 REMEMBER COLIN & SMILE H'CAP CHASE (18 fncs) 3m 110y
4:00 (4:01) (Class 4) (0-110,104) 5-Y-0+ **£2,276** (£668; £334; £166)

Form				RPR
63F5	**1**		**Jolly Boys Outing (IRE)**[27] 4413 8-9-10 **81**..... MrBJPoste(7)	92+
			(Rosemary Gasson) *hld up in tch: trckd ldrs 12th: led 15th: pushed clr bef 2 out: in command whn wnt rt last: hung lft flat: comf* **10/1**	
2223	**2**	*9*	**Filippo Lippi (IRE)**[60] 3764 6-11-9 **101**.....(b) APMcCoy	102
			(Jonjo O'Neill) *mstkes: in tch: jnd ldrs 10th: clr w wnr and ev ch whn j.lft 3 out: rdn and fnd nil bef next: j. awkwardly 2 out: one pce and no threat to wnr after* **7/2**[2]	
4-65	**3**	*1 3/4*	**Speed Bonnie Boat**[22] 4502 8-11-12 **104**.....(p) MarkBradburne	102
			(Henry Daly) *mstkes: nvr travelling wl in rr and rdn along at times: j.lft and rdn bnd after 9th: hdwy to chse ldrs u.p after 3 out: plugged on same pce fr next* **18/1**	
0PP4	**4**	*13*	**Silver Bay**[23] 4483 10-10-10 **88**..... SamJones	79
			(Oliver Sherwood) *hld up in last trio: mstke and rdn 10th: mstke 13th: drvn and chsng ldrs after 3 out: wknd after next* **11/2**	
4P12	**5**	*31*	**Von Galen (IRE)**[155] 2002 10-10-12 **90**.....(p) TomScudamore	49
			(Michael Scudamore) *chsd ldr after 2nd tl led 8th: mstke 12th: hdd 14th: wknd u.p after 3 out: t.o* **5/1**[3]	
5060	**6**	*5*	**Terrible Tenant**[102] 2980 12-11-0 **92**..... AndrewThornton	46
			(Seamus Mullins) *racd keenly: led after 1st tl 8th: dropped to rr 11th: wl bhd fr 14th: t.o fr 3 out* **25/1**	
-140	**P**		**Crank Hill**[16] 4718 9-10-9 **87**..... DarylJacob	—
			(Bob Buckler) *led tl after 1st: reminders after next: dropped to last and u.p 7th: wl detached fr 11th: t.o 14th tl p.u 2 out* **11/2**	
0P32	**P**		**Woodmore (IRE)**[17] 4694 7-11-4 **96**.....(p) AndrewTinkler	—
			(Charlie Longsdon) *chsd ldr: blnd and lost pl 1st: chsd ldr again 8th: mstke 12th: sn rdn: led and mstke 14th: hdd next: wknd rapidly after 3 out: wl bhd whn p.u next* **10/3**[1]	

6m 20.1s (-16.80) **Going Correction** -0.575s/f (Firm) 8 Ran SP% **110.9**

Speed ratings: **103,100,99,95,85 83,—,—**

toteswingers:1&2:£7.90, 1&3:£8.20, 2&3:£7.50 CSF £43.41 CT £600.85 TOTE £12.80: £3.40, £1.70, £3.80; EX 46.90.

Owner Mrs Rosemary Gasson **Bred** Tom Mullins **Trained** Banbury, Oxon

FOCUS

An ordinary handicap, run at a sound gallop. A big step up from the winner, with the second in line with his hurdles form.

NOTEBOOK

Jolly Boys Outing(IRE) opened his account under rules at the eighth time of asking and did the job in good style. He was well backed earlier in the day and, despite some deliberate early jumping, made smooth headway to lead from three out. He idled up the home straight but this triple point winner clearly had his optimum conditions here. (op 8-1 tchd 11-1)

Filippo Lippi(IRE) had blinkers back on for this chasing debut and was the only one to go with the winner nearing the final turn. He probably paid from the penultimate fence for taking time to settle and is not a simple horse to place successfully, but is entitled to improve for the experience. (op 4-1 tchd 11-4)

Speed Bonnie Boat would have given the winner something to think about had she not run so moodily, and it's not hard to see why connections reached for first-time cheekpieces. (op 10-1 tchd 22-1)

Silver Bay was never seriously in the hunt. (op 9-2 tchd 6-1)

Von Galen(IRE) shaped as though he needed this first outing since October. (op 9-2 tchd 11-2)

Woodmore(IRE) threw in the towel from three out. (op 9-2 tchd 3-1)

5061 SIS 1ST FOR FOOTBALL DATA H'CAP HURDLE (10 hdls 2 omitted) 3m
4:30 (4:30) (Class 3) (0-120,120) 4-Y-0+ **£3,252** (£955; £477; £238)

Form				RPR
2	**1**		**Connectivity (IRE)**[16] 4722 7-11-5 **118**..... MrTWeston(5)	139+
			(Dr Richard Newland) *a gng wl: hld up in tch: hdwy to trck ldrs bef 3 out: wnt 2nd sn after 3 out: led next: clr bef last: r.o wl: easily* **3/1**[2]	
3413	**2**	*11*	**Prophete De Guye (FR)**[16] 4726 8-10-6 **103**..... IanPopham(3)	106
			(James Evans) *t.k.h: hld up in tch in rr: mstke 8th: hdwy to chse ldrs next: drvn and outpcd bef 2 out: kpt on u.p flat to go 2nd nr fin: no ch w wnr* **7/1**	
230P	**3**	*3/4*	**Earcomesthedream (IRE)**[16] 4722 8-10-6 **100**.....(b) TomSiddall	102
			(Peter Pritchard) *chsd ldr tl led 3 out: sn rdn: hdd next: sn brushed aside by wnr: plugged on u.p: lost 2nd nr fin* **16/1**	
2-0P	**4**	*1/2*	**She's On The Case (IRE)**[20] 4536 6-10-7 **101**..... TomO'Brien	103
			(Grant Cann) *hld up in tch: blnd bdly 5th: sn dropped to last: hdwy to chse ldrs and in tch 3 out: outpcd bef next: plugged on to press for 2nd flat: no ch w wnr* **13/2**[3]	
-PP5	**5**	*80*	**Kilbeggan Blade**[20] 4537 12-10-9 **113**.....(v) ChristopherWard(10)	35
			(Robin Dickin) *mstkes: chsd ldrs: lost pl and rdr unbalanced 7th: sn drvn and no rspnse: wknd bef 3 out: looked like pulling up 2 out: continued wl t.o* **20/1**	
11-4	**P**		**Whitewater Dash**[126] 2571 11-11-1 **109**..... RhysFlint	—
			(Jim Old) *chsd ldrs: rdn and wknd qckly bef 3 out: wl bhd whn p.u 2 out* **12/1**	
-510	**P**		**Premier Des Marais (FR)**[23] 4464 8-11-9 **117**..... APMcCoy	—
			(Gary Moore) *hld up in tch: rdn and short-lived effrt after 8th: wknd bef next: wl bhd whn p.u 2 out* **13/2**[3]	
P022	**P**		**Lidar (FR)**[23] 4467 6-11-12 **120**..... RobertThornton	—
			(Alan King) *led j.lft 4th: hdd 3 out: sn rdn and wknd: 5th and wl btn whn p.u 2 out* **5/2**[1]	

6m 3.80s (-11.20) **Going Correction** -0.75s/f (Firm) 8 Ran SP% **111.1**

Speed ratings (Par 107): **88,84,84,83,57 —,—,—**

toteswingers:1&2:£4.40, 1&3:£12.50, 2&3:£7.30 CSF £22.76 CT £272.12 TOTE £5.30: £1.70, £1.80, £4.40; EX 23.60.

Owner D & D Coatings Ltd **Bred** Mrs K Healy **Trained** Claines, Worcs

FOCUS

This modest handicap was run at a steady gallop. The easy winner is on the upgrade but his rivals were all below their best.

NOTEBOOK

Connectivity(IRE) ◆ finished second on his debut for connections 16 days earlier and went one better with a bloodless success. He wasn't sure to appreciate the quicker ground on breeding, but it proved to be right up his street and he clearly stays very well. He would have to be of serious interest if turned out under a penalty, as the handicapper will now hike him up the weights, and he does hold an entry back at Chepstow on Saturday. (op 7-2 tchd 4-1)

Prophete De Guye(FR) also travelled nicely into contention, but was made to look laboured when the winner asserted. This was his first outing over hurdles since 2009 and, rated 10lb higher over fences, connections should be able to find him an opening in the coming weeks. (op 5-1 tchd 9-2)

Earcomesthedream(IRE) ran a game race under a prominent ride and looks to be coming back into form. (op 14-1)

She's On The Case(IRE) had looked totally out of sorts in two previous spins this term. However, she was well backed up in trip and shaped as though she would have enjoyed a stiffer test. (op 9-1 tchd 10-1)

Lidar(FR) found that the decision to send him out from the front on this big step up in trip on such a stiff track totally backfired. (tchd 9-4)

5062 RACING FORUM AT GG.COM H'CAP CHASE (14 fncs) 2m 3f 110y
5:00 (5:01) (Class 5) (0-90,89) 5-Y-O+ **£1,626** (£477; £238; £119)

Form RPR

P052 **1** **Lonesome Boatman (IRE)**[11] 4829 11-9-13 **69**...............(p) JoshWall(7) 83+
(Arthur Whitehead) *several slow jumps: in tch in midfield tl j. slowly and dropped to rr 6th: reminders bef next: hdwy to chse ldrs 10th: wnt 2nd bef 2 out: rdn to ld last: kpt on: rdn out* **11/4**[1]

236P **2** *3* **Monsieur Georges (FR)**[151] 2050 11-9-11 **63** oh2......... JohnKington(3) 72
(Violet M Jordan) *mostly chsd ldr: rdn 7th: ev ch 3 out: sn drvn ahd hdd last: styd on same pce flat* **20/1**

P433 **3** *15* **Bohemian Rock**[17] 4693 7-10-11 **74**...........................(t) AndrewThornton 69
(Caroline Bailey) *chsd ldrs tl 3rd: dropped towards rr and hmpd 7th: rdn 10th: drvn and hdwy to dispute 3rd 2 out: sn no prog and btn: wknd between last 2* **4/1**[2]

4233 **4** *4 1/2* **Crystal Prince**[22] 4504 7-11-7 **84**......................................(tp) FelixDeGiles 75
(Charlie Longsdon) *hld up in tch in rr: mstke 2nd: reminders after 5th: hdwy to chse ldrs 3 out: drvn and wknd next* **5/1**[3]

/6P6 **5** *5* **Carmond (GER)**[18] 4668 7-10-8 **71**....................................(b[1]) SamJones 57
(Oliver Sherwood) *hld up in tch in rr: hmpd 7th: rdn and effrt after 3 out: wkng whn j.rt 2 out: wl btn whn j.rt last* **12/1**

P06/ **6** *38* **Jolibob (IRE)**[1444] 4917 9-10-0 **63** oh1................................ CharliePoste 30
(Robin Dickin) *t.k.h: j.rt: in tch: hdwy to chse ldrs 6th: lft in ld next: hdd after 3 out: wknd qckly: wl bhd whn j.rt last: eased flat: t.o* **8/1**

5/43 **F** **Ilongue (FR)**[34] 4269 10-10-1 **67**... DavidBass(3) —
(Laura Hurley) *led tl fell 7th* **6/1**

05P3 **P** **Mister Watzisname (IRE)**[5] 4945 9-11-12 **89**............(tp) AndrewTinkler —
(Charlie Longsdon) *chsd ldrs tl bdly hmpd 7th: nt rcvr and bhd whn p.u bef next* **12/1**

3F50 **P** **Royial (FR)**[102] 2980 6-11-12 **89**... DarylJacob —
(Seamus Mullins) *in tch: lft 3rd 7th: rdn and struggling 10th: bhd 3 out: tailing off whn p.u next* **16/1**

5m 11.4s (-6.80) **Going Correction** -0.575s/f (Firm) **9** Ran SP% **114.8**
Speed ratings: **90,88,82,81,79 63,—,—,—**
toteswingers:1&2:£14.00, 1&3:£3.80, 2&3:£17.40 CSF £50.47 CT £219.32 TOTE £4.30: £1.60, £7.00, £1.40; EX 77.40.
Owner A J Whitehead **Bred** M Robinson **Trained** Aston on Clun, Shropshire
■ Josh Wall's first winner under rules.

FOCUS
A weak handicap, but it was competitive for the class and it saw a typical Towcester finish in the home straight. The first two are rated to their marks.

NOTEBOOK
Lonesome Boatman(IRE) was very well backed to go one better than his previous second here 11 days earlier and duly landed the bets, but made heavy weather of it. His jumping rather deserted him on the far side, but those in front began to wilt just as he got going from the 11th fence. He was always doing enough when in front against the stands' rail after the last and it was the veteran's first win under rules at the 16th attempt. (op 4-1)

Monsieur Georges(FR), another veteran, was last seen pulling up five months previously and so this was obviously a lot more like it from him. (op 25-1 tchd 28-1)

Bohemian Rock looked a tricky ride on his previous outing and that was again very much the case this time. (op 9-2)

Crystal Prince ran below his previous level and remains difficult to catch right. (op 10-3)

Ilongue(FR) was still going well prior to coming down, where she badly hampered Mister Watzisname. (op 8-1 tchd 9-2)

5063 GG.COM ALERTS STANDARD OPEN NATIONAL HUNT FLAT RACE 2m
5:30 (5:31) (Class 6) 4-6-Y-O **£1,301** (£382; £191; £95)

Form RPR

1 **1** **Make A Track (IRE)**[31] 4329 5-11-10 0................................ DarylJacob 110+
(David Arbuthnot) *hld up in tch: hdwy 6f out: chsd ldr ent fnl 2f: rdn over 1f out: led ins fnl f: r.o wl: rdn out* **7/4**[1]

2 *3 1/2* **Tony Dinozzo (FR)** 4-10-0 0.. JakeLoader(10) 92
(Nicky Henderson) *in tch: led over 3f out: rdn wl over 1f out: rn green ent fnl f: hdd and outpcd by wnr ins fnl f* **22/1**

3 **3** *1* **Willow's Saviour**[31] 4329 4-10-10 0...................................... FelixDeGiles 91
(Charlie Longsdon) *in tch in midfield: hdwy to chse ldrs and rdn over 2f out: styd on same pce and edgd rt fnl f* **16/1**

62- **4** *1 1/4* **No Substitute (IRE)**[353] 5122 6-11-3 0........................... RobertThornton 97
(Alan King) *t.k.h: in tch: shuffled bk and lost pl 6f out: hdwy to chse ldrs and rdn over 2f out: styd on same pce fnl 2f* **4/1**[2]

0 **5** *3/4* **So Fine (IRE)**[103] 2957 5-11-3 0.................................. RichieMcLernon 96
(Anabel L M King) *chsd ldrs: rdn and unable qck over 2f out: kpt on same pce fnl 2f* **100/1**

6 *4 1/2* **Trojan Sun** 5-11-0 0... DavidBass(3) 92
(Nicky Henderson) *in tch: chsd ldr over 3f out tl rdn 2f out: wknd over 1f out* **9/2**[3]

7 *4* **Cavite Eta (IRE)**[29] 4-10-3 0.................................... JeremiahMcGrath(7) 81
(Mark Bradstock) *in tch in rr: detached last 10f out: hanging and racing awkwardly 1/2-way: rallied on uphill run 3f out: styd on steadily past btn horses fnl 2f* **8/1**

300 **8** *7* **Vision Of Lights (IRE)**[14] 4780 6-11-0 0............................ TomMolloy(3) 81
(Graeme McPherson) *t.k.h: hld up in tch towards rr: pushed along and hdwy 6f out: wknd wl over 2f out* **40/1**

9 *1 3/4* **Ripoff** 6-11-3 0.. CharliePoste 79
(Robin Dickin) *t.k.h: chsd ldrs: wnt 2nd 10f out: led 1/2-way tl over 3f out: wknd over 2f out* **50/1**

10 *3 1/4* **Dartford Warbler (IRE)** 4-10-10 0................................ LeightonAspell 69
(Oliver Sherwood) *in rr: rdn and struggling 7f out: sme hdwy 4f out: no imp and wl btn over 2f out* **10/1**

500- **11** *9* **Alaccordion**[436] 3457 6-11-3 0... TomMessenger 67
(Violet M Jordan) *t.k.h: hld up in tch in rr: hdwy 6f out: wknd qckly 3f out* **100/1**

6 **12** *57* **Preferred Lies (IRE)**[36] 4239 6-11-3 0........................... TomScudamore 10
(Anabel L M King) *t.k.h: chsd ldr tl 10f out: wknd rapidly 4f out: t.o and virtually p.u fnl f* **33/1**

60 **13** *24* **Bally Gunner**[60] 3773 6-11-3 0.. HaddenFrost —
(Roger Curtis) *led tl 1/2-way: lost pl rapidly over 4f out: t.o and virtually p.u fnl 2f* **80/1**

3m 48.7s (-13.60) **Going Correction** -0.75s/f (Firm)
WFA 4 from 5yo+ 7lb **13** Ran SP% **115.5**
Speed ratings: **104,102,101,101,100 98,96,93,92,90 86,57,45**
toteswingers:1&2:£16.20, 1&3:£6.10, 2&3:£21.50. totesuper7: Win: Not won. Place: Not won CSF £48.18 TOTE £2.80: £1.60, £6.50, £2.80; EX 64.10.
Owner George Ward **Bred** Limetree Stud Ltd **Trained** Compton, Berks

FOCUS
An interesting bumper. It was run at a routine gallop. The winner is the sort to rate higher and the third sets the level.

NOTEBOOK
Make A Track(IRE) followed up his debut win at Sandown a month earlier with a workmanlike display. The winner responded to pressure leaving the back straight, but looked in trouble as the runner-up skipped into the lead off the home turn. To his credit he dug deep, though, and did look better the further he went. It must be remembered he was carrying a penalty and faced with contrasting ground here. His debut success also got a big boost when the runner-up there, Ambion Wood, hosed up next time and this 5-y-o looks a decent prospect for novice hurdling next season. (op 15-8 tchd 2-1 and 9-4 in places)
Tony Dinozzo(FR) ◆ was the seemingly lesser fancied of his trainer's pair here, but proved best. He showed his inexperience, but made a bold move off the home turn and this rates an encouraging debut as he should learn plenty. (op 16-1)
Willow's Saviour was 4lb better off with the winner for a six-length beating on his debut at Sandown. He posted another respectable effort on this quicker ground, but never threatened to reverse form. (op 12-1)
No Substitute(IRE) finished second in a useful field on his previous outing and the market suggested he was ready to do himself justice on this return from a 353-day layoff. He came under pressure a fair way out and really the run looked needed. (op 5-1 tchd 3-1)
So Fine(IRE) ◆ hit a flat spot before staying on promisingly in the closing stages and this was a big improvement on his debut form at Bangor in December. He is entitled to come on again.
Trojan Sun, Nicky Henderson's other runner, attracted support but took time to settle and was done with before the home straight. (op 8-1)
Cavite Eta(IRE) was in with every chance when falling at the last on his debut in a point this month and was well backed earlier in the day. However, having been held up out the back on this debut for new connections, he got taken off his feet and didn't look a straightforward ride. Official explanation: jockey said gelding hung left in the back straight (op 5-1)
Bally Gunner Official explanation: jockey said gelding stopped very quickly
T/Jkpt: Not won. T/Plt: £350.90 to a £1 stake. Pool:£105,029.37 - 218.48 winning tickets T/Qpdt: £16.70 to a £1 stake. Pool:£9,102.34 - 402.10 winning tickets SP

4781 TAUNTON (R-H)
Tuesday, March 29

OFFICIAL GOING: Good (good to firm in places)
Rail on bends moved reducing each circuit by 62metres.
Wind: virtually nil Weather: Sunny periods

5064 SOMERSET COUNTY GAZETTE LADIES DAY NOVICES' HURDLE (10 hdls) 2m 3f 110y
2:20 (2:21) (Class 4) 4-Y-O+ **£2,740** (£798; £399)

Form RPR

4401 **1** **Bold Addition (FR)**[18] 4706 6-11-8 122...................................... RWalsh 127+
(Paul Nicholls) *trckd ldrs: shkn up to trck ldr after 3 out: rdn to ld whn bmpd appr last: r.o to assert run-in* **2/11**[1]

0310 **2** *8* **Lucy's Perfect**[26] 4448 5-11-1 113...............................(b) TomScudamore 113
(David Pipe) *prom: led whn hit 3 out: sn qcknd pce: rdn and hdd whn edgd lft appr last: nt pce of wnr* **11/2**[2]

3 *29* **Be Kind**[49] 5-10-8 0.. AndrewThornton 75
(Karen George) *trckd ldrs: nt fluent 6th: struggling whn hit next: sn outpcd: wnt modest 3rd run-in* **100/1**

04 **4** *2* **Dolores Ortiz (IRE)**[7] 4924 5-10-8 0.. RhysFlint 73
(Philip Hobbs) *set stdy pce: hdd 3 out: sn rdn and outpcd: lost poor 3rd run-in* **28/1**[3]

4m 33.1s (-12.90) **Going Correction** -0.975s/f (Hard) **4** Ran SP% **104.4**
Speed ratings (Par 105): **86,82,71,70**
CSF £1.48 TOTE £1.30; EX 1.50.
Owner Mrs Sue Craven **Bred** Mme Jacques Thoreau **Trained** Ditcheat, Somerset

FOCUS
An uncompetitive novice hurdle and the first two are rated pretty much to their marks.

NOTEBOOK
Bold Addition(FR) ran out a ready enough, if not entirely convincing, winner. Held up, he joined the leader turning for home, but Ruby Walsh was forced to ride him out between the second-last and last, where a good jump allowed him to draw clear. While this was a decent enough effort under a penalty, we learnt little, though the impression lingers that he will not find it as easy in better company, nor does he appear the quickest, so may require a stiffer stamina test. He will be kept on the go and may end up chasing in the summer. (op 1-5)
Lucy's Perfect took it up down the far side, but was unable to go with the winner in the home straight. A C&D winner in December, this was better after a disappointing effort last time, and she can find opportunities in this grade. The front two finished well clear. (op 6-1)
Be Kind got up for third on this her hurdles debut and may come on a little for the experience, but will need a drop in grade.
Dolores Ortiz(IRE) will be best suited returning to selling company. (op 20-1)

5065 DI GAMBLE BIRTHDAY CELEBRATION NOVICES' CHASE (17 fncs) 2m 7f 110y
2:50 (2:50) (Class 4) 5-Y-O+ **£4,424**

Form RPR

3312 **1** **Qozak (FR)**[35] 4267 7-11-5 140..(t) RWalsh —
(Paul Nicholls) *led tl left alone 5th* **2/13**[1]

-50U **U** **Hudibras (IRE)**[11] 4855 7-10-9 117.................................(p) PeterToole(3) —
(Charlie Mann) *trckd wnr tl blnd and uns rdr 5th* **11/2**[2]

6m 33.7s (19.10) **Going Correction** +0.20s/f (Yiel) **2** Ran SP% **102.0**
Speed ratings: **76,—**
TOTE £1.20.
Owner The Stewart Family & Paul K Barber **Bred** Ivan Dumont **Trained** Ditcheat, Somerset

FOCUS
A simple task for course specialist Qozak and it turned into nothing more than a schooling session. Unrateable.

NOTEBOOK
Qozak(FR) was left alone after the mistake of the only other runner Hudibras at the fifth, he was allowed to complete the course in his own time, which was a slow one at that due to Ruby Walsh taking extra care to avoid the loose horse. He jumped well in the main, one slight mistake down the back straight the only worry for backers. Aside from that, there is nothing to read into this race, one which he would surely have won comfortably anyway. All his wins have come here and he is likely to return for the next meeting. (op 2-11)

Hudibras(IRE) unseated at the fifth, having jumped soundly enough up to that point, and failed to pick up any prize-money for connections in what looked a golden opportunity for a decent pot. (op 9-2)

5066 SIS LIVE H'CAP HURDLE (9 hdls) 2m 1f
3:20 (3:20) (Class 4) (0-110,110) 4-Y-0+ **£3,082** (£898; £449)

Form | | | | RPR
0504 **1** **Teshali (IRE)**[4] 4990 5-10-11 **105**..........(t) JamesCowley(10) 113+
(Paul Nicholls) *hld up in last pair: hdwy to join ldr 6th: led appr 2 out: rdn clr run-in* **3/1**[2]
3343 **2** *8* **Posh Emily**[18] 4697 8-10-13 **104**..........(b) JakeGreenall(7) 104
(Ron Hodges) *chsd ldrs tl lost pl u.p after 4th: regained 3rd after 3 out: styd on same pce fr next: wnt 2nd run-in* **11/2**
2123 **3** *4* **Woodlark Island (IRE)**[154] 2022 5-11-12 **110**..........(bt) TomScudamore 108
(David Pipe) *led: drvn along fr 6th: hdd appr 2 out: sn hld by wnr: no ex whn lost 2nd run-in* **4/1**[3]
P46 **4** *10* **Lang Shining (IRE)**[34] 4288 7-11-10 **108**.......... JimmyMcCarthy 97
(Jamie Osborne) *hld up in last but in tch: wnt 4th 3 out: sn rdn: one pce fr next: mstke last* **12/1**
-050 **5** *22* **Monopole (IRE)**[26] 4448 7-10-0 **94**.......... FrancisHayes(10) 58
(David Pipe) *racd wdst: j.lft: chsd ldrs: rdn after 6th: wknd after 3 out: t.o* **33/1**
02 **6** *23* **Giant O Murchu (IRE)**[19] 4670 7-10-13 **100**.......... DavidBass(3) 41
(Lawney Hill) *trckd ldr: rdn in 3rd after 6th: wknd after 3 out: t.o* **11/4**[1]
4406 **7** *25* **Foreign King (USA)**[5] 1912 7-10-13 **100**.......... JimmyDerham(3) 16
(Seamus Mullins) *trckd ldr: hit 4th: rdn after 5th: wknd 3 out: t.o* **13/2**

3m 54.8s (-13.20) **Going Correction** -0.975s/f (Hard) **7** Ran SP% **111.0**
Speed ratings (Par 105): **92,88,86,81,71 60,48**
Tote Swingers: 1&2 £3.70, 1&3 £2.90, 2&3 £3.00 CSF £18.58 TOTE £3.30: £1.50, £6.10; EX 18.70.
Owner D A Johnson **Bred** His Highness The Aga Khan's Studs S C **Trained** Ditcheat, Somerset

FOCUS
An open-looking handicap hurdle run at a good gallop. A step up from the winner with the next two close to their marks.

NOTEBOOK
Teshali(IRE) ended up a comfortable winner, travelling best of all, before drawing clear in the home straight. Having run well enough over 2m3f four days previous, the drop back in trip seems to have suited ideally and he remains an improving horse. Fast ground is important to him and he will be kept on the go in the coming months to take advantage. (op 7-2 tchd 11-4)
Posh Emily, under pressure with more than a circuit to go, ran a stormer to take second, shaping as though a step up in trip is essential. She can win if replicating this run, though she doesn't win as often as she perhaps should. (tchd 9-2)
Woodlark Island(IRE) ran his usual race, steaming off in front and responding when given reminders down the back straight, but may have been undone by his lack of fitness. This was his first run for 154 days and should put him right for a good ground campaign. (tchd 9-2 in places)
Lang Shining(IRE) was outpaced down the back straight, but did stay on a little and it may be that he needs more of a stamina test in this sphere. (op 9-1)
Giant O Murchu(IRE) was too keen early on and gave himself no chance of getting home. Official explanation: trainer said gelding bled from the nose (op 10-3)

5067 TAUNTON JAGUAR H'CAP CHASE (24 fncs) 4m 2f 110y
3:50 (3:50) (Class 3) (0-130,120) 5-Y-0+ **£6,851** (£1,997; £999)

Form | | | | RPR
6U6P **1** **Cold Mountain (IRE)**[135] 2395 9-11-9 **120**.......... JimmyDerham(3) 126
(Seamus Mullins) *trckd ldrs: hit 7th: chal 3 out: sn rdn: led last: styd on: drvn out* **9/2**
4U33 **2** *2 1/4* **Earth Planet (IRE)**[19] 4673 9-11-4 **117**..........(bt) MrRMahon(5) 121
(Paul Nicholls) *trckd ldrs: led 20th: rdn whn pressed fr 3 out: hdd last: no ex* **11/1**[3]
122B **3** *20* **Cashel Blue (USA)**[21] 4537 9-10-13 **110**..........(b) KeiranBurke(3) 98
(Patrick Rodford) *led: mstke 19th: hdd next: sn rdn: wknd after 4 out: b.b.v* **85/40**[1]
3PBP **4** *8* **Petite Margot**[104] 2953 12-10-9 **106**.......... SamTwiston-Davies(3) 82
(Nigel Twiston-Davies) *trckd ldr tl reminder after 17th: rdn after next: wknd after 4 out* **9/4**[2]

8m 59.0s (539.00) course record **4** Ran SP% **106.0**
CSF £16.33 TOTE £7.40; EX 15.30.
Owner Woodford Valley Racing **Bred** Skymarc Farm **Trained** Wilsford-Cum-Lake, Wilts

FOCUS
An interesting marathon handicap chase. Ordinary form with the first two close to their marks.

NOTEBOOK
Cold Mountain(IRE) got the better of the battle to end up a cosy enough winner. Only 1lb higher than his last win, he was suited by the return to a sound surface, having disappointed on heavy last time out. He has been entered in the Scottish Grand National, and although he'll struggle to get in, he would have an outside chance on quick ground if he does. (op 7-2)
Earth Planet(IRE) travelled well, as he often does, but failed to see out his race and always seems likely to come off second best once getting into a battle with the winner. He has not won since 2008, and while the ability is clearly there, it seems the attitude is not, so he's firmly one to avoid. (tchd 11-4)
Cashel Blue(USA) led for a long way, but a couple of mistakes down the back straight put paid to his chances. He's bled on two occasions of late, and looks best avoided at present. Official explanation: trainer said gelding bled from the nose (op 9-4 tchd 5-2 and 2-1)
Petite Margot is falling down the weights, but she isn't getting any younger and doesn't look like taking advantage anytime soon. (op 11-4)

5068 IZABY-WHITES' SPECIAL BIRTHDAYS H'CAP HURDLE (12 hdls) 3m 110y
4:20 (4:22) (Class 4) (0-100,100) 4-Y-0+ **£2,740** (£798; £399)

Form | | | | RPR
U606 **1** **Drumbeater (IRE)**[5] 4968 11-9-7 **74** oh10..........(p) MarkQuinlan(7) 76
(Bernard Scriven) *hld up: hdwy 7th: led 3 out: styd on gamely: drvn out* **5/1**
55 **2** *1 1/4* **Jewellery (IRE)**[19] 4675 4-10-2 **85**..........(t) JamieMoore 77
(Alison Thorpe) *trckd ldrs: chal 3 out: rdn and ev ch 2 out: swtchd rt bef last: styd on but a being hld* **3/1**[2]
-400 **3** *4 1/2* **Shacklesborough (IRE)**[54] 3907 7-11-11 **99**.......... RWalsh 96
(Paul Nicholls) *trckd ldrs tl dropped to last pair 5th: nudged along fr 8th: hdwy after 3 out: sn rdn: styd on same pce fr next* **9/4**[1]
/0P0 **4** *36* **Star Time (IRE)**[15] 4787 12-9-9 **74** oh15..........(v) COFarrell(5) 35
(Michael Scudamore) *in rr: reminders after 2nd: nvr threatened ldrs: lft modest 4th 2 out* **33/1**
6665 **U** **Orion Express**[173] 1741 10-10-7 **88**.......... MissLGardner(7) —
(Susan Gardner) *hld up: blnd and uns rdr 4th* **9/2**[3]
-00P **U** **Duffy Moon**[78] 3487 7-9-11 **74** oh10..........(t) PeterToole(3) 64
(Charlie Morlock) *trckd ldrs: led 9th tl 3 out: sn rdn: 4th and hld whn slipped bdly on landing and uns rdr 2 out* **20/1**
0000 **P** **Smoking (FR)**[46] 4052 5-11-9 **97**..........(b[1]) GerardTumelty —
(Jonathen de Giles) *led tl 9th: sn rdn: wknd next: bhd whn p.u bef 2 out* **14/1**
56 **P** **Iheardu**[26] 4445 5-11-12 **100**.......... AndrewThornton —
(Neil Mulholland) *trckd ldr: mstke 7th: rdn after 9th: blnd 3 out: sn wknd: bhd whn p.u bef next* **8/1**

5m 47.4s (-19.70) **Going Correction** -0.975s/f (Hard)
WFA 4 from 5yo+ 9lb **8** Ran SP% **116.1**
Speed ratings (Par 105): **92,91,90,78,— —,—,—**
Tote Swingers: 1&2 £4.60, 1&3 £3.90, 2&3 £1.80 CSF £21.24 CT £42.82 TOTE £12.20: £3.10, £1.02, £1.50; EX 23.70.
Owner B Scriven **Bred** Paul McDonnell **Trained** Creech Heathfield, Somerset
■ Bernard Scriven's first winner under rules for more than ten years.

FOCUS
No more than average handicap hurdle. The form is rated around the second and third.

NOTEBOOK
Drumbeater(IRE) again travelled well, from 10lb out of the handicap, before taking it up down the back and keeping up to his work in the straight. Jumping well in the main, he will receive a rise in the weights, and is not one to be too confident about repeating this effort, as he seems to have been prepared specifically for today. (op 6-1 tchd 7-1)
Jewellery(IRE) seemed to enjoy both the step up in trip and the decent ground. Although she is now 0-16 under both codes, she remains fairly unexposed and can find enough improvement to win a similar contest. (op 11-4)
Shacklesborough(IRE) was outpaced a long way from home, but kept on dourly for a remote third. He had previously been disappointing and it remains to be seen how long he remains in the care of the champion trainer. (op 10-3)
Star Time(IRE) was racing from more than two stone out of the handicap and has shown nothing in recent years. (tchd 40-1)
Orion Express departed too far out to know how he would fared. (op 18-1)
Duffy Moon, racing from 10lb wrong', was running a decent race on his handicap debut when unseating at the second-last. With a drop in grade, he may be able to find a weak race. (op 18-1)

5069 TOTAL STAR RADIO 102.4FM LADIES DAY H'CAP CHASE (14 fncs) 2m 3f
4:50 (4:50) (Class 4) (0-105,101) 5-Y-0+ **£3,675** (£1,248)

Form | | | | RPR
P351 **1** **Thunder Child**[15] 4784 11-10-1 **76**..........(t) AndrewGlassonbury 97+
(Simon Burrough) *mde all: rdn clr after 4 out: unchal* **6/4**[1]
P211 **2** *55* **Ours (FR)**[28] 4416 9-11-12 **101**.......... JasonMaguire 77
(Mark Rimell) *trckd wnr: rdn after 9th: lost 2nd next: no ch after: lft poor 2nd 3 out* **9/4**[2]
-40P **F** **Across The Straits (FR)**[46] 4052 7-10-11 **89**..........(t) JimmyDerham(3) 90
(Jonathan Geake) *hld up 4th: wnt 2nd 10th: rdn but no ch w wnr fr after 4 out: fell heavily next* **13/2**
3P54 **S** **Quetzal (IRE)**[15] 4768 6-11-9 **101**.......... CharlieHuxley(3) —
(Alan King) *trcking ldrs in cl 3rd whn slipped up on bnd appr 8th* **7/2**[3]

4m 43.9s (-12.60) **Going Correction** -0.575s/f (Firm) **4** Ran SP% **106.3**
Speed ratings: **103,79,—,—**
CSF £5.14 TOTE £2.90; EX 3.80.
Owner Richard Weeks **Bred** L Fuller **Trained** West Buckland, Somerset

FOCUS
What looked an open handicap chase was turned into a rout by an enterprising ride. The winner clocked a good time for the grade in the circumstances and looks very well treated at present.

NOTEBOOK
Thunder Child won the race with an injection of pace entering the back straight that allowed him to steal a 10l lead and put his rivals under pressure, from which they were never able to recover. He was ably assisted by the horse under him, who jumped enthusiastically and seems to love his racing, especially here. This was his second consecutive C&D victory (albeit fortunate last time), and if able to find another race to dominate, is likely to be able to handle a rise in mark if maintaining this rich vein of form. (op 13-8 tchd 15-8 in places)
Ours(FR) was unable to live with the change of pace by the winner and again wasn't the most fluent at his fences. Though he got away with his jumping last time, he really needs to sharpen up to be able to compete when races are run at a true pace. (tchd 5-2)
Across The Straits(FR) was merely racing for place money when taking a heavy fall three out, having never got involved. (tchd 10-3)
Quetzal(IRE) slipped around the turn entering the back straight on the flat, unseating his rider in an unfortunate incident. (tchd 10-3)

5070 WURZELS AFTER RACING - EVENING MEETING 12TH APRIL MARES' STANDARD OPEN NATIONAL HUNT FLAT RACE 2m 1f
5:20 (5:20) (Class 5) 4-6-Y-0 **£2,055** (£599; £299)

Form | | | | RPR
1 **Dancing Emily (IRE)** 5-11-0 0.......... JodieMogford 99+
(Graeme McPherson) *mid-div: smooth hdwy over 7f out: shkn up to ld over 2f out: kpt on wl: rdn out* **10/3**[3]
22 **2** *3* **Maid Of Silk (IRE)**[254] 1029 5-11-0 0.......... TomScudamore 93
(Neil Mulholland) *trckd ldrs: led 3f out: rdn and hdd over 2f out: kpt on but a being hld by wnr* **9/4**[1]
1 **3** *2* **Bahira (IRE)**[20] 4554 4-10-7 0.......... HenryBrooke(7) 91
(Donald McCain) *mid-div: hdwy 6f out: ev ch 4f out: sn rdn: kpt on same pce fnl 2f* **11/4**[2]
301 **4** *4* **Jaya Bella (IRE)**[50] 3979 6-11-7 0.......... WarrenMarston 94
(Milton Harris) *hld up: hdwy over 7f out: rdn to chse ldrs over 3f out: styd on same pce fnl 2f* **20/1**
0 **5** *3 1/2* **Tinagenic (FR)**[70] 3623 5-10-11 0.......... JimmyDerham(3) 84
(Seamus Mullins) *in tch: effrt 3f out: kpt on same pce* **33/1**
0 **6** *4 1/2* **Star Potential**[22] 4533 4-10-0 0.......... MarkQuinlan(7) 72
(Susan Gardner) *trckd ldrs: led 8f out tl 3f out: wknd 2f out* **100/1**
0 **7** *13* **Posh Totty**[22] 4533 4-10-7 0.......... DarylJacob 59
(Richard Price) *mid-div: rdn 4f out: wknd 2f out* **40/1**
5 **8** *1 1/2* **Titch Strider (IRE)**[18] 4709 6-11-0 0.......... DavidEngland 65
(John Panvert) *led tl 8f out: wknd over 3f out* **8/1**
0 **9** *5* **Sor Brook**[32] 4335 5-10-11 0.......... SamTwiston-Davies(3) 60
(Nigel Twiston-Davies) *t.k.h early: trckd ldrs: drvn along whn lost pl after 7f: wknd 6f out* **14/1**
0 **10** *19* **Calcot Rose**[39] 4184 5-11-0 0.......... GerardTumelty 41
(Alan King) *a towards rr: t.o* **28/1**
0 **11** *166* **Brandy N' Lovage**[160] 1920 6-11-0 0..........(p) JohnnyFarrelly —
(Richard Mitchell) *prom tl 1/2-way: t.o: virtually p.u* **100/1**

3m 51.9s (-10.50) **Going Correction** -0.975s/f (Hard)
WFA 4 from 5yo+ 7lb **11** Ran SP% **113.9**
Speed ratings: **85,83,82,80,79 77,70,70,67,58 —**
Tote Swingers: 1&2 £2.50, 1&3 £3.50, 2&3 £3.20, totesuper7: Win: Not won. Place: Not won CSF £10.20 TOTE £3.80: £1.10, £1.30, £1.10; EX 16.20.
Owner BPD Ltd **Bred** Pat Jones **Trained** Upper Oddington, Gloucs

FOCUS
Probably a fair mares' bumper with the market principals dominating. The winner has the potential to rate higher.
NOTEBOOK
Dancing Emily(IRE) ◆ ran out an easy winner having been backed into 100-30 from 10s in the morning. Although taking a little time to settle, she travelled best for a long way, before taking it up turning for home to draw clear in the home straight. Clearly well regarded by connections, she looks a decent prospect and seems sure to be even better with a stronger gallop. (op 5-1)
Maid Of Silk(IRE) has now finished runner-up on all three starts and would have won well here but for running into a good winner. Travelling nicely up the inside, this was a good run after a 254-day absence and she can win a race soon, over hurdles if not a bumper, with good ground essential. (op 11-4 tchd 3-1)
Bahira(IRE) won last time and put in a solid effort under the penalty. She's in good hands. (op 9-4)
Jaya Bella(IRE) ran a decent race under a penalty, but looks likely to struggle winning another bumper and will probably be best switched to hurdles sooner rather than later. (op 16-1)
Tinagenic(FR) ran a decent race under a penalty, but looks likely to struggle winning another bumper and will probably be best switched to hurdles sooner rather than later. (op 18-1)
T/Plt: £84.70 to a £1 stake. Pool:£58,317.78 - 502.08 winning tickets T/Qpdt: £48.70 to a £1 stake. Pool:£4,199.09 - 63.70 winning tickets TM

[4944]HEREFORD (R-H)
Wednesday, March 30

OFFICIAL GOING: Good (good to soft in places) changing to good to soft after race 1 (2.10)
Wind: Light Weather: Overcast

5071 LINDLEY CATERING NOVICES' HURDLE (8 hdls) 2m 1f
2:10 (2:10) (Class 4) 4-Y-0+ **£2,602** (£764; £382; £190)

Form RPR
3-24 **1** **Swift Lord (IRE)**[26] 4451 6-11-0 122 .... JamieMoore 130+
(Gary Moore) *led tl after 1st: chsd ldr tl regained ld 5th: drew clr fr 2 out: wl in command after: v easily* **5/2**[3]
2 *28* **Dashing Doc (IRE)**[201] 4-10-7 0 .... PaulMoloney 95
(Evan Williams) *nt fluent: hld up: hdwy appr 3rd: outpcd after 3 out: tk poor 2nd bef last where blnd: no ch w wnr* **28/1**
P-1P **3** *4* **Nobunaga**[43] 4129 6-11-6 0 .... AidanColeman 102
(Venetia Williams) *racd keenly: chsd ldr tl after 1st: remained prom: wnt 2nd appr 3 out: rdn and no imp on wnr after 2 out: sn no ch: lost 2nd whn wl btn bef last* **17/2**
2F1F **4** *1 ½* **Raya Star (IRE)**[8] 4930 5-11-0 0 .... RobertThornton 101
(Alan King) *hld up in rr: nt fluent 3 out: niggled along and no imp appr 2 out: tk poor 4th bef last: nvr a danger* **2/1**[2]
51 **5** *10* **Dubai Crest**[14] 4810 5-11-6 0 .... APMcCoy 92
(Nicky Henderson) *in tch: chsng ldrs whn nt fluent 3 out: pushed along appr 2 out: wl btn sn after* **15/8**[1]
-400 **6** *27* **Drumlang (IRE)**[79] 3489 5-11-0 0 .... DominicElsworth 62
(Henrietta Knight) *chsd ldrs: lost pl 4th: sn in rr: struggling appr 3 out: sn lost tch: t.o* **66/1**
P-PP **P** **Dark Haven**[90] 3227 8-10-0 0 .... RobertKirk[(7)] —
(James Evans) *plld hrd: hld up: hdwy to ld after 1st: hdd 5th: wkng qckly whn mstke 3 out: t.o whn p.u bef 2 out* **150/1**

4m 7.70s (8.30) **Going Correction** +0.55s/f (Soft)
WFA 4 from 5yo+ 7lb **7** Ran SP% **112.8**
Speed ratings (Par 105): **102,88,86,86,81 68,—**
toteswingers: 1&2 £4.50, 1&3 £6.50, 2&3 £20.70 CSF £42.80 TOTE £2.90: £1.70, £9.80; EX 32.30.
Owner R A Green **Bred** William J White **Trained** Lower Beeding, W Sussex
FOCUS
This looked to be a competitive novice hurdle, but did not turn out that way. The main reason for the poor form shown by his three major rivals was very likely down to the watered ground. It had been officially described as good, good to firm in places at the overnight stage, but due to 10-12mm of water applied over the previous two days, and morning rain, it was changed to good, good to soft in places prior to the opener. The jockey's came back in afterwards and described it more like soft and hard work. It certainly didn't look good and the form must be treated as suspect. A step up from the wide-margin winner.
NOTEBOOK
Swift Lord(IRE) hasn't seen much action since joining Gary Moore after winning his bumper in Ireland, but he was entitled to go close on the level of his previous outing at Doncaster and completed the task in good style. No doubt he is flattered by the winning margin as his main rivals all ran below par, but he will be high on confidence after this. (op 2-1 tchd 11-4)
Dashing Doc(IRE) won the battle for second, but didn't impress at all with his jumping on this hurdling debut for new connections. This dual Flat winner is entitled to improve on that front, though, and should be much sharper for the run. (op 25-1)
Nobunaga pulled up on two outings either side of winning at Huntingdon in January, again ran with the choke out and wasn't always fluent. He was some way below his best. (op 8-1 tchd 15-2 and 9-1)
Raya Star(IRE) took his second fall from three spins since going hurdling at Kempton last week, but was well backed to show his true colours again. He pulled hard out the back early, again putting in some deliberate leaps, and fell in a hole under pressure from three out. Official explanation: jockey said gelding ran too free (op 10-3)
Dubai Crest made his move nearing the third-last, but met it wrong and was soon under the pump. He looked a shadow of the horse that won well at Huntingdon a fortnight earlier and can be given another chance back on a sound surface. Official explanation: trainer's rep said gelding finished distressed (op 2-1 tchd 9-4)

5072 LINDLEY CATERING H'CAP HURDLE (10 hdls) 2m 4f
2:40 (2:40) (Class 5) (0-95,95) 4-Y-0+ **£1,723** (£506; £253; £126)

Form RPR
-PP0 **1** **Speedy Directa (GER)**[20] 4675 8-10-2 74 .... (vt) JimmyDerham[(3)] 84
(Milton Harris) *trckd ldrs: led 7th: rdn after 2 out: pressed whn edgd lft appr last: styd on wl and in command fnl 50yds* **4/1**[3]
/0-2 **2** *4* **Only Hope**[22] 4540 7-10-8 77 .... (tp) AidanColeman 85
(Rachel Hobbs) *hld up: hdwy to trck ldrs appr 7th: trying to chal whn blnd 2 out: moving into chalng 2nd whn bmpd bef last: stl ev ch jumping last: one pce fnl 50yds* **10/3**[2]
P-00 **3** *14* **Formedable (IRE)**[21] 4559 9-10-3 72 .... (p) WillKennedy 70
(Violet M Jordan) *prom: wnt cl 2nd 7th: blnd 3 out: rdn and ev ch 2 out: stl chalng but losing 2nd whn bmpd and pushed wd appr last: no ex sn after: wl btn run-in: eased towards fin* **17/2**
60-0 **4** *7* **Drawback (IRE)**[12] 4859 8-11-2 92 .... CDTimmons[(7)] 80
(Barry Brennan) *hld up: rdn after 5th: chsd ldrs appr 3 out: no imp on ldng trio bef 2 out: sn wl outpcd and lost tch w ldrs* **16/1**
3404 **5** *16* **Storm Command (IRE)**[10] 4899 4-10-3 80 .... (t) RichardJohnson 45
(Tim Vaughan) *in rr: struggling 3 out: nvr able to get on terms w ldrs* **3/1**[1]
2250 **6** *½* **Classic Fly (FR)**[19] 4698 8-11-12 95 .... (t) NickScholfield 68
(Arthur Whiting) *prom: pushed along appr 6th: struggling to hold on to pl bef 7th: wknd 3 out* **15/2**
-0PP **P** **Aymard Des Fieffes (FR)**[13] 4833 9-9-7 69 oh9 .... PeterHatton[(7)] —
(Nikki Evans) *led: hdd 7th: wknd appr 3 out: t.o whn p.u bef 2 out* **33/1**
-211 **P** **Chicago Alley**[295] 676 10-11-9 95 .... LeeEdwards[(3)] —
(Tony Carroll) *chsd ldrs: nt fluent 4th: niggled along whn nt fluent 7th: last whn wkng appr 3 out: t.o whn p.u bef 2 out* **13/2**

5m 7.80s (12.30) **Going Correction** +0.55s/f (Soft)
WFA 4 from 7yo+ 8lb **8** Ran SP% **112.5**
Speed ratings (Par 103): **97,95,89,87,80 80,—,—**
toteswingers: 1&2 £3.70, 1&3 £4.40, 2&3 £4.10 CSF £17.54 CT £104.42 TOTE £7.10: £2.20, £1.20, £3.60; EX 21.20.
Owner Robert Aplin **Bred** Gestut Graditz **Trained** Herridge, Wiltshire
■ Stewards' Enquiry : Jimmy Derham four-day ban: used whip with excessive force and frequency (Apr 13-16)
FOCUS
Not surprisingly the ground was changed to good to soft all over prior to this race and once again it looked hard work as the first three fought out a slow-motion finish from the second-last. A poor handicap. The winner was well in on his best form.
NOTEBOOK
Speedy Directa(GER) came out on top from the last flight and finally ended a losing run that dated back to March 2009. He arrived here looking out of sorts, but was the subject of a gamble and raced with a lot more enthusiasm. He was well treated on his previous best efforts but it was just his second win to date and he had a hard race, so wouldn't be one to confidently support for a follow up. Official explanation: trainer said, regarding apparent improvement in form, that the gelding had been dropped in the handicap and was better suited by the good to soft ground. (op 8-1)
Only Hope was just held on her return from a layoff at Exeter 22 days earlier and proved popular off 3lb higher. She travelled kindly into contention along with the winner and only gave way to that rival after the last, turning in another solid effort. (op 3-1 tchd 11-4)
Formedable(IRE) had been dropped 5lb since his previous outing and stepped up greatly on that with a much more encouraging effort in defeat. He is a longstanding maiden, however, and rather sums up the level of the form. (op 15-2 tchd 7-1 and 9-1)
Drawback(IRE) didn't look an easy ride, but at least posted a step in the right direction and appears to have now fallen to a workable mark. (op 14-1 tchd 12-1)
Storm Command(IRE) was well backed, but found nothing when asked for his effort and perhaps the ground wasn't for him. (op 9-2)
Chicago Alley, bidding for a fourth win from her last five outings, the wins coming over fences, proved easy to back on her return from a 295-day absence and was one of the first in trouble. She too wants better ground. (op 4-1)

5073 LINDLEY CATERING NOVICES' CHASE (19 fncs) 3m 1f 110y
3:10 (3:10) (Class 4) 5-Y-0+ **£3,252** (£955; £477)

Form RPR
1425 **1** **Balthazar King (IRE)**[109] 2883 7-11-12 140 .... RichardJohnson 133+
(Philip Hobbs) *mde all: blnd 5th: j.lft 3 out and 2 out: kicked clr appr last: in command after: r.o wl run-in* **1/2**[1]
1P3P **2** *4* **Acrai Rua (IRE)**[11] 4864 8-11-5 118 .... (v[1]) PaulMoloney 119
(Evan Williams) *hld up in last pl: mstke 10th and 12th: disputing 2nd whn stmbld 15th: sn def 2nd: abt 3 l down 3 out: sn rdn: no imp on wnr appr last: one pce run-in* **9/2**[3]
1 **3** *106* **Cottage Flyer (IRE)**[12] 4855 6-11-5 0 .... (p) JohnnyFarrelly —
(Paul John Gilligan, Ire) *chsd wnr: blnd 3rd: mstke 10th and 12th: hung rt bef 14th: jnd for 2nd 15th: sn dropped to last: lost tch bef 3 out: t.o* **4/1**[2]

6m 43.6s (11.80) **Going Correction** +0.40s/f (Soft) **3** Ran SP% **104.8**
Speed ratings: **97,95,—**
CSF £2.80 TOTE £1.50; EX 2.40.
Owner The Brushmakers **Bred** Sunnyhill Stud **Trained** Withycombe, Somerset
FOCUS
The cosy winner rated 10lb off his best with the second to his mark in this uncompetitive novice chase.
NOTEBOOK
Balthazar King(IRE) had a golden opportunity to register a third success over fences, which he duly accepted. He was last seen running below par at Cheltenham in December, but had run two decent races in classy company there beforehand and set the standard here even before the non-runner. He made all and, bar a mistake at the fifth, it was his jumping which won him the day. This ground probably wasn't ideal, which made him look more workmanlike than expected, and he is a likeable type. Whether he will be up to a mark of 140 in handicaps remains to be seen, but he is entitled to improve for the run and next month's Perth Festival is likely to be figure on his agenda. (op 2-5 tchd 8-13)
Acrai Rua(IRE) posted one of his better efforts in a first-time visor and clearly likes this venue. He is best on quick ground, but it isn't hard to see why he wears headgear and he still doesn't look a natural chaser. (op 6-1 tchd 7-2)
Cottage Flyer(IRE) looked progressive when making all on his chase debut under rules at Fakenham, but he turned in a shocker here. It may be that he sulks if not able to dominate, but this leaves him with plenty to prove. (tchd 3-1 and 9-2)

5074 LINDLEY CATERING MAIDEN HURDLE (10 hdls) 2m 4f
3:40 (3:40) (Class 4) 4-Y-0+ **£2,016** (£592; £296; £147)

Form RPR
1-06 **1** **Royal Riviera**[27] 4444 5-10-12 0 .... SamTwiston-Davies[(3)] 110+
(Nigel Twiston-Davies) *pom: j.rt and cannoned into rival 1st: led after 2nd: mde rest: pushed along appr last: styd on wl and in control run-in* **14/1**
464 **2** *2 ½* **Reginaldinho (UAE)**[35] 4288 5-11-1 111 .... AidanColeman 107
(Venetia Williams) *a.p: rdn and wandered whn ch and trying to press wnr appr last: nt qckn and no imp run-in but kpt on for press in duel for 2nd* **11/4**[2]
0-44 **3** *hd* **Sizing Ireland (IRE)**[24] 4500 5-11-1 0 .... APMcCoy 108
(Nicky Henderson) *led: bmpd 1st: hdd after 2nd: remained prom: rdn appr 2 out: stl ch bef last: kpt on u.p whn chalng for 2nd run-in: no imp on wnr* **6/4**[1]
004 **4** *16* **Cap Falco (IRE)**[17] 4739 6-11-1 0 .... TomO'Brien 92
(Anabel L M King) *chsd ldrs: rdn and outpcd appr 2 out: sn no threat* **8/1**[3]
1/P0 **5** *2 ¾* **Suburban Bay**[39] 4198 6-11-1 0 .... RobertThornton 90
(Alan King) *hld up: rdn and sme hdwy appr 2 out: nvr able to get on terms w ldrs* **9/1**
6 *16* **La Fille D'Oscar (IRE)** 7-10-1 0 .... PeterCarberry[(7)] 69
(Rachel Hobbs) *hld up: struggling after 3 out: wl btn* **40/1**
0P **7** *9* **Sam's Pride**[104] 2981 6-11-1 0 .... JackDoyle 72
(Peter Pritchard) *hld up: hdwy appr 3 out: rdn to chse ldrs bef 2 out but no imp: wknd sn after* **125/1**
5 **8** *9* **Thingathong (FR)**[21] 4552 4-10-0 0 .... AdrianLane 52
(Donald McCain) *midfield: nt fluent 7th: nt fluent 3 out: sn rdn and wknd* **17/2**

3-0 **9** *61* **Sir Cool (IRE)**[75] 3546 5-11-1 0......(t) AndrewThornton 4
(Tor Sturgis) *hld up in tch: reminder after 5th: pushed along appr 3 out: wknd long bef 2 out: t.o* **25/1**

0 **P** **Spieder Bay**[62] 3773 6-10-1 0...... RobertKirk(7) —
(James Evans) *midfield: lost pl bef 7th: bhd appr 3 out: t.o whn p.u bef 2 out* **125/1**

5m 9.10s (13.60) **Going Correction** +0.55s/f (Soft)
WFA 4 from 5yo+ 8lb **10** Ran SP% **112.8**
Speed ratings (Par 105): **94,93,92,86,85 79,75,71,47,—**
toteswingers:1&2 £4.10, 2&3 £1.80, 1&3 £4.10 CSF £51.58 TOTE £12.00: £4.10, £1.70, £1.10; EX 55.00.
Owner Tony Bloom **Bred** J L C Pearce **Trained** Naunton, Gloucs
■ Stewards' Enquiry : A P McCoy caution: careless riding.

FOCUS
A moderate novice hurdle, run at an ordinary gallop and there was a tight three-way finish in the home straight. The winner improved to the level of his bumper win with the next two to their marks.

NOTEBOOK
Royal Riviera was very hard to fancy after two lifeless efforts over hurdles since joining his current stable this year, but he was allowed to dominate and posted a massively improved effort to score. It was his first win since landing a heavy-ground bumper on debut in 2009 and he came out on top by proving more resolute than the placed horses, so it's hoped he can now build on this. (op 12-1 tchd 11-1)
Reginaldinho(UAE) was expected to enjoy stepping back up in trip but, while he held every chance, he looked reluctant to go through with his effort from the second-last. The tacky ground probably wasn't ideal for him, but this does leave him with something to prove temperament-wise. (op 5-2 tchd 3-1)
Sizing Ireland(IRE) is now looking one to avoid, but he too probably wasn't helped by the tacky surface. (op 9-4)
Cap Falco(IRE) failed to build on his encouraging hurdles debut at Market Rasen 17 days earlier. Perhaps he was yet another here that didn't act on the ground. (op 5-1)
Suburban Bay, who met support, did not look an easy ride but at least now qualifies for a handicap mark. (tchd 7-1)

5075 LINDLEY CATERING NOVICES' H'CAP HURDLE (11 hdls) 2m 6f 110y
4:10 (4:10) (Class 5) (0-95,93) 4-Y-O+ **£1,815** (£529; £264)

Form RPR
0041 **1** **E Street Boy**[3] 5040 5-11-7 **88**...... TomScudamore 97+
(David Pipe) *hld up and a travelling wl: hdwy to trck ldrs after 4th: led on bit 2 out: sn clr and wl in command: kpt up to work after last: comf* **5/6**[1]

2P02 **2** *2¾* **Monty's Moon (IRE)**[18] 4724 9-10-1 **75**......(p) PeterCarberry(7) 78
(Rachel Hobbs) *midfield: dropped in rr after 4th: kpt on again appr 2 out: wnt 2nd bef last: styd on towards fin: no ch w wnr* **16/1**

6331 **3** *2¼* **The Composer**[23] 4522 9-11-1 **82**...... JimmyMcCarthy 82
(Michael Blanshard) *hld up: stdy hdwy appr 3 out: kpt on u.p run-in wout threatening wnr* **7/1**[3]

-P23 **4** *nse* **Septos**[21] 4559 7-10-5 **75**......(p) PeterToole(3) 75
(Richard Price) *trckd ldrs: effrt appr 2 out: kpt on u.p run-in wout threatening wnr* **13/2**[2]

4510 **5** *6* **The Wee Midget**[162] 1911 6-11-12 **93**...... NickScholfield 90
(Arthur Whiting) *racd keenly: prom: stl wl there but u.p 2 out: sn outpcd by wnr: plugged on at one pce run-in* **33/1**

000P **6** *26* **Beau Colonel (FR)**[47] 4052 5-11-4 **85**...... HaddenFrost 56
(Henrietta Knight) *racd keenly: prom early: sn in midfield: nt fluent 3rd: outpcd appr 2 out: wl btn after 2 out* **66/1**

05U6 **7** *2¼* **Any Given Moment (IRE)**[28] 4422 5-11-11 **92**......(p) JasonMaguire 63
(Donald McCain) *led after 1st: rdn and hdd 2 out: sn wknd* **10/1**

F-50 **8** *1* **All The Fashion (IRE)**[147] 2144 7-10-1 **68**...... WillKennedy 36
(Violet M Jordan) *hld up: rdn appr 2 out: nvr able to get on terms* **28/1**

0000 **9** *½* **Sheezatreasure (IRE)**[16] 4787 6-9-10 **70**...... MarkQuinlan(7) 38
(James Evans) *in rr: hdwy into midfield after 4th: rdn and wknd 8th* **40/1**

0013 **10** *16* **Body Gold (ARG)**[29] 4405 8-11-5 **86**...... PaddyBrennan 39
(Nigel Twiston-Davies) *midfield: rdn and outpcd after 3 out: nvr a threat* **16/1**

P06P **11** *13* **Roi De Garde (FR)**[29] 4413 5-11-6 **87**......(b[1]) TomMessenger 29
(Chris Bealby) *racd keenly: led: hdd after 1st: remained handy: rdn and wknd appr 2 out* **50/1**

003F **P** **Artic Pride (IRE)**[38] 4238 7-11-2 **83**...... LeightonAspell —
(Oliver Sherwood) *nt fluent: hld up: struggling appr 8th: t.o whn p.u bef 2 out* **16/1**

5m 45.0s (7.00) **Going Correction** +0.40s/f (Soft) **12** Ran SP% **119.4**
Speed ratings (Par 103): **103,102,101,101,99 90,89,88,88,83 78,—**
toteswingers: 1&2 £3.40, 1&3 £2.80, 2&3 £10.40 CSF £15.05 CT £66.88 TOTE £2.20: £1.10, £3.60, £1.80; EX 16.90.
Owner Roger Stanley & Yvonne Reynolds **Bred** Kelanne Stud Ltd **Trained** Nicholashayne, Devon

FOCUS
This novice handicap was run at an average gallop. The cosy winner stood out on his recent win and is rated 8lb below that level.

NOTEBOOK
E Street Boy unsurprisingly followed up his effortless success at Wincanton on Sunday with another easy win. The only doubts about him beforehand was whether the tacky ground would blunt his stamina and he did drift out in the betting, but he was miles ahead of the handicapper having won a conditional riders' event last time. He travelled kindly and took it up going easily two out. He sauntered clear off the home turn and was in no danger thereafter, but looking at the way he tied up near the finish this is as far as he wants to go for now. His trainer has him entered up again later this week and he should again prove hard to stop if turning up under a penalty. (op 4-5 tchd 10-11 in places)
Monty's Moon(IRE), 3lb higher, went in snatches but kept responding to his rider's urgings and has now finished second on his last two outings. He sets the level. (tchd 14-1)
The Composer was up 10lb for finally getting off the mark 23 day earlier and could have done without the watering. He ran a fair race in defeat and remains on a workable mark. (op 15-2)
Septos, placed the last twice, didn't help his rider by running in snatches back up in trip and looks one to avoid for win-only purposes. (op 15-2 tchd 8-1)

5076 LINDLEY CATERING H'CAP CHASE (12 fncs) 2m
4:40 (4:40) (Class 4) (0-100,98) 5-Y-O+ **£2,602** (£764; £382; £190)

Form RPR
5F12 **1** **Bertenbar**[24] 4504 7-11-0 **86**...... AndrewThornton 102+
(Henrietta Knight) *mde all: rdn appr 2 out: asserted sn after: styd on wl* **11/8**[1]

64P4 **2** *9* **Roc De Guye (FR)**[17] 4744 6-10-11 **90**...... RobertKirk(7) 97
(James Evans) *in tch: chsd wnr after 9th: rdn and no imp whn nt fluent last: one pce* **9/2**[2]

3224 **3** *6* **Papradon**[11] 4863 7-11-9 **98**...... SamTwiston-Davies(3) 99
(Nigel Twiston-Davies) *prom: lost pl after 6th: rallied to chse ldrs after 9th: wknd 2 out* **9/2**[2]

5414 **4** *8* **Rince Donn (IRE)**[20] 4668 9-10-8 **80**...... HaddenFrost 75
(Roger Curtis) *hld up in tch: wnt 4th appr 3 out but unable to go pce to chal: wl btn fr 2 out* **7/1**[3]

FPPP **5** *18* **Builteoir (IRE)**[16] 4784 9-11-0 **93**......(p) MrJEngland(7) 73
(Evan Williams) *in tch: blnd 6th: rdn after 7th: wkng whn j.rt and awkwardly 9th: wl bhd and n.d whn hmpd and nrly knocked over last* **16/1**

P4FP **6** *1¼* **Sourchamp (FR)**[20] 4668 5-9-7 **72** oh3......(t) MrBJPoste(7) 48
(Arthur Whiting) *racd keenly: sn chsd wnr: hit 6th: lost 2nd after 9th: sn wknd: j.lft 3 out and last whn wl bhd* **12/1**

/0-6 **P** **Arthurs Dream (IRE)**[27] 4447 9-11-0 **86**...... JohnnyFarrelly —
(Nick Ayliffe) *hld up in last pl: detached bef 5th: struggling appr 9th: t.o whn p.u bef 3 out* **33/1**

4m 6.40s (2.80) **Going Correction** +0.40s/f (Soft) **7** Ran SP% **107.5**
Speed ratings: **109,104,101,97,88 87,—**
toteswingers: 1&2 £2.00, 1&3 £2.60, 2&3 £2.40 CSF £7.24 TOTE £2.80: £2.10, £2.80; EX 8.60.
Owner T J Wyatt **Bred** T J Wyatt **Trained** West Lockinge, Oxon

FOCUS
A moderate handicap, run at a fair gallop and only two mattered from four out. Bertenbar is on the upgrade and can win again, and the next pair were close to form.

NOTEBOOK
Bertenbar deservedly resumed winning ways and completed the task in game style from the front. He looked vulnerable nearing three out, but found more as the runner-up began to feel the pinch from there and was in no real danger in the home straight. This 7-y-o has developed into a likeable chaser of late, but life will be tougher once the handicapper reassesses him. (op 6-4 tchd 13-8)
Roc De Guye(FR) was backed to return to his best and it looked good for supporters on the back straight. However, he produced a limited response from the third-last and remains 7lb higher than when gaining his sole win at Fakenham in November. (op 5-1 tchd 4-1)
Papradon was easy to back down in trip and ideally wants a genuinely sound surface. (op 7-2)
Rince Donn(IRE) proved laboured from off the pace and remains hard to win with. (tchd 13-2 and 8-1)

5077 LINDLEY CATERING STANDARD OPEN NATIONAL HUNT FLAT RACE 2m 1f
5:10 (5:10) (Class 6) 4-6-Y-O **£1,507** (£439; £219)

Form RPR
3 **1** **Real Milan (IRE)**[24] 4505 6-11-3 0...... RichieMcLernon 101+
(Anabel L M King) *rn green thrght: w ldr: led after 2f: pushed along over 2f out: edgd lft and pressed fnl 50yds: plld out more fnl strides* **15/2**[3]

2 *¾* **Sparkling Air** 5-10-10 0...... RichardJohnson 92
(John Spearing) *hld up: reminders after 7f: hdwy 7f out: chsd wnr 5f out: chalng 3f out: lost 2nd over 2f out: outpcd over 1f out: rallied ins fnl f: pressed wnr fnl 50yds: hld fnl strides* **20/1**

2 **3** *2½* **Little Fritz (FR)**[27] 4443 4-10-10 0...... APMcCoy 90
(Nicky Henderson) *in tch: wnt 2nd over 2f out: chalng over 1f out: sn unable qck: kpt on u.p ins fnl f: no ex fnl 50yds* **11/10**[1]

4 *9* **Franklin Roosevelt (IRE)** 5-11-3 0...... RobertThornton 88
(Warren Greatrex) *led: hdd after 2f: remained prom: rdn over 3f out: outpcd over 2f out: one pce and no imp ins fnl f* **2/1**[2]

40 **5** *6* **Allerton (IRE)**[35] 4287 4-10-10 0...... PaddyBrennan 77
(Nigel Twiston-Davies) *hld up: rdn and outpcd 5f out: plugged on at one pce fnl 2f* **9/1**

0 **6** *17* **Before Bruce**[16] 4780 4-10-7 0...... TommyPhelan(3) 61
(Claire Dyson) *in tch: rdn and outpcd by ldrs over 3f out: dropped away over 2f out* **40/1**

00 **7** *79* **Go To The Edge**[139] 2328 5-10-10 0...... HarryChalloner(7) —
(John Bryan Groucott) *trckd ldrs: lost pl 6f out: sn pushed along: bhd after: t.o* **100/1**

4m 6.50s (12.70) **Going Correction** +0.55s/f (Soft)
WFA 4 from 5yo+ 7lb **7** Ran SP% **110.9**
Speed ratings: **92,91,90,86,83 75,38**
toteswingers: 1&2 £4.90, 1&3 £1.90, 2&3 £3.90 CSF £109.32 TOTE £4.90: £1.50, £17.10; EX 136.50.
Owner Mrs Diana L Whateley **Bred** Vincent And Jimmy Lawler **Trained** Wilmcote, Warwicks

FOCUS
A modest bumper, run at a sedate early gallop. A step up from the winner and there could be more to come.

NOTEBOOK
Real Milan(IRE) was something of an eye-catcher on his debut 24 days earlier, but he proved very easy to back here. He pulled his way to the front after a couple of furlongs and ran green. However, he kept responding to pressure as challenges mounted and there was plenty to like about his attitude in the home straight. He will get further once sent over hurdles. (op 6-1 tchd 8-1)
Sparkling Air ◆ is related to a bumper winner and some staying jumpers. She looked in trouble turning onto the far side, but picked up strongly on the back straight. Again she looked like fading 4f out, but rallied in the home straight and wasn't beaten far. A sounder surface can see her winning one of these, especially if turning out against her own sex. (op 12-1)
Little Fritz(FR) was too green when second at odds of 4/6 on his debut at Ludlow. He was produced with every chance here, but made heavy weather of it from 3f out and looked uneasy on the tacky surface. (op Evens tchd 5-4 in places)
Franklin Roosevelt(IRE) is bred to make his mark in this sphere and, from a bang in-form stable, attracted decent support for this racecourse debut. He was the first of leaders to feel the pinch on the back straight, however, and he too probably found the ground against him. (op 10-3)
T/Plt: £22.00 to a £1 stake. Pool of £74,495.68 - 2,464.47 winning tickets. T/Qpdt: £2.80 to a £1 stake. Pool of £5,948.04 - 1,539.38 winning tickets. DO

4437 LUDLOW (R-H)
Thursday, March 31

OFFICIAL GOING: Good (7.8)
Bends moved to fresh ground but impact on distances not notified.
Wind: very light Weather: bright and sunny

5078 EDGECLIFF HIGH SCHOOL RACING TO SCHOOL MARES' NOVICES' HURDLE (11 hdls) 2m 5f
2:35 (2:36) (Class 4) 4-Y-O+ **£2,602** (£764; £382; £190)

Form RPR
1F43 **1** **Kaituna (IRE)**[31] 4401 5-11-5 **105**...... LeightonAspell 123+
(Oliver Sherwood) *chsd ldrs: in last of three gng clr and pushed along bef 3 out: led next: clr whn j.lft last: comf* **11/4**[2]

535 **2** *14* **Kings Queen (IRE)**[27] 4454 5-10-12 **104**...... PaddyBrennan 102
(Tom George) *led at decent gallop tl rdn and hdd 2 out: sn outpcd: plugged on after jumping lft at last* **5/1**[3]

361P **3** *5* **Seren Cwmtudu (IRE)**[68] 3674 7-11-5 117 PaulMoloney 106
(Evan Williams) *nt jump wl: chsd wnr tl rdn 3 out: struggled on fr next* **13/8**[1]

P **4** *41* **Mrs Peacock (IRE)**[14] 4828 6-10-12 0 SamJones 61
(Norma Twomey) *chsd ldrs: rdn and lost tch in 20 l 5th wl bef 3 out: sn t.o* **40/1**

5 *5* **Emerald Glade (IRE)**[178] 4-10-4 0 DaveCrosse 49
(Milton Harris) *hld up wl in rr: blnd 5th: mstke 7th: gd prog after 8th to go fair 4th wl bef home turn: fading in poor 4th whn mstke 3 out: fin v weakly* **12/1**

00 **6** *14* **Dane Cottage**[17] 4781 4-10-2 0 ow1 LeeStephens(3) 37
(Katie Stephens) *hld up towards rr: nt jump wl: already struggling whn mstke 8th: 6th and t.o bef next* **100/1**

0 **7** *1 ¼* **Thorney Rose (IRE)**[28] 4437 7-10-12 0 CharliePoste 43
(Robin Dickin) *one-eyed: plld hrd in rr: lost tch after 6th: t.o after next* **150/1**

300P **8** *2 ¼* **Living Proof (IRE)**[35] 4309 6-10-5 0 StephenO'Donovan(7) 41
(Norma Twomey) *chsd ldrs: 5th and sing to weaken whn mstke 8th: stopped to nil and sn t.o* **33/1**

9 *33* **Bully Wuskers (IRE)**[131] 2537 6-10-5 93 BFCawley(7) 11
(Paul John Gilligan, Ire) *cl up: 4th and getting outpcd whn blnd 8th: stopped to nil and sn hopelessly t.o* **10/1**

0300 **P** **Enchanted Approach (IRE)**[284] 796 8-10-5 85 MissLBrooke(7) —
(Lady Susan Brooke) *walked to post v early: keen and prom to 5th: t.o 7th: p.u next* **33/1**

40- **P** **Shannons Firth (IRE)**[413] 3995 6-10-12 0 DarylJacob —
(Ben Case) *a bhd: struggling 7th: hopelessly t.o whn p.u 3 out* **28/1**

U-P0 **P** **Chestnut Lilly**[19] 4719 8-10-5 0 MrBJPoste(7) —
(Pam Ford) *20 l last at 1st: j. poorly: t.o 5th: p.u after scraping over next* **200/1**

00 **P** **Mew Gull**[52] 3979 6-10-12 0 WillKennedy —
(Henrietta Knight) *mstke 2nd: prom tl lost pl rapidly and mstke 6th: t.o next: p.u 8th* **50/1**

5m 12.1s (-2.70) **Going Correction** +0.075s/f (Yiel)
WFA 4 from 5yo+ 8lb **13** Ran SP% **114.1**
Speed ratings (Par 105): **108,102,100,85,83 77,77,76,64,— —,—,—**
toteswingers:1&2:£3.10, 1&3:£2.10, 2&3:£3.10 CSF £15.53 TOTE £4.80: £1.40, £1.90, £1.60; EX 20.40.
Owner P Deal & N Chamberlain **Bred** Miss Jane Mangan **Trained** Upper Lambourn, Berks

FOCUS
The front three finished well clear in this ordinary mares' novice. The winner is rated up a stone.

NOTEBOOK
Kaituna(IRE) continued her good form with a determined success. She was off the bridle a fair way out but responded well for pressure, and although she jumped left at the final hurdle, she powered clear on the run-in. By Flemensfirth, one would think she will get further and could go chasing in time. In the meantime connections will hope the handicapper doesn't put her up too much, especially considering the favourite underperformed. (op 7-2)
Kings Queen(IRE) put in an improved effort and the combination of a positive ride and better ground looked to suit. She kept on once headed by the ready winner. (tchd 9-2)
Seren Cwmtudu(IRE) proved a disappointment. She had the highest official rating of these but didn't run to that figure, finding little for pressure once asked by Paul Moloney. She handles the ground and maybe something was amiss. (op 15-8 tchd 2-1)
Mrs Peacock(IRE) finished a remote fourth but did plug on best of the rest.
Emerald Glade(IRE) showed a glimmer of promise on her first hurdles start. She was outpaced entering the backstraight before making good headway, but was unable to sustain that effort. She retains some ability from the Flat and a small race could be within her compass. (op 10-1)
Dane Cottage recovered from a mistake at the fourth to make headway down the back straight, but folded tamely rounding the home bend. She may appreciate a drop in trip.
Bully Wuskers(IRE) travelled better than most on the heels of the leaders but found nil when asked for maximum effort. Perhaps a shorter trip would suit too. (op 8-1)
Shannons Firth(IRE) Official explanation: jockey said mare had a breathing problem

5079 CHARITY DAY ON 21 APRIL NOVICES' CHASE (13 fncs) 2m
3:05 (3:05) (Class 4) 5-Y-0+ **£3,246** (£1,014; £546)

Form RPR

-4F1 **1** **Fahrisee (IRE)**[30] 4406 8-11-5 132 PaulMoloney 129+
(Evan Williams) *j.lft: chsd long ldr: clsd fr 7th: led and nt fluent 9th: drew clr 2 out: v easily* **8/11**[1]

1243 **2** *7* **Thumbs Up**[30] 4406 6-11-5 127 (p) JasonMaguire 125
(Donald McCain) *reluctant and s.s: often lacked fluency: wnt 3rd at 5th and 2nd after 9th: pressed wnr tl rdn and wl outpcd 2 out* **7/4**[2]

414 **3** *13* **Courella (IRE)**[20] 4695 7-11-7 114 AodhaganConlon(5) 119
(Evan Williams) *3rd tl last fr 5th: pushed along but nvr gng to win after being lft 3rd after 9th: nt fluent last* **17/2**[3]

-PPP **P** **Dark Haven**[1] 5071 8-9-12 0 (b[1]) RobertKirk(7) —
(James Evans) *bolted into 20 l ld: landed awkwardly 4th: stride shortening fr 6th: reminders after 8th: hdd and nt fluent next and stopped to nil: t.o and p.u 10th* **100/1**

4m 1.40s (2.90) **Going Correction** +0.15s/f (Yiel) **4** Ran SP% **105.8**
Speed ratings: **98,94,88,—**
CSF £2.32 TOTE £1.50; EX 2.00.
Owner Hugh Williams **Bred** I Williams **Trained** Llancarfan, Vale Of Glamorgan

FOCUS
Just the four runners for this moderate novices' chase. Straightforward form.

NOTEBOOK
Fahrisee(IRE) justified his short price and followed up his Ffos Las victory. He dictated matters once heading the tearaway leader and jumped adequately to run out a straightforward winner. Evan Williams reported the horse has had problems with his sinuses before but they have been ironed out now which could explain his improvement lately. A big, scopey individual, he looks on an upward curve and can win a similar novice event under a penalty, and should get further in time. (op 4-6 tchd 4-5)
Thumbs Up only just consented to line up. He lost several lengths at the start and lacked fluency at his fences. He was always going to find it hard to reverse placings with the winner on their previous meeting. Handicaps look the best option. (op 2-1 tchd 13-8)
Courella(IRE) struggled to shoulder his double penalty and needs a bit of cut in the ground to show his best. (op 8-1 tchd 9-1)
Dark Haven went off like a sprinter and was never going to finish her race.

5080 12 MAY IS LADIES DAY H'CAP HURDLE (11 hdls) 2m 5f
3:35 (3:35) (Class 3) (0-120,127) 4-Y-0+ **£4,618** (£1,356; £678; £338)

Form RPR

4312 **1** **Havingotascoobydo (IRE)**[20] 4700 6-11-7 115 WarrenMarston 126+
(Martin Keighley) *anchored in last and keen: rapid prog gng strly on outer after 8th: led 3 out: sn 3 l clr: wavered lft under driving after last: kpt on stoutly* **9/4**[1]

050F **2** *5* **Troubletimestwo (FR)**[24] 4524 5-10-12 109 LeeEdwards(3) 111
(Tony Carroll) *chsd ldr tl drvn 8th: dropped bk 5th bef next: rallied v gamely to regain 2nd after last: nt rch wnr* **16/1**

2531 **3** *3 ¼* **Mad Moose (IRE)**[8] 4940 7-11-12 127 7ex MrWTwiston-Davies(7) 126
(Nigel Twiston-Davies) *prom: lost pl 7th: rallied in 4th 3 out: rdn and wnt 2nd next tl no ex after last* **7/2**[2]

0006 **4** *nk* **Peaceful Means (IRE)**[47] 1556 8-10-10 104 PaulMoloney 103
(Evan Williams) *settled in rr: smooth prog 8th to ld bef 3 out where hdd: rdn and kpt on at one pce fr next* **33/1**

0304 **5** *10* **Briefcase (IRE)**[29] 4420 6-10-11 105 PaddyBrennan 96
(Nigel Twiston-Davies) *midfield: lost tch 8th: poor 7th bef 3 out: plugged on* **12/1**

5023 **6** *4* **Tom O'Tara**[21] 4672 7-10-12 106 CharliePoste 92
(Robin Dickin) *racd w awkward hd carriage: led: qcknd 6 l clr 6th tl hdd bef 3 out: immediately downed tools and dropped out* **11/1**

3-54 **7** *21* **Bedizen**[13] 4858 8-11-7 118 CPGeoghegan(3) 86
(Pam Sly) *towards rr: j. slowly 6th: rdn and struggling next: wl bhd after 8th* **40/1**

5332 **8** *1* **Silver Roque (FR)**[51] 3989 5-10-11 105 AndrewThornton 72
(Henrietta Knight) *settled 3rd: hit 7th: wnt 2nd next and ev ch tl rdn and dropped out qckly bef 3 out* **7/1**[3]

9 *65* **Rosangla (IRE)**[7] 4983 9-10-0 94 BarryKeniry 2
(Anthony James Costello, Ire) *chsd ldrs on outside tl 7th: struggling after next: hopelessly t.o* **80/1**

2252 **10** *47* **Kasbadali (FR)**[21] 4665 6-11-4 112 (b[1]) LeightonAspell —
(Oliver Sherwood) *towards rr: effrt to trck ldrs after 7th: v reluctant whn rdn after next and sn btn: hopelessly t.o and jumping wildly rt fr 3 out* **8/1**

33PP **P** **Accordingtoemandem (IRE)**[82] 3452 7-11-12 120 TomScudamore —
(Ian Williams) *t.k.h in rr: getting outpcd whn mstke 7th: t.o and p.u 3 out* **16/1**

0P45 **P** **Journeyman (IRE)**[22] 4557 5-10-6 100 AndrewTinkler —
(Nicky Henderson) *midfield: hit 7th and dropped out rapidly: t.o 8th: sn p.u* **28/1**

5m 12.5s (-2.30) **Going Correction** +0.075s/f (Yiel) **12** Ran SP% **114.5**
Speed ratings (Par 107): **107,105,103,103,99 98,90,90,65,47 —,—**
toteswingers:1&2:£22.90, 1&3:£2.10, 2&3:£20.90 CSF £35.32 CT £123.53 TOTE £3.60: £1.60, £5.90, £2.10; EX 49.50.
Owner D Bishop C Bowkley M Parker M Thornton **Bred** Daniel Kenneally **Trained** Condicote, Gloucs

FOCUS
A fair handicap hurdle run at a sound pace and won by a progressive type, who gives the impression there should be more to come.

NOTEBOOK
Havingotascoobydo(IRE), the only C&D winner in line-up, produced a good performance. He was given too much to do at Sandown recently but here he was produced at the right time, and despite idling on the run-in and edging left under pressure, he won with a bit in hand. This strong traveller is improving and looks up to winning off a higher mark. For now he may head to the Scottish National meeting for either a 2m4f or 3m hurdle. He has the size and scope for chasing in due course. (op 2-1)
Troubletimestwo(FR) put in an improved effort. He saw out the trip well but was just beaten by a better handicapped and more progressive horse. His yard continue in fine form. (op 20-1 tchd 25-1)
Mad Moose(IRE), penalised for winning emphatically at Haydock recently, was out quickly as he's due to go up 13lb. He wasn't fluent at many hurdles but responded for pressure and, although he couldn't go with the winner, won the battle for third. He's now 0-8 on right-handed tracks and may prefer going the other way round. (tchd 3-1 and 4-1 in a place)
Peaceful Means(IRE) got into contention rounding the home bend after pulling hard, holding every chance three out. She weakened thereafter and needs to relax during her races. (op 40-1)
Tom O'Tara was given a positive ride, kicking for home a long way out. He tried to battle once headed but was a spent force. Similar tactics could work if dropped in grade. (op 10-1)
Silver Roque(FR) held every chance in the home straight but got outstayed by his rivals. A drop in trip is likely to suit. (tchd 15-2)

5081 EDDIE MAPP MEMORIAL H'CAP CHASE (17 fncs) 2m 4f
4:05 (4:05) (Class 3) (0-120,120) 5-Y-O+ **£5,703** (£1,684; £842; £421; £210)

Form RPR

0023 **1** **Russian Epic**[20] 4704 7-10-9 103 (tp) RichardJohnson 122+
(Philip Hobbs) *bhd: blnd bdly 11th: stl 8th at 13th: rousted to cl fr next: led sn after last: drvn clr: gd ride* **8/1**

0F35 **2** *3 ¾* **Cruchain (IRE)**[33] 4355 8-11-5 113 DPFahy 126
(Dai Burchell) *prom: led 7th: gng easily bef 14th: rdn bef last: sn hdd flat: did nt find much and sn outpcd* **11/2**[2]

P362 **3** *3 ¾* **Akarshan (IRE)**[20] 4691 6-10-11 110 AodhaganConlon(5) 120
(Evan Williams) *chsd ldrs: effrt 11th: wnt 2nd bef 13th but drvn after 13th: stl on terms 2 out: no ex whn nt fluent last* **12/1**

4-53 **4** *7* **Shake The Barley (IRE)**[24] 4523 8-11-0 108 PaddyBrennan 112
(Tom George) *sn bhd: hdwy 11th: wnt 4th and rdn at 14th: no imp after: wl btn 2 out* **10/1**

5053 **5** *8* **Tyup Pompey (IRE)**[8] 4948 10-10-5 102 LeeStephens(3) 98
(Ann Price) *cl up tl rdn and outpcd 12th: no ch after but kpt trying* **33/1**

-431 **6** *22* **Up To The Mark**[17] 4775 6-11-4 112 AndrewTinkler 88
(Henry Daly) *t.k.h: led tl 7th: 2nd at 10th: cl up tl rdn and wknd after 13th: wl btn whn j.lft 3 out* **8/1**

U0-2 **7** *½* **Man From Highworth**[11] 4896 12-10-13 114 MrSParish(7) 97
(Audrey Manners) *settled towards rr tl gd prog gng wl in 3rd at 10th: 2nd and stl travelling sweetly 14th: suddenly lost pl: mstke 2 out: sn heavily eased* **7/1**[3]

F051 **8** *3* **Restezen D'Armor (FR)**[31] 4400 6-11-7 115 (p) TomScudamore 88
(Charlie Longsdon) *in tch tl rdn and lost tch tamely after 13th* **9/2**[1]

-PP5 **9** *3 ¼* **Leamington Lad (IRE)**[7] 4972 8-11-9 120 SamTwiston-Davies(3) 90
(Nigel Twiston-Davies) *w ldr tl j. slowly 1st: chsd ldr 4th tl 6th: lost pl under hrd driving 7th: nvr gng keenly after: t.o after 13th* **28/1**

5R05 **P** **The Snail**[28] 4440 8-11-10 118 PaulMoloney —
(Evan Williams) *hit 3rd and dropped himself bk to last at next: sn rdn and nt keen: t.o 8th: p.u after 13th* **7/1**[3]

0321 **P** **Azulada Bay (IRE)**[129] 2585 7-10-12 106 JasonMaguire —
(Mark Rimell) *in rr and drvn 7th: no rspnse: t.o 10th: p.u after 13th* **7/1**[3]

5m 3.80s (-0.60) **Going Correction** +0.15s/f (Yiel) **11** Ran SP% **116.5**
Speed ratings: **107,105,104,101,98 89,89,87,86,— —**
toteswingers:1&2:£13.00, 1&3:£23.30, 2&3:£14.10 CSF £52.14 CT £530.27 TOTE £11.30: £3.60, £3.20, £6.10; EX 60.20.
Owner Cromhall Stud **Bred** Derek R Price **Trained** Withycombe, Somerset

FOCUS
A tricky looking handicap on paper. Fair form. The winner is rated up a stone on his best hurdles figure.

NOTEBOOK

Russian Epic, on his chasing debut and wearing first-time cheekpieces, came under pressure a fair way out but responded well, sustaining a determined run on the outside of rivals to win going away. His jumping was far from fluent over hurdles but he gave the fences much more respect. He looks to have been on a good mark and can win again even with a guaranteed rise in the weights.
Cruchain(IRE), like the winner, has often jumped awkwardly but put in a more polished display this time and only went down to a better handicapped rival. He travels into his races well and is a consistent sort, but will go up in the weights for running well. (op 15-2)
Akarshan(IRE), hugged the rail throughout, and held every chance in the home straight. He needs a strongly run 2m to be seen at his best. (tchd 16-1)
Shake The Barley(IRE) couldn't go with the leaders for the majority of the race and, although he plugged on past beaten horses, he needs further these days. (tchd 9-1)
Tyup Pompey(IRE) was remarkably having his 31st race at Ludlow and travelled well for a long way. He doesn't have the speed at the business end of races which his younger rivals have.
Up To The Mark didn't jump with much enthusiasm which cost him any chance. (op 7-1)
Man From Highworth raced prominently but was caught for tow by younger horses in the home straight. (op 8-1)
Restezen D'Armor(FR) couldn't get into contention from a 8lb higher mark for winning last time. His form over fences is moderate (op 4-1)
Leamington Lad(IRE) has been moody lately and that didn't change here. (op 25-1)
The Snail, well supported all morning, jumped away on terms but didn't look in love with the game on this occasion. He's a risky betting proposition. (op 13-2 tchd 6-1)
Azulada Bay(IRE) Official explanation: jockey said gelding never travelled (op 13-2 tchd 6-1)

5082 LUDLOW POINT TO POINT ON 17TH APRIL NOVICES' CLAIMING HURDLE (9 hdls) 2m

4:35 (4:35) (Class 5) 4-Y-0+ **£1,788** (£525; £262; £131)

Form | | | | RPR
3P0P **1** **Supernoverre (IRE)**[176] 1726 5-10-9 100....................(p) DannyBurton(7) 104+
(Alan Jones) *one-eyed: settled in midfield: effrt and nt fluent 6th: shkn up to ld bef 3 out: sn in command but racing idly and kpt up to work* **4/1**[2]
000 **2** *7* **Second Brook (IRE)**[25] 4499 4-10-6 0.............................. PeterHatton(7) 95+
(Reg Hollinshead) *midfield: rdn and outpcd after 6th: styd on fr next: mstke 2 out: snatched 2nd but no ch w wnr* **7/2**[1]
450 **3** *hd* **Mister Fantastic**[89] 3304 5-10-9 99................................ OliverDayman(5) 94
(Dai Burchell) *hdwy to ld after 3rd: wnt 6 l clr after next: hdd bef 3 out: urged along and kpt on at same pce after: lost 2nd fnl strides* **11/1**
65-4 **4** *3 ½* **Goose Green (IRE)**[22] 1333 7-10-11 100.......................... IanPopham(3) 91
(Ron Hodges) *hld up: effrt after 6th: rdn and no imp fr 2 out* **7/1**
P0F5 **5** *hd* **Bahr Nothing (IRE)**[28] 4437 5-11-6 98.............................. RichardJohnson 98
(Henry Daly) *bhd: blnd 4th: drvn next: laboured prog bef 3 out: sn no imp: mstke last* **11/2**[3]
5045 **6** *1 ¾* **Ask The Oracle**[9] 4924 5-10-9 100....................(t) MissIsabelTompsett(5) 91
(Bernard Llewellyn) *t.k.h: led tl j. slowly 2nd: remained prom: 2nd after 6th: rdn and no ex 2 out: 3rd and btn whn mstke last* **6/1**
0U3- **7** *8* **Magnitude**[12] 2599 6-11-4 0..(p) JodieMogford 86
(Brian Baugh) *prom: 2nd at 6th: rdn and dropped out tamely bef next and hit it* **12/1**
0 **8** *2* **Polo Springs**[72] 3613 4-9-9 0..(t) MarkQuinlan(5) 66
(Bill Turner) *bhd: rdn after 6th: sn struggling* **100/1**
/0P4 **9** *17* **Barodine**[10] 4920 8-11-0 77...(t) TomScudamore 73
(Ron Hodges) *drvn to go prom 3rd: j. slowly 4th: downed tools in last after 6th: sn t.o* **20/1**
10 *68* **Count Of Tuscany (USA)**[227] 5-11-0 0................................. MarkGrant 4
(Charles Egerton) *led and j.lft and hit 2nd: hdd after 3rd: nt fluent 5th and rdn: rapidly dropped to rr next: nt keen and t.o: virtually p.u fr last* **9/1**

3m 52.4s (2.90) **Going Correction** +0.075s/f (Yiel)
WFA 4 from 5yo+ 7lb **10** Ran SP% **116.2**
Speed ratings (Par 103): **95,91,91,89,89 88,84,83,75,41**
toteswingers:1&2:£4.70, 1&3:£14.50, 2&3:£10.00 CSF £18.78 TOTE £6.00: £3.80, £1.10, £6.20; EX 22.30.
Owner Noel Glynn **Bred** Derek Veitch And Saleh Ali Hammadi **Trained** Coedkernew, Newport

FOCUS

A modest claiming hurdle run at a slow gallop. The winner is rated back to the level of last summer's Ffos Las run.

NOTEBOOK

Supernoverre(IRE), who is blind in one eye, was 0-8 over hurdles before this but put up an improved effort on this better ground. He was brought wide by Danny Burton in the straight and picked up well when asked for his effort to win handsomely. This was his first run for Alan Jones and the change of scenery looks to have rekindled his enthusiasm. He's a potential improver for a summer jumping campaign. (op 5-1)
Second Brook(IRE) ◆ is the horse to take out of the race. He was outpaced down the backstraight but stayed on relentlessly to nab second on the line. This isn't strong form but he could go close at this level over further. (tchd 3-1)
Mister Fantastic injected some much needed pace into the race after the third hurdle. The 5-y-o had shown precious little in three hurdle starts but this was a better performance. He was headed in the home straight but responded gamely and ran right to the line, just being denied for second. (op 12-1 tchd 10-1)
Goose Green(IRE) won four times on the Flat on fast ground and looked at home under these conditions, but was too slow at his hurdles to ever be in a challenging position. (op 8-1)
Bahr Nothing(IRE) made good headway in the second half of the race but paid for that effort when it mattered and had no more to give over the last hurdle. He may be suited by a stronger end-to-end gallop. (tchd 6-1)
Ask The Oracle was a bit keen in front and once restrained he performed well, holding every chance over the final two hurdles. He's only had five starts over hurdles and is entitled to improve with more outings. (op 8-1)

5083 BITTERLEY POINT TO POINT HUNTERS' CHASE (17 fncs) 2m 4f

5:05 (5:06) (Class 6) 5-Y-0+ **£936** (£290; £145; £72)

Form | | | | RPR
0-21 **1** **Double Mead**[14] 4832 9-11-6 119...................................... MrsAlexDunn(5) 123+
(Mrs K R Smith-Maxwell) *taken down early: taken steadily in rr: nt fluent 1st: effrt on outside 13th: blnd next: sn wnt 2nd: bmpd by rival but led jst after 2 out: sn forged clr: readily* **15/8**[1]
0044 **2** *4 ½* **Mccauley (IRE)**[8] 4950 8-11-3 96......................(p) MrMatthewHampton(7) 117+
(Paul Swaffield) *j. bdly lft: sme mstkes: led fr 3rd: 6 l clr at 10th: mstke 11th: rdn and hdd jst after 2 out: sn no ch w wnr: hung lft flat* **20/1**
3-33 **3** *1* **Almaydan**[41] 4197 13-11-13 122.......................................(b) MrWKinsey(5) 120
(Mrs K M Diggle) *chsd ldrs: effrt after 13th: sn rdn: chsd ldng pair fr 2 out: fnd little: no imp on runner-up and hung lft flat* **9/1**
1-0P **4** *17* **Caulkin (IRE)**[13] 4857 8-11-5 0... MrDKemp(5) 99
(David Kemp) *hdwy to 2nd at 9th tl pushed along 3 out: wknd tamely next* **10/1**
3-14 **5** *hd* **Emotional Article (IRE)**[18] 11-11-7 120................................ MrAWadlow(7) 101
(Mrs Belinda Clarke) *towards rr: rdn and struggling bef 10th: plodded on* **22/1**
05-5 **6** *15* **Give Me Love (FR)**[28] 4442 11-11-3 80.................... MrSWDrinkwater(7) 83
(Miss Louise Danton) *mstke 1st: outpcd 4th: blnd 8th: t.o 10th: passed two stragglers after 14th* **80/1**
/P-U **7** *9* **Gem Mill (IRE)**[18] 9-11-5 57..(b) MrPJTolman(5) 75
(Mrs Gillian Davies) *midfield: mstke 4th: rdn 9th: effrt u.p 13th: fading whn j.lft 3 out* **100/1**
0F6- **8** *12* **William Bonney (IRE)**[375] 4762 11-11-11 0...................(p) MrRHodges(7) 77
(Ann Price) *sn bhd: struggling after 11th: t.o* **33/1**
/11- **P** **Cedrus Libani (IRE)**[74] 10-12-4 130.. MrRBurton —
(Mrs A Rucker) *v reluctant to s and fnlly set off a fence bhd: continued pointlessly tl fnlly p.u bef 10th* **6/1**[3]
1F4F **P** **Otage De Brion (FR)**[25] 9-12-4 137........................... MrSWaley-Cohen —
(Robert Waley-Cohen) *j.lft: led tl 3rd: chsd ldr tl 9th: losing pl rapidly whn j. slowly next: blnd 11th: t.o and p.u 12th* **9/2**[2]
F6/1 **P** **Hivikos (FR)**[328] 195 8-11-11 0...(t) MrMWall(3) —
(Mrs P J Buckler) *chsd ldrs: rdn 9th: 3rd at next: wknd 12th: t.o and p.u last* **7/1**
0P-6 **P** **Cheapside (IRE)**[20] 4696 6-11-3 0....................................(t) MrOGarner(7) —
(D C Gannon) *cl up early: rdn 5th: hit 6th and dropped out rapidly: t.o and p.u after 9th* **150/1**

5m 8.40s (4.00) **Going Correction** +0.15s/f (Yiel) **12** Ran SP% **113.8**
Speed ratings: **98,96,95,89,88 82,79,74,—,— —,—**
toteswingers:1&2:£10.50, 1&3:£4.70, 2&3:£17.00 CSF £42.08 TOTE £3.10: £1.60, £7.30, £1.50; EX 50.80.
Owner Mrs K R Smith-Maxwell **Bred** Ashfield, Dawson And McGregor **Trained** Himbleton, Worcester

FOCUS

A decent hunters' chase.

NOTEBOOK

Double Mead has been in excellent form in points and won a hunter chase at Towcester in good fashion. She continued her progression this year with a good round of jumping under an uncomplicated ride from her jockey. She's a good-looking, reliable mare who will be kept on the go this summer and can win more races of this nature. (tchd 13-8 and 2-1 in a place)
Mccauley(IRE), tried in cheekpieces, ran a stormer. He's had problems with his jumping in similar events and again jumped markedly left. Losing many lengths throughout cost him vital ground, but to his credit he kept responding for pressure and even once headed he rallied well, finishing a game second. Another try on a left-handed course probably awaits. (op 25-1 tchd 28-1)
Almaydan rallied well from an unpromising position but was just too far off the pace to get closer to the winner. Ridden more positively he can go close next time. (op 16-1)
Caulkin(IRE) was soon prominent and travelled well but some jumping errors ended any realistic chance of winning. (op 16-1)
Emotional Article(IRE) had course experience but didn't travel with great enthusiasm. (op 25-1)
Cedrus Libani(IRE) won this race last year and was 2-2 in hunter chases, but had been reluctant to race in the past. This time he didn't want to line up and once he finally began to race the game was over. (op 11-2 tchd 9-2)
Otage De Brion(FR) stopped quickly on the final circuit, something presumably amiss. Official explanation: jockey said gelding never travelled (op 11-2 tchd 9-2)

5084 JP SEAFOODS STANDARD OPEN NATIONAL HUNT FLAT RACE 2m

5:35 (5:35) (Class 5) 4-6-Y-0 **£1,463** (£429; £214; £107)

Form | | | | RPR
1 **Sizing India (IRE)** 6-11-4 0.. APMcCoy 113+
(Nicky Henderson) *settled midfield: clsd 4f out: led gng best wl over 1f out: readily* **11/8**[1]
2 *5* **Castle Conflict (IRE)**[32] 6-11-4 0.................................... RichardJohnson 103
(Henry Daly) *led at stdy pce: rdn and hdd wl over 1f out: no ch w wnr but kpt gng steadily* **8/1**
3 *½* **Orangeaday** 4-10-11 0.. DarylJacob 96
(Ben Case) *bhd: effrt 1/2-way: chal 4f out: last of four w ch on home turn: nt qckn fnl 2f* **33/1**
4 *16* **Crescent Beach (IRE)** 4-10-11 0.. AlanO'Keeffe 81
(Jennie Candlish) *plld hrd in last: effrt 5f out: nt rch ldrs fnl 3f: should improve* **5/1**[2]
5 *7* **Milansbar (IRE)** 4-10-11 0.. AndrewThornton 75
(Henrietta Knight) *t.k.h: prom tl rdn and fdd over 2f out* **20/1**
6 *3 ¼* **Final Cast** 4-10-1 0.. DavidBass(3) 62
(Nicky Henderson) *rdn and outpcd 1/2-way: n.d after* **8/1**
7 *3* **Larkhall** 4-10-4 0.. HarryChalloner(7) 66
(John Bryan Groucott) *towards rr: rdn and no ch 5f out* **66/1**
8 *1* **Ainroe (IRE)** 4-10-11 0.. JohnnyFarrelly 65
(Paul John Gilligan, Ire) *hdwy 6f out: jnd ldr 4f out tl wknd qckly wl over 2f out* **16/1**
0 **9** *4 ½* **Kalantari (IRE)**[7] 4970 4-10-11 0.. PaulMoloney 61
(Evan Williams) *prom tl wknd over 3f out* **40/1**
10 *19* **Setters Gift** 4-10-1 0.. IanPopham(3) 35
(Ron Hodges) *t.k.h and cl up early: lost gd pl after 4f: rt out of contention wl over 3f out* **40/1**
11 *27* **Lara Dora (IRE)** 5-10-11 0... CharliePoste 15
(Robin Dickin) *struggling 6f out: t.o fnl 3f* **66/1**
12 *45* **Lambrini Belle** 5-10-11 0.. LeightonAspell —
(Lisa Williamson) *t.k.h early: cl up tl lost pl 1/2-way: t.o fnl 4f* **100/1**
1 **U** **Parsnip Pete**[28] 4443 5-11-11 0... PaddyBrennan —
(Tom George) *clipped heels and uns rdr sn after s* **7/1**[3]

3m 42.6s (-1.30) **Going Correction** +0.075s/f (Yiel)
WFA 4 from 5yo+ 7lb **13** Ran SP% **115.9**
Speed ratings: **106,103,103,95,91 90,88,88,85,76 62,40,—**
toteswingers:1&2:£14.10, 1&3:£4.20, 2&3:£15.90. totesuper7: Win: Not won. Place: £75.60 CSF £11.64 TOTE £3.40: £2.00, £3.70, £10.70; EX 13.80.
Owner Ann & Alan Potts **Bred** Diarmuid And Michael O'Connor **Trained** Upper Lambourn, Berks

FOCUS

A eventful bumper which produced an easy winner who should go on to rate a lot higher.

NOTEBOOK

Sizing India(IRE) justified strong support to run out a ready winner for the Nicky Henderson camp, who excel with their bumper runners at this track. McCoy held onto the Beneficial gelding for as long as he could before asking his mount to go and win the race, and he settled it with little effort. He could be a useful performer. (op 15-8 tchd 5-4)
Castle Conflict(IRE) led at a fair pace and did well to avoid trouble with the loose horse around a couple of the bends. He fought tenaciously in the last furlong to try and go with the winner but was always losing the battle. He looks a potential improver over a trip in due course. (op 15-2)
Orangeaday performed well on debut. He made rapid headway on the outside of the field down the back straight, and showed a willing attitude off the bridle. He will learn plenty for this and can go one better with this experience under his belt. (op 22-1)
Crescent Beach(IRE) finished well clear of the remainder. This was a good introduction as he was outpaced initially before staying on moderately up the straight. (op 9-2)
Milansbar(IRE) was keen early and wasn't given a hard ride once his chance of winning had gone. He's a half brother to useful hurdler/chaser Muhtenbar and will appreciate further in time, but could pick up a small bumper before stepping up in distance. (op 25-1)

Parsnip Pete, penalised for winning over C&D on debut, clipped heels with a rival soon after the start and came down. He can be given another chance to confirm his initial promise. (op 6-1)
T/Jkpt: £3,553.20 to a £1 stake. Pool:£35,031.86 - 7.00 winning tickets T/Plt: £33.70 to a £1 stake. Pool:£92,618.37 - 2,001.01 winning tickets T/Qpdt: £22.50 to a £1 stake. Pool:£5,909.37 - 193.68 w. tickets IM 5085a - 5090a (Foreign Racing) - See Raceform Interactive

4867 NEWCASTLE (L-H)

Friday, April 1

OFFICIAL GOING: Good to soft (soft in places; good in places last 3f)
All bends common with no dividing rails.
Wind: strong 1/2 against Weather: overcast, very breezy

5091 MOLSON COORS NOVICES' HURDLE (DIV I) (11 hdls) 2m 4f
2:30 (2:30) (Class 4) 4-Y-0+ **£1,886** (£553; £276; £138)

Form			Horse	Jockey	RPR
-112	1		**Lovey Dovey (IRE)**[65] 3747 7-10-7 0 (Simon West) *trckd ldr: led 6th: styd on wl fr 3 out: eased towards fin* **5/6**[1]	FearghalDavis	117+
4604	2	8	**Harris Hawk**[40] 4242 6-10-7 0 (John Wade) *chsd ldrs: wnt 2nd after 8th: rdn and hit next: kpt on same pce fr 2 out* **16/1**	MrJohnDawson(7)	113
3-2P	3	24	**Hannah Jacques (IRE)**[80] 3498 6-10-7 0 (Nicky Richards) *trckd ldrs: wnt 3rd after 8th: wknd fr next* **16/1**	JamesReveley	88
6122	4	32	**Eighteen Carat (IRE)**[26] 4506 7-11-6 117 (Donald McCain) *led to 6th: drvn next: wknd after 8th* **15/8**[2]	JasonMaguire	68
-F14	5	13	**Jago River (IRE)**[22] 4568 5-11-6 112 (Howard Johnson) *chsd ldrs: mstke 2nd: wknd after 8th: sn bhd* **8/1**[3]	BrianHughes	57
0	6	38	**Monty's Brig**[12] 4889 10-11-0 0 (Jane Clark) *in rr: bhd fr 6th: t.o 8th* **125/1**	PeterBuchanan	17
0	7	3/4	**Grey Locker**[12] 4889 8-10-7 0 (Lynn Siddall) *in rr: bhd fr 6th: t.o 8th* **100/1**	TomSiddall	9
5600	8	4 1/2	**Media Stars**[13] 4870 6-11-0 78 (Robert Johnson) *stdd s: in rr: reminders 5th: sn bhd: t.o 8th* **100/1**	KennyJohnson	12
00	9	51	**Indian Snow (IRE)**[36] 4304 6-11-0 0 (William Amos) *j. poorly in rr: reminders 4th: bhd fr 6th: t.o 8th: virtually p.u 3 out* **100/1**	CampbellGillies	—
0-P0	P		**Tommy Gun**[27] 4473 5-11-0 0 (Maurice Barnes) *in tch: drvn 5th: sn lost pl and bhd: t.o 8th: p.u bef next* **125/1**	(t) MichaelMcAlister	—

5m 21.0s (-0.10) **Going Correction** -0.05s/f (Good) **10** Ran SP% **116.8**
Speed ratings (Par 105): **98,94,85,72,67 52,51,49,29,—**
toteswingers: 1&2 £5.10, 1&3 £4.80, 2&3 £13.00. CSF £17.04 TOTE £1.40: £1.02, £2.90, £2.90; EX 17.60.
Owner J D Gordon **Bred** Hugh Suffern Bloodstock Ltd **Trained** Middleham Moor, N Yorks

FOCUS
No strength in depth to this opening novice event, which was run at an ordinary gallop, and the field came home well strung out. The easy winner can rate higher.

NOTEBOOK
Lovey Dovey(IRE) ◆ was unlucky not to have made a winning debut over hurdles at Musselburgh on her comeback in January, but she resumed winning ways with an emphatic success here. She took the race by the scruff of the neck leaving the back straight and was in no danger thereafter, despite idling from the second-last. It was just her second outing for connections and she has now won a point, three bumpers and over hurdles, so clearly has a touch of class about her. Connections will now have a look at a valuable mares' race at Ayr's Scottish National meeting for her later this month. (op 4-5 tchd 10-11)
Harris Hawk stayed on to look the only possible threat to the winner in the home straight, but he was never going to get to her. This was a nice bit of improvement from him, on just his second outing as a hurdler, and he was conceding 7lb to the winner.
Hannah Jacques(IRE), who got warm beforehand, took a step back in the right direction on her return from an 80-day break.
Eighteen Carat(IRE) looked to down tools once headed by the winner on the far side and was very disappointing. He is now due a break. Official explanation: trainer said, regarding running, that the gelding has had a long season and will benefit from a break (op 5-2)
Jago River(IRE) sweated up beforehand and posted a lifeless effort. (op 7-1)

5092 MOLSON COORS NOVICES' HURDLE (DIV II) (11 hdls) 2m 4f
3:00 (3:02) (Class 4) 4-Y-0+ **£1,886** (£553; £276; £138)

Form			Horse	Jockey	RPR
1	1		**Jammia (IRE)**[39] 4253 6-10-13 0 (Noel C Kelly, Ire) *mde all: clr 3 out: easily* **1/3**[1]	MrDRFox(7)	123+
2055	2	15	**Fill The Power (IRE)**[56] 3918 5-10-9 0 (Sue Smith) *chsd ldrs: outpcd appr 3 out: 4th last: styd on to take 2nd last 150yds* **8/1**[3]	ShaneByrne(5)	98+
F500	3	6	**Luso's Lad (IRE)**[37] 4281 7-10-11 105 (Howard Johnson) *hld up: hdwy to trck ldrs 4th: wnt 2nd 3 out: wknd run-in* **12/1**	(t) JamesO'Farrell(3)	92
00-P	4	shd	**Mocha (FR)**[80] 3498 6-10-4 0 (James Ewart) *chsd wnr: hit 6th: one pce fr 3 out* **66/1**	HarryHaynes(3)	86
36	5	4 1/2	**Dancing Art (IRE)**[12] 4889 5-11-0 0 (Keith Reveley) *in rr: blnd 7th: hdwy next: wknd 2 out* **15/2**[2]	JamesReveley	90
0-50	6	7	**Katapult (GER)**[36] 4304 8-11-0 0 (Kate Walton) *t.k.h: sn trcking ldrs: lost pl appr 3 out* **20/1**	RichieMcGrath	81
0	7	27	**Skybull (IRE)**[26] 4506 5-11-0 0 (Howard Johnson) *chsd ldrs: hit 4th: lost pl 6th: blnd 8th: sn wl bhd* **25/1**	BrianHughes	57
6P0	8	5	**No Way Hozay**[12] 4889 5-11-0 0 (Brian Storey) *nt jump wl: prom: lost pl 3rd: bhd fr 8th* **100/1**	(t) WilsonRenwick	52
00	9	35	**Rocky Bear (IRE)**[24] 4541 6-10-7 0 (Marjorie Fife) *in rr: sme hdwy 7th: sn wknd: bhd fr 3 out: t.o* **100/1**	KyleJames(7)	21
P	P		**Cherry Cake**[17] 4795 7-10-7 0 (Philip Kirby) *in rr: bhd fr 7th: t.o whn p.u next* **125/1**	TomMessenger	—

5m 21.9s (0.80) **Going Correction** -0.05s/f (Good) **10** Ran SP% **118.5**
Speed ratings (Par 105): **96,90,87,87,85 82,72,70,56,—**
toteswingers: 1&2 £1.40, 1&3 £3.80, 2&3 £4.40. CSF £3.73 TOTE £1.30: £1.10, £1.50, £1.80; EX 4.40.
Owner Mrs C Kelly **Bred** Mrs Catherine McCarthy **Trained** Draperstown, Co. Derry

FOCUS
This second division of the novice hurdle was even less competitive than the first. Ordinary form, with the easy winner rated 9lb off his Carlisle mark.

NOTEBOOK
Jammia(IRE) led from flag fall, following up his Carlisle success with a straightforward display. He has plenty of scope about him and appeals strongly as the sort to improve further once going chasing, but connections plan to up in him class with one more outing in this sphere before the season's end. That is likely to be at the Irish Grand National meeting at Fairyhouse later this month. (op 2-5 tchd 4-9)
Fill The Power(IRE) got markedly outpaced before staying on in the home straight to finish a clear second-best. He's one to look out for in handicaps over a stiffer test. (tchd 17-2)
Luso's Lad(IRE) just held on for third and posted a more encouraging effort in a first-time tongue tie, but is not going to prove simple to win with. (tchd 11-1)
Mocha(FR) was last seen pulling up on her hurdling debut over C&D in January. She was sweating through the race but should come on a deal for the experience. (op 50-1)
Dancing Art(IRE) looked nailed on for a place turning for home, but his effort proved short-lived and he failed to raise his game for the slightly sounder surface. It's a fair bet he will find a race when switching to handicaps. (op 9-1)

5093 KING STREET SOCIAL CLUB COORS LIGHT H'CAP CHASE (13 fncs) 2m 110y
3:30 (3:32) (Class 5) (0-95,92) 5-Y-0+ **£2,081** (£611; £305; £152)

Form			Horse	Jockey	RPR
5141	1		**Prince Tam**[13] 4868 7-11-6 86 (Lucinda Russell) *hld up: hdwy to trck ldrs 6th: wnt 2nd bef 4 out: led on bit 3 out: wnt clr between last 2: easily* **5/1**[1]	(p) CampbellGillies	107+
4234	2	11	**Catholic Hill (USA)**[5] 5036 6-10-9 82 (Mark Gillard) *chsd ldrs: reminders 6th: led and hit 9th: hdd and mstke 3 out: no ch w wnr* **7/1**[3]	MrTJCannon(7)	92+
4203	3	11	**The Green Hat (IRE)**[8] 4963 11-10-5 71 (Theresa Gibson) *chsd ldrs: lft modest 3rd 3 out: one pce* **11/2**[2]	BrianHughes	66
53P5	4	1 3/4	**More Shennanigans**[22] 4573 10-9-7 66 oh1 (Jean McGregor) *in rr: bhd fr 8th: kpt on to take modest 4th appr last* **14/1**	GaryRutherford(7)	60
2224	5	11	**Lerida**[17] 4800 9-11-2 89 (Sharon Watt) *chsd ldrs: drvn 8th: wnt modest 4th sn after 3 out: wknd between last 2* **11/2**[2]	(p) HenryBrooke(7)	73
5640	6	5	**Lindseyfield Lodge (IRE)**[26] 4511 10-11-4 84 (Robert Johnson) *hld up in rr: hdwy to chse ldrs whn hit 8th: sn wknd* **25/1**	(p) KennyJohnson	66
F3P4	7	8	**Native Coll**[22] 4573 11-10-11 77 (N W Alexander) *in rr: sme hdwy 6th: sn lost pl and bhd: t.o 2 out* **8/1**	PeterBuchanan	49
5463	U		**Poseidon (GER)**[17] 4796 9-11-3 90 (John Wade) *hld up: stmbld bdly landing and uns rdr 2nd* **5/1**[1]	(p) MrJohnDawson(7)	—
62-3	P		**Braddock Island**[17] 4800 8-11-12 92 (Mrs S Sunter) *led: hdd 9th: 3rd and wkng whn blnd 3 out: t.o last whn p.u appr last* **7/1**[3]	BarryKeniry	—

4m 18.8s (-2.30) **Going Correction** -0.05s/f (Good) **9** Ran SP% **110.7**
Speed ratings: **103,97,92,91,86 84,80,—,—**
toteswingers: 1&2 £5.00, 1&3 £6.10, 2&3 £8.00. CSF £37.37 CT £188.52 TOTE £3.90: £1.50, £2.00, £2.50; EX 26.20.
Owner Mrs L R Joughin **Bred** Miss Gail Joughin **Trained** Arlary, Perth & Kinross

FOCUS
An easy winner here who was value for further and seemingly produced a big step up. A small personal best from the second with the rest a stone+ off.

NOTEBOOK
Prince Tam could hardly have won any easier and he rates value for a deal further than the winning margin. It was his third success this season and each of them has come over C&D. He proved easy to back off his 4lb higher mark, probably on account of the quicker ground, but is clearly versatile on that front. Connections will probably do well to get him out under a penalty now. (op 9-2)
Catholic Hill(USA) went in snatches, but his rider produced him to lead nearing five out. He hit that, however, and it was his jumping thereafter that let him down. On the evidence of his career thus far over fences, he is anything but a natural chaser. (op 8-1)
The Green Hat(IRE), not the first time, plugged on after hitting a flat spot. He helps to set the level. (op 6-1 tchd 5-1)
More Shennanigans was never a player from off the pace and remains winless after 31 outings. (op 10-1)
Poseidon(GER), down in trip with cheekpieces applied, got no further than the second. (op 13-2 tchd 7-1)
Braddock Island paid for his early exertions and was held prior to whacking three out. (op 13-2 tchd 7-1)

5094 DUNSTON SOCIAL CLUB CAFFREYS H'CAP HURDLE (11 hdls) 2m 4f
4:00 (4:02) (Class 4) (0-100,100) 4-Y-0+ **£2,211** (£649; £324; £162)

Form			Horse	Jockey	RPR
0560	1		**Lisdonagh House (IRE)**[37] 4281 9-10-3 77 (Lynn Siddall) *t.k.h in rr: stdy hdwy 6th: wnt 2nd bef 3 out: led appr 2 out: jnd last: styd on: all out* **22/1**	TomSiddall	91
-043	2	1 1/4	**Lewlaur Supreme (IRE)**[21] 4686 8-11-2 90 (Jim Goldie) *hld up in rr: stdy hdwy7th: wnt handy 3rd appr 3 out: 2nd between last 2: upsides last: styd on same pce* **5/1**[1]	JamesReveley	104
0063	3	13	**Waltham Abbey**[8] 4960 10-9-13 80 (Lynsey Kendall) *chsd ldrs: led 6th: hdd appr 2 out: wknd last* **7/1**[3]	MrRUtley(7)	83
0000	4	1 3/4	**Ardesia (IRE)**[32] 4390 7-10-4 83 (Tina Jackson) *chsd ldrs: drvn 8th: one pce appr next* **10/1**	AlexanderVoy(5)	82
4P22	5	18	**Charming Knight (IRE)**[21] 4687 10-10-9 90 (Jane Walton) *chsd ldrs 3rd and outpcd whn mstke 3 out: sn wknd* **11/1**	AlistairFindlay(7)	75
0211	6	12	**Spice Bar**[129] 2603 7-11-1 89 (Declan Carroll) *hld up towards rr: hdwy 8th: rdn appr next: wknd appr 2 out* **5/1**[1]	BarryKeniry	68
2050	7	23	**Bubses Boy**[52] 3993 5-10-8 82 (Robert Johnson) *in rr: hit 6th: bhd whn blnd 8th: t.o 2 out* **33/1**	KennyJohnson	34
4534	8	1/2	**Blazing Bay (IRE)**[26] 4506 6-11-2 90 (James Moffatt) *mid-div: drvn 6th: bhd fr next: t.o 2 out* **25/1**	PaddyAspell	41
23-2	9	1 1/2	**Top Brass (IRE)**[21] 4688 10-11-4 99 (James H Black, Ire) *wnt prom 5th: drvn 8th: sn wknd: t.o 2 out* **12/1**	MrCCully(7)	49
0U62	10	37	**Artic Night (FR)**[20] 4712 5-11-7 95 (Nicky Richards) *towards rr: sme hdwy 6th: drvn 8th: sn wknd: bhd fr next: t.o 2 out: heavily eased* **11/2**[2]	FearghalDavis	12
0-00	P		**Ballamusic (IRE)**[8] 4960 9-11-2 90 (Andrew Parker) *in rr: p.u after 4th: lame* **33/1**	RichieMcGrath	—
0000	P		**Barbarian**[7] 4998 5-10-11 85 (Alan Brown) *chsd ldrs: reminders 5th: sn lost pl: t.o whn p.u bef next: lame* **22/1**	(p) JasonMaguire	—
-200	P		**Murrell (IRE)**[38] 4278 6-11-5 100 (Henry Hogarth) *in rr: sme hdwy 6th: sn wknd: bhd fr 8th: t.o whn p.u bef next* **40/1**	HenryBrooke(7)	—
504	P		**Short Supply (USA)**[50] 3637 5-11-4 92 (Tim Walford) *trckd ldrs: t.k.h: 7th whn mstke 7th: sn lost pl: t.o whn p.u bef 3 out* **20/1**	RobertWalford	—
0003	P		**Fightstar (FR)**[21] 4688 7-11-5 93 (Lucinda Russell) *w ldrs: wknd 3 out: poor 7th whn p.u after 2 out* **16/1**	(p) CampbellGillies	—

5m 17.3s (-3.80) **Going Correction** -0.05s/f (Good) **15** Ran SP% **117.8**
Speed ratings (Par 105): **105,104,99,98,91 86,77,77,76,61 —,—,—,—,—**
toteswingers: 1&2 £52.40, 1&3 £31.50, 2&3 £15.30. CSF £119.34 CT £870.45 TOTE £22.50: £5.50, £2.20, £3.40; EX 267.90.

Owner J P Cooke **Bred** Fintan Cronin And Barry Butler **Trained** Colton, N Yorks

■ Lynn Siddall's first winner for more than three years.

■ Stewards' Enquiry : Tom Siddall caution: used whip with excessive frequency.

FOCUS

This was a wide-open handicap. Few landed a serious blow, however, and the first pair came well clear from the penultimate flight. The winner is rated back to the level of his 2009 C&D best and the form looks sound. The time was good for the grade.

NOTEBOOK

Lisdonagh House(IRE), back up in trip, defied a walk in the market and finally shed his maiden tag with a gutsy effort. He moved nicely through the race and took it up going strongly after three out. He had to dig deep to repel the runner-up, but was always doing enough and this was a massively improved effort. Official explanation: trainer said, regarding apparent improvement in form, that the gelding benefited from a drop in class and step up in trip. (op 16-1)

Lewlaur Supreme(IRE) ◆, another up in trip, crept into contention off the home turn but hit something of a flat spot from two out. He rallied well and, a clear second-best, can surely be placed to get off the mark in the coming weeks. (op 6-1 tchd 9-2)

Waltham Abbey made a bold bid, but paid for his early exertions and would probably have fared even better had his amateur rider held onto him for longer. (op 10-1)

Ardesia(IRE) posted his best effort since winning at Cartmel last summer off 5lb higher and looks on his way back. (op 17-2 tchd 11-1)

Spice Bar was bidding for a hat-trick off a 7lb higher mark on this return from a 129-day break and shaped as though the run was needed. (op 6-1 tchd 9-2)

Ballamusic(IRE) Official explanation: trainer said gelding pulled up lame right-fore

Barbarian Official explanation: trainer said gelding pulled up lame left-fore

5095 LEMINGTON SOCIAL CLUB CARLING NOVICES' H'CAP CHASE (16 fncs) 2m 4f

4:30 (4:31) (Class 4) (0-110,109) 5-Y-0+ **£2,439** (£716; £358; £178)

Form				RPR
401B	1		**Allanard (IRE)**[58] 3886 7-10-13 **96**...(p) JamesReveley (Martin Todhunter) *chsd ldrs: led 12th: hdd 2 out: swtchd rt sn after last: rallied: led cl home* **7/1**	105+
4231	2	*hd*	**Finlay**[17] 4796 8-11-10 **107**...(t) JasonMaguire (Donald McCain) *hld up: hdwy to chse ldr 4 out: led 2 out: 1 1/2 l ahd: edgd lft last: hdd fnl strides* **2/1**[1]	115+
-631	3	*9*	**Apache Blue (IRE)**[19] 4741 7-10-5 **95**... MrJohnDawson[(7)] (John Wade) *hld up in tch: trckd ldrs 11th: one pce fr 3 out: tk modest 3rd last* **13/2**	96
04P5	4	*6*	**Soul Magic (IRE)**[36] 4302 9-9-7 **83** oh2... GaryRutherford[(7)] (Harriet Graham) *trckd ldrs: handy 3rd 3 out: wknd last* **7/1**	78
40U3	5	*6*	**Monsieur Jourdain (IRE)**[12] 4893 5-11-12 **109**...(p) RichieMcGrath (Tim Easterby) *hld up: hdwy to trck ldrs 10th: wknd after 3 out* **5/1**[3]	98
4521	6	*8*	**Innominate (IRE)**[21] 4690 9-10-12 **95**...(tp) CampbellGillies (Lucinda Russell) *led: hdd after 6th: wknd after 3 out* **4/1**[2]	78
25P3	7	*14*	**Still Calm**[7] 4996 7-10-0 **83** oh1...(t) MichaelMcAlister (Maurice Barnes) *nt fluent in rr 1st 2: hdwy 4th: led after 6th: j.rt and hit 8th: hdd 11th: lost pl 4 out* **33/1**	52

5m 29.5s (2.30) **Going Correction** -0.05s/f (Good) **7** Ran SP% **111.3**

Speed ratings: **93,92,89,86,84 81,75**

toteswingers: 1&2 £4.40, 1&3 £7.20, 2&3 £3.00 CSF £21.15 TOTE £10.40: £7.80, £1.10; EX 27.70.

Owner E Ron Madden **Bred** R Madden **Trained** Orton, Cumbria

FOCUS

A competitive handicap for the class. It was run at an ordinary gallop and the first pair came clear from two out. A step up from the winner to beat the well handicapped second.

NOTEBOOK

Allanard(IRE) was brought down over C&D two months earlier and he gained compensation with a last-gasp success. He looked held when the runner-up hit the front after the penultimate fence, but he battled most gamely for pressure and got back on top where it mattered. It was a career-best effort. (op 5-1)

Finlay finally shed his maiden tag at Sedgefield 17 days earlier and really should have followed up on this return to a handicap. Keen early, his rider confidently made his move from four out and he looked sure to collect once taking it up. He got there too soon, however, and was mugged near the line. He has a deal more talent than he has shown to date, but is clearly tricky. (op 5-2 tchd 7-4 tchd 11-4 in a place)

Apache Blue(IRE) was unable to go with the first pair when things got really serious, but still posted a sound effort off his 6lb higher mark and gives the form a solid look. (tchd 6-1 and 7-1)

Soul Magic(IRE) lacked the tactical pace to land a serious blow, but this was a step back in the right direction back over fences. (op 6-1 tchd 8-1)

Monsieur Jourdain(IRE) failed to see it out after travelling well enough into the home straight. (op 11-2 tchd 6-1)

Innominate(IRE) was well held off a 9lb higher mark on this quicker ground. (op 11-2)

5096 NEW DELAVAL AND NEWSHAM SOCIAL CLUB GROLSCH CONDITIONAL JOCKEYS NOVICES' H'CAP HURDLE (13 hdls) 3m

5:00 (5:01) (Class 5) (0-95,95) 4-Y-0+ **£1,951** (£573; £286; £143)

Form				RPR
0345	1		**Daasij (IRE)**[23] 4550 6-10-0 **69** oh2... HarryHaynes (N W Alexander) *chsd ldrs: upsides 2 out: n.m.r appr last: styd on to ld last 150yds: rdn rt out* **5/1**[3]	74
5412	2	*1 1/4*	**Easter Vic**[13] 4872 10-11-7 **90**...(p) AlexanderVoy (Robert Goldie) *chsd ldrs: led appr 3 out: edgd lft appr last: hdd and no ex last 150yds* **5/1**[3]	94
0P6	3	*4 1/2*	**Oh Landino (GER)**[21] 4686 6-9-10 **73**... PaulNorton[(8)] (Jim Goldie) *hld up in rr: stdy hdwy appr 3 out: sn chsng ldrs: kpt on one pce appr last* **17/2**	73+
5152	4	*3/4*	**Wheyaye**[15] 4822 9-11-7 **95**... CallumWhillans[(5)] (Valerie Jackson) *trckd ldrs: t.k.h: effrt 3 out: styd on same pce appr last* **9/2**[2]	94+
4600	5	*hd*	**Play The Rock (FR)**[44] 4144 8-9-11 **69** oh2...(p) HenryBrooke[(3)] (Philip Kirby) *hld up in rr: hdwy to chse ldrs 8th: outpcd between last 2: styd on clsng stages* **16/1**	68
0003	6	*11*	**Bach Street Girl (IRE)**[15] 4826 7-9-13 **71**... KyleJames[(3)] (Lynn Siddall) *in rr: outpcd 10th: no threat after* **22/1**	60
5215	7	*8*	**Vallani (IRE)**[21] 4687 6-11-5 **91**... CampbellGillies[(3)] (Lucinda Russell) *prom: outpcd appr 3 out: 6th and wl btn whn mstke 2 out* **4/1**[1]	73
/F26	8	*38*	**Wee George**[8] 4963 9-10-0 **79**... Zachery-JamesGaughan[(10)] (Sue Smith) *in rr div: sme hdwy 10th: sn wknd: t.o last* **11/1**	27
00FU	9	*nk*	**Froggy Lane**[7] 4997 8-11-6 **89**... FearghalDavis (Simon West) *t.k.h in rr: hdwy to trck ldrs 8th: led appr 10th: hdd appr next: hit 3 out: wknd rapidly: t.o whn heavily eased run-in* **16/1**	36
6060	10	*10*	**Morecambe Bay**[220] 1362 6-10-0 **72**... RobertMcCarth[(3)] (David Thompson) *chsd ldrs: wknd after 10th: t.o last* **33/1**	10
50P0	U		**Gun And More**[63] 3787 6-10-1 **80**... BenjaminStephens[(10)] (Sue Smith) *nt fluent: led: hdd appr 10th: wknd qckly: t.o whn mstke and uns rdr next* **14/1**	—

6m 24.5s (10.50) **Going Correction** -0.05s/f (Good) **11** Ran SP% **116.1**

Speed ratings (Par 103): **80,79,78,77,77 74,71,58,58,55** —

toteswingers: 1&2 £4.70, 1&3 £11.10, 2&3 £9.40. CSF £30.32 CT £208.65 TOTE £7.20: £3.10, £1.40, £3.70; EX 31.00.

Owner Liddle Philipps Stanistreet Robinson **Bred** Shadwell Estate Company Limited **Trained** Kinneston, Perth & Kinross

■ Stewards' Enquiry : Alexander Voy caution: careless riding.

FOCUS

A very weak novice handicap, confined to conditional riders. The first five all held every chance in the home straight. The first three are rated pretty close to their marks.

NOTEBOOK

Daasij(IRE) ◆ relished the step up to this longer distance and completed the task gamely, landing some decent bets in the process. It was this former useful Irish Flat winner's first success over hurdles, and an overdue one at that, so it's hoped he will now go on from this. (op 11-2)

Easter Vic came under pressure off the final turn, but kept battling away under maximum pressure and was only just held. She rates a solid benchmark. (op 13-2 tchd 9-2)

Oh Landino(GER) wasn't always foot perfect out the back early, but caught the eye making up his ground and this was by far his most encouraging display so far. The longer trip clearly helped. (op 9-1 tchd 12-1)

Wheyaye was bang there three out, but probably paid late on for running freely through the early parts. It was still a sound effort in defeat. (op 5-1 tchd 4-1)

Play The Rock(FR) didn't appear straightforward in first-time cheekpieces, but this rates his most encouraging effort to date and more positive handling may suit. (op 11-1)

Vallani(IRE) proved laboured and may now appreciate a break. (op 5-1 tchd 11-2)

5097 HEXHAM EX SERVICEMEN'S CLUB WORTHINGTONS H'CAP CHASE (18 fncs) 3m

5:30 (5:30) (Class 4) (0-105,98) 5-Y-0+ **£2,439** (£716; £358; £178)

Form				RPR
2P22	1		**Bear Dancing (IRE)**[24] 4543 7-11-12 **98**...(p) PeterBuchanan (Lucinda Russell) *hmpd and lost pl 4th: hdwy to chse ldrs 11th: outpcd appr 4 out: wnt 4 l 2nd 2 out: led appr last: drvn clr* **9/4**[2]	111+
UP2P	2	*6*	**Shrewd Investor (IRE)**[22] 4571 11-11-6 **92**...(b) RobertWalford (Henry Hogarth) *chsd ldr fr 4th: led briefly 12th: led 14th: hdd appr last: no ex* **16/1**	96
U36P	3	*1 1/2*	**Toulouse Express (IRE)**[15] 4827 12-10-8 **80**...(v) KennyJohnson (Robert Johnson) *led: briefly hdd and reminders 12th: hdd and mstke 14th: kpt on one pce fr 3 out* **40/1**	84
3444	4	*2*	**Sycho Fred (IRE)**[40] 4238 10-10-1 **73**...(t) CampbellGillies (Mike Sowersby) *in rr: hdwy to chse ldrs 11th: one pce 3rd whn mstke 2 out* **7/1**[3]	73
5-65	5	*4 1/2*	**Dollar Mick (IRE)**[23] 4551 6-11-1 **87**... PaddyAspell (James Moffatt) *in rr: hmpd 4th: pushed along 9th: outpcd 11th: kpt on fr 3 out: nvr a factor* **2/1**[1]	84
PPP3	6	*6*	**Panama At Once**[15] 4825 11-10-11 **83**...(p) TomMessenger (Philip Kirby) *mstke 3rd: chsd ldrs after next: lost pl 14th* **10/1**	73
0003	P		**Twelve Paces**[13] 4871 10-10-9 **88**...(p) MissLAlexander[(7)] (N W Alexander) *nt jump wl: chsd ldrs: mstke and dropped bk 4th: blnd 7th: bhd and drvn 9th: t.o whn p.u bef 4 out* **14/1**	—
0-0U	F		**Flaming Thistle (IRE)**[88] 3361 7-11-0 **86**...(v[1]) FearghalDavis (Nicky Richards) *reminders after 1st: fell 4th* **9/1**	—

6m 28.4s (5.90) **Going Correction** -0.05s/f (Good) **8** Ran SP% **110.7**

Speed ratings: **88,86,85,84,83 81,—,—**

toteswingers: 1&2 £6.50, 1&3 £14.80, 2&3 £17.40 CSF £32.36 CT £1051.72 TOTE £3.30: £1.50, £3.40, £4.30; EX 25.90.

Owner Peter J S Russell **Bred** Mrs E S Russell **Trained** Arlary, Perth & Kinross

FOCUS

This moderate handicap was run at a sound gallop and it saw changing fortunes in the home straight. The winner was better than the bare result and is on the upgrade.

NOTEBOOK

Bear Dancing(IRE) did really well to score having been all but brought to a standstill when badly hampered by the fall of Flaming Thistle. He unsurprisingly got outpaced as the leaders kicked for home around four out, but he is a very game horse and kept finding for his rider's urgings. His stamina kicked into play nearing the last and he was well on top at the finish. The quicker ground wasn't ideal for him, but first-time cheekpieces helped and this was a much-deserved first success. (op 2-1)

Shrewd Investor(IRE) was on a going day and made a bold bid in the home straight. His stamina began to empty from two out, however, and he was a sitting duck at the last. (op 14-1)

Toulouse Express(IRE) turned in one of his better efforts under a positive ride, over a trip that stretches him. He is well treated on his best form, but consistency is always an issue. (op 33-1)

Sycho Fred(IRE) travelled nicely into contention around five out, but not for the first time he proved laboured under pressure and remains very hard to win with. (tchd 15-2)

Dollar Mick(IRE), 8lb lower and very well backed, hit a wall from the tenth fence and looks as though he needs some form of headgear. (op 3-1)

5098 STONES H'CAP HURDLE (9 hdls) 2m

6:00 (6:01) (Class 4) (0-115,115) 4-Y-0+ **£2,211** (£649; £324; £162)

Form				RPR
0304	1		**Kai Broon (IRE)**[11] 4910 4-10-0 **93** oh7... PeterBuchanan (Lucinda Russell) *chsd ldrs: outpcd appr 3 out: wnt 3rd between last 2: led last 150yds: kpt on wl* **9/2**[2]	94+
0221	2	*2 1/4*	**Willie Hall**[24] 4544 7-11-8 **109**... CampbellGillies (William Amos) *hld up in rr: hdwy to trck ldrs 4th: led 2 out: hdd and no ex last 150yds* **15/8**[1]	114+
0051	3	*6*	**Hi Dancer**[7] 4998 8-11-7 **115** 7ex... JakeGreenall[(7)] (Ben Haslam) *trckd ldrs: led 3 out: hdd next: ev ch tl fdd last 200yds* **12/1**	115
00-1	4	*23*	**Lady Anne Nevill**[55] 3951 7-10-0 **87** oh3... BarryKeniry (Chris Fairhurst) *hld up in rr: hdwy 4th: rdn 6th: wknd appr next: lft poor 4th last* **8/1**	64
1F04	5	*1 1/2*	**Arisea (IRE)**[24] 4544 8-11-2 **103**... PaddyAspell (James Moffatt) *hld up in rr: hdwy 4th: sn chsng ldrs: drvn 6th: wknd appr next* **22/1**	79
3-01	6	*18*	**Shifting Gold (IRE)**[17] 4797 5-11-0 **106**...(b) BrianToomey[(5)] (Kevin Ryan) *prom: lost pl and mstke 5th: sn bhd* **6/1**[3]	66
00P0	7	*31*	**Daytime Dreamer (IRE)**[8] 4963 7-10-11 **98**... JamesReveley (Martin Todhunter) *w ldr: lost pl after 6th: sn bhd: t.o* **33/1**	30
1130	8	*3 1/4*	**Lady Willa (IRE)**[16] 4807 4-10-12 **112**... MrTJCannon[(7)] (Mark Gillard) *prom: reminders 5th: sn lost pl and bhd: t.o* **12/1**	35
/43-	F		**Anay Car (FR)**[510] 2121 7-11-4 **105**... WilsonRenwick (Howard Johnson) *hld up towards rr: hdwy to trck ldrs whn fell 4th* **25/1**	—

-0F5 **F** **Shadrack (IRE)**[18] 4778 7-11-12 **113** .... RichieMcGrath 108
(Sue Smith) *mde most: hdd 3 out: 4th and wkng whn fell heavily last* **10/1**

4m 8.30s (-1.70) **Going Correction** -0.05s/f (Good)
WFA 4 from 5yo+ 5lb **10** Ran SP% **114.0**
Speed ratings (Par 105): **102,100,97,86,85 76,61,59,—,—**
toteswingers:1&2 £3.10, 2&3 £6.70, 1&3 £7.20. totesuper7: Win: Not won. Place: £210.30. CSF £13.08 CT £92.46 TOTE £4.00: £1.30, £1.20, £3.70; EX 13.00.
Owner Mrs Elizabeth Ferguson **Bred** Philip Brady **Trained** Arlary, Perth & Kinross

FOCUS
Sound form for the class, with in-form horses dominating. The winner is rated 3lb off his improved Kelso run.

NOTEBOOK
Kai Broon(IRE) was still technically 9lb well in after his much-improved effort in defeat in novice company at Kelso 11 days earlier. He didn't look at all a straightforward ride under more restraint here, but to his credit he did his best work nearing the business end. It was his yard's third winner on the card. (op 7-2)
Willie Hall turned in a solid effort off his 6lb higher mark for winning over C&D 24 days earlier on softer ground and rates a decent benchmark. (op 9-4 tchd 11-4 in a place)
Hi Dancer travelled well under his penalty, but was done with after two out and failed to reverse previous C&D form with the runner-up.
Lady Anne Nevill was hiked up 10lb for opening her account at Wetherby on her belated seasonal return 55 days earlier, but was still 3lb wrong at the weights here. She came under pressure turning for home and probably needs easier ground. (op 13-2)
Shifting Gold(IRE) Official explanation: jockey said gelding never travelled
T/Plt: £67.30 to a £1 stake. Pool of £82,162.94 - 889.93 winning tickets. T/Qpdt: £26.80 to a £1 stake. Pool of £6,707.56 - 185.10 winning tickets. WG

5013 STRATFORD (L-H)

Friday, April 1

OFFICIAL GOING: Good (good to firm in places on hurdle course)
Both chase and hurdle bends moved to fresh ground but effect on distances not quantified.
Wind: Strong against Weather: cloudy and warm

5099 ST. DAVID'S PRIMARY SCHOOL NOVICES' HURDLE (9 hdls) 2m 110y
2:10 (2:10) (Class 4) 4-Y-0+ **£2,602** (£764; £382; £190)

Form RPR
052 **1** **Falcon Island**[12] 4895 6-10-13 112 .... (t) JoeTizzard 117+
(Colin Tizzard) *racd freely: led tl bef 3rd: led again 5th: gd jump next: rdn clr fr 2 out* **11/4**[1]

-321 **2** *1 ¼* **Grandads Horse**[222] 1349 5-10-13 0 .... TomO'Brien 117+
(Charlie Longsdon) *t.k.h: mstkes: led bef 3rd: hdd 5th: out j. next: chsd wnr after: rdn and nt qckn fr 2 out but easily beat rest* **11/2**[2]

0 **3** *7* **Laudatory**[27] 4478 5-10-13 0 .... (t) GerardTumelty 108
(Charlie Morlock) *t.k.h chsng ldrs: rdn and outpcd after 3 out: kpt on fr next: snatched 3rd* **25/1**

PP **4** *nk* **Spiritual Art**[33] 4370 5-10-6 0 .... JamieMoore 100
(Luke Dace) *prom: 3rd and hrd drvn bef 2 out: sn outpcd by ldng pair but kpt gng steadily although lost 3rd nr fin* **33/1**

0041 **5** *10* **Goodwood Starlight (IRE)**[14] 4859 6-10-13 118 .... (t) APMcCoy 99
(Jim Best) *plld hrd in rr: effrt 6th: chsd ldrs next: sn rdn: little rspnse: wl btn bef 2 out* **11/4**[1]

0 **6** *5* **Stevie Thunder**[156] 2038 6-10-13 0 .... (t) DaveCrosse 97
(Ian Williams) *cl up: rdn bef 3 out: wknd bef next* **25/1**

3 **7** *3* **Bow To No One (IRE)**[8] 4964 5-10-6 0 .... WillKennedy 84
(Alan Jarvis) *t.k.h: cl up: mstke 2nd and rdr lost iron: rdn bef 6th: wknd after next* **16/1**

50 **8** *nk* **Seven Summits (IRE)**[37] 4283 4-10-7 0 .... DenisO'Regan 85
(Barney Curley) *hld up and wl bhd: disputing last at 5th: pushed along and gd prog after 3 out: styng on nicely at fin* **80/1**

30 **9** *7* **Monroe Park (IRE)**[10] 4930 6-10-13 0 .... MattieBatchelor 85
(Noel Quinlan) *mstkes in rr: no ch fr 5th: hanging lft fr 2 out* **150/1**

10 *1 ¼* **Argaum (IRE)**[162] 4-10-7 0 .... PaulMoloney 77
(Evan Williams) *nt fluent 2nd: in rr div: lost tch 3 out* **28/1**

F43 **11** *9* **Omokoroa (IRE)**[20] 4711 5-10-13 0 .... AdrianLane 75
(Donald McCain) *mstke 1st: pressed ldrs: rdn 5th: wknd next: mstke last* **9/1**

00 **12** *12* **Lord Richie (IRE)**[54] 3964 5-10-10 0 .... MichaelMurphy(3) 65
(Pat Murphy) *plld v hrd in last: many mstkes: disputing last and struggling at 5th: t.o* **200/1**

U00 **13** *3 ¼* **December**[16] 4810 5-10-10 97 .... (vt) AlexMerriam(3) 62
(Christine Dunnett) *nt fluent 2nd: midfield: struggling after 5th: t.o* **150/1**

01 **14** *½* **The Hague**[32] 4397 5-11-5 0 .... RichardJohnson 67
(Tim Vaughan) *midfield: rdn 5th: sn btn: t.o* **7/1**[3]

U **15** *13* **Diamond Twister (USA)**[11] 4917 5-10-6 0 .... HarryChalloner(7) 49
(Lisa Williamson) *plld hrd: prom: faltered 1st: lost pl after 5th: hopelessly t.o* **80/1**

3m 54.1s (-1.90) **Going Correction** 0.0s/f (Good)
WFA 4 from 5yo+ 5lb **15** Ran SP% **115.5**
Speed ratings (Par 105): **104,103,100,99,95 92,91,91,88,87 83,77,76,75,69**
toteswingers: 1&2 £2.40, 1&3 £5.90, 2&3 £19.40 CSF £16.25 TOTE £3.80: £1.70, £1.60, £5.20; EX 18.90.
Owner The Butterwick Syndicate **Bred** Richard Mathias **Trained** Milborne Port, Dorset

FOCUS
Few got into this, the front pair disputing it throughout and finishing 7l clear. A fair novice hurdle for the track with the winner closing in on the best of his Irish form.

NOTEBOOK
Falcon Island stayed on the strongest, possibly due to the fact he had a fitness edge over his rival. Runner-up to a useful type at Newton Abbot last time, he also jumped the more fluently of the pair and deserved this first win at the 11th attempt over hurdles.
Grandads Horse ◆, withdrawn from his intended hurdles debut at Warwick last month on vet's advice, hadn't run since winning a Newton Abbot bumper late in the summer and was making his debut for Charlie Longsdon. Always up with the pace, he wasn't as fluent as the winner, and ultimately couldn't stay on as well, but it was a pleasing start and he looks the type to win his share in the spring/summer. Official explanation: vet said gelding lost an off-fore shoe (op 9-2)
Laudatory improved markedly on his initial hurdling effort, staying on despite racing keenly. (op 28-1)
Spiritual Art, pulled up on both previous attempts, benefited from a positive ride and showed much-improved form. She may have been flattered, but deserves a chance to prove otherwise. (op 28-1)
Goodwood Starlight(IRE) pulled hard early towards the rear and never threatened to mix it with the front pair. This wasn't his best form. (op 7-2 tchd 5-2)
Lord Richie(IRE) Official explanation: vet said gelding lost a shoe; jockey said gelding ran too freely
The Hague ran well below the form shown when winning at Plumpton last time. Official explanation: vet said gelding lost an off-fore shoe and was struck into. (op 15-2 tchd 8-1)

5100 RON SUMNER 80TH BIRTHDAY NOVICES' H'CAP CHASE (11 fncs 1 omitted) 2m 1f 110y
2:40 (2:40) (Class 4) (0-115,113) 5-Y-0+ **£3,252** (£955; £477; £238)

Form RPR
543F **1** **Marley Roca (IRE)**[107] 2961 7-11-6 **107** .... DominicElsworth 119+
(Paul Webber) *t.k.h in rr: hdwy on inner to ld 7th: drew clr on bridle appr last: pushed out* **4/1**[2]

1230 **2** *9* **Kack Handed**[27] 4490 8-11-12 **113** .... RichardJohnson 117
(Henry Daly) *led to 3rd: remained prom: mstke 6th: 2nd and rdn passing omitted 2 out: no ch w wnr* **9/2**[3]

0333 **3** *10* **Bathwick Quest (IRE)**[22] 4674 7-11-10 **111** .... TomScudamore 108+
(David Pipe) *led 4th: hdd 7th: terrible blunder and rdr lost both irons next: 3rd of ldng gp and drvn along passing omitted 2 out: wknd wl bef last* **11/4**[1]

1303 **4** *2 ½* **Amuse Me**[18] 4775 5-11-11 **112** .... APMcCoy 106
(Jonjo O'Neill) *settled in 4th: nt jump wl pushed along fr 4th: 6 l 4th and bad blunder 5th (water): nt travelling after: no ch fr next* **9/2**[3]

F565 **5** *5* **See You Jack**[42] 4182 6-11-4 **105** .... AndrewThornton 92
(Caroline Bailey) *settled in rr: pushed along after 7th: outpcd next: no ch after* **9/2**[3]

10F5 **F** **Babilu**[26] 4503 6-11-7 **108** .... (p) DPFahy —
(Dai Burchell) *t.k.h in last tl fell 3rd: fatally injured* **10/1**

4m 11.2s (4.10) **Going Correction** +0.075s/f (Yiel) **6** Ran SP% **110.3**
Speed ratings: **93,89,84,83,81** —
toteswingers: 1&2 £1.70, 1&3 £1.50, 2&3 £2.20. CSF £21.10 TOTE £4.80: £3.00, £1.30; EX 23.80.
Owner D G Carrington **Bred** Mrs M Lowry **Trained** Mollington, Oxon

FOCUS
The second-last fence was bypassed. An ordinary novices' handicap chase. The second sets the level.

NOTEBOOK
Marley Roca(IRE), having his fifth start over fences, won with ease. Beaten when falling in a better race than this at Newbury last time, the more restrained tactics clearly suited him well and he won in the style of a horse with more to offer. It'll be interesting to see how the handicapper reacts. (op 9-2 tchd 7-2)
Kack Handed went well for a long way, appreciating the drop in grade, but remains 7lb above his last successful mark. (op 11-2)
Bathwick Quest(IRE) was taken on for the lead and started jumping right down the back. Her race was over following a bad blunder at the eighth, but surely a small opening with present itself if she is kept on the go over the coming months. (op 5-2 tchd 3-1 in a place)
Amuse Me was never jumping, plodding on late. (op 5-1 tchd 11-2)
See You Jack was never out of last place. (op 11-2)
Babilu took a nasty fall at the third on this chasing debut and suffered a fatal injury. She had won once on the Flat and was also a dual scorer over hurdles. (op 7-1)

5101 JOHN BARNETT BIRTHDAY (S) HURDLE (9 hdls) 2m 110y
3:10 (3:10) (Class 5) 4-Y-0+ **£1,951** (£573; £286; £143)

Form RPR
3301 **1** **Leopard Hills (IRE)**[10] 4924 4-10-13 100 .... DPFahy 106+
(Alison Thorpe) *j. slowly 1st: prom in bunch chsng clr ldng pair: 6 l 4th and drvn bef 2 out where clsd to ld: clr and j.lft last: eased cl home* **6/1**

1605 **2** *1 ½* **Le Corvee (IRE)**[6] 4999 9-11-2 116 .... LeeEdwards(3) 108
(Tony Carroll) *prom in chsng gp: effrt 3 out: sn drvn: 3rd and ev ch bef 2 out: swtchd rt bef last and styd on at one pce: wnt 2nd flat but no ch w wnr* **4/1**[2]

0235 **3** *nse* **Olympian Boy (IRE)**[21] 4691 7-10-13 102 .... TomScudamore 102
(Anabel L M King) *led and sn clr w one rival tl 5th: cl 2nd tl drvn bef 2 out where ev ch: no ex appr last: wknd flat* **10/3**[1]

4P61 **4** *2* **Sole Bonne Femme (IRE)**[14] 4854 9-10-12 105 .... (tp) CharlieWallis(7) 107
(Gerard Butler) *cl 2nd tl led and j.rt 5th: drvn and hdd 2 out: lost 2nd after last: fnd nil and plodded on* **5/1**[3]

-00P **5** *14* **Shilpa (IRE)**[16] 4809 6-10-12 95 .... GerardTumelty 88
(Anabel L M King) *midfield: nt fluent 4th: effrt 6th: 8 l 5th and drvn bef 2 out: sn wknd: blnd last: hanging lft after* **25/1**

33UU **6** *1 ¼* **Turbo Shandy**[27] 4723 8-10-8 0 .... OliverDayman(5) 86
(Dai Burchell) *midfield: outpcd after 3 out: 10 l 6th bef next: no ch after* **15/2**

4460 **7** *3 ¼* **Morocchius (USA)**[90] 3302 6-10-10 94 .... AdamPogson(3) 86
(Charles Pogson) *plld v hrd: anchored in 20 l last at 1st: sme prog after 6th: 15 l 7th bef 2 out: no further imp: eased flat* **16/1**

4365 **8** *16* **Kasimali (IRE)**[11] 4919 8-10-13 95 .... (be) JamieMoore 74
(Gary Moore) *chsd clr ldng pair tl rdn bef 5th: reluctant and lost pl bef next: wl btn whn hmpd 3 out* **12/1**

35P6 **9** *2 ¼* **Maximix**[53] 3984 8-10-13 82 .... (p) AndrewGlassonbury 67
(Gary Moore) *midfield and n.d: drvn and lost tch bef 6th: t.o whn mstke 2 out* **33/1**

40F0 **10** *19* **Full Ov Beans**[18] 4776 7-10-13 0 .... DavidEngland 50
(Michael Gates) *bhd: drvn and struggling after 4th: t.o next* **40/1**

/0-U **P** **Carsington**[21] 4703 7-10-6 0 .... DaveCrosse —
(Lucinda Featherstone) *j. bdly in rr: t.o 4th: j. bdly rt 5th and p.u* **66/1**

U0FU **F** **Yourgolftravel Com**[22] 4676 6-10-8 0 .... (t) CO'Farrell(5) —
(David Pipe) *t.k.h: hld up: effrt bef 6th: 3 l 5th and clsng wl whn fell 3 out* **22/1**

0 **P** **Silver Astralis**[14] 4854 4-9-7 0 .... TrevorWhelan(7) —
(Christine Dunnett) *plld hrd in rr: lost tch 4th: t.o next: p.u 2 out* **100/1**

3m 56.3s (0.30) **Going Correction** 0.0s/f (Good)
WFA 4 from 5yo+ 5lb **13** Ran SP% **115.4**
Speed ratings (Par 103): **99,98,98,97,90 90,88,81,80,71** —,—,—
toteswingers: 1&2 £1.40, 1&3 £3.80, 2&3 £4.40. CSF £27.96 TOTE £5.30: £1.10, £2.60, £1.90; EX 27.00.The winner was bought in for 5,700gns.
Owner Mrs A M Thorpe **Bred** S And S Hubbard Rodwell **Trained** Bronwydd Arms, Carmarthens

FOCUS
No hanging around for this selling hurdle, Olympian Boy and Sole Bonne Femme taking each other on and surely hampering their chance of success. A big step up from the cosy winner, with the next three close to their marks.

NOTEBOOK
Leopard Hills(IRE), who had more upside to him than most, being a 4-y-o who had won last time, was always in a nice position, chasing the pace, and could be called the winner once switched out wide to challenge turning in. He readily drew clear, winning with more in hand than the official winning margin, and looks capable of victory outside this grade. (op 5-1)
Le Corvee(IRE) appreciated the drop in grade and kept on to just grab second. He's always respected around here. (op 9-2)
Olympian Boy(IRE) came back to form reverting to hurdles and dropping in grade, but could have done without being taken on for the lead. (op 4-1)

Sole Bonne Femme(IRE), an all-the-way winner at Fakenham last time, again gave it a good go, but had to do plenty of early running in a tussle with the third, and had nothing left off the final bend. (op 9-2)
Yourgolftravel Com was by no means out of it, keeping on in a close-up fifth, when taking a heavy fall three out. His form figures now read - U8FUF - and this will have done little to boost his confidence. (op 20-1 tchd 25-1)

5102 NIKLAS SARDANA III AND ANTHONY CIENA H'CAP HURDLE (9 hdls) 2m 110y

3:40 (3:40) (Class 3) (0-135,131) 4-Y-O+ **£3,903** (£1,146; £573; £286)

Form				RPR
0065	**1**		**Gifted Leader (USA)**[15] 4830 6-10-10 **115**..........(v[1]) DaveCrosse (Ian Williams) *chsd ldr: hmpd by loose horse jst bef 3 out: rdn and led sn after: 5 l clr bef 2 out: unchal* **10/1**	126+
3103	**2**	*12*	**Altan Khan**[18] 4778 6-10-1 **109**.......... JamesHalliday(3) (Malcolm Jefferson) *j. slowly 1st: sn pushed along: nt fluent 4th: 4th and effrt bef 6th: rdn to go 2nd bef 2 out: kpt on: no ch w wnr* **4/1**[2]	108
1000	**3**	*12*	**Crazy Bold (GER)**[28] 4025 8-9-11 **105** oh6.......... LeeEdwards(3) (Tony Carroll) *midfield: nt a fluent: rdn 3 out: sn outpcd: 4th and mstke 2 out: kpt on to go 3rd but no ch whn blnd last* **20/1**	91+
0200	**4**	*1 ½*	**King's Revenge**[27] 4488 8-10-2 **114**..........(b) MrOGarner(7) (Shaun Lycett) *chsd ldng pair tl 3 out: rdr lacked any urgency after: lost tch w ldng pair wl bef 2 out* **15/2**	99
3032	**5**	*nse*	**Tatispout (FR)**[18] 4778 4-10-0 **111** oh1.......... AndrewTinkler (Charlie Longsdon) *hld up: rdn 3 out: 6th and nt fluent 3 out: drvn to go 3rd bef 2 out: one pce and lost 3rd bef last* **9/4**[1]	90
0100	**6**	*hd*	**Ellerslie Tom**[14] 4848 9-11-1 **125**.......... OliverDayman(5) (Alison Thorpe) *led at str pce: hdd sn after 3 out: wknd qckly: wl btn 6th 2 out* **7/1**	110
25PP	**7**	*11*	**Bocamix (FR)**[39] 4257 5-11-1 **120**..........(t) SamThomas (Andrew Crook) *detached last early: rdn and no imp fr 6th: t.o* **28/1**	95
0-P0	**8**	*5*	**Kingsben**[177] 1731 8-11-0 **119**.......... GrahamLee (Malcolm Jefferson) *midfield: rdn after 4th and lost pl: nt fluent next: t.o 3 out* **25/1**	89
3F03	**U**		**Rivaliste (FR)**[27] 4470 6-11-2 **131**.......... JamesCowley(10) (Paul Nicholls) *3rd whn slt blunder and uns rdr 2nd* **5/1**[3]	—

3m 53.0s (-3.00) **Going Correction** 0.0s/f (Good)
WFA 4 from 5yo+ 5lb **9** Ran SP% **112.8**
Speed ratings (Par 107): **107,101,95,95,94 94,89,87,—**
toteswingers: 1&2 £14.10, 1&3 not won, 2&3 £34.10. CSF £48.07 CT £785.75 TOTE £11.50: £2.80, £1.60, £6.10; EX 46.80.
Owner Gifted Leader Partners **Bred** Juddmonte Farms Inc **Trained** Portway, Worcs
■ Stewards' Enquiry : Mr O Garner 14 day ban: failed to take all reasonable and permissable measures to obtain best possible placing (tba)

FOCUS
An ordinary enough handicap hurdle that was won emphatically by Gifted Leader. The winner is back to the level of his Haydock second, with the second to his mark.

NOTEBOOK
Gifted Leader(USA) was transformed by the first-time visor. He looked attractively weighted on the pick of his efforts and the headgear certainly brought out the best in him, enthusiastically bounding clear after three out and winging the last when the race was already in the bag. A rise will follow now, though, and there's always a doubt as to whether the headgear will work as well a second time, so it would be unwise to bank on a repeat of this effort next time. (op 8-1 tchd 15-2)
Altan Khan moved through to chase the winner, but always appeared booked for second. He continues to run well and looks worth another try at further (soft ground possibly to blame for previous failure at 2m4f). (op 9-2)
Crazy Bold(GER), racing from 6lb 'wrong', stayed on again for third, running easily his best race over jumps since winning last May. (op 16-1)
King's Revenge kept grinding away, but is something of a serial loser. His jockey was handed a 14-day ban for "an injudicious ride". Official explanation: jockey said, regarding running and riding, that his orders were to make his move halfway down the back and to take it up turning for home, the gelding travelled well but became unbalanced and he felt it prudent to hold it together; the trainer agreed but felt it could have finished closer. (op 10-1 tchd 7-1)
Tatispout(FR) never got into it, failing to confirm last-time-out form with the runner-up. (tchd 5-2)
Ellerslie Tom was quickly brushed aside from three out. (op 9-1)
Rivaliste(FR), reverting to hurdles, blundered at the second and James Cowley came off for a rather 'soft' unseat. (op 9-2)

5103 TED AND PEAR'S 40TH BIRTHDAY H'CAP HURDLE (12 hdls) 2m 6f 110y

4:10 (4:10) (Class 5) (0-95,95) 4-Y-O+ **£1,626** (£477; £238; £119)

Form				RPR
0402	**1**		**Boosha**[12] 4900 6-11-7 **90**.......... AidanColeman (Rachel Hobbs) *hld up towards rr: prog 8th: wnt 4th 3 out: sn hrd drvn: led bef next and hit it: drew wl clr bef last* **13/2**[2]	98+
UP0P	**2**	*12*	**Rossmill Lad (IRE)**[53] 3983 7-10-0 **69** oh1..........(t) JamieMoore (Luke Dace) *chsd ldrs: wnt 3rd after 7th and 2nd bef 9th: nt fluent next: sn led: drvn and hdd bef 2 out: tired 2nd but clr of rest whn mstke last* **8/1**[3]	68+
0506	**3**	*8*	**Direct Flo (IRE)**[57] 3906 4-11-4 **95**.......... SeanQuinlan (Kim Bailey) *hdwy to press ldrs 7th: wnt 3rd and hit 9th: drvn and mstke next: sn wknd: plodded home* **10/1**	78
3560	**4**	*6*	**Baby Car (FR)**[20] 4724 7-11-0 **83**..........(t) RichardJohnson (Noel Chance) *midfield: effrt to press ldrs 9th: rdn and outpcd bef next: sn wl btn: mod 5th bef 2 out* **16/1**	67
-4P4	**5**	*1 ½*	**Crack At Dawn (IRE)**[9] 4953 10-11-6 **89**..........(b) DavidEngland (Michael Gates) *prom: led bef 8th and hit it: drvn and mstke 3 out: sn hdd and fdd bdly* **12/1**	71
06P0	**6**	*1 ¼*	**Perjury**[28] 4454 7-9-11 **69** oh3.......... TommyPhelan(3) (Robin Mathew) *bhd: struggling 8th: plugged past btn horses: nvr anywhere nr ldrs* **100/1**	50
0040	**7**	*8*	**Watch Out**[25] 4532 7-11-4 **94**..........(tp) MrMGNolan(7) (Dai Burchell) *hld up: rdn and btn bef 3 out* **14/1**	68
-P00	**8**	*15*	**Petrus De Sormain (FR)**[212] 1451 8-10-4 **80**..........(t) RobertKirk(7) (James Evans) *a bhd: no ch after 8th: t.o 3 out* **11/1**	40
6056	**9**	*12*	**Drummers Drumming (USA)**[36] 4314 5-11-12 **95**...(t) JimmyMcCarthy (Charlie Morlock) *sn bhd: j. indifferently: drvn in 14th and nt looking keen 6th: t.o 8th* **16/1**	45
P62P	**10**	*8*	**Zi Missile (IRE)**[25] 4522 7-9-11 **69** oh3.......... DonalDevereux(3) (Mary Evans) *chsd ldr 4th tl 6th: dropped out qckly 8th: wl t.o 3 out* **20/1**	11
521U	**11**	*1*	**Cute N You Know It**[15] 4826 8-9-9 **69** oh1..........(p) CO'Farrell(5) (Andrew Crook) *cl up: wnt 2nd 6th tl mstke 7th: drvn and wknd bef 9th: t.o 3 out* **5/1**[1]	11
2FP0	**12**	*48*	**Kalulushi (IRE)**[30] 4422 6-11-5 **88**..........(p) AdrianLane (Donald McCain) *prom: u.p bef 7th: no rspnse: lost pl next: hopelessly t.o after 3 out* **25/1**	—
1/PP	**P**		**Lescer's Lad**[47] 4098 14-10-5 **81**..........(t) JeremiahMcGrath(7) (Mrs A M Woodrow) *j.v.slowly 1st: lumbered rnd in last: bdly t.o whn p.u 8th* **100/1**	—
	P		**The Antagonist (IRE)**[600] 1182 9-11-5 **95**.......... PeterCarberry(7) (Rachel Hobbs) *wnt wrong bef 1st: p.u after 2nd: fatally injured* **16/1**	—
26P2	**P**		**Hurricane Electric (IRE)**[23] 4559 6-11-5 **91**.......... TomMolloy(3) (Graeme McPherson) *towards rr whn mstke 4th: nvr gng wl after: t.o and p.u 8th* **5/1**[1]	—
PPPP	**P**		**Dancing Legend**[19] 4747 5-10-10 **79**.......... JodieMogford (Peter Hiatt) *led: mstke 7th: hdd and rdn bef 8th: lost pl rapidly: hopelessly t.o whn p.u after 3 out* **33/1**	—

5m 31.4s (3.30) **Going Correction** 0.0s/f (Good)
WFA 4 from 5yo+ 6lb **16** Ran SP% **120.7**
Speed ratings (Par 103): **94,89,87,84,84 84,81,76,71,69 68,52,—,—,— —**
toteswingers: 1&2 £14.10, 1&3 £8.30, 2&3 £17.50. CSF £55.09 CT £523.95 TOTE £8.70: £2.50, £2.60, £3.30, £4.60; EX 100.00.
Owner Three Counties Racing 2 **Bred** G L Edwards **Trained** Hanley Swan, Worcs

FOCUS
A rather weak big-field handicap. The winner is rated to the lvel of her Newton Abbot run.

NOTEBOOK
Boosha, representing the in-form Rachel Hobbs, had shown much-improved form when second at Newton Abbot the time before and built on that here off 2lb higher, appreciating the longer trip and staying on best in the straight. She's clearly on the up, although will need to be if she's to defy much of a rise. (tchd 6-1)
Rossmill Lad(IRE) had previously shown nothing over hurdles, but this much-improved display was clearly expected, as he was backed into 8-1 and travelled best down the back, but just couldn't stay on as well in the straight. (tchd 7-1)
Direct Flo(IRE) was helped by the step up in trip on this handicap debut, keeping on as though 3m will suit. (op 9-1)
Baby Car(FR) plugged on late.
Crack At Dawn(IRE) shaped better returned to hurdles. (op 14-1)
Perjury ran considerably better than she had done previously. (op 66-1)
Cute N You Know It was well below form. (op 11-2)
Lescer's Lad Official explanation: jockey said gelding lost its action behind (tchd 9-2 and 11-2)
The Antagonist(IRE), a stablemate of the winner, appeared to go wrong before the first hurdle and suffered fatal injuries. (tchd 9-2 and 11-2)
Hurricane Electric(IRE) was never travelling and pulled up with a circuit to run. Official explanation: jockey said gelding never travelled (tchd 9-2 and 11-2)

5104 HOOK NORTON BREWERY H'CAP CHASE (17 fncs) 2m 7f

4:40 (4:40) (Class 3) (0-135,133) 5-Y-O+ **£4,553** (£1,337; £668; £333)

Form				RPR
50P1	**1**		**Commemoration Day (IRE)**[18] 4777 10-10-9 **116**..........(p) FelixDeGiles (Charlie Longsdon) *sn pushed along in rr: last and reminders 10th: mstke 11th: drvn into 8 l 5th 2 out: surged past rivals to ld appr last: sn clr: hung lft flat: fine ride* **10/3**[2]	129+
1U55	**2**	*14*	**Rustarix (FR)**[61] 3832 10-11-0 **121**.......... RobertThornton (Alan King) *prom: mstke 12th: rdn 15th: 4th 2 out: drvn to go 2nd after 2 out: led briefly appr last: sn outpcd by wnr* **8/1**	120
100P	**3**	*11*	**Minella Theatre (IRE)**[15] 4821 8-11-7 **128**..........(p) SamThomas (Henrietta Knight) *prom early: rdn 11th where lost pl: 6th and wl bhd 2 out: kpt on to go 4th last: tk wl btn 3rd after last* **7/1**	118
61P4	**4**	*5*	**Royal Wedding**[14] 4856 9-10-10 **117**..........(p) LiamTreadwell (Nick Gifford) *led to 9th: remained prom: rdn 13th: 2nd and nt fluent 2 out: lost grnd qckly appr last where 5th and btn* **28/1**	103
11P/	**5**	*3 ½*	**Peter Pole (FR)**[727] 4847 8-11-4 **125**.......... RichardJohnson (Tim Vaughan) *in rr: slow 5th: nt fluent 8th: smooth hdwy 14th: led 2 out: rdn and hdd & wknd qckly appr last: 3rd and btn whn blnd last: lost 2 pls flat* **9/4**[1]	109+
4231	**6**	*2 ¼*	**Prince Des Marais (FR)**[14] 4856 8-11-5 **126**..........(t) AndrewThornton (Caroline Bailey) *t.k.h: hdwy to ld 9th: carried lft by loose horse 12th: rdn and hdd bef 2 out: sn wknd* **5/1**[3]	108
4P1P	**P**		**The Hollinwell**[76] 3575 8-11-12 **133**..........(b[1]) GrahamLee (Ferdy Murphy) *j.lft: lost pl 5th: dropped last next: nt keen: t.o whn p.u 12th* **11/1**	—
1230	**U**		**Job One (FR)**[125] 2670 8-10-4 **111**.......... HaddenFrost (Henrietta Knight) *mstke and uns rdr 1st* **17/2**	—

5m 39.2s (-2.40) **Going Correction** +0.075s/f (Yiel) **8** Ran SP% **116.4**
Speed ratings: **107,102,98,96,95 94,—,—**
toteswingers: 1&2 £4.90, 1&3 £7.00, 2&3 £5.30. CSF £30.12 CT £176.60 TOTE £5.50: £1.30, £2.60, £2.10; EX 34.00.
Owner Alan Bosley **Bred** Reg Griffin And Jim McGrath **Trained** Over Norton, Oxon

FOCUS
The picture changed quickly in this handicap chase, with the leaders stopping leaving the back. The winner is rated back to his 2009 best.

NOTEBOOK
Commemoration Day(IRE), who appeared to be struggling with a circuit to run, stormed around the outside of the field and took over two out. He duly sprinted clear, making it 2-2 since joining this yard, and it's easy to see why connections opted for the first-time cheekpieces, as he didn't travel at all. Although not straightforward, he was clearly well handicapped and one couldn't rule out a hat-trick if the handicapper doesn't overreact. (tchd 3-1)
Rustarix(FR) had evidently been freshened up by a short break and stayed on as though a return to 3m plus will suit. (tchd 9-1)
Minella Theatre(IRE) rallied to take third, having earlier lost his position. (op 15-2 tchd 13-2)
Royal Wedding ran well for a long way, albeit he was ultimately well held.
Peter Pole(FR) ◆ is surely the one to take from the race. A promising sort until getting injured two years ago, he jumped quickly on this return from 727 days off and got to the front down the back, but it was clear from the turn in that he was a tired horse. He should improve plenty and can win at least once this spring/summer. (op 11-4 tchd 3-1)
Prince Des Marais(FR) went best for much of the way, but had raced keenly and in the end those exertions took their toll. (op 7-1)
The Hollinwell looks to have completely lost the plot, quickly losing his position and receiving strong reminders in the first-time blinkers (which he had reportedly schooled well in at home), and being pulled up. A horse to avoid. (op 15-2)

5105 SWALLOW BOX STANDARD OPEN NATIONAL HUNT FLAT RACE 2m 110y

5:10 (5:12) (Class 5) 4-6-Y-O **£1,712** (£499; £249)

Form				RPR
	1		**Josh's Dreamway (IRE)** 5-10-11 0.......... NickScholfield (Jeremy Scott) *midfield: hdwy 6f out: wnt 2nd over 2f out: rdn and kpt on gamely to ld 100yds out: edgd clr* **50/1**	105+
34	**2**	*2*	**Karinga Dancer**[28] 4457 5-11-4 0..........(t) DarylJacob (Paul Nicholls) *led at fair pce: rdn over 2f out: hdd and nt qckn fnl 100yds* **3/1**[1]	111

	3	*7*	**Gumball** 6-11-4 0 ... DominicElsworth (Paul Webber) *pressed ldrs: 6th and outpcd 3f out: kpt on takingly to go 3rd ins fnl f: no ch w ldrs: promising* **25/1**	104
40	**4**	*2 ½*	**El Padrino (IRE)**[93] 3200 6-11-4 0 ... LeightonAspell (Nick Gifford) *pressed ldrs: 3rd and rdn wl over 2f out: nt qckn after: lost 3rd ins fnl f* **20/1**	102
	5	*2 ¼*	**The Goldmeister (IRE)** 4-10-12 0 ... TomScudamore (Ian Williams) *v keen to s: midfield: effrt 1/2-way: 5th and rdn and btn 3f out* **13/2**	94
2	**6**	*1 ¾*	**Getaway Driver (IRE)**[30] 4430 4-10-2 0 ... GeraldQuinn(10) (Charlie Longsdon) *mounted outside paddock and uns rdr: pressed ldr tl rdn and wknd over 2f out* **8/1**	92
2B5	**7**	*5*	**Traditional Bob (IRE)**[33] 4376 6-10-8 0 ... KillianMoore(10) (Graeme McPherson) *midfield: drvn 6f out: one pce and n.d after* **16/1**	94
	8	*10*	**Goonyella (IRE)** 4-10-9 0 ... SamTwiston-Davies(3) (Nigel Twiston-Davies) *sn drvn along and looked incredibly green: bhd: 13th 4f out: getting the hang of things fnl 2f and kpt on* **6/1**[3]	79
3	**9**	*3 ½*	**Kowloon (IRE)**[18] 4780 5-11-4 0 ... WayneHutchinson (Warren Greatrex) *towards rr: rdn 6f out: sn struggling* **9/2**[2]	82
043	**10**	*22*	**Twentyten (IRE)**[84] 3434 6-11-4 0 ... RichardJohnson (Paul Henderson) *sn rdn: prom tl stopped to nil 1/2-way: bdly t.o* **16/1**	62
45	**11**	*3*	**Cold Knight**[27] 4484 5-11-4 0 ... RobertThornton (Alan King) *cl up tl fdd tamely 7f out: bdly t.o* **14/1**	59
0	**12**	*15*	**Sussex Lass**[149] 2156 6-10-6 0 ... GemmaGracey-Davison(5) (Zoe Davison) *on her toes: plld hrd in rr: t.o fnl 6f* **200/1**	39
	13	*27*	**John's Oscar (IRE)** 4-10-12 0 ... MarkBradburne (Cecil Price) *bhd: rn wd and lost action after 6f: t.o after* **50/1**	15
00	**14**	*13*	**Sleeping Policeman (FR)**[28] 4457 5-11-4 0 ...(t) AndrewTinkler (Anna Bramall) *plld hrd in last but one: t.o fr 1/2-way* **100/1**	10
00	**P**		**Kala Patthar**[72] 3630 4-10-12 0 ... JoeTizzard (Colin Tizzard) *plld hrd in rr: prog 6f out: last of 8 w any ch over 4f out: lost pl qckly and eased 3f out: sn p.u* **12/1**	—
	U		**Rockbourne Rebel (IRE)** 5-10-11 0 ... TrevorWhelan(7) (Paul Henderson) *dumped rdr twice bef s: plld hrd in last: swvd rt and threw rdr off after 6f* **66/1**	—

3m 50.6s (0.20) **Going Correction** 0.0s/f (Good)
WFA 4 from 5yo+ 5lb **16** Ran SP% **123.5**
Speed ratings: **99,98,94,93,92 91,89,84,83,72 71,64,51,45,— —**
toteswingers:1&2 £55.70, 2&3 £32.00, 1&3 £233.30 CSF £195.50 TOTE £78.80: £18.00, £1.10, £12.00; EX 518.40.
Owner Ms Mary Miles **Bred** J P N Parker **Trained** Brompton Regis, Somerset

FOCUS
Something of a shock result for this fair bumper. A decent effort from the winner.

NOTEBOOK
Josh's Dreamway(IRE) got on top of the favourite in the closing stages to cause a shock. Her trainer Jeremy Scott (previously 0-10 in bumpers this season), had been amongst the winners recently and, having travelled nicely into contention, she picked up well close home when given a slap. She should stay further over hurdles.
Karinga Dancer was given a good ride from the front and had the rest well beaten off, but the winner proved too determined. (op 11-4 tchd 7-2)
Gumball, half-brother to a hurdles winner, caught the eye in a fast-finishing third. He ought to come on plenty and is the one to take from the race. (op 22-1 tchd 20-1)
El Padrino(IRE) took a step back in the right direction and should make his mark over hurdles. (op 16-1)
The Goldmeister(IRE) kept on dourly and looks a stayer in the making. (op 6-1 tchd 11-2)
Getaway Driver(IRE) finished weakly on this debut for the yard. (op 17-2 tchd 9-1)
Goonyella(IRE), a £55,000 son of Presenting, looked badly in need of the experience and kept on all too late. (op 10-1)
Kowloon(IRE), a promising third at the course on debut, being another to disappoint. He was never travelling and may have found the ground too lively. (op 6-1 tchd 4-1)
Kala Patthar Official explanation: jockey said gelding lost its action
T/Jkpt: Not won. T/Plt: £147.20 to a £1 stake. Pool of £86,075.22 - 426.79 winning tickets. T/Qpdt: £27.70 to a £1 stake. Pool of £6,705.01 - 178.92 winning tickets. IM

4964 CHEPSTOW (L-H)
Saturday, April 2

OFFICIAL GOING: Soft changing to good to soft (soft in places) after race 2 (2.15)
Wind: Virtually nil Weather: Sunny spells

5106 BRIDGEND DESIGNER OUTLET "NATIONAL HUNT" NOVICES' HURDLE (8 hdls) 2m 110y
2:15 (2:15) (Class 4) 4-Y-0+ **£2,341** (£687; £343; £171)

Form				RPR
-160	**1**		**Arthurian Legend**[70] 3691 6-11-6 123 ... TomO'Brien (Philip Hobbs) *hld up in rr: stdy hdwy appr 4 out: str run fr 2 out: drvn and qcknd run-in to ld nr fin* **16/1**	120+
5021	**2**	*¾*	**Bunclody**[46] 4132 6-11-6 118 ... JasonMaguire (Donald McCain) *led tl after 1st: styd pressing for ld tl slt advantage 2 out: rdn last: kpt on run-in: ct nr fin* **12/1**	119
1F04	**3**	*shd*	**High Benefit (IRE)**[29] 4454 6-10-13 106 ... RobertThornton (Alan King) *chsd ldrs: rdn and styd on fr 3 out: kpt on u.p and ev ch after last: nt qckn cl home* **20/1**	112
	4	*1*	**Priest Island (IRE)** 5-10-13 0 ... PaddyBrennan (Tom George) *mid-div: green and nt fluent: pushed along bef 4 out: j. slowly 3 out and next: stl green run-in kpt on encouragingly run-in: should improve* **66/1**	112+
3010	**5**	*nk*	**Bally Legend**[28] 4488 6-11-3 130 ... IanPopham(3) (Caroline Keevil) *chsd ldrs: rdn 2 out: disputing cl 2nd u.p last: kpt on same pce run-in* **11/2**[3]	118
5041	**6**	*3 ½*	**Street Dance (IRE)**[14] 4860 5-11-6 0 ... RhysFlint (Keith Goldsworthy) *chsd ldrs fr 4th: rdn 2 out: wknd run-in* **8/1**	114
	7	*2 ½*	**Twist Pistol (FR)**[69] 4-11-0 0 ... RWalsh (Paul Nicholls) *led after 1st: sn jnd but kpt slt advantage tl rdn and narrowly hdd 2 out: wknd bef last* **2/1**[1]	107
2321	**8**	*6*	**The Chazer (IRE)**[29] 4462 6-11-6 121 ... SamThomas (Richard Lee) *chsd ldrs: rdn bef 2 out: wknd next* **4/1**[2]	106
U314	**9**	*6*	**Grey Gold (IRE)**[44] 4159 6-11-6 127 ... JodieMogford (Richard Lee) *chsd ldrs to 3 out: wknd next* **9/1**	100
0601	**10**	*5*	**Cody Wyoming**[12] 4917 5-11-6 0 ... DominicElsworth (Heather Main) *chsd ldrs tl wknd 3 out* **40/1**	95
0-40	**11**	*8*	**Todareistodo**[14] 4881 5-10-13 0 ... MarkGrant (Jim Old) *hit 3 out: a bhd* **125/1**	80
6	**12**	*10*	**Grovemere (IRE)**[131] 2576 6-10-8 0 ... AodhaganConlon(5) (Debra Hamer) *a in rr* **100/1**	70
50	**13**	*11*	**Tickle Me (IRE)**[50] 4055 5-10-13 0 ... AndrewThornton (Henrietta Knight) *mid-div tl wknd and hit 4 out* **100/1**	59
S3	**14**	*9*	**Flyit Flora**[26] 4533 6-10-6 0 ... DenisO'Regan (Victor Dartnall) *hit 3rd: a in rr* **28/1**	43

4m 4.22s (-6.38) **Going Correction** -0.25s/f (Good)
WFA 4 from 5yo+ 5lb **14** Ran SP% **118.3**
Speed ratings (Par 105): **105,104,104,104,103 102,101,98,95,93 89,84,79,75**
toteswingers: 1&2 £33.20, 1&3 £56.50, 2&3 £27.70 CSF £181.01 TOTE £24.40: £4.70, £3.90, £5.00; EX 112.30.
Owner R T Kanter & A J Scrimgeour **Bred** Mrs L M Northover **Trained** Withycombe, Somerset

FOCUS
This proved most competitive, any number being in with a chance in the straight. The winner was the form pick but is rated below his best, with the time ordinary.

NOTEBOOK
Arthurian Legend, who had twice disappointed since winning over C&D in November, appreciated the return to a sounder surface and picked up best under pressure. He's likely to stay further and should make a chaser in time. Official explanation: trainer said, regarding apparent improvement in form, that the gelding settled better in the pre-race preliminaries. (op 22-1)
Bunclody posted improved form on this sounder surface under a penalty. He was always up there and looks another chasing type. (op 16-1)
High Benefit(IRE) has been a bit disappointing, so this effort will have pleased connections. She can probably pick up something small in the coming weeks.
Priest Island(IRE), a newcomer whose inexperience was evident, kept on takingly close home. He ought to improve plenty and looks a ready-made winner.
Bally Legend had his chance on this return to novice company. (op 6-1 tchd 13-2 and 5-1)
Twist Pistol(FR), ex-French, refused to settle early and was allowed to stride on. He was still in there fighting until two out, though, and can leave this form behind once settling better. (tchd 9-4)
The Chazer(IRE) had his chance and was below par under the penalty. (tchd 7-2)

5107 PIMM'S NOVICES' HURDLE (DIV I) (11 hdls) 2m 4f
2:45 (2:46) (Class 4) 4-Y-0+ **£2,016** (£592; £296; £147)

Form				RPR
23	**1**		**Rangitoto (IRE)**[28] 4489 6-11-0 0 ... RWalsh (Paul Nicholls) *chsd ldrs: reminder after 5th: rdn to chse ldr 2 out: led bef last rdn rt out* **5/2**[1]	117+
4U21	**2**	*2 ¾*	**Baile Anrai (IRE)**[23] 4665 7-11-6 120 ... RobertThornton (Ian Williams) *chsd ldrs: wnt 2nd and hit 4 out: rdn next: styng on same pce to chse wnr whn mstke last: no imp* **11/2**	122+
-223	**3**	*2 ½*	**Cresswell Crusader**[21] 4719 7-10-9 114 ... RachaelGreen(5) (Anthony Honeyball) *mde most tl rdn and hdd bef last: no ex run-in* **9/2**[3]	112
231	**4**	*8*	**Milo Milan (IRE)**[26] 4530 6-11-6 109 ... CharliePoste (Richard Lee) *chsd ldrs: no imp whn hit 3 out sn wknd: hit last* **16/1**	113
5	**5**	*16*	**Good Order**[29] 4459 6-11-0 0 ... PaddyBrennan (Tom George) *chsd ldrs: rdn after 4 out: sn wknd* **40/1**	90
1F	**6**	*8*	**Storming Gale (IRE)**[40] 4253 5-11-6 0 ... JasonMaguire (Donald McCain) *chsd ldrs: rdn 4 out: sn wknd* **4/1**[2]	89
-332	**7**	*3*	**Vincentian (IRE)**[34] 4376 6-11-0 0 ... DarylJacob (David Arbuthnot) *in rr: drvn along and sme prog 7th: sn dropped to rr: mod prog after 2 out* **14/1**	80
322/	**8**	*3 ¼*	**Ellerslie Ali (IRE)**[1126] 4240 9-10-7 0 ... SeanQuinlan (Kim Bailey) *in tch: rdn and btn whn hit 4 out* **50/1**	70
0	**9**	*2 ¼*	**Bob Lewis**[22] 4709 5-11-0 0 ... SamThomas (Chris Down) *t.k.h: hdwy after 7th: wknd 4 out* **50/1**	75
1-	**10**	*17*	**Manikon Eros (IRE)**[341] 20 6-11-0 0 ... APMcCoy (Rebecca Curtis) *w ldr: j.big 2nd: hit 2nd: j.big again at 3rd: 4th and 7th: wknd bef 4 out* **7/1**	60
0/-P	**11**	*63*	**Racing With Angels**[136] 2454 9-10-7 0 ... MrJMRidley(7) (Pam Ford) *j. slowly 6th: a wl bhd: t.o fr 7th* **200/1**	3
00-F	**P**		**Jays Cottage**[327] 249 8-11-0 0 ... RhysFlint (Jim Old) *a in rr: t.o whn p.u bef 4 out* **150/1**	—

4m 55.53s (-6.27) **Going Correction** -0.25s/f (Good)
WFA 4 from 5yo+ 6lb **12** Ran SP% **114.7**
Speed ratings (Par 105): **102,100,99,96,90 87,85,84,83,76 51,—**
toteswingers: 1&2 £1.90, 1&3 £2.80, 2&3 £5.50 CSF £15.92 TOTE £4.20: £1.50, £2.00, £1.80; EX 16.80.
Owner Charles Whittaker & P K Barber **Bred** Joe Doyle **Trained** Ditcheat, Somerset

FOCUS
The front three had this between them from quite a way out. Easy form to rate with the first three pretty much to their marks.

NOTEBOOK
Rangitoto(IRE) had twice run well since hurdling (former point winner), and coped well with the drop in trip, staying on strongest having gone to the front before the last. A fine, big type, he looks al over a chaser and could be a horse to keep on side. (op 9-4 tchd 11-4)
Baile Anrai(IRE) travelled well and had his chance, probably posting improved form under the penalty. He too looks a future chaser. (op 7-1 tchd 15-2 and 5-1)
Cresswell Crusader briefly looked to have them on the stretch, but was ultimately outstayed. He's proving consistent and should be reward before long. (op 5-1 tchd 4-1)
Milo Milan(IRE) found this a lot tougher than the lowly Newton Abbot handicap he won last time, but he did keep on and remains capable of better back down in grade. (tchd 14-1)
Good Order looks more of a long-term prospect.
Storming Gale(IRE) was disappointing and may have been feeling the affects of his last-time-out fall. Official explanation: jockey said, regarding running and riding, that his orders were to ride the gelding handily and give it every chance, it came off the bridle turning in and when it did not respond to a hit he felt it prudent to nurse it home. (op 9-2 tchd 7-2)
Manikon Eros(IRE) jumped big at his hurdles and finished well beaten. He had won a bumper, though, so probably deserves another chance. (op 8-1)

5108 PIMM'S NOVICES' HURDLE (DIV II) (11 hdls) 2m 4f
3:20 (3:21) (Class 4) 4-Y-0+ **£2,016** (£592; £296; £147)

Form				RPR
5241	**1**		**Super Directa (GER)**[31] 4424 7-11-6 120 ... DominicElsworth (Lucy Wadham) *mde all: stdd 5th: qcknd clr after 4 out: unchal* **4/5**[1]	123+
-346	**2**	*9*	**Thomas Wild**[21] 4719 6-11-0 0 ... RhysFlint (Philip Hobbs) *chsd ldrs: wnt 2nd and hit 3 out: kpt on but nvr any ch w wnr* **5/1**[2]	104
6F	**3**	*7*	**Ransson (FR)**[19] 4767 6-11-0 0 ... RobertThornton (Alan King) *in tch: hdwy 4 out: wnt 3rd fr 3 out: kpt on u.p but no ch w wnr and no imp on 2nd* **12/1**	95
10-4	**4**	*7*	**Deejan (IRE)**[10] 4944 6-10-0 0 ... MichaelByrne(7) (Tim Vaughan) *plld hrd: chsd wnr: hit 3rd: rdn 4 out: sn btn and lost 2nd next* **20/1**	84
650	**5**	*1*	**Carlos Gardel**[21] 4719 6-11-0 0 ... JasonMaguire (Mark Rimell) *in rr: drvn along and stl plenty to do fr 3 out: styd on wl to take 5th run-in and gng on cl home but nvr any ch* **66/1**	88

S415 **6** *10* **Hazy Dawn**[25] 4535 6-10-13 0 PaddyBrennan 78
(Michael Scudamore) *chsd ldrs to 4 out: wknd sn after* **14/1**

7 *20* **Ahwaak (USA)**[685] 7-11-0 0 FelixDeGiles 61
(Alastair Lidderdale) *in rr: hdwy after 7th: nvr on terms and wknd fr 4 out* **20/1**

8 *1 3/4* **Newlyn Bay**[20] 6-11-0 0 TomO'Brien 60
(Caroline Keevil) *chsd ldrs tl wknd and hit 4 out* **10/1**[3]

00 **9** *14* **Handford Henry (IRE)**[41] 4239 5-11-0 0 DavidEngland 47
(John Holt) *a in rr* **100/1**

06 **10** *4* **Waywood Princess**[31] 4423 6-10-7 0 SeanQuinlan 36
(John Bryan Groucott) *a in rr* **100/1**

224/ **11** *36* **Chesil Beach Boy**[712] 5123 8-11-0 0 DarylJacob 11
(John Coombe) *nt fluent: a in rr: t.o* **14/1**

454 **12** *13* **Brannoc (IRE)**[36] 4325 6-11-0 0 AndrewThornton —
(Tony Newcombe) *in tch: t.k.h: hit 5th: blnd and wknd 7th: t.o* **33/1**

0 **13** *52* **Private Patient (IRE)**[24] 4557 7-11-0 0 NickScholfield —
(Anna Newton-Smith) *hit 6th and 7th: a bhd: t.o* **100/1**

00 **P** **Harry Masters**[142] 2328 7-10-9 0 MattGriffiths(5) —
(Edward Bevan) *plld hrd: hit 2nd and 3rd: wknd rapidly 5th: t.o whn p.u bef next* **100/1**

4m 56.37s (-5.43) **Going Correction** -0.25s/f (Good) **14 Ran SP% 120.3**
Speed ratings (Par 105): **100,96,93,90,90 86,78,77,72,70 56,50,30,—**
toteswingers: 1&2 £1.10, 1&3 £5.40, 2&3 £36.00 CSF £4.46 TOTE £1.70: £1.10, £2.00, £2.00; EX 5.20.

Owner Richard S Keeley **Bred** Mrs I Bodewein **Trained** Newmarket, Suffolk

FOCUS
The weaker of the two divisions. the easy winner stood out and was value for further.

NOTEBOOK
Super Directa(GER), penalised for his last-time-out Folkestone success, readily drew clear down the straight and never looked in any danger. He's clearly progressing and could be of interest if tried in handicap company in the coming weeks. (op Evens tchd 11-10)

Thomas Wild stayed on without troubling the winner and should do better in handicaps. (op 4-1)

Ransson(FR), a faller on his hurdles debut, kept on late and this will have done plenty to restore confidence. He can improve on this.

Deejan(IRE) didn't fare badly considering how hard she pulled. (op 25-1)

Carlos Gardel kept on in eyecatching fashion on this second start over hurdles. He's sure to be of interest once sent handicapping when qualified.

Harry Masters Official explanation: trainer said gelding pulled up distressed

5109 JOHN IVOR ROGERS H'CAP CHASE (18 fncs) 3m
3:50 (3:52) (Class 5) (0-95,95) 5-Y-O+ **£2,439** (£716; £358; £178)

Form RPR

2005 **1** **Our Columbus (IRE)**[21] 4718 7-11-6 89 PaddyBrennan 103+
(Nigel Twiston-Davies) *chsd ldrs: blnd 9th: drvn along sn after and u.p fr 13th: chsd ldr but 5 l down fr 2 out and stl 4 l down at last: rallied u.str driving to ld cl home* **9/1**

4300 **2** *1/2* **Billy Murphy**[28] 4483 8-11-0 83 SamThomas 96
(Paul Cowley) *pressed ldr led: 4th: hdd after 7th: styd upsides: led again 8th: hdd 13th: chal next: led after 4 out: drvn 5 l clr 2 out: stl 4 l ahd last: wknd u.p fnl 50yds: hdd cl home* **12/1**

6344 **3** *8* **The Humbel Monk (IRE)**[14] 4865 9-11-1 84 JasonMaguire 91
(Lucy Jones) *led to 4th: styd pressing ldr: led after 7th: hdd 9th: styd chalng: led 13th: jnd 14th: hdd sn after 4 out: lost 2nd and btn 2 out* **22/1**

15-5 **4** *nk* **Quiet Bob (IRE)**[32] 4409 8-11-1 84 TomO'Brien 90
(Philip Hobbs) *in tch: pushed along and hdwy 14th: sn rdn: styd on same pce fr 3 out* **8/1**

P231 **5** *1 1/2* **Quazy De Joie (FR)**[21] 4718 7-11-11 94 (tp) APMcCoy 102+
(Jonjo O'Neill) *chsd ldrs: hit 8th: in tch whn blnd 4 out: no ch after and styd on one pce* **9/4**[1]

12P0 **6** *11* **Loco Grande (IRE)**[21] 4722 6-11-9 92 (p) AidanColeman 86
(Tim Vaughan) *in tch: chsd ldrs 13th: wknd 14th* **14/1**

62UP **7** *7* **Miss Fleur**[24] 4558 8-10-13 89 SClements(7) 77
(Nick Mitchell) *chsd ldrs tl rdn and wknd 14th* **16/1**

-113 **8** *2* **Clifden Boy (IRE)**[262] 987 9-11-12 95 NickScholfield 81
(Ron Hodges) *chsd ldrs to 13th: wknd bef next* **16/1**

2P06 **9** *25* **Oranger (FR)**[53] 3990 9-11-4 94 (p) MrAndrewMartin(7) 58
(Andrew J Martin) *a in rr* **25/1**

045P **U** **Top Tide (IRE)**[28] 10-11-2 90 (t) MattGriffiths(5) —
(Martin Hill) *hit 3rd: in rr tl blnd and uns rdr 9th* **50/1**

04/P **P** **Elton**[118] 2796 8-11-7 95 GilesHawkins(5) —
(Philip Hobbs) *hit 4th: in rr and rdn 8th: t.o 10th: p.u bef 12th* **25/1**

3400 **P** **Ballymorn (IRE)**[45] 4144 7-10-13 82 AndrewThornton —
(Henrietta Knight) *chsd ldrs to 8th: wknd 11th: t.o whn p.u bef 14th* **28/1**

P005 **P** **Just Unique**[13] 4890 7-10-8 77 (t) DarylJacob —
(Mark Rimell) *hit 2nd: sn bhd: t.o whn p.u bef 14th* **7/1**[2]

-045 **P** **Witch's Hat (IRE)**[88] 3391 8-11-9 92 (t) RhysFlint —
(Jim Old) *a in rr: t.o whn p.u bef 14th* **15/2**[3]

6m 13.91s (-8.09) **Going Correction** -0.20s/f (Good) **14 Ran SP% 119.7**
Speed ratings: **105,104,102,102,101 97,95,94,86,— —,—,—,—**
toteswingers: 1&2 £27.20, 1&3 £29.60, 2&3 £55.20 CSF £102.70 CT £2308.95 TOTE £14.30: £4.50, £3.20, £9.20; EX 145.50.

Owner Celia & Michael Baker **Bred** Cecil Ashe **Trained** Naunton, Gloucs

■ Stewards' Enquiry : Paddy Brennan four-day ban: used whip with excessive frequency (Apr 16-19)

FOCUS
Quite a competitive but low-grade handicap chase. The form is solid enough.

NOTEBOOK
Our Columbus(IRE), not out of it when making a race-ending blunder at the course last time, made no notable errors this time and stayed on strongly under a good ride from Paddy Brennan to get up close home. Having only his third start over fences, the 7-y-o clearly stays well and remains capable of better. (op 8-1)

Billy Murphy prospered under a positive ride and looked almost certain to lose his maiden tag when ridden into a clear lead. However, despite still holding a nice advantage at the last, he began to look vulnerable on the long run-in and was cruelly denied. He deserves to go one better. (op 14-1)

The Humbel Monk(IRE) disputed it with the runner-up throughout, but wasn't able to maintain the gallop in the straight. (tchd 25-1)

Quiet Bob(IRE) won over 3m5f at Warwick last season and this was always likely to prove inadequate, but he still stepped up on his last-time-out Ffos Las effort.

Quazy De Joie(FR), up 3lb for his recent course success, made a couple of mistakes in the first-time cheekpieces and was well held. (op 11-4)

Elton Official explanation: trainer said gelding pulled up distressed

Ballymorn(IRE) Official explanation: trainer said gelding pulled up distressed

5110 PLAY MECCA BINGO ON YOUR IPHONE H'CAP HURDLE (11 hdls) 2m 4f
4:25 (4:25) (Class 3) (0-135,132) 4-Y-O+ **£3,642** (£1,069; £534; £267)

Form RPR

3533 **1** **Roalco De Farges (FR)**[25] 4536 6-10-6 112 TomO'Brien 123+
(Philip Hobbs) *trckd ldrs: chal 4th: led next: c clr fr 3 out: easily* **7/1**[3]

0044 **2** *6* **William Hogarth**[7] 5003 6-11-2 122 RhysFlint 127
(Keith Goldsworthy) *hit 3rd: disp ld to 4th: chsd wnr fr 5th: no ch whn nt fluent 3 out but kpt on for clr 2nd* **13/2**[2]

0612 **3** *6* **Black Phantom (IRE)**[14] 4862 5-10-13 119 NickScholfield 119
(Andy Turnell) *in tch: hdwy fr 6th: drvn to chse ldrs 4 out but nvr on terms and no ch fr next but kpt on to take one pce 3rd fr 3 out* **8/1**

133 **4** *9* **On Trend (IRE)**[84] 3448 5-11-3 123 LiamTreadwell 115
(Nick Gifford) *led: jnd 4th: hdd next: styd chsng ldrs to 4 out: wknd after next and no ch whn blnd 2 out* **9/1**

310- **5** *16* **Makhzoon (USA)**[456] 3216 7-10-6 112 AidanColeman 88
(Tim Vaughan) *chsd ldrs: lost pl and in rr 7th: plenty to do 4 out: mod prog again after 2 out* **66/1**

113- **6** *2 1/4* **Natural Action**[481] 2751 7-10-10 119 (p) DonalDevereux(3) 93
(Peter Bowen) *chsd ldrs: hit 6th: wknd 4 out* **22/1**

1/2F **7** *6* **Phardessa**[44] 4167 10-10-11 117 SeanQuinlan 86
(Richard Phillips) *hld up in rr: smooth hdwy after 7th: wknd qckly 4 out* **20/1**

1P **8** *7* **Maxdelas (FR)**[77] 3567 5-11-0 120 PaddyBrennan 84
(Nigel Twiston-Davies) *t.k.h: chsd ldrs: hit 1st: drvn to go 3rd 4 out: wknd and blnd 2 out* **10/1**

3425 **9** *2* **Balzaccio (FR)**[49] 4077 6-11-9 129 RobertThornton 90
(Alan King) *in tch: rdn and wknd 4 out* **20/1**

2P0P **10** *4 1/2* **Awesome George**[28] 4470 7-11-9 132 CharlieHuxley(3) 89
(Alan King) *nvr beyond mid-div: wknd 4 out* **40/1**

22-F **11** *3/4* **R De Rien Sivola (FR)**[62] 3841 6-11-1 121 (t) RWalsh 77
(Paul Nicholls) *bhd fr 1/2-way* **8/1**

5201 **12** *11* **Aviador (GER)**[36] 4327 5-10-10 116 LeightonAspell 62
(Lucy Wadham) *mid-div: wknd bef 4 out* **10/1**

0034 **13** *2* **That'lldoboy (FR)**[51] 4034 5-9-7 109 JamesCowley(10) 53
(Paul Nicholls) *in tch 5th: rdn and wknd after 7th: wl bhd whn blnd last and rdr lost irons* **5/1**[1]

0-F0 **14** *16* **Maucaillou (GER)**[113] 2868 8-11-0 120 WarrenMarston 50
(Martin Keighley) *stdd: t.k.h: a bhd* **14/1**

2410 **P** **Daring Origyn (FR)**[28] 4485 6-10-8 121 (t) JakeGreenall(7) —
(Richard Lee) *rdn and in rr fr 5th: t.o whn p.u after 4 out* **28/1**

4m 48.04s (-13.76) **Going Correction** -0.25s/f (Good) **15 Ran SP% 120.8**
Speed ratings (Par 107): **117,114,112,108,102 101,98,96,95,93 93,88,88,81,—**
toteswingers: 1&2 £10.00, 1&3 £10.50, 2&3 £13.20 CSF £47.80 CT £380.01 TOTE £10.30: £2.70, £3.10, £1.90; EX 65.80.

Owner The Brushmakers **Bred** Regine Bollet **Trained** Withycombe, Somerset

FOCUS
Few got into this, the front pair having it between them from a long way out. The time was relatively good and the winner produced a step up.

NOTEBOOK
Roalco De Farges(FR) pressed on a long way from the finish and galloped on relentlessly. Although disappointing on his handicap debut at Exeter, he looked particularly interesting on his earlier third here and the way he did it suggests he'll get 3m in time. He can expect a hefty rise for this success and it will be interesting to see how he copes (op 17-2)

William Hogarth was never far away and looked a danger turning for home, but the winner was relentless and he always looked booked for second. (op 8-1)

Black Phantom(IRE), 34lb higher than when winning here earlier in the season, ran another reasonable race, keeping on, and gives the impression he can still win off this sort of mark.

On Trend(IRE) was unable to race on in the straight, but it's still early days for him. (op 12-1)

Makhzoon(USA) made notable late headway having got well behind on this return from 456 days off. He's entitled to come on plenty and will be of obvious interest next time. (op 50-1)

R De Rien Sivola(FR) was struggling from an early stage and may have had her confidence dented by a last-time-out fall over fences.

That'lldoboy(FR) was disappointing, finding nothing for pressure and fading tamely. He had shaped well on his handicap debut at Taunton and it's safe to assume this wasn't his true form. (tchd 9-2)

5111 BRIDGEND DESIGNER OUTLET FASHION H'CAP HURDLE (11 hdls) 2m 4f
5:00 (5:00) (Class 5) (0-95,95) 4-Y-O+ **£2,172** (£637; £318; £159)

Form RPR

0411 **1** **E Street Boy**[3] 5075 5-11-7 95 7ex CO'Farrell(5) 108+
(David Pipe) *hld up in rr: smooth hdwy 4 out to ld 3 out: sn clr: easily* **4/6**[1]

P000 **2** *4 1/2* **Big Knickers**[58] 3904 6-11-10 93 PaddyBrennan 94
(Neil Mulholland) *in tch: chsd ldrs 5th: rdn fr 4 out: styd on u.p in 3rd fr 3 out: kpt on to take 2nd fnl 50yds but nvr any ch w easy wnr* **7/1**[2]

1230 **3** *3/4* **Jeanry (FR)**[20] 4751 8-11-4 94 CDTimmons(7) 94
(Arthur Whitehead) *in tch: chsd ldrs 5th: rdn to ld 4 out: hdd next: styd chsng wnr but nvr any ch: lost 2nd fnl 50yds* **12/1**

6-P0 **4** *10* **King Kasyapa (IRE)**[21] 4724 9-10-8 80 DonalDevereux(3) 71
(Peter Bowen) *hit 4th: in rr: hdwy appr 4 out: nvr rchd ldrs no ch fr 3 out* **50/1**

0613 **5** *6* **Lightening Fire (IRE)**[9] 4965 9-10-10 84 (p) MarkQuinlan(5) 72
(Bernard Llewellyn) *led tl after 1st: styd w ldr: led again 4th: jnd 6th: hdd after next: rdn and ev ch 4 out: sn wknd: blnd 2 out* **20/1**

2P23 **6** *7* **Bob Casey (IRE)**[14] 4865 9-11-3 86 DenisO'Regan 65
(Keith Goldsworthy) *chsd ldrs: wnt 2nd 5th: chal fr next tl led after 7th: hdd 4 out: wknd sn after* **14/1**

0/00 **P** **Silent Jo (JPN)**[27] 4503 9-11-7 95 AnthonyFreeman(5) —
(Jonjo O'Neill) *hit 1st: a bhd: t.o whn p.u bef 2 out* **33/1**

PP01 **P** **Speedy Directa (GER)**[3] 5072 8-10-12 81 7ex (vt) WarrenMarston —
(Milton Harris) *plld hrd: chsd ldrs to 7th: t.o whn p.u bef 2 out* **9/1**[3]

-556 **P** **Immense (IRE)**[91] 3300 7-11-6 89 (vt) JasonMaguire —
(Ian Williams) *chsd ldrs and hit 3rd: wknd rapidly 5th: t.o next: p.u bef 4 out* **20/1**

0501 **P** **Gainsborough's Art (IRE)**[10] 4949 6-10-4 80 KillianMoore(7) —
(Harry Chisman) *hld up in rr: hdwy 5th: hit 7th: sn wknd: t.o whn p.u bef 3 out* **25/1**

030P **P** **Attainable**[51] 4032 5-11-6 89 (t) RhysFlint —
(Jim Old) *chsd ldrs tl wknd rapidly bef 5th: t.o and p.u bef next* **66/1**

04P2 **P** **Crackerjac Boy (USA)**[21] 4721 6-11-5 **95**.................(b) PeterCarberry(7) —
(Richard Phillips) *led after 1st: hdd 4th: wknd rapidly bef 4 out: t.o whn p.u bef 2 out* **25/1**

4m 56.86s (-4.94) **Going Correction** -0.25s/f (Good) 12 Ran SP% **120.5**
Speed ratings (Par 103): **99,97,96,92,90 87,—,—,—,— —,—**
toteswingers: 1&2 £1.20, 1&3 £2.90, 2&3 £16.30 CSF £5.53 CT £34.64 TOTE £1.90: £1.10, £1.60, £3.80; EX 11.30.
Owner Roger Stanley & Yvonne Reynolds **Bred** Kelanne Stud Ltd **Trained** Nicholashayne, Devon

FOCUS
An ordinary handicap hurdle. The easy winner is rated in line with his Wincanton victory.

NOTEBOOK
E Street Boy had no trouble registering his third win in the space of seven days, jumping quickly and cruising clear. He's improved markedly since going up to 2m4f and more, and holds numerous entries next week, so far all that things are going to get tougher, there's every chance he can complete a four-timer. The handicapper will have his say soon, however. (op 4-5 tchd 5-6 and Evens in places)
Big Knickers stayed on well to take second, and clearly benefited from the switch to handicap-company, although was flattered to finish so close to the winner.
Jeanry(FR) bounced back from a below-par run at Warwick last time, this run being more in keeping with his earlier efforts. (op 14-1)
King Kasyapa(IRE) ran easily his best race since returning from a lengthy absence and is well weighted on old form.
Lightening Fire(IRE) slowly faded having made a lot of the running. (tchd 22-1)

5112 FESTIVAL RACING ON THE RAILS H'CAP CHASE (12 fncs) 2m 110y
5:30 (5:31) (Class 4) (0-115,116) 5-Y-0+ **£2,602** (£764; £382; £190)

Form RPR

3111 **1** **Rileyev (FR)**[11] 4934 6-11-11 **114**....................................... AidanColeman 128+
(Venetia Williams) *led bnd after 1st: hdd next: styd trcking ldrs: qcknd to chal and mstke 8th: led bef 4 out: hrd drvn run-in and styd on wl* **7/2**[2]

3021 **2** *3 ¼* **Quipe Me Posted (FR)**[7] 5011 7-11-6 **116**.................... MrTJCannon(7) 124
(Suzy Smith) *chsd ldrs fr 3rd: chal 5th: led 6th: jnd and hit 8th: hdd bef 4 out: hit next: rallied u.p fr 2 out: kpt on run-in but a wl hld* **7/4**[1]

0643 **3** *6* **Amble Forge (IRE)**[9] 4967 9-10-12 **101**................................. JoeTizzard 104
(Colin Tizzard) *w ldrs: led 2nd: jnd 5th: hdd next: disp 2nd 7th: one pce fr 4 out: hit next and no imp fr 2 out* **13/2**

P053 **4** *6* **Our Bob (IRE)**[10] 4938 9-11-9 **112**......................................(t) TomO'Brien 112
(Philip Hobbs) *led tl rn wd and hdd bnd after 1st: styd chsng ldrs tl wknd after 4 out* **8/1**

3P54 **5** *34* **Smack That (IRE)**[14] 4873 9-11-12 **115**...........................(vt) DaveCrosse 94
(Milton Harris) *blnd 2nd: a towards rr: no ch fr 8th* **16/1**

2-PF **P** **Beherayn**[175] 1766 8-11-4 **114**... SClements(7) —
(Carroll Gray) *a in rr: t.o whn p.u bef 3 out* **28/1**

423 **P** **Rimini (FR)**[14] 4863 6-11-11 **114**.. PaddyBrennan —
(David Rees) *j. slowly and bhd 3rd: j. slowly 5th and in tch: chsd ldrs 7th: wknd rapidly and p.u bef 8th* **9/2**[3]

4m 11.38s (-5.72) **Going Correction** -0.20s/f (Good) 7 Ran SP% **110.5**
Speed ratings: **105,103,100,97,81 —,—**
toteswingers: 1&2 £1.40, 1&3 £3.50, 2&3 £2.20 CSF £9.83 TOTE £4.20: £1.90, £1.80; EX 5.10.
Owner John Mayne **Bred** Mme Laurence Barreaud & Claude Barreaud **Trained** Kings Caple, H'fords

FOCUS
Another thoroughly likeable effort from the rapidly progressive Rileyev, to beat the in-form runer-up who ran to his mark.

NOTEBOOK
Rileyev(FR) made it five wins in his last six with a gutsy effort. Although 25lb higher than when his winning run began in February, he appears to be thriving on racing, and just as had been the case at Kempton the time before, he kept pulling out extra once in front, going again having made a bit of a mess of the last. The form looks good and who's to say he won't go in again. (op 11-4)
Quipe Me Posted(FR), 11lb higher than when winning at Newbury, was never far away and had every chance to get past the winner, but was unable to do so. He'll probably be bumped up a couple of pounds for this. (op 15-8 tchd 13-8)
Amble Forge(IRE) ran a better race, losing no further ground on the front two over the last few fences. (op 11-2 tchd 7-1)
Our Bob(IRE) didn't jump as well as he had done at Haydock the time before and again looked in need of a stiffer test. (tchd 9-1)

5113 BRIDGEND DESIGNER OUTLET STANDARD OPEN NATIONAL HUNT FLAT RACE 2m 110y
6:05 (6:05) (Class 6) 4-6-Y-0 **£1,821** (£534; £267; £133)

Form RPR

4 **1** **Theatre Guide (IRE)**[49] 4082 4-10-12 0................................ JoeTizzard 114+
(Colin Tizzard) *hld up in tch: stdy hdwy fr 7f out: str chal fr over 3f out tl def advantage ins fnl f: styd on strly* **6/1**[3]

34 **2** *2* **Magnifique Etoile**[28] 4468 4-10-2 0.......................... GeraldQuinn(10) 113
(Charlie Longsdon) *in rr tl stdy hdwy fr 7f out: shkn up and styd on fnl 2f: drvn to take 2nd cl home but no imp on wnr* **22/1**

3 *nk* **Grove Pride**[139] 2410 6-11-4 0................................. AndrewTinkler 118
(Henry Daly) *chsd ldrs: chal 4f out: slt ld wl over 3f out but sn jnd by wnr: narrowly hdd ins fnl f: no ex and lost 2nd cl home* **6/1**[3]

41 **4** *5* **Themilanhorse (IRE)**[26] 4533 5-10-8 0........................ JamesCowley(10) 114
(Paul Nicholls) *chsd ldrs: drvn to chal 4 out: wknd ins fnl 2f* **7/2**[2]

2 **5** *5* **Global Fella (IRE)**[28] 4491 6-11-4 0.. APMcCoy 111
(Nicky Henderson) *chsd ldrs: drvn to take slt ld over 4f out: hdd and btn wl over 2f out* **11/5**[1]

02 **6** *7* **Slightly Hot**[14] 4879 5-11-4 0.. DaveCrosse 103
(Joanna Davis) *chsd ldrs: rdn over 4f out: wknd fr 3f out* **14/1**

2 **7** *7* **Great Gusto (IRE)**[48] 4097 5-11-4 0................................. DenisO'Regan 97
(Victor Dartnall) *led 2f: styd chsng ldrs: rdn 6f out: no ch fnl 4f* **12/1**

2 **8** *7* **I Know The Code (IRE)**[164] 1927 6-11-4 0.......................... TomSiddall 90
(Noel Chance) *plld hrd: bhd most of way* **25/1**

9 *¾* **Marshal Zhukov (IRE)**[84] 5-11-4 0................................ TomO'Brien 90
(Caroline Keevil) *racd wd bnd after 2f: led after 4f: hdd over 4f out: sn wknd* **14/1**

4 **10** *3 ¼* **Canopy Of Stars**[32] 4410 5-11-4 0.................................. PaddyBrennan 87
(Tom George) *led after 2f: hdd after 4f: wknd fr 4f out* **40/1**

2 **11** *36* **Noble Perk**[84] 3441 6-11-4 0... JodieMogford 54
(Adrian Wintle) *a in rr: t.o* **33/1**

3P **12** *50* **Gizzit (IRE)**[14] 4879 5-11-4 0....................................... AndrewThornton 9
(Karen George) *a in rr: t.o* **66/1**

4m 2.52s (-2.48) **Going Correction** -0.25s/f (Good) 12 Ran SP% **118.1**
Speed ratings: **95,94,93,91,89 85,82,79,78,77 60,36**
toteswingers: 1&2 £23.80, 1&3 £21.70, 2&3 £40.00 CSF £136.03 TOTE £6.90: £2.10, £5.80, £2.50; EX 135.10.
Owner Mrs Jean R Bishop **Bred** Kenilworth House Stud **Trained** Milborne Port, Dorset

FOCUS
Probably a decent bumper, all the field having made the frame previously. Steps up from the first three with the next four all rated to their marks.

NOTEBOOK
Theatre Guide(IRE) ◆, who shaped with an abundance of promise on his Warwick debut over 1m6f, built on that here. As was the case on debut, he travelled well into the straight and then ran green when first put under pressure, in fact he was all over the place here, hanging both ways and carrying his head awkwardly. Despite this, he kept finding, and stayed on strongly close home under hands and heels riding. In the same ownership and by the same sire as stable star Cue Card, he looks a very bright prospect with next season in mind and is most definitely a horse to keep on side. (op 15-2 tchd 8-1)
Magnifique Etoile, another 4-y-o, was last off the bridle but unable to quicken when coming under pressure and, for all that he stayed on right the way to the line, never really looked like winning. Improving all the time, he can win one of these before going hurdling, when he's likely to need further. (op 18-1)
Grove Pride, bought for £25,000 after finishing second in a Cork bumper on debut, edged on with over 3f to run and held every chance, but couldn't quicken late on and was just denied second. This was a promising effort and he looks a nice type for hurdles. (op 7-1 tchd 8-1)
Themilanhorse(IRE) found this a lot tougher than the Newton Abbot bumper he won, but it was still a fair effort under a penalty. (op 4-1 tchd 9-2)
Global Fella(IRE) was undoubtedly disappointing, having shaped with such promise on his debut at Newbury. Considering he looked green that day it was surprising he didn't build on it, but it would be folly to write him off and he should do much better hurdling next season. (op 15-8 tchd 13-8)
T/Plt: £937.20 to a £1 stake. Pool: £87,147.44. 67.88 winning tickets. T/Qpdt: £41.70 to a £1 stake. Pool: £6,921.79. 122.80 winning tickets. ST

4874 UTTOXETER (L-H)
Saturday, April 2

OFFICIAL GOING: Good (good to firm in places; chs 6.4, hdl 6.9)
Hurdles moved 6m off inside rail to fresh ground. Divided bends. Hurdle in the back straight was omitted on all circuits.
Wind: fresh, against Weather: bright and breezy

5114 BETFAIR RACING EXCELLENCE CONDITIONAL JOCKEYS' TRAINING SERIES H'CAP HURDLE (9 hdls 1 omitted) 2m
2:25 (2:25) (Class 5) (0-90,90) 4-Y-0+ **£2,172** (£637; £318; £159)

Form RPR

2000 **1** **Charles**[58] 3906 5-11-4 **90**..(p) EdCookson(8) 93+
(Kim Bailey) *chsd ldrs: ev ch after 3 out: pushed lft after 2 out: sn rdn to ld: mstke last: racing idly but a doing enough flat: rdn out* **15/2**

0053 **2** *1 ½* **Miss Champagne (IRE)**[33] 4395 8-9-11 **64**............... RobertMcCarth(3) 65
(Andrew Wilson) *t.k.h: chsd ldrs tl lost pl 4th: in tch in last trio next: n.m.r on inner bef 3 out: hdwy to chse ldrs 2 out: cl 3rd and mstke last: kpt on same pce flat: wnt 2nd nr fin* **4/1**[2]

4460 **3** *nse* **Daraybad (FR)**[24] 4548 9-10-0 **69**................................(v) TonyKelly(5) 70
(Andrew Crook) *hld up wl in tch towards rr: rdn and gd hdwy to ld 2 out: edgd lft and hdd between last 2: nt qckn u.p flat: lost 2nd nr fin* **14/1**

0060 **4** *¾* **Echo Dancer**[33] 3839 5-10-10 **82**..(t) JoshWall(8) 82
(Trevor Wall) *hld up wl in tch in rr: hdwy to chse ldrs 2 out: drvn between last 2: styd on same pce flat* **12/1**

4505 **5** *nse* **Secret Desert**[74] 3622 5-10-10 **82**............................. EdmondLinehan(8) 82
(Ferdy Murphy) *t.k.h: hld up wl in tch towards rr: hdwy 3 out: chsd ldrs next: n.m.r between last 2: cl 4th last: pushed along and kpt on same pce flat: b.b.v* **11/2**[3]

/0-0 **6** *12* **Top Achiever (IRE)**[307] 541 10-11-7 **90**........................(p) PeterHatton(5) 79
(Bill Moore) *chsd ldr tl led after 5th: rdn and hdd 2 out: wkng whn mstke last* **25/1**

4P44 **7** *1 ¼* **Youandme (IRE)**[131] 2588 9-10-1 **70**.............................(p) ChrisDavies(5) 59
(Ray Peacock) *led tl after 5th: sn rdn along: wknd 2 out* **16/1**

0556 **8** *1* **Stanley Bridge**[9] 4958 4-10-8 **83**................................. CallumWhillans(5) 64
(Barry Murtagh) *t.k.h: hld up in tch: hdwy bef 3 out: chsd ldrs and rdn bef 2 out: wknd between last 2: mstke last* **16/1**

P05- **9** *10* **Confide In Me**[38] 5285 7-11-1 **82**..........................(bt) JeremiahMcGrath(3) 60
(Jim Best) *chsd ldrs: mstke 1st and 4th: drvn and struggling after 6th: wknd bef 2 out* **8/1**

0002 **10** *4* **Tiger Dream**[10] 4947 6-11-6 **90**....................................(bt) DannyBurton(6) 79+
(Chris Down) *in tch: rdn and lost pl bef 3 out: last whn blnd and rdr lost irons 3 out: sn lost tch* **10/3**[1]

3m 53.7s (-1.50) **Going Correction** -0.25s/f (Good)
WFA 4 from 5yo+ 5lb 10 Ran SP% **111.3**
Speed ratings (Par 103): **93,92,92,91,91 85,85,84,79,77**
toteswingers:1&2 £6.80, 2&3 £12.30, 1&3 £19.50 CSF £36.40 CT £399.32 TOTE £7.20: £2.60, £1.20, £4.30; EX 39.20.
Owner T Rowe **Bred** T E Pocock **Trained** Andoversford, Gloucs

FOCUS
An open handicap, confined to conditional riders. Ordinary low-grade form, the first four rated to their marks.

NOTEBOOK
Charles, in first-time cheekpieces, came in for support earlier in the day on this handicap debut after a 58-day break and got off the mark at the fifth time of asking. He was suited by racing handily and showed a likeable attitude under pressure. It was a much-improved effort, but this was the first occasion he had met quick ground since finishing runner-up on his debut last October. Official explanation: trainer's rep said, regarding apparent improvement in form, that the gelding had appeared to benefit from the fast ground and first-time cheek pieces. (op 5-1)
Miss Champagne(IRE), 5lb lower, posted another improved effort in defeat and helps to set the level. Her turn isn't looking that far off. (tchd 9-2)
Daraybad(FR) had been beaten a long way in a seller last time, but that was his return from a break and he clearly improved here. Whether he will build on it is anyone's guess, however.
Echo Dancer, whose sole success was in a Fibresand maiden in 2009, posted his best effort yet as a hurdler on this return from the AW. The recent addition of a tongue-tie looks to have helped. (tchd 10-1)
Secret Desert closed to have every chance from two out, but rather flattened out under pressure and may need more positive handling on this ground. Official explanation: trainer's rep said gelding bled from the nose (op 8-1)

Tiger Dream was already beaten when his rider lost his iron three out. Official explanation: jockey said gelding resented coming under pressure (op 7-2)

5115 JENKINSONS CATERERS FIRST CHOICE FOR WEDDINGS MAIDEN HURDLE (10 hdls 2 omitted) 2m 4f 110y

3:00 (3:00) (Class 5) 4-Y-0+ **£2,211** (£649; £324; £162)

Form RPR

1 **Dancing Dude (IRE)**274 4-10-9 0 AndrewTinkler 115+
(Nicky Henderson) *chsd ldr tl 2nd: wnt 2nd again after 5th and clr w runner-up fr next: ev ch 2 out: led: wnt lft and mstke last: racd awkwardly flat: kpt on: pushed out* **8/1**

6F3 **2** 3 1/4 **Croan Rock (IRE)**11 [4930] 6-11-2 115 TomScudamore 117
(Ian Williams) *led tl 3rd: chsd ldr tl led again after 5th: clr w wnr fr next: rdn 3 out: hdd and sltly impeded last: kpt on same pce flat* **3/1**3

5233 **3** 14 **Robin De Creuse (FR)**27 [4499] 5-11-2 116 RichardJohnson 105
(Philip Hobbs) *racd wl off the pce in midfield: clsd and in tch 5th: outpcd by ldrs again next: wnt modest 3rd 7th: rdn and hit 3 out: no imp after* **85/40**1

60 **4** 4 **Gearbox (IRE)**23 [4676] 5-10-11 0 (t) MissLHorner(5) 102
(Liam Corcoran) *hld up wl off the pce in last trio: stdy hdwy after 7th: modest 5th after next: wnt 4th and mstke last: nvr trbld ldrs* **50/1**

0 **5** 1 1/4 **Wise Move (IRE)**70 [3678] 5-10-13 0 RichardKilloran(3) 103
(Nicky Henderson) *nt fluent 1st: chsd ldng pair tl 2nd: chsd ldng pair again after 5th: outpcd by ldng pair next: rdn and no hdwy bef 3 out: 6th and wl btn whn blnd 3 out* **5/2**2

4U33 **6** 24 **Four Strong Winds (IRE)**65 [3765] 7-11-2 0 RichieMcLernon 78
(Jonjo O'Neill) *t.k.h: hld up wl bhd in rr: hdwy into 4th but stl plenty to do bef 7th: no prog and btn whn mstke 3 out: wknd next: eased flat: t.o* **10/1**

00 **7** 17 **Thank The Groom**35 [4356] 5-11-2 0 HaddenFrost 63
(Martin Bosley) *t.k.h: hld up off the pce in midfield: mstke 3rd: clsd and in tch 5th: struggling next: t.o bef 3 out* **200/1**

3-66 **8** 9 **Yukon Quest (IRE)**50 [4051] 6-11-2 0 WayneHutchinson 55
(Alan King) *t.k.h: racd wl off the pce in midfield: struggling and outpcd by ldrs 6th: wl bhd after next: t.o 3 out* **16/1**

60 **9** 3/4 **Cool Steel (IRE)**56 [3957] 5-11-2 0 JimmyMcCarthy 54
(Alan King) *racd off the pce in midfield: blnd 2nd: clsd and in tch 5th: outpcd by ldrs in 4th next: wknd qckly after 7th: t.o 3 out* **40/1**

10 3/4 **Mojeerr**16 5-11-2 0 LiamHeard 53
(Laura Young) *t.k.h: hld up off the pce towards rr: hdwy and in tch in midfield 5th: outpcd next: lost tch 7th: t.o bef next* **66/1**

500- **11** 3 1/2 **Pensnett Bay**370 [4907] 6-10-6 0 JoshWall(10) 50
(Trevor Wall) *racd off the pce in midfield: hdwy and in tch 5th: rdn and toiling next: t.o after 7th* **80/1**

0 **12** 18 **Silver Seraph**283 [832] 7-10-2 0 HenryBrooke(7) 27
(Noel Wilson) *blnd 1st: a bhd: rdn and lost tch 6th: wl t.o after next* **100/1**

P **Crossbarry Breeze (IRE)**1062 9-11-2 0 TomMessenger —
(Violet M Jordan) *a towards rr: mstke and rdn 5th: lost tch next: wl t.o whn p.u 3 out* **100/1**

00 **F** **Praefectus (IRE)**14 [4881] 5-11-2 0 (t) JohnnyFarrelly —
(David Pipe) *plld hrd: stdd s: hld up in rr tl dashed up to chse ldr 2nd: led 3rd tl after 5th: losing pl rapidly whn fell next* **50/1**

4m 56.0s (-8.00) **Going Correction** -0.25s/f (Good)
WFA 4 from 5yo+ 6lb **14** Ran SP% **123.2**
Speed ratings (Par 103): **105,103,98,96,96 87,80,77,77,76 75,68,—,—**
toteswingers:1&2 £10.70, 2&3 £2.10, 1&3 £3.90 CSF £33.62 TOTE £8.10: £2.80, £1.60, £1.50; EX 42.30.

Owner A D Spence **Bred** Wadud Syndicate **Trained** Upper Lambourn, Berks

FOCUS
An ordinary novice event where it paid to race handily. The cosy winner is rated in line with his Flat form and the second sets the level.

NOTEBOOK
Dancing Dude(IRE) signed off on the Flat for Mark Johnston last year with just one win to his name and often ran below his official mark of 75 in that sphere. However, he didn't have many miles on the clock before this hurdling debut for his new, leading stable and his stamina was in no doubt having stayed 1m4f well on the level. It was therefore surprising that he proved so easy to back, but he got the job done in gutsy fashion and looks sure to improve for the experience. (op 11-2)
Croan Rock(IRE) is a point winner and so it wasn't surprising to see him out in front. He made the winner work, but would have been beaten further if that rival had jumped the last better. There ought to be a race for him before long, though, as he was well clear of the remainder. (op 9-2)
Robin De Creuse(FR), up in trip, found the leaders get away from him on the back straight and really wants more use made of him on such ground. He has become expensive to follow. (op 2-1 tchd 5-2)
Gearbox(IRE) ◆ had shown little in two previous spins over hurdles, but is a 62-rated 1m4f winner on the level and this was more encouraging back up in trip in a tongue strap. He is now eligible for handicaps. Official explanation: vet said gelding sustained a leg injury
Wise Move(IRE), something an eye-catcher on his hurdling bow at Ascot 70 days previously, was seemingly better fancied than his winning stablemate. He lacked any sort of gear change on this quicker surface, however, and was beat a long way out. (op 7-2)

5116 HOOPS AND JENKINSONS CATERERS NOVICES' CHASE (12 fncs) 2m

3:30 (3:30) (Class 4) 5-Y-0+ **£3,168** (£936; £468; £234; £117)

Form RPR

2110 **1** **Dan Breen (IRE)**18 [4789] 6-11-5 148 TomScudamore 138+
(David Pipe) *mde all and clr thrght: mstke 4th: wl in command last 2: eased towards fin: easily* **4/9**1

-113 **2** 11 **What's Up Doc (IRE)**16 [1163] 10-11-5 0 HarrySkelton 127
(Lawney Hill) *t.k.h: chsd ldrs: wnt 2nd bef 9th: effrt and 6 l down 2 out: no prog and btn last* **10/1**

-125 **3** 31 **Five Out Of Five (IRE)**223 [1343] 7-10-12 0 (t) PaulMoloney 92
(Evan Williams) *chsd wnr tl bef 9th: 3rd and wl btn 3 out: wknd* **9/2**2

200P **4** 28 **Causeway King (USA)**35 [4354] 5-10-12 0 (t) WayneHutchinson 77
(Alan King) *chsd ldrs: mstke 1st: j. slowly 6th and sn struggling: j.rt 8th: sn rdn and lost tch: t.o whn j. slowly next* **8/1**3

0-50 **5** 8 **Waldo Winchester (IRE)**24 [4550] 8-10-5 0 HenryBrooke(7) 60
(Noel Wilson) *several slow jumps: sn bhd: t.o fr 2nd* **66/1**

3m 56.7s (1.10) **Going Correction** -0.15s/f (Good) **5** Ran SP% **109.1**
Speed ratings: **91,85,70,56,52**
CSF £5.49 TOTE £1.30: £1.10, £1.90; EX 3.90.

Owner Stuart M Mercer **Bred** F Fitzgerald **Trained** Nicholashayne, Devon

FOCUS
A straightforward success for the very useful winner, with the form rated around the first two.

NOTEBOOK
Dan Breen(IRE) finished seventh in the Arkle on his previous outing last month and won pretty much as he was entitled to on this big drop in grade. He wasn't always convincing early on over his fences, but got better the further he went on that front. He was probably also idling as the runner-up closed a little in the home straight and, despite having won a bumper on quick ground before, this surface was probably faster than he ideally cares for. That said, he will be kept on the go and trips to both Sandown and Punchestown could figure. (op 2-5 tchd 1-2)
What's Up Doc(IRE) ◆ is a versatile sort and he posted a very pleasing effort seeing as he faced a very stiff task with the winner. He likes this ground and should be well up to defying his penalty before the season's end. (op 8-1)
Five Out Of Five(IRE) was a dual novice hurdle winner and rated 122 in that sphere. He shaped as though he needed a run on this switch to fences after a 223-day absence and ought to learn a deal for the experience. Slightly easier ground and a stiffer test ought to be ideal for him. (op 6-1 tchd 13-2)
Causeway King(USA) is rated 125 over hurdles, but he's lost his way in that sphere of late and never figured on this chase debut after meeting the first fence wrong. (op 9-1 tchd 7-1)

5117 CHEMTECH H'CAP HURDLE (10 hdls 2 omitted) 2m 4f 110y

4:05 (4:05) (Class 4) (0-115,113) 4-Y-0+ **£2,471** (£725; £362; £181)

Form RPR

2102 **1** **Be My Light (IRE)**27 [4501] 5-10-10 **104** (p) KielanWoods(7) 109+
(Charlie Longsdon) *in tch: swtchd to outer and effrt bef 3 out: chalng whn lft in ld next: sn rdn: styd on wl flat* **7/1**2

5145 **2** 4 1/2 **Marleno (GER)**56 [3950] 5-11-8 **112** (t) JimmyDerham(3) 114
(Milton Harris) *t.k.h: hld up wl bhd: hdwy after 7th: chsng ldrs whn lft 3rd 2 out: ch whn mstke last: drvn and no ex flat* **7/1**2

3-00 **3** 1/2 **Yeoman Spirit (IRE)**140 [2372] 8-11-4 **105** (tp) GrahamLee 106
(John Mackie) *chsd ldr tl after 2nd: racing awkwardly and lost pl 6th: sn rdn: lft 7th and plenty to do 2 out: stl awkward hd carriage but styd on wl between last 2: nt rch ldrs* **25/1**

252F **4** 4 **Switched Off**25 [4536] 6-11-4 **112** (vt) MrJHodson(7) 111+
(Ian Williams) *racd on outer: chsd ldrs: lft 2nd 7th: ev ch and j. awkwardly next: lft disputing ld next: racd awkwardly and nt qckn between last 2: cl 3rd and mstke last: wknd flat* **4/1**1

2440 **5** 11 **Father Probus**49 [4079] 5-11-6 **110** SamTwiston-Davies(3) 97
(Nigel Twiston-Davies) *chsd ldr after 2nd tl 7th: sn u.p: plugging on same pce and hld whn lft 4th sn after 2 out: wknd bef last* **12/1**

3404 **6** 8 **Wester Ross (IRE)**27 [4503] 7-11-12 **113** (b) MarkBradburne 97+
(James Eustace) *chsd ldrs: blnd 7th: rdn bef next: struggling and btn whn lft 6th and bdly hmpd 2 out: n.d and nt pushed after* **18/1**

506P **7** 4 1/2 **Drussell (IRE)**59 [3881] 5-10-11 **105** HenryBrooke(7) 83
(Richard Phillips) *hld up in tch: hdwy to chse ldrs 6th: rdn after 3 out: 5th and stl in tch whn bdly hmpd next: nt rcvr* **14/1**

-310 **8** 9 **Icy Colt (ARG)**140 [2375] 5-11-5 **106** (v) WillKennedy 74
(Paul Webber) *hld up in tch in midfield: hdwy and wl in tch 7th: rdn and struggling next: wkng whn hmpd next: no ch after* **20/1**

400P **9** 1 **Alhaque (USA)**36 [4327] 5-11-8 **109** (v) JamieMoore 76
(Gary Moore) *in tch towards rr: mstke 4th: rdn and no rspnse after 5th: lost tch 7th: styd on past btn horses fr 3 out: n.d* **16/1**

00F1 **10** 1/2 **Very Stylish (IRE)**270 [921] 7-11-11 **112** RichieMcLernon 78
(Jonjo O'Neill) *hld up in tch towards rr: hdwy after 5th: pushed along and struggling 7th: wl btn bef next* **14/1**

P01P **11** nk **Prince Louis (FR)**33 [4400] 8-10-9 **99** (t) PeterToole(3) 65
(Charlie Mann) *t.k.h: led tl blnd: pckd and hdd 7th: rdn and j. slowly next: wkng whn hmpd 2 out: fdd* **25/1**

P3-0 **12** nk **Kempley Green (IRE)**41 [4234] 8-11-6 **110** JohnKington(3) 76
(Michael Scudamore) *hld up towards rr: hdwy and in tch in midfield 6th: drvn and struggling after next: wknd on long run to 3 out* **50/1**

4502 **13** 50 **Spiritual Guidance (IRE)**23 [4667] 8-11-3 **104** TomScudamore 25
(Warren Greatrex) *chsd ldrs: hmpd and mstke 7th: wknd u.p wl bef next: t.o 2 out: eased after last: t.o* **12/1**

-460 **14** 13 **Soleil D'Avril (FR)**42 [4203] 5-11-7 **108** WayneHutchinson 17
(Alan King) *in tch in midfield: reminder after 5th: mstke and rdn next: sn toiling bdly: lost tch next: wl t.o bef 3 out* **12/1**

5030 **15** 2 1/2 **Elusive Muse**262 [986] 5-11-6 **112** (t) OliverDayman(5) 19
(Alison Thorpe) *a in rr: rdn and lost tch 6th: wl t.o after next* **25/1**

144- **16** 11 **Maria Antonia (IRE)**559 [1472] 8-11-4 **105** (t) RichardJohnson 2
(Alison Thorpe) *plld hrd: hld up wl in rr: dived rt 1st: lost tch after 6th: wl t.o bef 3 out* **10/1**3

0453 **F** **Kayfton Pete**14 [4874] 5-10-13 **107** PeterHatton(7) 105
(Reg Hollinshead) *t.k.h: hld up in tch: hdwy after 5th: lft in ld 7th: hrd pressed but stl travelling okay whn fell 2 out* **16/1**

4m 56.0s (-8.00) **Going Correction** -0.25s/f (Good) **17** Ran SP% **125.8**
Speed ratings (Par 105): **105,103,103,101,97 94,92,89,88,88 88,88,69,64,63 59,—**
toteswingers:1&2 £8.60, 2&3 £22.80, 1&3 £53.20 CSF £53.60 CT £1193.85 TOTE £8.10: £1.90, £2.80, £6.30, £1.60; EX 69.00.

Owner Foxtrot NH Racing Partnership IV **Bred** Mrs L Suenson-Taylor **Trained** Over Norton, Oxon

FOCUS
A wide-open handicap, run at a sound enough gallop. Fair form, the first two rated to their best.

NOTEBOOK
Be My Light(IRE) resumed winning ways in ready fashion. She looked in the handicapper's grip coming here, but the quicker ground evidently suited and there was plenty to like about her attitude when asked to seal the race.
Marleno(GER) is a confirmed hold-up performer and he cut his way through the pack on the back straight. He was still going sweetly nearing two out, but ultimately found the winner too resolute. He is entitled to come on a little for the run and may just prefer dropping back in trip. (op 17-2)
Yeoman Spirit(IRE) ◆, with a tongue-tie back on, didn't look the most straightforward and hit a flat spot at the crucial stage. That could have been down to blowing up, however, as it was his first outing for 140 days and he was motoring from the second-last. There could be improvement in him next time out.
Switched Off was not totally out of it before falling off this mark at Exeter last time. Well backed, he was produced with every chance, but not for the first time he didn't appear that willing under pressure and wilted after the last. (op 11-2)
Father Probus was in the process of running a bold race before crashing out in the home straight. (op 14-1)

5118 MARK CRANK MEMORIAL H'CAP HURDLE (10 hdls 2 omitted) 2m 6f 110y

4:40 (4:40) (Class 3) (0-130,125) 4-Y-0+ **£5,069** (£1,497; £748; £374; £187)

Form RPR

21 **1** **Connectivity (IRE)**5 [5061] 7-12-0 **125** 7ex TomScudamore 143+
(Dr Richard Newland) *nt fluent early: mde virtually all: wnt clr 7th: rdn bef 2 out: in command between last 2: styd on wl: eased towards fin* **2/1**1

5-22 **2** 18 **China Gold**36 [4327] 8-11-4 **115** WayneHutchinson 115
(Alan King) *hld up in tch: effrt to chse wnr 7th: rdn and mstke 2 out: btn whn j.rt last: wknd flat* **3/1**2

6016 **3** *2* **King Of Dubai**[57] 3931 6-10-8 **115** ThomasFlint(10) 111
(John Flint) *hld up in tch in rr: effrt and rdn to chse ldng trio wl bef 3 out: no imp and wl hld whn mstke 2 out: plugged on to go 3rd flat* **25/1**

00P3 **4** *2 1/4* **Pro Pell (IRE)**[22] 4700 6-10-10 **107** JamieMoore 100
(Gary Moore) *hld up in tch: rdn after 6th: chsd ldng pair and drvn after 7th: wknd 3 out: lost 3rd flat* **4/1**[3]

0106 **5** *2 1/2* **Snake Charmer**[14] 4869 8-10-9 **109** (v) PeterToole(3) 100
(Milton Harris) *chsd wnr tl 2nd: lost pl and dropped to rr after 5th: reminders next: drvn in 5th and wl hld after next: plugged on* **9/1**

0540 **6** *61* **County Zen (FR)**[35] 4354 8-11-12 **123** RichardJohnson 59
(Philip Hobbs) *chsd wnr 2nd: rdn after 6th: lost 2nd and struggling next: sn wknd: t.o bef 3 out: virtually p.u flat:* **7/1**

221 **7** *2* **Bobble Hat Bob (FR)**[262] 992 6-11-6 **117** RichieMcLernon 51
(Jonjo O'Neill) *chsd ldrs: struggling after 6th: lost tch and t.o bef 3 out: virtually p.u flat* **16/1**

-F00 **8** *40* **Song Of Songs**[17] 4806 9-11-6 **120** (v) MrAJBerry(3) 18
(Jonjo O'Neill) *chsd ldrs: rdn after 6th: dropped out rapidly next: wl t.o bef 3 out: virtually p.u flat* **20/1**

5m 18.0s (-12.90) **Going Correction** -0.25s/f (Good) **8** Ran SP% **115.3**
Speed ratings (Par 107): **112,105,105,104,103 82,81,67**
toteswingers:1&2 £2.30, 2&3 £16.00, 1&3 £11.80 CSF £8.86 CT £109.59 TOTE £3.70: £1.30, £1.50, £4.30; EX 6.20.
Owner D & D Coatings Ltd **Bred** Mrs K Healy **Trained** Claines, Worcs

FOCUS
A modest handicap and a fast-improving winner. The runner-up sets the level and the fourth was 12lb off his Sandown mark.

NOTEBOOK
Connectivity(IRE) hacked up on his second outing for connections at Towcester five days earlier and, well handicapped under his penalty, followed up with a bold display from the front. He lacked fluency early on, but that was likely due to the switch to front-running tactics and there was plenty to like about the manner in which he kept finding for pressure in the home straight. His yard is going very well and he has developed into a useful hurdler since getting on some decent ground. (op 9-4 tchd 5-2)
China Gold had posted two respectable efforts in defeat since resuming this term, but he again managed to find one too good here. It looked as though he was a massive threat to the winner three out, but he was shortly under the pump as that rival found more and perhaps this ground was that bit too lively for him. He deserves to go one better again. (tchd 5-2)
King Of Dubai stayed on off the home turn having been waited with out the back and probably needs more positive handling on this sort of ground. He has begun life in handicaps on a workable mark. (tchd 22-1)
Pro Pell(IRE) did his best to get involved on the back straight, but was under the pump turning for home and failed to raise his game for the quicker surface. (tchd 9-2)

5119 SILKS AND JENKINSONS CATERERS MARES' STANDARD OPEN NATIONAL HUNT FLAT RACE 2m
5:10 (5:10) (Class 6) 4-6-Y-0 **£1,821** (£534; £267; £133)

Form RPR

1 **Scholastica** 4-10-5 0 KielanWoods(7) 95+
(Charlie Longsdon) *hld up in midfield: lost pl 1/2-way: in last quartet whn shkn up and rn green 5f out: swtchd rt and gd hdwy 3f out: rdn and ev ch 1f out: led wl ins fnl f: r.o wl* **13/2**[3]

2 *1/2* **Flite (IRE)** 5-11-4 0 TomScudamore 100
(Warren Greatrex) *t.k.h early: hld up towards rr: sme hdwy 6f out: rdn and gd hdwy to chse ldrs wl over 2f out: rdn and ev ch over 1f out: led 1f out: hdd and no ex wl ins fnl f* **7/1**

160 **3** *4 1/2* **Dream Performance (IRE)**[51] 4027 6-11-8 0 PeterToole(3) 103
(G C Maundrell) *mde most: rdn and fnd ex over 2f out: hdd 1f out: sn drvn: wknd fnl 100yds* **9/1**

0 **4** *6* **Irene Kennet**[35] 4356 4-10-12 0 HaddenFrost 85
(Martin Bosley) *t.k.h: in tch: hdwy to chse ldr over 2f out tl over 1f out: outpcd by ldng trio ent fnl f: plugged on* **25/1**

5 *5* **Emily's Flyer (IRE)** 4-10-9 0 SamTwiston-Davies(3) 80
(Nigel Twiston-Davies) *w ldr tl rdn and unable qck wl over 2f out: wknd wl over 1f out* **7/2**[1]

10 **6** *2 3/4* **Genstone Trail**[51] 4027 5-11-11 0 WayneHutchinson 91
(Alan King) *t.k.h: hld up in tch in rr: hdwy into midfield 8f out: chsd ldrs and rdn 3f out: wknd 2f out* **10/1**

236 **7** *7* **Bathwick Junior**[26] 4527 4-10-2 0 ThomasFlint(10) 71
(John Flint) *t.k.h: chsd ldrs: rdn over 4f out: wknd ent fnl 2f* **16/1**

4 **8** *3 1/4* **Dancing Primo**[239] 1201 5-11-4 0 HarrySkelton 74
(Mark Brisbourne) *t.k.h: hld up wl in tch in midfield: rdn and wknd wl over 2f out* **8/1**

9 *3 1/4* **Set In Her Ways (IRE)** 5-10-11 0 EdCookson(7) 71
(Kim Bailey) *t.k.h: hld up in tch: hdwy 6f out: rdn and edgd rt wl over 2f out: sn wknd* **14/1**

0 **10** *25* **Charmouth Girl**[322] 333 5-11-4 0 GrahamLee 49
(John Mackie) *t.k.h: in tch: hdwy to press ldrs 6f out tl wknd qckly 3f out: t.o and virtually p.u ins fnl f* **50/1**

11 *1* **Surf Like A Lady (IRE)** 5-11-4 0 RichardJohnson 48
(Philip Hobbs) *t.k.h: hld up in tch in rr: rn wd bnd 8f out: rdn and struggling 6f out: lost tch over 4f out: t.o and eased ins fnl f* **6/1**[2]

0 **12** *21* **Wilkinson Court**[24] 4554 4-10-5 0 HenryBrooke(7) 23
(John Mackie) *t.k.h: hld up wl in tch tl rdn and wknd qckly 3f out: virtually p.u fnl f: t.o* **66/1**

13 *11* **Apolka** 4-10-12 0 JimmyMcCarthy 13
(Renee Robeson) *midfield tl dropped to rr after 6f: lost tch 5f out: t.o and virtually p.u ins fnl f* **16/1**

0- **14** *51* **Emmy (IRE)**[351] 5218 5-11-1 0 JohnKington(3) —
(Michael Scudamore) *t.k.h: hld up in rr: lost tch over 6f out: wl t.o fnl 3f: virtually p.u ins fnl f* **50/1**

3m 51.4s (1.80) **Going Correction** -0.25s/f (Good)
WFA 4 from 5yo+ 5lb **14** Ran SP% **120.2**
Speed ratings: **85,84,82,79,77 75,72,70,68,56 55,45,39,14**
toteswingers:1&2 £12.90, 2&3 £18.20, 1&3 £18.00 CSF £50.42 TOTE £7.10: £3.10, £3.20, £3.30; EX 66.80.
Owner David Redvers **Bred** Dr B Mayoh **Trained** Over Norton, Oxon

FOCUS
An average mares' bumper, rated around the penalised third and the sixth.

NOTEBOOK
Scholastica, whose dam won a bumper, hails from an in-form stable and got her career off to a perfect start. She took time to pick up for pressure in the home straight, but hit top gear from the furlong marker and was just on top at the business end. She clearly has a future and ought to enjoy stepping up in trip when sent hurdling. (op 8-1)
Flite(IRE) ◆, a little free in mid-field early on, made a bold bid in the home straight and was only picked off by the winner near the finish. This was a very pleasing debut effort and a sound surface looks right up her street, so she ought to be found an opening before long. (tchd 13-2)
Dream Performance(IRE) returned to her best on this return to a suitably sounder surface and rates a solid benchmark under her penalty. She should have little trouble adding to her tally once sent jumping. (op 12-1 tchd 8-1)
Irene Kennet got a positive ride, but lacked any sort of gear change and this racecourse debut looked needed.
Emily's Flyer(IRE) got a positive ride, but lacked any sort of gear change and this racecourse debut looked needed. (tchd 10-3 and 4-1)
Genstone Trail, free early on, looked a player leaving the back straight but her effort proved short-lived (op 9-1 tchd 11-1)

5120 JENKINSONS CATERERS FIRST CHOICE FOR CONFERENCES H'CAP CHASE (16 fncs) 2m 6f 110y
5:45 (5:45) (Class 4) (0-115,115) 5-Y-0+ **£3,168** (£936; £468; £234; £117)

Form RPR

0041 **1** **Willandrich (IRE)**[22] 4694 9-11-0 **106** MichaelMurphy(3) 114
(Ian Williams) *in tch in midfield: j. slowly 1st: chsd ldrs 11th: rdn bef 3 out: j. ahd last: kpt on wl flat: rdn out* **7/2**[2]

2P06 **2** *3/4* **Our Jim**[31] 4421 9-10-9 **105** HenryBrooke(7) 114+
(Donald McCain) *j.lft and mstkes: chsd ldrs: rdn after 12th: ev ch and mstke 2 out: no ex u.p fnl 100yds* **5/1**[3]

F426 **3** *2 3/4* **Moulin De La Croix**[95] 3157 7-11-9 **115** SamTwiston-Davies(3) 120
(Nigel Twiston-Davies) *t.k.h: chsd ldrs tl wnt 2nd 11th: ev ch and j.lft 3 out: led next: hdd last: no ex and btn fnl 100yds* **12/1**

1100 **4** *3* **Mister Wiseman**[21] 4723 9-11-6 **109** (p) LiamHeard 112
(Nigel Hawke) *led: mstke 9th: rdn and mstke 3 out: hdd next: wknd last* **20/1**

43RR **5** *10* **Blackpool Billy (IRE)**[9] 4961 9-11-3 **113** (be[1]) TonyKelly(7) 107
(Ferdy Murphy) *led into s: sn in midfield: mstke 5th: chsd ldrs 11th: wknd 2 out* **9/1**

FP33 **P** **Marc Of Brilliance (USA)**[27] 4502 8-11-3 **106** (v) JamieMoore —
(Gary Moore) *in tch towards rr: j. slowly 1st: mstke 4th: rdn and struggling 10th: lost tch after next: t.o whn p.u 3 out* **7/1**

43PP **P** **Lorum Leader (IRE)**[20] 4740 10-10-9 **98** (b) SamJones —
(Dr Richard Newland) *w ldr tl 10th: lost pl rapidly u.p 11th: wl t.o whn p.u bef 13th: b.b.v* **10/1**

-125 **P** **Extra Bold**[27] 4504 9-10-12 **101** JackDoyle —
(Emma Lavelle) *hld up in rr: mstke 7th: reminders after next: struggling and rdn after 10th: t.o wl bef 13th tl p.u 2 out* **3/1**[1]

1205 **P** **Nautical Approach (IRE)**[92] 3265 8-11-0 **103** (t) PaulMoloney —
(Alex Hales) *in tch in midfield: mstke 2nd: lost pl and last whn rdn after 8th: lost tch next: t.o whn p.u after 11th* **12/1**

5m 41.8s (-6.70) **Going Correction** -0.15s/f (Good) **9** Ran SP% **115.6**
Speed ratings: **105,104,103,102,99 —,—,—,—**
toteswingers:1&2 £3.60, 2&3 £6.30, 1&3 £6.80 CSF £21.95 CT £188.05 TOTE £3.90: £1.40, £2.50, £3.70; EX 24.10.
Owner Will Tyrrell Richard Tyrrell Andrew Dick **Bred** John Halliday **Trained** Portway, Worcs

FOCUS
A moderate handicap, run at a routine gallop and the first four were pretty much still upsides at the second-last fence. The winner is on the upgrade over fences.

NOTEBOOK
Willandrich(IRE) registered his first win for a year when scoring comfortably at Leicester last month and, despite a 7lb higher mark, he followed up with a game effort. He initially came under pressure on the back straight, but kept responding to his rider's urgings and saved his best jump for the last. Reverting to quicker ground of late has made all the difference to him and a bold bid for the hat-trick is now expected. (op 3-1)
Our Jim has been in and out since his last success in 2009, but he was well backed on this return to fences and would have probably ended his losing run had his fencing been more fluent. If he can brush up his jumping a little then there is no doubt a similar contest within his grasp. (op 8-1)
Moulin De La Croix ◆ was going best of all four out and posted a solid effort in defeat on her return from a 95-day break. She could take some beating next time. (op 11-1)
Mister Wiseman was taken on out in front, but that didn't stop him from running a brave race and he only gave way nearing the last. This was better again from him. (tchd 25-1)
Blackpool Billy(IRE) in the home straight, but he would have found the ground plenty quick enough and this was much more encouraging from him in first-time headgear. (op 7-1)
Lorum Leader(IRE) Official explanation: trainer said gelding bled from the nose (op 7-2)
Extra Bold proved popular back on quick ground, but got he got behind from before the final circuit and perhaps something went amiss. Official explanation: jockey said gelding never travelled (op 7-2)
T/Plt: £83.90 to a £1 stake. Pool of £71,108.57 - 618.25 winning tickets. T/Qpdt: £21.00 to a £1 stake. Pool of £4,294.92 - 151.24 winning tickets. SP

5121 - 5129a (Foreign Racing) - See Raceform Interactive

4738 MARKET RASEN (R-H)
Sunday, April 3

OFFICIAL GOING: Good (chs 7.4, hdl 7.3)
Rails moved out 2yds fro fresh ground increasing circuit distances by approximately 44yds.
Wind: moderate 1/2 against Weather: overcast, changeable, shower after race 2

5130 MY DAD SIMON BOURNE 50TH BIRTHDAY LADY RIDERS' (S) H'CAP HURDLE (8 hdls) 2m 1f
2:30 (2:30) (Class 5) (0-95,94) 4-Y-0+ **£1,712** (£499; £249)

Form RPR

P440 **1** **Solway Blue**[24] 4573 9-9-11 **72** (p) MissJRRichards(7) 77
(Lisa Harrison) *hdwy to trck ldrs 4th: led 2 out: drvn out* **14/1**

5-PP **2** *3 1/4* **Hi Ho Silvia**[18] 4814 6-10-1 **76** (tp) MissLAllan(7) 78
(Neil King) *chsd ldrs: wnt 2nd sn after last: styd on same pce* **16/1**

P435 **3** *hd* **Muntami (IRE)**[21] 4741 10-11-3 **92** MissKLMorgan(7) 94
(John Harris) *in rr: hdwy appr 2 out: styd on run-in* **10/1**

0606 **4** *1 1/4* **Hoar Frost**[24] 4572 6-11-1 **90** MissGTutty(7) 91
(Karen Tutty) *chsd ldrs: lost pl 3 out: rallied between last 2: fin wl* **13/2**[2]

0-40 **5** *1* **Sirjosh**[8] 4499 5-11-2 **91** MissCLWills(7) 92
(Des Donovan) *hld up in rr: t.k.h: hdwy 3 out: kpt on run-in* **9/1**

05 **6** *1/2* **Silver Lily (IRE)**[21] 4738 9-11-5 **94** (t) MissCareyWilliamson(7) 94
(Sarah Humphrey) *trckd ldrs: led briefly appr 2 out: 3 l 2nd whn blnd last: wknd towards fin* **10/1**

U3P0 **7** *shd* **Cosmetic**[26] 3993 6-10-1 **76** MissCWalton(7) 75
(Colin Teague) *hld up towards rr: hdwy appr 2 out: styd on run-in* **22/1**

P405 **8** *2* **Black Apache (IRE)**[15] 4873 7-11-4 **93** (b) MissLAlexander(7) 90
(Donald McCain) *trckd ldrs: rdn and upsides appr 2 out: wknd last 150yds* **14/1**

3060 **9** *5* **Mycenean Prince (USA)**[25] 4550 8-10-11 **86** MissPhillipaTutty(7) 78
(Karen Tutty) *chsd ldrs: drvn after 5th: wknd after next* **13/2**[2]

0P54 **10** *4* **Keep Guessing**[18] 4809 8-11-4 **93**......(p) MissZoeLilly(7) 81
(Warren Greatrex) *led 1st: hdd appr 2 out: sn wknd and mstke: fin lame* **5/1**[1]

-33P **11** *3 ¼* **The Iron Giant (IRE)**[301] 649 9-9-9 **68** oh5.. GemmaGracey-Davison(5) 53
(Neil King) *nt fluent: chsd ldrs: drvn and lost pl 4th: bhd fr 3 out* **15/2**[3]

0000 **12** *2 ½* **Simplified**[44] 4178 8-9-7 **68** oh9......(t) MissCBoxall(7) 50
(Michael Chapman) *in rr: bhd fr 3 out* **66/1**

/0P- **13** *15* **Noble Edge**[17] 12 8-9-9 **70**......(t) MissRJefferson(7) 37
(Lee James) *in rr: wl bhd fr 3 out* **28/1**

0/0P **14** *nk* **Dr Light (IRE)**[26] 4545 7-10-7 **80**...... MissLHorner(5) 47
(Anna Bramall) *in rr: wl bhd fr 3 out* **25/1**

4m 11.2s (4.50) **Going Correction** +0.225s/f (Yiel) **14** Ran SP% **115.6**
Speed ratings (Par 103): **98,96,96,95,95 95,95,94,91,89 88,87,80,79**
Tote Swingers: 1&2 £45.80, 1&3 £20.10, 2&3 £21.20 CSF £199.70 CT £2330.60 TOTE £17.30: £4.40, £5.50, £3.30; EX 255.20.There was no bid for the winner.

Owner David Alan Harrison **Bred** D A Harrison **Trained** Aldoth, Cumbria

FOCUS
The rails were moved out 2yds for fresh ground, increasing circuit distances by approximately 44yds. \n\x\x A tricky selling handicap, confined to lady amateur riders. There was a sound gallop on, but it still proved difficult to make up ground from off the pace. A number of these were well handicapped on their old form.

NOTEBOOK
Solway Blue had been out of sorts since finishing third in event last season, but was racing off a 17lb lower mark this time around and returned to his best with a clear-cut success. With cheekpieces reapplied, he was nicely placed in the race and hit top gear nearing the last flight. It was his first win at the 26th attempt. (op 12-1)

Hi Ho Silvia, pulled up the last two times, kept on to just hold on to second and this was her best effort so far. The first-time tongue tie evidently helped and a slightly stiffer test should be ideal. (op 18-1)

Muntami(IRE), a course specialist, appreciated this return to hurdling and was doing all of his best work at the finish, suggesting he might sharpen up for the outing. (op 17-2 tchd 8-1)

Hoar Frost ◆, well backed returning to more suitable ground, was another staying on too late in the day and needs more prominent handling. She's weighted to win at present. (op 9-1)

Sirjosh found himself too far back to land a blow in the home straight.

Keep Guessing, who is quirky, paid for his early exertions nearing two out. Official explanation: vet said gelding was lame right-hind (op 4-1)

5131 DAWN DOBINSON'S BIG 50TH BIRTHDAY NOVICES' HURDLE (8 hdls) 2m 1f

3:05 (3:05) (Class 4) 4-Y-0+ **£2,276** (£668; £334; £166)

Form RPR

1 **1** **Higgy's Ragazzo (FR)**[54] 3986 4-10-13 0...... APMcCoy 121+
(Nicky Henderson) *trckd ldrs: led after 3 out: nt fluent last: smoothly* **11/8**[1]

5146 **2** *2 ¼* **King Fingal (IRE)**[46] 4149 6-11-0 117...... BrianToomey(5) 116
(John Quinn) *hld up in midfield: effrt on ins whn hmpd after 5th: chsd wnr appr 2 out: kpt on same pce run-in* **9/4**[2]

5 **3** *6* **Strathcal**[11] 4952 5-10-13 0...... AndrewTinkler 103
(Anna Brooks) *trckd ldrs: wnt clr 3rd appr 2 out: kpt on same pce* **15/2**[3]

0255 **4** *7* **Kayaan**[18] 4809 4-10-7 95...... WarrenMarston 91
(Pam Sly) *stdd s: hld up in rr: stdy hdwy 3 out: poor 4th next: kpt on wl run-in* **9/1**

10 **5** *18* **Dica (FR)**[67] 3749 5-11-5 0...... TomScudamore 86
(Patrick Griffin, Ire) *w ldr: led 5th: hdd after next: wknd appr 2 out: hit last* **17/2**

P543 **6** *19* **Lochore (IRE)**[15] 4870 5-10-8 77...... AlexanderVoy(5) 59
(Lucy Normile) *led to 5th: lost pl appr 2 out* **66/1**

60 **7** *5* **Rebel Flag (IRE)**[87] 3406 4-10-7 0...... TomMessenger 48
(Chris Bealby) *t.k.h in midfield: effrt 3 out: sn wknd* **80/1**

PP06 **8** *1 ¾* **Solway Dornal**[15] 4870 6-10-10 0...... HarryHaynes(3) 52
(Lisa Harrison) *mid-div: drvn after 3rd: bhd fr 3 out* **200/1**

05 **9** *4 ½* **Bello Regalo (IRE)**[56] 3971 5-10-13 0...... GrahamLee 48
(Malcolm Jefferson) *t.k.h in rr: bhd fr 4th* **50/1**

10 *3* **Troopingthecolour**[492] 5-10-13 0......(t) RhysFlint 45
(Steve Gollings) *chsd ldrs: nt fluent 4th: drvn 3 out: wknd appr next: eased* **20/1**

00-0 **11** *28* **Poppy Lee Brown**[161] 1993 5-10-6 0...... CharliePoste 10
(Chris Bealby) *in rr: nt fluent 4th: wl bhd fr 3 out: t.o* **150/1**

12 *nk* **Into The Light**[173] 6-10-13 0...... JamesReveley 16
(Philip Kirby) *in rr: bdly hmpd 3rd: sn t.o* **50/1**

60 **F** **Pompan (IRE)**[128] 2660 5-10-13 0...... BrianHughes —
(Peter Niven) *towards rr: nt fluent 2nd: j. bdly lft and fell 3rd* **100/1**

U **Exit To Freedom** 5-10-13 0...... PaddyAspell —
(John Wainwright) *in rr: sn pushed along: last whn bdly hmpd and uns rdr 3rd* **100/1**

4m 7.00s (0.30) **Going Correction** +0.225s/f (Yiel)
WFA 4 from 5yo+ 5lb **14** Ran SP% **119.7**
Speed ratings (Par 105): **108,106,104,100,92 83,81,80,78,76 63,63,—,—**
Tote Swingers: 1&2 £2.00, 1&3 £4.50, 2&3 £4.70 CSF £4.42 TOTE £1.80: £1.10, £1.30, £2.10; EX 5.30.

Owner I Higginson **Bred** Thierry Grandsir & Patrick Bruneau **Trained** Upper Lambourn, Berks

■ Stewards' Enquiry : A P McCoy one-day ban: careless riding (Apr 17)
Warren Marston three-day ban: weighed in 2lb heavy (Apr 17-19)

FOCUS
This novice hurdle was run at a solid tempo and the form looks straightforward. The easy winner was value for further and should rate higher.

NOTEBOOK
Higgy's Ragazzo(FR) proved easy to back under his penalty, but could have been called the winner before the penultimate flight and readily made it 2-2 over hurdles (both over course and distance) since joining Nicky Henderson. He got warm beforehand and proved somewhat buzzy, but he is clearly improving and ought to get a stiffer test without much fuss. (op 10-11 tchd 6-4 and 13-8 in places)

King Fingal(IRE) was well supported back in novice company and set the standard. He tracked the winner, but didn't help his cause by running freely in the process and was held after a messy leap at the second-last. (op 3-1)

Strathcal stepped up on the level of his recent hurdling debut at Warwick and left the impression he can get the mark when faced with a stiffer test on similar ground. (op 13-2)

Kayaan had disappointed since finishing second to the winner over course and distance last March and again spoilt his cause by pulling hard under restraint. That saw him get well behind, but he caught the eye staying on late and he has more ability than he is currently advertising. (op 16-1 tchd 17-2)

Dica(FR) paid for doing too much early on. (op 18-1)

Troopingthecolour badly needed the run on this hurdling debut for his new connections and return from a lengthy absence.

5132 WEATHERBYS AINTREE FESTIVAL BETTING GUIDE H'CAP HURDLE (10 hdls) 2m 5f

3:40 (3:40) (Class 4) (0-115,114) 4-Y-0+ **£2,276** (£668; £334; £166)

Form RPR

4221 **1** **I Can Run Can You (IRE)**[25] 4559 5-10-12 **100**...... APMcCoy 106+
(Jonjo O'Neill) *2nd best away in ragged s: chsd ldr: led appr 2 out: sn briefly hdd: hrd rdn and hld on gamely* **11/4**[1]

2061 **2** *1 ¼* **Sail And Return**[8] 5016 7-10-4 **99**......(t) JosephAkehurst(7) 105+
(Philip Middleton) *trckd ldng pair: led narrowly and briefly 2 out: hit last: styd on same pce last 100yds* **4/1**[2]

152P **3** *23* **What's Occurrin**[80] 3523 7-11-1 **103**...... RobertWalford 87
(Tim Walford) *best away in ragged s: led: hdd bef 2 out: grad wknd* **10/1**

-312 **4** *½* **Quite The Man (IRE)**[42] 4234 6-11-12 **114**...... GrahamLee 98
(Malcolm Jefferson) *t.k.h in midfield: pushed along after 5th: outpcd whn nt fluent 7th: one pce 2 out* **4/1**[2]

1664 **5** *2 ¼* **Rushwee (IRE)**[24] 4667 9-11-8 **110**......(b[1]) DominicElsworth 92
(Lucy Wadham) *hld up in rr: hdwy 7th: outpcd next: one pce fr 2 out* **25/1**

0140 **6** *13* **Everaard (USA)**[13] 4914 5-11-1 **103**......(p) RichieMcGrath 73
(Kate Walton) *nt fluent in rr: bhd fr 4th* **20/1**

F504 **7** *24* **Royal And Ancient (IRE)**[14] 4892 4-10-9 **104**......(vt[1]) WarrenMarston 46
(Milton Harris) *towards rr: reminders 3rd: bhd fr 7th: t.o 2 out* **12/1**

266P **8** *24* **Solway Ally**[15] 4873 8-10-4 **95**...... HarryHaynes(3) 22
(Lisa Harrison) *in rr: bhd fr 4th: t.o 6th* **22/1**

265- **9** *57* **Lindy Lou**[380] 4721 7-11-1 **110**...... MissGAndrews(7) —
(Pam Sly) *worst away in ragged s: t.k.h in rr: hdwy 4th: wknd after 7th: t.o 2 out: eased* **10/1**

0/PP **P** **Cottam Grange**[21] 4741 11-10-0 **88** oh13......(p) PaddyAspell —
(John Wainwright) *in rr: bhd fr 6th: t.o 3 out: p.u bef 2 out* **150/1**

63 **P** **Strobe**[182] 1701 7-11-0 **107**......(p) AlexanderVoy(5) —
(Lucy Normile) *chsd ldrs: wknd bef 3 out: sn bhd: t.o whn p.u bef 2 out* **33/1**

33P0 **P** **Classic Contours (USA)**[4] 4797 5-11-3 **105**......(p) BrianHughes —
(Tracy Waggott) *mid-div: reminders 5th: sn lost pl and bhd: t.o 7th: p.u bef next* **40/1**

5404 **P** **The Laodicean**[21] 4745 5-11-6 **108**...... RobertThornton —
(Alan King) *chsd ldrs: wknd after 7th: t.o whn p.u bef 2 out* **8/1**[3]

5m 10.8s (2.00) **Going Correction** +0.225s/f (Yiel)
WFA 4 from 5yo+ 6lb **13** Ran SP% **122.7**
Speed ratings (Par 105): **105,104,95,95,94 89,80,71,49,— —,—,—**
Tote Swingers: 1&2 £2.50, 1&3 £12.40, 2&3 £12.70 CSF £13.64 CT £99.96 TOTE £2.40: £1.10, £2.10, £4.10.

Owner Mrs Gay Smith **Bred** Noel O'Brien **Trained** Cheltenham, Gloucs

■ Stewards' Enquiry : Joseph Akehurst caution: used whip with excessive frequency.

FOCUS
Not a bad handicap for the class. There was a decent gallop on and the first pair came well clear in the home straight. The winner is on the upgrade and there's a case for rating the form 10b+ higher.

NOTEBOOK
I Can Run Can You(IRE) looked an idle sort when off the mark under the champion jockey at Fontwell last month and, well backed, he followed up from a 5lb higher mark. He took it up turning for home, but again raced lazily and the runner-up looked like taking over nearing the last flight. He jumped it better than that rival, though, and once again his rider lifted him home thereafter. A sound surface is clearly important cause and he probably still has more to offer. (op 7-2)

Sail And Return was 6lb higher than when opening his account at Stratford eight days earlier under today's conditional rider, and he would have probably added to his tally had he not flattened the last. There was still plenty to like about this improved effort and he is obviously progressive. (op 13-2)

What's Occurrin, who attracted support, likes it out in front and posted a game effort on this first outing for 80 days. He can build on this and it appears as though his yard's runners are coming back to form. (op 14-1)

Quite The Man(IRE) failed to raise his game for the step up to this longer trip and was never a threat, but may want easier ground. (tchd 7-2 and 9-2 in places)

Rushwee(IRE) caught the eye creeping closer on the back straight, but he pulled under early restraint and had little to offer when push came to shove. (tchd 28-1)

5133 WEATHERBYS BLOODSTOCK INSURANCE NOVICES' CHASE (17 fncs) 3m 1f

4:10 (4:10) (Class 3) 5-Y-0+ **£5,197** (£1,613; £868)

Form RPR

1541 **1** **Dover's Hill**[24] 4673 9-11-5 136......(t) SamTwiston-Davies(3) 149+
(Mary Hambro) *mde all: drew clr appr 3 out: nt fluent 2 out: unchal* **15/8**[1]

20-3 **2** *12* **Helpston**[67] 3743 7-10-12 128...... DavidEngland 130
(Pam Sly) *rn in snatches: chsd ldng pair: shkn up 7th: drvn along 11th: wnt 2nd next: outpcd appr 3 out: kpt on run-in* **15/8**[1]

F211 **3** *41* **Fin Vin De Leu (GER)**[14] 4898 5-11-8 138......(p) DarylJacob 116
(Charlie Mann) *t.k.h: mstkes: chsd wnr: wknd 12th: bhd whn blnd 3 out and next: virtually p.u run-in: fin lame* **2/1**[2]

P4U0 **P** **Rester Vrai (FR)**[10] 4974 6-10-5 60...... JoeCornwall(7) —
(John Cornwall) *last: drvn 5th: reminders 7th: outpcd next: j. slowly and lost tch 11th: t.o whn p.u bef 4 out* **66/1**[3]

6m 15.3s (-16.00) **Going Correction** -0.40s/f (Good) **4** Ran SP% **104.4**
Speed ratings: **109,105,92,—**
CSF £5.46 TOTE £4.20; EX 6.20.

Owner Mrs Richard Hambro **Bred** Cotswold Stud **Trained** Bourton-on-the-Hill, Gloucs

FOCUS
The easy winner's recent Wincanton victory has been upped to this level, and the second is rated to his mark.

NOTEBOOK
Dover's Hill had the race sewn up off the home turn and he made all in tremendous fashion. He has really got his act together this season and showed his class when winning at Wincanton last month. Again he had his ideal conditions here and he jumped boldly in the main, his only semblance of an error coming two out. He could well be capable of winning off this mark in a handicap now his confidence will be sky high and surely connections will be tempted to look at something for him at the Punchestown Festival next month. That course on decent ground would be right up his street. There is also the option of going to Perth or Sandown later this month, however. (tchd 7-4)

Helpston posted a fair effort behind Master Of The Hall on his chasing/seasonal debut in January and unsurprisingly proved popular getting weight from his two main rivals here. He was never going that well, however, and the winner firmly put him in his place. He certainly has the scope to win races over fences, though, and easier ground is likely what he needs.

Fin Vin De Leu(GER) had really come good over fences the last twice, but he was flattered by his Newton Abbot success a fortnight earlier and his jumping badly let him down. Official explanation: vet said gelding returned lame having lost a shoe (op 15-8)

5134 BETFAIR'S IPHONE AND ANDROID APP H'CAP CHASE (14 fncs) 2m 4f
4:40 (4:40) (Class 4) (0-115,117) 5-Y-0+ **£4,683** (£1,375; £687; £343)

Form RPR

0235 **1** **Babysitter (IRE)**[30] 4461 8-11-5 **108**....(v[1]) APMcCoy 121+
(Jonjo O'Neill) *trckd ldrs: upsides whn nt fluent 3 out: led narrowly last: pushed out* **7/2**[2]

U033 **2** *5* **Karingreason**[21] 4740 8-10-4 **93**.... JamesReveley 100
(Keith Reveley) *trckd ldr: led after 11th: jnd next: hdd last: no ex* **9/2**[3]

4444 **3** *5* **Phoenix Des Mottes (FR)**[8] 5015 8-9-7 **89** oh6.... JoeCornwall(7) 91
(John Cornwall) *led tl after 11th: outpcd appr 3 out: kpt on to take 3rd 2 out: styd on run-in* **12/1**

6/05 **4** *7* **Park's Prodigy**[42] 4237 7-10-11 **105**.... MissLHorner(5) 102
(Chris Grant) *trckd ldrs: outpcd appr 3 out: wknd last* **12/1**

2632 **5** *18* **Knight Legend (IRE)**[16] 4856 12-11-5 **115**....(t) MrMEnnis(7) 95
(Sarah Humphrey) *in tch: outpcd 8th: lost pl next: lft poor 5th appr 3 out* **17/2**

20-P **6** *17* **Chicago Outfit (IRE)**[13] 4911 6-11-8 **111**.... CampbellGillies 75
(John Wade) *in tch: lost pl after 8th: sn bhd* **25/1**

5616 **P** **Pamak D'Airy (FR)**[34] 4392 8-11-11 **114**.... BrianHughes —
(Henry Hogarth) *in tch: lost pl after 8th: sn bhd: t.o whn p.u bef 3 out* **16/1**

011 **P** **Himrayn**[8] 5015 8-12-0 **117**.... RichieMcLernon —
(Anabel L M King) *trckd ldrs: drvn 8th: wknd after 10th: 5th and bhd whn p.u bef 3 out* **7/4**[1]

3243 **P** **Earl Grez (FR)**[38] 4305 6-10-6 **102**.... KyleJames(7) —
(Philip Kirby) *in rr but in tch: reminders after 1st: drvn 8th: sn lost tch: t.o whn p.u bef 3 out* **16/1**

4m 59.6s (-6.10) **Going Correction** -0.40s/f (Good) **9** Ran SP% **118.3**
Speed ratings: **96,94,92,89,82 75,—,—,—**
Tote Swingers: 1&2 £3.00, 1&3 £8.00, 2&3 £8.30 CSF £20.79 CT £171.95 TOTE £5.00: £1.80, £1.70, £3.50; EX 22.90.
Owner The Magnificent Six **Bred** Des Sunderland **Trained** Cheltenham, Gloucs

FOCUS
A moderate handicap, run at a fair gallop and another race where two came well clear. A big step up from the winner on his previous chase efforts.

NOTEBOOK
Babysitter(IRE) had an awful lot to prove coming here, but the application of a first-time visor worked the oracle and he opened his account over fences at the sixth attempt. He still didn't look the most willing and hampered his cause with an error three out, but to his credit he responded to McCoy's urgings. He was nicely on top at the finish and will still look well handicapped on his hurdles form after a rise for this, so it wouldn't be that surprising to see him follow up. (tchd 4-1 and 9-2 in places)
Karingreason travelled best of all through the race and looked the one to be on at the penultimate fence, but she failed to see it out like the winner. This was by some way her best effort so far over fences. (op 6-1)
Phoenix Des Mottes(FR) set out to make all and, although unable to live with the first pair, ran his race, helping to set the level. (op 16-1)
Park's Prodigy was very easy to back for his third outing as a chaser and never seriously got involved. Official explanation: jockey said gelding had a breathing problem (op 8-1 tchd 14-1)
Himrayn made it two out of two since going chasing at Stratford eight days earlier but he was hiked up 11lb. He was never really travelling here, however, and was pulled up with something going amiss on the final circuit. Official explanation: trainer said gelding ran flat (op 2-1tchd 9-4 in places)

5135 COUNTRYSIDE DAY 15TH MAY MARES' STANDARD OPEN NATIONAL HUNT FLAT RACE 2m 1f
5:10 (5:11) (Class 6) 4-6-Y-0 **£1,267** (£369; £184)

Form RPR

10 **1** **Toubeera**[22] 4728 5-11-5 0.... SamThomas 107
(Michael Smith) *hld up towards rr: hdwy 9f out: sn chsng ldrs: drvn 4f out: led 1f out: all out* **13/2**[3]

2 *hd* **Awesome Bella** 4-10-6 0.... RobertThornton 94
(Alan King) *mid-div: reminders 6f out: sn outpcd: hdwy over 3f out: styd on to chse wnr last 100yds: jst hld* **11/4**[1]

0 **3** *3 ¾* **Silver Wren**[44] 4184 4-10-6 0.... SamJones 90
(Renee Robeson) *in rr: drvn after 6f: outpcd 6f out: hdwy over 2f out: 6th 1f out: styd on wl to snatch 3rd nr fin* **50/1**

4 *½* **Skenakilla Cross (IRE)** 6-10-12 0.... DenisO'Regan 96
(David O'Meara) *trckd ldrs: t.k.h: chal over 4f out: kpt on same pce fnl f* **7/1**

220 **5** *3* **D'Gigi**[29] 4468 5-10-12 0.... JamesReveley 94
(Keith Reveley) *w ldr: led after 6f: hdd 1f out: wknd and eased towards fin* **4/1**[2]

0 **6** *hd* **Look Who's Talking**[37] 4335 4-10-6 0.... WayneHutchinson 87
(Alan King) *trckd ldrs: wknd over 1f out* **11/1**

7 *17* **Wendy'Sgreyhorse** 5-10-12 0.... PaddyAspell 78
(Geoffrey Harker) *led 6f: chsd ldrs: wknd 2f out* **20/1**

8 *3* **Bollin Tahini** 5-10-9 0.... AlexMerriam(3) 75
(Neil King) *mid-div: drvn after 6f: hdwy on outside 7f out: lost pl over 4f out* **25/1**

00 **9** *1 ½* **Stickaround**[75] 3623 6-10-12 0.... GrahamLee 74
(Malcolm Jefferson) *trckd ldrs: t.k.h: drvn and hung rt bnd after 6f: lost pl 6f out* **16/1**

10 *6* **Kinder Scout** 4-10-6 0.... CampbellGillies 62
(Chris Grant) *s.s: reminders after s: in rr: bhd fnl 6f* **18/1**

50 **11** *1* **Shan Valley (IRE)**[45] 4171 5-10-7 0.... AlexanderVoy(5) 67
(Lucy Normile) *mid-div: hmpd and lost pl bnd after 6f: bhd fnl 3f* **25/1**

12 *4 ½* **Jays Girl** 4-10-6 0.... DavidEngland 57
(Pam Sly) *trckd ldrs: reminders and lost pl 7f out: sn bhd* **16/1**

13 *71* **Lilirosa (IRE)** 5-10-12 0.... PaulMoloney —
(Des Donovan) *in rr: drvn after 6f: t.o 6f out: virtually p.u* **33/1**

4m 8.00s (6.90) **Going Correction** +0.225s/f (Yiel)
WFA 4 from 5yo+ 5lb **13** Ran SP% **115.2**
Speed ratings: **92,91,90,89,88 88,80,78,78,75 74,72,39**
Tote Swingers: 1&2 £4.90, 1&3 £34.00, 2&3 £24.80 CSF £22.08 TOTE £6.90: £2.00, £1.60, £8.40; EX 26.80.
Owner Mrs H I S Calzini **Bred** Mrs H I S Calzini **Trained** Kirkheaton, Northumberland

FOCUS
There was a cracking finish to this ordinary mares' bumper. The winner was back to the form of her debut win.

NOTEBOOK
Toubeera was outclassed in a Listed event at Sandown last month, but showed her true colours again and ran out a gutsy winner under her penalty. She took time to pick up, but found plenty from 2f out and her experience stood her in good stead nearing the business end. She ought to stay further over hurdles and, from a yard that does well here, is a fair prospect. (op 4-1 tchd 7-1)
Awesome Bella ◆ is from a family her stable knows all about and she so nearly made a winning debut. Well backed, she lost out by getting badly outpaced on the far side, but there was a lot to like about the way she finished. She really ought to be winning one of these before the season's end and should relish a stiffer track. (op 10-3 tchd 5-2)
Silver Wren did her best work late on and stepped up greatly on her debut effort at Fakenham in February. (op 40-1)
Skenakilla Cross(IRE), very green to post, was going best of all at the top of the home straight and clearly has a future. She ought to come on plenty. (op 8-1)
D'Gigi was given a positive ride, but paid for her early exertions from 2f out. She helps to set the standard. (op 9-2)
Look Who's Talking, the runner-up's stablemate, showed more than was the case on her debut in February and appreciated the better ground. (tchd 12-1)
T/Plt: £148.90 to a £1 stake. Pool of £79,175 - 387.95 winning tickets. T/Qpdt: £21.30 to a £1 stake. Pool of £6,933 - 240.10 winning tickets. WG

5136 - 5140a (Foreign Racing) - See Raceform Interactive

4752 LIMERICK (R-H)
Sunday, April 3

OFFICIAL GOING: Hurdle course - yielding to soft (soft in places); chase course - yielding (yielding to soft in places)

5141a HUGH MCMAHON MEMORIAL NOVICE CHASE (GRADE 2) (16 fncs) 3m
4:45 (4:45) 5-Y-0+ **£21,573** (£6,306; £2,987; £995)

RPR

1 **Mr Cracker (IRE)**[17] 4816 6-11-8 135.... APHeskin 150
(Michael Hourigan, Ire) *sn led and clr: j.w: slt mstke last: styd on wl* **4/1**[2]

2 *4* **Western Charmer (IRE)**[36] 4368 9-11-3 141....(p) AELynch 139+
(D T Hughes, Ire) *chsd ldrs: rdn in mod 3rd into st: kpt on wout troubling wnr fr bef last* **8/1**

3 *7* **Pontiac (FR)**[21] 4764 8-11-3 117.... RMPower 132
(Mrs John Harrington, Ire) *towards rr: hdwy to chse ldrs fr 3 out: u.p in mod 5th into st: sn no imp and kpt on wout threatening* **20/1**

4 *1 ¾* **Sebadee (IRE)**[168] 1893 7-11-3.... AndrewJMcNamara 130
(K J Condon, Ire) *chsd ldrs: mod 2nd 3 out: sn no imp u.p and kpt on same pce* **12/1**

5 *1* **Elysian Rock**[18] 4804 7-11-3 130.... MJFerris 129
(M F Morris, Ire) *mid-div: sme sltly slow jumps: mod 4th and no imp u.p into st: kpt on same pce* **14/1**

6 *11* **Slippers Percy (IRE)**[19] 4790 9-11-3.... DGHogan 118
(Denis Gerard Hogan, Ire) *chsd ldr: dropped to 3rd 3 out: sn wknd* **25/1**

7 *19* **Roi Du Mee (FR)**[42] 4250 6-11-8.... DJCondon 104
(Gordon Elliott, Ire) *towards rr: mod 7th 5 out: struggling 3 out: eased st* **6/4**[1]

P **Beau Michael**[28] 4515 7-11-6....(tp) BarryGeraghty —
(Adrian McGuinness, Ire) *chsd ldrs: slt mstke 7 out: sn no imp and p.u bef 3 out* **12/1**

P **Healys Bar (IRE)**[21] 4763 7-11-3 126.... TJDoyle —
(Oliver McKiernan, Ire) *mid-div: bad mstke 6th: p.u bef next* **16/1**

F **Hampshire Express (IRE)**[53] 4014 8-11-3....(t) RWalsh —
(W P Mullins, Ire) *towards rr: slow jump early and reminder: fell 6 out* **6/1**[3]

6m 20.6s (-14.40) **10** Ran SP% **121.9**
CSF £37.95 TOTE £4.80: £1.50, £1.90, £3.10; DF 31.40.
Owner Gigginstown House Stud **Bred** R Jenks **Trained** Patrickswell, Co Limerick

FOCUS
A decent contest won by a promising prospect. The standard is set around the fourth and fifth.

NOTEBOOK
Mr Cracker(IRE), stepping up to 3m for the first time, once again showed his love for this venue with an all-the-way success. Jumping brilliantly for Adrian Heskin, he had everything on the stretch half way up the back straight. There were no dangers other than a fall by the time they entered the home straight and a slight mistake at the last was the only anxious moment for his supporters. It was a fine jumping and galloping performance by a very likeable horse. (op 7/2)
Western Charmer(IRE) finished out his race very well and is a horse capable of winning a good race over fences. He raced close to the pace among the chasing group and, while trying to get to the winner proved futile, he certainly ran on by far the best of the remainder. His jumping stood up on this occasion as well. (op 7/1)
Pontiac(FR) was held up off the pace, but his jumping was a bit sticky at times. In the end, he ran on past beaten horses and looks to be an out-and-out stayer.
Sebadee(IRE) ran better than his finishing position suggests and he probably just failed to stay on the ground. He improved to chase the winner before the fourth-last and appeared to be travelling much better than the rest of the chasing group, but he couldn't make an impression and in the end he weakened from the second-last.
Elysian Rock could never really make an impression on ground which would have been softer than ideal and one would expect him to jump better on a sounder surface as well.
Slippers Percy(IRE) ran well for a long way before fading. (op 20/1)
Roi Du Mee(FR) started to struggle as his jumping went to pieces on the final circuit. After a couple of mistakes, he was being driven and could make no impression whatsoever. This was a very disappointing effort. (op 2/1)
Healys Bar(IRE) Official explanation: jockey said gelding made a bad mistake and lost its action

5142 - 5143a (Foreign Racing) - See Raceform Interactive

4910 KELSO (L-H)
Monday, April 4

OFFICIAL GOING: Good to soft (soft in places)
Wind: Fairly strong, half against Weather: Cloudy, raining

5144 ALI GILHOME CONDITIONAL JOCKEYS' H'CAP HURDLE (10 hdls) 2m 2f
2:30 (2:31) (Class 4) (0-115,115) 4-Y-0+ **£2,276** (£668; £334; £166)

Form RPR

U420 **1** **Rolecarr (IRE)**[8] 5030 8-11-2 **105**.... HarryHaynes 111
(Ann Hamilton) *trckd ldrs: pushed along 1/2-way: rdn to chse ldr bef 2 out: led run-in: hld on wl* **18/1**

2042 **2** *nk* **Latin Connection (IRE)**[14] 4912 5-10-13 **107**....(t) SClements(5) 113
(S R B Crawford, Ire) *hld up: stdy hdwy gng wl appr 3 out: 9 l down last: effrt and ev ch whn edgd rt last 100yds: kpt on: jst hld* **15/2**[3]

5521 **3** *4* **King Mak**[14] 4912 9-11-1 **107**.... KyleJames(3) 109
(Marjorie Fife) *mde most tl rdn and hdd run-in: kpt on same pce* **8/1**

042 **4** 2 1/2 **A Stones Throw (NZ)**[18] 4833 6-10-0 **92**......................(t) JakeGreenall(3) 92
(Ben Haslam) *hld up in midfield: hdwy after 4 out: rdn next: kpt on same pce run-in* **7/1**[2]

5-21 **5** 21 **Kykate**[26] 4552 5-11-7 **110**..(t) CharlieHuxley 92+
(Thomas Kinsey) *t.k.h: trckd ldrs: hit 4 out but sn chsng ldr: effrt bef 2 out: wknd fr last* **4/1**[1]

0060 **6** 6 **Cassius (IRE)**[46] 4169 9-11-7 **110**...................................... PaulGallagher 85
(Bruce Mactaggart) *in tch: drvn and outpcd after 3 out: no imp fr next* **14/1**

00F5 **7** 3 1/2 **Livvy Inn (USA)**[23] 4715 6-11-9 **115**............................ CampbellGillies(3) 87
(Lucinda Russell) *hld up on ins: outpcd 4 out: n.d after* **4/1**[1]

0-2F **8** 9 **Smarties Party**[60] 706 8-10-10 **99**.................................. JamesHalliday 63
(Clive Mulhall) *hld up: drvn and outpcd after 4 out: btn bef 2 out* **50/1**

0F43 **9** 3 1/4 **Scotswell**[18] 4824 5-10-8 **105**.. GaryRutherford(8) 66
(Harriet Graham) *hld up bhd ldng gp: outpcd whn hit 3 out: sn btn* **66/1**

645 **10** 20 **Thescottishsoldier**[30] 4473 4-9-11 **95** oh7.................. EwanWhillans(3) 32
(Alistair Whillans) *trckd ldrs: lost pl after 4 out: wknd fr next* **25/1**

40 **11** 14 **Benmadigan (IRE)**[136] 2506 9-11-4 **110**...................... FearghalDavis(3) 41
(Nicky Richards) *bhd: struggling fr 1/2-way: nvr on terms* **18/1**

036 **12** 4 **Battle Honour**[30] 4473 4-10-4 **102**.............................. RobertMcCarth(3) 23
(Sue Bradburne) *hld up on outside: struggling 1/2-way: sn btn* **20/1**

0P4P **P** **Bucephalus (IRE)**[46] 4169 7-10-8 **107**................(t) StephenMulqueen(10) —
(Maurice Barnes) *hld up: nt fluent 2nd: hdwy and prom next: rdn and wknd bef 4 out: t.o whn p.u bef 2 out* **33/1**

6P14 **P** **Just Maddie**[26] 4552 7-10-7 **96**......................................(p) AlexanderVoy —
(Rayson Nixon) *w ldr: reminders 1/2-way: wknd after 4 out: t.o whn p.u bef 2 out* **40/1**

4050 **P** **Miss Abbey**[24] 4688 7-9-11 **94**... PaulNorton(8) —
(Jim Goldie) *nt fluent: a bhd: struggling 1/2-way: t.o whn p.u bef 2 out* **12/1**

4m 33.0s (6.00) **Going Correction** +0.275s/f (Yiel)
WFA 4 from 5yo+ 5lb **15** Ran SP% **117.7**
Speed ratings (Par 105): **97,96,95,93,84 81,80,76,74,66 59,58,—,—,—**
toteswingers:1&2 £18.90, 2&3 £12.30, 1&3 £13.10 CSF £135.35 CT £1181.35 TOTE £28.00: £5.40, £2.50, £2.50; EX 181.80.
Owner Ian Hamilton **Bred** A W Buller **Trained** Great Bavington, Northumbland

FOCUS
A damp day and quite a strong headwind in the home straight. The ground was described as soft. A modest conditional jockeys' handicap hurdle run at a strong pace and four broke clear on the final turn. A good time compared with other races over the same trip, and steps up from the first two.

NOTEBOOK
Rolecarr(IRE), raised 13lb after his win at Hexham in November, has crept up another 10lb since. He put a poor effort last time behind him and did just enough under a very good ride. Official explanation: trainer said, regarding the apparent improvement of form, that the gelding settled better in this race (op 16-1)
Latin Connection(IRE), given a lot to do when 7l behind King Mak here last time, enjoyed an 8lb pull with that rival. Dropped right out in the early stages, he was set a very stiff task. Only fifth jumping the last, despite a tendency to hang left he only just failed to get there in the end. This looked like a winning opportunity which was allowed to get away. Official explanation: jockey stated that his instructions were to hold the horse up, get him relaxed and produce him with a late run. The trainer confirmed these instructions, adding that the gelding is a very difficult ride. (op 10-1)
King Mak, raised 9lb, tried hard to make all but in the end came up a fair bit short. He will return to fences at some point. (tchd 9-1)
A Stones Throw(NZ), improved since switching to this yard, might appreciate a return to a stiffer test. (op 11-2)
Kykate, who opened her account in novice company at Catterick, looked to have been allotted a stiff mark on her handicap debut and she weakened on the run-in. (tchd 3-1)
Cassius(IRE), well backed at long odds, continues to underperform. (op 20-1)
Livvy Inn(USA) is running out of excuses and again let down his dwindling band of supporters. (tchd 9-2)
Miss Abbey Official explanation: trainer's representative said that the mare bled from the nose

5145 PRINCESS ROYAL TRUST FOR CARERS H'CAP CHASE (12 fncs) 2m 1f
3:00 (3:00) (Class 4) (0-115,115) 5-Y-O+ **£3,903** (£1,146; £573; £286)

Form RPR

P253 **1** **Duke Of Malfi**[30] 4471 8-10-8 **97**....................................(p) PeterBuchanan 106+
(Lucinda Russell) *chsd ldr: led 7th to 2 out: rallied and regained ld appr last: drvn and kpt on gamely run-in* **4/1**[2]

0P00 **2** 3 1/4 **Bob's Dream (IRE)**[14] 4913 9-11-8 **111**.........................(t) CampbellGillies 117
(William Amos) *hld up: hdwy after 3 out: lft 4 l 3rd last: chsd wnr last 175yds: kpt on* **12/1**

1422 **3** 1 1/4 **Sheriff Hall (IRE)**[25] 4573 6-10-4 **93**...............................(t) JanFaltejsek 100+
(George Charlton) *cl up: led and j.rt 2 out: hdd whn j.rt 2f out: one pce last 200yds* **3/1**[1]

3-02 **4** 7 **Cabbyl Doo**[16] 4868 8-10-8 **97**.. PaddyAspell 98
(James Moffatt) *hld up in tch: blnd 4th: rdn 3 out: no imp fr next* **3/1**[1]

PP4 **5** 3 3/4 **Tooman Lane (IRE)**[35] 4392 7-10-11 **100**.........................(t) TomSiddall 95
(Patrick Holmes) *hld up in tch: stdy hdwy bef 3 out: rdn and outpcd after next* **22/1**

1300 **6** 40 **Heavenly Chorus**[14] 4913 9-11-7 **110**.............................. JamesReveley 69
(Keith Reveley) *hld up: hdwy bef 3 out: wknd next: eased whn btn run-in* **14/1**

P00U **7** 4 1/2 **Super Baby (FR)**[30] 4471 9-10-10 **102**......................(p) HarryHaynes(3) 57
(James Ewart) *prom: rdn and outpcd 4 out: wknd fr next* **16/1**

0064 **P** **Carrietau**[14] 4913 8-11-12 **115**...(bt) JasonMaguire —
(Barry Murtagh) *led: mstke 5th: hdd 7th: wknd after next: t.o whn p.u bef 3 out* **17/2**[3]

0050 **U** **Carters Rest**[43] 4237 8-10-4 **93**......................................(v[1]) DenisO'Regan 95
(Chris Grant) *hld up in tch: stdy hdwy and cl up 3 out: carried rt next: sn rdn: effrt and nrly 3 l 3rd whn mstke and uns rdr last* **10/1**

4m 26.6s (8.60) **Going Correction** +0.65s/f (Soft) **9** Ran SP% **114.2**
Speed ratings: **105,103,102,99,97 79,76,—,—**
toteswingers:1&2 £8.40, 2&3 £7.60, 1&3 £1.30 CSF £48.30 CT £162.38 TOTE £5.30: £1.70, £3.20, £1.30; EX 76.50.
Owner Miss G Joughin **Bred** Miss Gail Joughin **Trained** Arlary, Perth & Kinross

FOCUS
Three confirmed front runners in this modest handicap. The pace was strong over the first few fences but it steadied in the back straight. A small personal best from the winner, and the second has slipped to a good mark.

NOTEBOOK
Duke Of Malfi, who won three of his four starts over fences last season, likes soft ground and has run well round here before. Normally a front runner, he was happy to accept a lead over the first six fences. He looked to have a battle on his hands jumping the last but won going away in the end, confirming the fine form of his stable ahead of Aintree. (op 7-2)
Bob's Dream(IRE), a winner four times over hurdles and fences last season, has been in poor form this time and as a result his rating has slipped to 4lb below his last winning mark. He made up a fair amount of ground to be left third at the last but in the end the winner was going away from him. This was a vastly more encouraging effort. (op 11-1)
Sheriff Hall(IRE), having his third start over fences, was another unable to dominate. After getting to the front he tended to jump right-handed but to his credit was coming back for more at the line. He will surely break his duck over fences soon rather than later.
Cabbyl Doo, who has few miles on the clock, was runner-up at Newcastle on his chasing debut to a subsequent easy winner. Knocked back by an early blunder, he never threatened to take a hand. (op 9-2)
Tooman Lane(IRE), pulled up on his first two starts for this trainer, again hinted at a revival and this soft-ground performer appreciates a much stiffer test. (op 25-1)
Carrietau was harried in front and seemed to spit the dummy out altogether when headed before the halfway mark. Official explanation: jockey said that that the gelding made a mistake and lost interest thereafter (op 10-1 tchd 8-1)
Carters Rest in a first-time visor, survived a couple of jumping errors and was in the process of running a much more encouraging race when in third and giving his rider no chance at the final fence.\n (op 10-1 tchd 8-1)

5146 LE GARCON D'OR NOVICES' CHASE (19 fncs) 3m 1f
3:30 (3:30) (Class 4) 5-Y-O+ **£2,602** (£764; £382; £190)

Form RPR

4PP4 **1** **Soft Spoken Guy (IRE)**[35] 4394 8-10-12 0...............(t) MichaelMcAlister 130+
(Maurice Barnes) *nt fluent first circ: cl up: led 14th: mde rest: drew clr fr 2 out* **7/1**[3]

4240 **2** 25 **Flying Doctor**[40] 4285 8-11-2 127.................................... HarryHaynes(3) 117
(Elliott Cooper) *prom: niggled along whn blnd bdly 4 out: rallied to chse (clr) wnr after last: no imp* **9/1**

1U10 **3** nk **Chamirey (FR)**[19] 4802 8-11-12 135.............................(b) JasonMaguire 124
(Donald McCain) *nt fluent: in tch: pushed along 13th: outpcd whn hit 15th: sn struggling: sme late hdwy: nvr on terms* **8/11**[1]

-356 **4** 10 **Milans Man (IRE)**[15] 4890 6-10-7 0............................ PaulGallagher(5) 100
(Howard Johnson) *led tl hit and hdd 14th: nt fluent next: rdn and outpcd after 2 out: lost 2nd and wknd after last* **4/1**[2]

4-15 **P** **Club Class**[134] 2550 8-10-12 117....................................... MrDarylMillar(7) —
(John Wade) *chsd ldrs: outpcd bef 8th: lost tch fr 10th: t.o whn p.u bef 3 out* **12/1**

6m 47.3s (15.80) **Going Correction** +0.65s/f (Soft) **5** Ran SP% **108.1**
Speed ratings: **100,92,91,88,—**
CSF £51.31 TOTE £5.40: £3.40, £3.10; EX 59.30.
Owner Scott Lowther & The Whisperers **Bred** Brittas House Stud **Trained** Farlam, Cumbria

FOCUS
The winner improved to the level of his hurdles form but this form looks suspect. The finishing fractions were very slow.

NOTEBOOK
Soft Spoken Guy(IRE), pulled up and well beaten on his first two tries over fences, jumped much better. Keen early, he took a definite advantage two out and, soon out on his own, won easing down in the end. It was no fluke but his handicap mark could be harsh as a result. Official explanation: trainer said, regarding the apparent improvement of form, that the gelding was steadily improving over fences (tchd 13-2)
Flying Doctor, tailed off over hurdles six weeks earlier after a four-month break, took a liberty with the fourth last. He stuck on to claim a modest second spot but might struggle in handicaps from his current mark of 127. (op 7-1 tchd 13-2)
Chamirey(FR), who was already weakening when making a blunder when well beaten in the National Hunt Chase at Cheltenham, jumped very deliberately and was given some sharp reminders setting out on to the final circuit. A blunder five out sealed his fate, though he was just denied second spot in the end. He is not progressing as hoped and is one to be wary of. (op 5-6)
Milans Man(IRE), who took on the winner for the lead, ran poorly for the third time in succession. (op 5-1 tchd 7-2)
Club Class blundered his way round on his first start since November. He was losing touch with over a circuit to go. (op 11-1)

5147 DUNCAN SINCLAIR MEMORIAL NOVICES' HURDLE (DIV I) (10 hdls) 2m 2f
4:00 (4:00) (Class 4) 4-Y-O+ **£1,951** (£573; £286; £143)

Form RPR

F **1** **Realt Mor (IRE)**[24] 4684 6-10-13 0................................ DominicElsworth 123+
(Nicky Richards) *pressed ldr: led gng wl 3 out: pushed clr fr next* **8/11**[1]

2221 **2** 14 **Rupert Lamb**[18] 4824 5-11-0 119.................................... PaulGallagher(5) 113
(Howard Johnson) *t.k.h early: led to 3 out: sn rdn and rallied: no ch w wnr fr next* **3/1**[2]

5 **3** 3 3/4 **Tamanaco (IRE)**[52] 4056 4-10-7 0.................................... RobertWalford 98
(Tim Walford) *hld up in tch: effrt to chse clr ldrs appr 4 out: no imp bef next* **16/1**

00 **4** 19 **Nisaal (IRE)**[14] 4910 6-10-13 0... PaddyAspell 92
(Sandy Forster) *t.k.h in rr: pushed along and sme hdwy 4 out: nvr able to chal* **100/1**

40 **5** 19 **Brokethegate**[40] 4287 6-10-13 0... DenisO'Regan 69
(Chris Grant) *bhd: outpcd whn j.lft and plenty to do 6th: plugged on run-in: nvr on terms* **66/1**

-305 **6** 11 **Flaygray**[25] 4569 7-10-13 0.. CampbellGillies 60
(Chris Grant) *prom tl rdn and wknd fr 6th* **25/1**

-434 **7** nk **Four Fiddlers (IRE)**[39] 4308 6-10-6 0......................... MissLAlexander(7) 59
(N W Alexander) *chsd clr ldrs tl rdn and wknd appr 4 out* **66/1**

2320 **8** 6 **Kings Grey (IRE)**[22] 4739 7-10-13 114............................. JamesReveley 54
(Keith Reveley) *midfield: drvn and hdwy bef 4 out: wknd fr next* **9/2**[3]

0/36 **9** 9 **Dechiper (IRE)**[178] 1760 9-10-13 93.......................... MichaelMcAlister 46
(Robert Johnson) *midfield: drvn and outpcd 6th: n.d after* **100/1**

0P **10** 3 3/4 **Princess Cherry (IRE)**[25] 4569 6-9-13 0.................. GaryRutherford(7) 35
(Harriet Graham) *a bhd: no ch fr 6th* **200/1**

000 **11** 31 **Northern Acres**[46] 4165 5-10-13 95.................................. MarkBradburne 14
(Sue Bradburne) *midfield: outpcd whn blkd 6th: sn btn* **80/1**

00P/ **P** **Ashgrove Diamond (IRE)**[755] 4408 7-9-13 60................. KyleJames(7) —
(Lucy Normile) *sn wl bhd: t.o whn p.u bef 6th* **200/1**

/0-P **P** **Forrest Lemons**[146] 2297 7-10-13 0...........................(t) RichieMcGrath —
(Andrew Parker) *hld up: struggling 6th: nvr on terms: t.o whn p.u bef 2 out* **100/1**

0 **P** **King Kalium (IRE)**[27] 4547 5-10-13 0.............................. WilsonRenwick —
(Bruce Mactaggart) *bhd: struggling 1/2-way: t.o whn p.u after 4 out* **100/1**

4m 36.4s (9.40) **Going Correction** +0.275s/f (Yiel)
WFA 4 from 5yo+ 5lb **14** Ran SP% **120.0**
Speed ratings (Par 105): **90,83,82,73,65 60,60,57,53,51 38,—,—,—**
toteswingers:1&2 £2.00, 2&3 £6.90, 1&3 £4.70 CSF £3.12 TOTE £2.30: £1.30, £1.40, £3.40; EX 3.80.
Owner Mrs Pat Sloan **Bred** R Hartigan **Trained** Greystoke, Cumbria

FOCUS
Plenty of dead wood in the first division of this novices' hurdle. The easy winner can rate higher and the next three were all close to their marks.

NOTEBOOK
Realt Mor(IRE), winner of an Irish maiden point, had the race at his mercy when somewhat unluckily coming to grief three out at Ayr. He made no mistake this time, tracking the leader before taking charge on the home turn. Kept up to his work, he looks a decent prospect who will no doubt revert to fences next season. (op 5-6 tchd 4-6)
Rupert Lamb had it all to do under a 6lb penalty and his jumping was better than on some occasions in the past. (op 11-4 tchd 10-3 and 7-2 in a place)
Tamanaco(IRE), rated 78 on the Flat, settled a lot better than on his first try over hurdles at Musselburgh. He stayed on all the way to the line and will improve again and find a race. (op 18-1)
Nisaal(IRE), rated 72 on the level, again shaped with encouragement on his third try over hurdles and is one to bear in mind in modest handicap company.
Brokethegate, making his hurdling debut after a six-week break, appeared late on the scene and will appreciate a much stiffer test.
Kings Grey(IRE) moved up to dispute fourth four out but he stopped to nothing and was eased on the run-in. It had been the same story on his previous start at Market Rasen and he looks to have a problem. (op 6-1)

5148 BREWIN DOLPHIN BUCCLEUCH CUP MAIDEN HUNTERS' CHASE (19 fncs) 3m 1f
4:30 (4:30) (Class 5) 5-Y-0+ **£1,873** (£581; £290; £145)

Form RPR
PP/- **1** **Hold On Julio (IRE)**16 8-11-7 0 MrMEnnis(7) 113+
(Vicky Simpson) *cl up: hit 12th: led 14th tl hit and hdd next: led gng wl last: qcknd clr* **8/11**1
0/ **2** *28* **Marksmore**16 8-11-9 0 MissKBryson(5) 85
(Miss Katie Scott) *bhd: hdwy and in tch 13th: outpcd 4 out: lft modest 3rd next: plugged on fr last: wnt 2nd towards fin: no ch w wnr* **22/1**
503- **3** *2* **Putitawayforayear (IRE)**16 9-11-7 0 (t) MrDarylMillar(7) 85
(Miss V Renwick) *led to 14th: led again next: hdd last: sn outpcd: wknd: hung bdly rt and lost 2nd towards fin* **16/1**
F **4** *12* **Temple Green**16 9-11-2 0 MrJARichardson(5) 65
(Mrs J Martin-Mayland) *bhd: pushed along 1/2-way: outpcd 15th: sme hdwy whn mstke 3 out: nvr on terms* **25/1**
5400 **5** *9* **Ellandshe (IRE)**9 11-11-7 49 (b) MrRWilson(7) 67
(William Young) *in tch tl rdn and outpcd 14th: n.d after* **66/1**
05P/ **6** *95* **Zoren (FR)**16 7-11-7 83 (t) MrNOrpwood(7) —
(Raymond Shiels) *in tch tl rdn and wknd after 4 out: t.o* **40/1**
4/3- **P** **Stark Raven**16 11-11-7 82 (p) MrDHolmes(7) —
(R D Coupland) *prom: lost pl 6th: sn struggling: t.o whn p.u bef 10th* **16/1**
6P0/ **P** **Salveo (IRE)**9 9-11-7 79 MrGJCockburn(7) —
(Victor Thompson) *bhd: struggling fnl circ: no ch whn p.u bef last* **25/1**
4P-0 **F** **Silk Parasol (IRE)**16 9-11-0 71 MrRLindsay(7) —
(Alan J Brown) *trckd ldrs: 2 l 3rd and gng wl whn fell heavily 2 out: fatally injured* **15/2**3
5 **U** **Rakerin Lad (IRE)**30 8-11-9 0 MrGCrow(5) —
(Mrs S Taylor) *prom on outside: blnd and uns 4th* **9/2**2
6m 49.2s (17.70) **Going Correction** +0.65s/f (Soft) **10** Ran SP% **115.6**
Speed ratings: **97,88,87,83,80 50,—,—,—,—**
toteswingers:1&2 £8.20, 2&3 £15.70, 1&3 £4.00 CSF £23.22 TOTE £1.70: £1.60, £3.80, £1.70; EX 26.40.
Owner Miss Vicky Simpson **Bred** John Goodwin **Trained** North Berwick, East Lothian
■ Stewards' Enquiry : Mr Daryl Millar caution: used whip without giving time to repsond

FOCUS
A maiden hunters' chase where the second and third favourites failed to complete. The easy winner looks a decent hunter and can rate higher.

NOTEBOOK
Hold On Julio(IRE), pulled up in two starts over hurdles, has developed into a smart pointer and came here on the back of a hat-trick. He survived one mistake and a couple of errors to come right away on the run-in. He could take his chance in the intermediate race at Cheltenham's big hunter chase meeting next month. (op 5-6, tchd 10-11 in a place)
Marksmore, no match for Silk Parasol in a members' race at nearby Friars Haugh, stayed on to capture a remote second spot in the closing stages. (tchd 25-1)
Putitawayforayear(IRE), a giant individual who was a long way behind Hold On Julio in an intermediate point at Friars Haugh, helped force the pace, but he emptied badly on the run-in and looks a doubtful stayer.
Temple Green, who fell late on here in May, is not the soundest of jumpers and was struggling some way from home. (op 22-1)
Silk Parasol(IRE), having her second start in hunter chase company, was a handy third and seemingly full of running when suffering a fatal fall two out. (op 8-1 tchd 7-1)
Rakerin Lad(IRE), who had Silk Parasol back in fourth when taking the members' race at Corbridge, was out of the race at the first ditch. (op 8-1 tchd 7-1)

5149 JASON SWEENEY - SPORTING SCULPTURES IN STAINLESS STEEL H'CAP HURDLE (11 hdls) 2m 6f 110y
5:00 (5:14) (Class 3) (0-130,130) 4-Y-0+ **£2,602** (£764; £382; £190)

Form RPR
2424 **1** **Moon Indigo**30 4475 5-11-4 127 PaulGallagher(5) 128
(Howard Johnson) *prom: drvn 3 out: rallied and ev ch last: styd on gamely u.p to ld towards fin* **6/1**2
-U31 **2** *shd* **Hawaii Klass**15 4889 6-10-8 112 WilsonRenwick 113
(Donald Whillans) *hld up in midfield: hdwy and ev ch 3 out: led bef next to run-in: rallied to regain ld last 100yds: hdd cl home* **12/1**
51-0 **3** *nk* **Kilbrannish Hill (IRE)**22 4762 7-10-11 115 (p) AELynch 116
(I R Ferguson, Ire) *hld up: smooth hdwy appr 3 out: rdn to ld run-in: hdd last 100yds: hld towards fin* **8/1**3
0-01 **4** *2 1/4* **Sendali (FR)**14 4914 7-10-5 109 DenisO'Regan 109
(Chris Grant) *prom: effrt after 2 out: edgd rt: kpt on same pce run-in* **10/1**
3340 **5** *3 3/4* **Currahee**23 4715 7-10-3 107 (t) MichaelMcAlister 103
(Maurice Barnes) *cl up: led 4 out to bef 2 out: edgd rt and outpcd run-in* **14/1**
0130 **6** *8* **Stopped Out**44 4209 6-11-6 124 RichieMcGrath 112
(Kate Walton) *hld up: mstke 7th: rdn bef 3 out: effrt bef next: sn outpcd* **4/1**1
0340 **7** *7* **Political Paddy**16 4869 9-10-6 110 (p) JamesReveley 92
(Rayson Nixon) *cl up: ev ch 4 out to 2 out: sn wknd* **9/1**
3604 **8** *8* **Lawgiver (IRE)**14 4914 10-9-13 110 (p) KyleJames(7) 85
(Marjorie Fife) *hld up: drvn after 3 out: sn btn* **10/1**
U561 **9** *13* **Shooting Times**24 4688 6-10-0 104 oh1 GrahamLee 67
(Andrew Parker) *midfield on ins: drvn along 4 out: wknd after next* **8/1**3
26/P **10** *1* **Supreme Ruler (IRE)**8 5030 8-11-2 120 PaddyAspell 82
(Patrick Holmes) *hld up: shortlived effrt 3 out: btn next* **40/1**
45P4 **11** *1 1/4* **Glaced Over**20 4795 6-10-0 104 oh4 CampbellGillies 65
(Raymond Shiels) *hld up: blnd bdly 2nd: nt fluent after: effrt bef 3 out: sn wknd* **40/1**
0000 **12** *2* **The Shy Man (IRE)**9 5003 8-11-0 118 BarryKeniry 77
(George Moore) *cl up: ev ch 4 out: rdn and wknd fr next* **20/1**
1P-P **13** *26* **Middleton Dene (IRE)**149 2204 9-11-5 130 RobertMcCarth(7) 66
(Rose Dobbin) *trckd ldrs tl rdn and wknd bef 3 out* **50/1**
5426 **14** *11* **Chester Lad**23 4715 6-11-3 121 JanFaltejsek 47
(George Charlton) *chsd ldrs on outside: hit 4 out: sn rdn: wknd bef next* **25/1**
36P5 **15** *39* **Or De Grugy (FR)**46 4167 9-10-8 117 AlexanderVoy(5) 8
(Sue Bradburne) *mde most to 4 out: rdn and wknd bef next* **20/1**
5m 43.2s (2.20) **Going Correction** +0.275s/f (Yiel) **15** Ran SP% **119.3**
Speed ratings (Par 107): **107,106,106,106,104 101,99,96,92,91 91,90,81,77,64**
toteswingers:1&2 £10.80, 2&3 £28.90, 1&3 £6.90 CSF £67.72 CT £586.55 TOTE £3.10: £1.10, £5.20, £3.50; EX 63.00.
Owner Andrea & Graham Wylie **Bred** Britton House Stud Ltd **Trained** Billy Row, Co Durham
■ Stewards' Enquiry : Paul Gallagher caution:careless riding; one-day ban: used whip with excessive frequency
Wilson Renwick one-day ban: used hwip with excessive fequency (18 Apr)

FOCUS
A highly competitive stayers' handicap hurdle, and the form is solid if fairly ordinary. There were still eight in contention on the final turn and four almost upsides with a furlong left to run. The third, fourth and fifth have been rated close to their marks.

NOTEBOOK
Moon Indigo, rated 92 on the Flat, made his handicap debut from a possibly lenient mark of 127. Stepping up in trip, after a battle royal he poked his head in front right on the line. (op 11-2 tchd 5-1)
Hawaii Klass, another making his handicap bow, made the best of his way home and in the end was just touched off. He has a very good attitude and deserves to go one better. (op 16-1)
Kilbrannish Hill(IRE), who clipped heels and was pulled up at Navan on his previous start, was given a very patient ride. He moved up four out and was tracking the leading four still on the bridle setting out up the run-in. Level a furlong out, under severe pressure he could find no more near the finish. (tchd 7-1)
Sendali(FR), raised 4lb after his win here on his first outing for this trainer, ran right up to his best but the assessor has his measure now. (op 8-1 tchd 11-1)
Currahee has slipped 8lb in the ratings this time and helped force the pace until feeling the strain soon after the last. A slightly less stiff test will be in his favour. (op 18-1)
Stopped Out, down in trip, was 6lb higher than for his C&D success in November and could never land a telling blow. (op 9-1)

5150 MORE LIKELY MARES' H'CAP CHASE (17 fncs) 2m 6f 110y
5:30 (5:42) (Class 4) (0-115,112) 5-Y-0+ **£2,602** (£764; £382; £190)

Form RPR
0462 **1** **More Equity**19 4812 9-11-7 107 JamesReveley 115+
(Dianne Sayer) *cl up: led 2nd: mde rest: qcknd bef 2 out: styd on strly* **10/1**
0663 **2** *9* **Maid In Moscow (IRE)**14 4911 7-10-0 86 oh4 CampbellGillies 86
(S R B Crawford, Ire) *hld up in tch: effrt 3 out: rdn next: styd on to chse (clr) wnr last 100yds: no imp* **14/1**
-443 **3** *3* **Posh Bird (IRE)**22 4763 8-11-8 108 AELynch 107
(I R Ferguson, Ire) *led to 2nd: chsd wnr: hit and rdn 3 out: kpt on same pce fr last: lost 2nd last 100yds* **9/4**1
431 **4** *32* **Streamtown (IRE)**20 4795 7-11-3 103 PeterBuchanan 72
(S R B Crawford, Ire) *nt fluent on occasions: hld up in tch: effrt bef 3 out: wknd fr next* **4/1**2
U311 **5** *8* **Flighty Mist**20 4800 9-10-0 91 PaulGallagher(5) 55
(Sandy Forster) *prom: blnd 10th: hit 12th: effrt and rdn 3 out: wknd fr next* **6/1**
2505 **P** **Coldwells (IRE)**20 4799 11-10-0 86 oh6 GrahamLee —
(Martin Todhunter) *cl up: rdn and dropped in rr bef 12th: lost tch 4 out: p.u bef next* **8/1**
631V **P** **Identity Parade (IRE)**18 4831 7-11-12 112 JasonMaguire —
(Donald McCain) *cl up: blnd 2nd: lost pl 4th: hung lft and outpcd whn blnd 10th: sn p.u* **9/2**3
5m 56.8s (12.30) **Going Correction** +0.65s/f (Soft) **7** Ran SP% **110.1**
Speed ratings: **104,100,99,88,85 —,—**
toteswingers:1&2 £13.70, 2&3 £3.70, 1&3 £4.70 CSF £109.51 CT £400.01 TOTE £10.00: £3.00, £5.60; EX 61.70.
Owner Mrs Margaret Coppola **Bred** Mrs A F Tullie **Trained** Hackthorpe, Cumbria

FOCUS
A modest mares' handicap chase run at a sound pace. A small personal best from the winner, who is a better chaser than hurdler.

NOTEBOOK
More Equity, winner of three handicap hurdles in the past, came here on the back of a good effort when runner-up in a 3m2f handicap hurdle at Huntingdon. Her rider made sure her stamina came into play and, jumping really well, she came clear from three out. It was her first win over fences at the 12th attempt and on this showing further success should come her way over the coming months. (op 8-1)
Maid In Moscow(IRE), seemingly her trainer's second string, was running from 4lb out of the handicap. A point winner in the past, she too was returning to fences and, the way she finished, 3m will be right up her street. (op 12-1 tchd 11-1)
Posh Bird(IRE), runner-up in the Ulster Grand National, was hanging on to second spot when she crashed through the third last. That enabled the winner to give her the slip and she lost out on second spot in the final furlong. (op 11-4)
Streamtown(IRE), another point winner, had taken a novices' hurdle at Sedgefield on her previous start. Making her handicap bow, her jumping let her down and in the end she finished a distant fourth. (op 9-2)
Flighty Mist, hoisted another 6lb and stepping up in trip, made a couple of mistakes setting out on to the final circuit and her goose was cooked three out. This was her third start in less than a month and she may benefit from a short break. Official explanation: trainer said that the mare finished lame (tchd 13-2)
Identity Parade(IRE), who had the void Towcester race at her mercy when falling at the last, made her handicap bow. She never went a yard, jumping slowly, and was already out of touch when pulled up with a circuit to go. She has plenty to prove now. (op 7-2 tchd 5-1)

5151 DUNCAN SINCLAIR MEMORIAL NOVICES' HURDLE (DIV II) (10 hdls) 2m 2f
6:00 (6:10) (Class 4) 4-Y-0+ **£1,951** (£573; £286; £143)

Form RPR
6315 **1** **Bogside (IRE)**30 4475 7-11-5 118 JanFaltejsek 108+
(George Charlton) *t.k.h: cl up: led 4 out: hit last: shkn up briefly and drew clr run-in: readily* **2/5**1
00 **2** *7* **Mar Ocean (FR)**134 2553 5-10-13 0 JamesReveley 87
(Patrick Griffin, Ire) *hld up: hdwy on outside 3 out: effrt and chsd (clr) wnr run-in: no imp* **40/1**

4P **3** *7* **Master Performer (USA)**[162] 1984 4-10-7 0.................. DenisO'Regan 74
(Barry Murtagh) *hld up: smooth hdwy to trck ldrs bef 2 out: chsd wnr appr last to run-in: sn outpcd* **33/1**

0 **4** *2 3/4* **Hotgrove Boy**[30] 4473 4-10-0 0.. MrMEnnis(7) 71
(George Foster) *chsd ldr: hit 5th: ev ch 4 out: hit and rdn 2 out: edgd rt and no ex fr last* **50/1**

05-0 **5** *1* **Glingermill (IRE)**[177] 1783 8-10-13 0................................ FearghalDavis 76
(Nicky Richards) *in tch: nt fluent and pushed along 3 out: no imp fr next* **12/1**

0P0- **6** *6* **Tom's Toybox**[513] 2118 9-10-8 0..................................(p) MissLHorner(5) 70
(Chris Grant) *midfield: drvn and outpcd after 4 out: no imp bef 2 out* **13/2**[3]

600 **7** *3* **Little Fifi**[20] 4795 6-10-6 0... CampbellGillies 60
(Sandy Thomson) *cl up tl rdn and wknd bef 2 out* **100/1**

000 **8** *5* **Sleep In First (FR)**[27] 4541 5-10-13 0.......................... MarkBradburne 62
(Anna Bramall) *midfield: drvn and outpcd bef 3 out: sn btn* **125/1**

0000 **9** *hd* **Overpriced**[8] 5027 5-9-13 0..................................(t) MissAngelaBarnes(7) 55
(Maurice Barnes) *hld up: short lived effrt bef 3 out: sn btn* **125/1**

0000 **10** *3* **Isla Patriot**[14] 4910 5-10-13 0.. PeterBuchanan 59
(N W Alexander) *bhd: pushed along 7th: sn outpcd: n.d after* **100/1**

11 *1 3/4* **French Seventyfive**[276] 4-10-7 0.................................... RobertWalford 51
(Tim Walford) *hld up in tch: drvn after 3 out: wknd bef next* **25/1**

003 **12** *1 1/4* **Foot The Bill**[25] 4569 6-10-13 0.. TomSiddall 56
(Patrick Holmes) *led to 4 out: rdn and wknd fr next* **11/2**[2]

0P-P **13** *dist* **Boston Lad (IRE)**[24] 4684 7-10-8 0.......................... AlexanderVoy(5) —
(Lucy Normile) *cl up tl lost pl qckly appr 4 out: sn struggling: t.o* **100/1**

4m 42.7s (15.70) **Going Correction** +0.275s/f (Yiel)
WFA 4 from 5yo+ 5lb **13** Ran SP% **123.6**
Speed ratings (Par 105): **76,72,69,68,68 65,64,61,61,60 59,59,—**
toteswingers:1&2:£9.10, 2&3:£53.50, 1&3:£3.90. totesuper7: Win: Not won. Place: Not won. CSF £33.71 TOTE £1.60: £1.10, £6.30, £4.90; EX 34.20.
Owner Mrs A R Wood **Bred** Pat O'Donovan **Trained** Stocksfield, Northumberland

FOCUS
Again plenty of dead wood in division two of this novices' hurdle and on paper a simple task for the heavy odds-on favourite. It was the weaker vision and the easy winner was value for further but still rated below his best.

NOTEBOOK
Bogside(IRE), off the mark here in February and not disgraced in a Grade 2 event also here, is a headstrong type. In charge four out, after hitting the last he powered clear and won easing down, value double the official margin. He has plenty of size about him and will certainly make a decent novice chaser next term. (op 1-2 tchd 8-15, 4-7 in places)
Mar Ocean(FR), absent since November, was making his hurdling debut. He stayed on from off the pace to finish clear second best and a modest event should come his way.
Master Performer(USA), rated 73 on the Flat in Ireland, showed little in two starts over hurdles before the turn of the year. He travelled strongly much of the way and low-grade handicaps now beckon.
Hotgrove Boy, who showed little first time, pulled very hard and hung right as he tired on the run-in. He will need to learn to settle better. (op 66-1)
Glingermill(IRE), having his first start since October, was hard at work three out and looked very one paced. He should make a better chaser in time.
Tom's Toybox, a winner of four chases, was having his first start for 17 months. He kept on in his own time from four out and the outing will not be lost on him. (op 7-1)
T/Jkpt: Part won. £29,248.70. Pool of £41,195.39 - 0.50 winning units. T/Plt: £135.40 to a £1 stake. Pool of £103,712.47 - 559.05 winning tickets. T/Qpdt: £19.90 to a £1 stake. Pool of £6,793.10 - 252.50 winning tickets. RY

4924 EXETER (R-H)

Tuesday, April 5

OFFICIAL GOING: Good (good to firm in the back straight; chs 7.9, hdl 8.0)
Wind: mild half-behind Weather: overcast

5152 WOOD FARM STUD NOVICES' HURDLE (12 hdls) 2m 7f 110y
2:30 (2:30) (Class 4) 4-Y-O+ **£4,228** (£1,241; £620; £310)

Form RPR

-1F2 **1** **Vincitore (FR)**[27] 4555 5-11-1 117.................................. KielanWoods(7) 116+
(Charlie Longsdon) *trckd ldrs: rdn to ld narrowly 3 out: styd on wl to assert fr last: rdn out* **6/4**[1]

-450 **2** *2* **How's My Friend**[33] 4444 6-11-1 0.. NickScholfield 106
(Grant Cann) *hld up in mid-div: hdwy after 9th: ev ch last: sn rdn: styd on but no ex* **20/1**

-335 **3** *7* **Knighton Combe**[25] 4699 11-11-1 0...................................... DarylJacob 102
(Jamie Snowden) *led: rdn and narrowly hdd 3 out: ev ch next: styd on same pce* **7/4**[2]

0 **4** *6* **The Tatkin (IRE)**[51] 4097 5-10-8 0................................(t) TomScudamore 89+
(David Pipe) *mid-div: rdn appr 3 out: styd on same pce: wnt 4th run-in: nvr trbld ldrs* **25/1**

6-16 **5** *3 1/2* **Spock (FR)**[145] 2325 6-11-8 0.. HarrySkelton 103+
(Paul Nicholls) *hld up in mid-div: hit 5th: hdwy after 9th: rdn to dispute cl 3rd whn short of room and blnd 2 out: wknd last* **6/1**[3]

04 **6** *11* **Guam (IRE)**[9] 5038 6-10-8 0.. SClements(7) 84
(Nick Mitchell) *hld up towards rr: sme prog after 9th: sn rdn: nvr trbld ldrs* **40/1**

00 **7** *23* **Pretty Penny**[12] 4974 7-10-8 0.. GerardTumelty 59
(Martin Keighley) *trckd ldr tl reminders on long run after 5th: rdn bef 9th: wknd bef 3 out: t.o* **50/1**

8 *1/2* **Skating Home (IRE)**[149] 5-11-1 0...................................... WillKennedy 65
(Neil Mulholland) *j.lft: trckd ldr: rdn after 9th: wknd bef next: t.o* **28/1**

9 *41* **Identimin**[758] 7-10-5 0... IanPopham(3) 25
(Caroline Keevil) *stmbld bdly 1st: a towards rr: wknd bef 3 out: t.o* **16/1**

P **P** **Maxi's Dream**[51] 4094 6-10-12 0...................................... PeterToole(3) —
(Stuart Howe) *in tch tl dropped in rr after 5th: lost tch fr next: t.o whn p.u after 9th* **100/1**

0-P **P** **Alfie Brown**[51] 4091 8-10-12 0.. ChrisHonour(3) —
(Jacqueline Retter) *hld up towards rr: hdwy to trck ldrs after 5th: mstke next: sn wknd: t.o whn p.u after 9th* **100/1**

5m 53.5s (-5.50) **Going Correction** -0.55s/f (Firm) **11** Ran SP% **115.0**
Speed ratings (Par 105): **87,86,84,82,80 77,69,69,55,— —**
toteswingers:1&2:£20.00, 1&3:£1.80, 2&3:£9.10 CSF £33.02 TOTE £2.50: £1.40, £6.30, £1.10; EX 23.70.
Owner The Veni, Vidi, Vici Partnership **Bred** Mme Isabelle Garcon **Trained** Over Norton, Oxon

FOCUS
The ground was officially described as good, good to firm in the back straight. Tom Scudamore called it "basically good with a few softer bits, but there is no firm out there in my opinion." This novice hurdle was significantly weakened by the defections of the likely favourite Handy Andy and the fancied Rif, Ace High and Lundy Sky. The pace was steady. Ordinary form rated through the fourth and fifth.

NOTEBOOK
Vincitore(FR), second at Fontwell on his previous outing, built on that display to score a comfortable victory under a penalty. Confidently ridden, he tracked the pace and travelled nicely on the inside before staying on after the last. His trainer reported he will go for a novice chase next and, despite not being the biggest, should make a fair chaser. (op 11-8 tchd 6-5)
How's My Friend improved markedly for this step up in trip to run a creditable race. Having travelled kindly, he failed to match the winner on the run-in. Clearly suited by a stamina test, this rates his best run to date.
Knighton Combe was reverting to hurdles and led the field turning for home, but once pushed along he could only stay on at the one pace. The 11-y-o gave his all but looks vulnerable to less exposed rivals. (op 5-2)
The Tatkin(IRE) stayed on from a fair way back having been under pressure sooner than most on this hurdles debut. She should improve for the experience. (op 20-1)
Spock(FR), a winner at Worcester before disappointing at Ludlow last time, ran well for a long way before failing to see out the trip. He travelled strongly until a mistake at the second last and did not pick up when asked. He will benefit from a drop in distance. (op 5-1)
Alfie Brown Official explanation: jockey said gelding had a breathing problem

5153 NEWQUAY TRETHERRAS RACING TO SCHOOL H'CAP HURDLE (12 hdls) 2m 7f 110y
3:00 (3:00) (Class 3) (0-130,129) 4-Y-O+ **£4,293** (£1,260; £630; £314)

Form RPR

2304 **1** **Sir Kezbaah (IRE)**[17] 4875 7-11-8 **125**............................... NickScholfield 145+
(Jeremy Scott) *mid-div: hdwy 6th: led 3 out: sn in command: v easily* **5/1**[2]

5313 **2** *11* **Mauricetheathlete (IRE)**[14] 4929 8-9-7 **103** oh2............(b) MrNSlatter(7) 106
(Martin Keighley) *trckd ldrs 3rd: rdn along fr after 5th: dropped to last pair 8th: styd on again fr 3 out: wnt 2nd run-in: no ch w wnr* **8/1**

23-2 **3** *3 3/4* **Nemetan (FR)**[31] 4481 10-9-10 **106** oh4 ow3.............. EdGlassonbury(7) 107
(Victor Dartnall) *trckd ldr: led 9th: sn rdn: hdd bef next: styd on same pce: lost 2nd run-in* **10/3**[1]

3061 **4** *1* **Devon Native (IRE)**[29] 4532 8-11-3 **120**.......................(t) TomScudamore 119
(Chris Down) *hld up towards rr: hdwy fr 6th: rdn to chse ldng pair after 9th: styd on again fr 3 out: wnt 2nd run-in: no ch w wnr* **9/1**

0526 **5** *3 1/4* **Boomtown Kat**[29] 4532 7-10-12 **115**............................ AndrewThornton 114
(Karen George) *mid-div: blnd 5th: rdn in 4th after 9th: one pce fr next* **22/1**

5006 **6** *2* **Racing Demon (IRE)**[45] 4201 11-11-8 **125**........................ PaulMoloney 120
(Henrietta Knight) *mid-div: rdn after 9th: nvr any imp on ldrs* **6/1**[3]

431 **7** *nk* **Sum Laff (IRE)**[27] 4555 7-10-7 **113**................................... PeterToole(3) 111+
(Charlie Mann) *trckd ldrs tl 8th: rdn after next: one pce fr 3 out* **5/1**[2]

-F04 **8** *43* **Crannaghmore Boy (IRE)**[17] 4862 6-9-11 **103** oh1... DonalDevereux(3) 63
(Keith Goldsworthy) *led tl 9th: sn rdn and wknd: t.o* **16/1**

5235 **9** *4 1/2* **Or Bleu (FR)**[17] 4864 9-11-9 **126**.................................. RichardJohnson 83
(Philip Hobbs) *mid-div: pushed along after 5th: in last pair fr 8th: wknd bef 3 out: t.o* **16/1**

4406 **10** *11* **Made In Japan (JPN)**[41] 4285 11-11-0 **120**........ SamTwiston-Davies(3) 68
(Nigel Twiston-Davies) *trckd ldrs: rdn after 7th: sn wknd: t.o* **12/1**

5m 41.2s (-17.80) **Going Correction** -0.55s/f (Firm) **10** Ran SP% **115.6**
Speed ratings (Par 107): **107,103,102,101,100 100,99,85,84,80**
toteswingers:1&2:£6.40, 1&3:£3.90, 2&3:£2.30 CSF £44.31 CT £152.07 TOTE £4.50: £1.90, £2.50, £1.60; EX 31.30.
Owner Andrew & Vanessa Maddox **Bred** Joseph J O'Connor **Trained** Brompton Regis, Somerset

FOCUS
A highly competitive handicap hurdle, and solid form rated through the second, fourth and fifth.

NOTEBOOK
Sir Kezbaah(IRE) completely outclassed his rivals with an effortless victory. Travelling ominously well, he cruised clear entering the straight and won easing down. Having shown a solid level of form in similar contests, this was a deserved win and he should continue to go well, albeit the handicapper will have his say. He relishes this better ground and will embark on a chasing career in the autumn. (op 9-2 tchd 4-1)
Mauricetheathlete(IRE), running from 2lb out of the handicap, stayed on strongly for pressure without getting near the winner. He ran with credit and will appreciate a return to further. (op 10-1)
Nemetan(FR), second at Kempton on his return from a lengthy absence, raced on the inside and, having tried to go with the winner, tired quickly in the straight. He likes it round here and this was a fair effort from 4lb out of the weights. (op 9-2)
Devon Native(IRE), raised 10lb for her Newton Abbot success last time, was held up and could not muster a serious effort. (op 11-1 tchd 12-1)
Boomtown Kat was never able to land a blow and plugged on at one pace. (tchd 20-1)
Sum Laff(IRE), up in trip on this handicap debut, never got seriously involved after a mistake at the third-last. He is lightly raced so may prove better than this. (op 11-2 tchd 9-2)

5154 CHILDREN'S HOSPICE SOUTH WEST MARATHON H'CAP CHASE (21 fncs) 3m 6f 110y
3:30 (3:30) (Class 3) (0-120,118) 5-Y-O+ **£6,337** (£1,872; £936; £468; £234)

Form RPR

243P **1** **Drybrook Bedouin**[9] 5037 9-11-1 **114**.................................. SClements(7) 132+
(Nick Mitchell) *patiently rdn in rr: stdy prog fr 14th: sltly hmpd 17th: chal and wnt rt 4 out: rdn to ld and j. bdly rt last 2: styd on strly* **9/1**

F3PP **2** *13* **Pass Me By**[80] 3568 12-10-13 **112**.................................... MrTJCannon(7) 115
(Suzy Smith) *towards rr: reminders after 4th: drvn 14th: hdwy next: lft cl 3rd 17th: styd on same pce fr next: wnt 2nd run-in: no ch w wnr* **25/1**

4P11 **3** *3/4* **Theophrastus (IRE)**[14] 4927 9-11-9 **115**......................... LiamTreadwell 118
(Nick Gifford) *hld up: rdn 14th: hdwy after 17th: styd on same pce fr 4 out: wnt 3rd run-in* **13/2**[2]

-534 **4** *3 1/4* **Priors Glen (IRE)**[12] 4966 7-11-2 **115**................... StephenO'Donovan(7) 116
(Emma Lavelle) *led: j.rt at times: rdn after 4 out: hdd appr 2 out: no ex and lost 2 pls run-in* **13/2**[2]

PP55 **5** *3 1/2* **Kilbeggan Blade**[8] 5061 12-11-7 **113**.................................(v) CharliePoste 110
(Robin Dickin) *mid-div: struggling 14th: styd on same pce fr 4 out* **33/1**

-1P3 **P** **Martha's Kinsman (IRE)**[33] 4442 12-11-6 **112**............ RichardJohnson —
(Henry Daly) *w ldr: rdn appr 4 out: wknd qckly: bhd whn p.u bef 2 out* **7/1**[3]

3-00 **P** **Wind Instrument (IRE)**[76] 3629 10-11-12 **118**.............. RobertThornton —
(Alan King) *trckd ldrs: rdn after 14th: wknd bef 17th: bhd whn p.u bef 4 out* **12/1**

-413 **P** **Choumakeur (FR)**[9] 5037 9-11-6 **112**.......................(bt) TomScudamore —
(David Pipe) *in tch: rdn appr 14th: sn wknd: t.o whn p.u after 17th* **9/1**

-40F **P** **Jaunty Journey**[45] 4208 8-11-12 **118**................................ JasonMaguire —
(Nigel Twiston-Davies) *nvr fluent: sn struggling in rr: bhd whn p.u after 13th* **16/1**

23P2 **F** **Vamizi (IRE)**[28] 4537 8-11-12 **118** .... MattieBatchelor —
(Mark Bradstock) *mid-div: mstke 1st: awkward 2nd: fell 12th* **4/1**[1]

1044 **F** **Darstardly Dick (IRE)**[22] 4777 8-11-11 **117** ....(b) AndrewGlassonbury —
(Victor Dartnall) *in tch: rdn 14th: sn lost pl: fell 16th* **14/1**

500U **F** **Rhum (FR)**[28] 4538 6-11-6 **115** .... SamTwiston-Davies(3) —
(Nigel Twiston-Davies) *trckd ldrs: drvn along fr 14th: disputing 3rd whn fell 17th* **10/1**

7m 49.9s (1.30) **Going Correction** -0.375s/f (Good) **12** Ran SP% **115.3**
Speed ratings: **83,79,79,78,77** —,—,—,—,—,—
toteswingers:1&2:£33.70, 1&3:£22.60, 2&3:£33.70 CSF £190.75 CT £1556.23 TOTE £10.80: £4.30, £8.60, £2.40; EX 324.70.
Owner A Willmington **Bred** N And Mrs S Cook **Trained** Piddletrenthide, Dorset

FOCUS
A tight marathon handicap chase with just five finishers. The winner was value for further and the second and third have been rated close to their marks.

NOTEBOOK
Drybrook Bedouin, third in the Devon National on his penultimate outing before disappointing last time, bounced back to form to outstay and outjump his rivals. He travelled kindly and, despite jumping right in the straight, kicked clear to land an easy victory. He goes well around here and should continue to go well over extreme distances. His trainer said he is not easy to place and will hopefully go for the Summer National. Official explanation: trainer said, regarding apparent improvement in form, that on its previous run the gelding appeared unsuited by being ridden handily and sulked in cheek pieces. (op 11-1)
Pass Me By was under pressure very early on and kept finding for his rider's urgings without getting near the facile winner. He stays strongly and this was a much-improved display. (op 28-1)
Theophrastus(IRE) raced towards the inside and was ridden patiently before staying on for pressure. He never threatened, but saw out this extra distance better than he had previously. He remains in good heart. (op 7-1)
Priors Glen(IRE), up in trip, led the field going to four out but got tired and could not muster an effort thereafter. He remains unexposed over this sort of trip, but looks better suited by shorter. (op 7-1 tchd 6-1)
Kilbeggan Blade looks a shadow of his former self, but did complete the course. (op 28-1)
Vamizi(IRE), runner-up off this mark in the Devon National here last month, made a few errors and fell at the 12th fence.
Rhum(FR) unseated when going well here on his last start and fell at the 17th fence this time. He is one to treat with caution and needs to improve his jumping to have any chance.

5155 TONY HADLEY LIVE HERE MAY 3RD NOVICES' CHASE (15 fncs) 2m 3f 110y
4:00 (4:00) (Class 4) 5-Y-0+ **£3,187** (£935; £467; £233)

Form RPR

2101 **1** **Hidden Keel**[14] 4926 6-11-12 **145** .... PaddyBrennan 153+
(Charlie Longsdon) *mde all: j rt: mstke 7th: in command whn mstke 3 out: comf* **11/8**[1]

231P **2** *21* **Rougham**[21] 4794 5-11-5 **135** .... RichardJohnson 124
(Philip Hobbs) *trckd wnr: rdn appr 4 out: no ch w wnr fr 3 out: kpt on same pce* **4/1**[3]

1021 **3** *1* **Requin (FR)**[24] 4723 6-11-5 **132** .... DenisO'Regan 121
(Victor Dartnall) *trckd ldng pair: rdn to chal for 2nd appr 4 out: kpt on same pce fr 3 out: no ch w wnr* **13/8**[2]

4450 **4** *23* **Mangonel**[65] 3840 7-10-5 0 ....(v) JodieMogford 85
(Stuart Howe) *led chsng gp in 4th: no ch fr 9th: t.o* **66/1**

0414 **5** *1 ¾* **Lupita (IRE)**[14] 4926 7-10-2 0 ....(t) JimmyDerham(3) 83
(Derrick Scott) *in chsng gp: no ch fr 9th: t.o* **40/1**

23FF **6** *13* **Solitary Palm (IRE)**[121] 2796 8-10-9 **102** .... IanPopham(3) 79
(Brian Forsey) *a in rr of chsng gp: mstke 8th: sn no ch: t.o* **40/1**

044 **P** **Secret Shared (IRE)**[22] 4782 7-10-12 0 ....(tp) JohnnyFarrelly —
(Richard Mitchell) *j.rt at times: bmpd 1st: bhd fr 8th: t.o whn p.u after 11th* **100/1**

1P4U **P** **Humbel Ben (IRE)**[30] 4507 8-10-12 **118** .... WillKennedy —
(Alan Jones) *a towards rr of chsng gp: no ch fr 9th: t.o whn p.u bef 4 out* **16/1**

4m 44.9s (-12.40) **Going Correction** -0.375s/f (Good) **8** Ran SP% **113.4**
Speed ratings: **109,100,100,91,90 85**,—,—
toteswingers:1&2:£1.30, 1&3:£1.02, 2&3:£2.00 CSF £7.44 TOTE £1.70: £1.02, £1.50, £1.10; EX 6.40.
Owner Mrs Peter Matthey & John F Horn **Bred** Mrs M J Matthey **Trained** Over Norton, Oxon

FOCUS
A decent novice chase run at a good clip with the first three pulling well clear. The second and third have been rated a stone off their best and the fourth and fifth are probably better guides to the level.

NOTEBOOK
Hidden Keel, an easy winner over the C&D on his last start, made all to follow up in good style. Jumping boldly, he made the odd mistake but never saw another rival as he eased clear to score under a double penalty. This was his third chase victory and he is clearly an exciting horse, but may struggle in handicap company off his current mark. His trainer reported that he is finished for the season and he rates him as the best young horse in his yard. (op 6-4 tchd 13-8)
Rougham failed to cope with the rise in class at the Cheltenham Festival, but ran a better race here without looking like catching the winner. He made several errors and needs to jump better if he is to improve. (op 3-1 tchd 11-4)
Requin(FR), successful in handicap company at Chepstow on his latest outing, travelled into contention but never really picked up once entering the straight. He will find easier opportunities and may win a race under his penalty. (op 15-8 tchd 2-1)

5156 EXETER INN AT TOPSHAM NOVICES' HUNTERS' CHASE (18 fncs) 3m
4:30 (4:30) (Class 6) 5-Y-0+ **£936** (£290; £145; £72)

Form RPR

1 **Blackstaff (IRE)**[31] 6-11-3 0 .... MissEKelly(7) 123+
(Mrs Jane Williams) *j. sltly rt at times: racd keenly: hld up: hdwy to ld after 7th: 24 l clr 11th: unchal after: mstke last: pushed out* **4/1**[2]

3111 **2** *9* **Oca De Thaix (FR)**[12] 4969 9-11-11 **116** .... MissCharlotteEvans(7) 125+
(Keith Goldsworthy) *hld up: plld way through to ld after 3rd: hdd after 7th: chsd clr ldr/wnr: 24 l down 11th: rdn 4 out: sme imp on wnr next but alwtys being hld* **6/5**[1]

-421 **3** *23* **Louis Pasteur (IRE)**[29] 4534 6-11-9 **105** .... MrRGHenderson(5) 101
(Nick Mitchell) *led 2nd tl after 3rd: lost pl after 10th: sn plenty to do: plugged on fr 4 out: wnt modest 3rd sn after last:* **4/1**[2]

-212 **4** *4* **What Of It (IRE)**[29] 4526 8-11-9 **106** .... MrTWCEdwards(5) 97
(Tom George) *led tl 2nd: chsd ldrs: prom in chsng gp fr 10th: pushed along in 3rd after 14th: fdd fr 4 out: lost 3rd sn after the last* **8/1**[3]

5 *1 ¼* **King Of The Road**[23] 9-11-3 0 .... MrMatthewHampton(7) 92
(Mrs Janet Ackner) *trckd ldrs: chsd clr ldr/wnr fr 10th: rdn appr 4 out: fdd* **50/1**

-330 **P** **Thirtytwo Red (IRE)**[14] 4928 10-11-10 **85** .... MrWBiddick —
(R J Alford) *prom early: bhd fr 11th: t.o whn p.u bef 4 out* **20/1**

3-2 **P** **Brook Castle (IRE)**[31] 9-11-10 **82** ....(p) MrJoshuaGuerriero —
(Mrs Jill Dennis) *a towards rr: t.o whn p.u bef 3 out* **25/1**

P **Princesse De Rome**[16] 7-11-3 0 ....(t) MrNickWilliams —
(R Scrine) *in tch: mstke 2nd: lost tch fr 10th: p.u after 13th* **28/1**

6m 10.8s (1.50) **Going Correction** -0.375s/f (Good) **8** Ran SP% **110.6**
Speed ratings: **82,79,71,70,69** —,—,—
toteswingers:1&2:£1.30, 1&3:£5.20, 2&3:£1.90 CSF £9.00 TOTE £4.30: £1.90, £1.10, £1.60; EX 12.70.
Owner Mrs Jane Williams **Bred** P Magill **Trained** George Nympton, Devon
■ Stewards' Enquiry : Mr R G Henderson two-day ban: used whip with excessive frequency (tbn)

FOCUS
A strong race for the grade. The second has been rated to his mark.

NOTEBOOK
Blackstaff(IRE) was given an enterprising ride and survived a mistake at the last to land a comfortable success. Taking the advantage, she kicked on into a 15l lead and maintained the distance to make a successful rules debut. Following three point wins, this is his fourth victory in a row and he is open to any amount of improvement. This rates an impressive performance, despite never being challenged, and his jockey reported he would appreciate a bit of cut in the ground. (op 7-2)
Oca De Thaix(FR) lost many lengths at the start and pulled hard early on. Having chased the long-time leader, he made the odd mistake and could not get on terms, pulling well clear of the rest. A revelation this season for this trainer, he should pick up another similar contest if settling better. (op Evens tchd 5-6)
Louis Pasteur(IRE), up in trip, raced a little freely and plugged on into a modest third. (op 5-1 tchd 11-2)
What Of It(IRE) got outpaced when the pace lifted and was beaten a long way from home on this step up in trip.

5157 WOOD FARM STUD INTERMEDIATE OPEN NATIONAL HUNT FLAT RACE (DIV I) 2m 1f
5:00 (5:00) (Class 6) 4-6-Y-0 **£1,370** (£399; £199)

Form RPR

1 **Aland Islands (IRE)** 5-11-2 0 .... APMcCoy 113+
(Tim Vaughan) *in tch: hdwy 4f out: led over 2f out: styd on wl to assert fnl f: pushed out* **10/11**[1]

00- **2** *5* **Russie With Love**[388] 4592 5-10-2 0 .... DannyBurton(7) 101+
(Chris Down) *in tch: rdn to chal fr over 2f out: kpt on but hld by wnr ent fnl f* **50/1**

3 *10* **Moorland Sunset** 4-10-7 0 .... IanPopham(3) 93
(Caroline Keevil) *hld up towards rr: hdwy over 4f out: rdn over 3f out: styd on same pce: wnt 3rd over 1f out* **100/1**

4 *1* **Vic Legend (IRE)** 5-11-2 0 .... TomScudamore 98
(Rebecca Curtis) *in tch: outpcd 4f out: styd on again fnl 2f* **11/1**[3]

0 **5** *4 ½* **War Of The World (FR)**[38] 4356 5-11-2 0 ....(t) NickScholfield 94
(Paul Nicholls) *hld up towards rr: sme prog over 3f out: one pce fnl 2f* **20/1**

0-05 **6** *shd* **Night Rose**[39] 4335 5-10-9 0 .... RobertThornton 87
(Alan King) *hld up towards rr: prog over 4f out: sn rdn: one pce fnl 2f* **16/1**

00 **7** *nk* **Withy Mills**[153] 2156 6-10-9 0 .... JohnnyFarrelly 87
(Kevin Bishop) *trckd ldr: led over 3f out tl rdn over 2f out: fdd fnl f* **80/1**

0 **8** *6* **Mystic Appeal (IRE)**[31] 4468 5-11-2 0 .... WillKennedy 89
(Jeremy Scott) *led tl rdn over 3f out: grad wknd* **14/1**

2 **9** *½* **Harry Le Fise Lake (IRE)**[150] 2222 5-11-2 0 .... RichardJohnson 89
(Philip Hobbs) *t.k.h: hld up: hdwy over 4f out: effrt over 3f out: wknd over 1f out* **9/4**[2]

10 *26* **Royal Villan (IRE)** 5-11-2 0 .... MattieBatchelor 68
(Mark Bradstock) *trckd ldrs tl wknd 4f out: t.o* **33/1**

11 *31* **Lyphin' Legend** 4-10-3 0 .... HarrySkelton 30
(Nick Mitchell) *in tch on outer: pushed along 1/2-way: wknd over 4f out: t.o* **66/1**

4m 4.50s (-4.30) **Going Correction** -0.55s/f (Firm)
WFA 4 from 5yo+ 5lb **11** Ran SP% **117.4**
Speed ratings: **88,85,80,80,78 78,78,75,75,62 48**
toteswingers:1&2:£20.50 CSF £78.85 TOTE £2.20: £1.40, £9.50, £16.70; EX 105.50.
Owner Grand Designs Syndicate **Bred** Ms Debbie O'Neill **Trained** Aberthin, Vale of Glamorgan

FOCUS
A low-grade bumper won by the odds-on favourite, who looks above average. The sixth, seventh and eighth set the level.

NOTEBOOK
Aland Islands(IRE), heavily supported and the ride of Tony McCoy, justified market support to make a winning debut. Always going well in behind the pace, he led over 3f out before staying on nicely to land a cosy win. The champion jockey is now 11-40 for this trainer and this grand-looking sort rates an exciting prospect. He will go to the Cheltenham sales next week. (op Evens tchd 11-10 in places)
Russie With Love, returning from a 388-day absence, ran a much improved race, having every chance before failing to match the winner in the last furlong. She had been thought good enough to run in the Mares' Listed bumper at Sandown last year and showed her ability here. She should go close in similar company.
Moorland Sunset was held up before making good headway to run on for third. He can be expected be improve for this outing as his trainer doesn't usually have his runners fully wound up for their debuts (0-18 with newcomers).
Vic Legend(IRE), overlooked by McCoy, made a fair debut, keeping on for pressure having been outpaced. He should benefit from this experience. (op 12-1 tchd 10-1)
Harry Le Fise Lake(IRE), runner-up at Wincanton in November, raced keenly and was never able to strike a blow. (op 11-4)

5158 WOOD FARM STUD INTERMEDIATE OPEN NATIONAL HUNT FLAT RACE (DIV II) 2m 1f
5:30 (5:30) (Class 6) 4-6-Y-0 **£1,370** (£399; £199)

Form RPR

430 **1** **Golden Gael**[24] 4728 5-10-9 0 .... NickScholfield 107+
(Jeremy Scott) *in tch: wnt 2nd 4f out: led 3f out: styd on wl: pushed out* **13/2**[3]

2 *2* **Swaling (IRE)** 5-11-2 0 .... DenisO'Regan 115+
(Victor Dartnall) *in tch: wnt 2nd travelling wl 3f out: rdn and rn v green over 1f out: hung rt and hld fnl f* **7/2**[1]

3 *1 ½* **Wiffy Chatsby (IRE)** 4-10-5 0 .... MrRMahon(5) 105
(Paul Nicholls) *hld up towards rr: hdwy over 4f out: rdn 3f out: styd on fnl 2f* **7/2**[1]

4 *15* **Cosway Spirit (IRE)** 4-10-10 0 .... RobertThornton 93
(Alan King) *mid-div: hdwy into 4th over 3f out: sn rdn: wknd over 1f out* **6/1**[2]

504 **5** *1 ¾* **Champagne Rosie**[25] 4709 5-10-2 0 .... NathanSweeney(7) 91
(Bob Buckler) *trckd ldr: led 4f out tl rdn 3f out: wknd over 1f out* **22/1**

0 **6** *11* **Zava River (IRE)**[58] 3964 4-10-10 0 .... DarylJacob 83
(Jamie Snowden) *mid-div on outer tl lost pl after 5f: nvr bk on terms* **66/1**

0 **7** *3/4* **On The Raz**[111] 2965 4-10-3 0 JamesMillman 76
(Jacqueline Retter) *a towards rr* **100/1**
0 **8** *nk* **Key To Milan**[31] 4484 5-11-2 0 JamesDavies 88
(Chris Down) *mid-div: rdn over 4f out: little imp: wknd over 1f out* **50/1**
3 **9** *2 1/2* **Queen's Grove**[51] 4097 5-10-4 0 GilesHawkins(5) 79
(Kevin Bishop) *a towards rr* **16/1**
5 **10** *1 3/4* **Bob Emmet (IRE)**[51] 4097 6-11-2 0 RichardJohnson 85
(Philip Hobbs) *in tch tl wknd 4f out* **12/1**
5 **11** *16* **Fox Appeal (IRE)**[17] 4879 4-10-10 0 JackDoyle 66
(Emma Lavelle) *led tl 4f out: sn rdn: wknd 3f out* **7/1**
0 **12** *1 1/2* **Cobbler's Rest (IRE)**[59] 3957 5-11-2 0 APMcCoy 71
(Jonjo O'Neill) *trckd ldr: rdn 1/2-way: wknd over 5f out* **16/1**
13 *18* **Fleet Dawn** 5-11-2 0 DominicElsworth 57
(John Coombe) *in tch: rdn 1/2-way: wknd 4f out* **14/1**
0 **14** *35* **Moorlands Jack**[174] 1824 6-11-2 0 TomScudamore 29
(Tim Vaughan) *chsd ldrs tl wknd over 4f out* **16/1**

4m 2.60s (-6.20) **Going Correction** -0.55s/f (Firm)
WFA 4 from 5yo+ 5lb **14** Ran SP% **125.4**
Speed ratings: **92,91,90,83,82 77,76,76,75,74 67,66,58,41**
toteswingers:1&2:£13.60, 1&3:£9.20, 2&3:£7.00 CSF £30.21 TOTE £5.60: £1.60, £2.40, £1.80; EX 37.00.
Owner The Wild Bunch **Bred** R J & S A Carter **Trained** Brompton Regis, Somerset

FOCUS
The second division of the bumper had a wide open look to it. The winner has been rated as stepping up on her previous form and the fifth has been rated as running to her C&D mark.

NOTEBOOK
Golden Gael had shown ability in her three starts to date, and built on those displays to score a ready success. She found for pressure and her experience counted for plenty as she stayed on strongly in the straight. (op 15-2 tchd 6-1)
Swaling(IRE) cruised into contention 1f out but, having come under pressure, hung left and ran extremely green, throwing away the race in the process. He traded at 1.07 on Betfair and looked the likely winner 3f from home before wandering around. He will improve for this experience and, with normal progress, can go one better before long. (tchd 10-3)
Wiffy Chatsby(IRE), related to useful hurdlers, stayed on nicely from the rear. He should build on this display and can land a similar contest. (op 15-2)
Cosway Spirit(IRE) kept on at the same pace having come under the pump over 4f out. (op 11-2 tchd 5-1)
Champagne Rosie who had hinted at ability in her three bumpers to date, showed up for a long way and just faded once entering the straight. This is probably as good as she is. (tchd 20-1)
Fox Appeal(IRE) led early before fading tamely once headed. (op 6-1)
T/Plt: £20.30 to a £1 stake. Pool:£95,635.30 - 3,425.52 winning tickets T/Qpdt: £10.60 to a £1 stake. Pool:£6,186.34 - 429.76 winning tickets TM

5127 AUTEUIL (L-H)
Wednesday, April 6

OFFICIAL GOING: Turf: very soft

5159a PRIX ARTHUR VEIL-PICARD (HURDLE) (CONDITIONS) (5YO+) (TURF) 2m 2f
3:10 (12:00) 5-Y-0+ **£19,862** (£9,931; £5,793; £3,931; £1,862)

RPR
1 **Zanir (FR)**[19] 4848 7-10-8 0 PaddyBrennan —
(Tom George) *hld up in midfield: tk clsr order 5 out: 5th on stands' rail 2 out: styng on and 3rd at last: r.o wl flat to ld cl home* **31/1**
2 *hd* **Rameur (FR)**[663] 6-10-8 0 PACarberry —
(F-M Cottin, France) **30/1**
3 *1* **Un Certainmonsieur (FR)**[31] 5-10-8 0 ow2 DavidCottin —
(M Seror, France) **5/1**[2]
4 *snk* **Saint Renan (FR)**[572] 7-10-8 0 SebastienZuliani —
(D Sourdeau De Beauregard, France) **33/1**
5 *6* **Onatello (FR)**[1614] 2038 9-10-12 0 DavidBerra —
(L Viel, France) **33/10**[1]
6 *1/2* **Sphinx Du Lukka (FR)**[24] 5-10-4 0 ow1 ArnaudDuchene —
(T Trapenard, France) **22/1**
7 *nse* **Isnos (FR)**[493] 2605 8-10-8 0 ChristophePieux —
(J Bertran De Balanda, France) **63/10**
8 *2* **Soleil De Sivola (FR)**[17] 5-10-3 0 (b) AlainDeChitray —
(T Trapenard, France) **6/1**[3]
9 *3* **Klark (FR)**[143] 7-10-10 0 GregoryAdam —
(M Rolland, France) **15/1**
10 *2* **Sire Des Aulnays (FR)**[567] 5-10-1 0 AlbanDesvaux(3) —
(E Leray, France) **116/1**
0 **Chant De Lune (FR)**[364] 9-10-10 0 AlexisAcker —
(M Rolland, France) **44/5**
0 **Kipik (FR)**[147] 8-10-10 0 RaymondO'Brien —
(R Le Gal, France) **28/1**
0 **Masters Royal (FR)**[31] 6-10-10 0 (b) ElwisLequesne —
(B Barbier, France) **31/1**
0 **The Wonder Land (FR)**[77] 7-10-3 0 EricMichel —
(J-P Perruchot, France) **146/1**
0 **Katkopoly (FR)**[31] 5-10-6 0 JonathanViard(4) —
(C Diard, France) **23/1**
0 **Green Day (FR)**[133] 5-10-6 0 RegisSchmidlin —
(M Rolland, France) **14/1**

4m 25.4s (265.40) **16** Ran SP% **116.9**
PARI-MUTUEL (all including 1 euro stakes): WIN 31.60; PLACE 7.70, 7.30, 2.70; DF 342.90; SF 297.80.
Owner Mrs Laura Day **Bred** Jean Biraben & Mme Daniele Biraben **Trained** Slad, Gloucs

2540 AINTREE (L-H)
Thursday, April 7

OFFICIAL GOING: Mildmay course - good to soft changing to good to soft (good in places) after race 5 (4:15); hurdle course - good to soft (soft in places; 7.1); national course - soft (good to soft in places; 6.5)
moderate 1/2 againstfine and sunny

5160 BGC PARTNERS LIVERPOOL HURDLE (GRADE 1) (13 hdls) 3m 110y
2:00 (2:01) (Class 1) 4-Y-0+
£57,010 (£21,390; £10,710; £5,340; £2,680; £1,340)

Form RPR
-111 **1** **Big Buck's (FR)**[21] 4819 8-11-7 174 RWalsh 178+
(Paul Nicholls) *trckd ldrs: led appr 3 out: briefly hdd 2 out: shkn up and drew clr run-in* **4/6**[1]
1112 **2** *5* **Grands Crus (FR)**[21] 4819 6-11-7 169 (t) TomScudamore 169+
(David Pipe) *hld up in rr: hdwy to trck ldrs 7th: upsides 3 out: led briefly next: styd on same pce: no imp* **3/1**[2]
-554 **3** *7* **Won In The Dark (IRE)**[18] 4905 7-11-7 147 AELynch 161
(Sabrina J Harty, Ire) *trckd ldrs: kpt on fr 3 out: tk 3rd between last 2: one pce* **66/1**
-101 **4** *12* **Carlito Brigante (IRE)**[22] 4806 5-11-7 160 (t) DNRussell 154+
(Gordon Elliott, Ire) *trckd ldrs: 3rd and one pce whn hit 2 out: sn wknd* **10/1**[3]
0214 **5** *12* **Knockara Beau (IRE)**[21] 4817 8-11-7 155 JanFaltejsek 141
(George Charlton) *led tl appr 3 out: sn lost pl: hit 2 out* **33/1**
1-40 **6** *5* **Khyber Kim**[23] 4791 9-11-7 159 PaddyBrennan 136
(Nigel Twiston-Davies) *hld up towards rr: hdwy 8th: lost pl after 10th* **16/1**
32-0 **7** *28* **Possol (FR)**[159] 2084 8-11-7 147 RichardJohnson 120
(Henry Daly) *chsd ldrs: nt fluent 9th: sn drvn: hit 10th: lost pl appr next: sn bhd* **80/1**
P040 **8** *19* **Markington**[132] 2663 8-11-7 125 (b) TomO'Brien 95
(Peter Bowen) *in rr: nt fluent and reminders 4th: sn lost tch: t.o 8th* **200/1**
1P-0 **9** *35* **Sentry Duty (FR)**[117] 2884 9-11-7 154 BarryGeraghty 61
(Nicky Henderson) *in tch: drvn and outpcd 8th: bhd fr next: t.o 3 out* **25/1**
F400 **10** *16* **Gwanako (FR)**[21] 4817 8-11-7 137 DarylJacob 47
(Paul Nicholls) *chsd ldr: lost pl and hit 10th: t.o next* **100/1**
2144 **P** **Karabak (FR)**[39] 4373 8-11-7 160 (b[1]) APMcCoy —
(Alan King) *mid-div: lost pl and reminders 9th: sn bhd: t.o whn p.u bef 3 out* **20/1**

6m 10.2s (-6.10) **Going Correction** -0.05s/f (Good) **11** Ran SP% **115.7**
Speed ratings (Par 117): **107,105,103,99,95 93,84,78,67,62** —
toteswingers:1&2:£1.20, 1&3:£12.40, 2&3:£17.60 CSF £2.59 CT £57.12 TOTE £1.70: £1.02, £1.60, £10.60; EX 2.40 Trifecta £55.30 Pool: £11,003.94 - 147.20 winning units..
Owner The Stewart Family **Bred** Henri Poulat **Trained** Ditcheat, Somerset

FOCUS
The first day of the Grand National meeting and the ground was on the soft side of good on the Mildmay course and hurdle track, following light rain in the morning. The winning time suggested the going was just on the soft side of good, and this was backed up by the jockeys. This race looked a rematch of the World Hurdle, with the first two meeting again and it lived up to all expectations, the principals having it between them in the straight and coming right away from the rest. Big Buck's was value for 10l and this rates the best performance by a hurdler since Istabraq in 1999. Grands Crus was close to his Cleeve Hurdle mark.

NOTEBOOK
Big Buck's(FR) was bidding for a hat-trick in this race, to supplement his three successes at Cheltenham, and ran out a comfortable winner. He was always travelling within himself, although he flashed his tail when his main rival got too close to his rear end on the first circuit. He moved into the lead on the run round to the straight and was never off the bridle, as both he and the runner-up quickened. He is probably the best staying hurdler of modern times and, being only an 8-y-o, could well reign in this discipline for the foreseeable future; connections have stated that he will not be returning to fences. (tchd 8-13)
Grands Crus(FR) gave the winner a race at Cheltenham, despite the ground not being entirely in his favour, and the easier surface here was expected to help. He tracked the favourite throughout before striking for home going to three out. However, he could never get his rival off the bit and had to give best on the run-in. This performance did nothing to diminish his reputation, but he is clearly second-best in this division and so is likely to go chasing next season. He is capable of going to the top over fences if he takes to them and is none the worse for two tough battles. (op 7-2)
Won In The Dark(IRE) finished fourth in the 2m4f Grade 1 Hurdle here last season, but had struggled since until running better last time. Trying this trip for the first time, he moved up to the heels of the leaders leaving the back straight and, although he could not stay with the first two, drew well clear of the rest.
Carlito Brigante(IRE), a clear winner of the Coral Cup at Cheltenham, was stepping up in both trip and grade but travelled well until tiring from three out, as if finding the distance beyond him.
Knockara Beau(IRE) has been in good form in staying handicap hurdles recently and set off in front. He was no match for these top-class rivals, however, and was seen off before the home turn, although he did stay on again.
Khyber Kim, so disappointing in the Champion Hurdle, has had his problems and has looked a shadow of the horse that won the Grade 1 Aintree Hurdle here last season. Another trying a new trip, he moved up from the back but was left behind in the straight and was another who appeared not to stay. (op 18-1 tchd 20-1)
Possol(FR) finished third in this last year and again ran with credit to a point, despite being beaten a long way. He was allowed to come home in his own time once beaten turning for home.

5161 MATALAN ANNIVERSARY 4-Y-O JUVENILE HURDLE (GRADE 1) (9 hdls) 2m 110y
2:30 (2:32) (Class 1) 4-Y-0
£56,631 (£21,421; £10,761; £5,431; £2,781; £1,441)

Form RPR
11 **1** **Zarkandar (IRE)**[20] 4847 4-11-0 154 RWalsh 147+
(Paul Nicholls) *hld up in tch: hdwy to go 3rd at 4th: pushed along appr 3 out: chalng whn lft in narrow ld 2 out: hld on: drvn out* **4/6**[1]
1332 **2** *1 1/4* **Kumbeshwar**[22] 4807 4-11-0 141 RobertThornton 143
(Alan King) *chsd ldr: rdn appr 3 out: chal 2 out: sn drvn: kpt on but a jst hld by wnr flat* **11/1**[3]
210 **3** *29* **Houblon Des Obeaux (FR)**[20] 4847 4-11-0 147 AidanColeman 117
(Venetia Williams) *hld up: rdn after 4 out and sn no imp: lft remote 3rd 2 out* **28/1**
160 **4** *8* **Maoi Chinn Tire (IRE)**[40] 4350 4-11-0 128 AlanO'Keeffe 116+
(Jennie Candlish) *hld up: mstke 5th: rdn after 4 out: sn no imp: lft remote 4th 2 out: wnt lft last* **100/1**

1140 **5** *20* **Local Hero (GER)**[20] 4847 4-11-0 143 .... APMcCoy 97
(Steve Gollings) *in tch: nt fluent 3rd: rdn after 4 out: wknd appr next* **14/1**
6 *3* **Launchpad**[14] 4980 4-11-0 122 .... DNRussell 89
(D T Hughes, Ire) *in tch: lost pl appr 4 out: sn rdn: wknd appr 3 out* **28/1**
0211 **F** **Palawi (IRE)**[24] 4774 4-11-0 127 .... JasonMaguire 140+
(John Quinn) *led: clr 2nd: hit 4th: nt so far clr after 4 out: rdn in narrow ld whn fell 2 out* **25/1**
P **Oriental Cat**[166] 4-11-0 0 .... SamThomas —
(Venetia Williams) *hld up: keen tl j.v.slowly 1st: slow again 2nd and sn t.o: p.u bef 4th* **50/1**
2113 **B** **Grandouet (FR)**[20] 4847 4-11-0 148 .... BarryGeraghty 143+
(Nicky Henderson) *hld up: hdwy appr 4 out: trckd ldrs bef 3 out: effrt and ev ch whn b.d 2 out* **3/1**[2]
4m 2.80s (-3.40) **Going Correction** -0.05s/f (Good) **9** Ran SP% **113.7**
Speed ratings: **106,105,91,88,78 77,—,—,—**
toteswingers:1&2:£3.00, 1&3:£5.60, 2&3:£14.90 CSF £8.49 CT £109.26 TOTE £1.70: £1.20, £1.90, £4.60; EX 9.80 Trifecta £104.30 Pool: £12,030.29 - 85.28 winning units..
Owner Potensis Limited & Chris Giles **Bred** His Highness The Aga Khan's Studs S C **Trained** Ditcheat, Somerset

FOCUS
Last year's winner Orsippus caused a surprise, but before that many of the recent renewals had gone to the favourite. There was a five-year stretch where Faasel, Detroit City, Katchit, Binocular and Walkon all came here after good performances at Cheltenham and won this decent prize. This field was weakened slightly when Third Intention was a late withdrawal. The idling Zarkandar was value for further and rates similar to his Triumph Hurdle mark. Another step up from Kumbeshwar.

NOTEBOOK
Zarkandar(IRE) took the Triumph Hurdle on his second start over hurdles, which meant he held many he met here, and the horse he had beaten into second at Cheltenham, Unaccompanied, has gone on to win a Listed race on the Flat in Ireland. Well backed, his supporters were made to sweat as he took a long time to get on top and then wasn't able to lengthen away once in command. He did show good determination to hold off the persistent challenge of the runner-up, maintaining his unbeaten profile, but it does look as though the return of some headgear (he wore blinkers on all three of his Flat starts) will do him some good. That said, he had been suffering with a huge mouth abscess that had to be lanced in the previous week, which was where the bit would have been, so he was entitled to have not been feeling at his absolute best. The Champion Hurdle will be the target next season. (op 4-5)
Kumbeshwar was beaten a lot further by Zarkandar at Sandown than here (he gave the winner 4lb that day), so it is clear that he has improved since then, as his effort in the Fred Winter went some way to proving. He has taken well to hurdling and can make up into a decent handicapper. Punchestown is possibly on the agenda. (op 10-1)
Houblon Des Obeaux(FR) got a little bit behind at one point, but ran on. (tchd 25-1)
Maoi Chinn Tire(IRE) also made late progress before running into the horses that fell two out, which momentarily stopped him. (op 80-1)
Local Hero(GER) didn't always jump fluently, but wasn't in the same league as his rivals. (op 16-1)
Palawi(IRE) put plenty of pace into the contest and appeared to be in the process of running a personal best when he met the second-last flight all wrong and hit the deck. (op 20-1)
Oriental Cat, a hurdling newcomer, showed little inclination to even jump the hurdles early on and his rider didn't persevere for too long afterwards. (op 20-1)
Grandouet(FR) travelled well into contention and was still going fairly well at the second-last, but the prone Palawi gave him nowhere to go after jumping the hurdle and he also came down. It would have given the race a completely different complexion had the incident not happened. (op 20-1)

5162 TOTESPORT BOWL CHASE (GRADE 1) (19 fncs) 3m 1f
3:05 (3:06) (Class 1) 5-Y-0+

£84,780 (£31,965; £15,975; £7,980; £4,005; £1,995)

Form RPR
1443 **1** **Nacarat (FR)**[40] 4352 10-11-7 155 .... (t) PaddyBrennan 168+
(Tom George) *mde virtually all: j. boldly: drew clr 3 out: styd on wl: readily* **7/2**[2]
1222 **2** *6* **Carole's Legacy**[23] 4790 7-11-0 153 .... APMcCoy 154
(Nicky Henderson) *chsd ldrs: drvn 15th: chsd wnr bef 2 out: kpt on same pce appr last: no imp* **4/1**[3]
U015 **3** *3 ¾* **Follow The Plan (IRE)**[39] 4388 8-11-7 146 .... TJDoyle 156
(Oliver McKiernan, Ire) *hld up in rr: hdwy 15th: wnt 3rd bef 2 out: kpt on same pce* **40/1**
-3U3 **4** *7* **Deep Purple**[47] 4201 10-11-7 157 .... PaulMoloney 151
(Evan Williams) *w ldr: outpcd and lost pl appr 3 out: 5th whn hit 2 out: tk modest 4th sn after last* **12/1**
4-32 **5** *8* **Denman (IRE)**[20] 4850 11-11-7 177 .... RWalsh 149
(Paul Nicholls) *rn in snatches: chsd ldrs: reminders 15th: wnt 2nd appr 3 out: sn btn: 4th whn hit last: eased clsng stages* **5/4**[1]
-231 **6** *14* **Punchestowns (FR)**[55] 4053 8-11-7 158 .... BarryGeraghty 134
(Nicky Henderson) *in tch: lost pl 15th: sn bhd: lame* **6/1**
6m 31.7s (1.70) **Going Correction** +0.175s/f (Yiel) **6** Ran SP% **111.1**
Speed ratings: **104,102,100,98,96 91**
toteswingers:1&2:£2.50, 1&3:£11.30, 2&3:£12.20 CSF £17.43 TOTE £5.10: £2.30, £2.70; EX 23.30.
Owner Simon W Clarke **Bred** Francis Maze **Trained** Slad, Gloucs

FOCUS
A slightly disappointing turnout for this Grade 1 which was steadily run. Nacarat is rated back to his best with Carole's Legacy a bit below her Cheltenham run.

NOTEBOOK
Nacarat(FR) is a very useful performer given good ground and a flat track, although he made mistakes when third in this last season. He disputed the lead from the start but did not go too fast, and then wound it up from halfway down the back straight second time. Clear three out, he galloped on well and a bold leap at the final fence settled the issue. He will be aimed at the Charlie Hall Chase first next season and then be campaigned with a view to returning here in 12 months' time. (op 9-2)
Carole's Legacy is a really consistent mare over both hurdles and fences. She tracked the pace throughout and gamely went in pursuit of the winner three out, but could never reel him in. She has the option of going for the bet365 Gold Cup at the end of the month, but might be retired to stud now and should make a wonderful broodmare if she can pass on her qualities. (op 5-1)
Follow The Plan(IRE) had the lowest official rating of these, but was settled out the back and briefly looked as if he might play a hand early in the straight before being unable to find extra. He seems to run above himself in these graded events, having been a surprise winner of a Grade 1 novice chase last season and a Grade 2 this time around. (op 33-1)
Deep Purple disputed the lead for a circuit and a half, but began to struggle once the winner kicked on. He is not the horse he was, but his rating means he has to continue to compete in graded company. (tchd 10-1)
Denman(IRE) looked to have the ideal opportunity to get back to winning form following his gallant second in the Cheltenham Gold Cup. However, he was never travelling that well, being niggled on the first circuit and then coming under pressure at the end of the back straight on the second lap. He was beaten after a slow jump three out and the return to this course - he fell in this race two years ago - was not to his liking. Official explanation: trainer said gelding was unsuited by the track (op 6-5 tchd 11-8)
Punchestowns(FR), generally unconvincing since switching to fences, was again less than fluent and was well beaten jumping the cross fence. His trainer feels he has some sort of problem which is causing his jumping to suffer, and it was later reported that the gelding was lame. He might be better switched to back to hurdles, but that will mean taking on Big Buck's again. Official explanation: vet said gelding returned lame (op 11-2 tchd 5-1)

5163 JOHN SMITH'S FOX HUNTERS' () (18 fncs) 2m 5f 110y
3:40 (3:42) (Class 2) 6-Y-0+

£21,007 (£6,562; £3,279; £1,641; £819; £413)

Form RPR
-11U **1** **Baby Run (FR)**[20] 4851 11-12-0 136 .... MrWTwiston-Davies 138+
(Nigel Twiston-Davies) *led to 5th: lft in ld 8th: kpt on run-in: hld on towards fin* **3/1**[1]
2 *¾* **Boxer Georg (IRE)**[33] 4496 9-12-0 106 .... MrPWMullins 137+
(W P Mullins, Ire) *in rr: hdwy 8th: sn chsng ldrs: mstke 12th (Canal Turn): 4th whn mstke 2 out: wnt cl 2nd last: no ex fnl 75yds* **25/1**
0-33 **3** *13* **Offshore Account (IRE)**[43] 4286 11-12-0 119 .... (tp) MrNSutton 125+
(Mrs T L Bailey) *mid-div: blnd 4 out: styng on whn hit 2 out: tk modest 3rd elbow* **25/1**
3-21 **4** *1 ¼* **Mister Apple's (FR)**[27] 4701 11-12-0 120 .... (p) MrRMahon 121
(Ian Williams) *mid-div: hdwy after 3 out: kpt on wl run-in* **16/1**
11 **5** *½* **Fort View (IRE)**[34] 4463 7-12-0 124 .... (p) MrRGHenderson 121
(Polly Gundry) *in rr: pckd 8th: hdwy 12th (Canal Turn): one pce fr 2 out* **16/1**
314- **6** *19* **Van Ness (IRE)**[12] 12-12-0 106 .... MrRHunnisett 104
(G T H Bailey) *towards rr: sme hdwy 10th (Becher's): one pce fr 3 out* **66/1**
P36U **7** *5* **Silver Adonis (IRE)**[16] 4936 10-12-0 124 .... (p) MrTWeston 103
(Dr Richard Newland) *chsd ldrs: 3rd last: wknd qckly elbow: eased towards fin* **16/1**
2F63 **8** *7* **Dead Or Alive (IRE)**[27] 4695 8-12-0 119 .... (t) MrTomDavid 89
(Tim Vaughan) *chsd ldrs: wknd after 2 out* **50/1**
U4-5 **9** *1 ¾* **Belem Ranger (IRE)**[328] 317 11-12-0 104 .... MrJohnDawson 87
(Mrs J Warwick) *mid-div: hdwy 8th: chsng ldrs 10th (Becher's) wknd appr 2 out* **100/1**
1123 **10** *31* **Good Company (IRE)**[15] 4950 11-12-0 122 .... MrPJTolman 56
(S Flook) *in rr: blnd 10th (Becher's): bhd whn mstke 3 out: t.o* **33/1**
11 *42* **Kanesh (IRE)**[36] 4435 8-12-0 103 .... (p) MrJJCodd 14
(Mark L Fagan, Ire) *chsd ldrs: bdly hmpd 8th: nt rcvr and sn bhd: wl t.o* **20/1**
32 **12** *8* **Captain Knock (IRE)**[20] 4857 8-12-0 93 .... MrTJCannon 6
(David Phelan) *chsd ldrs: mstke 3rd (Chair): blnd 13th (Valentine's): sn wknd: t.o 3 out* **100/1**
22U6 **U** **Fairwood Present (IRE)**[15] 4950 13-12-0 117 .... MrRJarrett —
(John Buxton) *in rr: blnd and uns rdr 7th* **100/1**
-21P **U** **Mount Benger**[20] 4851 11-12-0 126 .... (p) MrSKeating —
(H Whittington) *mid-div: outpcd whn blnd and uns rdr 9th* **100/1**
/22- **F** **Kilty Storm (IRE)**[11] 12-12-0 131 .... MrDLQueally —
(Roger Joseph McGrath, Ire) *w ldrs: mstke 3rd (Chair): led 5th: fell 8th* **12/1**
-642 **B** **Moncadou (FR)**[25] 4750 11-12-0 120 .... (t) MrAJBerry —
(Jonjo O'Neill) *in rr: mstke 3rd (Chair): hdwy 5th: mid-div whn b.d 8th* **8/1**[3]
1612 **F** **Ice Tea (IRE)**[11] 11-12-0 127 .... (p) MrJHamer —
(Mrs S K McCain) *w ldrs: fell 6th* **11/1**
-0P2 **F** **Launde (IRE)**[48] 4197 12-12-0 101 .... MrPYork —
(Mrs Jenny Gordon) *mid-div: hdwy 13th (Valentine's): 5th whn fell 3 out* **100/1**
/2U1 **F** **Turko (FR)**[13] 4991 9-12-0 135 .... (t) MrSWaley-Cohen —
(Mrs L Borradaile) *chsd ldrs: fell 8th* **9/2**[2]
1110 **P** **Massini Man (IRE)**[21] 4821 10-12-0 126 .... MissCLWills —
(Brendan Powell) *mid-div: hmpd 8th: bhd whn hmpd 11th (Foinavon): t.o whn p.u after next (Canal Turn)* **25/1**
621U **F** **Herons Well**[20] 4851 8-12-0 135 .... (p) MrJoshHalley —
(Rebecca Curtis) *chsd ldrs: hmpd and fell 8th* **11/1**
1661 **U** **Call Me Mulligan (IRE)**[29] 4553 7-12-0 110 .... MrMEnnis —
(John Hellens) *in rr: bhd whn blnd and uns rdr 7th* **66/1**
5m 36.9s (0.90) **Going Correction** +0.275s/f (Yiel) **22** Ran SP% **125.4**
Speed ratings: **109,108,104,103,103 96,94,92,91,80 64,62,—,—,— —,—,—,—,— —,—**
toteswingers:1&2:£48.90, 1&3:£26.00, 2&3:£139.70 CSF £83.91 TOTE £3.60: £2.00, £7.00, £8.30; EX 141.00 Trifecta £3945.10 Part won. Pool: £5,331.27 - 0.10 winning units..
Owner N A Twiston-Davies **Bred** Haras De Preaux **Trained** Naunton, Gloucs
■ Stewards' Enquiry : Mr D L Queally four-day ban: breach of Rule (B)46.2, remounted (Apr 21,23-25)
Mr A J Berry four-day ban: breach of Rule (B)46.2, remounted (Apr 21,23-25)
Mr S Waley-Cohen four-day ban: breach of Rule (B)46.2, remounted (Apr 21,23-25)
Mr T Weston two-day ban: failed to ride out for 6th (Apr 21,23)
Mr Josh Halley four-day ban: breach of Rule (B)46.2, remounted (Apr 21,23-25)

FOCUS
The usual big field of hunters lined up for one of the most prestigious races in their calendar, and three of the first four home last season took their chance again. The field jumped nicely in the early stages and it wasn't until the sixth fence that Ice Tea became the first to depart, but the turning point of the race came at the eight fence where four departed. This rates an ordinary renewal, with Baby Run 10lb off his best.

NOTEBOOK
Baby Run(FR), undoubtedly the best horse in the race, had unseated when favourite for this last year and also when leading in the Cheltenham Foxhunter last month, but he assumed total command in front after the melee at the eighth fence. His jumping was decent throughout, as it can be, and he was brave after the last fence to repel his final challenger. It will be fascinating to see whether his bet365 Gold Cup entry is taken up if he gets in, as one could easily see him running well there off a low weight. (tchd 5-2)
Boxer Georg(IRE) was travelling strongly for much of the race but made the odd error, the worst of which came at the Canal Turn, and he just came up short. He hadn't run particularly well in the lead up to this contest, so the big fences may have inspired him. (op 33-1)
Offshore Account(IRE) was running for the third time over these fences and put up his best performance despite crashing through the15th. (op 22-1)
Mister Apple's(FR) stayed on from a midfield position, and really wants further. (op 14-1)
Fort View(IRE) ◆ got behind before The Chair (3rd fence) and was last jumping the next. He made his ground steadily and put up a most pleasing performance. Considering his age and experience, he is probably the one to take for the future for another crack at this race. (op 14-1)
Van Ness(IRE) once again did himself proud on his third try at this race. (op 50-1)
Silver Adonis(IRE), last year's victor, weakened quickly after holding every chance rounding the final bend. (op 14-1)
Kilty Storm(IRE) slithered and fell on landing at the eighth and hampered both Herons Well and Kanesh. (tchd 14-1)
Moncadou(FR) was hampered and brought down when Turko fell. (tchd 14-1)

Launde(IRE) looked seriously unlucky not to get involved in the finish. He made good progress into a challenging position and was still moving strongly when falling three out. (tchd 14-1)

5164 MATALAN.CO.UK RED RUM H'CAP CHASE (GRADE 3) (12 fncs) 2m
4:15 (4:16) (Class 1) 5-Y-0+

£34,206 (£12,834; £6,426; £3,204; £1,608; £804)

Form RPR

2-U5 **1** **Silk Drum (IRE)**[33] 4470 6-9-9 **141** oh9 PaulGallagher(5) 147+
(Howard Johnson) *in tch: wnt 2nd 5th: led after 8th: 4 l clr 3 out: rdn after next: styd on* **9/1**

4031 **2** 4 ½ **Oiseau De Nuit (FR)**[20] 4853 9-10-6 **154** (t) SClements(7) 160+
(Colin Tizzard) *hld up: blnd 2nd and rdr lost irons briefly: bhd after tl hdwy fr 4 out: chsd wnr 2 out: kpt on but a hld run-in* **8/1**

F062 **3** 4 **I'm Delilah**[33] 4470 9-10-0 **141** oh3 JamesReveley 144+
(Ferdy Murphy) *trckd ldrs: lost pl appr 6th: hmpd 8th and again next: styd on again after 3 out: wnt 3rd run-in: fin wl* **10/1**

-131 **4** 4 **Mamlook (IRE)**[26] 4729 7-9-9 **141** oh6 CO'Farrell(5) 134
(David Pipe) *in tch: j. slowly and lost pl 2nd: hdwy after 4 out: wnt 3rd bef 2 out: one pce and no imp on ldrs bef last: lost 3rd run-in* **13/2**[3]

F202 **5** 1 ½ **Tchico Polos (FR)**[48] 4187 7-11-3 **158** (t) RWalsh 149
(Paul Nicholls) *in tch: mstke 1st: hit 4th: rdn appr 3 out: one pce and no imp fr next* **5/1**[2]

-140 **6** 1 **Safari Journey (USA)**[117] 2881 7-10-1 **142** (b) RichardJohnson 133
(Philip Hobbs) *in tch: slow 3rd: hit 6th and 8th: chsd wnr 4 out tl 2 out: no ex appr last* **10/1**

-110 **7** 14 **Woolcombe Folly (IRE)**[22] 4805 8-11-7 **167** MrRMahon(5) 145
(Paul Nicholls) *hld up: hdwy 8th: rdn 4 out: wkng whn hit 3 out* **8/1**

055- **8** *hd* **Pepsyrock (FR)**[355] 5225 8-9-11 **141** oh11 DavidBass(3) 117
(Nicky Henderson) *midfield: hdwy 6th: chsd wnr briefly 4 out: wkng appr 2 out* **33/1**

0F30 **9** 14 **Enlightenment (IRE)**[67] 3841 11-9-7 **141** oh9 (p) NathanSweeney(7) 107
(Evan Williams) *w ldr led after 1st tl hit next: nt fluent 5th and lost 2nd: sn struggling: bhd whn mstke 8th* **100/1**

P-0U **10** 2 ¾ **Beggars Cap (IRE)**[20] 4853 9-10-0 **141** oh14 GrahamLee 102
(Ferdy Murphy) *hld up: hit 1st: a bhd* **18/1**

P04R **R** **Chaninbar (FR)**[20] 4853 8-10-10 **151** (bt) SeanQuinlan —
(Milton Harris) *ref to r* **28/1**

-253 **F** **Leo's Lucky Star (USA)**[20] 4853 9-10-0 **141** (t) TomScudamore —
(David Pipe) *hld up on inner: hdwy into 5th and stl gng wl whn fell 8th* **9/2**[1]

-450 **F** **Sports Line (IRE)**[20] 4853 8-9-7 **141** oh1 (t) HenryBrooke(7) —
(Donald McCain) *led tl hit 1st: led next: hit 8th: sn hdd: disputing 2nd whn fell 4 out* **10/1**

3m 57.3s (-2.70) **Going Correction** +0.175s/f (Yiel) **13 Ran SP% 120.3**
Speed ratings: **113,110,108,106,106 105,98,98,91,90 —,—,—**
toteswingers:1&2:£27.30, 1&3:£32.10, 2&3:£21.00 CSF £79.49 CT £745.94 TOTE £13.80: £3.90, £3.00, £3.40; EX 197.70 Trifecta £1955.20 Pool: £3,434.82 - 1.30 winning units..
Owner Andrea & Graham Wylie **Bred** Mrs Cherry Faeste **Trained** Billy Row, Co Durham

FOCUS
This usually competitive handicap chase was made less so by the presence of Woolcombe Folly, resulting in more than half the field racing from out of the weights. There should be more to come from the lightly raced winner, and the next two are rated a lot higher than the bare result.

NOTEBOOK
Silk Drum(IRE) was well beaten by I'm Delilah at Doncaster last time and was racing from 9lb out of the handicap. However, having just his fifth start over fences, he was a market springer and justified the support in decisive fashion. Always travelling strongly, he took the race by the scruff of the neck going to the cross fence and, clear at the next, was always holding the runner-up. Official explanation: trainer had no explanation for the apparent improvement in form other than the yard was previously under a cloud (op 20-1)

Oiseau De Nuit(FR) ◆, a surprise winner of the Grand Annual last time and 9lb higher, made a mistake at the second fence which cost him at least five lengths and a good deal of impetus, though his rider made a good recovery. He stayed on really well to chase the winner in the straight, but the effort of making up the ground told going to the last. He has to go down as unlucky in view of the official margin, and while in such good form can gain compensation if kept on the go. (op 7-1)

I'm Delilah ◆, well suited by a flat track and good ground, was 5lb higher than when narrowly beaten at Doncaster on her previous start, but was another who can be regarded as unlucky. Racing from 3lb out of the weights, she was a fair way back but still going well when badly hampered by the fall of the favourite five from home. Still eighth jumping the second last, she ran on really strongly to take the minor placing. Given her favoured conditions - she needs to go left-handed - she is another who can make up for this. Official explanation: jockey said mare was hampered in running (op 9-1 tchd 11-1)

Mamlook(IRE), high class on the Flat and over hurdles, has taken well to fences. Racing from 6lb wrong, he made headway to chase the leader early in the straight but was soon running on empty. (op 6-1)

Tchico Polos(FR), runner-up in a Grade 2 at Newbury, had not been raised for that on this return to handicaps. He was never far away, but had nothing more to give in the straight. (op 11-2)

Safari Journey(USA), well beaten in this last year and best on good ground, was 12lb higher than for his win in first-time blinkers in the autumn. He moved up to chase the winner turning in, but then faded.

Woolcombe Folly(IRE) has a very good strike rate, but finished well beaten in the Queen Mother. Effective on fast and easy ground and a flat track, he was 13lb higher than for his last success and ran a rather flat race having been held up.

Pepsyrock(FR) had not won since 2009, but has been lightly raced since. Racing from well out of the weights, he made a forward move down the back before dropping away in the straight. (tchd 40-1)

Chaninbar(FR) won this last year when making all in a first-time visor, but had refused to start on his previous outing and showed no inclination to take part again. (op 25-1 tchd 33-1)

Leo's Lucky Star(USA), a useful novice who ran third in the Grand Annual and was 7lb better off with Oiseau De Nuit, was tracking the leaders when taking a heavy fall five out. The result suggests he would not have been far away had he stood up. (op 5-1 tchd 11-2)

5165 TOTEPOOL MANIFESTO NOVICES' CHASE (GRADE 2) (16 fncs) 2m 4f
4:50 (4:50) (Class 1) 5-Y-0+ **£42,958** (£16,243; £8,233; £4,206; £2,211)

Form RPR

1212 **1** **Wishfull Thinking**[21] 4816 8-11-4 155 (t) RichardJohnson 163+
(Philip Hobbs) *j.w: trckd ldr: led 3rd: clr after 7th: rdn after 2 out: kpt on wl* **9/4**[2]

1214 **2** 10 **Medermit (FR)**[23] 4789 7-11-4 155 RobertThornton 155
(Alan King) *in tch: wnt 2nd after 8th: rdn after 3 out: kpt on but no ch w wnr* **15/8**[1]

3-11 **3** 23 **Royal Charm (FR)**[112] 2976 6-11-4 145 RWalsh 134
(Paul Nicholls) *in tch: wnt 3rd after 9th: hit 5 out: rdn 3 out: sn no imp* **10/3**[3]

3-26 **4** 7 **Tharawaat (IRE)**[23] 4794 6-11-4 137 (bt) DNRussell 130
(Gordon Elliott, Ire) *led to 3rd: in 3rd whn mstke 9th: wknd after 5 out* **10/1**

4150 **5** 41 **Hollo Ladies (IRE)**[21] 4820 6-11-4 138 GrahamLee 89
(Ferdy Murphy) *j. slowly in rr: reminders after 5th: a bhd* **33/1**

/2-4 **F** **Shirley Casper (IRE)**[32] 4514 10-10-11 127 (p) AELynch —
(D T Hughes, Ire) *hld up: in 5th whn fell 5 out* **16/1**

1-41 **U** **Hold Fast (IRE)**[92] 3393 7-11-4 0 BrianHughes —
(Howard Johnson) *hld up: mstke 8th: in 6th whn blnd bdly and uns rdr 5 out* **25/1**

5m 4.10s (-4.10) **Going Correction** +0.175s/f (Yiel) **7 Ran SP% 110.4**
Speed ratings: **115,111,101,99,82 —,—**
toteswingers:1&2:£1.40, 1&3:£2.50, 2&3:£3.00 CSF £6.70 TOTE £2.90: £2.10, £1.50; EX 5.10.
Owner Mrs Diana L Whateley **Bred** Cobhall Court Stud **Trained** Withycombe, Somerset

FOCUS
Not many runners, but a strong-looking contest. The winner ensured the pace was sound and he looks a serious contender for some major prizes next season. This was a slight step up on his run at Cheltenham.

NOTEBOOK
Wishfull Thinking ◆ ran really well at Cheltenham last time when putting up a bold display of jumping until weakening late on, but there was no repeat of the petrol running out here as he once again bounded off in front and made no jumping errors at all. What is so pleasing about him is that you can tell the horse is intelligent. He picked up and flew the first in the back straight on the final circuit, when Richard Johnson asked him for a big one, but also helped the jockey out when it didn't look obvious that he could see a stride. This certainly wasn't bad for a horse re-routed from the longer Grade 2 race the following day after this contest was reopened. Considering he appeared to enjoy this flat track, it wouldn't be a surprise to see him return in the Old Roan Chase at this course next season and he must merit serious respect for the King George if continuing his progression. That said, it wouldn't be a massive surprise if he proved good enough to take in a top-flight 2m race either, given the amount of pace he shows. If connections felt that was the way to go, the Tingle Creek may well suit his aggressive and courageous style. There is little doubt he is an extremely exciting prospect with many options. (op 2-1)

Medermit(FR) has endured an up-and-down time of it over fences, and failed to get competitive in the Arkle last time when strongly fancied to run well. The trainer reported afterwards that with hindsight he should have run his horse in the Jewson instead and he ran well here back up in trip, but simply bumped into a classier individual. (op 2-1)

Royal Charm(FR) had a bit to find with the market leaders on official figures, but hadn't been beaten over fences and represented a top stable. Trying this trip for the first time since going chasing, he had his chance but hit the final fence in the back straight quite hard and was never able to get to the runaway leader. One couldn't be sure he stayed the trip, but he possesses a big engine considering the way he travelled until he made the error, so a drop in trip may well be in order. (op 3-1)

Tharawaat(IRE) wasn't disgraced in the Centenary Novices' Chase last month, but was outclassed here. (op 12-1 tchd 14-1)

Hollo Ladies(IRE) looked very difficult to fancy on what he had done on his previous two starts and gave himself little chance here after getting behind from the start. (op 40-1 tchd 25-1)

Shirley Casper(IRE) probably wouldn't have troubled the winner, but she was still moving comfortably when taking a heavy fall five from home. (op 20-1 tchd 25-1)

5166 SILVER CROSS H'CAP HURDLE (LISTED RACE) (11 hdls) 2m 4f
5:25 (5:25) (Class 1) 4-Y-0+

£22,804 (£8,556; £4,284; £2,136; £1,072; £536)

Form RPR

0110 **1** **Russian War (IRE)**[144] 2387 8-10-1 **128** (t) PCarberry 134+
(Gordon Elliott, Ire) *hld up in rr: stdy hdwy 3 out: led last: drvn rt out towards fin* **16/1**

0110 **2** 1 ¼ **Reindeer Dippin**[19] 4875 9-9-12 **132** HenryBrooke(7) 136
(Donald McCain) *hld up in tch: smooth hdwy 8th: led 3 out: hdd last: kpt on wl towards fin* **40/1**

3131 **3** *nse* **Wyse Hill Teabags**[17] 4910 6-10-6 **133** RichieMcGrath 138+
(Jim Goldie) *chsd ldrs: 3rd whn blnd last: styd on towards fin* **20/1**

-240 **4** 2 ¾ **Micheal Flips (IRE)**[21] 4817 7-11-4 **145** NickScholfield 148+
(Andy Turnell) *mid-div: hdwy 8th: chsng ldrs next: kpt on same pce fr 2 out* **20/1**

-430 **5** 2 ¾ **Notus De La Tour (FR)**[20] 4848 5-11-1 **142** AELynch 142
(David Pipe) *chsd ldrs: outpcd 8th: kpt on fr 2 out* **20/1**

-343 **6** ¾ **First Point (GER)**[20] 4852 8-10-10 **144** JeremiahMcGrath(7) 142
(Nicky Henderson) *mid-div: hdwy to chse ldrs 8th: one pce fr 3 out* **25/1**

2522 **7** 7 **Bothy**[22] 4806 5-10-8 **140** CO'Farrell(5) 132
(Brian Ellison) *t.k.h: trckd ldrs: wknd fr 2 out* **9/1**

1114 **8** 1 ¼ **Problema Tic (FR)**[47] 4198 5-10-5 **132** BarryGeraghty 122
(Nicky Henderson) *chsd ldrs: one pce fr 3 out* **12/1**

6043 **9** 4 **Orsippus (USA)**[22] 4806 5-10-10 **137** DJCondon 130+
(Michael Smith) *hld up in rr: hdwy appr 3 out: 9th whn mstke and hmpd last* **10/1**

0/10 **10** 3 ¼ **Ski Sunday**[20] 4848 6-11-2 **143** SamThomas 129
(Lawney Hill) *in rr: drvn 7th: sme hdwy 3 out: hmpd last* **16/1**

2123 **11** 12 **Pateese (FR)**[26] 4727 6-10-2 **129** RichardJohnson 117+
(Philip Hobbs) *trckd ldrs: wknd appr 3 out: eased* **12/1**

2 **12** 6 **Cass Bligh (IRE)**[21] 4842 7-10-8 **135** PaddyBrennan 103
(Adrian Murray, Ire) *hld up in rr: hdwy 8th: wknd and mstke 2 out* **33/1**

1301 **13** 1 ¾ **Rio Gael (IRE)**[13] 4992 5-10-4 **131** (p) TomO'Brien 97
(Peter Bowen) *led after 1st: hdd 3 out: sn wknd* **25/1**

02F5 **14** 20 **Sophies Trophy (IRE)**[16] 4933 6-10-0 **127** (t) ColinBolger 75
(Pat Phelan) *led tl after 1st: t.k.h: w ldrs: wknd 3 out* **50/1**

0B53 **15** ¾ **Afsoun (FR)**[39] 4373 9-10-7 **137** AlexMerriam(3) 84
(Neil King) *chsd ldrs: hmpd bnd after 8th: sn wknd* **50/1**

0-22 **16** 16 **Nafaath (IRE)**[60] 3968 5-10-13 **140** BrianHughes 73
(Howard Johnson) *chsd ldrs: drvn and lost pl appr 3 out: sn bhd* **66/1**

2235 **17** 15 **Megastar**[22] 4803 6-11-0 **141** JamieMoore 61
(Gary Moore) *mid-div: lost pl 8th: sn bhd* **7/1**[2]

1040 **F** **Inventor (IRE)**[20] 4848 6-10-11 **138** (t) GrahamLee —
(Donald McCain) *mid-div: sn drvn: lost 4th: sme hdwy and mid-div whn fell 3 out: fatally injured* **33/1**

3126 **P** **Lake Legend**[19] 4864 7-10-10 **137** RobertThornton —
(Alan King) *prom: wkng whn mstke 8th: wl bhd whn p.u bef 2 out* **33/1**

1311 **P** **Russian George (IRE)**[15] 1466 5-10-2 **129** AidanColeman —
(Steve Gollings) *in rr: drvn 5th: sn bhd: t.o whn p.u bef 3 out* **33/1**

0602 **P** **Get Me Out Of Here (IRE)**[20] 4848 7-11-12 **153** (t) APMcCoy —
(Jonjo O'Neill) *in rr: sme hdwy on outside 7th: sn wknd: bhd whn p.u bef 2 out* **7/2**[1]

03 **F** **Sire Collonges (FR)**[33] 4488 5-10-2 129 RWalsh 119
(Paul Nicholls) *mid-div: rdn appr 3 out: j.lft 2 out: 8th whn fell last* **8/1**[3]
4m 54.1s (-6.60) **Going Correction** -0.05s/f (Good) **22** Ran SP% **133.7**
Speed ratings (Par 111): **111,110,110,109,108 107,105,104,103,101 96,94,93,85,85 79,73,—,—,— —,—**
toteswingers:1&2:£150.80, 1&3:£301.70, 2&3:£181.00. totesuper7: Win: Not won. Place: Not won CSF £560.54 CT £12159.75 TOTE £26.50: £4.80, £9.80, £4.20, £5.30; EX 1320.80 TRIFECTA Not won..
Owner T D Howley Jnr **Bred** Tommy Howley **Trained** Trim, Co Meath

FOCUS
A good competitive handicap hurdle and a big field, but the early pace steadied after half a circuit. Pretty solid form, the winner up 6lb on his early-season Cheltenham win.

NOTEBOOK
Russian War(IRE) ◆, progressive in the autumn but 6lb higher than when scoring at Cheltenham in October, was having his first run since the following month. Held up at the back, he was still last of all at the final flight in the back straight, but made up his ground to challenge going to the last and ultimately won comfortably. Presumably connections will be aiming for Punchestown next month providing he gets good ground, with his ability to stay 3m giving connections more options. (op 12-1)
Reindeer Dippin has been mixing hurdling and chasing of late and handles any ground. Although well beaten off this mark last month, he travelled much better in the pack and looked as though he might have stolen the race when kicking on in the straight. However, he had no answer when the winner arrived on the scene. (op 33-1)
Wyse Hill Teabags ◆, a decent novice who won well last month, was making his handicap debut. He tracked the pace on the inside and got rather squeezed up on the rail leaving the back straight. However, he came through to have every chance between the last two, only for a mistake at the last to cost him the runner-up spot. There should be more to come. (op 22-1 tchd 25-1)
Micheal Flips(IRE), well beaten in two runs at around 3m over hurdles since finishing runner-up on his chasing debut in the autumn, was back to a trip he is proven at on a track that suits. He travelled well off the pace, but was also caught up in the scrimmaging leaving the back straight before running on to chase the leaders in the straight. This was better from him. (tchd 22-1)
Notus De La Tour(FR) disappointed in the County Hurdle, but posted a good effort when third in the totesport Trophy before that. He ran much better ridden less positively this time and was staying on well enough in the straight. He looks ideally suited by 2m and softer ground.
First Point(GER) put up good efforts when fourth in the Lanzarote and third in the Martin Pipe at Cheltenham, and ran well again from 6lb higher. He has not won over hurdles for the best part of two years, though, and will not find things easy off his current mark. (tchd 28-1)
Bothy, a tough and genuine sort who has been runner-up in the Greatwood, totesport Trophy and Coral Cup this season, was 2lb higher today and, although he again ran creditably, may be in the handicapper's grip. (op 10-1)
Problema Tic(FR), unbeaten in two bumpers and two hurdles before being well held last time, was making his handicap debut off 132. He never really got into contention, but this was a fair effort. (op 10-1)
Ursippus(USA), a surprise Grade 1 winner here last season, had not scored since but was a good third in Coral Cup last time and was 1lb better off with Bothy. He ran reasonably on a course he likes and was staying on when hampered by the faller at the last.
Ski Sunday put up a decent effort in the County Hurdle and was better off with today's favourite. However, he was being niggled fairly early on before keeping on late.
Pateese(FR), usually a consistent sort on good and softer ground and best at 2m, was 4lb higher for finishing a good third in the Imperial Cup. He moved into contention at the end of the back straight, but faded once in line for home and was eased as though something was amiss, although it may have been that his stamina ran out.
Megastar has not quite lived up to early expectations, but has been running reasonably well in graded company. He was well supported having won a Grade 2 bumper at this meeting last year, but failed to figure on this handicap debut.
Get Me Out Of Here(IRE), whose trainer had won this twice in the previous four years, was well backed to gain compensation for his narrow defeat in the County Hurdle but, having been held up, he was struggling turning for home and was pulled up before two out. Official explanation: jockey said, regarding running, that the gelding felt amiss. (op 11-2)
Sire Collonges(FR) was 5lb better off with Pateese for 6l compared with Newbury last month and was staying on, although he would not have made the frame, when departing at the final flight. (op 11-2)
T/Jkpt: £10,217.40 to a £1 stake. Pool:£35,976.84 - 2.50 winning tickets T/Plt: £107.40 to a £1 stake. Pool:£356,860.38 - 2,423.48 winning tickets T/Qpdt: £75.80 to a £1 stake. Pool:£14,836.96 - 144.80 winning tickets WG

5071 HEREFORD (R-H)
Thursday, April 7

OFFICIAL GOING: Good (good to soft in places; watered; chs 7.0, hdl 7.3)
Wind: mild breeze across Weather: sunny with patchy cloud

5167 PLAY CASINO AT VICTORCHANDLER.COM MAIDEN HURDLE (DIV I) (8 hdls) 2m 1f
2:20 (2:20) (Class 5) 4-Y-0+ **£1,398** (£410; £205; £102)

Form RPR
14 **1** **Eastlake (IRE)**[19] 4881 5-11-0 0 RichieMcLernon 102+
(Jonjo O'Neill) *trckd ldr: chal after 2 out: led sn after last: pushed out: comf* **16/1**
2566 **2** *2 ¼* **Koup De Kanon (FR)**[38] 4397 5-11-0 0 JackDoyle 96+
(Emma Lavelle) *mid-div: hdwy 4th: rdn after 2 out: ch sn after last whn short of room: styd on* **9/2**[3]
0004 **3** *½* **Countess Susy**[15] 4946 6-10-0 0 PeterHatton(7) 88
(Phillip Dando) *mid-div: rdn after 2 out: little imp tl styd on wl fr last to go 3rd nr fin: nt rch ldrs* **66/1**
4520 **4** *1 ½* **Don't Turn Bach (IRE)**[34] 4462 7-11-0 106 (t) HarrySkelton 94
(Paul Nicholls) *led tl after 3 out: chsd ldr: rdn after 2 out: rallied briefly last: no ex fnl 120yds* **4/1**[2]
0 **5** *nk* **Sirdave**[15] 4952 5-11-0 0 JodieMogford 94
(Peter Hiatt) *trckd ldr: led after 3 out: rdn after next: hdd sn after last: no ex* **66/1**
P **6** *11* **Ogmore Junction (IRE)**[304] 662 6-10-4 0 (t) ThomasFlint(10) 86
(John Flint) *mid-div: hdwy after 3 out to chse ldrs: rdn after next: wknd last* **100/1**
0060 **7** *2 ¾* **North Stack**[37] 4404 5-11-0 0 SamJones 81
(Michael Scudamore) *hld up towards rr: sme late prog: nvr trbld ldrs* **50/1**
400 **8** *4* **Storm Survivor (IRE)**[17] 4917 5-10-9 0 AnthonyFreeman(5) 77
(Jonjo O'Neill) *nt fluent early: in rr whn struggling 3rd: nvr a factor* **7/1**
00 **9** *2 ¼* **Rajeeva (IRE)**[31] 4528 5-10-7 0 HarryChalloner(7) 75
(Venetia Williams) *mid-div: rdn after 3 out: wknd after next* **50/1**
6 **10** *1 ¾* **By Command**[139] 2495 6-11-0 0 LiamHeard 74
(Laura Young) *trckd ldr: rdn after 3 out: wknd after next* **50/1**
06 **11** *1* **Jacko's Boy**[17] 4917 8-11-0 0 WarrenMarston 73
(Martin Keighley) *trckd ldrs tl rdn after 4th: sn bhd* **8/1**
1-F **12** *hd* **Instabella**[154] 2168 5-10-7 0 RhysFlint 66
(Philip Hobbs) *t.k.h in mid-div: rdn after 3 out: sn wknd* **15/8**[1]
13 *6* **Resplendent Ace (IRE)**[180] 7-11-0 0 TomMessenger 67
(John Price) *mid-div tl 3rd: sn bhd* **33/1**
0/00 **14** *½* **Termon Boy**[12] 5013 7-10-11 0 (t) MichaelMurphy(3) 67
(Rob Summers) *a towards rr* **200/1**
005 **15** *¾* **Seventh Hussar**[35] 4443 5-11-0 0 AndrewThornton 66
(Henrietta Knight) *mid-div tl 3 out: sn rdn and wknd* **50/1**
50 **16** *22* **Call Me Frankie (IRE)**[19] 4860 5-11-0 0 TimmyMurphy 46
(Lucy Jones) *mid-div tl rdn 3 out: sn wknd: t.o* **66/1**
3m 57.7s (-1.70) **Going Correction** -0.175s/f (Good) **16** Ran SP% **119.2**
Speed ratings (Par 103): **97,95,95,95,94 89,88,86,85,84 84,84,81,81,80 70**
toteswingers:1&2:£11.20, 1&3:£41.30, 2&3:£41.30 CSF £84.18 TOTE £10.40: £3.40, £2.40, £10.70; EX 78.50.
Owner John P McManus **Bred** Mrs Eleanor Hadden **Trained** Cheltenham, Gloucs

FOCUS
This ordinary maiden proved a lively betting heat. It saw plenty of chances from the penultimate flight and there was a tight finish.

NOTEBOOK
Eastlake(IRE) showed the benefit of his return in a bumper at Uttoxeter 19 days earlier and won readily on this switch to hurdles. The big talking point here was his incredible drift in the market as he simply could not be given away. A sound surface looks important to his cause and, while his future lies over fences, there should really be improvement in him in this sphere. (op 17-2 tchd 18-1)
Koup De Kanon(FR) got a more positive ride this time and posted an improved effort as a result, as it helped him settle. He didn't get the clearest passage late on, but it made no difference to the result. (op 15-2)
Countess Susy's proximity holds the form down as she had been beaten out of sight in her four previous outings. Her connections have advertised in the past they can improve mares, however, so she is given a chance to prove she is progressing.
Don't Turn Bach(IRE) was equipped with a first-time tongue tie and looked slow. This was a step back in the right direction, though. (op 3-1 tchd 11-4)
Sirdave ran a bold race under a positive ride and only wilted on the run-in. This was a big improvement on his debut effort 15 days earlier. (op 80-1)
Instabella fell on her hurdling debut in November but looked very interesting on her bumper win at Cheltenham last season. She again took a keen hold and was beaten from halfway. Official explanation: jockey said mare ran too freely and was unsuited by the good (good to soft places) ground (op 5-2)

5168 PLAY CASINO AT VICTORCHANDLER.COM MAIDEN HURDLE (DIV II) (8 hdls) 2m 1f
2:55 (2:55) (Class 5) 4-Y-0+ **£1,398** (£410; £205; £102)

Form RPR
1-02 **1** **Sizing Santiago (IRE)**[27] 4706 5-11-0 0 SamTwiston-Davies 107+
(Nigel Twiston-Davies) *mde all: rdn after 2 out: hrd pressed last: kpt on u.str.p: edgd lft: hld on gamely* **12/1**
2 *nk* **Pippa Greene**[178] 7-11-0 0 AndrewTinkler 107+
(Nicky Henderson) *mid-div: hdwy appr 3 out: rdn to chse ldng pair after 3 out: chalng whn mstke last: kpt on: edgd rt: jst hld* **11/2**[3]
0642 **3** *2* **Robin Will (FR)**[28] 4672 6-11-0 118 HarrySkelton 106+
(Paul Nicholls) *mid-div: hdwy appr 3 out: cl 2nd whn mstke 2 out: sn rdn: hung lft: kpt on same pce* **9/4**[2]
56B0 **4** *9* **Cygnet**[85] 3505 5-11-0 113 AdrianLane 96
(Donald McCain) *mid-div: hdwy on inner appr 5th: rdn appr 2 out: sn one pce* **12/1**
0-05 **5** *8* **Domos Boy (IRE)**[18] 4895 8-11-0 0 RichieMcLernon 89
(Jonjo O'Neill) *in tch: rdn after 3 out: wknd bef last* **22/1**
0044 **6** *1* **Zambuka (FR)**[24] 4774 4-9-10 0 (t) MissLHorner(5) 75
(Pat Murphy) *mstke 4th: hld up towaqrds rr: rdn after 3 out: styd on past btn horses fr after next: nvr trbld ldrs* **50/1**
542 **7** *3 ¾* **Allerford Jack**[29] 4557 7-10-11 118 IanPopham(3) 84
(Caroline Keevil) *trckd ldrs: rdn after 3 out: wknd after next* **7/4**[1]
600 **8** *18* **Homer Run (IRE)**[16] 4930 4-10-5 0 JimmyDerham(3) 62
(Seamus Mullins) *a towards rr: t.o* **125/1**
300 **9** *1 ¾* **Midnight King**[35] 4443 5-10-7 0 TrevorWhelan(7) 67
(George Baker) *bhd fr 3rd* **50/1**
4044 **10** *1* **Sleeping Du Granit (FR)**[12] 5000 5-10-11 0 (t) TommyPhelan(3) 66
(Claire Dyson) *trckd ldrs: rdn 3 out: wknd next* **100/1**
0-0P **11** *14* **Lucky Lukey**[38] 4393 5-10-7 0 (p) HarryChalloner(7) 53
(Richard Ford) *trckd ldrs: pckd 2nd: wknd after 5th* **150/1**
0 **12** *27* **Hey Nineteen (IRE)**[46] 4239 5-11-0 0 FelixDeGiles 29
(Charlie Longsdon) *racd keenly: prom: rdn after 3 out: sn wknd* **33/1**
0P0 **13** *4 ½* **Sam's Pride**[8] 5074 6-11-0 0 JackDoyle 25
(Peter Pritchard) *a towards rr: t.o* **100/1**
PP **P** **Rageon (IRE)**[47] 4225 8-11-0 0 (t) WarrenMarston —
(Milton Harris) *mid-div tl 3rd: sn bhd: t.o whn p.u bef last* **80/1**
202 **P** **Optimistic Duke (IRE)**[152] 2211 4-10-8 108 JimmyMcCarthy —
(William Muir) *mid-div tl v bdly hmpd on bnd appr 3rd: nvr rcvrd and bhd thereafter: p.u bef 3 out* **22/1**
3m 56.2s (-3.20) **Going Correction** -0.175s/f (Good)
WFA 4 from 5yo+ 5lb **15** Ran SP% **118.1**
Speed ratings (Par 103): **100,99,98,94,90 90,88,80,79,78 72,59,57,—,—**
toteswingers:1&2:£10.20, 1&3:£6.70, 2&3:£3.50 CSF £72.04 TOTE £10.70: £2.20, £2.30, £1.60; EX 58.80.
Owner Ann & Alan Potts **Bred** Michael Ronayne **Trained** Naunton, Gloucs

FOCUS
This second division of the maiden saw the principals come clear from two out and the form looks straightforward enough.

NOTEBOOK
Sizing Santiago(IRE), down in trip, ran out a very gutsy winner and made it third time lucky as a hurdler. He got very warm beforehand and took time to settle, but there was no faulting his attitude under pressure. He looks just modest, but should be open to some improvement. (op 11-1)
Pippa Greene, rated 97 at his peak on the Flat, met support on this belated hurdling debut for Nicky Henderson. He was returning from a 178-day absence and proved free early, but made a bold bid off the home turn. He didn't help his cause by hitting the final flight and was done with soon after, but this was a pleasing introduction. (op 9-2 tchd 7-2)
Robin Will(FR) had every chance, but not for the first time he didn't look willing when it mattered and is one to tread carefully with. (op 5-2)
Cygnet shaped as though he would come on for this return from an 85-day break and will be better off in handicaps. (tchd 14-1)
Zambuka(FR) Official explanation: jockey said filly suffered interference in runing
Allerford Jack endured a hard race on his previous outing and was beaten a fair way out. This test probably wasn't for him, though. Official explanation: jockey said gelding was unsuited by the good (good to soft places) ground (op 9-4 tchd 5-2)
Homer Run(IRE) Official explanation: jockey said gelding pulled hard early
Hey Nineteen(IRE) Official explanation: jockey said gelding was unsteady on pulling up; vet said gelding was lame

Optimistic Duke(IRE) Official explanation: trainer's rep said gelding suffered interference in running

5169 BET MOBILE AT VICTORCHANDLER.COM H'CAP HURDLE (13 hdls) 3m 2f

3:30 (3:31) (Class 5) (0-95,95) 4-Y-0+ **£1,723** (£506; £253; £126)

Form RPR

P014 **1** **Bernard**[24] 4787 11-10-6 **80**.....(p) GilesHawkins(5) 87+
(Kevin Bishop) *in tch: led 10th: rdn after 2 out: styd on gamely: rdn out* **14/1**

004U **2** 2 3/4 **Gallimaufry**[24] 4787 5-10-2 **71**..... FelixDeGiles 76+
(Neil Mulholland) *mid-div: hdwy after 9th: rdn to chse wnr after 3 out: nodded on landing last: styd on* **14/1**

000P **3** 7 **Filimoss**[16] 4929 6-10-11 **80**..... JimmyMcCarthy 76
(Charlie Morlock) *mid-div: hdwy 7th: rdn in cl 3rd after 3 out: styd on same pce fr after next* **100/1**

P234 **4** 1 1/4 **Septos**[8] 5075 7-10-3 **75**.....(p) PeterToole(3) 70
(Richard Price) *mid-div: lost pl 10th: sn rdn: styd on again fr after 2 out:* **5/1**[2]

001P **5** 38 **Woodlands Gem (IRE)**[84] 3530 9-10-10 **79**.....(bt) JackDoyle 40
(Peter Pritchard) *racd wd: towards rr: drvn along and hdwy 6th: sn chsng ldrs: wknd after 2 out* **25/1**

0002 **6** 1 **Rivermouth**[28] 4675 6-11-0 **83**.....(b) WayneHutchinson 43
(Alan King) *mid-div: hdwy whn hit 9th: rdn after 3 out: wknd next* **6/1**[3]

2235 **7** 4 1/2 **Bounds And Leaps**[16] 4929 6-11-12 **95**.....(p) JohnnyFarrelly 51
(Michael Scudamore) *prom: led 5th tl 10th: sn rdn: wkng whn nt fluent 3 out* **12/1**

041 **8** 7 **Burnthill (IRE)**[22] 4812 6-11-4 **90**.....(t) TommyPhelan(3) 40
(Claire Dyson) *hld up towards rr: hdwy after 5th: rdn in 3rd after 3 out: wknd next* **8/1**

-3P4 **9** 21 **Glamorous Gg**[26] 4724 6-10-9 **78**.....(tp) DaveCrosse 9
(Ian Williams) *in tch: reminders after 6th: wknd 9th: t.o* **22/1**

2162 **10** 40 **Ukrainian Star (IRE)**[26] 4718 8-11-8 **91**.....(p) WarrenMarston —
(Martin Keighley) *led tl 5th: chsd ldrs: rdn 10th: wknd after next: t.o* **9/2**[1]

0-30 **P** **Normally**[44] 4273 7-11-7 **90**.....(b1) RhysFlint —
(John Flint) *trckd ldrs: rdn after 9th: wknd next: t.o whn p.u after 2 out* **10/1**

5P5P **P** **Fillyofthevalley**[29] 4560 8-10-0 **69** oh9..... MarkGrant —
(Peter Jones) *a bhd: t.o whn p.u bef 3 out* **50/1**

P-00 **P** **Doctor Kilbride (IRE)**[56] 4021 8-11-2 **85**..... TomMessenger —
(Chris Bealby) *rdn 4th: a in rr: t.o whn p.u bef 3 out* **22/1**

1446 **U** **Can't Remember**[15] 4955 6-11-2 **90**..... OliverDayman(5) —
(Alison Thorpe) *blnd and virtually fell whn uns rdr 2nd* **25/1**

02P6 **P** **Tiger Line**[78] 3635 7-11-4 **87**..... TomSiddall —
(Richard Phillips) *a bhd: t.o whn p.u bef 3 out* **28/1**

0P53 **P** **Rathconrath (FR)**[25] 4747 6-11-8 **94**..... TomMolloy(3) —
(Althea Barclay) *trckd ldrs tl after 7th: wknd bef 3 out: t.o whn p.u bef 2 out* **14/1**

00P0 **P** **Our Flora**[28] 4675 6-10-7 **76**.....(p) SamTwiston-Davies —
(Kim Bailey) *mid-div: rdn after 9th: sn wknd: bhd whn p.u after 2 out* **33/1**

6m 24.9s (-6.80) **Going Correction** -0.175s/f (Good) **17** Ran SP% **122.8**
Speed ratings (Par 103): **103,102,100,99,87 87,86,84,77,65 —,—,—,—,— —,—**
toteswingers:1&2:£29.70, 1&3:£54.40, 2&3:£54.40 CSF £176.95 CT £17354.19 TOTE £18.00: £3.30, £4.30, £36.10, £2.40; EX 406.70.
Owner K Bishop **Bred** Mountgrange Stud Ltd **Trained** Spaxton, Somerset

FOCUS
A very weak staying handicap, run at an average pace and the first four came clear.

NOTEBOOK
Bernard was sent off a big price considering he won over C&D on his penultimate outing and was sure to come on for his recent comeback last month. He took it up a fair way out and refused to give in thereafter. It rates his best effort over hurdles so far and the easier ground helped.
Gallimaufry was disappointing behind the winner on his previous start, but he posted by far his most encouraging effort and would've gone even closer had he not made a mess of the third-last. (op 16-1)
Filimoss was held from two out, but kept on gamely and she too posted a clear personal best in defeat.
Septos got the longer trip, but again didn't look that willing. (op 6-1)
Woodlands Gem(IRE) went in snatches from the off.
Rivermouth sports headgear for a reason and she was held before stamina became an issue. (op 17-2)
Ukrainian Star(IRE) dropped out tamely on this return to hurdling. (op 4-1 tchd 7-2)
Rathconrath(FR) Official explanation: vet said gelding pulled up lame
Our Flora Official explanation: vet said mare pulled up lame

5170 US MASTERS IN RUNNING AT VICTORCHANDLER.COM NOVICES' CHASE (14 fncs) 2m 3f

4:05 (4:06) (Class 4) 5-Y-0+ **£2,602** (£764; £382; £190)

Form RPR

-04F **1** **Our Bomber Harris**[16] 4926 7-11-0 0..... HarrySkelton 131+
(Paul Nicholls) *trckd ldr: led 4 out: sn pushed clr: comf* **11/8**[1]

413P **2** 23 **Quo Video (FR)**[23] 4794 7-11-4 134.....(t) MichaelMurphy(3) 117
(Tim Vaughan) *trckd ldrs: pckd 4 out: sn rdn: wnt 2nd after 3 out but no ch w wnr* **3/1**[2]

1006 **3** 13 **Ellerslie Tom**[6] 5102 9-11-7 0..... JohnnyFarrelly 106
(Alison Thorpe) *j.lft: led tl 4 out: sn rdn: wkng whn lost 2nd bef 2 out* **5/1**

64P0 **4** 34 **Sagunt (GER)**[16] 4925 8-11-0 0.....(t) TomSiddall 68
(Joanna Davis) *lost tch fr 5th: t.o* **40/1**

3041 **P** **Gentleman Anshan (IRE)**[15] 4948 7-11-0 109... MissHannahWatson(7) —
(Rosemary Gasson) *hld up in cl 5th: blnd and virtually fell 4th: immediately lost tch: nvr rcvrd: p.u bef 10th* **7/2**[3]

4m 42.5s (-4.20) **Going Correction** +0.025s/f (Yiel) **5** Ran SP% **108.4**
Speed ratings: **109,99,93,79,—**
CSF £5.83 TOTE £1.90: £1.02, £4.00; EX 4.40.
Owner Phil Fry **Bred** N D Cronin **Trained** Ditcheat, Somerset

FOCUS
An easy win for the favourite.

NOTEBOOK
Our Bomber Harris ◆ ran out an easy winner and gained a deserved first success over fences. He still didn't always look a natural over his fences at times, but in fairness he saved his best jump for the last and was far too strong for his two penalised rivals from the fourth-last. He can defy a double penalty at this stage of the season now his confidence will be high. (op 13-8 tchd 5-4)
Quo Video(FR) was pulled up in the Centenary Novices' Handicap at Cheltenham at odds of 100-1 on his previous outing last month, but was the one to beat if reproducing the level of his win at Market Rasen the time before. He didn't jump the seventh and eighth well here and was soon in trouble. A stiffer test is what he wants, but he will not be simple to place now. (op 10-3 tchd 11-4)
Ellerslie Tom ran with more enthusiasm over hurdles at Stratford six days earlier and had scored on his previous start over fences last year. He had his own way out in front, but tended to jump left in the main and folded tamely once taken on by the winner. (op 9-2 tchd 6-1)
Gentleman Anshan(IRE) came good in a moderate handicap here last time out and had lots to find. His chance was immediately ended when he all but came down at the fourth. (tchd 10-3 and 4-1)

5171 BEST ODDS GUARANTEED AT VICTORCHANDLER.COM H'CAP HURDLE (8 hdls) 2m 1f

4:40 (4:40) (Class 4) (0-115,114) 4-Y-0+ **£2,602** (£764; £382; £190)

Form RPR

531- **1** **Ministerofinterior**[504] 2377 6-10-9 **100**.....(b) PeterToole(3) 109+
(Barry Leavy) *hld up towards rr: hdwy on outer appr 5th: wnt 3rd 3 out: led after 2 out: rdn clr: idled flat* **14/1**

03P **2** 4 1/2 **Big Robert**[13] 4990 7-10-12 **105**.....(tp) GilesHawkins(5) 108
(Matt Sheppard) *trckd ldr: slt advantage whn nt fluent 2 out: sn rdn and hdd: kpt on same pce* **11/1**

0254 **3** 1 3/4 **Olympian (FR)**[21] 4830 9-11-3 **110**.....(tp) JoshuaMoore(5) 110
(Philip Middleton) *mid-div: hdwy after 4th: rdn after 3 out: styd on same pce* **6/1**[1]

-046 **4** 3 1/4 **General Ting (IRE)**[13] 4992 6-11-12 **114**..... LeightonAspell 112
(Lucy Wadham) *hld up towards rr: stdy prog u.p fr after 3 out: wnt 4th bef last: nvr trbld ldrs* **6/1**[1]

0-06 **5** 3 3/4 **Top Achiever (IRE)**[5] 5114 10-9-9 **90**.....(p) MrBJPoste(7) 84
(Bill Moore) *trckd ldr: led 4th: rdn and hdd after 3 out: fdd bef last* **14/1**

121F **6** 4 1/2 **Lean Burn (USA)**[107] 2643 5-10-11 **99**..... LiamHeard 89
(Barry Leavy) *in tch: rdn after 3 out: wknd bef last* **11/1**

3101 **7** 2 **Dormouse**[41] 4330 6-11-2 **111**.....(p) MrOJMurphy(7) 101
(Anabel L M King) *in tch tl outpcd after 3 out: wknd bef last* **8/1**[2]

0003 **8** 1 3/4 **Crazy Bold (GER)**[6] 5102 8-10-8 **99**..... LeeEdwards(3) 86
(Tony Carroll) *mid-div: rdn after 3 out: wknd after next* **9/1**[3]

5464 **9** 3 1/2 **Bun Oir (USA)**[16] 4935 4-10-0 **104**.....(bt) GeraldQuinn(10) 82
(Charlie Longsdon) *mid-div: hdwy 5th: rdn after 3 out:* **9/1**[3]

504 **10** 3 1/4 **Only Witness (IRE)**[12] 5010 6-10-12 **100**..... SamJones 81
(Brendan Powell) *drvn along fr 3rd: a towards rr* **16/1**

UF66 **11** 20 **Backstreet Billy (IRE)**[32] 4499 7-11-7 **109**..... AndrewThornton 72
(Richard Lee) *led: hit 1st: hdd 4th: rdn after next: wknd after 3 out* **14/1**

460F **12** 13 **Twentynineblack (FR)**[52] 4113 7-11-8 **110**..... AdrianLane 61
(Donald McCain) *hld up towards rr: hdwy after 3rd: mstke next: rdn after 5th: wknd after 3 out* **20/1**

-005 **P** **Mister New York (USA)**[40] 3302 6-10-5 **93**..... WillKennedy —
(Noel Chance) *trckd ldrs tl 5th: sn bhd: t.o whn p.u after 2 out* **12/1**

3m 56.0s (-3.40) **Going Correction** -0.175s/f (Good)
WFA 4 from 5yo+ 5lb **13** Ran SP% **114.7**
Speed ratings (Par 105): **101,98,98,96,94 92,91,90,89,87 78,72,—**
toteswingers:1&2:£43.60, 1&3:£13.80, 2&3:£15.90 CSF £153.09 CT £1027.01 TOTE £17.70: £5.20, £4.30, £2.20; EX 257.60.
Owner D E Simpson & R Farrington-Kirkham **Bred** Deerfield Farm **Trained** Forsbrook, Staffs

FOCUS
An open-looking handicap in which the majority had something to prove. It was run at an average sort of gallop and the first pair had it to themselves from two out.

NOTEBOOK
Ministerofinterior ran out a ready winner and picked up where he left off in November 2009 when landing a C&D seller. The absence was an obvious concern, but he moved best of all through the race and found plenty turning for home. This was a welcome winner for the stable. (tchd 16-1)
Big Robert posted a moody looking effort at Newbury on his previous outing, but went with plenty more enthusiasm here and was a clear second-best. He just left the impression a stiffer test is required. (op 14-1)
Olympian(FR), with cheekpieces replacing blinkers, is weighted to win at present but has become difficult to predict. (tchd 11-2)
General Ting(IRE) came under pressure a fair way out and never looked like taking advantage of the drop in grade. (op 13-2 tchd 11-2)
Top Achiever(IRE) improved on his previous effort at Uttoxeter at the weekend and could find another race back down in class.
Lean Burn(USA) shaped as though this first outing for 107 days was needed. (op 17-2 tchd 8-1)
Mister New York(USA) Official explanation: vet said gelding pulled up lame right-hind

5172 LINDLEY GROUP NOVICES' H'CAP HURDLE (10 hdls) 2m 4f

5:15 (5:15) (Class 5) (0-95,95) 4-Y-0+ **£1,723** (£506; £253; £126)

Form RPR

6560 **1** **Shoudhavenownbettr (IRE)**[53] 4098 7-10-2 **78**.....(b) MrJMRidley(7) 80+
(Matt Sheppard) *trckd ldrs tl lost pl and reminders after 4th: hdwy u.p after 3 out: chal after 2 out: ldng whn wnt rt at last: styd on wl* **33/1**

P005 **2** 6 **Rolline (IRE)**[14] 4964 6-11-3 **89**..... DonalDevereux(3) 86+
(Stuart Kittow) *trckd ldrs: led after 3 out: rdn whn hit next: hdd appr last no ex* **40/1**

0300 **3** 14 **Misstaysia (IRE)**[25] 4751 6-11-8 **91**..... AndrewTinkler 75
(Henry Daly) *hld up towards rr: hdwy after 6th: rdn and ch appr 2 out: sn hld by front 2* **16/1**

0-P0 **4** 3 1/4 **Little Eaglet (IRE)**[16] 4929 7-11-12 **95**.....(b) LiamHeard 76
(Colin Heard) *led tl after 6th: rdn after 3 out: grad fdd after next* **10/1**

-661 **5** 8 **Diddley Dee**[15] 4947 7-11-2 **92**..... MrBJPoste(7) 66
(Bill Moore) *mid-div tl dropped to rr u.p 4th: nvr a threat after* **12/1**

1132 **6** 12 **Decent Lord (IRE)**[18] 4892 7-11-4 **94**..... PeterCarberry(7) 59
(Jennie Candlish) *hld up towards rr: hdwy 7th: rdn after 3 out: wknd after next* **9/4**[1]

0054 **7** 12 **China House (IRE)**[27] 4684 8-11-4 **87**..... DenisO'Regan 39
(Lisa Williamson) *a towards rr* **20/1**

600P **8** 14 **Everdon Brook (IRE)**[22] 4814 6-10-12 **81**.....(vt1) CharliePoste 21
(Ben Case) *trckd ldr: led after 6th tl after 3 out: sn wknd* **20/1**

0005 **9** 20 **Summer De Baune (FR)**[12] 5000 6-9-7 **69** oh3..... HarryChalloner(7) —
(John Bryan Groucott) *trckd ldrs tl wknd after 6th: t.o* **66/1**

032P **P** **Bright Decision**[31] 4522 5-11-3 **86**.....(p) DaveCrosse —
(Joanna Davis) *mid-div tl wknd after 6th: t.o whn p.u bef last* **7/1**[3]

PP-P **P** **Ruttan Lake (IRE)**[62] 3931 8-10-6 **75**..... WillKennedy —
(Violet M Jordan) *mid-div tl wknd qckly 5th: t.o whn p.u bef 7th* **22/1**

0001 **P** **Charles**[5] 5114 5-11-0 **90**.....(p) EdCookson(7) —
(Kim Bailey) *mid-div tl wknd after 7th: t.o whn p.u bef last* **3/1**[2]

0000 **P** **Turf Legends (IRE)**[63] 3906 5-10-10 **79**.....(b1) RhysFlint —
(Philip Hobbs) *p.u after 1st: fatally injured* **20/1**

4m 50.8s (-4.70) **Going Correction** -0.175s/f (Good) **13** Ran SP% **116.4**
Speed ratings (Par 103): **102,99,94,92,89 84,79,74,66,— —,—,—**
toteswingers:1&2:£56.80, 1&3:£50.90, 2&3:£59.20 CSF £900.26 CT £19744.41 TOTE £47.80: £14.10, £19.60, £7.40; EX 1249.40.
Owner Will Gaskins **Bred** John Lynch **Trained** Eastnor, H'fords
■ James Ridley's first winner under rules.

■ Stewards' Enquiry : Mr J M Ridley six-day ban: used whip with excessive frequency (Apr 21,23-25,27-28)

FOCUS
A moderate novice handicap and most had cried enough before the back straight.

NOTEBOOK
Shoudhavenownbettr(IRE) opened his account for connections at the fifth time of asking despite proving awfully hard work for his rider. This was his first success since winning a good-ground Irish point in 2009 and it's hard to recommend him as one to follow up. This was his stable's first winner of the season. (op 28-1)
Rolline(IRE) showed much-improved form on this step back up in trip and finished well clear of the remainder. She wouldn't be certain to build on this. (op 33-1 tchd 50-1)
Misstaysia(IRE) travelled nicely into contention, but found little when push came to shove and a drop back in trip looks on the cards. Official explanation: jockey said mare hung left (op 14-1 tchd 18-1)
Little Eaglet(IRE) pulled too hard, but kept on for pressure. (op 16-1)
Decent Lord(IRE), back up in trip, was another that came unstuck as soon as he was put under pressure and perhaps the tacky ground was not for him. (op 15-8 tchd 13-8)
Charles had to be of interest off the same mark as when winning at Uttoxeter last weekend, but he fell in a hole under pressure and surely the run came too soon. (op 11-4 tchd 5-2 and 10-3 in places)

5173 BET ON THE NATIONAL AT VICTORCHANDLER.COM H'CAP CHASE (12 fncs) 2m
5:45 (5:45) (Class 4) (0-105,104) 5-Y-O+ **£2,927** (£859; £429; £214)

Form RPR
0453 **1** **Gilt Free (IRE)**[18] 4899 9-11-0 **92**............(v) AndrewTinkler 105+
(George Baker) *in tch: rdn after 8th: hdwy after 3 out: led after 2 out: r.o wl* **7/1**[3]
2554 **2** 7 **Bushwacker (IRE)**[14] 4967 7-11-5 **100**............(tp) JimmyDerham(3) 111+
(Seamus Mullins) *nt a fluent: trckd ldr: lft in ld 2nd: hit 6th: hdd 4 out: mstke 3 out: ldng whn awkward 2 out: sn hdd and hld* **10/1**
16P **3** 4 **Carrig An Uisce (IRE)**[56] 4022 10-11-4 **96**............(p) CharliePoste 98
(Anna Brooks) *outpcd in rr early: rdn after 8th: hdwy 3 out: wnt 3rd after 2 out: styd on same pce* **16/1**
-FP6 **4** ¾ **This Way (IRE)**[18] 4896 9-10-9 **87**............(t) GerardTumelty 90
(John Ryall) *hld up: rdn after 3 out: wnt 4th whn mstke 2 out: no further imp* **10/1**
552P **5** 7 **Coach Lane**[12] 5011 10-11-12 **104**............(p) AndrewThornton 99
(Nick Mitchell) *sn pushed along: chsd ldrs tl 8th: plugged on but n.d after* **10/1**
4063 **6** 2½ **Salybia Bay**[11] 5036 5-10-8 **93**............(t) MrBJPoste(7) 88
(Andy Turnell) *in tch: tk clsr order after 6th: led 4 out: sn rdn: hdd next: cl 3rd whn hmpd 2 out: wknd* **14/1**
4P42 **7** 12 **Roc De Guye (FR)**[8] 5076 6-10-5 **90**............ RobertKirk(7) 72
(James Evans) *raced keenly: trckd ldrs: jnd ldr 5th tl 4 out: sn rdn: wknd next* **7/2**[2]
P450 **P** **Showtime Annie**[10] 5057 10-9-7 **78** oh18............ PeterCarberry(7) —
(Jennie Candlish) *sn t.o: p.u after 9th* **25/1**
-444 **U** **Riddleofthesands (IRE)**[16] 4934 7-11-10 **102**............ SamTwiston-Davies —
(Nigel Twiston-Davies) *led tl mstke and uns rdr 2nd* **15/8**[1]

4m 1.70s (-1.90) **Going Correction** +0.025s/f (Yiel) **9** Ran SP% **113.2**
Speed ratings: **105,101,99,99,95 94,88,—,—**
toteswingers:1&2:£8.70, 1&3:£12.10, 2&3:£17.40 CSF £70.74 CT £1071.94 TOTE £5.30: £1.10, £1.50, £7.70; EX 61.00.
Owner Jeremy Dougall & Will Watt **Bred** C Lilburn **Trained** Whitsbury, Hants

FOCUS
A very ordinary handicap and again it is suspect form.

NOTEBOOK
Gilt Free(IRE) hit top gear nearing three out and was in no serious danger after hitting the front, despite her rider needing to be at his strongest. This was her first outing over fences since joining her present trainer from Ireland and the switch of discipline clearly rejuvenated her, as this was her first success. (op 13-2)
Bushwacker(IRE), equipped with cheekpieces and a tongue tie, would have gone a deal closer had he not hit the last four fences. He could defy this mark if getting his act together on that front. (op 17-2 tchd 11-1)
Carrig An Uisce(IRE) plugged on to post a more encouraging effort on his return from a 56-day break. (op 12-1)
This Way(IRE) found it all too sharp. (op 11-1 tchd 12-1)
Roc De Guye(FR) found nothing after travelling up enthusiastically on the final circuit. (op 4-1)
Riddleofthesands(IRE) gave his rider no chance of maintaining the partnership at the second. He galloped on loose and caused problems on the back straight. (op 5-2 tchd 13-8)

5174 LINDLEY CATERING STANDARD OPEN NATIONAL HUNT FLAT RACE 2m 1f
6:15 (6:17) (Class 6) 4-6-Y-O **£1,431** (£420; £210; £104)

Form RPR
1 **Harry Topper** 4-10-5 0............ MrCGreene(7) 112+
(Kim Bailey) *mid-div: hdwy over 3f out: rdn to chse ldrs over 1f out: r.o wl to ld ins fnl f: readily* **28/1**
1 **2** 2¾ **Speed Master (IRE)**[31] 4527 5-11-11 0............ AndrewTinkler 120
(Nicky Henderson) *trckd ldrs: rdn to chal over 1f out: led ent fnl f: sn hdd: kpt on but no ex* **9/4**[2]
3 4½ **One Term (IRE)** 4-10-7 0............ AodhaganConlon(5) 103
(Rebecca Curtis) *trckd ldr: led 4f out: rdn over 1f out: hdd ent fnl f: no ex* **10/1**[3]
4 **4** nse **Kusadiki (IRE)**[47] 4204 5-11-4 0............ JackDoyle 108
(Emma Lavelle) *in tch: rdn 2f out: effrt over 1f out: kpt on same pce fnl f* **14/1**
5 nse **Sleeping City (FR)** 4-10-12 0............ DenisO'Regan 106+
(Victor Dartnall) *mid-div on inner: making hdwy whn bdly hmpd 3f out: shkn up to chal whn hung lft over 1f out: kpt on same pce* **11/8**[1]
6 7 **Allthegear No Idea (IRE)** 4-10-12 0............ SamTwiston-Davies 96
(Nigel Twiston-Davies) *hung lft and slowly away: towards rr: styd on fnl 2f: nvr trbld ldrs* **20/1**
7 ½ **Overafrica (IRE)** 5-11-4 0............ AdrianLane 101
(Donald McCain) *trckd ldrs: rdn over 2f out: sn one pce* **16/1**
0 **8** 7 **Spring Bay**[53] 4097 6-10-8 0............ JimmyDerham(3) 87
(John Ryall) *led tl rdn 4f out: wknd over 1f out* **150/1**
9 4½ **Secret Legend** 6-11-4 0............ JohnnyFarrelly 89
(Kevin Bishop) *a towards rr* **50/1**
10 2¼ **Tiger's Jacey (IRE)** 4-10-1 0 ow3............ MrMatthewBarber(7) 77
(V J Hughes) *a towards rr* **33/1**
6 **11** 2¾ **Mousenikov**[63] 3909 5-11-1 0............ IanPopham(3) 84
(Paul Nicholls) *mid-div: rdn over 2f out: wknd over 1f out* **12/1**
12 3½ **Ama Jima** 4-9-12 0............ MrLRPayter(7) 68
(Henry Daly) *mid-div tl wknd over 4f out* **50/1**
6 **13** 75 **Camelloe**[39] 4376 5-10-11 0............ DaveCrosse —
(Colin Tizzard) *mid-div tl 5f out: t.o* **66/1**
0 **P** **Fanzee Man**[19] 4866 4-10-12 0............ JamesMillman —
(Rod Millman) *hld up towards rr: pushed along 1/2-way: stl in rr whn p.u 3f out* **100/1**
P **Smirfys Eric (IRE)** 5-11-4 0............ MarkBradburne —
(Michael Mullineaux) *mid-div tl 1/2-way: bhd whn p.u 3f out: dismntd* **100/1**

3m 56.7s (2.90) **Going Correction** -0.175s/f (Good)
WFA 4 from 5yo+ 5lb **15** Ran SP% **121.4**
Speed ratings: **86,84,82,82,82 79,79,75,73,72 71,69,34,—,—**
toteswingers:1&2:£13.60, 1&3:£42.60, 2&3:£4.50 CSF £88.64 TOTE £41.90: £14.60, £1.50, £1.10; EX 91.60.
Owner D J Keyte **Bred** The Round Oak Partnership **Trained** Andoversford, Gloucs

FOCUS
There's every chance this will work out to be a fair bumper.

NOTEBOOK
Harry Topper is bred to make his mark as a staying jumper in due course and was seemingly unfancied, but he ran out a ready debut winner. He travelled nicely and knuckled down gamely when asked for maximum effort. Connections evidently have a nice prospect on their hands. (tchd 25-1 and 33-1)
Speed Master(IRE) ran a solid race under his penalty and gives the form a sound look. (op 2-1 tchd 7-4)
One Term(IRE), from a yard with an outstanding record in bumpers here, made a bold bid leaving the back straight and posted a respectable debut display. (op 8-1)
Kusadiki(IRE) still looked green when put under pressure, but this was an improved effort in defeat and he is going the right way. (tchd 16-1)
Sleeping City(FR), who came here in preference to a Grade 2 at Aintree at the weekend, proved all the rage for this racecourse debut and, despite being hampered, travelled like the most probable winner until coming under pressure. He proved far too green when push came to shove, something which can often be the case with debutants from his stable, and he should really go close next time. (op 9-4)
T/Plt: £8,792.30 to a £1 stake. Pool:£56,006.15 - 4.65 winning tickets T/Qpdt: £451.80 to a £1 stake. Pool:£5,556.46 - 9.10 winning tickets TM

5175 - 5181a (Foreign Racing) - See Raceform Interactive

5160 AINTREE (L-H)
Friday, April 8

OFFICIAL GOING: Good (good to soft in places on grand national course; mildmay 7.8 hurdle 8.0 national 7.2)
Wind: light across Weather: fine and sunny

5182 JOHN SMITH'S TOP NOVICES' HURDLE GRADE 2 (9 hdls) 2m 110y
2:00 (2:00) (Class 1) 4-Y-O+
£31,355 (£11,764; £5,890; £2,937; £1,474; £737)

Form RPR
11 **1** **Topolski (IRE)**[19] 4895 5-11-4 145............ DarylJacob 149+
(David Arbuthnot) *swtg: hld up in rr: hdwy appr 3 out: 3rd and upsides whn hit last: sn led: hld on towards fin* **11/2**[2]
2-12 **2** ¾ **Oilily (IRE)**[154] 2196 8-10-11 135............ ADLeigh 141+
(Sean Byrne, Ire) *hld up in rr: hdwy and hit 6th: nt clr run and forced wd appr next: gd hdwy to ld 2 out: hdd sn after last: rallied: kpt on gamely last 100yds* **14/1**
4111 **3** 6 **Sire De Grugy (FR)**[41] 4353 5-11-4 138............ JamieMoore 141
(Gary Moore) *lw: mid-div: hdwy 6th: chsng ldrs after next: upsides last: styd on same pce run-in* **9/2**[1]
2210 **4** 7 **Alarazi (IRE)**[21] 4848 7-11-4 137............ DominicElsworth 135
(Lucy Wadham) *in rr: hdwy 3 out: chsng ldrs and swtchd rt after 2 out: sn wknd* **7/1**[3]
5212 **5** 2 **Desert Cry (IRE)**[34] 4475 5-11-4 135............ JasonMaguire 133
(Donald McCain) *trckd ldrs: one pce fr 2 out* **7/1**[3]
2-34 **6** nse **Perfect Smile (IRE)**[100] 3203 6-11-4 135............ PCarberry 133
(Noel Meade, Ire) *mid-div: drvn 6th: one pce fr next* **8/1**
2 **7** 3 **Polisky (FR)**[48] 4203 4-10-12 0............ NickScholfield 124
(Paul Nicholls) *lw: trckd ldrs: t.k.h: wknd 2 out* **40/1**
3522 **8** 4½ **Maggio (FR)**[40] 4377 6-11-4 125............(p) AndrewTinkler 127
(Patrick Griffin, Ire) *led: hdd after 3 out: wknd next* **80/1**
310 **9** ½ **Brampour (IRE)**[21] 4847 4-10-12 142............ RWalsh 122
(Paul Nicholls) *nt fluent: chsd ldr: mstke 4th: led after 3 out: hdd next: wknd between last 2* **7/1**[3]
2F1P **10** 4 **A Media Luz (FR)**[21] 4847 4-10-5 137............ BarryGeraghty 111
(Nicky Henderson) *lw: hld up in rr: hdwy on outside after 8th: chsng ldrs next: wknd 2 out* **8/1**
113 **11** 1 **Andhaar**[70] 3783 5-11-4 131............ RhysFlint 124
(Steve Gollings) *in rr: hdwy to chse ldrs 6th: lost pl next: bhd whn j.lft last 2* **50/1**
B1 **12** 10 **First In The Queue (IRE)**[33] 4499 4-10-12 0............ APMcCoy 106
(Nicky Henderson) *chsd ldrs: drvn 6th: wknd next: bhd whn hmpd appr 2 out* **18/1**
-115 **P** **Iolith (GER)**[45] 4270 6-11-4 130............ RobertThornton —
(Alan King) *chsd ldrs: drvn 5th: sn lost pl: wl bhd whn p.u bef 2 out* **33/1**

3m 59.7s (-6.50) **Going Correction** -0.30s/f (Good)
WFA 4 from 5yo+ 5lb **13** Ran SP% **113.8**
Speed ratings (Par 115): **103,102,99,96,95 95,94,92,91,89 89,84,—**
toteswingers:1&2:£14.70, 1&3:£3.00, 2&3:£12.10 CSF £73.10 TOTE £5.90: £2.40, £3.80, £2.20; EX 91.80 Trifecta £220.50 Pool: £3278.55 - 11 winning units..
Owner P M Claydon **Bred** C H Wacker Iii **Trained** Compton, Berks
■ Stewards' Enquiry : Barry Geraghty two-day ban: careless riding (Apr 23-24)

FOCUS
A wide-open Grade 2 hurdle run at a good clip, although in all honesty the result suggests it wasn't the strongest event. There's a case for rating the race higher, but the seventh and eighth finished close enough and limit the level.

NOTEBOOK
Topolski(IRE), 2-2 over hurdles coming into this, picked up best on the run-in. Well on top at the finish when defying a penalty at Newton Abbot last time, this formerly useful staying Flat handicapper readily made headway to reach a challenging position in the straight and, although not overly fluent at the last, showed a willing attitude to assert late on. This was a thoroughly likeable effort and it's not hard to see him doing well in all the top 2m handicap hurdles next season. He's likely to be seen on the Flat again first, though, with races such as the Old Newton Cup and Ebor likely to come under consideration. (op 5-1)
Oilily(IRE), never out the first two in ten previous starts (six bumpers/four hurdles), appeared to have plenty on if ratings were anything to go by, but she relished the conditions and overcame trouble in running to take the lead two out. She didn't give in once headed after the last, keeping on right the way to the line, but was just found wanting. (op 12-1)

Sire De Grugy(FR), so impressive when easily winning the Grade 2 Dovecote at Kempton, bypassed Cheltenham and was understandably made favourite. Despite the drying ground counting against him, he ran an absolute stormer, just getting done for speed by two nippier rivals from the last. He's a fine prospect with fences in mind next season.
Alarazi(IRE) ran well whilst coming up short switched to graded company. He remains capable of better in handicaps. (op 8-1)
Desert Cry(IRE) was not good enough on this rise in grade and is another who will find better opportunities in handicaps. (op 8-1)
Perfect Smile(IRE) had some smart form to his name in Ireland, but was lacking for pace in the straight and may prove suited by further.
Polisky(FR), runner-up to Sprinter Sacre at Ascot on his hurdles debut, travelled well, if a little keen, but couldn't race on in the straight. He'll find easier opportunities and looks a chaser. (tchd 33-1)
Maggio(FR) was on his toes beforehand. (op 66-1)
Brampour(IRE) ran well in the Triumph but jumped poorly here. (op 8-1)
A Media Luz(FR) travelled strongly before finding little. She again got wound up beforehand and is left with a bit to prove. (op 15-2)
Iolith(GER) has the look of a chaser. (op 25-1)

5183 JOHN SMITH'S MILDMAY NOVICES' CHASE GRADE 2 (19 fncs) 3m 1f
2:30 (2:30) (Class 1) 5-Y-O+ **£42,958** (£16,243; £8,233; £4,206; £2,211)

Form				RPR
211	1		**Quito De La Roque (FR)**[54] 4109 7-11-4 152 DNRussell (C A Murphy, Ire) *hld up in tch: sltly hmpd 5th: mstke 13th: hdwy after 5 out: j. into narrow ld 3 out: hdd whn stmbld on landing 2 out: led again last: drvn and hld on wl run-in* **6/1**[3]	151+
012F	2	nk	**Sarando**[20] 4877 6-11-4 130 (tp) WillKennedy (Paul Webber) *w ldr: led briefly bef 3rd: led 5 out: rdn whn hdd 3 out: led again after 2 out: hdd last: kpt on but a jst hld run-in* **50/1**	145
-141	3	2 3/4	**Golan Way**[139] 2527 7-11-4 146 LeightonAspell (Sheena West) *j.rt: trckd ldrs: led after 3rd: mstke 8th: blnd 13th: hdd 5 out: rdn after 3 out: kpt on* **8/1**	148+
1113	4	4 1/2	**Wayward Prince**[23] 4804 7-11-4 150 (v[1]) APMcCoy (Ian Williams) *in tch: nt fluent 12th and 14th: drvn after 4 out: kpt on same pce* **7/4**[1]	144+
5B14	5	1 1/2	**Radium (FR)**[22] 4816 6-11-4 147 FelixDeGiles (Nicky Henderson) *lw: trckd ldrs on inner: hit 5 out and lost pl: rdn bef 3 out: kpt on but no imp on ldrs* **11/1**	139
1F1U	F		**The Giant Bolster**[23] 4804 6-11-4 146 TomScudamore (David Bridgwater) *led tl 2nd: trcking ldrs whn fell 5th* **15/2**	—
5116	F		**Master Of The Hall (IRE)**[23] 4804 7-11-4 144 BarryGeraghty (Nicky Henderson) *lw: hld up: wknd qckly after 4 out: wl bhd whn fell 2 out* **9/2**[2]	—
F10P	P		**Robinson Collonges (FR)**[22] 4816 6-11-4 146 RWalsh (Paul Nicholls) *hld up: hit 8th: pushed along after 11th: hit 12th and sn struggling: p.u after next* **15/2**	—

6m 20.2s (-9.80) **Going Correction** -0.10s/f (Good) **8** Ran SP% **113.8**
Speed ratings: **111,110,110,108,108** —,—,—
toteswingers:1&2 £18.90, 2&3 £39.00, 1&3 £5.00 CSF £162.16 TOTE £4.90: £1.50, £7.20, £2.70; EX 270.10 Trifecta £1177.90 Pool: £3703.71 - 2.32 winning units..
Owner Gigginstown House Stud **Bred** Robert Mongin **Trained** Gorey, Co Wexford
■ Stewards' Enquiry : D N Russell one-day ban: used whip in incorrect place (Apr 23)
Will Kennedy three-day ban: used whip with excessive frequency without giving gelding time to respond (Apr 23-25)

FOCUS
A interesting staying novice chase. Jumping let down several of them and many will question the form, with 50-1 shot Sarando going down by just a neck. It's also fairly safe to assume RSA third Wayward Prince was below his best back in fourth. The winner has been rated below the level of his soft-ground form.

NOTEBOOK
Quito De La Roque(FR) bypassed Cheltenham on account of the ground being deemed too lively, so it was slightly surprising he lined up here on going that was probably even quicker. One thing that couldn't be questioned was the horse's quality, though, having won three from four over fences - his only defeat coming at the hands of RSA winner Bostons Angel. He had far from a smooth trip through the race, being hampered by the fall of The Giant Bolster at the fifth and making one notable blunder down the back, but he moved through well to take it up at the third-last and, not for the first time, showed admirable battling qualities under a strong ride from Davy Russell. He could have a big say in the top staying races in England and Ireland next season, and may leave this form behind under more suitable conditions. (op 9-2 tchd 13-2)
Sarando was only rated 130 and had fallen last time at Uttoxeter. His jumping kept him in it, gaining ground at his fences on several occasions, and it looked for much of the straight as though he would pull off a major shock. Ultimately, though, he was just denied by a classier rival. His handicap mark will suffer as a result of this, but he deserves a chance to show it wasn't a fluke. Punchestown could be next.
Golan Way may have won but for costly errors. The blunder which he made at the eighth would have stopped most horses in their tracks, but he made an even worse mistake at the 13th. It says a lot about his attitude that he hung in there and was still battling away in the straight, keeping on surprisingly well considering he has never won over a trip this far. Although not the biggest, he's clearly smart, and could win a decent handicap next season, when a return to right-handed tracks will help. Connections were talking of running him in a National one day. (op 7-1 tchd 9-1)
Wayward Prince set the standard and had the potential to improve for the fitting of a first-time visor. He did have a very hard race at Cheltenham, though, and for all that he moved well for the first half of the race, he was soon in trouble following a mistake and proved laboured under pressure. He is better than this and could be a player in something like the Hennessy later in the year, where potentially softer ground will help. (op 9-4)
Radium(FR), whose Jewson fourth received a boost when Wishfull Thinking bolted up here the previous day, ran well for a long way without suggesting he's anything other than a handicapper, albeit a potentially good one. (op 12-1 tchd 14-1)
The Giant Bolster came down at the fifth and has now failed to complete back-to-back. (op 4-1 tchd 5-1)
Master Of The Hall(IRE), a fine sixth in the RSA, promised to be suited by this flatter track, but made a couple of mistakes before failing to respond when asked for maximum effort, dropping away quickly after four out. He was well beaten when falling two out and has probably had enough for the season. (op 4-1 tchd 5-1)
Robinson Collonges(FR) failed to benefit from the rise in trip and looks to have lost his confidence. (op 4-1 tchd 5-1)

5184 JOHN SMITH'S MELLING CHASE GRADE 1 (16 fncs) 2m 4f
3:05 (3:06) (Class 1) 5-Y-O+
£98,910 (£37,292; £18,637; £9,310; £4,672; £2,327)

Form				RPR
1110	1		**Master Minded (FR)**[23] 4805 8-11-10 172 RWalsh (Paul Nicholls) *lw: trckd ldrs gng wl: smooth hdwy appr 3 out: led on bit between last 2: pushed out: impressive* **11/2**	176+
4FP1	2	9	**Albertas Run (IRE)**[22] 4818 10-11-10 168 APMcCoy (Jonjo O'Neill) *chsd ldrs: drvn 11th: hung lft and kpt on to chse wnr last: no imp* **11/4**[1]	168
3325	3	1/2	**Somersby (IRE)**[23] 4805 7-11-10 170 RobertThornton (Henrietta Knight) *lw: chsd ldrs: pushed along 9th: hung lft and kpt on same pce fr 2 out* **5/1**[3]	166
1150	4	2 3/4	**Tartak (FR)**[22] 4818 8-11-10 156 (t) PaddyBrennan (Tom George) *chsd ldrs: upsides 10th: hit 4 out: one pce fr next* **14/1**	166+
-016	5	3 3/4	**French Opera**[23] 4805 8-11-10 164 BarryGeraghty (Nicky Henderson) *nt fluent: led to 1st: chsd ldrs: outpcd 3 out: kpt on one pce* **11/1**	162
4630	6	3/4	**Mad Max (IRE)**[23] 4805 9-11-10 153 PCarberry (Nicky Henderson) *lw: led 1st: mde most: hdd between last 2: 5th and one pce whn j.rt last* **11/1**	159
6-11	7	31	**Tranquil Sea (IRE)**[114] 2970 9-11-10 159 AndrewJMcNamara (E J O'Grady, Ire) *prom: chsd ldrs 12th: wknd 3 out: bhd whn eased run-in* **8/1**	142
0526	8	10	**Made In Taipan (IRE)**[13] 5025 9-11-10 149 RMPower (Thomas Mullins, Ire) *in rr: nt fluent: bhd friom 8th: t.o 3 out* **40/1**	122
04RR	R		**Chaninbar (FR)**[1] 5164 8-11-10 151 (bt) SeanQuinlan (Milton Harris) *ref to r: lft at s* **100/1**	—
0542	P		**Kalahari King (FR)**[22] 4818 10-11-10 166 GrahamLee (Ferdy Murphy) *in rr: drvn 10th: outpcd whn mstke 12th: sn bhd: t.o whn p.u bef 2 out* **9/2**[2]	—

4m 57.5s (-10.70) **Going Correction** -0.10s/f (Good) **10** Ran SP% **114.8**
Speed ratings: **117,113,113,112,110 110,97,93,**—,—
toteswingers:1&2 £4.00, 2&3 £3.50, 1&3 £5.60 CSF £21.48 CT £80.23 TOTE £5.40: £2.00, £1.30, £2.20; EX 15.50 Trifecta £76.90 Pool: £10513.43 - 101.15 winning units..
Owner Clive D Smith **Bred** Marie-Christine Gabeur **Trained** Ditcheat, Somerset

FOCUS
This year's Melling Chase was well up to scratch - last year's winner Albertas Run again came into the race after winning the Ryanair, while Tartak was fourth once again - and Master Minded proved he's still top class. The pace was good. The winner has been given his best figure since early 2009, but that is still 10lb below his very best. The second and third have been rated in line with their recent Cheltenham runs.

NOTEBOOK
Master Minded(FR) was below form in the Champion Chase on his previous start (even allowing for a bad mistake two out), a performance that saw him deserted by many punters, with this the first time that he was not sent off favourite since March 2008. He had his stamina to prove, but his easy win over 2m3f at Ascot in November suggested he'd be well worth another try at this distance, and the longer trip helped him get into a good rhythm. So too did a patient ride from Ruby Walsh. On the turn out of the back straight it was clear he was absolutely tanking along and he eased his way to the front well before the last. A sound leap there sealed a victory that looked inevitable from some way out and he didn't have anything like a hard race. Master Minded is now set for a break before being aimed at the same Ascot race he won this season, ahead of a possible tilt at the King George. He should have no trouble staying 3m at Kempton, provided the ground is not a bog. (op 5-1 tchd 6-1)
Albertas Run(IRE) was unable to follow up his victory of 12 months ago, but this was an admirable effort. He lacks the natural talent of a real top notcher like Master Minded, and looked in serious trouble when under pressure down the back straight for the final time, but he kept responding to fare best of the rest. Unlikely to be getting any better, it would be understandable were he pointed towards Punchestown. (op 3-1)
Somersby(IRE) probably found this trip more suitable than the 2m of the Champion Chase, but he was one-paced and basically wasn't good enough. There's talk of him being aimed at next season's King George, but while he might benefit from the further increase in distance, it's doubtful he's up to winning such a race. (tchd 11-2)
Tartak(FR) did well to stay on into fourth (for the second year running) considering he lost momentum with mistakes at both the fifth last and fourth from the finish. He didn't convince on his two previous starts over 3m, but he wears a tongue-tie these days and looks in desperate need of a step up in trip. (op 16-1)
French Opera didn't jump fast enough when well held in the Champion Chase on his previous start and it was the same story this time. (tchd 12-1)
Mad Max(IRE) had conditions to suit (defeated Somersby in Grade 2 novice event over C&D last April) and ran well to a point under a positive ride, but he's ultimately struggled this season. He's been tubed, but it's hard to know if breathing issues are still affecting him. (op 14-1)
Tranquil Sea(IRE), who missed the Cheltenham festival following an unsatisfactory scope, did not have his favoured soft ground and was consequently well below form. (op 15-2)
Kalahari King(FR), a faller in this race last year, seemed to travel strongly through the early stages but was laboured going down the back straight for the final time was eventually pulled up. Official explanation: trainer said gelding bled from the nose (tchd 5-1)

5185 JOHN SMITH'S TOPHAM CHASE H'CAP (LISTED RACE) (18 fncs) 2m 5f 110y
3:40 (3:42) (Class 1) 5-Y-O+
£56,330 (£21,220; £10,620; £5,310; £2,660; £1,330)

Form				RPR
6004	1		**Always Waining (IRE)**[15] 4968 10-10-4 133 (p) TomO'Brien (Peter Bowen) *in rr: hdwy to chse ldrs 10th (Becher's): wnt 2nd 2 out: styd on to ld elbow: kpt on wl* **14/1**	149
1	2	4	**Mon Parrain (FR)**[27] 4726 5-11-6 149 RWalsh (Paul Nicholls) *trckd ldrs: wnt 2nd 11th (Foinavon): led appr 2 out: hdd elbow: no ex* **7/2**[1]	161
5344	3	6	**Scotsirish (IRE)**[48] 4227 10-11-10 153 DJCondon (W P Mullins, Ire) *hld up in rr: hdwy 13th (Valentine's): 6th appr 2 out: wnt 3rd appr last: styd on same pce* **20/1**	160
1-2P	4	10	**Gonebeyondrecall (IRE)**[118] 2886 8-10-7 136 (v) AELynch (N F Glynn, Ire) *chsd ldrs: one pce fr 2 out* **33/1**	134
5130	5	nk	**Swing Bill (FR)**[24] 4794 10-10-8 137 TimmyMurphy (David Pipe) *hld up in midfield: hdwy 10th (Becher's): trcking ldrs 4 out: one pce fr 2 out* **25/1**	135
-P1U	6	nse	**Frankie Figg (IRE)**[62] 3953 9-10-7 136 BrianHughes (Howard Johnson) *lw: lw: led: hdd appr 2 out: wknd run-in* **10/1**[3]	134
1100	7	6	**Shakalakaboomboom (IRE)**[24] 4794 7-10-5 134 BarryGeraghty (Nicky Henderson) *mid-div: prom 14th (Valentine's): wknd appr 2 out* **25/1**	126
F001	8	hd	**Stormin Exit (IRE)**[27] 4714 8-10-4 133 JamesReveley (Jim Goldie) *mid-div: hdwy 12th (Canal Turn): blnd 14th: one pce fr 3 out* **20/1**	125
01-6	9	1 3/4	**Chasing Cars (IRE)**[40] 4388 9-10-7 136 RMPower (Mrs John Harrington, Ire) *towards rr: sme hdwy 3 out: nvr on terms* **25/1**	127
P11P	10	16	**Sagalyrique (FR)**[41] 4352 7-10-4 133 (tp) PaddyBrennan (Donald McCain) *mid-div: mstke 9th: wkng whn mstke 3 out* **33/1**	119+
31-2	11	9	**Forzy Origny (FR)**[342] 98 9-10-11 140 FelixDeGiles (Nicky Henderson) *mid-div: wknd 4 out: sn bhd* **28/1**	108
10P-	12	2 3/4	**Ballyholland (IRE)**[30] 4563 10-11-1 144 AndrewJMcNamara (C A McBratney, Ire) *in rr: blnd 2 out* **16/1**	110
0530	13	17	**Edgbriar (FR)**[22] 4820 9-10-11 140 DominicElsworth (Paul Webber) *mid-div: wkng whn mstke 4 out: sn t.o* **40/1**	90

P313 **14** *16* **Isn't That Lucky**[20] 4864 8-10-0 **129**........ RichieMcGrath 65
(Jonjo O'Neill) *in: tch: lost pl 8th: in rr: t.o whn hmpd 12th (Canal Turn)* **16/1**

5-1P **15** *9* **Fistral Beach (IRE)**[41] 4352 8-10-9 **138**........ NickScholfield 66
(Paul Nicholls) *chsd ldrs: bdly hmpd 14th: sn lost pl* **28/1**

4064 **16** *2 ½* **Consigliere (FR)**[22] 4820 8-11-2 **145**........(bt) JasonMaguire 71
(David Pipe) *prom to 5th: sn in rr: t.o 10th (Becher's)* **33/1**

221- **F** **Dev (IRE)**[19] 4906 11-10-0 **129**........(p) PCarberry —
(Gordon Elliott, Ire) *chsd ldr: fell 8th* **6/1**[2]

2P32 **F** **Postmaster**[20] 4864 9-10-2 **134**........(t) RichardKilloran(3) —
(Tim Vaughan) *mid-div: fell 1st* **100/1**

1/63 **B** **Nevada Royale (FR)**[41] 4357 10-10-5 **134**........(tp) DenisO'Regan —
(Tim Pitt) *in rr: blnd 7th: bhd whn b.d 8th* **33/1**

3020 **F** **Bible Lord (IRE)**[22] 4820 10-9-11 **129** oh3........ HarryHaynes(3) —
(Andy Turnell) *mstkes: towards rr: fell 8th* **50/1**

3015 **F** **Siegemaster (IRE)**[44] 4298 10-11-12 **155**........(p) DNRussell —
(D T Hughes, Ire) *in rr: bhd whn fell 8th* **33/1**

-201 **U** **Calusa Caldera (IRE)**[14] 4987 9-10-0 **129** oh1........(p) RichardJohnson —
(Philip Hobbs) *in rr whn bdly hmpd and uns rdr 2nd* **33/1**

F010 **F** **Gansey (IRE)**[22] 4820 9-10-6 **135**........ PeterBuchanan —
(Sue Smith) *in rr: fell 1st* **33/1**

5F06 **F** **Pickamus (FR)**[36] 4440 8-10-2 **131**........ WillKennedy —
(Henry Daly) *mid-div: fell 10th (Becher's)* **50/1**

1465 **F** **Buffalo Bob (IRE)**[49] 4193 8-10-2 **131**........ SeanQuinlan —
(Kim Bailey) *chsd ldrs: fell 8th* **50/1**

1005 **F** **Passato (GER)**[133] 2665 7-10-6 **135**........(t) DaveCrosse —
(Joanna Davis) *in rr div: fell 8th* **50/1**

1P1P **F** **Polyfast (FR)**[41] 4352 8-10-3 **132**........ AndrewTinkler —
(Nicky Henderson) *in rr: fell 2nd* **50/1**

1021 **U** **Fine Parchment (IRE)**[34] 4487 8-10-3 **135**........(t) PeterToole(3) —
(Charlie Mann) *lw: prom: mid-div whn blnd and uns rdr 6th* **16/1**

-20P **F** **Free World (FR)**[41] 4352 7-11-3 **146**........ HarrySkelton —
(Paul Nicholls) *in rr: fell 10th* **66/1**

4-14 **F** **Alfa Beat (IRE)**[23] 4802 7-10-12 **146**........(v[1]) APHeskin(5) —
(C Byrnes, Ire) *in rr div: mstke 10th (Becher's): mid-div whn fell 4 out* **11/1**

5m 19.3s (-16.70) **Going Correction** -0.425s/f (Good) course record **30** Ran SP% **141.5**
Speed ratings: **113,111,109,105,105 105,103,103,102,96 93,92,86,80,77 76,—,—,—,— —,—,—,E**
toteswingers:1&2 £15.30, 2&3 £27.80, 1&3 £21.30 CSF £55.08 CT £1068.80 TOTE £17.20: £3.40, £2.10, £4.70, £9.40 Trifecta £789.70 Pool: £6409.45 - 6.0 winning units..
Owner Mr & Mrs Peter James Douglas **Bred** Barouche Stud Ireland Ltd **Trained** Little Newcastle, Pembrokes

FOCUS
A cracking handicap. The pace was fierce, resulting in the track record being broken by some 6.3secs, and it looked a really good edition of the race, with a 155-rated top weight and a favourite in Mon Parrain, who many had thought could develop into a championship horse for next season. The winner has been rated 5lb superior to last season's winning mark, while the second has been rated in line with his Sandown romp.

NOTEBOOK
Always Waining(IRE), just as was the case 12 months ago, sprang back to life on the return to these unique fences. His only credible effort since last year's victory off 5lb lower had come on this course in November's Grand Sefton, and he'd been warming up over hurdles, as recently as 15 days earlier, but once again he looked in love with the place, in fact he had been a reserve for the Grand National and would probably have run in that instead had he got in. He'll now stand more chance of getting into next year's big race and we'll presumably see him back here in November for the Grand Sefton.
Mon Parrain(FR), deeply impressive off 16lb lower over 3m at Sandown on his British debut, came into this race with a similar look to Cyfor Malta, who was of the same age when winning in 1998, and had the scope to progress on to better things. As natural a jumper as you'll see, especially of these fences, he looked the winner a long way out and Ruby Walsh appeared full of confidence as he sent him into the lead before two out, but there was no response when asked to go and settle it, keeping on at the one pace. It's hard to believe he failed through lack of stamina and perhaps it was something to do with his breathing that prevented him winning. He fully deserves another chance to enhance his reputation, and perhaps that'll come in the Paddy Power at Cheltenham's Open meeting in November. (tchd 4-1, 9-2 in places)
Scotsirish(IRE), runner-up in the race off 1lb higher last year, clearly likes these fences and it was somewhat surprising Willie Mullins turned down the opportunity to run him in the National, as he's always looked as though he wants further than this. He stayed on well in third and continues to be a good money-spinner, for all that he doesn't win often.
Gonebeyondrecall(IRE), returning from 118 days off, travelled better than all bar Mon Parrain, the visor having more effect second time, but he could stay on nowhere near strongly enough once under pressure. (tchd 28-1)
Swing Bill(FR) continues to run well despite having had a busy campaign. Although 12lb higher than when last winning, he had finished a fine seventh in the Centenary at last month's festival and jumped round safely to record an effort up there with his best.
Frankie Figg(IRE), who'd have been second in this last year but for unseating two out, won the Grand Sefton in November and is another who saves his best for these fences. He ran really well considering the pace he was forced to go, but just couldn't stay on as strongly as some. (op 12-1)
Shakalakaboomboom(IRE) jumped better than expected, but never posed a serious threat. (op 33-1)
Stormin Exit(IRE) got round safely but seemed to find it a bit too competitive. (tchd 22-1)
Chasing Cars(IRE) ideally likes to lead, but couldn't do so in this and could be one to watch out for when he bids for a repeat win at this year's Punchestown Festival. (op 22-1)
Ballyholland(IRE) had completed the course in the Grand National before, but never left the rear here. (op 20-1)
Dev(IRE), a winner over these fences in the 2009 Sefton, looked on a good mark but, having duelled for the early lead, took a chance with the eighth and got it wrong. (op 7-1 tchd 11-2)
Bible Lord(IRE) reportedly damaged his neck in his fall. (op 7-1 tchd 11-2)
Fine Parchment(IRE), usually a good jumper, got no further than the sixth. (op 7-1 tchd 11-2)
Alfa Beat(IRE) didn't look in love with the fences and eventually came down. (op 7-1 tchd 11-2)

5186 JOHN SMITH'S SEFTON NOVICES' HURDLE GRADE 1 (13 hdls) 3m 110y
4:15 (4:15) (Class 1) 4-Y-0+

£56,520 (£21,310; £10,650; £5,320; £2,670; £1,330)

Form RPR
02F3 **1** **Saint Are (FR)**[34] 4485 5-11-4 **129**........ RichardJohnson 145+
(Tim Vaughan) *midfield: hdwy 7th: led after 4 out: drvn after 2 out: kpt on run-in* **33/1**

41 **2** *4* **Cantlow (IRE)**[44] 4294 6-11-4 **125**........ DominicElsworth 142+
(Paul Webber) *midfield: hdwy after 4 out: hit 3 out: sn wnt 3rd: nt fluent 2 out: styd on to go 2nd run-in: nt trble wnr* **28/1**

1112 **3** *2 ¼* **Sparky May**[24] 4793 6-10-11 **148**........ KeiranBurke 131
(Patrick Rodford) *racd keenly: hld up: stdy hdwy after 7th: wnt 2nd after 4 out: chal 3 out: sn rdn: hung lft and lost 2nd run-in: no ex* **4/1**[1]

22 **4** *3 ¼* **Fists Of Fury (IRE)**[26] 4760 7-11-4 **133**........ AndrewJMcNamara 135
(C Byrnes, Ire) *w ldr: led 4 out: sn hdd: rdn bef 3 out: styd on same pce* **25/1**

-143 **5** *4 ½* **Muldoon's Picnic (IRE)**[86] 3505 5-11-4 **127**........ JasonMaguire 130
(Kim Bailey) *hld up: rdn and styd on fr 3 out: nvr threatened ldrs* **40/1**

2110 **6** *8* **Aikman (IRE)**[23] 4803 7-11-4 **138**........ RichieMcGrath 125
(James Ewart) *led narrowly: hdd appr 4 out: wknd gng to next* **28/1**

161F **7** *6* **Jetnova (IRE)**[21] 4849 6-11-4 **136**........ RobertThornton 118
(Alan King) *midfield: hdwy after 7th: wnt 3rd bef 3 out: wknd appr last* **18/1**

1 **8** *27* **Back In Focus (IRE)**[48] 4206 6-11-4 **0**........ BrianHughes 105+
(Howard Johnson) *trckd ldrs: rdn and wknd after 4 out* **8/1**

P31 **9** *14* **Cloudy Too (IRE)**[33] 4506 5-11-4 **124**........ ShaneByrne 80
(Sue Smith) *hld up in midfield: mstke 9th whn losing tch: bhd after 4 out* **100/1**

124F **10** *37* **For Non Stop (IRE)**[23] 4806 6-11-4 **140**........ DarylJacob 47
(Nick Williams) *in tch on inner: rdn and wknd after 4 out: t.o: b.b.v* **12/1**

0341 **P** **Russian Song (IRE)**[34] 4489 7-11-4 **121**........(p) AidanColeman —
(Colin Tizzard) *hld up in midfield: lost pl after 7th: wknd after 4 out: t.o whn p.u bef 3 outr* **100/1**

2123 **F** **Court In Motion (IRE)**[21] 4849 6-11-4 **146**........ JackDoyle 138
(Emma Lavelle) *lw: midfield: hdwy gng to 3 out: styng on in dispute of 3rd whn bmpd and fell 2 out* **7/1**[3]

2321 **P** **Basford Bob (IRE)**[17] 4932 6-11-4 **123**........ AlanO'Keeffe —
(Jennie Candlish) *trckd ldrs: nt fluent 8th and sn lost pl: wknd after 4 out: t.o whn p.u bef 3 out* **33/1**

P **Westmeath**[40] 4383 6-11-4 **125**........(t) DNRussell —
(Paul Nolan, Ire) *hld up: nt fluent 4th: hdwy after 4 out: wkng whn bad mstke 3 out: p.u bef next* **12/1**

1152 **P** **Mossley (IRE)**[21] 4849 5-11-4 **149**........ BarryGeraghty —
(Nicky Henderson) *in tch tl wknd qckly gng to 3 out: p.u bef 3 out* **9/2**[2]

12 **P** **Listenlook (FR)**[46] 4262 5-11-4 **128**........ SamTwiston-Davies —
(Nigel Twiston-Davies) *hld up: mstke 6th: rdn and wknd after 9th: t.o whn p.u bef 3 out* **50/1**

-122 **P** **Yurok (IRE)**[41] 4359 7-11-4 **130**........ PeterBuchanan —
(Sue Smith) *in tch: hit 2nd: slow 7th and sn lost pl: wknd after 8th: bhd whn p.u bef 3 out: lame* **33/1**

354 **F** **Indian Daudaie (FR)**[21] 4862 4-10-10 **140**........ RWalsh 127
(Paul Nicholls) *lw: hld up: styng on in 8th whn fell 2 out* **12/1**

1 **P** **Handy Andy (IRE)**[35] 4459 5-11-4 **0**........ JoeTizzard —
(Colin Tizzard) *midfield: rdn and wknd after 4 out: bhd whn p.u bef next* **11/1**

6m 9.60s (-6.70) **Going Correction** -0.30s/f (Good)
WFA 4 from 5yo+ 7lb **19** Ran SP% **124.4**
Speed ratings (Par 117): **98,96,96,94,93 90,89,80,75,64 —,—,—,—,— —,—,—,—**
toteswingers:1&2 £142.90, 2&3 £48.80, 1&3 £37.90 CSF £734.67 CT £4464.53 TOTE £48.20: £12.60, £12.50, £2.00; EX 1840.00 TRIFECTA Not won..
Owner D W Fox **Bred** Jacques Cypres **Trained** Aberthin, Vale of Glamorgan

FOCUS
This has been won by some quality types in recent years - no better example than Iris's Gift in 2003 - but the race has also produced a few shock results and Saint Are was yet another surprise, going in at odds of 33-1. The first two finishers came into this rated in the 120s and this looks ordinary form by Grade 1 standards. They went a modest pace for much of the journey (time 9.20 seconds slower than following handicap) and it paid to be prominent on the final circuit. The first two have been rated a stone up on their previous form, and the fourth and fifth help set the level.

NOTEBOOK
Saint Are(FR) had gained his only previous success in the French provinces last June and was beaten in a handicap off just 125 at Newbury on his previous start, although admittedly that was a promising run, staying on from well back over 2m5f. It also followed on from a fall at Ffos Las (still going well when hitting the deck) and his connections felt he might have needed the outing to rebuild his confidence. This longer trip clearly helped and so too did a sensible ride from Richard Johnson, who moved the 5-y-o into a handy position before the race got serious, aware there hadn't been much pace on, and the winner showed a fine attitude. While it would be unwise to get carried away (Sparky May some way below form), Saint Are is a nice type physically with plenty of size, and he's still lightly raced. He should make a smart novice chaser.
Cantlow(IRE) should have gone even closer as he was apparently travelling strongly when held up in an unpromising position - stuck behind rivals who were not going as well - leaving the back straight. At the same time the winner and third filled the front two positions. He stayed on dourly, despite not hurdling fluently under pressure, and this was a fine effort on just his third start under rules, following on from a win at Ludlow. He's expected to make a chaser. (op 25-1)
Sparky May, no match for the supremely talented Quevega in the Grade 2 Mares' Hurdle at Cheltenham but still the form pick on these terms, ruined her chance by refusing to settle. She was fairly tanking along for most of the journey, and having looked the winner leaving the back straight, she was one-paced when forced off the bridle soon after and simply ran out of energy. It transpired that the horsebox transporting her to the track broke down, and instead of arriving at Aintree at 9.30am, as planned, she didn't get there until 1pm. That cannot have helped, especially on a hot day. (op 5-1)
Fists Of Fury(IRE) seemed to handle the ground, which was quicker than he's been racing on, and this was a solid performance. (op 33-1 tchd 22-1)
Muldoon's Picnic(IRE) had the ground to suit but stamina to prove. He was ridden patiently, presumably to help him get the trip, but such tactics were no use considering how the race unfolded. (op 33-1)
Aikman(IRE) ran okay, but he's been busy and might have found this coming too soon after Cheltenham. (op 25-1)
Back In Focus(IRE) is very much a chaser and deserves another chance back on softer ground. Official explanation: trainer said gelding was unsuited by the good ground
For Non Stop(IRE) Official explanation: trainer said gelding bled from the nose
Court In Motion(IRE), third in the Albert Bartlett on his previous start, fell soon after jumping the second-last having been bumped on landing by runner-up Cantlow. He still had a few lengths to find with the winner, but was keeping on and gave the impression he might have had slightly more to offer than the runner-up. (op 15-2)
Basford Bob(IRE) Official explanation: jockey said gelding hung left-handed throughout (op 15-2)
Mossley(IRE) found nothing for pressure, stopping quickly approaching the third-last, and was pulled up sharply before that hurdle. Something looked to have gone amiss. Official explanation: jockey said gelding lost its action (op 15-2)
Yurok(IRE) Official explanation: trainer said gelding pulled up lame (op 15-2)

Indian Daudaie(FR) was no doubt put off when Court In Motion fell in front of him, himself falling moments afterwards before clattering into his stricken rival. (op 15-2)

5187 JOHN SMITH'S SMITHYTHEHORSE.COM H'CAP HURDLE GRADE 3 (11 hdls 2 omitted) 3m 110y

4:50 (4:50) (Class 1) 4-Y-0+

£28,505 (£10,695; £5,355; £2,670; £1,340; £670)

Form			Horse	RPR
4414	**1**		**Battle Group**[23] 4806 6-11-1 **137** .... BarryGeraghty (David Pipe) *midfield: hdwy after 6th: trckd ldrs 4 out: led after 2 out: pushed clr extended run-in: comf* **16/1**	148+
1-0P	**2**	*5*	**Ringaroses**[34] 4466 10-11-0 **136** .... (t) APMcCoy (Jonjo O'Neill) *lw: hld up: nt fluent 4 out: hdwy sn after: rdn after 3 out: styd on wl extended run-in: wnt 2nd fnl 150yds: no ch w wnr* **7/1**[2]	142
-0F6	**3**	*3 ¼*	**Sir Harry Ormesher**[146] 2360 8-11-8 **144** .... RobertThornton (Alan King) *midfield: hdwy after 4 out: chsd ldrs 3 out: ev ch 2 out: kpt on extended run-in* **14/1**	147
3411	**4**	*5*	**Cloudy Spirit**[13] 5003 6-10-10 **132** .... PaulMoloney (Reg Hollinshead) *hld up in rr: hmpd 1st: gd hdwy gng to 3 out: rdn bef 2 out: kpt on extended run-in* **17/2**[3]	134+
0011	**5**	*5*	**Golden Chieftain (IRE)**[20] 4875 6-11-4 **140** .... JoeTizzard (Colin Tizzard) *lw: midfield on outer: hdwy to trck ldrs gng after 4 out: chal 3 out: sn rdn: wknd extended run-in* **9/1**	134
0001	**6**	*hd*	**Buena Vista (IRE)**[22] 4817 10-11-6 **147** .... (b) CO'Farrell[(5)] (David Pipe) *led: hit 4th: rdn after 4 out: hdd after 2 out: wknd extended run-in* **12/1**	142+
321	**7**	*8*	**Swingkeel (IRE)**[20] 4861 6-10-11 **133** .... JasonMaguire (Nigel Twiston-Davies) *trckd ldrs: nt fluent 4 out: sn rdn: wknd after 3 out* **10/1**	121
1515	**8**	*2*	**Kilcrea Kim (IRE)**[21] 4849 6-11-3 **139** .... RichardJohnson (Philip Hobbs) *trckd ldrs: hit 9th: rdn gng to 3 out: wknd after 2 out* **6/1**[1]	127
1514	**9**	*5*	**Carpincho (FR)**[48] 4206 7-10-13 **135** .... JackDoyle (Sarah Humphrey) *t.k.h in midfield: rdn gng to 3 out: sn wknd* **33/1**	114
B026	**10**	*7*	**Ackertac (IRE)**[21] 4849 6-10-11 **133** .... PaddyBrennan (Nigel Twiston-Davies) *midfield: hdwy to trck ldrs after 6th: rdn gng to 3 out: sn wknd* **10/1**	108
14P0	**11**	*6*	**Mobaasher (USA)**[22] 4817 8-11-11 **147** .... (tp) AidanColeman (Venetia Williams) *midfield: lost pl after 6th: bhd after 8th* **40/1**	115
2160	**12**	*1 ¾*	**Mr Moonshine (IRE)**[22] 4817 7-10-13 **135** .... HenryOliver (Sue Smith) *trckd ldrs: w ldrs 6th: rdn after 4 out: wknd appr next* **50/1**	101
40P1	**13**	*3 ½*	**Al Co (FR)**[44] 4285 6-11-3 **139** .... DominicElsworth (Jonjo O'Neill) *hld up: rdn 4 out: a towards rr* **20/1**	102
-01F	**14**	*11*	**Superior Wisdom (IRE)**[119] 2870 11-10-10 **132** .... DenisO'Regan (Alex Hales) *midfield on outer: hdwy to trck ldrs 4 out: rdn gng to 3 out: sn wknd* **33/1**	85
0F40	**15**	*3 ½*	**Pistolet Noir (FR)**[23] 4806 5-10-13 **135** .... RWalsh (Paul Nicholls) *hld up: hmpd 1st: sme hdwy after 4 out: rdn gng to 3 out: sn wknd* **14/1**	85
2300	**16**	*7*	**Viking Blond (FR)**[22] 4817 6-11-0 **136** .... (b) SamTwiston-Davies (Nigel Twiston-Davies) *in tch: pushed along after 8th: wknd bef 4 out* **33/1**	80
36-0	**17**	*4*	**Whodoyouthink (IRE)**[26] 4762 6-11-2 **138** .... TJDoyle (Oliver McKiernan, Ire) *hld up in midfield on outer: rdn after 4 out: wknd gng to 3 out* **28/1**	78
22-0	**P**		**Souffleur**[22] 4819 8-11-11 **147** .... TomO'Brien (Peter Bowen) *midfield: p.u bef 8th:* **14/1**	—
1405	**B**		**Barnhill Brownie (IRE)**[175] 1855 8-10-3 **130** .... (t) GilesHawkins[(5)] (Philip Hobbs) *midfield: b.d 1st* **33/1**	—
5322	**F**		**Son Of Flicka**[21] 4852 7-11-5 **148** .... HenryBrooke[(7)] (Donald McCain) *midfield: fell 1st* **16/1**	—

6m 0.40s (-15.90) **Going Correction** -0.30s/f (Good) **20** Ran SP% **129.3**

Speed ratings (Par 113): **113,111,110,108,107 107,104,103,102,100 98,97,96,92,91 89,88,—,—,—**

toteswingers:1&2 £67.10, 2&3 £33.30, 1&3 £93.30 CSF £119.68 CT £1656.01 TOTE £23.50: £4.80, £1.80, £4.30, £2.20; EX 160.00 Trifecta £2550.50 Part won. Pool of £3446.73 - 0.60 winning units..

Owner Jolly Boys Outing **Bred** Juddmonte Farms Ltd **Trained** Nicholashayne, Devon

FOCUS

This race was won by Albertas Run in 2007 and Time For Rupert in 2009. This year's contest was predictably competitive and a solid pace resulted in a final time 9.20 seconds quicker than the earlier Grade 1 novice event. Following an incident on the first circuit in which two horses failed to safely negotiate the opening hurdle, the last flight in the straight was omitted on the final two laps. The second and third have been rated in line with their previous course form.

NOTEBOOK

Battle Group hasn't always looked straightforward, but he came into this in fine form - a winner at Newcastle before finishing fourth in the Coral Cup - and won well under late jockey change Barry Geraghty. He's had plenty of racing but this was only his second start at around 3m and he could be open to further improvement.

Ringaroses ran a fine race off a 6lb higher mark than when winning this last year, finishing nicely clear of the remainder. (op 8-1 tchd 13-2)

Sir Harry Ormesher was fresh after a 146-day break and had the ground to suit. This was a decent effort off a mark 5lb higher than when winning over 2m4f at this meeting last year.

Cloudy Spirit, bidding for a hat-trick off an 8lb higher mark, travelled well for a long way but was one-paced on the long run-in. This was a good performance stepped up in class. (op 11-1)

Golden Chieftain(IRE) was another aiming for a hat-trick but he was up 11lb and not proven over this trip. He went well for a fair way but didn't see his race out, perhaps finding conditions quicker than ideal. His long-term future probably lies over fences. (op 8-1)

Buena Vista(IRE), up 9lb for his second win in the Pertemps Final, was 6lb higher than when fourth in this 12 months ago. He ran well for a long way, although hitting the fourth hurdle didn't help and he ultimately found a few too strong.

Kilcrea Kim(IRE), fifth in the Albert Bartlett on his previous start, was reported to have run flat in the closing stages. Official explanation: jockey said gelding ran flat latter stages (op 13-2 tchd 7-1)

5188 JOHN SMITH'S MARES' STANDARD OPEN NATIONAL HUNT FLAT RACE (LISTED RACE) 2m 1f

5:25 (5:26) (Class 1) 4-6-Y-0

£17,103 (£6,417; £3,213; £1,602; £804; £402)

Form			Horse	RPR
334	**1**		**Tempest River (IRE)**[27] 4728 5-11-0 0 .... DarylJacob (Ben Case) *lw: prom: wnt 3rd 5f out: chal over 3f out: led 2f out: styd on wl* **20/1**	119+
	2	*2 ¼*	**Ceol Rua (IRE)**[98] 3274 6-11-4 0 .... MrPWMullins (W P Mullins, Ire) *mid-div: hdwy to chse ldrs 6f out: disp 2nd over 1f out: crowded and styd on ins fnl f* **5/1**[2]	121
11-6	**3**	*1 ¾*	**Big Time Billy (IRE)**[20] 4866 5-10-11 0 .... MichaelByrne[(7)] (Peter Bowen) *in rr: hdwy on outside 7f out: chsng ldrs over 3f out: disp 2nd over 1f out: edgd lft and kpt on same pce* **9/1**	120
113	**4**	*7*	**Baby Shine (IRE)**[27] 4728 5-11-4 0 .... LeightonAspell (Lucy Wadham) *trckd ldr: led over 3f out: hdd 2f out: sn wknd* **9/2**[1]	114
16	**5**	*4 ½*	**Heather Royal**[57] 4027 5-11-4 0 .... BarryGeraghty (Nicky Henderson) *lw: str: hld up in mid-div: hdwy 4f out: one pce fnl 2f* **14/1**	109
5230	**6**	*4*	**Miss Hippy (IRE)**[27] 4728 6-10-7 0 .... JakeGreenall[(7)] (Milton Harris) *in rr: reminders after 6f: sme hdwy 6f out: wknd over 2f out* **40/1**	101
115	**7**	*¾*	**Zhakiera Spirit**[27] 4728 5-11-4 0 .... BrianHughes (Howard Johnson) *lw: trckd ldrs: led 5f out: hdd over 3f out: wknd 2f out* **17/2**[3]	105+
0-	**8**	*4*	**Eyesontheprize (IRE)**[42] 4342 5-11-4 0 .... RWalsh (P A Fahy, Ire) *in rr: hdwy 7f out: wknd over 2f out* **12/1**	101
	9	*½*	**Thynetocatcher (IRE)**[34] 4498 5-11-4 0 .... RichardJohnson (Roger McGrath, Ire) *mid-div: kpt on fnl 3f: nvr a factor* **12/1**	101
100	**10**	*¾*	**Monnow Made (IRE)**[27] 4728 6-11-4 0 .... JimmyMcCarthy (Charles Egerton) *in rr: sme hdwy 6f out: wknd over 2f out* **66/1**	100
312	**11**	*9*	**Tante Sissi (FR)**[27] 4728 4-10-12 0 .... RobertThornton (Alan King) *mid-div: hdwy to chse ldrs over 4f out: wknd over 2f out* **5/1**[2]	86
1	**12**	*4*	**Keyaza (IRE)**[23] 4815 4-10-5 0 .... (p) TrevorWhelan[(7)] (Tobias B P Coles) *in rr: hdwy on outer 7f out: sn lost pl: bhd fnl 3f* **12/1**	82
514	**13**	*3*	**Sharlene's Quest (IRE)**[42] 4335 5-10-11 0 .... MrMatthewBarber[(7)] (V J Hughes) *led: hdd 5f out: sn wknd* **66/1**	86
	14	*1 ¼*	**Lady Knightess (IRE)**[22] 4846 5-10-13 0 .... BryanJCooper[(5)] (Thomas Cooper, Ire) *mid-div: lost pl 4f out* **20/1**	84
102	**15**	*49*	**Sparkling Hand**[30] 4554 5-10-13 0 .... PaulGallagher[(5)] (Peter Atkinson) *chsd ldrs: lost pl 6f out: bhd 3f out: t.o* **50/1**	40
10	**16**	*½*	**Elegant Touch (IRE)**[55] 4082 5-11-4 0 .... JackDoyle (Emma Lavelle) *chsd ldrs: j. path 6f out: sn lost pl and bhd: t.o* **33/1**	40
113	**17**	*31*	**With Grace**[138] 2546 6-11-1 0 .... DonalDevereux[(3)] (Peter Bowen) *chsd ldrs: lost pl 6f out: sn bhd: t.o 4f out: virtually p.u* **25/1**	12
14	**18**	*51*	**La Belle Au Bois (IRE)**[188] 1680 5-10-11 0 .... MrJBanks[(7)] (Nick Lampard) *in rr: bhd and rdn 6f out: t.o 4f: virtually p.u: eventually completed* **40/1**	—

4m 2.40s (-5.00) **Going Correction** -0.30s/f (Good)

WFA 4 from 5yo+ 5lb **18** Ran SP% **127.9**

Speed ratings: **99,97,97,93,91 89,89,87,87,87 82,80,79,78,55 55,41,17**

toteswingers:1&2 £31.60, 2&3 £11.70, 1&3 £63.10 CSF £113.66 TOTE £26.60: £6.80, £3.00, £2.40; EX 193.30 TRIFECTA Not won..

Owner Fly Like The Wind Partnership **Bred** Eileen, Countess of Mount Charles **Trained** Edgcote, Northants

■ Stewards' Enquiry : Michael Byrne one-day ban: careless riding (Apr 23); three-day ban: used whip with excessive frequency (Apr 24-26)

FOCUS

A race that can throw a shock result, as we saw last year with Big Time Billy, who ran another stormer this time round, and it again went to one of the outsiders. The first three have all been rated as having taken steps up, while the fourth has been rated below her Sandown form.

NOTEBOOK

Tempest River(IRE) had finished fourth in a Listed bumper at Sandown last month, behind a couple of these, and clearly prospered for the drier ground. Bred to stay, she looks a nice hurdling prospect and should win her share. (tchd 25-1)

Ceol Rua(IRE), a lengthy type who had been under consideration for the Cheltenham bumper, took this easier option and travelled strongly into contention, but was unable to quicken under pressure, staying on as though a return to slower conditions would suit. She too looks a nice hurdles prospect. (op 8-1)

Big Time Billy(IRE) ran for the first time since last year's success at Ffos Las last month, looking to need it, but she again showed herself to be a decent mare by returning right back to something like her best. She's still got plenty of time on her side, being just a 5-y-o, and should stay further over hurdles. (op 11-1 tchd 17-2)

Baby Shine(IRE), ahead of the winner at Sandown, travelled strongly into the straight, but perhaps had exerted a little too much energy in the early stages, and she was readily seen off from 2f out. (op 11-2)

Heather Royal, free to post, returned to something like her debut form, having disappointed in soft last time. She'll do better once learning to settle. (op 12-1)

Miss Hippy(IRE), who received a relatively early reminder, made some headway to record a creditable effort, taking her previous efforts into account. (op 66-1)

Zhakiera Spirit has got a big engine but needs to relax in her races. (op 8-1 tchd 9-1)

Tante Sissi(FR), runner-up in the Listed Sandown bumper ahead of today's winner, failed to settle early and never looked like justifying her prominent market position. (op 4-1)

Keyaza(IRE) was a bit disappointing in first-time cheekpieces, but probably deserves another chance, being just a 4-y-o. (op 11-1)

T/Jkpt: Not won. T/Plt: £250.10 to a £1 stake. Pool of £442,544.00 - 1,291.43 winning tickets. T/Qpdt: £36.50 to a £1 stake. Pool of £25,851.00 - 523.76 winning tickets. WG

4555 FONTWELL (L-H)

Friday, April 8

OFFICIAL GOING: Good (7.3)

Wind: virtually nil Weather: sunny

5189 BUTLINS CONFERENCE AND EVENTS MARES' NOVICES' HURDLE (9 hdls) 2m 2f 110y

2:10 (2:10) (Class 4) 4-Y-0+ **£2,276** (£668; £334; £166)

Form			Horse	RPR
2232	**1**		**American Ladie**[15] 4964 5-10-12 114 .... (b[1]) WayneHutchinson (Alan King) *trckd ldrs: squeezed up on inner and stmbld quite bdly on bnd after 3 out: led next: rdn whn mstke last: fnd ex u.p fnl 100yds: drvn out* **4/6**[1]	111+
2133	**2**	*1 ¾*	**The Bishops Baby (IRE)**[25] 4769 8-10-12 107 .... MrTJCannon[(7)] (Richard Rowe) *hld up: hdwy appr 3 out: cl 3rd 2 out: sn rdn to chse wnr: flattered briefly after last: no ex fnl 100yds* **17/2**	112
3U56	**3**	*17*	**Good Faloue (FR)**[64] 3901 6-10-9 100 .... AlexMerriam[(3)] (Neil King) *prom: mstke 6th: led after 3 out: rdn and hdd bef next: wknd bef last* **6/1**[3]	91
3102	**4**	*12*	**Lucy's Perfect**[10] 5064 5-11-5 113 .... (b) JohnnyFarrelly (David Pipe) *led tl rdn afer 3 out: sn edgd lft and btn* **4/1**[2]	90
0	**5**	*13*	**Belle De Fontenay (FR)**[50] 4164 6-10-12 0 .... MarkBradburne (George Baker) *trckd ldrs: nt fluent 2nd: losing pl whn hit 5th: wknd 3 out: t.o* **66/1**	68
00	**6**	*3 ¼*	**Bestwood Lodge**[54] 4097 5-10-7 0 .... JoshuaMoore[(5)] (Helen Nelmes) *struggling 4th: a in last pair: wknd 3 out: t.o* **100/1**	65

53F **7** *11* **Mekong Miss**[37] 4425 5-10-9 97 ow2 .... MrPYork(5) 57
(Raymond York) *rdn after 3 out: a in last pair: t.o* **33/1**

4m 16.6s (-17.70) **Going Correction** -0.675s/f (Firm) **7** Ran SP% **110.2**
Speed ratings (Par 105): **110,109,102,97,91 90,85**
toteswingers:1&2 £1.50, 2&3 £4.00, 1&3 £2.80 CSF £6.68 TOTE £1.40: £1.10, £4.20; EX 7.00.
Owner Million In Mind Partnership **Bred** Edy Srl **Trained** Barbury Castle, Wilts

FOCUS
There was a lush covering of grass on the course and the going was good on a watered track. The winning rider reported that the ground was riding on the livelier side of good. Most of the interest in this mares' novice event revolved around the hot favourite who finally delivered on her sixth hurdle start.

NOTEBOOK
American Ladie has been frustrating and had to settle for more minor money when turned over by a rival rated 14lb inferior at Chepstow last time. She set a clear standard again and this time she got the job done, despite not finding as much as expected after a mistake at the last. This form is still a few notches below her best and some doubts about her ability to find for pressure remain, but the plus side is that she travelled more smoothly in first-time blinkers and this 114-rated mare could go on to make an impact in handicaps if the headgear continues to work. (op 8-11 tchd 4-5)
The Bishops Baby(IRE), third off 107 in a Plumpton handicap last time, gave it a good try at running down the leading form contender considering she was faced with a tricky task under a penalty back in novice company. (tchd 7-1 and 10-1)
Good Faloue(FR) was under pressure some way out before being left behind by the front two. The ground was probably faster than ideal, but she has lost her way since finishing runner-up in this race last year. (op 17-2 tchd 5-1)
Lucy's Perfect looked the main form danger to the hot favourite and things seemed to be going well under a prominent ride for a long way, but she raced very awkwardly when coming under pressure and dropped away tamely. (op 10-3)

5190 PETER BOUGHTON MEMORIAL NOVICES' CHASE (SUPPORTED BY T I ENGINEERING) (16 fncs) 2m 6f
2:45 (2:45) (Class 4) 5-Y-0+ **£2,439** (£716; £358)

Form RPR
2210 **1** **Alderley Rover (IRE)**[22] 4821 7-11-7 128 .... SamThomas 136+
(Donald McCain) *mde all: shkn up appr last: comf* **11/10**[1]
-312 **2** *8* **Aldertune (IRE)**[19] 4898 7-11-4 129 ....(b) IanPopham(3) 131
(Paul Nicholls) *trckd ldrs: wnt 2nd 11th: stmbld whn mstke 4 out: sn rdn: kpt on but hld fr next* **7/4**[2]
PP5F **3** *34* **Vagrant Emperor (IRE)**[34] 4485 8-10-7 0 .... StephenO'Donovan(7) 100
(Emma Lavelle) *j. sltly rt getting progively worse fr 4 out: trckd wnr: hit 8th: lost 2nd 11th: wknd after 4 out* **7/2**[3]

5m 34.8s (-8.20) **Going Correction** -0.475s/f (Good) **3** Ran SP% **106.2**
Speed ratings: **95,92,79**
CSF £3.28 TOTE £1.80; EX 2.30.
Owner Alec Craig & Andrew Dick **Bred** Miss Kitty O'Connor **Trained** Cholmondeley, Cheshire

FOCUS
This novices' chase was weakened by the withdrawal of Quo Video but it still looked an intriguing event and there was a professional display by the 128-rated favourite.

NOTEBOOK
Alderley Rover(IRE) found things tough in the Kim Muir, but he bounced back with an impressive front-running effort to get back in the groove and improve Donald McCain's strike-rate to 4-6 at this track in recent seasons. This likeable type has already proved a better chaser than hurdler and looks an accurate and straight jumper. He should continue to do well in this sphere and looks fairly treated for handicaps on the pick of his form. (op 11-8 tchd 6-4 in a place)
Aldertune(IRE) made hard work of a good opportunity at Chepstow before not finding as much as expected when second upped to 3m2f in a similar novice chase at Newton Abbot last time. A similar scenario unfolded here, but a mistake four out did put a major dent in his momentum. Some doubts about his application and jumping technique remain, but this lightly raced type has achieved fairly useful form and could be more potent when getting a stronger pace to aim at in bigger-field handicaps. (op 11-8)
Vagrant Emperor(IRE) was a close second off 115 over hurdles at Newbury in November, but his form had slumped since and he made several hesitant and erratic jumps before trailing home faced with a stiff task on this chase debut. (tchd 11-4)

5191 PREMIER FOOD COURT NOVICES' H'CAP HURDLE (10 hdls) 2m 4f
3:20 (3:20) (Class 5) (0-95,102) 4-Y-0+ **£1,951** (£573; £286; £143)

Form RPR
4111 **1** **E Street Boy**[6] 5111 5-11-13 102 14ex .... SClements(7) 112+
(David Pipe) *travelled wl: hld up: effrtless hdwy 2 out: led whn nt fluent last: hung sltly rt: pushed out* **8/13**[1]
P5-0 **2** *2 ½* **Island News**[162] 2051 7-11-0 85 .... MarcGoldstein(3) 87
(Michael Madgwick) *in tch: rdn after 3 out: ev ch next: kpt on same pce fr last* **33/1**
0P12 **3** *nk* **Rossbrin (IRE)**[20] 4878 6-11-6 91 ....(t) IanPopham(3) 93
(Anna Brooks) *in tch: effrt after 3 out: kpt on same pce fr last* **7/2**[2]
55P0 **4** *1 ½* **Keckerrockernixes (IRE)**[30] 4559 5-9-13 74 ....(p) MrTJCannon(7) 76
(Richard Rowe) *chsd ldrs: drvn after 5th: lost pl 3 out: hdwy to ld next: hdd bef last: no ex* **20/1**
0201 **5** *13* **Curragh Dancer (FR)**[11] 5051 8-10-13 81 .... AndrewGlassonbury 71
(Paddy Butler) *in tch: reminders after 2nd: rdn after 5th: wknd after 2 out: wnt rt last* **14/1**
06U6 **6** *10* **Karingabay Queen**[22] 4828 6-9-7 68 ....(b) MrBJPoste(7) 48
(Kevin Tork) *trckd ldr: rdn after 3 out: ev ch whn faltered bef next: wknd bef last* **50/1**
P002 **7** *8* **Graylyn Amber**[11] 5057 6-11-2 84 .... CharliePoste 57
(Robin Dickin) *led: rdn after 3 out: hdd bef next: sn wknd* **7/1**[3]
0PPF **P** **Quelclasse (FR)**[45] 4269 7-10-10 85 .... RobertKirk(7) —
(Steven Dixon) *nvr travelling in rr but in tch: reminders fr after 2nd: wknd bef 3 out: p.u bef 2 out* **20/1**

4m 46.3s (-13.10) **Going Correction** -0.675s/f (Firm) **8** Ran SP% **117.7**
Speed ratings (Par 103): **99,98,97,97,92 88,84,—**
toteswingers:1&2 £27.90, 2&3 £12.80, 1&3 £1.30 CSF £27.84 CT £52.63 TOTE £1.50: £1.40, £5.70, £1.10; EX 36.20.
Owner Roger Stanley & Yvonne Reynolds **Bred** Kelanne Stud Ltd **Trained** Nicholashayne, Devon

FOCUS
The progressive hot favourite did the job in smooth style in this novices' handicap.

NOTEBOOK
E Street Boy proved a revelation when comfortably winning three times in the space of seven days recently. Officially 9lb well-in here despite a double penalty, he put in a slick display to complete a four-timer with more in hand than the margin suggests. Things will get a lot tougher when the handicapper reacts again, but this smooth traveller has improved significantly since sent upped to 2m4f-plus and could continue his golden spell. (op 4-6 tchd 8-11)
Island News was well held in bumpers/novice hurdles, but he showed a lot more dropped in trip on his handicap debut back from 162 days off.
Rossbrin(IRE) was well backed and ran a solid race, but couldn't match the finishing kick of the winner. He has got back to form with a win and two placed efforts with a tongue tie applied since a soft palate operation, and should continue to go well. (op 4-1)
Keckerrockernixes(IRE) showed nothing in blinkers last time, but cheekpieces helped inspire a positive response in this contest and he was not far off recording his first placed effort on his 13th start. (op 25-1)
Curragh Dancer(FR) capitalised on the jumping errors of others when a fortunate winner of a Plumpton handicap chase, but he was in trouble at an early stage in this very laboured run off 2lb higher back over hurdles.
Graylyn Amber found improvement switched to quicker ground when second in a 2m Towcester handicap, but she cut out quickly under a prominent ride here and probably had stamina issues. (tchd 13-2 and 8-1)

5192 HORSES FOR FORCES LONDON MARATHON H'CAP CHASE (21 fncs) 3m 4f
3:55 (3:55) (Class 4) (0-110,110) 5-Y-0+ **£2,439** (£716; £358; £178)

Form RPR
0264 **1** **River Indus**[31] 4537 11-10-6 95 .... JoshuaMoore(5) 105+
(Bob Buckler) *disp ld tl clr ldr 4 out: styd on gamely: rdn out* **10/3**[1]
215F **2** *1 ¾* **Abbey Dore (IRE)**[31] 4537 8-10-11 98 .... JimmyDerham(3) 105
(Seamus Mullins) *trckd ldrs: wnt 2nd 4 out: rdn after 3 out: styd on but unable to mount chal* **4/1**[2]
3443 **3** *27* **Lavenoak Lad**[26] 4749 11-11-1 99 ....(t) ColinBolger 82
(Simon Burrough) *disp ld: hit 3rd and 9th: rdn whn hdd 4 out: chsd ldng pair fr 3 out: wknd last* **11/2**
4632 **4** *8* **Rebel Melody (IRE)**[15] 4971 10-11-6 104 ....(bt) JamesDavies 80
(Charlie Mann) *trckd ldrs: rdn after 17th: nt pce to chal: wknd last* **5/1**
3142 **5** *36* **Lady De La Vega (FR)**[17] 4927 7-11-12 110 ....(vt) SamThomas 83
(Tim Vaughan) *trckd ldrs: jnd ldrs briefly 12th tl next: rdn after 4 out: 4th and wkng whn mstke last: virtually p.u* **9/2**[3]
4RP4 **P** **Celian (FR)**[29] 4669 8-10-7 94 .... AlexMerriam(3) —
(Neil King) *trckd ldrs: struggling in last pair 13th: wnt rt and slow jump 16th: sn p.u* **8/1**
PP-P **P** **Doc Reason (IRE)**[23] 4811 8-9-8 85 .... MrJMQuinlan(7) —
(Patrick Gilligan) *hld up bhd ldrs: hit 9th: lost tch fr 15th: p.u after next* **14/1**

7m 13.0s (-14.30) **Going Correction** -0.475s/f (Good) course record **7** Ran SP% **111.1**
Speed ratings: **101,100,92,90,80 —,—**
toteswingers:1&2 £4.50, 2&3 £4.90, 1&3 £3.10 CSF £16.36 TOTE £4.20: £1.80, £3.50; EX 17.60.
Owner Mrs C J Dunn **Bred** Mrs H R Dunn **Trained** Henley, Somerset

FOCUS
A competitive long-distance handicap chase. The five market leaders were in contention at the third last before the first two pulled clear.

NOTEBOOK
River Indus had not really been firing since December, but he got back to form with a gutsy front-running display to take advantage of a slipping mark. This generally reliable 11-y-o could back this up with another big run, but he has never won back-to-back races and has a modest strike-rate of 5-46. (op 7-2)
Abbey Dore(IRE) had a bit to prove after a submission and a fall on his last two runs, but he put up a good fight behind the well-treated winner. He is 34lb higher than the first of his four chase wins, but is not fully exposed over marathon trips and may be able to strike again. (tchd 3-1)
Lavenoak Lad was in the firing line for a long way, but couldn't hang in there when the front two forged clear. (op 9-2)
Rebel Melody(IRE) ran well to a point, but was ultimately well held and is struggling to rediscover the form of his 3m3f Wincanton win off 2lb higher in November. (op 9-2)
Lady De La Vega(FR), a close second off 4lb lower on good ground at Exeter last time, was under pressure some way out and couldn't find a decisive response before dropping away. (op 5-1 tchd 11-2)
Celian(FR) attracted support, but was in serious trouble at a relatively early stage before being pulled up. (op 12-1)

5193 MARY BROSNAN H'CAP HURDLE (9 hdls) 2m 2f 110y
4:30 (4:30) (Class 4) (0-115,114) 4-Y-0+ **£2,276** (£668; £334; £166)

Form RPR
32-1 **1** **Devil To Pay**[146] 2361 5-11-12 114 .... WayneHutchinson 126+
(Alan King) *trckd ldrs: rdn to ld sn after last: r.o wl* **5/2**[1]
3230 **2** *2* **Minneapolis**[160] 2081 6-10-12 105 .... MarkQuinlan(5) 111
(Alison Batchelor) *hld up: hdwy 5th: rdn to ld after 2 out: hdd sn after last: no ex* **33/1**
4046 **3** *6* **Wester Ross (IRE)**[6] 5117 7-11-11 113 ....(b) MarkBradburne 114
(James Eustace) *sn drvn to dispute ld: hdd 3 out: ev ch appr 2 out: 4th whn nt fluent last: kpt on same pce* **10/1**
0-06 **4** *1 ¼* **Home**[18] 4922 6-10-5 93 .... SamJones 91
(Brendan Powell) *chsd ldrs: led 3 out: rdn and hdd after 2 out: no ex fr last* **15/2**
20P3 **5** *4* **Kylenoe Fairy (IRE)**[14] 4990 7-11-3 105 ....(t) SamThomas 107+
(Paul Henderson) *outpcd in rr early: hdwy after 3 out: chsng ldrs whn squeezed out and snatched up jst bef next: no ch after* **11/2**[3]
P351 **6** *15* **De Welsh Wizzard**[11] 5054 8-10-9 104 .... StephenO'Donovan(7) 85
(Emma Lavelle) *rdn bef 3 out: a towards rr* **9/2**[2]
0006 **7** *11* **King Of The Titans (IRE)**[15] 4977 8-10-5 100 .... MrJMQuinlan(7) 71
(Patrick Gilligan) *mid-div: rdn appr 6th: wknd bef 2 out: hit last* **50/1**
0/5- **8** *1 ½* **Cossack Prince**[78] 5045 6-10-7 105 .... NathanAdams(10) 75
(Laura Mongan) *disp ld tl rdn 3 out: wknd bef next* **16/1**
0F1P **9** *12* **Balustrade (IRE)**[49] 4182 5-11-4 106 .... ColinBolger 65
(Chris Gordon) *mid-div tl 5th: sn pushed along: wknd 3 out* **12/1**
054 **10** *3 ½* **Benozzo Gozzoli**[49] 4195 5-11-0 105 .... JimmyDerham(3) 61
(Seamus Mullins) *mid-div: rdn after 4th: wknd bef 3 out* **20/1**
42F1 **11** *nse* **Watergate (IRE)**[29] 4670 5-11-0 102 .... AndrewThornton 58
(Richard Rowe) *chsd ldrs tl 6th: wknd next* **10/1**

4m 19.0s (-15.30) **Going Correction** -0.675s/f (Firm) **11** Ran SP% **115.3**
Speed ratings (Par 105): **105,104,101,101,99 93,88,87,82,81 81**
toteswingers:1&2 £19.70, 2&3 £42.30, 1&3 £7.60 CSF £83.34 CT £713.71 TOTE £2.10: £1.20, £6.30, £4.60; EX 53.10.
Owner Horace 5 **Bred** G Russell **Trained** Barbury Castle, Wilts

FOCUS
An unexposed last-time-out winner travelled very smoothly for most of the way and was value for more than the winning margin in this fairly competitive handicap.

NOTEBOOK
Devil To Pay made a successful handicap debut over hurdles when swooping late to beat a very consistent rival over 2m at Cheltenham in November. He had a 7lb higher mark to deal with back from a spin in a charity race at the Cheltenham Festival, but cruised into contention before knuckling down to overhaul the runner-up and make it 2-2 in handicaps. A fair stayer on the Flat, he has plenty of scope for further improvement and should appreciate taking another step up in trip. (op 2-1)
Minneapolis was disappointing at Ascot when last seen in October, but this generally reliable type was back on song on his return from 160 days off and looks fairly treated on the pick of his fast-ground form last summer. (op 28-1)

Wester Ross(IRE) put in a better effort, but he looks high enough in the weights on the balance of his recent form and his sole success in this sphere was in a maiden hurdle in October 2009. (op 11-1 tchd 12-1)
Home, a market mover in the morning, looked a possible winner when seizing the initiative around the final bend but he couldn't sustain his effort. (op 10-1)
Kylenoe Fairy(IRE) finished a 5l third behind a Nicky Henderson-trained improver at Newbury last time. There were early warning signs here, but she worked her way into it before running into some damaging traffic problems. (op 6-1 tchd 9-2)
De Welsh Wizzard was disappointing off the same mark as his commanding display in a conditional riders' handicap at Plumpton 11 days earlier. Official explanation: jockey said gelding never travelled (op 11-2 tchd 6-1)
Watergate(IRE) didn't find much before dropping away in his bid to defy a 12lb rise for his Folkestone win last month. (op 9-1 tchd 11-1)

5194 HARDINGS CATERING H'CAP CHASE (15 fncs) 2m 4f
5:05 (5:05) (Class 4) (0-115,115) 5-Y-0+ **£2,439** (£716; £358; £178)

Form RPR
0P12 **1** **Ready Or Not (IRE)**[15] 4967 8-10-10 **99** AndrewGlassonbury 111+
(Bob Buckler) *trckd ldrs: led 3 out: styd on strly fr last: comf* **3/1**[1]
2P22 **2** *6* **Psi (USA)**[17] 4931 6-11-0 **108** (b) JoshuaMoore(5) 115+
(Gary Moore) *hld up: hdwy 4 out: sn rdn to chse ldrs: wnt 3rd sn after last: snatched 2nd fnl stride* **3/1**[1]
322F **3** *nse* **Take A Mile (IRE)**[17] 4927 9-11-3 **109** JimmyDerham(3) 115
(Seamus Mullins) *hld up: hdwy whn nt fluent 4 out: sn rdn to chse ldrs: wnt 2nd jst bef last but no ch w wnr: lost 2nd fnl stride* **11/1**
336F **4** *12* **Molanna View (IRE)**[16] 4948 6-10-9 **105** StephenO'Donovan(7) 100
(Emma Lavelle) *trckd ldr: reminders after 5th: led 10th: rdn and hdd 3 out: hld in 3rd whn nt fluent last: fdd* **6/1**[2]
3116 **5** *11* **Silver Dollars (FR)**[57] 4022 10-10-12 **101** AndrewThornton 85
(David Arbuthnot) *cl up tl lost pl 8th: rdn in tch after 4 out: wknd bef last* **17/2**
20P3 **6** *14* **High Oscar**[25] 4770 10-9-12 **94** MrTJCannon(7) 66
(Richard Rowe) *in tch: wnt cl 3rd 11th: rdn after 4 out: wknd next* **8/1**[3]
4-FP **7** *2 1/4* **Senor Shane (IRE)**[14] 4988 8-11-5 **115** (vt) SClements(7) 85
(Chris Gordon) *a in last pair: rdn 4 out: wknd next* **16/1**
5530 **8** *32* **Cousin Maggie (IRE)**[14] 4990 7-10-6 **95** SamJones 36
(Brendan Powell) *in tch: pushed along after 6th: bhd fr 10th: t.o* **11/1**
510P **P** **Jeczmien (POL)**[25] 4770 8-11-7 **110** (p) LiamTreadwell —
(Nick Gifford) *led tl 10th: rdn after next: wknd 4 out: t.o whn p.u bef last* **20/1**

4m 55.2s (-12.10) **Going Correction** -0.475s/f (Good) **9** Ran SP% **113.2**
Speed ratings: **105,102,102,97,93 87,86,74,—**
toteswingers:1&2 £1.20, 2&3 £5.40, 1&3 £5.30 CSF £12.69 CT £83.53 TOTE £3.90: £1.70, £1.60, £3.00; EX 9.20.
Owner Christopher And Anne Collier **Bred** James T Williams **Trained** Henley, Somerset

FOCUS
A competitive handicap chase.

NOTEBOOK
Ready Or Not(IRE) was always travelling well and forged clear after the third-last to improve his record to 2-4 over fences. This former point winner drew a blank over hurdles, but has looked a more formidable force since sent chasing and should be capable of further progress. (op 7-2 tchd 11-4)
Psi(USA) needed a few reminders along the way, but he deserves some credit for grinding his way into second. He is not entirely straightforward and is still chasing a first win since coming to Britain, but he has been knocking on the door off similar ratings recently and probably has the ability to justify this mark. (op 11-4 tchd 10-3)
Take A Mile(IRE) ran respectably, but he is 11lb higher than his last win and may continue to be vulnerable off this sort of rating. (op 17-2)
Molanna View(IRE) got off to a bad start over fences when taking a heavy fall at Hereford, but he put that setback behind him with a fair front-running effort and shaped like a drop in trip could work in his favour. (op 15-2 tchd 8-1)
Silver Dollars(FR) completed a double on soft ground at around the turn of the year, but this 10-y-o has been found out by this 6lb higher mark on good ground in two runs since. (op 9-1)
Jeczmien(POL) was reported to have had a breathing problem. Official explanation: jockey said gelding had a breathing problem (tchd 25-1)

5195 ARUNDEL EQUINE HOSPITAL RACING EXCELLENCE "HANDS AND HEELS" H'CAP HURDLE (CONDITIONALS/AMATEURS) (13 hdls) 3m 3f
5:35 (5:36) (Class 4) (0-110,110) 4-Y-0+ **£2,276** (£668; £334; £166)

Form RPR
0031 **1** **Easement**[66] 3870 8-10-10 **97** (v) MrTGarner(3) 103+
(Charlie Morlock) *trckd ldng pair fr 5th: led 3 out: styd on wl: pushed out* **6/1**
22/0 **2** *3 3/4* **Ommega (FR)**[14] 4990 9-11-2 **105** (p) MrMatthewHampton(5) 107
(Gerald Ham) *hld up: hdwy 3 out: sn pushed along: styd on to take 2nd run-in* **40/1**
2002 **3** *1/2* **Inner Steel (IRE)**[25] 4767 6-11-3 **104** MrOJMurphy(3) 105
(Lydia Richards) *trckd ldr: led after 5th: hdd 3 out: styd on same pce fr next: lost 2nd run-in* **7/2**[1]
344P **4** *15* **Duneen Point (IRE)**[38] 4407 7-11-5 **108** JPKiely(5) 94
(Tim Vaughan) *hld up: hit 2nd: pushed along after 10th: plugged on past btn horses fr 3 out: n.d* **9/1**
3P02 **5** *2 1/4* **Latin America (IRE)**[53] 4121 6-11-12 **110** (v) PeterCarberry 94
(Nick Gifford) *cl up early tl dropped in last pair 5th: pushed along and hdwy after 9th: styd on same pce fr 3 out* **7/2**[1]
4003 **6** *2 1/2* **Shacklesborough (IRE)**[10] 5068 7-11-1 **99** MrDGPrichard 81
(Paul Nicholls) *nvr travelling: a in rr* **11/2**[3]
4434 **7** *3/4* **Nobby Kivambo (IRE)**[23] 4812 6-11-1 **102** (p) MrBJPowell(3) 83
(Brendan Powell) *led tl 5th: styd prom tl wknd 3 out* **4/1**[2]
53P6 **8** *40* **Power Lord (IRE)**[31] 4539 6-11-2 **100** NathanSweeney 45
(Bob Buckler) *chsd ldrs tl 9th: sn wknd: t.o* **11/1**
0P04 **F** **Star Time (IRE)**[10] 5068 12-10-0 **84** oh25 (v) AodhaganConlon —
(Michael Scudamore) *hld up: fell 2nd* **40/1**

6m 34.5s (-18.30) **Going Correction** -0.675s/f (Firm) **9** Ran SP% **117.3**
Speed ratings (Par 105): **100,98,98,94,93 92,92,80,—**
toteswingers:1&2 £36.00, 2&3 £13.70, 1&3 £6.70 CSF £174.02 CT £962.74 TOTE £7.80: £1.60, £5.10, £1.70; EX 216.20.
Owner Miss J Houston **Bred** C A Cyzer **Trained** Upper Lambourn, Berks
■ Stewards' Enquiry : J P Kiely seven-day ban: used whip in hands and heels (tbn)

FOCUS
The first three pulled clear in this staying handicap hurdle for conditional/amateur riders.

NOTEBOOK
Easement showed improved form when off the mark over 3m at Taunton in February. He had a 7lb rise to defy, but this longer trip was a plus point and he completed the double in smooth style. He has some quirks and an up and down profile, but is on a roll and could make it three in a row next time. (op 7-1)
Ommega(FR) finished tailed off back from a long absence on his recent debut for a new yard, but this ex-French performer bounced back with a solid staying-on effort with cheekpieces reapplied stepped up significantly in trip.
Inner Steel(IRE) ran a decent race up in trip on handicap debut. He is gradually learning to settle better and could find the extra needed to justify this mark. (op 9-2)
Duneen Point(IRE) had run in snatches and finished lame in two previous tries in handicaps, but this time he compromised his chance by taking a keen hold and could only plug on. A drop back in trip should suit. Official explanation: jockey said gelding hung right throughout (op 8-1 tchd 7-1)
Latin America(IRE) returned to form when having the run of things in a first-time visor at Plumpton, but he couldn't get an easy lead this time and his stamina seemed to crack stepped up 6f in trip. (op 9-2 tchd 5-1 and 10-3)
Shacklesborough(IRE) was disappointing in his attempt to build on his third back hurdling at Taunton last time. (op 9-2 tchd 6-1)
Nobby Kivambo(IRE) is a consistent type, but he failed to see out this trip and his record now stands at 0-22. (op 9-2)
T/Plt: £24.90 to a £1 stake. Pool: of £43,201.00 - 1,265.11 winning tickets. T/Qpdt: £12.80 to a £1 stake. Pool of £3,216.00 - 185.50 winning tickets. TM

5182 AINTREE (L-H)
Saturday, April 9

OFFICIAL GOING: Good (good to soft in places on grand national course; mildmay 7.8 hurdle 8.0 national 7.2)
The meeting began with the Aintree Legends Charity Flat race, over 1m5f, won by Tony Dobbin on Fortuni.
Wind: light 1/2 against Weather: fine and sunny, warm

5196 JOHN SMITH'S MERSEY NOVICES' HURDLE GRADE 2 (11 hdls) 2m 4f
1:45 (1:45) (Class 1) 4-Y-0+
£31,355 (£11,764; £5,890; £2,937; £1,474; £737)

Form RPR
112 **1** **Spirit Son (FR)**[25] 4788 5-11-4 149 BarryGeraghty 160+
(Nicky Henderson) *lw: trckd ldrs: led after 3 out: wnt clr appr last: impressive* **3/1**[2]
1124 **2** *13* **Cue Card**[25] 4788 5-11-4 154 JoeTizzard 148+
(Colin Tizzard) *t.k.h in rr: mstke 7th: hdwy appr 3 out: chsd wnr bef 2 out: no imp* **5/2**[1]
1122 **3** *8* **Rock On Ruby (IRE)**[24] 4803 6-11-4 148 (t) DarylJacob 142+
(Paul Nicholls) *swtg: edgy: t.k.h early: trckd ldrs: mstke 3rd: kpt on same pce fr 3 out: hit last* **9/2**
0B30 **4** *1/2* **Drill Sergeant**[28] 4727 6-11-4 128 (bt) JasonMaguire 138
(Donald McCain) *chsd ldrs: pushed along 8th: one pce fr 3 out* **40/1**
-110 **5** *4* **Storm Brig**[35] 4475 6-11-4 132 EwanWhillans 138
(Alistair Whillans) *edgy: nt fluent in rr: hdwy appr 3 out: sn drvn: nvr trbld ldrs* **25/1**
1144 **6** *hd* **Sam Winner (FR)**[22] 4847 4-10-11 148 RWalsh 129
(Paul Nicholls) *lw: j. boldly: led: hdd after 3 out: fdd run-in* **7/2**[3]
2-41 **7** *32* **Bold Sir Brian (IRE)**[35] 4475 5-11-4 135 PeterBuchanan 126
(Lucinda Russell) *in rr: outpcd whn sltly hmpd 3 out: bhd whn j.lft last 2* **12/1**
031 **8** *73* **Maringo Bay (IRE)**[51] 4159 6-11-4 138 PeterToole 40
(Charlie Mann) *lw: chsd ldrs: outpcd whn hit 8th: sn lost pl: t.o whn blnd 2 out: eventually completed* **28/1**
1P1 **F** **Drive Time (USA)**[35] 4467 6-11-4 125 BrianHughes —
(Howard Johnson) *trckd ldrs: rdn and outpcd whn fell 3 out* **28/1**

4m 52.2s (-8.50) **Going Correction** -0.325s/f (Good)
WFA 4 from 5yo+ 6lb **9** Ran SP% **114.8**
Speed ratings (Par 115): **104,98,95,95,93 93,80,51,—**
toteswingers:1&2:£2.90, 1&3:£2.90, 2&3:£3.30 CSF £10.74 TOTE £3.70: £1.50, £1.60, £1.40; EX 9.00 Trifecta £24.60 Pool: £3,000.39 - 90.20 winning units..
Owner Michael Buckley **Bred** Anne Baudrelle & Jean-Marc Baudrelle **Trained** Upper Lambourn, Berks

FOCUS
Tidal Bay and Peddlers Cross would be the better recent winners of this contest and this year's renewal looked well up to scratch, with the form of the main Cheltenham novice hurdles well represented. The only disappointing aspect to the race was that they went a crawl early, until Sam Winner went to the front and set just a respectable gallop. The winner deserves to be rated the season's top novice, while the third and sixth were well below their Cheltenham runs.

NOTEBOOK
Spirit Son(FR) could hardly have been more impressive. Stepping up to this trip for the first time after achieving a career-best when runner-up in the Supreme Novices', he was travelling like a winner in the slipstream of the leader throughout and, once taking it up after jumping three out, the result was never in doubt. He was immediately given quotes of between 8-1 and 14-1 for next year's Champion Hurdle and is likely to be aimed at the bigger hurdle contests before that. (tchd 11-4 and 100-30 in places)
Cue Card started off the season as the brightest novice talent around, but defeat by Menorah in the International Hurdle and only finishing fourth when a warm favourite for the Supreme Novices' had checked his progression. Back up in trip for the first time since winning over C&D on his seasonal reappearance, he took a strong hold in rear early and tended to race in snatches (a clumsy mistake at the seventh not helping), but he still loomed large straightening up for home. However, he couldn't match the pace of the winner over the last two flights and started to hang away to his left under pressure. He finished 4l behind Spirit Son at Cheltenham, but the margin was extended to 13l here and this may be as good as he is over hurdles. He is likely to go novice chasing next. (op 11-4 tchd 3-1)
Rock On Ruby(IRE) has had a fine season, even though he was beaten by the subsequent Albert Bartlett winner Bobs Worth at Cheltenham in January and by a whisker in the Neptune at the Festival last month, but despite that he was rejected by Ruby Walsh in favour of Sam Winner. Having taken a grip early, he travelled well but lacked speed when the sprint for home started and was beaten when clattering through the last. He is also likely to go over fences next season. (tchd 4-1)
Drill Sergeant had plenty to find on ratings so this wasn't a bad effort at all, but he hasn't really progressed over hurdles and has also shown his quirks.
Storm Brig had looked an exciting prospect before running a stinker (nearly 35l behind Bold Sir Brian) at Kelso last time. He didn't look happy from some way out and hung over the last three flights. (op 33-1)
Sam Winner(FR) was trying to match the exploits of Bouggler, who won this race as a 4-y-o two years ago. The preferred mount of Ruby Walsh, he had looked as though he would relish this extra 3f when coming from another parish to finish fourth in the Triumph Hurdle, but if the plan was to make the running here it didn't work. He had the run of the race out in front, but was easily picked off by the winner after three out and ran like a non-stayer, which means he now has questions to answer. (op 3-1)
Bold Sir Brian(IRE) was impressive at Kelso last time, but had plenty to find with several of these on official ratings and probably found the ground too quick. (tchd 10-1)

Maringo Bay(IRE) was very impressive when winning at Ffos Las last time, but although Saint Are (a faller at Ffos Las) won the Grade 1 novice here the previous day, the form of that race hasn't worked out very well and he dropped right out after a slow jump four from home. (op 25-1 tchd 33-1)

Drive Time(USA) was one of the least exposed in the field, but also held the lowest official rating and he was just starting to struggle to stay in touch when falling three out. (op 33-1 tchd 25-1)

5197 JOHN SMITH'S MAGHULL NOVICES' CHASE GRADE 1 (11 fncs 1 omitted) 2m

2:15 (2:15) (Class 1) 5-Y-0+

£56,631 (£21,421; £10,761; £5,431; £2,781; £1,441)

Form RPR

1112 **1** **Finian's Rainbow (IRE)**[25] 4789 8-11-4 157................... BarryGeraghty 161+
(Nicky Henderson) *mde all: hit 6th and next: kpt on u.p fr 2 out: hld on towards fin* **10/11**[1]

2115 **2** *2* **Ghizao (GER)**[25] 4789 7-11-4 155.. RWalsh 161+
(Paul Nicholls) *lw: chsd wnr: drvn to chal whn blnd 2 out: kpt on run-in* **3/1**[2]

1101 **3** *22* **Dan Breen (IRE)**[7] 5116 6-11-4 148.................................. JasonMaguire 139
(David Pipe) *chsd ldng pair: drvn 8th: one pce fr 3 out: nvr on terms* **8/1**

2313 **4** *18* **Starluck (IRE)**[28] 4729 6-11-4 0.. APMcCoy 126
(Alan Fleming) *nt fluent: chsd ldrs: hit 5th and next: wknd 3 out* **9/2**[3]

1-13 **5** *3 3/4* **Gilbarry (IRE)**[115] 2951 6-11-4 134.. GrahamLee 121
(Malcolm Jefferson) *rangy: sn outpcd and nt fluent: mstke 2nd: mstke and reminders 4th: lost tch 8th* **22/1**

6 *70* **Romanesco (FR)**[70] 3828 6-11-4 125...................... SamTwiston-Davies 54
(Alison Thorpe) *blnd bdly and lost tch 1st: continued t.o: mstkes: eventually completed* **50/1**

2506 **F** **Classic Fly (FR)**[10] 5072 8-11-4 104......................................(t) PeterToole —
(Arthur Whiting) *chsd ldrs: fell 1st* **100/1**

3m 54.6s (-5.40) **Going Correction** +0.05s/f (Yiel) **7** Ran SP% **114.0**
Speed ratings: **115,114,103,94,92 57,—**
toteswingers:1&2:£1.50, 1&3:£2.40, 2&3:£3.10 CSF £4.16 TOTE £1.90: £1.10, £2.20; EX 2.90.
Owner Michael Buckley **Bred** J O'Keeffe **Trained** Upper Lambourn, Berks

FOCUS

The key to this was always likely to be the Arkle with the second, fifth and seventh horses from Cheltenham lining up here. There was drama at the first fence when the complete outsider Classic Fly took a crashing fall and Romanesco was all but put out of the race. The pace was decent and the field were soon well spread out. The winner has been rated 2lb below his Cheltenham mark, while the runner-up has been rated to his best, but there's a case for rating the race higher.

NOTEBOOK

Finian's Rainbow(IRE) had lost his unbeaten record over fences when runner-up in the Arkle, but that was still the best form on offer here. Racing with the same exuberance that he showed at Cheltenham, he set a solid pace but did get a bit low at a couple of the fences on the far side. It looked as though he would face a stern challenge from the runner-up coming to two out but, unlike his main rival, he jumped the last two cleanly and that made all the difference. He was quoted a top-priced 10-1 for next year's Queen Mother Champion Chase. (op 4-5 tchd Evens)

Ghizao(GER) would undoubtedly have finished much closer to Finian's Rainbow in the Arkle had it not been for a serious blunder four out, and only 2lb separated them on official ratings. His trainer felt that 2m4f might suit him better on this ground, but he nonetheless travelled nicely behind the favourite and looked a big danger to his old rival when he got the second-last all wrong and lost a good 4l in the process. He tried to rally afterwards, but had insufficient time to do so. He was quoted a top-priced 25-1 for next season's Champion Chase which, although not that tempting, does look big when compared to the price of the winner. If all is well he may go to Punchestown.

Dan Breen(IRE), on his toes beforehand, disappointed in the Arkle when blinkered for the first time and had since enjoyed a confidence-booster without them at Uttoxeter. He was being niggled along from some way out here, but plugged on for a remote third and probably bettered his Arkle performance. He may not have finished for the season yet. (op 10-1)

Starluck(IRE), a high-class hurdler, had questions to answer after blundering his chance away when sent off at 2-5 at Sandown last month. He had been given a couple of sessions with Yogi Breisner in the meantime but, despite that, his jumping flaws were again there for all to see, especially over a couple on the far side, and he was a beaten horse three out. It looks a case of back to the drawing board with him. (op 11-2)

Gilbarry(IRE), not seen since finishing third behind Dan Breen at Bangor in December and 7lb better off, needed to improve plenty in order to be competitive here and found it all too much. (op 28-1 tchd 20-1)

5198 JOHN SMITH'S AINTREE HURDLE GRADE 1 (11 hdls) 2m 4f

2:50 (2:50) (Class 1) 4-Y-0+

£90,432 (£34,096; £17,040; £8,512; £4,272; £2,128)

Form RPR

-113 **1** **Oscar Whisky (IRE)**[25] 4791 6-11-7 165.......................... BarryGeraghty 165
(Nicky Henderson) *lw: chsd ldr: led 7th: styd on strly fr 3 out: 3 l ahd last: jst hld on* **6/1**[3]

-434 **2** *nk* **Thousand Stars (FR)**[25] 4791 7-11-7 163............................. MsKWalsh 165
(W P Mullins, Ire) *t.k.h towards rr: hdwy appr 3 out: wnt 2nd last: styd on wl: jst hld nr fin* **16/1**

-1B5 **3** *10* **Salden Licht**[22] 4848 7-11-7 156...................................... RobertThornton 157
(Alan King) *chsd ldrs: hit 1st: wnt 2nd appr 3 out: kpt on same pce appr last* **25/1**

-311 **4** *2 1/2* **Binocular (FR)**[63] 3945 7-11-7 171... APMcCoy 156
(Nicky Henderson) *hld up in tch: effrt appr 2 out: kpt on same pce appr last* **7/4**[2]

4033 **5** *hd* **Oscar Dan Dan (IRE)**[55] 4107 9-11-7 151.............................. PCarberry 155
(Thomas Mullins, Ire) *hld up in last: mstke 5th: hdwy appr 3 out: sn wl outpcd: styd on appr last: kpt on wl towards fin* **40/1**

0-3F **6** *2 3/4* **Ronaldo Des Mottes (FR)**[28] 4727 6-11-7 149.............. TimmyMurphy 152
(David Pipe) *hld up: stdy hdwy 8th: chsng ldrs next: wknd and j.lft last* **50/1**

-112 **7** *7* **Peddlers Cross (IRE)**[25] 4791 6-11-7 170.......................... JasonMaguire 148
(Donald McCain) *trckd ldrs: effrt appr 3 out: 5th whn hit last: sn wknd* **11/8**[1]

3321 **8** *3* **Celestial Halo (IRE)**[41] 4373 7-11-7 162................................(bt) RWalsh 144
(Paul Nicholls) *led to 7th: nt fluent next: sn rdn: lost pl 3 out: sn bhd* **8/1**

4m 45.3s (-15.40) **Going Correction** -0.325s/f (Good) **8** Ran SP% **118.0**
Speed ratings (Par 117): **117,116,112,111,111 110,107,106**
toteswingers:1&2:£8.80, 1&3:£11.60, 2&3:£14.80 CSF £83.51 CT £2230.95 TOTE £6.40: £1.70, £1.60, £5.10; EX 61.30 Trifecta £1004.10 Pool: £11,280.84 - 8.31 winning units..
Owner Walters Plant Hire Ltd **Bred** Stephanie Hanly **Trained** Upper Lambourn, Berks
■ Stewards' Enquiry : Ms K Walsh six-day ban: used whip with excessive frequency in incorrect place (tbn)

FOCUS

This year's line-up looked stronger than last year's with the 2010 champion hurdler taking on the runner-up, third and fourth in this year's running of that race. The pace was sound with the time being nearly 7secs faster than the opening novice hurdle, but it produced something of a surprise result, with both the market leaders running below par. It has been rated a solid renewal, with small personal bests from the first and second. The third, fifth and sixth help set the level.

NOTEBOOK

Oscar Whisky(IRE), a progressive sort who finished third in the Champion Hurdle when today's favourite was second, was likely to appreciate the return to a flatter track and longer trip and was given a positive ride by Barry Geraghty, who was completing a hat-trick on the afternoon. After tracking the leader, he went to the front five out and set sail for home at the third-last. He soon opened up an advantage and battled on well to hold off the strong-finishing winner. He will stick to hurdles next season when he will either be aimed at the Champion Hurdle again or step up in trip for the World Hurdle.

Thousand Stars(FR) had been running well behind stable companion Hurricane Fly in Ireland and finished a good fourth behind that gelding in the Champion Hurdle, two lengths behind today's winner. Already a winner over 2m3f on good ground, he was held up off the pace and was quite keen early, but came out of the pack and, under an inspired ride, very nearly wore down the winner. He will probably go to Punchestown next. (op 14-1)

Salden Licht had put up good efforts in two big handicap hurdles since winning at Exeter in January, but was up in trip and grade. He travelled nicely off the pace before moving up on the home turn looking a distinct threat, before being left behind when the winner quickened. He is also a very capable perfomer on the Flat and could be campaigned with something like the Ebor in mind. He might go chasing in the autumn.

Binocular(FR), the champion hurdler of 2010, missed this year's race due to drugs being used to clear up an infection still being in his system. He had shown he was in good form prior to that, though, when winning the Christmas Hurdle. He had a bit to find with today's favourite on early-season form, though, and he was trying this longer trip for the first time. He was keen under restraint early but still appeared to be travelling well enough turning for home. However, after a sloppy jump and a coming together with Salden Licht three out, he had no more to offer and the impression was that he did not stay, although connections are likely to have him scoped. (op 15-8 tchd 2-1 in places)

Oscar Dan Dan(IRE) had been running well in mostly graded company since winning a Grade 2 in the autumn and had a lot to find on the official ratings. He stays further than this and, best on softer ground, it was no surprise to see him struggling early on the second circuit before running on well past beaten horses in the straight. (tchd 33-1)

Ronaldo Des Mottes(FR) had not recovered his form since finishing second in the 2010 Totesport Trophy, and was stepping up in trip with lots to find judged on official ratings. However, he travelled well off the pace and only faded when his stamina began to ebb from the second-last. He clearly has talent when everything goes right.

Peddlers Cross(IRE) sustained his first defeat when runner-up in the Champion Hurdle but was clear of the first two here in that race and had beaten Binocular earlier in the season. A winner over C&D last year, he travelled well enough in the wake of the leaders but, when his rider asked him for more on the home turn, the response was limited. It can only be assumed that his hard race at Cheltenham had left its mark. Connections must now be thinking in terms of sending him over fences next season, as he is already an Irish point winner. (op 13-8 tchd 7-4)

Celestial Halo(IRE) had been running well back over hurdles since returning from an unsuccessful spell over fences in the autumn, winning a Grade 2 at this trip on his previous start. However, after making the running he was brushed aside by the winner at the end of the back straight and dropped right away. These days he is probably happier on softer ground. (op 9-1 tchd 15-2)

5199 JOHN SMITH'S H'CAP CHASE (LISTED RACE) (19 fncs) 3m 1f

3:25 (3:25) (Class 1) 5-Y-0+

£34,206 (£12,834; £6,426; £3,204; £1,608; £804)

Form RPR

U535 **1** **Prince De Beauchene (FR)**[35] 4487 8-10-5 **138**.......... PaulGallagher(5) 143+
(Howard Johnson) *lw: in tch: hdwy 10th: led narrowly fr 12th: rdn whn hdd 2 out: led again last: drvn and hld on wl run-in* **10/1**

3321 **2** *1 1/2* **Categorical**[32] 4546 8-10-0 **128** oh1................................... JamesReveley 131
(Keith Reveley) *hld up in rr: hdwy after 4 out: chsd ldrs after 2 out: wnt 2nd run-in: kpt on* **20/1**

1303 **3** *nk* **Reve De Sivola (FR)**[25] 4790 6-10-12 **140**.........................(p) DarylJacob 145+
(Nick Williams) *trckd ldrs: hit 13th: rdn after 4 out: chal 3 out: led 2 out: j.rt and hdd last: kpt on run-in* **7/1**

1201 **4** *hd* **Tarablaze**[14] 5001 8-10-10 **138**... RichardJohnson 144+
(Philip Hobbs) *lw: midfield: hit 8th: hdwy 12th: cl up whn mstke 5 out: rdn after 3 out: kpt on* **11/2**[3]

-521 **5** *6* **Bensalem (IRE)**[25] 4790 8-11-10 **152**............................. RobertThornton 156+
(Alan King) *lw: midfield: nt fluent 12th and 13th: hdwy gng to 4 out: cl 4th whn blnd bdly 2 out: mstke last: no ex run-in* **9/2**[2]

-62F **6** *16* **Great Endeavour (IRE)**[25] 4790 7-11-6 **148**.................... TimmyMurphy 134
(David Pipe) *hld up: hdwy 12th: rdn after 5 out: sn no imp: wknd after 2 out* **4/1**[1]

P203 **7** *29* **Saphir Des Bois (FR)**[17] 4941 7-10-6 **134**.....................(p) BrianHughes 90
(Peter Bowen) *w ldr: led appr 8th: hdd 11th: lost pl whn hit 3 out: sn wknd* **50/1**

244F **U** **Take The Breeze (FR)**[35] 4487 8-11-5 **147**................................. RWalsh —
(Paul Nicholls) *hld up: bdly hmpd and uns rdr 2nd* **12/1**

36UF **P** **Just Smudge**[23] 4820 9-10-0 **128** oh7.................................. AidanColeman —
(Venetia Williams) *hld up: bhd fr 10th: p.u bef 12th* **50/1**

3110 **P** **Silmi**[161] 2084 7-10-3 **131**.. PaulMoloney —
(Sophie Leech) *hld up: bdly hmpd 2nd: sn bhd: mstke 7th and 9th: t.o whn p.u bef 13th* **33/1**

-01P **U** **Rare Bob (IRE)**[25] 4790 9-11-4 **151**..........................(tp) BryanJCooper(5) 157
(D T Hughes, Ire) *led tl 2nd: w ldr: led briefly again 11th: blnd 14th: chalng whn blnd and uns rdr 2 out* **12/1**

6140 **U** **Carrickmines (IRE)**[25] 4790 9-10-0 **128** oh2.................(b) PaddyBrennan —
(Dr Richard Newland) *w ldr: led 2nd tl 8th: reminders and lost pl 10th: blnd and uns rdr next* **40/1**

P/15 **U** **Crescent Island (IRE)**[42] 4352 8-10-13 **141**.......... SamTwiston-Davies —
(Nigel Twiston-Davies) *trckd ldrs: blnd and uns rdr 2nd* **25/1**

0140 **P** **Hey Big Spender (IRE)**[23] 4818 8-11-12 **154**.................. JoeTizzard —
(Colin Tizzard) *hld up: bdly hmpd 2nd: mstke next and sn lost tch: t.o whn p.u bef 6th* **14/1**

1132 **P** **Invisible Man (FR)**[17] 4941 6-9-13 **132**..........................(t) MrRMahon(5) —
(Ian Williams) *midfield: rdn and wknd after 5 out: bhd whn p.u bef 2 out* **10/1**

6m 24.3s (-5.70) **Going Correction** +0.05s/f (Yiel) **15** Ran SP% **124.2**
Speed ratings: **111,110,110,110,108 103,94,—,—,— —,—,—,—,—**
toteswingers:1&2:£2.90, 1&3:£2.90, 2&3:£3.30 CSF £196.34 CT £1505.79 TOTE £17.60: £4.00, £5.60, £3.00; EX 277.50 Trifecta £1659.20 Pool: £3,527.05 - 1.57 winning units..
Owner Andrea & Graham Wylie **Bred** Raymond Bellanger **Trained** Billy Row, Co Durham

FOCUS
A fiercely competitive staying handicap chase with Carrickmines and Saphir Des Bois making sure there was no hanging about. The size of the field was virtually reduced by four when Crescent Island came down at the second fence, badly hampering Take The Breeze, whose rider Ruby Walsh was knocked out of the saddle, and also seriously inconveniencing Hey Big Spender, who was pulled up a couple of fences later, and Silmi. The winner was well in based on his best form on softer ground, while there's a case for thinking the third, fourth or fifth might have won but for errors/being hampered.

NOTEBOOK
Prince De Beauchene(FR) had shown all his very best previous form on soft ground over shorter trips, so these conditions were an obvious question mark. In front with a circuit left, he looked sure to finish second when Reve De Sivola headed him between the last two fences, but he rallied splendidly and removed any doubts over his stamina or his ability to handle a sound surface. His rider continues to impress. (op 12-1)
Categorical had no problem with these conditions, but a 3lb rise for his recent Newcastle win left him on a career-high mark. Given a patient ride, he stayed on strongly up the far rail over the last three fences to just snatch second and could be a Scottish National type in the future. (op 16-1)
Reve De Sivola(FR), who only made his chasing debut in November, was entitled to finish much closer to Bensalem than at Cheltenham last month on 9lb better terms, but he hadn't looked the most natural of jumpers. His jumping stood up this time and he looked to have done everything right when taking over in front between the last two fences, but he jumped violently out to his right at the last and basically threw it away. (op 8-1)
Tarablaze had won a couple of novice chases this season and was having just his fifth start over fences on this handicap debut. He travelled well behind the leaders and had every chance over the last couple of fences, but lacked a killer punch. His best days are still ahead of him. (op 15-2)
Bensalem(IRE) was 9lb higher than when winning the Grade 3 handicap chase over 3m at the festival last month though the runner-up Carole's Legacy didn't let the form down in the Totesport Bowl here on Thursday. Unfortunately he didn't help himself with some less-than-fluent jumping and, although he would have finished closer had Reve De Sivola not jumped across him at the last, he wouldn't have won. (tchd 5-1)
Great Endeavour(IRE) just looked to be getting the worst of it when falling two out in Bensalem's race at the festival. He was being ridden along at various stages on the final circuit here and is still to truly prove himself over this far. (op 7-2 tchd 100-30)
Rare Bob(IRE), 4lb higher than when third in this last year, went off far too fast when eventually pulled up behind Bensalem at the festival. With cheekpieces and a first-time tongue tie replacing the blinkers here, he made mistakes at crucial stages, and another one at the second-last when still bang there proved one too many. (op 16-1)
Hey Big Spender(IRE) Official explanation: jockey said gelding was hampered in running; vet said gelding finished lame (op 16-1)

5200 JOHN SMITH'S GRAND NATIONAL CHASE (H'CAP) GRADE 3 (28 fncs 2 omitted) 4m 4f

4:15 (4:18) (Class 1) 6-Y-0+

£535,135 (£201,590; £100,890; £50,445; £25,270; £12,635)

Form				RPR
-112	1		**Ballabriggs (IRE)**[35] 4474 10-11-0 **150** ... JasonMaguire (Donald McCain) *lw: w ldrs: led 3rd: hdd next: led 15th (Chair): blnd and hdd 6 out (2nd Valentine's): led next: styd on wl run-in* **14/1**	164
12-3	2	2 1/4	**Oscar Time (IRE)**[45] 4298 10-10-9 **145** ... MrSWaley-Cohen (M M Lynch, Ire) *trckd ldrs: chsd wnr after 2 out: chalng elbow: kpt on same pce* **14/1**	156
P000	3	12	**Don't Push It (IRE)**[23] 4817 11-11-10 **160** ... APMcCoy (Jonjo O'Neill) *mid-div: hdwy 6 out (Valentine's) hit 3 out: 5th next: styd on to take modest 3rd elbow* **9/1**[2]	162
/P3-	4	2	**State Of Play**[364] 5127 11-10-6 **142** ... PaulMoloney (Evan Williams) *chsd ldrs to 13th: outpcd 8 out (2nd Foinavon): hdwy appr 2 out: modest 7th last: styd on wl to take 4th last 100yds* **28/1**	142
-F50	5	7	**Niche Market (IRE)**[35] 4487 10-10-13 **149** ... HarrySkelton (Paul Nicholls) *trckd ldrs: lft in ld 6 out (2nd Valentine's) hdd next: wknd appr elbow* **16/1**	142
3-21	6	4	**The Midnight Club (IRE)**[45] 4298 10-10-13 **149** ... RWalsh (W P Mullins, Ire) *lw: trckd ldrs: blnd 3rd: struggling whn badly hmpd 4 out: kpt on fr 2 out* **15/2**[1]	143+
2F44	7	13	**Big Fella Thanks**[35] 4487 9-11-1 **151** ... GrahamLee (Ferdy Murphy) *hld up towards rr: hdwy whn bdly hmpd bnd after 16th (water): gd hdwy 4 out: trcking ldrs 2 out: 3rd last: wknd bdly elbow* **12/1**[3]	134+
11/0	8	hd	**Surface To Air**[27] 4742 10-10-4 **140** ... TomMessenger (Chris Bealby) *s.s: hdwy to chse ldrs 3rd: wknd 3 out* **100/1**	116
-011	9	19	**Skippers Brig (IRE)**[35] 4474 10-10-2 **138** ... DominicElsworth (Nicky Richards) *hld up in mid-div: hdwy 6 out (2nd Valentine's): hmpd 4 out: wknd bef 2 out* **33/1**	109+
UP-0	10	8	**Backstage (FR)**[34] 9-10-12 **148** ... (t) PCarberry (Gordon Elliott, Ire) *in rr: blnd 9 out: nvr on terms* **16/1**	100
11P5	11	1/2	**King Fontaine (IRE)**[25] 4790 8-10-6 **142** ... DenisO'Regan (Malcolm Jefferson) *lw: in rr: badly hmpd 6th (1st Becher's) bhd fr 13th* **80/1**	94
-001	12	25	**Silver By Nature**[49] 4208 9-10-12 **148** ... PeterBuchanan (Lucinda Russell) *towards rr: hmpd 13th: hdwy and mid-div 15th (Chair): lost pl 17th: sn bhd* **9/1**[2]	77
66U-	13	5	**In Compliance (IRE)**[20] 4906 11-10-5 **141** ... (p) LeightonAspell (D T Hughes, Ire) *hld up in rr: badly hmpd 2nd: mstke 15th (Chair): stdy hdwy 8 out (2nd Foinavon): wknd 4 out* **66/1**	66
1-46	14	8	**Bluesea Cracker (IRE)**[45] 4298 9-10-4 **140** ... AndrewJMcNamara (J Motherway, Ire) *rr-div: nvr on terms* **25/1**	57
0563	15	16	**Character Building (IRE)**[35] 4466 11-10-4 **140** ... MissNCarberry (John Quinn) *in rr: bhd whn bdly hmpd 6th (1st Becher's): t.o fr 17th* **25/1**	43
/F-0	16	12	**Golden Kite (IRE)**[27] 4762 9-10-2 **138** ... SJHassett (Adrian Maguire, Ire) *chsd ldrs to 5th: lost pl and blnd 12th: bhd after* **66/1**	30
053F	17	30	**Chief Dan George (IRE)**[25] 4790 11-10-12 **148** ... (p) PaddyAspell (James Moffatt) *in rr: bhd fr 9 out* **40/1**	13
-42P	18	20	**Royal Rosa (FR)**[91] 3437 12-10-3 **139** ... (p) PaulGallagher (Howard Johnson) *in rr: bhd 7 out (2nd Canal Turn)* **100/1**	—
34PP	19	46	**Piraya (FR)**[23] 4820 8-10-4 **140** ... (tp) JohnnyFarrelly (David Pipe) *in rr: sn wl bhd: t.o 17th* **100/1**	—
-524	P		**What A Friend**[22] 4850 8-11-6 **156** ... (b) DarylJacob (Paul Nicholls) *in rr-div: sme hdwy 17th: hit next: lost pl 19th: bhd fr 6 out (Valentine's): p.u bef 4 out* **12/1**[3]	—
P-1P	P		**Hello Bud (IRE)**[84] 3568 13-10-5 **141** ... (t) SamTwiston-Davies (Nigel Twiston-Davies) *led to 3rd: wknd 19th: bhd whn mstke 3 out: t.o whn p.u bef next* **20/1**	—
-06P	P		**Comply Or Die (IRE)**[42] 4360 12-10-8 **144** ... (b) TimmyMurphy (David Pipe) *in rr: bhd fr 7 out (2nd Canal Turn): lost tch 4 out: t.o whn p.u bef 2 out* **25/1**	—
0010	P		**Santa's Son (IRE)**[22] 4853 11-10-5 **141** ... (t) JamieMoore (Howard Johnson) *led 4th: hdd 10th: led 13th: mstke and hdd 15th (Chair): wknd 5 out: p.u bef next* **100/1**	—
1050	F		**That's Rhythm (FR)**[120] 2871 11-10-4 **140** ... JamesReveley (Martin Todhunter) *s.s: bhd whn fell 1st* **50/1**	—
-004	B		**Vic Venturi (IRE)**[23] 4837 11-11-6 **156** ... (p) AELynch (D T Hughes, Ire) *trckd ldrs: b.d 2nd* **50/1**	—
P/52	F		**Ornais (FR)**[36] 4463 9-10-4 **140** ... (t) NickScholfield (Paul Nicholls) *in rr: fell 4th: fatally injured* **100/1**	—
6/31	U		**Majestic Concorde (IRE)**[101] 3206 8-11-5 **155** ... MrRPMcNamara (D K Weld, Ire) *t.k.h: sn trcking ldrs: led 10th: hdd 13th: losing pl whn mstke and uns rdr 7 out (2nd Canal Turn)* **20/1**	—
F04/	F		**Or Noir De Somoza (FR)**[76] 9-11-5 **155** ... (tp) BarryGeraghty (David Pipe) *mid-div: fell 6th (1st Becher's)* **50/1**	—
P10P	F		**Grand Slam Hero (IRE)**[63] 3940 10-10-7 **143** ... (t) AidanColeman (Nigel Twiston-Davies) *mid-div: fell 13th* **66/1**	—
3226	U		**Tidal Bay (IRE)**[22] 4850 10-11-9 **159** ... BrianHughes (Howard Johnson) *rr-div: blnd and uns rdr 10th* **28/1**	—
04-4	F		**Dooneys Gate (IRE)**[65] 3915 10-11-4 **154** ... MrPWMullins (W P Mullins, Ire) *prom: fell 6th (1st Becher's): fatally injured* **50/1**	—
U-P2	F		**Arbor Supreme (IRE)**[45] 4298 9-10-3 **139** ... DJCasey (W P Mullins, Ire) *mstks: mid-div: bhd fr 19th: fell 3 out* **20/1**	—
-244	F		**The Tother One (IRE)**[70] 3805 10-11-0 **150** ... MrRMahon (Paul Nicholls) *mid-div: fell 6th (Becher's)* **50/1**	—
52-2	F		**Becauseicouldntsee (IRE)**[101] 3206 8-10-8 **144** ... DNRussell (N F Glynn, Ire) *lw: t.k.h: trckd ldrs: fell 2nd* **16/1**	—
-11P	B		**West End Rocker (IRE)**[49] 4208 9-10-5 **141** ... RobertThornton (Alan King) *lw: mid-div: b.d 6th (1st Becher's)* **33/1**	—
0P5P	F		**Can't Buy Time (IRE)**[23] 4821 9-10-4 **140** ... RichieMcLernon (Jonjo O'Neill) *in rr: fell 18th* **33/1**	—
P-56	F		**Killyglen (IRE)**[35] 4466 9-10-10 **146** ... RMPower (S R B Crawford, Ire) *w ldrs: led 9th (1st Valentine's): hdd next: blnd 5 out: disputing 3rd and styng on whn fell next* **66/1**	—
6242	F		**Calgary Bay (IRE)**[70] 3804 8-10-10 **146** ... HaddenFrost (Henrietta Knight) *w ldrs: fell 4th* **33/1**	—
4/P	U		**Quolibet (FR)**[25] 4792 7-10-8 **144** ... (b) MPWalsh (Jonjo O'Neill) *in rr: mstke 3rd: blnd 6th (1st Becher's): blnd and uns rdr 11th* **100/1**	—
1131	P		**Quinz (FR)**[42] 4352 7-10-8 **144** ... RichardJohnson (Philip Hobbs) *chsd ldrs: blnd 9th (1st Valentine's): sn lost pl: t.o whn p.u bef 16th (water): b.b.v* **14/1**	—

9m 1.20s (-19.30) **Going Correction** -0.20s/f (Good) **40** Ran SP% **154.7**
Speed ratings: **113,112,109,109,107 106,104,104,99,98 97,92,91,89,85 83,76,72,61,—**
—,—,—,—,—
toteswingers:1&2:£48.40, 1&3:£34.70, 2&3:£27.20 CSF £181.25 CT £1934.42 TOTE £14.50: £3.80, £3.50, £3.90, £7.30; EX 225.30 Trifecta £4686.20 Pool: £126,584.67 - 19.98 winning units..
Owner Trevor Hemmings **Bred** Mrs S L Jackson **Trained** Cholmondeley, Cheshire
■ Stewards' Enquiry : Jason Maguire five-day ban: used whip with excessive frequency (Apr 23-27)

FOCUS
The ground had been drying out all week and only limited watering was possible overnight, causing the ground to ride on the quick side and the time was fast. For the first time, fences were bypassed in this race, the 20th and 22nd, which was due to be Becher's second time. Very few got into the race having been held up. The winner has been rated 10lb higher than for last season's Cheltenham win, with the second another rated as being on the upgrade. The third has been rated 5lb off last season's winning mark, with the fourth 4lb up on last season's mark when third in this race.

NOTEBOOK
Ballabriggs(IRE), who was in front jumping the water, kept galloping to score in really game fashion, enabling Donald McCain to emulate his father Ginger in winning the race. A progressive chaser who won the Kim Muir at the 2010 festival off top weight, he had won twice over hurdles this season before being beaten by Skipper's Brig on his return to chasing. He really took well to the fences and was in the firing line throughout, only losing the lead on the second circuit when making a mistake and pecking at Valentine's second time. He was in front again soon after though and battled on gamely having been there to be shot at all the way up the straight. Unsurprisingly, he was exhausted after the race and was quickly dismounted, but will no doubt be given plenty of time to recover. (op 16-1)
Oscar Time(IRE), who is only medium-sized, was 4lb better off with The Midnight Club compared with their running in the Bobbyjo Chase last time, and had shown all his form on soft ground. Never far away, he came to challenge in the straight but could never get by and was always being held from the elbow. (op 12-1)
Don't Push It(IRE), last year's winner, had been campaigned over hurdles since, but was 7lb higher than for last year's win. He was soon chasing the leaders and responded well to pressure after three out, but had no more to give from the next. (op 11-1 tchd 12-1 in places)
State Of Play was having only his fourth run since December 2008, although two of the previous three were in this race, finishing third last year (his sole start of the season) and fourth in 2009. Racing off 3lb lower than last year, he was out the back early and still only ninth jumping the last, but ran on really well to again make the frame. This was a fine feat of training of a fragile but talented stayer.
Niche Market(IRE), pulled up in this last year, won the 2009 Irish Grand National on good ground. He was another who was always in the front rank and only tired going to the second-last. (op 20-1)
The Midnight Club(IRE), who favourite for this on the strength of his win over Arbor Supreme in a Grade 2 at Fairyhouse, was never far behind the leaders but made errors and was nearly stopped in his tracks by the fall of his old rival four out. He did well to keep going let alone run on again for sixth, and looks one of the most likely to improve on this performance if returning next season. (op 9-1 tchd 7-1)
Big Fella Thanks, sixth in 2009 and fourth last season when his stamina appeared to ebb away quickly in the closing stages, was running for different connections. Given a superb ride by Graham Lee, he gradually crept into contention turning for home. However, just as last year, he was legless on the run-in, losing several places having jumped the last in third. (op 16-1)
Surface To Air had endured a long absence since completing a hat-trick back in 2008 until finishing well beaten on his return last month. He was rather slowly away but was soon chasing the leaders and had his chance before fading over the last two.
Skippers Brig(IRE) beat Ballabriggs last time and was 8lb better off here. He ran well for a long way without ever looking as if he might win but appeared to pull up rather sore, and it is to be hoped he soon recovers.
Backstage(FR), who unseated at the 20th last year, had won two points this year. He was held up towards the rear and never got into contention. (tchd 18-1)
King Fontaine(IRE) won four successive races in 2010 on good and easy ground but finished fifth last time out in a 3m handicap at the festival when making a number of mistakes. He was out the back for a long way following an early mistake and being hampered at Bechers, but did run on past beaten horses in the straight.
Silver By Nature, an impressive winner of the totesport Grand National Trial at Haydock on his previous start, relishes heavy going. He was always struggling to go the pace and was hampered by the fall of Grand Slam Hero at the 13th. He can be expected to do better if he gets his ground here next season. (op 11-1 tchd 12-1)

In Compliance(IRE) had shown all his winning form at shorter and finished sixth in the Topham last season. He made headway on the second circuit before tiring from the fourth-last.
Bluesea Cracker(IRE) won the Irish Grand National last season from Oscar Time, but most of her form has been on testing ground. She was always towards the rear but is another who can fare better if she gets a softer surface next year. (op 20-1)
Character Building(IRE), seventh in this last year under this rider, encountered trouble in running racing towards the rear and was unable to make an impact.
Golden Kite(IRE), who likes good and fast ground, made several bad errors and it is to his credit that he managed to complete at all.
What A Friend finished fourth in the Gold Cup in first-time blinkers last time. Reasonably treated compared with his normal BHA rating, he travelled well enough in the pack, but got tired from Becher's second time and was sensibly pulled up before the last ditch. (op 33-1 tchd 40-1 in places)
Comply Or Die(IRE), the 2008 winner, gradually got further behind and his rider sensibly did not ask him to jump the last two. (op 33-1 tchd 40-1 in places)
Santa's Son(IRE) had had only one run over fences in the last year. However, he jumped well with the leaders for a circuit and a half before tiring. (op 33-1 tchd 40-1 in places)
Majestic Concorde(IRE) showed up well for a circuit, but had dropped back a little when making a mistake at the Canal Turn second time, unshipping his rider. (op 33-1 tchd 40-1 in places)
Tidal Bay(IRE), runner-up in the Grade 1 Betfair Chase and a Grade 2 this season, was racing over the big fences for the first time, but made a mistake at the tenth which gave his jockey no chance. (op 33-1 tchd 40-1 in places)
Becauseicouldntsee(IRE), who has plenty of size about him, came down early, but remains a very promising staying chaser. (op 33-1 tchd 40-1 in places)
Killyglen(IRE) looked one of the unluckiest in the race. He was always in the leading group and still appeared to be going well enough when departing at the last ditch. (op 33-1 tchd 40-1 in places)
Quinz(FR) showed up early but was pulled up before the Chair. His rider reported that the gelding had burst a blood-vessel. Official explanation: jockey said gelding pulled up distressed (op 33-1 tchd 40-1 in places)

5201 JOHN SMITH'S H'CAP HURDLE (FOR CONDITIONAL JOCKEYS AND AMATEUR RIDERS) (9 hdls) — 2m 110y

5:00 (5:00) (Class 2) 4-Y-0+

£25,048 (£7,400; £3,700; £1,852; £924; £464)

Form — RPR

-000 **1** **Far Away So Close (IRE)**[25] 4788 6-9-10 **130**.................. MNDoran(7) 146+
(Paul Nolan, Ire) *racd keenly: trckd ldrs: hdwy to ld 5th: rdn whn hdd after 2 out: kpt on wl u.str.p to ld again nr fin* **14/1**

4 **2** *nk* **Jack Cool (IRE)**[6] 5138 5-10-4 **136** 5ex..............................(p) APHeskin(5) 151
(C Byrnes, Ire) *lw: prom: chal 2 out: sn led narrowly: drvn and kpt on run-in: hdd towards fin* **7/1**[2]

0212 **3** *14* **Via Galilei (IRE)**[28] 4727 6-10-4 **136**........................ JoshuaMoore(5) 138
(Gary Moore) *hld up in midfield: hdwy gng to 3 out: rdn 2 out: kpt on yo 3rd run-in: no threat to ldng pair* **7/1**[2]

6/ **4** *3 ¼* **Total Excitement (IRE)**[20] 4903 9-9-13 **131**..............(p) BryanJCooper(5) 131
(Thomas Cooper, Ire) *hld up: midfield 3rd: hdwy 4 out: rdn 3 out: kpt on: nvr threatened ldrs* **40/1**

1503 **5** *¾* **Nearby**[22] 4848 7-11-5 **153**.. ChrisDavies(7) 151
(Philip Hobbs) *lw: midfield: hdwy 4 out: rdn 3 out: kpt on same pce* **14/1**

-500 **6** *½* **Conquisto**[48] 4235 6-10-4 **131**.. MsKWalsh 129
(Steve Gollings) *midfield on inner: rdn gng to 3 out: kpt on same pce* **66/1**

2466 **7** *1* **Eradicate (IRE)**[28] 4727 7-10-12 **142**................................. DavidBass(3) 140
(Nicky Henderson) *in tch: chsd ldrs whn nt fluent 4 out: sn pushed along: one pce after 3 out* **14/1**

0651 **8** *1* **Gifted Leader (USA)**[8] 5102 6-10-0 **130**.................(v) MichaelMurphy(3) 126
(Ian Williams) *midfield on outer: hdwy appr 4 out: rdn 3 out: one pce* **40/1**

111- **9** *hd* **Orzare (IRE)**[418] 4077 5-9-7 **130**................................ JosephAkehurst(10) 126
(Gary Moore) *hld up: sme hdwy gng to 3 out: sn rdn: kpt on: nvr threatened* **33/1**

0022 **10** *3 ¾* **Amazing King (IRE)**[22] 4858 7-10-1 **128**................ SamTwiston-Davies 121
(Philip Kirby) *trckd ldrs: lost pl 3rd: hdwy gng to 3 out: no imp after 2 out* **20/1**

P **11** *7* **Gorge (AUS)**[42] 4358 9-9-10 **130**..(t) MrJHamer(7) 116
(Anthony Cosgriff) *hld up in rr: sme hdwy 4 out: rdn bef next: sn no imp* **100/1**

234 **12** *1* **Plan A (IRE)**[24] 4807 4-10-0 **133** oh1..............................(t) MissNCarberry 115
(Gordon Elliott, Ire) *hld up in rr: nt fluent 4th: hdwy gng to 3 out: hit 3 out: no further imp fr 2 out* **7/2**[1]

-230 **13** *½* **Tito Bustillo (FR)**[28] 4727 6-10-3 **135**................................ MrRMahon(5) 120
(Paul Nicholls) *midfield on outer: rdn appr 3 out: no imp* **33/1**

162U **14** *3* **Praxiteles (IRE)**[22] 4848 7-9-9 **127**..........................(t) AodhaganConlon(5) 109
(Rebecca Curtis) *prom towards outer: rdn 3 out: stl 3rd 2 out: wknd sn after* **25/1**

2010 **15** *5* **Caught By Witness (IRE)**[50] 4180 6-9-7 **127** oh2..........(t) MrTGarner(7) 105
(Milton Harris) *midfield: rdn after 4 out: hit 3 out: wknd after 2 out* **100/1**

-B00 **16** *nse* **Caravel (IRE)**[28] 4727 7-9-9 **127**...................................... PaulGallagher(5) 105
(Howard Johnson) *hld up: rdn 3 out: n.d* **20/1**

411F **17** *2 ½* **Ciceron (IRE)**[22] 4848 5-10-3 **137**................................. HarryChalloner(7) 112
(Venetia Williams) *hld up: rdn after 3 out: sn no imp* **40/1**

3141 **18** *10* **Alazan (IRE)**[168] 1311 5-9-13 **129**................................ CPGeoghegan(3) 95
(Philip Hobbs) *hld up in midfield: hit 4 out: rdn bef 3 out: wknd after 2 out* **7/1**[2]

1240 **19** *¾* **Hibiki (IRE)**[120] 2868 7-9-8 **128**..(p) MrMEnnis(7) 94
(Sarah Humphrey) *hld up: a towards rr* **100/1**

30F4 **20** *1 ¼* **Lucaindubai (IRE)**[28] 4727 5-9-7 **127** oh2......................... MrJEngland(7) 92
(Evan Williams) *led: hdd whn nt fluent 5th: wknd after 2 out* **8/1**[3]

5035 **P** **Ultimate**[28] 4727 5-10-2 **129**.. RichieMcLernon —
(Brian Ellison) *w ldr: rdn and wknd after 4 out: p.u bef 3 out* **14/1**

3m 50.8s (-15.40) **Going Correction** -0.325s/f (Good)
WFA 4 from 5yo+ 5lb — **21** Ran SP% **129.0**
Speed ratings (Par 109): **123,122,116,114,114 114,113,113,113,111 108,107,107,105,103 103,102,97,97,96** —
toteswingers:1&2:£200.60, 1&3:£71.60, 2&3:£24.80 CSF £101.77 CT £769.57 TOTE £22.40: £5.10, £1.70, £1.90, £5.60; EX 247.70 Trifecta £1608.60 Part won. Pool: £2,173.88 - 0.44 winning units..
Owner Gigginstown House Stud **Bred** B Higgins **Trained** Enniscorthy, Co. Wexford
■ Stewards' Enquiry : M N Doran seven-day ban: used whip with excessive frequency (Apr 23-29)

FOCUS

A big field for this competitive handicap hurdle and they went an unrelenting gallop. The front pair, who pulled a long way clear at the line, were always close to the pace. The race provided a 1-2-4 for Ireland. Those placed fourth down to ninth have been rated close to their marks and the form looks pretty solid.

NOTEBOOK

Far Away So Close(IRE)'s last two starts had been in Grade 1 novice company and he found this easier. Taking quite a grip early on, he had carted himself to the front at halfway but a mistake two from home looked as though it might cost him dear. However, when it came down to a battle on the run-in he proved that much more determined.
Jack Cool(IRE), winner of three of his previous four starts, had a 5lb penalty to carry for his Limerick success six days earlier. Despite the application of cheekpieces, he spent plenty of time looking around at the scenery during the race, but appeared to have been presented with the race at the second-last. However, he didn't do a lot once in front and was worried out of it on the run-in. (op 10-1 tchd 6-1)
Via Galilei(IRE), shoved up 7lb after finishing second in the Imperial Cup, looked a possible player when moving into contention on the home bend, but could make no impression on the front pair. (op 9-2)
Total Excitement(IRE) travelled into the race like a dream turning for home, but didn't find as much off the bridle as looked likely. It may be no coincidence that he gained his only win over hurdles in August 2009. (op 50-1)
Nearby tried to get into it from the home bend, but couldn't land a blow. He was put up 4lb after finishing third in the County Hurdle and now finds himself off a career-high mark as a result. (op 12-1)
Conquisto had the ground in his favour and was entitled to need his most recent start when returning from a seven-month absence. This was another step forward and he could be the type for a race like the Swinton.
Eradicate(IRE) should have found the ground coming in his favour, but he is 10lb higher now and looks held.
Gifted Leader(USA) wasn't disgraced considering he was seriously off the bridle a fair way out, but he was put up 15lb for winning in the first-time visor at Stratford eight days earlier, so will need to improve plenty.
Orzare(IRE), not seen since going a perfect 3-3 in novice hurdles more than a year ago, couldn't get involved and could have done without the ground drying out.
Plan A(IRE), the only 4-y-o in the field and completely unexposed, ran a fine race to finish fourth in the Fred Winter (even though he was the beaten favourite) but he didn't look happy in last place from an early stage on this occasion and was never in the race. (op 5-1 tchd 11-2 in a place)
Alazan(IRE) looked fit enough, but never featured. (op 5-1)

5202 JOHN SMITH'S CHAMPION STANDARD OPEN NATIONAL HUNT FLAT RACE GRADE 2 — 2m 1f

5:35 (5:35) (Class 1) 4-6-Y-0

£17,103 (£6,417; £3,213; £1,602; £804; £402)

Form — RPR

1 **Steps To Freedom (IRE)**[279] 900 5-11-4 0.......................(t) PCarberry 130+
(Gordon Elliott, Ire) *hld up in rr: smooth hdwy 4f out: chal on bit wl over 1f out: rdn to ld appr fnl f: sn hung lft and kpt on wl* **12/1**

21 **2** *2* **Montbazon (FR)**[25] 4408 4-10-12 0................................ RobertThornton 122+
(Alan King) *hld up: smooth hdwy to trck ldrs over 4f out: effrt to chal 2f out: ev ch tl rdn and one pce ins fnl f* **5/2**[1]

3 *8* **Allure Of Illusion (IRE)**[233] 1307 5-11-4 0..................(t) MrPWMullins 120
(W P Mullins, Ire) *hld up: hdwy on outer 4f out: chsd ldrs over 2f out: rdn and ev ch over 1f out: sn one pce* **9/2**[2]

132 **4** *1 ½* **Matthew Riley (IRE)**[25] 4801 4-10-12 0.......................... RichieMcGrath 112
(Kate Walton) *trckd ldrs: effrt over 3f out: rdn along over 2f out: n.m.r and swtchd lft over 1f out: kpt on u.p fnl f* **40/1**

2110 **5** *¾* **Saint Luke (IRE)**[24] 4808 6-11-4 0.................................... AidanColeman 117
(Peter Bowen) *midfield: hdwy on outer to trck ldrs over 6f out: effrt to chal 3f out: rdn to ld 2f out: drvn and hdd over 1f out: one pce* **33/1**

1 **6** *nk* **Broadbackbob (IRE)**[86] 3525 6-10-13 0.............. MrStevenCrawford(5) 119+
(S R B Crawford, Ire) *lengthy: hld up and bhd: hdwy over 3f out: swtchd rt to outer 2f out: sn rdn and kpt on: nrst fin* **66/1**

1 **7** *¾* **Jonny Delta**[28] 4717 4-10-12 0.. JamesReveley 110
(Jim Goldie) *hld up and bhd: hdwy over 3f out: rdn to chse ldrs 2f out: sn drvn and no imp* **28/1**

13 **8** *2 ¾* **Ebanour (IRE)**[17] 4943 4-10-12 0....................................(t) TimmyMurphy 107
(Donald McCain) *hld up in rr: rdn along and green over 4f out: kpt on u.p fnl 2f: nvr nr ldrs* **66/1**

1 **9** *2* **Grandioso (IRE)**[52] 4151 4-10-7 0................................. PaulGallagher(5) 105
(Howard Johnson) *lw: hld up in midfield: rapid hdwy on outer over 3f out and sn cl up: ev ch tl rdn 2f out and sn wknd* **50/1**

1125 **10** *½* **Cinders And Ashes**[24] 4808 4-10-12 0.............................. JasonMaguire 105
(Donald McCain) *hld up in rr: hdwy 3f out: rdn along over 2f out: nvr nr ldrs* **8/1**

10 **11** *1* **Oscar Magic (IRE)**[24] 4808 4-10-12 0..................... SamTwiston-Davies 104
(Nigel Twiston-Davies) *midfield: effrt 3f out: rdn along over 2f out: n.d* **12/1**

310 **12** *5* **Distime (IRE)**[36] 4457 5-10-13 0.................................. BryanJCooper(5) 105
(John Quinn) *cl up: rdn along over 3f out: drvn wl over 2f out and grad wknd* **100/1**

1-3 **13** *5* **Nuts N Bolts**[36] 4457 5-11-4 0.. BarryKeniry 100
(Alan Swinbank) *hld up towards rr: hdwy and in tch 1/2-way: rdn along over 3f out and grad wknd* **10/1**

13 **14** *9* **Persian Snow (IRE)**[49] 4204 5-11-4 0..........................(t) RichardJohnson 91
(Philip Hobbs) *athletic: hld up towards rr: effrt and sme hdwy 3f out: sn rdn and nvr a factor* **7/1**[3]

21 **15** *½* **Richie Rob**[47] 4259 5-10-13 0... BrianToomey(5) 90
(Neville Bycroft) *in tch to 1/2-way: sn outpcd* **40/1**

12 **16** *3 ¼* **Tour D'Argent (FR)**[42] 4356 4-10-12 0................................. BarryGeraghty 81
(Nicky Henderson) *chsd ldrs: rdn along over 5f out: wknd 4f out* **14/1**

1- **17** *4* **Gallox Bridge**[426] 3915 6-11-4 0....................................(t) WarrenMarston 86
(Milton Harris) *lengthy: trckd ldrs on inner: rdn along whn n.m.r 5f out: sn wknd* **100/1**

13 **18** *14* **Peckhamecho (IRE)**[50] 4191 5-11-4 0..................................... APMcCoy 69
(Rebecca Curtis) *lw: cl up on inner: rdn along to ld briefly over 3f out: sn hdd: drvn and wknd fr over 2f out* **25/1**

0-3 **19** *14* **Real Tempo (FR)**[57] 4055 6-10-11 0.......................... TayronDevolder(7) 55
(J-M Plasschaert, Belgium) *t.k.h: sn led: rdn along over 5f out: hdd over 3f out and wknd qckly* **40/1**

6-12 **20** *27* **Laveroque (FR)**[146] 2389 5-11-4 0.. FelixDeGiles 28
(Charlie Longsdon) *athletic: midfield: rdn along along over 4f out: sn lost pl and bhd* **20/1**

3m 59.5s (-7.90) **Going Correction** -0.325s/f (Good)
WFA 4 from 5yo+ 5lb — **20** Ran SP% **130.7**
Speed ratings: **105,104,100,99,99 99,98,97,96,96 95,93,91,86,86 85,83,76,70,57**
toteswingers: 1&2:£9.70, 1&3:£20.90, 2&3:£3.70; totesuper7: Win: Not won. Place: £1,315.18 CSF £40.19 CT £238.70 TOTE £12.80: £3.70, £1.80, £2.50; EX 50.20 Trifecta £238.70 Pool: £2,052.99 - 6.36 winning units..
Owner Mrs Sean Hussey **Bred** Michael Thornton **Trained** Trim, Co Meath
■ Stewards' Enquiry : Tayron Devolder four-day ban: careless riding (Apr 23-26); one-day ban: used whip down shoulder in the forehand (Apr 27)

FOCUS
A very hot bumper with only one of these having not scored before. However, they went no pace which meant that the field remained tightly packed for a long way and several met trouble in running. The first two are undoubtedly nice prospects, but many of the beaten horses shouldn't be judged too harshly. The fourth, fifth, seventh and ninth help set the level.
NOTEBOOK
Steps To Freedom(IRE) ◆ and Montbazon arrived simultaneously with their efforts halfway up the home straight, with their respective riders sitting motionless, but with other horses between the pair they may not have seen each other. When they eventually did and were asked to quicken, it was Steps To Freedom who just found the better turn of speed. Not seen since clipping heels and falling at Bellewstown last July, he obviously has a bright future. (op 10-1)
Montbazon(FR) ◆ arguably had the best form on offer having run the subsequent Champion Bumper-winner Cheltenian close on his Kempton debut before beating a big field in a nice race at Doncaster. The way he travelled here marked him as a classy horse and he also has a big future despite this defeat. (op 9-4 tchd 3-1)
Allure Of Illusion(IRE) ◆, not seen since winning on his Killarney debut last August (form not worked out) can be rated a few lengths better than this, as he lost his place racing down the back straight and had to be taken very wide rounding the home bend in order to get back into contention. He still had every chance before his exertions started to tell and we will be hearing a lot more of him. (tchd 5-1 and 11-2 in a place)
Matthew Riley(IRE), from the stable that sent out the 66-1 winner of this race two years ago, also covered himself in glory as he fared best of those that were handy from the start. (op 50-1)
Saint Luke(IRE), winner of three bumpers and 12th in the Champion Bumper at the Festival, was bang there until entering the last 2f and ran really well, as he may prefer slower ground. (op 40-1)
Broadbackbob(IRE) ◆, who beat a subsequent winner at Catterick on his most recent start, ran an extraordinary race. Stone last starting the turn for home, he was badly hampered on the inside rounding the bend and was nearly brought down. Still with plenty to do starting up the straight, he was dramatically switched to his right 2f from home and finished with quite a flourish. Already placed in three Irish points, he is one to watch out for back over obstacles. (op 100-1)
Jonny Delta ◆ dismissed his four rivals with ease in a heavy ground bumper on his debut at Ayr last month and would have found these conditions very different, but he stayed on nicely in the latter stages having been given plenty to do and is a nice prospect for the future. (tchd 33-1)
Grandioso(IRE) ◆ ran better than his final position as he was still battling for the lead passing the 2f pole.
Distime(IRE) was another to run better than his finishing position might suggest.
Nuts N Bolts has the look of a jumper. (op 16-1)
Gallox Bridge was on his toes beforehand.
T/Jkpt: Not won. T/Plt: £574.00 to a £1 stake. Pool £451,565.59 - 574.29 winning units. T/Qpdt: £258.10 to a £1 stake. Pool £18,700.68 - 53.60 winning units. WG

4999 BANGOR-ON-DEE (L-H)
Saturday, April 9
OFFICIAL GOING: Good changing to good (good to firm in places) after race 4 (3:05)
Wind: light, across Weather: warm and sunny

5203 BET TOTEPOOL ON THE GRAND NATIONAL NOVICES' HURDLE (12 hdls) 3m
1:25 (1:25) (Class 4) 4-Y-O+ **£2,081** (£611; £305; £152)

Form				RPR
1256	1		**Tullyraine (IRE)**[51] 4159 7-11-0 132 MrWTwiston-Davies(7)	115+
			(Nigel Twiston-Davies) *chsd ldrs: rdn after 7th: ev ch 9th: drvn bef 2 out: led between last 2: styd on wl flat: rdn out* **1/1**[1]	
P52	2	5	**Areuwitmenow (IRE)**[27] 4747 6-11-1 0 AndrewTinkler	106+
			(Charlie Longsdon) *led at slow gallop tl qcknd after 2nd: blnd bdly and hdd 9th: 4th and looked wl hld bef 2 out: rallied u.p to chse wnr last: no imp flat* **13/8**[2]	
555U	3	3 ¾	**Sous Mix (FR)**[13] 5031 5-10-8 0 JakeGreenall(7)	101
			(Michael Easterby) *hld up wl in tch: hdwy to join ldrs 8th: lft in ld next: rdn bef 2 out: hdd between last 2: lost 2nd and blnd last: wknd flat* **20/1**	
-0P4	4	6	**Amroth Bay**[16] 4974 7-11-1 0 AlanO'Keeffe	95
			(Jennie Candlish) *t.k.h early: hld up in detached last trio: pushed along and effrt 8th: modest 5th bef 2 out: styd on steadily u.p fr between last 2: wnt 4th nr fin: nvr trbld ldrs* **10/1**[3]	
0330	5	hd	**Sunny Ledgend**[50] 4191 6-10-8 0 MrSWDrinkwater(7)	96
			(Andrew J Martin) *chsd ldrs: wnt 2nd after 7th: ev ch 9th: cl 3rd whn mstke next: drvn and struggling bef next: wknd 2 out* **33/1**	
-235	6	18	**Cocacobana (IRE)**[31] 4555 6-11-1 0 JodieMogford	86+
			(Graeme McPherson) *t.k.h: hld up in detached last trio: mstke 3rd: clsd and in tch 1/2-way: chsd ldrs and rdn after 3 out: wknd next* **20/1**	
000	7	43	**Go To The Edge**[10] 5077 5-10-8 0 HarryChalloner(7)	40
			(John Bryan Groucott) *nt fluent: hld up in detached last trio: rdn and struggling after 6th: wl t.o fr 9th* **100/1**	
0	8	36	**Farewell Bluebell (IRE)**[32] 4547 4-10-4 0 RichardKilloran(3)	—
			(Tim Vaughan) *chsd ldr tl mstke 8th: wknd rapidly next: wl t.o whn j.v.slowly last* **18/1**	
00/P	9	dist	**Northorsouth**[135] 2642 9-10-8 0 MrBJPoste(7)	—
			(Bill Moore) *t.k.h: in tch: mstke 1st: rdn and lost pl qckly bef 7th: wl t.o fr next: blnd 3 out* **150/1**	

5m 50.8s (-0.20) **Going Correction** -0.225s/f (Good)
WFA 4 from 5yo+ 7lb **9** Ran SP% **116.6**
Speed ratings (Par 105): **91,89,88,86,86 80,65,53,—**
toteswingers:1&2:£1.02, 1&3:£10.00, 2&3:£10.00 CSF £2.80 TOTE £2.20: £1.10, £1.70, £3.60; EX 2.60.
Owner Geoffrey & Donna Keeys **Bred** Mrs Judith Todd **Trained** Naunton, Gloucs
FOCUS
Bright and sunny conditions for this fixture on ground officially described as good but thought closer to good to firm down the back straight by Andrew Tinkler after the opener. There was no gallop early on in this moderate staying novice hurdle and several were instantly outpaced as soon as the gallop lifted with around a mile to travel. The third and sixth are the best guide to the level.
NOTEBOOK
Tullyraine(IRE) was driven into a closer position four out having not travelled especially well up to then. It was hard work ultimately and he'd not make ready appeal under a double penalty in this sphere, but a switch to chasing instead for this former Irish pointer may not be too far off in any event. (op 6-5 tchd 10-11)
Areuwitmenow(IRE)'s blunder four out lost him initiative and momentum he never fully clawed back, despite charging home again up the straight. He looks an out-and-out stayer and could pinch one of these around a Worcester or Ffos Las this summer. (tchd 15-8)
Sous Mix(FR) would have lost second position to the rallying Areuwitmenow even without nodding at the last. He hadn't convinced as the strongest finisher in bumpers and didn't here either, but he's good enough to take a small summer handicap if having the matter already settled far enough out to hold on.
Amroth Bay, as at Southwell (2m4f) last time, never threatened to get there after being raced well in rear to halfway. He remains capable of better. (op 8-1)
Sunny Ledgend's mistake came at the worst possible moment, leaving him irretrievably outpaced just as the race began in earnest, but he shaped with a little promise on this hurdling debut despite that.
Northorsouth Official explanation: trainer said gelding finished lame and bled from the nose

5204 TOTEPOOL A BETTER WAY TO BET NOVICES' CHASE (13 fncs 2 omitted) 2m 4f 110y
1:55 (1:55) (Class 3) 5-Y-O+ **£4,887** (£1,671)

Form				RPR
0111	1		**Midnight Appeal**[20] 4896 6-10-12 120 WayneHutchinson	132+
			(Alan King) *chsd ldr: hit 9th: rdn to chal 2 out: led bef last: in command whn idled last: kpt on wl flat* **1/1**[1]	
522	2	3	**Mud Monkey**[16] 4972 7-10-9 118 (t) TommyPhelan(3)	126
			(Claire Dyson) *j.rt: nt a fluent: led: rdn bef 2 out: drvn and hdd between last 2: styd on same pce after* **9/4**[2]	
1U3P	U		**Miss Sarenne (FR)**[134] 2662 6-10-5 118 AndrewTinkler	—
			(Nicky Henderson) *hld up in tch in 3rd tl blnd and uns rdr 7th* **3/1**[3]	

5m 4.40s (-4.70) **Going Correction** -0.725s/f (Firm) **3** Ran SP% **105.8**
Speed ratings: **79,77,—**
CSF £3.39 TOTE £1.80; EX 2.10.
Owner David Sewell **Bred** William Wilkinson **Trained** Barbury Castle, Wilts
FOCUS
The second in the back straight was omitted from all chases on the card. Just the three runners for this 0-120 novice chase and they were reduced to two at halfway. The second has been rated in line with his recent Southwell run.
NOTEBOOK
Midnight Appeal idled once heading and passing the long-time leader two out and made it four from four over fences with a bit up his sleeve again. He's not quite yet on the sort of mark that would guarantee him a run in something like the Summer Plate, should connections want to keep him on the go that long, but he can continue to be found opportunities at the right level with ground both firmer and softer than this no inconvenience. (op 11-10 tchd 6-5)
Mud Monkey won a juvenile hurdle around here some years back, but he races mostly right-handed nowadays and was jumping out to his right throughout this contest. He's proved pretty game and consistent when kept away from deep ground this season, though, and there is another handicap to be won with him back around a clockwise track while that remains the case. (op 11-4 tchd 3-1)
Miss Sarenne(FR) left her hind legs in the second ditch and gave Andrew Tinkler no chance. She had jumped pretty tidily up to that point, but that's not always a given with her, and she remains on balance one to tread a little carefully with over fences. (op 2-1)

5205 BET TOTEPOOL AT TOTESPORT.COM H'CAP HURDLE (12 hdls) 3m
2:25 (2:26) (Class 3) (0-120,119) 4-Y-O+ **£3,707** (£1,088; £544; £271)

Form				RPR
P01P	1		**Borero (FR)**[28] 4722 8-10-13 **113** (b) JakeGreenall(7)	114
			(Michael Easterby) *mde all: rdn between last 2: hrd pressed and hld on wl fnl 100yds: all out* **14/1**	
U602	2	½	**Crop Walker (IRE)**[21] 4869 9-10-9 **102** RichieMcGrath	103+
			(Kate Walton) *chsd wnr thrght: mstke 6th: rdn and j. awkwardly 2 out: ev ch flat: hld fnl 100yds* **9/2**[1]	
6033	3	½	**Calusa Shadow**[37] 4441 7-10-7 **100** (b[1]) TomO'Brien	101
			(Philip Hobbs) *hld up in last trio: mstke 3rd: hdwy to chse ldrs 9th: mstke next: cl 3rd last: styd on same pce flat* **6/1**[2]	
2U11	4	8	**Abstract Art (USA)**[16] 4975 8-11-5 **119** (p) PeterCarberry(7)	114
			(Rachel Hobbs) *chsd ldrs: hit 5th: rdn and struggling whn mstke 2 out: wknd bef last* **6/1**[2]	
0300	5	29	**Worth A King'S**[56] 4079 5-11-5 **112** AdrianLane	79
			(Donald McCain) *hld up in tch in midfield: dropped to rr and mstke 8th: sn lost tch: t.o bef 2 out* **14/1**	
512F	6	3 ½	**Wor Rom (IRE)**[34] 4508 7-10-6 **106** (p) MrNHalley(7)	70
			(Elliott Cooper) *in tch in midfield: rdn after 7th: 5th and btn 3 out: sn lost tch: t.o between last 2* **15/2**	
0F14	7	2 ½	**Copsehill Girl (IRE)**[38] 4418 6-10-12 **105** WillKennedy	66
			(Ian Williams) *hld up in tch in last pair: rdn and struggling after 8th: sn lost tch: t.o after 3 out* **13/2**[3]	
6PP6	8	10	**Love Of Tara**[27] 4742 9-11-1 **115** MrPMason(7)	67
			(Jennifer Mason) *chsd ldrs tl wknd rapidly bef 9th: t.o after 3 out* **9/1**	
0-4P	9	32	**Good For Blue (IRE)**[46] 4276 8-11-3 **110** TomSiddall	34
			(Richard Phillips) *hld up in tch in rr: hdwy 7th: chsd ldrs after next: wknd qckly bef 3 out: t.o bef 2 out: eased flat* **16/1**	

5m 41.3s (-9.70) **Going Correction** -0.225s/f (Good) **9** Ran SP% **101.1**
Speed ratings (Par 107): **107,106,106,104,94 93,92,89,78**
toteswingers:1&2:£0.00, 1&3:£15.80, 2&3:£2.40 CSF £60.25 CT £299.11 TOTE £14.00: £5.00, £2.30, £1.10; EX 63.80.
Owner N W A Bannister & M J R Bannister **Bred** Eric Becq **Trained** Sheriff Hutton, N Yorks
FOCUS
There was a decent pace on from flagfall. The form looks ordinary rated around the first four.
NOTEBOOK
Borero(FR) ultimately held on really gamely to record a fifth career win but first on going faster than good to soft. Jake Greenall reasoned afterwards that the intention was always to make plenty of use of the 8-y-o as he was likely to prove free in the blinkers, which were being reapplied for the first time since his final French start in November 2007. How much more there is to come may depend on this headgear inspiring him for longer than cheekpieces did two seasons earlier. Official explanation: trainer said, regarding apparent improvement in form, that the gelding was better suited by the application of the first-time blinkers. (tchd 12-1)
Crop Walker(IRE) might have worn down the determined winner without having hit the penultimate flight, but this looked another career-best effort for the nine-race maiden. He is standing his racing much better this season, and on the basis of this effort and the soft-ground Newcastle second which preceded it looks versatile enough as regards ground conditions to be placed to advantage this spring. (op 5-1 tchd 4-1)
Calusa Shadow proved amenable to first-time blinkers and was the only one to make a significant impact from the rear without ever quite looking like getting there. He can find a small opening in the coming weeks. (op 13-2 tchd 7-1)
Abstract Art(USA)'s recent gains have been in a non-handicap seller and claiming grade. He remains winless in handicap company over hurdles and, on this evidence, is too high in the weights to rectify that in the short term. (op 7-1 tchd 11-2)
Wor Rom(IRE) wasn't travelling well from some way out and defying a mark 16lb above his highest winning one may be beyond him. (op 7-1)
Copsehill Girl(IRE)'s forward move just after halfway proved pretty short-lived. (op 5-1)

5206 BET ON THE GRAND NATIONAL AT TOTESPORT.COM H'CAP CHASE (16 fncs 2 omitted) 3m 110y
3:05 (3:05) (Class 3) (0-135,130) 5-Y-O+ **£4,553** (£1,337; £668; £333)

Form				RPR
3011	1		**Garleton (IRE)**[29] 4689 10-10-8 **117** (t) AlexanderVoy(5)	134+
			(Maurice Barnes) *chsd ldrs: wnt 2nd bef 11th: led wl bef 2 out: rdn clr and in command last: eased flat: comf* **8/1**	

5-0P **2** *8* **Dom D'Orgeval (FR)**[63] 3940 11-11-1 **119**................ WayneHutchinson 128
(Nick Williams) *in tch: blnd 9th: drvn and struggling after next: rallied u.p bef 2 out: chsd clr wnr sn after last: styd on but no imp* **9/1**

5114 **3** *2* **Three Chords (IRE)**[50] 4181 7-11-8 **126**...................... AndrewThornton 129
(Caroline Bailey) *chsd ldrs: mstke 11th: chsd wnr after 3 out: mstke next: outpcd by wnr and btn between last 2: lost 2nd sn after last* **4/1**[1]

4/P2 **4** *1 1/2* **Tamadot (IRE)**[49] 4223 9-11-1 **119**...................................... TomO'Brien 127+
(Philip Hobbs) *hld up in tch in rr: mstke 7th: blnd 9th: detached last next: hdwy and nt clr after 3 out: swtchd wd and hdwy 2 out: pressing for 2nd but no ch w wnr last: no ex flat* **4/1**[1]

U344 **5** *3 3/4* **I'moncloudnine (IRE)**[50] 4193 8-11-12 **130**....................(p) WillKennedy 127
(Neil Mulholland) *in tch towards rr: reminders 1/2-way: struggling u.p 10th: rallied bef 2 out: imp between last 2* **6/1**[2]

4052 **6** *1/2* **Royal Kicks (FR)**[26] 4777 10-10-2 **109**............................ KeiranBurke(3) 109
(Suzy Smith) *mstkes: several positions: bmpd rival 5th: hdwy to chse ldrs 1/2-way: mstke and lost pl 9th: one pce and no threat to ldrs fr 3 out* **6/1**[2]

3F50 **7** *3/4* **Khachaturian (IRE)**[23] 4821 8-11-11 **129**............................ AdrianLane 127
(Donald McCain) *led: mstke 3rd: hdd and rdn sn after 3 out: wknd u.p next* **15/2**[3]

054P **8** *1 1/2* **Noun De La Thinte (FR)**[50] 4193 8-10-8 **117**..................... RTDunne(5) 112
(Venetia Williams) *chsd ldr tl 11th: 4th and struggling u.p after 3 out: wknd next* **9/1**

0305 **9** *3* **Tramantano**[119] 2881 12-11-0 **125**......................(t) MrWTwiston-Davies(7) 117
(Nigel Twiston-Davies) *bhd: bmpd rival 5th: hdwy next: 5th and unable qck whn mstke 3 out: wknd bef next* **16/1**

5m 57.1s (-22.70) **Going Correction** -0.725s/f (Firm) course record **9** Ran SP% **117.3**
Speed ratings: **107,104,103,103,102 101,101,101,100**
toteswingers:1&2:£6.70, 1&3:£21.10, 2&3:£21.10 CSF £76.73 CT £333.66 TOTE £10.10: £4.10, £4.00, £2.10; EX 270.60.

Owner East-West Partnership **Bred** Thomas And Mrs Bridget Buckley **Trained** Farlam, Cumbria

FOCUS

The feature race on the afternoon's card, but the early gallop looked just fair. The winner was value for further, while the second has been rated to his mark, and the third has been rated in line with his recent form.

NOTEBOOK

Garleton(IRE) is thriving and, having always travelled well just off the pace, powered clear up the straight to run up the hat-trick. This raises his highest winning mark by a further 6lb as well as serving a reminder that he's not entirely dependent on softer surfaces, and he may not be finished with for the time being even after reassessment. (op 7-1 tchd 13-2)

Dom D'Orgeval(FR)'s best form in 2010 was recorded during late March and April, and the same may prove to be true this term judged on this much-improved effort on his first outing for two months. He remains fabulously handicapped on the pick of his older chasing form and deserves to find another opening. (op 10-1)

Three Chords(IRE) was still close enough to land a blow on the winner turning for home but was eventually well held. This may have been slightly quicker ground than ideal, but he has it to prove after two straight defeats that the handicapper isn't on top. (op 5-1)

Tamadot(IRE) always had a bit too much to do after a couple of mistakes around halfway. (tchd 7-2)

I'moncloudnine(IRE), the Welsh National third, missed the cut in the Grand National and never threatened to gain any small compensation here, receiving reminders with a circuit to go. (op 13-2 tchd 7-1)

Royal Kicks(FR) won off just 3lb lower on his last C&D visit in October (I'moncloudnine second on 6lb worse terms that day including rider's claims), but his jumping isn't always the most assured and backers knew their fate early on after some less than convincing leaps. Official explanation: jockey said gelding hung left (op 8-1)

Khachaturian(IRE) curled up soon after being headed, and aside from one third in a jumpers' bumper has endured a most disappointing campaign. (op 8-1 tchd 17-2)

5207 BET ON TODAY'S FOOTBALL AT TOTESPORT.COM HUNTERS' CHASE (16 fncs 2 omitted) 3m 110y

3:40 (3:41) (Class 6) 6-Y-0+ **£758** (£233; £116)

Form RPR

32-2 **1** **Keenan's Future (IRE)**[18] 4928 10-11-7 115................(tp) MrJHodson(7) 127+
(Ian Williams) *hld up in tch towards rr: mstke 1st: hdwy 1/2-way: hmpd and lft 2nd 11th: upsides ldr on bit whn dived and blnd last: urged ahd flat: racd v awkwardly and drvn out fnl 100yds* **5/4**[1]

2FP6 **2** *1 1/2* **Lisadell King (IRE)**[36] 4463 11-12-1 114............................ MrJBanks(7) 129
(G C Maundrell) *chsd ldrs: j. slowly 2nd: led after 10th: rdn and jnd last: sn hdd: styd on same pce flat* **18/1**

-344 **3** *8* **Oopsmylord (IRE)**[16] 4969 9-11-7 112.............................(p) MrRJarrett(7) 118+
(S Flook) *chsd ldr tl 3rd: styd prom: hmpd and lft 3rd 11th tl after next: plugged on same pce and no imp bef 2 out: wnt 3rd again flat* **14/1**

2156 **4** *1 3/4* **It's Like That (IRE)**[17] 4937 11-12-4 110............................... MrAJBerry 119+
(Jonjo O'Neill) *hld up in last pair: j. awkwardly 1st: mstke 7th and sn pushed along: hdwy and lft 4th 11th: chsd ldng pair and rdn bef 2 out: no prog: wknd between last 2* **9/1**

01/3 **5** *10* **You Do The Math (IRE)**[18] 4928 11-11-7 0.......................... MrJSHorton(7) 109+
(William Hayes, Ire) *in tch: mstke and lost pl 8th: rallied after next: struggling whn hmpd 11th: wknd next* **9/2**[2]

0/41 **6** *29* **Locksmith**[16] 4973 11-11-11 112.......................... MrRichardCollinson(7) 81
(Mrs S J Stilgoe) *hld up in rr: hdwy into midfield 9th: wkng and in rr whn hmpd 11th: sn lost tch: t.o* **8/1**[3]

42F3 **7** *3* **Ice Bucket (IRE)**[15] 4991 11-11-7 101............................(p) MrLRPayter(7) 74
(A Phillips) *j.rt: led tl after 10th: bdly hmpd and lost pl next: sn wknd: t.o whn mstke 2 out* **14/1**

0P-0 **P** **Kalmo Bay (FR)**[13] 8-11-7 86.. MissLBrooke(7) —
(R A Owen) *t.k.h: hdwy to chse ldrs 3rd: mstke and lost pl 11th: last and wkng whn mstke 3 out: sn eased and p.u* **8/1**[3]

30P- **P** **Quentin D'Ex (FR)**[27] 7-11-11 98....................................(t) MrOGarner(7) —
(Mrs K M Diggle) *t.k.h: racd wd: chsd ldr 3rd: ev ch whn j.lft and blnd bdly 11th: sn lost pl: bhd whn eased and p.u bef 2 out: dismntd* **40/1**

6m 1.20s (-18.60) **Going Correction** -0.725s/f (Firm) **9** Ran SP% **115.9**
Speed ratings: **100,99,96,96,93 83,82,—,—**
toteswingers:1&2:£0.00, 1&3:£7.40, 2&3:£7.60 CSF £25.38 TOTE £2.00: £2.20, £2.80, £1.90; EX 41.80.

Owner Patrick Kelly **Bred** Charles Micheal Gildea **Trained** Portway, Worcs

FOCUS

The defection of Mad Victor, Fresh Air And Fun and particularly My Flora robbed this hunter chase of much of its competitiveness. In addition, Ice Bucket and Oopsmylord's chances were dealt a terminal blow at the final ditch, where Quentin D'Ex blundered badly (smashing the frame) and impeded them both. The third and fourth help set the level.

NOTEBOOK

Keenan's Future(IRE) ◆ was the winner on merit, travelling supremely well throughout and value for further than the final margin, having idled and drifted up the run-in. Clearly much of the ability which saw him place in a Summer National and Becher Chase during 2009 remains, and his proven stamina over further than this might make him one to consider for the marathon on Cheltenham's hunter chase evening, or even the Stratford Foxhunters' at the end of the hunter chase season. (op 6-4 tchd 13-8)

Lisadell King(IRE) had been jumping like a horse short on confidence in two previous starts since taking a crashing fall in last season's John Corbet Cup. A high, awkward leap at the last ditch suggests he's still not entirely over that experience, but this was still easily his most encouraging effort of 2011 and he's not for deserting just yet if building on this. (op 16-1)

Oopsmylord(IRE) could have done without the shunting four out but it's over two years now since he's won a hunter in any case. He might be worth stepping back up in trip in this sphere. (op 16-1)

It's Like That(IRE), a former C&D winner, owed his finishing position to his rider's perseverance, and he's operating some way below his best hunter-chase form of the last three years at present. (op 8-1)

You Do The Math(IRE) had run the winner to just over 3l at Exeter last time, but disappointed on this occasion, for all that he was a little short of room in the incident at the ditch. (tchd 4-1 and 5-1)

5208 BEAT THE BOOKIES WITH TOTEPOOL H'CAP HURDLE (11 hdls) 2m 4f

4:45 (4:47) (Class 4) (0-105,105) 4-Y-0+ **£2,192** (£639; £319)

Form RPR

600F **1** **Moufatango (FR)**[35] 4477 5-11-4 **97**............................... CampbellGillies 101+
(Nicky Richards) *chsd ldr: led sn after 3 out: clr next: pushed along and styd on wl flat* **9/2**[2]

F502 **2** *2 3/4* **Petit Fleur**[26] 4769 9-11-5 **98**.. WayneHutchinson 98
(Julian Smith) *hld up in rr: mstke 5th: stdy prog fr 7th: chsd wnr 2 out: swtchd rt bef last: styd on same pce flat* **17/2**

3052 **3** *6* **Diktalina**[45] 4289 5-11-9 **105**.. RichardKilloran(3) 102+
(Tim Vaughan) *in tch in midfield: rdn after 6th: chsd ldrs and mstke 3 out: no ex and btn 2 out: wknd last* **12/1**

561 **4** *7* **Winged Farasi**[16] 4960 7-11-2 **100**................. GemmaGracey-Davison(5) 88
(Joanne Foster) *hld up in tch: hdwy to chse ldrs after 7th: drvn and wknd 2 out* **17/2**

23F0 **5** *3/4* **Vin Rose**[30] 4675 6-10-4 **83**... AndrewTinkler 71
(Mark Rimell) *in tch towards rr: effrt bef 3 out: drvn and btn bef next* **12/1**

0606 **6** *6* **Peqeno Diablo (IRE)**[29] 4697 6-11-0 **100**....................... GeraldQuinn(7) 82
(Claire Dyson) *j.rt: led tl sn after 3 out: sn drvn: wknd next* **16/1**

0343 **7** *1 1/2* **Jaques Vert (FR)**[35] 4465 5-11-10 **103**................................ TomO'Brien 84
(Robert Wylie) *t.k.h: hld up in tch towards rr: hdwy after 6th: chsd ldrs gng wl bef 3 out: rdn and fnd little bef 2 out: swtchd rt and btn 2 out: wknd* **4/1**[1]

5-2F **8** *6* **Bright Sparky (GER)**[24] 4809 8-10-4 **90**........................ JakeGreenall(7) 65
(Michael Easterby) *in tch towards rr: rdn after 6th: struggling u.p bef 3 out: wknd wl bef 2 out* **9/2**[2]

PU00 **9** *3* **Still Royal**[40] 4390 5-9-11 **79** oh5..................................... JohnKington(3) 52
(John Davies) *chsd ldrs tl lost pl and mstke 5th: reminders bef next: struggling after 7th: wl btn 3 out* **25/1**

4150 **10** *37* **King Benny (IRE)**[54] 4115 7-11-3 **96**................................... TomSiddall 35
(Elliott Cooper) *t.k.h: in tch tl wknd qckly 8th: t.o bef 2 out* **7/1**[3]

0P0P **P** **King Gabriel (IRE)**[16] 4968 9-11-0 **100**.....................(t) MissJennyCarr(7) —
(Tracey Watkins) *racd wd: in tch: mstke 6th: sn rdn and struggling: t.o whn p.u 3 out* **50/1**

4m 43.7s (-8.30) **Going Correction** -0.225s/f (Good) **11** Ran SP% **117.0**
Speed ratings (Par 105): **107,105,103,100,100 98,97,95,93,79** —
toteswingers:1&2:£18.70, 1&3:£8.90, 2&3:£8.80 CSF £42.53 CT £432.16 TOTE £8.30: £2.10, £2.30, £5.40; EX 64.30.

Owner Jimmy Dudgeon **Bred** Olivier Le Quere **Trained** Greystoke, Cumbria

FOCUS

A moderate but still competitive handicap hurdle. The second has been rated to her mark.

NOTEBOOK

Moufatango(FR), who attracted support, was never far away and always had matters under control after hitting the front. Evidently none the worse for a fall on his handicap debut last time out, he jumped tidily here and can be found another of these granted a similar trip and ground. This performance was referred to the BHA, as the gelding had never previously been placed over hurdles. Official explanation: trainer said he had no explanation regarding the apparent improvement in form (op 11-2 tchd 6-1)

Petit Fleur gave the most meaningful chase from the turn in and posted another solid effort without ever looking like usurping the winner. Already a stone above her sole winning handicap mark though, she is starting to creep up the handicap again without winning (raced off 3lb higher than when second last time). (op 15-2)

Diktalina had never run in a handicap off this low before, but the race didn't appear to be run at a searching enough test for her to capitalise. She remains capable of better. (op 10-1 tchd 14-1)

Winged Farasi briefly thought twice about setting off and had his rider hard at work from some way out. He has placed off 5lb higher than his current mark in the past and is in the form to do so again, but only if he feels like it. (tchd 10-1)

Jaques Vert(FR) travelled strongly for a long way but backed out of things very quickly turning in. Too one-paced to nail a 2m handicap on the evidence of his three most recent previous outings, a race over an intermediate trip will need to be found, as he's not ready for 2m4f yet on this showing. Official explanation: jockey said gelding pulled up lame (op 9-2 tchd 5-1)

Bright Sparky(GER) produced just a short-lived effort leaving the back straight and disappointed. (tchd 3-1 and 5-1)

5209 BET ON THE MASTERS AT TOTESPORT.COM STANDARD NH FLAT RACE (CONDITIONALS/AMATEURS) (DIV I) 2m 1f

5:15 (5:16) (Class 5) 4-6-Y-0 **£1,370** (£399; £199)

Form RPR

1 **Super Duty (IRE)** 5-11-1 0... JohnKington(3) 101+
(Donald McCain) *t.k.h: in tch: chsd ldrs 7f out: drvn to ld and rn green wl over 1f out: kpt on and a holding runner-up fnl f* **14/1**

2 *3/4* **Charlie Wingnut (IRE)** 4-10-9 0.............................. RichardKilloran(3) 92
(Nicky Henderson) *t.k.h: chsd ldrs: rdn ent fnl 3f: chsd wnr over 1f out: hld hd high and nt qckn fnl f* **15/8**[1]

30 **3** *7* **Blue Blooded**[45] 4287 5-10-11 0.......................... JeremiahMcGrath(7) 91
(Alan Swinbank) *t.k.h: hld up in rr: stdy hdwy 5f out: chsd ldng quartet ent fnl 2f: unable qck and btn over 1f out: wnt 3rd and hung lft 1f out* **11/2**[3]

4 *3 1/4* **King Caractacus**[55] 6-10-11 0.. MrJFMathias(7) 88
(Lawney Hill) *led: rdn and hdd wl over 1f out: wknd over 1f out* **6/1**

0 **5** *2 1/2* **Pas Trop Tard (FR)**[73] 3752 4-10-7 0............................ AlexanderVoy(5) 79
(Maurice Barnes) *t.k.h: chsd ldr: ev ch over 2f out: wknd wl over 1f out* **40/1**

0 **6** *20* **Jamaddji**[45] 4287 4-9-12 0.. GeraldQuinn(7) 52
(Elliott Cooper) *t.k.h: hld up wl in tch in rr: swtchd rt and hdwy into midfield 10f out: wknd 5f out* **66/1**

7 *10* **Minor Chord** 5-10-4 0 .... MrJBanks(7) 48
(G C Maundrell) *t.k.h: hld up wl in tch in midfield: dropped to last and struggling 1/2-way: wl bhd fnl 3f: t.o* **20/1**

0 8 *4 ½* **Mill Mick**[26] 4780 4-10-12 0 .... CampbellGillies 45
(John Mackie) *t.k.h: hld up in tch: chsd ldrs 10f out: wknd qckly over 5f out: wl bhd fnl 3f: t.o* **16/1**

9 *½* **Fiorenza** 5-10-4 0 .... MrWTwiston-Davies(7) 43
(Nigel Twiston-Davies) *t.k.h: chsd ldrs: pushed along and struggling 7f out: bhd and lost tch 5f out: t.o fnl 3f* **11/4**[2]

4m 4.20s (-1.10) **Going Correction** -0.225s/f (Good)
WFA 4 from 5yo+ 5lb 9 Ran SP% **112.4**
Speed ratings: **93,92,89,87,86 77,72,70,70**
toteswingers:1&2:£9.50, 1&3:£6.70, 2&3:£1.50 CSF £39.09 TOTE £17.50: £2.10, £1.30, £1.70; EX 34.70.
Owner D McCain **Bred** Mrs A Connolly **Trained** Cholmondeley, Cheshire

FOCUS
There was a muddling early pace to division one of the bumper and several participants, not least Mill Mick and Jamaddji, were loathe to settle. The front two finished clear and it has been rated through the third.

NOTEBOOK
Super Duty(IRE)'s pedigree suggests stamina rather more than it does speed, but he worked his way through the field quickly enough when asked and held on well, despite the race being run as more of a speed test than most likely ideal. Green and wandering round inside the last couple of furlongs, he can prove capable of better as he matures and should have something to offer over hurdles in due course. (op 12-1 tchd 9-1)
Charlie Wingnut(IRE), a £40,000 purchase last May, travelled well during the race and nearly got upsides over a furlong out without ever forcing his way in front after that. This was a decent first effort, and compensation can follow in a small spring heat before attentions are turned to hurdling. (op 7-4)
Blue Blooded, for whom easier going and a longer track may not have suited at Doncaster last time, had no such excuses here and he just looks a bit too slow to land a bumper. Judged on the exploits of his half-siblings though, he will have plenty to offer in 2m hurdles. (op 5-1 tchd 6-1)
King Caractacus won a point around Cottenham's speedy 2m4f track in February, but John Mathias waited with him that day and his charge burned himself out in front on this occasion. He remains capable of better under a return to more patient tactics. (op 4-1)
Fiorenza never looked like emulating her dam in winning a Bangor bumper on debut, and she may need more time. (op 5-1)

5210 BET ON THE MASTERS AT TOTESPORT.COM STANDARD NH FLAT RACE (CONDITIONALS/AMATEURS) (DIV II) 2m 1f
5:45 (5:46) (Class 5) 4-6-Y-O £1,370 (£399; £199)

Form RPR

1 **Hazy Tom (IRE)**[55] 5-10-11 0 .... KielanWoods(7) 110+
(Charlie Longsdon) *hld up wl in tch: nt clr run on inner fr 4f out tl squeezed between rail and rival to ld wl over 1f out: r.o wl: comf* **7/4**[1]

2 *3 ½* **Pampanito** 5-11-1 0 .... JohnKington(3) 102
(Donald McCain) *chsd ldr tl led over 2f out: rdn and hdd wl over 1f out: kpt on but nt pce of wnr after* **15/2**

3 *2 ½* **Rob Conti (FR)** 6-10-11 0 .... MrJABest(7) 99
(Philip Hobbs) *in tch: rdn and effrt 4f out: chsd ldng pair wl over 1f out: kpt on but no imp after* **6/1**

4 *8* **Lady Gongar** 5-10-4 0 .... MrRJarrett(7) 84
(Thomas Kinsey) *plld hrd: hld up in tch: hdwy to chse ldrs 9f out: outpcd over 3f out: no ch w ldrs but kpt on again fnl f* **18/1**

40 5 *nk* **Hightown (IRE)**[150] 2315 4-10-5 0 .... MrJMQuinlan(7) 85
(Don Cantillon) *led tl over 2f out: wknd wl over 1f out* **9/2**[2]

2 6 *13* **Tiradia (FR)**[24] 4815 4-10-5 0 .... JakeGreenall(7) 75
(Michael Easterby) *chsd ldr: rdn and unable qck 4f out: wknd wl over 2f out* **11/2**[3]

7 *2* **High Road (IRE)** 4-10-9 0 .... MrAJBerry(3) 76+
(Jonjo O'Neill) *hld up in tch in rr: hdwy 1/2-way: rdn and wknd wl over 2f out* **8/1**

U **Snow Alert** 5-10-11 0 .... MrPHardy(7) —
(John Norton) *in tch on outer tl hung rt and uns rdr 1/2-way* **25/1**

3m 58.7s (-6.60) **Going Correction** -0.225s/f (Good)
WFA 4 from 5yo+ 5lb 8 Ran SP% **116.2**
Speed ratings: **106,104,103,99,99 93,92,—**
toteswingers:1&2:£1.50, 1&3:£1.30, 2&3:£2.00 CSF £16.11 TOTE £2.40: £1.30, £2.50, £1.90; EX 17.20.
Owner Charles Horton **Bred** Messrs T & J Hayes **Trained** Over Norton, Oxon

FOCUS
The quicker of the two bumpers by 5.5 seconds. The winner was value for further.

NOTEBOOK
Hazy Tom(IRE) produced a taking performance to score in this grade at the first attempt. A winner of a maiden point on dead going (same ownership) in February , he needed to be brave and persistent to force his way through on the inner early in the straight, but the response once granted a clear run was very pleasing. Staying chases are likely to prove his forte on breeding eventually, but he can make a mark in 2m4f-3m hurdles first. (op 9-4)
Pampanito, a £5,000 half-brother to Ashley Brook, responded quite well to pressure once headed but never looked like reeling the winner back in. He may just have run into a decent prospect here and can make amends in an ordinary event. (op 7-1)
Rob Conti(FR) was under pressure to maintain his position earlier than either of those that beat him, and already looks in need of a more substantial stamina test. (tchd 11-2)
Lady Gongar looks to have ability, and it's to her credit that she had enough in reserve to stay on again, having fought her rider throughout the first half of the race. She'll need to settle far better to rate a winning proposition in this or any sphere, though. (tchd 16-1)
Hightown(IRE) proved no more able to see out the trip than in two junior bumpers last autumn and may still need more time. (tchd 5-1)
Tiradia(FR) finished a fair second on debut at Huntingdon on similar ground, so this fading effort has to rate as a disappointment. (op 5-1)
T/Plt: £75.80 to a £1 stake. Pool:£37,458.64 - 360.65 winning tickets T/Qpdt: £34.30 to a £1 stake. Pool:£2,114.44 - 45.60 winning tickets SP

5106 CHEPSTOW (L-H)
Saturday, April 9

OFFICIAL GOING: Good
Wind: Light against Weather: Sunny

5211 JOHN SMITH'S NOVICES' HURDLE (8 hdls) 2m 110y
2:05 (2:05) (Class 4) 4-Y-0+ £2,341 (£687; £343; £171)

Form RPR

56 1 **Street Entertainer (IRE)**[55] 4092 4-10-2 0 .... CO'Farrell(5) 121+
(David Pipe) *prom: nt a fluent: hdwy to go 3rd 4 out: wnt 2nd next and gng wl: lft in ld 2 out: sauntered clr: mstke last: impressive* **11/4**[2]

311P 2 *9* **Pret A Thou (FR)**[35] 4487 8-11-4 130 .... KyleJames(7) 126
(John Bryan Groucott) *led at str pce: clr fr 2nd tl strly pressed fr 4 out: hdd next: 3rd and rdn 2 out where lft 2nd: nt pce of wnr* **5/1**[3]

04P5 3 *12* **Generous Bob**[37] 4444 4-10-4 0 .... WayneKavanagh(3) 97
(Seamus Mullins) *mounted outside paddock: in rr: niggled along 2nd: hdwy to chse ldrs 5th but nvr ldrs: lft mod 3rd 2 out* **22/1**

P440 4 *8* **Ballagio (IRE)**[16] 4974 6-10-13 109 .... SeanQuinlan 96
(Kim Bailey) *in rr: hdwy after 4th to chse ldrs next: rdn and no ch fr 3 out* **8/1**

0300 5 *10* **Don't Hang About**[47] 4260 6-10-6 0 .... SClements(7) 87
(Richard Mitchell) *chsd ldrs tl rdn and fdd qckly 5th: sn t.o* **33/1**

000 6 *37* **Cluain Alainn (IRE)**[98] 3296 5-10-13 0 .... DaveCrosse 54
(Ian Williams) *towards rr: hdwy 3rd: rdn after 4th: lost tch bef 3 out: wl t.o but nt hrd pushed* **50/1**

60 7 *37* **Grovemere (IRE)**[7] 5106 6-10-10 0 .... DonalDevereux(3) 20
(Debra Hamer) *rdn and labouring after 1st: bdly t.o fr 4th: fin eventually* **66/1**

0P0 8 *13* **Semelay (FR)**[37] 4444 5-10-13 0 .... (t) LiamHeard 9
(Laura Young) *nvr fluent: blnd bdly 1st: wl bhd fr 2nd: t.o next: completed eventually* **100/1**

22-0 9 *6* **Swing State**[338] 167 6-10-13 0 .... MattieBatchelor 3
(Tony Carroll) *chsd ldr to 3rd: rdn and wknd rapidly 4th: t.o next* **8/1**

500 10 *8* **Johnny Owen (IRE)**[58] 4029 5-10-10 0 .... LeeStephens(3) —
(David Brace) *t.k.h in midfield: nt fluent 4th: sn lost tch: t.o next: fin eventually* **50/1**

0452 F **Richmond (FR)**[99] 3261 6-10-13 115 .... LiamTreadwell 114
(Ian Williams) *prom: chsd ldr 3rd: led 3 out: stl gng wl (as was eventual wnr) and slt advantage whn fell 2 out* **11/8**[1]

00 P **Gracious Beau**[21] 4866 5-10-13 0 .... JackDoyle —
(Keith Goldsworthy) *nt fluent in rr: reminders 2nd: wl bhd fr 3rd: t.o and p.u 2 out* **50/1**

3m 54.6s (-16.00) **Going Correction** -0.775s/f (Firm)
WFA 4 from 5yo+ 5lb 12 Ran SP% **123.3**
Speed ratings (Par 105): **106,101,96,92,87 70,52,46,43,40 —,—**
toteswingers:1&2:£14.60, 1&3:£14.60, 2&3:£14.60 CSF £17.34 TOTE £5.70: £2.10, £1.10, £3.80; EX 17.00.
Owner Barnett, Manasseh & Partners **Bred** Marston Stud And Fleming Thoroughbreds **Trained** Nicholashayne, Devon

FOCUS
The course had been lightly watered overnight to help ease the fast conditions. This was a fair novice event dominated by a market plunge on the winner.

NOTEBOOK
Street Entertainer(IRE), the subject of a big gamble, travelled strongly and, although novicey in the home straight, could be called the winner from the home turn and won as expected. He had been beaten out of sight on his last start, but that was in a hot contest that has thrown up two Aintree festival winners in Spirit Son and stablemate Battle Group. He is inexperienced and still learning, but showed a lot of potential here. (op 13-2)
Pret A Thou(FR), in contrast to the winner, drifted markedly in the betting. Setting off at a good clip, he stuck to the task for as long as he could, but may have paid for the early pace. Connections have done well to exploit opportunities in novice hurdles for this experienced multiple-winning handicap chaser. This was another good run considering he prefers softer ground. (op 7-2 tchd 11-2)
Generous Bob was up with the leading bunch until the home turn, but his effort began to flatten out in the straight, suggesting a step back up in trip might be in his favour. (op 20-1)
Ballagio(IRE) got outpaced in the back straight, but made steady progress from an unpromising position. He lasted only a year with Paul Nicholls and has still to justify his £50,000 price tag for new connections, but this effort suggests he could pick up a handicap.
Johnny Owen(IRE) Official explanation: jockey said gelding ran too freely
Richmond(FR), having his first run since narrowly beaten at Warwick in December, was a bit keen but had just edged into the lead in a three-way battle up the straight when he stepped at the second-last and came down. However, he looked booked for second at the time. (op 6-4 tchd 7-4)

5212 JOHN SMITH'S NOVICES' H'CAP HURDLE (8 hdls) 2m 110y
2:35 (2:35) (Class 5) (0-95,94) 4-Y-0+ £2,172 (£637; £318; £159)

Form RPR

-400 1 **Taste The Wine (IRE)**[6] 4540 5-11-5 92 .... MarkQuinlan(5) 104+
(Bernard Llewellyn) *midfield: wnt 2nd 4 out: rdn to ld next and hung lft: drew clr fr 2 out* **6/1**[3]

0040 2 *9* **Special Cuvee**[14] 4999 5-11-5 92 .... (t) OliverDayman(5) 95
(Alison Thorpe) *in rr: hrd rdn after 4th: 14 l 6th and hrd rdn 2 out: styd on wl to go 3rd bef last: tk 2nd flat: no ch w wnr* **25/1**

5P0- 3 *2 ¾* **Gross Prophet**[179] 5072 6-11-3 90 .... CO'Farrell(5) 90
(Alastair Lidderdale) *led to 2nd and again 4th: rdn 4 out: hdd next: sn outpcd by wnr: lost 2nd flat* **15/2**

0000 4 *3 ¾* **Jomade (IRE)**[56] 4076 5-11-10 92 .... (p) SeanQuinlan 90
(Kim Bailey) *prom: rdn and outpcd bef 4 out: plugged on fr 3 out: nvr a danger* **11/1**

5630 5 *hd* **Reg's Ruby**[43] 4330 5-11-9 91 .... ColinBolger 88
(David Bridgwater) *prom: drvn and 2nd 4 out: wknd fr 3 out* **20/1**

61P6 6 *hd* **Time To Think**[32] 4535 6-11-9 94 .... JimmyDerham(3) 91
(Seamus Mullins) *midfield: hdwy to chse ldrs after 4th: rdn 4 out: one pce fr next* **11/1**

/PF0 7 *27* **Driving Miss Suzie**[14] 5016 7-10-13 84 .... DonalDevereux(3) 56
(Debra Hamer) *in rr: hdwy to join ldrs 4th: lost tch qckly 3 out* **33/1**

4P06 8 *5* **Tar (IRE)**[21] 4874 7-11-3 88 .... (t) WayneKavanagh(3) 56
(Matt Sheppard) *prom: led 2nd to 4th where nt fluent: sn wknd: t.o* **20/1**

6000 9 *7* **Calusa Catrina (IRE)**[77] 3691 6-10-12 80 .... CharliePoste 42
(Robin Dickin) *in rr: niggled along after 4th: struggling fr next: t.o* **25/1**

400 10 *1 ¼* **Tae Kwon Do (USA)**[134] 2658 5-11-5 92 .... (t) MrTomDavid(5) 52
(Tim Vaughan) *in rr: hdwy to midfield after 3rd: rdn and wknd bef 4 out: t.o fr next: carried lft last* **17/2**

P0 11 *11* **Captain Sully (IRE)**[138] 2577 6-11-12 94 .... LiamTreadwell 45
(Jim Wilson) *t.k.h in midfield: nt fluent 3rd: rdn and no imp fr 4 out: btn whn hmpd 2 out* **12/1**

6U00 12 *hd* **Cruise In Style (IRE)**[172] 1910 5-10-11 84 .... MattGriffiths(5) 34
(Kevin Bishop) *t.k.h in rr: mstke 1st: brief effrt 4th: rdn and wknd bef next: t.o whn j. violently lft last* **28/1**

000P 13 *10* **Terra Bleu (IRE)**[50] 4192 4-9-7 74 oh6 .... (t) PeterHatton(7) 9
(Milton Harris) *a in rr: rn wd on bnd after 1st and rdn: t.o fr 3rd* **11/2**[2]

0064 14 *3 ½* **Carbon Print (USA)**[36] 4266 6-11-5 90 .... (t) IanPopham(3) 28
(James Evans) *midfield: rdn after 4th: grad wknd fr 4 out: t.o* **16/1**

4231 **F** **Owner Occupier**[29] 4698 6-11-5 94 ...... MrTJCannon(7) 88
(Chris Gordon) *midfield: nt gng wl fr 3rd and str reminders: brief effrt bef 4 out: btn and 15 l 7th whn fell 2 out* **5/1**[1]

3m 57.2s (-13.40) **Going Correction** -0.775s/f (Firm) **15** Ran SP% **122.5**
WFA 4 from 5yo+ 5lb
Speed ratings (Par 103): **100,95,94,92,92 92,79,77,74,73 68,68,63,61,—**
toteswingers:1&2:£3.30, 1&3:£17.20, 2&3:£17.20 CSF £155.68 CT £1158.00 TOTE £5.10: £2.00, £7.20, £4.80; EX 86.30.
Owner Alan J Williams **Bred** Trevor Reilly **Trained** Fochriw, Caerphilly

FOCUS
A moderate event producing a runaway winner to outclass the rest.

NOTEBOOK
Taste The Wine(IRE) was ridden confidently, improving his position in the back straight before pouncing from the third-last, and although he did not jump too well there he had plenty left and stretched clear for a wide-margin success. He won on the AW last November after switching to his current stable and had excuses for his latest poor runs. He looked likely to go close when getting the last wrong at Catterick in December, and that form gave him every chance in this contest. (op 5-1 tchd 9-2)
Special Cuvee got going too late, but made good headway to pass four horses up the straight, although by that time the winner was clear. He has struggled to make any impact over hurdles so far and, although this was a better effort, he remains on a long losing run over hurdles and on the Flat.
Gross Prophet disputed the lead until the third-last, but could find no more once passed. A 66-rated winner at around a mile on the Flat last summer, he improved for the faster ground here after being beaten in three soft-ground hurdles this winter, but does not look a certain stayer at 2m. (op 10-1)
Jomade(IRE), a drifter in the market, lost ground with a slow jump at the fourth but recovered to maintain a prominent position until finding little in reserve from the turn in. However, this was a small step in the right direction after some poor efforts. (op 17-2 tchd 8-1 in place)
Reg's Ruby helped cut out the pace, but faded up the home straight. (op 22-1)
Time To Think was again ridden prominently, but was outpaced on this faster ground. (op 12-1)

5213 JOHN SMITH'S EXTRA SMOOTH NOVICES' CHASE (22 fncs) 3m 2f 110y
3:10 (3:10) (Class 3) 5-Y-0+ **£4,943** (£1,451; £725)

Form RPR
13-F **1** **Valentine Vic (IRE)**[50] 4185 7-10-9 0 ...... IanPopham(3) 130+
(Paul Nicholls) *t.k.h in last: nt fluent 14: rdn and outpcd 18th: rallied to chse ldr next: led 2 out: styd on dourly* **6/4**[2]
2221 **2** *5* **Fruity O'Rooney**[41] 4371 8-11-8 131 ...... AndrewGlassonbury 136+
(Gary Moore) *t.k.h in 2nd: mstke 13th: jnd ldr 16th: mstke 18th: led next: rdn and hdd 2 out: no imp on wnr fr last* **11/8**[1]
602P **3** *5* **Moleskin (IRE)**[43] 4328 8-10-12 117 ...... (p) JackDoyle 121
(Victor Dartnall) *led and racd lazily: jnd 16th: hrd drvn and hdd 4 out: lost 2nd next and sn wknd* **10/3**[3]

6m 53.8s (-8.20) **Going Correction** -0.625s/f (Firm) **3** Ran SP% **105.2**
Speed ratings: **87,85,83**
CSF £3.79 TOTE £2.40; EX 3.20.
Owner Mrs Ann Fulton & Paul Barber **Bred** Mrs H Clarke **Trained** Ditcheat, Somerset

FOCUS
They crawled along until the race began in earnest from the home turn.

NOTEBOOK
Valentine Vic(IRE) was caught out by the lifting of the pace, but once he got going he stayed on strongly to win comfortably. He fell on his first start in over a year in a hurdle at Newbury last time, but had been given time to get over that and his jumping was fluent enough. He is a big strapping sort who brushes through his fences with disdain and he looks to have a future in marathon chases in time. (op 7-4)
Fruity O'Rooney lost some momentum with a mistake at the first in the home straight as the pace began to quicken, but he was firmly put in his place. He is not that big and, with his high knee action, just lacks a bit of momentum off fast ground, but he remains effective on softer. (op 11-10)
Moleskin(IRE) did nothing wrong and ran as well as could be expected against two higher-rated rivals. However, he still has yet to run up to his rating over fences, and the slow early pace here inevitably flattered him somewhat. (op 7-2 tchd 3-1)

5214 JOHN SMITH'S "NO NONSENSE RACING" H'CAP CHASE (16 fncs) 2m 3f 110y
3:45 (3:45) (Class 4) (0-110,109) 5-Y-0+ **£2,602** (£764; £382; £190)

Form RPR
P-32 **1** **Digital Media (IRE)**[12] 5058 9-9-11 87 ...... (t) NathanSweeney(7) 93
(Simon Burrough) *midfield: hdwy to go 2nd 12th: rdn next: 10 l 2nd and looked btn whn lft 8 l clr 2 out: rdn out* **6/1**[3]
5P3P **2** *12* **Mister Watzisname (IRE)**[12] 5062 9-10-0 83 ...... (tp) SeanQuinlan 78
(Charlie Longsdon) *t.k.h in rr: hdwy 11th: 4th and rdn 12th: carried hd high and nt looking keen whn lft mod 2nd 2 out: mstke last* **8/1**
0FU **3** *2 ¾* **Kap West (FR)**[46] 4267 6-11-0 97 ...... LiamHeard 90
(Laura Young) *t.k.h: dropped out last: 8th appr 12th: hdwy next: kpt on fr 3 out: nvr a threat: promising* **33/1**
26P5 **4** *3* **Its Crucial (IRE)**[36] 4460 11-11-6 106 ...... TomMolloy(3) 96
(Nigel Twiston-Davies) *in rr: dropped to last and slow 7th: mstke 13th: kpt on one pce* **8/1**
F033 **5** *4* **Manmoon (FR)**[14] 5017 8-10-9 97 ...... (t) MattGriffiths(5) 83
(Nigel Hawke) *prom: jnd ldr 7th: led next: rdn and hdd and lost 2 pls 12th: grad wknd fr next* **9/1**
00P4 **6** *4 ½* **Jayjay Valentine**[28] 4718 8-9-13 89 ...... EdGlassonbury(7) 71
(Victor Dartnall) *t.k.h: nt a fluent: brief effrt 11th: rdn and fnd little 12th: sn btn* **9/4**[1]
6013 **7** *15* **Laneguy (FR)**[30] 4671 6-11-3 100 ...... (t) RhysFlint 69
(Tom George) *midfield: slow 6th: rdn bef 12th: wknd qckly: dismntd sn after fin* **9/1**
0050 **8** *13* **American World (FR)**[20] 4896 7-11-12 109 ...... JimmyMcCarthy 66
(Brendan Powell) *prom: dropped to rr 8th: t.o fr 12th* **16/1**
1233 **P** **Sultan Fontenaille (FR)**[26] 4777 9-11-6 108 ...... (bt) CO'Farrell(5) 124
(David Pipe) *led tl jnd 7th: hdd next: led again 12th: qcknd clr 4 out: 10 l advantage and in full command whn wnt bdly wrong bef 2 out: p.u: fatally injured* **9/2**[2]

5m 0.40s (-10.90) **Going Correction** -0.625s/f (Firm) **9** Ran SP% **114.3**
Speed ratings: **96,91,90,88,87 85,79,74,—**
toteswingers:1&2:£15.60, 1&3: not won, 2&3:£16.40 CSF £51.96 CT £1448.66 TOTE £6.00: £1.90, £2.90, £7.60; EX 86.20.
Owner Mrs Elizabeth Heal **Bred** D Delahunty **Trained** West Buckland, Somerset

NOTEBOOK
Digital Media(IRE), who was several lengths down when Sultan Fontenaille broke down, inherited the win. He still finished clear of the rest, but it was a somewhat hollow victory. However, his second in a competitive time at Towcester last month suggested he was on the verge of adding to his sole chase success and the combination of a low weight and easier finish here certainly helped. (op 7-1)
Mister Watzisname(IRE), who always held a prominent position, plugged on into second. He is sliding down the weights, but is not necessarily likely to break his chasing duck on faster ground. (op 10-1 tchd 15-2)
Kap West(FR) showed more aptitude for fences than he has to date, but after making some good headway around the final turn his effort flattened out. (op 22-1)
Its Crucial(IRE) never looked happy racing wide at the rear of the field, and though he made up some ground he gives the impression that his form is beginning to decline, despite slipping in the handicap to an exploitable mark. (op 15-2)
Manmoon(FR) disputed the lead until fading out of it in the straight. He has dropped back down to his last winning mark following several comprehensive defeats this winter, but might need a break to freshen him up. (tchd 17-2)
Jayjay Valentine theoretically held a chance based on the value of the form of his last start over 3m at this track and was backed to find improvement for the drop in trip and faster ground, but he was outpaced in the back straight and never picked up. Official explanation: jockey said gelding never travelled (op 11-4 tchd 3-1 in a place)
Sultan Fontenaille(FR) sadly broke down when clear of the field looking a certain winner. (op 4-1)

5215 JOHN SMITH'S GRAND NATIONAL DAY H'CAP HURDLE (8 hdls) 2m 110y
4:50 (4:50) (Class 4) (0-115,115) 4-Y-0+ **£2,341** (£687; £343; £171)

Form RPR
P05 **1** **Knight In Purple**[26] 4783 7-11-2 108 ...... (vt) DonalDevereux(3) 115+
(John Mackie) *chsd ldng pair: blunder 4th: wnt 2nd 4 out: led on bit 3 out: qcknd clr: easily* **15/2**
3541 **2** *6* **Spinning Waters**[16] 4965 5-10-6 100 ...... (p) OliverDayman(5) 100
(Dai Burchell) *t.k.h briefly: rdn after 2nd and dropped to rr: hdwy after 4th to chse ldrs: wnt mod 3rd and hrd rdn 3 out: hit 2 out: styd on to take 2nd bef last: no ch w wnr* **10/1**
1233 **3** *9* **Woodlark Island (IRE)**[11] 5066 5-11-2 110 ...... (bt) CO'Farrell(5) 104
(David Pipe) *chsd ldr tl led 2nd: qcknd 5 l clr appr 4 out: rdn and hdd 3 out: fnd little: lost 2nd bef last and mstke* **3/1**[1]
5F23 **4** *½* **J'Adhere (FR)**[18] 4925 6-11-1 109 ...... MrTomDavid(5) 99
(Tim Vaughan) *settled in detached last: 8th and stl nt asked for effrt appr 4 out: wnt 3rd briefly and pushed along bef 3 out: kpt on one pce fr next* **6/1**[3]
4052 **5** *15* **Sweet World**[58] 4028 7-10-11 105 ...... MarkQuinlan(5) 82
(Bernard Llewellyn) *t.k.h in rr: hdwy to chse ldrs after 4th: rdn and no imp fr 3 out* **7/1**
20-1 **6** *1 ½* **Wake Board (FR)**[31] 4548 6-11-12 115 ...... (t) SamThomas 91
(Dr Richard Newland) *t.k.h and led tl hdd 2nd: remained 2nd tl rdn and carried hd high 4 out: wknd qckly* **9/2**[2]
4022 **7** *4 ½* **Tenby Jewel (IRE)**[33] 4521 6-11-7 110 ...... JackDoyle 82
(Keith Goldsworthy) *in rr: effrt to go 3rd after 4th: rdn bef 4 out and mstke: sn btn: t.o whn blnd 2 out* **12/1**
-102 **8** *16* **Vertueux (FR)**[8] 4697 6-11-2 108 ...... LeeEdwards(3) 65
(Tony Carroll) *midfield: rdn and lost pl 4th: sn btn: t.o* **6/1**[3]
P50P **9** *45* **Award Winner**[33] 4523 8-11-4 107 ...... JimmyMcCarthy 24
(Brendan Powell) *midfield: nt fluent 3rd: rdn and sulking fr 4th: sn t.o* **40/1**

3m 55.9s (-14.70) **Going Correction** -0.775s/f (Firm) **9** Ran SP% **115.2**
Speed ratings (Par 105): **103,100,95,95,88 87,85,78,57**
toteswingers:1&2:£18.70, 1&3:£8.90, 2&3:£8.80 CSF £77.59 CT £274.78 TOTE £8.80: £2.60, £4.30, £2.00; EX 84.90.
Owner A J Wall, G Hicks & N Hooper **Bred** Wood Farm Stud **Trained** Church Broughton , Derbys

FOCUS
The two market leaders initially took each other on, and although the pace slowed markedly down the back, that early pace proved their undoing.

NOTEBOOK
Knight In Purple kept tabs on the leaders from a safe distance and, although he only began to jump fluently in the home straight, he stayed on strongly for a decisive success. He had come on for his first run back from a winter break last month and, on the decent ground he needs, was able to show his best. He was winning off a 5lb higher mark than his last victory and there might not be much leeway for future handicaps. (op 7-1 tchd 8-1)
Spinning Waters was stepping up in class and racing off a 7lb higher mark following his C&D win last month. He ran as well as could be expected, staying on under pressure. (op 9-1)
Woodlark Island(IRE) was travelling comfortably and made a strong-looking move when kicking clear again from the home turn. However, after being hassled for the early lead he found very little in the closing stages. If able to get an uncontested lead he is still a danger off this mark on fast ground. (op 4-1)
J'Adhere(FR) plugged on into fourth, but ideally needs a stiffer test than this to perform near the level of his current career-high mark. (op 13-2)
Sweet World has won only one hurdle from 31 attempts, but is gradually slipping down the weights again. (op 8-1 tchd 13-2)
Wake Board(FR) raced keenly as usual and was taken on for the lead which did not help, so he unsurprisingly faded out of it. He might need some slackening of his rating to make an impact in handicaps for his new connections. (tchd 7-2)

5216 JOHN SMITH'S H'CAP CHASE (18 fncs) 3m
5:20 (5:22) (Class 5) (0-95,91) 5-Y-0+ **£2,439** (£716; £358; £178)

Form RPR
5012 **1** **Ilewin Tom**[62] 3959 8-10-10 82 ...... SClements(7) 101+
(Gary Brown) *midfield: hdwy 10th: cl up 3rd and gng wl next: pressed ldr 14th: led 15th: slt advantage whn mstke 3 out: pushed 1 l ahd last: rdn out* **8/1**[2]
PP **2** *3* **Caspar Of Tarsus (IRE)**[62] 3961 8-10-11 76 ...... (tp) AndrewGlassonbury 91
(Gerald Ham) *drvn along to get gng: midfield: mstke 3rd: hdwy after 10th: led and j.rt and blnd 12th: hdd and hrd drvn 15th: kpt trying but nvr looked like passing wnr fr 3 out* **10/1**
0P53 **3** *3* **Kiltimoney (IRE)**[31] 4560 11-9-9 65 oh2 ...... (b) CO'Farrell(5) 78
(Richard Mitchell) *midfield: hdwy to chse ldrs after 7th: lft in ld after 9th: hdd 12th: hrd drvn and 3rd of clr ldng trio 14th: no imp on ldng pair fr 2 out: one pce* **12/1**
6343 **4** *32* **Portrait Royale (IRE)**[30] 4669 9-11-5 91 ...... MrTJCannon(7) 71
(Anna Newton-Smith) *prom: hrd drvn 12th: lost tch w ldng trio bef 14th and j.rt: t.o whn j.rt 3 out* **8/1**[2]
FPP4 **5** *1 ½* **Wham Bang**[33] 4522 7-9-13 67 ...... (p) JimmyDerham(3) 46
(Robin Mathew) *a towards rr and nt a fluent and smetimes jumping rt: t.o fr 10th: passed floundering rivals fr 4 out* **20/1**
0064 **6** *10* **Lions In Law**[18] 4927 7-10-0 68 ...... (bt) IanPopham(3) 38
(Richard Hawker) *t.k.h bhd ldrs: reminders and carried hd high 7th: nt looking willing after: sn btn: t.o* **20/1**
35P3 **7** *21* **Sieglinde (FR)**[12] 5051 5-10-1 71 ...... MarkQuinlan(5) 22
(Alison Batchelor) *in rr: mstke 3rd: lost pl 9th: struggling 10th: t.o next: plodded on past btn horses fr 3 out* **25/1**
62P0 **8** *¾* **Zi Missile (IRE)**[8] 5103 7-9-11 65 oh2 ...... DonalDevereux(3) 15
(Mary Evans) *t.k.h in midfield: hdwy 11th: ev ch next: hrd rdn and grad wknd fr next* **28/1**

P1P3 **9** *27* **Wide Receiver (IRE)**[23] 4829 8-10-13 **78**................(vt) JimmyMcCarthy 4
(Charlie Morlock) *cl up: lost pl 9th: downed tools and t.o 11th* **14/1**

0340 **10** *25* **Grey Cruzene (USA)**[19] 4922 5-11-0 **79**............................ ColinBolger —
(Chris Gordon) *prom: mstke 5th: rdn and lost pl after 7th: t.o 11th: blnd 13th* **40/1**

3P-6 **P** **Chamacco (FR)**[39] 4413 11-10-2 **67**.................................. CharliePoste —
(Sophie Leech) *midfield: hdwy to chse ldrs 13th: ev ch 14th: rdn and lost pl next: wkng whn p.u 2 out: lost action* **17/2**[3]

1413 **P** **Marias Rock**[28] 4718 9-11-4 **88**.. MattGriffiths[(5)] —
(Jeremy Scott) *towards rr: mstke 5th: hrd rdn and dropped to rr 7th: wl bhd next: continued t.o tl p.u 3 out: b.b.v* **11/4**[1]

3443 **P** **The Humbel Monk (IRE)**[7] 5109 9-11-5 **84**........................... RhysFlint —
(Lucy Jones) *led: terrible blunder and nrly fell 9th: sn p.u* **8/1**[2]

000P **P** **Lucius Fabeo (IRE)**[30] 4666 7-10-4 **69**.......................(p) MattieBatchelor —
(Anna Newton-Smith) *midfield and blunder 1st: reminders 4th: dropped to rr 7th: sn t.o: p.u 3 out* **66/1**

0600 **P** **Bridge Street Boy**[51] 4159 6-11-6 **88**..........................(t) CharlieHuxley[(3)] —
(Richard Lee) *in rr: j. bdly rt 5th and dropped to last: sn t.o: p.u 13th* **16/1**

6m 5.00s (-17.00) **Going Correction** -0.625s/f (Firm) **15** Ran SP% **120.6**
Speed ratings: **103,102,100,89,88 85,78,78,69,60 —,—,—,—,—**
toteswingers:1&2:£11.50, 1&3:£20.20, 2&3:£22.60 CSF £77.64 CT £968.35 TOTE £9.70: £4.10, £3.70, £3.90; EX 98.80.
Owner Tom Segrue **Bred** T J Segrue **Trained** East Garston, Berks

FOCUS
Three pulled clear of the field in this moderate contest.

NOTEBOOK
Ilewin Tom travelled well throughout, biding his time against the inside rail and finding enough to repel the sustained challenge of the runner-up, doing it rather comfortably in the end. Opening at 16-1, he attracted strong market support and when the money is down for a representative from this shrewd stable it is usually significant. However, with a win and second from two runs this year, the form was there to be seen and with a two-month break to freshen him up, he proved fully up to defying a 16lb rise in the weights. (tchd 7-1 and 17-2)
Caspar Of Tarsus(IRE) kept on under pressure to make the winner work all the way up the straight. He evidently improved for the re-fitting of headgear and a tongue-tie and left his previous soft-ground efforts behind. He is on an attractive mark if able to reproduce this effort. (op 14-1)
Kiltimoney(IRE) made progress to tack onto the leaders round the final turn, but lost momentum when pecking at the first in the home straight and could not make up the ground. He is largely consistent and appears well handicapped, but has managed just one win to date as he just lacks a bit of pace.
Portrait Royale(IRE) went with the leaders as they began to pull clear leaving the back straight, but he was soon struggling to keep up and eventually weakened. He does not usually race that far away from his East Sussex base and that might have been a factor. (op 15-2)
Wham Bang jumped right at several fences and struggled at the rear of the field before eventually staying on past beaten horses. (op 25-1 tchd 28-1)
Chamacco(FR) Official explanation: jockey said gelding lost its action (tchd 5-2 and 3-1)
Marias Rock was under pressure from an early stage and was never travelling. Official explanation: jockey said mare had bled from the nose (tchd 5-2 and 3-1)
The Humbel Monk(IRE) Official explanation: jockey said gelding had made a mistake (tchd 5-2 and 3-1)

5217 JOHN SMITH'S STANDARD OPEN NATIONAL HUNT FLAT RACE 2m 110y
5:55 (5:56) (Class 6) 4-6-Y-0 **£1,821** (£534; £267; £133)

Form RPR

1 **Sin Bin (IRE)** 5-11-1 0.. IanPopham[(3)] 118+
(Paul Nicholls) *midfield: smooth hdwy 6f out: pushed along to chse ldr 4f out: styd on and grad wore down ldr: led fnl 50yds* **7/4**[1]

2 **2** *½* **Chance Encounter (IRE)**[29] 4709 5-11-4 0.......... AndrewGlassonbury 117
(Linda Blackford) *j. out of paddock bef r: led: kicked clr 4f out: fnd plenty for press: edgd lft fr over 1f out: eventually overhauled fnl 50yds* **6/1**[2]

03 **3** *18* **All For Cash**[51] 4164 6-10-11 0.. MrCGreene[(7)] 101
(Kim Bailey) *chsd ldr and inclined to hang lft thrght: reminders after 5f: hrd drvn 7f out: lost 2nd 4f out: sn no ch w ldng pair* **8/1**[3]

0 **4** *10* **Cavite Eta (IRE)**[12] 5063 4-10-12 0.................................. GerardTumelty 86
(Mark Bradstock) *t.k.h in midfield: lost pl and wl bhd 6f out: t.o 5f out: mod prog to pass btn rivals* **10/1**

5 *3* **Ali Baba** 5-11-1 0... CharlieHuxley[(3)] 89
(Alan King) *midfield: 4th and gng wl 5f out: rdn and rn green: wl btn 3f out* **17/2**

6 *8* **Conellie** 5-10-13 0... MarkQuinlan[(5)] 82
(Bernard Llewellyn) *in rr: hdwy 7f out: rdn over 4f out and rn green: no further hdwy fr 3f out* **18/1**

0 **7** *9* **Marshal Zhukov (IRE)**[7] 5113 5-11-1 0................... WayneKavanagh[(3)] 74
(Caroline Keevil) *s.s and a in rr: t.o 6f out* **20/1**

8 *3 ¼* **Kings Lad (IRE)** 4-10-12 0.. DaveCrosse 65
(Colin Tizzard) *cl up: 3rd and ev ch 6f out: rdn 5f out: sn wknd: t.o* **11/1**

9 *16* **Looking Hopeful (IRE)** 5-11-4 0................................. JimmyMcCarthy 57
(Charlie Morlock) *wl in rr and nvr travelling: t.o after 7f* **40/1**

10 *10* **Divide And Conquer (IRE)** 6-11-4 0.................................. RhysFlint 48
(Warren Greatrex) *v quirky bef r and eventually led to s rdrless: prom: rdn and wknd qckly 6f out: hopelessly t.o* **8/1**[3]

0 **11** *9* **Top Rose**[67] 3876 5-10-11 0...................................(t) CharliePoste 33
(Robin Dickin) *nvr on terms and rn v green: reminders after 6f: sn t.o* **33/1**

12 *dist* **Bob Bank Boy** 6-10-13 0.. MattGriffiths[(5)] —
(Bernard Llewellyn) *green in rr: lost tch after 7f: sn hopelessly t.o: completed eventually* **33/1**

3m 45.0s (-20.00) **Going Correction** -0.775s/f (Firm)
WFA 4 from 5yo+ 5lb **12** Ran SP% **119.2**
Speed ratings: **116,115,107,102,101 97,93,91,84,79 75,—**
toteswingers:1&2:£9.70, 1&3:£20.90, 2&3:£3.70 CSF £11.34 TOTE £2.50: £1.70, £3.00, £1.10; EX 17.10.
Owner Trevor Hemmings **Bred** G T Morrow **Trained** Ditcheat, Somerset

FOCUS
The first two pulled clear of the field and look to have some potential.

NOTEBOOK
Sin Bin(IRE), a £65,000 purchase in November, looked to have been caught flat-footed as the runner-up went clear and he showed his greenness as he became unbalanced in the straight, but his jockey gave him plenty of time to get the hang of things and it just paid off. He needed the length of the straight to get on top and only managed to do so near the line, suggesting that stamina rather than speed will be his strong suit in time. (op 3-1)
Chance Encounter(IRE) went for home at the top of the straight and soon stretched clear of the field, but it was a long way home from there and he was eventually overhauled. He looks a big chasing sort and, though he has now finished second twice, he showed enough speed here to be able to go one better in a bumper. (op 7-1 tchd 5-1)
All For Cash wandered a little in the home straight and was readily outpaced, once again suggesting that he is all stamina not speed. (op 6-1)
Cavite Eta(IRE), following a somewhat errant display last week at Towcester, appears to be gradually getting the hang of racing but he was never a factor here. (tchd 12-1)
Ali Baba did not look that happy on the track and could not pick up, weakening over a furlong from home. He is related to some Flat winners at middle and staying trips, but cost just 5,500 guineas in July 2009. (op 8-1 tchd 7-1)
Top Rose Official explanation: jockey said mare resented the tongue tie
T/Plt: £4,863.30 to a £1 stake. Pool: £48,300.39 - 7.25 winning tickets T/Qpdt: £177.10 to a £1 stake. Pool: £3,495.66 - 14.60 winning tickets CS

5218 - 5224a (Foreign Racing) - See Raceform Interactive

4198 ASCOT (R-H)
Sunday, April 10

OFFICIAL GOING: Good (chs 8.4, hdl 8.0)
Wind: Almost nil Weather: Sunny and warm

5225 COLTS & FILLIES CLUB MAIDEN HURDLE (11 hdls) 2m 3f 110y
2:00 (2:00) (Class 3) 4-Y-0+
£4,383 (£1,295; £647; £324; £161; £81)

Form RPR

4U30 **1** **Invictus (IRE)**[29] 4725 5-11-0 122.................................... RobertThornton 124
(Alan King) *chsd ldrs: led appr last: narrow ld run-in: hld on gamely: all out* **7/2**[3]

555 **2** *shd* **Barbatos (FR)**[22] 4875 5-11-0 112............................... PaddyBrennan 123
(Ian Williams) *hld up towards rr: stdy hdwy fr 8th: str chal run-in: r.o wl* **5/2**[1]

2332 **3** *15* **Milgen Bay**[72] 3783 5-11-0 117.. LeightonAspell 112
(Oliver Sherwood) *mid-div: hdwy 7th: led 8th tl wknd appr last* **10/3**[2]

-132 **4** *12* **Mawsem (IRE)**[31] 4677 5-11-0 .... AndrewTinkler 99
(George Baker) *towards rr: hdwy 7th: hrd rdn and wknd 3 out* **9/2**

203 **5** *1 ¼* **Spirit Is Needed (IRE)**[31] 4676 5-11-0 114.............(vt[1]) WarrenMarston 99
(Milton Harris) *w ldrs: led 3rd: nt fluent and hdd 8th: wknd qckly appr 2 out* **8/1**

6 **6** *23* **Halucha (IRE)**[22] 4879 6-11-0 .... DominicElsworth 77
(Paul Webber) *bhd most of way: passed btn horses fr 3 out* **100/1**

033 **7** *16* **Abayaan**[15] 5013 5-11-0 105.......................................(t) DenisO'Regan 63
(Charlie Mann) *chsd ldrs: lost pl 6th: struggling towards rr after* **50/1**

1 **8** *nk* **Chasing Aces**[150] 2328 5-11-0 .... JamieMoore 63
(Gary Brown) *led tl 3rd: w ldrs tl wknd 3 out: 6th and no ch whn j.rt last* **25/1**

35 **9** *¾* **Cheney Manor**[15] 5010 6-10-7 .... MrNdeBoinville[(7)] 62
(Nicky Henderson) *hld up towards rr: hdwy and in tch 8th: wknd 3 out* **22/1**

06 **10** *31* **Joinedupwriting**[13] 5050 6-10-11 .... EamonDehdashti[(3)] 34
(Raymond York) *mid-div: outpcd 6th: bhd fr next* **100/1**

000 **11** *6* **Topthorn**[86] 3546 5-10-9 .... AnthonyFreeman[(5)] 29
(Martin Bosley) *plld hrd: sn chsng ldrs: mstke 6th: wknd after next: bhd whn blnd 3 out* **100/1**

0 **P** **The Gurner (IRE)**[36] 4491 4-10-7 .... AidanColeman —
(Charlie Longsdon) *in tch: dropped to rr 5th: wl bhd whn p.u bef 8th* **66/1**

4m 37.0s (-11.00) **Going Correction** -0.40s/f (Good)
WFA 4 from 5yo+ 5lb **12** Ran SP% **117.8**
Speed ratings (Par 107): **106,105,99,95,94 85,79,78,78,66 63,—**
toteswingers: 1&2 £1.90, 1&3 £2.10, 2&3 £2.40. CSF £12.51 TOTE £4.90: £2.00, £1.70, £1.80; EX 14.40 Trifecta £62.00 Pool: £454.71 - 5.42 winning units..
Owner Mr & Mrs R Kelvin Hughes **Bred** J O'Connell **Trained** Barbury Castle, Wilts

FOCUS
Following a dry night the going was given as good on both tracks, with the GoingStick recording 8.4 on the chase track and 8.0 on the hurdles track. Jockeys reported the ground to be on the quick side after this maiden hurdle. The first two came clear in the closing stages.

NOTEBOOK
Invictus(IRE) just edged things close home. Unlucky to still be a maiden coming into this, he coped fine with the quicker ground (point winner on good to firm) and will get further next year when presumably chasing will be on his agenda. (tchd 4-1)
Barbatos(FR) was nicely supported and clearly expected to improve for the quicker surface. He did just that, but came up a little short. A reproduction of this effort should be good enough to win a similar race in the next few weeks. (tchd 9-4 and 3-1)
Milgen Bay led them into the straight and came clear with the first two before being beaten off approaching the last. It's difficult to know his best trip. (op 4-1 tchd 11-4)
Mawsem(IRE) was under pressure some way out but kept going to take fourth. This was a step up in class for him and he could do with being dropped in grade. (op 11-2 tchd 4-1)
Spirit Is Needed(IRE), who wore a visor and a tongue-tie for the first time (won twice in blinkers on the Flat), ran well for a long way and would be of more interest in modest handicap company. (tchd 9-1)

5226 ASCOT ALL AREAS NOVICES' CHASE (17 fncs) 2m 5f 110y
2:35 (2:35) (Class 3) 5-Y-0+ **£6,262** (£1,850; £925; £463)

Form RPR

6030 **1** **Gee Dee Nen**[19] 4933 8-11-4 119.................................(v) JamieMoore 140+
(Gary Moore) *mde all: rdn after 3 out: drew clr appr last: comf* **12/1**

1 **2** *6* **Aerial (FR)**[50] 4223 5-11-3 140.....................................(t) MrRMahon[(5)] 138
(Paul Nicholls) *blnd 1st: pressed wnr next tl outpcd 2 out* **5/6**[1]

2312 **3** *1 ¼* **Squadron**[36] 4480 7-11-4 129.. RobertThornton 133
(Alan King) *in tch in 3rd tl outpcd 4 out: styd on fr 2 out* **11/4**[2]

3122 **4** *42* **Pascha Bere (FR)**[19] 4926 8-11-4 0...........................(p) LiamTreadwell 101
(Nick Gifford) *hld up in tch in rr: rdn and wknd 13th* **4/1**[3]

5m 21.0s (-5.00) **Going Correction** -0.40s/f (Good) **4** Ran SP% **108.9**
Speed ratings: **93,90,90,75**
CSF £23.80 TOTE £11.10; EX 30.40.
Owner Chris Duggan & Brendan Gilligan **Bred** Kingwood Bloodstock **Trained** Lower Beeding, W Sussex

FOCUS
This looked a good opportunity for Aerial to follow up his Wincanton success, but there was something of a shock result.

NOTEBOOK
Gee Dee Nen had 17lb to find with Aerial based on adjusted ratings, but he made just about every yard and saw off the favourite's challenge in the straight. He has been a little in and out this season, but likes to make the running, is at his best on decent ground and, perhaps crucially, is very effective at this track (has run well on the Flat and over hurdles here in the past). However, given the excuse for the favourite the form might not stand up. Official explanation: trainer said, regarding apparent improvement in form, that the gelding had been sweetened up by running it over hurdles. (op 11-1 tchd 14-1)
Aerial(FR) was disappointing, but he was racing on quicker ground and the fitting of a tongue-tie for the first time hinted at a breathing problem. It was later reported that the gelding had choked during the race and he'll apparently have a breathing operation now. Official explanation: jockey said gelding had a breathing problem; vet said gelding finished distressed (tchd 4-5 and evens in places)
Squadron ran on late to challenge for second, but he was never a real threat. He's Flat-bred and jumping fences has always looked quite an effort for him. (op 3-1)

Pascha Bere(FR) is at his best over shorter with more cut in the ground. (op 9-2 tchd 7-2)

5227 DAVID AUSTIN ROSES JUVENILE H'CAP HURDLE (9 hdls) 2m
3:10 (3:10) (Class 2) 4-Y-O

£8,140 (£2,405; £1,202; £601; £300; £150)

Form RPR
3441 **1** **Ultravox (USA)**[15] 5006 4-10-5 **121**............................ NathanSweeney[(7)] 124
(Jeremy Scott) *w ldr: led and nt fluent 6th: narrowly hdd 2 out: drvn to ld again run-in: gamely* **6/1**[3]
1445 **2** *nk* **Jubail (IRE)**[25] 4807 4-10-12 **121**................................ WayneHutchinson 124
(Alan King) *in tch: slt ld 2 out: hrd rdn and hdd run-in: rallied wl* **7/2**[2]
2551 **3** *24* **Pullyourfingerout (IRE)**[18] 4954 4-11-5 **135**........(t) JeremiahMcGrath[(7)] 120+
(Brendan Powell) *led tl 6th: w ldrs tl sltly hmpd and wknd 2 out* **10/1**
5200 **4** *1 1/2* **Gulf Punch**[12] 2639 4-9-11 **109** oh2............................(p) JimmyDerham[(3)] 89
(Milton Harris) *sn bhd: hrd rdn 3 out: wnt modest 4th run-in* **28/1**
5123 **5** *3* **Dhaafer**[25] 4807 4-10-13 **122**..(p) RobertThornton 106
(Alan King) *chsd ldrs tl wknd 3 out: lft modest 4th and side-stepped 2 fallers 2 out* **5/2**[1]
1100 **6** *dist* **Architrave**[23] 4847 4-11-10 **133**.. JohnnyFarrelly —
(Tim Vaughan) *chsd ldrs tl 4th: bhd fr 6th* **16/1**
P010 **B** **Whitby Jack**[25] 4807 4-11-7 **130**... JamieMoore 115
(Gary Moore) *t.k.h: in tch: rdn 3 out: lft 4th and no imp whn swvd to avoid faller and b.d next* **8/1**
3356 **F** **Rock Of Deauville (IRE)**[25] 4807 4-10-3 **112**..................(t) HarrySkelton 115+
(Paul Nicholls) *hld up towards rr: hdwy 6th: chalng whn fell 2 out* **7/2**[2]

3m 40.1s (-8.90) **Going Correction** -0.40s/f (Good) **8** Ran SP% **116.8**
Speed ratings: **106,105,93,93,91** —,—,—
toteswingers: 1&2 £6.40, 1&3 £3.80, 2&3 £12.90. CSF £28.45 CT £209.00 TOTE £8.30: £2.20, £2.40, £1.30; EX 51.50 Trifecta £408.50 Part won. Pool: £649.85 - 0.23 winning units..
Owner G T Lever **Bred** Hascombe Stud **Trained** Brompton Regis, Somerset

FOCUS
The complexion of this handicap changed when Rock Of Deauville, who was coming to challenge going well, fell at the second-last, hampering Pullyourfingerout in the process, and also clipping Whitby Jack, causing him to be brought down on the flat as well.

NOTEBOOK
Ultravox(USA), left clear with Jubail following the incident at the second-last, showed the most determination and just came out on top. He had made much of the running and, despite being ridden along from some way out and headed approaching the final flight, not for the first time he showed he's a really tough fighter and kept finding more for pressure. He wants further than this and can do better again back up in trip. Incidentally, the winning time was a course record and Ultravox provided his trainer with his eighth winner from 19 runners since the beginning of March. (tchd 11-2)
Jubail(IRE), fifth in the Fred Winter last time out, ran off the same mark here and had his favoured conditions. He had every chance, but the winner wanted it more. (op 9-2)
Pullyourfingerout(IRE), who kept the winner company up front for much of the race, looked booked for a place at best when hampered at the second-last. The incident merely accentuated the distance he was beaten. (op 9-1)
Gulf Punch, who was racing from 2lb out of the handicap, was struggling from a fair way out and is flattered by her finishing position. (op 33-1)
Dhaafer was also slightly hampered after the second-last, but he was never a threat to the principals. Perhaps he was still feeling the effects of a hard race at Cheltenham, and/or he doesn't want the ground this quick. (op 11-4 tchd 3-1 in a place)
Whitby Jack, disappointing in the Fred Winter, was running a better race here but still looked booked for fifth prior to the incident at the second-last. (op 4-1)
Rock Of Deauville(IRE) looked to be travelling best of all when coming down at the second-last. Whether he would have found as much as he promised off the bridle is open to question as he has disappointed before, but he looked sure to play a hand in the finish. (op 4-1)

5228 READING POST H'CAP CHASE (16 fncs) 2m 3f
3:45 (3:45) (Class 3) (0-130,127) 5-Y-O+

£6,262 (£1,850; £925; £463; £231; £116)

Form RPR
0121 **1** **Bedarra Boy**[80] 3648 5-10-11 **112**...................................... AidanColeman 128+
(David Arbuthnot) *hld up in rr: hdwy 10th: led 4 out: qcknd clr after next: comf* **9/2**[3]
4112 **2** *6* **Qianshan Leader (IRE)**[15] 5011 7-11-9 **124**.............................. JackDoyle 135
(Emma Lavelle) *w ldrs: mstke 10th: led 12th tl 4 out: nt pce of wnr fr next* **10/3**[1]
0255 **3** *19* **Double Vodka (IRE)**[29] 4730 10-11-6 **121**......................... DenisO'Regan 113
(Chris Grant) *towards rr: rdn 11th: styd on to snatch modest 3rd nr fin* **7/1**
1566 **4** *3/4* **Pilgrims Lane (IRE)**[176] 1863 7-11-9 **127**................(tp) JimmyDerham[(3)] 118
(Milton Harris) *in tch: mstke 3rd: outpcd fr 12th* **25/1**
2P21 **5** *1 1/4* **Fiftyonefiftyone (IRE)**[27] 4782 7-11-9 **124**...................... LeightonAspell 115
(Oliver Sherwood) *prom: mstke 10th: outpcd 4 out: 3rd and btn whn j.lft 2 out* **4/1**[2]
4062 **6** *1 3/4* **Tempting Paradise (IRE)**[30] 4698 8-10-9 **110**................... JamieMoore 98
(Evan Williams) *chsd ldrs: niggled along fr 6th: wknd 11th* **10/1**
5060 **7** *29* **Soulard (USA)**[43] 4355 8-11-10 **125**................................. PaddyBrennan 102
(Sophie Leech) *led: mstke 8th: hdd 12th: lft modest 4th and wkng whn hmpd 3 out* **8/1**
4231 **F** **Lordsbridge (USA)**[19] 4931 9-10-8 **116**............................ MrBJPoste[(7)] —
(Andy Turnell) *in tch: blnd 1st: cl 3rd whn fell 3 out* **7/1**

4m 40.1s (-6.90) **Going Correction** -0.40s/f (Good) **8** Ran SP% **110.3**
Speed ratings: **98,95,87,87,86 85,73**,—
toteswingers: 1&2 £1.30, 1&3 £5.20, 2&3 £1.10. CSF £19.05 CT £96.00 TOTE £5.70: £1.70, £1.60, £1.70; EX 15.40 Trifecta £53.50 Pool: £658.07 - 9.09 winning units..
Owner P M Claydon **Bred** Mickley Stud & E Kent **Trained** Compton, Berks

FOCUS
Quite a competitive handicap on paper, but Bedarra Boy ran out a fairly convincing winner.

NOTEBOOK
Bedarra Boy, a neat jumper who has now won three of his four starts over fences, appreciates a decent surface (won on firm ground at Bath on the Flat) and the extra 2f proved no trouble at all. The valuable Summer Plate at Market Rasen was mentioned as his big summer target and, providing the ground is suitable, he could be aimed at the Grand Sefton in November with a view to aiming him for the Topham next spring. (op 4-1)
Qianshan Leader(IRE) apparently wasn't suited by the watered ground at Newbury last time and this proper quick surface was much more to his liking. He bumped into an improving rival, but beat the rest comfortably and can win a similar race off this sort of mark. (op 7-2 tchd 11-4 and 4-1 in a place)
Double Vodka(IRE) looks held by the handicapper for the time being. (op 15-2 tchd 13-2)
Pilgrims Lane(IRE) is also on a stiff enough mark, but he's entitled to come on for this first outing since October. (tchd 28-1)
Fiftyonefiftyone(IRE), not for the first time, tended to jump out to his left and might prefer going the other way round. (tchd 7-2)
Soulard(USA), well supported on his debut for a new stable and running off a tempting-looking mark, has winning form round here and likes fast ground, so it was easy to see why the money came for him. He was off the leading group and had been given a couple of reminders prior to being hampered.
Lordsbridge(USA) was just in behind the first two when he came down at the third-last. He was the only other one who looked like having any sort of chance at the time and he badly hampered Soulard in the process. (tchd 15-2)

5229 ASCOT VETERANS H'CAP CHASE (20 fncs) 3m
4:20 (4:20) (Class 2) (0-145,135) 10-Y-O+

£10,056 (£2,997; £1,517; £777; £406)

Form RPR
PF40 **1** **Magic Sky (FR)**[36] 4486 11-10-6 **118**..........................(p) JimmyDerham[(3)] 125
(Milton Harris) *hld up in rr: hdwy 16th: led last: narrowly hdd 100yds out: rallied gamely to get bck up fnl strides* **12/1**
U452 **2** *hd* **Appleaday (IRE)**[29] 4726 10-10-6 **115**.......................(p) DominicElsworth 123
(Paul Webber) *prom: pressed ldr 11th: led after 3 out tl last: regained narrow ld 100yds out: hdd fnl strides* **4/1**[3]
4-36 **3** *14* **Wogan**[46] 4284 11-11-8 **131**.. AndrewTinkler 127
(Nicky Henderson) *led: mstke 16th: hdd & wknd after 3 out* **6/1**
334P **4** *11* **Ma Yahab**[22] 4876 10-10-9 **118**...(b) AidanColeman 103
(Venetia Williams) *in tch: rdn whn mstke 13th: sn outpcd* **7/1**
1U32 **5** *6* **Alderburn**[36] 4486 12-11-12 **135**....................................... PaddyBrennan 116
(Henry Daly) *mstke 7th: chsd ldr tl 11th: mstke and wknd 16th* **3/1**[2]
35-P **F** **Laskari (FR)**[169] 1960 12-11-12 **135**.................................... DenisO'Regan —
(Paul Webber) *hld up in 6th: hdwy to dispute 3rd after 14th: mstke and wknd next: 7th and no ch whn fell 4 out* **16/1**
-221 **P** **Blu Teen (FR)**[30] 4699 11-10-10 **124**................................(t) MrRMahon[(5)] —
(Paul Nicholls) *in tch: outpcd and struggling in rr 14th: bhd whn hmpd 4 out: t.o whn p.u bef 2 out* **11/4**[1]

5m 53.9s (-15.10) **Going Correction** -0.40s/f (Good) **7** Ran SP% **112.0**
Speed ratings: **109,108,104,100,98** —,—
toteswingers: 1&2 £13.00, 1&3 £7.10, 2&3 £6.10. CSF £57.21 TOTE £16.50: £5.40, £2.20; EX 75.10.
Owner Mrs D J Brown **Bred** Jean-Claude Mugain **Trained** Herridge, Wiltshire
■ Stewards' Enquiry : Jimmy Derham one-day ban: used whip with excessive frequency (Apr 24)

FOCUS
A veterans chase in which the top-weight weighed in 10lb below the ceiling.

NOTEBOOK
Magic Sky(FR) eventually came out on top in what was a duel from the second-last. The 11-y-o didn't jump well at Newbury last time, but he'd been dropped 6lb since and had the cheekpieces back on here. His jumping was much better and, ridden with a bit of patience, was delivered with a well-timed challenge, although he was made to fight by the runner-up.
Appleaday(IRE) was trying the impossible last time out when up against up-and-coming chasing star Mon Parrain at Sandown. Back against more exposed opposition, he was given a positive ride and saw off his fellow pace-setter Wogan, but couldn't quite hold off the more patiently ridden winner, hard though he tried. This was a solid effort. (op 9-2)
Wogan hasn't been at his best this season, but he likes a decent surface to run on and he put up a decent performance from the front here. He remains above his last winning mark, though, and could do with being eased a few pounds. (op 5-1 tchd 13-2)
Ma Yahab reversed Newbury form from last month with Alderburn, but neither proved quite as effective on this quick ground. (op 15-2 tchd 8-1)
Blu Teen(FR) didn't look badly handicapped on paper, but he was well behind when hampered at the fourth-last and proved disappointing. Official explanation: jockey said gelding never travelled (op 5-2 tchd 9-4 and 3-1 in a place)

5230 WOODSTOCK CONDITIONAL JOCKEYS' H'CAP HURDLE (13 hdls) 3m
4:55 (4:55) (Class 3) (0-135,128) 4-Y-O+

£4,508 (£1,332; £666; £333; £166; £83)

Form RPR
00P6 **1** **Puzzlemaster**[30] 4700 5-10-4 **109**..............................(t) EdGlassonbury[(3)] 111
(Hughie Morrison) *in tch: wnt prom 8th: slt ld last: plld out ex whn jnd run-in: gamely* **8/1**
4060 **2** *1/2* **Miss Overdrive**[26] 4793 7-10-13 **120**................................ EdCookson[(5)] 122
(Andy Turnell) *hdwy to ld 4th: hdd 2 out: rallied to join wnr run-in: jst outpcd nr fin* **5/1**[2]
0660 **3** *2* **Arkose (IRE)**[64] 3947 7-11-1 **120**.................................(p) PeterCarberry[(3)] 121
(Oliver Sherwood) *mde most tl 4th: outpcd 3 out: rallied and chal last: nt qckn* **8/1**
3-PU **4** *nk* **Georgian King**[19] 4933 8-10-10 **115**................................ MattCrawley[(3)] 117+
(Suzy Smith) *travelled wl in rr: gd hdwy on bit to ld 2 out: blnd and hdd last: one pce* **9/1**
231P **5** *7* **Like A Hurricane (IRE)**[64] 3947 8-11-1 **122**.................... PeterHatton[(5)] 118
(Alan King) *t.k.h: in tch: jnd ldrs 2 out: wknd last* **4/1**[1]
415 **6** *4 1/2* **Kasban**[16] 4988 7-10-7 **112**..(t) TrevorWhelan[(3)] 102
(Luke Dace) *chsd ldrs tl hrd rdn and wknd after 3 out* **11/2**[3]
3224 **7** *11* **Lupanar (IRE)**[55] 4121 7-11-0 **121**...........................(p) JosephAkehurst[(5)] 104
(Gary Moore) *chsd ldrs: lost pl 6th: rdn to stay in tch fr 9th: btn 3 out* **5/1**[2]
650F **8** *12* **Quickbeam (IRE)**[22] 4875 9-11-9 **128**............................. HarryChalloner[(3)] 97
(Venetia Williams) *prom: mstke 8th: sn lost pl and struggling* **11/1**
0F20 **F** **Go Amwell**[36] 4464 8-10-13 **118**...................................(v) CharlieWallis[(3)] —
(J R Jenkins) *hld up: in tch tl fell 6th* **14/1**

5m 52.5s (-3.50) **Going Correction** -0.40s/f (Good) **9** Ran SP% **115.9**
Speed ratings (Par 107): **91,90,90,90,87 86,82,78**,—
toteswingers: 1&2 £14.30, 1&3 £16.30, 2&3 £6.00. CSF £48.37 CT £333.71 TOTE £7.90: £2.90, £2.10, £2.20; EX 69.10 Trifecta £372.80 Part won. Pool: £503.88 - 0.50 winning units..
Owner Mr & Mrs Rory Sweet **Bred** Norcroft Park Stud **Trained** East Ilsley, Berks

FOCUS
An open handicap run at a fairly steady early pace. The top-weight was rated 7lb below the ceiling.

NOTEBOOK
Puzzlemaster began the season rated 127 and running against Menorah et al in the Greatwood Hurdle, but following a series of heavy defeats he found himself competing here off a mark of 109. Clearly well handicapped if recapturing the form he showed as a novice last season, he appreciated the step up to 3m on good ground and found plenty for pressure in the straight. He shouldn't go up too much for this and perhaps he can build on it. (op 10-1)
Miss Overdrive looked handicapped up to her best but she's tough, goes on any ground and is fairly consistent, and ran another fine race in defeat. (op 6-1)
Arkose(IRE) ran a better race in the first-time cheekpieces and he got the trip well, albeit off a steady early gallop. (tchd 15-2)
Georgian King led going to the final flight but blundered at it and couldn't get his momentum back. He's well handicapped on his best form for Alan King and looks the type to keep on the go over the summer as he likes quick ground. (op 15-2)
Like A Hurricane(IRE) could have done with a stronger pace as he was keen early and looked to pay for that in the closing stages. (tchd 7-2)

Kasban disappointed at Newbury last time and again he failed to perform to the level he showed at Kempton last month. (op 7-1tched 15-2 in places)

5231 GUY SALMON ASCOT LAND ROVER HUNTERS' CHASE (17 fncs) 2m 5f 110y
5:30 (5:30) (Class 4) 5-Y-0+ **£2,810** (£871; £435; £217)

Form RPR
-11P **1** **Just Amazing (IRE)**[23] 4851 8-12-6 136..............................(t) MrRMahon 114+
(Paul Nicholls) *mde virt all: idled and jnd run-in: rallied to get bk on top nr fin* **1/2**[1]
0-P2 **2** ½ **Sovereign King**[19] 4936 9-11-9 108.. MrMWall(3) 102
(Miss C Herrington) *sn pressing wnr: outpcd appr 2 out: rallied and stmbld last: drvn level run-in: jst hld nr fin* **9/1**[3]
34-2 **3** *31* **Oracle Des Mottes (FR)**[30] 4708 12-11-5 116................(t) MrDCollins(7) 71
(R Barber) *drpd to last and t.o fr 7th: regained remote 3rd at last* **11/4**[2]
00 **4** 1 ¼ **Orphelin Collonges (FR)**[32] 4560 9-11-7 68...................(p) MrMPrice(5) 70
(Richard Price) *t.o and no ch w 2 ldrs fr 7th, lost remote 3rd at last* **20/1**
5m 25.0s (-1.00) **Going Correction** -0.40s/f (Good) 4 Ran SP% **108.1**
Speed ratings: **85,84,73,73**
CSF £5.11 TOTE £1.60; EX 5.10.
Owner Mrs Catherine Penny **Bred** R J Powell **Trained** Ditcheat, Somerset

FOCUS
Just the four runners, and in truth a two-horse race from quite early on.

NOTEBOOK
Just Amazing(IRE) and Sovereign King duelled for the lead from some way out and the former looked to have finally justified his market position when jumping clear at the second-last, but he soon began to idle heading to the last and was again joined by the runner-up. Despite nodding on landing, Sovereign King has his chance to come back at the winner but, once he drew up alongside, Just Amazing found extra and showed he had more left in the tank than it had appeared. (op 8-13 tched 4-5 in places)
Sovereign King is flattered to have finished so close, but it was still a good effort in defeat and he beat the other two a country mile. (op 8-1)
Oracle Des Mottes(FR) could not match the pace of the two up front from an early stage and was never a factor in the race. (op 9-4)
T/Plt: £1,668.50 to a £1 stake. Pool:£95,658.04 - 41.85 winning tickets. T/Qpdt: £127.20 to a £1 stake. Pool:£8,237.89 - 47.90 winning tickets. LM

5078 LUDLOW (R-H)
Sunday, April 10

OFFICIAL GOING: Good (7.8)
Wind: Nil Weather: Warm and Sunny

5232 LUDLOW GOLF CLUB CLAIMING HURDLE (9 hdls) 2m
2:20 (2:20) (Class 4) 4-Y-0+ **£1,951** (£573; £286; £143)

Form RPR
11P1 **1** **Chrysander**[15] 4999 9-11-2 116..(vt) PaulMoloney 117+
(Evan Williams) *w ldr: led 4th: wnt abt 4 l clr appr 3 out: r.o wl and a in command: eased down towards fin* **1/1**[1]
24-0 **2** 2 ¾ **Bundle Up**[136] 2639 8-10-9 103.. RhysFlint 105
(John Flint) *in tch: clsd 5th: rdn to chse wnr appr 3 out: kpt on but no imp* **17/2**
6052 **3** *16* **Le Corvee (IRE)**[9] 5101 9-11-3 110.................................. LeeEdwards(3) 104
(Tony Carroll) *trckd ldrs: wnt 2nd appr 6th: rdn and lost 2nd bef 3 out: wknd fr 2 out* **9/1**
U403 **4** *7* **Claimant (IRE)**[15] 5014 4-10-8 101......................................(bt) SamJones 84
(Paul Fitzsimons) *in tch: outpcd by ldrs after 5th: clsd after 6th: rdn and outpcd appr 3 out where j.rt: no imp whn nt fluent and j.rt again 2 out* **25/1**
1160 **5** *5* **Tayarat (IRE)**[11] 4778 6-11-3 118.......................................(bt) MrOGarner(7) 94
(Michael Chapman) *led: hdd 4th: w ldr tl rdn appr 6th: wknd sn after* **20/1**
F12U **6** 3 ¼ **Hypnotic Gaze (IRE)**[15] 5014 5-11-8 107.........................(p) JamesDavies 91
(Andrew Haynes) *bhd: struggling 4th: sme hdwy appr 6th but no real threat: wknd 3 out* **20/1**
6441 **7** *5* **Master Fong (IRE)**[18] 4939 5-11-10 115...............................(b) AdrianLane 88
(Donald McCain) *trckd ldrs: blnd 6th: sn rdn and wknd: n.d whn stmbld 2 out* **9/2**[2]
00 **8** *10* **Polo Springs**[10] 5082 4-9-8 0...(t) GaryDerwin(7) 57
(Bill Turner) *stmbld after 1st: bhd: struggling 4th: nvr able to get on terms* **150/1**
0-PP **P** **Singapore Reef (FR)**[150] 2333 5-11-0 105............................ DarylJacob —
(Nick Williams) *bhd: struggling 4th: t.o after 5th: p.u bef 3 out* **8/1**[3]
3m 43.4s (-6.10) **Going Correction** -0.35s/f (Good)
WFA 4 from 5yo+ 5lb 9 Ran SP% **113.9**
Speed ratings (Par 105): **101,99,91,88,85 84,81,76,—**
toteswingers: 1&2 £3.10, 1&3 £3.50, 2&3 £14.40. CSF £9.56 TOTE £2.20: £1.20, £1.60, £1.60; EX 9.60.
Owner R E R Williams **Bred** Darley **Trained** Llancarfan, Vale Of Glamorgan

FOCUS
This was a moderate, uncompetitive claiming hurdle.

NOTEBOOK
Chrysander was the best off at the weights. Eased after the last, he was value for more than double the margin and has now won his last four starts in claimers. (op 5-4)
Bundle Up ran respectably after a 136-day break considering she had 6lb to find with the winner on the figures, but she was always held and is flattered to get so close. (op 7-1 tchd 13-2)
Le Corvee(IRE) had conditions to suit and seemed to go okay to a point, but he hung under pressure in the straight and did not look keen.
Claimant(IRE), in second-time blinkers, didn't improve for having a tongue-tie. (tchd 28-1)
Master Fong(IRE), successful in a seller at Haydock last time, had no easy task on these terms, but even so this was a poor show. (tchd 5-1)

5233 FREE RACING POST FORM AT TOTESPORT.COM NOVICES' CHASE (13 fncs) 2m
2:55 (2:55) (Class 3) 5-Y-0+ **£5,544** (£1,638; £819)

Form RPR
1230 **1** **Pepe Simo (IRE)**[23] 4853 7-11-4 140.. DarylJacob 133+
(Paul Nicholls) *led to 2nd: nt fluent 3rd: led again after 5th (water): mde rest: in command fr 4 out: effrtlessly drew clr run-in* **1/5**[1]
4143 **2** *13* **Courella (IRE)**[10] 5079 7-11-8 114.................................... PaulMoloney 122
(Evan Williams) *hld up in last pl: wnt 2nd 9th: no imp on wnr fr 4 out: eased whn one pce run-in* **6/1**[2]
-002 **3** *40* **Bay Central (IRE)**[27] 4782 7-10-12 0...................................... SamJones 76
(Evan Williams) *pressed ldr: led 2nd: hdd after 5th (water): dropped to last 9th: lost tch w front 2 bef 4 out* **9/1**[3]
3m 51.8s (-6.70) **Going Correction** -0.25s/f (Good) 3 Ran SP% **107.6**
Speed ratings: **106,99,92**
CSF £1.94 TOTE £1.10; EX 1.40.
Owner Highclere Thoroughbred Racing-Pepe Simo **Bred** Grange Stud **Trained** Ditcheat, Somerset

FOCUS
An uncompetitive novice chase.

NOTEBOOK
Pepe Simo(IRE), eighth in the Grand Annual on his previous start, outclassed his two rivals despite not jumping well. He made an error at the third fence and generally just didn't get that high at most of his obstacles. This was a good opportunity for him and he won't appeal back in better company. (op 1-3)
Courella(IRE) would have been 30lb better off with the winner in a handicap. (op 5-1)
Bay Central(IRE) was totally outclassed on just his second chase start. (op 8-1)

5234 BET ON LIVE FOOTBALL AT TOTESPORT.COM NOVICES' H'CAP HURDLE (11 hdls) 2m 5f
3:30 (3:32) (Class 3) (0-125,125) 4-Y-0+ **£5,069** (£1,497; £748; £374; £187)

Form RPR
1021 **1** **Badgers Cove (IRE)**[90] 3485 7-11-10 123.......................... CharliePoste 127+
(Robin Dickin) *a.p: led on long run to 3 out: sn jnd: carried rt fr bef 2 out: conitinued to duel for ld: gained upper hand fnl 75yds: r.o: dismntd after line* **4/1**[1]
1030 **2** ½ **Apache Chant (USA)**[19] 4935 7-9-11 99.......................(p) LeeEdwards(3) 102
(Tony Carroll) *hld up: rdn along after 6th: hdwy u.p on long run to 3 out: jnd wnr 3 out: edgd rt whn duelling for ld bef 2 out: hit last: hdd fnl 75yds: hld fnl strides* **12/1**
5306 **3** *13* **Thoresby (IRE)**[23] 4859 5-10-5 104.. DarylJacob 97
(Ben Case) *hld up: hdwy 8th: rdn to chse ldrs appr 3 out: kpt on same pce and no imp on front pair bef last* **11/1**
3546 **4** *8* **Loch Ba (IRE)**[35] 4500 5-10-3 102.. PaulMoloney 87
(Henrietta Knight) *midfield: lost pl 4th: hdwy to chse ldrs appr 3 out: one pce fr 2 out* **11/2**[3]
5U30 **5** *12* **Admiral Dundas (IRE)**[139] 2581 6-10-11 110...................(t) SeanQuinlan 83
(Kim Bailey) *in tch: lost pl appr 8th: toiling sn after: plugged on modly but n.d fr 3 out* **9/1**
00/3 **6** *18* **Rock Salmon**[20] 4922 8-10-1 103 ow2.................................. DavidBass(3) 60
(Lucy Wadham) *hld up: niggled along fr bef 6th: nvr on terms* **9/2**[2]
02P6 **7** 1 ½ **Puerto Azul (IRE)**[19] 4933 7-11-1 114...................................... SamJones 70
(Oliver Sherwood) *hld up in rr: hdwy to chse ldrs appr 8th: wknd bef 3 out: n.d whn mstke 2 out* **10/1**
F122 **8** *23* **Penyfan Dawn (IRE)**[234] 1289 7-11-4 120...................... RichardKilloran(3) 55
(Tim Vaughan) *hld up: mstke 3rd and 7th: hdwy sn after: chalng after 8th: wknd bef 3 out* **14/1**
2F30 **9** *16* **Red Rouble (IRE)**[44] 4327 6-10-9 108...................... SamTwiston-Davies 29
(Nigel Twiston-Davies) *in tch: rdn and wknd after 8th* **10/1**
2414 **10** *27* **Diamond MM (IRE)**[71] 3816 5-10-5 104...................................(t) RhysFlint —
(Alison Thorpe) *prom tl mstke 8th: sn wknd* **20/1**
0645 **11** *7* **Somewhatinevitable (IRE)**[19] 4930 6-10-9 108................ WillKennedy —
(Paul Webber) *led: hit 8th: hdd on long run to 3 out: sn wknd* **10/1**
5m 3.30s (-11.50) **Going Correction** -0.35s/f (Good) 11 Ran SP% **118.3**
Speed ratings (Par 107): **107,106,101,98,94 87,86,78,71,61 59**
toteswingers: 1&2 £25.80, 1&3 £9.60, 2&3 £31.40. CSF £51.39 CT £496.00 TOTE £5.40: £1.60, £5.30, £4.50; EX 60.30.
Owner E R C Beech & B Wilkinson **Bred** Miss Lillian Barry **Trained** Atherstone on Stour, Warwicks
■ Stewards' Enquiry : David Bass two-day ban: weighed in 2lb heavy (Apr 24-25)

FOCUS
A fair handicap hurdle for novices.

NOTEBOOK
Badgers Cove(IRE), a winner over 3m on soft ground at Towcester on his previous start, did well to follow up faced with a vastly different test on this handicap debut after a three-month break. He was dismounted soon after the race but that seemed to be owing to the heat and there didn't look to be much wrong with him. A horse with a fine attitude, he has plenty of size and may now be given a break before going chasing next season. He's a useful prospect. (op 6-1)
Apache Chant(USA) was getting a lot of weight from the winner and just failed to make it count. He had conditions to suit and this looked a career best. (op 11-1)
Thoresby(IRE), although not seeing his race out as well as the front two on this step up in trip, shaped as though he can win off this sort of mark. (tchd 12-1)
Loch Ba(IRE) ran creditably and is expected to do better when going chasing. (op 7-1)
Admiral Dundas(IRE) is a bit more exposed than some of these. (op 11-1)
Rock Salmon was having his second run after a lengthy absence and might have found the ground too fast. (op 11-2)

5235 WELSH GUARDS ASSOCIATION NOVICES' HURDLE (9 hdls) 2m
4:05 (4:05) (Class 4) 4-Y-0+ **£2,927** (£859; £429; £214)

Form RPR
-612 **1** **Lifestyle**[51] 4195 5-10-12 134.. FelixDeGiles 112+
(Nicky Henderson) *in tch: moved upsides gng wl 3 out: led on bit 2 out: readily drew clr run-in* **4/11**[1]
06 **2** *4* **Stevie Thunder**[9] 5099 6-10-13 0.......................................(t) DaveCrosse 100
(Ian Williams) *chsd ldr: mstke 5th: led appr 3 out: sn jnd: hdd 2 out: one pce and no ch w wnr run-in* **13/2**[2]
6330 **3** *17* **Tignello (IRE)**[160] 2128 6-11-5 111.......................................(t) DarylJacob 92
(Emma Baker) *led: hdd appr 3 out where j.lft and mstke: wl btn fr next* **8/1**[3]
0604 **4** *13* **Echo Dancer**[8] 5114 5-10-13 82.............................(t) SamTwiston-Davies 75
(Trevor Wall) *bhd: nt fluent and nrly uns rdr 4th: pushed along whn attempting to cl appr 3 out: no real imp: wl btn 2 out* **20/1**
0 **5** *58* **Cast Of Stars (IRE)**[25] 4810 4-10-7 0..................................... PaulMoloney 14
(Evan Williams) *a bhd: struggling 5th: nvr on terms: t.o* **10/1**
1626 **F** **Roxane Bruere (FR)**[13] 5057 6-10-2 75................(t) ChristopherWard(10) 77
(Robin Dickin) *chsd ldrs: nt fluent 2nd: niggled along in 4th whn fell 2 out* **33/1**
3m 44.3s (-5.20) **Going Correction** -0.35s/f (Good)
WFA 4 from 5yo+ 5lb 6 Ran SP% **114.6**
Speed ratings (Par 105): **99,97,88,82,53 —**
toteswingers: 1&2 £1.40, 1&3 £2.10, 2&3 £3.20. CSF £3.72 TOTE £1.30: £1.30, £2.60; EX 3.10.
Owner The Turf Club & David Ford **Bred** David G Ford **Trained** Upper Lambourn, Berks

FOCUS
Not much depth to this novice hurdle.

NOTEBOOK
Lifestyle, runner-up to the smart Topolski last time, didn't have to be at her best, winning with plenty in hand in a time 0.90 seconds slower than the earlier claiming hurdle. Fitted with earplugs for the first time, she was too good for this lot and deserves a step up in a class. (op 3-10)
Stevie Thunder was useful on the Flat and seems to be gradually getting the idea over hurdles. His handicap mark might suffer as a result of this effort, but he should find his level. (op 9-1)
Tignello(IRE) is entitled to come on for this first start in 160 days (op 14-1)

Roxane Bruere(FR) was in the process of running well but was held when falling at the second-last. (tchd 25-1)

5236 BET ON LIVE GOLF AT TOTESPORT.COM H'CAP CHASE (17 fncs) 2m 4f
4:40 (4:40) (Class 3) (0-135,131) 5-Y-O+

£6,262 (£1,850; £925; £463; £231; £116)

Form				RPR
0535	1		**Tyup Pompey (IRE)**[10] 5081 10-10-0 **108** oh8 ow3........ LeeStephens(3) (Ann Price) *prom: racd off the pce 10th: blnd 13th: hdwy to chse ldr appr 4 out: sn chalng: led 3 out: styd on wl to draw clr run-in* **14/1**	115+
1262	2	6	**Rockiteer (IRE)**[166] 2022 8-11-0 **119**.................................(p) WillKennedy (Henry Daly) *racd keenly: sn chsd ldr: led after 9th (water): jnd 4 out: hdd 3 out: stl chalng u.p abt 1 l down whn hit last: no ex run-in* **5/1**	120
2206	3	1 1/4	**Five Dream (FR)**[29] 4726 7-11-2 **131**.........................(b) JamesCowley(10) (Paul Nicholls) *in tch: lost pl 9th (water): effrt 12th: chsd ldrs appr 4 out: styd on same pce bef last* **4/1**[3]	128
5PUP	4	15	**Fit To Drive**[22] 4864 9-11-3 **122**...................................(tp) JimmyMcCarthy (Brendan Powell) *hld up: pushed along after 13th: wnt 4th 4 out: one pce fr 3 out* **8/1**	106
0011	5	30	**Patman Du Charmil (FR)**[40] 4408 9-11-6 **125**....(b) SamTwiston-Davies (Nigel Twiston-Davies) *j.lft: led: hdd after 9th (water): continued to chse ldr: rdn appr 13th: lost 2nd bef 4 out: sn wknd* **10/3**[1]	82
R05P	6	61	**The Snail**[10] 5081 8-10-10 **115**.. PaulMoloney (Evan Williams) *a bhd: wl adrift fnl circ: t.o* **17/2**	17
-0P2	P		**Bradford Boris**[30] 4695 7-10-8 **113**.. DarylJacob (Nick Williams) *hld up in tch: mstke 3rd: chsd ldrs after 9th (water): wnt 2nd and rdn after 13th: lost 2nd appr 4 out: wknd qckly: p.u bef 3 out* **7/2**[2]	—

4m 55.8s (-8.60) **Going Correction** -0.25s/f (Good) **7** Ran SP% **110.3**
Speed ratings: **107,104,104,98,86 61,—**
toteswingers: 1&2 £7.30, 1&3 £10.40, 2&3 £3.00. CSF £75.30 TOTE £17.00: £6.10, £2.80; EX 103.50.
Owner Mrs A Price **Bred** Rosetown Syndicate **Trained** Norton, Powys

FOCUS
Some of the likely types underperformed.

NOTEBOOK
Tyup Pompey(IRE) improved his record at the track to 4-32, despite being 8lb out of the handicap and carrying 3lb overweight. Not only that, but he made a bad mistake five from the finish yet was able to recover and take this in decisive fashion. This was the winner's fifth win in total and all of them have come in either April or May. He may try and follow up back here later in the month and could look well handicapped under a penalty. (tchd 16-1)
Rockiteer(IRE), returning from a 166-day break, raced enthusiastically under a positive ride and didn't have enough left to resist the winner's strong challenge. (op 11-2)
Five Dream(FR) offered a bit more than of late, finishing clear of the others. (tchd 7-2)
Patman Du Charmil(FR) was looking for a hat-trick but his recent wins had been gained on ground softer than this and he was up a further 3lb. (op 3-1 tchd 7-2)
Bradford Boris found nothing when off the bridle before the straight and was eventually pulled up. Perhaps something was amiss. (op 4-1 tchd 10-3)

5237 LUDLOW GOLD CUP HUNTERS' CHASE (17 fncs) 2m 4f
5:15 (5:15) (Class 6) 6-Y-O+ £999 (£309; £154; £77)

Form				RPR
1-4U	1		**Theatre Diva (IRE)**[23] 4851 10-11-4 120............................. MrJABest(7) (Miss J Du Plessis) *hld up: hdwy to take 2nd 10th: led appr 4 out: jst under 2 l up 2 out: pressed after last: on top fnl 50yds* **7/4**[1]	123+
2U6U	2	1 1/2	**Fairwood Present (IRE)**[3] 5163 13-11-3 117.................. MrTGarner(7) (John Buxton) *prom: led 7th: hdd appr 4 out where mstke: stl ev ch next: under 2 l down 2 out: rallied to press wnr run-in: no ex fnl 50yds* **9/1**[3]	119
-145	3	23	**Emotional Article (IRE)**[10] 5083 11-11-7 118.................. MrAWadlow(7) (Mrs Belinda Clarke) *hld up: pushed along appr 13th: sn outpcd: kpt on fr 3 out: styd on to take 3rd run-in: no ch w front 2* **16/1**	102
-550	4	1 1/4	**Little Rocker (IRE)**[18] 4950 10-11-3 94................... MrOscarChurton(7) (R Smart) *bhd: pushed along appr 8th: kpt on fr 3 out: styd on towards fin: nt gng pce to threaten ldrs* **50/1**	97
-F35	5	hd	**Port Talbot (IRE)**[284] 867 10-11-7 105............................. MrPMason(7) (Jennifer Mason) *hld up: hdwy 11th: mstke 13th: outpcd by ldrs bef 4 out: kpt on to take mod 3rd appr last: no imp: lost 3rd run-in* **14/1**	103
0-5U	6	17	**Jaamid**[30] 4696 9-11-3 0... MrJSHorton(7) (William Hayes, Ire) *racd keenly: prom tl wknd appr 4 out* **16/1**	81
1-25	7	1 1/4	**Spellchecker (IRE)**[36] 4476 7-11-7 102............................. MrMEnnis(7) (Mrs S J Stilgoe) *chsd ldrs: bmpd after 10th: outpcd by ldrs appr 4 out: no imp after: wknd bef last* **12/1**	84
5-56	8	shd	**Give Me Love (FR)**[10] 5083 11-11-3 80......................(b) MrDRogerson(7) (Miss Louise Danton) *chsd ldrs: lost pl bef 5th: bhd after* **33/1**	80
-333	P		**Almaydan**[10] 5083 13-11-3 122...(b) MrOGarner(7) (Mrs K M Diggle) *j.lft a few times: led: hdd 7th: hit 10th and wnt lft: losing pl whn blnd 12th: t.o whn p.u bef 4 out* **15/8**[2]	—
F6-0	U		**William Bonney (IRE)**[10] 5083 11-11-3 106.............(p) MrGHMBartlett(7) (Ann Price) *uns rdr 1st* **25/1**	—

4m 58.3s (-6.10) **Going Correction** -0.25s/f (Good) **10** Ran SP% **116.0**
Speed ratings: **102,101,92,91,91 84,84,84,—,—**
toteswingers: 1&2 £4.60, 1&3 £7.80, 2&3 £12.60. CSF £18.02 TOTE £2.90: £1.50, £2.50, £2.30; EX 24.70.
Owner Miss J Du Plessis **Bred** K J Manning **Trained** Saltash, Cornwall

FOCUS
The front two finished well clear in this ordinary hunter chase.

NOTEBOOK
Theatre Diva(IRE), who had unseated at the Cheltenham Festival on her previous start, is a decent enough sort at this level at her best, but she was made to work for her victory. She landed a similar race here in this month last year and has now won four times at Ludlow. (op 15-8 tchd 13-8)
Fairwood Present(IRE), like the winner, had unseated last time - in this one's case just three days earlier in the Aintree Fox Hunters'. However, he completed this time and ran well with conditions to suit. (op 12-1)
Emotional Article(IRE) had Fairwood Present behind when winning under similar conditions here last May, but he wasn't in quite the same form this time. (tchd 14-1)
Almaydan didn't jump well enough to get involved and was eventually pulled up. (tchd 2-1)

5238 JENKINSONS CATERERS "NEWCOMERS" STANDARD OPEN NATIONAL HUNT FLAT RACE 2m
5:45 (5:45) (Class 6) 4-6-Y-O £1,691 (£496; £248; £124)

Form				RPR
	1		**Featherintheattic (IRE)** 6-11-4 0.. FelixDeGiles (Nicky Henderson) *trckd ldrs gng wl: led on bit over 1f out: effrtlessly wnt clr ins fnl f: v easily* **7/4**[1]	105+
	2	7	**Reyes Magos (IRE)** 5-11-4 0... WillKennedy (Seamus Durack) *hld up: hdwy 5f out: chalng 3f out: rdn and ev ch over 2f out: wnt 2nd 1f out: no ch w wnr* **6/1**[3]	90
	3	3 1/4	**Saxon House (IRE)** 5-11-4 0....................................... JimmyMcCarthy (Mark Usher) *hld up: hdwy 5f out: chalng 3f out: rdn and edgd rt over 1f out: one pce* **20/1**	87
	4	1 3/4	**Cydonia (IRE)** 4-10-12 0... CharliePoste (Robin Dickin) *midfield: hdwy 5f out: led 4f out: rdn over 2f out: hdd over 1f out: wknd fnl f* **5/1**[2]	79
	5	5	**Staccato Valtat (FR)** 5-11-4 0................................ SamTwiston-Davies (Henry Daly) *prom tl rdn and outpcd 3f out: n.d after* **9/1**	80
	6	hd	**Gingers Reflection** 5-11-4 0... PaulMoloney (Henrietta Knight) *in tch: outpcd 6f out and bhd: kpt on modly fnl 2f: nt pce to trble ldrs* **12/1**	80
	7	32	**The Bootle Blitz** 5-11-4 0... MarkBradburne (Cecil Price) *bhd: pushed along on bnd after 4f: nvr on terms* **25/1**	48
	8	2 1/2	**Rock Of Fife** 4-10-12 0.. SamJones (Oliver Sherwood) *trckd ldrs: led 5f out: hdd 4f out: wknd 3f out* **13/2**	39
	9	20	**Generous Kenny** 5-11-4 0.. RhysFlint (John Flint) *led: hdd 5f out: rdn and wknd over 4f out: t.o* **14/1**	25

3m 41.3s (-2.60) **Going Correction** -0.35s/f (Good)
WFA 4 from 5yo+ 5lb **9** Ran SP% **113.6**
Speed ratings: **92,88,86,86,83 83,67,66,56**
toteswingers: 1&2 £2.50, 1&3 £7.20, 2&3 £24.60. totesuper7: WIN: Not won. PLACE: £1165.50. CSF £12.07 TOTE £2.40: £1.10, £2.20, £4.20; EX 8.00.
Owner Joseph Patrick Byrne & Finbar Kelleher **Bred** Jerry O'Sullivan **Trained** Upper Lambourn, Berks

FOCUS
No form to go on but probably an alright bumper and the winner looks decent. They went a steady pace.

NOTEBOOK
Featherintheattic(IRE) cost 60,000 euros as a yearling but only 20,000 euros as a 3yo. He's bred for the Flat but has plenty of size and obviously needed time. Having travelled easily, he found plenty when shaken up. There's no telling just how good he is, but he has potential. (op 6-4 tchd 11-8)
Reyes Magos(IRE), picked up for £38,000 last November, kept responding to pressure in a likeable fashion, but was no match for the classy winner. He should be up to winning one of these. (tchd 11-2)
Saxon House(IRE), a £16,000 purchase as a 2yo, was another who showed enough to suggest he can make his mark. (op 28-1)
Cydonia(IRE) cost 16,500 euros and is a half-brother to, among others, high-class jumper Keen Leader. He can build on this. (op 6-1 tchd 13-2)
Staccato Valtat(FR) shaped as though he'd be better for the experience and should make a nice enough jumper in due course.
T/Plt: £28.40 to a £1 stake. Pool:£48,048.99 - 1,230.81 winning tickets. T/Qpdt: £18.90 to a £1 stake. Pool:£3,294.13 - 128.30 winning tickets. DO

5035 WINCANTON (R-H)
Sunday, April 10

OFFICIAL GOING: Good (good to firm in places in the back straight)
Racing delayed by 35 minutes; insufficient medical cover.
Wind: Virtually nil Weather: Sunny

5239 BATHWICK TYRES YEOVIL "NATIONAL HUNT" NOVICES' HURDLE (10 hdls) 2m 4f
2:10 (2:45) (Class 4) 4-Y-O+ £2,406 (£706; £353; £176)

Form				RPR
4150	1		**Spanish Treasure (GER)**[26] 4788 5-11-6 134................. NickScholfield (Andy Turnell) *cl up: led after 3 out: sn clr: heavily eased run-in* **1/5**[1]	105+
1-00	2	7	**Custer Of The West (IRE)**[94] 3405 6-10-11 0............. CharlieHuxley(3) (Alan King) *hld up: rdn and stdy prog after 3 out: chsd wnr fr next but nvr any ch: b.b.v* **5/1**[2]	83
0/P-	3	4	**Little Fee**[394] 4569 6-10-7 0.. AndrewGlassonbury (Colin Mitchell) *hld up: mstke 5th: rdn after 3 out: styd on past btn horses fr next: wnt 3rd whn hmpd last* **50/1**	73
000	4	12	**Fran's Folly**[21] 4897 5-10-7 0.. TomO'Brien (Neil Mulholland) *trckd ldr: chal 3 out: sn rdn: one pce fr next: lft 4th last* **33/1**	61
050	5	4	**Absolution (IRE)**[94] 3403 5-11-0 0.................................. GerardTumelty (Henrietta Knight) *trckd ldr: led 5th: rdn and hdd after 3 out: wknd next* **10/1**[3]	65
0000	6	8	**Tenitemsplustoast**[31] 4677 5-11-0 0.................................(p) LiamHeard (Patrick Rodford) *racd keenly: j.lft: led tl 5th: prom tl 3 out: sn rdn: wknd bef next* **50/1**	57
3-00	P		**Sir Cool (IRE)**[11] 5074 5-11-0 0....................................(t) AndrewThornton (Tor Sturgis) *in tch: reminders after 3rd: dropped to last and rdn after 5th: wknd 3 out: p.u bef next* **16/1**	—
06	F		**Great Kicker (IRE)**[39] 4430 6-11-0 0.. JoeTizzard (Colin Tizzard) *in tch: tk clsr order 7th: rdn and hung bdly lft after 3 out: btn 4th whn fell last* **12/1**	70

4m 51.4s (-5.40) **Going Correction** -0.65s/f (Firm) **8** Ran SP% **129.5**
Speed ratings (Par 105): **84,81,79,74,73 70,—,—**
toteswingers: 1&2 £1.10, 1&3 £10.30, 2&3 £20.10. CSF £2.66 TOTE £1.30: £1.02, £1.20, £10.10; EX 2.30.
Owner M Tedham **Bred** M Beining **Trained** Broad Hinton, Wilts

FOCUS
The going was good, good to firm in places in the back straight, with 5mm of water having been applied to the track the previous day but the jockeys reckoned it was riding on the fast side. The first race was delayed by 30 minutes due to lack of medical cover. A fairly decent novice hurdle was weakened by late withdrawals and became an uncompetitive affair.

NOTEBOOK
Spanish Treasure(GER) had finished a reasonable eighth in the Supreme Novices' at Cheltenham and this step up in trip was expected to suit. He went on running round towards the straight and, soon clear before being eased near the line, this was little more than a schooling session. He can pick up another of these before the season's end and could well go chasing next season. (op 1-4 tchd 1-3 in a place)
Custer Of The West(IRE) won his bumper on fast ground but had failed to handle easy ground in two starts since. He ran on from the rear to chase home the winner, but the winning margin flatters him. Official explanation: vet said gelding had bled from the nose
Little Fee, who had managed only two runs in two years before this, ran on from the back and managed to grab the minor placing, which is more than connections could have expected.
Fran's Folly, beaten a long way in three previous starts, faded from the home turn. (tchd 40-1)
Absolution(IRE), the only one supported against the winner, faded tamely having been prominent from the start.

Great Kicker(IRE), who did not look a straightforward ride, was vying for a place when coming down at the last. Official explanation: jockey said gelding hung badly left

5240 BATHWICK TYRES SALISBURY NOVICES' H'CAP CHASE (21 fncs) 3m 1f 110y
2:45 (3:20) (Class 4) (0-110,109) 5-Y-0+ £3,447 (£1,012; £506; £252)

Form				RPR
PU44	1		**Victory Parade (IRE)**[33] 4538 8-11-3 **105**.............(p) AodhaganConlon(5) (Rebecca Curtis) *j.lft quite bdly at times: trckd ldr: led 9th: hdd 11th tl after next: mstke 15th: hdd next: led after 17th: mstke 4 out: clr next: styd on wl* **4/1**[2]	124+
1304	2	21	**Gentleman Jimmy**[41] 4402 11-10-8 **91**.................................. TomO'Brien (Hughie Morrison) *nt a fluent: in tch: pushed along at times: rdn 15th: styd on fr 4 out: wnt 2nd next: no further imp on wnr fr 2 out* **13/2**	84
56PP	3	2 ¾	**El Diego (IRE)**[19] 4927 7-10-13 **96**.................................. RichieMcLernon (Jamie Snowden) *hld up last: rdn after 15th: wnt 4th 17th: plugged on fr next: wnt 3rd 3 out: nvr trbld ldrs* **18/1**	84
5U14	4	43	**Ratify**[19] 4931 7-11-5 **109**.. SClements(7) (Brendan Powell) *led tl 9th: w ldr: led 11th tl after next: led 16th tl rdn after next: mstke 4 out: wkng whn lost 2nd 3 out: t.o* **9/2**[3]	74
1301	P		**Justabout**[28] 4749 8-11-3 **100**...(t) JoeTizzard (Colin Tizzard) *j.lft: trckd ldr: reminders after 12th: bhd after next: t.o whn p.u bef 17th* **7/2**[1]	—
2121	P		**Local Present (IRE)**[235] 1281 8-11-11 **108**............................. APMcCoy (Ron Hodges) *sn pushed along in tch: rdn after 15th: wknd next: p.u bef 4 out* **7/2**[1]	—
044	P		**Tom Bach (IRE)**[15] 5001 7-10-7 **90**.................................. GerardTumelty (Richard Price) *in tch whn p.u bef 13th: dismntd* **9/1**	—

6m 33.1s (-6.40) **Going Correction** -0.175s/f (Good) 7 Ran SP% **111.2**
Speed ratings: **102,95,94,81,—** —,—
toteswingers: 1&2 £2.50, 1&3 £4.00, 2&3 £15.10. CSF £27.63 TOTE £5.70: £2.70, £3.20; EX 37.00.
Owner Frank Davies **Bred** Robbie Supple And Tom Byrne **Trained** Newport, Dyfed

FOCUS
A modest handicap chase notable for some less than fluent jumping.

NOTEBOOK
Victory Parade(IRE), whose only previous win was on fast ground, had been given a real chance by the handicapper, as he was racing off 13lb lower than his hurdles mark. He appreciated this surface more than most and responded to a most positive ride to score easily, despite several mistakes. He eventually won the battle for the lead with the fourth turning out of the back straight, coming home unchallenged. (op 9-2)
Gentleman Jimmy was never going that well but did run on to chase home the winner without threatening him. (op 15-2)
El Diego(IRE) had shown little over hurdles and fences before this but stayed on from the back to take the minor placing. Official explanation: vet said gelding lost a shoe (tchd 16-1)
Ratify made the early running but lost out in a battle with the winner from before halfway, and got very tired in the straight. (tchd 4-1)
Justabout, the most recent winner in the race, came under pressure with a circuit to go and was soon beaten. Official explanation: jockey said gelding was unsuited by the good (good to firm places) ground (op 3-1 tchd 4-1)
Local Present(IRE) had a good spell over hurdles last summer and was sent off favourite on this first run since August. However, he was struggling down the back on the second circuit and eventually pulled up. Official explanation: jockey said gelding was unsuited by the good (good to firm places) ground (op 3-1 tchd 4-1)
Tom Bach(IRE) Official explanation: jockey said gelding was unsuited by the good (good to firm places) ground (op 3-1 tchd 4-1)

5241 BATHWICK TYRES DORCHESTER H'CAP HURDLE (11 hdls) 2m 6f
3:20 (3:55) (Class 4) (0-110,110) 4-Y-0+ £4,683 (£1,375; £687; £343)

Form				RPR
001	1		**Flying Award (IRE)**[21] 4900 7-10-11 **100**......................... MarkQuinlan(5) (Susan Gardner) *mid-div: shkn up and hdwy after 3 out: led appr last: styd on wl: rdn out* **6/1**[2]	110
-P04	2	2	**King Kasyapa (IRE)**[8] 5111 9-9-11 **84** oh7................. DonalDevereux(3) (Peter Bowen) *in tch: rdn after 3 out: styd on u.p to hold ch last: kpt on same pce* **14/1**	93
0612	3	3 ¼	**Sail And Return**[7] 5132 7-10-8 **99**................................(t) KielanWoods(7) (Philip Middleton) *trckd ldrs: chal after 3 out: sn rdn: kpt on same pce fr next* **5/4**[1]	105
U4P0	4	3	**Festival Dreams**[44] 4327 6-10-1 **92**................................(p) KyleJames(7) (Joanna Davis) *chsd ldr: rdn to ld after 3 out: hdd bef last: no ex* **25/1**	95
3256	5	2 ¾	**Unleashed (IRE)**[141] 2530 6-11-8 **106**........................... TimmyMurphy (Charlie Mann) *hld up towards rr: hdwy after 3 out: sn rdn: 4 l 5th whn hit last: no ex* **9/1**	109
3432	6	7	**Posh Emily**[12] 5066 8-11-2 **105**.......................................(b) MattGriffiths(5) (Ron Hodges) *hld up towards rr: rdn 3 out: sme imp next: nvr trbld ldrs* **12/1**	99
31F0	7	7	**Ruby Valentine (FR)**[15] 5016 8-9-11 **84** oh1............. MichaelMurphy(3) (Jim Wilson) *hld up towards rr: hdwy after 7th: rdn to chse ldrs after 3 out: wknd next* **33/1**	74
350	8	7	**Party Palace**[17] 1911 7-11-2 **100**.. JodieMogford (Stuart Howe) *led: rdn after 8th: hdd after 3 out: grad fdd* **33/1**	82
4434	9	20	**Lost Two Stars (IRE)**[30] 4703 6-10-7 **98**...................... SClements(7) (Colin Tizzard) *in tch: rdn 8th: sn wknd: t.o* **16/1**	62
2632	P		**Man Of Leisure**[14] 5040 7-10-3 **90**................................. KeiranBurke(3) (Nerys Dutfield) *trckd ldrs: rdn after 3 out: wknd qckly appr next and p.u* **8/1**[3]	—
/0-P	P		**Shardakhan (IRE)**[36] 9-11-5 **110**.................................(b) DannyBurton(7) (Sophie Leech) *mid-div: rdn appr 3 out: sn wknd: p.u bef next* **50/1**	—
P310	P		**Matako (FR)**[22] 4874 8-11-7 **108**.. IanPopham(3) (Caroline Keevil) *towards rr of mid-div: rdn after 3 out: wkng whn hit 2 out: p.u bef last* **20/1**	—
5050	P		**The Clyda Rover (IRE)**[65] 3934 7-10-6 **95**................... JoshuaMoore(5) (Helen Nelmes) *sn struggling in rr: t.o whn p.u bef 8th* **25/1**	—
-020	P		**Blakeneys Pet (IRE)**[152] 2289 5-10-11 **100**.................. TomO'Connor(5) (John Berwick) *a towards rr: bhd whn p.u bef last* **50/1**	—

5m 9.00s (-17.50) 14 Ran SP% **122.3**
toteswingers: 1&2 £24.20, 1&3 £4.60, 2&3 £7.00. CSF £79.39 CT £172.00 TOTE £9.10: £2.70, £4.10, £1.60; EX 79.39.
Owner Mr & Mrs P George & Mrs B Russell **Bred** James V Neville **Trained** Longdown, Devon
■ Stewards' Enquiry : Timmy Murphy two-day ban: used whip when out of contention (Apr 24-25)

FOCUS
A modest but fairly competitive staying handicap hurdle that was run at an even gallop.

NOTEBOOK
Flying Award(IRE), a good-ground point winner, had shown next to nothing over hurdles on easier ground before scoring on his handicap debut last time. Raised 16lb for that, it was not enough to stop him, and he might be able to complete the hat-trick as he should not go up too much for this. (tchd 13-2)
King Kasyapa(IRE) has dropped to a plater's mark after a long absence and loss of form and this was more like it. He might be able to pick up a small race off a similar rating. (op 12-1)
Sail And Return, who has improved for a sounder surface, travelled well in the slipstream of the leaders but had no more to offer from the second-last. He looks high enough in the weights now. (op 13-8 tchd 7-4 in a place)
Festival Dreams handles the ground and stays further and his rider made his bid for home at the last on the far side, but his mount could not sustain it.
Unleashed(IRE) has been unable to translate his Flat form to hurdles but ran his best race at this track in the autumn. He got to the heels of the leaders at the second-last before his effort flattened out. (op 10-1 tchd 11-1)
Posh Emily, stepping back up in trip, only ran on late and seems more effective at shorter. (op 11-1 tchd 10-1)
Ruby Valentine(FR) ran much better this time than she had done behind today's favourite on her previous appearance, but faded tamely having looked a threat early in the straight. (tchd 28-1)
Man Of Leisure was close up until weakening pretty quickly from the third last and being pulled up. Official explanation: jockey said gelding was unsuited by the good (good to firm places) ground (op 9-1)
Shardakhan(IRE) Official explanation: jockey said gelding was unsuited by the good (good to firm places) ground (op 9-1)
Matako(FR) Official explanation: jockey said gelding was unsuited by the good (good to firm places) ground (op 9-1)

5242 BATHWICK TYRES TAUNTON H'CAP CHASE (13 fncs) 2m
3:55 (4:30) (Class 3) (0-135,135) 5-Y-0+ £5,529 (£1,623; £811; £405)

Form				RPR
451P	1		**Russian Flag (FR)**[36] 4487 8-11-8 **134**............................ AlexMerriam(3) (Neil King) *hld up off str early pce: clsd on ldrs 5th: rdn after 4 out: lft in ld after next: kpt on: rdn out* **7/1**[3]	140
4064	2	2 ½	**King Edmund**[36] 4470 8-11-12 **135**... TomO'Brien (Chris Gordon) *w ldr: led after 5th: rdn and hdd after 4 out: kpt on fr next: sn regained 2nd but a being hld by wnr* **11/4**[2]	140
F03U	3	3	**Rivaliste (FR)**[9] 5102 6-11-7 **133**....................................... IanPopham(3) (Paul Nicholls) *hld up off str early pce: hdwy 5th: led after 4 out: stmbld v bdly 3 out: sn hdd and rdn: awkward last 2 fences: nt rcvr* **9/4**[1]	140+
4105	4	48	**Marodima (FR)**[30] 4698 8-10-9 **118**...........................(p) RichieMcLernon (Jamie Snowden) *led at gd pce tl 5th: sn struggling in last: lost tch after 9th: t.o* **7/1**[3]	76
3333	F		**Bathwick Quest (IRE)**[9] 5100 7-9-10 **110**......................(b[1]) CO'Farrell(5) (David Pipe) *hld up off str early pce: mstke and stmbld bdly 2nd: rdr lost iron and sddle looked to slip: hrdly rcvrd whn fell next* **11/4**[2]	—

3m 54.3s (-5.60) **Going Correction** -0.175s/f (Good) 5 Ran SP% **109.1**
Speed ratings: **107,105,104,80,—**
toteswinger: 1&2 £6.30. CSF £25.76 TOTE £6.70: £3.90, £3.10; EX 23.60.
Owner The Drovers & Drifters **Bred** Bernard Le Roux **Trained** Newmarket, Suffolk

FOCUS
The feature race on the card and a decent contest despite the small field. It was run at a good gallop and proved to be a race of changing fortunes.

NOTEBOOK
Russian Flag(FR) bounced back to form on soft ground at Sandown in February but was 9lb higher here as a result. He chased the leaders throughout but looked held when left in front after the favourite's mistake at the third-last. He did enough to hold on as his rivals could not rally. (op 9-2)
King Edmund took on the fourth for the lead and won that battle at the fifth. However, it left him vulnerable in the closing stages and he could only keep on at one pace up the straight. He could go to the Perth festival if the ground is good or softer. (op 3-1)
Rivaliste(FR) was well backed and looked set to justify the support when cruising to the front early in the straight, having jumped fairly well. However, he was unlucky as he sprawled badly on landing at the third last and could not recover. (op 11-4)
Marodima(FR) set off in front as usual, but was taken on for the lead by the runner-up and quickly lost interest once losing the advantage at the fifth. (op 15-2 tchd 8-1)
Bathwick Quest(IRE), in first-time blinkers, blundered badly at the second causing her rider to lose an iron. He struggled to get it back and the partnership was unbalanced going into the next, where they fell heavily. (op 3-1 tchd 5-2)

5243 BATHWICK TYRES BRIDGWATER MAIDEN HURDLE (8 hdls) 2m
4:30 (5:06) (Class 4) 4-Y-0+ £2,406 (£706; £353; £176)

Form				RPR
POP	1		**Surf And Turf (IRE)**[15] 5010 5-11-0 0........................... RichieMcLernon (Jonjo O'Neill) *mid-div: smooth hdwy to trck front pair 2 out: chal last: led run-in: r.o: pushed out* **22/1**	110+
PP42	2	¾	**Final Flyer (IRE)**[15] 4999 7-10-9 107............................ OliverDayman(5) (Alison Thorpe) *led tl 2nd: trckd ldr: led wl after 3 out: wnt lft next: sn rdn: hdd run-in: kpt on but no ex* **5/1**[3]	107
-233	3	3 ¼	**Penchesco (IRE)**[32] 4557 6-11-0 110.................................. APMcCoy (Amanda Perrett) *trckd ldrs: chal 2 out: sn rdn: ev ch last: kpt on same pce* **8/11**[1]	106
540	4	10	**Ebony Diamond (IRE)**[121] 2873 7-11-0 0.......................... TimmyMurphy (Charlie Mann) *hld up towards rr: hdwy after 3 out: rdn to chse ldrs next: sn one pce* **4/1**[2]	94
	5	11	**Encompassing (IRE)**[198] 4-10-8 0....................................... TomO'Brien (Sophie Leech) *hld up towards rr: sme prog 2 out: no further imp whn hit last* **12/1**	77
6UF	6	2 ¾	**Caunay**[14] 5035 4-10-3 0...(t) MarkQuinlan(5) (Neil Mulholland) *trckd ldr tl blnd 1st: in tch: rdn after 3 out: wknd bef last* **100/1**	74
3	7	6	**Hatchet Man**[14] 5035 5-10-11 0.. IanPopham(3) (Carroll Gray) *hld up towards rr: shortlived effrt after 3 out* **50/1**	74
530	8	1 ¼	**Oscar Charlie (IRE)**[255] 1124 6-11-0 0............................ GerardTumelty (Jamie Snowden) *t.k.h: led 2nd: rdn and hdd appr 2 out: wknd bef last* **20/1**	73
	9	1 ½	**Sponge**[625] 6-11-0 0.. MarkGrant (Norma Twomey) *trckd ldrs: hit 4th and next: rdn appr 2 out: wknd bef last* **50/1**	74
	10	18	**Softly Killing Me**[67] 6-10-4 0...................................... WayneKavanagh(3) (Brian Forsey) *mstke 2 out: a towards rr* **66/1**	46

3m 41.1s (-7.80) **Going Correction** -0.65s/f (Firm)
WFA 4 from 5yo+ 5lb 10 Ran SP% **117.8**
Speed ratings (Par 105): **93,92,91,86,80 79,76,75,74,65**
toteswingers: 1&2 £14.30, 1&3 £7.30, 2&3 £2.50. CSF £123.53 TOTE £25.00: £5.40, £1.90, £1.02; EX 200.10.
Owner John P McManus **Bred** J P Murphy & M Barry Murphy **Trained** Cheltenham, Gloucs

FOCUS
At best a modest maiden hurdle and a surprise result.

NOTEBOOK

Surf And Turf(IRE) had shown nothing in three previous starts and was discarded by the champion jockey in order to ride the favourite. However, the gelding travelled well throughout and, once produced after the last, ran on to score a shade comfortably. This was clearly unexpected. Official explanation: trainer's rep said, regarding apparent improvement in form, that the gelding was better suited by the good (good to firm places) ground. (op 20-1)

Final Flyer(IRE) finished second to Chrysander, who won a claimer earlier in the afternoon at Ludlow, in a similar race on his previous start. He ran his race, battling back past the favourite but being unable to hold the winner, and sets a modest standard. (op 6-1 tchd 13-2)

Penchesco(IRE) had shown a reasonable level of form in his three starts over hurdles this season and was sent off an odds-on favourite. He came through to lead at the second-last but was run out of it jumping the last. (op 4-6)

Ebony Diamond(IRE), an Irish bumper winner, had taken on better company on his first two starts over hurdles and travelled well under restraint. However, he could never get close enough to land a serious blow in the straight. (op 5-1)

Encompassing(IRE), a 92-rated Flat performer but bought cheaply out of Aidan O'Brien's stable, showed a measure of ability on this hurdling debut without getting involved. (op 10-1)

Hatchet Man Official explanation: jockey said gelding hung left

5244 BATHWICK TYRES MIDSOMER NORTON CONDITIONAL JOCKEYS' H'CAP HURDLE (8 hdls) 2m

5:05 (5:36) (Class 4) (0-105,105) 4-Y-0+ **£2,341** (£687; £343; £171)

Form RPR

0600 **1** **Mauritino (GER)**[67] 3882 7-10-13 **93** .... RichieMcLernon(3) 101+
(Jonjo O'Neill) *trckd ldr: led 2 out: pushed clr run-in: readily* **11/4**[1]

/FOU **2** *2 ¼* **No To Trident**[31] 4672 6-10-13 **100** .... ThomasFlint(10) 103
(John Flint) *trckd ldrs: ev ch whn hit 2 out: sn rdn: kpt on same pce* **15/2**

-P50 **3** *2* **Holden Caulfield (IRE)**[178] 1844 6-10-10 **87** .... MattGriffiths 87
(Nick Ayliffe) *trckd ldrs: rdn after 2 out: kpt on same pce* **33/1**

6500 **4** *nk* **Gtaab**[36] 4465 5-11-11 **102** ....(b[1]) CO'Farrell 102
(Paul Webber) *led tl rdn 2 out: kpt on same pce* **9/1**

5532 **5** *1 ½* **Magic Prospect (FR)**[23] 4859 4-11-5 **105** .... CharlieHuxley(3) 98
(Charlie Mann) *in tch: effrt 2 out: kpt on same pce fr last* **7/1**

60U4 **6** *1 ¼* **Mayberry**[37] 4455 6-11-4 **103** .... StephenO'Donovan(8) 102+
(Emma Lavelle) *hld up towards rr: hdwy appr 2 out to trck ldrs rdn and hung lft appr last: kpt on same pce* **7/2**[2]

5000 **7** *1 ¼* **Aine's Delight (IRE)**[18] 3387 5-10-10 **90** .... KyleJames(3) 86
(Andy Turnell) *racd keenly: mid-div: hdwy after 3 out: ev ch 2 out: sn rdn: kpt on same pce* **14/1**

5-44 **8** *1 ¾* **Goose Green (IRE)**[10] 5082 7-11-5 **96** .... IanPopham 90
(Ron Hodges) *in tch: hdwy 3 out: ev ch 2 out: sn rdn: fdd last* **22/1**

FU06 **9** *hd* **Al Amaan**[19] 4935 6-11-10 **101** .... MichaelMurphy 98+
(Gary Moore) *hld up bhd: hdwy after 3 out: rdn after next: wknd last* **20/1**

0550 **10** *13* **Fishoutofwater (IRE)**[22] 4860 7-11-0 **94** .... AodhaganConlon(3) 75
(Rebecca Curtis) *mstkes 1st and 3rd: sn struggling: a towards rr* **11/2**[3]

3013 **11** *29* **Galantos (GER)**[48] 4266 10-10-7 **89** .... SClements(5) 41
(Helen Nelmes) *mid-div tl 3 out: t.o* **16/1**

3m 45.6s (-3.30) **Going Correction** -0.65s/f (Firm)

WFA 4 from 5yo+ 5lb **11** Ran SP% **123.1**

Speed ratings (Par 105): **82,80,79,79,78 78,77,76,76,70 55**

toteswingers: 1&2 £7.30, 1&3 £28.80, 2&3 £22.40. CSF £24.77 CT £582.67 TOTE £6.30: £1.90, £3.00, £11.90; EX 42.90.

Owner P A Byrne **Bred** Werner Klein **Trained** Cheltenham, Gloucs

FOCUS

A moderate conditionals' handicap hurdle run at a steady pace but a second success on the afternoon for trainer and jockey with the well-backed winner.

NOTEBOOK

Mauritino(GER), a fast-ground winner in the summer, had shown little in five subsequent starts over the winter but was always close up and travelling. He asserted after the last and it would be no surprise if he was turned out quickly, as he gets no penalty for this. Official explanation: trainer's rep said, regarding apparent improvement in form, that the gelding was better suited by the good (good to firm places) ground (op 9-2)

No To Trident, who fell when having a seller in the bag in October, had failed to run to that in two subsequent starts. He was also never far away but just found the winner too strong. There is another small race in him on a sharp track. (op 8-1 tchd 7-1)

Holden Caulfield(IRE) struggled to find his form in the autumn after a ten-month absence. However, returning from a winter break, he rallied well in the straight to take the minor placing and can build on this. (op 50-1)

Gtaab, wearing blinkers for the first time, made the running and stuck to his task under pressure to post a better effort than of late. (tchd 8-1)

Magic Prospect(FR) had shown a fair amount of ability in previous starts and looked reasonably treated for this handicap debut. However, he failed to pick up in the straight and may have found the ground faster than ideal. (op 11-2)

Mayberry moved up off the home turn looking a big threat but tended to hang left and faded before the last. Official explanation: trainer's rep said mare bled from the nose (op 9-2 tchd 5-1)

Aine's Delight(IRE) took a really keen hold but was still there turning in and was not beaten far. If she settles better she might be able to add to her two Flat successes. (op 16-1)

T/Jkpt: Not won. T/Plt: £57.40 to a £1 stake. Pool:£67,957.09 - 863.40 winning tickets. T/Qpdt: £24.40 to a £1 stake. Pool:£3,723.99 - 112.90 winning tickets. TM

5245 - 5251a (Foreign Racing) - See Raceform Interactive

[4860]FFOS LAS (L-H)

Monday, April 11

OFFICIAL GOING: Good (watering; 7.6)

Wind: moderate against Weather: sunny spells

5252 COTTS EQUINE CONDITIONAL JOCKEYS' (S) HURDLE (12 hdls) 3m

5:10 (5:10) (Class 5) 4-Y-0+ **£1,951** (£573; £286; £143)

Form RPR

32P1 **1** **Sun Tzu (IRE)**[16] 5014 7-11-5 103 ....(b) SamTwiston-Davies 109+
(Dr Richard Newland) *j. fluently: mde all: rdn after 2 out: idled and styd on flat* **5/1**[3]

0400 **2** *3 ¼* **Yetholm (USA)**[38] 4456 6-11-1 108 ....(p) IanPopham 100
(Bernard Llewellyn) *in tch: clsd u.p after 9th: chsd wnr appr next: styd on same pce: hld flat* **7/1**

2FP0 **3** *hd* **Vivarini**[19] 4939 7-11-5 110 ....(p) CharlieWallis(6) 110
(John O'Shea) *hld up in last: niggled along fr 5th: hdwy 8th: sn rdn: j.lft last 3: styd on flat* **9/1**

552 **4** *8* **Jewellery (IRE)**[13] 5068 4-9-11 87 ....(t) EdGlassonbury(3) 80
(Alison Thorpe) *hld up in rr: hdwy after 6th: chsd wnr 8th: sn rdn: lost 2nd appr 3 out: kpt on same pce* **5/2**[1]

233P **5** *4* **Pocket Too**[51] 4224 8-10-10 103 ....(b) ChrisDavies(5) 89
(Matthew Salaman) *midfield: rdn and hdwy after 7th: disp 2nd u.p 9th: wknd after next* **8/1**

5440 **6** *3 ¼* **Always Bold (IRE)**[29] 4742 6-10-12 110 ....(tp) JohnKington(3) 87
(Donald McCain) *chsd ldrs: wnt 2nd after 6th: mstke and lost pl 8th: sn wknd* **9/2**[2]

221P **7** *59* **Cannon Fire (FR)**[91] 3483 10-11-11 109 ....(p) AodhaganConlon 43
(Evan Williams) *trckd ldr tl after 6th: sn rdn: wknd 8th: t.o* **5/1**[3]

6m 9.40s (22.40) **Going Correction** +0.625s/f (Soft)

WFA 4 from 6yo+ 7lb **7** Ran SP% **113.7**

Speed ratings (Par 103): **87,85,85,83,81 80,61**

toteswingers:1&2:£4.60, 1&3:£8.60, 2&3:£8.90 CSF £37.83 TOTE £5.70: £2.00, £9.60; EX 42.20.The winner was sold to Mr L H Evans for 6,300gns. Always Bold was claimed by M Keighley for £6,000.

Owner Too Easy Racing & Dr R D P Newland **Bred** Paul Ryan **Trained** Claines, Worcs

■ Stewards' Enquiry : Charlie Wallis three-day ban: used whip with excessive frequency (Apr 25-27)

FOCUS

The course had been watered over the past week, and the ground looked good with some give in it. This was an ordinary seller that was dictated throughout by the winner. He's rated in line with his best chase 2011 form.

NOTEBOOK

Sun Tzu(IRE) set a steady pace initially, but once he increased the tempo in the back straight he broke the resistance of most of his rivals, but it was still a long way home from the turn in and he and he got a bit tired, but stuck to the task grimly. He had scrambled home at Stratford last month, and there was some doubt if his resolution would hold up again, but if anything he showed superior stamina and looked as if he could go on for the hat-trick. (op 9-2)

Yetholm(USA) emerged from the pack to chase down the winner in the straight. He got tired near the finish but saw out the step up in trip well enough on his first start for his new stable. (tchd 6-1)

Vivarini was under pressure for the last mile but kept plugging on to make some modest late gains. He has looked short of confidence since falling at Warwick in January but this was a bit better and he should improve for softer ground. (op 10-1 tchd 7-1)

Jewellery(IRE) lost a couple of lengths going wide of the pack into the back straight, but was driven up to improve in the straight, before tiring from the second last. She came into this in good form but had something to find on official ratings, and might be better exploiting her mark in a handicap. (op 7-2)

Pocket Too did not get home. (op 7-1 tchd 6-1)

Always Bold(IRE) chased the winner until the pace quickened and he was done for, and he looks to be on the decline. (tchd 11-2)

Cannon Fire(FR) tracked the winner but was the first beaten and this was a disappointing effort, although he may have just needed this first run since January. (op 9-2 tchd 11-2)

5253 LINDLEY HERITAGE MAIDEN HURDLE (10 hdls) 2m 4f

5:40 (5:40) (Class 4) 4-Y-0+ **£2,027** (£860; £420; £214)

Form RPR

1 **Beneficial Reform (IRE)**[29] 6-11-0 0 .... NickScholfield 105+
(Dermot Day, Ire) *t.k.h in midfield: hdwy to trck ldrs 7th: chal 2 out: sn led: hung rt flat: comf* **6/1**

2 *5* **Mountainous (IRE)**[43] 6-11-0 0 .... RobertThornton 99
(Richard Lee) *trckd ldr tl led 6th: jnd next: rdn 2 out: sn hdd: edgd lft: one pce flat* **15/8**[1]

3 *31* **Taroum (IRE)**[187] 4-10-7 0 .... PaulMoloney 69
(Evan Williams) *hld up in rr: stdy hdwy 6th: trckd ldng pair bef 3 out: sn shkn up: fnd little: wknd 2 out* **12/1**

600 **4** *48* **Ammo Away**[23] 4860 5-10-11 0 ....(t) RichardKilloran(3) 27
(Tim Vaughan) *hld up in rr: mstke 5th: sn struggling: wnt poor 4th 3 out* **50/1**

5 *2 ¾* **Strictly (FR)**[371] 6-11-0 0 .... SamTwiston-Davies 25
(V J Hughes) *t.k.h: led tl mstke and hdd 6th: wknd qckly bef 3 out: t.o* **28/1**

0600 **6** *17* **The Merry Giant (IRE)**[23] 4860 5-11-0 0 .... RichieMcLernon 10
(Rebecca Curtis) *midfield: mstke 3rd: rdn 6th: sn wknd: t.o* **20/1**

0 **7** *3 ¾* **Florence May**[65] 3942 7-10-4 0 .... DonalDevereux(3) —
(Lucy Jones) *t.k.h in rr: struggling 5th: sn lost tch: t.o* **50/1**

323/ **P** **Grand Schlem (FR)**[658] 4427 7-11-0 122 .... RhysFlint —
(David Rees) *chsd ldrs: wkng qckly whn blnd 7th: wl bhd whn p.u next* **3/1**[2]

00P- **P** **Kericho**[23] 6-10-11 0 ....(t) KeiranBurke(3) —
(Patrick Rodford) *chsd ldrs: rdn along after 4th: wknd 6th: t.o whn p.u bef 3 out* **50/1**

4-43 **P** **Sothisisit (FR)**[183] 1799 5-11-0 0 ....(t) APMcCoy —
(Jonjo O'Neill) *in tch tl rdn and wknd after 7th: t.o whn p.u bef 2 out* **7/2**[3]

5m 2.30s (13.30) **Going Correction** +0.625s/f (Soft)

WFA 4 from 5yo+ 6lb **10** Ran SP% **118.1**

Speed ratings (Par 105): **98,96,83,64,63 56,55,—,—,—**

toteswingers:1&2:£5.00, 1&3:£7.20, 2&3:£5.80 CSF £17.79 TOTE £4.80: £1.40, £3.30, £1.10; EX 25.70.

Owner Kieran Doyle **Bred** Micheal Woodlock **Trained** Ballycogley, Co Wexford

FOCUS

An interesting maiden with the first three drawing clear of the rest. The time was relatively slow and this is not form to get carried away with.

NOTEBOOK

Beneficial Reform(IRE) was given the ideal ride, given time to make steady progress down the back straight before emerging upsides the leader, and once he had hung over to the rail he kept on strongly for a decisive success. The Irish raider won just a modest point in Ireland but looks to have some potential. (op 5-1)

Mountainous(IRE) was making his debut for Richard Lee after winning an Irish point in February and subsequently changing hands for £50,000. Racing prominently against the inside rail, he kept up to the task but was just outpaced on the day, and looks all over a chasing type. (op 5-2 tchd 11-4)

Taroum(IRE) made some good progress under a bit of pressure and got on terms with the leaders before fading up the straight. He was only a cheap purchase after racing for John Oxx on the Flat, but showed some promise on this hurdling debut and could be interesting dropped in trip. (tchd 11-1 and 14-1)

Ammo Away, in a first time tongue-tie, was held up in an attempt to help him settle but was never a factor. (op 66-1)

Strictly(FR) was too keen early on and pulled his way into the lead, but he was never going to last home after that. (op 20-1 tchd 16-1)

The Merry Giant(IRE) plugged on but was under pressure throughout the final circuit and the former bumper winner has not looked as good since suffering an electric shock in the unfortunate notorious incident at Newbury in February. (op 16-1)

Grand Schlem(FR), third in the Fred Winter at Cheltenham three years ago when trained by Francois Doumen, was returning for new connections after two years off the track, but he weakened quickly four out and does not look anywhere near the horse of old. (tchd 11-4 and 7-2)

Sothisisit(FR)was not too fluent at the second and never travelled that well, eventually being pulled up once beaten. He showed some ability in moderate bumpers last year and should eventually be better than the evidence of this hurdling debut. Official explanation: jockey said gelding bled from the nose (tchd 11-4 and 7-2)

5254 BARRY WALTERS CATERING NOVICES' CHASE (18 fncs) 3m
6:15 (6:15) (Class 4) 5-Y-0+ **£3,903** (£1,146; £573; £286)

Form RPR

2544 **1** **Ballyvesey (IRE)**[36] 4502 6-11-5 118..............................(v) TomO'Brien 125
(Peter Bowen) *led: increased pce 10th: rdn along after 14th: 3 l clr last: drvn out* **11/4**[2]

3220 **2** *3/4* **The Rainbow Hunter**[27] 4790 7-10-12 132....................... EdCookson(7) 126+
(Andy Turnell) *racd in 3rd tl trckd wnr 8th: chal and mstke 3 out: sn rdn: 3 l down last: r.o u.p flat* **4/6**[1]

4315 **3** *60* **Cold Harbour**[16] 5017 7-11-5 101.. PaulMoloney 85
(Evan Williams) *cl up bhd wnr tl relegated to 3rd 8th: wknd 4 out: eased next: t.o* **8/1**[3]

4 *81* **Another Puzzle**[323] 7-10-12 0.. MarkGrant —
(Dominic Ffrench Davis) *in rr: mstke 8th: struggling 11th: mstke 14th: sn t.o* **33/1**

6m 16.8s (-6.20) **Going Correction** +0.025s/f (Yiel) **4** Ran SP% **100.7**
Speed ratings: **111,110,90,63**
CSF £4.54 TOTE £2.80; EX 4.10.
Owner Roddy Owen & Paul Fullagar **Bred** Kevin Neville **Trained** Little Newcastle, Pembrokes

FOCUS
The small field was further reduced with the late withdrawal of ex-Irish pointer Gotoyourplay on veterinary advice at the start, but a good battle ensued between the two main protagonists. The fortm could be rated up to 10lb higher using he second.

NOTEBOOK
Ballyvesey(IRE) put up a thoroughly professional display, jumping fluently in the lead and staying on stoutly. His jockey did have to scrub along to keep the momentum going around the final turn, and that was a shrewd move as it just stretched the favourite into a couple of costly errors. He took a while to get the hang of jumping fences, but has plenty of experience behind him now (including over the National fences last November) and, having come on for his reappearance run last month, was able to exploit that edge in experience. He is slightly quirky but responds well to headgear and should find some more exploitable opportunities in the near future. (tchd 8-13 in a place)
The Rainbow Hunter has developed into a fair chaser this season, winning his first chase at this track and going on to place in several handicaps. He was out of his depth a bit in the heat of a Cheltenham Festival handicap, but back at this level had something in hand with a 14lb superior rating. However, he put in a couple of slow jumps at the first two fences and though he travelled strongly, once the winner had kicked on he was stretched into a mistake at the final open ditch. He closed again on the flat, but his less fluent jumping proved costly.
Cold Harbour goes well at this track, having won two chases here already, but was outclassed today. (tchd 15-2)
Another Puzzlefailed to win a point last year and was up against it on his rules debut.

5255 LINDLEY VENUE CATERING H'CAP HURDLE (10 hdls) 2m 4f
6:45 (6:45) (Class 3) (0-135,126) 4-Y-0+ **£4,878** (£1,432; £716; £357)

Form RPR

2013 **1** **Pure Faith (IRE)**[142] 2519 7-11-10 124................................ TomO'Brien 130+
(Peter Bowen) *hld up: racd keenly: hdwy 5th: wnt 2nd after 7th: led 3 out: clr last: styd on strly* **4/1**[3]

0442 **2** *3 1/2* **William Hogarth**[9] 5110 6-11-11 125.. RhysFlint 126
(Keith Goldsworthy) *led tl 6th: sn rdn and lost pl: rallied into 2nd last but a being hld by wnr* **5/2**[1]

-006 **3** *2 3/4* **Open Day (IRE)**[40] 4420 5-11-6 120.. APMcCoy 120
(Jonjo O'Neill) *hld up in rr: clsd 3 out: rdn next: kpt on same pce* **5/2**[1]

0440 **4** *3/4* **Gus Macrae (IRE)**[37] 4490 7-11-12 126..........................(t) JasonMaguire 124
(Rebecca Curtis) *trckd ldrs: rdn 3 out: kpt on same pce* **8/1**

0011 **5** *3/4* **Mickmacmagoole (IRE)**[35] 4524 9-11-0 119.......(p) AodhaganConlon(5) 116
(Evan Williams) *trckd ldr: led 6th: rdn bef 3 out: sn hdd: wknd last* **3/1**[2]

4m 57.9s (8.90) **Going Correction** +0.625s/f (Soft) **5** Ran SP% **113.3**
Speed ratings (Par 107): **107,105,104,104,103**
CSF £14.88 TOTE £4.70: £2.70, £1.40; EX 12.10.
Owner P Bowling,S Scott,R Harvey & K Bowen **Bred** P J Carmody **Trained** Little Newcastle, Pembrokes

FOCUS
A tight handicap run at a fair pace, and though there were questions about most of the runners, they finished close together to suggest the form should work out. The best of the winner's form from last summer could be rated to this sort of level.

NOTEBOOK
Pure Faith(IRE) looked fresh for his return from a winter break and travelled well, taking up the running three out and keeping his rivals at bay in behind. Despite winning four novice hurdles with ease last year he had not fared that well when pitched into handicaps and looked rated up to his best. However, those handicaps on tighter tracks would not have been best suited as stamina looks more his strong suit, and on this showing he looked to be a bit ahead of the handicapper here. (op 10-3)
William Hogarth led until feeling the pace in the back straight, but he rallied well under pressure to keep again on for second. He has been kept on the go since the autumn and has been reasonably consistent, but his two hurdling successes have come when he has been fresher than this. (op 9-4 tchd 11-4)
Open Day(IRE) has been gradually slipping down the weights from an ungenerous beginning after a successful juvenile campaign last season, but although he was held up in contention he did not pick up that well and never looked likely to win. (op 4-1)
Gus Macrae(IRE) was reverting to hurdles after an unsuccessful spell in novice chases this winter. He did not have an easy task on the ratings and got outpaced, but he should do better for this experience. (op 7-1 tchd 9-1)
Mickmacmagoole(IRE) came into this in top form having won a handicap over C&D a month ago following success in a seller a month before that, and although he ran well he was just found out by the step up in class. (tchd 7-2)

5256 THELINDLEYGROUP.COM H'CAP CHASE (17 fncs) 2m 5f
7:20 (7:20) (Class 5) (0-95,94) 5-Y-0+ **£2,602** (£764; £382; £190)

Form RPR

0114 **1** **Isle Of Inishmore (IRE)**[216] 1500 8-11-7 94................(t) MrTomDavid(5) 109+
(Tim Vaughan) *hld up in rr: mstke 11th: hdwy next: led bef 3 out: clr last: rdn out* **7/2**[2]

P600 **2** *3 3/4* **Lucky Dancer**[71] 3840 6-11-12 94....................................(v[1]) PaulMoloney 103
(Evan Williams) *hld up in rr: stdy hdwy 13th: rdn bef 4 out: chsd wnr after 2 out: hit last: unable qck flat* **15/2**

-046 **3** *8* **Reymysterio (IRE)**[31] 4706 10-10-10 81................(tp) KeiranBurke(3) 82
(Patrick Rodford) *trckd ldr: led 6th tl 8th: led 9th tl bef 3 out: kpt on same pce* **20/1**

F42F **4** *nse* **Mr Bond (IRE)**[31] 4693 8-11-1 83.. NickScholfield 86
(Andy Turnell) *chsd ldrs tl rdn and lost pl 12th: rallied 4 out: one pce fr next: hit last* **3/1**[1]

53P0 **5** *3 1/4* **Magnetic Pole**[68] 3878 10-11-9 94..............................(b) CharlieHuxley(3) 95
(Richard Lee) *in rr tl hdwy 3rd: ev ch whn mstke 4 out: sn rdn: wknd 2 out* **7/2**[2]

4PU5 **6** *7* **Gunship (IRE)**[22] 4900 10-11-1 90..........................(b) MrRGHenderson(7) 83
(Cathy Hamilton) *chsd ldrs: led 8th tl next: styd cl up tl wknd 3 out* **8/1**

2653 **P** **Rash Moment (FR)**[31] 4694 12-11-7 89...............................(p) RhysFlint —
(Michael Scudamore) *led tl 6th: mstke 10th: wknd 12th: t.o whn p.u bef last* **5/1**[3]

5m 30.6s (0.60) **Going Correction** +0.025s/f (Yiel) **7** Ran SP% **113.7**
Speed ratings: **99,97,94,94,93 90,—**
toteswingers:1&2:£17.40, 1&3:£7.60, 2&3:£9.20 CSF £28.28 TOTE £4.80: £2.50, £6.70; EX 36.80.
Owner J H Frost **Bred** Garry Hadden **Trained** Aberthin, Vale of Glamorgan

FOCUS
A very moderate handicap chase. A step up from the cosy winner and there should be more to come.

NOTEBOOK
Isle Of Inishmore(IRE) looked well for his first start since September and, ridden with quiet confidence, he struck the front three out with his ears pricked and looked to enjoy this return to action. He won two handicap hurdles last summer, the latter off the same mark as his chase rating today, and made his chasing debut just a week later. He did not improve for the switch to fences last year, but it might be that he is better when fresh. (op 3-1 tchd 4-1)
Lucky Dancer, in a first-time visor, was a bit low at several fences until getting the hang of things and was making up ground over the fences in the back straight, but he could not get to the winner. His form is somewhat inconsistent following a maiden hurdle win back in August 2009, but he has been given a chance by the handicapper over fences. (op 8-1)
Reymysterio(IRE) raced enthusiastically in or near the lead and despite fading in the closing stages the cheekpieces and tongue-tie seemed to have some effect as he finished much closer than in his three previous starts. Whether that is enough to suggest future winning form though is questionable. (op 16-1)
Mr Bond(IRE) is a long-standing maiden, so the fact he started favourite puts this race into context. He jumped better than at Leicester last time and is better going left-handed, but he got outpaced in the back straight so despite rallying under his jockey's urgings he was always fighting a losing battle. (op 7-2 tchd 9-4)
Magnetic Pole was making some headway until a mistake at the fourth-last stopped his momentum and his run petered out from there. (op 4-1)

5257 FFOS LAS ON COURSE BOOKMAKERS INTERMEDIATE OPEN NATIONAL HUNT FLAT RACE 2m
7:50 (7:50) (Class 6) 4-5-Y-O **£1,712** (£499; £249)

Form RPR

1 **Wheres The Hare (IRE)** 4-10-12 .... JasonMaguire 108+
(Rebecca Curtis) *trckd ldrs: led over 2f out: sn rdn and edgd lft: r.o wl fnl f: comf* **10/11**[1]

2 *2* **Sentimentaljourney (IRE)** 4-10-12 .... APMcCoy 103+
(Jonjo O'Neill) *hld up in rr: hdwy 4f out: rdn 3f out: ev ch 2f out: one pce fnl f* **4/1**[3]

3 *21* **Birchwood Lad** 5-11-1 .... TomMalone(3) 90
(Ian Patrick Browne, Ire) *racd keenly: led: pushed along and hdd over 2f out: sn wknd* **22/1**

5 **4** *9* **Special Vintage**[51] 4204 5-11-4 .... AndrewTinkler 82
(Nicky Henderson) *in tch tl outpcd by ldrs over 3f out* **7/2**[2]

5 *25* **Benefit Of Youth (IRE)** 4-10-7 .... MrTomDavid(5) 54
(Tim Vaughan) *towards rr: pushed along 1/2-way: wknd over 5f out: t.o* **10/1**

6 *40* **Sir Frog (IRE)**[308] 5-11-4 .... TomO'Brien 24
(Keith Goldsworthy) *plld hrd early: trckd ldr tl over 4f out: sn wknd: t.o* **12/1**

3m 49.2s (5.80) **Going Correction** +0.625s/f (Soft)
WFA 4 from 5yo 5lb **6** Ran SP% **115.7**
Speed ratings: **110,109,98,94,81 61**
toteswingers:1&2:£1.10, 1&3:£10.00, 2&3:£10.20 CSF £5.21 TOTE £1.90: £1.70, £2.00; EX 6.50.
Owner G Costelloe, C Trembath & D Owen **Bred** Seamus Braddish **Trained** Newport, Dyfed

FOCUS
Not a strong contest, but the winner looks a decent prospect and the second should improve.

NOTEBOOK
Wheres The Hare(IRE) readily quickened when asked and always had too much in hand for his nearest pursuer, going on for a comfortable success. The Flemensfirth gelding, whose dam won over hurdles and chases at around 2m4f, looks a sizeable 4yo who should make up into a promising hurdler given a summer to strengthen up. (op 5-4 tchd 11-8)
Sentimentaljourney(IRE) quickened with the winner initially but was never able to quite go that one's pace, and he settled for second before the line. He had to be mounted in the saddling boxes and went down to the start adrift of the others, but this half-brother to 2m4f winning hurdler Elliptic should be all right once he matures. (op 7-2 tchd 3-1)
Birchwood Lad, an Irish newcomer, was keen to get on with things and led until swamped by the market principals. (op 20-1 tchd 18-1)
Special Vintage had been readily outpaced on his debut in a small-field bumper at Ascot in February. This time he made some progress under pressure but was soon beaten and does not look that promising at this stage. (op 3-1)
Benefit Of Youth(IRE) was fractious beforehand and did not travel well through the race, struggling with half a circuit left. (op 8-1)
Sir Frog(IRE), a maiden ex-pointer, was up with the early pace but weakened tamely before the race began to hot up. (tchd 9-1)
T/Plt: £187.30 to a £1 stake. Pool:£47,854.60 - 186.48 winning tickets T/Qpdt: £23.10 to a£1 stake. Pool:£5,359.36 - 171.57 winning tickets RL

5027 HEXHAM (L-H)
Monday, April 11

OFFICIAL GOING: Good (good to soft in places back straight; good to firm in places last 2f; watering; 7.8)
All bends moved but impact on distances not notified.
Wind: Fresh, half behind Weather: Cloudy

5258 HAYDON H'CAP CHASE (19 fncs) 3m 1f
2:00 (2:00) (Class 5) (0-90,90) 5-Y-0+ **£1,951** (£573; £286; £143)

Form RPR

0-43 **1** **Nicky Tam (IRE)**[27] 4799 9-10-13 77..............................(t) RobertWalford 87
(Henry Hogarth) *in tch: hdwy to ld bef 3 out: rdn next: kpt on strly run-in* **8/1**[3]

P225 **2** *3 1/4* **Charming Knight (IRE)**[10] 5094 10-10-13 84.............. AlistairFindlay(7) 91
(Jane Walton) *midfield: hdwy and cl up 4 out: effrt after 2 out: chsd wnr last: r.o run-in* **14/1**

4444 **3** *hd* **Sycho Fred (IRE)**[10] 5097 10-10-7 **71**..........(t) PeterBuchanan 78
(Mike Sowersby) *hld up: hdwy bef 3 out: kpt on fr last: nrst fin* **14/1**
4 *5* **Carlanstown (IRE)**[15] 5044 7-10-11 **82**.......... MrJAJenkins(7) 86
(Mrs C De Montmorency, Ire) *in tch: hdwy to ld 4 out: hdd bef next: cl up: chsd wnr briefly bef last: rdn and no ex fnl 100yds* **6/1**[1]
2U5P **5** *5* **Hasper**[50] 4241 13-10-12 **81**.......... PaulGallagher(5) 79
(Sandy Forster) *hld up in midfield: hdwy and prom 1/2-way: chsd ldr 13th: ev ch 4 out: rdn 2 out: wknd last* **12/1**
6444 **6** *16* **Seek The Truth (IRE)**[82] 3636 8-10-8 **72**.......... MarkBradburne 56
(Sue Bradburne) *t.k.h: in tch: hit and rdn 4 out: outpcd fr next* **9/1**
5362 **7** *2* **Manoubi**[25] 4827 12-11-6 **84**.......... JamesReveley 66
(Martin Todhunter) *hld up: stdy hdwy bef 3 out: rdn bef next: no imp* **16/1**
P64P **8** *1* **Norminster**[49] 4258 10-10-7 **74**..........(p) EwanWhillans(3) 55
(Rayson Nixon) *nt fluent: bhd: drvn after 4 out: nvr able to chal* **50/1**
0521 **9** *1 3/4* **Lonesome Boatman (IRE)**[14] 5062 11-10-5 **76**..........(p) JoshWall(7) 55
(Arthur Whitehead) *towards rr: rdn along fr 1/2-way: nvr on terms* **6/1**[1]
2245 **10** *3 1/4* **Panthers Run**[25] 4827 11-10-1 **65** ow1..........(t) BrianHughes 41
(Jonathan Haynes) *cl up: ev ch 4 out: rdn and wknd after 2 out* **28/1**
0034 **11** *1 1/2* **Nifty Roy**[25] 4827 11-11-0 **78**..........(p) RichieMcGrath 53
(Brian Storey) *midfield on ins: lost pl qckly 13th: n.d fr next* **66/1**
/0P3 **12** *7* **Nick The Silver**[15] 5029 10-10-6 **77**..........(p) MissEYoung(7) 46
(Robert Johnson) *plld hrd in midfield: hdwy and prom 6th: outpcd whn hit 14th: sn btn* **25/1**
P125 **13** *6* **Von Galen (IRE)**[14] 5060 10-11-12 **90**..........(p) JohnnyFarrelly 53
(Michael Scudamore) *led to 12th: led next to 4 out: rdn and wknd 3 out* **14/1**
P36- **P** **Lethem Present (IRE)**[503] 2496 11-10-7 **78**.......... MrMEnnis(7) —
(Tim Butt) *cl up tl wknd 14th: tailing off whn p.u bef 4 out* **25/1**
/035 **P** **Kyathos (GER)**[18] 4975 10-10-13 **77**.......... CampbellGillies —
(David Thompson) *t.k.h: prom: led 12th to next: wknd 4 out: t.o whn p.u bef last* **50/1**
03P5 **U** **Teenando (IRE)**[17] 4997 11-9-13 **73**.......... NathanCook(10) —
(Sue Smith) *cl up: hit and uns rdr 6th* **20/1**
-5U3 **F** **Bubbly Breeze (IRE)**[31] 4687 6-11-7 **85**.......... GrahamLee —
(Pauline Robson) *hld up: niggled along whn fell 13th* **15/2**[2]

6m 31.1s (-1.10) **Going Correction** 0.0s/f (Good) **17** Ran SP% **116.3**
Speed ratings: **101,99,99,98,96 91,90,90,90,89 88,86,84,—,— —,—**
toteswingers:1&2:£26.10, 1&3:£27.90, 2&3:£17.60 CSF £99.86 CT £1540.73 TOTE £12.80: £3.80, £6.10, £3.90, £1.50; EX 158.90.
Owner Hogarth Racing **Bred** Noel O'Brien **Trained** Stillington, N Yorks

FOCUS
A low-grade handicap chase run at a steady pace. The first five home drew clear over the final three fences and there was a decisive winner. The first three are rated pretty close to their marks.

NOTEBOOK
Nicky Tam(IRE), who missed all of last season, had run well on both his two previous starts this term. Back up in trip, he took charge three out and had it won jumping the last, his first success on his ninth start over fences.
Charming Knight(IRE), a multiple winning pointer, was back over fences after two spins over hurdles. He stuck to his guns on the run-in without ever threatening the winner. (op 16-1)
Sycho Fred(IRE), hard to win with, keeps giving a good account of himself without ever threatening to hit the target. (op 16-1)
Carlanstown(IRE), winner of five points, put two poor efforts behind him. He tended to run with the choke out and after looking a big threat faded on the run-in. (tchd 4-1 and 7-1 in a place)
Hasper, who took a couple of hunter chases in 2009, was another to return to form well suited by this better ground. (op 16-1 tchd 18-1)
Lonesome Boatman(IRE), raised 7lb for his Towcester success, was never travelling. Official explanation: trainer had no explanation for the poor form shown (op 13-2)
Bubbly Breeze(IRE), making his chase debut, had not been asked a question when crashing out early on the final circuit. (op 13-2)

5259 THORNTON - FIRKIN NOVICES' HURDLE (DIV I) (10 hdls) 2m 4f 110y
2:30 (2:30) (Class 4) 4-Y-0+ **£2,055** (£599; £299)

Form RPR
654P **1** **Mister Wall Street (FR)**[64] 3966 6-11-0 110.......... GrahamLee 105
(Ferdy Murphy) *mde all: rdn along after 2 out: kpt on strly run-in* **15/8**[1]
0P23 **2** *2* **Alpha One (IRE)**[17] 4993 5-11-0 108.......... CampbellGillies 103
(Chris Grant) *trckd ldrs: wnt 2nd 2 out: effrt and ch last: kpt on same pce run-in* **7/2**[2]
0662 **3** *19* **Silent Snow (IRE)**[32] 4569 6-10-7 105.......... MissHBethell(7) 89
(Malcolm Jefferson) *t.k.h: w wnr: rdn whn hit and lost 2nd 2 out: wknd bef last* **4/1**[3]
00 **4** *5* **Quelle Chance (IRE)**[42] 4393 5-11-0 0.......... BrianHughes 82
(Howard Johnson) *hld up: stdy hdwy 3 out: rdn next: wknd bef last* **20/1**
605/ **5** *14* **Tipsy Dara (IRE)**[742] 4801 7-10-7 0.......... MarkBradburne 62
(Sue Bradburne) *t.k.h: hld up in tch: rdn and outpcd 3 out: sn btn* **33/1**
0/P0 **6** *4 1/2* **Some Lad (IRE)**[15] 5028 6-11-0 0.......... PeterBuchanan 65
(Mrs A C Hamilton) *t.k.h: trckd ldrs tl wknd fr 2 out* **25/1**
5646 **7** *23* **Floraclock**[27] 4795 6-10-7 0.......... HenryOliver 37
(Sue Smith) *bhd: reminders 1/2-way: rdn and wknd fr 4 out* **25/1**
00U0 **8** *8* **Grey Assassin**[42] 4396 4-10-4 0.......... EwanWhillans(3) 30
(Simon West) *bhd: hmpd 3rd: rdn and outpcd bef 3 out: sn btn* **200/1**
00-P **P** **Sweetaboutme**[46] 4303 6-9-11 0..........(t) StephenMulqueen(10) —
(Maurice Barnes) *prom tl rdn and wknd after 3 out: t.o whn p.u bef last* **50/1**
3350 **F** **Along Came Rosie**[38] 4455 7-10-13 105.......... FearghalDavis —
(Andrew Crook) *hld up in tch: fell 3rd* **5/1**

5m 10.3s (-2.20) **Going Correction** +0.10s/f (Yiel)
WFA 4 from 5yo+ 6lb **10** Ran SP% **111.5**
Speed ratings (Par 105): **108,107,100,98,92 91,82,79,—,—**
toteswingers:1&2:£1.60, 1&3:£1.90, 2&3:£11.10 CSF £7.56 TOTE £2.80: £1.20, £1.20, £2.10; EX 7.80.
Owner Gay And Peter Hartley **Bred** Simon Cocozza **Trained** West Witton, N Yorks

FOCUS
Just four could be seriously fancied beforehand for this modest novices' hurdle and one of the quartet Along Came Rosie was out of the contest at an early stage. The pace was very steady. The first two were close to their marks.

NOTEBOOK
Mister Wall Street(FR), best in on official ratings, has struggled since making a winning bumper debut two years ago. He was able to set his own pace and in the end did just enough. Connections will be hoping that he makes a better chaser next time round. (tchd 7-4 and 5-2)
Alpha One(IRE), placed at Newcastle and Sedgefield and on the up, went in pursuit of the winner up the final hill and went down fighting. He deserves to go one better. (op 3-1 tchd 11-4)
Silent Snow(IRE), who seemed to show much-improved form when runner-up in bad ground at Carlisle, took on the winner but was hard at work early on the final circuit. A clumsy jump two out settled his fate. (op 9-2 tchd 5-1)
Quelle Chance(IRE), who made an early blunder and was given some sharp remainders at the halfway mark, showed his first signs of ability. He looks more of a long term chasing prospect. (op 28-1)
Tipsy Dara(IRE), having her third start over hurdles on her first outing for two years, was by no means knocked about and is now qualified for handicaps. Official explanation: jockey said, regarding running and riding, that his orders were to jump the mare off mid-division, get a bit of light over the first couple of hurdles and to do his best, it was keen early on off a steady gallop but as the pace quickened turning down the back straight final circuit, it began to hang badly right-handed going down the hill and he was unable to ride vigorously because of this.
Some Lad(IRE), who had shown little on his two previous starts over hurdles, the latest just two weeks earlier, shaped a fraction better but he was given almost a year between his first three starts. (op 28-1 tchd 18-1)

5260 THORNTON - FIRKIN NOVICES' HURDLE (DIV II) (10 hdls) 2m 4f 110y
3:00 (3:00) (Class 4) 4-Y-0+ **£2,055** (£599; £299)

Form RPR
-640 **1** **Mr Supreme (IRE)**[86] 3572 6-11-0 0.......... RichieMcGrath 106+
(Kate Walton) *hld up in tch: smooth hdwy bef 3 out: led after next: asserted run-in: comf* **4/1**[3]
440- **2** *8* **River Music (IRE)**[394] 4580 6-11-0 91.......... DenisO'Regan 99
(John Wade) *prom: led 3 out to after next: rallied: nt fluent last: hung lft and sn no ex* **33/1**
02 **3** *10* **Masterful Act (USA)**[26] 4810 4-10-7 0.......... GrahamLee 82
(Ferdy Murphy) *in tch: stdy hdwy 4 out: rdn after next: nt fluent 2 out: sn no imp* **13/8**[2]
0 **4** *6* **Into The Light**[8] 5131 6-11-0 0.......... JamesReveley 83
(Philip Kirby) *hld up: stdy hdwy 1/2-way: outpcd after 3 out: sn n.d* **66/1**
-5P5 **5** *1 1/2* **Izzy Bella**[31] 4684 5-10-7 75.......... MarkBradburne 75
(Sue Bradburne) *chsd clr ldr to 3 out: sn outpcd: n.d after* **50/1**
-451 **U** **Scriptwriter (IRE)**[17] 4993 9-11-1 119.......... PaulGallagher(5) —
(Howard Johnson) *trckd ldrs: blnd and uns rdr 5th* **11/8**[1]
60 **P** **The Dagda (IRE)**[22] 4889 7-10-11 0.......... EwanWhillans(3) —
(Kevin Hunter) *bhd: struggling bef 4 out: sn btn: t.o whn p.u bef last* **80/1**
000 **P** **Saga Surprise (FR)**[21] 4910 6-11-0 78..........(t) MichaelMcAlister —
(Maurice Barnes) *mstkes: t.k.h: led and sn clr: hdd 3 out: sn wknd: t.o whn p.u bef last* **66/1**
PU **P** **Tipsy Nipper**[22] 4889 6-10-7 0.......... CampbellGillies —
(William Amos) *a bhd: t.o whn p.u 3 out* **150/1**
00 **U** **Nalim (IRE)**[32] 4574 5-10-11 0.......... JamesHalliday(3) —
(Malcolm Jefferson) *hld up: jinked lft and uns rdr 1st* **40/1**

5m 16.8s (4.30) **Going Correction** +0.10s/f (Yiel)
WFA 4 from 5yo+ 6lb **10** Ran SP% **112.4**
Speed ratings (Par 105): **95,91,88,85,85 —,—,—,—,—**
toteswingers:1&2:£20.30, 1&3:£1.10, 2&3:£16.60 CSF £89.77 TOTE £4.10: £1.40, £2.70, £1.20; EX 61.40.
Owner Mrs Susan Granger **Bred** James Cousins **Trained** Middleham Moor, N Yorks

FOCUS
Any price bar three. The early pace was very steady until the ultimately well-beaten tearaway leader took off after the second flight. The time was relatively slow and the form is suspect.

NOTEBOOK
Mr Supreme(IRE), who survived a blunder at the second flight, travelled strongly and proved much too strong for his sole challenger on the run-in. Suited by this much better ground, he should make a fair novice chaser next season. (op 5-1 tchd 11-2)
River Music(IRE), having his first race for a year and his first start for this yard, gave a good account of himself and this one-time expensive purchase has hopefully turned over a new leaf in his new surroundings. He can surely find an opening. (op 28-1)
Masterful Act(USA) had run out a wide-margin winner of a 1m6f AW maiden in November. Runner-up at Huntingdon on his second outing over hurdles, he suddenly came under strong pressure three from home and looked woefully one-paced. He is surely better than he showed here. (tchd 6-4)
Into The Light, a 63-rated maiden on the level, had been badly hampered at an early stage when tailed off on his hurdling debut. (op 50-1)
Scriptwriter(IRE) was out of the contest at the halfway mark. (op 5-4 tchd 6-4 and 13-8 in a place)

5261 BONNIE & CLIVE H'CAP CHASE (15 fncs) 2m 4f 110y
3:30 (3:30) (Class 4) (0-115,115) 5-Y-0+ **£2,602** (£764; £382; £190)

Form RPR
-122 **1** **Harry Flashman**[285] 859 10-11-6 **109**.......... PeterBuchanan 121+
(Donald Whillans) *prom: effrt and wnt 2nd after 2 out: led last: edgd lft: drvn out* **6/1**[2]
1026 **2** *2 1/2* **Montoya's Son (IRE)**[89] 3509 6-11-7 **115**.......... PaulGallagher(5) 124
(Howard Johnson) *cl up: chal 1/2-way: led bef 3 out: rdn and hdd last: kpt on same pce run-in* **6/1**[2]
-035 **3** *7* **Or D'Oudairies (FR)**[64] 3970 9-11-3 **106**..........(t) GrahamLee 109
(Ferdy Murphy) *hld up: nt fluent 10th: effrt 3 out: kpt on fr last: nt rch first two* **10/1**
13P4 **4** *1 1/2* **Ocarina (FR)**[18] 4961 9-10-11 **107**..........(p) NathanMoscrop(7) 108
(James Ewart) *towards rr: hdwy and in tch whn nt fluent 4 out: rdn next: one pce after 2 out* **12/1**
-0P1 **5** *1/2* **Mr Goofy (IRE)**[31] 4693 10-10-10 **99**.......... JohnnyFarrelly 102
(Michael Scudamore) *mde most to bef 3 out: sddle slippd & rdr lost irons and lost 2nd after next: wknd fr last* **12/1**
6FP2 **6** *19* **Baltic Pathfinder (IRE)**[18] 4962 7-10-9 **103**.......... ShaneByrne(5) 86
(Sue Smith) *t.k.h: midfield: outpcd 10th: wknd fr 4 out* **7/1**[3]
4245 **7** *44* **Guns And Butter (IRE)**[37] 4471 9-10-8 **97**.......... WilsonRenwick 40
(Rose Dobbin) *midfield: drvn 1/2-way: struggilng 10th: t.o* **22/1**
3022 **8** *3/4* **Bene Lad (IRE)**[18] 4961 9-10-8 **97**.......... RichieMcGrath 39
(Jim Goldie) *cl up: hit 3rd: drvn and outpcd after 8th: rallied 10th: wknd bef 3 out: t.o* **9/2**[1]
1325 **P** **Persian Prince (IRE)**[29] 4744 11-10-9 **98**.......... DenisO'Regan —
(John Wade) *cl up tl rdn and wknd 10th: t.o whn p.u bef 4 out* **8/1**
P0-6 **P** **Tot O'Whiskey**[155] 2249 10-11-7 **113**.......... JamesHalliday(3) —
(Malcolm Jefferson) *sn pushed along in rr: struggling fnl circ: t.o whn p.u bef 3 out* **11/1**
2FP2 **P** **King Of Castile**[72] 3818 7-11-6 **109**..........(p) LiamHeard —
(Barry Leavy) *sn towards rr: reminders 1/2-way: wknd 9th: t.o whn p.u bef 4 out* **18/1**

5m 11.9s (-1.60) **Going Correction** 0.0s/f (Good) **11** Ran SP% **112.8**
Speed ratings: **103,102,99,98,98 91,74,74,—,— —**
toteswingers:1&2:£5.20, 1&3:£17.40, 2&3:£4.50 CSF £40.86 CT £351.02 TOTE £6.50: £2.20, £3.00, £4.80; EX 36.80.
Owner A Gilchrist M Kent P Wylie **Bred** Allan Gilchrist **Trained** Hawick, Borders

FOCUS
A competitive handicap chase run at a sound pace, but only five still in contention jumping the third last. The form looks solid.

NOTEBOOK

Harry Flashman, a winner three times here previously, was having his first start since finishing runner-up at Perth in June. He travelled strongly and, produced to challenge at the final fence, soon put his mark on the race. He ran here from 109, 11lb below his hurdle-race mark, and seeing as he's suited by decent ground, he looks set for a profitable early summer. (op 11-2)

Montoya's Son(IRE), hit and miss over hurdles, was making his chase debut. He jumped soundly and his young rider had the confidence to send him to the front some way from home. In the end the winner was too quick for him on the run-in, but he should certainly be able to go one better. (op 15-2)

Or D'Oudairies(FR), without a win for over two years, is a keen-going sort and was dropped in at the start. Moving up at halfway, he stuck on up the final hill to claim third spot on the run-in. He may be worth a step up in trip.

Ocarina(FR), twice a winner over the C&D, did well to finish as close as he did after being given reminders as early as the sixth fence. (op 11-1)

Mr Goofy(IRE), who ended a three-year drought at Leicester from a 6lb lower mark, helped force the pace but looked booked for third spot at best when his rider lost his irons at the second-last fence. Official explanation: jockey said saddle slipped (op 10-1)

Bene Lad(IRE) was thought to not have any problem coping with the drying ground, but after a hesitant jump or two he was under strong pressure and struggling to keep up at the halfway mark. Official explanation: trainer had no explanation for the poor form shown (tchd 5-1)

Persian Prince(IRE) Official explanation: jockey said gelding lost its action but returned sound

5262 PRIMARY WEBSITES LTD H'CAP HURDLE (10 hdls) 2m 4f 110y

4:00 (4:00) (Class 3) (0-125,120) 4-Y-0+ **£3,252** (£955; £477; £238)

Form RPR

-532 **1** **Andreo Bambaleo**[23] 4870 7-10-11 **105** TomSiddall 111
(Simon West) *hld up in tch: hdwy to ld after 2 out: sn rdn: hld on wl fr last* **14/1**

6013 **2** *½* **San Deng**[42] 4391 9-9-9 **99** JoeColliver[(10)] 105
(Micky Hammond) *trckd ldrs: effrt and ev ch between last 2: kpt on towards fin* **4/1**[2]

6110 **3** *18* **The Magic Bishop**[50] 4235 6-11-7 **118** JamesHalliday[(3)] 107
(Malcolm Jefferson) *hld up: smooth hdwy and ev ch between last 2: sn rdn: wknd bef last* **7/1**[3]

P665 **4** *1½* **Bywell Beau (IRE)**[21] 4912 12-10-11 **112** AlistairFindlay[(7)] 100
(George Charlton) *t.k.h: prom: led after 2nd to after 2 out: wknd bef last* **8/1**

4000 **5** *9* **Woody Valentine (USA)**[17] 4998 10-10-3 **100** JamesO'Farrell[(3)] 80
(Evelyn Slack) *trckd ldrs: pushed along after 3 out: wknd fr next* **33/1**

4012 **6** *10* **Kempski**[23] 4873 11-10-8 **107** PaulGallagher[(5)] 78
(Rayson Nixon) *led to after 2nd: cl up: rdn bef 4 out: wknd fr 2 out* **17/2**

4313 **B** **Texas Holdem (IRE)**[15] 5030 12-11-8 **116** DenisO'Regan —
(Michael Smith) *hld up in tch: gng wl whn b.d 3 out* **15/8**[1]

42F4 **F** **Degas Art (IRE)**[49] 4257 8-11-12 **120** BrianHughes —
(Howard Johnson) *trckd ldrs: gng wl whn fell heavily 3 out* **7/1**[3]

5m 10.5s (-2.00) **Going Correction** +0.10s/f (Yiel) **8** Ran SP% **111.0**

Speed ratings (Par 107): **107,106,99,99,95 92,—,—**

toteswingers:1&2:£7.50, 1&3:£15.80, 2&3:£3.30 CSF £66.03 CT £416.83 TOTE £17.00: £4.20, £2.20, £2.90; EX 47.70.

Owner P Andries **Bred** Mrs V McKie **Trained** Middleham Moor, N Yorks

FOCUS

Quite a competitive handicap hurdle run at a steady pace and the complexion changed three out. The first two finished clear and this was a big step forward from the winner.

NOTEBOOK

Andreo Bambaleo looked to have a lot on his plate on his handicap bow. He slipped through on the inner to show ahead after two out but, after jumping the last in a useful lead, he was all out to hold on. (op 12-1)

San Deng, who goes well for this rider, went in pursuit of the winner up the final hill. He stuck on really well and would have made it in a few more strides. He is clearly in great heart. (op 9-2)

The Magic Bishop, back after a seven-week break, couldn't live with the first two. After winning twice in the winter he is now high in the weights but should make a fair chaser next season. (tchd 15-2)

Bywell Beau(IRE), without a win for over three years, retains plenty of enthusiasm but age looks to have caught up with the old boy. (op 17-2)

Texas Holdem(IRE), another pensioner, came into this in good form and had not been asked a question when he was brought down by the fall of Degas Art. (op 9-4)

Degas Art(IRE), a smart juvenile, has not won since. He was poised to challenge when falling three out but how much zest there would have been in his finishing effort is open to doubt. (op 9-4)

5263 HEXHAM SUNSHINE HUNTERS' CHASE (19 fncs) 3m 1f

4:30 (4:31) (Class 6) 5-Y-0+ **£936** (£290; £145; £72)

Form RPR

P434 **1** **Thunder Hawk (IRE)**[21] 4915 11-11-11 92 (v) MissLAlexander[(7)] 114
(Mrs L A Coltherd) *mde virtually all: hrd pressed fr 3 out: hld on gamely run-in* **20/1**

1F32 **2** *nk* **Ardnaclancy (IRE)**[21] 4915 8-12-3 116 MrJARichardson[(5)] 118
(Andrew Richardson) *t.k.h: a cl up: ev ch 4 out: outpcd bef 2 out: rallied to dispute ld bef last: kpt on run-in: jst hld* **7/4**[1]

13-P **3** *6* **Abragante (IRE)**[21] 4915 10-11-7 125 MrMEnnis[(7)] 105
(Mrs D Monteith) *cl up: chal after 2 out: rdn and no ex run-in* **7/1**

20P- **4** *20* **Aggie's Lad (IRE)**[71] 9-11-9 0 MrWKinsey[(5)] 87
(J P G Hamilton) *plld hrd: in tch tl rdn and wknd fr 2 out* **6/1**[3]

261- **5** *2¾* **Canada Street (IRE)**[23] 10-11-11 MissEStead[(7)] 90
(Miss E Stead) *prom: rdn after 4 out: wknd fr next* **20/1**

33-2 **6** *28* **Stagecoach Diamond**[8] 12-11-7 95 (b) MissHBethell[(7)] 59
(W A Bethell) *trckd ldrs tl rdn and wknd fr 15th* **12/1**

3-5P **P** **Nocatee (IRE)**[21] 4915 10-11-11 82 MrMSeston[(3)] —
(C Rae) *cl up: lost pl 6th: struggling fr 1/2-way: t.o whn p.u bef 4 out* **80/1**

P-U2 **P** **Optimistic Harry**[9] 12-11-11 86 MissSamanthaDrake[(7)] —
(Miss S A Drake) *nt fluent: sn wl bhd: shortlived effrt 1/2-way: sn btn: t.o whn p.u bef 4 out* **5/1**[2]

1310 **P** **Simply Smashing (IRE)**[169] 1999 11-12-1 119 MrJMThomas[(7)] —
(Philip Kirby) *hld up on outside: hit 4th: p.u after next* **17/2**

-P00 **F** **Bewery Man (IRE)**[230] 1362 10-11-7 96 MissCWalton[(7)] —
(Miss V E Hayter) *sn wl bhd: stdy hdwy 1/2-way: 6 l seventh and styng on whn fell 14th* **50/1**

5P/6 **P** **Zoren (FR)**[7] 5148 7-11-7 83 (t) MrNOrpwood[(7)] —
(Raymond Shiels) *in tch tl rdn and wknd fr 12th: t.o whn p.u bef 4 out* **125/1**

6m 27.7s (-4.50) **Going Correction** 0.0s/f (Good) **11** Ran SP% **111.5**

Speed ratings: **107,106,104,98,97 88,—,—,—,— —**

toteswingers:1&2:£10.40, 1&3:£46.90, 2&3:£9.10 CSF £53.69 TOTE £17.90: £3.80, £1.10, £2.70; EX 69.80.

Owner Robert Miller-Bakewell **Bred** J P N Parker **Trained** Selkirk, Borders

FOCUS

A modest hunter chase run at a sound pace and three in line jumping the last. The surprise winner is rated back to the level of his 2008 best.

NOTEBOOK

Thunder Hawk(IRE) took a similar event at Cartmel in June. On his previous start he had finished some way behind Ardnaclancy at Kelso, but jumping soundly and under a very tidy ride, he was persuaded to do just enough. (op 28-1)

Ardnaclancy(IRE), a prolific point winner, improved to take two hunter chases last summer. Runner-up behind a smart sort at Kelso on his previous start, well ahead of Thunder Hawk in fourth, he edged wide between the last two. Level at the last, he could not quite get there under what is best described as an enthusiastic ride. Other opportunities will come his way. (op 9-4 tchd 13-8)

Abragante(IRE), pulled up in that Kelso race after a five-month month absence, ran much better and was only found lacking on the run-in. (op 13-2 tchd 6-1)

Aggie's Lad(IRE), clear when running out at the last in a Ladies' Open at Friars Haugh on his first start for this yard, found this company much tougher. (op 5-1)

Optimistic Harry, winner of three points and runner-up behind smart sort at Kelso in his last four starts, never went a yard, jumping poorly. His busy season looks to have caught up with him. Official explanation: jockey said gelding never travelled (op 9-2)

5264 DURHAM C.C.C. STANDARD OPEN NATIONAL HUNT FLAT RACE 2m 110y

5:05 (5:05) (Class 6) 4-5-Y-O **£1,370** (£399; £199)

Form RPR

1 **Find A Key (IRE)** 4-10-7 0 PaulGallagher[(5)] 93
(Howard Johnson) *prom: hdwy to ld over 2f out: rdn and hld on wl fnl f* **4/1**[1]

2 *hd* **No Planning** 4-10-2 0 NathanCook[(10)] 93
(Sue Smith) *w ldr: rdn over 2f out: pushed along and styd on fnl f: jst hld* **17/2**

14 **3** *1* **Tricksofthetrade (IRE)**[30] 4717 5-11-1 0 BarryKeniry 105
(Alan Swinbank) *trckd ldrs: effrt 2f out: kpt on ins fnl f* **5/1**[3]

51 **4** *½* **Sinfield (IRE)**[42] 4396 5-11-1 0 JoeColliver[(10)] 105
(Micky Hammond) *prom: rdn 3f out: rallied wl over 1f out: edgd lft and kpt on fnl f* **9/2**[2]

10 **5** *¾* **Opera North**[68] 3889 4-11-5 0 JamesReveley 98
(Tom Tate) *midfield: effrt over 2f out: kpt on u.p fnl f* **14/1**

0-62 **6** *3¾* **Shannagarry (IRE)**[64] 3971 5-11-4 0 JanFaltejsek 93
(George Charlton) *midfield: pushed along over 6f out: rallied over 3f out: no imp fr 2f out* **15/2**

7 *12* **Nahneh (IRE)** 5-11-4 0 DenisO'Regan 81
(John Wade) *midfield: effrt and rdn over 4f out: wknd fr 2f out* **22/1**

8 *1¾* **Alba King (IRE)** 5-11-4 0 HenryOliver 79
(Sue Smith) *led at stdy pce: rdn and hdd over 2f out: wknd over 1f out* **14/1**

9 *5* **Kealshore** 4-10-2 0 SamuelWelton[(10)] 68
(George Moore) *hld up: outpcd over 6f out: shkn up and sme late hdwy: nvr nrr* **12/1**

10 *2¾* **Grey Danbys** 5-10-8 0 JamesHalliday[(3)] 65
(Malcolm Jefferson) *bhd: outpcd over 6f out: n.d after* **14/1**

0 **11** *½* **Tekthelot (IRE)**[47] 4287 5-11-4 0 JohnnyFarrelly 71
(Elliott Cooper) *hld up on ins: stmbld after 7f: struggling fr over 6f out* **50/1**

12 *14* **Vic's Witch (IRE)** 5-10-4 0 StevenGagan[(7)] 50
(Elliott Cooper) *in tch on outside: struggling 1/2-way: sn btn* **33/1**

13 *6* **My Friend George** 5-11-1 0 JamesO'Farrell[(3)] 51
(Dianne Sayer) *towards rr: rdn after 6f: wknd fr 7f out* **22/1**

4m 16.1s (3.40) **Going Correction** +0.10s/f (Yiel)

WFA 4 from 5yo 5lb **13** Ran SP% **118.4**

Speed ratings: **96,95,95,95,94 93,87,86,84,82 82,76,73**

toteswingers:1&2:£10.40, 1&3:£46.90, 2&3:£9.10 CSF £36.05 TOTE £3.60: £1.30, £5.70, £1.10; EX 40.00.

Owner Andrea & Graham Wylie **Bred** James Kinsella **Trained** Billy Row, Co Durham

■ Stewards' Enquiry : Paul Gallagher caution: careless riding.

FOCUS

No gallop at all until the halfway mark and a large blanket would have covered the first five home at the line. The third to sixth were all within 3lb of their pre-race marks.

NOTEBOOK

Find A Key(IRE), well touted beforehand, rather cut across his rivals when taking charge coming off the final turn. Ending up racing hard against the stands' side rail, he just gained the verdict. (op 6-1)

No Planning, well fancied on his debut, was in the thick of things throughout. He stuck to his task in willing fashion and was only just denied. He deserves to go one better. (op 11-1)

Tricksofthetrade(IRE), a ready Catterick winner on his debut, disappointed in bad ground at Ayr next time. Given four weeks off, he ran really well under his penalty. (op 3-1 tchd 11-4)

Sinfield(IRE), a decisive winner at Catterick on his second start, was another to acquit himself with credit under his penalty. (op 13-2 tchd 7-1)

Opera North won at Carlisle but didn't give his running at Newcastle next time for no obvious reason. A big type, he looked in grand trim and stayed on in determined fashion after being driven along half a mile out. If he tries his hand on the Flat proper he will need a real test. (op 11-1)

Shannagarry(IRE) was having his fourth start and will have to go hurdling now. He looks limited. (tchd 8-1)

Nahneh(IRE), from a yard with a poor record in bumpers, made a pleasing introduction, shaping well until tiring up the final hill.

T/Jkpt: Not won. T/Plt: £43.10 to a £1 stake. Pool:£85,164.24 - 1,439.85 winning tickets T/Qpdt: £12.00 to a £1 stake. Pool:£5,507.95 - 337.10 winning tickets RY

5050 PLUMPTON (L-H)

Monday, April 11

OFFICIAL GOING: Good to firm (good in places) changing to good to firm after race 1 (2:00)

Wind: Fine, warm Weather: Moderate, across

5265 PLUMPTON ANNUAL MEMBERS H'CAP HURDLE (14 hdls) 3m 1f 110y

2:20 (2:22) (Class 5) (0-95,95) 4-Y-0+ **£1,815** (£529; £264)

Form RPR

0426 **1** **Champs De Bleu (FR)**[25] 4833 8-10-13 **82** (b[1]) JamieMoore 92+
(Gary Moore) *hld up in rr: stdy prog fr 7th: trckd ldrs 11th: wnt 2nd after 3 out: jnd ldr gng strly whn lft clr 2 out* **7/1**

0604 **2** *13* **Petroupetrov (FR)**[28] 4773 8-11-7 **90** SeanQuinlan 90
(Richard Phillips) *prom in chsng gp: hmpd 3rd: rdn to chse ldr after 4 out tl after next: one pce whn lft 2nd 2 out* **5/1**[1]

-003 **3** *11* **Formedable (IRE)**[12] 5072 9-10-1 **70** (p) WillKennedy 58
(Violet M Jordan) *hld up in rr: rdn and outpcd by ldrs fr 11th: kpt on and lft modest 3rd 2 out* **9/1**

FPF **4** *6* **Sonus Weld (IRE)**[63] 3983 6-10-8 **77**....................(p) AndrewGlassonbury 59
(Paddy Butler) *reluctant to line up and led in s: mostly chsd ldng pair to 7th: rdn and stl in tch bef 3 out: wknd* **33/1**

3630 **5** *11* **Chouromanesco (FR)**[34] 4540 8-11-1 **84**....................(b) MattieBatchelor 56
(Mark Bradstock) *led after 1st: reminder after 5th (passing horsebox park): drvn 9th: hdd & wknd 11th* **10/1**

F410 **U** **Albert Park (IRE)**[224] 1434 10-9-13 **73**....................(p) AnthonyFreeman(5) —
(John Upson) *blnd and uns rdr 2nd: fell next whn loose* **14/1**

5560 **P** **Pursuit Of Purpose**[175] 1900 5-10-4 **80** ow1............... MrJackSalmon(7) —
(Philip Sharp) *trckd ldrs: wnt 2nd briefly 10th gng wl: immediately rdn and dropped out rapidly: t.o whn p.u bef 2 out* **66/1**

0135 **P** **Queenstown Lad**[49] 4263 6-10-5 **74**.................................. PaddyBrennan —
(Gary Brown) *j.rt: a in rr: hmpd 3rd: t.o fr 11th: p.u bef 2 out* **8/1**

5-P3 **F** **Willow Wren**[26] 4812 6-11-12 **95**..(tp) SamJones 98+
(Renee Robeson) *led tl after 1st: chsd ldr: j.lft 3rd: led again 11th (4 out): drvn and jnd whn fell 2 out* **6/1**[3]

0604 **P** **Drink Up**[14] 5057 7-10-8 **77**... AndrewThornton —
(John O'Neill) *a wl in rr: t.o whn p.u bef 11th* **11/2**[2]

403P **P** **Downe Payment (IRE)**[40] 4427 6-10-2 **78**.................... MissHGrissell(7) —
(Diana Grissell) *hld up in last trio: hmpd 3rd: nvr a factor: t.o after 11th: p.u bef 2 out* **5/1**[1]

6m 13.7s (-15.10) **Going Correction** -0.725s/f (Firm) **11** Ran SP% **116.8**
Speed ratings (Par 103): **94,90,86,84,81** —,—,—,—,— —
toteswingers:1&2:£7.30, 1&3:£14.20, 2&3:£6.50 CSF £42.28 CT £321.20 TOTE £9.80: £3.00, £2.30, £4.50; EX 47.20.
Owner A G Russell **Bred** Anthony Georges Russell **Trained** Lower Beeding, W Sussex

FOCUS
A weak handicap hurdle. The winner produced a big step up in the blinkers and the faller is rated as finishing second.

NOTEBOOK
Champs De Bleu(FR) looked to be gaining the upper hand before being left in a clear lead two out. He had run respectably over C&D previously but had failed to build on that and connections had reached for first-time blinkers. He is open to further improvement and has the size and scope to make his presence felt when jumping a fence. Unfortunately, he pulled up a little sore. (op 13-2 tchd 15-2)
Petroupetrov(FR) ran well enough off a reasonable mark, but this two-time winner over fences in 2010 remains a maiden over hurdles. Not out of the question to see him opening his account over hurdles, but he has had plenty of chances. (op 6-1)
Formedable(IRE) looked booked for fourth before being gifted the third spot and is exposed as modest. (tchd 10-1)
Willow Wren raced up with the pace and travelled better in first-time cheekpieces. She was still holding a narrow advantage under pressure when coming down at the second last. She looks capable of landing a similar contest, if none the worse. (op 8-1)
Drink Up was fancied to go well now stepped up in trip but was struggling from an early stage and was tailing off before being pulled up. (op 8-1)
Downe Payment(IRE) was in rear after being hampered early and eventually cried enough. Official explanation: vet said mare pulled up distressed (op 8-1)

5266 FOLLOW PLUMPTON RACECOURSE ON TWITTER CONDITIONAL JOCKEYS' H'CAP CHASE (14 fncs) 2m 4f
2:50 (2:50) (Class 5) (0-95,92) 5-Y-O+ **£1,952** (£569; £284)

Form RPR
36P2 **1** **Monsieur Georges (FR)**[14] 5062 11-9-11 **66**.............. PeterCarberry(3) 75+
(Violet M Jordan) *trckd ldr 4th to 6th: reminders after 8th but stl cl up: effrt to chal after 10th: rdn to ld 3 out: nt fluent last 2: styd on* **2/1**[2]

/43F **2** *6* **Ilongue (FR)**[14] 5062 10-10-1 **67**... DavidBass 69
(Laura Hurley) *led: pressed fr 9th: hdd 3 out: one pce whn pckd 2 out* **7/4**[1]

2015 **3** *35* **Curragh Dancer (FR)**[3] 5191 8-10-11 **80**................. NathanSweeney(3) 50
(Paddy Butler) *sloppy rnd of jumping and often wnt rt: chsd ldr to 4th: last fr 6th and sn in trble: t.o* **7/2**[3]

4466 **F** **Vasodilator (IRE)**[18] 4975 8-11-9 **92**.......................(v[1]) MichaelMurphy(3) —
(Pat Murphy) *hld up: prog to trck ldr 6th: chal 9th and next: sn lost 2nd: 5 l bhd ldng pair and losing grnd whn fell 4 out* **11/2**

5m 2.10s (-5.20) **Going Correction** -0.575s/f (Firm) **4** Ran SP% **107.3**
Speed ratings: **87,84,70,**—
CSF £5.93 TOTE £2.70; EX 5.10.
Owner Near & Far Racing **Bred** Georges Pelot Et Al **Trained** Quainton, Bucks

FOCUS
A poor low-grade conditional jockeys' handicap, rated around the first two.

NOTEBOOK
Monsieur Georges(FR) gaining a deserved success. He is in the frame more often than not and can continue to give his connections some fun, but his overall strike-rate is hardly encouraging. (op 5-2 tchd 15-8)
Ilongue(FR), who had been placed in two of his three runs over fences, looked to have solid claims in this weak contest. He had his chance but could only keep on at the same pace. (op 2-1 tchd 9-4)
Curragh Dancer(FR) ran poorly four days earlier back over hurdles after gaining a fortunate success over C&D. He needs plenty of encouragement and will need to be sharper at his fences in the future. Perhaps headgear will help. (op 3-1)
Vasodilator(IRE), racing in first-time visor after disappointing in a claiming hurdle recently, was just feeling the pinch when crashing out. He had lost his way over fences and can only be watched at present. (op 4-1 tchd 6-1)

5267 FRP NOVICES' HURDLE (12 hdls) 2m 5f
3:20 (3:20) (Class 4) 4-Y-O+ **£2,055** (£599; £299)

Form RPR
2100 **1** **Mr Muddle**[26] 4807 4-10-10 115...................................(p) MarcGoldstein(3) 101+
(Sheena West) *trckd ldr after 2nd: hit 7th: led next: rdn and jnd after 3 out: styd on to draw clr fr next: dismntd after fin* **10/11**[1]

P04 **2** *5* **Rebel High (IRE)**[19] 4951 7-11-0 0.................................... LiamTreadwell 96
(Derek Frankland) *led to 2nd: styd prom: chsd wnr after 9th: upsides after 3 out: rdn and nt qckn next: wl hld after* **6/1**[3]

P4 **3** *6* **Mrs Peacock (IRE)**[11] 5078 6-10-7 0.. SamJones 82
(Norma Twomey) *hld up: cl enough fr 8th: chsd ldng pair after 3 out: no imp but kpt on* **20/1**

-005 **4** *23* **Royal Mile (IRE)**[45] 4325 7-11-0 0............................... WayneHutchinson 68
(Warren Greatrex) *hld up in tch: pushed along after 9th: wnt 3rd briefly 3 out: sn fdd* **14/1**

-000 **5** *2* **Late Red**[21] 4918 6-11-0 0.. MattieBatchelor 66
(Jamie Poulton) *hld up last: cl enough fr 8th: bmpd 3 out and sn outpcd: wknd* **50/1**

404 **6** *76* **Fennis Ted (IRE)**[22] 4895 5-10-7 0... SClements(7) —
(Liam Corcoran) *trckd ldrs: wnt 2nd after 8th: upsides whn hit next: sn rdn and dropped away: virtually p.u flat* **5/1**[2]

-600 **7** *nk* **Castle Myth (USA)**[42] 4397 5-10-4 0.................................. AshleyBird(10) —
(Jim Best) *led 2nd and set decent pce: mstke 4th: hdd 8th: wknd rapidly: t.o 3 out: virtually p.u flat* **33/1**

05 **P** **Candlefort Lady (IRE)**[146] 2440 6-10-7 0........................... PaddyBrennan —
(Jim Best) *hld up in last pair: dropped out after 8th: t.o whn p.u bef 2 out* **8/1**

5m 6.80s (-15.50) **Going Correction** -0.725s/f (Firm)
WFA 4 from 5yo+ 6lb **8** Ran SP% **110.8**
Speed ratings (Par 105): **100,98,95,87,86 57,57,**—
toteswingers:1&2:£1.80, 1&3:£4.80, 2&3:£15.70 CSF £6.28 TOTE £2.50: £1.10, £1.30, £5.00; EX 7.20.
Owner Saloop **Bred** Saloop Ltd **Trained** Falmer, E Sussex

FOCUS
The ground was changed to good to firm prior to this weak novice hurdle. The first two are rated pretty much to their marks.

NOTEBOOK
Mr Muddle regained the winning thread on this dropped back in class after a couple of stiff tasks of late. Equipped with first-time cheekpieces, he had to be ridden out to assert going to the last but looked to be idling. Although dismounted after the winning post, he appeared to handle the quicker surface and connections will see how he comes out of this before deciding if he can return to the course on Easter Monday for a similar contest. (op 5-4 tchd 11-8 and 6-4 in a place)
Rebel High(IRE) probably ran to the same level of form as when finishing fourth in a maiden hurdle at Warwick last time. He kept to his task well and could be of interest when switching to handicaps. (op 7-1 tchd 8-1)
Mrs Peacock(IRE), a winner of two Irish point-to-points, is another who could be of interest when handicapping and stepped up further in trip, as she could only stay on at the same pace. (op 25-1)
Royal Mile(IRE) flattered briefly after three out before his effort petered out rather tamely. (op 16-1 tchd 12-1)
Fennis Ted(IRE), stepped back up in trip after an encouraging run at Newton Abbot last time, failed to build upon that and was soundly beaten. (op 7-2 tchd 3-1)

5268 PADDOCK RESTAURANT H'CAP CHASE (18 fncs) 3m 2f
3:50 (3:50) (Class 5) (0-95,90) 5-Y-O+ **£1,853** (£544; £272; £135)

Form RPR
5000 **1** **Wait No More (IRE)**[36] 4500 6-10-11 **75**.............................(tp) JackDoyle 85+
(Sarah Humphrey) *occasionally j.rt: in tch gng wl: led and mstke 13th: blnd next: drew clr fr 3 out: pushed out* **9/4**[2]

4006 **2** *7* **Knight Woodsman**[60] 4021 7-11-9 **90**..........................(p) AlexMerriam(3) 90
(Neil King) *hld up and last early: nt fluent 9th: cl up 12th: outpcd fr 4 out: kpt on to take 2nd last* **4/1**[3]

6646 **3** *2 1/4* **Front Street (IRE)**[31] 4705 7-10-10 **77**......................(b) MichaelMurphy(3) 76
(Pat Murphy) *racd wd: led to 9th: upsides after 12th: w wnr 4 out: one pce fr next: lost 2nd last* **8/1**

PPP5 **4** *19* **Allterrain (IRE)**[14] 5053 8-11-11 **89**................................... LeightonAspell 70
(Murty McGrath) *trckd ldr: led 9th to 13th: steadily wknd fr 4 out* **6/1**

P441 **5** *9* **Absolute Shambles**[14] 5053 7-11-4 **82**................................ JamieMoore 56
(Chris Gordon) *dropped to last and rdn 5th: lost tch 8th: kpt toiling on* **2/1**[1]

5-0P **P** **Toni Alcala**[26] 4812 12-11-4 **87**.....................(p) GemmaGracey-Davison(5) —
(Neil King) *in tch: mstke 6th: sn pushed along: lost tch 13th: t.o whn j. slowly 4 out: qckly p.u and dismntd* **18/1**

6m 42.8s (-7.90) **Going Correction** -0.575s/f (Firm) **6** Ran SP% **114.8**
Speed ratings: **89,86,86,80,77** —
toteswingers:1&2:£1.70, 1&3:£4.00, 2&3:£4.60 CSF £12.21 TOTE £4.40: £2.60, £3.10; EX 11.60.
Owner P & C Chapman & S Humphrey **Bred** Sean Naughton **Trained** West Wratting, Cambs

FOCUS
A tricky staying handicap chase with question marks surrounding most of the runners. Poor form, but a big step up from the winner on his hurdles level.

NOTEBOOK
Wait No More(IRE) ◆'s previous success had been on fast ground in an Irish point-to-point last year and he had shown little in three runs over hurdles this season on an easier surface. He attracted plenty of support now switched to fences on his handicap debut with cheekpieces and a tongue-tie also being applied. He jumped well on the whole, apart from a serious blunder at the top of the hill, and outstayed his rivals in good fashion. Connections were a little disappointed with him over hurdles, but he looks to be one to keep on the right side of over fences at present. (op 10-3)
Knight Woodsman had gone off the boil over hurdles so this was a welcome return to form on his chasing debut. He jumped well and stayed on to take second at the last, but had no answers against the well-handicapped winner. (op 11-2)
Front Street(IRE), the winner of a maiden point-to-point last May, had shown little under rules to date but ran respectably with blinkers replacing a visor. This was a step in the right direction, but he will have to repeat this effort if he is to get off the mark. (op 7-1)
Absolute Shambles takes an awful lot of stoking and was up just 2lb since a battling success over C&D last time. This was not one of his going days and he dropped away with a circuit to run. (tchd 11-4)

5269 HEART H'CAP CHASE (12 fncs) 2m 1f
4:20 (4:20) (Class 4) (0-105,101) 5-Y-O+ **£2,602** (£764; £382; £190)

Form RPR
U4P3 **1** **Health Is Wealth (IRE)**[22] 4896 6-11-3 **92**............................. JoeTizzard 103+
(Colin Tizzard) *led to 8th: rdn to ld again bef 2 out where lft in command: styd on wl* **7/5**[1]

0343 **2** *6* **Mister Matt (IRE)**[16] 5011 8-11-5 **101**........................(t) NathanSweeney(7) 108
(Bob Buckler) *w.w: pushed along to chse ldng pair after 8th: rdn to chal whn stmbld 2 out and lost impetus: one pce after* **11/4**[2]

1021 **3** *10* **She's Humble (IRE)**[14] 5055 9-11-8 **97**......................... AndrewThornton 93
(Linda Jewell) *unable to ld: chsd ldr to 7th: dropped to last after next and sn bhd: plugged on to take 3rd flat* **11/4**[2]

5542 **4** *4 1/2* **Bushwacker (IRE)**[4] 5173 7-11-8 **100**.......................(tp) JimmyDerham(3) 95+
(Seamus Mullins) *hld up: prog to chal 7th: led next: 2 l clr whn nt fluent 3 out: hdd & wknd bdly bef next* **6/1**[3]

4m 14.0s (-11.90) **Going Correction** -0.575s/f (Firm) **4** Ran SP% **109.3**
Speed ratings: **105,102,97,95**
CSF £5.66 TOTE £2.10; EX 5.00.
Owner Gale Force Five **Bred** Bernard Fenton **Trained** Milborne Port, Dorset

FOCUS
A tight handicap and modest form, rated around the front two.

NOTEBOOK
Health Is Wealth(IRE) ◆ asserted at the second last. He has always shaped as though a contest of this nature was within his compass since switching to handicaps/fences and he appreciated the drop back to 2m1f after a fair effort over further last time. There are plenty of similar opportunities in this division over the coming months with connections having the option of stepping him back up in distance. (op 7-4 tchd 15-8 and 11-8)
Mister Matt(IRE) ran with credit when third in a better race than this last time and again ran respectably here. A stumble at the second last did not aid his cause, but he should be capable of finding a similar contest to go one better before long. (op 5-2 tchd 3-1)

She's Humble(IRE) likes it around here but she has been creeping up the weights and the ground was probably livelier than ideal. She was struggling to hold her position with a circuit to run but to her credit kept on to regain third from the last. (op 3-1 tchd 7-2)

Bushwacker(IRE) ran well with cheekpieces and tongue-tie applied last time, but he jumps indifferently and ran out of petrol after being headed turning in. He might have found this coming too soon after his decent effort at Hereford. (op 5-1 tchd 9-2)

5270 PLUMPTONRACECOURSE.CO.UK H'CAP HURDLE (10 hdls) 2m 2f
4:50 (4:50) (Class 5) (0-95,95) 4-Y-O+ **£1,815** (£396; £396)

Form RPR

0503 **1** **Airedale Lad (IRE)**[28] 4771 10-9-8 **70** oh5 ow1..............(p) MrJBanks(7) 72
(Zoe Davison) *pressed ldr: led 7th: rdn 3 out: hrd pressed fr next: hld on wl* **17/2**

4542 **2** *1* **Just Beware**[28] 4771 9-11-7 **95**...................(p) GemmaGracey-Davison(5) 97
(Zoe Davison) *prom: rdn to go 2nd after 7th: drvn to chal 2 out: nrly upsides whn nt fluent last: nt qckn* **9/2**[3]

0001 **2** *dht* **Citrus Mark**[19] 4956 6-11-8 **91**... WillKennedy 96+
(Paul Webber) *hld up in last pair: pushed along after 6th: no prog tl after next: wnt 3rd after 3 out: clsng whn stmbld 2 out: rallied fr last: nt rch wnr* **9/4**[1]

0054 **4** *7* **Sovereign Spirit (IRE)**[25] 4833 9-10-13 **82**................(tp) GerardTumelty 77
(Chris Gordon) *in tch: rdn and struggling after 6th: dropped to last and mstke next: sn detached: styd on bef 2 out to take 4th flat* **10/3**[2]

4320 **5** *4 1/2* **Cloonavery (IRE)**[16] 5016 9-10-0 **69** oh2......................(v) LiamTreadwell 61
(Derek Frankland) *prom: rdn in 3rd 3 out: steadily outpcd* **7/1**

0-04 **6** *2 3/4* **Drawback (IRE)**[12] 5072 8-10-13 **89**.............................(p) CDTimmons(7) 77
(Barry Brennan) *in tch: reminder 4th: nt gng wl fr 1/2-way but stl in tch 3 out: wknd* **8/1**

U000 **7** *11* **December**[10] 5099 5-11-6 **92**..(t) AlexMerriam(3) 70
(Christine Dunnett) *w.w in tch: stl chsng ldrs 3 out: shkn up and fdd* **20/1**

-PPP **8** *6* **Bridge Of Fermoy (IRE)**[78] 3703 6-10-0 **69** oh5.......(bt) MattieBatchelor 42
(Daniel O'Brien) *led to 7th: steadily lost pl: eased after 3 out: mstke 2 out: shkn up flat* **20/1**

4m 25.5s (265.50) **8** Ran SP% **115.7**
Place: Just Beware £1.30, Citrus Mark £1.10 EX: AL&JB £18.80, AL&CM £20.30 CSF: AL&JB £23.71, AL&CM £14.58: TC: AL&JB&CM £57.19, AL&CM&JB £48.55. toteswingers: AL&JB £6.40. AL&CM £3.10, JB&CM £5.50. TOTE £11.50: £3.80.

Owner Mrs S E Colville **Bred** John Malone **Trained** Hammerwood, E Sussex

FOCUS
A weak handicap, run at a decent gallop. The winner's best run since 2009, with Citrus Mark arguably unlucky and Just Beware to her mark.

NOTEBOOK
Airedale Lad(IRE) had not scored since landing back-to-back sellers in 2009 but showed a return to some sort of form when cheekpieces were refitted last time, albeit being beaten nearly 20l by Just Beware. He was racing from 5lb out of the handicap but was reported to be coming to himself of late. Connections will be thinking of turning him out again quickly, with Fontwell at the end of next week on the cards. (op 8-1 tchd 9-1)

Just Beware is admirably consistent and this was another good effort, but she holds few secrets. (op 2-1 tchd 3-1)

Citrus Mark left previous hurdle form behind when scoring on his handicap debut over 2m at Warwick last time and was fancied to follow up off only 4lb higher. He was being shoved along at the top of the hill before coming back on an even keel at the third last. Although he kept on well enough to dead-heat for the runner-up spot, he could not find the pace to make a serious challenge. (op 2-1 tchd 3-1)

Sovereign Spirit(IRE) was staying on best in the straight but was never going to reach the leaders and ran better than the bare form suggests. He should be suited by a step back in trip. (op 11-2)

5271 DRIVE IN MOVIE ON 6TH AUGUST H'CAP HURDLE (12 hdls) 2m 5f
5:25 (5:25) (Class 4) (0-115,110) 4-Y-O+ **£2,397** (£698; £349)

Form RPR

4421 **1** **Top Smart**[63] 3985 5-11-7 **108**.. JimmyDerham(3) 118+
(Seamus Mullins) *cl up: led 8th: drew clr after 3 out: briefly pressed last: shkn up and styd on wl* **9/5**[1]

2 *3 3/4* **Knocklayde Vic (IRE)**[337] 242 7-11-12 **110**...................... DaveCrosse 112+
(Ian Williams) *t.k.h: trckd ldr to 8th: effrt to chse wnr 3 out: outpcd bef next: tried to cl last: readily hld* **5/2**[2]

3600 **3** *24* **Shropshirelass**[21] 4922 8-10-6 **95**................. GemmaGracey-Davison(5) 75
(Zoe Davison) *hld up in last: pushed along 8th: outpcd fr next: n.d after: tk 3rd bef last* **9/2**

2PP- **4** *12* **Highest Esteem**[350] 21 7-11-0 **105**.......................... MrJackSalmon(7) 75
(Philip Sharp) *cl up: chsd wnr after 8th to 3 out: wknd* **25/1**

54P1 **5** *60* **Horseshoe Reef (AUS)**[28] 4768 8-11-11 **109**.......................... DarylJacob 25
(Jamie Snowden) *led to 8th: wknd and last fr next: eased and t.o* **7/2**[3]

5m 4.00s (-18.30) **Going Correction** -0.725s/f (Firm) **5** Ran SP% **108.5**
Speed ratings (Par 105): **105,103,94,89,67**
totesuper7: Win: Not won. Place: £173.90. CSF £6.64 TOTE £2.80: £1.80, £1.70; EX 5.40.

Owner The Calvera Partnership No 2 **Bred** A Price **Trained** Wilsford-Cum-Lake, Wilts

FOCUS
An ordinary handicap. The easy winner is on the upgrade.

NOTEBOOK
Top Smart was the obvious improver in the line-up and duly followed up his Lingfield success off 7lb higher in a good manner. The main concern for connections was the faster ground after some niggling problems, but he seemed to handle the surface well. Considering he saw out this further step up in trip well and has plenty of scope for improvement, he looks a horse for the future. (op 2-1 tchd 9-4 and 7-4)

Knocklayde Vic(IRE) had been well supported on his return to action after a 337-day absence and on his debut for Ian Williams. He ran with plenty of credit in defeat and was unlucky to have bumped into an unexposed type. He can go on from this. (op 11-4)

Shropshirelass, winner of this last season, ran well enough before tiring after three out and should come on again. She remains on a fair mark. (tchd 4-1)

Highest Esteem, racing without usual headgear on his debut for new connections, could never land a serious blow but has been generally disappointing since scoring at Fontwell in 2009. (op 22-1)

Horseshoe Reef(AUS) was disappointing reverting to hurdles off only a 5lb higher mark than when winning a chase around here last time. Official explanation: jockey said gelding ran flat (op 3-1 tchd 11-4)

T/Plt: £169.60 to a £1 stake. Pool:£52,750.22 - 226.93 winning tickets T/Qpdt: £29.80 to a £1 stake. Pool:£4,519.90 - 111.90 winning tickets JN

5064 TAUNTON (R-H)
Tuesday, April 12

OFFICIAL GOING: Firm (good to firm in a few places) changing to firm after race 1 (4.45)
Rail moved on bends reducing distances by 6m each circuit.
Wind: fresh across Weather: sunny

5272 BET ON TOTEPLACEPOT AT TOTESPORT.COM (S) H'CAP HURDLE (8 hdls 1 omitted) 2m 1f
4:45 (4:46) (Class 5) (0-90,90) 4-7-Y-O **£2,055** (£599; £299)

Form RPR

4423 **1** **Stravita**[22] 4920 7-10-5 **79**..(b) AshleyBird(10) 87
(Jim Best) *trckd ldr: led 2 out: sn rdn: 3 l clr whn hit last: hld on: all out* **9/2**[1]

0060 **2** *nk* **Ostaadi**[22] 4920 5-10-7 **76**...(p) MarkQuinlan(5) 83
(Bernard Llewellyn) *in tch: wnt 2nd after 2 out: rdn bef last: styd on run-in: str run fnl 75yds: jst hld* **15/2**

P403 **3** *7* **A P Ling**[20] 4947 4-9-7 **70**..(p) MrTGarner(7) 64
(Christopher Kellett) *mid-div: hdwy after 2 out: sn rdn to chse ldng pair: kpt on same pce fr last* **14/1**

P050 **4** *3 1/2* **Whatshallwedo**[23] 4899 6-10-8 **72**... LiamHeard 69
(Chris Down) *trckd ldrs: rdn after 2 out: one pce fr last* **25/1**

000P **5** *1* **Rolanta (FR)**[84] 3611 6-10-7 **71**.. HaddenFrost 67
(James Frost) *led tl 2 out: sn rdn: one pce fr last* **7/1**

044 **6** *nk* **Dolores Ortiz (IRE)**[14] 5064 5-11-5 **83**.................................. RhysFlint 78
(Philip Hobbs) *hld up towards rr: rdn after 2 out: plugged on: nvr threatened ldrs* **11/2**[3]

6P2U **7** *24* **Motor Home**[20] 4956 5-11-9 **87**.....................................(t) JimmyMcCarthy 58
(Charlie Morlock) *mid-div: rdn whn wknd 2 out* **11/1**

5601 **8** *4 1/2* **Shoudhavenownbettr (IRE)**[5] 5172 7-11-0 **85** 7ex.....(p) MrJMRidley(7) 52
(Matt Sheppard) *sn struggling in rr: t.o fr 5th* **5/1**[2]

33P6 **9** *66* **Bari Bay**[84] 3619 5-10-4 **68**...(b) NickScholfield —
(Michael Blake) *sn struggling in rr: t.o fr 5th* **7/1**

650P **10** *5* **Southway Star**[29] 4785 6-11-0 **78**....................................... JamesDavies —
(Susan Gardner) *bhd fr 5th: t.o* **28/1**

0020 **F** **Tiger Dream**[10] 5114 6-11-5 **90**.......................................(bt) MrRHawkins(7) —
(Chris Down) *trcking ldr whn fell heavily 4th* **10/1**

3m 51.6s (-16.40) **Going Correction** -0.975s/f (Hard)
WFA 4 from 5yo+ 5lb **11** Ran SP% **118.4**
Speed ratings: **99,98,95,93,93 93,82,79,48,46** —
Tote Swingers: 1&2 £21.00, 1&3 £5.90, 2&3 £18.60 CSF £38.84 CT £442.60 TOTE £5.50: £1.70, £3.60, £4.10; EX 50.60.There was no bid for the winner.

Owner The Prophets **Bred** Eric Bennion And Miss Sarah Hollinshead **Trained** Lewes, E Sussex

FOCUS
This typically weak selling handicap was run at a sound gallop and those racing handily were at an advantage due to the rattling fast ground. A step up from the winner with the second back to form. The last flight was bypassed.

NOTEBOOK
Stravita was given too much to do at Lingfield under today's rider on her penultimate outing, but adopted a prominent position this time and finally got off the mark over hurdles. She took it up turning for home, but hit what was to be the final flight in the home straight and had to be kept right up to her work thereafter. It was her first success since 2008 and this is very much her sort of level. (op 5-1 tchd 11-2)

Ostaadi ◆, well backed, finished well behind the winner at Lingfield last time and had looked totally out of sorts since joining his yard. This was a lot more like it, however, and he looks well up to winning something similar over a stiffer test. (op 11-1)

A P Ling did his best to close from a mid-field position and is a bit better than the bare form as he was hampered by Tiger Dream falling at the fourth. (op 12-1)

Whatshallwedo has now found his sort of level.

Dolores Ortiz(IRE) found herself too far back to make a serious impact on her handicap debut. (op 6-1 tchd 7-1)

Shoudhavenownbettr(IRE) looked a fiendishly tricky sort despite getting off the mark at Hereford last week and was the first beaten here under his penalty. (op 9-2)

5273 FREE RACING POST FORM AT TOTESPORT.COM NOVICES' CHASE (17 fncs) 2m 7f 110y
5:15 (5:17) (Class 4) 5-Y-O+ **£4,453** (£1,298; £649)

Form RPR

3121 **1** **Qozak (FR)**[14] 5065 7-11-12 140.......................................(t) NickScholfield 123+
(Paul Nicholls) *j.w: mde most: narrowly hdd 11th tl next: drew clr after 4 out: v easily* **1/8**[1]

BP0P **2** *30* **Lansdowne Princess**[55] 4144 9-10-12 73....................... JohnnyFarrelly 79
(Gerald Ham) *disp ld 5th tl 7th: led 11th tl mstke next: no ch fr after 4 out: stmbld next: fin lame* **11/1**[2]

/P-V **3** *88* **Cengiz (IRE)**[26] 4831 9-10-9 79.......................................(t) LeeEdwards(3) —
(Aytach Sadik) *j.lft getting progively worse: chsd ldrs tl lost tch fr 10th: t.o* **16/1**[3]

6m 0.70s (-13.90) **Going Correction** -0.925s/f (Hard) **3** Ran SP% **103.1**
Speed ratings: **86,76,46**
CSF £1.81 TOTE £1.10; EX 1.70.

Owner The Stewart Family & Paul K Barber **Bred** Ivan Dumont **Trained** Ditcheat, Somerset

FOCUS
Another simple task for the winner, who had little to beat. The race has been given a token rating through the second.

NOTEBOOK
Qozak(FR) was faced with another easy task and he completed his sixth success over jumps, all of which have come at this venue. He was hassled by the 73-rated runner-up until that one hit the 11th fence and it was plain sailing from then on. His jumping wasn't so fluent on this ground, but that's understandable and when he eventually tackles something more valuable again, he will arrive full of confidence. His mark of 140 leaves little room for manoeuvre, but he remains open to some improvement over this sort of trip.

Lansdowne Princess appeared to lose her confidence after hitting the 11th and, although she wouldn't have beat the winner with the clear round, there was plenty to like about her effort in defeat. Official explanation: vet said the mare was lame right fore (op 10-1)

Cengiz(IRE) wasn't fluent at the first and immediately got behind before completing with a messy round of fencing. (op 14-1)

5274 P4 MARKETING NOVICES' HURDLE (10 hdls) 2m 3f 110y
5:45 (5:45) (Class 4) 4-Y-0+ **£3,768** (£1,098; £549)

Form				RPR
1134	1		**Vertige Dore (FR)**[38] 4467 6-11-6 0 TimmyMurphy (Paul Nicholls) *cl up: mstke 3rd: led 2 out: 1 l up but a looked in command: pushed out* **1/5**[1]	96+
3	2	1	**Be Kind**[14] 5064 5-10-4 0 EamonDehdashti(3) (Karen George) *cl up: wnt 3rd 3 out: rdn to chse wnr after 2 out: kpt on but a being hld* **20/1**	78
4B	3	13	**Murdoch**[16] 5035 7-11-0 0 JoeTizzard (Colin Tizzard) *t.k.h: trckd ldr: led 3rd: mstke 6th: hit 3 out: hdd next: sn rdn and one pce: hit last* **11/1**[3]	72
02	4	50	**Campden Society (IRE)**[16] 5038 8-10-7 0 JodieMogford (Peter Hiatt) *led tl 3rd: dropped to last after 5th: no ch fr next: regained poor 4th after 2 out: t.o* **8/1**[2]	15
PP	5	18	**Maxi's Dream**[7] 5152 6-10-11 0 IanPopham(3) (Stuart Howe) *clup: wnt 2nd 4th: pckd 6th: rdn in 4th 3 out: wknd bef 2 out: t.o* **66/1**	4

4m 38.9s (-7.10) **Going Correction** -0.97s/f (Hard) 5 Ran SP% **109.0**
Speed ratings (Par 105): **75,74,69,49,42**
CSF £5.58 TOTE £1.50: £1.10, £3.50; EX 4.20.
Owner The Ives & Johnson Families **Bred** Chantal Becq **Trained** Ditcheat, Somerset

FOCUS
An uncompetitive novice hurdle and weak form with the cosy winner rated two stone off his best. The time was very slow.

NOTEBOOK
Vertige Dore(FR) resumed winning ways in what transpired to be a very uncompetitive event. His only danger on paper was withdrawn earlier in the day and that ensured he faced a simple task if running anywhere near his previous best. He duly got the job done, but was workmanlike in doing so and perhaps the firm ground wasn't really for him. There should be more to come from him as he matures, though, and it will be interesting to see what mark he is allotted. (op 2-9 tchd 2-11 and 1-4 in a place)
Be Kind hit the third-last, but gave her all off the home turn and ensured the winner had to work for his prize. This was a nice improvement on her hurdling debut behind another odds-on shot from Paul Nicholls' stable over C&D a fortnight earlier. (op 16-1)
Murdoch showed his first worthwhile form since going close on his Flat debut way back in 2006. (op 10-1 tchd 12-1)
Campden Society(IRE) was beaten a long way out on this drop in trip. Official explanation: jockey said that the mare was unsuited by the firm ground (op 15-2)

5275 BET ON LIVE SPORT AT TOTESPORT.COM H'CAP CHASE (14 fncs) 2m 3f
6:15 (6:15) (Class 4) (0-105,102) 5-Y-0+ **£4,110** (£1,198; £599)

Form				RPR
3511	1		**Thunder Child**[14] 5069 11-10-12 **88** (t) AndrewGlassonbury (Simon Burrough) *j.w: mde all: styd on gamely fr 3 out: comf* **15/8**[1]	100+
514F	2	11	**Kirbys Glen (IRE)**[29] 4784 9-10-9 **88** KeiranBurke(3) (Patrick Rodford) *hld up bhd ldrs: rdn and ev ch after 4 out: kpt on same pce fr next* **3/1**[2]	91+
/F-5	3	11	**Run For Moor (IRE)**[32] 4708 10-11-9 **99** FelixDeGiles (Jennifer Mason) *hld up bhd ldrs: rdn after 10th: wl hld after 4 out: lft 4th next: kpt on to regain 3rd after next* **9/2**[3]	87
0U4R	4	5	**Star Galaxy (IRE)**[19] 4967 11-11-12 **102** (b) RhysFlint (John Flint) *trckd ldr tl rdn 4 out: wkng whn lft 3rd 3 out: lost 3rd after next* **22/1**	85
3FF6	P		**Solitary Palm (IRE)**[7] 5155 8-11-9 **102** IanPopham(3) (Brian Forsey) *trckd ldr: rdn and ch after 4 out: styng on same pce whn virtually fell next: great rcvry but no ch after and immediately p.u* **11/2**	100
P-1P	P		**Marsh Court**[33] 4671 8-11-10 **100** AidanColeman (Jamie Snowden) *reluctant to s: nvr gng: p.u after 1st* **8/1**	—

4m 43.8s (-12.70) **Going Correction** -0.925s/f (Hard) 6 Ran SP% **108.8**
Speed ratings: **89,84,79,77,—** —
Tote Swingers: 1&2 £2.00, 1&3 £2.20, 2&3 £2.80 CSF £7.67 TOTE £2.80: £1.40, £2.50; EX 6.60.
Owner Richard Weeks **Bred** L Fuller **Trained** West Buckland, Somerset

FOCUS
A moderate handicap. Straightforward form and the winner could still be ahead of the handicapper. The second ran to form.

NOTEBOOK
Thunder Child ◆ is in cracking form at present and he completed a C&D hat-trick with a gutsy effort. He certainly could have got more than a mark of 88 after winning his second handicap here a fortnight earlier and, while he isn't the most straightforward character, there could well be more still to come from the veteran. (op 9-4, tchd 3-1 in a place)
Kirbys Glen(IRE) was still in there fighting with the winner prior to falling over C&D last time and he held every chance to gain revenge here. The winner held too many guns for him when he challenged off the home turn, though, and while this ground would have been quick enough for him the handicapper looks to have his measure. (op 11-4)
Run For Moor(IRE) was making heavy weather of it before hitting the fifth and fourth-last fences and remains one to tread carefully with. (op 4-1)
Star Galaxy(IRE) continues to struggle for form. (op 18-1)
Solitary Palm(IRE) had made errors prior to whacking the third-last, at which his rider performed miracles to stay aboard. He would have very likely placed but for that. (op 13-2)

5276 GARY GABRIEL ASSOCIATES H'CAP HURDLE (10 hdls) 2m 3f 110y
6:45 (6:45) (Class 4) (0-115,115) 4-Y-0+ **£3,425** (£998; £499)

Form				RPR
4512	1		**Decision**[21] 4935 5-11-0 **106** (t) DavidBass(3) (Lawney Hill) *trckd ldr: led after 6th: rdn whn hrd pressed 2 out: narrowly hdd last: dug deep to regain ld sn after r.o gamely: drvn out* **13/8**[2]	108
5041	2	½	**Teshali (IRE)**[14] 5066 5-11-2 **115** (t) JamesCowley(10) (Paul Nicholls) *trckd ldrs: chal 2 out: sn rdn: slt ld last: sn hdd: kpt on but no ex* **8/11**[1]	116
6012	3	51	**Heir To Be**[168] 2023 12-11-7 **110** (b) NickScholfield (Michael Blake) *led tl after 6th: sn rdn: wknd after 3 out* **9/1**[3]	76

4m 27.4s (-18.60) **Going Correction** -0.975s/f (Hard) 3 Ran SP% **106.0**
Speed ratings (Par 105): **98,97,77**
CSF £3.23 TOTE £2.50; EX 3.90.
Owner The Go 90 Partnership **Bred** D D And Mrs Jean P Clee **Trained** Aston Rowant, Oxon

FOCUS
A modest little handicap, run at a fair gallop. The first two are rated pretty much to their marks.

NOTEBOOK
Decision, 4lb higher, resumed winning ways with a game effort on ground he loves under strong handling from the talented David Bass. He travelled just about best of all and, jumping economically in the home straight, showed a terrier-like attitude to shake off the runner-up. It rates a career-best over hurdles and he is another advert for his trainer's skills. (op 7-4)
Teshali(IRE) was hiked up 10lb for belatedly showing his true colours when switched to quick ground under today's pilot over C&D a fortnight earlier. He raced upsides the winner throughout, but found him too resolute at the business end. There is another handicap or two in him on similar ground this summer. (op 4-5 tchd 4-6 and 5-6 in places)
Heir To Be was in decent heart when last seen in 2010 and ensured this was a sound test. He did his best to rally once headed and should come on plenty. (op 7-1)

5277 RONNIE WALLACE HUNTERS' CHASE (17 fncs) 2m 7f 110y
7:15 (7:15) (Class 5) 5-Y-0+ **£1,977** (£608; £304)

Form				RPR
05P-	1		**Armoury House**[17] 10-11-5 0 MissCBoxall(7) (D Buckett) *hld up last but in tch: hdwy 12th: narrow advantage 3 out: styd on wl to assert bef last: rdn out* **10/1**	119+
0-20	2	4	**Man From Highworth**[12] 5081 12-11-5 118 (t) MrSParish(7) (Audrey Manners) *hld up bhd ldrs: wnt 3rd 11th: cl 2nd whn blnd 4 out: chal 3 out: sn rdn: ev ch next: no ex appr last* **1/1**[1]	118+
0P/	3	2¼	**Sheknowsyouknow**[17] 10-11-2 0 (p) MrMWall(3) (Michael Hawker) *trckd ldr: led after 10th: nt fluent next 2: rdn appr 4 out: narrowly hdd 3 out: ev ch next: kpt on same pce* **5/2**[2]	106
20-5	4	14	**Doof (IRE)**[9] 11-11-5 95 MissJBuck(7) (L Jefford) *led tl after 10th: rdn after 13th: one pce fr after next* **9/2**[3]	98
P-05	5	14	**Celestial Dragon (IRE)**[19] 4969 10-11-5 85 MissRachelKing(7) (James Richardson) *trckd ldr: rdn after 11th: wkng whn wnt lft 4 out* **22/1**	86

5m 50.3s (-24.30) **Going Correction** -0.925s/f (Hard) 5 Ran SP% **110.2**
Speed ratings: **103,101,100,96,91**
CSF £21.79 TOTE £11.20: £3.40, £1.10; EX 18.50.
Owner Miss A M Reed **Bred** Mrs H J Houghton **Trained** Upham, Hampshire

FOCUS
A modest hunter chase, run at a decent gallop. Seemingly a step up from the winner.

NOTEBOOK
Armoury House shook off the two market leaders from the third-last and ran out a ready enough winner. This 10-y-o had won his first open point 17 days earlier on firm ground and was given a lovely ride en route to this second hunter chase success. If able to maintain this mood there may be another one of these within his compass. (op 12-1 tchd 9-1)
Man From Highworth, rated 118, was equipped with a first-time tongue tie on this return to hunter chasing and met solid support. He was going best prior to meeting the fourth-last all wrong and, while he recovered, that mistake did look to cost him a first win in this sphere. (op 11-8)
Sheknowsyouknow is a progressive pointer and was well backed for this hunter chase debut. She jumped somewhat deliberately over these regulation fences and paid for running freely late on, but is capable of winning something similar with the experience now under her belt. (op 13-8)
Doof(IRE) came into this having been in good form between the flags and was a game second in the race last year. He like it out in front and ensured a decent gallop, but was quickly beaten when headed nearing the final circuit on ground quicker than he ideally cares for. (op 11-2)

5278 BET ON TONIGHT'S FOOTBALL AT TOTESPORT.COM H'CAP HURDLE (12 hdls) 3m 110y
7:45 (7:45) (Class 4) (0-115,114) 4-Y-0+ **£3,425** (£998; £499)

Form				RPR
665U	1		**Orion Express**[14] 5068 10-9-9 **88** MarkQuinlan(5) (Susan Gardner) *hld up in last pair: stdy prog fr 8th: chal 3 out: sn led: in command whn mstke last: readily* **5/1**[3]	91+
6-25	2	3	**Perception (IRE)**[112] 3058 5-11-4 **106** WayneHutchinson (Alan King) *trckd ldrs: rdn to chse wnr apporoaching 2 out: kpt on but a being hld* **7/2**[2]	105
0024	3	5	**Talenti (IRE)**[17] 5017 8-10-13 **108** (tp) KielanWoods(7) (Charlie Longsdon) *led tl slow jump 1st: prom: slow 3rd: led after 6th tl after next: rdn after 8th: styd on same pce fr 2 out* **3/1**[1]	101
446U	4	2¾	**Can't Remember**[5] 5169 6-9-11 **90** OliverDayman(5) (Alison Thorpe) *trckd ldrs: gd jump to join ldrs 6th: led after next: rdn and hdd after 3 out: kpt on same pce: no ex whn lost 3rd run-in* **13/2**	80
5001	5	43	**Captain Becket**[29] 4787 8-10-7 **95** HaddenFrost (James Frost) *hld up: rdn after 8th: nvr pce to get on terms: wknd after 3 out: t.o* **5/1**[3]	42
F140	P		**Pairc Na Gcapall (IRE)**[138] 2637 9-11-5 **110** (p) AlexMerriam(3) (Neil King) *led 1st tl after 6th: lost pl after next: rdn after 8th: sn bhd: p.u after 3 out* **13/2**	—
-006	F		**Anak (IRE)**[26] 4830 5-11-12 **114** (b) PaulMoloney (Jim Best) *hld up bhd: fell 3rd* **16/1**	—

5m 39.1s (-28.00) **Going Correction** -0.975s/f (Hard) 7 Ran SP% **113.1**
Speed ratings (Par 105): **105,104,102,101,87** —,—
Tote Swingers: 1&2 £2.00, 1&3 £2.20, 2&3 £2.80 CSF £22.60 CT £60.41 TOTE £4.70: £2.40, £2.80; EX 20.30.
Owner The Barley Mow Syndicate **Bred** Raffin Bloodstock **Trained** Longdown, Devon

FOCUS
An ordinary handicap and another race run at a decent tempo. The winner is rated in line with his best form of last year.

NOTEBOOK
Orion Express had been well backed when unseating on his previous outing over C&D a fortnight earlier and he made amends with a ready success. He moved nicely through the race and went to the front full of running three out. He was in control before hitting the final flight. This was his first win since 2009, when he scored off a 20lb higher mark and he is capable of holding his form well when in the mood. (tchd 9-2)
Perception(IRE), returning from a 110-day absence, looked well worth a try over this longer trip and she had her chance. She has yet to score over hurdles, but is worth persevering with over the distance. (op 10-3 tchd 3-1)
Talenti(IRE) came in for support back over hurdles and got a positive ride. He hit a flat spot before rallying in the home straight and was well held. (op 10-3)
Can't Remember all but fell when unseating at Hereford last week, so this was clearly more encouraging. She does look held by the handicapper, though. (op 8-1)
Captain Becket was up 10lb for resuming winning ways on his previous outing and, while he has scored off 5lb higher before, that came in 2008 so it wasn't surprising to see him drift in the market. He proved keen and was beaten well before his new mark came into play, however. (tchd 9-2)

T/Plt: £24.30 to a £1 stake. Pool:£40,986.00 - 1,230.51 winning tickets T/Qpdt: £9.30 to a £1 stake. Pool:£3,989.77 - 316.78 winning tickets TM

5057 TOWCESTER (R-H)

Tuesday, April 12

OFFICIAL GOING: Good to firm (good in places; 10.2)

Wind: brisk across Weather: sunny but with a chilly wind

5279 JENKINSONS CATERERS H'CAP CHASE (12 fncs) 2m 110y

5:00 (5:00) (Class 4) (0-115,111) 5-Y-0+ **£2,602** (£764; £382; £190)

Form RPR

6436 **1** **Kikos (FR)**[143] 2529 9-11-12 **111** SamJones 119+
(Renee Robeson) *narrow ld tl rdn and hdd sn after slt mstke 2 out: drvn ahd again after last: gng slowly up hill and all out* **11/4**[3]

5553 **2** *½* **Red Jester**[160] 2152 10-10-9 **97** MarcGoldstein(3) 104
(Laura Young) *cl 2nd tl drvn to ld sn after 2 out: hdd after last but kpt plugging on* **9/4**[2]

-PFP **3** *7* **Beherayn**[10] 5112 8-11-1 **107** SClements(7) 109
(Carroll Gray) *stdd s: plld hrd in last pair: tended to lack fluency: outpcd 9th: plugged on but no threat* **8/1**

1P32 **4** *65* **Irish Guard**[51] 4237 10-11-10 **109** AndrewThornton 86
(John O'Neill) *last pair: outpcd 8th: 10 l last whn hit 3 out: no ch after: t.o and eased 2 out: virtually p.u flat* **7/4**[1]

4m 2.30s (-13.80) **Going Correction** -0.675s/f (Firm) **4** Ran SP% **104.9**
Speed ratings: **105,104,101,70**
CSF £8.67 TOTE £3.40; EX 10.90.

Owner Nick Brown Racing **Bred** Roger Frieh And Sylvie Ringler **Trained** Tyringham, Bucks

FOCUS

On a bright but very breezy evening the watered ground was described as "fast but safe". A sensible pace and just the first two closely involved up the final hill. They are rated to their marks.

NOTEBOOK

Kikos(FR), back after a winter break, was able to race from a mark 9lb below his last success at Uttoxeter a year ago. Suited by quick ground, a clumsy jump two out put him on his back foot, but back level at the last he did just enough to gain the verdict. He looks ideal summer jumping material. (op 9-4)

Red Jester, who came into this with three wins from four round here, was back with his former yard. Having his first start since November and with the ground to suit he took a narrow lead between the last two only to miss out narrowly in the end. He should be able to record a sixth career success from this sort of mark. (op 5-2 tchd 2-1)

Beherayn, whose last success came for getting on for two years ago now, had failed to complete on his three previous starts this time. Dropped in at the start and very fre, he made a couple of jumping errors and could not match the first two from three out. (op 15-2 tchd 6-1)

Irish Guard, the first to feel the strain, stopped to nothing three out and completed in his own time. With him it seems it is either good or bad. (op 15-8 tchd 9-4)

5280 HAYGAIN HAY STEAMERS MARES' NOVICES' HURDLE (8 hdls) 2m

5:30 (5:31) (Class 4) 4-Y-0+ **£2,276** (£668; £334; £166)

Form RPR

640- **1** **Businessmoney Judi**[231] 5114 5-10-11 0 APMcCoy 94+
(David Pipe) *t.k.h whn pressing ldr: veered bdly lft 3rd and did best to dislodge rdr: sn chsng new ldr: rdn to ld 2 out: gng best whn mstke last: kpt on wl* **11/4**[3]

1-0F **2** *¾* **The Strawberry One**[22] 4917 6-10-11 0 DarylJacob 91
(David Arbuthnot) *prom: hmpd 3rd: 3rd bef 4th: outpcd briefly 3 out: drvn and tried to chal fr 2 out: nt fluent last: kpt on gamely to snatch 2nd but nt quite rch wnr* **2/1**[1]

3 *nse* **Beech View (IRE)**[33] 1822 6-10-6 0 AnthonyFreeman(5) 91
(Martin Bosley) *plld hrd: mstkes 1st and 2nd: bhd: bdly hmpd 3rd: lft 5th bef 4th: clsd after 3 out: sustained effrt fr next: wnt 2nd bef last: no ex fnl 100yds and relegated 3rd nr fin* **100/1**

0-1P **4** *15* **Osmosia (FR)**[58] 4101 6-10-11 0 (t) DominicElsworth 80
(Paul Webber) *t.k.h: wnt lft but sn lft in front after chaos at 3rd: rdn and hdd 2 out: fdd tamely bef last* **11/1**

0- **5** *25* **Prime Design (IRE)**[338] 6-10-11 0 LiamTreadwell 54
(Neale Dalton) *dropped out last: hmpd 3rd: t.o 5th: modest prog after next: plugged on but no hope of rching ldrs* **150/1**

30 **6** *hd* **Bow To No One (IRE)**[11] 5099 5-10-11 0 WillKennedy 54
(Alan Jarvis) *towards rr: hmpd 3rd: struggling fr 5th* **12/1**

0 **7** *18* **Lady Treacle (IRE)**[24] 4881 5-10-11 0 AndrewThornton 38
(Caroline Bailey) *midfield: lft in ld briefly 3rd as all but one other were involved in sme form of scrimmaging: lost pl bef next: rdn 3 out: sn fdd: t.o 2 out* **100/1**

4-05 **8** *1¼* **Landenstown Rose (IRE)**[34] 4554 5-10-11 0 AdrianLane 36
(Donald McCain) *midfield and keen: carried violently lft after 3rd: lost all ch: j. slowly 4th: t.o fr 5th* **50/1**

P **9** *3¾* **Truly Magic**[50] 3967 4-10-0 0 MissLHorner(5) 27
(Liam Corcoran) *a bhd: t.o whn mstke 5th* **100/1**

0321 **U** **Sara's Smile**[19] 4964 5-11-4 116 JasonMaguire —
(Donald McCain) *led tl veered bdly lft, almost ref and uns rdr 3rd* **9/4**[2]

3m 59.8s (-8.10) **Going Correction** -0.45s/f (Good)
WFA 4 from 5yo+ 5lb **10** Ran SP% **112.4**
Speed ratings (Par 105): **102,101,101,94,81 81,72,71,70,—**
Tote Swingers: 1&2 £1.10, 2&3 £30.60 CSF £8.62 TOTE £5.00: £2.20, £1.60, £14.70; EX 14.20.

Owner Business Money Promotions Limited **Bred** Mrs I Lefroy **Trained** Nicholashayne, Devon

FOCUS

A weak mares' novice hurdle, and there was drama at the third flight when the leader Sara's Smile swerved violently left giving Jason Maguire no chance and causing mayhem. The winner is rated 5lb off her best bumper figure.

NOTEBOOK

Businessmoney Judi, who showed fair form in bumper races, was having her first outing for this yard. Unsighted by Sara's Smile, AP McCoy had to sit tight at the third. In the end she had to be kept right up to her work. (op 9-4 tchd 2-1)

The Strawberry One, a winner of two bumpers with the second of those on fast ground here, was nearly knocked over by the errant Sara's Smile. Driven on the heels of the leaders three out, she stayed on from the last to snatch second spot. She clearly stays well and can go one better. (tchd 15-8)

Beech View(IRE), very limited under both codes in Ireland, had been well beaten from a mark of just 45 on her first start for this yard on the Flat at Kempton last month. She kept on stoutly up the hill to jump the last on the heels of the winner and this marked a vast improvement on anything she had achieved in the past.

Osmosia(FR), a fast-ground bumper winner at Worcester, took a keen hold in the rear. Racing on the inner, she avoided the mayhem and found herself at the head of affairs at the third flight but she weakened badly from two out. She will need to learn to settle better. (tchd 12-1)

Sara's Smile veered badly and unseated her rider at the third. (op 5-2 tchd 11-4 tchd 3-1 in places)

5281 WINNING IT BACK AUTOBIOGRAPHY BY GARY WILTSHIRE NOVICES' H'CAP CHASE (14 fncs) 2m 3f 110y

6:00 (6:01) (Class 4) (0-115,115) 5-Y-0+ **£2,602** (£764; £382; £190)

Form RPR

2620 **1** **Sonny Mullen (IRE)**[74] 3784 7-11-5 **115** (p) EdCookson(7) 128+
(Kim Bailey) *led after 1st: j. erratically: rdn clr bef 2 out: j.rt fnl two* **2/1**[1]

P115 **2** *16* **Victory Surge (IRE)**[153] 2311 7-11-8 **111** (p) APMcCoy 106
(Jonjo O'Neill) *led tl after 1st: cl up: nt fluent 8th: 2nd next: mstke 11th: ev ch 3 out: drvn and outpcd bef next: j.rt fnl two* **9/4**[2]

3036 **3** *½* **Global Flyer**[75] 3772 7-10-13 **102** (p) AndrewThornton 96
(Caroline Bailey) *mostly 2nd tl 9th: 2 l 3rd and drvn 3 out: sn lost tch w wnr and plodded on* **10/3**[3]

F456 **4** *4½* **Don't Tell Nina (IRE)**[69] 3878 7-10-8 **97** DominicElsworth 90
(Paul Webber) *last whn reminder 4th and nvr looking happy after: u.p after 5th: blnd 7th and lost tch: t.o 10th: plugged on fr 3 out to take 4th bef last* **5/1**

6PV0 **5** *11* **Zhukov (IRE)**[22] 4919 9-9-7 **89** MrBJPoste(7) 69
(Kevin Tork) *pressed ldrs tl rdn and fdd qckly sn after 3 out* **28/1**

5m 4.80s (-13.40) **Going Correction** -0.675s/f (Firm) course record **5** Ran SP% **107.3**
Speed ratings: **99,92,92,90,86**
CSF £6.74 TOTE £2.10: £1.10, £2.10; EX 6.10.

Owner Clive Washbourn **Bred** Richard And Marie Hennessy **Trained** Andoversford, Gloucs

FOCUS

A weak novice handicap chase. A small step up from the winner and he is probably still capable of better.

NOTEBOOK

Sonny Mullen(IRE), back after a ten-week break, had finished runner-up twice on his four previous starts over fences. Despite a tendency to jump right he made virtually all the running, and relishing the quick ground he skipped clear up the final hill. His jumping will need to improve if he is to progress. (tchd 13-8 and 9-4 tchd 5-2 in places)

Victory Surge(IRE), another suited by a fast surface, was having his first start since November. Here 9lb higher than his last success at Kempton, he was dropping back half a mile in trip and couldn't match the winner from two out. The outing will not be lost on him. (op 11-4)

Global Flyer, another back after a break, had shown little in two previous starts over fences and sported cheekpieces for the first time. He struggled to keep up three out. (op 3-1 tchd 11-4 and 7-2)

Don't Tell Nina(IRE), down a stone after two poor efforts, found this too sharp and his jumping suffered. He was soon struggling. (op 9-2 tchd 11-2)

Zhukov(IRE) came into this on the back of four poor efforts and there was little encouragement here. (op 22-1 tchd 33-1)

5282 BETFAIR CONDITIONAL JOCKEYS' TRAINING SERIES H'CAP HURDLE (RACING EXCELLENCE INITIATIVE) (8 hdls) 2m

6:30 (6:30) (Class 5) (0-95,95) 4-Y-0+ **£2,276** (£668; £334; £166)

Form RPR

0-05 **1** **Edgebury**[17] 5016 8-10-13 **85** PeterCarberry(3) 88
(Paul Webber) *set v slow pce tl 2nd: pressed ldr tl led 3 out: hdd bef next: kpt on for driving and lft in front last: all out* **6/1**[3]

004U **2** *½* **Mossmann Gorge**[15] 5057 9-11-10 **93** (p) MattGriffiths 96
(Anthony Middleton) *settled in rr: rdn and lost tch in 7th at 4th: hdwy bef 2 out where 5th and nt fluent: drvn and styd on flat: nt rch wnr* **6/1**[3]

5-63 **3** *nk* **Golden Button (IRE)**[19] 4977 6-11-4 **92** (t) EdCookson(5) 95
(Kim Bailey) *hld up: effrt 3 out: chal and hit next: led bef last: faltered into last and bungled it: sn hdd and fnd nthing* **5/2**[1]

6500 **4** *4½* **Cadeaux Cerise (IRE)**[219] 1479 7-11-2 **85** AodhaganConlon 84
(Andrew Haynes) *pressed ldrs: rdn to ld bef 2 out: sn hdd: wknd bef last* **6/1**[3]

2305 **5** *4½* **Ton-Chee**[20] 4956 12-11-7 **95** (e[1]) JoshWall(5) 89
(Arthur Whitehead) *hld up at rr of main bunch: effrt 3 out: rdn and wknd next* **11/1**

05-4 **6** *4* **Jessica**[19] 4965 6-9-13 **75** ow1 DarrenO'Keeffe(7) 65
(Seamus Mullins) *disorganised over jumps: dropped out last: lost tch 4th: plugged on valiantly fr bef 2 out: nvr rchd ldrs* **16/1**

2525 **7** *1¼* **Bollywood (IRE)**[138] 2638 8-10-10 **82** (t) NathanSweeney(3) 72
(Alison Batchelor) *plld hrd in 3rd: lost pl 3 out: racing w awkward carriage in poor last by next* **11/2**[2]

0350 **8** *3¼* **Sumner (IRE)**[138] 2468 7-11-4 **90** (t) KyleJames(3) 76
(William Davies) *t.k.h: hdd 3 out: gave up qckly and fdd bef next* **10/1**

4m 5.20s (-2.70) **Going Correction** -0.45s/f (Good) **8** Ran SP% **110.1**
Speed ratings (Par 103): **88,87,87,85,83 81,80,78**
Tote Swingers: 1&2 £2.10, 1&3 £6.00, 2&3 £5.60 CSF £38.49 CT £105.02 TOTE £8.40: £3.10, £1.40, £1.30; EX 26.90.

Owner D Allen **Bred** Mrs J K M Oliver **Trained** Mollington, Oxon

FOCUS

A modest handicap hurdle and the pace was very steady to the halfway mark. Ordinary form and a slow time. The winner was well in on his 2009 form.

NOTEBOOK

Edgebury, having his third start after two years on the sidelines, went on three out. He regained the lead at the last and did just enough. He has taken an age to gain full strength and may well be capable of building on this. (op 13-2 tchd 5-1)

Mossmann Gorge, put to sleep at the back, was seeking his first win since Boxing Day 2007. He made up a lot of ground up the final hill and was fast closing the winner down at the line, but he is far from reliable. (op 8-1)

Golden Button(IRE) travelled strongly and looked the likely winner when showing ahead between the last two. She lost momentum at the final flight and had no more to give near the line. She looks a shade tricky. (op 2-1 tchd 11-4)

Cadeaux Cerise(IRE), a maiden after seven previous attempts, was having his first start since September. He put three poor efforts behind him but it remains to be seen if he can build on this respectable return. (op 13-2 tchd 5-1)

Ton-Chee, a spring horse, was having his second outing in three weeks after an eight-month absence. He threatened to enter the argument two out but has always been something of a weak finisher and he does not have time on his side now. (op 12-1 tchd 14-1)

5283 HAYGAIN HAY STEAMERS MAIDEN HUNTERS' CHASE (14 fncs) 2m 3f 110y

7:00 (7:02) (Class 6) 6-Y-0+ **£988** (£304; £152)

Form RPR

5400 **1** **Plenty Of Chat (IRE)**[16] 7-11-7 78 MrRWinks(7) 90
(P Winks) *settled towards rr: str run fr 3 out: led next and sn surged clr: readily* **5/1**[3]

4-P0 **2** *4* **Goscar Rock (IRE)**[10] 10-11-9 85 MrPJTolman(5) 87
(P Hall) *pressed ldr: led 7th: hdd 2 out where wl clr of rest: hld whn mstke last: nt qckn after* **7/2**[2]

3 25 **Autumn's Over**[10] 10-11-7 0 ......(p) MrRGRSpencer(7) 64
(W M Wanless) *midfield: wknd after 11th: poor 5th 2 out: overtk two toiling rivals after last* **50/1**

5U4/ 4 3/4 **Kandelin (IRE)**[17] 8-11-7 0 ...... MrJonathanBailey(7) 63
(G T H Bailey) *rn in snatches and nt a fluent: rdn and dropped to rr 7th: slow next: rallied to press ldrs 3 out: fdd bdly bef next: remote 3rd briefly at last* **7/2**[2]

5 2 1/4 **Ballyshambles**[16] 8-11-7 0 ...... MissBAndrews(7) 63
(S R Andrews) *rn in snatches: wnt 3rd at 6th: pckd next: jnd wnr at 10th: drvn and ev ch 3 out: floundered up hill: lost poor 3rd after last* **28/1**

2533 6 15 **Battlefield Bob (IRE)**[32] 4696 7-11-7 87 ...... MrGGreenock(7) 48
(G T H Bailey) *led tl 7th: lost pl bdly 11th: t.o bef 2 out* **3/1**[1]

05U 7 67 **Westcoat Lad**[17] 6-11-9 0 ...... MrGGallagher(5) —
(Kevin Tork) *pressed ldrs: blnd 7th: lost tch and mstke 11th: t.o next: continued in ridiculous pursuit w much swishing of the tail: stl at the last after the 3rd had fin* **9/1**

05/0 P **High Rank**[16] 12-11-7 78 ...... MissHannahWatson(7) —
(H J Franklin) *nvr wnt a yard: sn last and jumping slowly: t.o fr 5th tl p.u 3 out* **20/1**

P **Cats In The Cradle**[30] 8-11-7 0 ...... MrFMitchell(7) —
(Miss V Collins) *mstkes in last but one: sn gng bdly: t.o fr 9th tl p.u 3 out* **11/1**

5m 2.00s (-16.20) **Going Correction** -0.675s/f (Firm) **9** Ran SP% **114.6**
Speed ratings: **105,103,93,93,92 86,59,—,—**
Tote Swingers: 1&2 £4.10, 2&3 £15.00 CSF £22.90 TOTE £6.40: £1.90, £1.30, £11.50; EX 27.50.
Owner P Winks **Bred** Denis Cleary **Trained** Little Houghton, S Yorks

FOCUS
A weak hunter chase and the first two came right away up the final hill.

NOTEBOOK
Plenty Of Chat(IRE) has done well in points since joining this yard last back end. A wide-margin winner of a restricted at Whitcliffe Grange (Ripon) two weeks earlier after a narrow defeat at Dalton Park, he came with a rattle to lead at the second-last and his enthusiastic rider simply had to keep him up to his work on the run-in. (op 4-1 tchd 11-2)
Goscar Rock(IRE), an all-the-way winner of an intermediate point ten days earlier, took it up but in the end was very much second best. (op 4-1 tchd 10-3)
Autumn's Over, making his debut under rules, had failed to get round in his six previous starts in points. He snatched a modest third near the line. (op 66-1)
Kandelin(IRE), who showed temperament over hurdles, came into this on the back of a hard-fought win in a restricted at Garthorpe and he seemed to be found out by the drop back in trip. (tchd 4-1)
Ballyshambles, pulled up on his next five starts in points after a maiden success, was making his hunter chase debut and he weakened quickly after the foot of the final hill after racing in the front rank on the way round. (op 33 1)
Battlefield Bob(IRE), a maiden point winner and placed in two hunter chases at Leicester, helped set the pace but he seemed to hang to his left before dropping right away. (tchd 5-2 and 10-3)

5284 HAYGAIN HAY STEAMERS MAIDEN OPEN NATIONAL HUNT FLAT RACE 2m
7:30 (7:30) (Class 5) 4-6-Y-O **£1,626** (£477; £238; £119)

Form RPR

30 1 **Jackstown (IRE)**[22] 4923 4-10-9 ...... JimmyDerham(3) 91+
(Seamus Mullins) *plld hrd in crawl: trckd ldrs: led wl over 1f out: urged along and styd on gamely to maintain advantage* **7/1**[3]

05 2 1 1/4 **So Fine (IRE)**[15] 5063 5-11-4 ...... RichieMcLernon 96
(Anabel L M King) *mde most at funereal pce tl rdn and hdd wl over 1f out: kpt on but a jst hld after* **1/1**[1]

6 3 10 **Money Bridge**[146] 2458 4-10-12 ...... TomMessenger 80
(Derek Shaw) *hld up last: effrt 3f out: threatened briefly 2f out: rdn and sn fdd* **28/1**

00 4 2 **Struanmore**[38] 4484 4-10-12 ...... DominicElsworth 78
(Paul Webber) *bhd: rdn 4f out: labouring after* **9/1**

0 5 2 **Well Sprung (IRE)**[61] 4027 5-10-11 ...... LeightonAspell 75
(Peter Winkworth) *kpt up for 13f: struggled on after* **5/1**[2]

P **Arewenearlythere** 5-11-4 ...... DenisO'Regan —
(Paul Webber) *w ldr tl p.u wl over 3f out: fatally injured* **5/1**[2]

4m 7.90s (5.60) **Going Correction** -0.45s/f (Good)
WFA 4 from 5yo 5lb **6** Ran SP% **109.3**
Speed ratings: **68,67,62,61,60** —
Tote Swingers: 1&2 £5.00, 1&3 £4.20, 2&3 £4.80 CSF £13.81 TOTE £6.60: £1.30, £1.50; EX 10.30.
Owner Ms J Chadwick **Bred** Richard O' Hara **Trained** Wilsford-Cum-Lake, Wilts

FOCUS
A modest bumper and with no one wanting to jump off in front the gallop was steady until the final three-quarters of a mile. The first two are rated to their marks.

NOTEBOOK
Jackstown(IRE), third on heavy ground here first time, was well beaten on Polytrack next time. He took a fierce grip early on but moved up to take charge with just less than two furlongs less to run. He has a fast-ground action and was always holding the runner-up. (op 15-2 tchd 8-1 and 6-1)
So Fine(IRE), who improved on his second start to finish a respectable fifth here, was left in command but in the end was very much second best. (op 11-8)
Money Bridge, who was trained in another yard when well beaten on his debut in a junior bumper at Warwick in November, was dropped in at the start. He kept on up the final hill to take a never-dangerous third and can improve again. (op 20-1)
Struanmore, well beaten on his two previous starts, was in big trouble the moment the pace was lifted. (op 7-1)
Well Sprung(IRE) showed a very scratchy action and dropped out of contention at the foot of the final hill. (op 9-2)
T/Plt: £22.00 to a £1 stake. Pool:£51,420.35 - 1,704.59 winning tickets T/Qpdt: £5.00 to a £1 stake. Pool:£6,574.33 - 110.38 winning tickets IM

4847 CHELTENHAM (L-H)
Wednesday, April 13

OFFICIAL GOING: Good (good to firm in places; watered; 8.5)
Wind: quite strong breeze half-across Weather: cloudy with light rain at times

5285 DOWNLOAD CHELTENHAM APP FREE TODAY NOVICES' HURDLE (10 hdls) 2m 4f 110y
2:10 (2:12) (Class 2) 4-Y-O+ **£6,262** (£1,850; £925; £463; £231)

Form RPR

4011 1 **Bold Addition (FR)**[15] 5064 6-11-4 125 ...... RWalsh 138+
(Paul Nicholls) *disp 3rd tl dropped to last but travelling wl after 7th: smooth hdwy on inner after 2 out: led last: rdn clr* **11/4**[2]

315 2 3 1/4 **Bottman (IRE)**[64] 3987 6-11-4 121 ...... RichardJohnson 134
(Tim Vaughan) *trckd ldr: led 6th: wnt lft and hit 2 out: sn rdn: drifted lft and hdd last: no ex* **11/1**

1330 3 9 **Habbie Simpson**[28] 4803 6-11-4 136 ...... RobertThornton 125
(Alan King) *hld up in cl 5th: tk clsr order 7th: ev ch after 2 out: sn rdn and hld: fdd last* **5/4**[1]

1F24 4 5 **Global Power (IRE)**[32] 4725 5-11-4 130 ...... LeightonAspell 122
(Oliver Sherwood) *disp 3rd: nt fluent 4th: hit 5th: rdn after 2 out: sn hld: wkng whn hit last* **7/2**[3]

-621 5 7 **E Major**[265] 1065 6-11-4 130 ...... JimmyMcCarthy 114
(Renee Robeson) *led tl 6th: pressed ldr: rdn whn sltly hmpd 2 out: wknd bef last* **14/1**

4m 56.8s (-8.20) **Going Correction** -0.125s/f (Good)
WFA 4 from 5yo+ 6lb **5** Ran SP% **108.3**
Speed ratings (Par 109): **110,108,105,103,100**
CSF £25.21 TOTE £3.30: £1.60, £2.20; EX 17.10.
Owner Mrs Sue Craven **Bred** Mme Jacques Thoreau **Trained** Ditcheat, Somerset

FOCUS
This opening novice hurdle often attracts a clear market leader, but this year it was a tight affair. They went a fair enough gallop, with all of the runners still having a chance two out, but they got sorted out up the rising finish.

NOTEBOOK
Bold Addition(FR) had readily beaten inferior opposition on his two previous outings at Wincanton and Taunton and this represented a much stiffer task on paper. He completed the hat-trick with a much-improved effort, however, under a very confident ride from Ruby Walsh. It was clear as he ate up the ground on the inside turning for home he was going to collect and this once again underlines the importance of a sound surface to his cause. His official rating will now shoot up, but he will be going chasing next term and has been very well prepared by Paul Nicholls for that new discipline. His trainer believes he will improve for fences and 3m, but didn't rule out looking to get him out again in a handicap on Swinton Hurdle day at Haydock next month. (op 3-1 tchd 9-4 and 7-2 in a place)
Bottman(IRE) was officially rated 121 prior to this, so it was surprising connections did not look for a handicap for him as he was open to improvement. He duly posted a career-best in defeat on this return from a 64-day break and, while his mark will also now suffer, his future lies as a chaser. A step up in trip won't bother him in that sphere and he's a likeable sort. (op 9-1)
Habbie Simpson, who had run decent races in defeat behind Bobs Worth over C&D prior to a respectable ninth in the Neptune (would've been closer had he not hit two out). He made his move around two out, but found very little once put under pressure and ran well below par. Perhaps this was one run too many, and it was the quickest ground he had faced to date, so he's given the benefit of the doubt for now. (op 11-8 tchd 6-4 and 13-8 in a place)
Global Power(IRE) brought useful handicap form into the race, but he once again didn't jump that well on this sound surface and was done with after the second-last. He has the scope to rate higher over fences on easy ground. (tchd 10-3 and 4-1)
E Major got hiked up to a mark of 130 despite winning easily on his previous outing last July. He found this an insufficient test and should come on plenty, but needs to come down in the handicap. (op 11-1 tchd 10-1)

5286 RUNDLE AND CO H'CAP CHASE (24 fncs) 3m 4f 110y
2:45 (2:47) (Class 3) (0-130,129) 5-Y-O+ **£6,319** (£1,907; £982; £520)

Form RPR

U114 1 **Galaxy Rock (IRE)**[27] 4821 7-11-7 124 ......(b) APMcCoy 133+
(Jonjo O'Neill) *mde all: wnt lft 6th (water): in command after 3 out: pushed out flat: comf* **2/1**[1]

25R1 2 14 **Shammy Buskins**[20] 4971 9-11-5 122 ......(p) AndrewThornton 120+
(Lawney Hill) *sn trcking ldrs: wnt 2nd after 5 out: chal briefly 3 out: sn rdn and hld: styd on same pce* **9/1**

3060 3 55 **Regal Approach (IRE)**[28] 4802 8-11-4 121 ......(p) JasonMaguire 68
(Kim Bailey) *w wnr most of way tl nudged along after 16th: rdn after 19th: lost 2nd after next: sn wknd: t.o* **9/2**

11F1 4 39 **Ammunition (IRE)**[36] 4537 11-10-13 116 ...... SamTwiston-Davies 27
(Nigel Twiston-Davies) *j.rt getting progively worse on fnl circ: trckd ldrs: nudged along 17th: wknd 5 out: t.o* **7/2**[3]

20-P F **Toby Jug**[25] 4876 10-11-12 129 ......(b) AidanColeman —
(Sarah Humphrey) *trcking ldrs whn fell 13th* **3/1**[2]

7m 18.1s (-6.90) **Going Correction** -0.125s/f (Good) **5** Ran SP% **108.7**
Speed ratings: **104,100,84,74,—**
CSF £16.70 TOTE £3.00: £1.90, £2.20; EX 16.10.
Owner Michael & John O'Flynn **Bred** Arctic Tack Stud **Trained** Cheltenham, Gloucs

FOCUS
Not the strongest of staying handicaps for the class. There was an ordinary gallop on and the first pair had it to themselves after the fourth-last.

NOTEBOOK
Galaxy Rock(IRE) was something of an eye-catcher when seventh in the Kim Muir at last month's festival and he made it three wins from his last four outings with a clear-cut display over this stiffer test. He struggled to get 3m over hurdles earlier in his career, but he has developed into a stayer over fences. A sound surface is right up his street, although he does handle it when the mud is flying, and he could be the sort for one of the minor Nationals next term. (op 9-4)
Shammy Buskins was hiked up 9lb for posting a career-best success at Southwell 20 days earlier and this dour stayer recorded another improved effort in defeat here. He again gave some trouble at the start, causing his rider to lose an iron nearing the first, but got into a nice rhythm and was the only one to give the winner a serious race. He sets the level, but the handicapper does now look to have his measure. (op 8-1 tchd 10-1)
Regal Approach(IRE), racing over his furthest trip to date, isn't the most straightforward ride and was in trouble around five out. He remains one to tread carefully with. (op 5-1)
Ammunition(IRE) was 4lb higher than when making it three wins from his last four starts at Exeter over 3m6f last month. He proved a nightmare to settle here and was well beaten prior to walking through the sixth-last fence. (op 3-1 tchd 4-1)
Toby Jug, pulled up in the Midlands National on his belated seasonal return 25 days earlier, made his first semblance of an error at the 12th and then came down at the next. He was quickly to his feet. (op 7-2)

5287 CHELTENHAM COLLECTION H'CAP HURDLE (10 hdls) 2m 4f 110y
3:20 (3:22) (Class 2) 4-Y-O+
£8,453 (£2,497; £1,248; £625; £311; £156)

Form RPR

-001 1 **My Shamwari (IRE)**[25] 4862 7-10-3 124 ......(t) RichardJohnson 132+
(Philip Hobbs) *hld up: hdwy appr 2 out: rdn to ld appr last: styd on strly to drew clr run-in* **15/2**

U-30 2 5 **King's Legacy (IRE)**[102] 3293 7-10-10 131 ...... RWalsh 136+
(Paul Nicholls) *patiently rdn: hld up: hit 4th: dropped to last after 3 out: outpcd briefly 2 out: rdn and hdwy appr last: styd on to go 2nd but no further imp on wnr fr last* **4/1**[1]

0050 3 2 1/4 **Secret Dancer (IRE)**[26] 4848 6-10-6 127 ...... TomO'Brien 130
(Alan Jones) *hld up: hdwy 2 out: rdn in 4th whn nt fluent last: styd on* **9/2**[2]

-U42 **4** ¾ **Ostland (GER)**[22] 4933 6-9-9 **123** oh1 ow2...................... KielanWoods(7) 124
(Charlie Longsdon) *in tch: stmbld on bnd after 7th: hdwy to ld after 2 out: rdn and hdd bef last: no ex: lost 3rd towards fin* **11/2**

FF-0 **5** ½ **Kangaroo Court (IRE)**[32] 4727 7-11-0 **135**............................ JackDoyle 136
(Emma Lavelle) *hld up: rdn whn ct flat-footed 2 out: styd on appr last: nrst fin* **12/1**

5025 **6** *8* **Kauto Relko (FR)**[26] 4852 7-9-13 **127**............................ PeterCarberry(7) 120
(Rachel Hobbs) *racd keenly: trckd ldr: ev ch 2 out: sn rdn: wknd bef last* **7/1**

6110 **7** ½ **Great Mates (IRE)**[179] 1864 7-9-11 **121** oh3...................... IanPopham(3) 115
(Paul Nicholls) *in tch: effrt 2 out: wknd bef last* **33/1**

1550 **8** *10* **Made In Time (IRE)**[39] 4488 6-10-0 **121**......................(t) RichieMcLernon 110+
(Rebecca Curtis) *racd keenly in tch: travelling ok whn swtchd wd and blnd 2 out: sn btn: nt rcvr* **5/1**[3]

1062 **9** *nk* **Black Jack Blues (IRE)**[67] 3939 8-11-7 **147**.........(t) AodhaganConlon(5) 131
(Rebecca Curtis) *led: nt fluent 6th: rdn after 3 out: hdd after 2 out: wknd appr last* **14/1**

3P60 **10** *7* **Tasheba**[53] 4202 6-11-6 **141**..(t) APMcCoy 120
(David Pipe) *trckd ldr: reminder after 7th: rdn after 3 out: ev ch 2 out: sn wknd* **16/1**

4m 58.2s (-6.80) **Going Correction** -0.125s/f (Good) **10** Ran SP% **117.7**
Speed ratings (Par 109): **107,105,104,103,103 100,100,96,96,93**
toteswingers:1&2:£7.60, 1&3:£16.20, 2&3:£3.40 CSF £38.67 CT £153.51 TOTE £9.20: £2.50, £2.10, £2.00; EX 36.30 Trifecta £339.50 Pool: £825.98 - 1.80 winning units..
Owner Mrs Julie Phillips **Bred** Mrs Catherine And Michael Norris **Trained** Withycombe, Somerset

FOCUS
This was a fair and competitive handicap even with the two withdrawals. Confirmed front-runner Black Jack Blues was allowed to dictate at an uneven gallop and that resulted in plenty of horses holding chances turning for home. The overall form should therefore be treated with a degree of caution.

NOTEBOOK
My Shamwari(IRE) comfortably followed up his success at Ffos Las last month despite a 5lb higher mark. He made up ground from off the pace easily three out and could have been called the winner nearing the last. It's fair to say he has improved a bundle since joining Phillip Hobbs and the addition of a first-time tongue-tie proved a positive. There could well be more to come on this sort of ground and connections will now look to a handicap at Sandown on the final Saturday of the season later this month. (op 9-1)
King's Legacy(IRE) ◆ was having his third consecutive run at the course and was last seen flopping upped to 3m on New Year's Day. He found himself well back nearing three out and once asked for an effort it looked as though something was again amiss. However, he motored after the next and was eating into the winner's advantage near the finish. It's not at all hard to see why he was tried over further last time and he should improve plenty for the run, so no doubt connections will be keen to get him out again in the coming weeks. (op 7-2, tchd 9-2 in place)
Secret Dancer(IRE) nearly always seems to run here, and regularly attracts support, which was again the case on this step back up in trip. He looked a big player on the home turn, but his stamina gave way before he made a mess of the last. It really looks as though he needs a sharper track over this trip. (op 7-1)
Ostland(GER) ◆ made a bold bid once meeting the climb for home, but he looked to pay for failing to settle off the uneven gallop. His turn is probably not far off and he helps to set the standard. (op 7-1)
Kangaroo Court(IRE) stayed on nicely late in the day and is one to keep an eye on. (op 10-1)
Kauto Relko(FR) looks to have nothing in hand on the handicapper. (op 11-1 tchd 13-2)
Made In Time(IRE) proved far too keen back up in trip and, while he made a mess of the second-last, has become disappointing. (op 9-2 tchd 4-1 and 6-1 in a plce)

5288 MASTERSON HOLDINGS SILVER TROPHY CHASE (LIMITED H'CAP) GRADE 2 (17 fncs) 2m 5f

3:55 (3:55) (Class 1) 5-Y-0+ **£22,804** (£8,556; £4,284; £2,136; £1,072)

Form RPR

2514 **1** **Poquelin (FR)**[27] 4818 8-11-10 **170**.. RWalsh 167+
(Paul Nicholls) *led: hdd whn hit 3 out: sn rdn: kpt chalng: regained narrow ld whn blnd last: kpt on gamely: all out* **11/10**[1]

2F11 **2** ½ **Holmwood Legend**[27] 4820 10-10-1 **150** oh10............... KeiranBurke(3) 146+
(Patrick Rodford) *trckd wnr: nt fluent 9th: jnd wnr 10th: stmbld whn reminder 4 out: led sn after 3 out: sn rdn: hdd whn hit last: kpt on gamely: hld nr fin* **4/1**[2]

-024 **3** *10* **De Boitron (FR)**[26] 4853 7-9-11 **150** oh13................. EdmondLinehan(7) 136
(Ferdy Murphy) *settled in last early: racd keenly in 3rd at the 5th: rdn after 3 out: 1 l 3rd 2 out: fdd fr last* **6/1**[3]

0030 **4** *62* **Pigeon Island**[26] 4853 8-10-4 **150** oh18.........................(b) PaddyBrennan 79
(Nigel Twiston-Davies) *trckd ldrs tl wknd appr 5 out: t.o* **16/1**

1P-0 **5** *48* **Copper Bleu (IRE)**[53] 4202 9-10-4 **150** oh7................(t) RichardJohnson 36
(Philip Hobbs) *trckd ldrs tl nt fluent 7th: last whn mstke next: sn t.o* **4/1**[2]

5m 8.40s (-11.00) **Going Correction** -0.125s/f (Good) **5** Ran SP% **107.8**
Speed ratings: **115,114,111,87,69**
CSF £5.74 TOTE £1.90: £1.30, £2.00; EX 5.10.
Owner The Stewart Family **Bred** Georges Sandor And Eric Becq **Trained** Ditcheat, Somerset
■ Stewards' Enquiry : Keiran Burke one-day ban: used whip with excessive frequency (Apr 27)

FOCUS
The meeting's feature race this season had a totally lopsided look about it due to the attendance of high-class course specialist Poquelin, who scared off plenty that were entered at the five-day stage, and ensured his four rivals all had to compete from out of the handicap.

NOTEBOOK
Poquelin(FR) was believed by his leading trainer to have run flat when returning from his customary winter break to finish fourth in the Grade 1 Ryanair Chase last month and appeared to have plenty in his favour here, so it was surprising to see him drift out in the market. Ruby Walsh didn't mess about and set out to make all, but he wasn't left alone for that spot by the progressive Holmwood Legend. He was still looking in command prior to that rival hitting the fourth-last, but he then hit three out and was just headed. Walsh held him together and regained the lead after the penultimate fence, but he made a right mess of the last. That didn't cost him too much momentum, however, and he was lifted home up the run-in by his brilliant jockey. It was the 8-y-o's sixth win over fences, five of which have come here and three of them over the C&D. It would be surprising were he not to come back in December and try and land a hat-trick of wins in the big C&D handicap that month, where he would probably again carry top weight. However, connections are now keen to try him over 3m and intend to start him off next term in the Charlie Hall at Wetherby. (op 10-11 tchd 5-6 and 6-5 in a place)
Holmwood Legend, who posted a clear personal best when winning the Byrne Group Plate at the festival last month, emerges with plenty of credit. He was hiked up 10lb for that success, but having to race from the same amount out of the weights in effect saw him racing off a 20lb higher mark, and he ran a blinder. Surely the Paddy Power Gold Cup back here at the Open meeting is the race for him next season. (op 5-1)
De Boitron(FR) has scored over this trip before but that was at Stratford, a much sharper track, and having travelled sweetly here his stamina bottomed out from the second-last. He deserves to land a decent pot and this was a decent effort from 13lb out of the handicap, but really he needs a prominent ride over a stiff 2m to be seen at his best. (op 7-1 tchd 8-1)
Pigeon Island went in snatches back up in trip and was done with five from home.
Copper Bleu(IRE) landed the old Jewson Novices' Chase over C&D at the 2010 Festival and has reportedly had problems with his wind. His stable wasn't in good form when he made his belated return over hurdles at Ascot in February, but he looked very fit that day and was still beaten from an early stage. He too went in snatches on this comeback over fences and did his cause no good with errors at the sixth and seventh. Richard Johnson eased him right off on the far side and this 9-y-o is now booked for retirement. Official explanation: jockey said gelding had a breathing problem (op 9-2)

5289 CITIPOST NOVICES' H'CAP HURDLE (12 hdls) 3m

4:30 (4:31) (Class 3) (0-120,120) 4-Y-0+
£6,262 (£1,850; £925; £463; £231; £116)

Form RPR

4021 **1** **Paint The Clouds**[17] 5038 6-11-10 **118**.................................. APMcCoy 132+
(Warren Greatrex) *trckd ldrs: led 2 out: in command whn jinked lft last: pushed out: comf* **3/1**[1]

6123 **2** *5* **Sail And Return**[3] 5241 7-9-13 **100** ow1.......................(t) KielanWoods(7) 104
(Philip Middleton) *mid-div: hdwy 3 out to trck ldrs: rdn to chse wnr after 3 out: kpt on but a comf hld* **4/1**[2]

4132 **3** *1* **Prophete De Guye (FR)**[16] 5061 8-10-6 **103**.................. IanPopham(3) 106
(James Evans) *t.k.h in rr: hdwy after 3 out: rdn into 4th appr last: styd on: wnt 3rd towards fin* **16/1**

1P5U **4** ¾ **Phare Isle (IRE)**[26] 4855 6-11-9 **117**.................................... DarylJacob 119
(Ben Case) *mid-div: hdwy appr 2 out: rdn to dispute 2nd appr last: no ex and lost 3rd nr fin* **16/1**

323 **5** *7* **Life Of A Luso (IRE)**[17] 5039 7-11-0 **108**...................(t) RichardJohnson 105
(Paul Henderson) *towards rr of mid-div: hdwy after 3 out: rdn after next: sn one pce* **14/1**

0401 **6** *6* **Madame Jasmine**[30] 4773 6-10-1 **102**............................ MrTJCannon(7) 93
(Suzy Smith) *mid-div: rdn and hdwy appr 3 out: wknd bef last* **16/1**

0032 **7** 2 ½ **Total Submission**[25] 4861 6-11-10 **118**.......................(t) WarrenMarston 106
(Martin Keighley) *trckd ldrs: rdn after 2 out: wknd bef last* **11/1**

5444 **8** 1 ½ **Rooftop Rainbow (IRE)**[22] 4929 7-10-6 **100**......... AndrewGlassonbury 87
(Linda Blackford) *in tch tl rdn 3 out* **8/1**[3]

2-24 **9** *hd* **Vico (IRE)**[45] 4370 7-11-12 **120**...(t) RWalsh 107
(Paul Nicholls) *hld up towards rr: sme prog u.p into midfield after 2 out: wknd bef last* **10/1**

35B1 **10** *10* **Rebel Swing**[32] 4712 5-10-8 **102**... HenryOliver 80
(Sue Smith) *prom tl 9th: sn bhd: t.o* **20/1**

/030 **11** *20* **Noddies Way**[22] 4929 8-10-6 **100**.. DavidEngland 60
(John Panvert) *nt fluent 2nd: a towards rr: t.o fr 8th* **66/1**

1445 **12** 2 ¾ **Educated Evans (IRE)**[33] 4700 6-11-5 **113**............ SamTwiston-Davies 70
(Nigel Twiston-Davies) *racd keenly: trckd ldrs: jnd ldrs 6th: hit 9th: sn led: hdd 2 out: rdn and wknd sn after* **10/1**

F023 **P** **Divy (FR)**[32] 4722 6-11-4 **112**... AndrewTinkler —
(George Baker) *disp ld tl rdn appr 3 out: wknd bef 2 out: t.o whn p.u bef last* **9/1**

2150 **P** **Jay J**[41] 4439 7-11-4 **115**.. TomMolloy(3) —
(Andrew Price) *towards rr whn hit 6th: losing tch whn blnd bdly next: immediately p.u and dismntd* **50/1**

5m 58.1s (-2.90) **Going Correction** -0.125s/f (Good) **14** Ran SP% **125.2**
Speed ratings (Par 107): **99,97,97,96,94 92,91,91,91,87 81,80,—,—**
toteswingers:1&2:£4.60, 1&3:£11.90, 2&3:£11.80 CSF £15.91 CT £174.14 TOTE £4.00: £2.30, £1.30, £5.50; EX 18.50 Trifecta £539.10 Pool: £801.36 - 1.10 winning units..
Owner Peter Deal & Jill & Robin Eynon **Bred** Guy Reed And Mrs A H Daniels **Trained** Upper Lambourn, Berks

FOCUS
This was a fair novice handicap for the class. There was an average gallop on and the form is rated around the placed horses.

NOTEBOOK
Paint The Clouds was left alone by the handicapper after winning a weak novice hurdle with ease at Wincanton last month and he followed up on this return to handicap company with a taking display. Well backed, he relished this further step up in trip and could really have been called the winner a fair way out. This "spring" horse remains capable of improvement as a stayer and has the scope to make into a chaser, so there may be a nice handicap over fences at this venue in him down the line. (op 7-2 tchd 4-1)
Sail And Return was having his third run in quick succession and he ran a brave race in defeat on this first attempt at 3m. He was already due to race off an 8lb higher future rating, but it would be surprising were he not capable of defying that sort of mark. (op 6-1 tchd 7-2)
Prophete De Guye(FR) is a versatile performer and arrived here in decent heart. Rated 10lb lower hurdles than fences, he got going late in the day from well off the pace and would have been better off under more positive handling. He rates a sound benchmark and deserves to find another opening.
Phare Isle(IRE), who unseated on his chasing debut last time, met some support and, not for the first time, travelled sweetly from off the pace. He couldn't raise his game when it mattered most and is probably held by the handicapper in this sphere, but it should tee him up nicely for a return to fences.
Life Of A Luso(IRE) was another that moved nicely through the race on his return from chasing. There is surely a race for him back over a sharper test. (op 18-1)
Vico(IRE) was making his handicap debut up in trip in a first-time tongue tie. He was never a factor from off the pace and, for all that he probably wants to jump fences, this former promising pointer looks firmly one of his trainer's lesser lights. (op 8-1 tchd 15-2)

5290 SQUAREINTHEAIR.COM NOVICES' CHASE (21 fncs) 3m 1f 110y

5:05 (5:05) (Class 2) 5-Y-0+ **£9,479** (£2,861; £1,472; £781)

Form RPR

4251 **1** **Balthazar King (IRE)**[14] 5073 7-11-8 140...................... RichardJohnson 142+
(Philip Hobbs) *led tl 11th: prom: led 5 out: rdn whn pressed after 3 out: 2 l clr next: styd on: drvn out* **1/1**[1]

102U **2** 1 ½ **Adams Island (IRE)**[29] 4790 7-11-8 133..............................(p) APMcCoy 142+
(Rebecca Curtis) *hld up bhd ldng trio: nt particularly fluent at times 1st circ: rdn in cl 3rd after 3 out: styd on to go 2nd run-in: a being hld* **9/4**[2]

1315 **3** 2 ¾ **Earth Dream (IRE)**[186] 1776 8-11-8 130...................................... RWalsh 137
(Paul Nicholls) *trckd ldrs: jnd wnr gng wl after 3 out: sn rdn: 2 l down next: styd on same pce: lost 2nd run-in* **4/1**[3]

00-P **4** *63* **Hunt Ball (IRE)**[25] 6-11-0 0.. KeiranBurke 71
(Patrick Rodford) *prom: led 11th tl 5 out: nodded on landing 4 out: sn rdn: wknd next: t.o* **100/1**

1252 **F** **Magical Legend**[18] 5007 10-10-12 117...........................(t) PaddyBrennan —
(Sophie Leech) *hld up: fell 6th* **9/1**

6m 30.3s (-7.90) **Going Correction** -0.125s/f (Good) **5** Ran SP% **111.8**
Speed ratings: **107,106,105,86,—**
CSF £3.90 TOTE £1.80: £1.02, £3.20; EX 3.80.
Owner The Brushmakers **Bred** Sunnyhill Stud **Trained** Withycombe, Somerset

FOCUS
This good staying novice chase saw the principals fight it out up the home straight and the form is straightforward enough.

NOTEBOOK

Balthazar King(IRE) had some decent placed form to his name here, but this was his first success at the course. He was workmanlike when long odds-on to win on his comeback at Hereford a fortnight earlier, but the very tacky ground there was responsible and this should rate a career-best display. He deserves credit as he was hassled for the lead and looked vulnerable after four out. His jumping was also tight at times, but in fairness he found a superb stride three from home and really produced for his rider over the final two fences. It was probably a case of him idling on the run-in that caused his supporters a few worries, and he looks value for a bit further. He was entitled to win at the weights here, but he looks well up to his current mark of 140. Trainer Phillip Hobbs came here instead of the Scottish National at the weekend and will now look to the bet365 Gold Cup at Sandown the following Saturday, as he gets no penalty for that. He wouldn't look out of place there and was cut into 10/1 by the sponsors in the ante-post betting. (op 11-10 tchd 10-11)

Adams Island(IRE) is a talented 7-y-o, but jumping has often been an issue for him as a chaser and he unseated when quietly fancied for the ultra-competitive Spinal Research Handicap over C&D at the festival on his previous outing. He was making inroads on the winner after the last, but once again spoilt his chance with some deliberate jumping. Providing he irons out the errors he definitely has a future as a staying handicap chaser back on flatter tracks. (op 5-2, tchd 11-4 in a place)

Earth Dream(IRE) was having his first outing since being well held over hurdles in October. A winner of two of his four previous chase runs, he did things smoothly in the race and looked likely to master the winner turning for home. However, that rival found extra and he hit a flat spot, suggesting his stamina for the longer trip was emptying. However, he rallied nearing the last and it was surely a case of him needing the run. He can improve over fences, but will have to go handicapping now. (op 9-2 tchd 5-1)

5291 RACEODDS.COM H'CAP HURDLE (8 hdls) 2m 1f

5:40 (5:43) (Class 2) (0-140,130) 4-Y-0+

£7,514 (£2,220; £1,110; £555; £277; £139)

Form				RPR
2610	**1**		**Paintball (IRE)**[28] 4807 4-10-13 **123** .... RichardJohnson (Charlie Longsdon) *hld up: hit 2 out: hdwy to chal last: sn rdn to ld: kpt on wl* **4/1**[1]	122+
2063	**2**	*1*	**Salontyre (GER)**[30] 4783 5-11-0 **123** ....(p) MarkQuinlan(5) (Bernard Llewellyn) *trckd ldr: led after 2 out: rdn whn wandered bef last: hdd run-in: kpt on but hld towards fin* **14/1**	125
1140	**3**	*4*	**Owen Glendower (IRE)**[32] 4725 6-11-5 **130** .... JeremiahMcGrath(7) (Nicky Henderson) *trckd ldrs: rdn after 2 out: styd on same pce* **5/1**[3]	128
03F0	**4**	*2 ¼*	**Forty Thirty (IRE)**[137] 2671 5-11-4 **125** .... MarcGoldstein(3) (Sheena West) *hld up: tk clsr order 2 out: sn rdn: styd on same pce: wnt 4th run-in* **12/1**	121
0521	**5**	*2 ½*	**Falcon Island**[12] 5099 6-11-0 **118** ....(t) JoeTizzard (Colin Tizzard) *led: rdn and hdd sn after 2 out: no ex fr last* **9/2**[2]	113
-100	**6**	*½*	**Robain (FR)**[61] 4049 6-10-6 **110** .... TomO'Brien (Philip Hobbs) *mid-div: effrt after 2 out: styd on same pce* **20/1**	104
34P3	**7**	*7*	**Gilded Age**[30] 4783 5-11-5 **123** .... RobertThornton (Alan King) *trckd ldrs: rdn after 2 out: 7th and hld whn stmbld last: fdd* **6/1**	112
0540	**8**	*3*	**Gloucester**[26] 4848 8-11-6 **129** .... CO'Farrell(5) (Michael Scudamore) *hld up: short lived effrt after 2 out: wknd bef last* **8/1**	116
1452	**9**	*7*	**Marleno (GER)**[11] 5117 5-10-10 **114** ....(t) WarrenMarston (Milton Harris) *hld up in last: rdn after 2 out: no imp* **5/1**[3]	92
1002	**10**	*16*	**Celticello (IRE)**[26] 4854 9-10-10 **114** .... HarrySkelton (Jamie Snowden) *in tch: pushed along after 3 out: rdn after 2 out: wknd bef last* **33/1**	78

4m 7.20s (-4.10) **Going Correction** -0.125s/f (Good)

WFA 4 from 5yo+ 5lb **10** Ran SP% **119.0**

Speed ratings (Par 109): **104,103,101,100,99 99,95,94,91,83**

toteswingers:1&2:£11.10, 1&3:£3.10, 2&3:£17.10 CSF £58.40 CT £290.13 TOTE £4.40: £2.30, £4.40, £2.40; EX 91.20 Trifecta £633.90 Part won. Pool: £856.70 - 0.10 winning units..

Owner Alan Halsall **Bred** James Waldron **Trained** Over Norton, Oxon

FOCUS

A moderate handicap for the class with the top weight rated 10lb lower than the race ceiling. It was run at a steady gallop and those racing handily proved at an advantage.

NOTEBOOK

Paintball(IRE) ◆ was well fancied when making his handicap debut over hurdles in the Fred Winter over C&D last month, but he did far too much early on that day and it was no surprise whatsoever to see him held up this time. He got back to winning ways with a gutsy effort, doing well to overcome an error two from home, and rates better than the bare form as he would have enjoyed a stronger pace. The valuable Swinton Hurdle at Haydock next month looks a viable target as he was a useful middle-distance handicapper on the Flat last year and this was just his fifth outing over hurdles. He probably wouldn't want the ground much quicker than it was here, though, and his trainer may opt to put him away.

Salontyre(GER) returned to form on his previous outing a month earlier and, well suited by racing up with the pace here, made a bold bid to resume winning ways. He was a sitting duck for the winner after the last, but rates a good benchmark and shouldn't be too long in going one better again.

Owen Glendower(IRE), back down in trip, was another that raced handily and he turned in a respectable effort under top weight. The handicapper looks to have his measure in this sphere, but he should win a novice chase or two next term. (tchd 9-2)

Forty Thirty(IRE) ◆ was another that came from off the pace and this was a pleasing return from his 137-day break. He needs quick ground and should build on this next time out. (tchd 11-1)

Falcon Island, who found only subsequent Grade 2 winner Topolski too good on his penultimate outing, finally came good over hurdles at Stratford 12 days earlier. The handicapper raised him 6lb for that, however, and he could offer no more after turning for home. (op 5-1 tchd 11-2)

Robain(FR) is entitled to come on for the run and should be more at home back down in class. (tchd 18-1)

Gilded Age ran well below the level that saw him dead-heat for a place with the runner-up on identical terms last time out. (tchd 13-2)

T/Plt: £19.30 to a £1 stake. Pool:£86,604.88 - 3,266.64 winning tickets T/Qpdt: £3.20 to a £1 stake. Pool:£8,167.44 - 1,835.47 winning tickets TM

4971 SOUTHWELL (L-H)

Wednesday, April 13

OFFICIAL GOING: Good (8.1)

Golf Club bend on outside bend into home straight on inside, fences on outside rail.

Wind: Moderate, across Weather: Overcast, very cool

5292 BET ON TOTEPLACEPOT AT TOTESPORT.COM H'CAP CHASE (19 fncs) 3m 110y

4:40 (4:40) (Class 4) (0-115,114) 5-Y-0+ **£2,276** (£668; £334; £166)

Form				RPR
1045	**1**		**Columbus Secret (IRE)**[40] 4456 6-11-6 **108** .... JamesReveley (Keith Reveley) *nt fluent: hld up wl in tch: mstke 7th: lft cl 2nd 4 out: led appr 2 out: sn drew clr: eased towards fin* **10/3**[2]	124+
U-43	**2**	*22*	**King Jack**[48] 4313 9-11-7 **109** ....(p) SeanQuinlan (Richard Phillips) *led: hdd appr 2 out: sn wknd* **13/2**	107
3265	**3**	*11*	**Dunkelly Castle (IRE)**[42] 4428 7-11-9 **111** .... HaddenFrost (Roger Curtis) *chsd ldrs: lft 3rd 4 out: wknd appr next* **5/1**[3]	97
PPP1	**4**	*28*	**Grenoli (FR)**[18] 5017 10-10-0 **95** ....(bt) JoeCornwall(7) (John Cornwall) *chsd ldrs: outpcd 13th: sn lost pl: bhd fr 4 out: t.o* **5/1**[3]	56
0505	**P**		**Tisfreetdream (IRE)**[30] 4777 10-10-11 **99** ....(p) TomSiddall (Peter Pritchard) *chsd ldrs: dropped bk last and drvn 12th: sn bhd: t.o whn p.u bef 4 out* **7/1**	—
4PU0	**F**		**Double Pride**[28] 4802 7-11-12 **114** ....(b) WayneHutchinson (Alan King) *jnd ldrs 11th: cl 2nd whn fell 4 out* **3/1**[1]	—

6m 29.6s (3.60) **Going Correction** +0.025s/f (Yiel) **6** Ran SP% **107.2**

Speed ratings: **95,87,84,75,—** —

toteswingers: 1&2 £4.80, 1&3 £3.90, 2&3 £2.80 CSF £21.61 TOTE £3.50: £1.50, £3.90; EX 42.70.

Owner Richard Collins **Bred** W E McCluskey **Trained** Lingdale, Redcar & Cleveland

FOCUS

A modest handicap chase.

NOTEBOOK

Columbus Secret(IRE) had his task simplified by the departure of Double Pride four out. He had run well in better races the last twice and proved well suited by the return to 3m, although he'll now be faced with a higher mark. (op 4-1)

King Jack, 1lb below his last winning mark, ideally prefers more cut in the ground and was readily swept aside.

Dunkelly Castle(IRE) remains 6lb above his last winning mark and was again well held.

Double Pride, still a maiden over fences, had run well when ninth at 100-1 in the 4m National Hunt Chase at Cheltenham last month and was in with every chance here when departing, giving his rider a particularly heavy fall. (tchd 5-2)

5293 FREE RACING POST FORM AT TOTESPORT.COM H'CAP CHASE (16 fncs) 2m 4f 110y

5:15 (5:15) (Class 4) (0-100,98) 5-Y-0+ **£2,211** (£649; £324; £162)

Form				RPR
6224	**1**		**Persian Gates (IRE)**[31] 4740 7-11-12 **98** ....(b) TomMessenger (Chris Bealby) *t.k.h: led 2nd: j.rt: jnd 2 out: kpt on wl run-in: drew clr clsng stages* **6/1**[3]	109+
0332	**2**	*3 ¼*	**Karingreason**[10] 5134 8-11-7 **93** .... JamesReveley (Keith Reveley) *hld up: hdwy to chse ldrs 10th: drvn appr 3 out: sn chsng wnr: upsides 2 out: kpt on same pce run-in* **3/1**[1]	100
6232	**3**	*11*	**Donald Will Do (IRE)**[56] 4144 11-9-11 **76** .... JakeGreenall(7) (Caroline Bailey) *chsd ldrs: one pce fr 4 out* **4/1**[2]	73
2134	**4**	*23*	**Guns Of Love (IRE)**[34] 4671 9-11-0 **86** .... CharliePoste (Robin Dickin) *hdwy to chse ldrs 7th: blnd 4 out: wknd appr 2 out* **10/1**	64
-42P	**5**	*3 ¼*	**Overlaw**[75] 3792 9-11-6 **92** .... DenisO'Regan (Tom George) *led to 2nd: chsd ldrs: wnt briefly 2nd appr 3 out: wknd appr 2 out* **8/1**	65
5061	**6**	*10*	**Peak Seasons (IRE)**[18] 5018 8-9-11 **72** oh4 .... CharlieStudd(3) (Michael Chapman) *prom: mstke 5th: lost pl and blnd 8th: t.o 10th* **14/1**	36
1124	**7**	*21*	**Phar Again (IRE)**[33] 4694 8-11-8 **97** ....(vt) TommyPhelan(3) (Claire Dyson) *chsd ldrs: blnd 8th: drvn 10th: sn lost pl: t.o 4 out* **8/1**	43
36P6	**8**	*6*	**Kinkeel (IRE)**[18] 5015 12-10-5 **80** .... EamonDehdashti(3) (Tony Carroll) *prom: hit 3rd: lost pl and drvn 6th: bhd whn mstke 10th: sn t.o* **14/1**	20
P4P5	**P**		**Ortega (FR)**[21] 4949 9-9-7 **72** oh6 ....(p) JoeCornwall(7) (John Cornwall) *chsd ldrs: outpcd 10th: in rr whn hit 4 out: sn t.o: p.u bef last* **14/1**	—

5m 23.7s (8.70) **Going Correction** +0.025s/f (Yiel) **9** Ran SP% **110.6**

Speed ratings: **84,82,78,69,68 64,56,54,—**

toteswingers: 1&2 £3.20, 1&3 £3.30, 2&3 £2.10 CSF £23.62 CT £75.68 TOTE £11.40: £3.30, £1.10, £1.80; EX 30.30 Trifecta £192.60 Pool: £9,981.36 - 38.34 winning units..

Owner Mrs Robert Bingley & Mrs Bryan Spooner **Bred** Thistletown Stud **Trained** Barrowby, Lincs

FOCUS

The front pair drew clear in the straight for this handicap chase.

NOTEBOOK

Persian Gates(IRE) put up a particularly game effort. He took over early, jumped well and found plenty when joined by the runner-up to assert on the run-in. This was a step up on his recent efforts, although he wouldn't want much of a rise. (op 7-1)

Karingreason made good headway to challenge and looked the winner coming to two out, but couldn't get past the winner, whose determination was the greater. She's holding her form and deserves to find a race. (op 7-2)

Donald Will Do(IRE) finds winning hard (just 1-34) and he was no match for the front pair. (op 9-2 tchd 7-2)

Overlaw looked all over the winner turning in, but stopped to nothing once asked for his effort and coasted home in his own time. (op 6-1)

5294 BET TOTEPOOL AT TOTESPORT.COM NOVICES' H'CAP CHASE (13 fncs) 2m

5:45 (5:47) (Class 4) (0-110,103) 5-Y-0+ **£2,211** (£649; £324; £162)

Form				RPR
0062	**1**		**Seigneur Des Bois (FR)**[18] 5004 5-11-12 **103** .... GrahamLee (Ferdy Murphy) *chsd ldrs: hit 4th and reminders: drvn after 6th: outpcd 4 out: hdwy 2 out: sn chsng ldr: kpt on to ld towards fin* **5/1**[3]	113+
P344	**2**	*½*	**Haka Dancer (USA)**[202] 1587 8-10-5 **89** .... KyleJames(7) (Philip Kirby) *t.k.h: j.rt: led 3rd: hrd rdn appr 3 out: hdd and no ex towards fin* **10/1**	97
0413	**3**	*8*	**Saddlers Deal (IRE)**[25] 4868 6-11-11 **102** ....(p) DenisO'Regan (Chris Grant) *hld up: hdwy to trck ldrs 4 out: chsng ldr whn j.rt 2 out: one pce* **4/1**[2]	104

050U **4** *5* **Carters Rest**[9] 5145 8-10-11 **93**....(v) ShaneByrne(5) 88
(Chris Grant) *jnd ldrs 7th: drvn 4 out: one pce whn hit next* **5/1**[3]

0650 **5** *34* **Jersey Boys**[28] 4809 5-10-5 **87**.... PaulGallagher(5) 64
(Howard Johnson) *led to 3rd: w ldr 9th: wknd after next: sn bhd: t.o last: virtually p.u nr fin* **7/2**[1]

P4 **F** **Back To Paris (IRE)**[18] 5018 9-10-7 **84**.... JamesReveley 82
(Philip Kirby) *w ldrs: dsiputing 3rd whn hmpd and fell 2 out* **20/1**

2252 **P** **The Darling Boy**[30] 4775 6-11-10 **101**....(tp) AidanColeman —
(Tom George) *chsd ldrs: blnd 3rd: lost pl and reminders 6th: bhd next: t.o whn p.u bef 8th* **7/2**[1]

4m 8.40s (-1.60) **Going Correction** +0.025s/f (Yiel) **7** Ran SP% **111.6**
Speed ratings: **105,104,100,98,81** —,—
toteswingers: 1&2 £3.20, 1&3 £15.10, 2&3 £12.80 CSF £46.64 TOTE £6.20: £3.30, £5.30; EX 55.00.

Owner Crossed Fingers Partnership **Bred** Jean-Christophe Froc **Trained** West Witton, N Yorks

FOCUS
Just a moderate handicap chase.

NOTEBOOK
Seigneur Des Bois(FR) didn't look to be going well with a circuit to run. He was under pressure and receiving reminders and there wew several going better leaving the back. However, just as had been the case at Bangor last time, he came strong in the straight and despite being less than fluent at the last, always looked to be getting up on the run-in. He'll stay further and there should be more to come. (op 7-2)
Haka Dancer(USA) improved to run his best race yet over fences. He's on a good mark in this sphere and can go one better. (op 11-1)
Saddlers Deal(IRE), below par on soft ground last time, travelled strongly, but couldn't go through with his effort having challenged in the straight. (tchd 3-1)
Carters Rest has still to win over jumps. (op 9-2)
Jersey Boys stopped to nothing and is left with a bit to prove. (op 6-1)
Back To Paris(IRE) had run well, but was beaten, when jumping into the back of Sadlers Deal and coming down two out. (op 18-1 tchd 16-1)
The Darling Boy was never travelling after an early blunder and pulled up. (op 18-1 tchd 16-1)

5295 TOTESPORT 0800 221 221 CONDITIONAL JOCKEYS' NOVICES' H'CAP HURDLE (13 hdls) 3m 110y
6:15 (6:15) (Class 5) (0-95,93) 4-Y-0+ **£1,541** (£449; £224)

Form RPR
P022 **1** **Monty's Moon (IRE)**[14] 5075 9-10-7 **77**....(p) PeterCarberry(3) 81
(Rachel Hobbs) *chsd ldrs: drvn 8th: sn lost pl: hdwy to chse ldrs 4 out: led last: kpt on wl* **9/2**[1]

3400 **2** *1* **Auberge (IRE)**[23] 4914 7-11-9 **90**.... RyanMania 93
(Dianne Sayer) *chsd ldrs: upsides last: styd on same pce* **13/2**

600P **3** *¾* **Life Long (IRE)**[31] 4741 7-11-12 **93**.... DavidBass 95
(Anabel L M King) *chsd ldrs: drvn along 9th: narrow ld between last 2: hdd last: kpt on same pce* **16/1**

0410 **4** *2 ¼* **Burnthill (IRE)**[6] 5169 6-11-4 **90**....(t) GeraldQuinn(5) 90
(Claire Dyson) *w ldr: led 4th: hdd between last 2: one pce* **10/1**

4004 **5** *17* **Kings Story (IRE)**[17] 5040 7-10-0 **67** oh3....(b) JamesHalliday 54
(Sophie Leech) *in tch: outpcd 3 out: blnd 2 out: heavily eased and lost 4th towards fin* **9/1**

2532 **6** *3* **Jacarado (IRE)**[30] 4787 13-9-10 **71**....(v) ChristopherWard(8) 53
(Robin Dickin) *rn in snatches: chsd ldrs: lost pl 10th* **11/2**[3]

0P23 **7** *6* **Feeling Peckish (USA)**[8] 4953 7-10-6 **76**....(t) KyleJames(3) 53
(Michael Chapman) *led to 4th: lost pl 10th: sn bhd* **20/1**

003P **8** *22* **Borderhopper**[28] 4814 7-10-9 **84**.... TonyKelly(8) 41
(Ferdy Murphy) *in rr: drvn 8th: bhd fr 9th: t.o 2 out* **10/1**

3030 **F** **Treason Trial**[8] 3951 10-11-11 **92**....(p) PaulGallagher —
(Andrew Crook) *in rr: hdwy to chse ldrs 7th: fell 9th* **20/1**

3P40 **F** **Glamorous Gg**[6] 5169 6-10-11 **78**....(b[1]) MichaelMurphy —
(Ian Williams) *hld up in rr: fell 4th* **16/1**

0543 **U** **Not A Bob (IRE)**[32] 4724 6-11-8 **92**.... RichieMcLernon(3) —+
(Jonjo O'Neill) *hld up: stdy hdwy 8th: trcking ldrs and gng wl whn blnd and uns rdr 3 out* **5/1**[2]

6m 29.1s (21.60) **Going Correction** +0.025s/f (Yiel) **11** Ran SP% **113.0**
Speed ratings (Par 103): **66,65,65,64,59 58,56,49**,—,— —
toteswingers: 1&2 £7.00, 1&3 £16.10, 2&3 £28.60 CSF £32.78 CT £421.46 TOTE £2.60: £1.10, £3.20, £7.20; EX 31.30 Trifecta £378.70 Pool: £2,763.98 - 5.40 winning units..

Owner The Full Monty Racing Club **Bred** Eugene Buckley **Trained** Hanley Swan, Worcs

FOCUS
A low-grade handicap hurdle.

NOTEBOOK
Monty's Moon(IRE) stayed on best after the last for a deserved first success under rules, having finished runner-up the last twice. He bumped into a rapid improver last time and overcame the 2lb higher mark. (tchd 4-1)
Auberge(IRE) remains 13lb higher than when gaining her sole previous victory, but this effort very much suggests she is capable off this mark. (op 6-1 tchd 11-2)
Life Long(IRE) kept finding for pressure and stayed on to record easily his best effort to date over hurdles. (op 20-1 tchd 25-1)
Burnthill(IRE) ran well without being able to match the front trio in the straight. (op 14-1)
Jacarado(IRE) was never travelling. (tchd 5-1 and 6-1)
Not A Bob(IRE) was still travelling and very much in the race when blundering badly and giving his rider no chance. He'll be of interest in future if none the worse for this. (tchd 9-2 and 11-2)

5296 GOLF AND RACING AT SOUTHWELL NOVICES' HURDLE (9 hdls) 2m
6:45 (6:45) (Class 4) 4-Y-0+ **£2,055** (£599; £299)

Form RPR
U1F **1** **Laterly (IRE)**[26] 4858 6-11-6 114.... RhysFlint 109
(Steve Gollings) *mde all: jnd last: hrd rdn: all out* **11/4**[2]

4600 **2** *hd* **Morocchius (USA)**[12] 5101 6-10-13 91.... AdamPogson 102+
(Charles Pogson) *t.k.h towards rr: hdwy to go handy 3rd bef 2 out: rdr dropped whip between last 2: chal last: no ex nr fin* **66/1**

4-44 **3** *5* **Theredballoon**[28] 4810 5-10-6 0.... OliverWilliams(7) 97
(Chris Bealby) *hld up: wnt prom 4th: lft 2nd 6th: ev ch 2 out: one pce* **10/1**

555 **4** *25* **Ibn Hiyyan (USA)**[95] 3443 4-10-7 99.... GrahamLee 69
(Ferdy Murphy) *chsd wnr to 3rd: rdn and wknd 3 out: sn bhd* **8/1**[3]

5 *3 ½* **Achimota (IRE)** 5-10-13 0.... DenisO'Regan 74
(Matt Sheppard) *in rr: nt fluent 4th: hmpd 6th: sn bhd* **40/1**

102 **F** **Get It On (IRE)**[66] 3960 6-11-13 125.... PaulMoloney —
(Evan Williams) *trckd ldrs: chsd wnr 3rd: fell 6th* **4/6**[1]

0-PP **P** **Solo Roma (IRE)**[73] 3836 7-10-13 0....(b[1]) WillKennedy —
(Violet M Jordan) *chsd ldrs: drvn and lost pl bef 5th: t.o whn p.u bef next: b.b.v* **125/1**

3m 55.9s (-1.20) **Going Correction** +0.025s/f (Yiel)
WFA 4 from 5yo+ 5lb **7** Ran SP% **111.6**
Speed ratings (Par 105): **104,103,101,88,87** —,—
toteswingers: 1&2 £15.30, 1&3 £2.40, 2&3 £11.30 CSF £94.41 TOTE £4.00: £2.30, £2.70; EX 29.60.

Owner P J Martin **Bred** Gestut Fahrhof Stiftung **Trained** Scamblesby, Lincs

FOCUS
This was thrown wide open when red-hot favourite Get It On fell at the sixth.

NOTEBOOK
Laterly(IRE) capitalised on the favourite's departure, although whether he'd have won had Adam Pogson, aboard the 66-1 runner-up, not dropped his whip remains to be seen. He's had his jumping troubles over hurdles, falling last time, was better in that department but proved particularly laboured in victory. He'll struggle under a double penalty and is best switched to handicaps. (op 5-2 tchd 9-4)
Morocchius(USA) has had problems settling, but wasn't as bad and loomed as a threat on entering the straight. His rider dropping his whip definitely had an effect, though, and he was unable to quite get up. He should win a small race before long. (op 50-1)
Theredballoon improved on his first outing over hurdles and looks a likely winner at some stage this summer, assuming he's kept on the go. (op 12-1 tchd 9-1)
Ibn Hiyyan(USA) can do better once handicapping. (op 11-1 tchd 14-1)
Get It On(IRE) set the standard and looked the one to beat, despite his double penalty. Not all horses take to hurdles on this course, though, and he'd had already made a couple of small mistakes before falling. It remains to be seen how this affects his confidence. (tchd 8-13 and 4-5)

5297 MEMBERSHIP AT SOUTHWELL GOLF CLUB MARES' NOVICES' HURDLE (11 hdls) 2m 4f 110y
7:15 (7:16) (Class 4) 4-Y-0+ **£1,541** (£449; £224)

Form RPR
115F **1** **Alpine Breeze (IRE)**[103] 3264 5-11-5 120.... PeterCarberry(7) 116+
(Don Cantillon) *hld up: t.k.h: trckd ldrs 6th: led on bit 2 out: shkn up and wnt clr run-in* **4/6**[1]

44R2 **2** *7* **Accordingtoeileen (IRE)**[24] 4897 6-10-7 0.... MrWTwiston-Davies(7) 97
(Nigel Twiston-Davies) *w ldrs: hit 2 out: wnt 2nd and kpt on same pce appr last: no imp* **10/3**[2]

3522 **3** *7* **Landenstown Pearl (IRE)**[193] 1680 5-10-11 0.... AlexMerriam(3) 90
(Neil King) *led tl 2 out: 3rd and wl hld whn hit last* **12/1**

0-05 **4** *43* **Bonnie Baloo**[24] 4894 5-11-0 0.... BarryKeniry 50
(Alan Swinbank) *chsd ldrs: rdn 3 out: sn wknd and bhd* **17/2**[3]

06/4 **5** *4* **Personal Flair**[34] 4665 8-11-0 0.... AidanColeman 46
(Sarah Humphrey) *kicked s: stdd s: wnt prom 6th: drvn 3 out: sn lost pl and bhd* **66/1**

0600 **6** *16* **Lilac Belle**[41] 4437 5-11-0 0....(t) WillKennedy 32
(Alex Hales) *stdd s: hld up: t.k.h: wnt prom 6th: wknd 3 out: sn bhd* **33/1**

U **Kitchen Loan (IRE)**[1144] 8-11-0 0.... LeightonAspell —
(Oliver Sherwood) *trckd ldrs: clipped heels and uns rdr bnd after 1st* **12/1**

R **Granny Kanzi**[66] 7-11-0 0....(p) FelixDeGiles —
(Charlie Longsdon) *towards rr whn ref and uns rdr 1st* **33/1**

0-0P **P** **Fleetstone**[23] 4918 6-11-0 0....(t) SeanQuinlan —
(Richard Phillips) *chsd ldrs: hit 3rd: drvn 6th: blnd and rdr briefly lost irons 7th: sn t.o: p.u bef 2 out* **66/1**

5m 21.8s (11.10) **Going Correction** +0.025s/f (Yiel) **9** Ran SP% **117.8**
Speed ratings (Par 105): **79,76,73,57,55 49**,—,—,—
toteswingers: 1&2 £1.10, 1&3 £1.60, 2&3 £4.70 CSF £3.23 TOTE £1.80: £1.90, £1.10, £2.50; EX 3.70 Trifecta £13.10 Pool: £4,473.66 - 250.84 winning units..

Owner Don Cantillon **Bred** D E Cantillon **Trained** Newmarket, Suffolk

FOCUS
A weak mares' hurdle.

NOTEBOOK
Alpine Breeze(IRE), who hadn't run since falling at Warwick in late December, ran out an easy winner. A C&D winner last summer, she jumped safely and readily asserted, suggesting she'll be up to defying a double penalty in the right company over the coming months. (op 11-10 tchd 5-4 in places)
Accordingtoeileen(IRE) ran another sound race in defeat and memories of her refusal to race on hurdles debut are now banished. She looks in need of 3m and fences wouldn't go amiss either. (tchd 3-1 and 7-2)
Landenstown Pearl(IRE) ran well for a long way off the front end on this hurdles debut and should improve. (op 11-1)
Bonnie Baloo was comfortably held. (op 7-1)
Kitchen Loan(IRE), off for 1144 days since winning a point-to-point, clipped heels early and unshipped Leighton Aspell. (op 8-1)

5298 CALL 01636 814481 TO SPONSOR A RACE H'CAP HURDLE (11 hdls) 2m 4f 110y
7:45 (7:45) (Class 5) (0-90,90) 4-Y-0+ **£1,541** (£449; £224)

Form RPR
0002 **1** **Pickworth (IRE)**[20] 4976 6-11-12 **90**.... JamesReveley 97+
(Philip Kirby) *w ldrs: led 2 out: kpt on wl run-in* **9/2**[1]

0-22 **2** *2 ¾* **Only Hope**[14] 5072 7-11-2 **80**....(tp) AidanColeman 85
(Rachel Hobbs) *mid-div: chsd ldrs 6th: wnt 2nd between last 2: styd on same pce* **8/1**

00U **3** *3 ¼* **Fairhaven (IRE)**[28] 4813 7-11-12 **90**.... FelixDeGiles 91
(Charlie Longsdon) *hld up in rr: hdwy 3 out: wnt 3rd appr 2 out: kpt on one pce* **25/1**

P036 **4** *3 ¼* **Qualitee**[24] 4900 6-11-8 **89**.... TommyPhelan(3) 87
(Claire Dyson) *led to 2nd: w ldrs: led 7th: hdd 2 out: wknd appr last* **25/1**

3336 **5** *5* **Home She Goes (IRE)**[20] 4976 9-11-7 **85**.... AdamPogson 80
(Charles Pogson) *in rr: nt fluent 2nd: bhd 7th: hdwy 2 out: styd on wl run-in* **20/1**

424U **6** *1 ¼* **Present Your Case (IRE)**[85] 3622 6-11-10 **88**....(t) DarylJacob 81
(Ben Case) *w ldr: led 2nd: hdd 7th: wknd appr 2 out* **15/2**[3]

040 **7** *2* **Mission Complete (IRE)**[23] 4917 5-11-12 **90**.... RichieMcLernon 81
(Jonjo O'Neill) *in rr: drvn 7th: nvr a factor* **8/1**

0345 **8** *19* **Chadwell Spring (IRE)**[20] 4976 5-9-9 **64**....(b) PaulGallagher(5) 38
(Mike Sowersby) *trckd ldrs: wknd qckly 3 out* **9/2**[1]

600P **9** *17* **Upper Deck (IRE)**[66] 3960 6-11-11 **89**.... SeanQuinlan 47
(Richard Phillips) *in rr: sme hdwy 8th: drvn and wknd after next: eased between last 2* **50/1**

0000 **10** *1* **Bach To Back (IRE)**[100] 3365 6-11-5 **83**.... SamTwiston-Davies 40
(Nigel Twiston-Davies) *in rr: drvn 6th: bhd whn j.rt 3 out* **8/1**

P462 **11** *28* **Yes Mate**[29] 4799 7-10-0 **67**.... JamesHalliday(3) —
(Dianne Sayer) *chsd ldrs: lost pl 8th: sn bhd: t.o* **7/1**[2]

FP0P **12** *¾* **Kilbready Star (IRE)**[28] 4814 11-10-2 **66**.... CharliePoste —
(Peter Pritchard) *chsd ldrs: lost pl 8th: sn bhd: t.o* **33/1**

600P **P** **Are Olive**[58] 4112 8-11-0 **78** RobertWalford —
(Tim Walford) *trckd ldrs: pckd 6th: lost pl 8th: bhd whn p.u bef 2 out* **40/1**
5m 19.3s (8.60) **Going Correction** +0.025s/f (Yiel) **13** Ran SP% **113.8**
Speed ratings (Par 103): **84,82,81,80,78 78,77,70,63,63 52,52,—**
toteswingers: 1&2 £2.90, 1&3 £97.70, 2&3 £55.20 CSF £34.79 CT £800.27 TOTE £8.50: £2.50, £1.10, £5.30; EX 32.10 Trifecta £351.40 Part won. Pool: £474.87 - 0.10 winning units..
Owner Keith Sivills **Bred** Andrew Kavanagh **Trained** Castleton, N Yorks

FOCUS
An open-looking handicap hurdle.

NOTEBOOK
Pickworth(IRE) showed much-improved form when second over 3m at the course last time and seemed helped by the drop in trip, again travelling well and staying on best for pressure. She's going the right way and looks to have more to offer. (op 5-1 tchd 4-1)
Only Hope continues to creep up the handicap, but again ran her race, just finding the one too good.
Fairhaven(IRE) appreciated the return to hurdles and the way he finished suggests a more positive ride will help in future. (op 20-1)
Qualitee ran an improved race and has scope to do better again. (op 20-1)
Home She Goes(IRE) finished well and would have been closer had she jumped more fluently early on. (op 16-1 tchd 22-1)
Chadwell Spring(IRE) failed to run her race and was disappointing. (op 11-2)
T/Plt: £128.60 to a £1 stake. Pool: £46,579.95. 264.36 winning tickets. T/Qpdt: £21.80 to a £1 stake. Pool: £6,588.39. 223.10 winning tickets. WG

5285 CHELTENHAM (L-H)
Thursday, April 14

OFFICIAL GOING: Good (good to firm in places; watered; 8.5)
Wind: mild breeze across Weather: overcast but dry

5300 GLOUCESTERSHIRE TRAINERS CHAMPIONSHIP NOVICES' HURDLE (8 hdls) 2m 1f
2:10 (2:11) (Class 2) 4-Y-0+ **£6,262** (£1,850; £925; £463; £231)

Form RPR
1220 **1** **Third Intention (IRE)**[27] 4847 4-10-12 143 JoeTizzard 140+
(Colin Tizzard) *hld up bhd ldrs: tk clsr order 3 out: chal gng wl after 2 out: shkn up to ld appr last: pushed clr: readily* **5/4**[1]
11 **2** *8* **Higgy's Ragazzo (FR)**[11] 5131 4-10-12 0 APMcCoy 135+
(Nicky Henderson) *trckd ldr: tk narrow advantage after 2 out gng jst as wl as wnr: rdn and hdd whn hit last: nt gng pce of wnr* **9/2**[3]
61 **3** *14* **Current Event (FR)**[19] 5010 4-10-12 139 RWalsh 120
(Paul Nicholls) *led: hdd after 2 out: sn rdn: fnd little* **7/4**[2]
3343 **4** *9* **Occasionally Yours (IRE)**[33] 4725 7-11-4 123 MrJMQuinlan 118
(Alan Blackmore) *trckd ldr: pushed along after 3 out: outpcd after 2 out: regained 4th sn after last* **20/1**
5012 **5** *8* **Smart Catch (IRE)**[23] 4930 5-11-4 127 LeeEdwards 112
(Tony Carroll) *trckd ldr: rdn after 2 out: wknd bef last* **25/1**
4m 0.30s (-11.00) **Going Correction** -0.30s/f (Good)
WFA 4 from 5yo+ 5lb **5** Ran SP% **107.6**
Speed ratings (Par 109): **113,109,102,98,94**
CSF £6.97 TOTE £2.00: £1.10, £2.60; EX 7.60.
Owner Robert And Sarah Tizzard **Bred** Richard Klay And Dr M Klay **Trained** Milborne Port, Dorset

FOCUS
An interesting novice hurdle, despite only three being given a chance. The winner was the form pick but this rates a small step up.

NOTEBOOK
Third Intention(IRE), the Triumph seventh and a late withdrawal from Aintree last week, came out much the best. This strong-traveller appreciates a sound surface and stayed on well having began to assert from the last. He's the type to progress further and it's possible he'll now head to Punchestown, where he may go close. He could make his mark in decent handicap hurdles next season. (op 13-8 tchd 7-4 in places)
Higgy's Ragazzo(FR), 2-2 over hurdles, both wins coming at Market Rasen, shaped well for a long way, but just lacked the speed, or indeed class, of the winner. He too will be a handicapper. (op 4-1 tchd 7-2)
Current Event(FR), impressive at Newbury on his first run since having a breathing operation, stopped quickly in the straight, clearly failing to match that form, and doesn't look one to place much faith in. (op 13-8 tchd 15-8)
Occasionally Yours(IRE) was outpaced. (tchd 18-1 and 22-1)

5301 NICHOLSON HOLMAN NOVICES' LIMITED H'CAP CHASE (17 fncs) 2m 5f
2:45 (2:45) (Class 3) (0-135,135) 5-Y-0+
£6,262 (£1,850; £925; £463; £231; £116)

Form RPR
252F **1** **Magical Legend**[1] 5290 10-10-6 117 (t) TomO'Brien 127+
(Sophie Leech) *hld up in last trio but in tch: tk clsr order 3 out: chal next: slt ld last: styd on wl: rdn out* **10/1**
1243 **2** *1* **Have You Seen Me (IRE)**[87] 3605 8-11-7 132 SamTwiston-Davies 140
(Nigel Twiston-Davies) *led: rdn after 3 out: hdd last: styd on but no ex* **5/1**[2]
1120 **3** *2* **Classic Swain (USA)**[180] 1861 6-11-10 135 (bt) RWalsh 141
(Paul Nicholls) *hld up last but in tch: pushed along after 11th: rdn and no imp 3 out: styd on fr 2 out: wnt 3rd towards fin* **7/2**[1]
P042 **4** *shd* **Simarian (IRE)**[19] 5002 6-10-6 122 (p) AodhaganConlon[(5)] 130+
(Evan Williams) *trckd ldr: reminder after 12th: stmbld 4 out: sn rdn: ev ch whn mstke 2 out: 3rd and hld last: no ex whn lost 3rd towards fin* **7/1**[3]
2420 **5** *8* **On Borrowed Wings (IRE)**[30] 4794 8-11-2 134 (p) MrTJCannon[(7)] 135
(Alan Fleming) *trckd ldrs: nudged along after 11th: rdn whn nt fluent 5 out: nt gng pce to chal: wknd last* **7/2**[1]
2F22 **6** *9* **Ravethebrave (IRE)**[20] 4987 7-11-2 127 (b[1]) RobertThornton 121
(Alan King) *nt a fluent: in tch: hit 6th: rdn after 12th: brief effrt 3 out: wknd bef last* **5/1**[2]
2144 **7** *8* **Cool Friend (IRE)**[19] 5007 8-10-12 123 NickScholfield 110
(Jeremy Scott) *hld up in last trio in tch: rdn after nodding on landing 4 out: nvr threatened: wknd after 2 out* **9/1**
20F1 **8** *42* **Mr Syntax (IRE)**[51] 4275 7-10-11 122 AndrewThornton 88
(Tim Fitzgerald) *in tch: hit 5th: rdn after 4 out: wknd after 3 out: t.o* **25/1**
5m 12.3s (-7.10) **Going Correction** -0.30s/f (Good) **8** Ran SP% **113.2**
Speed ratings: **101,100,99,99,96 93,90,74**
toteswingers:1&2 £25.40, 2&3 £7.30, 1&3 £8.90 CSF £58.34 CT £210.86 TOTE £13.80: £3.40, £2.00, £1.40; EX 83.40 Trifecta £438.20 Pool: £657.40 - 1.11 winning units..
Owner R H Kerswell **Bred** R H And Mrs Kerswell **Trained** Kingsbridge, Devon

FOCUS
A fair novice handicap chase. The winner improved towards her hurdles mark.

NOTEBOOK
Magical Legend, an early faller at the course 24 hours earlier, has been racing over further, but that stood her in good stead here as stamina proved vital in the straight. She was clearly none the worse for the previous day's incident and could win again if kept on the go. (tchd 12-1)
Have You Seen Me(IRE), returning from 87 days off, was given a good, positive ride, and jumped well throughout, but wasn't good enough to fend off the winner. (op 11-2 tchd 6-1)
Classic Swain(USA), off since disappointing at the October meeting here, had been given a big chance by the handicapper but never got close enough, staying on all too late. He should be sharper next time (tchd 3-1)
Simarian(IRE) could find no extra in the straight and will do better returned to a lesser track. (op 13-2 tchd 6-1)
On Borrowed Wings(IRE) could have been expected to fare better considering he finished a running-on eighth in the Centenary last time. (op 9-2)
Ravethebrave(IRE) made mistakes and didn't get home in the first-time blinkers. (tchd 9-2)

5302 MOBILE BETTING AT VICTOR CHANDLER MARES' H'CAP HURDLE (LISTED RACE) (10 hdls) 2m 5f 110y
3:20 (3:21) (Class 1) 4-Y-0+
£11,402 (£4,278; £2,142; £1,068; £536; £268)

Form RPR
4-61 **1** **Veiled**[22] 4955 5-9-11 125 oh5 DavidBass[(3)] 136+
(Nicky Henderson) *mid-div: hdwy appr 2 out: led after 2 out: wnt sltly lft last: r.o strly: readily* **17/2**
5234 **2** *5* **Alasi**[30] 4793 7-10-11 136 DominicElsworth 139
(Paul Webber) *hld up towards rr: hdwy after 3 out: led briefly after 2 out: sn rdn: kpt on but nt gng pce of wnr fr last* **4/1**[2]
2212 **3** *6* **Violin Davis (FR)**[19] 5008 5-9-9 125 oh3 MrRMahon[(5)] 123
(Paul Nicholls) *mid-div: smooth hdwy after 2 out: rdn bef last: kpt on but nt gng pce of ldng pair* **10/3**[1]
F310 **4** *1* **Naughty Naughty**[26] 4875 6-10-0 125 AidanColeman 122
(Brendan Powell) *mid-div: rdn and hdwy after 2 out: styd on fr last: wnt 4th nr fin* **20/1**
2010 **5** *½* **Banjaxed Girl**[30] 4793 7-11-3 149 MrWTwiston-Davies[(7)] 146
(Nigel Twiston-Davies) *trckd ldrs: rdn after 3 out: styd on same pce fr next: lost 4th nr fin* **8/1**
-022 **6** *nk* **Chilli Rose**[34] 4703 6-9-11 125 oh10 CharlieHuxley[(3)] 122
(Alan King) *mid-div: rdn appr 2 out: styd on wl appr last but nvr gng to rch ldrs* **22/1**
0113 **7** *14* **Ocean Transit (IRE)**[30] 4793 6-10-12 137 RichardJohnson 123
(Richard Price) *rdn along fr 7th: nvr bttr than mid-div* **9/1**
-120 **8** *3* **Ambrose Princess (IRE)**[200] 1626 6-9-9 125 oh5 (p) CO'Farrell[(5)] 107
(Michael Scudamore) *led: rdn and hdd after 2 out: wknd bef last* **50/1**
-154 **9** *nk* **Diklers Oscar (IRE)**[22] 4940 8-10-0 125 oh2 SamTwiston-Davies 106
(Keith Reveley) *hld up towards rr: nt fluent 6th: sn pushed along: rdn after 3 out: nvr a threat* **13/2**[3]
P114 **10** *1½* **Dorabelle (IRE)**[68] 3945 6-10-0 125 oh3 AdrianLane 104
(Donald McCain) *mid-div tl dropped in rr 5th: nvr bk on terms* **40/1**
3130 **11** *9* **Santera (IRE)**[30] 4793 7-10-10 135 (p) WillKennedy 106
(Bernard Llewellyn) *trckd ldrs: rdn after 2 out: sn wknd* **20/1**
0110 **12** *7* **Emmaslegend**[19] 5008 6-9-7 125 oh10 (t) MrTJCannon[(7)] 90
(Suzy Smith) *trckd ldr: rdn after 3 out: wknd sn after next* **20/1**
F431 **13** *8* **Kaituna (IRE)**[14] 5078 5-10-0 125 oh2 SamJones 85
(Oliver Sherwood) *in tch: rdn whn blnd 2 out: sn btn* **16/1**
2300 **14** *22* **Boogie Dancer**[21] 2347 7-10-0 125 oh16 HarrySkelton 63
(Stuart Howe) *a towards rr: t.o* **100/1**
2465 **P** **Je Ne Sais Plus (FR)**[68] 3941 7-10-0 125 oh12 (t) PaddyBrennan —
(Tom George) *mid-div tl hit 4th: bhd and struggling fr next: t.o whn p.u 3 out* **50/1**
1630 **P** **Sway (FR)**[30] 4794 5-10-11 136 APMcCoy —
(Jonjo O'Neill) *hld up towards rr: pushed along after 3 out: rdn and little imp after 2 out: lost action whn p.u bef last* **25/1**
5m 7.60s (-9.00) **Going Correction** -0.30s/f (Good) course record **16** Ran SP% **123.8**
Speed ratings (Par 111): **104,102,100,99,99 99,94,93,93,92 89,86,83,75,— —**
toteswingers:1&2 £10.10, 2&3 £4.10, 1&3 £6.40 CSF £38.90 CT £141.80 TOTE £12.80: £2.80, £1.80, £1.10, £5.30; EX 42.30 Trifecta £125.10 Pool: £1438.87 - 8.51 winning units..
Owner Pump & Plant Services Ltd **Bred** Cheveley Park Stud Ltd **Trained** Upper Lambourn, Berks

FOCUS
This is often a competitive mares' handicap hurdle and there was plenty of pace on, the race very much working out for those who were ridden under restraint. No fewer than ten of the runners were forced to race from out of the handicap. The easy winner improved to the level expected from her Flat form, with a small personal best from the second.

NOTEBOOK
Veiled, a recent Warwick winner and racing from 5lb out of the handicap, represented a yard that took the big mares' race at Newbury a few weeks ago, and she looks a useful sort in the making judged by the manner of this performance. Always travelling strongly, this lightly raced hurdler readily asserted before staying on strongly and looks capable of holding her own in good handicaps. (op 8-1 tchd 9-1)
Alasi, last year's runner-up who ran a fine race when fourth to Quevega at the festival, again travelled well, but couldn't match the winner's acceleration. She deserves to win a decent race. (op 6-1)
Violin Davis(FR), runner-up in the mares' finale at Newbury, was 8lb higher today (including 3lb out of the handicap) and continues to progress, running well in a stronger race. (op 9-2 tchd 3-1)
Naughty Naughty bounced back from a below-par effort at Towcester, keeping on well up the hill. (op 16-1)
Banjaxed Girl, last year's winner \bBanjaxed Girl\p, who again gave her all but wasn't good enough from 9lb higher this time around. (tchd 9-1)
Chilli Rose remains winless over hurdles and will surely appreciate 3m. (tchd 20-1)
Ocean Transit(IRE) ran a career-best to finish third to Quevega at the festival, but couldn't reproduce that level of form this time. (op 8-1)
Ambrose Princess(IRE) ran well for a long way on this return from 200 days off and should strip fitter next time. (op 66-1)

5303 PYMENTS CHARTERED QUANTITY SURVEYORS H'CAP CHASE (21 fncs) 3m 1f 110y
3:55 (3:55) (Class 2) (0-150,148) 5-Y-0+
£11,271 (£3,330; £1,665; £833; £415; £208)

Form RPR
FF3R **1** **Triggerman**[26] 4876 9-10-10 132 (p) RichardJohnson 146+
(Philip Hobbs) *hld up: wnt 4th 16th: nt fluent next: wnt 2nd after 4 out: rdn to ld 2 out: nt fluent last: styd on: drvn out* **9/2**[3]
/F4- **2** *1* **Benefit Night (IRE)**[39] 4516 11-10-4 126 (bt) DenisO'Regan 137
(Daniel William O'Sullivan, Ire) *led: rdn and hdd appr 2 out: ev ch whn edgd rt sn after last: styd on: no ex fnl 75yds* **13/2**

1131 **3** *20* **Bellflower Boy (IRE)**[26] 4864 8-10-0 **122** oh1............(tp) TimmyMurphy 122+
(Dr Richard Newland) *nvr travelling or fluent 1st circ: detached in last: latched on to bk of gp 13th: wnt 4th after 4 out: wnt 3rd after 3 out: rdn and 3 l down whn mstke 2 out: hld after: wknd last* **11/4**[1]

230P **4** *1* **Breedsbreeze (IRE)**[28] 4818 9-11-12 **148**.................................. RWalsh 140
(Paul Nicholls) *hld up: nudged along fr 12th: rdn after 4 out: wnt modest 4th after 3 out: nvr a factor* **15/2**

5025 **5** *22* **Beat The Boys (IRE)**[40] 4466 10-11-3 **139**............. SamTwiston-Davies 111
(Nigel Twiston-Davies) *trckd ldr tl 12th: sn pushed along: rdn after 15th: wknd after 4 out: t.o* **9/1**

-151 **6** *96* **Bai Zhu (IRE)**[20] 4989 7-10-10 **132**.............................. FelixDeGiles 18
(Nicky Henderson) *trckd ldrs: wnt 2nd 12th tl after rdn 4 out: wkng whn lost 3rd sn after next: fin v tired* **4/1**[2]

F12U **P** **Frankie Anson (IRE)**[20] 4989 7-10-0 **122** oh1................ PaddyBrennan —
(Micky Hammond) *trckd ldrs: hit 11th and 15th: rdn after 17th: stmbld 4 out: sn wknd: t.o whn p.u bef 2 out* **10/1**

6m 23.4s (-14.80) **Going Correction** -0.30s/f (Good) **7** Ran SP% **109.0**
Speed ratings: **110,109,103,103,96 66,—**
toteswingers:1&2 £3.80, 2&3 £2.70, 1&3 £1.50 CSF £29.69 TOTE £5.40: £2.80, £3.40; EX 29.70.
Owner M G St Quinton **Bred** M J Roberts **Trained** Withycombe, Somerset
■ This race was formerly run for the Golden Miller Trophy.

FOCUS
The front pair drew clear in this staying handicap chase. A good effort from the winner to beat the well handicapped second.

NOTEBOOK
Triggerman ran his heart out prior to refusing at the last through sheer exhaustion in the Midlands Grand National, and the considerably better ground here was to his advantage. He briefly looked to hand the momentum back to the runner-up when getting in close at the last, but readily found more and fully deserved it. (tchd 5-1)
Benefit Night(IRE), 6lb higher than when winning at Naas last month, was ridden aggressively and looked to have plenty in trouble running down the hill, but he couldn't get away from the winner and had to settle for second-best. (op 7-1 tchd 15-2)
Bellflower Boy(IRE), bidding for a fifth win in six, was never really travelling in rear, making many mistakes, so it's to his credit that he managed to drag himself into contention by he top of the hill. He couldn't race on in the end, but it's unwise to think he can't win off this mark with a more fluent round of jumping. (tchd 5-2)
Breedsbreeze(IRE), down in grade having pulled up in the Ryanair, has developed a habit of struggling in the early part of races before plodding on late, and that's exactly what he did here. (op 13-2 tchd 8-1)
Bai Zhu(IRE) is a fine, big, attractive sort, but he didn't exactly look to be crying out for this trip when just lasting home over 3m at Newbury last time, and he finished tired. He's a nice prospect for next season, when a shorter trip will suit, and he already appeals as a likely type for races over the National fences, with the Grand Sefton and Topham looking suitable aims. (tchd 7-2)

5304 MOLSON COORS H'CAP HURDLE (12 hdls) 3m
4:30 (4:31) (Class 2) (0-140,140) 4-Y-0+
£7,514 (£2,220; £1,110; £555; £277; £139)

Form RPR

3041 **1** **Sir Kezbaah (IRE)**[9] 5153 7-11-4 **132** 7ex........................ NickScholfield 148+
(Jeremy Scott) *mid-div: hdwy appr 2 out: led appr last: rdn and styd on strly run-in: a holding on fnl 75yds* **9/4**[1]

113 **2** *½* **There's No Panic (IRE)**[181] 1853 6-11-0 **128**............................ RWalsh 144+
(Paul Nicholls) *patiently rdn in rr: smooth hdwy after 2 out: chalng whn a little awkward last: rdn and styd on wl to draw wl clr of remainder: hld fnl 75yds* **7/1**[3]

-0F5 **3** *16* **Benbane Head (USA)**[40] 4485 7-10-9 **123**...................(t) WarrenMarston 124
(Martin Keighley) *mid-div: hdwy to trck ldrs 7th: chal 2 out: led sn after: rdn and hdd bef last: nt gng pce of front pair* **11/2**[2]

P-05 **4** *3 ¼* **Merrydown (IRE)**[19] 5003 8-11-2 **130**.......................... DominicElsworth 128
(Nicky Richards) *hld up towards rr: hdwy whn nt fluent 2 out: sn rdn: wnt 4th appr last: styd on same pce* **14/1**

5-36 **5** *1 ¾* **Hollins**[27] 4852 7-11-2 **130**... PaddyBrennan 128
(Micky Hammond) *mid-div: hdwy after 3 out: 1 l down next: sn rdn: styd on same pce* **16/1**

/601 **6** *1 ¼* **Counting House (IRE)**[20] 4988 8-10-9 **123**............................ RhysFlint 119
(Jim Old) *hld up towards rr: rdn after 3 out: styd on past btn horses fr jst bef last* **12/1**

1063 **7** *1 ¾* **Nicene Creed**[22] 4940 6-10-9 **123**.......................................(p) TomO'Brien 118
(Philip Hobbs) *trckd ldrs: hit 7th: struggling in rr 9th: nvr bk on terms: styd on past btn horses fr last* **7/1**[3]

4030 **8** *2* **Kayf Aramis**[28] 4817 9-11-12 **140**............................. SamTwiston-Davies 132
(Nigel Twiston-Davies) *led tl 7th: remained prom: rdn after 3 out: ev ch next: wknd bef last* **20/1**

5536 **9** *2 ¾* **Dantari (IRE)**[29] 4806 6-10-4 **125**.. MrJEngland(7) 115
(Evan Williams) *prom: hit 1st: led 7th: rdn and hdd sn after 2 out: wknd bef last* **17/2**

13-6 **10** *3 ¾* **Natural Action**[12] 5110 7-9-13 **116**..........................(v[1]) DonalDevereux(3) 102
(Peter Bowen) *trckd ldrs: nt fluent 2nd: ev ch 2 out: sn rdn: wknd bef last* **16/1**

4430 **11** *33* **Busker Royal**[29] 4806 8-10-13 **130**.............................. RichardKilloran(3) 100
(Nicky Henderson) *mid-div: hdwy to trck ldrs 9th: blnd bdly 3 out: sn lost pl u.p: wknd next: eased bef last* **28/1**

5m 48.2s (-12.80) **Going Correction** -0.30s/f (Good) **11** Ran SP% **116.0**
Speed ratings (Par 109): **109,108,103,102,101 101,100,100,99,98 87**
toteswingers:1&2 £4.40, 2&3 £7.30, 1&3 £3.90 CSF £18.53 CT £77.85 TOTE £3.50: £2.10, £1.30, £2.30; EX 17.00 Trifecta £60.40 Pool: £1043.83 - 12.77 winning units..
Owner Andrew & Vanessa Maddox **Bred** Joseph J O'Connor **Trained** Brompton Regis, Somerset

FOCUS
Quite a decent handicap hurdle in which two drew clear. The winner is rated up another 3lb, while the second was arguably unlucky.

NOTEBOOK
Sir Kezbaah(IRE) was perhaps fortunate as the runner-up was challenging when awkward at the last. Shouldering a 7lb penalty for his recent Exeter victory, he stays this trip well and it would have gone down as a good effort even if he had met with defeat. He remains progressive and should jump a fence. (op 5-2 tchd 11-4)
There's No Panic(IRE), a progressive sort last spring/summer, winning three times on a sound surface, hadn't run since finishing third here in October, but promised to be well suited by the trip and fitness was unlikely to be a problem. Ridden with extreme confidence by Walsh, he was hard on the bridle turning in and still seemed full of confidence coming into the last, but didn't get the best of jumps, costing him momentum, and was then unable to get past the winner. He'd have won had he been sent on earlier and should gain compensation despite an inevitable rise. He's the type to do well in staying chases further down the line. (op 8-1 tchd 9-1 in a place)
Benbane Head(USA) appreciated the return to a sound surface and ran better. (op 9-2 tchd 4-1)
Merrydown(IRE) had looked to need his two runs since returning from a year off, but ran better. He will be of interest in the coming weeks. (op 12-1 tchd 16-1)
Hollins was made to look very one-paced on this ground, and may prefer it easier. (op 14-1)
Counting House(IRE) was never involved off 8lb higher, but did keep on late. (op 10-1 tchd 9-1)
Nicene Creed hasn't gone on as expected and was again a bit disappointing. (op 8-1)

5305 AURIGA NETWORK CONDITIONAL JOCKEYS' H'CAP CHASE (14 fncs) 2m 110y
5:05 (5:06) (Class 3) (0-135,132) 5-Y-0+
£6,262 (£1,850; £925; £463; £231; £116)

Form RPR

F352 **1** **Cruchain (IRE)**[14] 5081 8-10-10 **116**................................ DonalDevereux 129+
(Dai Burchell) *disp tl clr ldr 4th: rdn and hdd after 3 out: regained ld whn awkward 2 out: hdd jst bef last: rallied to ld again run-in: drvn out: hld on gamely* **7/1**

2400 **2** *nk* **Riguez Dancer**[27] 4853 7-11-1 **129**............................ EdmondLinehan(8) 141+
(Ferdy Murphy) *in tch: hdwy after 4 out: rdn after next: chal 2 out: ldng whn hit last: hdd run-in: kpt on: no ex* **14/1**

0212 **3** *14* **Quipe Me Posted (FR)**[12] 5112 7-11-0 **120**......................... KeiranBurke 119
(Suzy Smith) *disp tl 4th: chsd wnr: pckd 4 out: rdn to ld after 3 out: hdd bef next: sn no ex* **11/2**[3]

1630 **4** *8* **Mam Ratagan**[124] 2881 10-11-0 **123**........................ JeremiahMcGrath(3) 116
(Heather Main) *trckd ldrs: pckd 4 out: sn rdn: wknd after 2 out: wnt lft last* **7/1**

6F02 **5** *7* **My Moment (IRE)**[24] 4913 8-11-4 **130**........................(b[1]) JakeGreenall(6) 116
(Henry Daly) *in tch: pckd 4 out: sn rdn: wknd bef 2 out* **16/1**

3460 **6** *2 ¼* **Cootehill (IRE)**[28] 4816 7-11-2 **125**.................. SamTwiston-Davies(3) 108
(Nigel Twiston-Davies) *in tch: rdn whn hit 4 out: wknd next* **11/1**

4116 **7** *7* **Anquetta (IRE)**[27] 4853 7-11-9 **132**............................... DavidBass(3) 108
(Nicky Henderson) *in tch: mstke 9th: sn struggling: pckd 4 out: wknd next* **11/4**[1]

0203 **8** *7* **Qulinton (FR)**[41] 4460 7-11-4 **127**... CO'Farrell(3) 97
(David Pipe) *nvr gng pce to get on terms: a towards rr* **4/1**[2]

3032 **9** *39* **Cortinas (GER)**[23] 4934 9-10-9 **115**....................................(t) IanPopham 60
(Claire Dyson) *a towards rr: t.o fr 4 out* **16/1**

4m 1.40s (-5.30) **Going Correction** -0.30s/f (Good) **9** Ran SP% **113.8**
Speed ratings: **100,99,93,89,86 85,81,78,60**
toteswingers:1&2 £15.80, 2&3 £10.70, 1&3 £7.20 CSF £91.47 CT £576.09 TOTE £8.30: £2.90, £4.20, £1.90; EX 118.70 Trifecta £417.80 Pool: £790.55 - 1.40 winning units..
Owner Mr & Mrs A J Mutch **Bred** Dunmanway Breeding Club **Trained** Briery Hill, Blaenau Gwent

FOCUS
Two came clear in the straight in this fair handicap chase. The form is solid and the winner is rated to his best.

NOTEBOOK
Cruchain(IRE) got the better jump of the pair at the last, holding on well for his first success since joining Dai Burchell. Back to form when second off 3lb lower at Ludlow last time, he jumped much better than he has done in the past and seemed helped by the return to 2m. (tchd 8-1)
Riguez Dancer may well have won but for getting the last wrong. He had struggled in more competitive races the last twice and, despite receiving little relief from the handicapper, almost pulled this off. (op 12-1)
Quipe Me Posted(FR) was 4lb higher than when finishing second at Chepstow and looks in the handicapper's grip now. (op 5-1 tchd 6-1)
Mam Ratagan ran well for a long way on this return from 124 days off. (op 8-1)
My Moment(IRE) Official explanation: trainer said gelding finished distressed
Anquetta(IRE), who ran well when sixth off this mark in the Grand Annual, failed to repeat the form and may have had enough for the season. (op 3-1)
Cortinas(GER) Official explanation: jockey said gelding hung and jumped right-handed

5306 ENDSLEIGH INSURANCE MARES' STANDARD OPEN NATIONAL HUNT FLAT RACE 2m 1f
5:40 (5:41) (Class 4) 4-6-Y-0 **£4,878** (£1,432; £716; £357)

Form RPR

1 **Golden Firebird (IRE)** 4-10-7 0.................................. RobertThornton 108+
(Alan King) *mid-div: hdwy over 3f out: nt clr run and swtchd rt 2f out: led ent fnl f: styd on wl to assert fnl 75yds* **10/1**

22 **2** *1 ¾* **Florafern**[48] 4335 6-10-10 0... CharlieHuxley(3) 112+
(Oliver Sherwood) *hld up towards rr: stdy prog fr over 6f out: led over 2f out: sn rdn: narrowly hdd ent fnl f: kpt on but no ex fnl 75yds* **11/2**[3]

3 *1 ½* **Carole's Destiny** 4-10-0 0...................................... JeremiahMcGrath(7) 105
(Nicky Henderson) *mid-div: hdwy to trck ldrs 5f out: rdn and ev ch over 2f out: styd on same pce fr over 1f out* **7/2**[1]

4 *1 ¾* **Flat Cap Thursday** 4-10-7 0... TimmyMurphy 103
(Murty McGrath) *mid-div: hdwy 3f out: sn rdn: styd on wout rching ldrs* **33/1**

5 *9* **One More Cookie (IRE)** 5-10-13 0.. JoeTizzard 101
(Colin Tizzard) *mid-div tl dropped in rr over 7f out u.p: wl bhd 3f out: styd on wl fnl 2f: wnt 5th ins fnl f* **6/1**

56 **6** *3* **Ballyquin Queen (IRE)**[33] 4728 5-10-13 0.................. RichardJohnson 98
(Philip Hobbs) *led tl 5f out: prom: rdn to ld again briefly over 2f out: hung lft and fdd ent fnl f* **4/1**[2]

0 **7** *hd* **Double Silver**[63] 4027 4-10-7 0... DarylJacob 92
(Keith Reveley) *hld up towards rr: styd on fnl 2f: nvr trbld ldrs* **40/1**

222 **8** *6* **Maid Of Silk (IRE)**[16] 5070 5-10-13 0...................................... APMcCoy 93
(Neil Mulholland) *trckd ldr: led 5f out: rdn and hdd over 2f out: sn wknd: dismntd after fin* **8/1**

9 *¾* **Oak Apple (IRE)** 5-10-13 0... RhysFlint 92
(Philip Hobbs) *in tch on outer: rdn over 2f out: wknd over 1f out* **28/1**

10 **10** *4 ½* **Who's Afraid**[72] 3876 4-11-0 0.. GerardTumelty 89
(Alan King) *rdn 4f out: nvr bttr than mid-div* **33/1**

236 **11** *3 ¾* **Young Mags (IRE)**[48] 4335 4-10-7 0........................ SamTwiston-Davies 80
(Nigel Twiston-Davies) *in tch: rdn 4f out: wknd over 1f out* **20/1**

06 **12** *½* **Star Potential**[16] 5070 4-10-2 0.. MarkQuinlan(5) 78
(Susan Gardner) *chsd ldrs tl wknd over 3f out* **100/1**

13 *6* **Legendary Hop**[39] 5-10-13 0... TomMessenger 79
(Chris Bealby) *trckd ldrs tl wknd over 2f out* **16/1**

14 *14* **Fruit Yoghurt** 5-10-13 0.. AndrewThornton 66
(Simon Earle) *a towards rr* **33/1**

00 **15** *nse* **On The Raz**[9] 5158 4-10-7 0... NickScholfield 60
(Jacqueline Retter) *mid-div tl wknd over 4f out* **100/1**

5-00 **16** *21* **Call Me Friday**[52] 4055 5-10-6 0.......................................(t) MrJBanks(7) 47
(Matthew Salaman) *mid-div tl wknd over 4f out* **50/1**

4 **P** **Timeforagin**[19] 5005 4-10-2 0... CO'Farrell(5) —
(Brian Eckley) *chsd ldrs tl over 5f out: sn wknd: eased and p.u 2f out* **66/1**

3m 59.1s (-6.60) **Going Correction** -0.30s/f (Good) **17** Ran SP% **122.9**
Speed ratings: **103,102,101,100,96 95,94,92,91,89 87,87,84,78,78 68,—**
toteswingers: 1&2 £7.40, 1&3 £9.20, 2&3 £5.60 CSF £59.65 TOTE £13.60: £3.50, £2.40, £2.00; EX 104.00 Trifecta £234.10 Pool: £474.71 - 1.50 winning units..
Owner Mel Fordham **Bred** Christopher Maye **Trained** Barbury Castle, Wilts

FOCUS
This is often a competitive mares' bumper. There were several performances of note and the race should produce its share of winners. The winner should go on to rate higher.

NOTEBOOK
Golden Firebird(IRE), whose dam is a half-sister to Trabolgan, was the chosen mount of Robert Thornton and she very much travelled like a decent filly. One may have expected the more experienced runner-up to get the better of her racing into the final furlong, but she showed a willing attitude and is the type to do well over hurdles next season. (op 11-1 tchd 12-1)
Florafern, representing last year's winning stable, had finished runner-up on both previous starts and was again forced to settle for that position. She too travelled well and looks a ready-made winner once hurdling.\n\x\x This was a pleasing debut from \bCarole's Destiny\p, a half-sister to the admirable Carole's Legacy. She couldn't quicken on with the front pair, but should have learnt plenty and can win a bumper before going hurdling.\n (op 5-1)
Carole's Destiny, a half-sister to the admirable Carole's Legacy as well as Mad Max, made a pleasing debut. She couldn't quicken on with the front pair, but should have learnt plenty and can win a bumper before going hurdling. (tchd 3-1 and 4-1)
Flat Cap Thursday was going on nicely at the finish and should improve plenty for the experience.
One More Cookie(IRE) caught the eye as, having been outpaced, finished with a real flourish to take fifth. She's going to want a stiffer test over hurdles. (tchd 8-1)
Ballyquin Queen(IRE), sixth in a valuable mares' Listed bumper at Sandown last time, was ridden positively, but was completely found wanting for pace in the straight. She'll want at least 2m4f over hurdles. (tchd 9-2)
Double Silver built on her debut effort, showing plenty of promise in keeping on late.
Oak Apple(IRE), a half-sister to Kicks For Free, showed ability before fading and could be of interest in something similar before hurdling. (op 22-1)
Timeforagin Official explanation: jockey said filly lost its action behind
T/Plt: £146.90 to a £1 stake. Pool of £99,370.97 - 493.80 winning units. T/Qpdt: £37.40 to a £1 stake. Pool of £119.00 - 6023.15 winning units. TM

4993 SEDGEFIELD (L-H)
Thursday, April 14

OFFICIAL GOING: Good to firm (firm in places on hurdle course; chs 7.8, hdl 8.7)
Wind: moderate 1/2 behind Weather: overcast

5307 SIS LIVE H'CAP HURDLE (8 hdls) 2m 1f
4:50 (4:52) (Class 5) (0-95,95) 4-Y-O+ **£1,821** (£534; £267; £133)

Form RPR
0600 **1** **Mycenean Prince (USA)**[11] 5130 8-10-12 **86**............... BrianToomey(5) 92
(Karen Tutty) *mde all: reminders 4th: jnd 2 out: hld on gamely run-in* **20/1**
6052 **2** ½ **The Tiddly Tadpole**[21] 4977 6-11-5 **95**........................... MrSFMagee(7) 101
(Simon West) *trckd ldrs: chsd wnr 3 out: upsides next: no ex towards fin* **13/2**[2]
F600 **3** 4 **Veronicas Boy**[39] 4508 5-11-10 **93**...............................(v) JasonMaguire 95
(George Moore) *chsd wnr: kpt on one pce fr 3 out* **8/1**
0102 **4** 18 **Won More Night**[21] 4965 9-11-3 **86**..................................(t) TomSiddall 73
(Martin Keighley) *hld up in rr: hmpd 3rd: hdwy 3 out: tk modest 4th last* **7/1**[3]
/056 **5** 1½ **Danny Cool**[20] 4995 8-11-3 **86**.. JamesReveley 70
(Keith Reveley) *hld up in rr: bhd and drvn 5th: sme hdwy appr 2 out: nvr a factor* **16/1**
0-04 **6** 1¼ **Lisbon Lion (IRE)**[21] 4958 6-11-5 **88**................................. PaddyAspell 71
(James Moffatt) *in rr: sme hdwy 5th: wknd after next* **33/1**
4-30 **7** nk **Whaston (IRE)**[13] 3855 6-11-12 **95**...............................(vt) BrianHughes 78
(Pauline Robson) *chsd ldrs: mstke 3rd: wknd appr 2 out* **8/1**
0000 **8** ½ **Darkan Road**[57] 4145 6-11-2 **85**....................................... JanFaltejsek 69
(George Charlton) *in rr: bhd and drvn 5th* **33/1**
3000 **9** 42 **Wicked Streak (IRE)**[153] 2349 6-10-11 **90**................. JoeCollivier(10) 35
(Micky Hammond) *chsd ldrs: lost pl 3 out: bhd whn heavily eased run-in: t.o* **11/1**
-000 **B** **Faith And Reason (USA)**[146] 2508 8-11-7 **95**...........(p) MissLHorner(5) —
(Chris Grant) *hld up towards rr: b.d 3 out* **33/1**
400U **U** **Danehillsundance (IRE)**[43] 4422 7-11-3 **86**.....................(t) BarryKeniry —
(Philip Kirby) *trckd ldrs: blnd and uns rdr 3rd* **9/4**[1]
0F04 **F** **Sheepclose (IRE)**[32] 4743 6-11-2 **85**.................................. GrahamLee —
(Michael Easterby) *trckd ldrs: 5th whn fell 3 out* **8/1**
4m 2.50s (-4.40) **Going Correction** -0.175s/f (Good) **12** Ran SP% **117.7**
Speed ratings (Par 103): **103,102,100,92,91 91,90,90,70,— —,—**
toteswingers:1&2 £35.00, 2&3 £15.30, 1&3 £20.00 CSF £140.66 CT £1132.62 TOTE £32.50: £6.70, £1.02, £3.40; EX 91.10.
Owner N D Tutty **Bred** Benjamin W Berger And Shadwell Farm Llc **Trained** Osmotherley, N Yorks
■ Stewards' Enquiry : Brian Toomey five-day ban: use of whip (TBA)

FOCUS
A moderate but competitive contest. The early pace looked to be sound. The winner is rated to his C&D mark in January, 3lb below his best.

NOTEBOOK
Mycenean Prince(USA) was allowed an easy lead and stayed on well as the challengers stacked up. Perhaps the change of jockey made the difference, as he certainly wasn't easy to fancy on recent form. (op 16-1)
The Tiddly Tadpole shaped well on his handicap debut last time and tracked the leader here. Travelling nicely, he seemed sure to go past but couldn't or wouldn't. (op 11-2 tchd 7-1)
Veronicas Boy was taking a big drop in trip here and wisely sat close to the lead considering the distance. He kept on under pressure after holding every chance but couldn't raise his game. (op 15-2 tchd 13-2)
Won More Night ran a couple of good races in March, but never threatened here after being restrained in rear. (op 9-2 tchd 15-2)
Whaston(IRE) isn't that exposed over hurdles but hit the third hurdle hard just before the plunge horse departed. He got back into things but became outpaced turning in. (op 6-1)
Danehillsundance(IRE), making his handicap debut over hurdles, looked to have a great chance if returning to his best Flat performances for David Brown, and attracted an avalanche of support from an opening show of 11-1. Settled in midfield, he took off too early at the third and unshipped his jockey. (op 7-1)
Sheepclose(IRE) fell when looking held and brought down Faith And Reason. (op 7-1)

5308 CLEANER AIR SOLUTIONS FREE SOLAR ELECTRICITY H'CAP HURDLE (10 hdls) 2m 5f 110y
5:25 (5:27) (Class 5) (0-95,95) 4-Y-O+ **£1,723** (£506; £253; £126)

Form RPR
2226 **1** **Classic Henri**[21] 4960 7-11-0 **88**.................................... PaulGallagher(5) 92+
(Barry Murtagh) *trckd ldrs: mstke 6th: led 2 out: hld on towards fin: lame* **8/1**
6064 **2** ¾ **Hoar Frost**[11] 5130 6-11-0 **90**.. MissGTutty(7) 91
(Karen Tutty) *mid-div: lost pl and reminders 6th: hdwy 3 out: wnt 2nd sn after last: kpt on wl: no ex towards fin* **18/1**
0053 **3** 2¾ **Border Tale**[36] 4550 11-11-2 **85**.......................................(v) BrianHughes 85
(James Moffatt) *in rr div: hdwy appr 3 out: styd on fr 2 out: 5th last: tk 3rd nr fin* **5/1**[2]
0333 **4** nse **The Fox's Decree**[18] 5040 7-11-12 **95**..........................(tp) JasonMaguire 95
(Martin Keighley) *chsd ldrs: reminders after 5th: outpcd after 3 out: hrd rdn and rallied: cl 4th whn hit last: kpt on same pce* **5/1**[2]
2602 **5** 1¼ **I'm Your Man**[20] 4994 12-11-4 **90**...............................(p) JamesHalliday(3) 89
(Evelyn Slack) *w ldrs: led after 4th: hdd after next: led after 3 out: hdd 2 out: one pce run-in* **18/1**
5600 **6** ¾ **Tears From Heaven (USA)**[18] 5027 5-10-13 **82**................ BarryKeniry 79
(Mrs S Sunter) *reluctant and led to s: last whn j. slowly 1st: hrd drvn 7th: hdwy appr next: kpt on fr 2 out: nvr a threat* **50/1**
0633 **7** 2¼ **Waltham Abbey**[13] 5094 10-10-4 **80**....................................... MrRUtley(7) 76
(Lynsey Kendall) *w ldrs: led after 5th: hdd after 3 out: hung lft and fdd appr last* **9/2**[1]
2542 **8** ¾ **Sambelucky (IRE)**[29] 4814 6-11-3 **86**................................ JamesReveley 80
(Keith Reveley) *in rr: hdwy appr 2 out: nvr trbld ldrs* **7/1**[3]
P001 **9** ½ **Mardood**[20] 4994 6-10-13 **87**...(v) AlexanderVoy(5) 81
(Chris Grant) *mid-div: hdwy 4th: lost pl 7th: hdwy appr 2 out: no threat* **10/1**
0/30 **10** 15 **Harps Counsel (IRE)**[18] 5042 9-11-5 **95**.......................(t) MrSFMagee(7) 80
(J K Magee, Ire) *led tl after 4th: lost pl appr 2 out: eased run-in* **16/1**
0U44 **11** 10 **I Witness (IRE)**[26] 4872 9-10-10 **86**...........................(t) AlistairFindlay(7) 57
(Jane Walton) *chsd ldrs 3rd: lost pl 7th: bhd whn eased fr 2 out* **25/1**
2103 **12** 20 **Scrum V**[32] 4738 7-11-12 **95**.. PaddyAspell 48
(John Davies) *in rr div: sme hdwy 6th: sn wknd: t.o 2 out: eased run-in* **20/1**
60/P **13** 39 **Pumboo (FR)**[40] 4465 8-11-0 **83**....................................(t) CampbellGillies 1
(Geoffrey Harker) *in rr: hdwy 6th: lost pl next: t.o 2 out: virtually p.u* **66/1**
0505 **R** **Buckden (IRE)**[266] 1065 7-10-13 **82**....................................... HenryOliver —
(Sue Smith) *in rr: sn pushed along: rn out 5th* **20/1**
5m 14.7s (0.10) **Going Correction** -0.175s/f (Good) **14** Ran SP% **117.4**
Speed ratings (Par 103): **92,91,90,90,90 89,89,88,88,83 79,72,58,—**
toteswingers:1&2 £37.80, 2&3 £37.10, 1&3 £4.40 CSF £126.32 CT £796.74 TOTE £11.10: £3.90, £8.60, £3.10; EX 158.70.
Owner Anthony White **Bred** Wood Farm Stud **Trained** Low Braithwaite, Cumbria

FOCUS
The bookmakers made it 9-2 the field, showing how open this low-grade affair was. Solid enough form, the winner rated in line with last month's course run.

NOTEBOOK
Classic Henri made a forward move down the back straight and really got going heading towards two out. He got to the front but took his time to get away, and hit the last hard before staying on well enough to gain success. His best two performances prior to this success came at Sedgefield, so he clearly likes this track. That said, he finished sore. (tchd 17-2)
Hoar Frost needed some strong driving after losing her place, but almost won. She found the winner too resilient in the final stages but did well to get as close as she did. (op 12-1)
Border Tale made late progress after needing to be pushed along. (op 13-2)
The Fox's Decree didn't make his jockey's life easy under pressure, but the pair still had a chance of victory coming to the last before knocking that hurdle out of the ground. (op 7-1)
I'm Your Man was one of three that dominated early, and ran a belter for his advancing years. (op 16-1 tchd 14-1)
Tears From Heaven(USA), who was reluctant to go to the start, made late progress after needing to be pushed along.
Waltham Abbey helped to share the early work, but didn't get home after appearing to hang left coming to the final hurdle. (op 7-1)
I Witness(IRE) Official explanation: jockey said gelding finished distressed
Pumboo(FR) travelled strongly while held up and doesn't look totally devoid of ability despite his final position. (op 50-1)
Buckden(IRE) took his time to get out on the course, and caused one of the two false starts. Racing in rear, he ran out before the fifth and isn't one to trust. (op 22-1)

5309 JOHN WADE EARTHWORKS & DEMOLITION MAIDEN HURDLE (QUALIFIER) (8 hdls) 2m 1f
5:55 (5:57) (Class 5) 4-Y-O+ **£1,951** (£573; £286; £143)

Form RPR
03 **1** **Odin's Raven (IRE)**[27] 4859 6-10-9 0............................ BrianToomey(5) 103
(Brian Ellison) *hld up in rr: stdy hdwy 5th: chsng ldng pair appr 2 out: 2nd and swtchd rt last: edgd lft and led run-in: cleverley* **8/1**[3]
53 **2** 1 **Strathcal**[11] 5131 5-11-0 0... AndrewTinkler 103
(Anna Brooks) *nt fluent: trckd ldrs: led 3 out: hdd briefly appr next: hit last: crowded: hdd and no ex run-in* **10/11**[1]
043 **3** 4 **Rear Admiral (IRE)**[32] 4743 5-11-0 0..................................... GrahamLee 98
(Michael Easterby) *t.k.h: sn trcking ldrs: upsides 3 out: led appr next: hit 2 out and hdd: wknd last* **11/4**[2]
5344 **4** 16 **Think Green**[36] 4554 5-10-7 0... FearghalDavis 76
(James Ewart) *chsd ldrs: outpcd and lost pl after 5th: poor 6th 2 out: kpt on to take modest 4th nr fin* **25/1**
5 1 **Cause For Applause (IRE)**[49] 5-10-7 0................................ PaddyAspell 75
(Ray Craggs) *hld up in rr: hdwy 5th: modest 4th appr 2 out: one pce* **100/1**
6 4½ **Castlebury (IRE)**[14] 6-11-0 0...(b) BrianHughes 78
(Ruth Carr) *trckd ldrs: t.k.h: outpcd and 5th whn hit 2 out: sn wknd* **80/1**
4030 **7** shd **Dizzy River (IRE)**[18] 5028 6-11-0 0...................................... JanFaltejsek 78
(George Charlton) *chsd ldrs: outpcd 5th: lost pl next* **25/1**
8 1¼ **Twisted**[15] 5-11-0 0.. RobertWalford 76
(Michael Easterby) *t.k.h in rr: bhd and drvn 5th* **33/1**
4 **9** 8 **It's A Mans World**[18] 5028 5-11-0 0....................................... TomSiddall 69
(Kevin M Prendergast) *sn trcking ldrs: led 3rd: hdd 3 out: sn lost pl* **20/1**
0 **10** 2½ **Cauldron**[59] 4117 4-10-8 0.. RichieMcGrath 61
(Tim Easterby) *in rr: bhd fr 3 out* **100/1**
0 **11** 15 **Eco Boxer (IRE)**[21] 4974 7-10-7 0..................................... MrCGreene(7) 53
(Nick Kent) *led to 4th: rdn and lost pl after 3 out: sn bhd* **150/1**
P **12** ½ **Baralaka**[101] 3358 4-10-8 0.. WilsonRenwick 47
(Rose Dobbin) *in tch: outpcd and lost pl 5th: bhd fr next: eased* **16/1**
4m 6.40s (-0.50) **Going Correction** -0.175s/f (Good)
WFA 4 from 5yo+ 5lb **12** Ran SP% **115.3**
Speed ratings (Par 103): **94,93,91,84,83 81,81,80,77,75 68,68**
toteswingers:1&2 £1.20, 2&3 £1.80, 1&3 £2.80 CSF £15.12 TOTE £4.10: £1.10, £1.40, £1.70; EX 19.20.
Owner Racing Management & Training Ltd **Bred** Newberry Stud Company **Trained** Norton, N Yorks

FOCUS
A maiden lacking any depth and run at a steady pace. Modest form, the first three rated pretty much to their marks.

NOTEBOOK

Odin's Raven(IRE), having his third start over hurdles, wasn't disgraced at a big price last time at Fakenham (form is ordinary) and, despite weaving from one side of the course to the other down the home straight, he won this comfortably. He'll presumably now head into handicaps. (tchd 17-2)

Strathcal appeared to be going in the right direction. Punters certainly felt he was, as he attracted strong support at short odds, and after tracking the leaders he got to the front after three out but couldn't hold the late thrust of the winner. (op 5-4)

Rear Admiral(IRE) showed promise on his initial try over hurdles last month, and again here before finding the final stages just a bit too much. He has plenty of size about him and surely has improvement to come. (op 5-2 tchd 3-1)

Think Green didn't look devoid of ability in bumpers and will surely find opportunities over hurdles in time.

Castlebury(IRE), plating class on the Flat, showed up really well until three out.

Baralaka was really disappointing on his debut for these connections after showing plenty on the Flat for Sir Mark Prescott, and didn't do much better here. (op 12-1)

5310 COLLINS SEAFOODS NOVICES' CHASE (QUALIFIER) (PART OF COLLINS SEAFOOD YOUNG CHASERS SERIES) (16 fncs) 2m 5f

6:25 (6:25) (Class 4) 5-Y-0+ **£2,992** (£878; £439; £219)

Form RPR

23U4 **1** **Benny Be Good**[26] 4867 8-11-5 127 .... JamesReveley 135+
(Keith Reveley) *trckd ldrs: led 12th: styd on strly fr 2 out* **11/4**[1]

1505 **2** *4* **Hollo Ladies (IRE)**[7] 5165 6-11-5 138 .... GrahamLee 127
(Ferdy Murphy) *t.k.h: trckd ldrs: lft cl 2nd 12th: rdn appr 2 out: kpt on same pce: no imp* **7/2**[2]

P50P **3** *32* **Frosty Spring**[21] 4975 8-10-5 0 .... DaveCrosse 87
(David Thompson) *w ldr: led 2nd: hdd 9th: wknd bef 3 out* **200/1**

3405 **4** *3 ¾* **Currahee**[10] 5149 7-10-12 0 .... (t) MichaelMcAlister 88
(Maurice Barnes) *hit 2nd: mstke 7th: drvn to chse ldrs after next: nt fluent 10th: wknd 13th* **16/1**

2402 **5** *9* **Flying Doctor**[10] 5146 8-10-12 127 .... PeterCarberry[(7)] 90
(Elliott Cooper) *chsd ldrs: drvn 9th: blnd 11th: sn wknd* **8/1**

0-00 **U** **Sadler's Cove (FR)**[79] 3728 13-10-9 71 .... (t) JamesO'Farrell[(3)] —
(J K Magee, Ire) *bdly hmpd and uns rdr bnd bef 1st* **250/1**

0310 **U** **Film Festival (USA)**[27] 4853 8-11-7 131 .... PaulGallagher[(5)] —
(Brian Ellison) *led to 2nd: w ldr: led 9th: hdd whn blnd and uns rdr 12th* **4/1**[3]

2-3P **S** **Pontop (IRE)**[330] 396 8-10-12 0 .... JanFaltejsek —
(George Charlton) *trcking ldrs: clipped heels and slipped up on bnd bef 1st* **7/2**[2]

5m 11.5s (-6.50) **Going Correction** -0.175s/f (Good) **8** Ran SP% **109.0**

Speed ratings: **105,103,91,89,86** —,—,—

toteswingers:1&2: £4.10, 2&3: Not won. 1&3: Not won. CSF £11.86 TOTE £4.20: £3.30, £1.02, £46.50; EX 16.20.

Owner John Wade **Bred** Maurice Ramshaw **Trained** Lingdale, Redcar & Cleveland

FOCUS

There was early drama in this useful contest with two out before the first fence. The form is rated around the first two.

NOTEBOOK

Benny Be Good, returning to fences, travelled smoothly in behind and showed a good attitude under pressure to maintain the advantage he gained over the runner-up. His record at this course reads an impressive 131211. (op 3-1 tchd 5-2)

Hollo Ladies(IRE), who was miles behind the winner at this course last November, hasn't shown a lot after landing a race at Southwell, but this looked a bit better after racing more handily than of late. (op 3-1 tchd 11-4)

Frosty Spring, whose dam loved to get her head in front, and went without the cheekpieces she tried last time, ran respectably considering her odds. She should be able to make an impact in a low-grade chase in due course. (op 150-1)

Currahee needed plenty of driving from an early stage and failed to get competitive. (tchd 20-1)

Flying Doctor was dropping in trip for this and probably ended any chance he had with a mistake at the 11th. (op 13-2 tchd 6-1)

Film Festival(USA), taking an drop in grade after being tried in the Grand Annual last time, lost his rider at the 12th when jumping into the back of the winner, who had just edged past him. The horse lost his footing momentarily and gave his jockey no chance of staying in the saddle. (op 5-1)

Pontop(IRE), absent since pulling up at Hexham last year, tripped rounding the first bend before any fences had been jumped, sending his rider to the ground. (op 5-1)

5311 KNOWLEDGE IT 30TH ANNIVERSARY H'CAP CHASE (21 fncs) 3m 3f

6:55 (6:55) (Class 5) (0-95,95) 5-Y-0+ **£2,211** (£649; £324; £162)

Form RPR

3-06 **1** **Esme Rides A Gaine**[298] 804 9-11-2 85 .... PaddyAspell 100+
(Christopher Wilson) *led to 2nd: chsd ldrs 11th: led after 3 out: drew wl clr between last 2: 17 l ahd last: heavily eased* **9/1**

36P3 **2** *13* **Toulouse Express (IRE)**[13] 5097 12-10-10 79 .... (v) KennyJohnson 74
(Robert Johnson) *led 2nd: jnd 3 out: sn hdd: one pce* **9/2**

32P0 **3** *9* **Moon Melody (GER)**[20] 4994 8-10-13 82 .... CampbellGillies 69
(Mike Sowersby) *in rr: sme hdwy 15th: poor 3rd 3 out* **8/1**

6005 **4** *nk* **Play The Rock (FR)**[13] 5096 8-10-3 72 .... (p) JamesReveley 61
(Philip Kirby) *j.rt in rr: blnd 14th: disp poor 3rd 2 out: one pce* **10/3**[2]

/22- **5** *46* **Snake Rave (IRE)**[396] 9-11-7 95 .... PaulGallagher[(5)] 56
(Henry Hogarth) *mstke 4th: wnt modest 13 13th: hit next: hit 16th: wknd 3 out: sn bhd: virtually p.u run-in: t.o* **4/1**[3]

2222 **P** **Jeringa**[20] 4997 12-11-9 92 .... (b) BrianHughes —
(John Wade) *chsd ldr 3rd: struggling 11th: lost pl and bhd whn p.u after 13th* **11/4**[1]

6m 52.1s (3.10) **Going Correction** -0.175s/f (Good) **6** Ran SP% **109.0**

Speed ratings: **88,84,81,81,67** —

toteswingers:1&2 £12.40, 2&3 £10.70, 1&3 £5.60 CSF £44.86 TOTE £10.30: £12.90, £4.10; EX 63.90.

Owner Mrs J Wilson (durham) **Bred** Mrs H M Woods **Trained** Manfield, N Yorks

FOCUS

Even though the six runners had 3m3f to travel, the pace throughout looked sound. The easy winner is rated up 7lb on her best 2009 form.

NOTEBOOK

Esme Rides A Gaine, absent since June, is a low-grade performer and needed a reminder relatively early here, so the fact she won this easily confirms how weak this contest was. One can only guess what to expect from her next time considering her race record, but she does handle this firmish ground when others may not. (tchd 10-1)

Toulouse Express(IRE) is well handicapped on his winning form and likes this course. He soon assumed command, gaining a decent advantage, and got every runner stretched before losing his lead to the staying-on winner. (tchd 5-1)

Moon Melody(GER), back over fences after three runs over hurdles but without cheekpieces this time, got behind and was never involved. (op 11-2)

Play The Rock(FR) didn't look straightforward last time and made no impression here. (op 4-1)

Jeringa travelled strongly chasing the leader early but steadily lost his place and was swiftly pulled up with a circuit to go. Official explanation: jockey said gelding never travelled and became distressed (op 3-1 tchd 5-2)

5312 COLLINS SEAFOODS H'CAP CHASE (13 fncs) 2m 110y

7:25 (7:25) (Class 4) (0-115,115) 5-Y-0+ **£2,992** (£878; £439; £219)

Form RPR

46U4 **1** **Tranos (USA)**[139] 2656 8-10-0 89 oh3 .... WilsonRenwick 99+
(Micky Hammond) *in rr: hit 3rd: hdwy 10th: sn trcking ldrs: wnt 2nd 2 out: shkn up to ld appr last: j.lft and hit last: pushed clr: eased towards fin* **10/1**

2315 **2** *13* **Schinken Otto (IRE)**[142] 2601 10-10-8 100 .... JamesHalliday[(3)] 103
(Malcolm Jefferson) *w ldr: led 4th: hdd after next: led 10th: hdd appr last: eased whn no ch w wnr last 100yds* **7/1**[3]

3F12 **3** *8* **Gavroche Gaugain (FR)**[30] 4800 7-10-2 98 .... TonyKelly[(7)] 92
(Ferdy Murphy) *trckd ldrs: wl outpcd appr 2 out: tk modest 3rd last* **7/2**[1]

22-P **4** *19* **Sea Venture (IRE)**[333] 352 9-11-6 109 .... RobertWalford 93
(Tim Walford) *t.k.h: trckd ldrs 7th: wknd between last 2: fdd bdly run-in* **15/2**

463U **P** **Poseidon (GER)**[13] 5093 9-10-1 90 .... (p) BrianHughes —
(John Wade) *led to 4th: reminders after next: led after 6th: nt fluent next: hdd 10th: sn lost pl and bhd: t.o whn p.u bef 2 out* **7/2**[1]

2-3P **F** **Braddock Island**[13] 5093 8-10-3 92 .... BarryKeniry —
(Mrs S Sunter) *t.k.h: trckd ldrs 3rd: 3rd and ev ch whn fell 3 out* **7/1**[3]

0104 **B** **Cranky Corner**[33] 4716 7-11-7 115 .... ShaneByrne[(5)] —
(Sue Smith) *chsd ldrs: reminders 6th: drvn 8th: 6th and drvn whn b.d 3 out* **4/1**[2]

4m 7.40s (-1.20) **Going Correction** -0.175s/f (Good) **7** Ran SP% **110.3**

Speed ratings: **95,88,85,76,**— —,—

toteswingers:1&2 £12.40, 2&3 £10.70, 1&3 £5.60 CSF £68.80 CT £278.87 TOTE £14.20: £3.60, £1.50; EX 55.60.

Owner Joe Buzzeo **Bred** Green Gates Farm **Trained** Middleham Moor, N Yorks

FOCUS

The field ran in a bunch for much of the race, as nothing seemed to want to go on, and this isn't reliable form. The winner is rated in line with his early-season efforts.

NOTEBOOK

Tranos(USA), without a success since July 2008, settled in the rear before passing all of his rivals and winning easily. He was 3lb out of the handicap for this returning from a long break, so it remains to be seen whether he can claim a second win over fences next time. (op 11-1)

Schinken Otto(IRE) enjoys this course but looked a little high in the weights. He helped to set the early fractions and almost stole it from the front. (op 11-2)

Gavroche Gaugain(FR), 9lb higher than his win in March, raced close up but came under pressure after four out and found only the one pace. (op 3-1)

Sea Venture(IRE), off since May last year, travelled smoothly wide of the field but may have needed the run. He ideally wants further. (op 7-1 tchd 8-1)

Poseidon(GER) had the cheekpieces kept on and attracted market support despite some ordinary efforts. It wasn't a massive surprise to see him run below expectations considering his chasing form. (op 11-2)

Braddock Island was still in with every chance when falling. (op 11-2)

Cranky Corner was sat behind a wall of horses throughout, causing him to have little room to manoeuvre at the fences. He was tripped over by Braddock Island when he fell in front of him three from home. (op 11-2)

5313 CLEANERAIRSOLUTIONS.CO.UK SOLAR POWERED STANDARD OPEN NATIONAL HUNT FLAT RACE 2m 1f

7:55 (7:55) (Class 6) 4-6-Y-0 **£1,431** (£420; £210; £104)

Form RPR

13 **1** **Bahira (IRE)**[16] 5070 4-10-12 0 .... JasonMaguire 96+
(Donald McCain) *led early: trckd ldrs: led 3f out: rdn 8 l clr 1f out: eased clsng stages* **7/4**[1]

2 *3 ½* **An Capall Mor (IRE)** 5-10-11 0 .... MrSFMagee[(7)] 95+
(Simon West) *hld up in rr: hdwy 6f out: wnt 3rd over 2f out: chsd wnr over 1f out: kpt on wl* **11/1**

3 *12* **Swaledale Lad (IRE)** 4-10-2 0 .... JoeColliver[(10)] 78+
(Micky Hammond) *trckd ldrs: t.k.h: sddle slipped after 7f: one pce fnl 3f* **12/1**

4 *2 ½* **Walser (IRE)** 4-10-7 0 .... PaulGallagher[(5)] 76
(Howard Johnson) *mid-div: drvn 7f out: one pce fnl 3f* **3/1**[2]

1 **5** *1* **Solaise (IRE)**[124] 2896 6-11-8 0 .... JamesO'Farrell[(3)] 88
(Liam Corcoran) *trckd ldrs: wnt 2nd over 2f out: wknd over 1f out* **10/1**

6 *1 ½* **Tikkandemickey (IRE)** 5-11-4 0 .... WilsonRenwick 80
(Raymond Shiels) *t.k.h in rr: hdwy 9f out: hung lft and one pce fnl 3f* **50/1**

7 *14* **Saut Du Cerf (FR)** 5-11-4 0 .... JamesReveley 67
(Andrew Crook) *sn led: hdd 3f out: lost pl over 1f out* **33/1**

1/5- **8** *1 ½* **Chickini (IRE)**[388] 4785 6-10-11 0 .... KyleJames[(7)] 66
(Simon Waugh) *t.k.h: trckd ldrs: drvn over 4f out: lost pl over 2f out* **25/1**

9 *1 ¼* **Little Missmoffatt** 6-10-11 0 .... BrianHughes 57
(Ann Hamilton) *trckd ldrs: rdn over 4f out: wknd over 2f out* **8/1**[3]

10 *2* **King Of Thorns (IRE)** 4-10-12 0 .... BarryKeniry 57
(George Moore) *in rr: drvn 7f out: lost pl over 4f out: sn wl bhd* **16/1**

30 **11** *34* **Count Vettori (IRE)**[31] 4780 5-11-4 0 .... CampbellGillies 32
(David Thompson) *in rr: bhd fnl 5f: sn t.o* **40/1**

12 *5* **Westendjack** 4-10-5 0 .... MissAngelaBarnes[(7)] 22
(Maurice Barnes) *mid-div: lost pl over 3f out: sn wl bhd: t.o: lame* **40/1**

4m 4.20s (2.90) **Going Correction** -0.175s/f (Good)

WFA 4 from 5yo+ 5lb **12** Ran SP% **117.1**

Speed ratings: **86,84,78,77,77 76,69,69,68,67 51,49**

toteswingers:1&2 £8.40, 2&3 £25.30, 1&3 £7.50 CSF £21.24 TOTE £3.20: £1.50, £4.50, £4.70; EX 26.30.

Owner Blue Belle Bud **Bred** Tom Cross **Trained** Cholmondeley, Cheshire

FOCUS

A really ordinary race of its type. Arguably a small step up from the cosy winner.

NOTEBOOK

Bahira(IRE) was strongly supported and sat in an ideal stalking position as the race unfolded. She got the break when needed in the home straight and flew clear to record an easy success. (op 2-1 tchd 11-8)

An Capall Mor(IRE) showed lots of potential after staying on strongly from the rear. He would have been a clear and impressive winner without Bahira. (op 12-1)

Swaledale Lad(IRE)'s saddle slipped forward quite early but that still didn't stop him getting into third. (op 9-1)

Walser(IRE) seemed a bit green in midfield while the race was taking shape and will no doubt be wiser next time. (op 9-2)

Solaise(IRE) looked to have obvious claims in a race of this nature, but he was friendless in the betting for some reason and weakened tamely in the final furlong. (op 15-2 tchd 11-1)

Little Missmoffatt, a daughter of the tough mare Deb's Ball, doesn't look very big. (op 10-1)

Westendjack Official explanation: vet said returned lame right-fore

T/Plt: £356.40 to a £1 stake. Pool of £60,548.42 - 124.00 winning tickets. T/Qpdt: £39.90 to a £1 state. Pool of £6,601.39 - 122.18 winning tickets. WG

4711 AYR (L-H)

Friday, April 15

OFFICIAL GOING: Good (good to soft in places; chs 7.7, hdl 7.8)

Wind: Slight, half against Weather: Overcast, dry

5314 WEST SOUND JUVENILE HURDLE (9 hdls) 2m

1:45 (1:46) (Class 3) 4-Y-O **£4,878** (£1,432; £716; £357)

Form				RPR
4	1		**Tonic Mellysse (FR)**[48] 4350 4-11-8 134 RWalsh (Paul Nicholls) *trckd ldrs: led on bit 3 out: qcknd clr bef last: v easily* 1/10[1]	128+
10	2	10	**Mason Hindmarsh**[16] 2356 4-11-8 0 GrahamLee (Karen McLintock) *cl up: led 4th: rdn and hdd 3 out: no ch w wnr fr next* 14/1[2]	109
	3	3 ½	**Sir Walter Raleigh**[13] 5122 4-10-12 0 PCarberry (C A McBratney, Ire) *hld up in tch: effrt whn hit 2 out: sn no imp: nt fluent last* 18/1[3]	98
2134	4	30	**Miereveld**[20] 4999 4-10-13 106 (v) PaulGallagher(5) (Brian Ellison) *led to 4th: cl up tl rdn and wknd 3 out* 14/1[2]	75
00	5	3	**Sixties Rock**[41] 4473 4-10-9 0 JamesHalliday(3) (William Young) *hld up: hit and rdn 4th: no ch fr 4 out* 150/1	66

3m 52.8s (-10.30) **Going Correction** -1.20s/f (Hard) **5** Ran SP% **110.2**

Speed ratings: **77,72,70,55,53**

CSF £2.91 TOTE £1.10: £1.10, £2.70; EX 2.40.

Owner Simon Munir **Bred** Armand Humeau **Trained** Ditcheat, Somerset

■ Stewards' Enquiry : R Walsh

FOCUS

The hurdles and chase tracks were on their innermost line, in order to provide fresh ground for the start of the two-day fixture. One rider in the first described the going as "slow", while another thought it was "beautiful" ground.\n\x\x This was a rather uncompetitive juvenile hurdle and the pace was fairly steady, contributing to a time nearly 14 seconds outside the standard. The easy winner was value for a lot further, with the second to his mark.

NOTEBOOK

Tonic Mellysse(FR) was also sent off favourite when fourth behind stablemate Zarkandar on his British debut in the Adonis at Kempton. Faced with a much simper task, he travelled strongly, impressed with his nimble jumping and ran out a very fluent winner, value for further. He proved in France that he handles testing ground well, but he appeared very much at home on this soundor surface too. Capable of stepping up considerably on the bare form, he could go for the Swinton Hurdle at Haydock next month. (op 2-13)

Mason Hindmarsh, a winner at Aintree first time out, was having his first run in this sphere since November. The best guide to this form's worth, he took over at halfway but the winner was in a different league on these terms.

Sir Walter Raleigh, a disappointing maiden on the Flat for Sir Michael Stoute, was well held on his hurdles debut at Gowran. He moved into third place approaching the second-last, but was immediately beaten after rapping the flight and probably needs a return to further. (op 16-1)

Miereveld has been beaten in selling and claiming company and looks something of a hard ride. The runner-up gave him competition for the lead and he was in trouble before the home turn.

Sixties Rock has now been soundly beaten on all three starts. (op 100-1)

5315 TAM O'SHANTER POPPYSCOTLAND H'CAP HURDLE (9 hdls) 2m

2:20 (2:20) (Class 3) (0-125,125) 4-Y-O+ **£4,878** (£1,432; £716; £357)

Form				RPR
021	1		**Remember Now (IRE)**[32] 4778 5-11-4 117 APMcCoy (Nicky Henderson) *t.k.h: hld up: stdy hdwy 4 out: led after 2 out: rdn and drew clr after last* 11/2[1]	128+
1-06	2	4	**Sure Josie Sure (FR)**[141] 2626 6-11-7 125 (t) CO'Farrell(5) (David Pipe) *chsd ldrs: wnt 2nd after 4 out: effrt and ev ch 2 out: rdn and blnd last: kpt on same pce* 6/1[2]	129+
12F4	3	1	**Teenage Idol (IRE)**[19] 5030 7-11-7 120 RyanMania (Evelyn Slack) *cl up: led 3rd tl rdn and hdd after 2 out: kpt on same pce fr last* 20/1	121
3311	4	hd	**Fujin Dancer (FR)**[28] 4858 6-10-11 117 MissHBethell(7) (Brian Ellison) *hld up: hdwy after 3 out: styd on wl run-in: nrst fin* 10/1	119
1543	5	1 ½	**Freddie Brown**[25] 4910 7-10-6 105 JanFaltejsek (George Charlton) *plld hrd: hld up in tch: effrt bef 2 out: kpt on same pce run-in* 9/1	105
F045	6	1	**Arisea (IRE)**[14] 5098 8-10-2 101 PaddyAspell (James Moffatt) *hld up: hdwy 3 out: styd on run-in: nrst fin* 66/1	100
-00P	7	1	**Toshi (USA)**[68] 3969 9-11-9 122 JasonMaguire (Jim Goldie) *hld up: smooth hdwy on outside and in tch 3 out: shkn up next: no imp whn hit last: no ex* 20/1	121
0042	8	3	**Culcabock (IRE)**[27] 4867 11-11-7 120 CampbellGillies (Lucinda Russell) *trckd ldrs: drvn and outpcd bef 3 out: plugged on run-in: no imp* 10/1	115
0606	9	nk	**Cassius (IRE)**[11] 5144 9-10-6 110 PaulGallagher(5) (Bruce Mactaggart) *midfield: drvn 4 out: outpcd bef next: n.d after* 50/1	105
2212	10	nk	**Willie Hall**[14] 5098 7-11-2 115 BrianHughes (William Amos) *t.k.h: trckd ldrs tl rdn and wknd bef 2 out* 16/1	112+
3311	11	hd	**Lady Bluesky**[22] 4958 8-10-8 110 EwanWhillans(3) (Alistair Whillans) *in tch on outside: lost pl bef 4 out: n.d after* 14/1	104
222	12	¾	**Kaolak (USA)**[42] 4451 5-11-1 114 JamesReveley (Keith Reveley) *hld up: rdn bef 3 out: nvr rchd ldrs* 11/2[1]	108
0332	13	1 ½	**Grand Diamond (IRE)**[14] 4939 7-10-7 113 PeterCarberry(7) (Jim Goldie) *hld up: stdy hdwy bef 3 out: sn rdn and no imp* 20/1	105
1160	14	½	**Maska Pony (IRE)**[23] 4940 7-11-12 125 TimmyMurphy (George Moore) *led to 3rd: cl up tl rdn and wknd bef 3 out* 28/1	119
234U	15	nk	**Enfant De Lune (FR)**[32] 4775 7-11-3 123 PeterHatton(7) (Alan King) *midfield: rdn 4 out: wknd bef next* 40/1	115
-112	16	3	**Circus Clown (IRE)**[34] 4715 6-11-0 113 GrahamLee (Jim Goldie) *in tch on ins: mstke and rdn 5th: wknd fr next* 8/1[3]	103
2300	P		**Sunarri (IRE)**[41] 4475 7-10-11 117 (p) AlistairFindlay(7) (Jane Walton) *cl up tl rdn and wknd 4 out: t.o whn p.u bef 2 out* 50/1	—

3m 44.6s (-18.50) **Going Correction** -1.20s/f (Hard) **17** Ran SP% **122.5**

Speed ratings (Par 107): **98,96,95,95,94 94,93,92,92,91 91,91,90,90,90 88,—**

toteswingers: 1&2 £19.40, 1&3 £18.80, 2&3 £27.70 CSF £34.66 CT £631.34 TOTE £4.40: £1.80, £1.30, £5.20, £3.60; EX 31.00.

Owner John P McManus **Bred** Elie Lellouche **Trained** Upper Lambourn, Berks

■ Stewards' Enquiry : A P McCoy two days ban: careless riding (Apr 29-30)

FOCUS

A competitive handicap hurdle, but they didn't go a great pace and finished in a bit of a heap. The form is solid and the easy winner can rate higher again.

NOTEBOOK

Remember Now(IRE) continues on the upgrade and he defied a 6lb rise for his narrow Stratford win, pulling away after the last to score in comfortable style. Still rather keen but not to the same extent as he had been earlier in his career, he is likely to head for a handicap at the Punchestown festival next. (op 9-2)

Sure Josie Sure(FR) had not run since November but has gone well fresh before. She looked a threat two from home, but met the last flight wrong and could not prevent the winner from pulling away. This was a solid effort under her big weight and she was declared to run again here the next day. (op 13-2)

Teenage Idol(IRE) ran well on this drop back in trip, but was able to set his own fairly modest gallop. He remains 15lb above his last winning mark. (tchd 22-1 and 25-1 in a place)

Fujin Dancer(FR) ◆, 7lb higher on this hat-trick bid, was again held up before finishing strongly. He would have been third in another stride and remains in top form.

Freddie Brown pulled hard yet again on this handicap debut and deserves credit for finishing as near as he did. There is plenty of potential there. (op 11-1)

Arisea(IRE) had ground conditions to suit and was another running on from the back. She was declared to run again here over 2m4f the next day. (op 50-1)

Toshi(USA) made progress up the straight but could not sustain it. (op 18-1)

Culcabock(IRE) might have been a bit closer had he not been hampered on the home turn. (op 9-1)

Willie Hall ran well for a long way but was fading when stumbling at the last. (op 18-1)

Kaolak(USA) reverted to hold-up tactics on this handicap debut and was never a factor. (op 13-2)

Circus Clown(IRE) was in trouble not long after halfway on this different ground. (op 17-2)

5316 ARTEMIS INVESTMENT MANAGEMENT SUPPORTING POPPYSCOTLAND NOVICES' H'CAP HURDLE (12 hdls) 3m 110y

2:50 (2:50) (Class 3) (0-135,130) 4-Y-O+ **£5,204** (£1,528; £764; £381)

Form				RPR
1P23	1		**Arctic Court (IRE)**[34] 4715 7-10-10 114 TimmyMurphy (Jim Goldie) *led 1st: hit 3rd: clr 4th to 6th: qcknd after 4 out: styd on strly fr next: unchal* 11/2	127+
1100	2	10	**Lively Baron (IRE)**[34] 4725 6-11-4 122 (t) JasonMaguire (Donald McCain) *prom: pushed along 1/2-way: chsd wnr 4 out: kpt on same pce fr next: no imp whn mstke last* 5/1[3]	122
2631	3	11	**Master Fiddle**[21] 4990 6-11-4 122 (t) BarryGeraghty (Nicky Henderson) *hld up towards rr: outpcd whn nt fluent 7th: rallied bef 3 out: tk 3rd run-in: no ch w first two* 7/2[2]	110
-321	4	2	**Yes Tom (IRE)**[62] 4062 6-11-7 125 APMcCoy (R T J Wilson, Ire) *prom: effrt and rdn 4 out: nt fluent next: sn outpcd: lost modest 3rd run-in* 2/1[1]	115+
4110	5	nk	**Lackamon**[55] 4209 6-11-7 130 ShaneByrne(5) (Sue Smith) *led to 1st: chsd wnr to 4 out: sn outpcd: n.d after* 16/1	117
4B02	6	35	**Majestic Mayhem (IRE)**[19] 5031 8-11-5 123 BarryKeniry (George Moore) *prom: outpcd 8th: n.d after* 12/1	78
20	7	18	**Rathnaroughy (IRE)**[20] 5020 7-10-7 111 PCarberry (S R B Crawford, Ire) *hld up and bhd: stdy hdwy 7th: rdn and no imp fr 4 out: btn fr next* 33/1	49
6020	P		**Nodforms Violet (IRE)**[90] 3556 7-11-5 123 GrahamLee (Karen McLintock) *towards rr: drvn and struggling 1/2-way: t.o whn p.u bef 8th* 25/1	—
2623	P		**Charlie Bucket**[27] 4869 8-9-10 110 CallumWhillans(10) (Donald Whillans) *hld up towards rr: reminders and drvn 1/2-way: struggling fr 7th: t.o whn p.u after 4 out* 20/1	—
0-5	P		**Drop Anchor (IRE)**[221] 1496 8-9-9 106 PeterCarberry(7) (Edward Cawley, Ire) *hld up: outpcd 7th: sn btn: t.o whn p.u bef 4 out* 20/1	—

6m 1.40s (-30.40) **Going Correction** -1.20s/f (Hard) **10** Ran SP% **117.5**

Speed ratings (Par 107): **100,96,93,92,92 81,75,—,—,—**

toteswingers: 1&2 £11.50, 1&3 £4.80, 2&3 £15.40 CSF £31.86 CT £110.87 TOTE £5.70: £2.00, £1.80, £1.80.

Owner Mr & Mrs Raymond Anderson Green **Bred** Paul Doyle **Trained** Uplawmoor, E Renfrews

FOCUS

A fair handicap hurdle in which not many got home. It was run at a steady pace early. The winner rates a big step up, with the second settting the level and the next pair a stone off their recent winning form.

NOTEBOOK

Arctic Court(IRE) was soon sent to the front. Pressing on before the straight, the gelding kept up the gallop and was never seriously challenged. Giving his trainer back-to-back wins in this race, he was helped by this better ground and could run in a conditions hurdle at Perth later in the month. He should make a name for himself over fences next season. (tchd 5-1)

Lively Baron(IRE) ran his race in second, but was struggling to make any meaningful impression on the winner from the home turn. Trip and ground were fine for him. (tchd 11-2 in a place)

Master Fiddle was put up 8lb for his win at Newbury. He was being niggled along a good mile out and was never a threat, but he did plug on late for a well-beaten third. He coped with this longer trip, but may appreciate easier ground. (tchd 4-1)

Yes Tom(IRE) has a good record on his trips over the water to Ayr and had Arctic Court 14l behind when winning a novice event here last time, but was 18lb worse off. The grey travelled quite well just off the pace, but weakened markedly from the second-last. (op 9-4 tchd 5-2 in places)

Lackamon is 19lb higher than when scoring at Southwell two starts back and was well held. (op 18-1 tchd 14-1)

5317 HILLHOUSE QUARRY H'CAP CHASE (17 fncs) 2m 4f

3:25 (3:25) (Class 2) 5-Y-O+

£15,655 (£4,625; £2,312; £1,157; £577; £290)

Form				RPR
U-54	1		**Watch My Back**[41] 4474 10-11-6 137 GrahamLee (Ferdy Murphy) *hld up in tch: hdwy to chse ldrs 5 out: effrt and led after 2 out: drew clr run-in* 11/1	149+
4060	2	7	**I'msingingtheblues (IRE)**[28] 4853 9-11-12 143 (t) APMcCoy (David Pipe) *hld up: effrt and rdn 4 out: chsd (clr) wnr run-in: no imp* 5/2[1]	149
3P0P	3	2	**Door Boy (IRE)**[48] 4352 8-10-5 127 PaulGallagher(5) (Howard Johnson) *chsd ldrs: chal 12th: rdn and led briefly 2 out: one pce and lost 2nd run-in* 5/1[3]	133
3P0	4	¾	**Premier Dane (IRE)**[28] 4848 9-10-3 120 DominicElsworth (Nicky Richards) *t.k.h: prom: led after 8th to 12th: effrt 4 out: kpt on same pce fr 2 out* 11/1	125
FP-2	5	2 ½	**Mighty Massini (IRE)**[34] 4716 8-10-5 122 PCarberry (C A McBratney, Ire) *led to after 8th: regained ld 12th: hdd 2 out: wknd last* 33/1	123
-5F1	6	½	**Nikos Extra (FR)**[23] 4941 7-11-4 135 RobertThornton (Alan King) *hld up: niggled whn mstke 12th: sn drvn: outpcd 3 out: n.d after* 11/4[2]	138
0156	7	7	**Lease Lend**[41] 4470 8-11-4 135 (tp) RichieMcGrath (Tim Easterby) *hld up: rdn after 5 out: wknd fr next* 16/1	130

12FP **8** *28* **Osric (IRE)**[31] 4794 8-11-1 **132**.. BarryGeraghty 116
(Nicky Henderson) *hld up in tch: drvn bef 4 out: wknd next: no ch whn bind bdly last* **15/2**

1U14 **9** *13* **Douglas Julian**[26] 4893 9-10-0 **117** oh2................................ HenryOliver 75
(Sue Smith) *chsd ldrs tl wknd bef 5 out: t.o* **20/1**

021U **U** **Raysrock (IRE)**[25] 4913 9-10-13 **130**............................(t) CampbellGillies —
(Lucinda Russell) *chsd ldr: mstke and uns rdr 2nd* **16/1**

5m 1.70s (-21.20) **Going Correction** -0.825s/f (Firm) **10** Ran SP% **119.8**
Speed ratings: **109,106,105,105,104 103,101,89,84,—**
toteswingers:1&2 £10.50, 2&3 £1.40, 1&3 £15.80 CSF £41.42 CT £162.16 TOTE £11.00: £2.80, £1.40, £1.90; EX 56.10.

Owner Tony Ambler **Bred** B Johnston **Trained** West Witton, N Yorks

FOCUS
Quite a valuable handicap chase, this was run at a fairly steady pace until halfway. The time was just under 14 seconds outside the standard but the form looks believable. A personal best from the winner.

NOTEBOOK
Watch My Back has done well to recover from a serious tendon injury sustained first time out this season. Well suited by this spring ground, he gradually worked his way into it under a patient ride and came away on the run-in to win emphatically. Ferdy Murphy won back-to-back editions of this race with Three Mirrors and it would be no surprise to see Watch My Back return for this event in 12 months' time. (op 12-1)

I'msingingtheblues(IRE), held up again, was slightly outpaced by the leaders early in the straight, but ran on well to grab second on the flat. Able but frustrating, he is perhaps best suited by around 2m2f, but races over that trip are in short supply. (op 11-4 tchd 3-1 and 10-3 in a place)

Door Boy(IRE) ◆ has been contesting some warm contests and has been eased 10lb since the autumn. He ran a better race, joining issue down the back straight and only giving best between the last two fences. Although he is still to win a handicap, he is capable of finding a race off this sort of mark. (op 6-1 tchd 7-1)

Premier Dane(IRE), running over fences for the first time in two years, went on with a circuit left. After jumping out to his right a couple of times, he was headed six from home but kept going quite well to hold fourth. (op 10-1)

Mighty Massini(IRE) had been second to Raysrock (an early unseater here) over 2m at this track last time. A pound well in, he regained his lead down the back straight, but could not hold on from the second-last.

Nikos Extra(FR), an easy Haydock winner, was comfortably held off this 10lb higher mark, in last place when making an error down the back and never a serious threat after. (op 3-1)

5318 BULMERS CRISP BLEND NOVICES' LIMITED H'CAP CHASE (12 fncs) 2m

4:00 (4:00) (Class 3) (0-130,130) 5-Y-0+ **£5,854** (£1,719; £859; £429)

Form RPR

1212 **1** **Kosta Brava (FR)**[80] 3730 7-10-6 **117**............................ WilsonRenwick 119
(Howard Johnson) *hld up: hit and rdn 5 out: rallied and lft 5 l 3rd 3 out: swtchd rt and led jst after last: r.o wl* **4/1**[2]

3130 **2** *5* **Mister Stickler (IRE)**[28] 4853 7-11-4 **129**....................(t) RobertThornton 126
(Alan King) *nt fluent on occasions: prom: rdn after 5 out: 16 l down and no imp whn lft in narrow ld 3 out: hdd jst after last: kpt on same pce* **4/1**[2]

1135 **3** *½* **Wind Shuffle (GER)**[41] 4472 8-11-5 **130**............................ GrahamLee 127
(Jim Goldie) *w ldr to 4th: rdn after 5 out: lft 2nd and ev ch 3 out to last: one pce run-in* **9/1**[3]

1F2B **4** *26* **Lightening Rod**[21] 4996 6-10-8 **126**................................ JakeGreenall[(7)] 108
(Michael Easterby) *t.k.h: hld up: mstke and rdn 7th: outpcd 5 out: lft modest 4th 3 out: no imp: eased whn no ch run-in* **7/2**[1]

4120 **5** *19* **Present To You (IRE)**[120] 2975 6-10-7 **118**............(b[1]) RichardJohnson 73
(Philip Hobbs) *prom tl wknd qckly 5 out: t.o* **4/1**[2]

5222 **F** **Ruthenoise (FR)**[45] 4406 6-10-11 **125**................................ DavidBass[(3)] 139+
(Nicky Henderson) *t.k.h: led: qcknd clr 1/2-way: 16 l in front whn fell 3 out* **4/1**[2]

3m 53.9s (-16.80) **Going Correction** -0.825s/f (Firm) **6** Ran SP% **112.2**
Speed ratings: **109,106,106,93,83 —**
totswingers:1&2 £5.40, 2&3 £2.00, 1&3 £10.10 CSF £20.18 TOTE £6.20: £3.20, £2.70; EX 18.00.

Owner Andrea & Graham Wylie **Bred** Guy Blasco **Trained** Billy Row, Co Durham

FOCUS
A fair limited handicap for novices and a race where the picture changed dramatically at the third-last when clear leader Ruthenoise fell. She was heading for a personal best. The fortunate winner is rated to his mark, with the next pair below their best.

NOTEBOOK
Kosta Brava(FR) was a fortunate winner. Left in third place by the mare's fall three out, he was switched going to the final fence and cut down the pair in front of him to win going away. Given a break since late January and resuming off a 5lb higher mark, he continues on an upward curve and is well suited by decent ground. (op 9-2)

Mister Stickler(IRE) was down in grade after contesting the Grand Annual at Cheltenham. He jumped somewhat stickily at times and was left a long way behind by Ruthenoise, only to find himself in front at the third-last when she fell. Battling on, he could not hold the winner after the last. (op 9-2)

Wind Shuffle(GER) was unable to lead as he usually does. He was left in there fighting when the clear leader departed, but was running on empty from the final fence. (op 7-1)

Lightening Rod failed to give his running and was struggling at the back throughout. Jake Greenall reported that he ran flat. Official explanation: jockey said gelding ran flat (op 3-1 tchd 4-1)

Present To You(IRE), having his second run over fences, was disappointing in the first-time blinkers. (op 7-1)

Ruthenoise(FR), running over fences for the second time, was keen early on but soon settled in front. She had compiled a clear lead, and was showing no signs of stopping, when she fell foul of the third-last. Undoubtedly an unlucky loser, she seemed none the worse and can gain compensation. (op 10-3 tchd 3-1)

5319 CORAL BACKING POPPYSCOTLAND MARES' H'CAP HURDLE (12 hdls) 3m 110y

4:35 (4:35) (Class 2) 4-Y-0+

£10,019 (£2,960; £1,480; £740; £369; £185)

Form RPR

3411 **1** **Bunglasha Lady (IRE)**[47] 4370 6-11-4 **120**............................ APMcCoy 130+
(Warren Greatrex) *prom: hdwy 4 out: effrt and ev ch 2 out: led and hung lft run-in: styd on strly towards fin* **13/8**[1]

5035 **2** *1 ¾* **Catleen (IRE)**[25] 4914 7-10-0 **102** oh3.................................. PCarberry 107
(S R B Crawford, Ire) *hld up: smooth hdwy to ld 2 out: rdn last: hdd and carried lft run-in: no ex towards fin* **7/1**

4122 **3** *9* **Easter Vic**[14] 5096 10-9-9 **102** oh7..............................(p) PaulGallagher[(5)] 99
(Robert Goldie) *hld up: hdwy 1/2-way: sn rdn: outpcd 4 out: styd on fr 2 out: no ch w first two* **20/1**

5PP1 **4** *1 ¼* **Elzahann (IRE)**[21] 4997 9-11-4 **120**..................................... GrahamLee 114
(Ferdy Murphy) *led to 2 out: sn drvn and outpcd* **6/1**[2]

4621 **5** *9* **More Equity**[11] 5150 9-10-3 **105**.. JamesReveley 93
(Dianne Sayer) *prom: lost pl 1/2-way: struggling 4 out: n.d after* **13/2**[3]

2032 **6** *33* **Bollin Ruth**[19] 5030 9-9-4 **102**.................................. CallumWhillans[(10)] 60
(Donald Whillans) *hld up: rdn 4 out: sn wknd* **15/2**

12P3 **7** *28* **Cailin Na Ri (IRE)**[147] 2506 8-10-12 **119**....................... AlexanderVoy[(5)] 52
(Martin Todhunter) *cl up tl rdn and wknd bef 3 out* **12/1**

4111 **P** **Alexander Road (IRE)**[36] 4568 6-11-12 **128**..................(t) JasonMaguire —
(Donald McCain) *cl up: rdn 4 out: sn wknd: p.u bef next* **7/1**

5m 56.0s (-35.80) **Going Correction** -1.20s/f (Hard) **8** Ran SP% **114.9**
Speed ratings (Par 109): **109,108,105,105,102 91,82,—**
toteswingers: 1&2 £4.00, 1&3 £12.90, 2&3 £8.20 CSF £13.90 CT £164.96 TOTE £3.00: £1.50, £1.90, £3.10; EX 19.70.

Owner Mrs T Brown **Bred** Desmond Devereux **Trained** Upper Lambourn, Berks

FOCUS
A decent handicap for mares, run in a time five seconds quicker than the earlier novices' handicap. The second and third were out of the weights, which lends a doubt to the form, but both ran to their mark. The winner is on the upgrade.

NOTEBOOK
Bunglasha Lady(IRE) completed a hat-trick on this handicap debut. Upped in trip, she joined issue at the first in the straight and, despite hanging quite badly to her left under pressure, got on top after the last. A tough mare who has more to offer, she would ideally prefer softer ground. (op 15-8 tchd 2-1 in places)

Catleen(IRE) remains a maiden under rules, but she ran a big race from 3lb out of the weights. Picking up ground under a trademark waiting ride from Carberry, she took a narrow lead going better than the winner but did not find as much as her rival on the run-in, where Bunglasha Lady drifted into her. The better ground appeared to help. (op 13-2)

Easter Vic is a difficult ride and Paul Gallagher was hard at work on her for most of the final circuit, but she rewarded his efforts by staying on for third. She was racing from 7lb out of the weights.

Elzahann(IRE), successful in this race from a 5lb higher mark two years ago, was reverting to hurdles after winning a handicap chase off 16lb lower last time. She made a lot of the running, but could not hold on between the last two flights.

More Equity, another who won over fences lastest, was officially 2lb well in. She lost her place down the far side and made only modest late progress. (op 8-1)

Alexander Road(IRE), bidding for a four-timer on her handicap debut, dropped away quickly down the back before pulling up. Jason Maguire reported that she had a breathing problem. Official explanation: jockey said mare had a breathing problem (op 13-2)

5320 NMT PLANT H'CAP HURDLE (12 hdls) 3m 110y

5:05 (5:05) (Class 3) (0-125,125) 4-Y-0+ **£4,878** (£1,432; £716; £357)

Form RPR

11- **1** **Aibrean (IRE)**[495] 2726 7-11-11 **124**.. PCarberry 135+
(S R B Crawford, Ire) *hld up: smooth hdwy to trck ldrs bef 3 out: led gng wl run-in: cheekily* **14/1**

42R5 **2** *½* **Aghill (IRE)**[19] 5032 7-10-0 **99** oh1.................................... WilsonRenwick 103
(Rose Dobbin) *hld up: hdwy 1/2-way: led after 3 out to run-in: kpt on but flattered by proximity to wnr* **12/1**

-PP4 **3** *4 ½* **Seven Is Lucky (IRE)**[34] 4712 9-9-9 **99** oh5................. PaulGallagher[(5)] 99
(Jim Goldie) *prom: led briefly 3 out: sn rdn: ev ch tl no ex fr last* **16/1**

3400 **4** *8* **Political Paddy**[11] 5149 9-10-11 **110**.................................(p) RyanMania 104
(Rayson Nixon) *hld up: rdn and outpcd bef 4 out: rallied whn hit 2 out: no imp* **25/1**

6344 **5** *9* **Sunnyside**[27] 4869 6-10-8 **112**.. AlexanderVoy[(5)] 100
(Lucy Normile) *mstkes: cl up: led briefly bef 3 out: wknd fr next* **7/1**[3]

1110 **6** *4 ½* **Jurisdiction**[146] 2512 7-11-12 **125**.....................................(p) GrahamLee 106
(Rose Dobbin) *led to bef 3 out: wknd bef next* **10/1**

P035 **7** *1* **Bollin Fiona**[40] 4508 7-9-5 **100**................................(b[1]) CallumWhillans[(10)] 80
(Donald Whillans) *hld up: rdn 7th: blnd 4 out: sn btn* **12/1**

F-02 **8** *1 ¼* **Larks Lad (IRE)**[20] 5003 7-11-12 **125**.................................. BarryGeraghty 105
(Nicky Henderson) *cl up: chal gng wl 3 out: mstke and rdn next: sn btn* **9/5**[1]

0053 **9** *7* **Forcefield**[27] 4873 5-9-9 **101**.. MissLAlexander[(7)] 73
(N W Alexander) *bhd: struggling 7th: nvr on terms* **25/1**

0113 **10** *16* **Stagecoach Opal**[20] 5003 10-10-12 **111**.............................. HenryOliver 69
(Sue Smith) *t.k.h: cl up tl wknd after 8th* **5/1**[2]

4410 **11** *½* **Soubriquet (IRE)**[181] 1871 8-10-13 **112**....................(t) MichaelMcAlister 69
(Maurice Barnes) *in tch: rdn 7th: wknd fr 8th* **28/1**

-P50 **12** *1 ¾* **Chief Bucaneer (IRE)**[60] 4115 8-10-7 **106**............................ JanFaltejsek 62
(George Charlton) *bhd: struggling 7th: nvr on terms* **20/1**

0-34 **P** **Foxes Delight (IRE)**[60] 4112 7-9-9 **101** ow1...............(t) AlistairFindlay[(7)] —
(Jane Walton) *midfield: lost pl 5th: struggling after next: t.o whn p.u bef 7th* **20/1**

5m 55.6s (-36.20) **Going Correction** -1.20s/f (Hard) **13** Ran SP% **122.6**
Speed ratings (Par 107): **109,108,107,104,101 100,100,99,97,92 92,91,—**
toteswingers: 1&2 £19.70, 1&3 £62.30, 2&3 £53.20 CSF £158.81 CT £2728.83 TOTE £10.70: £3.70, £3.50, £4.30; EX 313.20.

Owner Miss Patricia Duffin **Bred** Miss Patricia Duffin **Trained** Larne, Co Antrim

FOCUS
This fair handicap hurdle was just about the quickest of the three races over C&D. The winner was very progressive when last seen and was value for further. The second was well in on his recent chase form.

NOTEBOOK
Aibrean(IRE) was unbeaten in two previous hurdles starts, but had not been seen since December 2009 due to niggly problems. Paul Carberry replicated the tactics he'd used aboard her stablemate Catleen in the previous race and the mare made steady progress before leading on the flat to score on the bridle. This proved her effectiveness on better ground, and it will be interesting to see how the handicapper reacts. There is a possibility she may go to Punchestown, but she won't if conditions are too quick. (tchd 16-1)

Aghill(IRE), who was a pound out of the weights, ran well on this return to hurdles but the winner was toying with him on the run-in and he is flattered by the margin of defeat. Good ground suits. (op 10-1)

Seven Is Lucky(IRE) sweated up badly beforehand, but it didn't stop him running a solid race from 5lb out of the handicap. He still awaits his first win over hurdles. (op 14-1)

Political Paddy stayed on without ever posing a real threat. He is currently 5lb below his last winning mark and is due to be dropped a further 3lb.

Sunnyside couldn't quite get to the front and he put in a sketchy round of hurdling before dropping away two from home. (tchd 13-2)

Larks Lad(IRE) was having just his third run since being hurt in a fall on this card a year ago. He looked a threat turning in, but mistakes at the first two flights in the straight soon saw him on the retreat. (op 5-2)

Foxes Delight(IRE) Official explanation: jockey said gelding had a breathing problem

T/Plt: £36.70 to a £1 stake. Pool of £70,826.31 - 1406.35 winning units. T/Qpdt: £21.10 to a £1 stake. Pool of £5,681.00 - 198.90 - winning units. RY

5211 **CHEPSTOW** (L-H)

Friday, April 15

OFFICIAL GOING: Good (watered; 6.6)

Wind: almost nil Weather: overcast but warm

5321 DUNRAVEN WINDOWS NOVICES' HURDLE (11 hdls) 2m 4f

4:40 (4:40) (Class 4) 4-Y-0+ £2,276 (£668; £334; £166)

Form RPR

2-12 **1** **Lion On The Prowl (IRE)**[24] 4932 7-11-6 127..................(t) SeanQuinlan 124+
(Kim Bailey) *mde all: drew 6 l clr 7th nt fluent fr next: only had one serious pursuer fr after 2 out: drvn and hld on wl cl home* **5/4**[1]

4134 **2** ½ **Awesome Freddie**[41] 4464 6-11-3 123.......................... CharlieHuxley(3) 123+
(Alan King) *chsd ldrs: effrt 8th: rdn to go 2nd after 3 out: stl over 2 l bhd at last: kpt on stoutly but a jst hld* **11/8**[2]

3 11 **Satou (FR)**[138] 5-11-0 119... RhysFlint 108
(Philip Hobbs) *chsd ldrs: nt fluent 4th: wnt 12 l 2nd at 8th tl after next: rdn and wknd 2 out* **25/1**

50 **4** 21 **Two Bob (IRE)**[21] 4986 6-11-0 0.. TomO'Brien 90
(Philip Hobbs) *disp 2nd tl rdn bef 8th: sn wl outpcd by ldng trio: plugged on* **22/1**

-00P **5** 7 **Keltic Crisis (IRE)**[23] 4951 7-11-0 0..................................... DarylJacob 88
(Jonathan Geake) *nvr bttr than midfield: plugged on into 22 l: 4th whn mstke 2 out: struggling after* **100/1**

6 15 **Tastevin (FR)**[175] 4-10-2 0... MattGriffiths(5) 66
(Philip Hobbs) *towards rr and t.k.h: nt fluent 5th: sme prog after 7th to rr of main bunch: lost tch next: sn t.o* **22/1**

424- **7** 4½ **Rhythm Seeker**[82] 8-11-0 0.. HarrySkelton 69
(Anabel L M King) *disp 2nd tl rdn and lost pl after 7th: t.o 3 out* **20/1**

/-P0 **8** 1¾ **Racing With Angels**[13] 5107 9-10-7 64............................. MrBJPoste(7) 68
(Pam Ford) *a wl in rr: struggling 7th: t.o next* **200/1**

03 **9** 6 **That's Mine (IRE)**[23] 4942 5-11-0 0.............................. RichieMcLernon 63
(Jonjo O'Neill) *midfield but nvr on terms w ldrs: in tch after 7th: t.o next* **40/1**

10 3¾ **Before The War (USA)**[56] 4-10-0 0......................... MrRGHenderson(7) 53
(Polly Gundry) *wl bhd: rdn 6th: t.o 8th* **80/1**

P6 **11** 42 **Ogmore Junction (IRE)**[8] 5167 6-10-2 0...................(t) ThomasFlint(10) 24
(John Flint) *wl bhd: hopelessly t.o bef 8th* **66/1**

062P **12** 2 **Saffron Lord**[73] 3866 6-11-0 114...(t) TomSiddall 25
(Martin Keighley) *chsd ldrs: wkng whn mstke 3 out: virtually p.u after* **16/1**[3]

P **P** **Aboukir**[36] 4667 5-11-0 0.. SamJones —
(Oliver Sherwood) *bhd and nvr travelling: last whn nt fluent 5th: hopelessly t.o whn p.u 8th* **100/1**

2 **P** **Fitobust (IRE)**[60] 4124 5-11-0 0....................................... AndrewThornton —
(Seamus Mullins) *towards rr whn hung rt after 4th and rdn: sn last: p.u 5th: b.b.v* **20/1**

4m 57.3s (-4.50) **Going Correction** -0.425s/f (Good)
WFA 4 from 5yo+ 6lb **14** Ran SP% **122.1**
Speed ratings (Par 105): **92,91,87,79,76 70,68,67,65,63 47,46,—,—**
toteswingers:1&2:£1.20, 1&3:£11.90, 2&3:£6.30 CSF £2.91 TOTE £2.50: £1.30, £1.10, £3.30; EX 3.20.
Owner Kim Bailey Racing Partnership II **Bred** Abergwaun Farms **Trained** Andoversford, Gloucs

FOCUS

As a contest this was rather unsatisfactory as the field let the winner get away, only setting down to close the gap once it was too late. The winner was the form pick but was gifted quite a long lead. The first two are rated pretty close to their pre-race marks.

NOTEBOOK

Lion On The Prowl(IRE) raced freely at the head of affairs and, facing no semblance of a challenge, he injected a bit of pace at the end of the back straight and soon stretched the gap to ten lengths. He got tired in the straight and made his first couple of errors but kept going to hold off the late challenge of his market rival. He was the best horse on the day and looks progressive but he rather stole the race here and full credit to connections for exploiting this. (op 13-8 tchd 6-5)

Awesome Freddie has been racing over 3m this year, so it was a little surprising that he gave the winner so much leeway. To be fair, he did not look completely at ease early on but he was ready to make a little headway in the back straight, although it was only once they had turned in and his jockey realised how much gap had opened up that he got serious. He did close in on the tiring winner but had too much ground to make up. (op 7-4 tchd 5-4)

Satou(FR) showed some ability on his first start since leaving the Thierry Doumen yard, where he had put up a couple of reasonable efforts over hurdles before flopping when switched to fences. He raced on softer ground in France and gave the impression he could do with more give in the ground but this suggested there was something to build on. (op 18-1)

Two Bob(IRE), a negative in the paddock, made some inroads into the winner's lead in the back straight but did not get home. (op 18-1)

Rhythm Seeker was at the head of the chasing pack turning in but soon got outpaced and this maiden point winner should do better over further.

Fitobust(IRE) Official explanation: vet said gelding bled from the nose

5322 SUN TRADE WINDOWS H'CAP HURDLE (11 hdls) 2m 4f

5:10 (5:11) (Class 5) (0-105,103) 4-Y-0+ £1,951 (£573; £286; £143)

Form RPR

34F5 **1** **Not So Sure Dick (IRE)**[64] 4022 6-11-5 96...................... AndrewTinkler 104+
(George Baker) *chsd ldrs: wnt 2nd and nt fluent 3 out: rdn after: led last: drvn to assert: all out* **16/1**

3-10 **2** 2¼ **Spanish Cruise (IRE)**[77] 3791 7-11-11 102.................(p) JohnnyFarrelly 111+
(David Pipe) *cl 2nd: nt fluent 6th and 7th: led sn after: drvn whn hit 2 out: hdd last: nt qckn* **12/1**

F024 **3** 8 **Timetoring**[39] 4532 9-11-6 102.......................................(p) MarkQuinlan(5) 103
(Bernard Llewellyn) *slt ld tl 7th: rdn in 3rd and clr of rest 2 out: wknd bef last* **15/2**[2]

0004 **4** nk **Highland Legacy**[80] 3719 7-11-2 103..............................(p) AshleyBird(10) 103
(Jim Best) *midfield: mstke 5th and rdn: lost pl and tentative again next: rdn and styd on again but w little zest fr 3 out: tk 4th cl home: no ch w ldrs* **16/1**

U240 **5** 5 **Erdeli (IRE)**[68] 3962 7-11-12 103.......................................(tp) SamThomas 102+
(Tim Vaughan) *pressed ldrs: rdn and nt looking wnr after getting outpcd fr 8th: 4th and wl hld 2 out* **14/1**

5000 **6** 20 **Hard Tackle (IRE)**[26] 4895 5-11-11 102........................ RichieMcLernon 82
(Jonjo O'Neill) *chsd ldrs: rdn after 7th: sn lost tch* **20/1**

P065 **7** shd **Be Ashored**[18] 5054 6-11-1 95.. RichardKilloran(3) 75
(Tim Vaughan) *midfield: rdn after 7th: wl btn next* **50/1**

0560 **8** 3½ **Drummers Drumming (USA)**[14] 5103 5-10-13 90.(tp) JimmyMcCarthy 67
(Charlie Morlock) *prom: rn wd after 4th: 8 l 5th and wkng 8th: blnd 2 out* **50/1**

1465 **9** ¾ **Lyster (IRE)**[22] 4968 12-11-9 103...................................... LeeStephens(3) 80
(Graeme McPherson) *a bhd: lost tch after 7th* **50/1**

3004 **10** 11 **Lemon Silk (IRE)**[18] 5054 7-11-6 97...................................... TomO'Brien 65
(Alex Hales) *wl bhd: last at 5th: t.o bef 8th* **14/1**

60PP **11** 15 **Always Cruising (USA)**[237] 1335 6-9-11 77 oh3............ JohnKington(3) 33
(Linda Blackford) *a bhd: t.o bef 8th* **66/1**

0/P1 **12** 9 **Pepito Collonges (FR)**[25] 4922 8-10-11 98............(b) NathanAdams(10) 47
(Laura Mongan) *nvr nr front rnk: lost tch bef 8th: sn t.o* **16/1**

3P/P **P** **Manners (IRE)**[38] 4536 13-11-2 100...................................... MrSParish(7) —
(Audrey Manners) *bhd: sltly hmpd 3rd: t.o and p.u 8th* **100/1**

0P1U **F** **Louis Ludwig (IRE)**[234] 1361 6-11-4 100........................ MrTomDavid(5) —
(Tim Vaughan) *towards rr whn stmbld and fell 3rd* **10/1**[3]

0P64 **R** **Spirit Of Barbados (IRE)**[43] 4444 5-11-5 96........................(t) RhysFlint —
(David Pipe) *ducked lft and rn out and dumped rdr into 1st* **1/1**[1]

4m 57.7s (-4.10) **Going Correction** -0.425s/f (Good) **15** Ran SP% **122.7**
Speed ratings (Par 103): **91,90,86,86,84 76,76,75,75,70 64,61,—,—,—**
toteswingers:1&2:£20.00, 1&3:£17.60, 2&3:£9.20 CSF £188.02 CT £1578.27 TOTE £23.20: £5.80, £3.20, £1.70; EX 269.70.
Owner Peter Earl, Lin Baker & Irene Paterson **Bred** Oliver Maguire **Trained** Whitsbury, Hants

■ Stewards' Enquiry : Ashley Bird five-day ban: used whip in manner to cause wealing (Apr 29-30, May 3-5)

FOCUS

Early drama as the red-hot favourite Spirit Of Barbados departed. Still, a good battle ensued between the winner and long-time leader. The winner is rated in line with his chase form, with a big step up from the second.

NOTEBOOK

Not So Sure Dick(IRE) has been a disappointment over fences but he showed some battling qualities to win over hurdles at the first attempt. He was a little outpaced as they turned into the straight but rallied under pressure and was on top well before the line. (tchd 14-1)

Spanish Cruise(IRE), stablemate of the errant favourite, disputed the lead throughout and was tiring by the second-last but rallied to challenge the winner one more time. He failed to cope with the heavy ground at Fontwell last time but has regained his form and his willing attitude should see him win more races despite his climbing mark. He wore cheekpieces for the first time. (op 10-1)

Timetoring disputed the lead until they turned for home and plugged on once passed but he found the ground a bit too lively. (op 10-1)

Highland Legacy was slow to pick up from the back straight but eventually got going to make some good late progress. He has not achieved much over hurdles but finally looks to be going in the right direction. (op 12-1)

Erdeli(IRE) travelled well to the home turn but did not pick up from there but this was an improvement on his return to action at Fontwell in February. (op 11-1)

Spirit Of Barbados(IRE) jinked before the first, tried to jump the rail before the flight and ran out. He will have much to prove next time. (op 11-10)

5323 BRACEYS BUILDERS MERCHANT H'CAP CHASE (16 fncs) 2m 3f 110y

5:45 (5:45) (Class 3) (0-130,129) 5-Y-0+ £4,553 (£1,337; £668; £333)

Form RPR

P-62 **1** **Down The Stretch**[34] 4723 11-10-12 115......................... LiamTreadwell 124+
(James Payne) *sn led: dived at 5th: jnd 6th tl next: mde rest: drew 4 l clr 12th: a looked like holding rivals and kpt on gamely: rdn out* **4/1**[2]

2311 **2** 3¼ **Double The Trouble**[22] 4972 10-11-1 118.......................... NickScholfield 124
(Andy Turnell) *t.k.h and hld up: wnt 3rd at 11th: no real imp on wnr fr next: nt fluent last: wnt 2nd fnl 100yds* **3/1**[1]

1231 **3** ¾ **Pouvoir (FR)**[20] 5002 8-11-12 129.. SamThomas 134
(Alan King) *nt fluent: trckd ldrs: wnt 2nd at 13th: cajoled along w no great rspnse after: a hld by wnr and lost 2nd 100yds out* **3/1**[1]

1150 **4** 32 **Diamond Brook (IRE)**[49] 4328 6-11-3 120........................(v[1]) DarylJacob 98
(Nick Williams) *2nd tl 5th: pushed along and nvr happy fr next: plenty of reminders after: last at 8th: toiled on: hit 3 out* **4/1**[2]

13P1 **5** 32 **Take It There**[53] 4265 9-11-5 122.......................................(tp) FelixDeGiles 75
(Alastair Lidderdale) *wnt 2nd at 5th: jnd wnr but reminders 6th: level tl hdd 8th: mstke 11th: fdd bdly 13th: t.o* **10/1**

112P **P** **Peplum (FR)**[29] 4820 8-11-12 129.. JamieMoore —
(Gary Moore) *rn in snatches: nt fluent 2nd: often getting reminders fr 6th: drvn to go 2nd briefly at 11th: nt run on and sn lost pl: t.o and p.u 3 out* **8/1**[3]

5m 0.10s (-11.20) **Going Correction** -0.425s/f (Good) **6** Ran SP% **110.2**
Speed ratings: **105,103,103,90,77** —
toteswingers:1&2:£3.30, 1&3:£3.30, 2&3:£2.70 CSF £16.07 TOTE £5.40: £2.70, £2.00; EX 18.00.
Owner J R Payne **Bred** M J Roberts **Trained** Brompton Regis, Somerset

FOCUS

A tricky handicap in which case could be made for all the runners. Solid form, the winner rated back towards his best.

NOTEBOOK

Down The Stretch benefited from some enterprising tactics as he went for home at the top of the straight and got first run on his pursuers. He jumped well in the main, racing at the head of the field and found a bit more after the last. He attracted some market support when second over C&D a month ago and faced a 3lb rise in a better contest but he is a capable performer on his day and his jumping put his rivals under pressure. (op 11-2)

Double The Trouble, held up early, battled all the way to the line but he could not match the pace of the winner in his bid for a hat-trick. He is back up to a career-high mark after being raised 2lb further for his most recent win and might not withstand any more upward movement but that would be a shame as he blossoms at this time of year. (op 7-2)

Pouvoir(FR) has struggled with setbacks over the past few years but looked to be back to form with a comfortable success at Bangor last time. He was slow at the first open ditch but jumped adequately thereafter, if sometimes a bit low, and was given every chance to pick off the winner but could not find that extra gear. The 7lb rise might have had an effect but it might be that, in view of his previous problems, he will struggle for consistency. (op 5-2 tchd 9-4)

Diamond Brook(IRE) struggled from some way out when stepped up to three miles at Sandown seven weeks ago and, visored for the first time, found the pace a bit much with half a circuit left to go on this first run since. His three wins to date have come at Exeter and he seems to need a stiff test. (tchd 9-2)

Take It There faced a stiff task off an 8lb higher mark and stepping up in class following her heavy-ground win at Hereford in February, and some jumping errors cost her valuable ground. (op 11-1)

Peplum(FR) had an easier task than when coming unstuck in the heat of a Cheltenham Festival handicap last time but his jumping was never that fluent and he failed to give his running. (op 6-1 tchd 11-2)

5324 SUN TRADE WINDOWS H'CAP CHASE (22 fncs) 3m 2f 110y

6:20 (6:20) (Class 5) (0-95,90) 5-Y-0+ £2,081 (£611; £305; £152)

Form RPR

6634 **1** **Ethiopia**[18] 5053 8-11-3 81..................................(b[1]) AndrewGlassonbury 100
(Bob Buckler) *pressed ldrs: 3rd and rdn 14th: qcknd to ld bef 18th: nrly 3 l clr next: forced along and v idle: hdd between last two and dropped 2 l bhd rival: rallied under heavy driving to snatch verdict* **9/1**

0621 **2** *shd* **Midnight Diamond (IRE)**[80] 3729 8-10-8 77..............(v) MrTomDavid(5) 96
(Tim Vaughan) *t.k.h and hld up: qcknd to ld 12th: hdd bef 18th: sn clr w wnr: urged ahd again between last two: wnt 2 l clr: idled flat: jst pipped* **6/4**[1]

P533 **3** *15* **Kiltimoney (IRE)**[6] 5216 11-10-0 64 oh1..............(b) SamTwiston-Davies 72
(Richard Mitchell) *mstkes: 2nd 6th tl led 7th: hdd 11th: led again bef 12th where blnd and hdd: nt fluent 13th: disp 2nd but rdn after 17th: plodded on in modest 3rd fr next* **5/1**[2]

5342 **4** *24* **Ballyman (IRE)**[25] 4919 10-10-10 74.............................. AndrewThornton 61
(Jonathan Geake) *nvr bttr than 5th: nt fluent 13th: easily lft bhd bef 18th* **13/2**[3]

2242 **5** *8* **You Can Of Course (IRE)**[150] 2444 8-10-5 74...........(p) MarkQuinlan(5) 54
(Neil Mulholland) *towards rr but wl in tch tl rdn 17th: struggling whn hit next: sn remote* **7/1**

4P23 **P** **Zimbabwe (FR)**[18] 5053 11-10-0 64 oh2...........................(p) JamieMoore —
(Nigel Hawke) *pushed along in ld: hdd 7th: led again and nt fluent 11th: hdd bef 12th: sn strly rousted and downed tools: t.o 16th: p.u 19th* **12/1**

6443 **P** **Bobby Donald (IRE)**[37] 4551 9-10-13 77.............................. TomSiddall —
(Richard Phillips) *prom: rdn bef 12th: fnd nthing: t.o 15th: p.u next* **14/1**

6404 **P** **Casual Garcia**[26] 4898 6-11-9 90...................................(t) TommyPhelan(3) —
(Mark Gillard) *pushed along early: bhd: handled bnd after 11th poorly: wknd 12th: t.o 15th: p.u 18th* **40/1**

7m 3.70s (1.70) **Going Correction** -0.425s/f (Good) **8** Ran SP% **109.3**
Speed ratings: **80,79,75,68,66** —,—,—
toteswingers:1&2:£4.00, 1&3:£4.00, 2&3:£1.70 CSF £22.03 CT £68.70 TOTE £10.50: £2.20, £1.40, £1.80; EX 32.80.
Owner Nick Elliott **Bred** Mrs C Van Straubenzee & Mrs J N Humphreys **Trained** Henley, Somerset
■ Stewards' Enquiry : Andrew Glassonbury 12-day ban: used whip with excessive frequency (Apr 29-30, May 3-12)

FOCUS
Just a modest handicap but it produced an exciting finish with fortunes veering to and fro all the way up the straight with a head bob deciding matters on the line. The winner is rated back to his 2010 form, with the second similar to his old chase best.

NOTEBOOK
Ethiopia received a strong ride. Even when the favourite loomed up and beyond going to the last, his jockey was not going to give up and galvanised his mount for one decisive effort to snatch victory on the line. He had been struggling to find any form this term and blinkers were applied for this last-ditch attempt. Both his previous wins came at Plumpton last spring off higher marks but this was his eighth run since a break last summer, so he is not an obvious candidate to follow up. (op 15-2)
Midnight Diamond(IRE) had to surrender the lead entering the straight but rallied to regain what looked a winning advantage from the last but he began to flatten out near the line and just got pipped. His form has been resurgent since moving to Tim Vaughan's yard and he looked less reluctant over fences today but may lack a bit of resolution at the death. (op 5-4)
Kiltimoney(IRE) ran another consistent race but was done for pace from the home turn and this soft ground lover ran a little feelingly in the closing stages. (op 8-1)
Ballyman(IRE) made good progress in the back straight but found nil from there and did cope with the step up in trip. (op 15-2)
You Can Of Course(IRE), having his first run since November, made an effort in the back straight but it was short-lived. (op 6-1)

5325 DUNRAVEN WINDOWS H'CAP HURDLE (12 hdls) 3m
6:55 (6:55) (Class 2) 4-Y-0+ **£8,326** (£2,444; £1,222; £610)

Form RPR

0010 **1** **Thelobstercatcher**[65] 4003 7-10-11 128..................(v) DonalDevereux(3) 135+
(Peter Bowen) *led bef 2nd tl 7th: led again bef 9th: rdn clr 2 out: hanging lft after: 7 l in ld whn pitched and pckd last: kpt on wl and a looked like holding on* **9/1**

2361 **2** *4* **Five Star Wilsham (IRE)**[41] 4464 7-10-11 125............... NickScholfield 125
(Jeremy Scott) *travelled wl trcking ldrs: bit to do bef 9th: wnt 2nd bef 3 out: rdn next: sn outpcd: kpt on but flattered by proximity to wnr* **11/8**[1]

40FP **3** *4 ½* **Jaunty Journey**[10] 5154 8-10-4 118......................... SamTwiston-Davies 115
(Nigel Twiston-Davies) *sn 2nd: hit 4th and reminder: led narrowly 7th tl hdd and hit 9th: drvn and outpcd in 3rd fr bef 3 out: hit last* **22/1**

6302 **4** *20* **Heathcliff (IRE)**[65] 4003 9-11-2 130...............................(b) SamThomas 110
(Richard Lee) *led tl bef 2nd: chsd ldrs: mstke 6th: lost tch bef 9th: plodded on* **13/2**[3]

1F30 **5** *3 ¼* **Grafite**[34] 4725 6-10-2 123...(t) MrCGreene(7) 101
(Milton Harris) *towards rr: struggling bef 9th: continued wl bhd* **8/1**

-55S **6** *2* **Shalone**[28] 4852 7-11-11 139.. JimmyMcCarthy 115
(Alan King) *chsd ldrs: pushed along fr bef 5th: hit 7th: 4th and rdn and outpcd bef 9th: sn wl bhd* **6/1**[2]

4000 **7** *18* **Pause And Clause (IRE)**[29] 4817 7-11-12 140..................... JackDoyle 102
(Emma Lavelle) *15 l last at 1st: a wl in rr: t.o fr 9th* **16/1**

510P **8** *32* **Premier Des Marais (FR)**[18] 5061 8-10-1 115.................. JamieMoore 51
(Gary Moore) *towards rr: pushed along bef 6th: nvr travelling after: t.o bef 9th* **14/1**

P32F **P** **Postmaster**[7] 5185 9-10-8 125....................................(t) RichardKilloran(3) —
(Tim Vaughan) *nvr bttr than midfield: rdn after 8th: sn wknd: t.o and p.u 3 out* **14/1**

6m 3.80s (-16.00) **Going Correction** -0.425s/f (Good) **9** Ran SP% **114.4**
Speed ratings (Par 109): **109,107,106,99,98 97,91,81,**—
toteswingers:1&2:£7.50, 1&3:£18.70, 2&3:£14.50 CSF £22.31 CT £271.24 TOTE £9.40: £2.50, £1.60, £4.30; EX 29.30.
Owner G A Moore **Bred** J H Ray, M Mulholland & A M Varmen **Trained** Little Newcastle, Pembrokes

FOCUS
Just a steady pace for this competitive handicap and only those who raced near the front were able to make any impact. A step up from the winner who is better than the bare result.

NOTEBOOK
Thelobstercatcher set a comfortable pace, kicked for home and outstayed his rivals. He got in close to several flights and knuckled at the last when taking off too early but still had enough in hand. He flopped when stepped up in grade at Carlisle in February but that was on heavy ground and, given a break since then and back at a track where he has won before, he looked much more at ease. (tchd 8-1)
Five Star Wilsham(IRE) looked ahead of the handicapper when winning at Doncaster last month, and the previous course winner still looked reasonably treated, but he could not quite get to the winner and it might be that the 8lb higher mark made the difference. (op 13-8 tchd 15-8 in a place)
Jaunty Journey looked to be on a retrieval mission after failing to complete his last two chases. He disputed the lead for much of the way until finding it a bit too much, as he really needs softer ground but this will have boosted his confidence no end. (tchd 20-1)
Heathcliff(IRE) raced near the lead until losing his position with half a circuit to go but he ran as well as could be expected on ground faster than ideal. (op 15-2)
Grafite rallied under pressure down the back but did not fully see out the trip. He has been kept on the go over the winter, winning once over a shorter trip at Towcester in soft ground, but might appreciate a break now. (op 9-1 tchd 15-2)
Shalone was still in touch when falling in the conditionals' hurdle at the Cheltenham Festival and faced an easier task here if able to handle the step up in trip. He travelled well to the home turn but his stride soon began to shorten and he did not see out the 3m. (op 11-2)

5326 DUNRAVEN BOWL NOVICES' HUNTERS' CHASE (FOR DUNRAVEN WINDOWS SOUTH AND WEST WALES P-T-P CHAMPIONSHIP) (18 fncs) 3m
7:25 (7:27) (Class 5) 5-Y-0+ **£2,186** (£677; £338; £169)

Form RPR

1 **Bobs Law (IRE)**[13] 7-11-12 0.. MrNickWilliams 118+
(R Scrine) *racd enthusiastically: prom: led 8th: drew clr w runner-up after 13th: rdn next: kpt responding: untidy 2 out: plld out ex to take def advantage sn after last: gamely* **13/2**[2]

54-3 **2** *1* **Pathian Prince**[26] 8-11-7 100... MrPJTolman(5) 115
(E R Clough) *t.k.h towards rr: effrt 10th: wnt 2nd at 13th and sn clr w wnr: rdn 14th: stl ev ch at last: kpt on but jst outpcd flat* **8/1**[3]

1112 **3** *17* **Oca De Thaix (FR)**[10] 5156 9-11-13 116............. MrWTwiston-Davies(7) 109
(Keith Goldsworthy) *taken down early: plld hrd: hdwy 3rd: wnt 2nd at 5th: led after 7th tl 8th: lost pl tamely 10th and mod 5th at 13th: plugged on into 15 l 3rd at 15th but no further prog* **11/10**[1]

035- **4** *20* **Rich Nomad**[20] 9-10-12 75... MissSallyRandell(7) 78
(Miss Sally Randell) *t.k.h in midfield: outpcd by ldng pair 13th: wnt 12 l 3rd bef 14th where nt fluent: sn 4th and v wl btn* **50/1**

44F- **5** *24* **Doc Wells (IRE)**[33] 8-11-12 0... MrWBiddick 66
(Ms D C Faulkner) *nvr bttr than midfield: rdn and lost tch 13th: t.o next* **12/1**

32-4 **6** *2 ¾* **Minsgill Mans**[26] 13-11-12 98... MrJETudor 64
(J W Tudor) *set v slow pce: hdd after 7th: rdn and outpcd after 13th: t.o next* **20/1**

06/ **7** *6* **Cutlass Silver**[13] 7-11-5 0... MrBMoorcroft 52
(S A Jones) *mstke 6th: in tch tl wknd 11th: t.o fr 15th* **66/1**

0P **8** *6* **Diddle'Em**[5] 10-11-5 0... MrMatthewBarber(7) 54
(Mrs A Clarke) *midfield: getting outpcd whn mstke 11th: mod 4th at 13th: t.o next* **100/1**

P/ **P** **Get Off The Table (IRE)**[13] 10-11-5 0.......................... MrRJWilliams(7) —
(A Jeffries) *bhd: rdn and lost tch 11th: t.o and p.u 14th* **100/1**

P **Bayridge Mick (IRE)**[13] 8-11-5 0.................................. MrJoshuaHarris(7) —
(R Williams) *bhd: rdn bef 8th: t.o 12th: p.u 14th* **66/1**

6m 20.8s (-1.20) **Going Correction** -0.425s/f (Good) **10** Ran SP% **91.4**
Speed ratings: **85,84,79,72,64 63,61,59,**—,—
toteswingers:1&2:£5.50, 1&3:£2.90, 2&3:£1.70 CSF £29.44 TOTE £5.50: £2.00, £1.60, £1.02; EX 27.40.
Owner Grant Lewis **Bred** Stephen Lanigan O'Keeffe & Frank Clarke **Trained** Bridgend, Bridgend
■ Rosies Peacock (3/1) was withdrawn (rider unseated and injured leaving paddock). R4 applies, deduct 25p in the £.

FOCUS
They set off at a crawl with the pace picking up only towards the end of the back straight, from where the first two were locked in battle to the line and drew clear of the remainder. Not form to be confident about, with the winner a rules debutant.

NOTEBOOK
Bobs Law(IRE) held the ideal position, dictating the pace on a tight rein, and was fully up to the task when asked to pick up the tempo in a charge up the straight. He jumped slowly at a couple of fences but overall this was a thoroughly commendable debut under rules and he continued the progression he has shown this year in winning a couple of points. (tchd 11-2)
Pathian Prince was a bit keen held up off the early pace but he made up ground in eye-catching fashion to go eye-to-eye with the winner all the way up the straight until just tiring when making a mistake at the second-last. (op 9-1)
Oca De Thaix(FR) was a strong favourite to add to his three wins in hunter chases this year. He went down to the start early and was keen as normal but seemed to be going well within himself until getting caught flat-footed once the pace lifted in the back straight. He stayed on a from there but finished adrift and there is a suspicion that his good recent form has now peaked. (op 5-4 tchd 11-8 in places)
Rich Nomad raced prominently but was readily outpaced by the first two and could do no more than plug on. He was a maiden over hurdles and fences when last seen under rules a couple of years ago but has found his level in points. (op 66-1)

5327 BRACEYS "THE FRIENDLY BUILDERS MERCHANT" 'NATIONAL HUNT' MAIDEN HURDLE (8 hdls) 2m 110y
7:55 (7:55) (Class 5) 4-Y-0+ **£1,951** (£573; £286; £143)

Form RPR

-406 **1** **There And Then**[24] 4930 5-11-0 0.................................. AndrewThornton 106+
(Seamus Mullins) *mde virtually all: set stdy pce: rdn bef last: gd jump and kpt finding ex* **25/1**

254 **2** *2* **Varkala (IRE)**[87] 3616 5-10-7 0....................................... JimmyMcCarthy 96
(Charles Egerton) *settled towards rr: hdwy 5th: rdn 2 out: 3rd and keeping on same pce whn crossed by veering rival bef last: wnt 2nd flat but nt rch wnr* **14/1**[3]

00 **3** *3 ¾* **Bob Lewis**[13] 5107 5-11-0 0.. SamThomas 102+
(Chris Down) *2nd or 3rd: chal wnr fr 5th: ev ch but rdn tl suddenly veered bdly lft bef last: nt qckn after and kpt hanging lft flat: threw it away* **18/1**

4022 **4** *2 ¾* **Fontano (FR)**[20] 5010 5-10-11 119... AlexMerriam(3) 98
(Emma Lavelle) *settled trcking ldrs: wnt 4th and rdn 3 out: no imp between last two* **4/7**[1]

42F5 **5** *11* **Alwaysonthemove**[59] 4129 7-11-0 102.................................(p) ColinBolger 89
(Laura Mongan) *chsd ldrs: rdn 5th: fnd nil and no ch after* **16/1**

500 **6** *¾* **Call Me Frankie (IRE)**[8] 5167 5-11-0 0.................................. LiamHeard 88
(Lucy Jones) *midfield: rdn 5th: no ch after* **100/1**

-060 **7** *9* **Yorkshire Knight (IRE)**[40] 4500 6-11-0 0................................. TomO'Brien 81
(Peter Bowen) *midfield: dropped to rr 4th: lft last next where j. awkwardly: plodded on* **40/1**

0/ **8** *9* **Kayfrou**[738] 4897 6-11-0 0... RichieMcLernon 74
(Jonjo O'Neill) *mounted outside paddock: nvr bttr than midfield: rdn and btn 5th* **33/1**

5623 **9** *3* **Behindcloseddoors (IRE)**[36] 4667 5-11-0 114.................. SeanQuinlan 75
(Kim Bailey) *2nd or 3rd tl rdn and chal wnr 5th where nt fluent: wkng tamely in 5th whn mstke 2 out: eased and t.o* **3/1**[2]

560 **10** *5* **Trade On**[27] 4860 4-10-8 0.. GerardTumelty 62
(Alan King) *bhd: reminder 4th: lost tch next: t.o* **33/1**

00P **P** **Harry Masters**[13] 5108 7-11-0 0.. WillKennedy —
(Edward Bevan) *a last: drvn and lost tch rapidly after 4th: t.o and p.u next: b.b.v* **100/1**

4m 7.30s (-3.30) **Going Correction** -0.425s/f (Good)
WFA 4 from 5yo+ 5lb **11** Ran SP% **120.6**
Speed ratings (Par 103): **90,89,87,86,80 80,76,72,70,68** —
toteswingers:1&2:£18.80, 1&3:£25.20, 2&3:£26.90 CSF £303.82 TOTE £37.20: £6.00, £2.70, £5.70; EX 574.50.
Owner G B Balding **Bred** Miss B Swire **Trained** Wilsford-Cum-Lake, Wilts

The Form Book, Raceform Ltd, Compton, RG20 6NL

FOCUS
Four drew clear in this ordinary maiden hurdle and once again the best place to be was up with the pace. The first two are rated in line with their bumper marks but the fourth was a stone off.
NOTEBOOK
There And Then jumped well at the head of affairs and found more when asked to tough it out to the line. He had shown enough ability to win a Southwell bumper on the AW over a year ago but this season had floundered in his first two attempts on soft ground before running a bit better at Kempton last time on good ground. Given his ground, he looks to have a bit of ability and jumped as if he has already been schooled over fences. (op 20-1)
Varkala(IRE) was held up wide of the pack and took a long while to get going but once she did she ran on well, despite being a bit green on her hurdles debut. She had failed to progress from her bumper debut when running second to subsequent hurdle winner Semi Colon but had raced only on soft ground in two subsequent starts. There should be more to come now she is getting to grips with the task. (op 10-1)
Bob Lewis challenged round the final turn but veered left going to the last and just lacked a bit of pace at the finish. (op 20-1)
Fontano(FR)'s Newbury second last month gave him the best chance on form but, although he finished in the leading quartet and clear of the field, he never looked a serious threat. He may need faster ground, but ran a bit flat here. (op 4-6 tchd 8-11)
Behindcloseddoors(IRE) held every chance in the leading group up the straight but he was beginning to struggle when making a mistake at the second-last and he weakened tamely. (op 7-2)
Harry Masters Official explanation: jockey said gelding bled from the nose
T/Plt: £52.60 to a £1 stake. Pool:£55,735.50 - 772.28 winning tickets T/Qpdt: £7.10 to a £1 stake. Pool:£6,546.31 - 678.20 winning tickets IM

5328 - 5334a (Foreign Racing) - See Raceform Interactive

5314 AYR (L-H)
Saturday, April 16

OFFICIAL GOING: Good (chs 7.9, hdl 8.0)
Chase track on innermost line and hurdles track moved out 3m.
Wind: Breezy, half against Weather: Cloudy

5335 PURVIS MARQUEES RACING EXCELLENCE "HANDS AND HEELS" FINALE H'CAP HURDLE (CONDITIONALS) (11 hdls) 2m 4f
1:50 (1:50) (Class 3) (0-125,125) 4-Y-0+ **£4,878** (£1,432; £716; £357)

Form			Horse	RPR
3212	1		**Knight Valliant**[38] 4550 8-9-11 **99** oh4 MissEButterworth(3) (Barbara Butterworth) *hld up: hdwy and prom 7th: ev ch 3 out: led next: hit last: pushed out* **14/1**	104+
3064	2	nk	**Rain Stops Play (IRE)**[26] 4912 9-10-1 **105** MrCBewley(5) (Nicky Richards) *hld up: hdwy to chse ldrs 7th: led bef 3 out to next: nt fluent last: kpt on towards fin* **16/1**	110
313B	3	5	**Texas Holdem (IRE)**[5] 5262 12-11-3 **116** AodhaganConlon (Michael Smith) *hld up in tch: effrt bef 3 out: kpt on same pce fr next* **13/2**[3]	115
2210	4	6	**Pokfulham (IRE)**[26] 4912 5-11-2 **115** (v) GaryRutherford (Jim Goldie) *hld up: stmbld bnd bef 3rd: n.m.r bnd after 5th: effrt bef 3 out: no imp fr next* **16/1**	109
0242	5	1 ½	**Franklino (FR)**[21] 5006 4-10-7 **112** PeterHatton (Alan King) *hld up in midfield: effrt after 4 out: no imp fr next* **7/1**	98
0PU1	6	1 ¼	**Charingworth (IRE)**[20] 5030 8-11-4 **117** EdmondLinehan (Ferdy Murphy) *hld up: effrt after 4 out: plugged on fr last: nvr able to chal* **11/1**	109
2023	7	3 ¾	**Leith Walk (IRE)**[26] 4914 8-9-11 **99** CallumWhillans(3) (Donald Whillans) *in tch: n.m.r bnd after 5th: rdn and outpcd after 4 out: n.d after* **16/1**	87
P300	8	hd	**Lago Verde (SWI)**[23] 4958 6-9-12 **102** (tp) MrDOckenden(5) (Lucinda Russell) *chsd ldr: ev ch after 4 out: outpcd whn hit next: sn no ex* **100/1**	90
0550	9	1	**Grandad Bill (IRE)**[26] 4914 8-10-9 **108** PeterCarberry (Jim Goldie) *in tch: lost pl after 5th: sme late hdwy: nvr on terms* **6/1**[2]	96
3315	10	7	**Semi Colon (FR)**[21] 5008 5-11-0 **113** (t) JeremiahMcGrath (Nicky Henderson) *prom: pushed along bef 3 out: sn wknd* **3/1**[1]	94
5020	11	¾	**Quacity (FR)**[58] 4166 7-10-3 **105** MrGJCockburn(3) (Lucinda Russell) *bhd: outpcd 1/2-way: nvr on terms* **20/1**	85
41F2	12	14	**Locked Inthepocket (IRE)**[35] 4714 7-10-9 **108** PaulGallagher (Pauline Robson) *hld up in tch: pushed along after 4 out: wknd fr next* **12/1**	75
12P3	13	16	**Tout Regulier**[224] 1466 7-11-7 **120** MichaelByrne (Peter Bowen) *led to bef 3 out: sn rdn and btn* **16/1**	73
6500	P		**Melange (USA)**[58] 4166 5-10-1 **100** (t) JakeGreenall (George Charlton) *chsd ldrs: blkd bnd after 5th: sn struggling: p.u after next* **40/1**	—

4m 46.63s (-25.37) **Going Correction** -1.225s/f (Hard)
WFA 4 from 5yo+ 6lb **14** Ran SP% **119.5**
Speed ratings (Par 107): **101,100,98,96,95 95,93,93,93,90 90,84,78,—**
Tote Swingers: 1&2 £31.70, 1&3 £18.20, 2&3 £30.20 CSF £212.42 CT £1604.11 TOTE £14.50: £5.40, £5.90, £2.60; EX 246.70 TRIFECTA Not won..
Owner Mrs Barbara Butterworth **Bred** P E Clinton **Trained** Bolton, Cumbria
■ Aodhagan Conlon was the series winner.
FOCUS
The bends were out three metres from Friday's line on the hurdles course, but the chase track remained the same. The ground appeared to be riding as per the official description, backed up by a time for the opener which was 7.7sec over the Racing Post standard. Just a fair handicap hurdle. Riders weren't permitted to use their whips and the form should be treated with a little caution.
NOTEBOOK
Knight Valliant was 4lb out of the weights so in effect 15lb higher than when winning under this rider at Catterick two starts back. Held up and kept wide, he made smooth progress to lead and and, although only nudged along on the flat, was always just about holding the runner-up. He is in fine heart and could go for a ladies' race on the Flat next. (op 16-1)
Rain Stops Play(IRE) might have found himself in front a shade earlier than desirable. After meeting neither of the last two flights right he rallied on the run-in. He saw out the trip well enough but is still looking for his first win over hurdles.
Texas Holdem(IRE) is admirably consistent and kept on for third, showing no ill effects from being brought down last Monday. (op 9-1)
Pokfulham(IRE) was a shade reluctant to line up and stumbled early on. He was being pushed along some way out and plugged on for fourth.
Franklino(FR), racing from a 5lb higher mark, lost his pitch before keeping on at the same pace. He is not one to give up on yet. (op 13-2)
Charingworth(IRE) ran respectably off 4lb higher than when winning at Hexham. (op 10-1 tchd 12-1)
Grandad Bill(IRE) has slipped to a good mark but is not running well enough to take advantage. (op 15-2)
Semi Colon(FR) ran well off the same mark in a competitive mares' race at Newbury latest, but she was disappointing in a first-time tongue tie. Likely to go chasing in the new season, she has questions to answer over this trip. She was reported to have run flat. Official explanation: jockey said mare ran flat (op 11-4 tchd 10-3)

5336 SCOTTISH SUN FUTURE CHAMPION NOVICES' CHASE (GRADE 2) (17 fncs) 2m 4f
2:20 (2:20) (Class 1) 5-Y-0+
£17,103 (£6,417; £3,213; £1,602; £804; £402)

Form			Horse	RPR
-135	1		**Gilbarry (IRE)**[7] 5197 6-11-4 134 GrahamLee (Malcolm Jefferson) *hld up: hdwy and cl up whn nt fluent 12th: led bef 3 out: gng clr whn lft 14 l in front last: kpt on wl* **8/1**	152+
-012	2	16	**Sam Lord**[23] 4959 7-11-0 128 PaddyAspell (James Moffatt) *hld up: hdwy to chse clr ldrs 4 out: no imp fr next: lft 14 l 2nd last: no imp* **22/1**	134+
1160	3	2 ¼	**Nadiya De La Vega (FR)**[32] 4794 5-11-0 137 AndrewTinkler (Nicky Henderson) *hld up in tch: nt fluent 8th: rdn and outpcd 5 out: plugged on fr 2 out: lft modest 3rd last: nvr able to chal* **4/1**[3]	128
PP41	4	7	**Soft Spoken Guy (IRE)**[12] 5146 8-11-0 125 (t) MichaelMcAlister (Maurice Barnes) *prom: drvn and outpcd bef 5 out: btn next: lft modest 4th last* **14/1**	123
F126	5	22	**Giorgio Quercus (FR)**[32] 4789 6-11-7 148 BarryGeraghty (Nicky Henderson) *sn chsng ldr: led 4th tl mstke and hdd 8th: lost pl next: rallied 10th: hit and wknd 5 out* **5/2**[1]	112
211P	6	3 ¼	**Premier Sagas (FR)**[32] 4794 7-11-7 139 FearghalDavis (Nicky Richards) *led to 4th: cl up tl rdn and wknd bef 4 out* **9/2**	105
1120	F		**Stagecoach Pearl**[32] 4789 7-11-7 145 ShaneByrne (Sue Smith) *t.k.h: cl up: led 8th: hdd bef 3 out: no ex fr next: 9 l 2nd and hld whn fell last* **7/2**[2]	143

4m 57.9s (-25.00) **Going Correction** -1.20s/f (Hard) **7** Ran SP% **111.1**
Speed ratings: **102,95,94,91,83 81,—**
Tote Swingers: 1&2 £46.60, 1&3 £4.10, 2&3 £58.70 CSF £118.47 TOTE £9.30: £3.30, £4.60; EX 125.50.
Owner Highbank Stud **Bred** Colin Kennedy **Trained** Norton, N Yorks
FOCUS
A decent edition on paper of a Grade 2 which has been won by some smart novices, with Deep Purple and French Opera the previous two winners. Some of the fancied contenders disappointed though, and the form may not prove that solid. The time was around 10sec outside the standard.
NOTEBOOK
Gilbarry(IRE) was well held in Finian's Rainbow's race at Aintree last week, his first start since Dooombor having been kept away from soft ground, but was a different proposition over this longer trip. He made notable headway before the home turn and was never in any danger once jumping to the front three from home. A big individual, he can still be a little clumsy at his fences but there is more improvement to come from him as he builds experience. He may go for an intermediate chase at the Perth festival later this month.
Sam Lord made most when winning at Sedgefield but was ridden more conservatively here. Improving to turn into the home straight in third, he kept on steadily over the last line of fences and was presented with second at the last, but never threatened the winner. Not the sort to find much for pressure, he still has room for improvement in his jumping. (op 16-1)
Nadiya De La Vega(FR) was given a reminder with a circuit to run and had dropped to the back of the field on the home turn. This scopey mare did stay on when it was all over and may get further than this. She has a date at the sales next month. (tchd 9-2)
Soft Spoken Guy(IRE), a Kelso winner latest, faced a stiff task in this much warmer company, back in trip and on different ground. He was struggling down the far side, but plugged on for a well-beaten fourth. (tchd 12-1)
Giorgio Quercus(FR), the Arkle sixth, was expected to improve for this longer trip and jumped well in front until clouting the last with a lap to run and losing his lead. Never particularly happy afterwards, he had been seen off before the fourth-last. This was not his running. Official explanation: jockey said gelding made a mistake and never travelled (tchd 9-4)
Premier Sagas(FR), whose connections won this with Monet's Garden in 2006, was another to drop away rather tamely when the pressure was on. There had been excuses at Cheltenham but this was disappointing. (op 4-1)
Stagecoach Pearl was last of nine finishers in the Arkle. Tracking the pace this time, he was keen and had pulled his way to the front with a circuit left. He had a lot of these in trouble turning into the straight, the winner being an exception, and though he was tired he was still in second place when he knuckled over at the last. (op 5-1)

5337 ISLE OF SKYE BLENDED WHISKY SCOTTISH CHAMPION HURDLE LIMITED H'CAP (GRADE 2) (9 hdls) 2m
2:50 (2:50) (Class 1) 4-Y-0+
£28,505 (£10,695; £5,355; £2,670; £1,340; £670)

Form			Horse	RPR
-F30	1		**Sanctuaire (FR)**[86] 3649 5-10-8 **144** RWalsh (Paul Nicholls) *hld up: smooth hdwy to trck ldrs 3 out: plld out to ld last: sn rdn: edgd rt and kpt on wl* **9/2**[1]	150+
U020	2	1 ¾	**Bygones Of Brid (IRE)**[32] 4791 8-10-8 **144** GrahamLee (Karen McLintock) *prom: hdwy to press ldr bef 4th: effrt and ev ch 3 out to last: kpt on same pce run-in* **14/1**	147
1250	3	1 ½	**Overturn (IRE)**[32] 4791 7-11-10 **160** JasonMaguire (Donald McCain) *led: rdn bef 3 out: sn hrd pressed: hdd last: kpt on same pce* **13/2**	161
6342	4	4 ½	**Cockney Trucker (IRE)**[22] 4992 9-10-4 **140** oh3 RichardJohnson (Philip Hobbs) *hld up in tch: drvn and outpcd bef 3 out: rallied next: no imp* **8/1**	138
2123	5	3	**Via Galilei (IRE)**[7] 5201 6-10-4 **140** oh4 JamieMoore (Gary Moore) *hld up: effrt and rdn bef 3 out: nvr able to chal* **11/2**[3]	135
0310	6	5	**Hunterview**[29] 4848 5-9-13 **140** oh2 (b) CO'Farrell(5) (David Pipe) *chsd ldr to bef 4th: cl up tl rdn and wknd bef 3 out* **5/1**[2]	131
5035	7	2 ½	**Nearby**[7] 5201 7-10-10 **153** ChrisDavies(7) (Philip Hobbs) *hld up in tch: effrt bef 3 out: sn rdn and wknd* **8/1**	142
4-F4	P		**Apartman (CZE)**[285] 909 6-10-4 **140** oh5 JanFaltejsek (George Charlton) *nt fluent: bhd: lost tch 4th: t.o whn p.u bef 3 out* **40/1**	—
2110	P		**Mille Chief (FR)**[32] 4791 5-11-8 **158** RobertThornton (Alan King) *t.k.h: chsd ldrs: hit 5th: rdn and wknd 3 out: p.u bef next* **9/2**[1]	—

3m 38.1s (-25.00) **Going Correction** -1.225s/f (Hard) **9** Ran SP% **113.1**
Speed ratings (Par 115): **113,112,111,109,107 105,103,—,—**
Tote Swingers: 1&2 £23.70, 1&3 £3.90, 2&3 £24.50 CSF £61.07 CT £404.54 TOTE £5.10: £1.50, £4.80, £1.30; EX 79.70 Trifecta £548.20 Pool: £6741.62 - 9.10 winning units..
Owner Jared Sullivan **Bred** S C A De Lageneste-Har De St Voir **Trained** Ditcheat, Somerset
FOCUS
A decent edition of this limited handicap, run at a strong early tempo before the pace slackened a little down the far side. Four of the field were out of the weights but the form should prove sound.

NOTEBOOK

Sanctuaire(FR) was a promising juvenile a year ago, but had disappointed in three runs this term. Given a break to wait for this better ground, during which he had a breathing operation, he was settled by Ruby Walsh after a couple of flights and that enabled this often headstrong gelding to show his true colours. Given a nice tow into the race and cruising through on the bridle to challenge, he found plenty after the last. He may be supplemented for the Shell Champion Hurdle at Punchestown or could run at Sandown next weekend. (op 11-2)

Bygones Of Brid(IRE) ran creditably in the Champion Hurdle and this was another pleasing effort. Challenging Overturn for the lead from midway down the back straight, he could not hold off the strong-travelling winner but battled well to secure second close home.

Overturn(IRE) was bidding to extend an unbeaten record over C&D, but was 30lb higher than when winning this race 12 months ago having established himself in the interim as a very smart hurdler. Seeing off early competition for the lead from Hunterview, and taken on by Bygones Of Brid from halfway, he fought on well but had to give best on the run-in. He may go for the Chester Cup. (op 11-2)

Cockney Trucker(IRE) was 3lb wrong at the weights and could never get in a blow, although he was running on at the end.

Via Galilei(IRE), who was 4lb out of the weights and effectively 11lb higher than when second in the Imperial Cup last month, was another who was never able to mount a challenge. (op 9-2 tchd 6-1)

Hunterview was back on a flat, speed-favouring track which should have been to his advantage, but he was unable to get to the front and was in trouble before the home turn. (tchd 9-2)

Nearby travelled well into the race but could not sustain his effort, and this may have come too soon for him. (op 10-1)

Mille Chief(FR), who had Overturn behind in the Kingwell at Wincanton, dragged his hind legs through consecutive flights down the back and, fading in the straight, was pulled up. This followed a lacklustre effort at Cheltenham and he now has a bit to prove. (op 5-1)

5338 CORAL SCOTTISH GRAND NATIONAL H'CAP CHASE (GRADE 3)

(27 fncs) **4m 110y**

3:25 (3:28) (Class 1) 5-Y-O+

£102,618 (£38,502; £19,278; £9,612; £4,824; £2,412)

Form RPR

-B12 **1** **Beshabar (IRE)**[31] 4802 9-10-4 **146**................................ RichardJohnson 155+
(Tim Vaughan) *cl up: led 7th: mde rest: nt fluent 20th: rdn 3 out: kpt on wl u.p fr next: idled nr fin* **15/2**[2]

-0F0 **2** *3/4* **Merigo (FR)**[42] 4466 10-10-0 **142** oh12............................. TimmyMurphy 149
(Andrew Parker) *chsd ldrs: hdwy to chal fnl circ: effrt and edgd lft after 3 out: j.rt and sltly outpcd next: styd on wl run-in* **20/1**

-211 **3** *nk* **Always Right (IRE)**[42] 4466 9-10-0 **142** oh3.................... JamesReveley 149
(John Wade) *hld up: stdy hdwy fnl circ: chsd ldrs bef 4 out: effrt next: hit 2 out: kpt on u.p run-in* **15/2**[2]

0P52 **4** *30* **Lothian Falcon**[42] 4466 12-9-7 **142** oh15....................... PeterCarberry(7) 120
(Peter Maddison) *prom: rdn along after 5 out: wknd after next* **33/1**

24U2 **5** *3/4* **Heez A Steel (IRE)**[36] 4689 10-9-9 **144** oh14 ow2........ AlistairFindlay(7) 123
(George Charlton) *hld up in midfield: hdwy and in tch bef 15th: blnd and rdn 22nd: wknd after 4 out* **66/1**

B010 **6** *1 3/4* **Neptune Collonges (FR)**[29] 4850 10-11-12 **168**.................. APMcCoy 143
(Paul Nicholls) *midfield: rdn and outpcd 18th: rallied u.p 5 out: no imp fr next* **16/1**

52-6 **7** *4 1/2* **Gone To Lunch (IRE)**[29] 4851 11-10-0 **142** oh10.........(p) NickScholfield 113
(Jeremy Scott) *led to 7th: cl up: outpcd 5 out: rdn and wknd fr next* **14/1**

F251 **8** *12* **Chicago Grey (IRE)**[31] 4802 8-10-9 **151**..............................(t) PCarberry 112
(Gordon Elliott, Ire) *bhd: struggling bef 19th: sme hdwy bef 4 out: nvr on terms* **11/2**[1]

3221 **9** *6* **Regal Heights (IRE)**[42] 4486 10-10-0 **142** oh12...........(p) AidanColeman 97
(Tom George) *hld up in midfield: drvn and outpcd 19th: sn btn: collapsed and died after line* **33/1**

3P00 **10** *17* **No Panic (IRE)**[32] 4790 8-10-0 **142** oh17............................(p) TomO'Brien 82
(Peter Bowen) *in tch: rdn and outpcd whn hit 5 out: sn wknd* **50/1**

F423 **11** *8* **Neptune Equester**[56] 4206 8-9-9 **142** oh14.................. PaulGallagher(5) 75
(Brian Ellison) *prom: pushed along 19th: blnd 22nd: sn rdn: wknd fr 4 out* **14/1**

050F **12** *4* **That's Rhythm (FR)**[7] 5200 11-10-0 **142** oh2...............(v) CampbellGillies 71
(Martin Todhunter) *in tcouch: rdn after 19th: wknd fr 21st* **40/1**

1300 **13** *16* **Ouzbeck (FR)**[21] 5003 9-10-5 **147**.. JackDoyle 62
(Emma Lavelle) *hld up towards rr: rdn and outpcd whn nt fluent 20th: sn btn* **16/1**

50P- **P** **Iris De Balme (FR)**[392] 4740 11-9-11 **142** oh14...........(t) CharlieHuxley(3) —
(Joanna Davis) *a bhd: t.o whn p.u bef 22nd* **66/1**

4-P6 **P** **Roll Along (IRE)**[56] 4200 11-10-0 **142** oh9.............. SamTwiston-Davies —
(Nigel Twiston-Davies) *towards rr: struggling fr 15th: tailedoff whn p.u bef 20th* **50/1**

4522 **P** **Ballyfitz**[28] 4876 11-10-0 **142** oh11...................................... DavidEngland —
(Nigel Twiston-Davies) *prom: rdn 10th: struggling 15th: t.o whn p.u bef 21st* **28/1**

U6P1 **F** **Cold Mountain (IRE)**[18] 5067 9-10-0 **142** oh18.................... BarryKeniry —
(Seamus Mullins) *in tch: lost pl whn fell 11th* **66/1**

6110 **P** **Blazing Bailey**[32] 4790 9-10-11 **153**................................ RobertThornton —
(Alan King) *bhd: struggling and p.u bef 19th* **20/1**

-331 **P** **Morgan Be**[20] 5032 11-10-0 **142** oh19.............................. RichieMcGrath —
(Kate Walton) *a bhd: lost tch and p.u bef 19th* **80/1**

6P-3 **P** **Hot 'N' Holy**[26] 4915 12-9-11 **142** oh42......................... TommyPhelan(3) —
(David Thompson) *sn bhd: hmpd 11th: t.o whn p.u bef 17th* **200/1**

P-06 **U** **Poker De Sivola (FR)**[32] 4792 8-10-0 **142** oh6.................... GrahamLee —
(Ferdy Murphy) *hld up and bhd: hmpd and uns rdr 11th* **11/1**

010F **P** **Gansey (IRE)**[8] 5185 9-10-0 **142** oh7.............................. PeterBuchanan —
(Sue Smith) *a bhd: no ch fnl circ: t.o whn p.u bef 3 out* **66/1**

2216 **P** **Fredo (IRE)**[30] 4821 7-9-9 **142** oh12.................................(p) MrRMahon(5) —
(Ian Williams) *in tch tl wknd after 18th: t.o whn p.u bef 20th* **40/1**

42P1 **P** **Minella Four Star (IRE)**[28] 4876 8-9-11 **144**....................... CO'Farrell(5) —
(David Pipe) *nt fluent on occasions: in tch: mstke 18th: outpcd whn blnd 22nd: sn btn: p.u and dismntd after 4 out: collapsed and died* **16/1**

/0-U **P** **Long Strand (IRE)**[23] 4979 7-10-0 **142** oh19............................ DJCasey —
(C F Swan, Ire) *midfield: drvn 18th: sn lost pl: t.o whn p.u bef 22nd* **66/1**

3F32 **P** **Silent Cliche (IRE)**[20] 5029 7-10-0 **142** oh24...................(b) BrianHughes —
(Howard Johnson) *a bhd: struggling after 18th: t.o whn p.u bef 20th* **100/1**

2513 **P** **Be There In Five (IRE)**[31] 4802 7-10-0 **142** oh4................. FelixDeGiles —
(Nicky Henderson) *mstkes: in tch tl wknd 22nd: p.u after next* **22/1**

-113 **P** **The Minack (IRE)**[56] 4199 7-10-1 **143**.. RWalsh —
(Paul Nicholls) *hld up in midfield: mstke 14th: outpcd 19th: sn btn: p.u bef 22nd* **8/1**[3]

8m 2.50s (-50.50) **Going Correction** -1.20s/f (Hard) **28** Ran SP% **131.5**
Speed ratings: **113,112,112,105,105 104,103,100,99,95 93,92,88,—,— —,—,—,—,— —,—,E**
Tote Swingers: 1&2 £63.20, 1&3 £22.60, 2&3 £51.60 CSF £154.45 CT £1200.46 TOTE £9.40: £3.40, £4.90, £2.50, £7.20; EX 318.30 Trifecta £2833.60 Pool: £28107.04 - 7.34 winning units..
Owner Mrs M Findlay & Middleham Park Racing X **Bred** John Cotter **Trained** Aberthin, Vale of Glamorgan

FOCUS

The presence of the 168-rated Neptune Collonges in topweight meant that only a quarter of the field were able to race off their correct handicap marks. It still looked a competitive edition of this historic marathon chase. It was run at a solid pace and only a handful were still in contention facing up to the final four fences. The first three fought out a good finish, well clear of the rest.

NOTEBOOK

Beshabar(IRE), one of the few in the handicap proper, produced a fine staying performance on just his fifth run over fences. Forcing the pace from an early stage, he jumped well all the way and kept finding for pressure, although he was all out in the end as the second and third close on him. A rangy chaser who stayed the 4m well when runner-up to Chicago Grey in the National Hunt Chase at Cheltenham, he is old for a novice at nine but has a relatively low mileage and he looks just the type for the Grand National next spring. His campaign will be geared towards that race. (op 8-1)

Merigo(FR), last year's winner, was 15lb higher this time round as he was racing from 12lb out of the weights. He failed to make the cut at Aintree, but this provided a very suitable alternative and he ran a big race, always chasing the pace. His tendency to jump out to his right cost him ground two out and he looked held in third landing over the last, but stayed on well to go down fighting. There is no reason why he should not be competitive in races like this again next season, although Aintree will not be on the agenda.

Always Right(IRE) has made big strides this term since switching from hunter chases and beat Lothian Falcon and Merigo when taking the Grimthorpe at Doncaster latest. Racing from 12lb higher, being 3lb wrong, he made stealthy progress and loomed up as a big threat, but walked through the second-last and and was always just being held from there. He stayed this longer trip well. (op 8-1 tchd 9-1 in a place)

Lothian Falcon weakened before the home straight but kept going for a remote fourth. Now at the veteran stage but clearly still in fine heart, he was over a stone higher than at Doncaster, and wasn't fitted with the cheekpieces he wore there.

Heez A Steel(IRE) stayed on well over 3m6f at Catterick earlier this term and showed improved form over this marathon trip, albeit beaten a long way. A blunder on the final circuit could have cost him fourth and this was a decent effort from more than a stone wrong.

Neptune Collonges(FR), eighth in the Gold Cup when last seen, was never a threat to the leaders but did plug on for a respectable sixth under his big weight. (tchd 20-1)

Gone To Lunch(IRE), runner-up the last two years, was unable to build on that but he ran well for a long way from 10lb out of the handicap. (op 16-1)

Chicago Grey(IRE) beat Beshabar in the Cheltenham four-miler and was closely matched with him at the revised weights. He was slow to jump off though (at the second attempt following a false start) and was always near the back of the field before making late progress through beaten rivals. Cheltenham festival winners have a poor record in this race. He was reported to have run flat. Official explanation: jockey said, regarding running, that the gelding ran flat (op 6-1)

Regal Heights(IRE), who won eight times in a lengthy career, got round but sadly collapsed and died after the race.

Neptune Equester has been kept to hurdles during the winter and looked interesting on this return to chasing, but after making good progress to track the leaders prior to the final circuit he failed to get home. (op 16-1)

Iris De Balme(FR), the 2009 winner, effectively just a pound lower on this first start for his new yard, was always towards the back before pulling up. (op 10-1)

Blazing Bailey was well held in the Spinal Research Handicap Chase at Cheltenham and was in trouble with a full circuit to go here. (op 10-1)

Morgan Be was reported to have bled from the nose. Official explanation: jockey said gelding bled from the nose (op 10-1)

Poker De Sivola(FR) had been primed for this, but was put out of the race when Cold Mountain fell in front of him at the eleventh. (op 10-1)

Minella Four Star(IRE), the Midlands National winner, was pulled up and sadly died from internal bleeding. (op 10-1)

Be There In Five(IRE), third to Chicago Grey and Beshabar at Cheltenham, found this too hot and made mistakes. He dropped away on the final circuit. (op 10-1)

The Minack(IRE), a very useful novice running for only the fourth time over fences, was struggling and pulled up before his stamina for this trip could be tested. (op 10-1)

5339 AYRSHIRE HOSPICE H'CAP HURDLE (12 hdls) 2m 5f 110y

4:00 (4:00) (Class 2) (0-155,135) 4-Y-O+ **£9,757** (£2,865; £1,432; £715)

Form RPR

1101 **1** **Russian War (IRE)**[9] 5166 8-11-12 **135**..................................(t) PCarberry 144+
(Gordon Elliott, Ire) *stdd s: hld up in rr: stdy hdwy 9th: upsides on bit 2 out: led between last 2: v cheekily* **2/1**[1]

4161 **2** *1* **Attaglance**[20] 5028 5-10-8 **120**......................................(t) JamesHalliday(3) 121
(Malcolm Jefferson) *t.k.h: trckd ldrs: narrow ld 2 out: sn hdd: kpt on wl: no imp* **12/1**

3 *3/4* **Molly's Boy**[16] 5088 10-10-13 **122**....................................(t) BarryGeraghty 122
(Edward Cawley, Ire) *hld up wl in tch: upsides 9th: kpt on wl run-in* **8/1**

3566 **4** *7* **Los Nadis (GER)**[24] 4940 7-11-0 **123**..................................... GrahamLee 117
(Jim Goldie) *t.k.h: trckd ldr: led 6th: hdd 2 out: wknd appr last* **11/2**[2]

-420 **5** *2 3/4* **Arctic Wings (IRE)**[35] 4727 7-10-13 **125**........................ LeeEdwards(3) 116
(Tony Carroll) *trckd ldrs: nt fluent 7th: drvn next: sn outpcd: rallied appr 2 out: one pce* **14/1**

3151 **6** *4 1/2* **Bogside (IRE)**[12] 5151 7-10-9 **118**... JanFaltejsek 106
(George Charlton) *t.k.h: trckd ldrs: rdn 9th: wknd next* **7/1**

1-03 **7** *1* **Kilbrannish Hill (IRE)**[12] 5149 7-10-8 **117**.............................(p) AELynch 104
(I R Ferguson, Ire) *stdd s: hld up in rr: hdwy 9th: hit next: chasinng ldrs appr 2 out: sn wknd* **6/1**[3]

-521 **8** *3* **Cool Operator**[54] 4255 8-11-1 **129**.................................. PaulGallagher(5) 115
(Howard Johnson) *led: mstke 3rd: hdd 6th: rdn 9th: wknd appr 2 out* **7/1**

5m 22.4s (-17.90) **Going Correction** -1.225s/f (Hard) **8** Ran SP% **113.5**
Speed ratings (Par 109): **83,82,82,79,78 77,76,75**
Tote Swingers: 1&2 £8.30, 1&3 £8.60, 2&3 £18.20 CSF £25.07 CT £158.19 TOTE £2.90: £1.40, £3.90, £1.60; EX 22.50 Trifecta £331.10 Pool: £532.45 - 1.19 winning units..
Owner T D Howley Jnr **Bred** Tommy Howley **Trained** Trim, Co Meath

■ Stewards' Enquiry : James Halliday one-day ban: careless riding (Apr 30)

FOCUS

Not a strong race for the class with the top weight - the winner - running from 20lb below the race ceiling. The pace was steady and it became something of a sprint in the home straight.

NOTEBOOK

Russian War(IRE) impressed when winning a more competitive handicap than this last weekend and he shrugged off a 7lb rise to record his fifth win from his last eight starts. As at Aintree he was dropped out the back before coming from last to first, winning with plenty in hand. He was value for a lot further and there is probably more to come, but the handicapper will catch up with him at some point. (tchd 9-4)

Attaglance ran well on this handicap debut, running on willingly to secure second, albeit flattered to finish as close as he did to the easy winner. He had his tongue tied for the first time. (op 10-1 tchd 14-1)

Molly's Boy, an Irish raider, had the tongue-tie back on. He travelled well and was only shaken up going to the final flight, but found nothing like as much as the winner. (op 15-2)

Los Nadis(GER) had caught the eye on his two starts for this yard. Ridden differently and setting a modest pace, he was swallowed up two from home. (op 7-1)

Arctic Wings(IRE) was the first under pressure and was never a factor afterwards. (op 10-1)

Bogside(IRE), a Kelso novice winner last time, was too keen on this handicap debut. (op 8-1 tchd 13-2)

Kilbrannish Hill(IRE) faded between the last two flights. (op 13-2 tchd 7-1)

Cool Operator was disappointing off a 9lb higher mark than when winning well in heavy ground at Carlisle. (op 8-1)

5340 SCOTTY BRAND H'CAP CHASE (12 fncs) 2m
4:30 (4:30) (Class 2) 5-Y-O+ **£14,311** (£4,202; £2,101; £1,049)

Form				RPR
-0U0	1		**Beggars Cap (IRE)**[9] 5164 9-10-9 **127** GrahamLee (Ferdy Murphy) *t.k.h in rr: hdwy 4th: trcking ldrs 8th: led last: sn hdd: rallied to ld fnl strides* **14/1**	137
0602	2	nk	**I'msingingtheblues (IRE)**[1] 5317 9-11-11 **143** (t) APMcCoy (David Pipe) *trckd ldrs: chal 2 out: led sn after last: hdd and no ex nr fin* **4/1**[1]	153
4200	3	6	**Tanks For That (IRE)**[29] 4853 8-11-8 **140** BarryGeraghty (Nicky Henderson) *w ldrs: led 4th: hdd last: sn wknd* **9/1**	146
0035	4	3	**Quito Du Tresor (FR)**[29] 4853 7-10-12 **130** CampbellGillies (Lucinda Russell) *in tch: hdwy to chse ldrs 8th: wknd between last 2* **5/1**[2]	133
0623	5	3	**I'm Delilah**[9] 5164 9-11-6 **138** JamesReveley (Ferdy Murphy) *prom: lost pl 4th: hdwy to chse ldrs 9th: hit 3 out: sn wknd* **5/1**[2]	140
6630	6	17	**Oh Crick (FR)**[29] 4853 8-11-12 **144** RobertThornton (Alan King) *in rr: bhd fr 8th* **10/1**	131
64-4	7	3	**Professor Higgins (IRE)**[78] 3786 8-9-11 **120** PaulGallagher(5) (Howard Johnson) *w ldrs: rdn and lost pl appr 9th* **15/2**	105
0155	8	3 ¾	**Quicuyo (GER)**[26] 4913 8-10-2 **120** (t) RichieMcGrath (James Ewart) *led: pckd bdly 1st: hdd 4th: lost pl 7th* **22/1**	100
004	9	1 ¾	**Fred Bojangals (IRE)**[24] 4941 9-10-5 **123** (p) BrianHughes (Ann Hamilton) *chsd ldrs: lost pl 7th: sn bhd* **11/1**	99
4411	P		**Elite Land**[42] 4470 8-10-12 **130** JasonMaguire (Brian Ellison) *in rr: drvn 3rd: lost tch 6th: p.u bef next* **7/1**[3]	—

3m 46.8s (-23.00) **Going Correction** -1.20s/f (Hard) **10 Ran SP% 110.0**
Speed ratings: **111,110,107,106,104 96,94,92,92,—**
Tote Swingers: 1&2 £17.30, 1&3 £9.20, 2&3 £6.70 CSF £70.91 CT £543.28 TOTE £15.20: £4.60, £1.80, £1.90; EX 132.10 Trifecta £546.20 Part won. Pool of £738.11 - 0.40 winning units..

Owner Trevor Hemmings **Bred** Nicholas O'Neill **Trained** West Witton, N Yorks

FOCUS
A decent and competitive handicap chase, and the form should prove solid.

NOTEBOOK
Beggars Cap(IRE) had not won since scoring at Aintree in May 2009, having finished second in this race on his previous run. He was fancied for the Grand Annual two starts back, only to unseat his rider, and was never a factor from a stone out of the weights in the Red Rum Chase at Aintree. Able to race from his correct mark, he improved to track the leaders down the far side. Showing just ahead at the last, he was quickly headed but rallied to snatch the race near the line. Official explanation: trainer said, regarding apparent improvement in form, that the gelding was better suited by the track and the way the race was run. (op 12-1)

I'msingingtheblues(IRE), runner-up over 2m4f here on Friday, was ridden much more prominently than usual. The change of tactics appeared set to work as he went a neck up after the last, but he was worried out of it. He has gone 16 races since his last victory in January 2009, but is 4lb below his last winning mark. (op 5-1)

Tanks For That(IRE), who reportedly found the preliminaries too much for him in the Grand Annual at Cheltenham, where he dropped away to finish last, was 2lb lower here. Jumping his way to the front at the fourth, he was only collared at the last before weakening on the run-in. (op 17-2)

Quito Du Tresor(FR), fifth in the Grand Annual, is in the same ownership as I'msingingtheblues. Back on a flat track, he came to have his chance but weakened between the last two fences. (op 6-1)

I'm Delilah faded from the third-last and was unable to build on her good run at Aintree, where she was out of the weights and finished well for third. (op 4-1)

Oh Crick(FR) was rather disappointing. (op 8-1)

Professor Higgins(IRE), who is lightly raced, was well held on this return to 2m. (op 8-1)

Fred Bojangals(IRE) finished runner-up in this last year but never looked like going one better. (op 10-1)

Elite Land, another 6lb higher on this hat-trick bid, did not look too keen in rear prior to pulling up. Official explanation: jockey said gelding never travelled (op 8-1 tchd 13-2)

5341 WEATHERBYS BLOODSTOCK INSURANCE NOVICES' H'CAP CHASE (19 fncs) 3m 1f
5:05 (5:06) (Class 2) 5-Y-O+ **£10,408** (£3,056; £1,528; £763)

Form				RPR
414P	1		**On His Own (IRE)**[31] 4802 7-10-7 **116** PaulGallagher(5) (Howard Johnson) *cl up: chal and j.rt fnl circ: led 2 out: styd on strly fr last* **9/2**[2]	127+
-125	2	4 ½	**The Shoe (NZ)**[189] 1774 9-11-5 **123** BarryGeraghty (Nicky Henderson) *hld up in tch: hdwy to chse ldrs bef 4 out: effrt and ev ch 2 out to run-in: one pce* **8/1**	128
2212	3	6	**Cool Mission (IRE)**[21] 5001 7-11-12 **130** (p) JasonMaguire (Donald McCain) *cl up: led 10th: rdn and hdd 2 out: sn outpcd* **8/1**	131
14U3	4	2 ¼	**Misstree Dancer**[28] 4877 7-11-8 **126** HarrySkelton (Nick Mitchell) *hld up in tch: effrt 4 out: no ex fr 2 out* **20/1**	126
6621	5	26	**Humbie (IRE)**[24] 4938 7-11-2 **120** TimmyMurphy (Pauline Robson) *hld up in tch: hdwy to trck ldrs bef 11th: rdn bef 4 out: edgd lft and wknd bef next* **4/1**[1]	106+
024-	6	12	**Carsonstown Boy (IRE)**[28] 4884 7-11-4 **122** PCarberry (C A McBratney, Ire) *bhd: outpcd and drvn 11th: nvr on terms* **8/1**	85
4433	7	8	**Posh Bird (IRE)**[12] 5150 8-10-2 **106** (p) AELynch (I R Ferguson, Ire) *bhd and detached: mstke 11th: sn struggling* **9/1**	62
P121	8	8	**You Know Yourself (IRE)**[23] 4961 8-11-0 **118** HenryOliver (Sue Smith) *led to 9th: outpcd after 12th: sn wknd* **7/1**[3]	67
512	P		**Winterwood (IRE)**[22] 4989 8-11-1 **119** (v) SamThomas (Tim Vaughan) *prom: blnd 5th: rdn 13th: wknd bef 4 out: t.o whn p.u bef 2 out* **8/1**	—
2F3P	P		**Ballymacduff (IRE)**[20] 5032 7-10-0 **104** (t) JanFaltejsek (George Charlton) *prom: lost pl 12th: sn struggling: t.o whn p.u bef 3 out* **11/1**	—

6m 12.1s (-37.80) **Going Correction** -1.20s/f (Hard) **10 Ran SP% 118.2**
Speed ratings: **112,110,108,107,99 95,93,90,—,—**
Tote Swingers: 1&2 £8.80, 1&3 £21.60, 2&3 £10.20 CSF £41.04 CT £283.26 TOTE £7.30: £2.10, £2.60, £2.60; EX 48.70 TRIFECTA Not won..

Owner Andrea & Graham Wylie **Bred** Ms Margaret Treacy **Trained** Billy Row, Co Durham

FOCUS
A fair novice handicap chase which was won by Merigo in 2008.

NOTEBOOK
On His Own(IRE) ◆ was making his handicap bow after finishing fourth to Wayward Prince in a Wetherby Grade 2 and pulling up in the National Hunt Chase at Cheltenham. Forging clear of the runner-up on the flat, he had jumped out to his right throughout the final circuit and is value for a greater margin of victory. A rangy type, he is lightly raced and is one to keep on the right side, with more progress to come from him. Connections could offer no explanation for the improvement in form compared with Cheltenham. Official explanation: trainer's rep had no explanation for the improvement in form (op 7-1 tchd 15-2)

The Shoe(NZ) travelled well and jumped to the front two out, but could not hold off the winner. Not seen since a disappointing effort in October, this was a sound handicap debut. He handles easier ground too. (tchd 7-1)

Cool Mission(IRE) is a tough customer and he ran well under his big weight, only conceding defeat on the run down to the final fence. He looks a decent marker to the form.

Misstree Dancer ran creditably but perhaps could have done with some softer ground. (op 16-1)

Humbie(IRE), 6lb higher than at Haydock, made a mistake at the last down the back and faded up the home straight. There is still room for improvement in his jumping. (tchd 7-2)

5342 ASHLEYBANK INVESTMENTS STANDARD OPEN NATIONAL HUNT FLAT RACE 2m
5:35 (5:36) (Class 4) 4-6-Y-O **£3,252** (£955; £477; £238)

Form				RPR
1	1		**Fourth Estate (IRE)**[43] 4457 5-11-9 0 BarryGeraghty (Nicky Henderson) *in tch gng wl: smooth hdwy to ld over 1f out: sn shkn up briefly: comf* **5/4**[1]	123+
101	2	¾	**Toubeera**[13] 5135 5-11-5 0 SamThomas (Michael Smith) *bhd: effrt and hdwy over 2f out: chsd wnr last 100yds: r.o* **10/1**	111
222	3	1 ¼	**Pyjama Game (IRE)**[26] 4916 5-11-2 0 WilsonRenwick (Rose Dobbin) *trckd ldrs: rdn and led over 2f out: hdd over 1f out: kpt on ins fnl f* **13/2**[2]	108
3	4	2 ½	**Wild Child Lucy**[39] 4547 5-10-6 0 EwanWhillans(3) (Alistair Whillans) *t.k.h: cl up: led after 4f to 1/2-way: effrt and led briefly over 2f out: one pce fr over 1f out* **22/1**	98
	5	1	**Frizzo (FR)** 4-10-11 0 RobertThornton (Alan King) *hld up: hmpd 1/2-way: effrt and in tch wl over 3f out: drvn and outpcd over 2f out: rallied over 1f out: no imp* **7/1**[3]	99
	6	6	**Bury Parade (IRE)** 5-11-2 0 RyanMania (Robert Bewley) *hld up: hdwy and in tch over 3f out: rdn and outpcd fr 2f out* **66/1**	98
4	7	¾	**Oscar Baby (IRE)**[47] 4396 5-10-2 0 (p) MrNHalley(7) (Elliott Cooper) *prom: led 1/2-way to over 2f out: rdn and wknd over 1f out* **22/1**	92
00-5	8	6	**Santiago Boy**[35] 4717 5-10-11 0 PaulGallagher(5) (Linda Perratt) *bhd: hmpd 1/2-way: effrt u.p over 3f out: nvr able to chal* **40/1**	92
6	9	¾	**Balivernier**[26] 4916 5-11-2 0 JanFaltejsek (George Charlton) *prom: drvn along over 4f out: sn outpcd: no imp fnl 3f* **16/1**	92
665	10	4 ½	**Monashee (IRE)**[26] 4916 6-11-2 0 FearghalDavis (George Charlton) *hld up: stdy hdwy and prom over 3f out: rdn and wknd over 2f out* **40/1**	88
501	11	3 ½	**Scales (IRE)**[33] 4780 5-11-9 0 GrahamLee (Malcolm Jefferson) *t.k.h: hld up: hdwy on outside and in tch 1/2-way: rdn and wknd over 2f out* **12/1**	92
-206	12	22	**Pasture Bay (IRE)**[94] 3511 5-11-2 0 TimmyMurphy (George Charlton) *t.k.h: in tch tl wknd wl over 1f out: eased whn btn* **16/1**	90+
605	13	13	**My Idea**[20] 5033 5-11-2 0 MichaelMcAlister (Maurice Barnes) *in tch: drvn and outpcd over 6f out: sn wknd: t.o* **66/1**	53
	14	33	**Carsonstown Rock (IRE)**[28] 4888 4-10-11 0 PCarberry (C A McBratney, Ire) *led: hung rt and hdd bnd after 4f: lost pl 1/2-way: sn struggling: virtually p.u* **33/1**	48+
0	15	nk	**Aye Well**[75] 3856 6-11-2 0 BrianHughes (Elliott Cooper) *t.k.h: in tch: lost pl after 5f: lost tch fnl 6f: virtually p.u* **20/1**	23
2	F		**Rudemeister (IRE)**[35] 4717 5-11-2 0 RichieMcGrath (Andrew Parker) *hld up: hdwy into midfield whn clipped heels and fell 1/2-way* **14/1**	—

3m 39.2s (-21.50) **Going Correction** -1.225s/f (Hard)
WFA 4 from 5yo+ 5lb **16 Ran SP% 129.8**
Speed ratings: **104,103,103,101,101 98,97,94,94,92 90,79,73,56,56 —**
Tote Swingers: 1&2 £2.20, 1&3 £3.20, 2&3 £3.70 CSF £14.16 TOTE £2.30: £1.80, £3.20, £2.10; EX 13.10 Trifecta £51.90 Pool: £548.80 - 7.82 winning units.

Owner Out The Box Racing **Bred** Darley **Trained** Upper Lambourn, Berks

FOCUS
A reasonable bumper run at a truer pace than a lot of these races are.

NOTEBOOK
Fourth Estate(IRE) travelled strongly through the race and cruised to the front inside the last with his rider barely moving a muscle, although how aware Barry Geraghty was of the staying-on runner-up is open to conjecture. Aimed at this event since his Doncaster debut win, he is a promising recruit but at this stage it is difficult to make comparisons with Sprinter Sacre, who won this for Henderson last year. (op 11-8 tchd 6-4)

Toubeera stayed on well for second but was flattered to finish as close as she did to the winner. She had won two of her three starts against her own sex and is a decent hurdles prospect. (op 12-1)

Pyjama Game(IRE) was runner-up on each of his first three starts and he is a good guide to the merit of this form. He ran his race and showed ahead briefly, but lacked the pace of the winner and second late on. (op 6-1)

Wild Child Lucy ◆ followed up her debut third with another good run and handled the better ground well. A strong mare, she should make her mark when going hurdling. (op 25-1 tchd 28-1)

Frizzo(FR) comes from a decent French family and he showed ability on this debut. (op 6-1)

Bury Parade(IRE), who is out of a half-sister to a pair of winning jumpers, ran creditably first time. (tchd 50-1)

Pasture Bay(IRE) was still travelling comfortably on the inner halfway up the home straight, before Timmy Murphy eased off as if something may have been amiss. Official explanation: jockey said gelding lost its action (op 20-1)

Aye Well Official explanation: jockey said gelding finished distressed

Rudemeister(IRE) came down in the back straight, but fortunately he appeared to incur no lasting damage. (op 12-1)

T/Plt: £8,196.60 to a £1 stake. Pool of £171,230.78 - 15.25 winning units. T/Qpdt: £107.20 to a £1 stake. Pool of £13,442.25 - 92.79 winning units. RY

5099 STRATFORD (L-H)

Sunday, April 17

OFFICIAL GOING: Good to firm (good in places; watered; 9.7)

All bends moved d to provide fresh ground but impact on distances not quantified.
Wind: Nil Weather: Fine and sunny

5343 TOTEPLACEPOT NOVICES' HURDLE (12 hdls) 2m 6f 110y

2:15 (2:15) (Class 3) 4-Y-O+ **£3,903** (£1,146; £573; £286)

Form				RPR
	1		**Black Tor Figarro (IRE)**[103] 6-10-11 0 DavidBass(3) (Lawney Hill) *chsd ldr tl led 3rd: pushed clr after 3 out: comf* **4/1**[3]	112+
6645	**2**	*12*	**Rushwee (IRE)**[14] 5132 9-11-6 107 (b) DominicElsworth (Lucy Wadham) *hld up in tch: chsd ldr and mstke 3 out: styd on same pce* **11/4**[1]	109
10P	**3**	*8*	**Vicpol (ITY)**[95] 3506 5-11-0 0 (p) MarkBradburne (Tom Gretton) *hld up: pushed along after 3rd: wknd appr 9th* **7/1**	92
4556	**4**	*1/2*	**Tribal Dance (IRE)**[24] 4974 5-11-0 0 DarylJacob (Ben Case) *prom: wnt 2nd briefly appr 3 out: sn wknd* **4/1**[3]	93
5300	**5**	*30*	**William Percival (IRE)**[36] 4719 5-11-0 0 RichardJohnson (Henry Daly) *chsd ldrs: drvn along 7th: wknd after 9th: t.o* **10/1**	65
54	**6**	*19*	**Stapleton (IRE)**[20] 5059 6-11-0 0 JamieMoore (Philip Middleton) *led to 3rd: chsd wnr tl wknd appr 3 out: t.o whn j.rt last* **7/2**[2]	48
0-P	**P**		**Lombardy Breeze (IRE)**[104] 3366 6-11-0 0 DenisO'Regan (Henrietta Knight) *hld up: a in rr: wknd 8th: t.o whn p.u bef 2 out* **25/1**	—

5m 30.6s (2.50) **Going Correction** +0.25s/f (Yiel) **7 Ran SP% 114.3**
Speed ratings (Par 107): **105,100,98,97,87 80,—**
toteswingers:1&2:£2.20, 1&3:£5.60, 2&3:£4.70 CSF £15.80 TOTE £5.10: £2.30, £2.20; EX 15.80.
Owner Ruth Tupper & Tom Fletcher **Bred** Sweetmans Bloodstock **Trained** Aston Rowant, Oxon

FOCUS
This weak novice hurdle was run at an ordinary gallop and it proved highly uncompetitive.

NOTEBOOK
Black Tor Figarro(IRE), who looked hard fit, made a winning debut over hurdles for his new yard and completed the task in most decisive fashion. He looked something of a reluctant leader after pulling his way to the front, but really began to enjoy the new discipline on the final circuit and could have been called the winner nearing the home turn. He got 2m well enough on the Flat so it was a wise move introducing him over this distance and he won't mind some easier ground in future, having registered his sole success in that sphere on soft. (op 6-1)
Rushwee(IRE) wasn't suited by the way the race was run, but it's hard to imagine he would have got all that much closer to the winner even if things had gone more his way. He helps to set the level, but remains one to tread carefully with. (tchd 3-1)
Vicpol(ITY) attracted support, but he wasn't fluent early on and went in snatches after the fourth flight. He was plugging on late and this was better back at the course where he won his bumper, but he doesn't look that willing. (op 14-1)
Tribal Dance(IRE) came under pressure a fair way out and at least now qualifies for a handicap mark. (op 9-2)
Stapleton(IRE) was well backed earlier in the day and was expected to relish the longer trip. He didn't really impress in the paddock, though, and drifted right out before turning in a tame effort. Something may have gone amiss. (op 9-4)

5344 TOTEEXACTA FLEXI BETTING NOVICES' CHASE (17 fncs) 2m 7f

2:45 (2:46) (Class 4) 5-Y-O+ **£3,332** (£1,034; £557)

Form				RPR
56P1	**1**		**Indian Pipe Dream (IRE)**[43] 4469 9-11-2 101 LeeEdwards(3) (Aytach Sadik) *led to 6th: led again 10th: rdn appr last: styd on wl* **5/1**	110
3062	**2**	*4*	**Like Ice**[22] 5017 6-10-12 99 JamieMoore (Philip Middleton) *hld up: hdwy 12th: rdn to chse wnr last: no imp flat* **9/4**[2]	100
P15P	**3**	*2 3/4*	**Chevy To The Levy (IRE)**[165] 2146 9-10-12 107 CharlieWallis(7) (John O'Shea) *chsd wnr tl led 6th to 10th: chsd wnr again tl chal 3 out: rdn after next: lost 2nd last: no ex* **7/2**[3]	106
230U	**P**		**Job One (FR)**[16] 5104 8-11-5 111 DenisO'Regan (Henrietta Knight) *chsd ldrs: mstke 5th: lost pl 12th: reminders after next: wknd appr 2 out: t.o whn p.u flat* **13/8**[1]	—

5m 45.5s (3.90) **Going Correction** +0.15s/f (Yiel) **4 Ran SP% 107.8**
Speed ratings: **99,97,96,—**
CSF £15.90 TOTE £6.60; EX 10.80.
Owner A Sadik **Bred** Roger A Ryan **Trained** Wolverley, Worcs

FOCUS
A moderate novice chase.

NOTEBOOK
Indian Pipe Dream(IRE) was flattered by his Doncaster success last month, but that was still the best recent form on offer here and so it was surprising he was sent off the outsider of the four. He made most with a gutsy effort and is clearly starting to get the hang of chasing. Another likely rise will make his life harder in handicap company, but he was a useful hurdler in his heyday and so a bold bid for the hat-trick is not ruled out. (op 9-2)
Like Ice finished second in a very weak handicap over C&D on his chase debut 22 days earlier. He again ran freely and lost out with by jumping to his right over the second-last, something he did at numerous fences here last time. He no doubt has the ability to win in low-grade events as a chaser, but does look worth trying back on a right-handed circuit. (op 2-1 tchd 5-2)
Chevy To The Levy(IRE) raced enthusiastically on this first outing since pulling up last November and paid the price late on. He could build on this. (op 4-1 tchd 3-1)
Job One(FR) got no further than the first on his return last time and it was again his jumping which hampered him here. It later transpired he was lame. Official explanation: jockey said gelding finished lame (op 7-4 tchd 15-8 in places)

5345 TOTESWINGER FLEXI BETTING H'CAP CHASE (14 fncs) 2m 4f

3:15 (3:15) (Class 3) (0-130,120) 5-Y-O+ **£6,319** (£1,907; £982; £520)

Form				RPR
02P5	**1**		**High Jack (IRE)**[28] 4896 9-10-13 107 NickScholfield (Andy Turnell) *led to 4th: led again 7th: rdn appr last: styd on wl* **4/1**[3]	114
2542	**2**	*3 1/2*	**Storm Of Applause (IRE)**[29] 4863 10-11-12 120 RichardJohnson (Philip Hobbs) *a.p: rdn after 3 out: wnt 2nd last: no imp flat* **13/8**[1]	124
5566	**3**	*5*	**Rory Boy (USA)**[25] 4941 6-11-7 115 (b[1]) SamTwiston-Davies (Nigel Twiston-Davies) *chsd ldr to 4th: remained handy: drvn along after 6th: outpcd 8th: rallied appr 3 out: styd on same pce fr next: wnt 3rd towards fin* **6/1**	113
1432	**4**	*2 1/4*	**Courella (IRE)**[7] 5233 7-11-1 114 (p) AodhaganConlon(5) (Evan Williams) *chsd ldrs: led 4th to 7th: chsd wnr: rdn appr 2 out: lost 2nd and wknd last* **5/2**[2]	110
P653	**P**		**Sweet Seville (FR)**[30] 4855 7-9-9 94 CO'Farrell(5) (Terry Clement) *nt jump wl: sn t.o: p.u bef 4th* **14/1**	—

4m 53.3s (-0.90) **Going Correction** +0.15s/f (Yiel) **5 Ran SP% 107.6**
Speed ratings: **107,105,103,102,—**
CSF £10.84 TOTE £4.40: £1.70, £1.20; EX 11.10.
Owner M Tedham **Bred** Mrs Maura McSweeney **Trained** Broad Hinton, Wilts

FOCUS
A weak handicap for the class, run at a sound enough gallop.

NOTEBOOK
High Jack(IRE) made most of the running and finally bounced back to winning ways. He came into this with fairly inauspicious recent form figures, but he does enjoy a quick surface and showed plenty more enthusiasm for it. This was his first success since winning in this month last year and so he does look a real spring horse. (op 9-2 tchd 7-2)
Storm Of Applause(IRE) was beaten by the smallest margin on his return to action at Ffos Las last month. He was raised 5lb for that, which took him to the same amount above his last winning mark. However, it looked to be this sharper track down slightly in trip which found him out and he may not be weighted out of success again when reverting to a stiffer test. (op 7-4 tchd 15-8 and 2-1 in places)
Rory Boy(USA) has fallen in the handicap courtesy of a horrid season, but there were reasons to expect a revival here. He had won his only previous outing on good to firm and had first-time blinkers replacing cheekpieces. He didn't help his rider at any stage, however, and has obviously lost the plot. (op 11-2)
Courella(IRE) looked sure to enjoy the return to further and was equipped with cheekpieces for the first time since coming over from Ireland. He posted a fairly laboured effort, though, and may have found the run coming too soon. (op 9-4 tchd 11-4)

5346 BET TOTEPOOL ON 0800 221 221 MARES' H'CAP HURDLE (9 hdls 1 omitted) 2m 3f

3:50 (3:50) (Class 3) (0-120,113) 4-Y-O+ **£3,903** (£1,146; £573; £286)

Form				RPR
2331	**1**		**Illysantachristina**[34] 4769 8-10-3 95 MarkQuinlan(5) (Bernard Llewellyn) *a.p: chsd ldr 4th: led 3 out: rdn out* **7/1**[3]	99+
1120	**2**	*2 1/4*	**Empress Orchid**[22] 5008 6-11-12 113 AdrianLane (Donald McCain) *mde most tl hdd 3 out: rdn appr last: styd on same pce flat* **5/1**[2]	114
5055	**3**	*1 1/4*	**Laureate Des Loges (FR)**[25] 4955 7-11-2 103 RichardJohnson (Henry Daly) *hld up: hdwy after 3 out: rdn appr last: styd on same pce flat* **4/1**[1]	104+
3524	**4**	*4*	**Lesanda**[29] 4874 5-11-2 103 GrahamLee (Richard Fahey) *prom: rdn appr 2 out: styd on same pce* **5/1**[2]	99
0236	**5**	*4*	**Edgefour (IRE)**[169] 2089 7-11-6 107 DarylJacob (Ben Case) *hld up: hdwy appr 7th: rdn and wknd bef last* **7/1**[3]	98
2004	**6**	*11*	**Verde Goodwood**[24] 4964 5-10-3 95 PeterCarberry(5) (Oliver Sherwood) *prom: blnd 1st: lost pl after 3rd: hdwy appr 7th: rdn and wknd after 3 out* **8/1**	78
2004	**7**	*3 1/4*	**Gulf Punch**[7] 5227 4-11-0 107 (p) SeanQuinlan (Milton Harris) *chsd ldrs tl blnd 3 out: sn wknd:* **11/1**	81
44-0	**8**	*3/4*	**Maria Antonia (IRE)**[15] 5117 8-11-4 105 (t) JamieMoore (Alison Thorpe) *hld up: racd keenly: hdwy appr 7th: wknd 3 out* **16/1**	85
615P	**9**	*10*	**Monkhair (IRE)**[31] 4830 6-10-7 97 LeeEdwards(3) (Tony Carroll) *hld up: wknd 7th: t.o* **20/1**	66
064	**U**		**Mavalenta (IRE)**[34] 4781 4-10-5 98 SamTwiston-Davies (Nigel Twiston-Davies) *a.p: disputing cl 3rd but looked hld whn blnd and uns rdr last* **12/1**	91

4m 36.6s (5.10) **Going Correction** +0.25s/f (Yiel)
WFA 4 from 5yo+ 5lb **10 Ran SP% 116.1**
Speed ratings (Par 107): **99,98,97,95,94 89,88,87,83,—**
toteswingers:1&2:£3.50, 1&3:£3.80, 2&3:£5.60 CSF £42.33 CT £160.28 TOTE £4.60: £1.10, £1.80, £2.60; EX 31.80 Trifecta £103.10 Pool: £494.83 - 3.55 winning units..
Owner Marc Cohen **Bred** R And Mrs S Edwards **Trained** Fochriw, Caerphilly

FOCUS
The hurdle on the side of the course was bypassed on the second circuit. An ordinary mares' handicap, rated around the runner-up.

NOTEBOOK
Illysantachristina ◆ followed up her Plumpton success last month despite an 8lb hike in the weights and again completed the task readily. She would have enjoyed more of a gallop here too, so is clearly now coming good and there is little reason to think she will not go very close to landing a hat-trick while in her current mood. (op 5-1)
Empress Orchid was always up there and posted a solid effort in defeat under top weight on this return to a sensibly lower grade. She deserves to go one better again. (op 6-1)
Laureate Des Loges(FR) was back down in trip and really one again looked to be crying out for a more prominent ride. (tchd 5-1 in places)
Lesanda, up in trip, didn't look the most straightforward. Official explanation: jockey said mare had a breathing problem (op 7-1)
Edgefour(IRE) shaped encouragingly on her return from a 169-day break and ought to come on a good deal. (op 8-1)
Gulf Punch Official explanation: jockey said filly lost a shoe

5347 BET TOTEPOOL AT TOTESPORT.COM HUNTERS' CHASE (FOR THE JOHN AND NIGEL THORNE MEMORIAL CUP) (17 fncs) 2m 7f

4:25 (4:25) (Class 5) 6-Y-O+ **£1,249** (£387; £193; £96)

Form				RPR
3/1P	**1**		**Moment Of Madness (IRE)**[14] 13-11-11 106 MrMWalford(3) (Mrs M Stirk) *mde all: directed on to the hurdles crse after 2 out to bef last: sn clr easily* **7/2**[3]	110+
00-	**2**	*7*	**Trifollet**[28] 6-11-0 0 MrAndrewMartin(3) (Mrs J A Martin (Oxfordshire)) *prom: lost pl after 3rd: bhd and drvn along whn hit 9th: directed on to the hurdles crse after 2 out to bef last: styd on to go 2nd flat: no ch w wnr* **22/1**	92
132-	**3**	*7*	**Chapel Flowers (IRE)**[42] 9-11-7 0 MrDGwyn-Jones(7) (Miss Sally Duckett) *chsd ldrs: rdn whn directed on to the hurdles trck after 2 out tl bef last: wkng whn lost 2nd flat* **16/1**	98+
	4	*13*	**Jack's The Lad (IRE)**[21] 7-11-3 0 MrRHatch(7) (Miss Alice Reader) *hld up: hdwy 10th: wknd 13th: bhd whn directed on to the hurdles trck after 2 out tl bef last* **25/1**	80
FP02	**5**	*1 1/2*	**Seymar Lad (IRE)**[37] 4701 11-11-3 117 MrFMitchell(7) (Miss V Collins) *hld up: hdwy 4th: lost pl 8th: in rr and drvn along fr next: wknd 13th: bhd whn directed on to the hurdles trck after 2 out tl bef last* **11/4**[2]	78
P322	**S**		**Battlecry**[23] 4991 10-11-3 116 MrWTwiston-Davies(7) (Nigel Twiston-Davies) *chsd ldr tl j. slowly 5th and 6th: disputing cl 2nd whn slipped up bnd after 8th* **1/1**[1]	—

5m 48.0s (6.40) **Going Correction** +0.15s/f (Yiel) **6 Ran SP% 113.0**
Speed ratings: **94,91,89,84,84 —**
toteswingers:1&2:£12.20, 1&3:£3.80, 2&3:£11.70 CSF £52.88 TOTE £4.10: £1.70, £7.00; EX 80.30.
Owner Mrs R A G Haggie **Bred** William Hubbert **Trained** Laverton, N Yorks

FOCUS
The complexion of this hunter chase changed dramatically when the well-backed Battlecry slipped up nearing the home turn for the penultimate time. With his rider still on the deck on the final circuit the runners were re-routed on to the inner course.
NOTEBOOK
Moment Of Madness(IRE) arrived here having finished second on his last two outings in points and he made all for a decisive success. He loves it out in front and found plenty when asked for maximum effort in the home straight. It was his second win in this sphere. (tchd 3-1 tchd 4-1 in places)
Trifollet never seriously threatened, but was doing some decent late work on this debut over regulation fences. She has plenty of time on her side and ought to enjoy a more galloping circuit. (tchd 25-1)
Chapel Flowers(IRE) shaped more encouragingly than had been the case in points this year, but didn't do enough to suggest he will be winning anytime soon. (op 20-1)
Seymar Lad(IRE) ran a cracker at Sandown on his previous outing and his career-best when trained by Emma Lavelle had come over this course and distance. It was clear from halfway he didn't fancy it, however. (op 5-2 tchd 10-3)
Battlecry looked to have a decent chance here, but slipped up on the penultimate turn into the home straight and his winless run in this sphere goes on. Willie Twiston-Davies suffered a broken leg. (op 11-8 tchd 6-4 in places)

5348 BET TOTEPOOL ON ALL UK RACING NOVICES' H'CAP HURDLE (9 hdls) 2m 110y
5:00 (5:04) (Class 3) (0-125,119) 4-Y-0+ **£3,903** (£1,146; £573; £286)

Form				RPR
0325	1		**Tatispout (FR)**[16] 5102 4-11-3 **110** FelixDeGiles (Charlie Longsdon) *chsd ldrs: hit 2 out: led last: styd on* **3/1**[1]	112+
-316	2	2 ¼	**Katchmore (IRE)**[22] 5010 4-11-12 **119** JimmyMcCarthy (Michael Blanshard) *chsd ldr: rdn to ld after 2 out: hdd last: styd on same pce flat* **16/1**	112
-360	3	6	**James Pollard (IRE)**[14] 4330 6-10-6 **99** (t) MarkQuinlan(5) (Bernard Llewellyn) *hld up: hdwy 5th: rdn after 3 out: wnt 3rd last: nt trble ldrs* **9/2**[2]	92
3011	4	8	**Leopard Hills (IRE)**[16] 5101 4-11-4 **111** DarylJacob (Alison Thorpe) *chsd ldrs: drvn along after 5th: mstke 3 out: wknd next* **5/1**[3]	93
335P	5	5	**Apache Dawn**[210] 1552 7-10-4 **95** (t) EamonDehdashti(3) (Aytach Sadik) *chsd ldrs: rdn after 5th: wkng whn hit 3 out* **22/1**	77
F0FU	6	6	**Cityar (FR)**[25] 4944 7-10-3 **98** CharlieWallis(7) (John O'Shea) *hld up: rdn after 3 out: nvr on terms* **33/1**	74
300	7	27	**Monroe Park (IRE)**[16] 5099 6-10-4 **99** MrJMQuinlan(7) (Noel Quinlan) *hld up: a in rr: t.o* **12/1**	50
S03	8	34	**Ursus**[21] 5027 6-10-7 **95** PaddyAspell (Christopher Wilson) *hld up in tch: wknd 5th: t.o* **9/1**	16
F	F		**Pin D'Estruval (FR)**[34] 4775 8-10-10 **98** (t) AidanColeman (Matt Sheppard) *led: rdn and hdd appr 2 out: disputing 4th and wkng whn fell last* **8/1**	87
006	U		**Hail Caesar (IRE)**[34] 4783 5-10-9 **102** AodhaganConlon(5) (Evan Williams) *hld up: hdwy appr 2 out: 6th and styng on although no ch whn hmpd and uns rdr last* **11/2**	84

3m 57.8s (1.80) **Going Correction** +0.25s/f (Yiel) **10** Ran SP% **117.2**
Speed ratings (Par 107): **105,103,101,97,95 92,79,63,—,—**
toteswingers:1&2:£8.20, 1&3:£4.20, 2&3:£15.70 CSF £49.18 CT £216.54 TOTE £4.40: £1.70, £3.70, £1.90; EX 47.20.
Owner Mrs B J Lockhart **Bred** Mlle Tatiana Puitg & Guy Cherel **Trained** Over Norton, Oxon
FOCUS
A moderate handicap and an easy winner.
NOTEBOOK
Tatispout(FR) ◆ was very disappointing here last time out, but her narrow defeat to a subsequent winner over course and distance on her penultimate outing gave her a big shout and she belatedly came good with a taking display. The decision to ride her more positively worked the oracle, although she again ran freely and was still pulling for her head turning into the home straight. She took over on the run-in with ease and rates value for a lot further. She will be full of confidence and so it will be interesting to see how much she goes up for this. (op 10-3 tchd 7-2 in places)
Katchmore(IRE), winner of a weak maiden two runs back, returned to something like his best form but the winner toyed with him from three out. He helps to set the level.
James Pollard(IRE), not disgraced back on the Flat last time, lacked the required change of gear to get seriously involved. He did fare best of those coming from off the pace, though, and it looks as though he needs a longer trip on this ground. (tchd 5-1)
Leopard Hills(IRE) found it a lot tougher than the two sellers had he won before this. (tchd 11-2)

5349 BET TOTEPOOL ON ALL IRISH RACING H'CAP CHASE (20 fncs) 3m 4f
5:30 (5:31) (Class 5) (0-95,84) 5-Y-0+ **£1,951** (£573; £286; £143)

Form				RPR
-P0P	1		**Katalak (IRE)**[89] 3614 8-11-12 **84** (bt) FelixDeGiles (Jonathen de Giles) *sn chsng ldrs: outpcd 13th: hdwy 17th: wnt 2nd 2 out: rdn to ld last: styd on* **9/2**	93+
PP05	2	1 ½	**Fourpointone**[41] 4525 10-10-8 **66** (p) LiamTreadwell (Ed de Giles) *led: rdn after 2 out: hdd last: styd on same pce* **9/4**[2]	73
33P0	3	2	**The Iron Giant (IRE)**[14] 5130 9-10-2 **63** AlexMerriam(3) (Neil King) *chsd ldr: mstke 13th (water): rdn 17th: lost 2nd 2 out: styd on same pce appr last* **4/1**[3]	67
5052	4	24	**Heezagrey (IRE)**[25] 4953 8-10-13 **76** MarkQuinlan(5) (James Evans) *sn pushed along in rr: drvn along 8th: lost tch 14th* **6/4**[1]	63

7m 12.5s (9.50) **Going Correction** +0.15s/f (Yiel) **4** Ran SP% **109.0**
Speed ratings: **92,91,91,84**
CSF £14.54 TOTE £5.20; EX 17.80.
Owner Gavin MacEchern & Jonathen de Giles **Bred** His Highness The Aga Khan's Studs S C **Trained** Stanton Fitzwarren, Wilts
FOCUS
A very weak marathon handicap, but there was a cracking finish.
NOTEBOOK
Katalak(IRE) bided his time as the two leaders kicked on going out onto the final circuit and arrived to them going strongly nearing three out. It was a question of how his stamina would hold out against the proven runner-up when he came under pressure and he looked in trouble in the home straight. De Giles found extra from him, however, and if anything he got to the front too soon on the run-in as he idled. This 8-y-o relishes quick ground and is talented enough to defy a higher mark, but it was his first win since 2008. (op 4-1)
Fourpointone's last win in 2010 came over this trip and he is versatile regards ground, but he came here out of sorts. This was a much more encouraging effort in defeat, though, and it's hoped he can hold his form now as he is well treated. (op 5-2)
The Iron Giant(IRE) went enthusiastically for a long way back over fences and posted one of his better efforts.
Heezagrey(IRE) is a notoriously tricky character and had downed tools before the final lap. (op 13-8)
T/Plt: £494.90 to a £1 stake. Pool £87,056.72 - 128.40 winning units. T/Qpdt: £53.80 to a £1 stake. Pool £7,689.45 - 105.73 winning units CR

[4274]WETHERBY (L-H)
Sunday, April 17
OFFICIAL GOING: Good to firm (good in places; hdl 7.8, chs 8.0)
Wind: moderate 1/2 behind Weather: fine and sunny

5350 NATIONAL FESTIVAL CIRCUS IS HERE TODAY LADY RIDERS' H'CAP HURDLE (9 hdls) 2m 110y
2:25 (2:31) (Class 5) (0-95,95) 4-Y-0+ **£2,055** (£599; £299)

Form				RPR
-PP2	1		**Hi Ho Silvia**[14] 5130 6-10-5 **77** (tp) GemmaGracey-Davison(5) (Neil King) *led to 2nd: w ldrs: led after 6th: styd on wl: drvn rt out* **7/1**[2]	82
4605	2	2	**Petrocelli**[9] 4998 4-10-6 **85** MissSMDoolan(7) (Wilf Storey) *t.k.h: sn trcking ldrs: outpcd appr 3 out: styd on fr 2 out: tk 2nd last: no imp* **8/1**[3]	83
4353	3	1 ½	**Muntami (IRE)**[14] 5130 10-11-5 **93** (p) MissKLMorgan(7) (John Harris) *wnt prom 4th: kpt on same pce fr 2 out* **10/1**	94
0424	4	2	**A Stones Throw (NZ)**[13] 5144 6-11-4 **92** (t) MissJennyCarr(7) (Ben Haslam) *t.k.h: w ldr: led 2nd: hdd after 6th: fdd last* **10/3**[1]	92
0-14	5	3 ¼	**Lady Anne Nevill**[16] 5098 7-10-10 **84** MissEStead(7) (Chris Fairhurst) *chsd ldrs: outpcd appr 3 out: kpt on between last 2* **8/1**[3]	80
505	6	nk	**Waldo Winchester (IRE)**[15] 5116 8-10-1 **75** (p) MissKBannon(7) (Noel Wilson) *nt fluent in last: styd on fr 3 out: nt rch ldrs* **8/1**[3]	70
0155	7	3 ½	**Perez (IRE)**[222] 1504 9-10-6 **80** (vt) MissLAlexander(7) (Wilf Storey) *chsd ldrs: wkng whn hit last* **16/1**	73
4603	8	1 ½	**Daraybad (FR)**[15] 5114 9-9-10 **70** (v) MissCareyWilliamson(7) (Andrew Crook) *in rr: sn pushed along: nvr a factor* **14/1**	60
4401	9	1 ¼	**Solway Blue**[14] 5130 9-10-3 **77** (p) MissKHobbs(7) (Lisa Harrison) *hld up: hdwy to trck ldrs 6th: wknd 2 out* **8/1**[3]	67
0442	10	14	**Baraathen (USA)**[33] 4798 4-11-2 **95** MissBAndrews(7) (Donald McCain) *mid-div: no imp whn blnd 2 out: eased* **8/1**[3]	75
0/PP	11	8	**Mickwell Bay**[82] 3720 10-9-10 **70** (p) MissHBethell(7) (Tim Pitt) *in rr: bhd fr 6th* **20/1**	37

3m 46.1s (-9.70) **Going Correction** -0.85s/f (Firm)
WFA 4 from 5yo+ 5lb **11** Ran SP% **117.5**
Speed ratings (Par 103): **88,87,86,85,83 83,82,81,80,74 70**
toteswingers:1&2:£5.50, 1&3:£8.60, 2&3:£15.40 CSF £62.11 CT £564.23 TOTE £8.10: £2.60, £2.50, £2.90; EX 53.10.
Owner N J Catterwell **Bred** David Brace **Trained** Newmarket, Suffolk
FOCUS
The whole course received 90-110mm of water during the previous two days and the ground appeared to be riding as advertised. The pace was solid and the time beat the standard by nearly two seconds. \n\x\x A low-grade handicap confined to lady riders, and essentially plating-class form. The race was delayed after Dollar Express (66/1), who was eventually withdrawn, bolted on his way to post.
NOTEBOOK
Hi Ho Silvia had run an improved race in a tongue tie last time, splitting Solway Blue and Muntami in a ladies' seller at Market Rasen. She had the services of the only professional rider in this race and was in command after showing ahead before three out. She should cope with a return to slightly further.
Petrocelli, who has had a run on the Flat since his previous hurdles outing, came in for support. He emerged as the final threat to the winner and seemed to get the trip well enough. (op 14-1)
Muntami(IRE) ran a solid race in reapplied cheekpieces and this consistent grey could find a little race, most likely back at Market Rasen. (op 11-1)
A Stones Throw(NZ) sweated up badly during the delay to the start. This keen type was always prominent but lacked any change of pace from the second-last. Coping with this faster ground well enough, he's capable of finding a small race, probably back up in trip. (op 4-1)
Lady Anne Nevill remains rather high in the handicap. (op 7-1)
Waldo Winchester(IRE) made late gains in the first-time cheekpieces. (op 9-1)
Perez(IRE), who threw this race away a year ago when swerving and unshipping this rider, is a stablemate of the runner-up. Off the track since September, he was close enough turning for home but was fading when untidy at the last. He should strip fitter for the outing. (op 14-1)
Solway Blue, raised 5lb after Market Rasen, disappointed but was another who became warm down at the start.

5351 BOOK TICKETS ON-LINE @ WETHERBYRACING.CO.UK H'CAP CHASE (16 fncs) 2m 4f 110y
3:00 (3:00) (Class 4) (0-100,98) 5-Y-0+ **£2,602** (£764; £382; £190)

Form				RPR
1452	1		**Border Reiver**[27] 4911 7-11-12 **98** (t) RichieMcGrath (Tim Easterby) *w ldr: led 5th: styd on strly fr 4 out: 7 l ahd last: eased nr fin* **9/4**[1]	111+
3P3P	2	4 ½	**Ginger's Lad**[35] 4741 7-10-0 **79** (tp) JakeGreenall(7) (Michael Easterby) *t.k.h: trckd ldrs: rdn 11th: outpcd next: styd on fr 3 out: tk modest 2nd last* **5/1**	84
0132	3	2 ¼	**Ponchatrain (IRE)**[37] 4693 11-11-8 **94** (v) GerardTumelty (Martin Keighley) *trckd ldrs: 3rd: mstke 8th: rdn and outpcd whn hit 4 out: kpt on run-in: snatched 3rd nr fin* **3/1**[2]	101+
1435	4	hd	**Authentic Act (IRE)**[33] 4800 7-10-10 **82** JamesReveley (Martin Todhunter) *hld up in tch on outer: wnt prom 6th: chsd wnr 10th: wknd last* **15/2**	85
0PP3	5	10	**Ravenscar**[22] 5018 13-9-7 **72** oh10 JoeCornwall(7) (Charles Pogson) *led to 5th: reminders 10th: wknd appr 4 out* **20/1**	66
233P	6	2 ¾	**Archie's Wish**[56] 4241 7-10-7 **79** BarryKeniry (Micky Hammond) *j.lft and nt fluent in rr: hit 2nd: pushed along 11th: sn btn* **7/2**[3]	70

4m 58.9s (-8.90) **Going Correction** -0.375s/f (Good) **6** Ran SP% **111.2**
Speed ratings: **101,99,98,98,94 93**
toteswingers:1&2:£3.30, 1&3:£1.80, 2&3:£2.30 CSF £13.51 TOTE £3.10: £1.50, £3.00; EX 18.10.
Owner C H Stevens **Bred** M H Easterby **Trained** Great Habton, N Yorks
FOCUS
A modest handicap chase. The pace wasn't strong and the time was nearly nine seconds outside the standard.
NOTEBOOK
Border Reiver was always in the front rank and he drew away over the final line of fences to win comfortably, possibly idling a little and value for further. All three of his wins have come at this venue and he had dropped to a mark only 2lb higher than for his last success in January. He reportedly has wind issues and this better ground helped in that respect. (op 5-2 tchd 11-4)
Ginger's Lad, tried in a new headgear combination and keen in the early stages, seemed booked for fourth two from home but stayed on well from that point. He could be worth stepping up in trip. (op 13-2)
Ponchatrain(IRE), whose yard won this race two years ago, made rather too many jumping errors and has now been held three times from this mark since his Lingfield win. (op 9-4)

Authentic Act(IRE), a novice, was kept wide of his rivals, giving him a clear look at his fences. He travelled well on this faster surface and challenged for the lead turning out of the back straight, but was soon giving vain pursuit of the winner. His stamina was failing him near the finish and he gave the impression that he isn't straightforward. (op 7-1)

Ravenscar (tchd 22-1)

Archie's Wish, who didn't jump with much fluency on the faster ground, was always bringing up the rear. (op 9-2)

5352 WETHERBY RACECOURSE FOR CONFERENCES & EVENTS MAIDEN HURDLE (12 hdls) 2m 6f

3:35 (3:38) (Class 5) 4-Y-0+ **£2,055** (£599; £299)

Form					RPR
	1		**Oscar Barton (IRE)**[63] 4108 6-11-0 0 ... (tp) TomO'Brien (Paul W Flynn, Ire) *trckd ldrs: led 3rd: j.rt 9th: sn drvn: 7 l clr next: c rt away: kpt rt up to work*	**15/8**[1]	110+
33P	2	19	**Milano Supremo (IRE)**[92] 3572 6-10-9 0 ... (t) AlexanderVoy[(5)] (Chris Grant) *hld up: hdwy 7th: chsd wnr 3 out: no imp*	**17/2**	91
U	3	7	**Philasonic**[63] 8-10-7 0 ... MrMGarnett[(7)] (George Moore) *t.k.h: led to 3rd: lost pl appr 3 out: poor 5th whn blnd 2 out: kpt on to take 3rd nr fin*	**8/1**	87
5	4	3/4	**Tower**[21] 5027 4-10-8 0 ... CampbellGillies (Chris Grant) *chsd ldrs: modest 3rd 3 out: wknd run-in*	**7/1**[3]	78
55U3	5	3/4	**Sous Mix (FR)**[8] 5203 5-10-7 111 ... JakeGreenall[(7)] (Michael Easterby) *mid-div: hdwy 6th: drvn 9th: sn outpcd*	**5/2**[2]	83
000	6	41	**Rocky Bear (IRE)**[16] 5092 6-10-7 0 ... KyleJames[(7)] (Marjorie Fife) *nt fluent in rr: bhd fr 9th: sn t.o*	**100/1**	42
0-6	7	1/2	**Touz Master (FR)**[25] 4951 7-10-11 0 ... DonalDevereux[(3)] (Nick Kent) *chsd ldrs: hit 7th: wknd 9th: sn bhd: t.o*	**9/1**	41
0-00	8	67	**Knickerbokerglory**[21] 5033 5-10-4 0 ... JamesO'Farrell[(3)] (Barbara Butterworth) *chsd ldrs: lost pl 8th: sn bhd: t.o 3 out: eventually completed*	**50/1**	—
U00P	P		**Aitch Factor**[40] 4542 5-11-0 80 ... RobertWalford (Henry Hogarth) *chsd ldrs 4th: lost pl and mstke 8th: sn bhd: t.o 3 out: p.u bef last*	**40/1**	—
00	P		**Silver Seraph**[15] 5115 7-10-7 0 ... WilsonRenwick (Noel Wilson) *stdd s: in rr: bhd whn mstke 5th: t.o whn p.u bef next: lame*	**100/1**	—
0000	U		**Overpriced**[13] 5151 5-10-0 0 ... (t) MissAngelaBarnes[(7)] (Maurice Barnes) *in rr whn uns rdr 2nd*	**100/1**	—

5m 5.70s (-21.10) **Going Correction** -0.85s/f (Firm)
WFA 4 from 5yo+ 6lb 11 Ran SP% **114.9**
Speed ratings (Par 103): **104,97,94,94,94 79,78,54,—,— —**
toteswingers:1&2:£3.80, 1&3:£4.30 , 2&3:£7.40 CSF £18.19 TOTE £3.40: £1.70, £1.90, £2.60; EX 17.00.
Owner Miss C Howes **Bred** Rachel Ryan **Trained** Colehill, Co Longford

FOCUS

Not a strong event by any means, but the wide-margin winner clocked a quick time.

NOTEBOOK

Oscar Barton(IRE), the only Irish-trained runner on the card, made much of the running and, kicking off the home turn, came right away to slam his field. Fitted with cheekpieces to accompany the tongue tie, he was encountering fast ground for the first time and clearly relished it. Out of a decent chaser who was successful in the valuable Paddy Power Handicap chase over 3m at Leopardstown's Christmas meeting, he looks to have further improvement in him as he gains experience. (op 7-4 tchd 13-8)

Milano Supremo(IRE) ran respectably on this first start for three months, picking up ground down the back but left with a distant view of the winner from the home turn. He had run well on fast ground before and saw out the longer trip well enough. (tchd 8-1 and 9-1)

Philasonic, the early leader, was outpaced by the principals before the home turn but stayed on well late on to snatch third. Making his hurdles debut for a new yard, this winning pointer needs 3m. (op 14-1)

Tower, upped in trip, duelled for second spot with stablemate Milano Supremo turning in but was soon one-paced. (op 5-1)

Sous Mix(FR), rated 111 by the BHA, was disappointing, failing to pick up after coming under pressure leaving the back, and has something to prove now. He landed awkwardly at the last flight with a circuit to run and might not have been happy on the sound surface afterwards. (op 3-1)

Silver Seraph Official explanation: trainer said mare returned sore

5353 YORKSHIRE POST LADIES DAY - 19TH MAY H'CAP CHASE (17 fncs 1 omitted) 3m 1f

4:10 (4:10) (Class 3) (0-130,121) 5-Y-0+ **£3,332** (£1,034; £557)

Form					RPR
634P	1		**Western Gale (IRE)**[170] 2079 8-10-10 105 ... JamesReveley (Martin Todhunter) *j. soundly: trckd ldrs: hit 9th: led after next: drvn 7 l clr 4 out: styd on: eased towards fin*	**4/1**[3]	117+
4V21	2	5	**Matmata De Tendron (FR)**[31] 4825 11-10-1 96 ... (p) BrianHughes (Andrew Crook) *j. slowly: chsd ldrs: lft cl 2nd sn after omitted 11th: kpt on one pce friom 4 out*	**13/2**	100
26P4	3	11	**Dawn Ride (IRE)**[21] 5032 10-11-5 114 ... (p) BarryKeniry (Micky Hammond) *hld up: chsd ldrs 9th: hmpd and lft handy 3rd after omitted 11th: outpcd whn blnd 5 out: no threat after*	**7/2**[2]	111
6/5P	U		**Raining Horse (FR)**[74] 3888 9-10-2 100 ... (p) HarryHaynes[(3)] (James Ewart) *chsd ldrs: uns rdr 2nd*	**5/1**	—
10-6	P		**Checkerboard (IRE)**[36] 4730 8-11-5 119 ... PaulGallagher[(5)] (Howard Johnson) *jnd ldrs 7th: led next: hdd 10th: tk wrong crse after next: eased after 13th: t.o whn p.u after next*	**11/2**	—
5100	P		**Wolf Moon (IRE)**[22] 5003 8-11-12 121 ... (b[1]) JasonMaguire (Martin Keighley) *led: nt fluent 1st 4: hdd 8th: led 10th: sn hdd: chsng ldrs whn forced to take wrong crse after omitted 11th: eased after 13th: t.o whn p.u after next*	**10/3**[1]	—

5m 55.6s (-13.80) **Going Correction** -0.375s/f (Good) course record 6 Ran SP% **110.7**
Speed ratings: **107,105,101,—,— —**
toteswingers:1&2:£3.10, 1&3:£2.80, 2&3:£2.50 CSF £27.27 TOTE £5.80: £2.50, £2.20; EX 27.80.
Owner Mr & Mrs Ian Hall **Bred** Kate Gale Syndicate **Trained** Orton, Cumbria
■ Stewards' Enquiry : Paul Gallagher ten-day ban: took wrong course (May 3-12)
Jason Maguire ten-day ban: took wrong course (May 3-12)

FOCUS

There was drama on the second circuit as two horses took the wrong course after the field had been waved around the second fence in the back straight, where Harry Haynes was being attended to. The two jockeys had very little time in which to react, but both were given ten-day bans.

NOTEBOOK

Western Gale(IRE) was left with a definite advantage when two opponents took the wrong course in the back straight and, clear on the home turn, he was never in much danger despite slowing into the last. Dropped 3lb since his last run back in October, he jumped and travelled pretty well but this was a fairly bloodless success. (op 9-2)

Matmata De Tendron(FR) won over 4m in a bog at Hexham last time, and this admirably tough grey ran thoroughly respectably in these different and not entirely suitable conditions. (op 6-1 tchd 7-1)

Dawn Ride(IRE) has had plenty of success here and won this contest last year, when it was run on the first day of the current season. His rider's quick thinking took him the right side of the 2m4f start after the field had bypassed the second in the back straight, but his jumping let him down and he was soon no threat to the first two.

Checkerboard(IRE) was very much in contention when his jockey steered him the wrong side of a set of rails after the field had been waved around the second fence in the back straight. (op 5-1)

Wolf Moon(IRE), the long-time leader, was close up when he went the wrong side of a set of rails marking the 2m4f hurdle start just after the field had been waved around the second fence in the back straight. (op 5-1)

5354 BOOK YOUR LADIES DAY HOSPITALITY MARQUEE PACKAGE (S) H'CAP HURDLE (10 hdls 1 omitted) 2m 4f

4:40 (4:46) (Class 5) (0-90,90) 4-7-Y-0 **£2,055** (£599; £299)

Form					RPR
2002	1		**Pugnacity**[236] 1360 7-11-5 80 ... RyanMania (Dianne Sayer) *trckd ldrs: wnt cl 2nd after 4 out: led on bit appr next: drew wl clr between last 2: eased towards fin*	**4/1**[1]	96+
004P	2	12	**Some Catch (IRE)**[42] 4511 5-10-0 61 oh1 ... TomSiddall (Elliott Cooper) *chsd ldrs: drvn 6th: led after 4 out: hdd appr next: kpt on: no ch w wnr*	**8/1**	65
5000	3	9	**Knock Three Times (IRE)**[48] 4390 5-11-5 87 ... (t) MissLAlexander[(7)] (Wilf Storey) *in rr: hdwy whn hit 4 out: wnt modest 3rd next: one pce*	**7/1**[3]	82
P060	4	5	**Solway Dornal**[14] 5131 6-10-6 67 ... CampbellGillies (Lisa Harrison) *hmpd 1st: hld up in midfield: chsd ldrs 5th: sn drvn along: outpcd 4 out: kpt on fr last: tk 4th last strides*	**12/1**	56
44P5	5	nse	**Cornish Castle (USA)**[23] 4994 5-10-8 76 ... (p) JoeColliver[(7)] (Andrew Crook) *in rr: hdwy 6th: sn chsng ldrs: wnt 4th 3 out: one pce*	**6/1**[2]	67
1356	6	4	**Lady Pacha**[60] 4148 4-11-4 90 ... BrianToomey[(5)] (Tim Pitt) *nt fluent in rr: bhd and reminders 4 out: sme hdwy appr next: sn wknd*	**9/1**	73
6000	7	5	**Media Stars**[16] 5091 6-11-1 76 ... KennyJohnson (Robert Johnson) *hld up in rr: hmpd 1st: bhd fr 4 out*	**33/1**	56
0PP-	P		**Carlton Mac**[26] 3867 6-10-3 64 ... (p) RobertWalford (Simon Griffiths) *in rr: hmpd 1st: bhd and drvn 6th: sn t.o: p.u bef 3 out*	**66/1**	—
466U	F		**Railway Park (IRE)**[33] 4796 7-10-12 78 ... (p) PaulGallagher[(5)] (John Wainwright) *chsd ldrs: fell 1st*	**7/1**[3]	—
3P00	P		**Cosmetic**[14] 5130 6-11-0 75 ... WilsonRenwick (Colin Teague) *chsd ldrs: lost pl 4th: t.o 4 out: p.u bef next*	**9/1**	—
FP00	P		**Kalulushi (IRE)**[16] 5103 6-11-7 82 ... (b[1]) JasonMaguire (Donald McCain) *w ldr: led 3rd: hdd after 4 out: sn lost pl: t.o next: p.u bef 2 out*	**12/1**	—
P000	F		**Cloudy Joe (IRE)**[35] 4739 5-11-0 75 ... (b[1]) AdamPogson (Charles Pogson) *led to 3rd: chsd ldrs: 5th and wkng whn fell 3 out*	**14/1**	—

4m 41.0s (-18.50) **Going Correction** -0.85s/f (Firm)
WFA 4 from 5yo+ 6lb 12 Ran SP% **116.9**
Speed ratings: **103,98,94,92,92 90,88,—,—,— —,—**
toteswingers:1&2:£5.20, 1&3:£6.90, 2&3:£9.40 CSF £35.82 CT £218.80 TOTE £4.00: £1.60, £2.60, £3.10; EX 29.00.There was no bid for the winner.
Owner Anthony White **Bred** Old Mill Stud And S C Williams **Trained** Hackthorpe, Cumbria

FOCUS

The middle flight in the back straight was bypassed on the second circuit. A very ordinary seller run at a solid pace. There were only three previous hurdles scorers in the line-up, one of them the winner.

NOTEBOOK

Pugnacity ran out a very comfortable winner after taking it up approaching the first in the straight. A versatile mare who was runner-up over fences when last seen back in August, she was well backed for this. (op 6-1)

Some Catch(IRE) was a pound out of the weights. Her stint in the lead was short-lived and she was left trailing by the winner after clattering through the third-last. She had run respectably here two starts back and this better ground was probably in her favour. (op 7-1)

Knock Three Times(IRE) hasn't scored since her debut success but has dropped 18lb since moving into handicaps. She moved into third three from home but made no impression from there. (op 8-1)

Solway Dornal was staying on at the end on this handicap debut, just snatching fourth. (op 10-1)

Cornish Castle(USA) was well held with the cheekpieces back on. (op 11-2)

5355 MINSTER JAGUAR LEEDS BEGINNERS' CHASE (18 fncs) 2m 6f 110y

5:15 (5:25) (Class 4) 5-Y-0+ **£2,602** (£764; £382)

Form					RPR
-100	1		**Riptide**[30] 4852 5-11-0 0 ... (p) JasonMaguire (Donald McCain) *nt jump wl: j. slowly: reminders 5th and 9th: wnt 2nd after 14th: upsides 3 out: led last: drvn clr: eased towards fin*	**2/5**[1]	115+
-46F	2	13	**Le Commencement (IRE)**[40] 4538 9-11-0 112 ... JohnnyFarrelly (Sophie Leech) *led to 2nd: led 6th: mstke 4 out: jnd 3 out: hdd and hit last*	**11/4**[2]	102
00	3	44	**The Bravetraveller (IRE)**[23] 4993 8-10-11 0 ... JamesO'Farrell[(3)] (Barbara Butterworth) *led 2nd: hdd 6th: wknd 14th: sn bhd: t.o whn blnd 2 out: eased run-in*	**10/1**[3]	67

5m 34.3s (-2.70) **Going Correction** -0.375s/f (Good) 3 Ran SP% **107.2**
Speed ratings: **89,84,69**
CSF £1.91 TOTE £1.40; EX 1.80.
Owner Gone To The Bar Racing **Bred** D Robb **Trained** Cholmondeley, Cheshire

FOCUS

A weak beginners' chase, run in a time around 13sec outside standard.

NOTEBOOK

Riptide, a 131-rated hurdler, appeared to face a straightforward task on this chasing debut, but it turned out to be anything but. He didn't take to the fences at all, jumping slowly and sloppily in rear, and was being cajoled and pushed along from an early stage. Remarkably, Jason Maguire's persistence paid off in the end, as the reluctant gelding closed on the home turn and finally got on top after the last for an unlikely win. He had little to beat with the runner-up also making errors, and cannot be backed with any confidence to follow this up. (op 4-9 tchd 4-11)

Le Commencement(IRE), a faller on his recent debut for the yard, made a lot of the running. Getting in too close to the fourth-last when attempting to kick clear, he met each of the last three fences wrong too and had no more to offer on the run-in. He is not the biggest for fences. (tchd 3-1)

The Bravetraveller(IRE), a winning pointer, jumped well enough on this chase debut, but stopped worryingly quickly turning out of the back straight and was allowed to come home in his own time. (op 9-1 tchd 8-1)

5356 ROYAL PIGEON RACING ASSOCIATION NOVICES' HURDLE (DIV I) (9 hdls) 2m 110y

5:45 (5:53) (Class 4) 4-Y-O+ **£2,397** (£698; £349)

Form				RPR
5011	1		**Red Merlin (IRE)**[25] 4944 6-10-12 130 JasonMaguire — (Donald McCain) *trckd ldrs: led on bit after 6th: wnt clr 2 out: v easily* **4/7**[1]	123+
121	2	17	**Little Hercules (IRE)**[65] 4059 5-11-5 0 BrianHughes — (Howard Johnson) *chsd ldng trio: mstke 5th: tk 3rd 2 out: kpt on to take modest 2nd nr fin* **4/1**[2]	108
1335	3	3/4	**Jack The Gent (IRE)**[35] 4739 7-11-5 121 BarryKeniry — (George Moore) *led: hdd after 6th: hit 2 out: one pce* **9/2**[3]	108
0-30	4	8	**Toledo Gold (IRE)**[52] 4303 5-10-12 100 (t) MichaelMcAlister — (Maurice Barnes) *t.k.h: trckd ldr: 4th and weakning whn hit 2 out* **16/1**	94
00	5	9	**Provost**[23] 4995 7-10-5 0 JakeGreenall(7) — (Michael Easterby) *in rr: bhd 5th: kpt on fr 2 out* **50/1**	83
0	6	1 1/2	**French Seventyfive**[13] 5151 4-10-7 0 RobertWalford — (Tim Walford) *t.k.h: prom: lost pl 3rd: wnt poor 5th 3 out: nvr on terms* **66/1**	78
0000	7	25	**Wicked Streak (IRE)**[3] 5307 6-10-9 90 JamesHalliday(3) — (Micky Hammond) *hld up in rr: sme hdwy 6th: mstke and wknd next: sn bhd: t.o* **50/1**	57
P000	8	1 1/2	**Fred Grass**[21] 5027 5-10-9 72 JamesO'Farrell(3) — (Jonathan Haynes) *sn in rr: bhd fr 5th: t.o* **100/1**	55
-100	9	21	**Seam Of Diamonds**[147] 2547 6-10-5 0 JamesReveley — (Martin Todhunter) *in rr: bhd fr 5th: wl t.o* **25/1**	27

3m 45.0s (-10.80) **Going Correction** -0.85s/f (Firm)
WFA 4 from 5yo+ 5lb **9** Ran SP% **118.0**
Speed ratings (Par 105): **91,83,82,78,74 73,62,61,51**
toteswingers:1&2:£2.50, 1&3:£2.40, 2&3:£2.20 CSF £3.38 TOTE £1.70: £1.02, £1.30, £1.70; EX 3.30.
Owner Timeform Betfair Racing Club & M Taylor **Bred** Keatly Overseas Ltd **Trained** Cholmondeley, Cheshire

FOCUS
Not much depth to this novices' hurdle, but it produced a very taking winner.

NOTEBOOK
Red Merlin(IRE) ,unpenalised for two wins in races confined to conditional jockeys, streaked clear between the last two flights to land a hat-trick and is improving all the time. He goes very well on a sound surface and looks just the type for the Swinton Handicap Hurdle at Haydock next month, where the likely strong pace would play into his hands. Alternatively, he could go for a novice race at the Punchestown festival. (op 4-9 tchd 8-13)
Little Hercules(IRE) was pulled out of a Grade 2 at Aintree last week. Racing in fourth position, a little way off the front three, he came under pressure on the home turn as the winner made his move. He did stay on to grab second on the run-in, but was never a real threat to Red Merlin and may be ready for a step up in trip. (op 5-1)
Jack The Gent(IRE) ran respectably back on a left-handed track, and has had a perfectly acceptable season given that he is a real chasing type. (op 11-2 tchd 4-1)
Toledo Gold(IRE), keen again, finished a bit further behind Little Hercules than he had at Musselburgh and may have stamina limitations. (op 25-1)
Provost was one of those adrift of the first four from an early stage, but did come through for a remote fifth. He may do better in handicaps. (op 66-1)

5357 ROYAL PIGEON RACING ASSOCIATION NOVICES' HURDLE (DIV II) (9 hdls) 2m 110y

6:15 (6:22) (Class 4) 4-Y-O+ **£2,397** (£698; £349)

Form				RPR
14/5	1		**Hunters Belt (IRE)**[23] 4995 7-10-12 0 WilsonRenwick — (Noel Wilson) *in tch: hdwy to trck ldrs 6th: led appr last: hld on towards fin* **9/1**	108
443	2	3/4	**Archie Rice (USA)**[27] 4917 5-10-5 0 MattCrawley(7) — (Tom Keddy) *stdd s: hld up in rr: drvn: hdwy and modest 5th 3 out: 3rd last: kpt on: nt rch wnr* **7/2**[2]	107
0162	3	nk	**Solis**[25] 4942 5-10-9 115 JoeColliver(10) — (Micky Hammond) *chsd ldrs: rdn appr 3 out: kpt on same pce run-in* **9/2**[3]	114
5	4	1	**Enjoy Your Life (IRE)**[29] 4870 4-10-7 0 BrianHughes — (Andrew Crook) *trckd ldrs: led 3 out: blnd next: hdd and hit last: kpt on same pce run-in* **33/1**	103
412	5	shd	**Waldvogel (IRE)**[21] 5035 7-11-5 130 DominicElsworth — (Nicky Richards) *stdd s: hld up in rr: bdly hmpd 4th: hdwy and modest 6th 3 out: j.lft there and next: 5th last: kpt on same pce run-in* **Evs**[1]	116+
B	6	20	**Brink**[68] 3986 4-9-10 0 ow1 BrianToomey(5) — (Tim Pitt) *led to 2nd: led 5th: hdd 3 out: wknd: j.lft and blnd last: rdr lost irons: eased* **66/1**	83+
P	7	67	**Cayo**[56] 4242 4-10-7 0 KennyJohnson — (Robert Johnson) *in rr: bhd whn hmpd 4th: t.o 6th: eventually completed* **100/1**	14
U406	P		**High Hoylander**[23] 4998 5-10-12 103 JasonMaguire — (Sue Smith) *t.k.h: w ldrs: led 2nd: hdd 5th: 4th whn j.rt and blnd next: hung bdly rt and lost pl bnd: t.o whn p.u bef 3 out* **12/1**	—
60F	P		**Pompan (IRE)**[14] 5131 5-10-12 0 CampbellGillies — (Peter Niven) *chsd ldrs to 3rd: sddle slipped and lost pl whn blnd next: sn p.u* **66/1**	—

3m 55.6s (-0.20) **Going Correction** -0.85s/f (Firm)
WFA 4 from 5yo+ 5lb **9** Ran SP% **115.0**
Speed ratings (Par 105): **66,65,65,65,64 55,24,—,—**
toteswingers:1&2:£6.20, 1&3:£6.10, 2&3:£2.50. Tote Super 7: Win: Not won. Place: Not won. CSF £40.58 TOTE £9.70: £2.40, £1.30, £1.30; EX 30.10.
Owner Mrs N C Wilson **Bred** Charlie Purcell **Trained** Sandhutton, N Yorks

FOCUS
This was a most unsatisfactory affair, run at a very steady pace and featuring some decidedly novicey jumping. The first five finished in a heap and the time was more than ten seconds slower than the first division, so this is form to treat with a good deal of caution.

NOTEBOOK
Hunters Belt(IRE) built on the promise he had shown first time over hurdles at Sedgefield. Picking up ground on the home turn, he showed in front going to the last and held on in the sprint to the line. He may prove vulnerable under a penalty. (op 15-2)
Archie Rice(USA) was held up at the back as usual, which left him with plenty of work to do in this slowly run race. In the end he did well to be beaten under a length, and he is capable of landing a small race when things go his way. (op 10-3 tchd 4-1)
Solis, under a penalty, ran his race back down in trip but errors three out and again at the next didn't help his cause. (op 5-1 tchd 4-1)
Enjoy Your Life(IRE) was in front when bundering two out and met the last flight wrong too. He has still to prove his stamina in a truly-run race.
Waldvogel(IRE) was already towards the rear when he jumped into the back of Pompan at the fourth. Never hurdling with much fluency anyway, he did make up ground from a long way back but the damage had been done. Things went against him here but he is starting to look disappointing. (op 11-10)
T/Jkpt: £2,840.00 to a £1 stake. Pool £10,000.00 - 2.50 winning units. T/Plt: £100.80 to a £1 stake. Pool £78,245.86 - 566.51 winning units. T/Qpdt: £13.30 to a £1 stake. Pool £6,400.46 - 354.51 winning units. WG

5358 - 5366a (Foreign Racing) - See Raceform Interactive

5299 AUTEUIL (L-H)
Sunday, April 17

OFFICIAL GOING: Turf: very soft

5367a PRIX MURAT (CHASE) (GRADE 2) (5YO+) (TURF) 2m 6f

3:15 (12:00) 5-Y-O+

£93,103 (£45,517; £26,896; £18,620; £10,344; £7,241)

			RPR
1		**Polar Rochelais (FR)**[21] 5048 8-11-5 0 (p) JeromeZuliani — (P Quinton, France) **103/10**	—
2	nk	**Doumaja (FR)**[21] 5048 9-11-5 0 (p) CyrilleGombeau — (G Cherel, France) **17/2**[3]	—
3	3	**Pistolet Rouge (FR)**[21] 5-10-6 0 (p) ChristophePieux — (G Cherel, France) **5/1**[2]	—
4	2 1/2	**Pibrac (FR)**[21] 5048 7-10-10 0 PACarberry — (F-M Cottin, France) **51/1**	—
5	10	**Frolon (FR)**[21] 6-10-8 0 JonathanPlouganou — (F-M Cottin, France) **31/1**	—
6	1 1/2	**Odeillo Du Mathan (FR)**[21] 9-10-10 0 (b) BenoitGicquel — (G Cherel, France) **93/1**	—
7	dist	**Objectif Special (FR)**[21] 5048 9-10-6 0 (p) BertrandThelier — (G Cherel, France) **70/1**	—
R		**The Sawyer (BEL)**[33] 4790 11-10-8 0 NathanSweeney — (Bob Buckler) *wl away and pressed ldr early: sn settled in 2nd bhd clr ldr: slt mstke 2nd: j.v.slowly 5th and dropped to 6th pl: bhd fr 5 out: ref 3 out* **96/1**	—
P		**Deus Ex Machina (FR)**[21] 5048 7-10-8 0 ElwisLequesne — (B De Watrigant, France) **42/1**	—
F		**Rubi Ball (FR)**[21] 5048 6-11-5 0 (p) DavidCottin — (J Ortet, France) **2/5**[1]	—

5m 35.49s (-8.51) **10** Ran SP% **118.3**
PARI-MUTUEL (all including 1 euro stakes): WIN 11.30; PLACE 2.70, 2.70, 2.10; DF 14.70; SF 37.50.
Owner Ecurie Des Dunes **Bred** S Esnouf **Trained** France

5152 EXETER (R-H)
Monday, April 18

OFFICIAL GOING: Good to firm (chase 7.9, hurdle 8.0)
Wind: fresh across Weather: sunny

5368 FINLAKE HOLIDAY PARK NOVICES' (S) HURDLE (10 hdls) 2m 3f

2:30 (2:31) (Class 5) 4-Y-O+ **£1,951** (£573; £286; £143)

Form				RPR
00P5	1		**Rolanta (FR)**[6] 5272 6-10-6 71 HaddenFrost — (James Frost) *hld up: smooth hdwy after 7th: wnt 3rd next: led appr last: sn clr: rdn out* **5/1**	91+
524	2	8	**Jewellery (IRE)**[7] 5252 4-10-0 87 (t) JamieMoore — (Alison Thorpe) *led tl 2nd: prom: led after 7th: rdn and hdd bef 3 out: kpt on same pce: regained 2nd nr fin* **5/2**[1]	78
3002	3	hd	**Rhyton (IRE)**[23] 5014 4-10-4 95 (p) JohnKington(3) — (Donald McCain) *led 2nd: nt fluent 3rd: mstke 7th: sn hdd: rdn to regain ld bef next: nt fluent 2 out: sn hdd: kpt on same pce: lost 2nd nr fin* **3/1**[2]	88
0002	4	17	**Robello**[23] 5000 7-10-6 81 (p) CharlieWallis(7) — (John O'Shea) *trckd ldrs: rdn after 7th: wknd 3 out: fatally collapsed after fin* **16/1**	76
0	5	3/4	**Resplendent Ace (IRE)**[11] 5167 7-10-8 0 OliverDayman(5) — (John Price) *trckd ldrs: reminder after 5th: rdn after 7th: wknd next* **12/1**	75
5	6	86	**Emerald Glade (IRE)**[18] 5078 4-10-0 0 DaveCrosse — (Milton Harris) *trckd ldrs: nt fluent 6th: sn rdn: wknd after next: t.o* **10/3**[3]	—
F	P		**Fraamtaaztiic**[95] 3526 4-9-11 0 WayneKavanagh(3) — (Ron Hodges) *hld up: struggling 5th: t.o after 7th: p.u after 3 out* **25/1**	—
0	P		**Phlorian**[28] 4923 5-10-10 0 (t) JamesO'Farrell(3) — (Ian Patrick Browne, Ire) *hld up: blnd bdly 7th: sn wknd: t.o whn p.u after 3 out* **33/1**	—

4m 31.4s (-11.30) **Going Correction** -0.775s/f (Firm)
WFA 4 from 5yo+ 5lb **8** Ran SP% **113.7**
Speed ratings (Par 103): **92,88,88,81,81 44,—,—**
toteswingers:1&2:£4.60, 1&3:£6.30, 2&3:£1.30 CSF £18.19 TOTE £5.30: £1.90, £1.10, £1.60; EX 19.60.There was no bid for the winner.
Owner Mrs J McCormack **Bred** Roland Madiot **Trained** Scorriton, Devon

FOCUS
An ordinary seller and a big step up from the winner. It was run at an average sort of gallop and the placed horses attempted to catch their rivals napping when kicking on four out.

NOTEBOOK
Rolanta(FR) readily came through to mow down the leaders in the home straight. She faded from the front in this class last week, but the switch in tactics worked out nicely and this is clearly her level. (op 6-1)
Jewellery(IRE) failed to raise her game for the drop back in trip and is going to prove tricky to place successfully. (tchd 11-4)
Rhyton(IRE) no doubt has more talent than he's currently showing over hurdles and needs to learn to respect his jumps if he is to progress at all. He will likely pop up at some stage during the summer. (op 5-2 tchd 10-3)
Robello plugged on for a never dangerous fourth. He suddenly collapsed after the line with tragic consequences. (op 18-1 tchd 20-1)

5369 ELITE RACING CLUB H'CAP HURDLE (10 hdls) 2m 3f

3:00 (3:00) (Class 3) (0-125,125) 4-Y-O+ **£4,293** (£1,260; £630; £314)

Form				RPR
0521	1		**Laustra Bad (FR)**[27] 4925 8-11-7 **125** (bt) CO'Farrell(5) — (David Pipe) *trckd ldr: shkn up to ld 2 out: clr last: readily* **15/8**[1]	133+
2151	2	10	**Midnight Opera**[22] 5035 5-11-2 **120** MarkQuinlan(5) — (Neil Mulholland) *led: rdn and hdd whn nt fluent 2 out: sn hld by wnr* **2/1**[2]	117

44F6 **3** 2½ **Forest Rhythm (IRE)**[24] 4990 7-10-0 **102**................ WayneKavanagh(3) 97
(Seamus Mullins) *trckd ldrs: rdn appr 3 out: styd on same pce* **15/8**[1]

0-PP **4** 24 **Shardakhan (IRE)**[8] 5241 9-10-4 **110**........................(bt) DannyBurton(7) 83
(Sophie Leech) *trckd ldrs: pushed along after 5th: rdn after 7th: wknd 3 out: t.o* **25/1**[3]

4m 24.4s (-18.30) **Going Correction** -0.775s/f (Firm) 4 Ran SP% **106.7**
Speed ratings (Par 107): **107,102,101,91**
CSF £5.92 TOTE £2.00; EX 3.90.

Owner Mrs Sarah Ling **Bred** Jean Pierre Dubois **Trained** Nicholashayne, Devon

FOCUS

An open-looking little handicap. There was a fair gallop on and the winner is rated back to the level of his old form.

NOTEBOOK

Laustra Bad(FR) ended his losing run at this venue last month and followed up with a comfortable success despite a 10lb higher mark. The quicker ground was of some concern beforehand, but it proved no bother to him and he has more options now he has fully proved his stamina. Another hike in the handicap is forthcoming, however, so it would not surprise to see him out under a penalty at Sandown this weekend. (op 9-4)

Midnight Opera was up 3lb for winning his second novice event last month and was sure to enjoy the surface. He again set out to make all, but ultimately got outstayed by the winner over this longer trip. (op 15-8 tchd 7-4, tchd 85-40 in a place)

Forest Rhythm(IRE) was well supported, but he didn't settle that well and jumped somewhat deliberately. He was always being held in the home straight and probably needs to drop back down in class. (tchd 7-4)

Shardakhan(IRE), in a first-time tongue tie, was predictably outpaced but at least got home this time. (op 22-1)

5370 FINLAKE HOLIDAY PARK H'CAP CHASE (18 fncs) 3m
3:30 (3:31) (Class 4) (0-115,112) 5-Y-0+ **£3,065** (£951; £512)

Form RPR

300P **1** **Foynes Island (IRE)**[24] 4988 5-11-7 **100**..................(tp) RichardJohnson 116+
(Philip Hobbs) *trckd ldrs: nt fluent 11th: pushed along briefly: led 4 out: sn rdn: 1 1/2 up whn awkward and lft clr last: styd on* **9/4**[2]

4213 **2** 14 **Louis Pasteur (IRE)**[13] 5156 6-11-5 **105**........................... SClements(7) 109
(Nick Mitchell) *trckd ldrs: led briefly 9th: nt fluent 12th: sn u.p: styd on same pce fr 4 out: lft 2nd at the last* **3/1**[3]

2112 **3** 21 **Ours (FR)**[20] 5069 9-11-8 **101**... NickScholfield 86
(Mark Rimell) *led tl 9th: led after 10th: hdd 14th: rdn bef 4 out: fdd fr 3 out: lft 3rd at the last* **7/1**

U441 **F** **Victory Parade (IRE)**[8] 5240 8-12-0 **112** 7ex........(p) AodhaganConlon(5) 124
(Rebecca Curtis) *trckd ldr: led briefly 10th: led 14th: rdn and hdd 4 out: ev ch whn nt fluent 2 out: 1 1/2 down whn fell last* **6/4**[1]

5m 45.4s (-23.90) **Going Correction** -0.975s/f (Hard) 4 Ran SP% **108.3**
Speed ratings: **100,95,88,—**
CSF £8.92 TOTE £4.00; EX 11.80.

Owner M G St Quinton **Bred** William Ryan **Trained** Withycombe, Somerset

FOCUS

A moderate little handicap, run at a sound gallop. The winner is rated up 7lb on his best hurdles form with the faller heading for a figuer in line with his recent win.

NOTEBOOK

Foynes Island(IRE) had disappointed since joining Phillip Hobbs, but he won an Irish point before joining him and this was his chasing debut. He also went in first-time cheekpieces and came in for good support. Richard Johnson had to keep him going in front coming to the last, where his only rival at the time Victory Parade came down when still in with a fighting chance. He would have probably scored whatever as he did look to markedly idle once hitting the front and the switch to fences is clearly what he has been waiting for. There is still plenty of room for improvement with his jumping, but he's entitled to improve on that score. (op 7-2)

Louis Pasteur(IRE) went with more enthusiasm under today's rider, but was put in his place before the home turn. (op 10-3 tchd 5-2)

Ours(FR) went well for a long way, but had no more to give once headed. (op 13-2 tchd 15-2)

Victory Parade(IRE) came good over fences at Wincanton eight days earlier and was well treated under his penalty. His jumping under pressure was again his downfall, though, and he did take a heavy fall. (op 11-10 tchd 13-8)

5371 ELITE RACING CLUB NOVICES' CHASE (15 fncs) 2m 3f 110y
4:00 (4:00) (Class 3) 5-Y-0+ **£5,334** (£1,566; £783; £391)

Form RPR

1354 **1** **Rebel Du Maquis (FR)**[42] 4531 6-11-3 134........................ MrRMahon(5) 137+
(Paul Nicholls) *mde all: hrd pressed 3 out tl asserted after 2 out: wnt sltly rt last: r.o: pushed out* **4/7**[1]

6-20 **2** 9 **Lady Hillingdon**[217] 1519 8-10-11 129...................................(t) AELynch 117
(Paul John Gilligan, Ire) *trckd wnr: swtchd rt to chal 3 out tl after next: sn rdn: styd on same pce* **7/4**[2]

P444 **3** 23 **Chase Gate**[70] 3985 6-10-12 0... HaddenFrost 95
(James Frost) *trckd ldng trio: outpcd after 11th: r.o fr last to snatch modest 3rd towards fin* **16/1**[3]

4 **4** 1¾ **Another Puzzle**[7] 5254 7-10-12 0... MarkGrant 93
(Dominic Ffrench Davis) *trckd ldng pair: rdn after 11th: hld fr next: lost modest 3rd towards fin* **40/1**

4m 38.5s (-18.80) **Going Correction** -0.975s/f (Hard) 4 Ran SP% **108.3**
Speed ratings: **98,94,85,84**
CSF £2.01 TOTE £1.70; EX 2.10.

Owner Mrs Kathy Stuart **Bred** Daniel & Mme Jeannine Laupretre **Trained** Ditcheat, Somerset

FOCUS

This novice was slower than the later hunter chase and the first two are rated below their best. The race has been given a token rating through the third.

NOTEBOOK

Rebel Du Maquis(FR) made it 3-6 over fences with a ready effort under top weight on ground that really suits him. He unsurprisingly set out to make all, but his rider didn't overdo things and that made his jumping a touch sticky early on. He cranked it up from the ninth, however, and his jumping at proper speed over the next two was impressive. The runner-up ensured he had to be kept up to his work, but he came right away nearing the last and is a very useful sort on his day. There could be a decent handicap in him on a sound surface next season. (op 4-6 tchd 8-11, tchd 4-5 in a place)

Lady Hillingdon had a solid chance at the weights on her return from a 217-day break. He held every chance, but was always being held in the home straight and the winner is a class above. She ought to come on nicely, though, and should be capable of winning a handicap this summer. (tchd 6-4)

Chase Gate, a good-ground point winner, appeared to blow up on his return from a 70-day break before rallying and should enjoy a stiffer test once handicapping in this sphere. (op 14-1)

Another Puzzle did his best to stick with the first two off the home turn, but paid the price from the second-last. (op 50-1 tchd 28-1)

5372 TOTNES AND BRIDGETOWN OPEN HUNTERS' CHASE (15 fncs) 2m 3f 110y
4:30 (4:30) (Class 6) 5-Y-0+ **£936** (£290; £145; £72)

Form RPR

345- **1** **Lord Henry (IRE)**[357] 18 12-11-5 140............................... MrJABest(7) 133+
(Philip Hobbs) *in tch: trckd ldrs after 10th: led 4 out: in command next: awkward last: comf* **2/1**[2]

-412 **2** 9 **Takeroc (FR)**[26] 4950 8-11-9 140..................................(t) MrHDerham(7) 125+
(Paul Nicholls) *hld up towards rr: hdwy 9th: trckd ldrs 11th: rdn after 4 out: wnt 2nd 2 out: kpt on same pce* **5/4**[1]

13-1 **3** 10 **King Cyrus (IRE)**[35] 4786 9-11-9 118......................... MrMWoodward(7) 116
(Ms Emma Oliver) *prom: led 8th tl rdn appr 4 out: styd on same pce fr 3 out: hit last* **13/2**[3]

153U **4** 4½ **Ryeman**[27] 4936 9-12-2 112....................................(bt) MrJoshuaGuerriero 111
(Andrew Jackson) *trckd ldrs: rdn appr 4 out: sn one pce* **14/1**

0RUU **5** 6 **Cloud Nine (IRE)**[27] 4936 8-11-7 106....................(p) MrRGHenderson(5) 101
(Miss Jane Western) *led tl 8th: chsd ldrs: rdn after 11th: wknd 3 out* **25/1**

054P **6** 8 **Pearly Star**[15] 10-11-5 85..(b) MissAliceMills(7) 92
(D Bryant) *prom tl 9th: wknd after 11th* **100/1**

P0/6 **7** 11 **Glenary (IRE)**[16] 9-11-5 0.. MrRobertHawker(7) 81
(Mrs Sarah Hawker) *struggling 9th: a towards rr* **80/1**

60/P **8** 18 **Miss Nut Nut**[15] 8-10-12 0.. MrNdeBoinville(7) 56
(D Bryant) *a towards rr: struggling 8th: t.o* **100/1**

4040 **9** 19 **No Greater Love (FR)**[26] 4950 9-11-5 80.............................. MrJPark(7) 44
(Mrs T Porter) *mid-div: struggling 8th: mistke 10th: sn bhd: t.o* **100/1**

/5-0 **P** **Waziri (IRE)**[325] 499 10-11-9 0.. MrRWoollacott(3) —
(A S T Holdsworth) *mid-div tl wknd after 9th: p.u bef 11th* **100/1**

U-60 **P** **Triple Bluff**[336] 374 8-11-5 0.. MissJBuck(7) —
(Miss J Du Plessis) *p.u after 1st whn nt fluent and rdr lost irons* **100/1**

43P2 **F** **Quaddick Lake (IRE)**[29] 4901 8-11-12 95.......................... MrWBiddick —
(A J Farrant) *in tch whn fell 7th* **10/1**

4m 33.3s (-24.00) **Going Correction** -0.975s/f (Hard) 12 Ran SP% **116.9**
Speed ratings: **109,105,101,99,97 94,89,82,74,— —,—**
toteswingers:1&2:£1.80, 1&3:£3.40, 2&3:£2.80 CSF £4.99 TOTE £2.40: £1.30, £1.10, £1.50; EX 6.10.

Owner Mrs Karola Vann **Bred** Mrs Ann Maxwell **Trained** Withycombe, Somerset

FOCUS

Sound form for the division, with the first two high-class hunters. The next two set the level.

NOTEBOOK

Lord Henry(IRE) was making his hunter chase debut after a 357-day layoff and he bolted up. His jumping was rusty through the first half, although in fairness he was crowded over the first three. The further he went the better he was, though, and once again he advertised his liking for quick ground. Perhaps connections will be tempted to look at something for him at Stratford next month, while there is also the hunter chase meeting at Cheltenham too. (op 15-8, tchd 9-4 in a place)

Takeroc(FR) was outstayed by My Way De Solzen at Hereford last month and stamina was again the big worry at this venue, despite the quicker ground. He came through with his effort in the home straight, but it was apparent from two out the winner had his measure. He is a real 2m specialist. (op 7-4)

King Cyrus(IRE) defied a lengthy absence when winning on his debut in this sphere last month and, against two superior rivals, he posted a sound effort in defeat down in trip. (op 5-1)

Ryeman had his chance and wasn't at all disgraced, but is one to avoid for win-only purposes. (op 12-1 tchd 16-1)

5373 CITY OF EXETER CHALLENGE CUP NOVICES' H'CAP HURDLE (8 hdls) 2m 1f
5:00 (5:00) (Class 4) (0-110,110) 4-Y-0+ **£2,341** (£687; £343; £171)

Form RPR

6001 **1** **Mauritino (GER)**[8] 5244 7-10-9 **93**.. APMcCoy 104+
(Jonjo O'Neill) *trckd ldr: led on bit appr 3 out: sn jnd but a travelling best: eased into ld after last: unextended* **1/2**[1]

-414 **2** 1¼ **Allformary**[23] 5016 5-9-13 **90**..(t) EdCookson(7) 92
(Kim Bailey) *trckd ldrs: chal 3 out: sn rdn: stuck on gamely but a fighting losing battle* **6/1**[2]

0340 **3** 7 **That'lldoboy (FR)**[16] 5110 5-11-6 **109**................................ MrRMahon(5) 106
(Paul Nicholls) *hld up in last pair but wl in tch: hdwy after 5th: sn rdn: wnt 3rd and awkward 2 out: nt pce to threaten front 2* **17/2**[3]

2P5P **4** 7 **Risk Challenge (USA)**[193] 1740 9-10-8 **92**........................(t) TomO'Brien 80
(Sophie Leech) *hld up in last but wl in tch: rdn appr 3 out: kpt on same pce* **33/1**

0402 **5** 4 **Special Cuvee**[9] 5212 5-10-10 **94**..(t) JamieMoore 79
(Alison Thorpe) *trckd ldrs: pushed along after 3rd: rdn after 5th: wknd after 2 out* **16/1**

P/03 **6** 7 **Kiama**[15] 9-9-12 **85**... IanPopham(3) 62
(Ron Hodges) *led tl rdn appr 3 out: sn btn* **17/2**[3]

4m 0.30s (-15.20) **Going Correction** -0.775s/f (Firm) 6 Ran SP% **110.8**
Speed ratings (Par 105): **104,103,100,96,94 91**
toteswingers:1&2:£1.90, 1&3:£1.60, 2&3:£2.30 CSF £4.19 TOTE £1.60: £1.20, £2.50; EX 3.10.

Owner P A Byrne **Bred** Werner Klein **Trained** Cheltenham, Gloucs

FOCUS

An uncompetitive novice handicap, run at a solid gallop. The winner was value for further and there was another step up from the second.

NOTEBOOK

Mauritino(GER) ◆ confirmed his need for quick ground when resuming winning ways at Wincanton eight days earlier and escaped a penalty for that. Therefore, it was unsurprising he proved all the rage to follow up, being Tony McCoy's sole ride of the day, and he completed the task with an effortless success. He is evidently well ahead of the handicapper now the ground has come in his favour and he will surely be out under a penalty in search of the hat-trick. (op 4-7)

Allformary was the only one to keep with the winner from three out, but that rival was cantering all over her nearing the business end and she is well flattered by her proximity. This does confirm she is up to her current mark, though. (op 7-1 tchd 11-2)

That'lldoboy(FR) travelled nicely into the home straight, but wasn't fluent under pressure and was well held. He is very much one of his leading yard's lesser lights, but should appreciate being sent chasing over a stiffer test. (op 15-2)

Risk Challenge(USA), who can be tricky, was making his debut for new connections after a 193-day break and ought to come on plenty. (op 28-1)

T/Plt: £60.80 to a £1 stake. Pool:£51,892.51 - 622.34 winning tickets T/Qpdt: £8.40 to a £1 stake. Pool:£3,369.58 - 295.79 winning tickets TM

5279 TOWCESTER (R-H)

Monday, April 18

OFFICIAL GOING: Good to firm (watered; 9.4)

Hurdle course dolled out wide, shared bends.

Wind: moderate across Weather: overcast but warm

5374 FREE TIPS AT GG.COM H'CAP HURDLE (11 hdls) 2m 5f
2:10 (2:10) (Class 5) (0-90,90) 4-Y-0+ **£1,712** (£499; £249)

Form RPR

P01P **1** **Speedy Directa (GER)**[16] 5111 8-11-3 **81**.....................(vt) CharliePoste 88+
(Milton Harris) *hld up in midfield: effrt 8th: led 3 out: sn rdn: edging rt up st: 4 l clr last: drvn and all out* **11/2**[1]

2P6P **2** *2* **Tiger Line**[11] 5169 7-11-6 **84**...(b[1]) SeanQuinlan 88
(Richard Phillips) *prom: 3rd and rdn and outpcd briefly bef 3 out: drvn to chse wnr next: plugged on flat but a hld* **8/1**[3]

4P45 **3** *12* **Crack At Dawn (IRE)**[17] 5103 10-11-8 **86**...................(vt[1]) DavidEngland 80
(Michael Gates) *plld hrd: led bef 3rd tl drvn and hdd 3 out: lost 2nd at next: sn fnd nil* **17/2**

4003 **4** *13* **Radmores Oscar**[26] 4946 5-10-13 **82**.........................(p) PeterCarberry[(5)] 64
(John O'Shea) *midfield: rdn and struggling 8th: wnt v poor 4th after 3 out* **11/1**

6-10 **5** *2 1/2* **Tavalu (USA)**[41] 4540 9-11-3 **84**.................................(p) DonalDevereux[(3)] 63
(Gerald Ham) *nvr bttr than midfield: mstke 7th: 7th and struggling whn blnd next* **10/1**

564B **6** *11* **Earl Of Thomond (IRE)**[21] 5057 6-10-11 **82**.......(p) MrJonathanBailey[(7)] 52
(Caroline Bailey) *midfield: 5th and rdn 8th: fnd nthing and sn lost tch* **11/2**[1]

01P5 **7** *23* **Woodlands Gem (IRE)**[11] 5169 9-10-13 **77**......................(bt) JackDoyle 26
(Peter Pritchard) *prom: mstke 4th: rdn and downed tools 6th: t.o bef next* **8/1**[3]

PP0R **R** **Orpen Bid (IRE)**[18] 4976 6-10-0 **67**..............................(p) CharlieStudd[(3)] —
(Michael Mullineaux) *ref to r* **25/1**

00P/ **P** **Killer Jim**[875] 2411 9-10-0 **64** oh4..................................... TomMessenger —
(William Davies) *t.k.h in last: hanging lft: p.u after 5th: dismntd* **66/1**

5-46 **P** **Jessica**[6] 5282 6-10-7 **74**.. JimmyDerham[(3)] —
(Seamus Mullins) *mstkes and nvr travelling in rr: rdn 4th: lost tch 7th: wl t.o whn p.u 2 out* **17/2**

0-44 **P** **Deejan (IRE)**[16] 5108 6-11-5 **90**....................................... MichaelByrne[(7)] —
(Tim Vaughan) *led tl bef 3rd: prom tl rdn and wknd 8th: 12 l 4th whn mstke 3 out: p.u next* **7/1**[2]

-00P **P** **Midnight Trix**[108] 3261 5-10-11 **75**..................................... FelixDeGiles —
(Alex Hales) *bhd and nvr travelling: t.o bef 7th: p.u after 3 out* **20/1**

5m 23.8s (-3.40) **Going Correction** -0.85s/f (Firm) **12** Ran SP% **114.1**

Speed ratings (Par 103): **72,71,66,61,60 56,47,—,—,— —,—**

toteswingers:1&2:£13.10, 1&3:£14.20, 2&3:£16.60 CSF £46.26 CT £368.59 TOTE £7.20: £2.30, £3.70, £3.20; EX 53.30.

Owner Robert Aplin **Bred** Gestut Graditz **Trained** Herridge, Wiltshire

FOCUS

A low-grade handicap that was run a decent gallop on ground jockeys described as riding on the 'good' side of good to firm. The second, third and fourth were all close to their marks.

NOTEBOOK

Speedy Directa(GER) landed a touch two starts ago (off 7lb lower), and was again well backed. Always travelling best, he took matters in hand climbing the hill for home, and although driven right out, was always holding the runner-up. He had disappointed on his previous start (off this mark), and is likely to remain hard to predict. His next engagement is likely to be at the sales. Official explanation: Trainer's rep said, regarding apparent improvement in form, that the gelding's last run at Chepstow appeared to come too soon after it's previous outing on March 30. (op 13-2)

Tiger Line posted one of her better efforts in the first-time blinkers. She handled the quicker ground and will stay 3m. She has been very inconsistent this season, as opposed to last season, but should find a similar contest, if building on this. (op 12-1)

Crack At Dawn(IRE) ran freely, with a visor replacing the blinkers. He is a winning pointer at 2m4f, but is still winless under rules after 20 starts. (op 9-1 tchd 10-1 and 8-1)

Radmores Oscar had been tailed off on his most recent start, so this was a step forward. Maybe an easier track would suit. (op 12-1 tchd 10-1)

Tavalu(USA) has not looked like repeating his shock win at huge odds in a seller here two starts back. He never got competitive here and was well beaten entering the straight. (op 9-1 tchd 17-2)

Earl Of Thomond(IRE) continues to frustrate his supporters. He was off the bridle with a circuit to go, and never looked like taking a hand at the business end. Official explanation: trainer said gelding bled from the nose (tchd 5-1)

Woodlands Gem(IRE) is a course winner, but dropped out with over a mile to run. (op 13-2)

Killer Jim Official explanation: jockey said gelding hung badly left causing saddle to slip (op 6-1)

Jessica had shown a little promise under a 7lb claimer here last time. However, her jumping let her down and she never looked like getting involved. (op 6-1)

Deejan(IRE) was a drifter in the market and this bumper winner once again spoilt her chance by racing to keenly. An easier track may help. (op 6-1)

5375 PERRYS PEUGEOT OF MILTON KEYNES BEGINNERS' CHASE (12 fncs) 2m 110y
2:40 (2:40) (Class 4) 5-Y-0+ **£2,276** (£668; £334; £166)

Form RPR

2300 **1** **Ballabrook (IRE)**[54] 4292 9-11-0 96.............................(b[1]) JasonMaguire 111+
(Donald McCain) *mde all and sn clr: j.lft: 20 l ld 1/2-way: nvr looked remotely like being chal: hacked up* **1/3**[1]

0PPP **2** *31* **Mr Johnson (IRE)**[36] 4751 8-11-0 0.................................. DavidEngland 73
(Michael Gates) *t.k.h early: settled in modest 3rd tl wnt 20 l 2nd at 7th: rdn bef 3 out: wnr a totally different class* **12/1**[3]

4P04 **3** *7* **Sagunt (GER)**[11] 5170 8-11-0 0... TomSiddall 67
(Joanna Davis) *often j. slowly: mstke 4th: chsd wnr (who was clr) tl slow again 7th: rdn bef 3 out: plodded on* **7/2**[2]

6P0/ **4** *56* **Cash 'n Carrots**[29] 12-10-7 0... MissCLWills[(7)] 32
(Richard Harper) *a last w wnr clr: mstke 3rd: nvr gng wl: t.o bef 3 out: hanging lft bef next* **33/1**

4m 3.90s (-12.20) **Going Correction** -0.85s/f (Firm) **4** Ran SP% **107.9**

Speed ratings: **94,79,76,49**

CSF £4.64 TOTE £1.20; EX 3.50.

Owner Ray Pattison **Bred** J P Hand **Trained** Cholmondeley, Cheshire

■ Donald McCain's 100th winner of the season, his first century.

FOCUS

A poor beginners' chase which took little winning. Ballabrook was value for further.

NOTEBOOK

Ballabrook(IRE) took this modest chase on his 13th start over fences. He was always clear and, despite jumping left, scored unchallenged. Having been well beaten in recent starts, this confidence boost will do him good. (op 3-10 tchd 4-11 and 2-5 in places)

Mr Johnson(IRE) ended his sequence of being pulled up by finishing a remote second. He'll find easier opportunities in handicaps. (op 14-1 tchd 10-1)

Sagunt(GER) raced without the tongue-tie he had worn in his last two starts. Even so, it was disappointing he failed to claim second. He doesn't look a natural at this game. (op 9-2)

Cash 'n Carrots achieved no more than a clear round of jumping to claim some prize-money. (op 25-1 tchd 22-1)

5376 GG.COM H'CAP HURDLE (8 hdls) 2m
3:10 (3:11) (Class 4) (0-110,110) 4-Y-0+ **£2,602** (£764; £382; £190)

Form RPR

5005 **1** **Haarth Sovereign (IRE)**[50] 4375 7-11-0 **101**...................(t) DavidBass[(3)] 107
(Lawney Hill) *racd keenly: led tl 3rd: 2nd after: rejnd ldr 5th tl bef 2 out: rdn and rallied fr 2 out despite edging rt: led last: r.o gamely to forge clr* **9/2**[2]

2543 **2** *2 1/4* **Olympian (FR)**[11] 5171 9-11-5 **110**.............................(bt) KielanWoods[(7)] 114
(Philip Middleton) *trckd clr ldng trio bef 4th: effrt to chal between ldng pair and ld bef 2 out: drvn and hdd last: nt qckn flat* **4/1**[1]

0512 **3** *8* **Kadouchski (FR)**[13] 4830 7-11-4 **102**................................. WillKennedy 99
(John Berry) *wnt 2nd at 2nd: led next: jnd for ld 5th tl rdn appr 2 out: wknd between last two* **5/1**[3]

2F10 **4** *6* **Watergate (IRE)**[10] 5193 5-11-4 **102**................................. LeightonAspell 94
(Richard Rowe) *hld up in midfield: pushed along bef 3 out where lft 4th and mstke: no ch w ldng trio after* **20/1**

5040 **5** *10* **Only Witness (IRE)**[11] 5171 6-10-10 **94**................................ SamJones 77
(Brendan Powell) *bhd: rdn and btn 5th: plugged on* **12/1**

266 **6** *6* **Glorybe (GER)**[53] 4309 5-11-2 **100**................................ TomMessenger 78
(Chris Bealby) *plld hrd early: hld up in rr: outpcd 5th: 8th and struggling bef next where hmpd* **33/1**

2231 **7** *7* **Rawaaj**[29] 4892 5-11-9 **107**.. JasonMaguire 78
(Donald McCain) *pushed along and lost pl after 3rd: detached last bef next: nvr gng wl after: t.o 3 out* **6/1**

P422 **8** *25* **Final Flyer (IRE)**[8] 5243 7-11-9 **107**...................................... DarylJacob 55
(Alison Thorpe) *chsd ldrs tl rdn and fdd bef 3 out: t.o and eased last* **8/1**

65-0 **9** *13* **Lindy Lou**[15] 5132 7-11-3 **108**.. MissGAndrews[(7)] 45
(Pam Sly) *t.k.h: hld up and mostly in midfield: 6th bef 3 out: fdd tamely up hill: t.o and virtually p.u last* **14/1**

2426 **P** **Sadler's Star (GER)**[194] 1723 8-11-12 **110**..................(p) DenisO'Regan —
(Michael Blake) *t.k.h in midfield: shkn up 5th: sn fnd nthing: t.o and p.u 2 out* **14/1**

5335 **U** **Tri Nations (UAE)**[31] 4854 6-11-7 **105**..........................(tp) CharliePoste 97
(Milton Harris) *hld up in rr: nt fluent 2nd: hdwy 5th: 6 l 4th whn mstke and uns rdr 2 out* **16/1**

3m 52.2s (-15.70) **Going Correction** -0.85s/f (Firm) **11** Ran SP% **114.9**

Speed ratings (Par 105): **105,103,99,96,91 88,85,72,66,— —**

toteswingers:1&2:£5.70, 1&3:£6.10, 2&3:£4.20 CSF £22.73 CT £92.69 TOTE £7.00: £2.30, £1.90, £2.80; EX 30.60.

Owner Dr Joan H Manley **Bred** Hardys Of Kilkeel Ltd **Trained** Aston Rowant, Oxon

FOCUS

An ordinary but competitive handicap. The winner is rated back to the best of his 2010 form.

NOTEBOOK

Haarth Sovereign(IRE) was well backed and returned to form, dismissing any doubts over his ability to handle this quicker surface. He outbattled the runner-up, having looked beaten entering the straight, and can cope with a smallish rise in the weights. He should pay his way this summer. (op 5-1)

Olympian(FR)'s only win over hurdles was on heavy ground, but he handles all surfaces. He reversed recent course form with Kadouchski and looked the winner going to the second last, only to be worried out of it. He's more than capable of winning a similar race, and probably needs holding up for longer. (op 11-2)

Kadouchski(FR) ran another solid race. He handled the quicker ground absolutely fine, but the handicapper looks to have him spot on off this mark. (tchd 11-2)

Watergate(IRE) again failed to cope with what is now looking a harsh 12lb rise for his win at Folkestone. He was looking to be fighting a losing battle when a blunder three out sealed his fate.

Only Witness(IRE) beat Cantlow (subsequently placed in a Grade 1 at Aintree) in an Irish point last November. He hasn't cut much ice yet, but was plugging on steadily and a step up in trip looks required. He is on a very workable mark if that Irish form is reliable. (op 16-1)

Glorybe(GER) ran respectably on her first try in handicaps. A middle-distance winner on the Flat in Germany, she will improve with experience.

Rawaaj failed to give his running on quicker ground than he has encountered before. He can be excused this effort. Official explanation: trainer said gelding was unsuited by the good to firm ground (op 9-2)

Lindy Lou, well backed in the morning, but a drifter on course, was on the retreat three out. She has now posted two poor efforts since her return. (tchd 12-1)

Tri Nations(UAE) had made good headway to track the leaders when departing two out. It was too early to tell if he could have maintained the effort, especially as he had been keen during the early part of the race. (op 20-1)

5377 SAFENAMES.NET H'CAP CHASE (18 fncs) 3m 110y
3:40 (3:41) (Class 4) (0-105,104) 5-Y-0+ **£2,602** (£764; £382; £190)

Form RPR

0200 **1** **Arctic Echo**[40] 4551 12-10-10 91................................(t) MichaelMurphy[(3)] 100+
(Rob Summers) *in rr and nt a fluent: rdn and effrt 15th: chal on outside next: sn hrd drvn: lft in ld sn after last: styd on wl* **12/1**

3F51 **2** *2 1/4* **Jolly Boys Outing (IRE)**[21] 5060 8-10-7 92...................... MrBJPoste[(7)] 99+
(Rosemary Gasson) *t.k.h and gng wl in rr: in last at 5th: hdwy to trck ldrs 8th: chal 3 out: led bef next: racing awkwardly after but looked wnr tl shifted bdly rt last: sn hdd flat and outstyd* **11/2**[3]

P10P **3** *17* **Autumn Red (IRE)**[38] 4705 11-11-5 97.........................(tp) DenisO'Regan 89
(Paul Webber) *prom: coaxed into narrow ld fr 8th: mstke 13th: hdd 3 out: btn next: fin slowly* **14/1**

30P3 **4** *3* **Earcomesthedream (IRE)**[21] 5061 8-11-1 93...................(b) JackDoyle 79
(Peter Pritchard) *rn in snatches: often rdn fr 6th: in last at 8th: mstke 10th and 15th whn btn: plodded into poor 4th flat* **5/1**[2]

6FU3 **5** *1 3/4* **Or Sing About (FR)**[50] 4381 9-11-7 99.....................(p) AndrewThornton 83
(Seamus Mullins) *prom: led 5th tl 8th: pressed ldr tl pckd 15th: rdn to ld again 3 out: hdd & wknd bef next: mod 4th at last* **9/2**[1]

1503 **6** *1 1/4* **De Bansha Man (IRE)**[38] 4705 6-11-9 101............. SamTwiston-Davies 84
(Nigel Twiston-Davies) *trckd ldrs in midfield: j. indifferently at times: effrt 13th: nt fluent 15th: ev ch next: drvn and fdd in 5th bef 2 out* **5/1**[2]

-653 **7** *21* **Speed Bonnie Boat**[21] 5060 8-11-10 102.................(b[1]) MarkBradburne 75
(Henry Daly) *rn in snatches and on outer: rapid prog to go prom 5th: drvn and nt keen 11th: sn rallied: pressing ldrs bef 3 out: reluctant after: t.o* **15/2**

0154 **P** **Antonius Caesar (FR)**[36] 4749 8-11-7 104.................... PeterCarberry[(5)] —
(Alex Hales) *led tl 5th: drvn and lost pl 8th: struggling whn mstke 12th: t.o and p.u 2 out* **9/2**[1]

PP0P **P** **Wheretheres A Will**[36] 4741 9-9-9 78 oh14.................... BrianToomey(5) —
(Michael Mullineaux) *j. slowly 3rd: chsd ldrs and wl in tch tl p.u qckly 11th* **40/1**

6m 13.4s (-23.50) **Going Correction** -0.85s/f (Firm) **9** Ran SP% **113.6**
Speed ratings: **103,102,96,95,95 94,88,—,—**
toteswingers:1&2:£11.70, 1&3:£19.20, 2&3:£12.20 CSF £75.98 CT £938.04 TOTE £17.60: £4.30, £2.70, £4.90; EX 117.60.
Owner R P Dineen **Bred** R P Dineen **Trained** Tanworth-in-Arden, Warwicks

FOCUS
A modest handicap chase where the first two were clear. The winner didn't need to run near his best

NOTEBOOK
Arctic Echo scored his first win over fences under a patient ride. He has been inconsistent over fences, this win coming on the back of two modest efforts (in blinkers first-time last time). The fast pace helped set this up for the hold-up horses, though, so he may struggle to follow up. He'll probably head to Stratford next.
Jolly Boys Outing(IRE) looked like defying the 11lb rise for his recent course win, travelling strongly when taking up the running going to two out. However, he jumped notably right-handed at the last, and that lack of momentum cost him. He can gain compensation, but looks to have his quirks. (op 5-1 tchd 6-1)
Autumn Red(IRE) raced prominently, but the climb to home here probably stretched his stamina too far. He jumped left-handed and again looked a very tricky ride.
Earcomesthedream(IRE) stayed on dourly up the hill, but lacked the pace to make a challenge. This course winner is inexperienced over fences, so it was a fair effort in this company. (op 7-1)
Or Sing About(FR) ran his best race over fences, but paid late on for helping to force the gallop. Having failed to complete in two of his previous three runs over fences, this was a step forward. (op 5-1)
De Bansha Man(IRE) was hunting up the leaders at the bottom of the hill, but he ran out of gas on the climb to the second last. A less testing 3m would be more suitable. (tchd 11-2)
Speed Bonnie Boat gave another poor round of jumping here and the first-time blinkers failed to work the oracle. (op 13-2 tchd 6-1)
Antonius Caesar(FR) was never given his way in front and consequently waved the white flag. (tchd 5-1)
Wheretheres A Will Official explanation: vet said gelding pulled up lame (tchd 5-1)

5378 TCA ENGINEERING LTD NOVICES' HURDLE (8 hdls) 2m
4:10 (4:10) (Class 4) 4-Y-O+ **£2,276** (£668; £334; £166)

Form RPR
6121 **1** **Lifestyle**[8] 5235 5-11-5 134.................... FelixDeGiles 124+
(Nicky Henderson) *racd keenly in v slow r: hld up tl wnt 2nd after 3 out: drvn next: clsd to ld and best jump last: pushed clr: comf in end* **2/11**[1]
F430 **2** 3¾ **Omokoroa (IRE)**[17] 5099 5-10-12 114.................... JasonMaguire 115+
(Donald McCain) *taken down early: led at v sedate pce: nt fluent 3rd: drvn bef 2 out: hdd and mstke last: immediately outpcd* **13/2**[2]
3 4½ **Gordy Bee (USA)**[18] 5-10-12 0.................... PaddyAspell 108
(Richard Guest) *t.k.h in v slow r: 4 l last and rdn bef 3 out: chsd ldng pair vainly and hd in air fr next* **28/1**
06 **4** 20 **Red Whisper**[26] 4952 7-10-9 0.................... MichaelMurphy(3) 88
(Rob Summers) *plld hrd in last: 6 l bhd 1/2-way: effrt 5th: wl in tch tl fdd after next* **22/1**[3]
600 **5** 3 **Rebel Flag (IRE)**[15] 5131 4-10-7 0.................... TomMessenger 81
(Chris Bealby) *prom tl 3 out: rdn and fdd bef next* **66/1**
U0 **6** 13 **Diamond Twister (USA)**[17] 5099 5-10-5 0.................... HarryChalloner(7) 72
(Lisa Williamson) *taken down early: jnd ldr bef 4th tl bef 3 out: sn stopped to nil* **100/1**

3m 59.6s (-8.30) **Going Correction** -0.85s/f (Firm)
WFA 4 from 5yo+ 5lb **6** Ran SP% **108.2**
Speed ratings (Par 105): **86,84,81,71,70 63**
toteswingers:1&2:£1.30, 1&3:£2.10, 2&3:£1.50 CSF £1.56 TOTE £1.10: £1.10, £1.20; EX 1.80.
Owner The Turf Club & David Ford **Bred** David G Ford **Trained** Upper Lambourn, Berks

FOCUS
An uncompetitive novice hurdle run in a poor time. The form makes some sense.

NOTEBOOK
Lifestyle didn't have it easy, although she always looked to be doing enough. The slow gallop and her desire to take a keen hold meant her having to be ridden to find an extra gear between the last two flights, but a fast jump at the last soon had her in command. This is the quickest surface she has encountered and she got the job done in the end. Her trainer is keen to get her some black-type in due course, but she'll need to learn to settle before taking a step up in trip. (op 1-6 tchd 2-9 and 1-5 in places)
Omokoroa(IRE) went in short at the last and was out-jumped by the winner. He should be competitive in handicaps, assuming this form isn't taken literally. (op 7-1)
Gordy Bee(USA) is a fairly modest performer at around 1m on the Flat. This was a perfectly good start to his hurdling career. (op 33-1 tchd 40-1 and 25-1)
Red Whisper was too keen early on and weakened when the pace quickened up the hill. He still looks short of win material.
Rebel Flag(IRE) dropped away once the pace increased after the third-last. (op 100-1)
Diamond Twister(USA) Official explanation: trainer's rep said horse finished distressed

5379 HAYGAIN HAY STEAMERS H'CAP CHASE (12 fncs) 2m 110y
4:40 (4:41) (Class 4) (0-105,103) 5-Y-O+ **£2,602** (£764; £382; £190)

Form RPR
FF04 **1** **Beauchamp Viking**[59] 3875 7-10-4 **84**....................(t) JimmyDerham(3) 91
(Simon Burrough) *stdd s: keen in last: effrt in 3rd 3 out: delayed effrt tl rdn to ld after last: all out to hang on* **3/1**[2]
5532 **2** nk **Red Jester**[6] 5279 10-11-3 **97**.................... MarcGoldstein(3) 105
(Laura Young) *led 2nd: rdn and hung lft bef 2 out: hdd after last: kpt on gamely cl home* **11/4**[1]
6P60 **3** 2 **Kinkeel (IRE)**[5] 5293 12-10-1 **80** ow1.................... EamonDehdashti(3) 87
(Tony Carroll) *led tl 2nd: nt a fluent: lft 2nd briefly at 6th: dropped bk last after next: rdn and outpcd 3 out: styd on again fr last: unable to chal* **16/1**
2243 **4** 1 **Papradon**[19] 5076 7-11-5 **96**.................... SamTwiston-Davies 101
(Nigel Twiston-Davies) *prom: often getting reminders fr 5th: v slow next: pressed ldr after: ev ch u.p 2 out: fnd nthing last* **9/2**
0P02 **5** ¾ **Wee Ziggy**[26] 4945 8-9-9 **78** oh4.................... BrianToomey(5) 81
(Michael Mullineaux) *hld up in cl tch: racd keenly: nt fluent 7th: effrt on ins 3 out: tenderly handled to chal next: fnd nthing last* **13/2**
5655 **6** 9 **See You Jack**[17] 5100 6-11-12 **103**.................... AndrewThornton 98
(Caroline Bailey) *shied lft s: nt fluent 2nd: t.k.h: a last trio: rdn and wknd 3 out* **4/1**[3]

4m 3.40s (-12.70) **Going Correction** -0.85s/f (Firm) **6** Ran SP% **109.1**
Speed ratings: **95,94,93,93,93 88**
toteswingers:1&2:£2.40, 1&3:£13.40, 2&3:£5.90 CSF £11.30 TOTE £4.00: £2.30, £2.10; EX 8.60.
Owner Mrs Maureen Emery **Bred** E Penser **Trained** West Buckland, Somerset

FOCUS
A tight handicap.

NOTEBOOK
Beauchamp Viking has now achieved both his chase wins here. He still takes the odd liberty at the fences, but battled on well to lead after the last. He was well supported today and won't be too harshly dealt with for this success. He will always remain a risky betting proposition, though, because of his jumping. (op 7-2 tchd 4-1 in places)
Red Jester, a three-time course winner, probably would have held on but for drifting left up the straight. He will have more opportunities. (op 2-1)
Kinkeel(IRE) showed a return to form, staying on dourly after being outpaced going to three out. He has only won five from 101 starts under rules. (op 12-1)
Papradon needs decent ground and posted a fair effort after helping to force the gallop. He's still 10lb higher than for his last win and needs some respite from the assessor. (tchd 4-1 and 5-1)
Wee Ziggy is now winless in 45 starts. (op 8-1)
See You Jack is proving disappointing under rules after a promising start over hurdles here. (op 11-2 tchd 7-2)

5380 GG.COM MARES' STANDARD OPEN NATIONAL HUNT FLAT RACE 2m
5:10 (5:11) (Class 5) 4-6-Y-O **£1,712** (£499; £249)

Form RPR
1 **Wilde Ruby (IRE)** 4-10-4 0.................... JimmyDerham(3) 95+
(Seamus Mullins) *stdd in last in slow run r: stl 8 l last 6f out: clsd steadily up hill and rdn to ld 2f out: sn clr: styd on gamely* **6/1**
4 **2** 3¾ **Skenakilla Cross (IRE)**[15] 5135 6-10-12 0.................... DenisO'Regan 96
(David O'Meara) *midfield: effrt 4f out: gng wl whn led over 2f out: rdn and sn hdd: plugged on but a hld by wnr after* **10/3**[1]
3 1 **Splendid Blue (IRE)** 5-10-9 0.................... LeeEdwards(3) 95
(Tony Carroll) *prom: led 5f out: rdn and hung lft home turn: hdd over 2f out: kpt on same pce after* **16/1**
4 3½ **Shrewd Decision** 4-10-7 0.................... TomSiddall 87
(Dave Morris) *settled in rr: effrt 4f out: rdn and outpcd over 2f out: wnt 4th ins fnl f* **9/2**[2]
6 **5** 4 **Final Cast**[18] 5084 4-10-7 0.................... AndrewTinkler 83
(Nicky Henderson) *t.k.h chsng ldrs: rdn 3f out: btn 2f out: mod 4th over 1f out* **9/2**[2]
0 **6** 8 **Jays Girl**[15] 5135 4-10-7 0.................... SeanQuinlan 75
(Pam Sly) *cl up: drvn and fdd wl over 2f out: t.o* **33/1**
7 ½ **Velvet Shadow (IRE)** 4-10-0 0.................... MrBJPoste(7) 74
(Mrs Pauline Harkin) *t.k.h in rr: sme prog 4f out: wknd over 2f out: t.o* **40/1**
00 **8** 14 **Sor Brook**[20] 5070 5-10-12 0.................... SamTwiston-Davies 65
(Nigel Twiston-Davies) *w ldr tl 5f out: sn lost pl: t.o* **22/1**
9 8 **Bunny Girl (IRE)**[16] 6-10-5 0.................... MrMWall(7) 57
(Giles Smyly) *slt ld 11f: wknd qckly: t.o fnl 2f* **50/1**
0 **10** 11 **Katys Jools**[30] 4866 4-10-4 0.................... RichardKilloran(3) 41
(Tim Vaughan) *hld up in tight bunch tl hung lft and fdd 3f out: t.o and eased 2f out* **10/1**
11 3½ **Water Rose** 4-10-7 0.................... DarylJacob 38
(Ben Case) *rrd and uns bef s: stdd s: bhd: lost tch 4f out: bdly t.o* **5/1**[3]
00 **12** 11 **Sussex Lass**[17] 5105 6-10-7 0.................... GemmaGracey-Davison(5) 32
(Zoe Davison) *t.k.h in bunch tl lost pl 5f out: hopelessly t.o* **100/1**

3m 49.6s (-12.70) **Going Correction** -0.85s/f (Firm)
WFA 4 from 5yo+ 5lb **12** Ran SP% **118.0**
Speed ratings: **97,95,94,92,90 86,86,79,75,70 68,62**
toteswingers:1&2:£5.70, 1&3:£18.40, 2&3:£9.30 CSF £25.22 TOTE £8.50: £3.10, £1.20, £5.10; EX 37.00.
Owner Seamus Mullins **Bred** Mrs Valerie Dalgetty **Trained** Wilsford-Cum-Lake, Wilts

FOCUS
A fairly modest mares' bumper.

NOTEBOOK
Wilde Ruby(IRE) made her move on the rising ground turning for home and stayed on well after hitting the front. Her yard have been patient with her, giving her time to come to herself after an autumn campaign was shelved due to her immaturity. There's plenty of chasing blood in her pedigree, and she will get further in future. (op 7-1)
Skenakilla Cross(IRE) probably improved on her debut effort at Market Rasen. She was on her toes at the start, but showed no wayward tendencies in the race. She should find a similar contest. (op 5-2)
Splendid Blue(IRE) hung left and ran wide off the home turn, this proving costly as she rallied inside the final furlong. This was an encouraging debut from a yard not noted for bumper winners. (op 14-1)
Shrewd Decision, a cheap purchase at the Newmarket December sales, came in for plenty of support. Although never looking likely to collect, supporters will have been encouraged with the determined way she stayed on having met traffic problems on the climb before the straight. (op 12-1)
Final Cast was too keen early and paid the price late on. This sister to useful chaser Flying Instructor needs to settle. (op 4-1)
Jays Girl finished much closer Skenakilla Cross than she had done when both made their debuts at Market Rasen. She needs to improve further if she's to be winning, though.
Water Rose was well supported, but faded up the hill and finished well beaten. (op 6-1 tchd 9-2)
T/Plt: £77.20 to a £1 stake. Pool:£52,948.70 - 500.06 winning tickets T/Qpdt: £13.80 to a £1 stake. Pool:£5,185.81 - 276.35 winning tickets IM

5189 FONTWELL (L-H)
Tuesday, April 19

OFFICIAL GOING: Good
Rail movement added 55yds per circuit on chases and 35yds per circuit on hurdles.
Wind: nil Weather: very hot and sunny

5381 BULMERS CRISP BLEND NOVICES' HURDLE (11 hdls) 2m 6f 110y
2:20 (2:20) (Class 4) 4-Y-O+ **£2,016** (£592; £296; £147)

Form RPR
1325 **1** **Camden (IRE)**[31] 4861 5-11-6 125.................... LeightonAspell 126+
(Oliver Sherwood) *led 2nd: jnd briefly bef 2 out and nt fluent: drvn and asserted sn after: kpt plugging on: all out* **7/2**[3]
2 **2** 12 **Rossmore Lad (IRE)**[27] 4951 6-11-0 0.................... FelixDeGiles 110
(Charlie Longsdon) *prom tl 3rd and rdn and outpcd 8th: rallied bef 2 out where wnt 2nd: wl hld by wnr after* **3/1**[2]
2235 **3** 13 **Raduis Bleu (FR)**[25] 4990 6-11-0 115.................... RobertThornton 99
(Alan King) *prom: wnt 2nd at 6th: jnd wnr briefly bef 2 out: mstke and lost 2nd: rdn and fdd tamely* **5/4**[1]
5420 **4** 5 **Allerford Jack**[12] 5168 7-10-11 118.................... IanPopham(3) 92
(Caroline Keevil) *t.k.h early: chsd ldrs tl drvn after 7th: no rspnse: struggled on wout much enthusiasm fr 3 out* **11/2**
0 **5** 67 **Trepalo (FR)**[34] 4810 4-10-2 0.................... MarkQuinlan(5) 25
(Alison Batchelor) *stdd s: t.k.h in rr: impeded 3rd: rdn and mstke 7th: sn t.o: blnd 3 out: virtually p.u after next* **66/1**

The Form Book, Raceform Ltd, Compton, RG20 6NL

5P-5 **P** **Saltara**[92] 3607 7-10-7 0 MattieBatchelor —
(Mark Bradstock) *blnd 1st: led tl slow 2nd: terrible blunder 3rd and rdr lost iron for sme while and continued last: t.o and climbed 4th and 5th: p.u 6th* **100/1**

0 **P** **Bluemoonandstars (IRE)**[82] 3773 6-11-0 0 AndrewTinkler —
(George Baker) *chsd ldr to 5th: nt fluent next: rdn and wknd bef 8th: t.o and p.u 3 out* **22/1**

0P00 **P** **Semelay (FR)**[10] 5211 5-11-0 0 (t) LiamHeard —
(Laura Young) *stdd s: t.k.h early: in last pair: lost tch 7th: sn hopelessly t.o: eventually p.u 2 out* **150/1**

5m 19.7s (-22.80) **Going Correction** -0.65s/f (Firm)
WFA 4 from 5yo+ 6lb **8** Ran SP% **114.5**
Speed ratings (Par 105): **113,108,104,102,79** —,—,—
toteswingers:1&2 £1.60, 2&3 £1.10, 1&3 £1.70 CSF £14.54 TOTE £3.50: £1.40, £1.10, £1.30; EX 15.70.
Owner T D J Syder **Bred** Fran Kavanagh **Trained** Upper Lambourn, Berks

FOCUS
The ground had been watered and was officially described as good. Just a modest novice hurdle. The winner was the form pick and is rated back to his best.

NOTEBOOK
Camden(IRE), below par at Ffos Las on his latest outing, had shown all his best form with cut in the ground, but proved more than capable on this faster surface and won in the manner of a dour stayer. This was a fair effort with the penalty and he'll make a chaser next season. (op 10-3 tchd 4-1)
Rossmore Lad(IRE), runner-up at Warwick on his recent hurdles debut, confirmed that promise with another reasonable effort, although there's little doubt this former point winner will be at his best once chasing. (op 11-4 tchd 5-2)
Raduis Bleu(FR) remains hard to win with. He should have done better considering he came into the race with the best recent form, and is left with plenty to prove for the time being. (op 15-8)
Allerford Jack probably isn't up to winning a hurdle and is best switched to fences now. (tchd 6-1)
Bluemoonandstars(IRE) Official explanation: jockey said gelding had a breathing problem

5382 3663 FIRST FOR FOOD SERVICE NOVICES' CHASE (16 fncs) 2m 6f
2:50 (2:50) (Class 4) 5-Y-O+ **£2,602** (£764; £382; £190)

Form RPR

2212 **1** **Fruity O'Rooney**[10] 5213 8-11-12 131 JamieMoore 136
(Gary Moore) *mde all: rdn after 12th: u.p fr 2 out: hld on wl to outbattle rival flat* **11/10**[1]

513P **2** *2* **American Trilogy (IRE)**[35] 4794 7-11-5 132 (b) NickScholfield 127
(Paul Nicholls) *hld up gng easily: chsd wnr fr 8th: drvn 2 out: almost upsides last: declined to overtake flat* **11/8**[2]

-01U **3** *3 ¾* **Topsham Belle (IRE)**[68] 4023 7-10-12 118 AndrewTinkler 117
(Nicky Henderson) *drvn virtually fr s and plentiful reminders: tending to balloon jumps: chsd wnr tl 8th: 3rd after: no imp u.p fr 12th* **11/2**[3]

0/PP **4** *dist* **Midsummer Legend**[40] 4666 7-10-5 0 (t) SamJones —
(Norma Twomey) *hit 8th: cl up tl dropped out qckly bef 10th: hopelessly t.o* **66/1**

R **Over The Page**[24] 5-10-9 0 TommyPhelan(3) —
(Mark Gillard) *a in last: j. modly: outpcd 6th: u.p 8th: t.o 10th tl ref and threw rdr over 3 out* **50/1**

5m 35.1s (-7.90) **Going Correction** -0.45s/f (Good) **5** Ran SP% **108.6**
Speed ratings: **96,95,93**,—,—
CSF £3.02 TOTE £2.40: £1.10, £1.80; EX 3.20.
Owner Heart Of The South Racing **Bred** R W Russell **Trained** Lower Beeding, W Sussex

FOCUS
An easy-to-rate novice chase.

NOTEBOOK
Fruity O'Rooney produced a thoroughly likeable effort, as he kept finding for strong pressure to defy the double penalty. Despite being stalked by the runner-up into the straight, he had the greater resolution and deserved another win on account of his consistency. He could be a decent handicapper next season. (op 11-8 tched 13-8 in a place and 6-4 in places)
American Trilogy(IRE) is undeniably talented, but he's been unable to match the form shown in February's Kempton win, including at Cheltenham last time, and found nowhere near as much as expected once coming under pressure. (op 6-4 tchd 13-8)
Topsham Belle(IRE), bidding for a follow up when unseating at Huntingdon last time, was never going, giving her fences plenty of air and losing ground. She did keep plodding away, but never looked like winning. (op 7-2)

5383 SOL SUNSHINE BEER H'CAP HURDLE (11 hdls) 2m 6f 110y
3:20 (3:24) (Class 5) (0-85,85) 4-Y-O+ **£1,756** (£515; £257; £128)

Form RPR

06F0 **1** **Insignia (IRE)**[30] 4900 9-11-8 81 (b[1]) DenisO'Regan 97
(Victor Dartnall) *wl in rr early: prog to midfield after 7th: wnt 2nd after 3 out: no imp and hanging rt bef last and hit it: hung lft flat: cajoled ahd fnl 100yds: looked v unwilling and fine ride* **7/1**[3]

-F04 **2** *4 ½* **Diamanpeg (IRE)**[40] 4675 7-10-8 67 (v) RhysFlint 78
(David Rees) *led tl 2nd: chsd ldr tl led again 5th: wnt 6 l clr 3 out: nt fluent next: stl nrly 5 l ahd but idling and rdn urgently whn mstke last: hdd and sn outpcd fnl 100yds* **5/1**[2]

0544 **3** *10* **Sovereign Spirit (IRE)**[8] 5270 9-11-9 82 (tp) GerardTumelty 85
(Chris Gordon) *hdwy to chse ldrs 7th: 8 l 4th and drvn bef 2 out: plodded on into 3rd at last* **16/1**

P101 **4** *4 ½* **Brilliant (GER)**[60] 4178 8-10-9 73 AodhaganConlon(5) 72
(Debra Hamer) *drvn along thrght: in midfield: struggling 8th: 18 l 5th bef 2 out: no imp: hit last: tk 4th flat* **12/1**

5P04 **5** *3 ¼* **Keckerrockernixes (IRE)**[11] 5191 5-10-6 72 (p) MrTJCannon(7) 67
(Richard Rowe) *sn drvn along: towards rr: struggling 8th: plugged on fr 2 out but no hope of rching ldrs* **18/1**

5031 **6** *2 ½* **Airedale Lad (IRE)**[8] 5270 10-10-5 71 7ex (p) MrJBanks(7) 64
(Zoe Davison) *racd keenly and prom: chsd ldr 6th tl 3 out: rdn and wkng in 6 l 3rd bef next: wl btn whn hit last* **12/1**

0130 **7** *25* **Body Gold (ARG)**[20] 5075 8-11-11 84 SamTwiston-Davies 54
(Nigel Twiston-Davies) *bhd: rdn and struggling 7th: t.o next* **25/1**

2-05 **8** *7* **Hereditary**[15] 4559 9-11-7 85 (tp) MarkQuinlan(5) 49
(Linda Jewell) *hld up in rr: terrible mstke 6th and lost all ch: t.o fr 8th* **20/1**

6U66 **9** *3 ¾* **Karingabay Queen**[11] 5191 6-9-12 64 (b) MrBJPoste(7) 25
(Kevin Tork) *j. slowly and modly in rr: rdn and t.o after 7th* **66/1**

02P- **10** *dist* **So Extreme**[685] 580 9-11-4 84 MrJackSalmon(7) —
(Philip Sharp) *racd keenly and trckd ldrs tl bmpd along fr 7th: struggling next: hopelessly t.o 2 out* **66/1**

P042 **F** **King Kasyapa (IRE)**[9] 5241 9-11-1 77 DonalDevereux(3) —
(Peter Bowen) *chsd ldrs: reminders 7th and nt looking to be gng v wl: tk 6 l 4th and fell 8th* **10/11**[1]

4000 **P** **Fun Guy**[40] 4675 6-11-11 84 AndrewGlassonbury —
(Bob Buckler) *t.k.h: chsng ldrs: pushed along after 7th: 3rd and rdn whn stmbld 3 out: lost pl qckly and p.u next* **33/1**

03-0 **F** **Classic Bavard**[326] 500 9-11-12 85 JimmyMcCarthy —
(Geoffrey Deacon) *plld hrd in last tl 4th: rapid prog after next: 3rd whn fell 6th* **50/1**

0000 **P** **Kidajo**[51] 4370 5-11-3 76 (b[1]) HaddenFrost —
(Roger Curtis) *t.k.h: led 2nd: clr briefly 3rd: hdd and rdn 5th: stopped to nil 7th: p.u next* **100/1**

5m 25.3s (-17.20) **Going Correction** -0.65s/f (Firm) **14** Ran SP% **125.6**
Speed ratings (Par 103): **103,101,97,96,95 94,85,83,81**,— —,—,—,—
toteswingers:1&2 £1.60, 2&3 £1.10, 1&3 £1.70 CSF £42.51 TOTE £9.00: £2.70, £1.30, £3.70; EX 43.10.
Owner V R A Dartnall **Bred** Ennistown Stud **Trained** Brayford, Devon

FOCUS
A low-grade handicap hurdle. The winner is rated back to the level of his 2009 form.

NOTEBOOK
Insignia(IRE)'s last victory came in a selling hurdle way back in October 2008, and his most recent efforts haven't been up to much, but the application of first-time blinkers made a huge difference, taking over up the hill despite looking far from enthused. There's a major doubt as to whether he'll repeat this next time, though. (op 10-1)
Diamanpeg(IRE) travelled best for much of the race, and was still a few lengths clear coming to the last, but he was untidy there and readily swept aside. (op 7-1 tchd 15-2 and 8-1 in a place)
Sovereign Spirit(IRE) was helped by the step up in trip, plugging on into third.
Brilliant(GER), successful on two of his last three starts, both at 2m, was never travelling and beaten before the trip became an issue. (tchd 11-1 and 14-1 in a place)
King Kasyapa(IRE), the red-hot favourite, didn't appear to be going overly well, although was trying to close, when falling at the eighth. It remains to be seen how this affects his confidence. (op Evens tchd 5-6)
Fun Guy Official explanation: jockey said gelding had a breathing problem (op Evens tchd 5-6)

5384 FULLERS LONDON PRIDE H'CAP CHASE (19 fncs) 3m 2f 110y
3:50 (3:50) (Class 4) (0-110,109) 5-Y-O+ **£2,536** (£744; £372; £186)

Form RPR

6603 **1** **Troy Tempest (IRE)**[26] 4966 6-11-7 104 JackDoyle 117+
(Emma Lavelle) *hld up last tl 13th but wl in tch: wnt 3rd and hit 15th: chsd ldr next: chal 2 out: led last: sn rdn clr* **2/1**[1]

4161 **2** *12* **Ere Alfie (IRE)**[55] 4292 7-11-12 109 (p) DarylJacob 111
(Nick Williams) *led: mstke 9th: rdn after 16th: hrd pressed 2 out: hdd last: sn btn* **11/4**[3]

FP22 **3** *9* **Arturo Uno (IRE)**[37] 4749 8-11-12 109 SamTwiston-Davies 104
(Nigel Twiston-Davies) *mstke 8th: mostly 2nd tl hrd drvn 16th: readily outpcd bef next* **9/4**[2]

02P0 **4** *35* **Dusky Bob (IRE)**[48] 4427 6-11-3 100 LiamTreadwell 64
(Nick Gifford) *j. indifferently and nvr travelling: often rdn along: in tch tl landed bdly 13th: j. slowly 14th and struggling: t.o 16th* **12/1**

-PP1 **P** **Dust In Time**[48] 4429 6-10-9 97 (b) MarkQuinlan(5) —
(Bill Turner) *mstke 3rd: reminders 4th and 10th: nvr looked happy: in tch tl downed tools 15th: t.o and p.u after next* **8/1**

6m 45.3s (-15.80) **Going Correction** -0.45s/f (Good) **5** Ran SP% **109.6**
Speed ratings: **105,101,98,88**,—
CSF £7.99 TOTE £2.70: £1.20, £2.10; EX 8.50.
Owner T D J Syder **Bred** Mary Fanning McCormack **Trained** Wildhern, Hants

FOCUS
An ordinary handicap chase. A step up from the easy winner and there should be more to come.

NOTEBOOK
Troy Tempest(IRE) had shaped as though this trip would suit when third over 3m on his recent chasing debut at Chepstow. Jumping well in the main, he always looked the likely winner in the straight and readily asserted from the last. This was only his sixth start and it's reasonable to expect further progress, with him having the potential to make a nice staying handicapper next term. (op 9-4)
Ere Alfie(IRE), up 11lb for his Ludlow victory, again ran well but wasn't up to conceding 5lb to the winner. (op 5-2 tchd 3-1)
Arturo Uno(IRE), runner-up each of the last twice, was up another 2lb and probably failed to run right up to his best. (tchd 2-1)

5385 SPORTING APPOINTMENTS MARES' MAIDEN HURDLE (9 hdls) 2m 2f 110y
4:20 (4:20) (Class 4) 4-Y-O+ **£2,016** (£592; £296; £147)

Form RPR

666F **1** **Spe Salvi (IRE)**[48] 4417 7-10-13 0 DarylJacob 107+
(David Arbuthnot) *prom: led and nt fluent 2 out: nt fluent last: stl hrd pressed and rdn whn hung rt flat: stened and kpt on steadily* **5/1**

05 **2** *¾* **Belle De Fontenay (FR)**[11] 5189 6-10-13 0 AndrewTinkler 103
(George Baker) *led: drvn and hung rt fr after 3 out: hdd next: drvn and kpt on wl flat: a jst hld* **33/1**

335 **3** *4* **Yvonne Evelyn (USA)**[30] 4897 6-10-13 101 RobertThornton 102
(Alan King) *trckd ldrs: wnt prom 3rd: 3rd whn nt fluent 3 out: sn wnt 2nd tl lost pl home turn: hit 2 out: plugged on: n.d after* **9/2**[3]

-1P4 **4** *13* **Osmosia (FR)**[7] 5280 6-10-13 0 (t) DominicElsworth 90
(Paul Webber) *last tl 1/2-way: stdy prog fr 3 out: 6 l 5th bef next: rdn and btn 2 out* **9/1**

0363 **5** *2* **Sawpit Solitaire**[30] 4897 6-10-13 102 AidanColeman 86
(Venetia Williams) *pressed ldr tl 3rd and rdn bef 2 out: sn fdd* **3/1**[1]

1256 **6** *12* **Midnight Macarena**[92] 3607 6-10-13 109 LeightonAspell 78
(Lucy Wadham) *chsd ldrs: nt fluent 3 out and rdn: sn btn: j.rt next* **4/1**[2]

302 **7** *2 ¼* **Sorcillera**[73] 3937 5-10-13 110 RhysFlint 73
(John Flint) *t.k.h trcking ldrs: hit 6th: rdn after 3 out: sn wknd* **9/2**[3]

560P **8** *4 ½* **Pursuit Of Purpose**[8] 5265 5-10-6 79 MrJackSalmon(7) 69
(Philip Sharp) *midfield tl rdn and wknd 6th* **100/1**

-000 **9** *6* **Marvelous**[27] 4952 6-10-8 0 AodhaganConlon(5) 64
(Evan Williams) *bhd: pushed along and lost tch 6th: sn remote* **80/1**

04/- **10** *17* **Galathea**[1091] 5160 9-10-13 0 (t) JimmyMcCarthy 49
(Brendan Powell) *mounted on crse: bhd: lost tch 6th: sn t.o* **100/1**

0 **P** **Pursestrings**[144] 2047 4-10-7 0 ColinBolger —
(Laura Mongan) *midfield: rdn and btn 6th: t.o and p.u 2 out* **100/1**

0 **P** **Ravanchi**[93] 3590 7-10-10 0 JamesO'Farrell(3) —
(Ian Patrick Browne, Ire) *plld hrd: blnd 2nd and p.u: sddle slipped* **100/1**

4m 22.5s (-11.80) **Going Correction** -0.65s/f (Firm)
WFA 4 from 5yo+ 5lb **12** Ran SP% **116.2**
Speed ratings (Par 105): **98,97,96,90,89 84,83,81,79,72** —,—
toteswingers:1&2 £44.50, 2&3 £18.30, 1&3 £5.60 CSF £137.26 TOTE £7.90: £2.60, £11.30, £2.00; EX 174.80.
Owner George Ward **Bred** Sandwell Old Manor Syndicate **Trained** Compton, Berks

FOCUS
A typically modest mares' hurdle. A big step up from the easy winner, but in line with her bumper form.

NOTEBOOK
Spe Salvi(IRE), running well but held when falling at Bangor last time, was clearly none the worse for that spill and, despite wandering right after the last, she always looked to be doing enough. She'll need improvement if she's to defy a penalty. (op 6-1)

Belle De Fontenay(FR) showed much-improved form on this second run over hurdles. Having only her third start in total, she would appear to be a ready-made winner of something similar. (op 22-1)
Yvonne Evelyn(USA) bounced back from a poor effort at Newton Abbot last month, but was always being held in the straight. (tchd 5-1)
Osmosia(FR), a former point winner, is improving with experience over hurdles and should stay further. (op 8-1)
Sawpit Solitaire is exposed compared with most of these, but was still entitled to run much better than she did. (op 7-2 tchd 4-1)
Midnight Macarena was another to disappoint, quickly being beaten off at the end of the back straight. (op 9-2)
Pursestrings Official explanation: jockey said filly had a breathing problem

5386 HARDINGS CATERING H'CAP CHASE (13 fncs) 2m 2f
4:50 (4:51) (Class 5) (0-95,95) 5-Y-O+ **£1,886** (£553; £276; £138)

Form				RPR
-064	**1**		**Home**[11] 5193 6-11-7 **90** ... APMcCoy (Brendan Powell) *settled 3rd and gng wl: led on bit 10th: drew clr next: nt fluent 2 out: heavily eased flat* **13/8**[1]	103+
4004	**2**	*9*	**Kilvergan Boy (IRE)**[39] 4693 7-11-4 **87** ... SamTwiston-Davies (Nigel Twiston-Davies) *rn in snatches: reminders at several stages: hit 6th and 9th: 12 l 3rd and btn bef 3 out: wnt poor 2nd at last* **6/1**[3]	88
P453	**3**	*13*	**Sumdancer (NZ)**[22] 5055 9-11-2 **88** ... MarcGoldstein(3) (Michael Madgwick) *pressed ldr tl led 7th tl mstke 8th: led 9th tl next: rdn and lost tch w wnr after 3 out: lost 2nd at last and fin tired* **14/1**	75
202F	**4**	*15*	**Bid Art (IRE)**[22] 5055 6-11-0 **83** ... (tp) DarylJacob (Jamie Snowden) *t.k.h: and set decent gallop: hdd 7th: led again 8th tl 9th: lost tch w ldng pair 3 out: sn wl bhd* **7/4**[2]	56
560P	**5**	*47*	**Lepido (ITY)**[36] 4768 7-11-12 **95** ... (v) JamieMoore (Gary Moore) *j. slowly and nvr looked happy in last: drvn 7th: struggling 9th: t.o whn j.rt last* **13/2**	25

4m 34.7s **Going Correction** -0.45s/f (Good) **5** Ran SP% **108.7**
Speed ratings: **82,78,72,65,44**
CSF £10.79 TOTE £2.80: £1.10, £2.40; EX 9.90.
Owner Mrs Lynn Chapman **Bred** A T Macdonald **Trained** Upper Lambourn, Berks

FOCUS
A moderate handicap chase. The winner is rated in line with his best form over hurdles.

NOTEBOOK
Home, making his debut over fences, always looked to be travelling best under McCoy and readily asserted down the straight, a slight error two out being his only moment of worry. He jumped soundly on the whole and it'll be disappointing if he can't go in again. (op 2-1 tchd 6-4)
Kilvergan Boy(IRE) was under pressure with over a circuit to go, but kept responding and stayed on well up the straight for second. A stiffer test will probably help. (op 9-2)
Sumdancer(NZ) ran his best race in a while and is well weighted on old form, but hardly strikes as a winner waiting to happen. (op 9-1 tchd 17-2)
Bid Art(IRE), in front when falling at Plumpton last time, looked the one to beat if repeating that form, but he was unable to do so, and has clearly been affected by that fall. (op 2-1)
Lepido(ITY) never really got into a challenging position and remains winless over fences. (op 7-1 tchd 17-2)

5387 SIS LIVE STANDARD OPEN NATIONAL HUNT FLAT RACE (DIV I) 2m 2f 110y
5:20 (5:20) (Class 6) 4-6-Y-O **£1,301** (£382; £191; £95)

Form				RPR
4	**1**		**Victor Echo (IRE)**[31] 4866 5-11-4 0 ... APMcCoy (Nicky Henderson) *t.k.h pressing ldrs: rdn to ld 2f out: sn in command: pushed out* **3/1**[1]	115+
20	**2**	*8*	**Majorica King (FR)**[45] 4468 5-11-4 0 ... LeightonAspell (Oliver Sherwood) *bhd: prog 1/2-way: 2 l 3rd 4f out: rdn and chsd wnr vainly fnl 2f* **4/1**[2]	108
	3	*7*	**Farbreaga (IRE)**[44] 5-11-4 0 ... AndrewThornton (Anna Newton-Smith) *bhd early: styd on steadily fnl 3f: snatched mod 3rd* **15/2**	101
	4	*shd*	**Silsula** 5-10-6 0 ... MarkQuinlan(5) (Neil Mulholland) *t.k.h in midfield: rdn and outpcd in 15 l 5th 4f out: plugged on and snatched 4th* **33/1**	94
202	**5**	*½*	**Kaylif Aramis**[44] 4505 4-10-12 0 ... SamTwiston-Davies (Nigel Twiston-Davies) *led and t.k.h: mod pce early: qcknd 8 l clr 7f out: rdn and hdd 2 f out: sn btn: lost two pls nr fin* **5/1**[3]	95+
06	**6**	*13*	**Zava River (IRE)**[14] 5158 4-10-12 0 ... DarylJacob (Jamie Snowden) *last and looked rather cumbersme tl 1/2-way: picked off sme toiling rivals after* **66/1**	83
	7	*14*	**Churchfield Champ (IRE)** 5-11-4 0 ... JohnnyFarrelly (Laura Young) *t.k.h early: chsd ldrs: 10 l 4th 4f out: rdn and sn racing awkwardly: t.o* **12/1**	76
6	**8**	*4 ½*	**Chartplan (IRE)**[22] 5056 5-10-11 0 ... MrTJCannon(7) (Roger Teal) *shkn up after 5f: struggling 5f out: t.o* **66/1**	72
	9	*11*	**Themanfromcork** 4-10-7 0 ... (t) MrRMahon(5) (Paul Nicholls) *midfield: rdn 1/2-way: sn btn: t.o* **6/1**	56
0-0	**10**	*¾*	**Seffier**[49] 4410 6-10-8 0 ... JamesO'Farrell(3) (Ian Patrick Browne, Ire) *last in pair: t.o fnl 7f* **100/1**	55
	11	*2*	**Grape Expectations** 4-10-8 0 ow1 ... MrPYork(5) (Raymond York) *lost tch 7f out: sn t.o* **66/1**	55
4	**12**	*35*	**Jimmy The Brave**[342] 284 5-11-4 0 ... ColinBolger (Gerry Enright) *plld v hrd: wnt prom after 3f: wknd 5f out: t.o and heavily eased* **40/1**	28
3	**13**	*23*	**Western High**[48] 4423 6-11-4 0 ... RichardJohnson (Jim Best) *plld hrd: w ldrs tl lost pl 1/2-way: t.o fnl 4f: heavily eased* **11/1**	8
	14	*1 ¼*	**Gallowgate Lad** 5-10-8 0 ... JosephAkehurst(10) (Gary Moore) *nvr bttr than midfield: lost tch 7f out: t.o fnl 4f: heavily eased* **18/1**	7

4m 18.6s (-10.10) **Going Correction** -0.65s/f (Firm)
WFA 4 from 5yo+ 5lb **14** Ran SP% **119.9**
Speed ratings: **95,91,88,88,88 82,77,75,70,70 69,54,44,44**
toteswingers:1&2:£1.10, 2&3:£5.50, 1&3:£4.70 CSF £14.11 TOTE £2.60: £1.10, £1.60, £3.80; EX 15.90.
Owner Walters Plant Hire Ltd **Bred** Roger Ryan **Trained** Upper Lambourn, Berks

FOCUS
A fair bumper for the time of year and a big step up from the winner.

NOTEBOOK
Victor Echo(IRE) had to be driven along to keep tabs on Kaylif Aramis at one stage, but responded well and went to the front quite readily. Once there he pricked his ears and still looked green, suggesting he had plenty left. This confirmed the promise of his Ffos Las debut and he should do well over further once sent over obstacles. (tchd 5-2)
Majorica King(FR) was the only other runner to emerge from the pack and throw down a serious challenge, but he was always being held by the winner. (tchd 9-2)
Farbreaga(IRE) had shown plenty of ability in Irish points and narrowly fared best of those from off the pace. (op 10-1)
Silsula, a half-sister to a couple of winning chasers, was another to keep on nicely and can do better when there is more emphasis on stamina.
Kaylif Aramis, who had the form to go close, looked to be well ridden, gradually increasing a pace that had been steady early, and he opened up a lead of a few lengths at one stage. However, he had been a bit keen and didn't find as much as one might have hoped, finishing tired and losing two places late on. This was especially disappointing considering he's a brother to strong stayer Kayf Aramis. (op 9-2)
Churchfield Champ(IRE) was too keen early. (op 20-1)
Jimmy The Brave Official explanation: jockey said gelding ran to free

5388 SIS LIVE STANDARD OPEN NATIONAL HUNT FLAT RACE (DIV II) 2m 2f 110y
5:50 (5:51) (Class 6) 4-6-Y-O **£1,301** (£382; £191; £95)

Form				RPR
	1		**Royal Guardsman (IRE)** 4-10-12 0 ... JoeTizzard (Colin Tizzard) *a gng wl: racd enthusiastically: trckd ldrs tl led on bit over 2f out: sn qcknd clr: impressive in slow time* **15/2**	122+
3	**2**	*11*	**Grab The Glory (IRE)**[52] 4356 5-11-4 0 ... JamieMoore (Gary Moore) *midfield: effrt 4f out: rdn and chsd wnr vainly fr over 2f out* **6/4**[1]	113+
2	**3**	*7*	**Gores Island (IRE)**[104] 3399 5-11-4 0 ... RichardJohnson (Noel Chance) *bhd: effrt 4f out: tried to chal 3f out: sn rdn and one pce and no imp* **9/2**[3]	105
	4	*3 ¾*	**Cashallgone (IRE)** 4-10-9 0 ... JimmyDerham(3) (Seamus Mullins) *settled in rr: effrt 4f out: rdn and wknd over 2f out* **14/1**	95
5	**5**	*6*	**City Press (IRE)**[27] 4943 5-11-4 0 ... APMcCoy (Nicky Henderson) *pressed ldrs: rdn over 3f out: sn outpcd: t.o* **10/3**[2]	95
03	**6**	*1*	**Black Cache (IRE)**[27] 4957 5-11-4 0 ... SamTwiston-Davies (Nigel Twiston-Davies) *plld hrd: slt ld tl rdn and hdd over 2f out: sn wknd: t.o* **28/1**	94
6	**7**	*2 ¼*	**Pinkneys Prince**[39] 4709 4-10-12 0 ... DarylJacob (Nick Williams) *nvr bttr than midfield: rdn and wknd 3f out: t.o* **20/1**	86
6	**8**	*½*	**Aaly**[41] 4561 4-10-12 0 ... MarkBradburne (Lydia Richards) *prom tl rdn and lost pl qckly over 2f out: t.o* **100/1**	85
	9	*hd*	**Specialagent Alfie** 5-11-4 0 ... LiamTreadwell (Nick Gifford) *midfield: wknd over 3f out: t.o* **25/1**	91
0	**10**	*3 ¾*	**Proper Villan (IRE)**[52] 4356 6-11-4 0 ... JasonMaguire (Mark Bradstock) *pressed ldr tl drvn and fdd over 2f out: t.o* **66/1**	87
	11	*1 ½*	**Cariboo Lady** 5-10-11 0 ... HaddenFrost (Roger Curtis) *last pair: struggling 3f out: t.o* **100/1**	79
	12	*3 ¼*	**Burnt Orchid (IRE)** 6-10-11 0 ... JimmyMcCarthy (Geoffrey Deacon) *midfield tl 1/2-way: t.o fnl 3f* **100/1**	76
	P		**Cold Blow Lane (IRE)** 5-11-4 0 ... TomSiddall (Joanna Davis) *last and rdn 1/2-way: t.o 6f out: p.u 3f out* **80/1**	—
	P		**Shantou Breeze (IRE)** 4-10-2 0 ... MarcGoldstein(3) (Michael Madgwick) *last pair: sme prog 6f out: hung violently rt and unsteerable on bnd out of bk st: p.u 3f out* **66/1**	—

4m 21.4s (-7.30) **Going Correction** -0.65s/f (Firm)
WFA 4 from 5yo+ 5lb **14** Ran SP% **118.9**
Speed ratings: **89,84,81,79,77 76,75,75,75,74 73,72,—,—**
toteswingers:1&2:£2.60, 2&3:£1.20, 1&3:£8.70 CSF £17.98 TOTE £11.30: £2.60, £1.10, £2.20; EX 22.20.
Owner Camilla & Rosie Nock **Bred** Gerard Nock **Trained** Milborne Port, Dorset

FOCUS
The early pace was slow (time 2.80 seconds slower than the first division), but the runner-up and third-placed finisher, both of whom had shown plenty of ability on their respective debuts, give this form a solid look and there was a deeply impressive winner. He is sure to rate higher and win more races.

NOTEBOOK
Royal Guardsman(IRE) ◆ travelled strongly for much of the way, was still going easily when sent to the front and he quickened clear when pushed out without having to be seriously asked. He understandably looked green in the closing stages, so there should be plenty more to come, and it may be significant that Fontwell was the track his trainer chose to introduce Cue Card, a 6l winner of a bumper in January 2010. It's likely we'll be hearing a lot more of Royal Guardsman, who rates a smart prospect. (op 6-1 tchd 8-1)
Grab The Glory(IRE) shaped well on his debut at Kempton and time is likely to show this was another solid effort. (op 15-8 tched 2-1 in places)
Gores Island(IRE), who was runner-up at Southwell on his first start, was well held in this possibly stronger contest. (op 7-1)
Cashallgone(IRE), an 11,000euros purchase, made a pleasing start. (op 16-1)
City Press(IRE) didn't really run on for pressure and failed to build on his Haydock debut effort. (op 9-4 tchd 7-2)
Black Cache(IRE) pulled much too hard. (op 33-1 tchd 40-1)
Pinkneys Prince ◆ travelled well through the race and has ability. (op 25-1)
T/Plt: £63.40 to a £1 stake. Pool of £60,887.73 - 700 winning units. T/Qpdt: £36.70 to a £1 stake. Pool of £3,680.07 - 74.10 winning units. IM

5167 HEREFORD (R-H)
Wednesday, April 20

OFFICIAL GOING: Good to firm
Wind: almost nil Weather: very hot and sunny

5389 BET MOBILE AT VICTORCHANDLER.COM MAIDEN HURDLE (10 hdls) 2m 4f
2:20 (2:20) (Class 5) 4-Y-O+ **£1,723** (£506; £253; £126)

Form				RPR
0043	**1**		**Countess Susy**[13] 5167 6-10-2 101 ... MrTomDavid(5) (Phillip Dando) *mde all: racd enthusiastically: pushed along bef 2 out: clung on tenaciously flat* **7/2**[2]	93+
0	**2**	*1 ¼*	**Before The War (USA)**[5] 5321 4-10-1 0 ... MrRGHenderson(7) (Polly Gundry) *hld up towards rr: pushed along and hdwy bef 7th: nt fluent 2 out: sn 2nd: tried to chal fr bef last but nvr as resolute as wnr and a hld flat* **22/1**	92
0440	**3**	*10*	**Sleeping Du Granit (FR)**[13] 5168 5-10-11 0 ... (t) TommyPhelan(3) (Claire Dyson) *prom: wnt 2nd 3 out: rdn and ev ch next: wknd u.p bef last where nt fluent* **28/1**	90
-443	**4**	*14*	**Sizing Ireland (IRE)**[21] 5074 5-11-0 110 ... APMcCoy (Nicky Henderson) *cl up: hrd rdn 3 out: sn no rspnse but continued to be rousted to no avail tl wknd between last two* **2/5**[1]	76
0	**5**	*4*	**Grindy (IRE)**[32] 4866 5-11-0 0 ... TomMessenger (Evan Williams) *midfield: rdn and outpcd 6th: wl btn after: plugged on flat* **28/1**	73
0-5	**6**	*18*	**Prime Design (IRE)**[8] 5280 6-10-7 0 ... LiamTreadwell (Neale Dalton) *mstkes in last trio: lost tch and mstke 6th: t.o 3 out* **33/1**	50

00 **7** *29* **Florence May**[9] [5253] 7-10-4 0 DonalDevereux(3) 24
(Lucy Jones) *plld hrd in last pair: j. bdly lft 5th and lost tch: sn t.o: eased last* **100/1**

2P **P** **Border Station (IRE)**[162] [2291] 5-11-0 0 LeightonAspell —
(Alison Batchelor) *sn bhd: rdn and fading rapidly whn mstke 6th: sn p.u* **11/1**[3]

005 **P** **San Salito (FR)**[40] [4706] 5-11-0 0 DavidEngland —
(Giles Smyly) *t.k.h: nt jump wl: sn 2nd: mstke 4th: losing 2nd whn mstke 3 out: stopped rapidly and p.u next* **33/1**

4m 55.9s (0.40) **Going Correction** -0.225s/f (Good)
WFA 4 from 5yo+ 6lb **9** Ran SP% **120.1**
Speed ratings (Par 103): **90,89,85,79,78 71,59,—,—**
toteswingers:1&2: £13.80, 2&3: £30.10, 1&3: £13.80 CSF £64.63 TOTE £5.00: £1.80, £7.80, £12.90; EX 68.50.
Owner P Dando **Bred** H J Manners **Trained** Peterston-Super-Ely, S Glamorg

FOCUS
The going was good to firm on a watered track. The ground looked patchy and seemed to be kicking up in places. The hot favourite was in serious trouble a long way out before being left behind in this maiden hurdle which lacked strength in depth. The form is rated around the winner and third.

NOTEBOOK
Countess Susy showed much improved form when a strong finishing 66-1 third in a 2m1f maiden hurdle here last time. She had quite a bit to find with the leading form contender but confirmed her latest promise with a determined front-running success stepped up to 2m4f. She looks a tough sort who should continue to go the right way but this form looks suspect with the favourite disappointing and an opening mark of 101 looks on the high side on what she has achieved so far. (op 9-2)
Before The War(USA) is a modest maiden on the Flat and showed little at 80-1 on her hurdles debut last Saturday, but she left that run behind with a fair effort to try and get to grips with the resolute trailblazing winner. (op 20-1)
Sleeping Du Granit(FR) seemed to find a better rhythm and a bit of improvement stepped up to 2m4f on his third hurdle run and has probably got back somewhere near his respectable bumper form. (op 33-1)
Sizing Ireland(IRE) was fairly useful in bumpers and improved on his hurdling debut when a close third in a C&D event last month. He set a clear standard but held his head at a slightly awkward angle early on and there were severe warning signs and a limited response some way out. This was his first try on ground with firm in the description, so it is likely that the fast conditions caused his downfall, but he has now been beaten as favourite in four of six starts and some questions are mounting up. Official explanation: trainers rep said, regarding running, that the gelding finished distressed (op 4-11 tchd 4-9)

5390 BET FOOTBALL AT VICTORCHANDLER.COM NOVICES' H'CAP HURDLE (8 hdls) 2m 1f
2:55 (2:55) (Class 5) (0-95,92) 4-Y-O+ **£1,723** (£506; £253; £126)

Form RPR
00UU **1** **Danehillsundance (IRE)**[6] [5307] 7-11-6 **86** (t) BarryKeniry 93+
(Philip Kirby) *midfield and hld up: 6th and rdn 3 out: hit next: stl nt gng v wl between last two: styd on u.p as the opposition gave up: led fnl 100yds: all out and unimpressive* **2/1**[1]

0602 **2** *½* **Ostaadi**[8] [5272] 5-10-5 **76** MarkQuinlan(5) 82
(Bernard Llewellyn) *pressed ldrs: rdn bef 4th: outpcd 3 out: rallied u.p after 2 out: lft w ev ch after last: put hd in air and n.g.t cl home* **3/1**[2]

3UU6 **3** *1½* **Turbo Shandy**[19] [5101] 8-11-5 **90** OliverDayman(5) 94
(Dai Burchell) *hld up and bhd: effrt in 5th and rdn 2 out: nt clr run and nt qckn fr last: wnt 3rd cl home* **14/1**

-633 **4** *2* **Golden Button (IRE)**[8] [5282] 6-11-12 **92** (t) JasonMaguire 96
(Kim Bailey) *t.k.h: 2nd or 3rd: wnt 4 l 2nd and rdn 3 out: chal and lft in ld last: cajoled and fnd nthing: hdd and overwhelmed by three rivals ins fnl 100yds* **5/1**[3]

P042 **5** *1¾* **Sir Clad**[25] [5016] 5-9-13 **72** (vt) GeraldQuinn(7) 77+
(Claire Dyson) *led at brisk pce: hdd 5th: led again bef last and blnd and hdd and nt rcvr* **7/1**

U330 **6** *2½* **Carhue Princess (IRE)**[231] [1450] 5-11-5 **85** RhysFlint 84
(John Flint) *chsd ldrs: pushed along after 4th: outpcd and hit 3 out: drvn and sme prog bef last: no ch* **25/1**

/0-P **7** *1* **Limestone Boy (IRE)**[346] [223] 9-10-1 **70** (t) MichaelMurphy(3) 68
(Rob Summers) *towards rr: outpcd 5th: plugged on between last two: nt rch ldrs* **80/1**

055P **8** *1½* **Kyoto (GER)**[160] [2334] 7-10-5 **71** (p) LiamHeard 68
(Nigel Hawke) *racd freely: 2nd tl led 5th: 4 l clr 2 out: hdd bef last: nt run on* **25/1**

-350 **9** *90* **Ask Archer**[304] [793] 6-11-12 **92** TomMessenger 8
(Evan Williams) *j. stickily in last: rdn and t.o after 4th* **33/1**

000P **F** **Pegasus Lad (USA)**[226] [1489] 5-10-4 **70** AndrewGlassonbury —
(Linda Blackford) *struggling towards rr whn fell 5th: fatally injured* **40/1**

00F **F** **Steptoe**[46] [4465] 6-11-1 **81** AndrewTinkler —
(Nicky Henderson) *a bhd: struggling bdly whn stmbld and fell 3 out* **14/1**

3m 59.1s (-0.30) **Going Correction** -0.225s/f (Good) **11** Ran SP% **115.1**
Speed ratings (Par 103): **91,90,90,89,88 87,86,85,43,—** —
toteswingers: 1&2 £1.10, 1&3 £46.70, 2&3 £10.10 CSF £7.93 CT £63.09 TOTE £3.60: £2.10, £1.50, £3.80; EX 9.30.
Owner L & D Racing **Bred** J P Hardiman **Trained** Castleton, N Yorks
■ Stewards' Enquiry : Barry Keniry one-day ban: used whip with excessive frequency (May 4)

FOCUS
The market leaders filled the first two positions in this strongly run minor handicap but both were matched at around 280-1 in-running in a race of changing fortunes. The form looks reliable with the five immediaitely behind the winner all close to their marks.

NOTEBOOK
Danehillsundance(IRE) attracted an avalanche of support when unseating on his handicap hurdle debut at Sedgefield last time. He was strong in the market again and managed to keep grinding away to deliver off what looked a lenient mark relative to his Flat form last summer, which included a 1m2f Beverley win off 80. He has scope for improvement in this sphere but he did have to work really hard to get to the front here, and there was a suspicion that the leaders may have gone off a bit too fast which allowed the hold-up runners to pick up the pieces. (op 9-4 tchd 15-8)
Ostaadi sprang back to form with a close second in a selling handicap at Taunton last week. Due to go up 6lb in the future, he had strong claims off the same mark and did well to finish a close second after being one of the first under pressure.However, the slight negative is that he did hold his head a bit high in the closing stages. (op 4-1)
Turbo Shandy has had some jumping problems over fences since a smooth Market Rasen win off this mark last summer and he is still winless in 20 runs over hurdles, but he returned to form with a creditable third behind of a couple of well handicapped rivals. (tchd 18-1)
Golden Button(IRE) has just faltered when looking likely to strike on her last two starts but she deserves some credit for this run because she raced closer to the strong pace than the front three. She looks a bit tricky but is generally progressive and should be able to get her timing right in a minor handicap hurdle. (tchd 9-2 and 11-2)

Sir Clad set a good pace and made a dash for home around the final turn but the game was up after he ploughed into the last flight. This free-going sort has found improvement in a visor on his last two runs and rates a bit better than this finishing position. (op 15-2 tchd 8-1 and 6-1)

5391 GREEN DRAGON HOTEL NOVICES' H'CAP CHASE (14 fncs) 2m 3f
3:30 (3:30) (Class 4) (0-115,114) 5-Y-O+ **£2,439** (£716; £358; £178)

Form RPR
1636 **1** **Intac (IRE)**[151] [2513] 9-11-12 **114** JoeTizzard 123+
(Colin Tizzard) *j. neatly: led tl 3rd: led 5th tl hdd momentarily 3 out: wnt 3 l clr next: rdn between last two: wl in command after last* **9/4**[2]

041P **2** *6* **Gentleman Anshan (IRE)**[13] [5170] 7-11-0 **109** MissHannahWatson(7) 112
(Rosemary Gasson) *racd keenly: hld up trcking ldrs tl effrt 10th: wnt 2nd next: led briefly 3 out: rdn and wl hld next* **7/2**[3]

PPP5 **3** *3* **Builteoir (IRE)**[21] [5076] 9-9-7 **88** MrJEngland(7) 87
(Evan Williams) *led 3rd tl 5th: lost 2nd and rdn 11th: btn next: snatched mod 3rd on line* **9/1**

2312 **4** *hd* **Finlay**[19] [5095] 8-11-10 **112** (t) JasonMaguire 112
(Donald McCain) *sn last pair: rdn and awkward hd carriage bef 11th: outpcd u.p 3 out: wnt mod 3rd bef next tl fnl stride* **13/8**[1]

0023 **5** *11* **Bay Central (IRE)**[10] [5233] 7-10-12 **100** SamJones 91
(Evan Williams) *t.k.h: in last pair: nt fluent 8th: lost tch bef 11th: mstke last* **9/1**

4m 40.7s (-6.00) **Going Correction** -0.175s/f (Good) **5** Ran SP% **111.1**
Speed ratings: **105,102,101,101,96**
CSF £10.56 TOTE £3.90: £2.00, £2.00; EX 11.80.
Owner Stranger, Mogridge, Romans **Bred** Patrick A Keogh **Trained** Milborne Port, Dorset

FOCUS
There were not many runners but this looked fairly competitive and the form could work out, with the first two rated to their marks.

NOTEBOOK
Intac(IRE) put in a fluent and commanding front-running display to land a gamble on return from five months off. Ideally suited by fast ground, this enthusiastic type was a triple winner at similar trips over hurdles and fences last year and looks set for another very profitable spell. (op 10-3)
Gentleman Anshan(IRE) ruined his chance with a bad mistake last time, but this dual winning pointer jumped well and got back on track with a decent effort behind the well backed winner. This big, scopey 7-y-o still has some untapped potential over fences and should be able to add to his 2m5f handicap win here last month. (op 4-1)
Builteoir(IRE) was ridden prominently and gave a fair hint of a revival before fading. There are a number of letters in his form figures, but this was his first run on favoured fast ground for a while and he is well treated off 2lb lower than his last win. (tchd 7-1)
Finlay was a bit hesitant at some of the fences before being caught out when the pace increased. This was a bit disappointing from a generally progressive chaser who just failed at Newcastle last time, but it is a possible that the quick ground was against him. (op 11-8 tchd 7-4)
Bay Central(IRE) was a bit keen and couldn't get involved. This former Galway bumper winner has ability but he also has a very patchy profile and a temperamental side. (op 8-1 tchd 15-2 and 10-1)

5392 PERTEMPS PEOPLE DEVELOPMENT GROUP H'CAP HURDLE (10 hdls) 2m 4f
4:05 (4:05) (Class 4) (0-115,115) 4-Y-O+ **£2,016** (£592; £296; £147)

Form RPR
03P2 **1** **Big Robert**[13] [5171] 7-11-4 **107** (tp) AidanColeman 120+
(Matt Sheppard) *midfield: clsd gng wl in 2nd at 7th: led next: drew 6 l clr on bit after 2 out: eased flat* **4/1**[2]

3504 **2** *10* **Hadron Collider (FR)**[149] [2586] 6-10-11 **107** MrBJPoste(7) 106
(Chris Nenadich) *hld up trcking ldrs: effrt 3 out: rdn and outpcd by wnr next and 10 l 3rd between last two: clsd on eventual 3rd bef last where disp 2nd: kpt on wout threatening* **11/1**

1633 **3** *nk* **Topenhall (IRE)**[147] [1972] 10-11-10 **113** (t) CharliePoste 113
(Ben Case) *t.k.h and prom: chsd wnr 3 out: rdn and lost tch w him after next: lost duel for 2nd nr fin* **14/1**

1120 **4** *5* **Am I Blue**[27] [2514] 5-11-5 **108** RichardJohnson 103
(Mrs D Thomas) *led tl 3 out: lost pl fr next but kpt on quite nicely* **5/1**

0F10 **5** *¾* **Very Stylish (IRE)**[18] [5117] 7-11-7 **111** RichieMcLernon 105
(Jonjo O'Neill) *pressed ldr tl drvn 3 out: sn btn: wnt lft bef last* **7/2**[1]

0400 **6** *7* **Watch Out**[19] [5103] 7-9-11 **90** ow1 (tp) OliverDayman(5) 79
(Dai Burchell) *settled in rr: wl in tch in v tight gp 7th: btn next* **9/2**[3]

1PPU **7** *1* **City Heights (IRE)**[37] [4786] 9-11-7 **113** TomMolloy(3) 100
(Giles Smyly) *racd v wd: nt fluent 7th and rdn: wkng whn j. slowly next* **20/1**

06P0 **8** *27* **Drussell (IRE)**[18] [5117] 5-11-2 **105** WarrenMarston 79
(Richard Phillips) *chsd ldrs: pushed along bef 7th: btn next: eased last: t.o* **7/1**

2F-0 **9** *46* **Share Option**[47] [196] 9-11-9 **115** LeeEdwards(3) 36
(Tony Carroll) *plld hrd: prom tl lost pl 7th: t.o after next* **25/1**

3-00 **P** **Kempley Green (IRE)**[18] [5117] 8-10-13 **105** (tp) JohnKington(3) —
(Michael Scudamore) *in rr of bunch but wl in tch tl 7th: sn wknd: t.o and p.u after 2 out* **22/1**

4m 48.5s (-7.00) **Going Correction** -0.225s/f (Good) **10** Ran SP% **117.5**
Speed ratings (Par 105): **105,101,100,98,98 95,95,84,66,—**
toteswingers: 1&2 £4.90, 1&3 £8.70, 2&3 £21.20 CSF £45.28 CT £565.47 TOTE £3.70: £1.40, £3.10, £3.70; EX 36.60.
Owner Simon Gegg **Bred** Deerfield Farm **Trained** Eastnor, H'fords

FOCUS
They were tightly grouped for a long way in this fair handicap hurdle before the winner stormed clear off the steady pace. The third is the best guide to the level.

NOTEBOOK
Big Robert had stamina to prove, but his second here last time looked solid and he surged clear after making a decisive move after the second last. This first hurdle win should provide a good confidence boost for this former useful triple 7f-1m2f Flat winner. He could face a big rise in mark after this romp but should remain fairly handicapped on his best Irish form and may be able to strike again. (op 3-1 tchd 9-2 and 5-1 in places)
Hadron Collider(FR) shaped with promise on favoured quick ground back from five months off. He was in good form for Charlie Mann at around this time last year and looks fairly treated on his 2m4f Uttoxeter maiden hurdle win last June. (tchd 12-1)
Topenhall(IRE) moved well for a long way but couldn't hang in there when the winner kicked on. He did well after joining his current yard from Ireland last summer and should improve for this promising return from 147 days off. (tchd 16-1)
Am I Blue ran respectably under a prominent ride switched back from the Flat to hurdles, but she is 18lb higher than when completing a double at Newton Abbot last September and needs to find another jolt of improvement to be a big factor off this mark. (op 9-2 tchd 4-1)
Very Stylish(IRE) struggled when the pace picked up in a steadily run race over a trip shorter than ideal. He has a very erratic profile but landed a gamble when recording a standout effort off 5lb lower over 3m at Uttoxeter last July and should appreciate a return to that trip. (op 11-2 tchd 3-1)

Watch Out attracted support but was very laboured. (op 8-1)

5393 BEST ODDS GUARANTEED AT VICTORCHANDLER.COM H'CAP HURDLE (11 hdls) 2m 6f 110y

4:40 (4:40) (Class 5) (0-95,95) 4-Y-0+ **£1,723** (£506; £253; £126)

Form				RPR
5105	1		**The Wee Midget**[21] 5075 6-11-9 **92** NickScholfield (Arthur Whiting) *pressed ldng pair tl 7 l 3rd and pushed along bef 8th: chsd clr ldr bef 3 out: stl looked hld home turn: drvn and clsd gamely fr last: got up cl home* **11/4**[1]	93
0113	2	nk	**Border Lad**[44] 4522 7-11-0 **83** DarylJacob (Alison Thorpe) *led: wnt clr 6th: nt fluent next: 6 l advantage but racing awkwardly bef last: drvn and idled bdly: jst ct* **9/2**[2]	86+
5250	3	1 3/4	**Bollywood (IRE)**[8] 5282 8-10-13 **82** (t) LeightonAspell (Alison Batchelor) *chsd ldrs: dropped in rr 7th: sn wl bhd in 8th pl: rallied 2 out: wnt 3rd and drvn and trying to cl between last two: no real imp flat* **8/1**[3]	81
6615	4	4 1/2	**Diddley Dee**[13] 5172 7-11-2 **92** MrBJPoste(7) (Bill Moore) *towards rr: outpcd bef 8th: last of five w ch 3 out: 4th bef last and kpt on steadily but n.d* **11/1**	89
5F03	5	3/4	**Carys's Lad**[28] 4949 8-10-5 **74** MarkBradburne (Michael Mullineaux) *midfield: hit 4th: pushed along 5th: outpcd 8th: slt late prog but nvr plcd to chal* **9/2**[2]	68
6066	6	8	**Peqeno Diablo (IRE)**[11] 5208 6-11-5 **95** GeraldQuinn(7) (Claire Dyson) *mstke 4th: nt a fluent: chsd ldr (who wnt clr 6th) tl bef 3 out: lost pl rapidly* **8/1**[3]	82
3500	7	4 1/2	**Sumner (IRE)**[8] 5282 7-11-0 **90** (t) AndrewGlassonbury(7) (William Davies) *chsd ldrs: effrt 8th: 3rd 3 out: rdn and btn next: fnd nthing* **40/1**	77
0P40	8	52	**Ginolad (AUS)**[30] 4921 11-11-12 **95** AidanColeman (Venetia Williams) *reluctant and bking off all the hurdles: dropped bk last and drvn 5th: continued hopelessly t.o: kpt taking the mickey tl passed two in clsng stages* **17/2**	31
0P00	9	12	**Sam's Pride**[13] 5168 6-10-10 **79** JackDoyle (Peter Pritchard) *towards rr: struggling after mstke 6th: sn last and t.o* **33/1**	5
6-P	10	2 1/2	**Grand Fella (IRE)**[52] 4378 6-10-13 **85** (p) LeeEdwards(3) (Ken Wingrove) *bhd: hit 3rd and 4th: rdn 7th: sn t.o: eased last* **22/1**	8

5m 23.6s (-14.40) **Going Correction** -0.55s/f (Firm) **10** Ran SP% **113.8**
Speed ratings (Par 103): **103,102,102,100,100 97,96,78,73,72**
toteswingers: 1&2 £2.60, 1&3 £5.40, 2&3 £6.80 CSF £15.13 CT £86.12 TOTE £4.80: £2.10, £2.30, £2.50; EX 18.20.
Owner A J Whiting **Bred** David Jenks **Trained** North Nibley, Gloucs

FOCUS
An ordinary handicap hurdle. It was run at a good pace and there was a tight finish involving two of the market leaders. The form looks sound enough with the winner to form and the third, fourth and fifth close to their marks.

NOTEBOOK
The Wee Midget looked fairly treated off 3lb higher than when taking advantage of the runner-up's last-flight blunder at Towcester last October and showed a strong will to reel in the breakaway pacesetting runner-up on his second run back from a break. (op 7-2)
Border Lad turned the corner with back-to-back handicap wins on testing ground earlier in the year. He dispelled the theory that the handicapper may have quickly caught up with him by putting in a bold front-running display. He could find further progress and should be able to gain compensation for this last-gasp defeat. (op 4-1)
Bollywood(IRE) found 2m an insufficient test on his comeback at Towcester last week and quickly got back on song with a big run returned to 2m6f. He should continue to pose a threat but he has a modest career record of 2-81. (op 15-2)
Diddley Dee came with a powerful late run to land a 2m1f handicap here last month but that wasn't a strong heat and he has found life tough in both tries over further since. (op 12-1)
Carys's Lad flashed home for third over 2m4f here last month and again caught the eye staying on late over this stiffer test. He has come a long way down the weights but has had plenty of problems in recent years and his habit of getting behind could continue to hold him back. (op 5-1)

5394 LEVEL PEAKS ASSOCIATES H'CAP CHASE (12 fncs) 2m

5:10 (5:10) (Class 3) (0-130,116) 5-Y-0+ **£4,553** (£1,337; £668; £333)

Form				RPR
4324	1		**Courella (IRE)**[3] 5345 7-11-3 **114** MrJEngland(7) (Evan Williams) *settled 4th: outpcd and nt fluent 5th: rdn 8th: clsd and ct ldng pair who had gone off far too fast bef 3 out: pushed clr after next: sn in command: rdn out* **4/1**[3]	126+
6424	2	15	**Mibleu (FR)**[176] 2022 11-11-5 **116** SClements(7) (Colin Tizzard) *plld hrd: led at breakneck pce 4th: hdd but lft in ld again 9th: passed by wnr bef 3 out: btn sn after next but clung on to poor 2nd* **11/4**[2]	115
6-0U	3	1/2	**William Bonney (IRE)**[10] 5237 11-10-13 **106** (p) LeeStephens(3) (Ann Price) *lost tch 2nd: big jump 3rd: 15 l last at 7th: wnt 3rd bef 3 out and rdn: trying to catch 2nd fr after next but nt quite get there flat (w wnr wl clr)* **33/1**	104
0320	4	6	**Cortinas (GER)**[6] 5305 9-11-8 **115** (t) IanPopham(3) (Claire Dyson) *3rd early: 10 lrngths 4th at 7th: struggled on* **4/1**[3]	108
1P11	5	20	**Chrysander**[10] 5232 9-11-7 **116** (vt) AodhaganConlon(5) (Evan Williams) *set v fast pce tl 4th: blnd next: sn rcvrd: led again but blnd 9th and hdd: sn dropped out: mstke last* **6/4**[1]	106+

(-3.60) **Going Correction** -0.175s/f (Good) **5** Ran SP% **109.6**
Speed ratings: **102,94,94,91,81**
CSF £15.23 TOTE £4.30: £2.00, £2.40; EX 13.20.
Owner R E R Williams **Bred** Thomas Kinsella **Trained** Llancarfan, Vale Of Glamorgan

FOCUS
A decent handicap chase. It was run at furious pace and the two front-runners got involved in a destructive duel. The form could be rated higher but the winner to his mark is the best guide form now.

NOTEBOOK
Courella(IRE) appreciated the fast pace and powered his to victory with cheekpieces removed on his third run in the last ten days. Equally effective at 2m-2m4f, he was successful twice on good ground at Fontwell during an improved spell last summer and may be able to repeat that dual winning trend when getting another strong pace to aim at. (op 3-1)
Mibleu(FR), well backed in the morning, did quite well to hang on for second after getting involved a sustained battle up front on return from 176 days off. He has a modest strike-rate of 4-43 over fences but should be more potent under a bit more restraint on his second run back. (op 9-4)
William Bonney(IRE) stayed on late from a long way back but it is hard to rate this as a revival from a horse who has been in the doldrums since completing a double at Ludlow two years ago. (op 16-1)
Cortinas(GER) got outpaced before plugging on when it was all over. (op 11-2)
Chrysander has been in unstoppable form in claiming hurdles this year and had plenty in hand when winning at Ludlow last time. He looked on a fair mark switched back to fences but paid the price for getting involved in a blistering battle for the lead. (op 9-4)

5395 LINDLEY CATERING INTERMEDIATE OPEN NATIONAL HUNT FLAT RACE 2m 1f

5:45 (5:45) (Class 6) 4-6-Y-0 **£1,431** (£420; £210; £104)

Form				RPR
0-23	1		**Mike Towey (IRE)**[27] 4970 6-11-3 0 TomO'Brien (Peter Bowen) *in 2nd tl led 9f out: clr and rdn 2f out: a looked wnr after but racing lazily and kpt up to work* **5/6**[1]	105+
03	2	6	**Bollistick**[25] 5019 5-11-3 0 MarkBradburne (Michael Mullineaux) *wnt 2nd 6f out tl 5f out: v wd after: regained 2nd and drvn over 2f out: v one pce and nvr trbld wnr* **33/1**	96
2	3	8	**Sparkling Air**[21] 5077 5-10-10 0 RichardJohnson (John Spearing) *settled in 3rd: wnt 2nd 5f out: rdn and outpcd by wnr over 2f out and sn lost 2nd* **7/4**[2]	81
00-0	4	14	**Love Love Me Do**[301] 832 6-10-7 0 IanPopham(3) (Carroll Gray) *towards rr: lost tch tamely 4f out: t.o* **20/1**	69
0	5	dist	**Bathwick Tigger (IRE)**[167] 2173 4-10-5 0 RhysFlint (John Flint) *t.k.h: led for 7f: stopped to nil 7f out: sn hopelessly t.o: virtually p.u 3f out* **8/1**[3]	—

3m 54.8s (1.00) **Going Correction** -0.225s/f (Good)
WFA 4 from 5yo+ 5lb **5** Ran SP% **109.7**
Speed ratings: **88,85,81,74,—**
Tote Super 7: Win: Not won. Place: £323.00 CSF £24.99 TOTE £1.80: £1.10, £7.40; EX 33.70.
Owner Roddy Owen & Paul Fullagar **Bred** John Gallagher **Trained** Little Newcastle, Pembrokes

FOCUS
There were six withdrawals in this bumper and the hot favourite had no trouble cashing in on a straightforward opportunity. He is rated to his mark but is value for further.

NOTEBOOK
Mike Towey(IRE) won a heavy-ground maiden point in 2009 and set the standard on his placed form in bumpers at Ffos Las and Chepstow last month. Always prominent, he gradually wound things up after moving into the lead and scored with plenty in hand. This 6-y-o should stay well as he learns to settle a bit better and looks a fair prospect. (op 6-5)
Bollistick, a 7l third in a slowly run three-runner bumper at Southwell on his second start, stuck to his task quite well and seems to be improving with experience. (op 14-1)
Sparkling Air needed quite a bit of motivating along the way and has failed to build on her close second here on debut last month. However, it is encouraging that this half-sister to the same connections 3m hurdle winner Starlight Air is showing form in bumpers, as her future probably lies in staying hurdle events. (op 15-8 tchd 6-4)
Love Love Me Do struggled to get competitive in three previous bumper starts and it was a similar story back from 301 days off.
Bathwick Tigger(IRE) who has plenty of speed on her dam's side, was a bit disappointing when favourite at Towcester on debut and she dropped away at a relatively early stage before being being virtually pulled up this time. (op 6-1)
T/Plt: £116.10 to a £1 stake. Pool of £58,207.37 - 365.81 winning tickets. T/Qpdt: £10.90 to a £1 stake. Pool of £7,110.79 - 481.18 winning tickets. IM

5232 LUDLOW (R-H)

Thursday, April 21

OFFICIAL GOING: Good (watered; 7.7)
All bends moved to provide fresh ground.
Wind: Nil Weather: Hot and sunny

5396 MARCHES CARE (S) HURDLE (9 hdls) 2m

2:20 (2:20) (Class 5) 4-8-Y-0 **£1,723** (£506; £253; £126)

Form				RPR
060P	1		**Baccalaureate (FR)**[27] 4988 5-10-12 100 (t) SamTwiston-Davies (Nigel Twiston-Davies) *in tch: led appr 3 out: asserted 2 out: styd on wl to draw clr run-in* **8/1**	102+
4231	2	8	**Mut'Ab (USA)**[6] 4920 6-11-4 99 (b) TimmyMurphy (Edward Creighton) *chsd ldrs: effrt to take 2nd appr 3 out: j.rt 2 out: one pce whn j.rt again last: no imp on wnr* **11/2**[3]	101
126-	3	15	**Hucking Hero (IRE)**[376] 5130 6-10-12 0 RichardJohnson (Tim Vaughan) *in tch: effrt appr 3 out: sn eased: lost tch w front 2 bef 2 out: pushed along but unable to get on terms run-in* **2/1**[1]	89+
-F00	4	14	**Maucaillou (GER)**[19] 5110 8-10-5 115 (b) StephenO'Donovan(7) (Martin Keighley) *chsd ldr: lft in ld 6th: hdd appr 3 out: sn wknd: n.d whn nt fluent last* **6/1**	69
0F55	5	25	**Bahr Nothing (IRE)**[21] 5082 5-10-5 100 (b[1]) JakeGreenall(7) (Henry Daly) *in rr: u.p fr 5th: nvr gng after and n.d: lost tch 3 out: t.o* **17/2**	58
2353	F		**Olympian Boy (IRE)**[20] 5101 7-10-12 102 RichieMcLernon (Anabel L M King) *led tl fell 6th* **3/1**[2]	—
66-	P		**Graycliffe (IRE)**[12] 1105 5-10-12 0 AlanO'Keeffe (Patrick Morris) *a bhd: lot tch bef 5th: t.o whn p.u bef 3 out* **16/1**	—

3m 43.4s (-6.10) **Going Correction** -0.425s/f (Good) **7** Ran SP% **115.5**
Speed ratings: **98,94,86,79,67 —,—**
toteswingers:1&2:£3.70, 1&3:£3.50, 2&3:£2.50 CSF £51.29 TOTE £7.70: £3.30, £2.90; EX 24.70.There was no bid for the winner.
Owner The Yes No Wait Sorries **Bred** Elevage Fouchet Loick & Coolmore Stud **Trained** Naunton, Gloucs

FOCUS
Over half of these couldn't be fancied on anything they had done recently, so it remains to be seen whether this is solid form for the level with the runner-up the best guide.

NOTEBOOK
Baccalaureate(FR), dropped into this grade for the first time and with a tongue-tie back, took this but it's unlikely he beat much here. A former Grade 2-winning hurdler down a mile in trip, he is probably the type to win a few at this level if connections keep to this grade. There was no bid for him at the subsequent auction. (tchd 15-2)
Mut'Ab(USA), last of five recently on the Flat, easily landed a Lingfield seller on his last start over hurdles, and moved up to look a big danger here. However, he didn't appear to show the same resolve as the winner under pressure and was readily held. (op 6-1 tchd 5-1)
Hucking Hero(IRE), absent for over a year, travelled okay while chasing the leaders but one always felt that the jockey didn't have a great deal left under him when the tempo lifted. Richard Johnson seemed to ease right off after jumping three from home, almost as though he was about to pull his mount up, but he kept going and the pair ran on again after the final hurdle. (op 5-2 tchd 11-4 in places)

Maucaillou(GER) was well treated on official figures but doesn't win very often. With blinkers tried for the first time over jumps, he inherited the lead when the front-runner Olympian Boy came down, but showed little inclination to run on when his jockey got after him to quicken. (op 11-2)

5397 ALFA AGGREGATES PRODUCTS NOVICES' CHASE (17 fncs) 2m 4f
2:50 (2:50) (Class 3) 5-Y-O+ **£5,954** (£2,047)

Form RPR
3F04 **1** **Othermix (FR)**[85] 3743 7-10-12 134 DaveCrosse 114+
(Ian Williams) *led fr 2nd: mde rest: nt fluent 9th (water): jnd 12th: rdn after 13th: lft clr whn nrest rival stmbld on bnd appr 4 out: styd on wl and unchal after* **5/4**[1]
0-PP **2** *7* **Benartic (IRE)**[57] 4282 7-10-12 0 AndrewTinkler 112+
(Nicky Henderson) *j.lft a few times: hld up: chsd wnr fr 3rd: lost 2nd briefly 10th: upsides fr 12th tl stmbld on bnd and lost abt 6 l appr 4 out: no imp after* **4/1**[3]
4422 **P** **William Hogarth**[10] 5255 6-10-12 0 (v[1]) RhysFlint —
(Keith Goldsworthy) *led to 2nd: dropped to rr fr 3rd: nvr looked happy after: drvn to cl and tk 2nd briefly 10th: toiling whn blnd 12th: t.o after: p.u bef 3 out* **11/8**[2]

5m 1.60s (-2.80) **Going Correction** -0.175s/f (Good) **3** Ran SP% **106.5**
Speed ratings: **98,95,—**
CSF £5.34 TOTE £2.30; EX 4.50.
Owner Power Panels Electrical Systems Ltd **Bred** Jean Pierre Dubois **Trained** Portway, Worcs

FOCUS
Two non-runners meant that, although it wasn't a bad contest, this race was difficult to work out, as all of the runners those left had negatives to overcome. The pace was modest and it is not form to be confident about.

NOTEBOOK
Othermix(FR), who recently had a soft palate operation and was without the blinkers and tongue-tie he wore last time, was thrown in on official figures and soon got handed the lead. He appeared to enjoy himself for much of the contest but was caught by the runner-up, who was going well, and looked set to finish second. However, that horse didn't go on and slipped while challenging, and Othermix kept on dourly to secure success. It wasn't an impressive victory but the owner said afterwards that he feels his horse needs quick ground. (tchd 6-4)
Benartic(IRE), a previous course winner, had been disappointing this season, albeit in better company, and this looked a much more realistic opportunity. He sat in behind through the early stages but seemed certain to win as he closed up to Othermix, who was being ridden. It probably would have been wise for his jockey to kick on while travelling so well immediately after the final fence in the back straight, but there was little he could have done about his mount slipping on the final bend. He will win over fences judged on this effort. (op 7-2)
William Hogarth, returning to fences, had a visor fitted for the first time and wasn't overly keen early, going from first to last quite quickly. He made his jockey work hard just to keep in touch with his two rivals thereafter and, after momentarily getting back into contention, dropped out quickly down the back straight. He isn't a betting proposition over fences until he proves he is enjoys the experience. (op 6-4 tchd 5-4)

5398 ROBERT HOLDEN NOVICES' HURDLE (12 hdls) 3m
3:20 (3:20) (Class 4) 4-Y-O+ **£2,862** (£840)

Form RPR
-133 **1** **Buck Mulligan**[33] 4861 6-11-6 128 PaulMoloney 130+
(Evan Williams) *racd w plenty of zest: trckd ldr: chalng 2 out: led last: r.o wl: readily* **15/8**[2]
152 **2** *2 1/4* **Bottman (IRE)**[8] 5285 6-11-6 121 RichardJohnson 130+
(Tim Vaughan) *j.lft: led: wnt violently lft fnl 3: hdd last: hung lft run-in and nt qckn: drifted rt fnl 110yds: wl hld at fin* **4/9**[1]

5m 56.2s (3.90) **Going Correction** -0.425s/f (Good) **2** Ran SP% **104.0**
Speed ratings (Par 105): **76,75**
TOTE £2.20.
Owner L Fell **Bred** Peter Botham **Trained** Llancarfan, Vale Of Glamorgan

FOCUS
Only three were declared for this interesting contest, so it was disappointing that the promising Turtlethomas was announced a non-runner. This developed into a sprint up the straight and the form is not sure to be upheld.

NOTEBOOK
Buck Mulligan sat in behind the leader, taking a strong hold, before keeping much straighter than that rival down the home straight. This isn't form to take too seriously, but he looks to be in good heart and will be interesting if taking up any of his two forthcoming entries. (op 7-4)
Bottman(IRE), up in trip after a good effort at Cheltenham last time, was the hare to catch but gave victory away over the final three hurdles by jumping badly left at a couple of them - he was noted to have moved the same way on his previous outing at Cheltenham. He didn't have the pace of the winner in the sprint and couldn't get back to the front. (tchd 1-2 in places)

5399 BROMFIELD SAND & GRAVEL H'CAP CHASE (FOR THE OAKLY PARK CHALLENGE CUP) (17 fncs) 2m 4f
3:50 (3:50) (Class 3) (0-135,127) 5-Y-O+ **£6,337** (£1,872; £936; £468; £234)

Form RPR
5351 **1** **Tyup Pompey (IRE)**[11] 5236 10-10-0 104 7ex LeeStephens(3) 115+
(Ann Price) *led: hdd appr 5th: mstke 8th and sn towards rr: hdwy 13th: led appr 4 out: j.lft fnl 3: styd on wl to draw clr run-in* **2/1**[1]
05P6 **2** *8* **The Snail**[11] 5236 8-11-0 115 PaulMoloney 118
(Evan Williams) *prom: lost pl bef 5th: bhd 7th: pushed along after 9th (water): hdwy to go 2nd appr 4 out: no imp on wnr bef last: no ch run-in* **16/1**
2316 **3** *13* **Prince Des Marais (FR)**[20] 5104 8-11-10 125 (t) AndrewThornton 119
(Caroline Bailey) *racd keenly: in tch: led appr 5th: mstke 9th (water): hdd bef 4 out: one pce whn hit 2 out: no ch whn hit last* **9/2**[3]
6212 **4** *2 1/2* **Sunday City (JPN)**[165] 2234 10-11-12 127 JamieMoore 122+
(Peter Bowen) *hld up in tch: blnd 5th: effrt disputing 2nd abt 2 l off the pce whn stmbld on bnd appr 4 out: lost grnd and n.d after* **7/2**[2]
4263 **5** *11* **Moulin De La Croix**[19] 5120 7-11-0 115 (t) SamTwiston-Davies 93
(Nigel Twiston-Davies) *hld up in rr: hdwy to go prom appr 9th (water): rdn and wknd bef 4 out* **9/2**[3]
-14P **6** *28* **Noble Crusader (USA)**[26] 5009 8-11-11 126 (tp) SamThomas 79
(Richard Lee) *prom: rdn appr 13th: wknd bef 4 out: t.o* **8/1**

5m 0.70s (-3.70) **Going Correction** -0.175s/f (Good) **6** Ran SP% **108.9**
Speed ratings: **100,96,91,90,86 75**
toteswingers:1&2:£8.20, 1&3:£1.10, 2&3:£13.50 CSF £25.53 TOTE £3.20: £1.60, £3.00; EX 32.10.
Owner Mrs A Price **Bred** Rosetown Syndicate **Trained** Norton, Powys

FOCUS
An open-looking handicap which could be rated a few pounds higher but is best assessed through the winner.

NOTEBOOK
Tyup Pompey(IRE), running under a 7lb penalty, has spent a lot of his career running around this track and obviously knows his way home when in contention. Due to go up another 4lb from the weekend, he was on a handy mark so he is probably one to oppose next time. (tchd 9-4)
The Snail, who was kept on the go at the start, got towards the head of affairs quite swiftly but soon dropped in behind. He stayed on well after making ground but couldn't get to the winner. (op 14-1)
Prince Des Marais(FR) led for a lot of the race but offered little when challenged. (op 5-1)
Sunday City(JPN), off since early November, was ridden with restraint and made a mistake quite early. However, he was bang in contention when slipping on the home bend and couldn't recover. (op 3-1)
Moulin De La Croix raced with plenty of enthusiasm, but offered little after coming under pressure rounding the final bend. (tchd 5-1)
Noble Crusader(USA) had cheekpieces back on in an attempt to get back on the winning trail, but minor mistakes down the back straight effectively knocked him out of it. (op 10-1)

5400 GREENHOUS VOLKSWAGEN COMMERCIAL VEHICLES H'CAP HURDLE (9 hdls) 2m
4:20 (4:20) (Class 3) (0-125,117) 4-Y-O+ **£4,683** (£1,375; £687; £343)

Form RPR
3065 **1** **Joker Choker (IRE)**[42] 4677 6-10-13 107 RichardKilloran(3) 120+
(Nicky Henderson) *sn chsd clr ldrs: led appr 3 out: styd on wl after last: wl in command fnl 50yds* **10/1**
0362 **2** *2 1/2* **Art Broker (IRE)**[38] 4783 5-10-7 105 JakeGreenall(7) 115+
(Henry Daly) *hld up: hdwy 6th: effrt to chse wnr appr 3 out: wanted to lugg rt bef last and abt 2 l down: no ex fnl 50yds* **3/1**[2]
0030 **3** *19* **Crazy Bold (GER)**[14] 5171 8-10-3 97 LeeEdwards(3) 90
(Tony Carroll) *hld up: effrt to chse ldrs 3 out: one pce whn j.lft 2 out: no ch w ldrs after: plugged on to take 3rd run-in* **11/2**[3]
0332 **4** *1 1/4* **Lap Of Honour (IRE)**[27] 4998 7-10-3 101 RobertMcCarth(7) 92
(Ferdy Murphy) *hld up: hdwy after 6th: chsd ldrs 3 out: edgd rt bef 2 out: no imp and outpcd by ldrs bef last: wknd run-in* **9/4**[1]
1F55 **5** *20* **Three Ships**[176] 2035 10-11-12 117 RobertThornton 90
(Richard Lee) *in rr: unable to go pce of ldrs bef 2 out: nvr a threat* **15/2**
303F **6** *4* **Just One Thing (IRE)**[45] 4530 6-10-10 101 PaulMoloney 70
(Evan Williams) *led and clr w rival: hdd appr 5th: nt fluent 6th whn stl w ldr: wknd bef 3 out* **15/2**
P-5 **P** **Lightening Sky (IRE)**[177] 2029 8-11-5 110 (p) JohnnyFarrelly —
(Joseph Fox, Ire) *w ldr and clr of others: led appr 5th where nt fluent: nt fluent 6th: hdd appr 3 out: wknd bef 2 out: t.o whn p.u bef last* **9/1**

3m 39.8s (-9.70) **Going Correction** -0.425s/f (Good) **7** Ran SP% **113.8**
Speed ratings (Par 107): **107,105,96,95,85 83,—**
toteswingers:1&2:£6.40, 1&3:£9.80, 2&3:£4.80 CSF £40.30 TOTE £15.60: £4.80, £2.10; EX 45.70.
Owner Bradley Partnership **Bred** Michael Heskin **Trained** Upper Lambourn, Berks

FOCUS
Just One Thing went off with Lightening Sky in front and the pair appeared to go too fast. That proved to be the case as they both retreated quickly, at different stages, as their rivals loomed up. The first two are rated big improvers with the third rated in line with recent form.

NOTEBOOK
Joker Choker(IRE) doesn't look one of his powerful stable's superstars, but he collected his first success here in good style on his handicap debut. Lightly raced, he should have a bit more to come. (op 9-1 tchd 11-1)
Art Broker(IRE) came into the race on the back of a good performance, so he helps to uphold the form. He ought to win something similar in the coming weeks. (op 11-4)
Crazy Bold(GER) was back down to his last winning mark, but wasn't able to capitalise on it. (op 8-1)
Lap Of Honour(IRE) has been running to a reasonable level, so this was a little disappointing. (op 11-4)
Three Ships, a previous C&D winner, has now disappointed on his last three starts after what was a promising debut for the Richard Lee stable. (op 7-1 tchd 13-2)

5401 MCCONNEL NOVICES' H'CAP HURDLE (11 hdls) 2m 5f
4:50 (4:50) (Class 4) (0-115,113) 4-Y-O+ **£2,862** (£840; £420; £209)

Form RPR
4346 **1** **Ben Cee Pee M (IRE)**[30] 4929 6-10-10 97 (b[1]) LeightonAspell 106+
(Oliver Sherwood) *hld up: hdwy 8th: led 2 out: r.o wl to draw clr run-in* **5/2**[1]
0P56 **2** *5* **Eldred (IRE)**[47] 4479 5-11-8 112 DavidBass(3) 114
(Nicky Henderson) *trckd ldrs: chalng appr 3 out: rdn and ev ch 2 out: outpcd by wnr run-in* **7/1**[3]
0302 **3** *1/2* **Apache Chant (USA)**[11] 5234 7-10-9 99 (p) LeeEdwards(3) 102
(Tony Carroll) *trckd ldrs: pushed along after 8th: kpt on same pce u.p fr 2 out* **5/2**[1]
-061 **4** *15* **Royal Riviera**[22] 5074 5-11-12 113 SamTwiston-Davies 104+
(Nigel Twiston-Davies) *prom: led 5th: hdd and nt fluent 2 out: wknd appr last* **5/1**[2]
0002 **5** *31* **Second Brook (IRE)**[21] 5082 4-10-5 105 PeterHatton(7) 80
(Reg Hollinshead) *hld up: hdwy after 8th: chsd effrt to chse ldrs bef 3 out: btn whn hit 2 out: sn eased* **17/2**
11P **6** *59* **Eastwell Smiles**[82] 3820 7-11-6 107 (bt) PaulMoloney 15
(Sophie Leech) *led: hdd 5th: remained handy tl wknd appr 3 out: t.o* **15/2**
0/ **P** **Van Boxtal (IRE)**[572] 1541 8-10-3 90 JohnnyFarrelly —
(Joseph Fox, Ire) *hld up in tch: hdwy after 6th: wknd after 8th: t.o whn p.u bef 3 out* **25/1**

5m 8.10s (-6.70) **Going Correction** -0.425s/f (Good)
WFA 4 from 5yo+ 6lb **7** Ran SP% **112.4**
Speed ratings (Par 105): **95,93,92,87,75 52,—**
toteswingers:1&2:£5.10, 1&3:£1.70, 2&3:£4.90 CSF £19.32 CT £46.40 TOTE £3.10: £2.00, £3.60; EX 22.40.
Owner CPM Group Limited **Bred** Daniel Fogarty **Trained** Upper Lambourn, Berks

FOCUS
The early pace was modest to say the least, so this probably isn't solid form. The winner is rated to his bumper mark with the third to recent course form.

NOTEBOOK
Ben Cee Pee M(IRE), wearing blinkers for the first time, was the subject of sustained support throughout the day and won with a bit to spare once getting to the front. His only previous victory had come on officially good to firm ground, so maybe that is why he was so heavily punted after an ordinary performance on his previous outing. (op 7-2)
Eldred(IRE) got as close as he has done to winning on this handicap debut and is probably still open to more improvement. (op 6-1)
Apache Chant(USA), due to go up 6lb, needed strong riding to stay in contention but was easily held. (op 11-4)
Royal Riviera travelled nicely in front once there, but was made to look woefully one paced by the three that finished in front of him down the home straight. (op 9-2 tchd 11-2)
Second Brook(IRE), beaten in a claimer last time, found no improvement for the step up in distance. (op 8-1)

Eastwell Smiles took a strong hold while the gallop wasn't strong and weakened right out of it. His record suggests he prefers much easier ground. (op 13-2 tchd 8-1)

5402 ABBERLEY HALL OLD BOYS ASSOCIATION HUNTERS' CHASE (17 fncs) 2m 4f
5:15 (5:15) (Class 5) 5-Y-O+ **£1,623** (£503; £251; £125)

Form RPR
-4U1 **1** **Theatre Diva (IRE)**[11] 5237 10-11-4 120 MissJBuck(7) 117+
(Miss J Du Plessis) *in rr: hdwy 10th: led 3 out: j.lft 2 out and last: r.o wl to draw clr run-in* **11/10**[1]

2P53 **2** *16* **Captain Marlon (IRE)**[38] 4786 10-11-10 92 MrJoshuaGuerriero 101
(Miss C Wright) *hld up: hdwy 7th: chsng ldrs whn mstke 4 out: wnt 2nd appr 2 out: one pce bef last* **16/1**

U6U2 **3** *3* **Fairwood Present (IRE)**[11] 5237 13-11-3 117 MrTGarner(7) 96
(John Buxton) *chsd ldrs: wnt 2nd 7th: ev ch appr 4 out tl bef 2 out: one pce bef last* **7/2**[3]

-60P **4** *1* **Triple Bluff**[3] 5372 8-11-3 0 MrJABest(7) 97
(Miss J Du Plessis) *led: mstke 13th: rdn and hdd 3 out: wknd bef last* **33/1**

5504 **5** *14* **Little Rocker (IRE)**[11] 5237 10-11-3 94 MrOscarChurton(7) 84
(R Smart) *in tch: bhd fr 5th: toiling fnl circ* **33/1**

333P **6** *nk* **Almaydan**[11] 5237 13-11-5 122 (b) MrWKinsey(5) 83
(Mrs K M Diggle) *chsd ldrs: rdn and wknd appr 13th* **3/1**[2]

1453 **P** **Emotional Article (IRE)**[11] 5237 11-11-7 118 MrAWadlow(7) —
(Mrs Belinda Clarke) *prom: lost pl 3rd: bhd fr 7th: toiling fnl circ: wnt wrong and p.u bef last: dismntd* **16/1**

524/ **P** **Bougoure (IRE)**[11] 12-11-5 0 MrGCrow(5) —
(Miss N Higham) *midfield: lost pl bef 7th: bhd and struggling after 9th (water): p.u bef 11th* **20/1**

P **Commadore Barry (IRE)**[308] 779 10-11-5 0 MrJBanks(5) —
(Mrs Trish Cleverdon Lucy) *prom: wkng whn stmbld 10th: wl bhd whn p.u bef 11th* **66/1**

4m 58.3s (-6.10) **Going Correction** -0.175s/f (Good) **9** Ran SP% **118.7**
Speed ratings: **105,98,97,97,91 91,—,—,—**
toteswingers:1&2:£5.10, 1&3:£1.70, 2&3:£4.90. Tote Super 7: Win: Not won. Place: Not won CSF £19.43 TOTE £1.80: £1.10, £2.60, £1.20; EX 12.40.
Owner Miss J Du Plessis **Bred** K J Manning **Trained** Saltash, Cornwall

FOCUS
The gallop set by Triple Bluff, among others, was strong, which would have helped his stablemate the winner. The runner-up sets the level backed up by the fourth.

NOTEBOOK
Theatre Diva(IRE) does stay further than this distance. Given a wonderfully confident ride, her run was timed to perfection and the pair won clearly, meaning a second successive victory in the race. (op 8-11)
Captain Marlon(IRE) is often a strong traveller but doesn't always do it at the end. He probably would have been beaten by Theatre Diva, but a mistake four out didn't help his cause. (op 12-1)
Fairwood Present(IRE) ran a fantastic race for a 13-y-o, showing plenty of enthusiasm towards the head of affairs. Being a son on Presenting, the quick ground was probably to his advantage despite the fact he has winning form on an easier surface. (op 4-1)
Almaydan, another 13-y-o, appeared to go well for the majority of the race but quickly dropped out after coming under pressure down the back straight on their final circuit. He generally wanted ease in the ground when winning under rules. (op 7-1)
T/Jkpt: £33,494.90 to a £1 stake. Pool:£47,176.02 - 1.00 winning ticket T/Plt: £968.50 to a £1 stake. Pool:£53,878.31 - 40.61 winning tickets T/Qpdt: £79.60 to a £1 stake. Pool:£3,940.93 - 36.60 winning tickets DO

5239 WINCANTON (R-H)
Thursday, April 21

OFFICIAL GOING: Good to firm (watered; chase 8.8, hurdle 9.1)
Both courses at inner configuration on ground not used since October.
Wind: Moderate ahead Weather: Sunny

5403 HIGOS INSURANCE GLASTONBURY MARES' NOVICES' HURDLE (11 hdls) 2m 6f
2:10 (2:11) (Class 4) 4-Y-O+ **£4,293** (£1,260; £630; £314)

Form RPR
0602 **1** **Miss Overdrive**[11] 5230 7-11-5 120 NickScholfield 112+
(Andy Turnell) *mde all at mod early pce: hit 4th: stdd and nt fluent 6th: c clr again 3 out: in n.d whn hit last: won easing down* **1/3**[1]

32 **2** *20* **Be Kind**[9] 5274 5-10-9 0 EamonDehdashti(3) 78
(Karen George) *t.k.h off mod pce: trckd wnr to 5th and again 7th: no ch fr 3 out but stl clr 2nd: drvn next: mstke and rdr lost irons last* **5/1**[2]

/P-3 **3** *13* **Little Fee**[11] 5239 6-10-12 0 AndrewGlassonbury 66
(Colin Mitchell) *t.k.h off mod pce: chsd wnr 5th to 6th: wknd qckly after 3 out: poor 3rd whn blnd 2 out* **9/1**[3]

06 **4** *67* **Poetic Beat**[32] 4897 6-10-5 0 (t) MissCLWills(7) 5
(Seamus Durack) *in rr tl clsd w ldrs as pce stdd 6th: wknd after 4 out: t.o* **50/1**

54-0 **P** **My Legal Lady**[76] 3936 6-10-12 0 JodieMogford —
(Stuart Howe) *nvr jumping wl: a wl bhd: t.o whn p.u bef 4 out* **16/1**

5m 8.20s (-18.30) **Going Correction** -0.925s/f (Hard) **5** Ran SP% **109.5**
Speed ratings (Par 105): **96,88,84,59,—**
CSF £2.53 TOTE £1.30: £1.10, £1.40; EX 2.10.
Owner Partners In Wine **Bred** R And J Micklethwait **Trained** Broad Hinton, Wilts

FOCUS
The going was good to firm. On a dry, sunny day, it was only going to get quicker, though there was a good covering. An uncompetitive mares' hurdle with the second rated to her mark.

NOTEBOOK
Miss Overdrive was offered a golden opportunity and she always had things under control, reasserting towards the end of the back and galloping clear in the straight for a second career victory. (op 1-2 tchd 3-10)
Be Kind kept tabs on the winner until the straight, but was soon left behind. She may need a drop in grade. (op 7-2)
Little Fee kept on for a remote third but was well beaten. (op 11-1 tchd 12-1)
My Legal Lady didn't look a natural on this hurdles debut, jumping badly left and eventually pulling up. (tchd 14-1 and 22-1)

5404 AXMINSTER CARPETS H'CAP HURDLE (11 hdls) 2m 6f
2:40 (2:40) (Class 3) (0-125,121) 4-Y-O+ **£4,293** (£1,260; £630; £314)

Form RPR
1000 **1** **Moghaayer**[47] 4464 6-11-6 115 (b[1]) APMcCoy 120
(Nicky Henderson) *led: jnd 4th to 5th: hdd appr 2 out: rallied u.p appr last: styd on to ld nr fin* **7/4**[1]

4F63 **2** *¾* **Forest Rhythm (IRE)**[3] 5369 7-10-4 102 (t) WayneKavanagh(3) 107
(Seamus Mullins) *t.k.h towards rr but in tch: hdwy to trckd wnr 7th: led appr 2 out: sn rdn: kpt on tl hdd nr fin* **5/2**[2]

2240 **3** *16* **Lupanar (IRE)**[11] 5230 7-11-2 121 (p) JosephAkehurst(10) 111
(Gary Moore) *in rr but in tch: rdn 3 out: drvn to take 3rd appr 2 out but nvr any ch w ldng trio* **10/3**[3]

0300 **4** *5* **Noddies Way**[8] 5289 8-10-5 100 DarylJacob 88
(John Panvert) *trckd wnr: chal 4th to 5th: reminders after 6th: hit 7th and lost 2nd: wknd after 3 out and lost 3rd appr 2 out* **12/1**

006F **5** *5* **Anak (IRE)**[9] 5278 5-11-5 114 (b) DenisO'Regan 96
(Jim Best) *j. slowly 1st: cl up to 4th: sn in rr but in tch: j. slowly 4 out: rdn and n.m.r on rails after 3 out: wknd rapidly* **7/1**

5m 6.34s (-20.16) **Going Correction** -0.925s/f (Hard) **5** Ran SP% **108.2**
Speed ratings (Par 107): **99,98,92,91,89**
CSF £6.42 TOTE £2.60: £2.00, £1.80; EX 7.50.
Owner The Ten From Seven **Bred** Goldford Stud **Trained** Upper Lambourn, Berks

FOCUS
The front pair drew clear in what was an ordinary handicap hurdle. They are rated to form although it is not a contest to be confident about.

NOTEBOOK
Moghaayer has been proving inconsistent, but the application of first-time blinkers and persuasion of McCoy were enough for him to get his head back in front, simply outstaying the runner-up close home. It remains to be see whether he builds on this. (op 5-2)
Forest Rhythm(IRE), up in trip and making a quick reappearance, pulled hard early and was sent on plenty soon enough, those two factors ultimately leading to his defeat. He travelled much the best with the tongue-tie back on and perhaps 2m4f is his trip. (op 2-1)
Lupanar(IRE) kept on for pressure, but remains too high in the weights. (op 11-4)
Noddies Way, for whom there were nibbles in the market jumped hesitantly at times, and notably left, and was left trailing down the back. (op 16-1 tchd 11-1)
Anak(IRE) needs softer ground than this and was well held. (op 8-1 tchd 13-2)

5405 HIGOS SOMERSET NATIONAL H'CAP CHASE (22 fncs) 3m 3f 110y
3:10 (3:10) (Class 3) (0-130,124) 5-Y-O+ **£5,259** (£1,553; £776; £388; £194)

Form RPR
2423 **1** **The Ferbane Man (IRE)**[44] 4543 7-11-2 114 (v[1]) APMcCoy 122+
(Tim Vaughan) *trckd ldrs: mstke 17th and 18th: drvn and styd on to chal 3 out: led sn after: kpt on u.p run-in: strly chal in triple fin: jst lasted* **10/3**[2]

4321 **2** *nse* **Upham Atom**[25] 5037 8-11-4 116 LiamTreadwell 124+
(Kate Buckett) *in rr but in tch: hit 16th: hdwy and mstke 18th: stl 4th after 4 out: rallied fr 2 out but stl 3 l 3rd last: str run u.p fnl 25yds: jst failed in triple fin* **2/1**[1]

3353 **3** *shd* **Knighton Combe**[16] 5152 11-11-11 123 DarylJacob 128
(Jamie Snowden) *trckd ldr: chal fr 17th and stl chalng fr 4 out tl led appr 3 out but sn jnd: styd on to press wnr fnl 20yds: jst failed in triple fin* **8/1**

51P6 **4** *7* **Double Dizzy**[26] 5009 10-11-3 115 (bt) AndrewGlassonbury 114
(Bob Buckler) *led: jnd fr 17th: stl slt ld 4 out: hdd appr 3 out: wknd fr next* **15/2**

U332 **5** *12* **Earth Planet (IRE)**[23] 5067 9-11-0 117 (bt) MrRMahon(5) 105
(Paul Nicholls) *in rr but in tch: hdwy to cl on ldrs 17th: wknd 4 out* **5/1**[3]

6P1F **P** **Cold Mountain (IRE)**[5] 5338 9-11-9 124 JimmyDerham(3) —
(Seamus Mullins) *in tch: hdwy to chal 17th to next: wknd qckly 4 out: t.o and p.u bef 2 out* **13/2**

6m 45.24s (-22.96) **Going Correction** -0.625s/f (Firm) **6** Ran SP% **109.3**
Speed ratings: **107,106,106,104,101 —**
toteswingers:1&2:£1.10, 1&3:£2.20, 2&3:£8.60 CSF £10.28 TOTE £4.40: £2.00, £1.60; EX 8.10.
Owner Aidan & Gerard Flynn **Bred** Oliver Loughlin **Trained** Aberthin, Vale of Glamorgan

FOCUS
The best race on the card and it produced a thrilling finish, anyone of three being in with a chance on the run to the line. The winner and third are rated back to form.

NOTEBOOK
The Ferbane Man(IRE), wearing a first-time visor, who emerged victorious, just holding on under an all-out McCoy ride. He had started to lose his form, but the return to a lively surface enabled him to recapture his best and he may win again in the coming months. (op 7-2)
Upham Atom should have won, some shoddy jumping down the back ultimately costing him victory. This progressive sort fairly flew home after the last, and clearly stays well, so will surely being ridden more positively in future. This was only his fifth chase start and there's more to come. (op 9-4)
Knighton Combe was more at home back over fences and he took a narrow lead three out, but despite sticking on right the way to the line, came up just short. (op 11-2)
Double Dizzy, for whom the ground would have been on the quick side, ran well considering. (op 14-1)
Earth Planet(IRE) again travelled before failing to make any impression on the leaders. (tchd 9-2 and 11-2)
Cold Mountain(IRE), reappearing just five days after falling in the Scottish National, failed to give his true running. (op 5-1)

5406 HIGOS FOR ALL YOUR COMMERCIAL INSURANCE NOVICES' H'CAP HURDLE (8 hdls) 2m
3:40 (3:41) (Class 4) (0-105,104) 4-Y-O+ **£2,341** (£687; £343; £171)

Form RPR
0000 **1** **Aine's Delight (IRE)**[11] 5244 5-10-12 90 NickScholfield 102+
(Andy Turnell) *hld up in rr: stdy hdwy fr 3 out to chal 2 out: pushed clr last: easily* **3/1**[2]

4001 **2** *5* **Taste The Wine (IRE)**[12] 5212 5-11-7 104 MarkQuinlan(5) 110+
(Bernard Llewellyn) *trckd ldrs: hdwy to take slt ld and nt fluent 2 out: hdd sn after: no ch w wnr last: one pce* **13/8**[1]

5020 **3** *7* **Raise Again (IRE)**[161] 2333 8-10-8 89 KeiranBurke(3) 87
(Nerys Dutfield) *chsd ldrs: rdn 3 out: chal 2 out: sn outpcd by ldng duo: kpt on same pce for wl-hld 3rd* **7/1**

24P **4** *hd* **Moonbalej**[48] 4452 4-10-4 90 (vt) JimmyDerham(3) 83
(Milton Harris) *w ldr 2nd: led sn after: rdn and narrowly hdd 2 out: sn no ch w ldng duo and outpcd for wl-hld 3rd run-in* **6/1**[3]

0/ **5** *22* **Capdalight (IRE)**[25] 8-10-0 85 MrJHodson(7) 63
(A J Kennedy, Ire) *j. slowly 4 out: a bhd* **12/1**

P3PP **P** **Medicine Man (IRE)**[25] 5036 7-11-10 102 DarylJacob —
(Ben De Haan) *led: jnd 2nd: hdd sn after: chsd ldr tl after 4 out: wknd qckly after 3 out: t.o whn p.u bef next* **8/1**

3m 31.73s (-17.17) **Going Correction** -0.925s/f (Hard)
WFA 4 from 5yo+ 5lb **6** Ran SP% **108.7**
Speed ratings (Par 105): **105,102,99,98,87 —**
toteswingers:1&2:£1.10, 1&3:£7.00, 2&3:£5.80 CSF £8.01 TOTE £4.70: £1.50, £2.00; EX 5.50.
Owner Andrew Turnell **Bred** Dr John Hollowood And Aiden Murphy **Trained** Broad Hinton, Wilts

FOCUS
No Mauritino, who would have been a red-hot favourite, so this became quite an open novice handicap. The first two are on the upgrade and the third and fourth are rated close to their marks.

NOTEBOOK
Aine's Delight(IRE), who had finished behind late defector Mauritino last time, proved much the best, travelling strongly and readily asserting on the run to the last. Having only her fifth hurdles start, she clearly bounces off a fast surface and it will be both disappointing and surprising if she can't go in again. (op 7-2 tchd 11-4)

Taste The Wine(IRE), up 12lb for his Chepstow win, needed to pull out more and wasn't up to it, a mistake two out not helping. He still held every chance, though. (op 7-4 tchd 11-8)

Raise Again(IRE) travelled well but couldn't race on, making it 0-24 over hurdles. (op 13-2)

Moonbalej made a lot of the running before being swept aside from two out. (op 7-1)

Medicine Man(IRE) made one notable blunder that did for his chance on this return to hurdles. (op 15-2)

5407 RED RUBY DEVONS BIRTHDAY H'CAP CHASE (21 fncs) 3m 1f 110y
4:10 (4:10) (Class 4) (0-100,93) 5-Y-0+ **£3,265** (£1,013; £545)

Form				RPR
4506	1		**Classic Clover**[28] 4969 11-10-13 **87**.....(t) SClements(7) (Colin Tizzard) *trckd ldr: chal 9th: led next and reminders sn after: and again 17th: idling fr 3 out and pushed along fr 2 out: rousted and faltering run-in but a jst doing enough: (carried 2lb more - ex plate inadvertently added to sddle)* **8/1**	96+
0463	2	1 ½	**Reymysterio (IRE)**[10] 5256 10-10-11 **81**.....(tp) KeiranBurke(3) (Patrick Rodford) *racd in 3rd: chsd wnr fr 13th: outstyd 3 out: rallied fr 2 out as wnr idled: kpt on run-in but a hld* **11/2**[3]	84
0606	3	34	**Terrible Tenant**[24] 5060 12-10-13 **83**.....(p) JimmyDerham(3) (Seamus Mullins) *led to 10th: dropped to 3rd 13th: sn no ch w ldng duo* **7/2**[2]	61
P422	U		**Skipper's Lad (IRE)**[25] 5037 9-11-12 **93**.....(bt) JoeTizzard (Colin Tizzard) *nvr travelling in last pl: hit 7th: reminders 8th: brief effrt 14th but nvr anywhere nr ldrs: sn t.o: ref and uns rdr 2 out* **8/11**[1]	—

6m 22.81s (-16.69) **Going Correction** -0.625s/f (Firm) 4 Ran SP% **106.6**
Speed ratings: **100,99,89,—**
CSF £38.93 TOTE £12.00; EX 57.60.

Owner John and Heather Snook **Bred** M H Ings **Trained** Milborne Port, Dorset

FOCUS
A strange race, with red-hot favourite Skipper's Lad never going a yard, and his stablemate scoring. The first two set the level in a weak race.

NOTEBOOK
Classic Clover, who has been completely out-of-sorts, held on despite dossing under pressure from the end of the back straight. His recent form in hunter chases has been atrocious, but he was well weighted if returning to anything like his best, and his useful rider got the best out of him. One wouldn't want to bank on him repeating this form next time, however. (op 15-2 tchd 17-2)

Reymysterio(IRE) ran a bit better at Ffos Las the time before and he looked the likely winner starting out down the back, but was beaten before they reached the straight and only got as close as they did due to the winner idling. (op 4-1)

Terrible Tenant is well handicapped, but was taken on for the lead by the winner and that affected his performance, losing touch with the front two down the back. He remains below his best. (op 4-1)

Skipper's Lad(IRE), runner-up each of the last twice, looked a solid favourite, but he jumped slowly early on and was beaten after about a mile, ultimately getting rid of his rider when trying to refuse two out. This clearly wasn't his form, but it's no coincidence he hasn't won since 2009. (op 5-6 tchd 10-11 in a place)

5408 HIGOS THATCHED INSURANCE "NEWCOMERS" STANDARD OPEN NATIONAL HUNT FLAT RACE 2m
4:40 (4:40) (Class 6) 4-6-Y-0 **£1,370** (£399; £199)

Form				RPR
	1		**Indie Go (IRE)** 5-10-12 0..... CO'Farrell(5) (Cathy Hamilton) *trckd ldrs: drvn and qcknd to ld appr fnl f: pushed out: readily* **33/1**	95+
	2	5	**Chuckery (IRE)** 5-11-3 0.....(t) APMcCoy (Tim Vaughan) *led at mod pce: jnd 4f out: narrowly hdd ins fnl 3f: styd chalng tl outpcd by wnr fnl f but rallied to retake 2nd nr fin* **7/2**[3]	91
	3	¾	**Ambrose Hill Lad** 5-10-12 0..... MrRMahon(5) (Paul Nicholls) *pressed ldr: chal 4f out: slt ld ins fnl 3f: green over 2f out: hdd appr fnl f: sn outpcd by wnr: no ex and lost 2nd nr fin* **5/2**[2]	90
	4	3	**Shufflewing (IRE)** 4-10-5 0..... TomO'Brien (Hughie Morrison) *t.k.h off mod pce: trckd ldrs: drvn to chal over 2f out: wknd appr fnl f* **6/4**[1]	75
	5	5	**Midnight Lira** 4-10-2 0..... IanPopham(3) (Caroline Keevil) *in rr but in tch: rdn and effrt to cl on ldrs 3f out: wknd over 2f out* **9/1**	71
	6	4	**Tula Tots** 5-10-7 0..... WayneKavanagh(3) (Caroline Keevil) *in rr but in tch: sme hdwy to cl one ldrs 3f out: sn wknd* **11/1**	72

3m 45.57s (2.27) **Going Correction** -0.925s/f (Hard)
WFA 4 from 5yo 5lb 6 Ran SP% **112.1**
Speed ratings: **57,54,54,52,50 48**
toteswingers:1&2:£9.60, 1&3:£9.60, 2&3:£2.80 CSF £141.92 TOTE £46.10: £9.90, £2.80; EX 141.20.

Owner Family Goes Racing **Bred** J Kennedy **Trained** Kington Magna, Dorset

FOCUS
An interesting contest on paper, but the pace was very slow, even for a bumper, and it produced a shock result.

NOTEBOOK
Indie Go(IRE), the complete outsider, picked up strongly and came right away close home, providing his trainer with a first bumper winner at the first attempt. Picked up for just £1,100, it'll be nice to see him build on this in a more truly-run race, as he looks a nice prospect. (op 28-1 tchd 25-1)

Chuckery(IRE), the pick of the paddock, cost £8,000 and had the assistance of McCoy. He kept on well for second, but couldn't match the winner's acceleration. He should improve. (op 11-4 tchd 4-1)

Ambrose Hill Lad, whose dam was an Irish point and bumper winner, and also successful over fences, travelled strongly, but ran green once coming under pressure and was ultimately outpaced. He's probably the one to take from the race with the future in mind. (op 10-3 tchd 7-2)

Shufflewing(IRE), from a yard that is 5-13 in bumpers in recent years, was solid in the market, but her trainer wasn't overly confident about her chance beforehand and she could find no extra inside the final 2f. (op 7-4)

Midnight Lira, who played up and unseated her rider in the paddock, looked in need of the experience. (op 8-1 tchd 6-1)

T/Plt: £121.80 to a £1 stake. Pool:£46,034.99 - 275.73 winning tickets T/Qpdt: £75.00 to a £1 stake. Pool:£2,443.52 - 24.10 winning tickets ST

5409 - 5412a (Foreign Racing) - See Raceform Interactive

4958 CARLISLE (R-H)
Saturday, April 23

OFFICIAL GOING: Good to firm (good in places) changing to good after race 5 (4.35)
Wind: Light 1/2 against Weather: Overcast, rain race 4 onwards

5413 BET ON TOTEPLACEPOT AT TOTESPORT.COM NOVICES' CHASE (12 fncs) 2m
2:10 (2:10) (Class 4) 5-Y-0+ **£3,252** (£955; £477; £238)

Form				RPR
-U23	1		**Indian Groom (IRE)**[44] 4570 6-10-12 128..... WilsonRenwick (Howard Johnson) *trckd ldrs: j.rt: wnt cl 2nd 3 out: upsides next: hit last: rdn to forge clr fnl 150yds* **5/6**[1]	110+
P0FP	2	4	**Steel Man (IRE)**[48] 4510 9-10-12 48..... TomMessenger (Bruce Mactaggart) *led: jnd 2 out: hdd and no ex run-in* **100/1**	103
3321	3	4 ½	**Lord Villez (FR)**[34] 4890 7-10-12 125..... TonyKelly(7) (Ferdy Murphy) *chsd ldr: reminders after 6th: rdn 4 out: one pce* **6/4**[2]	106
5P30	4	37	**Still Calm**[22] 5095 7-10-12 74.....(t) MichaelMcAlister (Maurice Barnes) *nt fluent: in tch: blnd 6th: hit 4 out: sn lost pl and bhd: mstke 2 out* **25/1**	66
/360	P		**Dechiper (IRE)**[19] 5147 9-10-12 0..... KennyJohnson (Robert Johnson) *nt jump wl: sn detached in last: t.o 5th: p.u bef last* **10/1**[3]	—

4m 8.20s (-7.90) **Going Correction** -0.825s/f (Firm) 5 Ran SP% **108.5**
Speed ratings: **86,84,81,63,—**
CSF £24.91 TOTE £1.60: £1.10, £7.70; EX 64.10.

Owner J Howard Johnson **Bred** Tallyho Stud, J Delahooke & P Twoomey **Trained** Billy Row, Co Durham

FOCUS
Underfoot conditions were officially described as good to firm, good in places (down the hill), with a GoingStick reading of 8.5. A novice chase in which only two had obvious form claims, the time was slow and it is not a race to be confident about.

NOTEBOOK
Indian Groom(IRE), behind Lord Villez on his latest start but 7lb better off, comprehensively turned the form around. He raced in third for much of the journey, but quickened into second turning for home and took the lead just before the final fence. He was not entirely fluent there, but still had easily enough in the tank to draw away from the runner-up. (tchd 10-11)

Steel Man(IRE), well beaten on his only completed outing over fences before this, attempted to make all. The gallop he set was not especially fast, with the rest content to follow in Indian file, but he jumped adequately and was still in front between the last two fences. Once the winner eased into a higher gear, however, he was always fighting a losing battle. (tchd 80-1)

Lord Villez(FR), who had broken his duck over fences at the 24th attempt here last time out, was disappointing. He raced in second until four out, but made a mistake at that fence and could not up his game subsequently. (tchd 11-8)

Still Calm, with an official mark of 74, was always fourth. A mistake two from home put paid to any chance of his improving on that position.

5414 BET ON TOTESCOOP6 AT TOTESPORT.COM H'CAP CHASE (19 fncs) 3m 2f
2:45 (2:45) (Class 5) (0-95,92) 5-Y-0+ **£1,626** (£477; £238; £119)

Form				RPR
3P5U	1		**Teenando (IRE)**[12] 5258 11-10-7 **73**..... TomMessenger (Sue Smith) *mde all: styd on strly to forge clr gng to 2 out: kpt on wl* **9/2**[3]	85+
250F	2	7	**Almond Court (IRE)**[37] 4826 8-10-0 **66** oh2.....(p) KennyJohnson (Robert Johnson) *trckd ldr: outpcd 4 out: kpt on to chse wnr appr 2 out: no imp* **6/1**	72
U046	3	15	**Devil Water**[44] 4573 8-11-1 **88**.....(t) NathanMoscrop(7) (James Ewart) *t.k.h: jnd ldrs 11th: chal 4 out: wknd fr next* **17/2**	83
PP36	4	1 ¾	**Panama At Once**[22] 5097 11-10-13 **79**.....(p) RichieMcGrath (Philip Kirby) *hmpd bnd after 1st: chsd ldrs: outpcd and lost pl 14th: kpt on fr last* **4/1**[2]	70
P2P2	P		**Shrewd Investor (IRE)**[22] 5097 11-11-12 **92**.....(b) RobertWalford (Henry Hogarth) *hmpd bnd after 1st: chsd ldrs: hit 5th: reminders and lost pl 10th: t.o whn p.u bef next* **7/2**[1]	—
64P0	U		**Norminster**[12] 5258 10-10-0 **69**.....(p) EwanWhillans(3) (Rayson Nixon) *hit 3rd: wnt prom 10th: blnd and uns rdr next* **15/2**	—
563-	P		**Bayfirth (IRE)**[512] 2543 8-10-3 **76**..... GaryRutherford(7) (Tim Butt) *hdwy to chse ldrs 11th: sn lost pl and bhd: t.o 13th: p.u bef 4 out* **5/1**	—

6m 43.6s (-23.60) **Going Correction** -0.825s/f (Firm) 7 Ran SP% **113.6**
Speed ratings: **103,100,96,95,— —,—**
toteswingers: 1&2 £2.00, 1&3 £22.70, 2&3 £17.60. CSF £30.44 TOTE £4.50: £2.70, £3.90; EX 26.30.

Owner Mrs S Smith **Bred** Noel Collins **Trained** High Eldwick, W Yorks

FOCUS
A low-grade handicap chase, with the top weight rated a mere 92. The runner-up looks the best guide.

NOTEBOOK
Teenando(IRE), a winner off 93 in 2009 but without a success since, notched his fourth course victory thanks to a fine round of jumping. Headed briefly at the start, he was soon out in front and led all the way to the fourth-last. Overtaken by the eventual third at that point, he responded generously when asked to rally and was back at the head of affairs before two out. He was always in command thereafter. (op 7-2)

Almond Court(IRE), making her first appearance in a handicap chase from 2lb out of the weights, ran a fine race in the circumstances. In front for the first couple of hundred yards, she raced in second when the winner took over and chased the pace gamely until tiring slightly on the run-in. (op 9-1)

Devil Water, an 88-rated maiden under rules, was another to post a game display, even if he never seemed likely to collect. Patiently ridden on the first circuit, he got into contention four out, before fading in the closing stages. (op 8-1)

Panama At Once, well behind the pulled-up Shrewd Investor on his most recent start, was always in about the same place. He lacked the pace to get seriously involved in the home straight.

Shrewd Investor(IRE) was reportedly never travelling. (tchd 4-1)

5415 FREE RACING POST FORM AT TOTESPORT.COM NOVICES' CHASE (16 fncs) 2m 4f
3:20 (3:20) (Class 3) 5-Y-0+ **£4,878** (£1,432; £716; £357)

Form				RPR
0262	1		**Montoya's Son (IRE)**[12] 5261 6-10-7 120..... PaulGallagher(5) (Howard Johnson) *j.lft: mde virtually all: styd on fr 3 out: eased towards fin* **8/13**[1]	108+

4054 **2** *2* **Currahee**[9] 5310 7-10-12 0 (t) MichaelMcAlister 103
(Maurice Barnes) *chsd ldrs: bmpd 1st: hit 6th: outpcd 9th: wnt 2nd 11th: rdn 4 out: kpt on same pce run-in* **11/2**[3]

235- **3** *18* **Lord Samposin**[661] 834 10-10-12 0 (t) RichieMcGrath 89
(Maurice Barnes) *w wnr: hmpd 2nd: t.k.h: 3rd whn hmpd bnd bef 4 out: wkng whn hit 4 out* **11/1**

5P5P **4** *5* **Just Posh**[45] 4550 9-10-5 0 (p) RyanMania 74
(Rayson Nixon) *prom: outpcd 9th: bhd fr 12th: eased clsng stages* **25/1**

U40P **U** **Big Burrows (IRE)**[28] 5001 9-10-11 119 TonyKelly(7) —
(Ferdy Murphy) *chsd ldrs: j.lft 1st: blnd and uns rdr 2nd* **4/1**[2]

5m 13.6s (-13.80) **Going Correction** -0.825s/f (Firm) **5** Ran SP% **109.5**
Speed ratings: **94,93,86,84,—**
CSF £4.57 TOTE £1.70: £1.10, £3.60; EX 3.20.

Owner Andrea & Graham Wylie **Bred** Dr Marie Madden **Trained** Billy Row, Co Durham

FOCUS
Just a run-of-the-mill novice chase, but the winner seems to have the scope to progress. The second looks the best guide in a weak contest.

NOTEBOOK
Montoya's Son(IRE), second from a mark of 115 in a Hexham handicap chase 12 days earlier, made virtually all the running. Awkward at the first few fences, where he showed a tendency to jump left, he soon warmed to his task and won with something to spare. The form he showed here is far from outstanding, but this should not be the last time he collects. (op 4-7)

Currahee, whose jumping has not always been convincing, negotiated most of the fences adequately here. He raced in third for more than half the contest, but went second before the fourth-last and kept the winner honest until comfortably outpaced on the run-in. (op 15-2)

Lord Samposin, making his first appearance for 661 days, ran as if the outing would bring him on. He was keen in the early stages and, after disputing second for much of the journey, tired quickly in the home straight. (op 12-1 tchd 10-1)

Just Posh, a 71-rated hurdler who had looked modest over fences on previous attempts in this sphere, was always trailing. (op 22-1)

5416 BET TOTEPOOL AT TOTESPORT.COM H'CAP CHASE (18 fncs) 3m 110y
3:55 (3:55) (Class 3) (0-130,129) 5-Y-0+ **£13,010** (£3,820; £1,910; £954)

Form RPR

6525 **1** **Go Silver Bullet (FR)**[44] 4572 10-10-12 **115** CampbellGillies 123+
(Lucinda Russell) *trckd ldrs: nt fluent and dropped bk 3 out: styd on to take modest 4th last: str run fnl 150yds to ld nr fin* **5/1**[1]

0603 **2** *nk* **Storymaker**[28] 5002 10-11-8 **125** PaddyAspell 131
(Sandy Forster) *prom: jnd ldrs 11th: led last: idled and hdd towards fin* **8/1**

F401 **3** *nk* **Magic Sky (FR)**[13] 5229 11-11-7 **124** (p) CharliePoste 129
(Milton Harris) *hld up in last: hdwy to trck ldrs 10th: upsides 3 out: kpt on same pce last 100yds* **5/1**[1]

-RF6 **4** *1* **Bay Cherry (IRE)**[27] 5031 9-11-8 **125** WilsonRenwick 129
(Howard Johnson) *t.k.h: sn led: hdd 8th: led again after next: hdd 4 out: led 2 out: hdd last: kpt on same pce* **13/2**

0-6P **5** *25* **Checkerboard (IRE)**[6] 5353 8-10-11 **119** PaulGallagher(5) 108
(Howard Johnson) *hld up: jnd ldrs 9th: led 4 out: hdd and stmbld landing 2 out: 5th and wkng whn mstke last: sn eased* **11/2**[2]

0526 **6** *9* **Leac An Scail (IRE)**[43] 4689 10-10-12 **115** TomMessenger 88
(Sue Smith) *w ldrs: lost pl appr 4 out: sn bhd* **6/1**[3]

P3P2 **7** *19* **Acrai Rua (IRE)**[24] 5073 8-11-1 **118** TomSiddall 74
(Kevin M Prendergast) *led early: chsd ldrs: lost pl 10th: bhd fr 13th: sn t.o* **8/1**

144P **P** **Sheriff Hutton (IRE)**[37] 4821 8-11-12 **129** RobertWalford —
(Tim Walford) *t.k.h: trckd ldrs: led 8th: hdd after next: lost pl 11th: p.u bef 13th* **6/1**[3]

6m 21.1s (-21.50) **Going Correction** -0.825s/f (Firm) **8** Ran SP% **112.8**
Speed ratings: **101,100,100,100,92 89,83,—**
toteswingers: 1&2 £21.80, 1&3 £2.80, 2&3 £14.70. CSF £42.12 CT £208.02 TOTE £5.50: £1.90, £2.80, £2.10; EX 33.00.

Owner John R Adam & Sons **Bred** Jean-Marc Lucas **Trained** Arlary, Perth & Kinross

FOCUS
A competitive handicap chase in which not one could be confidently discounted. The form looks reasonably sound with the first four close to their marks.

NOTEBOOK
Go Silver Bullet(FR), second off a 2lb higher rating at Musselburgh in February, produced a powerful late run to get the best of a blanket finish. Held up towards the rear in the early stages, he began to make progress halfway round the second circuit and had eased into third with four fences to jump. Disputing that position negotiating the last, he then quickened under pressure to overhaul his main rivals on the run-in. On this evidence, he might handle a longer trip. (tchd 9-2)

Storymaker, third off this mark at Bangor on his most recent run, looks the most feasible guide to the standard achieved. In midfield early on, he had made progress into second by three out and led after the last. He briefly looked set to collect, but was caught in the dying strides. (op 15-2)

Magic Sky(FR) was 6lb higher than when scoring at Ascot 13 day previously and the extra proved just too much. Ridden patiently for the much of the race, he closed on the leaders after three out and jumped the last in third. He could not, however, engage a higher gear on the run-in. (tchd 11-2)

Bay Cherry(IRE), who had failed to complete on his two previous starts over fences this term, showed much better form here. He led for a good deal of the contest and was still ahead at the second-last, but faded late on. (op 8-1 tchd 6-1)

Checkerboard(IRE), lightly raced since collecting here in October 2009, showed he can still be competitive, even if he never serious threatened to come home in front. Second four out, he made a mistake two from home that took some of the stuffing out of him. (op 6-1 tchd 13-2)

Leac An Scail(IRE), 1lb higher than when second at Sandown two outings ago, was ultimately a little disappointing. He was prominent for at least half the race, but could not raise his game in the home straight.

5417 BET TOTEPOOL ON 0800 221 221 NOVICES' H'CAP CHASE (18 fncs) 3m 110y
4:30 (4:30) (Class 4) (0-100,98) 5-Y-0+ **£2,602** (£764; £382; £190)

Form RPR

-431 **1** **Nicky Tam (IRE)**[12] 5258 9-10-10 **82** (t) RobertWalford 105+
(Henry Hogarth) *j. soundly: trckd ldrs: led 11th: drew clr appr 2 out: 20l ahd last: heavily eased* **7/4**[1]

21P0 **2** *16* **Sierra Victor (IRE)**[162] 2354 8-11-10 **96** RyanMania 97
(Andrew Parker) *trckd ldrs: hit 3 out: chsd wnr appr next: no imp* **6/1**[3]

/6P3 **3** *18* **Craicneasy (IRE)**[30] 4962 8-10-0 **72** oh3 TomMessenger 56
(Bruce Mactaggart) *hit 1st: led 3rd: hdd 11th: wknd bef 2 out* **17/2**

0545 **4** *3 ¾* **Conflictofinterest**[30] 4963 9-11-1 **90** EwanWhillans(3) 70
(Kevin Hunter) *hld up in rr: mstke 1st: j.lft 5th: hdwy to trck ldrs 9th: drvn 14th: wknd and hit 3 out* **11/1**

PU31 **P** **Final Veto**[27] 5029 8-11-5 **98** TonyKelly(7) —
(Sue Smith) *in tch: nvr travelling wl: drvn along 8th: outpcd 14th: wknd appr 3 out: bhd whn eased next: t.o whn p.u bef last* **11/4**[2]

055 **F** **Frontier Boy (IRE)**[70] 4062 7-11-3 **96** NathanMoscrop(7) —
(James Ewart) *led to 3rd: chsd ldrs: fell 10th* **7/1**

6m 26.4s (-16.20) **Going Correction** -0.825s/f (Firm) **6** Ran SP% **108.7**
Speed ratings: **92,86,81,79,—,—**
toteswingers: 1&2 £1.60, 1&3 £2.00, 2&3 £6.40. TOTE £2.60: £1.70, £2.30; EX 11.00.

Owner Hogarth Racing **Bred** Noel O'Brien **Trained** Stillington, N Yorks

FOCUS
A modest handicap chase, lacking depth. Light rain fell beforehand, but the jockeys did not believe it affected the ground. The winner looked a big improver but is given the benefit of the doubt with the runner-up is rated to his mark.

NOTEBOOK
Nicky Tam(IRE) had been raised 5lb since winning at Hexham 12 days previously, but shrugged off that rise with ease. In the leading trio after the first couple of fences, he went to the front at the 11th and was never seriously threatened thereafter. He drew well clear on the run-in and will surely take another handicap rise as a result. He seems to be progressive, but this form is not strong. (op 15-8)

Sierra Victor(IRE), having his first start for new connections after a 162-day layoff, did enough to suggest his current yard can have some fun with him. He got tired late on and was no match for the winner in the closing stages, but beat the rest comfortably enough. (tchd 11-2 and 13-2)

Craicneasy(IRE), third when well out of the handicap here on his latest start, got to front early on and set a steady pace. He had been passed by the 11th, though, and could not quicken once the winner established an advantage. (op 9-1)

Conflictofinterest, fifth off a 2lb higher mark here a month earlier, was never in the hunt. He made a mistake at the first and jumped markedly left at the fifth, after which he was always in rear.

5418 BET ON TODAY'S FOOTBALL AT TOTESPORT.COM H'CAP CHASE (12 fncs) 2m
5:00 (5:03) (Class 4) (0-115,112) 5-Y-0+ **£2,602** (£764; £382; £190)

Form RPR

064P **1** **Carrietau**[19] 5145 8-11-10 **110** (bt) RyanMania 122+
(Barry Murtagh) *mde all: clr after 3rd: eased towards fin: unchal* **11/4**[1]

0P00 **2** *13* **Balnagore**[148] 2658 7-10-3 **92** (t) EwanWhillans(3) 93+
(Lucinda Russell) *hdwy to chse clr ldr 4 out: 12 l down whn blnd 2 out: one pce* **10/3**[3]

3RR5 **3** *½* **Blackpool Billy (IRE)**[21] 5120 9-11-5 **112** (be) TonyKelly(7) 109
(Ferdy Murphy) *wnt modest 2nd 5th: rdn after 8th: hesitant: j.rt and lost 2nd 4 out: kpt on run-in* **7/2**

114F **4** *12* **Samizdat (FR)**[29] 4998 8-10-5 **94** JamesO'Farrell(3) 80
(Dianne Sayer) *j.rt in rr: outpcd 5th: tk modest 4th 2 out* **3/1**[2]

-5U4 **5** *31* **Frith (IRE)**[30] 4963 9-9-7 **86** oh9 EdmondLinehan(7) 44
(Lucy Normile) *chsd wnr to 5th: hit next: 4th and wkng whn hmpd 4 out: last whn hmpd 2 out: blnd last: sn eased: t.o* **6/1**

4m 1.80s (-14.30) **Going Correction** -0.825s/f (Firm) **5** Ran SP% **111.3**
Speed ratings: **102,95,95,89,73**
CSF £12.32 TOTE £2.90: £1.60, £2.50; EX 15.60.

Owner Anthony White **Bred** John Ellis **Trained** Low Braithwaite, Cumbria

FOCUS
The ground was officially changed to good before the fifth, though the jockeys said there was no difference. Just a handful of runners in this moderate handicap chase. Two attempts were needed to get the race under way due to the third playing up. The form is rated around the first two.

NOTEBOOK
Carrietau, beaten a length off 8lb higher here in October but disappointing since, returned to form thanks to a fine exhibition of front-running. He was fastest away when the tapes went up, had established a ten-length advantage by halfway and was always in command. The runner-up tried to close on him in the home straight, but he was not stopping and scored easily despite being eased in the last few strides. (tchd 5-2 and 3-1)

Balnagore, fitted with a tongue-tie for this chasing debut, was not foot-perfect, but ran a decent race nonetheless. He might have finished a fair bit closer had he not clouted the second-last just as he was starting to make ground on the winner. (tchd 7-2)

Blackpool Billy(IRE), whose recent efforts had been well below his best, ran a little better here. He was always in the first three, but never close enough to the winner to land a meaningful blow. (op 10-3)

Samizdat(FR), a dual course winner over hurdles having his first chasing start, jumped right at the second and was not fluent at other fences. He will need to improve on this in order break his duck in this discipline. (op 7-2)

Frith(IRE) was 8lb higher than when fourth here a month previously and the rise proved well beyond him. He lost touch from the fourth-last. (op 15-2)

5419 GET LIVE FOOTBALL STATS AT TOTESPORT.COM OPEN HUNTERS' CHASE (18 fncs) 3m 110y
5:35 (5:35) (Class 6) 5-Y-0+ **£791** (£243; £121)

Form RPR

0P-4 **1** **Aggie's Lad (IRE)**[12] 5263 9-11-7 102 MrWKinsey(5) 113+
(Mrs A C Hamilton) *j. soundly: trckd ldr: led 4 out: drvn out run-in* **11/2**[3]

F322 **2** *3* **Ardnaclancy (IRE)**[12] 5263 8-12-1 116 MrJARichardson(5) 119
(Andrew Richardson) *led: hdd and rdn 4 out: kpt on to take 2nd last 150yds* **8/13**[1]

3-P3 **3** *1 ¾* **Abragante (IRE)**[12] 5263 10-11-5 119 MrMEnnis(7) 108
(Mrs D Monteith) *hld up in last: wnt 2nd 2 out: sn drvn: kpt on one pce* **5/2**[2]

6m 29.5s (-13.10) **Going Correction** -0.825s/f (Firm) **3** Ran SP% **105.9**
Speed ratings: **87,86,85**
CSF £9.44 TOTE £5.90; EX 10.10.

Owner J P G Hamilton **Bred** The Three Rivers Racing Syndicate **Trained** Cavers, Borders

FOCUS
A poor turnout for this moderate hunter chase and a surprise result. The second and third are rated in line with their previous Hexham form.

NOTEBOOK
Aggie's Lad(IRE) pulled hard when a well-beaten fourth behind these two rivals last time out, but was much more amenable to restraint here and collected cosily. He kept tabs on the front-running second from the start, before quickening into the lead at the fourth-last and easing away. (op 5-1)

Ardnaclancy(IRE), who had beaten both Aggie's Lad and Abragante when second at Hexham 12 days earlier, was below that form in this. He tried to make all, setting a steady gallop, but was overtaken four out and quickly out-speeded. He rallied on the run-in, having briefly been third after the final fence, but it was nothing like enough to trouble the winner. (op 8-11)

Abragante(IRE), 6l behind Ardnaclancy last time out, got a lot closer to him in this. He never looked remotely like collecting, though, and the best position he held was the second he took briefly after the last. (op 9-4)

T/Plt: £22.50 to a £1 stake. Pool:£37,315.05 - 1,209.01 winning tickets. T/Qpdt: £6.00 to a £1 stake. Pool:£1,844.60 - 226.90 winning tickets. WG

[4937]HAYDOCK (L-H)

Saturday, April 23

OFFICIAL GOING: Chase, brush hurdle & nh flat course - good (good to firm in places on bends); traditional hurdle course - good to firm (good in places; watered 6.0)

Rail realignment on bends added 38m to distance of race 1 and 19m to all others.
Wind: Light, against Weather: Cloudy with bright intervals

5420 YOU'RE BETTER OFF WITH BETFAIR H'CAP HURDLE 2m
2:20 (2:20) (Class 3) (0-135,130) 4-Y-O+ £6,505 (£1,910; £955; £477)

Form RPR

051 1 **Knight In Purple**[14] 5215 7-10-9 118..........................(vt) PeterCarberry(5) 130+
(John Mackie) *in tch: wnt 2nd 6th: upsides 3 out: led 2 out: asserted after last: styd on wl to draw clr* 5/1[2]

B304 2 5 **Drill Sergeant**[14] 5196 6-11-3 128..............................(bt) HenryBrooke(7) 136+
(Donald McCain) *trckd ldrs: led narrowly jst bef 3 out: hdd 2 out: u.p jst over 2 l down whn hit last: no ex fnl 150yds* 5/2[1]

1604 3 17 **Maoi Chinn Tire (IRE)**[16] 5161 4-11-5 128........................ AlanO'Keeffe 116
(Jennie Candlish) *nt fluent: hld up in rr: pushed along after 6th: mod prog u.p appr 2 out: wnt 3rd bef last: n.d to front 2* 14/1

2601 4 13 **Tharaya**[35] 4874 6-10-11 118.................................. TommyPhelan(3) 98
(Claire Dyson) *in tch: chsng ldrs whn hit 3 out: u.p and outpcd next: dropped away after* 8/1

5401 5 ¾ **Royal Max (IRE)**[149] 2076 5-10-7 111..........................(tp) DaveCrosse 91
(Ian Williams) *led: pushed along after 6th: rdn and hdd jst bef 3 out: wknd bef 2 out* 11/1

2U-0 6 11 **Dominican Monk (IRE)**[123] 3059 12-10-13 117................... DarylJacob 87
(David Arbuthnot) *hld up: u.p and unable to chal bef 2 out: wknd sn after* 9/1

6P3P 7 43 **Fiendish Flame (IRE)**[36] 4853 7-11-12 130......................... AdrianLane 61
(Donald McCain) *j.rt and nt fluent: chsd ldr: upsides fr 3rd to 4th: lost pl bef 6th: sn wknd: lost tch bef 3 out: t.o* 11/2[3]

5035 P **Crosby Jemma**[50] 4455 7-10-1 105....................................... GrahamLee —
(Mike Sowersby) *hld up: pushed along after 6th: nvr able to get on terms: wl bhd whn p.u bef last* 13/2

3m 48.1s (-16.10) **Going Correction** -0.825s/f (Firm)
WFA 4 from 5yo+ 5lb 8 Ran SP% **110.1**
Speed ratings (Par 107): **107,104,96,89,89 83,62,—**
toteswingers:1&2:£1.10, 1&3:£16.60, 2&3:£8.40 CSF £16.99 CT £149.36 TOTE £5.90: £1.80, £1.50, £2.80; EX 13.00 Trifecta £87.30.
Owner A J Wall, G Hicks & N Hooper **Bred** Wood Farm Stud **Trained** Church Broughton , Derbys

FOCUS
This was the only jump race of the day run on the normal hurdles course, with the chases and brush hurdles run on the chase course. A fair handicap hurdle in which the previous four runnings have been shared by six and 7-y-o, and it was one of the latter group who continued the sequence. The race could be rated a shade higher, but is assessed through the third to recent Aintree form.

NOTEBOOK
Knight In Purple ◆, who scored twice on good ground at around this time last season, had returned to form when winning at Chepstow earlier in the month, and defied a 10lb rise to follow up in this better race. He was always in control here and, although he will go up the weights again, there is good reason to believe he can complete the hat-trick. (op 9-2)
Drill Sergeant, taking a drop in grade, was never far off the pace and was upsides the winner three out but could not stay with that rival from the next. A flat track and sound surface suits him best. (op 3-1)
Maoi Chinn Tire(IRE), who had not gone on from a surprise win on his hurdling debut, was dropping into handicap company after being outclassed in graded races. He ran better but was beaten a long way in the end. (op 16-1 tchd 12-1)
Tharaya, who made a successful first appearance for this year last time, was 10lb higher in this better contest. She travelled well enough but could not pick up from the home turn. (op 7-1 tchd 9-1)
Royal Max(IRE) made the running but was brushed aside by the principals at the third last. (op 9-1 tchd 12-1)
Fiendish Flame(IRE) was unable to win the early duel for the lead and appeared to down tools down the back straight. (op 13-2 tchd 5-1)

5421 MICHAEL CONLON 50TH BIRTHDAY NOVICES' CHASE (18 fncs) 3m
2:55 (2:55) (Class 3) 5-Y-O+ £6,505 (£1,910; £955; £477)

Form RPR

6201 1 **Sonny Mullen (IRE)**[11] 5281 7-10-5 123........................(p) EdCookson(7) 138+
(Kim Bailey) *j.rt several times: prom: pckd 2nd: led 3rd: mde rest: clr fr 9th: slowed on approach to 4 out and 3 out: hrd at work but stl clr last: fin tired* 10/3[2]

5441 2 11 **Ballyvesey (IRE)**[12] 5254 6-10-12 125...............................(v) TomO'Brien 125
(Peter Bowen) *led to 3rd: racd in 2nd after: nt fluent 11th: u.p whn chsng clr wnr bef 3 out: no imp* 11/4[1]

0-63 3 4 **River D'Or (FR)**[29] 4989 6-10-12 116..............................(b[1]) DarylJacob 121
(Paul Nicholls) *hld up: mstke 10th: niggled along after 14th: wnt 3rd appr 3 out: plugged on at one pce and no imp after* 9/2

2115 4 1 ¼ **Asturienne**[28] 5007 7-10-5 125.......................................(p) RobertThornton 114
(Alan King) *nt fluent several times: hld up: impr to chse ldrs bef 6th: btn bef 3 out* 4/1[3]

100P P **Wolf Moon (IRE)**[6] 5353 8-10-12 121...........................(b) WarrenMarston —
(Martin Keighley) *racd keenly: prom: blnd bdly 1st: nt rcvr: wl bhd whn p.u bef 5th* 11/2

P **Renard (FR)**[160] 6-10-12 124.. SamThomas —
(Venetia Williams) *in tch: lost pl and bhd bef 10th: j. slowly 11th and 12th: lost tch: t.o whn p.u bef 13th* 14/1

6m 11.1s (-2.90) **Going Correction** -0.575s/f (Firm) 6 Ran SP% **110.0**
Speed ratings: **81,77,76,75,— —**
toteswingers:1&2:£1.10, 1&3:£2.90, 2&3:£1.50 CSF £12.71 TOTE £4.50: £2.30, £1.90; EX 13.20.
Owner Clive Washbourn **Bred** Richard And Marie Hennessy **Trained** Andoversford, Gloucs

FOCUS
A competitive novice chase on paper despite the relatively small field, but the winner came home unchallenged. They did not appear to go that fast but the finishers were all very tired. The placed horses set the level for the form.

NOTEBOOK
Sonny Mullen(IRE), the winner of a novice handicap chase over shorter on fast ground last time, was already proven at this trip. Despite pecking at the second fence, he jumped to the front at the next and was clear by the end of the back straight. He led for the rest although tending to jump right at some fences, and then got very tired up the finishing straight, but was always holding on. (op 7-2 tchd 3-1)
Ballyvesey(IRE) was the reluctant early leader and quite keen. Once headed he chased the winner the rest of the way, but got a reminder early on the second circuit and was only slowly getting closer to the winner from four out. (op 3-1tched 7-2 in places)
River D'Or(FR), in blinkers for the first time, was held up but was struggling from the last on the far side and just kept going at the one pace up the straight. (op 5-1)
Asturienne, trying this trip for the first time, still appeared to have something left on the home turn but was beaten soon afterwards, suggesting she did not get the trip. (op 7-2)
Wolf Moon(IRE) was in second place when making a bad blunder at the first which dropped him back to last and, awkward at the next, he was pulled up after the fourth. (op 13-2 tchd 7-1)
Renard(FR), ex-French and making his debut for new connections, dropped away quickly early on the second circuit. (op 13-2 tchd 7-1)

5422 BETFAIR.COM/PAULNICHOLLS H'CAP CHASE (15 fncs) 2m 4f
3:30 (3:30) (Class 2) 5-Y-O+
£21,917 (£6,475; £3,237; £1,620; £808; £406)

Form RPR

2066 1 **Matuhi**[37] 4820 8-11-2 135..(t) HaddenFrost 141
(David Pipe) *hld up: hdwy to trck ldrs after 6th: wnt 2nd appr 3 out: led bef 2 out: rdn after last: a doing jst enough towards fin* 3/1[1]

-541 2 1 **Watch My Back**[8] 5317 10-11-12 145.................................... GrahamLee 150
(Ferdy Murphy) *hld up in rr: pushed along and hdwy to chse ldrs 4 out: wnt 2nd appr 2 out: kpt on u.p run-in but unable to get to wnr* 3/1[1]

21UU 3 19 **Raysrock (IRE)**[8] 5317 9-10-11 130..............................(t) PeterBuchanan 121
(Lucinda Russell) *prom: led 7th to 9th: lost pl 11th: tried to get on bk on terms 2 out but no imp: tk mod 3rd run-in* 18/1

2101 4 3 ¼ **Alderley Rover (IRE)**[15] 5190 7-11-1 134.......................... SamThomas 121
(Donald McCain) *in tch: wnt prom 9th: led appr 4 out: hdd bef 2 out: wknd bef last* 8/1

3212 5 18 **Categorical**[14] 5199 8-10-12 131... JamesReveley 104
(Keith Reveley) *led to 7th: led again 9th: hdd appr 4 out: wknd bef 2 out* 13/2[3]

2063 6 37 **Five Dream (FR)**[13] 5236 7-10-11 130..............................(b) DarylJacob 65
(Paul Nicholls) *trckd ldrs: lost pl bef 10th: bhd after: toiling bef 4 out: t.o* 13/2[3]

60-2 P **Kealshore Boy**[50] 4456 8-9-7 119.................................... HenryBrooke(7) —
(Howard Johnson) *hld up in rr: blnd 10th and 11th: clsd to chse ldrs after: blnd 4 out: sn wknd: t.o whn p.u bef 2 out: lame* 9/2[2]

4m 54.0s (-16.00) **Going Correction** -0.575s/f (Firm) course record 7 Ran SP% **111.2**
Speed ratings: **109,108,101,99,92 77,—**
toteswingers:1&2:£1.50, 1&3:£5.90, 2&3:£16.70 CSF £12.15 TOTE £3.60: £1.40, £3.00; EX 11.60.
Owner Willsford Racing Incorporated **Bred** Mrs A Yearley **Trained** Nicholashayne, Devon

FOCUS
Decent prize-money resulted in a pretty good field for this handicap chase, but the top weights came clear from the second-last. The form is best rated around the principals, although several behind were below form.

NOTEBOOK
Matuhi has been running well enough in Grade 3 handicaps recently since his good start to the season and appreciated the drop in grade. He was made to work by the runner-up but found enough and could be the sort his trainer might send for the Galway Plate. (tchd 11-4 and 10-3)
Watch My Back, 8lb higher for his win in a similar contest at Ayr, had conditions to suit but did not travel that well early. He got into contention turning for home though and pushed the winner all the way to the line. (op 4-1 tchd 9-2)
Raysrock(IRE), who has had his jumping problems of late, was well up there early but lost his place before the end of the back straight and looked beaten. However, he rallied well despite an error at the third from home. (op 16-1 tchd 14-1)
Alderley Rover(IRE) has been in pretty good form of late and stays further than this. He went on at the first in the straight but stopped pretty quickly once the winner went by. He may have found the ground quicker than ideal.
Categorical made the running but was taken on down the back on the second circuit and was beaten off turning for home. (op 5-1)
Five Dream(FR) tracked the leaders until losing his place going to the last on the far side. (op 15-2)
Kealshore Boy, who ran well on his return from a year off last time, had been given seven weeks to recover. He was making headway when hitting the last on the far side and another mistake at the next finished his chance. The vet reported that the gelding finished lame. (op 4-1)

5423 TIM MOLONY H'CAP CHASE (22 fncs) 3m 4f
4:00 (4:02) (Class 3) (0-130,129) 5-Y-O+ £9,757 (£2,865; £1,432; £715)

Form RPR

-0P2 1 **Dom D'Orgeval (FR)**[14] 5206 11-11-2 119............................ DarylJacob 134+
(Nick Williams) *trckd ldrs: led appr 3 out: clr bef last: styd on wl: eased down towards fin* 7/1

5634 2 6 **Seize**[31] 4937 9-10-3 106... GrahamLee 112
(James Moffatt) *in rr: hdwy appr 14th: rdn and nt qckn bef 3 out: kpt on to take 2nd bef last: no ch w wnr* 14/1

140P 3 11 **Etxalar (FR)**[63] 4208 8-11-8 125.................................. PeterBuchanan 123
(Lucinda Russell) *trckd ldrs: niggled along after 18th: effrt 4 out: chsd wnr appr 2 out: lost 2nd bef last: sn wknd* 14/1

F121 4 7 **Eyre Square (IRE)**[27] 5031 8-11-3 120............................ JamesReveley 114
(Keith Reveley) *led to 5th: remained prom: regained ld appr 4 out: hdd bef 3 out where nt fluent: wknd bef last* 5/2[1]

0P11 5 3 **Commemoration Day (IRE)**[22] 5104 10-11-12 129........... FelixDeGiles 116
(Charlie Longsdon) *hld up: outpcd and toiling 18th: plugged on modly fr 2 out but n.d* 9/1

2064 6 17 **Quattrocento (FR)**[35] 4864 7-10-10 113..........................(v) TomO'Brien 93
(Peter Bowen) *midfield: hdwy 14th: chsng ldrs disputing 4th jst over 2 l off pce whn mstke 4 out: sn wknd* 10/1

0-PF 7 36 **Toby Jug**[10] 5286 10-11-12 129.......................................(b) JackDoyle 68
(Sarah Humphrey) *prom: led 5th: hdd appr 4 out: wknd qckly bef 3 out: t.o* 15/2

303F P **Theatre Dance (IRE)**[28] 5009 10-11-2 119.......................... SamThomas —
(David Arbuthnot) *hld up: hdwy whn blnd 15th: sn lost pl: bhd whn p.u bef 18th* 13/2[3]

1132 P **Incentivise (IRE)**[57] 4333 8-11-6 123.......................... RobertThornton —
(Richard Lee) *midfield: mstke 12th and 13th: lost pl 15th: bhd whn p.u bef 18th* 5/1[2]

7m 26.6s (-14.40) **Going Correction** -0.575s/f (Firm) 9 Ran SP% **115.3**
Speed ratings: **97,95,92,90,89 84,74,—,—**
toteswingers:1&2:£8.50, 1&3:£10.60, 2&3:£26.90 CSF £92.49 CT £1329.97 TOTE £10.00: £2.70, £2.00, £5.90; EX 82.90.
Owner A J White and Mrs A Underhill **Bred** Max De Minden **Trained** George Nympton, Devon

FOCUS
A fair long-distance handicap chase and the early pace was pedestrian, but they still finished tired. The form is rated around the first two.

NOTEBOOK

Dom D'Orgeval(FR), a veteran who had not won since February 2007, when he seemed best on soft ground, has since proved he handles a sound surface and travelled well throughout before going on at the first in the straight and scoring with a fair amount in hand. He will be kept on the go and, as this was only his fourth race in the last year, he should be fresh enough to win again, as he is well treated on his old form. (tchd 15-2)

Seize stays well and likes a sound surface and gradually picked his way through the field to chase the winner, but never looked like troubling him. He could be one for a race at Perth later this spring. (op 16-1)

Etxalar(FR), having his first run since pulled up over C&D in February, was never far away but had no more to offer from early in the straight. (op 16-1)

Eyre Square(IRE), relatively lightly raced but progressive over both hurdles and fences, was 8lb higher than for his last success but was a well-backed favourite. He helped cut out the running until fading in the straight. He probably found this trip too far. (op 9-2)

Commemoration Day(IRE), bidding for a hat-trick off 19lb higher than for the first of his two previous successes, had the cheekpieces he wore on his previous start left off. He was struggling with a circuit to go but did run on past beaten rivals. The vet reported that the gelding was later found to be suffering from heat stress. (op 6-1)

Quattrocento(FR) was close enough turning for home but the last of several mistakes, at the fourth-last, ended his chance. (op 17-2)

Toby Jug, who had failed to complete since returning from a long absence earlier this spring, helped make the running but faded quickly once headed at the first in the straight. (op 6-1 tchd 11-2)

Theatre Dance(IRE) was another whose jumping went to pieces in the second half of the race and was also pulled up down the far side. (tchd 11-2)

Incentivise(IRE)'s jumping rather went to pieces in the second half of the race and he was pulled up down the far side. He was reported to have run flat by his rider, and to have been unsuited by the ground by his trainer. (tchd 11-2)

5424 WATCH RACING UK ON SKY432 "FIXED BRUSH" NOVICES' H'CAP HURDLE (10 hdls) 2m 4f

4:35 (4:38) (Class 2) 4-8-Y-O **£13,010** (£3,820; £1,910; £954)

Form				RPR
4411	**1**		**Ultravox (USA)**[13] 5227 4-10-10 **127** NathanSweeney(7) (Jeremy Scott) *a.p: chalng and rdn fr 3 out: styd on to ld fnl 110yds: kpt on gamley cl home* **7/1**[3]	127+
2121	**2**	*3/4*	**A Bridge Too Far (IRE)**[31] 4942 5-10-13 **124** HenryBrooke(7) (Donald McCain) *led: rdn appr 2 out: hdd fnl 110yds: hld fnl strides* **7/2**[1]	130+
4211	**3**	*2 1/4*	**Top Smart**[12] 5271 5-10-6 **113** JimmyDerham(3) (Seamus Mullins) *midfield: hdwy 6th: chsd ldrs after 7th: rdn appr 2 out: styd on towards fin but nt get to front 2* **8/1**	117
1053	**4**	*6*	**Dark Ranger**[18] 4858 5-9-13 **108** BrianToomey(5) (Tim Pitt) *hld up: hdwy after 7th: chsd ldrs appr 3 out: swtchd lft bef last: oen pce run-in* **20/1**	106
3121	**5**	*6*	**Havingotascoobydo (IRE)**[23] 5080 6-11-9 **127** WarrenMarston (Martin Keighley) *hld up: niggled along after 4th: hdwy 6th: chsd ldrs bef 3 out: wknd 2 out* **9/2**[2]	120
6123	**6**	*11*	**Black Phantom (IRE)**[21] 5110 5-10-8 **119** EdCookson(7) (Andy Turnell) *trckd ldrs: rdn after 7th: wknd appr 3 out* **8/1**	107
01P0	**P**		**Wild Desert (FR)**[29] 4990 6-10-10 **114** (p) FelixDeGiles (Charlie Longsdon) *midfield: hdwy 5th: wknd bef 7th: t.o whn p.u bef 3 out* **11/1**	—
0131	**P**		**Pure Faith (IRE)**[12] 5255 7-11-12 **130** TomO'Brien (Peter Bowen) *hld up: in last and struggling 5th: t.o whn p.u bef 3 out* **8/1**	—
6065	**P**		**Niceonefrankie**[51] 4439 5-10-0 **108** ow1 RTDunne(5) (Venetia Williams) *hld up: wknd after 7th: t.o whn p.u bef 2 out* **16/1**	—
3321	**P**		**Tiptoeaway (IRE)**[46] 4545 6-11-0 **118** GrahamLee (Tim Easterby) *prom: rdn and wknd after 7th: t.o whn p.u bef 3 out* **8/1**	—

4m 47.1s (-26.40) **Going Correction** -1.175s/f (Hard)
WFA 4 from 5yo+ 6lb **10** Ran SP% **116.3**
Speed ratings: **105,104,103,101,99 94,—,—,—,—**
CSF £32.33 CT £202.72 TOTE £7.70: £2.60, £2.10, £3.10; EX 24.20.

Owner G T Lever **Bred** Hascombe Stud **Trained** Brompton Regis, Somerset

FOCUS

A decent prize resulted in a fair 'fixed brush' novice hurdle featuring six last-time-out winners and three of them filled the placings. The winner stepped up again and the third and fourth set the level.

NOTEBOOK

Ultravox(USA) ◆ has developed into a real battler since encountering a sound surface over hurdles and completed the hat-trick in the game and resolute fashion that is becoming his trademark. Always in the front rank, he looked held when the runner-up went a couple of lengths clear but would not go away and forced his way to the front after the last. He looks one to keep on-side when getting his ground. (op 6-1)

A Bridge Too Far(IRE), a C&D winner here on his last start in March when he made all, set off to do the same again and looked set to score halfway up the straight. However, he began to falter going to the last and was run out of it by a tough customer, so lost little in defeat. (op 9-2)

Top Smart, another bidding for a hat-trick, was 12lb higher than for the first of those successes but ran a decent race before being seen off in the straight. (tchd 9-1)

Dark Ranger likes good ground and was given a patient ride but could never quite land a blow at the leaders. (op 16-1)

Havingotascoobydo(IRE) has been in good form but was 12lb high than for his last success. He was getting reminders with a circuit to go but got into contention turning for home before fading. The handicapper may have him now. (tched 5-1 in places)

Pure Faith(IRE) was well-supported but was always at the back and was beaten early on the second circuit. This was not his running but the trainer could offer no explanation. (op 11-1)

Tiptoeaway(IRE) showed up for a fair way. (op 11-1)

5425 JASON TOMLINSON 40TH BIRTHDAY "FIXED BRUSH" H'CAP HURDLE (10 hdls) 2m 4f

5:10 (5:10) (Class 3) (0-125,120) 4-Y-0+ **£4,878** (£1,432; £716; £357)

Form				RPR
-054	**1**		**Agglestone Rock**[15] 4797 6-10-10 **111** KyleJames(7) (Philip Kirby) *hld up: hdwy 5th: led appr 6th: clr bef 3 out: wl in command after: r.o wl* **11/8**[1]	128+
0F50	**2**	*12*	**Livvy Inn (USA)**[19] 5144 6-11-4 **112** PeterBuchanan (Lucinda Russell) *hld up: nt fluent 4th: struggling after 7th: hdwy after 3 out: wnt 2nd appr 2 out: n.d to wnr* **25/1**	118+
-003	**3**	*6*	**Yeoman Spirit (IRE)**[21] 5117 8-10-13 **107** (p) GrahamLee (John Mackie) *in tch: rdn and outpcd 6th: kpt on to take mod 3rd appr last: no imp on front 2* **7/1**	108
-12P	**4**	*13*	**Restart (IRE)**[43] 4704 10-10-12 **106** DaveCrosse (Lucinda Featherstone) *hld up: hdwy to chse ldrs appr 5th: u.p and outpcd bef 3 out: dropped away bef 2 out* **20/1**	95
3005	**5**	*21*	**Worth A King'S**[14] 5205 5-11-2 **110** (b) AdrianLane (Donald McCain) *prom tl rdn and wknd bef 6th* **22/1**	80
26U1	**6**	*10*	**Perfect Reward**[40] 4776 7-11-0 **115** (p) KielanWoods(7) (Charlie Longsdon) *chsd ldrs: wnt 2nd 7th: rdn and outpcd by wnr whn mstke 3 out: lost 2nd appr 2 out: sn wknd* **9/2**[2]	76
5324	**7**	*46*	**Rifleman (IRE)**[163] 2324 11-11-2 **110** (t) RobertThornton (Richard Lee) *hld up: struggling after 5th: t.o* **16/1**	30
0110	**P**		**Pie At Midnight**[28] 5003 5-11-5 **120** HenryBrooke(7) (Donald McCain) *led: mstke 3rd: hdd 5th: wknd 6th: t.o whn p.u bef 3 out* **9/1**	—
1320	**P**		**Thanks For Coming**[31] 4940 5-11-11 **119** AndrewTinkler (Nicky Henderson) *w ldr: led 5th: hdd appr 6th: wknd after 7th: wl bhd whn p.u bef 3 out* **11/2**[3]	—

4m 46.1s (-27.40) **Going Correction** -1.175s/f (Hard) **9** Ran SP% **117.0**
Speed ratings (Par 107): **107,102,99,94,86 82,63,—,—**
toteswingers:1&2:£14.10, 1&3:£2.90, 2&3:£27.60 CSF £38.59 CT £191.94 TOTE £2.50: £1.30, £6.50, £1.90; EX 48.00.

Owner Geoff Kirby Basil Holian Michael Buckley **Bred** Mrs Fiona Denniff **Trained** Castleton, N Yorks

FOCUS

An ordinary 'fixed brush' handicap hurdle run exactly a second faster than the preceding novices' hurdle. The placed horses ran close to their marks and set the standard.

NOTEBOOK

Agglestone Rock was a warm favourite on the strength of running away with a handicap on the Flat earlier in the month. He was very keen that day but it it did not stop him, and that was the case once again, as he pulled early before taking charge halfway down the back straight. He put his rivals to the sword from that point and came home to score at his leisure. He is well treated over hurdles compared with fences and the level, but is sure to go up quite a lot as a result of this. He is clearly in fine fettle though and the hat-trick is possible, providing his exertions have not taken their toll. (tchd 13-8)

Livvy Inn(USA) gained his sole previous success on soft ground but handled this surface well and came from the rear to chase the winner home. He gave the impression that he will stay further than this.

Yeoman Spirit(IRE) having his second start following a break, was being urged along early on the final circuit but at least kept going past beaten rivals. He has had a recent wind operation and it seems to have helped. (op 15-2 tchd 9-1)

Restart(IRE), another having his second start following a break, was also being urged along early on the final circuit but at least kept going past beaten rivals. (op 25-1)

Perfect Reward, having his first start for new connections having won a seller last time and with the cheekpieces back on, was never far away but dropped back after chasing the winner into the straight. (op 5-1)

Pie At Midnight, the early pace-setters was done with before leaving the back straight. (op 6-1 tchd 13-2)

Thanks For Coming, another early pace-setter was also done with before leaving the back straight. (op 6-1 tchd 13-2)

5426 TURFTV.CO.UK STANDARD OPEN NATIONAL HUNT FLAT RACE 2m

5:45 (5:45) (Class 5) 4-6-Y-O **£1,712** (£499; £249)

Form				RPR
	1		**Darlan** 4-10-12 0 AndrewTinkler (Nicky Henderson) *hld up: hdwy 6f out: led over 3f out: clr over 1f out: v easily* **4/6**[1]	117+
5	**2**	*27*	**Highrate (IRE)**[46] 4547 5-11-3 0 HenryOliver (Sue Smith) *prom: pushed along 5f out: chsd wnr in vain fr over 2f out: wl outpcd over 1f out* **12/1**	92
	3	*2 1/2*	**Patricias Pride** 4-10-5 0 MrJPFeatherstone(7) (Lucinda Featherstone) *racd keenly in midfield: hdwy 1/2-way: led over 4f out: hdd over 3f out: u.p over 2f out: wl btn fnl f* **33/1**	85
4	**4**	*1 1/4*	**Boruler (IRE)**[34] 4894 5-11-3 0 AdrianLane (Donald McCain) *trckd ldrs: rdn and outpcd 3f out: rdn and hung lft over 2f out: n.d after* **14/1**	88
02	**5**	*1*	**Smart Ruler (IRE)**[33] 4923 5-11-3 0 DarylJacob (David Arbuthnot) *hld up: hdwy 4f out: rdn to chse ldrs 2f out: outpcd over 1f out: wl btn fnl f* **5/1**[2]	87
	6	*36*	**Nowurhurlin (IRE)** 4-10-9 0 JohnKington(3) (Donald McCain) *hld up: outpcd over 3f out: nvr a danger* **16/1**	46
3	**7**	*11*	**No Idea**[26] 5056 6-10-10 0 RobertThornton (Tim Vaughan) *racd keenly: prom: led after 3f: hdd 5f out: wknd 4f out* **8/1**[3]	33
	8	*2 1/4*	**Driftwood Lad (IRE)**[42] 5-11-3 0 SamThomas (Venetia Williams) *led: hdd after 3f: remained prom: led again 5f out: hdd over 4f out: wknd over 3f out* **25/1**	38

3m 57.8s (-0.80) **Going Correction** -1.175s/f (Hard)
WFA 4 from 5yo+ 5lb **8** Ran SP% **114.8**
Speed ratings: **55,41,40,39,39 21,15,14**
toteswingers:1&2:£14.10, 1&3:£2.90, 2&3:£27.60 CSF £10.41 TOTE £1.80: £1.10, £2.70, £4.00; EX 11.60.

Owner Paul Murphy **Bred** M G Kilroe **Trained** Upper Lambourn, Berks

FOCUS

Three newcomers in this bumper, and some major yards were represented. The early pace was very steady but the winner looks decent, while the runner-up and fourth appear the best guides to the level.

NOTEBOOK

Darlan ◆ went off favourite on this debut and, once he asserted over 2f out, the result was never in doubt. He looks a decent prospect, being out of a Flat and hurdles winner who stayed well. (op 10-11)

Highrate(IRE) ran well enough on soft ground on his debut but his breeding suggested that this better ground should suit. He had every chance 3f out but was left standing by the winner from that point. (tchd 14-1)

Patricias Pride is related to three winners, including one over hurdles, and his dam stayed well on the Flat. He ran pretty well on this racecourse debut, showing in front briefly turning for home. (op 20-1)

Boruler(IRE) was easy in the market but ran reasonably on very different ground from on his debut. (op 10-1)

No Idea was very keen early on when the gallop was pedestrian, and after getting to the front she paid for her exertions from the end of the back straight. (tchd 15-2)

T/Plt: £123.10 to a £1 stake. Pool:£83,817.15 - 497.02 winning tickets T/Qpdt: £44.50 to a £1 stake. Pool:£4,107.93 - 68.20 winning tickets DO

5144KELSO (L-H)

Saturday, April 23

OFFICIAL GOING: Good to firm (good in places) changing to good after race 3 (6.45)

Hurdle rail at innermost position.

Wind: Virtually nil Weather: Cloudy rain half hour before 1st until 2nd

5427 BORDER FACILITIES NOVICES' H'CAP CHASE (17 fncs) 2m 6f 110y

5:40 (5:40) (Class 3) (0-135,125) 5-Y-0+ **£4,553** (£1,337; £668; £333)

Form RPR

0U35 **1** **Monsieur Jourdain (IRE)**22 5095 5-10-8 **107**............(p) RichieMcGrath 113
(Tim Easterby) *led narrowly: hdd 12th: nt fluent next: hit 3 out: sn outpcd: styd on after last: led again nr fin* **11/4**3

12UP **2** ½ **Frankie Anson (IRE)**9 5303 7-11-7 **120**............................ BrianHughes 126
(Micky Hammond) *w ldr: led 12th: clr after 3 out: stl 7 l up last: wknd long run-in: hdd nr fin* **11/8**1

5664 **3** *19* **Pilgrims Lane (IRE)**13 5228 7-11-12 **125**......................(tp) SeanQuinlan 117
(Milton Harris) *in tch in 3rd: rdn to chal for 2nd 2 out: wknd appr last* **5/2**2

30P **4** *47* **Appeal Denied (IRE)**82 3853 9-10-0 **99** oh28................... JanFaltejsek 45
(Sandy Forster) *hld up: nt fluent 1st and 2nd: reminders after 3rd: sn bhd: t.o after 5 out* **9/1**

5m 47.43s (2.93) **Going Correction** +0.05s/f (Yiel) **4** Ran SP% **107.3**
Speed ratings: **96,95,89,72**
CSF £7.06 TOTE £3.50; EX 4.80.
Owner C H Stevens **Bred** Jim McCormack **Trained** Great Habton, N Yorks

FOCUS
It began to rain half an hour before racing, and after the course was watered earlier in the week the going had eased in places. A race of changing fortunes after the last. The winner is rated to his hurdles form with the second to form.

NOTEBOOK
Monsieur Jourdain(IRE) vied for the lead, but as the pace began to increase he hit the middle one in the back straight and looked as if he had run his race. However, full credit to a determined jockey who kept him going so that when the favourite began to falter he had enough momentum to battle past that rival for a well-earned first chasing success. He has not looked a natural over fences, but was more at home at this steady pace on faster ground, at least until things quickened up, but could remain vulnerable in bigger fields. (tchd 3-1)

Frankie Anson(IRE) has been found out since stepping up in grade at Cheltenham and Newbury latest, but prior to that was competitive over 3m on fastish ground at Doncaster. With the benefit of that experience he travelled comfortably, readily stretched clear down the back straight and looked to be going on for victory until reaching the elbow where his stride began to shorten markedly, so that he had nothing left once the winner went by. He does race with a slightly high head carriage, which could be a hint towards his resolution. (op 13-8)

Pilgrims Lane(IRE) chased the leaders but was never able to get in a position to challenge. He may have needed this second run back from a winter break but looks weighted up to his best and ran as if needing further. (op 2-1)

Appeal Denied(IRE) jumped slowly over the first four fences and, with ears pinned back, gradually lost touch. He was a moderate maiden over hurdles and looks no better over fences. (op 12-1)

5428 NSPCC SCHOOL SERVICE MAIDEN HURDLE (8 hdls) 2m 110y

6:15 (6:16) (Class 4) 4-Y-0+ **£2,602** (£764; £382; £190)

Form RPR

-040 **1** **Nelson's Chief**54 4393 5-11-0 100.................................. RichieMcGrath 106
(James Ewart) *mde all: rdn after 2 out: kpt on wl run-in* **12/1**

-235 **2** *1* **Inoogoo (IRE)**33 4910 6-11-0 0.. BarryKeniry 105
(George Bewley) *trckd ldrs: drvn after last: kpt on: wnt 2nd fnl 75yds* **11/4**2

555 **3** ¾ **Fortuni (IRE)**87 3749 5-11-0 110....................................(t) WilsonRenwick 104
(Rose Dobbin) *trckd ldr in 2nd: drvn and one pce run-in: lost 2nd fnl 75yds* **5/6**1

-006 **4** 2¾ **Agricultural**27 5028 5-10-9 75.. AlexanderVoy(5) 102
(Lucy Normile) *hld up in tch: hdwy gng to 4th: rdn after 3 out: kpt on* **80/1**

5 1¼ **Oh So Beautiful (IRE)**247 1301 4-10-2 0...................... CampbellGillies 89
(Lucinda Russell) *hld up in tch: rdn after 3 out: kpt on same pce run-in* **11/2**3

04 **6** *26* **Hotgrove Boy**19 5151 4-10-2 0.................................... RobertMcCarth(7) 74
(George Foster) *trckd ldrs: mstke 4th: rdn 3 out: wkng whn hit 2 out* **25/1**

P0P **7** *44* **Why Are You Asking (IRE)**49 4473 6-11-0 0.................... SeanQuinlan 38
(Rose Dobbin) *hld up: rdn after 5th: sn wknd* **66/1**

0P0 **8** *52* **Princess Cherry (IRE)**19 5147 6-10-0 0................... GaryRutherford(7) —
(Harriet Graham) *hld up: reminders after 3rd: sn bhd: nt fluent 5th: t.o* **100/1**

0360 **P** **Battle Honour**19 5144 4-10-4 99................................(p) PaulGallagher(5) —
(Sue Bradburne) *hld up: bhd after 4th: nt fluent 5th: t.o whn p.u bef last* **9/1**

F **Golden Emperor (IRE)**568 4-10-9 0.................................. JanFaltejsek —
(R MacDonald) *hld up: fell 1st* **33/1**

0P **P** **Lucky Belle (IRE)**58 4303 4-9-9 0............................... MrGJCockburn(7) —
(William Young) *nt fluent in rr: a bhd: t.o whn p.u bef last* **100/1**

0P **P** **King Kalium (IRE)**19 5147 5-11-0 0..................................... BrianHughes —
(Bruce Mactaggart) *trckd ldrs on outer: lost pl qckly after 3rd: bhd whn p.u bef 5th* **100/1**

3m 53.1s (-8.70) **Going Correction** -0.50s/f (Good)
WFA 4 from 5yo+ 5lb **12** Ran SP% **126.8**
Speed ratings (Par 105): **100,99,99,97,97 85,64,39,—,— —,—**
toteswingers: 1&2 £6.70, 1&3 £2.70, 2&3 £1.80. CSF £48.87 TOTE £13.60: £2.50, £1.50, £1.10; EX 54.30.
Owner Longlands Racing **Bred** Longlands Racing **Trained** Langholm, Dumfries & G'way

■ Stewards' Enquiry : Wilson Renwick two-day ban: careless riding (May 7 & 8)

FOCUS
A weak maiden with just four in with a chance from the home turn. The form is rated around the third, fifth and sixth.

NOTEBOOK
Nelson's Chief led throughout, was still full of energy when flying the second last, and stayed on for a game success. He had not sparkled on softer ground in bumpers and hurdles, but settled better on this faster ground, which clearly suits.

Inoogoo(IRE) got outpaced from the home turn but stayed on to be closing again at the finish. He did not make much impact in two soft-ground hurdles over the winter, but had been backed to improve for better going. He could go well over further. (op 11-2)

Fortuni(IRE) was well backed following his ready success in the legends' race at the Aintree festival earlier this month. He was given every chance to make a challenge, but when it came to the crunch his effort was laboured. He weakened in his three previous hurdle starts, all in January, but has improved for a tongue-tie and his runs on the Flat suggested he would be suited by this better ground. However, he did not look a hurdles winner in waiting on this showing. (tchd 4-5 and Evens)

Agricultural was driven along to tack onto the leading pack as they went clear, but could only finish at one pace. Considering he had 35lb to find on official ratings with Fortuni there was some encouragement in this effort. (op 66-1)

Oh So Beautiful(IRE), having her first run since her hurdling debut at Killarney last August, made some late progress and should come on for the run, especially as she has joined a yard whose runners usually fare better with a recent outing. (op 5-1)

5429 ARFURMINUTE BULLDOG H'CAP HURDLE (10 hdls) 2m 2f

6:45 (6:46) (Class 4) (0-115,112) 4-Y-0+ **£2,602** (£764; £382; £190)

Form RPR

4201 **1** **Rolecarr (IRE)**19 5144 8-11-6 **111**................................ PaulGallagher(5) 119+
(Ann Hamilton) *trckd ldrs: chsd wnr 3 out: rdn 2 out: led run-in: kpt on wl* **10/3**1

3040 **2** 2¾ **Bow School (IRE)**27 5030 10-11-0 **100**....................(b1) CampbellGillies 107+
(Mrs A C Hamilton) *led: hit 3 out: rdn last: hdd run-in: one pce* **12/1**

4223 **3** *5* **Sheriff Hall (IRE)**19 5145 6-10-4 **90**..................................(t) JanFaltejsek 90
(George Charlton) *trckd ldrs: rdn after 3 out: edgd lft run-in: kpt on one pce* **7/2**2

6000 **4** 3¼ **Barron Watlass (IRE)**39 4797 7-10-11 **97**.......................(p) BarryKeniry 94
(George Moore) *hld up in tch and t.k.h: rdn after 3 out: styd on fr last: wnt 4th run-in: nvr threatened* **14/1**

004 **5** 3½ **Nisaal (IRE)**19 5147 6-10-10 **96**...................................... PaddyAspell 90
(Sandy Forster) *midfield: rdn and outpcd after 4 out: hit 3 out: kpt on run-in* **12/1**

400 **6** *18* **Benmadigan (IRE)**19 5144 9-11-8 **108**.............................. FearghalDavis 86
(Nicky Richards) *hld up: rdn after 6th: wknd after 3 out* **14/1**

44P5 **7** ¾ **Trumpstoo (USA)**36 4858 5-11-12 **112**..........................(p) BrianHughes 89
(Richard Fahey) *trckd ldrs: reminders after 5th: rdn after 4 out: wknd after next* **16/1**

1032 **8** *1* **Altan Khan**22 5102 6-11-6 **109**...................................... JamesHalliday(3) 87
(Malcolm Jefferson) *hld up: hit 6th: mstke 3 out: sn rdn: wknd after 2 out* **4/1**3

F430 **9** *nk* **Scotswell**19 5144 5-10-2 **95**.. GaryRutherford(7) 71
(Harriet Graham) *hld up in tch: hdwy 6th: rdn 3 out: sn wknd* **40/1**

63P **10** *46* **Strobe**20 5132 7-10-10 **101**..(p) AlexanderVoy(5) 36
(Lucy Normile) *w ldr: rdn and outpcd after 4 out: wknd after 2 out* **22/1**

5213 **11** *8* **Patriot (IRE)**315 729 7-11-8 **108**...................................... WilsonRenwick 35
(Martin Todhunter) *hld up: rdn after 5th: sn bhd: t.o* **8/1**

4m 19.3s (-7.70) **Going Correction** -0.50s/f (Good) **11** Ran SP% **117.8**
Speed ratings (Par 105): **97,95,93,92,90 82,82,81,81,61 57**
toteswingers: 1&2 £6.60, 1&3 £3.40, 2&3 £15.30. CSF £43.10 CT £150.52 TOTE £5.20: £1.90, £3.80, £1.80; EX 67.20.
Owner Ian Hamilton **Bred** A W Buller **Trained** Great Bavington, Northumbland

FOCUS
The ground had eased to good for this competitive handicap, in which only those racing prominently got into it.

NOTEBOOK
Rolecarr(IRE) tracked the leader, got a bit outpaced as that rival went for home, but came home strongly up the straight to gain his second C&D success within a month. His previous best efforts have been on softer ground, so he was one that was suited by the easing conditions, and that helped offset the 6lb rise. He may not have anything in hand once the handicapper gets hold though. (op 4-1 tchd 5-1)

Bow School(IRE) is better known as a chaser but, lit up in first-time blinkers, made a bold show from the front, getting the field on the stretch around the final turn, but in the end he may have just gone for home too soon. However, on this evidence he should be up to breaking his duck over hurdles.

Sheriff Hall(IRE) has run with credit in three chases on softish ground over the past couple of months, but was better on faster going as a hurdler. He raced prominently and theoretically had every chance, even off a career-high hurdles mark, but he is now 0-5 at this track. (op 4-1)

Barron Watlass(IRE) made some late progress but was never a threat. He has been below his best since the turn of the year, but even then needed to improve on his best to feature here, so ran as well as could be expected. (op 20-1 tchd 22-1)

Nisaal(IRE)'s three novice hurdle runs had been on softer ground at this track, and he did not look particularly well treated for his first handicap, but could improve on faster ground. (op 11-1)

Benmadigan(IRE) ran a bit better than on his return from a winter break earlier this month, but he seems to be a stuffy horse who needs a couple of runs to put him straight. (op 12-1)

Altan Khan made up some ground from the rear of the field, but it was asking a lot to reel in the front-runners, especially since the ground had gone against him. (op 11-4)

5430 TOTEPOOL H'CAP CHASE (19 fncs) 3m 1f

7:15 (7:15) (Class 3) (0-120,115) 5-Y-0+ **£4,553** (£1,337; £668; £333)

Form RPR

2035 **1** **Zitenka (IRE)**41 4742 9-11-9 **115**...............................(b) JamesHalliday(3) 126+
(Tim Easterby) *w ldr: led 9th: hit 2 out: rdn clr after last* **5/2**1

6215 **2** *7* **More Equity**8 5319 9-11-9 **112**.. RyanMania 115
(Dianne Sayer) *prom: hit 12th: rdn after 4 out: outpcd after 2 out: kpt on run-in: wnt 2nd fnl 150yds: no ch w wnr* **11/4**2

2450 **3** *19* **Guns And Butter (IRE)**12 5261 9-10-3 **92**................(b1) WilsonRenwick 77
(Rose Dobbin) *in tch: hdwy 5 out: pckd 4 out: sn wnt 2nd: rdn to chal after 2 out: wknd run-in: lost 2nd fnl 150yds* **11/1**

621P **4** *35* **Copper's Gold (IRE)**27 5032 7-11-3 **106**...................(b) CampbellGillies 59
(Lucinda Russell) *led narrowly: hdd 9th: rdn bef 3 out: wknd after 2 out* **7/2**3

/5PU **P** **Raining Horse (FR)**6 5353 9-10-11 **100**.....................(p) RichieMcGrath —
(James Ewart) *hld up in tch: nt fluent 2nd: hit 14th: sn pushed along: wknd after next: t.o whn p.u bef 2 out* **7/2**3

6m 28.3s (-3.20) **Going Correction** +0.05s/f (Yiel) **5** Ran SP% **108.0**
Speed ratings: **107,104,98,87,—**
toteswinger: 1&2 £8.70. CSF £9.51 TOTE £3.80: £2.80, £1.60; EX 10.10.
Owner Mrs Jennifer E Pallister **Bred** Thomas Kinsella **Trained** Great Habton, N Yorks

FOCUS
A tricky race with question marks over all the runners.

NOTEBOOK
Zitenka(IRE) disputed the lead throughout and, despite hitting the last ditch, he jumped better than his rivals, meaning he had more left in reserve after the last. His handicap mark has taken a dive since a high of 132 a year ago, but there had been a couple of more encouraging runs in the meantime and he had to capitalise off just 115 today. (op 11-4 tchd 3-1)

More Equity often runs well round here and the 8lb rise for her maiden chase win looked fair. She was under pressure for much of the final circuit but stayed on again after getting outpaced and ran a creditable race, although she has been on the go since last August and might just need a break now. (tchd 5-2)

Guns And Butter(IRE) put in several slow jumps but put up a brief challenge before fading up the straight. He is a chasing maiden who might need a right-handed track if he is to capitalise on a sliding handicap mark. (tchd 14-1)

Copper's Gold(IRE) matched strides with the winner until fading from the home turn. He is best when relatively fresh, and though he looks on a reasonable mark following his win at Newcastle in March, this will have done no harm to his future prospects. (tchd 4-1)

Raining Horse(FR) jumped hesitantly early on. Although he warmed to the fences a bit, he was soon a spent force. (op 10-3 tchd 11-4)

5431 PHARMISTICE AT 20 H'CAP HURDLE (11 hdls) 2m 6f 110y

7:45 (7:45) (Class 3) (0-130,123) 4-Y-0+ **£4,553** (£1,337; £668; £333)

Form				RPR
1306	**1**		**Stopped Out**[19] 5149 6-11-12 **123** RichieMcGrath (Kate Walton) *mde all: rdn bef last: drvn and hld on wl run-in* **5/1**[2]	125
00	**2**	*1*	**Premier Grand Cru (FR)**[59] 4285 5-11-2 **120** NathanMoscrop(7) (James Ewart) *hld up on inner: hdwy 4 out: wnt 3rd 3 out: rdn after 2 out: kpt on run-in: wnt 2nd fnl 75yds* **20/1**	121
-014	**3**	*½*	**Sendali (FR)**[19] 5149 7-10-12 **109** BrianHughes (Chris Grant) *trckd ldrs: wnt 2nd 4 out: chal last: sn rdn: one pce: lost 2nd fnl 75yds* **9/2**[1]	110
4004	**4**	*24*	**Political Paddy**[8] 5320 9-10-10 **107** (p) RyanMania (Rayson Nixon) *trckd ldrs: rdn and outpcd after 3 out: wnt modest 4th fnl 150yds* **5/1**[2]	86
1103	**5**	*1 ¾*	**The Magic Bishop**[12] 5262 6-11-2 **116** JamesHalliday(3) (Malcolm Jefferson) *hld up: hdwy after 4 out: 4th 3 out: sn rdn: wknd run-in* **9/1**	93
-002	**6**	*7*	**Glingerbank (IRE)**[31] 4940 11-11-8 **119** FearghalDavis (Nicky Richards) *midfield: mstke 4 out: sn rdn: wknd bef 2 out* **9/2**[1]	90
0000	**7**	*17*	**The Shy Man (IRE)**[19] 5149 8-11-4 **115** BarryKeniry (George Moore) *prom tl wknd qckly after 4 out* **12/1**	71
500P	**8**	*21*	**Melange (USA)**[7] 5335 5-10-0 **97** (t) JanFaltejsek (George Charlton) *in tch: rdn and wknd after 4 out* **16/1**	34
4025	**9**	*38*	**Flying Doctor**[9] 5310 8-11-7 **118** TomSiddall (Elliott Cooper) *midfield on outer: pushed along after 7th: sn lost pl: t.o after 3 out* **25/1**	21
/2-1	**P**		**Whispering Death**[85] 3783 9-11-6 **117** WilsonRenwick (Howard Johnson) *hld up: rdn and wknd qckly after 3 out: p.u bef next* **11/2**[3]	—

5m 25.1s (-15.90) **Going Correction** -0.50s/f (Good) **10** Ran SP% **117.3**
Speed ratings (Par 107): **107,106,106,98,97 95,89,81,68,—**
toteswingers: 1&2 £31.20, 1&3 £5.20, 2&3 £21.90. CSF £93.90 CT £484.95 TOTE £7.60: £2.60, £6.20, £2.30; EX 148.60.

Owner The Well Oiled Partnership **Bred** J And T Shally **Trained** Middleham Moor, N Yorks

FOCUS

Once again, only those racing up with the pace got into it, with three drawing clear up the straight.

NOTEBOOK

Stopped Out was given a finely-judged ride from the front, winding up the tempo down the back, saving a bit for the finish and having enough left to rally. This dual course winner pulled too hard when held up off a steady pace over C&D last time, but he settles better near the front, and he showed how useful he can be when able to get to the lead. (op 6-1)

Premier Grand Cru(FR) stayed on well to the line, but just found the winner too speedy. He has taken time to acclimatise since leaving France, where he won a juvenile hurdle at Pau in December 2009, and on his efforts this year he had around 20lb of improvement to find. This was a much better effort and he should be able to build on this. (tchd 22-1)

Sendali(FR) won over C&D a month ago and again gave his best, but this was a step up in grade and he was just found out in the closing stages, but nevertheless ran right up to his new mark. (tchd 5-1)

Political Paddy has won twice over C&D in the past, but his last victory was two years ago. (op 8-1)

The Magic Bishop won twice earlier this year and acts on a variety of going, but he is still 9lb higher than his last winning mark and that seems to have stopped him. (op 10-1)

Glingerbank(IRE) usually goes well at this track, but needs to be fresh and might have left his race behind at Haydock a month ago. (tchd 4-1)

Whispering Death made a winning return from a layoff at Doncaster in January and had been absent again since. He made some progress but never really picked up when it mattered and never looked comfortable. (op 9-2 tchd 6-1)

5432 RADIO BORDERS CASH FOR KIDS STANDARD OPEN NATIONAL HUNT FLAT RACE 2m 110y

8:15 (8:15) (Class 6) 4-6-Y-0 **£1,301** (£382; £191; £95)

Form				RPR
544	**1**		**Capital Venture (IRE)**[27] 5034 5-10-9 0 NathanMoscrop(7) (James Ewart) *led: rdn whn hdd 2f out: rallied to ld again 1f out: hld on all out* **17/2**	111+
	2	*nk*	**Simply Ned (IRE)** 4-10-11 0 FearghalDavis (Nicky Richards) *midfield: hdwy over 4f out: chal 3f out: led narrowly 2f out: hdd 1f out: kpt on: jst hld* **8/1**	105
3/42	**3**	*13*	**Thirty Days Out (IRE)**[27] 5033 6-9-13 0 CallumWhillans(10) (Donald Whillans) *midfield: rdn over 4f out: kpt on fr over 1f out: wnt 3rd towards fin* **11/4**[1]	91
5	**4**	*nk*	**Venitzia (IRE)**[101] 3511 5-11-2 0 BrianHughes (Howard Johnson) *trckd ldrs: rdn over 3f out: one pce: lost 3rd towards fin* **3/1**[2]	98
0	**5**	*6*	**Kinder Scout**[20] 5135 4-10-4 0 WilsonRenwick (Chris Grant) *prom: rdn over 3f out: wknd over 1f out* **66/1**	81
06	**6**	*nk*	**Jamaddji**[14] 5209 4-10-4 0 TomSiddall (Elliott Cooper) *in tch: rdn over 5f out: one pce* **100/1**	80
	7	*1 ½*	**Rhymers Ha'** 4-10-11 0 CampbellGillies (Lucinda Russell) *hld up: rdn over 4f out: one pce* **16/1**	86
66	**8**	*6*	**Tartan Tiger (IRE)**[50] 4457 5-11-2 0 RichieMcGrath (John Quinn) *trckd ldrs: wknd over 3f out* **11/2**	86
	9	*½*	**Megamix** 5-10-4 0 PaulGallagher(5) (Robert Bewley) *midfield: rdn over 4f out: sn no imp* **40/1**	78
P-P	**10**	*7*	**Crosstek (IRE)**[68] 4117 5-10-13 0 EwanWhillans(3) (Alistair Whillans) *midfield on inner: rdn over 4f out: no imp* **50/1**	79
00	**11**	*38*	**Supreme Dawn**[44] 4574 6-10-9 0 PaddyAspell (Shelley Johnstone) *midfield: pushed along over 7f out: wknd 4f out* **80/1**	38
	12	*1 ¾*	**Hollyrock** 5-10-9 0 RyanMania (Rayson Nixon) *hld up: a bhd* **40/1**	36
	13	*15*	**John Crabbies (FR)** 4-10-11 0 BarryKeniry (Lisa Williamson) *trckd ldrs: wknd fnl 4f: t.o* **5/1**[3]	25
0	**14**	*16*	**Grey Danbys**[12] 5264 5-10-6 0 JamesHalliday(3) (Malcolm Jefferson) *hld up: t.k.h early: rdn over 5f out: wknd fnl 4f: t.o* **33/1**	8

3m 52.9s (-3.30) **Going Correction** -0.50s/f (Good)
WFA 4 from 5yo+ 5lb **14** Ran SP% **124.7**
Speed ratings: **87,86,80,80,77 77,76,74,73,70 52,51,44,37**
toteswingers: 1&2 £20.30, 1&3 £5.10, 2&3 £8.90. CSF £75.71 TOTE £11.30: £3.20, £3.50, £1.50; EX 84.40.

Owner Mrs Ray Calder & Mrs Jan Scott **Bred** Gerald Mitchell **Trained** Langholm, Dumfries & G'way

FOCUS

Yet another race dominated from the front this evening, with two pulling clear off the customary steady early pace.

NOTEBOOK

Capital Venture(IRE) set off in the lead and, despite looking green, he rallied well once passed up the straight to get up near the line. He looks a bit of a slow learner, as he still looked novicey despite having raced in three bumpers previously. Given a summer to grow into his sizeable frame, he looks a future chasing prospect. (op 8-1 tchd 15-2)

Simply Ned(IRE) made good progress from a rear position to get first run on the winner against the rail, but it was not enough to help him as he was eventually outstayed. This was still a thoroughly creditable debut, especially as he was a bit green near the finish, showing a bit of pace which he will be able to put to good use with the benefit of this experience behind him. (op 13-2)

Thirty Days Out(IRE) could not go with the leading pair but won a separate battle for third. She is becoming a consistent performer in bumpers, but just not good enough, though to be fair she is with a yard that rarely has a bumper winner. (op 4-1 tchd 5-2)

Venitzia(IRE) was expected to build on his debut at Doncaster in January, but in the end he could only find the one pace and was somewhat disappointing. (op 11-4 tchd 4-1)

Tartan Tiger(IRE) attracted some support to build on his two sixth-placed finishes to-date, but after being right there he found nothing when asked and weakened tamely. (op 6-1 tchd 15-2 tchd 8-1 in a place)

T/Plt: £95.40 to a £1 stake. Pool:£42,778.97 - 327.20 winning tickets. T/Qpdt: £15.50 to a £1 stake. Pool:£6,147.11 - 291.95 winning tickets. AS

4895 NEWTON ABBOT (L-H)

Saturday, April 23

OFFICIAL GOING: Good (good to firm in places)

All bends moved since last meeting but impact on distances not notified.

Wind: virtually nil with mild breeze from 4.00 Weather: sunny and very warm

5433 CHICKS CHILDREN'S CHARITY NOVICES' H'CAP HURDLE (10 hdls) 2m 6f

2:00 (2:00) (Class 5) (0-95,94) 4-Y-0+ **£1,658** (£487; £243; £121)

Form				RPR
3313	**1**		**The Composer**[24] 5075 9-11-0 **82** JimmyMcCarthy (Michael Blanshard) *mde all: set dawdle tl steadily upped tempo appr 7th: rdn whn chal after 3 out: styd on wl fr next: mstke last: rdn out* **9/4**[1]	85
-P04	**2**	*3 ¼*	**Little Eaglet (IRE)**[16] 5172 7-11-8 **90** LiamHeard (Colin Heard) *hld up in cl 5th: wnt 4th after 3 out: sn u.p: chsd wnr and hung lft after 2 out: mstke last: no further imp* **8/1**	90
65F3	**3**	*4 ½*	**Ladies Best**[32] 4924 7-11-3 **90** (t) MattGriffiths(5) (Gordon Edwards) *w wnr tl rdn after 3 out: kpt on same pce fr next* **13/2**[3]	85
0002	**4**	*½*	**Big Knickers**[21] 5111 6-11-12 **94** PaddyBrennan (Neil Mulholland) *trckd ldrs: chalng whn nt fluent 7th: rdn and ev ch after 3 out: one pce fr next* **9/4**[1]	89
P0P2	**5**	*4*	**Rossmill Lad (IRE)**[22] 5103 7-10-2 **70** (t) NickScholfield (Luke Dace) *trckd ldrs: rdn after 3 out: one pce whn nt fluent next* **3/1**[2]	62

5m 58.7s (38.50) **Going Correction** -0.075s/f (Good) **5** Ran SP% **111.0**
Speed ratings (Par 103): **27,25,24,24,22**
CSF £18.05 TOTE £3.20: £1.30, £3.00; EX 18.70.

Owner A D Jones **Bred** D A And Mrs Hicks **Trained** Upper Lambourn, Berks

FOCUS

The time was exceedingly slow and the form is probably worthless.

NOTEBOOK

The Composer was allowed to take them along at a virtual walk and, having increased the tempo down the back on the second circuit, kept finding to supplement his Ffos Las win in March, despite being 10lb higher. (op 5-2 tchd 11-4)

Little Eaglet(IRE) has often front-run but his jockey was keen not to do so this time and, while he finished well, he never really looked like breaking his duck. (op 15-2 tchd 7-1)

Ladies Best took his record over hurdles to 0-14 and is going to need to drop on a weak contest to end that run. (op 8-1)

Big Knickers looked a big threat half a mile out but her effort petered out. It's impossible to be too critical of her, or indeed any of the beaten runners, given how things panned out. (op 5-2 tchd 2-1)

5434 NEWTON ABBOT RACES H'CAP CHASE (16 fncs) 2m 5f 110y

2:40 (2:40) (Class 5) (0-95,91) 5-Y-0+ **£2,021** (£589; £294)

Form				RPR
PU56	**1**		**Gunship (IRE)**[12] 5256 10-11-2 **86** (b) MarkQuinlan(5) (Cathy Hamilton) *led 2nd: mde rest: in command fr 3 out: styd on strly* **8/1**	104+
P0P2	**2**	*12*	**Lansdowne Princess**[11] 5273 9-10-8 **73** AndrewThornton (Gerald Ham) *hld up in last pair but in tch: hdwy 11th: rdn in 3rd after 4 out: styd on to take 2nd run-in: no ch w wnr* **7/1**	79
-321	**3**	*3 ¼*	**Digital Media (IRE)**[14] 5214 9-11-3 **89** (t) SClements(7) (Simon Burrough) *trckd ldrs: wnt 2nd after 11th: rdn after 4 out: nvr any imp on wnr: no ex whn lost 2nd run-in* **10/3**[1]	94
1423	**4**	*22*	**Sir Bumble (IRE)**[230] 1474 11-11-12 **91** (t) DominicElsworth (Michael Blake) *led tl 2nd: chsd ldrs: dropped to last pair but in tch 7th: rdn after 4 out: nt pce to get bk on terms: wknd after 2 out* **9/2**[3]	79
3512	**5**	*32*	**Normandy Landings**[40] 4784 8-11-7 **86** (p) PaddyBrennan (Neil Mulholland) *trckd ldrs: effrt 11th: wknd 4 out: t.o* **5/1**	40
42F4	**P**		**Mr Bond (IRE)**[12] 5256 8-11-3 **82** (p) NickScholfield (Andy Turnell) *trckd wnr fr 3rd: prom whn hit 8th: mstke 11th: sn rdn: wkng whn nt fluent next: bhd whn p.u bef 3 out* **7/2**[2]	—
4504	**P**		**Mangonel**[18] 5155 7-11-3 **82** HarrySkelton (Stuart Howe) *nvr travelling or fluent in rr: t.o after 9th: p.u bef 3 out* **9/1**	—

5m 18.0s (-3.40) **Going Correction** -0.075s/f (Good) **7** Ran SP% **113.8**
Speed ratings: **103,98,97,89,77 —,—**
toteswingers: 1&2 £3.80, 1&3 £2.90, 2&3 £2.00 CSF £58.82 TOTE £11.40: £5.60, £3.00; EX 49.80.

Owner M W Hoskins **Bred** Thomas Abbey **Trained** Kington Magna, Dorset

FOCUS

A very modest handicap chase with the winner rated to last year's winning form and the placed horses to their marks.

NOTEBOOK

Gunship(IRE) led them a merry dance in front and, given he stays 3m, it was no surprise he kept on rolling and nothing got close to challenging. He clearly loves to bowl along, his jumping was sound and there is no reason why he can't win again in similar company.

Lansdowne Princess has a poor strike-rate and was beaten a long way at Taunton last time so this was better, without ever really threatening. She can probably win again but it will be a weak contest. (op 8-1)

Digital Media(IRE) looked like being a major threat on the second circuit but soon began to struggle to keep tabs on the winner and could plug on at only that one pace. This trip appears to stretch him. (op 7-2)

Sir Bumble(IRE) was nowhere near his best on his return from a 230-day break. He is entitled to strip fitter for this. (op 4-1)

5435 P4 MARKETING MARES' MAIDEN HURDLE (8 hdls) 2m 1f

3:15 (3:19) (Class 5) 4-Y-0+ **£1,747** (£509; £254)

Form RPR

PP4 **1** **Spiritual Art**[22] 5099 5-11-0 0 .... DominicElsworth 100+
(Luke Dace) *travelled wl bhd ldrs: smooth prog to ld 2 out: rn green and wandered bef last: r.o strly: readily* **11/8**[1]

400 **2** *6* **Blue Lovell (FR)**[30] 4970 5-10-11 0 .... WayneKavanagh(3) 91
(Caroline Keevil) *in tch: pushed along after 2nd: rdn and hdwy 5th: ev ch after 3 out: styd on same pce and sn hld in 3rd: regained 2nd run-in:* **25/1**

340 **3** *1 3/4* **Anaya**[31] 4952 4-10-9 97 .... PaddyBrennan 86
(David Bourton) *trckd ldrs: led 3 out: rdn and hdd next: sn hld by wnr: no ex whn lost 2nd run-in* **9/2**[3]

0000 **4** *22* **Gypsy Moth (IRE)**[30] 4970 5-10-11 0 .... (t) IanPopham(3) 69
(Caroline Keevil) *prom tl stmbld 3rd: trckd ldrs: ev ch 3 out: sn rdn: wknd bef next* **10/1**

455/ **P** **Adorabella (IRE)**[249] 4312 8-11-0 0 .... GerardTumelty —
(Simon Earle) *tubed: hld up and a last: wknd 5th: t.o whn p.u bef 2 out* **16/1**

P **Humor Me Rene (USA)**[37] 4-10-2 0 .... TrevorWhelan(7) —
(George Baker) *led: awkward 1st: hdd 3 out: sn rdn: wknd qckly: p.u bef next* **9/4**[2]

P **P** **Weebitevil**[43] 4709 4-10-2 0 .... MrJBanks(7) —
(Matthew Salaman) *awkward 1st: trckd ldrs: rdn appr 5th: sn wknd: t.o whn p.u bef 2 out* **40/1**

4m 4.10s (-1.60) **Going Correction** -0.075s/f (Good)
WFA 4 from 5yo+ 5lb **7** Ran SP% **112.3**
Speed ratings (Par 103): **100,97,96,86,— —,—**
toteswingers: 1&2 £13.60, 1&3 £1.40, 2&3 £19.20. CSF £31.89 TOTE £2.40: £1.60, £6.60; EX 36.30.
Owner Miss Ruth Kennedy **Bred** R Haim **Trained** Five Oaks, W Sussex

FOCUS

A weak mares' maiden event rated around the winner and third.

NOTEBOOK

Spiritual Art fairly bolted up, always travelling well under a patient ride before cruising through to jump to the front at the second-last and clear away from her rivals. She apparently works like a good horse at home and, although all her Flat wins came on the all-weather, she proved fully effective on this quick ground and looks the type who can hold her own in better company. (tchd 13-8)

Blue Lovell(FR) kept responding to pressure to make good headway down the back but then looked to have run her race turning for home. However, she picked up once again and finished well to pass Anaya for second in the closing stages. This was an improvement on her poor bumper runs and she looks the type who can do better again when there is less emphasis on speed. (op 16-1)

Anaya jumped to the front down the back but was always a sitting duck for the winner and couldn't sustain her effort in the straight. (op 4-1 tchd 5-1)

Gypsy Moth(IRE) lost touch on the leaders leaving the back and is beginning to look decidedly modest. (op 12-1 tchd 7-1)

Humor Me Rene(USA), a 72-rated Flat performer who came into this in good form in that sphere, attracted market support but couldn't justify it, dropping away tamely once headed. (op 3-1 tchd 2-1)

5436 SIS H'CAP CHASE (13 fncs) 2m 110y

3:50 (3:50) (Class 2) (0-150,140) 5-Y-0+ **£12,674** (£3,744; £1,872; £936; £468)

Form RPR

2301 **1** **Pepe Simo (IRE)**[13] 5233 7-11-7 **140** .... MrRMahon(5) 147+
(Paul Nicholls) *tendency to jump rt: chsd ldrs: led 3 out: qcknd clr after 2 out: wnt rt and hit last: r.o: rdn out* **5/2**[1]

1406 **2** *2 1/4* **Safari Journey (USA)**[16] 5164 7-11-7 **140** .... (p) MattGriffiths(5) 146+
(Philip Hobbs) *cl up tl v awkward 3rd: in last pair: wnt 2nd after 7th tl next: sn rdn: styd on fr 2 out: wnt 2nd at the last: a being hld* **10/3**[3]

3521 **3** *8* **Cruchain (IRE)**[9] 5305 8-10-6 **123** .... DonalDevereux(3) 120
(Dai Burchell) *led: wnt rt 5th: rdn and hdd 3 out: hld next: no ex whn lost 2nd at the last* **3/1**[2]

P240 **4** *5* **Moon Over Miami (GER)**[49] 4470 10-11-6 **134** .... (t) DominicElsworth 124
(Charlie Mann) *trckd ldr 3rd tl after 7th: rdn after 4 out: one pce fr next* **8/1**

4242 **5** *1 1/2* **Mibleu (FR)**[3] 5394 11-9-13 **116** .... KeiranBurke(3) 108
(Colin Tizzard) *racd keenly: hld up: wnt 3rd after 4 out: sn rdn: no further imp whn hit 2 out: fading whn wnt rt last* **13/2**

5F50 **6** *29* **Frosted Grape (IRE)**[149] 2630 5-10-9 **130** .... (b) SClements(7) 93
(David Pipe) *trckd ldr tl 3rd: sn dropped to last and rdn: no ch fr 7th: t.o* **10/1**

4m 1.20s (-5.30) **Going Correction** -0.075s/f (Good) **6** Ran SP% **110.2**
Speed ratings: **109,107,104,101,101 87**
toteswingers: 1&2 £1.30, 1&3 £1.40, 2&3 £1.10. CSF £11.05 TOTE £3.90: £3.40, £1.80; EX 11.00.
Owner Highclere Thoroughbred Racing-Pepe Simo **Bred** Grange Stud **Trained** Ditcheat, Somerset

FOCUS

A good-quality handicap chase and a slight personal best from the winner.

NOTEBOOK

Pepe Simo(IRE) had the profile of one who might prefer going right-handed (four of his five previous wins that way round) but proved he can handle going the in this direction. He caught the eye with a super leap down the back that took him within a couple of lengths of the lead and, upsides Cruchain approaching the second-last, showed a cracking change of speed to quicken away after that fence. A mistake at the last, where he went to his right, allowed the strong-finishing Safari Journey to close but the result was never in doubt. This was the first time he had won on ground quicker than good and this success opens up options over the summer if connections so wish. (op 11-4)

Safari Journey(USA) looked outpaced leaving the back, but saw his race out in strong style and ran well in defeat. (op 3-1)

Cruchain(IRE) dropped away once headed and is vulnerable off this sort of mark. He can be found easier opportunities than this. (op 7-2)

Moon Over Miami(GER) travelled with a good deal of zest for a long way, but couldn't land a blow when push came to shove and this ground is probably too quick for him.

Mibleu(FR) looked a major threat leaving the back but faded disappointingly and this may have come a little too soon, given he returned from an absence only three days previously. (op 6-1)

Frosted Grape(IRE) was never a factor and the 149-day break clearly hasn't revitalised her. (op 9-1)

5437 CHRISTOPHER SINGLETON 18TH BIRTHDAY CELEBRATION "NATIONAL HUNT" NOVICES' HURDLE (8 hdls) 2m 3f

4:25 (4:25) (Class 4) 4-Y-0+ **£2,706** (£788; £394)

Form RPR

P0P1 **1** **Surf And Turf (IRE)**[13] 5243 5-11-6 112 .... RichieMcLernon 96+
(Jonjo O'Neill) *confidently rdn: sn trcking ldr: led 2 out: hld on: pushed out* **8/11**[1]

40P **2** *nk* **Malibu Sun**[43] 4702 4-10-7 0 .... SamJones 83+
(Oliver Sherwood) *hld up bhd: stdy prog fr after 5th: disputing cl 3rd whn short of room 2 out: swtchd lft bef last: kpt on wl run-in* **16/1**

3 *4 1/2* **Storm Jack (FR)**[42] 6-10-13 0 .... NickScholfield 85
(Jeremy Scott) *tubed: trckd ldng pair: rdn and ev ch after 3 out: styd on same pce fr next* **11/4**[2]

0 **4** *1 1/4* **Newlyn Bay**[21] 5108 6-10-10 0 .... WayneKavanagh(3) 84
(Caroline Keevil) *led: rdn whn pressed after 3 out: hdd next: styd on same pce* **8/1**[3]

-0U **5** *31* **Mr Redwood**[49] 9-10-8 0 .... MarkQuinlan(5) 56
(Susan Gardner) *hld up in last pair: lost tch fr after 6th: t.o* **20/1**

6 *58* **My Runaway (IRE)**[34] 5-10-13 0 .... DominicElsworth 4
(Michael Blake) *chsd ldrs tl rdn sn after 3 out: wknd qckly: t.o* **12/1**

PP5 **7** *17* **Maxi's Dream**[11] 5274 6-10-10 0 .... IanPopham(3) —
(Stuart Howe) *in tch tl wknd appr 6th: t.o* **50/1**

4m 30.3s (-3.60) **Going Correction** -0.075s/f (Good)
WFA 4 from 5yo+ 5lb **7** Ran SP% **116.0**
Speed ratings (Par 105): **104,103,101,101,88 63,56**
toteswingers: 1&2 £3.90, 1&3 £1.10, 2&3 £5.90. CSF £15.13 TOTE £2.30: £1.10, £6.70; EX 18.30.
Owner John P McManus **Bred** J P Murphy & M Barry Murphy **Trained** Cheltenham, Gloucs

FOCUS

Little depth to this event and not form to be confident about.

NOTEBOOK

Surf And Turf(IRE) got the job done, but he was all out to hold the late thrust of Malibu Sun after the last. He took a huge step forward when getting off the market at Wincanton and handled the quicker ground well enough, but was made to work hard to concede the penalty. Still, he's clearly going the right way and it wouldn't be a surprise if he were well placed to complete the hat-trick next time. (op Evens)

Malibu Sun ♣ is the one to take out of the race having left his previous efforts miles behind and he looks a certain future winner on this evidence. He made eye-catching headway from well off the pace and was forced to switch to the inside before the final hurdle. He picked up strongly but the line came in time for the winner. (op 12-1 tchd 20-1)

Storm Jack(FR) didn't fare too badly but lacked a change of gear at the business end. He should do better over further in time. (op 10-3 tchd 7-2)

Newlyn Bay was also not disgraced but is out of a mare who improved with age, so we may not see the best of him until further down the line. (tchd 17-2)

5438 AJ BOOTH BUILDING & CARPENTRY H'CAP CHASE (20 fncs) 3m 2f 110y

4:55 (4:55) (Class 4) (0-110,108) 5-Y-0+ **£3,057** (£897; £448; £224)

Form RPR

F06U **1** **Estates Recovery (IRE)**[27] 5037 6-11-4 **107** .... MrJABest(7) 119+
(Philip Hobbs) *trckd ldr: chal 4 out: rdn after next: pckd 2 out: sn led: styd on strly to draw clr* **9/4**[1]

P255 **2** *9* **Porta Vogie (IRE)**[59] 4292 9-11-9 **105** .... JodieMogford 110+
(Graeme McPherson) *j.w: sn trcking ldng pair: led 15th: rdn after 3 out: hdd after next: sn hld: styd on same pce* **7/1**

6F55 **3** *11* **Cullahill (IRE)**[27] 5037 9-11-7 **103** .... AndrewThornton 94
(Bob Buckler) *j.rt: led tl 15th: outpcd 4 out: styd on to regain 3rd at the last but nvr any ch* **3/1**[2]

0P22 **4** *2 3/4* **Ban Uisce (IRE)**[27] 5039 6-11-12 **108** .... (tp) PaddyBrennan 97
(Neil Mulholland) *hld up bhd ldrs: outpcd 4 out: wnt 3rd sn after but no ch w ldrs: lost 3rd at the last* **10/3**[3]

4433 **P** **Lavenoak Lad**[15] 5192 11-10-12 **99** .... (t) MattGriffiths(5) —
(Simon Burrough) *chsd ldrs early: dropped to last after 6th: pushed along after next: losing tch whn p.u after 13th* **9/2**

6m 39.4s (-5.20) **Going Correction** -0.075s/f (Good) **5** Ran SP% **109.5**
Speed ratings: **104,101,98,97,—**
CSF £16.08 TOTE £3.00: £1.60, £3.00; EX 34.40.
Owner James Drummond **Bred** Damien Landy **Trained** Withycombe, Somerset

FOCUS

Modest stuff and it concerned only two leaving the back straight. The winner is rated to his best hurdles form with the second to his mark

NOTEBOOK

Estates Recovery(IRE) edged ahead before the last fence and although he went through the final obstacle, he came clear to win his first chase. He was low at a number of his fences throughout, which is a concern, but has got an engine and maybe this will be the confidence-booster he needs to go on and be as good in this sphere as over hurdles. (op 11-4)

Porta Vogie(IRE) jumped with much more relish and ran a blinder in defeat, being just outstayed by the winner. A return to slightly shorter and easier ground can see this 9-y-o back in the winner's enclosure. (op 13-2)

Cullahill(IRE) set a good gallop but weakened away once headed and once again didn't shape like he was ready to take advantage of his declining handicap mark. (op 7-2 tchd 11-4)

Ban Uisce(IRE) was never a factor. (op 7-2)

5439 SOUTH WEST RACING CLUB H'CAP HURDLE (10 hdls) 2m 6f

5:25 (5:25) (Class 4) (0-115,111) 4-Y-0+ **£2,569** (£754; £377; £188)

Form RPR

6066 **1** **Vintage Fabric (USA)**[181] 2001 9-10-3 **95** .... (t) MsLO'Neill(7) 100+
(Nigel Hawke) *chsd ldrs: pushed along after 6th: rdn whn lft 3rd next: led 2 out: styd on gamely* **15/2**

310P **2** *3 3/4* **Matako (FR)**[13] 5241 8-11-6 **108** .... IanPopham(3) 110
(Caroline Keevil) *travelled wl: sn trcking ldrs: led after 3 out: rdn and hdd bef next: styd on same pce* **16/1**

156 **3** *2 1/4* **Kasban**[13] 5230 7-11-12 **111** .... DominicElsworth 111
(Luke Dace) *hld up bhd: rdn after 6th: hdwy after 3 out: wnt 3rd next: styd on same pce* **11/2**[3]

3462 **4** *10* **Thomas Wild**[21] 5108 6-10-13 **105** .... ChrisDavies(7) 98
(Philip Hobbs) *mid-div: pushed along to hold pl fr 4th: hdwy 7th where lft disputing 4th: nvr gng pce to get on terms* **10/3**[1]

0123 **5** *26* **Heir To Be**[11] 5276 12-11-10 **109** .... (b) NickScholfield 77
(Michael Blake) *led tl 6th: sn rdn: wknd qckly: t.o bef 2 out* **9/1**

FP03 **6** *23* **Vivarini**[12] 5252 7-11-4 **110** CharlieWallis(7) 57
(John O'Shea) *mid-div tl dropped to last pair 3rd: rdn after 5th: no ch fr 7th: t.o bef 2 out* **8/1**

0-6P **P** **Arthurs Dream (IRE)**[24] 5076 9-10-0 **85** oh2 LiamTreadwell —
(Nick Ayliffe) *hld up towards rr: hdwy appr 7th where lft disputing 4th: sn rdn: wknd after 3 out: bhd whn p.u bef next* **28/1**

FF6P **P** **Solitary Palm (IRE)**[11] 5275 8-10-11 **96** PaddyBrennan —
(Brian Forsey) *trckd ldrs: led whn nt fluent 6th: rdn and hdd bef next: sn wknd: t.o whn p.u bef 2 out* **14/1**

-034 **F** **Teenage Kicks (IRE)**[161] 2372 6-11-5 **109** MattGriffiths(5) —
(Polly Gundry) *trckd ldrs: disputing ld and travelling wl whn fell 7th* **7/2**[2]

605 **F** **Luck'N'Thanks (IRE)**[28] 5013 8-10-4 **99** KillianMoore(10) 79
(Graeme McPherson) *mid-div: hdwy 6th: lft in clr ld next: rdn and hdd after 3 out: wkng in 5th whn fell next* **14/1**

5m 15.2s (-5.00) **Going Correction** -0.075s/f (Good) **10** Ran SP% **116.2**
Speed ratings (Par 105): **106,104,103,100,90 82,—,—,—,—**
toteswingers: 1&2 £9.10, 1&3 £9.10, 2&3 not won. CSF £114.45 CT £713.87 TOTE £8.60: £1.50, £3.30, £2.20; EX 251.20.
Owner N J McMullan and S H Bryant **Bred** Juddmonte Farms Inc **Trained** Woolminstone, Somerset

FOCUS
Another ordinary affair with the winner rated to last year's course form and the third to his mark.

NOTEBOOK
Vintage Fabric(USA) looked in trouble leaving the back but kept battling away and he showed much more resolution than Matako, who went to the front full of running, to come away up the straight. This was his first win beyond 2m3f but he loves this track and was back down to the same mark as when scoring here last June. (op 8-1)
Matako(FR) had shown little on his last two starts but this was a major improvement, although it was slightly disappointing to see him find so little. (op 14-1)
Kasban kept on steadily from a long way back and shapes as if he needs a stiffer stamina test to show his best, his sole previous win over hurdles having come at 3m+. This was an encouraging run. (tchd 6-1)
Thomas Wild kept plugging away but never looked likely to threaten and was slightly disappointing given he looked reasonably treated on handicap debut. (op 3-1 tchd 7-2)
Teenage Kicks(IRE) looked as if he would play a big part before crashing out on his first start for Polly Gundry. (op 9-2)
T/Plt: £206.30 to a £1 stake. Pool:£42,038.27 - 148.70 winning tickets. T/Qpdt: £7.50 to a £1 stake. Pool:£2,779.58 - 272.63 winning tickets. TM

4725 SANDOWN (R-H)

Saturday, April 23

OFFICIAL GOING: Flat and hurdles course - good (good to firm in places; flat 8.1, hurdle 7.8) chase course - good to firm (good in places: 8.4)
Other races under the rules of Flat racing.
Wind: Almost nil Weather: Sunny, warm

5440 BET365.COM HURDLE (LISTED RACE) (8 hdls) 2m
1:30 (1:30) (Class 1) 4-Y-0+ **£9,406** (£3,707; £1,998)

Form RPR
1310 **1** **The Jigsaw Man (IRE)**[244] 1346 7-11-0 139 AidanColeman 146
(Rebecca Curtis) *mde all and sn clr: nt fluent 4th: stl gng strly 2 out: shkn up whn pressed last: styd on wl flat* **15/2**[3]

1446 **2** *1 3/4* **Clerk's Choice (IRE)**[39] 4791 5-11-4 160 APMcCoy 150+
(Michael Banks) *trckd clr ldr (and wnr): nt fluent 2nd: mstke next: nt fluent 4th: clsd bef 2 out: rdn to chal after last: nt qckn* **4/6**[1]

1140 **3** *26* **Dorabelle (IRE)**[9] 5302 6-10-7 122 TimmyMurphy 116
(Donald McCain) *last fr 3rd: lft bhd fr 3 out: tk poor 3rd bef next* **33/1**

F301 **P** **Sanctuaire (FR)**[7] 5337 5-11-4 150 RWalsh —
(Paul Nicholls) *free to post: led in s and veered lft: heavily restrained in last: chsd ldng pair and in tch 3rd: nt fluent next: mstke 3 out: wknd rapidly: p.u bef next* **15/8**[2]

3m 47.2s (-12.60) **Going Correction** -0.625s/f (Firm) **4** Ran SP% **109.5**
Speed ratings (Par 111): **106,105,92,—**
CSF £13.86 TOTE £7.20; EX 13.70.
Owner LL R P Racing **Bred** P J O'Connor **Trained** Newport, Dyfed

FOCUS
This opening 2m hurdle is usually poorly contested, and it surely must be in danger of losing its Listed status following this years measly turnout. The result was an unsatisfactory one and the form, rated around the first two, is difficult to be confident about.

NOTEBOOK
The Jigsaw Man(IRE) made all and finding too much up the hill for favourite Clerk's Choice, who was rated 21lb his superior. Add in the fact Sanctuaire failed to give anything like his true running, and the form looks worthless. To the winner's credit, he kept up the gallop well and showed a likeable attitude, but his handicap mark is sure to suffer as a result. He's likely to turn out in the Swinton at Haydock early next month, though, before a possible return to fences - he won two of his three starts in novice chases last summer. (op 11-1 tchd 12-1)
Clerk's Choice(IRE), sixth in the Champion Hurdle and the pick at the weights, had conditions in his favour and McCoy seemed full of confidence as they wheeled into the straight, but he wasn't the quickest two out and, having jumped the last, was unable to stay on as strongly as the winner. This clearly wasn't his best form, but he's going to be tough to place next season unless sent chasing. (op 5-6, tchd 10-11 in places)
Dorabelle(IRE) completed in her own time to pick up some minor prize-money, and of more value, some black-type. (op 40-1)
Sanctuaire(FR) looked like the horse that won last season's Fred Winter when bolting up in last weekend's Scottish Champion Hurdle. That was his first run since having a breathing operation and he also settled a bit better, but this time, in such a small field, he wanted to go much quicker early than Walsh would allow and had to be restrained to such extent that he had lost many lengths by the time he was allowed to jump off, having swerved out to the left. These early exertions were always likely to take their toll and, having been a beaten horse by the end of the back, he was pulled up before the last. He'll presumably try chasing next season, but has it all to prove unless he settles. (op 11-8)

5441 BET365 H'CAP HURDLE (9 hdls) 2m 3f 110y
2:05 (2:05) (Class 2) (0-145,142) 4-Y-0+
£7,514 (£2,220; £1,110; £555; £277; £139)

Form RPR
P215 **1** **Sunley Peace**[29] 4992 7-10-3 **119** JamieMoore 126+
(Gary Moore) *trckd ldrs: effrt bef 2 out: rdn and clsd to ld last: drvn clr flat* **12/1**

3434 **2** *3* **Occasionally Yours (IRE)**[9] 5300 7-10-0 **123** MrJMQuinlan(7) 125
(Alan Blackmore) *hld up in last trio: sme prog fr 6th: stl only 9th on long run after 3 out and rdn: prog bef 2 out: wnt 3rd last: battled on wl to take 2nd nr fin* **12/1**

2430 **3** *1* **Monetary Fund (USA)**[36] 4852 5-10-10 **129** RichardKilloran(3) 130
(Nicky Henderson) *trckd ldrs: prog to ld 2 out: hdd and nt fluent last: nt qckn and lost 2nd nr fin* **9/1**

5360 **4** *5* **Dantari (IRE)**[9] 5304 6-10-7 **123** PaulMoloney 120
(Evan Williams) *chsd clr ldr: nt fluent 4th and lost 2nd: styd chsng ldrs: u.p bef 2 out: one pce* **6/1**[3]

B015 **5** *1 3/4* **Tobago Bay**[31] 4940 6-10-2 **128** (b) JosephAkehurst(10) 124
(Gary Moore) *led and sn clr: 15 l up after 3rd: c bk to field 3 out: hdd and fdd 2 out* **16/1**

5200 **6** *4* **Mohanad (IRE)**[18] 4806 5-10-6 **125** MarcGoldstein(3) 116
(Sheena West) *in tch in midfield: effrt 3 out: rdn to dispute 4th 2 out: nt qckn and sn outpcd* **12/1**

P0P0 **7** *3* **Awesome George**[21] 5110 7-10-8 **127** CharlieHuxley(3) 119+
(Alan King) *nt gng or jumping w any fluency and sn last: reminders after 2nd: kpt on bef 2 out: nrst fin* **25/1**

4404 **8** *7* **Gus Macrae (IRE)**[12] 5255 7-10-7 **123** (t) APMcCoy 105
(Rebecca Curtis) *wl in tch in midfield: rdn and fdd bef 2 out* **20/1**

5400 **9** *hd* **Raslan**[112] 3293 8-11-7 **142** (tp) CO'Farrell(5) 125
(David Pipe) *chsd ldng pair to 3rd: steadily lost pl: in last pair fr 6th: n.d after 3 out* **40/1**

1161 **10** *1 3/4* **Extreme Conviction (IRE)**[210] 1608 7-10-10 **126** RhysFlint 107
(John Berry) *hld up in rr: effrt after 3 out: chsng ldrs but no imp bef 2 out: sn wknd* **12/1**

151F **11** *nk* **King Of The Night (GER)**[36] 4852 7-11-8 **138** RWalsh 118
(Paul Nicholls) *hld up in rr: pushed along in 11th after 3 out: no prog and wl btn fr 2 out* **7/2**[1]

241- **12** *shd* **Stratigic Gale (IRE)**[392] 4894 7-10-3 **122** DavidBass(3) 104
(Nicky Henderson) *prom: chsd clr ldr 4th: mstke 6th: lost 2nd and wknd bef 2 out: mstke last* **12/1**

130 **13** *8* **Kazzene (USA)**[56] 4350 4-10-1 **123** (bt[1]) JohnnyFarrelly 93
(David Pipe) *t.k.h: hld up in last trio: blnd 1st: effrt after 3 out: sn wknd qckly* **5/1**[2]

4m 44.4s (-17.40) **Going Correction** -0.625s/f (Firm)
WFA 4 from 5yo+ 5lb **13** Ran SP% **118.6**
Speed ratings (Par 109): **109,107,107,105,104 103,101,99,99,98 98,98,94**
toteswingers:1&2:£26.90, 1&3:£22.70, 2&3:£22.00 CSF £142.56 CT £1366.54 TOTE £14.90: £3.80, £3.80, £3.20; EX 180.70 Trifecta £1087.70 Pool: £1,469.96 - 0.10 winning units..
Owner Davies, Sunley and Manley **Bred** Milton Park Stud Partnership **Trained** Lower Beeding, W Sussex

FOCUS
Often a competitive handicap hurdle and this year was no different. Tobago Bay went tearing into a clear early lead and ensured there was no hanging around. The form looks solid rated around the placed horses.

NOTEBOOK
Sunley Peace, who had disappointed a bit on his handicap debut at Newbury, appreciated the extra 3f and quick ground and stayed on well to win with a bit in hand. Having only his fifth start jumping, he's with the right stable to plunder a big pot over hurdles, although can expect a considerable hike. His trainer indicated afterwards that we're likely to see him back on the Flat this season. (op 11-1)
Occasionally Yours(IRE), who ran a cracker in the EBF Final here before being well held at Cheltenham last time, appreciated the return to handicaps/step back up in trip, keeping on dourly after the last. He ought to stay 3m and could make a half-decent chaser. (op 16-1)
Monetary Fund(USA), well beaten in the Martin Pipe at Cheltenham, found this easier and moved through to hold every chance, but couldn't race on up the hill. (op 10-1 tchd 17-2)
Dantari(IRE) led the main pack and kept on best he could, but his losing run continues. (op 7-1 tchd 11-2)
Tobago Bay did well to keep going the way he did, having raced into such a clear early lead, (op 18-1)
Mohanad(IRE) stayed on at the one pace. (op 14-1)
Awesome George was never travelling and jumped big at his hurdles, but did finish better than most. (op 40-1)
Extreme Conviction(IRE) appeared to get tired on this return from 206 days off.
King Of The Night(GER) was quickly beaten towards the end of the back and perhaps his last-time-out fall has left its mark. (op 4-1)
Stratigic Gale(IRE) stopped very quickly, but it was his first start in 392 days and he deserves another chance. He should make a fine chaser next season. (op 11-1)
Kazzene(USA) had little weight to carry on this handicap debut, but he was keen under restraint in the first-time blinkers and stopped very quickly. He's left with a bit to prove. (op 4-1 tchd 11-2)

5442 BET365.COM CELEBRATION CHASE GRADE 2 (13 fncs) 2m
2:35 (2:35) (Class 1) 5-Y-0+
£28,505 (£10,695; £5,355; £2,670; £1,340; £670)

Form RPR
0165 **1** **French Opera**[15] 5184 8-11-2 162 APMcCoy 159+
(Nicky Henderson) *led or disp thrght: def advantage 3 out: hrd pressed next and stl under threat last: drvn and asserted flat* **2/1**[2]

4RRR **2** *2* **Chaninbar (FR)**[15] 5184 8-11-2 151 (tp) SamTwiston-Davies 155
(Milton Harris) *j. off on terms and disp ld to 2nd: lost pl next: reminders and urged along in last after 6th: rallied 3 out: wnt 2nd sn after last: styd on but no imp on wnr* **33/1**

4100 **3** *1 3/4* **Cornas (NZ)**[38] 4805 9-11-2 152 LeightonAspell 153
(Nick Williams) *set off last and styd there tl 6th: wl in tch after: effrt fr 3 out: tried to cl next: one pce bef last* **15/2**

0312 **4** *nk* **Oiseau De Nuit (FR)**[16] 5164 9-11-2 154 (t) JoeTizzard 155+
(Colin Tizzard) *trckd ldng pair fr 3rd gng wl: wnt 2nd 2 out and chal: stl pressing wnr last: fdd flat* **4/1**[3]

21-3 **5** *nk* **Tataniano (FR)**[160] 2385 7-11-6 160 RWalsh 157
(Paul Nicholls) *disp ld after 2nd tl hdd bef 3 out: lost 2nd 2 out: one pce after* **6/4**[1]

51P1 **6** *32* **Russian Flag (FR)**[13] 5242 8-11-2 138 AlexMerriam 129
(Neil King) *in tch in rr tl lft bhd fr 4 out: t.o* **20/1**

3m 48.9s (-12.90) **Going Correction** -0.625s/f (Firm) **6** Ran SP% **112.8**
Speed ratings: **107,106,105,104,104 88**
toteswingers:1&2:£9.30, 1&3:£2.00, 2&3:£12.10 CSF £40.29 TOTE £3.80: £2.10, £4.20; EX 53.60.
Owner Mrs Judy Wilson & Martin Landau **Bred** N P Bloodstock Ltd **Trained** Upper Lambourn, Berks

FOCUS
Not up to Grade 2 status, but an interesting 2m chase. It produced a good finish, any one of five being in with a chance down the straight and the third and fourth offer the best guide to the level.

NOTEBOOK
French Opera gained a deserved victory, appreciating the drop in grade having contested the Champion Chase and Melling Chase on his last two starts. For all he shaped creditably in both, it's clear he isn't up to championship standard, and races such as this are where he's now most effective. Ridden aggressively by McCoy, this strong-galloping type kept pulling out more for pressure and, although he tended to jump left, he was in no mood to taste defeat. (op 11-4)

Chaninbar(FR) will have surprised many with this good performance, although the ability to win a race such as this has always been there, it's largely his shocking attitude of late that led to his price. Having refused to race on each of his last three starts, this was his last chance (would have been referred to the BHA had he planted again), so it was a relief to see him jump off. For all that he raced lazily, losing his early pitch, he kept responding to pressure and briefly looked like coming with a winning run. He's clearly talented, but it remains to be seen whether he can build on this. (op 40-1)

Cornas(NZ) is capable on his day and likes it here. He appeared to give his running, keeping on without having the pace to win on this sort of ground. (op 11-1)

Oiseau De Nuit(FR), who looked unlucky not to follow up his Grand Annual win at Aintree, was second in this last year and ran every bit as well in a stronger heat this time round. (tchd 9-2)

Tataniano(FR), conceding 4lb all round and not seen since disappointing at Cheltenham in November, jumped slickly and travelled strongly until the end of the railway fences, at which point he appeared to get a little tired before rallying again. This was a satisfactory effort, although he's still below the form shown at Aintree last April. (op 6-5)

Russian Flag(FR) was out of his depth and never posed a threat. (op 22-1)

5443 BET365 GOLD CUP CHASE H'CAP (GRADE 3) (24 fncs) 3m 5f 110y

3:10 (3:11) (Class 1) 5-Y-O+

£79,814 (£29,946; £14,994; £7,476; £3,752; £1,876)

Form				RPR
-06U	**1**		**Poker De Sivola (FR)**[7] 5338 8-10-12 **136**...(p) TimmyMurphy (Ferdy Murphy) *rdn w exaggerated waiting tactics: mstke 1st: detached last after 10th: stl only 12th at 15th: rchd modest 8th after 4 out and 6th 3 out: clsd on ldrs fr next: wnt 4th last: r.o wl to ld last 100yds* **11/1**	148+
P-02	**2**	*2 ¼*	**Faasel (IRE)**[37] 4821 10-10-7 **136**...(bt) CO'Farrell[(5)] (David Pipe) *prom: rousted along in 5th after 4 out: responded to go 2nd bef next: led bef 2 out gng strly: idled after last: hdd and outpcd last 100yds* **14/1**	145
11U1	**3**	*1 ¼*	**Baby Run (FR)**[16] 5163 11-10-12 **136**... SamTwiston-Davies (Nigel Twiston-Davies) *mde most to 4 out: rallied to ld again bef 3 out: hdd bef 2 out: kpt on but no ex* **6/1**[1]	145
F3R1	**4**	*1*	**Triggerman**[9] 5303 9-10-8 **132**...(p) RhysFlint (Philip Hobbs) *settled midfield: j.big 2nd and slowly 4th: prog to trck ldrs fr 11th: cl up in 4th whn mstke 20th: effrt after 3 out: wnt 2nd after next: nt fluent last: edgd lft and fdd flat* **10/1**	141+
31PU	**5**	*1 ½*	**Major Malarkey (IRE)**[38] 4802 8-10-4 **128**... AidanColeman (Nigel Twiston-Davies) *settled midfield: prog and prom fr 11th: jnd ldrs 18th: led 4 out gng strly hdd bef next: nt qckn* **16/1**	134
5002	**6**	*9*	**Maktu**[28] 5009 9-10-12 **136**... LeightonAspell (Pat Murphy) *settled midfield: prog to trck ldrs 15th: 6th and wl in tch whn blnd 20th: stl cl enough bef 3 out: wknd* **10/1**	138+
2640	**7**	*28*	**Briery Fox (IRE)**[28] 5009 13-10-2 **126**... MarkBradburne (Henry Daly) *settled wl in rr: nvr a threat: poor 12th at 19th and similarly far bhd in 9th bef 3 out* **50/1**	103
2-P2	**8**	*41*	**Aimigayle**[37] 4820 8-10-9 **133**... ColinBolger (Suzy Smith) *prom: pressed ldr fr 13th tl 4 out: wknd qckly: virtually p.u flat* **7/1**[2]	103
0P-P	**P**		**Iris De Balme (FR)**[7] 5338 11-10-1 **128**...(t) CharlieHuxley[(3)] (Joanna Davis) *nt a fluent and nvr beyond midfield: struggling fr 15th: t.o whn p.u bef 19th* **50/1**	—
541-	**P**		**Church Island (IRE)**[9] 5123 12-11-7 **150**...(b) APHeskin[(5)] (Michael Hourigan, Ire) *chsd ldrs: struggling to hold pl fr 15th: wkng whn mstke 19th: poor 12th after 4 out: p.u bef next* **22/1**	—
10-5	**P**		**Fire And Rain (FR)**[27] 5038 8-10-2 **126**... PaulMoloney (Emma Lavelle) *prom to 10th: wknd qckly next: tailing off in last whn p.u bef 14th* **33/1**	—
36U0	**P**		**Silver Adonis (IRE)**[16] 5163 10-9-7 **124**...(p) MrTJCannon[(7)] (Dr Richard Newland) *hld up in last trio: nvr remotely involved: wl t.o fr 16th: p.u bef 2 out* **40/1**	—
02PU	**P**		**Richard's Sundance (IRE)**[37] 4821 9-10-12 **136**... AndrewGlassonbury (Victor Dartnall) *chsd ldrs: wl in tch in 6th whn mstke 17th: 8th and wkng whn mstke 20th: t.o in 9th whn p.u bef 2 out* **33/1**	—
30U6	**P**		**Exmoor Ranger (IRE)**[39] 4790 9-11-6 **144**... DenisO'Regan (Victor Dartnall) *settled wl in rr: blnd 12th and rdr nrly off: dropped to last and nvr a factor after: t.o whn p.u bef 3 out* **20/1**	—
-PP4	**P**		**Gentle Ranger (IRE)**[35] 4876 9-10-5 **129**...(bt[1]) JohnnyFarrelly (David Pipe) *mostly pressed ldr to 13th: lost pl qckly next: t.o whn p.u bef 19th* **12/1**	—
P5PF	**P**		**Can't Buy Time (IRE)**[14] 5200 9-10-9 **133**... APMcCoy (Jonjo O'Neill) *settled in midfield: wl in tch if off the pce fr 15th: 7th whn nt fluent 4 out: wknd: poor 8th whn p.u bef 2 out* **14/1**	—
41U0	**P**		**Meanus Dandy (IRE)**[49] 4466 8-10-12 **136**...(b) RWalsh (Paul Nicholls) *nvr really gng wl in midfield: lost pl u.p fr 15th: wl bhd in 10th 4 out: p.u bef next* **9/1**	—
2511	**P**		**Balthazar King (IRE)**[10] 5290 7-11-2 **140**... RichardJohnson (Philip Hobbs) *nvr really gng wl in midfield: mstke 15th and lost several pls: wl bhd whn p.u bef 19th* **8/1**[3]	—

7m 16.3s (-27.70) **Going Correction** -0.625s/f (Firm) **18** Ran SP% **122.7**

Speed ratings: **111,110,110,109,109 107,99,88,**—,— —,—,—,—,— —,—,—

toteswingers:1&2:£34.30, 1&3:£12.70, 2&3:£20.50 CSF £143.69 CT £1022.45 TOTE £10.30: £3.20, £3.50, £1.10, £3.90; EX 105.60 Trifecta £1883.80 Pool: £31,566.62 - 12.40 winning units..

Owner D A Johnson **Bred** Gilles Trapenard **Trained** West Witton, N Yorks

FOCUS

The final major race of the jumps season, and it was as competitive as ever, even if the standard had dropped in terms of class, with only two of the runners being rated higher than 140. Plenty of front-runners in opposition, but they didn't go overly fast, and there were still six in with a shout taking the Pond fence. The runner-up and fifth are the best guides to the form.

NOTEBOOK

Poker De Sivola(FR) trailed for much of the race and was last with a circuit to run, but as last season's 4m National Hunt Chase win shows, all he does is stay, and Murphy must have been licking his lips when he saw the horse they had to chase down on the run-in was Faasel, who does little in front. The result was inevitable after the last and the first-time cheekpieces clearly helped the horse, who had largely struggled for form this season and unseated having been hampered in the Scottish National a week earlier. As for next season, this quirky individual is likely to be a contender in all the top marathon handicaps and few would stay better if he took his chance in the Grand National, although whether he jumps well enough remains to be seen. (op 12-1)

Faasel(IRE) wouldn't have been begrudged victory, and maybe he'd have been better having his challenge been delayed a touch longer. Runner-up in the Kim Muir for the second consecutive season last month, he gave the impression this sort of test would suit and he stuck on better than many would have expected having taken it up two out. As has all too often been the case for the 10-y-o, though, it wasn't to be. (op 16-1)

Baby Run(FR), who made up for his Cheltenham mishap with victory in the Aintree Foxhunters', hadn't run in a handicap since 2006, but appeared on a good mark, and was soon sent to the front. Having been headed by a stable companion over the Railway fences, he battled back to lead at the Pond fence, but was passed at the next and despite sticking on willingly, was always just coming up short. His trainer mentioned the Hennessy as a possible early-season target. (op 11-2)

Triggerman, due to go up 7lb in future, had probably never run on ground this quick before and was feeling it late on, edging under pressure as he tried to rally after the last. He's clearly on the up, but will find it tougher going in future. (op 12-1)

Major Malarkey(IRE) travelled well through the contest and looked to have plenty left in the tank when taking over at the middle of the Railway fences. However, he was soon passed again, and could only keep on at the one pace. This was still a good effort. (tchd 18-1)

Maktu's shown a preference for soft ground in the past, so this was a good run. He stays well and kept plugging on, despite having made a mess of the second of the Railway fences. (op 11-1)

Briery Fox(IRE) plugged on to complete in his own time, never getting competitive.

Aimigayle, who ran a cracker to be second off 6lb lower in the Festival Plate, was soon prominent, but her stamina didn't last and she was beaten by the last of the Railway fences, eventually being eased right down. (tchd 15-2 in a place)

Church Island(IRE), last year's winner and up 8lb, wasn't ridden as positively this time and seemed to sulk. (op 25-1)

Exmoor Ranger(IRE) never recovered from a bad blunder at the 12th. (op 25-1)

Gentle Ranger(IRE) appeared to do a bit too much too soon in the first-time blinkers and failed to run up to anything like his best. (op 25-1)

Can't Buy Time(IRE) briefly tacked on the leading group and looked likely to get involved, but his challenge petered out over the Railway fences. (op 25-1)

Meanus Dandy(IRE) never threatened to make a winning challenge. (op 25-1)

Balthazar King(IRE), who loves a fast surface, was beaten even before stamina came into play. This was the most competitive field he had faced over fences, and perhaps the third run in the space of little over three week's took its toll. (op 25-1)

INDEX TO MEETINGS JUMPS 2010-2011

*AW bumper meeting
† Abandoned
(M) Mixed meeting

INDEX TO STEEPLECHASING & HURDLE RACING

Figure underneath the horse's name indicates its age. The figures following the pedigree refer to the numbers of the races (steeplechases are in bold) in which the horse has run; parentheses () indicate a win; superscript figures denote other placings. Foreign races are denoted by the suffix 'a'. Horses withdrawn (not under orders) are shown with the suffix 'w'. The figures within arrows indicate Raceform Private Handicap MASTER ratings. The ratings are based on a scale of 0-175. The following symbols are used: 'h' hurdle rating, 'c' chase rating, '+' on the upgrade, 'd' disappointing, '?' questionable form. 't' tentative rating based on time.

Aachen *Venetia Williams* 137h
7 b g Rainbow Quest(USA) —Anna Of Saxony (Ela-Mana-Mou)
4806[10]
Aah Haa *Nick Gifford* 61h
6 b g King's Best(USA) —Snowtop (Thatching)
1289[6] 1547[11]
Aaly *Lydia Richards* 85b
4 b g Milan—Leyaaly (Night Shift (USA))
4561[6] 5388[8]
Aather (IRE) *Alan Fleming* 130h
6 b g Key Of Luck(USA) —Alkaffeyeh (IRE) (Sadler's Wells (USA))
2071[2] 2085[4] 2868[7] 3557[5] 3808[6] 4933[8]
Abayaan *Charlie Mann* 88h
5 gr g Sadler's Wells(USA) —Showdown (Darshaan)
4051[8] 4706[3] 5013[3] 5225[7]
Abbey Dore (IRE) *Seamus Mullins* 78h 105c
8 ch g Alderbrook—Bone Of Contention (IRE) (Buckskin (FR))
(2555)
2930[2] (3431)
3646[5] 4537[F] 5192[2]
Abbey Lane (IRE) *Gordon Elliott* 136h
6 b g Flemensfirth(USA) —Hazel Sylph (IRE) (Executive Perk)
(856)
Abbotts Mount *Michael Scudamore*
7 b g Terimon—The Nuns Secret (Petoski)
4499[F]
Abby Belle (IRE) *Mrs H Parrott* 40h
5 gr m Verglas(IRE) —Abbey Park (USA) (Known Fact (USA))
1921[P] 4854[7]
A Beat So Far *Robert Johnson* 72b
5 b m Beat All(USA) —Only So Far (Teenoso (USA))
2511[9] 3504[8]
Aberdale (IRE) *Jonjo O'Neill* 123h 133c
7 b g Oscar(IRE) —Some News (IRE) (Be My Native (USA))
(225) **1774[3]**
◆ 2110[2] ◆ (2615)
4802[P]
Aberdeen Park *David Evans* 109h 82c
9 gr m Environment Friend—Michelee (Merdon Melody)
3482[4]
Abey M'Boy *Oliver Sherwood* 117h 114c
8 b g Alflora(IRE) —See More Furrows (Seymour Hicks (FR))
(2071)
2429[3] ◆ 3257[4] 3628[U] 3869[4] 4265[F]
A Bid Too Far (IRE) *Lawney Hill* 77h
7 b g Lear Spear(USA) —Gentle Lady (IRE) (Strong Gale)
4878[4]
Abitofargybargy (IRE) *Richard Price* 85h
9 b g Dr Massini(IRE) —Gretchen's Castle (IRE) (Carlingford Castle)
3698[9] 4459[8] 4719[F]
Aboukir *Oliver Sherwood*
5 b g Almutawakel—Conquestadora (Hernando (FR))
4667[P] 5321[P]
Aboukir Bay (IRE) *John Cornwall* 71h 92c
7 b g Desert Sun—Tamarsiya (USA) (Shahrastani (USA))
1996[P]
2276[P] 2951[P] 3392[8]
3544[P] 3697[9] 3882[8]
Abragante (IRE) *Mrs D Monteith* 78h 108c
10 b g Saddlers' Hall(IRE) —Joli's Girl (Mansingh (USA))
4915[P] 5263[3] 5419[3]
A Bridge Too Far (IRE) *Donald McCain* 130h
5 b g Oscar(IRE) —Private Rose (IRE) (Roselier (FR))
2590[2] (3715) 4393[2] (4942) 5424[2]
Absolute Shambles *Chris Gordon* 86h 99c
7 b g Shambo—Brass Castle (IRE) (Carlingford Castle)
1550[5] 3431[P] 3867[4] 4811[4] (5053)
5268[5]
Absolution (IRE) *Henrietta Knight* 65h
5 b g Craigsteel—Legal Statement (IRE) (Strong Statement (USA))
2309[7] *2896[5]* 3403[15] 5239[5]
Abstinence (IRE) *Howard Johnson* 89h
8 b g Spectrum(IRE) —Ballerina Gold (USA) (Slew O'Gold (USA))
210[P]
Abstract Art (USA) *Rachel Hobbs* 114h 56c
8 ch g Distorted Humor(USA) —Code From Heaven (USA) (Lost Code (USA))
2330[P] 2471[3] 2983[9] 3299[P] 3493[2] 4028[U] (4289)
(4975) 5205[4]
Abulharith *Ronald Harris* 85h
5 b g Medicean—Limuru (Salse (USA))
4[6] 228[5] 441[2] 698[U] 826[10] 1451[10] 1798[6] 4028[5]
Acambo (GER) *David Pipe* 140h 132c
10 gr g Acambaro(GER) —Artic Lady (FR) (No Pass No Sale)
207[22] 627[12] 756[12] 1017[8] 1346[10]
Acceptance *Laura Mongan* 37b
6 b m Acclamation—Appleacre (Polar Falcon (USA))
284[9]
Accidental Outlaw (IRE) *Charles O'Brien* 122h
4 b g High Chaparral(IRE) —Nwaahil (IRE) (Nashwan (USA))
3239a[3] 4295a[6] (Dead)
Acclaimed (IRE) *John Joseph Hanlon* 125h
6 b g Hawk Wing(USA) —Park Charger (Tirol)
1155a[2] (Dead)
Acclaim To Fame (IRE) *Donald Whillans* 73h
5 b g Acclamation—Khafaya (Unfuwain (USA))
397[P]
According *Nicky Henderson* 101h
5 gr g Dalakhani(IRE) —Amaryllis (IRE) (Sadler's Wells (USA))
2122[4] 2960[17] 4049[12]
Accordingtoeileen (IRE) *Nigel Twiston-Davies* 97h
6 ch m Accordion—Hannigan's Lodger (IRE) (Be My Native (USA))
2987[4] 3842[4] 4703[RR] 4897[2] 5297[2]
Accordingtoemandem (IRE) *Ian Williams* 120h
7 b g Accordion—Merilena (IRE) (Roselier (FR))
76[3] 2035[3] ◆ 2387[P] 3452[P] 5080[P]
Accordingtojodie (IRE) *Nicky Henderson* 114b
5 b g Accordion—La Fiamma (FR) (General Assembly (USA))
3200[8]
According To Pete *Malcolm Jefferson* 137h 139c
10 b g Accordion—Magic Bloom (Full Of Hope)
2077[4] 2523[11] 3293[7] **3522[2]** 4209[2]
Accordingtotheboss (IRE) *Nicky Richards* 89h
6 b g Accordion—Wooden Pass (IRE) (Woodborough (USA))
457[6] 1867[7] 2208[8] 2654[10] 3728[9]
Accordintolawrence (IRE) *Charlie Longsdon* 123h
5 b g Accordion—Giolldante (IRE) (Phardante (FR))
1866[6] (2499) 3295[6] (3789) 4803[F]
Accordion To Paddy (IRE) *Michael O'Hare* 123h
7 b g Accordion—Missymp (IRE) (Mi Selecto (USA))
1757[5] 2302[5]
Accumulate *Bill Moore* 98h
8 b g Second Empire(IRE) —Bee-Bee-Gee (IRE) (Lake Coniston (IRE))
539[3]
Accumulus *Miss Sally Duckett* 106h 108c
11 b g Cloudings(IRE) —Norstock (Norwick (USA))
79[P] 4271[7]
Ace High *Victor Dartnall* 114h 125c
7 b g Kayf Tara—Celtic Native (IRE) (Be My Native (USA))
2136[3] 3448[7] **4096[2] 4531[2]**
Ace High Blue (IRE) *R W J Willcox* 102h 102c
9 b g Pistolet Bleu(IRE) —Derring Lass (Derring Rose)
36[2] **183[3]**
564[P] 1003[2]
1283[6] 1430[3] 4526[P]
Acey (IRE) *Nigel Twiston-Davies* 115h
6 b g Milan—Bonnie And Bright (IRE) (Topanoora)
1860[F]
Achieved *Daniel O'Brien* 47h
8 b g Lahib(USA) —Equity's Darling (IRE) (Law Society (USA))
292[F]
Achiltibuie (IRE) *Dai Burchell* 37h
6 b g Anshan—Sweet Innocence (IRE) (King's Ride)
407[6] 693[P]
Achimota (IRE) *Matt Sheppard* 74h
5 b g Double Eclipse(IRE) —Tullyfoyle (IRE) (Montelimar (USA))
5296[5]
Ackertac (IRE) *Nigel Twiston-Davies* 132h
6 ch g Anshan—Clonsingle Native (IRE) (Be My Native (USA))
(1553) (1821) 2360[5] 2870[B] 3561[14] 4285[2] 4849[6] 5187[10]
Acol *George Foster* 54h
4 ch g Domedriver(IRE) —Bridge Pal (First Trump)
1696[6] 1825[7]
Aconitum (GER) *Neil Mulholland* 106h 105c
6 b g Monsun(GER) —Akanta (GER) (Wolfhound (USA))
2585[5] 3230[3] 3646[7] 4219[U] 4380[5] 4773[3]
Acosta *Dr Jeremy Naylor* 78h
7 b g Foxhound(USA) —Dancing Heights (IRE) (High Estate)
2183[6] 2532[2] 3300[3] 3530[5] (4273)
Acquisitive (FR) *Nigel Twiston-Davies* 82h
5 b g April Night(FR) —American Glory (Baby Turk)
327[6] 3837[8] 4833[P]
Acrai Rua (IRE) *Kevin M Prendergast* 119h 119c
8 ch g Rock Hopper—Dontbelieveaword (IRE) (Be My Native (USA))
15[2] 266[2] **(797)** 3428[P] **3938[3] 4864[P] 5073[2] 5416[7]**
Across The Bay (IRE) *Noel Meade* 136h 135c
7 b g Bob's Return(IRE) —The Southern (IRE) (Glacial Storm (USA))
3206a[P] (3475a)
3798a[P]
Across The Straits (FR) *Jonathan Geake* 95h 90c
7 b g Dansili—Skipnight (Ashkalani (IRE))
2430[4] 3449[11] 4052[P]
5069[F]
Across The Tweed (IRE) *Sue Smith* 56b
5 bb g Alderbrook—Cash Chase (IRE) (Sexton Blake)
3957[13]
Action Hawk (GER) *Ben Pollock* 40h
7 b g Dashing Blade—Action Fire (GER) (Nebos (GER))
1819[8] 2419[9] 2594[10] 3487[P] 3495[9]
3819[P]
Action Impact (ARG) *Gary Moore* 119h
7 b g Bernstein(USA) —Valeur (ARG) (Lode (USA))
500[5]
Action Master *D T Hughes* 130h
5 b g Domedriver(IRE) —All Is Fair (Selkirk (USA))
3709a[6]
Act Of Kalanisi (IRE) *Dr Richard Newland* 134h
5 b g Kalanisi(IRE) —Act Of The Pace (IRE) (King's Theatre (IRE))
(2667) ◆ 3197[7] 3445[4] (4202)
Act Of Kindness (IRE) *Ben De Haan* 90b
6 b g Beneficial—Kemchee (Kemal (FR))
4164[6] ◆
Adage *Jim Best* 82h
8 b m Vettori(IRE) —Aymara (Darshaan)
1549[3] 2433[8]
Adajal (IRE) *Jonjo O'Neill* 120h 130c
8 b g Zilzal(USA) —Adalya (IRE) (Darshaan)
1131a[3] 1676[4] 1957[7] 2272[P] 2587[4] 3531[6] 3935[6]
Adams Island (IRE) *Rebecca Curtis* 128h 142c
7 b g Beneficial—Eoin's Orchestra (IRE) (Orchestra)
1985[2] (2363)
2979[3] (3508)
3940[9] 4351[2] 4790[U] 5290[2]
Adare Manor (IRE) *Jonjo O'Neill* 99h
7 b g Galileo(IRE) —Gravieres (FR) (Saint Estephe (FR))
566[4] 798[10] 1608[7] 1677[8]
Adare Prince (IRE) *Peter Salmon* 30h 97c
10 b g Supreme Leader—Legal Challenge (IRE) (Strong Gale)
3884[P] 4277[P]
Addiction *Oliver Sherwood* 100b
6 b m Alflora(IRE) —Premier Princess (Hard Fought)
2472[4] 2987[2] 4425[P]
Addwaitya *Laura Mongan* 100h
6 br g Xaar—Three White Sox (Most Welcome)
1466[4] 1899[2] 2083[5]
Adeus Ayrton (IRE) *Philip Hobbs* 93h
7 b g Definite Article—Flawless Finish (IRE) (Le Bavard (FR))
129[6]
Ad Idem *Mrs Pauline Gavin* 141h 147c
7 b g Kayf Tara—Major Hoolihan (Soldier Rose)
4250a[2]
Adieu Mari (FR) *Mrs C A Coward* 76h 78c
8 gr g Adieu Au Roi(IRE) —Mariwonder (FR) (The Wonder (FR))
150[6]
Adin Abroad (IRE) *John Wainwright* 48b
6 b m Turtle Island(IRE) —Hi Fasliyev (IRE) (Fasliyev (USA))
1785[8]
Adjami (IRE) *John Harris* 76h 64c
10 b g Entrepreneur—Adjriyna (Top Ville)
717[F] 1085[5] 1300[9]
1558[5]
Admirable Duque (IRE) *Dominic Ffrench Davis* 79h
5 b g Selkirk(USA) —Stunning (USA) (Nureyev (USA))
2181[4] 2960[13]
Admiral Breese *Evan Williams* 66h
4 b g Halling(USA) —Covet (Polish Precedent (USA))
1818[4]
Admiral Dundas (IRE) *Kim Bailey* 111h
6 b g Noverre(USA) —Brandish (Warning)
827[4] 932[2] (1083) 1282[4] 1726[5] 2023[U] 2161[3] 2581[9] 5234[5]
Admirals Way *Christopher Kellett*
6 ch g Observatory(USA) —Dockage (CAN) (Riverman (USA))
2282[P]
Admission *Sophie Leech* 86h
4 b g Azamour(IRE) —Eve (Rainbow Quest (USA))
2466[11] 3519[5] 3906[10] 4225[7] 4956[6]
Adorabella (IRE) *Simon Earle* 89b
8 b m Revoque(IRE) —Febrile (USA) (Trempolino (USA))
5435[P]
A Dream Come True *Graeme McPherson* 95h
6 b m Where Or When(IRE) —Katy Ivory (IRE) (Night Shift (USA))
358[3] (555) 760[3] 1479[P]
Adrenalin Flight (IRE) *Seamus Mullins* 90b
5 b g Dr Massini(IRE) —Chapel Queen (IRE) (Jolly Jake (NZ))
4382[5] 4561[4]
Adrianeo (IRE) *S R B Crawford* 91b 98c
8 ch g Blueprint(IRE) —Try Le Reste (IRE) (Le Moss)
944[3] 1068[4] 1341[3] 1784[P]
Advancement *Sophie Leech* 122h
8 b g Second Empire(IRE) —Lambast (Relkino)
(4783)
Advisor (FR) *Paul Nicholls* 124h
5 gr g Anabaa(USA) —Armilina (FR) (Linamix (FR))
2671[B] *(3058)* 3298[10] 3676[12]
Aega *Neil King* 91h
6 b m Kayf Tara—Circe (Main Reef)
140[4] 436[P]
Aegean Dawn *Nicky Henderson* 146h
6 b g Alflora(IRE) —Wychnor Dawn (IRE) (Broken Hearted)
(2347) ◆ (2498) ◆ 4806[16]
Aeneid *Brian Rothwell* 107b
6 b g Rainbow Quest(USA) —Grecian Slipper (Sadler's Wells (USA))
2646[5] 2943[9] 3572[P]
Aerial (FR) *Paul Nicholls* 117h 148c
5 b g Turgeon(USA) —Fille Formidable (USA) (Trempolino (USA))
(4223)
5226[2]
Aeronautica (IRE) *Tor Sturgis* 80h
8 b m Exit To Nowhere(USA) —Ida Melba (Idiots Delight)
2554[3] 2981[8] 3837[5] 4032[3]
Aerospace *Nick Mitchell* 94h
7 b g Lahib(USA) —Ida Melba (Idiots Delight)
2181[9]
Afistfullofpebbles *Jonjo O'Neill* 105h 129c
7 br g Sonus(IRE) —Lady Margaretta (Rolfe (USA))
3157[P] 3488[6] 3922[7]
A Fistful Of Euros *Chris Down* 90h
7 ch m East Wood—Europa (SPA) (Legend Of France (USA))
225[4] 2144[12] 3400[3] 3870[4]
A French Horse (FR) *Venetia Williams* 123h 138c
8 b g Astarabad(USA) —Ma Chance (FR) (Dancehall (USA))
3156[3] 3902[F]
African Broadway (IRE) *David Pipe* 119b
5 b g Broadway Flyer(USA) —African Lily (IRE) (Clearly Bust)
(3200)
Afsoun (FR) *Neil King* 147h 133c
9 b g Kahyasi—Afragha (IRE) (Darshaan)
94[3] 2498[10] 2870[B] 3199[5] 4373[3] 5166[15]
Against The Wind *Lucinda Russell* 84h 108c
8 b g Anshan—Harvest Memories (Oats)
1665[2] 2194[2] 2450[F] (4573)
4961[3]
Agapanthus (GER) *Barney Curley* 54h
6 b g Tiger Hill(IRE) —Astilbe (GER) (Monsun (GER))
2310[9] 3599[P] 3831[6]
Agente Romano (USA) *Evan Williams* 116h 107c
6 br g Street Cry(IRE) —Dixie Bay (USA) (Dixieland Band (USA))
170[4] 736[5] 1019[7]
1432[F] ◆ 1794[4] 2022[P] 2234[3]
Aggie's Lad (IRE) *Mrs A C Hamilton* 120h 113c
9 b g Saddlers' Hall(IRE) —Grangemills (Strong Gale)
5263[4] (5419)
Agglestone Rock *Philip Kirby* 128h 138c
6 b g Josr Algarhoud(IRE) —Royalty (IRE) (Fairy King (USA))
1155a[7] 3500[5] 4797[4] (5425)
Aggravation *Chris Grant* 104h
9 b g Sure Blade(USA) —Confection (Formidable (USA))
350[3] 748[P] (837)
Aghill (IRE) *Rose Dobbin* 103h 109c
7 ch g Denel(FR) —Hannah's Pet (IRE) (Fidel)
2080[7] 3336[2] **(3748)**
4004[4] 4306[2] 4825[R] 5032[5] 5320[2]
Agoodun *Mrs F Johnson* 91h 90c
10 b g Parthian Springs—God Is Good (River God (USA))
4534[3]
Agricultural *Lucy Normile* 102h
5 b g Daylami(IRE) —Rustic (IRE) (Grand Lodge (USA))
3850[8] 4686[8] 5028[6] 5428[4]
Agus A Vic (IRE) *Patrick Martin* 112h 137c
10 b g Old Vic—Marovia (IRE) (Montelimar (USA))
3206a[4] 3798a[P]
A Haon A Do (IRE) *Gerald Ham* 104h
9 b m Taipan(IRE) —Adelante (IRE) (Roselier (FR))
267[P] 432[5] 532[4] 660[5] 826[U]
Ah Come On Tom (IRE) *Mrs J Quinlan* 79h 98c
12 b g Distinctly North(USA) —Gooseneck (Try My Best (USA))
296[7]
Ahhdehken *Alistair Whillans* 86b
6 b g Cloudings(IRE) —Swazi Princess (IRE) (Brush Aside (USA))
5034[5]
Ahmedy (IRE) *John Quinn* 110h
8 b g Polish Precedent(USA) —Nawaji (USA) (Trempolino (USA))
1827[5]
Ahwaak (USA) *Alastair Lidderdale* 61h
7 b g Dynaformer(USA) —Saudia (USA) (Gone West (USA))
5108[7]
Aibrean (IRE) *S R B Crawford* 135h
7 b m Winged Love(IRE) —Bealtaine (IRE) (Zaffaran (USA))
(5320)
Aigle D'Or *Nicky Henderson* 150h 143c
8 b g Halling(USA) —Epistole (IRE) (Alzao (USA))
(2665)
4820[13]
Aikideau (FR) *Richard Rowe* 132h
4 b g Le Balafre(FR) —Kizitso (FR) (En Calcat (FR))
4350[6] 4847[11]
Aikman (IRE) *James Ewart* 139h
7 b g Rudimentary(USA) —Omas Lady (IRE) (Be My Native (USA))
(311) ◆ 3547[F] ◆ 3749[2] ◆ (4061) (4312) 4803[7] 5186[6]

Aim'Ees Star *John Harris* 56h
4 ch f Trade Fair—Star Cast (IRE) (In The Wings)
3507[4] 4283[10]
Aimigayle *Suzy Smith* 126h 141c
8 b m Midnight Legend—Cherrygayle (IRE) (Strong Gale)
3948[P] 4820[2] 5443[8]
Aine's Delight (IRE) *Andy Turnell* 102h
5 b m King's Best(USA) —Gentle Thoughts (Darshaan)
1921[5] 2331[7] *3057[8]* 3387[9] 5244[7] (5406)
Ainm Spartacus (IRE) *Kieran Purcell* 125h
4 b g Spartacus(IRE) —Hasainm (IRE) (Grand Lodge (USA))
2966a[9]
Ainroe (IRE) *Paul John Gilligan* 65b
4 ch g Oscar Schindler(IRE) —Inca Lady (IRE) (Pistolet Bleu (IRE))
5084[8]
Aint She The Lady (IRE) *Tim Vaughan* 105h
7 b m King's Theatre(IRE) —Gunner Marc (Gunner B)
2144 713[7] 1035[F]
Airdrie (IRE) *Henrietta Knight* 98h
5 b g Oscar(IRE) —Smokey Began It (IRE) (Supreme Leader)
3200[5] 3542[5] 3960[6] 4500[8]
Airedale Lad (IRE) *Zoe Davison* 72h 50c
10 b g Charnwood Forest(IRE) —Tamarsiya (USA) (Shahrastani (USA))
1761[0] 1199[6] 1361[8] 3985[5] 4399[8] 4771[3] (5270) 5383[6]
Airey Scarey *James Ewart*
8 b m Missed Flight—Terrorisa (Alias Smith (USA))
2353[P]
Airmen's Friend (IRE) *Charlie Mann* 108h
5 b g Craigsteel—High Academy (IRE) (Insan (USA))
3200[10] 3678[P] 4128[3] 4500[3]
Aisemma (IRE) *Peter Bowen* 87h
7 ch m Flemensfirth(USA) —Keen Waters (Keen)
522[P] 630[10] 826[3] 920[9] 1057[2]
Aitch Doubleyou (IRE) *Henry Hogarth* 61h 107c
11 ch g Classic Memory—Bucksreward (IRE) (Buckskin (FR))
4871[2]
Aitch Factor *Henry Hogarth* 70h
5 b g Beat All(USA) —Farmers Girl (Classic Cliche (IRE))
2612[8] 2954[U] 3715[15] 3885[8] 4542[P] 5352[P]
Aiteen Thirtythree (IRE) *Paul Nicholls* 137h 158c
7 b g Old Vic—Prudent View (IRE) (Supreme Leader)
(1860)
(2631) (4190)
4804[P]
Aitmatov (GER) *Noel Meade* 156h
10 b g Lomitas—Atoka (GER) (Kaiseradler)
1711a[2] 2259a[F] 2968a[10] 3030a[6] 3578a[8]
Ajman (IRE) *Evan Williams* 114h
6 b g Orpen(USA) —Grand Madam (Grand Lodge (USA))
(298) (566) 675[U] (798) 829[2] 1127[F] 1282[U] 1333[3] 1548[5] 2423[3] 4031[9] 4672[P]
Ajzal (IRE) *Ed de Giles* 111h 88c
7 b g Alhaarth(IRE) —Alkaffeyeh (IRE) (Sadler's Wells (USA))
48[3] 183[6] 3492[P]
Akarshan (IRE) *Evan Williams* 123h 120c
6 b g Intikhab(USA) —Akdara (IRE) (Sadler's Wells (USA))
372[3] 627[3] 1019[3] 1346[7] **3156[P] 3598[3] 4033[6] 4691[2] 5081[3]**
Akbabend *Charlie Mann* 109h
5 b g Refuse To Bend(IRE) —Akdariya (IRE) (Shirley Heights)
3781[6] 4467[6]
Akinndi (IRE) *Evan Williams* 75h
4 b g Intikhab(USA) —Akaliya (IRE) (Daylami (IRE))
4478[F]
Akula (IRE) *Mark H Tompkins* 118h
4 ch g Soviet Star(USA) —Danielli (IRE) (Danehill (USA))
1610[5] ◆ (1728) 2528[2] 2882[3] 3802[4] 4807[15]
Alaccordion *Violet M Jordan* 77b
6 br g Alflora(IRE) —Song For Jess (IRE) (Accordion)
5063[11]
Alaghiraar (IRE) *Emma Lavelle* 114h 117c
7 b g Act One—Tarsheeh (USA) (Mr Prospector (USA))
281[P] 463[6]
Alaivan (IRE) *E J O'Grady* 150h
5 b g Kalanisi(IRE) —Alaya (IRE) (Ela-Mana-Mou)
4848[6]
Al Amaan *Gary Moore* 101h
6 b g Nayef(USA) —Siobhan (Generous (IRE))
216[3] 823[F] 2081[U] 2294[8] 4935[6] 5244[9]
Alambique (IRE) *T W Dennis* 95c
12 b g Alderbrook—Calora (USA) (Private Account (USA))
173[2]
Aland Islands (IRE) *Tim Vaughan* 113b
5 b g Stowaway—Champagne Lady (IRE) (Turtle Island (IRE))
(5157)
Alarazi (IRE) *Lucy Wadham* 138h
7 b g Spectrum(IRE) —Alaya (IRE) (Ela-Mana-Mou)
(2419) 2944[3] 3386[2] 3808[2] ◆ (4727) ◆ 4848[15] 5182[4]
Alarming Alacrity (IRE) *Evan Williams* 33h
5 b g Bach(IRE) —More Dash (IRE) (Strong Gale)
1567[6]
Alasi *Paul Webber* 139h
7 b m Alflora(IRE) —Anamasi (Idiots Delight)
2218[5] 3442[2] 3674[3] 4793[4] 5302[2]
Alaskan Prince (IRE) *Peter Salmon* 51b 86c
6 b g Exit To Nowhere(USA) —Alaskan Princess (IRE) (Prince Rupert (FR))
847[P] **1779[P]**
1961[2] 2088[4] 3618[9]

Alaska River (IRE) *Brendan Duke* 92b
5 b m Whitmore's Conn(USA) —Unalaska (IRE) (High Estate)
412[3] 686[2] 1572[3] 1724[8]
Alazan (IRE) *Philip Hobbs* 128h
5 ch g Dubai Destination(USA) —Marion Haste (IRE) (Ali-Royal (IRE))
235[3] (331) 1017[4] (1311) 5201[18]
Alba King (IRE) *Sue Smith* 79b
5 b g Beauchamp King—Alba Dancer (Gran Alba (USA))
5264[8]
Albertas Run (IRE) *Jonjo O'Neill* 135h 170c
10 b g Accordion—Holly Grove Lass (Le Moss)
1958[4] 2515[F] 3560[P] (4818)
5184[2]
Albert Park (IRE) *John Upson* 73h
10 ch g Presenting—Victoria Belle (IRE) (Black Minstrel)
59[0] 336[F] 587[4] (1141) 1434[9] 5265[U]
Albert Saxe *Miss J R Tooth* 60b
5 b g Bertolini(USA) —Pooka's Daughter (IRE) (Eagle Eyed (USA))
2432[8]
Alcalde *John Berry* 115h
5 b g Hernando(FR) —Alexandrine (IRE) (Nashwan (USA))
2944[5] 3344[7] (3831) 4462[2] 4990[U]
Alcatras (IRE) *John Ryall* 76h 85c
14 bb g Corrouge(USA) —Kisco (IRE) (Henbit (USA))
24[P]
Alchester (IRE) *Seamus G O'Donnell* 11h 82c
11 bb m Arctic Lord—Cash Chase (IRE) (Sexton Blake)
990[13]
Al Co (FR) *Jonjo O'Neill* 134h 112c
6 ch g Dom Alco(FR) —Carama (FR) (Tip Moss (FR))
206[4] 2235[9] 3561[P] (4285) 5187[13]
Aldaado (IRE) *Paul Midgley* 42h
5 b g Alhaarth(IRE) —Zobaida (IRE) (Green Desert (USA))
3521[12]
Al Dafa (USA) *Gordon Elliott* 96h
4 ch g Kingmambo(USA) —Crimson Conquest (USA) (Diesis)
(1576) (1935) 2600[2] 3239a[10]
Alderburn *Henry Daly* 134h 139c
12 b g Alderbrook—Threewaygirl (Orange Bay)
(1960)
2531[U] 4054[3] 4486[2] 5229[5]
Alderley Rover (IRE) *Donald McCain* 121h 137c
7 gr g Beneficial—St Anne's Lady (IRE) (Roselier (FR))
(193) **1759[4]**
2165[2] 2670[6] 3368[2] 3694[2] (4057)
4821[16] (5190)
5422[4]
Alderluck (IRE) *Nick Gifford* 135h 135c
6 ch g Alderbrook—Cecelia's Charm (IRE) (Mister Lord (USA))
206[P] 2125[F] **3390[5] 3743[2] (4119)**
4480[3]
Aldertune (IRE) *Paul Nicholls* 125h 131c
7 ch g Alderbrook—Frankies Tune (IRE) (Accordion)
3368[3] (4720)
4898[2] 5190[2]
Aldiruos (IRE) *Tony Carroll* 111h 65c
11 ch g Bigstone(IRE) —Ball Cat (FR) (Cricket Ball (USA))
21[9] 606[7] 921[2] 1094[7] 1372[7] 1556[7]
Aldiva *Alan King* 104b
5 b g Alflora(IRE) —Diva (Exit To Nowhere (USA))
3054[3] 3842[13] 4943[7]
Aldorable *Roger Teal*
4 ch f Starcraft(NZ) —Aldora (Magic Ring (IRE))
3554[U] 4028[7]
Alegralil *Donald McCain* 129h
6 b m King's Theatre(IRE) —Lucy Glitters (Ardross)
(2089) 2671[F] 3442[6] 4793[10]
Aleron (IRE) *John Quinn* 134h 129c
13 b g Sadler's Wells(USA) —High Hawk (Shirley Heights)
314[P]
Alesandro Mantegna (IRE) *Keith Goldsworthy* 109h 130c
6 b g Peintre Celebre(USA) —Mantua (Mtoto)
1372[3]
(1676) 1926[2] 2212[2] ◆ 2674[U] 3686[11] 4159[5] 4439[6] 4524[F] **4730[7]**
Alexander Beetle *Henrietta Knight* 100h 108c
6 b g Beat All(USA) —Fleeting Affair (Hotfoot I)
62[3] **2303[6]**
2662[F]
Alexander Oats *Robert Goldie* 79h 119c
8 b g Insan(USA) —Easter Oats (Oats)
214[7] **(4063)**
4689[3]
Alexander Road (IRE) *Donald McCain* 115h
6 bb m Kaldounevees(FR) —Trinity Belle (FR) (Tel Quel (FR))
230[8] 1934[3] 3721[4] (4000) (4245) (4568) 5319[P]
Alexanderthegreat (IRE) *Venetia Williams* 129h 116c
13 b g Supreme Leader—Sandy Jayne (IRE) (Royal Fountain)
229[2] 431[3] 501[3]
Alfa Beat (IRE) *C Byrnes* 129h 146c
7 gr g Environment Friend—Belle D'Anjou (FR) (Saint Cyrien (FR))
(1527a) ◆ 4802[4] 5185[F]
Alfabet Souk *Bernard Llewellyn* 82h 62c
10 b g Alflora(IRE) —Levantine Rose (Levanter)
218[P]
Alfadora *Milton Harris* 98h 111c
11 ch g Alflora(IRE) —Dorazine (Kalaglow)
359[5] **540[4]**
(867) 993[2]
1059[5]
Alfatrix (IRE) *M G Miller* 97h 99c
8 b g Alflora(IRE) —Dutch Majesty (Homing)
4708[P]

Al Ferof (FR) *Paul Nicholls* 155h
6 gr g Dom Alco(FR) —Maralta (FR) (Altayan)
2873[F] 3197[3] (3647) (4069) (4788) ◆
Alfie Bet *Maurice Barnes* 85h
7 b g Alflora(IRE) —Brass Buckle (IRE) (Buckskin (FR))
30[4]
Alfie Brown *Jacqueline Retter*
8 b g Alflora(IRE) —Broughton Manor (Dubassoff (USA))
4091[P] 5152[P]
Alfie Flits *Alan Swinbank* 141h 120c
9 b g Machiavellian(USA) —Elhilmeya (IRE) (Unfuwain (USA))
(2548) *3092[5]* 3571[4] 4168[2] 4472[3] 5002[4]
Alfie Sherrin *Jonjo O'Neill* 147h 135c
8 b g Kayf Tara—Mandys Native (IRE) (Be My Native (USA))
2303[4] (3714)
4080[3] 4876[P]
Alfie's Pearl *Charles Pogson* 73h
6 b m Alflora(IRE) —Wild Dream (Derrylin)
3721[9] 4454[7] 4795[3]
Alfie Spinner (IRE) *Nick Williams* 137h
6 b g Alflora(IRE) —Little Red Spider (Bustino)
3298[4] 3566[2] ◆ 3947[2] ◆ 4817[19]
Alfie's Sun *Don Cantillon* 120c
12 b g Alflora(IRE) —Sun Dante (IRE) (Phardante (FR))
1509[P] 1725[5] 1885[P]
Alfinski *C W Thornton* 60b
6 b g Alflora(IRE) —Auntie Alice (Uncle Pokey)
1069[12]
Alflorabunda *Michael Roberts*
5 b m Alflora(IRE) —Appley Dapply (Broadsword (USA))
3964[10]
Alfloramoor *Charles Pogson* 104h 97c
9 b g Alflora(IRE) —Diamond Wind (USA) (Wind And Wuthering (USA))
64[7] 1084[6] 1259[6]
1358[3] 1430[6] 1646[7] 1816[5]
Al Gregg (IRE) *I A Duncan* 86b
5 b g Luso—Glasslacken Beauty (IRE) (The Bart (USA))
3856[7] 4308[7]
Alhaque (USA) *Gary Moore* 109h
5 ch g Galileo(IRE) —Safeen (USA) (Storm Cat (USA))
662[4] 2498[12] 3557[12] 4327[P] 5117[9]
Alhudhud (USA) *Kevin Morgan*
5 b g Swain(IRE) —Wasnah (USA) (Nijinsky (CAN))
602[11]
Ali Baba *Alan King* 89b
5 ch g Nayef(USA) —Alligram (USA) (Alysheba (USA))
5217[5]
Alimure *C W Thornton* 77b
5 b m Tamure(IRE) —Auntie Alice (Uncle Pokey)
841[9] 1629[7] 1764[6]
Alittlebitmore *Tom Gretton*
8 b g Parthian Springs—Scally Jenks (Scallywag)
992[7] 1196[8]
Alivad (IRE) *Peter Hedger* 60b
4 b f Milan—Icy Breeze (IRE) (Glacial Storm (USA))
4097[4] 4376[8]
Allamonty (IRE) *Martin Todhunter* 52b
5 b g Celtic Swing—Allatrim (IRE) (Montelimar (USA))
1764[10]
Allanard (IRE) *Martin Todhunter* 84h 105c
7 b g Oscar(IRE) —Allatrim (IRE) (Montelimar (USA))
2271[P] 2941[4] 3336[7]
(3712) 3886[8] (5095)
Alla Svelta (IRE) *Evan Williams* 115h
5 b g Milan—Miss Greinton (GER) (Greinton)
2137[2] 3762[2] ◆ (4528)
Allbarkanobite *Kate Walton* 50h
6 b m Kadastrof(FR) —Come The Dawn (Gunner B)
2355[7] 2616[3] 3498[P] 4000[7] 5031[7]
All But Beat *Ron Hodges* 92b
6 b g Beat All(USA) —Butleigh Rose (Nicholas Bill)
1029[4] 2186[13]
Alldunnandusted (IRE) *Seamus Mullins* 116h 111c
7 b g Rudimentary(USA) —Megans Dreamer (IRE) (Elbio)
(84) 382[2] (522)
1970[6] 2441[4] 2959[10] 3450[6] 3963[5] 5051[2]
Allee Garde (FR) *W P Mullins* 133h
6 b g Kapgarde(FR) —Allee Du Port (FR) (Port Etienne (FR))
4849[9]
Alleged Vanity (IRE) *Chris Grant* 39h
5 ch g Flemensfirth(USA) —Vanity Jane (IRE) (Revoque (IRE))
3525[6] 4541[9]
Allerford Jack *Caroline Keevil* 116h
7 br g Overbury(IRE) —Jiggiwithit (Distant Relative)
3960[5] 4268[4] 4557[2] 5168[7] 5381[4]
Allerton (IRE) *Nigel Twiston-Davies* 89b
4 b g Flemensfirth(USA) —Bonny Hall (IRE) (Saddlers' Hall (IRE))
3766[4] 4287[9] 5077[5]
Allez Les Rouges (IRE) *Andrew Balding* 89b
4 b g Saffron Walden(FR) —Louve Secrete (IRE) (Fasliyev (USA))
2797[5] ◆ 3294[8]
All For Cash *Kim Bailey* 101b
6 b g Alflora(IRE) —Mrs Moneypenny (Relkino)
3773[8] 4164[3] 5217[3]
All For Free (IRE) *Milton Harris* 119h
5 b g Atraf—Milain (IRE) (Unfuwain (USA))
2109[6] 2362[U] 3304[2] (3601) 3831[4] 4270[7] 4488[11]
Allformary *Kim Bailey* 92h
5 b m Tobougg(IRE) —Bollin Rita (Rambo Dancer (CAN))
224[4] (4707) 5016[4] 5373[2]

All For The Cause (IRE) *John Davies* 126h 120c
9 b g Gothland(FR) —Hurricane Hattie (Strong Gale)
290[3] 444[P] 857[4] (1329) 1501[2]
All Moving Parts (USA) *John Wainwright* 64h
4 bb g Forest Camp(USA) —Smooth Player (USA) (Bertrando (USA))
836[10]
Alloro *Alan Kirtley* 93h
7 ch g Auction House(USA) —Minette (Bishop Of Cashel)
210[7]
Allterrain (IRE) *Murty McGrath* 77h 99c
8 b g Almutawakel—Queen Of Art (IRE) (Royal Academy (USA))
218[4] 695[3] 911[3] 1027[P] 1093[P] 3982[P] 5053[5] 5268[4]
All That Remains (IRE) *Steve Gollings* 112b
6 b g King's Theatre(IRE) —Morning Breeze (IRE) (Bigstone (IRE))
(3835) (3992) 4457[5]
All The Cousins (IRE) *A J Martin* 117h 73c
11 b g Needle Gun(IRE) —Four Moons (IRE) (Cardinal Flower)
291[P]
All The Fashion (IRE) *Violet M Jordan* 71h
7 br m Alflora(IRE) —Fashion Day (Environment Friend)
1679[5] 2144[7] 5075[8]
Allthegear No Idea (IRE) *Nigel Twiston-Davies* 96b
4 b g Sayarshan(FR) —All The Gear (IRE) (Nashamaa)
5174[6]
All Things Equal (IRE) *Claire Dyson* 99h 96c
12 b g Supreme Leader—Angel's Dream (King's Ride)
1925[P]
All Thyne Greats (IRE) *Rachel Hobbs* 54h
9 br g Good Thyne(USA) —Cush Maid (Black Minstrel)
992[5]
Allure Of Illusion (IRE) *W P Mullins* 120b
5 ch g Captain Rio—Sixhills (FR) (Sabrehill (USA))
5202[3] ◆
Almanyan (IRE) *Adrian McGuinness* 119h
7 b g Anabaa(USA) —Alaiyda (USA) (Shahrastani (USA))
2506[10]
Almaydan *Mrs K M Diggle* 94h 137c
13 b g Marju(IRE) —Cunning (Bustino)
57[3] 4197[3] 5083[3] 5237[P] 5402[6]
Almond Court (IRE) *Robert Johnson* 78h 72c
8 ch m Accordion—Glencairn Fox (IRE) (Le Moss)
8[6] 212[4] 461[4] 2353[P] **3499[4] 3726[3] 4114[2] 4254[5]** 4508[9] 4826[F] **5414[2]**
Almost Blue (IRE) *N W Alexander* 108c
9 b g City Honours(USA) —Rahanine Melody (IRE) (Orchestra)
398[11]
Almutaham (USA) *James Moffatt* 90h
4 bb c Dynaformer(USA) —Forest Lady (USA) (Woodman (USA))
1696[2] 1984[4] 2655[6] 3711[7] 4146[9] 4960[2]
Alnwick *Peter Cundell* 95h
7 b g Kylian(USA) —Cebwob (Rock City)
1734[8] 1922[2]
Alone They Stand (IRE) *Jonjo O'Neill* 38h
6 ch g Flemensfirth(USA) —Have At It (IRE) (Supreme Leader)
4422[8] 4918[8]
Along Came Rosie *Andrew Crook* 106h
7 b m Alflora(IRE) —Seraphim (FR) (Lashkari)
2092[6] (2353) 3308[3] 3498[3] 4000[5] 4455[8] 5259[F]
Along The Nile *Graham Smith* 122h
9 b g Desert Prince(IRE) —Golden Fortune (Forzando)
(87) 235[7] 537[6]
Alonso De Guzman (IRE) *Tim Vaughan* 97h
7 b g Docksider(USA) —Addaya (IRE) (Persian Bold)
2246[9] 3833[2] 4404[4]
Alph *Roger Teal* 128h 135c
14 b g Alflora(IRE) —Royal Birthday (St Paddy)
(23) 521[5] 853[2] (1084) 1470[9] 1548[2] 2213[5] (2596)
Alphacino *Ben Haslam* 65h
4 b g Hunting Lion(IRE) —Fading Away (Fraam)
743[4] 851[4]
Alpha One (IRE) *Chris Grant* 103h
5 b g Fruits Of Love(USA) —Dunedin Lass (IRE) (Alphabatim (USA))
2553[6] 3525[10] 3952[P] 4541[2] 4993[3] 5259[2]
Alpha Ridge (IRE) *Paul Nolan* 154h 150c
9 b g Glacial Storm(USA) —Be My Soul Mate (IRE) (Be My Native (USA))
3798a[4] 4250a[3]
Alpine Breeze (IRE) *Don Cantillon* 123h
5 b m King's Theatre(IRE) —Alpine Gale (IRE) (Strong Gale)
327[3] (684) (2232) 2571[5] 3264[F] (5297)
Alpine Eagle (IRE) *Mrs John Harrington* 147h
7 b g Golan(IRE) —Alpine Symphony (Northern Dancer (CAN))
3474a[8] 4727[12]
Alpine Glade (IRE) *W McCreery* 140h
9 b m Oscar(IRE) —Stony View (IRE) (Tirol)
1133a[13] 3030a[3]
Al Qeddaaf (IRE) *Donald McCain* 124h
5 b g Alhaarth(IRE) —Just Special (Cadeaux Genereux)
42[2] 349[3] (1664) ◆ (2162)
Alrafid (IRE) *Gary Moore* 96h 80c
12 ch g Halling(USA) —Ginger Tree (USA) (Dayjur (USA))
172[8] 530[7] 821[7] 1294[3] **1474[6]**
Alroyal (GER) *Phillip Dando* 108h 112c
12 ch g Royal Solo(IRE) —Alamel (USA) (Shadeed (USA))
148[7] 663[2] 824[4]
Alsadaa (USA) *Laura Mongan* 141h
8 b g Kingmambo(USA) —Aljawza (USA) (Riverman (USA))
2085[6] *3058[3]*

Alsahil (USA) *Micky Hammond* 68h
5 ch g Diesis—Tayibah (IRE) (Sadler's Wells (USA))
2349[9]

Al Sirat *Brendan Powell* 77b
5 b g Josr Algarhoud(IRE) —Toleration (Petong)
7[7]

Also Jo *William Amos* 94h 86c
8 gr g Cloudings(IRE) —Forgotten Empress (Dowsing (USA))
2275[3] 2448[P] 3335[11] 3631[10] 4068[6]
4510[F] 4963[7]

Altan Khan *Malcolm Jefferson* 110h
6 b g Kayf Tara—Anabranch (Kind Of Hush)
1613[2] 1832[3] (2508) 3966[9] 4778[3] 5102[2] 5429[8]

Alta Rock (IRE) *Sue Smith* 108h
6 b g Luso—Princess Lulu (IRE) (Carroll House)
731[6] 1153[3] 3511[11] 4242[P] (4739)

Alteranthela (IRE) *Richard Rowe* 104h 94c
7 br g Alderbrook—Anthela (GER) (Orfano (GER))
2124[4] 2513[7] 2796[3] 3431[P] 4669[6]

Altilhar (USA) *Gary Moore* 91h 110c
8 b g Dynaformer(USA) —Al Desima (Emperor Jones (USA))
2126[6] 2662[5] 3198[P] 3947[10]

Altos Reales *Michael Scudamore* 89h
7 b m Mark Of Esteem(IRE) —Karsiyaka (IRE) (Kahyasi)
792[6] 1233[6]

Alvarado (IRE) *Howard Johnson* 129h 147c
6 ch g Goldmark(USA) —Mrs Jones (IRE) (Roselier (FR))
(1759)
(3571) (4891)

Alverstone *Lawney Hill* 125h
8 br m Alflora(IRE) —Sounds Familiar (IRE) (Orchestra)
(1963) 2627[2] (3264) 3674[4] 5008[U]

Always Baileys (IRE) *Pam Ford* 75h 72c
8 ch g Mister Baileys—Dubiously (USA) (Jolie Jo (USA))
1554[8] 1704[7]

Always Best *Dick Allan* 86h
7 b g Best Of The Bests(IRE) —Come To The Point (Pursuit Of Love)
875[11]

Always Bold (IRE) *Donald McCain* 135h 124c
6 ch g King's Best(USA) —Tarakana (USA) (Shahrastani (USA))
329[2] 605[3] 802[3] 1727[5] 2125[5] 3092[4] 3954[4] 4742[9]
5252[6]

Always Cruising (USA) *Linda Blackford* 80h
6 b g Fusaichi Pegasus(USA) —Mrs Marcos (USA) (Private Account (USA))
273[7] 532[6] 825[6] 1059[7] 1237[P] 1335[P] 5322[11]

Always De One *K F Clutterbuck* 70h
4 b f Fruits Of Love(USA) —Yes Virginia (USA) (Roanoke (USA))
3986[4] 4810[7]

Alwaysonthemove *Laura Mongan* 96h
7 b g Mujahid(USA) —Royal Roulette (Risk Me (FR))
215[4] 3056[2] 3864[F] 4129[5] 5327[5]

Always Right (IRE) *John Wade* 149c
9 ch g Right Win(IRE) —Kemal Brave (IRE) (Kemal (FR))
1871[2] ◆ (4167) ◆ (4466) ◆ 5338[3]

Always Roses *Chris Bealby* 65h
4 ch f Generous(IRE) —Arcady (Slip Anchor)
1691[6] 1825[4] 2068[6]

Always Waining (IRE) *Peter Bowen* 106h 149c
10 b g Unfuwain(USA) —Glenarff (USA) (Irish River (FR))
1611[11] 2084[11] 2541[6] 4285[7] 4464[11] 4968[4]
(5185)

Alwood Flora *Andrew Crook* 4b
8 b m Alflora(IRE) —Oriel Dream (Oats)
858[P]

Alystar (IRE) *Nicky Henderson* 87h
5 ch m Rock Of Gibraltar(IRE) —Arpege (IRE) (Sadler's Wells (USA))
3739[4] 4397[2]

Ama Jima *Henry Daly* 68b
4 b f Bollin Eric—Silken Pearls (Leading Counsel (USA))
5174[12]

Amalfi Coast *Karen Tutty* 107h 115c
12 b g Emperor Jones(USA) —Legend's Daughter (USA) (Alleged (USA))
1377[2] (1645)
1868[F]

Amant Gris (FR) *R Holcak* 143c
12 gr g House Rules(USA) —Amande Praline (FR) (Rusticaro (FR))
1811a[2]

Amarjit (IRE) *James McAuley* 125h
10 b g Bahhare(USA) —Dungeon Princess (IRE) (Danehill (USA))
1121a[17]

Amaury De Lusignan (IRE) *Gary Moore* 106h
5 b g Dushyantor(USA) —Celtic Sails (IRE) (M Double M (USA))
3626[5] 4180[5] 4767[3]

Amazing King (IRE) *Philip Kirby* 130h
7 b g King Charlemagne(USA) —Kraemer (USA) (Lyphard (USA))
1133a[18] 1609[7] 1827[2] 4858[2] 5201[10]

Amazing Request *Bernard Llewellyn* 89h
7 b g Rainbow Quest(USA) —Maze Garden (USA) (Riverman (USA))
2279[3] 380[U] 593[2] 757[2] 990[6] 1164[5] 1335[2] 1489[4]

Amazingreyce *Owen Brennan* 64b
6 gr m Rainbow High—Lightning Belle (Belfort (FR))
1201[9] 1955[8]

Amazing Valour (IRE) *Peter Bowen* 98h 67c
9 b g Sinndar(IRE) —Flabbergasted (IRE) (Sadler's Wells (USA))
3764[6]

Amber Brook (IRE) *Nigel Twiston-Davies* 114h 113c
10 ch m Alderbrook—Me Grannys Endoors (IRE) (Tremblant)
206[3] (1855) 2089[3] 2579[5]
2978[3]

Ambion Wood (IRE) *Victor Dartnall* 112b
5 b g Oscar(IRE) —Dorans Grove (Gildoran)
4329[2] ◆ (4879) ◆

Amble Forge (IRE) *Colin Tizzard* 86h 125c
9 b g Needle Gun(IRE) —La Mode Lady (Mandalus)
236[P] 2429[8] 2961[10] 3628[6] 4723[4] 4967[3] 5112[3]

Ambobo (USA) *Martin Brassil* 120h 137c
11 b g Kingmambo(USA) —Bold Bold (IRE) (Sadler's Wells (USA))
3206a[6] 3475a[9]

Ambrose Hill Lad *Paul Nicholls* 90b
5 b g Pilsudski(IRE) —Myblackthorn (IRE) (Mandalus)
5408[3]

Ambrose Princess (IRE) *Michael Scudamore* 120h
6 b m Chevalier(IRE) —Mark One (Mark Of Esteem (IRE))
(340) 1391[2] 1626[7] 5302[8]

Ambrosinni *P York* 115h 102c
9 b g Dr Massini(IRE) —Macfarly (IRE) (Phardante (FR))
292[3]

A Media Luz (FR) *Nicky Henderson* 131h
4 b f Johann Quatz(FR) —Immensement (FR) (Garde Royale)
2882[7] 3194[2] ◆ 3554[F] (4024) 4847[P] 5182[10]

Ameeq (USA) *Dr Richard Newland* 130h 118c
9 bb g Silver Hawk(USA) —Haniya (IRE) (Caerleon (USA))
45[10]

American Cricket (IRE) *Alex Hales* 115h
10 b g Lord Americo—Dixons Dutchess (IRE) (Over The River (FR))
62[2]

American Ladie *Alan King* 119h
5 b m Monashee Mountain(USA) —Dounine (Kaldoun (FR))
2289[2] ◆ 2944[2] 3481[2] ◆ 4451[3] 4964[2] (5189)

American Lover (FR) *John Wainwright* 37b
4 b f American Post—Lovarisk (FR) (Take Risks (FR))
4280[9]

American Trilogy (IRE) *Paul Nicholls* 133h 120c
7 gr g Sendawar(IRE) —Affaire Classee (FR) (Anabaa (USA))
2219[F]
2926[F] 3059[5] (4050)
4351[3] 4794[P] 5382[2]

American World (FR) *Brendan Powell* 117h 117c
7 bb g Lost World(IRE) —Rose Laura (FR) (Rose Laurel)
(65) (409) 1108[2] 2171[10] 2361[15] 2596[8] 3228[9]
3628[7] 4265[5] 4896[7] 5214[8]

Am I Blue *Mrs D Thomas* 107h
5 b m Dubai Destination(USA) —Seal Indigo (IRE) (Glenstal (USA))
646[7] 1164[10] 1272[12] (1451) (1494) 2329[2] 2514[7]
5392[4]

Amical Risks (FR) *Joss Saville* 101h
7 bl g Take Risks(FR) —Miss High (FR) (Concorde Jr (USA))
1357[4] 1553[9]

Amicelli (GER) *Mrs C A Coward* 125h 104c
12 b g Goofalik(USA) —Arratonia (GER) (Arratos (FR))
4851[9]

Amirico (IRE) *Venetia Williams* 115h
6 b g Lord Americo—Maori's Delight (Idiots Delight)
(2396) 2925[7] 3405[7] 3950[7] 4427[4]

Amir Pasha (UAE) *Micky Hammond* 112h
6 br g Halling(USA) —Clarinda (IRE) (Lomond (USA))
(1931) 2076[2] 2373[4] 3966[3] 4058[2] 4358[10] 4940[11]

Amjad *Simon West* 78h 58c
14 ch g Cadeaux Genereux—Babita (Habitat)
745[5] 1362[9] 1666[12] (4511)

Ammo Away *Tim Vaughan* 27h
5 b g Deploy—Miss Caitlin (IRE) (Over The River (FR))
3835[6] 4491[7] 4860[10] 5253[4]

Ammunition (IRE) *Nigel Twiston-Davies* 82h 124c
11 b g Needle Gun(IRE) —Flapping Freda (IRE) (Carlingford Castle)
(1738)
(1992) 2984[F] (4537)
5286[4]

Amore Mio (GER) *Richard Phillips* 130h 124c
6 b g Trempolino(USA) —Amore (GER) (Lando (GER))
2347[8] 2977[15] 3299[8] 3724[P] 3962[6] 4427[3]

Amroth Bay *Jennie Candlish* 95h
7 b g Alflora(IRE) —La Bella Villa (Relkino)
2791[12] 3678[P] 4974[4] 5203[4]

Amtired *Brian Ellison* 90b
5 gr g Beauchamp King—Rising Talisker (Primitive Rising (USA))
4287[6] 4801[5]

Amulree *N W Alexander* 87b 62c
8 b m Dancing High—Harrietfield (Nicholas Bill)
4254[6] 4570[4]

Amuse Me *Jonjo O'Neill* 117h 106c
5 gr g Daylami(IRE) —Have Fun (Indian Ridge)
1487[7] 1613[6] 1734[9] (1996) (2114) (2185) 3306[3]
3881[12]
4775[3] 5100[4]

Amwell Brave *J R Jenkins* 97h
10 b g Pyramus(USA) —Passage Creeping (IRE) (Persian Bold)
228[9] 697[10]

A M Xpress *Sue Smith* 82b
6 b g Kayf Tara—Shalateeno (Teenoso (USA))
2074[10]

Amylyn *John Holt*
4 b f Starcraft(NZ) —Skirt Around (Deploy)
2369[P]

Ana Buachaill Dana *Tom Gretton* 91h
9 b g Spadoun(FR) —Silva Linda (Precipice Wood)
432[2]

Anadama (IRE) *Alan King* 92h
7 br m Anshan—Welsh Chorus (IRE) (Decent Fellow)
223[3] 660[4]

Anak (IRE) *Jim Best* 122h
5 b g Sinndar(IRE) —Akdara (IRE) (Sadler's Wells (USA))
2606[9] 3306[8] 4830[6] 5278[F] 5404[5]

Ananda Kanda (USA) *Brian Ellison* 35h
4 bb f Hero's Tribute(USA) —Roja (USA) (L'Enjoleur (CAN))
3967[5] 4240[3] 4361[6]

Anaya *David Bourton* 88h
4 b f Tobougg(IRE) —Nacho Venture (FR) (Rainbow Quest (USA))
2528[3] 3519[4] 4952[7] 5435[3]

Anay Car (FR) *Howard Johnson* 110h
7 b g Sleeping Car(FR) —Anayette (FR) (Vaguely Pleasant (FR))
5098[F]

An Capall Mor (IRE) *Simon West* 95b
5 b g Flemensfirth(USA) —Corravilla (IRE) (Yashgan)
5313[2]

Anchorage Boy (USA) *Amy Weaver* 77h
4 b g Southern Image(USA) —Alaskan Winter (USA) (Gulch (USA))
629[3] 743[8] 851[2]

Ancient Times (USA) *Joss Saville* 84h
4 bb g Smart Strike(CAN) —Histoire Sainte (FR) (Kendor (FR))
1576[2]

Anderson McAuley (IRE) *W P Mullins* 110h
7 ch g Blueprint(IRE) —Southern Run (Deep Run)
1146a[6]

Andhaar *Steve Gollings* 129h
5 b g Bahri(USA) —Deraasaat (Nashwan (USA))
548[2] 712[4] (2092) (2397) 3783[3] 5182[11]

Andreo Bambaleo *Simon West* 111h
7 ch g Silver Patriarch(IRE) —Time And A Place (IRE) (Phardante (FR))
4061[5] 4541[3] 4870[2] (5262)

Andrew Nick (IRE) *Matt Hazell* 114h 119c
9 b g Riberetto—Legal Tour (IRE) (Legal Circles (USA))
(599)
3400[P] 4333[6]

And The Man *Nicky Richards* 120h
5 ch g Generous(IRE) —Retro's Lady (IRE) (Zaffaran (USA))
2246[7] 3330[6] (4304) 4910[P]

Andy Gin (FR) *Evelyn England* 68h
12 b g Ski Chief(USA) —Love Love Kate (FR) (Saint Andrews (FR))
3899[3] 4378[4]

Andytown (IRE) *Nicky Henderson* 149h 79c
8 ch g Old Vic—Pitfire (IRE) (Parliament)
2580[3]

Andy Vic (IRE) *Ian Brown* 68h
8 b g Old Vic—Garranard Ros (IRE) (Roselier (FR))
4112[8] 4393[10]

A New Story (IRE) *Michael Hourigan* 129h 142c
13 b g Fourstars Allstar(USA) —Diyala (FR) (Direct Flight)
3206a[15] 4792[3]

Aneyeforaneye (IRE) *Malcolm Jefferson* 109h
5 ch m Definite Article—Resolute Approach (IRE) (Toulon)
2167[2] 2616[2] 3498[2] (3747) ◆ 4454[3] 5008[15]

Ange Guerrier (FR) *Paul Nicholls* 95h
6 gr g Ange Gabriel(FR) —Quelle Diva (FR) (Tel Quel (FR))
3225[5] 3760[13]

Angel Sun (FR) *Ferdy Murphy* 98b
5 b g Astarabad(USA) —Five Rivers (FR) (Cadoudal (FR))
3731[7] 3998[2] 4801[4]

Angle Of Attack (IRE) *Alan Brown* 61h
6 b g Acclamation—Travel Spot Girl (Primo Dominie)
2509[12]

Angus's Antics *Kevin Morgan*
8 ch g Karinga Bay—Nessfield (Tumble Wind)
766[P]

Annibale Caro *Jim Goldie* 106h 100c
9 b g Mtoto—Isabella Gonzaga (Rock Hopper)
166[2] 444[P]
861[5] 1115[2] 1338[P]

Annie's Pride *George Moore* 60b
4 ch f Loup Sauvage(USA) —Whatagale (Strong Gale)
4171[8] 5034[6]

Annimation (IRE) *Seamus Mullins* 112h
7 b m Accordion—Euro Breeze (IRE) (Roselier (FR))
(2288) 2627[3] 3264[P] 4536[U] 5008[10]

A Nod And A Wink (IRE) *Shaun Lycett* 31h
7 b m Raise A Grand(IRE) —Earth Charter (Slip Anchor)
224[F]

Another Ambition (IRE) *A J Martin* 121h 132c
10 b g Oscar(IRE) —Reluctant Scholar (IRE) (Buckskin (FR))
874[P]

Another Brother (IRE) *Gerald Ham* 124h 104c
9 b g Supreme Leader—Sister Rosza (IRE) (Roselier (FR))
866[P]

Anothercoppercoast (IRE) *Paul A Roche* 121h 137c
11 ch g Presenting—Parsee (IRE) (Persian Mews)
4227a[3]

Another Dark Rum *John Weymes* 91h 98c
7 br g Beat All(USA) —Gourmet (IRE) (Homo Sapien)
32[3] ◆ 306[4] ◆ 477[4] 747[7]

Another Dimension (IRE) *Nigel Dunger* 115h
5 b g Overbury(IRE) —Freshwater (IRE) (Commanche Run)
3200[12] 3651[5] 4051[7] (4500)

Another Flint (IRE) *Lady Susan Brooke* 69h
11 ch g Accordion—Island Run (Deep Run)
1196[P]

Another Grand (IRE) *Ruth Carr* 65h
4 b g Statue Of Liberty(USA) —Fallacy (Selkirk (USA))
629[P] 743[5] 851[6]

Another Jewel (IRE) *Denis Paul Murphy* 95h 135c
9 b g Saddlers' Hall(IRE) —Sapphire Eile (Mujtahid (USA))
(312a)
4792[7]

Another Kate (IRE) *David Richards* 93h
7 gr m Norwich—Cracking Kate (IRE) (Roselier (FR))
2145[5] 2607[6] 3365[7] 3439[12]

Another Mystery *Evelyn Slack* 60h
6 b m Beat All(USA) —Mariner's Air (Julio Mariner)
2473[9] 3637[12] 3725[6] 4278[P]

Another Puzzle *Dominic Ffrench Davis* 93c
7 b g Another Hoarwithy—Jerpoint Jigsaw (Shaab)
5254[4] 5371[4]

Another Round (IRE) *Laura Young* 47h
7 b g Bach(IRE) —Another Sirrah (IRE) (Buckskin (FR))
2560[12] 2946[P] 3647[7] 4539[7]

Another Storm *Ben Case* 103h
9 gr m Shambo—Stormswift (Neltino)
(140)

Another Trump (NZ) *Jonjo O'Neill* 125h 118c
7 b g Montjeu(IRE) —She's A Trump (NZ) (Centro (NZ))
408[4] 714[6] 909[3] 1045[6] 1311[8]
(1481) 1926[3] 2184[6] 2961[P] 3154[7] 3494[8]

Anquetta (IRE) *Nicky Henderson* 119h 135c
7 b g Anshan—Quetta (IRE) (Alphabatim (USA))
303[2] 1952[2]
2330[4] (3494)
(3949) 4853[6] 5305[7]

Anshan Spirit (IRE) *R W Green* 105c
13 ch m Anshan—Saffron Spirit (Town And Country)
398[2]

Answer Me (IRE) *John Spearing* 84h
8 b g Sassanian(USA) —Answer That (IRE) (Mandalus)
59[6] 228[6]

Ant Music (IRE) *Evan Williams*
4 b g Antonius Pius(USA) —Day Is Dawning (IRE) (Green Forest (USA))
851[P]

Antoella (IRE) *Philip Kirby* 94h
4 gr f Antonius Pius(USA) —Bella Estella (GER) (Sternkoenig (IRE))
1984[6] 2369[3] 2556[5] (4148) 4419[2] 4892[5]

Antonius Caesar (FR) *Alex Hales* 84h 123c
8 b g Mansonnien(FR) —Kandania (FR) (Cadoudal (FR))
1950[P] 2214[3] 2940[10] 3263[8] (3723)
4328[5] 4749[4] 5377[P]

A Nun With A Gun (IRE) *Alan Jones* 112h
7 b m Presenting—Glacial Field (IRE) (Glacial Storm (USA))
(1343)

Anyauldiron (IRE) *Charlie Longsdon* 73h 80c
8 b g Lord Americo—Bodalmore Rose (IRE) (Roselier (FR))
3698[P] 4081[9] 4556[5]

Anychancedave (IRE) *Alan Swinbank* 109b
4 ro g Act One—Nabadhaat (USA) (Mr Prospector (USA))
3166[3] (3856) (4239)

Any Currency (IRE) *Martin Keighley* 116h 143c
8 b g Moscow Society(USA) —Native Bavard (IRE) (Be My Native (USA))
1990[3] 2358[2]

Any Given Day (IRE) *Donald McCain* 159h
6 gr g Clodovil(IRE) —Five Of Wands (Caerleon (USA))
1698[2] (1967) 2386[4] 2884[2] 3289[2] 4207[4] 4819[7]

Any Given Moment (IRE) *Donald McCain* 88h
5 b g Alhaarth(IRE) —Shastri (USA) (Alleged (USA))
3491[9] 3994[5] 4233[U] 4422[6] 5075[7]

Aohna (FR) *Alan King* 120h
6 b m Astarabad(USA) —Touques (FR) (Tip Moss (FR))
331[2] 736[3] ◆ 958[5] 1692[2] 1864[4] 2089[7]

Apache Blue (IRE) *John Wade* 91h 96c
7 b g Presenting—La Eile (IRE) (Brief Truce (USA))
176[6] 2656[3]
(4741)
5095[3]

Apache Brave (IRE) *Henry Hogarth* 65h 65c
8 ch g Kahtan—Glenstal Forest (IRE) (Glenstal (USA))
552[5] 955[9] 2301[P] 3503[4] 3712[4] 3884[P]

Apache Chant (USA) *Tony Carroll* 105h
7 b g War Chant(USA) —Sterling Pound (USA) (Seeking The Gold (USA))
554[3] 678[4] 1776[7] 2209[11] 3392[4] (3693) 3881[9]
4501[3] 4935[7] 5234[2] 5401[3]

Apache Country *Gordon Elliott* 102h 98c
7 b g Overbury(IRE) —Dara's Course (IRE) (Crash Course)
289[10]

Apache Dawn *Aytach Sadik* 97h 100c
7 ch g Pursuit Of Love—Taza (Persian Bold)
360[2] 479[3] ◆ 554[5] 768[2] 825[5] 983[3] 1083[3] 1296[3]
1405[5] 1552[P] 5348[5]

Apalachicola (IRE) *Eugene M O'Sullivan* 123h
5 b m Beneficial—Colleen Easpick (IRE) (Flemensfirth (USA))
3904[11]

Apartman (CZE) *George Charlton* 104h 80c
6 b g Scater(POL) —Apartma (CZE) (Dara Monarch)
647[F] 909[4] 5337[P]

A Patchy Dancer (IRE) *Sue Smith* 67h
6 b g Darnay—Amerindian (Commanche Run)
2074[8] 2525[6] 2939[9] 3506[9] 3725[8]

Aperitif *Michael Scudamore* 60h
10 ch g Pivotal—Art Deco Lady (Master Willie)
4260[11]
A P Ling *Christopher Kellett* 65h
4 b f Antonius Pius(USA) —Spain (Polar Falcon (USA))
836[11] 960[P] 1018[7] 1279[2] 1442[7] 1691[10] 1935[7] 2556[6] 3396[6] 3703[P] 4178[4] 4395[7] 4947[3] 5272[3]
Apolka *Renee Robeson* 13b
4 b f Pilsudski(IRE) —Amidst (Midyan (USA))
5119[13]
Apollo Blaze (IRE) *Mrs P J Shaw* 98c
10 ch g Lord Of Appeal—Molly Blaney (Kemal (FR))
(173) **502[7]**
3908[12] 4163[P] 4928[12]
Appeal Denied (IRE) *Sandy Forster* 117h 45c
9 ch g Lord Of Appeal—Cothu Na Slaine (IRE) (Roselier (FR))
405[7] 1762[10] 1929[3] 2351[7] **3853[P] 5427[4]**
Appeal To Paddy (IRE) *Matt Sheppard*
7 ch g Lord Of Appeal—Griffinstown Lady (Over The River (FR))
693[P] 792[11]
Appleaday (IRE) *Paul Webber* 96h 130c
10 gr g Beneficial—Hello Aris (IRE) (Aristocracy)
2214[4] 2871[14] 3444[U] 3629[4] 4486[5] 4726[2] 5229[2]
Appointment *Sheena West* 95h
6 ch m Where Or When(IRE) —Shoshone (Be My Chief (USA))
688[2] 826[9]
Approved Force (USA) *Lucy Wadham* 118h 118c
7 gr g With Approval(CAN) —Kinetic Force (USA) (Holy Bull (USA))
4931[3]
Apt Approach (IRE) *W P Mullins* 130h 143c
8 ch g Bob Back(USA) —Imminent Approach (IRE) (Lord Americo)
2227a[5]
Apt To Run (USA) *David Rees* 103h
8 bb g Aptitude(USA) —Tufa (Warning)
1115[4] 1370[2] 1723[2]
Apurna *John Harris*
6 ch m Rock Of Gibraltar(IRE) —Dance Lesson (In The Wings)
2421[P]
Aqualung (FR) *Claire Dyson* 124h
7 b g Port Lyautey(FR) —Verosa (FR) (Saint Estephe (FR))
359[4]
Arabella Boy (IRE) *E Bolger* 138h 135c
6 ch g Beneficial—Dasdilemma (IRE) (Furry Glen)
4802[10]
Arabian Silk (IRE) *Donald McCain* 86h
5 b m Barathea(IRE) —Anthyllis (IRE) (Night Shift (USA))
161[14] 577[P]
Arabian Spirit *Richard Fahey* 72h
6 b g Oasis Dream—Royal Flame (IRE) (Royal Academy (USA))
2509[8]
Aragall (GER) *George Baker* 96h
6 gr g Black Sam Bellamy(IRE) —A J Bear (USA) (Slew City Slew (USA))
1547[9] 1914[12] 4225[3] 4672[P]
Araldur (FR) *Alan King* 127h 155c
7 ch g Spadoun(FR) —Aimessa (FR) (Tropular)
1915 3387[2] 3739[2] 4091[2] (4479) (5059)
Araucaria (IRE) *John E Kiely* 131h
7 b m Accordion—Native Artist (IRE) (Be My Native (USA))
2196a[3] 2912a[5] 3592a[6]
Arbayoun (IRE) *Frederick Sutherland* 84h
6 b g Daylami(IRE) —Arameen (IRE) (Halling (USA))
2667[9] 3348[11]
Arbeo (IRE) *Diana Grissell* 110b
5 b g Brian Boru—Don't Waste It (IRE) (Mister Lord (USA))
(3434) (4430)
Arbor Supreme (IRE) *W P Mullins* 118h 154c
9 b g Supreme Leader—Peter's Well (IRE) (Electric)
3437[P] 4298a[2] 5200[F]
Arcadia Boy (IRE) *Donald McCain* 101h
8 b g King's Theatre(IRE) —Future Treasure (Habitat)
1138[4] (1295) 1505[P] **1823[P]**
Arcalis *Howard Johnson* 142h 98c
11 gr g Lear Fan(USA) —Aristocratique (Cadeaux Genereux)
207[6] 2672[3] 3807[6] 4806[8]
Arceye *William Davies* 85c
14 b g Weld—Flower Of Tintern (Free State)
251[4] 383[7] 1733[8] 1969[P] 2170[P]
Arch *Sandy Forster* 81h
8 ch g Arkadian Hero(USA) —Loriner's Lass (Saddlers' Hall (IRE))
678[9] 1340[2] 1700[8]
Archdale Lady (IRE) *Ferdy Murphy* 69h
7 gr m Great Palm(USA) —Daika (FR) (Argument (FR))
1760[P] 3635[7] 3883[4]
Archie Boy (IRE) *Paul W Flynn* 127h 148c
9 b g Basanta(IRE) —Darial Mill (IRE) (Salluceva)
1527a[F] ◆ 2096a[2]
Archie Rice (USA) *Tom Keddy* 107h
5 b g Arch(USA) —Gold Bowl (USA) (Seeking The Gold (USA))
4069[4] 4499[4] ◆ 4917[3] 5357[2]
Archie's Wish *Micky Hammond* 65h 89c
7 br g Beat All(USA) —Marlands (Henbit (USA))
10[5] 176[P] 490[8] 604[11] **(1360)**
1423[F] (1503)
1663[U] 1826[2] 2371[3] 3748[3] 4241[P] 5351[6]
Architrave *Tim Vaughan* 121h
4 ch g Hernando(FR) —White Palace (Shirley Heights)
(1298) (1473) (1610) 2356[13] 4847[19] 5227[6]
Arctic Actress *Nicky Henderson* 62b
4 b f King's Theatre(IRE) —Blast Freeze (IRE) (Lafontaine (USA))
3920[7]
Arctic Ben (IRE) *Henry Daly* 115h 107c
7 gr g Beneficial—Hurst Flyer (Neltino)
2112[7] 2635[2] 3765[4] 4482[F]
Arctic Court (IRE) *Jim Goldie* 127h
7 b g Arctic Lord—Polls Joy (Pollerton)
2202[2] 2545[7] (3362) 3742[P] 4062[2] 4715[3] (5316)
Arctic Echo *Rob Summers* 110h 115c
12 b g Alderbrook—Arctic Oats (Oats)
2171[P] 2372[11] 3713[2] 4079[8] **4551[7] (5377)**
Arctic Fashion (IRE) *Seamus Mullins* 17h
6 b m Milan—Penguin (Arctic Lord)
3904[12]
Arctic Flow *Caroline Keevil* 82h
7 b m Alflora(IRE) —Flow (Over The River (FR))
684[7] (3350) 3703[2] 4032[7] (4401) 4559[8]
Arctic Ghost *Philip Hobbs* 90h 103c
11 gr g Environment Friend—Saxon Gift (Saxon Farm)
587[3] 737[11]
Arctic Gunner *Geoffrey Deacon* 85h
7 gr g Alflora(IRE) —Arctic Chick (Henbit (USA))
3088[3] 4370[5]
Arctic Mick (IRE) *Michael O'Hare* 118h 116c
10 b g Arctic Lord—Lana Tee (IRE) (Kemal (FR))
2298[F] 3501[2]
Arctic Rock *Geoffrey Harker* 77h 62c
8 ch g Prince Daniel(USA) —Celtic Tern (Celtic Cone)
9[P] 161[6] 402[3] 490[11] 745[9]
Arctic Shadow *Tim Vaughan* 114h 97c
9 b g Bonny Scot(IRE) —Dickies Girl (Saxon Farm)
158[P] 695[P]
Arctic Watch *Brendan Duke* 90h
6 gr g Accondy(IRE) —Watcha (USA) (Blushing Stage (USA))
231[8]
Arctic Wings (IRE) *Tony Carroll* 126h 100c
7 b g In The Wings—Arctic Hunt (IRE) (Bering)
3520[4] 4485[2] 4727[14] 5339[5]
Arc Warrior (FR) *Andrew Parker* 100h
7 b g Even Top(IRE) —What The Hell (IRE) (Henbit (USA))
2107[P] 3854[P] 4062[P]
Ardesia (IRE) *Tina Jackson* 95h
7 b g Red Sunset—Lowtown (Camden Town)
(520) (582) 727[5] 1147[7] 1328[8] 3500[13] 3782[13] 4390[9] 5094[4]
Ardilaun (IRE) *John W Nicholson* 96h 74c
8 b m Darnay—Magic Glen (IRE) (Magical Wonder (USA))
1137[6]
Ardistan (IRE) *Jonjo O'Neill* 101h
7 b g Selkirk(USA) —Asmara (USA) (Lear Fan (USA))
853[9] 1084[9] 1443[2]
Ardkilly Gunner (IRE) *Ian Williams* 94b
6 b g Milan—Ardkilly Comet (IRE) (Montelimar (USA))
4970[6]
Ardkilly Rebel (IRE) *Philip Hobbs* 111h
7 b g Witness Box(USA) —Ardkilly Comet (IRE) (Montelimar (USA))
3153[6] 4012[4] 4462[10]
Ardmaddy (IRE) *Gary Moore* 105h
7 b g Generous(IRE) —Yazmin (IRE) (Green Desert (USA))
(215) 430[8] 534[7]
Ardnaclancy (IRE) *Andrew Richardson* 121c
8 br g Darnay—Ardnataggle (IRE) (Aristocracy)
90[4] 398[5] (551)
(628) 4211[F] 4476[3] 4915[2] 5263[2] 5419[2]
Are Olive *Tim Walford* 74h
8 b m Alflora(IRE) —Nasowas (IRE) (Cardinal Flower)
1613[7] 1780[6] 2075[7] *3167[10]* 4112[P] 5298[P]
Areuwitmenow (IRE) *Charlie Longsdon* 114h
6 b g Beneficial—Clonartic (IRE) (Be My Native (USA))
3719[P] 4233[5] 4747[2] ◆ 5203[2]
Arewenearlythere *Paul Webber*
5 ch g Millkom—Fiesta (Most Welcome)
5284[P]
Areyacoddinmee (IRE) *Mrs Elaine Smith* 105c
11 bb g Good Thyne(USA) —Fine Affair (IRE) (Fine Blade (USA))
398[4] 580[5]
Argaum (IRE) *Evan Williams* 77h
4 ch g Medicean—Poppy Carew (IRE) (Danehill (USA))
5099[10]
Argentia *Lucy Wadham* 90h 90c
6 b m Silver Patriarch(IRE) —Ludoviciana (Oats)
2554[10] 3721[5] 4118[4] 4380[P] **4741[4]**
Argentis (FR) *Charlie Morlock* 93h
6 b g Agent Bleu(FR) —Line Congre (FR) (Le Nain Jaune (FR))
157[P]
Argyll *Jeff Pearce*
4 b c Xaar—Vitesse (IRE) (Royal Academy (USA))
960[P]
Ariel Bender *Donald McCain* 67h
4 gr g Needwood Blade—Wandering Stranger (Petong)
960[6] 1135[P] 1234[6]
Arikinui *Stuart Coltherd* 11h
6 b m Noverre(USA) —Off The Blocks (Salse (USA))
3850[15] 4165[15] 4473[P]
Arisea (IRE) *James Moffatt* 104h
8 b m Cape Cross(IRE) —Castelfranca (IRE) (Scenic)
(470) 745[F] 3966[7] 4544[4] 5098[5] 5315[6]
Arizona River *George Moore* 92b
5 b m Fair Mix(IRE) —Halo Flora (Alflora (IRE))
4280[2]
Arkendale (IRE) *J P Fogarty* 98h 122c
9 b g Portrait Gallery(IRE) —Baby Alice (IRE) (Top Of The World)
1121a[11]
Arklow Ger (IRE) *Paul Nolan* 111h 122c
9 b g Presenting—Miss Rose (IRE) (Phardante (FR))
3706a[F]
Arkose (IRE) *Oliver Sherwood* 123h 96c
7 b g Luso—Endless Patience (IRE) (Miner's Lamp)
94[10] **2110[6]**
2441[6] 3947[12] 5230[3]
Armagnac Empress *Seamus Mullins*
7 ch m Emperor Fountain—Armagnac Messenger (Pony Express)
910[5]
Armaramak (IRE) *E J O'Grady* 132h 127c
7 b g Mark Of Esteem(IRE) —Armarama (Persian Bold)
1131a[2] ◆
Armedanddangerous (IRE) *Tom Gretton* 106h
6 b g Kris Kin(USA) —Lucky Fountain (IRE) (Lafontaine (USA))
2445[2] 3998[5] (4569)
Armenian Boy (FR) *David Pipe* 114h 125c
8 b g Simon Du Desert(FR) —Jade D'Eau (IRE) (Lion Cavern (USA))
170[8] 771[4] 994[9] 1556[2] 1726[2] 1937[2]
Armoury House *D Buckett* 91h 119c
10 ch g Gunner B—Coire Vannich (Celtic Cone)
(5277)
Arniecoco *Emma McWilliam* 102h
6 b g Dr Fong(USA) —Groovy (Shareef Dancer (USA))
765[P]
Arnold Layne (IRE) *Caroline Bailey* 88h 107c
12 gr g Roselier(FR) —Cotton Gale (Strong Gale)
1769[9] 1992[5] 2420[2] 2928[5] 3263[3] 3768[3] 4238[5]
(4953)
Arran Law (IRE) *Lucinda Russell* 103h
7 ch g Flemensfirth(USA) —Windy Run (Deep Run)
4303[6] 4686[4]
Arrayan *David Pipe* 134h
6 b g Catcher In The Rye(IRE) —Ganga (IRE) (Generous (IRE))
2137[7] 2504[2] (3449) (3532) 4031[U] 4727[21]
Arrow Barrow (IRE) *John Wade* 94h
6 b g Moscow Society(USA) —Miss Nee (IRE) (Strong Gale)
2552[6] 3725[4] 4253[7] 4914[6]
Art Bank *Sue Bradburne* 65h 49c
8 b g Saddlers' Hall(IRE) —Langton Lass (Nearly A Hand)
287[P]
Art Broker (IRE) *Henry Daly* 115h
5 b g Pivotal—La Gandilie (FR) (Highest Honor (FR))
1962[5] ◆ 2540[8] 3495[3] 4076[6] 4783[2] 5400[2]
Art Deco (IRE) *Charles Egerton* 97h
8 ch h Peintre Celebre(USA) —Sometime (IRE) (Royal Academy (USA))
1138[3] 1732[12]
Art Exhibition (IRE) *Charlie Mann* 101h
6 ch g Captain Rio—Miss Dilletante (Primo Dominie)
282[9] 2247[P] 3308[6]
Art Gallery *David Thompson* 95h 95c
7 ch g Indian Ridge—Party Doll (Be My Guest (USA))
1428[P] **2434[F]**
Arthurian (IRE) *Anthony Middleton* 84h
6 b g Daylami(IRE) —Kiltubber (IRE) (Sadler's Wells (USA))
2169[F] 2558[10] 3532[5]
Arthurian Legend *Philip Hobbs* 127h
6 b g Alflora(IRE) —Be My Adelina (IRE) (Be My Native (USA))
(2145) ◆ 2791[6] 3691[18] (5106)
Arthurs Dream (IRE) *Nick Ayliffe* 66h 51c
9 b g Desert Prince(IRE) —Blueprint (USA) (Shadeed (USA))
4447[6] 5076[P] 5439[P]
Arthur's Pass *Tom George* 114h
7 b g Midnight Legend—Bella Coola (Northern State (USA))
237[2] 637[2] 833[3] 3556[15] (4437)
Artic Bliss *Charlie Longsdon* 63h
9 ch m Fraam—Eskimo Nel (IRE) (Shy Groom (USA))
600[3] 920[8]
Artic Fire (IRE) *Craig Pilgrim* 82c
12 b g Arctic Cider(USA) —Upwitfireandflames (Bulldozer)
151[7]
Artic Journey (IRE) *Linda Blackford*
7 b g Kasmayo—Bella Blue (Artaius (USA))
4029[11] 4706[P]
Artic Night (FR) *Nicky Richards* 93h
5 gr g Kaldoun(FR) —Just Win (FR) (Homme De Loi (IRE))
2296[7] 2612[9] 3330[11] 3783[U] 3850[6] 4712[2] 5094[10]
Artic Pride (IRE) *Oliver Sherwood* 72h
7 b g Definite Article—Tricias Pride (IRE) (Broken Hearted)
2454[12] 2981[9] 3153[9] 3837[3] **4238[F]** 5075[P]
Articulate (IRE) *Henry Daly* 88b
6 b g Definite Article—Quare Dream'S (IRE) (Strong Gale)
1069[6]
Artist's Return (IRE) *William Stone* 29h 102c
9 br g Bob's Return(IRE) —Artist's Jewel (Le Moss)
955[6] 1105[4]
Art Man *James Frost* 98h 78c
8 b g Dansili—Persuasion (Batshoof)
171[3] 762[2] 1124[4] 1484[7] 1601[5] 1925[7] **2334[4]**
2605[F] 3449[7] 4178[6]
Art Professor (IRE) *Venetia Williams* 132h
7 b g In The Wings—Itab (USA) (Dayjur (USA))
2868[9] 3229[7] (3808)
Arturo Uno (IRE) *Nigel Twiston-Davies* 100h 120c
8 b g Bob's Return(IRE) —Aiguille (IRE) (Lancastrian)
2513[F] 3562[P] 4160[2] 4749[2] 5384[3]
Art Value *Carroll Gray* 85h
6 ch g Barathea(IRE) —Empty Purse (Pennine Walk)
1552[5] 1723[7] 1976[6] 2331[5] 2609[P]
Arumun (IRE) *Michael Scudamore* 95h 111c
10 b g Posidonas—Adwoa (IRE) (Eurobus)
99[4] (460)
848[P] 919[6] 1139[7]
Ascendant *Howard Johnson* 115h
5 ch g Medicean—Ascendancy (Sadler's Wells (USA))
1931[4] 3334[9] 4572[2]
As Cold As Ice *Linda Blackford*
11 b m Millkom—Miss Krispy (FR) (Bellypha)
129[P]
As De Fer (FR) *Anthony Honeyball* 106h 140c
5 b g Passing Sale(FR) —Miss Hollywood (FR) (True Brave (USA))
3056[8] 3299[9]
(3765) (4095)
4891[3]
Ashammar (FR) *Paul Webber* 122h 120c
6 b g King's Best(USA) —Asharna (IRE) (Darshaan)
(1641) 1827[7]
2153[4] 2548[U] 3620[3]
Ashbourne Folly (IRE) *Bob Buckler* 73b
5 b g Milan—Time To Ask (IRE) (Be My Native (USA))
3651[8] 4970[P]
Ashes House (IRE) *Tim Vaughan* 101b
5 b g Dushyantor(USA) —Cailinclover (IRE) (Ajraas (USA))
4561[2]
Ashfield's Dream *Evan Williams* 116h 127c
7 b g Alflora(IRE) —Colonial Princess (Roscoe Blake)
(2248)
3198[9] ◆ 3605[4]
Ashgrove Diamond (IRE) *Lucy Normile* 21h
7 b m Desert Sun—Nurses Run (IRE) (Turkoman (USA))
5147[P]
Ash High (IRE) *Nigel Twiston-Davies* 95h 73c
8 br g Rashar(USA) —Gothic Ash (IRE) (Yashgan)
251[6] 694[4] 872[P] 994[10]
Ash Holt *Charles Smith*
5 ch g Yoshka—Jawleyford Court (Moshaajir (USA))
2403[10]
Ashkazar (FR) *David Pipe* 161h 141c
7 b g Sadler's Wells(USA) —Asharna (IRE) (Darshaan)
2219[4] 2516[8] 2884[5] (3293) 4819[13]
Ashmolian (IRE) *Zoe Davison* 98h
8 b g Grand Lodge(USA) —Animatrice (USA) (Alleged (USA))
137[6] (382) (436) 708[9] 1129[6] 1291[3]
Asigh Pearl (IRE) *Noel Meade* 133h
7 ch m Lord Of Appeal—Graphic Lady (IRE) (Phardante (FR))
3474a[6]
Ask Again *Miss Sarah West* 123c
12 ch g Rakaposhi King—Boreen's Glory (Boreen (FR))
(184) **4928[4]**
Askanna (IRE) *Colin Bowe* 125h
6 b m Old Vic—All The Roses (IRE) (Roselier (FR))
2912a[3]
Ask Archer *Evan Williams* 90h
6 b g Sir Harry Lewis(USA) —Swing Bar (Sadeem (USA))
360[3] 563[5] 793[11] 5390[9]
Ask Bobby *Mrs M Sowersby* 83c
12 b g Primitive Rising(USA) —Ask Jean (Ascertain (USA))
3991[4]
Askmeroe (IRE) *A J Martin* 112h 125c
8 b g Rudimentary(USA) —Mill Lady (IRE) (Jurado (USA))
192[3] 3473a[10]
Askthemaster (IRE) *Robert Tyner* 129h 146c
11 b g Oscar(IRE) —Nicola Mac (IRE) (King's Ride)
4853[2]
Ask The Oracle *Bernard Llewellyn* 94h
5 ch g Where Or When(IRE) —Delphic Way (Warning)
1736[5] ◆ 2145[14] 2323[4] 4924[5] 5082[6]
A Special Lady (IRE) *I A Duncan*
6 ch m Samraan(USA) —Fleetmead (IRE) (Jamesmead)
2505[P] **4254[P]**
Aspirant (POL) *F Holcak*
8 b g In Camera(IRE) —Aspiracja (POL) (Jape (USA))
1811a[7]
A Splash Of Green (IRE) *Jonathan Portman* 28h
6 gr g Great Palm(USA) —Lottobuck (Buckskin (FR))
1778[12] 2985[P] 3781[11]
Aspolan (GER) *Rachel Hobbs* 96h 40c
8 b g Spectrum(IRE) —Arkona (GER) (Aspros (GER))
1959[12]
2332[4] 2645[P] 2930[11] 3260[P] 3622[P]
Astania *Philip Hobbs*
6 b m Shahrastani(USA) —So Ambitious (Teenoso (USA))
733[P]
Astarador (FR) *Howard Johnson* 128h 132c
9 b g Astarabad(USA) —Touques (FR) (Tip Moss (FR))
309[9] 1626[5]
A Stones Throw (NZ) *Ben Haslam* 95h
6 b g Montjeu(IRE) —Subject Matter (NZ) (Grosvenor (NZ))
3951[7] 4390[4] 4833[2] 5144[4] 5350[4]
Astracad (FR) *Nigel Twiston-Davies* 143h
5 br g Cadoudal(FR) —Astre Eria (FR) (Garde Royale)
(55) (196) 1609[3] (1859) 2386[8] 2887[6] 3288[6] 4852[14]

Astralogical (IRE) *Alan King* 83b
6 ch m Fourstars Allstar(USA) —Grainne Geal (General Ironside)
3159[4] 3876[11] 5056[8]

Astrodiva *Mark H Tompkins* 93h
5 b m Where Or When(IRE) —Astromancer (USA) (Silver Hawk (USA))
4952[2]

Astroleo *Mark H Tompkins* 22h
5 ch g Groom Dancer(USA) —Astrolove (USA) (Bigstone (IRE))
1829[12] 4951[8]

Astrolibra *Mark H Tompkins* 110h
7 b m Sakhee(USA) —Optimistic (Reprimand)
(421) 488[2] 1017[14] 1233[2] 1475[2] 1724[6] 1951[4]

Astrovenus *Mark H Tompkins* 37h
4 ch f Tobougg(IRE) —Astrolove (IRE) (Bigstone (IRE))
1818[5] 3958[8]

Asturienne *Alan King* 124h 134c
7 br m Sleeping Car(FR) —Asturias (FR) (Pistolet Bleu (IRE))
2242[3] 2514[3] 2983[7]
3627[2] (4127)
(4398) 5007[5] 5421[4]

Atabaas Allure (FR) *Chris Gordon* 66h
5 b m Alhaarth(IRE) —Atabaa (FR) (Anabaa (USA))
82[6] 379[5] 585[8] 1479[4] 1679[6] 1915[5] 2433[3]

Ataraxia *Mrs Sue Popham* 50b
9 b m Kayf Tara—Page Of Gold (Goldhill)
152[P]

Atared *Pam Sly* 97h
5 b m Nayef(USA) —Hawriyah (USA) (Dayjur (USA))
2168[13] 2456[6] 3987[12] 4310[P] 4809[2] 5057[5]

Atherstone Hill (IRE) *Robin Dickin* 103h 108c
9 b g Presenting—Mystic Madam (IRE) (Lafontaine (USA))
2457[2] (3700)
3900[2] (4829)

Athoss *Robert Smith* 40h 103c
9 gr g Environment Friend—Lady Flora (Alflora (IRE))
90[5] 306[3] 443[2] 551[7] 860[10] 4147[P]

Atlantic Coast (IRE) *Peter Bowen* 116h
7 b g In The Wings—Reasonably Devout (CAN) (St Jovite (USA))
514[5] 763[4] (820)

Atlantic Pearl *David Pipe* 78b
5 bg g Fair Mix(IRE) —Proper Posh (Rakaposhi King)
3569[9] 4097[11] 4468[11]

Atouchbetweenacara (IRE) *Venetia Williams* 116h 124c
10 bb g Lord Americo—Rosie Lil (IRE) (Roselier (FR))
2304[F] 2524[6] 3804[U] 4206[6]

Attaglance *Malcolm Jefferson* 121h
5 b g Passing Glance—Our Ethel (Be My Chief (USA))
209[4] 2038[7] 2162[4] (2473) 2954[6] (5028) 5339[2]

Attainable *Jim Old* 81h
5 bb m Kalanisi(IRE) —Balleta (USA) (Lyphard (USA))
2068[11] 2331[3] 2960[20] 4032[P] 5111[P]

Attorney General (IRE) *Neil King* 122h
12 b g Sadler's Wells(USA) —Her Ladyship (Polish Precedent (USA))
66[5]

Auberge (IRE) *Dianne Sayer* 96h
7 ch m Blueprint(IRE) —Castlegrace (IRE) (Kemal (FR))
212[3] 749[5] 871[P] 1119[4] 1362[2] (1428) 1507[2]
1559[3] 2080[3] 2654[4] 4276[7] 4914[8] 5295[2]

Au Courant (IRE) *Sophie Leech* 104h 136c
11 b g Zaffaran(USA) —Thatsthefashion (IRE) (Roselier (FR))
1332[10] 1557[P] 1858[7] 2543[7] 2794[P]

Auditor *Simon Lewis* 56h 69c
12 b g Polish Precedent(USA) —Annaba (IRE) (In The Wings)
1106[9] 1273[8] 1283[10] 1483[8]

Aughaloor (IRE) *W P Mullins* 130h
8 b g Supreme Leader—Awbeg Flower (IRE) (Alphabatim (USA))
4249a[4]

Aughcarra (IRE) *Harry Chisman* 82h
6 b g High Chaparral(IRE) —Pearly Brooks (Efisio)
154[11] 711[6] 793[9] (1552) 1704[6] 2467[7]

Aughnacurraveel (IRE) *Garry Ducey* 130h
7 b g Tajraasi(USA) —Water Ore (IRE) (Ore)
2562a[4] 3029a[4]

Auld Farmer *Christopher Wilson* 75b
7 br g Fraam—M'Auld Segoisha (IRE) (Dolphin Street (FR))
35[8] 474[10]

Aupcharlie (IRE) *P E Collins* 126b
5 b g Daliapour(IRE) —Lirfa (USA) (Lear Fan (USA))
731[2] 4808[3] ◆

Aura *John Flint*
6 b m Barathea(IRE) —Finger Of Light (Green Desert (USA))
1090[U] 1457[6]

Aura About You (IRE) *Paul Nolan* 138h 137c
8 b m Supreme Leader—Windswept Lady (IRE) (Strong Gale)
3779a[8] (4755a)

Aureate *Brian Forsey* 57h
7 ch g Jade Robbery(USA) —Anne D'Autriche (IRE) (Rainbow Quest (USA))
2021[8] 4446[P]

Aurifex (IRE) *Paul Murphy* 67c
7 b g Goldmark(USA) —River Rose (IRE) (Roselier (FR))
13[P] 873[7] 999[P]

Auroras Encore (IRE) *Sue Smith* 135h 150c
9 b g Second Empire(IRE) —Sama Veda (IRE) (Rainbow Quest (USA))
(98) **844[P]**
2399[5] 2523[14]

Australia Day (IRE) *Paul Webber* 156h
8 gr g Key Of Luck(USA) —Atalina (FR) (Linamix (FR))
(1017) ◆ (1886) 2219[9]

Authentic Act (IRE) *Martin Todhunter* 84h 85c
7 ch g Pivotal—All In All (Halling (USA))
(402) 490[3] 1005[5] 1504[7] 1700[2] 2302[6] (3727)
3997[4] 4510[3] 4800[5] 5351[4]

Automaticman (IRE) *Henry Daly* 68h
5 b g Craigsteel—Lora Lady (IRE) (Lord Americo)
2328[5] 3403[14] 3897[P] 4437[9]

Autumm Spirit *Robin Dickin* 84h 86c
7 ch m Kadastrof(FR) —Dickies Girl (Saxon Farm)
1737[P] 2425[4] 3430[2] 3545[2] 3745[7]
(4691) 5058[3]

Autumn Harvest *William Young* 81h
7 b g Beat Hollow—Welsh Autumn (Tenby)
3551[P] 3631[12] 3855[9] 3993[11] 4548[P]

Autumn Haze *Evan Williams* 75h
6 b g Chaddleworth(IRE) —Kristal Haze (Krisinsky (USA))
2640[4] 3626[6]

Autumn Red (IRE) *Paul Webber* 103h 101c
11 ch g Zaffaran(USA) —Ballygullen River (IRE) (Over The River (FR))
1276[4] 1483[3] 1747[2] 1939[4] 2155[P] (3388)
3723[8] 4705[P] 5377[3]

Autumn's Over *W M Wanless* 64c
10 b g Overbury(IRE) —Angel Falling (Scottish Reel)
5283[3]

Autumn's Quest *Teresa Spearing*
8 ch m Raheen(USA) —Sea-Belle (IRE) (Mukaddamah (USA))
635[P] 953[P]

Avanos (FR) *Philip Kirby* 101h
6 b g Kaldounevees(FR) —Annee De La Femme (IRE) (Common Grounds)
697[4] (886)

Avec Moi Ce Soir (IRE) *Colin Tizzard* 103h
8 b g Marignan(USA) —Claregary (IRE) (Brush Aside (USA))
266[5]

Avenue Marceau (FR) *Y Fouin* 136h 105c
6 b m Enrique—Transatlantique (FR) (Saint Estephe (FR))
2230a[4]

Avesomeofthat (IRE) *Miss Hannah Lewis* 116h 86c
10 b g Lahib(USA) —Lacinia (Groom Dancer (USA))
406[5]

Aviador (GER) *Lucy Wadham* 116h
5 b g Paolini(GER) —Albarana (GER) (Sure Blade (USA))
2074[3] 2426[3] 2925[5] 3302[2] 3696[9] (4327) ◆
5110[12]

Avoca Promise (IRE) *Charles Egerton* 111h
6 b g Oscar(IRE) —High Ace (IRE) (Good Thyne (USA))
2518[3] ◆ (2957) 3399[4] 4424[2]

Avon Gale *John Allen* 55b
7 gr m Silver Patriarch(IRE) —Severn Gale (Strong Gale)
1472[4] 1748[9]

Award Winner *Brendan Powell* 110h 121c
8 b g Alflora(IRE) —Blackwater Bay (IRE) (Supreme Leader)
1676[5] 2112[5] 2429[7] 3157[P] 3648[5] 3962[10]
4523[P] 5215[9]

Award Winning (IRE) *John Berwick* 77h 98c
10 b g Oscar(IRE) —Mum's Pride (IRE) (Phardante (FR))
272[5] 757[3] 1028[P] 1335[P]

Awareiness (IRE) *Chris Bealby* 100h
5 b g Flemensfirth(USA) —Special Case (IRE) (Be My Native (USA))
2281[3]

Away We Go (IRE) *Timothy Cleary* 119h 142c
8 ch g Stowaway—Margurites Pet (IRE) (Roselier (FR))
3206a[P]

Awaywiththegreys (IRE) *Peter Bowen* 95b
4 gr g Whipper(USA) —Silver Sash (GER) (Mark Of Esteem (IRE))
2237[3] 4491[5] 4943[8]

Awesome Bella *Alan King* 94b
4 b f Karinga Bay—Awesome Aunt (IRE) (Vestris Abu)
5135[2] ◆

Awesome Freddie *Alan King* 123h
6 b g Karinga Bay—Awesome Aunt (IRE) (Vestris Abu)
2143[4] 2946[4] (3483) 4185[3] 4464[4] 5321[2]

Awesome George *Alan King* 119h 141c
7 b g Exit To Nowhere(USA) —Awesome Aunt (IRE) (Vestris Abu)
1987[2] 2359[P] *3060[7]* **4470[P]** 5110[10] 5441[7]

Ayemdee (IRE) *Jonjo O'Neill* 79h 117c
8 b g Flemensfirth(USA) —Deep Coral (IRE) (Buckskin (FR))
2366[4] 2953[4] 3900[P]

Aye Well *Elliott Cooper* 28b
6 bb g Overbury(IRE) —Squeeze Box (IRE) (Accordion)
3856[10] 5342[15]

Aymard Des Fieffes (FR) *Nikki Evans* 14h
9 ch g Lute Antique(FR) —Margot Des Fieffes (FR) (Magistros (FR))
2244[8] 2589[P] 4833[P] 5072[P]

Azebra *Lynn Siddall* 15b
6 b m Picea—Bonita Joana (IRE) (Sri Pekan (USA))
4239[14] 4801[9]

Azione *Pat Murphy* 85h
8 b m Exit To Nowhere(USA) —Little Feat (Terimon)
2927[4] 3155[6] 3822[2] 4330[11] 4724[7]

Aztec Treasure (NZ) *Jonjo O'Neill* 88h 119c
7 b g Montjeu(IRE) —Big Belle (NZ) (Zabeel (NZ))
1708[2] (2170)
2595[2] (2982)
4538[5]

Aztec Warrior (IRE) *Mrs Antonia Bealby* 119h 91c
10 b g Taipan(IRE) —Eurocurrency (IRE) (Brush Aside (USA))
4026[3]

Azulada Bay (IRE) *Mark Rimell* 113h 109c
7 ch g Karinga Bay—Azulada (FR) (Pistolet Bleu (IRE))
232[5] 494[6] 1601[8]
1991[3] 2172[2] (2585)
5081[P]

Baaher (USA) *Jim Goldie* 118h 105c
7 b g War Chant(USA) —Raajiya (USA) (Gulch (USA))
196[2] 288[2] 447[8] (943)
1116[3] 1342[2]
1595[3] 1767[4] 1957[6] 2164[8]
2510[F] 2656[P] 3335[10]

Baan (USA) *James Eustace* 115h
8 ch g Diesis—Madaen (USA) (Nureyev (USA))
3719[6] 4012[2] 4500[5]

Babe Heffron (IRE) *Tom George* 78h 121c
10 ch g Topanoora—Yellow Ochre (IRE) (Ore)
213[6] (3375)
3574[3] 4460[6]

Babe Maccool (IRE) *David Pipe* 62h
9 ch g Giant's Causeway(USA) —Kotama (USA) (Shahrastani (USA))
792[12] 1199[10] 1552[P]

Babilu *Dai Burchell* 109h
6 ch m Lomitas—Creeking (Persian Bold)
1822[2] (2070) 2242[2] (2639) 3557[13] 3874[F] 4503[5]
5100[F] (Dead)

Baby Car (FR) *Noel Chance* 85h
7 b g Sleeping Car(FR) —Babycia (FR) (Baby Turk)
2131[6] 2452[4] 2980[3] 3297[5] 3837[6] 4724[9] 5103[4]

Baby Judge (IRE) *Michael Chapman*
4 ch g Captain Rio—Darling Clementine (Lion Cavern (USA))
1610[P]

Baby Run (FR) *Nigel Twiston-Davies* 134h 148c
11 b g Baby Turk—Run For Laborie (FR) (Lesotho (USA))
(3956)
(4211) 4851[U] (5163)
5443[3]

Baby Shine (IRE) *Lucy Wadham* 119b
5 b m King's Theatre(IRE) —Brambleshine (IRE) (Phardante (FR))
(3623) (4027) 4728[3] ◆ 5188[4]

Babysitter (IRE) *Jonjo O'Neill* 127h 121c
8 b g Rashar(USA) —Pil Eagle (FR) (Piling (USA))
1863[7] 3193[8] 3625[2] 3838[3] 4461[5] (5134)

Baccalaureate (FR) *Nigel Twiston-Davies* 124h
5 b g High Chaparral(IRE) —Rose D'Or (IRE) (Polish Precedent (USA))
372[12] 1609[12] 1986[13] 4235[6] 4536[8] 4988[P] (5396)

Bacher Boy (IRE) *Gordon Elliott* 126h
7 b g Bach(IRE) —Lady Sipash (Erin's Hope)
2562a[5]

Bachley Gale *Keith Goldsworthy* 56h
6 b m Bach(IRE) —Raise A Gale (IRE) (Strong Gale)
568[3] 686[7] 935[2] 1228[7] 1296[4] 1937[6] 2231[6]
2575[U]

Bach Protector (IRE) *Rebecca Curtis* 86b
5 b g Bach(IRE) —Cappamore Girl (IRE) (Commanche Run)
1029[6]

Bach Street Girl (IRE) *Lynn Siddall* 73h
7 ch m Bach(IRE) —Millmount (IRE) (Be My Guest (USA))
2148[5] 2353[8] 2554[9] 3498[8] 4826[3] 5096[6]

Bach To Back (IRE) *Nigel Twiston-Davies* 75h
6 b g Bach(IRE) —Prudent Princess (Puissance)
1817[3] 2389[12] 2577[12] 2944[9] 3365[12] 5298[10]

Bach To Front (IRE) *Sarah Wall* 93b
6 b m Bach(IRE) —Celtic Leader (IRE) (Supreme Leader)
3616[6] 4055[7] 4376[7] (5056)

Back Bob Back (IRE) *Tom George* 101h 104c
6 b g Bob Back(USA) —Joyney (Harlow (USA))
2069[2] 2642[4] **4504[6]**

Backbord (GER) *Lucy Wadham* 128h 129c
9 b g Platini(GER) —Bukowina (GER) (Windwurf (GER))
1312[2] 1404[4] 1611[7] 1769[P] 2125[2] 2360[3] 2523[12]

Back Exit (IRE) *Philip Hobbs* 103h 121c
8 b g Exit To Nowhere(USA) —Petite Galerie (IRE) (Pips Pride)
314[P]

Backfromthebrink (IRE) *Paul Webber* 102h 89c
7 b g Deploy—Time Of The Lord (IRE) (Lord Americo)
1567[5]
1747[P] 1991[F] 3230[9]

Backfromthecongo (IRE) *Richard Lee* 79h 112c
10 bb g Bob Back(USA) —Market Lass (IRE) (Orchestra)
(17) **769[P]**
1747[6] (2420)
4313[2] 4971[4]

Back In Business (IRE) *Evan Williams* 99h 94c
11 bb g Bob Back(USA) —Rose Of Burnett (IRE) (Be My Native (USA))
16[2] **549[3]**
1027[3] 1348[P] 1434[6]

Back In Focus (IRE) *Howard Johnson* 142h
6 ch g Bob Back(USA) —Dun Belle (IRE) (Over The River (FR))
(4206) 5186[8]

Back Is Back (IRE) *Miss Jane Western* 99h 102c
7 b g Bob Back(USA) —Kings Gap (IRE) (King's Ride)
4194[7] 4526[6] 4969[F]

Back Nine (IRE) *Miss Jane Western* 119c
14 b g Bob Back(USA) —Sylvia Fox (Deep Run)
253[4]

Back Of The Pack (IRE) *Colin Kidd* 107h 135c
9 b m Anshan—Wakt (Akarad (FR))
(2119a)
3268a[7] 3779a[9]

Backspin (IRE) *Jonjo O'Neill* 147h
6 ch g Flemensfirth(USA) —Oscars Princess (IRE) (Oscar (IRE))
(2954) (3197) ◆ 3806[4] (Dead)

Backstage (FR) *Gordon Elliott* 124h 136c
9 b g Passing Sale(FR) —Madame Nathalie (FR) (Dreams To Reality (USA))
1123a[10] 5200[10]

Backstreet Billy (IRE) *Richard Lee* 104h
7 br g Presenting—Basically (IRE) (Strong Gale)
3489[U] 3917[F] 4260[6] 4499[6] 5171[11]

Backstreet Lad *Wyn Morris* 66h 76c
9 b g Fraam—Forest Fantasy (Rambo Dancer (CAN))
4526[8]

Back The Rock (IRE) *Roy Brotherton* 91h
8 b g Luso—Quick Pick (IRE) (Alphabatim (USA))
2469[P]

Back To Bid (IRE) *James Danahar* 131h 132c
11 b g Mujadil(USA) —Cut It Fine (USA) (Big Spruce (USA))
4463[4] 4750[F] 4969[P]

Back To Normality (IRE) *B R Hamilton*
8 b m Bob Back(USA) —Miss Normania (FR) (Iron Duke (FR))
577[P]

Back To Paris (IRE) *Philip Kirby* 97h 82c
9 b g Lil's Boy(USA) —Alisco (IRE) (Shalford (IRE))
1552[P]
5018[4] 5294[F]

Back To The Wind (IRE) *David Pipe* 110h
9 ch g Bob Back(USA) —Saucy Gale (IRE) (Strong Gale)
746[P]

Baddam *Ian Williams* 133h 128c
9 b g Mujahid(USA) —Aude La Belle (FR) (Ela-Mana-Mou)
(408) **1274[2]**

Badger *Mrs C L Dennis* 68h 97c
11 b g Classic Cliche(IRE) —Tyrilda (FR) (Saint Cyrien (FR))
296[3]

Badger Foot (IRE) *Jonjo O'Neill* 103h 115c
6 bb g Beneficial—Droim Alton Gale (IRE) (Strong Gale)
(56) **352[3]**
1255[6] 1509[P] 2034[3]

Badgers Cove (IRE) *Robin Dickin* 127h
7 b g Witness Box(USA) —Celestial Rose (IRE) (Roselier (FR))
(2584) 2888[8] 2981[2] (3485) (5234)

Badly Bruised (IRE) *Martin Keighley* 100h
10 b g Tiraaz(USA) —Krissykiss (Gildoran)
645[P]

Bad Sir Brian (IRE) *Nick Gifford* 80h
6 b g Bach(IRE) —Ballyverane Pride (IRE) (Presenting)
(1906) 2181[P] 2577[13] 3789[U] 4859[7]

Baggsy (IRE) *Patrick Clinton* 74h
4 b f Statue Of Liberty(USA) —Nisibis (In The Wings)
1691[8] 2133[10] (2556) 3484[P] 4878[P]

Baguenaud (FR) *Stephen Clark* 110h 110c
6 b g Double Bed(FR) —Aigle D'Illyria (FR) (Subotica (FR))
917[7] 1147[14] 1258[8]

Bagutta Sun *Barry Leavy* 90h
5 b m Diktat—Valhalla Moon (USA) (Sadler's Wells (USA))
1832[5] 2038[4] ◆ 2282[3] 4874[8]

Bahira (IRE) *Donald McCain* 96b
4 b f Kalanisi(IRE) —Biagiotti (GER) (Winged Love (IRE))
(4554) 5070[3] (5313)

Bahrain Storm (IRE) *Patrick J Flynn* 159h 121c
8 b g Bahhare(USA) —Dance Up A Storm (USA) (Storm Bird (CAN))
(1038a) 1133a[2] 1711a[5]

Bahr Nothing (IRE) *Henry Daly* 98h
5 b g Bahri(USA) —Glen Innes (IRE) (Selkirk (USA))
60[5] 1974[P] 2322[10] 3739[F] 4437[5] 5082[5] 5396[5]

Baile Anrai (IRE) *Ian Williams* 122h
7 b g Norwich—Rose Ana (IRE) (Roselier (FR))
2985[4] 3366[4] 3789[U] 4196[2] ◆ (4665) 5107[2]

Baileys Encore *Valentine Donoghue* 75h
8 b g Mister Baileys—Exclusive Life (USA) (Exclusive Native (USA))
291[10]

Baileys Ruffit (IRE) *Neil McKnight* 26h
6 gr m Revoque(IRE) —Miss Ruffit (IRE) (Phardante (FR))
1934[5] 2353[10]

Baileys Surprise (IRE) *Tracy Waggott* 77h
9 ch g Mister Baileys—Sight'n Sound (Chief Singer)
8[5]

Bailey Street (IRE) *Andrew Slattery* 79b
5 b g Saffron Walden(FR) —Butterfly Morning (IRE) (Distinctly North (USA))
1146a[7]

Baily Storm (IRE) *Tim Vaughan* 131h 131c
9 br g Anshan—Euroblend (IRE) (The Parson)
(357) **(625)**
(828)
1968[P]

Bai Zhu (IRE) *Nicky Henderson* 117h 134c
7 bb g Anshan—Cool Thistle (IRE) (Mandalus)
(2046)
2670[5] (4989) ◆ **5303[6]**

Bajan Sunshine (IRE) *Gary Brown* 36h 68c
10 b g Presenting—Tina's Charm (IRE) (Hatim (USA))
1511[5] 1646[8] 3402[4] 3492[4] 3609[3] 3700[4]

Bakbenscher *Alan King* 136h 153c
8 gr g Bob Back(USA) —Jessolle (Scallywag)
2126[5] 3804[3] ◆ **(4093)**
4352[U]

Balableu (FR) *Mrs Diane Broad* 73h 54c
9 b g Epervier Bleu—Bajabala (FR) (Nikos)
292[6]

Balamory Dan (IRE) *Geoffrey Harker* 71h
10 b g Fort Morgan(USA) —Musical Horn (Music Boy)
1929[11]

Balding Banker (IRE) *Paul Nicholls* 120b
5 b g Accordion—What A Breeze (IRE) (Naheez (USA))
2087[2] (2632) 4191[7]

Bale O'Shea (IRE) *Michael O'Hare* 136h 117c
7 b g Bob Back(USA) —Pharney Fox (IRE) (Phardante (FR))
(608) 2300[3]

Balerina (FR) *Alan King* 111h
4 b f Della Francesca(USA) —Santa Marina (FR) (Kendor (FR))
2211[5] 2924[6] 3401[6] ◆ (4049) 4455[3] (4781)

Balivernier *George Charlton* 92b
5 b g Beat All(USA) —Keep Ikis (Anshan)
4916[6] 5342[9]

Ballabrace (IRE) *Venetia Williams* 15h
6 b g Bob Back(USA) —Presuming (Mtoto)
2432[3] 4097[8] 4422[9]

Ballabriggs (IRE) *Donald McCain* 130h 164c
10 b g Presenting—Papoose (IRE) (Little Bighorn)
(3454) (3851)
4474[2] ◆ (5200)

Ballabrook (IRE) *Donald McCain* 105h 111c
9 b g Alderbrook—Summer Holiday (IRE) (Kambalda)
1645[3] ◆ 2034[6] 2401[2] 2940[3] 3552[7] 4292[9] (5375)

Balladeer (IRE) *Lawney Hill* 107h 110c
13 b g King's Theatre(IRE) —Carousel Music (On Your Mark)
986[2] 1230[7] 1477[5]
2055[2]

Ballagio (IRE) *Kim Bailey* 100h
6 b g Beneficial—Leos Holiday (IRE) (Commanche Run)
2241[P] 3365[4] 4437[4] 4974[8] 5211[4]

Ballamusic (IRE) *Andrew Parker* 83h
9 b g Accordion—Hazy Fiddler (IRE) (Orchestra)
4390[15] 4960[8] 5094[P]

Ballestra (IRE) *Venetia Williams* 85h
7 gr m Alflora(IRE) —Sparkling Sword (Broadsword (USA))
2288[P] 2791[8] 2974[10]

Ballet D'Anges (FR) *Lucy Normile* 66h
5 bb g Ange Gabriel(FR) —Balm (FR) (Tel Quel (FR))
1702[4] 2297[4]

Ballinahow Lady (IRE) *David M O'Brien* 129h
6 b m Beneficial—Ballinahowliss (IRE) (Supreme Leader)
3181a[3]

Ballinasloe (IRE) *Donald McCain* 84b
7 b g Lord Of Appeal—Kilmana (IRE) (Castle Keep)
1764[7]

Ballinderry Park (FR) *Charlie Mann* 105h 76c
8 b g Maresca Sorrento(FR) —Nationale Du Rosay (FR) (Dom Louis (FR))
2049[5] 2364[5]

Ballingaddy (IRE) *Lawney Hill* 83h 91c
8 b g Stowaway—Afsana (IRE) (Bluebird (USA))
645[8]

Ballinhassig (IRE) *Sarah Wall* 56h 25c
6 ch g Beneficial—Dear Polly (IRE) (Germany (USA))
3346[7] 3485[7] **3865[5] 4119[5]**

Ballinruane (IRE) *S Wynne* 97c
12 br g Norwich—Katie Dick (IRE) (Roselier (FR))
599[7]

Ballinteni *Colin Tizzard* 109h 88c
9 b g Machiavellian(USA) —Silabteni (USA) (Nureyev (USA))
2021[2] 2122[2] 2361[11] 3760[2] **4050[5]**

Ballyadam Brook (IRE) *Terence O'Brien* 139h
7 b g Alderbrook—Luna Fleur (IRE) (Shardari)
1713a[2] 2344[3]

Ballyagran (IRE) *Tim Vaughan* 128h 62c
11 b g Pierre—Promalady (IRE) (Homo Sapien)
1020[11] 1312[P]

Ballybach (IRE) *Nick Gifford* 127h 120c
7 b g Bach(IRE) —Croom River (IRE) (Over The River (FR))
2081[2]
(3339)

Ballyboe Boy (IRE) *Shaun Harris* 34h 52c
12 b g Flying Spur(AUS) —Born To Fly (IRE) (Last Tycoon)
83[P] 136[6] 404[P]

Ballybriggan (IRE) *John Quinn* 124h
7 b g Flemensfirth(USA) —Shean Hill (IRE) (Bar Dexter (USA))
(1962) 2361[3] *3168[6]* 4235[4] (4743)

Ballyburke (IRE) *P J Rothwell* 126h
6 b g Tikkanen(USA) —Moonshee (IRE) (Le Moss)
2562a[3] ◆

Ballycarney (IRE) *Emma Lavelle* 114h 141c
7 b g Classic Cliche(IRE) —Rhythm Hill (IRE) (Orchestra)
(274) **735[2]**
844[7] 1178[5] (1469)
(1777)

Ballycarron Lad (IRE) *S R B Crawford* 91h 119c
9 b g Snurge—Ballycarron Lass (IRE) (Roselier (FR))
4304[5] 4712[3] **(4962)**

Ballyclough (IRE) *Jonjo O'Neill* 106b
4 b g Heron Island(IRE) —That's The Bonus (IRE) (Executive Perk)
(4943)

Ballycolin *I A Duncan* 112h 114c
8 ch g Alflora(IRE) —Shift Changeover (Saxon Farm)
550[5] 2507[3] 3852[4]

Bally Conn (IRE) *Martin Hill* 87h
9 br g Supreme Leader—Gladtogetit (Green Shoon)
2141[11] 3744[P] 4224[10] 4441[7]

Ballycracken (IRE) *Nicky Henderson* 112h
7 b g Flemensfirth(USA) —Cons Dual Sale (IRE) (Tidaro (USA))
1740[P] 2630[P]

Ballydonagh (IRE) *Emma Baker* 97c
8 b g Accordion—Little Elk (IRE) (Be My Native (USA))
4445[5]

Ballydub (IRE) *Philip Hobbs* 149h 128c
8 b g Presenting—Sovereign Leader (IRE) (Supreme Leader)
1769[6] 1923[3]

Ballyegan (IRE) *Bob Buckler* 103h 113c
6 b g Saddlers' Hall(IRE) —Knapping Princess (IRE) (Prince Of Birds (USA))
2136[8] 2396[2] **2670[8] 3230[2] 3488[2] 3900[U] 4119[3]**
4407[6]

Ballyeightra Cross (IRE) *G D Hanmer* 64b 103c
7 ch g Anshan—Riancoir Alainn (Strong Gale)
79[3]

Ballyfitz *Nigel Twiston-Davies* 149h 151c
11 b g Overbury(IRE) —Running For Gold (Rymer)
2358[8] 2523[4]
3437[4] 3940[5] 4208[2] 4876[2] 5338[P]

Ballyfoy (IRE) *Jamie Poulton* 113h 142c
10 bb g Alderbrook—Okanagan Valley (IRE) (Decent Fellow)
2512[5]
3437[8] 4051[4]
4360[P]

Ballygalley Bob (IRE) *Miss Caroline Fryer* 83h 115c
10 br g Bob Back(USA) —Follow The Guide (IRE) (Strong Gale)
229[P] 4832[4]

Bally Gunner *Roger Curtis* 77b
6 br g Needle Gun(IRE) —Rich Pickings (Dominion)
3259[6] 3773[12] 5063[13]

Ballyhaunis *W P Mullins* 137h
6 b g Daylami(IRE) —Ballet (Sharrood (USA))
3708a[2] 4806[17]

Ballyholland (IRE) *C A McBratney* 132h 147c
10 b g Tiraaz(USA) —Lilly Bolero (Fearless Action (USA))
5185[12]

Ballylanigan (IRE) *Gordon Elliott* 95h 125c
9 ch g Shahrastani(USA) —Logstown (IRE) (Keen)
458[F]

Bally Legend *Caroline Keevil* 127h
6 b g Midnight Legend—Bally Lira (Lir)
1736[4] 2145[7] 2634[2] 3228[3] 3688[9] (4291) 4488[9]
5106[5]

Ballymacduff (IRE) *George Charlton* 110h 110c
7 b g Strategic Choice(USA) —Ashpark Rose (IRE) (Roselier (FR))
(291) 2549[3] 3362[3] 3750[P]
4057[2] 4362[F] 4685[3] 5032[P] 5341[P]

Ballyman (IRE) *Jonathan Geake* 88b 81c
10 gr g Accordion—Sliabhin Rose (Roselier (FR))
2638[7] 4144[5] 4413[3] 4560[4] 4919[2] 5324[4]

Ballymorn (IRE) *Henrietta Knight* 82h 85c
7 b g Alderbrook—Morning Blush (IRE) (Glow (USA))
2170[3] 2555[4] 3527[8] 4144[11] 5109[P]

Ballyoliver *Venetia Williams* 99h
7 b g Kayf Tara—Macklette (IRE) (Buckskin (FR))
225[3] 2058[8] 2480[3]

Ballyquin Queen (IRE) *Philip Hobbs* 106b
5 br m King's Theatre(IRE) —One Swoop (IRE) (Be My Native (USA))
4027[5] 4728[6] 5306[6]

Ballyrock (IRE) *Tim Vaughan* 95b
5 b g Milan—Ardent Love (IRE) (Ardross)
3766[6]

Bally Sands (IRE) *Robin Mathew* 108h
7 b g Luso—Sandwell Old Rose (IRE) (Roselier (FR))
631[F] 763[5] 2347[20]

Ballyshambles *S R Andrews* 63c
8 b g Shambo—Ballyquintet (IRE) (Orchestra)
5283[5]

Ballysimon (IRE) *James Ewart* 98h
7 b g Great Palm(USA) —Sister Mary (IRE) (Erin's Hope)
179[2] ◆ 328[4]

Ballytober *Philip Hobbs* 108b
5 b g Kahyasi—Full Of Birds (FR) (Epervier Bleu)
(3766) 4329[4]

Ballytrim (IRE) *W P Mullins* 100h 151c
10 b g Luso—Helynsar (Fidel)
3798a[3]

Ballyveeney (IRE) *Venetia Williams* 104h
7 b g Lord Americo—Miss Agarbie (IRE) (Tremblant)
4922[8]

Ballyvesey (IRE) *Peter Bowen* 106h 125c
6 ch g Anshan—Bridgequarter Lady (IRE) (King's Ride)
193[5] 318[10] **909[2] (1022)**
1200[2] 1255[2] 1444[2] 1661[3] 1999[2] 2248[5] 2543[4]
4502[4]
(5254) 5421[2]

Ballyvoge (IRE) *R J Bevis* 111h 108c
10 b g Presenting—Ardnurcher (IRE) (King's Ride)
334[4]

Bally Wall (IRE) *I R Ferguson* 114h 117c
8 ch g Moscow Society(USA) —Carminda Thyne (IRE) (Good Thyne (USA))
308[5] 2269[2]
3552[3]

Balnagore *Lucinda Russell* 93h 93c
7 bb g Tobougg(IRE) —Bogus Mix (IRE) (Linamix (FR))
(397) 713[8] 1596[P] 1762[8] ◆ 2658[13] **5418[2]**

Balthazar King (IRE) *Philip Hobbs* 138h 144c
7 b g King's Theatre(IRE) —Afdala (IRE) (Hernando (FR))
(1602)
(1774) 1863[4] 2357[2] 2883[5] (5073)
(5290) 5443[P]

Baltic Ben (USA) *Alison Thorpe* 76h
4 b g Johannesburg(USA) —Baltic Dip (IRE) (Benny The Dip (USA))
1234[7] 1330[4] 1442[4] 4899[9]

Baltic Pathfinder (IRE) *Sue Smith* 108h 113c
7 b g Alflora(IRE) —Boro Bow (IRE) (Buckskin (FR))
(88) **608[9]**
2298[2] 2940[F] 3574[6] 3886[F] 4135[P] 4962[2] 5261[6]

Baltimore Jack (IRE) *Tim Walford* 95h
7 b g Night Shift(USA) —Itsibitsi (IRE) (Brief Truce (USA))
1325[4]

Baltimore Patriot (IRE) *Barry Brennan* 89h
8 b g Tiger Hill(IRE) —Berenice (Groom Dancer (USA))
480[6] 849[U]

Baltrap (FR) *Clarissa Caroe* 12h
6 b m True Brave(USA) —Bal De Foire (FR) (Always Fair (USA))
1147[P] 1816[P] 1993[10] 2398[P] 2554[P] 4309[P] 4771[7]
4920[10]

Balustrade (IRE) *Chris Gordon* 105h
5 b g Barathea(IRE) —Haladiya (IRE) (Darshaan)
1675[4] 1914[5] 2396[7] 3260[F] (3791) 4182[P] 5193[9]

Balwyllo (IRE) *Ben Haslam* 36b
6 ch g Hubbly Bubbly(USA) —Silver Gala (Gala Performance)
731[10] 1003[P] 2092[18]

Balzaccio (FR) *Alan King* 129h 138c
6 b g Marchand De Sable(USA) —Baliyna (USA) (Woodman (USA))
2046[2] 2527[3] ◆ 3193[4] 3770[2] 4077[5] 5110[9]

Banco Busto (IRE) *Stuart Howe*
4 b f Chineur(FR) —Banco Solo (Distant Relative)
1279[F]

Bandanaman (IRE) *Alan Swinbank* 112h
5 b g Danehill Dancer(IRE) —Band Of Angels (IRE) (Alzao (USA))
(835) (1359)

Bandra Bullet (IRE) *John C McConnell* 109b
5 b g Val Royal(FR) —Hakone (IRE) (Alzao (USA))
3208a[8]

Banellie (IRE) *Noel C Kelly* 109h
7 ch g Beneficial—Emily Bishop (IRE) (The Parson)
1119[3]

Banjaxed Girl *Nigel Twiston-Davies* 152h
7 b m King's Theatre(IRE) —Belle Magello (FR) (Exit To Nowhere (USA))
2218[2] 2579[2] 2884[10] (3442) 4793[7] 5302[5]

Bankers Bonus (IRE) *Martin Hill* 76h
6 b g Anshan—Candy Gale (IRE) (Strong Gale)
2001[P]

Bankstair (FR) *Nigel Twiston-Davies* 93h 112c
7 b g Astair(FR) —Idylle D'Estruval (FR) (Cadoudal (FR))
328[7] **(584)**
(689) **772[3]**

Bank The Bucks (IRE) *Aidan Anthony Howard* 93h
5 b g Beneficial—Mattie's Mulligan (IRE) (Lancastrian)
1963[P] 2080[14]

Banoge (IRE) *Rose Dobbin* 91h 104c
9 b g Flemensfirth(USA) —Prove It (IRE) (Black Monday)
1762[6]
2298[P] 3361[6] 4001[F] 4573[3]

Banquet (IRE) *Tim Walford* 111h
6 ch g Dr Fong(USA) —Barbera (Barathea (IRE))
2094[P]

Bansha (IRE) *Alan Bailey*
5 b g Indian Haven—Cha Cha (IRE) (Charnwood Forest (IRE))
75[P]

Bantry Bere (IRE) *Mrs Fleur Hawes* 126h 118c
7 b g Distant Music(USA) —Tirana (USA) (Fappiano (USA))
4750[4]

Ban Uisce (IRE) *Neil Mulholland* 107h 112c
6 b g Lahib(USA) —Scolboa Gold (IRE) (Accordion)
(2430) 3256[3] 3481[10] 3791[4] 4025[8] 4380[P]
4768[2] 5039[2] ◆ 5438[4]

Baraathen (USA) *Donald McCain* 83h
4 b g Sakhee(USA) —Attaared (USA) (Gulch (USA))
1135[3] 1298[F] 1498[2] 1699[5] 3951[8] 4148[4] 4419[4]
4798[2] 5350[10]

Baracas (FR) *Eoin Griffin* 131h
6 b g Miesque's Son(USA) —Sara Baras (IRE) (Turtle Island (IRE))
2387[12]

Barafundle (IRE) *Jennie Candlish* 143h
7 ch g Flemensfirth(USA) —Different Dee (IRE) (Beau Sher)
206[2] 2523[2] (2663) 4817[16]

Baralaka *Rose Dobbin* 47h
4 ch g Barathea(IRE) —Shakalaka Baby (Nashwan (USA))
3358[P] 5309[12]

Baraquet *Chris Down* 74h
5 b m Generous(IRE) —Pechaubar (FR) (Alesso (USA))
2137[8]

Barbarian *Alan Brown* 92h
5 b g Noverre(USA) —Love In The Mist (USA) (Silver Hawk (USA))
400[6] 604[6] 697[11] 2302[3] 2603[2] 3523[15] 3728[10]
4302[10] 4998[8] 5094[P]

Barbatos (FR) *Ian Williams* 123h
5 gr g Martaline—Peace Bay (FR) (Alamo Bay (USA))
3288[5] 3877[5] 4875[5] 5225[2]

Barbers Shop *Nicky Henderson* 135h 159c
9 b g Saddlers' Hall(IRE) —Close Harmony (Bustino)
2091[7] 2673[P]

Bardolet (IRE) *Keith Reveley* 97h 99c
8 b g Snurge—Bonne Atthenagh (IRE) (Rontino)
88[7] (2103) 2941[6] 3336[11] **4238[2] (4551)**
4811[3]

Bardolf (IRE) *Alan King* 107h
5 gr g Oscar(IRE) —Navale (FR) (Baryshnikov (AUS))
375[12] 2560[2] ◆ 3301[4] 4332[4] 4986[4]

Barello Road *Lucinda Russell* 47h
5 b m Grape Tree Road—Haudello (FR) (Marignan (USA))
2511[5] 3547[11] 4165[13]

Baren De Doc (IRE) *Tim Vaughan* 122h 119c
8 b g Dr Massini(IRE) —Barenises Rose (IRE) (Roselier (FR))
(556) **681[2]**
838[5]

Bari Bay *Michael Blake* 89h
5 b m Bahri(USA) —Sea Nymph (IRE) (Spectrum (IRE))
250[4] 380[2] 557[5] 762[5] 1340[5] 1361[P] 1489[5] 1949[3]
2070[3] 2367[3] 3338[P] 3619[6] 5272[9]

Bariolo (FR) *Noel Chance* 93h
7 b g Priolo(USA) —La Bardane (FR) (Marignan (USA))
4917[4]

Barizan (IRE) *Evan Williams* 145h
5 b g Kalanisi(IRE) —Behra (IRE) (Grand Lodge (USA))
1862[3] 2219[7] 2521[3] 3289[6] 3939[5] 4852[7]

Barlin Bay *David Pipe* 72h
7 ch m Karinga Bay—Aubade (Henbit (USA))
157[6] 708[11] 955[3] 1057[P] 1259[3] 1592[8] 1694[6]
1745[11]

Barna Bay (IRE) *V T O'Brien* 71h 145c
12 b g Oscar(IRE) —Barna Lass (IRE) (Lafontaine (USA))
1113a[3] 1527a[P]

Barnack *Pam Sly* 103h
5 b g Karinga Bay—Ima Delight (Idiots Delight)
254[9] 841[7] 2612[7] 3787[8] 4180[6] 4974[2]

Barnhill Brownie (IRE) *Philip Hobbs* 132h 94c
8 b g Presenting—In The Brownies (IRE) (Lafontaine (USA))
131[11] 302[6] 503[3] 685[3] (1108) (1198) 1391[4]
1626[10] 1855[5] 5187[B]

Barodine *Ron Hodges* 73h
8 ch g Barathea(IRE) —Granted (FR) (Cadeaux Genereux)
793[12] 3224[P] 4920[4] 5082[9]

Baron De Feypo (IRE) *Patrick O Brady* 133h 112c
13 b g Simply Great(FR) —Fete Champetre (Welsh Pageant)
2259a[4] 3475a[16]

Baron De'L (IRE) *Edward P Harty* 130h
8 ch g In The Wings—Lightstorm (IRE) (Darshaan)
1847a[4]

Barrel Of Fun (IRE) *Jim Best* 113h
5 b g Sadler's Wells(USA) —Mabrova (Prince Mab (FR))
(182) 400[3] 798[11] 2312[9]

Barr Head (IRE) *Lucy Normile* 59b
7 b g Anshan—Doolin Lake (IRE) (Salluceva)
1783[P]

Barrie Burn (IRE) *Jonjo O'Neill* 106h
5 ch g Flemensfirth(USA) —Phardester (IRE) (Phardante (FR))
1768[7] 1962[11] 2307[11] 2640[2] 3296[10] 4421[5]

Barrison *Simon Earle* 50b
4 gr g Baryshnikov(AUS) —Good Skills (Bustino)
4970[12]

Barron Watlass (IRE) *George Moore* 105h
7 b g Accordion—Lantys Luck (IRE) (Un Desperado (FR))
161[3] (400) 576[5] 2506[9] *3168[7]* 3500[6] 4115[9]
4738[7] 4797[7] 5429[4]

Barry The Cracker *Stephen Melrose* 49b 61c
8 gr g Baryshnikov(AUS) —Kins Token (Relkino)
310[3] 551[9] 4147[P]

Barseventytwo (IRE) *Alan Swinbank* 18b
6 b g Dernier Empereur(USA) —Woodram Delight (Idiots Delight)
3889[13]

Barthelemy *Nicky Henderson* 99b
6 b g Kyllachy—Quilt (Terimon)
(7) (Dead)

Bartleny Native (IRE) *Tom Gretton* 56b
6 b m Revoque(IRE) —Mello Native (IRE) (Be My Native (USA))
1934[7]

Barton Alf *Neil Mulholland* 92h
7 b g Alflora(IRE) —Home From The Hill (IRE) (Jareer (USA))
371[P] 1335[P]

Barton Bounty *Peter Niven* 50h
4 b g Bahamian Bounty—Tenebrae (IRE) (In The Wings)
2655[8]

Barton Cliche *Neil Mulholland* 102h
6 b g Classic Cliche(IRE) —Barton Dante (Phardante (FR))
3647[4] 4444[7] 4895[6]

Barton Felix *Neil Mulholland* 78b
4 gr g Fair Mix(IRE) —Home From The Hill (IRE) (Jareer (USA))
4881[8]

Barton Sun (IRE) *Alison Batchelor* 69h 83c
12 b g Indian Ridge—Sun Screen (Caerleon (USA))
(961) **1231[4]**
1430[4]

Barwell Bridge *Warren Greatrex* 138h
5 b g Red Ransom(USA) —Sentimental Value (USA) (Diesis)
1775[5] 2035[2] 2870[2] 3561[12] 4817[6]

Baseball Ted (IRE) *Charlie Longsdon* 96h 123c
9 b g Beneficial—Lishpower (Master Buck)
(2503)
3375[3] 3648[3] (4142)
(4460)

Basford Bob (IRE) *Jennie Candlish* 122h
6 b g Bob's Return(IRE) —El Monica (IRE) (Kahyasi)
2473[4] 3620[2] 3787[2] 4332[3] 4875[2] (4932) 5186[P]

Basford Lady (IRE) *Jennie Candlish* 99b
7 br m Accordion—Clarin River (IRE) (Mandalus)
2353[P] 4101[P]

Basford Lass *Jennie Candlish* 106h
6 b m Tobougg(IRE) —Exclusive Davis (USA) (Our Native (USA))
410^{2} (577) 737^{U} 826^{5} 920^{3} 1094^{8} (1347) 1556^{8} 1746^{P}

Basford Tara *Jennie Candlish* 90h
6 b m Kayf Tara—Cabriole Legs (Handsome Sailor)
412^{5} 693^{9} 842^{2} 989^{P} 1090^{6} 1236^{P}

Basic Fact (IRE) *J M Turner* 107h 99c
9 b g Rudimentary(USA) —Native Emma (IRE) (Be My Native (USA))
4315^{P} 4696^{2}

Basil Fawlty (IRE) *Warren Greatrex*
6 b g Balakheri(IRE) —Laughing Lesa (IRE) (Bob Back (USA))
3054^{5} ◆

Basoda *Kim Bailey* 112h 123c
8 b g Karinga Bay—Another Wag (Scallywag)
(24) **229^{P}**
(1885)

Bateau Bleu *Ben Haslam* 79h
4 b g Auction House(USA) —Fresh Look (IRE) (Alzao (USA))
1324^{2} 3519^{7}

Bathcounty (IRE) *Barry Brennan* 96b
4 ch c Tobougg(IRE) —Seasons Estates (Mark Of Esteem (IRE))
1913^{2} 2315^{3} *2824^{5}*

Bathwick Brave (IRE) *David Pipe* 93b
4 b g Westerner—Dorans Grove (Gildoran)
3651^{2} 4410^{3}

Bathwick Breeze *David Pipe* 103h 90c
7 ch g Sugarfoot—She's A Breeze (Crofthall)
517^{5} 921^{13} 1057^{5} 1232^{2}
1331^{4} 1483^{5}

Bathwick Junior *John Flint* 82b
4 b f Reset(AUS) —Bathwick Babe (IRE) (Sri Pekan (USA))
3159^{2} 3616^{3} 4527^{6} 5119^{7}

Bathwick Man *David Pipe* 118h
6 b g Mark Of Esteem(IRE) —Local Abbey (IRE) (Primo Dominie)
447^{3} 715^{4} 1364^{9} 1508^{8} 1569^{7} 1740^{P}

Bathwick Quest (IRE) *David Pipe* 115h 115c
7 b m Barathea(IRE) —Ninth Quest (USA) (Quest For Fame)
1740^{9} 1998^{5} **2139^{4} 2978^{2} 3531^{7} 3871^{3} 4140^{3} 4674^{3} 5100^{3} 5242^{F}**

Bathwick Tigger (IRE) *John Flint* 61h
4 b f Tiger Hill(IRE) —Bolshaya (Cadeaux Genereux)
2173^{7} 5395^{5}

Batonnier (FR) *Alan King* 98h
5 ch g Spadoun(FR) —La Bazine (FR) (Dreams To Reality (USA))
(284) 3200^{3} 3794^{5} 4239^{5} 4743^{2}

Battle Axe (IRE) *J J Lennon* 81h 127c
11 bb g Arctic Lord—Merry Magic (IRE) (Glen Quaich)
1113a^{S} (Dead)

Battle Bridge (IRE) *Nick Mitchell* 38h
6 br g Amilynx(FR) —Hells Angel (IRE) (Kambalda)
1739^{P} 1907^{8} 2054^{6}

Battlecry *Nigel Twiston-Davies* 139h 134c
10 bb g Accordion—Miss Orchestra (IRE) (Orchestra)
236^{P} 314^{P} 4141^{3} 4293^{2} 4991^{2} 5347^{S}

Battlefield Bob (IRE) *G T H Bailey* 80h 93c
7 b g Bob's Return(IRE) —Comkilred (IRE) (Mandalus)
283^{2} 477^{5} 4143^{3} 4696^{3} 5283^{6}

Battlefront (IRE) *T M Walsh* 67h 129c
9 b g Pistolet Bleu(IRE) —Penguin (Arctic Lord)
2541^{U}

Battle Group *David Pipe* 148h
6 b g Beat Hollow—Cantanta (Top Ville)
(360) ◆ (664) 842^{RR} 914^{2} (1150) 1346^{2} 1526a^{3} 1855^{4} 4092^{4} (4359) 4806^{4} (5187)

Battle Honour *Sue Bradburne* 95h
4 b g Mark Of Esteem(IRE) —Proserpine (Robellino (USA))
3749^{7} 4056^{3} 4473^{6} 5144^{12} 5428^{P}

Battleoftrafalgar *Michael Attwater* 79h
4 b c Galileo(IRE) —Pink Stone (FR) (Bigstone (IRE))
4458^{4}

Baulon (FR) *C Lerner* 98h 109c
7 b g Poliglote—Balladine (USA) (Trempolino (USA))
(190a)

Bavard Court (IRE) *Tim Vaughan* 119h
5 b g Court Cave(IRE) —Theyllallwin (IRE) (Le Bavard (FR))
1526a^{4} 1829^{4}

Bay Central (IRE) *Evan Williams* 8h 104c
7 b g Exit To Nowhere(USA) —Pretty Beau (IRE) (Beau Charmeur (FR))
3526^{12} 4260^{13} **4782^{2} 5233^{3} 5391^{5}**

Bay Cherry (IRE) *Howard Johnson* 83h 129c
9 b g Saddlers' Hall(IRE) —Cherry Black (IRE) (Roselier (FR))
2106^{R} 3522^{F} 5031^{6}
5416^{4}

Bayfirth (IRE) *Tim Butt* 83h
8 b g Flemensfirth(USA) —Baylough Lady (IRE) (Lancastrian)
5414^{P}

Baynes Cross (IRE) *David Bourton* 100h
8 b g Namid—Flying Clouds (Batshoof)
(2054) 2452^{12}

Bayridge Mick (IRE) *R Williams*
8 ch g Sonus(IRE) —Guernsey Girl (Deep Run)
5326^{P}

Bayross (IRE) *J Larkin* 127h
6 b g Karinga Bay—Produzione (FR) (Baby Turk)
3208a^{6} (Dead)

Bazart *Bernard Llewellyn* 104h
9 b g Highest Honor(FR) —Summer Exhibition (Royal Academy (USA))
40^{4} 219^{2} 430^{7} 566^{6} 914^{6} 1295^{6} 1450^{9}

Beamazed *Malcolm Jefferson* 115h 118c
7 ch g Silver Patriarch(IRE) —Gotogeton (Le Moss)
2955^{9} 3881^{10} **(4004)**
4546^{5}

Beano Boy *Brian Storey* 41h
6 b g Erhaab(USA) —Life Is Life (FR) (Mansonnien (FR))
732^{9} 800^{6} 2939^{P} 3715^{17} 3850^{12} 4302^{11} 4687^{P}

Bear Dancing (IRE) *Lucinda Russell* 87h 111c
7 b g Dancing High—Sandholes (IRE) (Tirol)
1662^{3} 2192^{2} 3260^{P}
4066^{2} 4543^{2} (5097)

Bearneen Boy (IRE) *Neil King* 48h 63c
8 b g Reprimand—Moyheez (IRE) (Naheez (USA))
2314^{10}
2645^{P} 3341^{4} 3611^{5} **4426^{3} 4668^{5}**

Bear's Affair (IRE) *Nicky Henderson* 125h
5 b g Presenting—Gladtogetit (Green Shoon)
(1824) (3620) (5000)

Bear Witness (IRE) *S R B Crawford* 121c
9 b g Witness Box(USA) —Anyone's Fancy (Callernish)
308^{2} ◆ 859^{4}

Be Ashored *Tim Vaughan* 102h
6 b g Beat All(USA) —Burning Shore (IRE) (Desert King (IRE))
227^{6} 538^{7} 710^{5} 990^{4} 1049^{2} (1333) 1730^{4} 3529^{P} 3934^{12} 4785^{6} 5054^{5} 5322^{7}

Beat All Odds *William Clay* 1b
5 b m Beat All(USA) —Bint St James (Shareef Dancer (USA))
1071^{10} 1705^{P}

Beat All Out *Dai Burchell* 100h
6 b g Beat All(USA) —Help Yourself (IRE) (Roselier (FR))
3441^{5} 3930^{9} 4288^{11} 4500^{7}

Beat In Time *John Mackie* 70h
5 b m Beat All(USA) —Corn Bunting (Teenoso (USA))
327^{10} 2109^{11} 4233^{8}

Beat The Band *Lucinda Russell* 104b
6 br m Beat All(USA) —Blue Gallery (IRE) (Bluebird (USA))
2505^{P} 4245^{P} 4552^{P}

Beat The Boys (IRE) *Nigel Twiston-Davies* [illegible]h 147c
10 gr g Portrait Gallery(IRE) —Portia's Delight (IRE) (The Parson)
1777^{5} 2871^{7} 3948^{2} 4466^{5} 5303^{5}

Beat The Devil *Tom George* 89h
5 ch g Nayef(USA) —Proud Titania (IRE) (Fairy King (USA))
3376^{5} 3782^{P}

Beat The Shower *Peter Niven* 104h
5 b g Beat Hollow—Crimson Shower (Dowsing (USA))
519^{3} (727)

Beattie Green *Stuart Kittow* 106b
4 b f Beat Hollow—Shades Of Green (Loup Sauvage (USA))
(3794)

Beaubrav *Michael Madgwick* 110h
5 b g Falbrav(IRE) —Wavy Up (IRE) (Brustolon)
1547^{3} (1899)

Beauchamp Viking *Simon Burrough* 8h 92c
7 b g Compton Admiral—Beauchamp Jade (Kalaglow)
183^{4} (381)
558^{2} 755^{9} 1912^{9} 2334^{2} ◆ 2484^{F} 2559^{F} 3255^{11}
3875^{4} (5379)

Beau Colonel (FR) *Henrietta Knight* 74h
5 gr g Colonel Collins(USA) —Brave Lola (FR) (Dom Pasquini (FR))
2056^{11} 2577^{10} 3366^{10} 4052^{P} 5075^{6}

Beau D'Argent *Ferdy Murphy* 79h
5 br m Alflora(IRE) —Ela D'Argent (IRE) (Ela-Mana-Mou)
1764^{15} 1989^{11} 2370^{4} 2547^{10} *3167^{5}* 3505^{9} 3781^{10}

Beau Fighter *Gary Moore* 113h
6 b g Tobougg(IRE) —Belle De Jour (Exit To Nowhere (USA))
2426^{2}

Beau Lake (IRE) *Suzy Smith* 109h
7 bb g Heron Island(IRE) —Brennan For Audits (IRE) (Creative Plan (USA))
2291^{5} 2630^{8} 3261^{7} 3745^{5} (4120) (4399) 4874^{2}

Beau Michael *Adrian McGuinness* 141h 143c
7 b g Medicean—Tender Moment (IRE) (Caerleon (USA))
(1131a) ◆ **(1712a) 2119a^{2} 5141a^{P}**

Beau Peak *Donald Whillans* 70h
12 ch m Meadowbrook—Peak A Boo (Le Coq D'Or)
3729^{P} 4245^{7} 4506^{9} 4826^{2}

Beau Supreme (IRE) *Kathleen Sanderson* 40h 75c
14 b g Supreme Leader—Miss Sabreur (Avocat)
173^{4} 758^{7}

Beautiful Sound (IRE) *Gordon Elliott* 139c
9 ch g Presenting—Croom River (IRE) (Over The River (FR))
3206a^{9} 4820^{3} ◆

Beautiful Vision (IRE) *Evan Williams* 111h 128c
11 ch g Moscow Society(USA) —Rumi (Nishapour (FR))
264^{P}

Beau Traveller *Miss Bianca Dunk* 30c
8 b g Beauchamp King—Steady Woman (IRE) (Aristocracy)
310^{4}

Be Back In Time (IRE) *Derek Frankland*
9 ch g Sharifabad(IRE) —Round By Boulea (IRE) (Roselier (FR))
2111^{11}

Be Bapalupa (IRE) *Gordon Elliott*
8 b g Deploy—Lasting Leader (IRE) (Supreme Leader)
1099^{P} (Dead)

Becauseicouldntsee (IRE) *N F Glynn* 104h 148c
8 ch g Beneficial—Ath Dara (Duky)
3206a^{2} 5200^{F}

Beck's Bolero (IRE) *Evan Williams* 86b
5 ch g Haafhd—Prealpina (IRE) (Indian Ridge)
7^{8} 277^{3}

Bedarra Boy *David Arbuthnot* 98h 128c
5 ch g Needwood Blade—Roonah Quay (IRE) (Soviet Lad (USA))
983^{4} 1160^{4} ◆ 1429^{7}
(2468) 3494^{2} (3648)
(5228)

Be Definite (IRE) *Tom George* 107h
7 b g Definite Article—Etoile Margot (FR) (Garde Royale)
3693^{13} 4354^{P} 4697^{4} 4925^{2}

Bed Fellow (IRE) *P Monteith* 65h
7 b g Trans Island—Moonlight Partner (IRE) (Red Sunset)
1700^{7}

Bedgebury Knight *Brett Johnson* 64h
6 b g Kayf Tara—Ell Gee (Ra Nova)
5050^{7}

Bedizen *Pam Sly* 122h 99c
8 b g Fantastic Light(USA) —Barboukh (Night Shift (USA))
4235^{5} 4858^{4} 5080^{7}

Beech View (IRE) *Martin Bosley* 91h
6 b m Desert Prince(IRE) —Karakapa (FR) (Subotica (FR))
5280^{3}

Beefeater (IRE) *Philip Hobbs*
6 br g Oscar Schindler(IRE) —Toulon Days (IRE) (Toulon)
2493^{F}

Beehawk *Bob Buckler* 108c
12 b g Gunner B—Cupids Bower (Owen Dudley)
911^{P}

Be Extraordinary (IRE) *Sarah Humphrey* 92b
5 b g Subtle Power(IRE) —Wise Native (IRE) (Be My Native (USA))
2186^{3}

Before Bruce *Claire Dyson* 78b
4 b g Danbird(AUS) —Bisque (Inchinor)
4780^{9} 5077^{6}

Before The War (USA) *Polly Gundry* 92h
4 ch g El Corredor(USA) —Adrenalin Running (USA) (A.P. Indy (USA))
5321^{10} 5389^{2}

Beggars Cap (IRE) *Ferdy Murphy* 102h 137c
9 ch g Lord Of Appeal—Ann's Cap (IRE) (Cardinal Flower)
4470^{7} 4853^{U} 5164^{10} (5340)

Beherayn *Carroll Gray* 126h 111c
8 b g Dansili—Behera (Mill Reef (USA))
1110^{P} 1766^{F}
5112^{P} 5279^{3}

Behest *Robin Mathew* 64h
6 b m Rainbow Quest(USA) —Keyboogie (USA) (Lyphard (USA))
1450^{8} 1505^{6}

Behindcloseddoors (IRE) *Kim Bailey* 98h
5 b g Tillerman—Vivacious Lass (IRE) (Common Grounds)
3365^{5} ◆ 3542^{6} 3691^{2} 4667^{3} 5327^{9}

Behind The Scenes (IRE) *Tim McCarthy* 93h 102c
9 br g Presenting—Run For Cover (IRE) (Lafontaine (USA))
293^{2} 913^{2} 1126^{F} 1478^{2} 4669^{2}

Behtarini (IRE) *Evan Williams* 88h
4 b g Dalakhani(IRE) —Behkiyra (IRE) (Entrepreneur)
4944^{3}

Beidh Tine Anseo (IRE) *Lucinda Russell* 121h
5 b g Rock Of Gibraltar(IRE) —Siamsa (USA) (Quest For Fame)
(161) (288) (548) 870^{3} 1859^{4} 2361^{13} 3969^{9}

Bejrut (POL) *Jiri Janda*
10 b g Who Knows—Bella's Gorl (GER) (Alkalde (GER))
1811a^{11}

Be Kind *Karen George* 78h
5 b m Generous(IRE) —Aquavita (Kalaglow)
5064^{3} 5274^{2} 5403^{2}

Belanak (IRE) *Michael Cunningham* 94h
8 b g Sinndar(IRE) —Balanka (IRE) (Alzao (USA))
459^{7}

Belavard (IRE) *Mrs J Quinlan* 93b 76c
11 b g Almaarad—Beloved (IRE) (Beau Sher)
(61)

Belcantista (FR) *Philip Hobbs* 135h 104c
9 b g Unfuwain(USA) —Opera Prima (USA) (Alleged (USA))
2286^{6} 4926^{3}

Belem Ranger (IRE) *Mrs J Warwick* 105c
11 gr g Presenting—Rosie Fort (IRE) (Roselier (FR))
317^{5} 5163^{9}

Bellaboosh (IRE) *Nicky Henderson* 106h
5 b m Dushyantor(USA) —Ara Blend (IRE) (Persian Mews)
230^{2} 3876^{7} (4417)

Bella Haze *Phillip Dando* 146h
9 b m Midnight Legend—Kristal Haze (Krisinsky (USA))
(94)

Bella Mana Mou (IRE) *Michael Cullen* 123h 131c
9 b m Snurge—How Provincial (IRE) (Be My Native (USA))
3798a^{5}

Bella Medici *Pat Murphy* 76h
6 ch m Medicean—Missouri (Charnwood Forest (IRE))
2130^{6} 2639^{5} 4771^{5}

Belle Brook (IRE) *Michael Cullen* 128h
7 b m Alderbrook—River Lodge (IRE) (Over The River (FR))
3592a^{2}

Belle De Fontenay (FR) *George Baker* 103h
6 b m Spadoun(FR) —Friendly Hostess (Environment Friend)
4164^{9} 5189^{5} 5385^{2}

Bellflower Boy (IRE) *Dr Richard Newland* 128h 125c
8 b g Old Vic—Dante's Arrow (IRE) (Phardante (FR))
1708^{3} 2171^{4} (2532) ◆ (2644) (2955) 4464^{3}
(4864) 5303^{3}

Bell Harbour (IRE) *Evan Williams* 102h
9 b g Insan(USA) —Broken Boots (IRE) (King's Ride)
3497^{7} 4956^{2}

Bello Regalo (IRE) *Malcolm Jefferson* 48h
5 b g Presenting—Simple Dame (IRE) (Simply Great (FR))
2511^{10} 3971^{5} 5131^{9}

Bellvano (GER) *Nicky Henderson* 145h 132c
7 b g Silvano(GER) —Bella Vista (GER) (Konigsstuhl (GER))
3393^{2} 4848^{P}

Belmore Baron *Sue Smith* 98h
9 ch g Double Trigger(IRE) —Belmore Cloud (Baron Blakeney)
1553^{12} 2202^{U} 2375^{4} 3485^{5}

Belon Gale (IRE) *Howard Johnson* 143c
8 b g Hubbly Bubbly(USA) —Belon Breeze (IRE) (Strong Gale)
(2449)
4360^{F} 4876^{P}

Belord (GER) *John J Walsh* 123h
8 ch g Lord Of Men—Belmoda (GER) (Jalmood (USA))
3474a^{10}

Below The Deck (IRE) *Barbara Butterworth* 101h 91c
8 b m Stowaway—Clear Bid (IRE) (Executive Perk)
2598^{P} 4572^{12} 5028^{2}

Beluga (IRE) *Miss Rose Grissell* 86h 45c
12 gr g John French—Mesena (Pals Passage)
296^{5} 466^{P}

Belvidera *Tony Carroll* 41h
5 b m Golden Snake(USA) —Satiric (IRE) (Doyoun)
2145^{12}

Bemused (IRE) *Simon Earle* 42h 32c
6 b g Spartacus(IRE) —Arab Scimetar (IRE) (Sure Blade (USA))
1773^{9} 2056^{14} 2291^{8}
3543^{3} 3790^{P}

Be My Deputy (IRE) *Richard Guest* 110h
6 b g Oscar(IRE) —Have A Myth (IRE) (Roselier (FR))
732^{2} 1989^{7} 2246^{3} 4112^{5}

Be My Light (IRE) *Charlie Longsdon* 109h
5 b m Oscar(IRE) —Simply Divine (IRE) (Be My Native (USA))
50^{5} 263^{3} 1724^{5} 2072^{4} 2478^{2} 3392^{2} (3745) 4034^{8} 4501^{2} (5117)

Be My Present *Charlie Longsdon* 98b
4 b f Presenting—Simply Divine (IRE) (Be My Native (USA))
(4484)

Benarchat (FR) *Paul Nicholls* 83h
6 b g Nikos—Brume (FR) (Courtroom (FR))
1887^{4} 2056^{13}

Benartic (IRE) *Nicky Henderson* 112h 112c
7 b g Beneficial—Glacial Queen (IRE) (Glacial Storm (USA))
1864^{P}
4282^{P} 5397^{2}

Benbane Head (USA) *Martin Keighley* 130h
7 ch g Giant's Causeway(USA) —Prospectress (USA) (Mining (USA))
1967^{7} 3575^{F} 4485^{5} 5304^{3}

Benbeoch *Sandy Thomson* 99c
12 ch g Hatim(USA) —Phantom Singer (Relkino)
(165) **398^{8}**
1784^{3} 2274^{2} 2602^{P}

Benbradagh (IRE) *I R Ferguson* 90b 109c
8 b g Mister Mat(FR) —Lough Hill Lass (IRE) (Erdelistan (FR))
524^{P}

Ben Brierley *Bruce Hellier* 48b
4 b g Tobougg(IRE) —Princess Perfect (IRE) (Danehill Dancer (IRE))
2309^{9} 3525^{12}

Ben Cee Pee M (IRE) *Oliver Sherwood* 106h
6 ch g Beneficial—Supreme Magical (Supreme Leader)
(254) 1812^{8} 3505^{13} 3645^{4} 3897^{3} 4224^{4} 4929^{6} (5401)

Ben Chorley *Tim Vaughan* 64h
7 gr g Inchinor—Arantxa (Sharpo)
1962^{10} ◆ 2331^{P}

Bench Warrent (IRE) *Charlie Mann* 124h 139c
8 b g Witness Box(USA) —Tee Aitch Kay (IRE) (War Hero)
2395^{F} 3437^{F} 3832^{2} 4093^{3} 4333^{3} 4876^{P}

Beneath *Kevin Ryan* 86h
4 b g Dansili—Neath (Rainbow Quest (USA))
2306^{6} 2614^{7}

Benedict Spirit (IRE) *John Flint* 118h
6 b g Invincible Spirit(IRE) —Kathy Caerleon (IRE) (Caerleon (USA))
3^{9} 693^{2} (843) 1347^{2} (1443) 1864^{14}

Beneficial Reform (IRE) *Dermot Day* 105h
6 ch g Beneficial—Miss Performance (IRE) (Lancastrian)
(5253)

Benefit Game (IRE) *Richard Hawker* 44h 107c
7 b g Beneficial—Glenarb Molly (IRE) (Phardante (FR))
233^{P} 734^{U} 1309^{7} 1708^{4} 1823^{3} 2054^{7}

Benefit Night (IRE) *Daniel William O'Sullivan* 129h 139c
11 b g Beneficial—Broomhill Star (IRE) (Deep Society)
5303^{2}

Benefit Of Youth (IRE) *Tim Vaughan* 54b
4 b g Beneficial—Persian Avenue (IRE) (Persian Mews)
5257^{5}

Benefit Scheme (IRE) *Miss Bernadette A K Murphy* 117h
7 b m Beneficial—Supreme Schemer (IRE) (Supreme Leader)
2196a^6

Bene Lad (IRE) *Jim Goldie* 94h 103c
9 bb g Beneficial—Sandwell Old Rose (IRE) (Roselier (FR))
2208^{11} 2941^9 (3363) 3635^3 4067^9 **4471^2 4961^2 5261^8**

Ben Eva (IRE) *Barry Brennan* 81b
5 b m Beneficial—Little Talk (Le Bavard (FR))
2432^5

Benfleet Boy *Brendan Powell* 136h 108c
7 gr g Fasliyev(USA) —Nicely (IRE) (Bustino)
1883^4 2233^4 2498^7 3649^4 3941^2 4354^7

Benheir (IRE) *Henry Daly* 91b
5 b g Beneficial—Vicford (IRE) (Old Vic)
319^6 3766^7

Benluna (IRE) *Alistair Whillans* 82h
7 b g Bob's Return(IRE) —Roseland (IRE) (Roselier (FR))
2349^{12} 3697^8

Benmadigan (IRE) *Nicky Richards* 115h 70c
9 ch g Presenting—Dont Tell Nell (IRE) (Denel (FR))
166^9 (393) 494^4 (767) 888^2 1118^6 1870^4 2506^7 5144^{11} 5429^6

Benmore Boy (IRE) *Henrietta Knight* 115h 71c
8 b g Old Vic—Proudstown Lady (IRE) (Ashford (USA))
22^3 382^5 530^P

Bennative (IRE) *S Donohoe* 103h
6 b g Beneficial—Which Is Which (IRE) (Be My Native (USA))
4684^3

Benny Be Good *Keith Reveley* 127h 135c
8 b g Benny The Dip(USA) —Hembane (FR) (Kenmare (FR))
1930^6 (2299) ◆ 3852^2 4210^3 4453^U 4867^4 **(5310)**

Bennynthejets (IRE) *Chris Bealby* 99h 109c
9 b g Beneficial—Lucky Adventure (IRE) (Hymns On High)
1991^8 2529^3 4022^7 4237^4 4813^4

Bennys Mist (IRE) *Venetia Williams* 91h
5 b g Beneficial—Dark Mist (IRE) (Mister Lord (USA))
2309^{10} 3528^8 3836^4 4100^6

Benny The Piler (IRE) *Carol Ferguson* 98h 89c
11 bb g Beneficial—An Charraig Mhor (IRE) (Tremblant)
211^P 405^P **517^P**

Benny The Swinger (IRE) *Henrietta Knight* 81h
6 b g Beneficial—The Olde Swinger (IRE) (Lord Americo)
1736^{11} 2241^{13} 3365^{10} 4314^{10}

Benozzo Gozzoli *Seamus Mullins* 92h
5 ch g Medicean—Star Precision (Shavian)
3344^{11} 3906^5 4195^4 5193^{10}

Ben Ryan (IRE) *S Rea* 99h 74c
12 ch g Presenting—Isoldes Tower (Balliol)
152^P 3991^P

Bensalem (IRE) *Alan King* 154h 156c
8 b g Turtle Island(IRE) —Peace Time Girl (IRE) (Buckskin (FR))
3807^5 ◆ 4207^2 **(4790) 5199^5**

Ben's Folly (IRE) *Tim Vaughan* 124h
6 ch g Beneficial—Daddy's Folly (Le Moss)
1254^6 (1401) (1507) (1626)

Bens Moor (IRE) *Tim Vaughan* 56h
6 b g Beneficial—Moor Lady (Primitive Rising (USA))
1963^5

Ben The Horse (IRE) *Henry Daly* 52h
5 b g Beneficial—Charwin (IRE) (Commanche Run)
2238^8 2981^P

Bentley Brook (IRE) *Barry Brennan* 76h
9 ch g Singspiel(IRE) —Gay Bentley (USA) (Riverman (USA))
2396^5

Bentota (IRE) *Michael Scudamore* 95c
10 b g Alflora(IRE) —Tasmin Gayle (IRE) (Strong Gale)
2436^3 2883^P

Ben Trovato (IRE) *John Upson* 38h 18c
5 ch g Subtle Power(IRE) —Dawn Eile (IRE) (Good Thyne (USA))
2518^{12} 3572^{10} 3698^7 4081^{14} **4772^5**

Benwell *G T Sunter* 77c
10 ch g Bien Bien(USA) —Amaretto Flame (IRE) (First Trump)
628^P

Bergonzi (IRE) *Howard Johnson* 80h
7 ch g Indian Ridge—Lady Windley (Baillamont (USA))
1832^6

Bermuda Boy (FR) *Paul Nicholls* 111h
6 b g Anabaa Blue—Fast Reema (IRE) (Fast Topaze (USA))
3057^2 ◆ (3296) 3645^3

Bermuda Pointe (IRE) *Nigel Twiston-Davies* 73h 118c
9 ch g Lahib(USA) —Milain (IRE) (Unfuwain (USA))
985^5 (1334) 1486^P 1676^6

Bernard *Kevin Bishop* 87h 106c
11 b g Nashwan(USA) —Tabyan (USA) (Topsider (USA))
540^7 868^P 1741^7 (2239) 4787^4 (5169)

Bernie'Stheboss (IRE) *David Anthony O'Brien*
6 ch m Old Vic—Laois Lottie (IRE) (Husyan (USA))
289^P

Bernie The Banker *W W Dennis* 81h
7 b g Alflora(IRE) —Just A Minute (Derrylin)
371^P

Bernshaw *James Turner* 24h
6 b g Fantastic Light(USA) —Lauren (GER) (Lightning (FR))
224^7

Berriedale *Ann Duffield* 82h
5 ch m Fraam—Carradale (Pursuit Of Love)
600^8

Berry Hill Lass (IRE) *John O'Shea* 64h
7 b m Alhaarth(IRE) —Gold Mist (Darshaan)
358^5 632^U 989^6

Bertenbar *Henrietta Knight* 87h 102c
7 b g Bertolini(USA) —Ardenbar (Ardross)
95^2 3492^5 3772^F (3959) 4504^2 (5076)

Bertie May *Kevin Bishop* 121h 118c
9 gr g Terimon—Kalogy (Kalaglow)
3440^P **3629^8 4095^P 4537^P**

Bertie Milan (IRE) *Sue Bradburne* 105h 95c
6 b g Milan—Miss Bertaine (IRE) (Denel (FR))
311^6 1698^6 2202^6 3330^5 **3852^6** 4477^5 4914^2

Berties Dream (IRE) *Paul John Gilligan* 160h 132c
8 b g Golden Tornado(IRE) —Orla's Pride (IRE) (Brush Aside (USA))
2357^4 2971a^5 4107a^6 4819^6

Bescot Springs (IRE) *Lucinda Russell* 120h 115c
6 b g Saddlers' Hall(IRE) —Silver Glen (IRE) (Roselier (FR))
1931^3 (1578) 1959^6 **2191^2**

Beshabar (IRE) *Tim Vaughan* 147h 155c
9 ch g Flemensfirth(USA) —In Our Intrest (IRE) (Buckskin (FR))
2357^8 ◆ (4282) 4802^2 (5338)

Beshairt *Dai Burchell* 112h
7 b m Silver Wizard(USA) —Irja (Minshaanshu Amad (USA))
1067^3 **1509^P**

Besi *Lisa Harrison* 69h
9 b g Lavirco(GER) —Brangane (IRE) (Anita's Prince)
228^{10} 552^P 1647^5

Beside The Fire *Colin Tizzard* 110h
6 b g Cois Na Tine(IRE) —Champagne N Dreams (Rambo Dancer (CAN))
1773^4 1974^2 2361^{10} 3348^2 3589^3 4034^7 4375^9

Be Smart (IRE) *Valentine Donoghue* 85h
6 b m Statue Of Liberty(USA) —Alaynia (IRE) (Hamas (IRE))
285^6

Best Catch (USA) *Gary Moore* 81h
4 b g Western Pride(USA) —Majestical (USA) (Garthorn (USA))
2133^7

Best Horse (FR) *Ferdy Murphy* 98h 91c
9 b g Xaar—Poplife (FR) (Zino)
1426^6
1575^3 1872^5 2301^2 2942^5 3307^P

Best Lover (FR) *James Ewart* 110h 130c
9 ch g Great Palm(USA) —Droid (FR) (Belgio (FR))
(2447)

Bestowed *Tim Vaughan* 96h
6 b g Kyllachy—Granted (FR) (Cadeaux Genereux)
3760^6

Best Prospect (IRE) *Michael Dods* 131h
9 b g Orpen(USA) —Bright Prospect (USA) (Miswaki (USA))
2551^3 *3169^8* 4358^2 (4867)

Best Start *Claire Dyson* 79b
5 ch g Medicean—Preference (Efisio)
4881^{10} 5005^6

Bestwood Lodge *Helen Nelmes* 65h
5 ch m Dubai Destination(USA) —Three Green Leaves (IRE) (Environment Friend)
2186^{10} 4097^9 5189^6

Betabob (IRE) *Nick Mitchell* 110h 121c
8 b g Bob's Return(IRE) —Cellatica (USA) (Sir Ivor (USA))
1688^2 1900^2 **(2572) 3154^2 3905^2 (4140) 4934^6**

Be There In Five (IRE) *Nicky Henderson* 138h 141c
7 b g Indian Danehill(IRE) —Marwa (IRE) (Shahrastani (USA))
2631^3 3394^2 3694^5 (4480) 4802^3 5338^P

Be True (IRE) *Donald McCain* 106h
7 b g Strategic Choice(USA) —Miss Perky (IRE) (Creative Plan (USA))
2368^8 2985^B 3439^4 4359^P

Betty Browneyes *Tom George* 66h 95c
6 bb m Classic Cliche(IRE) —Corn Bunting (Teenoso (USA))
501^2 2310^{11} 3480^8 **3875^6 4264^3 (4668) 5018^U**

Betty's Run *Lynn Siddall* 18h
9 b m Overbury(IRE) —Not So Prim (Primitive Rising (USA))
92^8 679^5 3498^P 3717^9 4112^P 4542^P

Between Dreams *Andy Turnell* 37h
8 br m Silver Wizard(USA) —I Have A Dream (SWE) (Mango Express)
1689^P 1997^{10}

Beverly Hill Billy *Sandy Forster* 100h
7 b g Primo Valentino(IRE) —Miss Beverley (Beveled (USA))
2551^5 3855^4 4686^{10}

Beware Chalk Pit (IRE) *Jonathan Geake* 94h 103c
7 b g Anshan—Rakiura (IRE) (Good Thyne (USA))
(2431) ◆ 3450^P 4139^6 4412^2 4558^P

Bewery Man (IRE) *Miss V E Hayter* 104h 107c
10 b g Heron Island(IRE) —Rumi (Nishapour (FR))
(31) 745^P 1118^9 1362^7
5263^F

Beyond (IRE) *Evan Williams* 113h
4 ch g Galileo(IRE) —Run To Jane (IRE) (Doyoun)
(674) (960) 1330^2 1610^4 4807^{13}

Beyond The Tweed *James Ewart* 85b
5 b g And Beyond(IRE) —Over The Tweed (Presidium)
3553^8 4396^7

Bianco Fuji *Oliver Sherwood* 121h
6 gr m Kayf Tara—Dissolve (Sharrood (USA))
332^5 2068^5 (3389)

Bible Lord (IRE) *Andy Turnell* 46h 140c
10 ch g Mister Lord(USA) —Pharisee (IRE) (Phardante (FR))
2212^6 2674^7 2984^4 3157^3 3558^7 4010^2 4820^8 5185^F

Bid Art (IRE) *Jamie Snowden* 82h 91c
6 b g Hawk Wing(USA) —Crystal Theatre (IRE) (King's Theatre (IRE))
63^4 283^3 533^P 961^6 1231^5 1290^3 1474^2 1591^7 5018^2 5055^F 5386^4

Big Bertie (IRE) *Anna Newton-Smith* 61h 86c
7 b g Luso—Next Venture (IRE) (Zaffaran (USA))
3556^{14}
3865^3 4426^2

Big Buck's (FR) *Paul Nicholls* 178h 164c
8 bb g Cadoudal(FR) —Buck's (FR) (Le Glorieux)
(2672) (3199) (4819) (5160)

Big Burrows (IRE) *Ferdy Murphy* 118h 123c
9 b g Supreme Leader—Bula Vogue (IRE) (Phardante (FR))
32^8 (401) 1957^U 2507^4 3953^7 5001^P 5415^U

Big Fella Thanks *Ferdy Murphy* 138h 156c
9 b g Primitive Rising(USA) —Nunsdream (Derrylin)
2273^2 2673^F 4201^4 ◆ 4487^4 ◆ 5200^7

Big Game Hunter (IRE) *M F Morris* 131h
5 b g Sadler's Wells(USA) —Hill Of Snow (Reference Point)
3846a^7

Big Geordie *Alan Kirtley*
6 gr g Prince Daniel(USA) —An Cailin Ban Vii (Damsire Unregistered)
3889^{14} 4117^{13}

Big Guns (IRE) *Warren Greatrex* 70b
7 b g Luso—Little Anna (IRE) (Lord Americo)
3448^U

Big Knickers *Neil Mulholland* 94h
6 b m Bob Back(USA) —Island Hopper (Be My Native (USA))
1629^4 1922^P 3439^8 3647^8 3904^7 5111^2 5433^4

Big Red Cat (IRE) *John Daniel Moore* 70b
5 b m Bishop Of Cashel—Queensland Bay (Primitive Rising (USA))
4151^6

Big Robert *Matt Sheppard* 121h
7 b h Medicean—Top Flight Queen (Mark Of Esteem (IRE))
3557^{14} 4291^3 4990^P 5171^2 (5392)

Big Sam *Bruce Hellier* 98b
6 b g Conclude(USA) —Geegee Emmarr (Rakaposhi King)
474^8 2660^2 3752^6

Big Talk *David Bridgwater* 101h
4 b g Selkirk(USA) —Common Request (USA) (Lear Fan (USA))
1674^3 1882^7 2151^6 (2421) 2556^2 (3818) 4079^{10}

Big Time Billy (IRE) *Peter Bowen* 120b
5 b m Definite Article—Zaratu (IRE) (Key Of Luck (USA))
4866^6 5188^3

Big Zeb (IRE) *C A Murphy* 148h 172c
10 b g Oscar(IRE) —Our Siveen (Deep Run)
(2262a)
(3204a) ◆ 3844a^2 4805^2

Bijou Dan *George Moore* 117h
10 ch g Bijou D'Inde—Cal Norma's Lady (IRE) (Lyphard's Special (USA))
34^7 351^6

Bilbo Boggart (IRE) *Ian McInnes* 82h
7 b g Imperial Ballet(IRE) —Skatt (Caerleon (USA))
1085^6 1258^5

Billie Magern *Nigel Twiston-Davies* 128h 143c
7 b g Alderbrook—Outfield (Monksfield)
476^F ◆ (738) (873) (944) (1627) 1863^3 2357^5 3291^{10} 4199^2 4821^8

Bill's Echo *Alistair Whillans* 29h 124c
12 br g Double Eclipse(IRE) —Bit On Edge (Henbit (USA))
46^7 524^5 680^3 (859)

Billsgrey (IRE) *William Amos* 53h 88c
9 gr g Pistolet Bleu(IRE) —Grouse-N-Heather (Grey Desire)
(2602) 4571^2 4825^P

Billy Beetroot (USA) *Katie Stephens* 83h
5 b g Rossini(USA) —Grazia (Sharpo)
58^9 356^8 555^2 696^6 845^8 1064^{10}

Billy Merriott (IRE) *Paul Nicholls* 108b
5 b g Dr Massini(IRE) —Hurricane Bella (IRE) (Taipan (IRE))
589^2 2335^2 3301^2

Billy Murphy *Paul Cowley* 101h 96c
8 gr g Silver Patriarch(IRE) —Sperrin View (Fidel)
2608^3 2950^2 3377^4 3933^3 4412^0 4483^7 5109^2

Billys Flyer (IRE) *Evan Williams*
6 b g Sinndar(IRE) —Beeper The Great (USA) (Whadjathink (USA))
1083^P

Billy Smith *John Upson* 74h
8 b g Suluk(USA) —Sams Queen (Another Sam)
559^P

Billy Teal *G P Kelly* 12b
6 ch g Keen—Morcat (Morston (FR))
1817^{12} 4801^{10}

Billyvoddan (IRE) *Phillip Rowley* 86h 112c
12 b g Accordion—Derryclare (Pollerton)
149^6

Bingo Des Mottes (FR) *Patrick Griffin* 97h
6 bb g April Night(FR) —Royale Bee (FR) (Matahawk)
792^8 862^{11}

Binocular (FR) *Nicky Henderson* 172h
7 b g Enrique—Bleu Ciel Et Blanc (FR) (Pistolet Bleu (IRE))
2668^3 (3559) ◆ (3945) 5198^4

Birchwood Lad *Ian Patrick Browne* 90b
5 b g Sakhee(USA) —Tyne Angel (Sabrehill (USA))
5257^3

Birnies Boy *Brian Storey* 94h
7 b g Thowra(FR) —Drumkilly Lilly (IRE) (Executive Perk)
92^6 461^2 624^3 871^6 1062^{12}

Birthday Star (IRE) *Linda Jewell* 27h
9 b g Desert King(IRE) —White Paper (IRE) (Marignan (USA))
3604^P 4125^6 4670^6

Bishophill Jack (IRE) *Kim Bailey* 104h
5 b g Tikkanen(USA) —Kerrys Cross (IRE) (Phardante (FR))
2456^3 3158^{11} 3448^5 4021^5 4968^3

Bishopsfurze (IRE) *W P Mullins* 143h
6 b g Broadway Flyer(USA) —Supreme Dipper (IRE) (Supreme Leader)
3353a^5 4319a^4

Bishops Heir *James Ewart* 113h
6 b g Turbo Speed—Linns Heir (Leading Counsel (USA))
4255^P

Bishy Barnaby (IRE) *G Chambers* 30b 105c
10 b g Flemensfirth(USA) —Brief Gaiety (IRE) (Be My Native (USA))
4271^4

Bit Of A Clown (IRE) *Caroline Bailey* 104h
5 b g Anshan—Dead Right Too (IRE) (Good Thyne (USA))
2295^{10} 3166^7 3491^3 3897^7

Bitta Dash *Jim Wilson* 78h
11 ch g Bandmaster(USA) —Letitica (Deep Run)
4189^P 4539^8

Bivouac (UAE) *Alan Swinbank* 114h
7 b g Jade Robbery(USA) —Tentpole (USA) (Rainbow Quest (USA))
(3091) 3169^2

Blackanblue *Alan Hollingsworth* 85c
12 b g Alflora(IRE) —Emmabella (True Song)
49^P

Black Annie (IRE) *Paul Webber* 108h
6 ch m Anshan—Black Zena (IRE) (Supreme Leader)
(841) 989^2 (1233) 1505^2 1724^3

Black Apache (IRE) *Donald McCain* 107h 39c
7 bb g Indian Danehill(IRE) —Cathy Garcia (IRE) (Be My Guest (USA))
175^5 522^P 2275^4 2644^7 4873^5 5130^8

Black Beauty *Mrs T Porter* 118h 12c
8 b g Diktat—Euridice (IRE) (Woodman (USA))
4969^7

Black Cache (IRE) *Nigel Twiston-Davies* 94b
5 b g Cachet Noir(USA) —Hindi (FR) (Cadoudal (FR))
2368^{11} 4957^3 5388^6

Black Coffee *Nicky Henderson* 123h
6 br g Vettori(IRE) —In The Woods (You And I (USA))
80^F 316^4

Black Jacari (IRE) *Philip Kirby* 116h
6 b g Black Sam Bellamy(IRE) —Amalia (IRE) (Danehill (USA))
447^7 (715) 1121a^{16}

Black Jack Blues (IRE) *Rebecca Curtis* 151h
8 b g Definite Article—Melody Maid (Strong Gale)
207^P (1797) 2219^8 2516^6 3939^2 5287^9

Black Noddy (IRE) *Emma Lavelle* 105h
5 b g Heron Island(IRE) —Shady's Wish (IRE) (Lancastrian)
2368^3 ◆

Black Phantom (IRE) *Andy Turnell* 119h
5 br g Alderbrook—Blenheim Blinder (IRE) (Mandalus)
(2149) 3348^7 3724^6 (4536) 4862^2 5110^3 5424^6

Blackpool Billy (IRE) *Ferdy Murphy* 117h 118c
9 br g Overbury(IRE) —Ina's Farewell (Random Shot)
2548^2 3524^2 3854^4 4546^3 4911^R 4961^{RR} 5120^5 5418^3

Black Rock Lake (IRE) *T G McCourt* 101h
5 gr m Daylami(IRE) —God Speed (IRE) (Be My Guest (USA))
2505^5

Blackstaff (IRE) *Mrs Jane Williams* 123c
6 b g Needle Gun(IRE) —Sister Swing (Arctic Lord)
(5156)

Blackstairmountain (IRE) *W P Mullins* 150h
6 b g Imperial Ballet(IRE) —Sixhills (FR) (Sabrehill (USA))
2197a^5 4848^7

Blackstone Vegas *Derek Shaw* 92h
5 ch g Nayef(USA) —Waqood (USA) (Riverman (USA))
1552^2 1953^3

Blackthirteen (IRE) *Joanne Foster*
7 br g Key Of Luck(USA) —Jenny May (IRE) (Orchestra)
492^4

Black Thunder (FR) *Paul Nicholls* 97b
4 bl g Malinas(GER) —Blackmika (FR) (Subotica (FR))
4970^4

Blacktoft (USA) *Evan Williams* 114h 132c
8 b g Theatrical—Black Truffle (USA) (Mt. Livermore (USA))
1^2 **422^3 (822) 1131a^5 1371^2 1485^2 1796^F 2233^3 3156^4 3393^U 3949^{11}**

Black Tor Figarro (IRE) *Lawney Hill* 112h
6 b g Rock Of Gibraltar(IRE) —Will Be Blue (IRE) (Darshaan)
(5343)

Blackwater Sparkle (IRE) *A J Kennedy* 89h
7 b g Sunshine Street(USA) —Severine (USA) (Trempolino (USA))
1822^{13}

Blakeneys Pet (IRE) *John Berwick* 93h
5 b m Celtic Swing—Kathryn's Pet (Blakeney)
1736^7 1994^2 2289^8 5241^P

Blandings Castle *Karen Tutty* 79h 64c
10 ro g Cloudings(IRE) —Country House (Town And Country)
178^4
Blantyre *Henrietta Knight* 42b
5 b g Generous(IRE) —Bella Macrae (Bustino)
2186^11 2957^17 3542^P
Blaqjack (IRE) *Michael Smith* 63b
7 br g Anshan—Mrs Byrne (IRE) (Mandalus)
42^P
Blast The Past *Dai Burchell* 102h 117c
9 b m Past Glories—Yours Or Mine (IRE) (Exhibitioner)
1023^5 1161^3 1283^P (1471) 1606^7 1767^5 1975^4
Blaze Ahead (IRE) *Brendan Powell* 108h 104c
11 ch g Mohaajir(USA) —Flaxen Queen (Peacock (FR))
296^2 (466) 4442^P 4832^5
Blaze Trailer (IRE) *T G McCourt* 116h 120c
8 b g Indian Danehill(IRE) —Moonlight Melody (Merdon Melody)
1871^U
Blazing Bailey *Alan King* 137h 156c
9 b g Mister Baileys—Wannaplantatree (Niniski (USA))
2090^6
(3290) (3940) 4790^9 5338^P
Blazing Bay (IRE) *James Moffatt* 85h
6 b m Luso—Blazing Missile (IRE) (Durgam (USA))
319^9 1989^12 2660^4 3856^5 4145^3 4506^4 5094^8
Blazing Bolte *Sheena West* 94h
6 b m Karinga Bay—Tis Gromit (Bedford (USA))
3434^2 5052^2
Blazing Buck *Tony Carroll* 120h
5 ch g Fraam—Anapola (GER) (Polish Precedent (USA))
1776^6 2347^21
Blazing Desert *John Quinn* 101h
7 b g Beat All(USA) —Kingsfold Blaze (Mazilier (USA))
1766^6 2094^11
Blazing Diva (IRE) *Sandy Thomson* 92h 111c
8 gr m Blueprint(IRE) —Irene's Call (IRE) (Cardinal Flower)
1763^7 2354^5 3716^P 4066^3 4256 (4571) 4825^6
Blazing Empress *Sarah Humphrey* 81h
6 b m Emperor Fountain—Gale Blazer (Strong Gale)
2156^8 3264^4 3607^4 4130^2 4773^P
Blazing Sun (IRE) *Kim Bailey* 89h
8 b g Tel Quel(FR) —Sparkling Light (IRE) (Torenaga)
1822^5
Blazing Tempo (IRE) *W P Mullins* 133h 143c
7 b m Accordion—Leading Duke (IRE) (Supreme Leader)
(3268a) 3779a^2 4816^5
Blazing Tommy *Kim Bailey* 54h
8 b g Terimon—Suilven (Teenoso (USA))
341^9 1063^6
Bleak House (IRE) *Howard Johnson* 126h 129c
9 b g Rudimentary(USA) —Dannkalia (IRE) (Shernazar)
2400^P
Bled (FR) *Donald McCain* 108h
6 b g Antarctique(IRE) —Morosa (USA) (Theatrical)
318^5 766^2 1782^5 (2364) 2642^6 3633^6
4004^P 4380^P
Blejan Eyhre *Tom George* 77h
9 b m Silver Patriarch(IRE) —Coire Vannich (Celtic Cone)
649^P
Blenheim Brook (IRE) *Lucinda Russell* 129h
6 br g Alderbrook—Blenheim Blinder (IRE) (Mandalus)
319^8 1783^2 ◆ 2102^5 (2446) 3335^2 3820^2 ◆ (4145) 4725^P
Bless My Soul *Ron Hodges* 82h 87c
8 b g Kayf Tara—Reve En Rose (Revlow)
2633^8 3224^7 3477^9
3873^6 4099^2 4560^6
Bless The Wings (IRE) *Alan King* 120h
6 b g Winged Love(IRE) —Silva Venture (IRE) (Mandalus)
2375^2 3877^4 4189^6 4986^2
Bleu Pois (IRE) *Howard Johnson* 102h 117c
9 ch g Pistolet Bleu(IRE) —Peas (IRE) (Little Wolf)
213^P
Blindspin *Andrew Lee* 116h 122c
6 b g Intikhab(USA) —Blinding (IRE) (High Top)
2008a^4
Blinka Me *Alex Hales* 82h
4 b g Tiger Hill(IRE) —Easy To Love (USA) (Diesis)
2882^11 3767^5 3958^6 5057^11
Bloodyburn Bay (IRE) *Graeme McPherson* 13h
7 b g Needle Gun(IRE) —Serpentine Artiste (Buckskin (FR))
3719^8 4500^14 4719^15
Blossom King (FR) *Tom George* 104h 113c
7 b g King's Best(USA) —Red Blossom (USA) (Silver Hawk (USA))
634^2 889^3 1139^5 1767^3 2037^B 2276^3
Blue Bell House (IRE) *Tracey Watkins* 82b
5 b g Great Palm(USA) —Copper Cailin (IRE) (Lord Americo)
4164^8 4443^6
Blue Bertie *Chris Grant* 14h
5 gr g Terimon—Den Is Over (IRE) (Denel (FR))
2102^15
Bluebird Chariot *Milton Bradley*
8 b g Bluebird(USA) —Boadicea's Chariot (Commanche Run)
760^U 1238^P
Blue Blooded *Alan Swinbank* 91b
5 b g Nayef(USA) —Aristocratique (Cadeaux Genereux)
2511^3 4287^12 5209^3
Blue Dark (FR) *Edward Creighton* 102h 102c
7 ch g Dark Moondancer—Windsor Blue (FR) (Epervier Bleu)
4429^P
Blue Express (IRE) *Evan Williams* 98h 89c
12 ch g Woodpas(USA) —Coill Mhor (IRE) (Cataldi)
566^8 962^5 1295^4
1474^7 1940^4
Blue Eyed Eloise *Brian McMath* 105h
9 b m Overbury(IRE) —Galix (FR) (Sissoo)
(216) 886^4 1083^2
Bluegun (IRE) *Philip Hobbs* 126h 135c
9 b g Pistolet Bleu(IRE) —Supreme Spice (IRE) (Supreme Leader)
208^3 329^4
Blue Jet (USA) *Mike Sowersby* 81h
7 b g Black Minnaloushe(USA) —Clickety Click (USA) (Sovereign Dancer (USA))
12^P 713^P
Blue Lovell (FR) *Caroline Keevil* 91h
5 gr m Loup Solitaire(USA) —Wackie (USA) (Spectacular Bid (USA))
1920^4 4124^7 4970^9 5435^2
Blue Monster (IRE) *Nicky Henderson* 108h
7 b g Flemensfirth(USA) —Millies Girl (IRE) (Millfontaine)
93^2 *(3055)*
Bluemoonandstars (IRE) *George Baker* 81b
6 ch g Moonax(IRE) —My Alanna (Dalsaan)
3773^11 5381^P
Blue Nymph *John Quinn* 126h
5 ch m Selkirk(USA) —Blue Icon (Peintre Celebre (USA))
4009^8 (4455)
Blues And Twos *Emma Lavelle* 66b
5 b g Presenting—Blue Gallery (IRE) (Bluebird (USA))
1778^8
Bluesea Cracker (IRE) *J Motherway* 114h 147c
9 b m Buster King—Zelies Pet (IRE) (Black Minstrel)
2358^4 4298a^6 5200^14
Blue Shark (FR) *Malcolm Jefferson* 126h 119c
9 bb g Cadoudal(FR) —Sweet Beauty (FR) (Tip Moss (FR))
91^3
Blue Shirt Lily *R K Watson* 59b
6 b m Val Royal(FR) —Lily Dale (IRE) (Distinctly North (USA))
876^4
Blue Signal (IRE) *Tom George* 104h
6 b g Blueprint(IRE) —Signal Lizzy (IRE) (Petorius)
1729^2 2058^P 4719^4
Blue Spartan (IRE) *Charlie Mann* 108h
6 gr g Spartacus(IRE) —Bridelina (FR) (Linamix (FR))
58^4 465^F
Blu Teen (FR) *Paul Nicholls* 117h 131c
11 ch g Epervier Bleu—Teene Hawk (FR) (Matahawk)
268^2 4194^2 (4699) 5229^P
Boardroom Dancer (IRE) *Suzy Smith* 72c
14 b g Executive Perk—Dancing Course (IRE) (Crash Course)
(83) 531^P
Bob Bank Boy *Bernard Llewellyn*
6 b g Alflora(IRE) —Gilded Lily (Gildoran)
5217^12
Bobbie Magern *Nigel Twiston-Davies* 114h
6 b g Alderbrook—Outfield (Monksfield)
1625^2 1963^3 2630^5
Bobbisox (IRE) *Alex Hales* 98h
6 ch m Bob Back(USA) —Swift Approach (IRE) (Dry Dock)
249^P 1821^5 2425^7 2514^13 3745^P 3989^3 4481^9 4955^10
Bobbits Way *Alan Jones* 68h
6 b g Overbury(IRE) —Bit Of A Chick (Henbit (USA))
167^9
Bobble Hat Bob (FR) *Jonjo O'Neill* 114h
6 b g Lost World(IRE) —Bisette (FR) (Star Maite (FR))
351^2 771^2 (992) 5118^7
Bobby Bullock (IRE) *Nigel Twiston-Davies* 113h 113c
9 b g Old Vic—Miss Chickabee (IRE) (Jolly Jake (NZ))
24^F (2172) (2240)
Bobby Donald (IRE) *Richard Phillips* 105h 96c
9 b g Lord Americo—River Rescue (Over The River (FR))
2152^F 2292^6 2930^4 3606^4 4551^3 5324^P
Bobby Gee *Renee Robeson* 118h 135c
10 ch g Bob's Return(IRE) —Country Orchid (Town And Country)
1612^F 2146^2 (2595) (2984) 3568^7
Bob Casey (IRE) *Keith Goldsworthy* 71h 94c
9 b g Bob Back(USA) —Casey Jane (IRE) (Mandalus)
1742^7 2081^13 **2236^3 3431^P 3790^2 4483^P 4525^2 4865^3** 5111^6
Bob Emmet (IRE) *Philip Hobbs* 85b
6 b g Robert Emmet(IRE) —Secret Pound (IRE) (Namaqualand (USA))
4097^5 5158^10
Bobering *Brian Baugh* 20h
11 b g Bob's Return(IRE) —Ring The Rafters (Batshoof)
338^P
Bob Hall (IRE) *Jonjo O'Neill* 122h 128c
10 b g Sadler's Wells(USA) —Be My Hope (IRE) (Be My Native (USA))
(153) 4197^P 4748^5
Bob Jackson (IRE) *Elliott Cooper* 73b
9 b g Bob's Return(IRE) —Frantesa (Red Sunset)
2162^9 2657^P
Bob Lewis *Chris Down* 102h
5 b g Sir Harry Lewis(USA) —Teelyna (Teenoso (USA))
4709^8 5107^9 5327^3
Bob Lingo (IRE) *Thomas Mullins* 145h 146c
9 b g Bob's Return(IRE) —Pharlingo (IRE) (Phardante (FR))
2971a^F
Bob 'N' You (IRE) *Ian Williams* 132h 132c
8 b g Bob Back(USA) —Hue 'N' Cry (IRE) (Denel (FR))
1923^2
Bob's Dream (IRE) *William Amos* 101h 122c
9 b g Bob's Return(IRE) —Back In Kansas (IRE) (Mister Lord (USA))
1987^P 2300^P 2551^11 3500^P 3855^7 **4913^7 5145^2**
Bobs Law (IRE) *R Scrine* 118c
7 b g Bob Back(USA) —Retinue (IRE) (Mister Lord (USA))
(5326)
Bobs Pride (IRE) *D K Weld* 139h 151c
9 b g Marju(IRE) —Vyatka (Lion Cavern (USA))
1123a^F ◆
Bob's Sister (IRE) *Martin Bosley* 81h
8 b m Pasternak—Sousse (Warrshan (USA))
52^6
Bob's Temptation *Jim Wilson* 44h 73c
12 br g Bob's Return(IRE) —Temptation (IRE) (Clearly Bust)
329^P
Bobs Worth (IRE) *Nicky Henderson* 153h
6 b g Bob Back(USA) —Fashionista (IRE) (King's Theatre (IRE))
(2577) ◆ (3288) (3806) (4849) ◆
Bob Will (IRE) *Chris Grant* 85h 96c
6 b g Bob's Return(IRE) —Mini Moo Min (Ardross)
1757^9 2351^6 2937^5 3363^8 4138^P
4549^2
Bocamix (FR) *Andrew Crook* 130h
5 gr g Linamix(FR) —Bocanegra (FR) (Night Shift (USA))
1931^9 2521^2 3559^5 3969^P 4257^P 5102^7
Bocciani (GER) *Dianne Sayer* 116h 53c
6 b g Banyumanik(IRE) —Baila (Lando (GER))
1005^6 1104^8 **1360^8** 1504^4 1552^3 1700^9 1997^2 2658^11 2937^3 3335^5 3523^3 (4115) (4243) 4995^3
Body Gold (ARG) *Nigel Twiston-Davies* 86h
8 b g Body Glove(ARG) —Aurifera (ARG) (Climber (USA))
1812^10 2059^7 2281^8 3386^11 (4272) ◆ 4405^3 5075^10 5383^7
Bogside (IRE) *George Charlton* 115h
7 ch g Commander Collins(IRE) —Miss Henrietta (IRE) (Step Together (USA))
2943^6 3749^3 ◆ (4165) 4475^5 (5151) 5339^6
Bogside Theatre (IRE) *George Moore* 123h
7 b m Fruits Of Love(USA) —Royal Jubilee (IRE) (King's Theatre (IRE))
2089^F 2551^4 *3169^14* 4202^F
Bohemian Lass (IRE) *T Hogan* 91h 135c
8 b m Moscow Society(USA) —Gypsy Lass (King's Ride)
3206a^P
Bohemian Rock *Caroline Bailey* 42h 83c
7 b g Alflora(IRE) —Karolina (FR) (Pistolet Bleu (IRE))
1821^12
2172^P 3880^4 4126^3 4693^3 5062^3
Bojangles Andrews *Tim Pitt* 76h
4 b g Avonbridge—Polished Up (Polish Precedent (USA))
1498^3 1818^P 2369^P
Bolachoir (IRE) *S Slevin* 116c
9 b g Hubbly Bubbly(USA) —Boolindrum Lady (IRE) (Meneval (USA))
4197^P
Bolanderi (USA) *Andy Turnell* 66h
6 ch g Seeking The Gold(USA) —Lilium (Nashwan (USA))
182^10 1238^5 1333^5
Bold Addition (FR) *Paul Nicholls* 138h
6 b g Cadoudal(FR) —Kaldona (FR) (Kaldoun (FR))
2361^4 ◆ 3228^4 3686^7 (4706) (5064) (5285)
Bold Adventure *Willie Musson* 94h
7 ch g Arkadian Hero(USA) —Impatiente (USA) (Vaguely Noble)
3495^5
Bold Exit (IRE) *Maurice Barnes* 106h
6 b g Exit To Nowhere(USA) —Lady Marguerrite (Blakeney)
167^11 (1003) 1196^P
Bold Identity (IRE) *Richard Phillips* 109h
5 b g Tagula(IRE) —Identify (IRE) (Persian Bold)
4029^3
Bold Indian (IRE) *Mike Sowersby* 75h
7 b g Indian Danehill(IRE) —Desert Gift (Green Desert (USA))
402^6 607^6 837^11 3951^11 4274^2 4548^6
Bold Pioneer (USA) *Zoe Davison* 78h 79c
8 b g Pioneering(USA) —Uber Alyce (USA) (Bold Forbes (USA))
402^9 **578^2**
745^6 **1587^5**
1883^U 2292^5 2392^4 2947^6
Bold Policy (IRE) *Milton Harris* 97h 104c
8 b g Shernazar—Lady Vic (IRE) (Old Vic)
135^4 250^8 **677^3 (694)** 825^2 888^6
Bold Punt (IRE) *Tom George* 118h 111c
9 ch g Hubbly Bubbly(USA) —Bold Shilling (IRE) (Meneval (USA))
156^P
Bold Sir Brian (IRE) *Lucinda Russell* 131h
5 b g Brian Boru—Black Queen (IRE) (Bob Back (USA))
2612^4 (4475) ◆ 5196^7
Bold Warning *Alex Hales* 73h
7 b g Erhaab(USA) —Celandine (Warning)
1629^6 1900^6
Bollin Felix *Tim Easterby* 119h
7 br g Generous(IRE) —Bollin Magdalene (Teenoso (USA))
2540^5 3506^8 3885^3 (4361) 4824^2
Bollin Fiona *Donald Whillans* 104h
7 ch m Silver Patriarch(IRE) —Bollin Nellie (Rock Hopper)
193^P 2448^8 4257^3 4508^5 5320^7
Bollin Ruth *Donald Whillans* 101h
9 gr m Silver Patriarch(IRE) —Bollin Roberta (Bob's Return (IRE))
313^8 582^6 727^2 3500^7 4822^3 5030^2 5319^6
Bollin Tahini *Neil King* 75b
5 b m Bollin Eric—Cinnamon Club (Derrylin)
5135^8
Bollistick *Michael Mullineaux* 96b
5 b g Bollin Eric—Slip Killick (Cosmonaut)
2368^13 5019^3 5395^2
Bollitree Bob *Jamie Snowden* 83h 41c
10 b g Bob's Return(IRE) —Lady Prunella (IRE) (Supreme Leader)
276^P
Bollywood (IRE) *Alison Batchelor* 85h 94c
8 ch g Indian Rocket—La Fille De Cirque (Cadeaux Genereux)
(36) 1592^6 1735^5 1840^3 2001^2 **2290^5 2332^2 2638^5** 5282^7 5393^3
Bolton Hall (IRE) *Keith Goldsworthy* 112h 56c
9 b g Imperial Ballet(IRE) —Muneera (USA) (Green Dancer (USA))
86^2 282^2 530^5 821^6 **1227^P** (1370) 1797^6
1936^6 3793^P
Bombie Boy *Brian Storey* 3h
6 b g Tobougg(IRE) —Waraqa (USA) (Red Ransom (USA))
2190^P 3336^P 3883^P
Bond Cruz *Olivia Maylam* 76h
8 b g King's Best(USA) —Arabis (Arazi (USA))
917^P 1095^8 1236^7 1300^6 1451^4 1551^9 1735^11
Bond Kathleen *Ian Williams* 89b
5 b g Kayf Tara—Con's Nurse (IRE) (Crowning Honors (CAN))
4287^11 4957^4
Bonfire Knight *John Quinn* 101h
4 b g Red Ransom(USA) —Attune (Singspiel (IRE))
2078^6 2306^4
Bonnie Baloo *Alan Swinbank* 50h
5 ch m Kirkwall—Bellabaloo (Seymour Hicks (FR))
609^7 4894^5 5297^4
Bonny Isle (IRE) *D McNamara* 99c
8 b m Heron Island(IRE) —Curraheigh (IRE) (Carlingford Castle)
2573^5
Bonny Prince Luso (IRE) *Stuart Kittow* 49b
6 b g Luso—Outofocus (IRE) (Be My Native (USA))
3751^3
Bon Spiel *Chris Gordon* 103h
7 b g Singspiel(IRE) —L'Affaire Monique (Machiavellian (USA))
82^3 1291^2 1918^4 2081^8
Bonzeno Queen (IRE) *Evan Williams* 96h
6 b m Old Vic—Shanesia (IRE) (Erins Isle)
(358) 547^3 1005^2 1253^5
Boo *James Unett* 90h
9 b g Namaqualand(USA) —Violet (IRE) (Mukaddamah (USA))
527^7 845^3 1066^4 1313^5 4809^8
Boo Boo Booyakasha *Arthur Whiting* 84h
7 b g Forzando—Miss Roberto (IRE) (Don Roberto (USA))
4100^5 4444^P
Boogie Dancer *Stuart Howe* 111h
7 b m Tobougg(IRE) —Bolero (Rainbow Quest (USA))
19^2 313^2 706^6 914^7 (1282) 1406^2 1548^3 1859^7 2347^9 5302^14
Books Review *Debra Hamer* 83h
7 b g Karinga Bay—In A Whirl (USA) (Island Whirl (USA))
23^5 100^5
Boomshakalaka (IRE) *Nicky Henderson* 109h 88c
11 ch g Anshan—Fairy Gale (IRE) (Strong Gale)
78^P
Boomtown *Claire Dyson* 85h
6 b g Fantastic Light(USA) —Ville D'Amore (USA) (Irish River (FR))
54^2 272^4
Boomtown Kat *Karen George* 114h 68c
7 b g Double Trigger(IRE) —Storm Kitten (IRE) (Catrail (USA))
1109^4 1740^3 2141^10 3688^5 ◆ 4220^2 4532^6 5153^5
Boosha *Rachel Hobbs* 103h
6 ch m Sir Harry Lewis(USA) —Musical Vocation (IRE) (Orchestra)
1749^8 2241^8 2454^7 3153^8 3540^DSQ 3791^8 4900^2 (5103)
Boragh Princess (IRE) *Gordon Elliott* 120h
7 b m King's Theatre(IRE) —Thats Luck (IRE) (Posen (USA))
1724^2 1921^2 2598^2 (Dead)
Border Castle *Michael Blake* 125h
10 b g Grand Lodge(USA) —Tempting Prospect (Shirley Heights)
521^8 **2071^P**
2326^R 2633^6
Border Flora *William Amos* 93h
6 br m Alflora(IRE) —Faucon (Polar Falcon (USA))
2271^2 3336^3 3729^P
Border Fox *Peter Salmon* 80h
8 b g Foxhound(USA) —Vado Via (Ardross)
598^P **1257^P**
Border Fusion *G D Hanmer* 130c
12 b g Weld—Monteviot (Scallywag)
334^2 525^P
Borderhopper *Ferdy Murphy* 85h
7 ch g Zaha(CAN) —Tom's Influence (Pitpan)
2446^6 *3171^11* 3994^8 4508^3 4814^P 5295^8
Border Lad *Alison Thorpe* 86h
7 ch g Double Trigger(IRE) —Rosevear (IRE) (Contract Law (USA))
3530^P 3870^7 (4263) (4405) 4522^3 5393^2

Border Reiver *Tim Easterby* 119h 112c
7 ch g Erhaab(USA) —Cumbrian Rhapsody (Sharrood (USA))
43[3] 1868[4] 2093[3] 2354[6] (3574) 3751[4] 4392[5] 4911[2] (5351)

Border Station (IRE) *Alison Batchelor* 99b
5 b g Shantou(USA) —Telemania (IRE) (Mujtahid (USA))
1906[2] 2291[P] 5389[P]

Border Tale *James Moffatt* 114h 94c
11 b g Selkirk(USA) —Likely Story (IRE) (Night Shift (USA))
288[4] 472[5] 1870[10] 2094[10] 2372[5] 4550[3] 5308[3]

Borero (FR) *Michael Easterby* 114h 127c
8 ch g Discover D'Auteuil(FR) —Harmonique (FR) (Exit To Nowhere (USA))
2611[P] *3169[7]* (3713) 4722[P] (5205)

Born Again (IRE) *Jonjo O'Neill* 127h 129c
6 b g Presenting—Merilena (IRE) (Roselier (FR))
1759[5] (2165)

Born To Be Wilde (IRE) *Evan Williams* 86h
6 b g Oscar(IRE) —Let The River Run (Over The River (FR))
2003[4] 2609[7] 3367[5] 4104[9] **4865[F]**

Borora *Richard Lee* 132h 126c
12 gr g Shareef Dancer(USA) —Bustling Nelly (Bustino)
427[4] 867[F]

Borouj (IRE) *Miss C D Richardson* 103h 65c
9 ch g Unfuwain(USA) —Amanah (USA) (Mr Prospector (USA))
499[U]

Boruler (IRE) *Donald McCain* 92b
5 b g Brian Boru—Lulus Ride (IRE) (King's Ride)
4894[4] 5426[4]

Bosamcliff (IRE) *David Evans* 107h 111c
6 b m Daylami(IRE) —L'Animee (Green Tune (USA))
1746[4] 2150[5] 2329[7]
2481[2] 2927[9] *3092[10]*

Boston Bob (IRE) *Howard Johnson* 112b
6 b g Bob Back(USA) —Bavaway (Le Bavard (FR))
(5033)

Boston Lad (IRE) *Lucy Normile* 86b
7 b g Winged Love(IRE) —Jinglers Court (Jamesmead)
4684[P] 5151[13]

Bostons Angel (IRE) *Mrs John Harrington* 132h 158c
7 b g Winged Love(IRE) —Lady Boston (FR) (Mansonnien (FR))
2971a[4] (3174a)
(4084a) (4804)

Both Ends Burning (IRE) *John Wainwright*
4 ch f Choisir(AUS) —Giadamar (IRE) (Be My Guest (USA))
1691[P]

Bothy *Brian Ellison* 142h
5 ch g Pivotal—Villa Carlotta (Rainbow Quest (USA))
2386[2] ◆ *3169[5]* 4188[2] 4806[2] 5166[7]

Bottman (IRE) *Tim Vaughan* 134h
6 gr g Milan—Dipped In Silver (IRE) (Roselier (FR))
2003[3] (3487) 3987[5] ◆ 5285[2] 5398[2]

Bouggler *Emma Lavelle* 150h 143c
6 b g Tobougg(IRE) —Rush Hour (IRE) (Night Shift (USA))
(2427)
3451[2] 3921[2] 4816[9]

Bougoure (IRE) *Miss N Higham* 123h 119c
12 b g Oscar(IRE) —Jasmine Melody (Jasmine Star)
5402[P]

Bouncing Bob *Miss Jo Pearson* 61b
10 ch g Florida Son—Dancing Dove (IRE) (Denel (FR))
253[P]

Bounds And Leaps *Michael Scudamore* 96h
6 b m Laveron—Geisha (Royal Vulcan)
2156[5] 2554[2] 3698[2] 4418[3] 4929[5] 5169[7]

Bow Badger *Howard Johnson* 124h
5 b g Sadler's Wells(USA) —Biloxi (Caerleon (USA))
(1758) 2397[3] 3572[P] 3999[2]

Bower Island (IRE) *Chris Gordon* 69b
7 ch g Oscar Schindler(IRE) —Flighty Sinead (IRE) (Mister Lord (USA))
279[P]

Bowmore Rock (IRE) *Mark Michael McNiff* 10b
6 br g Kris Kin(USA) —Forest Blade (IRE) (Charnwood Forest (IRE))
3553[11]

Bowntobebad (IRE) *Jeremy Scott* 110b
6 b g Alderbrook—Angels Flame (IRE) (Un Desperado (FR))
2222[3]

Bow School (IRE) *Mrs A C Hamilton* 107h 120c
10 b g New Frontier(IRE) —Sallaghan (IRE) (Hays)
(493) **628[U]**
805[2] **947[P]**
1869[3] 2080[13] **4147[4]** 5030[8] 5429[2]

Bow To No One (IRE) *Alan Jarvis* 87h
5 b m Refuse To Bend(IRE) —Deadly Buzz (IRE) (Darshaan)
4964[3] 5099[7] 5280[6]

Boxer Georg (IRE) *W P Mullins* 137c
9 b g Taipan(IRE) —Country Course (IRE) (Crash Course)
5163[2]

Boychuk (IRE) *Philip Hobbs* 137h 136c
10 b g Insan(USA) —Golden Flower (GER) (Highland Chieftain)
300[6]

Boyoboy (IRE) *George Moore* 104h
7 b g Saddlers' Hall(IRE) —Run Supreme (IRE) (Supreme Leader)
176[2] ◆ (318) 553[F]

Brackenwood *James Frost*
5 b g Morpeth—Sarena Pride (IRE) (Persian Bold)
1448[7]

Brackloon High (IRE) *Noel Chance* 130h
6 b g Bob Back(USA) —Homebird (IRE) (Be My Native (USA))
(2129) 2594[2] 2925[11]

Braddock (IRE) *Bill Turner* 92h
8 b g Pivotal—Sedna (FR) (Bering)
4899[6]

Braddock Island *Mrs S Sunter* 94h 98c
8 b g Rock City—Bally Small (Sunyboy)
48[2] 4800[3] 5093[P] 5312[F]

Braden Brook (IRE) *John Wade* 78h 89c
8 ch g Alderbrook—Templebraden Silky (IRE) (Eurobus)
32[7] 1663[5] 1826[F] 1933[3] 4553[4]

Bradford Boris *Nick Williams* 92h 127c
7 ch g Shernazar—Beauchamp Grace (Ardross)
3453[9] 3689[P] 4695[2] 5236[P]

Bradley *F M O'Brien* 86b 113c
7 ch g Karinga Bay—Good Taste (Handsome Sailor)
(150) **502[2]**

Brad's Luck (IRE) *Michael Blanshard* 82h
5 ch g Lucky Story(USA) —Seymour (IRE) (Eagle Eyed (USA))
548[8]

Brainwave (IRE) *Jonjo O'Neill* 60h
6 b g Flemensfirth(USA) —Dawn Native (IRE) (Be My Native (USA))
3253[9]

Brambley *Seamus Mullins* 48h
4 b f Domedriver(IRE) —Eternelle (Green Desert (USA))
2052[7] 2173[5] 2965[11] 3607[7] 3958[10] 4458[8]

Brampour (IRE) *Paul Nicholls* 135h
4 b g Daylami(IRE) —Brusca (USA) (Grindstone (USA))
3554[3] (4029) 4847[9] 5182[9]

Brandy And Pep (IRE) *Miss J Lightholder* 82h 72c
7 b g Lord Americo—Furry Hope (Furry Glen)
132[5]

Brandy Butter *David Pipe* 105h
5 ch g Domedriver(IRE) —Brand (Shareef Dancer (USA))
180[3] 760[6]

Brandy N' Lovage *Richard Mitchell* 13b
6 ch m Wared(USA) —Came Cottage (Nearly A Hand)
1920[7] 5070[11]

Brannoc (IRE) *Tony Newcombe* 89h
6 b g Pilsudski(IRE) —Ned's Choice (IRE) (Montelimar (USA))
1749[4] 2186[5] 4325[4] 5108[12]

Brass Tax (IRE) *Charlie Morlock* 50h
5 b g Morozov(USA) —Cry Before Dawn (IRE) (Roselier (FR))
3434[5] 4081[13]

Brave Beauty (IRE) *Gordon Elliott* 124h
7 ch m Accordion—Helens Dreamgirl (Caerleon (USA))
3747[7]

Brave Betsy (IRE) *Ms Joanna Morgan* 123h 125c
9 b m Pistolet Bleu(IRE) —Marias The One (IRE) (Ala Hounak)
3709a[14]

Brave Bugsy (IRE) *Graham Smith* 82h
8 b g Mujadil(USA) —Advancing (IRE) (Ela-Mana-Mou)
1434[2] 1798[3]

Brave Enough (USA) *Roger Curtis* 62h
4 b g Yes It's True(USA) —Courageous (USA) (Kingmambo (USA))
2047[8] 3344[10] 3958[9] 5057[8]

Bravello (IRE) *Howard Johnson* 63h
6 b g Exit To Nowhere(USA) —Be My Belle (IRE) (Be My Native (USA))
2297[6] 3952[P]

Brave Rebellion *Keith Reveley* 127h 126c
12 b g Primitive Rising(USA) —Grand Queen (Grand Conde (FR))
608[10]

Bravery Scotch (IRE) *Miss S M Taylor* 112c
9 b g Gothland(FR) —Aokay (IRE) (Roselier (FR))
4197[P]

Brave Spartacus (IRE) *Chris Grant* 67h
5 b g Spartacus(IRE) —Peaches Polly (Slip Anchor)
2355[5] ◆ 3525[3] 3887[8] 4393[11]

Brave Talk *Nigel Hawke* 57h
4 ch g Avonbridge—Zyzania (Zafonic (USA))
1024[6] 1234[8]

Bravo Riquet (FR) *Robin Mathew* 49h
5 br g Laveron—Jeroline (FR) (Cadoudal (FR))
3936[6] 4719[10] 4986[9]

Breadstick *Jeremy Scott* 62h
5 br m Diktat—Poilane (Kris)
4[P] 2282[10] 2499[13]

Breaking Silence (IRE) *Jonjo O'Neill* 131h 123c
10 b g Simply Great(FR) —Lady Of Tara (Deep Run)
149[P] 3956[2] 4286[4] 4973[5]

Breaking Storm (IRE) *Kate Walton* 120h
8 ch g Eurobus—Lisdoylelady (IRE) (Glacial Storm (USA))
(34) 627[7] (846) 1019[4]

Break The Chain *Caroline Bailey* 110h
5 b g Barathea(IRE) —Mesange Royale (FR) (Garde Royale)
(2282) 3386[7] 3831[2] 4234[3] 5059[3]

Breedsbreeze (IRE) *Paul Nicholls* 143h 155c
9 b g Fresh Breeze(USA) —Godfreys Cross (IRE) (Fine Blade (USA))
2964[2] 3677[3] 4200[7] 4818[P] 5303[4]

Breeze With Ease (IRE) *J J Lambe* 105h 105c
7 b g Fourstars Allstar(USA) —Roses Return (IRE) (Bob's Return (IRE))
338[P]

Bremen Plan (POL) *R Holcak* 105c
8 br h Enjoy Plan(USA) —Bremen Rose (USA) (Shadeed (USA))
1811a[U]

Brenin Cwmtudu *Evan Williams* 117h 113c
8 b g Saddlers' Hall(IRE) —Keel Row (Relkino)
17[2] (3371)
4102[2] 4863[F] (Dead)

Brett Vale (IRE) *Peter Hedger* 108h
5 br g Sinndar(IRE) —Pinta (IRE) (Ahonoora)
(1289) 1475[3]

Brian's Journey *Barbara Butterworth* 82h
9 b g Benny The Dip(USA) —Soviet Cry (Soviet Star (USA))
1760[P] 2603[P]

Bricos Boy (IRE) *Miss C J Williams*
10 b g Executive Perk—Moy Farina (Derrylin)
828[P]

Bridge Of Fermoy (IRE) *Daniel O'Brien* 78h
6 b g Danetime(IRE) —Banco Solo (Distant Relative)
3341[P] 3611[P] 3703[P] 5270[8]

Bridge Street Boy *Richard Lee* 82h
6 b g Alflora(IRE) —Celtic Bridge (Celtic Cone)
60[7] 412[13] 3495[6] 3836[7] 4159[8]
5216[P]

Bridlingtonbygones (IRE) *Karen McLintock* 108h
6 br g Bob's Return(IRE) —Slaney Athlete (IRE) (Warcraft (USA))
35[5] 2296[2] 3965[4] 4993[2]

Briefcase (IRE) *Nigel Twiston-Davies* 102h
6 b g Witness Box(USA) —Another Tycoon (IRE) (Phardante (FR))
2954[7] 3604[3] 4029[7] 4420[4] 5080[5]

Briery Fox (IRE) *Henry Daly* 115h 134c
13 ch g Phardante(FR) —Briery Gale (Strong Gale)
314[2] 3687[6] 4284[4] 5009[7] 5443[7]

Brigadore (USA) *Alan Jones* 95h
8 rg g Sandpit(BRZ) —Mersey I (Crystal Palace (FR))
264[5] 2135[10] 4178[3] 4378[5]

Bright Decision *Joanna Davis* 88h
5 b g Thowra(FR) —Bright Spangle (IRE) (General Monash (USA))
1588[P] 1705[7] 2181[5] 2607[13] 3367[3] 4272[2] 4522[P] 5172[P]

Bright Sparky (GER) *Michael Easterby* 93h 100c
8 ch g Dashing Blade—Braissim (Dancing Brave (USA))
48[5] 4390[2] 4809[F] 5208[8]

Brightwell *Miss P C Lownds* 68b
10 b g Charnwood Forest(IRE) —Ski Blade (Niniski (USA))
1602[U] 4832[F]

Brilliant (GER) *Debra Hamer* 76h
8 ch g Risk Me(FR) —Belle Orfana (GER) (Orfano (GER))
1745[P] (1949) 2135[9] (4178) 5383[4]

Brimham Boy *Martin Keighley* 98h 110c
9 ch g Minster Son—Winnie Lorraine (St Columbus)
(156) 409[4] **2453[5] 3772[3] 4740[P]**

Brimley *Ann Price* 96h 86c
8 b g Bandmaster(USA) —Tinkers Night (Layal)
3[P] 1449[3] 1726[15]
2471[2] 3368[5] 3837[7]
4007[5] 4945[P]

Bringbackthebiff (NZ) *E J O'Grady* 127c
9 b g Colombia(NZ) —Ellena Dawn (NZ) (Drums Of Time (USA))
1123a[13]

Bringewood Belle *John Needham* 98h
8 b m Kayf Tara—Carlingford Belle (Carlingford Castle)
223[5] 2072[3] ◆ 4009[14]

Bringewood Bunny *John Needham* 64b
7 b m King's Theatre(IRE) —Native Fox (Be My Native (USA))
3590[8]

Bringewood Fox *John Needham* 100h 21c
9 gr g Cloudings(IRE) —Leinthall Fox (Deep Run)
2457[5] 4144[13]

Bringewood Moll *John Needham* 83h
8 b m Kayf Tara—Callindoe (IRE) (Callernish)
3585[5]

Bring It On Home *Sophie Leech* 98h
7 b g Beat Hollow—Dernier Cri (Slip Anchor)
273[3] 1141[5] 1232[6]

Bring On The Judge (IRE) *Nigel Twiston-Davies* 114h
8 b g Witness Box(USA) —Turnpike Junction (Henbit (USA))
2269[3] 3621[7] 4407[5]

Bring Sweets (IRE) *Brian Ellison* 90h
4 b g Firebreak—Missperon (IRE) (Orpen (USA))
836[3] 1018[3] (1825) 4939[5]

Brink *Tim Pitt* 83h
4 b f Powerscourt—Fonage (Zafonic (USA))
3986[B] 5357[6]

Brisbane (IRE) *Dianne Sayer* 19h
4 b g Kheleyf(USA) —Waroonga (IRE) (Brief Truce (USA))
1699[10] 4240[P]

Bristol Delauriere (FR) *Natalie Lloyd-Beavis* 68b
7 b g Epistolaire(IRE) —Shenedova (FR) (Hellios (USA))
2241[U]

Brixen (IRE) *Lucy Wadham* 103h
7 b m Heron Island(IRE) —Rythem Ofthe Night (IRE) (Over The River (FR))
(1994) 2289[3] 2983[10]

Broadbackbob (IRE) *S R B Crawford* 119b
6 b g Broadway Flyer(USA) —Back Home (IRE) (Bob Back (USA))
(3525) 5202[6] ◆

Broadway Allstar (IRE) *Karen Tutty* 89h
6 b m Beneficial—O'Dwyers Field (IRE) (Fourstars Allstar (USA))
171[5] 358[4] 887[2] 1147[8] 1379[2]

Broadway Star (FR) *Tim Vaughan* 98h 99c
8 b g Broadway Flyer(USA) —Starry Dust (FR) (Zino)
746[4] 860[9] 3430[3] 3837[2]

Brockton Scrumpy *Lisa Williamson* 19h
6 b g Sir Harry Lewis(USA) —Oyster Bay (Mandalus)
2059[8]
2363[P] 3252[P]

Broken Reed (IRE) *R Hirons* 105h 99c
12 b g Broken Hearted—Kings Reserve (King's Ride)
4750[5] 4973[6]

Brokethegate *Chris Grant* 69h
6 b g Presenting—Briery Ann (Anshan)
3957[4] 4287[13] 5147[5]

Bromhead (USA) *Kevin Morgan* 99h
5 ch g Johannesburg(USA) —Caramel Queen (NZ) (Turbulent Dancer (USA))
1624[P] 1953[6] 2114[6] (3397) 3497[2] 4548[3] 4977[5]

Bronte Bay (IRE) *Paul W Flynn* 116h 132c
8 ch g Karinga Bay—Clever Kelly (Alflora (IRE))
98[6] 4109a[4]

Bronx Boy (IRE) *Martin Todhunter* 98h
8 b g Snurge—Young Preacher (Decent Fellow)
875[8] 946[6] 1101[P]

Bronze Dancer (IRE) *Brian Storey* 57h
9 b g Entrepreneur—Scrimshaw (Selkirk (USA))
1647[6] 1662[P]

Brook Castle (IRE) *Mrs Jill Dennis* 92c
9 ch g Windsor Castle—Brook Project (IRE) (Project Manager)
133[2] 5156[P]

Brookfieldshector (IRE) *Mike Hammond* 52h 53c
7 b g Oscar(IRE) —Goody Choo Choo (IRE) (Orchestra)
280[4] 665[P]

Brooklyn Bay *Malcolm Jefferson* 95h
6 ch g Karinga Bay—Wuchowsen (IRE) (King's Ride)
254[4] 1643[5] 1829[7]

Brooklyn Brownie (IRE) *Malcolm Jefferson* 116h 146c
12 b g Presenting—In The Brownies (IRE) (Lafontaine (USA))
844[2] 1020[P] 3290[6] 4284[2]

Brookview Lad (IRE) *R Smart* 84b 50c
8 b g Parthian Springs—Another Shuil (IRE) (Duky)
79[6] 334[5]

Broom Battalion (IRE) *Henry De Bromhead* 91h 117c
10 b g Oscar(IRE) —Insan Call (IRE) (Insan (USA))
1038a[P]

Broomfield *Paul Nicholls* 106b
4 b g Selkirk(USA) —Behera (Mill Reef (USA))
4491[3] ◆ 5012[2]

Brootommity (IRE) *P Monteith*
4 b f Azamour(IRE) —Polyandry (IRE) (Pennekamp (USA))
2451[P]

Brother Bob (IRE) *Charlie Longsdon* 118h
5 b g Robert Emmet(IRE) —Noon Performance (Strong Gale)
1688[3] ◆ 2038[2] 2540[2] 4467[9]

Broughton Green (IRE) *Jim Old* 118h
10 b g Shernazar—Lucy Walters (IRE) (King's Ride)
3771[8] 4079[14]

Broughtons Star *Willie Musson* 102b
4 ch g Starcraft(NZ) —Marrakech (IRE) (Barathea (IRE))
(2315) 3294[12]

Browneyes Blue (IRE) *James Moffatt* 72h 102c
13 b g Satco(FR) —Bawnard Lady (Ragapan)
45[11] 291[8] **491[3] 1093[2]**

Bruach Na Mara (IRE) *W Harney* 129h
8 ch g Pasternak—Slievenanee (Avocat)
1526a[7] 3709a[2]

Bruff Academy (IRE) *Nick Gifford* 96h
8 ch g Beneficial—Galballygirl (IRE) (Roselier (FR))
82[7]

Brunette'Sonly (IRE) *Seamus Mullins* 92h
6 ch m Flemensfirth(USA) —Pride Of St Gallen (IRE) (Orchestra)
1993[6] 2168[11] 2592[6] 3297[2] 4098[U] 4403[P]

Brunston *Nicky Henderson* 115h
5 gr g High Chaparral(IRE) —Molly Mello (GER) (Big Shuffle (USA))
3783[4] 4288[3]

Brunswick Gold (IRE) *Steve Gollings* 123h
6 ch g Moscow Society(USA) —Tranbu (IRE) (Buckskin (FR))
2403[4] 3506[2] 3806[5] (4180) 4725[12]

Brushford (IRE) *Chris Gordon* 61h 89c
7 b g High Roller(IRE) —Vesper Time (The Parson)
2048[P] 2292[7] 2608[P] 2930[7] 3377[3] 3792[3] 3961[P] 4921[F]

Buailteoir (IRE) *Evan Williams* 14h 101c
9 b g Humbel(USA) —Mona Curra Gale (IRE) (Strong Gale)
436[F] **(1126)**
1200[5] 1281[U] 1509[2] (1546)
1591[8] 2236[F] 3482[P] 4160[P] 4784[P] 5076[5]
5391[3]

Bubble Boy (IRE) *Brendan Powell* 121c
12 ch g Hubbly Bubbly(USA) —Cool Charm (Beau Charmeur (FR))
431[P] 1200[P]

Bubbly Braveheart (IRE) *Alan Bailey* 89h
4 b g Cape Cross(IRE) —Infinity (FR) (Bering)
1298[2] 1691[4]

Bubbly Breeze (IRE) *Pauline Robson* 79h
6 br g Hubbly Bubbly(USA) —Belon Breeze (IRE) (Strong Gale)
3502[5] 3883[U] 4687[3]
5258[F]

Bubbly Bruce (IRE) *Charlie Mann* 95h
7 br g Quws—Oakleaf Express (IRE) (John French)
2396[3] 2946[13]

Bubbs *Nick Ayliffe* 93h
9 b m Robellino(USA) —Llancillo Lady (IRE) (Be My Native (USA))
172[7] 660[2] 1232[11]

Bubses Boy *Robert Johnson* 87h
5 ch g Needwood Blade—Welcome Home (Most Welcome)
1258[6] 2188[2] 3631[11] 3697[5] 3993[7] 5094[7]

Bucephalus (IRE) *Maurice Barnes* 119h
7 b g Montjeu(IRE) —Flyleaf (FR) (Persian Bold)
14[3] (468) 712[2] 803[4] (945) 1641[7] 2300[P] 4058[4] 4169[P] 5144[P]

Buckden (IRE) *Sue Smith* 67h
7 b g Luso—Sleeven Lady (Crash Course)
238[8] 683[5] 843[8] 1065[5] 5308[0]

Buckie Boy (IRE) *Nicky Henderson* 114h
5 b g Bahri(USA) —Woodren (USA) (Woodman (USA))
(3740)

Buckie Massa *S Arthur*
7 ch g Best Of The Bests(IRE) —Up On Points (Royal Academy (USA))
915a[2]

Buckingham Bill (IRE) *Mrs C Wilesmith* 96c
11 bb g Flemensfirth(USA) —Miss River (IRE) (Lord Americo)
150[F]

Buck Magic (IRE) *Patrick Rodford* 119h
5 b g Albano(IRE) —Green Sea (Groom Dancer (USA))
(2025) (2482)

Buck Mulligan *Evan Williams* 130h 136c
6 b g Robellino(USA) —Music Park (IRE) (Common Grounds)
(3448) 4479[3] 4861[3] (5398)

Buckstruther (IRE) *Andrew Parker* 90h 90c
9 ch g Anshan—Immediate Action (Roselier (FR))
90[6] (1873) 2351[9] (2654)

Buck The Legend (IRE) *Nigel Twiston-Davies* 118h 136c
9 bb g Anshan—Patience Of Angels (IRE) (Distinctly North (USA))
524[6] 735[6] 2948[9]

Buddy Holly *Violet M Jordan* 123h
6 b g Reel Buddy(USA) —Night Symphonie (Cloudings (IRE))
1832[2] 3196[5] (3489) 4377[3] 4858[8]

Buds Dilemma *Peter Bowen* 86h 79c
7 b m Anabaa(USA) —Lady Thynn (FR) (Crystal Glitters (USA))
1479[6] 1559[F] **1646[4] ◆ 1678[P] (1924)**
2113[6]

Buena Vista (IRE) *David Pipe* 148h 145c
10 b g In The Wings—Park Special (Relkino)
1855[7]
2221[2] 2663[8] 2870[7] 3293[10] 3561[15] (4817) 5187[6]

Buffalo Bob (IRE) *Kim Bailey* 118h 139c
8 b g Bob's Return(IRE) —Back In Kansas (IRE) (Mister Lord (USA))
2305[2] (2629)
3290[4] 3804[6] 4193[5] 5185[F]

Buffalo Creek (FR) *Giles Smyly*
7 b g Indian River(FR) —Mealasta (FR) (Ti King (FR))
2493[P] **3702[P]**

Buffalo Stampede (IRE) *Venetia Williams* 103h
8 b g Accordion—Killoughey Fairy (IRE) (Torus)
4265[P] 4504[P] 4989[P]

Bugsy's Boy *George Baker* 126h 125c
7 b g Double Trigger(IRE) —Bugsy's Sister (Aragon)
401[3] 1952[3] (3689)
4053[P]

Bulas Boy *Edwin Tuer* 74h
6 ch g Exit To Nowhere(USA) —Bula Rose (IRE) (Alphabatim (USA))
1660[P]

Bullies Acre (IRE) *Barry Murtagh* 60h 72c
11 b g Arctic Cider(USA) —Clonminch Lady (Le Bavard (FR))
160[8]

Bullring (FR) *Peter Niven* 30h
5 ch g Green Tune(USA) —Capework (USA) (El Gran Senor (USA))
1086[5] 1201[8] 3749[12]

Bully Wuskers (IRE) *Paul John Gilligan* 98h
6 b m Witness Box(USA) —Clonloo Lady (IRE) (Nearly A Nose (USA))
5078[9]

Bumblebee (IRE) *Warren Greatrex* 59h
6 b g Revoque(IRE) —Dikler Gale (IRE) (Strong Gale)
2518[10] 3542[9]

Bunacurry *Barry Murtagh* 78h
6 b g Best Of The Bests(IRE) —Miss Doody (Gorytus (USA))
1664[6] 1867[11] 2349[10] 3855[P] 4274[P] 4798[P]

Bunclody *Donald McCain* 119h
6 b g Overbury(IRE) —Wahiba Reason (IRE) (Robellino (USA))
2368[4] *2826[2]* 2943[5] 3572[7] 3885[2] (4132) 5106[2]

Bundle Up *John Flint* 108h
8 b m Diktat—Bundle (Cadeaux Genereux)
2639[10] 5232[2]

Bunglasha Lady (IRE) *Warren Greatrex* 130h
6 b m Snurge—Enchanted Valley (IRE) (Glacial Storm (USA))
2168[3] 2925[4] ◆ (3901) (4370) (5319)

Bunny Girl (IRE) *Giles Smyly* 57b
6 b m Laveron—Chopins Revolution (Rakaposhi King)
5380[9]

Bun Oir (USA) *Charlie Longsdon* 109h
4 bb g Seeking The Gold(USA) —Fraulein (Acatenango (GER))
2211[6] 2924[5] 3491[4] 4672[6] 4935[4] 5171[9]

Bunratty (IRE) *Robert Johnson* 96h
5 b g Rudimentary(USA) —Miss Huff N Puff (IRE) (Grand Plaisir (IRE))
2553[9] 4259[8] 4506[P] 4824[4] 5027[2]

Buona Sarah (IRE) *Sheena West*
4 ch f Bertolini(USA) —Midnight Partner (IRE) (Marju (IRE))
4917[F]

Buraimi Oasis *Karen McLintock* 85b
6 ch g Kirkwall—Rhiann (Anshan)
949[4] 1989[8]

Bureaucrat *Kate Walton* 121h 128c
9 b g Machiavellian(USA) —Lajna (Be My Guest (USA))
3306[6] 3969[5] 4255[7] 4797[6]

Burgundy Beau *William Amos* 92b
5 br g Grape Tree Road—Chantilly Rose (Primitive Rising (USA))
5033[3]

Burnbrake *Les Hall*
6 b g Mujahid(USA) —Duena (Grand Lodge (USA))
1433[P]

Burning Light (IRE) *Andrew Haynes* 42b
4 b g Fantastic Light(USA) —Alashaan (Darshaan)
1913[13]

Burnthill (IRE) *Claire Dyson* 92h
6 b g Winged Love(IRE) —Kilcorig (IRE) (Niels)
58[6] 337[3] 847[6] 3989[7] 4441[4] (4812) 5169[8] 5295[4]

Burnt Oak (UAE) *Chris Fairhurst* 118h
9 b g Timber Country(USA) —Anaam (Caerleon (USA))
2373[7] 3509[3] 4025[4] 4875[7]

Burntoakboy *David Griffiths* 138h 107c
13 b g Sir Harry Lewis(USA) —Sainte Martine (Martinmas)
4928[6]

Burnt Orchid (IRE) *Geoffrey Deacon* 76b
6 ch m Subtle Power(IRE) —Native Orchid (IRE) (Be My Native (USA))
5388[12]

Burren Legend (IRE) *Richard Rowe* 121h 135c
10 b g Flying Legend(USA) —Burren View (IRE) (Mazaad)
98[U] 2084[P] 2221[P] 3948[3] 4200[5] 4821[P] 5009[5]

Burton Port (IRE) *Nicky Henderson* 142h 171c
7 b g Bob Back(USA) —Despute (IRE) (Be My Native (USA))
2673[2] ◆

Bury Parade (IRE) *Robert Bewley* 98b
5 br g Overbury(IRE) —Alexandra Parade (IRE) (Mister Lord (USA))
5342[6]

Bury The Hatchet (IRE) *Alan Swinbank* 79b
5 gr g Sesaro(USA) —Royal Myth (USA) (Sir Ivor (USA))
892[4] 1153[5]

Busby Berkeley (IRE) *Martin Keighley* 61b
5 b g Broadway Flyer(USA) —Upton Lodge (IRE) (Clearly Bust)
4457[10]

Bushlark *Renee Robeson* 64b
5 b m Bollin Eric—Mountain Lory (Ardross)
3266[13] 4027[16]

Bushwacker (IRE) *Seamus Mullins* 105h 119c
7 b g Top Of The World—Tender Pearl (Prince Tenderfoot (USA))
81[U] 130[2] (429)
681[P] 1161[F] 1471[2] 1888[5] 2124[5] 4967[4] 5173[2]
5269[4]

Businessmoney Judi *David Pipe* 94h
5 ch m Kirkwall—Cloverjay (Lir)
(5280)

Busker Royal *Nicky Henderson* 126h 137c
8 ch g Shahrastani(USA) —Close Harmony (Bustino)
94[4] 633[4] 3688[4] 4202[3] 4806[14] 5304[11]

Busy Times *John Spearing* 101h 38c
9 ch g Busy Flight—Jilly Wig (IRE) (Strong Gale)
226[6]

Bute Street *Ron Hodges* 55h
6 b g Superior Premium—Hard To Follow (Dilum (USA))
4917[11]

Butlers Glen (IRE) *Evan Williams* 85h
8 b m Shernazar—Belcamp Belle (IRE) (Nashamaa)
1308[2] 1600[4]

Buymequick (IRE) *Ron Barr*
6 b m Mr Combustible(IRE) —Boyne Judy (IRE) (Boyne Valley)
474[11]

Byblos *Warren Greatrex* 88h
6 ch g Tobougg(IRE) —My Girl (Mon Tresor)
1164[4]

By Command *Laura Young* 74h
6 b g Red Ransom(USA) —Rafha (Kris)
2495[6] 5167[10]

Byerley Bear (IRE) *Henry De Bromhead* 129h
6 ch g Exit To Nowhere(USA) —Miss Kamsy (Kambalda)
3846a[5]

Bygones In Brid (IRE) *Alan King* 120b
5 b g Old Vic—St Carol (IRE) (Orchestra)
(2511) 4191[2] ◆ 4808[18]

Bygones Of Brid (IRE) *Karen McLintock* 148h
8 b g Alderbrook—Glenadore (Furry Glen)
2447[P] 2668[4] *3170[6]* 3561[U] 3676[10] 4169[2] 4791[10]
5337[2]

Bygones Sovereign (IRE) *Karen McLintock* 115b
5 b g Old Vic—Miss Hollygrove (IRE) (King's Ride)
3731[4] 4308[2] ◆ (5034)

Bynack Mhor (IRE) *Lawney Hill* 82h 83c
10 b g Taipan(IRE) —Pride Of Poznan (IRE) (Buzzards Bay)
(987) **1093[4]**
1425[6] 1733[F] 1820[4] 2132[6]

Byron Bay *Robert Johnson* 72h 79c
9 b g My Best Valentine—Candarela (Damister (USA))
2603[P]
3632[3] 3884[P]

Bythehokey (IRE) *Brian Baugh* 80c
10 b g Barathea(IRE) —Regal Portrait (IRE) (Royal Academy (USA))
799[8] 891[9]

By The Hour (IRE) *Robert Tyner* 112h 126c
8 ch m Flemensfirth(USA) —Lucky Hour (IRE) (Mansooj)
(3706a)

Byways Boy *Caroline Bailey* 5h 34c
8 ch g Groom Dancer(USA) —Fuwala (Unfuwain (USA))
1747[P] 2555[5] 3388[8]

Bywell Beau (IRE) *George Charlton* 109h 129c
12 b g Lord Americo—Early Dalus (IRE) (Mandalus)
2076[P] 3334[6] 4169[6] 4912[5] 5262[4]

Byzantina Fair *Henrietta Knight* 43h
9 br m Contract Law(USA) —Harvest Fair (Oats)
429[P] 583[5]

Bzhamij Ai (SLO) *George Charlton* 75b
7 b m Almaz(RUS) —Bellona (RUS) (Enterprise Ru (IRE))
8[P]

Cabal *Andrew Crook* 57h
4 br f Kyllachy—Secret Flame (Machiavellian (USA))
3785[6] 4283[P] 4552[9]

Cabbyl Doo *James Moffatt* 81h 105c
8 b h Killer Instinct—Chipewyas (FR) (Bering)
3850[7]
4868[2] 5145[4]

Cabernet Sauvignon *Gordon Elliott* 123h
5 br g Dansili—Halcyon Daze (Halling (USA))
445[2] (Dead)

Caddie Master (IRE) *Jonjo O'Neill* 90h
5 ch g Old Vic—Clody Girl (IRE) (Zaffaran (USA))
3526[11] 3701[4] 3864[4]

Cadeaux Cerise (IRE) *Andrew Haynes* 92h
7 b m Cadeaux Genereux—Cerisette (IRE) (Polar Falcon (USA))
182[6] 384[5] 1062[11] 1479[7] 5282[4]

Cadoudalas (FR) *Richard Lee* 111h 140c
8 b g Cadoudal(FR) —Popie D'Ecorcei (FR) (Balsamo (FR))
234[7] (2148)
(3531) ◆ (4002)

Cadoulitique (FR) *Tina Jackson* 89h 80c
8 b g Antarctique(IRE) —Cadoulie Wood (FR) (Cadoudal (FR))
985[P] 1152[P]

Cadwell *Tim Pitt* 75h 44c
7 b g Pivotal—Sur Les Pointes (IRE) (Sadler's Wells (USA))
950[7]

Caerlaverock (IRE) *Rose Dobbin* 117h
6 br g Statue Of Liberty(USA) —Daziyra (IRE) (Doyoun)
305[2]

Caged Tiger *Mrs H M Kemp* 103h 86c
12 b g Classic Cliche(IRE) —Run Tiger (IRE) (Commanche Run)
4183[4]

Caheerloch (IRE) *Nigel Twiston-Davies* 100h
9 b g Sinndar(IRE) —Pharmacist (IRE) (Machiavellian (USA))
(1232) (1336) 1490[2] 1605[5] 1959[10] 2279[2] 2532[7]

Cailin Ceol (IRE) *Michael C Griffin* 92h
6 b m Bach(IRE) —Pugets Sister (IRE) (Lord Americo)
1793[3]

Cailin Maghnailbhe (IRE) *Seamus Mullins* 77b
4 b f Exit To Nowhere(USA) —Opera Lover (IRE) (Sadler's Wells (USA))
2965[6] ◆ *3979[10]* 5012[14]

Cailin Na Ri (IRE) *Martin Todhunter* 117h
8 b m King's Theatre(IRE) —Kings Gap (IRE) (King's Ride)
(30) 488[3] 744[2] 1149[2] 1357[2] (1499) 1643[2]
1959[P] 2506[3] 5319[7]

Caislean Na Deirge (IRE) *Neil Mulholland* 89h 71c
13 b g Boyne Valley—Bramble Lane (Boreen (FR))
650[P]

Calaficial (IRE) *Charles Pogson* 105h
8 br g Beneficial—Calamaire (Callernish)
1953[10] 2312[8] *3090[7]*

Calatagan (IRE) *Malcolm Jefferson* 116h 139c
12 ch g Danzig Connection(USA) —Calachuchi (Martinmas)
314[U] 606[5] 2076[4] 2423[4]
4116[9]

Calcot Rose *Alan King* 41b
5 b m Moscow Society(USA) —Be My Shuile (IRE) (Be My Native (USA))
4184[10] 5070[10]

Calculaite *Martin Todhunter* 116h 124c
10 b g Komaite(USA) —Miss Calculate (Mummy's Game)
34[9] **290[6]**
515[7] **(1502)**

Calfraz *Micky Hammond* 98h 58c
9 bb g Tamure(IRE) —Pas De Chat (Relko)
2610[P]

Calgary Bay (IRE) *Henrietta Knight* 133h 154c
8 b g Taipan(IRE) —Dante's Thatch (IRE) (Phardante (FR))
1856[5] 2091[6] 2304[2] 2886[4] 3804[2] 5200[F]

Calgary Jock *Mrs J Marles* 106h 85c
10 ch g Rakaposhi King—Lily Of The West (True Song)
148[8] 499[5] 4293[5] 4936[4]

Caliban (IRE) *Sally-Anne Wheelwright* 60h 109c
13 ch g Rainbows For Life(CAN) —Amour Toujours (IRE) (Law Society (USA))
233[U] 490[13]

Calico Rose *Victor Dartnall* 103h
7 ch m Karinga Bay—Sprig Muslin (Ra Nova)
2288[6] 2974[12] 3691[8] (4034) 4530[2]

Call At Midnight *Sarah Humphrey* 109h
6 b m Midnight Legend—Second Call (Kind Of Hush)
988[3] (1124) 1233[3] (1477) 1726[4]

Callisto Moon *Barry Brennan* 120h 98c
7 b g Mujahid(USA) —Nursling (IRE) (Kahyasi)
1364[3] 1626[11]

Call It On (IRE) *Philip Kirby* 104h
5 ch g Raise A Grand(IRE) —Birthday Present (Cadeaux Genereux)
2419[2] 3490[2] 3950[14] 4243[3]

Call Me A Legend *Alan King* 117h 141c
7 ch m Midnight Legend—Second Call (Kind Of Hush)
2665[4] ◆ (3565) ◆ 3949[9] 4820[5]

Call Me Bill (IRE) *Peter Bowen* 74h
5 b g Brian Boru—Roaming (IRE) (Be My Native (USA))
35[2] ◆ 448[2] (609) 1553[10] 1703[P] 1795[3] 2232[7]
2589[4]

Call Me Dave *John E Long* 52h
10 b g Bin Ajwaad(IRE) —Heckle (In The Wings)
25[8]

Call Me Frankie (IRE) *Lucy Jones* 88h
5 b g Indian Danehill(IRE) —Violets Wild (IRE) (Imperial Frontier (USA))
3943[5] 4860[9] 5167[16] 5327[6]

Call Me Friday *Matthew Salaman* 88b
5 b m Best Of The Bests(IRE) —Mistress Polly (Polish Precedent (USA))
332[8] 4055[15] 5306[16]

Call Me Mulligan (IRE) *John Hellens* 108h 108c
7 ch g Bach(IRE) —They Call Me Molly (CAN) (Charlie Barley (USA))
1045[4] (1109) 1357[6] **1661[6] (4553)**
5163[U]

Call Me Sir (IRE) *Susan Gardner* 79h
9 b g Lord Americo—Crash Call (Crash Course)
441[7]

Call The Police (IRE) *W P Mullins* 147h
8 b g Accordion—Evangelica (USA) (Dahar (USA))
3474a[2] 4806[11]

Call To Arms (IRE) *Peter Bowen* 103h
4 br g Shamardal(USA) —Requesting (Rainbow Quest (USA))
2020[4] 2306[2] 3519[2] 4925[6]

Calon *Evan Williams* 76h
5 b m Muhtarram(USA) —Merch Rhyd-Y-Grug (Sabrehill (USA))
648[5]

Calon Crwbin *Alison Thorpe* 132h
6 b g First Trump—Sweets (IRE) (Persian Heights)
(82) ◆ 591[2] (887) 1346[P] (1505)

Calow Green (IRE) *Ollie Pears* 74h
9 bb m Lord Americo—Wake Me Gently (IRE) (Be My Native (USA))
2598[P]

Calusa Caldera (IRE) *Philip Hobbs* 113h 134c
9 b g Presenting—Stormy Sea (IRE) (Strong Gale)
2582[2] 4440[8] (4987)
5185[U]

Calusa Catrina (IRE) *Robin Dickin* 74h
6 bb m Lahib(USA) —Bukowina (GER) (Windwurf (GER))
332[6] 2577[15] 3296[9] 3691[13] 5212[9]

Calusa Shadow *Philip Hobbs* 106h
7 br g Beat All(USA) —Tina Gee (Orchestra)
2577[6] 2949[9] 3297[3] 4441[3] 5205[3]

Calypso Bay (IRE) *Jonjo O'Neill* 113h
5 b g Galileo(IRE) —Poule De Luxe (IRE) (Cadeaux Genereux)
97[10] 356[6] 1111[11] 1392[6] 1559[2] 1798[2] (2183)
2941[3] 3589[2] 4079[13]

Calzaghe (IRE) *D Bryant* 119h
7 ch g Galileo(IRE) —Novelette (Darshaan)
598[3] 835[3] 1092[5]
4901[P]

Camas Bridge *Emma Lavelle* 86b
5 ch g Alflora(IRE) —Bobupandown (Bob's Return (IRE))
4376[4] ◆

Camden (IRE) *Oliver Sherwood* 126h
5 b g Old Vic—Electric View (IRE) (Electric)
(2186) 2944[7] (3599) 4180[3] 4489[2] ◆ 4861[5]
(5381)

Camden George (IRE) *Sue Smith* 114h 125c
10 b g Pasternak—Triple Town Lass (IRE) (Camden Town)
1761[10] 2106[5] 2449[2] 3488[5] 3695[2] 4167[2] 4546[6]
5032[3]

Camelloe *Colin Tizzard* 6b
5 ch m Kirkwall—Balula's Girl (Gildoran)
4376[6] 5174[13]

Camino Real *Jim Old* 81h
8 ch m Benny The Dip(USA) —Kingdom Ruby (IRE) (Bluebird (USA))
50[4] 432[4] 1450[P]

Camomile *Tracy Waggott* 70h
5 b m Xaar—Pretty Davis (USA) (Trempolino (USA))
14[P] 400[4] 470[10] 835[4]

Campden Society (IRE) *Peter Hiatt* 79h
8 ch m Moscow Society(USA) —Native Woodfire (IRE) (Mister Majestic)
4479[8] 5038[2] 5274[4]

Canada Street (IRE) *Miss E Stead* 108h 119c
10 b g Old Vic—Saucy Sprite (Balliol)
5263[5]

Canal Bank (IRE) *Jonjo O'Neill* 72h 109c
7 b g Heron Island(IRE) —Sudden Inspiration (IRE) (Good Thyne (USA))
1091[4] 1197[5] 1257[5] 1485[5] 1710[P] (1969)
2274[4] (2796)
3716[F] 4409[3]

Canal Cottage (IRE) *Lucinda Russell* 95h
7 b g Winged Love(IRE) —Toreena (IRE) (Torus)
2349[8] 3999[4] 4686[5]

Canalturn (FR) *Charles Egerton* 122h
9 b g Assessor(IRE) —Caline De Froment (FR) (Grand Tresor (FR))
2670[U]

Candleford *Sally Hall* 101h
6 b g Vettori(IRE) —Second Affair (IRE) (Pursuit Of Love)
3572[4] 3787[6] 4233[11]

Candlefort Lady (IRE) *Jim Best* 50b
6 b m Beneficial—Lady Blayney (IRE) (Mazaad)
2087[10] 2440[5] 5267[P]

Cane Brake (IRE) *Conor O'Dwyer* 137h 147c
12 b g Sadler's Wells(USA) —Be My Hope (IRE) (Be My Native (USA))
3798a[P] 4486[P]

Cannington Brook (IRE) *Colin Tizzard* 137h 133c
7 b g Winged Love(IRE) —Rosie Brook (IRE) (Be My Native (USA))
2357[3] 2883[6] 3342[2] 4080[2]

Canni Thinkaar (IRE) *Zoe Davison* 108h 122c
10 b g Alhaarth(IRE) —Cannikin (IRE) (Lahib (USA))
220^{2} 601^{6} 1590^{6} 1904^{9} **2441^{2} 2945^{6} 3628^{P} 4127^{2} 4666^{2} 4856^{5}**

Cannon Bridge (IRE) *P S Davies* 38h 108c
13 ch g Definite Article—Hit For Six (Tap On Wood)
(526)

Cannon Fire (FR) *Evan Williams* 109h 115c
10 ch g Grand Lodge(USA) —Muirfield (FR) (Crystal Glitters (USA))
(645) (682) 692^{F} 765^{2} 1004^{2} (1259) 3483^{P} 5252^{7}

Canny Lad *John Ryan* 42b
5 ch g Zaha(CAN) —Lady At Leisure (IRE) (Dolphin Street (FR))
1029^{11}

Canongate *Emma Lavelle*
7 gr g Highest Honor(FR) —Tremiere (FR) (Anabaa (USA))
279^{P}

Canon's Corner (IRE) *Rachel Hobbs* 102c
8 br g Flemensfirth(USA) —Deciding Dance (IRE) (Orchestra)
951^{3} 1109^{5} 1274^{3} 1452^{3} 1747^{4}

Canopy Of Stars *Tom George* 90b
5 gr g Fair Mix(IRE) —Maid Equal (Pragmatic)
4410^{4} 5113^{10}

Canshebemine *James Frost* 83h
7 b m Morpeth—Pigeon Loft (IRE) (Bellypha)
3983^{3} 4900^{4}

Cantabilly (IRE) *Ron Hodges* 116h 116c
8 b g Distant Music(USA) —Cantaloupe (Priolo (USA))
264^{2} (1740) 1972^{5} 2147^{7}
2502^{3} 2636^{3}
3531^{4} 3648^{F}

Can't Buy Time (IRE) *Jonjo O'Neill* 108h 153c
9 b g Supreme Leader—Sales Centre (Deep Run)
2084^{8} 2359^{P} 3292^{5} 4821^{P} 5200^{F} 5443^{P}

Cantgeton (IRE) *P Monteith* 76h 122c
11 b g Germany(USA) —Lahana (IRE) (Rising)
1761^{2} 2206^{4}

Canticle *Chris Bealby* 98c
6 b g Helissio(FR) —Litany (Colonel Collins (USA))
1815^{3} 2475^{5} 3390^{P}

Cantlow (IRE) *Paul Webber* 142h
6 b g Kayf Tara—Winnowing (IRE) (Strong Gale)
3960^{4} (4294) 5186^{2}

Cantrell (IRE) *H Smyth* 108h 34c
8 b g High Roller(IRE) —Executive Seat (IRE) (Executive Perk)
89^{8}

Can't Remember *Alison Thorpe* 93h
6 b m Overbury(IRE) —Myrtilla (Beldale Flutter (USA))
525 210^{P} 402^{2} 470^{5} (875) 1062^{10} 1479^{5} 1590^{3} 2244^{4} 2609^{5} 3155^{2} (3432) 4401^{4} 4704^{4} 4955^{6} 5169^{U} 5278^{4}

Canyouseeme *Claire Dyson* 77h
8 ch g Emperor Fountain—Speckyfoureyes (Blue Cashmere)
1736^{8} 1887^{5} 2144^{4}

Capable Guest (IRE) *George Moore* 44h
9 bb g Cape Cross(IRE) —Alexander Confranc (IRE) (Magical Wonder (USA))
887^{7}

Capall Eile (IRE) *Paul John Gilligan* 106h
8 b g Turtle Island(IRE) —Laurens Pet (IRE) (Glacial Storm (USA))
1121a^{6}

Capdalight (IRE) *A J Kennedy* 63h 103c
8 b g Simply Great(FR) —A Rare One (IRE) (Mandalus)
5406^{5}

Cape Breton *Patrick Chamings* 107b
5 b g Cape Cross(IRE) —Red Bouquet (Reference Point)
4484^{2} *4923^{4}*

Capeleira (IRE) *Richard Rowe* 43h
6 b g Tagula(IRE) —Agent Scully (IRE) (Simply Great (FR))
532^{P} 688^{P}

Capellanus (IRE) *E J O'Grady* 128h
5 b g Montjeu(IRE) —Secret Dream (IRE) (Zafonic (USA))
3474a^{11}

Cap Elorn (FR) *Paul Nicholls* 87h
5 b g Kapgarde(FR) —Legretta (USA) (Al Nasr (FR))
1748^{4} 2607^{7} 3691^{6} ◆ 4091^{10}

Cape Schanck *Alan Coogan* 94h
7 b g Observatory(USA) —Sally Gardens (Alzao (USA))
4952^{4}

Cape Secret (IRE) *Gordon Elliott* 107h
8 b g Cape Cross(IRE) —Baylands Sunshine (IRE) (Classic Secret (USA))
4428 (1092) 1339^{2}

Cape Tribulation *Malcolm Jefferson* 153h 147c
7 b g Hernando(FR) —Gay Fantastic (Ela-Mana-Mou)
(1661) ◆ **2105^{P} 3955^{2} 4236^{2}**

Cap Falco (IRE) *Anabel L M King* 97h
6 ch g Beneficial—Banderole (IRE) (Roselier (FR))
2957^{8} 3511^{9} 4739^{4} 5074^{4}

Capital Venture (IRE) *James Ewart* 111b
5 b g Moscow Society(USA) —Benrue Adventure (IRE) (Broken Hearted)
3525^{5} 3889^{4} 5034^{4} (5432)

Cappagh (IRE) *Philip Hobbs* 121h 124c
6 ch g Presenting—Random Bless (IRE) (Montelimar (USA))
134^{U} (273)
(1575) (1794) ◆ 2387^{5} 4185^{5}

Capricornus (USA) *Ferdy Murphy* 93h
4 ch c Rahy(USA) —Silent Partner (USA) (Capote (USA))
1696^{8} 2033^{5} 2655^{4} 3358^{5} 3550^{4} 4148^{3} 4465^{4}

Captain Americo (IRE) *James Ewart* 131h 131c
9 b g Lord Americo—Excitable Lady (Buckskin (FR))
(2205) 2523^{8}
(3499) 3955^{3} 4802^{P}

Captain Becket *James Frost* 101h 69c
8 b g Access Ski—Sporting Annie (Teamster)
273^{2} 410^{7} (661) 1443^{6} 1490^{7} 1740^{7} 1911^{2} 2023^{3} 2284^{5} 3493^{5} 3791^{7} 4224^{8} (4787) 5278^{5}

Captain Cee Bee (IRE) *Edward P Harty* 159h 166c
10 b g Germany(USA) —Elea Victoria (IRE) (Sharp Victor (USA))
(2096a) ◆ **3204a^{4} 4805^{3}**

Captain Chris (IRE) *Philip Hobbs* 151h 166c
7 b g King's Theatre(IRE) —Function Dream (IRE) (Strong Gale)
1966^{2}
2384^{2} 3193^{2} 3946^{2} (4351) (4789)

Captain Clint (IRE) *Mark H Tompkins*
4 b g Captain Rio—Lake Poopo (IRE) (Persian Heights)
1473^{P}

Captain Cool (IRE) *Richard Hannon* 92h
4 ch g Captain Rio—Aiaie (Zafonic (USA))
2958^{11} 4676^{6} 4951^{3}

Captain Flack *Giles Bravery*
5 ch g Lucky Story(USA) —Au Contraire (Groom Dancer (USA))
554^{0}

Captain Jack Black *Edward Bevan*
6 br g Superior Premium—La Volta (Komaite (USA))
2054^{P}

Captain John Smith *Tom George* 77b
6 b g Hernando(FR) —Lady Rebecca (Rolfe (USA))
2590^{6}

Captain Kirkton (IRE) *Gary Moore* 131h
5 b g Flemensfirth(USA) —What A Mewsment (IRE) (Persian Mews)
3054^{2} (3374) (3960) 4312^{4} 4725^{P}

Captain Knock (IRE) *David Phelan* 109c
8 bb g Busy Flight—Alien Jane (IRE) (Weavers Web)
4429^{3} 4857^{2} 5163^{12}

Captain Marlon (IRE) *Miss C Wright* 97h 101c
10 b g Supreme Leader—Marlonette (IRE) (Jareer (USA))
539^{7} **652^{6}**
755^{7} 913^{3} 1106^{2} 1161^{2} 1277^{P} 1447^{5} 4786^{3} 5402^{2}

Captains Dilemma (IRE) *T Hogan* 113h
4 ch g Captain Rio—Meas (IRE) (Mark Of Esteem (IRE))
2966a^{7}

Captain's Legacy *Miss E Leppard* 107h 91c
10 b g Bob's Return(IRE) —Tuppence In Clover (Petoski)
294^{2}

Captain Smoothy *Neil King* 93h 102c
11 b g Charmer—The Lady Captain (Neltino)
1992^{3} 2420^{P} 3305^{F} 4130^{P}

Captain Sully (IRE) *Jim Wilson* 108h
6 b g Pairumani Star(IRE) —Ginger Lily (IRE) (Lucky Guest)
2361^{P} 2577^{16} 5212^{11}

Captain Sunshine *Emma Lavelle* 120b
5 b g Oscar(IRE) —Gaye Fame (Ardross)
4468^{3} ◆

Captain Tee Gee *Michael Chapman*
5 b g Shahrastani(USA) —Amy Lewis (Sir Harry Lewis (USA))
718^{10} 892^{7}

Captain Tidds (IRE) *Richard Phillips* 107h 129c
10 b g Presenting—Kilmana (IRE) (Castle Keep)
2293^{6} 3634^{P}

Captain Walcot *Carroll Gray* 59h
5 b g Fantastic Light(USA) —Princess Minnie (Mistertopogigo (IRE))
2641^{1}

Captive Audience (IRE) *Rebecca Curtis* 140h 119c
8 b g Saddlers' Hall(IRE) —Silent Run (Deep Run)
206^{10}
1865^{4} 2057^{4} 2494^{5}

Capybara (IRE) *Henry Hogarth* 57h 109c
13 b g Commanche Run—The Pledger (Strong Gale)
212^{10}

Carabinier (FR) *Nicky Henderson* 93h
5 b g Martaline—Incorrigible (FR) (Septieme Ciel (USA))
2215^{6} 4198^{6}

Caracal *Gordon Elliott* 85h
4 b g Dubai Destination(USA) —Desert Lynx (IRE) (Green Desert (USA))
1728^{2}

Caramia (FR) *Miss S Klug* 62h 118c
10 ch g Medaaly—Ciqui (IRE) (Shernazar)
354^{6}

Caravan Queen (IRE) *Norma Twomey* 102b
7 b m Dushyantor(USA) —Gypsys Girl (IRE) (Husyan (USA))
1455^{2}

Caravel (IRE) *Howard Johnson* 131h
7 ch g Medicean—Caraiyma (IRE) (Shahrastani (USA))
1956^{8} 3969^{7} 4727^{9} 5201^{16}

Carbis Bay *Zoe Davison* 67b
5 b g Deploy—Hi Lily (Jupiter Island)
2432^{7} 3546^{P}

Carbon Print (USA) *James Evans* 99h
6 ch g Johannesburg(USA) —Caithness (USA) (Roberto (USA))
850^{2} 1111^{7} 2322^{11} 3563^{6} 4266^{4} 5212^{14}

Cardigan Island (IRE) *Peter Bowen* 55b
6 br g Winged Love(IRE) —Wollongong (IRE) (King Persian)
3551^{3}

Cardinal James (IRE) *Tor Sturgis* 104h
7 br g Bishop Of Cashel—Dilwara (IRE) (Lashkari)
1740^{2} 2185^{6} 2630^{7}

Cardinal Rose *Jonjo O'Neill* 87b
4 ch g Karinga Bay—Miniature Rose (Anshan)
2458^{2} 3294^{13}

Carhue Princess (IRE) *John Flint* 88h
5 b m Desert Prince(IRE) —Carhue Journey (IRE) (Barathea (IRE))
358^{U} 768^{3} 1030^{3} 1450^{14} 5390^{6}

Cariboo Lady *Roger Curtis* 79b
5 bb m Carisbrooke—Mandalady (IRE) (Mandalus)
5388^{11}

Carlanstown (IRE) *Mrs C De Montmorency* 97c
7 b g Winged Love(IRE) —Clever Kelly (Alflora (IRE))
5258^{4}

Carlas Dream (IRE) *Denis Paul Murphy* 105h 108c
9 b m Supreme Leader—Orchestral View (IRE) (Orchestra)
4802^{8}

Carlicue (IRE) *Paul Nicholls* 121h
6 b g King's Theatre(IRE) —Woodville Star (IRE) (Phardante (FR))
1963^{2} (3584) 4220^{P}

Carlito Brigante (IRE) *Gordon Elliott* 157h
5 b g Haafhd—Desert Magic (IRE) (Green Desert (USA))
(2521) 2884^{11} (4806) 5160^{4}

Carlos Gardel *Mark Rimell* 88h
6 b g Beat All(USA) —Melody Princess (Ardross)
2309^{6} 3842^{5} 4719^{11} 5108^{5}

Carloswayback (IRE) *Paul Nolan* 118h
6 b g Bob Back(USA) —Mandysway (IRE) (Mandalus)
2967a^{5} 3181a^{F} ◆ 3708a^{5}

Carlton Mac *Simon Griffiths* 64h
6 ch g Timeless Times(USA) —Julie's Gift (Presidium)
5354^{P}

Carlton Scroop (FR) *J Jay* 91h
8 ch g Priolo(USA) —Elms Schooldays (Emarati (USA))
539^{P}

Carmela Maria *Mike Sowersby* 90h
6 b m Medicean—Carmela Owen (Owington)
8^{3} 157^{9} 424^{7}

Carmond (GER) *Oliver Sherwood* 64h 65c
7 ch g Kornado—Cachira (GER) (Windwurf (GER))
3343^{6} 3724^{P} **4668^{6} 5062^{5}**

Carndonagh (IRE) *Malcolm Jefferson* 107h
7 b g Old Vic—T T Two (IRE) (Bin Ajwaad (IRE))
2296^{4} 3693^{15}

Carole's Destiny *Nicky Henderson* 105b
4 ch f Hernando(FR) —Carole's Crusader (Faustus (USA))
5306^{3}

Carole's Legacy *Nicky Henderson* 150h 158c
7 ch m Sir Harry Lewis(USA) —Carole's Crusader (Faustus (USA))
(2579)
3292^{2} 3674^{2}
4790^{2} 5162^{2}

Carpincho (FR) *Sarah Humphrey* 135h
7 bb g Jimble(FR) —La Rapaille (IRE) (Mandalus)
(2297) 2939^{5} (3866) 4206^{4} 5187^{9}

Carraigh Na Loine *Jonjo O'Neill* 77h
6 b g High-Rise(IRE) —Miss Betsy (IRE) (Pollerton)
596^{4}

Carribs Leap (IRE) *Charles Egerton* 123h
6 b g Old Vic—Majister Ludi (IRE) (Be My Native (USA))
(1951) 3346^{3} 3678^{4}

Carrickboy (IRE) *Venetia Williams* 133h 123c
7 b g Silver Patriarch(IRE) —Alaskan Princess (IRE) (Prince Rupert (FR))
2286^{2} 2869^{U} 2948^{8} 3690^{3}

Carrickmines (IRE) *Dr Richard Newland* 104h 135c
9 b g Saddlers' Hall(IRE) —Orlas Castle (IRE) (Bulldozer)
1821^{8}
2221^{8} 2522^{P} 2669^{3} 2962^{F} 3693^{6}
(4054) ◆ **4200^{4} 4790^{10} 5199^{U}**

Carrick Oscar (IRE) *Tim Vaughan* 110h 127c
11 b g Oscar(IRE) —Regents Prancer (Prince Regent (FR))
195^{U} 772^{4} 1200^{3} (1431)

Carrietau *Barry Murtagh* 106h 122c
8 b g Key Of Luck(USA) —Carreamia (Weldnaas (USA))
(395) **1761^{3}**
2613^{7} 4116^{7} 4456^{6} 4913^{4} 5145^{P} (5418)

Carrifran (IRE) *Malcolm Jefferson* 71h
6 b m Definite Article—Shuildante (IRE) (Phardante (FR))
718^{8} 916^{6} 1021^{8} 1090^{7} 1361^{P}

Carrig An Uisce (IRE) *Anna Brooks* 99h 98c
10 ch g Portrait Gallery(IRE) —Yarra Glen (Known Fact (USA))
1996^{U} 2114^{2} (2294)
3769^{6} 4022^{P} 5173^{3}

Carrigeen King (IRE) *George Baker* 117h 115c
10 b g Beneficial—Carrigeen Kerria (IRE) (Kemal (FR))
4034^{P}

Carrigleade (IRE) *Matt Sheppard* 86h
11 ch g Safety Catch(USA) —Tolaytala (Be My Guest (USA))
1111^{14}

Carrigmartin (IRE) *Edward P Harty* 128h 131c
6 b g King's Theatre(IRE) —Donna's Princess (IRE) (Supreme Leader)
1526a^{8}

Carroll Grey (IRE) *John Upson* 35h 36c
10 gr g Carroll House—Katie's Castle (IRE) (Celio Rufo)
1059^{9}

Carronhills (IRE) *Rebecca Curtis* 138c
9 b g Old Vic—Too Sharp (True Song)
4186^{4} 4333^{F}

Carrowbehy Lad (IRE) *Paul John Gilligan* 47h
7 ch g Deploy—Pamela's Princess (Black Minstrel)
768^{5} (Dead)

Carruthers *Mark Bradstock* 150h 160c
8 b g Kayf Tara—Plaid Maid (IRE) (Executive Perk)
2084^{6} 2673^{6} 4208^{4} 4850^{9}

Carry Duff *Ferdy Murphy* 85h 96c
10 b g Deploy—Pink Brief (IRE) (Ela-Mana-Mou)
2449^{P} 2940^{11} 3712^{6}

Carsington *Lucinda Featherstone* 84b
7 ch m And Beyond(IRE) —Nutmeg Point (Nashwan (USA))
4703^{U} 5101^{P}

Carsonstown Boy (IRE) *C A McBratney* 93h 121c
7 b g Golden Tornado(IRE) —Elbonne (IRE) (Supreme Leader)
5341^{6}

Carsonstown Rock (IRE) *C A McBratney* 48b
4 b g Rock Of Gibraltar(IRE) —Magical Cliche (USA) (Affirmed (USA))
5342^{14}

Carters Rest *Chris Grant* 101h 99c
8 gr g Rock City—Yemaail (IRE) (Shaadi (USA))
2508^{14}
3520^{7} 3854^{5} 4237^{7} 5145^{U} 5294^{4}

Carthalawn (IRE) *Gordon Elliott* 136h 153c
10 ch g Foxhound(USA) —Pohutakawa (FR) (Affirmed (USA))
2262a^{3} 2972a^{4}

Carys's Lad *Michael Mullineaux* 68h
8 b g Exit To Nowhere(USA) —Dawn Spinner (Arctic Lord)
1822^{12} 2314^{8} 3258^{5} 3622^{F} 3728^{8} 4949^{3} 5393^{5}

Casadei (IRE) *T G McCourt* 103h 107c
12 ch g Great Commotion(USA) —Inishmot (IRE) (Glenstal (USA))
1697^{2} 1871^{4}

Casey Top (IRE) *Leonard Whitmore* 134h
8 b g Topanoora—Royal Ruler (IRE) (Strong Gale)
1526a^{2} 3474a^{19}

Cashallgone (IRE) *Seamus Mullins* 95b
4 b g Dushyantor(USA) —Ring Ouzel (Deep Run)
5388^{4}

Cash Back *Anthony Honeyball* 94h
11 b g Bob's Return(IRE) —Connie's Pet (National Trust)
(410) 826^{4} 3300^{5}

Cash Crisis (IRE) *Mike Hammond*
6 ch m Ridgewood Ben—Miscall (IRE) (Commanche Run)
583^{P}

Cashel Blue (USA) *Patrick Rodford* 110h 114c
9 b g Aljabr(USA) —Al Saqiya (USA) (Woodman (USA))
1347^{9} (1490)
1908^{2} 4219^{2} 4537^{B} 5067^{3}

Cash In Hand (IRE) *R Harvey* 94c
11 b g Charente River(IRE) —Fern Fields (IRE) (Be My Native (USA))
79^{4} 335^{P} 4143^{P} 4415^{7} 4750^{6} 4973^{P}

Cash Man (IRE) *Evelyn Slack* 113h 117c
10 b g Flemensfirth(USA) —Bollero (IRE) (Topanoora)
(89) **213^{2}**
581^{3}

Cash 'n Carrots *Richard Harper* 21h 32c
12 b g Missed Flight—Rhiannon (Welsh Pageant)
5375^{4}

Cash On Friday *P Monteith* 84h 99c
10 b g Bishop Of Cashel—Til Friday (Scottish Reel)
160^{6} 626^{4}

Cashwell *David Evans* 43b
4 b g Saddlers' Hall(IRE) —Cashmere Lady (Hubbly Bubbly (USA))
4780^{13}

Caspar Of Tarsus (IRE) *Gerald Ham* 98h 93c
8 ch g Moonax(IRE) —Another Thurn (IRE) (Trimmingham)
2513 2557^{P} 3961^{P} 5216^{2}

Casper's Shadow (IRE) *Keith Goldsworthy* 55h
5 gr g Great Palm(USA) —Kambaya (IRE) (Kambalda)
1374^{6} 1680^{5} 1922^{6} 2634^{10}

Cass Bligh (IRE) *Adrian Murray* 139h
7 b g Witness Box(USA) —Fleur De Tal (Primitive Rising (USA))
1310^{2} 5166^{12}

Cassius (IRE) *Bruce Mactaggart* 122h
9 b g Pistolet Bleu(IRE) —L'Enfant Unique (IRE) (Phardante (FR))
44^{5} 196^{9} 2035^{11} 2551^{6} 4169^{7} 5144^{6} 5315^{9}

Cast Cada (IRE) *Charlie Mann* 130h 127c
8 b g Exit To Nowhere(USA) —Inch Rose (IRE) (Eurobus)
281^{2} (476)

Castelli (IRE) *Howard Johnson* 23h
5 b g Galileo(IRE) —Manger Square (IRE) (Danehill (USA))
307^{3}

Cast Iron Casey (IRE) *Howard Johnson* 115h 129c
9 ch g Carroll House—Ashie's Friend (IRE) (Over The River (FR))
1695^{4}
1871^{3} 2204^{2} 3522^{P} 4277^{5}

Castlebury (IRE) *Ruth Carr* 78h
6 b g Spartacus(IRE) —La Vie En Rouge (IRE) (College Chapel)
5309^{6}

Castle Conflict (IRE) *Henry Daly* 103b
6 b g Close Conflict(USA) —Renty (IRE) (Carlingford Castle)
5084^{2}

Castle Craigs (IRE) *Tim Vaughan* 74h 58c
9 b g Bob's Return(IRE) —Graigue Glen (Glen Quaich)
1294^{8} 1468^{5} ◆ 1592^{9}

Castle Legend *Simon Lewis* 1b
6 ch g Midnight Legend—Morstoncastle Rose (Carlingford Castle)
60^{9} 2389^{14} 3372^{10}

Castlemaine Vic (IRE) *Adrian Wintle* 98h
8 b g Old Vic—Dusky Walk (IRE) (Conquering Hero (USA))
3530^{P} 4522^{P}

Castle Myth (USA) *Jim Best* 64h
5 bb g Johannesburg(USA) —Castlemania (CAN) (Bold Ruckus (USA))
470^{6} 607^{9} 4397^{12} 5267^{7}

Castlerock *Jonjo O'Neill* 109h
7 gr g Kayf Tara—Jessolle (Scallywag)
1988[5] ◆ 3299[12]

Castlerock Rose (IRE) *D Rohan* 59h 100c
7 b m Presenting—Belgrove Girl (IRE) (Supreme Leader)
4755a[6]

Castletown Cross (IRE) *R Hirons* 96h 97c
10 b m City Honours(USA) —Fleetfoot (IRE) (Bravefoot)
4748[U]

Castletown Lass (IRE) *J M Kiernan* 89h
6 gr m Luso—Cullenstown Lady (IRE) (Wood Chanter)
1146a[U]

Cast Of Stars (IRE) *Evan Williams* 72h
4 b g Nayef(USA) —Scarpe Rosse (IRE) (Sadler's Wells (USA))
4810[10] 5235[5]

Casual Garcia *Mark Gillard* 106h 92c
6 gr g Hernando(FR) —Frosty Welcome (USA) (With Approval (CAN))
374[4] 467[2] 1230[8] 1918[6] 2284[4] 4272[9] **4898[4] 5324[P]**

Casual Style *David Pipe* 91h
5 ch m Bahamian Bounty—Artistry (Night Shift (USA))
185[4] 358[2] 462[7] 661[6]

Catawollow *Richard Guest* 9h
4 b f Beat Hollow—Catalonia (IRE) (Catrail (USA))
2068[P] 2245[9] 2369[U]

Catch Bob (IRE) *Ferdy Murphy* 115h 123c
7 ch g Bob Back(USA) —Catch The Breeze (IRE) (Denel (FR))
2037[F] 2299[2] 3852[3] 4507[3] (4996)

Catcherinscratcher (IRE) *Henry De Bromhead* 108h
6 b m Catcher In The Rye(IRE) —Maiden Over (IRE) (Bowling Pin)
3592a[7]

Catch Me (GER) *E J O'Grady* 146h 147c
9 b g Law Society(USA) —Calcida (GER) (Konigsstuhl (GER))
2096a[3] 2359[10] 3206a[5]

Catch The Perk (IRE) *Lucinda Russell* 107h 123c
14 b g Executive Perk—Kilbally Quilty (IRE) (Montelimar (USA))
308[P] 446[6] 946[7] **1577[4] 2036[4]**

Catch The Rascal (IRE) *Seamus Mullins* 84h
5 b m Presenting—Eneeymeenymineeymo (IRE) (Pistolet Bleu (IRE))
589[7] 1994[6] 2554[6] 2974[F] 3338[3]

Categorical *Keith Reveley* 106h 131c
8 b g Diktat—Zibet (Kris)
2163[3] 2544[3] 4357[2] (4546) 5199[2] 5422[5]

Cathedral Rock (IRE) *Ms A E Embiricos* 69h 126c
9 b g New Frontier(IRE) —Cathadubh (IRE) (Naheez (USA))
2209[14] 3744[P]

Catholic Hill (USA) *Mark Gillard* 88h 92c
6 rg g Pleasant Tap(USA) —Celestial Bliss (USA) (Relaunch (USA))
1158[7] 1450[4] 1489[3] 2149[3] 2583[5] 3611[6] **3932[5] 4133[4] 4264[2] 4447[3] 5036[4] 5093[2]**

Catleen (IRE) *S R B Crawford* 107h 102c
7 b m Craigsteel—The Plud (IRE) (Lord Americo)
285[5] 442[6] 577[5] 1782[10] 2353[3] 4914[5] 5319[2]

Cats In The Cradle *Miss V Collins* 86b
8 b g Shahrastani(USA) —Shirl (Shirley Heights)
5283[P]

Cat Six (USA) *Tom Gretton* 120h
7 b m Tale Of The Cat(USA) —Hurricane Warning (USA) (Thunder Gulch (USA))
2514[9]

Catspan (FR) *Charles Egerton* 108h
5 gr g Turgeon(USA) —Royale Pour Moi (FR) (Cadoudal (FR))
(1955) 2296[5] 2944[6] 3366[12]

Caught By Witness (IRE) *Milton Harris* 122h
6 b g Witness Box(USA) —Donegans Daughter (Auction Ring (USA))
168[2] 1857[3] 2246[5] 2361[7] *3060[4]* 3306[2] 3440[10] (3833) 4180[7] 5201[15]

Cauldron *Tim Easterby* 61h
4 b g Bollin Eric—Witch's Brew (Simply Great (FR))
4117[11] 5309[10]

Caulkin (IRE) *David Kemp* 111h 99c
8 b g King's Theatre(IRE) —Alice Brennan (IRE) (Good Thyne (USA))
288[7] **4857[P] 5083[4]**

Caunay *Neil Mulholland* 74h
4 ch g Generous(IRE) —Chantilly Lady (Rising)
3794[6] 4677[U] 5035[F] 5243[6]

Cause For Applause (IRE) *Ray Craggs* 75h
5 b m Royal Applause—Polyandry (IRE) (Pennekamp (USA))
5309[5]

Causeway King (USA) *Alan King* 125h 77c
5 ch g Giant's Causeway(USA) —A P Petal (USA) (A.P. Indy (USA))
2792[2] 3229[9] 3874[9] 4354[P] **5116[4]**

Causing Chaos (IRE) *Nigel Twiston-Davies* 107h
5 b g Alderbrook—Sue's Song (Alflora (IRE))
1734[2] 2238[4] 2983[P]

Cave Of The Giant (IRE) *Tim McCarthy* 78h 117c
9 b g Giant's Causeway(USA) —Maroussie (FR) (Saumarez)
64[5] 692[5] 1094[P] 1232[10] 1294[7]

Cavers Glen *Alistair Whillans* 99h 123c
9 b g Overbury(IRE) —Thorterdykes Lass (IRE) (Zaffaran (USA))
1761[5] (2544) (3634)

Cavite Beta (IRE) *Nicky Henderson* 121h
5 ch g Old Vic—Kinnegads Pride (IRE) (Be My Native (USA))
1966[6] (2325) 3787[5]

Cavite Eta (IRE) *Mark Bradstock* 86b
4 br g Spadoun(FR) —Samarinnda (IRE) (Akarad (FR))
5063[7] 5217[4]

Cawthorne *Michael Easterby* 38b
5 b g Mark Of Esteem(IRE) —Oh Whataknight (Primo Dominie)
1764[13]

Cayo *Robert Johnson* 14h
4 ch g Danroad(AUS) —Caysue (Cayman Kai (IRE))
4242[P] 5357[7]

Ceannline (IRE) *Venetia Williams* 50h
5 b m Lil's Boy(USA) —Scarpetta (USA) (Seattle Dancer (USA))
3604[7]

Ceasar's Return *George Moore* 109h
6 b g Kayf Tara—Supreme Lass (IRE) (Supreme Leader)
1643[6] 1829[6] 2446[2] 2939[10] 3633[F] 3996[P] 4276[RR]

Cebonne (FR) *Sophie Leech* 115c
10 b g Pistolet Bleu(IRE) —Northine (FR) (Northern Treat (USA))
1309[2] 1725[4] 2036[P]

Cedar Falls (USA) *Gary Brown* 35h
6 b g Giant's Causeway(USA) —J. D. Flowers (USA) (Dixieland Band (USA))
490[U] 632[P]

Cedre Bleu (FR) *Paul Nicholls* 123h
4 b g Le Fou(IRE) —Arvoire (IRE) (Exit To Nowhere (USA))
(3624) ◆ 4092[2]

Cedrus Libani (IRE) *Mrs A Rucker* 136h 136c
10 b g Beneficial—Cedar Castle (IRE) (Castle Keep)
5083[P]

Ceepeegee (IRE) *Colin Tizzard* 110h
6 b g Karinga Bay—That's Holly (Alflora (IRE))
1853[6] 2482[12] 3299[3] 3688[17] **4023[P]**

Ceilidh Royal *Nicky Henderson* 81b
5 b m Erhaab(USA) —Close Harmony (Bustino)
1955[4]

Celestial Dragon (IRE) *James Richardson* 86c
10 b g Taipan(IRE) —Ann's Cap (IRE) (Cardinal Flower)
466[7] 4969[5] 5277[5]

Celestial Halo (IRE) *Paul Nicholls* 167h 131c
7 b g Galileo(IRE) —Pay The Bank (High Top)
1909[F] 2664[3] 2884[3] 3289[3] 4222[2] (4373) 5198[8]

Celian (FR) *Neil King* 108h 110c
8 b g Indian River(FR) —Celinda (FR) (Bering)
2949[P] (3258) 3369[4] 3996[R] **4313[P] 4669[4] 5192[P]**

Celtic Ballad (IRE) *Colin Tizzard* 86h
5 br g Celtic Swing—Birdsong (IRE) (Dolphin Street (FR))
1737[P] 2185[7] 3343[3] 3839[5] **4269[F]** 4675[11] 4920[2]

Celtic Boy (IRE) *Miss R Dando* 125h 129c
13 b g Arctic Lord—Laugh Away (Furry Glen)
4163[P]

Celtic Dragon *David Evans* 108h
6 b g Fantastic Light(USA) —Zanzibar (IRE) (In The Wings)
1466[5]

Celticello (IRE) *Jamie Snowden* 122h 113c
9 bb g Celtic Swing—Viola Royale (IRE) (Royal Academy (USA))
96[4] 803[2] 958[3] 1084[2] (1254) 1609[4] 1692[3] **2588[F]** (3303) 3808[8] 4235[7] 4854[2] 5291[10]

Celtic Intrigue (IRE) *Tom George* 81h
4 b g Celtic Swing—Macca Luna (IRE) (Kahyasi)
1442[6] 2306[7] 2466[8]

Celtic Mystique *Christopher Wilson*
4 b f Beckett(IRE) —Kungfu Kerry (Celtic Swing)
5033[11]

Celtic Star (IRE) *Miss J Wickens* 52h 17c
13 b g Celtic Swing—Recherchee (Rainbow Quest (USA))
297[P] 4991[0]

Celtic Warrior (IRE) *John Harris* 76h 110c
8 b g Celtic Swing—Notable Dear (ITY) (Last Tycoon)
598[5]

Celts Espere *Chris Bealby* 68h
8 ch g Samraan(USA) —Celtic Dream (Celtic Cone)
337[6] 538[9] 3622[3]

Celtus (FR) *Nicky Henderson* 124h
4 b g Keltos(FR) —Infiltrate (IRE) (Bering)
4353[3] 4807[P]

Cengiz (IRE) *Aytach Sadik* 93h 93c
9 b g Taipan(IRE) —Gypsy Kelly (IRE) (Roselier (FR))
4831 5273[3]

Ceol Rua (IRE) *W P Mullins* 121b
6 ch m Bob Back(USA) —Glens Music (IRE) (Orchestra)
5188[2]

Cerium (FR) *Paul Murphy* 137h 127c
10 b g Vaguely Pleasant(FR) —Tantatura (FR) (Akarad (FR))
33[P]

Cesium (FR) *Tom George* 85h 118c
6 b g Green Tune(USA) —Tantatura (FR) (Akarad (FR))
3371[7] 3695[P] 4022[10] 4694[P]

C'Est Ca *W P Mullins* 139h 128c
7 b g Groom Dancer(USA) —Known Class (USA) (Known Fact (USA))
3210a[2]

Chablais (FR) *Nicky Henderson* 136h
6 b g Saint Des Saints(FR) —Malandra (Mtoto)
(3556)

Chadwell Spring (IRE) *Mike Sowersby* 82h
5 b m Statue Of Liberty(USA) —Cresalin (Coquelin (USA))
1325[5] 1466[7] 1613[9] 2114[9] 2398[5] 3989[10] 4274[3] 4548[4] 4976[5] 5298[8]

Chaim (IRE) *Lucy Wadham* 122h 71c
9 bb g Lord Americo—Furry Gran (Furry Glen)
2171[P] 3744[12] **4022[9]**

Chain Of Command (IRE) *Warren Greatrex* 115h 124c
8 bb g Sonus(IRE) —Come Along (IRE) (King's Ride)
(1883) 2233[2] *(3056)* **3555[P] 3905[3]**

Chain Of Events *Neil King* 53h
4 ch g Nayef(USA) —Ermine (IRE) (Cadeaux Genereux)
1610[11]

Chalice Welcome *Neil King* 97h 56c
8 b g Most Welcome—Blue Peru (IRE) (Perugino (USA))
439[U] 1976[7] 2114[3] 2314[11] 2438[4]

Chamacco (FR) *Sophie Leech* 32h 76c
11 b g Cadoudal(FR) —Awentina (FR) (Caerwent)
4413[6] 5216[P]

Chamirey (FR) *Donald McCain* 138h 128c
8 b g Cadoudal(FR) —Guigone (FR) (Esprit Du Nord (USA))
2599[3] ◆ (3702) 4114[U] (4362) 4802[11] 5146[3]

Champagne Mary *Raymond York* 33b
4 b f Erhaab(USA) —Nearly A Bay (Nearly A Hand)
2052[9]

Champagne Rosie *Bob Buckler* 91b
5 b m Shambo—Sharp Dance (Dance Of Life (USA))
3301[5] 3909[12] 4709[4] 5158[5]

Champion Court (IRE) *Martin Keighley* 139h
6 b g Court Cave(IRE) —Mooneys Hill (IRE) (Supreme Leader)
1824[2] (2388) ◆ 3806[9] 4849[4] ◆

Champs De Bleu (FR) *Gary Moore* 92h
8 b g Shambo—Flashing Silks (Kind Of Hush)
2667[11] *3055[11]* 3196[10] 3789[9] 4130[4] 4403[2] 4833[6] (5265)

Champtho (FR) *Oliver Sherwood* 100h 107c
6 bb g Lesotho(USA) —Champagnepourlolo (FR) (Pistolet Bleu (IRE))
353[4]

Chance Du Roy (FR) *Philip Hobbs* 121h 144c
7 ch g Morespeed—La Chance Au Roy (FR) (Rex Magna (FR))
2347[7] **2948[3] (3438) 4077[3] 4487[P]**

Chance Encounter (IRE) *Linda Blackford* 117h
5 br g Anshan—Glittering Grit (IRE) (Sheer Grit)
4709[2] 5217[2]

Changing Course (IRE) *Henry De Bromhead* 73h 125c
9 b g Luso—Triswell (IRE) (Rashar (USA))
2346[8] 3844a[5]

Changing Lanes *John Flint* 118h 120c
8 b g Overbury(IRE) —Snowdon Lily (Town And Country)
(1094) 1198[2] 1346[6] **1550[P]**

Chaninbar (FR) *Milton Harris* 127h 155c
8 b g Milford Track(IRE) —Logicia (FR) (Homme De Loi (IRE))
1861[2] 2138[P] 2385[7] 2515[4] 4853[RR] 5164[RR] 5184[RR] 5442[2]

Chant De Lune (FR) *M Rolland*
9 gr g Cadoudal(FR) —Tikidoun (FR) (Kaldoun (FR))
5159a[0]

Chapel Flowers (IRE) *Miss Sally Duckett* 102h 114c
9 b g Pistolet Bleu(IRE) —Stormweather Girl (IRE) (Strong Gale)
5347[3]

Chaperoned (IRE) *Mrs John Harrington* 123h
4 b f High Chaparral(IRE) —La Stravaganza (USA) (Rainbow Quest (USA))
4083a[4] ◆ 4295a[2]

Chapmans Peak (IRE) *C T Dawson* 91h 62c
8 b g Beneficial—Archetype (Over The River (FR))
310[2]

Chapolimoss (FR) *Martin Todhunter* 98h 95c
7 ch g Trempolino(USA) —Chamoss (FR) (Tip Moss (FR))
180[5] 1758[2] ◆ 2545[5] **4394[F] 4796[4]**

Chapoturgeon (FR) *Paul Nicholls* 125h 163c
7 gr g Turgeon(USA) —Chapohio (FR) (Script Ohio (USA))
2976[3] 3804[7]

Chapter (IRE) *Simon Sherwood* 90h
9 ch g Sinndar(IRE) —Web Of Intrigue (Machiavellian (USA))
2322[8]

Chapter Five *Keith Reveley* 90b
4 b f Grape Tree Road—Northern Shadows (Rock Hopper)
(4547)

Character Building (IRE) *John Quinn* 129h 143c
11 gr g Accordion—Mrs Jones (IRE) (Roselier (FR))
1960[3] 2358[12] 3290[5] 3940[6] 4466[3] 5200[15]

Charingworth (IRE) *Ferdy Murphy* 115h 131c
8 b g Supreme Leader—Quinnsboro Guest (IRE) (Be My Guest (USA))
194[6] ◆ 1956[4] *3168[9]* 3306[P] **3953[U]** (5030) 5335[6]

Charles *Kim Bailey* 93h
5 b g Loup Sauvage(USA) —Broom Isle (Damister (USA))
1799[2] 3196[12] 3398[10] 3906[8] (5114) 5172[P]

Charles Street *Mrs T Porter* 113h 102c
9 gr g Cois Na Tine(IRE) —Yemaail (IRE) (Shaadi (USA))
173[5]

Charlie Bucket *Donald Whillans* 106h
8 ch g Sugarfoot—Stoproveritate (Scorpio (FR))
318[6] 2549[2] 3502[6] 4067[2] 4869[3] 5316[P]

Charlie's Boy *Tobias B P Coles*
5 gr g Mutamarkiz(IRE) —Lavender Della (IRE) (Shernazar)
2646[7] *3054[11]*

Charlie Wingnut (IRE) *Nicky Henderson* 92b
4 br g Westerner—Back To Stay (IRE) (Supreme Leader)
5209[2]

Charlie Yardbird (IRE) *Tim Vaughan* 61h 125c
10 ch g Accordion—Reine Berengere (FR) (Esprit Du Nord (USA))
80[8] 479[P]

Charlotte's Ball (IRE) *Raymond York* 84b
5 b m Presenting—Thats The Girl (IRE) (Old Vic)
2186[4] 2987[9] 3616[8]

Charlotte Street (IRE) *Warren Greatrex* 78h
9 b g Sassanian(USA) —Street Peddler (Boreen (FR))
134[P]

Charmeur (USA) *Philip Hobbs* 59h
4 b c War Chant(USA) —Arme Ancienne (Sillery (USA))
1135[7] 1330[7] 1473[U] 1586[9]

Charming Knight (IRE) *Jane Walton* 91h 91c
10 b g Mohaajir(USA) —Arctic Laura (Le Bavard (FR))
91[4] 1341[P] 1423[4] 1701[P] 3883[2] 4687[2] 5094[5] **5258[2]**

Charming Lad (IRE) *Charlie Mann* 115h
6 b g Dushyantor(USA) —Glens Lady (IRE) (Mister Lord (USA))
2051[4] 3346[2] 3761[4] 4182[2] 4481[4]

Charming Oscar (IRE) *Bob Buckler* 31h 93c
9 b g Oscar Schindler(IRE) —Lady Of The West (IRE) (Mister Lord (USA))
1912[10] 2243[6]

Charminster (IRE) *Donald McCain* 126h
5 b g Broadway Flyer(USA) —Monteleena (IRE) (Montelimar (USA))
1989[2] (2525) 3365[2] ◆ (3725) ◆

Charmouth Girl *John Mackie* 49b
5 b m Makbul—Impish Jude (Imp Society (USA))
333[11] 5119[10]

Chartplan (IRE) *Roger Teal* 72b
5 ch g Marignan(USA) —Classic Moments (IRE) (Classic Memory)
5056[6] 5387[8]

Chartreux (FR) *David Pipe* 136h
6 ro g Colonel Collins(USA) —Ruaha River (FR) (Villez (USA))
3293[3] ◆ 4817[13]

Chase Gate *James Frost* 95h 95c
6 ch g Arkadian Hero(USA) —Carlingford Lass (IRE) (Carlingford Castle)
1736[9] 2137[P] 2594[3] 3495[4] 3985[4] **5371[3]**

Chaser's War (IRE) *Nikki Evans* 44h
7 b m Needle Gun(IRE) —Whisky Chaser (Never So Bold)
929[5] 1275[9] 2069[6] 2469[P]

Chasing Aces *Gary Brown* 63h
5 ch g Definite Article—Daprika (FR) (Epervier Bleu)
(2328) 5225[8]

Chasing Cars (IRE) *Mrs John Harrington* 144h 136c
9 b g Supreme Leader—Great Outlook (IRE) (Simply Great (FR))
4227a[6] 5185[9]

Cheapside (IRE) *D C Gannon* 64h 3c
6 b g Beckett(IRE) —Annahala (IRE) (Ridgewood Ben)
4696[6] 5083[P]

Cheatingsideoftown (IRE) *Sue Bradburne* 95h
5 b g Flemensfirth(USA) —My Baloo (On Your Mark)
(1153) 3851[11] 4059[5]

Checkerboard (IRE) *Howard Johnson* 109h 108c
8 b g Alderbrook—Jamie's Lady (Ashmore (FR))
4730[6] 5353[P] 5416[5]

Checklow (USA) *Howard Johnson* 92h
6 b g Street Cry(IRE) —Comstock Queen (USA) (Silver Hawk (USA))
3331[8]

Cheeky Boy *Steve Gollings* 62b
4 b g Barathea(IRE) —Darayna (IRE) (Shernazar)
2315[12] 2458[5]

Cheeky Lad *T M Stephenson* 70h 126c
11 b g Bering—Cheeky Charm (USA) (Nureyev (USA))
6[P]

Cheekyrun (IRE) *Paul Henderson* 36h
8 b g Runyon(IRE) —Lady On The Hill (IRE) (Commanche Run)
1030[7] 1196[U]

Chef De Cour (FR) *J P Owen* 126h 83c
10 b g Pistolet Bleu(IRE) —Cour De Rome (FR) (Cadoudal (FR))
4857[5]

Cheltenian (FR) *Philip Hobbs* 138b
5 b g Astarabad(USA) —Salamaite (FR) (Mansonnien (FR))
(4055) (4808) ◆

Cheney Manor *Nicky Henderson* 113h
6 b g Piccolo—One For Philip (Blushing Flame (USA))
3405[3] 5010[5] 5225[9]

Chernik (IRE) *Micky Hammond* 106h 117c
10 b g Norwich—Sue Pickering (IRE) (Tremblant)
608[3] 804[U] 1326[4] 1612[P]

Cherokee Star *Mike Hammond* 103h 102c
6 br g Primo Valentino(IRE) —Me Cherokee (Persian Bold)
761[6] 854[4] 957[S] 1034[3]

Cherokee Story *Chris Bealby* 88h
5 bl m Lucky Story(USA) —Me Cherokee (Persian Bold)
1689[P] 1994[4] 2526[7] 3397[P] 4178[P]

Cherry Cake *Philip Kirby*
7 ch m Executive Perk—Cherry Sip (Nearly A Hand)
4795[P] 5092[P]

Cherryland *Philip Kirby* 98c
8 b g Turtle Island(IRE) —Cherry Lane (Buckley)
90[8] 1654[4] 473[P]

Cherry On Top *Anthony Honeyball*
5 ch m Alflora(IRE) —Triggered (Gunner B)
3979[9]
Cherry Star (FR) *Noel Chance* 85b
7 gr g Marathon(USA) —Sharing (FR) (Kashmir Ring)
53[7]
Chervonet (IRE) *Nick Gifford* 80h
5 ch g Moscow Society(USA) —Cashla (IRE) (Duky)
2440[3] 2960[16] 3599[4] 4052[P]
Chesapeake (IRE) *Jonjo O'Neill* 120h
7 b g Sadler's Wells(USA) —Khoruna (GER) (Lagunas)
538[2] 763[2] (863) 1065[2]
Cheshire Prince *Neil King* 127h
7 br g Desert Prince(IRE) —Bundle Up (USA) (Miner's Mark (USA))
316[P] 1956[6] (2213) 4727[P]
Chesil Beach Boy *John Coombe* 11h
8 b g Commanche Run—Eatons (Daring March)
5108[11]
Chesnut Annie (IRE) *Miss H E Roberts* 77h 130c
10 ch m Weld—Leaden Sky (IRE) (Roselier (FR))
4449[2]
Chester Lad *George Charlton* 124h
6 ch g Fraam—Our Krissie (Kris)
1855[9] 2523[16] 3334[5] 3575[4] 3954[2] 4715[6] 5149[14]
Chester Ridge *William Amos* 34c
7 b g Alflora(IRE) —Scarlet Ember (Nearly A Hand)
2350[3]
Chestnut Ben (IRE) *Gary Brown* 78h 57c
6 ch g Ridgewood Ben—Betseale (IRE) (Step Together (USA))
(1489) 1647[P] 3611[2] 4675[8]
4919[4]
Chestnut Lilly *Pam Ford*
8 ch m Alflora(IRE) —Be In Space (Gunner B)
763[P] 4719[14] 5078[P]
Chevy To The Levy (IRE) *John O'Shea* 121h 114c
9 b g Saddlers' Hall(IRE) —Be The One (IRE) (Supreme Leader)
647[3] 951[2] 1034[P] (1452)
1794[5] 2146[P] 5344[3]
Chiaro (FR) *Philip Hobbs* 112h 118c
9 b g Hamas(IRE) —Link Diamond (FR) (Diamond Prospect (USA))
300[4]
Chicago Alley *Tony Carroll* 46h 112c
10 br m Bob Back(USA) —Winnetka Gal (IRE) (Phardante (FR))
77[2] (353)
(676) 5072[P]
Chicago Grey (IRE) *Gordon Elliott* 149h 155c
8 gr g Luso—Carrigeen Acer (IRE) (Lord Americo)
873[3] (1863)
2357[F] ◆ **2883[2] 3174a[5] (4802)**
5338[8]
Chicago Outfit (IRE) *John Wade* 108h 75c
6 b g Old Vic—Lambourne Lace (IRE) (Un Desperado (FR))
4911[P] 5134[6]
Chichina (USA) *Tracy Waggott* 51h
4 b f Afleet Alex(USA) —St Aye (USA) (Nureyev (USA))
3637[6] 3994[10] 4132[10]
Chickini (IRE) *Simon Waugh* 94b
6 b m Rossini(USA) —Fast Chick (Henbit (USA))
5313[8]
Chicklemix *Pam Sly* 97h
5 gr m Fair Mix(IRE) —Chichell's Hurst (Oats)
2370[3] 3599[3] 4330[3] 4501[4]
Chico Time (IRE) *Norma Twomey* 103h 102c
10 b m Presenting—Hilldalus (IRE) (Mandalus)
1027[P] 1094[9] 1336[2] **(2155)**
(2402) 3260[6] 3483[7] **3646[F] 3768[9]**
Chief Bucaneer (IRE) *George Charlton* 115h
8 b g Lord Americo—Fiery Buck (IRE) (Buckskin (FR))
(14) 214[P] 3715[5] 4115[14] 5320[12]
Chief Dan George (IRE) *James Moffatt* 114h 153c
11 b g Lord Americo—Colleen Donn (Le Moss)
2524[7] 4207[5]
4474[3] 4790[F] 5200[17]
Chief Lady Olwyn *Lynn Siddall* 48h 43c
12 ch m Alderbrook—Chief Lady Nicola (Nicholas Bill)
4101[P]
Chief Yeoman *Venetia Williams* 134h 124c
11 br g Machiavellian(USA) —Step Aloft (Shirley Heights)
94[11] 1967[6] **3438[5]** 3561[10]
3948[5]
Chigorin *James Sheppard* 63h 84c
10 b g Pivotal—Belle Vue (Petong)
4771[4] 5057[9]
Chilbury Hill (IRE) *Kevin Bishop* 98h 99c
8 b g Bahhare(USA) —Fire Goddess (Magic Ring (IRE))
183[2] 634[3] 848[P] 1841[6] 2243[P] 3481[8] 3686[6]
3840[2] 4272[6]
Chilla Cilla *Anthony Honeyball* 82h 85c
8 ch m Glacial Storm(USA) —Priscilla (Teenoso (USA))
2144[13]
2334[F] 2468[5] 3226[2] 3720[F] 3873[3] 4784[U]
Chilli Rose *Alan King* 122h
6 gr m Classic Cliche(IRE) —Solo Rose (Roselier (FR))
3227[9] 4025[2] 4703[2] 5302[6]
China Gold *Alan King* 117h
8 br g Bob's Return(IRE) —Oh So Bright (Celtic Cone)
3509[2] 4327[2] 5118[2]
China House (IRE) *Lisa Williamson* 73h
8 ch g Flemensfirth(USA) —Chancy Gal (Al Sirat)
3171[9] 3952[9] 4278[5] 4684[4] 5172[7]
China Rock (IRE) *M F Morris* 150h 160c
8 ch g Presenting—Kigali (IRE) (Torus)
(1684a)
(1850a) 2226a[3] 4087a[4] 4850[P]

China Sky (IRE) *Nicky Henderson* 80h
6 b m Definite Article—Katday (FR) (Miller's Mate)
333[8] 3480[4] 3904[P]
Chip N Pin *Tim Easterby* 96h
7 b m Erhaab(USA) —Vallauris (Faustus (USA))
50[2] 179[4]
Chit Chat *Jonjo O'Neill* 83h
6 b m Bob Back(USA) —Consuelo (Supreme Leader)
59[P] 3258[6]
Chocolat (IRE) *Susan Nock* 90h
6 b m King's Theatre(IRE) —Lisa Du Chenet (FR) (Garde Royale)
340[P] 796[6] 933[7] 4399[4] 4769[F]
Chocolate Caramel (USA) *Richard Fahey* 103h
9 b g Storm Creek(USA) —Sandhill (BRZ) (Baynoun)
2657[2] 2939[8] 3547[6]
Choctaw Nation *Malcolm Jefferson* 99h
7 b g Sadler's Wells(USA) —Space Quest (Rainbow Quest (USA))
3973 (713) 888[4] 1147[3] 1614[8] 1762[9]
Chookie Hamilton *Keith Dalgleish* 90h
7 ch g Compton Place—Lady Of Windsor (IRE) (Woods Of Windsor (USA))
4711[4]
Chord *Simon Earle* 93h 98c
7 ch g Pivotal—Choirgirl (Unfuwain (USA))
1095[11] 1735[P] **(1901)**
4413[4] 4945[P]
Chorizo (IRE) *Richard Guest* 93h 121c
10 b g Kahyasi—Bayariyka (IRE) (Slip Anchor)
229[8] 352[5] (716)
839[2] 890[2] 1103[4] 1570[7] 1932[P]
Choumakeur (FR) *David Pipe* 92h 120c
9 ch g Mansonnien(FR) —Feuille De Chou (FR) (Faucon Noir (FR))
3764[4]
(4705) 5037[3] 5154[P]
Chouromanesco (FR) *Mark Bradstock* 83h
8 ch g Maresca Sorrento(FR) —Fleur De Chou (FR) (Faucon Noir (FR))
249[0] 538[6] 863[7] 3432[3] 3717[6] 4403[3] 4540[7]
5265[5]
Chriseti (FR) *E Leenders* 120h
11 gr g April Night(FR) —L'Allier (FR) (Rose Laurel)
312a[F]
Christy Ring (IRE) *John Berry* 96b
6 b g Cape Cross(IRE) —Chater (Alhaarth (IRE))
362[5]
Chrysander *Evan Williams* 117h 106c
9 b g Cadeaux Genereux—Jumairah Sun (IRE) (Scenic)
1429[3]
2324[P] (3477) (4028) 4291[P] (4999) (5232) **5394[5]**
Chuckery (IRE) *Tim Vaughan* 91b
5 b g Snurge—Fair Conquest (IRE) (Be My Native (USA))
5408[2]
Churchfield Champ (IRE) *Laura Young* 76b
5 b g Norwich—Ash Dame (IRE) (Strong Gale)
5387[7]
Church Island (IRE) *Michael Hourigan* 87h 156c
12 ch g Erins Isle—Just Possible (Kalaglow)
5443[P]
Church Outing *Susan Gardner* 45h
7 ch m Minster Son—House Deed (Presidium)
1344[P] 1553[P]
Ciannte (IRE) *S R B Crawford* 87b
6 b m Definite Article—Barnish River (IRE) (Riverhead (USA))
731[3] (949)
Ciceron (IRE) *Venetia Williams* 134h
5 b g Pivotal—Aiglonne (USA) (Silver Hawk (USA))
2071[7] 2085[10] 2671[5] 2792[4] (3649) (4270) 4848[F]
5201[17]
Cider Lolly *Colin Tizzard* 71b
5 ch m Loup Sauvage(USA) —Lady Turk (FR) (Baby Turk)
3266[10]
Cigalas *Jean McGregor* 59h
6 ch g Selkirk(USA) —Langoustine (AUS) (Danehill (USA))
2349[P] 4165[11] 4303[8]
Cilrhiwviv *Sue Wilson* 88h 70c
8 ch g Lahib(USA) —Trefelyn Snowdrop (Buckley)
1600[5] 1730[7] **1939[P] 2250[5]**
Cils Blancs (IRE) *Michael Scudamore* 8h
5 b m Barathea(IRE) —Immortelle (Arazi (USA))
2960[19] 4129[P]
Cinaman (IRE) *Tim Vaughan* 76h 84c
7 b g Key Of Luck(USA) —Madame Nureyev (USA) (Nureyev (USA))
211[5] 987[2] 1100[5] 1331[P] 1446[6]
Cinderella Rose *Kim Bailey* 117h
5 ch m Midnight Legend—Miniature Rose (Anshan)
(1734) 1994[3] (2514)
Cinders And Ashes *Donald McCain* 114b
4 b g Beat Hollow—Moon Search (Rainbow Quest (USA))
(2052) *(2824)* 3294[2] 4808[5] ◆ 5202[10]
Cinnamon Hill *Nick Ayliffe* 39h
7 ch m Compton Place—Cajole (IRE) (Barathea (IRE))
4528[8] 4899[10]
Circus Clown (IRE) *Jim Goldie* 114h
6 b g Vettori(IRE) —Comic (IRE) (Be My Chief (USA))
(4068) (4166) 4715[2] 5315[16]
Circus Of Dreams *Oliver Sherwood* 120h 128c
8 b g Kayf Tara—Foehn Gale (IRE) (Strong Gale)
(155) **1952[5]**
2293[3] 2674[8] 3689[6] 4181[3] 4726[4]
Citrus Mark *Paul Webber* 96h
6 b g Mark Of Esteem(IRE) —Lemon's Mill (USA) (Roberto (USA))
1689[7] 1974[9] 3604[9] (4956) 5270[2]
Cityar (FR) *John O'Shea* 91h
7 b g Sagacity(FR) —Starry Dust (FR) (Zino)
304[2] 591[F] 2056[7] 2322[F] 4944[U] 5348[6]

City Ground (USA) *Michael Easterby* 98h
4 bb g Orientate(USA) —Magnet (USA) (Seeking The Gold (USA))
4283[9] (4995)
City Heights (IRE) *Giles Smyly* 115h 131c
9 ch g City Honours(USA) —Andy's Fancy (IRE) (Andretti)
738[7] (957)
1274[P] 1469[P] 4786[U] 5392[7]
City In The Sky *Mike Sowersby* 11b
5 b m Rock City—Celtic Sky (Celtic Swing)
174[P]
City Of Doral *J J Lambe* 123h 87c
9 b g Double Trigger(IRE) —Double Resolve (Gildoran)
45[8] **5029[4]**
City Press (IRE) *Nicky Henderson* 106b
5 b g Presenting—Phargara (IRE) (Phardante (FR))
4943[5] 5388[5]
City Theatre (IRE) *Jonjo O'Neill* 128h 114c
7 b g Oscar(IRE) —O Mio My (IRE) (Roselier (FR))
1964[4] 2945[5] 3368[4]
City Well *Laura Young* 58h
8 b g Sadler's Wells(USA) —City Dance (USA) (Seattle Slew (USA))
4539[U]
Civil Servant *Nigel Twiston-Davies* 111h 84c
6 gr g Diktat—Zafadola (IRE) (Darshaan)
1938 798[P] **1454[5]**
Civil Unrest (IRE) *James Ewart* 90b
5 ch g Blueprint(IRE) —Yore (IRE) (Ore)
3752[8] 4287[10]
Cladding *John Panvert* 67b
5 b g Deploy—Sharway Lady (Shareef Dancer (USA))
1927[10] 2025[7]
Claimant (IRE) *Paul Fitzsimons* 84h
4 b g Acclamation—Between The Winds (USA) (Diesis)
2047[U] 2151[4] 3958[7] 5014[3] 5232[4]
Clan Tara (IRE) *Paul Nolan* 136h 140c
9 b g Kayf Tara—Alpine Gale (IRE) (Strong Gale)
3206a[F] 3415a[F]
Clarach (IRE) *Tim Vaughan* 114h
6 b m Beneficial—Claramanda (IRE) (Mandalus)
1643[3] 1793[2] 1993[3] 2289[9]
Clash (IRE) *Miss L Thomas*
8 b g Bob Back(USA) —Alpine Gale (IRE) (Strong Gale)
148[P]
Classicality *Michael Mullineaux* 68b
6 ch m Classic Cliche(IRE) —Lissadell (IRE) (Zaffaran (USA))
869[6] 1196[U] 1449[P]
Classically (IRE) *Hughie Morrison* 75h
5 b g Indian Haven—Specifically (USA) (Sky Classic (CAN))
2021[6]
Classical Mist *David O'Meara* 92h
7 ch m Classic Cliche(IRE) —Mademist Jaz (Lord Bud)
4145[6] 4454[6] 4889[4]
Classic Bavard *Geoffrey Deacon* 89h
9 ch g Classic Cliche(IRE) —Anne Bavard (Le Bavard (FR))
15[3] 500[9] 5383[F]
Classic Chance *Miss A Ray* 81c
11 b g Classic Cliche(IRE) —Chance Again (Balinger)
4293[F] 4526[7]
Classic Clover *Colin Tizzard* 69h 107c
11 ch g Classic Cliche(IRE) —National Clover (National Trust)
181[4] 540[6] (665)
758[5] 1027[7] 1093[9] 1366[2] 1550[3] 1843[5] 1939[6]
2024[4]
4163[5] 4708[7]
4969[6] (5407)
Classic Contours (USA) *Tracy Waggott* 96h
5 b g Najran(USA) —What's Up Kittycat (USA) (Tabasco Cat (USA))
5483 1148[3] 2375[P] 4797[8] 5132[P]
Classic Cut *James Ewart* 115h 121c
7 b g Classic Cliche(IRE) —Leading Line (Leading Man)
2449[F]
Classic Fly (FR) *Arthur Whiting* 99h 109c
8 ch g Broadway Flyer(USA) —Guirlande (USA) (Rahy (USA))
23[9] 350[P] 1084[11] 1295[3] 1484[4] 1492[4] **1558[2]**
1628[2] 1731[5] 4698[7] 5072[6]
5197[F]
Classic Frontier (IRE) *C Byrnes* 52h 130c
9 b g New Frontier(IRE) —Classic Habit (IRE) (Aristocracy)
844[6] 1113a[F]
Classic Henri *Barry Murtagh* 92h
7 ch g Classic Cliche(IRE) —Sainte Etoile (FR) (Saint Cyrien (FR))
3363[3] 3728[2] 4302[2] 4511[2] 4960[6] (5308)
Classic Port (FR) *Suzy Smith* 62h
7 gr g Slickly(FR) —Portella (GER) (Protektor (GER))
2944[11] 4424[6]
Classic Rock *James Unett* 74h 93c
12 b g Classic Cliche(IRE) —Ruby Vision (IRE) (Vision (USA))
649[2] 931[P] 1061[P]
Classic Swain (USA) *Paul Nicholls* 133h 143c
6 ch g Swain(IRE) —Affirm Miss (USA) (Sky Classic (CAN))
357[2] 594[2] (1025)
(1229) 1332[2] 1861[9] 5301[3]
Classic Vintage (USA) *Amanda Perrett* 63h
5 b g El Prado(IRE) —Cellars Shiraz (USA) (Kissin Kris (USA))
2667[12]
Classy Crewella *Brian Eckley* 16b
5 b m Lahib(USA) —Karowna (Karinga Bay)
3590[11]
Claude Carter *Alistair Whillans* 100h
7 b g Elmaamul(USA) —Cruz Santa (Lord Bud)
161[7] 582[P] 1115[7] 4243[4] 4686[7]

Clayton Flick (IRE) *Andrew Haynes* 58h
4 b g Kheleyf(USA) —Mambodorga (USA) (Kingmambo (USA))
674[4] 851[5]
Clear Alternative (IRE) *Terry Clement*
4 ch g Indian Ridge—Token Gesture (IRE) (Alzao (USA))
3507[F]
Clearly Now (IRE) *Michael O'Hare* 96h
13 b g Clearly Bust—Paico Lane (Paico)
2301[P]
Clear Sailing *Ian Williams* 113h
8 b g Selkirk(USA) —Welsh Autumn (Tenby)
356[3] (500) (827)
Cleaver *Lady Herries* 114h
10 ch g Kris—Much Too Risky (Bustino)
2594[5] 3556[13] 4478[2] 4918[2]
Clee Hill Wind *Bill Turner*
4 ch f Sly—Golden Wind (Blaze O'Gold (USA))
2597[14]
Cleni Boy (FR) *P Grindrod* 77h 126c
9 b g Panoramic—Kailasa (FR) (R B Chesne)
3956[U]
Clerk's Choice (IRE) *Michael Banks* 160h
5 b g Bachelor Duke(USA) —Credit Crunch (IRE) (Caerleon (USA))
(154) (356) (1862) 2521[4] 2887[4] 4791[6] 5440[2]
Clever Dick (IRE) *Warren Greatrex*
5 b g Presenting—Amitge (FR) (Vaguely Pleasant (FR))
4329[7]
Clew Bay Cove (IRE) *C A Murphy* 103h 128c
11 ch g Anshan—Crashrun (Crash Course)
3706a[9]
Clifden Boy (IRE) *Ron Hodges* 95h 100c
9 br g Anshan—Pharandom (IRE) (Phardante (FR))
(649) **(758)**
987[3] 5109[8]
Clifton Debut *Kim Bailey* 117h 133c
8 ch g Bob Back(USA) —Quinag (Tina's Pet)
844[P] 1904[5]
Clifton Pier (IRE) *Mrs Prunella Dobbs* 97h 75c
7 br g Presenting—Chapel Queen (IRE) (Jolly Jake (NZ))
2644[4]
Cloonavery (IRE) *Derek Frankland* 72h 82c
9 b g Xaar—Hero's Pride (FR) (Hero's Honor (USA))
961[5] 991[4] 1106[3] 1237[U] ◆ **1290[5]** 1468[F] 1552[4]
1704[3] **1995[2]**
5016[11] 5270[5]
Cloonawillin Lady (IRE) *Elliott Cooper* 94c
8 b m Taipan(IRE) —Yasbee (IRE) (Yashgan)
3632[2] 4002[4] 4254[3] 4543[4]
Cloran Jack (IRE) *Marc Barber* 69h 91c
7 ch g Moonax(IRE) —Kerry Leitrim (IRE) (Supreme Leader)
4526[5]
Close House *David Pipe* 119b
4 b g Generous(IRE) —Not Now Nellie (Saddlers' Hall (IRE))
2315[2] (3364) 4468[2]
Closesthingtocrazy *Sarah Humphrey* 102h 116c
7 b g King's Theatre(IRE) —Cheyenne Squaw (IRE) (Night Shift (USA))
1996[6] 2280[P]
Cloudier *Tim Vaughan* 96h 59c
10 b m Cloudings(IRE) —Hutcel Loch (Lochnager)
52[2]
Cloudmor (IRE) *Alistair Whillans* 100h 125c
10 b g Cloudings(IRE) —Glen Morvern (Carlingford Castle)
2189[P]
Cloud Nine (IRE) *Miss Jane Western* 76h 114c
8 b g Saddlers' Hall(IRE) —Park Breeze (IRE) (Strong Gale)
169[3] 3908[13] 4197[R] 4708[U] 4936[U] 5372[5]
Cloudy Dawn *Sue Smith* 74h 92c
6 gr g Cloudings(IRE) —Persistent Gunner (Gunner B)
847[5] 988[5] 1149[5] 3392[3] 3622[P]
4996[2]
Cloudy Joe (IRE) *Charles Pogson* 67h
5 b g Cloudings(IRE) —Be My Citizen (IRE) (Be My Native (USA))
355[12] *2826[7] 3166[9]* 3485[P] 3787[10] 3952[10]
4739[10] 5354[F]
Cloudy Spirit *Reg Hollinshead* 134h
6 gr m Silver Patriarch(IRE) —Miss Lacroix (Picea)
2242[6] 2514[10] *(3090) 3168[3]* 4009[4] (4501)
(5003) 5187[4]
Cloudy Too (IRE) *Sue Smith* 126h
5 b g Cloudings(IRE) —Curra Citizen (IRE) (Phardante (FR))
2075[P] 3994[3] (4506) 5186[9]
Cloudy Wager *Anna Newton-Smith* 95h
6 b m Cloudings(IRE) —Gemma's Wager (IRE) (Phardante (FR))
222[4] 2526[6] 3374[7] 3607[2] 4052[7] 4773[2]
Clouseau (NZ) *Nick Williams* 109h 119c
7 ch g Riviera(FR) —Miss Marple (NZ) (March Hywel (USA))
(2635)
3531[3] 4324[4] 4934[5]
Clowance House *Venetia Williams* 111h
5 ch g Galileo(IRE) —Corsican Sunset (USA) (Thunder Gulch (USA))
2960[12] 3491[2] 4029[2] 4555[4]
Clu Agus Cail (IRE) *Alison Batchelor* 109h
6 b m Rock Of Gibraltar(IRE) —Political Society (IRE) (Law Society (USA))
(1900) 2329[15] 2639[11]
Cluain Alainn (IRE) *Ian Williams* 66h
5 b g Dalakhani(IRE) —Josh's Pearl (IRE) (Sadler's Wells (USA))
2310[13] 2640[10] 3296[14] 5211[6]
Club Class *John Wade* 102h 112c
8 b g Emperor Fountain—Four Leaf Clover (Sunyboy)
(2191)
2550[5] 5146[P]

Clueless *Carol Ferguson* 54h 85c
9 b g Royal Applause—Pure (Slip Anchor)
212[P] **404[7]**
473[4] 730[7] 860[6] 1049[4] 1380[5]

Cluthe Boy (IRE) *Miss S Sharratt* 111h 92c
8 ch g Anshan—Townhall (IRE) (Roselier (FR))
150[7] 551[5] 4143[4] 4415[4]

Clyffe Hanger (IRE) *Bob Buckler* 119h 116c
11 b g Taipan(IRE) —French Thistle (Kemal (FR))
1774[4] 2140[4]

Clyffe Top *Jonathan Portman* 89h
4 b f Turgeon(USA) —Chandni (IRE) (Ahonoora)
2965[5] 3616[9] 4781[3]

C'Monthehammers (IRE) *Nigel Twiston-Davies* 119h 134c
8 ch g Snurge—Mounthenry Lady (IRE) (Le Moss)
1759[3] 2248[3] (2794)
3568[P] 4333[6]

Cnoc An Einn (IRE) *W J Burke* 101h 62c
12 b g Supreme Leader—Casualty Madame (Buckskin (FR))
1121a[12]

Cnoc Moy (IRE) *Helen Rees* 40h
7 b g Mull Of Kintyre(USA) —Ewar Sunrise (Shavian)
4049[13]

Coach And Four (USA) *Michael Gates* 92h
6 bl h Storm Cat(USA) —Tacha (USA) (Mr Prospector (USA))
850[10] 1278[5] 1487[U] 1600[6] 1938[5]

Coach Lane *Nick Mitchell* 115h 115c
10 b g Barathea(IRE) —Emplane (USA) (Irish River (FR))
26[2] (99)
233[3] 444[3] 676[5] 847[7] 919[9] 2961[2] 3433[P] 3648[4]
4142[5]
4529[5] 4671[2]
5011[P] 5173[5]

Coastley (IRE) *David Carr* 130h 87c
9 b g Lord Americo—Cosima (IRE) (Over The River (FR))
(45) 396[2] 627[9] 2090[P]

Cobbler's Queen (IRE) *Henry Daly* 114h 114c
7 br m Presenting—Lareine D'Anjou (FR) (Panoramic)
2182[2] 2978[5] 3763[2] 4538[3] 5007[U]

Cobbler's Rest (IRE) *Jonjo O'Neill* 71b
5 b g Snurge—Jrred Up (IRE) (Jurado (USA))
3957[14] 5158[12]

Cocacobana (IRE) *Graeme McPherson* 93h
6 ch g Snurge—Dun Dun (IRE) (Saddlers' Hall (IRE))
3842[2] 4262[3] 4555[5] 5203[6]

Cockatoo (USA) *Gary Moore* 109h 121c
8 b g Dynaformer(USA) —Enticed (USA) (Stage Door Johnny (USA))
85[6] 2124[6] 2529[9] 3477[2] ◆

Cockleshell Road (IRE) *Martin Todhunter* 124h 79c
8 b g Sinndar(IRE) —Soeur Ti (FR) (Kaldoun (FR))
1759[9] 2299[6] 2940[P]

Cockney Prince (IRE) *Jonjo O'Neill* 90h
6 ch g Old Vic—Pharney Fox (IRE) (Phardante (FR))
100[4] 2144[3] 2558[9]

Cockney Trucker (IRE) *Philip Hobbs* 138h 146c
9 b g Presenting—Kiltiernan Easter (IRE) (Broken Hearted)
(265)
(1693) 2517[P] 2868[6] 3229[6] 3808[3] 4848[4] 4992[2]
5337[4]

Cock Of The Rock (IRE) *Keith Goldsworthy* 116b
6 b g Pierre—Glynn View (IRE) (Pistolet Bleu (IRE))
(833)

Cocoa Key (IRE) *Richard Guest* 102h 102c
7 br g Key Of Luck(USA) —Renvyle Rose (IRE) (Rainbows For Life (CAN))
350[11] (2104) 2506[5] **3730[4]**

Cocoa Minnie (IRE) *Paul Webber* 67b
5 ch m Presenting—Native Lucy (IRE) (Be My Native (USA))
4957[5]

Coda Agency *David Arbuthnot* 118h 100c
8 b g Agnes World(USA) —The Frog Lady (IRE) (Al Hareb (USA))
4447[5]

Code Blue *Donald McCain* 90h
8 b g Sir Harry Lewis(USA) —Nevermind Hey (Teenoso (USA))
1703[5] (2192)

Cody Wyoming *Heather Main* 103h
5 b g Passing Glance—Tenderfoot (Be My Chief (USA))
3766[8] 4082[6] 4677[8] (4917) 5106[10]

Coeur Brule (FR) *Sam Davison* 96h
5 b g Polish Summer—Sally's Cry (FR) (Freedom Cry)
886[7] 1059[4] 1291[7] 1446[2] 1551[3] 2469[5] 2980[7]

Coeur De Fou (FR) *Tom George* 109h
6 ch g Limnos(JPN) —Folly Lady (FR) (Saint Estephe (FR))
(4465)

Coeur De Lionne (IRE) *Mrs Pauline Harkin* 98h
7 b g Invincible Spirit(IRE) —Lionne (Darshaan)
754[2] 1278[6] 1344[7] 4310[8] 4977[P]

Cois Farraig *Paul Webber* 123h 131c
6 b g Karinga Bay—Oriel Dream (Oats)
2082[3] ◆ (2664)
3291[7] 3946[8] 4699[6]

Cold Blow Lane (IRE) *Joanna Davis*
5 ch g Bienamado(USA) —Queensland (IRE) (Dr Devious (IRE))
5388[P]

Cold Harbour *Evan Williams* 111h 102c
7 b g Classic Cliche(IRE) —Anchorage (IRE) (Slip Anchor)
2073[5] (2575)
3527[5] 3933[4] 4160[3] (4865)
5017[5] 5254[3]

Colditz (IRE) *Richard Ford* 72h 76c
7 ch g Noverre(USA) —West Escape (Gone West (USA))
(1378)

Cold Knight *Alan King* 101b
5 b g Sir Harry Lewis(USA) —Arctic Chick (Henbit (USA))
3569[4] 4484[5] 5105[11]

Cold Mountain (IRE) *Seamus Mullins* 113h 126c
9 b g Inchinor—Streak Of Silver (USA) (Dynaformer (USA))
131[3] 503[8] **(691)**
(911) 1570[6] 1858[U] 1999[6] 2395[P] (5067)
5338[F] 5405[P]

Coldwells (IRE) *Martin Todhunter* 98h 101c
11 b m Presenting—Coolmoonan (Le Moss)
1697[3] 2940[P] 3360[2] 3503[5] 3853[8] 4799[5] 5150[P]

Colinette *Robin Dickin* 17h 48c
8 b m Groom Dancer(USA) —Collide (High Line)
3882[6] 4032[8]

Colleens Pride (IRE) *Jonjo O'Neill*
8 b m Cut The Mustard(IRE) —Carrickaduff Girl (IRE) (Satco (FR))
3698[P] 3830[4] 3901[P]

College Ace (IRE) *Renee Robeson* 109h 129c
10 b g Taipan(IRE) —Frantesa (Red Sunset)
314[6]

College Green *Howard Johnson* 47b
4 b g Beat All(USA) —Velvet Leaf (Rakaposhi King)
4005[6]

Colleoni (IRE) *Evan Williams* 127h
6 b g Sadler's Wells(USA) —Francfurter (Legend Of France (USA))
(2322)

Colliers Castle (IRE) *Lisa Williamson* 77b
5 b m Karinga Bay—Aneeza (IRE) (Charnwood Forest (IRE))
4280[5] 4554[11]

Colliers Court *Lisa Williamson* 24h 102c
14 b g Puget(USA) —Rag Time Belle (Raga Navarro (ITY))
1552[6]
1823[P] 1940[5] 2334[3] 3404[P]

Collyns Avenue *James Ewart* 95h 110c
8 ch g Bal Harbour—Flower Of Dunblane (Ardross)
2552[7] 3851[10] **4275[3]**

Colonel Alf *Alex Hales* 23h
6 b g Alflora(IRE) —Re-Spin (Gildoran)
2111[10] 2464[13]

Colonel Arthur (IRE) *Sophie Leech* 113h 94c
10 b g Darazari(IRE) —Loch Na Mona (IRE) (King's Ride)
3650[P]

Colonial Harry *Neil Mulholland* 45b
4 b g Sir Harry Lewis(USA) —Shaadin (USA) (Sharpen Up)
3301[13] 3909[13]

Colonial Jim (IRE) *Neil Mulholland* 84h 93c
8 b g Rudimentary(USA) —Jenny May (IRE) (Orchestra)
692[2] 1048[F]

Colorado Kid (IRE) *Howard Johnson* 35h
5 b g Presenting—Silent Orders (IRE) (Bob Back (USA))
2553[7] 3399[10] 4995[8]

Colour Clash *Rose Dobbin* 115h
8 b g Rainbow Quest(USA) —Ancara (Dancing Brave (USA))
3500[11] 3820[3]

Colours Of Autumn (IRE) *D J Ryan* 34h 83c
10 ch m Carroll House—Couleurs d'Automne (FR) (Galant Vert (FR))
1500[5]

Colour Trooper (IRE) *David Pipe* 28h
6 ch g Traditionally(USA) —Viola Royale (IRE) (Royal Academy (USA))
754[12] 820[7] 914[10] 1179[11]

Columbus Secret (IRE) *Keith Reveley* 70h 124c
6 b g Luso—Bid For Fun (IRE) (Auction Ring (USA))
2191[P] 2615[3] (2938)
3333[9] 4116[4] 4456[5] (5292)

Comanche Kriek *George Yardley* 9b
8 ch g Commanche Run—Cherry Sip (Nearly A Hand)
1773[P]

Combat King (IRE) *Norma Twomey* 72b
7 b g Commander Collins(IRE) —Native Gift (IRE) (Be My Native (USA))
222[9]

Comedy Act *Philip Hobbs* 111h
4 b g Motivator—Comic (IRE) (Be My Chief (USA))
(2924) 3443[6] 4283[5] 5006[6]

Comehomequietly (IRE) *David Rees* 121h
7 b g King's Theatre(IRE) —Windswept Lady (IRE) (Strong Gale)
(1111) (1372) 1864[P] 4524[4] 4862[7]

Come On Eddie *Anabel L M King* 75h
8 b g Deploy—Arusha (IRE) (Dance Of Life (USA))
539[5]

Come Out Firing (IRE) *Michael Blake* 107h 101c
9 b g Supreme Leader—Thegirlfromslane (IRE) (Mandalus)
606[6] 756[9] 962[11] 4034[6] **4265[2]** 4536[4]

Comeragh King *Tim Fitzgerald* 107h
7 b g Kayf Tara—Velcro Girl (IRE) (Be My Native (USA))
2403[6] 3572[6] 4467[5]

Comeththehour (IRE) *James Moffatt* 87h
8 b g Oscar(IRE) —Bobs My Uncle (Deep Run)
2552[5] 3887[6] 4391[6] 4712[5]

Cometotheboardroom (IRE) *Alan Swinbank*
5 b g Where Or When(IRE) —Seabound (Prince Sabo)
4259[9]

Come What Augustus *R M Woollacott* 90h 113c
9 b g Mujahid(USA) —Sky Red (Night Shift (USA))
4271[2]

Comhla Ri Coig *Donald McCain* 138h 137c
10 b g Sir Harry Lewis(USA) —Analogical (Teenoso (USA))
2542[4] ◆

Commadore Barry (IRE) *Mrs Trish Cleverdon Lucy* 67h 45c
10 b g Gothland(FR) —Diane's Glen (Furry Glen)
5402[P]

Commanche Dawn *Gerry Enright* 55h 63c
9 b m Commanche Run—Charlycia (Good Times (ITY))
2183[F] 2391[3] **2950[4] 3377[5] 3609[U] 3867[5]**

Commanche Dream *Simon Lewis* 59h 106c
8 b g Commanche Run—Busy Girl (Bustiki)
251[U] 409[7] 1742[13] **1924[9]**

Commanche Luke *C Roberts* 81b
8 b g Commanche Run—Dawn O'Er Kells (IRE) (Pitskelly)
168[P] 1111[13]

Commander Jet *Brian Baugh* 73b
5 b g Kayf Tara—My Gal Ruby (Nalchik (USA))
2957[15] 3266[16]

Commander Kev (IRE) *Mrs K Hobbs* 118h 101c
10 b g Needle Gun(IRE) —Grange Park (IRE) (Warcraft (USA))
4901[3]

Command Marshal (FR) *Michael Scudamore* 102h
8 b g Commands(AUS) —Marsakara (IRE) (Turtle Island (IRE))
84[9] 336[4] (532) 645[2]

Commemoration Day (IRE) *Charlie Longsdon* 113h 129c
10 b g Daylami(IRE) —Bequeath (USA) (Lyphard (USA))
438[4] 2212[5] 2541[10] 3433[P] (4777) ◆ (5104)
5423[5]

Commit To Memory *Paul Henderson* 94h
6 br g Best Of The Bests(IRE) —Simonida (IRE) (Royal Academy (USA))
171[6] 2630[P] 3449[9] 4707[P]

Companero (IRE) *Howard Johnson* 81h 148c
11 b g Supreme Leader—Smart Decision (IRE) (Le Moss)
3568[P] 4003[6]
(4360) 4876[P]

Comply Or Die (IRE) *David Pipe* 116h 138c
12 b g Old Vic—Madam Madcap (Furry Glen)
2221[12] 3568[6] 4360[P] 5200[P]

Comprimario (IRE) *Nigel Twiston-Davies* 90h
5 b g Montjeu(IRE) —Soubrette (USA) (Opening Verse (USA))
232[7]

Compton Star *Ron Hodges* 78h 66c
11 ch g Compton Place—Darakah (Doulab (USA))
183[8] 276[P] 593[12]

Conellie *Bernard Llewellyn* 82b
5 ch g Hernando(FR) —Superstore (USA) (Blushing Groom (FR))
5217[6]

Conem (IRE) *W J Austin* 128h 130c
11 b g Oscar(IRE) —Dirty Diana (Boreen (FR))
3473a[7] 3706a[4]

Confide In Me *Jim Best* 79h
7 b g Medicean—Confidante (USA) (Dayjur (USA))
5114[9]

Conflictofinterest *Kevin Hunter* 132h 94c
9 b g Saddlers' Hall(IRE) —Fortune's Girl (Ardross)
528[7] **822[5]**
4549[4] 4963[5] 5417[4]

Congella *Tim Walford* 77b
6 b m Karinga Bay—Cool Shuil (IRE) (Glacial Storm (USA))
2167[8] 2612[P] 3389[P]

Conigre *Tor Sturgis* 84b
4 b g Selkirk(USA) —Mystify (Batshoof)
2237[6] 5012[12]

Coniston *Sue Smith* 79h
8 b m Cotation—Laughing Pet (Petoski)
488[6]

Conkering (USA) *Jonjo O'Neill* 98h 73c
8 ch g Horse Chestnut(SAF) —Nunbridled (USA) (Unbridled (USA))
100[P] **339[5]**

Connectivity (IRE) *Dr Richard Newland* 143h
7 b g Flemensfirth(USA) —Garden Town (IRE) (Un Desperado (FR))
4722[2] (5061) ◆ (5118)

Connie Beauchamp *Elliott Cooper* 82b
7 b m Commanche Run—Logani (Domynsky)
47[6] 399[7] 577[P]

Conquisto *Steve Gollings* 131h
6 ch g Hernando(FR) —Seal Indigo (IRE) (Glenstal (USA))
207[5] 1017[7] 4235[8] 5201[6]

Consigliere (FR) *David Pipe* 135h 152c
8 ch g Trempolino(USA) —Gianna Nannini (ITY) (Fire Of Life (USA))
2517[4] 2881[11] 3438[6] 4820[4] 5185[16]

Constant Cupid (IRE) *Graeme McPherson* 95h
7 b g Winged Love(IRE) —Eva Ross (IRE) (Furry Glen)
2469[3] (3837) 4722[10]

Consulate (IRE) *Gordon Edwards* 114h
7 b g Rock Of Gibraltar(IRE) —Soha (USA) (Dancing Brave (USA))
267[3] 534[3] 715[10] 994[2] 1372[5] 1972[6] 2333[3]
2636[8] 4925[5]

Contentwithmyluck (IRE) *Tom Gretton* 11h
5 b g Bach(IRE) —Rare Luck (Rare One)
1773[10] 2056[15] 3454[9] 5057[10]

Contrada *Jim Old* 92h
6 b g Medicean—Trounce (Barathea (IRE))
1258[2] 1453[6] 1601[9]

Contradiktive (IRE) *Tim Vaughan* 84h
5 b g Diktat—Additive (USA) (Devil's Bag (USA))
1280[3] 1433[9] 1641[8]

Converti *Simon Burrough* 108h 64c
7 b g Averti(IRE) —Conquestadora (Hernando (FR))
267[9] 1094[4] 1380[4] 1490[3] **1710[4] 1843[6]**

Cool Baranca (GER) *Dianne Sayer* 99h
5 b m Beat Hollow—Cool Storm (IRE) (Rainbow Quest (USA))
3547[7] 3746[5] 4242[6] 4912[0] ◆

Coolbeg (IRE) *Tom George* 106h
5 b g Oscar(IRE) —Dianeme (Primo Dominie)
2309[4] 3252[3] 3701[5] 4557[4]

Cool Bob (IRE) *Matt Sheppard* 98h 70c
8 b g Bob Back(USA) —Rosie Jaques (Doyoun)
3[5] 231[4] 630[4] 737[3] 849[5] 1035[2] 1601[4]
1991[U] 2327[2]

Coolcashin (IRE) *Michael J Bowe* 99h 143c
10 b g Taipan(IRE) —Daisy A Day (IRE) (Asir)
1684a[2] 2226a[4] 2970a[7] 4298a[P]

Cool Cliche *Evan Williams* 86h 101c
9 b g Classic Cliche(IRE) —Ardent Love (IRE) (Ardross)
737[P]

Cooldine (IRE) *W P Mullins* 151h 163c
9 b g Beneficial—Shean Alainn (IRE) (Le Moss)
2970a[5] 3176a[P]

Cool Doctor (IRE) *Kate Walton* 91b
5 b g Dr Massini(IRE) —Glacial Friend (IRE) (Glacial Storm (USA))
4280[4]

Coolefind (IRE) *W J Warner* 120c
13 b g Phardante(FR) —Greavesfind (The Parson)
(253) **525[8]**

Coolers Quest *Mrs R Ford* 84h 79c
12 b m Saddlers' Hall(IRE) —Lucidity (Vision (USA))
184[3] 466[5]

Cool Friend (IRE) *Jeremy Scott* 123h 129c
8 b m Anshan—Glacial Friend (IRE) (Glacial Storm (USA))
208[2] (1985)
4096[4] 5007[4] 5301[7]

Cool Mission (IRE) *Donald McCain* 131h 131c
7 ch g Definite Article—Mettlesome (Lomond (USA))
(305) 2235[6]
3332[3] 3586[4] 3902[2] 4282[2] (4685)
5001[2] 5341[3]

Coolnaharan (IRE) *S R B Crawford* 114h 106c
11 b g Blues Traveller(IRE) —Alma Assembly (General Assembly (USA))
1342[3] 1614[P] **1701[F]** (Dead)

Cool Operator *Howard Johnson* 132h 136c
8 b g Kahyasi—Gardana (FR) (Garde Royale)
34[5] 2104[5] 2506[2] (4255) 5339[8]

Cool Quest (IRE) *Terence O'Brien* 123h 134c
7 b m Turtle Island(IRE) —Solar Quest (IRE) (King's Ride)
3268a[2] 3779a[3]

Cool Roxy *Alan Blackmore* 128h 127c
14 b g Environment Friend—Roxy River (Ardross)
438[3]

Cool Running (IRE) *Jonjo O'Neill* 130h 130c
11 br g Glacial Storm(USA) —Strong Wings (Strong Gale)
139[4] 1404[2]

Cool Star (IRE) *David Carr* 41h
5 b g One Cool Cat(USA) —Pack Ice (USA) (Wekiva Springs (USA))
3885[9] 3999[8]

Cool Steel (IRE) *Alan King* 54h
5 br g Craigsteel—Coolafinka (IRE) (Strong Statement (USA))
3399[6] 3957[9] 5115[9]

Cool Strike (UAE) *Alex Hales* 101h
5 b g Halling(USA) —Velour (Mtoto)
3225[9] 3692[4] 4233[6] 4988[6]

Cool The Heels (IRE) *Emma Lavelle* 90h
6 b g Catcher In The Rye(IRE) —Alinea (USA) (Kingmambo (USA))
465[4] 635[8] 842[3]

Cool Touch (IRE) *Nigel Twiston-Davies* 118h
8 b g Marju(IRE) —Feather Star (Soviet Star (USA))
235[2] (428) 500[3] 733[5]

Cool Vic (IRE) *David Carr* 103b
7 b g Old Vic—Winterland Gale (IRE) (Strong Gale)
(1785)

Cool Water *John Wade* 76h
6 b m Classic Cliche(IRE) —Houselope Brook (Meadowbrook)
47[7] 474[5] 3504[4] 4059[12] 4552[12] 4993[4]

Cooper's Crest (IRE) *Sabrina J Harty* 129h
8 b m Deploy—Hillcrest (IRE) (Thatching)
207[14] 1038a[3]

Coosan Belle (IRE) *John Joseph Hanlon* 102h
5 b m Definite Article—Princess Of Zurich (IRE) (Law Society (USA))
1596[2]

Cootehill (IRE) *Nigel Twiston-Davies* 131h 131c
7 b g Alflora(IRE) —Dancing Dove (IRE) (Denel (FR))
(1371)
(1568) 1693[3] 2220[4] 3803[6] 4816[8] 5305[6]

Copper Bay (IRE) *Mrs C M James* 93h 122c
9 b g Revoque(IRE) —Bahia Laura (FR) (Bellypha)
4973[P]

Copper Bleu (IRE) *Philip Hobbs* 54h 152c
9 b g Pistolet Bleu(IRE) —Copper Supreme (IRE) (Supreme Leader)
4202[8] **5288[5]**

Copper Kate (IRE) *John Flint* 95b
7 b m Saddlers' Hall(IRE) —Ballycleary (IRE) (Phardante (FR))
333[3]

Copper's Gold (IRE) *Lucinda Russell* 89h 108c
7 b g Presenting—West Hill Rose (IRE) (Roselier (FR))
517[6] 1701[6] 3748[2] (4871)
5032[P] 5430[4]

Copper Sound *Michael Scudamore* 68h 81c
7 ch g Supreme Sound—Camorra (My Chopin)
2348[8] 2947[3] 3388[6] 3527[7] 3699[3] 4133[P] 4540[P]

Coppingers Court (IRE) *S Rea* 33h 84c
10 b g Accordion—Candalorea (IRE) (Satco (FR))
225[P] **3991[6]**
4415[5]

Copsehill Girl (IRE) *Ian Williams* 108h
6 bb m Carroll House—Merapi (Roi Guillaume (FR))
1146a^{9} 1505^{3} 2954^{12} 3487^{F} (4161) 4418^{4} 5205^{7}
Coq Hardi (FR) *Tim Vaughan* 127h 134c
10 b g Panoramic—Matagirl (FR) (Matahawk)
18^{P} (Dead)
Coral Cove *John Mackie* 100b
6 b g Karinga Bay—Herself (Hernando (FR))
602^{3}
Coralhasi (FR) *J-P Gallorini* 108h
9 b g Kahyasi—Coral Bird (FR) (Deep Roots)
2230a^{2}
Coral Point (IRE) *Alan Jessop* 69h
5 ch g Hawkeye(IRE) —Green Crystal (Green Dancer (USA))
2454^{11}
Coral Shores *Peter Hiatt* 51h
6 b m Carnival Dancer—Leading Role (Cadeaux Genereux)
1295^{7}
Cordier *John Mackie* 72h 101c
9 b g Desert Style(IRE) —Slipper (Suave Dancer (USA))
77^{P} 607^{5} 697^{8}
Corkage (IRE) *Lucinda Russell* 129h 121c
8 b g Second Empire(IRE) —Maslam (IRE) (Robellino (USA))
45^{5} 309^{7} 447^{2} 708^{3} 866^{7} 1019^{9}
Cork All Star (IRE) *Mrs J Quinlan* 146h 125c
9 b g Fasliyev(USA) —Lucky State (USA) (State Dinner (USA))
(4026)
(4779) ◆
Corker *Suzy Smith* 110h
9 ch g Grand Lodge(USA) —Immortelle (Arazi (USA))
1727^{F}
Corky Dancer *P Monteith* 51h
6 b g Groom Dancer(USA) —Cita Verda (FR) (Take Risks (FR))
311^{4} 731^{4} 876^{2} 2192^{6}
Corlande (IRE) *Donald McCain* 106h 104c
11 br g Teamster—Vaguely Deesse (USA) (Vaguely Noble)
2366^{3} 2610^{2} 3764^{5}
Cornas (NZ) *Nick Williams* 120h 156c
9 b g Prized(USA) —Duvessa (NZ) (Sound Reason (CAN))
(1801a)
2138^{6} 2881^{4} (3446)
4187^{7} 4805^{9} 5442^{3}
Cornish Castle (USA) *Andrew Crook* 89h
5 ch g Mizzen Mast(USA) —Rouwaki (USA) (Miswaki (USA))
14^{4} 228^{11} 459^{10} 1361^{4} 1407^{4} 1559^{P} 4994^{5} 5354^{5}
Cornish Ice *Robin Dickin* 112h
7 b g Dolpour—Icelandic Poppy (Oats)
2067^{3}
Cornish Sett (IRE) *Caroline Keevil* 113h 136c
12 b g Accordion—Hue 'N' Cry (IRE) (Denel (FR))
1960^{7} 2343^{U} 2962^{2} (3687)
4486^{7} 4821^{9}
Corporation (IRE) *J J Lambe* 96h 71c
7 b g Alderbrook—Nicky's Dilemma (Kambalda)
516^{7}
Corredor Sun (USA) *Nigel Twiston-Davies* 96h 89c
5 b g El Corredor(USA) —Cozzie Maxine (USA) (Cozzene (USA))
1628^{9} 1813^{3} 2152^{2} 3226^{7} 3768^{6} 4372^{7}
Corrick Bridge (IRE) *A J Martin* 108h 123c
9 gr g In The Wings—Osirixa (FR) (Linamix (FR))
873^{4}
Corrigans Road (IRE) *Donald McCain* 44h
6 b g Luso—Roseboreen (IRE) (Roselier (FR))
2069^{5}
Corso Palladio (IRE) *Peter Bowen* 117h
9 b g Montjeu(IRE) —Falafil (FR) (Fabulous Dancer (USA))
849^{2} (1291) 1380^{2} (1959) 3575^{5}
Corston Star (IRE) *Malcolm Jefferson* 79b
6 b m Carroll House—Corston Dancer (IRE) (Lafontaine (USA))
1934^{8} 2156^{13}
Cortinas (GER) *Claire Dyson* 101h 126c
9 b g Lomitas—Cocorna (Night Shift (USA))
592^{6} 831^{4} 1084^{7} 1249^{3} **1471^{3} 1888^{2} 2276^{4}**
2633^{3} 3686^{15} **4698^{3} 4934^{2}** 5305^{9}
5394^{4}
Cosavita (FR) *David Rees* 114h
6 b m Comte Du Bourg(FR) —Savita (FR) (Sicyos (USA))
1726^{P} 3155^{4} 3610^{4} 3985^{P} 4272^{13}
Coscorrig (IRE) *D T Hughes* 129h 142c
9 b m Pistolet Bleu(IRE) —Ava Gale (IRE) (Supreme Leader)
1131a^{4} 3268a^{4}
Cosmetic *Colin Teague* 78h
6 ch m Where Or When(IRE) —Cosmology (USA) (Distant View (USA))
12^{2} 2302^{U} 2603^{3} 3502^{P} 3993^{10} 5130^{7} 5354^{P}
Cossack Dancer (IRE) *Mark Bradstock* 122h 126c
13 b g Moscow Society(USA) —Merry Lesa (Dalesa)
236^{4} 608^{6} 1486^{4} 1861^{P}
Cossack Prince *Laura Mongan* 83h
6 b g Dubai Destination(USA) —Danemere (IRE) (Danehill (USA))
5193^{8}
Costa Courta (FR) *Charlie Morlock* 111h 123c
9 b g Marly River(FR) —Tosca De Bellouet (FR) (Olmeto)
2305^{P} 3588^{P} 4502^{P}
Cosway Spirit (IRE) *Alan King* 93b
4 ch g Shantou(USA) —Annalisa (IRE) (Rhoman Rule (USA))
5158^{4}
Cote D'Argent *Chris Down* 73h 90c
8 b g Lujain(USA) —In The Groove (Night Shift (USA))
1164^{7}

Cotillion *Ian Williams* 126h
5 b g Sadler's Wells(USA) —Riberac (Efisio)
2960^{8} 3439^{2} ◆ 3866^{U} 4260^{2}
Cotswold Charmer (IRE) *Nigel Twiston-Davies* 117h
6 b g Alderbrook—Nordice Equity (IRE) (Project Manager)
(1703) (2154) 2663^{9}
Cottage Acre (IRE) *Tom George* 116h 124c
8 b g Shernazar—Quits (IRE) (Brief Truce (USA))
3789^{2} 4260^{4} **(4490)** ◆ **4877^{U}**
Cottage Flyer (IRE) *Paul John Gilligan* 125c
6 b g Broadway Flyer(USA) —Cottage Lord (IRE) (Mister Lord (USA))
(4855)
5073^{3}
Cottage River (IRE) *P Hall* 69c
11 b g Hubbly Bubbly(USA) —Boolindrum Lady (IRE) (Meneval (USA))
4973^{P}
Cottam Chocolate *Alan Lockwood* 3b
4 b f Tobougg(IRE) —Northern Bird (Interrex (CAN))
3576^{7}
Cottam Grange *John Wainwright* 93h
11 b g River Falls—Karminski (Pitskelly)
4236^{P} 4741^{P} 5132^{P}
Cottam Phantom *Mrs C A Coward* 100c
10 b g River Falls—William's Bird (USA) (Master Willie)
493^{4}
Cotton Bay (IRE) *Mrs C M Gorman*
8 b g Beauchamp King—Moya's Magic (IRE) (Phardante (FR))
292^{P}
Cottrelsbooley (IRE) *W P Mullins* 135h
7 b g Bravefoot—Valiyist (IRE) (Valiyar)
4086a^{5}
Coulter Lass *William Amos*
7 b m Karinga Bay—Line Of Fire (Henbit (USA))
4359^{P}
Countess Susy *Phillip Dando* 93h
6 b m Kier Park(IRE) —Gazelle De Thou (FR) (Quart De Vin (FR))
2472^{7} 3943^{7} 4719^{13} 4946^{4} 5167^{3} (5389)
Counting House (IRE) *Jim Old* 127h
8 ch g King's Best(USA) —Inforapenny (Deploy)
2574^{6} 2636^{9} (4988) 5304^{6}
Count Of Tuscany (USA) *Charles Egerton* 4h
5 b g Arch(USA) —Corsini (Machiavellian (USA))
5082^{10}
Counttoten (IRE) *Oliver Sherwood* 73b
6 ch g Presenting—Accountancy Lady (Capitano)
53^{8}
Count Vettori (IRE) *David Thompson* 97b
5 br g Vettori(IRE) —Alifandango (IRE) (Alzao (USA))
4280^{3} 4780^{14} 5313^{11}
County Colours (IRE) *Howard Johnson* 106h 105c
6 ch g Lord Of Appeal—Silk Style (Polish Precedent (USA))
1757^{2} 1867^{5} **2938^{3} 3751^{F}** 4912^{3}
County Hotel (IRE) *Barry Brennan* 73b
4 b f Sulamani(IRE) —Seasons Parks (Desert Prince (IRE))
2965^{8} 4184^{11}
County Zen (FR) *Philip Hobbs* 127h 127c
8 bb g Lost World(IRE) —Fair County (FR) (Armos)
2082^{5} 2494^{3} 2869^{10} 3566^{5} 3947^{4} 4354^{8} 5118^{6}
Coup De Tabac (FR) *Nigel Hawke* 103h 96c
7 b g Kaldounevees(FR) —Razzamatazz (FR) (Always Fair (USA))
663^{P} 767^{P} 912^{10}
Coup Royale (FR) *Colin Tizzard* 116h 135c
7 b g Balleroy(USA) —Coup De Rouge (FR) (Quart De Vin (FR))
2127^{2} ◆ **2662^{4} (4355)**
Courella (IRE) *Evan Williams* 104h 126c
7 b g Corrouge(USA) —Volobollea (IRE) (Baragoi)
(1290)
1454^{2} 1491^{4} (1589)
4695^{4} 5079^{3} 5233^{2} 5345^{4} (5394)
Court By Surprise (IRE) *Emma Lavelle* 125h
6 b g Beneficial—Garryduff Princess (IRE) (Husyan (USA))
(2241) 2963^{4} 4081^{10}
Court Gamble (IRE) *Nerys Dutfield* 19h
7 b m King's Theatre(IRE) —Black Queen (IRE) (Bob Back (USA))
277^{4} 759^{4} 4528^{5} 4946^{P}
Court In Motion (IRE) *Emma Lavelle* 147h
6 br g Fruits Of Love(USA) —Peace Time Girl (IRE) (Buckskin (FR))
(2142) 3197^{2} (3567) 4206^{2} 4849^{3} 5186^{F}
Court Minstrel (IRE) *Evan Williams* 102b
4 b g Court Cave(IRE) —Theatral (Orchestra)
4866^{3}
Court Oliver *Peter Purdy*
13 ch g One Voice(USA) —Tudor Sunset (Sunyboy)
763^{P}
Court Red Handed (IRE) *Rebecca Curtis* 117h
6 ch g Flemensfirth(USA) —Desert Gail (IRE) (Desert Style (IRE))
1291^{5} 1556^{4} (1726) 1959^{2}
Cousin John (IRE) *R Mitford-Slade* 18b
8 br g Anshan—Another Advantage (IRE) (Roselier (FR))
4143^{P}
Cousin Khee *Hughie Morrison* 112b
4 b g Sakhee(USA) —Cugina (Distant Relative)
(1913) ◆ 3294^{5} 4808^{8}
Cousin Maggie (IRE) *Brendan Powell* 97h 36c
7 b m Lahib(USA) —The Marching Lass (IRE) (Aristocracy)
3789^{5} 4051^{5} 4555^{3} 4990^{9} **5194^{8}**
Cousin Nicky *Giles Smyly* 115h 124c
10 ch g Bob Back(USA) —Little Red Spider (Bustino)
300^{5}

Covert Mission *David Evans* 114h
8 b m Overbury(IRE) —Peg's Permission (Ra Nova)
2242^{5}
Covey (IRE) *John O'Shea* 86h 80c
10 gr m Saddlers' Hall(IRE) —Nagillah (IRE) (Bob Back (USA))
358^{7}
Cowboyboots (IRE) *Audrey Manners* 115h 121c
13 b g Lord Americo—Little Welly (Little Buskins)
4537^{7}
Cozy Tiger (USA) *Willie Musson* 112h
6 gr g Hold That Tiger(USA) —Cozelia (USA) (Cozzene (USA))
3740^{2} 4424^{3}
Crabbies Court *Lisa Williamson*
6 b g Beat All(USA) —Miss Lambrini (Henbit (USA))
3093^{5} 3253^{P}
Cracboumwiz (FR) *Mark Shears* 125h 127c
11 b g Baby Turk—Ellapampa (FR) (Pampabird)
1346^{P}
Crack At Dawn (IRE) *Michael Gates* 80h 97c
10 bb g Insan(USA) —Ten Quid Short (IRE) (Colonel Godfrey (USA))
3510^{4} 4080^{P} 4953^{4} 5103^{5} 5374^{3}
Crack Away Jack *Emma Lavelle* 166h 155c
7 ch g Gold Away(IRE) —Jolly Harbour (Rudimentary (USA))
3675^{8} 4053^{P}
Crackentorp *Tim Easterby* 108h
6 b g Generous(IRE) —Raspberry Sauce (Niniski (USA))
2349^{3}
Crackerjac Boy (USA) *Richard Phillips* 98h
6 b g Catienus(USA) —Julie Apple (USA) (Conquistador Cielo (USA))
2456^{9} 3740^{14} 3897^{4} 4314^{P} 4721^{2} 5111^{P}
Crackerjack Lad (IRE) *Lucinda Russell* 87h
8 br g Exit To Nowhere(USA) —Crowther Homes (Neltino)
3363^{9} 4068^{4} 4302^{3} 4712^{P}
Crafti Bookie (IRE) *Sue Smith* 106h
5 bb g Winged Love(IRE) —Cerise De Totes (FR) (Champ Libre (FR))
2943^{8} 3399^{12} 3719^{5} 3952^{3}
Craicajack (IRE) *Edward Creighton* 69h
4 ch g Avonbridge—Rash Gift (Cadeaux Genereux)
4397^{8} 4917^{8}
Craicneasy (IRE) *Bruce Mactaggart* 60h 73c
8 br g Anshan—Craic Go Leor (Deep Run)
1869^{6}
4507^{P} 4962^{3} 5417^{3}
Craiglands (IRE) *Ian Williams* 80h 124c
9 b g Dushyantor(USA) —Fernhill (IRE) (Good Thyne (USA))
2541^{R} 4193^{3} 4730^{4}
Crank Hill *Bob Buckler* 104h 108c
9 b g Shambo—Mariner's Air (Julio Mariner)
(3297)
4102^{4} 4718^{8} 5060^{P}
Cranky Corner *Sue Smith* 107h 115c
7 b g Classic Cliche(IRE) —Pondimari (FR) (Marignan (USA))
1931^{7} 2300^{6} 3500^{9}
(3730) 4456^{7} 4716^{4} 5312^{B}
Crannaghmore Boy (IRE) *Keith Goldsworthy* 100h
6 b g Pilsudski(IRE) —Glencairn Mist (IRE) (Roselier (FR))
4407^{F} 4700^{8} 4862^{4} 5153^{8}
Crash (IRE) *Michael Hourigan* 133h
6 b g Milan—Mary Connors (IRE) (Mandalus)
4319a^{5}
Crathorne (IRE) *Alison Thorpe* 103h 113c
11 b g Alzao(USA) —Shirley Blue (IRE) (Shirley Heights)
2671^{2} (912)
Crazy Bold (GER) *Tony Carroll* 105h
8 ch g Erminius(GER) —Crazy Love (GER) (Presto)
40^{6} (350) 2150^{10} 2626^{9} 4025^{12} 5102^{3} 5171^{8}
5400^{3}
Crazy Colours *Zoe Davison* 74h
5 ch g Dalakhani(IRE) —Eternity Ring (Alzao (USA))
4917^{9}
Crazy Eyes (IRE) *Charlie Mann* 119h
6 b g Accordion—Clonboy Girl (IRE) (Lord Americo)
2235^{8} 2581^{6} 3744^{2} 4079^{2} 4742^{4}
Credit Crunched (IRE) *Alan King* 106h
6 ch g Humbel(USA) —Owenageera (IRE) (Riot Helmet)
3556^{6} ◆ 3918^{2} 4485^{6}
Credit Swap *Venetia Williams* 126h
6 b g Diktat—Locharia (Wolfhound (USA))
(3386) 3645^{2} 3917^{2} 4031^{5}
Crescent Beach (IRE) *Jennie Candlish* 81b
4 b g Presenting—Angelas Choice (IRE) (Saddlers' Hall (IRE))
5084^{4}
Crescent Island (IRE) *Nigel Twiston-Davies* 136h 148c
8 b g Presenting—Island Crest (Jupiter Island)
(3953)
4352^{5} 5199^{U}
Cresswell Bramble *Keith Goldsworthy* 98b
7 b m Witness Box(USA) —Cresswell Princess (IRE) (Supreme Leader)
3200^{2} 3590^{5} 3876^{4} 4728^{15} 4861^{P}
Cresswell Bubbles *Nigel Twiston-Davies* 89h
8 ch m Flemensfirth(USA) —Cresswell Princess (IRE) (Supreme Leader)
4^{4} 303^{P}
Cresswell Crusader *Anthony Honeyball* 114h
7 b g Overbury(IRE) —Sloe Hill (Le Moss)
3266^{2} 3981^{2} 4719^{3} 5107^{3}
Cresswell Melody (IRE) *Anthony Honeyball* 83b
4 b f Milan—Dawn Awakening (IRE) (Norwich)
3159^{3} (4124)

Cricket Boy *David Pipe* 89h
7 b g Alflora(IRE) —Lady Cricket (FR) (Cricket Ball (USA))
410^{P}
Cridda Boy *Simon Burrough* 99h
5 ch g Mark Of Esteem(IRE) —Second Affair (IRE) (Pursuit Of Love)
2137^{10} 2633^{5} 3386^{6}
Crimson Canyon (IRE) *Jonjo O'Neill* 88h
5 b g Montjeu(IRE) —Fleur (GER) (Perugino (USA))
528^{2} 754^{7} 932^{12} 1062^{7} 1164^{P}
Cripsey Brook *Keith Reveley* 82h
13 ch g Lycius(USA) —Duwon (IRE) (Polish Precedent (USA))
380^{5}
Criqtonic (FR) *G Macaire* 100h
4 ch g Green Tune(USA) —Criquetot (FR) (Epervier Bleu)
(1658a)
Cristal Bonus (FR) *Evan Williams* 150h
5 b g Della Francesca(USA) —Cristal Springs (FR) (Loup Solitaire (USA))
2887^{5} 3807^{7}
Croan Rock (IRE) *Ian Williams* 117h
6 b g Milan—Fiddlers Bar (IRE) (Un Desperado (FR))
2291^{6} 4159^{F} ◆ 4930^{3} 5115^{2}
Crofton Arch *John Dixon* 7h 77c
11 b g Jumbo Hirt(USA) —Joyful Imp (Import)
9^{6} 88^{9} 404^{4} 516^{3} (578)
747^{6} 947^{5} 1001^{6}
Crookshanks (IRE) *Tom George* 37b
5 b g Catcher In The Rye(IRE) —Sunset Park (IRE) (Red Sunset)
1455^{7}
Croon *Andy Turnell* 99h 95c
9 b g Sinndar(IRE) —Shy Minstrel (USA) (The Minstrel (CAN))
26^{5} 339^{7}
Crop Walker (IRE) *Kate Walton* 103h
9 bb g Kotashaan(FR) —Miss Mutley (Pitpan)
3509^{U} 4276^{6} 4477^{7} 4869^{2} 5205^{2}
Crosby Jemma *Mike Sowersby* 108h
7 ch m Lomitas—Gino's Spirits (Perugino (USA))
34^{3} 159^{6} (803) 958^{10} 1127^{5} 1470^{8} 1827^{9}
2089^{5} 2508^{7} 4113^{3} 4455^{5} 5420^{P}
Crossbarry Breeze (IRE) *Violet M Jordan*
9 b g Fresh Breeze(USA) —Northern Crusade (IRE) (Le Moss)
5115^{P}
Crosscannon (IRE) *John Flint* 76h
7 b g Anshan—Portphelia (Torus)
4776^{6}
Cross Kennon (IRE) *Jennie Candlish* 160h
7 b g Craigsteel—Gaelic Million (IRE) (Strong Gale)
1986^{6} (2360) 2870^{8} 3742^{2} (4207) 4819^{4}
Crosstek (IRE) *Alistair Whillans* 79b
5 gr g Intikhab(USA) —Tennessee Valley (USA) (Quiet American (USA))
4117^{P} 5432^{10}
Cross The Boss (IRE) *Ben Haslam*
4 b g Cape Cross(IRE) —Lady Salsa (IRE) (Gone West (USA))
4283^{P}
Crowning Jewel *Keith Reveley* 105b
5 b g Sulamani(IRE) —Pennys Pride (IRE) (Pips Pride)
2943^{4} ◆ 4117^{2} 4943^{6}
Crow Spinney *Michael Easterby* 102h 104c
8 b m Classic Cliche(IRE) —Ivengica (FR) (Roi De Rome (USA))
88^{3} 443^{4} 498^{2}
Cruchain (IRE) *Dai Burchell* 118h 129c
8 ch g Shernazar—Mack Tack (IRE) (Shardari)
735^{U} 954^{5} 1692^{6} (1816) 2213^{7} 2633^{F} **3558^{3}**
4355^{5} 5081^{2} (5305)
5436^{3}
Cruise Control *Richard Price* 90h
5 b g Piccolo—Urban Dancer (IRE) (Generous (IRE))
2322^{7} 3387^{5} 3526^{F} 4076^{4} 4530^{3} 4899^{P}
Cruise In Luxury (IRE) *Kevin Bishop* 67h
6 ch m Definite Article—Galvina (FR) (Northern Fashion (USA))
4091^{U} 4268^{U} 4535^{8}
Cruise In Style (IRE) *Kevin Bishop* 65h
5 b m Definite Article—Henrietta Street (IRE) (Royal Academy (USA))
935^{4} 1201^{6} 1487^{U} 1736^{10} 1910^{7} 5212^{12}
Cruising Bye *Jonjo O'Neill* 52h
5 b g Alflora(IRE) —Althrey Flame (IRE) (Torus)
3156^{F} 4500^{12}
Cruising Katie (IRE) *R A Cotter* 121h 131c
9 b m Beneficial—Kate Fisher (IRE) (Over The River (FR))
1131a^{F} 1801a^{2}
Crushed Ice *Malcolm Jefferson* 84b
5 gr g Silver Patriarch(IRE) —Altogether Now (IRE) (Step Together (USA))
3998^{8}
Crushing (IRE) *Julie Camacho* 19h
4 b g Kheleyf(USA) —Filmgame (IRE) (Be My Guest (USA))
1825^{12}
Crystal Cliche *Julian Smith* 58b
6 b m Classic Cliche(IRE) —Tirley Pop Eye (Cruise Missile)
3372^{7} 3651^{11}
Crystal D'Ainay (FR) *Miss Hannah Lewis* 131h 123c
12 b g Saint Preuil(FR) —Guendale (FR) (Cadoudal (FR))
4928^{10}
Crystal Prince *Charlie Longsdon* 95h 93c
7 b g Marju(IRE) —Crystal Ring (IRE) (Kris)
157^{U} 1735^{2} 2049^{4} 3350^{2} **3790^{3} 4504^{3} 5062^{4}**
Crystal Rock (IRE) *Nicky Henderson* 119h
6 br g Rock Of Gibraltar(IRE) —State Crystal (IRE) (High Estate)
1238^{4} 1487^{3} (1601) 1677^{3} 2128^{2} 2361^{2} 3225^{3}

Cuan Na Grai (IRE) *Paul Nolan* 143h 143c
10 b g Erins Isle—Volnost (USA) (Lyphard (USA))
1038a[2]
1123a[11]

Cubism *Milton Harris* 108h
5 b g Sulamani(IRE) —Diagonale (IRE) (Darshaan)
216[6] 360[7] (527) 595[4] 798[3] 1033[2] 1150[5] 1291[6] 1347[4] (1614) 1726[7] 1904[4] 1972[2] 2235[3] 2581[12]

Cuckoo Hill *Martin Brassil*
4 b g Mujahid(USA) —Noor El Houdah (IRE) (Fayruz)
2966a[8]

Cuckoo Pen *Mark Bradstock* 103h
7 b g Alflora(IRE) —Plaid Maid (IRE) (Executive Perk)
3981[4]

Cuckoo Rock (IRE) *Jonathan Portman* 92h
4 b g Refuse To Bend(IRE) —Ringmoor Down (Pivotal)
3554[6] 3958[11]

Cucumber Run (IRE) *Nicky Henderson* 136h
6 b g Oscar(IRE) —Back To Roost (IRE) (Presenting)
2389[5] 2963[2] (3403) (3836) 4725[15]

Cue Card *Colin Tizzard* 152h
5 b g King's Theatre(IRE) —Wicked Crack (IRE) (King's Ride)
(1988) ◆ (2344) ◆ 2887[2] 4788[4] 5196[2]

Cue To Cue *Keith Reveley* 103b
5 b m King's Theatre(IRE) —Marello (Supreme Leader)
2167[5] 3623[3] 4815[3]

Cuigny (FR) *Simon Shirley-Beavan* 98h
8 b g Freedom Cry—Kaolombe (FR) (Huntercombe)
161[10]

Culcabock (IRE) *Lucinda Russell* 123h
11 b g Unfuwain(USA) —Evidently (IRE) (Slip Anchor)
1956[8] 2386[13] 3334[4] 4867[2] 5315[8]

Cullahill (IRE) *Bob Buckler* 125h 123c
9 bb g Good Thyne(USA) —Rossacrowe Gale (IRE) (Strong Gale)
408[2] (631)
761[3] 911[2] 1606[5] 1777[6] 2221[7] 2395[P] 2869[6]
3347[F] 3479[5]
5037[5] 5438[3]

Cunning Clarets (IRE) *Richard Fahey* 120h
6 ch g Trans Island—Ellistown Lady (IRE) (Red Sunset)
(3335) 3808[10] 3969[8]

Cunning Plan (IRE) *Raymond York* 87h
4 ch g Bachelor Duke(USA) —Madamaa (IRE) (Alzao (USA))
4424[5] 4917[5]

Cunning Pursuit *Robin Mathew* 80h 110c
10 b g Pursuit Of Love—Mistitled (USA) (Miswaki (USA))
1094[11]

Curlew (IRE) *Chris Down*
5 b g Cape Cross(IRE) —Billbill (USA) (Storm Cat (USA))
4528[P]

Curragh Dancer (FR) *Paddy Butler* 81h 83c
8 ch g Grand Lodge(USA) —Native Twine (Be My Native (USA))
1735[13] (1915) 2135[4] 2390[3]
2930[9] 3337[2] 4560[8] (5051) 5191[5] **5266[3]**

Currahee *Maurice Barnes* 117h 103c
7 b g Efisio—Dixie Favor (USA) (Dixieland Band (USA))
309[6] **458[3]**
4067[3] 4285[4] 4715[7] 5149[5] **5310[4] 5415[2]**

Current Climate (IRE) *Richard Rowe* 96h
7 b g Luso—Kambaya (IRE) (Kambalda)
2291[4] 2946[11] 3346[9] 4427[2] 4773[P]

Current Event (FR) *Paul Nicholls* 130h
4 b g Muhtathir—La Curamalal (IRE) (Rainbow Quest (USA))
2540[6] (5010) ◆ 5300[3]

Cursum Perficio *Richard Lee* 98h
9 b g Tagula(IRE) —Simply Sooty (Absalom)
3477[7] 4008[3] 4999[8]

Custer Of The West (IRE) *Alan King* 83h
6 ch g Shernazar—Karlybelle (FR) (Sandhurst Prince)
2186[8] 3405[8] 5239[2]

Cute N You Know It *Andrew Crook* 71h 87c
8 b m Tamure(IRE) —Clodaigh Gale (Strong Gale)
176[P] 424[3] **1081[5] 1341[P]** 1694[5] 2351[5] 3717[2] (4542) 4826[U] 5103[11]

Cutlass Silver *S A Jones* 68b 52c
7 ch m Silver Patriarch(IRE) —Cutlass Princess (USA) (Cutlass (USA))
5326[7]

Cuts Both Ways (USA) *Matthew Salaman*
4 b g Johannesburg(USA) —Wise Investor (USA) (Belong To Me (USA))
2661[P]

Cybergenic (FR) *Tracey Watkins* 74h 113c
13 gr g Bering—Ciudadella (FR) (Highest Honor (FR))
2308[P] 2467[8] 4104[8] 4266[5]

Cybora (FR) *Ferdy Murphy* 100h 104c
9 ch m Cyborg(FR) —Jolie Rapide (FR) (Nikos)
2189[4] (2510)
3549[P]

Cydonia (IRE) *Robin Dickin* 79b
4 b g Westerner—Keen Gale (IRE) (Strong Gale)
5238[4]

Cygnet *Donald McCain* 115h
5 b g Dansili—Ballet Princess (Muhtarram (USA))
1705[5] 1962[6] 2939[8] 3505[7] 5168[4]

Cylindar Rattler (IRE) *Tim Vaughan* 113h 77c
8 b g Beauchamp King—Run Or Bust (IRE) (Commanche Run)
1370[4]

Cypress Grove (IRE) *John Ryall* 97h
8 b g Windsor Castle—Grecian Queen (Fairy King (USA))
2977[9] 3370[7] 4446[5]

Daarth *Brendan Duke* 89h
6 b g Alhaarth(IRE) —Glamorous Girl (IRE) (Darshaan)
12[9] **132[8]**

Daasij (IRE) *N W Alexander* 74h
6 b g Dalakhani(IRE) —Alyakkh (IRE) (Sadler's Wells (USA))
289[P] 442[9] 576[10] 870[8] 1361[3] 4302[4] 4550[5] (5096) ◆

Dabaratsa (FR) *Tim Vaughan* 110h
8 b m Astarabad(USA) —Miss Reddy (FR) (Agent Bleu (FR))
19[5] 179[6]

Daggerman *Barry Leavy* 75h
6 ch g Daggers Drawn(USA) —Another Mans Cause (FR) (Highest Honor (FR))
2038[11] 2307[12] 2640[8]

Dais Return (IRE) *Jonjo O'Neill* 116h 112c
7 b g Lahib(USA) —Bayazida (Bustino)
330[P] 463[2]

Daisy Dolittle *John Holt* 28h
4 b f Tagula(IRE) —Misty Cay (IRE) (Mujadil (USA))
1818[6]

Dakota Boy (IRE) *Alex Hales* 105h
9 ch g Flying Legend(USA) —Lisaleen River (Over The River (FR))
(765) 2094[8] 2581[7] 3744[P]

Dakota Hues *Julia Feilden*
5 b g Rainbow Quest(USA) —West Dakota (USA) (Gone West (USA))
2896[13]

Dalaram (IRE) *Sean Curran* 114h 75c
11 b g Sadler's Wells(USA) —Dalara (IRE) (Doyoun)
51[2]

Daldini *Sue Smith* 57h 125c
9 b g Josr Algarhoud(IRE) —Arianna Aldini (Habitat)
33[6] 1828[6] 2106[6] 2374[P] 3395[4] 3634[4] 4937[3]

Daliarose (FR) *David Pipe* 106h 75c
5 b m Daliapour(IRE) —Hever Rose (GER) (Dashing Blade)
910[3] **1023[9]**
1233[5] 2329[11]

Dallas Bell *Alistair Whillans* 95h 110c
9 ch g Minster Son—Eleanor May (Crofthall)
287[P] 730[5] 1002[3] 2107[2] 2354[2] 3395[3] 3853[3]

Dallas Doll (IRE) *J T R Dreaper* [illegible]5b
6 b m Bob Back(USA) —Coco Girl (Mystiko (USA))
4134[F]

Dalrymple (IRE) *Michael Madgwick* 88h
5 ch g Daylami(IRE) —Dallaah (Green Desert (USA))
1914[9] 2185[8] 2583[10] 3430[P]

Dan Breen (IRE) *David Pipe* 139h 148c
6 b g Mull Of Kintyre(USA) —Kunuz (Ela-Mana-Mou)
207[20]
2153[2] (2951)
4326[2] 4789[7] (5116)
5197[3]

Dan Buoy (FR) *Richard Guest* 114h
8 b g Slip Anchor—Bramosia (Forzando)
2171[9]

Dance For Julie (IRE) *Ben Haslam* 99h
4 b f Redback—Dancing Steps (Zafonic (USA))
(1018) ◆ 3386[4] 3550[3]

Danceintothelight *Micky Hammond* 110h
4 gr g Dansili—Kali (Linamix (FR))
1825[F] (2451) (3521) 3967[3] 4475[9]

Dance Island (IRE) *Ben Case* 121h 143c
8 b g Turtle Island(IRE) —Inse Na Rince (IRE) (Brush Aside (USA))
1986[8]
2522[2] 3437[P] 4186[5] 4821[12]

Dance Sauvage *Mike Sowersby* 88h
8 ch g Groom Dancer(USA) —Peace Dance (Bikala)
1829[9] 2080[9] 2280[3] 4390[5] 4550[8] 4977[P]

Dance Til Midnight *Richard Rowe* 54b
4 b f Imperial Dancer—Flinders (Henbit (USA))
2052[8] 3616[10] *4923[13]*

Dance With Chance (IRE) *Alan King*
4 b f Kalanisi(IRE) —Persian Lass (IRE) (Grand Lodge (USA))
1018[P]

Dancewiththedevil (IRE) *Peter Bowen* 122h 87c
10 bb g Dr Massini(IRE) —Hibba (IRE) (Doubletour (USA))
80[2] 331[3] 521[6]
952[3] 1127[6] 1311[7]

Dancing Art (IRE) *Keith Reveley* 93h
5 b g Definite Article—Seductive Dance (Groom Dancer (USA))
4363[3] 4889[6] 5092[5]

Dancing Belle *J R Jenkins* 50h
6 b m Fasliyev(USA) —May Ball (Cadeaux Genereux)
3302[7] 4499[13] 4810[12]

Dancing Daffodil *Robin Dickin* 77h
6 ch m Kadastrof(FR) —Whistling Song (True Song)
1735[9] 1915[3] 2390[4] (3396) (3540)

Dancing Dude (IRE) *Nicky Henderson* 115h
4 ch g Danehill Dancer(IRE) —Wadud (Nashwan (USA))
(5115)

Dancing Emily (IRE) *Graeme McPherson* 99b
5 ch m Anshan—Goodthyne Lady (IRE) (Good Thyne (USA))
(5070) ◆

Dancing Gizmo *Alistair Whillans* 70b
6 b g Where Or When(IRE) —Tactile (Groom Dancer (USA))
1702[8] 4151[7]

Dancing Hero (IRE) *Thomas Foley* 136h 129c
10 ch g Simply Great(FR) —Buck And Roll (Buckskin (FR))
3206a[P]

Dancing Hill *Kevin Bishop* 75h
12 b m Piccolo—Ryewater Dream (Touching Wood (USA))
522[P] 646[9] 955[P] 1064[6] 1179[P] 1232[P]

Dancing Legend *Peter Hiatt* 66h
5 b m Midnight Legend—Disco Danehill (IRE) (Danehill Dancer (IRE))
249[5] 3396[P] 3487[P] 3724[P] 4747[P] 5103[P]

Dancing Partner (USA) *Micky Hammond* 21h
10 b g Distant View(USA) —Bold Ballerina (Sadler's Wells (USA))
1375[5] 4274[P]

Dancing Primo *Mark Brisbourne* 97b
5 b m Primo Valentino(IRE) —Tycoon's Last (Nalchik (USA))
1201[4] 5119[8]

Dancing Teasel *Emma Lavelle* 74b
4 ch f Snurge—Cajole (IRE) (Barathea (IRE))
2965[7] 4780[6]

Dancing Tornado (IRE) *Michael Hourigan* 155h 154c
10 ch g Golden Tornado(IRE) —Lady Dante (IRE) (Phardante (FR))
1527a[2] ◆ 2359[2]

Danderdandan *Philip Sharp*
5 b g Fraam—Heneseys Leg (Sure Blade (USA))
426[4]

Danderry (IRE) *Lawney Hill* 125h
7 b g Dilshaan—Creggan Vale Lass (Simply Great (FR))
3771[P]

Dane Cottage *Katie Stephens* 51h
4 ch f Beat Hollow—Lady Soleas (Be My Guest (USA))
4288[10] 4781[8] 5078[6]

Danehill Silver *Brian Storey* 57h
7 b g Silver Patriarch(IRE) —Danehill Princess (IRE) (Danehill (USA))
161[P] 456[P] 520[7] 604[12] 805[P]

Danehillsundance (IRE) *Philip Kirby* 93h
7 b g Danehill Dancer(IRE) —Rosie's Guest (IRE) (Be My Guest (USA))
3551[4] 3715[11] 3887[9] 4422[U] 5307[U] (5390)

Danehill Willy (IRE) *Evan Williams* 133h 134c
9 b g Danehill Dancer(IRE) —Lowtown (Camden Town)
2086[P]

Dani (IRE) *Mark Rimell* 25h
5 b m Modigliani(USA) —Stargard (Polish Precedent (USA))
2156[14] 3651[9] 4100[11] 4535[11]

Daniel's Dream *John Dixon* 76h
11 b g Prince Daniel(USA) —Amber Holly (Import)
209[7] 400[7] 490[5] 519[11] 999[6] 3855[5] 4068[10]

Danimix (IRE) *Peter Bowen* 122h
6 b g Dr Massini(IRE) —Spring Blend (IRE) (Persian Mews)
733[3] 843[4] (988) 1118[2] 1372[P]

Dani's Girl (IRE) *Pat Phelan* 124h
8 bb m Second Empire(IRE) —Quench The Lamp (IRE) (Glow (USA))
2498[13]

Danish Rebel (IRE) *George Charlton* 114h
7 b g Danetime(IRE) —Wheatsheaf Lady (IRE) (Red Sunset)
627[4]

Dan Maguire (IRE) *Peter Pritchard* 96h
10 b g Dr Massini(IRE) —Glucose (IRE) (Electric)
1059[6] 1129[5]

Danny Cool *Keith Reveley* 81h
8 b g Dansili—Strictly Cool (USA) (Bering)
4233[12] 4743[5] 4995[6] 5307[5]

Danny Mags (IRE) *Tim Vaughan* 85b
4 b g Overbury(IRE) —Back To Favour (IRE) (Bob Back (USA))
4151[5]

Danny Zuko (IRE) *Donald McCain* 112h 118c
8 ch g Anshan—Lezies Last (IRE) (Ragapan)
96[10] 515[3] (675) 803[7] 1043[3]

Danse Macabre (IRE) *Tony Carroll* 85h 69c
12 b g Flemensfirth(USA) —My Romance (Green Shoon)
698[8]

Dan's Heir *Wilf Storey* 66h 48c
9 b g Dansili—Million Heiress (Auction Ring (USA))
4115[12]

Dansilver *Jim Best* 80h 71c
7 b g Dansili—Silver Gyre (IRE) (Silver Hawk (USA))
2149[6] 2433[2] 4771[6]

Dansimar *Venetia Williams* 132h
7 gr m Daylami(IRE) —Hylandra (USA) (Bering)
2182[F] 2481[U] 3452[4] 3947[P]

Dantari (IRE) *Evan Williams* 130h
6 b g Alhaarth(IRE) —Daniysha (IRE) (Doyoun)
316[2] 756[2] 1133a[8] 1864[7] 1967[2] 3229[5] 3561[5] 3947[3] 4806[5] 5304[9] 5441[4]

Dante's Lady (IRE) *Neil Mulholland*
6 b m Samraan(USA) —Fashions Dante (IRE) (Phardante (FR))
3943[8]

Dante's Storm *Alan Hill* 134c
9 ch g Glacial Storm(USA) —Juleit Jones (IRE) (Phardante (FR))
(4131) ◆ 4851[5]

Danzig Fox *Michael Mullineaux* 78h
6 b g Foxhound(USA) —Via Dolorosa (Chaddleworth (IRE))
299[U] 527[6] 678[6] 1049[P]

Dapple Prince (IRE) *Tom Gretton* 26h
6 gr g Environment Friend—Mitsy (IRE) (Supreme Leader)
2074[14] 3647[11] 4081[P]

Daraybad (FR) *Andrew Crook* 86h 85c
9 b g Octagonal(NZ) —Daraydala (IRE) (Royal Academy (USA))
800[P] 1085[4] 1340[4] 1949[6] 4548[8] 5114[3] 5350[8]

Daraz Rose (IRE) *Barry Brennan* 107h 112c
10 br m Darazari(IRE) —Miss Rose (IRE) (Phardante (FR))
3483[U] 4025[9] 4955[7]

Darby's Turn (IRE) *Richard Phillips* 120h 129c
9 br g Pistolet Bleu(IRE) —Money For Buttons (IRE) (Alphabatim (USA))
(2153)
2662[F] 3722[4] 4723[7] 4989[P]

Darceys Dancer (IRE) *Noel Meade* 134h 134c
8 b g Lear Spear(USA) —Dun Oengus (IRE) (Strong Gale)
1849a[2] ◆ 2412a[5]

Darden Burn (IRE) *David Carr* 57b
5 b g Pilsudski(IRE) —Pro Bono Nobis (IRE) (Commanche Run)
399[11] 2553[14]

Daredevil Dan *Tina Jackson* 58h
5 b g Golden Snake(USA) —Tiempo (King Of Spain)
3521[P] 3885[P] 4165[12] 5027[13]

Dareios (GER) *John Mackie* 73h
6 ch g Numerous(USA) —Desert Chiara (USA) (Desert King (IRE))
1990[P] 2111[7] 3261[P]
3990[P] 4144[P]

Dare Me (IRE) *Philip Hobbs* 130h
7 b g Bob Back(USA) —Gaye Chatelaine (IRE) (Castle Keep)
(1910) ◆ (2137)

Dare To Doubt *W P Mullins* 131h
7 b m King's Theatre(IRE) —Karawa (Karinga Bay)
(4249a)

Darfour *Martin Hill* 98h
7 b g Inchinor—Gai Bulga (Kris)
664[8]

Darina's Boy *Sue Smith* 112h 93c
15 b g Sula Bula—Glebelands Girl (Burslem)
425[6]

Daring Approach (IRE) *Helen Nelmes* 105h 73c
10 b g Saddlers' Hall(IRE) —Nicks Approach (IRE) (Dry Dock)
2046[6] 2392[3] 3933[P]

Daring Origyn (FR) *Richard Lee* 123h
6 ch g Blushing Flame(USA) —Forza Malta (FR) (Royal Charter (FR))
1959[4] 2283[2] 3490[4] (3881) 4485[11] 5110[P]

Darkan Road *George Charlton* 71h
6 bb g Beat All(USA) —Sister Seven (IRE) (Henbit (USA))
609[5] 2355[8] 3547[8] 3851[15] 4145[7] 5307[8]

Dark Ben (FR) *Simon West* 114h 120c
11 b g Solar One(FR) —Reine D'Auteuil (FR) (Cap Martin (FR))
2163[4] (4060)
4284[3]

Dark Dancer *Laura Mongan* 83b
7 br m Alflora(IRE) —Swift Conveyance (IRE) (Strong Gale)
1680[3] *3060[5]* 4667[5] 4918[P]

Dark Energy *Michael Scudamore* 112h
7 br g Observatory(USA) —Waterfowl Creek (IRE) (Be My Guest (USA))
350[6] 798[2] ◆ 1282[F] 1726[14] 1911[5] 2054[3] 2169[3] 2323[2] 2633[2] 2977[12]

Dark Gem *Simon West*
4 br f Makbul—Giffoine (Timeless Times (USA))
629[P] 743[P]

Dark Gentleman *Evelyn Slack* 49h 89c
8 bl g Rock City—Panic Button (IRE) (Simply Great (FR))
1644[10]
2194[5] 2479[2] 3360[6] (3636)
3884[5] 4509[5]

Dark Glacier (IRE) *Chris Grant* 121b
6 b g Flemensfirth(USA) —Glacier Lilly (IRE) (Glacial Storm (USA))
(2553) 3889[2] ◆ (4308) ◆ 4808[14]

Dark Halo (IRE) *C A McBratney* 87h
6 b m Winged Love(IRE) —Rosie Brook (IRE) (Be My Native (USA))
285[3] 749[3] ◆ 871[5] 1102[P]

Dark Haven *James Evans* 59b
8 b m Lugana Beach—American Pie (Lighter)
2456[P] 3227[P] 5071[P]
5079[P]

Dark Lover (GER) *Paul Nicholls* 115h
6 b g Zinaad—Dark Lady (GER) (Lagunas)
1866[2] ◆ (2331) ◆ *3055[2]* (4268)

Darkness *Simon Sherwood* 119h 113c
12 ch g Accordion—Winnowing (IRE) (Strong Gale)
4463[3]

Dark Ranger *Tim Pitt* 108h
5 br g Where Or When(IRE) —Dark Raider (IRE) (Definite Article)
(1689) 1862[7] 2375[5] 4858[3] 5424[4]

Dark Ruby *Les Hall* 87b
6 b m Overbury(IRE) —Glenda Ross (Furry Glen)
1480[2] *2896[9]*

Dark Sensation *Stuart Kittow* 29h
6 b m Alflora(IRE) —Black Secret (Gildoran)
3327[7] 2168[14]

Dark Shadow *Nicky Henderson* 92b
4 b g Royal Applause—Royal York (Bustino)
4082[10] 5012[6]

Darksideofthemoon (IRE) *Tim Vaughan* 118h 82c
9 b g Accordion—Supreme Valentine (IRE) (Supreme Leader)
888[P] 1254[2] 1372[8]
1642[4]

Darlan *Nicky Henderson* 117b
4 br g Milan—Darbela (IRE) (Doyoun)
(5426) ◆

Darna *William Amos* 125h
5 b g Alflora(IRE) —Dutch Dyane (Midyan (USA))
1702[6] (3331) (3850)

Darn Hot *Alex Hales* 97h 112c
7 b m Sir Harry Lewis(USA) —Hot Classic (Classic Cliche (IRE))
158[2] 2311[3] 2975[4] 3230[P] 3695[3]

Darstardly Dick (IRE) *Victor Dartnall* 122h 127c
8 b g Oscar(IRE) —Fiery Belle (IRE) (Brush Aside (USA))
708[P] **(1706)**
3229[12]
3687[4] 4777[4] 5154[F]

Dartford Warbler (IRE) *Oliver Sherwood* 69b
4 bb g Overbury(IRE) —Stony View (IRE) (Tirol)
5063[10]

Darwins Fox (FR) *Henry De Bromhead* 126h
5 bb g Kahyasi—Parcelle De Sou (FR) (Ajdayt (USA))
4249a[8]

Dasher Reilly (USA) *Aytach Sadik* 110h 79c
10 b g Ghazi(USA) —Kutira (USA) (Dixieland Band (USA))
381[6] 649[P] 952[5] 1080[9] 1159[P] 1256[U] 1277[5] 1366[4] 1425[4]

Dashing Bach (IRE) *Alison Thorpe* 84h
7 b g Bach(IRE) —One More Dash (IRE) (Glacial Storm (USA))
698[P] 849[8] 912[7] 1049[8]

Dashing Doc (IRE) *Evan Williams* 95h
4 ch g Dr Fong(USA) —Dashiba (Dashing Blade)
5071[2]

Dashing George (IRE) *Dr Richard Newland* 126h 145c
9 ch g Beneficial—Here It Is (Stanford)
2171[7]
2541[7] 3290[9] 3437[10] 3922[2] 4193[P] (4328)

Dashing John *Audrey Manners* 96h
9 b g My Best Valentine—Westerlands Queen (Afzal)
1734[10] 1963[4]

Dashing Patriarch *Malcolm Beck* 94b
6 b g Silver Patriarch(IRE) —Mezzo Princess (Remezzo)
2772[2]

Dashing Ruby (IRE) *Paul W Flynn* 126h 118c
7 gr g Portrait Gallery(IRE) —Aurliano (IRE) (Knesset (USA))
1121a[3]

Dash Of Salt *Charlie Longsdon* 72h
6 b g Fantastic Light(USA) —Granita (CHI) (Roy (USA))
1821[11] 2232[P]

Daurica *Renee Robeson* 117h
7 b m Dolpour—Ardeola (Ardross)
193[11] 633[11] 846[6] 986[7] 1368[8]

Dave's Dream (IRE) *Nicky Henderson* 144h 154c
8 b g Anshan—Native Success (IRE) (Be My Native (USA))
(2345)
2886[12]

Davids City (IRE) *Geoffrey Harker* 70h
7 b g Laveron—Irelands Own (IRE) (Commanche Run)
8[7]

Davis Street (IRE) *Jonjo O'Neill* 113h
7 b g Flemensfirth(USA) —Kala Supreme (IRE) (Supreme Leader)
1162[P]

Davy Boy Legend (IRE) *Josie Ross* 70h 98c
8 gr g Saint Preuil(FR) —Samarinnda (IRE) (Akarad (FR))
398[7] 2552[13] 3746[12] 4067[P]

Dawn At Sea *John Flint* 106h
9 b m Slip Anchor—Finger Of Light (Green Desert (USA))
1746[6] 2141[13] 3791[9]

Dawn Auction (IRE) *Anthony Middleton* 38b
4 b g Auction House(USA) —Isle Of Sodor (Cyrano De Bergerac)
4082[16] 4356[15]

Dawn Ride (IRE) *Micky Hammond* 78h 121c
10 b g New Frontier(IRE) —Atlantic Dawn (IRE) (Radical)
(11) **425[5]**
2036[F] 2374[2] 3574[2] 4167[6] 4360[P] 5032[4] 5353[3]

Dawn Storm (IRE) *Rachel Hobbs* 69h
6 ch g City On A Hill(USA) —Flames (Blushing Flame (USA))
635[5] 766[4]

Day Du Roy (FR) *Lynn Siddall* 52h 59c
13 b g Ajdayt(USA) —Rose Pomme (FR) (Rose Laurel)
649[5]

Daymar Bay (IRE) *Emma Lavelle* 114b
5 b g Oscar(IRE) —Sunset View (IRE) (Good Thyne (USA))
(2295) ◆ 3909[2]

Days Ahead (IRE) *Eoin Doyle* 116h
4 ch g Kheleyf(USA) —Hushaby (IRE) (Eurobus)
2966a[5] 3239a[9]

Days Of Pleasure (IRE) *Chris Gordon* 110h 98c
6 b g Fraam—Altizaf (Zafonic (USA))
2141[7] 3308[2] **4666[4] 4927[3]**

Daytime Dreamer (IRE) *Martin Todhunter* 113h 62c
7 b g Diktat—Tuppenny (Salse (USA))
803[3] 958[12] 1406[8] 1644[7] 2104[3] 3334[7] 3523[7]
4305[P] 4963[8] 5098[7]

Day Time Run (IRE) *Diana Grissell* 95h
7 ch g Rudimentary(USA) —Theatral (Orchestra)
154[6] 683[U] 932[5]

Dazeen *Paul Midgley* 28h
4 b g Zafeen(FR) —Bond Finesse (IRE) (Danehill Dancer (IRE))
1498[U] 2033[8]

Dazzling Rita *Shaun Lycett* 82b
5 b m Midnight Legend—Pytchley Dawn (Welsh Captain)
5019[2]

Deadline (UAE) *Alison Thorpe* 107h
7 ch g Machiavellian(USA) —Time Changes (USA) (Danzig (USA))
888[5] 1026[RR]

Dead Or Alive (IRE) *Tim Vaughan* 113h 130c
8 b g Exit To Nowhere(USA) —Avro Avian (Ardross)
(438) **1032[2]**
1103[2] 1332[F] 1404[6] 4695[3] 5163[8]

Deal Done (FR) *D T Hughes* 139h 143c
7 b g Vertical Speed(FR) —Five Rivers (FR) (Cadoudal (FR))
3706a[3] 4821[3]

Dealing River *Neil King* 75b
4 b g Avonbridge—Greensand (Green Desert (USA))
3964[4]

Dean's Grange *Colin Tizzard* 115h
6 br g Alflora(IRE) —Bobupandown (Bob's Return (IRE))
235[10] 1736[2] 1910[5] 2128[4] 2626[5]

Dear Sam (GER) *Steve Gollings* 117h
6 b g Black Sam Bellamy(IRE) —Douce France (IRE) (Fabulous Dancer (USA))
1988[2] ◆ 2473[2] 3692[0]

De Bansha Man (IRE) *Nigel Twiston-Davies* 105h 109c
6 br g Overbury(IRE) —Gleann Alainn (Teenoso (USA))
(1596)
1912[5] 3391[9] 4705[3] 5377[6]

De Boitron (FR) *Ferdy Murphy* 90h 142c
7 b g Sassanian(USA) —Pondiki (FR) (Sicyos (USA))
2345[10] 4116[2] 4853[4] 5288[3]

December *Christine Dunnett* 92h
5 b g Oasis Dream—Winter Solstice (Unfuwain (USA))
3783[U] 4499[8] 4810[11] 5099[13] 5270[7]

Decent Lord (IRE) *Jennie Candlish* 93h
7 b g Lord Of Appeal—Otorum (IRE) (Muroto)
224[F] 490[P] (4104) (4136) (4266) 4314[3] 4892[2] 5172[6]

Dechiper (IRE) *Robert Johnson* 103h
9 bb g Almutawakel—Safiya (USA) (Riverman (USA))
1664[3] 1760[6] 5147[9]
5413[P]

Deciding Moment (IRE) *Ben De Haan* 92b
5 b g Zagreb(USA) —Fontaine Jewel (IRE) (Lafontaine (USA))
2328[3] 2957[9] 4356[6] 4468[13]

Decimus Meridius (IRE) *Howard Johnson* 66h
4 ch g Danehill Dancer(IRE) —Simaat (USA) (Mr Prospector (USA))
1699[9]

Decision *Lawney Hill* 108h
5 b g Royal Applause—Corinium (IRE) (Turtle Island (IRE))
299[3] 541[2] 850[3] 886[3] 1160[5] 2312[6] 3306[4] 4034[5] (4785) 4935[2] (5276)

Declan Og (IRE) *Chris Down* 61b
6 b g Witness Box(USA) —Journey Home (IRE) (Supreme Leader)
4533[6]

Decoy (FR) *David Pipe* 115h
5 b h Della Francesca(USA) —Vagualame (FR) (Saint Estephe (FR))
3196[9] 3478[4] 3808[11] 4031[7] 4358[4] ◆

Decoy Daddy (IRE) *Anthony Mullins* 132h 136c
9 ch g Lord Of Appeal—Young Bebe (IRE) (M Double M (USA))
1113a[4]

Decree Nisi *P Kelsall* 95h 83c
8 ch g Compton Place—Palisandra (USA) (Chief's Crown (USA))
250[P]

De Danu (IRE) *Aidan Anthony Howard* 96h 68c
8 ch g Pierre—Nuan (IRE) (Teofane)
95[P] 1102[6]

Dee Cee Bolter (IRE) *Lucinda Russell* 78h
9 b g Supreme Leader—Kim's Choice (Le Bavard (FR))
1782[9] 2103[9]

Dee Cee Elle *John Flint* 97h
7 b m Groom Dancer(USA) —Missouri (Charnwood Forest (IRE))
1107[P] 1451[13]

Deed Poll *Chris Down* 67h
5 ch g Fleetwood(IRE) —Prideway (IRE) (Pips Pride)
4094[10] 4528[6] 4952[8]

Dee Ee Williams (IRE) *Nick Gifford* 147h 138c
8 b g Dushyantor(USA) —Fainne Oir (IRE) (Montelimar (USA))
207[19] 2219[3] **(2578)**
3193[F] 3555[5] 4848[P]

Deejan (IRE) *Tim Vaughan* 84h
6 b m Oscar(IRE) —Boleree (IRE) (Mandalus)
4944[4] 5108[4] 5374[P]

Deep Pockets (IRE) *Caroline Keevil* 115h 122c
12 b g Fourstars Allstar(USA) —Pocket Price (IRE) (Moscow Society (USA))
2147[10]
2928[3] 3347[U] 3483[2] 3771[2] 4079[12]
(4402)

Deep Purple *Evan Williams* 140h 170c
10 b g Halling(USA) —Seal Indigo (IRE) (Glenstal (USA))
2091[3] 2964[U] 4201[3] 5162[4]

Deep Quest *Simon Burrough* 66h 61c
12 b g El Conquistador—Ten Deep (Deep Run)
2140[7] 2503[F] 2794[P]

Deep Reflection *Martin Keighley* 106h 42c
11 b g Cloudings(IRE) —Tudor Thyne (IRE) (Good Thyne (USA))
651[5] (1062) 1137[P] 1195[11]
2475[7] 3256[6] 3493[7] 3724[8]

Deer Fin (IRE) *Andrew Wilson* 44h
9 b g Luso—Capallbeag (IRE) (Bravefoot)
32[F]

Definite All Star (IRE) *Gordon Elliott* 113h
7 b g Definite Article—Native Pine (IRE) (Be My Native (USA))
943 [2]

Definite Artist (IRE) *Venetia Williams* 102b
5 b m Definite Article—Lady Llancillo (IRE) (Alflora (IRE))
3876[2] 4335[10]

Definite Dawn (IRE) *Tim Vaughan* 113h
7 br g Definite Article—Good Dawn (IRE) (Good Thyne (USA))
7[5] 1990[5] 2232[4] 2642[2] 3428[3] 3942[6]

Definite Lady (IRE) *Mark Rimell* 75b
5 b m Definite Article—Phillis Hill (Karinga Bay)
2590[4]

Definitley Lovely *Nigel Twiston-Davies* 105h
6 b m Definite Article—Fair Maid Marion (IRE) (Executive Perk)
230[6] 1771[7] 2168[4] 3480[7] (4454) 5008[P]

Definity (IRE) *Paul Nicholls* 147h 141c
8 br g Definite Article—Ebony Jane (Roselier (FR))
2979[4] (3788)
4093[2] 4794[5]

De Forgotten Man (IRE) *Martin Keighley* 109h
6 b g Commander Collins(IRE) —Jrred Up (IRE) (Jurado (USA))
25[2] 2142[10] (2981) 3346[F]

Defying Gravity (IRE) *Trevor Horgan* 53h 104c
8 b g Old Vic—Night Escape (IRE) (Satco (FR))
1178[6]

Degas Art (IRE) *Howard Johnson* 120h 125c
8 b g Danehill Dancer(IRE) —Answer (Warning)
1827[4] 2399[2] **3632[F]** 4257[4] 5262[F]

Deise Dan (IRE) *C A McBratney* 117h
8 b g Presenting—Daraheen Diamond (IRE) (Husyan (USA))
870[6]

Delcombe *Richard Mitchell* 82h
10 b g Deltic(USA) —Nellie's Joy VII (Damsire Unregistered)
2144[10]
3226[P]

Delfinia *David Thompson* 68h
10 b m Kingsinger(IRE) —Delvecchia (Glint Of Gold)
801[P]

Delgany Diva *Ben Pollock*
6 b m Executive Perk—No Grandad (Strong Gale)
249[P]

Delgany Gunner *Ben Pollock* 92c
7 b g Commanche Run—No Grandad (Strong Gale)
155[7] 429[5] 795[7] 1694[P]
1733[5] 1820[P] 2290[4] 3819[3] (4126)
(4560) 4829[4]

Delgany Run *Ben Pollock*
8 b g Commanche Run—No Grandad (Strong Gale)
138[3]

Delightful Cliche *S R Andrews* 102h 109c
10 b g Classic Cliche(IRE) —Ima Delight (Idiots Delight)
(292) **466[4]**
580[2]

Delightfully (FR) *Lucinda Russell* 105h
7 br m Sagacity(FR) —Green House (FR) (Houston (FR))
212[P] 1782[2] 2448[6] 3362[5] 4067[7] (4826)

Delightful Touch (FR) *Gerald Ham* 59h
10 gr g Villez(USA) —Fagaras (FR) (Kenmare (FR))
698[F] 921[10] 1066[10]

Deloughtane (IRE) *R M Woollacott* 90c
11 b g Dr Massini(IRE) —Bonnies Glory (General Ironside)
133[3] 4901[P]

Delphi Mountain (IRE) *C F Swan* 114h
6 b g Oscar(IRE) —Summer Break (IRE) (Foxhound (USA))
(1832)

Del Rio (IRE) *J T R Dreaper* 122h 130c
8 ch g Cyborg(FR) —Giuletta (FR) (Petit Montmorency (USA))
(306) **873[2]**

De Luain Gorm (IRE) *Chris Down* 72h 132c
13 b g Beneficial—Call Catherine (IRE) (Strong Gale)
130[6] 373[3] 522[8]
(592) (734)
1229[P]

Denali Highway (IRE) *Alan King* 92b
4 ch g Governor Brown(USA) —Amaretto Flame (IRE) (First Trump)
(4881)

Denman (IRE) *Paul Nicholls* 157h 183c
11 ch g Presenting—Polly Puttens (Pollerton)
2673[3] 4850[2] 5162[5]

Den Maschine *John Flint* 115h
6 b g Sakhee(USA) —Flamingo Flower (USA) (Diesis)
(250) 500[4] 733[2]

Dennis Doyle (IRE) *Tom George* 42h
5 ch g Trans Island—Lucy Liu (IRE) (Grand Lodge (USA))
3783[8] 4006[14] 4437[15]

Dennis The Legend *Grant Cann* 79b 121c
10 b g Midnight Legend—Fly The Wind (Windjammer (USA))
152[3] 411[4] 525[P] 911[P]

Denny Mac (IRE) *Liam Corcoran* 83h 114c
10 b g Arctic Lord—Rusada (IRE) (Beau Sher)
56[P]

Den Of Iniquity *Warren Greatrex* 50h 142c
10 b g Supreme Leader—Divine Comedy (IRE) (Phardante (FR))
1968[2] 2497[P] *(3092)* 3293[16]
4821[13]

Denton Ryal *Sheena West* 95h
4 b f Trade Fair—My Valentina (Royal Academy (USA))
1545[2] 1882[3] 2294[5] 3348[8]

Departed (IRE) *Richard Phillips* 92h 28c
7 b g Oscar(IRE) —Same Token (Cheval)
100[8]

Deputy Dog (IRE) *Jonjo O'Neill* 105h
5 b g Kahyasi—Hirayna (Doyoun)
1824[8] 2419[8] 2985[8] 3304[3] 3542[4] 4745[7]

Derawar (IRE) *Lucy Jones* 85h 102c
12 b g Kahyasi—Denizliya (IRE) (Sadler's Wells (USA))
4102[5] 4409[2] (4525)
4772[4]

Dereks (IRE) *Sophie Leech* 120h
9 b g Dr Massini(IRE) —Top Drawer (IRE) (Topanoora)
(604) 697[3] 829[4] (953) (1160) 1260[2] 1859[0] 1884[2]

Dermey Bowler (IRE) *Tim Vaughan* 110h
8 b g Pierre—Quittern Express (IRE) (Supreme Leader)
3153[P]

Der Spieler (GER) *J G Coogan* 138h
6 b g Singspiel(IRE) —Dabara (IRE) (Shardari)
1847a[2] 2197a[2] 2887[8]

Descaro (USA) *David O'Meara* 104h
5 gr g Dr Fong(USA) —Miarixa (FR) (Linamix (FR))
2477[6] 4115[5] 4892[3]

Description (IRE) *Mrs Jenny Gordon* 117h 125c
9 b g Humbel(USA) —Magic User (Deep Run)
33[5] 839[6] 4851[F]

Desert Cry (IRE) *Donald McCain* 140h
5 bb g Desert Prince(IRE) —Hataana (USA) (Robellino (USA))
3386[5] 3850[2] (4242) ◆ 4475[2] ◆ 5182[5]

Desert Fairy *James Unett*
5 b m Tobougg(IRE) —Regal Fairy (IRE) (Desert King (IRE))
4309[P]

Desert Fever *Nigel Twiston-Davies* 21h
5 b g Dubai Destination(USA) —Gaijin (Caerleon (USA))
690[6]

Desert Forest (IRE) *Howard Johnson* 43h
4 b g Desert Style(IRE) —Minehostess (IRE) (Shernazar)
1324[3]

Desert Mirage (IRE) *P J Goodwin* 87h
7 b g Desert Style(IRE) —Minehostess (IRE) (Shernazar)
2070[P] 2114[8]

Desertmore Star (IRE) *J Smith* 77h 84c
10 b g Dr Massini(IRE) —Very Very Sweet (IRE) (Commanche Run)
4307[U]

Desert Soul *Maurice Barnes* 93h
7 b g Fantastic Light(USA) —Jalousie (IRE) (Barathea (IRE))
943 [5] 1340[3] 1596[4] (1647) 1873[F] (Dead)

Desolait *Nigel Twiston-Davies* 94h
6 b m Erhaab(USA) —Brambly Hedge (Teenoso (USA))
27[2] 684[P] 916[3]

De Soto *Paul Webber* 124h 133c
10 b g Hernando(FR) —Vanessa Bell (IRE) (Lahib (USA))
300[3] 567[2] 1108[3]
1312[P] 1469[F] 1769[P]

Desperate Dex (IRE) *Ferdy Murphy* 100h 105c
11 b g Un Desperado(FR) —Too Sharp (True Song)
(1701)
2034[P] (3544)
4716[3]

Destiny's Dancer *Ben Haslam* 90h
4 b f Dubai Destination(USA) —Cybinka (Selkirk (USA))
836[4] 960[3] (1279)

Destroyer Deployed *Tim Vaughan* 131b
5 b g Deploy—Supreme Cove (Supreme Leader)
(3903) (4376) 4808[2] ◆

Detroit Red *Martin Hill* 112h
5 b m Hamairi(IRE) —Kingston Black (Shaab)
263[4] 591[3] (910) (2329) 2514[8]

Deuce *Lawney Hill* 94h
5 ch m Where Or When(IRE) —Justbetweenfriends (USA) (Diesis)
1737[4]

Deus Ex Machina (FR) *B De Watrigant* 124c
7 b g Pelder(IRE) —Mea Maxima Culpa (FR) (Holst (USA))
5367a[P]

Deuteronomy (IRE) *John Wade* 75h 105c
10 b g Beneficial—Good Heavens (IRE) (Heavenly Manna)
(2034)
2366[2] 3574[5] 3853[7]

Deutschland (USA) *W P Mullins* 144h 143c
8 b g Red Ransom(USA) —Rhine Valley (USA) (Danzig (USA))
1123a[P] 1527a[F]

Deux Etoiles (IRE) *Gary Moore* 30h
4 b g Montjeu(IRE) —Onereuse (Sanglamore (USA))
2211[9]

Dev (IRE) *Gordon Elliott* 94h 133c
11 b g Anshan—Local Dream (Deep Run)
5185[F]

Devilfishpoker Com *Shaun Harris* 73h
7 ch g Dr Fong(USA) —Midnight Allure (Aragon)
1085[P] 1236[9] 1375[3] 1428[7] 1660[P]
1954[P] 2070[P]

Devils And Dust (IRE) *Karen Tutty* 90h 45c
10 b g Needle Gun(IRE) —Tartan Trouble (Warpath)
456[3] 887[5] 1149[4] 1249[4] 1407[7] 1625[P]

Devils Delight (IRE) *James Moffatt* 76h 72c
9 b m Desert King(IRE) —Devil's Crown (USA) (Chief's Crown (USA))
520[2] **1378[5]**
1762[4] 2190[4] 2367[4] 3631[3] 4136[4] 4822[P]

Devils River (IRE) *Anna Brooks* 78h 97c
8 b g Anabaa(USA) —Riviere Du Diable (USA) (Irish River (FR))
(26) **2152[5]**
2591[P] 2986[P] 3898[3] 4142[4]

Devil To Pay *Alan King* 126h
5 b g Red Ransom(USA) —My Way (IRE) (Marju (IRE))
(2361) (5193)

Devil Water *James Ewart* 108h 101c
8 bb g Maresca Sorrento(FR) —Craig Burn (Arkan)
42[3] **306[6]**
2107[8] 2656[U] 3549[7] 4057[4] 4573[6] 5414[3]

De Vine Memory *Peter Niven* 81b
4 b f Grape Tree Road—Mystic Memory (Ela-Mana-Mou)
3752[5] 4554[6]

Devito (FR) *John Panvert* 94h
10 ch g Trempolino(USA) —Snowy (FR) (Wollow)
(990)

Devon Native (IRE) *Chris Down* 120h
8 ch m Double Trigger(IRE) —My Native Girl (IRE) (Be My Native (USA))
340[3] 2514[2] 3483[3] 3688[15] 3881[6] (4532) 5153[4]

Devotion To Duty (IRE) *Lucinda Russell* 122h
5 b g Montjeu(IRE) —Charmante (USA) (Alydar (USA))
315[4] 943 [4] 1573[2] 2545[3] 3362[7] (4058) 4420[2] 4875[10]

De Welsh Wizzard *Emma Lavelle* 108h
8 b g Karinga Bay—Valls D'Andorra (Free State)
1740[8] 2983[P] 3840[3] 4745[5] (5054) 5193[6]

D'Gigi *Keith Reveley* 94b
5 ch m Beat Hollow—Strictly Cool (USA) (Bering)
2511[2] 3752[2] 4468[16] 5135[5]

Dhaafer *Alan King* 122h
4 b g Nayef(USA) —Almurooj (Zafonic (USA))
2306[5] 2614[2] 3401[5] ◆ (3767) 4331[2] 4807[3] 5227[5]

Dhaular Dhar (IRE) *Jim Goldie* 111h
9 b h Indian Ridge—Pescara (IRE) (Common Grounds)
1962[14] 2509[2]

Diablo (IRE) *Nigel Twiston-Davies* 123h 135c
9 br g Even Top(IRE) —Warren Wonder (IRE) (Miner's Lamp)
155[5] 1365[3] 1856[P]

Diaco (IRE) *Jonjo O'Neill* 99h 123c
7 b g Dr Massini(IRE) —Eurogal (IRE) (Strong Gale)
687[6] 889[6] 1025[3] 1252[6] 1334[2] (1628) 2248[U]

Diamanpeg (IRE) *David Rees* 78h
7 gr g Fusaichi Pegasus(USA) —Diamilina (FR) (Linamix (FR))
1049[F] 1199[11] 4675[4] 5383[2]

Diamond Brook (IRE) *Nick Williams* 121h 121c
6 b g Alderbrook—Hilda Howard (IRE) (Tidaro (USA))
(1909)
(2502) 3803[5] 4328[7] 5323[4]

Diamond D'Amour (IRE) *Howard Johnson* 101h
5 gr g Danehill Dancer(IRE) —Diamond Line (FR) (Linamix (FR))
2552[P] 4132[3] ◆ 4545[3]

Diamond Eclipse (IRE) *Nick Williams* 92h
5 b g Double Eclipse(IRE) —Glory-Glory (IRE) (Buckskin (FR))
41[3] 2469[6] 3348[10]

Diamond Frontier (IRE) *Howard Johnson* 126h 134c
8 gr g Sadler's Wells(USA) —Diamond Line (FR) (Linamix (FR))
2272[4] 2613[3] 4065[4] 4546[7]

Diamondgeezer Luke (IRE) *Patrick Morris* 23h
4 b g War Chant(USA) —Banquise (IRE) (Last Tycoon)
1728[6]

Diamond Harry *Nick Williams* 165h 171c
8 b g Sir Harry Lewis(USA) —Swift Conveyance (IRE) (Strong Gale)
(2673) ◆

Diamond MM (IRE) *Alison Thorpe* 93h
5 b m Sakhee(USA) —Equity Princess (Warning)
47[0] 333[2] 686[4] (1780) 3816[4] 5234[10]

Diamond Smiles *Paul Webber* 73b
4 b f Starcraft(NZ) —Seal Indigo (IRE) (Glenstal (USA))
3876[10]

Diamond Sweeper (IRE) *Alan King* 107b
5 b g Witness Box(USA) —Vinecroft (IRE) (Executive Perk)
3546[2] ◆ 4356[5]

Diamond Twister (USA) *Lisa Williamson* 72h
5 b h Omega Code(USA) —King's Pact (USA) (Slewacide (USA))
4917[U] 5099[15] 5378[6]

Diavoleria *Michael Easterby* 123h 119c
8 b m Slip Anchor—Markapen (IRE) (Classic Music (USA))
91[2] (394)
802[2]

Dica (FR) *Patrick Griffin* 97h
5 ch g Kapgarde(FR) —Easy World (FR) (Lost World (IRE))
(2509) 3749[9] 5131[5]

Dice (IRE) *Chris Grant* 102h
5 b g Kalanisi(IRE) —Rain Dancer (IRE) (Sadler's Wells (USA))
426[3]

Dickie Henderhoop (IRE) *Lucy Normile* 95h
6 b g Milan—Merry Breeze (Strong Gale)
1578[4] 2654[7] 4572[3]

Dickie Valentine *Richard Phillips* 82h
6 b g Diktat—Passionelle (Nashwan (USA))
341[10] 462[5]

Didbrook *Mary Hambro* 96h
9 b m Alzao(USA) —Nedaarah (Reference Point)
1196[3] 1623[7] 3904[10]

Diddle'Em *Mrs A Clarke* 54c
10 b g Accondy(IRE) —Morepatience (North Briton)
863[10]
1177[P] 5326[8]

Diddley Dee *Bill Moore* 91h
7 b g Riverhead(USA) —Ballydiddle (Abednego)
2367[6] 4008[6] (4947) 5172[5] 5393[4]

Diego Velasquez (IRE) *Patrick Griffin* 86h 89c
7 b g Sadler's Wells(USA) —Sharata (IRE) (Darshaan)
646[6] **794[8]**
1666[P]

Diesel Tom *Michael Appleby*
5 ch g Rock City—Polly Tino (Neltino)
4879[P]

Different Trades (IRE) *Bob Buckler* 89h 107c
7 b g Oscar(IRE) —Gale Tan (IRE) (Strong Gale)
4449[4]

Digger Gets Lucky (IRE) *Nick Gifford* 105h 117c
9 b g Lord Americo—Exclusive View (IRE) (Camden Town)
(1965)
2595[4] 2928[4] 3391[3] 3768[2]

Digg Whitaker *John Wade* 83h
6 b g Mounting Spendent—Function Dreamer (Overbury (IRE))
3633[8]

Digital Media (IRE) *Simon Burrough* 92h 94c
9 b g Taipan(IRE) —Cats Concert (IRE) (Montelimar (USA))
4529[3] 5058[2] (5214)
5434[3]

Di Kaprio (FR) *Evan Williams* 108h
5 b g Kapgarde(FR) —Miss Nousha (FR) (True Brave (USA))
3760[12] 4203[3] 4860[2]

Diklers Oscar (IRE) *Keith Reveley* 124h
8 b m Oscar(IRE) —Diklers Dante (IRE) (Phardante (FR))
(3334) 4003[5] 4940[4] 5302[9]

Diktalina *Tim Vaughan* 121h
5 b m Diktat—Oiselina (FR) (Linamix (FR))
1609[9] 2242[7] 2644[3] 3370[11] 3724[5] 4289[2] 5208[3]

Dinarius *Alex Hales* 116h 132c
6 b g Bertolini(USA) —Ambassadress (USA) (Alleged (USA))
2983[4] 3299[11] 3696[6]
3932[3] (4096)
4324[2]

Dineur (FR) *Alan King* 107h
5 ch g Discover D'Auteuil(FR) —Sky Rocket (FR) (Sky Lawyer (FR))
2335[3] 3372[2] ◆ 3835[3] 4268[2] 4739[2]

Dingat (IRE) *Tim Vaughan* 112h
6 b g Exit To Nowhere(USA) —Dianeme (Primo Dominie)
1864[6] ◆ 2141[5]

Dinkie Short *Ben De Haan* 67h
4 b g Reset(AUS) —Spring Sunrise (Robellino (USA))
674[U] 1024[7] 1135[5] 1234[4] 1363[3]

Diocles (IRE) *Donald McCain*
5 b g Bob Back(USA) —Ardrina (Ardross)
(2826)

Diophas (GER) *E J O'Grady* 129h 126c
8 b g Acatenango(GER) —Dadrala (IRE) (Be My Guest (USA))
3706a[5]

Dipity Doo Dah *Peter Bowen* 98h
7 b m Slip Anchor—Lyra (Blakeney)
(1629) 1793[4] 2246[8] 3158[5] 3696[5] 3989[4] 4407[7]

Dirar (IRE) *Gordon Elliott* 142h
6 b g King's Best(USA) —Dibiya (IRE) (Caerleon (USA))
1133a[3] 4848[8] ◆

Direct Approach (IRE) *Lynn Siddall* 72h
7 b g Tel Quel(FR) —Miss Telimar (IRE) (Montelimar (USA))
2454[P] 4278[6] 4545[P] 4878[P]

Direct Flight (IRE) *Jeremy Scott* 44h 127c
13 ch g Dry Dock—Midnight Mistress (Midsummer Night II)
314[P] 2975[F] 3483[P]
4777[P]

Direct Flo (IRE) *Kim Bailey* 78h
4 b f Mr Combustible(IRE) —Direct Pursuit (IRE) (Hubbly Bubbly (USA))
1913[7] 2570[5] 3691[10] 3906[6] 5103[3]

Dirleton (IRE) *George Charlton* 77h
5 b g Flemensfirth(USA) —Dego Dancer (Andretti)
1764[11] 3521[9] 3746[11] 4059[9]

Dirty Deal *John Flint* 93h
7 ch m Karinga Bay—Lady Confess (Backchat (USA))
(222) 792[5]

Dishdasha (IRE) *Alison Thorpe* 131h 132c
8 b g Desert Prince(IRE) —Counterplot (IRE) (Last Tycoon)
(96) 521[4] (736) 861[2] **959[3] 1229[6]** 1609[11] 1797[5]

Dispol Diva *Paul Midgley* 75h
5 b m Deportivo—Kingston Rose (GER) (Robellino (USA))
2370[5] 3620[P]

Distant Thunder (IRE) *Mrs A S Hodges* 125h 118c
13 b g Phardante(FR) —Park Breeze (IRE) (Strong Gale)
6[2] 153[2] (268)
3908[10] 4197[4] 4786[4] 4851[12]

Distiller (IRE) *Nigel Twiston-Davies* 129h 106c
7 b g Invincible Spirit(IRE) —Bobbydazzle (Rock Hopper)
498[3] 691[5] 993[3]

Distime (IRE) *John Quinn* 110b
5 b g Flemensfirth(USA) —Technohead (IRE) (Distinctly North (USA))
3752[3] (3957) 4457[7] 5202[12]

Divers (FR) *Ferdy Murphy* 130h 145c
7 gr g Highest Honor(FR) —Divination (FR) (Groom Dancer (USA))
316[11]
1731[3] (1930)
2348[5] *3169[9]* **(3968)**
(4794) ◆

Divide And Conquer (IRE) *Warren Greatrex* 48b
6 b g Winged Love(IRE) —Madam Rocher (IRE) (Roselier (FR))
5217[10]

Divine Eric *Peter Niven* 43b
4 ch g Elmaamul(USA) —Mercede (IRE) (Perugino (USA))
2315[15]

Divine Folly (IRE) *Lawney Hill* 106b
6 b g Kotashaan(FR) —Jennys Grove (IRE) (Strong Gale)
1927[3] 2432[2] (3651) 4191[4]

Divine Intavention (IRE) *Sue Wilson* 102b 99c
7 b g Exit To Nowhere(USA) —Merrill Gaye (IRE) (Roselier (FR))
293[3]

Divine Rhapsody (IRE) *P J Rothwell* 120b
5 b g City Honours(USA) —Cyrils Girle (IRE) (Top Of The World)
4808[7]

Divy (FR) *George Baker* 114h
6 b g Highest Honor(FR) —Divination (FR) (Groom Dancer (USA))
2081[F] 2630[10] 4021[2] 4722[3] 5289[P]

Dixie Bull (IRE) *Charles Egerton* 122h
6 br g Milan—Calora (USA) (Private Account (USA))
2666[F] 4459[P] 4932[7]

Dix Villez (FR) *Miss A Waugh* 113h 102c
12 b g Villez(USA) —Dix Huit Brumaire (FR) (General Assembly (USA))
398[9] 4286[P]

Diyla (IRE) *M Flannery* 124h
8 b m Bahhare(USA) —Deylviyna (IRE) (Doyoun)
2196a[9]

Dizzy Rascal *Michael Hourigan* 104h
7 br m Bob Back(USA) —City Times (IRE) (Last Tycoon)
706[4]

Dizzy River (IRE) *George Charlton* 78h
6 ch g Flemensfirth(USA) —Dizzy Dealer (Le Bavard (FR))
311[8] ◆ 3553[4] 3752[7] 4151[3] 5028[13] 5309[7]

Dizzy Whizz *Murty McGrath* 80b
7 b m Kayf Tara—Zaffre Bleu (IRE) (Zaffaran (USA))
3266[9]

Django Reinhardt *Sam Davison* 94h
5 b g Tobougg(IRE) —Alexander Ballet (Mind Games)
1445[2] 1547[5] 1734[4] 1902[10] 1997[8] 2467[10] 3255[7]

Djarouda (FR) *Howard Johnson* 69b
5 b g Garuda(IRE) —Darling Well (FR) (Welkin (CAN))
3887[P]

Dobravany (IRE) *Kevin Morgan* 98h
7 b g Danehill Dancer(IRE) —Eadaoin (USA) (King Of Kings (IRE))
10[8] 598[P]

Doc Reason (IRE) *Patrick Gilligan* 95h 99c
8 b g Dr Massini(IRE) —Name A Reason (IRE) (Buckskin (FR))
4811[P] 5192[P]

Doc Row (IRE) *Miss V Renwick* 111h 119c
11 b g Dr Massini(IRE) —Roberto Moss (Le Moss)
446[P] 580[3] 4476[F]

Doctor Disny *Kim Bailey* 96h 96c
8 ch g Alflora(IRE) —Levantine Rose (Levanter)
2172[3] 2557[P] 3529[7]

Doctored *Daniel O'Brien* 82h
10 ch g Dr Devious(IRE) —Polygueza (FR) (Be My Guest (USA))
2400[7] 3011[9] 4400[6]

Doctor Foxtrot (IRE) *Philip Hobbs* 123h
6 b g Milan—French Life (IRE) (Un Desperado (FR))
1907[6] 2209[3] (3761) 4196[3] 4464[2]

Doctor Kilbride (IRE) *Chris Bealby* 78h
8 ch g Fruits Of Love(USA) —Kilbride Lass (IRE) (Lahib (USA))
2558[7] 4021[12] 5169[P]

Doctor Pat (IRE) *Jonjo O'Neill* 121h 128c
7 b g Definite Article—Bilboa (FR) (Phantom Breeze)
1769[7] 2948[11] 3453[8]

Doc Wells (IRE) *Ms D C Faulkner* 111h 66c
8 b g Dr Massini(IRE) —Palmrock Donna (Quayside)
5326[5]

Doeslessthanme (IRE) *Howard Johnson* 130h 125c
7 ch g Definite Article—Damemill (IRE) (Danehill (USA))
(2551)

Doheny Bar (IRE) *Nikki Evans* 25h 94c
8 b g Freddie's Star—Old Fontaine (IRE) (Millfontaine)
992[6] **1091[5]**
1237[4] 1451[11]
1727[4] 1991[P] 2243[8]

Do It For Dalkey *Lucinda Russell* 89h 98c
9 b g Silver Patriarch(IRE) —Dalkey Sound (Crash Course)
2189[3] (3503)
3636[P] 4004[P]

Dolans Bay (IRE) *Jim Best* 70h 83c
10 b g Old Vic—Kyle House VII (Damsire Unregistered)
557[6]

Dolatulo (FR) *Paul Nicholls* 129h
4 ch g Le Fou(IRE) —La Perspective (FR) (Beyssac (FR))
(2211) ◆ 2661[2] 3436[5]

Dollar Express (USA) *Edwin Tuer* 83h
5 ch g Broken Vow(USA) —Feminine (USA) (Tale Of The Cat (USA))
1664[11] 2190[P] 2603[P]

Dollar Mick (IRE) *James Moffatt* 90h 85c
6 b g Presenting—Bula Beag (IRE) (Brush Aside (USA))
4112[6]
4551[5] 5097[5]

Dolly Grey *Grant Cann* 85h 39c
8 gr m Karinga Bay—Islandreagh (IRE) (Knesset (USA))
167[10] **371[7]**

Dolores Ortiz (IRE) *Philip Hobbs* 78h
5 b m High Chaparral(IRE) —Ma N'Ieme Biche (USA) (Key To The Kingdom (USA))
4444[9] 4924[4] 5064[4] 5272[6]

Dom D'Orgeval (FR) *Nick Williams* 109h 134c
11 b g Belmez(USA) —Marie D'Orgeval (FR) (Bourbon (FR))
1777[9] 3940[P] 5206[2] (5423)

Dome Run *Alan Swinbank* 94b
5 ch g Domedriver(IRE) —Kiruna (Northern Park (USA))
3998[3] 4916[4]

Dominican Monk (IRE) *David Arbuthnot* 87h 129c
12 b g Lord Americo—Ballybeg Katie (IRE) (Roselier (FR))
3059[7] 5420[6]

Domino Dancer (IRE) *Lucy Jones* 100h
7 b g Tagula(IRE) —Hazarama (IRE) (Kahyasi)
(762) 1236[3] 4049[4] 4375[4] 4809[3] 5016[3]

Domoly (FR) *Alison Batchelor* 75h 66c
8 b g Varese(FR) —Queen D'Ouilly (FR) (King Of Macedon)
1783[8] 2192[7] 2642[5]
3402[P] 4119[4] 4403[P]
4829[7]

Domos Boy (IRE) *Jonjo O'Neill* 103h
8 b g Oscar(IRE) —Don't Tutch Me (The Parson)
4404[8] 4895[5] ◆ 5168[5]

Domtaline (FR) *Paul Nicholls* 120h
4 gr g Martaline—Domna Noune (FR) (Dom Pasquini (FR))
(1772) 2078[8] 3194[F]

Dona *Alan King* 127h
7 b g Anabaa Blue—Dominicana (FR) (King's Theatre (IRE))
(2312) 2667[3] (3478) 3649[5] 4727[15]

Donald Will Do (IRE) *Caroline Bailey* 55h 88c
11 ch g Zaffaran(USA) —Jersey Pearl (Last Fandango)
136[5] 383[8] 2277[6] 2424[2] 3720[3] 4144[2] 5293[3]

Don Jose (USA) *Richard Lee* 83h
8 bb g Dynaformer(USA) —Panthera (USA) (Storm Cat (USA))
1445[5] 1773[8] 2307[8] 3532[P]

Donnas Palm (IRE) *Noel Meade* 159h
7 gr g Great Palm(USA) —Donna's Tarquin (IRE) (Husyan (USA))
(1711a) 2414a[3] 2968a[9] 3578a[2]

Donny Briggs *Tim Easterby* 87h
6 b g Orpen(USA) —Passionate Pursuit (Pursuit Of Love)
3993[3] 4465[5]

Donovan (NZ) *Richard Guest* 65h 90c
12 b g Stark South(USA) —Agent Jane (NZ) (Sound Reason (CAN))
6[P] 954[8] 1043[5] 1261[9]
1612[4] 1991[10] 2250[3] 2479[5]

Don Pietro *Barry Brennan* 88h
8 b g Bertolini(USA) —Silver Spell (Aragon)
1996[4]

Don Pooleoni (IRE) *David Arbuthnot* 99b
6 b g Catcher In The Rye(IRE) —Liss Rua (IRE) (Bob Back (USA))
1374[2] 1778[7] 2087[6]

Don Stefano *Bill Turner* 16h
4 b g Deportivo—Molly Music (Music Boy)
3613[6]

Don't Be Bitin (IRE) *C A Murphy* 126h 140c
10 b g Turtle Island(IRE) —Shonara's Way (Slip Anchor)
1123a[F] (Dead)

Don't Call Harry *Tim Walford* 39b
6 ch g Bollin William—Sans Rivale (Elmaamul (USA))
2403[7] 2612[P]

Dont Call Me Derek *Dr Richard Newland* 123h 116c
10 b g Sri Pekan(USA) —Cultural Role (Night Shift (USA))
(478) ◆ 830[2]

Don't Hang About *Richard Mitchell* 87h
6 ch g Alflora(IRE) —Althrey Flame (IRE) (Torus)
2560[13] 3441[3] 4094[0] 4260[10] 5211[5]

Don't Panic (IRE) *Ron Hodges* 101h
7 ch g Fath(USA) —Torrmana (IRE) (Ela-Mana-Mou)
2596[5] 2977[P]

Dontpaytheferryman (USA) *Brian Ellison* 121h 118c
6 ch g Wiseman's Ferry(USA) —Expletive Deleted (USA) (Dr Blum (USA))
32[2] ◆ **401[2]** 1614[7] 1827[3] 2094[4] 2399[3] (4149) 4358[9]

Don't Push It (IRE) *Jonjo O'Neill* 125h 167c
11 b g Old Vic—She's No Laugh Ben (USA) (Alleged (USA))
2870[P] 3293[12] 4185[7] 4817[10] **5200[3]**

Don't Rush It (IRE) *John Quinn* 110h
9 ch g Old Vic—Sarahs Music (IRE) (Orchestra)
2545[6]

Don't Tell Nina (IRE) *Paul Webber* 103h 101c
7 b g Beneficial—Orchard Lass (On Your Mark)
2299[F] 2641[4] 3395[5] 3878[6] 5281[4]

Dont Tell The Boys *P J Rothwell* 106h
5 gr g Silver Patriarch(IRE) —Deep C Diva (IRE) (Supreme Leader)
1713a[F]

Dont Tell The Wife (IRE) *Nicky Henderson* 85h 114c
8 br g Anshan—Dark Gale (IRE) (Strong Gale)
359[8] 651[P]

Don't Think Twice (IRE) *Miss Caroline Fryer* 108h 90c
8 b g Orpen(USA) —Popcorn (Pharly (FR))
1453[7] **4857[P]**

Don't Turn Bach (IRE) *Paul Nicholls* 110h
7 b g Bach(IRE) —Bobbie Magee (IRE) (Buckskin (FR))
2454[4] 3762[5] 4100[2] 4462[11] 5167[4]

Dontupsettherhythm (IRE) *Charles Pogson* 97h
6 bb g Anshan—Whatalady (IRE) (Executive Perk)
1629[3] 1955[2] 2281[5] *3089[3]* 3505[6] 4974[5]

Dont Worry *Richard Mitchell*
5 b g Bertolini(USA) —Persian Dream (IRE) (Mazaad)
3930[R]

Doodlebop (IRE) *Ann Hamilton* 75h 96c
8 ch g Carroll House—Polar Mistress (IRE) (Strong Gale)
163[6]

Doof (IRE) *L Jefford* 102c
11 b g Old Vic—Ashpark Rose (IRE) (Roselier (FR))
268[5] 5277[4]

Dooneys Gate (IRE) *W P Mullins* 134h 153c
10 b g Oscar(IRE) —Park Breeze (IRE) (Strong Gale)
3473a[4] 5200[F] (Dead)

Door Boy (IRE) *Howard Johnson* 135h 145c
8 bb g Dr Massini(IRE) —Door Stopper (IRE) (Flemensfirth (USA))
2105[3] 2359[P] 3292[9] 4352[P] 5317[3] ◆

Dorabelle (IRE) *Donald McCain* 120h
6 b m King's Theatre(IRE) —Stateable Case (IRE) (Be My Native (USA))
332[2] (726) 956[P] (2370) (2598) 3945[4] 5302[10] 5440[3]

Dora Explora *Linda Jewell* 63h 69c
7 br m Vettori(IRE) —Fredora (Inchinor)
1479[P] 1549[8] **2182[4]**

Doric Echo *Charlie Morlock* 72h
5 b g Bertolini(USA) —Latour (Sri Pekan (USA))
185[P]

Doris's Gift *T Glass* 105h 72c
10 gr g Environment Friend—Saxon Gift (Saxon Farm)
398[U]

Dorlesh Way (IRE) *Patrick Holmes* 54b
4 ch g Rakti—Patalavaca (GER) (Acatenango (GER))
4457[9] 5033[12]

Dormouse *Anabel L M King* 107h
6 b g Medicean—Black Fighter (USA) (Secretariat (USA))
827[6] 1046[3] 1138[5] 1484[9] (1624) 1732[2] 2131[3] 2504[3] (3497) 3696[10] (4330) 5171[7]

Dot's Delight *Mark Rimell* 107h
7 b m Golden Snake(USA) —Hotel California (IRE) (Last Tycoon)
340[4] 1746[7] 1972[F] 2442[3] 3962[5] 4327[6]

Double Banded (IRE) *Jim Best*
7 b g Mark Of Esteem(IRE) —Bronzewing (Beldale Flutter (USA))
2129[P]

Double Bank (IRE) *A J Kennedy* 110h 64c
8 b g Double Trigger(IRE) —Misty Silks (Scottish Reel)
536[4]

Double Chocolate *Matt Sheppard* 108h 92c
8 b g Doubletour(USA) —Matching Green (Green Ruby (USA))
1963[F]
2146[5] 2502[4]

Double Dash *George Baker* 116h 120c
7 b g Sir Harry Lewis(USA) —Dashing Executive (IRE) (Executive Perk)
1917[2] 2330[2] 4223[6]

Double Default (IRE) *Martin Todhunter* 107h 113c
10 ch g Beneficial—Over The Risc (IRE) (Over The River (FR))
2549[10] 2941[F] 3362[P] 3635[2] **4004[3] 4258[2] 4713[2]**

Double Dizzy *Bob Buckler* 119h 138c
10 b g Double Trigger(IRE) —Miss Diskin (IRE) (Sexton Blake)
1856[7] 2212[4] 2541[11] 2869[9] 3453[4] 3689[5] (4219) 4486[P] 5009[6] 5405[4]

Double Double (FR) *Charles O'Brien* 118b
5 b g Sakhee(USA) —Queen Sceptre (IRE) (Fairy King (USA))
4808[11]

Double Eagle *Donald McCain* 121h 126c
9 b g Silver Patriarch(IRE) —Grayrose Double (Celtic Cone)
2984[8] 3370[3] 3713[5] (4257) 4715[4]

Double Expresso *Howard Johnson* 130h
7 b g Kayf Tara—Sallys Lodge (Roscoe Blake)
2507[U] 3575[2] 3954[3]

Double Fun *Martin Hill* 66b
5 b m Double Trigger(IRE) —Girl Of Pleasure (IRE) (Namaqualand (USA))
1778[9] 2025[5]

Double Handful (GER) *Venetia Williams* 103h
5 bl g Pentire—Durania (GER) (Surumu (GER))
315[5] 3497[8] 4503[3] 4751[U]

Double Mead *Mrs K R Smith-Maxwell* 106h 130c
9 b m Double Trigger(IRE) —Normead Lass (Norwick (USA))
**2036[2] (4832)
(5083)**

Double Or Quitz *Bob Buckler* 75h
6 b g Relief Pitcher—Straight Courage (Straight Knight)
1448[5] 2143[6]

Double Pride *Alan King* 112h 116c
7 ch g Double Trigger(IRE) —Forest Pride (IRE) (Be My Native (USA))
2363[3] ◆ 2959[4] 3784[P] 4402[U] 4802[9] 5292[F]

Double Silver *Keith Reveley* 92b
4 gr f Silver Patriarch(IRE) —Shadows Of Silver (Carwhite)
4027[8] 5306[7]

Double Tangle *Peter Hiatt* 33h
8 b g Double Trigger(IRE) —Tangle Touch (Nader)
21[P]

Double The Trouble *Andy Turnell* 122h 126c
10 b g Double Trigger(IRE) —Upton Lass (IRE) (Crash Course)
(85) **1992[U]**
**2184[5] 3263[6] 3772[2] 4223[3] (4695)
(4972) 5323[2]**

Doubletoilntrouble (IRE) *Keith Goldsworthy* 101h
5 b g Hubbly Bubbly(USA) —Boolindrum Lady (IRE) (Meneval (USA))
832[6] 1029[3] 1158[3] 1369[3] 1860[5] 2235[5] 2574[3]

Double Vodka (IRE) *Chris Grant* 127h 128c
10 bb g Russian Revival(USA) —Silius (Junius (USA))
2520[7] 3786[2] 4116[5] 4730[5] 5228[3]

Double Whammy *Jamie Poulton* 116h
6 b g Systematic—Honor Rouge (IRE) (Highest Honor (FR))
2396[4] 2946[3] 3866[2] 4489[5]

Doubly Sharp (USA) *Caroline Bailey* 76h 80c
8 ch g Diesis—La Soberbia (ARG) (Octante (ARG))
95[P] 250[5] 462[10]

Douchkette (FR) *John Berry* 98h
5 b m Califet(FR) —Douchka (FR) (Fijar Tango (FR))
865[7] (1031) 1125[2]

Dougall (IRE) *Joanne Foster* 69c
8 b g Oscar(IRE) —Parting Company (IRE) (King's Ride)
802[5] 951[P] 1377[U] 1661[5] 1784[4]

Douglas *Barry Brennan* 91h
6 b g Beat All(USA) —Cromaboo Crown (Crowning Honors (CAN))
337[2] 538[4] 843[11]

Douglas Julian *Sue Smith* 90h 119c
9 br g Overbury(IRE) —Swing Quartet (IRE) (Orchestra)
459[P] 1554[2] (1666) (2271)
**(2450) (2952)
3784[U] (4210)
4893[4] 5317[9]**

Doumaja (FR) *G Cherel* 104h 147c
9 b g Cadoudal(FR) —Majamone (FR) (Carmont (FR))
5367a[2]

Douryna *Colin Tizzard* 79h 116c
8 b m Generous(IRE) —Dounya (USA) (Caro)
**2605[F] 3226[3] 3431[P] (4504)
5007[3] ◆**

Dovecote Wood *Caroline Keevil* 105h
6 b g Fleetwood(IRE) —Flakey Dove (Oats)
3153[3] 3836[6]

Dove Hill (IRE) *Howard Johnson* 117h 125c
8 b g Old Vic—Commanchey's Pet (IRE) (Commanche Run)
1869[2] (2269)
3499[3]

Dover's Hill *Mary Hambro* 130h 149c
9 b g Pistolet Bleu(IRE) —Classic Beauty (IRE) (Fairy King (USA))
**(1739)
2084[5] 4093[4] (4673)
(5133)**

Dowd's Destiny (IRE) *Nicky Richards* 116h
8 b g Flemensfirth(USA) —Windy Run (Deep Run)
(1149) ◆ 1367[3]

Downe Payment (IRE) *Diana Grissell* 86h
6 b m Saddlers' Hall(IRE) —Waterloo Park (IRE) (Alphabatim (USA))
589[10] 1680[6] 2181[8] 2428[8] 3340[4] 3745[8] 4130[3] 4427[P] 5265[P]

Downing Street (IRE) *Jennie Candlish* 116h 107c
10 b g Sadler's Wells(USA) —Photographie (USA) (Trempolino (USA))
473[P] 581[2] 708[8] 846[8]

Down In Neworleans (IRE) *Ms Margaret Mullins* 134h
6 b g Saddlers' Hall(IRE) —Miss Muppet (IRE) (Supreme Leader)
2912a[6] 4319a[6]

Down The Stretch *James Payne* 2h 124c
11 b g Rakaposhi King—Si-Gaoith (Strong Gale)
4095[6] 4723[2] (5323)

Downward Spiral (IRE) *Jennie Candlish* 110h
6 br g Windsor Castle—Misty Links (IRE) (Hushang (IRE))
303[4] (559) 863[2] 1105[3] 1367[4] 1625[4]

Doyen Diva *Peter Chapple-Hyam* 67b
4 ch f Doyen(IRE) —Zarma (FR) (Machiavellian (USA))
4184[8] 4728[20]

Doyenne Dream *James Eustace* 82h
4 b f Doyen(IRE) —Cribella (USA) (Robellino (USA))
1279[3] 1473[5] 1691[3] 2435[2] 3338[P] 3545[6]

Doynosaur *Mrs K Burke* 99b
4 b f Doyen(IRE) —Daring Destiny (Daring March)
(2173) 3576[2] 4171[6]

Draco Boy *Andy Turnell* 45h
4 gr g Silver Patriarch(IRE) —Miss Tehente (FR) (Tehente (FR))
3478[12]

Dragon's Den (IRE) *Chris Down* 91h
4 b g Antonius Pius(USA) —Tallassee (Indian Ridge)
2151[5] 2958[F]

Dramatic Jewel (USA) *Lucinda Russell* 76h
5 b g Diesis—Seeking The Jewel (USA) (Seeking The Gold (USA))
870[10] 1337[8] 2540[7] 3255[3] 3631[6]

Drawback (IRE) *Barry Brennan* 80h
8 b g Daggers Drawn(USA) —Sacred Heart (IRE) (Catrail (USA))
4859[8] 5072[4] 5270[6]

Dr Cerullo *E Walker* 107h 68c
10 b g Dr Fong(USA) —Precocious Miss (USA) (Diesis)
153[8]

Dr Dream (IRE) *John O'Shea* 42h
7 b g Dr Fong(USA) —Only In Dreams (Polar Falcon (USA))
359[10] 990[10]

Dream Alliance *Philip Hobbs* 127h 157c
10 ch g Bien Bien(USA) —Rewbell (Andy Rew)
2673[P] 3437[P] 4792[8]

Dream Catcher (SWE) *Jonjo O'Neill* 112h
8 b g Songline(SWE) —Queen Ida (SWE) (Diligo (FR))
534[10] (914) 1084[4] 1282[3] 1548[7] 1740[4] 2209[7]

Dreamers Of Dreams (IRE) *Malcolm Jefferson* 106b
6 b g Flemensfirth(USA) —Cushogan (IRE) (King's Ride)
3773[3] (4894)

Dream Esteem *David Pipe* 123h
6 b m Mark Of Esteem(IRE) —City Of Angels (Woodman (USA))
2977[3] 3228[2] 3808[7] 4455[2]

Dream Function (IRE) *Philip Hobbs* 111h
6 b m King's Theatre(IRE) —Function Dream (IRE) (Strong Gale)
2156[3] ◆ 3590[3] 3904[2] 4309[10]

Dream Performance (IRE) *G C Maundrell* 103b
6 b m Oscar(IRE) —Pharlen's Dream (IRE) (Phardante (FR))
(1771) 2987[6] 4027[7] 5119[3]

Dream Risk (FR) *Kate Walton* 109h
5 b m Dream Well(FR) —Lovarisk (FR) (Take Risks (FR))
(547) 706[7] (1115) 1427[2] 1695[6] 2076[5] 4166[11] 4455[9] 4797[P]

Dream Spinner *Dr Richard Newland* 58h
4 b g Royal Applause—Dream Quest (Rainbow Quest (USA))
2528[6] 2958[14]

Dreamwalk (IRE) *Roger Curtis* 110h
5 b g Bahri(USA) —Celtic Silhouette (FR) (Celtic Swing)
(932) (1058) 1160[P]

Dreamy Sweeney (IRE) *Nicky Henderson* 128h 95c
9 bb g Supreme Leader—Black Pit (Black Minstrel)
556[3]

Dreux (FR) *R J Rowsell* 127h 121c
9 b g Anabaa(USA) —Divination (FR) (Groom Dancer (USA))
4950[5]

Drever Route (IRE) *Howard Johnson* 123h 131c
8 b g Flemensfirth(USA) —I Remember It Well (IRE) (Don't Forget Me)
**194[2] (1828)
3804[8]**

Dr Finley (IRE) *Jeff Pearce* 90h
4 ch g Dr Fong(USA) —Farrfesheena (USA) (Rahy (USA))
1473[3] 1610[8] 2078[7] 2438[3] 2958[10]

Dr Flynn (IRE) *Howard Johnson* 102h
6 b g Tikkanen(USA) —Tallaquale (IRE) (Tale Quale)
1599[2] 1764[3] 2296[6] 3547[4] 4393[4] 4798[3]

Driftwood Lad (IRE) *Venetia Williams* 38b
5 b g Pilsudski(IRE) —Cappard Ridge (IRE) (Executive Perk)
5426[8]

Drill Sergeant *Donald McCain* 138h
6 br g Rock Of Gibraltar(IRE) —Dolydille (IRE) (Dolphin Street (FR))
(1487) 1765[2] (2038) 2519[2] 3561[8] 4202[B] 4420[3] 4727[16] 5196[4] 5420[2]

Drink Up *John O'Neill* 75h
7 b g Dolpour—Laced Up (IRE) (The Parson)
833[9] 2981[10] 3701[6] 4233[9] 5057[4] 5265[P]

Drive Time (USA) *Howard Johnson* 126h
6 b g King Cugat(USA) —Arbusha (USA) (Danzig (USA))
(3506) 3806[P] (4467) ◆ 5196[F]

Driving Miss Suzie *Debra Hamer* 56h
7 br m Diktat—Santa Isobel (Nashwan (USA))
3839[P] 4707[F] 5016[7] 5212[7]

Driving Onwards (IRE) *Ron Hodges* 74h
7 ch g Presenting—Sleepy Polly (Pollerton)
1748[5] 2136[7]

Driving Seat *Michael Mullineaux* 63h
7 b g Daylami(IRE) —Zorleni (Zafonic (USA))
349[11] 1148[9] 2310[P]

Dr Light (IRE) *Anna Bramall* 47h
7 b g Medicean—Allumette (Rainbow Quest (USA))
2166[8] 4545[P] 5130[14]

Dr Livingstone (IRE) *Charles Egerton* 129h
6 b g Dr Fong(USA) —Radhwa (FR) (Shining Steel)
2164[3] 2498[5] 2671[10] 3452[5] 3587[8]

Drom *P S Davies* 115c
8 b g Gildoran—Sabre Drom (Broadsword (USA))
4415[2]

Drombeg Pride (IRE) *Gerry Enright* 73h 82c
7 b g High Account(USA) —Proserpina (Most Welcome)
283[F] 1546[4] 1901[4] 2048[P]

Dromore Hill (IRE) *Charlie Morlock* 84h 93c
7 b g Flemensfirth(USA) —Tree Oaks (IRE) (Be My Native (USA))
1820[3] 2290[3] 2608[2] 2982[3] 3933[7] 4409[4] 4772[P]

Drop Anchor (IRE) *Edward Cawley* 108h
8 b g King's Theatre(IRE) —Ship's Twine (IRE) (Slip Anchor)
1308[5] 5316[P]

Drop The Hammer *David O'Meara* 67h
5 b m Lucky Story(USA) —Paperweight (In The Wings)
2370[7] 3783[7] 4278[4]

Drumbaloo (IRE) *J J Lambe* 111h
7 bb g Flemensfirth(USA) —Supreme Baloo (IRE) (Supreme Leader)
(4684)

Drumbeater (IRE) *Bernard Scriven* 76h
11 b g Supreme Leader—Ballydrummund (IRE) (Henbit (USA))
3873[U] 4273[6] 4787[7] 4968[6] (5068)

Drum Bustible (IRE) *J J Lambe* 97h
7 b g Mr Combustible(IRE) —Celtic Smiles (IRE) (Nucleon (USA))
2553[8] 3331[4] 5031[P]

Drumfire (IRE) *Eoin Griffin* 128h
7 b g Danehill Dancer(IRE) —Witch Of Fife (USA) (Lear Fan (USA))
2388[7]

Drumlang (IRE) *Henrietta Knight* 62h
5 b g Soviet Star(USA) —Sherekiya (IRE) (Lycius (USA))
2328[4] 2873[11] 3489[8] 5071[6]

Drumlargan Girl (IRE) *Martin Todhunter* 71h
6 b m Bob Back(USA) —Kings Gap (IRE) (King's Ride)
3637[11]

Drum Major (IRE) *Jim Best* 70h
6 b g Sadler's Wells(USA) —Phantom Gold (Machiavellian (USA))
842[7] 916[5]

Drummers Drumming (USA) *Charlie Morlock* 92h
5 b g Stroll(USA) —Afleet Summer (USA) (Afleet (CAN))
2426[6] 2960[10] 3604[5] 4314[6] 5103[9] 5322[8]

Drumshambo (USA) *Venetia Williams* 116h
5 b g Dynaformer(USA) —Gossamer (USA) (Seattle Slew (USA))
1956[P]

Drussell (IRE) *Richard Phillips* 116h
5 b g Orpen(USA) —Cahermee Queen (USA) (King Of Kings (IRE))
2213[10] 2423[5] 2977[13] 3299[6] 3881[P] 5117[7] 5392[8]

Dr Valentine (FR) *Ann Duffield* 101h
5 ch g Dr Fong(USA) —Red Roses Story (FR) (Pink (FR))
210[3] 2421[5]

Drybrook Bedouin *Nick Mitchell* 132c
9 b g Nomadic Way(USA) —Biddles (Norwick (USA))
**149[7] 525[F] 3558[P] 3907[2] 4328[4] 4537[3] 5037[P]
(5154)**

Dubai Crest *Nicky Henderson* 109h
5 b g Dubai Destination(USA) —On The Brink (Mind Games)
4451[5] (4810) 5071[5]

Dubrovnick (IRE) *Tim Vaughan* 94h
6 b g Montjeu(IRE) —Aquila Oculus (IRE) (Eagle Eyed (USA))
833[8] 953[4]

Duc De Regniere (FR) *Nicky Henderson* 155h 156c
9 b g Rajpoute(FR) —Gladys De Richerie (FR) (Le Pontet (FR))
2090[4] 2672[2] 3199[P]

Dudley Docker (IRE) *Daniel O'Brien*
9 b g Victory Note(USA) —Nordic Abu (IRE) (Nordico (USA))
3701[P]

Duers (IRE) *Paul Magnier* 126h 139c
9 b g Rudimentary(USA) —Sup A Whiskey (IRE) (Commanche Run)
2886[P] 5025a[4]

Duffy Moon *Charlie Morlock* 64h
7 gr g Presenting—Dawn Spinner (Arctic Lord)
1821[13] 3346[10] 3487[P] 5068[U]

Duke Of Burgundy (FR) *Jennie Candlish* 87h
8 b g Danehill(USA) —Valley Of Gold (FR) (Shirley Heights)
360[4] 576[11]

Dukeofchesterwood *Sandy Forster* 103h 107c
9 ch g Missed Flight—Gale Storm (Midland Gayle)
873[6] 1002[2] 1868[U] 2203[7]

Duke Of Lucca (IRE) *Philip Hobbs* 149h
6 b g Milan—Derravaragh Native (IRE) (Be My Native (USA))
1967[10] 2672[4] 2870[4] 3289[5] 4817[18]

Duke Of Malfi *Lucinda Russell* 91h 106c
8 b g Alflora(IRE) —Princess Maxine (IRE) (Horage)
88[10] 395[2] 1767[6] 2194[P] 3699[2] 4001[5] 4471[3] (5145)

Duke Of Monmouth (IRE) *Charlie Mann* 85b
4 b g Presenting—Hayley Cometh (IRE) (Supreme Leader)
5012[11]

Duke Of Normandy (IRE) *Brian Baugh* 37h
5 gr g Refuse To Bend(IRE) —Marie De Bayeux (FR) (Turgeon (USA))
1031[8]

Duke Of Ormond (IRE) *Anna Brooks* 84h 105c
8 ch g Flemensfirth(USA) —Supreme Alannah (IRE) (Supreme Leader)
2154[8] 2642[3] 2981[P] 3428[P] 3822[6]
(4238) 4412[3] 4921[2] ◆

Dulce Domum *Roger Curtis* 69h
5 b m Dansili—Enclave (USA) (Woodman (USA))
3604[U] 3866[7] 4129[4]

Dunaskin (IRE) *Richard Guest* 123h
11 b g Bahhare(USA) —Mirwara (IRE) (Darshaan)
(210) (515) 1017[11] 1249[6] (1375) 1609[16]

Dunbrody House *Peter Bowen* 97h 92c
7 b g Needle Gun(IRE) —Lucky Baloo (The Parson)
136[F] 517[P]

Dundock *Alistair Whillans* 100h
10 gr g Cloudings(IRE) —Rakajack (Rakaposhi King)
291[3]

Dun Drinan (IRE) *Eamonn Fehily* 94h 105c
12 b g Anshan—Smiles Again (IRE) (Brush Aside (USA))
1027[4]

Dundry *Philip Sharp* 97h
10 b g Bin Ajwaad(IRE) —China's Pearl (Shirley Heights)
1575[5] 380[4] 4128[8]

Duneen Point (IRE) *Tim Vaughan* 108h
7 b g Saddlers' Hall(IRE) —Miss Ogan (IRE) (Supreme Leader)
2571[3] 3584[4] 4182[4] 4407[P] 5195[4]

Dune Raider (USA) *David Evans* 100h 112c
10 b g Kingmambo(USA) —Glowing Honor (USA) (Seattle Slew (USA))
169[10]

Dune Shine *Oliver Sherwood* 112h
6 b g Karinga Bay—Caipirinha (IRE) (Strong Gale)
2307[9] 2985[2] 3158[14] (3793) 4375[3] 4988[4]

Dunguib (IRE) *Philip Fenton* 159h
8 b g Presenting—Edermine Berry (IRE) (Durgam (USA))
(4229a) 4791[8]

Dunkelly Castle (IRE) *Roger Curtis* 108h 122c
7 ch g Old Vic—Nanna's Joy (IRE) (Phardante (FR))
1043[2] 1230[2] **1281[3] (1747)
2146[3] 3450[2] 4023[6] 4428[5] 5292[3]**

Dunnicks County *Patrick Rodford*
8 ch m Sula Bula—Dunnicks Country (Town And Country)
263[9]

Dunnicks Spindle *Patrick Rodford*
5 b m Tamure(IRE) —Dunnicks Chance (Greensmith)
375[16]

Dunowen Point (IRE) *Donald McCain* 108h
5 b g Old Vic—Esbeggi (Sabrehill (USA))
1785[2] 2943[3] 3521[3]

Dunraven Storm (IRE) *Philip Hobbs* 143h
6 br g Presenting—Foxfire (Lord Americo)
(1736) ◆ (2083) 2344[2] 2519[4] 4788[P]

Dun See Dee (IRE) *Charlie Mann* 114h
7 b m Flemensfirth(USA) —Crafty Classy (IRE) (Warcraft (USA))
2288[3] 2974[2] 3389[3]

Duo Cubar (FR) *B Lefevre*
6 ch g Poplar Bluff—Soiree De Martine (FR) (Seurat)
190a[P]

Duroob *Patrick O Brady* 128h
9 b g Bahhare(USA) —Amaniy (USA) (Dayjur (USA))
3475a[18]

Dusk *Evan Williams* 77h 100c
6 b g Fantastic Light(USA) —Dark Veil (USA) (Gulch (USA))
2469[P]

Dusky Bob (IRE) *Nick Gifford* 100h 64c
6 br g Bob Back(USA) —Sunsets Girl (IRE) (The Parson)
2123[8] 3346[8] 3604[2] 3950[P] 4427[7]
5384[4]

Dust In Time *Bill Turner* 91h 94c
6 ch g Karinga Bay—Dusty Bankes (Greensmith)
373 217[P] **4011[P] (4429)**
5384[P]

Dusty Dane (IRE) *Bill Turner* 93h 114c
9 b g Indian Danehill(IRE) —Teer On Eer (IRE) (Persian Heights)
21[3] **274[4]**
(501) 1348[5]
1858[10]

Dusty Showbiz *Anthony Middleton* 52b
4 b f Passing Glance—Parsons Lass (IRE) (The Parson)
2173[8] 2556[P]

Dutch Bill *J Cole* 99c
10 b g Cloudings(IRE) —Double Dutch (Nicholas Bill)
268[4]

Duty Free (IRE) *James Moffatt* 110h
7 b g Rock Of Gibraltar(IRE) —Photographie (USA) (Trempolino (USA))
519[2] 627[6] 861[6] 1003[F] 1114[2] 1337[2] 1426[4]

Dynamic Approach (IRE) *Edward U Hales* 117b
5 b g Milan—Creative Approach (IRE) (Toulon)
4808[17]

Dynaste (FR) *David Pipe* 138h
5 gr g Martaline—Bellissima De Mai (FR) (Pistolet Bleu (IRE))
1743[3] 2347[2] ◆ (3229) 4725[6]

Dystonia's Revenge (IRE) *Mrs Sheena Walton*
6 b g Woods Of Windsor(USA) —Lady Isaac (IRE) (Le Bavard (FR))
90[P]

Eagle Nebula *Brett Johnson* 41h
7 ch g Observatory(USA) —Tarocchi (USA) (Affirmed (USA))
4917[12]

Eagle Owl (IRE) *Tim Easterby* 92h
5 b g Hawk Wing(USA) —Keepers Dawn (IRE) (Alzao (USA))
2075[4] 2296[P] 2612[10] 3951[P]

Earcomesthedream (IRE) *Peter Pritchard* 102h 79c
8 b g Marignan(USA) —Play It By Ear (IRE) (Be My Native (USA))
66[4] 318[7] 601[P] 2171[2] 2558[3]
4292[11] 4722[P] 5061[3] **5377[4]**

Earl Grez (FR) *Philip Kirby* 89h 104c
6 ch g Turgeon(USA) —Yoruba (FR) (Cyborg (FR))
349[4] 468[5] **2938[6] 3524[3] 3769[2] 3970[4] 4305[3]**
5134[P]

Earl Of Thomond (IRE) *Caroline Bailey* 89h
6 b g Milan—Jodella (IRE) (Executive Perk)
1734[7] 1997[3] 2314[2] 2929[5] 3392[6] 4125[4] 5057[8]
5374[6]

Earlson Gray (FR) *W P Mullins* 140h 137c
6 gr g Take Risks(FR) —Euadne (GER) (Acatenango (GER))
3846a[2]

Early Wings (GER) *Caroline Bailey* 93h 95c
9 b g Winged Love(IRE) —Emy Coasting (USA) (El Gran Senor (USA))
24[2] 251[2]

Earth Dream (IRE) *Paul Nicholls* 121h 137c
8 b g Old Vic—Barbaras Mews (IRE) (Persian Mews)
(373) 592[3]
(1345) 1776[5] **5290[3]**

Earth Magic (IRE) *Evan Williams* 138h 128c
11 b g Taipan(IRE) —Miss Pollerton (IRE) (Pollerton)
138[F] 208[4] (2188) 3493[4]

Earth Moving (IRE) *G E Burton* 89c
11 ch g Anshan—Jacks Sister (IRE) (Entitled I)
4271[P] 4463[U]

Earth Planet (IRE) *Paul Nicholls* 136h 124c
9 b g Kayf Tara—Arctic Rose (IRE) (Jamesmead)
1964[2] 2343[8] 3479[4] 4030[U] 4445[3] 4673[3] 5067[2]
5405[5]

Ease And Grace *Emma Lavelle* 91h
7 b m King's Theatre(IRE) —Swing Quartet (IRE) (Orchestra)
84[4] 273[P]

Easement *Charlie Morlock* 103h
8 b g Kayf Tara—Raspberry Sauce (Niniski (USA))
1555[2] 1907[5] 2143[8] 2532[8] 3369[3] (3870) (5195)

Easter Lad *Luke Dace* 69b
7 b g Shahrastani(USA) —Frozen Pipe (Majestic Maharaj)
3981[P]

Easter Legend *Emma Lavelle* 138h 148c
7 ch m Midnight Legend—Easter Comet (Gunner B)
(2182)
(2481) 2978[F] (5007)

Easter Meteor *Emma Lavelle* 123h
5 b g Midnight Legend—Easter Comet (Gunner B)
2493[4] ◆ 3288[13] 3836[2] 4986[3]

Eastern Chariot *Tobias B P Coles* 48b
4 b f Oscar(IRE) —Lifeguard (IRE) (Desert Prince (IRE))
2315[13]

Eastern Supreme (IRE) *Kim Bailey* 86h 92c
6 b g Norwich—Kitty Supreme (IRE) (Supreme Leader)
2310[8] 2512[11] 2667[10]
4668[3]

Easter Queen *Robert Goldie* 84h
9 b m Rakaposhi King—Easter Oats (Oats)
212[P]

Easter Vic *Robert Goldie* 99h
10 b m Old Vic—Easter Oats (Oats)
3729[5] 4062[4] (4687) 4872[2] 5096[2] 5319[3]

Eastlake (IRE) *Jonjo O'Neill* 102h
5 b g Beneficial—Guigone (FR) (Esprit Du Nord (USA))
(1749) 4881[4] (5167)

Easton Clump *Dominic Ffrench Davis* 98h
8 b g Dancing Spree(USA) —High Commotion (IRE) (Taufan (USA))
2607[12] *3167[3]* 3448[8] 3882[2] 4310[2] 4785[P]

Eastwell Smiles *Sophie Leech* 105h
7 gr g Erhaab(USA) —Miss University (USA) (Beau Genius (CAN))
587[6] 930[3] (1048) (3261) (3430) 3820[P] 5401[6]

Easyfix (IRE) *Brendan Powell* 83h
8 ch g Naheez(USA) —Eurolucy (IRE) (Shardari)
1482[5]

Ebanour (IRE) *Donald McCain* 108h
4 ch g Indian Ridge—Ebadiyla (IRE) (Sadler's Wells (USA))
(4280) 4943[3] 5202[8]

Ebony Diamond (IRE) *Charlie Mann* 99h
7 b g Marignan(USA) —Mrs Quigley (IRE) (Mandalus)
1817[5] 2495[4] 2873[8] 5243[4]

Ebony River (IRE) *Donald McCain* 108h
5 b g Alderbrook—Dishy (IRE) (Jurado (USA))
1757[4] 2296[3]

Echo Dancer *Trevor Wall* 84h
5 br g Danehill Dancer(IRE) —Entail (USA) (Riverman (USA))
711[U] 1058[4] 1705[6] 1962[8] 2149[13] 2467[6] 3839[10]
5114[4] 5235[4]

Echoes Of Dawn (IRE) *Howard Johnson* 91h
7 b g Definite Article—Falconera (IRE) (Tirol)
2080[11] 4994[6]

Echo Point (IRE) *Nicky Richards* 140h 132c
11 b g Luso—Lady Desart (IRE) (Buckskin (FR))
1577[P] 2106[P]

Eco Boxer (IRE) *Nick Kent* 53h
7 b g Rudimentary(USA) —Storm Lassie (IRE) (Glacial Storm (USA))
4974[11] 5309[11]

Eddie Boy *Rebecca Curtis* 78h
5 b g Tobougg(IRE) —Maristax (Reprimand)
1857[7] 2137[12] 3526[9]

Eddie Dowling *Milton Harris* 114h
6 b g High Chaparral(IRE) —Dans Delight (Machiavellian (USA))
252[7] 462[3] 593[P]

Eddystone (IRE) *Linda Jewell* 51h
7 ch g Fantastic Light(USA) —Far Reaching (USA) (Distant View (USA))
217[5] 587[9] 692[P]

Ede's *Pat Phelan* 67h 78c
11 ch g Bijou D'Inde—Ballagarrow Girl (North Stoke)
156[4] 3606[P] 4556[3]

Ede's The Best *Pat Phelan* 91h
7 b m Kayf Tara—Irish Impulse (USA) (Irish River (FR))
157[P]

Edgbriar (FR) *Paul Webber* 134h 145c
9 br g Brier Creek(USA) —Harmonie De Valtat (FR) (Video Rock (FR))
(1861)
2359[8] 3677[5] 3949[3] 4820[9] 5185[13]

Edgebury *Paul Webber* 88h
8 br g Overbury(IRE) —Dusky Dante (IRE) (Phardante (FR))
4751[12] 5016[5] (5282)

Edge End *Lisa Williamson*
7 ch g Bold Edge—Rag Time Belle (Raga Navarro (ITY))
2323[P]

Edgefour (IRE) *Ben Case* 109h
7 b m King's Best(USA) —Highshaan (Pistolet Bleu (IRE))
440[P] 682[P] 962[2] 1067[2] 1150[7] 1484[2] 1746[3]
2089[6] 5346[5]

Edgeover *Paul Webber* 112h 128c
9 br g Overbury(IRE) —Dusky Dante (IRE) (Phardante (FR))
(714)

Edgevine *Paul Webber* 91h
7 b m Grape Tree Road—Vieille Russie (Kenmare (FR))
645[6]

Edgeworth (IRE) *Brendan Powell* 27h
5 b g Pyrus(USA) —Credibility (Komaite (USA))
5050[9]

Edieskaia (IRE) *Tim Vaughan* 60b
5 b g Exit To Nowhere(USA) —Friendly Craic (IRE) (Mister Lord (USA))
3731[12] 4443[9]

Edinburgh Gin Time *Lucy Normile* 69b
5 b g Bollin Terry—Good Job (King's Ride)
4308[9] 5033[8]

Editors Rose (IRE) *Tim Walford* 89h 89c
8 ch m Publisher(USA) —Rosalisa (Hildenley)
211[P]

Edlomond (IRE) *Bill Turner* 82b
5 gr g Great Palm(USA) —Samardana (IRE) (Hernando (FR))
60[2]

Edmund (IRE) *Howard Johnson* 91b
4 b g Indian River(FR) —Awomansdream (IRE) (Beneficial)
3731[2] 4259[4]

Educated Evans (IRE) *Nigel Twiston-Davies* 118h
6 b g Bishop Of Cashel—Pavlova (IRE) (Montelimar (USA))
1594[U] (2058) 2607[4] 3881[4] 4700[5] 5289[12]

Eeny Mac (IRE) *Neville Bycroft* 70h
4 ch g Redback—Sally Green (IRE) (Common Grounds)
2369[6]

Egypt Mill Spirit (IRE) *Paul Nicholls* 96b
5 b g Overbury(IRE) —Miss Tickill (IRE) (Mandalus)
1729[3] 2328[7]

Eighteen Carat (IRE) *Donald McCain* 119h
7 b g Luso—Jemma's Gold (IRE) (Buckskin (FR))
289[6] (2545) 4112[2] 4506[2] 5091[4]

Elaala (USA) *Barry Leavy* 116h
9 ch m Aljabr(USA) —Nufuth (USA) (Nureyev (USA))
96[7]

El Batal (IRE) *Sean Curran* 95h 86c
10 b g Oscar(IRE) —Native Sunset (IRE) (Be My Native (USA))
83[5] 383[3] 665[2] 1159[P]

Elby *Eve Johnson Houghton*
4 b g Compton Place—Shall We Run (Hotfoot I)
2597[12]

Elcanos (GER) *A J Martin* 117h 80c
8 ch g Acatenango(GER) —Elisha (GER) (Konigsstuhl (GER))
442[4] 711[5]

El Diego (IRE) *Jamie Snowden* 97h 84c
7 b g Sadler's Wells(USA) —Goncharova (USA) (Gone West (USA))
1675[10] 1990[7] 2283[5] 3252[5] 3589[6] 4052[P] **4927[P]**
5240[3]

El Distintivo (ARG) *Venetia Williams* 109h
7 bb g Body Glove(ARG) —Shy Susana (ARG) (Shy Tom (USA))
2148[P] 2587[F]

Eldred (IRE) *Nicky Henderson* 114h
5 b g Beneficial—Miss Executive (IRE) (Executive Perk)
1989[5] 2963[14] 3678[P] 4203[5] 4479[6] 5401[2]

Electric City (IRE) *Michael Quinlan* 71h
4 b f Elusive City(USA) —Accell (IRE) (Magical Wonder (USA))
1674[5] 2068[9]

Elegant Olive *Roger Curtis* 88h
8 b m Alflora(IRE) —Strong Cloth (IRE) (Strong Gale)
1035[3] 1232[P] 1434[4] 2239[2] 2980[5] (3400)

Elegant Touch (IRE) *Emma Lavelle* 101b
5 b m Kayf Tara—Faucon (Polar Falcon (USA))
(2167) ◆ 4082[8] 5188[16]

Eleven Fifty Nine *Anthony Honeyball* 95b
5 b m Midnight Legend—Essex Bird (Primitive Rising (USA))
(832)

Elevenses *James Moffatt* 105h
7 b g Wellbeing—Tea Leaves (USA) (Twining (USA))
180[2] 1401[2] 1757[6] 1869[P]

Eliades Run (IRE) *Ferdy Murphy* 74h
5 b g Turtle Island(IRE) —Chancy Gal (Al Sirat)
1988[7] 2297[3] 3952[8]

Elie Shore *Maurice Barnes*
4 b f Tobougg(IRE) —Mitsuki (Puissance)
1696[10]

Elite Land *Brian Ellison* 118h 134c
8 b g Namaqualand(USA) —Petite Elite (Anfield)
(634) 1023[4]
1229[4] 2613[4] (3970)
(4470) 5340[P]

Eliza Doalott (IRE) *Mrs M Stirk* 66h 113c
9 b m Oscar(IRE) —Alottalady (IRE) (Mandalus)
(178) ◆ **398[F]** 1829[10] 1929[15] 2072[P]

Eljay's Boy *J Myerscough-Walker* 82h 107c
13 b g Sir Harry Lewis(USA) —Woodland Flower (Furry Glen)
1195[6]
1273[9] 4708[F]

El Jo (IRE) *Martin Bosley* 116h 97c
10 b g Oscar(IRE) —Gayla Orchestra (Lord Gayle (USA))
3602[5] 4102[3] 4558[3]

Elk Trail (IRE) *Michael Mullineaux* 114h
6 ch g Captain Rio—Panpipes (USA) (Woodman (USA))
3504 682[2]

Ellandshe (IRE) *William Young* 24h 74c
11 bb g Topanoora—Fox Glen (Furry Glen)
32[6] 625[5] 801[6]
944[4] 1100[4] 1360[6] 1423[5] 1595[4] 1701[7] 4476[9]
5148[5]

Ellen Tilley *Alan King* 106h
7 b m Overbury(IRE) —Fortunes Course (IRE) (Crash Course)
651[P]

Ellerslie Ali (IRE) *Kim Bailey* 70h
9 b m Zaffaran(USA) —Garrisker (IRE) (King's Ride)
5107[8]

Ellerslie George (IRE) *Nick Mitchell* 114h 148c
11 br g Presenting—Proud Polly (IRE) (Pollerton)
1611[13] 1777[8] 2221[3] 2531[P]

Ellerslie Tom *Alison Thorpe* 123h 123c
9 br g Octagonal(NZ) —Tetravella (IRE) (Groom Dancer (USA))
2079 **(469)**
4488[14] 4848[22] 5102[6]
5170[3]

Ellie Wiggins *Bob Buckler* 75b
5 br m Wace(USA) —River Reine (IRE) (Lahib (USA))
2377 *2295[5]* 2632[7] 3487[P]

Ellis *Christopher Kellett* 48b
4 ch g Central Park(IRE) —Precious Island (Jupiter Island)
2458[9] 4082[15] 4422[10]

El Padrino (IRE) *Nick Gifford* 102b
6 b g Definite Article—Nova Rose (Ra Nova)
2215[4] 3200[20] 5105[4]

El Pescadero (IRE) *Nick Ayliffe* 34b
5 b m Milan—Dantes Term (IRE) (Phardante (FR))
1778[11] 4535[13] 4897[P]

El Presidente (IRE) *Neil King* 109h 98c
6 gr g Daylami(IRE) —Todi (IRE) (Spinning World (USA))
440[2] 1000[5] 1150[3] 1254[5] 1329[3] 1555[P]

Eltheeb *George Moore* 102h
4 gr g Red Ransom(USA) —Snowdrops (Gulch (USA))
3507[3] 3967[F]

Elton *Philip Hobbs* 102h 86c
8 ch g Classic Cliche(IRE) —Happy Go Lucky (Teamster)
2796[P] 5109[P]

Elton Fox *John Needham* 99b
6 bb g Bob Back(USA) —Leinthall Fox (Deep Run)
2074[5] 2368[10]

Elusive Dream *Paul Nicholls* 133h 113c
10 b g Rainbow Quest(USA) —Dance A Dream (Sadler's Wells (USA))
281[3]

Elusive Muse *Alison Thorpe* 109h
5 ch g Exit To Nowhere(USA) —Dance A Dream (Sadler's Wells (USA))
1934 302[5] 503[9] 856[3] 986[10] 5117[15]

Elysian Rock *M F Morris* 126h 130c
7 b g King's Theatre(IRE) —Elaine Tully (IRE) (Persian Bold)
3174a[7] 3472a[3] 4804[7] 5141a[5]

Elzahann (IRE) *Ferdy Murphy* 114h 114c
9 b m Saddlers' Hall(IRE) —Serpentine Artiste (Buckskin (FR))
2061[4] 2205[7] **2507[2]** ◆ **(3332)**
3508[5] 3784[P] 4060[P] (4997) 5319[4]

El Zorro *Neil King* 122h 120c
10 b g El Conquistador—Miss Wrensborough (Buckskin (FR))
3821[2]

E Major *Renee Robeson* 124h
6 ch g Singspiel(IRE) —Crystal Cavern (USA) (Be My Guest (USA))
196[6] ◆ 601[2] (1065) 5285[5]

Emerald Glade (IRE) *Milton Harris* 49h
4 b f Azamour(IRE) —Woodland Glade (Mark Of Esteem (IRE))
5078[5] 5368[6]

Emergency Exit (IRE) *Philip Hobbs* 41h 130c
8 b g Exit To Nowhere(USA) —Scarlete (FR) (Cyborg (FR))
1973[3] 3157[4] 3689[3] 4223[7] 4532[8]

Emily's Flyer (IRE) *Nigel Twiston-Davies* 80b
4 b f Oscar(IRE) —Lady Rolfe (IRE) (Alzao (USA))
5119[5]

Emirate Isle *Brian Storey* 94h
7 b g Cois Na Tine(IRE) —Emmajoun (Emarati (USA))
421[2] (2302) 2603[5] 3855[P] 4068[F] **4800[P]**

Emirates World (IRE) *Alan Jessop* 103h
5 b g Exceed And Excel(AUS) —Enrich (USA) (Dynaformer (USA))
1292[5] (1484) 1688[4]

Emmaslegend *Suzy Smith* 114h
6 b m Midnight Legend—Cherrygayle (IRE) (Strong Gale)
1724[4] 1907[P] 2329[13] (4675) (4814) 5008[8]
5302[12]

Emmy (IRE) *Michael Scudamore*
5 b m Oscar(IRE) —Brogeen Lady (IRE) (Phardante (FR))
5119[14]

Emotional Article (IRE) *Mrs Belinda Clarke* 103h 111c
11 ch g Definite Article—Cairo Lady (IRE) (Persian Bold)
6[3] (301)
499[4] 5083[5] 5237[3] 5402[P]

Emotive *Barry Murtagh* 91h 104c
8 b g Pursuit Of Love—Ruby Julie (Clantime)
88[2] 287[4] 516[2] 728[3] 860[2] 1001[F] 1100[2] (1338)
1403[3] 1781[P] 2942[2]
3549[5] 4001[P]

Emperor Charlie *Ferdy Murphy* 99h
7 b g Emperor Fountain—State Lady (IRE) (Strong Statement (USA))
53[5] 2102[11] 2552[4] 3485[4] ◆ 3713[4] 4501[5]

Emperor Concerto *Lucy Wadham* 119h 129c
8 ch g Emperor Fountain—Busy Mittens (Nearly A Hand)
1950[4] 2395[P] 4987[P]

Emperor's Choice (IRE) *Venetia Williams* 80b
4 b g Flemensfirth(USA) —House-Of-Hearts (IRE) (Broken Hearted)
4124[3]

Empire Builder (IRE) *Caroline Bailey* 111h
5 b g Brian Boru—Fair Draw (IRE) (Mister Mat (FR))
2963[7] 3405[6] 3719[2] 4021[3] 4745[3]

Empire Levant (USA) *Paul Nicholls* 123h
4 rg g Empire Maker(USA) —Orellana (USA) (With Approval (CAN))
2958[3] ◆ (3785) 4353[2] ◆

Empire Seeker (USA) *Heather Main* 79h
6 br g Seeking The Gold(USA) —Lady From Shanghai (USA) (Storm Cat (USA))
1899[5] 2131[7] 3839[13]

Empire Theatre (IRE) *Noel Meade* 134h
7 b g King's Theatre(IRE) —Foreign Estates (IRE) (Be My Native (USA))
3709a[15]

Empress Chang (IRE) *Christopher Kellett* 38b
4 b f Revoque(IRE) —Belmarita (IRE) (Belmez (USA))
4879[10]

Empress Orchid *Donald McCain* 114h
6 b m Sir Harry Lewis(USA) —Empress Of China (IRE) (Anshan)
2353[2] 3389[4] (3637) (3816) 4417[2] 5008[9] 5346[2]

Empty Scabbard *Ron Hodges* 61h
7 b g Daggers Drawn(USA) —Feather-In-Her-Cap (Primo Dominie)
3478[11]

Emrani (USA) *Donald McCain* 2h
4 b g Rahy(USA) —Ebaza (IRE) (Sinndar (IRE))
4283[13] 4684[P]

Enchanted Approach (IRE) *Lady Susan Brooke* 93h
8 bb m Bob Back(USA) —Vics Approach (IRE) (Old Vic)
3[8] 59[4] 231[7] 303[3] 737[7] 796[7] 5078[P]

Encompassing (IRE) *Sophie Leech* 77h
4 b g Montjeu(IRE) —Sophisticat (USA) (Storm Cat (USA))
5243[5]

Endeavor *Dianne Sayer* 66h
6 ch g Selkirk(USA) —Midnight Mambo (USA) (Kingmambo (USA))
5027[12]

Endless Intrigue (IRE) *D K Weld* 129h
7 ch g In The Wings—Chill Seeking (USA) (Theatrical)
4086a[9]

Enfant De Lune (FR) *Alan King* 115h 120c
7 ch g Inchinor—Ombre De Lune (IRE) (Polish Precedent (USA))
194[4] *3059[6]* **3573[2] 3834[3] 4456[4] 4775[U]** 5315[15]

Englishtown (FR) *Jonjo O'Neill* 113h 121c
11 b g Mark Of Esteem(IRE) —English Spring (USA) (Grey Dawn II)
302[9] 708[10] 954[9] 1108[6] 1368[2] 1556[9] 1814[5] 2161[9] 2530[9] 2929[9]

Enigma Variations (IRE) *G J Tarry* 81h 93c
9 b g Presenting—Swinging Single (IRE) (Ashford (USA))
(4857)

Enitsag (FR) *S Flook* 88h 108c
12 ch g Pistolet Bleu(IRE) —Rosala (FR) (Lashkari)
6[P]

Enjoy Your Life (IRE) *Andrew Crook* 103h
4 ch g Zafeen(FR) —Queen Chief (IRE) (Grand Lodge (USA))
4870[5] 5357[4]

Enlightenment (IRE) *Evan Williams* 132h 140c
11 b g Presenting—Shaiybaniyda (He Loves Me)
1390[5] 1611[12] 1797[8]
2234[F] 2496[3] 3841[8] 5164[9]

Entertain Me *Robin Dickin* 117h
7 b m Kadastrof(FR) —Just The Ticket (IRE) (Jolly Jake (NZ))
100[2] ◆ (249) 432[3] (706) 2347[3]

Entre Vous Et Moi (FR) *Garvan Donnelly* 92h
6 bb g Sheyrann—Croque Ines (FR) (Monseigneur (USA))
871[P]

Ephorus (USA) *John Joseph Hanlon* 123h
6 b g Galileo(IRE) —No Frills (IRE) (Darshaan)
3709a[8]

Equity Release (IRE) *Louise Davis* 103h
10 b g Supreme Leader—Loshian (IRE) (Montelimar (USA))
3822[5] 4745[2] 4988[F]

Eradicate (IRE) *Nicky Henderson* 146h
7 b g Montjeu(IRE) —Coyote (Indian Ridge)
(207) *3058[2]* 3808[4] 4188[6] 4727[6] 5201[7]

Erdeli (IRE) *Tim Vaughan* 104h
7 b g Desert Prince(IRE) —Edabiya (IRE) (Rainbow Quest (USA))
233[U] 823[2] 988[4] 3962[8] 5322[5]

Ere Alfie (IRE) *Nick Williams* 70h 111c
7 b g High Roller(IRE) —Quench The Lamp (IRE) (Glow (USA))
1912[4] (2184)
3349[6] (4292)
5384[2]

Erehwon *Philip Hobbs* 74b
7 b g Exit To Nowhere(USA) —Lady Emm (Emarati (USA))
284[5]

Ergo (FR) *James Moffatt* 110h
7 b h Grand Lodge(USA) —Erhawah (Mark Of Esteem (IRE))
3855[C]

Ericaceous *Christine Dunnett*
4 b f Bollin Eric—Sealed Orders (Bustino)
3304[P] 3830[3]

Ericht (IRE) *Nicky Henderson* 125b
5 b g Alderbrook—Lady Orla (IRE) (Satco (FR))
2518[2] ◆ (3406) (4191) 4808[6]

Eric's Charm (FR) *Oliver Sherwood* 146h 151c
13 b g Nikos—Ladoun (FR) (Kaldoun (FR))
98[3] 2084[10] 2358[9] 3444[P] (3948)
4486[U]

Erin Dancer (IRE) *Ferdy Murphy* 107h
6 b g Chevalier(IRE) —Negria (IRE) (Al Hareb (USA))
1951[8] *3167[8]* 3304[5] 4059[6] (4798)

Erin Vogue *Nicky Richards* 90b
5 b m Mark Of Esteem(IRE) —Estrelinha (Sadler's Wells (USA))
1771[6] 2167[9]

Ernst Blofeld (IRE) *Donald McCain* 116h 136c
7 br g Flemensfirth(USA) —Estacado (IRE) (Dolphin Street (FR))
2163[R] 2500[3] 5003[13]

Eros Moon (IRE) *Alan King* 46h
7 b g Winged Love(IRE) —Kemal's Princess (Kemal (FR))
249[P]

Errington *Howard Johnson* 75h
6 ch g Karinga Bay—Saxon Gift (Saxon Farm)
1783[7] 2075[F] 2612[P]

Erritt Lake (IRE) *D T Hughes* 125h 127c
8 b g Bob Back(USA) —Bramdean (Niniski (USA))
2413a[U] 3706a[8]

Erzen (IRE) *Venetia Williams* 134h 124c
6 b g Daylami(IRE) —Ebaziya (IRE) (Darshaan)
206[8] **2664[4]**
◆ 4445[U] 4666[3] 4855[2]

Escape Artist *Tim Easterby* 59h
4 gr g Act One—Free At Last (Shirley Heights)
1984[8] 2245[6]

Escapee *Terry Caldwell* 47b
4 b f Lucky Owners(NZ) —Cap It If You Can (IRE) (Capitano)
2108[11]

Escape Exit *Tom George* 43b
6 b g Exit To Nowhere(USA) —La Feuillarde (FR) (Nikos)
2957[16] 3506[P]

Escardo (GER) *David Bridgwater* 78h
8 b g Silvano(GER) —Epik (GER) (Selkirk (USA))
762[10]

Escort'men (FR) *Paul Nicholls* 149h
5 ch g Robin Des Champs(FR) —Escortee (FR) (Cadoudal (FR))
(1775) 3559[6]

Eseej (USA) *Peter Hiatt* 96h
6 ch g Aljabr(USA) —Jinaan (USA) (Mr Prospector (USA))
4810[3]

Eskimo Pie (IRE) *Charles Pogson* 68h 124c
12 ch g Glacial Storm(USA) —Arctic Verb (Proverb)
66[P]

Esme Rides A Gaine *Christopher Wilson* 51h 100c
9 gr m Doubletour(USA) —Silver Penny (Silly Prices)
549[8] 804[6] (5311)

Esporao (IRE) *Gordon Elliott* 105h
5 b g Hawk Wing(USA) —Roman Love (IRE) (Perugino (USA))
(876)

Esprit De Fer (FR) *Rob Summers* 102h
7 b g Esprit Du Nord(USA) —Fernie (FR) (Valanour (IRE))
360[8]

Essex (IRE) *Denis W Cullen* 111h 129c
11 b g Sadler's Wells(USA) —Knight's Baroness (Rainbow Quest (USA))
1038a[9]
1712a[5] 4817[20]

Estate *David Pipe* 116h
9 b g Montjeu(IRE) —Fig Tree Drive (USA) (Miswaki (USA))
633[14]

Estates Recovery (IRE) *Philip Hobbs* 116h 119c
6 b g Luso—Jendam (IRE) (Fourstars Allstar (USA))
1725[10] 1908[F] 2663[7]
4538[6] 5037[U] (5438)

E Street Boy *David Pipe* 112h
5 b g Kayf Tara—Eau De Vie (Terimon)
589[4] 3225[10] 3691[17] 3906[7] 4272[10] 4450[4] (5040) ◆ (5075) (5111) (5191)

Estrica (IRE) *Tim Vaughan* 76h
8 b m Exit To Nowhere(USA) —Mrs Marples (IRE) (Sexton Blake)
1237[P]

Eterna *Alan McCabe* 79h
11 b m Terimon—Nothings Forever (Oats)
50[8]

Eternal City *Paul Webber* 87h
6 b g Hernando(FR) —Eversince (USA) (Foolish Pleasure (USA))
1941[3] 2946[P]

Ethan's Star (IRE) *William Young* 97h
9 b g Taipan(IRE) —Ethans Rose (IRE) (Roselier (FR))
166[P]

Ethiopia *Bob Buckler* 95h 106c
8 b g Silver Patriarch(IRE) —Anhaar (Ela-Mana-Mou)
(218) 3597 **588[4] 1452[4] 2431[U] 2794[5] 3527[6] 4292[6] 4772[3] 5053[4]** (5324)

Et Maintenant (FR) *Lucinda Russell* 108h 124c
9 ch g Johann Quatz(FR) —Dunlora (Sagaro)
1761[7] 2272[2] 2541[5] 3573[5] 4065[3] 4546[4]

Etoile Ardente *James Ewart* 88h
7 gr m Laveron—Burning Scally (Scallywag)
3498[7] 4000[3]

Etoile D'Or (IRE) *Tim Vaughan* 78h 78c
7 ch m Soviet Star(USA) —Christeningpresent (IRE) (Cadeaux Genereux)
762[P]

Etxalar (FR) *Lucinda Russell* 109h 133c
8 b g Kingsalsa(USA) —Tender To Love (Old Vic)
(2106)
2522[4] 3290[8] 4208[P] 5423[3]

Eurhythmic (IRE) *Jim Old* 27h
4 b g Danehill Dancer(IRE) —Russian Ballet (USA) (Nijinsky (CAN))
4029[10] 4458[9]

Euro American (GER) *Rose Dobbin* 98h 110c
11 br g Snurge—Egyptale (Crystal Glitters (USA))
2104[7] 2448[9] 3635[4]
4001[2] (4241) 4544[6] **4713[4]**

Euro One *Dianne Sayer* 24h
7 b m Beat All(USA) —Si Celia (Primitive Rising (USA))
2102[16] 2192[P] 2547[12]

European Dream (IRE) *Richard Fahey* 130h
8 br g Kalanisi(IRE) —Tereed Elhawa (Cadeaux Genereux)
2373[5] 3969[2] 4488[5]

Evans Wood *Michael Easterby* 90b
4 b g Gentleman's Deal(IRE) —Boulevard Rouge (USA) (Red Ransom (USA))
3406[3] 4396[5]

Evelith Regent (IRE) *John Davies* 84h
8 b g Imperial Ballet(IRE) —No Avail (IRE) (Imperial Frontier (USA))
10[4] 490[7] 1707[P]

Evella (IRE) *Neil King* 127h 134c
7 ch m Beneficial—Drimadrian (Gildoran)
2171[P]
2470[P] 3263[P] (3598)
(3817) 4398[2] (4746)
5007[P]

Even Homer Nods (IRE) *A F Gorman* 97h 71c
10 ch g Desert King(IRE) —Suaad (IRE) (Fools Holme (USA))
148[6] 4194[P]

Evening Haze *Phillip Dando* 89h
7 ch m Tumbleweed Ridge—Kristal Haze (Krisinsky (USA))
167[5] 275[3] 407[5]

Eventide *Sean Thornton* 104h
6 ch m Where Or When(IRE) —Evening Guest (FR) (Be My Guest (USA))
1695[10]

Everaard (USA) *Kate Walton* 102h
5 ch g Lion Heart(USA) —Via Gras (USA) (Montbrook (USA))
400[9] 604[2] 713[2] 3523[9] (3750) 4477[4] 4914[11] 5132[6]

Everdon Brook (IRE) *Ben Case* 82h
6 br g Laveron—Shean Rose (IRE) (Roselier (FR))
2058[10] 2985[6] 3252[8] 3989[9] 4814[P] 5172[8]

Ever Dreaming (USA) *J Morrison* 106h
6 b m Dynaformer(USA) —Slept Thru It (USA) (Sunny's Halo (CAN))
1155a[5]

Everkingly *Anna Brooks* 67b
5 b g Bollin Eric—Pink Mosaic (Safawan)
4055[16] 4239[12] 4780[15]

Everyman *John Bryan Groucott* 92h
7 gr g Act One—Maid To Dance (Pyramus (USA))
299[7] 2244[P] 2469[7] 3703[P]

Excape (IRE) *Nicky Henderson* 104h
6 b g Cape Cross(IRE) —Viscaria (IRE) (Barathea (IRE))
2083[6]

Executive's Hall (IRE) *Andrew Crook* 76b 78c
7 b g Saddlers' Hall(IRE) —Overtime (IRE) (Executive Perk)
422[4] 491[4] 804[5] 872[3] 1152[P] 1360[5] 1503[2] 1826[3] 1954[2]

Exeptional Girl *Peter Brookshaw*
5 b m Medicean—Crimson Rosella (Polar Falcon (USA))
3979[4]

Exiles Return (IRE) *Sue Wilson* 47h
9 b g Needle Gun(IRE) —Moores Girl (IRE) (Mandalus)
632[7]

Exit Forty Four (IRE) *Martin Todhunter* 91h
9 br g Exit To Nowhere(USA) —De Derri (IRE) (Denel (FR))
473[7]

Exit To Freedom *John Wainwright*
5 ch g Exit To Nowhere(USA) —Bobanvi (Timeless Times (USA))
5131[U]

Exit To Luck (GER) *S Robinson* 92h
10 b g Exit To Nowhere(USA) —Emy Coasting (USA) (El Gran Senor (USA))
3991[F]

Exmoor Ranger (IRE) *Victor Dartnall* 125h 149c
9 ch g Grand Plaisir(IRE) —Slyguff Torus (IRE) (Torus)
2084[4] ◆ 2871[3] 3437[9] 4200[U] 4790[6] 5443[P]

Exotic Man (FR) *John Wade* 111h
6 ch g Arvico(FR) —Northine (FR) (Northern Treat (USA))
1702[7] 2375[9] 3781[2] 4281[4] 4998[9]

Expensive Problem *Ralph Smith* 45h
8 b g Medicean—Dance Steppe (Rambo Dancer (CAN))
850[11]

Express Leader *Paul Nicholls* 120h
8 b g Supreme Leader—Karawa (Karinga Bay)
(167)

Extra Bold *Emma Lavelle* 77h 109c
9 b g Overbury(IRE) —Tellicherry (Strong Gale)
(2638)
3963[2] 4504[5] 5120[P]

Extracurricular (USA) *Steve Gollings*
5 ch m Thunder Gulch(USA) —Frans Lass (USA) (Shanekite (USA))
380[P]

Extra Smooth *Chris Bealby* 104h 96c
10 gr g Cloudings(IRE) —Miss Ondee (FR) (Dress Parade)
95[4]

Extreme Conviction (IRE) *John Berry* 129h
7 b g Danehill Dancer(IRE) —Nousaiyra (IRE) (Be My Guest (USA))
196[4] 767[6] (1043) (1129) 1372[6] (1608) 5441[10]

Extreme Impact *Evan Williams* 126h
5 b g Rock Of Gibraltar(IRE) —Soviet Moon (IRE) (Sadler's Wells (USA))
3881[7] (4722)

Extremely So *Philip McBride* 115h
5 ch m Kyllachy—Antigua (Selkirk (USA))
(2944) 3344[3] (3719) 4312[5]

Exulto (IRE) *Philip Hobbs* 115h
6 ch h Barathea(IRE) —All's Forgotten (USA) (Darshaan)
(51) 736[2] 798[4] 958[6] 1282[5] 1569[2] 1797[2] 2213[6]

Eyesontheprize (IRE) *P A Fahy* 107b
5 b m Shantou(USA) —Penny Fiction (IRE) (Welsh Term)
5188[8]

Eyre Square (IRE) *Keith Reveley* 119h 125c
8 b g Publisher(USA) —Eyre Eile (IRE) (Miner's Lamp)
(2354)
2962[F] (3361) 4568[2] (5031)
5423[4]

Ezdiyaad (IRE) *Kevin Morgan* 107h
7 b g Galileo(IRE) —Wijdan (USA) (Mr Prospector (USA))
1603[6] 3491[8] 3740[4] 4234[6] 4503[7]

Faasel (IRE) *David Pipe* 141h 145c
10 b g Unfuwain(USA) —Waqood (USA) (Riverman (USA))
2871[10] 4821[2] 5443[2]

Factotum *Jonjo O'Neill* 135h 64c
7 b g Sadler's Wells(USA) —Gift Of The Night (USA) (Slewpy (USA))
631[U] 738[8] 2057[7] 2475[6] 2869[P] 3562[5] 3935[5]

Fade To Grey (IRE) *Shaun Lycett* 107h
7 gr g Aljabr(USA) —Aly McBear (USA) (Alydeed (CAN))
994[5] 1282[8] 1477[3] 1590[F]

Fahrisee (IRE) *Evan Williams* 124h 129c
8 b g Fahris(IRE) —Vesper Time (The Parson)
2210[4] 3156[F] (4406)
(5079)

Failed The Test (IRE) *James McAuley* 81b
5 b m Dushyantor(USA) —Room To Room Magic (IRE) (Casteddu)
4239[8]

Fair Along (GER) *Philip Hobbs* 164h 151c
9 b g Alkalde(GER) —Fairy Tango (FR) (Acatenango (GER))
(2090) 3807[9]
4186[3] 4790[4]

Fairhaven (IRE) *Charlie Longsdon* 105h 36c
7 b g Exit To Nowhere(USA) —Rath Caola (Neltino)
4021[10]
4483[9] 4813[U] 5298[3]

Fairlea Bob (IRE) *Rose Dobbin* 53b
7 b g Bob's Return(IRE) —Condonstown (IRE) (Remainder Man)
1764[9] 2553[10] 3885[P]

Fairoak Lad (IRE) *Philip Hobbs* 132h 144c
8 br g Tiraaz(USA) —Flair Dante (IRE) (Phardante (FR))
1626[3] **1999[5]**

Fair Question (IRE) *Donald McCain* 121h 130c
13 b g Rainbow Quest(USA) —Fair Of The Furze (Ela-Mana-Mou)
152[P] 580[U]

Fair Rome *Peter Bowen*
7 ch m Roi De Rome(USA) —Fair Cruise (Cruise Missile)
3761[P] 3942[8] 4159[P]

Fair Spin *Micky Hammond* 98h
11 ch g Pivotal—Frankie Fair (IRE) (Red Sunset)
(459) (729) (2275) (2448)

Fairview Sue *Graeme McPherson* 104b
7 gr m Alflora(IRE) —Tall Story (Arzanni)
3599[6]

Fairwood Dante (IRE) *Simon Earle* 63h
7 b g Mr Combustible(IRE) —Lady De Hatton (IRE) (Phardante (FR))
1607[7] 1749[5] 1990[8]

Fairwood Present (IRE) *John Buxton* 119c
13 ch g Presenting—Ladys Wager (Girandole)
6[4] 301[2] 499[2] 4696[U] 4950[6] 5163[U] 5237[2] 5402[3]

Fairy Mist (IRE) *Brian Rothwell* 12b
4 b g Oratorio(IRE) —Prealpina (IRE) (Indian Ridge)
4287[16]

Fairynuff *Kate Walton* 101h
7 gr g Terimon—Hand Inn Glove (Alflora (IRE))
2349[7] 2612[5] 3403[11] 4146[3] 4572[7]

Fairy Trader (IRE) *Keith Goldsworthy* 83b
4 b f Hawk Wing(USA) —Magic Touch (Fairy King (USA))
2237[5] 2458[10]

Faith And Reason (USA) *Chris Grant* 86h 103c
8 b g Sunday Silence(USA) —Sheer Reason (USA) (Danzig (USA))
1929[14] 2094[14] 2508[15] 5307[8]

Faith Keeper (IRE) *Nigel Twiston-Davies* 91h
6 ch g Beneficial—Witney Girl (Le Bavard (FR))
3340[5] 4203[6] 4451[9]

Falcon Island *Colin Tizzard* 123h
6 b g Turtle Island(IRE) —Dolly Sparks (IRE) (Electric)
3709a[7] 4448[5] 4895[2] (5099) 5291[5]

Falcun *Micky Hammond* 95h
4 b g Danehill Dancer(IRE) —Fanofadiga (IRE) (Alzao (USA))
3885[U] 4056[4]

False Economy (IRE) *Michael Hourigan* 128h
6 b g Orpen(USA) —Ashanti Dancer (IRE) (Dancing Dissident (USA))
1713a[5]

False Evidence (IRE) *Mrs John Harrington* 126h
9 b g Witness Box(USA) —Merrys Delight (IRE) (Balinger)
1121a[8]

Famagusta *Peter Charalambous* 82b
4 b f Sakhee(USA) —Gitane (FR) (Grand Lodge (USA))
4184[5] 4728[14]

Fandor Chalet (FR) *J-L Henry*
9 b g Cachet Noir(USA) —Lettre De Balme (FR) (Solicitor (FR))
190a[9]

Fantastic Morning *Violet M Jordan* 38h
7 ch g Fantastic Light(USA) —Gombay Girl (USA) (Woodman (USA))
532[7] 3727[8] 4378[P]

Fantastic Sam (IRE) *Kate Walton* 43h
4 ch f Redback—Jellybeen (IRE) (Petardia)
2435[4]

Fanzee Man *Rod Millman* 46b
4 b g Zafeen(FR) —Mild Deception (IRE) (Glow (USA))
4866[12] 5174[P]

Faraway Downs *Gary Moore*
5 b g Golden Snake(USA) —Zaffaran Run (IRE) (Zaffaran (USA))
4923[3]

Far Away So Close (IRE) *Paul Nolan* 146h
6 b g Norwich—Ballyknock Lass (IRE) (Electric)
2344[7] 4086a[8] 4788[9] (5201)

Farbreaga (IRE) *Anna Newton-Smith* 101b
5 b g Shernazar—Gleann Alainn (Teenoso (USA))
5387[3]

Farewellatmidnight *Alex Hales* 93h
5 b m Midnight Legend—Fond Farewell (IRE) (Phardante (FR))
2156[6] 3266[11] (3830) 4703[F]

Farewell Bluebell (IRE) *Tim Vaughan* 66b
4 b g Milan—Bluebell Wedding (Henbit (USA))
4547[7] 5203[8]

Farleigh House (USA) *Neil King* 112h
7 b g Lear Fan(USA) —Verasina (USA) (Woodman (USA))
1886[4] 2076[7] 4778[8] 4858[P]

Farmer Frank *Nick Kent* 123c
8 b g Cotation—Carly-J (Cruise Missile)
148[4] (354)
493[2] 4141[P] 4856[3]

Farmer Henry *Sandy Forster* 46h
7 b g Killer Instinct—Liebside Lass (IRE) (Be My Guest (USA))
2297^{8} 3850^{11} 3994^{11}

Farmers Cross (IRE) *Ferdy Murphy* 103h
7 b g Old Vic—Ace Conqueror (IRE) (Lashkari)
1644^{8} 1827^{6} 2506^{6} ◆ 3693^{2} ◆ 4572^{9}

Farmers Glory *Neil King* 76h
4 b g Mujahid(USA) —Action De Grace (USA) (Riverman (USA))
3304^{8} 3401^{14} 3599^{P} 3785^{5}

Far More Serious (IRE) *Charlie Longsdon* 105h 143c
11 bb g Needle Gun(IRE) —Womans Heart (IRE) (Broken Hearted)
2497^{2} 3444^{U} 3687^{5} (3922)
4486^{3} 4821^{7}

Farm Pixie (IRE) *Ann Hamilton* 98b
5 b g Snurge—Blue Bobby (IRE) (Flemensfirth (USA))
1599^{5} 2355^{4} 4916^{3}

Farncombe (IRE) *Michael Scudamore* 35h
5 ch m Where Or When(IRE) —Promenade (Primo Dominie)
275^{5} 535^{6}

Farringdon *Mrs Prunella Dobbs* 153h 147c
8 b g Sadler's Wells(USA) —Rebecca Sharp (Machiavellian (USA))
2119a^{3}

Fashion Stakes *Chris Grant* 55b
5 ch m Fleetwood(IRE) —Glamour Game (Nashwan (USA))
2987^{12} 3504^{6}

Fasolo (GER) *C F Swan* 109b
5 b g Monsun(GER) —Flashing Green (Green Desert (USA))
4082^{14}

Father Murtagh (IRE) *Mrs Freya Brewer* 97c
11 b g Oscar(IRE) —Mullaghroe (Tarboosh (USA))
90^{3} 551^{4}

Father Probus *Nigel Twiston-Davies* 106h
5 ch h Fleetwood(IRE) —Nearly At Sea (Nearly A Hand)
1607^{3} 1824^{4} 2241^{2} 3153^{4} 3771^{4} 4079^{9} 5117^{5}

Faultless Feelings (IRE) *Philip Hobbs* 112h
5 b g Milan—Duchess Of Cork (IRE) (Satco (FR))
3405^{2} 4951^{5}

Favouring (IRE) *Michael Chapman* 49h
9 ch g Fayruz—Peace Dividend (IRE) (Alzao (USA))
135^{8}

Favours Brave *Tim Easterby* 111h
5 b g Galileo(IRE) —Tuning (Rainbow Quest (USA))
349^{2} 468^{4} 988^{2} (1325)

Fealing Real (IRE) *Rebecca Curtis* 101h 125c
9 ch g Woods Of Windsor(USA) —Bernelle (IRE) (Don't Forget Me)
(795) ◆ (849) **1136^{2} (1176)**
1312^{7} 1469^{6}

Fearless Falcon (IRE) *Adrian McGuinness* 129h
4 b g Pivotal—Juno Madonna (IRE) (Sadler's Wells (USA))
1699^{2} 2966a^{3} 3239a^{2} 4083a^{3} 4295a^{4}

Fearless Warrior *John Joseph Hanlon* 102h
6 br g Erhaab(USA) —Princess Genista (Ile De Bourbon (USA))
1155a^{10} (Dead)

Featherbed Lane (IRE) *Anabel L M King* 115h
6 b g Saddlers' Hall(IRE) —Frankly Native (IRE) (Be My Native (USA))
2310^{3} 2666^{5} (3495) 3960^{3} 4992^{U}

Featherintheattic (IRE) *Nicky Henderson* 105b
6 b g Bahri(USA) —Silk Feather (USA) (Silver Hawk (USA))
(5238)

Federstar (GER) *Milton Harris* 134h 119c
9 b g In A Tiff(IRE) —Federspeil (Konigsstuhl (GER))
94^{5} **1706^{4}**
2363^{2} ◆ **2544^{P} 3198^{F}** 3566^{6}
3832^{3} 4334^{3} 4461^{F}

Feeling (IRE) *Dai Burchell* 100h
7 b g Sadler's Wells(USA) —La Pitie (USA) (Devil's Bag (USA))
1569^{3} 1971^{6} 4751^{7}

Feeling Peckish (USA) *Michael Chapman* 53h 85c
7 ch g Point Given(USA) —Sunday Bazaar (USA) (Nureyev (USA))
49^{P} 136^{4} 437^{2} 549^{9} 1022^{3} 1081^{P} 1326^{5} 1425^{3}
1627^{4} 1826^{4}
(1939) 2277^{3}
2437^{3} 2585^{4} 3092^{7} 3170^{3}
3305^{3} 3402^{3}
3990^{8} 5295^{7} 4144^{8}
4292^{P} 4551^{2}
4953^{3}

Feel The Force (IRE) *Alan Fleming* 103h
7 br g Presenting—Shipping News (IRE) (Glacial Storm (USA))
2321^{0} 1709^{2}

Felix Da Housecat (IRE) *Ian Williams* 105h
8 br g Accordion—Collinstown Queen (IRE) (King's Ride)
1477^{2}

Felix Yonger (IRE) *Howard Johnson* 105b
5 b g Oscar(IRE) —Marble Sound (IRE) (Be My Native (USA))
(3752) 4808^{21}

Fencote Mystery *Malcolm Jefferson* 80h 71c
9 b g Classic Cliche(IRE) —Soupinette (FR) (Noblequest (FR))
1646^{9} 1733^{7}

Fenella Mere *Patricia Rigby* 42h
8 b m Sir Harry Lewis(USA) —Sharp Pet (Petong)
989^{9} 1140^{8} 1310^{3}

Fen Farm *Emma Baker* 63b
6 b g Luso—Regan (USA) (Lear Fan (USA))
362^{8} 1812^{13} 1990^{P}

Fennis Ted (IRE) *Liam Corcoran* 103h
5 b g Posidonas—Linen Fold (IRE) (Darnay)
4533^{4} 4767^{7} 4895^{4} 5267^{6}

Fentara *Tim Walford* 106h
6 b m Kayf Tara—Miss Fencote (Phardante (FR))
209^{6} (3498) 3822^{4} 4391^{9} 5030^{P}

Fergall (IRE) *Seamus Mullins* 92b
4 br g Norwich—Gaybrook Girl (IRE) (Alderbrook)
3909^{4}

Fergal's Find (IRE) *F M O'Brien* 92c
12 ch g Pierre—Nuan (IRE) (Teofane)
153^{11}

Fertiflirt *Ray Craggs*
5 b m Rock City—Miss Fleurie (Alzao (USA))
35^{P}

Festival Dreams *Joanna Davis* 95h 100c
6 ch g Largesse—Bright Spangle (IRE) (General Monash (USA))
646^{3} **(1708)**
2073^{4} 2961^{U} 3371^{4} 3819^{P} 4327^{10} 5241^{4}

Festival King (IRE) *Pauline Robson* 105h 105c
9 br g King's Theatre(IRE) —Mary Linda (Grand Lodge (USA))
1500^{2} 1697^{4} 3360^{3} 3552^{2} (3853) 4146^{2}

Ffos Las Diamond (IRE) *Nicky Henderson* 119h
7 b g Lahib(USA) —Viking Dream (IRE) (Vision (USA))
96^{5}

Fiachrua Lad (IRE) *Donal Hassett* 71b
7 b g Strategic Choice(USA) —Beautiful River (Over The River (FR))
1146a^{12}

Fiddledee (IRE) *Jonjo O'Neill* 96h
6 b m Beneficial—Betty Balfour (Decent Fellow)
1771^{2} 2168^{5} 3196^{8} 3761^{6}

Fidelis (IRE) *Ben De Haan* 107h 118c
7 gr g Great Palm(USA) —Americo Rescue (IRE) (Lord Americo)
182^{2} 299^{2} **(1813)**

Fidelor (FR) *Henry Daly* 94h
5 b g Sagacity(FR) —Fille Fidele (FR) (Lost World (IRE))
2058^{P} 2454^{10} 3366^{7} 3724^{4} 4310^{6}

Fiendish Flame (IRE) *Donald McCain* 131h 152c
7 ch g Beneficial—Deenish (IRE) (Callernish)
1766^{7}
2086^{2} (2304)
2881^{3} 3446^{6} 4077^{P} 4235^{3}
4853^{P} 5420^{7}

Fifi L'Amour (IRE) *Linda Jewell* 80b
5 ch m Flemensfirth(USA) —Supreme Adventure (IRE) (Supreme Leader)
4055^{9} 4780^{7}

Fifth Sea Lord (IRE) *Tom Gretton* 25h
6 ch g Right Win(IRE) —Venture To Heaven (IRE) (The Parson)
514^{9} 2985^{F} 3495^{8} 4100^{10} **4799^{F}**

Fiftyfive Degrees (IRE) *Pauline Robson* 127h 119c
10 b g Presenting—Streets (Furry Glen)
2205^{9}
3634^{P} 4060^{6} 4306^{P} 5032^{7}

Fiftyonefiftyone (IRE) *Oliver Sherwood* 118h 130c
7 b g Oscar(IRE) —Great Dante (IRE) (Phardante (FR))
2082^{7} 2593^{8} 3339^{2} 3690^{P} 4460^{2} (4782)
5228^{5}

Figairy (IRE) *Noel C Kelly* 97b
7 gr g Lord Of Appeal—Rosy Waters (Roselier (FR))
1116^{P}

Fight Club (GER) *Bernard Llewellyn* 96h
10 b h Lavirco(GER) —Flaming Song (IRE) (Darshaan)
2540^{10} 2667^{6} 3296^{8}

Fighting Chance (IRE) *Richard Lee* 106h 141c
11 b g Germany(USA) —Una Juna (IRE) (Good Thyne (USA))
2112^{P} 2665^{6} 3565^{P} 3841^{7} 4972^{3}

Fightstar (FR) *Lucinda Russell* 93h
7 b g Lord Of Men—Parla (GER) (Lagunas)
1573^{6} 2202^{10} 3331^{10} 4068^{8} 4688^{3} 5094^{P}

Filbert (IRE) *Philip Hobbs* 119h
5 b g Oscar(IRE) —Coca's Well (IRE) (Religiously (USA))
2291^{3} (3295)

Filimoss *Charlie Morlock* 76h
6 ch m Classic Cliche(IRE) —Fililode (Mossberry)
2222^{8} 2554^{8} 2985^{10} 4081^{15} 4929^{P} 5169^{3}

Filippo Lippi (IRE) *Jonjo O'Neill* 102h 102c
6 b g Oscar(IRE) —Marhabtain (Touching Wood (USA))
539^{8} 930^{2} 1094^{2} 3260^{2} 3764^{3}
5060^{2}

Fill The Power (IRE) *Sue Smith* 98h
5 b g Subtle Power(IRE) —Our Alma (IRE) (Be My Native (USA))
718^{2} 3399^{11} 3572^{5} 3918^{5} 5092^{2}

Fillyofthevalley *Peter Jones* 38h 68c
8 b m Wizard King—Slipmatic (Pragmatic)
2627^{5}
3627^{P} 3980^{5} 4560^{P} 5169^{P}

Film Festival (USA) *Brian Ellison* 107h 132c
8 ch g Diesis—To Act (USA) (Roberto (USA))
748^{2} **1502^{2}**
1606^{3} 1828^{2} (2093)
2436^{4} *3170^{7}* **3968^{3} (4453)**
4853^{15} 5310^{U}

Final Approach *W P Mullins* 145h
5 b g Pivotal—College Fund Girl (IRE) (Kahyasi)
(3474a) (4848)

Final Bid (IRE) *Tracey Barfoot-Saunt* 111h 83c
8 b g Mujadil(USA) —Dusky Virgin (Missed Flight)
95^{6} 231^{P} 698^{10}

Final Cast *Nicky Henderson* 83b
4 b f Presenting—Telmar Flyer (Neltino)
5084^{6} 5380^{5}

Final Day (IRE) *Gordon Elliott* 135h
7 b g Bob Back(USA) —First Strike (IRE) (Magical Strike (USA))
(1853) 2388^{5}

Final Flyer (IRE) *Alison Thorpe* 107h
7 br g Beneficial—Highways Daughter (IRE) (Phardante (FR))
1195^{P} 1344^{P} 4676^{4} 4999^{2} 5243^{2} 5376^{8}

Final Veto *Sue Smith* 95h 110c
8 ch g Vettori(IRE) —Robin Lane (Tenby)
3724^{P} 4390^{U} 4542^{3}
(5029) 5417^{P}

Financialregulator (IRE) *Gordon Elliott* 120h 120c
7 ro g City Honours(USA) —Notorious (Auction Ring (USA))
469^{2}

Finbin (IRE) *Henry Hogarth* 103h 106c
9 b g Presenting—More Dash (IRE) (Strong Gale)
(211) 424^{2} **(471)**
549^{6} 2274^{6}

Finch Flyer (IRE) *Gary Moore* 99h
4 ch g Indian Ridge—Imelda (USA) (Manila (USA))
1586^{2} 1674^{6} 3554^{4}

Find A Key (IRE) *Howard Johnson* 93b
4 b g Definite Article—Jims Leader (IRE) (Supreme Leader)
(5264)

Fine By Me (IRE) *Julian Smith* 102h 117c
12 b g Accordion—Girseach (Furry Glen)
1769^{8} 1960^{P} 2483^{P} 2953^{P} 4997^{P}

Fine Lace (IRE) *Evan Williams* 90h
4 b f Barathea(IRE) —Fine Detail (IRE) (Shirley Heights)
1772^{2} 2435^{P}

Finellas Fortune *George Moore* 89b
6 b m Elmaamul(USA) —Fortune's Filly (Nomination)
399^{6}

Fine Parchment (IRE) *Charlie Mann* 101h 137c
8 b g Presenting—Run For Cover (IRE) (Lafontaine (USA))
2036^{6} (2366)
2544^{2} (2869) ◆ **3438^{8} 4077^{2} (4487)** ◆
5185^{U}

Fingal Bay (IRE) *Philip Hobbs* 122b
5 b g King's Theatre(IRE) —Lady Marguerrite (Blakeney)
(4097)

Finger Onthe Pulse (IRE) *T J Taaffe* 147h 151c
10 b g Accordion—Quinnsboro Ice (IRE) (Glacial Storm (USA))
(1123a)
1527a^{3} 2359^{12} 2886^{11}

Finger Spin *Mark H Tompkins* 67h
5 b m Vettori(IRE) —Light Hand (Star Appeal)
1819^{6} 3960^{8}

Finian's Rainbow (IRE) *Nicky Henderson* 140h 163c
8 b g Tiraaz(USA) —Trinity Gale (IRE) (Strong Gale)
(2628)
(3625) (4078)
4789^{2} (5197)

Finlay *Donald McCain* 94h 115c
8 gr g Parthian Springs—Grey Scally (Scallywag)
2938^{4} 3723^{2} 4258^{3} (4796)
5095^{2} 5391^{4}

Finmerello *Kim Bailey* 55b
5 b m Definite Article—Belle Magello (FR) (Exit To Nowhere (USA))
4027^{12}

Finnbennach (IRE) *Liam Corcoran* 89h
6 b g Revoque(IRE) —South Queen Lady (IRE) (King's Ride)
4273^{11}

Finnish Melody *Andy Turnell* 90h 30c
7 ch m Karinga Bay—Myrtilla (Beldale Flutter (USA))
183^{7}

Fin Vin De Leu (GER) *Charlie Mann* 121h 140c
5 b g Dr Fong(USA) —Fairy Queen (IRE) (Fairy King (USA))
206^{7} 1864^{13} 2399^{4} 2955^{6} **3598^{F} 3988^{2} (4445)**
(4898) 5133^{3}

Finzi Contini (FR) *Tim Vaughan* 70h 61c
7 gr g Kaldounevees(FR) —Rainbird (Rainbow Quest (USA))
1326^{0} 1402^{5} 1424^{RR}

Fiorenza *Nigel Twiston-Davies* 43b
5 b m Kayf Tara—Priests Bridge (IRE) (Mr Ditton)
5209^{9}

Fire And Rain (FR) *Emma Lavelle* 56h 137c
8 b g Galileo(IRE) —Quatre Saisons (FR) (Homme De Loi (IRE))
5038^{5} **5443^{P}**

Firedog (IRE) *Venetia Williams* 88h
7 b g Bob Back(USA) —Avoca Vale (IRE) (Warcraft (USA))
539^{P} 4330^{P}

Fireitfromye (IRE) *Alan Fleming* 92h
6 b g Milan—Sweet Merenda (IRE) (Lancastrian)
3344^{6} 3864^{2} 4159^{9}

Firescent *Dominic Ffrench Davis* 75b
4 b g Firebreak—Milliscent (Primo Dominie)
1913^{6} 2237^{8}

Firm Foundations (IRE) *Michael Mulvany* 106h
5 b m Noverre(USA) —Battle Wiery (USA) (Schossberg (CAN))
2196a^{5}

Firm Order (IRE) *Paul Webber* 123h
6 b g Winged Love(IRE) —Fairylodge Scarlet (IRE) (Mister Lord (USA))
(303) (1904) 2581^{5} 3556^{4} (3950) 4464^{6}

First Avenue *Gary Moore* 125h
6 b g Montjeu(IRE) —Marciala (IRE) (Machiavellian (USA))
3447^{11} 3808^{13} 4323^{5} 4452^{5}

First Bay (IRE) *Keith Goldsworthy* 92h
5 b g Hawk Wing(USA) —Montmartre (IRE) (Grand Lodge (USA))
279^{7} 853^{5}

First Beauty (IRE) *D T Hughes* 117h
7 bb m Norwich—Alleged Beauty (IRE) (Jurado (USA))
1121a^{10}

First Boy *Sue Smith* 98h 102c
9 b g Polar Prince(IRE) —Seraphim (FR) (Lashkari)
1628^{7}

First Fandango *Tim Vaughan* 119h
4 b g Hernando(FR) —First Fantasy (Be My Chief (USA))
(2570) (3358) 4847^{15}

First Fought (IRE) *Joanne Foster* 14h 77c
9 b g Germany(USA) —Royal Flame (IRE) (Royal Academy (USA))
749^{7} **840^{9}**
1360^{3} 1642^{5} 1826^{7}

First Gunner *Tim Walford* 82h
6 ch g Alflora(IRE) —Gundreda (Gunner B)
4363^{5} 4569^{P} 5031^{5}

First In The Queue (IRE) *Nicky Henderson* 111h
4 b g Azamour(IRE) —Irina (IRE) (Polar Falcon (USA))
4029^{8} (4499) 5182^{12}

First Lieutenant (IRE) *M F Morris* 151h
6 ch g Presenting—Fourstargale (IRE) (Fourstars Allstar (USA))
(3203a) ◆ (4803) ◆

First Lord (FR) *Ronald O'Leary* 24h
7 b g Trempolino(USA) —Lightly Dancing (FR) (Groom Dancer (USA))
468^{7}

First Point (GER) *Nicky Henderson* 143h 143c
8 b g Trempolino(USA) —First Smile (Surumu (GER))
2665^{3} 3561^{4} 4852^{3} 5166^{6}

First Rock (IRE) *Alan Swinbank* 102b
5 b g Rock Of Gibraltar(IRE) —Sakkara (IRE) (Sadler's Wells (USA))
1702^{2} (2660) *(3089) 3171^{3}*

First Smash (GER) *Milton Harris* 101h
6 b g Monsun(GER) —First Smile (Surumu (GER))
3057^{3} 3491^{P} 4031^{4} 4448^{6}

First Spirit *Robin Dickin* 84h
5 ch m First Trump—Flaming Spirt (Blushing Flame (USA))
1994^{9} 2282^{5} 3620^{6} 4330^{14} 4976^{P}

First Stream (GER) *Howard Johnson* 129h
7 ch g Lomitas—First Class (GER) (Bustino)
2094^{2} 2870^{8} ◆ 3566^{P} 4354^{P} 4940^{8}

First Watch *Martin Keighley* 83b
6 b h Midnight Legend—My French Willow (Man Of France)
609^{6} 827^{P}

Fisher Bridge (IRE) *Noel Meade* 128h 145c
8 ch g Singspiel(IRE) —Kristal Bridge (Kris)
1133a^{6}

Fishoutofwater (IRE) *Rebecca Curtis* 94h
7 ch g Old Vic—Frost Bound (Hawaiian Return (USA))
3585^{6} 3937^{5} 4260^{5} 4860^{6} 5244^{10}

Fistral Beach (IRE) *Paul Nicholls* 125h 146c
8 b g Definite Article—Empress Of Light (Emperor Jones (USA))
(3453)
4352^{P} 5185^{15}

Fists Of Fury (IRE) *C Byrnes* 135h
7 ch g Beneficial—Shean Alainn (IRE) (Le Moss)
2912a^{2} 3353a^{2} 5186^{4}

Fitobust (IRE) *Seamus Mullins* 98b
5 b g Classic Cliche(IRE) —Noan Rose (IRE) (Roselier (FR))
4124^{2} 5321^{P}

Fit To Drive *Brendan Powell* 71h 132c
9 b m Kayf Tara—Fit For Firing (FR) (In Fijar (USA))
1828^{P} 1973^{4} (2214) 3674^{5} **4193^{P} 4726^{U} 4864^{P}**
5236^{4}

Fitzgutentyte (IRE) *C W J Farrell* 94h 99c
6 ch m Beneficial—Joyau (IRE) (Roselier (FR))
4264^{4}

Fiulin *Evan Williams* 136h
6 ch g Galileo(IRE) —Fafinta (IRE) (Indian Ridge)
1857^{2} 2083^{3} 4727^{10} 4849^{P}

Five Dream (FR) *Paul Nicholls* 148h 140c
7 b g Take Risks(FR) —Jenny Pous (FR) (Kaid Pous (FR))
1123a^{6} 1611^{2} 2496^{2} 3292^{11} 4726^{6} 5236^{3} 5422^{6}

Fiveforthree (IRE) *W P Mullins* 158h
9 gr g Arzanni—What A Queen (King's Ride)
4819^{8}

Five Jembs (IRE) *Adrian McGuinness* 92h
7 b g Commander Collins(IRE) —Thorn Tree (Zafonic (USA))
2508^{12}

Five Out Of Five (IRE) *Evan Williams* 122h 92c
7 b g Saddlers' Hall(IRE) —Grangemills (Strong Gale)
372^{2} (662) 1058^{2} 1343^{5}
5116^{3}

Five Rivers (IRE) *Warren Greatrex* 108b
5 ch g Accordion—Native Country (IRE) (Be My Native (USA))
2222^{4} 3266^{5} 4970^{5}

Five Star Wilsham (IRE) *Jeremy Scott* 125h
7 b g Bob's Return(IRE) —Riverpauper (IRE) (Over The River (FR))
370^{5} 2141^{2} 2284^{2} 3452^{3} 3688^{6} (4464) 5325^{2}

Flag Dancer *Christine Dunnett* 13b
5 b g Carnival Dancer—Bunty (Presidium)
2826^{8} 3088^{8} 3698^{P} 3833^{P}

Flag Flier *Bob Buckler* 87h
8 ch m Alflora(IRE) —Glenn's Slipper (Furry Glen)
273^{9} 660^{3} 930^{8} 1798^{4} 2239^{3}

Flag Hill *Peter Atkinson* 38h 68c
8 b g Minster Son—Dreamago (Sir Mago)
473^{P} 605^{4} 802^{6} 951^{U}

Flake *Sue Smith* 113h 125c
11 ch g Zilzal(USA) —Impatiente (USA) (Vaguely Noble)
236^{9} 2035^{9}
2163^{5}

Flamand (FR) *Nikki Evans* 15h
10 b g Double Bed(FR) —Rays Honor (Ahonoora)
1450^{13}

Flameproof (IRE) *Caroline Keevil*
6 b m Mr Combustible(IRE) —Mariussa (IRE) (Fools Holme (USA))
2288^{P} 2634^{13}

Flaming Breeze (IRE) *Henry Hogarth* 94h
6 b g Revoque(IRE) —Bitofabreeze (IRE) (Callernish)
2103[2] 3396[5] 4391[11]

Flaming Gorge (IRE) *Nick Williams* 123h 124c
6 ch g Alderbrook—Solmus (IRE) (Sexton Blake)
1853[4] 2213[11] **2503[2] 3628[2] 4782[3]**

Flaming Heck *Lucy Normile* 64h 99c
14 b g Dancing High—Heckley Spark (Electric)
290[5] 578[7] 730[P]

Flaming Thistle (IRE) *Nicky Richards* 85h 70c
7 b g Flemensfirth(USA) —Native Thistle (IRE) (Ovac (ITY))
2203[8] 3361[U] 5097[F]

Flanagan (IRE) *Venetia Williams* 112h
7 b g Old Vic—Fosterandallen (IRE) (Petoski)
2171[P]
3198[F] 3482[P]

Flapjack Crumbly *Sue Smith* 57h
8 b g Beat All(USA) —Megabucks (Buckskin (FR))
92[7] 1308[6] 1556[P] 1647[P]

Flash Flight (IRE) *Michael Smith* 63b
6 b g Busy Flight—Churchtown Colleen (IRE) (Buckskin (FR))
47[8]

Flash Harriet *John Mackie* 93h
7 ch m Classic Cliche(IRE) —Harry's Bride (Sir Harry Lewis (USA))
179[3] 328[11]

Flashy Conquest *Colin Tizzard* 81h 79c
9 b g El Conquistador—Craberi Flash Foot (Lighter)
3373[4]

Flashy Max *Jedd O'Keeffe* 75h
6 b g Primo Valentino(IRE) —Be Practical (Tragic Role (USA))
490[4] 748[P]

Flat Cap Thursday *Murty McGrath* 103b
4 ch f Erhaab(USA) —Zaffre Bleu (IRE) (Zaffaran (USA))
5306[4]

Flat Out (FR) *W P Mullins* 145h 146c
6 gr g Sagamix(FR) —Divine Rodney (FR) (Kendor (FR))
3705a[U]

Flaygray *Chris Grant* 96h
7 gr g Terimon—I'll Skin Them (IRE) (Buckskin (FR))
2525[3] 3987[10] 4569[5] 5147[6]

Fleet Dawn *John Coombe* 57b
5 b g Polish Precedent(USA) —Wychnor Dawn (IRE) (Broken Hearted)
5158[13]

Fleetstone *Richard Phillips* 40h
6 ch m Fleetwood(IRE) —Lamper's Light (Idiots Delight)
4397[11] 4918[P] 5297[P]

Fleetwood Daughter *Dai Burchell*
9 b m Fleetwood(IRE) —Mezza Luna (Distant Relative)
1158[P]

Flemish Invader (IRE) *Nigel Twiston-Davies* 108h 125c
8 b g Flemensfirth(USA) —Lite 'n Easy (IRE) (Buckskin (FR))
1747[3] (2453) ◆ 2629[6] 4010[7] (4502) 4987[4]

Flemi Two Toes (IRE) *Rebecca Curtis* 102b
5 b g Flemensfirth(USA) —Silva Venture (IRE) (Mandalus)
2309[3] 3936[2] 4164[2]

Flemross (IRE) *R T J Wilson* 105h 133c
8 b g Bravefoot—Grey Furey (IRE) (Roselier (FR))
446[7] 1118[8]

Fletch And Lenny (IRE) *Adrian Wintle* 105h
7 b g Bach(IRE) —Jennylee (IRE) (Lord Americo)
3563[7]

Fleur De Vallee *Alistair Whillans*
6 b m Rossini(USA) —Val De Fleurie (GER) (Mondrian (GER))
876[7]

Fleur De Vassy *Venetia Williams* 92h 95c
7 ch m Alflora(IRE) —Royale De Vassy (FR) (Royal Charter (FR))
2470[4] 2930[3] 3700[5] 4099[P]

Flexi Time (IRE) *Alison Thorpe* 106h
7 b g Environment Friend—Princess Perk (IRE) (Executive Perk)
232[11] 530[P]

Flichity (IRE) *Donald McCain* 112h 93c
6 br g Turtle Island(IRE) —Chancy Gal (Al Sirat)
827[2] 1003[6] 1310[F] 1567[2] 1867[3] 2584[2] *3089[7]* 4437[6] **4549[F]** 4999[6]

Flicka's Witness (IRE) *Donald McCain* 103h
6 b g Witness Box(USA) —Ballinard Sarah (IRE) (Phardante (FR))
93[3] 679[3] 4361[3] 4990[7]

Flight Leader (IRE) *Colin Tizzard* 147h 132c
11 b g Supreme Leader—Stormy Petrel (IRE) (Strong Gale)
2883[P] 2979[7] 3437[11] 3586[2] 4190[3] 4537[P]

Flighty Frances (IRE) *John Flint*
4 ch f Camacho—Moon Diamond (Unfuwain (USA))
3436[F]

Flighty Mist *Sandy Forster* 39h 100c
9 b m Missed Flight—Some Shiela (Remainder Man)
2202[12] 2547[11] **3997[U] 4244[3] (4509) (4800) 5150[5]**

Flinski (IRE) *Mrs Diane Wilson* 58c
16 b g Warcraft(USA) —Rose Almond (Stanford)
133[U]

Flintoff (USA) *Venetia Williams* 96h 29c
10 ch g Diesis—Sahibah (USA) (Deputy Minister (CAN))
2346[P] 2955[7] 3529[4] **4360[P] 4537[10]**

Flinty Bay (IRE) *Nicky Richards* 120h
6 b g King's Theatre(IRE) —Autumn Vixen (IRE) (Trigon)
1757[3] ◆ 2349[2] 2954[3] 3696[2] (4303) (5027)

Flite (IRE) *Warren Greatrex* 100b
5 b m Flemensfirth(USA) —Lite 'n Easy (IRE) (Buckskin (FR))
5119[2] ◆

Flixter *Zoe Davison*
4 b g King O' The Mana(IRE) —Freedom Weekend (USA) (Shahrastani (USA))
4561[P]

Floating Cloud *Trevor Wall* 21b
7 gr m Overbury(IRE) —Squirrellsdaughter (Black Minstrel)
60[8] 1071[9] 1724[0]

Float My Boat *Sean Regan* 87h
5 b g Beat All(USA) —Bit Of A Chick (Henbit (USA))
448[3] 949[3] 1099[5] 3601[6] 3740[9] 4314[5]

Flockton Tobouggie *Michael Easterby* 84b
5 b g Tobougg(IRE) —Johnson's Point (Sabrehill (USA))
53[10]

Floraclock *Sue Smith* 66h
6 gr m Alflora(IRE) —Rua Ros (IRE) (Roselier (FR))
1764[5] 1934[6] 2598[4] 4795[6] 5259[7]

Floradora Do *Ron Hodges* 46h 80c
9 b m Alflora(IRE) —Cream By Post (Torus)
3300[P]
4447[2] 4556[7] 4924[7]

Florafern *Oliver Sherwood* 112b
6 b m Alflora(IRE) —Mossy Fern (Le Moss)
3623[2] 4335[2] 5306[2]

Flora King *Anthony Honeyball* 19h
6 b g Alflora(IRE) —Made For A King (Roselier (FR))
1749[9] 2634[12]

Flora's Pride *Keith Reveley* 105h
7 b m Alflora(IRE) —Pennys Pride (IRE) (Pips Pride)
2370[6] 4552[6]

Floreana (GER) *Mrs A J Boswell* 107h 98c
10 b m Acatenango(GER) —Frille (FR) (Shareef Dancer (USA))
398[3]

Florence May *Lucy Jones* 24h
7 b m Alflora(IRE) —Cape Dubathriller (Dubassoff (USA))
3942[9] 5253[7] 5389[7]

Florida Dream (IRE) *Mrs C Twiston-Davies* 115h 112c
12 b g Florida Son—Ice Pearl (Flatbush)
152[5]

Floridahall (IRE) *Tim Vaughan* 68b
7 b g Saddlers' Hall(IRE) —Floruceva (IRE) (Florida Son)
1180[4]

Flowerdew (IRE) *Nicky Henderson* 96h
6 b g Old Vic—Gonearethedays (IRE) (Be My Native (USA))
2632[4] 4006[4] 4702[5]

Flower Haven *Victor Dartnall* 114h
9 b m Dr Fong(USA) —Daisy May (In The Wings)
(313) 706[3] 1067[F]

Flowersoftherarest (IRE) *David Phelan*
8 b g Hymns On High—What Thing (Riot Helmet)
295[U] 4131[U]

Flow Gently Along (IRE) *Michael Scudamore* 32h
8 b m Norwich—Over The Pond (IRE) (Over The River (FR))
4375[8]

Flowonlovelyriver (IRE) *Rachel Hobbs* 90h 69c
10 ch g Beneficial—Over The Pond (IRE) (Over The River (FR))
3934[P]
4282[3] 4718[6]

Fluters House *Gerald Ham* 55h
7 b g Piccolo—Little Tumbler (IRE) (Cyrano De Bergerac)
1031[7] 4924[10]

Fly Direct (IRE) *Lawney Hill* 77h
8 b g Dr Massini(IRE) —Hurst Flyer (Neltino)
84[10] 849[6]

Flyford Prince *Tony Carroll* 54h
6 b g Superior Premium—Bisquet-De-Bouche (Most Welcome)
850[9] 2985[B]

Flyford Princess *Tony Carroll* 43b
5 b m Superior Premium—Bisquet-De-Bouche (Most Welcome)
855[11]

Flyinflyout *Sheena West* 31h
4 b f Fath(USA) —Hana Dee (Cadeaux Genereux)
2528[9]

Flying Award (IRE) *Susan Gardner* 110h
7 b g Oscar(IRE) —Kate's Machine (IRE) (Farhaan)
2560[7] 3295[9] 3762[9] 4094[8] (4900) (5241)

Flying Bella *J J Lambe* 114h
5 b m Desert Prince(IRE) —La Belle Simone (IRE) (Grand Lodge (USA))
726[5] 2196a[8]

Flying Doctor *Elliott Cooper* 117h 128c
8 b g Mark Of Esteem(IRE) —Vice Vixen (CAN) (Vice Regent (CAN))
(176) ◆ (212) 318[2] (424) 461[3] (553) 708[5]
(802) ◆ 859[5] 951[F] 1198[9] 1405[2] 1508[9]
1661[4] 1759[2] 1932[4] 4285[13]
5146[2] 5310[5] 5431[9]

Flying Feathers (IRE) *James Moffatt* 91b
7 b m Stowaway—The Red One (IRE) (Camden Town)
577[P]

Flying Flagship *Chris Down* 79h
6 ch g Alflora(IRE) —Flagship Princess (IRE) (Topanoora)
2454[P]

Flying Johnny M (IRE) *Michael Hourigan* 111h 106c
11 ch g Flying Legend(USA) —How Doudo (Oats)
1452[U]

Flying Phento *Grant Cann* 87h
9 b m Lyphento(USA) —Fly The Wind (Windjammer (USA))
820[3]

Flying Squad (UAE) *Milton Harris* 101h 118c
7 b g Jade Robbery(USA) —Sandova (IRE) (Green Desert (USA))
850[13] 1344[6] 1487[4] 1608[8] **2555[2] 2604[2] (3305) (3488) 3602[3] 3687[P]** 4182[P]
4699[7] 4871[4]

Flyit Flora *Victor Dartnall* 43h
6 b m Alflora(IRE) —Be My Valentine (IRE) (Be My Native (USA))
3909[S] 4533[3] 5106[14]

Flyjack (USA) *Lisa Williamson*
4 b g Johannesburg(USA) —Let Fly (USA) (Flying Paster (USA))
4240[P]

Fly Tipper *Wilf Storey* 87h
11 ch g Environment Friend—Double Birthday (Cavo Doro)
163[4] 424[4] 805[3] 946[5] 999[5] 1102[5] (1339) 1700[11] 1929[6] 2080[P]

Fochabers *Bernard Llewellyn* 68h
4 b g Dr Fong(USA) —Celtic Cross (Selkirk (USA))
1772[5] 2556[8]

Fog Patches (IRE) *Lucinda Russell* 95b
5 br g Oscar(IRE) —Flash Parade (Boreen (FR))
4717[3]

Foildubh (IRE) *John Patrick Ryan* 129h
7 b g Woods Of Windsor(USA) —Bushey Glen (IRE) (Roselier (FR))
1713a[10]

Folie A Deux (IRE) *Dr Richard Newland* 104h 116c
9 b g Anshan—Flynn's Girl (IRE) (Mandalus)
99[2] ◆ 276[5] 689[2] (919) (1070) 1139[4] 1334[5] 1604[3] 1842[3]
1973[F] 2217[4] (3769)
3963[4] 4196[7] 4465[7]

Folk Tune (IRE) *John Quinn* 116h 123c
8 b h Danehill(USA) —Musk Lime (USA) (Private Account (USA))
1987[4] 2510[3] 3573[6] 3970[2] 4392[2] 4778[4]

Follow On *Maurice Barnes* 96h 76c
9 b h Barathea(IRE) —Handora (IRE) (Hernando (FR))
32[5] 291[5] 553[4] 801[F] 871[4] 946[8] 1428[6] 1507[7] 1666[5]

Follow The Plan (IRE) *Oliver McKiernan* 128h 156c
8 b g Accordion—Royal Rosy (IRE) (Dominion Royale)
3206a[U] 3473a[9] (3778a) 4227a[5] 5162[3]

Follow The Sun (IRE) *Peter Niven* 99h 99c
7 br g Tertullian(USA) —Sun Mate (IRE) (Miller's Mate)
932[9] 1062[F] **2301[P] 2659[4] 3404[3] (3618) 3970[6] 4392[U]**

Fongoli *Brendan Powell* 100h 78c
5 b m Dr Fong(USA) —Darmagi (IRE) (Desert King (IRE))
530[8] 661[3] 821[3]
918[4] 1126[3] 1331[5] 1468[6]
1678[4] 1745[10]
1924[3] 2187[2] 2434[2] 3226[5]

Font *Paul Nicholls* 103h 49c
8 b g Sadler's Wells(USA) —River Saint (USA) (Irish River (FR))
2869[12] 3786[6] 4289[3]

Fontano (FR) *Emma Lavelle* 114h
5 gr g Astarabad(USA) —Little Bud (FR) (Pampabird)
2791[4] 3678[8] 4499[2] 5010[2] 5327[4]

Font Froide (FR) *F Belmont*
6 b m Trempolino(USA) —Fontaine Guerard (FR) (Homme De Loi (IRE))
2265a[4]

Foodbroker Founder *N W Alexander* 91h
11 ch g Groom Dancer(USA) —Nemea (USA) (The Minstrel (CAN))
291[P]

Fools Mate *Alison Batchelor*
4 b g Best Of The Bests(IRE) —Millers Maid (Miller's Gilt)
5056[7]

Fool's Wildcat (USA) *Gordon Elliott* 124h
6 b g Forest Wildcat(USA) —Nine Flags (USA) (Forty Niner (USA))
289[4] 442[7] 1726[8]

Foot The Bill *Patrick Holmes* 98h
6 b g Generous(IRE) —Proudfoot (IRE) (Shareef Dancer (USA))
319[14] 3987[9] 4569[3] 5151[12]

Footy Facts (IRE) *Robert Tyner* 151h 138c
11 b g Oscar(IRE) —Princess Henry (IRE) (Callernish)
1527a[P] 3796a[6] 4107a[F]

For Bill (IRE) *Michael Winters* 139h 142c
8 b m Presenting—Bobalena (IRE) (Bob Back (USA))
(3779a)
4755a[2]

Forcefield *N W Alexander* 100h
5 b g Kalanisi(IRE) —Force Of Nature (USA) (Sadler's Wells (USA))
2525[4] 3330[12] 3851[7] 4303[5] 4873[3] 5320[9]

Forcryingoutloud (IRE) *Andrew Haynes* 106h
7 ch g Old Vic—Bijubu (IRE) (Buckskin (FR))
832[3] 1124[2] 1296[8]

Ford Of Wells (IRE) *Patrick Griffin* 41h 114c
10 b g Saddlers' Hall(IRE) —No Dunce (IRE) (Nordance (USA))
744[8] 826[12]

Foreign King (USA) *Seamus Mullins* 104h 114c
7 b g Kingmambo(USA) —Foreign Aid (USA) (Danzig (USA))
23[4] **(276)**
373[2] 734[5] 934[4] 1548[4] 1844[8] **1912[6]** 5066[7]

Forest Pennant (IRE) *Paul Nicholls* 144h 140c
9 bb g Accordion—Prudent View (IRE) (Supreme Leader)
2221[10] 2871[12]

Forest Rhythm (IRE) *Seamus Mullins* 113h
7 b g Great Palm(USA) —Eurythmic (Pharly (FR))
40[2] (185) 534[2] 690[3] 914[5] 1842[5] 2185[U] 2636[F] 3452[P] 3686[4] 4672[4] 4925[F] 4990[6] ◆ 5369[3] 5404[2]

Forestside (IRE) *J J Lambe* 113h
6 br g Zagreb(USA) —Silver Sunset (Arzanni)
4304[P]

Foretto (GER) *D J Ryan* 115h 103c
9 b g Lavirco(GER) —Fairwind (GER) (Andrang (GER))
4411[4]

Forever Emo (IRE) *Jonjo O'Neill* 108c
8 gr g Saddlers' Hall(IRE) —Blossom Rose (IRE) (Roselier (FR))
1917[5] 2303[7] 2942[F]

Forever Man (IRE) *Paul W Flynn* 65c
8 b g Luso—Annynat (Good Thyne (USA))
3880[5]

Forever Waining (IRE) *Peter Bowen* 99b
5 b g Choisir(AUS) —Dahoar (Charnwood Forest (IRE))
2328[2] 3766[5] 4287[3]

Forget It *Gary Moore* 113h 130c
6 b g Galileo(IRE) —Queens Way (FR) (Zafonic (USA))
(86) 196[F] 494[F] 1816[6]
(2124) (3690)
4355[3]

Forgotten Promise *Jo Crowley* 78b
4 b f Revoque(IRE) —Ivory's Promise (Pursuit Of Love)
5012[10]

Forlovenormoney (IRE) *Paul Nicholls* 101h
7 b g Flemensfirth(USA) —Ounavara Girl (IRE) (Hollow Hand)
2238[6] 4459[7]

Form And Beauty (IRE) *Bernard Llewellyn* 80h 81c
9 b g Orpen(USA) —Formezza (IRE) (Cyrano De Bergerac)
1049[6]
1106[8] 2468[4] 3350[5] 3839[2] 4104[5] 4266[2] (4721) 4965[5]

Formedable (IRE) *Violet M Jordan* 85h
9 ch g Moonax(IRE) —Castle Flame (IRE) (Carlingford Castle)
3728[11] 4559[7] 5072[3] 5265[3]

For Non Stop (IRE) *Nick Williams* 141h
6 b g Alderbrook—Lost Link (IRE) (Shernazar)
(1776) ◆ 2387[2] 3197[4] 4806[F] 5186[10]

Forpadydeplasterer (IRE) *Thomas Cooper* 143h 167c
9 b g Moscow Society(USA) —Run Artiste (Deep Run)
2385[2] 3560[P]

Forrest Lemons *Andrew Parker* 56h
7 ch g Supreme Sound—Barn Stripper (Germont)
2297[P] 5147[P]

Forsyth *Alan Swinbank* 79h
4 ch g Pursuit Of Love—Forsythia (Most Welcome)
1135[4] 1422[2] 1699[7]

Fortification (USA) *Michael Blake* 100h 141c
8 gr g With Approval(CAN) —Palisade (USA) (Gone West (USA))
2482[4]
3444[P] 4054[6] 4441[8]

Fort Royal (IRE) *Jeff Pearce* 34h 33c
12 b g Commanche Run—Grainne Geal (General Ironside)
436[4]

Fort Severn (IRE) *Brendan Powell* 97h 93c
7 gr g Saddlers' Hall(IRE) —La Cabrilla (Carwhite)
63[3] 283[P]

Fortunelini *Peter Brookshaw* 38b
6 b m Bertolini(USA) —River Of Fortune (IRE) (Lahib (USA))
3979[11]

Fortune's Fool *Ian Brown* 64h 69c
12 b g Zilzal(USA) —Peryllys (Warning)
424[P] 490[12]

Fortuni (IRE) *Rose Dobbin* 104h
5 b g Montjeu(IRE) —Desert Ease (IRE) (Green Desert (USA))
3331[5] 3547[5] 3749[5] ◆ 5428[3]

Fort View (IRE) *Polly Gundry* 121c
7 b g Ashley Park(IRE) —Laurens Pride (IRE) (Kambalda)
(293)
(4463) 5163[5] ◆

Forty Five (IRE) *Jonjo O'Neill* 133h 124c
9 b g Quws—Three In A Twist (IRE) (Meneval (USA))
1761[4] 2148[2] 2869[U]

Forty Knights *Chris Down* 93h
6 b m Sir Harry Lewis(USA) —Tinoforty (FR) (Saint Estephe (FR))
2137[4] 2558[13] 3745[9] 4032[6]

Fortysecond Street (IRE) *Howard Johnson* 120h 128c
7 ch g Flemensfirth(USA) —Miss Murtle (IRE) (Old Vic)
1957[4] 3333[8] 4116[8]

Forty Something (IRE) *William Amos* 71h
6 b g Moothyeb(USA) —Drumquin Girl (IRE) (Brush Aside (USA))
2102[9]

Forty Thirty (IRE) *Sheena West* 124h
5 b g Poliglote—Ciena (FR) (Gold Away (IRE))
316[3] 521[2] 756[4] 958[8] 1127[3] 2085[F] 2671[9] 5291[4] ◆

For Valour *Sabrina J Harty* 100b
7 b g King's Best(USA) —Intrepidity (Sadler's Wells (USA))
2389[13]

Forzy Origny (FR) *Nicky Henderson* 111h 144c
9 gr g Sleeping Car(FR) —Forza Malta (FR) (Royal Charter (FR))
98[2] ◆ 5185[11]

Fosters Cross (IRE) *Thomas Mullins* 148h 146c
9 b g Dr Massini(IRE) —Francie's Treble (Quayside)
1133a[15]
1527a[P] 3474a[9]

Fountains Flypast *Anthony Honeyball* 121h
7 b g Broadway Flyer(USA) —Miss Flower Girl (Petoski)
(1680) 2241[3] 2960[14] *3060[3]* ◆ 3366[6] (4448)

Four Chimneys (IRE) *W J Austin* 139h 133c
10 b g Denel(FR) —Treat A Lady (IRE) (Lord Americo)
3475a[6]

Four Commanders (IRE) *M F Morris* 125h
5 b g Old Vic—Fairy Blaze (IRE) (Good Thyne (USA))
4249a[5]

Four Fiddlers (IRE) *N W Alexander* 59h
6 br g Accordion—Folle Idee De Luz (FR) (Reve Bleu (FR))
2553[4] 3856[3] 4308[4] 5147[7]

Fourjacks *Tim Easterby* 117h
6 b g Karinga Bay—Jack's The Girl (IRE) (Supreme Leader)
2553[2] 2943[2] 3511[2] 3887[2]

Fourovakind *Matt Hazell* 103b
6 b g Sir Harry Lewis(USA) —Four M'S (Majestic Maharaj)
2632[3]

Fourpointone *Ed de Giles* 89h 96c
10 b g Overbury(IRE) —Praise The Lord (Lord Gayle (USA))
83[P] 2155[4] 2402[P] 3530[P]
3768[8] 4525[5] 5349[2]

Four Strong Winds (IRE) *Jonjo O'Neill* 124h 100c
7 b g Heron Island(IRE) —That's The Bonus (IRE) (Executive Perk)
2400[4] 2938[U] 3339[3] 3765[3] 5115[6]

Fourth Estate (IRE) *Nicky Henderson* 123b
5 b g Fantastic Light(USA) —Papering (IRE) (Shaadi (USA))
(4457) (5342)

Fourth In Line (IRE) *Anabel L M King* 53h
7 b g Flemensfirth(USA) —Lantern Line (The Parson)
3739[10]

Fourty Acers (IRE) *David Pipe* 127h 124c
11 ch g Bob Back(USA) —Guest Cailin (IRE) (Be My Guest (USA))
1723[3]

Fox Appeal (IRE) *Emma Lavelle* 90b
4 b g Brian Boru—Lady Appeal (IRE) (Phardante (FR))
4879[5] 5158[11]

Foxbridge (IRE) *Nigel Twiston-Davies* 95b
5 b g King's Theatre(IRE) —Fairy Native (IRE) (Be My Native (USA))
4866[5]

Foxesbow (IRE) *Jonjo O'Neill* 96h 111c
7 b g Beneficial—Bro Ella (IRE) (Cataldi)
599[5] 1763[9] 2170[P] (2479)
3230[6] (3695)
4102[P]

Foxes Delight (IRE) *Jane Walton* 96h
7 ch g Hubbly Bubbly(USA) —Paradiso (IRE) (Phardante (FR))
42[13] 3633[3] 4112[4] 5320[P]

Foxhill *Jacqueline Retter*
11 b g El Conquistador—Flying Cherub (Osiris)
763[P]

Foxtown Girl (IRE) *David Anthony O'Brien*
9 b m Basanta(IRE) —Ennel View (IRE) (Le Bavard (FR))
234[F]

Foynes Island (IRE) *Philip Hobbs* 109h 116c
5 b g Presenting—Lucy Lodge (IRE) (Moscow Society (USA))
1603[2] 2069[3] 2630[12] 4700[9] 4988[P]
(5370)

Fraam Lea *Andrew Price* 29h
5 b m Fraam—Castanet (Pennekamp (USA))
1921[P] 4964[6]

Fraamtaaztiic *Ron Hodges*
4 b f Fraam—Dahlawise (IRE) (Caerleon (USA))
3526[F] 5368[P]

Frame And Cover *Joanna Davis* 29h
5 b m Carnival Dancer—Fly In Style (Hernando (FR))
500[10] 792[10] 863[P]

Frameit (IRE) *Tim Vaughan* 95h
4 b g Antonius Pius(USA) —Delisha (Salse (USA))
1324[F] 1422[6] 1545[3] (1818) 1935[3] 2133[3]

Francesa *Henry Daly* 115h
6 b m Silver Patriarch(IRE) —Franciscaine (FR) (Legend Of France (USA))
2168[9] 3264[6] 3721[3] (4828) 5008[13]

Franchoek (IRE) *Alan King* 153h 121c
7 ch g Trempolino(USA) —Snow House (IRE) (Vacarme (USA))
536[U] 636[2]

Frankie Anson (IRE) *Micky Hammond* 117h 126c
7 b g Needle Gun(IRE) —Macha's Pet (IRE) (Montelimar (USA))
1151[4] ◆ **1251[F] (1402)**
3784[2] 4989[U] 5303[P] 5427[2]

Frankie Falco *Giuseppe Fierro* 75h
5 br h Bollin Eric—Marsh Marigold (Tina's Pet)
2111[9] 2419[6] 2640[11] 4949[6]

Frankie Figg (IRE) *Howard Johnson* 111h 142c
9 b g Portrait Gallery(IRE) —Ardnataggle (IRE) (Aristocracy)
2077[P] (2541)
3953[U] 5185[6]

Franklee *Harriet Graham* 61h
8 ch g Endoli(USA) —Gemma's Choice (Beveled (USA))
470[8] 945[5] 1362[F] 1666[10]

Franklino (FR) *Alan King* 110h
4 ch g Gold Away(IRE) —Amour Fatal (IRE) (Rainbows For Life (CAN))
1984[3] 2466[7] 3507[2] 3785[4] 5006[2] 5335[5]

Franklin Roosevelt (IRE) *Warren Greatrex* 88b
5 b g Beneficial—Glen's Gale (IRE) (Strong Gale)
5077[4]

Fran's Folly *Neil Mulholland* 61h
5 b m Baryshnikov(AUS) —Lansdowne Park (El Conquistador)
3872[9] 4225[11] 4897[7] 5239[4]

Frascati Park (IRE) *Nigel Twiston-Davies* 135h
7 b g Bach(IRE) —Hot Curry (IRE) (Beau Sher)
1966[3] (2493) (3387) 3676[8]

Frazers Fortune *Seamus Mullins* 60c
11 ch g Environment Friend—Safidar (Roan Rocket)
913[P]

Freckle Face *Bill Turner* 99h
4 br g Septieme Ciel(USA) —Wavet (Pursuit Of Love)
1442[P] 1674[4] 2047[2] 2466[5] 3366[8] 3958[4]

Fred Bojangals (IRE) *Ann Hamilton* 107h 128c
9 b g Scribano—Southern Princess (Black Minstrel)
1641[2] 2373[8] **4470[8] 4941[4] 5340[9]**

Freddie Brown *George Charlton* 105h
7 b g Missed Flight—Some Shiela (Remainder Man)
(399) 3850[5] 4473[4] 4910[3] 5315[5]

Freddy's Star (IRE) *Alan Jones* 115h
9 ch g Kris—Kutaisi (IRE) (Soviet Star (USA))
170[5] 331[7] 372[10] 2333[P] 3840[10] 4999[3]

Fred Grass *Jonathan Haynes* 73h
5 ch g And Beyond(IRE) —Tempted (IRE) (Invited (USA))
1867[10] 2349[P] 2612[P] 3999[11] 4550[13] 5027[9]
5356[8]

Fredo (IRE) *Ian Williams* 133h 133c
7 ch g Lomitas—Felina (GER) (Acatenango (GER))
2057[2] 2494[2] 3390[2] 3571[2] (3902)
4821[6] 5338[P]

Free As A Lark *Evan Williams* 77h
4 b f Oratorio(IRE) —Regal Magic (IRE) (Sadler's Wells (USA))
1935[4] 2020[F] 2570[F]

Freedom Fire (IRE) *Gary Moore* 116h
5 b g Alhaarth(IRE) —Feel Free (IRE) (Generous (IRE))
(465) 792[2] 983[2] 1083[6] (1453) 1547[2] 1998[4]
4778[7]

Freedom Flying *Lee James* 92h 76c
8 b m Kalanisi(IRE) —Free Spirit (IRE) (Caerleon (USA))
402[7] 745[2] 920[5] 1059[8] 1259[P] 3728[6]

Freedomofthecity (IRE) *Miss L Thomas* 55h 75c
9 b g City Honours(USA) —Cap D'Azure (Majority Blue)
151[8]

Free Falling *Alastair Lidderdale* 82h
5 ch m Selkirk(USA) —Free Flying (Groom Dancer (USA))
2289[7] 2960[11] 3389[6] 3703[P]

Free Gift *R H & Mrs S Alner* 120c
13 b g Presenting—Gladtogetit (Green Shoon)
236[P] 411[7] 636[6] 824[2]

Free Speech *Sarah Humphrey* 93h 89c
8 b g King's Best(USA) —Daring Miss (Sadler's Wells (USA))
955[11]
1081[2] 1152[3]

Free To Air *Oliver Sherwood* 77h
8 b g Generous(IRE) —Petonica (IRE) (Petoski)
84[7] 467[P] 1261[8]

Free World (FR) *Paul Nicholls* 121h 156c
7 b g Lost World(IRE) —Fautine (FR) (Fast Topaze (USA))
2126[2] 3446[7] 4352[P] 5185[F]

Free World (IRE) *Warren Greatrex* 115h 124c
9 b g Luso—Paddy's Dancer (Paddy's Stream)
1861[3] 2084[7] *(3059)* **3558[4] 3948[7]**

Freeze Up (IRE) *Philip Hobbs* 90h 118c
9 b g Presenting—Ballymacoda Lady (IRE) (Lord Ha Ha)
3263[9] 4966[P]

French Bey (IRE) *Mrs L Pomfret* 75c
11 b m Beyssac(FR) —Cerise De Totes (FR) (Champ Libre (FR))
4415[6]

French Leave (IRE) *Victor Dartnall* 96h
9 ch g Gunner B—La Kabyle (FR) (Bikala)
2144[8] 2504[5] 2980[10] 3791[11] 5057[3]

French Opera *Nicky Henderson* 138h 162c
8 b g Bering—On Fair Stage (IRE) (Sadler's Wells (USA))
3446[9] (4187)
4805[6] 5184[5] (5442)

French Seventyfive *Tim Walford* 78h
4 b g Pursuit Of Love—Miss Tun (Komaite (USA))
5151[11] 5356[6]

French Ties (IRE) *Jennie Candlish* 93h 93c
9 ch g John French—No Ties (IRE) (General View)
2452[9] 3729[0] 3996[3] 4263[6] **(4413)**
4827[3]

Freneys Well *E Bolger* 102h 137c
11 b g Primitive Rising(USA) —Betrothed (Aglojo)
1526a[11]
2346[4] 4792[11]

Frequency *Amy Weaver*
4 br g Starcraft(NZ) —Soundwave (Prince Sabo)
2245[P]

Fresh Air And Fun (IRE) *A G Hobbs* 109h 128c
8 bb g Trans Island—Executive Ellie (IRE) (Executive Perk)
232[2] **4293[3]**
4786[2]

Fresher Fishing (IRE) *Victor Dartnall* 63h
7 gr g Luso—Turbet Lass (IRE) (Carlingford Castle)
2560[8] 3295[14] 3930[11] 4895[11]

Friends Of Tina (IRE) *Alex Hales* 89h 82c
8 ch m Environment Friend—Runaway Tina (IRE) (Mandalus)
1918[2] 2314[6] 3697[7]

Fringe Theatre *Gary Moore*
5 b g King's Theatre(IRE) —Second Best (IRE) (Supreme Leader)
3060[6]

Frith (IRE) *Lucy Normile* 6h 80c
9 b g Benny The Dip(USA) —Melodist (USA) (The Minstrel (CAN))
4136[5]
4573[U] 4963[4] 5418[5]

Frizzo (FR) *Alan King* 99b
4 ch g Ballingarry(IRE) —Floridene (FR) (Saumarez)
5342[5]

Froggy Lane *Simon West* 90h 86c
8 b g Roi De Rome(USA) —Cullane Lake (IRE) (Strong Statement (USA))
2202[11] 3505[12] **3748[F] 4997[U]** 5096[9]

Frolic Along (IRE) *J R Jenkins* 87b
4 b f Medecis—High Glider (High Top)
5012[5]

Frolon (FR) *F-M Cottin* 93h 137c
6 b g Lavirco(GER) —Fourmille (FR) (Rose Laurel)
5367a[5]

From Dawn To Dusk *Philip Hobbs* 141h 151c
12 b g Afzal—Herald The Dawn (Dubassoff (USA))
2084[3] 2358[5] 2871[5]

Frontier Boy (IRE) *James Ewart* 91h
7 b g New Frontier(IRE) —Mary Bridie (IRE) (Meneval (USA))
2102[8] 3633[5] 4062[5]
5417[F]

Frontier Dancer (IRE) *Nigel Twiston-Davies* 136h 129c
7 b g New Frontier(IRE) —All The Gear (IRE) (Nashamaa)
94[6] **(1595)**
1854[2] 2527[4] 2979[5] 3672[5] 4461[4] 4864[U]

Frontier Spirit (IRE) *Nigel Twiston-Davies* 119h
7 b g New Frontier(IRE) —Psalmist (Mystiko (USA))
(1573) 1951[2] 2428[3] 3678[5] 4121[3] 4862[6]

Front Of House (IRE) *Ben Haslam* 122h 100c
9 b g King's Theatre(IRE) —Dancing Line (High Line)
(1296) 1703[P] 2075[2] (2281)
3520[5]

Front Rank (IRE) *Dianne Sayer* 114h
11 b g Sadler's Wells(USA) —Alignment (IRE) (Alzao (USA))
166[12] 582[4] 948[2] 1104[2] (1406) 1597[8] 1695[7]
2208[12] 2551[P] 3523[16] 4113[11] 4572[10] 5030[9]

Front Street (IRE) *Pat Murphy* 73h 76c
7 b g Saddlers' Hall(IRE) —Glebe Dream (IRE) (Be My Native (USA))
2154[6] 2571[6] 3428[4]
4705[6] 5268[3]

Frosted Grape (IRE) *David Pipe* 103h 126c
5 b m Kheleyf(USA) —Two Shonas (IRE) (Persian Heights)
275[2] 541[6] 754[3] (989) 1162[4] 1313[2]
(1454) 1481[2] (1509)
(1557) 1604[5] 1861[F] 2130[5] 2630[9] **5436[6]**

Frosty's Gift *Jimmy Fox* 78h
7 ch m Bold Edge—Coughlan's Gift (Alnasr Alwasheek)
384[10] 865[9] 1064[3] 1199[3] 1272[3] 1997[4] 2169[4]
2583[3]

Frosty Spring *David Thompson* 61h 87c
8 gr m Terimon—Springaleak (Lafontaine (USA))
3599[P] 4134[5] 4795[7] 4975[P] **5310[3]**

Fruitfull Citizen (IRE) *Simon Jones* 100c
11 ch m Anshan—Sweet Peach (IRE) (Glenstal (USA))
253[2]

Fruit Yoghurt *Simon Earle* 66b
5 b m Hernando(FR) —Diamant Noir (Sir Harry Lewis (USA))
5306[14]

Fruity O'Rooney *Gary Moore* 135h 136c
8 b g Kahyasi—Recipe (Bustino)
(1917) 2523[10] **3429[2] 3564[2] 4119[2] (4371)**
5213[2] (5382)

Fujin Dancer (FR) *Brian Ellison* 119h
6 ch g Storming Home—Badaayer (USA) (Silver Hawk (USA))
2308[3] 3696[3] ◆ (4113) (4858) 5315[4] ◆

Full Atraction (FR) *M Nicolau*
5 b m Poliglote—Full Contact (FR) (Cadoudal (FR))
2265a[6]

Full Of Joy (IRE) *Jonjo O'Neill* 120h
6 b g King's Theatre(IRE) —Penny Brae (IRE) (Montelimar (USA))
2477[2] ◆ (2630) 3771[6] 4988[P]

Full Ov Beans *Michael Gates* 50h
7 ch g Midnight Legend—Scarlet Baroness (Baron Blakeney)
855[4] 3266[15] 4081[F] 4776[7] 5101[10]

Fully Funded (USA) *Noel Meade* 134h
6 b g Aptitude(USA) —Fully Invested (USA) (Irish River (FR))
(2562a) 3029a[3] 3708a[4]

Fulofanoyance *Malcolm Jefferson* 88h
6 b g Rainbow High—More To Life (Northern Tempest (USA))
349[5] ◆

Ful Of Grace (IRE) *James Frost* 58h
7 b m Marju(IRE) —Mitawa (IRE) (Alhaarth (IRE))
912[9] 1164[P] 1707[6] 1949[7]

Fun Guy *Bob Buckler* 78h
6 ch g Fleetwood(IRE) —Aifung (IRE) (Bigstone (IRE))
2331[4] 2873[9] 3398[7] 4675[12] 5383[P]

Funky Beat *John Holt* 18b
5 b m Hamas(IRE) —Funky (Classic Music (USA))
355[14]

Funky Munky *Alistair Whillans* 78h
6 b g Talaash(IRE) —Chilibang Bang (Chilibang)
2552[9] 4824[5] 5027[6]

Funny Fellow *Richard Rowe* 96h 105c
9 b g Defacto(USA) —Royal Comedian (Jester)
985[P]

Furius *Sue Smith* 82h
5 b g Montjeu(IRE) —Frottola (Muhtarram (USA))
1629[10] 1831[7] 2282[8]

Furrows *Oliver Sherwood* 115h
6 b g Alflora(IRE) —See More Furrows (Seymour Hicks (FR))
2074[9] 2590[5] (3691) 4437[2]

Fushe Jo *Howard Johnson* 133h
7 gr g Act One—Aristocratique (Cadeaux Genereux)
3808[P] **4507[F]**

Fusilade (FR) *Warren Greatrex* 72b
8 ch g Nikos—Fulgina (FR) (Double Bed (FR))
1028[P]

Gabreselassie (IRE) *Jonjo O'Neill* 106h 115c
8 b g Old Vic—Montelisa (IRE) (Montelimar (USA))
(918)
(1081)

Gabrielle Da Vinci *David Evans* 51h
5 b m Erhaab(USA) —Gulshan (Batshoof)
275[4] *3089[9]*

Gaelic Flight (IRE) *Jeremy Scott* 66h 134c
13 bb g Norwich—Ash Dame (IRE) (Strong Gale)
78[P] 735[12] 1973[P]

Gafferdy Lane *Mike Sowersby*
8 ch g Classic—Aunt Gladys (IRE) (Glacial Storm (USA))
801[P]

Gagewell Flyer (IRE) *W P Mullins* 146h
7 br g Deploy—Drumcay Polly (IRE) (Le Bavard (FR))
(3353a) (3846a) 4849[P]

Gaining Ground (IRE) *Graeme McPherson* 42h 81c
11 ch g Presenting—Lorglane Lady (IRE) (Lancastrian)
(531) **931[8]**
1478[5] 1733[2]

Gainsborough's Art (IRE) *Harry Chisman* 79h 85c
6 ch g Desert Prince(IRE) —Cathy Garcia (IRE) (Be My Guest (USA))
63[7] 757[8] 4330[5] 4751[11] (4949) 5111[P]

Gala Evening *Jim Old* 126h
9 b g Daylami(IRE) —Balleta (USA) (Lyphard (USA))
2663[5]

Galandora *Dr Jeremy Naylor* 56h
11 b m Bijou D'Inde—Jelabna (Jalmood (USA))
4032[P] 4787[5] 4976[P]

Galant Eye (IRE) *Chris Down* 84h
12 ch g Eagle Eyed(USA) —Galandria (Sharpo)
264[10] 557[3] 593[8] 2149[9] 2467[4] 3622[P] 3839[12]

Galant Nuit (FR) *Ferdy Murphy* 102h 141c
7 b g Comte Du Bourg(FR) —Little Blue (FR) (Reve Bleu (FR))
2888[P] **4821[P]**

Galantos (GER) *Helen Nelmes* 92h 83c
10 b g Winged Love(IRE) —Grey Metal (GER) (Secret 'n Classy (CAN))
374[6] 557[P] 1679[3] 2049[9] (3839) 4266[3] 5244[11]

Galant Star (FR) *Gary Moore* 85h
5 b m Galileo(IRE) —La Norvegienne (Darshaan)
1914[6] 2209[6] 2592[6] 3338[6] 4559[4]

Gala Queen *William Young* 1h
11 gr m Accondy(IRE) —Miss Jedd (Scallywag)
31[7] 456[P]

Galathea *Brendan Powell* 49h
9 b m Gildoran—Belle VII (Damsire Unregistered)
5385[10]

Galaxy Rock (IRE) *Jonjo O'Neill* 129h 133c
7 b g Heron Island(IRE) —Blue Pool (Saddlers' Hall (IRE))
1985[F] 2663[4] 2955[5] **3342[U] (3586)**
(4414) 4821[4] (5286)

Galileo Figaro (AUS) *Joss Saville* 85h
7 b g Galileo(IRE) —Overnight (GER) (Windwurf (GER))
1250[6] 1359[5] 1574[3]

Galiotto (IRE) *Gary Moore* 106h
5 b g Galileo(IRE) —Welsh Motto (USA) (Mtoto)
(5050)

Gallant Approach (IRE) *Tim Billington* 110h 85c
12 ch g Roselier(FR) —Nicks Approach (IRE) (Dry Dock)
4991[4]

Gallant Oscar (IRE) *Rebecca Curtis* 104h
5 b g Oscar(IRE) —Park Wave (IRE) (Supreme Leader)
2368[5] 3528[4]

Gallego *Richard Price* 67h
9 br g Danzero(AUS) —Shafir (IRE) (Shaadi (USA))
1857[8]

Galley Slave (IRE) *Michael Chapman* 92h 83c
6 b g Spartacus(IRE) —Cimeterre (IRE) (Arazi (USA))
440[4] 552[2] 713[4] 886[6] 1005[4] 1253[2] 1328[7] (1407)
1428[3] 1554[5] 1624[3] 1953[2] 2280[P] 2438[5] 3697[4]
3989[6] 4854[4] 4956[3]

Gallimaufry *Neil Mulholland* 76h
5 b m Sir Harry Lewis(USA) —Hinemoa (IRE) (Mandalus)
1736[12] 2137[11] 2499[11] 3367[4] 4787[U] 5169[2]

Gallowgate Lad *Gary Moore* 7b
5 gr g Tobougg(IRE) —Moon Magic (Polish Precedent (USA))
5387[14]

Gallox Bridge *Milton Harris* 106b
6 b g Kayf Tara—Explorer (Krisinsky (USA))
5202[17]

Gambo (IRE) *Evan Williams* 115h
5 b g Oscar(IRE) —River Thyne (IRE) (Good Thyne (USA))
167[2] 1369[2] (1603) 3587[14] 4862[9]

Gamedor (FR) *Gary Moore* 84h
6 ch g Kendor(FR) —Garmeria (FR) (Kadrou (FR))
1292[10] 1549[7]

Games (IRE) *Christopher Kellett* 111h 60c
10 b g Lord Americo—Anns Run (Deep Run)
427[6] 652[P] 913[F] 1095[7]

Gamesters Lady *Jim Best* 113h
8 br m Almushtarak(IRE) —Tycoon Tina (Tina's Pet)
1506[3]

Gandalfe (FR) *Alan Fleming* 105h 135c
6 bb g Laveron—Goldville (FR) (Gold And Steel (FR))
2427[4] 4729[2]

Gan On *Anthony Honeyball* 121h
7 b m Missed Flight—Sayin Nowt (Nicholas Bill)
(1746) 4009[15]
4398[P]

Gansey (IRE) *Sue Smith* 133h 141c
9 br g Anshan—Ebony Jane (Roselier (FR))
2400[F] 3953[8] (4357)
4820[12] 5185[F] 5338[P]

Gaora Lane (IRE) *Charlie Mann* 100h 127c
10 ch g Anshan—Lisfuncheon Adage (Proverb)
1858[8] 2443[7] 2975[11] 3395[6] 3990[9]
Garafena *Richard Lee* 94h
8 b m Golden Snake(USA) —Eclipsing (IRE) (Baillamont (USA))
19[4] 384[P] 796[9]
Garde Champetre (FR) *E Bolger* 128h 165c
12 b g Garde Royale—Clementine Fleurie (FR) (Lionel (FR))
2346[2] 4792[2]
Garleton (IRE) *Maurice Barnes* 41h 134c
10 b g Anshan—Another Grouse (Pragmatic)
1763[6] 2036[3] ◆ 3853[9] (4066)
(4689) (5206)
Garrai Ard (IRE) *Laurence James Butler* 126h 125c
8 b m Idris(IRE) —Ceili Queen (IRE) (Shareef Dancer (USA))
3175a[P]
Garrulous (UAE) *Tim Vaughan* 101h
8 b g Lomitas—Friendly (USA) (Lear Fan (USA))
675[3] 853[P]
Garton King *Paul Nicholls* 117h
7 b g Sovereign Water(FR) —Country Choice (IRE) (Paean)
(1907)
Gaspara (FR) *David Pipe* 124h
8 b m Astarabad(USA) —Gaspaisie (FR) (Beyssac (FR))
1470[11] 1608[5]
Gates Of Rome (IRE) *C A Murphy* 138h 138c
7 b g Luso—Express Mail (IRE) (King's Ride)
2412a[2] 3241a[6]
Gatien Du Tertre (FR) *Frank Sheridan* 86h 99c
7 ch g Kutub(IRE) —Gardine Lass (FR) (Jeune Homme (USA))
480[10]
Gauvain (GER) *Nick Williams* 137h 166c
9 b g Sternkoenig(IRE) —Gamina (GER) (Dominion)
(2385)
2885[5] 3675[5] 4201[2] ◆ 4818[8]
Gavroche Gaugain (FR) *Ferdy Murphy* 83h 100c
7 b g Varese(FR) —Jobereine (FR) (Joberan (FR))
2194[F] 2434[F] 3307[F] 3730[3] 3997[F] (4510)
4800[2] 5312[3]
Gdynia Baba (FR) *Alison Batchelor*
7 b g Sassanian(USA) —Babacha (FR) (Latnahc (USA))
2896[8]
Gearbox (IRE) *Liam Corcoran* 102h
5 br g Tillerman—Persian Empress (IRE) (Persian Bold)
3965[6] 4676[7] 5115[4] ◆
Gee Dee (IRE) *Sue Smith* 106h
10 gr g Arzanni—Silver Haired (IRE) (General View)
193[12]
Gee Dee Nen *Gary Moore* 131h 140c
8 b g Mister Baileys—Special Beat (Bustino)
(594) **822[2]**
1345[2] 1854[4] 2427[3] 3479[6] 3947[15] 4354[3] ◆
4933[10]
(5226)
Geeveem (IRE) *Henry Hogarth* 117h 73c
11 b g Supreme Leader—Glacial Field (IRE) (Glacial Storm (USA))
2941[P]
Gemini June (IRE) *Martin Keighley* 48b
7 b m Alflora(IRE) —Miss Jamielou (IRE) (Be My Native (USA))
238[10]
Gem Mill (IRE) *Mrs Gillian Davies* 59h 75c
9 b g Exit To Nowhere(USA) —Cara Gail (IRE) (Strong Gale)
4526[U] 5083[7]
General Blackthorn *Norman G Crouch* 43c
12 b g General Gambul—Miss Blackthorn (Homeboy)
4901[8]
General Eliott (IRE) *Frederick Sutherland* 103h
6 b g Rock Of Gibraltar(IRE) —Marlene-D (Selkirk (USA))
2667[5] 3376[3]
General Hardi *John Wade* 88h 124c
10 b g In Command(IRE) —Hardiprincess (Keen)
(33) **746[2]**
1828[5] 2374[4] (3522)
General Kutuzov (IRE) *Nick Gifford* 109h 130c
7 b g Moscow Society(USA) —Bonnie Thynes (IRE) (Good Thyne (USA))
2441[5] 2945[4] 3435[U] (3980)
4461[2]
General Lygon *Peter Hiatt* 30h
8 br g Midnight Legend—Kayt Two (Kaytu)
4767[6]
General Melchett (IRE) *Giles Smyly* 103b
4 b g Broadway Flyer(USA) —Kept In The Dark (Kemal (FR))
4082[3] 5005[2]
General Miller *Nicky Henderson* 152h
6 b g Karinga Bay—Millers Action (Fearless Action (USA))
2386[10]
General Sam (USA) *Richard Mitchell*
5 ch g Trippi(USA) —Milagro Blue (USA) (Cure The Blues (USA))
2021[11]
General Simara *Tony Carroll* 76h
7 b g Baryshnikov(AUS) —Hinton Bairn (Balinger)
424[8] **918[U]**
1034[P] 1092[4] 1291[9] 1554[7]
Generals Love (IRE) *Donald McCain* 63b
5 b g Winged Love(IRE) —Always Happy (Sharrood (USA))
2560[11] 3259[8] 3999[10]
General Smith *James Evans* 99h
12 b g Greensmith—Second Call (Kind Of Hush)
228[4] 338[2] 541[5] (1147) 1484[P]
General Striker *Mrs L A Coltherd* 134h 67c
11 ch g Classic Cliche(IRE) —Springfield Girl (Royal Vulcan)
4170[3]

General Ting (IRE) *Lucy Wadham* 120h
6 b g Daylami(IRE) —Luana (Shaadi (USA))
1864[12] 2213[4] ◆ 4992[6] 5171[4]
General Willie *C J Lawson*
9 ch g Master Willie—General Comment (IRE) (Torus)
293[P]
Generous Bob *Seamus Mullins* 97h
4 ch g Generous(IRE) —Bob's Finesse (Gran Alba (USA))
1913[8] 2797[4] 3836[P] 4444[5] 5211[3]
Generous Kenny *John Flint* 25b
5 ch g Generous(IRE) —Lady Franpalm (IRE) (Danehill Dancer (IRE))
5238[9]
Generous Spender *Mrs H J Cobb* 88b
5 b g Spendent—Molly Dreamer (Rushmere)
3054[12] 4124[5]
Genies Lamp (IRE) *Warren Greatrex* 82h
7 ch m Snurge—Kyle Lamp (IRE) (Miner's Lamp)
23[10]
Genny Wren *Renee Robeson* 103h
5 ch m Generous(IRE) —Wren Warbler (Relkino)
1607[5] 1921[10] 2526[4] 3264[3] 3904[3] 4828[2]
Genstone Trail *Alan King* 95b
5 b m Generous(IRE) —Stoney Path (Petoski)
(3159) 4027[10] 5119[6]
Gentle Alice (IRE) *Daniel G Murphy* 122h 130c
7 b m Beneficial—Dear Polly (IRE) (Germany (USA))
3779a[4] 4755a[3]
Gentle Bob (IRE) *Tom George* 109h
6 b g Bob's Return(IRE) —Maraniza (IRE) (Akarad (FR))
2365[5] 2954[10] 3296[2] 3698[6] 4462[5]
Gentle George *S Flook* 130c
8 b g Roi De Rome(USA) —Madam's Walk (Ardross)
151[6] 3908[4] 4163[3] 4851[P]
Gentleman Anshan (IRE) *Rosemary Gasson* 112c
7 b g Anshan—Second Violin (IRE) (Cataldi)
153[F] 526[6] 2588[3] 3772[7] 4007[4] (4948)
5170[P] 5391[2]
Gentleman Jeff (USA) *Chris Grant* 121h
7 ch g Mr Greeley(USA) —Wooing (USA) (Stage Door Johnny (USA))
3521[4] 3965[5] **4938[U]**
Gentleman Jimmy *Hughie Morrison* 99h 104c
11 br g Alderbrook—Irish Orchid (Free State)
17[3] (2929) 3260[3] 3589[8] **4402[4] 5240[2]**
Gentle Ranger (IRE) *David Pipe* 120h 141c
9 br g Presenting—Gentle Lady (IRE) (Strong Gale)
2106[P] 2358[P] 4876[4] 5443[P]
Genuine Pearl (IRE) *Lawney Hill* 118h
9 b g Desert King(IRE) —Pearl Kite (USA) (Silver Hawk (USA))
(763)
Geography (IRE) *Jim Best* 83h
11 ch g Definite Article—Classic Ring (IRE) (Auction Ring (USA))
217[F] 587[P]
Geojimali *Jim Goldie* 66h
9 ch g Compton Place—Harrken Heights (IRE) (Belmez (USA))
2551[10] 3335[P]
George My Friend *Simon Waugh* 88b
5 b g River Falls—Mystical Madam (Teenoso (USA))
4916[7]
George Nympton (IRE) *Nick Williams* 117h
5 br g Alderbrook—Countess Camilla (Bob's Return (IRE))
1775[7] 2136[9] 2577[3] 3228[10]
Georgian King *Suzy Smith* 117h 109c
8 b g Overbury(IRE) —Roslin (Roscoe Blake)
4354[P] 4933[U] 5230[4]
Georgiebegood (IRE) *S R B Crawford* 40h
10 b m Florida Son—College Street (IRE) (Strong Gale)
4684[7]
Georgie's Grey *Diana Grissell*
9 gr g Terimon—Lake Tiberias (Kings Lake (USA))
528[P]
Gerrard (IRE) *Althea Barclay* 62h 100c
13 b g Jurado(USA) —Vienna Waltz (IRE) (Orchestra)
(251) **1969[6]**
(2277)
4292[7] 4483[2]
Gershwinner (IRE) *Ms Emma Oliver* 95h 110c
8 b g Classic Cliche(IRE) —Dalton Lady (Roscoe Blake)
24[6] 251[U] 517[4] 549[10] 872[2] 4271[5] 4449[3] 4928[8]
Getaway Driver (IRE) *Charlie Longsdon* 93b
4 br g Zagreb(USA) —Catch The Mouse (IRE) (Stalker)
4430[2] 5105[6]
Get It On (IRE) *Evan Williams* 127h
6 b g King's Theatre(IRE) —Keshia (Buckskin (FR))
1433[2] (1623) (2246) 3452[8] 3960[2] 5296[F]
Get Me Out Of Here (IRE) *Jonjo O'Neill* 153h
7 b g Accordion—Home At Last (IRE) (Mandalus)
2085[7] 2386[6] 4188[8] 4848[2] 5166[P]
Get Off The Table (IRE) *A Jeffries*
10 b g Darazari(IRE) —La Fairy (IRE) (Lafontaine (USA))
5326[P]
Get Ready To Go (IRE) *Neil King* 108h
7 b g Turtle Island(IRE) —Buckalong (IRE) (Buckskin (FR))
2646[6] 3200[9] 3506[7] 3833[4] 4128[2] 4427[5]
Ghaill Force *Paddy Butler* 82h
9 b g Piccolo—Coir 'A' Ghaill (Jalmood (USA))
54[3] 272[3] 441[8] 155[10] 2131[4] 2430[6]
Ghimaar *Nicky Henderson* 140h
6 b g Dubai Destination(USA) —Charlecote (IRE) (Caerleon (USA))
(648) (929)

Ghizao (GER) *Paul Nicholls* 138h 161c
7 b g Tiger Hill(IRE) —Glorosia (FR) (Bering)
1865[2] (2384)
(3193) ◆ 4789[5] 5197[2]
Giant O Murchu (IRE) *Lawney Hill* 99h
7 b g Carroll House—Centralspires Best (Nishapour (FR))
4128[7] 4670[2] 5066[6]
Giant Star (USA) *Jim Goldie* 83h
8 b g Giant's Causeway(USA) —Vogue Star (ARG) (Ringaro (USA))
161[12]
Gibb River (IRE) *Nicky Henderson* 138h
5 ch g Mr Greeley(USA) —Laurentine (USA) (Private Account (USA))
(2310) (3344) (3906) 4788[10]
Gifted Leader (USA) *Ian Williams* 126h
6 b g Diesis—Zaghruta (USA) (Gone West (USA))
1956[8] 2164[2] 3229[10] 3808[9] 4358[6] 4830[5] (5102)
5201[8]
Gift Of Dgab (IRE) *A J Martin* 134h
7 b g Winged Love(IRE) —Creative Princess (IRE) (Creative Plan (USA))
2562a[2]
Gift Of Freedom (IRE) *Nigel Twiston-Davies* 47b
6 b m Presenting—Decent Slave (Decent Fellow)
568[11]
Gift Of The Gods (IRE) *Tim Vaughan* 86h 91c
8 b m Presenting—Temple Heather (Faustus (USA))
1102[3]
1425[2] 1478[3] 1663[P] 1969[4]
Giggles O'Shea (IRE) *Richard Rowe* 20b
9 b g Clerkenwell(USA) —Carrick Shannon (Green Shoon)
2050[P]
Gilbarry (IRE) *Malcolm Jefferson* 122h 152c
6 b g Bahri(USA) —Starry Night (Sheikh Albadou)
(2088)
2951[3] 5197[5] (5336)
Gilded Age *Alan King* 130h 115c
5 b g Cape Cross(IRE) —Sweet Folly (IRE) (Singspiel (IRE))
1862[4] 2085[8] **2455[3]** 3229[4] 3808[P] 4783[3] 5291[7]
Gilded Youth *Simon Lewis* 100h 63c
7 b g Gorse—Nisha (Nishapour (FR))
252[P] 338[6] 554[9]
761[5] 1137[9]
Gilderoy *Dominic Ffrench Davis* 10h
4 b g Compton Place—Lola Sapola (IRE) (Benny The Dip (USA))
1586[8] 1728[P]
Giles Cross (IRE) *Victor Dartnall* 134h 143c
9 b g Saddlers' Hall(IRE) —Mystockings (Idiots Delight)
2358[P] 3437[2] 4360[2]
Gilsland (IRE) *Donald McCain* 108h 124c
8 b g Alderbrook—Credit Transfer (IRE) (Kemal (FR))
(162)
(2374) 2953[2]
Gilt Free (IRE) *George Baker* 95h 105c
9 b m Rudimentary(USA) —Gold Bracelet (Golden Fleece (USA))
3782[14] 4272[4] 4401[5] 4899[3] **(5173)**
Gilwen Glory (IRE) *Evan Williams* 114h
8 b m Saddlers' Hall(IRE) —Clowns Glory (Idiots Delight)
231[6] 3155[5] (3589) 4009[6] 4161[7] (4968)
Gilzean (IRE) *Nigel Twiston-Davies* 93b
5 b g Flemensfirth(USA) —Sheknowso (Teenoso (USA))
4124[6] 4970[7]
Gimli's Rock (IRE) *Mrs John Harrington* 145h
5 b g Rock Of Gibraltar(IRE) —Beltisaal (FR) (Belmez (USA))
(2197a) 4229a[3]
Gin Cobbler *Howard Johnson* 101h
5 b g Beneficial—Cassia (Be My Native (USA))
2511[11] 4165[7] 4993[5]
Ginger Fizz *Ben Case* 92b
4 ch f Haafhd—Valagalore (Generous (IRE))
5012[4]
Ginger Jalapeno *Edward Bevan* 40b
5 ch m Tobougg(IRE) —Hello Sweety (Shaamit (IRE))
568[12]
Ginger's Lad *Michael Easterby* 74h 85c
7 ch g Elmaamul(USA) —Chadwick's Ginger (Crofthall)
9[3] 403[F] (473)
730[3] 840[3] 950[3] 1080[P] 3997[3] 4741[P] 5351[2]
Gingers Reflection *Henrietta Knight* 80b
5 ch g Alflora(IRE) —Trassey Bridge (Strong Gale)
5238[6]
Ginolad (AUS) *Venetia Williams* 31h 125c
11 br g Perugino(USA) —Royale High (AUS) (King's High (AUS))
300[2] 446[5] 735[7] 911[P] 3629[7] 3907[P] 4313[4] 4921[7]
5393[8]
Giollacca (IRE) *Graeme McPherson* 76h
7 ch m Accordion—Giolldante (IRE) (Phardante (FR))
1675[7] 2144[5] 3540[2]
Giorgio Quercus (FR) *Nicky Henderson* 127h 148c
6 b g Starborough—Winter Breeze (FR) (Kaldoun (FR))
(3057)
3345[F] (3722)
(4326) 4789[6] 5336[5]
Giovanna *Richard Phillips* 126h
10 b m Orpen(USA) —Red Leggings (Shareef Dancer (USA))
193[7] 503[F] 830[7] 2514[4] 3483[8] 3934[P] 4327[P]
4745[6]
Giveabobback (IRE) *Eugene M O'Sullivan* 105h
6 ch g Bob Back(USA) —Hallatte (USA) (Trempolino (USA))
3942[5]

Give Me Love (FR) *Miss Louise Danton* 90h 88c
11 ch g Bering—Cout Contact (USA) (Septieme Ciel (USA))
6[5] 4442[5] 5083[6] 5237[8]
Gizzit (IRE) *Karen George* 97b
5 b g Son Of Sharp Shot(IRE) —Suez Canal (FR) (Exit To Nowhere (USA))
3842[3] 4879[P] 5113[12]
Glaced Over *Raymond Shiels* 105h
6 br m Overbury(IRE) —Brun Bess (IRE) (Glacial Storm (USA))
1499[U] 1593[P] 1698[4] 1869[5] 2547[P] 4795[4] 5149[11]
Glacial Call (IRE) *James Frost* 68h 95c
8 b m Glacial Storm(USA) —Crash Call (Crash Course)
(133) **502[P]**
1730[10]
1820[P]
Glacial Harry *Reg Hollinshead* 66h
5 b g Sir Harry Lewis(USA) —Glacial Wonder (IRE) (Glacial Storm (USA))
637[4] 739[7] 992[F]
Glacial Rambler (IRE) *Stuart Coltherd* 60h 70c
12 b g Glacial Storm(USA) —Rambling Ivy (Mandalus)
211[P] 318[11] 461[5]
Glad Big (GER) *Richard Phillips* 86h 108c
9 b g Big Shuffle(USA) —Glady Sum (GER) (Surumu (GER))
371[5]
Gladeemma *Paul Cowley* 19h
6 ch m Karinga Bay—Gladys Emmanuel (Idiots Delight)
847[8]
Glad Lion (GER) *J J Lambe* 85h 56c
10 b g Dashing Blade—Glady Beauty (GER) (Big Shuffle (USA))
3993[9] **4305[4]**
Glad Schipi (FR) *Tor Sturgis* 52b
6 b m Robin Des Pres(FR) —So Glad (FR) (Sir Brink (FR))
412[11]
Glam Gerry (IRE) *C A Murphy* 136h
7 b g Dr Massini(IRE) —Daraheen Diamond (IRE) (Husyan (USA))
(3709a)
Glamorous Gg *Ian Williams* 76h
6 ch m Classic Cliche(IRE) —Glamour Game (Nashwan (USA))
2365[3] 3258[P] 4724[4] 5169[9] 5295[F]
Glan Lady (IRE) *John Mackie* 80h
5 b m Court Cave(IRE) —Vanished (IRE) (Fayruz)
52[4] 358[3] 600[7] 862[5] 1137[5] 1199[4] 1272[8] 1554[F]
1732[9]
Glassawine *David Pipe* 94h
4 gr g Verglas(IRE) —Persian Ruby (IRE) (Grand Lodge (USA))
2797[8] 3630[4] 4268[3] 4528[3]
Glasson Lad (IRE) *Ferdy Murphy* 56h
4 b g Quws—Glasson House (IRE) (Supreme Leader)
2824[12] 3166[10] 4993[6]
Gleannacreim (IRE) *Tim Vaughan* 103h 33c
8 ch g Old Vic—Rosie Brook (IRE) (Be My Native (USA))
3369[5] 3530[P] 4522[2] 4787[6]
Gleann An Sagart *Michael Scudamore* 116h 117c
9 b g Groom Dancer(USA) —Dunkellin (USA) (Irish River (FR))
5[7] ◆ 373[F]
Gleann Eagas (IRE) *Emma Lavelle* 83b
4 b g Gold Well—Glen Princess (IRE) (Bob Back (USA))
3630[6] 4055[8]
Gleann Na Ndochais (IRE) *Alistair Whillans* 27b
5 b g Zagreb(USA) —Nissereen (USA) (Septieme Ciel (USA))
4574[9]
Glebehall Bay (IRE) *Venetia Williams* 106h 113c
8 b g Saddlers' Hall(IRE) —Glebe Dream (IRE) (Be My Native (USA))
2146[5] 2585[6] 2953[3] 3646[F] 3900[3]
Glenary (IRE) *Mrs Sarah Hawker* 104h 81c
9 ch g Presenting—My Native Glen (IRE) (Be My Native (USA))
4293[6] 5372[7]
Glencove Marina (IRE) *Eoin Griffin* 134h 162c
9 b g Spectrum(IRE) —Specifiedrisk (IRE) (Turtle Island (IRE))
1684a[P] 2970a[4] 3176a[4] 3778a[7] 4087a[2] (Dead)
Glencree (IRE) *Howard Johnson* 117h 128c
7 b g Presenting—Hidden Ability (IRE) (Alphabatim (USA))
(3520)
4453[3] 4938[2]
Glendue *Nicky Henderson* 91h
6 b g Kayf Tara—Mayfair Minx (St Columbus)
4012[6] 4437[13]
Glenfly (IRE) *Philip Hobbs* 61h 51c
6 b g Presenting—Dorans Glen (IRE) (Over The River (FR))
319[18] 2142[8] 3153[11] 3448[9] **3723[5] 4144[6]**
Glengap (IRE) *Elliott Cooper* 68h 52c
8 br g Needle Gun(IRE) —Miss Betsy (IRE) (Pollerton)
456[7] **578[9]**
3636[6] 3997[6] 4068[7]
Glengarra (IRE) *Liam Corcoran* 93h 111c
14 ch g Phardante(FR) —Glengarra Princess (Cardinal Flower)
734[P] 919[4] 1128[2] 1277[4] 1509[5] 1744[2] (2134)
2453[P]
Glen Lass *Jamie Snowden* 70h
4 ch f Zafeen(FR) —Welcome Aboard (Be My Guest (USA))
674[2] 960[P] 1226[5] 2133[11]
Glen Rhydian *Ian McInnes*
5 ch g Shinko Forest(IRE) —Bustling Around (Bustino)
5033[10]

Glen Rouge (IRE) *James Moffatt* 84h
10 ch g Fourstars Allstar(USA) —Charcol (Nicholas Bill)
318[9] 553[2] 749[2]

Glens Boy (IRE) *Henrietta Knight* 92h
7 b g Dushyantor(USA) —Glens Lady (IRE) (Mister Lord (USA))
1821[9] 2142[5] 2482[8]

Glenseskin *Eamonn Fehily* 66b
7 b g Kayf Tara—Minden Rose (Lord Bud)
1349[4]

Glenstal Abbey (IRE) *C F Swan* 140h 140c
7 b g Montjeu(IRE) —Almarai (USA) (Vaguely Noble)
1712a[3] 4794[10]

Glenturn (IRE) *Mrs Prunella Dobbs* 30h 90c
10 b g Taipan(IRE) —Tuney Blade (Fine Blade (USA))
2645[2]

Glen Vale *John Wade* 30h
8 ch g Karinga Bay—Furryvale (Furry Glen)
1359[6] 1499[5] 1928[P]

Glenwood Knight (IRE) *Donald McCain* 124h 127c
8 ch g Presenting—Glens Lady (IRE) (Mister Lord (USA))
2447[2] ◆ (3254)
3714[F] 4190[F]

Glimmer Of Light (IRE) *Dr Richard Newland* 88h 98c
11 b g Marju(IRE) —Church Light (Caerleon (USA))
99[P] 177[5] (339)
460[7] 799[7]

Glingerbank (IRE) *Nicky Richards* 121h 120c
11 b g Supreme Leader—Mauradante (IRE) (Phardante (FR))
2549[8] 3334[11] 4940[2] 5431[6]

Glingermill (IRE) *Nicky Richards* 92h
8 b g Mister Mat(FR) —Wonover (IRE) (Convinced)
1783[9] 5151[5]

Glitzy D'Ocala (FR) *Philip Hobbs* 116h
6 ch g Adnaan(IRE) —Diane D'Ocala (USA) (Arctic Tern (USA))
(3301) ◆ 3718[3] 4539[2]

Global *Brian Ellison* 95h
5 ch g Bahamian Bounty—Tuppenny Blue (Pennekamp (USA))
1278[3] 1831[3] 2076[6]

Global Fella (IRE) *Nicky Henderson* 113b
6 b g Chevalier(IRE) —Antapoura (IRE) (Bustino)
4491[2] ◆ 5113[5]

Global Flyer *Caroline Bailey* 119h 101c
7 b g Sir Harry Lewis(USA) —Flicker (Unfuwain (USA))
1904[8] 2171[3] 2347[17]
3394[3] 3772[6] 5281[3]

Global Power (IRE) *Oliver Sherwood* 132h
5 b g Subtle Power(IRE) —Bartelko (IRE) (The Bart (USA))
(2432) (2946) 3340[F] 3877[2] 4725[4] 5285[4]

Global Warming (IRE) *Emma Lavelle* 110h 113c
7 b g King's Theatre(IRE) —Croi Na Greine (IRE) (Broken Hearted)
2513[3]

Glorious Feeling (IRE) *Nicky Henderson* 104b
5 br m Old Vic—Supreme Touch (IRE) (Supreme Leader)
(4505) ◆

Glorybe (GER) *Chris Bealby* 94h
5 ch m Monsun(GER) —Glorosia (FR) (Bering)
2370[2] 3302[6] 4309[6] 5376[6]

Glory Nights *Dr Richard Newland* 52h
7 ch g Karinga Bay—Angel Falling (Scottish Reel)
589[6] 3692[10]

Gloucester *Michael Scudamore* 134h
8 b g Montjeu(IRE) —Birdlip (USA) (Sanglamore (USA))
207[18] 1017[2] 1133a[7] 1311[5] 1797[4] 4848[10] 5291[8]

Go All Out (IRE) *Richard Phillips* 102h
8 gr g Beauchamp King—Auburn Princess (IRE) (Arapahos (FR))
1571[11] 630[P]

Go All The Way (IRE) *Nigel Twiston-Davies* 122b
6 b g Milan—Kings Rose (IRE) (King's Ride)
4808[4] ◆

Go Amwell *J R Jenkins* 119h
8 b g Kayf Tara—Daarat Alayaam (IRE) (Reference Point)
(1814) 2581[11] 3742[F] 4185[2] ◆ 4464[12] 5230[F]

Goat Castle (IRE) *Nigel Twiston-Davies* 97h
7 b g Goldmark(USA) —Rolands Girl (IRE) (Soughaan (USA))
1179[3] 1601[2] 1704[2] 2150[2]

Goffa Crag *Nicky Richards* 94h
7 b g Tamayaz(CAN) —Chinook's Daughter (IRE) (Strong Gale)
1783[6] 2202[5] 2552[8] 3502[P] 4477[13]

Go Flo Go *Mark Hoad* 8b
4 b f Auction House(USA) —Present Warning (Cadeaux Genereux)
2173[11] *2597[13]*

Go Free *John O'Shea* 84h 114c
10 gr g Easycall—Miss Traxdata (Absalom)
264[4] 371[P]
593[9] 990[8]

Gogeo (IRE) *Alan Swinbank* 84b
4 b g Val Royal(FR) —Steal 'Em (Efisio)
4005[3]

Go Go Simon (IRE) *Noel G Hynds* 78b
7 b g Desert Millennium(IRE) —Jaldini (IRE) (Darshaan)
1099[P]

Going Nowhere Fast (IRE) *Alison Thorpe* 90h
6 b g Exit To Nowhere(USA) —Sister Gabrielle (IRE) (Buckskin (FR))
4404[10]

Going Twice *Steve Woodman*
6 b g Josr Algarhoud(IRE) —Its Your Bid (Dilum (USA))
4923[6]

Go Johnny Go (IRE) *Colin Tizzard* 58h 71c
9 b g Moonax(IRE) —The Helmet (IRE) (Riot Helmet)
821[8]

Golan Guy (IRE) *A J Martin* 115h
6 b g Golan(IRE) —Countess Marengo (IRE) (Revoque (IRE))
288[11] 3709a[3]

Golan Way *Sheena West* 146h 148c
7 b g Golan(IRE) —Silk Daisy (Barathea (IRE))
(1727)
2126[4] (2527) ◆ 5183[3]

Golbelini *Martin Keighley* 65h
6 ch m Bertolini(USA) —Final Faze (Chaddleworth (IRE))
2289[13] 3489[7] 3721[7]

Goldan Jess (IRE) *Philip Kirby* 106h
7 b g Golan(IRE) —Bendis (GER) (Danehill (USA))
166[7] 888[3] 1004[4] 1644[6]

Gold Cygnet (IRE) *James Joseph Mangan* 122h 119c
6 b g Beneficial—Windy Bee (IRE) (Aristocracy)
2971a[6]

Golden Alchemist *Mark Usher* 107h
8 ch g Woodborough(USA) —Pure Gold (Dilum (USA))
717[6]

Golden Button (IRE) *Kim Bailey* 96h
6 ch m Trans Island—Velvet Appeal (IRE) (Petorius)
4[5] 3367[6] 4977[3] 5282[3] 5390[4]

Golden Celebration *Chris Gordon* 84b
5 ch g Double Trigger(IRE) —Rose Thyne (IRE) (Good Thyne (USA))
254[6] 589[11]

Golden Chieftain (IRE) *Colin Tizzard* 138h
6 b g Tikkanen(USA) —Golden Flower (GER) (Highland Chieftain)
1778[2] (2607) 2888[7] 3288[9] (4094) (4875) 5187[5]

Golden Dream (IRE) *Caroline Bailey* 102h 89c
7 ch g Golden Tornado(IRE) —Orion Dream (Skyliner)
3386[8]
3741[4] 4691[3]

Golden Duck (IRE) *Nick Williams* 87h 118c
11 b g Turtle Island(IRE) —Mazeeka (IRE) (Glow (USA))
(2187)
3650[3] (4290)

Golden Emperor (IRE) *R MacDonald*
4 ro g Antonius Pius(USA) —Lily Shing Shang (Spectrum (IRE))
5428[F]

Golden Firebird (IRE) *Alan King* 108b
4 b f Old Vic—Kinnegads Pride (IRE) (Be My Native (USA))
(5306)

Golden Future *Peter Niven* 104h
8 b g Muhtarram(USA) —Nazca (Zilzal (USA))
350[5] 582[2] (748) 1406[5] 1695[8]

Golden Gael *Jeremy Scott* 107b
5 ch m Generous(IRE) —Gaelic Gold (IRE) (Good Thyne (USA))
2156[4] ◆ 3301[3] 4728[9] (5158)

Golden Games (IRE) *Daniel O'Brien* 78h
5 b m Montjeu(IRE) —Ski For Gold (Shirley Heights)
4397[5] 4707[3]

Golden Gem (IRE) *Rachel Hobbs* 104h 83c
9 ch g Golden Tornado(IRE) —Princess Gemma (IRE) (Orchestra)
862[10] 953[3] 1107[5] (1195)
1309[6] 1484[12] (1555) 1726[10]

Golden Globe (IRE) *Ferdy Murphy* 104h 87c
9 bb g Oscar(IRE) —Rich Desire (Grey Desire)
2450[P] 3549[6]

Golden Grimshaw (IRE) *J J Lambe* 126h
9 b g Grand Lodge(USA) —Daftiyna (IRE) (Darshaan)
1713a[9] (Dead)

Golden King (IRE) *Lisa Williamson* 10h
6 br g King's Theatre(IRE) —One Swoop (IRE) (Be My Native (USA))
3957[17] 4444[12]

Golden Kite (IRE) *Adrian Maguire* 132h 144c
9 b g Anshan—Miss Nee (IRE) (Strong Gale)
1527a[10] 5200[16]

Golden Partner *Matt Sheppard* 88h
6 ch g Where Or When(IRE) —Quite Happy (IRE) (Statoblest)
1709[7] 1997[6] 2244[9] 2467[9]

Golden Prospect *Paul Fitzsimons* 94h
7 b g Lujain(USA) —Petonellajill (Petong)
2426[4] 3879[4] 4310[5] 4956[4]

Golden Silver (FR) *W P Mullins* 118h 170c
9 b g Mansonnien(FR) —Gold Or Silver (FR) (Glint Of Gold)
2262a[2] (2972a) ◆ 3204a[2] (3594a)
(3844a) (4248a)
4805[4]

Golden Smog (IRE) *Ian Williams* 72h
5 ch m Anshan—Dante's Blaze (IRE) (Phardante (FR))
50[10] 360[6] 554[F] 762[7]

Golden Sparkle (IRE) *I A Duncan* 62b
5 ch m Samraan(USA) —Bye For Now (Abednego)
4308[8]

Golden Square *Tony Carroll* 92h
9 ch g Tomba—Cherish Me (Polar Falcon (USA))
54[10] 462[4] 762[4] 933[10] 1060[7]

Golden View (IRE) *J J Lambe* 95b
6 b g Goldmark(USA) —In Grace's View (IRE) (Shardari)
47[3]

Goldfinger (IRE) *Seamus Mullins* 110h 112c
9 ch g Giant's Causeway(USA) —Darya (USA) (Gulch (USA))
4194[R]

Gold Heart (FR) *Miss C P Holliday* 115h 123c
9 gr g Turgeon(USA) —Shannondore (FR) (Nashamaa)
297[P]

Gold Reef *Alan King* 126h
8 ch m Double Trigger(IRE) —Realms Of Gold (USA) (Gulch (USA))
(2209) 3452[2] 3674[P]

Gold Ring *Mark Gillard* 83h
11 ch g Groom Dancer(USA) —Indubitable (Sharpo)
1443[4]

Golfer's Crossing (IRE) *Lucinda Russell* 123h 86c
8 b g City Honours(USA) —Queens Rook (IRE) (Castle Keep)
2191[6] 3332[F] 3851[4] (4477) ◆ 5030[6]

Gonebeyondrecall (IRE) *N F Glynn* 125h 134c
8 b g Dr Massini(IRE) —Green Walk (Green Shoon)
1712a[2] 2886[P] 5185[4]

Gone To Lunch (IRE) *Jeremy Scott* 151h 153c
11 ch g Mohaajir(USA) —Jayells Dream (Space King)
4851[6] 5338[7]

Good Buy Dubai (USA) *Edward Creighton* 71h
5 gr g Essence Of Dubai(USA) —Sofisticada (USA) (Northern Jove (CAN))
2421[6] *3058[6]* 3376[7]

Good Bye Simon (FR) *T Doumen* 143h
8 gr g Simon Du Desert(FR) —Marie De Pharis (FR) (Pas De Seul)
2230a[3]

Good Company (IRE) *S Flook* 130h 128c
11 b g Among Men(USA) —Khatiynza (Nishapour (FR))
236[6] 499[7] 707[3] 852[7] 1044[4] (1277)
(4293) 4748[2] 4950[3] 5163[10]

Good Egg (IRE) *Lady J Fowler* 128c
8 b g Exit To Nowhere(USA) —Full Of Surprises (IRE) (Be My Native (USA))
502[P]

Good Faloue (FR) *Neil King* 109h
6 b m Kahyasi—Good Blend (FR) (Darshaan)
2526[3] 3264[U] 3599[5] 3901[6] 5189[3]

Good Fella (IRE) *Patrick Mooney* 126h 125c
10 b g Religiously(USA) —Bleanerville (Buckskin (FR))
3798a[P]

Good For Blue (IRE) *Richard Phillips* 110h
8 ch g Beneficial—Pixie Blue (IRE) (Henbit (USA))
3744[4] 4276[P] 5205[9]

Good Golly (IRE) *Tony Newcombe*
4 b f Golan(IRE) —Elsinore (IRE) (Danehill (USA))
2173[10]

Good Harvest (IRE) *Jonjo O'Neill* 113h 115c
8 ch g Elnadim(USA) —Summers End (USA) (Woodman (USA))
540[5] 868[2] 1093[8] (1348)
1550[2]

Goodison Park *Michael Quinlan* 74h
4 ch f Big Shuffle(USA) —Perfect Dream (Emperor Jones (USA))
3401[9] 3613[4]

Good Old Days (IRE) *Kim Bailey* 97h 108c
12 b g Bob Back(USA) —Idealist (Busted)
(81) 463[3]
1277[P] 1732[4]
1919[3] 2243[3] 3154[5] 5058[4]

Good Order *Tom George* 98h
6 b g Alflora(IRE) —Twinnings Grove (IRE) (Lord Americo)
4459[5] 5107[5]

Good Return (FR) *Mrs Kim Smyly* 66c
8 gr g Saint Preuil(FR) —Surfing France (FR) (Art Francais (USA))
293[5]

Good Tack (USA) *Richard Fahey* 95b
6 bb g Lycius(USA) —Chesa Plana (Niniski (USA))
1284[4]

Goodtimes A'Coming *Noel Chance* 81b
5 ch m Bob Back(USA) —Ollejess (Scallywag)
3159[5] 3623[10]

Goodtimetoby (IRE) *Richard Lee* 78h
8 b g Norwich—Clara Rose (IRE) (Good Thyne (USA))
2143[U] 2241[12] 2607[F] 3491[5] 4103[P] 4691[P]

Good To Be Grey *Reg Hollinshead* 93h
9 gr g Environment Friend—Jarin Rose (IRE) (Jareer (USA))
100[P] 557[0]

Goodwill Phil *Nigel Hawke* 64h
7 ch g Muhtarram(USA) —Phylian (Glint Of Gold)
1741[6]

Goodwood Starlight (IRE) *Jim Best* 110h
6 br g Mtoto—Starring (FR) (Ashkalani (IRE))
1884[8] 2607[14] 3302[4] (4859) 5099[5]

Googoobarabajagal (IRE) *Stuart Kittow* 98h
5 b g Almutawakel—Shamah (Unfuwain (USA))
129[4] 823[6] 1129[2] 1477[6] 1737[8]

Go On Arch (IRE) *Nigel Twiston-Davies* 104b
5 b g Oscar(IRE) —Good Aim (IRE) (Priolo (USA))
2389[7] 3200[19]

Go On Be A Lady *Alan Swinbank* 96h 84c
8 b m Commanche Run—Miss Moneypenny (Silly Prices)
2301[4] *3093[4] 3170[11]* 3712[3] 4064[3] 4551[6]

Goonyella (IRE) *Nigel Twiston-Davies* 79b
4 br g Presenting—Miss Fresher (FR) (Pampabird)
5105[8]

Goose Green (IRE) *Ron Hodges* 91h
7 b g Invincible Spirit(IRE) —Narbayda (IRE) (Kahyasi)
1333[4] 5082[4] 5244[8]

Gordon Road (IRE) *Michael Quinlan* 35h
5 b g Amilynx(FR) —Celtic Smiles (IRE) (Nucleon (USA))
607[10]

Gordy Bee (USA) *Richard Guest* 108h
5 b g More Than Ready(USA) —Honoria (USA) (Danzig (USA))
5378[3]

Gores Island (IRE) *Noel Chance* 107b
5 b g Beneficial—Just Leader (IRE) (Supreme Leader)
3399[2] 5388[3]

Gorge (AUS) *Anthony Cosgriff* 116h
9 b g Thunder Gulch(USA) —Heed Zamelina (AUS) (Serheed (USA))
4358[P] 5201[11]

Gorgehous Lliege (FR) *Venetia Williams* 83h
5 b g Lavirco(GER) —Charme D'Estruval (FR) (Mistigri)
3374[5] 3930[8]

Gorgeous Annie (IRE) *John G Carr* 65h
4 gr f Kheleyf(USA) —Secret Justice (USA) (Lit De Justice (USA))
1825[11]

Goring One (IRE) *Anna Newton-Smith* 95h 100c
6 b g Broadway Flyer(USA) —Brigette's Secret (Good Thyne (USA))
216[7] 2949[F] 3450[4] 3723[7] 4668[2] (4919) ◆
(5039)

Goring Two (IRE) *Anna Newton-Smith* 62h 66c
6 br g Needle Gun(IRE) —Kam Slave (Kambalda)
215[5] 4130[10] 4559[6]
5051[4]

Gortenbuie (IRE) *Henrietta Knight* 113h
6 b g Flemensfirth(USA) —Carnival Buck (IRE) (Buckskin (FR))
2325[4] 2946[P] 3295[7] 4439[2]

Gort Na Lea (IRE) *A J Kennedy* 104c
8 b g Fourstars Allstar(USA) —Canwestopit (IRE) (Commanche Run)
4857[U] 4973[3]

Go Ruby Go *Kevin Morgan* 79b
7 b m Karinga Bay—Nessfield (Tumble Wind)
237[8] 731[8] 3816[5] 4309[P]

Goscar Rock (IRE) *P Hall* 84h 103c
10 b g Synefos(USA) —Almost Regal (IRE) (Jurado (USA))
4857[P] 4973[7] 5283[2]

Go Set Go *James Eustace* 98b
4 b g Reset(AUS) —Dragon Star (Rudimentary (USA))
2052[3] 4082[5] 4484[3]

Go Silver Bullet (FR) *Lucinda Russell* 101h 125c
10 gr g Simon Du Desert(FR) —Bouge De La (USA) (Trempolino (USA))
446[3] 947[4] 3552[6] 3751[5] 4060[2] 4572[5]
(5416)

Gospel Preacher *Alan King* 111b
6 b g Kayf Tara—Gospel (IRE) (Le Bavard (FR))
2632[2] 3773[9] 4970[2]

Got Attitude (IRE) *Mrs John Harrington* 95h 134c
8 ch g Beneficial—Ilderton Road (Noalto)
3206a[17] 3473a[2]

Go Teescomponents *Keith Reveley* 51b
4 b g Septieme Ciel(USA) —Linea-G (Keen)
3525[11] 4117[10] 4396[10]

Gothic Charm (IRE) *Rachel Hobbs* 49b 102c
9 gr g Gothland(FR) —Tomgar Satisfy (IRE) (Satco (FR))
226[3] 556[2] 840[10] 2420[5] 2641[P]

Go To The Edge *John Bryan Groucott* 40h
5 b g Tobougg(IRE) —Gulsha (Glint Of Gold)
2074[12] 2328[10] 5077[7] 5203[7]

Gotoyourplay (IRE) *Andy Turnell* 108c
7 ch g Definite Article—Johnston's Flyer (IRE) (Orchestra)
4445[4]

Got The Gift (IRE) *Sue Smith* 80h 92c
10 b g Norwich—Kylemore Rose (IRE) (Roselier (FR))
1645[8]

Gougane (IRE) *Hugh McWilliams* 110h 110c
8 b g Luso—Gill's Honey (IRE) (Celio Rufo)
854[7] 1000[4] 1136[3]

Gouranga *Tony Carroll* 90h
8 b m Robellino(USA) —Hymne D'Amour (USA) (Dixieland Band (USA))
3934[11] 4032[4] 4273[8] 4508[P] (4833)

Go West (IRE) *Nigel Twiston-Davies* 113h 122c
10 b g Flemensfirth(USA) —Roaming (IRE) (Be My Native (USA))
314[3] 599[P] 1725[8]

Grab The Glory (IRE) *Gary Moore* 113b
5 b g Accordion—Full Of Surprises (IRE) (Be My Native (USA))
4356[3] ◆ 5388[2]

Graceful Fifi *Liam Corcoran*
5 b m Delta Dancer—Judy Gale (IRE) (Glacial Storm (USA))
910[P]

Graceful Spirit *Des Donovan* 69b
4 b f Reset(AUS) —Naemi (GER) (Tannenkonig (IRE))
4815[6]

Grace N' Favour (IRE) *B R Hamilton* 98h
8 ch m Exit To Nowhere(USA) —Reine Berengere (FR) (Esprit Du Nord (USA))
858[3]

Gracious Beau *Keith Goldsworthy* 76b
5 b g Beat All(USA) —Grace (Buzzards Bay)
4527[7] 4866[11] 5211[P]

Graduation Night *Jamie Snowden* 107h
5 br g Kayf Tara—Jadidh (Touching Wood (USA))
2136[6] 2634[4] 2944[4] 3370[5] 3934[4] 4427[P] 4929[9]

Grafite *Milton Harris* 125h
6 gr g Act One—Silver Gyre (IRE) (Silver Hawk (USA))
1768[2] 2067[5] 2307[5] 2596[F] (2983) 3229[F] 3877[3]
4725[8] 5325[5]

Graiguecullen (IRE) *Eoin Griffin* 100b
7 b g Bob Back(USA) —Sarahlee (Sayyaf)
2389[11]

Grams And Ounces *Amy Weaver* 98h
4 b g Royal Applause—Ashdown Princess (IRE) (King's Theatre (IRE))
3401[12] 3711[3] 4774[3]

Granakey (IRE) *Peter Bowen* 69h
8 b m Key Of Luck(USA) —Grand Morning (IRE) (King Of Clubs)
1392[5] 1487[9] 1613[8] 1949[5] 2070[7]

Grandad Bill (IRE) *Jim Goldie* 118h
8 ch g Intikhab(USA) —Matikanehanafubuki (IRE) (Caerleon (USA))
2506[4] 3334[8] 3709a[10] 3966[5] 4255[5] 4914[7] 5335[9]

Grandads Horse *Charlie Longsdon* 117h
5 bb g Bollin Eric—Solid Land (FR) (Solid Illusion (USA))
20^4 375^3 759^2 (1349) 5099^2 ◆

Grand Art (IRE) *Tim Vaughan* 100h
7 b g Raise A Grand(IRE) —Mulberry River (IRE) (Bluebird (USA))
875^2 1137^2 1362^5 2654^2

Grand Article (IRE) *Paul Cowley* 90h
7 ch g Definite Article—Grand Morning (IRE) (King Of Clubs)
137^7 436^3

Grand Award *Donald McCain* 106h 106c
6 b g Indian Danehill(IRE) —Rule Britannia (Night Shift (USA))
91^P 327^2 519^5 693^4 862^8 2231^F
2479^3 3524^4

Grand Bay (USA) *Jonjo O'Neill* 102h 99c
10 b g Coronado's Quest(USA) —Buckeye Gal (USA) (Good Counsel (USA))
156^5 (646) 986^3
1546^U 1842^6

Grand Diamond (IRE) *Jim Goldie* 115h
7 b g Grand Lodge(USA) —Winona (IRE) (Alzao (USA))
1574^2 1695^3 1766^2 (1870) 2164^7 2508^3 4149^3 4939^2 5315^{13}

Grande Bretagne (FR) *Mrs S Prouse* 69b
12 b g Legend Of France(USA) —L'Epicurienne (FR) (Rex Magna (FR))
133^P

Grand Fella (IRE) *Ken Wingrove* 100h
6 ch g Raise A Grand(IRE) —Mummys Best (Bustino)
4378^P 5393^{10}

Grandioso (IRE) *Howard Johnson* 105b
4 b g Westerner—Champagne Warrior (IRE) (Waajib)
(4151) ◆ 5202^9 ◆

Grand Lahou (FR) *Tim Vaughan* 100h 138c
8 ch g Cyborg(FR) —Yota (FR) (Galetto (FR))
1117^3 (1299)
1390^F 1609^{13}
1828^4 2112^2 2345^2 2881^{10} (3841)
4853^F 5002^6

Grand Opera (IRE) *Gordon Elliott* 118h 130c
8 b g City On A Hill(USA) —Victoria's Secret (IRE) (Law Society (USA))
857^3 1133a^{14}

Grandouet (FR) *Nicky Henderson* 143h
4 bb g Al Namix(FR) —Virginia River (FR) (Indian River (FR))
2078^5 2356^2 (3194) (3673) 4847^3 5161^B

Grand Schlem (FR) *David Rees* 136h
7 b g Astarabad(USA) —Forty Love (FR) (Maelstrom Lake)
5253^P

Grands Crus (FR) *David Pipe* 171h
6 gr g Dom Alco(FR) —Fee Magic (FR) (Phantom Breeze)
(2387) (2523) (3807) ◆ 4819^2 5160^2

Grand Silence (IRE) *S Joynes* 100c
8 ch g Grand Lodge(USA) —Why So Silent (Mill Reef (USA))
148^P

Grand Slam Hero (IRE) *Nigel Twiston-Davies* 131h 157c
10 ch g Anshan—Tidal Princess (IRE) (Good Thyne (USA))
(330) **(567)**
(1020) ◆ **1123a^F 1332^P (1373)**
1611^8 3940^P 5200^F

Grand Union (IRE) *John Wade* 97h 95c
7 b g Bob Back(USA) —Queens Mark (IRE) (Roselier (FR))
3750^5 ◆ 4276^F

Grand Vintage (IRE) *Howard Johnson* 84b
5 gr g Basanta(IRE) —Rivers Town Rosie (IRE) (Roselier (FR))
4117^4 4894^8

Grand Vision (IRE) *Colin Tizzard* 104b
5 gr g Old Vic—West Hill Rose (IRE) (Roselier (FR))
3766^2 4881^2 ◆

Grand Zouki (FR) *George Moore* 124h
6 b g Garuda(IRE) —Flaiha (FR) (Esprit Du Nord (USA))
92^3 (1357) 1499^3 1698^5

Granny Kanzi *Charlie Longsdon*
7 b m Dolpour—Great Granny Smith (Fine Blue)
5297^R

Gran Torino (IRE) *Noel Meade* 126h
6 b g Milan—Miss Greinton (GER) (Greinton)
3579a^P

Granville Island (IRE) *Jennie Candlish* 103b
4 b g Flemensfirth(USA) —Fox Glen (Furry Glen)
(5005)

Grape Expectations *Raymond York* 55b
4 gr g Grape Tree Road—Maid Equal (Pragmatic)
5387^{11}

Grasscutter (IRE) *Donald McCain* 106h 100c
7 b g Presenting—Cherry Black (IRE) (Roselier (FR))
760^5 **918^P**

Grassfinch *Renee Robeson* 86h
5 ch m Generous(IRE) —Stock Dove (Deploy)
1553^5

Gratification *Oliver Sherwood* 100h 36c
8 ch g Alflora(IRE) —Fun While It Lasts (Idiots Delight)
299^5 **716^7**
991^P 1735^{14}

Graycliffe (IRE) *Patrick Morris* 56h
5 gr g Val Royal(FR) —Popiplu (USA) (Cozzene (USA))
5396^P

Graylyn Amber *Robin Dickin* 91h
6 b m Nomadic Way(USA) —State Lady (IRE) (Strong Statement (USA))
2985^9 3542^P 3740^8 4310^7 5057^2 5191^7

Graylyn Ruby (FR) *Robin Dickin* 85h
6 b g Limnos(JPN) —Nandi (IRE) (Mujadil (USA))
1688^8 1734^6 2637^{11}

Gray Mountain (USA) *Lucinda Russell* 130h
8 rg g Lasting Approval(USA) —Cuando Quiere (USA) (Affirmed (USA))
2165^F

Great Bounder (CAN) *Michael Blake*
5 bb g Mr Greeley(USA) —Jo Zak (USA) (Vilzak (USA))
1475^F 1571^6

Great Endeavour (IRE) *David Pipe* 134h 154c
7 gr g Great Palm(USA) —Strong Irish (IRE) (Corrouge (USA))
2359^6 2886^2 4790^F 5199^6

Great Esteem (IRE) *Charles Egerton* 92h
6 b g Carnival Dancer—California Dreamin (Slip Anchor)
519^8 (2003) 2231^4

Great Gusto (IRE) *Victor Dartnall* 97b
5 ch g Moscow Society(USA) —Warm Front (Bustino)
4097^2 5113^7

Great Hero *Richard Phillips* 110h
6 ch g Arkadian Hero(USA) —Great Tern (Simply Great (FR))
1071^2 1284^9 2145^8 2456^8 3366^5 3840^4 4462^4

Great Kicker (IRE) *Colin Tizzard* 70h
6 b g Great Palm(USA) —Keep The Change (IRE) (Castle Keep)
3372^9 4430^6 5239^F

Great Mates (IRE) *Paul Nicholls* 119h
7 b g Bob's Return(IRE) —All Set (IRE) (Electric)
370^6 (632) (1196) 1864^{10} 5287^7

Great Ocean Road (IRE) *David Thompson* 72h 85c
8 ch g Shernazar—Princess Breda (IRE) (Long Pond)
83^3 529^4 931^P (1678)
1954^3 2437^2

Great Reason *Nicky Henderson* 116h 130c
7 b g Alflora(IRE) —Grignette (FR) (Video Rock (FR))
3390^3

Great Tsar (IRE) *Tim Vaughan* 94h 86c
8 b g Moscow Society(USA) —Simply Slippy (IRE) (Simply Great (FR))
136^U 652^4

Great Vintage (IRE) *Peter Niven* 57h
6 gr g Great Palm(USA) —Grape Love (FR) (Grape Tree Road)
12^P

Greek Star *H Hill* 92h 56c
10 b g Soviet Star(USA) —Graecia Magna (USA) (Private Account (USA))
293^6 466^9

Greenandredparson (IRE) *Patrick Griffin* 99h 103c
8 b g Pasternak—Parson's Run (The Parson)
49^U 162^3 471^B 3729^6 4112^P

Green Art (IRE) *Tracey Barfoot-Saunt* 19h
4 b g Dubai Destination(USA) —Seamstress (IRE) (Barathea (IRE))
2356^{15} 2882^{12} 2924^P

Greenbelt *George Moore* 78h 114c
10 b g Desert Prince(IRE) —Emerald (USA) (El Gran Senor (USA))
13^2 1642^6 1830^3 2093^P 2350^F 4115^8

Green Day (FR) *M Rolland*
5 b g Mansonnien(FR) —Kiluti (FR) (Solid Illusion (USA))
5159a^0

Green For Luck (IRE) *Sue Smith* 64h
4 b c Key Of Luck(USA) —Kasota (IRE) (Alzao (USA))
1825^6 2245^{10} 2369^P

Greengables (IRE) *Aidan Anthony Howard* 108h 97c
10 b m Darazari(IRE) —Clowater Buck (IRE) (Buckskin (FR))
1100^6

Green Gamble *Diana Grissell* 120c
11 gr g Environment Friend—Gemma's Wager (IRE) (Phardante (FR))
586^P

Gremlin *Dai Burchell* 109h
7 b g Mujahid(USA) —Fairy Free (Rousillon (USA))
41^2 (224)

Grenoli (FR) *John Cornwall* 93h 101c
10 b g Garde Royale—Pietrosella (FR) (Alias Smith (USA))
(49) **158^3**
501^P 1469^P 1952^P (5017)
5292^4

Grethel (IRE) *Alan Berry* 76h
7 b m Fruits Of Love(USA) —Stay Sharpe (USA) (Sharpen Up)
547^4 577^U 1003^4 1427^U

Grey Assassin *Simon West* 30h
4 gr g Timeless Times(USA) —Royal Comedian (Jester)
2511^8 3511^{10} 3992^U 4396^8 5259^8

Grey Bobby *Renee Robeson* 50b
4 gr g Silver Patriarch(IRE) —Country Orchid (Town And Country)
3957^{11}

Grey Cruzene (USA) *Chris Gordon* 92h
5 rg g Cozzene(USA) —Cruise Line (Rainbow Quest (USA))
2432^6 2944^P 3374^4 3604^8 3985^3 4403^4 4922^{10} **5216^{10}**

Grey Danbys *Malcolm Jefferson* 65b
5 gr m Terimon—Miss Danbys (Charmer)
5264^{10} 5432^{14}

Grey Garth (IRE) *James Bethell*
4 gr g Verglas(IRE) —Again Royale (IRE) (Royal Academy (USA))
4451^P

Grey Gold (IRE) *Richard Lee* 125h
6 gr g Strategic Choice(USA) —Grouse-N-Heather (Grey Desire)
238^4 869^4 2640^U 2985^3 (3526) ◆ 4159^4 ◆ 5106^9

Grey Locker *Lynn Siddall* 46h
8 gr m Silver Patriarch(IRE) —Not So Prim (Primitive Rising (USA))
4889^9 5091^7

Grey Missile *Jeremy Scott* 116h
6 gr g Terimon—Bonne Anniversaire (Alflora (IRE))
2059^5 2499^6 2791^3

Grey Soldier (IRE) *Gordon Elliott* 142h
6 gr g Galileo(IRE) —Crusch Alva (FR) (Unfuwain (USA))
1711a^4 4848^{21}

Greywell Boy *Nick Williams* 91b
4 gr g Fair Mix(IRE) —Rakajack (Rakaposhi King)
3909^5 4468^{12}

Grey Wulff (IRE) *Emma Lavelle* 106h
6 gr g Oscar(IRE) —Only A Rose (Glint Of Gold)
2136^4 2607^5 3528^2 4196^5

Grindy (IRE) *Evan Williams* 73h
5 b g Alderbrook—Blake's Fable (IRE) (Lafontaine (USA))
4866^{10} 5389^5

Gringo *Howard Johnson* 118h 132c
9 gr g Alzao(USA) —Glen Falls (Commanche Run)
2206^2 2520^5 4149^5
4913^3

Gripit N Tipit (IRE) *Sarah Humphrey* 120h 114c
10 b g Saddlers' Hall(IRE) —Savanagh (IRE) (Brush Aside (USA))
4026^P 4374^P

Gris Lord (IRE) *R T J Wilson* 107b
6 ch g Lord Of Appeal—Raveleen Rose (IRE) (Norwich)
3856^6 4253^8

Grit (IRE) *Nick Ayliffe* 87h
6 gr g Clodovil(IRE) —Lisa's Pride (IRE) (Pips Pride)
590^7

Gritti Palace (IRE) *John Upson* 112h 36c
11 b g Duky—Glittering Grit (IRE) (Sheer Grit)
3771^P

Groove Master *William Amos* 76h
4 b g Tobougg(IRE) —Magic Mistress (Magic Ring (IRE))
1772^3 2033^4 2528^F 4998^F

Gross Prophet *Alastair Lidderdale* 90h
6 b g Lujain(USA) —Done And Dusted (IRE) (Up And At 'Em)
5212^3

Group Leader (IRE) *J R Jenkins* 110h
5 ch g Noverre(USA) —Stem The Tide (USA) (Proud Truth (USA))
3718^8 4462^8 4874^5

Grovemere (IRE) *Debra Hamer* 70h
6 bb g Beneficial—Holly Grove Lass (Le Moss)
2576^6 5106^{12} 5211^7

Grove Pride *Henry Daly* 118b
6 b g Double Trigger(IRE) —Dara's Pride (IRE) (Darazari (IRE))
5113^3

Gtaab *Paul Webber* 102h
5 b g Cape Cross(IRE) —Nabadhaat (USA) (Mr Prospector (USA))
1899^6 2122^5 3386^{10} 4465^8 5244^4

Guam (IRE) *Nick Mitchell* 84h
6 br g Tamayaz(CAN) —Midway (IRE) (Warcraft (USA))
4677^7 5038^4 5152^6

Guarino (GER) *Gary Moore* 85h
7 b g Acatenango(GER) —Global World (GER) (Big Shuffle (USA))
3604^P 3872^6 4069^5 5057^F

Guerilla (AUS) *Lucy Normile* 57h 8c
11 bb g Octagonal(NZ) —Partisan (AUS) (Canny Lad (AUS))
626^P 948^{11} 1101^6 1578^P

Guess Again (IRE) *Warren Greatrex*
6 b g Milan—Guess Twice (Deep Run)
3088^4

Guga (IRE) *Dr Richard Newland* 80h
5 b g Rock Of Gibraltar(IRE) —Attitre (FR) (Mtoto)
1031^4

Gulf Of Aqaba (USA) *Ian Williams* 81h
5 bb g Mr Greeley(USA) —Ocean Jewel (USA) (Alleged (USA))
3296^{12} 3899^6 5016^P

Gulf President *Tim Vaughan* 114h
5 b g Polish Precedent(USA) —Gay Minette (IRE) (Peintre Celebre (USA))
216^2 554^4 (1099)

Gulf Punch *Milton Harris* 103h
4 b f Dubawi(IRE) —Fruit Punch (IRE) (Barathea (IRE))
674^3 836^6 (851) 960^4 (1024) 1279^4 (1330) 1610^7 1882^5 2033^2 2356^{11} 2639^7 5227^4 5346^7

Gullible Gordon (IRE) *Paul Nicholls* 138h 148c
8 ch g Anshan—Cronohill (IRE) (Mister Lord (USA))
1777^4 (1999)
2543^F 4792^9

Gumball *Paul Webber* 104b
6 ch g Karinga Bay—Little Dasi (IRE) (Mandalus)
5105^3

Gumlayloy *George Jones* 57h 20c
12 ch g Indian Ridge—Candide (USA) (Miswaki (USA))
75^P

Gun And More *Sue Smith* 54h
6 ch g Double Trigger(IRE) —Snowmore (Glacial Storm (USA))
1785^5 2281^{10} 3487^P 3787^{11} 5096^U

Gunna Be A Devil (IRE) *Jeremy Scott* 110h
7 b g Alflora(IRE) —Gunna Be Precious (Gunner B)
2482^6 2981^3 3295^4 3688^{14} 3919^3 4722^6

Gunnadoit (USA) *Ann Price* 96h 67c
6 bb g Almutawakel—Gharam (USA) (Green Dancer (USA))
66^8 441^9 467^P 1450^{11} **1727^6 4011^U 4293^P**

Gunner Be Quick *Mrs Monica Tory* 44c
9 b g Gunner B—At Long Last (John French)
296^6

Gunner Snow *Joanne Foster*
10 ch g Gunner B—Polar Belle (Arctic Lord)
802^P

Guns And Butter (IRE) *Rose Dobbin* 111h 100c
9 b g Definite Article—Clairification (IRE) (Shernazar)
2034^7 2371^4 3549^2 4150^4 4471^5 5261^7 5430^3

Gunship (IRE) *Cathy Hamilton* 72h 104c
10 b g Needle Gun(IRE) —Teejay's Future (IRE) (Buckskin (FR))
(95) **463^P**
2240^4 2645^P 4675^U 4900^5 **5256^6 (5434)**

Gunslinger (FR) *Michael Scudamore* 104h
6 b g High Chaparral(IRE) —Gamine (IRE) (High Estate)
823^5 3449^{10}

Gun Smith *Nick Kent* 100h 91c
9 b g Pistolet Bleu(IRE) —Bayariyka (IRE) (Slip Anchor)
90^7

Guns Of Love (IRE) *Robin Dickin* 36h 91c
9 b g Lord Of Appeal—Golden Seekers (Manado)
1924^6 (2334)
3388^4 3544^2 (3875)
4142^3 4671^4 5293^4

Guppy's Girl (IRE) *Sam Davison* 7h
4 b f Fantastic Light(USA) —Ninth Quest (USA) (Quest For Fame)
1845^P 2151^{11}

Gurtacrue (IRE) *Evan Williams* 118h
6 ch g Deploy—Biddy Early (IRE) (Sharp Charter)
1743^2 2145^2 ◆ 3365^3 (4557)

Gurteen Lass (IRE) *Miss G Lee* 96b
5 b m Misternando—Dark Sybil (IRE) (Warcraft (USA))
1146a^{11}

Gus Macrae (IRE) *Rebecca Curtis* 124h 114c
7 b g Accordion—Full Of Surprises (IRE) (Be My Native (USA))
2951^8 3555^4 3932^4 4490^9 5255^4 5441^8

Gutter Lane *Malcolm Jefferson* 76h
7 b g Saddlers' Hall(IRE) —Water Stratford (IRE) (Jurado (USA))
1071^6 1201^{11} 1357^9 1553^7

Guydus (IRE) *Venetia Williams* 99h 97c
7 b m Old Vic—Lady Mayday (IRE) (Strong Gale)
2982^4 3527^4 3961^3

Guzzle An Go (IRE) *E J O'Grady* 128h
6 b m King's Theatre(IRE) —Deemiss (IRE) (Buckskin (FR))
1121a^7 (Dead)

Gwanako (FR) *Paul Nicholls* 142h 153c
8 bb g Sin Kiang(FR) —Vaubecourt (FR) (Courtroom (FR))
1861^F 2359^F 3293^4 3807^{10} 4817^{15} 5160^{10}

Gwendraeth Girl (IRE) *Tony Carroll* 83b
6 b m Revoque(IRE) —Shes Elite (IRE) (Supreme Leader)
1069^5 1284^{11}

Gwyre (IRE) *Tim Easterby* 96h 84c
5 b m Mull Of Kintyre(USA) —Boadicea (Celtic Swing)
1870^{14} 3523^{11} 4115^7
4507^4 4822^4

Gypsy George *Mrs S M McPherson* 122h 141c
10 bb g Sovereign Water(FR) —Query Line (High Line)
3956^P

Gypsy Jazz (IRE) *Jennie Candlish*
4 b f Antonius Pius(USA) —Dawn's Folly (IRE) (Bluebird (USA))
674^P

Gypsy Moth (IRE) *Caroline Keevil* 69h
5 gr m Zagreb(USA) —Hurst Flyer (Neltino)
3301^7 3909^9 4561^8 4970^{11} 5435^4

Haar *Andy Turnell* 119h 132c
7 ch g Selkirk(USA) —Chilly Start (IRE) (Caerleon (USA))
234^B 1926^U

Haarth Sovereign (IRE) *Lawney Hill* 110h
7 b g Alhaarth(IRE) —Summer Queen (Robellino (USA))
331^5 3686^{14} 4025^7 4375^5 (5376)

Habbie Simpson *Alan King* 137h
6 b g Elmaamul(USA) —Hamanaka (USA) (Conquistador Cielo (USA))
(2075) (2454) ◆ 3288^3 3806^3 4803^9 5285^3

Hackpenbay *Lawney Hill* 87b
5 b g Karinga Bay—Peasedown Tofana (Teenoso (USA))
2896^2 3166^2 3903^7 4287^8

Hades (IRE) *Tim Easterby* 76h
4 b g Antonius Pius(USA) —Lady Lucre (IRE) (Last Tycoon)
2600^3 4283^{11}

Hadron Collider (FR) *Chris Nenadich* 109h
6 ch g Dubai Destination(USA) —Liver De Saron (USA) (Mt. Livermore (USA))
279^2 635^2 (847) 1065^3 1742^5 2241^7 2586^4 5392^2

Hail Caesar (IRE) *Evan Williams* 120h
5 gr g Montjeu(IRE) —Alabastrine (Green Desert (USA))
3481^{15} 4076^{12} 4783^6 5348^U

Hail The King (USA) *Roger Curtis* 81h 98c
11 gr g Allied Forces(USA) —Hail Kris (USA) (Kris S (USA))
2173 1477^{11}

Hair Of The Dog *William Amos* 68h
7 b g Foxhound(USA) —Bebe De Cham (Tragic Role (USA))
727^6 837^{12} 948^P 3631^9

Haka Dancer (USA) *Philip Kirby* 103h 97c
8 b g War Chant(USA) —Safe Return (USA) (Mr Prospector (USA))
472^P **1082^3**
1257^4 1587^4 5294^2

Halcon Genelardais (FR) *Alan King* 146h 150c
11 ch g Halcon—Francetphile (FR) (Farabi)
3908^3 4211^2 4876^P

Haldibari (IRE) *Shaun Lycett* 108h
7 b g Kahyasi—Haladiya (IRE) (Darshaan)
(232) 267^2 651^6 986^6 1198^7 1368^6

Half Cocked *Richard Rowe* 121h
9 b g Double Trigger(IRE) —Half Asleep (Quiet Fling (USA))
2123^4 2925^6 (3428) ◆ 3866^P

Haling Park (UAE) *Tim Vaughan* 82h
5 b m Halling(USA) —Friendly (USA) (Lear Fan (USA))
171[F] 384[P] 845[P]

Halla San *Richard Fahey* 89h
9 b g Halling(USA) —St Radegund (Green Desert (USA))
2868[U] 3566[P] **4453[U]**

Halling Gal *Evan Williams* 104h
5 b m Halling(USA) —Saik (USA) (Riverman (USA))
19[6] 1090[3] 1280[2] 1844[6] 1938[F]

Hallmark Harry *Michael Easterby* 92b
5 b g Silver Patriarch(IRE) —Society Girl (Shavian)
949[2] ◆ (1071)

Hallstatt (IRE) *John Mackie* 75h
5 ch g Halling(USA) —Last Resort (Lahib (USA))
2038[12]

Halucha (IRE) *Paul Webber* 77h
6 b g Luso—Rose Basket (IRE) (Roselier (FR))
4879[6] 5225[6]

Hamalac *Martin Keighley* 49h
5 b g Hamas(IRE) —Lac Marmot (FR) (Marju (IRE))
759[8] 1734[11] 1990[P]

Hamilton Hill *Terry Clement* 64b
4 b g Groom Dancer(USA) —Loriner's Lass (Saddlers' Hall (IRE))
3630[5]

Hammer *Alison Thorpe* 94h
6 b g Beat Hollow—Tranquil Moon (Deploy)
134[5] 298[2]

Hammerwood *Zoe Davison* 39b
5 br g Makbul—Havantadoubt (IRE) (Desert King (IRE))
1680[8] 2594[8]

Hampshire Express (IRE) *W P Mullins* 135h 132c
8 b g Dushyantor(USA) —Gypsys Girl (IRE) (Husyan (USA))
5141a[F]

Hampstead Heath (IRE) *David Marnane* 117h 125c
6 gr g Daylami(IRE) —Hedera (USA) (Woodman (USA))
1123a[RR]

Hampton Court *Seamus Mullins* 99h
6 ch g King's Best(USA) —Rafting (IRE) (Darshaan)
359[6] **631[U]**
691[P] 930[5]

Hanahoe *Alex Hales* 86b
6 b g Diktat—Shortfall (Last Tycoon)
1955[6]

Handford Henry (IRE) *John Holt* 47h
5 b g Brian Boru—Second Violin (IRE) (Cataldi)
3773[13] 4239[11] 5108[9]

Handsome Chap *Ian McInnes* 64h
6 b g Tumbleweed Ridge—Dolphin Beech (IRE) (Dolphin Street (FR))
1504[P]

Handtheprizeover *Ben Case* 92h 110c
6 b g Exit To Nowhere(USA) —Main Dans La Main (FR) (Pistolet Bleu (IRE))
2113[2] (2559)
2986[2] 3819[4] (4139)
4461[3]

Handy Andy (IRE) *Colin Tizzard* 130h
5 b g Beneficial—Maslam (IRE) (Robellino (USA))
(4459) ◆ 5186[P]

Hangover (IRE) *Conor O'Dwyer* 133h 142c
9 br g Presenting—Native Wood (IRE) (Be My Native (USA))
3206a[P] 3798a[11]

Hang Up My Boots (IRE) *James McAuley* 95b
5 gr g Great Palm(USA) —Carmenta (IRE) (Unfuwain (USA))
4239[7]

Hannah Jacques (IRE) *Nicky Richards* 88h
6 b m Flemensfirth(USA) —Richs Mermaid (IRE) (Saddlers' Hall (IRE))
1934[2] 3498[P] 5091[3]

Hannicean *Ian Williams* 85h
7 ch g Medicean—Hannah's Music (Music Boy)
224[F] 835[F]

Hannour (IRE) *Evan Williams* 72h
4 b g Kahyasi—Halawanda (IRE) (Ashkalani (IRE))
836[12] 1298[4] 1545[5]

Haoyunma (IRE) *Harry Chisman* 38h 75c
9 ch m Old Vic—A Bit Of Luck (IRE) (Good Thyne (USA))
56[2] 371[P] 597[5]

Happy Fleet *Roger Curtis* 70h
8 b m Beat All(USA) —Fleeting Affair (Hotfoot I)
920[7] 1179[6] (1479) 1592[4]

Hapthor *F Jestin* 94h 87c
12 ch m Zaffaran(USA) —My Goddess (Palm Track)
801[3] **1001[4]**
1360[RR] 1423[RR]

Harbour Way *John Wade* 76h 83c
8 b g Bal Harbour—Adjusting (IRE) (Busted)
1642[3]

Harcas (IRE) *Martin Todhunter* 77h
9 b g Priolo(USA) —Genetta (Green Desert (USA))
459[5] 948[5] 1361[5] 2302[P]

Hard Tackle (IRE) *Jonjo O'Neill* 92h
5 b g Milan—Penguin (Arctic Lord)
2518[5] ◆ 4091[8] 4268[10] 4895[7] 5322[6]

Hard To Name *Alan Mactaggart* 85h
8 b g Beat All(USA) —Hobbs Choice (Superpower)
2270[F] 2656[P]

Hard To Swallow (IRE) *Martin Keighley* 119b
5 b g Snurge—Nicat's Daughter (IRE) (Oscar (IRE))
(4866) ◆

Hard To Tell (IRE) *Bill Turner* 65b
5 b g Presenting—Superior Dawn (IRE) (Mandalus)
1729[10] 1906[5]

Hardwick Wood *Caroline Bailey* 72h
6 ch g Fleetwood(IRE) —Lizzy Lamb (Bustino)
1990[10] 2281[6] 2642[7] 3255[5]

Harinya (GER) *David Bridgwater*
4 b f Ransom O'War(USA) —Haraluna (GER) (Lagunas)
4335[P]

Harlequinn Danseur (IRE) *John Flint* 97h
6 b g Noverre(USA) —Nassma (IRE) (Sadler's Wells (USA))
534[8] 823[7]

Harley Fern *Terry Clement* 48h
5 b m Primo Valentino(IRE) —Its All Relative (Distant Relative)
1688[10]

Harley Road (IRE) *Gordon Elliott* 46h
8 b g Quws—Marble Desire (IRE) (Un Desperado (FR))
1573[P]

Harmony Brig (IRE) *Nicky Richards* 95h 132c
12 ch g Accordion—Bridges Daughter (IRE) (Montelimar (USA))
45[9]

Harouet (FR) *Paul Nicholls* 119h 122c
6 ch g Vertical Speed(FR) —Laïrna (FR) (Beaudelaire (USA))
(2235)

Harps Counsel (IRE) *J K Magee* 95h 107c
9 b g Leading Counsel(USA) —Up The Harps (IRE) (Lord Americo)
2654[3] 3729[7] 5308[10]

Harris Hawk *John Wade* 113h
6 b g Karinga Bay—Harristown Lady (Muscatite)
1764[4] 2355[6] 3715[9] 4242[4] 5091[2]

Harry Flashman *Donald Whillans* 121h 121c
10 ch g Minster Son—Youandi (Silver Season)
46[5] (626)
804[2] 859[2] (5261)

Harry Hunt *Graeme McPherson* 114h
4 b g Bertolini(USA) —Qasirah (IRE) (Machiavellian (USA))
2466[2] 3484[P] (3917) 4283[3] 4807[11]

Harry Le Fise Lake (IRE) *Philip Hobbs* 112b
5 b g Great Palm(USA) —Jennypenney (Arctic Lord)
2222[2] 5157[9]

Harry Masters *Edward Bevan* 76b
7 b g Alflora(IRE) —Dominant Duchess (Old Vic)
254[12] 2328[14] 5108[P] 5327[P]

Harry Oscar (IRE) *Ken Wingrove*
10 b g Oscar(IRE) —Kilcrea Breeze (IRE) (Fresh Breeze (USA))
1742[P] 2154[9] **2588[P]**

Harrys Double (IRE) *Joseph Bewley* 76b
7 ch g Double Eclipse(IRE) —Go Hunting (IRE) (Abednego)
42[P]

Harry The Viking *Paul Nicholls* 116h
6 ch g Sir Harry Lewis(USA) —Viking Flame (Viking (USA))
4719[2]

Harry Topper *Kim Bailey* 112b
4 b g Sir Harry Lewis(USA) —Indeed To Goodness (IRE) (Welsh Term)
(5174)

Harry Tricker *Gary Moore* 137h 133c
7 b g Hernando(FR) —Katy Nowaitee (Komaite (USA))
(1587)
(2313) *3059[4]* **4729[4]**

Harsh But Fair *Michael Easterby* 91b
5 br g Sakhee(USA) —Royal Distant (USA) (Distant View (USA))
474[4] (892)

Hartland Point *Malcolm Beck* 24b
6 b g Polish Precedent(USA) —Prickly Poppy (Lear Fan (USA))
375[15]

Harvest Song (IRE) *Henrietta Knight* 106h
5 b g Sadler's Wells(USA) —La Mouline (IRE) (Nashwan (USA))
(279) 2111[4] 2630[P] 4739[6]

Harvey May (IRE) *John Upson* 28c
9 b g New Frontier(IRE) —Dizzy Lady (IRE) (Sarab)
226[7] 556[5] 987[6]

Harvey's Hope *Keith Reveley* 108b
5 b g Sinndar(IRE) —Ancara (Dancing Brave (USA))
4457[2] 4916[9]

Harveys Spirit (IRE) *A J Martin* 81h
6 ch m Rossini(USA) —Ex-Imager (Exhibitioner)
285[F]

Harwood Dale *Mrs Freya Brewer* 55b
11 b g Past Glories—Scalby Clipper (Sir Mago)
90[P]

Hasper *Sandy Forster* 95c
13 b g Perpendicular—Hasland (Aragon)
211[3] 471[2] 730[2] 872[U] 3853[5] 4241[P] 5258[5]

Hassadin *Andrew Haynes* 96h
5 ch g Reset(AUS) —Crocolat (Croco Rouge (IRE))
1067[6]

Hatchet Man *Carroll Gray* 74h
5 ch g Needwood Blade—Mayfair (Green Desert (USA))
5035[3] 5243[7]

Hathamore *Allie Tullie* 75h
7 b m Classic Cliche(IRE) —Sillymore (Silly Prices)
999[7]

Hatton Flight *Andrew Balding* 100h
7 b g Kahyasi—Platonic (Zafonic (USA))
1884[6] 2322[6]

Haulage Lady (IRE) *Karen McLintock* 36h
5 b m Xaar—Blue Mantle (IRE) (Barathea (IRE))
3331[15]

Havenstone (IRE) *Evan Williams* 109h 95c
10 bb g Needle Gun(IRE) —Melodic Tune (IRE) (Roselier (FR))
1292[3]
1483[2] 1741[4]
1939[3] 2024[5] (4099)

Have You Seen Me (IRE) *Nigel Twiston-Davies* 119h 140c
8 b g Beneficial—Silent Supreme (IRE) (Supreme Leader)
(1731)
2427[2] 3291[4] 3605[3] 5301[2]

Having Nightmares (IRE) *A J Martin* 64c
7 bb g King's Theatre(IRE) —Quare Dream'S (IRE) (Strong Gale)
873[8]

Havingotascoobydo (IRE) *Martin Keighley* 126h
6 b g Witness Box(USA) —In Blue (IRE) (Executive Perk)
(1448) 3252[4] 3698[3] (4439) 4700[2] (5080) 5424[5]

Hawaii Klass *Donald Whillans* 113h
6 ch g Classic Cliche(IRE) —Youandi (Silver Season)
3633[U] 4359[3] (4889) 5149[2]

Hawkaller *Anthony Honeyball* 93h
6 gr g Cloudings(IRE) —Tone Mist (Absalom)
1778[6] 2493[8] 3225[6] 3691[4] 4225[4] 4536[6]

Hawkes Point *Paul Nicholls* 121h
6 b g Kayf Tara—Mandys Native (IRE) (Be My Native (USA))
4294[3] ◆ 4747[5]

Hawk Gold (IRE) *Michelle Bryant* 78h
7 ch g Tendulkar(USA) —Heiress Of Meath (IRE) (Imperial Frontier (USA))
688[4] 1592[5] 1915[6]

Hawk Run *Jonjo O'Neill* 77b
5 ch g Central Park(IRE) —Bobbie Black (IRE) (Bob's Return (IRE))
4970[10]

Hawksbury Heights *J J Lambe* 101h 90c
9 ch g Nashwan(USA) —Gentle Dame (Kris)
1660[5]

Haydens Mount *James Frost* 46h
6 ch g Bahamian Bounty—Tenderfoot (Be My Chief (USA))
1927[8] 2137[15] 2499[15] 3877[10] 4225[9] 4899[8]

Hayes Princess (IRE) *Tim Vaughan* 109h
7 bb m King's Theatre(IRE) —Celtic Angel (IRE) (Bob Back (USA))
1067[5]

Hayjack *Venetia Williams* 113b
6 b g Karinga Bay—Celtic Native (IRE) (Be My Native (USA))
2957[5] (3372) 4533[2]

Hazelbury *Nigel Hawke* 54h 87c
10 b m Overbury(IRE) —Mira Lady (Henbit (USA))
913[P] 1159[P] 1546[6] 1678[P] 1843[P] 2050[P]

Hazeldene *George Charlton* 111h 104c
9 ch g Dancing High—Gaelic Charm (IRE) (Deep Run)
(44) 309[4] 3966[8] **4472[4] 4913[6]**

Hazeymm (IRE) *E J O'Grady* 134h
8 b g Marju(IRE) —Shimna (Mr Prospector (USA))
1713a[6] 2260a[2] 3203a[5]

Hazy Bay *Michael Roberts* 86h
6 b g Zaha(CAN) —Barton Bay (IRE) (Kambalda)
3432[4] 3791[6] (4403)

Hazy Dawn *Michael Scudamore* 97h
6 b m Cloudings(IRE) —Quiet Dawn (Lighter)
2472[3] 2987[S] 3623[4] (4118) 4535[5] 5108[6]

Hazy Oaks *Kevin M Prendergast* 89h
8 gr m Classic Cliche(IRE) —Island Mist (Jupiter Island)
12[P] 3728[7] 4395[6] 4550[P]

Hazy Tom (IRE) *Charlie Longsdon* 110b
5 b g Heron Island(IRE) —The Wounded Cook (IRE) (Muroto)
(5210)

Head Hunted *Charlie Mann* 108h
4 b g Dubai Destination(USA) —Tropical Breeze (IRE) (Kris)
3767[2] 4192[4] 4954[3]

Head Of Chambers *Lawney Hill* 41b
5 gr g Terimon—Flaming Rose (IRE) (Roselier (FR))
1607[10]

Head Of The Posse (IRE) *John E Kiely* 151h 151c
8 b g Supreme Leader—Aussieannie (IRE) (Arapahos (FR))
(2008a)
2971a[3] 3174a[6]

Heads Onthe Ground (IRE) *E Bolger* 116h 133c
14 br g Be My Native(USA) —Strong Wings (Strong Gale)
2346[9]

Health Is Wealth (IRE) *Colin Tizzard* 92h 103c
6 br g Anshan—Cherry Black (IRE) (Roselier (FR))
2000[2] 2428[7] 2791[11]
3349[U] ◆ 3650[4] 4102[P] 4896[3] (5269) ◆

Healys Bar (IRE) *Oliver McKiernan* 146h 142c
7 b g Beneficial—River Rescue (Over The River (FR))
2413a[4] 3174a[P] 5141a[P]

Hear My Song (IRE) *Jonjo O'Neill* 114h
6 ch g Snurge—Siberiansdaughter (IRE) (Strong Gale)
1821[2] 2154[2]

Hearthstead Dream *Gordon Elliott* 126h 84c
10 ch g Dr Fong(USA) —Robin Lane (Tenby)
(309) **550[4]**
1372[2]

Heart Of Dubai (USA) *Micky Hammond* 100h
6 b g Outofthebox(USA) —Diablo's Blend (USA) (Diablo (USA))
400[2] 576[6] 800[2] 916[4] 1644[2] ◆ 1870[13] 2080[10] 2300[4] 2658[8]

Heart Of Tuscany *Jonathen de Giles* 35h
5 b m Falbrav(IRE) —Zarma (FR) (Machiavellian (USA))
989[7]

Heart O' The West (IRE) *Andrew Parker* 102h
7 b g Tamayaz(CAN) —She's All Heart (Broken Hearted)
2104[10] 2658[10]

Heart Springs *Dr Jeremy Naylor* 99h 96c
11 b m Parthian Springs—Metannee (The Brianstan)
2240[8]

Heathcliff (IRE) *Richard Lee* 129h 133c
9 b g Glacial Storm(USA) —Gaye Le Moss (Le Moss)
206[P] **2106[U]**
2606[6] 3440[3] ◆ 3566[7] 4003[2] 5325[4]

Heathcote *Gary Moore* 133h 139c
9 b g Unfuwain(USA) —Chere Amie (USA) (Mr Prospector (USA))
438[5]

Heather Glen (IRE) *Sue Smith* 62h
5 b m Luso—Kadara (IRE) (Slip Anchor)
2167[7] 3504[5] 4245[6] 4684[6]

Heather Royal *Nicky Henderson* 109b
5 ch m Medicean—Close Harmony (Bustino)
(332) 4027[6] 5188[5]

Heavenly Blues (GER) *T M Walsh* 132h
9 br g Kallisto(GER) —Heavenly Storm (USA) (Storm Bird (CAN))
4817[8]

Heavenly Chorus *Keith Reveley* 108h 115c
9 b m Key Of Luck(USA) —Celestial Choir (Celestial Storm (USA))
89[4] **460[4]**
728[5] 2208[9]
2656[2] (2942)
(3524) 4116[3] 4455[7]
4913[8] 5145[6]

Heavenly Saint *Lisa Day* 34h
6 b m Bertolini(USA) —Heavenly Glow (Shavian)
754[11] 843[12]

Hector's Choice (FR) *Richard Lee* 113h 138c
7 bb g Grey Risk(FR) —The Voice (FR) (Ski Chief (USA))
1956[11]
4010[3] (4438)
4941[P]

Hector's House *David Brace* 109h
5 b g Tobougg(IRE) —Thrasher (Hector Protector (USA))
1956[F] 4115[16] 4778[10]

Hector Spectre (IRE) *Nikki Evans* 46h
5 gr g Verglas(IRE) —Halicardia (Halling (USA))
1466[9]

Heez A Cracker (FR) *Emma Lavelle* 124h
5 b g Goldneyev(USA) —Jolly Harbour (Rudimentary (USA))
(1887) 2387[8] 3288[11] (3744) 3950[11]

Heezagrey (IRE) *James Evans* 74h 79c
8 gr g Naheez(USA) —Silver Belle (IRE) (Roselier (FR))
992[3] 1059[2] 1336[4]
1483[4] 1694[2]
(1820) 1939[2] 2239[5] 3530[4] **3961[5] 4483[8] 4829[5]**
4953[2] 5349[4]

Heez A Steel (IRE) *George Charlton* 131h 133c
10 b g Naheez(USA) —Ari's Fashion (Aristocracy)
162[2] 3522[4] 4167[U] 4689[2] 5338[5]

Hegrid (IRE) *A J Martin* 114h 114c
10 b g Lake Coniston(IRE) —Joyful Tidings (IRE) (Lycius (USA))
2507[8] 2599[U]

Heir To Be *Michael Blake* 110h
12 b g Elmaamul(USA) —Princess Genista (Ile De Bourbon (USA))
581[9] 821[4] 921[6] 1094[3] 1195[2] 1259[4] 1477[7] 1551[6] 1745[7] (1840) 2023[2] 5276[3] 5439[5]

Helena Of Troy *Sue Smith* 56h
5 b m Largesse—Just Julia (Natroun (FR))
686[6] 1086[2] 4117[6] 4552[10]

Helens Vision *James Evans* 120h
8 b m Alflora(IRE) —Kinlet Vision (IRE) (Vision (USA))
2514[5] 2955[10] 3686[P]

Helen Wood *David Pipe* 109h 120c
8 b m Lahib(USA) —Last Ambition (IRE) (Cadeaux Genereux)
23[2] (264)
444[2] 592[2]

Helieorbea *Alan Brown* 99h
5 b g Reset(AUS) —Rendition (Polish Precedent (USA))
1501[3] 1624[5] 2421[3] 3509[12]

Heliopsis (IRE) *Venetia Williams* 100b
6 b g Beneficial—Bright Note (Buckskin (FR))
1824[3] 3259[3]

Helium (FR) *Nick Gifford* 127h
6 b g Dream Well(FR) —Sure Harbour (SWI) (Surumu (GER))
2071[0]

He'Llberemembered (IRE) *P G Fahey* 129h
8 ch g Blue Ocean(USA) —Remember Rob (IRE) (Deep Society)
1526a[6]

Hello Bud (IRE) *Nigel Twiston-Davies* 49h 144c
13 b g Jurado(USA) —Orchestral Sport (IRE) (Orchestra)
(2543)
3568[P] 5200[P]

Hello Hector *Colin Tizzard* 86h
8 b g Overbury(IRE) —Hester Ann (Proverb)
370[7]

Hell's Bay (FR) *Colin Tizzard* 138h 156c
9 b g Supreme Leader—Queen's Flagship (IRE) (Accordion)
234[6] 909[0] (1444)
1863[5] 2348[2] 2628[2] (3291)

Helm (IRE) *Richard Rowe* 87h 102c
10 b g Alhaarth(IRE) —Pipers Pool (IRE) (Mtoto)
2055[4] 2794[F]

Helpston *Pam Sly* 130h 130c
7 b g Sir Harry Lewis(USA) —Chichell's Hurst (Oats)
3743[3] 5133[2]

Hemington *Michael Scudamore* 75h 108c
8 gr g Shahrastani(USA) —Race To The Rhythm (Deep Run)
218[5] (502)
911[P] 1057[6]

Hendaway *Chris Bealby*
7 b g Nomadic Way(USA) —Mindahen (Henbit (USA))
2069[P]

Hennerwood Beech *Richard Price* 35b
6 ch m Sly—Mother Goose (Alflora (IRE))
304^{9} 568^{13}

Henok (FR) *Nigel Twiston-Davies* 103b
5 ch g Kapgarde(FR) —Harkosa (FR) (Nikos)
3943^{3} 4527^{5}

Henry Havelock *Chris Grant* 79h
4 ch c Noverre(USA) —Burmese Princess (USA) (King Of Kings (IRE))
629^{5} 1696^{3} 1825^{10}

Henry Hook (IRE) *Victor Dartnall* 123h
7 ch g Presenting—Swing The Lead (IRE) (Good Thyne (USA))
282^{8} 527^{8} 664^{7} 1737^{3} 1976^{2} (2558) 3370^{10}
3686^{9} 3950^{4} (4446) 4700^{P}

Henry King (IRE) *Victor Dartnall* 126h
7 gr g Great Palm(USA) —Presenting Shares (IRE) (Presenting)
2148^{P} (3481) 3874^{5} (4444)

Henry's Hero *Gary Brown* 33b
5 b g Mujahid(USA) —Primavera (Anshan)
1284^{12}

Hepahepa Naeney (IRE) *D M Fogarty* 116h
7 b m In Yarak—Carrowmore Queen (IRE) (Montelimar (USA))
1155a^{8}

Herald Angel (FR) *Barry Brennan* 106h 93c
8 b g Priolo(USA) —Heavenly Music (USA) (Seattle Song (USA))
2401^{4} 3431^{P} 3741^{U} 4021^{9}

Heraldry (IRE) *Peter Brookshaw* 111h 58c
11 b g Mark Of Esteem(IRE) —Sorb Apple (IRE) (Kris)
4407^{4}

Herdsman (IRE) *Philip Hobbs* 101h
6 b g Flemensfirth(USA) —My Sunny South (Strong Gale)
(1989) 2525^{2} 3253^{2}

Herecomesthetruth (IRE) *Chris Gordon* 124h 160c
9 ch g Presenting—Beagan Rose (IRE) (Roselier (FR))
2138^{0} 2964^{3}

Hereditary *Linda Jewell* 70h
9 ch g Hernando(FR) —Eversince (USA) (Foolish Pleasure (USA))
4130^{7} 4559^{5} 5383^{8}

Here's Hockey *Mrs K Burke* 64b
5 b g Alflora(IRE) —Ella Falls (IRE) (Dancing Dissident (USA))
4280^{8}

Here's The Key (FR) *Paul Webber* 99h 39c
7 b m Dark Moondancer—Hereke (Blakeney)
2424^{F} 3338^{2} 3607^{3} **3817^{4}** 4401^{2} 4955^{9}

Here To Eternity (IRE) *Sarah Robinson* 40h 53c
10 b g In The Wings—Amnesty Bay (Thatching)
2731^{0} **758^{P}**
987^{P}

Herewearagain (IRE) *Philip Hobbs* 118c
8 b g Beneficial—Philipintown Queen (IRE) (Castle Keep)
85^{4} 429^{3} 663^{4} 1128^{6} 1491^{P} 1589^{4} 1841^{3} 1916^{3}

Hermoso (IRE) *Nigel Twiston-Davies* 112h
6 br g Jolly Jake(NZ) —Hang On (IRE) (Strong Gale)
693^{3} 871^{P} (946) 1391^{3}

Hernando Cortes *Martin Todhunter* 89h
7 b g Sadler's Wells(USA) —Houseproud (USA) (Riverman (USA))
161^{13} 456^{5} 520^{5} 604^{10}

Hernando's Boy *Keith Reveley* 111h 73c
10 b g Hernando(FR) —Leave At Dawn (Slip Anchor)
(2474)
2940^{9} 4975^{4}

Herne Bay (IRE) *Ian Williams* 106h
9 b g Hernando(FR) —Charita (IRE) (Lycius (USA))
846^{2} 1033^{5} 1364^{10} 1814^{6}

Heroic Lad *Andrew Haynes* 13h
6 ch g Arkadian Hero(USA) —Erith's Chill Wind (Be My Chief (USA))
1058^{6}

Heron Bay *Peter Bowen* 123h
7 b g Hernando(FR) —Wiener Wald (USA) (Woodman (USA))
315^{2} (711) 916^{2} 1017^{9} 1250^{2} 1372^{4} 1625^{6}
1956^{2} 2307^{3} 2542^{3} 3447^{10} 3620^{4} 4291^{8}

Herons Well *Rebecca Curtis* 119h 140c
8 b g Heron Island(IRE) —The Storm Bell (IRE) (Glacial Storm (USA))
18^{3} 524^{2} 4011^{6} 4163^{2} (4374)
4851^{U} 5163^{F}

Herschel (IRE) *Gary Moore* 118h
5 br g Dr Fong(USA) —Rafting (IRE) (Darshaan)
(1125) (1548)

He's A Hawker (IRE) *Michael Mullineaux* 93b
6 ch g Fourstars Allstar(USA) —Dromin Deel (IRE) (Lanfranco)
1284^{7} 1510^{3}

Hesaposer (IRE) *Gordon Elliott* 111h
5 b g Lucky Story(USA) —Naked Poser (IRE) (Night Shift (USA))
442^{5}

He's A Sheila *Trevor Wall* 80h
8 b g Overbury(IRE) —Dannistar (Puissance)
75^{2} 298^{8} 760^{8} 1137^{8} 1552^{7}

He's On His Way (IRE) *David Phelan* 117c
12 ch g Zaffaran(USA) —Soraway (Choral Society)
292^{2}

Hes Our Lad (IRE) *Anthony Honeyball* 98h
5 b g Rudimentary(USA) —Polyzar (IRE) (Shernazar)
1748^{3} (2335) 4468^{14} (5013)

He's Our Man (IRE) *Patrick O Brady* 122h
6 b g Statue Of Liberty(USA) —She's Our Mare (IRE) (Commanche Run)
2562a^{6} 3029a^{5}

Hever Road (IRE) *David Pearson* 93c
12 ch g Anshan—The Little Bag (True Song)
549^{5} 1826^{P} 2155^{5} 2420^{3} 2952^{P} 3723^{4}

Hey Big Spender (IRE) *Colin Tizzard* 121h 160c
8 b g Rudimentary(USA) —Jim's Monkey (Monksfield)
(2273)
2673^{F} 3292^{8} (4077)
4352^{4} 4818^{9} 5199^{P}

Hey Charlie (IRE) *Nicky Richards* 107h
9 b g Mister Mat(FR) —Reynards Run (Kemal (FR))
1339^{6} 1595^{5} 1762^{11}

Hey Nineteen (IRE) *Charlie Longsdon* 29h
5 b g Millkom—Scolboa Victoria (IRE) (Roselier (FR))
4239^{9} 5168^{12}

Hey There Tiger (IRE) *Alistair Whillans* 49b
6 ch m Ashkalani(IRE) —Cloone Swinger (Celtic Swing)
311^{10} 876^{5}

Hibiki (IRE) *Sarah Humphrey* 129h 104c
7 b g Montjeu(IRE) —White Queen (IRE) (Spectrum (IRE))
207^{16} **687^{5}**
(1971) 2085^{2} 2498^{4} 2868^{13} 5201^{19}

Hi Dancer *Ben Haslam* 115h 119c
8 b g Medicean—Sea Music (Inchinor)
(179) 2076^{8} 3500^{14} 4113^{10} 4544^{5} (4998) 5098^{3}

Hidden Cyclone (IRE) *John Joseph Hanlon* 148h
6 b g Stowaway—Hurricane Debbie (IRE) (Shahanndeh)
(2260a) 3203a^{3} (3708a) (4319a)

Hidden Harmony (IRE) *Rose Dobbin* 91b
5 b g Subtle Power(IRE) —Duffys Alpha (IRE) (Alphabatim (USA))
5034^{3}

Hidden In Time *Keith Reveley* 21h
6 b g Slip Anchor—Linea-G (Keen)
2296^{9} 2612^{P}

Hidden Keel *Charlie Longsdon* 133h 153c
6 gr g Kirkwall—Royal Keel (Long Leave)
(1972) 2387^{4}
2793^{2} ◆ (3390)
3946^{9} (4926)
(5155)

Hidden Pleasure *Nerys Dutfield* 88b
6 b m Karinga Bay—Girl Of Pleasure (IRE) (Namaqualand (USA))
237^{6} 820^{P}

Hidden Springs *Brian Baugh* 83b
6 b g Kayf Tara—Meole Brace (Starch Reduced)
1729^{7} 2328^{8}

Hidden Universe (IRE) *D K Weld* 140h
5 gr g Linamix(FR) —Hint Of Humour (USA) (Woodman (USA))
4086a^{4} 4788^{12}

Higgy's Boy (IRE) *Nicky Henderson* 131h
6 b g Choisir(AUS) —Pagan Rhythm (USA) (Joanie's Chief (USA))
1609^{14} 1859^{10} 2213^{3} 2868^{5} 4852^{12}

Higgy's Ragazzo (FR) *Nicky Henderson* 135h
4 b g Sinndar(IRE) —Super Crusty (IRE) (Namid)
(3986) (5131) 5300^{2}

High Benefit (IRE) *Alan King* 112h
6 b m Beneficial—Higher Again (IRE) (Strong Gale)
(2456) 2954^{F} 3403^{10} 4454^{4} 5106^{3}

High Bird Humphrey *Simon West* 109h 124c
12 ch g Nomadic Way(USA) —Miss Kewmill (Billion (USA))
316^{6} **1023^{2}**
1110^{3} 1328^{2} 1470^{10} **1761^{6}** 1931^{2}
2112^{P} 2213^{9}

High Dee Jay (IRE) *Dai Burchell* 22h
6 b g High Chaparral(IRE) —Brogan's Well (IRE) (Caerleon (USA))
792^{P} 1466^{10}

Highest Esteem *Philip Sharp* 100h
7 b g Mark Of Esteem(IRE) —For More (FR) (Sanglamore (USA))
21^{P} 5271^{4}

High Expectation *James Ewart* 31b
4 bb f Kayf Tara—Hazel Bank Lass (IRE) (Insan (USA))
3504^{7} 4005^{5}

Highheelsnhandbags *Michael P Hourigan* 90h
8 b m Roi De Rome(USA) —D'Egliere (FR) (Port Etienne (FR))
920^{10}

High Holborn (IRE) *David Pipe* 102h
4 b g Danehill Dancer(IRE) —Wedding Morn (IRE) (Sadler's Wells (USA))
674^{0} 1018^{13}

High Hoylander *Sue Smith* 110h
5 b g Aljabr(USA) —Ma-Arif (IRE) (Alzao (USA))
892^{2} 2355^{3} 2943^{0} 3387^{3} 3692^{U} 3739^{U} 3987^{4}
4323^{7} 4998^{6} 5357^{P}

High Jack (IRE) *Andy Turnell* 94h 114c
9 b g Supreme Leader—Pharisee (IRE) (Phardante (FR))
156^{3} (427)
2073^{F} 2453^{4} 3371^{10} 3878^{2} 4523^{P} 4896^{5} (5345)

High Kite (IRE) *Henrietta Knight* 84h
5 bb g High-Rise(IRE) —Sister Rose (IRE) (Roselier (FR))
1824^{9} 2518^{7} 3365^{8} 4006^{6}

Highland Cadett *Rod Millman* 83h
4 ch g Putra Sandhurst(IRE) —Highland Rossie (Pablond)
1772^{4} 1935^{5} 2133^{8} 2485^{6}

Highland Cathedral *James Walton* 33h
7 ch g Minster Son—Celtic Waters (Celtic Cone)
1785^{7} 5031^{9}

Highland Legacy *Jim Best* 103h
7 ch g Selkirk(USA) —Generous Lady (Generous (IRE))
2960^{18} 3340^{9} 3556^{12} 3719^{4} 5322^{4}

Highland Love *Jedd O'Keeffe* 107h
6 b g Fruits Of Love(USA) —Diabaig (Precocious)
2092^{3} 2361^{16}

Highland River *Aytach Sadik* 91h
5 b g Indian Creek—Bee One (IRE) (Catrail (USA))
3^{P} 382^{8} 932^{11} 1066^{P}

Highland Storm *Ben Pollock* 68h
5 b g Storming Home—Real Emotion (USA) (El Prado (IRE))
1693^{P}

Highland Valley (IRE) *Emma Lavelle* 133h
6 ch g Flemensfirth(USA) —Loch Lomond (IRE) (Dry Dock)
(2283) ◆ 2888^{4} (4091) 4803^{10}

Highly Elaborate (IRE) *James Bennett* 22h
6 b m Halling(USA) —Elaborate (Sadler's Wells (USA))
2054^{9}

Highly Regal (IRE) *Roger Teal* 100h
6 b g High Chaparral(IRE) —Regal Portrait (IRE) (Royal Academy (USA))
2495^{3} 5050^{3}

High Oscar *Richard Rowe* 110c
10 b g Oscar(IRE) —Highfrith (Deep Run)
(1916)
2134^{3} 2429^{2} 2928^{9} 3349^{P} 4770^{3} 5194^{6}

High Rank *H J Franklin* 84h 61c
12 b g Emperor Jones(USA) —Hotel Street (USA) (Alleged (USA))
4748^{7} 5283^{P}

High Ransom *Micky Hammond* 110h
4 b f Red Ransom(USA) —Shortfall (Last Tycoon)
3711^{2} (3999) 4847^{17}

Highrate (IRE) *Sue Smith* 92b
5 b g Presenting—Hollygrove Cliche (Classic Cliche (IRE))
4547^{5} 5426^{2}

High Road (IRE) *Jonjo O'Neill* 76b
4 b g Beneficial—The Long Bill (IRE) (Phardante (FR))
5210^{7}

High Rolling *Tim Easterby*
4 b g Fantastic Light(USA) —Roller Girl (Merdon Melody)
3711^{P}

High Skies *Dr Richard Newland* 109h 118c
8 b g Kahyasi—High Summer (USA) (Nureyev (USA))
354^{P} 767^{5} (865) 933^{9} **1070^{P}** 1258^{3} 1431^{4}
1555^{P} **1612^{P}**

High Stand Lad *Martin Todhunter* 103h 108c
9 gr g Rock City—Snowys Pet (Petong)
403^{3} 860^{7} (1001)
1403^{P}

High Toby *Raymond York* 69h 98c
12 b g Dancing High—Henny Penny (Le Coq D'Or)
294^{5} 4429^{6} 4829^{U}

Hightown (IRE) *Don Cantillon* 92b
4 b g King's Theatre(IRE) —Faucon (Polar Falcon (USA))
2052^{4} 2315^{9} 5210^{5}

Highway Code (USA) *Richard Lee* 126h
5 b g Street Cry(IRE) —Fairy Heights (IRE) (Fairy King (USA))
2322^{F} 2362^{2} 3563^{F} (4031) 4291^{7} (4952)

Highway Magic (IRE) *Alan Jarvis* 59h
5 ch g Rainbow Quest(USA) —Adultress (IRE) (Ela-Mana-Mou)
360^{11}

Hi Ho Silvia *Neil King* 82h
6 b m Silver Patriarch(IRE) —Dunraven Girl (Seymour Hicks (FR))
4401^{P} 4814^{P} 5130^{2} (5350)

Hijack The Duke (IRE) *John Ferguson* 60b
5 b g Exit To Nowhere(USA) —Pharleng (IRE) (Phardante (FR))
1817^{9} 1955^{7}

Hildisvini (IRE) *Charlie Longsdon* 121h
5 b g Milan—Site Mistress (IRE) (Remainder Man)
(3773) (4325) ◆ (4918)

Hilfiger (GER) *Ian Williams* 116h
6 b g Lando(GER) —Hollywood Dream (GER) (Master Willie)
97^{2} ◆ (733)

Hill Forts Gloria (IRE) *Seamus Mullins* 95h
6 b m King's Theatre(IRE) —Ad Gloria (IRE) (Shernazar)
27^{3} 1675^{2} 2130^{4} 2627^{4} 3227^{10} 4897^{4}

Hills Of Aran *Keith Goldsworthy* 143h 118c
9 b g Sadler's Wells(USA) —Danefair (Danehill (USA))
1855^{12} 1967^{4} 2523^{5}
2673^{9} 3195^{4} 3561^{11} 3807^{11} 4185^{8}

Himalayan Express *Charlie Longsdon* 67h 58c
7 b g Rakaposhi King—Street Magic (IRE) (Jolly Jake (NZ))
429^{6} 693^{8}

Himayna *Tim Vaughan* 96h
7 b m Generous(IRE) —Himaya (IRE) (Mouktar)
27^{4} 230^{7} 1308^{3} 1553^{6} 1703^{2} 2072^{5} 3155^{7}
3697^{3} 4263^{4}

Himba *Nick Gifford* 58h 60c
8 b g Vettori(IRE) —Be My Wish (Be My Chief (USA))
532^{P}

Himitas (FR) *Graeme McPherson* 87h
6 b m Lomitas—Himaya (IRE) (Mouktar)
684^{P} 843^{5} 910^{4} 1449^{4} 1559^{4} 1840^{5} 2244^{P}

Himrayn *Anabel L M King* 101h 122c
8 b g Generous(IRE) —Himaya (IRE) (Mouktar)
154^{2} 678^{3} 2927^{7} 3509^{7} **(4744)**
(5015) 5134^{P}

Hindon Road (IRE) *Alan King* 74b
4 b g Antonius Pius(USA) —Filoli Gardens (Sanglamore (USA))
4866^{9}

Hinton Indiana *Nicky Henderson* 106b
6 b g Kayf Tara—Hinton Grace (Vital Season)
3511^{3} 4491^{4}

Hinton Luciana *Nicky Henderson*
8 ch m Double Trigger(IRE) —Hinton Grace (Vital Season)
538^{P} 763^{P}

Hippodrome (IRE) *John Harris* 96h
9 b g Montjeu(IRE) —Moon Diamond (Unfuwain (USA))
1329^{5} 1555^{5} 1726^{11} 2247^{2} 2477^{4} 3693^{10}
4380^{4} 4833^{3}

Hippolytus *Lucinda Russell* 83h
6 ch g Observatory(USA) —Pasithea (IRE) (Celtic Swing)
397^{5} 604^{3}

His Lordship *Grant Cann* 98h
7 ch g Karinga Bay—Friendly Lady (New Member)
319^{11} 3647^{2} 4029^{6}

History Lesson *Alan Jones* 62h
5 ch g Golan(IRE) —Once Upon A Time (Teenoso (USA))
2283^{U} 4225^{P} 4528^{P}

Hi Tide (IRE) *J R Jenkins* 108h 119c
7 br g Idris(IRE) —High Glider (High Top)
1084^{8}
1485^{F} 1693^{4} 1883^{6} 2313^{3} 4311^{4}

Hit The Headlines (IRE) *Nicky Henderson* 121b
5 b g Flemensfirth(USA) —Heather Breeze (IRE) (Lord Americo)
(3546) ◆ 4491^{6}

Hivikos (FR) *Mrs P J Buckler* 117h 105c
8 ch g Nikos—Hijika (FR) (Silver Cape (FR))
(195) **5083^{P}**

Hi Wycombe (IRE) *David Bridgwater* 98h
7 b g Dr Massini(IRE) —Merric (IRE) (Electric)
711^{4} 932^{10} 1124^{U} 1249^{2} 1431^{7} 1506^{P} 1679^{8}
1857^{6} 1996^{10} 2054^{4}

Hoare Abbey (IRE) *Tom George* 90b
5 ch g Definite Article—Tourist Attraction (IRE) (Pollerton)
3372^{4} 4356^{12}

Hoar Frost *Karen Tutty* 99h
6 b m Fraam—Natalie Jay (Ballacashtal (CAN))
600^{2} (845) 984^{4} 1147^{4} 1732^{13} 2937^{9} 3951^{6}
4390^{11} 4572^{6} 5130^{4} ◆ 5308^{2}

Hoback Junction (IRE) *Lucy Wadham* 122h
7 b g Heron Island(IRE) —Lizzie Simms (IRE) (Phardante (FR))
1952^{P} 2111^{3} 2387^{14}

Hobb's Dream (IRE) *Neil Mulholland* 81h 102c
7 br m Winged Love(IRE) —La-Greine (Strong Gale)
1678^{P} 1969^{2} 2391^{2}
(3377) (3527)
3900^{5} 4219^{5}

Hobsons Bay (IRE) *Howard Johnson* 103h
6 b g Flemensfirth(USA) —Ou La La (IRE) (Be My Native (USA))
3885^{4} 4278^{2} 5028^{12}

Hocinail (FR) *P Goldsworthy* 55c
7 ch g Majorien—Flamme (FR) (Shining Steel)
301^{7}

Hockenheim (FR) *George Bewley* 126h 123c
10 b g Kadalko(FR) —L'Inka (FR) (R B Chesne)
2272^{5} 4167^{3} 4357^{P}

Hohlethelonely *Venetia Williams* 103h
7 ch g Medicean—Now And Forever (IRE) (Kris)
231^{3}

Hoh Viss *Caroline Bailey* 90h 132c
11 b g Rudimentary(USA) —Now And Forever (IRE) (Kris)
2477^{9} 2983^{F} 3303^{5} 3493^{P}

Holden Caulfield (IRE) *Nick Ayliffe* 87h
6 b g Catcher In The Rye(IRE) —God Speed Her (Pas De Seul)
1333^{P} 1488^{5} 1844^{12} 5244^{3}

Hold Fast (IRE) *Howard Johnson* 129h 130c
7 ch g Flemensfirth(USA) —Delko (Decent Fellow)
1930^{4} (3393)
5165^{U}

Hold On Julio (IRE) *Vicky Simpson* 113c
8 br g Blueprint(IRE) —Eileens Native (IRE) (Be My Native (USA))
(5148)

Hold The Bid (IRE) *Sue Smith* 102h 108c
11 bb g Luso—Killesk Castle (IRE) (Little Bighorn)
11^{3} 352^{6} 608^{4} 985^{6}

Hold The Pin (IRE) *A J Martin* 139h 133c
12 b g Oscar(IRE) —Carnbelle (IRE) (Electric)
3475a^{14}

Hole In One (IRE) *Lucinda Russell* 78h
5 b m Saddlers' Hall(IRE) —Shuildante (IRE) (Phardante (FR))
2353^{9} 3331^{6} 4000^{4}

Holiday Cocktail *John Quinn* 106h
9 b g Mister Baileys—Bermuda Lily (Dunbeath (USA))
1328^{5} (1660) 2169^{5}

Hollandia (IRE) *Kathleen Sanderson* 67h 28c
10 gr g Needle Gun(IRE) —Steel Mariner (Kambalda)
1494^{P}
1924^{10}

Hollies Favourite (IRE) *Louise Davis* 104h
8 b g Great Palm(USA) —Sweet Marie (IRE) (Archway (IRE))
582^{7} 837^{10} 917^{3} 1035^{7} 1450^{2} 1554^{6}

Hollins *Micky Hammond* 135h
7 b g Lost Soldier(USA) —Cutting Reef (IRE) (Kris)
4169^{3} 4852^{6} 5304^{5}

Hollo Ladies (IRE) *Ferdy Murphy* 132h 132c
6 ch g Captain Rio—Lace Flower (Old Vic)
2299^{U} 2475^{2} 2951^{2} *3169^{4}* **(3394)**
3955^{5} 4820^{14} 5165^{5} 5310^{2}

Hollow Blue Sky (FR) *Nigel Twiston-Davies* 100b
4 gr g Turgeon(USA) —Run For Laborie (FR) (Lesotho (USA))
3903^{4} 4943^{4}

Hollow Ranger (IRE) *Miss Sally Randell* 64h 46c
10 b g Norwich—Clarina Queen (IRE) (Orchestra)
4293^{7}

Hollows Gift (IRE) *Barry Murtagh* 54h
6 b g Darnay—Bellagrana (Belmez (USA))
42^{11}

Hollyrock *Rayson Nixon* 36b
5 b m Rock City—Delightfool (Idiots Delight)
5432^{12}

Holly Tree (IRE) *E Sheehy* 94h 129c
11 br g Accordion—Lime Tree (Bulldozer)
1123a^{9}

Holly Walk *J Cole* 90c
10 ch m Dr Fong(USA) —Holly Blue (Bluebird (USA))
4163[6]

Hollywood Law (IRE) *D M Leigh* 129h 124c
10 ch g Zaffaran(USA) —Whoareyoutoday (IRE) (Strong Gale)
1121a[5] 1346[4]

Holme Rose *Donald McCain* 95b
5 b m Bob Back(USA) —Disallowed (IRE) (Distinctly North (USA))
4468[17]

Holmwood Legend *Patrick Rodford* 100h 146c
10 b g Midnight Legend—West-Hatch-Spirit (Forzando)
1926[4] ◆ **2324[5] (2587)**
2869[5] 3689[2] 4221[F] (4730)
(4820) 5288[2]

Holoko Heights *Tim Vaughan* 116h 125c
6 br g Pivotal—Treble Heights (IRE) (Unfuwain (USA))
715[9] (984) (1085) 1406[3] **(1485)**
1558[P] 4406[4] 4939[4]

Holy Balloney *Anabel L M King* 34h
8 b g Kayf Tara—Ballon (Persian Bold)
1296[5]

Holy Joe (FR) *Mrs C A Coward* 107c
14 b g Pharly(FR) —Niffy Nora (Mandalus)
153[7]

Holyrood *Tim Vaughan* 100h 89c
5 b g Falbrav(IRE) —White Palace (Shirley Heights)
1574[4] 2583[7] 2795[2] 3297[7] **4033[5]**

Home *Brendan Powell* 91h 103c
6 b g Domedriver(IRE) —Swahili (IRE) (Kendor (FR))
2049[7] 4922[6] 5193[4]
(5386)

Homeleigh Sir *Shaun Harris*
7 b g Sir Harry Lewis(USA) —Give It A Bash (IRE) (Gianchi)
4974[12]

Homer Run (IRE) *Seamus Mullins* 62h
4 b g Classic Cliche(IRE) —Suir Native (IRE) (Be My Native (USA))
3964[6] 4444[10] 4930[8] 5168[8]

Home She Goes (IRE) *Charles Pogson* 96h 91c
9 br m Bob's Return(IRE) —Vague Resemblance (Furry Glen)
3392[7]
3817[3] 4238[3] 4741[3] 4976[6] 5298[5]

Hommage A Bach (IRE) *Paul John Gilligan* 64h 72c
6 b g Bach(IRE) —Elinor Glyn (IRE) (Glacial Storm (USA))
4179[3] 4394[P] 4414[2]

Honest *Karen George* 83h
8 b g Double Trigger(IRE) —Nothings Forever (Oats)
3691[14] 3906[9] **4269[F]** 4450[8] 4900[P]

Honeycombe *Mrs S P Stretton* 60h
10 b m Relief Pitcher—Hanglands (Bustino)
185[6] 384[7]

Honeycreeper *Renee Robeson* 83b
4 ch f Sir Harry Lewis(USA) —Hazel Grouse (Absalom)
4184[4]

Hong Kong Harry *Alan King* 115h
7 b g Sir Harry Lewis(USA) —Hong Kong Classic (Anshan)
2512[2] 3950[P] 4370[2] 4988[P]

Honorable Endeavor *Edward Vaughan* 60h
5 b g Law Society(USA) —Lilac Dance (Fabulous Dancer (USA))
843[7] 988[P]

Honorary Title (IRE) *Tim Vaughan* 117h
6 ch g Ashkalani(IRE) —Bramble Hall (IRE) (Saddlers' Hall (IRE))
(4)

Honourable Arthur (IRE) *Victor Dartnall* 95h 125c
8 br g Presenting—Ronkino (IRE) (Rising)
1912[8] 2146[4] (3450)
(3741) (4313) ◆ **4877[P]**

Honourable Dreamer (IRE) *Jonjo O'Neill* 76h
6 b g City Honours(USA) —Crucial Move (IRE) (Last Tycoon)
1741[P] 2244[6] 3400[5]

Honourable Spider *Mrs Suzy Bull* 25c
12 br g Nomadic Way(USA) —Baroness Spider (Baron Blakeney)
296[P]

Honour's Dream (FR) *Mrs Jenny Gordon* 83h 113c
8 ch g Acatenango(GER) —The Last Dream (FR) (Arazi (USA))
280[6] 4374[2] 4701[3]

Honour The King (IRE) *Peter Bowen* 74b
5 bb g Insan(USA) —Cassies Girl (IRE) (Mandalus)
3191[3]

Hoof It Harry (IRE) *Paul Henderson* 97h 109c
10 ch g City Honours(USA) —Miss Boots (IRE) (Brush Aside (USA))
181[3] (529)
691[2] 867[P] 1281[4]

Hooked On Line (IRE) *Pam Sly* 9h
6 b g Catcher In The Rye(IRE) —Pohutakawa (FR) (Affirmed (USA))
14[6]

Hooky's Hope *Harriet Graham* 77h
8 b m Endoli(USA) —Hooky's Treat (Dutch Treat)
212[9] 461[6] 871[8]

Hoopy (IRE) *Gordon Elliott* 128h 128c
9 ch g Presenting—Simply Joyful (Idiots Delight)
446[9] 1373[P] 3709a[18]

Hopatina (IRE) *Neil Mulholland*
5 b m Flemensfirth(USA) —Bonny Lass (Bonny Scot (IRE))
3979[7] 4535[12]

Hopeand *Charles Pogson* 98h
6 b m King's Theatre(IRE) —Land Of Glory (Supreme Leader)
50[6]

Hopeful Dream (IRE) *Seamus Mullins*
6 ch m Atraf—Brownsfield (IRE) (Ajraas (USA))
1201[14]

Hopeful Start (IRE) *Jonjo O'Neill* 132h 64c
7 b g Flemensfirth(USA) —Calishee (IRE) (Callernish)
2979[8] 3254[4] 3871[9] 4267[3]

Hopes Up *Ian Williams* 73b
4 ch f Trade Fair—Nursling (IRE) (Kahyasi)
2824[7] 3406[7] 4335[8]

Horatio Caine (FR) *Nick Williams* 115h
4 b g Assessor(IRE) —Red Flower (USA) (Trempolino (USA))
1658a[7] 2356[4] 2882[8] 5047a[7]

Horner Woods (IRE) *Nicky Henderson* 119h 134c
9 br g Presenting—Horner Water (IRE) (Over The River (FR))
2871[13] 3444[P]

Horseford Hill *Miss J R Tooth* 109h
7 b g In The Wings—Love Of Silver (USA) (Arctic Tern (USA))
503[P]

Horseshoe Reef (AUS) *Jamie Snowden* 105h 113c
8 b g Encosta De Lago(AUS) —Christies Beach (AUS) (Naturalism (NZ))
234[3] 594[5] 2580[4] 3306[P]
(4768) 5271[5]

Horsford (IRE) *David Pipe* 125h 122c
7 b g Winged Love(IRE) —Ecyba (FR) (Cyborg (FR))
2977[8] 3299[2] **3690[4] 4408[2]**

Horsham Lad (IRE) *F M O'Brien* 68h 122c
7 b g Muroto—Comeragh Queen (The Parson)
(79) **4374[P]**

Hot Candy *Reg Hollinshead*
7 ch m Classic Cliche(IRE) —Derring Floss (Derring Rose)
1821[P] 2069[P]

Hot Chipotle *Paul Henderson* 35h
5 b m Terimon—Fountain Well (Shambo)
1812[11] 2051[5]

Hot Choc (IRE) *John Ryall* 83h
9 br g Darnay—Vulcan Belle (Royal Vulcan)
185[P]

Hotgrove Boy *George Foster* 74h
4 b g Tobougg(IRE) —Tanwir (Unfuwain (USA))
4473[7] 5151[4] 5428[6]

Hot Head *Tim Vaughan*
4 b g Selkirk(USA) —Treble Heights (IRE) (Unfuwain (USA))
3166[6]

Hot 'N' Holy *David Thompson* 89h 90c
12 b g Supreme Leader—Clonmello (Le Bavard (FR))
4915[3] 5338[P]

Hot Tottie (IRE) *Jeremy Scott* 100h
7 b m Lahib(USA) —Midway (IRE) (Warcraft (USA))
313[9] 737[8] 1737[5] 2280[4] (2795) 2980[2]

Houblon Des Obeaux (FR) *Venetia Williams* 137h
4 b g Panoramic—Harkosa (FR) (Nikos)
3436[2] ◆ (4205) 4847[16] 5161[3]

House Of Bourbon (IRE) *Tim Vaughan* 116h 104c
8 ch g Rainbow Quest(USA) —Her Ladyship (Polish Precedent (USA))
(227) (771)
1570[P] 1992[4] 2483[2]

Howard's Legacy (IRE) *Venetia Williams* 107b
5 b g Generous(IRE) —Ismene (FR) (Bad Conduct (USA))
3546[4] 3903[2] 4561[S] 4879[4]

Howizee *Maurice Barnes* 92h
5 gr g Baryshnikov(AUS) —Sendai (Le Moss)
1764[8] 2075[3] 3851[P]

How Realee (IRE) *Nigel Hawke* 65h
8 br g Kotashaan(FR) —Lucky Diverse (IRE) (Lucky Guest)
264[P]

How's My Friend *Grant Cann* 106h
6 b g Karinga Bay—Friendly Lady (New Member)
3651[4] 3903[5] 4444[8] 5152[2]

Hows The Boy *Victor Dartnall*
8 ch g Bandmaster(USA) —Fashion Princess (Van Der Linden (FR))
167[P]

Hows Trix (IRE) *Ferdy Murphy* 86h 93c
11 b g Lord Americo—Bannow Drive (IRE) (Miner's Lamp)
552[9]

Hucking Hero (IRE) *Tim Vaughan* 117h
6 b g Iron Mask(USA) —Selkirk Flyer (Selkirk (USA))
5396[3]

Huckleberry (IRE) *James Unett* 80h 69c
9 b g Hubbly Bubbly(USA) —Laur's Melody (IRE) (Meneval (USA))
3527[2] 4238[8] 4829[6]

Hudibras (IRE) *Charlie Mann* 110h
7 b g Bluebird(USA) —Mannequin (IRE) (In The Wings)
3692[5] 4180[8] **4855[U] 5065[U]**

Hughies Grey (IRE) *Mervyn Torrens* 128h 136c
7 gr g Houmayoun(FR) —Newtown Rosie (IRE) (Roselier (FR))
(5025a) ◆

Huguenot (IRE) *Philip Hobbs* 103h 125c
8 b g King's Best(USA) —Kingsridge (IRE) (King's Theatre (IRE))
57[2] 361[3] 592[4] 831[F]

Humbel Ben (IRE) *Alan Jones* 116h 88c
8 br g Humbel(USA) —Donegans Daughter (Auction Ring (USA))
372[2] (756) 3440[P] **3838[4] 4507[U] 5155[P]**

Humbel Lad (IRE) *Richard Guest* 84h
7 ch g Humbel(USA) —Loughrealt (Carlingford Castle)
596[U] 683[3] 744[9] 1700[14] **1995[P]**

Humbel Times (IRE) *Neil King* 62h 73c
7 b g Humbel(USA) —Polleroo (IRE) (Pollerton)
2493[8] 3303[P] 3603[4] 3833[P] 4378[3]
4693[6] (4799)

Humbie (IRE) *Pauline Robson* 115h 126c
7 b g Karinga Bay—South Queen Lady (IRE) (King's Ride)
396[6] **3520[6]**
4275[2] (4938)
5341[5]

Hume River (IRE) *Mrs John Harrington* 66h 134c
9 b g Sassanian(USA) —Muchsorrylady (IRE) (Boreen (FR))
3798a[P]

Humor Me Rene (USA) *George Baker*
4 bb f Kitten's Joy(USA) —Star Of Humor (USA) (Distorted Humor (USA))
5435[P]

Humourous (IRE) *Brian Storey* 78h
9 b g Darshaan—Amusing Time (IRE) (Sadler's Wells (USA))
10[3] 176[P] 424[U] 861[9] 871[P] 1362[10] 1504[6]

Huncheon Wells (IRE) *R T J Wilson* 105h 104c
9 b g Clerkenwell(USA) —Waterland Lady (Strong Gale)
442[2]

Hungry For More *Mark Hoad* 84h
7 b g Silver Patriarch(IRE) —Plaything (High Top)
3611[P] 3983[P]

Hunt Ball (IRE) *Patrick Rodford* 50h 71c
6 b g Winged Love(IRE) —La Fandango (IRE) (Taufan (USA))
3908[P] 5290[4]

Hunters Belt (IRE) *Noel Wilson* 108h
7 b g Intikhab(USA) —Three Stars (Star Appeal)
4995[5] (5357)

Hunters Ploy (IRE) *Nigel Twiston-Davies* 117h 136c
9 ch g Deploy—Hunt The Thimble (FR) (Relkino)
2273[4] 3347[F]

Hunterview *David Pipe* 140h
5 ch g Reset(AUS) —Mount Elbrus (Barathea (IRE))
207[13] 2868[11] 3298[3] (3969) 4848[12] 5337[6]

Huntingford (IRE) *Tracey Barfoot-Saunt* 40c
8 b g Sassanian(USA) —Nancy Whiskey (IRE) (Alphabatim (USA))
2[4] 758[P]

Hunting Red *Jonathen de Giles* 74b
6 b m Hunting Lion(IRE) —Micklow Magic (Farfelu)
254[11] 589[14] 4268[F]

Hurricane Electric (IRE) *Graeme McPherson* 90h
6 b g Dansili—Heaven's Echo (USA) (Woodman (USA))
(328) 480[2] 2558[6] 3603[P] 4559[2] 5103[P]

Hurricane Fly (IRE) *W P Mullins* 170h
7 b g Montjeu(IRE) —Scandisk (IRE) (Kenmare (FR))
(2968a) ◆ (3205a) (3707a) (4791)

Hurricane Jack *Lucinda Russell* 97h 102c
8 gr g Silver Patriarch(IRE) —Gale (Strong Gale)
287[2] (872)

Hurryonharry *Brian Storey* 48b
5 b g Erhaab(USA) —Gypsy Race (IRE) (Good Thyne (USA))
311[15] 731[9]

Hurst Park (IRE) *Susan Gardner* 17h
9 b g Mtoto—Shotoski (Petoski)
1445[F] 1488[8] 1553[P]

Hustle (IRE) *Gay Kelleway* 98h
6 ch g Choisir(AUS) —Granny Kelly (USA) (Irish River (FR))
1433[4] 1832[4]

Hyde Place *Michael Dods* 79b
4 b g Tiger Hill(IRE) —Hyde Hall (Barathea (IRE))
3889[6] 4259[7]

Hypnotic Gaze (IRE) *Andrew Haynes* 109h
5 b g Chevalier(IRE) —Red Trance (IRE) (Soviet Star (USA))
97[4] ◆ 712[3] 983[5] 2477[F] (4452) 4776[2] 5014[U]
5232[6]

Ibn Hiyyan (USA) *Ferdy Murphy* 88h
4 rg g El Prado(IRE) —Lovely Later (USA) (Green Dancer (USA))
1984[5] 2614[5] 3443[5] 5296[4]

Ibrox (IRE) *Alan Brown* 91h
6 b g Mujahid(USA) —Ling Lane (Slip Anchor)
837[5]

I Can Run Can You (IRE) *Jonjo O'Neill* 106h
5 ch g Old Vic—Merry Batim (IRE) (Alphabatim (USA))
58[8] 224[3] 1046[5] 1294[2] 1592[P] 3256[4] 3622[2]
3745[2] (4559) (5132)

Icansayno (IRE) *Lawney Hill* 54b
5 gr m Environment Friend—Begsy's Bullet (Primitive Rising (USA))
2156[11]

Ice Boru (IRE) *Mike Hammond* 14b
5 br m Brian Boru—Glacial Field (IRE) (Glacial Storm (USA))
589[12] 935[12]

Ice Bucket (IRE) *A Phillips* 91h 121c
11 ch g Glacial Storm(USA) —Tranbu (IRE) (Buckskin (FR))
65[4] 4011[3] 4271[F] 4991[3] 5207[7]

Ice Image (IRE) *George Charlton* 93h 106c
9 b g Darnay—Ice Trix (IRE) (Glacial Storm (USA))
9[U] 88[4] 460[2] 578[8] 860[5] 1001[3] 1378[6] 3503[U] (3997)
4392[3] 4963[9]

Iceman George *Giles Bravery* 117h
7 b g Beat Hollow—Diebiedale (Dominion)
(1812) 2081[3] ◆

Ice 'N' Easy (IRE) *Richard Rowe* 45h
5 b g Dushyantor(USA) —Glacial Valley (IRE) (Glacial Storm (USA))
2445[4] 3434[P] 4329[5] 4918[6]

Ice Tea (IRE) *Mrs S K McCain* 124h 138c
11 ch g Glacial Storm(USA) —Kakemona (Kambalda)
(334) **525[6]**
(4286)
4699[2] 5163[F]

Ice Warrior (IRE) *Milton Harris* 127h 108c
9 b g New Frontier(IRE) —Quinnsboro Ice (IRE) (Glacial Storm (USA))
1227[2] 1297[3]

Iconic Rose *Pam Sly* 45b
4 ch f Sir Harry Lewis(USA) —Standing Bloom (Presidium)
4335[11]

Iconoclast (IRE) *Alex Hales* 123h 141c
10 bb g Topanoora—La Cigale (IRE) (Lafontaine (USA))
(2140)
(4200)

Icy Colt (ARG) *Paul Webber* 106h
5 br g Colonial Affair(USA) —Icy Desert (USA) (Desert Secret (IRE))
4[3] 1553[3] (1829) 2375[7] 5117[8]

Idarah (USA) *Paul Cashman* 126h 133c
8 gr g Aljabr(USA) —Fatina (Nashwan (USA))
3706a[U]

Identimin *Caroline Keevil* 25h
7 b m Tamure(IRE) —Minigale (Strong Gale)
5152[9]

Identity Parade (IRE) *Donald McCain* 107h 110c
7 b m Witness Box(USA) —New Line (IRE) (Roselier (FR))
(223) (514) 1959[P] 2552[3] **2978[6] 3763[3] (4254)**
4831 5150[P]

Idle Talk (IRE) *Mrs S K McCain* 130h 129c
12 br g Hubbly Bubbly(USA) —Belon Breeze (IRE) (Strong Gale)
4211[3]

Idol Deputy (FR) *James Bennett* 13h
5 gr g Silver Deputy(CAN) —Runaway Venus (USA) (Runaway Groom (CAN))
1705[P] 1914[11] 2129[11]

Idris (GER) *Philip Sharp* 95h 115c
10 ch g Generous(IRE) —Idraak (Kris)
1918[P] 2949[P] 4130[11]

I Feel Fine *Alan Kirtley* 38h
8 ch m Minster Son—Jendorcet (Grey Ghost)
421[7]

If I Had Him (IRE) *George Baker* 113h
7 b g City Honours(USA) —Our Valentine (IRE) (Be My Native (USA))
2058[4] (2633) 3686[5] 4008[2] 4503[2]

If I Were A Boy (IRE) *Dominic Ffrench Davis* 45h
4 b f Invincible Spirit(IRE) —Attymon Lill (IRE) (Marju (IRE))
2151[8]

If You Knew Suzy *Hon Barr* 16h
6 b m Efisio—Sioux (Kris)
12[P]

I Got Music *Keith Reveley* 88h
4 gr f Silver Patriarch(IRE) —I Got Rhythm (Lycius (USA))
2655[7] 3358[4] 3818[3] 4148[5] 4452[4]

I Have Dreamed (IRE) *S Flook* 134h 137c
9 b g Montjeu(IRE) —Diamond Field (USA) (Mr Prospector (USA))
2086[3] (4936)

Ihaventabob (IRE) *Aidan Anthony Howard* 78h 100c
7 b g Old Vic—Dame Daffodil (IRE) (Petorius)
(1425)
2079[5]

I Hear A Symphony (IRE) *J J Lambe* 131h 133c
9 b g Accordion—Annilogs Daughter (IRE) (Yashgan)
170[3] 3475a[17] **3706a[13] 5025a[5]**

Iheardu *Neil Mulholland* 101c
5 b g Overbury(IRE) —Tina Gee (Orchestra)
4096[5] 4445[6] 5068[P]

I Hear Thunder (IRE) *Nick Mitchell* 30h 123c
13 b g Montelimar(USA) —Carrigeen Gala (Strong Gale)
4701[4]

Ikidunot (IRE) *Mrs Maureen Danagher* 130h
7 br g Definite Article—Sweet Rocket (IRE) (Phardante (FR))
1121a[14]

I Know The Code (IRE) *Noel Chance* 100b
6 b g Viking Ruler(AUS) —Gentle Papoose (Commanche Run)
1927[2] 5113[8]

Ikorodu Road *Martin Keighley* 117h 142c
8 b g Double Trigger(IRE) —Cerisier (IRE) (Roselier (FR))
714[U] 1970[2] 2959[3] ◆ **3198[U] 4487[F] 4531[3]**

Il Duce (IRE) *Alan King* 130h 130c
11 br g Anshan—Glory-Glory (IRE) (Buckskin (FR))
1861[8] 2531[3] 3290[P] 4284[P]

Il En Reve (FR) *Milan Theimer* 101h 115c
13 b g Denham Red(FR) —Itaparica (FR) (Mistigri)
1811a[P]

Ilewin Dundee *Gary Brown* 80b
5 b g Loup Sauvage(USA) —Ilewin Janine (IRE) (Soughaan (USA))
759[3]

Ilewin Tom *Gary Brown* 25h 101c
8 b g Alflora(IRE) —Bridepark Rose (IRE) (Kemal (FR))
63[8] 650[P] 913[8] 1272[11]
1293[5] 1450[15]
(3867) 3959[2] (5216)

Illegale (IRE) *Venetia Williams* 35h
5 b m Poliglote—Pinkai (IRE) (Caerleon (USA))
263[8]

Illysantachristina *Bernard Llewellyn* 99h
8 b m Parthian Springs—Arian Spirit (IRE) (High Estate)
1921[11] 2068[10] 2231[5] 3255[2] 3839[3] 4161[3]
(4769) (5346) ◆

Ilongue (FR) *Laura Hurley* 45h 73c
10 b m Nononito(FR) —Marie De Geneve (FR) (Nishapour (FR))
3898[4] 4269[3] 5062[F] 5266[2]

Il Portico *Gary Moore* 95h
4 b g Zafeen(FR) —Diddymu (IRE) (Revoque (IRE))
1882[4] 2047[4] 2528[7]

I'm A Legend *Neil Mulholland* 114h 130c
9 b g Midnight Legend—I'm Maggy (NZ) (Danseur Etoile (FR))
1200[P] 1327[4] 1628[6] (1912)
(2217) (2484)
3453[2] 3677[2] 4223[4] 4820[15]
I'm Delilah *Ferdy Murphy* 112h 144c
9 b m Overbury(IRE) —Gallants Delight (Idiots Delight)
2206[F] 2881[12] 3953[6] 4470[2] 5164[3] ◆ 5340[5]
I'm Innocent *Mrs S Watson* 54h
10 b g Silver Patriarch(IRE) —Lady Confess (Backchat (USA))
4534[P]
I'm In The Pink (FR) *David Evans* 118h 92c
7 b g Garuda(IRE) —Ahwaki (FR) (River Mist (USA))
96[9] 500[6] **2153[7] 2330[6]** *3091[5]* (3224) 3477[3]
3818[4] 4008[4]
Immense (IRE) *Ian Williams* 94h
7 b g Montjeu(IRE) —Admiring (USA) (Woodman (USA))
630[5] 2532[5] 3300[6] 5111[P]
I'moncloudnine (IRE) *Neil Mulholland* 90h 138c
8 b g Cloudings(IRE) —I'm Maggy (NZ) (Danseur Etoile (FR))
1769[2] 2221[4] 2543[U] 3437[3] ◆ 3940[4] 4193[4] 5206[5]
Im Ova Ere Dad (IRE) *Don Cantillon* 87h
8 b g Second Empire(IRE) —Eurolink Profile (Prince Sabo)
349[7]
Impact Zone *Michael Easterby* 53h 84c
7 br g Erhaab(USA) —Stormy Gal (IRE) (Strong Gale)
24[3] 211[7]
Imperial Breeze (IRE) *J J Lambe* 104h
6 b g Mr Combustible(IRE) —Imperial Performer (IRE) (Pierre)
42[4] 337[P] 1928[2] 3523[6] (4686) 5028[10]
Imperial Circus (IRE) *Philip Hobbs* 114h
5 b g Beneficial—Aunty Dawn (IRE) (Strong Gale)
2493[6]
Imperial Commander (IRE) *Nigel Twiston-Davies* 135h 182c
10 b g Flemensfirth(USA) —Ballinlovane (Le Moss)
(2524)
4850[P]
Imperial Royale (IRE) *Patrick Clinton* 83h
10 ch g Ali-Royal(IRE) —God Speed Her (Pas De Seul)
2643[3] 3255[8] 3882[3] (4274)
Imperial Shabra (IRE) *Patrick O Brady* 126h
7 b g Imperial Ballet(IRE) —Jane Digby (IRE) (Magical Strike (USA))
1526[9] 1713a[7] 1847a[3] 2260a[5] 3029a[6]
Imperial Sun (IRE) *Mrs A S Hodges* 106h 96c
12 b g Un Desperado(FR) —Ashley's Princess (IRE) (Lafontaine (USA))
4928[9]
Impersonator *Anthony Mullins* 119h
11 b g Zafonic(USA) —Conspiracy (Rudimentary (USA))
(1155a)
Important Business (IRE) *Renee Robeson* 117h 117c
8 ch g Mutamam—Opus One (Slip Anchor)
155[3] 536[2] 838[2]
I'msingingtheblues (IRE) *David Pipe* 137h 158c
9 b g Pistolet Bleu(IRE) —Nova Rose (Ra Nova)
1958[F] 2138[4] 2515[2] 2881[8] 3292[4] 3446[8] 4187[6]
4853[7] 5317[2] 5340[2]
I'm So Lucky *David Pipe* 142h 159c
9 b g Zilzal(USA) —City Of Angels (Woodman (USA))
2885[4] 3675[6] 4805[7]
I'm So Special (IRE) *Noel Chance* 57b
5 b m Milan—Hudson Hope (IRE) (Topanoora)
4027[11]
I'm Supreme (IRE) *Philip Hobbs* 71h 58c
9 b g Supreme Leader—Imtheone (IRE) (Meneval (USA))
131[9] 3599[9] **599[6]**
I'm The Decider (IRE) *Jonjo O'Neill* 126h 108c
9 b g Presenting—Donegal Thyne (IRE) (Good Thyne (USA))
234[4] 476[3] 890[5] 1176[P] 1277[P] 1454[8] 1589[10]
2243[10]
I'm Your Man *Evelyn Slack* 92h 110c
12 gr g Bigstone(IRE) —Snowgirl (IRE) (Mazaad)
88[5] 403[2] 3730[6] 4390[12] 4994[2] 5308[5]
Inca Cave (IRE) *Patrick Rodford* 102h 25c
6 b g Court Cave(IRE) —Inca Hill (IRE) (Insan (USA))
3528[7] 3698[5] 4091[4]
4674[5]
Incendo *James Fanshawe* 89h
5 ch g King's Best(USA) —Kindle (Selkirk (USA))
1688[5]
Incentivise (IRE) *Richard Lee* 86h 129c
8 ch g Snurge—Festive Isle (IRE) (Erins Isle)
567[5] (1968)
(2953) 3568[3] 4333[2] 5423[P]
Inching Closer *R J Hewitt* 121h 99c
14 b g Inchinor—Maiyaasah (Kris)
334[F]
Inchloch *Claire Dyson* 91h
9 ch g Inchinor—Lake Pleasant (IRE) (Elegant Air)
593[5] 1959[P] 2280[7]
2585[F] 3870[5]
Inch Native (IRE) *Denis Paul Murphy* 80b 114c
9 br m Supreme Leader—Birdless Bush (IRE) (Be My Native (USA))
3268a[6] 3779a[P]
In Compliance (IRE) *D T Hughes* 140h 156c
11 b g Old Vic—Lady Bellingham (IRE) (Montelimar (USA))
5200[13]
Incy Wincy *Milton Bradley*
5 b g Zahran(IRE) —Miss Money Spider (IRE) (Statoblest)
1547[U]

Indiana Gold (FR) *Alison Thorpe* 106c
7 b g Sleeping Car(FR) —Gold Wine (FR) (Holst (USA))
746[5] 848[10] 961[3] 1047[5] (1161)
1252[2] 1334[3] 1454[6] 1589[5] 1888[6] 2127[P]
Indian Daudaie (FR) *Paul Nicholls* 131h
4 ch g Nicobar—Aldounia (FR) (Kaldoun (FR))
3802[3] 4083a[5] 4852[4] 5186[F]
Indian Groom (IRE) *Howard Johnson* 133h 130c
6 gr g High Chaparral(IRE) —Taatof (IRE) (Lahib (USA))
1779[U] 4002[2] 4570[3] (5413)
Indian Pipe Dream (IRE) *Aytach Sadik* 9h 117c
9 br g Indian Danehill(IRE) —Build A Dream (USA) (Runaway Groom (CAN))
353[2] 550[3] 716[5] 854[6] 1022[5] 1297[P] 1424[2] 1444[4]
1602[6] 1706[5]
1885[6] 1923[P]
(4469) (5344)
Indian Print (IRE) *V Thompson* 65c
7 ch g Blueprint(IRE) —Commanche Glen (IRE) (Commanche Run)
3991[5]
Indian Snow (IRE) *William Amos* 59h
6 b g Indian Lodge(IRE) —Wet And Windy (Cloudings (IRE))
3572[12] 4304[7] 5091[9]
Indian Spring (IRE) *Gary Moore* 126h
7 br g Indian Danehill(IRE) —Lille Hammer (Sadler's Wells (USA))
3059[12] 3493[P]
Indicco *Ruth Carr* 17b
4 ch f Carnival Dancer—Irish Light (USA) (Irish River (FR))
2824[11] 4801[8]
Indie Go (IRE) *Cathy Hamilton* 95b
5 b g Blueprint(IRE) —Bamji (IRE) (Dr Massini (IRE))
(5408)
Indienne Etoile *Robert Johnson* 33h
7 ch m Dom Alco(FR) —Indienne Efi (FR) (Passing Sale (FR))
14[P] 214[P]
Indigo Dancer *J D J Davies* 60h
8 b g Groom Dancer(USA) —Violet (IRE) (Mukaddamah (USA))
1060[5] 1468[7]
I Need A Hero (IRE) *Sarah Humphrey* 96h 121c
6 b g Oscar Schindler(IRE) —Old Fontaine (IRE) (Millfontaine)
(528) **687[3]**
1068[2] (1255)
1274[4] 1858[6]
Inga Bird *Henry Daly* 104h
6 ch g Karinga Bay—Girlzone (IRE) (Orchestra)
2181[3] 3153[12] 4081[11] 4745[P]
Ingenue *Paul Howling* 81h
5 b m Hernando(FR) —I Do (Selkirk (USA))
478[P] 684[P]
Inghwung *Oliver Sherwood* 109h
9 b m Kayf Tara—Mossy Fern (Le Moss)
1198[6] 1368[3] 1814[2]
In Good Hands *Alan Fleming* 69h
7 b g Oscar(IRE) —Hi Breda (IRE) (Camden Town)
4128[6]
Inishargie (IRE) *S R B Crawford* 100b
7 bb g Exit To Nowhere(USA) —Wilmott's Fancy (Buckley)
876[3]
Inishmor (IRE) *Jeremy Scott* 31b
7 gr g Great Palm(USA) —Kampa Island (IRE) (Turtle Island (IRE))
1989[15]
Inishrush (IRE) *Adrian Chamberlain* 37h
10 br g Presenting—Ballyknock Lass (IRE) (Electric)
1742[10] 1907[7] 2058[P]
Inishturk (IRE) *S R Andrews* 110h 93c
12 bb g Glacial Storm(USA) —Judy Henry (Orchestra)
295[P]
Inkberrow Rose (IRE) *Tom Gretton* 95h
7 b m Glacial Storm(USA) —Inuit (IRE) (Supreme Leader)
2288[7] 2554[5] 3485[6] (3822) 4273[3] (4418)
Inmate (IRE) *Robin Dickin* 81h 115c
10 b g Needle Gun(IRE) —Highland Spirit (Scottish Reel)
755[2] (1128)
1471[F]
In Media Res (FR) *Charlie Longsdon* 104h
10 b g Dushyantor(USA) —Colour Scheme (FR) (Perrault)
232[3] 530[P]
Inner Pride *Don Cantillon* 75b
6 gr m Silver Patriarch(IRE) —Plough Hill (North Briton)
230[10]
Inner Steel (IRE) *Lydia Richards* 109h
6 b g Zagreb(USA) —Mrs McClintock (IRE) (Arctic Lord)
92[2] 2123[7] 2482[10] 4767[2] 5195[3]
Inner Voice (USA) *J J Lambe* 108h
8 gr g Cozzene(USA) —Miss Henderson Co (USA) (Silver Hawk (USA))
1004[7] 1104[7] 1362[4] 1660[3] 1929[4] 3855[6]
Innocent Rebel (USA) *Mrs K Heard* 57h 103c
10 ch g Swain(IRE) —Cadeaux D'Amie (USA) (Lyphard (USA))
148[3] 526[9]
Innominate (IRE) *Lucinda Russell* 110h 99c
9 b g Saddlers' Hall(IRE) —Tip Marie (IRE) (Celio Rufo)
2450[2] 3574[4] 3819[5] 4064[2] (4690)
5095[6]
Inoogoo (IRE) *George Bewley* 105h
6 b g Great Palm(USA) —Ballindante (IRE) (Phardante (FR))
3856[2] 4304[3] 4910[5] 5428[2]

Inside Dealer (IRE) *Colin Tizzard* 99h 130c
7 b g Presenting—Sea Gale (IRE) (Strong Gale)
1912[3] (2243)
2484[2] (2975)
3479[2] ◆ 4095[4] 4730[3] 4987[F]
Insignia (IRE) *Victor Dartnall* 97h 69c
9 b g Royal Applause—Amathea (FR) (Exit To Nowhere (USA))
227[10] 424[6] 4273[F] 4900[7] (5383)
Instabella *Philip Hobbs* 66h
5 ch m Karinga Bay—Instabene (Mossberry)
2168[F] 5167[12]
Instant Decision (IRE) *Peter Bowen* 83b
5 b g Oscar(IRE) —Mrs Kelly (IRE) (Supreme Leader)
602[5] 892[3]
Instant Shot (IRE) *Jim Goldie* 71h 80c
8 b g Definite Article—Mistress Mine (IRE) (King Of Clubs)
160[2]
Instigator *S Donohoe* 100h 100c
8 b g Observatory(USA) —Imaginary (IRE) (Dancing Brave (USA))
4690[U]
Intac (IRE) *Colin Tizzard* 110h 123c
9 b g Dr Massini(IRE) —Nicat (Wolver Hollow)
264[3] 374[2] 651[7] (821) 912[6] **1025[2] (1091)**
1197[4] 1454[4] 1491[7] 1589[3] (1841)
1965[6] 2220[3] 2513[6]
(5391)
Integria *Venetia Williams* 87h
5 b g Intikhab(USA) —Alegria (Night Shift (USA))
1111[6] 1280[4]
Intense Suspense (IRE) *Robin Dickin* 74h 56c
8 ch g Bob's Return(IRE) —In Sin (IRE) (Insan (USA))
1126[5] 1237[P] 1300[8]
1481[F] 1558[P]
Intersky Music (USA) *Jonjo O'Neill* 106h
8 b g Victory Gallop(CAN) —Resounding Grace (USA) (Thunder Gulch (USA))
359[P]
Inthejungle (IRE) *Daniel O'Brien* 100h 110c
8 ch g Bob Back(USA) —Whizz (Salse (USA))
2429[5] 3982[2]
In The Sand (IRE) *Jonjo O'Neill* 39h
5 b g King's Theatre(IRE) —Hannigan's Lodger (IRE) (Be My Native (USA))
2145[13] 2397[P]
Inthesettlement *Donald McCain* 97b
6 gr m Alflora(IRE) —Cheeky Mare (Derrylin)
2546[2] ◆ *3088[5]* 4417[P]
In The System (IRE) *David Phelan*
9 b g Corrouge(USA) —Cover Story (Cut Above)
4131[P]
In The Tuns (IRE) *Kate Walton* 58b
5 b g Zagreb(USA) —Pomorie (IRE) (Be My Guest (USA))
3889[9] 4287[17]
In The Zone (IRE) *Jonjo O'Neill* 113h 121c
7 br g Bob Back(USA) —Fairy Native (IRE) (Be My Native (USA))
1136[5] 1283[9] (1493)
(1991) ◆ 2073[2] 2670[2] 3198[6] 4490[7] 4877[2] ◆
Into The Light *Philip Kirby* 83h
6 b g Fantastic Light(USA) —Boadicea's Chariot (Commanche Run)
5131[12] 5260[4]
Inventor (IRE) *Donald McCain* 142h
6 b g Alzao(USA) —Magnificent Bell (IRE) (Octagonal (NZ))
(627) 1017[13] 1311[4] 4848[16] 5166[F]
Inverclyde (IRE) *Bill Turner* 63b
4 bb g Westerner—Glenmoss Tara (IRE) (Zaffaran (USA))
4923[9] 5056[4]
Investment Affair (IRE) *Sarah Humphrey* 81h 87c
11 b g Sesaro(USA) —Superb Investment (IRE) (Hatim (USA))
3305[4] 3541[F] 3608[P] 4022[F] 4560[5] 4880[2]
Investment Wings (IRE) *P Kelsall* 84h
9 b g In The Wings—Superb Investment (IRE) (Hatim (USA))
232[P]
Invictus (IRE) *Alan King* 124h
5 b g Flemensfirth(USA) —Clashwilliam Girl (IRE) (Seymour Hicks (FR))
3346[4] 3719[U] ◆ 4159[3] 4725[10] (5225)
In Vigo (IRE) *William Jarvis* 73b
4 b g Hawk Wing(USA) —Marie De Blois (IRE) (Barathea (IRE))
3406[8] 3957[18]
Invisible Man (FR) *Ian Williams* 122h 139c
6 ch g Mansonnien(FR) —J'y Reste (FR) (Freedom Cry)
(838)
(1113a) ◆ 1627[3] 4941[2] 5199[P]
Iolith (GER) *Alan King* 127h
6 b g Monsun(GER) —Indian Jewel (GER) (Local Suitor (USA))
(2122) (3225) 4270[5] 5182[P]
Iona Days (IRE) *Henrietta Knight* 104h 96c
6 br g Epistolaire(IRE) —Miss Best (FR) (Grand Tresor (FR))
1675[F] 1988[6] 2322[5]
3494[4] 4744[6]
Iphar (FR) *Giles Smyly*
10 br g Panoramic—Ipharita (FR) (Dearling (FR))
156[P]
Irene Kennet *Martin Bosley* 85b
4 b f Kayf Tara—Evaporate (Insan (USA))
4356[9] 5119[4]
Iris De Balme (FR) *Joanna Davis* 104h 66c
11 ch g Phantom Breeze—Fleur D'Ecajeul (FR) (Cyborg (FR))
5338[P] 5443[P]
Irish Airman (IRE) *Paul Nicholls* 72h
6 b g Broadway Flyer(USA) —Ballinamona Lady (IRE) (Le Bavard (FR))
37[4]

Irish Chaperone (IRE) *Keith Reveley* 95b
4 b g High Chaparral(IRE) —Harry's Irish Rose (USA) (Sir Harry Lewis (USA))
4005[2] 4894[3]
Irish Guard *John O'Neill* 105h 116c
10 b g Infantry—Sharp Practice (Broadsword (USA))
24[8] (2424)
(2986) 3371[P] 3878[3] 4237[2] 5279[4]
Irish Joe (USA) *Ray Peacock* 56h
5 gr g Brahms(USA) —Morning Pearl (CAN) (Morning Bob (USA))
1974[7] 2322[12]
Irish Legend (IRE) *Bernard Llewellyn* 116h 121c
11 b g Sadler's Wells(USA) —Wedding Bouquet (Kings Lake (USA))
21[2] 503[F]
Irish Love *Roy Brotherton*
5 b g Pursuit Of Love—Miss Tun (Komaite (USA))
7[9]
Irish Raptor (IRE) *Nigel Twiston-Davies* 115h 135c
12 bb g Zaffaran(USA) —Brownskin (Buckskin (FR))
1960[6] 2221[6] 2543[6] 2871[6]
Irish Stream (USA) *Mrs E Mitchell* 82h 72c
13 ch g Irish River(FR) —Euphonic (USA) (The Minstrel (CAN))
499[11]
Irish Symphony (IRE) *John Mackie* 109h
7 ch m Bach(IRE) —Conna Dodger (IRE) (Kemal (FR))
51[P] 3509[11] 3696[F] 4076[10]
Iris Mary (IRE) *Shaun Lycett* 70b
10 ch m Flemensfirth(USA) —Here To-Day (King's Equity)
766[P] 3485[P]
Iris's Flyer *Brian Rothwell* 92h 97c
9 gr g Terimon—Miss Shaw (Cruise Missile)
2080[8]
2942[4] 3503[6]
Iron Chancellor (IRE) *Alan King* 118h
6 b g Alderbrook—Masriyna (IRE) (Shahrastani (USA))
2238[3] 3153[2] ◆ 3942[2] ◆
Iron Condor *James Eustace* 82h
4 b g Tobougg(IRE) —Coh Sho No (Old Vic)
3944[6]
Ironical (IRE) *Nigel Twiston-Davies* 85h
7 b g Bob's Return(IRE) —Cheryls Pet (IRE) (General Ironside)
249[P] **3265[F]**
Iron Man Of Mersey (FR) *Tony Carroll* 90h
5 b g Poliglote—Miss Echo (Chief Singer)
154[4] 465[5] 792[7] 1066[8] 1125[U]
Isario (GER) *Noel Chance* 84h
6 b g Sholokhov(IRE) —Iaskre (GER) (Slip Anchor)
97[7]
I See A Star *Miss E Stead* 103c
8 br g Dounba(FR) —Starana (FR) (Northern Crystal)
424[P] 456[S] **4476[DSQ]**
Isintshelovely (IRE) *Chris Gordon* 89h 72c
8 ch m Broken Hearted—Sarah Blue (IRE) (Bob Back (USA))
1294[4] 1479[9] (1679) 2391[4]
2947[4]
Isitcozimcool (IRE) *Barry Murtagh* 93h
6 b g Shinko Forest(IRE) —Hazarama (IRE) (Kahyasi)
1148[5] ◆ 1664[9] 1758[7]
Is It Me (USA) *Sophie Leech* 117h 120c
8 ch g Sky Classic(CAN) —Thea (GER) (Surumu (GER))
207[21] 521[7] 633[10] 756[P] 853[3] 1084[3] 1127[4]
1230[4] 1590[2] 1864[2] 2360[P]
Islamouth *Kim Bailey* 106b
7 ch g Karinga Bay—Saffron Delight (Idiots Delight)
238[2]
Island Arrow (IRE) *George Baker* 103h
10 b g Heron Island(IRE) —Fleeting Arrow (IRE) (Commanche Run)
651[P]
Island Chief *Kevin Ryan* 81h
5 b g Reel Buddy(USA) —Fisher Island (IRE) (Sri Pekan (USA))
400[5]
Island Flyer (IRE) *Tom George* 93h 101c
9 bb g Heron Island(IRE) —Lindas Statement (IRE) (Strong Statement (USA))
947[3] 1725[11] 2036[8]
Island Jim (IRE) *Charlie Longsdon* 99h 108c
7 b g Heron Island(IRE) —Jimmy The Bib (IRE) (Glacial Storm (USA))
2058[5]
2527[U] 2949[5]
3433[5] (3878)
Island News *Michael Madgwick* 87h
7 b g Carisbrooke—Sweet N' Twenty (High Top)
2051[7] 5191[2]
Island Oscar (IRE) *Paul A Roche* 126h
7 b g Oscar(IRE) —Paperwork Lady (IRE) (Jurado (USA))
(1175) 3474a[P]
Island Sprite (IRE) *Martin Todhunter* 91b
7 b m Heron Island(IRE) —Saucy Sprite (Balliol)
35[7] 474[2]
Isla Patriot *N W Alexander* 68h
5 b g Silver Patriarch(IRE) —Salem Beach (Strong Gale)
311[11] 3553[10] 4473[9] 4910[9] 5151[10]
Isla Pearl Fisher *N W Alexander* 89h 110c
8 br g Supreme Sound—Salem Beach (Strong Gale)
306[5] (1933)
(2203) 3361[F] (3552)
Isle Of Inishmore (IRE) *Tim Vaughan* 102h 109c
8 b g Tel Quel(FR) —Natidja (FR) (Shardari)
630[7] 826[8] (1253) (1446)
1500[4] (5256)
Isnos (FR) *J Bertran De Balanda* 114h 123c
8 ch g Limnos(JPN) —Isgala (FR) (Galetto (FR))
5159a[7]

Isn't That Lucky *Jonjo O'Neill* 116h 135c
8 b g Alflora(IRE) —Blast Freeze (IRE) (Lafontaine (USA))
1690[P] 3953[3] (4440)
4864[3] 5185[14]

Issaquah (IRE) *Malcolm Jefferson* 142h
9 b m Supreme Leader—Our Sioux (IRE) (Jolly Jake (NZ))
2073[2] 2089[2] 2386[15]

Istron Bay *Richard Lee* 87h 87c
9 b g Petoski—Annie Buckers (IRE) (Yashgan)
1995[5] 2605[F] 3497[4] 3724[P]

Itea Du Fau (FR) *Alan King* 68h 107c
6 b m Roakarad—Pointe Espiegle (FR) (Point Of No Return (FR))
353[P] 2124[7] 2470[P]

It Plays Itself (IRE) *Miss K Young* 61h 37c
12 bb g Naheez(USA) —Adabiya (IRE) (Akarad (FR))
466[8]

Its A Classic *Pat Murphy* 90h 124c
10 b g Classic Cliche(IRE) —Mcmahon's River (Over The River (FR))
5032[P]

It's A Date *Alan King* 96h
6 b g Kyllachy—By Arrangement (IRE) (Bold Arrangement)
2452[5] 3782[9]

It's A Discovery (IRE) *Donald McCain* 84h 89c
10 b m Grand Plaisir(IRE) —Kilnock Lass (Rymer)
212[8]

Its A Dream (IRE) *Nicky Henderson* 127h 144c
11 b g Oscar(IRE) —Gra-Bri (IRE) (Rashar (USA))
4193[F]

It's A Gimme (IRE) *Jonjo O'Neill* 109b
4 b g Beneficial—Sorcera (GER) (Zilzal (USA))
2237[4] (2797) 3294[4]

It's A Killer *Richard Rowe* 20b
6 b g Killer Instinct—Lykoa (Shirley Heights)
3406[15] 4376[9]

It's A Mans World *Kevin M Prendergast* 83h
5 b g Kyllachy—Exhibitor (USA) (Royal Academy (USA))
5028[4] 5309[9]

It's A Roofer (IRE) *Kate Walton* 104h 107c
11 b g Topanoora—Chelsea Belle (IRE) (Supreme Leader)
88[11] 353[10] 801[2]

Its Bobkat (IRE) *Robert Smith* 50h
5 b g Bob Back(USA) —Katieella (IRE) (King's Theatre (IRE))
1660[9] 1783[10]

Its Crucial (IRE) *Nigel Twiston-Davies* 101h 122c
11 b g Beneficial—Balda Girl (IRE) (Mandalus)
1957[2] 2531[2] 3558[6] 4223[P] 4460[5] 5214[4]

Its Danny Boy (IRE) *David Brace* 101h
8 ch g Beneficial—Storm Queen (IRE) (Le Bavard (FR))
1487[5] 1571[4]

It's Like That (IRE) *Jonjo O'Neill* 119c
11 b g Accordion—Hollygrove Cezanne (IRE) (King's Ride)
152[2] (406)
4463[5] 4937[6] 5207[4]

It's Molly *Simon Earle*
9 b m Thowra(FR) —Race Against Time (Latest Model)
1742[14] 1963[P]

Its Teescomponents (IRE) *Keith Reveley* 87h 115c
9 b m Saddlers' Hall(IRE) —Windswept Lady (IRE) (Strong Gale)
3498[4]
3888[3] 4137[P] 4571[P]

Itstooearly *James Moffatt* 93h 31c
8 br m Overbury(IRE) —Deb's Ball (Glenstal (USA))
313[7] 519[6] 582[8] 2208[3] 2658[9] 3717[10]

Its Tough (IRE) *P Montelth* 108h
8 b g Dushyantor(USA) —Parsons Brush (IRE) (Brush Aside (USA))
45[7]

Itzacliche (IRE) *Nicky Richards* 87h 102c
11 b g Classic Cliche(IRE) —Ower (IRE) (Lomond (USA))
354[5] 749[8] 1057[9]

I'Ve Been Framed (IRE) *Neil King* 122h
7 b g Portrait Gallery(IRE) —Sunday Surprise (IRE) (Black Monday)
2312[5] (2530) (3306) 3742[5] 4285[9] 4933[P]

Iveragh Lad (IRE) *Steven Dixon* 39h 25c
11 b g Teenoso(USA) —Cheryls Pet (IRE) (General Ironside)
585[P]

Ivor's King (IRE) *Colin Tizzard* 95b
4 b g King's Theatre(IRE) —Christelle (IRE) (Revoque (IRE))
4356[4]

Iwakuni (NZ) *Nigel Twiston-Davies* 11h
7 ch g Daggers Drawn(USA) —McCloud (NZ) (Sky Chase (NZ))
1857[9]

I Witness (IRE) *Jane Walton* 84h
9 br g Witness Box(USA) —Challenging Times (IRE) (Kemal (FR))
163[P] 2202[9] **4057[U]** 4688[4] 4872[4] 5308[11]

Ixora (IRE) *Jamie Snowden* 107h
5 gr m Milan—Tucacas (FR) (Highest Honor (FR))
(1793) 2168[10]

Izind An Affair (IRE) *C A McBratney* 85h
6 b m Zindabad(FR) —Formal Affair (Rousillon (USA))
4712[P]

Iznt Getting Court (IRE) *John Wainwright* 87b
5 b g Court Cave(IRE) —Iznitgreat (IRE) (Montelimar (USA))
1955[5] *3088[6]*

Izzy Bella *Sue Bradburne* 75h
5 b m Grape Tree Road—Shazal (Afzal)
1758[5] 3498[P] 4684[5] 5260[5]

Jaamid *William Hayes* 131h 134c
9 b g Desert Prince(IRE) —Strictly Cool (USA) (Bering)
4197[5] 4696[U] 5237[6]

Jabus (IRE) *B R Hamilton* 49b
5 b g Bob Back(USA) —Salsita (FR) (Fijar Tango (FR))
876[6]

Jacarado (IRE) *Robin Dickin* 71h 89c
13 b g Jurado(USA) —Lady Mearba (IRE) (Le Bavard (FR))
24[4] 251[5] 1733[P] 1991[4] 2589[3] 3400[2] **3720[5] 4144[3]**
4787[2] 5295[6]

Jack Apple (IRE) *C A McBratney* 105h
9 ch g Pistolet Bleu(IRE) —Terrific Temp (Kemal (FR))
1099[4]

Jack Cool (IRE) *C Byrnes* 151h
5 b g One Cool Cat(USA) —Rachrush (IRE) (Sadler's Wells (USA))
1155a[4] 5201[2]

Jack Fawaz (IRE) *Pat Phelan* 53h
5 b g Choisir(AUS) —Pretty Procida (USA) (Procida (USA))
82[8] 215[6]

Jack Jicaro *Nicky Vaughan*
5 b g Mind Games—Makeover (Priolo (USA))
4008[P]

Jacko's Boy *Martin Keighley* 83h
8 b g Kayf Tara—O My Love (Idiots Delight)
3526[8] 4917[6] 5167[11]

Jack Rio (IRE) *Laura Young* 76h
6 gr m Captain Rio—Order Of Success (USA) (With Approval (CAN))
3703[5] 3901[7] 4130[9] 4272[11]

Jacks Grey *I R Ferguson* 91h
6 gr g Karinga Bay—Arctic Chick (Henbit (USA))
448[4] 3553[7]

Jack's Lad (IRE) *Tim Vaughan* 76h 88c
12 ch g High Roller(IRE) —Captain's Covey (Captain James)
(2947)
3337[4] 3959[3] 4945[P]

Jackson (BRZ) *Richard Guest* 66h
9 ch g Clackson(BRZ) —More Luck (BRZ) (Baynoun)
2540[U] 4377[9]

Jackson Cage (IRE) *Donald McCain* 114b
6 b g Oscar(IRE) —Phenics Allstar (IRE) (Fourstars Allstar (USA))
4117[3] (4423) 5005[3]

Jack's Present (IRE) *N Pearce* 00c
9 b m Presenting—Sassy Sally (IRE) (Callernish)
4131[3]

Jack's Rocket *Richard Guest* 70b
4 b g Beckett(IRE) —Aybeegirl (Mazilier (USA))
2108[7] 2451[P]

Jack's The Lad (IRE) *Miss Alice Reader* 80c
7 b g Aahsaylad—Kate Ross (Salluceva)
5347[4]

Jackstown (IRE) *Seamus Mullins* 93b
4 b g Hawk Wing(USA) —Soltura (IRE) (Sadler's Wells (USA))
4382[3] *4923[8]* (5284)

Jack The Blaster *Howard Johnson* 124h 129c
11 b g Alflora(IRE) —Marsden Rock (Tina's Pet)
446[P] 2204[U] 2544[5]

Jack The Gent (IRE) *George Moore* 124h
7 b g Anshan—Asidewager (IRE) (Brush Aside (USA))
2612[6] *3167[2]* (3505) 3787[3] 4242[3] 4739[5] 5356[3]

Jack The Soldier (IRE) *Chris Gordon* 76h 88c
7 b g Oscar Schindler(IRE) —Frances Pet (IRE) (Mister Lord (USA))
1675[8] 2181[6] 2396[6]
2947[5] 3402[2] 3720[6] 4558[P]

Jadanli (IRE) *Paul John Gilligan* 130h 156c
9 b g Saddlers' Hall(IRE) —Testaway (IRE) (Commanche Run)
1850a[F] 2227a[6]

J'Adhere (FR) *Tim Vaughan* 109h 104c
6 b g Nikos—Lettre De Lune (FR) (Cadoudal (FR))
215[2] (432) 713[5] 837[9] 2485[2] *3169[6]* 3343[2]
3730[5] 3834[F] 4465[2] 4925[3] 5215[4]

Jago River (IRE) *Howard Johnson* 105h
5 b g Milan—Light And Airy (Linamix (FR))
2075[F] (2657) 4568[4] 5091[5]

Jamaddji *Elliott Cooper* 80b
4 b f Needwood Blade—Tintera (IRE) (King's Theatre (IRE))
4287[14] 5209[6] 5432[6]

Jamadiel (IRE) *S Slevin* 104c
10 ch g Kadastrof(FR) —Petal Dust (IRE) (Convinced)
4194[6]

James Caird (IRE) *J Clements* 83h 58c
11 ch g Catrail(USA) —Polish Saga (Polish Patriot (USA))
518[5]

James De Vassy (FR) *Nick Williams* 149h
6 b g Lavirco(GER) —Provenchere (FR) (Son Of Silver)
2523[13] (3561)

James Junior *Peter Niven* 19h
5 ch g Tobougg(IRE) —Celts Dawn (Celtic Swing)
3491[2] 835[P]

James Pine (IRE) *Sue Wilson* 116c
12 b g Jamesmead—Princess Astrid (IRE) (Mandalus)
151[4] 317[3] 540[2]

James Pollard (IRE) *Bernard Llewellyn* 105h
6 ch g Indian Ridge—Manuetti (IRE) (Sadler's Wells (USA))
3760[3] 4031[6] 4330[12] 5348[3]

Jammia (IRE) *Noel C Kelly* 132h
6 b g Rudimentary(USA) —The Bowlers Boreen (Boreen Beag)
(4253) (5092)

Jam Tomorrow (FR) *Ian Williams* 69h
6 b g Sagacity(FR) —Fida Kahlo (FR) (Cricket Ball (USA))
2166[7] 2666[8] 3365[13] 4100[9]

Janal (IRE) *Stuart Coltherd* 48h 83c
8 b m Taipan(IRE) —Ben Roseler (IRE) (Beneficial)
88[U] 211[4] 404[3] 473[5] 677[U] 872[P] 1080[7] 1100[3]
1360[7] 1378[4]
(1665) 1924[8]
(2194) 3631[8]
(3884) 4133[U]
4510[P] 4827[P]

Jane Doe *Harriet Graham* 89h
8 b m Emperor Fountain—Glorious Jane (Hittite Glory)
212[7] 318[P]

Janie's Encore *Malcolm Jefferson* 88b
6 ch m Muhtarram(USA) —Janie-O (Hittite Glory)
732[6]

Jan Jandura (IRE) *Tim Vaughan* 82h
6 b g Flemensfirth(USA) —Friends Of Friends (IRE) (Phardante (FR))
2646[3] 3253[4] 3585[9] 3761[7] 4675[6]

January *Liam Corcoran* 83h 108c
8 gr g Daylami(IRE) —Noushkey (Polish Precedent (USA))
(1283)
1493[2] 1569[8]
1888[3] 2022[F] 2484[4] 4671[P] (5036)

Jaques Vert (FR) *Robert Wylie* 104h
5 ch g Dr Fong(USA) —Sayuri (USA) (Sadler's Wells (USA))
1962[13] 2509[7] 3505[10] 3855[3] 4113[4] 4465[3] 5208[7]

Jardin De Vienne (FR) *Renee Robeson* 113h 102c
9 gr g Highest Honor(FR) —Vaguely Money (USA) (Vaguely Noble)
381[3] 634[7]

Jat Punjabi *Trevor Wall* 89h
7 b g Karinga Bay—Balmoral Princess (Thethingaboutitis (USA))
4377[5] 4747[P]

Jaunty Dove *Andrew Price* 86h
9 b m Atraf—Flossy Dove (Le Moss)
1746[9] 2425[5] 2589[7]

Jaunty Flight *David M Easterby* 147h 147c
9 b m Busy Flight—Jaunty June (Primitive Rising (USA))
206[P] **4851[P]**

Jaunty Journey *Nigel Twiston-Davies* 115h 126c
8 ch g Karinga Bay—Jaunty June (Primitive Rising (USA))
2106[4] 3440[9]
4208[F] 5154[P] 5325[3]

Jawaab (IRE) *Richard Guest* 93h
7 ch g King's Best(USA) —Canis Star (Wolfhound (USA))
2509[3] ◆

Jawhary *Philip Hobbs* 95b
4 bb g Pivotal—Moon's Whisper (USA) (Storm Cat (USA))
4780[2] ◆

Jaya Bella (IRE) *Milton Harris* 94b
6 gr m Tikkanen(USA) —Maxis Girl (IRE) (Mister Mat (FR))
1771[3] 2546[7] *(3979)* 5070[4]

Jay J *Andrew Price* 117h
7 b g Sovereign Water(FR) —Passing Cloud (IRE) (Accordion)
1743[5] 1887[2] (2123) 2584[5] 4439[8] 5289[P]

Jay Jays Lady *Bernard Llewellyn* 38b
4 b f Beat All(USA) —Tachometer (IRE) (Jurado (USA))
2237[10]

Jayjay Valentine *Victor Dartnall* 80h 90c
8 b g Double Trigger(IRE) —Magic Valentine (Magic Ring (IRE))
2142[6] 2499[8] 3366[9]
3768[P] 4718[4] 5214[6]

Jayne's Crusader *Mrs S Alner* 106h 113c
8 b g Lord Americo—Carole's Crusader (Faustus (USA))
3908[7] (4708)

Jayo (FR) *W P Mullins* 132h 149c
8 ch g Grape Tree Road—Joie De Nuit (USA) (Affirmed (USA))
3473a[8] 5025a[P]

Jays Cottage *Jim Old* 62b
8 b g Karinga Bay—Pendil's Niece (Roscoe Blake)
249[F] 5107[P]

Jays Girl *Pam Sly* 75b
4 b f Danbird(AUS) —Just Jay (Keen)
5135[12] 5380[6]

Jazrawy *Sue Smith* 12h
9 b g Dansili—Dalila Di Mare (IRE) (Bob Back (USA))
2080[P]

Jazz Age (IRE) *David Pipe* 90h
4 b g Shamardal(USA) —Tender Is Thenight (IRE) (Barathea (IRE))
1728[3] 2133[4] 2369[7]

Jazz Attack (IRE) *Miss M Tomlinson* 87c
12 b g Flemensfirth(USA) —Ballagh Riona (The Parson)
4429[4]

Jeanry (FR) *Arthur Whitehead* 97h
8 b g Marathon(USA) —Envergure (Kenmare (FR))
(1925) 2308[2] 2452[3] 4751[10] 5111[3]

Jeczmien (POL) *Nick Gifford* 89h 111c
8 b g Fourth Of June(USA) —Jetka (POL) (Five Star Camp (USA))
2591[5] (3612)
3769[5] (4033)
4290[7] 4770[P] 5194[P]

Je Ne Sais Plus (FR) *Tom George* 119h
7 gr m Spadoun(FR) —Sheer Drop (FR) (Kenmare (FR))
1746[2] 2089[4] 3490[6] 3941[5] 5302[P]

Jenny Potts *Chris Down* 104h
7 b m Robellino(USA) —Fleeting Vision (IRE) (Vision (USA))
40[3]

Jenny Soba *Lucinda Featherstone* 72h
8 b m Observatory(USA) —Majalis (Mujadil (USA))
3879[5] 4263[P]

Jered (IRE) *Noel Meade* 115h 151c
9 ch g Presenting—La Noire (IRE) (Phardante (FR))
3206a[13] 3473a[5] (Dead)

Jeringa *John Wade* 89h 99c
12 b g Karinga Bay—Jervandha (Strong Gale)
2371[P] 2602[2] 3503[2] 3888[2] 4135[2] 4997[2] 5311[P]

Jerry Lee (IRE) *F Jordan* 73h
8 b g Orpen(USA) —Vinicky (USA) (Kingmambo (USA))
341[7] 1735[10]

Jersey Boys *Howard Johnson* 88h 64c
5 gr g Fair Mix(IRE) —Princess Maxine (IRE) (Horage)
35[6] 1664[8] 2092[16] 3746[6] 4243[5] 4809[7] **5294[5]**

Jersey Joe (IRE) *Brian Ellison* 71b
4 br g Trans Island—Meigiu (IRE) (Catrail (USA))
2108[6] *3166[8]*

Jessica *Seamus Mullins* 65h
6 b m Karinga Bay—Pedrosa (IRE) (Petardia)
4965[4] 5282[6] 5374[P]

Jessie Gwendoline (IRE) *Donald McCain* 82b
5 b m King's Theatre(IRE) —Knocktartan (IRE) (King's Ride)
333[6] 1771[8]

Jessies Dream (IRE) *Gordon Elliott* 146h 156c
8 ch g Presenting—Lady Apprentice (IRE) (Phardante (FR))
(2971a) ◆ **3472a[2] 4804[2]** ◆

Jetnova (IRE) *Alan King* 138h
6 b g Luso—Yamashina (IRE) (Kahyasi)
370[3] 1990[6] (2428) (2925) 3567[6] (4220) 4849[F]
5186[7]

Jeu De Roseau (IRE) *Chris Grant* 112h
7 b g Montjeu(IRE) —Roseau (Nashwan (USA))
(252) 539[2] (1644)

Jewelled Dagger (IRE) *Jim Goldie* 111h
7 b g Daggers Drawn(USA) —Cappadoce (IRE) (General Monash (USA))
1104[3] (1337) 1594[3]

Jewellery (IRE) *Alison Thorpe* 80h
4 b f King's Best(USA) —Eilean Shona (Suave Dancer (USA))
2570[4] 2924[8] 3158[12] 3870[10] 4272[5] 4675[5]
5068[2] 5252[4] 5368[2]

Jigalo (IRE) *Ms Joanna Morgan* 139h 130c
10 b g Accordion—Kasterlee (FR) (Stay For Lunch (USA))
1133a[17]
2412a[3]

Jigsaw Financial (IRE) *Roger Curtis* 53h
5 b g Brian Boru—Ardcolm Cailin (IRE) (Beneficial)
1607[4] 1729[6] 2145[10] 2310[P]

Jilly Anne *Chris Grant*
4 ch f And Beyond(IRE) —Solway Dawn (Minster Son)
3364[7]

Jimbatai (IRE) *Barry Leavy* 109h 124c
8 ch g Moscow Society(USA) —Kouron (Pauper)
420[2] 846[5] **(1045)**
1424[4] 1557[2] 2305[5] 3558[F] 3820[8]

Jim Job Jones *Neil Mulholland* 58h
7 b g Tipsy Creek(USA) —Sulapuff (Sula Bula)
362[6] 1488[10] 1600[8] 1675[9] 1902[12]

Jimmy Bedney (IRE) *Sirrell Griffiths* 75h 77c
10 bb g Simply Great(FR) —Double Token (Furry Glen)
794[6]

Jimmy Bond *Kate Walton* 85h 122c
12 b g Primitive Rising(USA) —Miss Moneypenny (Silly Prices)
2272[P]

Jimmy The Brave *Gerry Enright* 74b
5 b g Josr Algarhoud(IRE) —Polly Minor (Sunley Builds)
284[4] 5387[12]

Jimmy The Hat (IRE) *Giles Smyly* 96b
5 b g Accordion—Pride 'N' Joy (IRE) (Lashkari)
2087[5] 4376[3]

Jimmy The Saint (IRE) *Donald McCain* 118h
8 b g Flemensfirth(USA) —Sheknowso (Teenoso (USA))
(3897) 4422[2] 4889[3]

Jim Tango (FR) *Donald McCain* 101h 118c
7 bb g Jimble(FR) —Fitanga (FR) (Fijar Tango (FR))
177[6] 395[3] 676[4]

Jim Will Fix It (IRE) *Seamus Roche* 129h
6 b g Lord Of Appeal—North County Lady (IRE) (Roselier (FR))
(3208a) 4249a[3]

Jingoism (USA) *Brian Ellison* 64h
5 b g Empire Maker(USA) —Pert Lady (USA) (Cox's Ridge (USA))
35[4] 732[7] 1153[4] 1250[5]

Jinksy Minx *Suzy Smith* 77h
4 b f Piccolo—Medway (IRE) (Shernazar)
1691[5] 2211[7] 2528[4] 4949[U]

Jinn And Tinick *Tony Carroll*
5 b m Kadastrof(FR) —Modesty Forbids (Formidable (USA))
1280[P]

Joaaci (IRE) *Mrs P J Shaw* 126h 117c
11 b g Presenting—Miss Sarajevo (IRE) (Brush Aside (USA))
4463[P] 4851[P]

Joan D'Arc (IRE) *Michael Quinlan* 92h
4 b f Invincible Spirit(IRE) —Prakara (IRE) (Indian Ridge)
(1442) 1610[9] (1691) 2133[9] (2435)

Joan's Legacy *Jimmy Fox*
4 b f Piccolo—CC Canova (Millkom)
2661[P]

Jobekani (IRE) *Lisa Williamson* 91h
5 b g Tagula(IRE) —Lyca Ballerina (Marju (IRE))
93[6] 519[10] 842[6]

Job One (FR) *Henrietta Knight* 109h 120c
8 gr g Kahyasi—Corrossol (FR) (Kaldounevees (FR))
(854) **1452[2]**
1570[3] 2670[9] 5104[U] 5344[P]

Jocheski (IRE) *Tony Newcombe* 115h 113c
7 b g Mull Of Kintyre(USA) —Ludovica (Bustino)
170[7] **1091[U]**
1345[U] 1909[2] 2330[5] 4529[4] 4972[4]

Jockies Burn (IRE) *Jonjo O'Neill* 11h
5 b g Milan—Badriya (IRE) (Be My Chief (USA))
1138[7]

Joe Lively (IRE) *Colin Tizzard* 125h 161c
12 b g Flemensfirth(USA) —Forest Gale (Strong Gale)
2346[6] 3290[P] (Dead)

Joe Rua (USA) *John Ryan* 83h
4 bb g Johannesburg(USA) —Red Tulle (USA) (A.P. Indy (USA))
960[5] 1024[3] (1324) 1473[U] 1610[12] 1691[7] 2047[6]

Joe Smooth *Noel Meade* 127h
5 ch g No Excuse Needed—Euippe (Air Express (IRE))
3846a[4]

Joe Soap (IRE) *Mrs C L Dennis* 15c
10 b g Germany(USA) —Lahana (IRE) (Rising)
4143[5] 4429[F]

Johann Sabestian (IRE) *Jonjo O'Neill* 96b
6 b g Bach(IRE) —Eskimo Kiss (IRE) (Distinctly North (USA))
609[RR] 637[5]

John Crabbies (FR) *Lisa Williamson* 25b
4 b g Super Celebre(FR) —Clelia La Belle (FR) (Rusticaro (FR))
5432[13]

John Diamond (IRE) *Helen Needham* 100h 79c
10 b g Un Desperado(FR) —Lessons Lass (IRE) (Doyoun)
153[6]

Johnmanderville *Noel Wilson* 95h
5 b g Kheleyf(USA) —Lady's Walk (IRE) (Charnwood Forest (IRE))
548[4]

Johnnycarpethead (IRE) *A J Martin* 100h
6 gr g Turtle Island(IRE) —Loughaderra Rose (IRE) (Roselier (FR))
870[11]

Johnny Kilawee (IRE) *M H Weston* 121h 111c
7 ch g Daggers Drawn(USA) —Jenny Jingle (IRE) (Digamist (USA))
4293[RR]

Johnny Mullen (IRE) *Paul Henderson* 118h
8 b g Bishop Of Cashel—Native Land (Be My Native (USA))
2393[5] 2977[6] 3557[15] 4448[P]

Johnny Owen (IRE) *David Brace* 24h
5 b g Danehill Dancer(IRE) —Makarova (IRE) (Sadler's Wells (USA))
3406[5] 3872[10] 4029[12] 5211[10]

Johnny Venture (IRE) *C C Pimlott* 44c
12 ch g Grand Plaisir(IRE) —Galaxy Fare (IRE) (Hollow Hand)
178[5]

John Potts *Brian Baugh* 59h
6 b g Josr Algarhoud(IRE) —Crown City (USA) (Coronado's Quest (USA))
2245 842[9]

John's Gift *Bob Buckler* 104h 105c
7 ch g Kadastrof(FR) —Connaught's Pride (Hubbly Bubbly (USA))
1911[3] 2141[3] **2979[6] 4096[P]**

John Sixteen (IRE) *Peter Bowen* 66b
6 ch g Anshan—Local Issue (IRE) (Phardante (FR))
1349[6] 1729[9] 1937[P] 3153[15] 3584[P]

John's Oscar (IRE) *Cecil Price* 15b
4 b g Oscar(IRE) —Vigna Maggio (FR) (Starborough)
5105[13]

John The Glass *Mark Wellings*
4 b g Deportivo—Brendas Nightmare (Tina's Pet)
2458[13] 4443[11]

Joinedupwriting *Raymond York* 69h
6 b g Desert Style(IRE) —Ink Pot (USA) (Green Dancer (USA))
4918[10] 5050[6] 5225[10]

Join Together (IRE) *Paul Nicholls* 139h
6 b g Old Vic—Open Cry (IRE) (Montelimar (USA))
2142[3] 2888[2] (3931) 4849[P]

Jojabean (IRE) *Alan King* 107b
4 b g Milan—Garden City (IRE) (Shernazar)
3294[11] 4082[2] ◆

Joker Choker (IRE) *Nicky Henderson* 120h
6 b g Oscar(IRE) —Stormy Lady (IRE) (Glacial Storm (USA))
2295[3] 3691[7] 4094[6] 4677[5] (5400)

Jokers Legacy (IRE) *Tim Vaughan* 109h
9 b g Fourstars Allstar(USA) —Sweet Charm (IRE) (Glacial Storm (USA))
3440[7]
3938[F] 4096[U]

Joli Al *Michael Roberts* 50b
7 b g Alflora(IRE) —Joline (IRE) (Roselier (FR))
249[P]

Jolibob (IRE) *Robin Dickin* 63h 30c
9 b g Bob's Return(IRE) —Short Of A Buck (IRE) (Buckskin (FR))
5062[6]

Jolly Boys Outing (IRE) *Rosemary Gasson* 99c
8 b g Glacial Storm(USA) —St Carol (IRE) (Orchestra)
150[P] 466[6] 3702[3] 3880[F] 4413[5] (5060)
5377[2]

Jolly Roger (IRE) *John Flint* 105h
4 b g Oratorio(IRE) —Chalice Wells (Sadler's Wells (USA))
2151[3] (2528) 3554[5] 3967[4] 4521[3]

Jomade (IRE) *Kim Bailey* 90h
5 b g Definite Article—Culmore Native (IRE) (Be My Native (USA))
355[9] 3158[10] 3478[8] 3645[11] 4076[13] 5212[4]

Joncol (IRE) *Paul Nolan* 124b 163c
8 b g Bob's Return(IRE) —Finemar Lady (IRE) (Montelimar (USA))
2262a[4] 3176a[3] ◆ 4087a[3]

Jonlahy (IRE) *Mrs J Quinlan* 51c
12 b g Beneficial—Beloved (IRE) (Beau Sher)
293[7]

Jonny Delta *Jim Goldie* 110b
4 ch g Sulamani(IRE) —Send Me An Angel (IRE) (Lycius (USA))
(4717) 5202[7] ◆

Jonny No Eyebrows *Patrick Leech*
4 br g Auction House(USA) —She's Expensive (IRE) (Spectrum (IRE))
1234[P]

Jordan *Suzy Smith* 94h
8 b m Golden Snake(USA) —Formula One Affair (Four Burrow)
2949[4] 3432[2] 3791[3] (4130) 4327[9]

Jordan's Light (USA) *David Evans* 108h 106c
8 rg g Aljabr(USA) —Western Friend (USA) (Gone West (USA))
135[5] **(463)**

Jordaura *John Holt* 46h
5 br g Primo Valentino(IRE) —Christina's Dream (Spectrum (IRE))
3495[7]

Josear *Chris Down* 92h 117c
9 b g Josr Algarhoud(IRE) —Real Popcorn (IRE) (Jareer (USA))
330[3] 2504[6]
2975[5] 3433[2] 3617[5]

Jose Bove *Henrietta Knight* 29h 84c
9 ch g So Factual(USA) —Dark Sirona (Pitskelly)
381[5] 1095[9]
1474[P]

Josephine Malines *John Flint* 105h 93c
7 b m Inchinor—Alrisha (IRE) (Persian Bold)
210[5] 515[5] 1236[2] 1429[2] **1511[3]** 2242[4] 2586[2]
3155[9]

Josh's Dreamway (IRE) *Jeremy Scott* 105b
5 b m Deploy—Midway (IRE) (Warcraft (USA))
(5105)

Josie's Set *George Charlton* 62b
4 ch f Reset(AUS) —Our Krissie (Kris)
2108[8]

Josr's Magic (IRE) *Peter Hedger* 80h
7 b g Josr Algarhoud(IRE) —Just The Trick (USA) (Phone Trick (USA))
2129[7]

Joueur D'Estruval (FR) *Wilf Storey* 120h 67c
14 gr g Perrault—Alrose (FR) (Kalyan (FR))
4476[6]

Journeyman (IRE) *Nicky Henderson* 92h
5 b g Anshan—Daizinni (Dr Massini (IRE))
238[3] *3054[10]* 3584[P] 3937[4] 4557[5] 5080[P]

Jovial Starry Nite *Carroll Gray* 33b
6 b m Shambo—Jovial Lass (Casteddu)
3651[12] 4533[9]

Jubail (IRE) *Alan King* 124h
4 ch g Redback—Daneville (IRE) (Danetime (IRE))
1610[3] ◆ (1882) 2078[4] 4283[4] 4807[5] 5227[2]

Jubilee George *Christopher Kellett* 64c
11 b g Parthian Springs—Miss Lawn (FR) (Lashkari)
2479[6] *3092[8]* **3404[P]**

Judge Davis *Caroline Keevil* 101b
4 b g Alflora(IRE) —Minimum (Terimon)
5012[3]

Jug Of Punch (IRE) *Simon Lewis* 76h
12 ch g In The Wings—Mysistra (FR) (Machiavellian (USA))
1199[P] 1468[10] 1605[6] 1735[6] 1855[10] 2239[6] 2589[2]

Jukebox Melody (IRE) *Malcolm Jefferson* 110h
5 b g Brian Boru—Carmels Cottage (IRE) (Riberetto)
355[4] (2403) (3553) 4165[P] (4541) 4870[F]

Julia Too *William Amos* 87b
4 b f King's Theatre(IRE) —Candello (Supreme Leader)
(4005) 4574[5]

Julius Caesar *Ferdy Murphy* 123h 119c
11 b g Sadler's Wells(USA) —Stiletta (Dancing Brave (USA))
1763[P] 2298[P]

July The Firth (IRE) *Alan Jones* 85b
5 b g Flemensfirth(USA) —Leader Of Fashion (IRE) (Supreme Leader)
1029[7]

Jumbo Rio (IRE) *E J O'Grady* 157h
6 b g Captain Rio—Nafzira (IRE) (Darshaan)
2259a[2] 2968a[6] 3796a[4]

Jumbul Sale *Mrs Alana Cowley* 90c
12 bl g Sula Bula—Confused Express (Confused)
139[3]

Jumeirah Jane *Sue Smith* 84h
8 br m Kayf Tara—Ace Girl (Stanford)
1005[P]

Jump City (FR) *Paul Nicholls* 128h
5 b g Muhtathir—Just Fizzy (Efisio)
4225[2]

Jumpjack Flint *David Brace* 88h
5 b g Definite Article—Bajan Girl (FR) (Emperor Jones (USA))
1743[7] 2021[4] 2322[U] 2456[14] **3544[P]** 3837[P] 4721[8]

Jump Jet (IRE) *Miss O Curl* 114h 129c
9 ch g Beneficial—Cherry In A Hurry (IRE) (Be My Native (USA))
4183[3]

Jumps Road *Colin Tizzard* 100b
4 b g Clerkenwell(USA) —Diletia (Dilum (USA))
3794[2] 4191[8] 5012[7]

Jump Up *Keith Goldsworthy* 100h
5 b g Carnival Dancer—Taylor Green (USA) (Green Dancer (USA))
739[3] 869[2] (1180) 1344[2] 1795[2] 3370[12] 3761[3]
4034[9] (4407)

Jung (POL) *Pavlina Bastova* 109c
11 br g Alywar(USA) —Jurata (POL) (Wolver Heights)
1811a[P]

Junior *David Pipe* 140h 157c
8 ch g Singspiel(IRE) —For More (FR) (Sanglamore (USA))
2358[3] 3293[2]
(4821) ◆

Junior Jack *Martin Keighley* 110h
6 b g Kayf Tara—O My Love (Idiots Delight)
589[3] 3585[3] 4918[5]

Jupiter Rex (FR) *Venetia Williams* 59h
4 ch g Dano-Mast—Creme Pralinee (FR) (Kashtan (FR))
2797[9] 3767[11] 4094[9]

Jurado Express (IRE) *Miss Michelle Bentham* 91h 120c
15 b g Jurado(USA) —Express Film (Ashmore (FR))
4936[3]

Jurisdiction *Rose Dobbin* 123h
7 b g Goldmark(USA) —Juris Prudence (IRE) (Law Society (USA))
(163) (1869) (2202) 2512[8] 5320[6]

Justabout *Colin Tizzard* 83h 110c
8 br g Classic Cliche(IRE) —Dubacilla (Dubassoff (USA))
171[4] **371[3]**
(650) 987[5]
(1159)
1331[2] 1738[6] 2146[7] (2332)
2638[3] 3230[11] (4749)
5240[P]

Justalittlebitmore (IRE) *Diana Grissell* 65b
8 b g Kahtan—Get Cracking (IRE) (Supreme Leader)
3981[P]

Just Amazing (IRE) *Paul Nicholls* 131h 148c
8 b g Presenting—Just Precious (Ela-Mana-Mou)
(4197)
(4271) 4851[P] (5231)

Just Benny (IRE) *Richard Phillips* 97h
6 bb g Beneficial—Artic Squaw (IRE) (Buckskin (FR))
2646[4] 3918[3] 4747[4]

Just Beware *Zoe Davison* 97h
9 b m Makbul—Bewails (IRE) (Caerleon (USA))
534[4] 1236[6] 1677[6] (2131) 2294[2] 2442[5] 3378[4]
3610[5] 3983[4] 4771[2] 5270[2]

Just Blue *Mark Rimell* 91b
5 gr g Silver Patriarch(IRE) —Miss Millie (Homeboy)
4287[5]

Just Cloudy *Anthony Honeyball* 81h
7 b g Cloudings(IRE) —Tycoon Tina (Tina's Pet)
(3259) 3762[7] 4091[5] 4557[6]

Just Dan *David Thompson* 72h
5 b g Best Of The Bests(IRE) —Scapavia (FR) (Alzao (USA))
30[3] 2227 420[5] 2433[7] 3603[5] 3883[P] **4509[P]**

Just Dave (IRE) *Evan Williams* 104h
5 br g Alflora(IRE) —Melody Maid (Strong Gale)
1824[5] 2216[4] ◆ 3366[13]

Just For Jean (IRE) *Donald McCain* 95h
6 b m Presenting—Meldrum Lass (Buckskin (FR))
100[6] 358[F]

Just For Men (IRE) *Martin Todhunter* 81h 122c
11 gr g Glacial Storm(USA) —Regents Ballerina (IRE) (Commanche Run)
213[5] 1781[8]

Just Jennings (IRE) *John Norton* 84b
6 b m Beneficial—Cameo Dawn (IRE) (Broken Hearted)
488[P] 1379[F]

Just Josie *Sheena West* 68h
5 b m Josr Algarhoud(IRE) —Spatham Rose (Environment Friend)
2594[6] 3556[8]

Just Lola *Michael Blake* 71h
7 b m Kadastrof(FR) —Plain Jane (Sula Bula)
263[7] 2974[P] 3620[12]

Just Maddie *Rayson Nixon* 99h
7 gr m Supreme Sound—Delightfool (Idiots Delight)
42[9] 163[9] 2547[6] 3727[P] (4395) 4552[4] 5144[P]

Just Mossie *Bill Turner* 96h
6 ch g Ishiguru(USA) —Marinsky (USA) (Diesis)
547 219[3] 2985 3747

Just One Thing (IRE) *Evan Williams* 104h
6 b g Zagreb(USA) —Blue Jumbo (IRE) (Bluebird (USA))
58[3] 2294[3] 3228[12] 3962[3] 4530[F] 5400[6]

Just Posh *Rayson Nixon* 77h 74c
9 b m Moshaajir(USA) —Split The Wind (Strong Gale)
1870[11] 2208[5] 4146[P] 4511[5] 4550[P]
5415[4]

Just Richie (IRE) *Arthur Whiting*
6 b g Jammaal—Righthand Lady (Buckskin (FR))
3546[11] 3836[P]

Just Sandy (IRE) *Denis P Quinn* 46b
8 ch m High Roller(IRE) —Cloona Lady (IRE) (Duky)
1146a[13]

Just Smudge *Venetia Williams* 98h 130c
9 b g Fraam—Flakey Dove (Oats)
78[4] ◆ (1957)
2582[3] 2674[6] 4440[U] 4820[F] ◆ 5199[P]

Just Talking (IRE) *Miss J Houldey* 95h 105c
9 br g Windsor Castle—Fam-E Fam-E (IRE) (King's Ride)
3991[3]

Just The Job (IRE) *Neil Mulholland* 108h
7 b g Religiously(USA) —Fashions Side (Quayside)
1343[P] 1488[7] 1741[10] (2135) ◆ 2244[2] (2314)
(2327) 3299[P] 3483[6] 3793[6] 4025[6] 4314[2] 4375[2]

Just Tootsie *Nick Mitchell* 93h
7 ch g Emperor Fountain—Thamesdown Tootsie (Comedy Star (USA))
3296[7] 3791[14] 4224[7] 4540[4] ◆ **5039[U]**

Just Unique *Mark Rimell* 66h 96c
7 ch g Sure Blade(USA) —Miss Millie (Homeboy)
1448[6] 1749[7] 2365[4] 2981[P] 3719[7]
4144[9] 4890[5] 5109[P]

Just Victor *Paul Webber* 112h
6 b g Revoque(IRE) —Villian (Kylian (USA))
522[2] 847[2] 1196[6] 1508[10]

Just Watch Ollie (IRE) *John Coombe*
5 b g Indian Danehill(IRE) —Westgate Run (Emperor Jones (USA))
4923[11]

Justwhateverulike (IRE) *Sandy Forster* 78h 116c
10 b g Courtship—Rose Of Summer (IRE) (Taufan (USA))
33[4] 3922[9] 4306[4]

Juventus (POL) *Josef Vana II* 125c
12 ch g Royal Court(IRE) —Julietta (POL) (Antrieb (GER))
1811a[10]

Juwireya *Peter Hiatt* 49h
4 b f Nayef(USA) —Katayeb (IRE) (Machiavellian (USA))
2047[F] 2245[7]

J'y Vole (FR) *W P Mullins* 104h 163c
8 ch m Mansonnien(FR) —J'y Reste (FR) (Freedom Cry)
2970a[2] 3176a[6] 3778a[3] 4818[6]

Kack Handed *Henry Daly* 117h 117c
8 b g Terimon—Hand Inn Glove (Alflora (IRE))
330[7] 634[5] 1734[5]
(2037) 2572[2] 3786[3] 4490[8] 5100[2]

Kadalkin (FR) *Nigel Hawke* 58h
5 b g Robin Des Champs(FR) —Kadalma (FR) (Cadoudal (FR))
3647[5]

Kadouchski (FR) *John Berry* 103h
7 b g Ski Chief(USA) —Douchka (FR) (Fijar Tango (FR))
2949[8] 3343[5] (4323) 4830[2] 5376[3]

Kadount (FR) *J M Turner* 134h 120c
13 b g Our Account(USA) —Une De Lann (FR) (Spoleto)
(139) (296)

Kaffie *Kim Bailey* 104b
6 b m Kayf Tara—Galix (FR) (Sissoo)
3259[4] (3590) 4728[17]

Kahfre *Gary Moore* 98h
4 ch g Peintre Celebre(USA) —Minerva (IRE) (Caerleon (USA))
(1545) 1691[2] 2078[9] 2439[2] 4196[6] 5006[5] ◆

Kai Broon (IRE) *Lucinda Russell* 96h
4 b g Marju(IRE) —Restiv Star (FR) (Soviet Star (USA))
2451[P] 3358[9] 3785[3] 4148[7] 4910[4] (5098)

Kaituna (IRE) *Oliver Sherwood* 123h
5 b m Flemensfirth(USA) —Southern Skies (IRE) (Dr Massini (IRE))
333[5] (2130) ◆ 2554[F] 3789[4] 4401[3] (5078)
5302[13]

Kakagh (IRE) *W Harney* 129h 127c
7 b g Tel Quel(FR) —Pheisty (Faustus (USA))
3210a[3]

Kalahari King (FR) *Ferdy Murphy* 147h 167c
10 bb g Kahyasi—Queen Of Warsaw (FR) (Assert)
2206[3] 2885[7] *3170[5]* **3675[4] 4818[2] 5184[P]**

Kalamill (IRE) *Shaun Lycett* 106h
4 b g Kalanisi(IRE) —Desert Pageant (IRE) (Desert King (IRE))
1674[2] 2356[6] 3436[7] 3985[2]

Kalann (IRE) *Sabrina J Harty* 118h
4 b g Barathea(IRE) —Karkiyla (IRE) (Darshaan)
2966a[2] 3239a[5] 4083a[8]

Kalantari (IRE) *Evan Williams* 71b
4 b g Kalanisi(IRE) —Khatela (IRE) (Shernazar)
4970[8] 5084[9]

Kala Patthar *Colin Tizzard* 63b
4 b g Tobougg(IRE) —Lady Emily (Alflora (IRE))
2458[7] 3630[7] 5105[P]

Kalatime (IRE) *William Young* 72h 30c
8 bb m Kalanisi(IRE) —Dream Time (Rainbow Quest (USA))
285[7] 603[4] 1049[9] 1101[5]

Kaliski (IRE) *John Flint* 82h
7 b m Kahyasi—Moonlight Saunter (USA) (Woodman (USA))
58[7] 410[P] 990[5]

Kalmo Bay (FR) *R A Owen* 104h 106c
8 b g Alamo Bay(USA) —Kermesse (USA) (Irish River (FR))
160[9] 5207[P]

Kalulushi (IRE) *Donald McCain* 76h
6 b g Environment Friend—Gilly's Dream (IRE) (Germany (USA))
832[12] 2297[2] **3726[F]** 4062[P] 4422[7] 5103[12] 5354[P]

Kanad *Milton Harris* 116h 115c
9 b g Bold Edge—Multi-Sofft (Northern State (USA))
135[2] **536[3]**
687[2] 797[3] 854[2] 1032[8] 1235[P]

Kandelin (IRE) *G T H Bailey* 61h 63c
8 b g Beneficial—Bright Moonbeam (IRE) (Celio Rufo)
5283[4]

Kanesh (IRE) *Mark L Fagan* 105c
8 b g Fruits Of Love(USA) —Annella (IRE) (Glenstal (USA))
5163[11]

Kangaroo Court (IRE) *Emma Lavelle* 136h 153c
7 b g Lahib(USA) —Tombazaan (IRE) (Good Thyne (USA))
4727[20] 5287[5]

Kanonkop *Charles Pogson* 100h
7 b m Observatory(USA) —Camcorder (Nashwan (USA))
1329[2] ◆

Kaolak (USA) *Keith Reveley* 113h
5 bb h Action This Day(USA) —Cerita (USA) (Magesterial (USA))
1962[4] ◆ 2960[9] 3331[3] 3547[2] ◆ 3746[2] 4451[2]
5315[12]

Kapborg (FR) *David Pipe* 71h
5 ch m Kapgarde(FR) —Dicta Borg (FR) (Cyborg (FR))
182[8] 263[6] 754[6] 1060[8] 1294[F]

Kapellmeister (IRE) *Philip Sharp*
8 b g Mozart(IRE) —March Hare (Groom Dancer (USA))
953[7]

Kappelhoff (IRE) *Lydia Richards* 3h 80c
14 b g Mukaddamah(USA) —Miss Penguin (General Assembly (USA))
280[P] 2048[2] (2394)
2950[10] 3790[5]

Kap West (FR) *Laura Young* 90c
6 b g Kapgarde(FR) —Themis Eria (FR) (Signe Divin (USA))
2975[12] 3628[F] 4267[U] 5214[3]

Karabak (FR) *Alan King* 166h
8 b g Kahyasi—Mosstraye (FR) (Tip Moss (FR))
2516[2] (2884) 3289[4] 4373[4] 5160[P]

Karanja *Simon Burrough* 125h 104c
12 b g Karinga Bay—Proverbial Rose (Proverb)
1316 2500[P] **3438[9]**

Karasakal (IRE) *Gary Moore* 115h 101c
8 b g Kahyasi—Karasta (IRE) (Lake Coniston (IRE))
5843 2453[7] 2986[P] 3612[2] (3898) 4411[3] 4919[7]

Karasenir (IRE) *Philip Hobbs* 136h
5 b g Sendawar(IRE) —Karasta (IRE) (Lake Coniston (IRE))
(1613) 1773[2] (1884) 2092[2] 3298[5] 3649[2] 4852[10]

Karelian *Ferdy Murphy* 117h 109c
10 gr g Linamix(FR) —Kalikala (Darshaan)
581[P] **746[P]**

Karingabay Queen *Kevin Tork* 65h 14c
6 b m Karinga Bay—Ower Farm (Coronash)
1480[4] 2265a[P] 2495[7]
3865[6] 4398[U] 4828[6] 5191[6] 5383[9]

Karinga Dancer *Paul Nicholls* 111b
5 b g Karinga Bay—Miss Flora (Alflora (IRE))
3766[3] 4457[4] 5105[2]

Karinga Dream *Venetia Williams* 80h
5 b m Karinga Bay—Function Dreamer (Overbury (IRE))
2168[8] 2974[15] 3227[5] 3540[P] 3870[6]

Karinga Madame *Richard Rowe* 48b
4 b f Karinga Bay—Black Secret (Gildoran)
2965[12]

Karingreason *Keith Reveley* 103h 100c
8 b m Karinga Bay—Noreasonatall (Lord David S (USA))
2942[8] 3520[U] 3695[7] 4237[3] 4740[3] 5134[2] 5293[2]

Karky Schultz (GER) *James Eustace* 125h
6 gr g Diktat—Kazoo (Shareef Dancer (USA))
80[7] 2423[6] 3557[3] (3874) 4488[F] (Dead)

Karley *Polly Gundry* 73c
10 b g Weldnaas(USA) —Future Romance (Distant Relative)
133[5]

Karoshdee *John E Long* 92b
8 ch m Fantastic Light(USA) —Larousse (Unfuwain (USA))
222[3]

Karrical *Donald McCain* 78b
6 b g Karinga Bay—Analogical (Teenoso (USA))
4879[7]

Kartanian (IRE) *Philip Hobbs* 108h
5 b g Kalanisi(IRE) —Katiykha (IRE) (Darshaan)
(1607) ◆ (1778) ◆ 2389[3] 2960[5] ◆ 3405[11]

Karzelle *Milton Harris* 74h
7 b g Karinga Bay—Gazelle De Thou (FR) (Quart De Vin (FR))
635[4] 863[6] 992[4] 1605[U] 2244[P]

Kasakovs Girl *Simon West* 68b
4 ch f Kasakov—Lady Magician (Lord Bud)
2511[4]

Kasbadali (FR) *Oliver Sherwood* 113h
6 b g Kahyasi—Nikalie (FR) (Nikos)
(355) 1910[2] ◆ 2281[2] 4012[5] 4665[2] 5080[10]

Kasban *Luke Dace* 111h
7 b g Kingmambo(USA) —Ebaraya (IRE) (Sadler's Wells (USA))
1588[2] 1742[11] 1914[7] 2581[3] (4481) 4988[5] 5230[6] 5439[3]

Kashmina *Sheena West* 104h
6 ch m Dr Fong(USA) —Lady Melbourne (IRE) (Indian Ridge)
853[P]

Kashubian Quest *Sue Smith* 81h
5 b g Rainbow Quest(USA) —Kartuzy (JPN) (Polish Precedent (USA))
97[8] 468[8] 713[F] 837[P]

Kasimali (IRE) *Gary Moore* 113h 107c
8 b g Soviet Star(USA) —Kassiyda (Mill Reef (USA))
3375[4] 3608[3] 3982[6] 4919[5] 5101[8]

Kassjan (IRE) *Nigel Hawke*
8 b m Saddlers' Hall(IRE) —Sirrah Madam (Tug Of War)
1107[P]

Kasthari (IRE) *Chris Grant* 138h 45c
12 gr g Vettori(IRE) —Karliyka (IRE) (Last Tycoon)
890[6]

Katalak (IRE) *Jonathen de Giles* 85h 104c
8 b g Desert Prince(IRE) —Katiykha (IRE) (Darshaan)
49[3] 2982[P] 3391[10] 3614[P] (5349)

Katapult (GER) *Kate Walton* 90h
8 b g Dashing Blade—Katharina (GER) (Esclavo (FR))
3887[5] 4304[8] 5092[6]

Katchit (IRE) *Alan King* 157h
8 b g Kalanisi(IRE) —Miracle (Ezzoud (IRE))
1886[2]

Katchmore (IRE) *Michael Blanshard* 112h
4 br g Catcher In The Rye(IRE) —One For Me (Tragic Role (USA))
2570[3] (4521) 5010[6] 5348[2]

Kathindi (IRE) *Neil King*
4 ch g Pearl Of Love(IRE) —Turfcare Flight (IRE) (Mujadil (USA))
1324[4] 1473[P]

Kathleen Kennet *Martin Bosley* 69h
11 b m Turtle Island(IRE) —Evaporate (Insan (USA))
1705[4] 2129[8]

Kathleens Pride (IRE) *Robin Dickin* 111h 108c
11 b g Broken Hearted—Cyprus Hill (IRE) (Bulldozer)
(2284)
3768[P]

Katie's Prince (IRE) *Chris Grant* 64b
7 b g Anshan—One Move (IRE) (Montelimar (USA))
1785[6]

Katkopoly (FR) *C Diard* 98c
5 b g Poliglote—Kitka (FR) (Epervier Bleu)
5159a[0]

Katys Jools *Tim Vaughan* 69b
4 b f King's Theatre(IRE) —Jessolle (Scallywag)
4866[8] 5380[10]

Kauto Cyreo (FR) *Claire Dyson* 78h
6 b g Saint Cyrien(FR) —Kauto Of Realm (FR) (Signe Divin (USA))
3718[6] 3918[8]

Kauto Relko (FR) *Rachel Hobbs* 127h
7 b g With The Flow(USA) —Kauto Relka (FR) (Port Etienne (FR))
1956[3] ◆ 2164[5] 2671[8] 4235[2] ◆ 4852[5] 5287[6]

Kauto Star (FR) *Paul Nicholls* 146h 191c
11 b g Village Star(FR) —Kauto Relka (FR) (Port Etienne (FR))
(2226a)
3560[3] 4850[3]

Kauto The Kid (FR) *Paul Nicholls*
6 ch g Saint Cyrien(FR) —Kauto Relka (FR) (Port Etienne (FR))
267[P] 661[P]

Kauto The Roc (FR) *Alan King* 123h
7 ch g With The Flow(USA) —Kauto Of Realm (FR) (Signe Divin (USA))
1907[3] ◆ (2181) (2581) 3566[F] 3742[6] 4421[2] 5003[12]

Kavaloti (IRE) *Gary Moore* 41h
7 b g Kahyasi—Just As Good (FR) (Kaldounevees (FR))
4025[13] 4310[P] 4922[12]

Kavatina *Lawney Hill* 50b
7 b m Overbury(IRE) —Auntie Dora (Idiots Delight)
935[10]

Kavegirl *John Panvert* 94h
8 b m Kayf Tara—Kolyas Girl (IRE) (Be My Native (USA))
1028[4] 1140[4] 1343[4] 1479[U] 1556[3]

Kavi (IRE) *Simon Earle* 35h 97c
11 ch g Perugino(USA) —Premier Leap (IRE) (Salmon Leap (USA))
1159[7]

Kawa (FR) *Robin Dickin* 106b
5 gr g Kouroun(FR) —Kulitch (FR) (Courtroom (FR))
(2590) ◆ 3936[3] 4468[10]

Kawagino (IRE) *Seamus Mullins* 122h 130c
11 b g Perugino(USA) —Sharakawa (IRE) (Darshaan)
2395[2] 3347[5] 3488[4]

Kayaan *Pam Sly* 97h
4 br g Marju(IRE) —Raheefa (USA) (Riverman (USA))
3739[8] 3986[2] 4192[5] 4809[5] 5131[4]

Kaybeew *Nigel Twiston-Davies* 112h
6 b g Alflora(IRE) —Lunareva (USA) (Nureyev (USA))
154[8] 2949[F] (3764) 4446[6]

Kaycee (IRE) *Roger Curtis* 89h
6 ch g King Charlemagne(USA) —Bollicina (USA) (Woodman (USA))
1902[9] 2314[9] 4272[7] 5040[6]

Kayef (GER) *Michael Scudamore* 112h
4 ch c Nayef(USA) —Kassna (IRE) (Ashkalani (IRE))
2882[9] 3443[4] (4192) 4807[14]

Kayf Aramis *Nigel Twiston-Davies* 150h
9 b g Kayf Tara—Ara (Birthright)
2090[2] 2672[5] 2884[6] 3199[4] 3807[8] 4207[3] 4817[14] 5304[8]

Kayf Commander *Mel Brittain* 97h
8 b g Kayf Tara—Silk Stockings (FR) (Trempolino (USA))
423[3] 494[7] 748[P]

Kayfontaine *Jonjo O'Neill* 82b
5 gr m Kayf Tara—Roufontaine (Rousillon (USA))
4866[7]

Kayf Paradis *John Spearing* 66b
6 b m Kayf Tara—Paris Fashion (FR) (Northern Fashion (USA))
1927[9] 2472[10]

Kayfrou *Jonjo O'Neill* 74h
6 b g Kayf Tara—Roufontaine (Rousillon (USA))
5327[8]

Kayfton Pete *Reg Hollinshead* 108h
5 b g Kayf Tara—Jonchee (FR) (Le Thuit Signol (FR))
1768[10] 2056[10] 2307[4] *3093[3]* 3481[14] 3917[4] 4076[5] 4874[3] 5117[F]

Kaygeekay (IRE) *Chris Down*
5 b m Erhaab(USA) —Rocheflamme (FR) (Snurge)
3930[P]

Kaylif Aramis *Nigel Twiston-Davies* 95b
4 b g Kayf Tara—Ara (Birthright)
2797[2] ◆ 3294[14] 4505[2] 5387[5]

Kazzene (USA) *David Pipe* 110h
4 b g Cozzene(USA) —Coconut Willamina (USA) (Pleasant Colony (USA))
(3554) 3937[3] 4350[9] 5441[13]

Kealshore *George Moore* 68b
4 ch g Alflora(IRE) —Top Of The Dee (Rakaposhi King)
5264[9]

Kealshore Boy *Howard Johnson* 124h 126c
8 br g Overbury(IRE) —Rippling Brook (Phardante (FR))
4456[2] 5422[P]

Keara *Amy Weaver*
6 b m Kayf Tara—Lavender Lady (IRE) (Lord Americo)
3616[11]

Kearn's Girl (IRE) *Barry Brennan* 20b
7 b m Gothenberg(IRE) —Grouse-N-Heather (Grey Desire)
2987[13]

Keckerrockernixes (IRE) *Richard Rowe* 79h
5 ch g Tomba—Dromhall Lady (IRE) (Imperial Frontier (USA))
215[U] 528[8] 690[4] 1592[11] 1918[5] 2390[5] 3611[P] 4559[10] 5191[4] 5383[5]

Keelaghan (IRE) *A J Martin* 123h 137c
11 ch g Accordion—New Legislation (IRE) (Dominion Royale)
2345[6]

Keel Road (IRE) *Giles Smyly* 79h 116c
9 b m Luso—Wiltreo (IRE) (Insan (USA))
1739[4] ◆ (1964)

Keenan's Future (IRE) *Ian Williams* 119h 131c
10 ch g Safety Catch(USA) —The Singer (IRE) (Accordion)
4928[2] (5207) ◆

Keenans Reserve (IRE) *Brian Baugh* 86c
10 b g Broken Hearted—Caoimhne (IRE) (Buckskin (FR))
79[5] 889[7]

Keen Whip *C Brader* 90c
9 ch g Keen—Magic Whip (Current Magic)
4553[3]

Keep Guessing *Warren Greatrex* 93h
8 b g Lord Americo—Wychnor Dawn (IRE) (Broken Hearted)
129[7] 2280[P] 2927[5] 4809[4] 5130[10]

Keep Gunin (IRE) *Sue Smith* 90h
6 br g Needle Gun(IRE) —Remoosh (Glint Of Gold)
350[8]

Keepitsecret (IRE) *Jonjo O'Neill* 115h 110c
10 b g Topanoora—Try Your Case (Proverb)
(335) 844[P]
1020[10] 1332[P] 1469[7] 1604[9] 1992[7] 2940[5]

Keep Kicking (IRE) *Clive Mulhall* 105b
4 b g Tiger Hill(IRE) —Dalannda (IRE) (Hernando (FR))
(4801)

Keep Silent *John Berry* 46h
4 gr f Largesse—Not A Word (Batshoof)
1279[6]

Keep Talking (IRE) *Neil King* 110h
7 b g Religiously(USA) —Celia Barros (IRE) (Insan (USA))
62[5] 1689[4] 1812[2] 2081[9]

Keepthebooton (IRE) *Noel Chance* 90h
8 b g Turtle Island(IRE) —Fair View (IRE) (Castle Keep)
3864[3] 4377[10]

Keeverfield (IRE) *Miss S A Drake* 93h 112c
10 b g Lord Americo—Quayfield (Monksfield)
(3991)

Keki Buku (FR) *Philip Hobbs* 139h 134c
8 b g Kadalko(FR) —Bigouden (What A Guest)
(2399) 2542[5]
3262[2] 3871[2] 4122[F] 4853[10]

Kells Belle (IRE) *Nicky Henderson* 123h
5 b m Alflora(IRE) —Clandestine (Saddlers' Hall (IRE))
(237) 3366[2] ◆ (4006) 4703[3] 5008[12]

Kells Castle *Gordon Elliott* 25h 102c
9 gr g Fraam—Bit O' May (Mummy's Pet)
308[P]

Kelly Manor (IRE) *Tony Carroll* 88h
7 b m Exit To Nowhere(USA) —Montelfolene (IRE) (Montelimar (USA))
250[F] 547[8] 697[5] 988[P]

Kellystown Lad (IRE) *Ferdy Murphy* 120h 131c
8 b g Old Vic—Kissangel (IRE) (Namaqualand (USA))
1779[3] 2270[2] (2599)
3390[6] 3672[6] 5002[P]

Keltic Crisis (IRE) *Jonathan Geake* 88h
7 b g Needle Gun(IRE) —Catch Ball (Prince Sabo)
3200[15] 4489[8] 4951[P] 5321[5]

Keltic Lord *Peter Hiatt* 79h 101c
15 b g Arctic Lord—Scarlet Dymond (Rymer)
431[7] 695[P] 868[4] 1061[2] 1152[4] (1235)
1297[5] 1550[4] 1843[3]

Kembla Grange (IRE) *C A McBratney* 111h
5 ch g Medecis—Mrs Kanning (Distant View (USA))
744[3] 856[2] ◆

Kempes (IRE) *W P Mullins* 146h 167c
8 b g Intikhab(USA) —Unicamp (Royal Academy (USA))
2972a[3] 3176a[U] (4087a)
4850[P]

Kempley Green (IRE) *Michael Scudamore* 76h 94c
8 b g Revoque(IRE) —Alaroos (IRE) (Persian Bold)
4234[8] 5117[12] 5392[P]

Kempski *Rayson Nixon* 107h 64c
11 b g Petoski—Little Katrina (Little Buskins)
309[10] 2104[11] (2448) 4067[4] 4169[8] (4715) 4873[2] 5262[6]

Kemsley Lass *Milton Bradley* 43h
6 b m Sooty Tern—Hayley's Lass (Royal Boxer)
760[10] 1090[P]

Kensington Oval *Jonjo O'Neill* 98h
6 b g Sadler's Wells(USA) —Request (Rainbow Quest (USA))
1160[7] 1333[P] 1484[11] 1601[7] (1997) 2247[5]

Kensix Star (IRE) *Howard Johnson* 67h
5 b g Zagreb(USA) —Beechberry (IRE) (Shernazar)
3398[8] 4112[P] 5027[11]

Kentford Grey Lady *Emma Lavelle* 111b
5 gr m Silver Patriarch(IRE) —Kentford Grebe (Teenoso (USA))
(3876) 4728[11]

Kentmere (IRE) *Paul Webber* 89h 102c
10 b g Efisio—Addaya (IRE) (Persian Bold)
410[4]

Kent Street (IRE) *Sue Smith* 99b
6 ch g Flemensfirth(USA) —Fernhill (IRE) (Good Thyne (USA))
2355[2] 2957[7]

Keoghs Bar (IRE) *Irene J Monaghan* 86h 100c
7 bb g Flemensfirth(USA) —What's Up Mary (IRE) (Mister Lord (USA))
1500[3] 1663[U] 1928[3]

Kerada (FR) *Nicky Henderson* 131h 141c
7 b m Astarabad(USA) —Mossita (FR) (Tip Moss (FR))
2218[4]
(3627) ◆ (3763)
(4162) ◆ 5007[F]

Kercabellec (FR) *John Cornwall* 94h 83c
13 bb g Useful(FR) —Marie De Geneve (FR) (Nishapour (FR))
156[7] 1483[P] 2250[7] 2402[5] 3388[P] 3541[4] 4238[7] 4744[3] (4811)
(4945)

Kericho *Patrick Rodford* 84b
6 b g Alflora(IRE) —Do It On Dani (Weld)
37[P] 5253[P]

Kew Jumper (IRE) *Andy Turnell* 100h 126c
12 b g Mister Lord(USA) —Pharisee (IRE) (Phardante (FR))
236[10]

Keyaza (IRE) *Tobias B P Coles* 105b
4 b f Azamour(IRE) —Key Change (IRE) (Darshaan)
(4815) 5188[12]

Key Cutter (FR) *Paul Webber* 116h 128c
7 b g Alderbrook—Two Roads (Boreen (FR))
3[7] **1727[2]**
2324[2] (2580)
2959[12]

Keyneema *Cathy Hamilton* 93h 93c
9 b g Kayf Tara—Nothings Forever (Oats)
1732[6] 2149[5] **2334[5]** 3611[7]
3792[2] 3959[4] 4693[7]

Keys (IRE) *Roger Charlton* 114b
4 b g Doyen(IRE) —Freni (GER) (Sternkoenig (IRE))
(2237) *(2597)* (3294)

Key Time (IRE) *Howard Johnson* 110h
9 b g Darshaan—Kasota (IRE) (Alzao (USA))
447[P]

Key To Milan *Chris Down* 88b
5 b g Milan—Key West (FR) (Highest Honor (FR))
4484[10] 5158[8]

Khachaturian (IRE) *Donald McCain* 116h 144c
8 b g Spectrum(IRE) —On Air (FR) (Chief Singer)
2523[15] *3092[3]* **3948[F]** 4209[5]
4821[10] 5206[7]

Khalashan (FR) *Peter Niven* 79b
5 gr g Sinndar(IRE) —Khalasha (FR) (Linamix (FR))
935[8] 3889[16] 4396[9]

Khayar (IRE) *E McNamara* 112h
5 b g Refuse To Bend(IRE) —Khatela (IRE) (Shernazar)
2361[5]

Khazar (FR) *Jonjo O'Neill* 128h 97c
8 bb g Anabaa(USA) —Khalisa (IRE) (Persian Bold)
251[P] (533)
689[5] 864[3] 1237[3] 1474[4] 1678[3]

Kheskianto (IRE) *Michael Chapman* 57h
5 b m Kheleyf(USA) —Gently (IRE) (Darshaan)
1613[10] 1723[P] 2323[5]

Khorun (GER) *Tim Vaughan* 114h 104c
6 ch g Lord Of Men—Kalata (GER) (Lando (GER))
(1260) 1392[2] 4145[4] **4692[2]**

Khyber Kim *Nigel Twiston-Davies* 168h 121c
9 b g Mujahid(USA) —Jungle Rose (Shirley Heights)
3559[4] 4791[9] 5160[6]

Kiama *Ron Hodges* 62h 100c
9 b m Dansili—Catriona (Bustino)
3908[9] 4271[3] 5373[6]

Kickahead (USA) *Ian Williams* 121h 108c
9 b g Danzig(USA) —Krissante (USA) (Kris)
934[2] 1025[4]

Kick Start *V C Ward*
6 ch g Observatory(USA) —Kamkova (USA) (Northern Dancer (CAN))
1146a[S]

Kidajo *Roger Curtis* 69h
5 gr g Terimon—Miss Muire (Scallywag)
1749[10] 2432[9] 3200[11] 3789[10] 3960[11] 4370[10] 5383[P]

Kid Cassidy (IRE) *Nicky Henderson* 137h
5 b g Beneficial—Shuil Na Lee (IRE) (Phardante (FR))
(2666) 3196[3] 4325[2]

Kielder Rise *Evan Williams* 56h
7 b m Classic Cliche(IRE) —Countessmarkievicz (IRE) (Elbio)
2425[8] 3532[8] 4098[6] 5040[5]

Kijivu *Alastair Lidderdale* 110h
6 gr m Erhaab(USA) —Alsiba (Northfields (USA))
282[4] 645[3] 796[3] (1292) (1492)

Kikos (FR) *Renee Robeson* 97h 123c
9 ch g Nikos—Balgarde (FR) (Garde Royale)
361[U] 709[2] 959[4] 1606[6] 1690[4] 1975[3] 2529[6] (5279)

Kilbeggan Blade *Robin Dickin* 35h 127c
12 b g Sure Blade(USA) —Moheli (Ardross)
2305[P] 3488[P] 4537[5] 5061[5]
5154[5]

Kilbrannish Hill (IRE) *I R Ferguson* 126h
7 br g Oscar(IRE) —Raheenbawn (IRE) (Be My Native (USA))
4149[7] 5149[3] 5339[7]

Kilbready Star (IRE) *Peter Pritchard* 81h 88c
11 bb g Germany(USA) —Rutger Move (SWE) (Imperial Fling (USA))
1822[10] 2111[5] **2243[F]** 3837[P] 4314[8] 4814[P] 5298[12]

Kilcascan *Rosemary Gasson* 74c
7 b g Alflora(IRE) —Peasedown Tofana (Teenoso (USA))
4973[8]

Kilcommon Pride (IRE) *Roger Curtis* 77h
6 bb g Catcher In The Rye(IRE) —Ballyhookeen Lass (IRE) (Balla Cove)
1455[3] 1607[6] 2122[10] 2607[11] 3491[7] 3839[8]

Kilcrea Kim (IRE) *Philip Hobbs* 143h
6 ch g Snurge—Kilcrea Deer (IRE) (Brush Aside (USA))
(1765) (2067) (2574) 3293[5] (3947) ◆ 4849[5] 5187[8]

Kildonnan *Jim Old* 91h 121c
12 b g Bob's Return(IRE) —Celtic Tore (IRE) (Torus)
3588[4] 4277[3]

Kilkenny All Star (IRE) *Sue Smith* 113h 123c
10 b g Alderbrook—Borris Bounty (IRE) (Treasure Hunter)
676[3] (1823)
(2276) 3573[F] 4324[7] 4470[P]

Killard Point (IRE) *Caroline Bailey* 110h 125c
12 b g Old Vic—Chic And Elite (Deep Run)
11[2] 608[5]

Killenaule Boy *Tim Vaughan* 104h 134c
9 b g Alflora(IRE) —Kellsboro Queen (Rakaposhi King)
1113a[8] 1332[P] 1390[7] 1555[P]

Killer Jim *William Davies* 52h
9 ch g Killer Instinct—Sister Jim (Oats)
5374[P]

Killfinnan Castle (IRE) *Violet M Jordan* 57h 86c
8 br g Arctic Lord—Golden Seekers (Manado)
1678[U] 2048[4] 3492[2] 3790[U] 3984[3] 4560[10]

Killiney Ranger (IRE) *P J Goodwin* 94h 71c
13 ch g Phardante(FR) —Sea Folly (IRE) (King's Ride)
2113[7]

Killing Me Softly *Brian Forsey* 83h 87c
10 b g Kingsinger(IRE) —Slims Lady (Theatrical Charmer)
371[6] 593[4] 757[P] 4273[4] 4522[5]

Killowenabbey (IRE) *Debra Hamer* 113h 56c
7 b g Oscar(IRE) —Boreen Belle (Boreen (FR))
21[P] (75) 2131[8] **3873[F] 4292[10] 4447[F]** 5014[F]

Killusty Fancy (IRE) *Dominic Ffrench Davis* 102h
4 b g Refuse To Bend(IRE) —Crafty Fancy (IRE) (Intikhab (USA))
2570[2] 2882[10] 3554[8] 3962[11] 4925[8]

Killyglen (IRE) *S R B Crawford* 128h 158c
9 b g Presenting—Tina Maria (IRE) (Phardante (FR))
2226a[5] 4466[6] ◆ 5200[F]

Kilmore West (IRE) *Tim Vaughan* 100h
6 b g Turtle Island(IRE) —Lincoln Green (IRE) (Ela-Mana-Mou)
20[2] 137[4] (766) 1296[F] 1709[3] 1925[5]

Kilmurry (IRE) *Colin Tizzard* 126h 152c
6 b g King's Theatre(IRE) —Mawly Day (IRE) (Fourstars Allstar (USA))
(1865)
2384[4] 4078[P] (Dead)

Kilshanna (IRE) *Daniel William O'Sullivan* 54h
6 b g Bach(IRE) —Mugazine (Kemal (FR))
2331[8]

Kilshannig (IRE) *Jonjo O'Neill* 117h 106c
6 ch g Galileo(IRE) —Surf The Web (IRE) (Ela-Mana-Mou)
532[3] 717[3] **867[2] 1034[4] 1509[3] 1747[F]** 2279[3] 2474[2]

Kiltartan (IRE) *Miss Clare Judith Macmahon*
6 bb g Tel Quel(FR) —Sharnad (IRE) (Shardari)
289[P]

Kiltimoney (IRE) *Richard Mitchell* 81b 82c
11 gr g Kasmayo—Rosie's Midge (General Ironside)
1969[3] 2394[2] 2950[9] 3377[7] 3609[P] 3933[5] 4560[3]
5216[3] 5324[3]

Kilty Storm (IRE) *Roger Joseph McGrath* 113h 134c
12 b g Glacial Storm(USA) —Hogan's Cherry (General Ironside)
5163[F]

Kilvergan Boy (IRE) *Nigel Twiston-Davies* 98h 106c
7 br g Zagreb(USA) —Brigante (IRE) (Grand Lodge (USA))
22[4] 273[6] 522[4] 698[2] 1925[8] **2557[4]** 2980[8]
3371[8] 4693[4] 5386[2]

Kilvoydansouth (IRE) *N F Glynn* 116h
7 b g Oscar(IRE) —Before (IRE) (Ore)
2325[3]

Kimberley Downs (USA) *Noel Wilson* 79h
5 gr g Giant's Causeway(USA) —Fountain Lake (USA) (Vigors (USA))
1832[7]

Kim Tian Road (IRE) *Martin Hill* 89h
5 b m King's Theatre(IRE) —Shaunies Lady (IRE) (Don't Forget Me)
3647[3]

Kinder Scout *Chris Grant* 81b
4 b f Tamure(IRE) —Riviere (Meadowbrook)
5135[10] 5432[5]

Kind Heart *Donald McCain* 105h 85c
5 b m Red Ransom(USA) —Portorosa (USA) (Irish River (FR))
331[F] 648[4] **1000[2] 1252[F]** 1427[4]

Kindlelight Soleil (FR) *Nick Littmoden* 59b
4 b g Anabaa(USA) —Fee Du Nord (Inchinor)
4055[11]

Kind Of Easy (IRE) *Emma Lavelle* 120h
5 b g Kalanisi(IRE) —Specifiedrisk (IRE) (Turtle Island (IRE))
2925[10] 4094[2]

Kinfayre Boy *S Bowden* 92h 95c
9 b g Grey Eagle—Amber Gambler (ITY) (Nijin (USA))
4147[P] 4696[P]

King Ar Aghaidh (IRE) *Charlie Longsdon* 101h 119c
10 b g King's Theatre(IRE) —Shuil Ar Aghaidh (The Parson)
138[F] 830[4] 1855[2]

Kingaroo (IRE) *Garry Woodward* 70h
5 b g King Charlemagne(USA) —Lady Naomi (USA) (Distant View (USA))
4499[12]

King Benny (IRE) *Elliott Cooper* 99h
7 br g Beneficial—Kindly Lass (Wolver Hollow)
727[7] 803[6] 1066[7] 3622[4] (3717) 3782[5] 4115[11]
5208[10]

King Brex (DEN) *Charlie Mann* 115h 122c
8 b g Primatico(USA) —Moon Shine (DEN) (Shining Steel)
1816[P]
2022[P] 4049[7] (4697) 4858[7]

King Caine (IRE) *Alan Jones* 122h 119c
9 b g King's Theatre(IRE) —Kadarassa (IRE) (Warning)
265[U] 329[U] 1045[U] 4265[U] 4975[P]

King Canute (IRE) *Neil Mulholland* 31h
7 b g Danehill(USA) —Mona Stella (USA) (Nureyev (USA))
1111[12]

King Caractacus *Lawney Hill* 88b
6 b g Fleetwood(IRE) —Go Tally-Ho (Gorytus (USA))
5209[4]

King Cyrus (IRE) *Ms Emma Oliver* 106h 120c
9 br g Anshan—Miss Eurolink (Touching Wood (USA))
(4786)
5372[3]

King Diamond (FR) *Violet M Jordan* 78c
10 b g Exit To Nowhere(USA) —Diamona (FR) (Diamond Shoal)
283[P] 4104[P]

Kingdom Of Munster (IRE) *Richard Fahey* 103h
4 b g Danehill Dancer(IRE) —Kitty O'Shea (Sadler's Wells (USA))
3358[7] 3519[3] 4056[2] 4358[7] 4807[8]

King Edmund *Chris Gordon* 113h 143c
8 b g Roi De Rome(USA) —Cadbury Castle (Midyan (USA))
2086[4] ◆ 2517[7] 3949[6] 4470[4] ◆ 5242[2]

King Fingal (IRE) *John Quinn* 116h
6 b g King's Best(USA) —Llia (Shirley Heights)
2162[5] (3547) 3781[4] 4149[6] 5131[2]

Kingfisher Niamh *Paul Cowley* 77h 95c
11 b m Cloudings(IRE) —Legata (IRE) (Orchestra)
849[P] **1061[P]**

King Fontaine (IRE) *Malcolm Jefferson* 120h 146c
8 b g King's Theatre(IRE) —Kerfontaine (Lafontaine (USA))
(2163)
(2522) 4208[P] 4790[5] 5200[11]

King Gabriel (IRE) *Tracey Watkins* 43h
9 b g Desert King(IRE) —Broken Spirit (IRE) (Slip Anchor)
534[11]
1025[P] 4441[9] 4968[P] 5208[P]

King Harald (IRE) *A Bradstock* 105h 84c
13 b g King's Ride—Cuilin Bui (IRE) (Kemal (FR))
501[P] 4991[6]

King High (IRE) *Eoin Doyle* 125h 125c
7 b g King's Theatre(IRE) —Tessano Queen (IRE) (Jurado (USA))
1121a[P]

King In Waiting (IRE) *David O'Meara* 115h 104c
8 b g Sadler's Wells(USA) —Ballerina (IRE) (Dancing Brave (USA))
4275[F] 4890[3]

King Jack *Richard Phillips* 126h 116c
9 b g Classic Cliche(IRE) —Hack On (Good Thyne (USA))
3617[4] 4313[3] 5292[2]

King Kalium (IRE) *Bruce Mactaggart* 65b
5 b g Kayf Tara—Hannah Park (IRE) (Lycius (USA))
4547[8] 5147[P] 5428[P]

King Kasyapa (IRE) *Peter Bowen* 93h
9 b g Darshaan—Ezana (Ela-Mana-Mou)
4098[P] 4724[8] 5111[4] 5241[2] 5383[F]

King Killone (IRE) *Henry Hogarth* 119h 132c
11 b g Moonax(IRE) —Killone Brae (King's Ride)
3509[P] **4137[P]**

King Mak *Marjorie Fife* 109h 128c
9 gr g Makbul—Miss Nova (Ra Nova)
2477[7] 3523[5] 3951[5] 4738[2] (4912) 5144[3]

King Maker (IRE) *John Joseph Murphy* 114h
7 ch g Strategic Choice(USA) —Rosies All The Way (Robellino (USA))
2116a[4]

Kingman Reef (IRE) *Chris Bealby* 61h
7 ch g Glacial Storm(USA) —Monadante (IRE) (Phardante (FR))
1990[9] 2375[10]

King Of Castile *Barry Leavy* 111h
7 ch g Hernando(FR) —Pato (High Top)
227[2] (420) 603[2] 953[2] 1092[F] 1555[P] 3818[2] **5261[P]**

King Of Dubai *John Flint* 117h
6 b g Dubai Destination(USA) —Pearl Barley (IRE) (Polish Precedent (USA))
2241[6] ◆ 2607[8] (3585) 3931[6] 5118[3]

King Of Leon (FR) *Emma Lavelle* 103h 103c
7 b g Kingsalsa(USA) —Dany Ohio (FR) (Script Ohio (USA))
353[9] 3745[3] 4224[P] **4811[2] 5051[F]**

King Of Magic *Bill Turner* 11h
7 b g King O' The Mana(IRE) —Mountain Magic (Magic Ring (IRE))
3224[8]

King Of The Beers (USA) *T J Bougourd* 85h
7 rg g Silver Deputy(CAN) —Pracer (USA) (Lyphard (USA))
(915a)

King Of The Moors (USA) *Richard Guest*
8 b g King Of Kings(IRE) —Araza (USA) (Arazi (USA))
1083[P]

King Of The Night (GER) *Paul Nicholls* 132h
7 b g Lomitas—Kaiserlerche (GER) (Subotica (FR))
(1857) 2344[5] (3787) 4852[F] 5441[11]

King Of The Road *Mrs Janet Ackner* 92c
9 ch g Romany Rye—Queen's Cross (Kinglet)
5156[5]

King Of The Titans (IRE) *Patrick Gilligan* 87h
8 b g Titus Livius(FR) —She's The Tops (Shernazar)
534[9] 1292[9] 2128[11] 4977[6] 5193[7]

King Of Thorns (IRE) *George Moore* 57b
4 b g Close Conflict(USA) —Rolled Thistle (IRE) (Carlingford Castle)
5313[10]

King Olav (UAE) *Tony Carroll* 121h
6 ch g Halling(USA) —Karamzin (USA) (Nureyev (USA))
2122[9]

King O'The Gypsies (IRE) *Howard Johnson* 125h 120c
6 b g Sadler's Wells(USA) —Love For Ever (IRE) (Darshaan)
(2300)
4002[U] 4168[3] 4823[3]

King Ozzy (IRE) *Martin Keighley* 111h 125c
7 b g King Charlemagne(USA) —Kingpin Delight (Emarati (USA))
715[11] **848[9]**
(1047)
1136[4] 1766[9]
2293[2] 3345[4] 3486[2]

King Penda (IRE) *Nicky Richards* 94h 36c
8 br g Presenting—Peacock Feather (Bustino)
42[5] 459[2] 1929[9]
3748[P] 4690[4]

King Puc *Barry Murtagh* 24h
6 gr g Karinga Bay—Squirrellsdaughter (Black Minstrel)
2446[10] 3850[13]

King Raven (IRE) *Mark Rimell* 107h 101c
9 b g Sea Raven(IRE) —Wee Norex (IRE) (Roselier (FR))
217[2] 467[4] (692) 737[4]

King Richard (IRE) *Richard Rowe* 33h
7 bb g Rashar(USA) —Garys Girl (Seclude (USA))
1914[13] 2440[6] 2594[9]

King Rocky *Shaun Lycett* 97h
10 b g Rakaposhi King—Jims Sister (Welsh Captain)
1105[2]

King Roonah *Gordon Elliott* 91h 131c
7 b g Wizard King—Roonah Quay (IRE) (Soviet Lad (USA))
287[3] 443[F] 459[3]
(860) 874[7] 1117[U] 1338[2] 1598[2] (1725)
1858[P]

King Sandor (IRE) *Nicky Richards* 87h
6 b g King's Theatre(IRE) —Irene Good-Night (IRE) (Shernazar)
2192[5] 3330[9] 3692[13] 4067[8]

Kingsben *Malcolm Jefferson* 111h 92c
8 b g King's Best(USA) —Bluebelle (Generous (IRE))
1642[P] 1731[8] 5102[8]

Kings Brook *John Cornwall* 107h 84c
11 br g Alderbrook—Kins Token (Relkino)
352[P]

Kings Canyon (IRE) *Howard Johnson* 92b
5 ch g Stowaway—Hurricane Debbie (IRE) (Shahanndeh)
3889[10] 4574[2]

King's Chorister *Barry Murtagh* 80h
5 ch g King's Best(USA) —Chorist (Pivotal)
161[5] 286[3] 604[4] 948[10] 1407[8] 1574[5] 3551[5]
3727[2] 3993[2] 4136[3] 4686[2] 4998[4]

King's Counsel (IRE) *David O'Meara* 107h
5 ch g Refuse To Bend(IRE) —Nesaah's Princess (Sinndar (IRE))
4113[5] 4452[2] 4797[2]

Kingscourt Lad (IRE) *Charles Pogson* 93h
13 b g Norwich—Mrs Minella (Deep Run)
2070[P] 2398[9]

King's Envoy (USA) *Jean McGregor* 60h 72c
12 b g Royal Academy(USA) —Island Of Silver (USA) (Forty Niner (USA))
1700[13] 2103[10]

Kings Flagship *Chris Down* 96h
6 b g Lahib(USA) —Queen's Flagship (IRE) (Accordion)
4676[5] 4986[7]

King's Forest (IRE) *Emma Lavelle* 109h 132c
7 b g Celtic Swing—Glen Princess (IRE) (Bob Back (USA))
1626[8] 1855[8] 2125[F]

King's Grace *Donald McCain* 111b
5 b g King's Theatre(IRE) —Beauchamp Grace (Ardross)
(2309) ◆

Kings Grey (IRE) *Keith Reveley* 113h
7 gr g King's Theatre(IRE) —Grey Mo (IRE) (Roselier (FR))
2349[5] 3330[2] ◆ 3851[3] 4281[2] 4739[9] 5147[8]

Kings Guard (IRE) *Alistair Whillans* 97h
8 b g Turtle Island(IRE) —Rose Of Stradbally (IRE) (Roselier (FR))
2104[9] 2448[4] ◆ (3635) 4068[2] 4477[3]

King's Icon (IRE) *Michael Wigham* 87h
6 b g King's Best(USA) —Pink Sovietstaia (FR) (Soviet Star (USA))
349[9]

Kings Lad (IRE) *Colin Tizzard* 65b
4 b g King's Theatre(IRE) —Festival Leader (IRE) (Supreme Leader)
5217[8]

King's Legacy (IRE) *Paul Nicholls* 136h
7 b g King's Theatre(IRE) —Kotton (FR) (Cyborg (FR))
2387[3] 3293[11] 5287[2] ◆

King's Lion (IRE) *Charles Pogson* 96h
7 b g King's Theatre(IRE) —Petite Galerie (IRE) (Pips Pride)
833[6] 1260[4] 1401[5]

Kings Lodge *Nicky Henderson* 107b
5 b g King's Theatre(IRE) —Mardello (Supreme Leader)
2957[4] ◆ 3835[4] 4468[5]

King's Majesty (IRE) *Tim Pitt* 93h 86c
9 b g King's Best(USA) —Tiavanita (USA) (J O Tobin (USA))
10[7] **177[3]**
491[2] 634[4] 747[3] 840[8]

Kingsmere *Henry Daly* 111h
6 b g King's Theatre(IRE) —Lady Emily (Alflora (IRE))
2241[4] 3405[4] 3919[2]
4461[P]

Kingsmoss (IRE) *J J Lambe* 118h 118c
6 b g Luso—Galamear (Strong Gale)
519[4] 3330[10] 3851[5]
4685[P]

Kingspark Boy (IRE) *David Rees*
4 b g Tillerman—Malacca (USA) (Danzig (USA))
1772[8] 2020[5]

Kings Queen (IRE) *Tom George* 102h
5 b m Wizard King—Muharib Lady (IRE) (Muharib (USA))
3389[5] 4101[3] 4454[5] 5078[2]

King's Realm (IRE) *Alison Thorpe* 106h
4 ch g King's Best(USA) —Sweet Home Alabama (IRE) (Desert Prince (IRE))
3158[7] 3484[3] 4288[2] 4488[4] 4925[4]

King's Revenge *Shaun Lycett* 121h
8 br g Wizard King—Retaliator (Rudimentary (USA))
1998[2] 2347[13] 3686[2] 3874[8] 4488[8] 5102[4]

Kings Riches (IRE) *Peter Bowen* 98h
6 ch g Anshan—Kaikoura Girl (IRE) (Desse Zenny (USA))
(277) 855[3] 935[6] 1124[6] 1158[6] 1228[2] 1401[4]
2161[4]

Kings Story (IRE) *Sophie Leech* 66h
7 b g Royal Applause—Poppy Carew (IRE) (Danehill (USA))
2795[4] 3400[7] 4522[7] 5040[4] 5295[5]

Kingston Folly *Andrew Haynes*
4 gr g Septieme Ciel(USA) —Napapijri (FR) (Highest Honor (FR))
4917[16]

Kingston Orla *Andrew Haynes* 73b
6 gr m Baryshnikov(AUS) —Tricata (Electric)
412[12] 1069[10] 1455[8]

Kingston Queen (IRE) *Rachel Hobbs* 81h 72c
8 b m Moscow Society(USA) —Lady Of Sonas (IRE) (Lancastrian)
931[P] 1059[3] 1232[P] 1559[6] 1694[4] 1745[3]

Kings Troop *Alan King* 110h
5 ch g Bertolini(USA) —Glorious Colours (Spectrum (IRE))
3228[8] 4049[3]

King Supreme (IRE) *Richard Hannon* 97h
6 b g King's Best(USA) —Oregon Trail (USA) (Gone West (USA))
4478[5]

King's Wood (IRE) *A J Farrant* 99c
10 b g Oscar(IRE) —Deep Bart (Deep Run)
152[4]

King Troy (IRE) *Alan King* 120h 153c
9 bb g Presenting—Les Mis (IRE) (Supreme Leader)
(524) **1020[3]**
◆

Kinkeel (IRE) *Tony Carroll* 66h 90c
12 b g Hubbly Bubbly(USA) —Bubbly Beau (Beau Charmeur (FR))
1997[P]
2437[P] 2515[5] 2885[9] 2986[5] 3265[7] 3388[5] 3492[7]
3618[3] (3699)
3898[2] 4099[3]
4269[6] 4379[P]
5015[6] 5293[8]
5379[3]

Kinsya *Mark H Tompkins* 105h
8 ch g Mister Baileys—Kimono (IRE) (Machiavellian (USA))
1953[5] 2294[4]

Kiosk (FR) *J T R Dreaper* 94h
7 gr g Take Risks(FR) —Grande Souveraine (FR) (Sillery (USA))
856[7]

Kipik (FR) *R Le Gal*
8 b m Welkin(CAN) —Kipartira (FR) (Magwal (FR))
5159a[0]

Kirbybroguelantern (IRE) *T Hogan* 122h 125c
10 br g Tidaro(USA) —Karline Ka (FR) (Franc Parler)
3709a[11]

Kirbys Glen (IRE) *Patrick Rodford* 85h 91c
9 b g Charente River(IRE) —Silence To Silence (IRE) (Salmon Leap (USA))
276[4] 3544[3] 3875[5] (4269)
4447[4] 4784[F] 5275[2]

Kirby's Vic (IRE) *Nigel Twiston-Davies* 72h 114c
11 b g Old Vic—Just Affable (IRE) (Phardante (FR))
361[4]

Kiristani *Caroline Keevil* 55h
6 b m Shahrastani(USA) —Kiri Te (Liboi (USA))
759[11] 908[7] 1063[4] 1158[11]

Kirkhammerton (IRE) *Barry Leavy* 103h 119c
9 ch g Grand Lodge(USA) —Nawara (Welsh Pageant)
250[3] **339[2]**
477[B] 848[3] 919[2] (1139)
(1252) 1486[P] 1690[2] 1828[3] 2093[4]

Kirkton *Jim Wilson* 36b
6 ch m Kirkwall—Futona (Fearless Action (USA))
637[U] 1455[P]

Kirkum (IRE) *Diana Weeden* 33h
6 b g Selkirk(USA) —Jumilla (USA) (El Gran Senor (USA))
847[P] 2054[8] 3599[P] 4812[6] 4976[P]

Kisha King (IRE) *David Rees* 100h 114c
10 b g Dr Massini(IRE) —Lady Elise (IRE) (Celio Rufo)
1094[5]
1200[U] 1255[4]

Kissing Lessons *Patrick Leech* 57b
6 b m Polish Precedent(USA) —Aquarelle (Kenmare (FR))
686[10]

Kiss Me Twice *Martin Keighley* 95b
5 br g Generous(IRE) —Kiss Me Du Cochet (FR) (Orival (FR))
1729[4]

Kit Carson (IRE) *R MacDonald* 119h 97c
11 b g Dr Massini(IRE) —Roses Niece (IRE) (Jeu De Paille (FR))
2301[6] 2659[2] 3970[P] 4510[4]

Kitchen Loan (IRE) *Oliver Sherwood*
8 b m Presenting—Greenfield Noora (IRE) (Topanoora)
5297[U]

Kitley Hassle *James Frost* 85b 112c
9 b g Morpeth—Celtic Land (Landyap (USA))
1706[3] 2046[5] 2286[5] 2794[2] 3768[7] 3982[5] 4179[F]

Kitty Koo (IRE) *Tony Carroll* 92h
4 ch f Dr Fong(USA) —Jesting (Muhtarram (USA))
2211[3] 3484[4] 3767[3]

Klampenborg *Michael Scudamore* 73h
6 b g Exit To Nowhere(USA) —Party Girl (Unfuwain (USA))
591[4] 843[10]

Klark (FR) *M Rolland* 118h 132c
7 b g Mansonnien(FR) —Kogina (FR) (Lyfko (FR))
5159a[9]

Knapp Bridge Boy *James Payne* 96h 90c
11 b g Wimbleball—Toll Bridge (New Member)
130[5] 755[P] 4529[2]

Knar Mardy *Charles Pogson* 108h
6 bb m Erhaab(USA) —Iborga (FR) (Cyborg (FR))
52[3] 250[7] 421[2] (488) (603) 863[9] 1357[3] 1625[5] 1829[8]

Knickerbokerglory *Barbara Butterworth* 75b
5 b m Saddlers' Hall(IRE) —Cashmere Lady (Hubbly Bubbly (USA))
4554[9] 5033[7] 5352[8]

Knight Blaze *David Brace* 27h
4 b f Bach(IRE) —Braceys Girl (IRE) (Be My Native (USA))
1913[10] 4164[10] 4781[9]

Knight In Purple *John Mackie* 130h
7 b g Sir Harry Lewis(USA) —Cerise Bleue (FR) (Port Lyautey (FR))
331[4] 2076[P] 2508[11] 4783[5] (5215) (5420) ◆

Knight Legend (IRE) *Sarah Humphrey* 115h 140c
12 b g Flying Legend(USA) —Well Trucked (IRE) (Dry Dock)
131[7] **523[F]**
764[4] 874[4] 1110[2] 1390[4] 2112[3] 2531[4] 2869[8]
3303[2] 3493[6] 4025[3]
4856[2] 5134[5]

Knighton Combe *Jamie Snowden* 116h 136c
11 b g Midnight Legend—Cindercombe (Ra Nova)
3866[3]
4194[3] 4699[5] 5152[3]
5405[3]

Knight Pass (IRE) *Warren Greatrex* 128b
5 b g Accordion—Toulon Pass (IRE) (Toulon)
(2215) ◆ (3399) 4808[19]

Knightsbridge Hill (IRE) *Patrick Rodford* 103h 60c
9 b g Raise A Grand(IRE) —Desert Gem (Green Desert (USA))
183[5] 665[7] 913[7]

Knightsbridgelives (IRE) *Lawney Hill* 107h
8 b g Taipan(IRE) —Shean Rose (IRE) (Roselier (FR))
379[4] 692[6] 912[3] 990[12] 1125[4] 1431[3] 1555[6] 1677[P]

Knight Valliant *Barbara Butterworth* 104h
8 bl g Dansili—Aristocratique (Cadeaux Genereux)
405[3] 520[4] 875[3] 948[8] 1762[3] 2190[2] (4390) 4550[2] (5335)

Knight Woodsman *Neil King* 101h 90c
7 ch g Sir Harry Lewis(USA) —Jowoody (Gunner B)
318[P] 2532[4] 3370[8] 3745[10] 4021[6]
5268[2]

Knockalongi *Oliver Sherwood* 113b
5 b g Fair Mix(IRE) —Understudy (In The Wings)
2957[3] (3511) 4808[16]

Knockando *Lucinda Russell* 98h
6 b g Milan—Cherry Lane (Buckley)
311[9] 2355[9] 3553[9] 3851[9] 4253[4] 4569[F]

Knockara Beau (IRE) *George Charlton* 153h 158c
8 b g Leading Counsel(USA) —Clairabell (IRE) (Buckskin (FR))
2091[P] 2871[4] 3292[7] 3807[2] (4003) 4817[4] 5160[5]

Knockaveen (IRE) *Andrew Crook* 76h
6 b m Flemensfirth(USA) —Kitty Maher (IRE) (Posen (USA))
174[5] 421[6] 1780[4] 2275[5] 2598[P] 4395[5] 4872[6]

Knockavilla (IRE) *Howard Johnson* 123h 127c
8 b g Saddlers' Hall(IRE) —Native Singer (IRE) (Be My Native (USA))
(32) 2088[3]
3714[2]

Knockbaun Prince (IRE) *John G Carr* 100h
7 b g Hubbly Bubbly(USA) —Carrigeen Lass (IRE) (Vaour (USA))
1574[F] 2104[12]

Knockdolian (IRE) *Roger Charlton* 86h
4 b g Montjeu(IRE) —Doula (USA) (Gone West (USA))
3194[7] 3613[5] 4521[5]

Knock Em Dead (IRE) *Jonjo O'Neill* 109h
7 b g Bob Back(USA) —Knocknagow (Buckskin (FR))
66[2] **695[P]**

Knockfierna (IRE) *C Byrnes* 143h
6 b m Flemensfirth(USA) —Garden Town (IRE) (Un Desperado (FR))
(3181a) ◆

Knocklayde Euro (IRE) *J J Lambe* 115h 110c
7 b g Beneficial—Eurolink Sea Baby (Deep Run)
3520[10]

Knocklayde Vic (IRE) *Ian Williams* 112h
7 ch g Old Vic—Laughing Lesa (IRE) (Bob Back (USA))
5271[2]

Knocknagow Leader (IRE) *Jonjo O'Neill* 82h 121c
9 b g Supreme Leader—Knocknagow (Buckskin (FR))
4695[F]

Knock On The Head (IRE) *A L T Moore* 112h 119c
9 b g Flemensfirth(USA) —Hilldalus (IRE) (Mandalus)
1113a[7]

Knock Three Times (IRE) *Wilf Storey* 94h
5 b m Hernando(FR) —Tawoos (FR) (Rainbow Quest (USA))
1695[11] 1870[5] 2094[9] 4113[12] 4390[14] 5354[3]

Knockvicar (IRE) *Richard Mitchell* 72h
9 b m Anshan—It Time To Run (IRE) (Buckskin (FR))
134[6] 272[9] 593[P] 1915[7] 2135[P]

Knottage Hill (IRE) *Reg Hollinshead* 63h
6 b g Woods Of Windsor(USA) —Indiana Journey (IRE) (Eurobus)
93[10] 1600[9] 1821[P]

Knowhere (IRE) *Nigel Twiston-Davies* 140h 148c
13 b g Lord Americo—Andarta (Ballymore)
844[P] 2343[3] 2871[15] 3290[P]

Knowsall *Ms A E Embiricos* 78b
6 ch g Kyllachy—Ecstatic (Nashwan (USA))
1817[6] 2445[8]

Know The Ropes (IRE) *Mrs L A Coltherd* 60c
11 b g Muroto—Bobs My Uncle (Deep Run)
90[10]

Know Your Place *Jonjo O'Neill* 89h
7 ch g Double Trigger(IRE) —Charossa (Ardross)
665[P]

Kobuz (POL) *Josef Vana II*
9 bb g Tioman Island—Koneksja (POL) (Who Knows)
1811a[8]

Kochanski (IRE) *John Weymes* 79h
5 ch m King's Best(USA) —Ascot Cyclone (USA) (Rahy (USA))
405[11]

Konigsbote (GER) *Sophie Leech* 94h 75c
9 b g Monsun(GER) —Karenina (GER) (Second Set (IRE))
66[7] **529[5]**
1126[6] 1331[P]

Kopylova *Tim Vaughan* 101h
8 ch m Moscow Society(USA) —Country Store (Sunyboy)
(757) (930) 1336[3] 1490[4] 1605[P]

Koralsdarling (IRE) *Alan Jones* 90b
7 b g Witness Box(USA) —Jenny's Jewel (IRE) (Be My Native (USA))
1866[8]

Kornati Kid *Anabel L M King* 112h 132c
9 b g Kayf Tara—Hiltonstown Lass (IRE) (Denel (FR))
98[P] (4928)

Kosta Brava (FR) *Howard Johnson* 110h 119c
7 ch g Nikos—Tamana (USA) (Northern Baby (CAN))
(174)
1575[0] (1872)
2207[2] (2659)
3730[2] (5318)

Kotkidy (FR) *Henry De Bromhead* 100h 111c
5 b g Anabaa Blue—Kotkita (FR) (Subotica (FR))
1038a[8]
1865[5]

Koultas King (IRE) *Tim Vaughan* 101b
4 b g Exit To Nowhere(USA) —Carrigmoorna Style (IRE) (Dr Massini (IRE))
3364[2] 3920[4] 4527[3]

Koup De Kanon (FR) *Emma Lavelle* 96h
5 b g Robin Des Pres(FR) —Coup De Sabre (FR) (Sabrehill (USA))
2074[2] 2495[5] 3604[6] 4397[6] 5167[2]

Kowloon (IRE) *Warren Greatrex* 101b
5 b g Flemensfirth(USA) —Kouron (Pauper)
4780[3] 5105[9]

Krackatara *Susan Gardner* 79h
9 b g Kayf Tara—Kolyas Girl (IRE) (Be My Native (USA))
1556[P] 1740[P] 2141[12] 3529[6]

Kris Kin Line (IRE) *Donald McCain* 93h
5 ch g Kris Kin(USA) —Shell Garland (USA) (Sadler's Wells (USA))
174[4] 328[P]

Kristal Komet (IRE) *Tracey Collins* 112h
4 b f High Chaparral(IRE) —Mad Madam Mym (Hernando (FR))
3239a[6]

Kristallo (GER) *Paul Webber* 107h 89c
6 ch g Lando(GER) —Key West (GER) (In The Wings)
64[4] 328[10] (962) 1035[3] 1507[P] 1692[8]
2053[7]

Kristoffersen *Helen Nelmes* 107h 107c
11 ch g Kris—Towaahi (IRE) (Caerleon (USA))
302[5] 503[6] 1347[6] 1490[5] (2023) 4481[7]

Kudu Country (IRE) *Tom Tate* 123h
5 gr g Captain Rio—Nirvavita (FR) (Highest Honor (FR))
3447[4] 3969[P] 4358[3]

Kuilsriver (IRE) *Alison Thorpe* 129h
4 b g Cape Cross(IRE) —Ripple Of Pride (IRE) (Sadler's Wells (USA))
2237[2] 3294[7] 3554[2] 3958[2] 4847[12]

Kumbeshwar *Alan King* 143h
4 b g Doyen(IRE) —Camp Fire (IRE) (Lahib (USA))
(3944) 4205[3] 4350[3] 4807[2] 5161[2]

Kusadiki (IRE) *Emma Lavelle* 108b
5 b g Tobougg(IRE) —Mother Molly (USA) (Irish River (FR))
4204[4] 5174[4]

Kvarner Riviera (IRE) *Malcolm Jefferson* 95h
5 b g Zagreb(USA) —Black Noir (IRE) (Boreen (FR))
47[2] 1764[14] 2446[F]

Kyathos (GER) *David Thompson* 88h 88c
10 br g Dashing Blade—Kajaana (Esclavo (FR))
3717[7]
4549[3] 4975[5]
5258[P]

Kyber *Jim Goldie* 103h 103c
10 ch g First Trump—Mahbob Dancer (FR) (Groom Dancer (USA))
1118[7]
1341[2] ◆ 1598[P] 1868[5] 2203[9] 2654[8]

Kykate *Thomas Kinsey* 101h
5 b m Hamas(IRE) —Coleham (Saddlers' Hall (IRE))
27[5] 4245[2] (4552) 5144[5]

Kylebeg Krystle (IRE) *Denis Gerard Hogan* 132h 124c
7 b m Oscar(IRE) —Sister Christian (IRE) (Satco (FR))
4755a[4]

Kylenoe Fairy (IRE) *Paul Henderson* 110h 106c
7 ch m Anshan—Supreme Stroke (IRE) (Supreme Leader)
1677[4]
1917[4] 2217[2] (2442) 2949[2] 3452[9] 4446[P] 4990[3] 5193[5]

Kyoto (GER) *Nigel Hawke* 94h
7 b g Monsun(GER) —Key West (GER) (In The Wings)
1232[9] 1707[5] 1976[5]
2334[P] 5390[8]

Kyte *Sue Smith* 35b
6 b g Josr Algarhoud(IRE) —Gold And Blue (IRE) (Bluebird (USA))
2943[11]

La Bacouetteuse (FR) *Simon Shirley-Beavan* 85b
6 b g Miesque's Son(USA) —Toryka (Vettori (IRE))
47[4] 731[5]

La Belle Au Bois (IRE) *Nick Lampard* 93b
5 b m Val Royal(FR) —Pomme Pomme (USA) (Dayjur (USA))
(1480) 1680[4] 5188[18]

La Belle Sauvage *Venetia Williams* 82b
4 ch f Old Vic—Lady Rebecca (Rolfe (USA))
4881[3]

La Bombonera (FR) *Venetia Williams* 118h 112c
5 bb m Mansonnien(FR) —Bab Khaldoun (FR) (Kaldoun (FR))
4420[7] 4852[P]

Laborec (IRE) *Neil King* 115h 115c
8 gr g Oscar(IRE) —Bere Science (IRE) (Roselier (FR))
2364[3] 2644[2] (3493) 4327[8]

Labretella (IRE) *Shaun Harris*
4 b f Bahamian Bounty—Known Class (USA) (Known Fact (USA))
1234[P] 1422[P]

L'Accordioniste (IRE) *Nigel Twiston-Davies* 139h
6 b m Tikkanen(USA) —Crystal Chord (IRE) (Accordion)
(2068) (2592) (2868) 3674[6] 4793[6]

Lacdoudal (FR) *Philip Hobbs* 87h 142c
12 gr g Cadoudal(FR) —Belfaster (FR) (Royal Charter (FR))
1856[2] (2346)

La Chemme *Reg Hollinshead* 58b
5 b m Ishiguru(USA) —Smartie Lee (Dominion)
304[8] 637[7] 1567[F] 1688[P] 1921[P]

Lackamon *Sue Smith* 132h
6 b g Fleetwood(IRE) —Pearlossa (Teenoso (USA))
457[5] 632[5] 1829[3] 2446[4] (3575) (3621) 4209[11] 5316[5]

Ladies Best *Gordon Edwards* 102h
7 b g King's Best(USA) —Lady Of The Lake (Caerleon (USA))
1124[3] 1443[3] 1605[8] 1741[9] 1971[5] 2144[6] 2367[5] 4675[F] 4924[3] 5433[3]

Ladies Dancing *Chris Down* 119h
5 b g Royal Applause—Queen Of Dance (IRE) (Sadler's Wells (USA))
2137[6] 3478[2] ◆

Ladies Pride (IRE) *Bruce Mactaggart* 81b
6 ch m Anshan—Craic Go Leor (Deep Run)
399[9]

Lady An Co (FR) *Paul Nicholls* 128c
6 b m Lavirco(GER) —Lady Start (FR) (Village Star (FR))
265[3]

Lady Anne Nevill *Chris Fairhurst* 86h
7 b m Nomadic Way(USA) —Prudent Pet (Distant Relative)
(3951) 5098[4] 5350[5]

Lady Bling Bling *Peter Jones* 112h 112c
10 b m Midnight Legend—Slipmatic (Pragmatic)
3690[2] 4009[9]
4355[4] 4674[P] 4931[5]

Lady Bluesky *Alistair Whillans* 105h
8 gr m Cloudings(IRE) —M N L Lady (Polar Falcon (USA))
2547[3] 4245[3] (4822) (4958) 5315[11]

Lady Brig *Mrs Wendy Hamilton* 72c
12 b m Overbury(IRE) —Birniebrig (New Brig)
165[2]

Lady Chorister *Simon West* 16b
6 b m Minster Son—Flip The Lid (IRE) (Orchestra)
3498[P] 3952[F] 4112[F]

Lady Counsellor *Alan Swinbank* 79b
5 b m Turbo Speed—Linns Heir (Leading Counsel (USA))
1785[4]

Lady De La Vega (FR) *Tim Vaughan* 94h 115c
7 b m Kizitca(FR) —Shinobie (FR) (Le Nain Jaune (FR))
2080[5]
2332[3] (3933) 4161[4] **4927[2] 5192[5]**

Lady Dixton *Tim Vaughan* 30b
5 b m Runyon(IRE) —Chopins Revolution (Rakaposhi King)
3590[10] 3942[P]

Lady Edina (IRE) *I A Duncan* 38b
8 b m Kotashaan(FR) —Tom's Folly (IRE) (Febrino)
858[6]

Lady Everywhere *Nick Williams* 87h
6 b m Exit To Nowhere(USA) —Lady Felix (Batshoof)
1920[2] 2167[3] 2472[5] 2974[9]

Lady Exe *Chris Down* 66b
6 b m Karinga Bay—Rempstone (Coronash)
2472[13] 3904[F] 4262[P]

Lady Florence *Alan Coogan* 83h
6 gr m Bollin Eric—Silver Fan (Lear Fan (USA))
585[5]

Lady From Ige (IRE) *Neil Mulholland* 70h
7 ch m Spinning World(USA) —Sofia Aurora (USA) (Chief Honcho (USA))
3296[11] 3645[9] 3937[8] 4450[11]

Lady Gongar *Thomas Kinsey* 84b
5 ch m Sir Harry Lewis(USA) —Kentford Fern (El Conquistador)
5210[4]

Lady Gower *David Evans*
5 br m Beat All(USA) —Tachometer (IRE) (Jurado (USA))
3088[7] 3434[P]

Lady Hetherington *Gary Brown*
4 b f Kyllachy—Silver Top Hat (USA) (Silver Hawk (USA))
836[U] 1024[P]

Lady Hight (FR) *Nicky Henderson* 94h
5 b m Take Risks(FR) —Miss High (FR) (Concorde Jr (USA))
2167[4] ◆ 2987[3] 3601[2]

Lady Hillingdon *Paul John Gilligan* 134h 131c
8 b m Overbury(IRE) —Ecologically Kind (Alleged (USA))
770[2] 1133a[10]
5371[2]

Lady Ida *Jennie Candlish* 97h
6 b m Dolpour—La Princesse (Le Bavard (FR))
2167[6] 2616[6] 4000[6] 4134[4] 4795[2]

Lady Jannina *Henry Daly* 89b
5 b m Sir Harry Lewis(USA) —Jannina (FR) (Useful (FR))
230[3] 2526[U]

Lady Jinks *Maurice Barnes* 112h
6 ch m Kirkwall—Art Deco Lady (Master Willie)
796[P] 1643[4] 2102[7]

Lady Karabaya *Henrietta Knight* 99h
6 b m Karinga Bay—Supreme Lady (IRE) (Supreme Leader)
2068[U] 3264[F] 3480[5] 4309[5]

Lady Karinga *David Evans* 94h
6 ch m Karinga Bay—Tachometer (IRE) (Jurado (USA))
1742[4] 1914[P] *3089[4]* 3428[P]

Lady Kathleen *Paul Webber* 79b
4 b f Hernando(FR) —Lady Of Fortune (IRE) (Sovereign Water (FR))
5012[9]

Lady Kayf *Mark Usher* 70h
7 b m Kayf Tara—Zany Lady (Arzanni)
2963[11]

Lady Knightess (IRE) *Thomas Cooper* 95b
5 br m Presenting—Soupinette (FR) (Noblequest (FR))
5188[14]

Lady Myfanwy *Mrs Myfanwy Miles* 100c
10 b m Sir Harry Lewis(USA) —Orange Princess (Cruise Missile)
526[2]

Lady Norlela *Brian Rothwell* 50h
5 b m Reset(AUS) —Lady Netbetsports (IRE) (In The Wings)
2370[9]

Lady Of Ashcott *Neil Mulholland* 60h
5 ch m Loup Sauvage(USA) —Pointlet (IRE) (Reference Point)
384[8] 645[9] 930[P] 1049[7] 2149[4] 2643[2] 3255[4] 3839[9] 4272[P]

Lady Pacha *Tim Pitt* 83h
4 b f Dubai Destination(USA) —St Radegund (Green Desert (USA))
836[2] 1018[9] (2369) 2435[3] 3545[5] 4148[6] 5354[6]

Lady Pilot *Jim Best* 109h 115c
9 b m Dansili—Mighty Flyer (IRE) (Mujtahid (USA))
2275[5] 661[5]

Lady Rapido (IRE) *J J Lambe* 84h 94c
9 bb m Presenting—Laban Lady (IRE) (Over The River (FR))
1379[F] 2547[5]

Lady Romanov (IRE) *Paddy Butler* 73h
8 br m Xaar—Mixremember (FR) (Linamix (FR))
1431[5]

Lady Rusty (IRE) *Lucinda Russell* 86h
5 gr m Verglas(IRE) —Patteness (FR) (General Holme (USA))
582[5] 948[4]

Lady Sambury *Maurice Barnes* 90h
9 b m Overbury(IRE) —Skiddaw Samba (Viking (USA))
4138[P] 4687[P]

Lady Shanakill (IRE) *James Joseph Mangan* 79c
7 bb m Witness Box(USA) —Shanakill River (IRE) (Anshan)
3779a[6]

Lady Sorcerer *Alan Jarvis* 93h
6 b m Diktat—Silk Law (IRE) (Barathea (IRE))
358[F]

Lady Soughton (IRE) *Tim Vaughan* 93h
6 gb m Daylami(IRE) —Indaba (IRE) (Indian Ridge)
(683)

Lady Treacle (IRE) *Caroline Bailey* 38h
5 b m Brian Boru—Got To Fly (IRE) (Kemal (FR))
4881[11] 5280[7]

Lady Willa (IRE) *Mark Gillard* 105h
4 b f Footstepsinthesand—Change Partners (IRE) (Hernando (FR))
1586[7] 1845[2] 2020[3] 2485[3] (3613) (3879) 4092[3] 4807[18] 5098[8]

Lady Wright (IRE) *Michael Easterby* 93h
8 b m King's Theatre(IRE) —Amelia Earhart (IRE) (Be My Native (USA))
494[5] 717[8] 871[P] 1147[6] ◆ 1328[6] 1361[2] 1644[9] 1929[13]

La Fille D'Oscar (IRE) *Rachel Hobbs* 69h
7 b m Oscar(IRE) —Ladoc Et Moi (IRE) (Weldnaas (USA))
5074[6]

Lagan Katie *Neil Mulholland* 81h
5 b m Kayf Tara—Bichette (Lidhame)
1455[5] 1821[10] 2142[7]

Lagosta (SAF) *S J Graham* 84h 104c
11 ch g Fort Wood(USA) —Rose Wine (Chilibang)
551[3]

Lago Verde (SWI) *Lucinda Russell* 90h
6 ch g Generous(IRE) —La Venta (USA) (Drone (USA))
327[P] 827[3] 1757[7] 4958[7] 5335[8]

Laharna *Lucy Wadham* 44h 98c
11 b g Overbury(IRE) —Royal Celt (Celtic Cone)
63[6]

Lahib The Fifth (IRE) *Nicky Richards* 105h 109c
11 br g Lahib(USA) —Bob's Girl (IRE) (Bob Back (USA))
2298[4] 3549[3] 3853[2] 4139[P] 4937[7]

Lahinch Lad (IRE) *Brendan Powell* 15h 52c
11 ch g Bigstone(IRE) —Classic Coral (USA) (Seattle Dancer (USA))
217[P] **280[5]**

Laish Ya Hajar (IRE) *Paul Webber* 103h
7 ch g Grand Lodge(USA) —Ya Hajar (Lycius (USA))
1429[4]

Lajidaal (USA) *Gary Moore* 77h
4 b c Dynaformer(USA) —Tayibah (IRE) (Sadler's Wells (USA))
3401[11] 4810[9] 5050[5]

Lake Legend *Alan King* 143h 128c
7 b g Midnight Legend—Lac Marmot (FR) (Marju (IRE))
2330[3] 3508[3] (4030)
4469[2] 4864[6] 5166[P]

Lakil House (IRE) *Jason Cairns* 97h 85c
11 bb g Accordion—Own Gale (IRE) (Strong Gale)
3551[3] (Dead)

Lakreg (CZE) *Jana Minarikova* 77c
11 b g Regulus(CZE) —Lakonka (CZE) (Wolver Heights)
1811a[9]

Lambertstown Lad (IRE) *Miss Clare Judith Macmahon* 46h
9 b g Heron Island(IRE) —Red Shoon (Salluceva)
856[6]

Lamboro Lad (IRE) *Peter Bowen* 125h
6 b g Milan—Orchard Spray (IRE) (Supreme Leader)
191[3] (538) ◆ 710[2] 929[2]

Lambrini Belle *Lisa Williamson*
5 ch m Bold Edge—Rag Time Belle (Raga Navarro (ITY))
5084[12]

Lambrini Classic *Lisa Williamson* 76h
8 gr g Classic Cliche(IRE) —Lizzy Lamb (Bustino)
1505[10] 1553[11] 1703[4]

Lambrini Lace (IRE) *Lisa Williamson* 49h
6 b m Namid—Feather 'n Lace (IRE) (Green Desert (USA))
3746[13] 4242[P] 4552[11]

Lambro River (IRE) *Alison Batchelor* 80h 90c
6 b g Milan—Chaparral Reef (IRE) (Simply Great (FR))
3055[8] 3374[9] 3405[13] **4483[3]**

Lamb's Cross *Nigel Twiston-Davies* 110h
5 b g Rainbow High—Angie Marinie (Sabrehill (USA))
1153[6] (1600) 3567[P] 4281[6]

L'Ami (FR) *E Bolger* 119h 157c
12 ch g Lute Antique(FR) —Voltige De Nievre (FR) (Brezzo (FR))
4792[P]

L'Ami Gaby (FR) *R Chotard*
4 ch g Muhtathir—Bonne Gargotte (FR) (Poliglote)
1658a[P]

La Milanaise *Anthony Honeyball* 80b
5 b m Milan—Dalticia (FR) (Cadoudal (FR))
1572[4]

Lampion Du Bost (FR) *Jim Goldie* 81h 120c
12 b g Mont Basile(FR) —Ballerine Du Bost (FR) (Fast (FR))
2541[8] 3333[5] 3853[6] (4306)
4689[5] 4937[5]

Lamps *Michael Blake* 114h
4 b g Dynaformer(USA) —Conspiring (USA) (Grand Slam (USA))
2306[8] 2661[5] 3443[2] 4240[2]

Lancetto (FR) *James J Hartnett* 135h
6 b g Dubai Destination(USA) —Lanciana (IRE) (Acatenango (GER))
3474a[15]

Landenstown Lad (IRE) *Seamus Mullins* 65b
5 b g Tamayaz(CAN) —Princess Roxanne (Prince Tenderfoot (USA))
5056[5]

Landenstown Pearl (IRE) *Neil King* 90h
5 b m Definite Article—Golden Moment (IRE) (Roselier (FR))
284[3] 686[5] 935[2] 1680[2] 5297[3]

Landenstown Rose (IRE) *Donald McCain* 36h
5 br m Definite Article—Returning (Bob's Return (IRE))
2167[11] 4554[5] 5280[8]

Landenstown Star (IRE) *Seamus Mullins* 80h 32c
6 ch g Bob's Return(IRE) —Slieve Bernagh (IRE) (Phardante (FR))
1742[6] **1908[4]**

Land Of Plenty (IRE) *Jamie Poulton*
4 b f Azamour(IRE) —Bring Plenty (USA) (Southern Halo (USA))
1674[P]

Landscape Lad *Ron Hodges*
6 b g Shambo—Sweet Symphony (IRE) (Orchestra)
3651[14]

Laneguy (FR) *Tom George* 99h 105c
6 b g Nikos—Aykoku Saky (FR) (Baby Turk)
171[P] **1813[P]**
2053[6] 4269[8] (4447)
4671[3] 5214[7]

Langley *Pat Murphy* 84h
4 b c Trempolino(USA) —Late Night (GER) (Groom Dancer (USA))
2958[8] 3194[6] 3767[12] 4751[8]

Lang Shining (IRE) *Jamie Osborne* 103h
7 ch g Dr Fong(USA) —Dragnet (IRE) (Rainbow Quest (USA))
2960[P] 3906[4] 4288[6] 5066[4]

Lan Na Lamh (IRE) *P S Davies* 81h 83c
11 b m Beneficial—Philipintown Queen (IRE) (Castle Keep)
148[P]

Lansdowne Princess *Gerald Ham* 83h 79c
9 b m Cloudings(IRE) —Premier Princess (Hard Fought)
134[4] 645[4] 737[5]
1273[7] (1447)
1733[8] 2240[P] 3870[8]
4144[P] 5273[2] 5434[2]

La Pantera Rosa (IRE) *Micky Hammond* 102h 114c
8 br g Tragic Role(USA) —Fortune Cookie (Selkirk (USA))
(1697)
2079[U] 2611[5] (3510)
3716[F] 4277[2]

Lapin Garou (FR) *Nick Williams* 78h
4 gr g Martaline—Belle Grande (FR) (Villez (USA))
3624[4] 3802[7]

Lap Of Honour (IRE) *Ferdy Murphy* 110h
7 b g Danehill Dancer(IRE) —Kingsridge (IRE) (King's Theatre (IRE))
2092[12] 3302[3] 3570[3] 4998[2] 5400[4]

L'Apprenti Sorcier (FR) *Joanna Davis* 75h
8 b g Phantom Breeze—Flower Of Dream (FR) (Mansonnien (FR))
3622[U] 4273[2] 4787[3]

Lara Dora (IRE) *Robin Dickin* 15b
5 b m Pasternak—Remember Dora (IRE) (Classic Memory)
5084[11]

Laredo Sound (IRE) *Alex Hales* 97h 129c
9 ch g Singspiel(IRE) —Lanelly (GER) (Shining Steel)
2164[9] 2626[7] 4235[11]

Lariat Sam (IRE) *Alan King* 97h
6 b g Flemensfirth(USA) —Nufemme (IRE) (Abednego)
2518[6] 3295[11] 3918[7] 4459[6]

Larkhall *John Bryan Groucott* 66b
4 b g Saddlers' Hall(IRE) —Larkbarrow (Kahyasi)
5084[7]

Larks Lad (IRE) *Nicky Henderson* 128h
7 b g Bob Back(USA) —Higher Again (IRE) (Strong Gale)
4185[9] 5003[2] 5320[8]

Larry Luso (IRE) *Daniel William O'Sullivan* 120h 124c
9 b g Luso—Princess Millicent (Proverb)
1858[14]

Laskari (FR) *Paul Webber* 114h 146c
12 b g Great Palm(USA) —Hatzarie (FR) (Cyborg (FR))
1960[P] 5229[F]

La Soie (IRE) *James Frost* 84h
5 b m Barathea(IRE) —Jomana (IRE) (Darshaan)
1344[5] 1445[3]

Last Chorus *Tracy Waggott*
5 b m Courteous—Wild Briar (Green Adventure (USA))
1934[14] 2297[P] 4795[P]

Last Flight (IRE) *Peter Bowen* 119h 119c
7 b m In The Wings—Fantastic Fantasy (IRE) (Lahib (USA))
550[2] 738[2] 854[F]

Last Of The Bunch *Alan Swinbank* 115h
6 ch m Silver Patriarch(IRE) —Elegant City (Scallywag)
313[6] 2300[7] 3570[2] (4067) 4742[3]

Lastoftheleaders (IRE) *A L T Moore* 125h 135c
8 b g Supreme Leader—Heather Breeze (IRE) (Lord Americo)
4794[12]

Last One Standing *Sheena West* 105h
7 b g Dancing Spree(USA) —It's Been Jilted (IRE) (Good Thyne (USA))
62[4] 847[3] ◆

Lastroseofsummer (IRE) *Rae Guest* 107h
5 ch m Haafhd—Broken Romance (IRE) (Ela-Mana-Mou)
2068[4] (2505) 3308[4] 4025[5]

Latalanta (FR) *Mrs P A Tetley* 103h
8 b g Lost World(IRE) —Belle De Saigon (FR) (Deep Roots)
297[P] 4197[P]

Latanier (FR) *Venetia Williams* 126h 143c
8 b g Cadoudal(FR) —Lattaquie (FR) (Fast Topaze (USA))
4077[7]

Late Red *Jamie Poulton* 66h
6 b g Anshan—Lady Naninsa (IRE) (Glacial Storm (USA))
222[8] *2295[9]* 4918[9] 5267[5]

Laterly (IRE) *Steve Gollings* 118h
6 b g Tiger Hill(IRE) —La Candela (GER) (Alzao (USA))
3831[U] (4310) ◆ 4858[F] (5296)

Lathyrus (FR) *John Needham* 69h 65c
11 b g Roi De Rome(USA) —Provenchere (FR) (Son Of Silver)
827[7]

Latin America (IRE) *Nick Gifford* 117h
6 b g Sadler's Wells(USA) —La Pitie (USA) (Devil's Bag (USA))
2209[13] 2594[3] 2983[P] 3744[7] 4121[2] 5195[5]

Latin Connection (IRE) *S R B Crawford* 113h
5 b g Soviet Star(USA) —Via Verbano (IRE) (Caerleon (USA))
1337[7] 2657[5] 3523[2] 3750[8] 4115[4] 4912[2] 5144[2]

L'Aubergiste (FR) *J-L Guillochon*
7 ch g King Fontenailles(FR) —La Savoyana (USA) (Bellypha)
312a[5]

Laudatory *Charlie Morlock* 108h
5 b g Royal Applause—Copy-Cat (Lion Cavern (USA))
4478[7] 5099[3]

Laughing Game *Laura Hurley* 86h
7 b m Classic Cliche(IRE) —Ground Game (Gildoran)
4098[5] 4833[F]

Launchpad *D T Hughes* 119h
4 ch g Starcraft(NZ) —Revival (Sadler's Wells (USA))
5161[6]

Launde (IRE) *Mrs Jenny Gordon* 69h 114c
12 b g Norwich—Carbia's Last (Palm Track)
26[4] 153[12] 463[P] 4197[2] 5163[F]

Laura's Light (IRE) *Alan J Brown* 88h 110c
9 b g Turtle Island(IRE) —Conditional Sale (IRE) (Petorius)
4476[P]

Laureate Des Loges (FR) *Henry Daly* 116h 97c
7 b m Marathon(USA) —The Paradis (FR) (R B Chesne)
313[3] **1936[5]**
3155[10] 4009[5] 4955[5] 5346[3]

Laureus (GER) *Rachel Hobbs* 53h
8 b g Tiger Hill(IRE) —Lauderdale (GER) (Nebos (GER))
1552[P] 1840[P] 3540[P] 3839[P]

Laurollie *Bill Moore* 41h
9 b m Makbul—Madonna Da Rossi (Mtoto)
711[P] 1308[8]

Laustra Bad (FR) *David Pipe* 133h 109c
8 b g Astarabad(USA) —Love Crazy (FR) (Loup Solitaire (USA))
2530[2] ◆ 2977[4] 3299[7] 3793[5] 4448[2] (4925) (5369)

Lava Lamp (GER) *Evan Williams* 112h
4 b g Shamardal(USA) —La Felicita (Shareef Dancer (USA))
4350[5]

Lavally Legend (IRE) *John Anthony Staunton* 80h 99c
8 b g Rainwatch—Kacy's Legend (IRE) (Mandalus)
2938[5]

Lava Steps (USA) *Paul Midgley* 85h
5 b g Giant's Causeway(USA) —Miznah (IRE) (Sadler's Wells (USA))
607[7] 3620[8] 3715[14]

La Vecchia Scuola (IRE) *Jim Goldie* 110h
7 b m Mull Of Kintyre(USA) —Force Divine (FR) (L'Emigrant (USA))
4793[11]

Lavender Grey *Tony Carroll* 40b
5 gr m Cape Town(IRE) —Erica Jayka (Golden Heights)
1284[14] 1472[5]

Lavenoak Lad *Simon Burrough* 83h 108c
11 b g Cloudings(IRE) —Halona (Pollerton)
549[4] 749[P]
3230[4] 3646[3] 3900[4] 4333[4] 4749[3] 5192[3] 5438[P]

Laveroque (FR) *Charlie Longsdon* 121b
5 b g Laveron—Six Fois Sept (FR) (Epervier Bleu)
(1748) 2389[2] 5202[20]

Lawaaheb (IRE) *Tim Walford* 100h 106c
10 b g Alhaarth(IRE) —Ajayib (USA) (Riverman (USA))
352[2]

Lawgiver (IRE) *Marjorie Fife* 113h 97c
10 b g Definite Article—Marylou Whitney (USA) (Fappiano (USA))
396[3] 1501[6] 3966[10] 4914[4] 5149[8]

Laybach (IRE) *Michael Quinlan* 70h
7 br g Bach(IRE) —River Breeze (IRE) (Sharifabad (IRE))
490[9]

Lay De Brook *Jim Goldie* 18h
6 b m Meadowbrook—Chaperall Lady (Mansingh (USA))
4304[P] 4684[8]

Layla's Boy *John Mackie* 79h
4 ch g Sakhee(USA) —Gay Romance (Singspiel (IRE))
2245[8] 4283[8] 4952[F]

Leac An Scail (IRE) *Sue Smith* 116h 124c
10 b g Lord Americo—Swings'N'Things (USA) (Shernazar)
33[3] 844[P] 2955[F]
3488[7] 3922[5] 4328[2] 4689[6] 5416[6]

Leading Contender (IRE) *Philip Hobbs* 140h 136c
10 b g Supreme Leader—Flair Dante (IRE) (Phardante (FR))
2962[U] 3444[3] ◆ 3948[U]

Leading Man (IRE) *Mrs V Dobbin* 111h 116c
11 b g Old Vic—Cudder Or Shudder (IRE) (The Parson)
335[4]

Lead On (IRE) *Philip Hobbs* 130h 135c
10 b g Supreme Leader—Dressed In Style (IRE) (Meneval (USA))
98[5] 1856[6] 2358[6] 2962[U] 3290[P]

Leamington Lad (IRE) *Nigel Twiston-Davies* 129h 130c
8 gr g Beckett(IRE) —Nicea (IRE) (Dominion)
523[P] 1690[P] 4972[5] 5081[9]

Lean Burn (USA) *Barry Leavy* 101h
5 b g Johannesburg(USA) —Anthelion (USA) (Stop The Music (USA))
182[7] 754[9] 821[9] 1066[3] 1164[9] (1976) 2070[2] (2478) 2643[F] 5171[6]

Leanne (IRE) *W Harney* 87h 139c
9 ch m Alderbrook—Nagillah (IRE) (Bob Back (USA))
3206a[11] 3778a[5]

Lease Lend *Tim Easterby* 133h 143c
8 ch g Zilzal(USA) —Moogie (Young Generation)
2077[8] (3573)
3953[5] 4470[6] 5317[7]

Leath Acra Mor (IRE) *Ian Williams* 42b
5 b g King's Theatre(IRE) —Happy Native (IRE) (Be My Native (USA))
3200[16]

Le Beau Bai (FR) *Richard Lee* 147h 150c
8 b g Cadoudal(FR) —Dame Blonde (FR) (Pampabird)
1777[7] 2500[2] 3293[15] **3568[4] 4208[3] 4876[P]**

Le Brocquy *Martin Keighley* 107h 98c
6 b g Pursuit Of Love—Catawba (Mill Reef (USA))
829[6] 917[4] 984[3]
1047[3] 1273[6] 1295[2]
1430[2] 1511[P]

Le Burf (FR) *Giles Smyly* 106h 142c
10 b g Lute Antique(FR) —Fripperie (FR) (Bojador (FR))
1968[3] 2497[3] 3453[5] 3689[F]

Le Commencement (IRE) *Sophie Leech* 115h 115c
9 b g Beneficial—Ballyduggan Queen (IRE) (King Luthier)
1557[4] ◆ 1739[6] 4538[F] 5355[2]

Le Corvee (IRE) *Tony Carroll* 114h 100c
9 b g Rossini(USA) —Elupa (IRE) (Mtoto)
(1127)
1731[6] 1972[8] 4999[5] 5101[2] 5232[3]

Ledbury Star (IRE) *Matt Sheppard* 39h
5 b g Mr Combustible(IRE) —Sapien Dame (IRE) (Homo Sapien)
3441[6] 3836[11] 3930[10]

Le Forezien (FR) *Carroll Gray* 91h 87c
12 b g Gunboat Diplomacy(FR) —Diane Du Forez (FR) (Quart De Vin (FR))
795[4] 913[8] 1057[7]
1159[3] 1348[3] 1447[3] 1733[U]

Legal Glory (IRE) *Ron Hodges* 75h 69c
11 b g Bob Back(USA) —Native Shore (IRE) (Be My Native (USA))
267[7] 467[5] 587[F]

Legbeforewicket *Lucinda Russell* 36h
5 gr m Silver Patriarch(IRE) —Shazana (Key Of Luck (USA))
1573[P] 4303[P] 4910[12]

Legendary Hop *Chris Bealby* 79b
5 b m Midnight Legend—Hopping Mad (Puget (USA))
5306[13]

Leggy Lad (IRE) *Stephen McConville* 113h 102c
8 ch g Denel(FR) —Tullyfoyle (IRE) (Montelimar (USA))
305[3]

Legion D'Honneur (UAE) *Chris Down* 117h
6 b g Halling(USA) —Renowned (IRE) (Darshaan)
(157) 3950[2] ◆ 4700[7]

Leith Walk (IRE) *Donald Whillans* 99h
8 ch m Posidonas—Gothic Shadow (IRE) (Mandalus)
393[5] 729[F] 2275[2] 3500[8] 4477[2] 4914[3] 5335[7]

Leitra House (IRE) *Jeremy Scott* 104h
8 gr g Environment Friend—Sister Nora (IRE) (The Parson)
583[4] 1028[0] 1196[2] 1308[4] 1821[6]

Leitzu (IRE) *Mick Channon* 89h
4 b f Barathea(IRE) —Ann's Annie (IRE) (Alzao (USA))
3906[3] 4676[2] 5050[4]

L'Eldorado (FR) *Chris Bealby* 117h
6 b g Urban Ocean(FR) —Little Warden (Bellman (FR))
1951[5] 2247[7] (4234) 4830[8]

L'Eminence Grise (IRE) *Nick Williams* 105h
4 gr g Kahyasi—Belle Innocence (FR) (Turgeon (USA))
2211[8] 3194[4] 3673[4] 4203[4] 4807[21]

Lemon Queen (IRE) *John Quinn* 5b
5 ch m Desert Sun—Calendula (Be My Guest (USA))
2167[15] 2660[9] 4239[15]

Lemon Silk (IRE) *Alex Hales* 103h
7 ch g Barathea(IRE) —Bois De Citron (USA) (Woodman (USA))
(1911) 2209[2] 2949[3] 3693[8] 4327[7] 5054[4] 5322[10]

Lem Putt (IRE) *Mrs N Naughton* 44c
8 b g Moonax(IRE) —Streaming Along (Paddy's Stream)
4553[5]

Lennon (IRE) *Howard Johnson* 113h 142c
11 bb g Beneficial—Stradbally Bay (Shackleton)
3551[2] 4115[15] **4284[P]**

Lennox Gardens *Warren Greatrex* 100h
7 ch g Anabaa Blue—Ariadne (GER) (Kings Lake (USA))
1232[8]

Leoballero *Stephen Hughes*
11 ch g Lion Cavern(USA) —Ball Gown (Jalmood (USA))
821[P]

Leo McGarry (IRE) *Miss Caroline Fryer* 112h 77c
8 ch g Fantastic Light(USA) —Lilissa (IRE) (Doyoun)
4183[6]

Leomode (USA) *Liam Corcoran* 59b
5 b g Cherokee Run(USA) —Twist Of Faith (USA) (Storm Cat (USA))
1029[10]

Leopard Hills (IRE) *Alison Thorpe* 106h
4 b g Acclamation—Sadler's Park (USA) (Sadler's Wells (USA))
1422[3] 1576[3] 3989[11] (4924) (5101) 5348[4]

Leo's Lucky Star (USA) *David Pipe* 141h 147c
9 b g Forestry(USA) —Leo's Lucky Lady (USA) (Seattle Slew (USA))
2976[2] 3446[5] 4853[3] 5164[F]

Le Petit Vigier *Patrick Holmes* 74h
5 b m Groom Dancer(USA) —Fallujah (Dr Fong (USA))
684[P] 1003[3] 1780[5] 2190[P]

Lepido (ITY) *Gary Moore* 108h 86c
7 b g Montjeu(IRE) —Luv Is For Sharing (USA) (Miswaki (USA))
235[9] 1677[5] 2049[2] 2185[2] 3348[3]
3650[5] 3963[6] 4504[8] 4768[P] 5386[5]

Le Platino (GER) *John Wade* 108h 125c
9 ch g Platini(GER) —La Paz (GER) (Roi Dagobert)
(13) **287[6]**
(2036)
(2611)

Lerida *Sharon Watt* 74h 92c
9 ch g Groom Dancer(USA) —Catalonia (IRE) (Catrail (USA))
1924[7] 2194[P] (3404)
3618[2] 3997[2] 4510[2] 4800[4] 5093[5]

Le Roi Max (FR) *Nigel Twiston-Davies* 82h
7 bb g Robin Des Champs(FR) —Violletta (FR) (Sheyrann)
375[9] 1594[6] 1910[9] 2216[8] 2583[8] 3261[8]

Le Roi Rouge (FR) *Ferdy Murphy* 106h 127c
9 ch g Bateau Rouge—Reine De Lutece (FR) (Synefos (USA))
1761[9] 2272[3] 3786[7] 4357[6]

Lerubis (FR) *Ken Wingrove* 99c
12 b g Ragmar(FR) —Perle De Saisy (FR) (Italic (FR))
1450[P] **1568[3]**

Lesanda *Richard Fahey* 99h
5 b m Hernando(FR) —Wardeh (Zafonic (USA))
3330[14] 3637[3] 4242[5] 4552[2] 4874[4] 5346[4]

Les Andelys *Terry Clement* 83b
5 b g Zieten(USA) —Oasis Song (IRE) (Selkirk (USA))
304[7]

Lescer's Lad *Mrs A M Woodrow* 71h 94c
14 b g Perpendicular—Grange Gracie (Oats)
3837[P] 4098[P] 5103[P]

Leslingtaylor (IRE) *John Quinn* 134h 138c
9 b g Orpen(USA) —Rite Of Spring (Niniski (USA))
2219[6] 2386[11] *3170[8]* 3969[4]

Lesmoir *Tony Newcombe* 91h
9 b g Wizard King—Paprika (IRE) (The Parson)
374[5]

Letcombe Brook *Charlie Morlock* 71b
5 b g Generous(IRE) —Segsbury Belle (Petoski)
180[U]

Lethal Glaze (IRE) *Brian Ellison* 122h
5 gr g Verglas(IRE) —Sticky Green (Lion Cavern (USA))
(2939) 3288[F]

Lethal Gun (IRE) *Richard Mitchell* 34h 84c
9 b g Needle Gun(IRE) —Bubbling (Tremblant)
148[P] 2021[10] 2633[P]

Lethal Weapon (IRE) *C Roche* 136h
6 ch g Hawk Wing(USA) —Lady Windley (Baillamont (USA))
1133a[F]

Letham Island (IRE) *Tony Carroll* 117h 65c
7 b m Trans Island—Common Cause (Polish Patriot (USA))
403[6] (537) (598) (796) 1067[4]

Lethem Present (IRE) *Tim Butt* 40h 90c
11 ch m Presenting—Present Tense (Proverb)
5258[P]

Letmespeak (IRE) *Donald McCain* 79h
6 b g Tikkanen(USA) —Ithastobesaid (IRE) (Lanfranco)
2074[6] 2640[3] 3584[6]

Le Toto *Oliver Sherwood* 91h
8 b g Mtoto—La Dolce Vita (Mazilier (USA))
36[7] 1732[8]

Lets Get Serious (IRE) *Nicky Henderson* 121b
5 b g Overbury(IRE) —Vendimia (Dominion)
(1866) ◆

Lets Go Girls *James Moffatt* 95h
7 b m Sir Harry Lewis(USA) —Bee Pushi (Rakaposhi King)
515[2] 748[4] 1004[8] 1115[6]

Letterpress (IRE) *Howard Johnson* 92h
7 b g King's Theatre(IRE) —Empress Of Light (Emperor Jones (USA))
212[P]

Let Yourself Go (IRE) *Adrian Maguire* 132h 157c
9 b g Zaffaran(USA) —Auburn Princess (IRE) (Arapahos (FR))
1801a[5] 2339a[2] 2972a[U] 3415a[3] 3594a[3] 4087a[P]

Leulahleulahlay *Evan Williams* 89h
5 ch g Dr Fong(USA) —Fidelio's Miracle (USA) (Mountain Cat (USA))
1313[3] 1549[4] 1976[8]

Levera *Alan King* 117h
8 b g Groom Dancer(USA) —Prancing (Prince Sabo)
2085[9]

Le Vert Galant (FR) *Ferdy Murphy* 98h 113c
8 b g Vertical Speed(FR) —Marie Prends Garde (FR) (Garde Royale)
2298[U]

Lewlaur Supreme (IRE) *Jim Goldie* 104h
8 b g Supreme Leader—Dark Dame (IRE) (Norwich)
3851[12] 4304[4] 4686[3] 5094[2] ◆

Lexicon Lad (IRE) *Tom George* 111h
6 ch g Presenting—Hazel's Glory (IRE) (Mister Lord (USA))
319[3] 1989[3] 2963[6] 3584[3] 4012[U] 4439[3]

L'Homme De Nuit (GER) *Jim Best* 109h 98c
7 b g Samum(GER) —La Bouche (GER) (In The Wings)
3788[3] 4122[U] 4140[4] 4379[4] 4697[P]

Liberate *Philip Hobbs* 124h
8 ch g Lomitas—Eversince (USA) (Foolish Pleasure (USA))
5003[6]

Liberty Girl (IRE) *Linda Jewell* 78h
4 b f Statue Of Liberty(USA) —La Mazya (IRE) (Mazaad)
1473[6]

Liberty Rock (FR) *Miss S Butler* 114h 38c
12 b g Video Rock(FR) —Calarie (FR) (Altayan)
4449[U]

Liberty Seeker (FR) *John Harris* 109h 92c
12 ch g Machiavellian(USA) —Samara (IRE) (Polish Patriot (USA))
846[P] (1249) 1328[4] 1938[4] (2169) 2474[3] 2887[9] 3303[3] 4830[3]
5058[5]

Lidar (FR) *Alan King* 122h
6 ch g Take Risks(FR) —Light Wave (FR) (Marignan (USA))
(25) 3153[3] 1966[P] 2493[7] 4031[2] 4467[2] 5061[P]

Lidjo De Rouge (FR) *Paul Henderson* 95h 115c
12 b g Murmure(FR) —Delijoe (FR) (Useful (FR))
586[4] 852[5] 1093[7] 2184[7] 3433[P] 3790[P] 4269[5] 4560[9]

Lieutenant Miller *Nicky Henderson* 109h
5 b g Beat All(USA) —Still Runs Deep (Karinga Bay)
375[7] 2328[6] 2667[4]

Life Long (IRE) *Anabel L M King* 97h
7 b g Old Vic—Be My Rainbow (IRE) (Be My Native (USA))
224[2] 2241[11] 2454[6] 3693[11] 4224[9]
4741[P] 5295[3]

Life Of A Luso (IRE) *Paul Henderson* 107h 93c
7 b g Luso—Life Of A Lady (IRE) (Insan (USA))
4052[3] 4704[2] **5039[3]** 5289[5]

Lifes A Mystery (IRE) *Pauline Robson* 63h
8 b g Luso—Life Of A Lady (IRE) (Insan (USA))
12[3] 341[8] 930[P]

Lifestyle *Nicky Henderson* 124h
5 b m Karinga Bay—Like Manner (Teenoso (USA))
2222[6] (3721) ◆ 4195[2] (5235) (5378)

Light Des Mulottes (FR) *S J Coady* 104c
12 gr g Solidoun(FR) —Tango Girl (FR) (Tip Moss (FR))
4708[4]

Light Dragoon *Evan Williams* 85h
6 ch g Alflora(IRE) —Colonial Princess (Roscoe Blake)
2456[7] 3478[P]

Lightening Fire (IRE) *Bernard Llewellyn* 87h
9 b g Woodborough(USA) —Glowlamp (IRE) (Glow (USA))
1996[3] 2980[15] 3717[8] 4378[6] (4724) 4965[3] 5111[5]

Lightening Rod *Michael Easterby* 127h 131c
6 b g Storming Home—Bolero (Rainbow Quest (USA))
2542[P] *(3171)*
3995[F] 4507[2] 4996[B] 5318[4]

Lightening Sky (IRE) *Joseph Fox* 112h 97c
8 b m Saddlers' Hall(IRE) —Claudia Electric (IRE) (Electric)
1104[5] 5400[P]

Lighting Larry (IRE) *Liam Corcoran*
6 br g Expelled(USA) —City Siege (IRE) (Jareer (USA))
863[P]

Lightning Moley (IRE) *Tracey Watkins* 65h
8 ch g Lord Of Appeal—Arabella Bee (Abednego)
409[6]

Lightning Strike (GER) *Venetia Williams* 131h 145c
8 ch g Danehill Dancer(IRE) —La Capilla (Machiavellian (USA))
4209[7] 4806[18]

Lights Of Broadway (IRE) *Barry Brennan* 78b
5 b m Broadway Flyer(USA) —Supreme Call (IRE) (Supreme Leader)
2472[6] *3166[4]*

Ligreta (CZE) *V Hrbacek*
11 ch m Sectori(USA) —Ligbara (CZE) (Gala Boy)
1811a[F]

Like A Duke (FR) *Colin Tizzard* 111h 123c
8 br g Kaldou Star—Belle Des As (FR) (Melypro (FR))
372[7] 664[6] 994[11]

Like A Hurricane (IRE) *Alan King* 124h
8 b g Simply Great(FR) —Legal Challenge (IRE) (Strong Gale)
583[2] 1821[3] (2081) 3947[P] 5230[5]

Like Ice *Philip Middleton* 100h 100c
6 b g Beat All(USA) —Susie's Money (Seymour Hicks (FR))
25[3] 379[P] 2181[7] 2558[12] 3610[3] 4330[8] 4809[6]
5017[2] 5344[2]

Like Minded *Paul Nicholls* 139h
7 b g Kayf Tara—Sun Dante (IRE) (Phardante (FR))
3561[9] 4202[4]

Lilac Belle *Alex Hales* 66h
5 b m Robellino(USA) —Lilac Dreams (Second Set (IRE))
2156[12] *2896[6]* 3721[8] 4437[7] 5297[6]

Lil Ella (IRE) *Patrick Holmes* 97h
4 b f Pearl Of Love(IRE) —Royal Jubilee (IRE) (King's Theatre (IRE))
3519[6] 3711[8] 4465[9]

Lilirosa (IRE) *Des Donovan*
5 b m Windsor Castle—Baby Brown (IRE) (Supreme Leader)
5135[13]

Lillie Lou *Ray Fielder* 65h 56c
8 b m Tomba—Tread Carefully (Sharpo)
4857[F]

Lilly De Rome *Mrs Edward Crow*
10 ch m Roi De Rome(USA) —Bishop's Folly (Weld)
79[P]

Lilly Royal (IRE) *Bryn Palling* 73h
5 b m Tillerman—Ervedya (IRE) (Doyoun)
1445[6]

Limbunya (IRE) *Ron Hodges* 75h
6 b m Oscar(IRE) —Europet (IRE) (Fourstars Allstar (USA))
869[5] 1029[5] 1158[9]

Limestone Boy (IRE) *Rob Summers* 68h
9 bb g Beneficial—Limestone Lady (IRE) (Boreen (FR))
223[P] 5390[7]

Lindengrove *Claire Dyson* 76h
6 ch g Executive Perk—Lady Blakeney (Baron Blakeney)
1910[P] 2111[6] 3253[5] 3837[4]

Lindoro *Kevin M Prendergast* 71h
6 b g Marju(IRE) —Floppie (FR) (Law Society (USA))
2092[13] 2540[11] 3781[9] 4465[P]

Lindsay's Dream *Zoe Davison* 99h
5 b m Montjeu(IRE) —Lady Lindsay (IRE) (Danehill Dancer (IRE))
1449[5] 1689[6] 1971[2] 4118[2] 4769[5]

Lindseyfield Lodge (IRE) *Robert Johnson* 92h 101c
10 br g Presenting—Missusan (IRE) (King's Ride)
9[4] (160)
353[7] 680[P] 749[P]
804[U] 955[F] 1504[8] **1575[0] 1701[5] (1868)** 2190[3]
2550[6] 2942[10]
3524[10] 3728[5]
4001[6] 4241[4] 4511[8] 5093[6]

Lindy Lou *Pam Sly* 115h
7 b m Hernando(FR) —Daylight Dreams (Indian Ridge)
5132[9] 5376[9]

Line Artic (FR) *Chris Down* 106h 130c
7 b m Freedom Cry—Si Jamais (FR) (Arctic Tern (USA))
57[4] 831[P]

Line Ball (IRE) *Jonjo O'Neill* 142h 128c
10 b g Good Thyne(USA) —Navaro (IRE) (Be My Native (USA))
493[3] 764[5]

Line Freedom (FR) *Nicky Henderson* 135h
6 b m Freedom Cry—Ilioucha (FR) (Synefos (USA))
(2168) 2627[F] 3830[U] 4309[2] (5008)

Lion On The Prowl (IRE) *Kim Bailey* 126h
7 b g Sadler's Wells(USA) —Ballerina (IRE) (Dancing Brave (USA))
(97) 4932[2] (5321)

Lions In Law *Richard Hawker* 88h 63c
7 ch g Double Trigger(IRE) —Water Flower (Environment Friend)
2981[7] 3374[6] 3870[13] 4273[10] **4525[6] 4927[4] 5216[6]**

Lirain (CZE) *Josef Vana II* 133c
10 b g Rainbows For Life(CAN) —Licitace (CZE) (Vilnius (POL))
1811a[6]

Lisadell King (IRE) *G C Maundrell* 129c
11 b g Flemensfirth(USA) —Reardans Fancy (Dramatic Bid (USA))
317[2] 502[F] 4011[P] 4463[6] 5207[2]

Lisa's Enigma *Shaun Harris* 17b
8 b g Nomadic Way(USA) —Groacher (Starch Reduced)
2985[P] 4974[P]

Lisbon Lion (IRE) *James Moffatt* 85h
6 bg g Mull Of Kintyre(USA) —Ludovica (Bustino)
3746[8] 4958[4] 5307[6]

Lisdonagh House (IRE) *Lynn Siddall* 91h
9 b g Little Bighorn—Lifinsa Barina (IRE) (Un Desperado (FR))
2098 2190[5] 2452[6] 4281[7] (5094)

Lisglynn Jim (IRE) *Mayne Kidd* 61h 80c
7 gr g Loup Sauvage(USA) —Seethrough (Scallywag)
1000[P]

Lisscow Lad (IRE) *Alison Batchelor* 55b
6 b g Moscow Society(USA) —Lisselan Lass (IRE) (Lancastrian)
4124[11]

Listenlook (FR) *Nigel Twiston-Davies* 127h
5 ch g Bering—Pacifiste (IRE) (Anabaa (USA))
(3930) 4262[2] 5186[P]

List Of Life (IRE) *Tim Walford*
6 b g Oscar Schindler(IRE) —Nancy Whiskey (IRE) (Alphabatim (USA))
4796[P]

Little Al *Oliver Sherwood* 104h
8 b g Alflora(IRE) —Mossy Fern (Le Moss)
694[P] 1559[P] 1730[3] 2558[4] 4427[P]

Little Bit Of Hush (IRE) *Neil King* 40h
11 b g Oscar(IRE) —Florenanti (Floriferous)
1571[0] **437[P]**

Little Blackbeetle *Paul Webber* 74h
6 br m Beat All(USA) —Mrs Barty (IRE) (King's Ride)
21[8]

Little Buddy *Richard Price*
4 ch g Reel Buddy(USA) —Little Kenny (Warning)
3526[14]

Little Carmela *Neil King* 110h
7 gr m Beat Hollow—Carmela Owen (Owington)
1373 ◆ 577[4] (2425) 3308[P] 3405[12] 4182[6] 4769[4] 4955[2]

Littledean Jimmy (IRE) *John O'Shea* 100h
6 b g Indian Danehill(IRE) —Gold Stamp (Golden Act (USA))
375[8] 935[7] 1455[0] (1472) 1567[4] 2143[9] 2666[6] 3760[4]

Little Dibber *Peter Pritchard* 102h
8 b g First Trump—Robert's Daughter (Robellino (USA))
1449[6] 1555[7] 1821[7] 2279[4]

Little Eaglet (IRE) *Colin Heard* 106h 108c
7 br g Dushyantor(USA) —Bagatelle (IRE) (Strong Gale)
4219[P] 4929[8] 5172[4] 5433[2]

Little Fee *Colin Mitchell* 73h
6 b m Emperor Fountain—Passing Fair (Pablond)
5239[3] 5403[3]

Little Fifi *Sandy Thomson* 60h
6 ch m Karinga Bay—Festival Fancy (Le Coq D'Or)
2660[6] 4363[7] 4795[8] 5151[7]

Little Frano (IRE) *Peter Bowen* 75h
7 b g Bob's Return(IRE) —Vicford (IRE) (Old Vic)
2368[12] 3585[10] 3762[8] 3942[7] 4405[4]

Little Fritz (FR) *Nicky Henderson* 90b
4 gr g Turgeon(USA) —Hunorisk (FR) (Mansonnien (FR))
4443[2] 5077[3]

Little George (IRE) *Alan King* 112h 130c
8 b g Heron Island(IRE) —Kyle Eile (IRE) (Callernish)
(2662)
3193[5]

Little Girl *Ray Peacock* 22h 65c
13 b m Homo Sapien—Dancing Returns (Bali Dancer)
226[4] 579[4] 797[P] 1377[4] 1747[U] 1820[6] 2608[P]

Little Glenshee (IRE) *N W Alexander* 61b
5 gr m Terimon—Harrietfield (Nicholas Bill)
4574[6]

Little Green (IRE) *E McNamara* 125h
4 b f Governor Brown(USA) —Megan's Bay (Muhtarram (USA))
(4295a)

Little Hercules (IRE) *Howard Johnson* 108h
5 b g King's Theatre(IRE) —Johnston's Crest (IRE) (Be My Native (USA))
(2943) 3525[2] (4059) 5356[2]

Little Josh (IRE) *Nigel Twiston-Davies* 132h 160c
9 ch g Pasternak—Miss Top (IRE) (Tremblant)
(2105)
(2359) 2886[5] 3804[5]

Little Justice *Paul Cowley* 69b
7 b m Witness Box(USA) —Little Time (Arctic Lord)
841[6] 1086[7] 1734[P]

Little Lily Morgan *Robin Bastiman* 56h
8 gr m Kayf Tara—Cool Grey (Absalom)
547[9]

Little Lu (IRE) *Alan Swinbank* 118h 118c
9 b m Danehill Dancer(IRE) —Tales Of Wisdom (Rousillon (USA))
45[P]

Little Miss Foozle *Peter Niven* 42b
7 b m Compton Admiral—Kingennie (Dunbeath (USA))
14[P] 174[P] 337[P] 488[5]

Little Missmoffatt *Ann Hamilton* 57b
6 b m Karinga Bay—Deb's Ball (Glenstal (USA))
5313[9]

Little Ms Piggie *Simon Burrough* 53b
5 br m Alflora(IRE) —Bobs Bay (IRE) (Bob's Return (IRE))
3651[10] 4097[14]

Little Rocker (IRE) *R Smart* 116h 101c
10 b g Rock Hopper—One Back (IRE) (Meneval (USA))
301[5] 4141[5] 4950[7] 5237[4] 5402[5]

Little Rort (IRE) *Simon Lewis* 76h
12 b g Ali-Royal(IRE) —Florinda (CAN) (Vice Regent (CAN))
3367[8] 3530[7] 3703[6]

Little Roxy (IRE) *Anna Newton-Smith* 85h
6 b m Dilshaan—Brunswick (Warning)
841[11] 1822[9] 2135[5] *3057[7]* 3350[3] (4123) (4771)

Littleton Aldor (IRE) *Mark Gillard* 59h 90c
11 b g Pennekamp(USA) —Belle Etoile (FR) (Lead On Time (USA))
1919[6] 2148[5] 2604[5] 3792[5] 3959[5]

Little Wizard (IRE) *George Charlton* 92h 86c
9 b g Oscar(IRE) —Ruby Lass (IRE) (Orchestra)
92[4] 456[2] 3336[P]
3524[F] 3854[7]

Lively Baron (IRE) *Donald McCain* 122h
6 b g Presenting—Greavesfind (The Parson)
319[7] (1764) (2166) (3330) 4206[7] 4725[7] 5316[2]

Lively Fling (USA) *Venetia Williams* 119h
5 b g Dynaformer(USA) —Creaking Board (Night Shift (USA))
2081[10] (3563) 3820[4] 4462[9]

Livingonaknifedge (IRE) *Richard Guest* 125h 107c
12 bb g Classic Memory—Duhallow Fiveo (Black Minstrel)
213[4] 383[6]

Living Proof (IRE) *Norma Twomey* 79h
6 b m Oscar(IRE) —Footsteps (IRE) (Broken Hearted)
1284[3] ◆ 2156[9] 4012[7] 4309[P] 5078[8]

Livvy Inn (USA) *Lucinda Russell* 118h
6 ch g Woodman(USA) —London Be Good (USA) (Storm Bird (CAN))
2551[8] 2868[14] 3334[13] 4257[F] 4715[5] 5144[7] 5425[2]

Liz's Dream *Lisa Harrison* 102h 70c
11 b g Alflora(IRE) —Spicey Cut (Cut Above)
(100) 1578[P] 1959[P]

Lizzie Bennett (IRE) *W McCreery* 118h
6 b m Bahri(USA) —Literary Lover (IRE) (Sadler's Wells (USA))
2196a[7]

Llama Farmer *Paul Webber* 124h 93c
6 bg g Sagamix(FR) —Quick Quick Sloe (Scallywag)
2662[6] 3198[P] 3494[7]

Llobo *F Jestin*
5 ch g Daylami(IRE) —Toffee Nosed (Selkirk (USA))
732[P]

Lobby Ludd *Philip Hobbs* 94h
6 b g Kirkwall—Zany Lady (Arzanni)
2143[5] 2791[5] 4006[5] 4439[P]

Local Hero (GER) *Steve Gollings* 135h
4 b g Lomitas—Lolli Pop (GER) (Cagliostro (GER))
(2614) ◆ (3507) (3802) 4205[4] 4847[8] 5161[5]

Local Present (IRE) *Ron Hodges* 97h 107c
8 ch g Presenting—Local Issue (IRE) (Phardante (FR))
132[2] (588)
1034[2] (1281)
5240[P]

Location *Ian Williams* 67h
5 b m Dansili—Well Away (IRE) (Sadler's Wells (USA))
600[6]

Loch Ba (IRE) *Henrietta Knight* 103h
5 b g Craigsteel—Lenmore Lisa (IRE) (Phardante (FR))
2215[3] 2954[5] 3487[4] 4500[6] 5234[4]

Loch Dhu (IRE) *Alistair Whillans* 72h
7 b m Oscar(IRE) —Shannon Juliette (Julio Mariner)
4552[P] 4889[7] 5028[5]

Loch Long (IRE) *Tracey Collins* 128h
5 b g Galileo(IRE) —Spinney (Unfuwain (USA))
1038a[6]

Lochore (IRE) *Lucy Normile* 77h
5 b g Morozov(USA) —Fulgina (FR) (Double Bed (FR))
1594[8] 2271[P] 4138[5] 4542[4] 4870[3] 5131[6]

Locked Inthepocket (IRE) *Pauline Robson* 106h 116c
7 b g Beneficial—Ruby Rubenstein (IRE) (Camden Town)
2107[6] 2450[4] (4064)
4150[F] 4714[2] 5335[12]

Locksmith *Mrs S J Stilgoe* 133h 106c
11 gr g Linamix(FR) —Zenith (Shirley Heights)
4748[4] (4973)
5207[6]

Lockstown *Ann Hamilton* 108h 115c
8 ch g Exit To Nowhere(USA) —Slaney Rose (IRE) (Roselier (FR))
1402[3] 2203[4] 2550[2] 3552[4] (3886)
4167[4] (4543)
4893[F] 5032[2]

Loco Grande (IRE) *Tim Vaughan* 103h 86c
6 ch g Raise A Grand(IRE) —Locorotondo (IRE) (Broken Hearted)
1996[7] 2314[4] **2575[4] 2930[5]** (3341) 3603[2] 3791[P]
4722[7] **5109[6]**

Lodgician (IRE) *Nigel Twiston-Davies* 105h
9 b g Grand Lodge(USA) —Dundel (IRE) (Machiavellian (USA))
(1236) 1261[4] 1470[5] 1597[5] 1938[2]

Lofthouse *Alistair Whillans*
4 b g Hunting Lion(IRE) —Noble Destiny (Dancing Brave (USA))
4132[P]

Lofty Leader (IRE) *Harriet Graham* 18h 110c
12 b g Norwich—Slaney Jazz (Orchestra)
948[12] 1695[13]

Logan Rock *Susan Gardner* 75b
7 br g Access Ski—Miss Foxy (High Season)
1572[5] 1778[13]

Logans Run (IRE) *Howard Johnson* 100h 121c
8 b g Shernazar—Toposki (FR) (Top Ville)
(91) 4060[5]

Loita Hills (IRE) *Philip Hobbs* 119h 123c
11 b g Norwich—Gleann Oisin (IRE) (Le Bavard (FR))
636[P]

Lola Jay *Malcolm Jefferson* 47b
5 b m Kayf Tara—Wuchowsen (IRE) (King's Ride)
1153[7]

Lombardy Boy (IRE) *Michael Banks* 99h
6 b g Milan—Horner Water (IRE) (Over The River (FR))
(3088) 3987[11] 4500[10] 5059[2]

Lombardy Breeze (IRE) *Henrietta Knight* 57b
6 b g Milan—Stormy Breeze (IRE) (Glacial Storm (USA))
3366[P] 5343[P]

Lombok *Gary Moore* 54h
5 b g Hernando(FR) —Miss Rinjani (Shirley Heights)
2667[13] 3344[13] 3739[11]

Lomitaar *Tony Newcombe* 103h
6 b g Lomitas—Owtaar (IRE) (Royal Applause)
(1028) 2440[4] 4121[P] 4929[11]

London Times (IRE) *Simon Lewis* 85h
6 ch g Lomitas—Vituisa (Bering)
380[P] 932[13] 990[P] 1031[5] 1199[2] 1272[2] 1450[5]
1601[F]

Lonely Sky (IRE) *W F Codd* 87h
6 ch m Blueprint(IRE) —Silver Valley (IRE) (Henbit (USA))
930[P]

Lonesome Boatman (IRE) *Arthur Whitehead* 67h 83c
11 b g Old Vic—Midnight Miss (NZ) (Princes Gate)
22[2] 383[P] 2239[9] 4273[5] **4829[2] (5062)**
5258[9]

Lonesome Dove (IRE) *C F Swan* 124h
6 b m Milan—Glen Empress (IRE) (Lancastrian)
3592a[3] 4793[13]

Longdale *Martin Todhunter* 99h 98c
13 b g Primitive Rising(USA) —Gunnerdale (Gunner B)
34[6] 288[6]

Long Distance (FR) *Lucinda Russell* 107h
6 bb g Storming Home—Lovers Luck (IRE) (Anabaa (USA))
166[13] 1484[8] 1695[5] 1870[3] ◆ 2208[6] 2658[4]

Long Range *Dianne Sayer* 44b
5 b g Pivotal—Flight Of Fancy (Sadler's Wells (USA))
4117[12] 4473[12]

Long Row *Stuart Howe* 92b
5 ch m Tobougg(IRE) —Stealthy (Kind Of Hush)
375[4] 2222[10] 3876[6]

Long Run (FR) *Nicky Henderson* 142h 183c
6 bb g Cadoudal(FR) —Libertina (FR) (Balsamo (FR))
2359[3] (3560)
(4850)

Long Strand (IRE) *C F Swan* 122h 127c
7 b g Saddlers' Hall(IRE) —Oh So Breezy (IRE) (Be My Native (USA))
1830[U] 5338[P]

Long Wait (IRE) *Gordon Elliott* 109h
5 ch g Viking Ruler(AUS) —Striking Style (IRE) (Catrail (USA))
(871) 946[4]

Looby Magoodle *Richard Fahey* 71b
5 b m Grape Tree Road—Folly Foster (Relkino)
3504[3] 4027[15]

Lookin Daggers (IRE) *George Bewley* 41b
7 ch g Daggers Drawn(USA) —Shefoog (Kefaah (USA))
448[7]

Looking Hopeful (IRE) *Charlie Morlock* 57b
5 b g Heron Island(IRE) —Mahaasin (Bellypha)
5217[9]

Look Officer (USA) *Mandy Rowland* 40h
5 b m Officer(USA) —Inn Between (USA) (Quiet American (USA))
3692[11]

Looks Like Slim *Ben De Haan* 110h
4 b c Passing Glance—Slims Lady (Theatrical Charmer)
2958[6] 3401[7] ◆ 3673[3] ◆ 4283[2] 4807[20]

Looks The Business (IRE) *Andrew Haynes* 87h 105c
10 b g Marju(IRE) —Business Centre (IRE) (Digamist (USA))
185[3] 490[10] 1199[8]

Look Who's Talking *Alan King* 87b
4 b f King's Theatre(IRE) —Makounji (FR) (Tip Moss (FR))
4335[9] 5135[6]

Loom (GER) *David Pipe* 90h
9 b g Tiger Hill(IRE) —La Curamalal (IRE) (Rainbow Quest (USA))
185[10]

Looselastic *John Panvert*
6 b m Kayf Tara—Kolyas Girl (IRE) (Be My Native (USA))
4533[10]

Loosen My Load (IRE) *Henry De Bromhead* 139h 155c
7 b g Dushyantor(USA) —The Kids Dante (IRE) (Phardante (FR))
(1849a)
2384[3] 3241a[4] 4816[3] ◆

Loose Preformer (IRE) *Nicky Henderson* 124h
5 b g Luso—Out Performer (IRE) (Persian Bold)
3505[2] 3942[4]

Lord Aldervale (IRE) *Richard Rowe* 37b
4 br g Alderbrook—Monavale (IRE) (Strong Gale)
2597[10] 4055[14]

Lord Arion (IRE) *Jeremy Scott*
6 b g Revoque(IRE) —Charvet (IRE) (Executive Perk)
2295[P]

Lord Brunello (IRE) *Lawney Hill* 67h 106c
9 br g Lord Americo—Tickhill (General Assembly (USA))
158[F] 431[4] 588[5] 921[12] 1094[10]

Lord Collingwood (IRE) *Nigel Tinkler* 101h 98c
10 ch g Accordion—Cracker Dawn (IRE) (Executive Perk)
175[U] 353[3] 630[P]

Lord Deevert *Bill Turner* 89h
6 br g Averti(IRE) —Dee-Lady (Deploy)
4008[8]

Lord Fitzroy *Mrs O Bush* 66c
12 ch g Afzal—Friendly Lady (New Member)
295[4]

Lord Francois (FR) *Tim Vaughan* 82h
6 b g Kapgarde(FR) —Bellambre (FR) (Ambroise (FR))
299[U] 595[8] 1295[5] 1504[P]

Lord Gale (IRE) *W P Mullins* 122b
5 ch g Bach(IRE) —Wire Lady (IRE) (Second Set (IRE))
4808[P]

Lord Generous *Nigel Twiston-Davies* 136h 91c
7 ch g Generous(IRE) —Lady Rebecca (Rolfe (USA))
1964[5] 2523[P]
3342[3] 3770[3]

Lord Gunnerslake (IRE) *Tim Vaughan* 80h 94c
11 ch g Flying Spur(AUS) —Cry In The Dark (Godswalk (USA))
(63) (278)
381[2] (475) 587[7] **769[4] 867[6]**

Lord Henry (IRE) *Philip Hobbs* 136h 150c
12 b g Lord Americo—Auntie Honnie (IRE) (Radical)
18[5] (5372)

Lord Hugo *Seamus Mullins* 69b
6 ch g Alflora(IRE) —Kentford Duchess (Jupiter Island)
277[5] 632[P]

Lord Jay Jay (IRE) *David Evans* 89h 118c
11 b g Lord Of Appeal—Mesena (Pals Passage)
524[10] 959[7]

Lord Kennedy (IRE) *Alex Hales* 50h
6 b g Saddlers' Hall(IRE) —Minstrel Madame (IRE) (Black Minstrel)
1749[2] *3054[7]* 3678[10]

Lord Landen (IRE) *Rachel Hobbs* 105h
6 br g Beneficial—Agua Caliente (IRE) (Old Vic)
167[4] 407[2] 1925[2]

Lord Larsson *Malcolm Jefferson* 116h 127c
8 b g Kayf Tara—Shuildante (IRE) (Phardante (FR))
226[2] 1642[2] ◆ **(2350)**
3573[U]

Lord Lescribaa (FR) *Philip Hobbs* 85h 89c
8 b g Ungaro(GER) —Manon Lescribaa (FR) (Trebrook (FR))
665[P] 758[3] 872[4] 1061[4] 1159[2] 1331[6] 1843[2] 2002[3]

Lord Liath (IRE) *Alan King* 118h
5 gr g Beneficial—Lady Blayney (IRE) (Mazaad)
2518[4] 2963[5] ◆ 3295[2] 3718[2] ◆

Lord Nellerie (FR) *David Peter Nagle* 122c
12 b g Panoramic—Epsom Nellerie (FR) (Carmont (FR))
4792[10]

Lord Ragnar (IRE) *Nicky Henderson* 123h 125c
8 b g King's Theatre(IRE) —Shaiymara (IRE) (Darshaan)
3451[4] 3938[2] 4806[21]

Lord Richie (IRE) *Pat Murphy* 65h
5 b g Lord Of Appeal—Borough Trail (IRE) (Woodborough (USA))
3434[8] 3964[9] 5099[12]

Lord Rudi (IRE) *R K Watson* 121h
7 b g Lord Americo—Emmodee (Bowling Pin)
4568[3]

Lord Ryeford (IRE) *Mrs S P George* 117h 79c
11 br g Arctic Lord—Killoskehan Queen (Bustineto)
4991[5]

Lord Samposin *Maurice Barnes* 96h 89c
10 b g I'm Supposin(IRE) —Skiddaw Samba (Viking (USA))
5415[3]

Lords Bridge *Tim Vaughan* 97h
10 b g Rakaposhi King—The Secret Seven (Balidar)
(1101)
1126[U] 1141[7]
1293[P] 1468[8]

Lordsbridge (USA) *Andy Turnell* 119h 124c
9 b g Lord Avie(USA) —Victorian Style (Nashwan (USA))
131[8] 1740[10] **2124[3] 2662[2] 2961[3] 3672[4] 4140[2]**
4490[3] (4931)
5228[F]

Lordship (IRE) *Tony Carroll* 44h
7 b g King's Best(USA) —Rahika Rose (Unfuwain (USA))
2640[7]

Lord Singer (FR) *Gary Moore* 121h 124c
6 b g Secret Singer(FR) —Cricale (FR) (Grand Tresor (FR))
2210[2] 2593[F] 3531[P] (3834)
4033[4] 4324[3] 4482[3] 5011[4]

Lord Snow (IRE) *N Pearce* 66c
10 br g Mister Lord(USA) —Snowdrifter (Strong Gale)
294[P]

Lord Villez (FR) *Ferdy Murphy* 114h 121c
7 b g Villez(USA) —Samina (FR) (Saint Cyrien (FR))
2447[3] 2951[6] 3359[3] 3486[U] 3520[3] 3995[3] 4570[2]
(4890)
5413[3]

Lorient Express (FR) *Venetia Williams* 106h 137c
12 b g Sleeping Car(FR) —Envie De Chalamont (FR) (Pamponi (FR))
4324[6]

Lorum Leader (IRE) *Dr Richard Newland* 65h 125c
10 bb g Supreme Leader—Whistling Doe (Whistling Deer)
1957[5] 2249[4] 2984[10] 3482[3] 3695[4] 3821[3] 4219[P]
4740[P] 5120[P]

Los Nadis (GER) *Jim Goldie* 127h 107c
7 ch g Hernando(FR) —La Estrella (GER) (Desert King (IRE))
309[3] 627[5] 3969[6] 4940[6] 5339[4]

Lost Glory (NZ) *Jonjo O'Neill* 108h
6 b g Montjeu(IRE) —Joie De Vivre (NZ) (Zabeel (NZ))
1477[10] 1726[3] 1959[7] 2637[6]

Lost Two Stars (IRE) *Colin Tizzard* 102h
6 gr m Fourstars Allstar(USA) —Beagan Rose (IRE) (Roselier (FR))
2896[7] 3227[4] 3904[4] 4370[3] 4703[4] 5241[9]

Lothian Falcon *Peter Maddison* 97h 131c
12 b g Relief Pitcher—Lothian Rose (Roscoe Blake)
446[8] 844[P] 4284[5] 4466[2] 5338[4]

Lots Of Fun (IRE) *Jonjo O'Neill* 66h
7 bb g Heron Island(IRE) —Clonroche Floods (Pauper)
1820[P] 2290[P]

Lotta Presents (IRE) *John Ferguson*
8 b g Presenting—Lotta Talk (IRE) (Le Moss)
150[F]

Lough Derg (FR) *David Pipe* 158h 140c
11 b g Apple Tree(FR) —Asturias (FR) (Pistolet Bleu (IRE))
1855[11] 2125[7] 2516[7] 3199[2] 3676[3] 4202[6]

Lough Rynn (IRE) *Richard Lee* 75c
13 b g Beneficial—Liffey Lady (Camden Town)
1159[6] 1483[6]

Louie's Lad *John Bridger*
5 gr g Compton Place—Silver Louie (IRE) (Titus Livius (FR))
2960[21]

Louisa (GER) *P Monteith* 92h
7 b m Seattle Dancer(USA) —La Ola (GER) (Dashing Blade)
1780[3] 2102[17]

Louis Ludwig (IRE) *Tim Vaughan* 108h
6 b g Mull Of Kintyre(USA) —Fantastic Bid (USA) (Auction Ring (USA))
338[7] **1231[P]**
(1272) 1361[U] 5322[F]

Louis Pasteur (IRE) *Nick Mitchell* 98h 115c
6 b g Luso—Aokay (IRE) (Roselier (FR))
232[4] **4143[2]**
(4534)
5156[3] 5370[2]

Louisville Lip (IRE) *Patrick J Flynn* 125h
4 b g Orpen(USA) —Former Drama (USA) (Dynaformer (USA))
4083a[11]

Loupy Loups *Brendan Powell* 44b
5 ch m Loup Sauvage(USA) —Digyourheelsin (IRE) (Mister Lord (USA))
759[10]

Love Love Me Do *Carroll Gray* 81b
6 b m Alflora(IRE) —Lady Turk (FR) (Baby Turk)
832[7] 5395[4]

Love Of Tara *Jennifer Mason* 129h
9 b m Kayf Tara—O My Love (Idiots Delight)
2061[3] 2218[6] 2579[6]
3254[P] 3566[P] 4742[6] 5205[8]

Lovey Dovey (IRE) *Simon West* 117h
7 b m Winged Love(IRE) —Dansana (IRE) (Insan (USA))
(448) (732) 3747[2] ◆ (5091) ◆

Low Delta (IRE) *Michael Blake* 96h 8c
11 ch g Old Vic—La-Greine (Strong Gale)
593[7] 990[3] 1232[5] 2980[4] 3341[3] 3703[4] 4378[2]
4920[8]

Loyal Knight (IRE) *Paul Midgley* 82h
6 ch g Choisir(AUS) —Always True (USA) (Geiger Counter (USA))
1021[6] 1148[7] 1613[5]

Lua De Itapoan *Malcolm Jefferson* 90h
6 gr m Silver Patriarch(IRE) —Gotogeton (Le Moss)
2616[5] 2987[7] 4000[2] 4545[2] 5031[4]

Lucaindubai (IRE) *Evan Williams* 128h
5 bb g Orpen(USA) —Singhana (IRE) (Mouktar)
4[2] (168) (1392) 1859[3] 2361[9] 3676[F] 4727[4]
5201[20]

Lucciolina *Robin Dickin* 66h
8 b m Hernando(FR) —Gastina (FR) (Pistolet Bleu (IRE))
1965[P] 2073[P]

Luccombe Chine *John Quinn* 63b
6 ch m Karinga Bay—Sounds Familiar (IRE) (Orchestra)
2167[12]

Luccombe Rose *Lawney Hill*
6 b m Alflora(IRE) —Flaming Rose (IRE) (Roselier (FR))
3876[13]

Luce Bay *Richard Phillips* 74h 9c
8 b g Picea—Mary Macblain (Damister (USA))
12[P]

Lucia Bay *Lucinda Russell* 99b
6 ch m Karinga Bay—Lucia Forte (Neltino)
4171[2] ◆

Lucius Fabeo (IRE) *Anna Newton-Smith* 21h
7 b g Alderbrook—Clontyglass Lass (IRE) (Leading Counsel (USA))
3556[16] 3719[9] 4128[10]
4666[P] 5216[P]

Luck'N'Thanks (IRE) *Graeme McPherson* 86h
8 bb g Kotashaan(FR) —Miss Mutley (Pitpan)
3918[6] 4370[8] 5013[5] 5439[F]

Lucky At Last (IRE) *Patrick Martin* 144h 144c
9 b g City Honours(USA) —Leixlip Belle (IRE) (Camden Town)
2227a[4]

Lucky Belle (IRE) *William Young*
4 ch f Barathea(IRE) —Borders Belle (IRE) (Pursuit Of Love)
3850[16] 4303[P] 5428[P]

Lucky Breeze (IRE) *Ed de Giles* 94h
4 b f Key Of Luck(USA) —Lasting Chance (USA) (American Chance (USA))
3401[10] 4192[2]

Lucky Dance (BRZ) *Mark Rimmer* 88h
9 b h Mutakddim(USA) —Linda Francesa (ARG) (Equalize (USA))
4129[7] 4397[3] 4810[6]

Lucky Dancer *Evan Williams* 109h 103c
6 ch g Selkirk(USA) —Spot Prize (USA) (Seattle Dancer (USA))
233[P] 530[6] 1477[8] 3840[11]
5256[2]

Lucky Decision *Chris Grant* 71b
6 b m Sir Harry Lewis(USA) —Twenty Winks (Gunner B)
4171[7]

Lucky Landing (IRE) *Donald McCain* 81h
5 bb g Well Chosen—Melville Rose (IRE) (Phardante (FR))
(2368) 3761[9] 4377[8]

Lucky Luk (FR) *Kim Bailey* 77h 121c
12 b g Lights Out(FR) —Citronelle II (FR) (Kedellic (FR))
(431) 599[4]
1858[5] 2346[7]

Lucky Lukey *Richard Ford* 53h
5 gr g Cape Town(IRE) —Imprevue (IRE) (Priolo (USA))
3398[9] 4393[P] 5168[11]

Lucky Mix *Alan King* 107h
5 b m Fair Mix(IRE) —Nicklup (Netherkelly)
3590[6] 4535[2] ◆

Lucky Nellerie (FR) *Ferdy Murphy* 82h 114c
12 ch g Grand Tresor(FR) —British Nellerie (FR) (Le Pontet (FR))
33[8]

Lucky Pearl *Tim Vaughan* 88h
10 b m Jendali(USA) —Fardella (ITY) (Molvedo)
1798[P] 2001[3] 2239[8] 2589[8] 3341[P]

Lucky Quay (IRE) *David Pipe* 91h
4 br g Key Of Luck(USA) —Lakatoi (Saddlers' Hall (IRE))
(629) 743[2] 1024[5]

Lucky Score (IRE) *Chris Grant* 97h
5 b m Lucky Story(USA) —Musical Score (Blushing Flame (USA))
140[P] (1379)

Lucky Sun *Brian Eckley* 86b
5 b g Lucky Owners(NZ) —Sun Bonnet (Grand Lodge (USA))
304[4] 2025[2]

Lucky Sunny (IRE) *Richard Phillips* 113h
8 b g Pasternak—Flying Fur (IRE) (Elbio)
2362[4] 2954[9] 3718[4] 4132[2] 4541[6]

Lucky To Be (FR) *G Macaire* 122h 132c
5 b g Poliglote—Haute Tension (FR) (Garde Royale)
3193[6]

Lucky William (IRE) *Thomas Cooper* 137h 136c
7 ch g All My Dreams(IRE) —Dantes Mile (IRE) (Phardante (FR))
2971a[8] 3578a[6]

Lucky Wish *Eoin Griffin* 134h 135c
8 b g Alhaarth(IRE) —All The Luck (USA) (Mr Prospector (USA))
1123a[F] 1527a[9]

Lucy's Perfect *David Pipe* 113h
5 ch m Systematic—Water Flower (Environment Friend)
1689[2] 1921[4] 2150[4] 2329[12] 2639[3] (3227) 4448[8]
5064[2] 5189[4]

Lukey Luke *James Turner* 78h
8 b g Kayf Tara—Skiddaw Samba (Viking (USA))
12[5] 176[4] 552[3] 2271[3] 3502[8]

Lukeys Luck *Richard Ford* 71b
5 b g Cape Town(IRE) —Vitelucy (Vettori (IRE))
602[6]

Lukie Victor (IRE) *Evan Williams* 78h 99c
10 ch g Old Vic—Chapanga (IRE) (Un Desperado (FR))
646[8] **950[5]**
1001[7] 1179[9]
1273[4] 2604[3] (3307)
3606[P] 3839[11]

Luksar (IRE) *Rose Dobbin* 37c
11 gr g Erins Isle—Just Possible (Kalaglow)
4170[5]

Lulu's Gift (IRE) *Michael Mullineaux* 51b
5 gr m Lahib(USA) —She's A Gift (Bob's Return (IRE))
1771[10]

Luna Landing *Jedd O'Keeffe* 58h
8 ch g Allied Forces(USA) —Macca Luna (IRE) (Kahyasi)
420[P]
Luna Lightning *Linda Jewell* 47b
7 b m Rainbow High—Wilomeno (Efisio)
2445[7] *2825[5] 3060[8]* 3607[P] 4665[5]
Lundy Sky *Tony Newcombe* 121h
6 b g Zaha(CAN) —Rosina Mae (Rousillon (USA))
4091[3] (4539) ◆
Lupanar (IRE) *Gary Moore* 121h 120c
7 ch g Galileo(IRE) —Louve Sacree (USA) (Seeking The Gold (USA))
1904[3] 2581[2] 3688[2] 4121[4] 5230[7] 5404[3]
Lupita (IRE) *Derrick Scott* 79h 83c
7 ch m Intikhab(USA) —Sarah (IRE) (Hernando (FR))
134[9] 2239[12] 2609[4] (4540)
4926[4] 5155[5]
Lure of The Night (IRE) *Brian Rothwell* 79b
4 b g Sadler's Wells(USA) —Moneefa (Darshaan)
2108[4] 4117[7]
Lureyno *Renee Robeson* 74h
5 br g Lujain(USA) —Tereyna (Terimon)
1812[12] 3740[11] 4467[10]
Lush Life (IRE) *Nicky Henderson* 141h
6 b g Indian Danehill(IRE) —Karmisymixa (FR) (Linamix (FR))
2387[9] (2870) 3947[11] 4817[P]
Luska Lad (IRE) *John Joseph Hanlon* 157h
7 ch g Flemensfirth(USA) —Notsophar (IRE) (Phardante (FR))
(1847a) 2197a[4] 3205a[3] 4229a[2]
Luso's Lad (IRE) *Howard Johnson* 112h
7 b g Luso—Sister Stephanie (IRE) (Phardante (FR))
1661[F] 2092[5] 3500[16] 4281[9] 5092[3]
Lusty (FR) *C Le Galliard*
10 b g Double Bed(FR) —Lutsine (FR) (Zino)
312a[6]
Luther (IRE) *Alan King* 67h
8 br g Anshan—Candy Gale (IRE) (Strong Gale)
225[P]
Luthien (IRE) *Alex Hales* 96h
5 b m Polish Precedent(USA) —Triplemoon (USA) (Trempolino (USA))
1902[3] 2438[F]
Lutin Collonges (FR) *Michael Roberts* 74c
12 b g Ragmar(FR) —Ariane Collonges (FR) (Quart De Vin (FR))
278[P] 4772[P]
Lutteur Bleu (FR) *Mrs Angela Davis*
12 b g Franc Bleu Argent(USA) —Sirene Du Lac (FR) (Missolonghi (USA))
184[P]
Lutteur Dancer (FR) *Y Fouin* 106h
6 gr g Chichicastenango(FR) —Lady De Loi (FR) (Homme De Loi (IRE))
190a[6]
Lydon House *Gordon Elliott* 119c
12 ch g Lancastrian—The Mount (Le Moss)
(579)
Lyes Green *Oliver Sherwood* 117h 130c
10 gr g Bien Bien(USA) —Dissolve (Sharrood (USA))
1198[4]
1373[10]
Lyford Lad *George Moore* 45b
4 ch g Bahamian Bounty—Carradale (Pursuit Of Love)
2315[14]
Lygon Legend *Peter Hiatt* 102h
8 b g Midnight Legend—Gold Nite (Nesselrode (USA))
428[3] 826[2]
Lying Eyes *Paul Henderson*
5 b g Beat All(USA) —Jeanne D'Arc (Highest Honor (FR))
1817[P]
Lynford Nakita *Caroline Keevil* 67b
5 ch m Baryshnikov(AUS) —Lynphord Girl (Lyphento (USA))
568[10] 3651[7]
Lynn's Lady *Michael Easterby*
4 b f Fantastic Light(USA) —Silvernus (Machiavellian (USA))
1324[U] 1610[P]
Lyphin' Legend *Nick Mitchell* 30b
4 b f Midnight Legend—A Lyph (USA) (Lypheor)
5157[11]
Lyrical Intent *Maurice Barnes* 70h
5 ch g Imperial Dancer—Magical Flute (Piccolo)
2162[7] 4059[11]
Lyster (IRE) *Graeme McPherson* 104h 91c
12 b g Oscar(IRE) —Sea Skin (Buckskin (FR))
3[6] (359) (467) 503[4] 4501[6] 4968[5] 5322[9]
Maadraa (IRE) *Bernard Llewellyn* 109h
6 br g Josr Algarhoud(IRE) —Del Deya (IRE) (Caerleon (USA))
3760[7] 4404[5] 4528[2]
Mac Aeda *Malcolm Jefferson* 123h
7 gr g Kayf Tara—Altogether Now (IRE) (Step Together (USA))
2246[2] 2983[P] 3509[4] ◆ (4112) 4464[5]
Macarthur *James McAuley* 97h
7 b g Montjeu(IRE) —Out West (USA) (Gone West (USA))
4233[7]
Mac Beattie *Evan Williams* 90h
5 b g Beat All(USA) —Macnance (IRE) (Mandalus)
2499[12] 3645[13] 4860[4] ◆
Maccool (IRE) *Barney Curley*
5 b g King's Best(USA) —Mellow Park (IRE) (In The Wings)
3833[P]
Macdougal (IRE) *Donald McCain* 86h 92c
7 b g Presenting—Accountancy Lady (Capitano)
1710[P]
Mac Halen (IRE) *Evan Williams* 111h
8 b g Lord Americo—Colleen Donn (Le Moss)
359[2] (660) 771[7] 1230[9] 4862[5]
Machu Picchu (FR) *Jamie Snowden* 105c
9 b g Sendawar(IRE) —Nabita (FR) (Akarad (FR))
824[5] 1992[6] 2638[P] 2949[P]
Macindi Starr *Zoe Davison* 4b
5 b m Bahamian Bounty—Millazure (USA) (Dayjur (USA))
739[14]
Macklycuddy (USA) *Patrick G Kelly* 71h
5 b g Monashee Mountain(USA) —Exellensea (USA) (Exbourne (USA))
1146a[8]
Maclean *Philip Sharp* 105h 87c
10 b g Machiavellian(USA) —Celtic Cross (Selkirk (USA))
424[P]
Macmar (FR) *John Coombe* 102h 72c
11 b g Ragmar(FR) —Ex Des Sacart (FR) (Balsamo (FR))
3933[P] 4224[5] 4675[F]
Mac's Haul (IRE) *Ian Williams* 45b
6 b g Saddlers' Hall(IRE) —Vallee Doree (FR) (Neverneyev (USA))
1989[13]
Macs Lad (IRE) *Liam Corcoran* 95h 109c
8 ch g Old Vic—Nanna's Joy (IRE) (Phardante (FR))
1830[U] (1903)
1939[7]
Macville (IRE) *Patrick Neville* 138h
7 b m Christophene(USA) —I'lltelimar (IRE) (Montelimar (USA))
(2196a)
Madame Allsorts *Willie Musson* 103b
6 b m Double Trigger(IRE) —Always A Pleasure (Chauve Souris)
(3616) 4184[6] 4728[10]
Madame Jasmine *Suzy Smith* 100h
6 gr m Karinga Bay—Roslin (Roscoe Blake)
2056[9] 2331[2] 2873[7] 3693[4] 4009[11] (4773) 5289[6]
Madame Mado (FR) *Nicky Henderson* 117h
7 b m Lost World(IRE) —Brume (FR) (Courtroom (FR))
(19)
Madamlily (IRE) *John Quinn* 102h
5 b m Refuse To Bend(IRE) —Rainbow Dream (Rainbow Quest (USA))
2505[2]
Maddoxtown (IRE) *Robert Alan Hennessy* 71h
5 b g Luso—Augusta Victoria (Callernish)
1146a[5] 4132[6]
Made In France (FR) *Miss Helen Herrick* 87h 30c
11 b g Luchiroverte(IRE) —Birgonde (FR) (Quart De Vin (FR))
6[6] 499[F]
Made In Japan (JPN) *Nigel Twiston-Davies* 127h 122c
11 b g Barathea(IRE) —Darrery (Darshaan)
1968[4] 2544[4] 3440[13] 4285[6] 5153[10]
Made In Montot (FR) *B J Clarke* 94h 89c
11 b g Video Rock(FR) —Deep Turple (FR) (Royal Charter (FR))
4293[P] 4696[7]
Made In Taipan (IRE) *Thomas Mullins* 137h 158c
9 br g Taipan(IRE) —No Easy Way (IRE) (Mandalus)
3578a[9]
4087a[5] 4248a[2] 5025a[6] 5184[8]
Made In Time (IRE) *Rebecca Curtis* 125h
6 bb g Zagreb(USA) —No Easy Way (IRE) (Mandalus)
(2059) 2493[5] 3556[5] 4488[7] 5287[8]
Maderson Blue (IRE) *Roger Curtis* 85h
9 b g Pistolet Bleu(IRE) —Not A Bid (IRE) (Buckskin (FR))
956[4]
Madison De Vonnas (FR) *Mrs Freya Brewer* 106h 99c
11 bb g Epervier Bleu—Carine De Neuvy (FR) (Shelley (FR))
493[6]
Madison Du Berlais (FR) *David Pipe* 120h 161c
10 b g Indian River(FR) —Anais Du Berlais (FR) (Dom Pasquini (FR))
2136[2]
2673[F] 3560[6] 3805[5] 4208[P]
Mad Jack Duncan (IRE) *Lawney Hill* 98h 113c
9 br g Presenting—My Native Gesture (IRE) (Be My Native (USA))
(985) 1126[2]
(1276)
(1486) 1858[P]
Madman (FR) *Christopher Kellett* 69h
7 br g Kaldou Star—Shirlauges (FR) (Port Lyautey (FR))
1487[10] 1689[8] 2114[7] 2367[P]
Mad Max (IRE) *Nicky Henderson* 144h 164c
9 b g Kayf Tara—Carole's Crusader (Faustus (USA))
2359[4] 2886[6] 3675[3] 4805[10] 5184[6]
Mad Moose (IRE) *Nigel Twiston-Davies* 132h
7 ch g Presenting—Sheshollystar (IRE) (Fourstars Allstar (USA))
566[7] 771[F] 1004[5] (1380) 1507[F] 1578[2] 1967[5]
2581[4] (4940) 5080[3]
Mad Professor (IRE) *John Cornwall* 80h 80c
8 b g Mull Of Kintyre(USA) —Fancy Theory (USA) (Quest For Fame)
(48) 136[U]
353[6] 477[3] 1481[6] 1744[4] 1954[5] 2113[5] 2956[10]
3404[6] 3618[6] 3720[7] 4178[2] 4741[2]
4813[2] 5016[6]
Mad Victor (IRE) *Miss S M Taylor* 115c
10 ch g Old Vic—Maddens Run VII (Damsire Unregistered)
151[U] 526[5] 4442[2]
Mae Cigan (FR) *Michael Blanshard* 114h
8 gr g Medaaly—Concert (Polar Falcon (USA))
372[5] 3587[11] 3934[7] 4524[5]
Magellan Straits *Sue Smith* 116h 99c
7 b g Nikos—Gaelic Gold (IRE) (Good Thyne (USA))
32[4] 353[F] 460[10] 681[3]
Magen's Star (IRE) *T Stack* 137h
6 b m Galileo(IRE) —Bluffing (IRE) (Darshaan)
4788[13]
Maggie Aron *V J Hughes* 52h
5 gr m Generous(IRE) —Pems Gift (Environment Friend)
375[5] (568) (759) 908[6] 2584[F]
Maggie Mathias (IRE) *Brendan Powell* 55h
10 b m Portrait Gallery(IRE) —The Marching Lady (IRE) (Archway (IRE))
81[P]
Maggio (FR) *Patrick Griffin* 129h
6 b g Trempolino(USA) —La Musardiere (FR) (Cadoudal (FR))
1664[2] 1867[2] 2260a[3] 3030a[5] 4242[2] 4377[2] 5182[8]
Magical Flight *Carroll Gray*
9 b m Busy Flight—Swansea Gold (IRE) (Torus)
820[6]
Magical Harry *Anthony Honeyball* 113c
11 b g Sir Harry Lewis(USA) —Magic (Sweet Revenge)
(169) 663[3]
Magical Island *Sophie Leech* 84h
8 gr g Thowra(FR) —Alice's Mirror (Magic Mirror)
318[8] 1048[2]
Magical Legend *Sophie Leech* 127h 127c
10 gr m Midnight Legend—Alice's Mirror (Magic Mirror)
89[2] 302[P] **838[3] 1045[3] 1197[2] (1377)**
1661[2] 2214[5] 5007[2] 5290[F] (5301)
Magical Man *Debra Hamer* 83b
4 b g Lahib(USA) —Majestic Di (IRE) (Zaffaran (USA))
2237[7] 4533[5]
Magical Maybe (IRE) *Matt Sheppard* 87h
6 b g Wizard King—Milwaukee (IRE) (Over The River (FR))
1567[8]
Magical Treasure *Sophie Leech* 101h
7 gr g Riverwise(USA) —Alice's Mirror (Magic Mirror)
167[3] 379[3] 1028[3]
Magic Marmalade (IRE) *Philip Hobbs* 94h 108c
8 ch g Mohaajir(USA) —Kylogue's Delight (Strong Gale)
3296[5]
(3650) 5039[F]
Magic Merlin *Charlie Morlock* 83h
10 b g Magic Ring(IRE) —St James's Antigua (IRE) (Law Society (USA))
5325 1049[P]
Magic Millie (IRE) *David O'Meara* 48h
4 bb f Marju(IRE) —Fille De La Terre (IRE) (Namaqualand (USA))
1825[8] 2078[P]
Magic Prospect (FR) *Charlie Mann* 98h
4 b g Miesque's Son(USA) —Clarissa Dalloway (FR) (Sillery (USA))
3673[5] 3944[5] ◆ 4458[3] 4859[2] 5244[5]
Magics Gold (IRE) *James Danahar* 4h
9 b m Bob Back(USA) —Sweet Harmony (IRE) (Altountash)
3581[0]
Magic Show *Peter Bowen* 70h
7 b g Marju(IRE) —White Rabbit (Zilzal (USA))
1910[8]
Magic Sky (FR) *Milton Harris* 120h 137c
11 b g Simon Du Desert(FR) —Kailasa (FR) (R B Chesne)
78[5] 1776[10]
1960[2] 2541[4] *3059[3]* **3437[P] 3568[P] 4077[F] 4221[4]**
4486[8] (5229)
5416[3]
Magic Spirit *Suzy Smith*
4 ch f Kirkwall—Flaming Spirt (Blushing Flame (USA))
1882[8] 2047[P]
Magistrate (IRE) *Andy Turnell* 84h
6 b g Nayef(USA) —Alabastrine (Green Desert (USA))
40[P]
Magnanimity (IRE) *D T Hughes* 140h 155c
7 bb g Winged Love(IRE) —Mossy Mistress (IRE) (Le Moss)
(3472a)
4084a[2] 4804[4]
Magnetic Pole *Richard Lee* 65h 109c
10 b g Machiavellian(USA) —Clear Attraction (USA) (Lear Fan (USA))
5[2] 475[4] 862[7]
1044[3] (1309)
1604[7] 2034[5] 2587[3] 2952[P] 3878[7] 5256[5]
Magnifico (FR) *Nikki Evans* 121h 91c
10 b g Solid Illusion(USA) —Born For Run (FR) (Pharly (FR))
3440[14]
4102[P]
Magnifique Etoile *Charlie Longsdon* 113b
4 b g Kayf Tara—Star Diva (IRE) (Toulon)
3794[3] 4468[4] 5113[2]
Magnitude *Brian Baugh* 86h
6 ch g Pivotal—Miswaki Belle (USA) (Miswaki (USA))
5082[7]
Magnum Force (IRE) *C A McBratney* 136h
7 b g Redback—Dalal (Cadeaux Genereux)
1133a[16] 2197a[U]
Magnushomesdotcom (IRE) *Maurice Barnes* 88h
7 b g Daylami(IRE) —Perfect Alibi (Law Society (USA))
349[8] 624[5] 805[P]
Magroom *Ron Hodges* 88h
7 b g Compton Place—Fudge (Polar Falcon (USA))
2021[5]
Magusta (GER) *Jamie Snowden* 87h 46c
7 b g Second Set(IRE) —Manhattan Girl (USA) (Vice Regent (CAN))
168[6] 1900[5] **2187[5] 2468[P]**
Mahogany Blaze (FR) *Nigel Twiston-Davies* 136h 157c
9 b g Kahyasi—Mahogany River (Irish River (FR))
2138[U] 2385[5] 2885[6] 3292[3] 3677[U]
Mahonia (IRE) *Paul Nicholls* 138h 138c
8 b g Turtle Island(IRE) —Bell Walks Run (IRE) (Commanche Run)
208[P]
Maid In Moscow (IRE) *S R B Crawford* 76h 86c
7 b m Moscow Society(USA) —Dromkeen Wood (Primitive Rising (USA))
4000[9] 4304[6] 4688[6]
4911[3] 5150[2]
Maid Of Silk (IRE) *Neil Mulholland* 94b
5 b m Blueprint(IRE) —Silk Style (Polish Precedent (USA))
832[2] 1029[2] 5070[2] 5306[8]
Maidstone Mixture (FR) *David Pipe* 100h 96c
6 gr h Linamix(FR) —Marie Jbeil (FR) (Double Bed (FR))
1500[6] 1969[P]
Main Beach *Tobias B P Coles*
4 ch g Starcraft(NZ) —Ocean View (USA) (Gone West (USA))
2597[4] 2824[3]
Maison Brillet (IRE) *Howard Johnson* 79h
4 b g Pyrus(USA) —Stormchaser (IRE) (Titus Livius (FR))
1696[4] 2078[11]
Maizy Missile (IRE) *Mary Evans* 96h
9 b m Executive Perk—Landsker Missile (Cruise Missile)
341[3] (1066) 1489[2] 2467[2] (4899)
Majaales (USA) *Tom George* 130h
8 b g Diesis—Roseate Tern (Blakeney)
1776[9]
Majd Aljazeera *Alison Thorpe*
5 b g King's Best(USA) —Tegwen (USA) (Nijinsky (CAN))
563[P]
Majestic Bull (USA) *Susan Gardner* 80h
5 bb g Holy Bull(USA) —Croissant (USA) (Lycius (USA))
171[9] 356[5] 585[9]
Majestic Concorde (IRE) *D K Weld* 141h 160c
8 b g Definite Article—Talina's Law (IRE) (Law Society (USA))
1123a[3] (3206a)
5200[U]
Majestic Mayhem (IRE) *George Moore* 123h
8 b g Luso—Florida Bay (IRE) (Florida Son)
(624) (805) 954[7] 1367[2] 1662[4] 1860[B] 2090[7]
5031[2] 5316[6]
Major Bob *Richard Mitchell*
5 b g Wared(USA) —Express Edition (Comedy Star (USA))
3964[12] 4709[10]
Major Euro (IRE) *S J Gilmore* 82h 83c
14 b g Lord Americo—Gold Bank (Over The River (FR))
95[P]
Majorica King (FR) *Oliver Sherwood* 108b
5 b g Kahyasi—Majorica Queen (FR) (Kaldoun (FR))
3406[2] 4468[7] 5387[2]
Major Kirk *Terry Clement* 27b
4 b g Kirkwall—Flying Wind (Forzando)
3835[7]
Major Malarkey (IRE) *Nigel Twiston-Davies* 118h 135c
8 b g Supreme Leader—Valley (IRE) (Flemensfirth (USA))
(2146)
2305[3] (2959) ◆ **4208[P] 4802[U] 5443[5]**
Major Miller *Nicky Henderson* 100h 119c
10 b g Opera Ghost—Millers Action (Fearless Action (USA))
994[4] 1129[3] 1590[5] 2080[P]
Major Payne (IRE) *Donald McCain* 113h
7 b g Deploy—Rikaba (IRE) (Kahyasi)
3585[8]
Major Potential (USA) *Venetia Williams* 79h
5 ch g Officer(USA) —Protea (USA) (Roanoke (USA))
3158[15] 3489[U] 3526[10] 3740[10] 4104[7]
Major Upset (IRE) *John Upson* 82h
8 b g Oscar(IRE) —Ikdam Valley (IRE) (Ikdam)
84[P]
Majy D'Auteuil (FR) *Alan Jessop* 89h 106c
9 b g Discover D'Auteuil(FR) —Majestic Dancer (FR) (What A Guest)
81[P] 2276[5]
Makbullet *Michael Smith* 103h
4 gr g Makbul—Gold Belt (IRE) (Bellypha)
1825[2] 2655[3] 3550[2]
Make A Track (IRE) *David Arbuthnot* 110b
5 ch g Hernando(FR) —Tracker (Bustino)
(4329) ◆ (5063)
Make It Blossom (IRE) *John G Carr* 72h
9 b m Bob Back(USA) —Strategic Ploy (Deploy)
552[7] 875[7] 1407[6] 1428[5] 1647[3] 2103[4]
Makena (FR) *David Rees* 110h 120c
9 b m Sky Swallow(FR) —Maiakovskaia (FR) (Bikala)
645[7] (955) ◆ (1057) **(1080)**
(1476) ◆ 1590[7] 1746[5] 1904[6]
Makhaaleb (IRE) *Gordon Elliott* 112h
5 b g Haafhd—Summerhill Parkes (Zafonic (USA))
1337[6] 1594[2] 1859[8]
Makhzoon (USA) *Tim Vaughan* 110h
7 bb g Dynaformer(USA) —Boubskaia (Niniski (USA))
5110[5]
Maktu *Pat Murphy* 121h 146c
9 ch g Bien Bien(USA) —Shalateeno (Teenoso (USA))
2163[2] ◆ **3437[5] 3940[8] 4487[7] 5009[2]** ◆ **5443[6]**
Malenfant *Michael Easterby* 37h
4 ch g Generous(IRE) —Markapen (IRE) (Classic Music (USA))
3399[13] 3542[11] 4233[P]
Maletton (FR) *P R M Philips* 112h 32c
11 b g Bulington(FR) —Reine Dougla (FR) (Faunus (FR))
4141[6]

Malibu Sun *Oliver Sherwood* 83h
4 ch g Needwood Blade—Lambadora (Suave Dancer (USA))
2824[4] 4055[12] 4702[P] 5437[2] ◆

Malin Bay (IRE) *Nicky Richards* 113h
6 b g Milan—Mirror Of Flowers (Artaius (USA))
289[2] 3500[3] 4067[U] 4506[3]

Malindi Bay *Kim Bailey* 115h
6 b m Alflora(IRE) —Rachel C (IRE) (Phardante (FR))
1768[3] (2072) (2554) 2983[8] 5008[14]

Maljimar (IRE) *Nick Williams* 93h 144c
11 b g Un Desperado(FR) —Marble Miller (IRE) (Mister Lord (USA))
2543[F] 3290[7] 4792[4]

Mallusk (IRE) *Kim Bailey* 106h 125c
6 b g Exit To Nowhere(USA) —Saucy Nun (IRE) (Orchestra)
(3257)
3562[P] 4490[6]

Malt Master (IRE) *Nicky Henderson* 100b
4 b g Milan—Dantes Profit (IRE) (Phardante (FR))
(4287)

Mamba (GER) *Chris Down* 63h 74c
9 b m Tannenkonig(IRE) —Mostly Sure (IRE) (Sure Blade (USA))
591[0] 2721[0] **2468[2] 3404[2] 3618[P] 3873[P]**

Mamlook (IRE) *David Pipe* 148h 142c
7 br g Key Of Luck(USA) —Cradle Brief (IRE) (Brief Truce (USA))
(3600)
4096[3] (4729)
5164[4]

Mam Ratagan *Heather Main* 90h 131c
10 b g Mtoto—Nika Nesgoda (Suave Dancer (USA))
(1467)
1568[2] (1796)
1975[6] 2662[3] 2881[7] 5305[4]

Manadam (FR) *Anthony Middleton* 114h 114c
8 b g Mansonnien(FR) —Cadoudame (FR) (Cadoudal (FR))
318[3] 685[8] **867[P]** 1092[3] 1259[5] 1368[5] 1555[3] 1814[3] 2171[5] 2532[6] 2929[6] 3530[3] 3870[9]

Management (IRE) *Alan King* 106h
5 b g True Brave(USA) —Princesse Ira (FR) (Less Ice)
2295[2] 3055[3] 3398[4] 4029[5] (4676)

Manathon (FR) *Alan Jones* 62h
8 b g Marathon(USA) —Fleurissante (FR) (Legend Of France (USA))
1489[6]

Mandalay Bay (IRE) *Chris Gordon* 71h 58c
11 b g Humbel(USA) —Molly Bigley (IRE) (Lancastrian)
531[4] 689[4] 913[P]

Mandalay Prince *Willie Musson* 71h
7 b g Tobougg(IRE) —Autumn Affair (Lugana Beach)
2310[12] 3491[10] 3882[9]

Mandarino (CZE) *S Popelka Jr* 137c
10 b g Bin Shaddad(USA) —Mest (RUS) (Mistnik)
1811a[4]

Mandingo Chief (IRE) *Miss C L Wills* 83h 99c
12 b g Flying Spur(AUS) —Elizabethan Air (Elegant Air)
4026[P] 4463[U]

Manele Bay *Richard Rowe* 113h
8 ch m Karinga Bay—Lacounsel (FR) (Leading Counsel (USA))
2081[7] ◆ 2514[11] 3881[3] 4327[5] 4700[P]

Man From Highworth *Audrey Manners* 120h 120c
12 b g Ballet Royal(USA) —Cavisoir (Afzal)
4896[2] 5081[7] 5277[2]

Man From Moscow *Mrs Alison Hickman* 77c
8 b g Gleaming(IRE) —Mosta (IRE) (Moscow Society (USA))
294[7] 4429[5]

Mangham (IRE) *David Brown* 48h
6 b g Montjeu(IRE) —Lovisa (USA) (Gone West (USA))
3304[9]

Mango Catcher (IRE) *Rebecca Curtis* 111h 113c
11 b g Personal Flag(USA) —Sun Shines East (USA) (Eastern Echo (USA))
1299[5]

Mangonel *Stuart Howe* 81h 85c
7 ch m Beckett(IRE) —Apachee Flower (Formidable (USA))
16[6] 263[5] 1164[P] 1335[5] 1451[5] 1551[5] 1741[2] 2001[4] 2329[4] 2480[5] 3840[9]
5155[4] 5434[P]

Manics Man *Helen Nelmes* 57h
6 ch g Double Trigger(IRE) —No Near Miss (Nearly A Hand)
3930[12] 4094[P] 4370[9]

Manikon Eros (IRE) *Rebecca Curtis* 60h
6 b g Old Vic—Cloughan Girl (IRE) (Yashgan)
(20) 5107[10]

Manjam (IRE) *Rebecca Curtis* 97h
7 b g Almutawakel—Mubkera (IRE) (Nashwan (USA))
55[4] 252[4] 566[5]

Manmoon (FR) *Nigel Hawke* 106h 109c
8 gr g Mansonnien(FR) —La Voix De La Lune (FR) (Less Ice)
1912[11] 2287[4] (2604)
2975[7] (3349)
3608[F] 4022[8] 4768[3] 5017[3] 5214[5]

Mannered *John Wade* 93h
6 b g Alflora(IRE) —Manettia (IRE) (Mandalus)
1829[11] 3633[4] 3887[F]

Manners (IRE) *Audrey Manners* 111h 101c
13 b g Topanoora—Maneree (Mandalus)
4536[P] 5322[P]

Mannlichen *Venetia Williams* 129h
5 ch g Selkirk(USA) —Robe Chinoise (Robellino (USA))
1857[4] 2129[3] 2983[2] (3840) 3881[5]

Man Of Leisure *Nerys Dutfield* 96h
7 b g Karinga Bay—Girl Of Pleasure (IRE) (Namaqualand (USA))
1742[9] 2607[15] 2791[13] 3367[2] 3532[2] 4104[2] 4540[6] 4785[3] 5040[2] 5241[P]

Man Of The Moment *Jim Best* 81h 97c
9 gr g Silver Patriarch(IRE) —Winnowing (IRE) (Strong Gale)
383[P]

Manolete (IRE) *Ralph Smith* 59b
5 b g Hawkeye(IRE) —Sainte Gig (FR) (Saint Cyrien (FR))
284[7]

Manoubi *Martin Todhunter* 88h 95c
12 b g Doyoun—Manuetti (IRE) (Sadler's Wells (USA))
88[8] 1666[2] ◆ 1782[6] **2189[2]** 2448[10] 2937[4] 3363[5]
3501[3] 3883[6]
4827[2] 5258[7]

Man Overboard *Gary Brown* 27h
9 b g Overbury(IRE) —Dublin Ferry (Celtic Cone)
374[P] 532[8]

Manshoor (IRE) *Lucy Wadham* 108h
6 gr g Linamix(FR) —Lady Wells (IRE) (Sadler's Wells (USA))
1624[2] (1732) 2312[3] 2558[P] (3348) 3793[P]

Mansolias (FR) *Sophie Leech* 79h
7 b g Mansonnien(FR) —Popie D'Ecorcei (FR) (Balsamo (FR))
36[P]

Mansonien L'As (FR) *Ferdy Murphy* 67h 75c
5 b g Mansonnien(FR) —Star Des As (FR) (Kaldou Star)
2192[4]
2938[7] *3171[10]* **3520[8] 3726[2] 4509[P]**

Mansony (FR) *A L T Moore* 88h 156c
12 b g Mansonnien(FR) —Hairly (FR) (Air De Cour (USA))
2339a[P] 4248a[3]

Manxman (IRE) *Ferdy Murphy* 97h
4 b c Celtic Swing—Viscaria (IRE) (Barathea (IRE))
1825[5] 2245[2] 2451[3]

Manyriverstocross (IRE) *Alan King* 145h
6 b g Cape Cross(IRE) —Alexandra S (IRE) (Sadler's Wells (USA))
2386[3]

Maoi Chinn Tire (IRE) *Jennie Candlish* 120h
4 b g Mull Of Kintyre(USA) —Primrose And Rose (Primo Dominie)
(2078) 3802[6] 4350[8] 5161[4] 5420[3]

Maolisa (IRE) *S R B Crawford* 96h 41c
9 b m Jamesmead—Wissey (IRE) (Florida Son)
291[2] 577[3] 871[3] (1119) 1339[5] 1782[7]

Maraafeq (USA) *Venetia Williams* 128h 123c
7 bb g Bahri(USA) —Tabrir (IRE) (Unfuwain (USA))
2125[4] 2393[6] 3440[8] 3688[18] **(4007)**
4210[4] 4438[3] 4877[P]

Maraased *Steve Gollings* 98h
6 b g Alhaarth(IRE) —Fleeting Rainbow (Rainbow Quest (USA))
3692[6] 4739[3]

Marado (IRE) *Simon Lewis* 31h 73c
10 ch g Un Desperado(FR) —Hi Marble (IRE) (Wylfa)
148[P] 1106[P] 1452[P]

Marblehead (IRE) *Nigel Twiston-Davies* 118h 135c
9 gr g Environment Friend—General Chase (Scottish Reel)
151[2] 525[P] 863[3] (1105)
1178[3] 1373[7] 1625[3]
1858[13]

Marc Aurele (IRE) *Milton Harris* 116h 115c
6 b g Trempolino(USA) —Ile Rousse (Danehill (USA))
(41) 675[2] ◆ 1160[3] 1488[4] (1547) 1884[P] **2153[5]**
2210[3] 2422[4] 3494[6] 3834[4]

Marching Song (USA) *Andy Turnell* 109h
5 b g War Chant(USA) —Tates Creek (USA) (Rahy (USA))
284[2] 3386[3] 3740[5] (Dead)

Marc Of Brilliance (USA) *Gary Moore* 114h 122c
8 ch g Sunday Silence(USA) —Rahcak (IRE) (Generous (IRE))
85[2] (281)
1676[P] 2112[6] 2513[F] 3482[P] 4023[3] 4502[3] 5120[P]

Mardood *Chris Grant* 94h
6 b g Oasis Dream—Gaelic Swan (IRE) (Nashwan (USA))
176[9] 393[3] 2603[8] 2941[10] 3635[P] 4390[7] 4550[11] (4994) 5308[9]

Maree Hall (IRE) *Martin Ward* 85h 67c
10 b g Saddlers' Hall(IRE) —My Sunny South (Strong Gale)
61[3]

Maree Prince (IRE) *Ferdy Murphy* 103h 88c
10 b g Taipan(IRE) —A Woman's Heart (IRE) (Supreme Leader)
1660[7] 2188[P]

Maria Antonia (IRE) *Alison Thorpe* 85h
8 ch m King's Best(USA) —Annieirwin (IRE) (Perugino (USA))
5117[16] 5346[8]

Marias Rock *Jeremy Scott* 87h 93c
9 b m I'm Supposin(IRE) —Our Lottie (Nearly A Hand)
(2930)
3790[4] (4409)
4718[3] 5216[P]

Marie De Laufon (FR) *Chris Bealby* 96h
6 ch m Kapgarde(FR) —Marie De Valois (FR) (Moulin)
1066[2] 1554[3] 1732[11]

Marieschi (USA) *Roger Fisher* 65h
7 b g Maria's Mon(USA) —Pennygown (Rainbow Quest (USA))
519[9]

Marigolds Way *Anthony Honeyball* 98h 101c
9 b m Nomadic Way(USA) —Miss Marigold (Norwick (USA))
36[3] **4560[2]**
5037[4]

Mariinsky (GER) *Tim Vaughan* 104h
5 b g Tiger Hill(IRE) —Mayada (USA) (The Minstrel (CAN))
847[4] 3481[9] 3840[8] 4860[3]

Marillos Proterras *Ann Duffield* 38h
5 b m Fraam—Legend Of Aragon (Aragon)
726[6]

Marina Bay *Christopher Kellett*
6 br m Karinga Bay—Marina Bird (Julio Mariner)
4423[7]

Maringo Bay (IRE) *Charlie Mann* 138h 134c
6 b g Old Vic—Waterland Lady (Strong Gale)
2181[10]
3600[3] (4159) ◆ 5196[8]

Marino Prince (FR) *Jim Best* 109h
6 b g Dr Fong(USA) —Hula Queen (USA) (Irish River (FR))
96[6] 228[F] 678[5] 2398[2] (2467) (2583) (2643) 4924[6]

Marjac (IRE) *Nigel Twiston-Davies*
4 b g Alderbrook—Silver Palm (FR) (Great Palm (USA))
4239[P]

Markadam *Ms Jackie Williamson* 21h
5 b g Mark Of Esteem(IRE) —Elucidate (Elmaamul (USA))
548[8] **4147[P]**

Marked Man (IRE) *Richard Lee* 98h 107c
15 b g Grand Plaisir(IRE) —Teazle (Quayside)
330[8] 795[3] (1061)
2240[F]

Market Bob (IRE) *Ann Price* 51h
9 br g Bob Back(USA) —Market Lass (IRE) (Orchestra)
635[6]

Markila (FR) *Henry Daly* 120h 116c
8 b m Mark Of Esteem(IRE) —Ile Mamou (IRE) (Ela-Mana-Mou)
5[5]

Markington *Peter Bowen* 130h
8 b g Medicean—Nemesia (Mill Reef (USA))
302[2] (708) 1855[P] 1986[11] 2235[4] 2663[10] 5160[8]

Mark Of Love (IRE) *Martin Keighley* 105h
7 ch g Mark Of Esteem(IRE) —Dazilyn Lady (USA) (Zilzal (USA))
(2128) 2361[P]

Marksman *George Margarson* 56b
4 b g Mark Of Esteem(IRE) —Thea (USA) (Marju (IRE))
3406[11]

Marksmore *Miss Katie Scott* 74h 85c
8 b g Shahrastani(USA) —Admire-A-More (Le Coq D'Or)
5148[2]

Mark Twain (IRE) *Kim Bailey* 116h
4 b g Rock Of Gibraltar(IRE) —Lady Windermere (IRE) (Lake Coniston (IRE))
3194[3] (3519) 3802[5] 4807[22]

Marlborough Sound *James Turner* 93h 63c
12 b g Overbury(IRE) —Dark City (Sweet Monday)
228[12] (557) 717[2] 3899[2] 4572[11]

Marlee Mourinho (IRE) *Lucy Normile* 70b
5 bl g Pushkin(IRE) —Spur Of The Moment (Montelimar (USA))
4308[6]

Marleno (GER) *Milton Harris* 114h
5 b g Lecroix(GER) —Mondalita (GER) (Alkalde (GER))
1884[3] 2362[3] *3056[5]* (3228) 3481[4] 3950[5] 5117[2] 5291[9]

Marleybow (IRE) *Richard Lee* 117h 120c
8 br g Presenting—Gaye Artiste (IRE) (Commanche Run)
1725[3] 2036[5] 4937[2]

Marley Roca (IRE) *Paul Webber* 119h 119c
7 bb g Tamayaz(CAN) —Gaye Gordon (Scottish Reel)
1770[5] 1970[4] 2298[3] 2961[F] (5100)

Mar Ocean (FR) *Patrick Griffin* 87h
5 b g Johann Quatz(FR) —Free Demo (FR) (Hero's Honor (USA))
1729[8] 2553[15] 5151[2]

Marodima (FR) *Jamie Snowden* 147h 144c
8 b g Robin Des Pres(FR) —Balbeyssac (FR) (Beyssac (FR))
(1) (219) 627[11]
831[5] 1044[5] 1195[5] 1370[3] **1676[2] 1975[5] 2293[5]**
2586[5] 3477[4] (3962) 4049[10]
4698[5] 5242[4]

Marshal Zhukov (IRE) *Caroline Keevil* 90b
5 b g Morozov(USA) —Artic Brush (IRE) (Brush Aside (USA))
5113[9] 5217[7]

Marsh Court *Jamie Snowden* 93h 102c
8 b m Overbury(IRE) —Lady Prunella (IRE) (Supreme Leader)
(3873)
4671[P] 5275[P]

Marsh Warbler *Brian Ellison* 140h
4 ch g Barathea(IRE) —Echo River (USA) (Irish River (FR))
2245[3] (2306) (2600) (3436) 4788[11]

Marsool *Donald McCain* 94h
5 br g Key Of Luck(USA) —Chatifa (IRE) (Titus Livius (FR))
1661[1] 393[7]

Martha Elizabeth (IRE) *Liam Lennon* 102h 85c
6 b m Orpen(USA) —Kaguyahime (Distant Relative)
(50) 1140[3]

Martha's Kinsman (IRE) *Henry Daly* 116h 122c
12 b g Petoski—Martha's Daughter (Majestic Maharaj)
(152) **525[P]**
4442[3] 5154[P]

Martin Scruff (IRE) *Michael Quinlan* 129h
5 b g Oscar(IRE) —Robo's Sister (IRE) (Strong Gale)
833[10] 1250[4] 1475[U] 1688[6] 1812[5] 2390[U]

Martys Mission (IRE) *Richard Rowe* 125h 135c
9 b g Zaffaran(USA) —Parson's Lodge (IRE) (The Parson)
2343[10] 2669[5] 2962[5] 3347[7]

Marufo (IRE) *Philip Hobbs* 110h 123c
9 b g Presenting—Bucks Cregg (IRE) (Buckskin (FR))
1348[2] ◆ **1469[3]**

Marvelous *Evan Williams* 64h
6 b m Beneficial—Keel Row (Relkino)
4006[13] 4288[14] 4952[10] 5385[9]

Marvo *Mark H Tompkins* 67h
7 b g Bahamian Bounty—Mega (IRE) (Petardia)
2495[8] 4859[10]

Marwan (IRE) *Ian Williams* 98h
7 b g Moscow Society(USA) —Cointosser (IRE) (Nordico (USA))
766[P]

Marybelle *Philip Hobbs*
9 b m Double Trigger(IRE) —Bellara (Thowra (FR))
2974[P]

Masdar (IRE) *D K Weld* 114b
5 ro g Dalakhani(IRE) —Balaabel (USA) (Sadler's Wells (USA))
(1146a)

Mashdood (USA) *Peter Hiatt* 77h
5 b g Sinndar(IRE) —Rahayeb (Arazi (USA))
2325[5]

Maska Pony (IRE) *George Moore* 129h
7 gr g Celtic Swing—Clotted Cream (USA) (Eagle Eyed (USA))
(166) 1253[3] (1426) (1501) (1827) 2344[6] 4940[9] 5315[14]

Masked Man (IRE) *Alan King* 120h 137c
8 ch g Alhaarth(IRE) —Misbegotten (IRE) (Baillamont (USA))
329[5]

Mason Hindmarsh *Karen McLintock* 109h
4 ch g Dr Fong(USA) —Sierra Virgen (USA) (Stack (USA))
(1984) 2356[14] 5314[2]

Masra *Alan Kirtley* 89h
8 b g Silver Patriarch(IRE) —Go Sally Go (IRE) (Elbio)
12[P]

Massachusetts *Brendan Powell* 75h
4 ch g Singspiel(IRE) —Royal Passion (Ahonoora)
1234[3] 1330[6] 1473[4] 2133[6]

Massams Lane *Carole Ikin* 107h
7 b g Lahib(USA) —Night Trader (USA) (Melyno)
853[6] 1147[9] 1236[8]

Massasoit (IRE) *Paul Nicholls* 151h 145c
9 br g Supreme Leader—Lady Margaretta (Rolfe (USA))
2273[3]

Massena (IRE) *Venetia Williams* 105h
4 b g Marju(IRE) —Mayara (IRE) (Ashkalani (IRE))
4192[P]

Massini Man (IRE) *Brendan Powell* 125c
10 b g Dr Massini(IRE) —Tina Torus (IRE) (Torus)
1045[P] 1109[2] (1227)
(3938) (4183)
4821[15] 5163[P]

Massini Moon (IRE) *Gary Moore* 102h
7 b g Dr Massini(IRE) —Sangan Court (IRE) (Yashgan)
2314[5] 2637[2] 2929[2] 3745[P]

Massini's Maguire (IRE) *David Pipe* 149h 158c
10 b g Dr Massini(IRE) —Molly Maguire (IRE) (Supreme Leader)
(2084)

Massini Sunset (IRE) *Richard Mitchell* 83h 123c
11 b g Dr Massini(IRE) —Burgundy Sunset (IRE) (Buckskin (FR))
2134[4] 2529[8] 2975[8] (3373)
(3608) 3935[4] 4265[4] 4372[2] 4723[5]

Master Act (IRE) *Alistair Whillans* 88b
6 bg g Act One—Celtic Fling (Lion Cavern (USA))
4308[5] 4894[6]

Master Alfredo *Susan Nock* 86h 89c
7 b g Alflora(IRE) —Frosty Mistress (Arctic Lord)
2283[P]
4453[5] 5001[F]

Master Beau *George Charlton* 103h
7 b g Beat All(USA) —Golden Aureole (Gildoran)
2873[4] ◆ 3288[12] 4059[2]

Master Brew *Mrs Alison Hickman* 69h 58c
13 b g Homo Sapien—Edithmead (IRE) (Shardari)
292[5]

Master Builder (FR) *Ferdy Murphy* 117h 107c
10 b g Lute Antique(FR) —Solaine (FR) (Pot D'Or (FR))
1556[P]

Master Cardor Visa (IRE) *Emma Baker* 79h
6 br g Alderbrook—Princess Moodyshoe (Jalmood (USA))
847[7] 992[2]

Master Charm (FR) *Tim Vaughan* 107h 118c
7 b g Smadoun(FR) —Kandania (FR) (Cadoudal (FR))
(477)

Master Conor (IRE) *Henry Hogarth*
5 b g Classic Cliche(IRE) —Shuil Iontach (IRE) (Oscar (IRE))
3259[9] 3505[14] 3952[P]

Master Dane (IRE) *Martin Bosley*
5 b g Indian Danehill(IRE) —Sarabi (Alzao (USA))
4356[17]

Master Darcy *Laura Mongan* 84h 86c
9 bb g Cloudings(IRE) —Swift Conveyance (IRE) (Strong Gale)
155[6] *3055[10]*

Master D'Or (FR) *Sophie Leech* 111h 111c
11 b g Cyborg(FR) —Une Pomme D'Or (FR) (Pot D'Or (FR))
3608[2] (3821)
3982[3] 4412[6] 4825[4]

Master Eddy *Shaun Lycett* 114h 111c
11 b g Alflora(IRE) —Mistress Star (Soldier Rose)
3621[4]
4004[2] 4538[F] 4988[2]

Master Fiddle *Nicky Henderson* 123h
6 ch g Alflora(IRE) —Fiddling The Facts (IRE) (Orchestra)
3158[2] 3678[6] 4281[3] (4990) 5316[3]

Master Fong (IRE) *Donald McCain* 113h
5 b g Dr Fong(USA) —Last Cry (FR) (Peintre Celebre (USA))
76^{2} 548^{5} 1956^{10} 2164^{6} *3091^{4}* 3966^{4} (4939) 5232^{7}
Masterful Act (USA) *Ferdy Murphy* 94h
4 ch g Pleasantly Perfect(USA) —Catnip (USA) (Flying Paster (USA))
4451^{7} 4810^{2} 5260^{3}
Master John (IRE) *E Walker* 103h 92c
10 b g Bob's Return(IRE) —B Greenhill (Gunner B)
4708^{6}
Masterly (FR) *Mlle M-L Mortier* 125c
8 b g Medaaly—Miss Waty (IRE) (Last Tycoon)
190a^{0}
Master Mahogany *Ron Hodges* 106h
10 b g Bandmaster(USA) —Impropriety (Law Society (USA))
1844^{7} 1998^{6}
Master Medic (IRE) *Tim Walford* 112h 159c
10 b g Dr Massini(IRE) —Name A Reason (IRE) (Buckskin (FR))
2964^{P}
Master Milan (IRE) *Jonjo O'Neill* 81h
5 b g Milan—English Clover (Tina's Pet)
2215^{5} 2873^{14} 3225^{13} 3489^{5} 3868^{6}
Master Minded (FR) *Paul Nicholls* 117h 176c
8 b g Nikos—Haute Tension (FR) (Garde Royale)
(2515)
(2885) (3675)
4805^{8} (5184)
Master Murphy (IRE) *Jane Walton* 101b
6 b g Flemensfirth(USA) —Awbeg Beauty (IRE) (Supreme Leader)
(2355) 4808^{20}
Master'n Commander *John Joseph Hanlon* 108h 94c
9 ch g Zafonic(USA) —Magical Retreat (USA) (Sir Ivor (USA))
1598^{U}
Master Nimbus *John Quinn* 48h 136c
11 b g Cloudings(IRE) —Miss Charlie (Pharly (FR))
194^{F} 1609^{17}
Master Of The Hall (IRE) *Nicky Henderson* 128h 148c
7 b g Saddlers' Hall(IRE) —Frankly Native (IRE) (Be My Native (USA))
(2494) ◆ 3291^{5} (3743)
(4199) 4804^{6} ◆ 5183^{F}
Master Overseer (IRE) *David Pipe* 101h 138c
8 b g Old Vic—Crogeen Lass (Strong Gale)
3347^{2}
Master Paddy (IRE) *Andy Turnell* 26h
7 b g Kahtan—Missy Gee (IRE) (Germany (USA))
2069^{P} 2456^{15} *3057^{9}* 3367^{7}
Master Performer (USA) *Barry Murtagh* 74h
4 b g Van Nistelrooy(USA) —Blarin Speed (USA) (Senor Speedy (USA))
1576^{4} 1984^{P} 5151^{3}
Masterpoint *Richard Harper* 76h 85c
11 ch g Mark Of Esteem(IRE) —Baize (Efisio)
462^{2} 557^{4} 757^{6}
961^{7} 1235^{5} 1434^{7} 1549^{5} 4814^{3} 5016^{10}
Master Sebastian *Lucinda Russell* 110h 109c
12 ch g Kasakov—Anchor Inn (Be My Guest (USA))
579^{3} 1763^{5} 2274^{5} 3501^{P} 4064^{6}
Master Somerville *Henry Daly* 96h 121c
9 b g Alflora(IRE) —Lucy Glitters (Ardross)
78^{F} 2034^{8} 2587^{P} 3935^{3} 4948^{2}
Masters Royal (FR) *B Barbier* 71h
6 ch g Vertical Speed(FR) —Royale Pauline (FR) (Garde Royale)
5159a^{0}
Master T (USA) *Mrs Suzy Bull* 85h 105c
12 b g Trempolino(USA) —Our Little C (USA) (Marquetry (USA))
297^{2}
Master Woodsman *Edwin Tuer* 77b
5 ch g Loup Sauvage(USA) —Jowoody (Gunner B)
399^{12}
Matako (FR) *Caroline Keevil* 110h 100c
8 b g Nikos—Verabatim (FR) (Pampabird)
1907^{P} 2058^{3} (2480) 4874^{9} 5241^{P} 5439^{2}
Mater Mater *Caroline Bailey* 78h
4 gr f Silver Patriarch(IRE) —Emily-Mou (IRE) (Cadeaux Genereux)
3401^{15} 3830^{2} 4309^{8} 4878^{7}
Matilda Highway (IRE) *John Halley* 87h
5 b m King's Theatre(IRE) —Winton Lass (IRE) (Glacial Storm (USA))
1146a^{4} (Dead)
Matilda's Folly (IRE) *Ben Haslam* 64h
6 ch m Exit To Nowhere(USA) —Hook's Close (Kemal (FR))
2616^{10} *2825^{6}* 3521^{U} 3715^{16} 4132^{9}
Matmata De Tendron (FR) *Andrew Crook* 88h 100c
11 gr g Badolato(USA) —Cora Des Tamarix (FR) (Iron Duke (FR))
1933^{9} (2193)
2402^{3} 2602^{4} 3996^{4}
4256 4508^{2}
(4825) 5353^{2}
Matrow's Lady (IRE) *Neil Mulholland* 84h
4 b f Cloudings(IRE) —I'm Maggy (NZ) (Danseur Etoile (FR))
2466^{6} 3365^{11} 3906^{12} 4263^{7}
Mattaking (IRE) *Renee Robeson* 84h 98c
8 br g Mister Mat(FR) —Kings Comfort (IRE) (King's Ride)
(136) **4375**
Matthew Riley (IRE) *Kate Walton* 112b
4 b g Dr Massini(IRE) —Helorhiwater (IRE) (Aristocracy)
(3731) 4239^{3} 4801^{2} 5202^{4}
Matuhi *David Pipe* 123h 141c
8 b g Dansili—Montserrat (Aragon)
(2496)
2665^{2} 2886^{10} 4487^{6} 4820^{6} (5422)
Maucaillou (GER) *Martin Keighley* 133h 128c
8 b g Tiger Hill(IRE) —Montserrat (GER) (Zilzal (USA))
2360^{F} 2868^{16} 5110^{14} 5396^{4}

Mauricetheathlete (IRE) *Martin Keighley* 111h
8 b g Sayarshan(FR) —Ardagh Princess (Proverb)
231^{5} 522^{6} 1730^{6} 2023^{5} 3529^{3} (4508) 4929^{3} 5153^{2}
Maurisca (FR) *Charlie Longsdon* 106h 127c
6 b g Maresca Sorrento(FR) —Maurise (FR) (April Night (FR))
169^{2} 1911^{4} 2209^{4} **2975^{3} (4740)**
(4937)
Mauritino (GER) *Jonjo O'Neill* 104h
7 b g Dashing Blade—Miss Page (Gorytus (USA))
(793) 2150^{9} 2504^{7} 2927^{6} 3261^{9} 3882^{7} (5244) (5373) ◆
Mavalenta (IRE) *Nigel Twiston-Davies* 91h
4 b f Montjeu(IRE) —Velouette (Darshaan)
3554^{7} 4118^{6} 4781^{4} 5346^{U}
Mawsem (IRE) *George Baker* 114h
5 ch g Monsun(GER) —Irtifa (Lahib (USA))
(53) (1817) 2322^{3} 4677^{2} ◆ 5225^{4}
Max Bygraves *Kim Bailey* 110h 130c
8 ch g Midnight Legend—Smokey Diva (IRE) (Orchestra)
2347^{5} 3299^{4} 3621^{6}
4010^{4} 4440^{2} 4987^{P}
Maxdelas (FR) *Nigel Twiston-Davies* 113h
5 ch g Sabrehill(USA) —Quendora (FR) (Kendor (FR))
(3252) ◆ 3567^{P} 5110^{8}
Maxford Lass *John Quinn* 97h
6 ch m Definite Article—Gaye Mercy (Petoski)
3787^{7} 4233^{4}
Maxim Gorky (IRE) *Noel Meade* 107h
4 b g Montjeu(IRE) —Altruiste (USA) (Diesis)
4083a^{10}
Maximix *Gary Moore* 67h 110c
8 gr g Linamix(FR) —Time Will Show (FR) (Exit To Nowhere (USA))
221^{4} 586^{6} 2134^{6} 2591^{3} 3349^{5} 3792^{P} 3984^{6}
5101^{9}
Maxi's Dream *Stuart Howe* 4h
6 b g Webberys Dream—Madame Maxi (Ron's Victory (USA))
4094^{P} 5152^{P} 5274^{5} 5437^{7}
Max Laurie (FR) *Michael Banks* 81h
6 bl g Ungaro(GER) —Laurie Mercurialle (FR) (Dom Pasquini (FR))
(2560) *2826^{3}* 4081^{7}
Max My Boy (IRE) *Geoffrey Harker* 49b
4 ch g Refuse To Bend(IRE) —Lucky Fountain (IRE) (Lafontaine (USA))
4363^{6}
Maxwil *Pat Phelan* 100h 114c
6 b g Storming Home—Lady Donatella (Last Tycoon)
81^{2} 584^{2} 957^{3}
Ma Yahab *Venetia Williams* 116h 134c
10 ch g Dr Fong(USA) —Bay Shade (USA) (Sharpen Up)
3444^{6} 3922^{3} 4221^{3} 4486^{4} ◆ 4876^{P} 5229^{4}
Maybe A Malt (IRE) *Richard Rowe* 49h 71c
9 b m Shernazar—Petite Deb (Cure The Blues (USA))
283^{5} 529^{3} 987^{P} 1126^{4}
Maybeme *Neville Bycroft* 23h
5 b m Lujain(USA) —Malvadilla (IRE) (Doyoun)
3637^{P} 3692^{12}
May Be Possible (IRE) *R Bryan* 112c
12 ch g Presenting—Definitely Maybe (IRE) (Brush Aside (USA))
4064^{4} 4779^{2} ◆
Mayberry *Emma Lavelle* 110h
6 b m Silver Patriarch(IRE) —Top Berry (High Top)
534^{5} 1844^{5} 2128^{6} 2329^{8} 4034^{U} 4455^{4} 5244^{6}
May Boy *Ron Hodges*
5 br g Bandmaster(USA) —Kathies Pet (Tina's Pet)
2633^{P}
Mayo Abbey (IRE) *Gordon Elliott* 122c
8 b g Sea Raven(IRE) —Tinerana Dancer (IRE) (Hatim (USA))
306^{2}
Mayolynn (USA) *Caroline Bailey* 108h
5 ch m Johannesburg(USA) —Civilynn (USA) (Lost Code (USA))
1994^{8} 2310^{6} 3387^{4} 3563^{2} (3882) 4310^{3} 4955^{8}
Mayor Of Kilcock *James Danahar* 109h
8 b g King's Theatre(IRE) —Disallowed (IRE) (Distinctly North (USA))
55^{F} 382^{3} 522^{9} 829^{8} 1726^{13} 2327^{5}
Mccauley (IRE) *Paul Swaffield* 92h 117c
8 b g Vettori(IRE) —Tintinara (Selkirk (USA))
129^{8} 3701^{0} **4526^{4} 4950^{4} 5083^{2}**
Mckyla (IRE) *Tony Carroll* 80b
6 b m Lord Americo—A Bit Of Luck (IRE) (Good Thyne (USA))
1071^{3}
Mcmurrough (IRE) *Malcolm Jefferson* 128h
7 b g Spectrum(IRE) —Sensitive (IRE) (Posen (USA))
396^{5}
Mcqueen (IRE) *Barry Leavy* 103h 98c
11 ch g Barathea(IRE) —Bibliotheque (USA) (Woodman (USA))
351^{4} 601^{3} 921^{9} 1033^{4} **1309^{4} 1481^{3} 1826^{5} (2113)**

Meadows Thyne (IRE) *A J Martin* 120h 102c
10 b g Good Thyne(USA) —Butlers Meadow (IRE) (Orchestra)
193^{3} **443^{3}**
708^{P}
Mealagh Valley (IRE) *Ben De Haan* 28h 106c
10 b g Darazari(IRE) —Sister Dympna (Grundy)
597^{4} 2959^{P}
Meanus Dandy (IRE) *Paul Nicholls* 141c
8 ch g Anshan—Geray Lady (IRE) (Roselier (FR))
1856^{4} (2221)
2543^{U} 4466^{7} 5443^{P}
Medellin (IRE) *Liam Corcoran* 99h 78c
7 b g Sunshine Street(USA) —Abadila (IRE) (Shernazar)
3838^{5} 3980^{7}

Medermit (FR) *Alan King* 158h 157c
7 gr g Medaaly—Miss D'Hermite (FR) (Solicitor (FR))
(1961)
2313^{R} (2926)
3291^{2} (3946) ◆ **4789^{4} 5165^{2}**
Media Man (IRE) *P Winks* 74h 37c
11 br g Presenting—Derravarragh Lady (IRE) (Radical)
499^{8}
Media Stars *Robert Johnson* 78h
6 gr g Green Desert(USA) —Starine (FR) (Mendocino (USA))
953^{5} 1660^{6} 2092^{11} 4870^{7} 5091^{8} 5354^{7}
Medicinal (IRE) *Michael Blake* 119h 103c
10 gr g Linamix(FR) —Pharmacist (IRE) (Machiavellian (USA))
798^{7} 914^{8}
Medicine Man (IRE) *Ben De Haan* 96h
7 b g Great Palm(USA) —Sorimak Gale (IRE) (Strong Gale)
2216^{7} 3403^{P} 4006^{3}
4691^{P} 5036^{P} 5406^{P}
Medinas (FR) *Alan King* 106b
4 bb g Malinas(GER) —Medicis (FR) (Sicyos (USA))
3957^{2} (4491)
Mediolanum (IRE) *Nigel Twiston-Davies* 109h
6 b g Milan—Pebble Hill (IRE) (Fourstars Allstar (USA))
1962^{2} ◆ (2231)
Meetings Man (IRE) *Micky Hammond* 115h
4 gr g Footstepsinthesand—Missella (IRE) (Danehill (USA))
(743) (1363) 1610^{10} 2078^{2} 2655^{2} 3967^{U}
Meet The Critics (IRE) *Brendan Powell* 110h 119c
8 b g Rashar(USA) —Rose Basket (IRE) (Roselier (FR))
1911^{0} 1603^{4} **(4461)**
Me Fein *Barney Curley* 88h
7 gr g Desert Prince(IRE) —Attachment (USA) (Trempolino (USA))
1688^{9} 1900^{9} 2310^{7} 3256^{6} 3563^{5} 3882^{10} 4314^{11}
Megagrace *Gary Moore* 35h
4 ch f Kirkwall—Megalex (Karinga Bay)
2315^{7} 2965^{9} 3944^{8}
Megamix *Robert Bewley* 78b
5 gr m Fair Mix(IRE) —Sabeel (Local Suitor (USA))
5432^{9}
Megan May *Ian Williams* 70b
5 b m Josr Algarhoud(IRE) —Jenny Rocket (Minster Son)
1927^{7} *2825^{3}*
Megastar *Gary Moore* 142h
6 b g Kayf Tara—Megalex (Karinga Bay)
(2495) ◆ 3196^{2} ◆ 3445^{2} 4195^{3} 4803^{5} 5166^{17}
Mega Watt (IRE) *Venetia Williams* 104h
6 b g Acclamation—Kilshanny (Groom Dancer (USA))
159^{3} 541^{P} 2927^{11} 3744^{10} 4076^{9}
Meglio Ancora *Jonathan Portman* 90h
4 ch g Best Of The Bests(IRE) —May Fox (Zilzal (USA))
2211^{4} 2661^{7} 3613^{3}
Meitheamh (IRE) *Mrs John Harrington* 113h
6 b m Beneficial—Gales Hill (IRE) (Beau Sher)
2260a^{U}
Me Julie *Arthur Whiting* 77h 100c
8 b m Kayf Tara—Miss Roberto (IRE) (Don Roberto (USA))
1730^{P}
2170^{4} 2470^{3} 2573^{4} 3230^{10}
Mekong Miss *Raymond York* 90h
5 ch m Mark Of Esteem(IRE) —Missouri (Charnwood Forest (IRE))
3818^{5} 4118^{3} 4425^{F} 5189^{7}
Melange (USA) *George Charlton* 117h
5 b g Alphabet Soup(USA) —Garendare (Vacarme (USA))
2373^{6} 2941^{5} 3509^{9} 4166^{12} 5335^{P} 5431^{8}
Melchizedek (IRE) *Rachel Hobbs* 104h 101c
7 b g Goldmark(USA) —Vic's Hope (IRE) (Old Vic)
4971^{3}
Melon Delta (IRE) *John Joseph Hanlon* 121h 128c
10 ch g Good Thyne(USA) —Little Talk (Le Bavard (FR))
1121a^{15}
Melua Maid (IRE) *Sue Smith* 71h
9 b m Flemensfirth(USA) —Chatty Lookalike (IRE) (Good Thyne (USA))
1783^{5} 2067^{8} 3389^{10} 3729^{3}
Melvino *John Price* 102h
9 b g Josr Algarhoud(IRE) —Safe Secret (Seclude (USA))
4008^{7} 4778^{6}
Menepresents (IRE) *Henrietta Knight* 59b
6 bb m Presenting—Menedreams (IRE) (Strong Gale)
2156^{10} 3200^{14} 3904^{P}
Meneur (FR) *Gary Moore* 107h 96c
9 gr g Septieme Ciel(USA) —Mamamia (FR) (Linamix (FR))
2662^{F} 2961^{9} 3869^{5} 4556^{2} 5055^{2}
Menorah (IRE) *Philip Hobbs* 165h
6 b g King's Theatre(IRE) —Maid For Adventure (IRE) (Strong Gale)
(2386) ◆ (2887) ◆ 4791^{5}
Merchant Red (USA) *Paul Webber* 114h 107c
8 bb g Red Ransom(USA) —Great Lady Slew (USA) (Seattle Slew (USA))
361^{U} 523^{P}
Mercury Bay (IRE) *Keith Goldsworthy* 105b
6 ch g Karinga Bay—Jolie Landaise (FR) (Beaudelaire (USA))
(855)
Merehead (FR) *Paul Nicholls* 112h
5 gr g Al Namix(FR) —Moneda (FR) (Cadoudal (FR))
1778^{3} 2666^{4} 3439^{3} 4444^{2}
Meridian City (IRE) *Howard Johnson* 128h
7 b g Presenting—Talk To The Missus (IRE) (Executive Perk)
4488^{12}

Meridiem *Sean Regan* 93h
7 b g Tamure(IRE) —Anatomic (Deerhound (USA))
254^{2} 2397^{4} 3601^{7} 3831^{3} 4465^{10} (5057)
Merigo (FR) *Andrew Parker* 112h 149c
10 ch g Pistolet Bleu(IRE) —Muleta (FR) (Air De Cour (USA))
2205^{8}
2543^{F} 4466^{8} 5338^{2}
Merrydown (IRE) *Nicky Richards* 132h
8 b g Oscar(IRE) —Euro Coin Lady (IRE) (Phardante (FR))
4209^{9} 5003^{5} 5304^{4}
Merry Music (IRE) *Julian Smith* 95h
12 b g Good Thyne(USA) —Sarah's Smile (Callernish)
2171^{8}
Merry Storm (IRE) *Lisa Day* 82c
12 b g Glacial Storm(USA) —Cap Reform (IRE) (Phardante (FR))
3870^{P}
Merry Terry *Colin Tizzard* 71h 98c
7 br g Terimon—In Memoriam (IRE) (Buckskin (FR))
918^{2} 1061^{B} 1227^{3} 1276^{5} 1546^{P}
Mersey *S R B Crawford* 99h 47c
7 b g Beat All(USA) —Deadly Dove (Little Wolf)
1099^{6}
Me Too (IRE) *Liam Corcoran* 79b
6 b m Beneficial—Pharwood (IRE) (Phardante (FR))
568^{7}
Mew Gull *Henrietta Knight* 64b
6 ch m Generous(IRE) —Ida Melba (Idiots Delight)
2987^{10} *3979^{8}* 5078^{P}
Mewstone *Tom George* 107h 82c
8 b m Supreme Leader—Carmel's Joy (IRE) (Carlingford Castle)
553^{P}
Mexican Pete *Ian Williams* 119h 120c
11 b g Atraf—Eskimo Nel (IRE) (Shy Groom (USA))
1970^{3} 2475^{3} 3784^{6} 4007^{2}
Mezuzah *Joanne Foster* 87h 46c
11 b g Barathea(IRE) —Mezzogiorno (Unfuwain (USA))
404^{8}
Mhilu (IRE) *John O'Shea* 128h 131c
9 b g Rock Hopper—Moohono (IRE) (Roselier (FR))
(374) 555^{0} (696)
839^{5} 1044^{P}
Mia's Vic (IRE) *Noel C Kelly* 99h
6 b g Old Vic—Mill Lane Flyer (IRE) (Un Desperado (FR))
4889^{5}
Mibleu (FR) *Colin Tizzard* 57h 126c
11 b g Agent Bleu(FR) —Eauseille (FR) (Un Numide (FR))
233^{2} 592^{P} (831)
848^{4} 959^{2} 1110^{5} 1299^{6} 1390^{6} 1606^{4} 1975^{2} 2022^{4}
5394^{2} 5436^{5}
Micadou (FR) *G Macaire*
11 b g Cadoudal(FR) —Minouche (FR) (Fill My Hopes (FR))
190a^{4}
Mic Aubin (FR) *Giles Smyly* 104h 115c
8 b g Broadway Flyer(USA) —Patney (FR) (Hasty Tudor (USA))
2051^{2} 2630^{3} 3260^{7}
Micheal Flips (IRE) *Andy Turnell* 148h 134c
7 b g Kayf Tara—Pianissimo (IRE) (Shernazar)
1731^{2} 3566^{4} 4817^{12} 5166^{4}
Michelle's Express (IRE) *A J Martin* 126h 116c
7 b g Oscar(IRE) —Euro Blazer (IRE) (Phardante (FR))
2509^{13}
Michigan Assassin (IRE) *Debra Hamer* 104h 121c
9 b g King's Theatre(IRE) —Shuil Ar Aghaidh (The Parson)
172^{5} **(564)**
694^{2} 769^{5} 1176^{P} 1277^{2} 1486^{7} 1794^{P}
Michigan D'Isop (FR) *John Ryall* 95h 118c
11 b g Cadoudal(FR) —Julie Du Berlais (FR) (Rose Laurel)
579^{P} 1769^{5} 2055^{P} 3265^{3}
Mickey Monk (IRE) *Gordon Elliott* 103h
6 b g Lil's Boy(USA) —Mega Drama (IRE) (King's Theatre (IRE))
447^{P}
Mickmacmagoole (IRE) *Evan Williams* 121h 81c
9 b g Sadler's Wells(USA) —Musk Lime (USA) (Private Account (USA))
80^{5} 1614^{2} 1864^{5} 2209^{9} 2347^{11} (4008) (4524) 5255^{5}
Mick's Dancer *Richard Phillips* 104h
6 b g Pivotal—La Piaf (FR) (Fabulous Dancer (USA))
2310^{10} 3872^{8} 4499^{5} ◆
Micks Prospect (IRE) *Tim Vaughan* 69h
8 b g Accordion—Supremely Deep (IRE) (Supreme Leader)
7638 956^{6} 1261^{10}
Mickwell Bay *Tim Pitt* 37h 89c
10 b g Bal Harbour—Katie's Kitty (Noble Patriarch)
2277^{P} 3720^{P} 5350^{11}
Mickytaker (IRE) *Alan King* 92h
6 b g Bach(IRE) —Aimees Princess (IRE) (Good Thyne (USA))
2957^{5} 3439^{11} 3918^{4} 4951^{7}
Mic's Delight (IRE) *Victor Dartnall* 134h
7 b g Witness Box(USA) —Warrior Princess (IRE) (Mister Lord (USA))
2067^{4} 2607^{3} (3299) (3877) 4725^{2}
Midas Way *Patrick Chamings* 124h
11 ch g Halling(USA) —Arietta's Way (IRE) (Darshaan)
131^{4} (503)
Mid Div And Creep *Alan Hill* 125c
11 b m Sovereign Water(FR) —Knightsbridge Bred (Montelimar (USA))
4851^{2}

Middlebrook (IRE) *Peter Niven* 66h
6 ch g Ashkalani(IRE) —Accordeon Royale (IRE) (Accordion)
1764[2] 2355[11] 3725[7]

Middlemarch (IRE) *Jim Goldie* 90h
11 ch g Grand Lodge(USA) —Blanche Dubois (Nashwan (USA))
286[4] 875[5]

Middleton Dene (IRE) *Rose Dobbin* 66h 127c
9 b g Oscar(IRE) —Sharonamar (IRE) (Merrymount)
2204[P] 5149[13]

Middleton Red (IRE) *Graham Smith* 28h
7 ch g Carroll House—Over The Sands (IRE) (Over The River (FR))
531[2] 1505[7] 1703[P] 1922[P]

Midies Prince (IRE) *Terry Clement* 105b
5 b g Basanta(IRE) —Mixed Up Lady (IRE) (Unblest)
1817[2] 2186[12]

Midnight Appeal *Alan King* 100h 132c
6 b g Midnight Legend—Lac Marmot (FR) (Marju (IRE))
2469[8]
(4022) (4674) ◆ (4896) (5204)

Midnight Charmer *Emma Baker* 23h
5 b g Midnight Legend—Dickies Girl (Saxon Farm)
2328[11] 4012[12] 4262[P] 4918[P]

Midnight Chase *Neil Mulholland* 136h 167c
9 b g Midnight Legend—Yamrah (Milford)
98[4] (458)
(1856) (2358)
(2871) 4850[5]

Midnight Choice *Mrs H Parrott* 54b
6 b g Midnight Legend—Pearl's Choice (IRE) (Deep Run)
4356[13] 5005[8]

Midnight Diamond (IRE) *Tim Vaughan* 103h 96c
8 b g Alzao(USA) —Derena (FR) (Crystal Palace (FR))
49[P] 597[7] 2135[6]
2290[2] (3729)
5324[2]

Midnight Dove *Andrew Price* 57b
6 ch g Karinga Bay—Flighty Dove (Cruise Missile)
2328[13]

Midnight Fun *Graham Smith* 84h
6 b m Midnight Legend—More Laughter (Oats)
855[5] 1046[4] 1233[4] 1559[10]

Midnight Gold *Peter Bowen* 107h 129c
11 ch g Midnight Legend—Yamrah (Milford)
(16) 467[3]
680[2] (769)
1032[9] 1178[2] 1373[2] 1769[3] 1960[P] 2543[U]

Midnight Haze *Kim Bailey* 98h 132c
9 b g Midnight Legend—Gypsy Haze (Romany Rye)
(2324)
2948[7] 3444[P]

Midnight Jack *Ben Pollock*
6 b g Tamayaz(CAN) —Casino Nell (Neltino)
135[P]

Midnight King *George Baker* 67h
5 b g Midnight Legend—Phar Breeze (IRE) (Phardante (FR))
254[3] 4124[10] 4443[7] 5168[9]

Midnight Lira *Caroline Keevil* 71b
4 ch f Midnight Legend—Bally Lira (Lir)
5408[5]

Midnight Macarena *Lucy Wadham* 106h
6 ch m Midnight Legend—Royal Tango (Petoski)
(589) 2526[2] 3264[5] 3607[6] 5385[6]

Midnight Maisie *Anna Brooks* 21b
4 ch f Midnight Legend—Persian Silk (IRE) (King Persian)
2597[11] 4239[13] 4918[P]

Midnight Molly *John Spearing* 66h
4 b f Midnight Legend—Timeless Chick (Timeless Times (USA))
1927[5] 2237[11] 3398[5] 4288[8] 4774[5]

Midnight Ocean *Julian Smith* 91h
10 br m Sovereign Water(FR) —Mascara VII (Damsire Unregistered)
4032[5] 4773[5]

Midnight Opera *Neil Mulholland* 121h
5 b g Midnight Legend—Ballad Opera (Sadler's Wells (USA))
1819[4] 2129[2] (2540) 4672[5] (5035) 5369[2]

Midnight Paradise *Neil Mulholland* 74b
5 b m Midnight Legend—Barton Dante (Phardante (FR))
2137[P] 3295[P] 3647[P]

Midnight Place *Richard Hawker* 90b
6 ch g Compton Place—Midnight Break (Night Shift (USA))
237[5] 602[10]

Midnight Prayer *Alan King* 75h
6 b g Midnight Legend—Onawing Andaprayer (Energist)
3556[9]

Midnight Socialite (IRE) *T Hogan* 94h
7 ch m Moscow Society(USA) —Midnight Light (IRE) (Roselier (FR))
3592a[P]

Midnight Spirit *Frederick Sutherland* 106h
11 b g Midnight Legend—West-Hatch-Spirit (Forzando)
252[3] 407[3] 430[5] 648[P] 956[5]

Midnight Trix *Alex Hales* 69h
5 b m Midnight Legend—Chilly Squaw (IRE) (Commanche Run)
1994[7] 2281[7] 3261[P] 5374[P]

Midnight Tuesday (FR) *Nigel Twiston-Davies* 113h
6 b g Kapgarde(FR) —Deat Heat (FR) (Volochine (IRE))
4860[5]

Midnight Uno *Bill Turner*
4 b g Desert Style(IRE) —Carati (Selkirk (USA))
1024[P]

Midnite Blews (IRE) *Maurice Barnes* 102h 78c
6 gr g Trans Island—Felicita (IRE) (Catrail (USA))
166[10] 472[3] 748[3]
1082[5] (1695) 1870[2] 2076[3]

Midsummer Legend *Norma Twomey* 5h
7 ch m Midnight Legend—Sabeel (Local Suitor (USA))
3264[P]
4666[P] 5382[4]

Mid Valley *J R Jenkins* 100h
8 ch g Zilzal(USA) —Isabella D'Este (IRE) (Irish River (FR))
25[F] (Dead)

Mid Wicket (USA) *Mouse Hamilton-Fairley* 92h
5 b g Strong Hope(USA) —Sunday Bazaar (USA) (Nureyev (USA))
216[9] 865[12] 1902[7] 2131[9] 5057[B]

Miereveld *Brian Ellison* 101h
4 b g Red Ransom(USA) —Mythic (Zafonic (USA))
1422[4] 1498[6] 3484[2] 3782[6] 4148[2] (4419) 4939[3] 4999[4] 5314[4]

Might As Well *Seamus Mullins* 111h 111c
8 gr g Terimon—Might Be (Gunner B)
(2002)

Mighty Magnus (IRE) *Martin Todhunter* 94h 92c
8 ch g Night Shift(USA) —Arbaletta (GER) (Surumu (GER))
2107[4] 2601[3] 2942[6] 3636[2] 3884[F] 4133[3] 4573[P]

Mighty Massini (IRE) *C A McBratney* 117h 127c
8 b g Dr Massini(IRE) —Chilly Morning (IRE) (Ovac (ITY))
4716[2] 5317[5]

Mighty Matters (IRE) *Charlie Longsdon* 97c
12 b g Muroto—Hasaway (IRE) (Executive Perk)
153[4] 707[4] 890[P]

Mighty Monty *Victor Dartnall* 86h
6 br g Overbury(IRE) —Ruby Star (IRE) (Grand Plaisir (IRE))
2518[9] 3295[12] 3789[8] 4195[5] 4929[10]

Mighty Moose (IRE) *Jeremy Scott* 96c
11 b g Mister Lord(USA) —Brief Pace (IRE) (Riot Helmet)
83[2]

Migigi *Michael Roberts* 74h
11 b m Alflora(IRE) —Barton Bay (IRE) (Kambalda)
84[P]

Mik *Dr Jeremy Naylor*
5 b g Baryshnikov(AUS) —Daphne's Doll (IRE) (Polish Patriot (USA))
180[U] 428[P]

Mikael D'Haguenet (FR) *W P Mullins* 158h 158c
7 b g Lavirco(GER) —Fleur D'Haguenet (FR) (Dark Stone (FR))
2971a[F] ◆ 3241a[5] 4084a[3] 4804[F]

Mike Towey (IRE) *Peter Bowen* 105b
6 ch g Ashkalani(IRE) —Cosy Lady (IRE) (Lord Americo)
4410[2] 4970[3] (5395)

Mikeys Sister *Tony Carroll* 37h
6 b m Dancing Maestro(USA) —Debbie's Darling (Baron Blakeney)
432[6]

Milandale (IRE) *Tom George* 95h
6 b g Milan—Sally Dale (Deep Run)
97[5] ◆ 327[P]

Milan Deux Mille (FR) *David Pipe* 104h 92c
9 b g Double Bed(FR) —Uberaba (FR) (Garde Royale)
3791[P]

Milaneen *Keith Goldsworthy* 79b
5 b m Milan—Kosheen (IRE) (Supreme Leader)
4443[4]

Milano Supremo (IRE) *Chris Grant* 91h
6 b g Milan—Lucy Popp (IRE) (Supreme Leader)
732[3] 1702[3] 3572[P] 5352[2]

Milansbar (IRE) *Henrietta Knight* 75b
4 b g Milan—Ardenbar (Ardross)
5084[5]

Milans Danielle (IRE) *Brian Storey*
5 b m Milan—Persian Argument (IRE) (Persian Mews)
2943[12] 3553[13]

Milans Man (IRE) *Howard Johnson* 127h 103c
6 b g Milan—Montanara (IRE) (Montelimar (USA))
2191[3] 3394[5] 4890[6] 5146[4]

Milarrow (IRE) *Colin Tizzard* 86b
4 b g Milan—Fleeting Arrow (IRE) (Commanche Run)
2797[6] 3630[2]

Milesian King (IRE) *Lawney Hill* 11b 107c
10 b g Saddlers' Hall(IRE) —Myglass (IRE) (Strong Gale)
425[4] 586[P] 1589[8]

Miles Of Sunshine *Ron Hodges* 87b
6 b g Thowra(FR) —Rainbow Nation (Rainbow Quest (USA))
4097[13]

Milgen Bay *Oliver Sherwood* 115h
5 br g Generous(IRE) —Lemon's Mill (USA) (Roberto (USA))
375[2] 2109[3] 2584[3] 3783[2] 5225[3]

Militant (FR) *Gordon Elliott* 118h 97c
11 b g Cyborg(FR) —Giuletta (FR) (Petit Montmorency (USA))
446[P]

Military Precision (IRE) *Warren Greatrex* 98b
5 b g Exit To Nowhere(USA) —Devil Leader (USA) (Diesis)
3406[6]

Mill Beattie *John Mackie* 73h
6 b m Beat All(USA) —Step On Degas (Superpower)
2162[6] 2421[7]

Mille Chief (FR) *Alan King* 159h
5 b g Ski Chief(USA) —Mille Flora (IRE) (Be My Guest (USA))
1956[5] 2498[2] (3447) (4222) 4791[11] 5337[P]

Miller's Dawn *Henrietta Knight* 100h 100c
7 ch g Karinga Bay—Dawn Gait (Fearless Action (USA))
64[3] 249[4] 1911[8]
2240[3] 2928[F] 3260[P]

Millers Saphire *Ken Wingrove*
6 b m Sly—So Welcome (Weld)
1723[P]

Millksheikh *Raymond York* 86b
4 b g Millkom—Shelayly (IRE) (Zaffaran (USA))
4430[3] *4923[5]*

Mill Mick *John Mackie* 70b
4 b g Karinga Bay—Step On Degas (Superpower)
4780[10] 5209[8]

Millrock Lady (IRE) *Gordon Elliott* 113h
6 b m Court Cave(IRE) —Mill Lady (IRE) (Jurado (USA))
858[2] 1155a[9]

Mill Run *Sean Regan* 29b
5 b m Tamure(IRE) —Seul Moi (IRE) (Denel (FR))
2403[9]

Mill Side *Donald McCain* 111h 134c
11 b g Milieu—Little Greyside (Nearly A Hand)
2669[8] 4060[P]

Milly Malone (IRE) *Oliver Sherwood* 101b
5 b m Milan—Sharp Single (IRE) (Supreme Leader)
4184[2] 4728[19]

Milo Milan (IRE) *Richard Lee* 113h
6 b g Milan—Simply Divine (IRE) (Be My Native (USA))
3526[2] 4100[3] (4530) 5107[4]

Miltara (IRE) *Diana Grissell* 82b
6 br m Milan—Nethertara (Netherkelly)
589[8]

Milton Des Bieffes (FR) *David Evans* 91h 113c
11 gr g Princeton(FR) —Rose Fuschia (FR) (Courtroom (FR))
993[4] 1057[10]

Milton Hill *Dominic Ffrench Davis*
4 ch g Compton Admiral—Stay With Me Baby (Nicholas Bill)
3794[9]

Mi Man Sam (IRE) *George Jones* 68b
6 ch g Exit To Nowhere(USA) —Brinawa (IRE) (Tate Gallery (USA))
1201[12] 1284[10] 2576[7]

Mi Money *David Pipe* 65h
6 ch m Alflora(IRE) —M I Babe (Celtic Cone)
2142[9] 2634[7]

Minden March *Peter Maddison* 73b
6 b m Baryshnikov(AUS) —Minden Rose (Lord Bud)
448[5] 609[8]

Minder *Jonathan Portman* 92h
5 b g Mind Games—Exotic Forest (Dominion)
4935[8]

Mind Shower (IRE) *Robert Wylie* 54h 48c
5 b g Bach(IRE) —Knockacool Breeze (Buckskin (FR))
1988[8] 2375[11] 3506[10] 3883[P] **3995[8] 4799[6]**

Minella (IRE) *Michael Appleby* 97b
7 b g Moscow Society(USA) —Castlefarm Leader (IRE) (Supreme Leader)
832[5] 855[6] **1045[P] 1274[P]**

Minella Boys (IRE) *Charlie Longsdon* 131h 139c
9 br g Bob's Return(IRE) —Ring-Em-All (Decent Fellow)
2305[4] 2794[3] (3347)
3568[2] 4360[P]

Minella Class (IRE) *Nicky Henderson* 143h
6 br g Oscar(IRE) —Louisas Dream (IRE) (Supreme Leader)
(2960) ◆ (3445) 4312[2] 4803[6]

Minella For Food (IRE) *Evan Williams* 96h 72c
8 b g Saddlers' Hall(IRE) —Minella Madam (The Parson)
49[P]

Minella Four Star (IRE) *David Pipe* 67h 149c
8 ch g Bob Back(USA) —Market Lass (IRE) (Orchestra)
38[F] 844[4] 3940[2] 4466[P] (4876)
5338[P]

Minella Stars (IRE) *Paul Nicholls* 121h
6 b g Accordion—V'Soske Gale (IRE) (Strong Gale)
(3528) 4189[3]

Minella Theatre (IRE) *Henrietta Knight* 122h 141c
8 b g King's Theatre(IRE) —Ring Of Water (USA) (Northern Baby (CAN))
(1973)
2674[9] 3677[7] 4821[P] 5104[3]

Mini Beck *Sandy Thomson* 116h 109c
12 ch g Meadowbrook—Minibrig (Le Coq D'Or)
163[2] ◆ 291[6] 2300[2] 2657[4] **3995[4] 4275[4]**

Mini Max *Brendan Duke* 64h
4 b f Tobougg(IRE) —Maxilla (IRE) (Lahib (USA))
1018[12] 1279[5] 1442[5] 1545[6] 1674[7]

Mini Melody *Stuart Coltherd*
5 ch m And Beyond(IRE) —Midlem Melody (Syrtos)
4171[14] 4473[P]

Mini Minster *Peter Atkinson* 105h
9 b m Minster Son—Dreamago (Sir Mago)
89[5] 313[4] (494) 606[P] 2549[7] 4115[6]

Minireturn (IRE) *M J Vanstone* 73h 56c
9 b m Bob's Return(IRE) —Minifortune (FR) (Kouban (FR))
4901[6]

Mini Shower *Norma Twomey* 94b
7 b m Terimon—Last Shower (Town And Country)
637[11] 759[13]

Ministerofinterior *Barry Leavy* 111h
6 b g Nayef(USA) —Maureen's Hope (USA) (Northern Baby (CAN))
(5171)

Mini The Minx (IRE) *Donald Whillans* 83b
5 br m Accordion—Gypsy Run (Nomadic Way (USA))
4574[3]

Minneapolis *Alison Batchelor* 111h
6 b g Sadler's Wells(USA) —Teggiano (IRE) (Mujtahid (USA))
500[7] 823[3] 908[2] 1343[3] 2081[14] 5193[2]

Minnie Hill (IRE) *Victor Dartnall* 115h
7 b m Oscar(IRE) —Greybrook Lass (IRE) (Roselier (FR))
(2504) ◆ 2639[4] (3686)

Minnigaff (IRE) *George Foster* 67h
11 b g Supreme Leader—Across The Pond (IRE) (Over The River (FR))
3851[P]

Minnis Bay (CAN) *Ferdy Murphy* 57h
7 b g Royal Academy(USA) —Aly's Daylite (USA) (Dayjur (USA))
14[P] 349[10]

Minor Chord *G C Maundrell* 48b
5 b m Alflora(IRE) —Minimum (Terimon)
5209[7]

Minortransgression (USA) *David Evans* 15h
4 ch g Yes It's True(USA) —Casting Pearls (USA) (Fusaichi Pegasus (USA))
3507[5]

Minouchka (FR) *Simon Shirley-Beavan* 101h 117c
11 bb m Bulington(FR) —Elbury (FR) (Royal Charter (FR))
46[4] (164)

Minsgill Mans *J W Tudor* 106c
13 b g Minster Son—Gilmanscleuch (IRE) (Mandalus)
502[4] 5326[6]

Minster Shadow *Chris Grant* 96h 128c
12 b g Minster Son—Polar Belle (Arctic Lord)
2106[2] 2543[F] 3634[P] 4869[P]

Mintiverdi *Noel Chance* 88b
7 br m Kayf Tara—Just Jodi (IRE) (Good Thyne (USA))
(3054) 4728[13]

Mioche D'Estruval (FR) *A J Farrant*
11 bl g Lute Antique(FR) —Charme D'Estruval (FR) (Mistigri)
173[R]

Miracle Wish (IRE) *Bernard Scriven*
4 b f One Cool Cat(USA) —Bentley's Bush (IRE) (Barathea (IRE))
1024[P]

Mirage Dore (FR) *Rose Dobbin* 145h 123c
8 b g Muhtathir—Rose Venitien (FR) (Bikala)
3333[4]

Misamon (FR) *David Rees* 92h 104c
8 b g Simon Du Desert(FR) —Misaline (FR) (Mister Sicy (FR))
650[3] 689[3] (755) 826[6] **919[5] (950)**
1047[2] (1060)
1283[2] 1334[6]

Mischief Man *Sue Smith* 90h 98c
9 b g Alflora(IRE) —Rascally (Scallywag)
404[5] 730[P] (1423)
2250[6]

Miss Abbey *Jim Goldie* 97h
7 ch m Missed Flight—Little Brockwell (IRE) (Nestor)
2505[4] 3330[8] 3747[5] 4688[7] 5144[P]

Miss Bellatrix *Neville Bycroft* 81b
4 b f Helissio(FR) —Canal Street (Oats)
4554[3]

Miss Bolte *Sheena West* 82b
6 b m Karinga Bay—Cherry Lee (Buckley)
4124[4] 4561[5]

Miss Champagne (IRE) *Andrew Wilson* 65h
8 b m Tagula(IRE) —Champagne Lady (IRE) (Turtle Island (IRE))
2398[7] 3631[7] 4068[5] 4395[3] 5114[2]

Miss Cruisecontrol *Jim Best* 75h
6 b m Hernando(FR) —Wenda (IRE) (Priolo (USA))
12[P]

Miss Fernietickles *Harriet Graham* 33b
4 ch f Grape Tree Road—Sabeel (Local Suitor (USA))
3364[6] 4171[12]

Miss Fleur *Nick Mitchell* 72b 92c
8 b m Bandmaster(USA) —Floral Park (Northern Park (USA))
2146[B] (2290)
2457[3] 2950[6] 3609[2] 4381[U] 4558[P] 5109[7]

Miss Franklin (IRE) *Adrian Murray* 91h
7 b m Orpen(USA) —Fire Flower (Sri Pekan (USA))
(1308)

Miss Galross (IRE) *Nicky Richards* 58h
7 bb m Overbury(IRE) —Mambo Music (FR) (Rusticaro (FR))
1071[P] 4000[10] 4393[P] 4870[4]

Miss Harriet *Rachel Hobbs* 60b
6 b m Sir Harry Lewis(USA) —Coddington Girl (Green Adventure (USA))
412[10]

Miss Hippy (IRE) *Milton Harris* 106b
6 b m Quws—Oakleaf Express (IRE) (John French)
2576[3] 3259[5] 3590[2] 4184[3] 4728[7] 5188[6]

Missing The Craic *Sean Curran*
5 b g Josr Algarhoud(IRE) —Missed Again (High Top)
53[14]

Missionaire (USA) *Tony Carroll* 82h
4 bb c El Corredor(USA) —Fapindy (USA) (A.P. Indy (USA))
2661[4] 3443[P] 4458[7]

Mission Complete (IRE) *Jonjo O'Neill* 81h
5 b g Milan—Kilmington Breeze (IRE) (Roselier (FR))
3872[7] 4424[4] 4917[10] 5298[7]

Mission Control (IRE) *Tim Vaughan* 133h 118c
6 ch g Dubai Destination(USA) —Stage Manner (In The Wings)
756[5] **(1251)**
1389[P]

Mission Possible (IRE) *P J Rothwell* 91h 129c
10 b g Beneficial—Coolavanny Queen (Furry Glen)
3709a[17]

Mississippian (IRE) *Rose Dobbin* 60h
7 b g Montjeu(IRE) —Swilly (USA) (Irish River (FR))
3331[14] 3551[7]

Mississippi River (IRE) *John E Kiely* 126b
6 b g Sadler's Wells(USA) —Dabiliya (Vayrann)
3208a[2]

Miss Kessie *Alan Lockwood*
5 b m Where Or When(IRE) —Ladies Day (Robellino (USA))
1629[P]

Miss Lala (IRE) *Nicholas Pomfret* 30b
6 b m Lahib(USA) —Frankford Leader (IRE) (Supreme Leader)
1817[11]

Miss Mamma Wagga (IRE) *Lawney Hill* 89h
8 b m Environment Friend—Deep Vision (Deep Run)
252[6]

Miss Mardy Pants (IRE) *Charlie Morlock*
6 b m Overbury(IRE) —Sparebit (Henbit (USA))
428[P]

Miss Markham (IRE) *Patricia Rigby* 58h
6 ch m Soviet Star(USA) —Dynamo Minsk (IRE) (Polish Precedent (USA))
535[7] 711[7] 1003[5] 1090[8] 1554[U] 1707[2]

Miss Milborne *Colin Tizzard* 103b
5 b m Tamure(IRE) —Motown Melody (IRE) (Detroit Sam (FR))
3266[6] 3616[2] 4027[2]

Miss Miracle *Jonjo O'Neill* 77h
4 gr f Motivator—Miracle (Ezzoud (IRE))
1818[3] 2033[3] 2439[4] 2956[9] 4675[3]

Miss Mitch (IRE) *P A Fahy* 122h 157c
10 b m King's Theatre(IRE) —Party Woman (IRE) (Sexton Blake)
1684a[5] 3798a[P]

Miss Molly Be Rude (IRE) *Tim Walford* 83h
9 b m Perugino(USA) —Ediyrna (IRE) (Doyoun)
600[5] 1048[3] (1137) 1261[5]
1360[P] 1647[4]

Miss Molly Moses *Laura Young* 72h
7 b m Karinga Bay—Brancepeth Belle (IRE) (Supreme Leader)
1343[9] 1445[8] 2609[8]

Miss Nightshade *Jamie Snowden* 109h
7 b m Alflora(IRE) —Black Secret (Gildoran)
555[4] **934[P]**

Miss Nut Nut *D Bryant* 76b 56c
8 br m Prince Daniel(USA) —French Spirit (FR) (Esprit Du Nord (USA))
2059[P] **5372[8]**

Miss Overdrive *Andy Turnell* 122h
7 b m Overbury(IRE) —Free Travel (Royalty)
(1724) 1993[4] 2218[U] 2663[2] 3440[4] 3947[13] 4185[6] 4793[9] 5230[2] (5403)

Miss Pepperpot (IRE) *F Flood* 115h 111c
7 b m Winged Love(IRE) —Celtic Serf (Celtic Cone)
1121a[4]
3779a[5]

Miss Phoebe (IRE) *Giles Smyly* 117h 87c
6 b m Catcher In The Rye(IRE) —Stroke Of Six (IRE) (Woodborough (USA))
330[P]

Miss Saffron *Susan Gardner* 97h
8 br m Access Ski—Saffron Lake (Shaab)
(737) 796[5] 1446[3] (1737) 2558[8]

Miss Sarenne (FR) *Nicky Henderson* 125h 125c
6 b m Robin Des Pres(FR) —Miss Palma (FR) (Great Palm (USA))
(192) **361[U]**
523[3] 2662[P] 5204[U]

Miss Sunflower *Tina Jackson* 17h 87c
9 ch m Keen—Ellfiedick (Alfie Dickins)
625[3] 802[4] 931[9] 987[P]

Miss Tarantella *Maurice Barnes* 87h
8 ch m Minster Son—Granham Charm (IRE) (Phardante (FR))
176[3] 424[P] 494[3] 749[9] 2372[6] 4146[10] 4542[2] 4999[4]

Misstaysia (IRE) *Henry Daly* 90h
6 ch m Moscow Society(USA) —See More Tricks (Seymour Hicks (FR))
869[U] 935[9] 1201[7] 2974[14] 3816[3] 4288[7] 4751[9] 5172[3]

Miss Teeny Bash (IRE) *Miss Katie Scott* 75b
7 b m Strategic Choice(USA) —Question Of Trust (IRE) (Tirol)
4307[F]

Miss Tilly Oscar (IRE) *Edward Bevan* 63b
5 b m Oscar(IRE) —Whisky Chaser (Never So Bold)
568[9]

Misstree Dancer *Nick Mitchell* 119h 133c
7 b m Bandmaster(USA) —Miss Match (Lighter)
2606[5]
2945[2] (3198)
3803[4] 4210[U] 4877[3] 5341[4]

Miss Vivian (IRE) *David Thompson* 19b
5 b m Exit To Nowhere(USA) —Acetylene (Miner's Lamp)
474[9]

Miss Wendy *Mark H Tompkins* 80h
4 b f Where Or When(IRE) —Grove Dancer (Reprimand)
2556[3] ◆ 3944[7] 4854[3] 5014[4]

Mista Rossa *Jamie Snowden* 91h
6 br g Red Ransom(USA) —Cloud Hill (Danehill (USA))
185[7] 441[4] 1232[3] (1434) 1490[6] 1694[P]

Mister Apple's (FR) *Ian Williams* 127c
11 ch g Video Rock(FR) —Doryane (FR) (Bayolidaan (FR))
4286[2] (4701)
5163[4]

Mister Benedictine *Brendan Duke* 121h 118c
8 b g Mister Baileys—Cultural Role (Night Shift (USA))
170[6] **523[2]**
715[2] 798[5] 954[3]
1023[8] 1364[8]
2961[5] 3299[10]

Mister Bishop (IRE) *Paul John Gilligan* 102h 122c
6 b g Bishop Of Cashel—Marlatara (IRE) (Marju (IRE))
565[3]

Mister Carter (IRE) *T Stack* 132h
4 b g Antonius Pius(USA) —Kotdiji (Mtoto)
4847[U]

Mister Castlefield (IRE) *John J Maguire* 106h
7 gr g Mujahid(USA) —Woodland Garden (Godswalk (USA))
1104[4] 1115[3]

Mister Chancer (IRE) *Alan King* 113h
6 b g Craigsteel—Cluain Chaoin (IRE) (Phardante (FR))
2241[5] 3405[P] 4233[3] (4946)

Mister Concussion *Peter Jones* 24h
7 b g Baryshnikov(AUS) —Slipmatic (Pragmatic)
2560[10] 3528[10] 4294[7]

Mister Daniel Dee *Richard Whitaker* 18b
6 br g One More Tiger—Primitive Lace (Primitive Rising (USA))
2355[15]

Mister Fantastic *Dai Burchell* 94h
5 ch g Green Tune(USA) —Lomapamar (Nashwan (USA))
1974[4] 2426[5] 3304[7] 5082[3]

Mister Farmer (FR) *Martin Brassil* 92h 122c
10 ch g Trempolino(USA) —Planoise (FR) (Pampabird)
3709a[9]

Mister Fizzbomb (IRE) *John Wainwright* 90h
8 b g Lend A Hand—Crocus (IRE) (Mister Baileys)
10[6] 402[5] 745[3] 1949[2] 3727[P] 3951[12]

Mister Frosty (IRE) *George Prodromou* 94h
5 gr g Verglas(IRE) —La Chinampina (FR) (Darshaan)
4859[5]

Mister Gold *David Evans* 22b
6 ch g Lomitas—Sur Le Fil (IRE) (Funambule (USA))
2335[7]

Mister Hyde (IRE) *Jonjo O'Neill* 130h
6 b g Beneficial—Solar Quest (IRE) (King's Ride)
2056[2] ◆ (2171) 2387[6] (3346) 3947[8] 4852[B]

Mister Kay Bee *Miss J Houldey*
10 b g Thowra(FR) —Rose Garden (Pragmatic)
406[P]

Mister Marker (IRE) *Nicky Richards* 119h 124c
7 ch g Beneficial—Bavards Girl (IRE) (Le Bavard (FR))
1759[7] 3499[P] 3852[7] 4137[U] (4570)
4893[2]

Mister Matt (IRE) *Bob Buckler* 106h 116c
8 b g Alflora(IRE) —Swing Quartet (IRE) (Orchestra)
2294[7]
2961[8] 4022[3] 4504[4] 5011[3] 5269[2]

Mister McGoldrick *Sue Smith* 105h 150c
14 b g Sabrehill(USA) —Anchor Inn (Be My Guest (USA))
2077[3] (2631)
3292[6]

Mister Micheau (IRE) *Joanna Davis* 103h 103c
8 b g Turtle Island(IRE) —Blenheim Run (IRE) (Remainder Man)
1546[2] 1901[3]

Mister Music Man (IRE) *Patrick J Flynn* 116b
7 b g Accordion—Site-Leader (IRE) (Supreme Leader)
1146a[3]

Mister New York (USA) *Noel Chance* 88h
6 b g Forest Wildcat(USA) —Shebane (USA) (Alysheba (USA))
1884[7] 2122[8] 3302[5] 5171[P]

Mister Pete (IRE) *Chris Grant* 111h
8 b g Piccolo—Whistfilly (First Trump)
89[7] 1762[7] 2448[3] 3502[2] 4257[2] (4873)

Mister Pink *Richard Rowe* 81h 87c
11 gr g Accordion—Place Stephanie (IRE) (Hatim (USA))
2132[4] 2431[3]

Mister Pous (FR) *Miss J Houldey* 106h 98c
12 b g Kaid Pous(FR) —Epson Lady (FR) (Mendez (FR))
4696[P]

Mister Quasimodo *Colin Tizzard* 104h 132c
11 b g Busy Flight—Dubacilla (Dubassoff (USA))
78[6]

Mister Right (IRE) *Dominic Ffrench Davis* 103h
10 ch g Barathea(IRE) —Broken Spirit (IRE) (Slip Anchor)
1569[P]

Mister Stickler (IRE) *Alan King* 111h 131c
7 b g Alflora(IRE) —Almost Trumps (Nearly A Hand)
(2429) ◆ **2951[7] 3672[3] (3905)**
4311[3] 4853[11] 5318[2]

Mister Two Fifty (IRE) *John Anthony Staunton* 98h 115c
8 ch g Anshan—Amarine (IRE) (Rainbow Quest (USA))
1402[2]

Mister Virginian (IRE) *Chris Gordon* 33h 83c
12 ch g Mister Lord(USA) —Ardglass Mist (Black Minstrel)
1676[3] 1916[5] 2051[6]
2950[7] 3609[6] 3700[6]

Mister Wall Street (FR) *Ferdy Murphy* 111h
6 bb g Take Risks(FR) —Miss Breezy (FR) (Sicyos (USA))
2038[6] 3506[5] 3749[4] 3966[P] (5259)

Mister Watzisname (IRE) *Charlie Longsdon* 104h 118c
9 b g King's Theatre(IRE) —Jambo Jambo (IRE) (Kafu)
986[4] **1992[F]**
2214[8] 3391[8] 3608[5] 4238[P] 4945[3] 5062[P] 5214[2]

Mister Wiseman *Nigel Hawke* 120h 114c
9 gr g Bal Harbour—Genie Spirit (Nishapour (FR))
1710[2] 1965[2] 2146[8] (3819)
(3990) 4223[8] 4723[9] 5120[4]

Mistress Eva *Sophie Leech* 81h
6 br m Diktat—Foreign Mistress (Darshaan)
1341[11] 2649[3]

Mistress To No One *Martin Keighley* 105h
8 b m Exit To Nowhere(USA) —Frosty Mistress (Arctic Lord)
157[F]

Misttori Belle *Philip Hobbs* 69h
8 b m Vettori(IRE) —Misbelief (Shirley Heights)
132[P] 650[P]

Misty Dancer *Venetia Williams* 112h 125c
12 gr g Vettori(IRE) —Light Fantastic (Deploy)
586[2] 707[2] 852[F]

Misty Gem (IRE) *Philip Kirby* 58h
10 b m General Monash(USA) —Jade's Gem (Sulaafah (USA))
441[6]

Mix N Match *Gerald Ham* 93h
7 b g Royal Applause—South Wind (Tina's Pet)
172[U] 410[9] 845[6] 1164[6]

Mizen Raven (IRE) *Peter Bowen* 116h 133c
8 b g Sea Raven(IRE) —Consproblem (IRE) (Mazaad)
411[3] 839[4] (1002)
1103[5] 1312[3] 1469[2] 1611[F] 2163[6]

Mizen Station (IRE) *Oliver Sherwood* 120h
6 bb g Presenting—Lonesome Lady (IRE) (Broken Hearted)
3506[6] 3952[P] (4986)

Mizzurka *Bob Buckler* 126h
7 b m Alflora(IRE) —Miss Diskin (IRE) (Sexton Blake)
2974[4] 3227[2] 3442[5] (4101) 5008[4]

M'Lady Eliza *Joanne Priest* 85h
6 b m Mtoto—Starboard Tack (FR) (Saddlers' Hall (IRE))
228[7] 600[4]

M'Lady Rousseur (IRE) *Chris Bealby* 92h
5 ch m Selkirk(USA) —Millay (Polish Precedent (USA))
2554[7] 3389[8] 3901[5] 4812[5]

Mlini (IRE) *Tim Etherington* 15b
5 ch g Bertolini(USA) —Sherkova (USA) (State Dinner (USA))
531[3]

Mobaasher (USA) *Venetia Williams* 148h 141c
8 ch g Rahy(USA) —Balistroika (USA) (Nijinsky (CAN))
3293[6] (3566) 3807[4] **4208[P]** 4817[17] 5187[11]

Mocambo (GER) *Colin Tizzard* 86b
5 gr g Acambaro(GER) —Mobos (GER) (Nebos (GER))
1778[5] 2025[6]

Mocha (FR) *James Ewart* 86h
6 b m Mansonnien(FR) —Pocahontas (FR) (Nikos)
3498[P] 5092[4]

Mocha Java *Seamus Mullins* 41h
8 b g Bertolini(USA) —Coffee Cream (Common Grounds)
1125[7]

Mocho (IRE) *Mrs H Parrott* 103h 107c
10 b g Accordion—Supreme Kellycarra (IRE) (Supreme Leader)
2638[F] 3772[P] 4718[7]

Modestine *Jane Walton* 49h
9 b m Theatrical Charmer—Camden Thistle (IRE) (Camden Town)
457[P] 577[P] 858[P] 1337[F] 1832[F]

Modicum (USA) *Rose Dobbin* 99h 153c
9 b g Chester House(USA) —Wandesta (Nashwan (USA))
44[7] 396[7]

Moghaayer *Nicky Henderson* 120h
6 b g Sinndar(IRE) —Guest Of Anchor (Slip Anchor)
(302) 2581[10] 3742[9] 4464[10] (5404)

Mohanad (IRE) *Sheena West* 121h
5 b g Invincible Spirit(IRE) —Irish Design (IRE) (Alhaarth (IRE))
372[4] 648[3] 1017[5] 1150[2] 1967[12] 4806[12] 5441[6]

Mohayer (IRE) *Jonjo O'Neill* 124h 123c
9 gr g Giant's Causeway(USA) —Karlafsha (Top Ville)
80[3] **2270[4]**
(2593)
2951[5] 3841[4] 4723[3]

Mohi Rahrere (IRE) *Barry Leavy* 102h 117c
8 b g New Frontier(IRE) —Collinstown Lady (IRE) (Welsh Term)
328[3] **(2073)**
3488[3] 3562[4] 3922[6]

Mojeerr *Laura Young* 53h
5 b g Royal Applause—Princess Miletrian (IRE) (Danehill (USA))
5115[10]

Mojo Moon (IRE) *D Darlix* 93h
5 gr m Slickly(FR) —Moonlight Melody (GER) (Law Society (USA))
2265a[7]

Mokum (FR) *Tony Carroll* 99h 96c
10 b g Octagonal(NZ) —Back On Top (FR) (Double Bed (FR))
695[7] 2961[12] 3371[9] 3695[5] 3878[5]

Molannarch *Keith Reveley* 92b
5 b m Old Vic—La Femme En Rouge (Slip Anchor)
4171[3] 4574[7]

Molanna View (IRE) *Emma Lavelle* 107h 100c
6 b g Old Vic—Sonnys Girl (IRE) (Broken Hearted)
1736[3] 2123[3] 3840[6]
4948[F] 5194[4]

Molesden Glen (IRE) *Simon Waugh* 86h
5 b g Spartacus(IRE) —Sea Glen (IRE) (Glenstal (USA))
8[P] 289[9] 468[3] 748[P] 837[P]

Moleskin (IRE) *Victor Dartnall* 120h 125c
8 b g Saddlers' Hall(IRE) —Magic Gale (IRE) (Strong Gale)
2140[6] 2959[8] 3562[2] 4328[P] 5213[3]

Mollyash (IRE) *S R B Crawford* 39b
6 b m Definite Article—Stormy (IRE) (Glacial Storm (USA))
1934[9]

Mollycarrs Dream *Bill Turner* 69b
4 br f Grape Tree Road—Eugenie (Primo Dominie)
1913[5] 2173[9]

Molly Round (IRE) *Grant Cann* 109h
7 b m Old Vic—Mondeo Rose (IRE) (Roselier (FR))
2499[7] 3227[7] (3703)
3898[U] (4032) (4224) 4446[2] 5008[6]

Molly's Boy *Edward Cawley* 127h
10 b g Parthian Springs—May Day Belle (Scallywag)
5339[3]

Molon Labe (IRE) *Tom Tate* 100h
4 ch g Footstepsinthesand—Pillars Of Society (IRE) (Caerleon (USA))
2451[2] 3401[16] 3767[U] 3999[5] 4253[5]

Molostiep (FR) *Susan Nock* 101h 107c
11 b g Video Rock(FR) —Unetiepy (FR) (Marasali)
1531[3]

Molotof (FR) *Nicky Henderson* 137h
4 gr g Smadoun(FR) —Memorial (FR) (Homme De Loi (IRE))
4350[2] 4847[14]

Moment Of Madness (IRE) *Mrs M Stirk* 88h 110c
13 ch g Treasure Hunter—Sip Of Orange (Celtic Cone)
(398)
3956[P] (5347)

Moment Of Magic (IRE) *Kathleen Sanderson* 100h 60c
8 b g Alderbrook—Pankhurst (IRE) (Radical)
133[7]

Moment Present (FR) *Charlie Mann* 120h 112c
6 gr g Enrique—Abigaila (FR) (River River (FR))
1961[6] **594[3]**
838[6]

Monaadi (IRE) *Bernard Llewellyn* 82h
6 b g Singspiel(IRE) —Bint Albaadiya (USA) (Woodman (USA))
1549[9]

Monashee (IRE) *George Charlton* 93b
6 bb g Monashee Mountain(USA) —On The Bridle (IRE) (Mandalus)
448[6] 3957[6] 4916[5] 5342[10]

Monash Lad (IRE) *Michelle Bryant* 61h
9 ch g General Monash(USA) —Story Time (IRE) (Mansooj)
220[7] 2135[8] 2430[5]

Monbeg Dude (IRE) *Michael Scudamore* 101b
6 b g Witness Box(USA) —Ten Dollar Bill (IRE) (Accordion)
3259[2] 3903[6]

Moncadou (FR) *Jonjo O'Neill* 132c
11 bb g Cadoudal(FR) —Palencia (FR) (Taj Dewan)
3908[6] 4163[4] 4750[2] 5163[B]

Monetary Fund (USA) *Nicky Henderson* 130h
5 b g Montjeu(IRE) —Maddie G (USA) (Blush Rambler (USA))
500[2] 792[4] 2626[2] 2868[4] 3229[3] 4852[11] 5441[3]

Monet's Garden (IRE) *Nicky Richards* 159h 165c
10 gr g Roselier(FR) —Royal Remainder (IRE) (Remainder Man)
(1958)

Monets Masterpiece (USA) *P Kelsall* 55h
8 b g Quiet American(USA) —Math (USA) (Devil's Bag (USA))
380[P]

Money Bridge *Derek Shaw* 80b
4 ch c Doyen(IRE) —Crochet (IRE) (Mark Of Esteem (IRE))
2458[6] 5284[3]

Money Dieu (IRE) *Stephen Marshall* 27b
6 b m Turtle Island(IRE) —Aon Suil Amhain (IRE) (Supreme Leader)
4916[13]

Money Finder *Trevor Wall* 94h
8 b m Karinga Bay—Balmoral Princess (Thethingaboutitis (USA))
227[3] 340[2] 553[3] 3919[9]

Money Order (IRE) *Brendan Powell* 132h 128c
9 b g Supreme Leader—Dipper's Gift (IRE) (Salluceva)
2235[7] 3440[12] **3588[3] 4256 (4333)**

Money Tree *Donald McCain* 88h
5 ch g Central Park(IRE) —Idiots Money (Idiots Delight)
311[13] 3920[9] 4545[4]

Money Trix (IRE) *Nicky Richards* 145h 163c
11 gr g Old Vic—Deer Trix (Buckskin (FR))
3176a[2] 4087a[P] (Dead)

Moneywise (IRE) *Jonjo O'Neill* 52c
7 b g Definite Article—Wealthy And Wise (IRE) (Camden Town)
634[8]

Monfils Monfils (USA) *Philip Kirby* 72h
9 b g Sahm(USA) —Sorpresa (USA) (Pleasant Tap (USA))
470[7] 745[7] 1468[9] 1976[4] 2478[4]

Monkhair (IRE) *Tony Carroll* 102h
6 b m Monashee Mountain(USA) —Khairka (IRE) (Tirol)
171[7] 384[2] 527[3] (600) (697) 793[6] (1005) 1066[5] 4830[P] 5346[9]

Mon Michel (IRE) *Gary Moore* 110h 69c
8 b g Montjeu(IRE) —Miniver (IRE) (Mujtahid (USA))
159[5] 479[9]

Monnow Made (IRE) *Charles Egerton* 110b
6 b m Bob Back(USA) —Lady Llancillo (IRE) (Alflora (IRE))
(2546) 3590[7] 4728[16] 5188[10]

Monn Royal (FR) *Venetia Williams* 115h 63c
7 bb g Rochesson(FR) —Miss Coco (FR) (Bay Comeau (FR))
2243[7] 2796[5]

Monogram *Howard Johnson* 118h
7 ch g Karinga Bay—Dusky Dante (IRE) (Phardante (FR))
1593[0] (1783) 3713[3]

Mon Oiseau (FR) *C A McBratney* 58h 113c
11 b g Port Lyautey(FR) —Amour D'Oiseau (FR) (Dirak Creiomin (FR))
1117[6]

Mono Man (IRE) *Nicky Henderson* 120b
5 b g Old Vic—Quadrennial (IRE) (Un Desperado (FR))
(3842) (4204)

Monopole (IRE) *David Pipe* 58h
7 b g Montjeu(IRE) —Pretty (IRE) (Darshaan)
3645[14] 4092[5] 4448[9] 5066[5]

Mon Parrain (FR) *Paul Nicholls* 162c
5 b g Trempolino(USA) —Kadaina (FR) (Kadalko (FR))
(4726) ◆ **5185[2]**

Monreale (GER) *David Pipe* 98h
7 b g Silvano(GER) —Maratea (USA) (Fast Play (USA))
554^{6} 917^{6}

Monroe Park (IRE) *Noel Quinlan* 98h
6 b g Spectrum(IRE) —Paloma Bay (IRE) (Alzao (USA))
1599^{3} 4930^{7} 5099^{9} 5348^{7}

Monsieur (FR) *Carroll Gray* 92h 77c
11 b g Cyborg(FR) —Quintessence III (FR) (El Condor (FR))
762^{8} 1064^{5} 1164^{3} 1272^{7} 1976^{9} 2149^{2} (2308) 2467^{3} 3532^{3} 3782^{4} 4104^{4} 4330^{2} 4450^{2} 4785^{F}

Monsieur Cadou (FR) *Tom George* 104h
6 b g Cadoudal(FR) —Dame De Trefles (FR) (Antheus (USA))
212^{P} 2141^{6} (2469) 3260^{4} 3745^{6} 4407^{2}

Monsieur Georges (FR) *Violet M Jordan* 76h 75c
11 b g Kadalko(FR) —Djoumi (FR) (Brezzo (FR))
83^{4} 280^{2} 531^{3} 1733^{6} 2050^{P} 5062^{2} (5266)

Monsieur Jourdain (IRE) *Tim Easterby* 113h 113c
5 b g Royal Applause—Palwina (FR) (Unfuwain (USA))
1931^{10} 2076^{9} **2299^{4} 2599^{4} 3524^{8} 3886^{U} 4893^{3}**
5095^{5} (5427)

Monsoon Music (IRE) *Lucinda Russell* 60h
7 b g Dushyantor(USA) —Stormey Tune (IRE) (Glacial Storm (USA))
2446^{8} 3850^{9} **4133^{F}** 4302^{9} 4688^{P}

Montan (FR) *A J Martin* 128h 143c
7 b g Trempolino(USA) —Mandchoue (FR) (Mansonnien (FR))
3474a^{12}

Montana Gold (IRE) *Tim Vaughan* 86h 97c
10 b g Bob Back(USA) —Tell A Tale (Le Bavard (FR))
132^{3} (280)

Montbazon (FR) *Alan King* 122b
4 bb g Alberto Giacometti(IRE) —Duchesse Pierji (FR) (Cadoudal (FR))
4055^{2} ◆ (4468) 5202^{2} ◆

Montero (IRE) *D T Hughes* 124h 143c
9 ch g Pistolet Bleu(IRE) —Wayward Queen (Alflora (IRE))
1123a^{F} 1527a^{7}

Montevetro *William Clay* 78h
6 b g Galileo(IRE) —Three Piece (Jaazeiro (USA))
717^{5} 1275^{8}

Montiboli (IRE) *Gordon Edwards* 33h
6 ch m Bahamian Bounty—Aunt Sadie (Pursuit Of Love)
358^{9}

Montiyra (IRE) *Lynn Siddall* 87h
7 b g Montjeu(IRE) —Shiyra (Darshaan)
713^{9} 4739^{12}

Montoya's Son (IRE) *Howard Johnson* 114h 124c
6 ch g Flemensfirth(USA) —Over The Grand (IRE) (Over The River (FR))
(209) 1594^{7} 1829^{2} 3509^{6}
5261^{2} (5415)

Mont Present (FR) *Philip Hobbs* 82h 127c
7 b g Marly River(FR) —Nice Donna (FR) (Nice Havrais (USA))
(234) **1858^{9}**

Montybella (IRE) *Evan Williams* 39b
4 b g Orpen(USA) —Larentia (Salse (USA))
4866^{13}

Monty's Brig *Jane Clark* 36h
10 ch g Minster Son—Minibrig (Le Coq D'Or)
4889^{10} 5091^{6}

Monty's Fortune *Mike Sowersby* 54b
6 br g Terimon—Islandreagh (IRE) (Knesset (USA))
718^{P} 841^{10}

Monty's Moon (IRE) *Rachel Hobbs* 81h 79c
9 b g Moonax(IRE) —Brett And Danny (IRE) (Yashgan)
278^{4} 650^{4} 757^{4}
1080^{4} 1237^{2} 1468^{3}
3388^{2} 3790^{P} 4413^{7} 4724^{2} 5075^{2} (5295)

Monty's Revenge (IRE) *Martin Keighley* 38h
6 b g Bob's Return(IRE) —Native Bavard (IRE) (Be My Native (USA))
1734^{12} 2123^{9} 3253^{8}

Monzon (FR) *Chris Gordon* 64h 105c
11 b g Kadalko(FR) —Queenly (FR) (Pot D'Or (FR))
522^{11}

Moonbalej *Milton Harris* 83h
4 ch g Motivator—Glam Rock (Nashwan (USA))
1728^{P} 1772^{6} 2133^{2} 2369^{4} 4452^{P} 5406^{4}

Moon Bear *Linda Blackford* 96h 83c
10 b g Petoski—Culm Country (Town And Country)
758^{6} 913^{5} 991^{3} 1231^{3} 1273^{10}

Moon Indigo *Howard Johnson* 128h
5 b g Sadler's Wells(USA) —Solo De Lune (IRE) (Law Society (USA))
1662^{2} (2375) 2939^{2} 3567^{4} 3965^{2} 4475^{4} (5149)

Moonlight Blaze *Chris Fairhurst* 75h
4 b g Barathea(IRE) —Moonlight (IRE) (Night Shift (USA))
1135^{P} 4393^{6} 4824^{7}

Moonlight Drive (IRE) *John Quinn* 126h
5 b g Oscar(IRE) —Perspex Queen (IRE) (Presenting)
(3952) 4849^{P}

Moon Lightning (IRE) *Tina Jackson*
5 b g Desert Prince(IRE) —Moon Tango (IRE) (Last Tycoon)
2349^{P}

Moonlight Rose *Christopher Kellett* 70b
7 b m Overbury(IRE) —Thistle Princess (Belfort (FR))
227^{P}

Moonlight Sapphire *J F O'Shea* 127h
6 b m High Chaparral(IRE) —Halska (Unfuwain (USA))
1121a^{13}

Moon Melody (GER) *Mike Sowersby* 89h 96c
8 b g Montjeu(IRE) —Midnight Fever (IRE) (Sure Blade (USA))
(441) **531^{2}**
913^{4} 1048^{P}
1331^{3} (1478)
1503^{3} 4115^{2} 4276^{P} 4994^{7}
5311^{3}

Moon Over Miami (GER) *Charlie Mann* 133h 147c
10 b g Dashing Blade—Miss Esther (GER) (Alkalde (GER))
1861^{11} (2234)
2541^{9} 3292^{P} 3565^{2} 3949^{4} 4470^{9} 5436^{4}

Moon Over Moscow (IRE) *T Hogan* 109h
7 ch m Moscow Society(USA) —Got No Choice (IRE) (Mandalus)
2116a^{5}

Moonset *Sean Regan*
7 gr g Silver Patriarch(IRE) —Zaffaran Run (IRE) (Zaffaran (USA))
1063° 1149^{R}

Moonshine Hall (IRE) *Richard Hawker* 26h
7 b m Saddlers' Hall(IRE) —Sno-Cat Lady (IRE) (Executive Perk)
855^{8} 1028^{5}

Moonslit (IRE) *Miss G Lee* 65b
5 ch g Pilsudski(IRE) —Marys Madera (IRE) (Toca Madera)
1146a^{14}

Moon Star (GER) *Barry Brennan* 110h 113c
10 b g Goofalik(USA) —Maria Magdalena (GER) (Alkalde (GER))
664^{5}

Moonstreaker *Charles Pogson* 116h
8 b g Foxhound(USA) —Ling Lane (Slip Anchor)
(439)

Moon Stream *David Brace* 5b
4 b g Kayf Tara—Moon Catcher (Kahyasi)
4164^{11}

Moonwolf (NZ) *Sheena West* 104h
7 b g Ustinov(AUS) —Moonrise (Grundy)
1433^{5} (1675) 1914^{4}

Moorland Picture *Mark Shears*
6 b g Relief Pitcher—Chasing The Groom (Petoski)
1607^{P}

Moorlands Jack *Tim Vaughan* 69b
6 b g Cloudings(IRE) —Sandford Springs (USA) (Robellino (USA))
1824^{10} 5158^{14}

Moorlands Teri *Tim Vaughan* 119h 107c
8 b m Terimon—Sandford Springs (USA) (Robellino (USA))
1986^{12}
2641^{3} *3171^{2}* **3435^{F} 3763^{4} 4160^{P}**

Moorland Sunset *Caroline Keevil* 93b
4 b g Pasternak—Lady Harriet Luis (Sir Harry Lewis (USA))
5157^{3}

Moose Moran (USA) *Nicky Henderson* 115h
4 rg g Lemon Drop Kid(USA) —After All (IRE) (Desert Story (IRE))
3944^{4} (4283) 4458^{5} 5006^{P}

Mootabar (IRE) *Chris Fairhurst* 87b
4 gr g Verglas(IRE) —Melanzane (Arazi (USA))
3399^{7} 3957^{8}

Morcambe *Nicky Henderson* 109h
6 b g Bollin Eric—Lunabelle (Idiots Delight)
1951^{6} 2454^{8} 3487^{3} 3919^{8} 4439^{4} 4988^{P}

Mordetta Road *James Turner* 43b
6 ch m Alflora(IRE) —Carbia's Last (Palm Track)
2616^{8} 3504^{9} 4000^{P}

Morecambe Bay *David Thompson* 72h
6 b g Luso—Gun Shot (Gunner B)
426^{F} 887^{6} 999^{8} 1149^{6} 1362^{8} 5096^{10}

More Claret (IRE) *Kevin F O'Donnell* 106h 112c
5 b m Beneficial—Sheryl Lynn (Miller's Mate)
2233^{5}

More Equity *Dianne Sayer* 106h 115c
9 b m Classic Cliche(IRE) —Sillymore (Silly Prices)
1338^{3} 1424^{6} 1598^{3} 1868^{2} 2203^{2} 2550^{3} 2940^{8}
3362^{4} 3750^{6} 4812^{2}
(5150) 5319^{5}
5430^{2}

More Like It (IRE) *Peter Niven* 95h 102c
11 b g Windsor Castle—Ms Brooks (IRE) (Lord Ha Ha)
(10) 252^{9}
460^{8} 716^{4} 952^{2} (1256)

Morenito (FR) *Tom George* 89h 109c
8 b g Nononito(FR) —Cohiba (FR) (Ti King (FR))
475^{2} 677^{5} 891^{6} 1061^{F} (1293)

More Shennanigans *Jean McGregor* 63h 81c
10 ch g Rock City—Blooming Spring (IRE) (Strong Gale)
306^{P} 460^{5} 652^{2} 1665^{3} 1872^{U} 1924^{5} 2548^{3} 3618^{P}
4573^{5} 5093^{4}

Morestead (IRE) *Brendan Powell* 78h 112c
6 ch g Traditionally(USA) —Itsy Bitsy Betsy (USA) (Beau Genius (CAN))
81^{5} 586^{5} 691^{4} 921^{8}
1128^{3} 1293^{3} 1430^{5} (1474)
1589^{2} 1841^{2} 1916^{4} 2127^{5}
2484^{3} 2961^{14}
3433^{4} 3791^{12}

More Trouble (IRE) *Alan Hill* 97h 97c
10 b g Zaffaran(USA) —Athas Liath (IRE) (Roselier (FR))
(294) **502^{3}**

Morgan Be *Kate Walton* 121h 127c
11 b g Alderbrook—Vicie (Old Vic)
3634^{3} 4360^{3} (5032)
5338^{P}

Morgan's Bay *Tom George* 16h
6 b g Karinga Bay—Dubai Dolly (IRE) (Law Society (USA))
319^{2} 3301^{6} 4100^{8} 4499^{P}

Morgan The Mighty (IRE) *Nigel Twiston-Davies* 48h
9 bb g Presenting—Another Grouse (Pragmatic)
2002^{P}

Morning Farewell *William Clay* 101h
7 br g Daylami(IRE) —Got To Go (Shareef Dancer (USA))
2038^{3} 4874^{F}

Morning Sunshine (IRE) *Donald McCain* 98h 114c
8 b g Presenting—Culfadda Girl (IRE) (Buckskin (FR))
864^{F} 991^{U} 1139^{6} 1260^{3}
(1403) (1767)
1872^{2} 2093^{5} 2635^{3}

Morning Supreme (IRE) *W P Mullins* 144h 141c
8 b m Supreme Leader—Portryan Native (IRE) (Be My Native (USA))
3779a^{F}

Morning Time (IRE) *Lucinda Russell* 105h
5 b g Hawk Wing(USA) —Desert Trail (IRE) (Desert Style (IRE))
1104^{9} 1337^{3} 1641^{5} 1870^{9}

Morocchius (USA) *Charles Pogson* 102h
6 b g Black Minnaloushe(USA) —Shakespearean (USA) (Theatrical)
1831^{4} 2282^{4} *3091^{6}* 3302^{9} 5101^{7} 5296^{2}

Mororless *Zoe Davison*
4 b f Exceed And Excel(AUS) —Final Pursuit (Pursuit Of Love)
2528^{P}

Mortimers Cross *John Needham* 122h 117c
10 b g Cloudings(IRE) —Leinthall Doe (Oats)
2363^{4} 3586^{3} 3902^{F} 4030^{P}

Moscow Chancer (IRE) *Tom George* 104h
5 b g Moscow Society(USA) —I'll See You Again (IRE) (Presenting)
3505^{5} 3987^{8} 4702^{4}

Moscow Court (IRE) *Mrs David Plunkett* 112h 91c
13 b g Moscow Society(USA) —Hogan Stand (Buckskin (FR))
4779^{4}

Moscow Jewel (IRE) *Richard Price* 95b
7 ch m Moscow Society(USA) —Sound Foundation (IRE) (Shardari)
684^{U}

Moscow Mischief *Lucinda Russell* 96h
7 ch m Moscow Society(USA) —Desperate Measures (Kasakov)
871^{7} 1119^{5} (2547) 3261^{5} 3747^{8}

Moscow Oznick *Des Donovan*
6 br g Auction House(USA) —Cozette (IRE) (Danehill Dancer (IRE))
887^{P}

Moscow Player (IRE) *John Wade*
6 ch g Moscow Society(USA) —Accordian's Choice (IRE) (Accordion)
30^{P}

Moskova (IRE) *Paul Nolan* 148h 142c
8 gr m Montjeu(IRE) —Russian Rebel (Machiavellian (USA))
2259a^{3} 3175a^{6} 3796a^{2} 4107a^{8}

Mossbank (IRE) *Michael Hourigan* 132h 132c
11 b g Kadeed(IRE) —Miromaid (Simply Great (FR))
2226a^{6} 2970a^{P} 3176a^{10} 3778a^{F} 4298a^{P}

Mossey Joe (IRE) *W J Austin* 142h 120c
8 ch g Moscow Society(USA) —Delmiano (IRE) (Henbit (USA))
(2912a) ◆ 3175a^{7}

Mossini (IRE) *Gary Moore* 109h
6 b g Dr Massini(IRE) —Ballylooby Moss (IRE) (Supreme Leader)
3789^{7} 4052^{9} (4427)

Mossley (IRE) *Nicky Henderson* 149h
5 b g Old Vic—Sorivera (Irish River (FR))
(637) (2111) (2888) 3567^{5} 4849^{2} 5186^{P}

Mossmann Gorge *Anthony Middleton* 96h
9 b g Lujain(USA) —North Pine (Import)
1085^{2} 1261^{7} 4330^{10} 4751^{4} 5057^{U} 5282^{2}

Mosstown (IRE) *Mrs John Harrington* 125h
5 b g Dilshaan—Tavildara (IRE) (Kahyasi)
3474a^{17}

Mostly Bob (IRE) *Philip Hobbs* 125h 140c
8 b g Bob Back(USA) —Town Gossip (IRE) (Indian Ridge)
(191) 2035^{8} 2663^{3} ◆ **2959^{F} 3508^{2} (3784)**
4352^{F} 4821^{P}

Motafarred (IRE) *Tina Jackson* 85h
9 ch g Machiavellian(USA) —Thurayya (Nashwan (USA))
2092^{9} 2373^{10}

Motarjm (USA) *Jeff Pearce* 107h
7 br g Elusive Quality(USA) —Agama (USA) (Nureyev (USA))
(1953) 2586^{6}

Motirani *Jeff Pearce* 62h
4 br g Motivator—Maharani (USA) (Red Ransom (USA))
1691^{9}

Motive (FR) *Howard Johnson* 108h 94c
10 ch g Machiavellian(USA) —Mistle Song (Nashwan (USA))
179^{7} 423^{4}

Motor Home *Charlie Morlock* 86h
5 b g Tobougg(IRE) —Desert Dawn (Belfort (FR))
850^{8} 1046^{7} 1125^{6} 1451^{P} 1902^{2} 4956^{U} 5272^{7}

Motou (FR) *Richard Phillips* 97b
6 b g Astarabad(USA) —Picoletta (FR) (Galetto (FR))
3773^{6} 4430^{4}

Moufatango (FR) *Nicky Richards* 101h
5 bb g Sagacity(FR) —Bold-E-Be (Persian Bold)
355^{3} 609^{3} 2246^{6} 3330^{13} 3851^{8} 4477^{F} (5208)

Moulin De La Croix *Nigel Twiston-Davies* 91h 120c
7 b m Muhtarram(USA) —Brambly Hedge (Teenoso (USA))
586^{3} 769^{3} 1256^{3} (1491)
1509^{F} 1604^{4} 2470^{2} 3157^{6} 5120^{3} ◆ **5399^{5}**

Mountainous (IRE) *Richard Lee* 99h
6 b g Milan—Mullaghcloga (IRE) (Glacial Storm (USA))
5253^{2}

Mount Benger *H Whittington* 130h 128c
11 ch g Selkirk(USA) —Vice Vixen (CAN) (Vice Regent (CAN))
4026^{2} (4315)
4851^{P} 5163^{U}

Mount Hadley (USA) *David Pipe* 92h
7 b g Elusive Quality(USA) —Fly To The Moon (USA) (Blushing Groom (FR))
1344^{3} 1723^{10}

Mount Helicon *T Hogan* 135h
6 b g Montjeu(IRE) —Model Queen (USA) (Kingmambo (USA))
(2116a) 2388^{3} 2967a^{6}

Mount Oscar (IRE) *Colin Tizzard* 135h 152c
12 b g Oscar(IRE) —Sweet Mount (IRE) (Mandalus)
1777^{3} (2674)
3453^{6} 4352^{2}

Mountrath *Brett Johnson*
4 b g Dubai Destination(USA) —Eurolink Sundance (Night Shift (USA))
3944° 4192^{P}

Mount Sandel (IRE) *Mrs Alison Hickman* 120h 98c
10 b g Supreme Leader—Droichidin (Good Thyne (USA))
4131^{2}

Mountskip *Rose Dobbin* 104h 95c
7 b g Beat All(USA) —Roman Uproar (Primitive Rising (USA))
161^{2} (456) 520^{10} 748^{U} 837^{2} 1104^{6}
1645^{5} 2208^{7} 2508^{6}

Mourad (IRE) *W P Mullins* 167h
6 ch g Sinndar(IRE) —Mouramara (IRE) (Kahyasi)
2968a^{4} (3175a) (3796a) ◆ 4819^{3}

Mouseen (IRE) *Lisa Day* 104h
8 ch g Alhaarth(IRE) —Marah (Machiavellian (USA))
962^{P} 1084^{12} 1162^{P}

Mousenikov *Paul Nicholls* 100b
5 b g Baryshnikov(AUS) —Mousiemay (El Conquistador)
3909^{6} 5174^{11}

Mous Of Men (FR) *David Pipe* 126h 121c
8 b g Lord Of Men—Mousmee (FR) (Kaldounevees (FR))
206^{12} **(536)**
828^{3} 1346^{8}

Moynalveylad (IRE) *David Anthony O'Brien* 100h 53c
11 b g Taipan(IRE) —Tirol's Luck (IRE) (Tirol)
234^{P}

Mr Bachster (IRE) *Victor Dartnall* 95h
6 b g Bach(IRE) —Warrior Princess (IRE) (Mister Lord (USA))
375^{10} 2499^{10} 3645^{6} 3789^{6} 4272^{8} 4899^{2}

Mr Bennett (IRE) *David Pipe* 108h 122c
8 b g Mister Mat(FR) —Miss Bobby Bennett (Kings Lake (USA))
2946^{10} 3771^{5} 4079^{P}
(4538)

Mr Big (IRE) *Charlie Mann* 86h 123c
10 ch g Eurobus—All A Struggle (IRE) (Carlingford Castle)
1570^{5} 1811a^{12} 2346^{5} 2984^{2} (3263)
3602^{2} 4194^{5} 4699^{8}

Mr Bond (IRE) *Andy Turnell* 84h 97c
8 ch g Moscow Society(USA) —Wise Wish (Baragoi)
1995^{F} 2292^{2} 2605^{4} 2982^{P} 3388^{F} 3720^{4} 3984^{2}
4693^{F} 5256^{4} 5434^{P}

Mr Bones (IRE) *J G Coogan* 127h 98c
9 b g Trans Island—Leaghillaun (IRE) (Turtle Island (IRE))
1121a^{2}

Mr Chamonick (IRE) *Valentine Donoghue*
7 ch g Marignan(USA) —Lucey Allen (Strong Gale)
945^{P}

Mr Chippy (IRE) *Ian Williams* 89h 92c
7 b g Laveron—Lady Denel (IRE) (Denel (FR))
93^{9} 596^{6} **3933^{2} 4292^{3}**

Mr Chow (IRE) *Warren Greatrex* 81h
7 b g King's Theatre(IRE) —Della Wee (IRE) (Fidel)
2145^{9} 2944^{8} *3091^{3}* 3739^{7}

Mr Clyde (IRE) *Patrick J Flynn* 125h
8 br g Turtle Island(IRE) —Grangemills (Strong Gale)
3474a^{18}

Mr Coates *Simon Waugh*
5 b g Forzando—Portacasa (Robellino (USA))
5034^{11}

Mr Cracker (IRE) *Michael Hourigan* 142h 151c
6 ch g Anshan—Sesame Cracker (Derrylin)
(3210a)
3705a^{3} 4816^{7} (5141a)

Mr Dass (IRE) *Matthew Smith* 106h
9 ch g Bob's Return(IRE) —Belle Babillard (IRE) (Le Bavard (FR))
4857^{P}

Mr Deal *Eve Johnson Houghton* 83h
5 b g King's Best(USA) —One Of The Family (Alzao (USA))
54^{P}

Mr Demister *Susan Gardner* 54h
8 b g Access Ski—Celtic Mist (Celtic Cone)
1445^{7} 1488^{6} 1567^{7}

Mr Ed (IRE) *Peter Bowen* 128h 115c
13 ch g In The Wings—Center Moriches (IRE) (Magical Wonder (USA))
152^{P} 579^{2} 911^{5}

Mr Fantozzi (IRE) *Des Donovan* 9h
6 br g Statue Of Liberty(USA) —Indian Sand (Indian King (USA))
850^{12}

Mr Floppy (IRE) *Alison Batchelor* 81h 81c
10 b g Un Desperado(FR) —Bright Future (IRE) (Satco (FR))
278^{5}

Mr Gardner (IRE) *Nicky Henderson* 150h 150c
8 b g Deploy—Lady Padivor (IRE) (Zaffaran (USA))
(3543)
3946^{3} ◆ **4816^{P}**

Mr Goofy (IRE) *Michael Scudamore* 103c
10 b g Rock Hopper—Jamie's Lady (Ashmore (FR))
148^{9} 824^{P} (4693)
5261^{5}

Mr Grumpalot *Bill Turner*
4 b g Grape Tree Road—Saffron Delight (Idiots Delight)
2052[10]

Mr Hooper *Victor Dartnall* 116b
5 b g Karinga Bay—Rempstone (Coronash)
(4970)

Mr Hudson (IRE) *Paul Nicholls* 124h
6 b g Old Vic—Esbeggi (Sabrehill (USA))
(375) (2136) 3295[3] 4354[F]

Mr Ironman *Alan Jones* 9h 77c
10 b g Jendali(USA) —Carly-J (Cruise Missile)
1991[6] 2170[P]

Mr Jay Dee (IRE) *Lucy Wadham* 119h
6 b g Lord Americo—Emmas Flyer (IRE) (Beneficial)
399[3] (1086) 1357[5] (1867) 3403[2] 3601[3] 3947[17]

Mr Johnson (IRE) *Michael Gates* 18h 73c
8 bb g Runyon(IRE) —Santosha (Wolver Hollow)
1275[10]
1467[P] 1922[P] 4751[P] **5375[2]**

Mr Logistics (IRE) *Charles Egerton* 105h
8 b g Simply Great(FR) —Midnight Light (IRE) (Roselier (FR))
918[P]

Mr Lu *Jim Goldie* 28h
6 b g Lujain(USA) —Libretta (Highest Honor (FR))
3331[16] 3551[P]

Mr Madeit (IRE) *Caroline Bailey* 28h
5 b g Brian Boru—Henrietta Howard (IRE) (King's Ride)
3740[13]

Mr Mansson (IRE) *Lucy Normile* 60b
4 b g Millenary—Supreme Dare (IRE) (Supreme Leader)
4151[8] 4916[14]

Mr Melodious *Nigel Twiston-Davies* 92h
5 ch g Green Tune(USA) —Moly (FR) (Anabaa (USA))
23[8] 172[4] 227[4] 607[2] 737[10] 984[6]

Mr Midaz *Donald Whillans* 74h
12 ch g Danzig Connection(USA) —Marmy (Midyan (USA))
459[8] 801[P] 1101[4] 1666[P]

Mr Mohican (IRE) *Ann Duffield* 66h
4 b g Barathea(IRE) —Tipi Squaw (King's Best (USA))
629[4] 743[3] 851[8]

Mr Moonshine (IRE) *Sue Smith* 136h 121c
7 b g Double Eclipse(IRE) —Kinross (Nearly A Hand)
(426) 805[6] 1988[3] **2248[2]** (3742) 4207[6] 4817[22] 5187[12]

Mr Moss (IRE) *Evan Williams* 95h
6 b g Moscow Society(USA) —Yesterdays Gorby (IRE) (Strong Gale)
3761[5] 4946[2]

Mr Muddle *Sheena West* 108h
4 gr g Imperial Dancer—Spatham Rose (Environment Friend)
2924[2] 3344[2] 3613[2] (4129) ◆ 4350[7] 4807[19] (5267)

Mr Nobody (IRE) *A J Martin* 94h
6 gr g Overbury(IRE) —Hifinanba (Gran Alba (USA))
870[4]

Mr One Too (IRE) *Keith Goldsworthy* 74h
6 b g Mr Combustible(IRE) —Too Back (IRE) (Toulon)
2525[5] 3760[11]

Mr Parson (IRE) *David Lewis* 52c
11 b g Bob Back(USA) —Queenie Kelly (The Parson)
22[5] 4832[6]

Mr Pointment (IRE) *Paul Murphy* 128h 84c
12 b g Old Vic—Bettyhill (Ardross)
33[9]

Mr Preacher Man *Lucinda Russell* 90h 119c
9 b g Sir Harry Lewis(USA) —Praise The Lord (Lord Gayle (USA))
4067[10]

Mr Presley (IRE) *Jonjo O'Neill* 82h 58c
7 ch g Sonus(IRE) —Fly Like A Bird (Keen)
531[P]

Mr Redwood *Susan Gardner* 56h
9 ch g Romany Rye—Wood Corner (Sit In The Corner (USA))
1553[13]
4315[U] 5437[5]

Mr Robert (IRE) *Evan Williams* 119h 136c
10 b g Dr Massini(IRE) —Langretta (IRE) (Lancastrian)
1486[P] 3157[P] 4864[7]

Mrs Eff *Kate Walton* 88h
5 b m Tamure(IRE) —Roman Uproar (Primitive Rising (USA))
355[5] 1934[4] 2598[3] 2939[13] 3498[5] 3883[8] 4390[13] 4872[3]

Mrs Fawlty (IRE) *Jim Old* 106h 92c
8 b m Kayf Tara—Hannigan's Lodger (IRE) (Be My Native (USA))
4127[P] 4381[2] 4880[3]

Mrsilverlining (IRE) *Miss I H Pickard*
9 gr g Turtle Island(IRE) —Sasset (GER) (Kalaglow)
79[P] 151[P] 4143[P]

Mrs Overall *Bob Buckler* 74h
6 br m Overbury(IRE) —Casciara (FR) (Lomond (USA))
134[7] 660[6] 849[P]

Mrs Peacock (IRE) *Norma Twomey* 82h
6 b m Dushyantor(USA) —Peacock Feather (Bustino)
4828[P] 5078[4] 5267[3]

Mr Straffan (IRE) *Martin Hill* 81h
8 ch g Exit To Nowhere(USA) —Cab In The Storm (IRE) (Glacial Storm (USA))
267[5] 593[P]

Mrs Trellis *Paul Webber* 76h
6 ch m Alflora(IRE) —Ardrom (Ardross)
2547[P]

Mr Supreme (IRE) *Kate Walton* 106h
6 b g Beneficial—Ardfallon (IRE) (Supreme Leader)
2826[6] 3330[4] 3572[8] (5260)

Mr Syntax (IRE) *Tim Fitzgerald* 114h 114c
7 b g King's Theatre(IRE) —Smile Awhile (USA) (Woodman (USA))
30[2] **2350[2]**
2938[8] 3886[F] (4275)
5301[8]

Mr Tallyman *Micky Hammond* 97h
5 b g Auction House(USA) —Island Colony (USA) (Pleasant Colony (USA))
289[8]

Mr Tambourine Man (IRE) *Katie Stephens* 80h 93c
10 b g Rainbow Quest(USA) —Girl From Ipanema (Salse (USA))
54[9] 557[8]

Mr Tee Pee (IRE) *Miss Rose Grissell* 75h 46c
11 b g Norwich—Msadi Mhulu (IRE) (Kambalda)
297[P]

Mr Thriller (FR) *David Pipe* 160h 147c
6 b g Kapgarde(FR) —Gaspaisie (FR) (Beyssac (FR))
2348[F] 3291[9] 4816[6]

Mr Tingle *Richard Phillips* 99h
7 br g Beat All(USA) —Dianthus (IRE) (Doyoun)
2150[6] 3540[DSQ] 3745[4]

Mr Tobias *C Roberts* 70h
14 b g Current Edition(IRE) —Matching Green (Green Ruby (USA))
1343[P]

Mr Valentino (IRE) *Lawney Hill* 95h
6 b g Dr Massini(IRE) —Miss Ranova (Giacometti)
2530[7] 3599[P] 4745[P]

Mr Windmill *Lisa Williamson* 76h
5 ch g Elmaamul(USA) —Mrs Oh (IRE) (Arctic Lord)
3836[F]

Mr Woods *Harriet Graham* 111h 131c
9 b g Then Again—Lucky Lievre (Nomadic Way (USA))
394[U] 2106[F] 2549[6] 4003[P] **425[6] 4689[P]**

Mtpockets (IRE) *Neil Mulholland* 109h
6 ch m Deploy—No Moore Bills (Nicholas Bill)
1675[5] 1907[4] (2051)
2395[P] 3483[4] 3713[8] 4021[4] 4722[8]

Mubrook (USA) *E J O'Grady* 128h
6 b g Alhaarth(IRE) —Zomaradah (Deploy)
3474a[21] 3709a[4]

Mucho Loco (IRE) *Roger Curtis* 81h 80c
8 ch g Tagula(IRE) —Mousseux (IRE) (Jareer (USA))
1732[15]

Mudita Moment (IRE) *Anna Brooks* 95h
6 b g Heron Island(IRE) —Woodville Leader (IRE) (Supreme Leader)
3556[10] 3836[5] 4281[5] 4922[4]

Mud Monkey *Claire Dyson* 82h 127c
7 ch g Muhtarram(USA) —Tenderfoot (Be My Chief (USA))
1911[11]
2243[2] (2529)
2587[F] 3690[5] 4095[5] 4502[2] 4972[2] 5204[2]

Muhtenbar *Ms A E Embiricos* 119h 100c
11 b g Muhtarram(USA) —Ardenbar (Ardross)
4696[5]

Muirhead (IRE) *Noel Meade* 157h 129c
8 b g Flemensfirth(USA) —Silaoce (FR) (Nikos)
2119a[5]

Mujada *David O'Meara*
6 b m Mujahid(USA) —Catriona (Bustino)
92[P] 2370[P]

Mujamead *Sally-Anne Wheelwright* 92h 92c
7 b g Mujahid(USA) —Island Mead (Pharly (FR))
410[3] 698[4] 845[9] 1049[3] (1095) 1137[3]
2326[5] 2468[3] 2930[10] 2986[P] 3618[4] 3875[2] 4103[3]
4264[5]

Mulaazem *Derek Frankland* 86h
8 b g King's Best(USA) —Harayir (USA) (Gulch (USA))
465[3] 793[3] 932[8] 1063[3] 1433[6] 1554[9] 1704[5] 1902[8] 2114[5]

Muldoon's Picnic (IRE) *Kim Bailey* 130h
5 b g King's Theatre(IRE) —Going My Way (Henbit (USA))
(2109) 3196[4] 3505[3] 5186[5]

Mulligan's Pride (IRE) *James Moffatt* 86h
10 b g Kahyasi—Babs Mulligan (IRE) (Le Bavard (FR))
604[5] 999[3] 1141[6] 1428[4] 1559[7] (1760)

Mulranny (IRE) *Nigel Twiston-Davies* 52h
6 br g Whitmore's Conn(USA) —Tirhala (IRE) (Chief Singer)
1071[4] 1284[8] 1603[7]

Mumbles Head (IRE) *Peter Bowen* 129h 140c
10 ch g Flemensfirth(USA) —Extra Mile (Torus)
844[F]

Mumbles Pier (IRE) *Peter Bowen* 115h 125c
6 b g Definite Article—Golden Jorden (IRE) (Cadeaux Genereux)
196[13] **357[F]**
565[4] 828[P] (1019)

Munching Mike (IRE) *Michael Scudamore* 75h
8 br g Orpen(USA) —Stargard (Polish Precedent (USA))
1232[P]

Munich (IRE) *Roger Curtis* 82h
7 b g Noverre(USA) —Mayara (IRE) (Ashkalani (IRE))
1111[8]

Munlochy Bay *Matt Sheppard* 105h
7 b m Karinga Bay—Meghdoot (Celestial Storm (USA))
2094[5] 2514[6] 2955[8] 4079[7] 4441[5]

Muntami (IRE) *John Harris* 101h 71c
10 gr g Daylami(IRE) —Bashashah (IRE) (Kris)
351[P] 888[7] 2247[6]
2422[5] 3305[P] 3694[4] 4236[3] 4741[5] 5130[3] 5350[3]

Muraqeb *Harry Chisman* 56h
11 ch g Grand Lodge(USA) —Oh So Well (IRE) (Sadler's Wells (USA))
697[P] 1745[P]

Murcar *Alison Thorpe* 116h
6 ch g Medicean—In Luck (In The Wings)
191[7] (379) 583[3] 744[5] 958[4] 1138[2] 1254[3] 1364[4] 3299[P] 3962[2] 4521[4]

Murchan High (IRE) *Jim Best* 82b
6 b m Rainbow High—Murchan Tyne (IRE) (Good Thyne (USA))
4505[5] *4923[7]* 5056[2]

Murdoch *Colin Tizzard* 72h
7 b g Mutamarkiz(IRE) —Miss Pharly (Pharly (FR))
4528[4] 5035[8] 5274[3]

Murfreesboro *Alan Jones* 44h
8 b g Bahamian Bounty—Merry Rous (Rousillon (USA))
2323[P] 3253[P] 3701[7]

Murphys Appeal (IRE) *Peter Bowen* 80h
7 b m Lord Of Appeal—Murphys Lady (IRE) (Over The River (FR))
1043[4] 1232[7] 1446[7] 1647[2] 4273[P]

Murphys Beau (IRE) *Mrs S Foster* 88h 68c
9 bb g Beau Sher—Royal Broderick (IRE) (Lancastrian)
1423[3] 1663[3] 1784[2] 1933[4] 4553[P]

Murphy's Choice *Paul Webber* 86b
4 b g Sakhee(USA) —Ballet Princess (Muhtarram (USA))
4457[8]

Murphys Future *Alan Berry* 61h
6 b g Where Or When(IRE) —Snaefell Heights (Suave Dancer (USA))
209[12] 945[4] 1115[10] 1375[4]

Murrell (IRE) *Henry Hogarth* 103h
6 b g Dushyantor(USA) —Lady Mayday (IRE) (Strong Gale)
2058[2] 3851[14] 4278[7] 5094[P]

Musashi (IRE) *Laura Mongan* 106h
6 ch g Hawk Wing(USA) —Soubrette (USA) (Opening Verse (USA))
(1549) 1971[7] 4670[3]

Musca (IRE) *John Wade* 70h
7 b g Tendulkar(USA) —Canary Bird (IRE) (Catrail (USA))
400[8] 468[6]

Musical Affair *F Jordan* 42h
7 b m Alflora(IRE) —Song For Jess (IRE) (Accordion)
250[F] 384[9] 585[P]

Musical Script (USA) *Mouse Hamilton-Fairley*
8 b g Stravinsky(USA) —Cyrillic (USA) (Irish River (FR))
1899[P]

Musical Wedge *Claire Dyson* 97h
7 ch g Sir Harry Lewis(USA) —Wedge Musical (What A Guest)
(59) 1959[11] 2469[4] 3297[6] 3919[7] 4481[6]

Music In The Air *Robin Dickin* 92b
7 ch m Kadastrof(FR) —Makin Whoopee (IRE) (Air Display (USA))
686[3] 1472[2] 2074[4]

Music Of The Moor (IRE) *Tom Tate* 118h
4 ch g Rock Of Gibraltar(IRE) —A La Longue (GER) (Mtoto)
(3443) 3885[P] 4165[2]

Mustakhlas (USA) *Brian Baugh* 89h
10 ch g Diesis—Katiba (USA) (Gulch (USA))
341[P]

Mustamad *Chris Gordon* 92h 80c
8 b g Anabaa(USA) —Nasanice (IRE) (Nashwan (USA))
652[7] 864[6] (991)
1106[5] 1290[4]

Mustangsallyrally (IRE) *R Barber* 125h 121c
10 br g Mister Lord(USA) —Castle Dante (IRE) (Phardante (FR))
153[3] (586)
4449[5]

Mut'Ab (USA) *Edward Creighton* 106h
6 b g Alhaarth(IRE) —Mistle Song (Nashwan (USA))
1899[3] 2129[6] 3376[6] 3882[4] 4125[2] 4450[3] (4920) 5396[2]

Mutadarek *Ms Joanna Morgan* 125h
10 b g Machiavellian(USA) —Nasheed (USA) (Riverman (USA))
3474a[3]

Mutadarrej (IRE) *Ian Williams* 111h
7 ch g Fantastic Light(USA) —Najayeb (USA) (Silver Hawk (USA))
1278[2] 1433[3] 1571[2] 1603[3]

Mutanaker *Ed de Giles* 80h
4 b g Cape Cross(IRE) —Purple Haze (IRE) (Spectrum (IRE))
3767[13] 5059[5]

Mutual Friend (USA) *David Pipe* 141h 134c
7 gr g Aljabr(USA) —Dubai Visit (USA) (Quiet American (USA))
207[8] **(422)**
518[2]

Mutual Respect (IRE) *Evan Williams* 85h 122c
9 b g Moscow Society(USA) —Deepest Thoughts (IRE) (Supreme Leader)
130[3] (437)
475[3] 680[4] (952)
1022[4] (Dead)

Muzak (IRE) *John Monroe* 110h
8 ro g Moscow Society(USA) —Shir Rose (IRE) (Roselier (FR))
1155a[6]

Muzey's Princess *Michael Mullineaux* 71b
5 b m Grape Tree Road—Premier Princess (Hard Fought)
27[7] 718[7] 1196[3] 1449[9] 1724[P]

Mvuto *Lucy Wadham* 104h
6 b m Mtoto—Cavina (Ardross)
157[3]

Mwaleshi *Donald McCain* 81h
6 b g Oscar(IRE) —Roxy River (Ardross)
319[15] 800[3]

My Arch *Ollie Pears* 123h 127c
9 b g Silver Patriarch(IRE) —My Desire (Grey Desire)
3092[2]

My Boy Paddy (IRE) *Nigel Twiston-Davies* 119h
7 ch g Accordion—Securon Rose (IRE) (Roselier (FR))
2067[2] (2642)

My Brother Sylvest *David Brace* 111h
5 b g Bach(IRE) —Senna Da Silva (Prince Of Birds (USA))
(1567) 1768[6] 1862[8] 2419[4] 2634[8] 4113[13] 4776[4]

Mycenean Prince (USA) *Karen Tutty* 95h 70c
8 b g Swain(IRE) —Nijinsky's Beauty (USA) (Nijinsky (CAN))
(1064) 1199[7] (1450)
1901[P] 2937[13] 3727[3] 3993[8] 4390[6] 4550[7] 5130[9] (5307)

My Clementine (IRE) *Michael Easterby* 78b
6 b m Classic Cliche(IRE) —Kimpour (FR) (Hawker's News (IRE))
50[13] 225[P]

My Condor (IRE) *Donald McCain* 90h 100c
10 b g Beneficial—Margellen's Castle (IRE) (Castle Keep)
(233) **404[F]**
652[3] 950[4] (1106)
1273[5]

My Destination (FR) *P Journiac*
6 b m Sleeping Car(FR) —Doree Du Pin (FR) (April Night (FR))
2265a[5]

My Fella (IRE) *Seamus Mullins* 109h
8 gr g Insatiable(IRE) —Deep Impact (Deep Run)
218[P] 647[F]

My Friend George *Dianne Sayer* 51b
5 ch g Alflora(IRE) —Snowgirl (IRE) (Mazaad)
5264[13]

My Friend Sandy *Jim Old* 122h 125c
10 ch g Anshan—Gaye Fame (Ardross)
4080[U]

My Idea *Maurice Barnes* 62b
5 b g Golan(IRE) —Ghana (GER) (Bigstone (IRE))
60[6] 637[8] 5033[5] 5342[13]

My Island Rose (IRE) *Julie Camacho* 42b
5 gr m Turtle Island(IRE) —Beagan Rose (IRE) (Roselier (FR))
4457[12] 5034[10]

My Kinda Guy *Andrew Crook*
4 b g Iktibas—Anneka (Among Men (USA))
4005[7]

My Legal Lady *Stuart Howe* 94b
6 b m Sir Harry Lewis(USA) —Clifton Mist (Lyphento (USA))
3936[7] 5403[P]

My Les *Jim Best* 84h
5 b m Josr Algarhoud(IRE) —Ashantiana (Ashkalani (IRE))
2070[P] 3397[P]

Mylo *Jonjo O'Neill* 108h 113c
13 gr g Faustus(USA) —Bellifontaine (FR) (Bellypha)
341[5]

Mylord Collonges (FR) *Susan Nock* 81h 108c
11 bl g Video Rock(FR) —Diane Collonges (FR) (El Badr)
2073[U] 2453[2] 4139[3]

My Lucky Lady (IRE) *Roger Curtis*
5 b m Bishop Of Cashel—The Flying Nun (IRE) (Torus)
4484[11]

Mymateeric *Jeff Pearce* 102h
5 b g Reset(AUS) —Ewenny (Warrshan (USA))
3303[6]

My Matilda *Lawney Hill* 87h
8 gr m Silver Patriarch(IRE) —Upton Lass (IRE) (Crash Course)
(217) 587[2]

My Moment (IRE) *Henry Daly* 126h 134c
8 ch g Presenting—Golden Moment (IRE) (Roselier (FR))
194[5] 2077[6] 2520[F] 3949[8] 4913[2] 5305[5]

My Only Boy *Michael Madgwick* 33b
6 b g Carisbrooke—Jaydeebee (Buckley)
1680[9] 1906[7]

My Pal Val (IRE) *John Panvert* 74h 104c
11 br g Classic Cliche(IRE) —Lessons Lass (IRE) (Doyoun)
755[5] 794[P] (864)
961[2] 1070[4] 1163[4]

My Rosie Ribbons (IRE) *Zoe Davison* 64h
12 b m Roselier(FR) —Georgic (Tumble Gold)
2183[4] 2391[P] 2532[P]

My Runaway (IRE) *Michael Blake* 4h
5 b g Luso—Arran Mews (IRE) (Persian Mews)
5437[6]

Mysaynoway *Lawney Hill* 49h 88c
9 br m Overbury(IRE) —Chinook's Daughter (IRE) (Strong Gale)
1057[8]

My Shamwari (IRE) *Philip Hobbs* 132h
7 b g Flemensfirth(USA) —Quilty Rose (Buckskin (FR))
2868[12] 3874[7] (4862) (5287)

Mystic Appeal (IRE) *Jeremy Scott* 91b
5 br g Alderbrook—Piseog (IRE) (Pistolet Bleu (IRE))
4468[8] 5157[8]

Mystic Echo *John Davies* 68b
5 b m Overbury(IRE) —Sunday News'N'Echo (USA) (Trempolino (USA))
230[11] 474[6] 732[8]

Mystic Touch *Andrew Haynes* 87h
5 b g Systematic—Lycius Touch (Lycius (USA))
850[4] 917[5] 1031[6] 1300[3] 1551[12]

Mytara *Pam Sly* 98h
6 br m Kayf Tara—Myumi (Charmer)
3715[7] 3987[6]

Mythical Prince *Evan Williams* 132h 103c
7 b g Alhaarth(IRE) —Mythical Girl (USA) (Gone West (USA))
1389[2]

My Viking Bay (IRE) *John O'Shea* 96h
7 b m Saddlers' Hall(IRE) —So Supreme (IRE) (Supreme Leader)
568[4] 1069[7] 1793[F] 2168[6] 2554[4] 3820[7] 4101[4] 4425[2] 4828[4]

My Way De Solzen (FR) *Gabe Mahon* 162h 125c
11 b g Assessor(IRE) —Agathe De Solzen (FR) (Chamberlin (FR))
(4950)

My Will (FR) *Paul Nicholls* 130h 151c
11 b g Saint Preuil(FR) —Gleep Will (FR) (Cadoudal (FR))
3290[10]

Mzuri Bay *Brendan Duke* 110h 108c
6 b g Arkadian Hero(USA) —Eyelet (IRE) (Satco (FR))
8[10] 168[3] 409[2] 559[4] (1033) 1196[5] 1275[7] 1507[8]
1568[4] 1903[2] 2669[F]

Nabouko (FR) *Susan Nock* 101h
10 br g Kadalko(FR) —Badrapette (FR) (Bad Conduct (USA))
359[3] 4021[P] **4718[P]**

Nacarat (FR) *Tom George* 130h 168c
10 gr g Smadoun(FR) —Gerbora (FR) (Art Bleu)
(2091)
2524[4] 3560[4] 4352[3] (5162)

Nadiya De La Vega (FR) *Nicky Henderson* 140c
5 bb m Lost World(IRE) —Shinobie (FR) (Le Nain Jaune (FR))
(2455)
(3555) 3946[6] 4794[11] 5336[3]

Nafaath (IRE) *Howard Johnson* 129h 132c
5 ch g Nayef(USA) —Alshakr (Bahri (USA))
3359[2] 3968[2] 5166[16]

Nagam (FR) *Alan Fleming* 96h 123c
10 b g Denham Red(FR) —Gamaytoise (FR) (Brezzo (FR))
1885[5]

Nahneh (IRE) *John Wade* 81b
5 b g Beneficial—Arusha Rose (IRE) (Supreme Leader)
5264[7]

Najca De Thaix (FR) *John Spearing* 121h 108c
10 bb g Marmato—Isca De Thaix (FR) (Cimon)
2280[5] (2609) 3529[5] (3724) 3934[RR]

Naledi *Richard Price* 43h
7 b g Indian Ridge—Red Carnation (IRE) (Polar Falcon (USA))
792[9]

Nalim (IRE) *Malcolm Jefferson* 74b
5 b g Milan—Hati Roy (IRE) (Lafontaine (USA))
4239[10] 4574[8] 5260[U]

Nampour (FR) *Philip Hobbs* 137h
6 gr g Daylami(IRE) —Nadira (FR) (Green Desert (USA))
94[U] 372[11]

Nanga Parbat (FR) *Paul Nicholls* 111h 116c
10 b g True Brave(USA) —Celeste (FR) (Amen (FR))
172[2]

Napoleons Mistress (IRE) *Nicky Henderson* 82h
4 ch f Peintre Celebre(USA) —State Crystal (IRE) (High Estate)
4781[F]

Napoletano (ITY) *Robert Johnson* 75h
5 b g Kyllachy—Nationality (Nashwan (USA))
3521[10] 3994[6] 4361[4] 4872[9]

Naranga *Richard Phillips* 76b
5 ch g Generous(IRE) —D'Egliere (FR) (Port Etienne (FR))
3920[8]

Narima (GER) *Mervyn Torrens* 106h
4 b f Sabiango(GER) —Nanouska (GER) (Dashing Blade)
3239a[8]

Narrandera (IRE) *J A Berry* 68b
8 b g Corrouge(USA) —Imlistening (IRE) (Tremblant)
3208a[10]

Nascar (FR) *Mlle M-L Mortier*
8 ch g Volochine(IRE) —Algazelle (FR) (Mister Sicy (FR))
190a[2]

Naseby (USA) *Sam Davison*
4 ch g Maria's Mon(USA) —Branchbury (USA) (Mt. Livermore (USA))
1772[P]

Natacha Rochelaise (FR) *P Quinton*
10 b m Assessor(IRE) —Gazelle Rochelaise (FR) (The Wonder (FR))
312a[F]

Natal (FR) *J J Lambe* 104h 154c
10 b g Funny Baby(FR) —Donitille (FR) (Italic (FR))
1113a[5]

National Heritage *Micky Hammond* 90h
6 b g High Chaparral(IRE) —French Quartet (IRE) (Lycius (USA))
837[6] 1329[7] 1624[8] 1700[3] **1995[R]**

National Obsession (IRE) *Venetia Williams* 85h
8 b g Bob Back(USA) —Retinue (IRE) (Mister Lord (USA))
76[5]

National Trust *Edward Creighton* 122h 97c
9 b g Sadler's Wells(USA) —National Treasure (Shirley Heights)
756[8] **1796[3]**
(1937) (2279) (2610) *3057[4]* 3303[4] 3947[16]

Native American *Tim McCarthy* 70h
9 b g Indian Lodge(IRE) —Summer Siren (FR) (Saint Cyrien (FR))
532[P] 1294[5]

Native Art (IRE) *Rachel Hobbs* 34h
6 br g Definite Article—Artic Native (IRE) (Be My Native (USA))
3842[7] 4719[12]

Native Bob (IRE) *J M Turner* 91h 94c
7 ch g Bob Back(USA) —Beaver Run (IRE) (Be My Native (USA))
61[F] 293[P]

Native Breeze (IRE) *Philip Hobbs* 95b
6 br m Flemensfirth(USA) —Roaming (IRE) (Be My Native (USA))
319[4] 1771[4]

Native Cherry *George Yardley*
10 b m Commanche Run—Cherry Sip (Nearly A Hand)
1742[P]

Native City (IRE) *Jonjo O'Neill* 110h 116c
9 b g City Honours(USA) —Fourroads-Native (IRE) (Be My Native (USA))
608[8] 769[7] 1200[P] 1276[6] 1476[2]

Native Coll *N W Alexander* 51h 92c
11 ch g Primitive Rising(USA) —Harrietfield (Nicholas Bill)
2103[6]
3360[F] 3636[F] 3884[3] 4064[P] 4573[4] 5093[7]

Native Coral (IRE) *Nicky Richards* 86h 125c
13 ch g Be My Native(USA) —Deep Coral (IRE) (Buckskin (FR))
308[6] (874) 1198[8] **1871[8]**

Native Gallery (IRE) *Ben De Haan* 114h 114c
6 gr g Portrait Gallery(IRE) —Native Bev (IRE) (Be My Native (USA))
2281[4] ◆ 2428[2] **(3865)**

Native Taipan (IRE) *Rebecca Curtis* 114h
9 b g Taipan(IRE) —Ryansnative (IRE) (Be My Native (USA))
(15) 409[3] 2147[12] 2574[7]

Natural Action *Peter Bowen* 125h
7 b g Diktat—Naskhi (Nashwan (USA))
5110[6] 5304[10]

Naturally Royal *Lawney Hill* 28h
8 bb g Naturalist—Tree Poppy (Rolfe (USA))
5381[2]

Natural Spring *Suzy Smith* 104h
6 b m Generous(IRE) —Highbrook (USA) (Alphabatim (USA))
332[3] 2087[4] 2526[5] *3168[2]* 3505[4]

Natureofthebeast (IRE) *Evan Williams* 119h
6 b g Definite Article—Mrs Battleaxe (IRE) (Supreme Leader)
(1729) (1941) ◆ 2584[4] 3454[F]

Natures Way (IRE) *Jonjo O'Neill* 62h
5 b g Old Vic—Furry Hope (Furry Glen)
1148[8] 1445[9]

Naughtyatiz (IRE) *Debra Hamer* 87h
5 b g Beneficial—My Miss Molly (IRE) (Entitled I)
1349[3] 1455[6] 2231[7] 3762[12] 4006[7] 4450[6] 4785[5]

Naughty By Nature *Rebecca Curtis* 101h 107c
5 b g Machiavellian(USA) —Rumpipumpy (Shirley Heights)
769[2] 867[3]

Naughty Diesel *Robert Johnson* 82h 59c
8 b g Killer Instinct—Scottish Royal (IRE) (Night Shift (USA))
12[4] 161[9] 552[6]
802[8] 955[7]

Naughty Naughty *Brendan Powell* 124h
6 b m Subotica(FR) —Rocheflamme (FR) (Snurge)
379[2] 684[P] 1601[6] (1993) 2288[2] 2514[F] 2974[3] (4309) 4875[9] 5302[4]

Nautical Approach (IRE) *Alex Hales* 102h 113c
8 b g Oscar(IRE) —Creative Approach (IRE) (Toulon)
843[6] **1919[2]**
(2437)
2591[2] 2961[11] 3265[5] 5120[P]

Navajo Nation (IRE) *Bill Turner* 99h
5 b g Indian Haven—Kathy Desert (Green Desert (USA))
216[4] 537[4] 661[2] 823[4] 912[8] 1125[5] 1333[2] 1488[3] 1547[4] 1723[4] 4530[P] 4895[10] 5014[5]

Naval Attache *Fred Kirby* 48h 93c
9 b g Slip Anchor—Cayla (Tumble Wind)
403[5]

Nawow *Matt Hazell* 75h 107c
11 b g Blushing Flame(USA) —Fair Test (Fair Season)
26[U] 339[3] 463[7] 799[U] 1283[3] 1471[F] 1589[9] 1841[4] 2170[5]

Naxox (FR) *Ms A Hardy* 110h 83c
10 ch g Cupidon(FR) —Frou Frou Lou (FR) (Groom Dancer (USA))
4696[4] 4950[9]

Nearby *Philip Hobbs* 153h
7 b g King's Best(USA) —Contiguous (USA) (Danzig (USA))
316[10] (1766) (1956) ◆ (2219) 2668[5] 4188[10] 4848[3] ◆ 5201[5] 5337[7]

Nearly A Breeze *Chris Down* 90h 80c
11 b m Thowra(FR) —Nearly At Sea (Nearly A Hand)
24[7] 273[11]
2172[P]

Nearly Sunday *Donald Whillans* 87h
6 ch m Where Or When(IRE) —Special (Polar Falcon (USA))
457[3] 624[4] 871[P]

Near The Water (IRE) *Richard Rowe* 112h 114c
7 b g Oscar(IRE) —The Dark One (IRE) (Mandalus)
281[F] 2185[5]
(2591) 2959[11] 3375[2] 3878[P]

Nebeltau (GER) *Jonjo O'Neill* 71c
9 ch g Platini(GER) —Nebelharfe (Sharrood (USA))
529[P]

Necessity *Simon Dow*
4 b g Empire Maker(USA) —Fully Invested (USA) (Irish River (FR))
2597[5]

Necromancer (IRE) *Venetia Williams* 103h
8 b g Broken Hearted—Black Trix (Peacock (FR))
538[3]

Ned Ludd (IRE) *Jonathan Portman* 124h
8 b g Montjeu(IRE) —Zanella (IRE) (Nordico (USA))
2393[2] 2868[15] 4488[13] 4933[7]

Nedzer's Return (IRE) *Gordon Elliott* 119h 140c
9 b g Bob's Return(IRE) —Moydanganrye (IRE) (Over The River (FR))
(442) 945[2]
1123a[8] 1527a[11]

Needwood Ridge *Frank Sheridan*
4 ch g Needwood Blade—Aspen Ridge (IRE) (Namid)
3166[11]

Negus De Beaumont (FR) *Ferdy Murphy* 105h 125c
10 b g Blushing Flame(USA) —Givry (FR) (Bayolidaan (FR))
2641[P] 3499[2] 3634[P] 4360[P]

Nehemiah *Henrietta Knight* 93h
7 b g Mtoto—Sharp Move (Night Shift (USA))
25[7] 528[4]

Neil Harvey (IRE) *Nick Gifford* 125h 127c
8 b g Winged Love(IRE) —At Dawn (IRE) (Lashkari)
3902[3] (4666)

Nelliedonethat (IRE) *Lucinda Russell* 101h 114c
11 b g Warcraft(USA) —Kilmana (IRE) (Castle Keep)
213[7] 1697[7] 1933[6] 2602[3] (3549)
4060[4] 4997[3]

Nelson Du Ronceray (FR) *P Monteith* 115h 125c
10 b g Lute Antique(FR) —Trieste (FR) (Quart De Vin (FR))
194[9] 393[4] 627[10]

Nelson's Chief *James Ewart* 106h
5 b g Kayf Tara—Lady Lenor (Presidium)
576[7] 4059[4] 4393[8] (5428)

Nelson's Spice (IRE) *Jonjo O'Neill* 94h 134c
10 b g Presenting—My Native Glen (IRE) (Be My Native (USA))
524[9] 764[P]

Neltara *Claire Dyson* 104h
7 b g Kayf Tara—Lucia Forte (Neltino)
4932[5]

Nemetan (FR) *Victor Dartnall* 107h 118c
10 ch g Port Lyautey(FR) —Annabelle Treveene (FR) (Spoleto)
4481[2] ◆ 5153[3]

Nemo Spirit (IRE) *Tim Vaughan* 105h
6 gr g Daylami(IRE) —La Bayadere (Sadler's Wells (USA))
3158[3] 3528[5] 3762[4]

Nephele (IRE) *Tim Easterby* 6h
4 gr f Antonius Pius(USA) —Grey Clouds (Cloudings (IRE))
2033[11]

Neptune Collonges (FR) *Paul Nicholls* 155h 169c
10 gr g Dom Alco(FR) —Castille Collonges (FR) (El Badr)
2673[8] 2871[11] (3805)
4850[8] 5338[6]

Neptune Equester *Brian Ellison* 133h 136c
8 b g Sovereign Water(FR) —All Things Nice (Sweet Monday)
33[2] ◆ (425)
(605) (2077) ◆ 2401[F] 2939[4] 3567[2] 4206[3]
◆ 5338[11]

Nesnaas (USA) *Mark Rimell* 83h 99c
10 ch g Gulch(USA) —Sedrah (USA) (Dixieland Band (USA))
26[3] 233[6] 463[5] 689[6] 891[2] 1023[7] 1152[2] 1327[5]
1493[3] 1589[7] 1732[7]

Nessa *P York* 76h 91c
8 b m Spendent—Lancastrianventure (IRE) (Lancastrian)
294[P]

Nether Stream (IRE) *Shaun Lycett* 104h
7 b g Blueprint(IRE) —Shuil Ub (Le Moss)
409[P] 763[6] 956[2] 1111[9] 1129[4] 1295[U] (1470) 1569[P]

Net Lovely (FR) *E Clayeux* 123h
5 b m Network(GER) —Line Lovely (FR) (Mansonnien (FR))
2265a[2]

Neutrino *David Bridgwater* 93h 120c
9 b g Mtoto—Fair Seas (General Assembly (USA))
5[4] 489[P] (677)
(764) 852[6] 1044[6] 1277[3]

Nevada Royale (FR) *Tim Pitt* 129h 140c
10 gr g Garde Royale—Ahhotep (FR) (Sambrezan (FR))
2522[6] 4357[3] 5185[B]

Nevertika (FR) *James Ewart* 117h 144c
10 b g Subotica(FR) —Griotte De Coddes (FR) (Silver Rainbow)
44[2]

Nevsky Bridge *Martin Todhunter* 100h 91c
9 b m Soviet Star(USA) —Pontressina (USA) (St Jovite (USA))
166[4]

New Alco (FR) *Ferdy Murphy* 120h 126c
10 bb g Dom Alco(FR) —Cabira Des Saccart (FR) (Quart De Vin (FR))
2358[P] 4357[5]

Newbay Bob *Nick Mitchell* 80h 115c
11 b g Bob Back(USA) —Guinda (IRE) (Corvaro (USA))
181[2] 2483[F]

New Code *Gary Moore* 48h
4 ch g Reset(AUS) —Illeana (GER) (Lomitas)
3554[9]

Newdane Dancer (IRE) *Howard Johnson* 68h
4 b f Golan(IRE) —Flagofconvienience (IRE) (Old Vic)
(3576) 4245[4]

New Den *Jim Boyle* 44h
4 ch g Piccolo—Den's-Joy (Archway (IRE))
4424[7] 4847[P]

Newgatehopeful *Mark Campion*
7 b g Elmaamul(USA) —Newgate Bubbles (Hubbly Bubbly (USA))
693[10] 3877[P] 4278[8]

Newlyn Bay *Caroline Keevil* 84h
6 b g Alflora(IRE) —Broughton Manor (Dubassoff (USA))
5108[8] 5437[4]

Newman Des Plages (FR) *Martin Todhunter* 34h 130c
10 b g Passing Sale(FR) —Reine Des Plages (FR) (Torvay (FR))
(1763)
2543[F] 3522[P] 4360[P] 4960[P]

Newmill (IRE) *James Daniel Dullea* 142h 161c
13 br g Norwich—Lady Kas (Pollerton)
3778a[4]

New Mill Moll *Kevin Bishop* 83h
8 b m Kayf Tara—Pretty Pride (IRE) (Doyoun)
132[7] 370[8]

New Phase (IRE) *D K Weld* 138h
7 b g Spectrum(IRE) —South Of Heaven (IRE) (Fairy King (USA))
1133a[12] 3474a[22]

Newport Rose *Ben Case* 87b
5 b m Alflora(IRE) —Newport (FR) (Hawker's News (IRE))
4505[4]

New Rackheath (IRE) *Mark Shears* 86h 90c
8 b g Norwich—Bonne Sante (IRE) (Tremblant)
54[4] **533[4]**
(652)
1273[P] 1335[P]
1474[P]

New Shuil (IRE) *John Wade* 97h 113c
7 b g New Frontier(IRE) —Shuil Ura (IRE) (Phardante (FR))
1645[P] 1830[2] (2507)
3552[P]

New Street Express (IRE) *Paul Blagg* 72h 80c
10 b g Portrait Gallery(IRE) —Toome Lady (Lord Gayle (USA))
153[9] 294[6]

New Team (FR) *Mrs T Porter* 115h 63c
10 ch g Green Tune(USA) —Fortuna Jet (FR) (Highest Honor (FR))
4011[8]

Newton Tonic *Alex Hales* 91h
6 b g Sir Harry Lewis(USA) —Wedidthat (IRE) (Moscow Society (USA))
53[6] 2560[4] 2925[9] 3701[3] 3897[5] 4721[P]

Newyearsresolution (IRE) *Nick Mitchell* 97h
7 b g Mr Combustible(IRE) —That's Magic (IRE) (Lord Americo)
1349[5] 1553[4] 1703[3] 2637[9] 2980[9] 3300[4]

Next Exit (IRE) *Tim Vaughan*
6 b g Exit To Nowhere(USA) —Pilgrim Star (IRE) (Marju (IRE))
3167[4]

Next Man In (IRE) *Alan King* 87b
5 b g Trans Island—I'Ll Be Waiting (Vettori (IRE))
2632[8] 3266[8] 3920[6] 4468[15]

Next To Nowhere (IRE) *Nicky Richards* 100h
6 ch g Exit To Nowhere(USA) —Zarote (IRE) (Mandalus)
4303[3] 4541[4]

Niamh's Way (IRE) *Liam Lennon* 102h
10 b m Oscar(IRE) —Zoria (IRE) (Tender King)
(858) 1140[5] (Dead)

Nicanor (FR) *Noel Meade* 142h 137c
10 b g Garde Royale—Uthane (FR) (Baly Rockette)
1038a[5]
1123a[12] 1801a[4]

Niceboy (IRE) *Nick Gifford* 66h
7 br g Environment Friend—Take The Catch (Relief Pitcher)
2456[10]

Nicene Creed *Philip Hobbs* 130h
6 b g Hernando(FR) —First Fantasy (Be My Chief (USA))
(1819) 1988[4] (2634) 2887[7] 4354[6] 4940[3] 5304[7]

Niceonefrankie *Venetia Williams* 113h
5 b g Ishiguru(USA) —Chesnut Ripple (Cosmonaut)
58[2] ◆ (554) 710[4] 3228[6] 3490[11] 4049[6] 4439[5] 5424[P]

Niche Market (IRE) *Paul Nicholls* 153c
10 b g Presenting—Juresse (IRE) (Jurado (USA))
2221[F] 2673[5] 4487[8] 5200[5]

Nicholas The Spark (IRE) *Mrs Angela Davis* 79b
9 b g Saddlers' Hall(IRE) —Merapi (Roi Guillaume (FR))
4901[P]

Nick The Silver *Robert Johnson* 74h 92c
10 gr g Nicolotte—Brillante (FR) (Green Dancer (USA))
4390[10]
4799[P] 5029[3] 5258[12]

Nicky Nutjob (GER) *John O'Shea* 102h
5 b g Fasliyev(USA) —Natalie Too (USA) (Irish River (FR))
159[8] 351[P] 555[3] 2054[10] 2323[3] 2421[4] 3818[7] 4008[9] 4999[9]

Nicky Tam (IRE) *Henry Hogarth* 83h 105c
9 bb g Presenting—Wigmore (IRE) (Denel (FR))
4551[4] 4799[3] (5258)
(5417)

Nicto De Beauchene (FR) *Victor Dartnall* 92h 143c
10 b g Nashamaa—Chipie D'Angron (FR) (Grand Tresor (FR))
2106[P] 2962[3] (3444)
4208[P] 4876[P]

Nifty Roy *Brian Storey* 39h 80c
11 b g Royal Applause—Nifty Fifty (IRE) (Runnett)
9[P] 2194[4] 2601[7] 4064[7] 4690[3] 4827[4] 5258[11]

Night Force *Howard Johnson* 110h
8 br g Sovereign Water(FR) —Oatis Rose (Oats)
89[6]

Night In Milan (IRE) *Keith Reveley* 112h
5 b g Milan—Chione (IRE) (Mandalus)
2202[8] 2939[7] 3398[6] (3622) 3728[3] (4138) 4358[5] 4869[5]

Night Knight (IRE) *Chris Grant* 88h
5 b g Bachelor Duke(USA) —Dark Albatross (USA) (Sheikh Albadou)
286[6] 604[8] 1380[6]

Night Orbit *Julia Feilden* 127h 121c
7 b g Observatory(USA) —Dansara (Dancing Brave (USA))
1432[3] 1602[3] 2278[2] 3598[P] 4285[8] 4742[8] 4975[2]

Night Rose *Alan King* 90b
5 b m Midnight Legend—Fortunes Course (IRE) (Crash Course)
4082[9] 4335[5] 5157[6]

Niki Royal (FR) *Barry Potts* 84h
6 b m Nikos—Balgarde (FR) (Garde Royale)
4134[2] ◆

Nik Nak Too *Seamus Mullins* 32h
5 b g Loup Sauvage(USA) —Colline De Feu (Sabrehill (USA))
3773[16] 4444[11] 4917[15]

Nikola (FR) *Nigel Twiston-Davies* 124h 132c
10 b g Roi De Rome(USA) —Envie De Chalamont (FR) (Pamponi (FR))
236[7] 1606[2] 2086[9] 2541[2] 3438[P] 4221[P]

Nikos Extra (FR) *Alan King* 122h 141c
7 b g Nikos—Madame Extra (FR) (Sir Brink (FR))
236[5] 1828[F] (4941)
5317[6]

Nile Moon (IRE) *Mrs C Sutcliffe* 93h 111c
10 b g Simply Great(FR) —Reasonable Time (IRE) (Reasonable (FR))
46[3] 213[3] 489[2] 746[3] 804[P] 4915[6]

Nine De Sivola (FR) *Ferdy Murphy* 127h 118c
10 b g Video Rock(FR) —Quine De Chalamont (FR) (Do Do (FR))
3548[2]

Nine Stories (IRE) *Howard Johnson* 129h 123c
6 b g Catcher In The Rye(IRE) —Irinatinvidio (Rudimentary (USA))
44[3] (2373)
(4472)

Ninogaro (FR) *Linda Blackford* 53h
6 b g Ungaro(GER) —Nina Bird (FR) (Rose Laurel)
134[10] 273[8]

Ninon De Grissay (FR) *F-H Hayeres*
10 b m Saint Preuil(FR) —Vemarvis (FR) (Djarvis (FR))
312a[2]

Nintytwo Team (IRE) *Paul John Gilligan* 138h 124c
9 ch g Golden Tornado(IRE) —Administer (Damister (USA))
(687) ◆ **1113a[U]**

Ni Plus Ni Moins (FR) *P Journiac*
10 gr m Kadalko(FR) —Almeida (FR) (Royal Charter (FR))
312a[3]

Nipper Nial *R MacDonald*
6 b g Overbury(IRE) —Pinch (Ardross)
47[P]

Nirvana Du Bourg (FR) *R A Wilson* 121h 84c
10 bb g Cadoudal(FR) —Gnosca (FR) (Matahawk)
493[7] 4147[5]

Nisaal (IRE) *Sandy Forster* 92h
6 b g Indian Ridge—Kahalah (IRE) (Darshaan)
4165[8] 4910[11] 5147[4] 5429[5]

Nisaro De Cimbre (FR) *L Viel*
4 b g Bonbon Rose(FR) —Belle De Liziere (FR) (Bojador (FR))
5047a[6]

Nishnash *Jim Wilson* 25h
8 b g Commanche Run—Rosehall (Ardross)
232[9] 436[6] 863[8] 1742[12]

Noakarad De Verzee (FR) *Mrs Kim Smyly* 131c
10 b g Roakarad—Taratata (FR) (Prove It Baby (USA))
4315[3] 4851[11]

Nobby Kivambo (IRE) *Brendan Powell* 103h
6 b g Anabaa(USA) —Kivavite (USA) (Kingmambo (USA))
407[4] 585[7] 688[3] 915a[4] 1137[4] 1261[2] **1360[F]**
1451[7] 1605[2] 1730[2] 2080[2] 2630[6] 3260[5] 3589[4]
4052[4] 4407[3] 4812[4] 5195[7]

Nobel (FR) *Brian Storey* 80h 68c
10 gr g Dadarissime(FR) —Eire Dancer (FR) (Useful (FR))
10[2] 490[2] 698[6] 1064[2] 1361[6]

Nobel Play *Debra Hamer* 17h
7 b m Silver Patriarch(IRE) —Mothers Help (Relief Pitcher)
168[P] 535[P]

Nobetter Buachaill (IRE) *J J Lambe* 95h
9 ch g Carroll House—Current Liability (Caribo)
514[4] 729[5]

Noble Alan (GER) *Nicky Richards* 133h 146c
8 gr g King's Theatre(IRE) —Nirvavita (FR) (Highest Honor (FR))
1886[3]
(2206) 2517[3] 2886[F] 3949[7]

Noble Aran (IRE) *Nigel Twiston-Davies* 88h 84c
7 b g Beneficial—Sue Pickering (IRE) (Tremblant)
2796[4] 3226[4] 3765[5]

Noble Bily (FR) *Neil King* 108h 115c
10 b g Signe Divin(USA) —Vaillante Bily (FR) (The Quiet Man (FR))
2529[5] 3347[P] 4428[2] 4705[5]

Noble Commander (IRE) *James Halpin* 116h 105c
8 b g Charente River(IRE) —Fern Fields (IRE) (Be My Native (USA))
860[8]

Noble Concorde *J H Culloty* 114h 132c
9 gr g Daylami(IRE) —Place De L'Opera (Sadler's Wells (USA))
4876[P]

Noble Crusader (USA) *Richard Lee* 116h 129c
8 b g Giant's Causeway(USA) —Suitably Discreet (USA) (Mr Prospector (USA))
(2293)
4460[4] 5009[P] 5399[6]

Noble Edge *Lee James* 62h
8 ch g Bold Edge—Noble Soul (Sayf El Arab (USA))
12[P] 5130[13]

Noble Future *Venetia Williams* 80h 93c
9 b g Averti(IRE) —Gold Luck (USA) (Slew O'Gold (USA))
156[2]

Noble Perk *Adrian Wintle* 105b
6 ch g Executive Perk—Far From Perfect (IRE) (Phardante (FR))
3441[2] 5113[11]

Noble Prince (GER) *Paul Nolan* 150h 164c
7 b g Montjeu(IRE) —Noble Pearl (GER) (Dashing Blade)
3241a[2] 3705a[2] (4816) ◆

Noble Request (FR) *Philip Hobbs* 117h 141c
10 gr g Highest Honor(FR) —Restless Mixa (IRE) (Linamix (FR))
207[15] **(464)**
770[U]

Noble Ruler *George Baker* 71h
5 b g Black Sam Bellamy(IRE) —Nobilissima (GER) (Bluebird (USA))
4029[9]

Noble Scholar (IRE) *Alan Swinbank* 105h
6 b g Anabaa(USA) —Lisieux Rose (IRE) (Generous (IRE))
(474) (731) 2102[4] 2446[3] *3090[3] 3168[10]*

Nobody's Business (IRE) *Zoe Davison* 38h
10 ch g Carroll House—Arctic Crush (IRE) (Phardante (FR))
4665[F] 4918[7]

Nobody Tells Me (FR) *E Walker* 116h 115c
10 bb g Lute Antique(FR) —Becebege (FR) (Iron Duke (FR))
151[3] 406[2] 4786[6]

Nobunaga *Venetia Williams* 119h
6 ch g Beat Hollow—Absolute Precision (USA) (Irish River (FR))
(3739) 4129[P] 5071[3]

Nocatee (IRE) *C Rae* 67h 46c
10 b g Vettori(IRE) —Rosy Sunset (IRE) (Red Sunset)
4286[5] 4915[P] 5263[P]

Nodanawink *Donald McCain* 77h 40c
10 b g Shahrastani(USA) —Twenty Winks (Gunner B)
97[9] 341[6] **597[P]**

Noddies Way *John Panvert* 96h
8 b g Nomadic Way(USA) —Sharway Lady (Shareef Dancer (USA))
2482[7] 4539[3] 4929[13] 5289[11] 5404[4]

Nodebateaboutit *Tom George* 94h
6 b g Alflora(IRE) —Mystere (IRE) (Montelimar (USA))
4719[7]

Nodform Richard *Karen McLintock* 109b
5 b g Groom Dancer(USA) —Shayzara (IRE) (Turtle Island (IRE))
(4916)

Nodforms Paula (IRE) *Milton Harris* 112h
8 b g Rashar(USA) —Monamandy (IRE) (Mandalus)
2147[6]
2670[U] 4179[U]

Nodforms Violet (IRE) *Karen McLintock* 123h
7 ch g Rashar(USA) —Whose Yer Wan (IRE) (Remainder Man)
710[3] 943 [3] 2361[6] *3169[12]* 3334[2] 3556[7] 5316[P]

Nodform William *Karen McLintock* 102h
9 b g Prince Sabo—Periwinkle (FR) (Perrault)
2448[P] *3169[3]* 3335[6]

No Greater Love (FR) *Mrs T Porter* 101h 84c
9 b g Take Risks(FR) —Desperate Virgin (BEL) (Chief Singer)
233[P] 689[P] 921[4] 1094[12] **1293[4] 4950[8] 5372[9]**

No Idea *Tim Vaughan* 81b
6 ch m Karinga Bay—Ollejess (Scallywag)
5056[3] 5426[7]

Noir Et Vert (FR) *N W Alexander* 112h 100c
10 b g Silver Rainbow—Danse Verte (FR) (Brezzo (FR))
4307[2]

Noir Noir *Anna Newton-Smith* 42h
6 bl m Gleaming(IRE) —Shengari (Tout Ensemble)
2130[7] 2428[F]

Noland *Paul Nicholls* 150h 150c
10 b g Exit To Nowhere(USA) —Molakai (USA) (Nureyev (USA))
3060[2] **3804[P] (4186)**

Nolecce *Richard Guest*
4 ch g Reset(AUS) —Ghassanah (Pas De Seul)
3885[P]

Nomad (FR) *Carroll Gray* 79h 35c
10 b g Brier Creek(USA) —Fortune V (FR) (Video Rock (FR))
(134) (272) 557[U] 826[11]

Nomadic Dreamer *Phillip Rowley*
8 ch g Nomadic Way(USA) —Nunsdream (Derrylin)
150[U]

Nomadic Warrior *John Holt* 99h 110c
6 b g Nomadic Way(USA) —Jesmund (Bishop Of Cashel)
351[S] 2373[9] **3612[U] 3869[3] (4237)**
(4880)

Nomansland (IRE) *Nicky Henderson* 86b
5 b g Indian Danehill(IRE) —Best Wait (IRE) (Insan (USA))
2632[6] 4484[7]

Nom De Guerre (IRE) *Ben De Haan* 115h 120c
9 b g Presenting—Asklynn (IRE) (Beau Sher)
(39)

Nomecheki (FR) *Nick Gifford* 64h 144c
9 b g Kalmoss(FR) —Kan A Dare (FR) (Apeldoorn (FR))
3808[14]
3949[2] 4853[P]

No More Prisoners (IRE) *Liam Corcoran* 101h 89c
11 b g Allstar Leader(IRE) —Kelly's Native (IRE) (Be My Native (USA))
3865[4] 4428[U] 4812[P]

Nomoretaxes (BRZ) *Debbie Mountain* 55h
9 b g First American(USA) —Raghida (BRZ) (Roi Normand (USA))
215[7]

No More Whispers (IRE) *Evan Williams* 87h 18c
6 b g Kahyasi—Dizzy's Whisper (IRE) (Supreme Leader)
59[5] **1747[7]**
2146[F] 2327[4]
2608[P] 3396[4]
3961[P]

Non Dom (IRE) *Hughie Morrison* 123h
5 br g Hawk Wing(USA) —Kafayef (USA) (Secreto (USA))
2960[15] 3344[4] ◆ (3491) (4422)

Nonobu (UAE) *George Baker* 82b
5 b m Halling(USA) —Japanese Whisper (UAE) (Machiavellian (USA))
686[8] 935[5] 1086[3]

Nono Le Sage (FR) *David Pipe* 99h
7 ch g Ultimately Lucky(IRE) —Altesse D'O (FR) (Tadj (FR))
(228) 338[4] 748[6] **1591[P]** 1741[P]

Nonotreally *Lynsey Kendall* 36h 58c
10 b g Rakaposhi King—Wellwotdouthink (Rymer)
2302[P]
4150[5] 4549[5]

No Obligation (IRE) *Brendan Powell* 105h
6 b g Oscar(IRE) —Sound Case (IRE) (Husyan (USA))
2632[5] 2963[15] 3295[10] 3454[6]

No One Tells Me *Mrs John Harrington* 137h 119c
6 ch m Dr Fong(USA) —Bajan Blue (Lycius (USA))
1133a[5]
3268a[5]

No Panic (IRE) *Peter Bowen* 122h 130c
8 b g Dushyantor(USA) —Afon Alwen (Henbit (USA))
(890) 1108[4] **(1404)**
1611[P] 1950[3] 2305[P] 4440[7] 4790[7] 5338[10]

No Planning *Sue Smith* 93b
4 b g Kayf Tara—Poor Celt (Impecunious)
5264[2]

No Principles *Julian Smith* 123h
8 b g Overbury(IRE) —Selective Rose (Derring Rose)
(2477) 4209[P]

Norborne Bandit (IRE) *Evan Williams* 100h 114c
10 b g Croco Rouge(IRE) —Saninka (IRE) (Doyoun)
361[2] 523[5] 831[3] 959[6] 1229[2] 1299[2] 1334[4] 1628[8]

Nordwind (IRE) *Evan Williams* 124h 117c
10 b g Acatenango(GER) —Narola (GER) (Nebos (GER))
736[6] 958[2] 1017[P] 1311[6] **1485[3] 1558[3]** 1827[11]

No Reception (IRE) *Lady Susan Brooke* 118h 115c
10 bb g Mister Mat(FR) —The Lar (IRE) (Remainder Man)
1136[P] 1602[4] 1725[9] 2057[5]

Norisan *Alan Jones* 97h
7 ch g Inchinor—Dream On Deya (IRE) (Dolphin Street (FR))
(267) 3483[P] 3793[P]

Normally *John Flint* 91h
7 b g Tobougg(IRE) —Constant Delight (Never So Bold)
3870[3] 4273[9] 5169[P]

Norman Beckett *Jim Best* 98h
8 b g Beckett(IRE) —Classic Coral (USA) (Seattle Dancer (USA))
402[P]

Normandy Landings *Neil Mulholland* 92h 92c
8 gr g Alflora(IRE) —Hinemoa (IRE) (Mandalus)
132[P] 1901[2] 2048[3] 2575[5] (3402)
4784[2] 5434[5]

Norman The Great *Alan King* 124h 124c
7 b g Night Shift(USA) —Encore Du Cristal (USA) (Quiet American (USA))
3345[2] 4122[2] ◆ **5011[P]**

Norminster *Rayson Nixon* 90h 84c
10 ch g Minster Son—Delightfool (Idiots Delight)
88[12] 290[7] 1781[P] 2194[6] 4001[4] 4258[P] 5258[8] 5414[U]

North Brook (IRE) *Alistair Whillans* 100h
6 b g Alderbrook—Nicola's News (IRE) (Buckskin (FR))
319[16] 3399[9] 3887[7] 4132[4] 4684[U] 4960[7]

Norther Bay (FR) *Eoin Griffin* 114h 132c
8 b g Alamo Bay(USA) —Northern Mixa (Linamix (FR))
1038a[7]
1849a[3]

Northern Acres *Sue Bradburne* 88h
5 b g Mtoto—Bunting (Shaadi (USA))
3746[9] 4059[8] 4165[9] 5147[11]

Northern Alliance (IRE) *A J Martin* 138h 154c
10 ch g Naheez(USA) —Lady Bettina (Bustino)
1123a[5] 1527a[5] 2886[8] 3474a[4]

Northern Cross (IRE) *Howard Johnson* 89h
7 br g Accordion—Gale Johnston (IRE) (Strong Gale)
3715[10] 4145[5] 4910[6]

Northern Flame (IRE) *N W Alexander* 82h
6 b g Luso—Gails Gift (IRE) (Alphabatim (USA))
2202[P] 3331[7] 3999[7] 4477[10] 4872[P]

Northern Lad (IRE) *Jim Best* 107h
9 ch g Lord Of Appeal—Deep Green (Deep Run)
713[6] 837[4] 1095[2] 1451[2] (1741) ◆ 1840[2] 2209[6]

Northern Quest (IRE) *Henry Hogarth* 74h 113c
10 ch g Un Desperado(FR) —Strong Heather (IRE) (Strong Gale)
2371[P] 2601[2] 2942[3] 3257[5]

Northern Revoque (IRE) *T Morrison* 60h 67c
9 b m Revoque(IRE) —Delia (IRE) (Darshaan)
4915[5]

North Island (IRE) *Peter Bowen* 112h 129c
9 bb g New Frontier(IRE) —Port-O-Call (Import)
(352) **524[4]**
772[2] 1105[F] (1367) 1482[4] 2023[4] 2232[6] **3453[P]**

Northorsouth *Bill Moore* 49h
9 b g Polar Prince(IRE) —What The Devil (Devil To Play)
2642[P] 5203[9]

North Shadow *Alan Brown* 48h
4 ch g Motivator—Matoaka (USA) (A.P. Indy (USA))
1825[9] 2033[7]

North Stack *Michael Scudamore* 81h
5 ch g Alflora(IRE) —Mandy Chat (IRE) (Mandalus)
2074[13] 3546[9] 3897[6] 4404[9] 5167[7]

Northumberland *Michael Chapman* 64h
5 b g Bertolini(USA) —Cal Norma's Lady (IRE) (Lyphard's Special (USA))
4859[9]

Northwold *Christopher Kellett* 60h
7 b g Cloudings(IRE) —Briery Gale (Strong Gale)
2111[8] *3089[5]* 3506[11] 3870[12]

Nortonthorpe Lad (IRE) *Alison Thorpe* 128h 91c
9 b g Charnwood Forest(IRE) —Tisima (FR) (Selkirk (USA))
(170) 4420[5]

No Rules *Mark H Tompkins* 118h
6 b g Fraam—Golden Daring (IRE) (Night Shift (USA))
1508[2] ◆

Norwest (IRE) *Tim Vaughan* 99h
8 br g Norwich—Chestnut Shoon (Green Shoon)
849[3] 1119[6] 4146[11]

Norwich Well (IRE) *Oliver Sherwood* 74h
6 b g Norwich—Allijess (USA) (Tom Rolfe)
2291[P] 3405[10] **4438[P]**

Nosecond Chance (IRE) *Charlie Mann* 102h
5 b g Classic Cliche(IRE) —Mandy's Treasure (IRE) (Mandalus)
2634[9] 2985[5] (3304) 3691[9] 4076[7] 4439[7]

No Secrets (IRE) *Warren Greatrex* 134h
7 b g King's Theatre(IRE) —Happy Native (IRE) (Be My Native (USA))
2087[3] 2963[8] (3340) 3678[2] 4849[11]

No Stopping Sarah (IRE) *P A Fahy* 127h
7 b m King's Theatre(IRE) —Bolly (IRE) (Jolly Jake (NZ))
1121a[P]

Nostringsattached (IRE) *Jonjo O'Neill* 111h 137c
10 b g Un Desperado(FR) —Site Mistress (IRE) (Remainder Man)
735[13] 1020[7] 1373[4] 2629[P] 2984[P] 3157[P]

No Substitute (IRE) *Alan King* 110b
6 b g Definite Article—Kindly Light (IRE) (Supreme Leader)
5063[4]

No Supper (IRE) *George Bewley* 97h
7 ch g Inchinor—Be Thankfull (IRE) (Linamix (FR))
1574[8] (1762) ◆ 2104[8] 2208[14] 3855[13] 4166[5]
4544[3] 4912[6]

Not A Bob (IRE) *Jonjo O'Neill* 91h
6 ch g Old Vic—Cab In The Storm (IRE) (Glacial Storm (USA))
62[6] 1021[7] 2070[5] 3261[4] 4724[3] 5295[U]

Notabotheronme (IRE) *Philip Hobbs* 103h 117c
9 b g Religiously(USA) —Kylogue's Delight (Strong Gale)
2343[7] 3687[8]

Not Another Barney (IRE) *Helen Nelmes* 43h
8 b g Beneficial—Hard Ecu (IRE) (King Persian)
2[P]

No Tears (IRE) *Alan King* 76h 106c
8 b g Saddlers' Hall(IRE) —Badsworth Rose (IRE) (Roselier (FR))
1963[P] 3505[8] **3880[2] 4483[5]**

Not For Diamonds (IRE) *Seamus Mullins* 95h 24c
11 b g Arctic Lord—Black-Crash (Crash Course)
217[6]

Nothingbutthetruth (IRE) *Tim Pitt* 112h 123c
7 b g Witness Box(USA) —Named And Shamed (IRE) (Electric)
(9) **(175)**
608[2] 839[7]

Nothing Is Forever (IRE) *Liam Corcoran* 100h
7 b g Daylami(IRE) —Bequeath (USA) (Lyphard (USA))
23[7] 430[6] 595[P] 798[8] 914[4] (1164) 1236[4] 1492[3]
(1844) 2333[5] 3481[13]

Nothing's Easy (IRE) *Liam Corcoran* 74h
7 b g Alflora(IRE) —Banusal (IRE) (Lord Americo)
1816[P] 1937[P]

Nothing Ventured *John Norton* 51h
6 b g Sir Harry Lewis(USA) —Sahara Reem (IRE) (Don't Forget Me)
2612[P] 3572[13] 4281[11] 4798[P]

No Through Road *Michael Scudamore* 69b
4 b g Grape Tree Road—Pendil's Delight (Scorpio (FR))
3842[9] 4739[11]

Not In The Clock (USA) *Charlie Mann* 109h
4 b g Chapel Royal(USA) —Bavarian Girl (USA) (Unbridled (USA))
3944[3] 4288[5] 4932[8]

Not Left Yet (IRE) *P Monteith* 128h 114c
10 bb g Old Vic—Dalus Dawn (Mandalus)
1697[5] 1932[P] 2079[P]

Notmorebrandy (IRE) *Diana Grissell* 83h
7 b g Alderbrook—April's Baby (Paico)
530[9] **1813[F]**
2046[P]

Not Now Later *Barry Murtagh* 40b
5 ch g Karinga Bay—Charlotte Gray (Rolfe (USA))
3889[15] 4894[10]

No To Trident *John Flint* 110h
6 b g Zilzal(USA) —Charmante Femme (Bin Ajwaad (IRE))
2054[F] 3793[7] 4672[U] 5244[2]

Notre Cyborg (FR) *Jonjo O'Neill* 110h 124c
10 ch g Cyborg(FR) —Cate Bleue (FR) (Katowice (FR))
772[P]

Notre Pere (FR) *J T R Dreaper* 95h 153c
10 b g Kadalko(FR) —Gloria IV (FR) (Video Rock (FR))
2543[5] 3176a[9]

Not So Prudent (IRE) *Nigel Twiston-Davies* 80h 111c
7 b g Flemensfirth(USA) —Prudent Princess (Puissance)
3254[2] 3702[P] 4414[U]

Not So Sure Dick (IRE) *George Baker* 104h 102c
6 b g Flemensfirth(USA) —The Peckaloo (IRE) (Buckskin (FR))
4743[3] 739[8] **1727[3] 2046[4] 3723[F] 4022[5]** (5322)

Not Talking (IRE) *John Quinn* 78h 23c
8 b g Supreme Leader—View Of The Hills (Croghan Hill)
1666[7] ◆ (2351) ◆ 3369[2]
3748[4] 4391[7]

Not Til Monday (IRE) *J R Jenkins* 121h
5 b g Spartacus(IRE) —Halomix (Linamix (FR))
1660[2] (3604) (3981) 4485[10] 4918[4]

Notus De La Tour (FR) *David Pipe* 146h
5 b g Kutub(IRE) —Ridiyla (IRE) (Akarad (FR))
3676[4] 4188[3] 4848[14] 5166[5]

Nouailhas *Reg Hollinshead* 96h
5 b g Mark Of Esteem(IRE) —Barachois Princess (USA) (Barachois (CAN))
1308[7] 1433[7] 1506[6] 2054[2] 2244[3] (2956) 4465[6]

Noun De La Thinte (FR) *Venetia Williams* 97h 131c
10 b m Oblat(FR) —Belis De La Thinte (FR) (Marasali)
2072[6]
2343[4] 2669[2] ◆ 2984[7] 3568[5] 3832[4] 4193[P] 5206[8]

Nous Voila (FR) *Alan Coogan* 101h 89c
10 b g Video Rock(FR) —Ability (FR) (Olmeto)
2643[4] 3899[7] 4178[5] 4330[7] **4411[2] 4691[7]**

Novel Investment (IRE) *John Brassil* 132h
10 b g Taipan(IRE) —Hi Sheree (IRE) (Beau Sher)
(1121a)

November Papa Golf (IRE) *A J Martin* 90h
11 b g Classic Cliche(IRE) —Gospel (IRE) (Le Bavard (FR))
286[2]

Novikov *David Evans* 122h 122c
7 ch g Danehill Dancer(IRE) —Ardisia (USA) (Affirmed (USA))
(934) **1163[2]**
(1257)
1606[8]

Novillero *Jimmy Fox*
4 b c Noverre(USA) —Fairy Story (IRE) (Persian Bold)
3944[10]

No Virtue *S Flook* 91c
8 b m Defacto(USA) —Easy Virtue (Northern Park (USA))
4011[5] 4442[4] 4779[5]

No Way Hozay *Brian Storey* 52h
5 b g Nomadic Way(USA) —Sweet Sensation (Carlingford Castle)
3998[6] 4569[P] 4889[11] 5092[8]

Now Listen To Me *Paul Nicholls* 112h 117c
8 br g Slip Anchor—Calendula (Be My Guest (USA))
39[2] 181[5] 824[3]

No Woman No Cry *Colin Tizzard* 85h
6 b g Kayf Tara—Motown Melody (IRE) (Detroit Sam (FR))
1860[6] 2154[7] 3261[6] 3870[2] 4098[3]

No Wonga *Katie Stephens* 100h
6 b g Where Or When(IRE) —Fizzy Fiona (Efisio)
2364[P]

Now Then Sam *Sharon Watt*
5 b g Presidium—Callace (Royal Palace)
1153[9]

Now This Is It (IRE) *S R B Crawford* 139h
7 ch g Accordion—Leitrim Bridge (IRE) (Earl Of Barking (IRE))
648[2] ◆ (866) 1038a[4] 1609[8] (1698)

Nowurhurlin (IRE) *Donald McCain* 46b
4 b g Saddlers' Hall(IRE) —Pint Taken (IRE) (Needle Gun (IRE))
5426[6]

Nowzdetime (IRE) *Caroline Bailey* 56h
6 b g Statue Of Liberty(USA) —Sensitive (IRE) (Posen (USA))
1196[7] 1554[P]

Nozic (FR) *Nick Gifford* 110h 154c
10 b g Port Lyautey(FR) —Grizilh (FR) (Spoleto)
2360[P]
2674[P] 2962[P] 3438[4]

Nudge And Nurdle (IRE) *Nigel Twiston-Davies* 123h 128c
10 b g Shernazar—Firey Comet (IRE) (Buckskin (FR))
1044[2] 1151[3] 1327[3] 1390[3] 1577[5] 1926[6]

Nulato (IRE) *Alan King* 107h 112c
8 b g Turtle Island(IRE) —Newtown Wonder (IRE) (Be My Native (USA))
267[6] **2611[3]**

Numbercruncher (IRE) *Brendan Powell* 78h
5 b g Beneficial—Josie's Turn (IRE) (Kambalda)
3200[13] 4091[6]

Numide (FR) *Rod Millman* 127h 121c
8 b g Highest Honor(FR) —Numidie (FR) (Baillamont (USA))
96[3] 2423[2] 2977[7] 3298[6] (3587) 3947[7] 4270[2] (4420) 4727[7]

Nuts N Bolts *Alan Swinbank* 115b
5 b g Marju(IRE) —Anniversary (Salse (USA))
4457[3] 5202[13]

Oak Apple (IRE) *Philip Hobbs* 92b
5 b m Great Palm(USA) —Keep The Change (IRE) (Castle Keep)
5306[9]

Oakapple Express *Geoffrey Harker* 52h
11 b g Alflora(IRE) —Royal Scarlet (Royal Fountain)
708[P] 1827[12]

Oakfield Legend *John Flint* 80h 130c
10 b g Midnight Legend—Kins Token (Relkino)
4440[4] 4864[P]

Oaklands Luis *R G Russ* 74c
12 b g Primitive Rising(USA) —Bally Small (Sunyboy)
580[P]

Oaklea *Liam Corcoran* 44h
7 br g Alflora(IRE) —Carry Me (IRE) (Lafontaine (USA))
690[5]

Oamaru Stone (IRE) *Paul Nicholls* 95h 109c
8 b g Presenting—Closing Thyne (IRE) (Good Thyne (USA))
218[2] 588[2] 1027[6]

Oasis Knight (IRE) *Nicky Henderson* 118h
5 b g Oasis Dream—Generous Lady (Generous (IRE))
4069[2] 4479[4] 4986[6]

Obara D'Avril (FR) *Simon West* 95h
9 gr m April Night(FR) —Baraka De Thaix II (FR) (Olmeto)
313[10] 675[5]

Oberon Moon (IRE) *Alan King* 116h
10 gr g New Frontier(IRE) —Kemal's Princess (Kemal (FR))
193[P]

Objectif Special (FR) *G Cherel* 135c
9 b g Ungaro(GER) —Edition Speciale (FR) (Useful (FR))
5367a[7]

Oca De Thaix (FR) *Keith Goldsworthy* 125c
9 b g Bulington(FR) —Fonseca De Thaix (FR) (Quart De Vin (FR))
150[3] (4011)
(4526) (4969)
5156[2] 5326[3]

O'Callaghan Strand (AUS) *Jonjo O'Neill* 79h
5 ch g Galileo(IRE) —New Gold Dream (AUS) (Alzao (USA))
596[3] 754[5] 1547[10] 1915[2] ◆ 2390[7]

Ocarina (FR) *James Ewart* 91h 114c
9 b g Bulington(FR) —Alconea (FR) (Brezzo (FR))
46[6] (213)
(2189) 2354[3] 3574[P] 4961[4] 5261[4]

Occasionally Yours (IRE) *Alan Blackmore* 125h
7 b g Moscow Society(USA) —Kristina's Lady (IRE) (Lafontaine (USA))
2671[0] 539[6] (826) 862[2] 994[6] (1688) 1951[3] 2393[3] 4180[4] 4725[3] 5300[4] 5441[2]

Oceana Gold *Emma Lavelle* 125h
7 ch g Primo Valentino(IRE) —Silken Dalliance (Rambo Dancer (CAN))
1609[15] 1859[6]

Ocean Club *Nigel Twiston-Davies*
4 ch g Storming Home—Strictly Cool (USA) (Bering)
1330[P]

Ocean Du Moulin (FR) *Jamie Snowden* 97h 125c
9 b g Robin Des Champs(FR) —Hacienda Du Moulin (FR) (Video Rock (FR))
84[5] 273[4]

Ocean Transit (IRE) *Richard Price* 136h
6 b m Trans Island—Wings Awarded (Shareef Dancer (USA))
80[6] 2442[2] 2639[6] 3490[3] 3874[10] (4009) (4354) 4793[3] 5302[7]

Ocheekobee (IRE) *Richard Phillips* 63h
8 b g Rashar(USA) —Whishtaminute (IRE) (Balboa)
695[P] 931[P]

Ockey De Neulliac (FR) *Ferdy Murphy* 112h 123c
9 ch g Cyborg(FR) —Graine De Neulliac (FR) (Le Nain Jaune (FR))
1987[5] 2520[6] 3573[4] 4065[P]

Oddjob (IRE) *Warren Greatrex* 101h
7 b g Bob's Return(IRE) —Bettyhill (Ardross)
2231[3] 2946[12] 3405[5]

Oddshoes (IRE) *Philip Hobbs* 128h
9 b g Mujadil(USA) —Another Baileys (Deploy)
1470[2] **2578[F]**

Odeillo Du Mathan (FR) *G Cherel* 111h 136c
9 b g Balleroy(USA) —Stone's Glow (USA) (Arctic Tern (USA))
5367a[6]

Odin's Raven (IRE) *Brian Ellison* 103h
6 ro g Dalakhani(IRE) —Oriane (Nashwan (USA))
3999[9] 4859[3] (5309)

Oedipe (FR) *Nicky Henderson* 121h 137c
9 ch g Chamberlin(FR) —Massada (FR) (Kashtan (FR))
137[2] (370)

Oeil Du Maitre (FR) *J-P Gallorini* 125h
9 b g Robin Des Champs(FR) —Stephanotis (FR) (Saint Estephe (FR))
2230a[5]

O Ellie (IRE) *Miss Katie Thory*
7 b g Odyle(USA) —Dinah B (IRE) (Yashgan)
61[U] 4315[P]

Oenologue (FR) *Alison Thorpe* 121h 98c
9 b g Ragmar(FR) —Cabira Des Saccart (FR) (Quart De Vin (FR))
2393[P]

O'Er And Beyond *Carol Ferguson* 53b
5 ch g And Beyond(IRE) —Hand On Heart (IRE) (Taufan (USA))
1510[8]

Of Course (FR) *Simon West* 109h
9 ch g Adnaan(IRE) —Intelectuelle (FR) (Montorselli)
1929[2] 2941[P]

Off By Heart (FR) *G Macaire* 101h
4 b g Kapgarde(FR) —Fassonwest (FR) (Dom Pasquini (FR))
5047a[4]

Off Gallivanting *Jonjo O'Neill* 107h
6 b g Karinga Bay—Princess Hotpot (IRE) (King's Ride)
409[5] (635) 1063[P]

Officer Mor (USA) *Evelyn Slack* 23h
5 ch g Officer(USA) —Hot August Nights (USA) (Summer Squall (USA))
3850[14]

Officier De Reserve (FR) *Venetia Williams* 127h 133c
9 br g Sleeping Car(FR) —Royaute (FR) (Signani (FR))
2106[P] 2962[4] 3290[3] 3568[P]

Offshore Account (IRE) *Mrs T L Bailey* 121h 140c
11 b g Oscar(IRE) —Park Breeze (IRE) (Strong Gale)
3956[3] 4286[3] 5163[3]

Ogee *Renee Robeson* 148h 149c
8 ch g Generous(IRE) —Aethra (USA) (Trempolino (USA))
2358[7] 4466[4] 5009[4]

Ogmore Junction (IRE) *John Flint* 86h
6 b g Catcher In The Rye(IRE) —Fairy Berry (IRE) (Fairy King (USA))
662[P] 5167[6] 5321[11]

Ogre D'Estruval (FR) *Paul John Gilligan* 102h 114c
9 b g Nononito(FR) —Pommette III (FR) (Trac)
1045[2]

Ohana *Alistair Whillans* 105h 120c
8 b g Mark Of Esteem(IRE) —Subya (Night Shift (USA))
1117[5] 1327[2] 1424[3]

Oh Crick (FR) *Alan King* 128h 158c
8 ch g Nikos—Other Crik (FR) (Bigstone (IRE))
2385[6] 2881[6] 3446[3] 4853[13] 5340[6]

Ohio Gold (IRE) *Colin Tizzard* 138h
5 b g Flemensfirth(USA) —Kiniohio (FR) (Script Ohio (USA))
2143[3] 2666[3] 2963[3] 3454[2] 3806[6] 4803[8]

Oh Landino (GER) *Jim Goldie* 73h
6 b g Lando(GER) —Oh La Belle (GER) (Dashing Blade)
576[9] 4303[P] 4686[6] 5096[3]

Oh No Not Harry (FR) *Ian Williams* 114h
6 b g Astarabad(USA) —La Pitchoun (FR) (Mansonnien (FR))
191[8] 3793[8]

Oh Right (IRE) *Dianne Sayer* 49h
7 b g Zagreb(USA) —Conna Bride Lady (IRE) (Phardante (FR))
732[5] 842[8]

Oh So Beautiful (IRE) *Lucinda Russell* 96h
4 b f Montjeu(IRE) —Dart Board (IRE) (Darshaan)
5428[5]

Oh Yah Dancer (IRE) *George Bewley* 89h 13c
9 ch g Portrait Gallery(IRE) —Croi Na Greine (IRE) (Broken Hearted)
31[2] 212[6]

Oil Burner *William Amos* 102h
6 b g Sir Harry Lewis(USA) —Quick Quote (Oats)
1783[4]
2191[U] 2448[7] 3362[2] 3633[B]

Oilily (IRE) *Sean Byrne* 141h
8 b m Dr Massini(IRE) —Be My Trump (IRE) (Be My Native (USA))
(1713a) ◆ 2196a[2] 5182[2]

Oiseau De Nuit (FR) *Colin Tizzard* 114h 160c
9 b g Evening World(FR) —Idylle Du Marais (FR) (Panoramic)
1861[U] 2086[6] 2385[4] 2885[8] 4187[3] (4853)
5164[2] ◆ 5442[4]

Okafranca (IRE) *Jim Old* 98h
6 b g Okawango(USA) —Villafranca (IRE) (In The Wings)
3489[4] 3724[7] 3919[4]

Okalydokely (IRE) *Andrew Crook* 35h
7 b g Shinko Forest(IRE) —Delirious Tantrum (IRE) (Taufan (USA))
3783[5]

Oke Prince (FR) *J Follain*
9 b g Princeton(FR) —Ugaina (FR) (Maiymad (IRE))
312a[F]

Okey Dokey *Evan Williams* 47h
5 b g Lujain(USA) —La Piazza (IRE) (Polish Patriot (USA))
1278[9]

Oklahoma Seven (FR) *J-L Gay* 104h
4 b f Saint Des Saints(FR) —Quick Ville (FR) (Villez (USA))
(5047a)

Olazuro Du Mou (FR) *M De Montfort* 102h 103c
9 b g Sleeping Car(FR) —Viviane Du Mou (FR) (Tin Soldier (FR))
190a[8]

Old Benny *Alan King* 99h 110c
10 b g Saddlers' Hall(IRE) —Jack's The Girl (IRE) (Supreme Leader)
2962[7] 3437[P] 4428[P]

Old Brigade (IRE) *Jonjo O'Neill* 92h 105c
7 br g Dushyantor(USA) —The Nurse (IRE) (Mujadil (USA))
157[P] **597[3]**
840[2] 1027[P] (1136)
1227[4]

Old Dungarvan Oak (IRE) *Gary Moore* 61h
5 b m Flemensfirth(USA) —Gandi's Dream (IRE) (Commanche Run)
2289[11] 2627[6] 2974[13]

Old Emily Rose *Althea Barclay* 78b
6 b m Kirkwall—My Little Doxie (IRE) (Supreme Leader)
254[8] 718[6]

Old McDonald *N F Glynn* 129h
6 b g King's Theatre(IRE) —Desperate Virgin (BEL) (Chief Singer)
563[3] 4086a[6]

Old Noddy (IRE) *A M Crow* 93h 87c
11 ch g Duky—General Run (General Ironside)
164[5] 461[P]

Oldrik (GER) *Philip Hobbs* 141h 110c
8 b g Tannenkonig(IRE) —Onestep (GER) (Konigsstuhl (GER))
2085[5]

Old Rusty Cross (IRE) *Nicky Henderson* 72b
6 ch g Old Vic—Rosa View (IRE) (Roselier (FR))
4561[7]

Old Si (IRE) *D T Hughes* 125h 137c
8 b g Saddlers' Hall(IRE) —Shaping (Deep Run)
3206a[8]

Old Style (IRE) *Jennie Candlish* 78h
6 b g Classic Cliche(IRE) —Granny Smith (IRE) (Mandalus)
3773[7] 4278[3] 4993[8]

Old Way (IRE) *Venetia Williams* 127h
5 b g Gold Away(IRE) —Brooklyn's Dance (FR) (Shirley Heights)
3478[5] 3701[2] (4260) 4727[18]

Old Wigmore (IRE) *Rebecca Curtis* 120h
6 ch g Old Vic—Wigmore (IRE) (Denel (FR))
1989[4] (2238) 2888[5] 4262[4] 4861[4]

Oleolat (FR) *William Amos* 62h 98c
9 ch g Art Bleu—Contessina (FR) (Mistigri)
3360[P] 4305[P]

Olifan D'Oudairies (FR) *J Larkin* 107h 105c
9 ch g Video Rock(FR) —Bouffonne (FR) (Shafoun (FR))
606[4]

Olivia Des Bordes (FR) *F-M Cottin* 91h 97c
9 b m Antarctique(IRE) —Gamine Royale (FR) (Garde Royale)
190a[7]

Olivino (GER) *Bernard Llewellyn* 111h
10 ch g Second Set(IRE) —Osdemona (GER) (Solarstern (FR))
595[3] 1162[2] 1282[6] 1492[2] (1569) 4028[3]

Ollie Magern *Nigel Twiston-Davies* 123h 156c
13 b g Alderbrook—Outfield (Monksfield)
(446) **2091[4]**
2964[4]

Olofi (FR) *Tom George* 138h
5 gr g Slickly(FR) —Dona Bella (FR) (Highest Honor (FR))
1775[2] 2386[5] 2671[3] 3229[8]

Olympian (FR) *Philip Middleton* 118h
9 b g Video Rock(FR) —Attualita (FR) (Master Thatch)
316[8] 2393[P] 2983[P] 3490[10] 4399[2] 4697[5] 4830[4] 5171[3] 5376[2]

Olympian Boy (IRE) *Anabel L M King* 102h 101c
7 b g Flemensfirth(USA) —Notanissue (IRE) (Buckskin (FR))
736[7] 2312[2] 2927[3]
4691[5] 5101[3] 5396[F]

O Malley's Oscar (IRE) *Suzy Smith* 103h
6 b g Oscar(IRE) —Notre Dame (IRE) (Classic Music (USA))
3866[4] 4128[4] 4462[6] 4922[2]

Omaruru (IRE) *Renee Robeson* 106h
4 b g Cape Cross(IRE) —Monturani (IRE) (Indian Ridge)
1691[11] 2151[2] ◆ 2924[3] 3401[4] 3958[3] (4458)

Omix D'Or (FR) *James Evans* 92h 117c
9 gr g Fragrant Mix(IRE) —Une Pomme D'Or (FR) (Pot D'Or (FR))
2141[9] 2532[9] **2794[6] 3482[2] 3687[F]**

Omme Antique (FR) *Venetia Williams* 105h 95c
9 b g Lute Antique(FR) —Saturbaine (FR) (Djarvis (FR))
49[P]

Ommega (FR) *Gerald Ham* 107h 117c
9 gr g Ragmar(FR) —Cathou (FR) (Quart De Vin (FR))
4990[11] 5195[2]

Omokoroa (IRE) *Donald McCain* 115h
5 b g Hawkeye(IRE) —Alycus (USA) (Atticus (USA))
2939[F] 3715[4] 4711[3] 5099[11] 5378[2]

Onatello (FR) *L Viel* 114h
9 b g Rajpoute(FR) —Glory De Foyt (FR) (Faucon Noir (FR))
5159a[5]

On Borrowed Wings (IRE) *Alan Fleming* 104h 136c
8 br g Quws—Ann's Pet (King's Signet (USA))
(1970)
2664[2] 3508[4] 4202[2] ◆ **4794[8] 5301[5]**

Oncle Kid (FR) *Paul Henderson* 50h 109c
9 b g Kidder(FR) —Hanoi City (FR) (Sky Lawyer (FR))
371[P] 2049[8]
2236[U] 2443[6] 3614[5] 4372[3]

Ondeafears (IRE) *Stuart Howe* 57b
4 b f Chineur(FR) —Irma La Douce (IRE) (Elbio)
1913[9]

One And All (IRE) *Nigel Hawke* 83h 76c
8 gr g Saddlers' Hall(IRE) —Rostarr (IRE) (Roselier (FR))
2283[6] 2980[F] **3765[2] 4483[F]**

One Cool Cookie (IRE) *C F Swan* 86h 154c
10 ch g Old Vic—Lady Bellingham (IRE) (Montelimar (USA))
2339a[5] 2543[3] 4792[0] (Dead)

One Cool Knight (IRE) *Mrs K Hobbs* 94h 84c
8 b g Blueprint(IRE) —Hurry Over (IRE) (Phardante (FR))
150[5]

One Cool Tornado (IRE) *Paul John Gilligan* 136h
6 b g Golden Tornado(IRE) —Ballycarron Lass (IRE) (Roselier (FR))
773[2] (1526a) ◆ 1713a[8] 2388[P]

One Cornetto (IRE) *Nick Gifford* 105h 107c
12 b g Eurobus—Costenetta (IRE) (Runnett)
81[6]

Oneeightofamile (IRE) *John E Kiely* 127h
6 b g Catcher In The Rye(IRE) —Punta Gorda (IRE) (Roi Danzig (USA))
1713a[3]

One Five Eight *Mrs C A Coward* 67c
12 b g Alflora(IRE) —Dark Nightingale (Strong Gale)
178[3]

One For Lou (IRE) *Ian Williams* 84b
5 b g Presenting—One Last Chance (Le Bavard (FR))
3773[10]

One Last Tipple (IRE) *Malcolm Jefferson*
5 b g Deploy—She's All Heart (Broken Hearted)
1510[10]

Onemix *Nicky Henderson* 105h
5 gr m Fair Mix(IRE) —One For Philip (Blushing Flame (USA))
215[U] (535) 706[P]

One More Cent *Dianne Sayer* 2h
6 b m Karinga Bay—One More Dime (IRE) (Mandalus)
30[5] 1049[P] 1101[P] 1361[P]

One More Cookie (IRE) *Colin Tizzard* 101b
5 b m Old Vic—Lady Bellingham (IRE) (Montelimar (USA))
5306[5]

One More Dinar *John Bryan Groucott* 46h 92c
8 b g Kayf Tara—One More Dime (IRE) (Mandalus)
1939[5] 2277[2] 2585[U] 2952[2] 3492[U] 3873[4] (4144)
4483[6]

One Of A Kind (FR) *John Daniel Moore* 33h
7 ch g Ultimately Lucky(IRE) —Jabalya (FR) (Tel Quel (FR))
1175[5] 1449[10]

One Of The Boys (IRE) *Tim Vaughan* 108c
10 ch g Shernazar—Easter Morning (FR) (Nice Havrais (USA))
276[P] 799[2] 848[2] 950[2] 1309[3] 1454[3]

One Shot Sheehan (IRE) *F M Hanley* 73h
15 b g Lord Americo—Alcmena's Last (Pauper)
1048[P]

One Term (IRE) *Rebecca Curtis* 103b
4 b g Beneficial—One Edge (IRE) (Welsh Term)
5174[3]

Onetokeep (IRE) *Anabel L M King* 53h
6 b g Accordion—Slaney Pal (IRE) (Supreme Leader)
1927[6] 2560[9] 4260[12]

One To Note (IRE) *David Phelan* 89h 88c
8 b g Definite Article—Timissa (IRE) (Kahyasi)
150[P]

Onetwobeat *Lisa Williamson* 64b
6 b m Beat All(USA) —Angel Falling (Scottish Reel)
1934[11]

One Under (IRE) *Nicky Richards* 49b
6 b m Tamayaz(CAN) —City Lights (Henbit (USA))
547[P]

Oneway (IRE) *Mark Rimell* 106h 130c
14 b g Bob's Return(IRE) —Rendezvous (Lorenzaccio)
(1606)

On Gossamer Wings (IRE) *Ferdy Murphy* 96c
7 b g Winged Love(IRE) —Katie Parson (The Parson)
43[4] 3361[3] 3522[P] 4004[P]

On His Own (IRE) *Howard Johnson* 116h 127c
7 b g Presenting—Shuil Na Mhuire (IRE) (Roselier (FR))
3288[4]
(3548) 3955[4] 4802[P] (5341) ◆

Oniz Tiptoes (IRE) *John Wainwright* 102h 100c
10 ch g Russian Revival(USA) —Edionda (IRE) (Magical Strike (USA))
352[8] 553[P] 1329[8] 1501[8] 1694[U] 1782[8] 2372[2] 2941[7] 3258[3] 3729[4] 3996[2] 4276[2] 4508[4] **4740[2]**
4997[6]

On Khee *Hughie Morrison* 96h
4 b f Sakhee(USA) —Star Precision (Shavian)
2661[3] ◆

Only Dreams (IRE) *Nick Lampard* 107c
10 b g Shahrastani(USA) —Shanamara (IRE) (Shernazar)
755[8]

Only Hope *Rachel Hobbs* 85h
7 b m Marju(IRE) —Sellette (IRE) (Selkirk (USA))
4540[2] 5072[2] 5298[2]

Only The Best *Ferdy Murphy* 123h 97c
8 b g Flemensfirth(USA) —Celtic Remorse (Celtic Cone)
2191[4] 3902[P] 4114[F] 4825[P]

Only Vintage (USA) *Paul Henderson* 112h 133c
11 b g Diesis—Wild Vintage (USA) (Alysheba (USA))
2147[11] 2606[8] **(2948)**
4328[P]

Only Witness (IRE) *Brendan Powell* 97h
6 b g Witness Box(USA) —Shiny Button (Bob's Return (IRE))
4479[5] 4895[9] 5010[4] 5171[10] 5376[5]

Ontario Lass (IRE) *Ferdy Murphy*
5 b m Bach(IRE) —Reoss (King's Ride)
731[P]

On The Fringe (IRE) *E Bolger* 133c
6 b g Exit To Nowhere(USA) —Love And Porter (IRE) (Sheer Grit)
4851[4]

Onthegoagain (IRE) *J J Lambe* 83h 94c
10 ch g Accordion—Annesley Lady (IRE) (Over The River (FR))
517[2] 1002[7] (Dead)

Onthelips (IRE) *Amy Weaver* 58h
7 ch g Moscow Society(USA) —Southern Mariner (IRE) (Le Bavard (FR))
3153[10] 3601[5] 4006[15] 4397[9]

On The Loose (IRE) *T G McCourt* 103h
7 gr g Great Palm(USA) —Marys Rival (IRE) (Soughaan (USA))
1596[3]

On The Raz *Jacqueline Retter* 76b
4 b f Rakaposhi King—Trillow (Pitpan)
2965[13] 5158[7] 5306[15]

On The Right Path *Alison Batchelor* 68h
4 b g Pursuit Of Love—Glen Falls (Commanche Run)
1422[5] 2047[7] 2439[6]

On The Way Out (IRE) *John E Kiely* 147h
8 b g Saddlers' Hall(IRE) —Two Sweets (IRE) (Good Thyne (USA))
1711a[3] 2968a[7] 3578a[4]

Ontrack (IRE) *Rose Dobbin* 90h
7 ch g Snurge—Tamed (Rusticaro (FR))
209[10] 3336[8] 3729[2] (3996) 4508[7]

On Trend (IRE) *Nick Gifford* 123h
5 b g Jammaal—Comrun (IRE) (Commanche Run)
(2291) ◆ 2925[3] 3448[3] 5110[4]

On You Go (IRE) *Jonjo O'Neill* 120c
10 b g Blue Ocean(USA) —Fern Fields (IRE) (Be My Native (USA))
663[P] 890[4] 1276[3] 1491[6] 1738[7]

Oodachee *C F Swan* 116h 123c
12 b g Marju(IRE) —Lady Marguerrite (Blakeney)
1113a[P]

Oojar *Jane Makin*
7 b g Kayf Tara—Madame La Claire (Superlative)
310[P]

Oopsmylord (IRE) *S Flook* 118c
9 br g Rock Hopper—Backfromthewest (IRE) (Cardinal Flower)
253[3] 4211[4] 4969[4] 5207[3]

Open Day (IRE) *Jonjo O'Neill* 126h
5 b g Oscar(IRE) —Shaping (Deep Run)
3298[8] 4202[7] 4420[6] 5255[3]

Open De L'Isle (FR) *James Ewart* 128h 104c
9 bb g Funny Baby(FR) —Gratiene de l'Isle (FR) (Altayan)
3573[3] 3821[P] 4358[8]

Openditch (FR) *Mrs C Wilesmith* 126h 106c
9 b g Video Rock(FR) —Enita (FR) (Brezzo (FR))
1444[3] 4779[3]

Opening Meet *Paul Nicholls* 107h
7 b g Classic Cliche(IRE) —On My Toes (Le Solaret (FR))
(908) 1158[5] 1347[7] 1555[8]

Open Range (IRE) *George Wareham* 42h 56c
11 b g Saddlers' Hall(IRE) —L'Enfant Unique (IRE) (Phardante (FR))
278[F] 533[P] 692[4]
2046[P]

Open The Light *Giles Bravery* 38b
4 b f Fantastic Light(USA) —Seed Al Maha (USA) (Seeking The Gold (USA))
4505[7]

Operachy *James Frost* 77h
6 b g Kyllachy—Sea Music (Inchinor)
1344[8] 1488[9] 2021[9] 2633[7]

Opera North *Tom Tate* 98b
4 ch g Nayef(USA) —Reveuse De Jour (IRE) (Sadler's Wells (USA))
(2108) 3889[11] 5264[5]

Opera Og (IRE) *Venetia Williams* 85h
5 b g Oscar(IRE) —Maspaloma (IRE) (Camden Town)
3252[7] 4332[P]

Opera Prince *Lady Herries*
6 b g Kyllachy—Optaria (Song)
2667[P]

Ophelia's Kiss *Brendan Powell* 81b
4 b f Karinga Bay—Baileys Baby (Puissance)
2173[4] 2458[11]

Oponce (FR) *Noel Chance* 75h 91c
9 b g Varxi(FR) —Fraxinelle (FR) (Lou Piguet (FR))
2292[3] 2930[8] 3305[2] 3867[3]

Optimaxer (IRE) *Jamie Snowden* 37b
6 b g Accordion—Magheracar Lady (IRE) (Montekin)
1971[F]

Optimistic Duke (IRE) *William Muir* 94h
4 ch g Bachelor Duke(USA) —Gronchi Rosa (IRE) (Nashwan (USA))
1473[2] 1674[8] 2211[2] 5168[P]

Optimistic Harry *Miss S A Drake* 79h 89c
12 b g Sir Harry Lewis(USA) —Miss Optimist (Relkino)
580[U] 4170[2] 5263[P]

Optimum (IRE) *Richard Ford* 97h
9 br g King's Best(USA) —Colour Dance (Rainbow Quest (USA))
(1049)
2952[P] 4390[16]

Optimus Maximus (IRE) *Claire Dyson* 80h
6 ch g Galileo(IRE) —Morning Welcome (IRE) (Be My Guest (USA))
3298[11] 3490[12] 4501[7]

Option Money (IRE) *Peter Salmon* 107h 104c
9 b g Kotashaan(FR) —Be My Bargain (IRE) (Be My Native (USA))
196[17] 331[U] 494[10] 682[4] **1255[P]**

Oracle Des Mottes (FR) *R Barber* 94h 133c
12 b g Signe Divin(USA) —Daisy Des Mottes (FR) (Abdonski (FR))
4708[2] 5231[3]

Orangeaday *Ben Case* 96b
4 b g Kayf Tara—One Of Those Days (Soviet Lad (USA))
5084[3]

Oranger (FR) *Andrew J Martin* 108c
9 b g Antarctique(IRE) —True Beauty (Sun Prince)
151[5] 354[2] 525[P] 3772[8] 3990[6] 5109[9]

Orang Outan (FR) *Laura Hurley* 100h 100c
9 b g Baby Turk—Ellapampa (FR) (Pampabird)
(3899) 4785[2]

Or Bleu (FR) *Philip Hobbs* 83h 138c
9 ch g Discover D'Auteuil(FR) —Kidibleue (FR) (Beyssac (FR))
2212[3] 2629[P] 2976[5] 3438[2] ◆ **4095[3] 4864[5]** 5153[9]

Orchard King (IRE) *Alison Thorpe* 119h 81c
10 ch g Beneficial—Evelyn Anthony (IRE) (Phardante (FR))
131[10] **408[3]**
631[2] 1348[P]

Or De Grugy (FR) *Sue Bradburne* 8h 129c
9 b g April Night(FR) —Girlish (FR) (Passing Sale (FR))
308[3] 1598[U] (1871)
2204[3] 3333[6] 3634[P] 4167[5] 5149[15]

Ordelia *Chris Bealby* 95h
7 b m Overbury(IRE) —Ardeal (Ardross)
1559[F] 1814[P]

Or D'Oudairies (FR) *Ferdy Murphy* 110h 112c
9 b g April Night(FR) —Belle Truval (FR) (Rose Laurel)
330[9] 3751[3] 3970[5] 5261[3]

Ordre De Bataille (FR) *Henry Daly* 65h 124c
9 gr g Ungaro(GER) —Hache De Guerre (FR) (Royal Charter (FR))
1973[P] 2324[P] 3157[P]

Orfeo Conti (FR) *Henrietta Knight* 95h 115c
9 ch g Bulington(FR) —Gazelle Lulu (FR) (Altayan)
586[P]

Organisateur (IRE) *Paul Nicholls* 157h
6 b g Highest Honor(FR) —Willamina (IRE) (Sadler's Wells (USA))
1859[2] (2021) 2083[4] (2636) 3229[2] 3561[2] 3807[13] 4270[6]

Organisedconfusion (IRE) *A L T Moore* 82h 135c
6 b g Laveron—Histologie (FR) (Quart De Vin (FR))
3473a[3]

Organiz (FR) *Robin Dickin* 98h 88c
9 bb g Mansonnien(FR) —Madame Illusion (FR) (Solid Illusion (USA))
1740[P]
2986[3] 3492[6] 3699[P]

Oriental Cat *Venetia Williams*
4 b g Tiger Hill(IRE) —Sentimental Value (USA) (Diesis)
5161[P]

Orient Legend *Miss Jennifer Pidgeon* 103c
8 b g Shambo—Hong Kong Classic (Anshan)
4832[2]

Original Fly (FR) *Donald McCain* 76h 109c
9 b g Chef De Clan(FR) —Ultim De Plaisance (FR) (Top Dancer I (FR))
227[P]

Original Option (IRE) *Noel Meade* 124h
6 br g Anshan—Deepest Thoughts (IRE) (Supreme Leader)
2116a[2]

Original Prankster (IRE) *Nigel Twiston-Davies* 103h
6 ch g Carroll House—Kinallen Lady (IRE) (Abednego)
238[11] 2166[4] 3158[9] 3542[7] 4052[F] 4330[6] 4922[7]

Orion Express *Susan Gardner* 91h 100c
10 b g Bahhare(USA) —Kaprisky (IRE) (Red Sunset)
771[6] 954[6] 1230[6] 1336[6] 1741[5] 5068[U] (5278)

Orion Star (IRE) *Seamus Mullins* 56h 89c
9 ch g Fourstars Allstar(USA) —Rosies Sister (IRE) (Deep Run)
39[3] (132)
1843[4] (2132)
2444[3]

Or Jaune (FR) *Gary Moore* 110h 130c
9 ch g Grand Tresor(FR) —Vancia (FR) (Top Dancer I (FR))
193[6]

Orkney (IRE) *Julie Camacho* 98h
6 b g Trans Island—Bitty Mary (Be My Chief (USA))
8[9]

Orlittlebylittle *Donald McCain* 51h
5 b g Bollin Eric—Davana Blue (FR) (Epervier Bleu)
602[7] 1758[8] 2069[P]

Ormello (FR) *Lucinda Russell* 88h 122c
9 b g Cyborg(FR) —Galante V (FR) (Vorias (USA))
831[2] 1117[2] 1339[3]
1598[4] 2034[U] 2510[4]

Ormus *Christopher Wilson* 109h 104c
8 b g Rambling Bear—Adar Jane (Ardar)
(728) **848[6]**
891[3] 2107[3] (2207)
2510[2]

Ornais (FR) *Paul Nicholls* 124h 118c
9 b g Michel Georges—Imperia II (FR) (Beyssac (FR))
3908[5] 4463[2] 5200[F]

Or Noir De Somoza (FR) *David Pipe* 134h 146c
9 bl g Discover D'Auteuil(FR) —Planete D'O (FR) (Son Of Silver)
5200[F]

Orpen Bid (IRE) *Michael Mullineaux* 75h
6 b m Orpen(USA) —Glorious Bid (IRE) (Horage)
726[4] 858[RR] 2068[P] 3367[P] 3727[7] 4976[RR] 5374[RR]

Orpen Wide (IRE) *Michael Chapman* 69h 57c
9 b g Orpen(USA) —Melba (IRE) (Namaqualand (USA))
1406[P] 1569[9] 1953[7] *3092[9]* **4142[6] 4290[P]**

Orphelin Collonges (FR) *Richard Price* 72h 70c
9 b g Video Rock(FR) —Altesse Collonges (FR) (Quart De Vin (FR))
4011[7] 4560[7] 5231[4]

Orraloon *Donald Whillans* 92b
5 ch g And Beyond(IRE) —Mortify (Prince Sabo)
399[5] 1599[6]

Or Sing About (FR) *Seamus Mullins* 120h 112c
9 b g Le Balafre(FR) —Grande Folie (FR) (Highlanders (FR))
2975[6] 3342[F] 3562[U] 4381[3] 5377[5]

Orsini Conti (FR) *Bill Turner*
9 ch g Limnos(JPN) —Dona Mirande (FR) (Pebble (FR))
908[P]

Orsippus (USA) *Michael Smith* 140h
5 bb g Sunday Break(JPN) —Mirror Dancing (USA) (Caveat (USA))
1862[6] 2386[7] 4169[4] 4806[3] ◆ 5166[9]

Orsm *Laura Mongan* 87b
4 b g Erhaab(USA) —Royal Roulette (Risk Me (FR))
4055[6] *4923[12]*

Ortega (FR) *John Cornwall* 60h 80c
9 b g Useful(FR) —Madame Dabrovine (FR) (Vacarme (USA))
2277[P] 2479[4] 3396[P] 4949[5] **5293[P]**

Orvita (FR) *K A Nelmes* 100h 82c
9 b g Lute Antique(FR) —Ulvita (FR) (Spoleto)
6[U] 301[4]

Orzare (IRE) *Gary Moore* 126h
5 b g Montjeu(IRE) —Contare (Shirley Heights)
5201[9]

Osana (FR) *E J O'Grady* 166h 163c
9 b g Video Rock(FR) —Voilette (FR) (Brezzo (FR))
2227a[3] 2972a[F]

Osbaldeston (IRE) *Rose Dobbin* 91h
8 b g Oscar(IRE) —Sharonamar (IRE) (Merrymount)
289[P] 514[8] 744[4] 999[P] 1099[3] 1362[6]

Oscara Dara (IRE) *Alan Fleming* 118b
6 b g Oscar(IRE) —Lisa's Storm (IRE) (Glacial Storm (USA))
(3166) 4204[2]

Oscar Baby (IRE) *Elliott Cooper* 94b
5 b m Oscar(IRE) —Snowbaby (IRE) (Be My Native (USA))
4396[4] 5342[7]

Oscar Barton (IRE) *Paul W Flynn* 110h
6 b g Oscar(IRE) —I Can Imagine (IRE) (Husyan (USA))
(5352)

Oscar Bay (IRE) *James Frost* 134h 142c
9 bb g Oscar(IRE) —Rabbit Sand (IRE) (Decent Fellow)
206[P] **(411)**
1373[8] 4792[P]

Oscar Brando (IRE) *Paddy Butler*
8 b g Oscar(IRE) —Lady Diamond (Tesoro Mio)
216[P]

Oscar Charlie (IRE) *Jamie Snowden* 88h
6 b g Oscar(IRE) —Leefen Queen (IRE) (King's Ride)
759[5] 929[3] 1124[7] 5243[8]

Oscar Close (IRE) *George Baker* 119h
6 br g Oscar(IRE) —Upham Close (Oats)
279[3] 2141[8] 3934[5] 4399[3]

Oscar Dan Dan (IRE) *Thomas Mullins* 156h
9 b g Oscar(IRE) —Warmley's Gem (IRE) (Phardante (FR))
(2259a) 2968a[5] 3175a[4] 3475a[15] 3796a[3] 4107a[3] 5198[5]

Oscar D'Angron (FR) *Mrs C J Robinson* 88c
9 b g Robin Des Pres(FR) —Quovaria D'Angron (FR) (Le Pontet (FR))
4293[P]

Oscar Delta (IRE) *James Joseph Mangan* 131c
8 b g Oscar(IRE) —Timerry (IRE) (Alphabatim (USA))
4851[3]

Oscar Flyer (IRE) *Tim Vaughan* 86b
4 b g Oscar(IRE) —Cointosser (IRE) (Nordico (USA))
3630[3] 4191[6]

Oscar Glory (IRE) *Edward Cawley* 116h 116c
11 b g Oscar(IRE) —Graf Spey (IRE) (Amazing Bust)
1312[4] 1858[3]

Oscargo (IRE) *Paul Nicholls* 115h
7 b g Oscar(IRE) —Broken Rein (IRE) (Orchestra)
(4719)

Oscar Gogo (IRE) *Evan Williams* 117h 122c
9 b g Oscar(IRE) —Ceolbridgequeen (IRE) (Executive Perk)
2148[3] 2572[3] (3154)
3531[2] 4723[P]

Oscar Honey (IRE) *Rose Dobbin* 99h 111c
10 b g Oscar Schindler(IRE) —Tanhoney (IRE) (Asir)
308[P] 1781[4] 2036[P] 4067[P]

Oscar Looby (IRE) *Noel Meade* 135h 152c
8 b g Oscar(IRE) —Ballylooby Moss (IRE) (Supreme Leader)
1527a[F] 1684a[3] 2339a[4] 3206a[P] 5025a[F]

Oscar Mac (IRE) *Tim Vaughan* 84h
5 b g Oscar(IRE) —Rossmill Native (IRE) (Be My Native (USA))
1906[3] (Dead)

Oscar Magic (IRE) *Nigel Twiston-Davies* 111b
4 bb g Oscar(IRE) —Just An Illusion (IRE) (Shernazar)
(4356) 4808[9] 5202[11]

Oscar Nominee (IRE) *Nicky Henderson* 83b
4 b g Old Vic—Native Bid (IRE) (Be My Native (USA))
4468[9]

Oscar Papa *Nick Gifford* 123h
6 ch g Presenting—Oso Special (Teenoso (USA))
2142[2] 2946[9] 3439[9] 4051[2] 4479[2]

Oscar Park (IRE) *David Arbuthnot* 120h 137c
12 b g Oscar(IRE) —Parkavoureen (Deep Run)
2663[P]

Oscar Prairie (IRE) *Warren Greatrex* 115h 118c
6 b g Oscar(IRE) —Silver Prairie (IRE) (Common Grounds)
(2440) 3378[2]
3772[5] 4538[F] (4966)

Oscar Royal (IRE) *Peter Hiatt* 120c
10 gr g Oscar(IRE) —Stonehill Princess (IRE) (King's Ride)
195[2] 694[P] (852)
957[2]

Oscar Sierra (IRE) *Tim Vaughan* 60b
5 b g Oscar(IRE) —Einaun (IRE) (Long Pond)
1989[14] *2295[6]* 3766[9]

Oscar Sunset (IRE) *Evan Williams* 104b
4 b g Oscar(IRE) —Derravarra Sunset (IRE) (Supreme Leader)
4866[2]

Oscars Well (IRE) *Mrs John Harrington* 153h
6 bb g Oscar(IRE) —Placid Willow (IRE) (Convinced)
(3029a) (4086a) ◆ 4803[4] ◆

Oscar The Myth (IRE) *Jamie Snowden* 83h
5 b g Oscar(IRE) —Have A Myth (IRE) (Roselier (FR))
3434[7] 3789[11] 3931[P] 4268[7] 4878[8]

Oscar Time (IRE) *M M Lynch* 138h 156c
10 b g Oscar(IRE) —Baywatch Star (IRE) (Supreme Leader)
4298a[3] ◆ **5200[2]**

Oscar Trial (IRE) *Sharon Watt* 75h 54c
9 b g Oscar(IRE) —The Polecat (IRE) (Supreme Leader)
1666[11] 1822[14] 3717[P]

Oscar Whisky (IRE) *Nicky Henderson* 165h
6 b g Oscar(IRE) —Ash Baloo (IRE) (Phardante (FR))
(3289) (3939) 4791[3] (5198)

Oscatello (USA) *Ross Oliver* 114h 129c
11 bb g Woodman(USA) —Galea Des Bois (FR) (Persian Bold)
(297) **4851[P]**

Oshkosh (IRE) *Kim Bailey* 81h
10 ch g Shernazar—Lucy Mews (IRE) (Persian Mews)
59[7] 467[6]

Oslot (FR) *Paul Nicholls* 80h 125c
9 b g Passing Sale(FR) —Une De Lann (FR) (Spoleto)
372[13]

Osmosia (FR) *Paul Webber* 90h
6 b m Mansonnien(FR) —Osmose (FR) (Cricket Ball (USA))
(935) 4101[P] 5280[4] 5385[4]

Osokenda *Jeremy Scott* 80h
11 b m Teenoso(USA) —Song Of Kenda (Rolfe (USA))
84^8

Osolomio (IRE) *Jennie Candlish* 111h 118c
8 b g Singspiel(IRE) —Inanna (Persian Bold)
636^7 764^P 866^2 994^8 1108^7 1501^5 1644^P 1929^{12} 2606^7 3621^P 4412^5 4880^P

Osric (IRE) *Nicky Henderson* 130h 141c
8 b g Mister Mat(FR) —Miss Ondee (FR) (Dress Parade)
(76) (591)
2088^2 (3156) ◆ 3672^2 3905^F 4794^P 5317^8

Ossmann (IRE) *Tom George* 91h 97c
11 b g Luso—Bit Of A Chance (Lord Ha Ha)
95^P

Ossmoses (IRE) *Mrs Alison Christmas* 126h 104c
14 gr g Roselier(FR) —Sugarstown (Sassafras (FR))
152^P

Ostaadi *Bernard Llewellyn* 83h
5 b g Nayef(USA) —Blodwen (USA) (Mister Baileys)
3439^P 3584^8 3761^8 4377^7 4721^6 4920^7 5272^2 ◆ 5390^2

Ostentation *Roger Teal* 91h
4 ch g Dubawi(IRE) —Oshiponga (Barathea (IRE))
3673^6 4192^3 4917^{13}

Ostland (GER) *Charlie Longsdon* 124h
6 b g Lando(GER) —Ost Tycoon (GER) (Last Tycoon)
3881^U 4354^4 4933^2 ◆ 5287^4 ◆

Otage De Brion (FR) *Robert Waley-Cohen* 120h 140c
9 b g Rajpoute(FR) —Gesse Parade (FR) (Dress Parade)
(329) 1345^F
1770^4 1970^F 5083^P

Othello (IRE) *Jonjo O'Neill* 61h
4 b g Azamour(IRE) —Bonheur (IRE) (Royal Academy (USA))
1330^5 1442^R 1545^9 2958^9 3255^P

Othermix (FR) *Ian Williams* 140h 146c
7 gr g Linamix(FR) —Other Crik (FR) (Bigstone (IRE))
2082^2 2348^3 2867^F 3291^8 3743^4 (5397)

Otis Tarda (IRE) *Philip Hobbs* 46h
5 b g Soviet Star(USA) —Top Ar Aghaidh (IRE) (Topanoora)
1748^6 3691^{16} 4437^{14}

O'Toole (IRE) *Caroline Keevil* 111h 120c
12 b g Toulon—Legs Burke (IRE) (Buckskin (FR))
664^3 846^3 1161^4 1277^P

Otterburn (IRE) *Alan Swinbank* 109b
5 b g Flemensfirth(USA) —Mrs Battle (IRE) (Be My Native (USA))
3992^2 ◆ 4308^3

Otter Mist *Victor Dartnall* 111h
6 gr g Karinga Bay—Absolutley Foxed (Absalom)
2074^7 2607^9 3295^8 3931^4 ◆

Otto Quercus (FR) *John Wade* 105h 106c
6 b g Saint Cyrien(FR) —La Haie Blanche (FR) (Sanglamore (USA))
1831^5 3500^{10}

Ouest Eclair (FR) *Ferdy Murphy* 104h
6 b g Sagacity(FR) —Kalistina (FR) (Sillery (USA))
1758^4 2080^4 2438^2 *3167^6* 3308^P 3951^2 (4751) 4958^2

Ouragan Lagrange (FR) *Gary Moore* 107h 86c
9 b g Panoramic—Fannie De Lagrange (FR) (Torence (FR))
156^6 280^P

Our Bob (IRE) *Philip Hobbs* 133h 120c
9 gr g Bob Back(USA) —Mondeo Rose (IRE) (Roselier (FR))
2165^3 3157^P 4355^8 4490^5 4938^3 5112^4

Our Bomber Harris *Paul Nicholls* 131h 131c
7 b g Saddlers' Hall(IRE) —Gaye Fame (Ardross)
2360^8
4453^4 4926^F (5170) ◆

Our Columbus (IRE) *Nigel Twiston-Davies* 95h 103c
7 b g Deploy—Phartoodeep (IRE) (Phardante (FR))
2365^2 2963^{10} 4292^8 4718^5 (5109)

Our Double Diamond *Jeremy Scott* 81b
6 ch m Double Trigger(IRE) —What A Gem (Karinga Bay)
3876^{12}

Our Father (IRE) *David Pipe* 131h
5 gr g Shantou(USA) —Rosepan (IRE) (Taipan (IRE))
(3439) ◆ 3930^2 4459^2

Our Flora *Kim Bailey* 61h
6 gr m Alflora(IRE) —Charlotte Gray (Rolfe (USA))
1768^8 3225^{11} 3480^P 4675^9 5169^P

Our Gar (IRE) *Mrs Prunella Dobbs* 132h 115c
8 bb g Rashar(USA) —Garys Girl (Seclude (USA))
1526a^5

Our Girl Salley (IRE) *Mrs Prunella Dobbs* 132h
6 b m Carroll House—Lenmore Lisa (IRE) (Phardante (FR))
(3592a)

Our Golden Boy (IRE) *Mark Usher* 85h
5 b g Milan—Just Little (Mtoto)
3054^4 3842^6 4459^9 5013^4

Our Guardian Angel (IRE) *Tim Vaughan* 94h
7 b m Dushyantor(USA) —Hearth (IRE) (King's Ride)
632^3 843^2 999^2 1140^2 1275^3

Our Hero (IRE) *Charlie Longsdon* 117h 125c
8 b g Oscar Schindler(IRE) —Miners Own (IRE) (Miner's Lamp)
425^2 735^{10} 911^6 1032^{10}

Our Island (IRE) *Tim Vaughan* 131h
6 b g Turtle Island(IRE) —Linda's Leader (IRE) (Supreme Leader)
(3942) ◆ (4189) 4849^7

Our Jasper *Donald McCain* 80h 131c
11 gr g Tina's Pet—Dawn's Della (Scottish Reel)
1725^2 1960^U

Our Jim *Donald McCain* 95h 115c
9 ch g Sir Harry Lewis(USA) —Dawn's Della (Scottish Reel)
352^4 501^F 695^2 804^P 3922^8 4421^6 5120^2

Our Little Dreamer (IRE) *Jeremy Scott* 81h
7 b g Lahib(USA) —Majestic Run (Deep Run)
223^P 2058^7 2390^8 3300^7

Our Matti *Chris Grant* 82h
10 b g Supreme Leader—Haudello (FR) (Marignan (USA))
2473^7

Our Mick *Donald McCain* 126h
5 gr g Karinga Bay—Dawn's Della (Scottish Reel)
2403^2 2954^2 3572^3 (4100) 4702^2 5000^F

Ours (FR) *Mark Rimell* 88h 107c
9 b g Discover D'Auteuil(FR) —Geographie (FR) (Petit Montmorency (USA))
2952^P 3618^P 3720^2 (4103)
(4416) 5069^2 5370^3

Oursininlaw (IRE) *Evan Williams* 111h
7 gr g Turgeon(USA) —Fontanalia (FR) (Rex Magna (FR))
(137) 514^6 683^2 (999) 1275^2 1391^U 1625^P 3941^4 4700^{10}

Ouste (FR) *Alison Thorpe* 31h 126c
9 ch g Ragmar(FR) —Elbe (FR) (Royal Charter (FR))
1961^5 430^P 994^{12}
1200^P 1335^P

Outaouais (FR) *George Baker* 120h 109c
9 b g Sleeping Car(FR) —Hatilade (FR) (Royal Charter (FR))
1816^P

Outclass *Harry Chisman* 70h 77c
9 b m Classic Cliche(IRE) —Winnetka Gal (IRE) (Phardante (FR))
371^4 797^4

Outlaw Tom (IRE) *Alex Hales* 112h 96c
7 b g Luso—Timely Approach (IRE) (Good Thyne (USA))
2110^5 2595^5 2941^2 3771^7 4988^P

Outside Investor (IRE) *Patrick Rodford* 89h 89c
11 bb g Cadeaux Genereux—Desert Ease (IRE) (Green Desert (USA))
931^7 1027^8 (1843)
2024^6 2483^3 2638^P

Outside The Box *Noel Chance* 114h 114c
7 b g Karinga Bay—Maydoo (IRE) (Mandalus)
2213^8 2626^U 2926^5 3393^3 3838^2 4355^F 4698^6

Out The Black (IRE) *Caroline Keevil* 139c
13 b g Presenting—Executive Wonder (IRE) (Executive Perk)
1769^{10}

Out To Impress (IRE) *Murty McGrath* 70h
6 b g Alzao(USA) —Dance Fontaine (IRE) (Danehill Dancer (IRE))
216^8 528^P 1900^7 2169^7

Ouzbeck (FR) *Emma Lavelle* 122h 153c
9 bb g Denham Red(FR) —Volodia (FR) (Dhausli (FR))
503^7 (844)
1856^3 2221^9 5003^8
5338^{13}

Overafrica (IRE) *Donald McCain* 101b
5 b g Overbury(IRE) —Siberiansdaughter (IRE) (Strong Gale)
5174^7

Overbranch *Malcolm Jefferson* 108h 100c
8 br m Overbury(IRE) —Anabranch (Kind Of Hush)
353^8 3524^7 4001^3 4254^2 4744^8

Overbury Pearl *I J Hooper* 52b
8 b m Overbury(IRE) —Vi's Delight (New Member)
4011^P

Overclear *Victor Dartnall* 124h 146c
9 b g Overbury(IRE) —Callope (USA) (Recitation (USA))
524^8 756^7

Overlady *James Ewart* 89c
9 bb m Overbury(IRE) —Chief Lady Nicola (Nicholas Bill)
3996^P 4256
4571^5 5032^6

Overlaw *Tom George* 65h 104c
9 br g Overbury(IRE) —Reprieve (Riberetto)
2952^4 ◆ 3541^2 3792^P 5293^5

Overlay *John O'Neill* 12h
7 br m Overbury(IRE) —Lay It Off (IRE) (Strong Gale)
5059^6

Overlut (FR) *R Scrine* 59h 105c
9 bl g Discover D'Auteuil(FR) —Lutsine (FR) (Zino)
4463^U 4748^3

Overnight Fame (IRE) *Tom George* 112h
7 b m Kayf Tara—Best Of The Girls (IRE) (Supreme Leader)
2288^5 2974^5 3485^2 3901^4 4418^2

Overpriced *Maurice Barnes* 65h
5 b m Chocolat De Meguro(USA) —One Stop (Silly Prices)
1510^7 1934^{10} 2167^{10} 5027^{10} 5151^9 5352^U

Overquest *Elliott Cooper* 114c
9 b g Overbury(IRE) —Foleys Quest (IRE) (River Falls)
1000^6 1068^3 1402^4 (1663) ◆ 1763^2 (2274)
2354^F 3522^6 4360^P

Overrule (USA) *Brian Ellison* 116h 42c
7 b g Diesis—Her Own Way (USA) (Danzig (USA))
34^4 ◆ 192^4

Overspin *Paul Webber* 90h 38c
8 b m Overbury(IRE) —Re-Spin (Gildoran)
477^F 799^P 864^5

Over The Clyde *William Young* 37b
6 b g Overbury(IRE) —La Dama (USA) (Known Fact (USA))
448^8 2553^{12} 3553^{12} 3856^9 4061^P

Over The Creek *M J Coate* 9h 124c
12 br g Over The River(FR) —Solo Girl (IRE) (Le Bavard (FR))
181^6 911^8 4928^7

Over The Flow *Bob Buckler* 105h 101c
9 br m Overbury(IRE) —Flow (Over The River (FR))
56^U 169^7 (371)

Over The Hill *Nigel Twiston-Davies* 89h
7 b g Overbury(IRE) —Nearlymissed Daisy (Presidium)
1567^9 2244^{10}

Over The Page *Mark Gillard*
5 b g Where Or When(IRE) —Snaefell Heights (Suave Dancer (USA))
5382^R

Over The Phone (IRE) *A G Hobbs* 120c
6 b g Heron Island(IRE) —Carry On Queen (IRE) (Cataldi)
(4415)
(4901)

Over To Joe *C C Pimlott* 73h 109c
11 br g Overbury(IRE) —Flo-Jo (DEN) (Pelton Lad)
493^P 4973^P

Overton Lad *Peter Pritchard* 69h 87c
10 gr g Overbury(IRE) —Safe Arrival (USA) (Shadeed (USA))
(383) 471^U
665^4 931^4 1159^8 1483^P 1733^P 2155^2 2457^4

Overturn (IRE) *Donald McCain* 163h
7 b g Barathea(IRE) —Kristal Bridge (Kris)
207^2 (1133a) ◆ 3559^2 4222^5 4791^7 5337^3

Overyou *Elliott Cooper* 89h
6 bl m Overbury(IRE) —Keep The Treasure (IRE) (Treasure Hunter)
93^7 174^2 519^7 706^P 2271^P 2658^{12} 3619^5 4138^2 ◆ 4302^8 4542^P

Ovthenight (IRE) *Pam Sly* 112h 115c
6 b g Noverre(USA) —Night Beauty (King Of Kings (IRE))
351^5 846^4 962^{10} 1556^5 1813^2 1952^4 (2311)
3784^7 4313^7 4971^5

Owen Glendower (IRE) *Nicky Henderson* 128h
6 br g Anshan—Native Success (IRE) (Be My Native (USA))
(1743) (2056) 2344^4 4725^9 5291^3

Owls FC (IRE) *Michael Chapman* 75h
5 b m King's Best(USA) —Sadinga (IRE) (Sadler's Wells (USA))
1329^6 1427^U 1555^9
1628^P 4233^{13}

Owlsley *Jim Old* 56h
9 b g Terimon—Black H'Penny (Town And Country)
2311^0

Owner Occupier *Chris Gordon* 88h 109c
6 ch g Foxhound(USA) —Miss Beverley (Beveled (USA))
(1995) ◆ 2429^F 2605^2 2986^F 3343^4
3869^2 4400^3 (4698) 5212^F

Own Line *Miss S L Gould* 49h 73c
12 b g Classic Cliche(IRE) —Cold Line (Exdirectory)
184^5

Oxford Circus *Anna Brooks* 82h
9 b g Loup Sauvage(USA) —Ideal Candidate (Celestial Storm (USA))
76^P

Oxford De Lagarde (FR) *Mrs Alison Christmas* 47h 99c
9 b g Sleeping Car(FR) —Gamine De Tanues (FR) (Fast (FR))
132^P 4553^F

Oxlea Lass *James Frost* 37h
6 b m Access Ski—Sporting Annie (Teamster)
591^5

Oxus (IRE) *William Clay* 12h
6 ch g Sinndar(IRE) —River Dancer (Irish River (FR))
224^P

Pablo Du Charmil (FR) *David Pipe* 121h 153c
10 ch g Lyphard's Wish(FR) —Pacifie Du Charmil (FR) (Dom Pasquini (FR))
98^7 1020^6 1332^6 1611^9

Pacco (FR) *Oliver Sherwood* 103h 123c
8 b g Assessor(IRE) —Uguette IV (FR) (Chamberlin (FR))
2073^6 (2557)
2928^6 (3615)
4277^4 4537^6

Pacha D'Oudairies (FR) *Michael Blake* 126h 110c
8 b g Ungaro(GER) —Forlane V (FR) (Quart De Vin (FR))
2217^5 2366^U 2587^2 3265^4 3819^2 4139^5 4744^7

Pacific Bay (IRE) *Richard Ford* 74h
5 b m Diktat—Wild Clover (Lomitas)
547^P

Paco Jack (IRE) *P J Rothwell* 128h 136c
7 b g Soviet Star(USA) —Tocade (IRE) (Kenmare (FR))
1123a^U 1527a^{12} 3473a^P

Pacte Noir (FR) *Tony Newcombe* 51h
8 gr g Morespeed—Diva Noire (FR) (Royal Charter (FR))
264^{12}

Paddington Bob (IRE) *Pauline Robson* 86h
7 b g Bob's Return(IRE) —Castlehaven (IRE) (Erins Isle)
163^3 (552) 729^2 946^P

Paddleyourowncanoe (IRE) *Emma Baker* 104h
10 b g Saddlers' Hall(IRE) —Little Paddle (IRE) (Remainder Man)
359^P 522^7 767^2 (994)

Paddy O Dee *P J Rothwell* 120h 120c
6 b g Kasakov—Baladiya (Darshaan)
3706a^{10}

Paddy Partridge *Tim Vaughan* 118h
5 b g Pivotal—Treble Heights (IRE) (Unfuwain (USA))
(983) 4361^2 4944^2

Paddy Rielly (IRE) *John Flint* 69h
6 b g Catcher In The Rye(IRE) —The Veil (IRE) (Barathea (IRE))
303^5

Paddys Honour (IRE) *Lucinda Russell* 85h
8 b g City Honours(USA) —Clara Petal (IRE) (Castle Keep)
2271^5 3336^6 3729^P

Paddys Unyoke (IRE) *Stuart Coltherd* 96c
10 b g Carroll House—Paddy's Dancer (Paddy's Stream)
2189^5 3503^3 3636^P

Paddy The Hare (IRE) *Dr Richard Newland* 88b
6 ch g Old Vic—Boragh Thyme (IRE) (Simply Great (FR))
3200^7 3842^{11}

Paddy The Piper (IRE) *J Heard* 125h 94c
14 b g Witness Box(USA) —Divine Dibs (Raise You Ten)
173^R

Paddy The Yank (IRE) *Richard Mitchell* 89c
8 b g Sassanian(USA) —Celias Fancy (IRE) (Mandalus)
3788^4 4122^3 4556^4 4770^4

Padre Eterno *Heather Main* 99b
6 b g Luso—Right On Target (IRE) (Presenting)
3200^{17}

Padys Arkle (IRE) *Brett Johnson* 28h
7 b g African Chimes—Ardnaglug Cross (Tug Of War)
1680^7 4397^P 4917^{14}

Pagan Lightning (USA) *Dianne Sayer* 88h
6 ch g Street Cry(IRE) —Bloomin Thunder (USA) (Thunder Gulch (USA))
1426^5 2446^7 3252^P 3749^{10} (3993)

Pagan Sword *David Bridgwater* 108h 105c
9 ch g Selkirk(USA) —Vanessa Bell (IRE) (Lahib (USA))
828^2 864^2 934^3 1091^3 1128^5 1481^5 1587^2

Paintball (IRE) *Charlie Longsdon* 122h
4 b g Le Vie Dei Colori—Camassina (IRE) (Taufan (USA))
3401^2 ◆ 3767^6 (4288) ◆ 4807^9 (5291) ◆

Painted Sky *Richard Fahey* 99h
8 ch g Rainbow Quest(USA) —Emplane (USA) (Irish River (FR))
166^3 462^F

Painted Tail (IRE) *James Frost* 83b
4 b f Mark Of Esteem(IRE) —Bronwen (IRE) (King's Best (USA))
2052^5 *2597^2* *3979^5*

Painter Man (FR) *David Pipe* 114h 122c
9 b g Double Bed(FR) —Diana La Belle (FR) (Synefos (USA))
501^7 735^3

Paint The Clouds *Warren Greatrex* 132h
6 b g Muhtarram(USA) —Preening (Persian Bold)
(1974) 2428^4 3452^7 4354^2 ◆ (5038) (5289)

Paint The Tape (IRE) *J T R Dreaper* 79h 69c
8 b m Oscar(IRE) —Heather Darling (IRE) (Be My Native (USA))
1338^4 (Dead)

Paint The Town Red *Hugh Collingridge*
6 b g Mujahid(USA) —Onefortheditch (USA) (With Approval (CAN))
1325^P

Pairc Na Gcapall (IRE) *Neil King* 107h 131c
9 b g Taipan(IRE) —Ballindante (IRE) (Phardante (FR))
65^2 225^2
501^4 1032^4 1252^4 (1326)
1469^5 1570^4 1814^F
(2024) 2127^4 2637^{10} 5278^P

Pair Of Kings (IRE) *Alan Swinbank* 93h
6 b g Revoque(IRE) —Valleymay (IRE) (King's Ride)
8^4 305^4 603^3

Pak Jack (FR) *Richard Phillips* 106h 134c
11 ch g Pitchounet(FR) —Miss Noir Et Or (FR) (Noir Et Or)
2123^6
2543^F 3588^2 (4277)

Palace Jester *Jonjo O'Neill* 125h
6 b g King's Theatre(IRE) —Jessolle (Scallywag)
2166^2 ◆ (2612) ◆ 3542^3 3917^3 4862^8

Palace Merano (FR) *Donald McCain* 134h 123c
8 b g Antarctique(IRE) —Domage II (FR) (Cyborg (FR))
2106^P 3522^P 4689^P

Palawi (IRE) *John Quinn* 140h
4 ch g Dubawi(IRE) —Palwina (FR) (Unfuwain (USA))
(2033) ◆ 2356^{10} 3785^2 (4240) (4774) 5161^F

Pallasmore (IRE) *Paul W Flynn* 80h 131c
8 gr g Ala Hounak—Pallas Lady (IRE) (Mister Lord (USA))
1332^8 1712a^F

Pallaton *Brendan Powell*
5 ch g Bertolini(USA) —Miss Honeypenny (IRE) (Old Vic)
583^P

Palmier (FR) *F-M Cottin* 112h
8 b g Brier Creek(USA) —Goguette II (FR) (Bayolidaan (FR))
2230a^8

Palmito (IRE) *Nigel Twiston-Davies* 111h
7 gr m Great Palm(USA) —Island Crest (Jupiter Island)
521^9

Palm Reader (IRE) *Donald McCain* 116h
8 b g Oscar(IRE) —Jasmine Melody (Jasmine Star)
2104^F 3256^P

Palomar (USA) *Brian Ellison* 134h 138c
9 bb g Chester House(USA) —Ball Gown (USA) (Silver Hawk (USA))
(1609) *(3170)* 3561^3 4188^9 4852^{16}

Palos Conti (FR) *Tim Pitt* 113h 118c
8 ch g Robin Des Champs(FR) —Dona Mirande (FR) (Pebble (FR))
(2079)
3510^6

Palypso De Creek (FR) *Charlie Longsdon* 134h 144c
8 b g Brier Creek(USA) —Belgheera (FR) (Vorias (USA))
2522^F 2871^P 3832^U (3954) 4209^6
4821^{14}

Pamak D'Airy (FR) *Henry Hogarth* 115h 120c
8 b g Cadoubel(FR) —Gamaska D'Airy (FR) (Marasali)
330^6 2352^U 2613^5 3854^6 (4279)
4392^6 5134^P

Pamoja *Martin Todhunter* 66h
5 b g Rock Of Gibraltar(IRE) —Royal York (Bustino)
1962[12] 2509[10]

Pampanito *Donald McCain* 102b
5 b g Bollin Eric—Seamill (IRE) (Lafontaine (USA))
5210[2]

Pampelonne (IRE) *Nicky Henderson* 91b
5 b m Oscar(IRE) —Bondi Storm (IRE) (Glacial Storm (USA))
1771[5]

Panache *Debra Hamer* 99b
6 b g King's Best(USA) —Exclusive (Polar Falcon (USA))
(1572) 2389[9]

Panama At Once *Philip Kirby* 53h 96c
11 ch g Commanche Run—Cherry Sip (Nearly A Hand)
626[P] 3888[P] 4306[P] 4825[3] 5097[6] 5414[4]

Panama Canal (IRE) *Charles Pogson* 82h 108c
6 b g Accordion—Maltese Lady (IRE) (Viking (USA))
1623[6] 1951[7] **2071[2] 2475[4]** *3171[5]* **3395[U] 3695[P] 3990[7]**

Panashka (IRE) *Mark Campion* 81b
6 ch m Ashkalani(IRE) —Dressed In Style (IRE) (Meneval (USA))
2546[5] 3992[5]

Pancake (FR) *Philip Hobbs* 84h 104c
8 ch g Cyborg(FR) —Six Fois Sept (FR) (Epervier Bleu)
2311[4] 2794[4] 3768[5]

Pandorama (IRE) *Noel Meade* 157h 169c
8 b g Flemensfirth(USA) —Gretchen's Castle (IRE) (Carlingford Castle)
2673[P] (3176a) ◆ **4850[7]**

Panjo Bere (FR) *Gary Moore* 127h 152c
8 b g Robin Des Pres(FR) —Honeymoon Suite (FR) (Double Bed (FR))
2086[8] 2515[3] 3677[10] 4077[4]

Pan Pan (FR) *Anna Bramall* 28h 65c
8 ch g Ragmar(FR) —Pin'Hup (FR) (Signani (FR))
4570[5] 5029[P]

Pantalaimon *Henry Daly* 77h 114c
10 b g Classic Cliche(IRE) —Threewaygirl (Orange Bay)
158[5]

Panthers Run *Jonathan Haynes* 48h 87c
11 b g Jendali(USA) —Dorado Beach (Lugana Beach)
459[P] **730[6]**
931[P] 1665[5] 1826[6] 2301[3] 2645[3] 3636[P] 3712[2] 4241[2] 4509[4]
4827[5] 5258[10]

Pantxoa (FR) *Alan King* 120h
4 b g Daliapour(IRE) —Palmeria (FR) (Great Palm (USA))
(2151) 2882[5] 4024[2] 4954[2]

Panzer (GER) *Donald McCain* 102h 105c
10 b g Vettori(IRE) —Prompt (Old Vic)
1137[5] 1380[3] (1745)
(2050) 2183[2]
4381[F] 4713[F]

Papa Caruso *Sue Smith* 112h 114c
7 b g Kayf Tara—Madonna Da Rossi (Mtoto)
1931[3]
2270[5] 2599[5] 3391[4]

Papa Drew (IRE) *Andrew Parker* 81h 58c
7 b g Anshan—Royal Shares (IRE) (Royal Fountain)
2125 2302[7] **2656[5] 3748[P]** 4146[8]

Papamoa *N W Alexander* 71h
6 gr g Terimon—Larksmore (Royal Fountain)
2192[3]

Papa Noel *Michael Mullineaux*
5 b g Paris House—Diamond Rouge (Puissance)
833[P]

Papa's Princess *James Moffatt*
7 b m Mujadil(USA) —Desert Flower (Green Desert (USA))
1375[6]

Paperboy *Mike Hammond* 56b
7 b g Double Trigger(IRE) —Paperweight (In The Wings)
766[P]

Papradon *Nigel Twiston-Davies* 89h 106c
7 b g Tobougg(IRE) —Salvezza (IRE) (Superpower)
318[12] (585) 697[2] 875[4]
991[2] (1231) 1272[6] **1471[5] 1710[3] 1940[2] 4290[2] 4863[4] 5076[3]** 5379[4]

Paquet Cadeau (FR) *Henry Daly* 63h 122c
6 ch g Robin Des Champs(FR) —Chantalouette (FR) (Royal Charter (FR))
2069[4] 2530[11] **3648[U]** 4874[P]

Paradise Ally (IRE) *P Budds* 90h
9 b m Presenting—Azaban (IRE) (Be My Native (USA))
1798[7]

Paradise Expected *Tim Vaughan* 94h 89c
8 ch m North Briton—Phenomenon (Unfuwain (USA))
16[4] 336[3] 3258[4]
3790[6] 4099[P] 4718[9]

Paradise Regained (FR) *Sophie Leech* 64h 94c
8 b g Lost World(IRE) —Bajabala (FR) (Nikos)
272[11] 5931[1] **822[4] 864[P]**

Parazar (FR) *Oliver Sherwood* 94h
6 b g Kutub(IRE) —Paraja (IRE) (Doyoun)
865[5] 1107[3] 1292[4] 1477[4] 1592[7] 1842[7]

Parc Des Princes (USA) *Nicky Richards* 79h
5 bb g Ten Most Wanted(USA) —Miss Orah (Unfuwain (USA))
2509[9] 3331[13] 3746[10] 4686[9]

Par Excellence *Jeremy Scott* 61h
8 gr m Wizard King—Great Intent (Aragon)
358[6] 535[5]

Parhelion *Evan Williams* 84h
4 b g Fantastic Light(USA) —Shamaiel (IRE) (Lycius (USA))
1226[2]

Parisian Dream *Tim Pitt* 40h
7 b g Sakhee(USA) —Boojum (Mujtahid (USA))
1688[11]

Parisian Knight (IRE) *A M Crow* 82h
8 ch g Moonax(IRE) —Dunelady (IRE) (Mister Lord (USA))
31[3] 405[6] 456[4] 875[P] 1101[P]

Parkhalkevi (FR) *Y Fouin*
6 b g Khalkevi(IRE) —Part Time (FR) (Lead On Time (USA))
190a[3]

Park Lane *Paul Fitzsimons* 117h
5 b g Royal Applause—Kazeem (Darshaan)
1773[6] (2150) 4049[9]

Park's Prodigy *Chris Grant* 91h 102c
7 b g Desert Prince(IRE) —Up And About (Barathea (IRE))
1695[12]
4237[5] 5134[4]

Parlesotho (FR) *Ben Case* 128h 80c
8 b m Lesotho(USA) —Shelba (FR) (Rolling Bowl (FR))
3[4] 633[7] 1364[7] 1986[4] 2579[4] 3575[6]

Parrain (FR) *J M Turner* 130h 82c
8 b g Brier Creek(USA) —Grenelle II (FR) (Quart De Vin (FR))
4183[5]

Parsnip Pete *Tom George* 96b
5 b g Pasternak—Bella Coola (Northern State (USA))
(4443) 5084[U]

Parson's Punch *Lucy Normile* 84h
6 b g Beat Hollow—Ordained (Mtoto)
4068[9] 4910[8]

Party Palace *Stuart Howe* 102h
7 b m Auction House(USA) —Lady-Love (Pursuit Of Love)
771[5] 1162[3] 1740[5] 1911[9] 5241[8]

Party Pictures (IRE) *A J Farrant* 85b 67c
8 b g Exit To Nowhere(USA) —Beccemma (IRE) (Over The River (FR))
133[6]

Pascha Bere (FR) *Nick Gifford* 137h 137c
8 gr g Verglas(IRE) —Ephelide (FR) (Count Pahlen)
(235) 633[5] 2085[3] **(4122)**
4311[2] 4926[2] 5226[4]

Pasco (SWI) *Paul Nicholls* 133h 152c
8 ro g Selkirk(USA) —Palena (Danehill (USA))
2674[2] 4053[2]

Passato (GER) *Joanna Davis* 114h 141c
7 b g Lando(GER) —Passata (FR) (Polar Falcon (USA))
(130) **(523)**
(959)
(1332) 1861[7] 2359[11] 2665[5] 5185[F]

Passive Interest *Ray Peacock* 27h
6 b m Sir Harry Lewis(USA) —Carole's Choir (Primo Dominie)
224[P] 635[7]

Pass Me By *Suzy Smith* 126h 115c
12 b g Balnibarbi—Errol Emerald (Dom Racine (FR))
312a[F] 2395[3] 3347[P] 3568[P] 5154[2]

Pass The Parsel (IRE) *G T H Bailey* 84b 107c
10 bb g Bob Back(USA) —My Lovely Rose (IRE) (Orchestra)
4832[3]

Pastek (FR) *Martin Peaty* 78b 99c
8 b g Ungaro(GER) —Capsolane (FR) (Son Of Silver)
335[3] 502[5] 3908[11] 4271[6]

Past Gambles (IRE) *Bill Moore* 70h
9 bb g Pasternak—Most Effective (IRE) (Lancastrian)
3917[8] 4006[9]

Past Heritage *Alan Jones* 71h 85c
12 b g Past Glories—Norman's Delight (IRE) (Idiots Delight)
1106[4] 1231[2] (1511)

Pas Trop Tard (FR) *Maurice Barnes* 79b
4 b g Caballo Raptor(CAN) —This Melody (FR) (Saint Preuil (FR))
3752[9] 5209[5]

Pasture Bay (IRE) *George Charlton* 97b
5 b g Flemensfirth(USA) —Silver Oak (IRE) (Anshan)
399[2] 2943[10] 3511[6] 5342[12]

Patavium (IRE) *Edwin Tuer* 97h
8 b g Titus Livius(FR) —Arcevia (IRE) (Archway (IRE))
4115[3] 4738[P] 4960[5]

Patchoulie Conti (FR) *Sue Smith* 90h 96c
8 b m Robin Des Champs(FR) —Lady In Love (FR) (Kadalko (FR))
473[P]

Pateese (FR) *Philip Hobbs* 130h
6 b g Priolo(USA) —Flyer (FR) (Highest Honor (FR))
2499[3] 2960[3] ◆ 3489[2] (3760) 4488[2] 4727[3]
5166[11]

Pathian Prince *E R Clough* 88h 115c
8 b g Parthian Springs—Smilingatstrangers (Macmillion)
4526[3] 5326[2]

Pathlow (IRE) *Anabel L M King* 81b
5 b g Old Vic—Rosa View (IRE) (Roselier (FR))
412[8] 602[8]

Patman Du Charmil (FR) *Nigel Twiston-Davies* 123h 132c
9 b g Robin Des Pres(FR) —Pacifie Du Charmil (FR) (Dom Pasquini (FR))
2374[5] 2869[11] 3292[12] (3617)
(4408) 5236[5]

Patricias Pride *Lucinda Featherstone* 85b
4 ch g Silver Patriarch(IRE) —Anniversary Guest (IRE) (Desert King (IRE))
5426[3]

Patrick Dee *Christine Dunnett* 61h
6 gr g Silver Patriarch(IRE) —Bunty (Presidium)
1541[2] 2109[9] 2577[14] *3090[6]* 3400[6] 3540[DSQ]
3833[P] 4403[P] 4920[5]

Patrick's Secret *Zoe Davison*
7 br g Wace(USA) —Miss Secret (El Conquistador)
5059[P]

Patriot (IRE) *Martin Todhunter* 105h
7 b g Sadler's Wells(USA) —Sweeten Up (Shirley Heights)
179[5] 214[2] (457) 729[3] 5429[11]

Patrixbourne *Tim Vaughan* 77h
8 ch m Double Trigger(IRE) —Lady Buck (Pollerton)
(749) ◆

Patrixtoo (FR) *Tim Fitzgerald* 69h
10 gr g Linamix(FR) —Maradadi (USA) (Shadeed (USA))
157[7] 4511[7]

Patsy Finnegan *Alan King* 127h 127c
9 b g Sir Harry Lewis(USA) —Bampton Fair (Free Boy)
3543[2] 4050[2] 4445[2] 4989[4]

Patterning *Chris Grant* 102h
4 b g Pivotal—Historian (IRE) (Pennekamp (USA))
(4056) 4473[3]

Pauillac (FR) *David Pipe* 100h 102c
8 b g Useful(FR) —Jolie Mome (FR) (Art Francais (USA))
274[P] 549[2] 1027[9]

Paul Revere (IRE) *Nicky Richards* 71h
7 b g Exit To Nowhere(USA) —Sharkezan (IRE) (Double Schwartz)
2192[P] 2552[11] 3850[P] 4910[P]

Pause And Clause (IRE) *Emma Lavelle* 146h 131c
7 b g Saddlers' Hall(IRE) —Silver Glen (IRE) (Roselier (FR))
1627[2] 2082[4] 2494[4] 2945[7] 3947[14] 4817[21] 5325[7]

Pavanne (IRE) *Martin Keighley* 87h
6 ch g Hawk Wing(USA) —Pillars Of Society (IRE) (Caerleon (USA))
100[7] 990[P]

Pavillon Bleu (FR) *Philip Hobbs* 121h 128c
8 b g Vaguely Pleasant(FR) —Isaure De Bussy (FR) (Bad Conduct (USA))
1776[2] 2147[2] 2500[P]
3453[P] 4220[4] 4875[3]

Paxford Junior *Milton Harris* 30b
5 b g Bollin Eric—Paxford Lady (Alflora (IRE))
1071[8]

Pay On (IRE) *Alistair Whillans* 81h
8 ch g Danehill Dancer(IRE) —Richly Deserved (IRE) (Kings Lake (USA))
405[9] 459[4] 875[10]

Pay The Bounty *Robert Tyner* 122h 137c
8 b g Karinga Bay—Jack's The Girl (IRE) (Supreme Leader)
2119a[6] 3241a[7]

Pay The Russian *Neil King* 25h
5 b g Auction House(USA) —Thabeh (Shareef Dancer (USA))
693[P] 835[5]

Peace Corps *Michael Gates* 101h
5 ch g Medicean—Tromond (Lomond (USA))
4076[3]

Peaceful Means (IRE) *Evan Williams* 108h
8 b m Witness Box(USA) —Princess Satco (IRE) (Satco (FR))
51[3] 140[2] 350[2] 479[2] ◆ 959[3] 1282[7] 1470[7] 1556[6]
5080[4]

Peachey Moment (USA) *Nicky Richards* 83h 101c
6 bb g Stormin Fever(USA) —Given Moment (USA) (Diesis)
1758[10]
2352[F] 3524[5]

Peak Seasons (IRE) *Michael Chapman* 46h 84c
8 ch g Raise A Grand(IRE) —Teresian Girl (IRE) (Glenstal (USA))
48[4] 136[2] 516[6] 891[4] 1001[2] 1080[5] 1378[2] 1423[2] 1628[5] 1940[3]
2276[2] 2434[U] 3091[8] 3307[3]
3404[5] 3618[8]
4238[6] (5018)
5293[6]

Pearl (IRE) *Alison Thorpe* 101h
7 b m Daylami(IRE) —Briery (IRE) (Salse (USA))
2574[P] 3529[9] 4161[6]

Pearl Mountain (IRE) *Jeff Pearce* 86b
4 b f Pearl Of Love(IRE) —Latest Chapter (IRE) (Ahonoora)
2173[2] *2597[8]* 2965[4] 3406[9]

Pearly Star *D Bryant* 97h 92c
10 br g Bob's Return(IRE) —Pearly-B (IRE) (Gunner B)
84[6] 410[8] 593[5] 1468[4] **4534[P] 5372[6]**

Pearlysteps *Henry Daly* 123h 141c
8 ch g Alflora(IRE) —Pearly-B (IRE) (Gunner B)
2303[2] ◆ **2527[2]** ◆ **(3368)**
3803[3] 4802[7]

Peasant Law *Tracy Waggott* 69b
5 gr g Cape Town(IRE) —Regal Academy (IRE) (Royal Academy (USA))
841[8]

Peccatorum (IRE) *A J McNamara* 107h
4 bb g Big Bad Bob(IRE) —Golden Skiis (IRE) (Hector Protector (USA))
4295a[8]

Peckhamecho (IRE) *Rebecca Curtis* 113b
5 b g Beneficial—Nolans Pride (IRE) (Good Thyne (USA))
(2222) 4191[3] 5202[18]

Pedasus (USA) *Ronald Harris* 38h
5 b g Fusaichi Pegasus(USA) —Butterfly Cove (USA) (Storm Cat (USA))
1238[6] 4924[8]

Peddlers Cross (IRE) *Donald McCain* 169h
6 b g Oscar(IRE) —Patscilla (Squill (USA))
(2668) ◆ (4169) 4791[2] 5198[7]

Peedeeque *Andy Turnell* 106h
5 b g Kayf Tara—Sister Kit (IRE) (Glacial Storm (USA))
4677[4] 5038[3]

Pegasus Lad (USA) *Linda Blackford* 70h
5 bb g Fusaichi Pegasus(USA) —Leo Girl (USA) (Seattle Slew (USA))
754[4] 908[5] 1066[11] 1164[8] 1272[9] 1489[P] 5390[F]

Pegasus Prince (USA) *Keith Reveley* 130h
7 b g Fusaichi Pegasus(USA) —Avian Eden (USA) (Storm Bird (CAN))
289[3] 2375[8] (3820) (4235) 4742[2]

Peintre Du Roi (USA) *Natalie Lloyd-Beavis* 98h
7 ch g El Prado(IRE) —Peinture Bleue (USA) (Alydar (USA))
1812[9] 4129[3] 4503[9]

Peintre Ster (IRE) *Neil King* 73b
4 ch g Peintre Celebre(USA) —Goldster (IRE) (Intikhab (USA))
2315[11] 3835[5] *(4923)*

Pekan Two *John Hellens* 68b
5 ch g Dr Fong(USA) —Carambola (IRE) (Danehill (USA))
3731[9] 3998[7]

Pelennor (FR) *R Scrine* 104h
7 b g River Bay(USA) —Alidami (GER) (Damister (USA))
4936[P]

Pelo Du Bief (FR) *John Cornwall* 99h 105c
8 b g Useful(FR) —Hopeful Of Silver (FR) (Son Of Silver)
1767[7] 2034[F]

Pemberton *David Pipe* 128h 109c
6 ch g Lomitas—Whitehaven (Top Ville)
756[6] 830[F]

Pembo *Mike Hammond* 68h
6 b g Choisir(AUS) —Focosa (ITY) (In The Wings)
338[8]

Pena Dorada (IRE) *Mrs K Burke* 114h
4 b g Key Of Luck(USA) —Uluwatu (IRE) (Unfuwain (USA))
(1699) ◆ 1984[2] 2356[9] 4083a[9] 4467[3]

Penchesco (IRE) *Amanda Perrett* 109h
6 b g Orpen(USA) —Francesca (IRE) (Perugino (USA))
1914[2] 2122[3] 4557[3] 5243[3]

Pendle Forest (IRE) *Miss E Young* 77h 77c
11 gr m Charnwood Forest(IRE) —Pride Of Pendle (Grey Desire)
4147[P]

Penelope Pips *Evan Williams* 75b
4 ch f Presenting—Chartridge Hill (Crested Lark)
(5019)

Pen Gwen (FR) *Kate Walton* 80h 109c
8 b g Le Balafre(FR) —Dans Dro (FR) (Spoleto (IRE))
178[2] 480[8]
628[3]

Penn Da Benn (FR) *Bernard Llewellyn* 138h 134c
8 b g Passing Sale(FR) —Gwen Ha Du (FR) (Djarvis (FR))
2501[3]

Pennek (FR) *Philip Kirby* 139h 121c
8 b g Grand Tresor(FR) —Annabelle Treveene (FR) (Spoleto)
2401[3] 2953[6] 4256 4394[2] 4891[2]

Pennellis (FR) *Paul Nicholls* 126h
7 bb g Alderbrook—Muchsorrylady (IRE) (Boreen (FR))
1773[3] (2333) 2626[4] 3229[11]
4782[P]

Penny Bazaar *Dianne Sayer* 40h
4 b f Mujahid(USA) —Femme Femme (USA) (Lyphard (USA))
2600[5] 3358[F] 3498[P]

Penny Doc (IRE) *P York* 119c
10 b g Dr Massini(IRE) —Penny Bride (IRE) (The Parson)
502[6]

Penny King *Ken Wingrove* 57h
10 b g Desert King(IRE) —Pennycairn (Last Tycoon)
1705[U] 1937[P]

Penny Max (IRE) *Emma Lavelle* 116h
5 b g Flemensfirth(USA) —Ballymartin Trix (IRE) (Buckskin (FR))
(2445) 3626[3] ◆ 4081[4]

Penny Queen *Paul Webber* 94h 98c
6 gr m Nayef(USA) —Pennycairn (Last Tycoon)
(1646)

Penny's Bill (IRE) *Miss Elizabeth Doyle* 120h 133c
9 ch g Rashar(USA) —Classical Wave (IRE) (Orchestra)
3706a[8]

Penric *Martin Bosley* 72h 43c
11 b g Marju(IRE) —Nafhaat (USA) (Roberto (USA))
410[6] 990[9] 1059[U]
1331[7] 1733[3]

Penshurst Lad (IRE) *Richard Phillips* 18h
4 gr g Bertolini(USA) —Nuit Chaud (USA) (Woodman (USA))
2151[10] 2614[P]

Pensnett Bay *Trevor Wall* 67h
6 ch g Karinga Bay—Balmoral Princess (Thethingaboutitis (USA))
5115[11]

Pentopyn Harry *Tony Newcombe* 91b
5 ch g Zaha(CAN) —Paprika (IRE) (The Parson)
1778[14] 4881[5]

Penyfan Dawn (IRE) *Tim Vaughan* 114h
7 ch g Bach(IRE) —Aillwee Dawn (Deep Run)
767[F] (1035) 1175[2] 1289[2] 5234[8]

Penylan Star (IRE) *Philip Hobbs* 121h
6 bb g Presenting—Northwood May (Teenoso (USA))
206[P] (1625)

Pepe Simo (IRE) *Paul Nicholls* 142h 147c
7 b g Victory Note(USA) —Vallee Doree (FR) (Neverneyev (USA))
1587[P] (2210) *(3060)* **3555[2] 4326[3] 4853[8] (5233)**
(5436)

Pepite Rose (FR) *Venetia Williams* 109h
4 bb f Bonbon Rose(FR) —Sambre (FR) (Turgeon (USA))
2068[7] (2439) 3401[3] 3789[3] (4331) 4535[4]

Pepito Collonges (FR) *Laura Mongan* 101h 82c
8 b g Brier Creek(USA) —Berceuse Collonges (FR) (Vorias (USA))
4130[P] (4922) 5322[12]

Peplum (FR) *Gary Moore* 51h 134c
8 b g Subotica(FR) —Great Filly (FR) (Murmure (FR))
2665[U] 2948[P] (3628)
(4010) 4730[2] 4820[P] 5323[P]

Pepporoni Pete (IRE) *Milton Harris* 118h 78c
10 b g Un Desperado(FR) —Sister Shot (Celtic Cone)
80[4] 521[3] 627[8] 866[5] *3056[7]* 3477[P] 4220[6] 4536[2]

Pepsyrock (FR) *Nicky Henderson* 106h 125c
8 b g Video Rock(FR) —La Baine (FR) (Ramouncho (FR))
5164[8]

Peqeno Diablo (IRE) *Claire Dyson* 115h
6 br g Alexius(IRE) —Miss Huro (IRE) (Mandalus)
3225[14] 3491[6] 3950[13] 4697[6] 5208[6] 5393[6]

Perazzi George (IRE) *Chris Gordon* 101b
5 b g High Roller(IRE) —Kit Kat Kate (IRE) (Moscow Society (USA))
3569[3] 4124[8]

Perception (IRE) *Alan King* 105h
5 b m Hawk Wing(USA) —Princesse Darsha (GER) (Darshaan)
2480[2] *3058[5]* 5278[2]

Perce Rock *Jonjo O'Neill* 150h 135c
9 b g Dansili—Twilight Secret (Vaigly Great)
2345[11] 2665[8] 2881[13]

Pere Blanc (IRE) *David Arbuthnot* 139h
6 b g King's Theatre(IRE) —Sunset Leader (IRE) (Supreme Leader)
2577[7] 2873[10] 3403[9] (4052) ◆ (4196) (4933) ◆

Perez (IRE) *Wilf Storey* 82h
9 b g Mujadil(USA) —Kahla (Green Desert (USA))
10[U] 161[15] 604[9] 948[7] (1340) 1407[5] 1504[5] 5350[7]

Perfect Deal *Michael Easterby* 50b
4 b g Gentleman's Deal(IRE) —Better Still (IRE) (Glenstal (USA))
4396[11]

Perfect Ending (IRE) *Richard Fahey* 79b
4 b g Lucky Story(USA) —Wheeler's Wonder (IRE) (Sure Blade (USA))
3525[4] 3957[15]

Perfect Reward *Charlie Longsdon* 120h
7 b g Cadeaux Genereux—Maid To Perfection (Sadler's Wells (USA))
2169[6] 2596[2] 3224[2] 3818[6] 4323[U] (4776) 5425[6]

Perfect Shot (IRE) *Jim Best*
5 b g High Chaparral(IRE) —Zoom Lens (IRE) (Caerleon (USA))
3344[F]

Perfect Smile (IRE) *Noel Meade* 140h
6 bb g Anshan—Mambo Music (FR) (Rusticaro (FR))
2967a[3] 3203a[4] 5182[6]

Perfectus (IRE) *Malcolm Jefferson* 88h
7 b g Sadler's Wells(USA) —Highest Accolade (Shirley Heights)
2448[P] 3523[14] 4548[2]

Pergamon (IRE) *Claire Dyson* 40h
5 b g Dalakhani(IRE) —Pinaflore (FR) (Formidable (USA))
1046[8] 1138[P]

Pericam *Simon Waugh* 36h
6 b g Bollin Eric—Petrea (St Ninian)
3852[P] 4281[12]

Perjury *Robin Mathew* 50h
7 b m Midnight Legend—Heresy (IRE) (Black Minstrel)
3266[14] 3783[6] 4101[P] 4454[9] 5103[6]

Perkin Warbeck *Mark Rimell* 101h
9 ch g Karinga Bay—Supreme Lady (IRE) (Supreme Leader)
2452[8] 4224[3]

Perlon (FR) *Gary Moore* 104h
6 b g Winning Smile(FR) —Perle Deux Mille (FR) (French Glory)
252[5] 430[9] 595[7]

Persian Forest *Alan King* 20h
5 br m Presenting—Forest Pride (IRE) (Be My Native (USA))
4027[14] 4454[8] 4946[P]

Persian Gates (IRE) *Chris Bealby* 95h 109c
7 ch g Anshan—Mrs Jenks (Gunner B)
1612[3] 1813[5] (2250)
3391[6] 3990[2] 4416[2] 4740[4] (5293)

Persian Present (IRE) *Sophie Leech* 78h
5 ch g Anshan—Cherry Sent (IRE) (Presenting)
2791[10] 3478[9]

Persian Prince (IRE) *John Wade* 74h 102c
11 br g Anshan—Real Decent (IRE) (Strong Gale)
175[3] (403)
473[3] 3751[2] 4744[5] 5261[P]

Persian Run (IRE) *Colin Tizzard* 121h 119c
7 b g Anshan—Billeragh Thyne (IRE) (Good Thyne (USA))
94[12] **1739[5]**
◆ 1908[3] 3451[P] 4030[2] 4445[P] 4989[5]

Persian Snow (IRE) *Philip Hobbs* 122b
5 b g Anshan—Alpine Message (Tirol)
(2087) ◆ 4204[3] 5202[14]

Persian Tomcat (IRE) *Julia Feilden*
5 gr g One Cool Cat(USA) —Persian Mistress (IRE) (Persian Bold)
135[F]

Personal Column *Tor Sturgis* 135h 101c
7 ch g Pursuit Of Love—Tromond (Lomond (USA))
475[P]

Personal Flair *Sarah Humphrey* 46h
8 ch m Alflora(IRE) —Lara's Princess (Pragmatic)
4665[4] 5297[5]

Pertinent (FR) *C R Whittaker* 111h 121c
8 b g Sleeping Car(FR) —Jamais De La Vie (FR) (Saint Preuil (FR))
173[F]

Pete *Barry Murtagh* 96h 44c
8 b g Overbury(IRE) —Fen Terrier (Emarati (USA))
2107[10] 2308[6] 3631[5] 3782[3] 4113[7]

Petelo D'Ha (FR) *L Postic*
8 b g Le Balafre(FR) —Miss Zayani (FR) (Zayyani)
190a[0]

Peter Grimes (IRE) *Alan King* 118h
5 ch g Alhaarth(IRE) —Aldburgh (Bluebird (USA))
2094[3] 2477[P]

Peter Pole (FR) *Tim Vaughan* 109c
8 ch g Garuda(IRE) —La Banize (FR) (Ski Chief (USA))
5104[5] ◆

Peter Sent *Tom George* 91h
9 b g Alflora(IRE) —Sabeel (Local Suitor (USA))
538[10]
2172[P] 3377[P]

Peters Star (IRE) *Donald McCain* 113h
9 b g Fourstars Allstar(USA) —Supreme View (Supreme Leader)
196[14] 708[P] 801[4] 1107[P]

Peter Tchaikovsky *Brian Rothwell* 64h
5 b g Dansili—Abbatiale (FR) (Kaldoun (FR))
1258[7] 1359[P]

Pete The Feat (IRE) *Anna Newton-Smith* 92h 105c
7 b g King's Theatre(IRE) —Tourist Attraction (IRE) (Pollerton)
84[3] 1679[4] 2135[7] (2390)
(2950) 3373[3] (3614)
4372[6] 4921[4]

Petit Ecuyer (FR) *Gary Moore* 101h
5 b g Equerry(USA) —Petite Majeste (FR) (Riverquest (FR))
4557[7] 4917[2]

Petit Margot *Nigel Twiston-Davies* 110h 122c
12 b m Alderbrook—Outfield (Monksfield)
501[5] 859[U] 1002[4] 1200[4] 1376[2] 1769[4] 2055[3]
2395[P] 2794[8] 2953[P]
5067[4]

Petit Fleur *Julian Smith* 101h
9 b m Nomadic Way(USA) —Sense Of Value (Trojan Fen)
384[6] 645[5] 829[3] 933[5] 1179[7] (1335) 2530[F]
2956[5] 4009[12] 4769[2] 5208[2]

Petito (IRE) *Mark Gillard* 103h
8 b g Imperial Ballet(IRE) —Fallacy (Selkirk (USA))
185[2]

Petit Robin (FR) *Nicky Henderson* 154h 167c
8 b g Robin Des Pres(FR) —Joie De Cotte (FR) (Lute Antique (FR))
2885[2] 3675[F]

Petrocelli *Wilf Storey* 86h
4 b g Piccolo—Sarcita (Primo Dominie)
743[P] 1699[4] 3711[6] 4113[8] 4998[5] 5350[2]

Petroglyph *Noel Quinlan* 108h
7 ch g Indian Ridge—Madame Dubois (Legend Of France (USA))
2150[P] 2364[P] 2644[P] 3255[9] 3603[3] 4900[3]

Petrosian *Lisa Williamson* 96h 110c
7 b g Sakhee(USA) —Arabis (Arazi (USA))
1506[5]
1731[7] 1937[4]
2326[4] 3257[6] 3524[9]

Petroupetrov (FR) *Richard Phillips* 97h 105c
8 br g Ungaro(GER) —Harlem (FR) (Garde Royale)
540[3] (695)
868[5] 2127[6] 2420[P] 2637[3] 3483[9] 3713[6] 4021[7]
4773[4] 5265[2]

Petrus De Sormain (FR) *James Evans* 78h
8 b g Milford Track(IRE) —Bialystok (FR) (Saint Henri)
359[P] 1254[8] 1451[9] 5103[8]

Peut Etre Sivola (FR) *David Pipe* 99h 122c
8 b g Robin Des Champs(FR) —Largentiere (FR) (Antheus (USA))
2055[5] (2395)
2794[P] 3347[3] 3687[9] 4537[8]

Peveril *Nicky Henderson* 139h 148c
7 b g Presenting—Starana (FR) (Northern Crystal)
2523[3]
(3342) 3564[F]

Peveril Pandora *Jimmy Fox* 88h
8 b m Kayf Tara—Spellbinder (IRE) (Magical Wonder (USA))
2168[7] 2499[5] 3449[6] 4052[6]

Pezula *Richard Phillips* 67h 60c
5 b m Diktat—Mashmoum (Lycius (USA))
336[8] 2956[8] 3622[P] 3882[5] **4746[2]**

Phakos (FR) *P Cottin*
8 b g Robin Des Champs(FR) —Tipperary II (FR) (Chamberlin (FR))
312a[4]

Phantom Serenade (IRE) *Michael Dods*
6 b g Orpen(USA) —Phantom Rain (Rainbow Quest (USA))
4995[P]

Phar Again (IRE) *Claire Dyson* 88h 116c
8 b g Beneficial—Phar From Men (IRE) (Phardante (FR))
1885[P] 2113[3] 2280[6]
2555[U] 3388[3] (3492)
(3720) 4139[2] 4694[4] 5293[7]

Phar Beyond *Maurice Barnes*
6 ch m And Beyond(IRE) —Granham Charm (IRE) (Phardante (FR))
1785[9] 1934[13]

Phardessa *Richard Phillips* 118h 138c
10 b m Pharly(FR) —Mardessa (Ardross)
3587[2]
4167[F] 5110[7]

Phare Isle (IRE) *Ben Case* 119h
6 b g Turtle Island(IRE) —Pharenna (IRE) (Phardante (FR))
66[3] 231[2] 1959[9] 2347[6] (3308) 3566[P] 4285[5]
4855[U] 5289[4]

Pheidias (IRE) *Pam Sly* 113h 129c
7 ch g Spectrum(IRE) —Danse Grecque (IRE) (Sadler's Wells (USA))
(138) 559[3] **735[5] 957[5] 1815[2] 1950[2] 2110[4] 2669[4]**
3602[4]

Philippides (IRE) *Evan Williams* 139h 139c
7 ch g Presenting—Sarah Blue (IRE) (Bob Back (USA))
2139[2] (2588)
3496[3] 4438[2]

Philasonic *George Moore* 87h
8 br g Classic Cliche(IRE) —Phildante (IRE) (Phardante (FR))
3956[U] 5352[3]

Phiroza *Mrs C Hobbs* 52b
8 b m Baryshnikov(AUS) —Niloufer (Nader)
4197[P]

Phlorian *Ian Patrick Browne*
5 b g Falbrav(IRE) —Ravishing (IRE) (Bigstone (IRE))
4923[10] 5368[P]

Phoenix Des Mottes (FR) *John Cornwall* 105h 105c
8 b g Useful(FR) —Camille Des Mottes (FR) (Abdonski (FR))
1612[6] 1747[U] 2161[8]
2437[4] 3395[P] 3617[3] 3695[6] 3878[4] 4139[4] 4412[4]
5015[4] 5134[3]

Phoenix Enforcer *George Baker* 75h
5 b m Bahamian Bounty—Kythia (IRE) (Kahyasi)
384[P] 462[9]

Phoenix Eye *Michael Mullineaux* 101h 92c
10 b g Tragic Role(USA) —Eye Sight (Roscoe Blake)
675[4] 798[9] 1147[5] ◆ 1254[4] 1328[3] 1429[5] 1644[4]
1732[5] 1816[2] 1938[6] 2312[7]

Phoenix Flight (IRE) *James Evans* 116h
6 b g Hawk Wing(USA) —Firecrest (IRE) (Darshaan)
711[2] 1111[4] 2081[4] 4933[3]

Phone In *Lucinda Russell* 104h 120c
8 b g Sinndar(IRE) —Patria (USA) (Mr Prospector (USA))
43[2] 443[P]

Photogenique (FR) *Rob Summers* 6h
8 b m Cyborg(FR) —Colombia (FR) (Le Riverain (FR))
3530[P] 4098[4] 4550[12]

Piano Star *Michael Cunningham* 120h 141c
11 b g Darshaan—De Stael (USA) (Nijinsky (CAN))
446[4]

Pibrac (FR) *F-M Cottin* 127h 126c
7 ch g Spadoun(FR) —Palissandre (FR) (Phantom Breeze)
5367a[4]

Picabo Kid (USA) *Mrs C H Covell* 97h 115c
8 b g Lemon Drop Kid(USA) —Picabo Street (USA) (Deputy Minister (CAN))
253[5]

Picaroon *Tim Vaughan* 126h 142c
7 b g Jade Robbery(USA) —Anaam (Caerleon (USA))
78[2] (491)
1020[U] 1116[2]

Piccolo Pride *Maurice Barnes* 97h
6 ch g Piccolo—Jaycat (IRE) (Catrail (USA))
161[4] 350[9] 800[4] 886[U] 1115[8] 1337[5]

Pickamus (FR) *Henry Daly* 121h 144c
8 gr g April Night(FR) —Duchesse Du Cochet (FR) (Native Guile (USA))
1967[8]
2517[5] 3292[F] 3677[9] 4440[6] 5185[F]

Pickworth (IRE) *Philip Kirby* 97h
6 b g Milan—Loshian (IRE) (Montelimar (USA))
684[3] *3089[6]* 3389[7] 3521[8] 3883[9] 4302[7] 4976[2]
(5298)

Picot De Say *Adrian Wintle* 123h 119c
9 b g Largesse—Facsimile (Superlative)
3874[P]

Picts Hill *Anthony Honeyball* 89h 128c
11 ch g Romany Rye—Nearly A Brook (Nearly A Hand)
1690[3] 4221[P]

Picture In The Sky (IRE) *Susan Nock* 123h 118c
10 ch g Portrait Gallery(IRE) —Little Bloom (Little Buskins)
234[2] 2057[6] 2580[U] 3568[P] 3907[U] 4313[5] 4927[5]

Picture This (IRE) *Paul Nicholls* 145h 137c
8 ch g Old Vic—Below The Wind (Gala Performance)
(206) **1863[2]**

Pie At Midnight *Donald McCain* 117h
5 ch g Midnight Legend—Bergerac Pie (Cyrano De Bergerac)
1768[4] 2307[7] 2473[5] 3509[8] (3919) (4421) 5003[11]
5425[P]

Piece Of Magic *Michael Easterby* 83b
6 b m Alflora(IRE) —Madame Illusion (FR) (Solid Illusion (USA))
3546[5]

Pigeon Island *Nigel Twiston-Davies* 141h 140c
8 gr g Daylami(IRE) —Morina (USA) (Lyphard (USA))
1865[3] 2359[9] 2886[7] 4440[3] 4853[9] 5288[4]

Piggy Back (IRE) *Jonjo O'Neill* 41b
5 b m Oscar(IRE) —Ar Muin Na Muice (IRE) (Executive Perk)
2546[8] 3227[P]

Pikasso (FR) *Pam Sly* 88h
8 bb g Sleeping Car(FR) —Roseraie (FR) (Quart De Vin (FR))
2075[5] 2452[P] 4052[P]

Pilgreen (FR) *Evan Williams* 106h
6 ch g Green Tune(USA) —Galinetta (FR) (Galetto (FR))
1974[3] (3158) 5013[2]

Pilgrims Lane (IRE) *Milton Harris* 120h 132c
7 b g Dr Massini(IRE) —Miss Mylette (IRE) (Torus)
221[2] (361)
(498) 592[5] 852[3] 1151[8] (1365)
1486[5] 1626[6]
1863[6] 5228[4] 5427[3]

Pillar Of Hercules (IRE) *Ferdy Murphy* 104h
7 b g Rock Of Gibraltar(IRE) —Sabreon (Caerleon (USA))
1870[6] 2508[2] ◆ 2658[5]

Pills Baby (IRE) *Adrian McGuinness* 45b
6 b m Pilsudski(IRE) —Back To Bavaria (IRE) (Bob Back (USA))
2511[12]

Pimbury (IRE) *Peter Shaw* 111h 79c
9 b g Pistolet Bleu(IRE) —Duchess Of Kinsale (IRE) (Montelimar (USA))
4271[U]

Piment D'Estruval (FR) *Tim Vaughan* 114h 103c
8 b g Sheyrann—Gabika De Keroger (FR) (Shafoun (FR))
3256[P]
4103[4] (4556)
5015[3]

Pin D'Estruval (FR) *Matt Sheppard* 87h 107c
8 ch g Lute Antique(FR) —Haie D'Estruval (FR) (Cyborg (FR))
4775[F] 5348[F]

Pineau De Re (FR) *Philip Fenton* 139h
8 b g Maresca Sorrento(FR) —Elfe Du Perche (FR) (Abdonski (FR))
2967a[2] 3353a[3] 4319a[2]

Pinerock (IRE) *Jonjo O'Neill* 112h 91c
7 b g Oscar(IRE) —Marhabtain (Touching Wood (USA))
431[6] 1308[U] (1482) 1709[P] 1814[P]

Pinerolo *Sue Smith* 61b
5 b g Milan—Hollybush (IRE) (Ali-Royal (IRE))
3957[10]

Pinewood Legend (IRE) *Peter Niven* 84h 84c
9 br g Idris(IRE) —Blue Infanta (Chief Singer)
520[9] **1001[5]**
2398[3] 3619[2] 3727[6]
3997[P]

Pingaro De La Vire (FR) *Giles Smyly* 109h 116c
8 br g Ungaro(GER) —Kina De La Vire (FR) (Nayoulat (FR))
352[P]

Pinkneys Prince *Nick Williams* 86b
4 b g Fair Mix(IRE) —Cool Run (Deep Run)
4709[6] 5388[7] ◆

Pipe Banner *Nicky Henderson* 118h
7 b g Silver Patriarch(IRE) —Bella Macrae (Bustino)
2035[6] 4285[P]

Piper Royal *Nicky Henderson* 95b
7 ch g Erhaab(USA) —Close Harmony (Bustino)
632[8]

Pipers Legend *Sarah Humphrey* 102h 101c
12 b g Midnight Legend—Pipers Reel (Palace Music (USA))
677[4] 795[2]

Pipes A'Calling *Sarah Humphrey*
10 b m Bonny Scot(IRE) —Second Call (Kind Of Hush)
3865[7] 4236[F]

Pippa Greene *Nicky Henderson* 107h
7 b g Galileo(IRE) —Funny Girl (IRE) (Darshaan)
5168[2]

Pipsacre *Henry Daly*
7 b m Kayf Tara—Miss Laid (Jupiter Island)
4746[P]

Pips Assertive Way *Tony Carroll* 94h
10 ch m Nomadic Way(USA) —Return To Brighton (Then Again)
172[9] 382[7] 522[3] 646[5]

Pirans Car *Nigel Hawke* 74b
5 b g Sleeping Car(FR) —Karolina (FR) (Pistolet Bleu (IRE))
2335[5]

Pirate Depp (IRE) *G J Tarry* 17c
7 b g Mohaajir(USA) —Reggie's Honour (IRE) (Nashamaa)
466[10]

Pirate D'Estruval (FR) *S J Robinson* 32h
8 b g Saint Preuil(FR) —Kermesse D'Estruval (FR) (Cadoudal (FR))
628[U]

Piraya (FR) *David Pipe* 121h 146c
8 gr g Lost World(IRE) —Ella Royale (FR) (Royal Charter (FR))
2517[2] 2674[3] 3677[4] 4352[P] 4820[P] 5200[19]

Piroulet (FR) *Philip Hobbs* 109h
5 b g Slickly(FR) —Pantelleria (IRE) (Barathea (IRE))
2322[4] 3296[0] 3505[11]

Pistol At Dawn (IRE) *Ian Williams* 80h
7 bb g Needle Gun(IRE) —Dawn Native (IRE) (Be My Native (USA))
1062[6]

Pistol Basc (FR) *Ferdy Murphy* 103c
7 ch g Maille Pistol(FR) —Moldane (FR) (Sicyos (USA))
9[2] 95[3] 1663[4] (1826)
2371[2] 2952[P]

Pistolet Dove (IRE) *Sophie Leech* 86h 107c
9 br g Pistolet Bleu(IRE) —Emerald Dove (Green Adventure (USA))
427[P] (1940)
2453[6] 2795[5]

Pistolet Noir (FR) *Paul Nicholls* 134h
5 b g Maille Pistol(FR) —Black Et Or (FR) (Noir Et Or)
1967[11] 2360[F] 4270[4] 4806[9] 5187[15]

Pistolet Rouge (FR) *G Cherel* 96h 141c
5 b g Polish Summer—Royale Antigua (FR) (Jimble (FR))
5367a[3]

Pitbull *Alan Berry*
8 b g Makbul—Piccolo Cativo (Komaite (USA))
1375[7]

Pitton General *Kevin Bishop*
10 b g So Factual(USA) —Olympic Run (Salse (USA))
1196[P]

Piverina (IRE) *Julie Camacho* 69h
6 b m Pivotal—Alassio (USA) (Gulch (USA))
4552[8] 5028[8]

Plaisir De Montot (FR) *Simon Shirley-Beavan* 42h
8 ch g Video Rock(FR) —Idylle De Montot (FR) (Luchiroverte (IRE))
1911[2]

Plan A (IRE) *Gordon Elliott* 132h
4 b g Le Vie Dei Colori—Heres The Plan (IRE) (Revoque (IRE))
1882[2] ◆ 2356[3] 4807[4] 5201[12]

Plane Painter (IRE) *Brendan Powell* 94h 112c
7 b g Orpen(USA) —Flight Sequence (Polar Falcon (USA))
218[3]

Pyjama Game (IRE) *Rose Dobbin* 108b
5 b g Hernando(FR) —Princess Claudia (IRE) (Kahyasi)
3553[2] 4151[2] 4916[2] 5342[3]

Pyleigh Lass *Jeremy Scott* 100b
5 bg m Silver Patriarch(IRE) —Lady Callernish (Callernish)
3876[3] 4728[8]

Pyracantha *Alan Swinbank* 120h 122c
6 b g Muhtarram(USA) —Forsythia (Most Welcome)
209[3] 468[2] 1870[7] 2104[2] (2506) *3090[5]* **3520[2] 3995[6]**

Qaasi (USA) *Ian Brown* 77h
9 ch g Rahy(USA) —Recording (USA) (Danzig (USA))
87[P] 490[14] 604[P]

Qalinas (FR) *David Pipe* 113h
4 b g Malinas(GER) —Tabletiere (FR) (Kaldounevees (FR))
3872[4] 4029[4] 4323[2] ◆ 4503[F]

Qaspal (FR) *Philip Hobbs* 138h
7 b g Subotica(FR) —Une Du Chatelier (FR) (Quart De Vin (FR))
4852[15]

Qbuster (IRE) *Sharon Watt* 111h 66c
10 b g Turtle Island(IRE) —Torbay (IRE) (Surumu (GER))
3502[12]
3712[5] 3995[7] 5029[5]

Qhilimar (FR) *Charlie Longsdon* 133c
7 b g Ragmar(FR) —Philida (FR) (Zelphi (USA))
2343[5] ◆ **3290[P] (4193) 4876[R]**

Qianshan Leader (IRE) *Emma Lavelle* 101h 135c
7 b g Anshan—Gaelic Leader (IRE) (Supreme Leader)
1604[8] 1885[4] (2022) ◆ **(4456) 5011[2] 5228[2]**

Qolliure (FR) *Simon Shirley-Beavan* 98h
7 b g Bulington(FR) —Bonne Bibine (FR) (Quart De Vin (FR))
163[P]

Qozak (FR) *Paul Nicholls* 146h 144c
7 b g Apple Tree(FR) —Good Girl (FR) (Vorias (USA))
2139[3] 3262[3] (3871) 4267[2] (5065) (5273)

Qrackers (FR) *Venetia Williams* 130h 129c
7 h g Lahint(USA) —Baholna (FR) (Tropular)
3689[P] ◆ **4010[6] 4723[6]**

Qroktou (FR) *Philip Hobbs* 124h
7 b g Fragrant Mix(IRE) —Cathou (FR) (Quart De Vin (FR))
1742[2]

Quacity (FR) *Lucinda Russell* 105h
7 b g Sagacity(FR) —Desert Show (IRE) (Desert Style (IRE))
1664[5] 3502[9] 3855[2] 4166[8] 5335[11]

Quaddick Lake (IRE) *A J Farrant* 89h 102c
8 br g Blueprint(IRE) —Wondermac (IRE) (Jeu De Paille (FR))
846[10] 1026[4] **1366[3] 1511[P] 4901[2] 5372[F]**

Quadrillon (FR) *W P Mullins* 133h 133c
7 b g Dounba(FR) —Gastibelza (FR) (Ecossais (FR))
3174a[8]

Quahadi (IRE) *Chris Gordon* 45b
5 b g Montjeu(IRE) —Kicking Bird (FR) (Darshaan)
1680[10] 1899[F]

Quai Du Roi (IRE) *T G McCourt* 125h 96c
9 ch g Desert King(IRE) —Emly Express (IRE) (High Estate)
1155a[3] 1870[8]

Qualitee *Claire Dyson* 89h
6 b m Superior Premium—Coco Loco (Bin Ajwaad (IRE))
2309[5] 2546[4] 3259[7] 3721[6] 3816[P] 4094[7] 4417[3] 4900[6] 5298[4]

Quality Control (IRE) *Ferdy Murphy* 119h 67c
10 b g Tiraaz(USA) —Booking Note (IRE) (Brush Aside (USA))
553[P]

Quality Mover (USA) *Edwin Tuer* 67h
4 bb f Elusive Quality(USA) —Katherine Seymour (Green Desert (USA))
2600[4]

Qualviro (FR) *J H Culloty* 129h 123c
7 b g Lavirco(GER) —French County (FR) (Cyborg (FR))
3475a[13]

Qualypso D'Allier (FR) *Andy Turnell* 86h 106c
7 b g Dark Moondancer—Miss Akarad (FR) (Akarad (FR))
1747[5] (2048)

Quam Celerrime *Roger Curtis* 80h
6 b g Xaar—Divine Secret (Hernando (FR))
(1707) 1822[3] 2070[4] 2367[2] 3611[4] 4125[7]

Quand Je Reve De Toi (FR) *Mrs Pauline Harkin* 34b
7 ch m Evening World(FR) —Betty Royale (FR) (Royal Charter (FR))
2472[11] *2825[7]*

Quantitativeeasing (IRE) *Nicky Henderson* 139h 147c
6 ch g Anshan—Mazuma (IRE) (Mazaad)
2348[7] (3429) (3988) 4794[2]

Quantocks Lastbrat *Miss G Langley* 42c
12 ch g Granache(FR) —Quantock Superbrat (Owen Anthony)
133[8]

Quapriland (FR) *Althea Barclay* 85h 98c
7 br m Dark Moondancer—Falkland III (FR) (Video Rock (FR))
2287[2] ◆ **4275[F] 4504[7]**

Quarrymount *Chris Gordon* 124h 110c
10 b g Polar Falcon(USA) —Quilt (Terimon)
438[2]

Quarry Town (IRE) *David Pipe* 120h 96c
9 b g Pistolet Bleu(IRE) —Dano Doo (IRE) (Orchestra)
769[6] 993[5]

Quartano (GER) *Warren Greatrex* 128h 111c
8 ch g Platini(GER) —Queen's Diamond (GER) (Konigsstuhl (GER))
2082[6] *3090[4]*

Quart Monde (FR) *F Nicolle* 116c
7 ch g Network(GER) —In Extremis (FR) (Quart De Vin (FR))
312a[F]

Quartz D'Anjou (FR) *Pat Phelan* 43h
7 b m Ungaro(GER) —Kiliane (FR) (Chamberlin (FR))
1600[7]

Quartz De Thaix (FR) *Venetia Williams* 148h 142c
7 b g Ragmar(FR) —Une Amie (FR) (Prove It Baby (USA))
(2542) 2884[9] 3561[6] 3947[6]
(4261) (4531) 4820[7]

Quartz Du Montceau (FR) *Anna Newton-Smith* 48h 100c
7 b g Robin Des Champs(FR) —Emeraude (FR) (Persifleur (USA))
2050[3] 2928[7] 3431[P] 3609[5] 3867[2] 4126[4]

Quasar D'Oudairies (FR) *Nick Williams* 126h
7 b g Epistolaire(IRE) —Hanebane (FR) (Djarvis (FR))
2578[U] 3555[P]

Quatre Huit (FR) *Tim Vaughan* 65h 92c
7 ch g Ragmar(FR) —Fasolasido (FR) (Balsamo (FR))
36[6]

Quatro Pierji (FR) *James Moffatt* 113h 81c
7 br g Robin Des Champs(FR) —Bebenefertiti (FR) (Le Nain Jaune (FR))
209[5] 576[3] **2037[P] 2270[U] 2447[P]** 3966[P]

Quattrocento (FR) *Peter Bowen* 105h 128c
7 b g Robin Des Champs(FR) —Quadrige Du Marais (FR) (Le Pontet (FR))
33[7] 1178[4] 1373[9] (1858)
2343[6] 2544[P] 3444[2] 3629[10] 4277[6] 4864[4] 5423[6]

Quatuor Collonges (FR) *David Bridgwater* 61h
7 ch g Video Rock(FR) —Elegante Collonges (FR) (Quart De Vin (FR))
1588[4] 1745[P]

Quay Meadow (IRE) *John Norton* 90h
9 bb g Alderbrook—Harp Song (Auction Ring (USA))
2351[4] 2589[P] 3258[P] 3729[P]

Quazy De Joie (FR) *Jonjo O'Neill* 105h 118c
7 b g Fado(FR) —Gerboise II (FR) (Dress Parade)
2982[P] 3377[2] 3723[3] (4718) 5109[5]

Quechua Des Obeaux (FR) *R D E Woodhouse* 85h 74c
7 b m Ungaro(GER) —Diese D'Estruval (FR) (Castle Guard)
4147[6]

Quedillac (FR) *Tim Vaughan* 111h 111c
7 b g Clerkenwell(USA) —Esmidanne (FR) (Dastaan (FR))
(37) **169[4]**
773[3] **1082[2]**
1235[3] 1587[3] 1796[2] 3589[10]

Queen Court (IRE) *R K Watson* 90c
9 b m Broken Hearted—Flaxen Queen (Peacock (FR))
873[5] 1402[6]

Queen Musa *Dr Jeremy Naylor* 78h
9 b m Parthian Springs—Metannee (The Brianstan)
2609[P] 3530[P]

Queen's Bay *Colin Tizzard* 96b
5 b m Karinga Bay—Minibelle (Macmillion)
1448[3] 3590[4] (3964)

Queen's Forest (IRE) *Emma Lavelle* 74b
6 b m King's Theatre(IRE) —Glen Princess (IRE) (Bob Back (USA))
3616[7]

Queen's Grove *Kevin Bishop* 88b
5 gr m Baryshnikov(AUS) —Just Jasmine (Nicholas Bill)
4097[3] 5158[9]

Queen's Pawn (IRE) *Raymond York* 58b
4 br g Strategic Choice(USA) —Curragh Queen (IRE) (Lord Americo)
3630[11] 4124[9]

Queenstown Lad *Gary Brown* 76h
6 b g Double Trigger(IRE) —Four-Legged Friend (Aragon)
1666[6] 2149[8] (2391) 3703[3] 4263[5] 5265[P]

Queiros Bleu (FR) *Henry De Bromhead* 134h 118c
7 b g Ungaro(GER) —Guibolle Bleue (FR) (Ghost Buster'S (FR))
1526a[10] 1853[2] 3475a[10] 4817[5] ◆

Quel Ballistic *John Wade* 91h
7 b g Kayf Tara—Herballistic (Rolfe (USA))
1644[3] 2247[3]

Quel Bruere (FR) *Graeme McPherson* 99h 117c
7 gr g Sassanian(USA) —Housseliere (FR) (April Night (FR))
233[5] 2529[F] 3510[2] 3695[P] 4022[2] 4372[P]

Quelclasse (FR) *Steven Dixon* 91h
7 b g Ultimately Lucky(IRE) —Huronne (FR) (Useful (FR))
266[7] **3720[P]**
3961[P] 4269[F] 5191[P]

Quel Elite (FR) *James Moffatt* 106h
7 b g Subotica(FR) —Jeenly (FR) (Kadalko (FR))
4165[6] 4393[5] 4910[2]

Quel Esprit (FR) *W P Mullins* 144h 144c
7 gr g Saint Des Saints(FR) —Jeune D'Esprit (FR) (Royal Charter (FR))
4084a[F] 4804[F]

Quelle Chance (IRE) *Howard Johnson* 82h
5 ch g Old Vic—Iona Flyer (IRE) (Montelimar (USA))
3725[9] 4393[9] 5259[4]

Quell The Storm (FR) *Milton Harris* 119h 121c
7 b g Sleeping Car(FR) —Hot D'Or (FR) (Shafoun (FR))
(1163) ◆ **1558[4] 2088[5] 2422[3] 2869[P]**

Quentin Collonges (FR) *Henry Daly* 135h 125c
7 gr g Dom Alco(FR) —Grace Collonges (FR) (Bayolidaan (FR))
2110[3]

Quentin D'Ex (FR) *Mrs K M Diggle* 71h 117c
7 b g Dark Moondancer—Ile D'Ex (FR) (Lute Antique (FR))
5207[P]

Que On Time (IRE) *Tim Vaughan* 79h
7 b m Revoque(IRE) —Nikiya (IRE) (Lead On Time (USA))
4521[6] 4920[9]

Querido (GER) *Gary Brown* 61h
7 b g Acatenango(GER) —Quest Of Fire (FR) (Rainbow Quest (USA))
4288[12] ◆

Querido (USA) *Simon Burrough* 93h 113c
9 b g Spectrum(IRE) —Polent (Polish Precedent (USA))
595[5] 661[4] 821[5]

Questarabad (FR) *M Rolland* 143h
7 b g Astarabad(USA) —Hatilade (FR) (Royal Charter (FR))
(2230a)

Questions Answered (IRE) *E McNamara* 138h 135c
6 ch g Old Vic—Sleetmore Gale (IRE) (Strong Gale)
3706a[2]

Quetzal (IRE) *Alan King* 105h 89c
6 b g Mr Combustible(IRE) —Auction Piece (IRE) (Auction Ring (USA))
2128[3] *3348[P]* 3989[5]
4768[4] 5069[S]

Quevega (FR) *W P Mullins* 157h
7 b m Robin Des Champs(FR) —Vega IV (FR) (Cap Martin (FR))
(4793) ◆

Quezac De La Roque (FR) *F-M Cottin* 94h 137c
7 b g Officiel(FR) —Shade Du Buhot (FR) (Pot D'Or (FR))
4792[5]

Quick Bay *G C Evans* 24c
7 b g Karinga Bay—Quick Profit (Formidable (USA))
4415[8]

Quickbeam (IRE) *Venetia Williams* 131h 142c
9 b g Lord Americo—Your Life (Le Bavard (FR))
2360[9] 2663[6] 2870[5] 4285[11] 4875[F] 5230[8]

Quick Fix (IRE) *Susan Nock* 111h 108c
9 b g Needle Gun(IRE) —Nice Little Earner (Warpath)
130[4] 2529[P] 4142[7] 4880[4]

Quick Man (FR) *Nicky Richards* 67h
7 ch g Agent Bleu(FR) —Honfleur (FR) (Murmure (FR))
552[P]

Quick Will (FR) *James Ewart* 113h 121c
7 b g Dark Moondancer—Beautiful Lady (FR) (Polonium (FR))
(43) 394[F]

Quicolai (FR) *Tom George* 91h 80c
7 ch g Ragmar(FR) —Alene (FR) (King Cyrus (USA))
2286[7] 4099[P] 4556[6]

Quicuyo (GER) *James Ewart* 94h 127c
8 ch g Acatenango(GER) —Quila (IRE) (Unfuwain (USA))
213[P] 2551[9] 3500[12] **(3854)**
4065[5] 4913[5] 5340[8]

Quidam Blue (FR) *Tim Vaughan* 96h
7 b g Lucky Dream(FR) —Etiane Bleue (FR) (Reve Bleu (FR))
222[6] 739[6] 956[3] 1030[2] 1295[F] 1624[10]

Quiditch D'Ouxy (FR) *Mark Hoad* 86h 63c
7 b g Dark Moondancer—Jaca De Bissy (FR) (Royal Charter (FR))
462[11] 585[P]

Quiet Alice *Neil Mulholland* 44h
6 ch m Silver Patriarch(IRE) —Quiet City (True Song)
2136[10] 2482[14] 3454[8]

Quiet Bob (IRE) *Philip Hobbs* 54h 95c
8 b g Bob Back(USA) —Quit The Noise (IRE) (Un Desperado (FR))
4409[5] 5109[4]

Quiet Whisper (IRE) *Kim Bailey* 100h
5 b g Quiet American(USA) —Relish (IRE) (Sadler's Wells (USA))
2162[3] 2577[8] 3158[4]

Quilip (IRE) *Nigel Tinkler*
5 b g Traditionally(USA) —Quittance (USA) (Riverman (USA))
1153[8]

Quilver Tatou (FR) *Charlie Mann* 79h 99c
7 b g Silver Rainbow—Canlastou (FR) (Tanlas (FR))
3373[2] 3612[4] 4265[P] 4738[6]

Quincy Des Pictons (FR) *Graeme McPherson* 109h 106c
7 b g Kadalko(FR) —Izabel Des Pictons (FR) (Bayolidaan (FR))
1070[5] 1227[5] 1509[6] (4375)

Quinder Spring (FR) *Lucinda Russell* 100h 119c
7 gr g Chef De Clan(FR) —Virginia Spring (FR) (Beaudelaire (USA))
310[U] (1781) ◆ **(2401) 2550[4] 3522[5] 4150[2] 4962[4]**

Quine Des Ormeaux (FR) *Stuart Coltherd* 69h
7 ch m Rochesson(FR) —Kezaque D'Ormeaux (FR) (Beyssac (FR))
42[7]

Quinola Des Obeaux (FR) *Frank Sheridan* 104h 52c
7 b g Useful(FR) —Zaouia (FR) (Cyborg (FR))
2527[5] *3170[10]* **3632[U] 4482[P]**

Quintero (FR) *Evan Williams* 105h 114c
7 bb g Video Rock(FR) —Fautrenne (FR) (Brezzo (FR))
3257[3] 3628[5] 3935[F] 4265[3] 5015[5]

Quintessentially (IRE) *Warren Greatrex* 101h 95c
9 ch g Bob's Return(IRE) —Four Moons (IRE) (Cardinal Flower)
1965[3] 2670[10]

Quintus (FR) *Chris Bealby* 82h 88c
7 gr g Myrakalu(FR) —Elisa De Mai (FR) (Video Rock (FR))
1820[U] 1995[3] 3402[5] 4741[P]

Quiny Boy (FR) *David Pipe* 106h
7 b g Franc Bleu Argent(USA) —Robern (FR) (Within Hail (USA))
984[8] 1092[2]

Quinz (FR) *Philip Hobbs* 141h 158c
7 b g Robin Des Champs(FR) —Altesse Du Mou (FR) (Tin Soldier (FR))
(1908)
(2497) ◆ **2883[3] (4352)** ◆ **5200[P]**

Quipe Me Posted (FR) *Suzy Smith* 109h 124c
7 b g Discover D'Auteuil(FR) —Harlem (FR) (Garde Royale)
(541) **1965[4]**
2453[3] ◆ **2961[13] 4744[2] (5011)** ◆ **5112[2] 5305[3]**

Quiqui De L'Isle (FR) *Anna Bramall* 95h 123c
7 gr g Fragrant Mix(IRE) —Ad Vitam Eternam (FR) (Cap Martin (FR))
4546[2]

Quiscover Fontaine (FR) *W P Mullins* 142h 152c
7 b g Antarctique(IRE) —Blanche Fontaine (FR) (Oakland (FR))
3415a[2]

Quitao (GER) *P Monteith* 75h
4 b g Monsun(GER) —Quest Of Fire (FR) (Rainbow Quest (USA))
1576[P] 1696[5]

Quite The Man (IRE) *Malcolm Jefferson* 116h
6 b g Zagreb(USA) —Ballinard Lizzie (IRE) (Beneficial)
1734[3] (3696) 4234[2] 5132[4]

Quito De La Roque (FR) *C A Murphy* 144h 154c
7 b g Saint Des Saints(FR) —Moody Cloud (FR) (Cyborg (FR))
3174a[2] (3579a) (4109a) (5183)

Quito Du Tresor (FR) *Lucinda Russell* 121h 141c
7 b g Jeune Homme(USA) —Itiga (FR) (Djarvis (FR))
(194) 709[3]
874[2] 1597[2]
(1975) 2345[7] 3292[10] 4058[3]
4853[5] 5340[4]

Quix *Bob Buckler* 99b
6 gr g Fair Mix(IRE) —Teeno Nell (Teenoso (USA))
2896[3] 3399[8] 3909[15]

Quizwork (FR) *Graeme McPherson* 112h
7 b g Network(GER) —Galene De Saisy (FR) (Montorselli)
3919[P]

Qulinton (FR) *David Pipe* 137h 137c
7 b g Bulington(FR) —Klef Du Bonheur (FR) (Lights Out (FR))
1332[5] 1611[3] 1856[8] 2077[2] 4095[7] 4460[3] 5305[8]

Quolibet (FR) *Jonjo O'Neill* 96h 132c
7 gr g Fragrant Mix(IRE) —Goguette II (FR) (Bayolidaan (FR))
4792[P] 5200[U]

Quotica De Poyans (FR) *Simon Shirley-Beavan* 130c
7 b g Subotica(FR) —Etole II (FR) (Pebble (FR))
195[F] (4170) (4476) (4915)

Quo Video (FR) *Tim Vaughan* 130h 135c
7 b g Video Rock(FR) —Badrapette (FR) (Bad Conduct (USA))
426[2] (690) 830[9] 1966[P]
3394[4] (3694) 4162[3] 4794[P] 5170[2]

Quo Vista (IRE) *John Wade* 31h
6 b g Anshan—Miss Cooline (IRE) (Flemensfirth (USA))
1357[P] 1499[4]

Quws Law (IRE) *Lucinda Russell* 122h 117c
9 b g Quws—Love For Lydia (IRE) (Law Society (USA))
3362[P]
3854[8] 4306[P]

Rabbitkettle Lake (IRE) *Michael Blanshard* 37b
7 ch g Double Eclipse(IRE) —Nahanni Gift (IRE) (Padre Pio)
375[14] 2283[P]

Rabbit Lewis *Tom Gretton* 59b
6 b m Sir Harry Lewis(USA) —Yorton Mint (Cloudings (IRE))
333[10] 686[12]

Racey Lacey *Chris Down* 99h
4 b f Loup Sauvage(USA) —La Feuillarde (FR) (Nikos)
2458[12] 4091[P] 4781[2]

Rachael's Ruby *Roger Teal* 72b
4 b f Joe Bear(IRE) —Fajjoura (IRE) (Fairy King (USA))
4356[7] 5012[15]

Racing Demon (IRE) *Henrietta Knight* 132h 136c
11 b g Old Vic—All Set (IRE) (Electric)
1986[2] 2663[5] 3293[9] 3561[7] **4201[6]** 5153[6]

Racingisdreaming (USA) *David Pipe* 95h
5 bb g Fusaichi Pegasus(USA) —Luna Wells (IRE) (Sadler's Wells (USA))
356[7] 595[9] 845[U] 908[3] 1066[9] 1179[2] 1232[F]

Racing With Angels *Pam Ford* 68h
9 ch g Alflora(IRE) —Murphy's Angel (Derrylin)
2454[P] 5107[11] 5321[8]

Rackham Lerouge (FR) *Nicky Henderson* 119h 135c
6 b g Fado(FR) —History (FR) (Alesso (USA))
2926[3] ◆ **(3486) 3921[3]**

Radetsky March (IRE) *Mark Bradstock* 129h 132c
8 b g Taipan(IRE) —Jane Jones (IRE) (Beau Sher)
314[5] (1044)
1332[8] 1557[6] 2674[F] (3405) 3626[2] (4081) 4849[P]

Radharc Na Mara (IRE) *J T R Draper* 108c
7 b m Balla Cove—Poor Reception (IRE) (Mandalus)
(3726) 4831

Radium (FR) *Nicky Henderson* 137h 152c
6 b g Fragrant Mix(IRE) —Kalgary (FR) (Hawker's News (IRE))
(2082) ◆ **2384[5] 2867[8] (4236)**
4816[4] 5183[5]

Radmores Oscar *John O'Shea* 64h
5 ch g Karinga Bay—Harvey's Sister (Le Moss)
2074[11] 2576[5] 3441[4] 3836[10] 4081[12] 4946[3] 5374[4]

Radmores Revenge *John O'Shea* 108h
8 b g Overbury(IRE) —Harvey's Sister (Le Moss)
2144[2] ◆ 2606[2] 3621[P]

Radmores Sam Evans *John O'Shea* 58b
6 ch g Karinga Bay—Harvey's Sister (Le Moss)
2087[9] 2389[0] 3773[17]

Raduis Bleu (FR) *Alan King* 116h 115c
6 gr g Dadarissime(FR) —Regence Bleue (FR) (Porto Rafti (FR))
2291[2] 3374[2] 3744[3] 4990[5] 5381[3]

Rafta (IRE) *Linda Perratt* 98h
5 b m Atraf—First Kiss (GER) (Night Shift (USA))
1030[6] 1090[2] 1238[3] 1392[3] 1427[3] 3855[P]

Ragador *Sue Smith* 91h 110c
10 b g El Conquistador—Ragsi (Amerian (USA))
1754[4] 4894[8] 634[6] (1327)
1557[P] 2034[9] 4740[P]

Ragdollianna *Murty McGrath* 105h
7 b m Kayf Tara—Jupiters Princess (Jupiter Island)
2592[4] 5050[2]

Rageon (IRE) *Milton Harris*
8 gr g Turgeon(USA) —County Kerry (FR) (Comrade In Arms)
2238[P] 4225[P] 5168[P]

Raggios Boy *Barry Murtagh* 59b
5 ch g Karinga Bay—Fen Terrier (Emarati (USA))
4916[11]

Rahaala (IRE) *Lucy Wadham* 89h
4 b f Indian Ridge—Mythie (FR) (Octagonal (NZ))
2047[5] 2245[4] 3389[P]

Rahood (IRE) *F Jestin*
9 b g Afif—Cawkwell Patricia (Boco (USA))
514[P] 624[8] 801[P]

Rahotep (FR) *Henry Daly* 31b
6 b g Ragmar(FR) —Savane III (FR) (Quart De Vin (FR))
2143[P] 3365[P]

Rahy's Crown (USA) *Philip Sharp* 66h
8 b g Rahy(USA) —Inca Princess (USA) (Big Spruce (USA))
420[4] 955[P]

Raifteiri (IRE) *Neil King* 88b
4 b g Galileo(IRE) —Naziriya (FR) (Darshaan)
3406[4] 4055[5]

Railway Dillon (IRE) *Donald McCain* 122h
6 b g Witness Box(USA) —Laura's Native (IRE) (Be My Native (USA))
2646[2] 3252[2] 3528[3] (3887) 4189[2]

Railway Diva (IRE) *Evan Williams* 72h
7 b m Laveron—Four Moons (IRE) (Cardinal Flower)
412[2] 684[4] 2607[10] 3584[7] **4863[P]**

Railway Park (IRE) *John Wainwright* 94h 67c
7 ch g Karinga Bay—High Park Lady (IRE) (Phardante (FR))
1624[6] 1831[6] 2247[4] 2433[5] 2937[P] 3697[6] 3727[4] 3993[6] **4510[6] 4796[U]** 5354[F]

Raincoat *Barry Brennan* 114h
7 b g Barathea(IRE) —Love The Rain (Rainbow Quest (USA))
1111[3]

Rainiers Girl *Roger Teal* 80h
5 b m Tobougg(IRE) —Premier Night (Old Vic)
2795 554[7]

Raining Horse (FR) *James Ewart* 110h 106c
9 b g Rainbow Reef—Gabatine (FR) (Garde Royale)
3361[5] 3888[P] 5353[U] 5430[P]

Rainsborough *Sean Curran*
4 b g Trans Island—Greeba (Fairy King (USA))
1024[P]

Rain Stops Play (IRE) *Nicky Richards* 111h
9 b g Desert Prince(IRE) —Pinta (IRE) (Ahonoora)
1337[4] 1499[2] 1641[4] 1829[5] 3335[3] 3523[12] 4166[6] 4912[4] 5335[2]

Raise Again (IRE) *Nerys Dutfield* 88h
8 b g Raise A Grand(IRE) —Paryiana (IRE) (Shernazar)
823[P] 853[4] 1236[5] 1592[10] 1844[2] 2333[7] 5406[3]

Raise The Beat *C A Murphy* 130b
6 b g Beat All(USA) —Autumn Leaf (Afzal)
4808[22]

Raise You Five (IRE) *Jonjo O'Neill* 113h 116c
7 b m Flemensfirth(USA) —Raise An Ace (Buckskin (FR))
2182[5] 2470[5] (3395)
4537[P]

Raise Your Hopes (IRE) *Linda Blackford* 32h
8 ch g Marignan(USA) —Valmai (Seaepic (USA))
168[P] 820[P]

Raisthorpe *Tim Fitzgerald* 75h
7 ch g Elmaamul(USA) —Campaspe (Dominion)
7131[0] 849[7]

Rajamand (FR) *Warren Greatrex* 114h
5 gr g Linamix(FR) —Ridafa (IRE) (Darshaan)
1884[5] 2361[F] ◆ 2630[F] 4323[8]

Rajeeva (IRE) *Venetia Williams* 75h
5 b g Rock Of Gibraltar(IRE) —Balade Russe (USA) (Gone West (USA))
4225[8] 4528[7] 5167[9]

Rajeh (IRE) *John Spearing* 131h
7 b g Key Of Luck(USA) —Saramacca (IRE) (Kahyasi)
633[2] 1019[5] 1198[5] 1864[9]

Rajnagan (IRE) *Paul Webber* 80h
7 ch g Muhtarram(USA) —Rajnagara (IRE) (Darshaan)
1884[9] 2322[9]

Rakerin Lad (IRE) *Mrs S Taylor* 91c
8 b g New Frontier(IRE) —Lotta (IRE) (Sharifabad (IRE))
628[5] 5148[U]

Raki Rose *Michael Scudamore* 62h 5c
9 b g Rakaposhi King—Fortria Rosie Dawn (Derring Rose)
2240[P] 2608[P] 2982[P] 3400[4] 4021[8] **4238[9]**

Ralahine (IRE) *Sirrell Griffiths* 96h 98c
8 b g Insan(USA) —Cracking Time (IRE) (Simply Great (FR))
148[5]

Raleagh House (IRE) *Miss E Alvis* 80c
9 ch g Carroll House—Pencil (Crash Course)
150[4]

Raleigh Quay (IRE) *Micky Hammond* 94h
4 b g Bachelor Duke(USA) —Speedbird (USA) (Sky Classic (CAN))
3746[3] ◆

Ramblees Holly *Robert Wood* 43h
13 ch g Alfie Dickins—Lucky Holly (General David)
405[8] 717[7]

Rambling Minster *Keith Reveley* 123h 139c
13 b g Minster Son—Howcleuch (Buckskin (FR))
2205[2]
3522[8] (4284)

Ramborob (IRE) *Mike Sowersby* 81c
6 b g Xaar—Annaletta (Belmez (USA))
1830[4] 2110[P] 2615[4] 4394[P] 4551[P]

Rameur (FR) *F-M Cottin* 100h
6 b g Shaanmer(IRE) —Imola II (FR) (Video Rock (FR))
5159a[2]

Rampant Ronnie (USA) *Alison Thorpe* 109h
6 b g Honor Glide(USA) —Jalfrezi (Jalmood (USA))
861[3]

Ramsden Boy (IRE) *R T J Wilson* 120h 90c
10 b g Saddlers' Hall(IRE) —Double Glazed (IRE) (Glacial Storm (USA))
2542[8]

Ramses De Marcigny (FR) *Paul Nicholls* 89h
6 bb g Subotica(FR) —Isca De Thaix (FR) (Cimon)
3691[3]

Ramvaswani (IRE) *Neil King* 95h 58c
8 b g Spectrum(IRE) —Caesarea (GER) (Generous (IRE))
1997[9] 2183[10] 2314[3] 2327[3] 2558[RR] 2929[RR] 3603[6]

Randjo (FR) *Victor Dartnall* 74h 114c
6 b g Network(GER) —Daytona II (FR) (Video Rock (FR))
(183) ◆ **1919[4] 2334[P] (3792)**
4142[2] 4674[4]

Randolph O'Brien (IRE) *Nigel Twiston-Davies* 94h 79c
11 b g Zaffaran(USA) —Gala's Pride (Gala Performance)
2155[P] 3541[3] 3933[F] 4144[4] 4921[6]

Randomer *Paddy Butler* 84h
8 b g Alflora(IRE) —Lavenham's Last (Rymer)
215[3] 532[P] **1290[P]** 1429[9] 1549[10]

Rangitoto (IRE) *Paul Nicholls* 117h
6 b g Old Vic—Kendos Dream (IRE) (Presenting)
3761[2] ◆ 4489[3] (5107)

Ranjobaie (FR) *Venetia Williams* 137h 128c
6 b g Crillon(FR) —Ilari Du Missellot (FR) (Brezzo (FR))
3291[U] 3605[2] 3871[P]

Ransson (FR) *Alan King* 95h
6 b g Subotica(FR) —Cathou (FR) (Quart De Vin (FR))
4204[6] 4767[F] 5108[3]

Rapide Plaisir (IRE) *Richard Lee* 104h 115c
13 b g Grand Plaisir(IRE) —Royal Well (Royal Vulcan)
1[3] **233[4]**
799[F] 865[6] 1107[2] 1195[7] 1451[6]

Rapid Exit (IRE) *Brendan Powell* 70b
6 ch g Alderbrook—Novaro Express (IRE) (Corvaro (USA))
222[7]

Rapid Increase (IRE) *Jonjo O'Neill* 123h 127c
8 br g Sonus(IRE) —Lady Margaretta (Rolfe (USA))
3263[5] 3821[P] (4558)

Rapid Return (IRE) *Richard Phillips* 43h 77c
8 b g Tel Quel(FR) —Emer's Breeze (Mandalus)
539[P] **650[P]**
1840[7] **2132[3]**
2332[P] 2638[U] 3723[P] 4772[P]

Rappel D'Estruval (FR) *Tom George* 107h
6 gr g Panoramic—Caro D'Estruval (FR) (Caramo (FR))
632[2]

Raptor (GER) *Mark Rimmer* 79h
8 b g Auenadler(GER) —Royal Cat (Royal Academy (USA))
850[7]

Raquel White *John Flint* 118h
7 b m Robellino(USA) —Spinella (Teenoso (USA))
2636[7]

Rare Bob (IRE) *D T Hughes* 135h 157c
9 bb g Bob Back(USA) —Cut Ahead (Kalaglow)
2871[8] (3473a)
4790[P] 5199[U]

Rare Coincidence *Roger Fisher* 110h
10 ch g Atraf—Green Seed (IRE) (Lead On Time (USA))
581[7] (1004) 2161[2] 2372[9] 4572[4]

Rare Commodity (IRE) *E J O'Grady* 130h 124c
7 b g Definite Article—Soul Mate (IRE) (Phardante (FR))
1526a[13]

Rare Malt (IRE) *Milton Harris* 86h
4 b f Intikhab(USA) —A'Bunadh (USA) (Diesis)
2245[5] 2435[5] 3484[5] 3782[7]

Rare Society (IRE) *Sue Smith* 97h 92c
13 b g Deep Society—Rare Glen (Glen Quaich)
1200[6] 1255[5] 1781[7] 2354[9] 2602[P]

Rare Symphony (IRE) *Philip Hobbs* 91h
4 br f Pastoral Pursuits—Rubileo (Galileo (IRE))
2958[12] 3401[13] 4225[5] 4751[2] (4935)

Rascella Bay *Charlie Mann* 78h
5 gr g Karinga Bay—Rascella (Scallywag)
2957[14] 4294[6]

Rash Call (IRE) *Evan Williams* 89h
7 b g Rashar(USA) —Twilight Katie (Stubbs Gazette)
1819[2] 3879[P]

Rash Moment (FR) *Michael Scudamore* 60h 94c
12 b g Rudimentary(USA) —Ashura (FR) (No Pass No Sale)
95[5] 649[P] 758[P] 1128[4] 1235[2] 1297[2] (1483)
1678[2] 1840[6]
2277[5] 4694[3] 5256[P]

Rash Move (IRE) *F A Hutsby* 119c
10 bb g Rashar(USA) —Lady Tarsel (Tarqogan)
4183[2] (4748)

Rash Oak (IRE) *P D Thomas* 46h
9 bb g Rashar(USA) —Oak Tavern Lady (Dublin Taxi)
4526[P]

Raslan *David Pipe* 142h 125c
8 b g Lomitas—Rosia (IRE) (Mr Prospector (USA))
94[9] 372[14] 633[13] 756[11] 1019[12] (1346) 1626[2] 1855[3] 2090[5] 2360[4] 2870[11] 3293[17] 5441[9]

Raspbary *Seamus Mullins* 90h 94c
5 gr g Baryshnikov(AUS) —Ruby Too (El Conquistador)
41[P] 1902[11] 2583[6]
3339[4] 3486[F] 3792[P]

Rateable Value *Colin Tizzard* 91h 107c
7 ch g Classic Cliche(IRE) —Dame Fonteyn (Suave Dancer (USA))
2925[8]
3265[2] 3615[2] ◆ **3935[2] (4372)**

Rate Field (IRE) *Emma Lavelle* 97h
7 b g Bob Back(USA) —Alone Tabankulu (IRE) (Phardante (FR))
760[4] 1094[6] 1291[4]

Rate Of Knots (IRE) *Jonjo O'Neill* 114h 126c
8 b m Saddlers' Hall(IRE) —Fast Time (IRE) (Be My Native (USA))
2305[6] 2984[3] 3263[2] 4428[3]

Rathconrath (FR) *Althea Barclay* 96h
6 b g Bulington(FR) —Algue Rouge (FR) (Perouges (FR))
2087[8] 3528[9] 3931[P] 4294[5] 4747[3] 5169[P]

Rathcor *Ian Williams* 132h
9 b g Overbury(IRE) —Brenig (Horage)
(1692) 2474[P]

Rathlin *P J Rothwell* 140h
6 b g Kayf Tara—Princess Timon (Terimon)
4788[6]

Rathmore Castle (IRE) *Mrs Maureen Danagher* 109h 136c
9 ch g Topanoora—Torgyl (Sayyaf)
1113a[9]

Rathnaroughy (IRE) *S R B Crawford* 106h
7 b g Bach(IRE) —Lee Valley Lady (IRE) (Boyne Valley)
4684[2] 4910[7] 5316[7]

Rathnaskillogue (IRE) *Paul A Roche* 61h 87c
10 b g Executive Perk—Soft Tone (IRE) (Buckskin (FR))
1176[P]

Rathrockscourt (IRE) *Victor Dartnall* 111h
8 b g Kotashaan(FR) —Bourbon Belle (IRE) (Roselier (FR))
598[P]

Ratify *Brendan Powell* 93h 116c
7 br g Rakaposhi King—Sea Sky (Oats)
2059[3] 2666[12] 2963[12] 3483[5] ◆ **3741[U] (4102)**
4931[4] 5240[4]

Rationing (IRE) *Tim Easterby* 82b
5 b g Hernando(FR) —Scarcity (USA) (Polish Numbers (USA))
892[6] 2375[P]

Rats *Alan Kirtley* 88b
8 b g Man Among Men(IRE) —Springside (IRE) (Brush Aside (USA))
3725[P]

Ravanchi *Ian Patrick Browne* 57b
7 br m Indian Danehill(IRE) —Ravishing (IRE) (Bigstone (IRE))
3590[9] 5385[P]

Ravastree (IRE) *Alan King* 108h
5 b g Lord Americo—Stonehill Princess (IRE) (King's Ride)
3626[4] 4094[3] 4489[6]

Ravati (IRE) *Liam Corcoran* 104h
5 b g Fasliyev(USA) —Amravati (IRE) (Project Manager)
331[8] 541[4] 715[6] 861[8] 3587[7] 3954[5] 4776[5]

Ravenclaw (IRE) *Emma Lavelle* 121h
8 b g Blueprint(IRE) —Enchanted Heart (IRE) (Good Thyne (USA))
1568[P] 1815[P]

Ravensbill (IRE) *William Amos* 76h 80c
9 b g Sea Raven(IRE) —Two Hills Folly (IRE) (Pollerton)
2351[P] 3363[6] 3635[5] 4138[4] **4509[3] 4799[U]**

Ravenscar *Charles Pogson* 98h 83c
13 b g Thethingaboutitis(USA) —Outcrop (Oats)
3618[7] 4378[P]
4799[P] 5018[3] 5351[5]

Ravethebrave (IRE) *Alan King* 114h 133c
7 b g Rashar(USA) —Mrs Blobby (IRE) (Rontino)
(2441)
2869[4] 3198[2] 3803[F] 4054[2] 4987[2] 5301[6]

Ravine Rose *Ben Case* 76h
5 b m Lomitas—Chine (Inchinor)
358[8] 762[9] 1064[7] 1199[13]

Ravi River (IRE) *Brian Ellison* 72h
7 ch g Barathea(IRE) —Echo River (USA) (Irish River (FR))
4059[10]

Rawaaj *Donald McCain* 103h
5 ro g Linamix(FR) —Inaaq (Lammtarra (USA))
59[3] 552[4] 1996[9] *3091[2]* (3367) 3540[DSQ] 3782[2] 4243[2] 4462[3] (4892) 5376[7]

Raya Star (IRE) *Alan King* 116h
5 b g Milan—Garden City (IRE) (Shernazar)
2957[2] 3789[F] (4281) 4930[F] 5071[4]

Ray Diamond *Michael Madgwick* 114h 104c
6 ch g Medicean—Musical Twist (USA) (Woodman (USA))
282[7] **1883[3]**
2427[5]

Ray Mond *Neil King* 74h 133c
10 b g Midnight Legend—Kinsale Florale (IRE) (Supreme Leader)
2443[2] (3602)
3832[P] 4181[P] 4987[3]

Rayon Vert (FR) *Philip Hobbs* 98h
6 bb g Ragmar(FR) —Danse Verte (FR) (Brezzo (FR))
2216[5] 4672[7] 4990[10]

Rayshan (IRE) *Rose Dobbin* 96h 97c
11 b g Darshaan—Rayseka (IRE) (Dancing Brave (USA))
1761[11]

Raysrock (IRE) *Lucinda Russell* 117h 132c
9 br g Anshan—Sovereign Leader (IRE) (Supreme Leader)
2035[10] 2551[2] **3333[7] 4065[2] (4716)**
4913[U] 5317[U] 5422[3]

Razor Royale (IRE) *Nigel Twiston-Davies* 136h 154c
9 b g Oscar(IRE) —Maypole Gayle (Strong Gale)
2358[11] 2673[P] 4352[6] 4790[U]

R'Cam (IRE) *Emma Lavelle* 87h 104c
9 br g Glacial Storm(USA) —Beann Ard (IRE) (Mandalus)
1483[P] (1591)

R De Rien Sivola (FR) *Paul Nicholls* 77h 116c
6 bb m Robin Des Champs(FR) —Gamine D'Ici (FR) (Cadoudal (FR))
3841[F] 5110[11]

Reach For The Top (IRE) *M J Tuckey* 106h 128c
10 br g Topanoora—Burren Gale (IRE) (Strong Gale)
4851[U]

Ready Or Not (IRE) *Bob Buckler* 102h 111c
8 b g Oscar(IRE) —Ou La La (IRE) (Be My Native (USA))
2049[6] 2637[8] **2982[P] (4523)**
4967[2] (5194)

Reai (IRE) *Richard Fahey*
4 gr g Verglas(IRE) —Sheen Falls (IRE) (Prince Rupert (FR))
2824[6]

Real Dandy *Lucinda Featherstone*
5 b g Bahamian Bounty—You Make Me Real (USA) (Give Me Strength (USA))
1821[P] 2454[P] **4261[P]**

Real Desire *P Monteith* 57h
5 ch g Haafhd—Stop Press (USA) (Sharpen Up)
2038[13] 2349[13] 2509[14]

Really Hurley (FR) *Mme P Alexanian* 103h
6 gr g Urban Ocean(FR) —Millie Hurley (FR) (Green Tune (USA))
2230a[9]

Real Milan (IRE) *Anabel L M King* 101b
6 b g Milan—The Real Athlete (IRE) (Presenting)
4505[3] ◆ (5077)

Realt Dubh (IRE) *Noel Meade* 146h 165c
7 b g Beneficial—Suez Canal (FR) (Exit To Nowhere (USA))
2008a[F] (2412a) ◆ **2971a[2] (3241a)**
(3705a) 4789[3]

Real Tempo (FR) *J-M Plasschaert* 109b
6 b g Trempolino(USA) —Vision Of Realm (FR) (Vision (USA))
4055[3] 5202[19]

Realt Mor (IRE) *Nicky Richards* 123h
6 b g Beneficial—Suez Canal (FR) (Exit To Nowhere (USA))
4684[F] (5147)

Real Treasure *Kim Bailey* 119h
7 b m Rainbow High—Karen's Lady Luck (Primitive Rising (USA))
(3155) 3587[10] 4009[7]

Rear Admiral (IRE) *Michael Easterby* 98h
5 b g Dushyantor(USA) —Ciaras Charm (IRE) (Phardante (FR))
3889[7] 4363[4] 4743[3] 5309[3]

Rear Gunner (IRE) *Diana Grissell* 124h 129c
9 b g Pistolet Bleu(IRE) —Nethertara (Netherkelly)
2441[3] 2945[3] (3562)
4023[2] 4726[5]

Reasonably Sure (IRE) *Patrick Morris* 105h 81c
11 b g Presenting—No Reason (Kemal (FR))
9[5] 160[7] 649[P]

Rebeccas Choice (IRE) *Mark Rimell* 115h 82c
8 b g Religiously(USA) —Carolin Lass (IRE) (Carlingford Castle)
2476[4]

Rebel Dancer (FR) *Ian Williams* 132h
6 b g Dark Moondancer—Poupee d'Ancyre (FR) (Brinkmanship (USA))
159[4] 299[U] (1429) 1470[3] 1766[F] 2671[2] 4188[F]

Rebel Du Maquis (FR) *Paul Nicholls* 125h 146c
6 b g Brier Creek(USA) —Jade De Chalamont (FR) (Royal Charter (FR))
(1854)
(2330) 2867[3] 3946[5] 4531[4] (5371)

Rebel Fitz (FR) *Michael Winters* 124b
6 b g Agent Bleu(FR) —Gesse Parade (FR) (Dress Parade)
3208a[4]

Rebel Flag (IRE) *Chris Bealby* 81h
4 br g Statue Of Liberty(USA) —Ibiza (GER) (Linamix (FR))
2597[6] 3406[14] 5131[7] 5378[5]

Rebel High (IRE) *Derek Frankland* 96h
7 ch g Hymns On High—Celia's Fountain (IRE) (Royal Fountain)
1922[P] 4479[7] 4951[4] 5267[2]

Rebel Hunter (IRE) *Steve Gollings* 93h 107c
6 b g Revoque(IRE) —Nebuliser (IRE) (Foxhound (USA))
843[3] 1065[4] 1148[4] 1325[3] ◆ **1467[2] 1645[2] 1813[F]**

Rebelious (IRE) *Seamus Mullins* 87h
6 b g Oscar(IRE) —Miss Executive (IRE) (Executive Perk)
2186[14] 4932[6]

Rebel Melody (IRE) *Charlie Mann* 112h 119c
10 b g Houmayoun(FR) —Queenford Melody (IRE) (Orchestra)
2249[2] (2483)
2928[2] 3347[4] 3907[6] 4402[3] 4971[2] 5192[4]
Rebel Rebellion (IRE) *Paul Nicholls* 132h
6 b g Lord Americo—Tourmaline Girl (IRE) (Toulon)
2512[10] (4051) ◆ (4702) ◆
Rebel Rock (IRE) *D P Keane* 68h 97c
9 b g Rock Hopper—Penstal Lady (IRE) (Glenstal (USA))
(2645)
Rebel Swing *Sue Smith* 99h
5 b g Robellino(USA) —Ninia (USA) (Affirmed (USA))
800[5] 1003[8] 1083[5] (1261) 1428[2] (1559) ◆ 1929[7] 2205[4] 2372[3] 3919[5] 4508[B] (4712) 5289[10]
Reblis (FR) *Gary Moore* 110h 115c
6 b g Assessor(IRE) —Silbere (FR) (Silver Rainbow)
2311[2] 2959[6] 3450[3] 3907[4] 4160[4] 5053[2]
Rebus (IRE) *Tom Gretton* 47h
7 b g Witness Box(USA) —Blackwater Babe (IRE) (Arctic Lord)
1963[P]
Recession Proof (FR) *John Quinn* 147h
5 ch g Rock Of Gibraltar(IRE) —Elevate (Ela-Mana-Mou)
(1757) 2083[2] (2594) *(3169)* (4188) 4788[5]
Reckless Venture (IRE) *Lucinda Russell* 78h 94c
10 ch g Carroll House—Satin Talker (Le Bavard (FR))
164[3] 1663[2] 1784[P] 2193[P]
Recurring Dream *John Flint* 87h
5 b m Beat All(USA) —Rewbell (Andy Rew)
129[5] 535[4] 853[8]
Red Army Commander (IRE) *Neil Mulholland* 89h
6 b g Soviet Star(USA) —Penny Fan (Nomination)
182[3] 360[9]
Red Barcelona (IRE) *Mark H Tompkins* 77h
4 ch c Indian Haven—Purepleasureseeker (IRE) (Grand Lodge (USA))
1586[5] 1825[P]
Red Birr (IRE) *Paul Webber* 98h 106c
10 b g Bahhare(USA) —Cappella (IRE) (College Chapel)
1273[2] (1430)
1767[8] 1888[4] 2243[9]
Redbridge Flyer (IRE) *Philip Hobbs* 114h
7 b g Broadway Flyer(USA) —Beechdale Nell (IRE) (Lord Americo)
1799[5] 2145[3] 3487[2]
Red Current *Michael Scudamore* 98h
7 b m Soviet Star(USA) —Fleet Amour (USA) (Afleet (CAN))
916[7] 1090[4] 1488[2] 1902[5] 2131[5]
Red Dagger (IRE) *Richard Price* 53h
5 b g Daggers Drawn(USA) —Dash Of Red (Red Sunset)
4[8] 224[6] 648[U]
Red Dynamite *Geoffrey Harker* 94h 106c
10 ch g Gunner B—Marsden Rock (Tina's Pet)
160[4] (489)
918[5] 1701[2] 1933[8]
Redgrave Dancer *Kevin Bishop* 52b
5 gr m Baryshnikov(AUS) —Redgrave Bay (Karinga Bay)
1029[9] 1349[7]
Red Harbour (IRE) *Paul Nicholls* 129h
7 ch g Old Vic—Auntie Honnie (IRE) (Radical)
2523[7] 3452[6] 4875[6]
Red In Bed (IRE) *Matthew Smith* 62c
7 b m Moscow Society(USA) —Secret Tryst (IRE) (Roi Danzig (USA))
61[2] 466[11]
Red Jester *Laura Young* 31h 105c
10 b g Thowra(FR) —Red Ebrel (IRE) (Red Sunset)
339[4] 728[6] 799[3] 919[3] 985[3] 1070[2] 1252[5] 1557[5]
2022[5] 2152[3]
5279[2] 5379[2]
Red Kingdom (IRE) *A J Martin* 100h 129c
7 b g Red Ransom(USA) —Eucalyptus Hill (USA) (Peaks And Valleys (USA))
(857)
Red Lancer *Jonathen de Giles* 93h
10 ch g Deploy—Miss Bussell (Sabrehill (USA))
1195[10] 1477[9] 1997[7] 3899[4] 4272[12]
Red Law (IRE) *Mark Gillard* 85h 91c
7 b g Reprimand—Trouville Lass (IRE) (Be My Native (USA))
1914[10] 2216[6] 2482[11]
3226[8] 3492[3] 3873[6] 4144[14] 4413[2] 4691[4] (4813)
Red Merlin (IRE) *Donald McCain* 136h
6 ch g Soviet Star(USA) —Truly Bewitched (USA) (Affirmed (USA))
2960[2] ◆ 3445[5] 3749[8] (4451) (4944) (5356)
Red Mile (FR) *Emma Lavelle* 115h
6 ch g Kapgarde(FR) —Katespeed (FR) (Vertical Speed (FR))
2946[5] 3340[3] 3688[16] 4079[4] 4446[3] 4988[3]
Red Not Blue (IRE) *Simon Earle* 110h
8 b g Blueprint(IRE) —Silent Valley (Forzando)
76[4] (336) (539) 3744[11]
Red Perfection *Tony Carroll* 81h
8 b m Lahib(USA) —Perfect Poppy (Shareef Dancer (USA))
2452[P] 2980[17] 3703[P] 4123[5]
Red Rocco (IRE) *George Moore* 102b
4 ch g Croco Rouge(IRE) —Youbetido (IRE) (Eurobus)
2511[7] 3511[4] 3957[3] 4943[2]
Red Rock (FR) *Tor Sturgis* 91h
6 b g Saint Cyrien(FR) —Ariloba De Brize (FR) (Roymel (FR))
3295[13] 3645[7] 4268[5] ◆ 4670[P]
Red Rouble (IRE) *Nigel Twiston-Davies* 104h 119c
6 ch g Moscow Society(USA) —Chirouble (IRE) (High Roller (IRE))
(1730)
1991[2] ◆ 2529[F] 3494[3] 4327[11] 5234[9]

Red Shuttle *Michael Quinlan* 37b
4 b g Starcraft(NZ) —Red Azalea (Shirley Heights)
3569[8]
Red Skipper (IRE) *Noel Wilson* 96h
6 ch g Captain Rio—Speed To Lead (IRE) (Darshaan)
576[8] 1426[3] 1831[2] 2438[6]
Redskyatnight *H J Franklin* 42c
10 br g Prince Of Darkness(IRE) —Red Rhapsody (Sizzling Melody)
148[P] 301[P]
Red Sparky (IRE) *J Larkin* 111h
4 b g Spartacus(IRE) —Cool Ann (IRE) (Up And At 'Em)
2882[4]
Red Tanber (IRE) *Bruce Mactaggart* 75h
8 ch g Karinga Bay—Dreamy Desire (Palm Track)
1919 2658[7] 4115[13] 4511[11]
Red Twist *Martin Hill* 112h
6 b g Red Ransom(USA) —Spinning The Yarn (Barathea (IRE))
(266) 662[2]
Redunderthebed (IRE) *Philip Hobbs* 96h
6 ch m Moscow Society(USA) —Niat Supreme (IRE) (Supreme Leader)
(1140)
Red Valerian Two (IRE) *George Moore* 58h
4 ch g Hawk Wing(USA) —La Turque (IRE) (Diesis)
3715[12]
Red Whisper *Rob Summers* 90h
7 ch g Midnight Legend—Secret Whisper (Infantry)
637[9] 4952[6] 5378[4]
Reefer Beefer (IRE) *Tony Newcombe* 105h
6 ch g Double Eclipse(IRE) —Sweet Laura (FR) (Vettori (IRE))
1910[6] 2331[6] 2634[5] 3378[P] (4976)
Reel Missile *Charles Pogson* 86h 90c
12 b g Weld—Landsker Missile (Cruise Missile)
351[7] **714[3]**
1085[3] 1147[13]
Reelwill (FR) *Chris Bealby* 62h 76c
6 gr m Dom Alco(FR) —Jeep Will (FR) (Royal Charter (FR))
(1954)
2277[4] 2559[3] 3388[7] 4144[10]
Reflex Blue *Rex Smith* 67h 67c
14 b g Ezzoud(IRE) —Briggsmaid (Elegant Air)
207[5]
Regain Du Charbonneau (FR) *David Pipe* 90h 77c
6 b g Arnaqueur(USA) —Fatima III (FR) (Bayolidaan (FR))
134[12] 272[6] 585[6]
794[5] 1447[6]
Regal Approach (IRE) *Kim Bailey* 116h 125c
8 b g Bob Back(USA) —Crash Approach (Crash Course)
2236[2] (2670) ◆ 2869[3] ◆ 3198[8] 3950[6]
4802[12] 5286[3]
Regal Heights (IRE) *Tom George* 137h 133c
10 b g Grand Plaisir(IRE) —Regal Hostess (King's Ride)
2629[P] 2948[2] 3453[3] 3953[2] 4221[2] (4486)
5338[9] (Dead)
Regal Lyric (IRE) *Gordon Elliott* 100h
5 b g Royal Applause—Alignment (IRE) (Alzao (USA))
1596[P]
Regent's Secret (USA) *Jim Goldie* 111h 113c
11 br g Cryptoclearance(USA) —Misty Regent (CAN) (Vice Regent (CAN))
288[3] (1597) 1956[9] 2506[11]
Reginaldinho (UAE) *Venetia Williams* 107h
5 b g Galileo(IRE) —River Patrol (Rousillon (USA))
3225[4] 4081[6] 4288[4] 5074[2]
Regional Counsel *Alex Hales* 102h
7 b g Medicean—Regency Rose (Danehill (USA)) (40)
Reg's Ruby *David Bridgwater* 90h
5 b m Pursuit Of Love—Sweets (IRE) (Persian Heights)
855[10] 1071[5] 1233[7] 1433[8] 1567[3] 1994[5] 2425[6] 4104[3] 4330[9] 5212[5]
Reindeer Dippin *Donald McCain* 136h 148c
9 b g Sir Harry Lewis(USA) —Analogical (Teenoso (USA))
3490[9]
(4065) (4358) 4875[8] 5166[2]
Reinriver *Brendan Powell* 99h
5 b m Barathea(IRE) —La Riveraine (USA) (Riverman (USA))
1793[5] 2577[5] 2791[9] 3155[8]
Reland (FR) *Nigel Twiston-Davies* 102h 108c
6 b g Shaanmer(IRE) —Falkland III (FR) (Video Rock (FR))
1575[2] 2243[4] 2585[3] 3646[6] 4865[5]
Remark (IRE) *Joanne Foster*
7 b g Machiavellian(USA) —Remuria (USA) (Theatrical)
835[P]
Remarkable Rocket (IRE) *Andrew Price* 25h
7 b g Oscar(IRE) —Miss Capella (IRE) (Invited (USA))
2590[7] 4810[14] 4951[U]
Remember Bampi *Simon Burrough* 100c
7 b g Baryshnikov(AUS) —Ruby Celebration (New Member)
2[2] 276[2] 594[6] 3226[6]
Remember Now (IRE) *Nicky Henderson* 128h
5 ch g Anabaa Blue—Bleu Ciel Et Blanc (FR) (Pistolet Bleu (IRE))
1736[6] 2122[7] 3376[2] (4778) ◆ (5315)
Remmyniss *Derek Shaw* 29b
7 b m Sea Freedom—Royal Lark (Royal Vulcan)
2403[8]
Renard (FR) *Venetia Williams* 93c
6 bb g Discover D'Auteuil(FR) —Kirmelia (FR) (Chamberlin (FR))
5421[P]

Renard D'Irlande (FR) *Venetia Williams* 135h
6 gr g April Night(FR) —Isati'S (FR) (Chamberlin (FR))
2056[5] 2499[4] 2954[U] (4128) ◆ (4667)
Rendezvous Bay (IRE) *A J Martin* 81h
7 b g Glacial Storm(USA) —Jmember (IRE) (Jurado (USA))
327[7]
Renege The Joker *Sean Regan* 73h
8 b g Alflora(IRE) —Bunty (Presidium)
135[7] 439[3] 760[9] 1953[9] 4854[6]
Renovatio (FR) *Anabel L M King* 37b
5 b g Cadoudal(FR) —Miss Energie (FR) (Kind Music)
4815[7]
Reportage (USA) *Robert Alan Hennessy* 114h
5 b g Elusive Quality(USA) —Journalist (IRE) (Night Shift (USA))
(1342) 1597[7]
Representingceltic (IRE) *Pat Phelan* 115h
6 ch g Presenting—Nobull (IRE) (Torus)
1607[2] 2123[2] 2512[3] 3950[8]
Requin (FR) *Victor Dartnall* 118h 134c
6 bb g Video Rock(FR) —Funkia (FR) (Royal Charter (FR))
(2977) 3688[8]
4095[2] (4723)
5155[3]
Rescindo (IRE) *C Roberts* 108h
12 b g Revoque(IRE) —Mystic Dispute (IRE) (Magical Strike (USA))
1035[P]
Resolute Road *Nigel Twiston-Davies* 19h
4 b c Medicean—Madam Ninette (Mark Of Esteem (IRE))
1576[P] 1728[7]
Resplendent Ace (IRE) *John Price* 75h
7 b g Trans Island—Persian Polly (Persian Bold)
5167[13] 5368[5]
Restart (IRE) *Lucinda Featherstone* 109h
10 b g Revoque(IRE) —Stargard (Polish Precedent (USA))
(480) 954[2] 4704[P] 5425[4]
Rester Vrai (FR) *John Cornwall* 85h 73c
6 gr g Cadoudal(FR) —Moulouya (FR) (Turgeon (USA))
2166[6]
2436[5] 3402[P] 4179[4] 4414[U] 4974[9]
5133[P]
Restezen D'Armor (FR) *Charlie Longsdon* 102h 127c
6 b g Grand Tresor(FR) —Lafrizen D'Armor (FR) (Africanus (FR))
2826 1737[2] **2034[2] 2502[F] 2948[12] 4010[5] (4400)**
5081[8]
Restless Harriet *Robin Dickin* 67h
5 b m Sir Harry Lewis(USA) —Fair Cruise (Cruise Missile)
254[7] 1480[3] 1607[9] 2168[12] 2556[7] 3389[11]
Restless Harry *Robin Dickin* 156h
7 b g Sir Harry Lewis(USA) —Restless Native (IRE) (Be My Native (USA))
1967[3] ◆ 2516[3] 2884[7] 3199[3] 3807[3] 4819[9]
Retrievethelegend (IRE) *J T R Dreaper* 120h 131c
12 gr g Flying Legend(USA) —Nellsway (Neltino)
874[5] (947)
1960[U]
Return Perk (IRE) *Jim Goldie* 103h
8 b g Bob's Return(IRE) —Lucky Perk (IRE) (Executive Perk)
1867[12] 2657[3]
Revani *Nick Mitchell* 94b
4 b g Sulamani(IRE) —Clotted Cream (USA) (Eagle Eyed (USA))
2458[3] 3294[9] 3909[3]
Reveal The Light *Garry Woodward* 83b
4 b f Fantastic Light(USA) —Paper Chase (FR) (Machiavellian (USA))
2173[3] ◆ 3576[6] 4027[13]
Reve De Sivola (FR) *Nick Williams* 155h 145c
6 b g Assessor(IRE) —Eva De Chalamont (FR) (Iron Duke (FR))
2348[4] (2867)
3291[3] 3946[7] 4790[3] 5199[3]
Revelator (IRE) *Paul Nicholls*
4 b g One Cool Cat(USA) —Capades Band (FR) (Chimes Band (USA))
1845[P]
Reverend Green (IRE) *Chris Down* 96h
5 b g Tagula(IRE) —Red Letter (Sri Pekan (USA))
315[P] 3478[6]
Rexmehead (IRE) *Andrew Wilson* 85h 82c
10 b g Fort Morgan(USA) —Moon Rose (IRE) (Imperial Frontier (USA))
211[8] 4994[F]
Reyes Magos (IRE) *Seamus Durack* 90b
5 b g Indian Danehill(IRE) —Cincuenta (IRE) (Bob Back (USA))
5238[2]
Reymysterio (IRE) *Patrick Rodford* 84h 84c
10 b g Luso—Rehey Lady (The Parson)
3871[8] 4028[4] 4706[6] **5256[3] 5407[2]**
Rey Nacarado (IRE) *Charlie Longsdon* 104h 122c
6 b g Posidonas—Ice Pearl (Flatbush)
(1694) 1959[3]
2611[2] (2928) ◆ 3562[3] 4181[2] (5009)
Rhum (FR) *Nigel Twiston-Davies* 117h 121c
6 ch g Dark Moondancer—Ireland (FR) (Kadalko (FR))
(1705) 2147[5] 2347[15] **2975[10] 4538[U] 5154[F]**
Rhymers Ha' *Lucinda Russell* 86b
4 br g Kasakov—Salu (Ardross)
5432[7]
Rhythm Seeker *Anabel L M King* 103h
8 b g Alflora(IRE) —Pearlossa (Teenoso (USA))
5321[7]
Rhyton (IRE) *Donald McCain* 88h
4 b g Rainbow Quest(USA) —Sea Picture (IRE) (Royal Academy (USA))
1363[4] 1586[6] 1696[7] 3387[6] 3717[3] 4068[11] 4550[9] 5014[2] 5368[3]

Richardlionheart (USA) *Michael Madgwick* 12h
5 ch g Lion Heart(USA) —Cleito (USA) (Unbridled's Song (USA))
2181[11]
Richard's Sundance (IRE) *Victor Dartnall* 124h 144c
9 b g Saddlers' Hall(IRE) —Celestial Rose (IRE) (Roselier (FR))
2343[9] 3290[2] 3568[P] 4821[U] 5443[P]
Richard The Third *John Harris* 95h
7 b g King's Best(USA) —Larousse (Unfuwain (USA))
100[3] 539[4] 849[4]
Rich Buddy *Richard Phillips* 105b
5 b g Kayf Tara—Silver Gyre (IRE) (Silver Hawk (USA))
3569[5] 4561[3]
Richie Rob *Neville Bycroft* 116b
5 b g Robellino(USA) —Friend For Life (Lahib (USA))
3088[2] (4259) 5202[15]
Rich Kayf *John O'Shea* 49h
7 b g Kayf Tara—Granny Rich (Ardross)
168[5] 338[9]
Rich Live (FR) *Lady Anne Connell* 79h
6 b g Subotica(FR) —Iona Will (FR) (Kadalko (FR))
3487[P] 3836[9] 4500[9]
Rich Lord *Ferdy Murphy* 43h
7 b g Zamindar(USA) —Al Corniche (IRE) (Bluebird (USA))
3881[11] 4503[F]
Richmond (FR) *Ian Williams* 114h
6 b g Assessor(IRE) —Hirondel De Serley (FR) (Royal Charter (FR))
2109[7] 2456[4] 2873[5] 3261[2] 5211[F]
Rich Nomad *Miss Sally Randell* 77h 78c
9 b m Nomadic Way(USA) —Weareagrandmother (Prince Tenderfoot (USA))
5326[4]
Richo *Shaun Harris* 87h
5 ch g Bertolini(USA) —Noble Water (FR) (Noblequest (FR))
837[7] 1005[3] 1066[6] 1407[3]
Rick (FR) *D T Hughes* 140h
7 b g Astarabad(USA) —Catty Jolie (FR) (Mansonnien (FR))
3175a[8]
Riddleofthesands (IRE) *Nigel Twiston-Davies* 105h 100c
7 bb g Oscar(IRE) —Flaxen Pride (IRE) (Pips Pride)
2148[4] 2986[4] 4934[5] 5173[U]
Ridley Taylor *Sean Regan* 85h
8 b m Karinga Bay—Saxon Gift (Saxon Farm)
1141[3] 1434[3]
Rien A Perdre (FR) *Graeme McPherson* 90h 126c
10 b g Nikos—Kamirish (FR) (Assert)
2311[1] 534[6] 682[3] 826[7]
Rif (FR) *Alex Hales* 124h
7 b g Byzantium(FR) —Isabellita (FR) (Cyborg (FR))
(1990) 2888[6]
Rifleman (IRE) *Richard Lee* 110h 114c
11 ch g Starborough—En Garde (USA) (Irish River (FR))
(231) 630[3]
(868) 1027[2] (1200)
1312[5] 1482[3]
1932[2] 2324[4] 5425[7]
Rigadin De Beauchene (FR) *Venetia Williams* 103h
6 bb g Visionary(FR) —Chipie D'Angron (FR) (Grand Tresor (FR))
2387[11]
Right Move (IRE) *Caroline Keevil* 65b
6 b g Golan(IRE) —Need You Badly (Robellino (USA))
3751[1] 637[10]
Right Or Wrong (IRE) *Gordon Elliott* 130h 113c
7 b g Key Of Luck(USA) —Sarifa (IRE) (Kahyasi)
(307) 470[2] 861[7] **944[2] (1116)**
Right Stuff (FR) *Gary Moore* 119h
8 bb g Dansili—Specificity (USA) (Alleged (USA))
4462[12] 4935[3]
Rigid *Tony Carroll* 74h
4 ch g Refuse To Bend(IRE) —Supersonic (Shirley Heights)
2151[7]
Rigour Back Bob (IRE) *E J O'Grady* 163h
6 ch g Bob Back(USA) —Rigorous (Generous (IRE))
(3030a) 3175a[3] 4107a[2] 4819[5]
Riguez Dancer *Ferdy Murphy* 126h 141c
7 b g Dansili—Tricoteuse (Kris)
2400[3] (2613) *3170[2]* **3446[3] 3949[10] 4853[12] 5305[2]**
Rileyev (FR) *Venetia Williams* 107h 128c
6 b g Goldneyev(USA) —Jiletta (FR) (Passing Sale (FR))
2187[3] 2604[4] 3741[3] 4103[2] (4264)
4290[3] (4529)
(4770) (4934) ◆ (5112)
Rimini (FR) *David Rees* 104h 118c
6 b g Bedawin(FR) —Ma'Am (FR) (Garde Royale)
528[3] 766[DSQ] (1902)
2053[4] (2605)
(2961) 3154[U] 3563[P] 3962[4] **4490[2] 4863[3] 5112[P]**
Rimsky (IRE) *Tina Jackson* 126h 123c
10 gr g Silver Patriarch(IRE) —Mistinguett (IRE) (Doyoun)
3956[4] 4170[4]
Rinca Deas (IRE) *Seamus Mullins* 82b
6 br m Beneficial—Hot Curry (IRE) (Beau Sher)
333[7]
Rince Donn (IRE) *Roger Curtis* 73h 102c
9 b g Imperial Ballet(IRE) —Arrow Field (USA) (Sunshine Forever (USA))
845[7] 1060[6] **1283[7] 1511[4] 1591[5] 1710[P] 2152[4]**
2559[2] 3404[4] 3875[3] 3898[5]
4269[4] (4426)
4668[4] 5076[4]
Ringadingadoo *Joanne Priest* 51b
6 b m Karinga Bay—Anamasi (Idiots Delight)
686[11]

Ringaroses *Jonjo O'Neill* 142h 134c
10 b g Karinga Bay—Rose Ravine (Deep Run)
3293^{8}
4466^{P} 5187^{2}

Ring Bo Ree (IRE) *Tom George* 115h
8 b g Topanoora—La Ronde (Common Grounds)
157^{2} (601) 1019^{6}

Ring For Time *John Flint* 113h
8 ch m Karinga Bay—Little Time (Arctic Lord)
235^{6} 494^{2} 756^{10} *3168^{8}* 3440^{5} 3688^{21}

Ring Street Roller (IRE) *W McCreery* 119h 96c
11 b m High Roller(IRE) —Eyre Street Lady (Carlingford Castle)
46^{P} 3709a^{5}

Rio Gael (IRE) *Peter Bowen* 129h
5 br g Captain Rio—Palavera (FR) (Bikala)
(917) 1160^{6} (1238) 1359^{2} 1426^{2} 1797^{3} (2164) 2373^{3} 4467^{7} (4992) 5166^{13}

Rio Laine *Tom George* 90h 101c
6 ch g Beat Hollow—Toffee (Midyan (USA))
4275

Ripalong Lad (IRE) *Peter Bowen* 130h 114c
10 b g Zaffaran(USA) —King's Concubine (King's Ride)
553^{5} 771^{3} 921^{5} (986) (1391) 1508^{3} 1626^{4}

Ripoff *Robin Dickin* 79b
6 b g Kadastrof(FR) —Just The Ticket (IRE) (Jolly Jake (NZ))
5063^{9}

Riptide *Donald McCain* 132h 115c
5 b g Val Royal(FR) —Glittering Image (IRE) (Sadler's Wells (USA))
(2035) 2387^{13} 4852^{17} **(5355)**

Riqaab (IRE) *Michael Easterby* 11h
6 b g Peintre Celebre(USA) —Jeed (IRE) (Mujtahid (USA))
887^{8} 945^{P}

Risaala *Pam Sly* 125h
5 b m Alhaarth(IRE) —Perfect Plum (IRE) (Darshaan)
2168^{2} ◆ (2526) 3721^{2} (3987) 4725^{13}

Risk Challenge (USA) *Sophie Leech* 100h 100c
9 ch g Mt. Livermore(USA) —Substance (USA) (Diesis)
541^{2} 298^{6} 428^{4} (462) 585^{4} 793^{7} 990^{2} 1035^{5} (1179) 1232^{4} **1237^{P} 1256^{2} 1481^{P} 1546^{5}** 1740^{P} 5373^{4}

Riskier *John Wade* 26h
6 gr g Kier Park(IRE) —Risky Girl (Risk Me (FR))
2192^{P}
3726^{F} 3995^{P} 4996^{U}

Risk Runner (IRE) *James Moffatt* 118h 112c
8 b g Mull Of Kintyre(USA) —Fizzygig (Efisio)
1000^{3} 1377^{3} 1661^{P} 1986^{9}

Rith Bob (IRE) *David Rees* 113h
8 b m Bob Back(USA) —Rith Ar Aghaidh (IRE) (Phardante (FR))
684^{2} 763^{3} 2051^{3} 2288^{P} (3607) 4161^{2} 4532^{5} (4897)

Rivage D'Or (FR) *D T Hughes* 146h
6 b g Visionary(FR) —Deesse D'Allier (FR) (Pure Hasard (FR))
4817^{11}

Rival D'Estruval (FR) *Pauline Robson* 118h
6 b g Khalkevi(IRE) —Kermesse D'Estruval (FR) (Cadoudal (FR))
319^{5} 2102^{2} 2939^{3} 4304^{2}

Rivaliste (FR) *Paul Nicholls* 112h 143c
6 b g Robin Des Champs(FR) —Idomale (FR) (Dom Alco (FR))
2345^{3} 2665^{F} 3438^{7} 4470^{3} 5102^{U}
5242^{3}

River Alder *J M Dun* 111h 115c
13 b m Alderbrook—River Pearl (Oats)
394^{2}

River Beauty *Barry Brennan* 97h
7 ch m Exit To Nowhere(USA) —Just Beautiful (FR) (Mansonnien (FR))
50^{7} 737^{P}

River Conquest *Neil Mulholland* 16b
7 b m Riverwise(USA) —Newman's Conquest (El Conquistador)
263^{P}

River D'Or (FR) *Paul Nicholls* 122h 121c
6 b g Saint Preuil(FR) —Une Pomme D'Or (FR) (Pot D'Or (FR))
4461^{6} 4989^{3} 5421^{3}

River Dragon (IRE) *Neville Bycroft* 103h
6 b g Sadler's Wells(USA) —Diarshana (GER) (Darshaan)
1629^{5} 1785^{3} 2246^{4} *3090^{2}* 3521^{5} 3952^{5} 4253^{2} (4629) 5030^{P}

River Indus *Bob Buckler* 91h 116c
11 b g Rakaposhi King—Flow (Over The River (FR))
274^{2} 431^{2} 586^{P} 3230^{8} 3646^{2} 4328^{6} 4537^{4} (5192)

River Logic (IRE) *J Hetherton* 125h 118c
8 b g Fasliyev(USA) —Grey Again (Unfuwain (USA))
193^{10}

Rivermouth *Alan King* 85h
6 ch g Karinga Bay—Rippling Brook (Phardante (FR))
53^{11} 3153^{13} 3572^{11} 3877^{9} 4675^{2} 5169^{6}

River Music (IRE) *John Wade* 99h
6 b g Flemensfirth(USA) —Shean Bracken (IRE) (Le Moss)
5260^{2}

River Rhapsody (IRE) *Evan Williams* 83h
5 ch g Alderbrook—Double Symphony (IRE) (Orchestra)
1504^{3} ◆ 1554^{4} 2149^{7} 3397^{2} 4724^{6}

River Ripples (IRE) *Tom George* 97h 104c
12 ch g Over The River(FR) —Aelia Paetina (Buckskin (FR))
169^{9}

Riverscape (IRE) *Gordon Elliott* 125h
6 ch m Peintre Celebre(USA) —Orinoco (IRE) (Darshaan)
(870) (1090) (1574)

Riverside Poppet *James Ewart* 67b
5 ch m Courteous—Topothenorthracing (IRE) (Tremblant)
4171^{9} 5033^{4}

Riverside Theatre *Nicky Henderson* 145h 172c
7 b g King's Theatre(IRE) —Disallowed (IRE) (Distinctly North (USA))
(2126) ◆ 3560^{2} (4201)

Rivers Run Free (IRE) *J J Lambe* 70h
6 b g No Excuse Needed—Peig Sayers (IRE) (Royal Academy (USA))
1361^{7} 1666^{4}

Roalco De Farges (FR) *Philip Hobbs* 123h
6 gr g Dom Alco(FR) —Vonaria (FR) (Vorias (USA))
2482^{3} 3584^{5} 3930^{3} 4536^{3} (5110)

Roaringwater (IRE) *Miss C M E Haydon* 108h 91c
12 b g Roselier(FR) —Supreme Cherry (Buckskin (FR))
292^{P} 4857^{3}

Robain (FR) *Philip Hobbs* 111h
6 b g Robin Des Champs(FR) —Landaise (FR) (Lando (GER))
(1998) 2361^{12} 4049^{14} 5291^{6}

Robbers Bridge (IRE) *Victor Dartnall* 84h 103c
7 b g Oscar(IRE) —Rainy Way (IRE) (Mister Lord (USA))
(2287) ◆

Robbers Glen (IRE) *Valerie Jackson* 112h 129c
11 b g Muroto—Dante's Thatch (IRE) (Phardante (FR))
4915^{F}

Robbie Dye *Donald Whillans* 30h 79c
9 ch g Minster Son—Youandi (Silver Season)
3635^{8} **4064^{F}**

Robbmaa (FR) *Tony Carroll* 71h
6 bl g Cape Cross(IRE) —Native Twine (Be My Native (USA))
698^{9} 1048^{5} (1199) 1272^{4}

Rob Conti (FR) *Philip Hobbs* 99b
6 b g Network(GER) —Initiale Royale (FR) (Video Rock (FR))
5210^{3}

Robello *John O'Shea* 76h
7 b g Robellino(USA) —Realms Of Gold (USA) (Gulch (USA))
718^{5} 869^{3} 1866^{7} 2328^{9} 4006^{11} 4288^{9} 5000^{2} 5368^{4} (Dead)

Robe Longue (FR) *F-M Cottin* 67h
6 b m Dark Moondancer—Shardazar (Shardari)
190a^{P}

Robertewenutter *Sue Smith* 82h 102c
7 b g Robertico—T O O Mamma'S (IRE) (Classic Secret (USA))
2038^{9} 2166^{5} 3487^{7} 3713^{9} **3995^{5} (4549) (5004)**

Roberto Goldback (IRE) *Mrs John Harrington* 146h 158c
9 b g Bob Back(USA) —Mandysway (IRE) (Mandalus)
2227a^{2} 2970a^{3} 3778a^{2} 4227a^{2} 4818^{10}

Robert The Brave *Dai Burchell* 30h 108c
7 b g Primo Valentino(IRE) —Sandicliffe (USA) (Imp Society (USA))
4291^{9} **4723^{8}**

Robin De Creuse (FR) *Philip Hobbs* 111h
5 bb g Robin Des Champs(FR) —Myrolix (FR) (Linamix (FR))
2310^{5} 2873^{2} 3739^{3} 4499^{3} 5115^{3}

Robinson Collonges (FR) *Paul Nicholls* 139h 146c
6 gr g Dom Alco(FR) —Grace Collonges (FR) (Bayolidaan (FR))
(1770)
2220^{F} (2471)
2886^{9} 4816^{P} 5183^{P}

Robin Will (FR) *Paul Nicholls* 116h
6 bl g Dark Moondancer—Gleep Will (FR) (Cadoudal (FR))
2143^{7} 2666^{7} 2873^{6} 3454^{4} 4672^{2} ◆ 5168^{3}

Robo (FR) *Renee Robeson* 114h 140c
6 br g Cadoudal(FR) —Garde De Nuit (FR) (Courtroom (FR))
170^{2} **(1952)**
(2436)
2883^{4}

Robougg (IRE) *Claire Dyson* 86b
5 b g Tobougg(IRE) —Robin Lane (Tenby)
3992^{6} 4484^{6}

Roc De Guye (FR) *James Evans* 35h 97c
6 b g Video Rock(FR) —Kasibelle De Guye (FR) (Scooter Bleu (IRE))
635^{9} 1058^{5} **1485^{6}** 2149^{15}
(2434) 2605^{6} 3769^{4} 4139^{P} 4744^{4} 5076^{2} 5173^{7}

Rockabilly (FR) *Nigel Twiston-Davies* 110h
6 ch g Robin Des Champs(FR) —Massada (FR) (Kashtan (FR))
2058^{6} 3439^{7} 4094^{5} (4929)

Rockandahardplace (IRE) *Tracey Barfoot-Saunt* 98h
8 b g Rock Hopper—Field Of Smiles (IRE) (Aylesfield)
4539^{5}

Rock And Ska (FR) *James Evans* 80b
6 b g Maresca Sorrento(FR) —Roxy Rocky (FR) (Star Maite (FR))
3842^{8} 4479^{9}

Rockbourne Rebel (IRE) *Paul Henderson*
5 gr g Great Palm(USA) —Gaye Chimes (IRE) (Un Desperado (FR))
5105^{U}

Rock County (IRE) *Sabrina J Harty* 130h
7 b g Subtle Power(IRE) —The Ostrich Blake (IRE) (Roselier (FR))
2387^{7}

Rock Diplomat (IRE) *Dr Richard Newland* 126h 118c
11 b g Oscar(IRE) —Pre-Let (IRE) (Supreme Leader)
1960^{P}

Rocking Blues (FR) *Rose Dobbin* 111b
6 b g Lavirco(GER) —Herbe De La Roque (FR) (Courtroom (FR))
(1702)

Rockiteer (IRE) *Henry Daly* 125h 122c
8 b g Rudimentary(USA) —Party Woman (IRE) (Sexton Blake)
427^{3} 957^{4} (1151)
1432^{2} 1604^{6} 2022^{2} 5236^{2}

Rocklandslad (IRE) *Rebecca Curtis* 108h
8 b g Darnay—Er In Doors (General Ironside)
1028^{P} 1111^{5} 1308^{9} 1569^{6} 1723^{9}

Rockman *Patricia Rigby*
10 b g Daywelpacificgold(NZ) —Broken Paws (Busted)
75^{P}

Rock Me (IRE) *Lawney Hill* 107h 78c
6 ch g Rock Of Gibraltar(IRE) —Final Farewell (USA) (Proud Truth (USA))
86^{4} 227^{P} 593^{3} 825^{4} 962^{4} (1162) 1292^{2} 1551^{4} 1886^{5}

Rock Noir (FR) *Jonjo O'Neill* 150h 150c
6 bb g Mansonnien(FR) —Keep Me (FR) (Kadalko (FR))
1693^{2} (2139)
2304^{3} (3262)
3946^{4} 4789^{8}

Rock 'N' Roller (FR) *Gary Moore* 102h
7 bb g Sagacity(FR) —Diamond Dance (FR) (Dancehall (USA))
2530^{5} 2983^{P} 4773^{P}

Rockoboy (IRE) *Zoe Davison*
10 ch g Rock Hopper—Smile On (IRE) (Aylesfield)
4371^{P} 4666^{P} 4855^{P} 5059^{P}

Rock Of Deauville (IRE) *Paul Nicholls* 115h
4 b g Rock Of Gibraltar(IRE) —Ruff Shod (USA) (Storm Boot (USA))
2466^{3} 3872^{3} 4291^{5} 4807^{6} 5227^{F}

Rock Of Fife *Oliver Sherwood* 39b
4 b g Erhaab(USA) —Foehn Gale (IRE) (Strong Gale)
5238^{8}

Rock On Ruby (IRE) *Paul Nicholls* 150h
6 b g Oscar(IRE) —Stony View (IRE) (Tirol)
(2389) (3196) ◆ 3806^{2} 4803^{2} 5196^{3}

Rock Port *James Walton* 69b
9 b m Rock City—Super Sandy (Import)
4134^{P} 4361^{P}

Rock Relief (IRE) *Chris Grant*
5 gr g Daylami(IRE) —Sheer Bliss (IRE) (Sadler's Wells (USA))
2297^{U}

Rock Salmon *Lucy Wadham* 100h
8 ch g Silver Patriarch(IRE) —The Lady Scores (IRE) (Orchestra)
4922^{3} 5234^{6}

Rocks Rule (IRE) *Alan Swinbank* 111b
6 b g Oguri Cap(JPN) —Waka Shirayuki (JPN) (Arazi (USA))
2403^{5} 4363^{2}

Rockstown *Paul Webber*
7 b g Beneficial—My Moona (Ballacashtal (CAN))
2075^{8}

Rock The Soul (IRE) *Seamus Mullins* 34b
7 b g Talkin Man(CAN) —City Siege (IRE) (Jareer (USA))
1467^{P}

Rock The Stars (IRE) *Colin Tizzard* 72h
4 ch g Rock Of Gibraltar(IRE) —Crimphill (IRE) (Sadler's Wells (USA))
4331^{5}

Rocky Bear (IRE) *Marjorie Fife* 62h
6 b g Alderbrook—Sprightly Sioux (IRE) (Little Bighorn)
3957^{16} 4541^{8} 5092^{9} 5352^{6}

Rocky Lane (IRE) *Victor Dartnall* 83h
7 ch g Great Palm(USA) —Green Thorn (IRE) (Ovac (ITY))
16^{5}

Rocky Wednesday (IRE) *Gordon Elliott* 128h
4 b g Rock Of Gibraltar(IRE) —Tuesday Morning (Sadler's Wells (USA))
4295a^{3}

Rodrigo Gonzales (IRE) *Martin Keighley* 67h 82c
9 b g Accordion—Newgate Beauty (IRE) (Beau Sher)
2125^{6} **2582^{5}**

Rody (FR) *Tom George* 105b
6 ch g Colonel Collins(USA) —Hamelie II (FR) (Dress Parade)
602^{2} 832^{8}

Roe Valley (IRE) *Linda Jewell* 43b
4 ch g Arakan(USA) —Waaedah (USA) (Halling (USA))
2315^{16} *2824^{8}* 3630^{10}

Roger Beantown (IRE) *Howard Johnson* 121b
6 b g Indian Danehill(IRE) —Best Wait (IRE) (Insan (USA))
4916^{12}

Rogue Dancer (FR) *Michael Banks* 96b
6 b g Dark Moondancer—Esperanza IV (FR) (Quart De Vin (FR))
2389^{8}

Roi De Garde (FR) *Chris Bealby* 85h
5 b g Kapgarde(FR) —Belle Du Roi (FR) (Adieu Au Roi (IRE))
2067^{P} 2282^{9} 2473^{6}
4413^{P} 5075^{11}

Roi De Rose (FR) *David Pipe* 93h 129c
7 b g Insatiable(IRE) —Couture Rose (IRE) (Ajraas (USA))
2948^{6} (3433) ◆ 3689^{4} 4357^{4}

Roi Du Mee (FR) *Gordon Elliott* 127h 154c
6 b g Lavirco(GER) —British Nellerie (FR) (Le Pontet (FR))
(4250a)
5141a^{7}

Roisin's Prince (IRE) *Matt Sheppard* 104h
9 br g Bold Fact(USA) —Rosie Jaques (Doyoun)
1^{4} 302^{8} 651^{4} 765^{4} 921^{11} 1062^{8} 1451^{8}

Roi's Last Runner *Barry Murtagh* 60b
6 ch g Roi De Rome(USA) —Running Frau (Deep Run)
399^{13} 1757^{F}

Rojabaa *Simon Burrough* 65h 72c
12 b g Anabaa(USA) —Slava (USA) (Diesis)
2239^{10}
2332^{P}

Rojo Vivo *Karen McLintock* 107b
5 b g Deploy—Shareef Walk (Shareef Dancer (USA))
2368^{7} 3889^{5} 4259^{2} (4574)

Rokinhorsescience (FR) *Jonjo O'Neill* 100h 109c
7 b g Raintrap—Rosacotte (FR) (Rose Laurel)
176^{5} **353^{11}**
919^{7} 1022^{2} (1152) ◆ 1235^{4} 1612^{2}

Roko Dancer (FR) *Alan King* 101h
6 bb g Dark Moondancer—Komunion (FR) (Luchiroverte (IRE))
2372^{10}

Rolanta (FR) *James Frost* 91h
6 b m Maresca Sorrento(FR) —Gazelle De Sou (FR) (Ajdayt (USA))
1343^{P} 1601^{10} 1844^{11} 2329^{9} 2639^{8} 3477^{10} 3611^{P} 5272^{5} (5368)

Rolecarr (IRE) *Ann Hamilton* 119h
8 b g Tragic Role(USA) —Nuit D'Ete (USA) (Super Concorde (USA))
748^{P} 1005^{7} (2190) 3500^{2} 4058^{U} 4255^{4} 4544^{2} 5030^{7} (5144) (5429)

Role On (IRE) *Rose Dobbin* 97h 86c
9 gr g Bob's Return(IRE) —Banderole (IRE) (Roselier (FR))
2549^{P}
3333^{P} 3751^{6} 4477^{6}

Roll Along (IRE) *Nigel Twiston-Davies* 132h 129c
11 b g Carroll House—Callmartel (IRE) (Montelimar (USA))
3947^{P}
4200^{6} 5338^{P}

Rolline (IRE) *Stuart Kittow* 90h
6 b m Revoque(IRE) —Fille D'Argent (IRE) (Desert Style (IRE))
238^{6} 568^{8} 2288^{P} 2974^{11} 3389^{9} 4964^{5} 5172^{2}

Roll Over Rose (IRE) *William Amos* 102h
6 b m Beneficial—Rockport Rosa (IRE) (Roselier (FR))
1662^{P} 2353^{4} 3637^{5}

Roll The Dice (IRE) *Philip Hobbs* 96h
5 b g Oscar(IRE) —Sallowglen Gale (IRE) (Strong Gale)
3569^{2} 4164^{4} 4974^{3}

Rollwiththepunches *Philip McBride* 126h
6 b g Hernando(FR) —Zarma (FR) (Machiavellian (USA))
3447^{9} 3941^{3} 4354^{5}

Romance Dance *Sophie Leech* 109h
8 b m Terimon—Run On Stirling (Celtic Cone)
340^{7} 706^{2} 910^{2} 3688^{19}

Romanesco (FR) *Alison Thorpe* 117h 127c
6 b g Epistolaire(IRE) —Kadrige (FR) (Video Rock (FR))
5197^{6}

Roman History (IRE) *Tracy Waggott* 92h
8 b g Titus Livius(FR) —Tetradonna (IRE) (Teenoso (USA))
(1361) 1644^{P}

Roman Landing *Peter Pritchard* 58h
7 ch g Roi De Rome(USA) —Safe Arrival (USA) (Shadeed (USA))
223^{U} 3836^{P} 4294^{P}

Romantic Lead *Paul John Gilligan* 114h
6 b g Sadler's Wells(USA) —Valentine Girl (Alzao (USA))
4422^{3}

Romany Quest *Linda Blackford* 84b
4 b g Nomadic Way(USA) —Dinkies Quest (Sergeant Drummer (USA))
3301^{9} 4709^{7}

Romeo Desbois (FR) *Rebecca Curtis* 96b
6 ch g Maresca Sorrento(FR) —Baraka De Thaix II (FR) (Olmeto)
1180^{2} 1284^{6}

Romeos Girl *Jennie Candlish*
4 b f Statue Of Liberty(USA) —Fadaki Hawaki (USA) (Vice Regent (CAN))
836^{13} 1018^{P}

Romney Marsh *Roger Curtis* 93h 88c
10 br m Glacial Storm(USA) —Mirador (Town And Country)
1479^{8} 1732^{3} 1918^{3}
2170^{2} 2444^{4} 3349^{2} 3700^{7} 4126^{P} 4669^{5}

Romping Home (IRE) *Evan Williams* 93h 118c
8 b m Rock Hopper—Euro Joy (IRE) (Eurobus)
181^{P} 601^{4}
1176^{3}

Romulus D'Artaix (FR) *Alan King* 121h
5 b g Sassanian(USA) —Kadisha (FR) (Always Fair (USA))
2222^{7} 4081^{2} 4444^{3} 4932^{3}

Ronaldo Des Mottes (FR) *David Pipe* 152h
6 b g Rifapour(IRE) —Gemma (FR) (Djarvis (FR))
4222^{3} 4727^{F} 5198^{6}

Ronnie Ronalde (IRE) *Nick Mitchell* 55h
6 b g Laveron—Carryonharriet (IRE) (Norwich)
3301^{8} 3647^{6} 4325^{6}

Roodolph *Eve Johnson Houghton* 118h
7 ch g Primo Valentino(IRE) —Roo (Rudimentary (USA))
(58) 356^{2} 465^{2}

Rooftop Rainbow (IRE) *Linda Blackford* 106h
7 b g Lord Americo—Rulleena (IRE) (Boreen (FR))
3295^{5} 3585^{4} 4294^{4} 4929^{4} 5289^{8}

Rookery Rebel (IRE) *C W J Farrell* 120h 120c
9 ch g Minster Son—Counterbalance (Orchestra)
2345^{8} 3706a^{11}

Root Cause *Donald McCain* 113h
8 gr g Linamix(FR) —Bolas (Unfuwain (USA))
55^{5} 601^{5} 801^{5}

Rootheday (IRE) *Michael Mullineaux* 54h
11 b g King Persian—The Porchfields (Furry Glen)
538^{8}

Roper (IRE) *Jonjo O'Neill* 110h
6 b g Beneficial—Lady Fancy (IRE) (Taipan (IRE))
1768^{5} 2109^{2} ◆ 2873^{F} 4159^{U}

Rory Boy (USA) *Nigel Twiston-Davies* 115h 138c
6 b g Aldebaran(USA) —Purr Pleasure (USA) (El Gran Senor (USA))
1861^6 2522^5 4054^5 4355^6 4941^6 5345^3

Rosangla (IRE) *Anthony James Costello* 106h
9 b m Sanglamore(USA) —Gorgeous Georgina (IRE) (Tirol)
5080^9

Rosenblatt (GER) *M S Tuck* 85h
9 b g Dashing Blade—Roseraie (GER) (Nebos (GER))
585^2

Roseneath (IRE) *Alex Hales* 92h 120c
7 b g Saddlers' Hall(IRE) —Vital Approach (IRE) (Mandalus)
(158)
(2249) 3395^F

Rose Of The Moon (IRE) *Milton Harris* 130h
6 gr g Moonax(IRE) —Little Rose (IRE) (Roselier (FR))
(2074) 2389^4 3288^2 ◆ 3806^8 4206^5 4852^8

Roses Legend *Reginald Brown* 67h
6 b g Midnight Legend—Graig Hill Rose (Rustingo)
3842^{12} 4100^7 4437^{10} 4719^8 5014^P

Rose Street (IRE) *Pauline Robson* 104h
7 b m Noverre(USA) —Archipova (IRE) (Ela-Mana-Mou)
535^2 945^3

Rosie All Over *Donald McCain* 105h 110c
9 br m Overbury(IRE) —Hallo Rosie (IRE) (Mister Lord (USA))
164^4

Rosie Larkin (IRE) *Joss Saville* 56h
7 br m Beneficial—Mull's Nag (IRE) (Lord Americo)
227^8 424^5 461^7 1057^P 1428^P

Rosies Peacock *D H Llewellyn* 60b
8 b g Peacock Jewel—Final Rose (Derring Rose)
150^U

Roslin Moss *Donald Whillans* 78h
5 ch g Loup Sauvage(USA) —Etourdie (USA) (Arctic Tern (USA))
3885^7 4361^7 5027^7

Rosoff (IRE) *Laura Mongan* 98h 99c
9 b g New Frontier(IRE) —Annida (IRE) (Torus)
219^U (3378) 3610^2 3868^5

Rossbrin (IRE) *Anna Brooks* 93h
6 b g Flemensfirth(USA) —Mustard Mor (IRE) (Norwich)
54^U 228^2 336^2 2937^8 3432^P (4314) 4878^2
5191^3

Rossini's Dancer *Sue Bradburne* 94h 115c
6 b g Rossini(USA) —Bint Alhabib (Nashwan (USA))
288^{10} 445^5 1573^5
1759^8 1933^2 2203^6 3332^2 3548^3 (4150)
(4911)

Ross Limestone (IRE) *T G McCourt* 104h
8 ch g Bob's Return(IRE) —Laprida (IRE) (Executive Perk)
1594^4

Rossmill Lad (IRE) *Luke Dace* 68h
7 ch g Definite Article—Rossmill Native (IRE) (Be My Native (USA))
1710^U 2002^U 2390^P 2594^7 3983^P 5103^2 5433^5

Rossmore Lad (IRE) *Charlie Longsdon* 110h
6 bb g Beneficial—Celestial Rose (IRE) (Roselier (FR))
4951^2 ◆ 5381^2

Roudoudou Ville (FR) *Victor Dartnall* 106h 138c
6 bb g Winning Smile(FR) —Jadoudy Ville (FR) (Cadoudal (FR))
2107^P (4671) ◆ (4967)

Rouge Et Blanc (FR) *Oliver Sherwood* 105h
6 ch g Mansonnien(FR) —Fidelety (FR) (Villez (USA))
2148^P 3608^P

Rougham *Philip Hobbs* 128h 138c
5 b g Red Ransom(USA) —Louella (USA) (El Gran Senor (USA))
1775^4
1909^F 2326^2 3451^3 (3672)
4794^P 5155^2

Roughing It (IRE) *Michael Scudamore* 52h 35c
8 ch g Beneficial—Castle Street (IRE) (Dolphin Street (FR))
1494^P 1915^4

Roulez Cool *Robert Waley-Cohen* 115h 151c
8 b g Classic Cliche(IRE) —Makounji (FR) (Tip Moss (FR))
(525)

Round About *Paul Nicholls* 63b
6 ch m Grape Tree Road—Rosie Ring (IRE) (Phardante (FR))
1920^5

Round The Horn (IRE) *Jim Old* 120h
11 ch g Master Willie—Gaye Fame (Ardross)
3934^6 (4276) (4380) 4532^2

Round Tom (FR) *Paul Nicholls* 112h
6 br g Sleeping Car(FR) —Mamie Bleue (FR) (Air Du Nord (USA))
2232^3 3448^2 4446^4 4722^9

Rowaad *Andrew Price* 10h
6 ch g Compton Place—Level Pegging (IRE) (Common Grounds)
1280^5 1831^P

Rowan River *Alison Thorpe* 91h
7 b m Invincible Spirit(IRE) —Lemon Tree (USA) (Zilzal (USA))
185^5 384^3 697^6 862^9

Rowlestone Lad *John Flint* 86b
4 b g Sulamani(IRE) —Charmante Femme (Bin Ajwaad (IRE))
3569^6 3936^4 4443^3

Roxane Bruere (FR) *Robin Dickin* 77h
6 b m Loup Solitaire(USA) —Ifranne (FR) (April Night (FR))
1768^9 1993^7 2244^7 (3545) 3839^6 4707^2 5057^6
5235^F

Royal And Ancient (IRE) *Milton Harris* 105h
4 b g Danehill Dancer(IRE) —Champaka (IRE) (Caerleon (USA))
1442^2 1545^4 1610^6 2020^2 2306^3 3436^6 3484^F
3820^5 4462^7 4892^4 5132^7

Royal Arms *C Roberts* 79h
9 b g Desert King(IRE) —Opus One (Slip Anchor)
167^7 225^P

Royal Box *Dai Burchell* 18h
4 b g Royal Applause—Diamond Lodge (Grand Lodge (USA))
2466^{10}

Royal Charm (FR) *Paul Nicholls* 147h 147c
6 bl g Cadoudal(FR) —Victoria Royale (FR) (Garde Royale)
(2286) ◆ (2976) 5165^3

Royal Chatelier (FR) *Michael Blake* 94h
6 b g Video Rock(FR) —Attualita (FR) (Master Thatch)
2308^7 2980^{14} 3297^4 3822^3 (4098) 4263^F 4878^5

Royal Choice (IRE) *Henry De Bromhead* 113h 129c
7 b m King's Theatre(IRE) —Mammy's Choice (IRE) (Mandalus)
1684a^4 2972a^P

Royal Collonges (FR) *Paul Nicholls* 114h 115c
6 gr g Fragrant Mix(IRE) —Castille Collonges (FR) (El Badr)
1907^2 **2513^5**

Royal Crystal *James Turner* 53h
8 ch m Weldnaas(USA) —Frixa (Bob's Return (IRE))
3167^7 3521^{11} 3901^P

Royal Daffodil *Donald McCain* 37b
5 b m Hamas(IRE) —Vado Via (Ardross)
2167^{13} 3920^{12}

Royal De La Thinte (FR) *J T R Dreaper* 18b 149c
6 b g Cachet Noir(USA) —Belis De La Thinte (FR) (Marasali)
3579a^F 4109a^2

Royal Entourage *Philip Kirby* 89h
6 b g Royal Applause—Trempkate (USA) (Trempolino (USA))
712^U 1021^4 1250^3 1700^4 2469^P

Royale's Charter *Nick Williams* 114h
5 ch g Karinga Bay—Royale De Vassy (FR) (Royal Charter (FR))
7^2 1743^4 2003^2 3449^2 3950^3 4327^4 4933^4

Royal Etiquette (IRE) *Lawney Hill* 73h
4 b g Royal Applause—Alpine Gold (IRE) (Montjeu (IRE))
1298^5 1845^3 2528^8

Royal Flynn *Kate Walton* 97h
9 b g Royal Applause—Shamriyna (IRE) (Darshaan)
520^3 1407^2 (1554) 2070^6 2603^6 3782^{15}

Royal Guardsman (IRE) *Colin Tizzard* 122b
4 b g King's Theatre(IRE) —Lisa Du Chenet (FR) (Garde Royale)
(5388) ◆

Royal Holiday (IRE) *Brian Ellison* 87h
4 ch g Captain Rio—Sunny Slope (Mujtahid (USA))
3711^5 3879^3

Royal Kicks (FR) *Suzy Smith* 100h 116c
10 b g Garde Royale—Al Kicks (FR) (Al Nasr (FR))
85^3 330^2 764^2 (1769)
1858^{12} 2582^4 3483^{10} 4052^5 **4777^2 5206^6**

Royal Mackintosh *Alan Mactaggart* 102h 109c
10 b g Sovereign Water(FR) —Quick Quote (Oats)
2354^8 4256 4571^3

Royal Master *Richard Ford* 60h 99c
9 b g Royal Applause—High Sevens (Master Willie)
762^6

Royal Max (IRE) *Ian Williams* 111h
5 b g Hawkeye(IRE) —Baccara (IRE) (Sri Pekan (USA))
479^{10} 1084^5 1508^5 1614^4 1911^7 (2076) 5420^5

Royal Mile (IRE) *Warren Greatrex* 68h
7 br g Bob's Return(IRE) —Country Style (Town And Country)
2281^9 3960^{10} 4325^5 5267^4

Royal Mix (FR) *Paul Nicholls* 137h
5 gr g Sagamix(FR) —Princesse Irena (FR) (Apple Tree (FR))
1862^2

Royal Patriot (IRE) *Paul Green* 84h
4 b g King's Best(USA) —Lady Ragazza (IRE) (Bering)
3917^6 4331^6 4939^6

Royal Penny (FR) *B Barbier* 122h
7 ch g Cyborg(FR) —Royale Pauline (FR) (Garde Royale)
2230a^7

Royal Prodigy (USA) *Ron Hodges* 86h
12 ch g Royal Academy(USA) —Prospector's Queen (USA) (Mr Prospector (USA))
462^P 585^P

Royal Riviera *Nigel Twiston-Davies* 110h
5 b g Nayef(USA) —Miss Cap Ferrat (Darshaan)
4012^{11} 4444^6 (5074) 5401^4

Royal Role *Peter Pritchard* 89h
7 b g Tragic Role(USA) —Manx Princess (Roscoe Blake)
1922^4 2154^5 2532^3

Royal Rosa (FR) *Howard Johnson* 157h 134c
12 ch g Garde Royale—Crystalza (FR) (Crystal Palace (FR))
1960^4 2543^2 3437^P 5200^{18}

Royal Scoundrel (IRE) *Peter Bowen* 99b
7 bb g Anshan—Bridgequarter Lady (IRE) (King's Ride)
1778^4 2215^{10}

Royal Tender (IRE) *Dai Williams* 52h 72c
7 gr m Woods Of Windsor(USA) —Tender Guest (IRE) (Be My Guest (USA))
502^P

Royal Torbo (ISR) *George Baker* 82h
4 b c Tabari(GER) —Royal Dutch (GER) (Monsun (GER))
1545^7 1818^2 2047^9 2421^P 2556^U

Royal Tune (FR) *G Macaire* 148c
6 b g Green Tune(USA) —Royale Sea (FR) (Garde Royale)
(3157)
4200^3 ◆

Royal Villan (IRE) *Mark Bradstock* 68b
5 b g Luso—Frantesa (Red Sunset)
5157^{10}

Royal Wedding *Nick Gifford* 117h 125c
9 b g King's Best(USA) —Liaison (USA) (Blushing Groom (FR))
2961^6 (3963)
4328^P 4856^4 5104^4

Royal Willy (IRE) *Chris Grant* 68h
5 b g Val Royal(FR) —Neat Dish (CAN) (Stalwart (USA))
3547^9 4393^{13} 4548^5

Royaume Bleu (FR) *Alex Hales* 84h
6 ch g Kapgarde(FR) —Dear Blue (FR) (Cyborg (FR))
2452^7 2929^4 3791^{10} 4263^P 4724^5

Royial (FR) *Seamus Mullins* 92h 94c
6 b g Ungaro(GER) —Kissmirial (FR) (Smadoun (FR))
1344^4 1494^3 **1901^F 2134^5** 2980^{11}
5062^P

Roznic (FR) *Tim Vaughan* 107h 124c
13 b g Nikos—Rozamie (FR) (Azimut (FR))
(801) 865^8 1195^8

Rozolenn (FR) *Venetia Williams* 104h
6 gr g Kaktoz D'Armor(FR) —Belle Indifference (FR) (Kendor (FR))
3153^7 4719^5

Rubi Ball (FR) *J Ortet* 109h 153c
6 ch g Network(GER) —Hygie (FR) (Lute Antique (FR))
5367a^F

Rubi Light (FR) *Robert Alan Hennessy* 138h 166c
6 b g Network(GER) —Genny Lights (FR) (Lights Out (FR))
3594a^2 (4227a)
4818^3 ◆

Rubin (CZE) *Martina Ruzickova*
9 b g Laten(CZE) —Rubi (CZE) (Amyndas)
1811a^U

Rubipresent (IRE) *Malcolm Jefferson* 124h
7 b g Presenting—Azaban (IRE) (Be My Native (USA))
(349) (712) 1623^2 2164^4

Ruby Bay (IRE) *Tim Vaughan* 38h
6 ch g Beneficial—Ruby Supreme (IRE) (Supreme Leader)
4091^9

Ruby Crown *Kim Bailey* 107h
9 b m Rakaposhi King—Suilven (Teenoso (USA))
252^2 (384) (472) 796^4

Ruby Delta *Alan Juckes* 58h
6 b g Delta Dancer—Picolette (Piccolo)
93^{11} 380^P

Ruby Isabel (IRE) *Tim Vaughan* 94h 107c
7 gr m Great Palm(USA) —Royal Lucy (IRE) (King's Ride)
441^3 **(558)**
(747) 755^3
886^2

Ruby Queen (IRE) *Geoffrey Harker* 39h
9 bb m King's Theatre(IRE) —Ardrina (Ardross)
8^8 3728^{14} 4826^F

Ruby Valentine (FR) *Jim Wilson* 88h 74c
8 b m Kayf Tara—A Ma Valentine (FR) (Caerwent)
77^4 440^3 864^P 1049^5 1300^2 1976^3 (2244) 2480^F
5016^8 5241^7

Rudanphast (IRE) *Peter Bowen* 124h
6 b g Rudimentary(USA) —Alpha Style (GER) (Saddlers' Hall (IRE))
(1284) (1488) 1623^3 3787^4 4206^8 4861^F

Rudemeister (IRE) *Andrew Parker* 95b
5 b g Rudimentary(USA) —Boardroom Belle (IRE) (Executive Perk)
4717^2 5342^F

Rudinero (IRE) *Barry Brennan* 73h 96c
9 gr g Rudimentary(USA) —Cash Chase (IRE) (Sexton Blake)
283^4 529^2 795^6 931^3 1159^5 (1331)
2402^2 2950^5 (3646)
4428^4 4953^P

Rudivale (IRE) *Colin Tizzard* 102h 98c
9 ch g Rudimentary(USA) —Conjure Up (IRE) (Jurado (USA))
498^P

Ruff Diamond (USA) *Milton Harris* 67h 51c
6 bb g Stormin Fever(USA) —Whalah (USA) (Dixieland Band (USA))
4235^{10}

Rugged Jem (IRE) *Richard Mathias* 100h 89c
10 b g Humbel(USA) —Glenastar VII (Damsire Unregistered)
4415^F

Ruling Party *Alan King* 100b
6 ch g Fleetwood(IRE) —My Tern (IRE) (Glacial Storm (USA))
53^3

Rumballina *Amy Weaver* 60h
4 ch f Trade Fair—Bravo Dancer (Acatenango (GER))
2068^8 2439^5 3302^8 3540^P 3883^P

Rumble Of Thunder (IRE) *Kate Walton* 122h
5 b g Fath(USA) —Honey Storm (IRE) (Mujadil (USA))
3304^P 3715^3 4165^5 (4870)

Rumreelic (IRE) *Miss Elizabeth Doyle* 85h 98c
9 b m Quws—Ballylime Again (IRE) (Le Bavard (FR))
795^5

Runaway Harry (IRE) *Peter Bowen* 94h
8 ch g Exit To Nowhere(USA) —Rosy Posy (IRE) (Roselier (FR))
1228^6 1369^F 1449^7 1723^5

Run For Moor (IRE) *Jennifer Mason* 111h 96c
10 b g Accordion—Run For Shelter (Strong Gale)
4708^5 5275^3

Running Upthathill (IRE) *Venetia Williams* 65h
7 ch g Marignan(USA) —Effelie (FR) (Son Of Silver)
2666^{10} 2873^{13} 2985^7 3530^P 4986^P

Runshan (IRE) *David Bridgwater* 79h 115c
11 ch g Anshan—Whitebarn Run (Pollerton)
1885^2 (2055)
2395^4 4102^6 4705^4

Runswick Relax *John Wade* 82b
5 ch g Generous(IRE) —Zany Lady (Arzanni)
4916^8

Run To Fly (IRE) *Peter Bowen* 74h 74c
6 b g Milan—Paper Money (IRE) (Supreme Leader)
3153^{14} 3585^7 3762^{10}
4126^2 4409^6 4865^2

Run To Space *Nicky Richards* 86h 114c
10 b g Zahran(IRE) —Need Some Space (Precocious)
839^P 947^2 1117^7

Rupert Bear *James Walton* 67b
5 b g Rambling Bear—Glittering Stone (Dancing High)
3889^{12} 4894^7

Rupert Lamb *Howard Johnson* 113h
5 gr g Central Park(IRE) —Charlotte Lamb (Pharly (FR))
2092^7 2612^2 ◆ 3331^2 4061^2 (4824) 5147^2

Rupin (FR) *Howard Johnson* 115h
6 bb g Panoramic—Divine D'Estruval (FR) (Reve Bleu (FR))
(1928) 3633^7

Rural Mag (FR) *M Rolland*
6 b g Shaanmer(IRE) —Feat (FR) (Cadoudal (FR))
190a^{10}

Rushing Nature (IRE) *David O'Meara* 75h
7 b g Mohaajir(USA) —Princess Gemma (IRE) (Orchestra)
2075^6

Rushwee (IRE) *Lucy Wadham* 110h
9 b g Oscar(IRE) —My Baloo (On Your Mark)
3497^U (3570) 3820^6 4399^6 4667^4 5132^5 5343^2

Russe Blanc (FR) *Richard Lee* 96b
4 wh g Machiavellian Tsar(FR) —Fleur De Mad (FR) (Maiymad (IRE))
(3569)

Russellstown Boy (IRE) *Evan Williams* 42h 95c
11 bb g Arctic Lord—Lough Borough (IRE) (Orchestra)
1559^9
(1710) 1965^U 2605^5 3337^3 3984^4

Russian Conquest *Seamus Mullins* 66h
5 gr g Baryshnikov(AUS) —Kellys Conquest (El Conquistador)
238^7 3372^6 3691^{11}

Russian Epic *Philip Hobbs* 106h 122c
7 b g Diktat—Russian Rhapsody (Cosmonaut)
1911^6 3452^{11} 3686^{12} 4052^2 4704^3
(5081)

Russian Flag (FR) *Neil King* 105h 140c
8 b g Kingsalsa(USA) —Nousa Nousa (FR) (Top Ville)
1690^5 1957^3 2496^4 3786^5 (4324)
4487^P (5242)
5442^6

Russian Genie (IRE) *Victor Dartnall* 29b
5 b m Generous(IRE) —Miss Fresher (FR) (Pampabird)
3301^{11}

Russian George (IRE) *Steve Gollings* 124h
5 ch g Sendawar(IRE) —Mannsara (IRE) (Royal Academy (USA))
711^3 (842) 1021^3 (1250) (1466) 5166^P

Russian Music (USA) *Ian Williams* 79h
6 b g Stravinsky(USA) —Private Seductress (USA) (Private Account (USA))
2307^{10} 2640^P

Russian Romance (IRE) *Robin Dickin* 48b
6 b m Moscow Society(USA) —My Romance (Green Shoon)
4335^{12}

Russian Song (IRE) *Colin Tizzard* 122h 111c
7 b g Moscow Society(USA) —Sweet Charm (IRE) (Glacial Storm (USA))
266^4 503^5 **2502^2 2959^F 3371^P** 3686^8 3931^3
4189^4 (4489) 5186^P

Russian War (IRE) *Gordon Elliott* 144h
8 b g Moscow Society(USA) —Oneofmegirls (IRE) (Supreme Leader)
(1369) 1526a^{12} (1643) (1864) 2387^{10} (5166) ◆
(5339)

Russie With Love *Chris Down* 101b
5 b m Alflora(IRE) —Vieille Russie (Kenmare (FR))
5157^2

Russinrudi (IRE) *Donald McCain*
8 b g Rudimentary(USA) —Lady Of Grange (IRE) (Phardante (FR))
2269^4

Rustarix (FR) *Alan King* 127h 128c
10 b g Housamix(FR) —Star Of Russia (FR) (Soviet Star (USA))
(2343)
2669^U 2984^5 3832^5 5104^2

Rustic John *Michael Hawker* 51h 63c
11 ch g Afzal—Spartiquick (Spartan General)
3991^P

Rustler *Mary Evans* 69h 99c
9 b g Green Desert(USA) —Borgia (Machiavellian (USA))
54^F

Rusty Red (IRE) *Chris Grant* 68h 97c
8 b g Brave Act—Earth Charter (Slip Anchor)
424^P

Ruthenoise (FR) *Nicky Henderson* 128h 139c
6 ch m Robin Des Champs(FR) —Rouge Amour (FR) (Cadoudal (FR))
1614^5 2242^P 3228^5 3945^2 4009^2
4406^2 5318^F

Ruttan Lake (IRE) *Violet M Jordan* 68h
8 b g Winged Love(IRE) —Crossmacahilly (IRE) (Executive Perk)
3931^P 5172^P

Ruze (FR) *John Mackie* 66b
6 b g Fragrant Mix(IRE) —Decibelle II (FR) (Quart De Vin (FR))
3920[10]

Ryans Good Time (IRE) *Nikki Evans* 80h
9 b g Good Thyne(USA) —Beth's Apparition (IRE) (Henbit (USA))
55[6] 336[P]

Ryeman *Andrew Jackson* 111c
9 b g Romany Rye—Night Bloomer (USA) (Told (USA))
148[2] 268[3] (499)
799[5] 4708[3] 4936[U] 5372[4]

Rye Park *Noel Chance* 39b
5 b m Central Park(IRE) —Diamond Vanessa (IRE) (Distinctly North (USA))
3979[3] 4184[9]

Rye Rocket *Richard Lee* 71h
6 b g Catcher In The Rye(IRE) —Platinum Michelle (Pivotal)
4260[7]

Saalback (USA) *Luke Price* 92h 63c
9 ch m King Of Kings(IRE) —Parker's Cove (USA) (Woodman (USA))
4526[U]

Sablazo (FR) *Andy Turnell* 77h
5 b g Ragmar(FR) —Daytona II (FR) (Video Rock (FR))
1743[6] 1974[8] 2216[9] *3058[7]* 3386[12]

Sacco D'Oro *Michael Mullineaux* 91h
5 b m Rainbow High—Speedy Native (IRE) (Be My Native (USA))
2162[P] 2362[6] 2640[6] 3255[6] (3619) 3840[5] 4738[4]

Sacred Mountain *James Walton* 29h 100c
10 b g Primitive Rising(USA) —Gone Astray (The Parson)
2102[13]

Sacre Toi (FR) *E Leray*
5 b g Network(GER) —Magicielle (FR) (Video Rock (FR))
1659a[5]
5049a[6]

Sacrilege *Daniel O'Brien* 121h
6 ch g Sakhee(USA) —Idolize (Polish Precedent (USA))
515[R] **2593[P]**
4992[3]

Saddlers Blaze (IRE) *Edward Creighton* 59h 67c
9 b g Saddlers' Hall(IRE) —Strong Profit (IRE) (Strong Gale)
152[P] 294[3]

Saddlers Deal (IRE) *Chris Grant* 103h 108c
6 b g Saddlers' Hall(IRE) —Native Deal (IRE) (Be My Native (USA))
1872[3] ◆ 2107[7] 2942[7] 3549[4] (4392)
4868[3] 5294[3]

Saddlers Mount (IRE) *J Jay* 56h 77c
7 b g Saddlers' Hall(IRE) —Be My Beauty (IRE) (Be My Native (USA))
95[P] 558[3]

Saddler's Native (IRE) *Patrick O Brady* 105h 117c
9 b g Saddlers' Hall(IRE) —Farney Girl (IRE) (Be My Native (USA))
4250a[4]

Saddlers' Secret (IRE) *Mark Campion* 79h
6 b m Saddlers' Hall(IRE) —Birdless Bush (IRE) (Be My Native (USA))
2355[10] 3952[7] 5031[3]

Saddlers Singer (IRE) *E N Cameron* 63h
8 b g Saddlers' Hall(IRE) —Parsons Law (The Parson)
4553[P]

Saddlers Storm (IRE) *A J Martin* 122h 136c
9 b g Saddlers' Hall(IRE) —Lisa's Storm (IRE) (Glacial Storm (USA))
4821[11]

Saddlers' Supreme (IRE) *Martin Todhunter* 88h
9 b m Saddlers' Hall(IRE) —Festival Leader (IRE) (Supreme Leader)
163[8] 286[F] 697[7] 875[6]

Saddler's Way (IRE) *A M Crow* 98c
8 b g Saddlers' Hall(IRE) —Waydante (IRE) (Phardante (FR))
549[P]

Saddlewood (IRE) *Jamie Snowden* 87h 87c
8 b m Saddlers' Hall(IRE) —Skipcarl (IRE) (Carlingford Castle)
528[6] 920[6] 1479[3] 1694[3] 1798[5] 2183[3] **2950[3]**
3614[4]

Sadler's Cove (FR) *J K Magee* 65h 65c
13 b g King's Theatre(IRE) —Mine D'Or (FR) (Posse (USA))
459[9] 3728[13] **5310[U]**

Sadler's Star (GER) *Michael Blake* 115h
8 b g Alwuhush(USA) —Sadlerella (IRE) (King's Theatre (IRE))
576[4] 712[5] (829) 962[9] 1158[2] 1359[4] 1506[2]
1723[6] 5376[P]

Safari Adventures (IRE) *Lucinda Russell* 111h 136c
9 b g King's Theatre(IRE) —Persian Walk (FR) (Persian Bold)
236[3] (707)
1957[F] 2204[6] 2869[2] 3333[3] 3558[2] 4352[P]

Safari Journey (USA) *Philip Hobbs* 120h 148c
7 ch h Johannesburg(USA) —Alvernia (USA) (Alydar (USA))
(2086)
2345[4] 2881[9] 5164[6] 5436[2]

Safe Catch (IRE) *Martin Hill* 103h 104c
9 b g Safety Catch(USA) —Lady Satco (IRE) (Satco (FR))
763[7] **854[3]**
(1158) 1228[3]

Safe Investment (USA) *Ben Pollock* 94h 96c
7 b g Gone West(USA) —Fully Invested (USA) (Irish River (FR))
63[5] 353[5] 597[2] 840[5] 987[4] 1612[5] 1733[4] 1954[P]

Saffron Lord *Martin Keighley* 114h
6 b g Alflora(IRE) —Jan's Dream (IRE) (Executive Perk)
2238[7] 3253[6] 3584[2] 3866[P] 5321[12]

Saffron Sam *Simon Burrough* 84b
4 b g Zamindar(USA) —Sally Gardens (Alzao (USA))
2797[7] 3294[16]

Saffron Spring *Mrs S P Stretton* 59h
8 b m Emperor Fountain—Cinnamon Cruise (Cruise Missile)
180[8] 379[6]

Safin (GER) *Sue Bradburne* 85h
11 b g Pennekamp(USA) —Sankt Johanna (GER) (High Game)
166[5] 405[5] **1575[F]**

Safran De Cotte (FR) *Henry Daly* 114h
5 gr g Dom Alco(FR) —Vanille De Cotte (FR) (Italic (FR))
(2307) ◆ 3288[10] 3567[3] 3877[6]

Sagalyrique (FR) *Donald McCain* 113h 140c
7 bb g Sagacity(FR) —Folklorique (FR) (Groom Dancer (USA))
314[P] 2305[P] (3333)
(3786) 4352[P] 5185[10]

Saga Surprise (FR) *Maurice Barnes* 71h
6 b g Sagacity(FR) —Vacaria (SWI) (Llandaff (USA))
3850[10] 4165[10] 4910[13] 5260[P]

Sagredo (USA) *Jonjo O'Neill* 112h
7 b g Diesis—Eternity (Suave Dancer (USA))
1705[2] 2294[6]

Sagunt (GER) *Joanna Davis* 99h 68c
8 ch g Tertullian(USA) —Suva (GER) (Arazi (USA))
480[5] 862[6] 1196[4] 4224[P] 4925[7]
5170[4] 5375[3]

Sahara Prince (IRE) *Matt Sheppard* 78h 84c
11 b g Desert King(IRE) —Chehana (Posse (USA))
762[3] **799[4]**
864[4] 961[4] 1080[P] 1106[7]

Sahara Sunshine *Laura Mongan* 51h
6 b m Hernando(FR) —Sahara Sunrise (USA) (Houston (USA))
3374[P]

Sahrati *Michael Blake* 123h
7 ch g In The Wings—Shimna (Mr Prospector (USA))
590[3] (693) (916) (1063) 1357[8] 4852[18]

Sail And Return *Philip Middleton* 105h
7 b g Kayf Tara—Maidwell (Broadsword (USA))
1689[5] 1900[4] 2185[4] 2390[2] 2949[7] 3532[6] (5016)
5132[2] 5241[3] 5289[2]

Sailor's Sovereign *Julian Smith* 67h 73c
10 b g Sovereign Water(FR) —Tirley Pop Eye (Cruise Missile)
2132[2] ◆ 2431[2] 2950[8] 3700[P]

Sailors Warn (IRE) *E J O'Grady* 136h
4 b g Redback—Coral Dawn (IRE) (Trempolino (USA))
2966a[4] (3239a) 4083a[2] 4847[6]

Saint Are (FR) *Tim Vaughan* 145h
5 bb g Network(GER) —Fortanea (FR) (Video Rock (FR))
3288[7] 3692[2] 4159[F] ◆ 4485[3] ◆ (5186)

Saint Ber Song (FR) *A Chaille-Chaille*
5 b g Bernebeau(FR) —Isterienne (FR) (Saint Cyrien (FR))
5049a[2]

Saint Denis (FR) *Alex Hales* 89h
5 b g Saint Des Saints(FR) —Imprevue (FR) (Beyssac (FR))
2143[10] *3089[2]* 3866[5] 4332[5]

Saint Des Fresnes (FR) *P Lenogue*
5 b g Double Heart(FR) —Gazelle Royale (FR) (Beyssac (FR))
1659a[P]

Saint Espiegle (FR) *Rob Summers* 85h
7 b g Saint Preuil(FR) —Pointe Espiegle (FR) (Point Of No Return (FR))
428[2] 630[P]

Saint Gratien (FR) *E Leenders* 125h
5 gr g Fragrant Mix(IRE) —Fregate De Nourry (FR) (Video Rock (FR))
(1659a)

Saint Guru *Natalie Lloyd-Beavis*
4 b g Ishiguru(USA) —St James's Antigua (IRE) (Law Society (USA))
2597[7]

Saint Luke (IRE) *Peter Bowen* 117b
6 b g Bob's Return(IRE) —Condonstown (IRE) (Remainder Man)
(1374) 1510[2] (3441) (3936) 4808[12] 5202[5]

Saintly Lady (IRE) *Peter Bowen* 111h
6 b m Old Vic—Ban Ri Ciara (IRE) (King's Ride)
1378 421[3] 577[2] 1379[3] 1507[3] 1605[3] 2072[2]
(2372) 2606[3] 3428[2] 3742[4]

Saint Renan (FR) *D Sourdeau De Beauregard* 82h
7 b g Saint Des Saints(FR) —Erdijiya (IRE) (Kahyasi)
5159a[4]

Saints Bay (IRE) *Steven Dixon*
5 b m Redback—Alexander Eliott (IRE) (Night Shift (USA))
2122[P]

Salden Licht *Alan King* 157h
7 b g Fantastic Light(USA) —Salde (GER) (Alkalde (GER))
(3298) ◆ 4188[8] 4848[5] 5198[3]

Salesin *Niall Madden* 146h 131c
8 ch g Lomitas—Elisita (ARG) (Ride The Rails (USA))
1801a[3] 2008a[3]

Salford Rose (IRE) *David Evans* 80h
5 ch m Salford Express(IRE) —Toppagale (IRE) (Topanoora)
1180[U] 1201[3] 1284[2] 1374[3] 1603[5] 1793[6]

Sally O'Malley (IRE) *Charles Smith*
5 b m Dilshaan—Mamborina (USA) (Kingmambo (USA))
1989[17] *2825[9]* 3623[13]

Sally's Idea *Donald McCain* 99h
5 gr m Fair Mix(IRE) —One Of Those Days (Soviet Lad (USA))
1921[3] 2505[3] 3545[4]

Salontyre (GER) *Bernard Llewellyn* 125h
5 b g Pentire—Salonrolle (IRE) (Tirol)
2574[4] (2792) 2977[2] 3298[7] 3941[6] 4783[3] 5291[2]

Salpierre (IRE) *Jonjo O'Neill* 126h
6 b g Pierre—Promalady (IRE) (Homo Sapien)
1822[8] (2280) ◆ (2452) (3370) 3742[3]

Saltagioo (ITY) *Milton Harris* 124h
7 b g Dr Devious(IRE) —Sces (Kris)
159[2] (590) 733[6] 1026[2] (1138) 1160[2] 1343[7]
1466[2]

Saltara *Mark Bradstock* 13h
7 b m Kayf Tara—Star Diva (IRE) (Toulon)
3607[5] 5381[P]

Salto Angel (FR) *Gary Moore* 81b
5 b g Sheyrann—Joie D'Amour (FR) (Cadoudal (FR))
2109[F] 2577[F]

Salto Des Mottes (FR) *Neil Mulholland* 71h
5 b g Useful(FR) —Julie Des Mottes (FR) (Puma Des Mottes (FR))
3715[18] 4225[13] 4676[8] 5040[7]

Salto Royal (FR) *P Peltier*
5 b g Kapgarde(FR) —Hymne Royale (FR) (Mistigri)
1659a[4]
5049a[F]

Saltrash (IRE) *B R Hamilton* 99h 56c
10 bb g Rashar(USA) —Salt Mills (Proverb)
857[5]

Saludos (IRE) *Mrs John Harrington* 138h 145c
7 b g Bob Back(USA) —Katie's Cracker (Rambo Dancer (CAN))
3241a[F] 3705a[5]

Salute Him (IRE) *A J Martin* 141h
8 b g Mull Of Kintyre(USA) —Living Legend (ITY) (Archway (IRE))
316[5]

Salut Honore (FR) *Alex Hales* 91h
5 b g Lost World(IRE) —Kadalkote (FR) (Kadalko (FR))
1906[4] 2963[9] 3346[6] 3833[3] 4745[P]

Salveo (IRE) *Victor Thompson* 100h
9 b g Saddlers' Hall(IRE) —Devil Worship (Yashgan)
5148[P]

Salybia Bay *Andy Turnell* 93h 90c
5 b m Fraam—Down The Valley (Kampala)
1773[5] 2289[5] 2639[9] *3058[8]* 3338[4] 4049[8] **4691[6]**
5036[3] 5173[6]

Sam Adams (IRE) *Paul Nolan* 143h 134c
8 b g Presenting—Lovely Snoopy (IRE) (Phardante (FR))
2119a[4] 2413a[3] 4084a[P]

Samaret *Harriet Graham* 62h
6 ch m And Beyond(IRE) —Nova Nita (Ra Nova)
42[8] 547[7] 2103[P] 3336[13]

Sambelucky (IRE) *Keith Reveley* 86h
6 b g Barathea(IRE) —Kalimar (IRE) (Bigstone (IRE))
92[5] 457[4] 1929[8] 2351[8] 2654[6] (2937) 3363[2]
3717[5] 4550[4] 4814[2] 5308[8]

Sambulando (FR) *Tom George* 123h 123c
8 gr g Kouroun(FR) —Somnambula (IRE) (Petoski)
1766[4]
2326[3] 2572[5] 3555[3] 3949[12]

Sam Cruise *Steve Gollings* 77h 98c
10 b g Lord Americo—Final Cruise (Cruise Missile)
383[5] 517[8] (931)
1061[U] 1152[5] 1273[3] 1511[2] 1591[2] 1665[4]

Sam D'Oc (FR) *Keith Reveley* 75h
5 b g Chef De Clan(FR) —Samarie (FR) (Donald Duck (FR))
2553[5] 3889[8] 4112[7] 4506[8] 4824[6]

Sam Hall (FR) *Patrick Griffin* 71h
6 ch g Kapgarde(FR) —Salsigne (FR) (Lost World (IRE))
1869[4] 2552[15]

Samizdat (FR) *Dianne Sayer* 108h 80c
8 b g Soviet Star(USA) —Secret Account (FR) (Bering)
34[2] 163[5] 309[8] 472[P] 745[8] 1405[6] 1501[P] 1597[6]
1762[5] 2103[8] 2603[U] 2937[10] 3255[10] 3727[5] (4550)
(4809) 4960[4] 4998[F] **5418[4]**

Sam Lord *James Moffatt* 116h 134c
7 ch g Observatory(USA) —My Mariam (Salse (USA))
4115[10]
(4507) 4959[2] 5336[2]

Sammy G *Kim Bailey*
4 b f Helissio(FR) —Castaigne (FR) (Pivotal)
2824[13]

Sammy Pat (IRE) *Michael O'Hare* 78h
7 ch g Anshan—Cappuccino Girl (Broadsword (USA))
603[6] 1758[9]

Sammy Spiderman *Alistair Whillans* 70h 95c
8 b g Karinga Bay—Thorterdykes Lass (IRE) (Zaffaran (USA))
2274[7] 3501[5] 3888[P] 4064[4] 4306[3] (4713)

Sam Patch *Donald Whillans* 84h
8 ch g Weldnaas(USA) —Youandi (Silver Season)
1700[10] 1959[F] 2351[11] 2654[9] 3728[4] 3993[5]
4511[3] (4872)

Samsons Son *Alan King* 114h
7 b g Primo Valentino(IRE) —Santiburi Girl (Casteddu)
3557[6]

Sam's Pride *Peter Pritchard* 72h
6 b g Needle Gun(IRE) —Bromley Supreme (IRE) (Supreme Leader)
2590[9] 2981[P] 5074[7] 5168[13] 5393[9]

Samstown *Lucinda Russell* 51b
4 b g Kingsalsa(USA) —Red Peony (Montjeu (IRE))
3364[4]

Samtheman *Chris Nenadich* 44b
6 b g Dancing Spree(USA) —Sisterly (Brotherly (USA))
1607[8] 1748[8]

Samurai Warrior *Jamie Snowden* 90h
6 br g Beat All(USA) —Ma Vie (Salse (USA))
990[P]

Samurai Way *Venetia Williams* 112h 132c
9 b g Darshaan—Truly Special (Caerleon (USA))
155[2]

Sam Whiskey (GER) *Diana Grissell* 76h 66c
8 b g Tiger Hill(IRE) —Schlenderaca (FR) (Monsun (GER))
1816[7] 2049[10]

Sam Winner (FR) *Paul Nicholls* 141h
4 b g Okawango(USA) —Noche (IRE) (Night Shift (USA))
(2356) (2882) 3436[4] 4847[4] 5196[6]

Sanctuaire (FR) *Paul Nicholls* 150h
5 bb g Kendor(FR) —Biblique (FR) (Saint Cyrien (FR))
2386[F] 2792[3] 3649[7] (5337) 5440[P]

Sanctuary *Michael Scudamore* 80h
5 ch g Dr Fong(USA) —Wondrous Maid (GER) (Mondrian (GER))
3620[13] 3937[6] 4225[6] 4707[5]

San Deng *Micky Hammond* 105h 95c
9 gr g Averti(IRE) —Miss Mirror (Magic Mirror)
918[3] 1358[U] 2094[6] 2372[7] (3523) 4391[3] 5262[2]

Sandman (GER) *William Amos* 66h
6 b g Auenadler(GER) —Scadiomare (Taufan (USA))
174[9]

Sandofthecolosseum (IRE) *Alex Hales* 109h
6 b g Bob Back(USA) —Shuil Again (IRE) (Good Thyne (USA))
2347[10] 2955[4] **3821[P]** 4722[4]

Sandynow (IRE) *Henry Daly* 116h 101c
6 ch g Old Vic—Kasterlee (FR) (Stay For Lunch (USA))
2588[2] 3496[4] 4023[5]

Sandy's Double *Jamie Snowden* 93h
5 ch g Double Trigger(IRE) —Skipcarl (IRE) (Carlingford Castle)
3930[7] 4665[3]

Sandyzar (IRE) *Nick Mitchell* 69h 94c
12 b g Shernazar—Sandy Jo (IRE) (Sandalay)
229[6]

Sang Bleu (FR) *Paul Nicholls* 130h 119c
5 gr g Lavirco(GER) —Formosa (FR) (Royal Charter (FR))
2628[3] 3291[F]

Sangfroid *Nick Williams* 130h
7 gr g With Approval(CAN) —Affaire D'Amour (Hernando (FR))
206[5] 1855[F] 2500[4] 3566[3] 4185[11] 5003[9]

Sanpor (IRE) *Miss J Lightholder* 87h 90c
8 b g Taipan(IRE) —Not A Bother Tohim (IRE) (Abednego)
134[3]

San Remo Bello (FR) *Paul Nicholls* 126h
5 ch g Ballingarry(IRE) —Tchi Tchi Bang Bang (FR) (Perrault)
2056[4] 4180[2] 4725[5]

San Salito (FR) *Giles Smyly* 39h
5 bb g Sassanian(USA) —Lita (FR) (Big John (FR))
2518[11] 3266[12] 4706[5] 5389[P]

Sans Histoire (FR) *A Adeline De Boisbrunet* 84h
5 gr m Blushing Flame(USA) —Fia Rosa (FR) (Royal Charter (FR))
5049a[3]

Sansili *Peter Bowen* 82h
4 gr g Dansili—Salinova (FR) (Linamix (FR))
629[2] 836[5] 1018[2] 1226[3] 1935[6] 2308[5] 3449[8]
3697[2] 4224[6]

San Silvestro (IRE) *Tim Vaughan* 97h
6 ch g Fayruz—Skehana (IRE) (Mukaddamah (USA))
4704 1902[6]

Sans Un Souci (FR) *John O'Shea* 63b
5 b g Shaanmer(IRE) —Lady Vernizy (FR) (Video Rock (FR))
832[11] 1284[13]

Santal D'Alene (FR) *M Rolland*
5 b g Fragrant Mix(IRE) —Joliette D'Alene (FR) (Garde Royale)
1659a[6]

Santamina (IRE) *Peter Bowen* 95h
5 ch g Anshan—Capotaormina (IRE) (Shardari)
20[5] 624[7] 887[4] 1028[2] 1925[4] 2209[12]

Santa's Son (IRE) *Howard Johnson* 130h 150c
11 ch g Basanta(IRE) —Rivers Town Rosie (IRE) (Roselier (FR))
309[2] 627[2] 1017[12] 1406[7] 1508[7] (3966)
4853[16] 5200[P]

Santera (IRE) *Bernard Llewellyn* 138h
7 br m Gold Away(IRE) —Sainte Gig (FR) (Saint Cyrien (FR))
170[P] 1125[3] 1258[4] (1556) 1608[2] 1776[3] (2218)
2579[3] 4793[8] 5302[11]

Santiago Boy *Linda Perratt* 92b
5 b g Silver Patriarch(IRE) —Gunner Marc (Gunner B)
4717[5] 5342[8]

Santo Subito (IRE) *Michael Chapman* 51h
10 b g Presenting—Shinora (IRE) (Black Minstrel)
2589[P]

Santo Thomas (FR) *Venetia Williams* 94h
5 gr g Chichicastenango(FR) —European Style (FR) (Ezzoud (IRE))
678[8]

Saoma (FR) *Lucy Wadham* 90h
5 bb m Laveron—Fleurissa (FR) (Dress Parade)
3816[2] 4309[7]

Saphir Des Bois (FR) *Peter Bowen* 105h 143c
7 b g Saint Des Saints(FR) —Studieuse (FR) (Snurge)
78[P] 3841[2] 4487[10] 4941[3] 5199[7]

Saphire Night *Tom George* 118h 121c
10 b m Sir Harry Lewis(USA) —Tyrilda (FR) (Saint Cyrien (FR))
2147[4] 2606[10] 3771[3] 4209[3] **4720[2] ◆**

Sapphire Rouge (IRE) *Seamus Mullins* 96h
5 ch m Alderbrook—Emerald Express (Bigstone (IRE))
332[4] 2592[3] 2974[8] 3480[U] 3901[3] 4380[2]

Sarah's Boy *David Pipe* 75h
6 ch g Nayef(USA) —Bella Bianca (IRE) (Barathea (IRE))
538[11] 1907[P] 2137[9] 2499[9] 3255[13]

Sarahs Gift (IRE) *Lawney Hill* 85h 116c
8 ch g Spectrum(IRE) —Trigger Happy (IRE) (Ela-Mana-Mou)
463[4] 868[6] 1434[5]
(1550) 1903[3] 2214[2] 2669[7]

Sarando *Paul Webber* 139h 145c
6 b g Hernando(FR) —Dansara (Dancing Brave (USA))
2926[6] 3293[14]
(3605) 4371[2] 4877[F] 5183[2]

Sara's Smile *Donald McCain* 103h
5 b m Presenting—Queen's Banquet (Glacial Storm (USA))
230[9] 1780[7] 2547[2] 2954[4] 3366[11] 3747[3] 4454[2] (4964) 5280[U]

Sarde (FR) *Kim Bailey* 116h 132c
7 b g Lost World(IRE) —Stenoree (FR) (Garde Royale)
(2476)
(2669) 4208[P] 4726[P]

Sarika (FR) *Nick Williams* 77h
5 b g Grand Tresor(FR) —Arika (FR) (Le Riverain (FR))
4[7]

Sarin *Venetia Williams* 72h 127c
13 b g Deploy—Secretilla (USA) (Secreto (USA))
1107[6] 1195[9]

Sarobar (IRE) *John Spearing* 51h 94c
11 gr g Sesaro(USA) —Khairka (IRE) (Tirol)
156[9] 383[4] 649[3] 794[P] 955[5]

Sarteano (FR) *D T Hughes* 120h 140c
8 gr g Kaldounevees(FR) —Sovereign Touch (IRE) (Pennine Walk)
1123a[7]

Sasharzy (FR) *B Barbier*
4 b g Country Reel(USA) —Rowat Arazi (Arazi (USA))
1658a[P]

Saskatoon Lily (IRE) *Malcolm Beck*
9 b m Beneficial—Rosemary Mac (IRE) (Supreme Leader)
1344[P]

Sassanian (IRE) *Tim Vaughan* 96h
4 b g Clodovil(IRE) —Persian Sally (IRE) (Persian Bold)
1024[2] 1135[2] 1363[2] 1442[3] (1498)

Sassenheim (FR) *G Macaire*
4 b g Sassanian(USA) —Floresca (FR) (Hellios (USA))
1658a[2]

Sassy Wren *Sarah Humphrey*
6 ch m Best Of The Bests(IRE) —Times Of Times (IRE) (Distinctly North (USA))
2554[F]

Sa Suffit (FR) *James Ewart* 111h 150c
8 b g Dolpour—Branceilles (FR) (Satin Wood)
4003[4]

Satch *Thomas Kinsey* 33b
5 ch g Shahrastani(USA) —Repunzel (Carlingford Castle)
602[9]

Satindra (IRE) *Carole Ikin* 86h 87c
7 b g Lil's Boy(USA) —Voronova (IRE) (Sadler's Wells (USA))
410[P] 478[3] 698[7]
794[7] 1080[6] 1735[3] 2144[9] 2433[6]

Satou (FR) *Philip Hobbs* 123h
5 b g Fragrant Mix(IRE) —Jonquiere (FR) (Trebrook (FR))
5321[3]

Saucy Bingo (IRE) *Miss Helen Herrick* 102h
9 gr g Supreme Leader—Tante Marie (Bruni)
6[U]

Saujana *Joseph Bewley* 96h
7 b g Benny The Dip(USA) —Silky Heights (IRE) (Head For Heights)
1611[11] 3938

Saulty Max (IRE) *Nigel Twiston-Davies* 93h
7 b m Exit To Nowhere(USA) —Mardeila (IRE) (Alphabatim (USA))
3530[2] 4032[2] 4403[F] 4976[P]

Saut Du Cerf (FR) *Andrew Crook* 67b
5 b g Rifapour(IRE) —Judelle Du Buard (FR) (April Night (FR))
5313[7]

Saute *Jim Best* 86h
5 br g Hawk Wing(USA) —Lifting (IRE) (Nordance (USA))
2944[10] 3340[8] 3439[10] 3866[8] 4330[13]

Savannah *Luke Comer* 57h
8 b h Sadler's Wells(USA) —La Papagena (Habitat)
82[5]

Savanna's Gold *Richard Rowe*
7 ch m Bold Edge—Midnight Romance (Inca Chief (USA))
500[P]

Savaronola (USA) *Barney Curley* 67h
6 ch g Pulpit(USA) —Running Debate (USA) (Open Forum (USA))
837[3]

Saveiro (FR) *Alan Swinbank* 122h 123c
7 b g Raintrap—Branceilles (FR) (Satin Wood)
(42) 315[6]
(1779) 1930[F] 3359[5] 3784[4]

Save My Blushes *Paul W Flynn* 123h 120c
5 ch g Tobougg(IRE) —American Rouge (IRE) (Grand Lodge (USA))
2260a[4]
2412a[4]

Savigny (FR) *E Clayeux*
5 b m Alberto Giacometti(IRE) —Montre En Main (FR) (Mansonnien (FR))
5049a[4]

Saville Row (IRE) *Mrs John Harrington* 123h
6 b g Snurge—Designer Lady (IRE) (Buckskin (FR))
2912a[4] 3181a[4] 3475a[8]

Sawago (FR) *Gary Moore* 103h
5 bb g Gold Away(IRE) —Maikawa (FR) (Green Tune (USA))
3962[7] 4375[7] 4830[7]

Sawpit Solitaire *Venetia Williams* 107h
6 ro m Daylami(IRE) —Balleta (USA) (Lyphard (USA))
2637[F] 3260[8] 4009[3] 4441[6] 4897[3] 5385[5]

Sawpit Supreme *Venetia Williams* 99h 100c
9 b m Cloudings(IRE) —Dara's Course (IRE) (Crash Course)
2172[4] 2986[P] 3402[F] (3772)
4379[2] 4896[4]

Saxon House (IRE) *Mark Usher* 87b
5 b g Flemensfirth(USA) —Suka (IRE) (Acceglio)
5238[3]

Scale Bank (IRE) *Alan Swinbank* 115h 115c
8 b g Indian Danehill(IRE) —Cory Everson (IRE) (Brief Truce (USA))
175[2] 469[3]

Scales (IRE) *Malcolm Jefferson* 103b
5 b g Bob Back(USA) —Mrs Avery (IRE) (Supreme Leader)
3399[5] 3856[8] (4780) 5342[11]

Scalini's (IRE) *Chris Nenadich* 60h 78c
11 ch g Peintre Celebre(USA) —Sistadari (Shardari)
5[P] 794[2] 931[6] 1080[P]

Scampi Boy (IRE) *Paul Webber* 119h
7 b g Flemensfirth(USA) —Loch Lomond (IRE) (Dry Dock)
1864[11] 2347[14]

Scaramouche *Ben De Haan* 95h 99c
11 b g Busy Flight—Laura Lye (IRE) (Carlingford Castle)
318[P]

Scarvagh Rose *Rose Dobbin* 89h
6 b m Exit To Nowhere(USA) —Lady Phyl (Northiam (USA))
1867[6] 2547[4] 3331[9] 3631[4] 4395[8] 4912[8]

Scene Two *Philip Hobbs* 118h
5 gr g Act One—Gleaming Water (Kalaglow)
554[2] 1111[2] ◆ 1343[2] 1859[5]

Schelm (GER) *Ronald O'Leary* 115h 148c
9 b g Alwuhush(USA) —Shoba (GER) (Local Suitor (USA))
1684a[P]

Schindlers Maze (IRE) *James H Black* 112c
9 ch g Oscar Schindler(IRE) —Raggleruss (IRE) (Orchestra)
4714[3]

Schindlers Society (IRE) *J J Lambe* 94h 104c
8 br g Moscow Society(USA) —Storm Call (Celestial Storm (USA))
(3360)
3853[P]

Schindlers Tune (IRE) *Daniel Mark Loughnane* 84h 107c
11 ch g Oscar Schindler(IRE) —Musical Millie (IRE) (Orchestra)
24[P]

Schinken Otto (IRE) *Malcolm Jefferson* 78h 105c
10 ch g Shinko Forest(IRE) —Athassel Rose (IRE) (Reasonable (FR))
(404) **578[6]**
747[4] 848[8] 1095[5]
1358[2] 1502[3] (2301)
2601[5] 5312[2]

Schmetterling (IRE) *Sophie Leech* 18b
7 b m Bob's Return(IRE) —Bridge Supreme (IRE) (Supreme Leader)
1920[6]

Scholastica *Charlie Longsdon* 95b
4 b f Old Vic—La Perrotine (FR) (Northern Crystal)
(5119)

Schumpters Lad (IRE) *Charlie Mann* 117h
6 gr g Beneficial—Stepfaster (Step Together (USA))
3306[P]

Scotch Warrior *Robert Smith* 71b 111c
7 ch g Karinga Bay—Tarda (Absalom)
(310) **628[6]**
4147[F] 4476[2]

Scoter Fontaine (FR) *Rebecca Curtis* 115h
5 b g Sleeping Car(FR) —Blanche Fontaine (FR) (Oakland (FR))
(60) ◆ 1962[3] ◆ 2307[2] 2977[10] 3587[6] 4291[4] 4862[3]

Scotland Yard (UAE) *Mrs Fleur Hawes* 110h 114c
8 b g Jade Robbery(USA) —Aqraba (Polish Precedent (USA))
354[4]

Scotmail Too (IRE) *Miss S Sharratt* 103h 83c
10 b g Saddlers' Hall(IRE) —Kam Slave (Kambalda)
526[8]

Scotsbrook Cloud *David Evans* 107h
6 gr g Cloudings(IRE) —Angie Marinie (Sabrehill (USA))
646[F] 793[P] 862[3] 930[7] 1062[9] 1179[4] 1300[5] 1468[2] (1798) (1918) ◆ (2161) 2284[6] *3093[2]*

Scots Dragoon *Nicky Henderson* 117h 130c
9 gr g Silver Patriarch(IRE) —Misowni (Niniski (USA))
1858[11] 2214[F] 2669[U] 2962[F] 3688[11]
4194[4] 4699[4] 5009[3]

Scotsirish (IRE) *W P Mullins* 147h 162c
10 b g Zaffaran(USA) —Serjitak (Saher)
2339a[3] ◆ 2972a[5] 3204a[3] ◆ 3844a[4] 4227a[4]
5185[3]

Scotswell *Harriet Graham* 88h
5 b g Endoli(USA) —Tofino Swell (Primitive Rising (USA))
1702[9] 2552[12] 3330[F] 4061[4] 4824[3] 5144[9] 5429[9]

Scottish Affair *J J Lambe* 107h
5 b g Selkirk(USA) —Southern Queen (Anabaa (USA))
4303[P]

Scottys *Rachel Hobbs* 47b
5 b g Beat All(USA) —Scottish Dance (Bustino)
3842[14]

Scrappie (IRE) *C R Whittaker* 91h 108c
11 b g Fourstars Allstar(USA) —Clonyn (Wolverlife)
3908[8]

Screaming Brave *Sheena West* 124h
5 br g Hunting Lion(IRE) —Hana Dee (Cadeaux Genereux)
566[2] 2636[U] 4049[2] 4727[8] 4992[4]

Screenscraper (IRE) *Evan Williams* 94h
6 br g Flemensfirth(USA) —House-Of-Hearts (IRE) (Broken Hearted)
3[P]

Scriptwriter (IRE) *Howard Johnson* 126h
9 b g Sadler's Wells(USA) —Dayanata (Shirley Heights)
3952[4] 4169[5] (4993) 5260[U]

Scrum V *John Davies* 92h
7 b g Sonus(IRE) —Miss The Post (Bustino)
2302[2] (3697) 4166[9] 4738[3] 5308[12]

Sea Cadet *Laura Mongan* 87h 115c
9 gr g Slip Anchor—Stormy Gal (IRE) (Strong Gale)
1885[3] 2127[3]

Sea Change (IRE) *David Pipe* 105h
4 b g Danehill Dancer(IRE) —Ibtikar (USA) (Private Account (USA))
3443[7] 4677[3]

Sea Cliff (IRE) *Andrew Crook* 91h 113c
7 b g Golan(IRE) —Prosaic Star (IRE) (Common Grounds)
155[8] 564[3] 888[8] 1033[6] 1162[7] 1336[5] 1451[3] (1605) 1745[8] (3728) 4511[12]

Sea Cove *Dianne Sayer* 93h 68c
11 b m Terimon—Regal Pursuit (IRE) (Roi Danzig (USA))
10[9] **160[10]**
288[9] **460[9]**
748[5] 948[6]

Sea Diva (IRE) *Rebecca Curtis* 78h 132c
11 b m Old Vic—Upsail (Top Ville)
3589[12]

Seafield (IRE) *Paul Nolan* 123h
6 ch g Tel Quel(FR) —Finemar Lady (IRE) (Montelimar (USA))
2562a[7] 3846a[6]

Seafire Lad (IRE) *Ms Jackie Williamson* 86h
10 b g Portrait Gallery(IRE) —Act The Fool (IRE) (Always Fair (USA))
4915[U]

Sea Fury (IRE) *Suzy Smith*
4 b f Hawk Wing(USA) —Scruple (IRE) (Catrail (USA))
3979[6]

Sea Land (FR) *Brian Ellison* 73h
7 ch g King's Best(USA) —Green Bonnet (IRE) (Green Desert (USA))
1249[7]

Seam Of Diamonds *Martin Todhunter* 75h
6 br m Montjoy(USA) —Diamond Rachael (IRE) (Shalford (IRE))
(602) 2296[8] 2547[7] 5356[9]

Sean Og (IRE) *Tim Vaughan* 65h 70c
9 gr g Definite Article—Miss Goodbody (Castle Keep)
278[3] 794[3] (1905)
1954[4] 2334[6]

Seaquel *Sally-Anne Wheelwright* 105h
5 b m Kyllachy—Broughton Singer (IRE) (Common Grounds)
1348 (380) 598[2] (678) 865[4] 1429[6] 1484[13]

Search My Soul (IRE) *Jennie Candlish* 76b
5 b g Luso—Scurlogue Again VII (Damsire Unregistered)
1510[6]

Searree *James Turner* 69h
6 b m Daylami(IRE) —Magongo (Be My Chief (USA))
355[11] 5475 805[5]

Sea Saffron *Susan Gardner* 96h 116c
10 b g Sea Raven(IRE) —Saffron Lake (Shaab)
130[P] 2980[6] 3300[2] **(3907)**
4313[6]

Seasonselite *Venetia Williams* 101h
6 b m Sagamix(FR) —Oleana (IRE) (Alzao (USA))
3724[F] 4266[6]

Sea Storm (IRE) *James Moffatt* 108h
13 b g Dolphin Street(FR) —Prime Interest (IRE) (Kings Lake (USA))
44[8]

Sea Venture (IRE) *Tim Walford* 101h 113c
9 b g Sea Raven(IRE) —Good Highlights (IRE) (Good Thyne (USA))
352[P] 5312[4]

Seaview Lad (IRE) *Bob Buckler* 42h
8 b g Sonus(IRE) —Nice Little Earner (Warpath)
168[7] 3701[2] 2051[8]
2608[P] 3609[P]

Sea Wall *Jonjo O'Neill* 121h 129c
9 b g Giant's Causeway(USA) —Spout (Salse (USA))
300[P] 567[3] 911[7] (1032)
(1178) 1373[3] 4442[P]

Sebadee (IRE) *K J Condon* 126h 130c
7 b g Cape Cross(IRE) —Phyllode (Pharly (FR))
5141a[4]

Sebastiano (FR) *Gary Moore* 117h 117c
8 ch g Ski Chief(USA) —Femme Rouge (IRE) (Elmaamul (USA))
170[P] 2596[7] 3378[3] 3793[3] 3868[3] 4399[5]

Sebennytos *Warren Greatrex* 67h
6 b g Beat All(USA) —Lady Benson (IRE) (Pennine Walk)
2056[12] 2577[11] *3089[8]*

Second Brook (IRE) *Reg Hollinshead* 95h
4 b g Celtic Swing—Mur Taasha (USA) (Riverman (USA))
3401[8] ◆ 4283[7] 4499[7] 5082[2] ◆ 5401[5]

Secret Cavern (USA) *Peter Pritchard* 58h 80c
9 b g Lion Cavern(USA) —River Dyna (USA) (Dynaformer (USA))
54[6] **339[6]**
1924[4] 2152[F]

Secret Dancer (IRE) *Alan Jones* 132h
6 b g Sadler's Wells(USA) —Discreet Brief (IRE) (Darshaan)
2498[11] 3289[7] 3808[5] 4848[18] 5287[3]

Secret Desert *Ferdy Murphy* 88h
5 b g Dubai Destination(USA) —Lady Bankes (IRE) (Alzao (USA))
14[F] 174[3] 2302[4] 2478[5] 2937[12] 3622[5] 5114[5]

Secret Legend *Kevin Bishop* 89b
6 ch g Midnight Legend—Grecian Bay (Vouchsafe)
5174[9]

Secret Palm (IRE) *Caroline Bailey*
6 gr g Great Palm(USA) —Proud Gayle (IRE) (Homo Sapien)
1325[6] 1819[7]

Secret Past (IRE) *Karen McLintock* 102b
6 b g Rudimentary(USA) —Lucifer's Way (Lucifer (USA))
2560[3] ◆ 3773[5]

Secret Shared (IRE) *Richard Mitchell* 12h
7 b g Secral(USA) —Geryea (USA) (Desert Wine (USA))
407[8] **4267[4]**
4782[4] 5155[P]

Secret Tune *Tom George* 132h 93c
7 b g Generous(IRE) —Sing For Fame (USA) (Quest For Fame)
1017[P] 1346[3] 1864[8] 2542[7]

Secret World (IRE) *Nicky Henderson* 126h
8 ch g Spinning World(USA) —Classic Park (Robellino (USA))
2667[2] ◆ 3478[3] 3872[2]

Securitisation (IRE) *Barney Curley* 31h
4 ch g Rock Of Gibraltar(IRE) —Maria Delfina (IRE) (Giant's Causeway (USA))
1018[11]

Sedano (FR) *Alan King* 53b
5 bb g Dark Moondancer—Kadalville (FR) (Kadalko (FR))
4879[9]

Seeability (IRE) *Patrick O Brady* 124h 110c
8 b g Bob Back(USA) —Tropical Lake (IRE) (Lomond (USA))
1712a[4]

Seeking Power (IRE) *N W Alexander* 82h 101c
10 b g Supreme Leader—Seeking Gold (IRE) (Lancastrian)
2193[2] 3501[4] 4066[P] 4306[5] 4825[2]

Seek The Truth (IRE) *Sue Bradburne* 68h 97c
8 b g Witness Box(USA) —Country Project (IRE) (Project Manager)
1701[U] 1781[6] 2354[4] 3360[4] 3636[4] 5258[6]

Seekwall *Seamus Mullins*
5 b g Kirkwall—Seem Of Gold (Gold Dust)
2000[P]

See The Legend *Sandy Forster* 83h
6 b m Midnight Legend—Amys Delight (Idiots Delight)
42[10] 2547[8] 4068[3] 4688[5] 4960[P]

See U Bob (IRE) *Paul Nolan* 134h 146c
8 b g Bob Back(USA) —Hidden Ability (IRE) (Alphabatim (USA))
2227a[F] 5025a[2]

Seeyaaj *Lucinda Russell* 107h 119c
11 b g Darshaan—Subya (Night Shift (USA))
(290) **676[2]**
1023[3] 3970[3] 4471[4] 5004[3]

See You Jack *Caroline Bailey* 103h 98c
6 b g Dolpour—Layston Pinzal (Afzal)
1812[4] 2111[2] 2530[F] 3487[5] 3744[6] 4182[5] **5100[5]**
5379[6]

See You Sunday *Seamus Mullins*
6 gr m Baryshnikov(AUS) —Shepani (New Member)
3301[14]

See You There (IRE) *Lucinda Russell* 70h 115c
12 br g Religiously(USA) —Bye For Now (Abednego)
2106[7] 2449[3] 3634[2] 4137[P] 4689[7]

Seffier *Ian Patrick Browne* 66b
6 b m Zamindar(USA) —Eujane (IRE) (Alzao (USA))
4410[8] 5387[10]

Sefton Park *Charles Egerton* 79h
4 b g Dansili—Optimistic (Reprimand)
674[U] 1024[4] 1135[6] 1234[5] 1442[8]

Seigneur Des Bois (FR) *Ferdy Murphy* 113c
5 b g Ballingarry(IRE) —Studieuse (FR) (Snurge)
1759[10] 1930[7] 2270[7] 2601[6] 5004[2] (5294)

Seize *James Moffatt* 88h 112c
9 gr g Silver Patriarch(IRE) —Sleepline Princess (Royal Palace)
46[2] 164[2] 608[7] (1103)
1404[5] 1697[6] 3716[3] 4937[4] 5423[2]

Selection Box (IRE) *C A McBratney* 105h 136c
10 b g Witness Box(USA) —Challenging Times (IRE) (Kemal (FR))
3798a[7]

Semah George *John Holt* 33b
5 ch g Central Park(IRE) —Semah's Dream (Gunner B)
3489[11] 3987[P]

Semelay (FR) *Laura Young* 9h
5 bb g Shaanmer(IRE) —La Menardiere (FR) (True Brave (USA))
3569[7] 3930[F] 4444[13] 5211[8] 5381[P]

Semi Colon (FR) *Nicky Henderson* 117h
5 ch m Robin Des Champs(FR) —Hi Colon (FR) (Nashamaa)
(2472) 3227[3] 3781[3] (4535) ◆ 5008[5] 5335[10]

Semi Detached (IRE) *James Unett* 102h
8 b g Distant Music(USA) —Relankina (IRE) (Broken Hearted)
4234[7] 4785[F]

Seminal Moment *William Amos* 57h
5 b m Sakhee(USA) —Thracian (Green Desert (USA))
2297[5] 2547[9] 3637[8] 4138[P] 4994[P]

Semiramiss (FR) *P Quinton*
7 b m Pennekamp(USA) —Vision De Ville (FR) (Comrade In Arms)
312a[P]

Sendali (FR) *Chris Grant* 110h
7 b g Daliapour(IRE) —Lady Senk (FR) (Pink (FR))
3500[15] (4914) 5149[4] 5431[3]

Sendeed (USA) *Peter Atkinson* 92c
9 bb g Gulch(USA) —Aghsaan (USA) (Wild Again (USA))
628[P] 889[5] 1000[7] 1255[P] 1500[P]

Sendefaa (IRE) *Michael Gates*
6 bb m Halling(USA) —Patruel (Rainbow Quest (USA))
3506[12] 4081[P] 4776[P]

Send For Tim (IRE) *F Jordan* 58h
8 b g Corrouge(USA) —Duneavey (IRE) (Mandalus)
541[11] 587[P]

Sendiym (FR) *Ferdy Murphy* 87h
4 b c Rainbow Quest(USA) —Seraya (FR) (Danehill (USA))
4059[7] 5028[3]

Senor Alco (FR) *Howard Johnson* 110h
5 gr g Dom Alco(FR) —Alconea (FR) (Brezzo (FR))
2202[3] 4253[3] 5031[F]

Senor Shane (IRE) *Chris Gordon* 93h 120c
8 b g Gothland(FR) —Cummin River (IRE) (Over The River (FR))
4745[F] 4988[P] **5194[7]**

Senses (USA) *David Pipe* 67h
5 ch g Rahy(USA) —Sweet And Steady (USA) (Steady Growth (CAN))
2944[12] 3526[7] ◆ 3645[10] 4069[7] 4707[P]

Sentimentaljourney (IRE) *Jonjo O'Neill* 103b
4 ch g Portrait Gallery(IRE) —Hazy Rose (IRE) (Roselier (FR))
5257[2]

Sentosa *Michael Blanshard* 67h
4 b f Dansili—Katrina (IRE) (Ela-Mana-Mou)
4781[7]

Sentry Duty (FR) *Nicky Henderson* 161h
9 b g Kahyasi—Standing Around (FR) (Garde Royale)
2884[8] 5160[9]

Septemberintherain *Robert Mills* 69h
4 gr g Verglas(IRE) —Gwyneth (Zafonic (USA))
1018[6]

September Moon *Michael Appleby* 61h 95c
13 b m Bustino—Lunabelle (Idiots Delight)
1434[8]
1903[U] 2155[3] 2532[P]
2953[P]

Septland (FR) *P Peltier*
5 b m Agent Bleu(FR) —Jubyland (FR) (Kadalko (FR))
(5049a)

Septos *Richard Price* 75h
7 b g Nikos—Tres Chic (IRE) (Bob Back (USA))
16[P] 3703[P] 4263[2] 4559[3] 5075[4] 5169[4]

Serenader *David O'Meara* 83b
4 ch g Singspiel(IRE) —Temora (IRE) (Ela-Mana-Mou)
2108[3] 3971[4] 4457[11]

Seren Cwmtudu (IRE) *Evan Williams* 112h
7 b m Glacial Storm(USA) —Keel Row (Relkino)
20[3] 2068[3] 3158[6] (3480) 3674[P] 5078[3]

Serenitatis (IRE) *Tim Easterby* 92b
5 ch m Alderbrook—Four Moons (IRE) (Cardinal Flower)
2825[4] 3504[2] 4171[5] 4554[7]

Seren Rouge *Keith Reveley* 113h
6 b g Old Vic—Bayrouge (IRE) (Gorytus (USA))
2102[3] 3887[4] 4285[3]

Sergeant Pink (IRE) *Steve Gollings* 120h 118c
5 b g Fasliyev(USA) —Ring Pink (USA) (Bering)
2313[2] 2455[5] 3694[3] 4050[4]

Seriatim (IRE) *R T J Wilson* 87b
6 b g Oscar(IRE) —Royale Boja (FR) (Kadalko (FR))
4259[5]

Sericina (FR) *Miss C Roddick* 132c
8 b m Colonel Collins(USA) —Pierrebrune (FR) (Cadoudal (FR))
(4163)
4851[P]

Serious Intent (IRE) *C A McBratney* 94h
9 ch g Lord Of Appeal—Marbleade (IRE) (Over The River (FR))
744[7]

Sertao (FR) *Tim Vaughan* 110b
5 b g Passing Sale(FR) —Etoile Bleu (FR) (Ghost Buster'S (FR))
3943[2] (4410)

Sesame Rambler (IRE) *Mrs S Alner* 114h 108c
12 gr g Roselier(FR) —Sesame Cracker (Derrylin)
229[5] 431[U] 4374[P]

Set In Her Ways (IRE) *Kim Bailey* 71b
5 b m Old Vic—Yes Your Honour (Carlingford Castle)
5119[9]

Setters Gift *Ron Hodges* 35b
4 b f Generous(IRE) —Setter Country (Town And Country)
5084[10]

Setter's Princess *Ron Hodges* 93h
5 ch m Generous(IRE) —Setter Country (Town And Country)
2499[U] 2592[2] 2974[6]

Seven Is Lucky (IRE) *Jim Goldie* 99h 101c
9 b g Old Vic—Green Legend (IRE) (Montekin)
3853[P] 4066[P] 4712[4] 5320[3]

Seven Summits (IRE) *Barney Curley* 85h
4 b g Danehill Dancer(IRE) —Mandavilla (IRE) (Sadler's Wells (USA))
4024[5] 4283[12] 5099[8]

Seventh Hussar *Henrietta Knight* 66h
5 b g Alflora(IRE) —Shuil Do (IRE) (Be My Native (USA))
3406[13] 3964[8] 4443[5] 5167[15]

Sevivon *Colin Tizzard* 27b
4 ch f Dubai Destination(USA) —Circle Of Light (Anshan)
4335[13]

Sexy Rexy (IRE) *Nigel Twiston-Davies* 78h
10 b g Mister Lord(USA) —Cab On Time (IRE) (Alphabatim (USA))
2171[6]
3768[P] 4524[P]

Seymar Lad (IRE) *Miss V Collins* 104h 123c
11 b g Oscar(IRE) —Far And Deep (IRE) (Phardante (FR))
300[7] 501[F] 844[P] 1032[7] 4701[2] 5347[5]

Seymour Eric *Michael Scudamore* 103h
6 b g Bollin Eric—Seymour Chance (Seymour Hicks (FR))
2143[F] 2365[P] 3439[5] 3918[10] 4722[11]

Seymour Weld *Charles Pogson* 104h 135c
11 ch g Weld—Seymour News (Seymour Hicks (FR))
1020[P] 1151[7] 1404[8]

Shacklesborough (IRE) *Paul Nicholls* 96h 106c
7 b g Presenting—Idiot's Gale (IRE) (Strong Gale)
2059[4]
3230[7] 3907[9] 5068[3] 5195[6]

Shadow Boxer *Donald Whillans* 80h
6 gr g Makbul—Shadows Of Silver (Carwhite)
3363[P] 3883[5] 4302[6]

Shadow Dancer (IRE) *Jonjo O'Neill* 127h 118c
6 b g Milan—Fox Burrow (IRE) (Supreme Leader)
947[7] **1706[2]**
2153[6] 2951[4] 3531[5] 4010[P]

Shadow's Gold (IRE) *Keith Goldsworthy* 95b
7 b g Moonax(IRE) —Katie Daly (IRE) (Lord Americo)
1180[3]

Shadows Lengthen *Michael Easterby* 120h
5 b g Dansili—Bay Shade (USA) (Sharpen Up)
3521[2] 3885[6] (4393) 4993[F]

Shadow Wood (IRE) *Patrick Griffin* 86h
7 b g Exit To Nowhere(USA) —Safariyna (FR) (Labus (FR))
768[4] 853[7] 1700[6]
1924[F] (Dead)

Shadrack (IRE) *Sue Smith* 110h
7 gr g Tamayaz(CAN) —Alba Dancer (Gran Alba (USA))
1827[8]
2037[F] 4778[5] 5098[F]

Shaftesbury Avenue (USA) *Ian McInnes*
8 ch g Fusaichi Pegasus(USA) —Little Firefly (IRE) (Danehill (USA))
14[P] 174[P]

Shahramore *P Monteith* 39h
6 b m Shahrastani(USA) —Sillymore (Silly Prices)
870[9] 943[6] 1340[P]

Shakalakaboomboom (IRE) *Nicky Henderson* 112h 140c
7 b g Anshan—Tia Maria (IRE) (Supreme Leader)
2153[3] (2582)
(3479) ◆ 3803[7] 4794[9] 5185[7]

Shake On It *Mark Hoad* 78h
7 b g Lomitas—Decision Maid (USA) (Diesis)
465[6]

Shake The Barley (IRE) *Tom George* 81h 124c
8 ch g Marignan(USA) —Glengarra Princess (Cardinal Flower)
4223[5] 4523[3] 5081[4]

Shaking Hands (IRE) *David Pipe* 96h 127c
7 b g Bach(IRE) —Picton Lass (Rymer)
2483[F] (3768)
4537[9]

Shalambar (IRE) *Tony Carroll* 110h
5 gr g Dalakhani(IRE) —Shalama (IRE) (Kahyasi)
2667[7] 3387[7] (3782) (4076) 4323[6] 4990[P]

Shalamiyr (FR) *Philip Hobbs* 110h 53c
6 gr g Linamix(FR) —Shamanara (IRE) (Danehill (USA))
(129) 372[8] 1859[9] 2150[7] 2626[11] **3494[9]**

Shalimar Fromentro (FR) *Nick Williams* 131h 133c
5 gr g Martaline—Miss Des Ormeaux (FR) (Glaieul (USA))
1659a[2] 1966[5] **2455[4] 2979[2] ◆ (3564)**
5049a[P]

Shalone *Alan King* 135h
7 ch g Tobougg(IRE) —Let Alone (Warning)
3676[5] 4202[5] ◆ 4852[5] 5325[6]

Shame The Devil (IRE) *James Evans* 78h
6 b g Danehill Dancer(IRE) —Iles Piece (Shirley Heights)
590[8]

Shammick Boy (IRE) *Victor Dartnall* 135h
6 b g Craigsteel—Dulcet Music (IRE) (Topanoora)
2368[9] 3225[7] (3645) (3872) 4895[3]

Shammy Buskins *Lawney Hill* 82h 125c
9 b g Shambo—Quistaquay (El Conquistador)
(229) **501[2]**
1032[5] 4749[RR] (4971)
5286[2]

Shamrock Bay (FR) *E Lecoiffier*
5 b g Al Namix(FR) —Hermine Du Butel (FR) (Cyborg (FR))
1659a[P]

Shamrogine (IRE) *Paul John Gilligan* 76h
5 b m Saddlers' Hall(IRE) —Marshys Mia (Alflora (IRE))
1289[5]

Shanahan (IRE) *Nikki Evans* 98h 110c
10 b g Little Bighorn—Thomastown Girl (Tekoah)
169[5] 437[P] 799[P] 1137[10]

Shan Blue (IRE) *Steve Gollings* 105h
6 ch g Anshan—River Runs Blue (IRE) (Over The River (FR))
1749[3] 3511[7] 3725[2] 3987[7] 4743[F]

Shanen (IRE) *George Charlton* 87b
5 b g Tikkanen(USA) —Ursha (IRE) (Shardari)
1702[5] ◆

Shane Rock *M F Morris* 130h 121c
6 b g King's Theatre(IRE) —Elaine Tully (IRE) (Persian Bold)
3475a[5]

Shannagarry (IRE) *George Charlton* 93b
5 b g Presenting—Tikrara (USA) (Assert)
3553[6] 3971[2] 5264[6]

Shannersburg (IRE) *Ian Williams* 86h
6 bb g Johannesburg(USA) —Shahoune (USA) (Blushing Groom (FR))
845[5]

Shannon Lodge (IRE) *Tracey Barfoot-Saunt* 83h 86c
13 gr g Aristocracy—Roseville Baroness (Sexton Blake)
913[P] 1106[P] 1259[P]

Shannons Boy (IRE) *Richard Lee* 81h 99c
9 b g Anshan—Dusky Lady (Black Minstrel)
(2608)
3527[F]

Shannons Firth (IRE) *Ben Case* 92b
6 ch m Flemensfirth(USA) —Collopy's Girl (IRE) (Be My Native (USA))
5078[P]

Shannon Spirit (IRE) *T Hogan* 123h
6 b g Snurge—Spirit Of The Nile (FR) (Generous (IRE))
3208a[5]

Shantou Breeze (IRE) *Michael Madgwick*
4 b f Shantou(USA) —Homersmare (IRE) (Shardari)
5388[P]

Shantour (IRE) *Joseph Fox* 64h
7 ch g Anshan—West Tour (Deep Run)
1115[9]

Shan Valley (IRE) *Lucy Normile* 85b
5 ch m Shantou(USA) —Statim (Marju (IRE))
311[5] 4171[11] 5135[11]

Sharabosky *Caroline Bailey*
7 ch m Shahrastani(USA) —Bosky (Petoski)
2987[14]

Sharadiyn *Clive Mulhall* 98h
8 b g Generous(IRE) —Sharadiya (IRE) (Akarad (FR))
405[4] 604[7] 3951[3] 4511[10]

Shara Like Magic *Dianne Sayer* 25h
8 gr m Baryshnikov(AUS) —Total Tropix (Saddlers' Hall (IRE))
1665[P] 1760[P] 1996[11]

Shardakhan (IRE) *Sophie Leech* 83h 140c
9 b g Dr Devious(IRE) —Sharamana (IRE) (Darshaan)
3908[P] 5241[P] 5369[4]

Shared Secret *Anthony Honeyball* 25h
7 ch m Riverwise(USA) —Shared-Interest (Interrex (CAN))
1742[8] 2288[P] 2634[P]

Share Option *Tony Carroll* 114h
9 b g Polish Precedent(USA) —Quota (Rainbow Quest (USA))
196[8] 5392[9]

Sharinga *Reg Hollinshead* 44b
4 ch f Karinga Bay—Forever Shineing (Glint Of Gold)
3569[10] 4082[13] 4500[P] 4747[P]

Shark Man (IRE) *Andrew Reid* 49h
4 b g Arakan(USA) —Sharkiyah (IRE) (Polish Precedent (USA))
1545[8] 1728[P]

Sharlene's Quest (IRE) *V J Hughes* 103b
5 b m Revoque(IRE) —Sanka (IRE) (Standiford (USA))
3623[5] (3943) 4335[4] 5188[13]

Shaw Cross *Robert Johnson*
4 b g Apprehension—Allegedly Red (Sabrehill (USA))
2108[12] 2451[P]

Sheepclose (IRE) *Michael Easterby* 74h
6 b g Beneficial—Returning (Bob's Return (IRE))
2612[P] *3167[9]* 3403[8] 3952[F] 4281[10] 4743[4] 5307[F]

Sheer Genius (IRE) *John Joseph Murphy* 122h
6 b g Norwich—Sheeghee (IRE) (Noalto)
4788[14]

Sheezatreasure (IRE) *James Evans* 77h
6 b m Naheez(USA) —Cottage Treasure (IRE) (Roselier (FR))
412[7] 855[7] 1743[9] 2241[9] 2634[11] 2956[7] 3532[7] 4787[8] 5075[9]

Sheikhman (IRE) *Brett Johnson* 99h
10 b g Sadler's Wells(USA) —Maria Isabella (USA) (Kris)
522[5] 757[5]

Sheila's Castle *Sean Regan* 90h
7 b m Karinga Bay—Candarela (Damister (USA))
4859[4]

Sheila's Rose (IRE) *Barry Brennan* 96b
6 ch m Golan(IRE) —Delilah's Unrest (Unfuwain (USA))
739[9] 2472[9]

She Is A Cracker (FR) *Gary Moore* 86h
6 b m Cadoudal(FR) —Douchka (FR) (Fijar Tango (FR))
1915[8]

Sheknowsyouknow *Michael Hawker* 106c
10 b m Petrizzo—Margaret Modes (Thatching)
5277[3]

Shelomoh (IRE) *James Turner* 84h 108c
10 b g Zaffaran(USA) —Parson's Run (The Parson)
3501[P] 4001[7] 4379[3]

Shergill (IRE) *Shaun Lycett* 77h
10 bb g Weld—Gaelic Holly (IRE) (Scenic)
66[6] 273[5] 467[P] (1059)
1366[P]

Sheriff Hall (IRE) *George Charlton* 93h 100c
6 b g Saddlers' Hall(IRE) —Derravarra Breeze (IRE) (Supreme Leader)
209[9] 397[7] 1505[11] 1700[12] (2658) 3335[4]
4305[2] 4573[2] 5145[3] 5429[3]

Sheriff Hutton (IRE) *Tim Walford* 129h 135c
8 b g Rudimentary(USA) —Will She What (IRE) (Lafontaine (USA))
(308) 708[2] **859[6] (2204)** *3171[4]* **3953[4] 4821[P]**
5416[P]

Sheriff Roscoe *R M Woollacott* 114h 104c
11 b g Roscoe Blake—Silva Linda (Precipice Wood)
4271[F] 4786[5]

Sherlock (FR) *E Clayeux*
5 ch g Shaanmer(IRE) —Ili Dancer (FR) (Missolonghi (USA))
1659a[P]

Sherwani Wolf (IRE) *Nigel Twiston-Davies* 126h
7 b g Loup Sauvage(USA) —Sherwani (IRE) (Shernazar)
2946[6] (3934) 4485[4]

Shesells Seashells *Donald McCain* 76h
4 b f Tiger Hill(IRE) —Brush Strokes (Cadeaux Genereux)
4781[6]

Sheshali (IRE) *Evan Williams* 128h 125c
7 b g Kalanisi(IRE) —Sheshara (IRE) (Kahyasi)
1627[F] (2278)
4030[4] 4673[P]

She's Humble (IRE) *Linda Jewell* 68h 102c
9 ch m Humbel(USA) —She's No Tourist (IRE) (Doubletour (USA))
2429[6] *3059[10]* 3338[6]
(3606) 3869[7] 4400[2] (5055)
5269[3]

She's Little Don *Stephen Hughes* 22h
11 b m Gran Alba(USA) —Doubting Donna (Tom Noddy)
992[8] 2070[8] 2144[P]

She'Solovely *Martin Wilesmith* 62h
7 b m Alflora(IRE) —Cashmere Lady (Hubbly Bubbly (USA))
327[9]

She's On The Case (IRE) *Grant Cann* 104h
6 b m Witness Box(USA) —New Line (IRE) (Roselier (FR))
4448[7] 4536[P] 5061[4]

She's Sassy (IRE) *Suzy Smith* 73b
6 bb m Sassanian(USA) —Fulgina (FR) (Double Bed (FR))
222[10]

Shianda *Gary Moore* 82h
4 b f Kyllachy—Limuru (Salse (USA))
4781[5]

Shifting Gold (IRE) *Kevin Ryan* 103h
5 b g Night Shift(USA) —Gold Bust (Nashwan (USA))
3523[8] (4797) 5098[6]

Shillingstone *G T H Bailey* 144c
9 ch g Emperor Fountain—Columcille (St Columbus)
4750[3]

Shilpa (IRE) *Anabel L M King* 103h
6 b m Medicean—Nature Girl (USA) (Green Dancer (USA))
350[10] 4234[9] 4809[P] 5101[5]

Shindig *John Flint* 92h 99c
9 b g Classic Cliche(IRE) —Cloud Cuckoo (Idiots Delight)
755[6] 1062[3] 1261[3] 1484[10]

Shinko Moon *Jo Crowley* 93b
4 b g Shinko Forest(IRE) —Silver Moon (Environment Friend)
1913[3] (4709)

Shinnecock Bay *Oliver Sherwood* 100h 108c
7 b g Selkirk(USA) —Lemon's Mill (USA) (Roberto (USA))
129[3] 272[8] **1139[3] 1290[2] 1888[7] 4139[U]** 4830[9]

Shinrock Hill (IRE) *Philip Hobbs* 116h
7 b g Turtle Island(IRE) —Clashdermot Lass (Cardinal Flower)
2791[2] (3376) 3587[9] 4031[8]

Shinrock Paddy (IRE) *Paul Nolan* 152h
7 b g Deploy—Arts Theater (IRE) (King's Theatre (IRE))
3175a[5] (3578a) 4107a[5]

Shipboard Romance (IRE) *Mark Rimell* 96h
6 b m Captain Rio—In Other Words (IRE) (Lake Coniston (IRE))
40[7] (338) 527[5] 845[4] 933[2] 2333[6]

Shirley Casper (IRE) *D T Hughes* 139h 127c
10 b m Presenting—Glen Empress (IRE) (Lancastrian)
3705a[4] 5165[F]

Shiyrman (IRE) *J T R Dreaper* 84h
5 gr g Dalakhani(IRE) —Shaiyzima (IRE) (Polish Precedent (USA))
1339[8]

Shoal Bay Dreamer *Dianne Sayer* 67h
5 b m Central Park(IRE) —Ninfa (IRE) (The Parson)
3572[P] 3851[13] 4253[P] 4795[5]

Shoegazer (IRE) *David Pipe* 132h
6 b g Bach(IRE) —American Native (IRE) (Lord Americo)
2868[8] 3688[3] (3941) 4852[9]

Shooters Wood (IRE) *Miss C Baylis* 12h 109c
7 b g Needle Gun(IRE) —Talbot's Hollow (IRE) (Strong Statement (USA))
(148)

Shooting Times *Andrew Parker* 101h
6 b g Commanche Run—Rainbow Times (IRE) (Jareer (USA))
311[7] 1664[4] 2296[U] 2446[5] 4255[6] (4688) 5149[9]

Shootin The Breeze (IRE) *David Pipe* 109h
6 b g Alderbrook—Magheraeagh Lady (IRE) (Old Vic)
2960[7] ◆ 4159[8] 4767[4]

Shop Dj (IRE) *Peter Fahey* 137h
6 b m Dushyantor(USA) —Shoplifter (IRE) (Presenting)
2196a[4] 5008[3]

Shopfrontspecialist (IRE) *Gordon Elliott* 125h 101c
8 b g Turtle Island(IRE) —Grange Classic (IRE) (Jurado (USA))
286[5] 445[3] (948) (1104) 1342[F]
(1642) 1865[F]

Shoreacres (IRE) *Brendan Powell* 138h 145c
8 b g Turtle Island(IRE) —Call Me Dara (IRE) (Arapahos (FR))
(4267)
4853[14]

Shore Thing (IRE) *Bernard Llewellyn* 129h 110c
8 b g Docksider(USA) —Spicebird (IRE) (Ela-Mana-Mou)
(21) 912[2]

Short Straw (IRE) *Barry Murtagh* 44h 60c
8 b g Lord Americo—Marita Ann (Crozier)
176^{11} **802^{7}**
872^{P}

Short Supply (USA) *Tim Walford* 76h
5 b m Point Given(USA) —Introducing (USA) (Deputy Minister (CAN))
2397^{5} 2640^{9} 3637^{4} 5094^{P}

Shot From The Hip (GER) *E J O'Grady* 144h
7 b g Monsun(GER) —Sopran Biro (IRE) (Roi Danzig (USA))
4086a^{3}

Shoudhavenownbettr (IRE) *Matt Sheppard* 84h
7 br g Churlish Charm—Windmillviewclaire (IRE) (Architect (USA))
2059^{6}
2588^{5} 3526^{6} 4098^{7} (5172) 5272^{8}

Shouldhavehadthat (IRE) *Nicky Henderson* 121h 113c
9 b g Definite Article—Keep The Pace (IRE) (Shardari)
300^{P}

Shouldntbethere (IRE) *Joanna Davis* 62h 73c
7 ch g Soviet Star(USA) —Octomone (USA) (Hennessy (USA))
1905^{U} 2187^{F} 2434^{3}

Showtime Annie *Jennie Candlish* 58h
10 b m Wizard King—Rebel County (IRE) (Maelstrom Lake)
3993^{P} 4395^{4} 4947^{5} 5057^{7} **5173^{P}**

Shraden Edition *P A Jones* 94c
14 b g Tina's Pet—Star Edition (Leading Man)
79^{7}

Shrewd Decision *Dave Morris* 87b
4 b f Motivator—Dilemma (Generous (IRE))
5380^{4}

Shrewd Investment *Alan King* 105h
5 ch g Beauchamp King—Zaffarimbi (IRE) (Zaffaran (USA))
2283^{4} *3056^{9}* 3952^{6} 4459^{U} 5054^{2}

Shrewd Investor (IRE) *Henry Hogarth* 123h 114c
11 ch g Mister Lord(USA) —Mens Buisiness (IRE) (Buckskin (FR))
425^{3} 716^{6} 2079^{6} 2420^{4} 2953^{U} 3501^{P} 3716^{2}
4571^{P} 5097^{2} 5414^{P}

Shropshirelass *Zoe Davison* 100h
8 b m Beat All(USA) —Emma-Lyne (Emarati (USA))
140^{3} 706^{5} 962^{3} 1292^{6} 1551^{7} 4922^{11} 5271^{3}

Shufflewing (IRE) *Hughie Morrison* 75b
4 ch f Sakhee(USA) —Hen Harrier (Polar Falcon (USA))
5408^{4}

Shuil Royale (IRE) *David Arbuthnot* 117h
6 b g King's Theatre(IRE) —Shuil Na Lee (IRE) (Phardante (FR))
(3266) (3909) 4325^{3} (4930)

Shulmin *Carol Ferguson* 56h 92c
11 ch m Minster Son—Shultan (IRE) (Rymer)
211^{2} (516)
(549) 1376^{5} 1503^{4}

Shut The Bar *George Baker* 112h
6 b g Midnight Legend—Time For A Glass (Timeless Times (USA))
765^{P}

Shuttle Diplomacy (IRE) *Elliott Cooper* 56h
6 b m Beneficial—Snowbaby (IRE) (Be My Native (USA))
1069^{9} 1426^{8} 1505^{8} 1594^{9} 1757^{8}

Shy Glance (USA) *P Monteith* 82h
9 b g Red Ransom(USA) —Royal Shyness (Royal Academy (USA))
2509^{6}

Siam De La Roque (FR) *J Follain*
5 gr g Maille Pistol(FR) —Corthalina (FR) (Saint Preuil (FR))
5049a^{F}

Sibenek (IRE) *Martin Todhunter* 117h 125c
7 b g Oscar(IRE) —Blaithin's Leader (IRE) (Supreme Leader)
1759^{U} (2272)
3571^{P} 4063^{2} 4689^{4}

Siberian Tiger (IRE) *Evan Williams* 137h
6 b g Xaar—Flying Millie (IRE) (Flying Spur (AUS))
3945^{3} 4852^{B}

Si Bien (FR) *James Ewart* 111h 116c
6 b g Solon(GER) —Secret Gold (GER) (Lemhi Gold (USA))
1867^{4}
2270^{3} 2938^{U} 3359^{4} (3632) 3999^{3} **4959^{3}**

Si C'Etait Vrai (FR) *D T Hughes* 131h
5 b g Robin Des Champs(FR) —Bleu Perle (FR) (Pistolet Bleu (IRE))
3353a^{F} 3708a^{3} 4086a^{7}

Sidney Melbourne (USA) *Charlie Mann* 120h
4 ch g Lemon Drop Kid(USA) —Tolltally Light (USA) (Majestic Light (USA))
4774^{2} ◆

Siegemaster (IRE) *D T Hughes* 140h 162c
10 b g Lord Americo—Shabra Princess (Buckskin (FR))
1850a^{3} 3176a^{8} (3798a)
4298a^{5} 5185^{F}

Sieglinde (FR) *Alison Batchelor* 79h 80c
5 b m Canyon Creek(IRE) —Heliette (FR) (Tropular)
1124^{5} 1291^{8} **2182^{3}** *3057^{10}* **3375^{5} 3606^{3} 3984^{5}**
4401^{P} **5051^{3}**
5216^{7}

Sierra Peak (IRE) *Martin Todhunter* 99h 84c
7 b g Needle Gun(IRE) —Maria Renata (Jaazeiro (USA))
160^{11} 517^{7}

Sierra Victor (IRE) *Andrew Parker* 70b 100c
8 b g Blueprint(IRE) —An Charraig Mhor (IRE) (Tremblant)
43^{P} 625^{2} (1784)
2079^{P} 2354^{7} 5417^{2}

Sieur De La Prise (FR) *F-M Cottin*
5 b g Smadoun(FR) —Koueen De La Prise (FR) (Dadarissime (FR))
5049a^{F}

Signalman *James Ewart* 116h 122c
7 gr g Silver Patriarch(IRE) —Kairine (IRE) (Kahyasi)
4472^{2} 4823^{2}

Signatory (USA) *Jonjo O'Neill* 125h 90c
9 b g Kris S(USA) —Escrow Agent (USA) (El Gran Senor (USA))
2961^{15} 3265^{6} 3615^{P}

Signs Of Love (FR) *Noel Chance* 87h 103c
8 b g Poliglote—Severina (Darshaan)
220^{6} 645^{10}

Silent Cliche (IRE) *Howard Johnson* 125h 127c
7 b g Classic Cliche(IRE) —Mini Moo Min (Ardross)
2205^{3}
2615^{2} 3254^{3} 3726^{F} 4394^{3} 5029^{2} 5338^{P}

Silent Creek (IRE) *C Roche* 132h 132c
9 b g Shernazar—Ask Breda (Ya Zaman (USA))
3473a^{6}

Silent Jo (JPN) *Jonjo O'Neill* 107h 100c
9 b g Sunday Silence(USA) —Jo Knows (USA) (The Minstrel (CAN))
3696^{8} 4503^{8} 5111^{P}

Silent Snow (IRE) *Malcolm Jefferson* 106h
6 ch g Moscow Society(USA) —Miss Ogan (IRE) (Supreme Leader)
3511^{8} 3999^{6} 4253^{6} 4569^{2} 5259^{3}

Silicium (FR) *Nicky Henderson* 110h
5 b g Shaanmer(IRE) —Kalgary (FR) (Hawker's News (IRE))
3599^{2} 4478^{3}

Silk Affair (IRE) *Patrick J Flynn* 131h
6 b m Barathea(IRE) —Uncertain Affair (IRE) (Darshaan)
3475a^{12}

Silk And Roses *David Thompson* 66h
8 gr m Roi De Rome(USA) —Joetta (IRE) (Roselier (FR))
225^{P} 577^{P}

Silk Drum (IRE) *Howard Johnson* 134h 147c
6 gr g Intikhab(USA) —Aneydia (IRE) (Kenmare (FR))
3565^{U} 4470^{5} (5164)

Silk Parasol (IRE) *Alan J Brown* 45c
9 b m Anshan—Callow Run (IRE) (Satco (FR))
90^{9} 5148^{F}

Silk Rose *Martin Wilesmith*
7 gr m Terimon—Silk Oats (Oats)
3321^{0}

Sillkom *Ben Pollock* 83b
4 b g Millkom—Satire (Terimon)
4815^{5}

Silly Wupple *Mrs H M Kemp* 97h 119c
9 b g Syrtos—Lily The Lark (Crested Lark)
4748^{6}

Silmi *Sophie Leech* 127h 134c
7 gr g Daylami(IRE) —Intimaa (IRE) (Caerleon (USA))
236^{8} 581^{5}
1139^{2} 1252^{3} (1424)
(1611) 2084^{12} 5199^{P}

Silsula *Neil Mulholland* 94b
5 rg m Silver Patriarch(IRE) —Sulapuff (Sula Bula)
5387^{4}

Silver Accord (IRE) *Oliver Sherwood* 117h
8 bb g Accordion—Mazza (Mazilier (USA))
328^{2} (2049) 2637^{7} 2955^{2} 3771^{10} 4932^{4}

Silver Adonis (IRE) *Dr Richard Newland* 100h 134c
10 gr g Portrait Gallery(IRE) —Fair Fontaine (IRE) (Lafontaine (USA))
184 525^{P} 839^{3} 1151^{6} 4936^{U} 5163^{7} 5443^{P}

Silver Astralis *Christine Dunnett* 32h
4 gr f Silver Patriarch(IRE) —Bunty (Presidium)
4854^{8} 5101^{P}

Silver Bay *Oliver Sherwood* 112h 112c
10 b g Silver Patriarch(IRE) —Mossy Fern (Le Moss)
234^{5} 1815^{4} 2214^{7} 2953^{P} 3510^{P} 4483^{4} 5060^{4}

Silver Breese *R Robinson* 82h 84c
9 gr g Silver Patriarch(IRE) —Rymolbreese (Rymer)
4307^{4} 4553^{P}

Silverburn (IRE) *Evan Williams* 130h 132c
10 b g Presenting—Polly Puttens (Pollerton)
131^{2} 302^{F} 685^{4}
1020^{4} 1332^{3}

Silver By Nature *Lucinda Russell* 116h 168c
9 gr g Silver Patriarch(IRE) —Gale (Strong Gale)
2673^{10} 3437^{7} (4208) ◆ **5200^{12}**

Silver Commander *Alison Thorpe* 59b
4 gr g Silver Patriarch(IRE) —New Dawn (Rakaposhi King)
2237^{9}

Silver Dollars (FR) *David Arbuthnot* 110h 105c
10 gr g Great Palm(USA) —Marie Olga (FR) (Dom Pasquini (FR))
734^{4} 891^{7} 1128^{7} 2555^{3} (3265)
(3541) 4022^{6} 5194^{5}

Silver Emblem *Colin Heard* 37h
6 gr m Silver Patriarch(IRE) —Ballyquintet (IRE) (Orchestra)
374^{P}

Silver Footnote *Emma Lavelle* 102h
6 gr g Silver Patriarch(IRE) —Mavourneen (IRE) (Strong Gale)
(2365) 3529^{8}

Silver Gypsy (IRE) *Kim Bailey* 135h
6 b m Luso—Your Life (Le Bavard (FR))
2068^{2} (2640) (2974) 3442^{3} 4793^{14}

Silverini *Milton Harris*
5 b m Bertolini(USA) —Silver Kristal (Kris)
855^{12}

Silver Kate (IRE) *David Richards* 142h 137c
8 gr m Insan(USA) —Cracking Kate (IRE) (Roselier (FR))
2303^{5} (3435)
(4080) 4673^{2}

Silver Lily (IRE) *Sarah Humphrey* 94h
9 gr m Gothland(FR) —Imlistening (IRE) (Tremblant)
4314^{9} 4738^{5} 5130^{6}

Silverlord (FR) *Gordon Elliott* 124h
7 ch g Numerous(USA) —Silverware (FR) (Polish Precedent (USA))
576^{2} 2322^{2} (3746)

Silver Monet *Matt Sheppard* 67b
7 gr m Silver Patriarch(IRE) —Hopperdante (IRE) (Phardante (FR))
2472^{12}

Silver Palm (IRE) *John Joseph Hanlon* 56h 105c
8 gr g Great Palm(USA) —Model Lady (Le Bavard (FR))
1575^{U}

Silver Palomino *Mrs L A Coltherd* 77c
10 ch g Double Trigger(IRE) —Mayfair Minx (St Columbus)
165^{3} 398^{10}

Silver Peninsula *Martin Hill*
6 gr m Silver Patriarch(IRE) —Hanukkah (Oats)
1778^{15}

Silver Phoenix *Caroline Keevil* 101h
7 gr m Silver Patriarch(IRE) —Flamebird (IRE) (Mukaddamah (USA))
249^{3} 532^{2} (630) 1605^{4}

Silver Roque (FR) *Henrietta Knight* 106h
5 b g Laveron—Bible Gun (FR) (Pistolet Bleu (IRE))
154^{7} 2137^{5} 2419^{3} 3449^{3} 3989^{2} 5080^{8}

Silver Sedge (IRE) *Ann Hamilton* 113h 126c
12 b g Aristocracy—Pollyfaster (Polyfoto)
398^{5}

Silver Seraph *Noel Wilson* 27h
7 b m Silver Patriarch(IRE) —On Golden Pond (IRE) (Bluebird (USA))
832^{10} 5115^{12} 5352^{P}

Silver Shuffle (IRE) *J G Coogan* 119h
4 ch g Big Shuffle(USA) —Silvetta (Lando (GER))
4295a^{5}

Silver Sonnet *Ben Case* 57h
8 br m Silver Patriarch(IRE) —Bella Macrae (Bustino)
535^{U} 684^{P} 929^{4} 989^{8} 1300^{P}

Silver Sophfire *Nick Gifford* 48b
5 gr m Silver Patriarch(IRE) —Princess Timon (Terimon)
3903^{8}

Silvers Spirit *Keith Reveley* 82b
5 b m Makbul—Shadows Of Silver (Carwhite)
2616^{9} 3525^{8} 4554^{8}

Silver Steel (FR) *Richard Ford* 92h 120c
8 b g Robin Des Pres(FR) —Oliver's Queen (FR) (King Cyrus (USA))
177^{4} 1299^{4} 1509^{4} 1645^{7} 3397^{3}
3751^{U}

Silver Stirrup (IRE) *Jonjo O'Neill* 90b
4 b g High Chaparral(IRE) —Meseta (Lion Cavern (USA))
5012^{8}

Silver Story *Tim Vaughan* 107h 118c
8 gr g Silver Patriarch(IRE) —Tall Story (Arzanni)
408^{U} (647)
985^{4} 1177^{P} 4523^{2} ◆ **4966^{5}**

Silver Sutton *Bob Buckler*
8 gb g Baryshnikov(AUS) —Quick Million (Thowra (FR))
3295^{P}

Silver Token *David Brace* 108h
6 gr g Silver Patriarch(IRE) —Commanche Token (IRE) (Commanche Run)
(1795) 4159^{7}

Silver Twilight *John Allen* 38h
6 gr m Silver Patriarch(IRE) —Cle De Lune (FR) (Kadalko (FR))
1455^{4} 2482^{15}

Silverwort *Mike Sowersby* 18b
5 b g Lujain(USA) —Cryptogam (Zamindar (USA))
609^{9} 841^{13}

Silver Wren *Renee Robeson* 90b
4 gr f Silver Patriarch(IRE) —Wren Warbler (Relkino)
4184^{7} 5135^{3}

Silvery Fox (IRE) *Evan Williams* 10h
7 gr g Anshan—Kingsmar (IRE) (King's Ride)
1487^{11}

Silviniaco Conti (FR) *Paul Nicholls* 163h
5 ch g Dom Alco(FR) —Gazelle Lulu (FR) (Altayan)
(1768) (1966) ◆ (2516) 2887^{3} 4222^{4}

Simarian (IRE) *Evan Williams* 140h 134c
6 b g Kalanisi(IRE) —Sinnariya (IRE) (Persian Bold)
265^{2} (550)
3291^{F} 3587^{13}
4162^{4} 5002^{2} 5301^{4}

Simbamead *Michael Mullineaux* 66h
6 b g Beat All(USA) —Quay Four (IRE) (Barathea (IRE))
407^{7} 596^{5} 955^{P}

Simhal *Clive Mulhall* 36h
7 b g Minster Son—Busky Girl (Wonderful Surprise)
8^{P} 624^{P} 4112^{P}

Simiola *Simon Lewis* 14h 57c
12 b m Shaamit(IRE) —Brave Vanessa (USA) (Private Account (USA))
558^{U} 864^{U} 934^{P} 991^{5} 1064^{9} 2169^{P} **2468^{6}**

Simone Martini (IRE) *Milton Harris* 84h
6 b g Montjeu(IRE) —Bona Dea (IRE) (Danehill (USA))
215^{P} 760^{7} 887^{9} (1704) 1741^{3} 1822^{6} 2308^{4}
(2367) 2643^{5}

Simonsberg (IRE) *I R Ferguson* 130c
8 b g Sonus(IRE) —Blue Rainbow (Balinger)
525^{7}

Simonside *Brian Ellison* 96h
8 b g Shahrastani(USA) —Only So Far (Teenoso (USA))
2104^{4} 2508^{4} ◆

Simple Jim (FR) *J Hetherton* 107h 99c
7 b g Jimble(FR) —Stop The Wedding (USA) (Stop The Music (USA))
196^{12}

Simplified *Michael Chapman* 56h
8 b m Lend A Hand—Houston Heiress (USA) (Houston (USA))
63^{F} 547^{6} 1249^{9} 1831^{8} 1949^{8} 4178^{7} 5130^{12}

Simply Ben (IRE) *Colin Tizzard* 98b
5 b g Pilsudski(IRE) —Peace Time Girl (IRE) (Buckskin (FR))
4055^{4} ◆

Simply Blue *Simon Burrough* 126h
7 b g Rainbow High—What A Scene (IRE) (Scenic)
2498^{6} 3557^{9} 3874^{4} 4220^{3} 4485^{U}

Simply Ned (IRE) *Nicky Richards*
4 ch g
5432^{2}

Simply Smashing (IRE) *Philip Kirby* 128c
11 b g Simply Great(FR) —Kitty Boggan (Roselier (FR))
680^{6} (804)
1376^{3} (1570)
1999^{7} 5263^{P}

Simply Strong (IRE) *Charlie Mann* 89h 77c
7 ch g Simply Great(FR) —Sheltered (IRE) (Strong Gale)
3391^{7} 3723^{6} 4741^{P}

Simply Wings (IRE) *Richard Lee* 120h
7 b g Winged Love(IRE) —Simply Deep (IRE) (Simply Great (FR))
2283^{3} 2630^{4} 2983^{3} 3529^{2} (4262)

Sinbad The Sailor *George Baker* 121h
6 b g Cape Cross(IRE) —Sinead (USA) (Irish River (FR))
1900^{3} (4012) 4700^{4}

Sin Bin (IRE) *Paul Nicholls* 118b
5 b g Presenting—Navaro (IRE) (Be My Native (USA))
(5217)

Sine Mora *Donald McCain* 65b
5 b g Beneficial—Fashion House (Homo Sapien)
4801^{6} 5005^{7}

Sinfield (IRE) *Micky Hammond* 108b
5 b g Oscar(IRE) —Leave Me Be (IRE) (Be My Native (USA))
3957^{5} (4396) 5264^{4}

Singapore Harbour (IRE) *Oliver Sherwood* 80h
5 b m Beneficial—Nanja Monja (IRE) (Bering)
3046 989^{4} 1140^{6} 1289^{4} 1840^{8}

Singapore Reef (FR) *Nick Williams* 102h
5 b g Sagacity(FR) —Mutual Consent (IRE) (Reference Point)
3^{10} 2164^{P} 2333^{P} 5232^{P}

Singapore Storm (FR) *Tom George* 62h
4 b g Sagacity(FR) —Castlevania (USA) (Slew City Slew (USA))
3673^{9} 4006^{12} 4268^{8} 4721^{7}

Sing Of Run *Peter Brookshaw* 89h
4 br g Singspiel(IRE) —Crimson Rosella (Polar Falcon (USA))
4404^{3}

Sing Sing Sing (FR) *Barry Brennan* 95b
5 b m Passing Sale(FR) —Caline So (FR) (Port Etienne (FR))
4382^{2}

Siouxme (IRE) *Alison Batchelor* 71h 87c
9 b m Little Bighorn—Winter Sunset (Celio Rufo)
280^{3} 691^{P} 1478^{4}

Sir Bathwick (IRE) *David Pipe* 107h 128c
12 b g Oscar(IRE) —Karenda (Kambalda)
(181) **446^{2}**
772^{P}

Sir Bere (FR) *Rebecca Curtis* 94h
5 b g Della Francesca(USA) —Known Alibi (USA) (Known Fact (USA))
58^{5} 1600^{3} 1842^{8}

Sir Boss (IRE) *Don Cantillon* 87h
6 b g Tagula(IRE) —Good Thought (IRE) (Mukaddamah (USA))
1114^{3}

Sir Bumble (IRE) *Michael Blake* 84h 97c
11 b g Humbel(USA) —Adelinas Leader (IRE) (Supreme Leader)
758^{2} (913)
931^{2} 1080^{3} (1237)
1360^{4} 1447^{2} 1474^{3} 5434^{4}

Sircharleswatford *Pat Phelan* 77b
4 ch g Bahamian Bounty—Marah (Machiavellian (USA))
3964^{3} 4484^{P}

Sir Charlie Hutch (GER) *Alan Swinbank* 103b
6 ch g Spartacus(IRE) —Susan (IRE) (Pips Pride)
4396^{3} 5005^{5}

Sir Clad *Claire Dyson* 77h
5 b g Fantastic Light(USA) —Katina (USA) (Danzig (USA))
1729^{11} 2590^{8} 3224^{6} 3493^{P} 3987^{13} 4814^{4}
5016^{2} 5390^{5}

Sir Cool (IRE) *Tor Sturgis* 4h
5 b g Selkirk(USA) —Legend Has It (IRE) (Sadler's Wells (USA))
3546^{8} 5074^{9} 5239^{P}

Sircozy (IRE) *Gary Moore* 123h
5 b g Celtic Swing—Furnish (Green Desert (USA))
(1433) 1689^{3} 1812^{3} 2213^{2} 3649^{6} (5052)

Sir Cycroid Hawk (IRE) *Alan Swinbank* 50b
5 b g Hawk Wing(USA) —Danccini (IRE) (Dancing Dissident (USA))
841^{11}

Sirdave *Peter Hiatt* 94h
5 ch g Where Or When(IRE) —Charming Tina (IRE) (Indian Ridge)
4952^{9} 5167^{5}

Sir Des Champs (FR) *W P Mullins* 143h
5 bb g Robin Des Champs(FR) —Liste En Tete (FR) (Video Rock (FR))
(4852)

Sir Du Bearn (FR) *Paul Nicholls* 134c
5 bb g Passing Sale(FR) —Girl Du Bearn (FR) (Sarpedon (FR))
2455^{2}

Sire Collonges (FR) *Paul Nicholls* 129h
5 gr g Dom Alco(FR) —Idylle Collonges (FR) (Quart De Vin (FR))
3676[9] 4488[3] 5166[F]

Sire De Grugy (FR) *Gary Moore* 141h
5 ch g My Risk(FR) —Hirlish (FR) (Passing Sale (FR))
2215[2] 2577[2] ◆ *3056[4]* (3302) (3864) (4353) 5182[3]

Sire Des Aulnays (FR) *E Leray*
5 gr g Rifapour(IRE) —Femme D'Honneur (FR) (Take Risks (FR))
5159a[10]

Sir Frank (IRE) *David Pipe* 117h
6 b g Old Vic—Leave Me Be (IRE) (Be My Native (USA))
(35) (519) 624[2] (1021) (1148) 3874[6]

Sir Frog (IRE) *Keith Goldsworthy* 24b
5 b g Orpen(USA) —Preen (Lion Cavern (USA))
5257[6]

Sir Harry Cash *Michael Mullineaux* 94b
5 b g Sir Harry Lewis(USA) —Miss Cashtal (IRE) (Ballacashtal (CAN))
832[4] 1069[3]

Sir Harry Cool *John Panvert* 96h 92c
8 b g Sir Harry Lewis(USA) —Cool Merenda (IRE) (Glacial Storm (USA))
267[11] **498[5]**
840[4] 1062[4] 2001[7] **2217[3]**

Sir Harry Ormesher *Alan King* 147h 135c
8 b g Sir Harry Lewis(USA) —Glamour Game (Nashwan (USA))
94[8] 1967[F] 2360[6] 5187[3]

Sir Ian (IRE) *Charlie Longsdon* 101h 134c
8 b g Turtle Island(IRE) —Bobby Hays (IRE) (Bob Back (USA))
(1604)
(1926) 2629[3] 5002[5]

Sir John *Jonjo O'Neill* 78h
5 ch g Sir Harry Lewis(USA) —Jenga (Minster Son)
2589[F] 3350[P]

Sirjosh *Des Donovan* 92h
5 b g Josr Algarhoud(IRE) —Special Gesture (IRE) (Brief Truce (USA))
842[4] 4499[9] 5130[5]

Sirkeel (FR) *James Ewart* 107h 71c
9 b g Dolphin Street(FR) —Sirkeela (FR) (Noir Et Or)
1868[7]

Sir Kezbaah (IRE) *Jeremy Scott* 148h
7 b g Oscar(IRE) —Madam Chloe (Dalsaan)
3298[2] 3587[3] 4209[10] 4875[4] (5153) (5304)

Sir Mark (IRE) *Anna Bramall* 85h
7 ch g In The Wings—Web Of Intrigue (Machiavellian (USA))
1974[5] 2282[7] 2603[7]

Sir Mattie (IRE) *David Rees* 60h
6 bb g Moscow Society(USA) —Manhattan Catch (IRE) (Safety Catch (USA))
1963[6] 2283[8]

Sir Monty (USA) *Peter Bowen* 99h 87c
9 ch g Cat's Career(USA) —Lady Of Meadowlane (USA) (Pancho Jay (USA))
17[4] (341) 581[6]

Sir Ocus *Colin Tizzard* 32h
5 b g Sir Harry Lewis(USA) —Go Tally-Ho (Gorytus (USA))
3647[9] 3872[12]

Sir Peter (IRE) *Henry Daly* 43h 102c
9 ch g City Honours(USA) —Any Offers (Paddy's Stream)
2170[6] 2557[2] 3527[P]

Sir Pitt *Alison Thorpe* 137h
4 b g Tiger Hill(IRE) —Rebecca Sharp (Machiavellian (USA))
3767[4] 3986[U] 4260[3] 4847[5]

Sir Quigley (IRE) *Mayne Kidd* 75h
9 b g Pistolet Bleu(IRE) —Elect Her (Jumbo Hirt (USA))
1666[8]

Sir Ronan *Lawney Hill* 101h
8 gr g Roi De Rome(USA) —Slack Alice (Derring Rose)
1063[2] (1275)

Sir Royal (USA) *Brendan Powell* 92h
6 b g Diesis—Only Royale (IRE) (Caerleon (USA))
4918[3]

Sir Tamburlane (IRE) *Sue Smith* 103h
6 ch g Tamayaz(CAN) —Lady Lupin (Derrylin)
1071[7] 3994[4] 4467[8] 4889[2]

Sir Tantallus Hawk *Alan Swinbank* 133h 133c
7 b g Overbury(IRE) —Mobile Miss (IRE) (Classic Secret (USA))
2399[6]
3714[3] 3995[2] (4244)
4453[2] 5001[3]

Sir Walter Raleigh *C A McBratney* 98h
4 b g Galileo(IRE) —Elizabethan Age (FR) (King's Best (USA))
5314[3]

Sir William Orpen *Pat Phelan* 24h
4 b g Orpen(USA) —Ashover Amber (Green Desert (USA))
4557[8]

Sir Winston (IRE) *Victor Dartnall* 84h 106c
9 b g Supreme Leader—Aliandbet Jewel (IRE) (Strong Gale)
2240[2] 2638[2] 3230[5] 3527[3] 3907[3]

Sissi De Teille (FR) *E Leray*
5 gr m Martaline—Princesse D'Orton (FR) (Saint Cyrien (FR))
2265a[3]

Sister Palma (FR) *J Bertran De Balanda* 89h
5 b m Kahyasi—Miss Palma (FR) (Great Palm (USA))
(2265a)

Sitting Tennant *Howard Johnson* 115h
8 b g Erhaab(USA) —Aeolina (FR) (Kaldoun (FR))
4057[F]

Sivola De Sivola (FR) *Tom George* 122h
5 gr g Martaline—Kerrana (FR) (Cadoudal (FR))
2954[8] 3542[2] 3806[7]

Sivota (IRE) *W P Mullins* 144h
7 b g Sakhee(USA) —Mamara Reef (Salse (USA))
3475a[4] 4817[3]

Sixteen (FR) *Josef Vana II* 136c
11 gr m Rainbows For Life(CAN) —Semantica (FR) (Tel Quel (FR))
1811a[3]

Sixties Rock *William Young* 66h
4 ch g Rock Of Gibraltar(IRE) —Scene (IRE) (Scenic)
4056[7] 4473[10] 5314[5]

Sizing Africa (IRE) *Henry De Bromhead* 122h 135c
9 b g Bob's Return(IRE) —Brown Forest (Brave Invader (USA))
2086[7]

Sizing Australia (IRE) *Henry De Bromhead* 117h 144c
9 b g New Frontier(IRE) —All The Gear (IRE) (Nashamaa)
2346[3] (4792)

Sizing Europe (IRE) *Henry De Bromhead* 168h 176c
9 b g Pistolet Bleu(IRE) —Jennie Dun (IRE) (Mandalus)
1850a[2] 2226a[2] 3844a[3] (4805)

Sizing India (IRE) *Nicky Henderson* 113b
6 b g Beneficial—Brown Forest (Brave Invader (USA))
(5084)

Sizing Ireland (IRE) *Nicky Henderson* 108h
5 b g Dushyantor(USA) —Buddy's Toy (IRE) (Be My Native (USA))
4239[4] 4500[4] 5074[3] 5389[4]

Sizing Mexico (IRE) *Henry De Bromhead* 132h
6 b g Snurge—Shyanne (IRE) (Mandalus)
3353a[4]

Sizing Santiago (IRE) *Nigel Twiston-Davies* 107h
5 br g Accordion—Denys Daughter (IRE) (Crash Course)
2059[9] 4706[2] (5168)

Skarloey *Tony Carroll* 84b
5 b g Alflora(IRE) —Stonebridge Rose (Fleetwood (IRE))
4082[11] 4443[10] 4957[6]

Skating Home (IRE) *Neil Mulholland* 65h
5 b g Luso—Wintry Day (IRE) (Presenting)
5152[8]

Skenakilla Cross (IRE) *David O'Meara* 96b
6 ch m Flemensfirth(USA) —Dun Ar Aill (IRE) (Supreme Leader)
5135[4] 5380[2]

Skenfrith *Sandy Forster* 118h 86c
12 b g Atraf—Hobbs Choice (Superpower)
3888[4] 4066[4] 4713[3]

Skiddaw Jones *Maurice Barnes* 24h 95c
11 b g Emperor Jones(USA) —Woodrising (Nomination)
460[11] 747[5] 891[5] 1116[4] 1358[U] 1502[P] 1573[P]

Skiddaw Secret *John Weymes* 84b
4 ch f Tobougg(IRE) —Stealthy (Kind Of Hush)
3576[4] 4171[13] 4554[12]

Skint *Nicky Henderson* 133h
5 b g King's Theatre(IRE) —No More Money (Alflora (IRE))
(2216) ◆ 2925[2] ◆ 3557[2] 3965[3] (4725)

Skipper Robin (FR) *Nigel Twiston-Davies* 96h
5 b g Loup Solitaire(USA) —L'Oceane (FR) (Epervier Bleu)
1623[4] 2283[U] 2981[4] 3693[14] 4704[5]

Skippers Brig (IRE) *Nicky Richards* 140h 148c
10 b g Zaffaran(USA) —Mathewsrose (IRE) (Roselier (FR))
3206a[14] (4209)
(4474) ◆ 5200[9]

Skipper's Lad (IRE) *Colin Tizzard* 97h 116c
9 br g Flemensfirth(USA) —Spin N' Win (Cardinal Flower)
274[5] 695[5] 867[7] 1230[3]
1348[4] 2928[10] 3687[7] 3907[P] 4372[4] 4705[2] 5037[2]
◆ 5407[U]

Skipping Chapel *N W Alexander* 78h 75c
10 ch g Minster Son—Harrietfield (Nicholas Bill)
160[5]

Skip The Present (IRE) *John Spearing* 87h
8 br g Presenting—Dante's Skip (IRE) (Phardante (FR))
645[11]

Skirlaw (IRE) *Howard Johnson* 69b
4 b g Gold Well—Lady Boufant (IRE) (Polykratis)
4280[6]

Ski Sunday *Lawney Hill* 146h
6 b g King's Best(USA) —Lille Hammer (Sadler's Wells (USA))
(3557) 4848[9] 5166[10]

Skorcher (IRE) *W P Mullins* 133h
7 b g Flemensfirth(USA) —River Clyde (IRE) (Presenting)
4319a[3]

Sky Artist (IRE) *Claire Dyson* 65b
6 b g Old Vic—Dancing Venus (Pursuit Of Love)
3920[11]

Skybull (IRE) *Howard Johnson* 78h
5 b g Milan—Elphis (IRE) (Supreme Leader)
4506[7] 5092[7]

Skye But N Ben *Michael Chapman* 121h
7 b g Auction House(USA) —Island Colony (USA) (Pleasant Colony (USA))
(54) (171) 298[7] (1723) (1938)

Skylancer *J J Lambe* 125h 116c
7 b g In The Wings—Moon Cactus (Kris)
1931[8]

Slam *Tom George* 92h
6 b g Beat Hollow—House Hunting (Zafonic (USA))
185[8] 1844[3]

Slash And Burn (IRE) *Gordon Elliott* 116h 114c
9 b g Presenting—Force Seven (Strong Gale)
1923[4]

Sleep In First (FR) *Anna Bramall* 67h
5 bb g Sleeping Car(FR) —First Union (FR) (Shafoun (FR))
1817[10] 2355[12] 4541[7] 5151[8]

Sleeping City (FR) *Victor Dartnall* 106b
4 bb g Sleeping Car(FR) —City Prospect (FR) (Diamond Prospect (USA))
5174[5]

Sleeping Du Granit (FR) *Claire Dyson* 90h
5 b g Sleeping Car(FR) —Broceliande Fine (FR) (Royal Charter (FR))
3992[4] 4443[8] 4815[4] 5000[4] 5168[10] 5389[3]

Sleeping Policeman (FR) *Anna Bramall* 43b
5 bb g Sleeping Car(FR) —Furika (FR) (Kadalko (FR))
1927[11] 4457[13] 5105[14]

Sleeping Tree (FR) *Paul Nicholls*
6 b g Sleeping Car(FR) —Doll Night (FR) (Karkour (FR))
4356[16]

Sleepy (FR) *Nicky Henderson* 96b
5 b g Sleeping Car(FR) —Haida IV (FR) (Passing Sale (FR))
3909[7]

Slew Charm (FR) *Noel Chance* 117h
9 b g Marathon(USA) —Slew Bay (FR) (Beaudelaire (USA))
2209[5] 2596[3] 3306[P]

Slieveardagh (IRE) *E J O'Grady* 145h
7 b g King's Theatre(IRE) —Gayephar (Phardante (FR))
1133a[4] ◆ 3474a[14]

Slightly Hot *Joanna Davis* 104b
5 b g Kayf Tara—Ginger Rogers (Gildoran)
4082[7] 4879[2] 5113[6]

Slip *Conor Dore* 115h
6 b g Fraam—Niggle (Night Shift (USA))
479[6]

Slip Duty (IRE) *Kate Buckett* 26h
9 ch g Moscow Society(USA) —Simply Slippy (IRE) (Simply Great (FR))
2666[13] 3489[10] 4128[11]

Slippers Percy (IRE) *Denis Gerard Hogan* 117h 129c
9 b g Sea Raven(IRE) —Lough Borough (IRE) (Orchestra)
3579a[3] 4109a[3] 4790[P] 5141a[6]

Smack That (IRE) *Milton Harris* 125h 129c
9 b g Rashar(USA) —Woolly (Giolla Mear)
(709) **822[3]**
959[U] 1390[P] 1485[4] 1970[5] 2520[3] 2948[P] 3345[3]
3438[P] 4008[5] 4873[4] 5112[5]

Smad Place (FR) *Alan King* 138h
4 gr g Smadoun(FR) —Bienna Star (FR) (Village Star (FR))
(2661) 3436[3] (4225) 4847[10]

Small Fly (IRE) *Bob Buckler* 99h
7 b g Humbel(USA) —Tworow (IRE) (Accordion)
4404[F] 5050[F]

Smart Boy Prince (IRE) *Miss C C Jones* 94h 81c
10 b g Princely Heir(IRE) —Miss Mulaz (FR) (Luthier)
148[10] 499[6]

Smart Catch (IRE) *Tony Carroll* 118h
5 b g Pivotal—Zafaraniya (IRE) (Doyoun)
1778[10] 2445[5] 4203[8] (4478) 4930[2] 5300[5]

Smart Command (IRE) *Ferdy Murphy* 22b
7 b g Deploy—Smart Rhythm (True Song)
319[19] 2375[P] 3633[P]

Smart Dwellie *Kevin Bishop* 111c
8 ch g Emperor Fountain—Cabbery Rose (IRE) (Lord Ha Ha)
408[5] 594[4] 647[U]

Smart Freddy *Lawney Hill* 115h
5 b g Groom Dancer(USA) —Smart Topsy (Oats)
412[6] 2577[4] 3398[2] 4198[5]

Smarties Party *Clive Mulhall* 102h
8 b m Tamure(IRE) —Maries Party (The Parson)
393[2] 706[F] 5144[8]

Smart John *Simon Lewis* 97h
11 b g Bin Ajwaad(IRE) —Katy-Q (IRE) (Taufan (USA))
341[2] **794[P]**
1141[9] 1195[4] 1451[P]

Smart Man *Evelyn Slack* 54h 72c
9 gr g Silver Patriarch(IRE) —Run Tiger (IRE) (Commanche Run)
160[3]

Smart Mistress *Ferdy Murphy* 102c
9 gb m Silver Patriarch(IRE) —Smart Rhythm (True Song)
2274[P]

Smart N Sharp (IRE) *Linda Jewell* 50h
8 ch m Quws—Imminent (IRE) (Nicolotte)
217[7] 436[5] 688[P]

Smart Ruler (IRE) *David Arbuthnot* 87b
5 ch g Viking Ruler(AUS) —Celebrated Smile (IRE) (Cadeaux Genereux)
4082[12] *4923[2]* 5426[5]

Smart Song *Ferdy Murphy*
6 b g Pilsudski(IRE) —Smart Rhythm (True Song)
3166[12]

Smiles Better *Chris Down* 34h
6 ch g Fleetwood(IRE) —Pondimari (FR) (Marignan (USA))
37[5] 168[8]

Smiling Applause *Harry Chisman* 68h
12 b g Royal Applause—Smilingatstrangers (Macmillion)
226[U] 478[4] 698[5] 930[4] 955[4] 1259[P] 1507[4] 1559[8]
1860[7] 4976[P]

Smirfys Eric (IRE) *Michael Mullineaux*
5 b g Bollin Eric—Smirfys Dance Hall (IRE) (Halling (USA))
5174[P]

Smithy The Horse (IRE) *Donald McCain* 97h
5 ch g Kris Kin(USA) —Priyanka (Last Tycoon)
1867[9] 4145[2]

Smokey George *Kim Bailey* 104h
6 ch g Kadastrof(FR) —Smokey Diva (IRE) (Orchestra)
1705[8] 2149[12] (3255) (3392) 3396[2] 4034[10]

Smokey Joe Joe (IRE) *Kieran Purcell* 137h
5 b g Snurge—Goldens Monkey (Monksfield)
4319a[P]

Smokey Oakey (IRE) *Mark H Tompkins* 104h
7 b g Tendulkar(USA) —Veronica (Persian Bold)
2122[6] 2495[2]

Smoking (FR) *Jonathen de Giles* 93h
5 b g Arnaqueur(USA) —Juppelongue (FR) (Trebrook (FR))
739[11] 2056[8] 2666[11] 3454[7] 4052[10] 5068[P]

Smooth Classic (IRE) *Warren Greatrex* 118h
7 b g Luso—Noan Rose (IRE) (Roselier (FR))
82[2] 1860[3] *3055[5]* 3454[5] 3950[P]

Smoothly Does It *Venetia Williams* 110h
10 b g Efisio—Exotic Forest (Dominion)
1282[P]

Smudger *Sue Smith* 76h
6 b g Alflora(IRE) —Debutante Days (Dominion)
3620[10] 5028[7]

Smugglers Bay (IRE) *Tim Easterby* 110h 110c
7 b g Celtic Swing—Princess Mood (GER) (Muhtarram (USA))
88[6]

Smuglin *Donald McCain* 116h 126c
8 gr m Sir Harry Lewis(USA) —Parslin (The Parson)
(285) **(2475)**
3571[3] 3817[2] 5007[P]

Snakebite (IRE) *Miss Grace Muir* 124h 135c
11 gr g Taipan(IRE) —Bee In The Rose (IRE) (Roselier (FR))
4131[P]

Snake Charmer *Milton Harris* 109h 117c
8 b g Golden Snake(USA) —Moly (Inchinor)
3059[9] 3452[10]
3598[2] 3881[8] (4079) 4464[7] 4869[6] 5118[5]

Snake Rave (IRE) *Henry Hogarth* 53h 56c
9 b g Taipan(IRE) —Raveleen Rose (IRE) (Norwich)
5311[5]

Snap Decision *Rayson Nixon* 59h
9 b m Glacial Storm(USA) —Dunraven Girl (Seymour Hicks (FR))
92[P]

Snark (IRE) *Simon Earle* 87h
8 b g Cape Cross(IRE) —Agoer (Hadeer)
341[4] 587[8]

Sninfia (IRE) *Kevin Bishop* 84h 99c
11 b m Hector Protector(USA) —Christmas Kiss (Taufan (USA))
169[8] 340[5]

Snope *Jamie Snowden* 40b
6 b g Sagamix(FR) —Chant De L'Aube (FR) (Bon Sang (FR))
739[12]

Snore No More (IRE) *Stuart Coltherd*
4 b g Spartacus(IRE) —Shinko Song (IRE) (Shinko Forest (IRE))
674[F]

Snow Alert *John Norton*
5 ch g Where Or When(IRE) —Ela Aphrodite (Halling (USA))
5210[U]

Snow Patrol *Nigel Dunger* 73h 65c
10 gr g Linamix(FR) —Overcast (IRE) (Caerleon (USA))
3056[6] 3350[U] 3611[3] 3983[2] 4125[3]

Snowy (IRE) *P Monteith* 99h 103c
13 gr g Pierre—Snowy Gunner (Gunner B)
46[P] 1701[4]

Sobrando Lodge (IRE) *Mark Michael McNiff* 64h
6 b g Hawk Wing(USA) —Madamaa (IRE) (Alzao (USA))
3547[F]

Sobre Tresor (FR) *Nigel Hawke* 89h
5 b g Grand Tresor(FR) —Gaie Anna (FR) (Art Bleu)
266[6] 538[5] 662[3] 820[5]

Soccerjackpot (USA) *Nigel Twiston-Davies* 69h
7 b g Mizzen Mast(USA) —Rahbaby (USA) (Rahy (USA))
97[P] 590[P] 5050[8]

Society Fashion *Noel Chance*
6 b m Moscow Society(USA) —Black Fashion (IRE) (Boreen (FR))
4692[3]

Society Shares (IRE) *Graeme McPherson* 106b
6 ch g Moscow Society(USA) —Presenting Shares (IRE) (Presenting)
2186[9]

Society Venue *Michael Scudamore* 109h
6 b g Where Or When(IRE) —Society Rose (Saddlers' Hall (IRE))
733[4] 842[5] 1021[2] 1148[2] 1487[6] 1844[4] 2128[8]

So Extreme *Philip Sharp* 88h
9 ch g Cayman Kai(IRE) —Go Gipsy (Move Off)
5383[10]

So Fine (IRE) *Anabel L M King* 96b
5 bb g Definite Article—Not So Green (IRE) (Roselier (FR))
2957[12] 5063[5] ◆ 5284[2]

Softly Killing Me *Brian Forsey* 46h
6 b m Umistim—Slims Lady (Theatrical Charmer)
5243[10]

Soft Spoken Guy (IRE) *Maurice Barnes* 133h 130c
8 b g Saddlers' Hall(IRE) —Pisa (IRE) (Carlingford Castle)
206[6] 1766[3] 2035[4] ◆ **2599[P]** 4003[P]
4394[4] (5146)
5336[4]

Soggy Dollar *Neil King* 96h
6 ch g Bahamian Bounty—Ninia (USA) (Affirmed (USA))
693[7] 850[5] 984[5] 1147[12]

Sohappyharry *Jane Mathias* 93b
5 ch g Sir Harry Lewis(USA) —Sohapara (Arapahos (FR))
362[3] 739[4] 855[2]

Soir D'Estruval (FR) *Alan King* 123h
5 bb g Sheyrann—Kob D'Estruval (FR) (Lute Antique (FR))
3987[3] 4459[F]

Soixante (IRE) *Henrietta Knight* 116h 135c
8 b g Old Vic—Dantes Serenade (IRE) (Phardante (FR))
3444[5] 4355[2]

So Jo Beach *Philip Sharp*
5 b m Josr Algarhoud(IRE) —Sylvia Beach (The Parson)
1920^{8}

Solaise (IRE) *Liam Corcoran* 88b
6 b g Alflora(IRE) —Keelaun Express (IRE) (Supreme Leader)
(2896) 5313^{5}

Solaise Express *Philip Hobbs* 93h
6 b g Kayf Tara—Solo Girl (IRE) (Le Bavard (FR))
4081^{5}

Solar Express *John Bridger* 60b
6 b g Fantastic Light(USA) —Jumairah Sun (IRE) (Scenic)
3056^{10} 3960^{P}

Soldatino (FR) *Nicky Henderson* 153h
5 gr g Graveron(FR) —Malory Du Chenay (FR) (Art Sebal (USA))
3676^{6} 4188^{5} 4848^{11}

Soldiers Tree (IRE) *Sue Bradburne* 79h
6 b g Norwich—Just Ginger (The Parson)
289^{5} 1760^{8} 2103^{7} 3336^{10} **3548^{P} 3884^{F} 4064^{P}**

Sole Agent (IRE) *Diana Grissell* 112h 109c
9 b g Trans Island—Seattle Siren (USA) (Seattle Slew (USA))
(4921)

Sole Bonne Femme (IRE) *Gerard Butler* 107h 110c
9 b g Rudimentary(USA) —Ardnacrusha (IRE) (Electric)
3170^{4} 3724^{P} 4503^{6} (4854) 5101^{4}

Soleil D'Avril (FR) *Alan King* 107h
5 bb g Laveron—Melanie Du Chenet (FR) (Nikos)
2310^{4} ◆ 3196^{6} 4203^{7} 5117^{14}

Soleil De Sivola (FR) *T Trapenard* 105h 126c
5 b g Discover D'Auteuil(FR) —Neva De Sivola (FR) (Blushing Flame (USA))
5159a^{8}

Soleil Du Mou (FR) *T Doumen*
5 b g Lesotho(USA) —Viviane Du Mou (FR) (Tin Soldier (FR))
1659a^{P}
5049a^{P}

Soleil Fix (FR) *Nick Gifford* 65c
10 b g Mansonnien(FR) —Ifaty (FR) (Rose Laurel)
190a^{F} 4197^{U}

Solent (IRE) *John Quinn* 116h
9 b g Montjeu(IRE) —Stylish (Anshan)
581^{P}

Sole Survivor (FR) *Paul Webber* 80b
4 gr g Smadoun(FR) —Sellaginella (Konigsstuhl (GER))
3294^{15} 4423^{2} 4943^{9}

Sole Witness (IRE) *C A McBratney* 119h
7 b g Witness Box(USA) —Deeco Valley (IRE) (Satco (FR))
4711^{2}

Solis *Micky Hammond* 115h
5 b g Josr Algarhoud(IRE) —Passiflora (Night Shift (USA))
2092^{4} ◆ 2423^{7} (3781) 4451^{6} 4942^{2} 5357^{3}

Solis (GER) *P Monteith* 99h
8 ch g In The Wings—Seringa (GER) (Acatenango (GER))
161^{8} (286) 397^{2}

Solitary Palm (IRE) *Brian Forsey* 97h 104c
8 rg g Great Palm(USA) —Grande Solitaire (FR) (Loup Solitaire (USA))
231^{9} **2124^{2}**
2286^{3} 2513^{F} 2796^{F} 5155^{6} 5275^{P} 5439^{P}

Solix (FR) *Nicky Henderson* 151h
5 bb g Al Namix(FR) —Solimade (FR) (Loup Solitaire (USA))
4188^{7} 4806^{5}

Soliya (FR) *David Pipe* 118h
7 b m Vaguely Pleasant(FR) —Solimade (FR) (Loup Solitaire (USA))
(530)

Soll *John Quinn* 116h
6 ch g Presenting—Montelfolene (IRE) (Montelimar (USA))
(3633)

Sollim (FR) *Paul Nicholls* 109h
4 b g Solon(GER) —Winkle (FR) (Turgeon (USA))
3366^{3}

Solo Choice *Ian McInnes* 76h
5 b g Needwood Blade—Top Of The Class (IRE) (Rudimentary (USA))
14^{5} 174^{6} 480^{7} 3619^{7} **4241^{F} 4510^{P}**

Solo Roma (IRE) *Violet M Jordan* 40b
7 br g Double Eclipse(IRE) —Cassies Girl (IRE) (Mandalus)
337^{P} 3836^{P} 5296^{P}

Solway Ally *Lisa Harrison* 102h
8 b m Alflora(IRE) —Rita Larkin (Mister Lord (USA))
212^{2} 340^{6} 553^{6} 4873^{P} 5132^{8}

Solway Bay *Lisa Harrison* 109h 118c
9 b g Cloudings(IRE) —No Problem Jac (Safawan)
(287) (396)

Solway Bee *Lisa Harrison* 93h
11 ch m Gunner B—Lady Mag (Silver Season)
291^{7} **471^{F}**
1666^{9} 1782^{3} 2941^{P}

Solway Blue *Lisa Harrison* 89h 77c
9 gr g Cloudings(IRE) —In Any Case (IRE) (Torus)
336^{6} **403^{U}**
445^{4} **473^{6}**
875^{P} 1102^{4} 1873^{4}
4573^{7} (5130) 5350^{9}

Solway Dornal *Lisa Harrison* 56h
6 b g Alflora(IRE) —Solway Donal (IRE) (Celio Rufo)
225^{P} 442^{P} 711^{8} 4870^{6} 5131^{8} 5354^{4}

Solway Flight *Lisa Harrison* 77h
8 b g Double Trigger(IRE) —Double Flight (Mtoto)
1962^{15} 2937^{15}

Solway Minstrel *Lisa Harrison* 109h
14 ch g Jumbo Hirt(USA) —Spicey Cut (Cut Above)
193^{2} 708^{7} 871^{P}

Solway Pete *Lisa Harrison*
5 br g And Beyond(IRE) —Rita Larkin (Mister Lord (USA))
1989^{16}

Solway Sam *Lisa Harrison* 134h 99c
8 b g Double Trigger(IRE) —Some Gale (Strong Gale)
(214) (710) 1986^{7} 2870^{10} 4464^{9}
4890^{4}

Solway Silver *Lisa Harrison* 66h
5 gr g Silver Patriarch(IRE) —Solway Rose (Minster Son)
1573^{8} 1664^{7} 1783^{11} 4872^{8}

Solwhit (FR) *C Byrnes* 165h
7 b g Solon(GER) —Toowhit Towhee (USA) (Lucky North (USA))
(2414a) 2968a^{2} 3205a^{2} 3707a^{2}

So Many Questions (IRE) *G C Evans* 72h 59c
11 b g Bob Back(USA) —Shuil Alanna (Furry Glen)
301^{6}

Some Catch (IRE) *Elliott Cooper* 65h
5 b m Shantou(USA) —Quiver Tree (Lion Cavern (USA))
2446^{9} 2612^{11} 3717^{4} 4511^{P} 5354^{2}

Some Craic (IRE) *Paul Henderson* 87h 120c
11 b g Presenting—The Branner (IRE) (The Parson)
1032^{6} 1178^{7} 1491^{3} 1589^{6} 1841^{P} 2024^{3}

Some Lad (IRE) *Mrs A C Hamilton* 65h
6 b g Beneficial—Some News (IRE) (Be My Native (USA))
442^{P} 5028^{11} 5259^{6}

Some Magic (IRE) *Edward Cawley* 91h 82c
11 b g Accordion—Ollatrim Lady (Strong Gale)
1309^{P}

Somersby (IRE) *Henrietta Knight* 147h 171c
7 b g Second Empire(IRE) —Back To Roost (IRE) (Presenting)
2138^{3} 2885^{3} 3675^{2} 4805^{5} 5184^{3}

Somerset Level *James Payne*
7 b m Wimbleball—Spirit Level (Sunley Builds)
759^{P}

Somervell *Tim Easterby*
4 ch g Sulamani(IRE) —Cumbrian Rhapsody (Sharrood (USA))
2824^{9}

Some Secret *Chris Down* 95h
6 b m Fleetwood(IRE) —Secret Dance (Sadler's Wells (USA))
230^{4} 2288^{P} 3480^{3} 3904^{9} 4535^{7} 4929^{2}

Some Slam (IRE) *David Marnane* 130h
6 b g Orpen(USA) —Diva Aldante (IRE) (Phardante (FR))
3474a^{P}

Some Target (IRE) *W P Mullins* 129h 142c
7 b g Witness Box(USA) —Bayloughbess (IRE) (Lancastrian)
4802^{5}

Somethingdifferent (IRE) *Mrs John Harrington* 116h
5 b g Distant Music(USA) —Valleya (FR) (Linamix (FR))
1146a^{2}

Something Silver *Jim Goldie* 91h 97c
10 gr g Silver Patriarch(IRE) —Phantom Singer (Relkino)
46^{P} 2352^{3} 3360^{7}

Some Timbering (IRE) *P S Davies* 94h 103c
12 b g Accordion—Hard Buns (IRE) (Mandalus)
153^{10} 268^{U}

Some Touch (IRE) *Howard Johnson* 118h 127c
11 b g Scribano—Sarahs Touch (IRE) (Mandalus)
361^{6}

Somewhatinevitable (IRE) *Paul Webber* 100h
6 b g Oscar(IRE) —Maspaloma (IRE) (Camden Town)
2666^{U} 3403^{13} 3740^{6} 4478^{4} 4930^{5} 5234^{11}

Sommersturm (GER) *Barney Curley* 99h
7 b g Tiger Hill(IRE) —Sommernacht (GER) (Monsun (GER))
1475^{4} 1547^{6} 1732^{10} 2312^{10} 2927^{10} 3255^{12}

Son Amix (FR) *Thomas Cooper* 142h
5 gr g Fragrant Mix(IRE) —Immage (FR) (Bad Conduct (USA))
3030a^{4} 3475a^{2} 4817^{2}

Sonara (IRE) *Howard Johnson* 91h
7 b g Peintre Celebre(USA) —Fay (IRE) (Polish Precedent (USA))
1929^{5} (2941) 3750^{4}

Sona Sasta (IRE) *David Pipe* 115h 134c
8 b g Sonus(IRE) —Derry Lark (IRE) (Lancastrian)
(3482) ◆ **(3629) 4802^{6}**

Soneva Gili (IRE) *Shelley Johnstone* 71h
7 ch g Sakhee(USA) —Navajo Love Song (IRE) (Dancing Brave (USA))
3883^{11} 4146^{P} 4511^{P}

Songe (FR) *Charlie Longsdon* 136h 145c
7 b g Hernando(FR) —Sierra (FR) (Anabaa (USA))
155^{U} 464^{2} (1690)
(2212) 3561^{F}
4794^{P}

Song In My Heart (IRE) *Jonjo O'Neill* 78h
6 b g Spartacus(IRE) —Joyfullness (USA) (Dixieland Band (USA))
490^{6} 1095^{P} 1335^{P}

Song Of Songs *Jonjo O'Neill* 135h 144c
9 b g Singspiel(IRE) —Thea (USA) (Marju (IRE))
4131^{F} 4727^{17} 4806^{19} 5118^{8}

Son Histoire (FR) *Philip Hobbs* 115h 117c
7 ch g Maresca Sorrento(FR) —Iskara (IRE) (Astronef)
1738^{5} 2140^{3} 2669^{6} 3263^{7} 3646^{4}

Sonic Anthem (USA) *John Mackie* 100h
9 b g Royal Anthem(USA) —Whisperifyoudare (USA) (Red Ransom (USA))
75^{3} 598^{4} 1569^{5} 1816^{4} 2956^{3} 3397^{4} 3782^{11}

Sonning Star (IRE) *Nick Gifford* 114h 120c
7 b g Desert Prince(IRE) —Fantazia (Zafonic (USA))
86^{3} 479^{5} **1883^{2} 2422^{2} 2582^{F} 3193^{7}**

Sonny Mullen (IRE) *Kim Bailey* 116h 138c
7 br g Bob's Return(IRE) —Agua Caliente (IRE) (Old Vic)
1794^{2} ◆ 2214^{6} 2513^{2} 3784^{8} (5281)
(5421)

Son Of Flicka *Donald McCain* 147h 130c
7 b g Groom Dancer(USA) —Calendula (Be My Guest (USA))
(80) 316^{9} (633) 1019^{8} 1311^{2} 1609^{5} 1864^{3}
2542^{2} 4852^{2} 5187^{F}

Son Of Oscar (IRE) *Philip Fenton* 137h 137c
10 b g Oscar(IRE) —Mistress Kyteler (Sallust)
2008a^{2}

Son Of Robain (FR) *Alison Batchelor*
5 ch g Robin Des Champs(FR) —Agathe De Beard (FR) (Faunus (FR))
2985^{P} 3340^{P}

Sonofvic (IRE) *Paul Nicholls* 141h
6 ch g Old Vic—Prudent View (IRE) (Supreme Leader)
(2143) ◆ (4198) ◆

Sonowyouno (IRE) *Jonjo O'Neill* 124h 120c
7 b g Oscar(IRE) —Bottle A Knock (IRE) (Le Moss)
1731^{9} (2270)

Sonus Weld (IRE) *Paddy Butler* 70h
6 gr m Sonus(IRE) —Buckners Girl (Weld)
2130^{F} 3607^{P} 3983^{F} 5265^{4}

Sophies Trophy (IRE) *Pat Phelan* 129h
6 b g Orpen(USA) —Ar Hyd Y Knos (Alzao (USA))
2387^{15} 3447^{2} 3676^{F} 4933^{5} 5166^{14}

Sophisticated Lady *Neil King* 74h
8 b m Prince Daniel(USA) —Sapling (Infantry)
140^{P} 441^{5}

Sophonie (FR) *Ferdy Murphy* 102h
5 b m Kapgarde(FR) —Kore Des Obeaux (FR) (Saint Cyrien (FR))
1780^{2} 2598^{F} 3498^{6}

Soprano (GER) *Jim Goldie* 93h 113c
9 b g Sendawar(IRE) —Spirit Lake (GER) (Surumu (GER))
3335^{9}
3552^{P} 3750^{3} 4146^{6} 4687^{P}

Soprano Vallis (FR) *G Chaignon* 110h
5 b g Sleeping Car(FR) —Bora Vallis (FR) (Le Pontet (FR))
5049a^{5}

Sor Brook *Nigel Twiston-Davies* 65b
5 b m Alderbrook—Rashaya (IRE) (Rashar (USA))
4335^{7} 5070^{9} 5380^{8}

Sorcillera *John Flint* 103h
5 b m Anzillero(GER) —Sorceress (FR) (Fabulous Dancer (USA))
2137^{3} 3158^{16} 3937^{2} ◆ 5385^{7}

Sordid Secret (IRE) *Evan Williams* 93h 107c
8 b m Flemensfirth(USA) —Anns Gift (IRE) (Decent Fellow)
169^{P} (597)
3433^{3} 3963^{3} 4160^{P}

Sorry Al (IRE) *S J Stearn* 104h 119c
11 ch g Anshan—Just A Second (Jimsun)
296^{4}

Sothisisit (FR) *Jonjo O'Neill* 94b
5 b g Sleeping Car(FR) —Une Etoile (FR) (Take Risks (FR))
412^{4} 1799^{3} 5253^{P}

Sotovik (IRE) *Alistair Whillans* 103h 112c
10 gr g Aahsaylad—Moenzi (IRE) (Paris House)
(443)
(1761) 2272^{P} 3361^{4} 3695^{8} 4065^{P} 4258^{4} 5032^{P}

Soubriquet (IRE) *Maurice Barnes* 107h 128c
8 b g Daylami(IRE) —Green Lucia (Green Dancer (USA))
288^{8} **(746)**
874^{6} 1004^{3} 1198^{3} 1405^{4} 1501^{4} **(1577)**
1871^{7} 5320^{11}

Souchang (IRE) *Susan Gardner* 46h
6 b m Basanta(IRE) —Afternoon Tea (IRE) (Decent Fellow)
439^{4}

Souffleur *Peter Bowen* 153h
8 b g In The Wings—Salinova (FR) (Linamix (FR))
4819^{11} 5187^{P}

Soul Angel *Sandy Forster* 94h 90c
7 ch g Tipsy Creek(USA) —Over Keen (Keen)
2194^{3} 3884^{2} 4064^{5} 4690^{2} (4827)

Soulard (USA) *Sophie Leech* 87h 137c
8 b g Arch(USA) —Bourbon Blues (USA) (Seeking The Gold (USA))
214^{6} **2077^{5}**
3677^{8} 3948^{6} 4355^{7} 5228^{7}

Soul Bid (IRE) *Chris Grant* 79h
5 b g Luso—Bid For Fun (IRE) (Auction Ring (USA))
3731^{8} 4259^{6} 4506^{6}

Soul Magic (IRE) *Harriet Graham* 86h 81c
9 b g Flemensfirth(USA) —Indian Legend (IRE) (Phardante (FR))
1339^{4} 1578^{3} 1760^{2} 2351^{10} **3853^{4} 4168^{P}** 4302^{5}
5095^{4}

Sound Accord (IRE) *Alex Hales* 134h 125c
10 br g Accordion—Shuil Na Lee (IRE) (Phardante (FR))
4208^{P}

Sound Judgment (IRE) *Mark Rimell* 80b
5 b g Lahib(USA) —Shadow Smile (IRE) (Slip Anchor)
1510^{5} 1817^{7}

Sound Of Silver *Andrew Crook* 50b
8 b g Supreme Sound—Silver's Girl (Sweet Monday)
1426^{P}

Sound Stage *Caroline Keevil* 122h 139c
8 b g Saddlers' Hall(IRE) —Re-Release (Baptism)
1986^{3} ◆ **2347^{4} 2629^{2}**

Sourchamp (FR) *Arthur Whiting* 48h 77c
5 b g Robin Des Pres(FR) —Jourie (FR) (Lute Antique (FR))
1922^{P} 2456^{13} 2795^{P}
4099^{4} 4447^{F} 4668^{P} 5076^{6}

Sous Mix (FR) *Michael Easterby* 101h
5 gr g Fragrant Mix(IRE) —Insoumise (FR) (Royal Charter (FR))
3166^{5} 4117^{5} 4810^{5} 5031^{U} 5203^{3} 5352^{5}

Souter Point (USA) *Nicky Henderson* 110h
5 bb g Giant's Causeway(USA) —Wires Crossed (USA) (Caller I.D. (USA))
590^{2} 3557^{8} 3950^{10} 4234^{5} 4935^{5}

South Bank (IRE) *Tim Vaughan* 30h 84c
9 b g Old Vic—Cluain-Ard (IRE) (Glacial Storm (USA))
2643^{6} **3527^{F}**

Southerness *David Pipe* 113h
7 ch g Halling(USA) —Teresa Balbi (Master Willie)
1641^{3} ◆

South O'The Border *Nigel Twiston-Davies* 128h 133c
9 b g Wolfhound(USA) —Abbey's Gal (Efisio)
2286^{4} 3444^{7} 3566^{9}
4261^{4} 4421^{3}

South Stack *Michael Scudamore* 79h
6 b g Alflora(IRE) —Mandy Chat (IRE) (Mandalus)
2109^{8} 2640^{5} 3403^{6} 3951^{9} 4465^{11}

Southway Star *Susan Gardner* 76h
6 b m Morpeth—Nearly A Score (Nearly A Hand)
850^{6} 1030^{5} 1158^{8} 4785^{P} 5272^{10}

Southwestern (IRE) *Jeremy Scott* 119c
12 br g Roselier(FR) —Catchthegoose (Tug Of War)
149^{3} 525^{5}

Soutine (IRE) *Alex Hales* 88b
5 b g Flemensfirth(USA) —Bells Chance (IRE) (Needle Gun (IRE))
4356^{8}

Sou'Wester *Colin Tizzard* 118h 133c
11 b g Fleetwood(IRE) —Mayfair (Green Desert (USA))
5^{6} 411^{2} 735^{8} 911^{4} 1110^{6} 1469^{P}

Sovereign King *Miss C Herrington* 125h 128c
9 bb g Sovereign Water(FR) —Bedwyn Bridge (Over The River (FR))
4463^{P} 4936^{2} 5231^{2}

Sovereign Spirit (IRE) *Chris Gordon* 92h
9 b g Desert Prince(IRE) —Sheer Spirit (IRE) (Caerleon (USA))
3540^{3} 3703^{7} 4540^{5} 4833^{4} 5270^{4} 5383^{3}

Soviet Cat (IRE) *Miss C J Williams* 84h
6 b g Soviet Star(USA) —Forest Kitten (IRE) (Marju (IRE))
823^{P} 1028^{P} 1164^{P}

So Young (FR) *W P Mullins* 148h
5 b g Lavirco(GER) —Honey (FR) (Highlanders (FR))
4803^{3}

Space Cowboy (IRE) *Gary Moore* 109h 80c
11 b g Anabaa(USA) —Lady Moranbon (USA) (Trempolino (USA))
81^{4} 278^{2} 533^{3} 689^{P} 1474^{8} 1591^{6} 1905^{2} 2048^{P}

Space Mission (IRE) *Paul Webber* 114h 103c
9 b g Kayf Tara—Jupiter's Message (Jupiter Island)
2959^{7} ◆

Space Star *Paul Webber* 77h 103c
11 b g Cosmonaut—Sophiesue (Balidar)
952^{4} 1744^{3} 1919^{5}

Space Telescope (IRE) *Jonjo O'Neill* 115h
5 b g Galileo(IRE) —Matikanehamatidori (JPN) (Sunday Silence (USA))
527^{2} 767^{3} (862) (933) 1150^{4}

Spanchil Hill *Mrs A S Hodges* 61h 92c
11 b g Sabrehill(USA) —War Shanty (Warrshan (USA))
466^{2}

Spanish Cruise (IRE) *David Pipe* 111h 98c
7 gr g Daylami(IRE) —Baldemara (FR) (Sanglamore (USA))
(3300) 3791^{13} 5322^{2}

Spanish Treasure (GER) *Andy Turnell* 138h
5 b g Black Sam Bellamy(IRE) —Santa Zinaada (GER) (Zinaad)
3055^{4} (3366) 3739^{5} 4788^{8} (5239)

Spare Change (IRE) *P J Rothwell* 98h 112c
10 gr g Portrait Gallery(IRE) —Goin Home (IRE) (Warcraft (USA))
1141^{2}

Spare Me *Milton Harris* 107h 113c
8 b g Cloudings(IRE) —Spare Set (IRE) (Second Set (IRE))
96^{2} (351) 581^{4}

Sparkbridge (IRE) *J Legg* 62h 72c
8 b g Mull Of Kintyre(USA) —Persian Velvet (IRE) (Distinctly North (USA))
4901^{9}

Sparkling Air *John Spearing* 92b
5 ch m Central Park(IRE) —Moonlight Air (Bold Owl)
5077^{2} ◆ 5395^{3}

Sparkling Brook (IRE) *Jennifer Mason* 83h
8 b m Alderbrook—Auntie Prickle Pin (IRE) (Sexton Blake)
25^{6} 480^{4} 793^{2} 862^{4} 1095^{3} 4450^{10} 4721^{3} 4947^{4}

Sparkling Hand *Peter Atkinson* 107b
5 b m Lend A Hand—Sparkling Yasmin (Derring Rose)
(1934) 2616^{7} 4554^{2} 5188^{15}

Sparkling Montjeu (IRE) *George Baker* 103h
6 b m Montjeu(IRE) —Dart Board (IRE) (Darshaan)
21^{4}

Sparkling Zola *Alistair Whillans* 99h
9 b m Double Trigger(IRE) —Sparkling Yasmin (Derring Rose)
318^{4} (461) 729^{4} 871^{U} 946^{2} 1782^{P}

Sparky May *Patrick Rodford* 149h
6 b m Midnight Legend—Glassy Appeal (USA) (Glassy Dip (USA))
(1921) (2289) (2627) (3674) 4793^{2} 5186^{3}

Sparrow Hills (IRE) *Steven Dixon* 125h 70c
7 b g Moscow Society(USA) —Glenstal Forest (IRE) (Glenstal (USA))
138^{U} 2393^{4} (3452) (3688) 4524^{2} 4933^{9}

Spartan Place *R Gurney* 106h 86c
11 b g Overbury(IRE) —Pennethorne Place (Deep Run)
293^{4}

Spate River *Jonjo O'Neill* 102h
6 b g Zaha(CAN) —Rion River (IRE) (Taufan (USA))
228[3] (698) 962[6] 1162[P]
Spa Wells (IRE) *C A McBratney* 109h
10 ch g Pasternak—La Tache (Namaqualand (USA))
861[4]
Speakers Corner *Barney Curley*
5 b g Dalakhani(IRE) —Abbey Strand (USA) (Shadeed (USA))
3877[P] 4281[P]
Spear Thistle *Charlie Mann* 129h 116c
9 ch g Selkirk(USA) —Ardisia (USA) (Affirmed (USA))
(2423) 3676[11]
3980[2] 4270[3]
Specialagent Alfie *Nick Gifford* 91b
5 b g Alflora(IRE) —Oso Special (Teenoso (USA))
5388[9]
Special Bond *Kevin Bishop* 63h
5 b m Monsieur Bond(IRE) —Fizzy Treat (Efisio)
275[P] 590[9] 754[8] 1060[9]
Special Catch (IRE) *Rose Dobbin* 94b
4 b g Catcher In The Rye(IRE) —Top Quality (Simply Great (FR))
3889[3]
Special Cuvee *Alison Thorpe* 95h
5 b g Diktat—Iris May (Brief Truce (USA))
3296[13] 3760[8] 3937[7] 4707[4] 4999[7] 5212[2] 5373[5]
Special Day (FR) *Lucy Wadham* 15h
7 gr g Daylami(IRE) —Plissetskaia (FR) (Caerleon (USA))
2393[P] 4025[14]
Special Envoy (FR) *Nicky Henderson* 117h 124c
9 gr g Linamix(FR) —Pawnee Dancer (IRE) (Dancing Brave (USA))
633[9] 1019[P]
Special Mate *Richard Lee* 106b
5 br g Generous(IRE) —Flying Iris (IRE) (Un Desperado (FR))
(4164)
Special Occasion *Caroline Keevil* 127h 120c
7 b g Inchinor—Special Beat (Bustino)
2636[5] 2868[10] **3722[3] 3871[4] 4490[4] 4987[5]**
Special Portrait (IRE) *Mark Hughes* 111c
7 rg g Portrait Gallery(IRE) —Goin Home (IRE) (Warcraft (USA))
(90) **(4307)**
4851[10]
Special Vintage *Nicky Henderson* 104b
5 br g Grape Tree Road—Special Beat (Bustino)
4204[5] 5257[4]
Speed Bonnie Boat *Henry Daly* 111h 102c
8 ch m Alflora(IRE) —Sail By The Stars (Celtic Cone)
3690[6] 4502[5] 5060[3] 5377[7]
Speed Dating *John Quinn* 102h
5 ch g Pivotal—Courting (Pursuit Of Love)
3387[8] 3521[6] 3692[7] 4874[7]
Speed Master (IRE) *Nicky Henderson* 120b
5 b g King's Theatre(IRE) —Handy Lass (Nicholas Bill)
(4527) 5174[2]
Speedy Directa (GER) *Milton Harris* 88h
8 b g Areion(GER) —Sourour (IRE) (Ahonoora)
2244[P] 4098[P] 4675[7] (5072) 5111[P] (5374)
Speedy Max (IRE) *George Stanley* 86h 107c
10 b g Supreme Leader—Bula Vogue (IRE) (Phardante (FR))
1404[7] 1424[7] (Dead)
Spellchecker (IRE) *Mrs S J Stilgoe* 107h 112c
7 ch g Alderbrook—Auntie Sally (IRE) (Bob Back (USA))
4147[2] 4476[5] 5237[7]
Spell Shot *Jimmy Fox* 45b
7 b g Double Trigger(IRE) —Spellbinder (IRE) (Magical Wonder (USA))
2087[12]
Spent *Alison Thorpe* 107h
6 b g Averti(IRE) —Top (Shirley Heights)
129[2] 1588[3] 1734[F]
Spe Salvi (IRE) *David Arbuthnot* 107h
7 b m Beneficial—Decent Preacher (Decent Fellow)
833[5] (1029) 1480[0] *3054[6]* 3480[6] 3904[6] 4417[F] (5385)
Sphere (IRE) *John Mackie* 93h
6 b m Daylami(IRE) —Apple Town (Warning)
93[5] ◆ 349[6] 837[8] 920[P]
Sphinx (FR) *Edwin Tuer* 123h
13 b g Snurge—Egyptale (Crystal Glitters (USA))
4285[12]
Sphinx Du Lukka (FR) *T Trapenard*
5 b g Dear Doctor(FR) —Io Du Lukka (FR) (Grand Tresor (FR))
5159a[6]
Spice Bar *Declan Carroll* 95h
7 b g Barathea(IRE) —Scottish Spice (Selkirk (USA))
990[7] 1199[9] 2280[2] (2398) (2603) 5094[6]
Spider Boy *Zoe Davison* 91h 79c
14 b g Jupiter Island—Great Dilemma (Vaigly Great)
23[6] 430[P] 587[5] 692[3] 1886[6] 1996[2] 2135[2] 2504[4] 2672[6] 3540[DSQ] 3868[2] (4125) 4670[5]
Spiders Tern *Milton Bradley* 80h
6 b g Sooty Tern—Miss Money Spider (IRE) (Statoblest)
760[11] 1547[7] 1723[13]
Spieder Bay *James Evans* 34b
6 b m Superior Premium—American Pie (Lighter)
3773[18] 5074[P]
Spinning Waters *Dai Burchell* 104h
5 b g Vettori(IRE) —Secret Waters (Pharly (FR))
2021[7] 3526[3] 3872[5] 4530[4] (4965) 5215[2]
Spirit Calling (IRE) *Lucinda Russell* 51h 109c
10 br g Lord Americo—Satco Street (IRE) (Satco (FR))
2448[P] 3336[12] **3549[P] (4963)**
Spirit D'Armor (FR) *Venetia Williams* 95h
5 b g Port Lyautey(FR) —For The Glen (FR) (Quitte Et Passe I (FR))
3964[2] 4478[6] 4917[U]

Spirit Diamond (IRE) *P A Fahy* 92b
5 ch m Sunshine Street(USA) —Fallon (IRE) (Arcane (USA))
1146a[10]
Spirit Is Needed (IRE) *Milton Harris* 99h
5 b g No Excuse Needed—The Spirit Of Pace (IRE) (In The Wings)
3225[2] 3781[7] 4676[3] 5225[5]
Spirit Of Adjisa (IRE) *Tim Vaughan* 128h
7 br g Invincible Spirit(IRE) —Adjisa (IRE) (Doyoun)
(679) (4233)
Spirit Of Barbados (IRE) *David Pipe* 93h
5 b g Oscar(IRE) —Finnisk Dream (IRE) (Phardante (FR))
2957[11] 4091[P] 4268[6] 4444[4] ◆ 5322[0]
Spirit Of Lake (IRE) *Karen George* 84h 90c
9 b g Sheer Danzig(IRE) —Rosheen (IRE) (Brush Aside (USA))
371[2]
Spirit Of The Mist (IRE) *James Moffatt* 107h
7 ch g Trans Island—Exciting (Mill Reef (USA))
1406[6] 2508[10]
Spiritonthemount (USA) *Peter Hiatt* 80h
6 bb g Pulpit(USA) —Stirling Bridge (USA) (Prized (USA))
21[P] **797[U]**
1922[3] 2183[9] 4929[P]
Spirit River (FR) *Nicky Henderson* 150h
6 b g Poliglote—Love River (FR) (Epervier Bleu)
2664[F] 2867[F] 3807[12]
Spirit Son (FR) *Nicky Henderson* 160h
5 b g Poliglote—Kirzinnia (FR) (Zino)
(3542) (4092) ◆ 4788[2] (5196)
Spiritual Art *Luke Dace* 100h
5 b m Invincible Spirit(IRE) —Oatey (Master Willie)
3981[P] 4370[P] 5099[4] (5435)
Spiritual Guidance (IRE) *Warren Greatrex* 100h
8 b g Broken Hearted—Native Tango (IRE) (Be My Native (USA))
3058[4] 3403[5] 3740[7] 4667[2] 5117[13]
Splendid Blue (IRE) *Tony Carroll* 95b
5 br m Blueprint(IRE) —Splendid Choice (IRE) (The Parson)
5380[3]
Spock (FR) *Paul Nicholls* 103h
6 b g Lost World(IRE) —Quark Top (FR) (Perrault)
(1922) 2325[6] 5152[5]
Sponge *Norma Twomey* 74h
6 b g Zaha(CAN) —Glensara (Petoski)
5243[9]
Sported And Played (IRE) *Lucy Normile* 48h
8 b m Saddlers' Hall(IRE) —Alice Freyne (IRE) (Lancastrian)
2353[7]
Sporting Rebel (IRE) *James Frost* 100h 127c
11 b g Zaffaran(USA) —High Church Annie (IRE) (Bustomi)
579[5] 1491[2] 1557[3] (1950)
2443[3] 3588[P]
Sports Line (IRE) *Donald McCain* 144h 155c
8 b g Norwich—Hot Line (IRE) (Riverhead (USA))
2976[4] 4187[5] 4853[17] 5164[F]
Sports Model (IRE) *Howard Johnson* 43h
5 ch g Presenting—Belmarita (IRE) (Belmez (USA))
3749[11]
Spot The Ball (IRE) *Jonjo O'Neill* 80h
6 b g Oscar(IRE) —Sudden Inspiration (IRE) (Good Thyne (USA))
1925[6] 2149[10] 2980[13]
Spring A Suprise *Ken Wingrove*
7 ch m Alflora(IRE) —River Springs (Parthian Springs)
1748[10] 2156[16]
Springaway *Simon West* 67h 60c
12 ch g Minster Son—Galway Gal (Proverb)
1760[3] ◆ **1933[5]**
Spring Bay *John Ryall* 87b
6 b m Karinga Bay—Spring Grass (Pardigras)
4097[10] 5174[8]
Springfield Dante *Nick Kent* 111c
10 b g Pharly(FR) —Mythical Storm (Strong Gale)
79[2] 502[P]
Springfield Raki *Steve Gollings* 119h 118c
7 b g Rakaposhi King—Springfield Rhyme (Idiots Delight)
351[3] **518[4]**
714[4] 3988[3] 4179[2] 4469[3] 4855[P]
Spring Haze *Phillip Dando* 74h
6 ch m Chaddleworth(IRE) —Gypsy Haze (Romany Rye)
272[7] 590[6] 989[5] 1060[4] 1369[5] 1450[10]
Spring Jim *James Fanshawe* 137h
10 b g First Trump—Spring Sixpence (Dowsing (USA))
2498[9] 4848[19]
Spring Moon (IRE) *Martin Keighley* 80b
6 b g Anshan—Toasted Oats (IRE) (Be My Native (USA))
1963[P]
Spring Snow (USA) *Alan Swinbank* 99b
5 b g Silver Deputy(CAN) —Starry Farrari (USA) (Inherent Star (USA))
53[2] 355[6] 732[4] 1284[5]
Sprint De Ferbet (FR) *Nicky Henderson* 114h
5 b g Dark Moondancer—Belle De Ferbet (FR) (Brezzo (FR))
4355[P] 4877[P]
Sprinter Sacre (FR) *Nicky Henderson* 151h
5 bb g Network(GER) —Fatima III (FR) (Bayolidaan (FR))
2493[2] ◆ (3937) ◆ (4203) ◆ 4788[3] ◆
Sprosser (IRE) *Oliver Sherwood* 108h 119c
11 b g Alflora(IRE) —Dark Nightingale (Strong Gale)
4021[11]
Sprowler *Joanna Davis* 101h
7 b g Peintre Celebre(USA) —Enlisted (IRE) (Sadler's Wells (USA))
408[U] 635[3]

Spruzzo *C W Thornton* 74h
5 b g Emperor Fountain—Ryewater Dream (Touching Wood (USA))
12[P] 31[5]
Squadron *Alan King* 141h 133c
7 b g Sakhee(USA) —Machaera (Machiavellian (USA))
155[4] 3156[2] 3479[3] (4023)
4480[2] 5226[3]
Squinch *Nigel Twiston-Davies* 90h
7 b h Kayf Tara—Alta (Arctic Lord)
4081[8]
Staccato Valtat (FR) *Henry Daly* 80b
5 gr g Fragrant Mix(IRE) —Harmonie De Valtat (FR) (Video Rock (FR))
5238[5]
Stadium Arcadium (IRE) *Emma Lavelle*
8 ch g Clerkenwell(USA) —Miles (Selkirk (USA))
2067[P] 2482[P]
Stafford Charlie *John O'Shea* 93h
5 ch g Silver Patriarch(IRE) —Miss Roberto (IRE) (Don Roberto (USA))
336[P] 863[5] 930[9] (1468) 1559[P] 1798[0] 2149[U] 2556[4] 2609[6] 3764[P] 4098[P]
Stage Acclaim (IRE) *Dr Richard Newland* 122h
6 b g Acclamation—Open Stage (IRE) (Sadler's Wells (USA))
(159) 715[5] 1017[3] 1609[10] 1692[5]
Stagecoach Amber (USA) *Sue Smith* 87h 123c
9 b g Bright Launch(USA) —Clan Lake (USA) (Navajo (USA))
636[4] 874[3] 1151[5] 1312[6] 1424[5] 1781[3] 1932[3] 2204[4]
Stagecoach Diamond *W A Bethell* 130h 116c
12 b g Classic Cliche(IRE) —Lyra (Blakeney)
4553[2] 5263[6]
Stagecoach Opal *Sue Smith* 114h 79c
10 b g Komaite(USA) —Rag Time Belle (Raga Navarro (ITY))
2036[P] 2477[8] 2941[8] 3883[7] (4391) (4742) 5003[3] 5320[10]
Stagecoach Pearl *Sue Smith* 111h 153c
7 gr g Classic Cliche(IRE) —Linwood (Ardross)
34[8] **422[2]** ◆
728[2] 857[2] (1000)
(1110) 1257[3] (1987)
(2520) 4078[2] 4789[8] 5336[F]
Stagehand (IRE) *Chris Down* 101h
7 b g Lend A Hand—Ridotto (Salse (USA))
2480[4]
Stage Right *Simon Lewis* 71h
10 b g In The Wings—Spot Prize (USA) (Seattle Dancer (USA))
1925[9] 1997[4] 2244[P] 3839[4]
Stags Leap (IRE) *P Monteith* 94h
4 b g Refuse To Bend(IRE) —Swingsky (IRE) (Indian Ridge)
1699[3] 1984[7]
Stan (NZ) *Venetia Williams* 85h 141c
12 b g Super Imposing(NZ) —Take Care (NZ) (Wham (AUS))
18[2] 194[3] 959[P] 1020[9]
Stance *Peter Hedger* 69h 66c
12 b g Salse(USA) —De Stael (USA) (Nijinsky (CAN))
1721[0] 4224[11] 4900[9]
Stand Clear *Ferdy Murphy* 104h
6 b m Sir Harry Lewis(USA) —Clair Valley (Ardross)
191[6] ◆ 514[2] (744)
Standing Order *Richard Ford* 75h
8 ch g Arkadian Hero(USA) —Simple Logic (Aragon)
984[9] 1046[6] 1300[P] 1760[5] 2433[4] 2956[6] 4522[6] 4920[6]
Stanley Bridge *Barry Murtagh* 68h
4 b g Avonbridge—Antonia's Folly (Music Boy)
3358[8] 4132[5] 4361[5] 4958[6] 5114[8]
Stanley's Choice *John Ferguson* 33h
5 b g Karinga Bay—Be My Babe (Be My Native (USA))
1955[3] 2560[5] 4180[9]
Stanroad *Robert Johnson*
4 b g Danroad(AUS) —Distinctly Laura (IRE) (Distinctly North (USA))
2824[14]
Stan's Cool Cat (IRE) *Alan King* 73h
5 b m One Cool Cat(USA) —Beautiful France (IRE) (Sadler's Wells (USA))
4118[5] 4677[6]
Stapleton (IRE) *Philip Middleton* 96h
6 br g Alflora(IRE) —Star Councel (IRE) (Leading Counsel (USA))
4780[5] 5059[4] 5343[6]
Star Beat *Kate Walton* 114h 124c
8 b g Beat All(USA) —Autumn Leaf (Afzal)
2079[4] 2374[3] (2940)
3522[3]
Starbird *Mike Sowersby* 59b
4 br g Danbird(AUS) —Tennessee Star (Teenoso (USA))
4280[7] 4801[7]
Starbougg *Keith Reveley* 107h 98c
7 b m Tobougg(IRE) —Celestial Welcome (Most Welcome)
420[3] 607[8]
Starburst *Brendan Powell* 81h
6 b m Fantastic Light(USA) —Rasmalai (Sadler's Wells (USA))
3477[6] 3879[2] 4028[6]
Starburst Diamond (IRE) *C R Whittaker* 128h 125c
9 ro g Old Vic—Camlin Rose (IRE) (Roselier (FR))
(4750)
Star Double (ITY) *Mrs Fleur Hawes* 107h 84c
11 ch g Bob Back(USA) —Among The Stars (Pharly (FR))
335[P] 4026[4] 4857[4]
Star Galaxy (IRE) *John Flint* 90h 112c
11 b g Fourstars Allstar(USA) —Raven Night (IRE) (Mandalus)
328[9] 646[2] 4034[12]
4265[U] 4523[4] 4967[R] 5275[4]

Star King (IRE) *Henrietta Knight* 93h
6 bb g Flemensfirth(USA) —Native Flutter (IRE) (Be My Native (USA))
3403[12] 4052[P]
Stark Raven *R D Coupland* 72h 89c
11 b g Sea Raven(IRE) —Hilly Path (Brave Invader (USA))
5148[P]
Starlet Mandy (IRE) *Nigel Twiston-Davies* 55h
8 br m Presenting—Actress Mandy (IRE) (Mandalus)
3264[7] 3762[11] 4260[9]
Starlight Air *John Spearing* 102h
8 ch m Karinga Bay—Moonlight Air (Bold Owl)
651[P] 921[3]
Starluck (IRE) *Alan Fleming* 160h 142c
6 gr g Key Of Luck(USA) —Sarifa (IRE) (Kahyasi)
2668[2] 3559[3] **(4311)** ◆ ***4729[3]* 5197[4]**
Star Neuville (FR) *John Joseph Hanlon* 125b
5 bl g East Of Heaven(IRE) —Danystar (FR) (Alycos (FR))
4808[13]
Star Of Germany (IRE) *Ian Williams* 105h 139c
11 b g Germany(USA) —Twinkle Bright (USA) (Star De Naskra (USA))
1332[P] 1861[12] 2077[7] 2345[9]
Star Of Kalani (IRE) *Robert Wylie* 81h
4 b g Ashkalani(IRE) —La Bekkah (FR) (Nononito (FR))
1234[2] 1422[P]
Star Of Raven *Joss Saville* 79h 47c
14 b m Sea Raven(IRE) —Lucy At The Minute (Silly Prices)
1140[7] **1425[5]**
Star Player (IRE) *Chris Grant* 100h 131c
9 ch g Accordion—Folle Idee De Luz (FR) (Reve Bleu (FR))
1763[3] 2274[3] (3501)
(3888) 4256 (Dead)
Star Potential *Susan Gardner* 78b
4 b f Starcraft(NZ) —Sharena (IRE) (Kahyasi)
4533[8] 5070[6] 5306[12]
Star Role *Richard Ford*
7 b g Tragic Role(USA) —Julie's Glen (IRE) (Good Thyne (USA))
832[U] 935[13] 1138[0]
Starry Mount *Andrew Haynes* 80h
4 ch g Observatory(USA) —Lady Lindsay (IRE) (Danehill Dancer (IRE))
4404[6]
Star Shuil (IRE) *David Arbuthnot* 65b
6 b m Soviet Star(USA) —Shuil Ar Aghaidh (The Parson)
2987[11] 3623[8]
Starstruck Peter (IRE) *Jim Best* 92h
7 b g Iron Mask(USA) —Daraliya (IRE) (Kahyasi)
757[P] 1335[6] 1468[8]
Star Tenor (IRE) *Sandy Forster* 103h 97c
9 b g Fourstars Allstar(USA) —Coco Opera (IRE) (Lafontaine (USA))
(77) **403[4]**
578[4] 747[8]
Star Time (IRE) *Michael Scudamore* 35h
12 b g Fourstars Allstar(USA) —Punctual (Lead On Time (USA))
4130[8] 4380[P] 4787[9] 5068[4] 5195[F]
Start Me Up (IRE) *C F Swan* 133h
7 b g Winged Love(IRE) —Go And Tell (Kemal (FR))
3181a[2] 4849[P]
State Benefit (IRE) *Nicky Henderson* 118h
6 b g Beneficial—Gifted (Shareef Dancer (USA))
(3153) ◆ 3931[5] 4489[4]
State Of Play *Evan Williams* 113h 142c
11 b g Hernando(FR) —Kaprice (GER) (Windwurf (GER))
5200[4]
State Visit *Amy Weaver* 77h
4 b g Dr Fong(USA) —Saint Ann (USA) (Geiger Counter (USA))
2133[5]
Stawell Gift (AUS) *Nick Littmoden*
7 br g Dash For Cash(AUS) —Lots Of Style (AUS) (Coalcliff (AUS))
1812[P]
Stays All Night (FR) *Tim Vaughan* 58h
5 ch g Marathon(USA) —Statyra (FR) (Double Bed (FR))
2896[12] 3406[12] 3760[U] 3917[7] 4397[7]
St Blazey (IRE) *Paul Nicholls* 73b
6 b g Bob Back(USA) —Baden (IRE) (Furry Glen)
3909[11]
St Devote (FR) *Eoin Griffin* 132h
6 b g Saint Des Saints(FR) —Battani (FR) (Top Ville)
2386[14]
Steadys Breeze *R MacDonald* 80h
7 b m Nomadic Way(USA) —Willies Witch (Bandmaster (USA))
2297[7] 2505[6]
Steady Tiger (IRE) *Nicky Richards* 115h 115c
9 b g Presenting—Mindyourown (IRE) (Town And Country)
3499[P] 3852[5] 4063[3] 4685[2]
Stealing Time (IRE) *Jonjo O'Neill* 33c
6 b g Oscar(IRE) —On The Hour (IRE) (Topanoora)
2963[16]
3339[5]
Steel Bullet (IRE) *Jennie Candlish* 82b
5 b g Craigsteel—Augusta Lucinda (IRE) (Luso)
7[3] 304[3] 739[10]
Steeldrivinman *Donald McCain* 77h
5 b g High-Rise(IRE) —Miss Betsy (IRE) (Pollerton)
2957[13] 4281[8] 5000[3]
Steel Edge (IRE) *Ferdy Murphy* 81h
6 b g Flemensfirth(USA) —River Valley Lady (IRE) (Salt Dome (USA))
35[3] 1962[9] 2939[12]

Steel Giant (USA) *Malcolm Jefferson* 79h
6 b g Giant's Causeway(USA) —Ride The Wind (USA) (Meadowlake (USA))
400[10]

Steel Magnate (IRE) *Gordon Elliott* 108c
8 ch g Presenting—Black Gayle (IRE) (Strong Gale)
1577[P] 1595[2] 1727[F]

Steel Man (IRE) *Bruce Mactaggart* 72h 103c
9 b g Anshan—One Edge (IRE) (Welsh Term)
1759[P] 1872[7] 2548[F] 4510[P] 5413[2]

Steel Park (IRE) *Sean Byrne* 123h
7 b g Craigsteel—Parkavoureen (Deep Run)
2260a[6]

Steely Bird *Richard Hawker* 72h
4 gr g Needwood Blade—La Cygne Blanche (IRE) (Saddlers' Hall (IRE))
2151[9] 2924[9] 3477[11] 4289[4] 4522[P]

Steeple D'Or (FR) *G Chaignon*
5 b g Sleeping Car(FR) —Hot D'Or (FR) (Shafoun (FR))
1659a[3]

Stellar Cause (USA) *Nick Ayliffe*
5 ch g Giant's Causeway(USA) —Stellar (USA) (Grand Slam (USA))
3872[13] 4924[11]

St Enoder *Brendan Powell* 83h
6 b m Terimon—Suntas (IRE) (Riberetto)
589[5] 1086[6] *3171[6]* 3620[7] 3901[P]

Stephanie Kate (IRE) *C F Swan* 130h
5 bb m King's Theatre(IRE) —Native Bid (IRE) (Be My Native (USA))
3592a[4] 4793[5] ◆

Stephie *Michael Easterby* 52b
5 b m Sulamani(IRE) —Bahirah (Ashkalani (IRE))
230[12]

Steps To Freedom (IRE) *Gordon Elliott* 130b
5 b g Statue Of Liberty(USA) —Dhakhirah (IRE) (Sadler's Wells (USA))
(5202) ◆

Steptoe *Nicky Henderson* 76h
6 b g Dark Moondancer—Cadoutene (FR) (Cadoudal (FR))
327[8] 3691[15] 4465[F] 5390[F]

Sterling Chief *Oliver Sherwood* 64b
7 b g Silver Patriarch(IRE) —Lady Callernish (Callernish)
2445[6]

Sterling Moll *W De Best-Turner* 76h
8 gr m Lord Of Men—Princess Maud (USA) (Irish River (FR))
217[8]

Sternenzelt (GER) *Michael Gates* 54h 124c
8 gr g Silvano(GER) —Sterlina (GER) (Linamix (FR))
1235[P] 1295[8]
1481[P] 1940[P]

Steveys Lad (IRE) *Philip Kirby* 86h
8 ch g Rainwatch—Inchy (IRE) (Roselier (FR))
749[4]

Stevie Bull (IRE) *Chris Gordon* 81h
6 b g Turtle Island(IRE) —Jodi (IRE) (Phardante (FR))
25[5] 279[6] 630[9]

Stevie Thunder *Ian Williams* 100h
6 ch g Storming Home—Social Storm (USA) (Future Storm (USA))
2038[8] 5099[6] 5235[2]

Stewarts House (IRE) *A L T Moore* 125h 137c
9 b g Overbury(IRE) —Osocool (Teenoso (USA))
3206a[12] 3798a[P]

Stickaround *Malcolm Jefferson* 80b
6 ch m Muhtarram(USA) —Altogether Now (IRE) (Step Together (USA))
2957[10] 3623[7] 5135[9]

Stick Together *Malcolm Jefferson* 111h 83c
8 gr m Kayf Tara—Altogether Now (IRE) (Step Together (USA))
1709[6] 2477[3] **3520[9] 3695[9]** 5030[5]

Still At Lunch (IRE) *Kate Walton* 121h
8 b g King's Theatre(IRE) —Class Society (IRE) (Lahib (USA))
196[10] **401[F]**

Still Calm *Maurice Barnes* 82h 87c
7 b g Zamindar(USA) —Shining Water (Kalaglow)
12[8] 31[4] 307[2]
714[5] 4304[P]
4996[3] 5095[7] 5413[4]

Still Royal *John Davies* 75h
5 b g Val Royal(FR) —On Till Morning (IRE) (Never So Bold)
154[9] 494[P] 1831[U] 2398[10] 4390[8] 5208[9]

Stir On The Sea (IRE) *James Frost* 102h
5 bb m Turtle Island(IRE) —Ballyroe Flash (IRE) (Don't Forget Me)
19[3] 250[2] 547[2] 1746[8] 1921[8] 2442[6] 2633[8] 3879[6] 4924[2]

Stitched Up (IRE) *Tim Walford* 27b
5 b g Needle Gun(IRE) —Kam Slave (Kambalda)
3525[13] 3725[P]

Stitchnick (IRE) *Stuart Kittow* 77b
6 b g Needle Gun(IRE) —American Chick (IRE) (Lord Americo)
759[7]

St Killian's Run (IRE) *P Monteith* 103h 111c
7 b g Beneficial—Make A Move (IRE) (Buckskin (FR))
88[F] 2208[10]

Stolen Light (IRE) *Andrew Crook* 40h 91c
10 ch g Grand Lodge(USA) —Spring To Light (USA) (Blushing Groom (FR))
13[3] 404[6] 860[3] 1378[3] (1500)
1646[2] 2107[5] 2250[2] 3503[U]

Stolen Moments (FR) *James Moffatt* 88h 135c
10 gr g Villez(USA) —Brave Lola (FR) (Dom Pasquini (FR))
214[5] 492[2] 514[7] 856[5]

Stolen Thunder *Emma Lavelle* 116h
6 b g Alflora(IRE) —Cullen Bay (IRE) (Supreme Leader)
(2069) 2981[P] 3836[3] 4539[4]

Stonehenge Lad (AUS) *Michael Appleby*
6 br g Hawk Wing(USA) —Aretha (AUS) (Sir Dapper (AUS))
833[P]

Stonemaster (IRE) *D T Hughes* 149h
6 br g Old Vic—Rose Of Stradbally (IRE) (Roselier (FR))
3030a[2] 3578a[3] 4107a[4]

Stoneraker (IRE) *G Chambers* 105h 115c
10 b g Beneficial—Orchardstown Lady (Le Moss)
4901[5]

Stonethrower (IRE) *Tim Vaughan* 113h
6 b g Dushyantor(USA) —Ciaras Charm (IRE) (Phardante (FR))
3370[4] 3693[U] 3919[6]

Stoney's Treasure *Alan King* 112h 134c
7 ch g Silver Patriarch(IRE) —Stoney Path (Petoski)
2184[3] 2670[4] 3628[3] (4334)
(4877) ◆

Stop On *Chris Grant* 94h
6 b g Fraam—Tourmalet (Night Shift (USA))
3887[F]

Stopped Out *Kate Walton* 125h
6 gr g Montjoy(USA) —Kiomi (Niniski (USA))
1608[6] 1766[8] (2549) 3334[3] 4209[8] 5149[6] (5431)

Stop The Show (IRE) *Richard Phillips* 116h 94c
10 b g King's Theatre(IRE) —Rathsallagh Tartan (Strong Gale)
549[7] 695[6] 2930[6] (3609)
3961[2] 4525[3]

Storm Brig *Alistair Whillans* 138h
6 b g Heron Island(IRE) —The Storm Bell (IRE) (Glacial Storm (USA))
(2349) ◆ (3885) 4475[7] 5196[5]

Storm Command (IRE) *Tim Vaughan* 75h
4 ch g Halling(USA) —Clarinda (IRE) (Lomond (USA))
960[7] 1226[4] 1330[3] 4123[4] 4450[7] 4899[4] 5072[5]

Stormin Exit (IRE) *Jim Goldie* 106h 137c
8 b g Exit To Nowhere(USA) —Stormin Norma (IRE) (Runnett)
2541[F] 3206a[7] 3706a[7] (4714)
5185[8]

Storming Gale (IRE) *Donald McCain* 120h
5 b g Revoque(IRE) —Dikler Gale (IRE) (Strong Gale)
(3762) ◆ 4253[F] 5107[6]

Storming Redd *James Eustace* 6h
4 gr g Storming Home—Bogus Mix (IRE) (Linamix (FR))
2245[11]

Stormion (IRE) *Lucinda Russell* 83h
6 b g Flemensfirth(USA) —El Moss (IRE) (Le Moss)
42[6] 1758[6] 2103[3] 2351[2]

Storm Jack (FR) *Jeremy Scott* 85h
6 bb g Lost World(IRE) —Line As (FR) (Cadoudal (FR))
5437[3]

Storm Kirk *Alistair Whillans* 88b
5 b g Heron Island(IRE) —The Storm Bell (IRE) (Glacial Storm (USA))
(47)

Storm Of Applause (IRE) *Philip Hobbs* 110h 124c
10 b g Accordion—Dolce Notte (IRE) (Strong Gale)
959[5] 1229[5] 1604[2] 1926[5] 2234[4] 4863[2] 5345[2]

Storm Prospect *Lucinda Russell* 98h 106c
8 b g Mujahid(USA) —Bajan Blue (Lycius (USA))
290[2] 460[6] 860[4] 1118[4] 1405[3] **1868[3] 2203[5] (2656)**

Storm Surge (IRE) *Martin Todhunter* 55h 107c
8 gr g Great Palm(USA) —Ashfield Rosie (IRE) (Roselier (FR))
(177) **516[5]**
4001[8]

Storm Survivor (IRE) *Jonjo O'Neill* 104h
5 b g Milan—Lindas Present (IRE) (Presenting)
4100[4] 4404[7] 4917[7] 5167[8]

Stormy Bob (IRE) *Mrs C Wilesmith* 90c
12 b g Bob's Return(IRE) —Stormweather Girl (IRE) (Strong Gale)
406[3]

Stormy Chance (IRE) *Miss Emma Crew*
10 b g Flemensfirth(USA) —Storm Trix (IRE) (Glacial Storm (USA))
151[P]

Stormyisland Ahead *Evan Williams* 113h
6 b g Turtle Island(IRE) —Queen's Banquet (Glacial Storm (USA))
1046[2] 1175[4] 1482[2] 1742[3] 2232[5] 2574[5]

Stormy Morning *Lawney Hill* 48h
5 ch g Nayef(USA) —Sokoa (USA) (Peintre Celebre (USA))
2129[9]

Stormy Weather (FR) *Howard Johnson* 120h
5 gr g Highest Honor(FR) —Stormy Moud (USA) (Storm Bird (CAN))
2671[7] 4058[F] 4485[9]

Storymaker *Sandy Forster* 118h 131c
10 b g Midnight Legend—Amys Delight (Idiots Delight)
(78) **524[7]**
874[8] 4116[6] 4820[10] 5002[3] 5416[2]

Story Malinas (FR) *A Chaille-Chaille*
4 ch g Malinas(GER) —Starry Dome (USA) (Conquistador Cielo (USA))
5047a[5]

Stow *Venetia Williams* 127h
6 ch g Selkirk(USA) —Spry (Suave Dancer (USA))
193[P] 2147[9] (2606) 3440[2] 3742[7] (4185)

Stoway (FR) *Richard Lee* 111c
9 b g Broadway Flyer(USA) —Stowe (FR) (Garde Royale)
3648[2] 4258[5]

Stowford Press (IRE) *Nikki Evans* 75h
8 br m Exit To Nowhere(USA) —Whisky Chaser (Never So Bold)
630[6] 1141[8] 1745[4] 2239[11]

Stradbrook (IRE) *Jonjo O'Neill* 123h 115c
9 b g Midhish—Bowland Park (Nicholas Bill)
2443[4] 2975[2] 3154[3] 3375[6]

Straight Face (IRE) *David Evans* 92h
7 b g Princely Heir(IRE) —Dakota Sioux (IRE) (College Chapel)
1506[4]

Strand Line (IRE) *Lisa Day* 97h 97c
11 b g Supreme Leader—Good Credentials (Take A Reef)
16[3]

Strategic Approach (IRE) *Warren Greatrex* 131h 122c
9 ch g Bob Back(USA) —Merrill Gaye (IRE) (Roselier (FR))
2580[2] 2945[P]

Stratford Stroller (IRE) *Jonjo O'Neill* 102h 96c
7 b g Beneficial—Kemchee (Kemal (FR))
86[5] **498[7]**
694[3]

Strathcal *Anna Brooks* 103h
5 b g Beat Hollow—Shall We Run (Hotfoot I)
4952[5] 5131[3] 5309[2]

Strath Gallant *Suzy Smith* 67h 75c
8 b g Alhaarth(IRE) —Brief Lullaby (IRE) (Brief Truce (USA))
529[6]

Stratigic Gale (IRE) *Nicky Henderson* 116h
7 b g Darnay—Stealth (Strong Gale)
5441[12]

Stravita *Jim Best* 87h
7 b m Weet-A-Minute(IRE) —Stravsea (Handsome Sailor)
298[3] 1704[4] 1949[4] 4123[2] ◆ 4920[3] (5272)

Straw Bear (USA) *Nick Gifford* 115h 130c
10 ch g Diesis—Highland Ceilidh (IRE) (Scottish Reel)
3429[3] 3788[2] 4221[5] 4806[15]

Streamtown (IRE) *S R B Crawford* 110h 72c
7 b m Bob Back(USA) —Kelly Gales (IRE) (Strong Gale)
3747[4] 4112[3] (4795)
5150[4]

Street Dance (IRE) *Keith Goldsworthy* 114h
5 b g Beneficial—Zvezda (IRE) (Soviet Lad (USA))
3731[3] 4191[5] 4410[7] 4527[4] (4860) 5106[6]

Street Devil (USA) *Pat Murphy* 95h
6 gr g Street Cry(IRE) —Math (USA) (Devil's Bag (USA))
2426[7] 4751[3] 5016[9]

Street Entertainer (IRE) *David Pipe* 121h
4 br g Danehill Dancer(IRE) —Opera Ridge (FR) (Indian Ridge)
3760[5] 4092[6] (5211)

Streets Of Gold (IRE) *C Roche* 138h 135c
9 b g Sadler's Wells(USA) —User Friendly (Slip Anchor)
3206a[P]

Strevelyn *Ann Duffield* 83h
5 br g Namid—Kali (Linamix (FR))
748[F] 1005[P]

Strictly (FR) *V J Hughes* 25h
6 gr g Slickly(FR) —Misallah (IRE) (Shirley Heights)
5253[5]

Strictly Business *Tom George* 93h
6 ch g Shahrastani(USA) —Top Notch (Alderbrook)
93[8] 168[4] 1453[P] 2149[P]

Strikemaster (IRE) *Brian Ellison* 106h
5 b g Xaar—Mas A Fuera (IRE) (Alzao (USA))
1230[10]

Stripe Me Blue *Peter Jones* 118h 43c
9 b g Miner's Lamp—Slipmatic (Pragmatic)
2347[16] 2626[8] 3587[12]
4007[U] 4538[7]

Strobe *Lucy Normile* 106h 98c
7 ch g Fantastic Light(USA) —Sadaka (USA) (Kingmambo (USA))
447[4] (717) 946[9] **(1100)**
1338[5] 1598[6] 1701[3] 5132[P] 5429[10]

Strolling Vagabond (IRE) *John Upson* 82h 65c
12 ch g Glacial Storm(USA) —Found Again (IRE) (Black Minstrel)
83[P] 280[P]

Strongbows Legend *Charlie Longsdon* 105h 114c
6 ch g Midnight Legend—Miss Crabapple (Sunyboy)
2310[2]
2961[7] 3371[2] 3784[3] 4402[F] 4966[2]

Strong Coffee *Oliver Sherwood* 116h 114c
9 b g Classic Cliche(IRE) —Foehn Gale (IRE) (Strong Gale)
274[F] 769[8] (1027)
1093[3] 1255[3] 1550[P] 1903[F]

Stronghaven (IRE) *Howard Johnson* 102h
7 b g Oscar(IRE) —Native Crystal (IRE) (Be My Native (USA))
4451[8]

Strong Market *Jeremy Scott* 95h
6 b g Piccolo—Bon Marche (Definite Article)
1035[10] 1313[6]

Strongpoint (IRE) *Patrick Griffin* 122h 122c
7 bb g Bob Back(USA) —Ceo Draiochta (IRE) (Erins Isle)
1698[3]
1849a[U] 2506[8]

Strong Weld *Mrs N Sheppard* 122c
14 br g Weld—Shoreham Lady (Strong Gale)
493[5]

Stroom Bank (IRE) *Simon Andrews* 92h 79c
11 b g Warcraft(USA) —All Alright (Alzao (USA))
354[P]

Struanmore *Paul Webber* 78b
4 ch g Doyen(IRE) —Burghmuir (IRE) (Cadeaux Genereux)
3957[12] 4484[8] 5284[4]

Strumble Head (IRE) *Peter Bowen* 101h
6 b g Anshan—Milan Moss (Le Moss)
552[8] 737[9] 1048[4] 1141[P] (1300) 1335[3] (1551)
1726[12] (2001) 2545[P]

Study Troubles (IRE) *Debra Hamer* 88h
7 b g Lord Americo—Ballinlee Lady (IRE) (Yashgan)
327[5] 766[3]

Stuff Of Dreams *Ferdy Murphy* 58h 84c
6 b m Groom Dancer(USA) —Best Of The Best (FR) (Cadoudal (FR))
48[6]

Stumped *Milton Harris* 114h 110c
8 b g Bertolini(USA) —So Saucy (Teenoso (USA))
479[8] (534) 664[2] 736[4] 958[7] **1161[5]** 1292[7] 1443[5]

Su Bleu (IRE) *Milton Harris* 78h
9 ch g Pistolet Bleu(IRE) —Local Issue (IRE) (Phardante (FR))
406[P] 3526[13] 4012[P]

Sublimity (FR) *Robert Alan Hennessy* 162h
11 b g Selkirk(USA) —Fig Tree Drive (USA) (Miswaki (USA))
2414a[4] 3707a[5]

Subtle Approach (IRE) *Emma Baker* 84b
6 b g Subtle Power(IRE) —Rotoruasprings (IRE) (Jurado (USA))
1749[6] *2295[8]*

Suburban Bay *Alan King* 90h
6 ch g Karinga Bay—Orchid House (Town And Country)
3678[P] 4198[8] 5074[5]

Suburbia (USA) *Lucinda Russell* 70h
5 b g Street Cry(IRE) —Green Lady (IRE) (Green Desert (USA))
3331[12] 3547[12]

Sucess River (FR) *G Cherel* 116h
6 b g Robin Des Champs(FR) —News Rivers (FR) (Cadoudal (FR))
2230a[P]

Sufficient Warning *Ralph Smith* 70h
7 b g Warningford—Efficacious (IRE) (Efisio)
154[10] 380[6]

Sula's Legend *Neil Mulholland* 17h 116c
10 ch g Midnight Legend—Sulapuff (Sula Bula)
169[6] 663[P] 868[7] 1107[7]

Sullivan's Cascade (IRE) *Edward Bevan* 51h
13 b g Spectrum(IRE) —Sombre Lady (Sharpen Up)
148[P] 594[F]

Sullumo (GER) *Charlie Mann* 118h 138c
8 b g Acatenango(GER) —Secret Of Salome (IRE) (Vision (USA))
2500[6] 3440[6] 3742[10] 4421[4]

Sulpius (GER) *Bob Buckler* 95h
6 b g Tertullian(USA) —Suva (GER) (Arazi (USA))
2215[8] 2791[7] 3196[7] 3556[P] 4397[10]

Sultan Fontenaille (FR) *David Pipe* 105h 124c
9 b g Kaldounevees(FR) —Diane Fontenaille (FR) (Tel Quel (FR))
(3230)
3650[2] 4219[3] 4777[3] 5214[P]

Sumak (FR) *Ferdy Murphy* 108h
7 b g Kahyasi—Lady Slave (IRE) (In The Wings)
1695[2] ◆

Sumdancer (NZ) *Michael Madgwick* 107h 107c
9 b g Summer Suspicion(JPN) —Epic Dancer (NZ) (Epidaurus (USA))
221[5] (1919)
2429[4] 2591[4] 3349[4] 3608[P] 4400[4] 4770[5] 5055[3]
5386[3]

Sum Laff (IRE) *Charlie Mann* 115h
7 ch g Publisher(USA) —Tiergarten (IRE) (Brief Truce (USA))
3448[4] 4081[3] (4555) 5153[7]

Summerandlightning (IRE) *Mark Usher*
5 gr m Great Palm(USA) —Young Love (FR) (Jeune Homme (USA))
3054[9] 3623[12]

Summer Blues (FR) *J-C Baudoin*
4 b g Polish Summer—Dancing Darby (IRE) (Highest Honor (FR))
1658a[9]

Summer De Baune (FR) *John Bryan Groucott* 59h
6 b g Saint Cyrien(FR) —Fee De Baune (FR) (En Calcat (FR))
2328[12] 3842[15] 4288[13] 4437[11] 5000[5] 5172[9]

Summer Soul (IRE) *Lucinda Russell* 124h 56c
9 b g Danehill(USA) —Blend Of Pace (IRE) (Sadler's Wells (USA))
291[4] (447) (581) 2035[7] 2205[5]

Summery Justice (IRE) *Venetia Williams* 119h 144c
7 b g Witness Box(USA) —Kinsella's Rose (IRE) (Roselier (FR))
(2305)

Summit Meeting *Mrs John Harrington* 149h
6 b g Sadler's Wells(USA) —Apogee (Shirley Heights)
2197a[3] ◆ 2968a[11] 3175a[P] 3475a[7]

Sumner (IRE) *William Davies* 88h 61c
7 b g Xaar—Black Jack Girl (IRE) (Ridgewood Ben)
1723[8] 1925[3] 2244[5]
2468[7] 5282[8] 5393[7]

Sunarri (IRE) *Jane Walton* 115h
7 b g Sonus(IRE) —Rosearro (IRE) (Roselier (FR))
44[P] (2208) 2545[2] 3330[3] 3966[11] 4475[10] 5315[P]

Sunblest *Lisa Williamson* 23b
5 b m Medicean—Invincible (Slip Anchor)
4280[10]

Sundae Best (IRE) *Howard Johnson* 101h
7 b g Oscar(IRE) —Celestial Dance (Scottish Reel)
2610[3] 3631[2] 3951[4]

Sunday City (JPN) *Peter Bowen* 100h 139c
10 ch g Sunday Silence(USA) —Diamond City (USA) (Mr Prospector (USA))
65[3] 330[P] 1044[U] (1117)
1176[2] 1486[6] 1611[6] 1973[2] (2112)
2234[2] 5399[4]

Sunday Sharpner (IRE) *Renee Robeson* 102h
5 ch g Ultimately Lucky(IRE) —Cent Prime (Hernando (FR))
2069[P] 3405[9] 3719[3] 4276[P] 4968[7]

Sun Des Mottes (FR) *David Pipe* 54h
5 ch m Adnaan(IRE) —Ingrid Des Mottes (FR) (Useful (FR))
2068[12] 2216[10] 3227[8] 3448[10] 3839[7]

Sundown Trail (IRE) *Nicky Richards* 92h 76c
6 ch g Old Vic—Mary's View (IRE) (Phardante (FR))
2107[U] 2250[4] 3336[9] (4302) 4687[4]

Sun Lady (FR) *Robert Johnson* 70b
5 b m Rifapour(IRE) —Vousseliere (FR) (Tourangeau (FR))
4547[6]

Sunley Peace *Gary Moore* 126h
7 ch g Lomitas—Messila Rose (Darshaan)
3626[P] 3906[2] (4677) 4992[5] (5441)

Sunnyhillboy (IRE) *Jonjo O'Neill* 144h 147c
8 b g Old Vic—Sizzle (High Line)
2359[7] 2886[3] 4790[F]

Sunnyhill Gal *Milton Harris* 71b
5 b m Beat All(USA) —Among Women (Common Grounds)
2541[0]

Sunny Ledgend *Andrew J Martin* 96h
6 b g Midnight Legend—Swordella (Broadsword (USA))
3266[7] 3546[3] 3992[3] 4191[9] 5203[5]

Sunnyside *Lucy Normile* 120h
6 gr g Silver Patriarch(IRE) —Gretton (Terimon)
(1662) ◆ 2102[6] 4062[3] 4359[4] 4869[4] 5320[5]

Sunny Spells *Julia Feilden* 29h
6 b g Zamindar(USA) —Bright Spells (Salse (USA))
3833[6]

Sun Quest *Steven Dixon* 106h
7 b g Groom Dancer(USA) —Icaressa (Anabaa (USA))
235[5] 2128[5] 2333[2] 2596[4] 3481[7] 3793[4] 4375[6]

Sunrise Court *Peter Purdy*
12 ch g One Voice(USA) —Tudor Sunset (Sunyboy)
266[P]

Sunsalve (IRE) *Rebecca Curtis* 91b 57c
7 ch g Definite Article—Mrs Battleaxe (IRE) (Supreme Leader)
602[4] **3435[P]**
3586[6] 3938[4]

Sunset Boulevard (IRE) *Jim Best* 79h
8 b g Montjeu(IRE) —Lucy In The Sky (IRE) (Lycius (USA))
1489[P] 4450[5]

Sunset Resort (IRE) *Maurice Barnes* 82h
6 b g King's Best(USA) —Summer Dreams (IRE) (Sadler's Wells (USA))
210[4] 397[6] 492[3] 887[3] 999[4] 1339[7]

Sunsetten (IRE) *Henry Daly* 123h 70c
7 b g Tendulkar(USA) —Rosy Affair (IRE) (Red Sunset)
2[3]

Sunshine Buddy *Chris Down* 62h
4 b f Reel Buddy(USA) —Bullion (Sabrehill (USA))
851[3]

Suntini (GER) *Emma Lavelle* 115h 142c
9 b g Platini(GER) —Sunita (GER) (Abary (GER))
2665[7]

Sun Tzu (IRE) *Dr Richard Newland* 109h 106c
7 br g Definite Article—Told You So (IRE) (Glacial Storm (USA))
3256[2] 3589[7] 3822[U]
3990[3] 4279[2] 4744[P] (5014) (5252)

Sunwise (USA) *Paul Nicholls* 97h
5 b g Arch(USA) —Turning Wheel (USA) (Seeking The Gold (USA))
1910[4] 2209[P]

Supa Tramp *Mrs Suzy Bull* 91h 94c
8 b g Kayf Tara—Shirley Superstar (Shirley Heights)
292[4] 4429[2] 4857[6]

Super Ally (IRE) *Andrew Parker* 87h
6 b g Flemensfirth(USA) —Strong Tide (Strong Gale)
3855[12]

Super Baby (FR) *James Ewart* 104h 117c
9 b g Baby Turk—Norma Jane (FR) (Rahotep (FR))
2207[3] 2942[P] 3523[10] 4166[7] **4471[U] 5145[7]**

Supercede (IRE) *Gordon Elliott* 145h 133c
9 b g Lahib(USA) —Super Zoe (Bustino)
(1102) 1119[2]
1373[11] (1593) 1860[2] 2360[7]

Super Directa (GER) *Lucy Wadham* 123h
7 b g Protektor(GER) —Summernight Dream (GER) (Highest Honor (FR))
3306[5] ◆ 4120[2] 4323[4] (4424) (5108)

Super Duty (IRE) *Donald McCain* 101b
5 b g Shantou(USA) —Sarah's Cottage (IRE) (Topanoora)
(5209)

Super Fly *Debra Hamer* 102h
9 b g Kayf Tara—Dawn Alarm (Warning)
374[3]

Superhoops *Stuart Howe*
4 b g Hunting Lion(IRE) —Colonial Lady (Dansili)
851[F] 1024[P]

Superior Knight *James Evans* 90h
7 b g Superior Premium—American Pie (Lighter)
739[5] 1069[4] 1374[5] 2456[12] 3225[12] 3365[6] 4076[8] 4263[3]

Superior Wisdom (IRE) *Alex Hales* 135h 130c
11 b g Pierre—Viva Las Vegas (IRE) (Pennine Walk)
206[9] (2500) 2870[F] 5187[14]

Superius (IRE) *Emma Lavelle* 108h
6 b g High Chaparral(IRE) —Zing Ping (IRE) (Thatching)
1470[12] 1816[3] 1998[3] 3228[11] 4025[10]

Super Kay (IRE) *Lawney Hill* 28h 86c
10 ch m Alderbrook—Another Vodka (IRE) (Moscow Society (USA))
1048[6]

Super Ken (IRE) *Chris Gordon* 96b
4 b g Amilynx(FR) —Tell The Country (IRE) (Good Thyne (USA))
2052[6] (4561)

Super Kenny (IRE) *Nicky Henderson* 121h
5 b g Kendor(FR) —Zalida (IRE) (Machiavellian (USA))
360[5] 2626[3] 3228[P] 4291[6]

Supernoverre (IRE) *Alan Jones* 104h
5 b g Noverre(USA) —Caviare (Cadeaux Genereux)
1175[3] 1289[3] 1492[P] 1590[8] 1726[P] (5082)

Super Sensation (GER) *K Kukk* 79h
10 ch g Platini(GER) —Studford Girl (Midyan (USA))
4374[U]

Super Villan *Mark Bradstock* 118h
6 ch g Alflora(IRE) —Country House (Town And Country)
1821[4] 2238[2] 2946[2] 3931[2]

Supply And Fix (IRE) *J J Lambe* 93h 101c
13 b g Supreme Leader—Hannies Girl (IRE) (Invited (USA))
1101[3]

Supralunary *Robin Mathew* 59b
5 b g Midnight Legend—Heresy (IRE) (Black Minstrel)
4527[8]

Supreme Dawn *Shelley Johnstone* 47b
6 b m Supreme Sound—Glorious Dawn (Distinct Native)
4171[10] 4574[11] 5432[11]

Supreme De Paille (IRE) *Nigel Twiston-Davies* 127h
9 b g Supreme Leader—Wondermac (IRE) (Jeu De Paille (FR))
(3256) 3947[9]

Supreme Keano (IRE) *Jonjo O'Neill* 115h 126c
9 b g Supreme Leader—Keen Gale (IRE) (Strong Gale)
2611[4] 3371[5]

Supreme Oscar (IRE) *Frederick Sutherland* 26h
8 br g Oscar(IRE) —Bula Supreme (IRE) (Supreme Leader)
2981[P] 3439[14]

Supreme Piper (IRE) *Claire Dyson* 70h 86c
13 b g Supreme Leader—Whistling Doe (Whistling Deer)
1745[6]

Supreme Plan (IRE) *Kim Bailey* 111h 122c
8 b g Flemensfirth(USA) —Castlehill Lady (IRE) (Supreme Leader)
223[4] 370[4] 651[2] ◆ **2073[3] 2595[3] 3821[P] 4334[5]**

Supreme Royal (IRE) *Philip Hobbs* 74h
9 b g Supreme Leader—View Of The Hills (Croghan Hill)
264[7]

Supreme Ruler (IRE) *Patrick Holmes* 82h
8 b g Supreme Leader—Twin Gale (IRE) (Strong Gale)
5030[P] 5149[10]

Supreme Team (IRE) *Louise Davis* 79h 66c
8 b g Supreme Leader—La Gazelle (IRE) (Executive Perk)
1745[2] 4098[2] 4976[3]

Suprendre Espere *Christopher Kellett* 19h 83c
11 b g Espere D'Or—Celtic Dream (Celtic Cone)
3699[P] 3875[P] 4263[P]

Suprise Vendor (IRE) *Stuart Coltherd* 110h
5 ch g Fath(USA) —Dispol Jazz (Alhijaz)
4166[10] 4477[11] 4914[9]

Surdoue *Michael Scudamore* 63h
11 b g Bishop Of Cashel—Chatter's Princess (Cadeaux Genereux)
554[8]

Sure Josie Sure (FR) *David Pipe* 131h
6 gr m Kalanisi(IRE) —Aerdee (FR) (Highest Honor (FR))
2386[9] 2626[6] 5315[2]

Surenaga (IRE) *Miss Sally Randell* 87h 133c
9 b g Arctic Lord—Surely Madam (Torenaga)
(4194)
4699[3]

Surface To Air *Chris Bealby* 74h 116c
10 b g Samraan(USA) —Travelling Lady (Almoojid)
4742[10]
5200[8]

Surf And Turf (IRE) *Jonjo O'Neill* 110h
5 ch g Beneficial—Clear Top Waltz (IRE) (Topanoora)
4094[P] 4437[8] 5010[P] (5243) (5437)

Surfing (FR) *Nicky Henderson* 117h 149c
5 b g Califet(FR) —Hawai De Vonnas (FR) (Cadoudal (FR))
3193[3] ◆ 3932[2]

Surf Like A Lady (IRE) *Philip Hobbs* 48b
5 b m Presenting—Midnight Light (IRE) (Roselier (FR))
5119[11]

Suspect (GER) *Paul Nicholls* 100b
5 b g Tiger Hill(IRE) —Shoah (GER) (Acatenango (GER))
3200[18] 4709[3]

Sussex Lass *Zoe Davison* 39b
6 b m Beat All(USA) —Emma-Lyne (Emarati (USA))
2156[15] 5105[12] 5380[12]

Sussex Sunset *Paul Webber* 99h
5 b m Milan—Deep Sunset (IRE) (Supreme Leader)
1887[F]

Sustainability (IRE) *Venetia Williams* 84h
6 ch g Old Vic—Over The Glen (IRE) (Over The River (FR))
3158[13] 4377[6]

Swains Meadow *Kevin Bishop* 81b
6 ch m First Trump—Level Headed (Beveled (USA))
4097[7] 4881[6]

Swainson (USA) *Helen Nelmes* 102h 102c
10 br g Swain(IRE) —Lyphard's Delta (USA) (Lyphard (USA))
281[4] 687[4] 1912[7] 2184[4] 2638[U] (3790)
4372[P]

Swaledale Lad (IRE) *Micky Hammond* 78b
4 b g Arakan(USA) —Tadjnama (USA) (Exceller (USA))
5313[3]

Swaling (IRE) *Victor Dartnall* 115b
5 b g Oscar(IRE) —Princess Supreme (IRE) (Supreme Leader)
5158[2]

Swallow (FR) *James Ewart* 79b
5 bb g Lavirco(GER) —Pocahontas (FR) (Nikos)
1989[10]

Swansbrook (IRE) *Alan King* 127h 128c
8 b g Alderbrook—Bobsyourdad (IRE) (Bob's Return (IRE))
3390[4] 3871[5] 4261[2] (4692)

Sway (FR) *Jonjo O'Neill* 137h 129c
5 b m Califet(FR) —Kadrige (FR) (Video Rock (FR))
2071[3] (2326)
(2978) 3291[6] 3627[3] 4794[13] 5302[P]

Sweden (IRE) *Evan Williams* 121c
7 b g Beneficial—Our Alma (IRE) (Be My Native (USA))
152[U] (1830)
2191[5] (3588)
4749[F]

Sweetaboutme *Maurice Barnes* 62b
6 b m Sir Harry Lewis(USA) —Bee-A-Scally (Scallywag)
4303[P] 5259[P]

Sweet Caroline (IRE) *Nicky Richards* 94h
4 b f Motivator—Figlette (Darshaan)
2655[5] 3358[3] 3747[9] 4552[7]

Sweet Irony (FR) *Alan King* 119h
5 b g Laveron—Medicis (FR) (Sicyos (USA))
355[2] 2216[3] ◆ 2612[3] 4051[3] (4951)

Sweet My Lord (FR) *W P Mullins* 134h
5 b g Johann Quatz(FR) —Hasta Manana (FR) (Useful (FR))
4188[12]

Sweet Request *Dr Jeremy Naylor* 47h
7 ch m Best Of The Bests(IRE) —Sweet Revival (Claude Monet (USA))
180[4]

Sweet Seville (FR) *Terry Clement* 105h 93c
7 b m Agnes World(USA) —Hispalis (IRE) (Barathea (IRE))
430[4] 767[P] 994[3] (3603) 3807[P] **3980[6]** 4161[5]
4855[3] 5345[P]

Sweet Shock (GER) *Michael O'Hare* 137h
6 b g Sholokhov(IRE) —Sweet Royale (GER) (Garde Royale)
3029a[2]

Sweet Sugar (FR) *Ferdy Murphy* 85h
5 ch g Loup Solitaire(USA) —Violette D'Avril (FR) (Olmeto)
3715[13] 3885[5]

Sweet World *Bernard Llewellyn* 112h
7 b g Agnes World(USA) —Douce Maison (IRE) (Fools Holme (USA))
1127[2] 1311[3] 1548[8] 2333[4] 3348[9] 3477[5] 4028[2] 5215[5]

Swift Counsel (IRE) *John O'Callaghan* 126h 139c
10 b g Leading Counsel(USA) —Small Iron (General Ironside)
1527a[4]

Swift Lord (IRE) *Gary Moore* 130h 107c
6 b g Spectrum(IRE) —Ediyrna (IRE) (Doyoun)
3865[2] 4451[4] (5071)

Swift Sailor *Derek Frankland* 45h 102c
10 gr g Slip Anchor—New Wind (GER) (Windwurf (GER))
5221[0]

Swincombe Flame *Nick Williams* 122b
5 b m Exit To Nowhere(USA) —Lady Felix (Batshoof)
(4335) (4728) ◆

Swincombe Rock *Nigel Twiston-Davies* 119h 142c
6 ch g Double Trigger(IRE) —Soloism (Sulaafah (USA))
(1598)
(1815) 2631[4] 4794[P]

Swing Bill (FR) *David Pipe* 130h 141c
10 gr g Grey Risk(FR) —Melodie Royale (FR) (Garde Royale)
(909) **1332[4]**
1611[4] 1858[2] 2140[5] 2343[2] 3198[5] (4221)
4487[3] ◆ 4794[7] 5185[5]

Swinging Hawk (GER) *Ian Williams* 117h
5 ch h Hawk Wing(USA) —Saldenschwinge (GER) (In The Wings)
2540[4] ◆ 3225[8]

Swinging Sultan *Keith Reveley* 103b
4 b g Sulamani(IRE) —Nobratinetta (FR) (Celtic Swing)
4239[2] ◆

Swingkeel (IRE) *Nigel Twiston-Davies* 128h
6 ch g Singspiel(IRE) —Anniversary (Salse (USA))
3942[3] ◆ 4294[2] (4861) 5187[7]

Swing State *Tony Carroll* 70h
6 b g Overbury(IRE) —Peg's Permission (Ra Nova)
1678[5] 5211[9]

Swinside Silver *Donald Whillans* 38h
7 gr m Silver Patriarch(IRE) —Ballyquintet (IRE) (Orchestra)
4000[8] 4359[P]

Swirl Tango *F Jordan*
5 b m Lujain(USA) —Tangolania (FR) (Ashkalani (IRE))
1899[P]

Swiss Art (IRE) *Nick Mitchell* 112h
5 b g One Cool Cat(USA) —Alpine Park (IRE) (Barathea (IRE))
693[5] 932[3] 1031[2] (1344) (1445) 1614[6] 1740[6] 2586[3] (2927)

Swiss Guard *Tim Vaughan* 115h
5 b h Montjeu(IRE) —Millennium Dash (Nashwan (USA))
154[5] 548[7] 733[8] 1278[4] 3256[5] 3497[5] (3983) 4104[6]

Switched Off *Ian Williams* 116h
6 b g Catcher In The Rye(IRE) —Button Hole Flower (IRE) (Fairy King (USA))
472[6] 2131[2] (2485) 2658[2] 3481[5] 4076[2] 4536[F] 5117[4]

Swordsman (GER) *Chris Gordon* 128h 111c
9 b g Acatenango(GER) —Saiga (Windwurf (GER))
530[3] **691[3]**
867[4] (1297)
1476[3] 1570[8]

Sworn Tigress (GER) *George Baker* 80h
6 b m Tiger Hill(IRE) —Sweet Tern (GER) (Arctic Tern (USA))
1921[7] 2289[10]

Sybarite (FR) *Nigel Twiston-Davies* 133h
5 bb g Dark Moondancer—Haida III (FR) (Video Rock (FR))
(1510) ◆ 1866[3] 2388[2] ◆ 3556[2] 4849[10]

Sycho Fred (IRE) *Mike Sowersby* 92h 91c
10 b g Buster King—Rebecca Steel (IRE) (Arapahos (FR))
158[4] 516[4] 716[3] 804[4] 931[5] 1152[P] 2079[3] 2402[4]
3990[4] 4238[4]
5097[4] 5258[3]

Sydney Cove (IRE) *William Amos* 85h
5 b g Cape Cross(IRE) —First Fleet (USA) (Woodman (USA))
3335[8] 3855[11] 4136[6] 4511[9]

Sydney Des Pictons (FR) *C A McBratney* 127h
5 b g Khalkevi(IRE) —Tchama Minda (FR) (Marchand De Sable (USA))
3208a[7]

Sydney Sling (IRE) *Evan Williams* 111h 108c
6 b g Xaar—Cherry Hills (IRE) (Anabaa (USA))
567[P]

Sykalino (FR) *Alan Fleming* 62h
8 b g Robin Des Champs(FR) —Et Que Ca Saute (FR) (Royal Charter (FR))
379[P]

Symphonica (IRE) *Gordon Elliott* 107h
8 ch m Definite Article—Double Symphony (IRE) (Orchestra)
457[2] 1099[2]

Symphonick (FR) *Paul Nicholls* 110c
5 b g Passing Sale(FR) —Cymphonie (FR) (Djarvis (FR))
3531[U] 3690[F]

Synchronised (IRE) *Jonjo O'Neill* 139h 165c
8 b g Sadler's Wells(USA) —Mayasta (IRE) (Bob Back (USA))
2500[5] 2870[6] **(3437)**
4876[3]

Syndication (IRE) *Venetia Williams* 95b
4 b g Accordion—Huit De Coeur (FR) (Cadoudal (FR))
(4382)

Synonymy *Michael Blanshard* 87h
8 b g Sinndar(IRE) —Peony (Lion Cavern (USA))
232[6] 1336[7] 1605[7] 2589[5]

Synthe Davis (FR) *Laura Mongan* 132h
6 b m Saint Des Saints(FR) —Trumpet Davis (FR) (Rose Laurel)
(263) 690[2] (1475) (1588) 3442[4] 4198[3]

Tabaran (FR) *Alison Thorpe* 124h
8 ch g Polish Precedent(USA) —Tabariya (IRE) (Doyoun)
3[2] 196[5] (372) 633[6] 830[6]

Tae Kwon Do (USA) *Tim Vaughan* 88h
5 b g Thunder Gulch(USA) —Judy's Magic (USA) (Wavering Monarch (USA))
1313[4] 1953[8] 2658[14] 5212[10]

Taffy Thomas *Peter Bowen* 106h
7 b g Alflora(IRE) —Tui (Tina's Pet)
846[7]

Tafika *Paul Webber* 100h 120c
7 b g Kayf Tara—Shiwa (Bustino)
2670[P] 3391[2] (3880)
4334[4]

Tahiti Pearl (IRE) *Sue Smith* 98h
7 b g Winged Love(IRE) —Clara's Dream (IRE) (Phardante (FR))
2162[2] 3490[8] 3693[12] 4477[8] 4942[4]

Tail Of The Bank (IRE) *Laura Young* 124h 139c
8 b g Flemensfirth(USA) —Dear Money (IRE) (Buckskin (FR))
2884[12]
3625[F] ◆ (3932)
4078[3] 4487[2] ◆

Tait's Clock (IRE) *Jonjo O'Neill* 67h
5 b g King's Theatre(IRE) —Tremplin (IRE) (Tremblant)
3692[9] 3831[7] 3917[5] 4128[9]

Takaatuf (IRE) *John Hellens* 104h
5 b g Dubai Destination(USA) —Karlaka (IRE) (Barathea (IRE))
4001[1] 548[6] 2508[13] 3509[10] 3746[4] 4113[9] 4797[5] 4977[4]

Takamaru (FR) *David Pipe* 96h
5 b g Kapgarde(FR) —Tamainia (FR) (Lashkari)
2482[5] 2954[11] 3252[6] 3589[9] 4034[11] 4878[P]

Take A Mile (IRE) *Seamus Mullins* 101h 115c
9 ch g Inchinor—Bu Hagab (IRE) (Royal Academy (USA))
(221) **498[4]**
957[S] 1481[4] 1546[3] 1916[2] 2184[2] 4927[F] 5194[3]

Take It There *Alastair Lidderdale* 98h 122c
9 ch m Cadeaux Genereux—Feel Free (IRE) (Generous (IRE))
(2470)
2573[3] 3482[P] (4265)
5323[5]

Takelli (IRE) *Evan Williams* 89h
5 b g Marju(IRE) —Takaliya (IRE) (Darshaan)
1095[4] **1511[P]**

Takeroc (FR) *Paul Nicholls* 145h 155c
8 gr g Take Risks(FR) —Rochambelle (FR) (Truculent (USA))
4293[4] (4696)
4950[2] 5372[2]

Takestan (IRE) *Patrick O Brady* 131h
8 b g Selkirk(USA) —Takariya (IRE) (Arazi (USA))
1038a[P] 1711a[6]

Take The Breeze (FR) *Paul Nicholls* 136h 156c
8 gr g Take Risks(FR) —Reine Breeze (FR) (Phantom Breeze)
2084[2] 3948[4] ◆ 4187[4] 4487[F] 5199[U]

Take The Profit *Chris Grant*
5 b g Domedriver(IRE) —Fantastic Belle (IRE) (Night Shift (USA))
1629[F]

Take The Stand (IRE) *Peter Bowen* 127h 135c
15 b g Witness Box(USA) —Denys Daughter (IRE) (Crash Course)
(149) (317)
525[3] 628[2] 844[8]
Taketimeout (IRE) *Jonjo O'Neill* 110h
6 b g Oscar(IRE) —Fast Time (IRE) (Be My Native (USA))
1819[3] 2109[5] 2397[2] 2983[6]
Takeyourcapoff (IRE) *Mrs John Harrington* 124h
6 b m King's Theatre(IRE) —Masriyna's Article (IRE) (Definite Article)
1713a[4]
Talenti (IRE) *Charlie Longsdon* 115h 87c
8 b g Sadler's Wells(USA) —Sumoto (Mtoto)
137[5] 478[2] 821[2] 912[4] 3744[9] 4025[11] 4441[2]
5017[4] 5278[3]
Tale Of Tanganyika (FR) *John Wade* 102h
5 b g King's Best(USA) —White Rose (GER) (Platini (GER))
319[10] 1989[6] 2509[4] 3521[7]
Talesofriverbank *Alistair Whillans* 72h
8 b m Minster Son—The White Lion (Flying Tyke)
2351[3] 3396[3] 3883[3] 4872[5]
Tales To Tell (IRE) *Alan King* 103b
6 b g Oscar(IRE) —What's The Story (Homeboy)
3266[4] 3584[P]
Talkin' Tough (IRE) *B R Hamilton* 122h 122c
9 ch g Zaffaran(USA) —Reine Dagoberte (FR) (The Wonder (FR))
3709a[13]
Talk Of Saafend (IRE) *Dianne Sayer* 46h
6 b m Barathea(IRE) —Sopran Marida (IRE) (Darshaan)
5028[9]
Talk Up Trouble *Mark Brisbourne* 64b
5 ch m Barathea(IRE) —Polish Rhythm (IRE) (Polish Patriot (USA))
1069[11] 1284[15]
Tallulah Mai *Matthew Salaman* 81h
4 b f Kayf Tara—Al Awaalah (Mukaddamah (USA))
1586[3]
Tally Em Up (IRE) *P J Rothwell* 118h 134c
8 gr m Flemensfirth(USA) —Tot Em Up (Strong Gale)
3594a[4] 3709a[12]
Tamadot (IRE) *Philip Hobbs* 130h 130c
9 b g Supreme Leader—Barenises Rose (IRE) (Roselier (FR))
3588[P] 4223[2] 5206[4]
Tamanaco (IRE) *Tim Walford* 98h
4 b g Catcher In The Rye(IRE) —Right After Moyne (IRE) (Imperial Ballet (IRE))
4056[5] 5147[3]
Tamayo (IRE) *I R Ferguson* 49h 109c
11 bb g In The Money(IRE) —Cassies Girl (IRE) (Mandalus)
305[6]
Taminkle (FR) *Caroline Keevil* 56h
5 b g Tamure(IRE) —Periwinkle (FR) (Perrault)
4706[4]
Tammys Hill (IRE) *Liam Lennon* 106h
6 b g Tamayaz(CAN) —Hillside Lass (Troy Fair)
53[4] 311[12]
Tampa Boy (IRE) *Milton Harris* 105h 117c
9 b g Montjeu(IRE) —Tirolean Dance (IRE) (Tirol)
734[2] 840[6] (1034)
1177[2] 1348[P] 1491[5] 1570[P] 1885[F] 1973[U]
Tancredi (SWE) *Gruffydd Jones* 85h 69c
9 b g Rossini(USA) —Begine (IRE) (Germany (USA))
762[P]
Tango Knight (IRE) *Mrs John Harrington* 122h
7 b g King's Theatre(IRE) —Anne Hathaway (IRE) (Definite Article)
2116a[3]
Tango Master *Mouse Hamilton-Fairley* 76b
4 ch g Doyen(IRE) —Silver Purse (Interrex (CAN))
2315[8] 3406[10]
Tanikos (FR) *Mrs A Malzard* 86h 130c
12 b g Nikos—Tamana (USA) (Northern Baby (CAN))
915a[3]
Tank Buster *Carroll Gray* 84h 106c
11 b g Executive Perk—Macfarly (IRE) (Phardante (FR))
181[P]
Tanks For That (IRE) *Nicky Henderson* 93h 146c
8 br g Beneficial—Lady Jurado (IRE) (Jurado (USA))
524[3] 709[4] 2881[2] 3808[12]
4853[18] 5340[3]
Tanmeya *Tim Vaughan* 75h 81c
10 gr m Linamix(FR) —Ta Awun (USA) (Housebuster (USA))
1450[12] 1601[U] **1744[P]**
Tanners Court *Claire Dyson* 111h 109c
14 b g Framlington Court—True Nell (Neltino)
49[2] 597[8]
Tanners Emperor *Claire Dyson* 29h
7 b g Emperor Fountain—La Vie En Primrose (Henbit (USA))
1824[7] 2143[P] 3647[10]
Tante Sissi (FR) *Alan King* 112b
4 b f Lesotho(USA) —Kadjara (FR) (Silver Rainbow)
2965[3] ◆ (4184) 4728[2] 5188[11]
Tantsor (FR) *Paul Midgley*
4 ch g Brier Creek(USA) —Norova (FR) (Hawker's News (IRE))
743[P]
Tanwood Boy (FR) *Venetia Williams* 63h
7 b g Marathon(USA) —Amie Jolie (FR) (Cadoudal (FR))
2456[11] 2873[12] 3253[7]
Tanzanite Bay *Lucinda Russell* 80h
6 b m Karinga Bay—Diamond Wind (USA) (Wind And Wuthering (USA))
3330[15] 4134[3] 4417[4]
Taoiri (FR) *Alan King* 114h
4 b g Khalkevi(IRE) —Josvalie (FR) (Panoramic)
4702[3]

Tar (IRE) *Matt Sheppard* 94h
7 b g Danzig(USA) —Royal Show (IRE) (Sadler's Wells (USA))
171[P] 402[4] **652[P]** 793[8] 4874[6] 5212[8]
Tarabela *Gerald Ham* 97h 97c
8 b m Kayf Tara—Rocky Revival (Roc Imp)
2203[3] 2329[14] 2558[P] 2980[12] **3871[7] (4381)**
4927[F]
Tarablaze *Philip Hobbs* 125h 144c
8 b g Kayf Tara—Princess Hotpot (IRE) (King's Ride)
2303[3] (2793)
4190[2] 4817[9]
(5001) 5199[4]
Tara Isle *Henry Daly* 66h
7 b m Kayf Tara—Island Gift (Jupiter Island)
50[11]
Taranis (FR) *Paul Nicholls* 135h 160c
10 ch g Mansonnien(FR) —Vikosa (FR) (Nikos)
2673[7] 3292[F]
Tara Rose *David Evans* 96b
6 br m Kayf Tara—True Rose (IRE) (Roselier (FR))
637[3]
Tara Royal *Donald McCain* 123h 137c
6 b g Kayf Tara—Poussetiere Deux (FR) (Garde Royale)
(208) ◆ 1770[U] 1930[2] 2220[2] 2520[2]
Tarashan *Ted Haynes* 60b
6 b m Kayf Tara—Rupert's Princess (IRE) (Prince Rupert (FR))
4780[11]
Taras Joy (IRE) *John Wade* 45h
6 b g Kayf Tara—Native Sylph (IRE) (Supreme Leader)
2102[12]
Tarateeno *Pat Murphy* 123h 126c
8 b g Kayf Tara—Shalateeno (Teenoso (USA))
2501[2] 3198[7] 3435[3] 3922[P]
Tara Warrior (IRE) *Tim Vaughan* 109h
5 b g Dilshaan—Dungeon Princess (IRE) (Danehill (USA))
1238[2] 1369[4] 4076[11] 4465[P]
Tarisandre Du Bosc (FR) *F-M Cottin*
4 b g Poplar Bluff—Larisandre (FR) (Le Nain Jaune (FR))
1658a[8]
Tarkani (IRE) *Valentine Donoghue* 121h 107c
8 ch g Spectrum(IRE) —Tarwila (IRE) (In The Wings)
309[5] 447[6] 708[4] 871[2] 946[3] 1118[3]
Tarkari (IRE) *Evan Williams* 141h
6 ch g Fantastic Light(USA) —Taraza (IRE) (Darshaan)
1609[2] 2386[F] 3939[3] ◆ 4373[5] 4848[20]
Tarkesar (IRE) *Carole Ikin* 80h
9 b g Desert Prince(IRE) —Tarwila (IRE) (In The Wings)
234[U] 865[11] 1048[7] 1259[P]
Tarn Hows (IRE) *Jennie Candlish* 104b
5 ch g Old Vic—Orchardstown Lady (Le Moss)
2309[2] (3920)
Taroum (IRE) *Evan Williams* 69h
4 b g Refuse To Bend(IRE) —Taraza (IRE) (Darshaan)
5253[3]
Tartak (FR) *Tom George* 127h 166c
8 b g Akhdari(USA) —Tartamuda (FR) (Tyrnavos)
1958[3] (2964)
(3292) 4201[5] 4818[7] 5184[4]
Tartan Snow *Stuart Coltherd* 126h 124c
11 b g Valseur(USA) —Whitemoss Leader (IRE) (Supreme Leader)
2450[F] 3854[2] (4001)
4305[F] 4471[U] (4913)
Tartan Tie *Alison Thorpe* 91h
7 b g Grand Lodge(USA) —Trois Graces (USA) (Alysheba (USA))
182[4] 744[6] 962[8]
Tartan Tiger (IRE) *John Quinn* 98b
5 ch g Flemensfirth(USA) —River Clyde (IRE) (Presenting)
3731[6] 4457[6] 5432[8]
Tarvini (IRE) *Jonjo O'Neill* 127h
6 b g Kalanisi(IRE) —Tarwila (IRE) (In The Wings)
302[S] (606) (830) 1346[5] 1508[11] 1776[11] 1986[10]
2347[12] 3306[7] 3452[12]
Tasheba *David Pipe* 148h 107c
6 ch g Dubai Destination(USA) —Tatanka (IRE) (Lear Fan (USA))
2125[3] 2523[P] **3871[6]** 4202[9] 5287[10]
Tasman (IRE) *Liam McAteer* 117h 139c
11 ch g Definite Article—Felin Special (Lyphard's Special (USA))
1113a[6]
Tasman Tiger *Kate Walton* 68b
4 b f Danbird(AUS) —Laylee (Deploy)
2108[5] 2173[10]
Tastes Like More (IRE) *Donald McCain* 85h 114c
9 b m Close Conflict(USA) —Fly Your Kite (IRE) (Silver Kite (USA))
340[P]
Taste The Wine (IRE) *Bernard Llewellyn* 110h
5 gr g Verglas(IRE) —Azia (IRE) (Desert Story (IRE))
2485[4] 2937[7] 4540[8] (5212) 5406[2]
Tastevin (FR) *Philip Hobbs* 66h
4 ch g Dark Moondancer—Donitille (FR) (Italic (FR))
5321[6]
Tataniano (FR) *Paul Nicholls* 148h 167c
7 b g Sassanian(USA) —Rosa Carola (FR) (Rose Laurel)
2385[3] 5442[5]
Tatenen (FR) *Richard Rowe* 89h 154c
7 b g Lost World(IRE) —Tamaziya (IRE) (Law Society (USA))
2126[3] 2517[8] 3195[3] (3677)
4352[7] 4820[11]
Tatispout (FR) *Charlie Longsdon* 112h
4 b f Califet(FR) —Larmonie (FR) (Great Palm (USA))
2356[12] 2614[3] 2958[7] 3403[3] 4778[2] ◆ 5102[5]
(5348) ◆

Tatsu (IRE) *L S Rowe* 61c
8 b g Kotashaan(FR) —Some-Friend (IRE) (Be My Native (USA))
4901[7]
Tavalu (USA) *Gerald Ham* 82h 61c
9 b g Kingmambo(USA) —Larrocha (IRE) (Sadler's Wells (USA))
(4378) 4540[12] 5374[5]
Tawnies (IRE) *Thomas Gerard O'Leary* 83h 131c
11 b g Norwich—Extra Chance (Pollerton)
1113a[P]
Tayarat (IRE) *Michael Chapman* 120h
6 b g Noverre(USA) —Sincere (IRE) (Bahhare (USA))
1971[3] (2323) (2586) 4452[6] 4778[9] 5232[5]
Taylors Secret *Shaun Lycett* 76h
5 b g Indian Haven—Top Tune (Victory Note (USA))
7[6] 2335[4] 3981[3] 4747[P] 5013[6]
Tayman (IRE) *Nigel Twiston-Davies* 104h 112c
9 bb g Sinndar(IRE) —Sweet Emotion (IRE) (Bering)
601[P] **868[P]**
1937[P] 2161[10]
Tazzarine (FR) *Charles Egerton* 68h
5 b m Astarabad(USA) —Belle Yepa (FR) (Mansonnien (FR))
(2825) 3227[6] 4828[5]
Tchico Polos (FR) *Paul Nicholls* 128h 161c
7 b g Sassanian(USA) —Miss Saint Germain (FR) (Pampabird)
(2138)
2359[F] 3446[2] 3675[7] 4187[2] 5164[5]
Tchikita (FR) *James Ewart* 100h 73c
8 b m April Night(FR) —Tchi Tchi Bang Bang (FR) (Perrault)
2107[9] 2353[6] 3637[7] 4395[P]
Teaforthree (IRE) *Rebecca Curtis* 136h
7 b g Oscar(IRE) —Ethel's Bay (IRE) (Strong Gale)
1866[4] 2143[2] (2571) 2888[3] 4159[2] ◆ 4849[8]
Tealissio *Lucy Wadham* 106b
5 b g Helissio(FR) —Tealby (Efisio)
718[3] 3835[2]
Teals Star *C I Ratcliffe* 91b
7 b g Gods Solution—Morcat (Morston (FR))
1086[4] 1629[9] 2074[15]
Team Allstar (IRE) *Jonjo O'Neill* 53h 123c
12 ch g Fourstars Allstar(USA) —Bint Alsarab (Rainbow Quest (USA))
1200[P] 1368[7]
Tear Drops (IRE) *P E Collins* 111h
7 b m Beneficial—Shuil Na Gale (Strong Gale)
858[4]
Tears From Heaven (USA) *Mrs S Sunter* 79h
5 bb g Street Cry(IRE) —Heavenly Aura (USA) (St Jovite (USA))
254[5] 712[6] 4506[10] 5027[8] 5308[6]
Tech Zinne *George Baker* 59h
5 ch m Zinaad—Technik (GER) (Nebos (GER))
1920[3] *2295[4]* 2560[6] 3904[8]
Tecktal (FR) *Pat Phelan* 76h
8 ch m Pivotal—Wenge (USA) (Housebuster (USA))
3430[P]
Teddy's Reflection (IRE) *Henrietta Knight* 129h 127c
8 b g Beneficial—Regal Pursuit (IRE) (Roi Danzig (USA))
(2513)
3496[2] 4199[4] 4821[P]
Teela *Ben Haslam* 69h
4 b f Motivator—Orange Sunset (IRE) (Roanoke (USA))
836[8] 1018[8] 1422[P] 1498[4] 2369[P]
Teeming Rain (IRE) *Jonjo O'Neill* 98h 123c
12 b g Supreme Leader—Lady Graduate (IRE) (Le Bavard (FR))
2794[P] 3629[P]
Teenage Idol (IRE) *Evelyn Slack* 121h
7 bb g Sadler's Wells(USA) —Kaaba (Darshaan)
1642[U] 1827[10] 1956[12] 2300[5] 2549[5] 3570[4] (3855)
4255[2] 4715[F] 5030[4] 5315[3]
Teenage Kicks (IRE) *Polly Gundry* 111h
6 ch g Giant's Causeway(USA) —Ruissec (USA) (Woodman (USA))
8[2] 1812[7] 2154[3] 2372[4] 5439[F]
Teenando (IRE) *Sue Smith* 69h 85c
11 b g Teenoso(USA) —Ananda (Majestic Maharaj)
456[5] **680[5]**
804[8] 3636[3] 3883[10]
4241[3] 4509[P] 4997[5] 5258[U] (5414)
Teerie Express *George Bewley* 106c
10 b g Sir Harry Lewis(USA) —Trecento (Precious Metal)
(4135)
4571[4] 5032[P]
Tee Shot (IRE) *Tim Vaughan* 13b
5 gr g Deploy—Carnoustie (USA) (Ezzoud (IRE))
2576[8] *3171[8]*
Teeton Bollinger *Mrs Joan Tice* 96c
10 b g Shambo—Sunday Champers (True Song)
(295) 502[F]
Tegan Lee *Liam Corcoran* 96h 99c
8 b m Midnight Legend—What Chance (IRE) (Buckskin (FR))
1179[10] (1294) 1451[12] 1592[2]
1901[F] 2187[P]
Tek A Deek *James Moffatt* 19b
7 ch g Zaha(CAN) —Lightning Blaze (Cosmonaut)
1003[P]
Tekthelot (IRE) *Elliott Cooper* 71b
5 b g Shantou(USA) —Bryna (IRE) (Ezzoud (IRE))
4287[15] 5264[11]
Telenor *J T R Dreaper* 124h 140c
8 ch g Bob Back(USA) —Ardent Love (IRE) (Ardross)
3798a[8] ◆
Tell Henry (IRE) *C I Ratcliffe* 108h 109c
11 ch g Broken Hearted—Valleymay (IRE) (King's Ride)
4975[U]

Telling Stories (IRE) *Barry Leavy* 76h
5 b m Lucky Story(USA) —Yes Virginia (USA) (Roanoke (USA))
337[4] 478[P]
Tell Massini (IRE) *Tom George* 151h 135c
7 b g Dr Massini(IRE) —Kissantell (IRE) (Broken Hearted)
(2057)
2631[F] (Dead)
Tell Me The Story (IRE) *Jonjo O'Neill* 109h 113c
7 b g Oscar(IRE) —What's The Story (Homeboy)
985[P] 1486[3] ◆ 1604[P]
Temoin *Richard Phillips* 144h 131c
11 b g Groom Dancer(USA) —Kowtow (USA) (Shadeed (USA))
4193[6] 4749[F]
Tempest River (IRE) *Ben Case* 119b
5 b m Old Vic—Dee-One-O-One (Slip Anchor)
3266[3] 4027[3] 4728[4] (5188)
Temple Green *Mrs J Martin-Mayland* 65c
9 b m Double Trigger(IRE) —Polly Leach (Pollerton)
165[F] 5148[4]
Temple Place (IRE) *Alan Jones* 87h 44c
10 b g Sadler's Wells(USA) —Puzzled Look (USA) (Gulch (USA))
520[6] 1164[2] 1707[4]
1905[3] 2243[5]
Templer (IRE) *Philip Hobbs* 133h 137c
10 ch g Charmer—Ballinamona Lady (IRE) (Le Bavard (FR))
149[2] 525[2] 844[5] 1373[5] 1570[2] 1777[2] 1999[4] 4315[2]
4851[7]
Tempsford (USA) *Jonjo O'Neill* 97h 131c
11 b g Bering—Nadra (IRE) (Sadler's Wells (USA))
(839) 1020[5]
1777[P]
Tempting Paradise (IRE) *Evan Williams* 94h 116c
8 ch g Grand Lodge(USA) —Summer Trysting (USA) (Alleged (USA))
523[4] 919[8] 3841[6] 4698[2] 5228[6]
Tenawa *Karen George* 87h
9 b m Commanche Run—Gypsy Blues (Sula Bula)
684[6]
Tenby Jewel (IRE) *Keith Goldsworthy* 105h
6 ch g Pilsudski(IRE) —Supreme Delight (IRE) (Supreme Leader)
2215[9] 2576[2] 3434[9] 3691[4] 4012[10] 4404[2] 4521[2]
5215[7]
Ten Fires (GER) *D T Hughes* 133h 125c
9 bb g Acambaro(GER) —Tosca Dona (GER) (Solo Dancer (GER))
4537[F]
Tenitemsplustoast *Patrick Rodford* 57h
5 ch g Midnight Legend—Ultra Pontem (Governor General)
2371[10] 3651[13] 4225[10] 4677[9] 5239[6]
Tenor Nivernais (FR) *Venetia Williams* 118h
4 b g Shaanmer(IRE) —Hosanna II (FR) (Marasali)
3686[3] 3874[3] 4807[7]
Ten Pole Tudor *Michael Scudamore* 105h
6 b g Royal Applause—Amaniy (USA) (Dayjur (USA))
299[6]
Tension Point *Chris Grant* 121h
7 b g Hernando(FR) —Blessed (IRE) (Jurado (USA))
45[6] 396[4] 685[2]
Tenth Avenue (IRE) *Donald McCain* 60h
6 b g Luso—Persian Honey (IRE) (Persian Mews)
1308[U] 1401[6] 1928[4]
Terenzium (IRE) *Micky Hammond* 115h 105c
9 br g Cape Cross(IRE) —Tatanka (ITY) (Luge)
494[8] 606[2] 717[4]
1759[11] 1930[5] 2299[P] 2477[5] 3575[3] 3713[7] 4276[4]
4914[10]
Teresina (GER) *F Zobal*
9 ch m General Assembly(USA) —Tsarina (GER) (Aspros (GER))
1811a[U]
Teri D Trixter (IRE) *Denis Paul Murphy* 95c
6 br g Oscar(IRE) —Cygnus (IRE) (Phardante (FR))
738[4]
Termon Boy *Rob Summers* 67h
7 b g Rainbow High—Killmacrennan Lady (IRE) (Gladden)
4100[13] 5013[7] 5167[14]
Terra Bleu (IRE) *Milton Harris* 63h
4 b g Azamour(IRE) —Pinaflore (FR) (Formidable (USA))
3443[10] 3767[9] 3944[9] 4192[P] 5212[13]
Terre De Grez (FR) *J Ortet*
4 b g Network(GER) —Luttica (FR) (Cadoudal (FR))
1658a[5]
Terrible Tenant *Seamus Mullins* 20h 106c
12 gr g Terimon—Rent Day (Town And Country)
38[2] 274[3] 431[5] 1991[7] 2638[6] 2980[16]
5060[6] 5407[3]
Teshali (IRE) *Paul Nicholls* 116h
5 bg g Anabaa(USA) —Tashiriya (IRE) (Kenmare (FR))
2145[6] 2667[8] 3344[5] 3874[11] 4990[4] (5066) 5276[2]
Tesserae *Andrew Haynes* 91h
5 b m Reset(AUS) —Moxby (Efisio)
796[8]
Tetouan *Gordon Elliott* 111h
7 b g Danehill Dancer(IRE) —Souk (IRE) (Ahonoora)
288[5]
Teutonic Knight (IRE) *Ian Williams*
4 ch c Daggers Drawn(USA) —Azyaa (Kris)
2597[3]
Teviot (CZE) *Jiri Janda* 134c
8 ch g Regulus(CZE) —Thessalonike (CZE) (Sharp End)
1811a[5]
Texas Holdem (IRE) *Michael Smith* 115h 82c
12 b g Topanoora—Lough N Uisce (IRE) (Boyne Valley)
2208[2] 2448[5] 3696[4] 4166[3] (4572) 5030[3] 5262[8]
5335[3]

Thackeray *Chris Fairhurst* 91b
4 b g Fasliyev(USA) —Chinon (IRE) (Entrepreneur)
2108^{2}
Thai Vango (IRE) *Nigel Twiston-Davies* 96h 116c
10 b g Religiously(USA) —Danesway (Be My Native (USA))
158^{P} (1612) 1814^{4} **2249^{5} 3695^{F}**
Thanks For Coming *Nicky Henderson* 119h
5 b g Helissio(FR) —Kyle Rhea (In The Wings)
(304) 3506^{3} ◆ 3987^{2} 4940^{10} 5425^{P}
Thank The Groom *Martin Bosley* 63h
5 b g Groom Dancer(USA) —Owtaar (IRE) (Royal Applause)
3773^{15} 4356^{14} 5115^{7}
Tharawaat (IRE) *Gordon Elliott* 140h 140c
6 b g Alhaarth(IRE) —Sevi's Choice (USA) (Sir Ivor (USA))
2413a^{2} 4794^{6} 5165^{4}
Tharaya *Claire Dyson* 117h
6 b m Choisir(AUS) —Karlaska (Lashkari)
(52) (423) 726^{2} 2282^{6} 2508^{8} (4874) 5420^{4}
That'Ll Do *Paul Nicholls* 130h
6 b g Beat All(USA) —Forever Shineing (Glint Of Gold)
(2000) ◆ 2634^{3} 3688^{13}
That'Ildoboy (FR) *Paul Nicholls* 109h
5 b g Turgeon(USA) —A Womans Heart (USA) (Star De Naskra (USA))
2283^{7} 3196^{11} 3296^{3} 4034^{4} 5110^{13} 5373^{3}
Thatildoforme *Alistair Whillans* 100h 106c
9 b g Dancing High—Bantel Bargain (Silly Prices)
2549^{F} 3502^{7}
That'Il Do Nicely (IRE) *Nicky Richards* 85h
8 b g Bahhare(USA) —Return Again (IRE) (Top Ville)
2509^{5}
That Look *Don Cantillon* 122h 91c
8 b g Compton Admiral—Mudflap (Slip Anchor)
526^{7}
That Man Fox *Tony Carroll* 49h 67c
10 b g Sovereign Water(FR) —Oh No Rosie (Vital Season)
1278^{8} 1429^{8} 1730^{9}
2113^{4}
That's All Right (IRE) *Kevin M Prendergast* 96h
8 b g Beneficial—Karnataka (IRE) (Lord Americo)
1499^{P} 1643^{P} 1832^{P}
That's For Sure *Debra Hamer* 73h
11 bb g Forzando—Sure Flyer (IRE) (Sure Blade (USA))
3870^{11}
That's Mine (IRE) *Jonjo O'Neill* 92h
5 ch g Kapgarde(FR) —Cherry Pie (FR) (Dolpour)
4499^{10} 4942^{3} 5321^{9}
That's Rhythm (FR) *Martin Todhunter* 123h 150c
11 b g Pistolet Bleu(IRE) —Madame Jean (FR) (Cricket Ball (USA))
98^{3} 844^{9} (1312)
1611^{10} 2091^{5} 2871^{9} 5200^{F} 5338^{12}
That's Some Milan (IRE) *Milton Harris* 85h
6 b g Milan—Ballinapierce Lady (IRE) (Glacial Storm (USA))
1466^{8} 1505^{5} 1705^{3}
That's The Deal (IRE) *John Cornwall* 84h 103c
7 bb g Turtle Island(IRE) —Sister Swing (Arctic Lord)
1627^{P} 1770^{6} 2037^{3} (2152)
Thatsthereasonwhy (IRE) *Ms Lucinda Broad* 87b
10 ch g Old Vic—Leafy Moss (Le Moss)
90^{P}
The Antagonist (IRE) *Rachel Hobbs* 102h
9 b g Anshan—Swarm Leader (IRE) (Supreme Leader)
5103^{P}
The Apprentice (IRE) *M J Vanstone* 121h 122c
9 b g Shernazar—Kate Farly (IRE) (Phardante (FR))
4534^{P}
The Artful Fox *Mike Sowersby* 98c
10 ch g Then Again—Dercanny (Derek H)
49^{P} 211^{6} 517^{3} (680)
1002^{5} 1081^{4} 3956^{P} 4412^{U} 4997^{4}
Theatre Dance (IRE) *David Arbuthnot* 115h 128c
10 b g King's Theatre(IRE) —Dance Alone (USA) (Monteverdi)
2581^{8}
2948^{5} 3687^{3} 3940^{7} 4328^{3} 5009^{F} 5423^{P}
Theatre Diva (IRE) *Miss J Du Plessis* 126h 123c
10 b m King's Theatre(IRE) —Rigobertha (IRE) (Nordico (USA))
149^{4} 4851^{U} (5237)
(5402)
Theatre Guide (IRE) *Colin Tizzard* 114b
4 b g King's Theatre(IRE) —Erintante (IRE) (Denel (FR))
4082^{4} ◆ (5113) ◆
Theatrical Moment (USA) *Jonjo O'Neill* 131h 146c
8 b g Royal Anthem(USA) —Given Moment (USA) (Diesis)
2343^{11} 3948^{8}
Theatrical Spirit *Robin Dickin*
6 b m Baryshnikov(AUS) —Dickies Girl (Saxon Farm)
833^{12} 1771^{11}
Theatrical Star *Colin Tizzard* 108b
5 b g King's Theatre(IRE) —Lucy Glitters (Ardross)
2389^{6} 3372^{3} 4468^{6}
Theballyedmondchap (IRE) *Evan Williams*
7 b g Tel Quel(FR) —Ten Past Ten (IRE) (Farhaan)
3586^{U} 3880^{U}
The Beat Is On *Tony Carroll* 53h
5 b m Beat All(USA) —Lady Ezzabella (Ezzoud (IRE))
2143^{11} 2556^{9}
The Betchworth Kid *Alan King* 143h
6 b g Tobougg(IRE) —Runelia (Runnett)
2671^{4} 3561^{13} 4188^{4} 4727^{11}
The Bishop Looney (IRE) *T J Nagle Jr* 134h 116c
7 b g Oscar(IRE) —Bright News (Buckskin (FR))
3475a^{3}

The Bishops Baby (IRE) *Richard Rowe* 112h
8 b m Bishop Of Cashel—Mystical Treat (IRE) (Be My Guest (USA))
1914^{3} 2289^{4} 2927^{2} 3348^{5} 3793^{2} (3868) 4120^{3} 4769^{3} 5189^{2}
The Boat (IRE) *Lawney Hill* 77h
9 b g Anshan—Sallowglen Gale (IRE) (Strong Gale)
632^{6} 930^{6}
The Boat Shed (IRE) *Brendan Duke* 74h
5 b g Barathea(IRE) —Silver Hut (USA) (Silver Hawk (USA))
557^{7} 955^{10}
The Bootle Blitz *Cecil Price* 48b
5 b g Fantastic Light(USA) —Khamsin (USA) (Mr Prospector (USA))
5238^{7}
The Boss (IRE) *Jeremy Scott* 109h 110c
6 ch g Accordion—Danjo's Lady (IRE) (Carlingford Castle)
2142^{4} 2454^{3} **3628^{4}** ◆ 3934^{3} 4446^{P} (4745)
The Boss Rock (IRE) *Jim Old* 68h
8 b g Shernazar—Lake Garden Park (Comedy Star (USA))
2328 2467^{11}
The Bravetraveller (IRE) *Barbara Butterworth* 5h 67c
8 b g Bravefoot—Morning Nurse (IRE) (Head For Heights)
4569^{7} 4993^{7} **5355^{3}**
The Brig At Ayr *John Weymes* 20h 74c
7 gr g Terimon—Rosie O'Keeffe (IRE) (Royal Fountain)
24^{U} 3883^{P}
4551^{P}
The Brimmer (IRE) *Seamus Mullins* 107h 107c
7 br g Luso—Office Antics (IRE) (Jolly Jake (NZ))
328^{6} 1484^{6} 1601^{3} 1737^{7} **1909^{3} 2053^{5}**
The Buddy Mole *Sean Curran*
10 b g Bonny Scot(IRE) —Gambling Linda (Park Row)
766^{5} 992^{P}
The Bull Hayes (IRE) *Mrs John Harrington* 134h
5 b g Sadler's Wells(USA) —No Review (USA) (Nodouble (USA))
4086a^{10}
The Burrow Vic (IRE) *D E Fitzgerald* 126h 116c
8 b g Old Vic—Any Old Music (IRE) (Montelimar (USA))
3206a^{16}
The Camerengo (IRE) *A R Corbett* 95c
11 ch g Glacial Storm(USA) —Lady Leona (Leander)
295^{2} 502^{P}
The Cayterers *Tony Carroll* 109h
9 b g Cayman Kai(IRE) —Silky Smooth (IRE) (Thatching)
2128^{7} (4672) 4992^{7}
The Chazer (IRE) *Richard Lee* 123h
6 gr g Witness Box(USA) —Saffron Holly (IRE) (Roselier (FR))
327^{4} 2499^{2} 3481^{3} ◆ 3897^{2} (4462) 5106^{8}
The Chisholm (IRE) *Adrian Wintle* 56b
9 b g Oscar(IRE) —Dipped In Silver (IRE) (Roselier (FR))
3528^{P}
Thecircleoftrust (FR) *Tom George* 111b
6 ch g Gold Away(IRE) —Dash (FR) (Sillery (USA))
(238)
The Client (IRE) *David Pearson* 38h 16c
10 b g Rakaposhi King—Woodram Delight (Idiots Delight)
1830^{P} 2641^{P}
The Clubhousebee (IRE) *Kevin Bishop* 111h
7 b m Jolly Jake(NZ) —Bemyhostess (IRE) (Bob Back (USA))
172^{6}
The Clyda Rover (IRE) *Helen Nelmes* 93h
7 ch g Moonax(IRE) —Pampered Molly (IRE) (Roselier (FR))
1675^{3} 2136^{5} 2482^{13} 3791^{5} 3934^{10} 5241^{P}
The Cockney Mackem (IRE) *Nigel Twiston-Davies* 112h
5 b g Milan—Divine Prospect (IRE) (Namaqualand (USA))
(1599) 3495^{2} 4006^{2} 4437^{3}
The Cockney Squire (IRE) *Lucinda Russell* 119h 119c
6 b g Bob Back(USA) —Mandalaw (IRE) (Mandalus)
1594^{5}
2207^{5} 2659^{3} 3257^{2} 3854^{3}
The Composer *Michael Blanshard* 85h 75c
9 b g Royal Applause—Superspring (Superlative)
132^{6} 2609^{3} 4272^{3} (4522) 5075^{3} (5433)
The Cool Guy (IRE) *Elliot Newman* 135h 133c
11 b g Zaffaran(USA) —Frostbite (Prince Tenderfoot (USA))
(151) **4011^{2}**
The Crafty Cuckoo (IRE) *Emma Lavelle*
6 b g Sadlers' Hall(IRE) —Curracloe Star (Over The River (FR))
3866^{P}
The Dagda (IRE) *Kevin Hunter* 56h
7 b g Turtle Island(IRE) —Stormweather Girl (IRE) (Strong Gale)
4569^{6} 4889^{8} 5260^{P}
The Dark Witch *Alan Blackmore* 67b
7 b m Tragic Role(USA) —Loch Scavaig (IRE) (The Parson)
2389 1812^{P} 2554^{P}
The Darling Boy *Tom George* 93h 107c
6 b g Medicean—Silver Top Hat (USA) (Silver Hawk (USA))
381^{8} (1744)
1841^{5} 2093^{2} 4033^{2} 4411^{5} 4775^{2} 5294^{P}
Thedeboftheyear *Chris Down* 118h
7 b m Sir Harry Lewis(USA) —Juste Belle (FR) (Mansonnien (FR))
1315 2218^{P} 4079^{6} 4481^{5} 4722^{5} 4955^{3}

The De Thaix (FR) *Robin Dickin* 51b
4 b g Polish Summer—Etoile De Thaix (FR) (Lute Antique (FR))
2309^{8} 3630^{8} 4331^{P}
The Duke's Speech (IRE) *Sophie Leech* 104h 125c
10 b g Saddlers' Hall(IRE) —Dannkalia (IRE) (Shernazar)
87^{2} **411^{6}**
735^{9} 985^{2} 1117^{4} 1738^{4} 2034^{4} 2484^{5}
The Dunion *R MacDonald* 76h
8 br g Beckett(IRE) —Dacian (USA) (Diesis)
286^{U}
The Ferbane Man (IRE) *Tim Vaughan* 113h 122c
7 b g Dr Massini(IRE) —Hi Up There (IRE) (Homo Sapien)
(22) **138^{2}**
(492) **605^{2}**
(951) **3347^{6}**
3764^{2} **4023^{4}**
4334^{2} 4543^{3} (5405)
The Fonze (IRE) *Eoin Doyle* 141h 157c
10 br g Desert Sun—Ultimate Beat (USA) (Go And Go)
1123a^{4}
The Fox's Decree *Martin Keighley* 100h
7 br g Diktat—Foxie Lady (Wolfhound (USA))
59^{8} 272^{2} 630^{2} 737^{2} 921^{7} 1449^{2} 1507^{6} 1730^{8} 2478^{3} 4540^{3} 5040^{3} 5308^{4}
The Galloping Shoe *Alistair Whillans* 105h
6 b g Observatory(USA) —My Way (IRE) (Marju (IRE))
3547^{10} 4165^{4} 4303^{P} 4912^{P}
The General Lee (IRE) *Phillip Rowley* 79h 109c
9 bb g Accordion—Catrionas Castle (IRE) (Orchestra)
526^{4} 4011^{4} (4442)
4973^{2}
The Giant Bolster *David Bridgwater* 148h 148c
6 b g Black Sam Bellamy(IRE) —Divisa (GER) (Lomitas)
(1923)
2348^{F} (3803) ◆ **4804^{U} 5183^{F}**
The Giggler (IRE) *Alan Swinbank* 79b
5 gr g Val Royal(FR) —Aneydia (IRE) (Kenmare (FR))
3525^{9} 4894^{9}
The Gloves Are Off (IRE) *Sue Smith* 119h 117c
8 b g Oscar(IRE) —Reapers Dream (IRE) (Electric)
45^{4} **401^{4}**
715^{8}
The Goldmeister (IRE) *Ian Williams* 94b
4 b g Craigsteel—M C A River (Tina's Pet)
5105^{5}
The Good Guy (IRE) *Graeme McPherson* 102h 103c
8 b g Lord Americo—Lady Farnham (IRE) (Farhaan)
331^{6} 715^{7} 994^{7} 1195^{3} 1347^{5} 1551^{2} (1677)
Thegreatjohnbrowne (IRE) *Noel Meade* 129h 148c
7 ch g Beneficial—Alltoplayfor (IRE) (Broken Hearted)
(2413a) ◆ **3174a^{4}**
The Great Outdoors (IRE) *Sarah Humphrey* 60h
7 b m Simply Great(FR) —Bobalena (IRE) (Bob Back (USA))
684^{5}
The Green Hat (IRE) *Theresa Gibson* 103h 95c
11 bb g Mister Lord(USA) —Dark Native (IRE) (Be My Native (USA))
211^{P} 625^{4} 730^{4} 804^{P} 2193^{3} 2449^{P} 3884^{4} 4133^{2}
4799^{7} 4963^{3}
5093^{3}
The Grey One (IRE) *Milton Bradley* 92h
8 gr g Dansili—Marie Dora (FR) (Kendor (FR))
182^{9} 356^{4} 590^{10} 793^{5} 1035^{8} 1095^{6} 1450^{3} 1489^{P}
The Grifter *John Ryall* 102h
9 b g Thowra(FR) —Spring Grass (Pardigras)
93^{4} ◆ 2136^{P} 2482^{9} 3449^{4}
The Gripper (IRE) *Rachel Hobbs* 102h
7 b g City Honours(USA) —Peacefull River (IRE) (Over The River (FR))
2469^{2} 3261^{3} (3529) 3771^{P}
The Gurner (IRE) *Charlie Longsdon*
4 b g Snurge—Celestial Queen (IRE) (Persian Mews)
4491^{8} 5225^{P}
The Hague *Tim Vaughan* 106h
5 b g Xaar—Cox Orange (USA) (Trempolino (USA))
3760^{10} (4397) 5099^{14}
The Hairy Mutt (IRE) *Lady Susan Brooke* 87h 80c
9 b g Presenting—Crash Approach (Crash Course)
738^{6} 797^{U} 1057^{3} 1275^{6} 1367^{0}
The Hardy Boy *Anna Newton-Smith* 20h 97c
11 br g Overbury(IRE) —Miss Nero (Crozier)
2134^{2} 2394^{3} 2949^{10}
3349^{3} 3608^{4} 3792^{4} 4400^{F} 4770^{2}
Thehillofuisneach (IRE) *Jonjo O'Neill* 106h
7 b g Flemensfirth(USA) —Miniconjou (IRE) (Be My Native (USA))
3930^{6} 4422^{4}
The Hollinwell *Ferdy Murphy* 120h 137c
8 b g Classic Cliche(IRE) —Action De Balle (FR) (Cricket Ball (USA))
2105^{4} 2674^{P} *(3168)* 3575^{P}
5104^{P}
The Hollow Bottom *Nigel Twiston-Davies* 89h 103c
10 b g Kadeed(IRE) —Leighten Lass (IRE) (Henbit (USA))
431^{P} 681^{4}
Thehonourablelady *John Flint* 103h
10 b m Prince Daniel(USA) —Sapling (Infantry)
55^{3} 220^{4} 530^{4} 796^{2} 920^{4} 1057^{4}
The Hon Tara *Charlie Longsdon* 96h
7 b m Kayf Tara—Marielou (FR) (Carwhite)
2130^{2} 2925^{12} 3718^{7}
The Hudnalls (IRE) *Jim Old* 100h
10 ch g Shernazar—Toposki (FR) (Top Ville)
2637^{5} (3369) 3589^{5}

The Humbel Monk (IRE) *Lucy Jones* 92c
9 b g Humbel(USA) —Miss Monks (IRE) (Phardante (FR))
3761^{F}
4007^{6} 4261^{3} 4438^{4} 4865^{4} 5109^{3} 5216^{P}
The Hurl (IRE) *M F Morris* 142h 142c
8 b g Supreme Leader—No Dunce (IRE) (Nordance (USA))
3210a^{F} 4109a^{5}
The Iron Giant (IRE) *Neil King* 53h 71c
9 b g Giant's Causeway(USA) —Shalimar (IRE) (Indian Ridge)
21^{P} **136^{3}**
437^{3} 649^{P} 5130^{11}
5349^{3}
The Jazz Musician (IRE) *Colin Tizzard* 92h 130c
9 b g Tiraaz(USA) —Royal Well (Royal Vulcan)
2163^{F}
The Jigsaw Man (IRE) *Rebecca Curtis* 146h 135c
7 ch g Bob Back(USA) —Native Sunset (IRE) (Be My Native (USA))
(316) **565^{2}**
(761) 830^{3} **(1197)** 1346^{9} (5440)
The Jolly Spoofer (IRE) *Diana Grissell* 82h 115c
9 b g Luso—Some News (IRE) (Be My Native (USA))
85^{P} 220^{P}
The Kealshore Kid (IRE) *George Moore* 97h 108c
7 gr g Saddlers' Hall(IRE) —Rongai (IRE) (Commanche Run)
177^{2} 460^{3} 848^{5}
The Knoxs (IRE) *Howard Johnson* 125h 145c
8 b g Close Conflict(USA) —Nicola Marie (IRE) (Cardinal Flower)
2350^{F} 3332^{F} (3995)
(4959)
The Languid One *Michael Quinlan* 57b
4 ch c Halling(USA) —Al Afreata (Bering)
2458^{8}
The Laodicean *Alan King* 109h
5 b g Midnight Legend—Sea Pearl (Derring Rose)
2123^{5} 3506^{4} 4051^{9} 4745^{4} 5132^{P}
The Last Derby (FR) *Eoin Griffin* 130h 141c
7 b g Anabaa(USA) —The Last Dream (FR) (Arazi (USA))
1123a^{8}
The Lemonpie (GER) *Milton Harris* 87h
6 b h Next Desert(IRE) —Terra Novalis (GER) (Astylos (GER))
1548^{9} 3563^{3}
The Listener (IRE) *Nick Mitchell* 132h 166c
12 gr g Roselier(FR) —Park Breeze (IRE) (Strong Gale)
3176a^{5} 4087a^{7}
Thelobstercatcher *Peter Bowen* 135h 107c
7 gr g Silver Patriarch(IRE) —Everything's Rosy (Ardross)
761^{F} 889^{2} 1177^{F} 1368^{4} 1501^{7} (2147) 2523^{9} 3440^{11} (3771) 4003^{7} (5325)
The Lollygagger (IRE) *Alex Hales* 93b
7 ch g Make No Mistake(IRE) —Mellon Lady (IRE) (Supreme Leader)
1201^{5}
The Magic Bishop *Malcolm Jefferson* 117h
6 b g Bishop Of Cashel—Magic Bloom (Full Of Hope)
14^{2} 174^{7} 1359^{3} ◆ 1556^{10} 2080^{6} (3500) (3989) 4235^{9} 5262^{3} 5431^{5}
Themanfromcork *Paul Nicholls* 56b
4 b g Overbury(IRE) —Country Choice (IRE) (Paean)
5387^{9}
The Masters Lesson *Keith Reveley* 45h 45c
8 ch g Minster Son—Japodene (Uncle Pokey)
840^{11}
The Merry Giant (IRE) *Rebecca Curtis* 64h
5 b g Curtain Time(IRE) —Laughing Lesa (IRE) (Bob Back (USA))
(412) 3439^{13} 4069^{6} 4332^{7} 4860^{8} 5253^{6}
The Midnight Club (IRE) *W P Mullins* 150h 156c
10 ch g Flemensfirth(USA) —Larry's Peach (Laurence O)
3798a^{2} (4298a) ◆ **5200^{6}**
The Mightie Quin *Terry Clement*
4 b c Reset(AUS) —Dance Light (IRE) (Lycius (USA))
2597^{9}
The Mighty Bard (IRE) *Tracey Watkins* 24h
8 b g Old Vic—Out Of Danger (IRE) (Darnay)
992^{P} 1063^{5} 1195^{P}
Themilanhorse (IRE) *Paul Nicholls* 114b
5 b g Milan—Sports Leader (IRE) (Supreme Leader)
3773^{4} (4533) 5113^{4}
The Minack (IRE) *Paul Nicholls* 146h 146c
7 b g King's Theatre(IRE) —Ebony Jane (Roselier (FR))
(3451)
(3770) 4199^{3} 5338^{P}
Themoonandsixpence (IRE) *W P Mullins* 135h 144c
8 ch g Presenting—Elphis (IRE) (Supreme Leader)
1123a^{2}
The Mouse Carroll (IRE) *Sean Curran* 68h
7 b g Barathea(IRE) —Grecian Glory (IRE) (Zafonic (USA))
1111^{10}
The Musical Guy (IRE) *Nigel Twiston-Davies* 91h
5 b g Lahib(USA) —Orchestral Sport (IRE) (Orchestra)
3877^{8} 4942^{5}
Thenameescapesme *Kim Bailey* 85h 114c
11 b g Alderbrook—Gaygo Lady (Gay Fandango (USA))
382^{4} **677^{P}**
(794) ◆ **868^{3} (1093)**
1276^{F}
Thenford Duke (IRE) *Ken Wingrove* 19h
11 b g Dr Massini(IRE) —Ring-Em-All (Decent Fellow)
934^{P}

The Nightingale (FR) *Paul Nicholls* 145h 160c
8 b g Cadoudal(FR) —Double Spring (FR) (Double Bed (FR))
(2227a)
3560[P]

The Old Buccaneer (IRE) *Jonjo O'Neill* 84h
8 b g Turtle Island(IRE) —Claycastle (IRE) (Carlingford Castle)
2954[13] 3344[8] 3601[4] 4052[P]

The Old Pretender (IRE) *Nigel Twiston-Davies* 103h
8 ch g Old Vic—Cluain-Ard (IRE) (Glacial Storm (USA))
2454[5]

Theologist (IRE) *Dr Richard Newland* 116h
5 b g Galileo(IRE) —Medina (IRE) (Pennekamp (USA))
(1571)

The Only Way *Chris Grant* 88h 69c
8 b m Yaheeb(USA) —Way Home (La Grange Music)
3520[11]

Theophrastus (IRE) *Nick Gifford* 120h 120c
9 b g Overbury(IRE) —Over The Glen (IRE) (Over The River (FR))
1964[3] 2285[F] 2670[7] 2984[9] 3347[P] 3615[4] 4219[P] (4669)
(4927) 5154[3]

The Package *David Pipe* 136h 151c
8 b g Kayf Tara—Ardent Bride (Ardross)
2221[5]

The Paddy Premium (IRE) *M A Molloy* 119h 107c
11 b g Glacial Storm(USA) —Miss Cripps (IRE) (Lafontaine (USA))
5015[2]

The Panama Kid (IRE) *Malcolm Jefferson* 104h 122c
7 b g Presenting—Mrs Jodi (Yaheeb (USA))
44[6] 3509[5]

The Pier (IRE) *Joseph G Murphy* 127h
5 ch g Alhaarth(IRE) —Cois Cuain (IRE) (Night Shift (USA))
4319a[7]

The Pious Prince (IRE) *David Pipe* 77h 49c
10 ch g Shahrastani(USA) —Ara Blend (IRE) (Persian Mews)
587[P]

The Portonion (IRE) *Malcolm Jefferson* 96h
7 br g Accordion—Mazza (Mazilier (USA))
1758[P] 2166[3] 3621[P]

The Pundit *Bill Turner* 1b
4 gr g Silver Patriarch(IRE) —Native Thatch (IRE) (Thatching)
2237[12]

The Quantum Kid *Robin Dickin* 98h
7 b g Desert Prince(IRE) —Al Hasnaa (Zafonic (USA))
3620[5] 4076[F] (4977)

The Rainbow Hunter *Andy Turnell* 117h 138c
7 b g Rainbow High—Sobranie (High Top)
1692[P] 1972[4] **(2236)**
2948[4] 3198[3] 3629[2] 4193[2] 4790[12] 5254[2]

The Randy Bishop *Tony Carroll* 91h 95c
11 b g Bishop Of Cashel—Fly South (Polar Falcon (USA))
75[4] 380[3] **437[4] 985[P]**

The Real Deal (IRE) *Nick Williams* 123h 112c
10 b g Taipan(IRE) —Forest Mist (Dalsaan)
372[9] 503[2] 830[P]

The Real Rupee (IRE) *Conor O'Dwyer* 89h 83c
8 b g Rudimentary(USA) —Parsee (IRE) (Persian Mews)
3700[2]

There And Then *Seamus Mullins* 106h
5 b g Where Or When(IRE) —Cugina (Distant Relative)
3434[4] 3836[8] 4930[6] (5327)

Theredballoon *Chris Bealby* 97h
5 ch g Sulamani(IRE) —Sovana (FR) (Kadounor (FR))
4287[4] 4810[4] 5296[3]

The Red Laird *Neil King* 101h
8 b g Kayf Tara—Sekhmet (Gunner B)
2929[3] (3260) 3698[4] 4391[4]

The Reformer (IRE) *Paul Nicholls* 128h
6 b g Pilsudski(IRE) —Tinogloria (FR) (Al Nasr (FR))
2216[2] (2791) 3556[3] 4725[14]

There's No Panic (IRE) *Paul Nicholls* 144h
6 ch g Presenting—Out Ranking (FR) (Le Glorieux)
(220) 530[2] (1026) (1228) 1853[3] 5304[2]

The Ridge *Michael Scudamore* 64b
7 ch g Tumbleweed Ridge—Race To The Rhythm (Deep Run)
222[11] 637[6] 1824[11] 1990[P]

The Rockies (IRE) *Evan Williams* 111b
4 b g Oscar(IRE) —Calling Classy (IRE) (Good Thyne (USA))
4527[2] ◆

The Rocking Dock (IRE) *Gordon Elliott* 128h 128c
10 gr g Dr Massini(IRE) —Ackle Backle (Furry Glen)
(444)

The Rustlin Rhino *Donald McCain* 89h
6 b g Overbury(IRE) —All Gone (Giolla Mear)
1760[4] 2103[5] **2645[P]** 3703[P]

The Saucy Snipe *Daniel O'Brien* 75h
5 b m Josr Algarhoud(IRE) —The Dark Eider (Superlative)
217[4]

The Sawyer (BEL) *Bob Buckler* 127h 152c
11 b g Fleetwood(IRE) —Green Land (BEL) (Hero's Honor (USA))
2138[5] 2359[13] 3677[6] 3804[4] 4200[2] 4486[6] 4790[8]
5367a[R]

Thescottishsoldier *Alistair Whillans* 82h
4 ch g Observatory(USA) —Twenty Seven (IRE) (Efisio)
4056[6] 4240[4] 4473[5] 5144[10]

The Sheepdipper *Lucy Normile* 72h
7 b g Weldnaas(USA) —Good Job (King's Ride)
305[5] 520[8] 875[P]

The Shepherd (IRE) *Gordon Elliott* 143h
7 b g Dilshaan—Silly Imp (IRE) (Imperial Frontier (USA))
1118[5] 3475a[11]

The Shepherd King (IRE) *Thomas Cooper* 136h
7 b g Marignan(USA) —Boolavogue (IRE) (Torus)
2967a[4]

The Shoe (NZ) *Nicky Henderson* 119h 128c
9 b g Montjeu(IRE) —Madiya (IRE) (Natroun (FR))
(1068)
1365[2] 1774[5] 5341[2]

The Shy Man (IRE) *George Moore* 123h 123c
8 b g Grand Plaisir(IRE) —Black Betty (Furry Glen)
(1986) 2523[6] 3566[8] 4209[12] 4742[7] 5003[14] 5149[12] 5431[7]

The Skanky Farmer *Sandy Thomson*
11 b g Royal Fountain—Cornkitty (Oats)
2202[P] **4685[P]**

The Sliotar (IRE) *Philip Hobbs* 131h 134c
10 ch g Presenting—Annie's Alkali (Strong Gale)
3290[P] 4093[P]

The Snail *Evan Williams* 117h 130c
8 b g Namaqualand(USA) —Moonshine Malt (Superlative)
2234[5] 3558[RR] 4010[8] 4440[5] 5081[P] 5236[6] 5399[2]

The Snatcher (IRE) *Richard Phillips* 82h
8 b g Indian Danehill(IRE) —Saninka (IRE) (Doyoun)
3601[0] 2122[11] 2419[5] 2927[8] 4125[5]

The Starboard Bow *Lucinda Russell* 119h
4 b g Observatory(USA) —Overboard (IRE) (Rainbow Quest (USA))
(2655) ◆ 3358[6] 3967[2] 4807[10]

The Stickler *Mrs Elaine Smith* 91c
12 ch g Weld—Bivadell (Bivouac)
551[6]

The Strawberry One *David Arbuthnot* 91h
6 ch m Kadastrof(FR) —Peppermint Plod (Kinglet)
(27) *3055[7]* 4917[F] 5280[2]

The Tailor Carey (IRE) *Mrs C M Gorman* 68c
12 b g Kadeed(IRE) —Secret Tryst (IRE) (Roi Danzig (USA))
294[4]

Thetasteofparadise *Bruce Hellier* 4b
4 b f Act One—Rose Bounty (Polar Falcon (USA))
4005[8] 5033[9]

The Tatkin (IRE) *David Pipe* 89h
6 b m Tikkanon(USA) —Miss Bobby Bennett (Kings Lake (USA))
4097[12] 5152[4]

The Thirsty Bricky (IRE) *John Daniel Moore* 111h 100c
9 b g Saddlers' Hall(IRE) —Splendid Choice (IRE) (The Parson)
1645[6]

The Tiddly Tadpole *Simon West* 101h
6 b g Tipsy Creek(USA) —Froglet (Shaamit (IRE))
1764[12] 1989[9] 2553[11] 3749[6] ◆ 4393[7] 4506[5] 4977[2] 5307[2]

The Tother One (IRE) *Paul Nicholls* 149h 163c
10 b g Accordion—Baden (IRE) (Furry Glen)
2091[2] 2673[4] 3805[4] 5200[F]

The Tracey Shuffle *David Pipe* 118b
5 br g Kapgarde(FR) —Gaspaisie (FR) (Beyssac (FR))
3054[8] (3971) (4363) 4808[10]

Thetwincamdrift (IRE) *Alan King* 100h 123c
9 b g Humbel(USA) —Air Hostess (IRE) (Supreme Leader)
2629[4] ◆

The Venetian (IRE) *Miss G G Haywood* 82h 80c
10 b g Presenting—Dashing March (Daring March)
152[7] 4708[P]

The Vicar (IRE) *Henrietta Knight* 125h 125c
8 b g Bob Back(USA) —Moon Storm (IRE) (Strong Gale)
2305[P] 2629[5] 2984[6] 3821[P]

The Viking *Mrs Sarah L Dent* 75c
12 ch g Primitive Rising(USA) —Duright (Dubassoff (USA))
4553[U]

The Walnut Tree (IRE) *Simon Lewis* 76h 84c
10 b g Mister Lord(USA) —Janet's Girl (IRE) (Mandalus)
1745[P]
1858[P] 1991[9] 2170[P] 2240[P] 2559[4] 2608[6] 3369[6]
3699[4]

The Wayward Lord *Michael Easterby* 96b
6 b g Emperor Fountain—Last House (Vital Season)
1153[2]

The Wee Midget *Arthur Whiting* 93h
6 b g Mtoto—Fragrant Rose (Alflora (IRE))
355[8] 792[U] 1028[P] 1158[10] 1228[4] 1446[4] 1559[5] (1735) 1911[13] 5075[5] (5393)

Thewellmeadow (IRE) *Paul Henderson* 82b
6 b g Oscar(IRE) —Portphelia (Torus)
2186[7] 2445[3]

The Whisperer (IRE) *Nicky Richards* 79h 121c
10 b g Supreme Leader—Ring Mam (IRE) (King's Ride)
193[P] 4869[8]

The White Admiral (IRE) *Nicky Henderson* 102h
6 wh g Revoque(IRE) —Stage Debut (Decent Fellow)
3288[14] 4198[7] 4459[4] ◆

The Wifes Pet (IRE) *Lawney Hill* 120h 116c
7 gr m Environment Friend—Badsworth Rose (IRE) (Roselier (FR))
1364[6]
1731[4] 2278[3] 2978[4]

The Wonder Land (FR) *J-P Perruchot*
7 b m Lord Of Men—Tel Reema (FR) (Tel Quel (FR))
5159a[0]

The Wonga Coup (IRE) *Pat Phelan* 36h
4 b g Northern Afleet(USA) —Quichesterbahn (USA) (Broad Brush (USA))
4478[9]

Thewritinonthewall *N F Glynn* 108h 91c
6 b g Red Ransom(USA) —Mystify (Batshoof)
564[4]

Thievery *Henry Daly* 76h 97c
10 gr g Terimon—Piracy (Jupiter Island)
48[U] 1940[6] 2334[U] 2559[F] 3532[4] 4721[5]

Thingathong (FR) *Donald McCain* 74h
4 b f Trempolino(USA) —Fontaine Guerard (FR) (Homme De Loi (IRE))
4552[5] 5074[8]

Think *Clive Mulhall* 82b
4 ch g Sulamani(IRE) —Natalie Jay (Ballacashtal (CAN))
3957[7] 4396[6]

Think Green *James Ewart* 76h
5 b m Montjeu(IRE) —Hasty Words (IRE) (Polish Patriot (USA))
3553[5] 3971[3] 4151[4] 4554[4] 5309[4]

Think Lucky *Mrs N Naughton* 93h 98c
8 br g Zafonic(USA) —Hyde Hall (Barathea (IRE))
354[3] 628[4] 4476[7]

Think On This (IRE) *Mrs C M Budd* 107c
8 b g Aboo Hom—Can't Think What (Saher)
4928[5]

Third Intention (IRE) *Colin Tizzard* 140h
4 b g Azamour(IRE) —Third Dimension (FR) (Suave Dancer (USA))
(2958) ◆ 3802[2] 4205[2] 4847[7] (5300)

Thirty Days Out (IRE) *Donald Whillans* 95b
6 b m Beneficial—Executive Move (IRE) (Executive Perk)
4171[4] 5033[2] 5432[3]

Thirtytwo Red (IRE) *R J Alford* 106c
10 b g Revoque(IRE) —Trouville Lass (IRE) (Be My Native (USA))
173[3] 4415[3] 4928[11] 5156[P]

This Masquerade *Warren Greatrex* 105h
8 b g Parthian Springs—Rose Rambler (Scallywag)
2512[9] *3057[5]* 3403[4]

Thistle *George Baker* 98h 74c
10 ch g Selkirk(USA) —Ardisia (USA) (Affirmed (USA))
865[10] 1062[5] 1107[4]

Thistlecraft (IRE) *Miss Laura Morgan* 114h 110c
12 b g Warcraft(USA) —Thistletopper (Le Bavard (FR))
139[2] 335[2] 580[4]

This Way (IRE) *John Ryall* 92h 98c
9 b g Exit To Nowhere(USA) —Hawthorn's Way (IRE) (Regular Guy)
3230[F] 3482[P] 4896[6] 5173[4]

Thomas Bell (IRE) *John O'Shea* 52h
7 b g Moscow Society(USA) —Cottage Girl (IRE) (Actinium (FR))
362[7] (869) 1086[9] 1572[2] 2145[11] 3761[10] 4100[12]

Thomas Crapper *Robin Dickin* 87b
4 b g Tamure(IRE) —Mollycarrs Gambul (General Gambul)
4382[4] 4957[2]

Thomas O'Malley (FR) *Robert Collet*
4 b g Turgeon(USA) —Pretty Kate (FR) (Pistolet Bleu (IRE))
1658a[P]

Thomas Wild *Philip Hobbs* 105h
6 ch g Muhtarram(USA) —Bisque (Inchinor)
2373 3930[4] 4719[6] 5108[2] 5439[4]

Thompson *Richard Phillips* 93h
7 br g Averti(IRE) —Sewards Folly (Rudimentary (USA))
157[4] 630[P] 4130[6] 4976[4]

Thoresby (IRE) *Ben Case* 103h
5 b g Milan—I Remember It Well (IRE) (Don't Forget Me)
2374 2456[5] 2873[3] 3403[7] 4859[6] 5234[3]

Thorney Rose (IRE) *Robin Dickin* 45h
7 ch m Jamesmead—Di's Wag (Scallywag)
4437[12] 5078[7]

Thornton Alice *Richard Phillips* 91h
6 b m Kayf Tara—Lindrick Lady (IRE) (Broken Hearted)
609[2] 2616[4] 3365[9] 3637[2] (4134)

Thorpey's Girl (IRE) *Alison Thorpe* 39h
6 b m Hernando(FR) —Pearl Shell (USA) (Bering)
568[5] 754[10] 858[P] 988[6]

Thousand Stars (FR) *W P Mullins* 165h
7 gr g Grey Risk(FR) —Livaniana (FR) (Saint Estephe (FR))
3205a[4] 3707a[3] 4791[4] 5198[2]

Three Boars *Claire Dyson* 88h
9 ch g Most Welcome—Precious Poppy (Polish Precedent (USA))
1494[P] 1735[4] 2114[10]

Three Chords (IRE) *Caroline Bailey* 77h 133c
7 b g Winged Love(IRE) —Crystal Chord (IRE) (Accordion)
1765[4]
2641[2] 2959[5] ◆ **(3391)**
(3832) 4181[4] 5206[3]

Three Ships *Richard Lee* 115h
10 ch g Dr Fong(USA) —River Lullaby (USA) (Riverman (USA))
159[7] 515[8] 698[3] 845[2] 865[2] 933[3] (1067) (1107) 1370[F] 1766[5] 2035[5] 5400[5]

Thumbprint (IRE) *Chris Down* 59h
9 b g Aahsaylad—Tinerana Girl (IRE) (Executive Perk)
2678 **1109[P]**
1738[U]

Thumbs Up *Donald McCain* 130h 125c
6 gr g Intikhab(USA) —Exclusive Approval (USA) (With Approval (CAN))
(518) **3722[2]**
4168[4] 4406[3] 5079[2]

Thunder Child *Simon Burrough* 46h 100c
11 gr g Cloudings(IRE) —Double Dutch (Nicholas Bill)
173[P] 3700[3] 4093[5] (4784)
(5069) (5275) ◆

Thunder Hawk (IRE) *Mrs L A Coltherd* 115c
11 b g Saddlers' Hall(IRE) —Final Peace (IRE) (Satco (FR))
317[4] (580)
1002[P] 1103[3] 1341[P] 1376[4] 4147[3] 4915[4] (5263)

Thundering Home *Michael Attwater* 78h
4 gr g Storming Home—Citrine Spirit (IRE) (Soviet Star (USA))
1135[P] 4024[4]

Thunderstorm (IRE) *Philip Hobbs* 92h
6 b g Milan—Elizabeth Tudor (IRE) (Supreme Leader)
3478[7] 3645[5] ◆ 3760[9] 4310[4]

Thurnham *Keith Reveley* 96b
5 b g Tobougg(IRE) —Nobratinetta (FR) (Celtic Swing)
399[4] 2355[13] 2660[3] 3553[3]

Thyne For Deploy (IRE) *Michael Hourigan* 122h
7 ch g Deploy—What Thyne (IRE) (Good Thyne (USA))
(8) (92) 1391[5]

Thyne Spirit (IRE) *Simon Lewis* 66h 73c
12 ch g Good Thyne(USA) —Friston (IRE) (Roselier (FR))
429[4] 556[4] 797[5] 1061[3] 1126[P] 1281[5] 1733[P] 1969[5]

Thynetocatcher (IRE) *Roger McGrath* 110b
5 b m Catcher In The Rye(IRE) —Randal Island (IRE) (Good Thyne (USA))
5188[9]

Tiagra *Paul Webber* 84b
4 b g Tiger Hill(IRE) —Shifting Mist (Night Shift (USA))
3909[10] 4484[4]

Tibetan Dragon (IRE) *Evan Williams* 108h
7 b g In The Wings—Private River (USA) (Private Account (USA))
1608[P] 1937[5]

Tickateal *Alan Lockwood* 59h 117c
11 ch g Emperor Fountain—Mary Hand (IRE) (Hollow Hand)
31[6]

Ticket To Ride (FR) *I J Hooper* 69h 69c
13 ch g Pistolet Bleu(IRE) —Have A Drink (FR) (Hasty Tudor (USA))
557[9] 1745[9] **4950[P]**

Tickle Me (IRE) *Henrietta Knight* 59h
5 ch g Definite Article—Coming Home (FR) (Exit To Nowhere (USA))
3372[5] 4055[10] 5106[13]

Tidal Bay (IRE) *Howard Johnson* 164h 170c
10 b g Flemensfirth(USA) —June's Bride (IRE) (Le Moss)
2090[3]
2524[3] 3005[3] 4850[6] 5200[U]

Tieptiep (FR) *Paul Nicholls* 36b
4 b g Ungaro(GER) —Unetiepy (FR) (Marasali)
3794[8]

Tiermore (IRE) *Sirrell Griffiths* 107h
7 br g Bob's Return(IRE) —Billmar (Kambalda)
(1449) 1553[8] 1844[9] 2241[10]

Tifernati *Gary Moore* 53h
7 b g Dansili—Pain Perdu (IRE) (Waajib)
3611[P]

Tiffany Jones *John Spearing* 77h
8 b m Kayf Tara—Juleit Jones (IRE) (Phardante (FR))
1922[8] 2469[P]

Tifoso (FR) *Richard Guest* 103h 103c
6 ch g Priolo(USA) —Tifosa (USA) (Hickman Creek (USA))
382[6] 888[P] 1254[7]
1628[4] 1781[2] 2450[3] 3617[7] (Dead)

Tiger Bay (IRE) *Noel Chance* 66h
7 b g Goldmark(USA) —Roussanne (IRE) (Satco (FR))
2666[9] 3344[12] 3542[8]

Tiger Breeze (USA) *Bob Buckler* 95h
5 b g Roar Of The Tiger(USA) —M. S. Gripsholm (USA) (Goldwater (USA))
2137[P] 2499[14] 3224[4] 3477[8] 4785[4]

Tiger Dream *Chris Down* 101h
6 b g Oasis Dream—Grey Way (USA) (Cozzene (USA))
328[8] 1996[5] 2452[11] 4450[9] 4540[10] 4947[2] 5114[10] 5272[F]

Tiger Hawk (USA) *David Evans* 6h
4 b g Tale Of The Cat(USA) —Aura Of Glory (CAN) (Halo (USA))
851[7]

Tiger King (GER) *P Monteith* 89h 82c
10 b g Tiger Hill(IRE) —Tennessee Girl (GER) (Big Shuffle (USA))
948[3] 1342[4] **1502[P]** 1695[9]
1872[6] 2194[P] 2302[P]

Tiger Line *Richard Phillips* 94h
7 b m Kayf Tara—Run Tiger (IRE) (Commanche Run)
2149[11] 2609[2] 2929[P] 3635[6] 5169[P] 5374[2]

Tiger O'Toole (IRE) *Evan Williams* 137h 98c
6 gr g King's Theatre(IRE) —Memsahib Ofesteem (Neltino)
(479) ◆ (521) 1017[6] 1133a[9] 3447[5] ◆ (3676) 4806[20]

Tiger Run (IRE) *John Queally* 92h 91c
8 b g Luso—Run Cat (IRE) (Lord Americo)
1177[3]

Tigers Charm *Milton Bradley*
4 b g Tiger Hill(IRE) —Amazing Dream (IRE) (Thatching)
1545[P]

Tiger's Jacey (IRE) *V J Hughes* 77b
4 b f Milan—Shes Elite (IRE) (Supreme Leader)
5174[10]

Tigh Bhruadair (IRE) *Evan Williams* 100h
7 br g Presenting—Mullaghcloga (IRE) (Glacial Storm (USA))
1031[3]
1256[F] 1493[P] 1551[11]

Tighe Caster *Graeme McPherson* 105h 114c
12 b g Makbul—Miss Fire (Gunner B)
330[4] 824[P] 1726[9] 1937[3] 2530[4]

Tignello (IRE) *Emma Baker* 114h
6 b g Kendor(FR) —La Genereuse (Generous (IRE))
182[F] 590[4] (1280) 1453[2] 1548[6] 1723[3] 2021[3] 2128[9] 5235[3]

Tigre D'Aron (FR) *Howard Johnson* 118h
4 gr g Dom Alco(FR) —Fleche Noir II (FR) (Quart De Vin (FR))
(3711) 4569^{4}

Tijuana Dancer (IRE) *A J Martin* 126h
7 b g Desert Prince(IRE) —Osirixa (FR) (Linamix (FR))
3474a^{13}

Tikkandemickey (IRE) *Raymond Shiels* 80b
5 br g Tikkanen(USA) —Miss Vikki (IRE) (Needle Gun (IRE))
5313^{6}

Tikram *Gary Moore* 128h 104c
14 ch g Lycius(USA) —Black Fighter (USA) (Secretariat (USA))
149^{5} 466^{3}

Tilabay (IRE) *S Buggy* 139h
6 b g Sadler's Wells(USA) —Tilimsana (IRE) (Darshaan)
1133a^{11}

Tild'Or Du Granit (FR) *James Evans* 65h
4 b f Polish Summer—Ile D'Or (FR) (Lute Antique (FR))
2173^{6} *2824^{10}* 3767^{10} 4006^{10} 4417^{5} 5016^{P}

Tillahow (IRE) *M F Morris* 124h
4 b g Tillerman—Ale' Ale' (USA) (Storm Cat (USA))
4083a^{7} 4847^{18}

Tillietudlem (FR) *Jim Goldie* 116h
5 gr g Kutub(IRE) —Queenhood (FR) (Linamix (FR))
2205^{P}

Tilly Shilling (IRE) *Kevin Bishop* 87h 69c
7 b m Montjeu(IRE) —Antiguan Jane (Shirley Heights)
276^{6} 590^{5}
652^{5} 755^{11}

Tilt *Brian Ellison* 127h
9 b g Daylami(IRE) —Tromond (Lomond (USA))
1019^{11} 1150^{0}

Timber Treasure (USA) *Paul Green*
7 bb g Forest Wildcat(USA) —Lady Ilsley (USA) (Trempolino (USA))
3917^{P}

Time Book (IRE) *Gary Moore* 95h
5 b g Galileo(IRE) —Pocket Book (IRE) (Reference Point)
3376^{4} 3645^{12}

Time Do (FR) *Caroline Keevil* 78b
4 ch g Grand Tresor(FR) —Demoiselle Do (FR) (Le Pontet (FR))
3794^{4} 4879^{8}

Timeforagin *Brian Eckley* 70b
4 b f Pasternak—Little Time (Arctic Lord)
5005^{4} 5306^{P}

Time For Rupert (IRE) *Paul Webber* 168h 163c
7 ch g Flemensfirth(USA) —Bell Walks Run (IRE) (Commanche Run)
(2348) ◆ (2883) ◆ 4804^{5}

Time For Spring (IRE) *Charlie Longsdon* 131h
7 b g Snurge—Burksie (IRE) (Supreme Leader)
2059^{2} (2512) 3346^{F} 3877^{7} (4700)

Time Legend *Martin Keighley* 70b
5 b m Midnight Legend—Time To Get Up (Puget (USA))
27^{8} 412^{9} 766^{P}

Time'Ll Tell *Fiona Kehoe*
6 b g Best Of The Bests(IRE) —Pearl Venture (Salse (USA))
631^{P}

Time Machine (UAE) *Robert Alan Hennessy* 122h
5 ch g Halling(USA) —Tempting Fate (IRE) (Persian Bold)
(1594)

Time Out (IRE) *James Ewart* 110h 112c
8 b g Alhaarth(IRE) —Waif (Groom Dancer (USA))
2450^{5} ◆ 2938^{2}

Timesawastin (IRE) *Evan Williams* 118h
5 b g Curtain Time(IRE) —Innocent Approach (IRE) (Dry Dock)
2056^{3} ◆ 3398^{3} (4404)

Time Square (FR) *Tony Carroll*
4 b g Westerner—Sainte Parfaite (FR) (Septieme Ciel (USA))
2958^{15}

Timetoring *Bernard Llewellyn* 108h
9 ch g Karinga Bay—Little Time (Arctic Lord)
2147^{8} 3256^{F} 3589^{11} 3934^{2} 4532^{4} 5322^{3}

Time To Think *Seamus Mullins* 94h
6 b m Alflora(IRE) —Shuil Do (IRE) (Be My Native (USA))
2329^{6} (3338) 4032^{P} 4535^{6} 5212^{6}

Tim Henry (IRE) *Patrick Rodford* 106h
8 b g Sonus(IRE) —Emesions Lady (IRE) (Bigstone (IRE))
266^{8}

Timoca (IRE) *Evan Williams* 93h
6 br m Marju(IRE) —Tara Gold (IRE) (Royal Academy (USA))
50^{3} 182^{5} 600^{P} 793^{4} 1035^{6} 1453^{3} 1844^{10}

Timocracy *Andrew Haynes* 100h
6 br g Cape Cross(IRE) —Tithcar (Cadeaux Genereux)
1453^{4}

Timpo (FR) *Henry Daly* 97h 102c
8 ch g Baby Turk—Faensa (FR) (Fabulous Dancer (USA))
55^{7} 651^{3} 1726^{6}
2079^{2} 2585^{2} 3741^{2} 4292^{2} 4953^{P}

Tim The Chair (IRE) *Emma Lavelle* 97h 118c
6 b g Pierre—Dinah B (IRE) (Yashgan)
2981^{6} 3340^{6} 3528^{6}
(4412)

Tinabianca (FR) *Seamus Mullins* 64h
5 b m Sleeping Car(FR) —Tinarctica (FR) (Arctic Tern (USA))
3616^{5} 5052^{3}

Tinagenic (FR) *Seamus Mullins* 84b
5 b m Sleeping Car(FR) —Cometina (FR) (Arctic Tern (USA))
3623^{9} 5070^{5}

Tinalliat (FR) *David Rees* 45h
8 b m Robin Des Champs(FR) —Cometina (FR) (Arctic Tern (USA))
16^{7} **283^{P}**
758^{8} 3792^{P} 4522^{P}

Tin Pot Man (IRE) *Evan Williams* 109h
5 br g Tillerman—White-Wash (Final Straw)
(754) 1776^{8} 2235^{2} 3370^{P} 3764^{7} 4407^{8}

Tinseltown *Brian Rothwell* 94h
5 b g Sadler's Wells(USA) —Peony (Lion Cavern (USA))
2939^{6} 3715^{8} 3887^{3} 4138^{3}

Tippering (IRE) *Sue Smith* 103h
6 b g Flemensfirth(USA) —Tart Of Tipp (IRE) (Saddlers' Hall (IRE))
355^{7} 2349^{6} 3489^{6} 3718^{5} 3989^{8} 4712^{U}

Tipsy Dara (IRE) *Sue Bradburne* 62h
7 gr m Dushyantor(USA) —Tara The Grey (IRE) (Supreme Leader)
5259^{5}

Tipsy Indian *Sue Smith* 95h
8 ch g Commanche Run—Dubelle (Dubassoff (USA))
179^{0}

Tipsy Nipper *William Amos*
6 b m And Beyond(IRE) —Homo Dorney (IRE) (Homo Sapien)
4000^{P} 4889^{U} 5260^{P}

Tiptoeaway (IRE) *Tim Easterby* 109h
6 b g Insan(USA) —My Blackbird (IRE) (Mandalus)
2102^{10} 2473^{3} 3725^{3} 4233^{2} (4545) 5424^{P}

Tiptronic (FR) *Reginald Brown* 107h
4 ch g Officiel(FR) —Canlastou (FR) (Tanlas (FR))
(2466)

Tiradia (FR) *Michael Easterby* 97b
4 bb g Without Connexion(IRE) —Jimanji (FR) (Kadalko (FR))
4815^{2} 5210^{6}

Tirol Livit (IRE) *John Wainwright* 16h
8 ch g Titus Livius(FR) —Orange Royale (IRE) (Exit To Nowhere (USA))
405^{10} 603^{5}

Tisfreetdream (IRE) *Peter Pritchard* 121h 123c
10 b g Oscar(IRE) —Gayley Gale (IRE) (Strong Gale)
(226) **738^{P}**
2324^{P} 2497^{P} 2955^{P} 3771^{9} 4079^{5}
4313^{8} 4777^{5} 5292^{P}

Titan De Sarti (FR) *Nicky Henderson* 113h
4 bb g Kapgarde(FR) —Copie Des Planches (FR) (Pot D'Or (FR))
2356^{5} 2958^{2} 3624^{2} 4807^{16}

Titch Strider (IRE) *John Panvert* 89b
6 b m Milan—Just Little (Mtoto)
4709^{5} 5070^{8}

Tito Bustillo (FR) *Paul Nicholls* 135h
6 b g Kahyasi—Litani Queen (Emperor Jones (USA))
2219^{2} 3649^{3} 4727^{19} 5201^{13}

Tiumen (POL) *Josef Vana II* 143c
10 b g Beaconsfield—Toskanella (POL) (Demon Club (POL))
(1811a)

To Arms *Lawney Hill* 132h 135c
9 b g Mujahid(USA) —Toffee (Midyan (USA))
196^{7} (954) 1019^{2} **(1177) ◆ (1389)**

Tobago Bay *Gary Moore* 129h 67c
6 b g Tobougg(IRE) —Perfect Dream (Emperor Jones (USA))
94^{2} 633^{12} **838^{7}** 2977^{11} 3229^{8} 3557^{11} (4485) 4940^{5} 5441^{5}

Tobayornottobay *Bruce Hellier* 70b
5 b m Tobougg(IRE) —Rose Bay (Shareef Dancer (USA))
2167^{14} 2660^{5}

Tobetall *Malcolm Jefferson* 81b
4 b f Tobougg(IRE) —Our Ethel (Be My Chief (USA))
3576^{5} 4554^{10} 5034^{7}

Tobizzy *Linda Blackford*
5 ch m Tobougg(IRE) —Isabella D'Este (IRE) (Irish River (FR))
754^{F} 821^{U}

Tobougg Welcome (IRE) *Miss Rose Grissell* 77h
7 ch g Tobougg(IRE) —Three White Sox (Most Welcome)
294^{P}

Toby Belch (IRE) *Henry Daly* 125h
8 ch g Presenting—Peptic Lady (IRE) (Royal Fountain)
302^{3}

Toby Jug *Sarah Humphrey* 115h 148c
10 b g Sovereign Water(FR) —Country Choice (IRE) (Paean)
4876^{P} 5286^{F} 5423^{7}

Toby Mac *Lee James* 50h
9 b g Presidium—Ski Path (Celtic Cone)
4274^{4}

Tocatchaprince (IRE) *Milton Harris* 76h
5 b g Catcher In The Rye(IRE) —Queen For A Day (Emperor Jones (USA))
238^{5} 1705^{9} 1899^{7} 1974^{6} (2433) 2583^{2} ◆ *3055^{6}*
3350^{P}

Tocca Ferro (FR) *Emma Lavelle* 146h
6 gr g April Night(FR) —La Pelode (FR) (Dress Parade)
(2085) ◆ (2671) ◆

Todareistodo *Jim Old* 80h
5 gr g Fair Mix(IRE) —Its Meant To Be (Gunner B)
2576^{4} 4881^{7} 5106^{11}

Tofta Tilly *Lee James* 82h
11 ch m Muhtarram(USA) —Budding Prospect (Rudimentary (USA))
801^{P}

Togiak (IRE) *David Pipe* 67h
4 b g Azamour(IRE) —Hawksbill Special (IRE) (Taufan (USA))
3526^{5} 3767^{8}

Toi Express (IRE) *Susan Gardner* 43h 101c
15 ch g Phardante(FR) —Toi Figures (Deep Run)
185^{9}

Toledo Gold (IRE) *Maurice Barnes* 99h
5 ch g Needwood Blade—Eman's Joy (Lion Cavern (USA))
4059^{3} 4303^{7} 5356^{4}

Tom Bach (IRE) *Richard Price* 95c
7 ch g Bach(IRE) —Fiovefontaine (IRE) (Lafontaine (USA))
2238^{9}
4720^{4} 5001^{4} 5240^{P}

Tombov (FR) *James Ewart* 61h
5 bb g Laveron—Zamsara (FR) (Zino)
210^{P}

Tomillielou *Miss H L Phizacklea* 89h 51c
10 gr g I'm Supposin(IRE) —Belle Rose (IRE) (Roselier (FR))
335^{5}

Tommy Gun *Maurice Barnes* 64b
5 b g Rainbow High—On The Bay (Carlton (GER))
2296^{P} 4473^{11} 5091^{P}

Tom O'Tara *Robin Dickin* 110h
7 b g Kayf Tara—Mrs May (Carlingford Castle)
252^{12} 1938^{3} ◆ 2150^{3} 2452^{2} 2983^{5} 3490^{7} 4291^{2} 4672^{3} 5080^{6}

Tom's Toybox *Chris Grant* 70h 134c
9 b g Classic Cliche(IRE) —Jobiska (Dunbeath (USA))
5151^{6}

Tom Wade (IRE) *John Harris* 99h
4 b g Rakti—Plutonia (Sadler's Wells (USA))
1728^{U} 1935^{2} 2882^{6} 3563^{4} 4419^{3} 4807^{12}

Tomzatackman (IRE) *Raymond Shiels* 69h
6 b g Saddlers' Hall(IRE) —Zafilly (Zafonic (USA))
1599^{4} 2202^{P} 2552^{14}

Ton-Chee *Arthur Whitehead* 98h 41c
12 b g Vettori(IRE) —Najariya (Northfields (USA))
338^{5} (490) 595^{2} 765^{3} 933^{8} 4956^{5} 5282^{5}

Toner D'Oudairies (FR) *Gordon Elliott* 122h
4 b g Polish Summer—Iroise D'Oudairies (FR) (Passing Sale (FR))
(2966a) ◆ 3239a^{4} 4083a^{6}

Toni Alcala *Neil King* 30h 39c
12 b g Ezzoud(IRE) —Etourdie (USA) (Arctic Tern (USA))
4021^{13} 4812^{P} **5268^{P}**

Tonic Mellysse (FR) *Paul Nicholls* 128h
4 b g Smadoun(FR) —Mellyssa (FR) (Panoramic)
4350^{4} (5314)

Tony Dinozzo (FR) *Nicky Henderson* 92b
4 b g Lavirco(GER) —Arika (FR) (Le Riverain (FR))
5063^{2} ◆

Tony Star (FR) *Philip Hobbs* 108h
4 b g Lone Bid(FR) —Effet De Star (FR) (Grand Tresor (FR))
(3401) ◆ 5010^{3}

Too Cool To Fool (IRE) *Jim Goldie* 96h 79c
8 b g Bob Back(USA) —Mandysway (IRE) (Mandalus)
287^{5} (3336) (3502)

Tooka *Anthony Middleton* 108h 101c
10 b g Sure Blade(USA) —Parsons Lass (IRE) (The Parson)
(5058)

Tooman Lane (IRE) *Patrick Holmes* 115h 115c
7 b g Close Conflict(USA) —Treasure Forecast (IRE) (Treasure Hunter)
3617^{P} 4135^{P} 4392^{4} 5145^{5}

Toomuchinformation *Anna Newton-Smith* 93h
7 b m Sonus(IRE) —Sight'n Sound (Chief Singer)
1679^{7} 2183^{8} *3060^{P}*

Toomyvara (IRE) *Nick Gifford* 68b
7 b g Midhish—Kilannadrum (IRE) (Tremblant)
60^{4} 3266^{P} 4370^{P}

Tooney Malooney *Neil Mulholland* 40h
6 gr m Silver Patriarch(IRE) —Sulapuff (Sula Bula)
333^{9} 2137^{14}

Too Tall *Tim Vaughan* 48h
5 b h Medicean—Embark (Soviet Star (USA))
174^{8}

Tootsie Too *Mike Hammond* 50h
9 b m Overbury(IRE) —Tap On Tootsie (Faustus (USA))
1294^{F}

Top Achiever (IRE) *Bill Moore* 86h
10 ch g Intikhab(USA) —Nancy Maloney (IRE) (Persian Bold)
541^{7} 5114^{6} 5171^{5}

Topalena (IRE) *Michael Banks* 41h
8 b g Even Top(IRE) —Soralena (IRE) (Persian Bold)
2109^{10}

Top Benefit (IRE) *Keith Goldsworthy* 112h 111c
9 gr g Beneficial—Cottage Lass (IRE) (Roselier (FR))
2571^{2} 3197^{P} 3585^{2}
3907^{5} 4030^{3} 4408^{4}

Top Bob (IRE) *Tracey Barfoot-Saunt* 15h
6 b m Bob Back(USA) —Top Ar Aghaidh (IRE) (Topanoora)
2472^{8} *2896^{10}* 4309^{9}

Top Brass (IRE) *James H Black* 98h
10 ch g Night Shift(USA) —Opus One (Slip Anchor)
4688^{2} 5094^{9}

Top Dawn (IRE) *Matt Sheppard* 67h 92c
11 b g Topanoora—Andros Dawn (IRE) (Buckskin (FR))
4693^{5}

Top Dressing (IRE) *Howard Johnson* 91h 122c
10 br g Rashar(USA) —Ross Gale (Strong Gale)
(46) **308^{4}**
1598^{5} 1871^{9} 2940^{6} 3552^{5} 4137^{2} 4571^{6}

Topenhall (IRE) *Ben Case* 113h 85c
10 b g Topanoora—Jrred Up (IRE) (Jurado (USA))
829^{7} 1062^{2} 1147^{2} ◆ (1328) 1470^{6} 1614^{3} 1972^{3} 5392^{3}

Topflight Wildbird *Alan King* 107h 91c
8 br m Diktat—Jamarj (Tyrnavos)
430^{2} 706^{U} 796^{P} 2329^{3} 2558^{11}

Top It All *Rose Dobbin* 98h 107c
8 b g Beat All(USA) —Forever Shineing (Glint Of Gold)
1762^{P} 1959^{5} **2203^{3} (2550)**
2940^{4} 3361^{2}

Topless (IRE) *Neil Mulholland* 99h 111c
10 gr m Presenting—Tara The Grey (IRE) (Supreme Leader)
85^{5} 2024^{2} 2573^{2} 2796^{2} 2982^{2} 3431^{2} 3982^{4} 4558^{2}

Top Mark *Alan King* 69h 91c
9 b g Mark Of Esteem(IRE) —Red White And Blue (Zafonic (USA))
2626^{10} 3557^{16} **4324^{8}**

Topofdemornintou (IRE) *Mrs C Cuff* 38h 110c
9 ch g Mister Lord(USA) —Templebredin (IRE) (Muharib (USA))
4271^{8}

Top Of The Rock (IRE) *Mrs John Harrington* 87h 141c
8 ch g Beneficial—One Last Cut (IRE) (Roselier (FR))
3706a^{6}

Topolski (IRE) *David Arbuthnot* 149h
5 b g Peintre Celebre(USA) —Witching Hour (IRE) (Alzao (USA))
(4195) (4895) (5182)

Topping The Bill *Michael Wigham* 77h
8 ch g Singspiel(IRE) —Ayunli (Chief Singer)
1149^{P} 1250^{7} 1433^{10} 1553^{14}

Top Ram (IRE) *Chris Gordon* 109h
11 ch g Topanoora—Aries Girl (Valiyar)
220^{U}

Top Rose *Robin Dickin* 85b
5 b m Sleeping Car(FR) —Quark Top (FR) (Perrault)
3876^{9} 5217^{11}

Topsham Belle (IRE) *Nicky Henderson* 117h 117c
7 b m Presenting—Ara Blend (IRE) (Persian Mews)
2959^{13} (3496)
4023^{U} 5382^{3}

Top Smart *Seamus Mullins* 118h
5 b g Karinga Bay—Clover Dove (Overbury (IRE))
1899^{4} 2129^{4} ◆ 2440^{2} (3985) (5271) 5424^{3}

Topthorn *Martin Bosley* 29h
5 gr g Silver Patriarch(IRE) —Miss Traxdata (Absalom)
2087^{11} 2518^{8} 3546^{10} 5225^{11}

Top Tide (IRE) *Martin Hill* 90h
10 br g Topanoora—Strong Tide (Strong Gale)
1028^{F} 1343^{8} 1445^{4} 1571^{5} 1737^{P}
5109^{U}

Tora Bora (GER) *Brendan Powell* 95h 74c
9 bb g Winged Love(IRE) —Tower Bridge (GER) (Big Shuffle (USA))
3170^{9} 3621^{2}
4292^{4} 4525^{4}

Tora Petcha (IRE) *Barry Leavy* 102h 95c
8 b g Bahhare(USA) —Magdalene (FR) (College Chapel)
252^{11} 537^{2} 696^{3} 865^{3} 984^{7}
1283^{5} 1481^{7} 1555^{P}

Toreador (FR) *Nigel Twiston-Davies* 75b
4 b g Epalo(GER) —Etoile D'Or II (FR) (Lute Antique (FR))
4410^{5}

Tornade Precieuse (FR) *Mme M Desvaux*
4 b f Network(GER) —Kerfournoise (FR) (Funny Baby (FR))
5047a^{2}

Tornado Bob (IRE) *Donald McCain* 143h
6 bb g Bob Back(USA) —Double Glazed (IRE) (Glacial Storm (USA))
2666^{2} ◆ (3253) ◆ (3718) 4198^{2} ◆ 4803^{P}

Tornedo Shay (IRE) *T J O'Mara* 129h
6 ch g Dr Fong(USA) —Pattimech (USA) (Nureyev (USA))
3846a^{3} 4249a^{6}

Torphichen *E J O'Grady* 145h 145c
6 ch g Alhaarth(IRE) —Genoa (Zafonic (USA))
3241a^{3}

Torran Sound *James Eustace* 91h
4 b g Tobougg(IRE) —Velvet Waters (Unfuwain (USA))
(836) 1018^{4} 4314^{4} 4929^{7}

Torta Nel Cielo *James Ewart* 103h
7 gr g Bertolini(USA) —Royal Keel (Long Leave)
(2552) 3362^{P}

Tory Hill Lad (IRE) *Mrs Hannah Lee* 113h 113c
12 b g Good Thyne(USA) —Lochda (Crash Course)
1113a^{2}

Toshi (USA) *Jim Goldie* 121h
9 b g Kingmambo(USA) —Majestic Role (FR) (Theatrical)
2551^{7} 3334^{10} 3969^{P} 5315^{7}

Toss The Caber (IRE) *Stephen Clark* 103h
9 ch g Dr Devious(IRE) —Celtic Fling (Lion Cavern (USA))
1147^{10} 1261^{6}

Total Effects (IRE) *Anabel L M King* 39b
7 b g Alderbrook—Bounty (IRE) (Cataldi)
739^{13}

Total Excitement (IRE) *Thomas Cooper* 137h 95c
9 b g Michelozzo(USA) —Oak Court (IRE) (Bustineto)
5201^{4}

Totally Beat *Ian Williams* 72h
6 b g Beat All(USA) —Aonia (Mummy's Pet)
1819^{5} 2314^{P}

Total Submission *Martin Keighley* 121h
6 gr g Kayf Tara—Ardentinny (Ardross)
(93) 1853^{5} 2388^{4} 2870^{9} 3288^{8} 4393^{3} 4861^{2} 5289^{7}

Tot Of The Knar *Peter Bowen* 136h 123c
9 b m Kayf Tara—Maggie Marne (Relkino)
330^{5} 626^{2} 735^{4}

Totoman *Tim Vaughan* 115h
6 b g Mtoto—Norcroft Lady (Mujtahid (USA))
607^{3} 768^{F} (1046) 1138^{6} 1392^{4} 1505^{F} 1660^{8}

Tot O'Whiskey *Malcolm Jefferson* 111h 140c
10 b g Saddlers' Hall(IRE) —Whatagale (Strong Gale)
2249^{6} 5261^{P}

Toubab (FR) *Paul Nicholls* 138h
5 gr g Martaline—Tabachines (FR) (Art Francais (USA))
207^{4} (2519) 3445^{3} 4353^{4}

Toubeera *Michael Smith* 111b
5 b m Tobougg(IRE) —Efizia (Efisio)
(4171) 4728[12] (5135) 5342[2]

Touch Of Flame *K J Cumings* 91c
12 b g Terimon—Flame O'Frensi (Tudor Flame)
4708[P]

Touch Of Spring *Alan Swinbank* 64b
4 ch g Pursuit Of Love—Blossom (Warning)
2108[10]

Tou Fou (FR) *G Macaire* 61h
4 b g Le Fou(IRE) —La Du Maine (FR) (Sleeping Car (FR))
1658a[4]

Tough Cookie (IRE) *Michael Gates* 86b
8 b g Rashar(USA) —Vam Cas (IRE) (Carlingford Castle)
847[P]

Toujours Souriante *Tracy Waggott* 71h
5 b m Lucky Story(USA) —Tous Les Jours (USA) (Dayjur (USA))
12[7] 176[8] 459[6]

Toulaman (GER) *Gary Moore* 100h
6 b g Black Sam Bellamy(IRE) —Theresina (IRE) (Vision (USA))
4930[4]

Toulouse Express (IRE) *Robert Johnson* 71h 107c
12 b g Toulon—Miss Ivy (IRE) (Le Bavard (FR))
352[7] 746[6] 804[7] 1697[8] 2298[5] 2601[4] 2937[11] 3502[11] **3695[10] 4135[U]** 4279[3] 4509[6] 4827[P] 5097[3] 5311[2]

Tour D'Argent (FR) *Nicky Henderson* 111b
4 b g Martaline—Keep Well (FR) (Agent Bleu (FR))
(3630) 4356[2] 5202[16]

Tout Ou Rien (FR) *M Rolland* 84h
4 b g Poliglote—Necessaire (FR) (Garde Royale)
1658a[3]

Tout Regulier *Peter Bowen* 120h
7 b m Beat All(USA) —Winnow (Oats)
(275) 488[4] (888) (958) (1030) 1296[2] 1346[P] 1466[3] 5335[13]

Touz Master (FR) *Nick Kent* 85h
7 ch g Wagon Master(FR) —Tressa (FR) (Assert)
4951[6] 5352[7]

Tovaria *Edward P Harty* 96h
7 b m Muhtarram(USA) —Budoor (IRE) (Darshaan)
2196a[10]

Tower *Chris Grant* 78h
4 b g Nayef(USA) —Palatial (Green Desert (USA))
5027[5] 5352[4]

Towmater *Charlie Longsdon* 53h
7 b g Overbury(IRE) —Bit Of A Chick (Henbit (USA))
82[P]

Toxic Asset *John Flint* 71b
6 b g Hernando(FR) —Language Of Love (Rock City)
60[3] 759[12]

Trachonitis (IRE) *J R Jenkins* 78h
7 b g Dansili—Hasina (IRE) (King's Theatre (IRE))
1688[7]

Track Star (IRE) *Luke Dace* 57h
6 b g Sadler's Wells(USA) —Angelica Tree (CAN) (Time For A Change (USA))
589[9] 759[9] 1743[8] 2594[P] 4478[8]

Tracy Road (FR) *Carroll Gray* 28h
7 br m Grape Tree Road—Lady Tracy (FR) (Perrault)
1736[13] 2288[P] 2586[8]

Trade Off (IRE) *Miss L Alner* 93h 78c
13 br g Roselier(FR) —Lady Owenette (IRE) (Salluceva)
184[4]

Trade On *Alan King* 76h
4 b g Trade Fair—Mystic Beauty (IRE) (Alzao (USA))
2315[5] 4097[6] 4860[7] 5327[10]

Trading Nation (USA) *Peter Hiatt*
5 b g Tiznow(USA) —Nidd (USA) (Known Fact (USA))
1238[P]

Traditional Bob (IRE) *Graeme McPherson* 99b
6 b g Saddlers' Hall(IRE) —Portia's Delight (IRE) (The Parson)
362[2] ◆ 3909[B] 4376[5] 5105[7]

Trafalgar Man (IRE) *Micky Hammond* 91h 105c
10 bb g Scribano—Call Over (Callernish)
177[P]

Traffic Article (IRE) *Gordon Elliott* 120h
7 b g Definite Article—Climbing Rose (USA) (Quest For Fame)
1573[3] 2347[F]

Traffic Chaos (IRE) *Charlie Mann* 105h
6 b g Zagreb(USA) —Classic Material (Classic Cliche (IRE))
3340[7] 3698[8] 4489[7] (4974)

Trafford Lad *Laurence James Butler* 146h 156c
9 b g Tragic Role(USA) —Another Shuil (IRE) (Duky)
2226a[P] 2970a[6] 3778a[6] 4087a[6]

Train Spotter (IRE) *John Wade*
6 ch g Anshan—Lotschberg Express (Rymer)
1359[P] 1499[6]

Tramantano *Nigel Twiston-Davies* 121h 144c
12 b g Muhtarram(USA) —Hatta Breeze (Night Shift (USA))
194[8] 1987[3] 2674[10] 2881[5] 5206[9]

Tram Express (FR) *Shaun Lycett* 87h
7 ch g Trempolino(USA) —Molly Dance (FR) (Groom Dancer (USA))
632[P] 827[5] 932[7] 1035[9] 1272[10]

Tramp Stamp (IRE) *Matthieu Palussiere* 133h 125c
7 b m King's Theatre(IRE) —Return Again (IRE) (Top Ville)
3268a[3]

Tranos (USA) *Micky Hammond* 97h 99c
8 b g Bahri(USA) —Balancoire (USA) (Diesis)
290[P] 1403[2] 1646[3] 1872[4] 2093[6] 2352[U] 2656[4] (5312)

Tranquil River (IRE) *John Upson*
6 b g Heron Island(IRE) —Halycon Day (IRE) (Satco (FR))
3936[8] 4951[P]

Tranquil Sea (IRE) *E J O'Grady* 146h 163c
9 b g Sea Raven(IRE) —Silver Valley (IRE) (Henbit (USA))
(2339a)
(2970a) ◆ **5184[7]**

Transact (IRE) *Martin Todhunter* 81h
6 ch g Trans Island—Khrisma (Kris)
209[11] 1647[P] 2271[6] 3363[7] (3631) 3993[4] 4136[2] 4302[P]

Transfered (IRE) *Lucinda Featherstone*
5 b m Trans Island—Second Omen (Rainbow Quest (USA))
478[P]

Transinski (IRE) *Alastair Lidderdale* 63b
5 b g Trans Island—Spinsky (USA) (Spinning World (USA))
284[6] 637[12]

Transparency *Sue Smith* 21h
6 b g Josr Algarhoud(IRE) —Scene (IRE) (Scenic)
2102[14]

Trans Sonic *David O'Meara* 88h
8 ch g Trans Island—Sankaty Light (USA) (Summer Squall (USA))
2398[4]

Transvestite (IRE) *Tor Sturgis* 100h 64c
9 b g Trans Island—Christoph's Girl (Efisio)
381[4] 650[U]

Treason Trial *Andrew Crook* 97h
10 b g Peintre Celebre(USA) —Pampabella (IRE) (High Estate)
1149[3] 1325[2] 1401[3] 1573[7] 2188[3] 3951[10] 5295[F]

Treasure's Girl *Michael Chapman*
6 b m Weet-A-Minute(IRE) —Trecento (Precious Metal)
1153[P]

Treasury Counsel (IRE) *Evan Williams* 102h 69c
9 br g Leading Counsel(USA) —Dunacarney (Random Shot)
955[2] 1336[P] 1551[8] 1798[P]

Treaty Flyer (IRE) *Alison Thorpe* 136h 134c
10 ch m Anshan—Highways Daughter (IRE) (Phardante (FR))
(440) **857[F]**

Treeko (IRE) *Philip Kirby* 97h 77c
6 b g Alhaarth(IRE) —Allegheny River (USA) (Lear Fan (USA))
835[2] 953[P] 1253[6]

Trempari *Mike Murphy* 71h
8 ch g Trempolino(USA) —Ariadne (GER) (Kings Lake (USA))
1990[0]

Trenchant *Alan King* 153h
6 b g Medicean—Tromond (Lomond (USA))
4373[2] 4806[13]

Trepalo (FR) *Alison Batchelor* 25h
4 b g Epalo(GER) —Bebenefertiti (FR) (Le Nain Jaune (FR))
4810[13] 5381[5]

Tresor De L'Isle (FR) *Anna Bramall* 15b
4 br g Dark Moondancer—Ad Vitam Eternam (FR) (Cap Martin (FR))
4574[10]

Trevis *Peter Bull* 71b
4 ch g Tobougg(IRE) —La Piazza (IRE) (Polish Patriot (USA))
3964[5] 4484[9] 5012[13]

Trew Style *David Rees* 74h
9 ch g Desert King(IRE) —Southern Psychic (USA) (Alwasmi (USA))
129[9] 298[F] 563[6]

Triagoz (FR) *F Belmont*
4 ch g Ragmar(FR) —Falkland III (FR) (Video Rock (FR))
1658a[6]

Tribal Dance (IRE) *Ben Case* 93h
5 br g Flemensfirth(USA) —Native Sparkle (IRE) (Be My Native (USA))
1510[4] 1729[5] 4422[5] 4974[6] 5343[4]

Tribal Rule *Evan Williams* 73h
5 gr g Daylami(IRE) —Native Justice (USA) (Alleged (USA))
439[5]

Tribe *Paul Webber* 128h 100c
9 b g Danehill(USA) —Leo Girl (USA) (Seattle Slew (USA))
193[9] **854[5]**
1109[3]

Tribes And Banner (IRE) *C F Swan* 128h 124c
7 br g Bob's Return(IRE) —Kaysdante (IRE) (Phardante (FR))
1131a[F]

Tribunel *Nigel Hawke* 82h
7 b g Diktat—Ring Of Love (Magic Ring (IRE))
410[10] **761[P]**
909[P]

Tricksofthetrade (IRE) *Alan Swinbank* 108b
5 b g Mull Of Kintyre(USA) —Soden (IRE) (Mujadil (USA))
(4117) 4717[4] 5264[3]

Tricky Tangler (IRE) *Mrs E Mitchell*
9 bb g Clerkenwell(USA) —Missile Lady (Paddy's Stream)
152[P]

Tricky Tree (IRE) *Pam Sly* 121h
5 b g Montjeu(IRE) —Ruissec (USA) (Woodman (USA))
25[4] 1953[4] 2375[3] 3693[5] (4025) 4332[2] 4725[11]

Tricky Trickster (IRE) *Paul Nicholls* 125h 147c
8 b g Oscar(IRE) —Pavlova (IRE) (Montelimar (USA))
2358[P] 4189[5]
4876[F]

Trifollet *Mrs J A Martin (Oxfordshire)* 63b 92c
6 b m Kirkwall—St Doughla'S (IRE) (Phardante (FR))
5347[2]

Triggerman *Philip Hobbs* 135h 146c
9 b g Double Trigger(IRE) —Carrikins (Buckskin (FR))
1602[2] 1739[2] 2057[3] 2221[11] (2945)
3479[F] 3687[F] 3940[3] 4876[R] (5303)
5443[4]

Triggernometry *Colin Tizzard* 96h 117c
10 b g Double Trigger(IRE) —Dubacilla (Dubassoff (USA))
(38) **501[6]**
691[P] 863[4] 986[8] 1490[P]
1738[9]

Trigger The Light *Alan King* 115h 119c
10 ch g Double Trigger(IRE) —Lamper's Light (Idiots Delight)
3629[5] ◆

Tri Nations (UAE) *Milton Harris* 111h
6 ch g Halling(USA) —Six Nations (USA) (Danzig (USA))
537[3] 696[2] 917[2] 984[2] 1249[5] 1375[2] (1506) 2054[5] 4452[3] 4776[3] 4854[5] 5376[U]

Triple Bluff *Miss J Du Plessis* 104h 97c
8 b g Medicean—Trinity Reef (Bustino)
264[6] 374[8] **5372[P] 5402[4]**

Triptico (FR) *Ronald O'Leary* 114b
5 gr g Turgeon(USA) —Al Kicks (FR) (Al Nasr (FR))
(3889)

Triton *Michael Easterby* 34h
8 ch g Observatory(USA) —Questionable (Rainbow Quest (USA))
1149[7]

Tritonville Lodge (IRE) *Emma Lavelle* 127h 122c
9 b g Grand Lodge(USA) —Olean (Sadler's Wells (USA))
170[P] 633[8] 830[5]
1091[2] 1276[2] 1725[P]

Trojan Sun *Nicky Henderson* 92b
5 b g Kayf Tara—Sun Dante (IRE) (Phardante (FR))
5063[6]

Troodos Jet *Dianne Sayer* 65h 85c
10 b g Atraf—Costa Verde (King Of Spain)
99[3] 404[2] 578[5] 747[2] 1001[F] 1047[6] (1358)
1646[5] 2301[P] 2942[9] 3618[5] 3997[5] 4510[5] 4813[3] 4963[2]

Trooper Clarence *Evan Williams* 100h 112c
7 b g Trempolino(USA) —Ten To Six (Night Shift (USA))
2236[4] 3154[4] 4290[4] ◆ **(4482)**
5036[2]

Troopingthecolour *Steve Gollings* 45h
5 b g Nayef(USA) —Hyperspectra (Rainbow Quest (USA))
5131[10]

Trop Fort (FR) *David Pipe* 112h
4 b g Bernebeau(FR) —Violeta (FR) (Rhapsodien)
4029[F] 4847[20]

Tropical Bachelor (IRE) *Tim Pitt* 96h 68c
5 b g Bachelor Duke(USA) —Tropical Coral (IRE) (Pennekamp (USA))
950[6]

Trotters Bottom *Edward Bevan* 60h
10 b g Mind Games—Fleeting Affair (Hotfoot I)
2149[14] 2467[5]

Trouble Digger *Kim Bailey* 47h
6 ch g Double Trigger(IRE) —Inesdela (Wolver Hollow)
2137[13]

Troubletimestwo (FR) *Tony Carroll* 114h
5 gr g Linamix(FR) —Time Of Trouble (FR) (Warning)
1775[6] 2213[F] 2977[14] 3490[5] 3874[12] 4524[F] 5080[2]

Troys Run (IRE) *Bill Moore* 75h
8 gr g Cloudings(IRE) —Troja (Troy)
2364[P] 2644[6] 3530[P] 4949[4]

Troys Steps *Sandy Forster* 72h
7 b m Cloudings(IRE) —Troys Guest (IRE) (Be My Guest (USA))
527[4] 875[9]

Troy Tempest (IRE) *Emma Lavelle* 105h 117c
6 b g Old Vic—Quinnsboro Native (IRE) (Be My Native (USA))
2512[6] 3448[6] 4370[7]
4966[3] (5384)

Trozulon (FR) *Nicky Henderson* 110b
4 b g Roli Abi(FR) —Manza (FR) (Bobinski)
3294[3] ◆

Truckers Storm (IRE) *A J Kennedy*
8 ch m Flemensfirth(USA) —Parsons Storm (IRE) (Glacial Storm (USA))
547[P]

Trucking Along (IRE) *S R B Crawford* 125h
5 br g Zagreb(USA) —Pegus Gold (Strong Gale)
2553[3] 4117[8] 4303[4] (4711)

True Blue Saga (IRE) *Tim Vaughan* 90h
6 b g Anabaa Blue—Saiga (FR) (Baryshnikov (AUS))
3256[P] 3497[6] 4178[8]

True Character (IRE) *Mrs John Harrington* 104b
5 b g Catcher In The Rye(IRE) —Harvest Gold (IRE) (Goldmark (USA))
3208a[9]

True Grit (NZ) *Lucinda Russell* 120h 82c
7 br g Istidaad(USA) —Damask (NZ) (Kohaylan (USA))
2171[P]

True To Form (IRE) *George Baker* 74h
4 b g Rock Of Gibraltar(IRE) —Truly Yours (IRE) (Barathea (IRE))
3767[7]

Truly Magic *Liam Corcoran* 27h
4 ch f Traditionally(USA) —Truly Bewitched (USA) (Affirmed (USA))
3967[P] 5280[9]

Trump Call (IRE) *Venetia Williams* 85h
7 b g Mull Of Kintyre(USA) —Trumped (IRE) (Last Tycoon)
2128[10] 2485[7] 2795[3]

Trumpstoo (USA) *Richard Fahey* 115h
5 b g Perfect Soul(IRE) —Cozzy Love (USA) (Cozzene (USA))
1017[F] 1282[2] 1406[4] 1597[4] 1931[P] 4858[5] 5429[7]

Trustan Times (IRE) *Tim Easterby* 130h
5 b g Heron Island(IRE) —Ballytrustan Maid (IRE) (Orchestra)
(3572) 3952[2]

Truxton King (IRE) *Paul Nicholls* 119h
6 gr g Clodovil(IRE) —Robinia (USA) (Roberto (USA))
1311[P]

Try Cat *Philip Hobbs* 99h
5 b m Mark Of Esteem(IRE) —French Spice (Cadeaux Genereux)
1600[2] 1724[7] 1921[6] 2329[10] 2633[4] 3155[3] 3224[3]

Tsarinova *Alan King* 101h
6 b m Alflora(IRE) —Dawn Spinner (Arctic Lord)
230[5] 2974[7] 3904[5] 4309[4] 4955[4]

Tuanku (IRE) *Alan King* 119h
6 b g Tagula(IRE) —Be My Lover (Pursuit Of Love)
2498[3] 3228[7] 3686[10]

Tuckers Treasure *Sue Smith* 57h
5 b g Trans Island—Shafaq (USA) (Dayjur (USA))
1201[10] 1426[7] 1664[10] 2092[15] 2398[6]

Tucumcari (IRE) *Brendan Powell* 90h 98c
6 b g Subtle Power(IRE) —Bright Day (IRE) (Phardante (FR))
337[5] 559[2] **828[4] 1081[3] 1281[2]** ◆

Tudor Beat *Ron Barr*
5 br m Beat All(USA) —Help Yourself (IRE) (Roselier (FR))
4554[13]

Tuilan *Peter Bowen* 59b
5 b m Milan—Tui (Tina's Pet)
4117[9]

Tula Tots *Caroline Keevil* 72b
5 ch m Pasternak—Royal Czarina (Czaravich (USA))
5408[6]

Tullamore Dew (IRE) *Nick Gifford* 139h 146c
9 ch g Pistolet Bleu(IRE) —Heather Point (Pollerton)
1967[9]
(2392) 2926[2] (3345)
3600[2] 4794[3]

Tully Hill *Kevin Hunter* 79c
10 b g Garde Royale—Bull Finch Aulmes (FR) (Rose Laurel)
88[P] (730)
804[P]

Tullyraine (IRE) *Nigel Twiston-Davies* 133h
7 b g Winged Love(IRE) —Struell Princess (Avocat)
319[12] (1742) 1990[2] 3197[5] 4159[6] (5203)

Tuppenny Piece *Alan King* 90h
5 ch m Sakhee(USA) —Tuppenny (Salse (USA))
50[9] 535[3] 908[4] 2131[P]

Turbo Du Ranch (FR) *Warren Greatrex* 107b
4 gr g Useful(FR) —Zoumba Du Ranch (FR) (Smadoun (FR))
(5012) ◆

Turbolinas (FR) *Kate Walton* 90b
4 b g Malinas(GER) —L'Orchidee (FR) (Gunboat Diplomacy (FR))
(3998) 4916[10]

Turbo Shandy *Dai Burchell* 94h 106c
8 b g Piccolo—Carn Maire (Northern Prospect (USA))
515[6] **578[3]**
755[4] (891)
1070[3] 1229[3] 1299[3] 4504[U] 4723[U] 5101[6] 5390[3]

Turbulance (IRE) *Jason Parfitt* 114h 107c
9 gr g Snurge—Full Deck (IRE) (Roselier (FR))
588[3] 769[P] 4141[P]

Turf Legends (IRE) *Philip Hobbs* 63h
5 b g Carroll House—Dunany Star (IRE) (Salluceva)
2087[7] 2791[14] 3478[10] 3906[13] 5172[P]

Turf Trivia *George Moore* 94h
4 gr g Alhaarth(IRE) —Exclusive Approval (USA) (With Approval (CAN))
(1422) (1696) 2078[10] 3570[F] 3994[9] 4998[7]

Turkish Sultan (IRE) *Milton Bradley* 81h
8 b g Anabaa(USA) —Odalisque (IRE) (Machiavellian (USA))
537[5] 593[6] 1450[6] 1549[6]

Turko (FR) *Mrs L Borradaile* 139h 140c
9 gr g Turgeon(USA) —Cambaria (FR) (Nice Havrais (USA))
4141[2] 4701[U] (4991)
5163[F]

Turner Brown (IRE) *Michael O'Hare* 135h
7 ch g Lahib(USA) —Inzamaam (IRE) (Zaffaran (USA))
607[4] 2347[F]

Turn Up (IRE) *Matt Sheppard* 91c
8 b g Saddlers' Hall(IRE) —Highland Chain (Furry Glen)
1710[F] 1924[2] 2053[3] 2468[F] 2605[3]

Turnworth (IRE) *R H & Mrs S Alner* 95c
8 b g Sunshine Street(USA) —Fourroads-Native (IRE) (Be My Native (USA))
132[P]

Turthen (FR) *C St V Fox* 115h 140c
10 ch g Turgeon(USA) —Majathen (FR) (Carmarthen (FR))
184[2] 525[4] (3908)
4141[4] 4851[8]

Turtle Gale (IRE) *P C O'Connor* 76h 114c
8 b g Turtle Island(IRE) —Cappagale (IRE) (Strong Gale)
2119a[7]

Turtlethomas (IRE) *Lawney Hill* 122h
5 br g Turtle Island(IRE) —Makingyourmindup (IRE) (Good Thyne (USA))
3546[7] (4767)

Tusa Eire (IRE) *W P Mullins* 116b
5 b g Turtle Island(IRE) —Neeto (IRE) (Over The River (FR))
4808[15]

Tuscany Star (IRE) *Edward Creighton* 112h 89c
8 ch g Fourstars Allstar(USA) —Merendas Sister (Pauper)
64[6] **429[2]**
556[P] 824[P] 918[6] 1080[8]

Tuskar Rock (FR) *Venetia Williams* 111h 112c
8 gr g Turgeon(USA) —Shannondore (FR) (Nashamaa)
2928[8] 3450[5] 3768[4] (3982)
4219[4] (4483)

Tutchec (FR) *James Ewart* 28b
4 gr g Turgeon(USA) —Pocahontas (FR) (Nikos)
5034[9]

Twelfth Of Never (IRE) *Miss Elizabeth Doyle* 113h 113c
8 b m Dushyantor(USA) —Native Chorus (IRE) (Be My Native (USA))
3779a[7]

Twelve Paces *N W Alexander* 114h 104c
10 b g Double Trigger(IRE) —Raise The Dawn (Rymer)
(1341)
1577[2] 1763[8] 2036[7] 4476[8] 4871[3] 5097[P]

Twentyfourcarat (IRE) *Ian Williams* 109b
6 b g Craigsteel—Romany River (Over The River (FR))
(2518) 4808[23]

Twentynineblack (FR) *Donald McCain* 111h 119c
7 b g Valanour(IRE) —Grange Cunault (FR) (Magwal (FR))
209[2] (327) (576)
1779[2] ◆ 1936[4] 2270[6] *3090[8]* 4113[F] 5171[12]

Twentypoundluck (IRE) *Andrew Crook* 103h
6 ch g Beneficial—Guitane Lady (IRE) (Commanche Run)
679[4] 1783[3] 1922[7] 3750[9]

Twentyten (IRE) *Paul Henderson* 90b
6 br g Busy Flight—Tullow Sunset (IRE) (Yashgan)
2222[9] *2896[4]* 3434[3] 5105[10]

Twice Lucky *Sue Smith* 80h
7 b g Mtoto—Foehn Gale (IRE) (Strong Gale)
2297[F] 2939[11] 3489[9] 3918[9] 4958[3]

Twigg Echoes (IRE) *Howard Johnson*
5 b g Milan—Echoes Of Erin (IRE) (Torus)
4112[P]

Twilight Star (IRE) *Roger Teal* 45h
7 b g Green Desert(USA) —Heavenly Whisper (IRE) (Halling (USA))
2129[10]

Twill (IRE) *Dai Burchell* 102h
8 ch g Barathea(IRE) —Khafaya (Unfuwain (USA))
2586[7]

Twin Barrels *Andrew Haynes* 79b
4 ch g Double Trigger(IRE) —Caballe (USA) (Opening Verse (USA))
3936[5] 4410[6]

Twin Bud *Anna Newton-Smith* 96h
6 b m Double Trigger(IRE) —Little Bud (Lord Bud)
2130[3] 2428[6] 2949[8] 3791[2] 4401[P] 4767[5] 5054[3]

Twin Edge *George Foster*
6 ch m Bold Edge—Sally's Twins (Dowsing (USA))
3991[4]

Twirling Magnet (IRE) *Jonjo O'Neill* 104b
5 b g Imperial Ballet(IRE) —Molly Maguire (IRE) (Supreme Leader)
(1927)

Twisted *Michael Easterby* 76h
5 ch g Selkirk(USA) —Winding (USA) (Irish River (FR))
5309[8]

Twist Magic (FR) *Paul Nicholls* 115h 174c
9 b g Winged Love(IRE) —Twist Scarlett (GER) (Lagunas)
2138[2] 2964[F] (Dead)

Twist Pistol (FR) *Paul Nicholls* 107h
4 b g Maille Pistol(FR) —Cypriere (FR) (Shafoun (FR))
5106[7]

Two Bob (IRE) *Philip Hobbs* 90h
6 ch g Bob Back(USA) —Double Symphony (IRE) (Orchestra)
2222[5] 4986[8] 5321[4]

Two Cloudy (IRE) *Pat Murphy* 99h
5 b g Cloudings(IRE) —Two Choices (IRE) (Persian Mews)
2368[6] 2946[8] 3604[4] 3960[7] 4767[P]

Two Kisses (IRE) *Brendan Powell* 113h
4 b f Spartacus(IRE) —Flight Sequence (Polar Falcon (USA))
960[2] (1135) (1226) 1610[2] 2078[3] 2356[7] 3673[2] 4024[3] 4458[2] 5006[3]

Two Left Boots (FR) *Tim Vaughan* 115h
7 b g Sagacity(FR) —Kemalina (FR) (Linamix (FR))
423[2] 798[6]

Two Mile Borris (IRE) *Michael Quinlan* 23h
5 b g Morozov(USA) —Rebel Heart (IRE) (Remainder Man)
855[9] 1086[8] 1289[7]

Two Miles West (IRE) *Jonjo O'Neill* 124h 104c
10 b g Sadler's Wells(USA) —User Friendly (Slip Anchor)
(651) 830[10] 1019[13] 1108[P] (1405) 2147[13]

Two Tone *Garry Woodward* 70h
5 bb g Diktat—Fireburst (Spectrum (IRE))
4499[11]

Two Wheel Drive (IRE) *J Cole*
11 ch m Mohaajir(USA) —Ashleys Sister (Fidel)
4901[P]

Tyko (FR) *P Peltier* 128h 140c
6 b g Robin Des Champs(FR) —Chikiwi (FR) (Saint Cyrien (FR))
2230a[6]

Ty Perrine (FR) *F Cheyer* 85h 105c
8 b m Assessor(IRE) —Mystere D'Un Soir (FR) (Mistigri)
190a[0]

Tyrone House (IRE) *John Wade* 102h 121c
7 b g Strategic Choice(USA) —Naughty Marietta (IRE) (Good Thyne (USA))
1759[6] (2298)
(3751) 4362[R] **4941[5]**

Tyrrhenian *Rose Dobbin* 64h
8 gr g Blueprint(IRE) —Calabria (Neltino)
494[9]

Tyup Pompey (IRE) *Ann Price* 81h 115c
10 ch g Docksider(USA) —Cindy's Baby (Bairn (USA))
5[3] (57)
(300) 636[5] 1454[7] 1725[7] 2324[P] 3371[6] 3841[5]
4010[9] 4290[5]
4948[3] 5081[5]
(5236) (5399)

Tzora *Philip Hobbs* 114h
6 b g Sakhee(USA) —Lucky Arrow (Indian Ridge)
756[8] 866[3] 1026[3] 1470[4]

U B Carefull *Sirrell Griffiths* 118h
8 ch g Roi De Rome(USA) —Harry's Bride (Sir Harry Lewis (USA))
(563) 773[U] 2636[6]

Ubi Ace *Tim Walford* 125h
5 b g First Trump—Faithful Beauty (IRE) (Last Tycoon)
3715[2] ◆ 4061[3] (4503)

Udaya Klum *Sue Smith* 77h
8 b g Minster Son—Wynyard Damsel (Silly Prices)
3781[8] 4132[6] 4473[8] 4798[4]

Uffa Fox (IRE) *Ben De Haan* 100h
8 b g Bravefoot—Ocean Mist (IRE) (Crash Course)
864[8] (1842)

Ukrainian Star (IRE) *Martin Keighley* 91h 99c
8 ch g Carrowkeel(IRE) —Gemmasdelemma (IRE) (Red Sunset)
1820[5] (2457) 3258[2] (3530)
3867[6] 4718[2] 5169[10]

Ultimate *Brian Ellison* 133h
5 b h Anabaa(USA) —Nirvana (Marju (IRE))
1862[5] 2219[5] 2521[5] 3447[7] 3969[3] 4727[5] 5201[P]

Ultimate Limit *Alan Fleming* 52h 118c
11 b g Bonny Scot(IRE) —Second Call (Kind Of Hush)
4701[P] 4969[3]

Ultimate Quest (IRE) *Michael Chapman* 100h
6 ch g Rainbow Quest(USA) —Crepe Ginger (IRE) (Sadler's Wells (USA))
2325[2] 2512[7] 3304[6] 3599[P] 4182[P]

Ultravox (USA) *Jeremy Scott* 127h
4 b g Lemon Drop Kid(USA) —Lynnwood Chase (USA) (Horse Chestnut (SAF))
2047[3] 2466[4] 2924[4] (3484) 3624[3] 4196[4] 4377[4]
(5006) (5227) (5424) ◆

Ulysees (IRE) *Jim Goldie* 71h
12 b g Turtle Island(IRE) —Tamasriya (IRE) (Doyoun)
3331[11] 3631[P] 3855[10]

Umverti *Joanne Foster* 62h
6 b m Averti(IRE) —Umbrian Gold (IRE) (Perugino (USA))
4393[12] 4995[F]

Unaccompanied (IRE) *D K Weld* 136h
4 b f Danehill Dancer(IRE) —Legend Has It (IRE) (Sadler's Wells (USA))
(4083a) 4847[2]

Un Autre Espere *Trevor Wall* 79h 84c
12 b g Golden Heights—Drummer's Dream (IRE) (Drumalis)
381[7] 558[F] 755[10] 864[7] 991[6] 1048[P]

Un Certainmonsieur (FR) *M Seror*
5 b g Timboroa—Maria Irena (FR) (Rahotep I (FR))
5159a[3]

Uncle Ant (IRE) *Paul Webber* 95h 85c
6 b g Alderbrook—Auntie Sally (IRE) (Bob Back (USA))
2310[14] 3304[4] **4140[5] 4934[P]**

Uncle Bunge (IRE) *Liam Corcoran* 99h
5 b g Rock Of Gibraltar(IRE) —Ouija's Sister (Groom Dancer (USA))
36[4] 1902[4] 2185[9] 2795[6] 4536[7]

Uncle Eli (IRE) *Richard Rowe* 113h 108c
9 b g Raintrap—Yosna (FR) (Sicyos (USA))
498[6]

Uncle Johnny *Anthony Honeyball* 91b
6 b g Alflora(IRE) —Lady Speckles (IRE) (Husyan (USA))
4709[9]

Uncle Keef (IRE) *Nicky Henderson* 100h
5 b g Sadler's Wells(USA) —Love For Ever (IRE) (Darshaan)
2129[5] 2512[12] 3833[5] 4182[3]

Uncommited (IRE) *Noel G Hynds* 110h 107c
11 b m Dr Massini(IRE) —Myra Gaye (Buckskin (FR))
1102[2]
4755a[5]

Under A Spell (IRE) *Sue Smith* 34b
6 b g Namid—Mystic Belle (IRE) (Thatching)
1510[9]

Undergraduate (IRE) *Michael E O'Callaghan* 114h 123c
9 b g Unfuwain(USA) —Starlet (Teenoso (USA))
3206a[P]

Under The Stars (IRE) *Nicky Richards* 94h
6 b g Beneficial—Flashy Gem (IRE) (Mister Lord (USA))
2375[6] 3330[7]

Un Hinged (IRE) *John J Coleman* 139h 129c
11 b g Danetime(IRE) —Classic Silk (IRE) (Classic Secret (USA))
3474a[P]

Union Island (IRE) *Alan King* 102h
5 b g Rock Of Gibraltar(IRE) —Daftiyna (IRE) (Darshaan)
1613[3] (2426) 4129[6]

Universal Soldier (IRE) *Lawney Hill* 146h
6 b g Winged Love(IRE) —Waterland Gale (IRE) (Fourstars Allstar (USA))
(3440)

Univoque (FR) *Alan King* 75b
4 gr g Turgeon(USA) —Us Et Coutumes (FR) (Shining Steel)
4329[6]

Unleashed (IRE) *Charlie Mann* 109h
6 br g Storming Home—Uriah (GER) (Acatenango (GER))
632[4] 908[P] 1466[6] 1571[3] 1842[2] 2081[5] 2530[6] 5241[5]

Unnecessary Xpense *Michael Scudamore* 68b
4 b g Grape Tree Road—Manque Pas D'Air (FR) (Kadalko (FR))
2458[4] 3301[10]

Unoitmakessense (IRE) *Mrs Pauline Harkin* 61h
9 b g Pistolet Bleu(IRE) —Tara The Grey (IRE) (Supreme Leader)
2929[7] 3369[P]

Until The Man (IRE) *Jim Best* 82h
4 b g Tillerman—Canoe Cove (IRE) (Grand Lodge (USA))
1728[4] (1845)

Unwanted Gift (IRE) *L J Archdeacon* 85h
6 b g Tendulkar(USA) —Slieverue (IRE) (Zieten (USA))
1069[2]

Up And Away (IRE) *Caroline Bailey* 56h
6 b g Saddlers' Hall(IRE) —Fairy Native (IRE) (Be My Native (USA))
718[4] 843[9] 2067[7]

Upham Atom *Kate Buckett* 113h 124c
8 b g Silver Patriarch(IRE) —Upham Lady (Bustino)
3485[P]
3980[4] 4127[3] 4538[2] (5037)
5405[2]

Upper Deck (IRE) *Richard Phillips* 80h
6 b g Beckett(IRE) —Princess Accord (USA) (D'Accord (USA))
759[6] 2473[8] 3542[10] 3960[P] 5298[9]

Upstairs *Paul Henderson*
7 ch g Sugarfoot—Laena (Roman Warrior)
662[P]

Upthemsteps (IRE) *Ian Williams* 119h
6 br g Beneficial—Carrigloss (IRE) (Roselier (FR))
2826[4] (2985) 3930[5] (4332)

Up The Pub (IRE) *Mrs J Weston* 67h 90c
13 ch g Carroll House—Brave Ruby (Proverb)
4750[7]

Up There (IRE) *Mrs N Sheppard* 103h 94c
10 b g Supreme Leader—Avro Avian (Ardross)
152[6]

Upton Mead (IRE) *Chris Down* 59b
4 b g Jimble(FR) —Inchinnan (Inchinor)
1913[11]

Up To The Mark *Henry Daly* 105h 117c
6 b g Mark Of Esteem(IRE) —Villella (Sadler's Wells (USA))
2109[4] 4031[3] **(4775)**
5081[6]

Urban Clubber *Howard Johnson* 48h
4 b g Dubai Destination(USA) —Surprise Visitor (IRE) (Be My Guest (USA))
1018[10]

Ursis (FR) *Steve Gollings* 113h 122c
10 b g Trempolino(USA) —Bold Virgin (USA) (Sadler's Wells (USA))
1019[10] 1150[6] **1577[3] 1690[6] (2400)**
3558[5] 4221[P]

Ursus *Christopher Wilson* 87h
6 ch g Rambling Bear—Adar Jane (Ardar)
4242[S] 4451[10] 5027[3] 5348[8]

Usquaebach *Pat Phelan* 11h
4 b f Trade Fair—Mashmoum (Lycius (USA))
3443[9]

Utern *Venetia Williams* 75h
7 br m Overbury(IRE) —My Tern (IRE) (Glacial Storm (USA))
21[6] 737[6] 1822[11]

Vacario (GER) *Mark Gillard* 111h
7 br g Acatenango(GER) —Vaillance (GER) (Dashing Blade)
250[6] 478[5] 1162[5] 1230[5] 1446[5] 1590[4] 1745[5] 1840[4] 2001[5] 2183[5] 3341[2] 3530[5] 4130[5] 4273[7]

Vadition (IRE) *John Bridger*
4 b f Halling(USA) —Retail Therapy (IRE) (Bahhare (USA))
1545[P] 1586[10]

Vagrant Emperor (IRE) *Emma Lavelle* 127h 100c
8 b g Oscar(IRE) —Dragonmist (IRE) (Digamist (USA))
2630[2] 3440[P] 3742[P] 4220[5] 4485[F]
5190[3]

Valantino Oyster (IRE) *Ben Haslam* 71h
4 b g Pearl Of Love(IRE) —Mishor (Slip Anchor)
1298[3] 1498[5] 2369[5]

Valdan (IRE) *Maurice Barnes*
7 b g Val Royal(FR) —Danedrop (IRE) (Danehill (USA))
1426[P]

Valdez *Alan King* 98b
4 ch g Doyen(IRE) —Skew (Niniski (USA))
(4957) ◆

Valentine Vic (IRE) *Paul Nicholls* 123h 130c
7 bb g Old Vic—Elleena Rose (IRE) (Roselier (FR))
4185[F]
(5213)

Valento *Kim Bailey* 123h
6 ch g Noverre(USA) —My Valentina (Royal Academy (USA))
(3) 633[3] 3447[8] 3688[12] 3881[2] ◆

Valerius (IRE) *Gordon Elliott* 110h 135c
7 b g Galileo(IRE) —Rainbow Dream (Rainbow Quest (USA))
1373[6] 1577[P]

Valiant Shadow (GER) *R A Wilson* 123h 18c
9 b g Winged Love(IRE) —Vangelis (Gorytus (USA))
4553[6]

Valid Point (IRE) *Jim Old* 105h
5 b g Val Royal(FR) —Ricadonna (Kris)
2145[15] 3386[9] (4830)

Valid Reason *Dean Ivory* 75h
4 b g Observatory(USA) —Real Trust (USA) (Danzig (USA))
4810[8]

Valkyrie (IRE) *Nick Littmoden* 89h
5 b m Danehill Dancer(IRE) —Ridotto (Salse (USA))
154[3] 421[4] 697[P]

Vallani (IRE) *Lucinda Russell* 91h
6 ch m Vettori(IRE) —Hecuba (Hector Protector (USA))
176[P] 2038[10] 2353[5] 2654[5] 3336[5] 3750[2] (4146) 4687[5] 5096[7]

Valldemoso (CZE) *J Uhl*
7 b g Mill Pond(FR) —Valdivia (CZE) (Justus (GER))
1811a[U]

Valley Lad (IRE) *Tim Vaughan* 105b
5 b g Flemensfirth(USA) —Old Moon (IRE) (Old Vic)
(2576) 3943[4]

Valleymount (IRE) *F Flood* 120b
5 b m Milan—Newhall (IRE) (Shernazar)
3208a[3]

Valley Of Giants *Gordon Elliott* 124h 122c
9 ch g Giant's Causeway(USA) —Karri Valley (USA) (Storm Bird (CAN))
291[9]

Valley Ride (IRE) *Peter Bowen* 132h 137c
11 bb g Glacial Storm(USA) —Royal Lucy (IRE) (King's Ride)
(685) **844[3]**
1020[8] 1332[9] 1508[U]
1611[5] 1960[5]

Valley View (IRE) *Jonjo O'Neill* 91h 106c
5 b g Anshan—Sweet Valley High (IRE) (Strong Gale)
2067[6] 3296[6] 3526[4]
(3869) ◆ 4880[F]

Valonty *Brian Storey*
9 b g Villez(USA) —Polly Verry (Politico (USA))
8[P] 174[P]

Valrene *George Jones* 70b
5 b m Grape Tree Road—Across The Water (Slip Anchor)
1771[9]

Valsesia (IRE) *Howard Johnson* 87b
4 b f Milan—Ballinapierce Lady (IRE) (Glacial Storm (USA))
4396[2] ◆ 4801[3]

Valsfirth (IRE) *Donald McCain* 82h
8 ch g Flemensfirth(USA) —Surfer Katie (IRE) (Be My Native (USA))
3487[6]

Vamizi (IRE) *Mark Bradstock* 105h 129c
8 b g Supreme Leader—Cuilin Bui (IRE) (Kemal (FR))
1738[2] ◆ 2140[2] 3629[3] 3922[P] 4537[2] 5154[F]

Van Boxtal (IRE) *Joseph Fox* 92h
8 b g Needle Gun(IRE) —Ask Mama (Mummy's Pet)
5401[P]

Van Ness (IRE) *G T H Bailey* 101h 116c
12 ch g Hubbly Bubbly(USA) —Brown Trout (IRE) (Beau Charmeur (FR))
5163[6]

Vannin (IRE) *Tim Easterby* 93h
5 b g Golan(IRE) —Khalsheva (Shirley Heights)
2540[P]

Varkala (IRE) *Charles Egerton* 96h
5 b m Old Vic—Liss Rua (IRE) (Bob Back (USA))
2472[2] 2987[5] 3616[4] 5327[2]

Vasodilator (IRE) *Pat Murphy* 106h 103c
8 ch g Beneficial—Late Call (IRE) (Callernish)
1068[P] 1476[4] 1813[4] 2152[6] 4975[6]
5266[F]

Va Vavoom (IRE) *Mrs Fleur Hawes* 113h 102c
13 b g Supreme Leader—Shalom Joy (Kemal (FR))
4183[P]

Veiled *Nicky Henderson* 136h
5 b m Sadler's Wells(USA) —Evasive Quality (FR) (Highest Honor (FR))
4455[6] (4955) (5302)

Veiled Applause *John Quinn* 123h
8 b g Royal Applause—Scarlet Veil (Tyrnavos)
4778[F]

Velvet Shadow (IRE) *Mrs Pauline Harkin* 74b
4 b f Needle Gun(IRE) —Meldrum Park (IRE) (Mandalus)
5380[7]

Velvet Vic (IRE) *Richard Guest* 72h
5 b g Old Vic—Elleena Rose (IRE) (Roselier (FR))
319[17] 2355[14] 2509[11] 3725[5] 3887[10]

Venalmar *M F Morris* 135h 136c
9 b g Kayf Tara—Elaine Tully (IRE) (Persian Bold)
3206a[P] 3473a[P] 4107a[7]

Venetian Dove (IRE) *Evan Williams* 100h
5 bl m One Cool Cat(USA) —Venetian Pearl (IRE) (Generous (IRE))
(2438)

Venetian Lad *Lydia Richards* 97h
6 ro g Midnight Legend—Henrietta Holmes (IRE) (Persian Bold)
2186[6] 2428[5] 3866[6] 4128[5] 4370[6] 4773[6]

Venir Rouge *Matthew Salaman* 102h 102c
7 ch g Dancing Spree(USA) —Al Awaalah (Mukaddamah (USA))
1197[3] 1471[4]

Venitzia (IRE) *Howard Johnson* 98b
5 bb g Presenting—Bloom Berry (Overbury (IRE))
3511[5] 5432[4]

Venture Girl (IRE) *Tim Easterby* 84h
4 ch f Footstepsinthesand—Bold Assumption (Observatory (USA))
1699[6] 1825[3] 2033[10] 2369[2]

Verasi *Gary Moore* 8h 74c
10 b g Kahyasi—Fair Verona (USA) (Alleged (USA))
2214[9] 2497[4] 2928[11] 3493[8]

Verde Goodwood *Oliver Sherwood* 84h
5 ch m Lomitas—Dissolve (Sharrood (USA))
7[4] 568[2] *2825[2]* 3787[9] 4535[10] 4964[4] 5346[6]

Veruga (IRE) *Tim Easterby* 85h
4 gr g Verglas(IRE) —Caviare (Cadeaux Genereux)
2614[6] 3986[3] 4240[5]

Veronicas Boy *George Moore* 104h
5 br g Diktat—Thamud (IRE) (Lahib (USA))
1641[6] 2508[5] *3169[13]* 3509[F] 4113[6] 4391[8] 4508[8] 5307[3]

Vertige Dore (FR) *Paul Nicholls* 123h
6 b g Kingsalsa(USA) —Princesa Elena (FR) (Esprit Du Nord (USA))
(1201) (1310) *3056[3]* 4467[4] (5274)

Vertueux (FR) *Tony Carroll* 109h
6 gr g Verglas(IRE) —Shahrazad (FR) (Bering)
(299) 2361[14] 4697[2] 5215[8]

Very Cool *David Pipe* 121h 56c
9 b g Sir Harry Lewis(USA) —Laurel Diver (Celtic Cone)
(131) 708[6] 830[8] **1738[8]**

Very Edgy (IRE) *Charles Egerton* 102h
7 ch g Accordion—Lady Llancillo (IRE) (Alflora (IRE))
3693[9] 4501[P]

Very Stylish (IRE) *Jonjo O'Neill* 113h
7 b g Winged Love(IRE) —Native Craft (IRE) (Be My Native (USA))
331[9] 479[7] 765[F] (921) 5117[10] 5392[5]

Vesey Lodge (IRE) *Jennie Candlish* 9h
5 b g City Honours(USA) —Boreen Perky (IRE) (Executive Perk)
(1069) 2667[14]

Via Archimede (USA) *Lucinda Russell* 88h
6 ch g Hussonet(USA) —Azarina (IRE) (Kenmare (FR))
1114[4] 3746[7] 4062[P]

Viable *Pam Sly* 120h 125c
9 b g Vettori(IRE) —Danseuse Davis (FR) (Glow (USA))
479[4] **838[4]**
(1023)
1690[7] 2112[4] 2613[2] 3573[7] 4324[5] 4934[3]

Via Galilei (IRE) *Gary Moore* 138h
6 b g Galileo(IRE) —Manger Square (IRE) (Danehill (USA))
(2626) 3557[7] 3874[2] (4488) ◆ 4727[2] 5201[3] 5337[5]

Vial De Kerdec (FR) *Mark Bradstock* 82h 110c
8 bb g Poliglote—Love For Ever (FR) (Kaldoun (FR))
586[P] 769[U] 868[P] 1476[5] 1678[P]

Vicario *Mrs S K McCain* 101h 113c
10 gr g Vettori(IRE) —Arantxa (Sharpo)
334[3]

Vicentio *Tim Fitzgerald* 63h 77c
12 br g Vettori(IRE) —Smah (Mtoto)
176[P] 461[8] 955[8]

Vic Legend (IRE) *Rebecca Curtis* 98b
5 b g Flying Legend(USA) —Rowlands Star (IRE) (Old Vic)
5157[4]

Vico (IRE) *Paul Nicholls* 118h
7 b g Old Vic—Over The Glen (IRE) (Over The River (FR))
2482[3] 4370[4] 5289[9]

Vico Road (IRE) *Jonjo O'Neill* 68h
6 b g Dushyantor(USA) —Serengeti Plains (IRE) (Toulon)
1866[5] 2162[8] 2419[7] 3296[15]

Vicpol (ITY) *Tom Gretton* 92h
5 b g Poliglote—Vehota Vic (Old Vic)
(739) 2215[11] 3506[P] 5343[3]

Vic's Witch (IRE) *Elliott Cooper* 50b
5 b m Old Vic—Bewitch (Idiots Delight)
5264[12]

Vic's World (IRE) *James Frost* 89h 101c
9 b m Old Vic—Marble World (Top Of The World)
647[2] 761[4] 3612[3] 3878[8] 4269[2]

Victor (IRE) *Miss Victoria Easterby* 72c
8 b g Old Vic—Missymp (IRE) (Mi Selecto (USA))
628[7]

Victor Daly (IRE) *Martin Keighley* 87h 125c
10 b g Old Vic—Murphys Lady (IRE) (Over The River (FR))
(314) **844[P]**
1275[4] **1856[F]**

Victor Echo (IRE) *Nicky Henderson* 115b
5 b g Old Vic—Lambourne Lace (IRE) (Un Desperado (FR))
4866[4] (5387)

Victor Hewgo *Keith Reveley* 102b
6 b g Old Vic—Pennys Pride (IRE) (Pips Pride)
4287[2] 5034[2]

Victoria Rose (IRE) *Simon Burrough* 110h
6 b m Old Vic—West Hill Rose (IRE) (Roselier (FR))
2288[8] 3389[2] 3678[3] ◆ 4459[3] ◆

Victorias *Andrew Crook* 75h
6 gr m Tamayaz(CAN) —Paper Flight (Petong)
713[P]

Victorias Groom (GER) *Lucy Wadham* 130h 140c
9 bb g Lavirco(GER) —Valda (RUS) (Dotsero (USA))
98[P] 2400[2] 2541[P] 2948[10] 3290[F] 3629[6] 4181[5] 4502[U]

Victor Leudorum (IRE) *Charlie Mann* 90b
4 b g Wareed(IRE) —Rock Garden (IRE) (Bigstone (IRE))
3399[3] 3794[7] 4780[4]

Victor Lynch (IRE) *Kate Walton* 98b
5 b g Old Vic—Jmember (IRE) (Jurado (USA))
2403[3]

Victors Serenade (IRE) *Anthony Honeyball* 124h 114c
6 b g Old Vic—Dantes Serenade (IRE) (Phardante (FR))
(2141) 2284[3] 3370[2] (3698)
4890[2]

Victory Bay *Simon Burrough* 70h
6 ch g Karinga Bay—Play It Down (Thethingaboutitis (USA))
1029[12] 3372[8] 3872[11] 4225[12] 4268[9] 4707[6] 4924[9]

Victory Gunner (IRE) *Richard Lee* 122h 120c
13 ch g Old Vic—Gunner B Sharp (Gunner B)
579[P] (3900)
4256 (4428)
4966[6]

Victory Parade (IRE) *Rebecca Curtis* 120h 124c
8 ch g Old Vic—Charlotte's Moss (Le Moss)
2140[P] 2285[U] 2513[4] 4538[4] (5240)
5370[F]

Victory Surge (IRE) *Jonjo O'Neill* 101h 118c
7 b g Old Vic—Quinnsboro Guest (IRE) (Be My Guest (USA))
55[2] **1061[P]**
(1366)
(2127) 2311[5] 5281[2]

Victrix Gale (IRE) *Nicky Henderson* 120h
5 b m Presenting—Ballyclough Gale (Strong Gale)
833[2] 3623[6] (4425) 4828[3]

Vic Venturi (IRE) *D T Hughes* 133h 160c
11 ch g Old Vic—Carmen Lady (Torus)
3176a[7] 3578a[7]
4298a[4] 5200[8]

Viel Gluck (IRE) *Ferdy Murphy* 95h 102c
8 b g Supreme Leader—Discerning Air (Ezzoud (IRE))
160[P]

Viking Affair (IRE) *Rebecca Curtis* 34h
7 b g Old Vic—Proudstown Lady (IRE) (Ashford (USA))
1296[6] **4526[P]**

Viking Blond (FR) *Nigel Twiston-Davies* 137h
6 ch g Varese(FR) —Sweet Jaune (FR) (Le Nain Jaune (FR))
206[P] 1855[6] 2360[2] 2870[3] 3293[13] 4817[7] 5187[16]

Viking Gold *Tim Vaughan* 79b
7 b m Bob Back(USA) —Queen's Flagship (IRE) (Accordion)
27[6] 370[11]

Viking Rebel (IRE) *W T Reed* 136h 129c
9 b g Taipan(IRE) —Clodagh's Dream (Whistling Deer)
3956[5] 4476[4]

Viking Visitor (IRE) *Jonjo O'Neill* 94h
6 b g Viking Ruler(AUS) —Clifton Lass (IRE) (Up And At 'Em)
3153[5] 4012[9]

Vincentian (IRE) *David Arbuthnot* 80h
6 ch g Bob Back(USA) —Native Sunset (IRE) (Be My Nativo (USA))
3651[3] 3903[3] 4376[2] 5107[7]

Vincent Pipe (IRE) *Michael O'Hare* 98h
9 ch g Presenting—Flawless Finish (IRE) (Le Bavard (FR))
606[3]

Vincitore (FR) *Charlie Longsdon* 116h
5 b g Starborough—Viva Vodka (FR) (Crystal Glitters (USA))
(62) 1675[F] ◆ 4555[2] (5152)

Vin De Roy (FR) *Rachel Hobbs* 110h
6 gr g Balleroy(USA) —Coup De Rouge (FR) (Quart De Vin (FR))
2238[5] 2454[9] 3370[6] 3621[3] 4079[3]

Vinmix De Bessy (FR) *Gary Moore* 83h 129c
10 gr g River Bay(USA) —Hesse (FR) (Linamix (FR))
194[7] 523[P] *3059[11]* **3834[F] 4698[4]**

Vinnes Friend (IRE) *Gordon Elliott* 118h
7 b m Beneficial—Sweet Mount (IRE) (Mandalus)
1597[3]

Vino Griego (FR) *Gary Moore* 140h 137c
6 b g Kahyasi—Vie De Reine (FR) (Mansonnien (FR))
1883[5] 2348[6] 2670[3] 3803[2] 3980[3] 4794[4] ◆

Vinomore *Shaun Lycett* 84b
5 b m Grape Tree Road—Sillymore (Silly Prices)
1927[4] 2389[10]

Vin Rose *Mark Rimell* 90h
6 ch m Alflora(IRE) —Miniature Rose (Anshan)
1253[4] 2956[2] 3545[3] 3951[F] 4675[10] 5208[5]

Vintage Fabric (USA) *Nigel Hawke* 101h 105c
9 b g Royal Anthem(USA) —Sandalwood (USA) (El Gran Senor (USA))
646[4] (825) 962[7] 1162[6] 1347[8] **1794[6]** 2001[6] (5439)

Vintage Quest *Dai Burchell* 69h
9 b m Diktat—Sadly Sober (IRE) (Roi Danzig (USA))
4721[4] 4947[6]

Vintage Star (IRE) *Sue Smith* 105b
5 b g Presenting—Rare Vintage (IRE) (Germany (USA))
3920[2] 4259[3] 4894[2]

Violin Davis (FR) *Paul Nicholls* 125h
5 b m Turgeon(USA) —Trumpet Davis (FR) (Rose Laurel)
(1920) 2577[9] 3480[2] ◆ 4101[2] (4703) 5008[2] ◆ 5302[3]

Viper *Dr Richard Newland* 12h 118c
9 b g Polar Prince(IRE) —Maradata (IRE) (Shardari)
714[2] 797[2] 890[3] 1023[P] 1109[P]

Virginia Rose Wood (IRE) *Peter Hedger* 5b
5 b m Reset(AUS) —Sandy Lady (IRE) (Desert King (IRE))
2632[9] *2896[11]*

Viscount Rossini *Steve Gollings* 113h 104c
9 bb g Rossini(USA) —Spain (Polar Falcon (USA))
(2247) 3500[4] 3596[8] 4234[4] 4544[F]

Viscount Victor (IRE) *Steve Gollings* 67b
5 b g Wizard King—Minstrels Daughter (IRE) (Magical Wonder (USA))
3998[8]

Vision Of Lights (IRE) *Graeme McPherson* 101b
6 b g Fantastic Light(USA) —Kadassa (IRE) (Shardari)
3920[3] 4287[7] 4780[12] 5063[8]

Vital Plot (USA) *S Weld* 137h
7 b g Theatrical—First Breeze (USA) (Woodman (USA))
3474a[16]

Vital Spark *O R Dukes* 89c
12 b g Primitive Rising(USA) —Enkindle (Relkino)
493[P]

Vito Volterra (IRE) *Michael Smith*
4 b g Antonius Pius(USA) —River Abouali (Bluebird (USA))
743[P]

Vitruvian Man *Sophie Leech* 87h
5 b g Montjeu(IRE) —Portrait Of A Lady (IRE) (Peintre Celebre (USA))
4029[8] 4451[11]

Vittachi *Alistair Whillans* 69h
4 b g Bertolini(USA) —Miss Lorilaw (FR) (Homme De Loi (IRE))
1699[8] 2033[9] 4910[10]

Viva Colonia (IRE) *David O'Meara* 119h
6 ch g Traditionally(USA) —Ansariya (USA) (Shahrastani (USA))
530[P] 846[12] 1292[8] (2094) ◆ 2373[2] 3966[6] 4149[4] 4940[7]

Vivaldi (IRE) *J J Lambe* 129h
6 b g Montjeu(IRE) —Parvenue (FR) (Ezzoud (IRE))
3850[3] 3994[2] 5027[4]

Vivarini *John O'Shea* 120h
7 b g Hernando(FR) —Venetian Red (USA) (Blushing Groom (FR))
1692[9] 2169[2] 2364[2] 2574[2] ◆ 3771[F] 4079[P] 4939[7] 5252[3] 5439[6]

Viva Taipan (IRE) *Alex Hales* 21h
8 b m Taipan(IRE) —Viva Las Vegas (IRE) (Pennine Walk)
1993[9] *3055[9]*

Viviani (IRE) *Amanda Perrett* 85h
4 ch g Galileo(IRE) —Bintalreef (USA) (Diesis)
2528[5] 2924[10]

Vivona Hill *Alan Swinbank* 100h
7 b g Overbury(IRE) —Lets Go Dutch (Nicholas Bill)
3851[6] 4569[P]

Vodka Brook (IRE) *Tim Walford* 128h 136c
8 b g Alderbrook—Another Vodka (IRE) (Moscow Society (USA))
2106[3] 2374[P] *3169[11]* **3488[P] 3634[F]**

Vogarth *Michael Chapman* 87h
7 ch g Arkadian Hero(USA) —Skara Brae (Inchinor)
135[6] 886[5] 1147[11] 1249[8] 1624[7] 1723[12] 2398[8]

Volcanic Rock (IRE) *John Anthony Staunton* 101h 119c
11 b g Shernazar—Down Town To-Night (Kambalda)
(517)
(1376) 1404[3] 2055[6] 2953[5]

Voler La Vedette (IRE) *C A Murphy* 154h
7 b m King's Theatre(IRE) —Steel Grey Lady (IRE) (Roselier (FR))
2414a[2] 2968a[3] 3707a[4] (4107a)

Von Galen (IRE) *Michael Scudamore* 75h 95c
10 b g Germany(USA) —Castle Carrig (IRE) (Le Bavard (FR))
383[2] 597[6] 804[3] 1027[5] 1159[4] 1331[P] (1733)
2002[2] 5060[5] 5258[13]

Von Origny (FR) *Mrs Corrine Wynne* 101h 104c
10 gr g Blushing Flame(USA) —Forza Malta (FR) (Royal Charter (FR))
334[P]

Voramar Two *Philip Hobbs* 150h 143c
8 b g Kayf Tara—Amaretto Flame (IRE) (First Trump)
2285[2] ◆ 2631[2] 3435[2] ◆ 3743[5] 4720[U] 4898[3]

Vosges (FR) *James Ewart* 113h
4 b g Turgeon(USA) —Vanilla Sky (FR) (Kaldounevees (FR))
2451[4] 3358[2] (3550) (3967) 4205[5] 4475[8]

Voy Por Ustedes (FR) *Nicky Henderson* 128h 167c
10 b g Villez(USA) —Nuit D'Ecajeul (FR) (Matahawk)
4818[5]

Vrondi (IRE) *William Davies* 63b
7 b g Dansili—Zapatista (Rainbow Quest (USA))
833[11]

Waarid *Gary Moore* 99h
6 b g Alhaarth(IRE) —Nibbs Point (IRE) (Sure Blade (USA))
134[2]

Wade Farm Billy (IRE) *Gary Moore* 121h 119c
7 b g Dr Massini(IRE) —Burgundy Sunset (IRE) (Buckskin (FR))
464[3] 687[7] 1693[5] 2209[15] *3057[6]*

Wadham Hill *William Reed* 81h
9 b m Bandmaster(USA) —Sport Of Fools (IRE) (Trojan Fen)
1228[P]

Wadnaan *Ferdy Murphy* 83h
4 ch g Shamardal(USA) —Australian Dreams (Magic Ring (IRE))
4995[4]

Wait For The Light *Sophie Leech* 78h
7 b g Fantastic Light(USA) —Lady In Waiting (Kylian (USA))
298[P]

Wait No More (IRE) *Sarah Humphrey* 61h 95c
6 ch g Strategic Choice(USA) —Tearaway Lady (IRE) (Tidaro (USA))
2826[5] 3572[9] 4112[8] 4500[11]
(5268) ◆

Wake Board (FR) *Dr Richard Newland* 106h 106c
6 b g Dansili—Criquetot (FR) (Epervier Bleu)
(4548) 5215[6]

Walamo (GER) *Tim Vaughan* 114h 121c
7 b g Mujahid(USA) —Walkona (IRE) (Local Suitor (USA))
738[5] (889)
1045[5] 1251[2] (1432)
1568[P]

Walden Prince (IRE) *P F McEnery* 104h
4 b g Saffron Walden(FR) —Kahyasi Princess (IRE) (Kahyasi)
2966a[6]

Waldo Winchester (IRE) *Noel Wilson* 95h 60c
8 b g Second Empire(IRE) —Zeddaana (FR) (Arctic Tern (USA))
423[5] 4550[10] **5116[5]** 5350[6]

Waldsee (GER) *Sean Curran* 2h
6 b g Xaar—Wurftaube (GER) (Acatenango (GER))
2283[P] 2667[15]

Waldvogel (IRE) *Nicky Richards* 122h
7 ch g Polish Precedent(USA) —Wurftaube (GER) (Acatenango (GER))
397[4] (3749) ◆ 5035[2] 5357[5]

Walkon (FR) *Alan King* 155h
6 gr g Take Risks(FR) —La Tirana (FR) (Akarad (FR))
3676[2] 4188[11] 4806[7]

Walkonabubble (IRE) *D J Barry* 76h
7 b g Hubbly Bubbly(USA) —Hazy Walk (IRE) (Henbit (USA))
856[4]

Walk Tall (IRE) *Venetia Williams* 102h 102c
8 b g Blueprint(IRE) —Dikler Gale (IRE) (Strong Gale)
2170[P] 2952[3] (3226)

Wallace Monument *Gary Brown* 73h
7 b g Mtoto—Misowni (Niniski (USA))
4268[11] 4676[9] 4947[U]

Wallbro (IRE) *Lawney Hill* 86b
6 ch g Bob's Return(IRE) —Dear Empress (IRE) (Buckskin (FR))
4780[8]

Walls Way *Tony Carroll* 91h
7 ch g Karinga Bay—Wilming (Komaite (USA))
16[P] 2144[11] 2589[9] 4522[P]

Walser (IRE) *Howard Johnson* 76b
4 b g Milan—Brass Neck (IRE) (Supreme Leader)
5313[4]

Walter De La Mare (IRE) *John Joseph Murphy* 125h
4 b c Barathea(IRE) —Banutan (IRE) (Charnwood Forest (IRE))
4847[13]

Walter De Wodeland *Miss J Du Plessis* 99c
10 b g Bandmaster(USA) —Kingsmill Quay (Noble Imp)
133[4] 499[3] 4534[2] 4901[4]

Walter's Laddie *Stuart Morris*
10 b g Classic Cliche(IRE) —Spalease (Strong Gale)
4553[F]

Waltham Abbey *Lynsey Kendall* 83h 77c
10 b g Relief Pitcher—Flash-By (Ilium)
1929[10] 2549[0] 4140[7] 4391[10] 4550[0] 4900[0] 5094[3] 5308[7]

Walton Way *Miss G Stephens* 48h 83c
11 b g Charmer—Needwood Poppy (Rolfe (USA))
152[P]

Wapiti Creek (IRE) *John G Carr* 77h 31c
7 gr m Great Palm(USA) —Swift Rose (IRE) (Roselier (FR))
1402[F] 1426[P]
1830[5]

Wardington Lad *Michael Appleby* 95h
9 b g Yaheeb(USA) —Lavenham's Last (Rymer)
2558[P] *3168[5]* 3523[13] 3782[8] 4559[9] 4833[5]

War Kitty *Roger Curtis* 69h
4 b f Largesse—Princess Of War (Warrshan (USA))
3964[11] 4430[5]

Warmaster (IRE) *Howard Johnson* 87h
7 bb g Definite Article—Queen Street (IRE) (King's Ride)
8[P]

Warnell View *Rayson Nixon* 33h
8 b g Weldnaas(USA) —Joyful Imp (Import)
394[P]

Warne's Way (IRE) *Brendan Powell* 132h 118c
8 ch g Spinning World(USA) —Kafayef (USA) (Secreto (USA))
(2393) 3298[9] (3490) 3676[7] 4185[10] 4485[7]

War Of The World (FR) *Paul Nicholls* 94b
5 b g Lost World(IRE) —Folklorique (FR) (Groom Dancer (USA))
4356[10] 5157[5]

War Of The World (IRE) *Tim Vaughan* 95h 143c
9 b g Shernazar—Fairpark (IRE) (Shardari)
1020[P] 3428[P]

War Party *Dr Richard Newland* 109h 123c
7 b g Fantastic Light(USA) —War Game (FR) (Caerleon (USA))
1484[3]
1628[3] 1828[P] 1971[4]
(2053) (2601)

Warpath (IRE) *Evan Williams* 110h 132c
10 b g Alderbrook—Blake's Fable (IRE) (Lafontaine (USA))
(5) **(236)**
411[5] 764[3]

Warren Bank *Mary Hambro* 84h
6 b g Nayef(USA) —Neptunalia (Slip Anchor)
3620[9] 4008[10]

Warren Chase (IRE) *Anabel L M King* 92b
6 b g Oscar(IRE) —Kilcash Cross (IRE) (Commanche Run)
4423[5]

Warrior One *Howard Johnson* 122h
5 gr g Act One—River Cara (USA) (Irish River (FR))
(1831) 2349[4] (3994)

Washango (IRE) *Shaun Lycett* 95h 21c
9 b m Presenting—Peptic Lady (IRE) (Royal Fountain)
(407) 1090[5] 2452[10] **4140[6] 4775[F]**

Washington Irving (IRE) *Howard Johnson* 129h
6 b g Montjeu(IRE) —Shouk (Shirley Heights)
2542[6] 4358[0] 4867[3]

Wasntme (IRE) *Colin Tizzard* 44h 96c
8 b g Flemensfirth(USA) —Spin N' Win (Cardinal Flower)
665[6] 795[P] 2608[5] (3337)
3614[3] 3933[6] 4269[7] 4718[P]

Wassailing Queen *Colin Tizzard* 109b
5 gr m Generous(IRE) —Absalom's Lady (Absalom)
(2156) ◆ 3876[5]

Watamu Bay (IRE) *Paul Nicholls* 134h 144c
8 b g Sunshine Street(USA) —Janzoe (IRE) (Phardante (FR))
1774[2] (2285)
(2501) 3437[6] (Dead)

Watch Closely Now (IRE) *I A Duncan* 16h
7 b m Winged Love(IRE) —Bye For Now (Abednego)
4304[9]

Watch My Back *Ferdy Murphy* 30h 150c
10 b g Bob Back(USA) —Gallants Delight (Idiots Delight)
1958[5] 4474[4] (5317)
5422[2]

Watch Out *Dai Burchell* 95h 112c
7 b g Observatory(USA) —Ballet Fame (USA) (Quest For Fame)
518[3] 761[2] 889[4] 2530[10] 3481[11] 3934[8] 4330[4] 4532[7] 5103[7] 5392[6]

Watch The Master *Ben Case*
5 b g Passing Glance—Fine Arts (Cadeaux Genereux)
538[P] 632[P]

Watch The Wind *James Walton* 74h 84c
10 ch m High Kicker(USA) —Marejo (Creetown)
163[7]

Watercolours (IRE) *Jim Goldie* 102h
6 b m High Chaparral(IRE) —Emerald Waters (Kings Lake (USA))
2161[6] 2549[4]

Water Garden (FR) *Paul Nicholls* 91h
5 gr g Turgeon(USA) —Queenstown (FR) (Cadoudal (FR))
2186[2] 3346[5] 4094[4] 4895[8]

Watergate (IRE) *Richard Rowe* 100h 102c
5 gr g Verglas(IRE) —Moy Water (IRE) (Tirol)
595[6] 914[9] 2294[P] 2583[4] **2947[2] 4426[F]** (4670) 5193[11] 5376[4]

Water King (USA) *Robert Stronge* 73h
12 b g Irish River(FR) —Brookshield Baby (IRE) (Sadler's Wells (USA))
264[8]

Waterloo Chateau (IRE) *Noel Meade* 124h
8 br g Presenting—Be My Flower (IRE) (Be My Native (USA))
1121a[9]

Waterloo Corner *Ray Craggs* 101h
9 b g Cayman Kai(IRE) —Rasin Luck (Primitive Rising (USA))
1870[12] 2208[13] 2658[6] 3523[4] 4113[2] 4797[3] 4998[3]

Waterloo Road (IRE) *Howard Johnson* 100h 104c
8 b g Old Vic—Struell Lady (IRE) (Mister Lord (USA))
3524[6]

Water Rose *Ben Case* 38b
4 b f Exit To Nowhere(USA) —Rhapsody Rose (Unfuwain (USA))
5380[11]

Waterski *Jean McGregor* 86h 108c
10 b g Petoski—Celtic Waters (Celtic Cone)
2354[F] 3361[P] 3617[6] 4066[5] 4474[5]

Water Taxi *Ferdy Murphy* 108h 117c
10 ch g Zafonic(USA) —Trellis Bay (Sadler's Wells (USA))
11[4] 352[9]

Watledge (FR) *Tom George* 88b
4 b g Lando(GER) —Flower Of Freedom (FR) (Sadler's Wells (USA))
1913[4] 2315[6]

Watoscar (IRE) *Rachel Hobbs* 65h
6 b g Oscar(IRE) —Arabella Supreme (IRE) (Supreme Leader)
180[7]

Wave Power (IRE) *Howard Johnson* 105h
7 ch g Definite Article—Romany Rose (IRE) (Montelimar (USA))
214[3]

Wavertree Bounty *John Ryan* 23h
4 b f Pastoral Pursuits—Grecian Halo (USA) (Southern Halo (USA))
2924[11] 3740[12]

Way Back When *Alan King* 113h
6 b m Phantom Breeze—Makounji (FR) (Tip Moss (FR))
263[2] 1993[2] 2288[4] 3264[2] (3904) 4481[8] 5008[11]

Waynesworld (IRE) *Mrs Marilyn Scudamore* 73h 95c
13 b g Petoski—Mariners Mirror (Julio Mariner)
152[P]

Waypost *David Bridgwater* 82b
5 b g Zamindar(USA) —Trellis Bay (Sadler's Wells (USA))
935[11] 1069[8] 1201[13]

Way To Finish *James Moffatt* 101b
5 b g Oasis Dream—Suedoise (Kris)
2511[6] 3752[4] ◆ 4943[P]

Wayward Prince *Ian Williams* 147h 155c
7 b g Alflora(IRE) —Bellino Spirit (IRE) (Robellino (USA))
(2110)
(2357) (3955)
4804[3] 5183[4]

Waywood Princess *John Bryan Groucott* 36h
6 b m Sir Harry Lewis(USA) —First Bee (Gunner B)
3842[10] 4423[6] 5108[10]

Waziri (IRE) *A S T Holdsworth* 67h 18c
10 b g Mtoto—Euphorie (GER) (Feenpark (GER))
499[9] 5372[P]

Weather Permitting (IRE) *David Pipe* 87h 4c
8 b g Glacial Storm(USA) —Star Mover (Move Off)
749[10] 849[9] **1093[P]**

Webbswood Lad (IRE) *Martin Bosley* 93h
10 b g Robellino(USA) —Poleaxe (Selkirk (USA))
(4450) 4899[5]

Weebitevil *Matthew Salaman*
4 b f Mark Of Esteem(IRE) —Kasamba (Salse (USA))
4709[P] 5435[P]

Wee Fly (FR) *Ross Oliver* 68c
9 b m Robin Des Pres(FR) —Harpyes (FR) (Quart De Vin (FR))
295[3]

Wee Forbees (IRE) *Michael Easterby* 100h 103c
9 b g Shernazar—Gender Gap (USA) (Shecky Greene (USA))
21[5] 87[4] 210[6] 472[4] **677[2] 891[8] 1023[6]**

Wee George *Sue Smith* 27h 87c
9 ch g Alflora(IRE) —Cherry Dee (Ardross)
4133[F] 4509[2] 4963[6] 5096[8]

Wee Ginge *Emma McWilliam*
4 ch g Cadeaux Genereux—Darya (USA) (Gulch (USA))
1234[R]

Weekend Millionair (IRE) *David Evans* 72h
4 ch g Arakan(USA) —Almi Ad (USA) (Silver Hawk (USA))
836[9]

Wee Sonny (IRE) *Liam Lennon* 100h 99c
5 b g Refuse To Bend(IRE) —Coup De Coeur (IRE) (Kahyasi)
51[5] 3551[6]

Weetentherty *Jim Goldie*
4 b g Bertolini(USA) —Binaa (IRE) (Marju (IRE))
1576[P] 1696[9]

Weetfromthechaff *Maurice Barnes* 100h
6 gr g Weet-A-Minute(IRE) —Weet Ees Girl (IRE) (Common Grounds)
727[3] (800) 2208[15]

Weet In Nerja *James Unett* 79h
5 b g Captain Rio—Persian Fortune (Forzando)
299[4] 462[8]

Wee Ziggy *Michael Mullineaux* 82h 88c
8 b g Ziggy's Dancer(USA) —Midnight Arrow (Robellino (USA))
54[5] 328[5] 480[3] ◆ 713[3] 849[P] 1064[8] 1450[7] 1647[P] 1732[14]
4945[2] 5379[5]

Weird Al (IRE) *Ian Williams* 122h 159c
8 b g Accordion—Bucks Gift (IRE) (Buckley)
(2105)
2673[8] 4850[P]

Welcome Stranger *Louise Davis* 98h
11 b g Most Welcome—Just Julia (Natroun (FR))
682[P] 829[5] 933[6] 1484[5] 1569[4] 4751[5] 4949[2]

Welcome Wonder *John Allen* 86h
7 ch m Most Welcome—Star Of Wonder (FR) (The Wonder (FR))
500[8] 733[7] 1689[9]

Weldone Honey *Peter Bowen* 77h
6 ch m Weld—Di's Last (Ra Nova)
375[6] 568[6] 841[4] 1275[5] 1369[U] 1482[F]

Well Chilled *Peter Winkworth*
6 b m Nikos—Cool Spring (IRE) (Zaffaran (USA))
3616[P]

Well Disguised (IRE) *Donald Whillans* 107h
9 b m Beneficial—Executive Move (IRE) (Executive Perk)
316[7] 4166[4]

Wellesley *Donald Whillans* 75h
5 b g Bertolini(USA) —Markova's Dance (Mark Of Esteem (IRE))
289[7] 748[7] 870[7] 948[9]

Wellforth (IRE) *Paul John Gilligan* 129h 123c
7 b g New Frontier(IRE) —Faitch's Lady (IRE) (Dock Leaf)
(4181)
4856[F]

Well Hello There (IRE) *Jonjo O'Neill* 104h
5 b g Oscar(IRE) —Bird Of Passage (Shambo)
1962[7] 2282[2] ◆ 3158[8] 3744[8]

Well Mick (IRE) *Jonathen de Giles* 72h 83c
10 b g Naheez(USA) —Commonary (IRE) (Commanche Run)
245 251[P] 4144[7]

Well Oiled (IRE) *Sandy Forster* 113h 90c
10 b g Supreme Leader—Mightyatom (Black Minstrel)
395[4] 728[4] 1001[8] 1646[6] 2301[5]

Well Refreshed *Peter Winkworth* 100h
7 b g Nikos—Cool Spring (IRE) (Zaffaran (USA))
3678[9] 4091[7] 4332[6] (4878)

Well Sprung (IRE) *Peter Winkworth* 81b
5 b m Generous(IRE) —Cool Spring (IRE) (Zaffaran (USA))
4027[9] 5284[5]

Welsh Jaunt *Dai Burchell* 75h
6 b m Laveron—Arcachon (GER) (Platini (GER))
16[8] 298[4] 757[F]

Wendel (GER) *Venetia Williams* 110h 116c
7 gr g Definite Article—Wild Side (GER) (Sternkoenig (IRE))
4720[3]

Wendy'Sgreyhorse *Geoffrey Harker* 78b
5 gr m Beneficial—Nearly Decent (Nearly A Hand)
5135[7]

Wenger (FR) *Shaun Lycett* 100h 96c
11 b g Unfuwain(USA) —Molly Dance (FR) (Groom Dancer (USA))
2249[F]

Wensleydale Web *Martin Todhunter* 95h 39c
9 b m Kayf Tara—Little Red Spider (Bustino)
166[8] 582[3] 727[4] (920)
1001[9]

We'Re Delighted *Michael Blake* 96h
6 b g Tobougg(IRE) —Samadilla (IRE) (Mujadil (USA))
462[6] 762[11] 1060[3] 1340[6] 1549[2] 1949[9] 2485[8]

Wessex King (IRE) *Henry Daly* 123h 124c
7 b g Second Empire(IRE) —Winchester Queen (IRE) (Persian Bold)
329[3] 1770[3] 1961[U] 3949[5] ◆ 4460[P] 4934[7]

West Bay Hoolie *Helen Nelmes* 21b
5 b g Nomadic Way(USA) —West Bay Breeze (Town And Country)
589[13] 4376[10]

Westcoat Lad *Kevin Tork* 14h
6 b g Lahib(USA) —Jabuka (Shareef Dancer (USA))
832[9] 1475[5] **4936[U] 5283[7]**

Westendjack *Maurice Barnes* 22b
4 b g Piccolo—Everdene (Bustino)
5313[12]

West End Rocker (IRE) *Alan King* 124h 148c
9 bb g Grand Plaisir(IRE) —Slyguff Lord (IRE) (Lord Americo)
(2962)
(3568) 4208[P] 5200[B]

Western Bound (IRE) *Gordon Elliott* 100h
10 ch g Presenting—Mid West Girl (IRE) (Commanche Run)
3750[7]

Western Charmer (IRE) *D T Hughes* 140h 141c
9 b g Good Thyne(USA) —Tulladante (IRE) (Phardante (FR))
3174a[3] 3579a[2] 4084a[4] 5141a[2]

Western Gale (IRE) *Martin Todhunter* 128h 118c
8 br g Presenting—Kate Gale (IRE) (Strong Gale)
314[4] 626[3] 859[3] 1002[6] 1326[3] 1763[4] 2079[P] (5353)

Western High *Jim Best* 94b
6 b g Rainbow High—Western Ploy (Deploy)
4423[3] 5387[13]

Western Palm (IRE) *Charlie Mann* 85h 73c
8 b g Great Palm(USA) —Haveafewmanners (IRE) (Celio Rufo)
82[4] 528[5] **840[7] 991[P]** 1179[8]

Western Pride *Richard Price* 71b 81c
8 b m Classic Cliche(IRE) —Llanfihangel Lass (Gildoran)
1106[6] (1273)
1481[P] 1744[P]

Western Whisky (FR) *Richard Lee* 119h 112c
9 b g Passing Sale(FR) —Winska Girl (FR) (Ashtar)
2366[F] 3371[3] 4402[2] 4502[P]

Wester Ross (IRE) *James Eustace* 119h
7 b g Fruits Of Love(USA) —Diabaig (Precocious)
1608[3] 2636[4] 3688[20] 4503[4] 5117[6] 5193[3]

Westlin' Winds (IRE) *Charles Egerton* 137h
5 b g Montjeu(IRE) —Uliana (USA) (Darshaan)
1775[3] 1956[7] 3229[P] 3447[6] 4220[P] 4485[8] 4975[3]

Westmeath *Paul Nolan* 128h
6 b g Kayf Tara—Squaw Talk (USA) (Gulch (USA))
5186[P]

Weststern (GER) *Gary Moore* 99h 102c
8 b g Dashing Blade—Westafrika (GER) (Aspros (GER))
40[5] **477[2]**
799[6] 1082[4]

Westwire Toby (IRE) *Lynn Siddall* 63h
9 ch g Anshan—Ware It Well (IRE) (Torus)
3994[12] 4233[10] 4878[3]

West With The Wind *Evan Williams* 121h 150c
6 b g Fasliyev(USA) —Midnight Angel (GER) (Acatenango (GER))
(2) **192[2]**
(565) **(770)**
(1390)
4789[P]

Wham Bang *Robin Mathew* 88h 46c
7 b g Double Trigger(IRE) —Idiot's Lady (Idiots Delight)
556[F] 3261[P] 3530[P] 4522[4]
5216[5]

Whaston (IRE) *Pauline Robson* 98h
6 b g Hawk Wing(USA) —Sharafanya (IRE) (Zafonic (USA))
2658[3] 3855[8] 5307[7]

Whataboutya (IRE) *Jonjo O'Neill* 123h 125c
10 br g Eve's Error—Tara's Tribe (Good Thyne (USA))
(6) **301[3]**
526[3] 772[P] 1032[3] 1178[F] 1469[4] 1725[6] 2055[F]
2249[3] 3347[P]
4102[F]

What A Charm (IRE) *A L T Moore* 121h
4 b f Key Of Luck(USA) —Atalina (FR) (Linamix (FR))
3239a[7] 4295a[7] (4807)

What A Cliche *E N Cameron* 72h
8 b g Classic Cliche(IRE) —Calametta (Oats)
165[P] 4748[P]

What A Dream *William Amos* 99h
5 ch g Supreme Sound—Ben Roseler (IRE) (Beneficial)
2202[4] 2552[2] 3362[8] 4067[5] 4477[9] 4892[P]

What A Friend *Paul Nicholls* 131h 172c
8 b g Alflora(IRE) —Friendly Lady (New Member)
2524[5] 4186[2] 4850[4] 5200[P]

What An Oscar (IRE) *Nigel Twiston-Davies* 104h
6 b g Oscar(IRE) —Katie Buckers (IRE) (Yashgan)
1367[5] 1765[3] 2056[6] 2630[11] 3228[P] 4990[2]

What A Riddle (IRE) *A J Martin* 112h
8 b g Turtle Island(IRE) —What An Answer (IRE) (Executive Perk)
(289) 760[2] 870[F] (Dead)

What A Scientist (IRE) *Nigel Twiston-Davies* 116h 88c
11 b g Karinga Bay—Half Irish (Carlingford Castle)
501[P] 695[8] 1093[5] (1230) (1368) 1626[P]
1903[4] 2140[P] 2606[11]

What A Steel (IRE) *Alistair Whillans* 94h
7 b g Craigsteel—Sonya's Pearl (IRE) (Conquering Hero (USA))
2545[4] 3502[4] 3693[3] 4067[6]

What A Warrior (IRE) *Nigel Twiston-Davies* 109b
4 b g Westerner—Be Right (IRE) (Be My Native (USA))
2797[3] 3294[10] (4082) ◆ 4879[3]

Whatcanisay *James Frost* 69h 82c
12 b g Morpeth—Supreme Daughter (Supreme Leader)
1324 650[2] 1710[P] 2287[3] 2608[4] 3492[P] 3614[2] 4919[6]

Whatcanyasay *Evelyn Slack* 84h 89c
10 gr g Prince Daniel(USA) —Snowys Pet (Petong)
1358[F] 1647[P]
4510[7] 4799[4]

Whatdoidowiththat *Sue Smith* 99h 92c
8 ch g Minster Son—Wynyard Lady (Say Primula)
1507[5] (1782) 4391[5]

Whatdoyoucallit (IRE) *Evan Williams* 113h
6 b g Snurge—Glamorous Gale (Strong Gale)
1278[7] 1487[2] ◆ 1547[F]

Whatever Next (IRE) *Edward Creighton* 7h 120c
9 br g Presenting—Parsons Broom (IRE) (Brush Aside (USA))
3059[8] **3263[4] 3615[5] 3878[P]** 4427[6]
4921[3]

Whateverthewheather *Sandy Forster* 67h
7 b g Classic Cliche(IRE) —Galix (FR) (Sissoo)
470[9] 1760[7] 2103[P] 4136[P] 4958[5]

What Luck (IRE) *Sean Curran* 78h
9 b g Taipan(IRE) —Kilbally Quilty (IRE) (Montelimar (USA))
2271[1]

What Mix (FR) *F-X De Chevigny*
4 gr g Sagamix(FR) —Life Watch (USA) (Highland Park (USA))
1658a[P]

What Of It (IRE) *Tom George* 112c
8 bb g Tel Quel(FR) —Whats The Trouble (IRE) (Alphabatim (USA))
551[2] (4143)
4526[2] 5156[4]

What's For Tea *Paddy Butler* 89h
6 b m Beat All(USA) —Come To Tea (IRE) (Be My Guest (USA))
140[5] 384[4] 585[3]

Whatshallwedo *Chris Down* 69h
6 b g Zindabad(FR) —Key West (FR) (Highest Honor (FR))
3405[P] 3739[9] 4530[5] 4899[7] 5272[4]

What's Occurrin *Tim Walford* 102h
7 b g Robertico—Tugra (FR) (Baby Turk)
176[7] (1929) 2558[5] 2937[2] 3523[P] 5132[3]

What's Up Doc (IRE) *Lawney Hill* 108h 127c
10 b g Dr Massini(IRE) —Surprise Treat (IRE) (Shalford (IRE))
(135) **(1082)**
1163[3] 5116[2] ◆

Whats Up Woody (IRE) *Howard Johnson* 116h 117c
6 b g Beneficial—Lady Noellel (IRE) (Step Together (USA))
3435[4] 4004[P] 4362[2] (4893)

Whatuthink (IRE) *Oliver McKiernan* 155h 150c
9 ch g Presenting—Glen's Encore (IRE) (Orchestra)
2543[F] 5025a[3]

Wheelavit (IRE) *Claire Dyson* 121h
8 b g Elnadim(USA) —Storm River (USA) (Riverman (USA))
51[6] 235[4] (595) (853) 958[11]

Wheels Up (IRE) *Jonjo O'Neill* 128h 127c
10 b g Oscar(IRE) —Woodville Princess (IRE) (Torus)
2503[3] 3157[5] 3488[F] 4095[P]

Whenever *Richard Phillips* 117h
7 ch g Medicean—Alessandra (Generous (IRE))
756[3] 866[4] 1364[5] 1904[7]

Whenwehadmoney (IRE) *Evan Williams* 106h
7 ch g Talkin Man(CAN) —Honest-Lady (IRE) (Hays)
180[6] 792[3] ◆

Wheresben (IRE) *Seamus Fahey* 138h 102c
12 b g Flemensfirth(USA) —Chataka Blues (IRE) (Sexton Blake)
4298a[P].

Wheres Johnny *Jamie Poulton* 100h 98c
10 gr g Touch Of Grey—Lady Poly (Dunbeath (USA))
2430[2] 2949[6] 3348[4] (3610) 3793[9] 4121[5] 4399[7] 4773[7]

Wheres The Hare (IRE) *Rebecca Curtis* 108b
4 b g Flemensfirth(USA) —Knocknabrogue (IRE) (Afzal)
(5257)

Wheretheres A Will *Michael Mullineaux* 19h
9 gr g Wizard King—Sian's Girl (Mystiko (USA))
2365[P] 3897[P] 4281[13]
4741[P] 5377[P]

Whereveryougoigo (IRE) *Peter Bowen* 96h
5 b g Flemensfirth(USA) —Lady Appeal (IRE) (Phardante (FR))
739[2] 833[4] (1455) 1472[3] 1795[F] 1922[5] 2231[2] 2545[8] 3497[3] 3745[11] 4929[12]

Wheyaye *Valerie Jackson* 96h
9 ch m Midnight Legend—Sayin Nowt (Nicholas Bill)
1644[5] (2080) 4276[5] 4822[2] 5096[4]

Which Pocket (IRE) *D Laverty* 106h 123c
13 br g Norwich—Toran Pocket (Proverb)
4183[P]

Whiepa Snappa (IRE) *Pat Phelan* 45h
4 b g Whipper(USA) —Boudica (IRE) (Alhaarth (IRE))
1772[7]

Whimper (FR) *Nigel Twiston-Davies* 94c
6 b g Numerous(USA) —Pasta Reale (FR) (Johann Quatz (FR))
1047[4] 1152[F] 1297[P]

Whinstone Boy (IRE) *James Joseph Mangan* 135h 144c
10 b g Supreme Leader—Deemiss (IRE) (Buckskin (FR))
3798a[9]

Whipperway (IRE) *Sheena West* 95h
4 b f Whipper(USA) —Prince's Passion (Brief Truce (USA))
(1586) 2078[F] 2439[3] 2958[5] 3348[6] 3793[U] 3962[9]

Whiskey Mist (IRE) *Stephen McConville* 22b
7 b g Darnay—Super Boreen (Boreen (FR))
311[14]

Whiskey Ridge (IRE) *Sue Smith* 92h
5 b g High-Rise(IRE) —Little Chartridge (Anshan)
355[10] 718[9] 3715[6] 4739[7] 5031[8]

Whisky Magic (FR) *Howard Johnson* 125h
7 b g Maresca Sorrento(FR) —Winska Girl (FR) (Ashtar)
5030[U]

Whispering Death *Howard Johnson* 115h
9 br g Pivotal—Lucky Arrow (Indian Ridge)
(3783) 5431[P]

Whispering Jack *Charlie Mann* 121h
6 b g Beat All(USA) —Ski Shot (Petoski)
2058[9] 2493[9] 3556[11] 3762[6] 4224[2] (4441) (4704)

Whistle Me (IRE) *Chris Grant* 93b
5 ch g Definite Article—Storm Whistle (IRE) (Toulon)
3998^4 4423^4

Whitby Jack *Gary Moore* 120h
4 b g Bering—Sablonne (USA) (Silver Hawk (USA))
3443^P 3673^7 (3958) 4807^17 5227^8

Whitcombe Spirit *Jamie Poulton* 90h
6 b g Diktat—L'Evangile (Danehill (USA))
2183^7 2390^6 3350^4 (3611) 3868^4 4123^3 4540^11 4922^5

Whiteadder *Rose Dobbin* 84b
6 ch g Golden Snake(USA) —Solo Buck (Buckskin (FR))
47^5 399^10

White Diamond *Malcolm Jefferson* 90h
4 b f Bertolini(USA) —Diamond White (Robellino (USA))
3711^4 4283^6 4552^3

White Lightening (IRE) *John Wade* 91h
8 ch g Indian Ridge—Mille Miglia (IRE) (Caerleon (USA))
179^U 402^8 470^3 745^10

White On Black (GER) *Steven Dixon* 54h
10 b g Lomitas—White On Red (GER) (Konigsstuhl (GER))
86^6

White Star Line (IRE) *D T Hughes* 129h
7 b g Saddlers' Hall(IRE) —Fairly Deep (Deep Run)
4249a^7

Whitewater Dash *Jim Old* 94h 121c
11 b g Bob Back(USA) —Skiddaw Samba (Viking (USA))
2571^4 5061^P

Whizzaar *R M Woollacott* 134c
11 ch g Sayaarr(USA) —Whitstar (Whitstead)
3908^2 (4449)

Whodoyouthink (IRE) *Oliver McKiernan* 145h
6 b g Court Cave(IRE) —Glen's Encore (IRE) (Orchestra)
3474a^23 5187^17

Whoops A Daisy *Nicky Henderson* 131h
5 b m Definite Article—Bayariyka (IRE) (Slip Anchor)
2156^2 ◆ (3365) (3918) (4377) 5008^16

Who's Afraid *Alan King* 94b
4 b f Loup Sauvage(USA) —Vis Comica (FR) (Fill My Hopes (FR))
(2965) 3876^8 5306^10

Whos Counting *Kevin Bishop* 63h
7 ch m Woodborough(USA) —Hard To Follow (Dilum (USA))
754^P 1058^3

Who's Deal (IRE) *Gerard J O'Keeffe* 104h 122c
9 b g Pistolet Bleu(IRE) —Native Deal (IRE) (Be My Native (USA))
1131a^P

Why Are You Asking (IRE) *Rose Dobbin* 44h
6 b g Needle Gun(IRE) —Tyrilda (FR) (Saint Cyrien (FR))
3887^P 4165^14 4473^P 5428^7

Why So Serious *Peter Salmon* 59h
5 ch g Falbrav(IRE) —Marrakech (IRE) (Barathea (IRE))
474^7 732^10 1962^16 2092^17 3620^11 3996^P

Wicked Streak (IRE) *Micky Hammond* 82h
6 b g Peintre Celebre(USA) —Peruvian Witch (IRE) (Perugino (USA))
609^4 841^3 1867^8 2092^10 2349^11 5307^9 5356^7

Wicked Times *Sue Smith* 68h
6 b g Olden Times—La Notte (Factual (USA))
1629^8 2092^14

Wicklewood *Christine Dunnett* 89h
5 b g Mujahid(USA) —Pinini (Pivotal)
135^3 439^2 697^9 2114^4 2438^P *3091^7* 3302^10

Wide Receiver (IRE) *Charlie Morlock* 80h 89c
8 b g Taipan(IRE) —The Plud (IRE) (Lord Americo)
1969^P 2170^7 2557^3 3377^P (3961)
4483^P 4829^3 5216^9

Wiesenfurst (GER) *John Berwick* 86h 92c
7 ch g Artan(IRE) —Wiesenblute (GER) (Big Shuffle (USA))
63^2 (283)
529^P 689^P 1991^5 2292^4 3699^P 4900^P

Wiesentraum (GER) *Lucy Wadham* 108h
5 ch g Next Desert(IRE) —Wiesenblute (GER) (Big Shuffle (USA))
3200^6 3546^6 4500^2 4986^5

Wiffy Chatsby (IRE) *Paul Nicholls* 105b
4 br g Presenting—Star Child (GER) (Neshad (USA))
5158^3

Wikaala (USA) *Gordon Elliott* 135h 119c
6 ch g Diesis—Roseate Tern (Blakeney)
(861) **1936^2**

Wilbury Star (IRE) *Nicky Henderson* 110h
5 br g Trans Island—Gold Blended (IRE) (Goldmark (USA))
315^7 563^4 (823) 914^3 1158^4 1453^5 2081^6

Wild Bay *Nick Gifford* 79h
8 b g Karinga Bay—Let's Park (IRE) (Brush Aside (USA))
1675^6 **2132^P**

Wild Cane Ridge (IRE) *Rose Dobbin* 89h 121c
12 gr g Roselier(FR) —Shuil Na Lee (IRE) (Phardante (FR))
2205^6 3362^6 **(4137)**
4689^P

Wild Child Lucy *Alistair Whillans* 98b
5 b m Karinga Bay—Thorterdykes Lass (IRE) (Zaffaran (USA))
4547^3 5342^4 ◆

Wild Desert (FR) *Charlie Longsdon* 118h
6 bb g Desert Prince(IRE) —Sallivera (IRE) (Sillery (USA))
1613^4 2038^5 2361^8 ◆ (3509) 4285^P 4990^8 5424^P

Wilde Ruby (IRE) *Seamus Mullins* 95b
4 b f Oscar(IRE) —Ruby Thewes (IRE) (Anshan)
(5380)

Wilde Wit Pleasure (IRE) *Sean O O'Brien* 188h 78c
8 b g Oscar(IRE) —Be My Pleasure (IRE) (Be My Native (USA))
3474a^5

Wild Geese (IRE) *Jonathan Portman* 28h
4 br g Cape Cross(IRE) —Intrepidity (Sadler's Wells (USA))
2958^13

Wild Ground (IRE) *Kevin Bishop* 82h 73c
10 ch m Simply Great(FR) —Rapid Ground (Over The River (FR))
3907^8

Wild Lyph *Neil Mulholland*
5 b g Loup Sauvage(USA) —A Lyph (USA) (Lypheor)
635^P

Wild Power (GER) *Helen Nelmes* 97h 90c
13 b g Turtle Island(IRE) —White On Red (GER) (Konigsstuhl (GER))
1231^U 1283^8 1493^4

Wild Rhubarb *Jonjo O'Neill* 86h
6 ch m Hernando(FR) —Diamant Noir (Sir Harry Lewis (USA))
3296^4 3952^8

Wild Side Of Life (IRE) *Tim Vaughan* 78h
8 gr g Exit To Nowhere(USA) —Gypsy Kelly (IRE) (Roselier (FR))
1368^9 1507^P 1707^3
1995^F

Wild Tango *Bob Buckler* 56b
5 ch g Loup Sauvage(USA) —Danse Slave (FR) (Broadway Flyer (USA))
3936^5

Wild Tonto (IRE) *Nigel Twiston-Davies* 116h 110c
8 b g Saddlers' Hall(IRE) —Shipping News (IRE) (Glacial Storm (USA))
3^3 (172) 302^7 696^5

Wilfie Wild *Mrs Lynne Ward* 90c
15 b g Nomadic Way(USA) —Wild Child (Grey Ghost)
551^8

Wilkinson Court *John Mackie* 23b
4 br f Karinga Bay—Do It On Dani (Weld)
4554^14 5119^12

Willandrich (IRE) *Ian Williams* 104h 114c
9 b g Insan(USA) —Cool Mary (Beau Charmeur (FR))
2161^5 3370^9 3693^7
4022^4 (4694)
(5120)

Willard *Tony Carroll* 56b
5 b g Hamas(IRE) —Flicker (Unfuwain (USA))
3773^14 4055^13

Willent *Julie Camacho*
5 b g Lend A Hand—Lapu-Lapu (Prince Sabo)
1832^P

William Bonney (IRE) *Ann Price* 114h 128c
11 br g Oscar(IRE) —Beaudel (Fidel)
5083^8 5237^U 5394^3

William Butler (IRE) *Evan Williams* 120h 127c
11 b g Safety Catch(USA) —Rosie Josie (Trombone)
567^4 (824)
852^4 1431^2

William Hogarth *Keith Goldsworthy* 129h 118c
6 b g High Chaparral(IRE) —Mountain Holly (Shirley Heights)
(1773) 1884^4 1966^4 **2572^4** 3557^10 3688^7 4185^4 5003^4 5110^2 5255^2 **5397^P**

William Percival (IRE) *Henry Daly* 74h
5 b g Presenting—Soy Alegre (IRE) (Night Shift (USA))
304^5 2590^3 4012^8 4719^9 5343^5

William Somers *T F Sage* 128c
10 b g Parthian Springs—Cautious Leader (Supreme Leader)
150^2 (4141)

William's Wishes (IRE) *Evan Williams* 131h 139c
6 b g Oscar(IRE) —Strong Wishes (IRE) (Strong Gale)
207^7 **(1936)**
(2422)
(3838)

William Womble *James Frost* 14b
4 b g Morpeth—Miracle Monarch (Elegant Monarch)
2797^10 3478^P

Willie Ever *D C Gannon* 6h
7 b g Agnes World(USA) —Miss Meltemi (IRE) (Miswaki Tern (USA))
75^P **4293^P**

Willie Hall *William Amos* 114h
7 b g Alflora(IRE) —G'Ime A Buzz (Electric)
2202^7 2552^10 3633^2 4166^2 (4544) 5098^2 5315^10

Willie Martin (IRE) *Michael O'Hare* 104b 101c
6 b g Beneficial—Coronea Sea Queen (IRE) (Bassompierre)
605^5 2299^5

Willie Wong (IRE) *W R Kinsey* 89h
9 ch g Anshan—Miss Aylesbury (IRE) (Le Moss)
79^P

Will If I Want (IRE) *Sophie Leech* 113h 25c
10 ch g Accordion—Kakemona (Kambalda)
1109^F 1739^7

Willing Weasel (IRE) *Miss M Chesterman* 91h 101c
9 b g Rudimentary(USA) —Final Peace (IRE) (Satco (FR))
4748^P

Will Jamie Run (IRE) *John C McConnell* 140h 140c
10 b g Dr Massini(IRE) —Fillo'srun (IRE) (Commanche Run)
1527a^6 3206a^10 3798a^10

Willos Silvergirl *Keith Goldsworthy* 32b
5 b m Silver Patriarch(IRE) —Ladyalder (Alderbrook)
686^13

Willowpattern *Martin Keighley* 65b
8 b m Young Buster(IRE) —My French Willow (Man Of France)
234^P

Willow's Saviour *Charlie Longsdon* 91b
4 ch g Septieme Ciel(USA) —Willow Gale (Strong Gale)
4329^3 5063^3

Willow The Rose *J R Jenkins* 73b
4 b f Zamindar(USA) —Lilac Lady (Weld)
2965^10 *3979^2* 4505^6

Willowthewizard *Shelley Johnstone*
7 b g Wizard King—Kashana (IRE) (Shahrastani (USA))
2553^13 3885^P

Willow Wren *Renee Robeson* 98h
6 ch m Alflora(IRE) —Wren Warbler (Relkino)
2532^P 4812^3 5265^F

Willy Be Lucky (IRE) *Seamus Mullins* 66h
5 b g Classic Cliche(IRE) —Hadaani (Mtoto)
222^2 2432^4 2963^13

Wilmington *Jean McGregor*
7 ch g Compton Place—Bahawir Pour (USA) (Green Dancer (USA))
870^P

Winbury *Ken Wingrove*
8 b g Overbury(IRE) —Winnetka Gal (IRE) (Phardante (FR))
1571^P 1705^10

Winchester Red *Evan Williams* 90h 119c
9 ch g Gunner B—M I Babe (Celtic Cone)
599^2 911^P 3840^7 4407^P

Wind Instrument (IRE) *Alan King* 130h 132c
10 ch g Accordion—Windy Bee (IRE) (Aristocracy)
2358^10 3629^9 5154^P

Windmill Cross (IRE) *D J Barry* 8h
9 b m Insatiable(IRE) —Windmill Theatre (IRE) (Beau Charmeur (FR))
858^5

Windpfeil (IRE) *Simon Burrough* 89h
5 bl g Indian Ridge—Flying Kiss (IRE) (Sadler's Wells (USA))
171^2 338^3 1844^P

Wind Prospect *Ray Craggs* 49b
5 b g Shinko Forest(IRE) —Rasin Luck (Primitive Rising (USA))
3731^10

Wind Shuffle (GER) *Jim Goldie* 121h 135c
8 b g Big Shuffle(USA) —Wiesensturmerin (GER) (Lagunas)
(445) 870^2 (1114)
(3359) 4002^3 4472^3 5318^3

Wind Star *Milton Harris* 81h
8 ch g Piccolo—Starfleet (Inchinor)
1030^4

Windy Hills *Nicky Richards* 115h 95c
11 bl g Overbury(IRE) —Chinook's Daughter (IRE) (Strong Gale)
164^6

Winged Farasi *Joanne Foster* 103h 99c
7 b g Desert Style(IRE) —Clara Vale (IRE) (In The Wings)
77^3 403^F 516^F (1362) 2644^5 2937^6 (4960) 5208^4

Wingman (IRE) *Gary Moore* 116h
9 b g In The Wings—Precedence (IRE) (Polish Precedent (USA))
2498^8 2977^17 3447^P

Wingull (IRE) *George Baker* 95h 101c
7 b g Darnay—Avro Avian (Ardross)
23^3 252^8 **1823^2 2053^2 2575^2**

Winner Takes Itall *T J Taaffe* 111h
7 b g Heron Island(IRE) —Persrolla (Persian Bold)
1847a^5

Winnetka Dancer *David Bridgwater* 14b
6 gr g Baryshnikov(AUS) —Winnetka Gal (IRE) (Phardante (FR))
3897^P 4747^P

Winning Counsel (IRE) *Miss A Smith-Maxwell* 116h 106c
9 br m Leading Counsel(USA) —Dainty Daisy (IRE) (Buckskin (FR))
406^P

Winning Show *Chris Gordon* 87h 86c
7 b g Muhtarram(USA) —Rose Show (Belmez (USA))
1293^2 1478^P (1592) 1915^F 2135^3

Winsley Hill *Neil Mulholland* 123h 130c
9 b m Midnight Legend—Hinemoa (IRE) (Mandalus)
300^P 708^12 846^3 986^9 1033^3 (1590) 1776^4 1904^2 2218^3 2514^P

Winter Alchemy (IRE) *Nicky Richards* 90h
6 b g Fruits Of Love(USA) —Native Land (Be My Native (USA))
1911^11 2208^4 3363^4 4390^3 **4911^U**

Winter Holly *Tim Walford* 84h
5 b m J B Quick—Nativus (IRE) (Be My Native (USA))
841^5 1140^P 1260^5 1499^P 1623^5 1822^P 2425^3 3392^5

Winter Star *Evan Williams* 130h
11 b g Overbury(IRE) —Pepper Star (IRE) (Salt Dome (USA))
1452^P

Winterwood (IRE) *Tim Vaughan* 124h 127c
8 b g Definite Article—Miss Dolly (IRE) (Alzao (USA))
1964^6 2278^4 3586^5 (4160)
4989^2 5341^P

Wise Hawk *Chris Down* 84h
6 b g Hawk Wing(USA) —Dombeya (IRE) (Danehill (USA))
2150^8 2485^5 3449^5 3619^3 4446^7 4536^5

Wise Move (IRE) *Nicky Henderson* 111h
5 b g Kalanisi(IRE) —Akariyda (IRE) (Salse (USA))
3678^7 ◆ 5115^5

Wise Princess *Bill Turner* 77h
5 ch m Riverwise(USA) —Princess Penny (King's Signet (USA))
1487^8 1549^P

Wishes Or Watches (IRE) *John Upson* 44h 70c
11 br g Bravefoot—Shadya's Amal (Shaadi (USA))
136^P 2187^4 2434^F 3397^5
3606^2 3792^P 4426^P

Wishfull Thinking *Philip Hobbs* 144h 163c
8 ch g Alflora(IRE) —Poussetiere Deux (FR) (Garde Royale)
1985^F (2220)
2867^2 ◆ (3804) ◆ 4816^2 ◆ (5165) ◆

Wisteria Lane (IRE) *Anabel L M King* 80h
8 b g In The Wings—Web Of Intrigue (Machiavellian (USA))
678^2 825^3 862^F 1272^5 1735^7 1822^7

Wistow *Pam Sly* 125h
7 b m Sir Harry Lewis(USA) —River Bay (IRE) (Over The River (FR))
3692^3 (4182) (4747) 5008^7

Witch Of The Wave (IRE) *Joanna Davis* 91h
5 ch m Dr Fong(USA) —Clipper (Salse (USA))
252^10 410^5 630^8

Witch's Hat (IRE) *Jim Old* 90h 95c
8 br g Hubbly Bubbly(USA) —Bold Shilling (IRE) (Meneval (USA))
2469^9 2637^4 **3391^5 5109^P**

Wither Hills (IRE) *I R Ferguson* 83h
5 b g Karinga Bay—Bonnie Article (IRE) (Definite Article)
311^3 ◆

With Grace *Peter Bowen* 110b
6 b m Alflora(IRE) —Rakajack (Rakaposhi King)
(333) (686) 2546^3 5188^17

With Speed (GER) *Ronald O'Leary* 99h
8 br g Spectrum(IRE) —Well Known (GER) (Konigsstuhl (GER))
1666^3

Withy Mills *Kevin Bishop* 87b
6 gr m Baryshnikov(AUS) —Gipsy Rose (Nicholas Bill)
1748^7 2156^7 5157^7

Witness Run (IRE) *Sandy Thomson* 83h 92c
11 b g Witness Box(USA) —Early Run (Deep Run)
160^P 393^6 875^P 4477^12

Wizaller *Henrietta Knight* 83h
6 b m Erhaab(USA) —Ardenbar (Ardross)
97^6

Wizard Of Edge *Ron Hodges* 117h 105c
11 b g Wizard King—Forever Shineing (Glint Of Gold)
1843^P 3646^8 3907^7

Wizard Of Odds *Tom Gretton* 115h
9 b g Wizard King—Chardon (IRE) (Camden Town)
270^4 706^5 4074^7

Wizard Of Us *Michael Mullineaux* 93h
11 b g Wizard King—Sian's Girl (Mystiko (USA))
96^8 336^7

Wizards Dust *Donald McCain* 75h 106c
9 gr g Environment Friend—Linoats (Derrylin)
489^3 599^3 867^8 1152^6

Wogan *Nicky Henderson* 126h 143c
11 b g Presenting—Fall About (Comedy Star (USA))
2522^3 4284^6 5229^3

Wolf Moon (IRE) *Martin Keighley* 128h 128c
8 b g Presenting—Toasted Oats (IRE) (Be My Native (USA))
1854^3 2357^6 2869^P 3784^5 (4394)
4790^11 5003^10
5353^P 5421^P

Wolf Rock *David Barron*
4 ch g Lomitas—Shore Light (USA) (Gulch (USA))
2614^P

Womaniser (IRE) *Clive Drew* 19h
7 br g Rock Of Gibraltar(IRE) —Top Table (Shirley Heights)
1505^9

Won In The Dark (IRE) *Sabrina J Harty* 161h
7 b g Montjeu(IRE) —Meseta (Lion Cavern (USA))
2516^5 3205a^5 3939^4 5160^3

Won More Night *Martin Keighley* 85h 87c
9 b m Kayf Tara—Wonderfall (FR) (The Wonder (FR))
2583^9 3782^10 (4738) 4922^9 4965^2 5307^4

Wonmorenomore (IRE) *Anthony Middleton* 75b
5 br g Bob's Return(IRE) —Marine Leader (IRE) (Supreme Leader)
1817^8 4468^18

Wood Burner *Chris Down* 62b
6 b m Fleetwood(IRE) —Hot Classic (Classic Cliche (IRE))
332^9

Woodfield Queen (IRE) *Joseph Fox* 64h
7 b m Arctic Lord—Woodfield Lass (IRE) (Bustineto)
1092^P

Woodhouse Mill (IRE) *Nigel Tinkler*
4 b f Oratorio(IRE) —Wurfklinge (GER) (Acatenango (GER))
1324^P

Woodlands Gem (IRE) *Peter Pritchard* 82h
9 b m Oscar(IRE) —Play It By Ear (IRE) (Be My Native (USA))
601^7 2239^7 (2589) 3530^P 5169^5 5374^7

Woodlands Genpower (IRE) *Peter Pritchard* 89h 93c
13 gr g Roselier(FR) —Cherished Princess (IRE) (Kemal (FR))
2557^P 3900^P

Woodlark Island (IRE) *David Pipe* 108h 112c
5 b g Tagula(IRE) —Be My Lover (Pursuit Of Love)
(430) 566^3 767^4 933^4
1767^2 (1888)
1912^2 2022^3 5066^3 5215^3

Wood Lily (IRE) *Mrs John Harrington* 123h
5 b m Definite Article—Sidalcea (IRE) (Oscar (IRE))
3592a^5

Woodmore (IRE) *Charlie Longsdon* 107h 104c
7 b g Luso—Supreme Stream (IRE) (Supreme Leader)
223^2 514^3 1692^4 2081^11 **2529^7** 3299^P
3880^3 4694^2 5060^P

Wood Yer (IRE) *Nigel Twiston-Davies* 95h
5 ch g Anshan—Glenasheen (IRE) (Presenting)
1593^2 3253^3 3724^2 4380^3

Woody Valentine (USA) *Evelyn Slack* 114h 114c
10 ch g Woodman(USA) —Mudslinger (USA) (El Gran Senor (USA))
87^5 515^4 846^11 4572^8 4998^10 5262^5

Woody Waller *Howard Johnson* 103h 124c
6 ch g Lomitas—Reamzafonic (Grand Lodge (USA))
3440^P
4063^4 (4823)

Woolcombe Folly (IRE) *Paul Nicholls* 143h 170c
8 bb g Presenting—Strong Gara (IRE) (Strong Gale)
(2517) ◆ (2881) 4805^10 5164^7

Word Of Warning *Martin Todhunter* 116h
7 gr g War Chant(USA) —Frosty Welcome (USA) (With Approval (CAN))
196^11 606^F 803^5 1004^6 (1118) 1364^2 1508^6

Work Boy *Sue Smith* 91h 117c
10 b g Nomadic Way(USA) —Swift Reward (Kinglet)
2476^3 2940^7 3510^3 (3716)
(4258) 4714^P

Working Title (IRE) *Nicky Henderson* 148h 141c
9 b g Oscar(IRE) —Dantes Term (IRE) (Phardante (FR))
372^6 (1508) (2125)
2674^4 *3059^2* **3453^7 4077^6**

World Of Events (USA) *Howard Johnson* 99h
6 br g Red Ransom(USA) —Sha Tha (USA) (Mr Prospector (USA))
1504^2 1762^2

World Watch (IRE) *Tom Gretton* 81h
6 b g Bob's Return(IRE) —Jessica's Pet (IRE) (King's Ride)
3489^3 3960^9 4377^11

Wor Rom (IRE) *Elliott Cooper* 107h
7 b g Subtle Power(IRE) —Snowbaby (IRE) (Be My Native (USA))
(66) 2941^11 3502^3 3621^5 (3883) 4391^2 4508^F 5205^6

Worship The Stars *Miss Sarah-Jayne Davies* 110c
10 gr g Silver Patriarch(IRE) —Sail By The Stars (Celtic Cone)
4969^2

Worth A King'S *Donald McCain* 115h
5 b g Red Ransom(USA) —Top Romance (IRE) (Entrepreneur)
191^2 (337) 679^2 1931^6 2542^9 2955^3 3334^12 4079^15 5205^5 5425^5

Wosayu *Colin Tizzard* 69h
5 b g Central Park(IRE) —Waltz On Air (Doc Marten)
2335^6 3301^12 3691^12 3906^11

Wotchalike (IRE) *Shelley Johnstone* 89h
9 ch g Spectrum(IRE) —Juno Madonna (IRE) (Sadler's Wells (USA))
405^2 4146^5

Wotsurpoison *Lucy Normile*
4 b g Exit To Nowhere(USA) —Misty View (Absalom)
3856^S

Wot Way Chief *Malcolm Jefferson* 111h 129c
10 b g Defacto(USA) —Wych Willow (Hard Fought)
45^3 715^3 2094^12

Wricksons Bridge (IRE) *Keith Goldsworthy* 98h
7 b g Moscow Society(USA) —Dan's Choice (IRE) (Spanish Place (USA))
220^5

Wujood *Laura Young* 91h 62c
9 b g Alzao(USA) —Rahayeb (Arazi (USA))
1095^10 1294^6 1446^8 1741^8 1996^8
2132^5 2608^P

Wulfrida (IRE) *Alison Thorpe* 79h
4 b f King's Best(USA) —Panna (Polish Precedent (USA))
2924^7

Wychwoods Kaddy *Graeme McPherson* 43h
5 ch g Kadastrof(FR) —Blackchurch Lass (IRE) (Taum Go Leor (IRE))
1729^12 2025^3 3920^5 4393^14 4767^8

Wychwoods Legend *Martin Keighley* 127h 130c
8 b m Midnight Legend—Miss Millbrook (Meadowbrook)
206^F

Wyck Hill (IRE) *David Bridgwater* 110h
7 b g Pierre—Willow Rose (IRE) (Roselier (FR))
1887^3 2154^4 2512^4 3950^9 4481^3

Wyeth *Gary Moore* 111h
7 ch g Grand Lodge(USA) —Bordighera (USA) (Alysheba (USA))
2169^P 4008^P

Wymott (IRE) *Donald McCain* 150h 155c
7 b g Witness Box(USA) —Tanya Thyne (IRE) (Good Thyne (USA))
(2303)
(2979) (3921)
4804^P

Wyse Hill Teabags *Jim Goldie* 138h
6 b g Theatrical Charmer—Mrs Tea (First Trump)
3547^3 (3965) 4475^3 (4910) 5166^3 ◆

Xtravaganza (IRE) *Jamie Snowden* 87h 41c
6 b m Xaar—Royal Jubilee (IRE) (King's Theatre (IRE))
340^8 **2287^5**

Yabora (FR) *Charlie Longsdon* 116h 134c
6 b g Timboroa—Hyacinthe (FR) (Epervier Bleu)
78^3 1990^4 ◆ 2388^6 3340^2
4355^P

Yachvili (IRE) *J J Lambe* 122h 114c
8 b g Xaar—Dananira (High Top)
729^6

Ya I Know (IRE) *Sarah Humphrey* 107c
10 b g Oscar(IRE) —Strong Rosejen (IRE) (Strong Gale)
3522^P 4402^U 4669^7

Yankee Holiday (IRE) *Sue Bradburne* 76h 98c
11 b g Oscar(IRE) —Parloop (IRE) (Buckley)
290^4

Yanky Sundown (FR) *P Bigot*
6 b g Until Sundown(USA) —Yanky Panky (USA) (Allen's Prospect (USA))
190a^5

Yarlington Mill *Edward Bevan* 77b
6 b g Fleetwood(IRE) —Dominant Duchess (Old Vic)
237^9 362^9

Yellow Flag *Jonjo O'Neill* 107h 130c
8 b g Halling(USA) —Bunting (Shaadi (USA))
(799) **(848)**
1151^2 1390^2 1861^F

Yeomanry *Ian Williams* 109h
6 b g High Chaparral(IRE) —Charming Life (NZ) (Sir Tristram)
596^2 805^4 932^4 2362^5

Yeoman Spirit (IRE) *John Mackie* 108h 116c
8 ch g Soviet Star(USA) —Hollywood Pearl (USA) (Phone Trick (USA))
2094^13 2372^8 5117^3 ◆ 5425^3

Yes I Can (IRE) *Miss Maria D Myco*
7 b g Great Palm(USA) —Rathcolman Queen (IRE) (Radical)
4553^P

Yes Man (IRE) *Peter Bowen* 100h 99c
6 b g Needle Gun(IRE) —Nut Touluze (IRE) (Toulon)
3154^6 3494^5 3873^2 4103^5

Yes Mate *Dianne Sayer* 68h 72c
7 ch g Alflora(IRE) —Sister's Choice (Lepanto (GER))
1757^10
1933^7 2602^P 3336^4 4511^6 **4799^2** 5298^11

Yes Minister (IRE) *Sophie Leech* 56h
7 b g Elnadim(USA) —Tahdid (Mtoto)
983^6 1114^5 1228^F 1592^3 1915^9

Yes Tom (IRE) *R T J Wilson* 126h
6 gr g Tikkanen(USA) —Ammieanne (IRE) (Zaffaran (USA))
2540^3 ◆ 3851^2 (4062) 5316^4

Yesyoucan (IRE) *Alan Fleming* 78h
6 b g Beneficial—Except Alice (IRE) (Orchestra)
1817^4 3344^9

Yetholm (USA) *Bernard Llewellyn* 117h 64c
6 rg g Dynaformer(USA) —Gypsy (USA) (Marfa (USA))
2530^8 *3169^10* 3587^4 3934^9 **4456^8** 5252^2

Yonder *Hughie Morrison* 102h
7 br m And Beyond(IRE) —Dominance (Dominion)
64^2 249^2

Yorgunnabelucky (USA) *Alan King* 108h
5 b h Giant's Causeway(USA) —Helsinki (Machiavellian (USA))
3781^5 ◆ 4069^3 4353^6

Yorkshire Knight (IRE) *Peter Bowen* 81h
6 b g Old Vic—Fosterandallen (IRE) (Petoski)
3525^7 3943^6 4500^13 5327^7

Yossi (IRE) *Richard Guest* 102h
7 b g Montjeu(IRE) —Raindancing (IRE) (Tirol)
1660^4 3899^5

Youandme (IRE) *Ray Peacock* 81h 24c
9 b g Norwich—Victorious Belle (IRE) (Crash Course)
1260^6 1449^8 1505^4 1730^P 1941^4
2588^4 5114^7

You Can Of Course (IRE) *Neil Mulholland* 82h 82c
8 b g Saddlers' Hall(IRE) —O'Dalaigh (IRE) (Tirol)
83^6 665^3 931^P 1423^6 1494^2 1679^2 **2050^2** 2239^4
2444^2 5324^5

You Do The Math (IRE) *William Hayes* 109h 117c
11 b g Carroll House—Ballymave (IRE) (Jareer (USA))
4928^3 5207^5

You Know Yourself (IRE) *Sue Smith* 102h 123c
8 b g Dr Massini(IRE) —Gift Of The Gab (IRE) (Orchestra)
1553^2 ◆ 1758^3 1959^8
(2371) 3695^P (4114)
4210^2 (4961)
5341^8

Youm Jamil (USA) *Henry Daly* 23h
4 rg g Mizzen Mast(USA) —Millie's Choice (IRE) (Taufan (USA))
3944^P 4774^6

You Mug *Sean Curran*
4 b g Denounce—Zaras Legend (Midnight Legend)
2047^P

You Never Said (IRE) *Charles Egerton* 104h
7 b g Dushyantor(USA) —Bramblehill Mandy (IRE) (Mandalus)
693^6

Young Albert (IRE) *Charlie Longsdon* 118h 118c
10 br g Taipan(IRE) —Smooth Leader (IRE) (Supreme Leader)
267^4 (1709) 2147^3 2606^4

Young Alfie *Keith Reveley* 41h
7 b g Alflora(IRE) —Keldholme (Derek H)
3885^10

Young Buddy *Malcolm Jefferson* 99h 31c
6 ch g Reel Buddy(USA) —Our Ethel (Be My Chief (USA))
2161^7
2450^6 3502^10

Young Firth *John Norton* 54h
4 b g Lucky Story(USA) —Le Petit Diable (IRE) (Trans Island)
3519^P 3994^7 4253^P 4878^6

Young Mags (IRE) *Nigel Twiston-Davies* 93b
4 ch f Presenting—Mags Benefit (IRE) (Beneficial)
2965^2 ◆ 3576^3 4335^6 5306^11

Youngstown (IRE) *Donald McCain* 115h 131c
8 b g Luso—Blue Approach (IRE) (Balinger)
1871^5 2476^2 3444^4 3922^4 4408^3 4937^P

Young Tot (IRE) *Carroll Gray* 86h 70c
13 b g Torus—Lady-K (IRE) (Rock Chanteur)
36^5 **373^4**
593^10 757^7 **1061^5** 1199^5 1300^4 1335^4
1447^4 1591^3

Young Valentino *Michael Appleby* 77h
9 ch g Komaite(USA) —Caprice (Mystiko (USA))
3882^P 4557^10 4814^P 5016^P

Young Victoria *Richard Lee* 109b
5 b m Old Vic—Siroyalta (FR) (Royal Charter (FR))
(2987) 3773^2 4335^3

Young Yozza *David Pearson* 92h 72c
9 b g Kayf Tara—Swift Messenger (Giolla Mear)
226^5 550^6

Youralltalk (IRE) *Keith Goldsworthy* 115h
7 b g Almaarad—Celtic Goblin (Swinging Rebel)
1349^2 1748^2 (1799) 2232^2 2454^2 3197^6

You're The Top (FR) *Nicky Henderson* 140h 141c
7 b g Poliglote—Lolly Lodge (FR) (Grand Lodge (USA))
1861^4 2086^5 4820^F ◆

Yourgolftravel Com *David Pipe* 97h
6 b g Fasliyev(USA) —Hiddnah (USA) (Affirmed (USA))
3477^U 3645^8 4028^F 4676^U 5101^F

Your Night Out (FR) *Matt Sheppard* 101h 75c
6 b m Dubai Destination(USA) —Happy Hour (GER) (Alzao (USA))
1283^P 1940^P

Yukon Quest (IRE) *Alan King* 90h
6 ch g Ashkalani(IRE) —Hidden Ability (IRE) (Alphabatim (USA))
2634^6 4051^6 5115^8

Yurok (IRE) *Sue Smith* 130h
7 b g Alflora(IRE) —Wigwam Mam (IRE) (Commanche Run)
(2102) 3572^2 4359^2 5186^P

Yu Tiger (IRE) *David Pipe* 84b
5 b g Haafhd—Pure (Slip Anchor)
833^7 1029^8

Yvonne Evelyn (USA) *Alan King* 102h
6 rg m Cozzene(USA) —One Great Lady (USA) (Fappiano (USA))
3740^3 4309^3 4897^5 5385^3

Zaarito (IRE) *C A Murphy* 131h 154c
9 b g Tiraaz(USA) —Coppenagh Girl (Kambalda)
2972a^2

Zacharova (IRE) *Venetia Williams* 64h 134c
8 b g Lil's Boy(USA) —Voronova (IRE) (Sadler's Wells (USA))
2358^P 2962^6 3949^RR 4460^RR

Zafar (IRE) *John Flint* 126h
8 b g Kalanisi(IRE) —Zafzala (IRE) (Kahyasi)
696^4 912^5 (1258) 1548^10

Zafeen Star *Susan Gardner*
4 ch f Zafeen(FR) —Rare Fling (USA) (Kris S (USA))
1913^14

Zaffarani's Star *Michael Gates* 65h 50c
10 b g Zaffaran(USA) —Slipstream Star (Slip Anchor)
930^P

Zaffman (IRE) *David Pritchard* 88h 98c
10 bb g Zaffaran(USA) —Cinderella's Dream (IRE) (Un Desperado (FR))
493^P 4286^P

Zafranagar (IRE) *Tony Carroll* 112h
6 b g Cape Cross(IRE) —Zafaraniya (IRE) (Doyoun)
2596^6 4049^5 4488^6

Zagova (IRE) *Philip Hobbs* 92b
5 b g Zagreb(USA) —Move Over Lucy (IRE) (Grand Plaisir (IRE))
3909^8

Zahara Joy *Maurice Barnes* 97h
8 ch m Cayman Kai(IRE) —Enjoy (IRE) (Mazaad)
870^5 1083^4 1357^7 (1504) (1700) 1931^5 2104^6

Zahirah Moon *Lady Herries* 91b
4 b f Grape Tree Road—Lunasa (IRE) (Don't Forget Me)
2052^2 4027^4 4728^18

Zahra's Place *Neil King* 118h
8 ch m Zaha(CAN) —La Piazza (IRE) (Polish Patriot (USA))
157^8

Zaidpour (FR) *W P Mullins* 150h
5 b g Red Ransom(USA) —Zainta (IRE) (Kahyasi)
(2967a) ◆ 3203a^2 4086a^2 4788^7

Zaif (IRE) *Dominic Ffrench Davis* 60h
8 b g Almutawakel—Colourful (FR) (Gay Mecene (USA))
1723^11

Zakatal *Philip Hobbs* 118h
5 gr g Kalanisi(IRE) —Zankara (FR) (Linamix (FR))
97^3 370^2 1941^2 3454^3 3762^3 4012^3 4524^3 5003^7

Zakeeta (IRE) *Oliver Sherwood* 105h
4 b f Intikhab(USA) —Julianne (IRE) (Persian Bold)
(1674) (2047) 2356^8 3374^8 4331^3 4555^6

Zama Zama *Nicky Henderson* 101b
4 b g Sakhee(USA) —Insinuation (IRE) (Danehill (USA))
(2458) 3294^6

Zambuka (FR) *Pat Murphy* 75h
4 gr f Zieten(USA) —Mercalle (FR) (Kaldoun (FR))
2466^9 3443^8 4331^4 4774^4 5168^6

Zanir (FR) *Tom George* 139h
7 b g Munir—Shahmy (USA) (Lear Fan (USA))
3557^4 4188^F 4848^13 (5159a)

Zanzibar Boy *Mrs K Fanshawe* 86h 118c
12 gr g Arzanni—Bampton Fair (Free Boy)
4271^P

Zarinava (IRE) *Mrs John Harrington* 136h
7 gr m Daylami(IRE) —Zariliya (IRE) (Darshaan)
2071^11

Zarinski (IRE) *Nicky Henderson* 105h
5 b g Dalakhani(IRE) —Zarafsha (IRE) (Alzao (USA))
2960^6 ◆ 3696^F

Zarkandar (IRE) *Paul Nicholls* 147h
4 b g Azamour(IRE) —Zarkasha (IRE) (Kahyasi)
(4350) ◆ (4847) ◆ (5161)

Zarrafakt (IRE) *Emma Lavelle* 125h 137c
7 b g Rudimentary(USA) —Carrick Glen (IRE) (Orchestra)
(2443)
2629^P 4877^P

Zaru (FR) *James Ewart* 96b
5 bb g Laveron—Zianini (FR) (Dom Pasquini (FR))
2943^7 3856^4 4574^4

Zava River (IRE) *Jamie Snowden* 83b
4 b g Zagreb(USA) —Great Accord (IRE) (Accordion)
3964^7 5158^6 5387^6

Zaynar (FR) *Nicky Henderson* 165h
6 gr g Daylami(IRE) —Zainta (IRE) (Kahyasi)
2516^4 2884^4 4819^12

Zazamix (FR) *Nicky Henderson* 118h 119c
6 b g Sagamix(FR) —Ombre Bleue (FR) (Agent Bleu (FR))
3447^3
4050^3 4461^7

Zed Candy (FR) *Richard Ford* 120h
8 b g Medicean—Intrum Morshaan (IRE) (Darshaan)
3821^P 4532^3 (4869)

Zefooha (FR) *Tim Walford* 83h
7 ch m Lomitas—Bezzaaf (Machiavellian (USA))
2092^8 2370^8 3637^9

Zelos (IRE) *David Bridgwater* 55h
7 b g Mujadil(USA) —First Degree (Sabrehill (USA))
171^8 490^P

Zelos Diktator *Gary Moore* 92h
5 br g Diktat—Chanterelle (IRE) (Indian Ridge)
(12) ◆ 212^P 552^10 1101^2 (3343) 4049^11 4670^4

Zemsky (IRE) *I R Ferguson* 128h 150c
8 ch g Presenting—Chic And Elite (Deep Run)
476^2 (4147) ◆ (4851)

Zepnove (IRE) *Neil King* 101h 76c
5 b m Noverre(USA) —Royal Zephyr (USA) (Royal Academy (USA))
313^11 1953^11 2514^12
3307^2 4955^P

Zero (IRE) *Emma Lavelle* 104h
8 b g Halling(USA) —Zonda (Fabulous Dancer (USA))
282^5 530^F

Zero Six Zoo (IRE) *Karen McLintock* 83h
8 b g Saddlers' Hall(IRE) —Miner's Twinkle (IRE) (Miner's Lamp)
2314^7 4511^4 4994^3

Zhakiera Spirit *Howard Johnson* 118b
5 b m Kayf Tara—Megalex (Karinga Bay)
(2616) ◆ (3504) 4728^5 5188^7

Zhukov (IRE) *Kevin Tork* 111h 93c
9 b g Saddlers' Hall(IRE) —Tamasriya (IRE) (Doyoun)
2230a^P
2392^2 2494^6 3869^6 4697^P
4831 4919^8 5281^5

Ziggy Zen *David Anthony O'Brien* 107h 98c
12 br g Muhtarram(USA) —Springs Welcome (Blakeney)
287^P

Zimbabwe (FR) *Nigel Hawke* 93h 85c
11 b g Turgeon(USA) —Razzamatazz (FR) (Always Fair (USA))
3609^4 3933^P 4772^2 5053^3 5324^P

Zi Missile (IRE) *Mary Evans* 63h 65c
7 b m Anshan—Landsker Missile (Cruise Missile)
665^5 795^P 1293^6 4405^2 4522^P 5103^10
5216^8

Zitenka (IRE) *Tim Easterby* 113h 138c
9 b g Beneficial—Volobollea (IRE) (Baragoi)
1871^6 2204^5 2374^6 2940^2 3522^7 4060^3 4742^5
(5430)

Zizou (IRE) *Sean Curran* 95h
8 b g Fantastic Light(USA) —Search Committee (USA) (Roberto (USA))
228^8 462^P 990^11 1199^12 1300^7 1431^6

Zoenicibel *Malcolm Jefferson* 92h
7 b m Kayf Tara—Romany Hill (Nomadic Way (USA))
726^3 920^2

Zoren (FR) *Raymond Shiels* 83h
7 b g Robin Des Champs(FR) —Zianini (FR) (Dom Pasquini (FR))
5148^6 5263^P

Zorro De La Vega (FR) *Sarah Humphrey* 98h 123c
8 b g Marathon(USA) —Shinobie (FR) (Le Nain Jaune (FR))
4858^6

Zuleta *Laura Young* 40h
10 ch m Vettori(IRE) —Victoria (Old Vic)
4032^P 4540^9 4900^8

Zuwaar *Paddy Butler* 82h
6 b g Nayef(USA) —Raheefa (USA) (Riverman (USA))
1547^8 1914^8

Season Statistics Owners - British Jumps 2010-2011

NAME	WINS-RUNS	2nd	3rd	4th	WIN PRIZE	TOTAL PRIZE
Trevor Hemmings	32 204 16%	27	23	10	£822,165	£951,635
John P McManus	84 650 13%	56	63	54	£430,611	£818,997
The Stewart Family	14 74 19%	12	10	5	£455,227	£549,563
Andrea & Graham Wylie	46 242 19%	35	28	20	£268,438	£439,553
Mrs Diana L Whateley	16 67 24%	16	6	7	£349,339	£425,532
Robert Waley-Cohen	3 14 21%	0	2	1	£405,674	£422,670
Clive D Smith	4 14 29%	1	4	0	£220,902	£300,026
T G Leslie	15 77 19%	21	12	8	£114,965	£294,039
Walters Plant Hire Ltd	21 80 26%	7	9	11	£222,939	£276,025
Gigginstown House Stud	6 29 21%	0	2	5	£218,151	£262,511
Michael Buckley	15 46 33%	7	1	2	£163,860	£245,153
D A Johnson	8 86 9%	9	6	8	£123,079	£222,271
Ann & Alan Potts Ptnrshp	2 6 33%	0	2	0	£207,480	£213,006
G Creighton/Mrs R Boyd	1 1 100%	0	0	0	£210,937	£210,937
R W-Cohen/M & S Br'ton	0 1	1	0	0	£0	£201,590
Simon W Clarke	2 14 14%	1	1	4	£141,790	£173,872
John Wade	22 156 14%	20	15	12	£118,626	£164,448
R Stanley/Y Reynolds III	3 5 60%	2	0	0	£78,086	£155,090
J Hales	6 32 19%	2	2	5	£136,654	£145,489
Paul Duffy Partnership	4 14 29%	0	3	2	£122,068	£140,695
Jimmy Nesbitt Ptnrship	2 3 67%	1	0	0	£100,315	£138,817
Paul Murphy	7 18 39%	6	2	0	£68,253	£136,845
Paul K Barber	0 3	1	1	0	£0	£129,698
Mrs Jean R Bishop	5 14 36%	4	1	3	£51,530	£125,731
Potensis Ltd & Chris Giles	3 3 100%	0	0	0	£125,728	£125,728
Our Friends In The North	1 4 25%	0	0	0	£112,660	£112,660
Simon Munir	9 66 14%	13	11	6	£38,808	£110,057
Mrs Findlay/Middleham Pk	1 1 100%	0	0	0	£102,618	£102,618
Alan Peterson	6 34 18%	0	5	3	£89,430	£101,795
Tony Bloom	3 12 25%	0	0	1	£95,947	£101,248
Potensis Limited	6 20 30%	2	3	5	£76,659	£100,815
Mrs T P Radford	1 42 2%	5	5	6	£2,277	£96,932
Hammer & Trowel Synd.	1 4 25%	1	0	1	£39,431	£96,926
Mr/Mrs R Anderson Green	9 104 9%	19	11	9	£31,986	£94,488
R E R Williams	24 98 24%	14	10	10	£73,989	£94,236
Andrew L Cohen	4 34 12%	2	6	5	£79,876	£90,491
Lady Clarke	5 13 38%	0	0	2	£72,804	£88,874
Terry Warner	1 37 3%	7	10	2	£42,758	£84,780
E A P Scouller	2 10 20%	0	1	3	£78,016	£84,150
Mr & Mrs William Rucker	7 40 18%	7	5	4	£24,360	£83,710
David Sewell	10 35 29%	5	3	0	£63,489	£82,197
C G Roach	5 36 14%	5	5	4	£29,957	£82,055

Season Statistics Trainers - British Jumps 2010-2011

NAME	WINS-RUNS	2nd	3rd	4th	WIN PRIZE	TOTAL PRIZE	£1 STAKE
Paul Nicholls	134 583 23%	89	81	55	£1,607,886	£2,424,059	-77.99
Nicky Henderson	153 612 25%	76	68	54	£1,591,676	£2,210,465	-77.66
Donald McCain	100 588 17%	97	64	54	£954,456	£1,286,133	-169.14
Philip Hobbs	86 556 15%	75	78	53	£817,243	£1,163,051	-154.06
David Pipe	65 504 13%	63	47	46	£545,872	£999,942	-99.39
Nigel Twiston-Davies	97 711 14%	74	81	77	£668,971	£988,425	+18.15
Alan King	84 600 14%	103	83	56	£528,023	£901,329	-180.82
Jonjo O'Neill	94 750 13%	70	75	64	£526,606	£861,735	-160.11
Evan Williams	90 595 15%	86	85	59	£355,650	£647,447	-75.90
Tim Vaughan	91 563 16%	82	59	66	£427,605	£574,061	-133.61
Howard Johnson	60 368 16%	50	39	35	£330,615	£524,195	-30.83
W P Mullins	4 35 11%	3	5	2	£318,454	£483,874	-12.92
Colin Tizzard	41 328 13%	50	36	35	£248,666	£436,281	-37.11
Peter Bowen	60 384 16%	60	39	43	£271,237	£396,962	+14.82
Ferdy Murphy	29 321 9%	39	32	34	£219,089	£392,034	-124.13
Gordon Elliott	35 123 28%	29	7	7	£280,026	£365,016	+46.24
Nick Williams	17 116 15%	15	13	19	£247,711	£352,498	+17.71
Tom George	18 224 8%	29	26	25	£228,764	£341,862	-103.27
Lucinda Russell	41 343 12%	43	40	38	£227,531	£323,903	-117.50
Gary Moore	45 390 12%	54	40	33	£171,450	£304,187	-30.36
Venetia Williams	38 372 10%	29	42	37	£164,601	£264,405	-83.62
Sue Smith	40 361 11%	29	31	22	£197,878	£258,496	-25.22
Charlie Longsdon	44 233 19%	38	27	23	£177,548	£258,091	+53.80
Emma Lavelle	30 206 15%	21	21	24	£188,293	£257,910	-41.04
Paul Webber	28 203 14%	23	19	25	£161,252	£256,818	-14.92
Henry De Bromhead	2 11 18%	1	3	0	£207,480	£228,602	+7.50
Brian Ellison	21 108 19%	12	17	16	£129,160	£223,407	+21.06
Milton Harris	32 311 10%	38	36	36	£114,520	£222,214	-34.83
Neil Mulholland	21 206 10%	33	10	24	£119,174	£202,968	-66.67
M M Lynch	0 1	1	0	0	£0	£201,590	-1.00
Malcolm Jefferson	26 208 13%	30	22	16	£105,581	£183,900	-6.20
Kim Bailey	38 200 19%	16	29	21	£141,015	£183,438	+54.19
Ian Williams	25 199 13%	33	19	19	£106,146	£175,966	-75.93
Victor Dartnall	26 145 18%	18	14	11	£92,197	£162,431	+9.75
Richard Lee	26 166 16%	19	21	18	£95,928	£151,872	+30.24
Patrick Rodford	12 60 20%	7	6	6	£101,658	£148,147	+73.60
Charlie Mann	20 202 10%	27	25	23	£91,852	£147,165	-42.50
Rebecca Curtis	28 150 19%	19	14	21	£89,872	£146,207	-53.98
Nicky Richards	18 189 10%	17	20	19	£108,204	£143,866	-68.66
Jennie Candlish	15 111 14%	14	12	13	£79,291	£138,637	+173.78
Henrietta Knight	6 150 4%	11	13	12	£25,899	£133,813	-63.88
Dr Richard Newland	22 108 20%	9	13	10	£102,200	£133,691	+23.17
John Wade	13 116 11%	13	12	12	£90,634	£128,270	-1.85
Brendan Powell	22 222 10%	25	24	28	£78,166	£128,175	-83.78
Lawney Hill	26 143 18%	21	11	21	£86,850	£121,933	+28.56
Oliver Sherwood	24 213 11%	26	22	25	£75,862	£117,058	+110.25
Martin Keighley	19 176 11%	22	19	13	£68,347	£116,840	-67.47
Keith Reveley	22 164 13%	25	23	15	£68,257	£112,832	+27.71
C A Murphy	1 3 33%	1	0	0	£42,959	£111,407	+4.00
Nick Gifford	17 128 13%	17	14	15	£64,552	£110,363	-27.25

Season Statistics Jockeys - British Jumps 2010-2011

NAME	WINS-RUNS	2nd	3rd	4th	WIN PRIZE	TOTAL PRIZE	£1 STAKE
A P McCoy	218 885 25%	137	91	82	£1,236,364	£1,871,512	-163.86
Richard Johnson	151 784 19%	116	110	67	£1,088,106	£1,442,329	-41.74
Jason Maguire	95 490 19%	79	62	44	£931,702	£1,233,428	-44.59
Paul Moloney	79 531 15%	76	75	60	£346,446	£606,001	-50.23
Paddy Brennan	78 535 15%	61	58	60	£534,540	£780,686	-42.80
Graham Lee	77 606 13%	80	67	70	£353,874	£599,951	-153.57
Tom O'Brien	74 466 16%	41	58	53	£357,580	£483,222	+2.60
Brian Hughes	65 541 12%	68	60	48	£245,205	£456,370	-176.36
Tom Scudamore	63 556 11%	84	55	62	£378,216	£717,038	-207.24
Aidan Coleman	61 491 12%	50	54	58	£266,986	£431,821	+12.74
Barry Geraghty	61 235 26%	40	18	23	£773,078	£1,225,058	-23.32
Sam Twiston-Davies	59 487 12%	50	52	47	£362,424	£514,108	-9.25
Dougie Costello	57 366 16%	55	36	35	£331,725	£444,400	-44.72
Daryl Jacob	56 427 13%	47	47	52	£456,976	£686,870	-88.46
Robert Thornton	52 375 14%	69	53	31	£325,698	£586,921	-120.84
Jamie Moore	47 417 11%	53	42	36	£179,255	£311,308	-19.02
Nick Scholfield	42 323 13%	36	31	30	£172,818	£270,747	-47.88
Wayne Hutchinson	41 284 14%	35	32	35	£205,386	£322,458	+12.80
Leighton Aspell	39 448 9%	46	56	52	£123,502	£230,720	-12.83
Felix De Giles	39 245 16%	20	31	18	£138,139	£204,266	+14.17
Sam Thomas	36 340 11%	38	30	35	£193,014	£406,645	-73.18
Jimmy Derham	36 319 11%	47	35	40	£126,172	£203,309	-83.49
Denis O'Regan	35 378 9%	42	34	42	£135,658	£229,460	-170.87
Richie McLernon	35 354 10%	21	40	25	£141,654	£210,855	-46.53
Andrew Tinkler	35 328 11%	40	42	28	£131,361	£217,757	-82.60
James Reveley	35 304 12%	46	36	28	£136,391	£240,288	-18.89
Barry Keniry	34 295 12%	34	44	27	£96,478	£154,116	-53.82
David Bass	33 234 14%	23	34	19	£174,570	£243,664	-22.43
Timmy Murphy	32 283 11%	29	20	19	£222,527	£424,210	-91.52
Noel Fehily	31 150 21%	23	17	11	£290,223	£383,732	-7.19
Peter Toole	30 285 11%	35	35	29	£120,158	£184,657	-60.04
Campbell Gillies	29 314 9%	33	41	29	£133,448	£197,997	-109.18
Harry Skelton	29 206 14%	29	28	24	£133,696	£291,629	+38.24
Peter Buchanan	28 304 9%	35	29	33	£155,444	£228,144	-129.09
Joe Tizzard	28 258 11%	37	28	27	£149,836	£281,436	-99.36
Jack Doyle	27 206 13%	14	21	22	£155,834	£213,822	-12.92
Richie McGrath	26 281 9%	22	32	26	£81,318	£133,945	-81.24
Paul Gallagher	26 193 13%	15	19	21	£143,614	£168,296	+13.57
R Walsh	26 106 25%	15	16	7	£875,583	£1,121,129	-11.10
Rhys Flint	25 309 8%	33	33	45	£92,778	£182,881	-92.17
Sean Quinlan	25 256 10%	16	30	26	£85,972	£135,355	-99.57
Ryan Mania	24 241 10%	29	18	24	£72,158	£122,823	-64.92
Charlie Poste	24 237 10%	25	24	22	£66,943	£113,851	+0.88
Donal Devereux	24 209 11%	28	22	18	£80,780	£131,966	+46.92
Warren Marston	23 224 10%	21	25	25	£82,724	£125,437	-59.80
Andrew Thornton	22 394 6%	32	48	41	£106,662	£182,030	-201.88
Will Kennedy	22 275 8%	22	31	14	£125,530	£193,456	+10.57
Wilson Renwick	22 235 9%	22	21	24	£85,432	£126,508	-100.14
Liam Treadwell	21 263 8%	31	26	29	£87,927	£160,252	-131.05
Johnny Farrelly	21 261 8%	23	19	13	£84,396	£129,993	-44.49

RACEFORM TOP RATED CHASERS AND HURDLERS 2010-2011

CHASERS

Long Run (FR)	183
Denman (IRE)	181
Sizing Europe (IRE)	176
Master Minded (FR)	176
Kauto Star (FR)	174
Twist Magic (FR)	174
What A Friend	172
Imperial Commander (IRE)	172
Poquelin (FR)	172
Riverside Theatre	172
Big Zeb (IRE)	171
Diamond Harry	171
Burton Port (IRE)	171
Somersby (IRE)	171
Golden Silver (FR)	170
Tidal Bay (IRE)	170
Woolcombe Folly (IRE)	170
Neptune Collonges (FR)	169
Pandorama (IRE)	169
Albertas Run (IRE)	168
Nacarat (FR)	168
Silver By Nature	168
Kalahari King (FR)	167
Kempes (IRE)	167
Midnight Chase	167
Petit Robin (FR)	167
Captain Cee Bee (IRE)	166
Gauvain (GER)	166
Tartak (FR)	166
Rubi Light (FR)	166
Captain Chris (IRE)	166

HURDLERS

Big Buck s (FR)	178
Grands Crus (FR)	171
Hurricane Fly (IRE)	170
Peddlers Cross (IRE)	169
Mourad (IRE)	167
Thousand Stars (FR)	165
Solwhit (FR)	165

RACEFORM JUMP MEDIAN TIMES 2010-2011

Some distances have been omitted where insufficient data exists to establish a reliable median times

AINTREE
Chase (Mildmay)
2m 4m 0.0
2m4f 5m 8.2
3m1f.................... 6m 30.0
Chase (National)
2m5f110y 5m 36.0
4m4f.................... 9m 20.5
Hurdles
2m110y 4m 4.6
2m4f.................... 5m 0.7
3m110y 6m 16.3

ASCOT
Chase
2m1f.................... 4m 15.0
2m3f.................... 4m 47.0
2m5f110y 5m 26.0
3m 6m 9.0
Hurdles
2m 3m 49.0
2m3f110y 4m 48.0
2m6f.................... 5m 27.0
3m 6m 11.0

AYR
Chase
2m 4m 10.7
2m4f.................... 5m 22.9
3m1f.................... 6m 49.9
4m1f.................... 8m 20.8
Hurdles
2m 4m 3.1
2m4f.................... 5m 12.0
3m110y 6m 31.8

BANGOR-ON-DEE
Chase
2m1f110y 4m 22.1
2m4f110y 5m 09.1
3m110y 6m 19.8
3m6f.................... 7m 55.0
Hurdles
2m1f.................... 4m 10.9
2m4f.................... 4m 57.4
3m 5m 51.0

CARLISLE
Chase
2m 4m 16.1
2m4f.................... 5m 27.4
3m110y 6m 42.4
3m2f.................... 7m 7.2
Hurdles
2m1f.................... 4m 29.8
2m4f.................... 5m 22.8
3m1f.................... 6m 38.2

CARTMEL
Chase
2m1f110y 4m 18.9
2m5f110y 5m 25.4
3m2f.................... 6m 34.9
3m6f.................... 7m 36.2
Hurdles
2m1f110y 4m 13.2
2m6f.................... 5m 29.3
3m2f.................... 6m 26.1

CATTERICK
Chase
2m 4m 0.1
2m3f.................... 4m 48.8
3m1f110y 6m 42.0
Hurdles
2m 3m 52.5
2m3f.................... 4m 46.8
3m1f110y 6m 27.6

CHELTENHAM (NEW)
Chase
2m110y 4m 6.7
2m5f.................... 5m 19.4
3m1f110y 6m 38.2
3m2f110y 6m 54.3
4m1f.................... 8m 49.9
Hurdles
2m1f.................. 4m 11.3
2m4f110y 5m 5.0
2m5f110y 5m 16.6
3m 6m 1.0

CHELTENHAM (OLD)
Chase
2m 3m 58.0
2m4f110y 5m 11.0
3m110y 6m 18.3
3m3f110y 7m 12.6
Hurdles
2m110y 4m 2.0
2m5f.................. 5m 13.4
3m1f110y 6m 30.9
Cross Country Chases
3m7f.................... 8m 38.0

CHEPSTOW
Chase
2m110y 4m 17.1
2m3f110y 5m 11.3
3m 6m 22.0
3m2f110y 7m 2.0
3m5f110y 7m 49.0
Hurdles
2m110y 4m 10.4
2m4f.................... 5m 2.7
3m 6m 16.8

DONCASTER
Chase
2m110y 4m 7.9
2m3f.................... 4m 49.0
3m 6m 12.7
3m2f.................... 6m 40.0
Hurdles
2m110y 4m 4.7
2m3f110y 4m 51.3
3m110y 6m 15.0

EXETER
Chase
2m1f110y 4m 19.0
2m3f110y 4m 57.3
2m7f110y 6m 0.1
3m1f110y 6m 41.1
4m 8m 28.7
Hurdles
2m1f.................. 4m 15.5
2m3f.................. 4m 42.7
2m6f110y 5m 48.0
3m110y 6m 14.4

FAKENHAM
Chase
2m110y 4m 16.6
2m5f110y 5m 41.8
3m110y 6m 35.7
Hurdles
2m 4m 5.4
2m4f.................... 5m 12.6
2m7f110y 6m 4.4

FFOS LAS
Chase
2m 4m 5.0
2m5f.................... 5m 34.0
3m 6m 23.0
Hurdles
2m 3m 54.0
2m4f.................... 4m 52.0
3m 6m 39.0

FOLKESTONE
Chase
2m 4m 7.2
2m5f.................... 5m 22.2
3m1f.................... 6m 35.8
3m2f.................... 6m 43.1
Hurdles
2m1f110y 4m 30.8
2m4f110y 5m 35.8
2m6f110y 6m 9.1

FONTWELL
Chase
2m2f.................... 4m 34.7
2m4f.................... 5m 7.3
2m6f.................... 5m 43.0
3m2f110y 7m 1.1
Hurdles
2m2f110y 4m 34.3
2m4f.................... 4m 59.4
2m6f110y 5m 42.5
3m3f.................... 6m 52.8

HAYDOCK
Chase
2m 4m 11.0
2m4f.................... 5m 10.0
3m 6m 14.0
3m4f.................... 7m 34.0
Hurdles
2m 4m 0.7
2m4f.................... 4m 56.0
3m 5m 52.0
3m1f.................... 6m 8.0

HEREFORD
Chase
2m 4m 3.6
2m3f.................... 4m 46.6
3m1f110y 6m 31.8
Hurdles
2m1f.................... 3m 59.4
2m3f110y 4m 47.9
3m2f.................... 6m 31.7

HEXHAM
Chase
2m110y 4m 9.8
2m4f110y 5m 13.5
3m1f.................... 6m 32.2
Hurdles
2m110y 4m 17.4
2m4f110y 5m 12.5
3m 6m 13.2

HUNTINGDON
Chase
2m110y 4m 10.2
2m4f110y 5m 5.3
3m 6m 10.3
Hurdles
2m110y 3m 54.9
2m4f110y 4m 59.0
2m5f110y 5m 10.6
3m2f.................... 6m 22.9

KELSO
Chase
2m1f.................... 4m 18.0
2m6f110y 5m 44.5
3m1f.................... 6m 31.5
3m4f.................... 7m 25.4
Hurdles
2m110y 4m 1.8
2m2f.................... 4m 27.0
2m6f110y 5m 41.0

KEMPTON
Chase
2m 3m 58.0
2m4f110y 5m 19.5
3m 6m 15.0
Hurdles
2m 4m 0.0
2m5f..................... 5m 24.0
3m 110y 6m 27.5

LEICESTER
Chase
2m 4m 8.2
2m4f110y 5m 18.9
2m7f110y 6m 4.0
Hurdles
2m 4m 1.0
2m4f110y 5m 24.7

LINGFIELD
Chase
2m 4m 7.8
2m4f110y 5m 18.2
3m 6m 23.7
Hurdles
2m110y 4m 14.1
2m3f110y 5m 6.7
2m7f..................... 6m 2.8

LUDLOW
Chase
2m 3m 58.5
2m4f..................... 5m 4.4
3m 6m 8.3
Hurdles
2m 3m 49.5
2m5f..................... 5m 14.8
3m 5m 52.3

MARKET RASEN
Chase
2m2f..................... 4m 35.0
2m4f..................... 5m 5.7
2m6f110y 5m 46.0
3m1f..................... 6m 31.3
3m4f110y 7m 47.1
Hurdles
2m1f110y 4m 19.0
2m3f110y 4m 51.7
2m6f..................... 5m 31.8
3m 6m 7.7

MUSSELBURGH
Chase
2m 3m 52.4
2m4f..................... 5m 1.2
3m 6m 3.4
Hurdles
2m 3m 48.4
2m4f..................... 4m 51.5
3m110y 5m 56.7

NEWBURY
Chase
2m1f..................... 4m 13.0
2m2f110y 4m 44.0
2m4f..................... 5m 12.0
2m6f110y 5m 50.3
3m 6m 11.0
3m2f110y 6m 56.0
Hurdles
2m110y 4m 9.9
2m3f..................... 4m 50.6
2m5f..................... 5m 19.0
3m110y 6m 8.3

NEWCASTLE
Chase
2m110y 4m 21.1
2m4f..................... 5m 27.2
3m 6m 22.5
3m6f..................... 8m 20.4
4m1f..................... 9m 7.8
Hurdles
2m 4m 10.0
2m4f..................... 5m 21.1
3m 6m 14.0

NEWTON ABBOT
Chase
2m110y 4m 6.5
2m5f110y 5m 21.4
3m2f110y 6m 44.6
Hurdles
2m1f..................... 4m 5.7
2m3f..................... 4m 33.9
2m6f..................... 5m 20.3
3m3f..................... 6m 41.0

PERTH
Chase
2m 4m 2.8
2m4f110y 5m 14.0
3m 6m 20.4
3m7f..................... 8m 11.6
Hurdles
2m110y 3m 59.7
2m4f110y 5m 6.9
3m110y 6m 9.9
3m3f..................... 6m 47.6

PLUMPTON
Chase
2m1f..................... 4m 25.9
2m4f..................... 5m 07.3
3m2f..................... 6m 50.7
3m5f..................... 7m 40.0
Hurdles
2m 4m 0.8
2m5f..................... 5m 22.3
3m1f110y 6m 28.8

SANDOWN
Chase
2m 4m 1.8
2m4f110y 5m 18.4
3m110y 6m 27.8
3m5f110y 7m 44.0
Hurdles
2m110y 4m 7.2
2m3f110y 5m 1.8
2m6f..................... 5m 30.0

SEDGEFIELD
Chase
2m110y 4m 8.6
2m4f..................... 5m 3.0
2m5f..................... 5m 18.0
3m3f..................... 6m 49.0
Hurdles
2m1f..................... 4m 6.9
2m4f..................... 4m 58.7
2m5f110y 5m 14.6
3m3f110y 6m 52.0

SOUTHWELL
Chase
2m1f.....................4m 7.7
2m4f110y 5m 15.0
3m110y 6m 26.0
3m2f..................... 6m 38.8
Hurdles
2m 3m 57.1
2m4f110y 5m 10.7
3m110y 6m 7.5

STRATFORD
Chase
2m1f110y 4m 7.1
2m4f..................... 4m 54.2
2m5f110y 5m 15.0
2m7f..................... 5m 41.6
3m4f..................... 7m 13.0
Hurdles
2m110y 3m 56.0
2m3f..................... 4m 35.3
2m6f110y 5m 28.1
3m3f..................... 6m 28.6

TAUNTON
Chase
2m110y 4m 10.0
2m3f..................... 4m 56.5
2m7f110y 6m 14.6
Hurdles
2m1f..................... 4m 8.0
2m3f110y 4m 46.0
3m110y 6m 7.1

TOWCESTER
Chase
2m110y 4m 16.1
2m3f110y 5m 18.2
2m6f..................... 5m 53.0
3m110y 6m 46.6
Hurdles
2m 4m 7.9
2m3f110y 4m 9.6
2m5f..................... 5m 38.9
3m 6m 15.0

UTTOXETER
Chase
2m 3m 55.6
2m5f..................... 5m 23.5
2m6f110y 5m 48.5
3m 6m 15.1
3m2f..................... 7m 4.0
4m1f110y 9m 0.0
Hurdles
2m 3m 55.2
2m4f110y 5m 4.0
2m6f110y 5m 30.9
3m 6m 5.0

WARWICK
Chase
2m 4m 5.6
2m4f110y 5m 21.0
3m110y 6m 27.0
3m2f..................... 6m 52.7
3m5f..................... 7m 41.0
Hurdles
2m 3m 56.5
2m3f..................... 4m 42.7
2m5f..................... 5m 15.0
3m1f..................... 6m 27.5

WETHERBY
Chase
2m 3m 55.8
2m4f110y 5m 7.8
2m7f110y 5m 58.5
3m1f..................... 6m 15.8
Hurdles
2m110y 3m 55.8
2m4f110y 5m 15.9
2m6f..................... 5m 28.6
3m1f..................... 6m 16.5

WINCANTON
Chase
2m 3m 59.9
2m5f..................... 5m 25.2
3m1f110y 6m 39.5
3m3f110y 7m 8.2
Hurdles
2m 3m 48.9
2m4f..................... 5m 0.0
2m6f..................... 5m 26.5

WORCESTER
Chase
2m 3m 51.6
2m4f110y 5m 5.6
2m7f110y 5m 55.7
Hurdles
2m 3m 47.3
2m4f..................... 4m 47.4
3m 5m 44.6

RACEFORM JUMPS RECORD TIMES 2010-2011

AINTREE

Distance	Time	Age	Weight	Going	Horse	Date
2m C	3m 45.2	9	10-7	Firm	Nohalmdun	Apr 7 ,1990
2m 110y H	3m 44.6	6	11-6	Firm	Spinning	Apr 3 ,1993
2m 4f C	4m 47.5	8	11-6	Gd to firm	Wind Force	Apr 2 ,1993
2m 4f H	4m 37.1	5	10-11	Gd to firm	Gallateen	Apr 2 ,1993
2m 5f 110y C	5m 19.3	10	10-4	Good	Always Waining	Apr 8 , 2011
3m 110y H	5m 50.6	6	10-2	Gd to firm	Andrew s First	Apr 1 ,1993
3m 1f C	6m 3.4	7	11-3	Gd to firm	Cab on Target	Apr 2 ,1993
4m 4f NC	8m 47.8	11	10-6	Firm	Mr Frisk	Apr 7 ,1990

ASCOT

Distance	Time	Age	Weight	Going	Horse	Date
2m H	3m 40.1	5	9-7	Gd to firm	Kanad	Nov 3, 2007
2m H	3m 40.1	4	10-5	Good	Ultravox (USA)	Apr 10, 2011
2m 1f C	4m 3.0	8	11-12	Gd to firm	Crossbow Creek	Oct 28, 2006
2m 3f C	4m 40.1	5	10-11	Good	Bedarra boy	Apr 10, 2011
2m 3f 110y H	4m 34.26	4	11-4	Good	Zaynar (FR)	Nov 21, 2009
2m 5f 110y C	5m 12.6	9	10-13	Good	Kew Jumper (IRE)	Apr 11, 2008
3m H	5m 46.6	6	10-11	Good	Scots Dragoon	Apr 11, 2008
3m C	5m 47.75	8	10-4	Good	Present Glory (IRE)	Mar 30, 2007
3m 1f H	5m 57.3	7	11-7	Gd to firm	Lough Derg	Dec 22, 2007

AYR

Distance	Time	Age	Weight	Going	Horse	Date
2m H	3m 27.4	6	10-7	Firm	Secret Ballot	Apr 19,1980
2m C	3m 38.7	6	11-0	Gd to firm	Clay County	Oct 12,1991
2m 4f C	4m 44.1	8	12-2	Firm	Chandigar	May 15,1972
2m 4f H	4m 35.0	8	9-10	Firm	Moss Royal	Apr 19,1974
2m 5f 110y H	5m 5.6	6	11-12	Good	The Polomoche (IRE)	Apr 18, 2009
3m 110y H	5m 42.0	13	10-11	Firm	Nautical Lad	Apr 6 ,1964
3m 1f C	5m 57.7	9	11-0	Gd to firm	Top N Tale	May 12,1982
4m1f C	7m 55.1	8	9-9	Gd to firm	Hot Weld	Apr 21, 2007

BANGOR-ON-DEE

Distance	Time	Age	Weight	Going	Horse	Date
2m 1f H	3m 44.5	9	10-2	Firm	Andy Rew	Apr 24, 1982
2m 1f 110y C	4m 5.0	6	11-11	Gd to firm	Beherayn	Jul 31, 2009
2m 4f H	4m 34.1	5	11-13	Good	Smithy s Choice	Apr 25, 1987
2m 4f 110y C	4m 52.5	6	11-5	Gd to firm	Apollo Creed (IRE)	Jul 22, 2008
3m H	5m 34.0	5	11-2	Gd to firm	General Pershing	Apr 20, 1991
3m 110y C	5m 50.6	8	11-3	Gd to firm	He's The Gaffer (IRE)	Aug 16, 2008
3m 6f C	7m 34.1	6	12-0	Good	Kaki Crazy (FR)	May 23, 2001
4m 1f C	8m 50.7	6	10-11	Gd to soft	Nazzaro	Dec 3, 1995

CARLISLE

Distance	Time	Age	Weight	Going	Horse	Date
2m C	3m 55.8	8	11-2	Firm	Cape Felix	Apr 20, 1981
2m 1f H	4m 2.6	9	11-3	Firm	Supertop	Oct 25, 1997
2m 4f C	5m 0.4	6	11-2	Good	New Alco (FR)	Nov 12, 2007
2m 4f 110y H	4m 45.4	4	10-12	Firm	Sujud (IRE)	Spt 21, 1996
3m 110y C	6m 0.7	8	10-13	Gd to firm	Ripalong Lad (IRE)	Oct 9, 2009
3m 1f H	6m 13.5	5	11-0	Good	Mr Preacher Man	Oct 25, 2007
3m 2f C	6m 40.4	8	11-3	Good	Lady of Gortmerron (IRE)	Oct 6, 2000

CARTMEL

Distance	Time	Age	Weight	Going	Horse	Date
2m 1f 110yH	3m 57.8	7	11-4	Good	Sayeh (IRE)	Aug 28, 1999
2m 1f 110yC	4m 7.5	12	11-13	Hard	Clever Folly	May 27, 1992
2m 5f 110y C	5m 6.1	10	10-10	Firm	Corrarder	May 30, 1994
2m 6f H	5m 13.9	9	10-3	Good	Browneyes Blue (IRE)	May 28, 2007
3m 2f C	6m 21.3	12	11-12	Good	Better Times Ahead	Aug 29, 1998
3m 2f H	5m 57.9	10	11-3	Firm	Portonia	May 30, 1994
3m6f C	7m12.0	10	11-4	Good	Chabrimal Minster	May 26, 2007

CATTERICK

Distance	Time	Age	Weight	Going	Horse	Date
2m C	3m 44.6	6	10-0	Firm	Preston Deal	Dec 18, 1971
2m H	3m 36.5	7	11-3	Firm	Lunar Wind	Apr 22, 1982
2m 3f C	4m 41.9	8	10-8	Gd to firm	Fear Shuil (IRE)	Nov 24, 2001
2m 3f H	4m 33.0	7	11-6	Gd to firm	Sovereign State (IRE)	Dec 1, 2004
3m 1f 110y C	6m 14.0	10	10-1	Gd to firm	Clever General	Nov 7 , 1981
3m 1f 110y H	6m 3.8	6	10-9	Gd to firm	Seamus O Flynn	Nov 7 , 1981
3m 6f C	7m 48.4	9	10-8	Good	Harlov (FR)	Jan 24, 2004

CHELTENHAM

Distance	Time	Age	Weight	Going	Horse	Date
2m OldC	3m 44.6	8	12-0	Good	Edredon Bleu (FR)	Mar 15, 2000
2m110y OldH	3m 48.1	8	12-0	Good	Istabraq (IRE)	Mar 14, 2000
2m110y NwC	3m 52.4	7	10-11	Gd to firm	Samakaan (IRE)	Mar 16, 2000
2m 1f NwH	3m 51.2	5	11-2	Gd to firm	Moody Man	Mar 15, 1990
2m1f NewH	3m 51.2	4	11-0	Good	Detroit City (USA)	Mar 17, 2006
2m4f110yNH	4m 45.0	6	10-4	Gd to firm	Sir Dante (IRE)	Apr 15, 1997
2m4f110yOC	4m 49.6	9	10-3	Good	Dark Stranger (FR)	Mar 15, 2000
2m 5f OldH	4m 52.0	6	11-7	Good	Monsignor (IRE)	Mar 15, 2000
2m 5f NwC	5m 1.6	9	11-10	Gd to firm	Barnbrook Again	Apr 18, 1990
2m 5f110yNH	4m 53.6	4	10-9	Good	Fashion House	Spt 19, 1968
3m 110yNwH	5m 36.6	6	11-10	Gd to firm	Bacchanal (IRE)	Mar 16, 2000
3m 1f OldC	5m 59.7	8	10-3	Good	Marlborough (IRE)	Mar 14, 2000
3m 1f110yNC	6m 13.4	9	10-11	Gd to firm	Bigsun	Mar 15, 1990
3m 1f110yOH	6m 3.4	9	11-2	Good	Rubhahunish (IRE)	Mar 14, 2000
3m 2f110yNC	6m 29.7	6	11-10	Good	Long Run (FR)	Mar 18, 2011
3m 3f110yOC	7m 1.0	6	10-2	Good	Shardam (IRE)	Nov 15, 2003
3m 7f XCC	8m 6.22	9	10-9	Gd to firm	Sizing Australia	Mar 15, 2011
4m 1f NwC	8m 33.2	7	11-11	Good	Hot Weld	Mar 16, 2006

CHEPSTOW

Distance	Time	Age	Weight	Going	Horse	Date
2m 110y H	3m 43.2	4	10-1	Firm	Tingle Bell	Oct 4 , 1986
2m 110y C	3m 54.1	8	12-0	Firm	Panto Prince	May 9 , 1989
2m 3f 110y C	4m 45.0	11	9-12	Firm	Armala	May 14 , 1996
2m 4f 110y H	4m 36.2	9	11-3	Firm	Aileen s Cacador	Apr 23 , 1957
3m H	5m 33.5	10	10-0	Firm	Chucklestone	May 11 , 1993
3m C	5m 47.9	9	10-11	Firm	Broadheath	Oct 4 , 1986
3m 2f 110y C	6m 39.4	7	12-0	Firm	Jaunty Jane	May 26, 1975
3m 5f 110y C	7m 24.0	9	10-5	Firm	Creeola	Apr 23 , 1957

DONCASTER

Distance	Time	Age	Weight	Going	Horse	Date
2m 110y H	3m 46.6	6	10-0	Gd to firm	Good for a Loan	Feb 24, 1993
2m 110y C	3m 51.9	12	10-9	Gd to firm	Itsgottabealright	Jan 28, 1989
2m 3f C	4m 41.8	8	11-4	Good	Watch My Back	Dec 12, 2009
2m 3f 110y H	4m 33.0	4	10-12	Good	Bobby Ewing (IRE)	Dec 11, 2009
3m C	5m 52.4	8	10-9	Good	Dalkey Sound	Jan 26, 1991
3m 110yH	5m 45.3	6	10-12	Firm	Pandolfi	Nov 4 , 1972
3m 2f C	6m 11.8	9	10-10	Good	Always Right	Mar 5, 2011

EXETER

Distance	Time	Age	Weight	Going	Horse	Date
2m 1f H	3m 52.2	4	10-10	Gd to firm	Made In France (FR)	Sep 28 , 2004
2m 1f 110y C	3m 58.7	6	11-5	Gd to firm	Passato (GER)	May 4, 2010
2m 3f H	4m 16.5	5	11-11	Firm	Il Capitano	Oct 9 , 2002
2m 3f 110y C	4m 34.8	8	11-4	Firm	Gay Edition	Oct 2, 1990
2m 5f 110y H	5m 15.2	7	10-13	Good	Miss Saffron	Oct 7, 2010
2m 6f 110y H	5m 18.5	7	11-10	Gd to firm	Presenting Express	Oct 4, 2006
2m 7f 110y H	5m 26.2	8	10-11	Gd to firm	Very Cool	May 4, 2010
2m 7f 110yC	5m 30.1	7	11-4	Gd to firm	Mister Gloss	May 14, 2008
3m C	5m 42.8	8	10-5	Gd to firm	Dennis The Legend	May 5, 2009
3m 110y H	5m 42.3	5	11-7	Firm	Il Capitano	Oct 1 , 2002
3m 1f 110yC	6m 3.0	8	11-4	Gd to firm	Radnor Lad	May 14, 2008

FAKENHAM

Distance	Time	Age	Weight	Going	Horse	Date
2m H	3m 45.7	5	10-9	Gd to firm	Cobbet (CZE)	May 9, 2001
2m 110y C	3m 44.9	11	12-4	Firm	Cheekio Ora	Apr 23, 1984
2m 4f H	4m 41.1	4	10-8	Gd to firm	Ayem (IRE)	May 16, 1999
2m 5f 110yC	5m 10.1	13	12-2	Gd to firm	Skipping Tim	May 25, 1992
2m 7f 110yH	5m 37.1	6	11-3	Good	Laughing Gas (IRE)	May 20, 1995
3m 110y C	5m 57.0	7	11-1	Gd to firm	Specialize	May 16, 1999

FFOS LAS

Distance	Time	Age	Weight	Going	Horse	Date
2m C	3m 46.60	5	11-8	Gd To firm	West With The Wind	Jun 17 2010
2m H	3m 33.60	6	10-11	Good	Valain (IRE)	Aug 28 2009
2m 3f 110y C	4m 45.60	8	10-7	Gd to firm	Feeling Real (IRE)	Aug 3 2010
2m 4f H	4m 39.40	6	10-9	Good	Plunkett (IRE)	Jun 18 2009
2m 5f C	5m 9.70	8	11-11	Gd To firm	Putney Bridge	Jun 17 2010
2m 6f H	5m 25.90	5	11-0	Good	Am I Blue	Apr 25 2011
3m C	5m 49.60	7	11-7	Good	Sea Wall	Jun 18 2009
3m H	5m 41.50	5	11-9	Good	Quattrocento (FR)	Jun 18 2009
3m 1f 110y C	6m 7.10	7	10-1	Good	Backstage (FR)	Aug 28 2009

FOLKESTONE

Distance	Time	Age	Weight	Going	Horse	Date
2m C	3m 48.7	7	12-0	Gd to firm	High Gale (IRE)	Apr 30, 1999
2m 1f 110yH	3m 56.2	5	11-5	Firm	Super Tek	Nov 14, 1983
2m 4f 110yH	4m 57.0	6	11-0	Gd to firm	Circus Colours	Apr 2 , 1996
2m 5f C	5m 6.0	9	11-5	Gd to firm	Free Gift	Oct 24, 2007
	5m 6.0	8	11-12	Gd to firm	Mr Boo (IRE)	Oct 24, 2007
2m 6f 110y H	5m 18.2	6	10-0	Firm	Royalty Miss	Apr 30, 1985
3m 1f Ch	6m 11.4	7	11-0	Gd to firm	Highland	May 23, 2001
3m 2f C	6m 23.1	9	10-13	Firm	Bolt Hole	Apr 26, 1988

FONTWELL

Distance	Time	Age	Weight	Going	Horse	Date
2m 2f C	4m 14.5	12	10-1	Gd to firm	A Thousand Dreams (IRE)	Jun 3 , 2002
2m 2f 110y H	4m 6.8	7	10-2	Gd to firm	Hyperion du Moulin II (FR)	Jun 3 , 2002
2m 6f C	5m 13.9	10	10-0	Gd to firm	Contes (IRE)	Jun 3, 2002
2m 6f 110y H	5m 6.7	7	10-1	Gd to firm	Mister Pickwick (IRE)	Jun 3, 2002
3m 2f 110y C	6m 24.3	5	10-2	Gd to firm	Il Capitano	May 6, 2002
3m 3f H	6m 21.6	5	11-2	Gd to firm	Lord Of The Track (IRE)	Aug 18, 2003
3m 4f C	7m 11.1	8	10-6	Good	Strolling Vagabond (IRE)	Mar 18, 2007

HAYDOCK

Distance	Time	Age	Weight	Going	Horse	Date
2m C	4m 0.10	10	10-5	Good	Incorporation	Oct 28 2009
2m 1y H	3m 32.30	6	10-0	Good	She s Our Mare (IRE)	May 1 1999
2m 4f H	4m 35.30	7	10-10	Gd To firm	Moving Out	May 6 1995
2m 4f C	4m 49.90	6	11-7	Good	Etxalar (FR)	Oct 28 2009
2m 6f H	5m 12.70	5	10-10	Firm	Peter the Butcher	May 3 1982
2m 7f 110y H	5m 32.30	9	11-0	Gd To firm	Boscean Chieftain	May 3 1993
3m C	5m 55.30	12	11-4	Good	Catch The Perk (IRE)	Oct 28 2009
3m 4f C	7m 26.60	11	11-2	Good	Dom D Orgeval	Apr 23 2011

HEREFORD

Distance	Time	Age	Weight	Going	Horse	Date
2m C	3m 46.0	6	10-9	Gd to firm	Smolensk (IRE)	Mar 21, 1998
2m 1f H	3m 42.2	10	10-1	Hard	Tasty Son	Spt 11, 1973
2m 3f C	4m 30.0	9	10-11	Good	Kings Wild	Sep 28, 1990
2m 4f H	4m 38.9	4	11-4	Gd to firm	Pigeon Island	Sep 5 , 2007
2m5f 110y C	5m 6.90	8	11-1	Gd to firm	Fealing Real	Jun 20, 2010

Distance	Time	Age	Weight	Going	Horse	Date
3m1f 110y C	6m 10.6	8	10-10	Firm	Gilston Lass	Apr 8, 1995
3m 2f H	6m 2.8	6	10-1	Gd to firm	Wee Danny (IRE)	Spt 10, 2003

HEXHAM

Distance	Time	Age	Weight	Going	Horse	Date
2m 110y H	3m 57.8	8	11-7	Gd to firm	Francies Fancy (IRE)	Jun 19, 2005
2m 110y C	3m 53.6	9	11-9	Gd to firm	Adamatic	Jun 17, 2000
2m 4f 110y H	4m 31.5	6	11-0	Gd to firm	Pappa Charlie (USA)	May 27, 1997
2m 4f 110y C	4m 55.4	8	9-11	Firm	Mr Laggan	Spt 14, 2003
3m H	5m 45.4	7	9-9	Firm	Fingers Crossed	Apr 29, 1991
3m 1f C	6m 7.6	9	9-11	Gd to firm	Silent Snipe	Jun 1, 2002
4m C	8m 34.0	10	10-12	Good	Simply Smashing (IRE)	Mar 18, 2010

HUNTINGDON

Distance	Time	Age	Weight	Going	Horse	Date
2m 110y H	3m 32.7	5	11-11	Gd to firm	Weather Front	Aug 31, 2009
2m 110y C	3m 53.3	5	10-0	Gd to firm	No Greater Love (FR)	May 23, 2007
2m 4f 110y C	4m 46.4	10	10-13	Gd to firm	Peccadillo	Sep 26, 2004
2m 4f 110y H	4m 32.9	6	10-12	Gd to firm	Richie's Delight (IRE)	Aug 30, 1999
2m 5f 110y H	4m 45.8	6	11-5	Firm	Sound of Laughter	Apr 14, 1984
3m C	5m 44.3	7	11-9	Gd to firm	Ozzie Jones	Spt 18, 1998
3m 2f H	5m 50.2	8	11-12	Gd to firm	Orchard King (IRE)	Aug 31, 2009
3m 6f 110y C	8m 2.7	9	10-4	Gd to soft	Kinnahalla (IRE)	Nov 24, 2001

KELSO

Distance	Time	Age	Weight	Going	Horse	Date
2m 110y H	3m 39.6	5	10-0	Firm	The Premier Expres	May 2, 1995
2m 1f C	4m 2.6	8	11-9	Firm	Mr Coggy	May 2, 1984
2m 2f H	4m 11.5	7	11-0	Firm	All Welcome	Oct 15, 1994
2m 6f 110y H	5m 12.2	4	11-3	Firm	Hit The Canvas (USA)	Sep 30, 1995
2m 6f 110y C	5m 29.6	10	10-13	Good	Bas De Laine (FR)	Nov 13, 1996
3m 1f C	6m 1.2	13	12-0	Gd to firm	Mcgregor The Third	Sept 19, 1999
3m 3f H	6m 10.1	8	11-5	Firm	Ambergate	Oct 21, 1989
3m 4f C	7m 2.3	7	10-6	Good	Seven Towers (IRE)	Dec 2, 1996
4m C	8m 7.4	8	10-0	Good	Seven Towers	Jan 17, 1997

KEMPTON

Distance	Time	Age	Weight	Going	Horse	Date
2m C	3m 48.3	6	10-9	Good	Hoo La Baloo (FR)	Oct 21, 2007
2m H	3m 40.40	7	11-8	Good	Australia Day (IRE)	Oct 17, 2010
2m 4f 110y C	5m 7.0	9	11-4	Good	Au Courant (IRE)	Apr 20, 2009
2m 5f H	5m 2.5	7	11-12	Good	Dover's Hill	Apr 20, 2009
3m C	5m 57.4	8	11-10	Good	Kauto Star (FR)	Dec 26, 2008
3m 110y H	6m 6.90	6	10-12	Good	Carole's Legacy	Nov 22, 2010

LEICESTER

Distance	Time	Age	Weight	Going	Horse	Date
2m H	3m 39.6	6	10-11	Gd to firm	Ryde Again	Nov 20, 1989
2m C	3m 54.5	5	11-7	Good	William's Wishes (IRE)	Nov 15, 2010
2m 4f 110y C	5m 0.5	9	9-6	Firm	Prairie Minstrel (USA)	Dec 4, 2003
2m 4f 110y H	4m 45.5	4	11-7	Gd to firm	Prince of Rheims	Dec 5, 1989
2m 7f 110y C	5m 47.7	10	11-4	Good	Bubble Boy (IRE)	Dec 9, 2009

LINGFIELD

Distance	Time	Age	Weight	Going	Horse	Date
2m C	3m 48.7	9	11-2	Gd to firm	Rapide Plaisir (IRE)	Sep 28, 2007
2m 110y H	3m 47.2	5	11-0	Firm	Va Utu	Mar 19, 1993
2m 3f 110y H	4m 37.4	6	10-3	Firm	Bellezza	Mar 20, 1993
2m 4f 110y C	5m 4.0	8	11-7	Good	Copsale Lad	Oct 29, 2005
2m 7f H	5m 31.9	8	11-6	Gd to firm	Herecomestanley	Sep 28, 2007
3m C	5m 58.4	6	11-3	Firm	Mighty Frolic	Mar 19, 1993

LUDLOW

Distance	Time	Age	Weight	Going	Horse	Date
2m C	3m 47.3	5	11-7	Gd to firm	Pearl King (IRE)	Apr 5, 2007
2m H	3m 36.4	10	10-11	Gd to firm	Desert Fighter	Oct 11, 2001
2m 4f C	4m 47.3	10	11-8	Gd to firm	Handy Money	Apr 5, 2007
2m 5f H	4m 54.7	8	11-0	Gd to firm	Willy Willy	Oct 11, 2001
3m H	5m 36.6	10	10-11	Gd to firm	Rift Valley (IRE)	May 12, 2005
3m C	5m 50.5	6	11-12	Good	Rodalko (FR)	Mar 4, 2004

MARKET RASEN

Distance	Time	Age	Weight	Going	Horse	Date
2m 1f 110yH	3m 57.4	7	11-5	Good	Australia Day (IRE)	Jly 17, 2010
2m 2f C	4m 17.2	8	11-1	Good	Viable	Jly 17, 2010
2m 3f 110yH	4m 30.7	7	10-10	Gd to firm	Coble Lane	May 29, 1999
2m 4f C	4m 42.8	7	10-13	Gd to firm	Fleeting Mandate (IRE)	Jly 24, 1999
2m 6f H	5m 12.2	6	9-8	Gd to firm	Fisby	Apr 15, 2007
2m 6f 110yC	5m 24.2	8	11-9	Good	Annas Prince	Oct 19, 1979
3m H	5m 38.8	6	12-5	Firm	Trustful	May 21, 1977
3m 1f C	6m 1.0	7	11-8	Gd to firm	Allerlea	May 1, 1985
3m 4f 110y C	7m 17.5	10	11-1	Good	Fin Bec (FR)	Nov 20, 2003

MUSSELBURGH

Distance	Time	Age	Weight	Going	Horse	Date
2m H	3m 35.9	3	10-7	Gd to firm	Joe Bumpas	Dec 11, 1989
2m C	3m 48.1	8	10-12	Gd to firm	Sonsie Mo	Dec 6, 1993
2m 4f C	4m 44.5	7	11-9	Gd to firm	Bohemian Spirit (IRE)	Dec 18, 2005
2m 4f H	4m 37.8	5	11-0	Good	Pyracantha	Nov 19, 2010
3m C	5m 47.7	7	11-10	Firm	Snowy (IRE)	Dec 18, 2005
3m 110y H	5m 39.5	6	11-8	Gd to firm	Percutant (FR)	Mar 1, 2009

NEWBURY

Distance	Time	Age	Weight	Going	Horse	Date
2m 110y H	3m 45.2	5	10-2	Gd to firm	Dhofar	Oct 25, 1985
2m 1f C	3m 58.2	8	12-0	Gd to firm	Barnbrook Again	Nov 25, 1989
2m 2f 110y C	4m 31.9	6	11-12	Gd to firm	Rubberdubber	Mar 4, 2006
2m 3f H	4m 30.5	4	11-11	Gd to soft	Schapiro (USA)	Apr 2, 2005
2m 4f C	4m 47.9	8	11-12	Gd to firm	Espy	Oct 25, 1991
2m 5f H	4m 48.63	6	11-0	Good	Argento Luna	Mar 21, 2009
2m 6f 110y C	5m 34.63	6	10-12	Good	Aimigayle	Mar 21, 2009
3m C	5m 43.5	7	11-3	Gd to soft	Red Devil Robert (IRE)	Apr 2, 2005
3m 110y H	5m 45.4	8	10-9	Good	Lansdowne	Oct 25, 1996
3m 2f 110y C	6m 27.1	10	12-0	Firm	Topsham Bay	Mar 26, 1993

NEWCASTLE

Distance	Time	Age	Weight	Going	Horse	Date
2m H	3m 40.7	7	10-10	Good	Padre Mio	Nov 25, 1995
2m 110y C	3m 56.7	7	11-12	Firm	Greenheart	May 7, 1990
2m 4f C	4m 46.7	7	9-13	Firm	Snow Blessed	May 19, 1984
2m 4f H	4m 42.0	4	10-10	Hard	Mils Mij	May 13, 1989
3m C	5m 48.1	8	10-4	Firm	Even Swell	Oct 30, 1975
3m H	5m 40.1	4	10-5	Gd to firm	Withy Bank	Nov 29, 1986
3m 6f C	7m 30.0	8	12-0	Good	Charlie Potheen	Apr 28, 1973
4m 1f C	8m 30.4	7	10-0	Good	Domaine de Pron (FR)	Feb 21, 1998

NEWTON ABBOT

Distance	Time	Age	Weight	Going	Horse	Date
2m 110y C	3m 53.2	8	11-3	Gd to firm	Norborne Bandit (IRE)	Aug 22, 2009
2m 1f H	3m 45.0	5	11-0	Firm	Windbound Lass	Aug 1, 1988
2m 3f H	4m 17.2	6	11-9	Good	Super Ross (IRE)	Jul 13, 2009
2m 5f 110y C	5m 2.1	7	11-0	Good	Mhilu (IRE)	Jul 13, 2009
2m 6f H	4m 55.4	7	10-0	Firm	Virbian	Jun 30, 1983
3m 2f 110y C	6m 17.6	8	10-3	Good	Spare Change (IRE)	Jul 13, 2009
3m 3f H	6m 16.7	8	10-13	Gd to firm	Celebrity Call (IRE)	Jun 4, 2009

PERTH

Distance	Time	Age	Weight	Going	Horse	Date
2m C	3m 47.5	7	11-10	Gd to firm	Beldine	Aug 22, 1992
2m 110y H	3m 40.4	4	11-8	Hard	Molly Fay	Spt 23, 1971
2m 4f 110y H	4m 41.2	8	10-2	Firm	Valiant Dash	May 19, 1994
2m 4f 110y C	4m 53.0	8	11-12	Gd to firm	Abragante (IRE)	Jul 2, 2009
3m C	5m 49.4	9	11-0	Gd to firm	Crozan (FR)	Jul 1, 2009
3m 110y H	5m 41.6	10	11-1	Gd to firm	Imtihan (IRE)	Jul 2, 2009

PLUMPTON

Distance	Time	Age	Weight	Going	Horse	Date
2m H	3m 31.0	3	11-1	Firm	Royal Derbi	Sep 19, 1988
2m 1f C	4m 5.00	7	11-12	Good	Gauvain (GER)	Apr 13, 2009
2m 4f C	4m 42.8	6	11-0	Gd to firm	Dead Or Alive (IRE)	May 10, 2009
2m 5f H	4m 46.8	4	11-2	Gd to firm	Urban Warrior	Sep 21, 2008
3m 1f 110y H	5m 57.6	10	11-12	Good	Take The Stand	Oct 16, 2006
3m 2f C	6m 23.5	9	9-7	Gd to firm	Sunday Habits	Apr 19, 2003
3m 5f C	7m 19.8	6	11-7	Gd to firm	Ecuyer Du Roi (FR)	Apr 15, 2002

SANDOWN

Distance	Time	Age	Weight	Going	Horse	Date
2m C	3m 43.4	9	11-6	Gd to firm	Dempsey (IRE)	Apr 28, 2007
2m 110yH	3m 42.0	6	10-0	Firm	Olympian	Mar 13, 1993
2m 4f 110y C	4m 57.2	8	11-7	Gd to firm	Coulton	Apr 29, 1995
2m 4f 110y H	4m 35.7	5	11-3	Gd to firm	Oslot (FR)	Apr 28, 2007
2m 6f H	5m 5.6	8	11-3	Firm	Kintbury	Nov 5, 1983
3m H	5m 39.1	6	11-5	Gd to firm	Rostropovich	Apr 27, 2002
3m 110y C	5m 59.0	8	12-7	Good	Arkle	Nov 6, 1965
3m 5f 110y C	7m 9.1	9	10-0	Gd to firm	Cache Fleur (FR)	Apr 29, 1995

SEDGEFIELD

Distance	Time	Age	Weight	Going	Horse	Date
2m 110y C	3m 53.6	7	10-7	Gd to firm	Suas Leat (IRE)	Sep 16, 1997
2m 1f H	3m 45.7	6	10-5	Gd to firm	Country Orchid	Sep 5, 1997
2m 4f H	4m 38.3	7	11-4	Gd to firm	Ad Murum (IRE)	Aug 11, 2006
2m 4f C	4m 48.0	7	10-8	Gd to firm	Polar Gale (IRE)	May 23, 2007
2m 5f C	4m 59.2	8	11-10	Gd to firm	Pennybridge	Spt 30, 1997
2m 5f 110y H	4m 46.3	7	10-0	Gd to firm	Palm House	Spt 4, 1992
3m 3f C	6m 29.3	7	11-8	Gd to firm	The Gallopin' Major	Sept 14, 1996
3m 3f 110y H	6m 19.7	7	9-13	Firm	Pikestaff (USA)	Jly 25, 2005

SOUTHWELL

Distance	Time	Age	Weight	Going	Horse	Date
2m 1f C	4m 0.9	9	11-5	Good	Master Nimbus	Aug 16, 2009
2m 1f H	3m 50.3	6	10-12	Good	Truly Fruitful (USA)	Aug 16, 2009
2m 4f 110y C	5m 2.8	9	10-0	Gd to firm	Bally Parson	May 8, 1995
2m 4f 110y H	4m 47.8	8	11-13	Gd to firm	Man of the Grange	May 2, 1994
3m 110y H	5m 46.5	5	10-0	Gd to firm	Soloman Springs (USA)	May 8, 1995
3m 110y C	6m 1.9	6	11-2	Gd to firm	Soloman Springs (USA)	May 6, 1996
3m 2f H	6m 10.2	6	10-7	Good	Super Ross (IRE)	Aug 16, 2009

STRATFORD-ON-AVON

Distance	Time	Age	Weight	Going	Horse	Date
2m 110y H	3m 40.4	6	11-12	Hard	Chusan	May 7, 1956
2m 110y C	3m 58.1	7	11-5	Gd to firm	Enlightenment (IRE)	Sep 9, 2007
2m 3f H	4m 19.7	7	9-11	Gd to firm	Mister Ermyn	Jly 29, 2000
2m 4f C	4m 41.0	9	10-7	Gd to firm	Inmate	Jul 29, 2010
2m 5f 110y C	4m 56.5	6	9-10	Gd to firm	Spare Change (IRE)	Sep 16, 2007
2m 6f 110y H	5m 6.8	6	11-0	Firm	Broken Wing	May 31, 1986
2m 7f C	5m 24.9	11	10-4	Good	Fieldsofclover (IRE)	Jun 15, 2008
3m 3f H	6m 13.1	7	10-8	Gd to firm	Burren Moonshine (IRE)	Jun 11, 2006
3m 4f C	6m 44.2	8	10-0	Gd to firm	Dusty Dane (IRE)	May 28, 2010

TAUNTON

Distance	Time	Age	Weight	Going	Horse	Date
2m 110y C	3m 49.5	8	10-9	Firm	I Have Him	Apr 28, 1995
2m 1f H	3m 39.5	4	12-0	Hard	Indian Jockey	Oct 3, 1996
2m 3f C	4m 30.7	9	11-7	Firm	Harik	Mar 24, 2003
2m 3f 110y H	4m 19.7	5	10-6	Firm	Prairie Spirit	Apr 2, 2009

2m 7f 110y C	5m 39.80	7	11-10	Firm	Glacial Delight (IRE)	Apr 24, 2006
3m 110y H	5m 30.4	7	10-4	Firm	On My Toes	Oct 15, 1998
3m 3f C	6m 40.1	8	11-8	Firm	Fourpointone	Mar 21, 2009
4m2f 110y C	8m 59.0	9	11-9	Good	Cold Mountain	Mar 29, 2011

TOWCESTER

Distance	Time	Age	Weight	Going	Horse	Date
2m H	3m 39.5	4	10-0	Firm	Nascracker (USA)	May 22, 1987
2m 110y C	3m 54.1	9	10-3	Gd to firm	Nawow	May 29, 2009
2m 3f 110y C	4m 57.8	6	11-0	Gd to firm	Mystic Storm	May 29, 2008
2m 3f 110y H	4m 40.9	6	10-5	Good	Anglicisme (FR)	Oct 8 , 2008
2m 5f H	5m 0.9	7	11-2	Gd to firm	Mailcom	May 3 , 1993
2m 6f C	5m 22.7	7	10-10	Gd to firm	Inaro (IRE)	Jun 19, 2008
3m H	5m 44.0	9	9-10	Firm	Dropshot	May 25, 1984
3m 110y C	5m 52.6	10	10-13	Gd to firm	Lucky Luk (FR)	May 29, 2009

UTTOXETER

Distance	Time	Age	Weight	Going	Horse	Date
2m H	3m 37.2	4	10-9	Gd to firm	Flying Eagle	Jun 11, 1995
2m C	3m 41.5	6	11-0	Good	Tapageur	Aug 8 , 1991
2m 4f 110y H	4m 39.1	8	10-9	Gd to firm	Chicago s Best	Jun 11, 1995
2m 5f C	4m 54.2	8	11-8	Firm	McKenzie	Apr 27, 1974
2m 6f 110y H	5m 6.8	8	11-8	Gd to firm	Fealing Real (IRE)	Jun 27, 2010
2m 6f 110y C	5m 39.5	8	11-5	Good	Coq Hardi (FR)	May 10, 2009
3m C	5m 56.8	6	11-2	Good	Always Waining (IRE)	May 5, 2007
3m H	5m 43.4	8	10-13	Gd to firm	Fourty Acers (IRE)	May 11, 2008
3m 2f C	6m 23.5	10	11-13	Gd to firm	Mcgregor the Third	Oct 5 , 1996
4m 2f C	8m 33.7	8	11-4	Good	Seven Towers (IRE)	Mar 15, 1997

WARWICK

Distance	Time	Age	Weight	Going	Horse	Date
2m H	3m 34.6	5	11-4	Gd to firm	Arabian Bold	May 22, 1993
2m 110y C	3m 46.3	6	11-0	Gd to firm	Bambi De L'Orme (FR)	May 7, 2005
2m 3f H	4m 14.9	6	11-7	Gd to firm	Runaway Pete	Nov 2, 1996
2m 4f 110y C	4m 53.3	9	9-12	Gd to firm	Dudie	May 16, 1987
2m 5f H	4m 43.6	5	10-10	Firm	Three Eagles (USA)	May 11, 2002
3m 110y Ch	6m 0.2	7	11-8	Good	Shining Gale (IRE)	Mar 18, 2009
3m 1f H	5m 53.5	7	11-0	Gd to firm	City Poser	Apr 2, 2002
3m 2f C	6m 16.1	12	10-12	Gd to firm	Castle Warden	May 6, 1989
3m 5f C	7m 12.00	12	11-7	Good	Arnold Layne (IRE)	Mar 23, 2011

WETHERBY

Distance	Time	Age	Weight	Going	Horse	Date
2m C	3m 44.9	6	10-12	Good	Mutual Friend (USA)	May 20, 2010
2m 110y H	3m 43.9	8	10-7	Gd to firm	Olivino (GER)	Apr 26, 2009
2m 4f H	4m 42.0	6	11-7	Gd to firm	Lady Wright (IRE)	Apr 26, 2009
2m 4f 110y C	4m 47.8	7	10-12	Good	Drever Route (IRE)	Oct 13, 2010
2m 6f H	5m 5.7	7	11-0	Gd to firm	San Deng	Apr 26, 2009
2m 6f H	5m 5.7	6	11-0	Gd to firm	Oscar Barton (IRE)	Apr 17, 2011
2m 6f 110y C	5m 24.9	6	11-3	Good	Pistol Basc (FR)	Oct 13, 2010
3m 1f C	5m 52.1	9	11-0	Good	Nacarat (FR)	Oct 30, 2010
3m 1f H	6m 1.9	7	11-4	Good	Fair Along	Oct 31, 2009

WINCANTON

Distance	Time	Age	Weight	Going	Horse	Date
2m H	3m 25.8	6	10-5	Good	Nearby	Nov 6, 2010
2m C	3m 43.7	8	12-7	Firm	Kescast	May 11, 1988
2m 4f H	4m 29.46	7	10-4	Gd to firm	Uffa Fox (IRE)	Oct 14, 2010
2m 5f C	4m 59.2	11	11-10	Firm	Edredon Bleu (FR)	Oct 26, 2003
2m 6f H	4m 57.0	6	10-0	Good	Santera (IRE)	Nov 6, 2010
3m 1f 110yC	6m 9.7	7	11-6	Gd to firm	Swansea Bay	Nov 8, 2003
3m 3f 110yC	6m 37.2	7	11-8	Good	Gullible Gordon (IRE)	Oct 24, 2010

WORCESTER

Distance	Time	Age	Weight	Going	Horse	Date
2m H	3m 33.8	5	11-5	Gd to firm	Factotum	Jun 24, 2009
2m C	3m 41.46	7	10-10	Good	Fit To Drive	Sep 25, 2009
2m 4f H	4m 31.5	6	11-6	Good	Son Of Flicka	Jun 5, 2010
2m 4f 110y C	4m 50.38	7	11-0	Good	Sir Ian (IRE)	Sep 24, 2010
2m 7f C	5m 34.2	8	11-8	Gd to firm	Oscar Bay (IRE)	May 19, 2010
3m H	5m 25.4	5	9-9	Gd to firm	Last Flight (IRE)	Jun 24 , 2009

SPLIT SECOND SPEED RATINGS

The following list shows the fastest performances of chasers and hurdlers which have recorded a speed figure of 105 or over during the 2010-2011 season. Additional information in parentheses following the speed figure shows the distance of the race in furlongs, course, state of going and the date on which the figure was achieved.

CHASING

A New Story 110 (31f,Chl,GF,Mar 15)
Abbey Dore 108 (19½f,Tow,S,Nov 21)
According To Pete 106 (30f,Cat,GS,Jan 13)
Acrai Rua 106 (25½f,Her,GF,Jun 20)
Adams Island 106 (25½f,Chl,G,Apr 13)
Against The Wind 105 (16f,Crl,S,Mar 10)
Agus A Vic 107 (24f,Leo,HY,Dec 29)
Aigle D Or 109 (17f,Nby,GS,Nov 26)
Aimigayle 107 (21f,Chl,G,Mar 17)
Aiteen Thirtythree 111 (24f,Nby,GS,Nov 25)
Albertas Run 113 (20f,Ain,G,Apr 8)
Alderburn 108 (26½f,Nby,GS,Mar 5)
Alderley Rover 111 (25½f,Her,S,Jan 3)
Alderluck 105 (24f,Hun,S,Jan 26)
Aldertune 108 (25½f,Her,S,Jan 3)
Alesandro Mantegna 107 (18f,Fon,S,Oct 2)
Alfa Beat 107 (32f,Chl,G,Mar 16)
Alfadora 105 (23f,Wor,GF,Jun 30)
Alfie Flits 109 (17f,Kel,S,Nov 21)
Alvarado 106 (24½f,Crl,S,Mar 20)
Always Bold 107 (25f,Wet,G,Jun 3)
Always Right 112 (32½f,Ayr,G,Apr 16)
Always Waining 113 (21½f,Ain,G,Apr 8)
Amalfi Coast 105 (20f,Sed,G,Sep 28)
Ambobo 107 (24f,Leo,HY,Dec 29)
Ammunition 105 (24f,Exe,G,Oct 7)
Andrew Nick 105 (26f,Utt,GF,Jun 3)
Another Jewel 106 (31f,Chl,GF,Mar 15)
Another Trump 105 (20½f,Wor,G,Sep 5)
Anquetta 110 (16½f,Chl,G,Mar 18)
Antonius Caesar 105 (23½f,Lei,G,Jan 25)
Any Currency 109 (27½f,Chl,GS,Nov 13)
Appleaday 108 (24f,Asc,G,Apr 10)
Arabella Boy 108 (20f,Pun,SH,Nov 13)
Arbor Supreme 112 (25f,Fai,HY,Feb 23)
Arturo Uno 106 (29f,War,G,Mar 13)
Arumun 105 (16½f,Hex,GF,May 25)
As De Fer 107 (19½f,Exe,HY,Feb 13)
Askthemaster 114 (16½f,Chl,G,Mar 18)
Asturienne 107 (20f,Nby,S,Jan 19)
Atherstone Hill 105 (24½f,Tow,GS,Mar 17)
Auroras Encore 111 (24f,Utt,S,May 1)
Aztec Treasure 105 (22f,Tow,GS,Nov 4)

Baby Run 110 (29½f,San,GF,Apr 23)
Backbord 107 (22½f,Mar,G,Sep 25)
Bai Zhu 109 (20f,Fon,GS,Oct 28)
Baily View 108 (25f,Fai,HY,Jan 16)
Bakbenscher 107 (21f,Chl,GS,Jan 29)
Bale O Shea 107 (22½f,Wet,G,Jun 3)
Ballabriggs 113 (36f,Ain,G,Apr 9)
Ballycarney 109 (24f,Chp,GS,Oct 9)
Ballyegan 106 (22f,Tow,S,Jan 10)
Ballyfitz 110 (33½f,Utt,GS,Mar 19)
Ballyvesey 111 (24f,Ffo,G,Apr 11)
Balthazar King 107 (25½f,Chl,G,Apr 13)
Baltic Pathfinder 105 (20½f,Hex,G,May 1)
Balzaccio 115 (20½f,Hun,GS,Nov 20)
Ban Uisce 106 (21f,Wcn,GF,Mar 27)
Bardolet 108 (25½f,Cat,G,Mar 9)
Baseball Ted 107 (17f,Nby,GS,Mar 4)
Basoda 105 (24½f,Tow,GF,Apr 26)
Be There In Five 107 (32f,Chl,G,Mar 16)
Bear Witness 106 (24f,Per,GF,May 13)
Beat The Boys 107 (25½f,Chl,G,Dec 10)
Beautiful Sound 109 (25f,Fai,HY,Jan 16)
Becauseicouldntsee 110 (24f,Leo,HY,Dec 29)
Beggars Cap 111 (16f,Ayr,G,Apr 16)
Bellflower Boy 107 (24f,Ffo,G,Mar 19)
Bench Warrent 106 (24½f,Fak,GS,Jan 30)
Bene Lad 106 (17f,Kel,GS,Mar 5)
Benefit Night 109 (25½f,Chl,G,Apr 14)
Benny Be Good 105 (21f,Sed,GF,Apr 14)
Bensalem 115 (24½f,Chl,G,Mar 15)
Bentota 106 (24½f,Fak,GS,Nov 16)
Bertenbar 109 (16f,Her,GS,Mar 30)
Bescot Springs 106 (25f,Hex,HY,Nov 5)
Beshabar 116 (24f,Don,GS,Feb 23)
Best Lover 107 (16½f,Hex,HY,Nov 17)
Betabob 108 (16f,Wcn,GS,Feb 3)
Bible Lord 106 (20f,Lud,G,Feb 9)
Big Burrows 107 (20f,Sed,GF,May 19)
Big Fella Thanks 111 (21½f,Asc,S,Feb 19)
Big Zeb 114 (16f,Chl,G,Mar 16)
Bill s Echo 112 (24f,Per,GF,Jun 30)
Blackpool Billy 106 (20f,Ncs,S,Mar 8)
Blacktoft 105 (16½f,Nab,GF,Jun 22)
Blazing Bailey 112 (26½f,Chl,GS,Jan 1)
Blazing Tempo 109 (20f,Chl,G,Mar 17)
Blu Teen 107 (24½f,San,G,Mar 11)
Bluegun 108 (20f,Hay,G,May 8)
Bob Lingo 109 (22f,Pun,HY,Feb 9)
Bobby Donald 105 (25½f,Cat,G,Mar 9)
Bobby Gee 107 (22f,Tow,S,Dec 16)
Bostons Angel 117 (21f,Leo,HY,Feb 12)
Breedsbreeze 107 (21½f,Asc,GS,Jan 22)
Brooklyn Brownie 110 (28f,Utt,GF,Jun 27)
Buena Vista 111 (25½f,Wcn,G,Nov 6)
Buffalo Bob 106 (26½f,Chl,GS,Jan 1)
Bugsy s Boy 107 (21f,Wcn,S,Jan 22)
Burren Legend 107 (24½f,San,G,Feb 5)
Burton Port 120 (26½f,Nby,GS,Nov 27)
By The Hour 111 (21f,Leo,S,Feb 27)

C Monthehammers 107 (32f,Exe,GS,Dec 5)
Cadoudalas 109 (16f,Her,HY,Jan 13)
Calculaite 105 (16½f,Sed,G,Sep 7)
Calgary Bay 113 (21f,Chl,GS,Dec 11)
Call Me A Legend 109 (16f,War,HY,Jan 15)
Can t Buy Time 105 (21f,Chl,GS,Jan 1)
Cannington Brook 109 (25f,Fol,S,Jan 2)
Cappagh 105 (21f,Ffo,G,Oct 10)
Captain Cee Bee 112 (16f,Chl,G,Mar 16)
Captain Chris 117 (16f,Chl,G,Mar 15)
Carole s Legacy 114 (24½f,Chl,G,Mar 15)
Carrigmartin 113 (21f,Leo,S,Feb 27)
Carruthers 115 (26½f,Nby,GS,Nov 27)
Carthalawn 112 (17f,Fai,S,Dec 15)
Cast Cada 105 (22f,Fon,G,May 12)
Cast Iron Casey 106 (25f,Kel,GF,Oct 16)
Catch Me 107 (24f,Leo,HY,Dec 29)
Categorical 110 (25f,Ain,G,Apr 9)
Cavers Glen 107 (25f,Ain,GS,Nov 21)
Chance Du Roy 109 (19½f,Chp,S,Jan 8)
Chaninbar 108 (20½f,Chl,G,Oct 16)
Chapolimoss 105 (20f,Sed,S,Mar 15)
Character Building 106 (28f,Ffo,GS,Feb 5)
Chernik 105 (22½f,Wet,G,Jun 3)
Chicago Alley 105 (20f,Mar,G,May 16)
Chicago Grey 111 (32f,Chl,G,Mar 16)
China Rock 107 (24f,Leo,HY,Feb 12)
Chorizo 106 (22½f,Mar,GF,Jun 25)
City Heights 109 (21½f,Str,GF,Jly 11)
Classic Frontier 107 (28f,Utt,GF,Jun 27)
Classic Swain 110 (21½f,Nab,GS,Aug 21)
Club Class 107 (25f,Hex,HY,Nov 5)
Cold Mountain 107 (26½f,Nab,GF,Jly 5)
Commemoration Day 107 (23f,Str,G,Mar 14)
Companero 113 (33f,Ncs,HY,Feb 26)
Conem 106 (19f,Leo,S,Jan 23)
Consigliere 105 (17f,Asc,GS,Nov 20)
Cool Friend 108 (20f,Hay,G,May 8)
Cool Mission 115 (24f,Don,GS,Feb 23)
Cool Roxy 105 (21½f,Fak,GF,May 23)
Cool Running 106 (26f,Crt,G,Aug 28)
Coolcashin 107 (28f,Pun,S,Jan 30)
Cornas 105 (16f,San,GF,Apr 23)
Coup Royale 107 (20½f,Kem,GS,Feb 26)
Courella 105 (20f,Fon,G,Sep 23)
Craiglands 106 (24½f,San,GS,Feb 18)
Cranky Corner 105 (16½f,Sed,GS,Jan 25)
Crescent Island 109 (20½f,Wet,GS,Feb 5)
Cruchain 106 (20½f,Kem,GS,Jan 15)
Cullahill 106 (26½f,Nab,GF,Jly 5)
Cybora 107 (20f,Mus,G,Nov 19)

Dallas Bell 106 (26f,Crt,GS,Jly 15)
Dan Breen 112 (16f,San,S,Feb 25)
Dancing Tornado 111 (20½f,Chl,GS,Nov 13)
Darby s Turn 107 (16f,War,G,Nov 3)
Dark Ben 107 (24f,Mus,S,Feb 11)
Dashing George 107 (24½f,San,S,Feb 25)
Dave s Dream 109 (16f,Chl,G,Nov 12)
Dawn Ride 107 (25f,Wet,G,Apr 25)
De Boitron 111 (21f,Chl,G,Apr 13)
De Luain Gorm 108 (20f,Str,G,Jun 13)
De Soto 106 (24f,Ffo,GF,Jun 1)
Dead Or Alive 107 (21½f,Fak,GF,May 23)
Deal Done 107 (19f,Leo,S,Jan 23)
Deep Purple 112 (25f,Wet,G,Oct 30)
Definity 109 (20f,Fon,GS,Jan 28)
Den Of Iniquity 106 (24f,Chp,S,Oct 23)
Denman 116 (26½f,Nby,GS,Nov 27)
Diaco 105 (18f,Mar,G,Sep 26)
Diamond Brook 107 (19½f,Exe,S,Nov 19)
Diamond Frontier 106 (16f,Wet,S,Nov 24)
Diamond Harry 121 (26½f,Nby,GS,Nov 27)
Diavoleria 105 (25f,Kel,GF,May 19)
Digger Gets Lucky 106 (19½f,Chp,S,Oct 23)
Dinarius 106 (19½f,Exe,HY,Feb 13)
Divers 108 (16½f,Tow,G,Oct 6)
Don t Push It 109 (36f,Ain,G,Apr 9)
Dontpaytheferryman 105 (20f,Sed,GF,Apr 27)
Door Boy 105 (20f,Crl,S,Oct 31)
Double Mead 106 (24f,Hay,G,Oct 27)
Double The Trouble 107 (20½f,Lei,GF,Mar 11)
Douglas Julian 105 (20½f,Hex,HY,Nov 17)
Douryna 107 (22½f,Nby,G,Mar 26)
Dover s Hill 109 (25f,Mar,G,Apr 3)
Down The Stretch 105 (19½f,Chp,G,Mar 12)
Dream Alliance 105 (31f,Chl,GF,Mar 15)
Drever Route 107 (20½f,Wet,G,Oct 13)
Duers 109 (20f,Pun,G,Oct 13)
Duke Of Malfi 106 (17f,Kel,GS,Mar 5)
Dukeofchesterwood 106 (26f,Crt,GS,Jly 15)
Dusty Dane 105 (28f,Str,GF,May 28)

Earth Dream 107 (21½f,Nab,S,Aug 22)
Easter Legend 111 (22½f,Nby,G,Mar 26)
Edgbriar 109 (20½f,Chl,G,Oct 16)
Edgeover 109 (20f,Mar,G,Jun 11)
Elite Land 109 (16f,Mus,S,Feb 6)
Ellerslie George 106 (25½f,Wcn,G,Nov 6)
Enfant De Lune 105 (19f,Don,G,Mar 4)
Ere Alfie 105 (22f,Fon,GS,Nov 5)
Eric s Charm 109 (24½f,San,G,Feb 5)
Et Maintenant 105 (21½f,Ain,S,Nov 21)
Ethiopia 105 (26f,Plu,GF,May 9)
Etxalar 107 (26f,Crl,S,Oct 31)
Exmoor Ranger 110 (25½f,Chl,G,Dec 10)
Extra Bold 105 (23½f,Tau,G,Nov 25)
Eyre Square 105 (24f,Ncs,GS,Nov 12)

Faasel 110 (29½f,San,GF,Apr 23)
Fahrisee 109 (16f,Ffo,S,Mar 1)
Fair Along 107 (24f,Nby,GS,Feb 18)
Fairoak Lad 105 (27½f,Wcn,G,Oct 24)
Far More Serious 107 (24½f,Ban,GS,Feb 4)
Fealing Real 105 (19½f,Ffo,GF,Aug 3)
Feeling Peckish 107 (25½f,Cat,G,Mar 9)
Festival King 105 (24f,Mus,GS,Jan 14)
Fiendish Flame 106 (17f,Asc,G,Oct 30)
Fiftyonefiftyone 106 (17f,Nby,GS,Mar 4)
Film Festival 107 (20½f,Wet,G,Oct 30)
Fine Parchment 111 (20f,Nby,GS,Mar 5)
Finian s Rainbow 115 (16f,Chl,G,Mar 15)
Finlay 111 (20f,Sed,S,Mar 15)
First Point 105 (17f,Nby,GS,Nov 26)
Fistral Beach 109 (21f,Wcn,S,Jan 8)
Fit To Drive 105 (24½f,San,G,Nov 6)
Five Dream 110 (22½f,Mar,G,Sep 25)
Flemish Invader 107 (24f,Hun,GS,Mar 6)
Flying Squad 107 (19½f,Tow,S,Nov 21)
Folie A Deux 105 (16f,Utt,G,Jly 22)
Folk Tune 107 (16f,Mus,S,Feb 6)
Forpadydeplasterer 106 (16f,Chl,GS,Nov 14)
Forzy Origny 109 (24f,Utt,S,May 1)
Foxesbow 105 (22½f,Mar,GS,Jan 23)
Frankie Anson 107 (21½f,Crt,G,Aug 28)
Frankie Figg 109 (21½f,Ain,S,Nov 21)
Fredo 105 (20½f,Lei,G,Jan 4)
Free World 114 (20½f,Kem,G,Nov 1)
French Opera 113 (17f,Nby,GS,Feb 18)
From Dawn To Dusk 109 (25½f,Chl,G,Dec 10)
Frontier Dancer 106 (20½f,Hun,GS,Nov 20)
Frosted Grape 107 (21f,Utt,GS,Sep 19)
Fruity O Rooney 105 (20f,Fon,G,Oct 20)

Gabreselassie 105 (21f,Utt,GF,Jly 6)
Galaxy Rock 106 (25½f,Chl,G,Mar 17)
Garde Champetre 110 (31f,Chl,GF,Mar 15)
Garleton 107 (25f,Ayr,S,Mar 11)
Gates Of Rome 112 (16f,Pun,SH,Nov 14)
Gauvain 116 (21½f,Asc,S,Feb 19)
Gee Dee Nen 106 (21½f,Nab,S,Aug 22)
General Hardi 107 (30f,Cat,GS,Jan 13)
General Kutuzov 106 (20½f,Lin,S,Feb 7)
Gentle Ranger 107 (33½f,Utt,GS,Mar 19)
Gerrard 105 (24½f,Tow,GF,May 10)
Ghizao 114 (16f,Ain,G,Apr 9)
Gilbarry 109 (16f,Wet,G,Oct 30)
Giles Cross 105 (33f,Ncs,HY,Feb 26)
Gilsland 107 (25f,Wet,GS,Nov 13)
Gilt Free 105 (16f,Her,G,Apr 7)
Ginolad 105 (25½f,Lud,G,May 13)
Giorgio Quercus 111 (16f,San,S,Feb 25)
Glencove Marina 113 (24f,Leo,HY,Dec 28)
Glengarra 105 (20f,Plu,G,Nov 1)
Glenwood Knight 108 (24f,Utt,HY,Dec 31)
Glimmer Of Light 105 (16f,Utt,GS,Jly 15)
Go Silver Bullet 105 (24f,Mus,S,Feb 11)
Golan Way 117 (20½f,Hun,GS,Nov 20)
Golden Silver 118 (17f,Fai,S,Dec 15)
Gonebeyondrecall 105 (21½f,Ain,G,Apr 8)
Good Company 105 (20½f,Wor,G,Aug 17)
Good Harvest 105 (26½f,Nab,S,Aug 22)
Goring One 107 (21f,Wcn,GF,Mar 27)
Got Attitude 109 (21f,Leo,S,Feb 27)
Grand Lahou 107 (19f,Her,S,Jan 30)
Grand Slam Hero 111 (22½f,Mar,G,Jly 17)
Great Endeavour 115 (21f,Chl,GS,Dec 11)
Gullible Gordon 109 (27½f,Wcn,G,Oct 24)

Harry Flashman 110 (24f,Per,GF,Jun 30)
Have You Seen Me 113 (16½f,Tow,G,Oct 6)
Health Is Wealth 105 (17f,Plu,GF,Apr 11)
Healys Bar 108 (22f,Pun,HY,Feb 9)
Hector s Choice 105 (20f,Lud,G,Feb 9)
Heez A Steel 106 (25f,Ayr,S,Mar 11)
Hell s Bay 114 (21f,Chl,GS,Jan 1)
Hello Bud 114 (26f,Ain,S,Nov 21)
Helpston 105 (25f,Mar,G,Apr 3)
Herons Well 108 (21½f,Str,G,May 29)
Hey Big Spender 111 (20½f,War,GS,Feb 12)
Hidden Keel 109 (20½f,Lei,G,Jan 4)
High Jack 107 (20f,Str,GF,Apr 17)
High Oscar 105 (17f,Plu,S,Nov 15)
High Stand Lad 105 (17½f,Crt,GS,Jly 15)
Himrayn 107 (20f,Str,G,Mar 26)
Hold Fast 105 (16f,Sth,GS,Jan 5)
Hollo Ladies 108 (22½f,Mar,GS,Nov 18)
Holmwood Legend 114 (21f,Chl,G,Apr 13)

I Have Dreamed 105 (17f,Asc,G,Oct 30)
I m A Legend 107 (21f,Wcn,S,Jan 8)
I m Delilah 108 (16½f,Don,G,Mar 5)
I moncloudnine 109 (28f,Ffo,GS,Feb 5)
I msingingtheblues 110 (21f,Chl,GS,Jan 1)
Ice Tea 106 (24½f,San,G,Mar 11)
Iconoclast 107 (24f,Exe,GS,Nov 2)
Ikorodu Road 109 (20f,Str,G,Oct 23)
Imperial Commander 118 (24f,Hay,GS,Nov 20)
Important Business 106 (20f,Mar,GF,Jun 25)
Incentivise 110 (29f,War,HY,Jan 15)
Indian Groom 105 (16f,Crl,HY,Feb 9)
Indian Pipe Dream 108 (21½f,Crt,G,May 31)
Indiana Gold 105 (16½f,Nab,G,Aug 2)
Inmate 105 (20f,Str,GF,Jly 29)
Inside Dealer 107 (19½f,Exe,GS,Dec 16)
Intac 105 (21f,Wcn,GF,Oct 14)
Invisible Man 112 (20f,Mar,GF,Jun 25)
Irish Raptor 109 (25½f,Chl,G,Dec 10)
Isla Pearl Fisher 107 (24f,Mus,GS,Jan 14)
Isn t That Lucky 107 (24f,Lud,G,Mar 3)

J y Vole 109 (24f,Leo,HY,Dec 28)
January 105 (16f,Her,G,Aug 18)
Jayo 108 (17f,Fai,S,Dec 15)
Jessies Dream 111 (24½f,Chl,G,Mar 16)
Jigalo 106 (16f,Pun,SH,Nov 14)
Jimbatai 105 (20½f,Ban,S,Jly 20)
Joncol 114 (24f,Leo,HY,Dec 28)
Jordan s Light 105 (20½f,Hun,GF,May 25)
Junior 115 (25½f,Chl,G,Mar 17)
Justabout 107 (29f,War,G,Mar 13)

Kalahari King 110 (21f,Chl,G,Mar 17)
Kauto Star 115 (26½f,Chl,G,Mar 18)
Kawagino 105 (28f,Fon,HY,Nov 14)
Kealshore Boy 106 (19f,Don,G,Mar 4)
Kellystown Lad 105 (20f,Sed,S,Nov 23)
Keltic Lord 105 (23f,Str,GF,Aug 12)
Kempes 115 (17f,Fai,S,Dec 15)
Kerada 110 (20f,Nby,S,Jan 19)
Kercabellec 105 (24f,Hun,G,Mar 16)
Key Cutter 105 (24f,Lud,GS,Nov 11)
Kikos 105 (16½f,Tow,GF,Apr 12)
Kilkenny All Star 105 (16f,Utt,GS,Oct 13)
Killard Point 106 (25f,Wet,G,Apr 25)
Kilmurry 108 (16f,Chl,G,Oct 16)
King Edmund 105 (17f,Asc,G,Oct 30)
King Fontaine 107 (24f,Hay,GS,Nov 4)
King Ozzy 106 (16f,Lin,GS,Nov 9)
King Roonah 107 (24f,Lud,G,Oct 6)
King Troy 109 (21½f,Str,G,May 29)
Kirkhammerton 105 (17½f,Ban,G,Jly 30)
Kitley Hassle 105 (32f,Exe,GS,Dec 5)
Knight Legend 105 (16f,Wor,G,Jly 27)
Knighton Combe 106 (27½f,Wcn,GF,Apr 21)
Knockara Beau 110 (25½f,Chl,G,Dec 10)
Knockavilla 107 (20f,Sed,GF,Apr 27)
Kosta Brava 109 (16f,Ayr,G,Apr 15)

La Pantera Rosa 105 (25f,Kel,G,Oct 3)
Lacdoudal 109 (31f,Chl,G,Nov 12)
Lady Hillingdon 106 (16f,Ffo,GF,Jun 17)
Lake Legend 108 (23½f,Tau,G,Feb 10)
Last Flight 109 (21½f,Crt,G,May 31)
Lastoftheleaders 108 (17f,Fai,S,Dec 15)
Lavenoak Lad 106 (29f,War,G,Mar 13)
Le Beau Bai 110 (29f,War,HY,Jan 15)
Le Platino 108 (24f,Hay,G,Oct 27)

Leac An Scail 105 (24½f,San,S,Feb 25)
Lead On 106 (24f,Utt,S,May 1)
Lease Lend 112 (16f,Wet,S,Jan 15)
Leo s Lucky Star 113 (16½f,Chl,G,Mar 18)
Little Josh 113 (20f,Crl,S,Oct 31)
Local Present 105 (26½f,Fon,G,Jun 2)
Long Run 120 (24f,Kem,GS,Jan 15)
Loosen My Load 112 (20f,Chl,G,Mar 17)
Lord Villez 106 (20f,Crl,S,Mar 10)
Lordsbridge 105 (20½f,Kem,G,Mar 22)
Lothian Falcon 110 (26f,Don,G,Mar 5)
Loup Du Saubouas 105 (17f,Fai,S,Dec 15)
Lucky Luk 105 (24½f,Tow,GF,May 21)
Lurgan 107 (28f,Pun,S,Jan 30)

Ma Yahab 107 (26½f,Nby,GS,Mar 5)
Macs Lad 105 (26f,Plu,GF,Oct 18)
Mad Jack Duncan 107 (20½f,Wor,G,Sep 5)
Mad Max 110 (20f,Ain,G,Apr 8)
Made In Taipan 106 (24f,Leo,HY,Feb 12)
Magic Marmalade 105 (19f,Tau,GS,Jan 20)
Magic Sky 109 (24f,Asc,G,Apr 10)
Magical Harry 105 (21½f,Nab,G,May 6)
Magical Legend 109 (22½f,Nby,G,Mar 26)
Magnanimity 116 (21f,Leo,HY,Feb 12)
Magnetic Pole 105 (20f,Lud,GF,Apr 25)
Mahogany Blaze 111 (21f,Chl,GS,Jan 1)
Majestic Concorde 111 (24f,Leo,HY,Dec 29)
Major Malarkey 109 (29½f,San,GF,Apr 23)
Maktu 109 (26½f,Nby,G,Mar 26)
Maljimar 110 (31f,Chl,GF,Mar 15)
Mallusk 105 (16f,Utt,HY,Dec 31)
Mamlook 107 (21½f,Fak,HY,Jan 17)
Maraafeq 111 (24f,Lud,G,Feb 9)
Marc Of Brilliance 106 (22f,Fon,G,May 12)
Maringo Bay 106 (21½f,Fak,HY,Jan 17)
Marodima 106 (18f,Fon,S,Oct 2)
Marufo 105 (23f,Str,GF,Sep 4)
Massini Sunset 105 (20f,Plu,HY,Jan 17)
Massini s Maguire 112 (24f,Asc,G,Oct 30)
Master Charm 105 (16f,Sth,G,May 26)
Master Minded 117 (20f,Ain,G,Apr 8)
Master Of The Hall 107 (24f,Hun,S,Jan 26)
Master Overseer 106 (29f,Plu,GS,Jan 2)
Matmata De Tendron 105 (32f,Hex,HY,Mar 17)
Matuhi 109 (20f,Nby,GS,Mar 5)
Max Bygraves 106 (24f,Lud,G,Mar 3)
Meanus Dandy 113 (25½f,Wcn,G,Nov 6)
Medermit 117 (20½f,San,G,Feb 5)
Meet The Critics 105 (22½f,Nby,GS,Mar 4)
Merigo 112 (32½f,Ayr,G,Apr 16)
Mexican Pete 110 (24f,Lud,G,Feb 9)
Micheal Flips 112 (16½f,Tow,G,Oct 6)
Midnight Appeal 107 (20½f,Hun,G,Feb 10)
Midnight Chase 113 (25½f,Chl,G,Dec 10)
Midnight Gold 109 (24f,Ffo,GF,Jun 17)
Midnight Haze 107 (24f,Lud,GS,Nov 11)
Mikael D Haguenet 114 (21f,Leo,HY,Feb 12)
Minella Boys 112 (29f,War,HY,Jan 15)
Minella Four Star 113 (33½f,Utt,GS,Mar 19)
Minella Theatre 107 (21½f,Str,G,Oct 23)
Minouchka 105 (28f,Kel,G,May 5)
Minster Shadow 106 (26f,Crl,S,Oct 31)
Misamon 105 (16f,Sth,GF,Jly 11)
Mischief Man 107 (21½f,Crt,G,Aug 30)
Miss Sarenne 111 (16f,Ain,G,May 7)
Misstree Dancer 108 (25f,Fol,GS,Dec 14)
Mister Marker 107 (20f,Crl,S,Mar 10)
Mister Matt 105 (20½f,Hun,G,Feb 10)
Mister McGoldrick 109 (20½f,Hun,GS,Nov 20)
Mister Stickler 109 (16f,Wcn,GS,Feb 3)
Mister Two Fifty 105 (21½f,Crt,G,Aug 28)
Mister Wiseman 105 (19½f,Chp,S,Oct 23)
Mizen Raven 107 (26f,Crt,GS,Jly 15)
Mohi Rahrere 105 (20f,Utt,HY,Oct 29)
Mon Parrain 112 (24½f,San,G,Mar 12)
Monet s Garden 119 (20f,Ain,GS,Oct 23)
Money Order 107 (29f,War,HY,Feb 25)
Money Trix 115 (24f,Leo,HY,Dec 28)
Moon Over Miami 111 (16f,Ffo,GS,Nov 7)
Morgan Be 105 (24f,Ncs,S,Jan 19)
Mostly Bob 107 (24f,Don,G,Jan 28)
Moulin De La Croix 107 (21½f,Nab,HY,Sep 6)
Mount Oscar 112 (24f,Kem,GS,Feb 26)
Mr Bennett 105 (24f,Exe,G,Mar 8)
Mr Cracker 105 (20f,Chl,G,Mar 17)
Mr Gardner 116 (20½f,Hun,S,Jan 14)
Mr Syntax 105 (20½f,Wet,S,Feb 22)
Mr Thriller 109 (20f,Chl,G,Mar 17)
Mud Monkey 106 (24f,Hun,GS,Mar 6)
Mustangsallyrally 105 (22f,Fon,G,Jun 2)
Mutual Friend 105 (16f,Wet,G,May 20)

Nacarat 115 (25f,Wet,G,Oct 30)
Nadiya De La Vega 117 (16f,War,GS,Nov 17)
Nafaath 110 (16f,Ayr,G,Jan 3)
Native Coral 108 (20½f,Per,G,Jly 1)
Naughty By Nature 108 (24f,Ffo,GF,Jun 17)
Neptune Collonges 111 (26½f,Chl,G,Mar 18)
Neptune Equester 111 (20½f,Wet,G,Oct 29)
Neutrino 107 (20½f,Wor,GF,Jun 16)
Newman Des Plages 105 (24½f,Crl,GS,Oct 8)
Niche Market 116 (26½f,Nby,GS,Nov 27)
Nicto De Beauchene 109 (24½f,San,S,Jan 8)
Nikola 107 (21½f,Ain,S,Nov 21)
Nikos Extra 107 (20f,Hay,G,Mar 23)
No Panic 107 (26f,Crt,G,Aug 28)
Noble Alan 105 (17f,Asc,GS,Nov 20)
Noble Concorde 110 (28f,Pun,S,Jan 30)
Noble Crusader 107 (16f,Lin,GS,Nov 9)
Noble Prince 116 (20f,Chl,G,Mar 17)
Noland 108 (24f,Nby,GS,Feb 18)
Nomadic Warrior 105 (18f,Mar,S,Feb 20)
Norborne Bandit 107 (16½f,Nab,G,Aug 10)
North Island 106 (21f,Ffo,GF,Jun 17)
Nostringsattached 106 (25½f,Ffo,GS,Aug 25)
Not Before Eight 108 (25f,Fai,HY,Jan 16)
Not So Prudent 105 (24f,Utt,HY,Dec 31)
Nothingbutthetruth 105 (20½f,Wet,G,Apr 25)
Notre Pere 106 (26f,Ain,S,Nov 21)
Noun De La Thinte 106 (29f,War,HY,Jan 15)
Novikov 109 (16f,Sth,G,Aug 15)
Nudge And Nurdle 105 (20f,Mar,G,Aug 1)

Oakfield Legend 105 (24f,Lud,G,Mar 3)
Ocarina 105 (20½f,Hex,G,May 8)
Officier De Reserve 108 (26½f,Chl,GS,Jan 1)
Ogee 105 (26f,Don,G,Mar 5)
Oiseau De Nuit 116 (16½f,Chl,G,Mar 18)
Old Si 107 (20f,Pun,G,Oct 13)
Ollie Magern 111 (25f,Wet,G,Oct 30)
On Borrowed Wings 110 (20f,Str,G,Oct 23)
On His Own 112 (25f,Ayr,G,Apr 16)
One Cool Cookie 110 (26f,Ain,S,Nov 21)
Or Bleu 108 (19½f,Chp,S,Jan 8)
Or De Grugy 107 (25f,Kel,GF,Oct 16)
Ormus 105 (16½f,Hex,GS,Jun 12)
Oscar Bay 107 (23f,Wor,GF,May 19)
Oscar Royal 111 (20f,Str,GF,Jun 29)
Oscar Time 112 (36f,Ain,G,Apr 9)
Osric 106 (16f,Wet,G,Oct 30)
Our Bomber Harris 109 (19f,Her,G,Apr 7)
Our Columbus 105 (24f,Chp,GS,Apr 2)
Our Jasper 105 (24f,Lud,G,Oct 6)
Ours 105 (20½f,Lei,HY,Mar 1)
Ouzbeck 111 (28f,Utt,GF,Jun 27)
Ovthenight 106 (24f,Hun,GS,Nov 10)

Pablo Du Charmil 107 (21½f,Nab,GS,Aug 21)
Pacco 105 (24½f,Tow,S,Nov 21)
Pairc Na Gcapall 105 (25f,Mar,G,Aug 21)
Pak Jack 105 (24f,Ffo,S,Jan 16)
Pamak D Airy 105 (16f,Wet,S,Feb 22)
Pandorama 117 (24f,Leo,HY,Dec 28)
Pascha Bere 111 (16½f,Hun,S,Feb 24)
Pasco 106 (20f,Nby,GS,Nov 27)
Passato 111 (21½f,Nab,GS,Aug 21)
Patman Du Charmil 107 (21f,Ffo,S,Mar 1)
Peak Raider 109 (17f,Fai,S,Dec 15)
Peak Seasons 106 (21½f,Crt,G,Aug 30)
Pearlysteps 116 (20½f,Hun,GS,Nov 20)
Pennek 105 (24½f,Crl,S,Mar 20)
Pepe Simo 109 (16½f,Nab,G,Apr 23)
Peplum 107 (20f,Lud,G,Feb 9)
Persian Prince 105 (20f,Sed,GF,May 19)
Persian Run 107 (23½f,Tau,G,Feb 10)
Petit Robin 107 (16½f,Chl,GS,Dec 11)
Petite Margot 106 (26f,Crt,GS,Jly 15)
Petroupetrov 105 (24f,Utt,G,Jun 10)
Peut Etre Sivola 107 (28f,Fon,HY,Nov 14)
Peveril 111 (25f,Fol,S,Jan 2)
Pheidias 107 (24½f,Fak,GF,May 4)
Picaroon 106 (20½f,Ban,S,Apr 30)
Pigeon Island 105 (24f,Lud,G,Mar 3)
Pilgrims Lane 107 (17½f,Str,G,May 16)
Piraya 106 (17f,Asc,GS,Nov 20)
Planet Of Sound 114 (24f,Hay,GS,Nov 20)
Playing The Field 110 (20f,Sed,S,Mar 15)
Plein Pouvoir 105 (19½f,Chp,S,Feb 4)
Plunkett 107 (24½f,Fak,GS,Nov 16)
Poker De Sivola 111 (29½f,San,GF,Apr 23)
Polar Gunner 107 (17f,Kel,GS,Mar 5)
Polyfast 107 (20½f,Wor,G,Jun 5)
Pomme Tiepy 108 (24f,Leo,HY,Dec 29)
Poquelin 118 (20f,Ain,GS,Oct 23)
Portrait Royale 105 (25f,Fol,S,Nov 16)
Poseidon 105 (20f,Sed,S,Mar 15)
Postmaster 109 (21f,Ffo,GF,Apr 26)
Potemkin 105 (16f,Ffo,GS,Nov 7)
Predictive 106 (20f,Sed,HY,Feb 20)
Premier Dane 105 (20f,Ayr,G,Apr 15)
Premier Sagas 106 (20f,Ayr,GS,Jan 2)
Present M Lord 106 (27½f,Wcn,G,Oct 24)
Presentandcorrect 107 (20f,Str,GF,Jun 29)
Presenting Forever 112 (25½f,Chl,G,Dec 10)
Pret A Thou 107 (19f,Cat,GS,Feb 14)
Primrose Time 109 (16f,Crl,S,Oct 31)
Prince De Beauchene 111 (25f,Ain,G,Apr 9)
Prince Des Marais 107 (21½f,Fak,G,Mar 18)
Private Be 107 (21½f,Ain,S,Nov 21)
Promising Anshan 106 (24f,Nby,G,Dec 15)
Prophete De Guye 105 (24f,Utt,G,May 30)
Prosecco 105 (16f,Ayr,S,Feb 24)
Punchestowns 109 (20½f,Kem,GS,Feb 11)
Pure Faith 107 (16f,Sth,G,Aug 15)
Putney Bridge 110 (22½f,Mar,G,Jly 17)

Qhilimar 107 (24½f,San,GS,Feb 18)
Qianshan Leader 107 (19f,Don,G,Mar 4)
Qozak 105 (19f,Tau,GS,Feb 1)
Quantitativeeasing 106 (20½f,Chl,G,Mar 15)
Quarrymount 106 (21½f,Fak,GF,May 23)
Quartz De Thaix 111 (21½f,Nab,GS,Mar 7)
Quel Bruere 106 (20½f,Hun,G,Feb 10)
Questions Answered 108 (19f,Leo,S,Jan 23)
Quezac De La Roque 110 (31f,Chl,GF,Mar 15)
Quicuyo 105 (16f,Ayr,G,Jan 31)
Quinz 113 (24f,Kem,GS,Feb 26)
Quiqui De L Isle 106 (20f,Ncs,S,Mar 8)
Quito De La Roque 111 (25f,Ain,G,Apr 8)
Quito Du Tresor 110 (16½f,Chl,G,Mar 18)
Qulinton 109 (22½f,Mar,G,Sep 25)

Rackham Lerouge 109 (17f,Plu,GS,Dec 13)
Radetsky March 107 (20½f,Ban,GS,Jly 20)
Radium 111 (20f,Chl,G,Mar 17)
Rahan De Marcigny 112 (21f,Leo,S,Feb 27)
Rambling Minster 109 (24f,Don,GS,Feb 23)
Randjo 105 (16f,Wcn,GF,May 6)
Rapid Increase 105 (26½f,Fon,GS,Mar 9)
Rare Bob 106 (25½f,Chl,G,Dec 10)
Rateable Value 105 (22f,Fon,S,Feb 27)
Ratify 105 (25½f,Her,S,Feb 13)
Ray Mond 107 (24½f,Fak,HY,Jan 17)
Raysrock 107 (16f,Ayr,HY,Mar 12)
Ready Or Not 105 (19½f,Ffo,GS,Mar 7)
Realt Dubh 115 (16f,Pun,SH,Nov 14)
Rear Gunner 105 (24f,Hun,G,Feb 10)
Rebel Du Maquis 107 (19f,Tau,G,Nov 11)
Rebel Melody 107 (25f,Mar,S,Nov 7)
Rebel Rock 105 (22½f,Utt,S,Nov 25)
Red Dynamite 105 (22½f,Wet,G,May 27)
Red Law 105 (16½f,Hun,G,Mar 16)
Regal Heights 109 (26½f,Nby,GS,Mar 5)
Reindeer Dippin 107 (16f,Ayr,HY,Feb 12)
Requin 107 (19½f,Chp,G,Mar 12)
Restezen D Armor 105 (17f,Plu,S,Feb 28)
Retrievethelegend 107 (20½f,Per,GF,Jly 11)
Reve De Sivola 111 (24½f,Chl,G,Mar 15)
Rey Nacarado 110 (26½f,Nby,G,Mar 26)
Richard s Sundance 108 (26½f,Chl,GS,Jan 1)
Rifleman 105 (24½f,Crl,G,Oct 21)
Riguez Dancer 107 (16f,Wet,S,Nov 24)
Rileyev 105 (16½f,Nab,GS,Mar 7)
Rimini 105 (16½f,Chp,S,Nov 24)
Riverside Theatre 120 (21½f,Asc,S,Feb 19)
Robinson Collonges 108 (21½f,Her,S,Nov 18)
Robo 118 (24½f,Fak,GS,Nov 16)
Rock Noir 114 (20½f,San,G,Feb 5)
Rockiteer 107 (20f,Mar,G,Aug 1)
Roi Du Mee 113 (22f,Pun,HY,Feb 9)
Roseneath 108 (25f,Mar,S,Nov 7)
Rossini s Dancer 105 (20f,Mus,S,Feb 16)
Royal Kicks 107 (24½f,Ban,G,Oct 9)
Royal Rosa 113 (26f,Ain,S,Nov 21)
Rubi Light 109 (21f,Chl,G,Mar 17)
Runshan 107 (28f,Str,GS,Oct 28)
Russian Epic 107 (20f,Lud,G,Mar 31)
Russian Flag 107 (16f,Wcn,G,Apr 10)
Russian Song 106 (19½f,Exe,S,Nov 19)
Ruthenoise 107 (16f,Ffo,S,Mar 1)

Safari Adventures 106 (20½f,Kem,GS,Jan 15)
Safari Journey 112 (17f,Asc,G,Oct 30)
Sagalyrique 107 (20f,Ayr,GS,Jan 2)
Sang Bleu 107 (28f,Pun,S,Jan 30)
Saphir Des Bois 106 (19f,Her,S,Jan 30)
Sarahs Gift 105 (26f,Plu,GF,Sep 19)
Sarando 110 (25f,Ain,G,Apr 8)
Saveiro 107 (16½f,Hex,S,Oct 9)
Scots Dragoon 105 (26½f,Nby,G,Mar 26)
Scotsirish 110 (17f,Fai,S,Dec 15)
Sea Saffron 105 (25½f,Wcn,GS,Feb 3)
Sea Wall 108 (23f,Str,GF,Jly 18)
See You There 105 (24f,Ncs,S,Jan 19)
Seigneur Des Bois 105 (16f,Sth,G,Apr 13)
Shakalakaboomboom 107 (20½f,Kem,G,Nov 22)
Shaking Hands 105 (26f,War,GS,Jan 27)
Shammy Buskins 106 (24½f,Sth,G,Mar 24)
She s Humble 106 (17f,Plu,GF,Mar 28)
Sheriff Hutton 107 (24f,Per,GF,May 13)
Shoreacres 109 (19f,Tau,S,Feb 22)
Shulmin 105 (21½f,Crt,G,May 29)
Siegemaster 106 (25f,Fai,HY,Feb 23)
Sierra Victor 107 (25f,Hex,S,Oct 9)
Silk Drum 113 (16f,Ain,GS,Apr 7)
Silmi 111 (22½f,Mar,G,Sep 25)
Silver Adonis 106 (22½f,Mar,GF,Jun 25)
Silver By Nature 114 (28f,Hay,HY,Feb 19)
Silver Kate 112 (24f,Chp,S,Jan 8)
Silverburn 109 (21½f,Nab,GS,Aug 21)
Simarian 110 (21½f,Crt,G,May 31)
Simply Smashing 109 (28f,Str,GF,Sep 21)
Sir Du Bearn 110 (16f,War,GS,Nov 17)
Sir Ian 107 (20½f,Wor,G,Sep 24)
Sir Tantallus Hawk 108 (20f,Sed,S,Feb 8)
Sizing Australia 111 (31f,Chl,GF,Mar 15)
Sizing Europe 117 (16f,Chl,G,Mar 16)
Smack That 107 (16f,Ain,G,Jun 11)
Smuglin 109 (22½f,Mar,GS,Nov 18)
Sole Agent 105 (24f,Lin,GS,Mar 21)
Solway Bay 105 (24f,Per,GF,May 12)
Some Craic 105 (21½f,Nab,HY,Sep 6)
Some Target 111 (28f,Pun,S,Jan 30)
Somersby 115 (17f,Asc,GS,Jan 22)
Songe 107 (20½f,Hun,G,Oct 3)
Sou Wester 106 (23f,Wor,GF,May 19)
Soubriquet 107 (24f,Per,S,Sep 22)
Sporting Rebel 107 (24½f,Fak,G,Oct 22)
Squadron 107 (24f,Hun,G,Feb 10)
Stagecoach Pearl 109 (16f,Hay,GS,Nov 20)
Stan 108 (21f,Ffo,GF,Apr 26)
Star Beat 107 (25½f,Cat,G,Dec 14)
Star Player 105 (24f,Ncs,S,Jan 11)
Starluck 114 (16½f,Hun,S,Feb 24)
State Of Play 109 (36f,Ain,G,Apr 9)
Storm Of Applause 105 (20½f,Wor,G,Sep 24)
Storm Prospect 105 (20f,Mus,G,Nov 26)
Storm Surge 112 (16f,Wet,G,May 6)
Stormin Exit 106 (24f,Leo,HY,Dec 29)
Storymaker 107 (20½f,Ban,S,Apr 30)
Straw Bear 106 (20f,Fon,GS,Jan 28)
Streets Of Gold 105 (28f,Pun,S,Jan 30)
Strong Coffee 105 (26½f,Nab,G,Jly 18)
Sultan Fontenaille 105 (23½f,Tau,GS,Dec 30)
Summery Justice 107 (24½f,Ban,S,Nov 10)
Sunday City 110 (16f,Ffo,GS,Nov 7)
Sunnyhillboy 113 (21f,Chl,GS,Dec 11)
Surenaga 105 (24½f,San,G,Mar 11)
Sweden 107 (24f,Ffo,S,Jan 16)
Swincombe Rock 107 (20½f,Per,S,Sep 23)
Swing Bill 110 (20f,Nby,GS,Mar 5)
Swordsman 105 (23f,Str,G,Aug 19)
Synchronised 110 (33½f,Utt,GS,Mar 19)

Tafika 106 (23½f,Lei,G,Feb 2)
Tail Of The Bank 110 (20f,Nby,GS,Mar 5)
Take The Breeze 111 (24f,Asc,G,Oct 30)
Tampa Boy 106 (20f,Str,G,Jun 13)
Tanks For That 110 (16½f,Chl,GS,Dec 11)
Tara Royal 109 (20f,Hay,G,May 8)
Tarablaze 110 (25f,Ain,G,Apr 9)
Taranis 113 (26½f,Nby,GS,Nov 27)
Tartak 113 (21f,Chl,GS,Jan 1)
Tartan Snow 107 (17f,Kel,GS,Mar 21)
Tatenen 114 (20½f,Kem,G,Nov 1)
Tawaagg 106 (17f,Leo,SH,Jan 9)
Tchico Polos 110 (17½f,Exe,GS,Nov 2)
Tell Me The Story 105 (20½f,Wor,G,Sep 5)
Templer 109 (28f,Utt,GF,Jun 27)
Tempsford 107 (22½f,Mar,GF,Jun 25)
Ten Fires 110 (21f,Leo,S,Feb 27)
Thai Vango 105 (22½f,Mar,G,Sep 25)
That s Rhythm 110 (25f,Wet,G,Oct 30)
The Ferbane Man 108 (25f,Wet,G,Jun 3)
The Kealshore Kid 111 (16f,Wet,G,May 6)
The Knoxs 109 (20f,Sed,S,Feb 8)
The Listener 112 (24f,Leo,HY,Dec 28)
The Midnight Club 113 (25f,Fai,HY,Feb 23)
The Minack 105 (20½f,War,GS,Jan 27)
The Rainbow Hunter 110 (24f,Ffo,G,Apr 11)
The Rocking Dock 105 (16f,Per,GS,May 23)
The Sawyer 105 (24f,Asc,S,Feb 19)
The Shoe 110 (25f,Ayr,G,Apr 16)
The Tother One 116 (26½f,Nby,GS,Nov 27)
The Wifes Pet 106 (16½f,Tow,G,Oct 6)
Thegreatjohnbrowne 109 (24f,Leo,HY,Dec 28)
Thenameescapesme 105 (24f,Utt,G,Jly 26)
Theophrastus 105 (25f,Fol,G,Mar 10)
Three Chords 107 (24½f,Fak,GS,Jan 30)
Tidal Bay 117 (24f,Hay,GS,Nov 20)
Time For Rupert 112 (25½f,Chl,GS,Dec 11)
Top Dressing 107 (25f,Kel,G,Apr 28)
Torphichen 109 (17f,Leo,HY,Dec 30)
Triggerman 110 (28f,Ffo,GS,Feb 5)
Troy Tempest 105 (26½f,Fon,G,Apr 19)
Tullamore Dew 109 (17f,Plu,GS,Dec 13)
Turbo Shandy 105 (18f,Mar,GF,Jly 4)
Tuskar Rock 105 (24f,Lin,S,Feb 7)
Twelve Paces 105 (24f,Per,G,Aug 21)
Twist Magic 109 (17½f,Exe,GS,Nov 2)
Tyrone House 107 (20f,Mus,G,Jan 26)
Tyup Pompey 107 (16f,Her,G,Apr 29)

Upham Atom 106 (27½f,Wcn,GF,Apr 21)
Ursis 107 (20f,Mar,S,Nov 14)

Valerius 105 (25½f,Ffo,GS,Aug 25)
Valley Ride 110 (28f,Utt,GF,Jun 27)
Valley View 105 (16f,Fol,G,Feb 1)

Vamizi 106 (24f,Exe,GS,Nov 2)
Viable 106 (18f,Mar,G,Jly 17)
Vic Venturi 109 (25f,Fai,HY,Feb 23)
Victor Daly 105 (25f,Ain,G,May 14)
Victory Gunner 105 (24½f,Tow,S,Feb 3)
Victory Surge 105 (24½f,Ban,G,Aug 25)
Vino Griego 105 (20½f,Chl,G,Mar 15)
Viper 105 (25½f,Her,GF,Jun 20)
Vodka Brook 105 (26f,Crl,S,Oct 31)
Volcanic Rock 105 (30f,Crt,G,Aug 26)
Voramar Two 111 (24f,Chp,S,Jan 8)
Voy Por Ustedes 108 (21f,Chl,G,Mar 17)

Walamo 105 (20½f,Hun,GF,Aug 30)
Warpath 107 (20f,Lud,GF,Apr 25)
Watch My Back 109 (20f,Ayr,G,Apr 15)
Wayward Prince 111 (24½f,Chl,G,Mar 16)
Weird Al 113 (20f,Crl,S,Oct 31)
Wellforth 107 (24½f,Fak,GS,Feb 18)
West End Rocker 113 (29f,War,HY,Jan 15)
West Ship Master 108 (25f,Fai,HY,Jan 16)
West With The Wind 110 (16f,Ain,G,May 7)
Western Charmer 110 (24f,Leo,HY,Dec 28)
Western Gale 110 (24f,Per,GF,Jun 30)
What A Friend 115 (26½f,Chl,G,Mar 18)
What s Up Doc 105 (16f,Sth,G,Jly 23)
Whataboutya 107 (25f,Mar,S,Nov 7)
Whats Up Woody 107 (20f,Crl,S,Mar 20)
Will Jamie Run 105 (24f,Leo,HY,Dec 29)
Willandrich 105 (22½f,Utt,G,Apr 2)
William s Wishes 109 (16f,Lei,G,Nov 15)
Wind Shuffle 111 (16f,Ayr,G,Jan 3)
Winterwood 105 (24f,Ffo,S,Feb 17)
Wishfull Thinking 115 (20f,Ain,GS,Apr 7)
Wolf Moon 105 (25½f,Cat,GS,Feb 28)
Woolcombe Folly 113 (16½f,Chl,GS,Dec 11)

Yabora 105 (20½f,Ban,S,Apr 30)
Yellow Flag 108 (16f,Ffo,G,Aug 27)
You Know Yourself 106 (20½f,Wet,GS,Nov 13)
You re The Top 106 (20½f,Chl,G,Oct 16)

Zaarito 115 (17f,Fai,S,Dec 15)
Zarrafakt 107 (21f,Fol,S,Nov 16)
Zitenka 107 (25f,Kel,G,Apr 23)

HURDLES

A Bridge Too Far 107 (20f,Hay,G,Mar 23)
A Media Luz 108 (16½f,Nby,GS,Dec 29)
Aberdale 107 (24f,Utt,GF,May 9)
Accidental Outlaw 111 (16f,Leo,SH,Dec 30)
According To Pete 108 (24f,Hay,HY,Feb 19)
Accordintolawrence 105 (17f,Exe,HY,Nov 19)
Ackertac 108 (24½f,Don,GS,Feb 23)
Act Of Kalanisi 111 (19½f,Asc,S,Feb 19)
Action Impact 105 (16½f,Str,GF,May 28)
Action Master 108 (16f,Leo,HY,Feb 12)
Advancement 107 (17f,Tau,G,Mar 14)
Aegean Dawn 107 (21f,Chl,GS,Nov 12)
Afsoun 108 (20f,Fon,S,Feb 27)
Agglestone Rock 107 (20f,Hay,G,Apr 23)
Aggravation 105 (17f,Mar,GF,Jun 25)
Aghill 108 (24½f,Ayr,G,Apr 15)
Aibrean 109 (24½f,Ayr,G,Apr 15)
Aikideau 109 (17f,Chl,G,Mar 18)
Aikman 111 (20½f,Hun,S,Feb 24)
Ainama 105 (16f,Leo,HY,Feb 12)
Aine s Delight 105 (16f,Wcn,GF,Apr 21)
Airmen s Friend 105 (20½f,Hun,GS,Mar 6)
Aisemma 108 (24f,Wor,GF,Jly 21)
Ajman 107 (17f,Her,GF,Jun 20)
Al Co 109 (24½f,Don,GS,Feb 23)
Al Ferof 120 (16½f,Chl,G,Mar 15)
Al Qeddaaf 106 (16½f,Kel,G,Apr 28)
Alaivan 111 (17f,Chl,G,Mar 18)
Alarazi 111 (16½f,San,G,Mar 12)
Alasi 107 (24f,Asc,GS,Jan 22)
Alazan 109 (17f,Ban,G,Aug 20)
Alcalde 110 (16f,Fak,GS,Jan 30)
Alderley Rover 109 (24½f,Ain,G,May 7)
Alegralil 113 (16½f,Wet,G,Oct 30)
Alfie Spinner 112 (22f,San,G,Feb 5)
All For The Cause 105 (20f,Sed,G,Sep 7)
Alla Svelta 105 (17f,Nab,GS,Mar 7)
Alldunnandusted 105 (19f,Str,G,May 29)
Allerford Jack 106 (18½f,Fon,G,Mar 9)
Allformary 107 (19f,Str,G,Mar 26)
Alph 107 (16½f,Lin,HY,Nov 23)
Alpha One 107 (20½f,Hex,G,Apr 11)
Alpine Breeze 109 (20½f,Sth,G,Jun 8)
Alpine Eagle 108 (16f,Leo,S,Jan 9)
Altan Khan 105 (16f,Mus,G,Nov 19)
Alverstone 117 (24f,Chp,GS,Oct 23)
Amaury De Lusignan 105 (20f,Fak,GS,Feb 18)
Amazing King 111 (16½f,Ain,G,Apr 9)
Amber Brook 109 (24f,Chl,G,Oct 15)
Ambrose Princess 105 (24f,Utt,G,May 15)

American Ladie 110 (18½f,Fon,G,Apr 8)
American World 105 (24f,Wor,G,Jly 27)
Amuse Me 105 (16f,Tow,G,Oct 24)
Andhaar 106 (16½f,Don,G,Jan 28)
Andrea s Answer 106 (24f,Pun,HY,Feb 9)
Andreo Bambaleo 107 (20½f,Hex,G,Apr 11)
Aneyeforaneye 105 (19½f,Don,G,Mar 4)
Annimation 110 (19f,Exe,S,Nov 9)
Another Dimension 109 (20½f,Hun,GS,Mar 6)
Anothercoppercoast 105 (22f,Pun,SH,Nov 14)
Anquetta 107 (21f,Lud,G,May 13)
Any Given Day 122 (20½f,Chl,GS,Dec 11)
Aohna 105 (17f,Ban,G,May 15)
Apache Chant 106 (21f,Lud,G,Apr 10)
Apt To Run 105 (16f,Lud,G,Oct 6)
Araldur 107 (16f,Lei,S,Jan 4)
Araucaria 105 (18f,Fai,HY,Jan 16)
Arcalis 108 (16½f,Hay,G,May 8)
Arctic Court 105 (24½f,Ayr,G,Jan 3)
Ardesia 105 (17½f,Crt,G,Jun 2)
Areuwitmenow 108 (25f,War,G,Mar 13)
Armedanddangerous 106 (20f,Crl,S,Mar 10)
Armenian Boy 106 (21f,Lud,G,Oct 21)
Art Broker 106 (17f,Tau,G,Mar 14)
Art Professor 111 (17f,Chl,GS,Jan 29)
Arthur s Pass 108 (16f,Lud,G,Mar 3)
Arthurian Legend 105 (16½f,Chp,S,Apr 2)
Ashkazar 117 (20½f,Chl,GS,Dec 11)
Ashmolian 105 (19½f,Tow,GF,May 18)
Asigh Pearl 112 (16f,Fai,S,Dec 15)
Askanna 109 (22f,Pun,SH,Nov 14)
Astracad 109 (17f,Chl,GS,Dec 11)
Astrolibra 105 (18½f,Fon,G,Sep 5)
Attaglance 106 (19f,Mar,GS,Nov 18)
Auberge 106 (24f,Utt,G,Sep 19)
Australia Day 121 (16f,Kem,G,Oct 17)
Awesome Freddie 106 (24½f,Don,G,Mar 5)

Baahor 106 (20f,Ain,G,May 7)
Back In Focus 108 (24f,Hay,HY,Feb 19)
Backbord 107 (21f,Kem,G,Nov 1)
Backspin 113 (21f,Nby,GS,Dec 29)
Badgers Cove 107 (21f,Lud,G,Apr 10)
Baggsy 107 (16f,Tow,S,Nov 21)
Balerina 105 (16f,Kem,GS,Feb 11)
Ballinahow Lady 106 (24f,Pun,HY,Feb 9)
Bally Legend 107 (16f,Lud,GS,Feb 23)
Ballyadam Brook 106 (16½f,Chl,G,Nov 12)
Ballybach 106 (19½f,Asc,G,Oct 30)
Balustrade 105 (22½f,Fon,GS,Jan 28)
Banjaxed Girl 107 (22f,Wcn,G,Nov 6)
Barafundle 107 (24f,Hay,GS,Nov 20)
Barbatos 107 (22½f,Utt,GS,Mar 19)
Bari Bay 106 (16f,Tow,GF,May 18)
Barizan 110 (16f,Hay,GS,Nov 20)
Barnhill Brownie 107 (24f,Wor,G,Jly 27)
Baron De L 107 (16f,Pun,G,Oct 14)
Barwell Bridge 107 (24f,Chl,G,Mar 17)
Basford Bob 107 (22½f,Utt,GS,Mar 19)
Battle Group 113 (24½f,Ain,G,Apr 8)
Bayross 105 (20f,Fai,HY,Jan 16)
Be My Light 105 (20½f,Hun,S,Jan 26)
Beau Lake 106 (16f,Plu,HY,Feb 14)
Beaubrav 105 (16f,Plu,GF,Oct 18)
Beidh Tine Anseo 107 (16½f,Per,GF,May 12)
Bella Haze 109 (20½f,Utt,GS,May 1)
Bellaboosh 110 (17f,Ban,S,Mar 2)
Belle Brook 111 (18f,Fai,HY,Jan 16)
Bellflower Boy 107 (24f,Ban,G,Dec 15)
Belord 107 (16f,Leo,S,Jan 9)
Ben s Folly 109 (24f,Mar,G,Sep 26)
Benedict Spirit 105 (19f,Nab,GS,Aug 31)
Bensalem 113 (24f,Hay,HY,Feb 19)
Bescot Springs 105 (24½f,Per,S,Sep 22)
Best Prospect 108 (16f,Ncs,HY,Feb 26)
Betabob 107 (16f,Plu,GF,Oct 18)
Big Buck s 107 (24½f,Ain,GS,Apr 7)
Big Robert 105 (20f,Her,GF,Apr 20)
Big Talk 106 (16f,Tow,S,Nov 21)
Binocular 117 (16f,Kem,GS,Jan 15)
Black Jacari 107 (19f,Mar,G,Jun 11)
Black Jack Blues 111 (16f,Ffo,GS,Feb 5)
Black Phantom 112 (20f,Chp,GS,Apr 2)
Black Tor Figarro 105 (22½f,Str,GF,Apr 17)
Blackstairmountain 111 (17f,Chl,G,Mar 18)
Bled 105 (20½f,Utt,HY,Nov 13)
Blenheim Brook 106 (16f,Utt,S,Jan 29)
Bobbie Magern 108 (24f,Chp,GS,Oct 23)
Bobble Hat Bob 106 (24f,Ffo,GF,Jun 17)
Bobs Worth 115 (20½f,Chl,GS,Jan 1)
Bocamix 112 (16f,Hay,GS,Nov 20)
Bold Addition 110 (20½f,Chl,G,Apr 13)
Bollin Felix 108 (16½f,Hex,HY,Mar 17)
Bollywood 105 (20f,Wcn,GF,Apr 27)
Bonzeno Queen 107 (16½f,Str,G,May 16)
Boogie Dancer 107 (17f,Her,G,Aug 18)
Boragh Princess 111 (16f,Wor,G,Oct 20)
Borero 107 (24f,Ban,G,Apr 9)
Bothy 112 (16½f,Chl,GS,Nov 14)
Bottman 108 (20½f,Chl,G,Apr 13)
Brackloon High 112 (16f,Plu,G,Nov 1)
Brampour 110 (17f,Tau,G,Feb 10)
Breaking Storm 107 (17f,Sed,GF,Apr 27)

Broadway Allstar 106 (19f,Mar,GF,Jly 4)
Brunswick Gold 110 (20f,Fak,GS,Feb 18)
Bucephalus 105 (17f,Sed,GF,May 26)
Buck Barrow 114 (16f,Leo,HY,Dec 29)
Buck Magic 111 (22f,Wcn,G,Nov 18)
Buck Mulligan 105 (21f,Kem,G,Mar 5)
Buddy Holly 105 (16f,Tow,S,Jan 10)
Buena Vista 113 (24f,Chl,G,Mar 17)
Bunglasha Lady 112 (22½f,Fon,GS,Feb 27)
Busker Royal 110 (19½f,Asc,S,Feb 19)
Bygones Of Brid 112 (16f,Ayr,G,Apr 16)

Cailin Na Ri 112 (20f,Sed,GF,Apr 27)
Call At Midnight 105 (22½f,Fon,G,Sep 5)
Call The Police 112 (16f,Leo,S,Jan 9)
Calon Crwbin 114 (19f,Mar,GF,Jly 4)
Calusa Shadow 106 (24f,Ban,G,Apr 9)
Calypso Bay 107 (24f,Utt,G,Sep 19)
Camden 113 (22½f,Fon,G,Apr 19)
Canaly 107 (16f,Leo,HY,Dec 29)
Cannon Fire 105 (20f,Wor,G,Jun 6)
Cantabilly 108 (19f,Nab,G,May 11)
Capellanus 107 (16f,Fai,S,Dec 15)
Cappagh 109 (23½f,Exe,GF,May 12)
Captain Americo 107 (27f,Kel,G,Nov 6)
Captain Becket 107 (23½f,Exe,GF,May 12)
Captain Chris 107 (20f,Chp,S,Oct 23)
Captain Kirkton 111 (18½f,Fon,S,Feb 6)
Captain Paulie 108 (16f,Leo,HY,Dec 29)
Carlicue 112 (24f,Chp,GS,Oct 23)
Carlito Brigante 113 (16f,Hay,GS,Nov 20)
Carole s Legacy 110 (24f,Asc,GS,Jan 22)
Carpincho 108 (22½f,Fol,S,Feb 1)
Carribs Leap 108 (20f,Fak,G,Oct 22)
Carrig An Uisce 105 (16½f,Lin,GS,Nov 9)
Cash Man 107 (20½f,Hex,G,May 1)
Cass Bligh 107 (16f,Leo,S,Feb 27)
Casual Style 106 (16½f,Str,G,May 16)
Catch Me 105 (18f,Leo,S,Feb 27)
Catleen 108 (24½f,Ayr,G,Apr 15)
Caught By Witness 106 (20f,Fak,G,Jan 1)
Cedre Bleu 108 (16½f,Nby,S,Jan 19)
Celestial Halo 120 (20½f,Chl,GS,Dec 11)
Celticello 107 (17f,Mar,G,Sep 25)
Changing Lanes 106 (24f,Wor,G,Aug 6)
Charlie Bucket 106 (22½f,Kel,S,Nov 21)
Charminster 110 (17f,Sed,GS,Jan 25)
Chartreux 110 (24f,Chl,GS,Jan 1)
Cheshire Prince 107 (16½f,San,GS,Nov 6)
Chestnut Charlie 105 (20f,Pun,HY,Feb 16)
China Gold 105 (22½f,Utt,G,Apr 2)
Chrysander 105 (17f,Tau,G,Feb 10)
Ciceron 109 (17f,Tau,GS,Jan 20)
Circus Clown 106 (20f,Ayr,HY,Mar 12)
Clan Tara 105 (20f,Pun,HY,Feb 16)
Classical Mist 105 (20f,Crl,S,Mar 20)
Clear Sailing 107 (16½f,Str,GF,May 28)
Clerk s Choice 118 (16½f,Chl,G,Oct 16)
Clifton Debut 106 (25½f,Plu,GF,Oct 18)
Cloudy Spirit 108 (24½f,Ain,G,Apr 8)
Clu Agus Cail 109 (16f,Plu,GF,Oct 18)
Coastley 108 (22½f,Kel,GF,May 19)
Cockney Trucker 112 (17f,Chl,G,Mar 18)
Cocoa Key 105 (17f,Crl,S,Oct 31)
Cody Wyoming 107 (16½f,Lin,GS,Mar 21)
Colleoni 107 (16f,Lud,GS,Nov 11)
Comhla Ri Coig 105 (20f,Ain,S,Nov 21)
Connectivity 112 (22½f,Utt,G,Apr 2)
Conquisto 114 (16½f,Ain,G,Apr 9)
Cool Operator 107 (17f,Crl,HY,Feb 21)
Cool Touch 106 (16f,Wor,G,May 9)
Cornish Ice 110 (20½f,Utt,HY,Oct 29)
Corso Palladio 105 (22½f,Fon,G,Aug 19)
Cotswold Charmer 108 (22½f,Utt,HY,Oct 3)
Cottrelsbooley 117 (16f,Leo,HY,Dec 29)
County Zen 109 (22f,San,G,Feb 5)
Court In Motion 109 (21f,Nby,GS,Dec 29)
Court Red Handed 105 (21f,Lud,G,Oct 6)
Crackentorp 105 (16f,Ncs,GS,Nov 12)
Crathorne 107 (19f,Nab,GF,Jly 5)
Crazy Eyes 106 (25f,War,GS,Feb 12)
Credit Swap 107 (16f,Lei,S,Jan 4)
Cristal Bonus 109 (17f,Chl,GS,Dec 11)
Crom Abu 107 (16f,Pun,G,Oct 14)
Crop Walker 106 (24f,Ban,G,Apr 9)
Crosby Jemma 105 (17f,Sed,GF,Apr 27)
Cross Appeal 105 (22f,Pun,SH,Nov 14)
Cross Kennon 115 (24f,Hay,HY,Feb 19)
Crystal Rock 105 (16f,Wor,G,Sep 24)
Cubism 106 (25½f,Plu,GF,Oct 18)
Cucumber Run 106 (16½f,Hun,GS,Jan 6)
Cue Card 116 (16½f,Chl,G,Mar 15)
Cunning Clarets 105 (16f,Ayr,GS,Jan 2)

Danceintothelight 107 (16f,Cat,GS,Jan 13)
Dancewiththedevil 105 (17f,Ban,S,Apr 30)
Dancing Dude 105 (20½f,Utt,G,Apr 2)
Danny Zuko 107 (17f,Ban,G,Jun 8)
Dansimar 105 (20f,Wcn,S,Jan 8)
Dantari 109 (22f,San,G,Feb 5)
Dare Me 111 (17f,Exe,G,Oct 19)
Daring Origyn 108 (20½f,Lei,HY,Feb 2)
Day Of A Lifetime 105 (16f,Leo,S,Jan 23)
Days Ahead 105 (16f,Fai,S,Dec 15)

Dear Sam 105 (19f,Mar,GS,Nov 18)
Dee Ee Williams 109 (16f,Wcn,G,Nov 6)
Deep Pockets 106 (25f,War,GS,Jan 27)
Deep Reflection 105 (20f,Wor,GF,Jly 21)
Define 105 (16f,Leo,S,Feb 27)
Definite Dawn 105 (24f,Utt,S,Nov 25)
Definitley Lovely 110 (16f,Tow,GS,Nov 4)
Den Maschine 105 (16½f,Str,GF,May 28)
Der Spieler 110 (16f,Pun,G,Oct 14)
Desert Cry 112 (17f,Sed,HY,Feb 20)
Devil To Pay 105 (16½f,Chl,GS,Nov 13)
Devito 106 (20f,Wor,G,Jly 14)
Devotion To Duty 107 (20f,Mus,S,Feb 11)
Dhaafer 110 (16½f,Chl,G,Mar 16)
Dirar 111 (17f,Chl,G,Mar 18)
Dishdasha 105 (16½f,Str,GF,Jun 13)
Doctor Deejay 109 (16f,Fai,S,Dec 15)
Doctor Foxtrot 110 (24½f,Don,G,Mar 5)
Domino Dancer 110 (19f,Str,G,Mar 26)
Don t Push It 105 (24f,Chl,G,Mar 17)
Dona 105 (17f,Tau,GS,Jan 10)
Donnas Palm 115 (16f,Pun,SH,Nov 14)
Donny Briggs 105 (17f,Sed,S,Feb 8)
Dont Call Me Derek 111 (24f,Wor,GF,Jun 23)
Dontpaytheferryman 107 (16f,Mus,S,Feb 16)
Dorabelle 105 (16½f,Wet,GS,Nov 13)
Double Whammy 105 (22½f,Fol,S,Feb 1)
Dove Hill 105 (25f,Crl,HY,Nov 8)
Downward Spiral 105 (21f,Lud,G,May 13)
Dream Catcher 107 (17f,Nab,GF,Jly 5)
Dream Risk 106 (17½f,Crt,G,May 31)
Drill Sergeant 105 (21f,Kem,GS,Jan 15)
Drive Time 106 (19½f,Don,G,Jan 12)
Duc De Regniere 110 (25f,Wet,G,Oct 30)
Duke Of Lucca 110 (20½f,Chl,GS,Jan 1)
Dun See Dee 105 (19f,Exe,GS,Dec 16)
Dunaskin 112 (17½f,Crt,G,Aug 26)
Dunguib 107 (16½f,Chl,G,Mar 15)
Dunraven Storm 111 (16½f,Chl,G,Nov 12)
Dynaste 109 (19½f,Tau,GS,Dec 30)

Earcomesthedream 106 (21f,Tow,GS,Nov 4)
Easter Meteor 112 (19½f,Asc,GS,Nov 19)
Easter Vic 105 (24½f,Ayr,G,Apr 15)
Eastwell Smiles 105 (19f,War,S,Dec 31)
Edgefour 106 (19f,Str,GF,Jly 11)
Educated Evans 105 (20½f,Lei,HY,Feb 2)
Elusive Muse 106 (24½f,Ain,G,May 7)
Elzahann 105 (24½f,Ayr,G,Apr 15)
Emmaslegend 106 (20f,Wcn,GF,Mar 10)
Empire Levant 107 (16½f,Nby,G,Dec 15)
Empress Orchid 107 (17f,Ban,S,Mar 2)
Enchanted Approach 106 (21f,Lud,G,May 13)
Eradicate 113 (16½f,Hay,G,May 8)
Escort men 109 (16½f,Chp,GS,Oct 9)
Estrela Brage 106 (16f,Leo,HY,Dec 29)
European Dream 106 (16f,Mus,S,Feb 6)
Everaard 105 (24½f,Mus,G,Jan 26)
Express Leader 106 (19f,Nab,G,May 6)
Extreme Conviction 105 (20f,Ain,G,May 7)
Extreme Impact 105 (24f,Chp,G,Mar 12)
Extremely So 106 (20½f,Hun,S,Feb 24)
Exulto 105 (16f,Sth,G,Apr 28)
Eyre Square 106 (24f,Hex,GS,Mar 27)

Fair Along 115 (25f,Wet,G,Oct 30)
Fair Spin 105 (20½f,Hex,GS,Jun 12)
Fairoak Lad 105 (24f,Mar,G,Sep 26)
Falcon Island 107 (17f,Nab,GS,Mar 20)
Far Away So Close 123 (16½f,Ain,G,Apr 9)
Farewellatmidnight 105 (20f,Fak,GS,Jan 30)
Favours Brave 105 (17f,Mar,G,Aug 21)
Fearless Falcon 113 (16f,Fai,S,Dec 15)
Fiddledee 109 (16f,Tow,GS,Nov 4)
Final Approach 113 (16f,Leo,S,Jan 9)
Firm Order 111 (21f,Lud,G,May 13)
First Fandango 107 (16½f,Ffo,GS,Nov 22)
First Lieutenant 110 (21f,Chl,G,Mar 16)
First Point 111 (20½f,Chl,G,Mar 18)
First Stream 105 (20f,Wet,G,Oct 30)
Five Out Of Five 105 (19f,Nab,G,Jun 7)
Five Star Wilsham 111 (24½f,Don,G,Mar 5)
Fiveforthree 111 (16f,Pun,HY,Feb 16)
Flinty Bay 112 (16f,Ayr,S,Feb 24)
Flower Haven 105 (20f,Ain,G,May 14)
Fly Tipper 105 (20½f,Per,G,Aug 21)
Flying Doctor 105 (22f,Wet,G,May 6)
For Non Stop 108 (21f,Nby,GS,Dec 29)
Forest Rhythm 105 (16f,Wcn,GF,May 6)
Forty Foot Tom 106 (16f,Leo,HY,Feb 12)
Forty Thirty 107 (17f,Ain,G,May 14)
Fosters Cross 111 (16f,Fai,S,Dec 15)
Fountains Flypast 105 (19½f,Tau,GS,Mar 3)
Frascati Park 117 (19½f,Asc,GS,Nov 19)
Front Of House 105 (22½f,Str,GF,Aug 19)
Front Rank 107 (17½f,Crt,G,Aug 28)
Frontier Spirit 107 (20f,Fak,G,Oct 22)
Fujin Dancer 107 (16f,Fak,G,Mar 18)
Full Of Joy 107 (21f,Nby,GS,Nov 25)
Furrows 105 (16f,Lud,G,Mar 3)

Galiotto 110 (16f,Plu,GF,Mar 28)
Gee Dee Nen 105 (21f,Kem,GS,Feb 26)

Genuine Pearl 105 (24f,Wor,GF,Jun 16)
Get It On 107 (18½f,Fon,S,Feb 6)
Get Me Out Of Here 112 (17f,Chl,G,Mar 18)
Ghimaar 106 (16f,Wor,GS,Jun 6)
Gibb River 108 (16½f,Chl,G,Mar 15)
Gifted Leader 113 (16½f,Ain,G,Apr 9)
Gilded Age 106 (17f,Tau,G,Mar 14)
Glitzy D Ocala 108 (20½f,Lei,S,Jan 25)
Global Power 106 (22½f,Fol,S,Dec 14)
Gloucester 110 (17f,Chl,G,Mar 18)
Go Amwell 105 (26f,Hun,G,Oct 12)
Gold Reef 106 (20f,Wcn,S,Jan 8)
Golden Chieftain 110 (22½f,Utt,GS,Mar 19)
Golfer s Crossing 105 (22½f,Kel,GS,Mar 5)
Good Time Donie 109 (20f,Fai,HY,Feb 23)
Gorge 108 (16½f,Ain,G,Apr 9)
Gormanstown Cuckoo 111 (16f,Leo,HY,Dec 29)
Gortenbuie 106 (21f,Lud,G,Mar 3)
Grafite 107 (19½f,Tow,S,Dec 16)
Grand Diamond 107 (16½f,Per,S,Sep 22)
Grand Zouki 106 (20f,Sed,GF,Aug 24)
Grandouet 112 (17f,Chl,G,Mar 18)
Grands Crus 111 (24f,Hay,GS,Nov 20)
Gulf President 105 (16f,Tow,G,May 31)
Gurtacrue 107 (18½f,Fon,G,Mar 9)
Gwanako 110 (24f,Chl,GS,Jan 1)

Haarth Sovereign 105 (16f,Tow,GF,Apr 18)
Habbie Simpson 113 (20½f,Chl,GS,Jan 1)
Half Cocked 105 (27f,Fon,HY,Jan 7)
Harry Hunt 107 (17f,Ban,GS,Feb 4)
Havingotascoobydo 107 (21f,Lud,G,Mar 3)
Hawaii Klass 107 (20f,Crl,S,Mar 20)
Hearthstead Dream 107 (20½f,Per,GF,May 13)
Heathcliff 112 (25f,Crl,HY,Feb 9)
Heavenly Blues 106 (20f,Pun,HY,Feb 16)
Heavenly Chorus 105 (20½f,Hex,G,May 1)
Heez A Cracker 105 (21f,Kem,G,Oct 17)
Helen Wood 109 (19f,Nab,G,May 11)
Henry Hook 105 (21f,Tow,S,Nov 21)
Henry King 105 (17f,Tau,GS,Jan 10)
Heron Bay 107 (16½f,Ain,GS,Oct 23)
Herschel 107 (16f,Plu,GF,Sep 19)
Hidden Cyclone 105 (16f,Leo,HY,Dec 29)
Hidden Keel 107 (19f,Str,G,Oct 23)
Hidden Universe 115 (18f,Leo,HY,Feb 12)
Higgy s Boy 105 (16½f,San,GS,Nov 6)
Higgy s Ragazzo 109 (17f,Chl,G,Apr 14)
High Ransom 105 (16½f,Wet,GS,Jan 24)
High Skies 106 (16f,Wor,GF,Jun 30)
Highland Valley 107 (19f,Exe,HY,Feb 13)
Hildisvini 109 (16½f,San,S,Feb 25)
Hilfiger 105 (16½f,Str,GF,Jun 13)
Hills Of Aran 105 (20f,Chp,S,Oct 23)
Hoback Junction 106 (20½f,Hun,G,Oct 31)
Hong Kong Harry 110 (22½f,Fon,GS,Feb 27)
Horsford 105 (19f,Exe,GS,Jan 1)
Houblon Des Obeaux 112 (16f,Hay,HY,Feb 19)
House Of Bourbon 107 (24f,Ffo,GF,Jun 17)
Humbel Ben 107 (19f,Nab,GF,Jun 15)
Hunterview 109 (17f,Exe,GS,Jan 1)
Hurricane Electric 105 (20f,Ban,G,May 15)
Hurricane Fly 121 (16f,Leo,S,Jan 23)

I Can Run Can You 105 (21f,Mar,G,Apr 3)
I Ve Been Framed 107 (20½f,Hun,GS,Nov 20)
Iceman George 109 (20½f,Hun,G,Oct 12)
Imperial Breeze 105 (16f,Ayr,S,Mar 11)
Imperial Circus 109 (19½f,Asc,GS,Nov 19)
Imperial Shabra 109 (16f,Pun,G,Oct 14)
Indian Daudaie 109 (20½f,Chl,G,Mar 18)
Inspector Clouseau 109 (16f,Pun,G,Oct 14)
Intac 108 (19f,Nab,GF,Jun 22)
Inventor 109 (16½f,Hex,GF,Jun 5)
Invictus 106 (19½f,Asc,G,Apr 10)
Iolith 107 (17f,Tau,S,Feb 22)
Island Oscar 109 (16f,Ffo,GF,Aug 3)
Issaquah 112 (16½f,Wet,G,Oct 30)

Jack Cool 122 (16½f,Ain,G,Apr 9)
Jack The Gent 108 (19½f,Don,G,Jan 12)
James De Vassy 113 (21f,Kem,GS,Jan 15)
Jammia 108 (20f,Crl,HY,Feb 21)
Jaunty Journey 106 (24f,Chp,G,Apr 15)
Jayo 106 (20f,Pun,HY,Feb 16)
Je Ne Sais Plus 106 (16½f,Wet,G,Oct 30)
Jetnova 106 (22f,Wcn,GS,Feb 19)
Jimmy The Saint 107 (16f,Tow,S,Feb 3)
Joe Smooth 105 (16f,Leo,SH,Dec 30)
Join Together 109 (24f,Chp,S,Feb 4)
Joker Choker 107 (16f,Lud,G,Apr 21)
Josephine Malines 105 (17½f,Crt,G,May 29)
Jubail 108 (16½f,Chl,G,Mar 16)
Jumbo Rio 112 (20f,Fai,S,Dec 15)
Junior 111 (24f,Chl,GS,Jan 1)
Just Beware 105 (16f,Plu,G,Nov 1)

Kadouchski 105 (16½f,San,S,Feb 25)
Kaituna 108 (21f,Lud,G,Mar 31)
Kalann 114 (16f,Fai,S,Dec 15)
Karabak 123 (20½f,Chl,GS,Dec 11)
Karasenir 108 (17f,Mar,G,Sep 25)
Karky Schultz 107 (17f,Tau,GS,Feb 1)
Kasbadali 105 (17f,Exe,G,Oct 19)
Kasban 105 (24½f,Kem,G,Mar 5)
Katchit 116 (16f,Kem,G,Oct 17)
Katchmore 110 (16f,Ffo,GS,Mar 7)
Kathleens Pride 105 (23½f,Exe,S,Nov 9)
Katys Girl 107 (20f,Pun,S,Nov 13)
Kauto Relko 106 (19f,Mar,GS,Feb 20)
Kayanna s Back 105 (20f,Pun,G,Oct 14)
Kayef 111 (16½f,San,GS,Feb 18)
Kayf Aramis 116 (20½f,Chl,GS,Dec 11)
Keep Talking 108 (20½f,Hun,G,Oct 12)
Keki Buku 107 (19f,Mar,S,Nov 14)
Kempski 107 (20f,Ayr,HY,Mar 12)
Kerb Appeal 106 (24f,Pun,S,Jan 30)
Khyber Kim 110 (16f,Kem,GS,Jan 15)
Kid Cassidy 107 (16½f,San,S,Feb 25)
Kilbrannish Hill 106 (22½f,Kel,GS,Apr 4)
Kilcrea Kim 114 (20½f,Utt,HY,Oct 29)
Killusty Fancy 105 (16f,Ffo,GS,Nov 22)
King Ar Aghaidh 109 (24f,Wor,GF,Jun 23)
King Brex 107 (16½f,San,G,Mar 11)
King Fingal 107 (16f,Mus,GS,Jan 14)
King Mak 107 (16½f,Kel,GS,Mar 21)
King Of Castile 105 (22f,Wet,G,Jun 3)
King Of Dubai 105 (22½f,Utt,G,Apr 2)
King Of The Night 107 (19½f,Don,G,Jan 28)
King s Chorister 107 (17f,Sed,S,Feb 8)
King s Legacy 105 (20½f,Chl,G,Apr 13)
King s Revenge 106 (16f,Wcn,S,Jan 22)
Kingdom Of Munster 106 (16½f,Chl,G,Mar 16)
Kings Grey 105 (16f,Ncs,GS,Nov 12)
Kings Riches 105 (19f,Nab,G,Aug 10)
Knar Mardy 106 (20f,Wet,G,May 27)
Knight In Purple 107 (16f,Hay,GF,Apr 23)
Knight Legend 106 (20f,Fak,GS,Jan 1)
Knighton Combe 105 (22½f,Fol,S,Feb 1)
Knightsbridgelives 105 (19f,Nab,GF,Jly 5)
Knockara Beau 113 (25f,Crl,HY,Feb 9)
Kristal Komet 107 (16f,Leo,SH,Dec 30)
Kristallo 107 (19f,Str,GF,Jly 11)
Kristoffersen 105 (24½f,Tau,GF,Oct 26)
Kudu Country 107 (16f,Ncs,HY,Feb 26)
Kuilsriver 107 (17f,Chl,G,Mar 18)
Kumbeshwar 112 (16½f,Chl,G,Mar 16)
Kylenoe Fairy 107 (19f,Nby,G,Mar 25)

L Accordioniste 107 (17f,Chl,G,Dec 10)
Laborec 105 (20½f,Lei,HY,Jan 11)
Lady Anne Nevill 105 (16½f,Wet,GS,Feb 5)
Lamboro Lad 108 (20½f,Utt,G,May 30)
Laterly 105 (16½f,Hun,S,Feb 24)
Laustra Bad 107 (19f,Exe,GF,Apr 18)
Lawgiver 107 (22½f,Kel,GF,May 19)
Le Beau Bai 108 (23½f,Exe,HY,Nov 19)
Legion D Honneur 107 (21½f,Hun,GS,May 5)
Lethal Glaze 107 (19f,Cat,G,Dec 14)
Letham Island 111 (16f,Utt,GF,Jun 3)
Lets Go Girls 107 (17½f,Crt,G,May 29)
Liberty Seeker 106 (16f,Tow,GS,Nov 4)
Lidar 106 (16½f,Ain,G,May 14)
Lifestyle 105 (16f,Lei,S,Jan 25)
Like A Hurricane 107 (19½f,Asc,G,Oct 30)
Like Minded 108 (19½f,Asc,S,Feb 19)
Lilywhitedancer 106 (16f,Leo,S,Feb 27)
Line Freedom 115 (16f,Tow,GS,Nov 4)
Lisdonagh House 105 (20f,Ncs,GS,Apr 1)
Listenlook 107 (20f,Chp,S,Feb 4)
Little Carmela 106 (23½f,Fak,GF,May 4)
Lively Fling 105 (16f,War,HY,Jan 15)
Local Hero 110 (17f,Chl,G,Mar 18)
Lodgician 105 (16½f,Str,GF,Aug 12)
Lonesome Dove 109 (18f,Fai,HY,Jan 16)
Long Wait 105 (24½f,Per,GF,Jly 1)
Loose Preformer 107 (19½f,Don,G,Jan 12)
Lord Liath 108 (20½f,Lei,S,Jan 25)
Lucaindubai 107 (16½f,San,G,Mar 12)
Lucky Breeze 105 (16½f,San,GS,Feb 18)
Lucky Sunny 107 (20½f,Lei,S,Jan 25)
Lupanar 106 (25½f,Plu,GF,Oct 18)
Luska Lad 112 (16f,Pun,G,Oct 14)
Lyster 105 (27f,Str,G,May 16)

Mac Aeda 108 (25½f,Cat,GS,Feb 14)
Mackeys Forge 107 (16f,Pun,G,Oct 14)
Mad Moose 107 (20f,Hay,G,Mar 23)
Made In Taipan 110 (18f,Leo,S,Feb 27)
Made In Time 111 (19½f,Asc,GS,Nov 19)
Madison Du Berlais 106 (21½f,Exe,S,Nov 2)
Maggio 107 (16f,Tow,HY,Feb 27)
Magical Legend 106 (20½f,Hex,G,May 1)
Makena 111 (24f,Wor,GF,Jly 21)
Malindi Bay 106 (21f,Tow,S,Nov 21)
Manele Bay 105 (20½f,Lei,HY,Feb 2)
Mannlichen 109 (16f,Plu,G,Nov 1)
Manshoor 105 (16f,Tow,G,Oct 6)
Manyriverstocross 110 (16½f,Chl,GS,Nov 14)
Marc Aurele 106 (17f,Ban,G,Jun 8)
Maringo Bay 113 (20f,Ffo,S,Feb 17)
Markington 107 (24½f,Ain,G,Jun 11)
Marlay Park 105 (20f,Fai,HY,Feb 23)
Maska Pony 108 (17½f,Crt,G,Aug 30)
Master Fiddle 110 (19f,Nby,G,Mar 25)
Master Fong 105 (16f,Hay,G,Mar 23)
Matako 105 (20f,Wcn,G,Nov 18)
Mauricetheathlete 105 (27½f,Sed,GS,Mar 6)
Mcmurrough 105 (22½f,Kel,GF,May 19)
Meadows Thyne 107 (24½f,Ain,G,May 7)
Megastar 106 (21f,Chl,G,Mar 16)
Menorah 115 (17f,Chl,GS,Dec 11)
Mic s Delight 110 (20½f,Utt,HY,Oct 29)
Micheal Flips 109 (20f,Ain,GS,Apr 7)
Mickmacmagoole 107 (20f,Ffo,GS,Mar 7)
Midnight Diamond 105 (27½f,Sed,GS,Jan 25)
Midnight Gold 105 (24f,Ffo,GF,Apr 26)
Midnight Macarena 105 (20½f,Hun,GS,Nov 20)
Midnight Opera 115 (16f,Wcn,GF,Mar 27)
Milgen Bay 106 (16½f,Don,G,Jan 28)
Mille Chief 115 (16f,Wcn,GS,Feb 19)
Minella Class 109 (20½f,Hun,S,Feb 24)
Mini Minster 105 (20½f,Hex,G,May 1)
Minnie Hill 107 (16f,Wcn,S,Jan 22)
Miss Molly Be Rude 105 (20f,Ban,G,Jly 30)
Miss Overdrive 105 (24f,Chp,S,Jan 8)
Miss Saffron 105 (22½f,Str,GF,Jun 13)
Miss Wendy 106 (16f,Tow,S,Nov 21)
Misstree Dancer 105 (24f,Chp,S,Nov 24)
Mister Benedictine 106 (19f,Mar,G,Jun 11)
Mister Chancer 110 (20f,Her,G,Mar 23)
Mister Hyde 107 (21f,Tow,GS,Nov 4)
Mister Wall Street 108 (20½f,Hex,G,Apr 11)
Mizzurka 111 (21f,Nby,G,Mar 26)
Mobaasher 105 (24f,Chl,GS,Jan 1)
Moghaayer 107 (24f,Lud,G,May 13)
Mohanad 105 (19f,Mar,G,Aug 1)
Mohayer 105 (17f,Ban,S,Apr 30)
Molly Round 107 (21f,Nby,G,Mar 26)
Molotof 111 (16f,Kem,GS,Feb 26)
Monetary Fund 107 (19½f,San,G,Apr 23)
Monkhair 105 (17½f,Crt,GS,Jly 15)
Montan 108 (16f,Fai,S,Dec 15)
Moon Indigo 109 (24f,Hex,GS,Oct 1)
Moonlight Drive 109 (22f,Wet,GS,Feb 5)
Mossini 105 (22½f,Fol,S,Mar 2)
Mossley 110 (20½f,Hun,G,Oct 31)
Moufatango 107 (20f,Ban,G,Apr 9)
Mourad 114 (20f,Fai,S,Dec 15)
Mr Hudson 107 (21½f,Exe,S,Nov 2)
Mr Muddle 106 (17½f,Fol,S,Feb 15)
Mr Syntax 109 (20f,Sed,GF,Apr 27)
Muldoon s Picnic 107 (19½f,Don,G,Jan 12)
Mutadarek 111 (16f,Leo,S,Jan 9)
My Boy Paddy 113 (20½f,Utt,HY,Oct 29)
My Brother Sylvest 107 (16½f,Str,GF,Sep 21)
My Shamwari 107 (20½f,Chl,G,Apr 13)
My Viking Bay 109 (16f,Tow,GS,Nov 4)

National Trust 109 (21f,Lud,G,Oct 21)
Naughty Naughty 109 (19f,Exe,S,Nov 9)
Nearby 114 (16½f,Ain,G,Apr 9)
Ned Ludd 106 (18½f,Fon,HY,Nov 14)
Ned Of The Hill 105 (18f,Leo,SH,Dec 30)
Nedzer s Return 107 (20½f,Per,GS,May 23)
Neptune Equester 105 (24f,Hay,HY,Feb 19)
Newmill 109 (16f,Pun,HY,Feb 16)
Nicene Creed 105 (19½f,Tau,G,Nov 25)
Niceonefrankie 111 (16f,Tow,G,May 31)
Nine Stories 107 (16½f,Wet,GS,Nov 13)
No Principles 105 (21f,Mar,GS,Nov 18)
No Secrets 110 (22½f,Fol,HY,Jan 2)
Noble Alan 115 (16f,Kem,G,Oct 17)
Nordwind 105 (16½f,Str,GF,Jly 11)
Norisan 105 (22f,Nab,G,May 11)
Northern Alliance 111 (16f,Leo,S,Jan 9)
Nortonthorpe Lad 107 (19f,Nab,G,May 6)
Not Til Monday 105 (16f,Plu,HY,Jan 17)
Notus De La Tour 112 (16½f,Nby,S,Feb 18)
Now This Is It 109 (22½f,Kel,G,Oct 3)
Numide 109 (20f,Ffo,S,Jan 16)

Occasionally Yours 107 (20f,Fak,GS,Feb 18)
Ocean Transit 107 (21f,Lud,G,Feb 9)
Oedipe 106 (23½f,Fak,GF,May 4)
Ohio Gold 106 (20f,Chp,GS,Nov 3)
Old McDonald 109 (18f,Leo,HY,Feb 12)
Olofi 109 (16½f,Chl,GS,Nov 14)
On Borrowed Wings 110 (19½f,Asc,S,Feb 19)
On His Own 108 (20½f,Chl,GS,Jan 1)
On The Way Out 110 (20f,Fai,S,Dec 15)
On Trend 108 (20f,Chp,GS,Apr 2)
Ontrack 105 (27½f,Sed,S,Feb 8)
Organisateur 112 (21f,Kem,GS,Jan 15)
Orion Express 105 (24½f,Tau,F,Apr 12)
Orsippus 109 (21f,Chl,G,Mar 16)
Orzare 113 (16½f,Ain,G,Apr 9)
Oscar Dan Dan 112 (20f,Fai,S,Dec 15)
Oscar Papa 106 (21f,Kem,G,Mar 5)
Oscar Prairie 110 (17½f,Fol,HY,Nov 16)
Oscar Whisky 118 (20½f,Chl,GS,Jan 1)
Oscars Well 120 (18f,Leo,HY,Feb 12)
Osolomio 106 (20f,Wor,GF,Jun 30)
Osric 111 (19f,Nab,G,Jun 3)
Ostland 105 (21f,Kem,G,Mar 22)
Ouest Eclair 105 (16f,War,G,Mar 13)
Our Father 106 (20f,Chp,S,Feb 4)
Our Girl Salley 112 (18f,Fai,HY,Jan 16)
Our Mick 110 (17f,Ban,G,Dec 15)
Oursininlaw 107 (23½f,Fak,GF,May 4)
Overrule 105 (17f,Sed,GF,Apr 27)
Overturn 115 (16f,Kem,GS,Jan 15)

Paddleyourowncanoe 105 (20f,Wor,G,Jly 14)
Pagan Lightning 108 (17f,Sed,S,Feb 8)
Paint The Clouds 105 (21f,Kem,GS,Feb 26)
Paintball 105 (16½f,Chl,G,Mar 16)
Pairc Na Gcapall 105 (24f,Utt,GF,May 9)
Palace Jester 107 (16½f,Hun,S,Jan 14)
Palawi 109 (16½f,Str,G,Mar 14)
Palomar 112 (21f,Kem,GS,Jan 15)
Park Lane 105 (16f,War,G,Nov 3)
Pascha Bere 109 (16f,Wor,G,May 9)
Pateese 108 (16½f,San,G,Mar 12)
Pavillon Bleu 107 (22½f,Utt,GS,Mar 19)
Peaceful Means 106 (16f,Sth,G,May 26)
Peak Raider 109 (16f,Leo,HY,Feb 12)
Peddlers Cross 115 (16½f,Chl,G,Mar 15)
Pegasus Prince 107 (16f,Utt,S,Jan 29)
Penchesco 106 (18½f,Fon,G,Oct 20)
Pennellis 105 (17f,Tau,G,Nov 11)
Penyfan Dawn 108 (16f,Ffo,GF,Aug 3)
Pepite Rose 107 (16f,War,HY,Feb 25)
Pere Blanc 107 (21f,Kem,G,Mar 22)
Perfect Reward 105 (16½f,Lin,HY,Nov 23)
Perfect Smile 108 (16f,Fai,S,Dec 15)
Pete The Feat 105 (22½f,Fon,HY,Nov 14)
Petit Ecuyer 106 (16½f,Lin,GS,Mar 21)
Petit Fleur 105 (20f,Ban,G,Apr 9)
Phardessa 108 (20f,Ffo,S,Jan 16)
Pineau De Re 109 (16f,Fai,S,Dec 15)
Pistolet Noir 107 (17f,Tau,S,Feb 22)
Pittoni 109 (16f,Leo,S,Feb 27)
Plan A 109 (16½f,Chl,G,Mar 16)
Players Please 105 (16f,Wor,GF,Jun 16)
Points Of View 107 (20f,Ban,G,Aug 25)
Pokfulham 105 (16f,Mus,S,Feb 16)
Political Paddy 105 (25f,Crl,HY,Feb 9)
Pontop 106 (20½f,Hex,G,May 1)
Popcorn 106 (16f,Pun,HY,Feb 9)
Poungach 113 (19½f,Asc,GS,Nov 19)
Powerstation 109 (20f,Fai,S,Dec 15)
Praxiteles 111 (16½f,Ain,G,May 14)
Premier Dane 107 (17f,Chl,G,Mar 18)
Premier Des Marais 105 (26f,Hun,G,Feb 10)
Premier Grand Cru 106 (22½f,Kel,G,Apr 23)
Present To You 107 (18½f,Fon,G,Oct 20)
Pride In Battle 109 (20½f,Hun,S,Feb 24)
Prima Vista 111 (16f,Leo,HY,Dec 28)
Prince Du Seuil 107 (21f,Plu,HY,Feb 14)
Prince Tom 106 (22f,San,G,Feb 5)
Pro Pell 105 (20f,Fon,G,May 12)
Problema Tic 110 (19f,Mar,G,Jan 23)
Professeur Emery 106 (16½f,Nby,G,Dec 15)
Proud Times 111 (16f,Ayr,S,Feb 24)
Pure Faith 107 (20f,Ffo,G,Apr 11)
Pyracantha 107 (20f,Mus,G,Nov 19)

Qroktou 108 (24f,Wor,GS,Oct 7)
Quartz De Thaix 114 (20½f,Chl,GS,Dec 11)
Quatro Pierji 106 (17½f,Crt,G,Jun 2)
Quedillac 110 (20f,Wcn,GF,Apr 27)
Queiros Bleu 108 (24f,Chl,G,Mar 17)
Quito Du Tresor 106 (16½f,Per,S,Sep 23)

Racing Demon 105 (21f,Kem,GS,Jan 15)
Radmores Revenge 106 (24f,Chp,S,Nov 24)
Raduis Bleu 106 (19f,Nby,G,Mar 25)
Ragdollianna 108 (16f,Plu,GF,Mar 28)
Railway Dillon 105 (20f,Ncs,S,Feb 2)
Rajeh 106 (20f,Wor,G,Jun 5)
Raslan 109 (22f,Nab,S,Aug 22)
Rathcor 107 (20½f,Hun,G,Oct 3)
Rathlin 112 (16½f,Chl,G,Mar 15)
Rawaaj 106 (16½f,Nby,S,Mar 4)
Real Treasure 107 (16f,Ffo,S,Dec 28)
Rebel Dancer 107 (16½f,Nby,GS,Nov 27)
Rebel Swing 109 (24f,Utt,G,Sep 19)
Recession Proof 116 (16½f,Chl,G,Mar 15)
Red Harbour 106 (22½f,Utt,GS,Mar 19)
Red Merlin 107 (17f,Her,G,Mar 23)
Red Mile 105 (22½f,Fol,HY,Jan 2)
Red Not Blue 105 (20½f,Utt,G,May 30)
Regent s Secret 107 (16½f,Per,S,Sep 23)
Reindeer Dippin 110 (20f,Ain,GS,Apr 7)
Remember Now 106 (16½f,Lin,HY,Jan 3)
Renard D Irlande 108 (17½f,Fol,G,Mar 10)
Requin 106 (17f,Exe,GS,Dec 16)
Restart 105 (20½f,Sth,GF,Jly 11)
Restless Harry 116 (20½f,Chl,GS,Dec 11)
Rhum 107 (16f,Utt,HY,Oct 3)
Rimini 105 (16f,Plu,GF,Oct 18)
Ring Bo Ree 106 (21½f,Hun,GS,May 5)

Ringaroses 111 (24½f,Ain,G,Apr 8)
Rio Gael 106 (16½f,Nby,G,Mar 25)
Ripalong Lad 107 (24f,Ffo,G,Aug 27)
Risaala 114 (16f,Tow,GS,Nov 4)
Risk Challenge 105 (20f,Wor,G,Jly 14)
Rith Bob 108 (20½f,Sth,G,Jun 8)
Rivage D Or 108 (24f,Pun,S,Jan 30)
River Dragon 105 (20f,Wet,S,Feb 22)
Riverscape 109 (16½f,Per,S,Sep 22)
Roalco De Farges 117 (20f,Chp,GS,Apr 2)
Rock County 108 (16f,Fai,S,Dec 15)
Rock Me 105 (19f,Str,GF,Jly 11)
Rock Of Deauville 107 (16½f,Chl,G,Mar 16)
Rock On Ruby 109 (21f,Chl,G,Mar 16)
Rockabilly 105 (23½f,Exe,G,Mar 22)
Ronaldo Des Mottes 110 (20f,Ain,G,Apr 9)
Rose Of The Moon 114 (20½f,Chl,GS,Jan 1)
Rosoff 105 (16½f,Lin,HY,Jan 3)
Rossmore Lad 108 (22½f,Fon,G,Apr 19)
Rougham 105 (16½f,Chp,GS,Oct 9)
Round The Horn 105 (22f,Wet,S,Feb 22)
Royal Mix 108 (16½f,Chl,G,Oct 16)
Ruby Crown 105 (17f,Sed,GF,May 26)
Rudanphast 105 (17f,Nab,S,Sep 6)
Rupert Lamb 109 (16½f,Hex,HY,Mar 17)
Russian War 111 (20f,Ain,GS,Apr 7)
Ruthenoise 106 (16½f,San,G,Feb 5)

Sadler s Star 105 (16f,Wor,GF,Jun 23)
Safe Catch 105 (19f,Nab,G,Aug 10)
Sail And Return 112 (19f,Str,G,Mar 26)
Sailors Warn 114 (16f,Leo,SH,Dec 30)
Saint Are 109 (19f,Mar,G,Jan 23)
Saintly Lady 106 (24f,Chp,S,Nov 24)
Salden Licht 112 (20f,Ain,G,Apr 9)
Salontyre 106 (17f,Tau,G,Mar 14)
Salpierre 105 (20½f,Sth,G,Nov 8)
Sam Winner 116 (16½f,Chl,GS,Nov 13)
Samizdat 106 (17f,Sed,GF,Apr 27)
San Deng 106 (20½f,Hex,G,Apr 11)
San Remo Bello 109 (20f,Fak,GS,Feb 10)
Sanctuaire 113 (16f,Ayr,G,Apr 16)
Santa s Son 106 (16½f,Hex,GF,Jun 5)
Santera 109 (22f,Wcn,G,Nov 6)
Saphire Night 105 (25f,War,GS,Jan 27)
Sara s Smile 107 (19½f,Don,G,Mar 4)
Saveiro 107 (16½f,Kel,G,Apr 28)
Scene Two 106 (16f,Tow,G,May 31)
Scotsbrook Cloud 105 (22½f,Fon,G,Oct 20)
Seaquel 110 (16f,Tow,GF,May 18)
Secret Dancer 107 (17f,Chl,G,Mar 18)
See U Bob 109 (16f,Fai,S,Dec 15)
See You Jack 108 (20½f,Hun,G,Oct 31)
Semi Colon 110 (21f,Nby,G,Mar 26)
Sendali 106 (22½f,Kel,GS,Apr 4)
Sentry Duty 115 (20½f,Chl,GS,Dec 11)
Seren Rouge 108 (24½f,Don,GS,Feb 23)
Seven Is Lucky 107 (24½f,Ayr,G,Apr 15)
Shadows Lengthen 107 (19f,Cat,GS,Feb 28)
Shalambar 105 (16½f,Don,G,Jan 28)
Shalone 108 (19½f,Asc,S,Feb 19)
Sheriff Hall 105 (16f,Mus,G,Nov 26)
Shinrock Hill 108 (16½f,Lin,HY,Jan 3)
Shop Dj 112 (21f,Nby,G,Mar 26)
Shore Thing 106 (19f,Nab,GF,Jly 5)
Shot From The Hip 116 (18f,Leo,HY,Feb 12)
Shropshirelass 105 (19f,Str,GF,Jly 11)
Si C Etait Vrai 107 (18f,Leo,HY,Feb 12)
Sidney Melbourne 107 (16½f,Str,G,Mar 14)
Silent Snow 105 (20f,Crl,S,Mar 10)
Silver Accord 106 (24f,Ban,G,Dec 15)
Silver Friend 106 (16f,Leo,HY,Feb 12)
Silver Gypsy 108 (19f,Exe,GS,Dec 16)
Silverburn 106 (23½f,Exe,GF,May 4)
Silverlord 106 (17½f,Crt,G,Jun 2)
Silviniaco Conti 116 (19½f,Asc,GS,Nov 20)
Sinbad The Sailor 107 (16f,Plu,GF,Oct 18)
Sir Clad 110 (19f,Str,G,Mar 26)
Sir Des Champs 112 (20½f,Chl,G,Mar 18)
Sir Harry Ormesher 110 (24½f,Ain,G,Apr 8)
Sir Kezbaah 110 (17f,Exe,GS,Jan 1)
Sir Pitt 111 (17f,Chl,G,Mar 18)
Sir Tamburlane 106 (20f,Crl,S,Mar 20)
Sircozy 106 (16½f,San,GS,Nov 6)
Sire De Grugy 112 (16f,Fak,GS,Jan 1)
Sivola De Sivola 109 (16½f,Hun,S,Jan 14)
Sivota 111 (24f,Chl,G,Mar 17)
Sizing Ireland 105 (20½f,Hun,GS,Mar 6)
Ski Sunday 110 (17f,Chl,G,Mar 18)
Skint 106 (16f,Kem,GS,Jan 15)
Skippers Brig 109 (24f,Hay,HY,Feb 19)
Skye But N Ben 106 (16f,Lud,G,Oct 6)
Smad Place 109 (17f,Chl,G,Mar 18)
Smooth Classic 107 (20f,Fon,G,Apr 30)
Snake Charmer 107 (25f,War,GS,Feb 12)
So Young 108 (21f,Chl,G,Mar 16)
Soldatino 111 (16½f,Nby,S,Feb 18)
Solix 107 (16½f,Nby,S,Feb 18)
Soliya 105 (22½f,Fon,G,May 30)
Solway Bay 109 (22½f,Kel,GF,May 19)
Solway Minstrel 107 (24½f,Ain,G,May 7)
Solwhit 119 (16f,Leo,S,Jan 23)
Son Amix 111 (24f,Chl,G,Mar 17)
Son Of Flicka 111 (20½f,Chl,G,Mar 18)
Sonofvic 109 (20f,Chp,GS,Nov 3)

Sophies Trophy 106 (16½f,San,HY,Jan 8)
Space Telescope 105 (16f,Wor,GF,Jly 7)
Spanish Treasure 111 (16½f,Chl,G,Mar 15)
Spare Me 105 (21f,Mar,G,May 16)
Sparky May 112 (16f,Wor,G,Oct 20)
Sparrow Hills 107 (20f,Wcn,S,Jan 8)
Spear Thistle 107 (16f,Lei,S,Nov 15)
Spirit Son 119 (16½f,Chl,G,Mar 15)
Spock 105 (20f,Wor,G,Oct 20)
Sprinter Sacre 117 (16½f,Chl,G,Mar 15)
Square Sphere 109 (24f,Pun,S,Jan 30)
Stafford Charlie 105 (16f,Tow,S,Nov 21)
Stage Acclaim 105 (16½f,Hun,GS,May 5)
Stagecoach Opal 108 (24f,Mar,G,Mar 13)
Starluck 114 (16f,Kem,GS,Jan 15)
Start Me Up 108 (16f,Pun,G,Oct 14)
Stephanie Kate 109 (18f,Fai,HY,Jan 16)
Stonemaster 111 (18f,Leo,S,Feb 27)
Stopped Out 107 (22½f,Kel,S,Nov 21)
Storm Brig 112 (16f,Ncs,GS,Nov 12)
Stormyisland Ahead 105 (24f,Wor,GS,Oct 7)
Stow 107 (24f,Chp,S,Nov 24)
Street Dance 106 (16f,Ffo,G,Mar 19)
Street Entertainer 106 (16½f,Chp,G,Apr 9)
Strobe 105 (21f,Mar,G,Jun 11)
Strongpoint 107 (22½f,Kel,G,Oct 3)
Strumble Head 105 (22f,Wcn,G,Oct 24)
Sum Laff 107 (22½f,Fon,G,Mar 9)
Summer Soul 107 (20½f,Per,GS,May 23)
Sunley Peace 109 (19½f,San,G,Apr 23)
Sunnyside 111 (24f,Hex,GS,Oct 1)
Super Villan 105 (22½f,Fol,S,Dec 14)
Superior Wisdom 109 (23½f,Exe,HY,Nov 19)
Supernoverre 106 (16f,Ffo,GF,Aug 3)
Supreme De Paille 105 (20½f,Utt,HY,Dec 31)
Sweet My Lord 108 (22f,Pun,SH,Nov 14)
Sweet World 105 (17f,Ban,G,Aug 20)
Synthe Davis 113 (18½f,Fon,G,Sep 5)

Tabaran 107 (19f,Nab,G,May 17)
Taking Stock 107 (16f,Leo,HY,Dec 20)
Talenti 107 (19f,Nab,GF,Jun 22)
Tarablaze 105 (24f,Chl,G,Mar 17)
Tarkari 109 (16f,Ffo,GS,Feb 5)
Tarvini 113 (24f,Wor,GF,Jun 23)
Tatispout 105 (16½f,Str,GF,Apr 17)
Tayarat 109 (16f,Lud,GS,Nov 22)
Teaforthree 109 (20f,Ffo,S,Feb 17)
Teenage Kicks 105 (22f,Wet,G,Apr 25)
Tenby Jewel 105 (16f,Ffo,GS,Mar 7)
Tenor Nivernais 106 (17f,Tau,GS,Feb 1)
Tension Point 106 (22½f,Kel,GF,May 19)
Terenzium 106 (22f,Wet,G,Jun 3)
Teshali 106 (19f,Nby,G,Mar 25)
Thanks For Coming 106 (19f,Mar,G,Feb 8)
The Betchworth Kid 112 (16½f,Nby,S,Feb 18)
The Bishops Baby 109 (18½f,Fon,G,Apr 8)
The Burrow Vic 106 (24f,Pun,HY,Feb 9)
The Chazer 107 (16½f,Nby,S,Mar 4)
The Cockney Mackem 105 (16f,Lud,G,Mar 3)
The Good Guy 105 (18½f,Fon,S,Oct 2)
The Gripper 105 (22½f,Her,HY,Jan 13)
The Hairy Mutt 107 (24f,Wor,GF,Jly 21)
The Jigsaw Man 113 (17f,Ain,G,May 14)
The Magic Bishop 105 (16f,Ncs,S,Jan 11)
The Reformer 105 (17f,Exe,GS,Dec 5)
The Shepherd King 106 (16f,Leo,S,Feb 27)
The Shy Man 108 (24½f,Ain,GS,Oct 24)
The Starboard Bow 105 (16½f,Chl,G,Mar 16)
The Wee Midget 105 (19½f,Tow,G,Oct 6)
Thelobstercatcher 109 (24f,Chp,G,Apr 15)
There s No Panic 108 (24f,Chl,G,Apr 14)
Third Intention 113 (17f,Chl,G,Apr 14)
Thousand Stars 118 (16f,Leo,S,Jan 23)
Three Ships 105 (20½f,Utt,G,Jly 22)
Thyne For Deploy 106 (22f,Wet,G,Apr 25)
Tidal Bay 112 (25f,Wet,G,Oct 30)
Tiger O Toole 107 (16f,Sth,G,May 26)
Tighe Caster 106 (21f,Lud,G,Oct 21)
Tignello 106 (17f,Her,G,Aug 18)
Tigre D Aron 106 (16½f,Wet,GS,Jan 24)
Tijuana Dancer 108 (16f,Leo,HY,Dec 28)
Time For Spring 107 (22f,San,G,Mar 11)
Time Machine 106 (16½f,Per,S,Sep 23)
Tiptoeaway 106 (20f,Ncs,S,Mar 8)
Tiptronic 105 (17f,Her,GS,Nov 18)
Titan De Sarti 110 (16½f,Nby,G,Dec 15)
Tito Bustillo 110 (16f,Wcn,G,Nov 6)
To Arms 107 (20½f,Sth,GF,Jly 11)
Tobago Bay 105 (20½f,Utt,GS,May 1)
Toby Belch 105 (24f,Lud,G,May 13)
Tocca Ferro 109 (16½f,Nby,GS,Nov 27)
Tofino Bay 108 (16f,Leo,HY,Dec 29)
Ton-Chee 106 (16½f,Wet,G,May 27)
Toner D Oudairies 116 (16f,Fai,S,Dec 15)
Top Smart 107 (17½f,Fol,HY,Nov 16)
Topolski 109 (17f,Nab,GS,Mar 20)
Tornado Bob 112 (20½f,Lei,S,Jan 25)
Total Excitement 114 (16½f,Ain,G,Apr 9)
Total Submission 105 (20½f,Chl,GS,Jan 1)
Totoman 105 (17f,Ban,S,Jly 20)
Toubab 109 (16½f,Hay,G,May 8)
Tout Regulier 107 (16½f,Str,GF,Jly 11)
Traffic Chaos 105 (20½f,Sth,G,Mar 24)

Trenchant 111 (20f,Fon,S,Feb 27)
Tri Nations 105 (17½f,Crt,G,Aug 26)
Tritonville Lodge 109 (24f,Wor,GF,Jun 23)
Troubletimestwo 105 (21f,Lud,G,Mar 31)
Trumpstoo 105 (17f,Her,G,Aug 18)
Trustan Times 109 (20f,Wet,S,Jan 15)
Tullyraine 111 (24f,Wor,GS,Oct 7)
Turner Brown 107 (24f,Pun,HY,Feb 9)
Turtlethomas 110 (21f,Plu,GS,Mar 14)
Twentynineblack 108 (17½f,Crt,G,Jun 2)
Two Miles West 105 (24f,Wor,GS,Jun 6)
Tzora 106 (20f,Wor,GF,Jun 30)

Uffa Fox 105 (20f,Wcn,GF,Oct 14)
Ultimate 110 (16f,Hay,GS,Nov 20)
Ultravox 106 (16f,Asc,G,Apr 10)
Unaccompanied 113 (17f,Chl,G,Mar 18)
Universal Soldier 112 (24f,Chp,S,Jan 8)

Vagrant Emperor 106 (21f,Nby,GS,Nov 25)
Valento 107 (21f,Lud,GF,Apr 25)
Valid Point 107 (16f,Tow,GS,Mar 17)
Vallani 105 (24½f,Mus,S,Feb 16)
Vertueux 105 (16f,Lud,G,May 13)
Very Cool 107 (23½f,Exe,GF,May 4)
Very Stylish 105 (24f,Utt,GF,Jly 6)
Via Galilei 116 (16½f,Ain,G,Apr 9)
Vico 110 (22f,Wcn,G,Nov 18)
Victors Serenade 105 (23½f,Exe,S,Nov 2)
Viking Blond 107 (24f,Chl,G,Mar 17)
Vin De Roy 106 (25f,War,GS,Feb 12)
Vincitore 106 (22½f,Fon,G,Mar 9)
Vintage Fabric 106 (22f,Nab,G,Apr 23)
Violin Davis 113 (21f,Nby,G,Mar 26)
Vital Plot 106 (16f,Fai,S,Dec 15)
Viva Colonia 107 (20f,Wet,G,Oct 30)
Voler La Vedette 115 (16f,Pun,SH,Nov 14)

Waldvogel 109 (16f,Wcn,GF,Mar 27)
Walkon 105 (21f,Chl,G,Mar 16)
Walter De La Mare 105 (17f,Chl,G,Mar 18)
Wango 106 (16f,Pun,G,Oct 14)
Warne s Way 107 (18½f,Fon,HY,Nov 14)
Warrior One 105 (16f,Ncs,GS,Nov 12)
Way Back When 105 (16f,Tow,G,Oct 24)
Westlin Winds 108 (16½f,Chp,GS,Oct 9)
What A Charm 113 (16½f,Chl,G,Mar 16)
What An Oscar 108 (19f,Nby,G,Mar 25)
What s Occurrin 105 (20f,Crl,G,Oct 21)
Whatdoidowiththat 105 (24f,Hex,S,Oct 9)
Wheelavit 105 (17f,Nab,G,Jun 3)
Whenever 106 (19f,Nab,GF,Jun 15)
Wheyaye 105 (22f,Wet,G,Oct 29)
Whispering Death 107 (16½f,Don,G,Jan 28)
Whispering Jack 105 (22f,Wcn,GF,Mar 11)
Whitby Jack 109 (18½f,Fon,GS,Feb 6)
Whodoyouthink 106 (16f,Fai,S,Dec 15)
Whoops A Daisy 109 (16f,Tow,HY,Feb 27)
Wiesentraum 105 (20½f,Hun,GS,Mar 6)
Wikaala 105 (16½f,Per,GF,Jun 30)
Wilbury Star 105 (17f,Nab,GF,Jun 22)
Wild Desert 105 (19½f,Don,G,Jan 12)
Wilde Wit Pleasure 110 (16f,Leo,S,Jan 9)
William Hogarth 114 (20f,Chp,GS,Apr 2)
William s Wishes 106 (16½f,Hay,G,May 8)
Wind Shuffle 105 (16½f,Per,GS,May 23)
Winged Farasi 105 (21½f,Sed,G,Aug 24)
Winner Takes Itall 106 (16f,Pun,G,Oct 14)
Winsley Hill 106 (25½f,Plu,GF,Oct 18)
Wistow 110 (25f,War,G,Mar 13)
Won In The Dark 105 (16f,Ffo,GS,Feb 5)
Wood Lily 109 (18f,Fai,HY,Jan 16)
Woodlark Island 105 (16f,Tow,GF,May 21)
Woody Valentine 105 (17½f,Crt,G,May 29)
Wor Rom 105 (26f,Hun,G,Apr 29)
Working Title 109 (21f,Kem,G,Nov 1)
Wot Way Chief 105 (19f,Mar,G,Jun 11)
Wyse Hill Teabags 110 (20f,Ain,GS,Apr 7)

Yabora 105 (22½f,Fol,HY,Jan 2)
Yes Tom 109 (24½f,Ayr,HY,Feb 12)
Yetholm 107 (20f,Ffo,S,Jan 16)
Young Albert 106 (24f,Chp,S,Nov 24)
Yurok 107 (20f,Wet,S,Jan 15)

Zaidpour 117 (18f,Leo,HY,Feb 12)
Zakatal 105 (20f,Ffo,GS,Mar 7)
Zanir 109 (17f,Chl,G,Mar 18)
Zarkandar 115 (17f,Chl,G,Mar 18)
Zaynar 117 (20½f,Chl,GS,Dec 11)
Zed Candy 107 (24f,Ncs,S,Mar 19)